All Music Guide to

THE DEFINITIVE GUIDE

TO ROCK, POP, AND SOUL

Edited by

Vladimir Bogdanov

Chris Woodstra

Stephen Thomas Erlewine

AMG
All Media Guide

Backbeat
Books

◗AMG
All Media Guide   **All Media Guide** has created the world's largest and most comprehensive information databases for music, videos, DVDs, and video games. With coverage of both in-print and out-of-print titles, the massive AMG archive includes reviews, plot synopses, biographies, ratings, images, titles, credits, essays, and thousands of descriptive categories. All content is original, written expressly for AMG by a worldwide network of professional staff and freelance writers specializing in music, movies, and games. The AMG databases – **All Music Guide**®, **All Movie Guide**®, and **All Game Guide**™ – are licensed by major retailers and Internet content sites and are available to the public through its websites (www.allmusic.com, www.allmovie.com, www.allgame.com) and through its series of books: *All Music Guide, All Music Guide to Rock, All Music Guide to Country, All Music Guide to Jazz, All Music Guide to Blues,* and *All Music Guide to Electronica.*

All Media Guide 301 E. Liberty Street, Suite 400, Ann Arbor, MI 48104
T: 734/887-5600 F: 734/827-2492
www. allmediaguide.com email: feedback@allmediaguide.com

Published by Backbeat Books
600 Harrison Street, San Francisco, CA 94105
www.backbeatbooks.com
Email: books@musicplayer.com
An imprint of Music Player Network
www.musicplayer.com
United Entertainment Media, Inc.

◗AMG
All Media Guide

Distributed to the book trade in the U.S and Canada by Publishers Group West 1700 Fourth Street, Berkeley, CA 94710

Distributed to the music trade in the U.S. and Canada by Hal Leonard Publishing P.O. Box 13819, Milwaukee, WI 53213

Cover Design: Wagner Design, Ann Arbor, MI
AMG – All Music Guide Founder: Michael Erlewine
Text Composition: Interactive Composition Corporation

Library of Congress Cataloging-in-Publication Data

All music guide to rock : the experts' guide to the best recordings in rock, pop, soul,
R&B, and rap / edited by Vladimir Bogdanov, Chris Woodstra, Stephen Thomas
Erlewine. – 3rd ed.
         p.   cm. – (All music guide)
      Includex index.
      ISBN 0-87930-653-X
      1. Sound recordings–Reviews.   2. Rock music–Discography.   3. Popular
music–Discography.   4. Rock music–Bio-bibliography.   5. Rock music–History and
criticism.   I. Bogdanov, Vladimir, 1965-.   II. Woodstra, Chris.   III. Erlewine, Stephen
Thomas.   IV. AMG all music guide series.

ML156.9 .A39   2002
016.78164'0266–dc21   2002018397

Printed in the United States of America
02 03 04 05 06 5 4 3 2 1

Contents

How to Use This Book	iv
Contributors	v
Introduction	vii

Artists — 1

A	1
B	47
C	170
D	278
E	346
F	384
G	444
H	497
I	551
J	568
K	609
L	635
M	684
N	781
O	811
P	836
Q	903
R	910
S	971
T	1113
U	1169
V	1181
W	1197
X	1249
Y	1253
Z	1264
Various Artists	1273

Essays — 1303

Birth of Rock & Roll	1303
Music Map: The Birth of Rock & Roll	1304
Early Rhythm & Blues	1304
New Orleans R&B	1305
Music Map: New Orleans R&B	1305
Doo Wop	1306
Music Map: Doo Wop	1306
Rockabilly	1307
Music Map: Rockabilly	1307
Rock & Roll	1308
Instrumental Rock	1308
Music Map: Instrumental Rock	1309
Teen Idols	1309
Music Map: Teen Idols	1310
British Rock & Roll Before the Beatles	1310
Music Map: British Rock & Roll Before the Beatles	1311
Brill Building Sound	1311
Music Map: Brill Building Sound	1312
Girl Groups	1312
Music Map: Girl Groups	1313
Surf Music	1313
Music Map: Surf Music	1314
Motown	1314
Music Map: Motown	1315
Early British R&B	1315
British Invasion	1316
Music Map: British Invasion	1317
Folk-Rock	1318
Music Map: Folk-Rock	1318
Merseybeat	1319
Garage Rock	1320
Music Map: Garage Rock	1321
Mod	1321
Psychedelic Rock	1322
Music Map: Psychedelic Rock	1323
Soul	1323
Music Map: Soul	1324
Blue-Eyed Soul	1325
Music Map: Blue-Eyed Soul	1325
Blues Rock	1325
Music Map: Blues Rock	1326
Country Rock	1327
Music Map: Country Rock	1327
Singer/Songwriters	1328
Music Map: Singer/Songwriters	1328
Jazz Rock	1328
Music Map: Jazz Rock	1329
Progressive Rock	1330
Music Map: Progressive Rock	1330
Bubblegum	1331
Music Map: Bubblegum	1331
Heavy Metal	1332
Southern Rock	1332
Music Map: Southern Rock	1332
Funk	1333
Music Map: Funk	1333
Philly Soul	1334
Pub Rock	1335
Punk Music	1335
American Punk Rock	1336
Music Map: American Punk Rock	1336
British Punk	1336
Music Map: British Punk	1337
Post-Punk	1337
New Wave	1338
Power Pop	1339
Hardcore & Thrash	1339
Music Map: Hardcore	1340
Australian Rock	1341
New Zealand Rock	1342
Jangle Pop	1343
American Alternative Rock/Post-Punk	1344
British Alternative Rock	1346
Rap	1347
Music Map: Rap	1347

Non-Rock Styles that Influenced Rock — 1350

Acoustic Blues	1350
Gospel	1351
Electric Blues	1351
American Folk	1353
British Isles Folk Music	1354
Reggae	1355

Index	**1357**

How to Use This Book

ARTIST NAME ──────────────────

VITAL STATISTICS: For groups, **f.** indicates date and place of formation; **db.** indicated date disbanded. For individual performers, date and place of birth (**b.**) and death (**d.**), if known, are given.

PERFORMER(S) / STYLE: Indicates a group, musician, DJ, or producer, followed by the styles of music associated with the performer or group.

BIOGRAPHY: A quick view of the artist's life and musical career. For major performers, proportionally longer biographies are provided.

ALBUM REVIEWS: These are the albums selected by our editors and contributors.

KEY TO SYMBOLS: ● ☆ ★ ───────────────

☆ ESSENTIAL RECORDINGS: Albums marked with a star should be part of any good collection of the genre. Often, these are also a good first purchase (filled star). By hearing these albums, you can get a good overview of the entire genre. These are must-hear and must-have recordings. You can't go wrong with them.

●★ FIRST PURCHASE: Albums marked with either a filled circle or a filled star should be your first purchase. This is where to begin to find out if you like this particular artist. These albums are representative of the best this artist has to offer. If you don't like these picks, chances are this artist is not for you. In the case of an artist who has a number of distinct periods, you will find an essential pick marked for each period. Albums are listed chronologically when possible.

ALBUM TITLE: The name of the album is listed in bold as it appears on the original when possible. Very long titles have been abbreviated, or repeated in full as part of the comment, where needed.

DATE: The year of an album's first recording or release, if known.

RECORD LABEL: Record labels indicate the current (or most recent) release of this recording. Label numbers are not included because they change frequently.

ALBUM RATINGS: ✦ TO ✦✦✦✦✦ In addition to the stars and circles used to distinguish exceptional noteworthy albums, as explained above, all albums are rated on a scale from one to five diamonds.

REVIEWERS: The name of each review's author are given at the end of the review.

David Bowie (David Robert Jones)

b. Jan. 8, 1947, Brixton, England

Vocals, Saxophone, Keyboards, Guitar / Experimental Rock, Blue-Eyed Soul, Proto-Punk, Pop/Rock, Glam Rock, Prog-Rock/Art Rock, Hard Rock

The cliche about David Bowie says he's a musical chameleon, adapting himself according to fashion and trends. While such a criticism is too glib, there's no denying that Bowie demonstrated remarkable skill for perceiving musical trends at his peak in the '70s. After spending several years in the late '60s as a mod and as an all-around music-hall entertainer, Bowie reinvented himself as a hippie singer/songwriter. Prior to his breakthrough in 1972, he recorded a proto-metal record and a pop-rock album, eventually redefining glam-rock with his ambiguously sexy Ziggy Stardust persona. By the mid-'70s, he developed an effete, sophisticated version of Philly soul that he dubbed "plastic soul," which eventually morphed into the eerie avant-pop of 1976's *Station to Station*. Shortly afterward, he recorded three experimental electronic albums with Brian Eno. At the dawn of the '80s, Bowie was still at the height of his powers, he slowly sank into mediocrity before salvaging his career in the early '90s. Even when he was out of fashion in the '80s and '90s, it was clear that Bowie was one of the most influential musicians in rock, for better and for worse. Each one of his phases in the '70s sparked a number of subgenres, including punk, new wave, goth-rock, the New Romantics, and electronica. Few rockers ever had such lasting impact. —*Stephen Thomas Erlewine*

☆ **The Rise & Fall of Ziggy Stardust** / 1972 / Virgin ✦✦✦✦

Borrowing heavily from Marc Bolan's glam rock and the future shock of *A Clockwork Orange*, David Bowie reached back to the heavy rock of *The Man Who Sold the World* for *The Rise & Fall of Ziggy Stardust and the Spiders From Mars*. Constructed as a loose concept album about an androgynous alien rock star named Ziggy Stardust, the story falls apart quickly, yet Bowie's fractured, paranoid lyrics are evocative of a decadent, decaying future, and the music echoes an apocalyptic, nuclear dread. Fleshing out the off-kilter metallic mix with fatter guitars, genuine pop songs, string sections, keyboards, and a cinematic flourish, *Ziggy Stardust* is a glitzy array of riffs, hooks, melodrama, and style and the logical culmination of glam. Bowie succeeds not in spite of his pretensions but because of them, and *Ziggy Stardust*—familiar in structure, but alien in performance—is the first time his vision and execution met in such a grand, sweeping fashion. —*Stephen Thomas Erlewine*

David Live / 1974 / Rykodisc ✦✦

The supporting tour for *Diamond Dogs* was supposed to be a theatrical extravaganza, yet as he headed out on the road, David Bowie became infatuated with Philly soul and changed his entire approach to reflect his new interest, as well as his backing band in the process. As a result, the double-album *David Live* captures Bowie in transition, as he moves from glam-rock to plastic soul. The set list draws heavily from *Ziggy Stardust*-era songs, yet a few surprises, like a stilted cover of "Knock on Wood" and an inspired version of "All the Young Dudes," a song Bowie gave Mott the Hoople. Since Bowie's attempts at soul are a little awkward at this stage, *David Live* is primarily of interest as a historical document, yet there's enough good material to make it worthwhile for fanatics. —*Stephen Thomas Erlewine*

● **Best of David Bowie: 1969-1974** / Oct. 7, 1997 / Virgin ✦✦✦✦

Early in 1997, David Bowie sold the rights to his RCA catalog to EMI, and the first release to appear under the new agreement was *The Best of 1969-1974*, which was part of EMI's limited-edition 100th Birthday series. Instead of playing it straight, the 20-track set offers both the predictable classics—"The Jean Genie," "Space Oddity," "Starman," "Drive In Saturday," "Ziggy Stardust," "Suffragette City," "Changes," "Sorrow," "The Man Who Sold the World"—and relative obscurities, like the B-side "Velvet Goldmine," Bowie's version of "All the Young Dudes" and alternate takes of "John, I'm Only Dancing" and "The Prettiest Star." There are also album tracks like "Oh! You Pretty Things" and "Life on Mars" that have become classics, making *The Best of 1969-1974* an impressive, reasonably thorough overview of Bowie's glam years. —*Stephen Thomas Erlewine*

Hours / Oct. 5, 1999 / Virgin ✦✦✦

Since David Bowie spent the '90s jumping from style to style, it comes as a shock that *Hours*, his final album of the decade, is a relatively straightforward affair. *Hours* is a relaxed, natural departure from this method. Arriving after two labored albums, the shift in tone is quite refreshing. "Thursday's Child," the album's engaging mid-tempo opener, is a good indication of what lays ahead. It feels like classic Bowie, yet recalls no specific era of his career. That doesn't mean *Hours* is on par with his earlier masterworks; it never attempts to be that bold. What it does mean is that it's the first album where he has accepted his past and is willing to use it as a foundation for new music. That's the reason why *Hours* feels open, even organic—he's no longer self-conscious, either about living up to his past or creating a new future. And that's what's appealing about *Hours*—it may not be one of Bowie's classics, but it's the work of a masterful musician who has begun to enjoy his craft again and isn't afraid to let things develop naturally. —*Stephen Thomas Erlewine*

Contributors

All Music Guide Editors

Vladimir Bogdanov, President
Chris Woodstra, Vice President of
  Content Development
Stephen Thomas Erlewine, Director
  of Content, Pop Music
John Bush, Senior Editor, Pop Music

AMG Pop Editors

Al Campbell
Steve Huey
Zac Johnson
Joslyn Layne
Heather Phares
Stacia Proefrock
Tim Sendra
Sean Westergaard
MacKenzie Wilson

Contributors

Nitsuh Abebe
Bret Adams
Greg Adams
Steve Aldrich
Mark Allan
Rick Anderson
Jason Ankeny
Jennifer Ansbach
William Ashford
Glenn Astarita
Jon Azpiri
Susan Bachner
Aaron Badgley
Gautam Baksi
Jonathan Ball
Ashley S. Battel
Bart Bealmear
George Bedard
Fred Beldin
Jason Birchmeier
Tyson Bjorge
Vladimir Bogdanov
Myles Boisen
Ross Boissoneau
Gina Boldman
John Book
Rob Bowman
Daniel Browne
Rick A. Bueche
Scott Bultman
Jeff Burger
Nick Burton
John Bush
Nathan Bush
Bryan Buss
Blake Butler
Becky Byrkit
Rob Caldwell
Al Campbell
Dean Carlson
Matt Carlson

Bil Carpenter
Troy Carpenter
Bryan Carroll
Sean Carruthers
Phil Carter
Bill Cassel
Kenneth M. Cassidy
Darryl Cater
Evan Cater
Eugene Chadbourne
David M. Childers
James Chrispell
Andy Claps
David Cleary
Jonathan Cohen
Paul Collins
Matt Conaway
David Connolly
Stephen Constantelos
Stephen Cook
Sean Cooper
William Cooper
Kristi Coulter
François Couture
Erik Crawford
Jeff Crooke
Michelle Cross
Susan Cruickshank
Rosalind Cummings-Yeates
Zachary Curd
Michael Cusanelli
Bill Dahl
Jason Damas
Peter J. D'Angelo
Mike DaRonco
Ben Davies
Hank Davis
Michael P. Dawson
Mike DeGagne
Tom Demalon
Mark Deming
Ron DePasquale
Michael Di Bella
Tim DiGravina
Charlotte Dillon
Kirk Dombek
Charles Donovan
John Dougan
Jimmy Draper
Jonathan Druy
John Duffy
Bruce Eder
Brian Christopher Egan
Jason Elias
Iotis Erlewine
Meredith Erlewine
Michael Erlewine
Stephen Thomas Erlewine
Alan Esher
Peter Fawthrop
Kathleen C. Fennessy

Christopher Fielder
Matt Fink
Brian Flota
John Floyd
Luke Forrest
Dan Forte
Patrick Foster
John Franck
Michael Freedberg
Michael Frey
Tracy Frey
Paul Fucito
Michael Gallucci
Alex S. Garcia
James A. Gardner
Brandon Gentry
Marc Gilman
Richard S. Ginell
Geoff Ginsberg
Daniel Gioffre
Dan Gizzi
Ryan Randall Goble
Robert Gordon
Bob Gottlieb
Michael Gowan
Mary Grady
Tom Graves
Adam Greenberg
Jo-Ann Greene
Matthew Greenwald
JT Griffith
Tim Griggs
Donald A. Guarisco
Romain Guillou
James Haag
Erik Hage
Tom Hallett
Andrew Hamilton
Chris Handyside
Shawn Haney
Jim Harper
Craig Harris
Brett Hartenbach
Michael Hastings
Kelvin Hayes
Ralph Heibutzki
Dan Heilman
Alex Henderson
Robert Hicks
Matthew Hilburn
Gary Hill
Melinda Hill
Andy Hinds
John Hinrichsen
Christian Hoard
Ed Hogan
Hal Horowitz
Stephen Howell
Steve Huey
Eddie Huffman
Jason Hundey

Jaime Ikeda
Jack L.V. Isles
Vik Iyengar
Qa'id Jacobs
Vincent Jeffries
Daevid Jehnzen
Dale Jensen
Jessica Jernigan
Zac Johnson
Liana Jonas
Michael Jourdan
Thom Jurek
Jason Kane
Matthew Isaac Kantor
Michael Katz
Jason Kaufman
Andy Kelllman
Nick Kemper
Patrick Kennedy
David Kent-Abbott
Kit Kiefer
Joshua Klein
Don Kline
Cub Koda
Linda Kohanov
Brad Kohlenstein
Paul Kott
Todd Kristel
Peter Kurtz
Steve Kurutz
Joshua Landau
Keir Langley
Ronnie Lankford, Jr.
Sanz Lashley
Theresa E. LaVeck
Joslyn Layne
Jack Leaver
Dan Lee
Dan LeRoy
Jonathan Lewis
Bret Love
John Lowe
Jacob N. Lunders
Craig Lytle
Dennis MacDonald
Jason MacNeil
Brian Mansfield
Dave Marsh
Stewart Mason
Greg Matherly
Leslie Mathew
Greg Maurer
Kieran McCarthy
Kelly McCartney
Joseph McCombs
Steven McDonald
Dean McFarlane
Kembrew McLeod
Steve McMullen
Bill Meredith
Richard Meyer

Terry Miles
Jon Mojo Mills
Ted Mills
Josh Modell
Tim Monger
Martin Monkman
Jeri Montesano
Stansted Montfichet
Mark Morgenstein
Brian Musich
Michael G. Nastos
Opal Louis Nations
Alvaro Neder
Jim Newsom
Dale Nicholls
Shawn Nicholls
Jason Nickey
Chris Nickson
Ed Nimmervoll
Alex Ogg
Christine Ohlman
Brian Olewnick
J.P. Ollio
Jim O'Neal
Geoff Orens
Pat Padua
Roch Parisien
Chris Parker
Archie Patterson
Dan Pavlides
Paul Pearson
Jana Pendragon
Keith Pettipas
Heather Phares
Richard Pierson
Lindsay Planer
Robin Platts
Matthew Plichta
J. Poet

Bob Porter
Jim Powers
Greg Prato
Stacia Proefrock
Jose Promis
Jon Pruett
Jack Rabid
Nathan Rabin
Brian Raftery
Ned Raggett
Stephen Raiteri
Darren Ratner
Matt Reasor
Michael Ribas
Mark Richardson
Vince Ripol
Ed Rivadavia
Pemberton Roach
Matthew Robinson
Gregg Rounds
Arthur Rowe
William Ruhlmann
Marc Ruxin
Jeremy Salmon
Stephen Spaz Schnee
Amy Schroeder
Tom Schulte
Linda Seida
Tom Semioli
Tim Sendra
Scott Sepich
David Serra
Mathias Sheaks
Joe Silva
Richard Skelly
Chris Slawecki
Dave Sleger
Craig Robert Smith
David Ross Smith

Jim Smith
Kerry L. Smith
Michael B. Smith
Charles Spano
Matthew Springer
Leo Stanley
Peter Stepek
Alex Stimmel
Doug Stone
Yancey Strickler
Denise Sullivan
Kim Summers
Michael Sutton
Glen Swann
Stanton Swihart
Sara Sytsma
Jeff Tamarkin
Ken Taylor
Robert Taylor
Rob Theakston
Bryan Thomas
David Thomas
Dave Thompson
William Tilland
Paul Tinelli
Bradley Torreano
Chris True
Blue Gene Tyranny
Jeremy Ulrey
Neal Umphred
Richie Unterberger
Victor W. Valdivia
Elmer Valo
Andrew Vance
Mark Vanderhoff
Marc van der Pol
Joe Viglione
Barry Weber
Sean Westergaard

MacKenzie Wilson
Steve Winick
Ari Wiznitzer
Kurt Wolff
Cary Wolfson
Jan Mark Wolkin
Chris Woodstra
Jim Worbois
Ron Wynn
Scott Yanow
Curtis Zimmermann

AMG Technical Editors

Jonathan Ball
Joseph Cobb
Matt Collar
George Davis
Maestro Mark Donkers
Heather Humphrey
Jack L.V. Isles
Andy Kellman
Corwin Moore
Rob Theakston
Chris True

AMG Copy Editors

Jason Birchmeier
Amy Cloud
Elizabeth Erlewine
Margaret Erlewine
Benjamin Goldstein
Jennifer Jones
Kim Kunoff
David Lynch
Amber Melosi
Stephanie Somerville
Rachel Sprovtsoff-Mangus

Introduction

Rock 'n' roll is entering its fifth decade of existence. In that time, stacks of worthwhile recordings have piled up, and while live rock 'n' roll is electrifying, the history of the music is, for better or worse, passed on through recordings. With that in mind, *The All Music Guide to Rock* doesn't attempt to tell the history of rock 'n' roll, it offers a guide to performers and their recordings. Like the previous books in the All Music Guide series, the intent of *The All Music Guide to Rock* is not to draw comparisons between the artists, but to provide a guide to the artists themselves. It helps readers find the best recordings by everyone from Pat Boone to Michael Bolton, from Elvis Presley to Madonna, judging each artist's music on its own terms.

Given our space limitations, certain artists had to be excluded, yet we included a broad range of musicians reflecting the wide range of stylistic variations rock 'n' roll has taken over the years. Stylistically, rock 'n' roll encompasses blues, R&B, country, traditional pop, folk, vaudeville, British music hall, electronica–nearly every form of music finds its way into rock 'n' roll, and every subgenre of rock 'n' roll has found its way into *The All Music Guide to Rock*. That doesn't mean every rockabilly or doo wop singer, or every heavy metal or punk band has been included. Nevertheless, you'll find scores of rockabilly, doo wop, metal, and punk records in here, along with psychedelia, garage rock, British Invasion, pub rock, lo-fi, post-punk, techno, house, Brill Building pop, Southern rock…the vast variety of styles that make popular music so intriguing.

What makes rock 'n' roll so interesting is the sheer amount of variety it offers. It's been a long road from Chuck Berry and Elvis Presley to the Wu-Tang Clan and Pavement, and all the side roads have something interesting to offer. It may be the songcraft of Neil Diamond or it could be the trance-inducing electronics of the Orb. It could be the driving heartland rock 'n' roll of Bob Seger and John Mellencamp or the minimalist rock of the Ramones, AC/DC and Unrest, who all take simplicity in different sonic directions. Is it all rock and roll? In the conventional sense it's not, but it is all popular music that owes its existence to rock 'n' roll. There's not an obvious link between Sonic Youth and Chuck Berry, yet there are links between Chuck Berry and the Velvet Underground, and the Velvets and Sonic Youth.

The All Music Guide to Rock tries to explain Sonic Youth to Chuck Berry fans and, just as importantly, Chuck Berry to Sonic Youth fans. In the meantime, the book explores unheralded subgenres like garage and surf rock that rarely get space in conventional rock books. It also spotlights cult figures from the Celibate Rifles to Scott Walker that may have never gotten popular recognition, yet they had a small impact in shaping popular music–or they simply made intriguing, interesting music. *The All Music Guide to Rock* may not explore every genre of rock 'n' roll in depth, yet it helps make sense of the ever-changing entity that is rock 'n' roll. If the book does anything, it should open you up to some terrific music you may not have heard before.

As the decades have passed, the music has changed and so have the recording formats. For the past decade, the compact disc has been the dominant medium, replacing the long-playing vinyl album. However, in the early years of rock 'n' roll, the single was the dominant format. Artists like Elvis Presley, Chuck Berry, Fats Domino, Buddy Holly, the Everly Brothers, and Jerry Lee Lewis didn't think in terms of making cohesive full-length albums–they were making their next hit single. Around 1966, long-playing albums became the dominant musical format in rock 'n' roll, with British Invasion bands like the Beatles and the Kinks crafting records that were tied together by both lyrical and musical themes. Soon, artists were putting more thought into making cohesive albums. Initially, this meant "concept albums"–records like The Who's *Tommy*, The Kinks' *Arthur*, or the Moody Blues' *Days of Future Passed* –that told specific stories with their songs. Concept albums gave way to a wave of progressive rock bands that wrote music that could only be told over the course of a full-length album. As the British Invasion groups explored conceptual records, American psychedelic bands like the Grateful Dead and Jefferson Airplane were making music that could not be confined to a three-minute single, so they also concentrated on full-length albums. Eventually, hard rock bands like Led Zeppelin had hit albums, not singles, which helped inaugurate the era of album-rock. Ever since the late '60s, the majority of rock bands focused their creative attentions on full-length albums and several groups had long, successful careers without the benefit of hit singles. Consequently, albums were more important to the careers of '70s rockers like David Bowie and Queen than they were to the careers of Duane Eddy or the Ventures, which explains why Bowie and Queen have more albums listed than Eddy or the Ventures. It's not a critical judgment about which band is more important, it's a reflection of their particular era.

Within the text are biographies and reviews of 2,500 artists. The goal of *The All Music Guide* is not to draw comparisons between Carpenters and Mötley Crüe albums, or pit the Beatles against the Clash. Rather, the intent of *The All Music Guide to Rock* is to provide a guide to the recordings of a particular artist, offering a biography and description of the music, as well as to capsule reviews of their albums. If the description of a musician intrigues you, the book also provides a starting point for each artist, in the form of a filled-in circle or star. Each entry in the book has a filled-in circle, with the possible exception of artists with only one album. Within each entry, to the right of the album's title, is a rating for the album itself, on a scale from one to five. These ratings are based on the artist themselves, not of their overall worth (for instance, a four-star Whitney Houston album is not necessarily the same as a four-star Nirvana album). The only global rating in the book is a star, which signals an album that is the best of its genre–in other words, it's essential listening.

Many of the artists included in *The All Music Guide to Rock* have a complete discography–on occasion, significant bootlegs and rarities have been included, as well–but some records were not reviewed because of space constraints. Similarly, some artists have selected listings, particularly acts that only had a handful of hits. On the other hand, musicians like James Brown and Elvis Presley have simply released too many albums for each album to be reviewed in our allotted space. In this case, all of their major records have been included, along with some interesting minor albums that illustrate the depth of their artistry. Also, hard-rock bands like Deep Purple and Black Sabbath, who continued to tour and record similar albums for nearly 30 years, have selected listings because their latter-day records proved the law of diminishing returns, both commercially and creatively. By listing the highlights, we are attempting to sort out the highlights in their lengthy, occasionally convoluted discography. When records haven't been reviewed, they have been rated, providing a guideline to the album's worth. By providing both an artist's biography and a reviewed discography, *The All Music Guide to Rock* provides enough information to satisfy both the curious and the collector. There's a wildly diverse selection of artists and records within the book, showcasing the unpredictable evolutions of rock 'n' roll over its 40 years of existence. No matter your taste, you'll find something of interest within the book, and if you don't, take a look at our internet site (www.allmusic.com), which provides thorough discographies and extensive biographies for an even larger variety of artists.

The All Music Guide to Rock has been culled from a much larger database that is available in several electronic formats. *The All Music Guide* is constantly updated and corrected, so if you spot any mistakes or inconsistencies, please contact us.

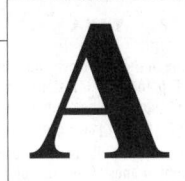

Aaliyah (Aaliyah Haughton)

b. Jan. 16, 1979, Brooklyn, NY, d. Aug. 25, 2001, Abaco, The Bahamas
Vocals / Contemporary R&B, Urban, Dance-Pop, Hip-Hop
Contemporary R&B singer Aaliyah (born Aaliyah Haughton) became an overnight sensation in 1994 with her debut album, *Age Ain't Nothing But a Number*, and its two hit singles, "Back and Forth" and "At Your Best (You Are Love)." Born in Brooklyn but raised in Detroit, she was influenced by an entertainment background—her mother was a singer, her uncle an entertainment lawyer once married to Gladys Knight. She appeared in concert with Knight at the age of 11, and released her first album just four years later. Paced by the Top Ten hits "Back & Forth" and "At Your Best (You Are Love)" (the latter an Isley Brothers cover), 1994's *Age Ain't Nothing But a Number* became a multi-platinum smash. She endured controversy near the end of the year, however, when news broke of her marriage at the age of 15 to her producer, R. Kelly.

After severing her ties with Kelly, Aaliyah resurfaced in 1996 with her second album, *One in a Million*. Collaborating with rising production stars Timbaland and Missy Misdemeanor Elliott, Aaliyah pointed the way for the minimalist hip-hop of the late '90s with hits like "One in a Million" and "If Your Girl Only Knew." By the end of the decade, she'd made the move to film, starring in *Romeo Must Die* with Jet Li and agreeing to appear in the projected pair of sequels to *The Matrix*. Just one month after her self-titled third album appeared in 2001, though, she died in a private-plane crash while returning from a video shoot in the Bahamas. —*Stephen Thomas Erlewine*

Age Ain't Nothing But a Number / 1994 / Blackground/Jive ✦✦✦✦

Aaliyah has a pleasant voice, but the real reason the teenager's debut album, *Age Ain't Nothing But A Number*, was a hit is the radio-ready production courtesy of R. Kelly, her husband. Kelly wraps Aaliyah's voice in layers of lush synths and deep grooves, while adding songs that are frequently better than the ones on his own album, *12 Play*. *Age* may have its share of filler, but its singles are slyly seductive. —*Stephen Thomas Erlewine*

One in a Million / Aug. 27, 1996 / Blackground ✦✦✦✦✦

Aaliyah's second album doesn't necessarily prove that she is indeed *One In A Million* but it does showcase more depth and talent than her acclaimed debut. That's not only due to the greater variety of material on *One In A Million*, or to the way that her producers (Vincent Herbert, Jermaine Dupri, and many others) immaculately produce each track, but it is also due to the fact that Aaliyah's singing is smoother, more seductive, and stronger than before. It might not be the commercial juggernaut of *Age Ain't Nothin' But A Number*, but *One In A Million* is a more consistently satisfying album. —*Leo Stanley*

- ### Aaliyah / Jul. 17, 2001 / Blackground ✦✦✦✦✦

Aaliyah waited nearly five years to deliver her third album, but considering that she was essentially growing up—it was the equivalent of spending time in college—when she came back with an eponymous record in the summer of 2001, she came back strong. *Aaliyah* isn't just a statement of maturity and a stunning artistic leap forward, it is one of the strongest urban soul records of its time. Where such peers as Macy Gray and Jill Scott work too hard to establish their ties with classic soul, Aaliyah revels in the present, turning out a pan-cultural array of sounds, styles, and emotions. This sound is entirely unfamiliar—part of the pleasure is how contemporary it sounds—but she sounds just as comfortable within the sonicscapes of Timbaland as Missy Misdemeanor Elliott and, possibly, less self-conscious. Aaliyah never oversings, never oversells the songs—this comes on easy and sultry, and there's a lot of substance here, in terms of the songwriting and the songs themselves. Urban albums rarely come any better than this, and there haven't been many records better than this in 2001, period. —*Stephen Thomas Erlewine*

ABBA

f. 1971, Stockholm, Sweden, db. 1983
Swedish Pop/Rock, Euro-Dance, Pop/Rock, Euro-Pop
The most commercially successful pop group of the 1970s, ABBA comprised singer Agnetha Faltskog, keyboardist/vocalist Benny Andersson, guitarist/vocalist Bjorn Ulvaeus, and singer Anni-Frid Lyngstad. In 1972, the duo of Andersson and Ulvaeus had scored a massive international hit with "People Need Love," which featured Faltskog and Lyngstad on backing vocals. The record's success earned them an invitation to enter the Swedish leg of the 1973 Eurovision song contest, where, under the unwieldy name of Bjorn, Benny, Agnetha & Frida, they submitted "Ring Ring," which proved extremely popular with audiences but placed only third in the judges' ballots. The next year, rechristened ABBA (an acronym of the members' first names), the quartet submitted the single "Waterloo," and became the first Swedish act to win the Eurovision competition. In 1975, ABBA issued "S.O.S.," a smash not only in America and Britain but also in non-English speaking countries such as Spain, Germany, and the Benelux nations, where the group's success was fairly unprecedented. A string of hits followed, including "Mamma Mia,"

"Fernando," and "Dancing Queen" (ABBA's sole U.S. chart-topper), further honing their lush, buoyant sound. ABBA's popularity continued in 1977, when both "Knowing Me, Knowing You" and "The Name of the Game" dominated airwaves. A year later, Andersson and Lyngstad married, as had Ulvaeus and Faltskog in 1971, although the latter couple separated a few months later; in fact, romantic suffering was the subject of many songs on the quartet's next LP, 1979's *Voulez-Vous*. Shortly after the release of 1980's *Super Trouper*, Andersson and Lyngstad divorced as well, further straining the group dynamic; *The Visitors*, issued the following year, was the final LP of new ABBA material, and the foursome officially disbanded after the December 1982 release of the "Under Attack" single. —*Jason Ankeny*

Ring Ring / 1973 / Polygram ✦✦

This, the first album by the group later called ABBA (they were called Bjorn, Benny, Agnetha & Frida at the time), originally was released only in Sweden; England and America didn't show any interest until the group won the Eurovision Song Contest with "Waterloo" the following year, although "Ring Ring" had been a hit in several other countries. It's clear that this team has spent a lot of time listening to albums like *Abbey Road* and *Honky Chateau*, not to mention *Sweet Baby James*. But they've also been absorbing a broad range of the pop charts of the late '60s and early '70s. At the same time, they haven't put together the ABBA sound yet. For one thing, the men sing almost as much as the women, and for another, Benny Andersson and Bjorn Ulvaeus have underproduced the recordings, even as they have overarranged the music. [Eventually released in Europe, *Ring Ring* has not been released officially in the U.S., although import copies are readily available.] —*William Ruhlmann*

Waterloo / 1974 / Polygram ✦✦✦

ABBA's second (and U.S. debut) album contains the American Top Ten title track, as well as "Honey, Honey," a minor U.S. hit that deserved better. This album is rather unusual in the group's output, however, for the fact that the guys are still featured fairly prominently in some of the vocals, and for the variety of sounds, including reggae, folk-rock, and hard rock, embraced by its 11 songs. The reggae number "Sitting in the Palm Tree" is quite remarkable to hear, with its perfect Caribbean beat and those radiant female voices carrying the chorus behind the beat. "King Kong Song" is a good example of hard rock by rote, going through the motions of screaming vocals and over-amplified guitar (courtesy of Janne Schaffer), although even here, when the womens' voices jump in on the choruses, it's hard not to listen attentively; the quartet knew what a powerful weapon they had, but not quite how to use it. They get a little closer to their winning formula on the catchy, folky-textured pop song "Hasta Manana," which sounds like a lost Mary Hopkin number. "Dance (While the Music Still Goes On)" is on the money, as the embodiment of the Euro-disco sound that the group would move in the millions on their coming albums, although it also embraces a vague oldies sound, with a melody that somehow reminds this listener of both the Four Seasons' "Dawn" and the Beach Boys' "Don't Worry Baby." [The 1999 PolyGram remastering adds no songs but is still a significant improvement over the original LP or earlier CD editions—the vocals are stunningly clear and glistening ("Honey, Honey" is particularly ravishing), and the instruments finally get their due.] —*Bruce Eder*

ABBA / 1975 / Polygram ✦✦✦

ABBA appears on the cover of this album sitting in the back of a limousine and drinking champagne, which may have been intended as an ironic comment on their one-hit wonder status at the time but became an apt reflection of their status after this record's success. The lead-off track is the irresistible "Mamma Mia," their second U.K. chart topper and a U.S. Top 40 hit, and also included are the equally catchy "SOS" (Top Ten in Britain, Top 40 in America) and the minor U.K. hit "I Do, I Do, I Do, I Do, I Do," which actually did better in the U.S. —*William Ruhlmann*

Arrival / Jan. 1977 / Polygram ✦✦✦✦✦

ABBA's fourth album of new material appeared after the group had "arrived" as major stars. It featured "Dancing Queen," a tame disco number that went number one in both the U.S. and U.K., as well as "Knowing Me, Knowing You (another U.K. number one that hit the Top 40 in the U.S.) and a third single, "Money Money Money." The 1999 remastered edition (part of Polydor's *The ABBA Remasters* series) in 24-bit digital audio is a significant improvement over earlier CD or LP editions, bringing out not only stunning richness and radiance in the vocals by Faltskog and Lyngstad, but also Rutger Gunnarsson's especially muscular bass playing throughout the album and the rich texture of Bjorn Ulvaeus' acoustic guitar on "When I Kissed the Teacher," Lasse Wellander's acoustic rhythm guitar on "Dum Dum Diddle," and the rippling electric guitar and keyboard textures of "Knowing Me, Knowing You"—Wellander's power chords over the chorus of the latter song is one of those dramatic musical effects that this group played for maximum effect and gave their music a raw power that their detractors usually overlooked. Some of this clarity is wasted on disco numbers that now seem to have relatively little point, though they are catchy and have a relentless beat, but that's what the group was about at this point in their history—and the sheer presence of the bass drums behind the choruses on "Tiger" will be pretty impressive to any noise freaks. — *William Ruhlmann/Bruce Eder*

The Album / Feb. 1978 / Polygram ◆◆◆◆

ABBA's fifth album continued its phenomenal international success, featuring the U.K. number ones "The Name of the Game" and "Take a Chance on Me" and achieving ABBA's highest ever showing in the U.S. LP charts: it reached the Top 20 and sold a million copies in six months. *The Album* was unusually progressive by the standards of this group, opening with the decidedly dramatic, six-minute long synthesizer-dominated "Eagle" (almost an art rock track), before giving way to the hit "Take a Chance on Me." Even the latter, with its luminous a cappella opening, was rather bold in its exploiting of the group's established strengths. Despite its hit status, "The Name of the Game" was never as strong or interesting a cut as "Take a Chance on Me," and there are better tracks surrounding it, including "Move On," which has a better beat and more impressive harmonizing, and "Hole in Your Soul" (which is a rare guitar showcase for Lasse Wellander's lead electric playing). "Girl With the Golden Hair" shows ABBA move into the realm of Broadway-style material, courtesy of Andersson and Ulvaeus's aspirations to compose in that direction: "Thank You for the Music" became a popular stage number, but is rather flat as a studio recording; "I Wonder" is rather dullish; and "I'm a Marionette" seems like an attempt (only partly successful) to recast the vague influence of Kurt Weill in a hard rock mode. — *Bruce Eder & William Ruhlmann*

Voulez-Vous / Jun. 1979 / Polygram ◆◆

Internationally, it was business as usual for ABBA on its sixth studio album, which included the hits "Voulez-Vous," "I Have a Dream," "Angeleyes," "Does Your Mother Know," and "Chiquitita," all of which made the U.K. Top Five. But America had begun to lose interest; the album stopped at gold (500, 000 copies), with only "Chiquitita" getting into the Top 40. — *William Ruhlmann*

Super Trouper / Dec. 1980 / Polygram ◆◆◆◆

Always pop-savvy, ABBA took account of the passing of disco with this release and moved back toward the pop-rock sound more typical of their early albums with this, their seventh. They were rewarded with their last big U.S. hit, "The Winner Takes It All," plus two more American chart entries and an uptick in album sales. In the U.K., they continued to roll along, with the title track becoming their final NumberOne single. — *William Ruhlmann*

The Visitors / 1981 / Polygram ◆◆◆◆

ABBA's swan song was also perhaps their most musically sophisticated album. Although it was short on big hits ("The Visitors" and "When All Is Said and Done" charted in the U.S., "One of Us" and "Head Over Heels" in the U.K., with only "One of Us" making the Top Ten), it was a consistent record imbued with a sense of the pressures that were splitting the group (the title track was subtitled "Crackin' Up"). — *William Ruhlmann*

The Singles: The First Ten Years / 1982 / Polygram ◆◆◆◆◆

This 23-track double LP contains 16 of ABBA's 20 U.S. chart entries and 22 of their 25 U.K. hits. Especially notable are the group's final new single, "Under Attack," and the terrific ballad "The Day Before You Came," which had previously appeared in the U.S. only as a non-LP B-side. This collection supersedes the previous *Greatest Hits* albums, and, since ABBA was a singles band, captures their essence. — *William Ruhlmann*

ABBA Live / 1986 / Polygram ◆◆◆◆

This recording is often underrated, and might seem superfluous in the wake of the release of the group's various hits compilations on CD, but it does have merits. Drawn from three distinct sets of performances, in Australia (1977), London's Wembley Arena (1979), and the television special *Dick Cavett Meets ABBA* (1981), the quartet proves that they could recreate their recordings on stage with a few improvements. The beat is more urgent on most of the numbers (most especially "Dancing Queen," "Take a Chance on Me," and "Does Your Mother Know"—the live version of the latter, in particular, puts the studio rendition to shame), and the singers lose none of their elegance, even as they benefit from the immediacy of live work (albeit in front of upwards of 50,000 people, rather impersonal). The song selection on this 14-track CD makes it virtually a live greatest-hits package, and at mid-price that's not a bad thing. Further, the 1999 Polydor remastering, as part of "The ABBA Remasters" series, brings out the same rippling instrumental textures that highlighted their studio sides, from the acoustic opening of "I Have a Dream" to the throbbing bass of "Gimme Gimme Gimme," except that the arrangements are all tighter here, and the singing is never less than stunning (and none of it sounds redubbed). This is the kind of recording that CDs were created to enhance. — *Bruce Eder*

More ABBA Gold / Jun. 1, 1993 / Polygram ◆◆◆

The multi-million unit sales of *ABBA Gold* led to the creation of this 20-song compilation, containing the remaining singles from the group plus other notable tracks. None of what's here is as tuneful or compelling as the group's most successful recordings—though the arrangements and, especially, the vocals are, as always, almost idealized in their crystalline purity—and most of the tracks won't be familiar to listeners in all countries, since a number were hits in specific limited national markets. At the time, in 1993, the sound was an improvement over the existing CDs on which the tracks appeared, although, like *ABBA Gold*, this collection is crying for fresh remastering in 24-bit audio. — *Bruce Eder*

★ **Gold: Greatest Hits** / Aug. 9, 1993 / Polygram ◆◆◆◆◆

This 19-song collection was the first hits compilation prepared specifically for the CD format by the 1970s supergroup, and, appearing after a period of several years in which ABBA's music had been off the market, was a welcome addition to the catalog. It is still the simplest and most straightforward collection of the group's material that it is possible to buy, but there is a negative consideration—for reasons best understood by their record label, in contrast to virtually the entire rest of the group's CD catalog (even the Spanish-

language compilation *Oro: Grand Exitos* and the live album), it has never been remastered to modern standards. Thus, the songs that most fans and casual listeners want to hear—all of the worldwide international hits—are present, but don't sound remotely as good as they do on the upgraded individual CDs (in cases where they appear on those CDs). And lest anyone think that considerations of 24-bit sound aren't too important with a group like this, most of ABBA's songs featured meticulous productions, arrangements, and playing, and very strong singing, all of which are enhanced on the remasterings that have surfaced. — *Bruce Eder*

Thank You for the Music [Box] / Apr. 18, 1995 / Polygram ◆◆◆◆◆

Released in Europe in October 1994 and in the U.S. six months later, *Thank You for the Music* is the ABBA box-set retrospective, tracing their 10 years of record making, 1972-1982, including 52 previously released tracks on the first three discs, plus a fourth disc of rarities. Listening to all the singles, plus scattered album tracks and B-sides, provides a clear picture of the group's development. Early on, there is considerable stylistic experimentation, as these pop dabblers ape everything from Phil Spector's "Wall of Sound" rock to big-band swing. But after "Dancing Queen," they find their niche in disco, and the second disc is loaded with hit songs anchored to the familiar bass-heavy walking beat and swooping synths-meant-to-sound-like-strings that defined that most '70s of genres. On the third disc, covering their last years, ABBA returns to the more propulsive pop/rock of early classics like "SOS" and "Mamma Mia," revving up the tempo in acknowledgment of the arrival of new wave. Wracked by romantic discord, they also achieve somewhat more meaningful lyrics before calling it a day. In the album's liner notes, the band members register mild protest at the inclusion of unreleased material on the fourth disc—what they finished and liked, they released, they note. Fair warning. Most prominent in a collection of alternate takes, miscellaneous B-sides, foreign-language recordings, and TV soundtracks is the 23-and-a-half-minute "ABBA Undeleted," a medley of 15 song fragments and Swedish studio chatter that suggests ABBA had a few more hits in them if they had found the time to finish them off. Nevertheless, this remains fan-only material. [This album is not to be confused with the 1983 compilation of the same title released by Epic Records in the U.K.] — *William Ruhlmann*

20th Century Masters—The Millennium Collection: The Best of ABBA / Sep. 26, 2000 / Polydor ◆◆◆

The Millennium Collection: The Best of ABBA condenses the group's hits into an 11-song best-of-the-best compilation that includes "Waterloo," "Dancing Queen," "Take a Chance on Me," and "S.O.S." "Mamma Mia," "Fernando," and "The Winner Takes It All" are some of the other highlights of this brief but enjoyable collection, which may please casual fans that lack the patience for *Gold*'s 19 tracks. — *Heather Phares*

ABC

f. 1980, Sheffield, Yorkshire, England
New Romantic, Pop/Rock, New Wave, Synth Pop, Dance-Pop

One of the more popular new wave bands of the early '80s, the British group ABC built upon the detached, synthesized R&B pop of David Bowie and Roxy Music, adding a self-conscious, campy sense of theatrics and style. Under the direction of vocalist Martin Fry, the group scored several catchy, synth-driven dance-pop hits in the early '80s, including "Poison Arrow," "Look of Love," and "Be Near Me." ABC formed when Fry joined a pre-existing band including guitarist Mark White, then steered it in a more pop-oriented direction. By the fall of 1981, ABC hit the British charts with their first single, "Tears Are Not Enough." Two singles, "Poison Arrow" and "The Look of Love," became Top Ten hits one year later, paving the way for their debut album, *The Lexicon of Love*, to enter the charts at number one. The harder, guitar-driven *Beauty Stab* didn't perform as well as the debut, and by 1985, Fry and White had moved to New York. Released at the beginning of 1985, the light, catchy "Be Near Me" became a hit single in both Britain and America, pushing the third ABC LP *How to Be A . . . Zillionaire!* into the charts as well. In the summer of 1987, ABC released the Motown tribute "When Smokey Sings," their biggest hit in America. *Alphabet City* followed that fall, and in 1989, they released *Up*, which only charted in the U.K. Following an extended break, Fry returned in 1997 with a revamped ABC and a new album, *Skyscraping*. — *Stephen Thomas Erlewine*

★ **The Lexicon of Love** / 1982 / Mercury ◆◆◆◆◆

ABC's stylish debut successfuly melded the cool detachment of Bryan Ferry and David Bowie with a more pop-oriented production than either Roxy Music or Bowie. Even if the songs tended to blend together over the course of the album, the record was successful, scoring two hits with "The Look of Love" and "Poison Arrow." — *Stephen Thomas Erlewine*

Beauty Stab / 1983 / Mercury ◆◆◆

For their second album, ABC toned down the synths and turned up the guitars, making an inconsistent set of rocking, Roxy-styled pop that does have its impressive moments, particularly the single "That Was Then but This Is Now." — *Stephen Thomas Erlewine*

How to Be A . . . Zillionaire! / 1985 / Mercury ◆◆◆◆◆

Moving away from the guitar histrionics of *Beauty Stab*, Martin Fry reduced ABC to a duo of himself and Mark White for 1985's danceable *How to Be a . . . Zillionaire!* Incorporating light hip-hop rhythms, ABC made sure *Zillionaire* sounded contemporary for mid-'80s dance clubs, and, as a result, some of the record sounds stiff and dated. Still, when Fry's sense of melody is on, as on the catchy single "Be Near Me," or when he works in his vicious, cynical wit, as on "How to Be a Millionaire" and "So Hip It Hurts," the record rivals the peaks of *Lexicon of Love*. — *Stephen Thomas Erlewine*

Alphabet City / 1987 / Mercury ◆◆◆

Returning to the Motown and Northern soul that provided the basis of their debut album, ABC turned to the pop songcraft on their fifth album, *Alphabet City*. The increased songcraft is certainly engaging, particularly on the hit "When Smokey Sings," but the songs are usually indistinguishable from each other, resulting in a sleek, stylish, and thoroughly entertaining album that leaves no lasting memory. *—Stephen Thomas Erlewine*

Up / Oct. 30, 1989 / Mercury ✦✦

Absolutely ABC: The Best of ABC / Aug. 1990 / Mercury ✦✦✦✦✦
Absolutely ABC: The Best of ABC is a terrific 13-track collection of the synth-pop band's greatest hits, featuring all of the group's necessary singles. Without concentrating too heavily on any particular album, each of the group's first five albums are represented by their highlights, so *Absolutely ABC* functions as a fine overview, containing every song a casual fan could want ("Poison Arrow," "The Look of Love," "Tears Are Not Enough," "That Was Then But This Is Now," "How to Be a Millionaire," "Be Near Me," "When Smokey Sings"), even if *The Lexicon of Love* remains a better encapsulation of what the band was all about. [The CD version of *Absolutely* contains four unnecessary remixes of four of the group's biggest hits.] *—Stephen Thomas Erlewine*

Abracadabra / Oct. 1991 / MCA ✦✦

Skyscraping / Mar. 1997 / Deconstruction ✦✦✦
After spending half the better part of a decade in semi-retirement, Martin Fry regrouped ABC for the surprisingly successful comeback *Skyscraping*. Instead of pursuing the dance-pop inclinations of ABC's late-'80s records, Fry returns to the grandly theatrical new romantic pop of *Lexicon of Love*, cutting it with some contemporary dance production techniques. Collaborating with Heaven 17's Glenn Gregory, Fry constructs a number of shiny pop gems, highlighted by glammy guitars and shining synthesizers. While *Skyscraping* isn't as consistently thrilling as his best '80s singles, it has a number of fine moments, and is ABC's best record since *How to Be a Zillionaire*. *—Stephen Thomas Erlewine*

20th Century Masters—The Millennium Collection: The Best of ABC / Jun. 27, 2000 / Mercury ✦✦✦✦
The Millennium Collection: The Best of ABC gathers the tracks that defined their witty, theatrical synth-pop sound. All the expected hits are here, including the *Lexicon of Love* singles "Poison Arrow," "The Look of Love (Part One)," "All of My Heart," and "Tears Are Not Enough," as well as the Top Ten hits "Be Near Me" and "When Smokey Sings." Album tracks like "S.O.S." and remixes such as "Vanity Kills (The Abigails Party Mix)" round out this concise retrospective, which wisely concentrates on ABC's first four albums. Though it's not as complete a look at the band as *Absolutely ABC*, *The Best of ABC* is a worthwhile option for casual fans. *—Heather Phares*

Paula Abdul

b. Jun. 19, 1962, Los Angeles, CA
Vocals / Club/Dance, Adult Contemporary, Urban, Dance-Pop
In the wake of Madonna's success, many dance-pop divas filled the charts, but out of them all, Paula Abdul was the only one that sustained a career. The former L.A. Lakers cheerleader and choreographer began to make inroads in pop music when she was hired as an assistant dance director on the Jacksons' "Victory" tour, which led to a job choreographing Janet Jackson's videos for *Control*. Abdul's work on Jackson's videos helped make the album a hit, making her a sought-after choreographer. She released her debut album, *Forever Your Girl*, in 1988; the single "Straight Up" made her a superstar, beginning a string of six number one singles that ran through the summer of 1991. Abdul's singles were hits not because her singing was exceptional—her voice is thin and transparent—but because she worked with savvy producers who had a knack for picking songs with solid pop and dance hooks. Abdul's spectacular big-budget videos helped push the sales of *Forever Your Girl* past seven million in the U.S. alone. While her second album, 1991's *Spellbound*, wasn't as successful, it still sold over three million copies and spent two weeks at number one. *—Stephen Thomas Erlewine*

Forever Your Girl / Jun. 1988 / Virgin ✦✦✦✦
Singer/dancer/choreographer Paula Abdul hit the big time with the third single, "Straight Up," off this album, which sparked a string of hits that carried through to her follow-up. Despite having a slight voice, her voice is distinct and perfectly suited to this synthesized type of late-'80s dance-pop. "Cold Hearted" is insistent and catchy, "Forever Your Girl" is sweet and accessible, and "Opposites Attract" gives Abdul a chance to spar with the Wild Pair. There is some filler—"Next to You," for example—that doesn't age as well as the better material, but overall this is a consistent album with some great pop-dance songs. Unfortunately, as Abdul and her material matured, her audience waned. *—Bryan Buss*

Spellbound / May 1991 / Captive/Virgin ✦✦✦
The reason Paula Abdul was one of the handful of pop-dance artists of her time to actually have a career is that her production is so good that 10-15 years later it stands as the embodiment of late-'80s pop without being a parody of itself. And with this, her second album, she reinforces the upbeat personality she expressed on *Forever Your Girl* while showing growth as well. "Promise of a New Day," "Rock House," and John Hiatt's "Alright Tonight" are bouncy and joyous, much like some of the bright hits from her debut, but she adds a funky techno edge with "Vibeology," and "Will You Marry Me?" skates that thin line between sweet and precious. Additionally, Abdul adds better and more ballads to this CD. Smartly, her production team has put together sweeping, adult love songs (the hits "Rush Rush" and "Blowing Kisses in the Wind") that help give her strong crossover appeal to adult contemporary without alienating her original fan base. Not many artists hit the mark twice in terms of commercial and critical appeal, but Abdul was savvy enough to choose strong material (much of which was co-written by Abdul herself, Peter Lord, Sandra St. Victor, and V. Jeffrey Smith) and smart producers (including Lord, Smith, and Don Was). This was a safe follow-up to a massively successful debut, and surprisingly enough for a pop star, the baby steps she took toward becoming a respected artist were sure and solidly embraced. *—Bryan Buss*

Head over Heels / Jun. 13, 1995 / Captive/Virgin ✦✦

● **The Greatest Hits** / Sep. 26, 2000 / Virgin ✦✦✦✦
The only Paula Abdul album most listeners will need, *Greatest Hits* gathers *almost* all the singles from her first three albums in one place. The 16 tracks here include an amazing run of eight consecutive Top Ten hits, six of which reached number one, over a span of approximately three years (before more soulful, urban sounds began to conquer Abdul's audience). In most cases, the versions included are the 7" single edits, which often differed from the album cuts and are hence quite nice to have collected. The only questionable choice is that the Top 20 single "Will You Marry Me?" was left off in favor of an unnecessary "Megamix Medley," but it's hard to imagine most fans finding this anything more than a minor flaw. The songs still sound as slick and hyper-produced as ever, but they're also catchy and well-constructed, and it's no surprise they were hits in their era (which, nostalgia buffs will find, they evoke very well). All in all, a nicely executed package. *—Steve Huey*

AC/DC

f. 1973, Sydney, Australia
Aussie Rock, Album Rock, Arena Rock, Heavy Metal, Hard Rock
AC/DC's mammoth power-chord roar became one of the most influential hard rock sounds of the '70s. In its own way, it was a reaction against the pompous art rock and lumbering stadium rock of the early '70s. AC/DC's rock was minimalist—no matter how huge and bludgeoning the guitar chords were, there was a clear sense of space and restraint. Combined with Bon Scott's larynx-shredding vocals, the band spawned countless imitators over the next two decades. AC/DC was formed in 1973 in Australia by guitarist Malcolm Young, with his younger brother Angus as lead guitarist. When Scott joined in 1974 (the year the group released its first album in Australia), he helped cement the group's image as brutes—he had several convictions on minor criminal offenses and was rejected by the Australian army for being "socially maladjusted." And AC/DC *was* socially maladjusted. Throughout their career, they favored crude double entendres and violent imagery, all spiked with a mischievous sense of fun. What really broke the doors down for the band was 1979's *Highway to Hell*, which became their first million-seller. However, AC/DC's train was nearly derailed when Bon Scott died on February 20, 1980. The official coroner's report stated that he had "drunk himself to death." The band quickly replaced Scott with Brian Johnson and recorded *Back in Black*, which would prove to be their biggest album, selling over ten million copies in the U.S. alone. For the next few years, AC/DC was one of the biggest rock bands in the world, with *For Those About to Rock We Salute You* topping the charts in the U.S. After 1983's *Flick of the Switch*, the band's commercial standing began to slip; they were able to reverse their slide with 1990's *The Razor's Edge*, which spawned the hits "Moneytalks" and "Thunderstruck." While they haven't proved to be the commercial powerhouse they were during the late '70s and early '80s, the '90s have seen them maintain their status as a top international concert draw, and they continued to record into the new millennium. *—Stephen Thomas Erlewine*

High Voltage / Oct. 1976 / Atco ✦✦✦✦✦
AC/DC's debut album, *High Voltage*, is a stripped-down collection of loud, raw, rude rockers, mostly odes to rock & roll and its attendant hard-partying lifestyle—to paraphrase the leadoff track "It's a Long Way to the Top (If You Wanna Rock & Roll)," getting drunk, stoned, beat up, and laid. The band reveled in its own macho obnoxiousness, particularly Bon Scott; at the end of the gleefully sexist, double-entendre-filled "The Jack," Scott grandiosely thanks a hostile, booing dubbed-in crowd. While their sense of humor and clever wordplay made early AC/DC a great deal of sleazy, infectious fun, the band's revolutionary musical attack could not be overlooked—Angus Young's manic guitar solos overlaid a series of simple, basic boogie grooves delivered with ferocious power and volume, a sound that made the band a popular attraction at British punk clubs around this same time. The formula would be refined on subsequent albums, but *High Voltage* proves that AC/DC was already in the big leagues. *—Steve Huey*

Let There Be Rock / Jun. 1977 / Atco ✦✦✦✦✦
Let There Be Rock kicks up the energy level a notch from its predecessor, making for a bracing hard rock record of blasting guitar and basic, aggressive grooves. While slightly more metallic, AC/DC's sound was still bluesier than it would be by the time of their commercial breakthrough. Appealing in spite of himself, Bon Scott delivers his leering double entendres and humorous asides with typical panache, while the Young brothers' guitars bite, kick, and scratch behind him. While the music still meanders on occasion, the songwriting is overall a bit more memorable; AC/DC classics on hand include "Problem Child," "Whole Lotta Rosie," and "Bad Boy Boogie." *—Steve Huey*

Powerage / May 1978 / Atco ✦✦✦
AC/DC's third U.S. release, 1978's *Powerage*, followed the blueprint set by 1977's *Let There Be Rock*—tales of the hard life merged with lethal, cranked-to-ten, unpolished hard rock. It also marked the studio debut of bassist Cliff Williams (who replaced Mark Evans), which would unfortunately prove not to be the last time a member of the band would be replaced—due to either choice, or in Bon Scott's case, death. Although *Powerage* contains only one true AC/DC classic, the gloriously sleazy anthem "Sin City," the album's lesser-known material is often just as exhilarating. Both "Rock & Roll Damnation" and "Riff Raff" would be featured in concert on the ensuing tour, while "Down Payment Blues," "Gimme a Bullet," and especially "What's Next to the Moon" remain among AC/DC's most underrated rockers. The album's last few songs are obviously filler, but it doesn't prevent *Powerage* from being an early AC/DC classic. *Powerage* would also prove to be the last album produced by Vanda and Young for nearly ten years; the band's next few

mega-hit releases featured newcomer Robert John "Mutt" Lange behind the boards. —*Greg Prato*

If You Want Blood You've Got It / Dec. 1978 / Atco ✦✦✦

AC/DC was fast becoming one of rock's top live acts by the late '70s. Few others could match the band's electrifying live performances: Angus Young's never-ending energy and wise-ass antics, Bon Scott's whiskey-soaked vocals, and the rest of the band's penchant for nailing simple, yet extremely effective and memorable, riffs and grooves. While most other rock bands of the era were busy experimenting with disco or creating studio-perfected epics, AC/DC was one of the few specializing in raw and bluesy hard rock, as evidenced by 1978's live set, *If You Want Blood You've Got It*. Recorded during their world tour in support of their *Powerage* album, *If You Want Blood* contains many of AC/DC's best compositions up until that point: "Bad Boy Boogie" (complete with the break-down section in which Young would "strip"), "The Jack," "Problem Child," "Whole Lotta Rosie," "High Voltage," "Let There Be Rock," and "Rocker." Strangely, their early anthem "Sin City" was not included, and there's a slight sense of studio enhancement on certain tracks. While the first disc of the 1997 box set *Bonfire* is the best document of live Bon Scott-era AC/DC ("Live From the Atlantic Studios"), *If You Want Blood You've Got It* is highly recommended. —*Greg Prato*

☆ Highway to Hell / Aug. 1979 / Atco ✦✦✦✦✦

Given that Bon Scott's hard-partying, sex-booze-and-brawls lifestyle tragically caught up with him some six months after *Highway to Hell* was released, the album-opening title track—one of hard rock's all-time classics—now takes on an eerie resonance. It's not just a snotty, nihilistic party anthem, but a moment of unrepentant self-recognition from a rowdy ruffian who, for better or worse, exulted in what he was. The rest of the songs on *Highway to Hell* don't lend themselves to any deep readings, but of course, that's not the point. *Highway to Hell* distilled all the virtues of AC/DC's signature minimalism—loud, simple, pounding riffs and grooving backbeats—into the tightest batch of songs the group had written to that point, barreling along at a take-no-prisoners rate and producing a handful of gems ["Girl's Got Rhythm," "If You Want Blood (You've Got It)"] along the way. *Highway to Hell* is not only a fitting epitaph for Bon Scott, it's also a classic rock & roll album. —*Steve Huey*

★ Back in Black / Aug. 1980 / Atco ✦✦✦✦✦

Bon Scott's alcohol-related death in early 1980 couldn't have come at a worse time for AC/DC; the band was poised for worldwide breakthrough success, as their last album, *Highway to Hell*, was Angus and company's first gold-certified stateside release. They made an excellent choice in selecting Brian Johnson as their new vocalist; while he had the same bluesy edge as Scott, Johnson sang with more power and conviction. The first album from the new group, *Back in Black*, was issued only five months after Scott's passing but immediately rocketed up the charts, eventually becoming one of rock's all-time classics. By 1997, it had sold an astounding 16 million copies in the U.S. alone. Musically, the band hadn't changed much, although producer "Mutt" Lange helped the group focus their high voltage rock. The result was such perennial rock anthems as the stomping title track, the eerie "Hell's Bells," the melodic "Shoot to Thrill," the album-closing battle cry "Rock & Roll Ain't Noise Pollution," and one of AC/DC's best and most recognizable tracks, "You Shook Me All Night Long." Not a single weak track is included, even the lesser-known album tracks are strong ("Have a Drink on Me," "Shake a Leg,"). *Back in Black* is the ultimate example of a band turning a career-threatening negative into a remarkable positive and stands alongside such landmark albums as *Van Halen*, *Led Zeppelin II*, *Are You Experienced?*, and *Paranoid* as hard rock's greatest achievements. Rock music rarely gets better than *Back in Black*. —*Greg Prato*

☆ Dirty Deeds Done Dirt Cheap / Apr. 1981 / Atco ✦✦✦✦✦

Originally released in 1975, *Dirty Deeds Done Dirt Cheap* did not hit the U.S. until 1981, when AC/DC became rock icons the previous year and fans were growing hungry for more material featuring the band's late singer, Bon Scott. Overall, the record is worth the wait, even if there is absolutely no reason to place "Problem Child" on the album since it was placed on *Let There Be Rock*. The title track became a concert staple for the band, but *Dirty Deeds*' most well-known track is arguably "Big Balls," a sleazy, ambiguous number that would become one of the band's most well-recognized songs. The album's greatest artistic moment, however, comes in the form of "Ride On," where AC/DC experiments with a slow, rhythmic blues ballad. The song, highlighted by the Keith Richards-inspired licks of Angus Young and the haunting, melancholy lyrics of Bon Scott, shows AC/DC in a rare sensitive form yet manages to retain the raw power that has since become the band's trademark ("Ride On" would be the only Bon Scott-era song to be placed on the 1986 compilation *Who Made Who*). On the whole, *Dirty Deeds* is a fine album with some nice treats for diehards. Though it may not be as well-crafted as the in-memory-of-Bon classic *Back in Black*, *Dirty Deeds Done Dirt Cheap* is another fitting eulogy to one of hard rock's most influential vocalists. —*Barry Weber*

For Those About to Rock We Salute You / Nov. 1981 / Atco ✦✦✦

AC/DC's hot streak began to draw to a close with *For Those About to Rock We Salute You*. While *Back in Black* was infused with the energy and spirit of paying tribute to Bon Scott, it became apparent on the follow-up that the group really did miss Scott more than it initially indicated. Brian Johnson's lyrics started to seem more calculated and a bit cliched, lacking Scott's devil-may-care sense of humor. And the band itself slows down the tempo frequently, sounding less aggressive and inspired. There is still some decent material here—the title track became a concert staple with cannon-firing sound effects—but overall, *For Those About to Rock* ushers in the band's long '80s slump. —*Steve Huey*

Flick of the Switch / Aug. 1983 / Atco ✦✦

For *Flick of the Switch*, AC/DC jettisoned producer "Mutt" Lange in an attempt to recapture the rawness and simplicity of their early records. While they more or less succeed

in terms of the record's sound, and show more energy than on the preceding *For Those About to Rock (We Salute You)*, the songs themselves suffer—AC/DC's music has always been simple, but here it sounds underdeveloped and unmemorable. As perhaps indicated by the record's idiotic original title, the utterly generic *I Like to Rock*, AC/DC seemed to be running out of ideas at an alarming rate, and their record sales began to reflect that fact. —*Steve Huey*

'74 Jailbreak / 1984 / Atco ✦✦✦

Despite longtime AC/DC fans' immediate acceptance of replacement singer Brian Johnson (resulting in one of rock's all-time best sellers, 1980's *Back in Black*), there was still demand for Bon Scott-era unreleased tracks. Several of their early albums in Australia and Europe (such as *T.N.T.*) were later combined together for their first U.S. release, 1976's *High Voltage*, while several tracks were cut from the original versions and never issued stateside. 1984's five-song EP, *'74 Jailbreak*, features these forgotten tracks from the band's early days. "Jailbreak" automatically became a concert standard when the EP came out, and it remains a mystery why it wasn't released earlier. Also included is the largely instrumental "Soul Stripper," a cover of "Baby Please Don't Go," plus a pair of Angus Young-Malcolm Young-Scott originals: "You Ain't Got a Hold on Me" and the autobiographical "Show Business." Although *'74 Jailbreak* is by no means a definitive collection of early rarities (such compositions as "Fling Thing," "Love Song," "Stick Around," "R.I.P.-Rock in Peace," and "School Days" remain unreleased in the States), it is a worthwhile, brief snapshot of early AC/DC. —*Greg Prato*

Fly on the Wall / Jul. 1985 / Atco ✦✦

Who Made Who / May 1986 / Atco ✦✦✦

On paper, *Who Made Who* is just a cheap soundtrack to a cheap movie (Stephen King's disastrous *Maximum Overdrive*), but it's actually much more than that. It serves as a ripping AC/DC retrospective, tearing through such classics as "You Shook Me All Night Long" and "For Those About to Rock," adding the pounding title track to their canon, and rescuing overlooked songs like "Sink the Pink" from otherwise mediocre albums. It's not a perfect retrospective—there's no "Back in Black," "Highway to Hell," or "Dirty Deeds Done Dirt Cheap"—but what is here is terrific. —*Stephen Thomas Erlewine*

Blow Up Your Video / Feb. 1988 / Atco ✦✦✦

AC/DC remained a popular concert draw throughout the '80s, although such albums as *Flick of the Switch* and *Fly on the Wall* failed to replicate their mass U.S. commercial success of 1980-1981 (*Back in Black*, *For Those About to Rock*, a reissue of *Dirty Deeds*). But the successful soundtrack for Stephen King's lackluster movie *Maximum Overdrive*, titled *Who Made Who*, put AC/DC back on the right track commercially. Their first new studio album of all-new material in three years, 1988's *Blow Up Your Video* turned out to be their most successful album since 1981's *For Those About To Rock*, even though it was chock full of filler. The driving album opener, "Heatseeker," turned out to be a surprising Top Ten single in the U.K., while the anthemic "That's the Way I Want to Rock & Roll" proved to be another highlight (video clips were filmed for both songs, as well). But from there on (with the exception of "Kissin' Dynamite" and "This Means War"), it gets pretty unfocused. The album is glutted with such throwaways as "Nick of Time," "Ruff Stuff," and "Two's Up"—completely missing the point of what made such previous albums as *Back in Black* so great (they simply did not contain a weak moment). *Blow Up Your Video* also marked the return of AC/DC's early production team, Harry Vanda and George Young, who man the boards for the first time since 1978's *If You Want Blood*. —*Greg Prato*

The Razor's Edge / Sep. 1990 / Atco ✦✦✦

Although AC/DC's popularity had decreased by the early '90s, the band still had a lot of life left in it. Arguably the Australian headbangers' strongest album in over half a decade, *Razor's Edge* is quintessential AC/DC—rowdy, abrasive, unapologetically fun metal full of blistering power chords, memorable hooks and testosterone-driven lyrics. Lead singer Brian Johnson sounds more inspired than he had since 1983's *Flick of the Switch*, and lead guitarist Angus Young isn't about to take any prisoners on such hard-hitting material as "Shot of Love," the menacing title song and the appropriately titled "Got You by the Balls." Although not quite in a class with *Back in Black*, *Highway to Hell* or *Let There Be Rock*—all of which would, for novices, serve as fine introductions to the distinctive band—*Razor's Edge* was a welcome addition to AC/DC's catalogue. —*Alex Henderson*

AC/DC Live / Oct. 27, 1992 / Atco ✦✦✦

Despite the fact that the band's best days were obviously behind them, a live album for AC/DC was all but completely necessary. After all, the group's first live release, *If You Want Blood You've Got It*, was recorded at a time when AC/DC was nothing more than a cult act who had yet to produce many of its future rock staples. Though recorded well into their career on the *Razor's Edge* 1991 tour, *AC/DC Live* surprisingly captures the hype and excitement that made AC/DC such a hit in their heyday. The set list wisely overlooks the songs from the band's mid-'80s slump and concentrates on hard rock hits such as "Hells Bells," "Back in Black," "Highway to Hell," and "Dirty Deeds Done Dirt Cheap." Brian Johnson's voice may not be as strong as in the early '80s, but he still sounds competent in his role. All too often, a live album is a cheaply made, rushed recording that only serves as a testament to a band's decline. *AC/DC Live*, however, shows what makes this band different from their peers—here they are still entirely capable of pulling off a great live show. This ranks among the best live metal albums of the '90s. —*Barry Weber*

Ballbreaker / Sep. 26, 1995 / East West ✦✦✦

In over 20 years, AC/DC have never changed their minimalist, bone-crunching hard rock. During their first ten years, that wasn't a problem, since they were still finding ways to expand and subvert the pattern, but ever since *For Those About to Rock*, they've had trouble coming up with consistent material. Consequently, their performances tended to be a little lazy and their records didn't deliver a reliable knockout punch. Released in 1990, *The Razor's Edge* showed some signs of life, and their comeback culminated in the Rick Rubin-produced *Ballbreaker*. What makes *Ballbreaker* different than the albums AC/DC churned out during the '80s is simple—it's a matter of focus. Although "Hard as a Rock" comes close, there aren't any songs as immediately memorable as any of their '70s classics, or even "Moneytalks." However, unlike any record since *Back in Black*, there are no bad songs on the album. Surprisingly, Rubin's production is a bit too dry, lacking the muscle needed to make the riffs sound truly earthshaking. Nevertheless, Angus Young's riffs are powerful and catchy, showcasing every element that makes him one of hard rock and heavy metal's greatest guitarists. Throughout the album, the band sounds committed and professional, making *Ballbreaker* the best late-period AC/DC album to date. —*Stephen Thomas Erlewine*

Bonfire / Nov. 11, 1997 / East West ✦✦✦
Oddly, the legend of Bon Scott never haunted AC/DC. They grieved, certainly, but they were able to move on, releasing *Back in Black* as a tribute in 1980. The record became their biggest hit and helped them become one of the biggest rock & roll bands in the world. By the late '90s, the group remained popular, and a strange phenomenon had happened—there were generations of AC/DC fans who came of age after Scott's death, and had only a passing familiarity with the rocker. Perhaps that's one of the reasons why they lovingly assembled the five-disc box set *Bonfire* in 1997. The set is a tribute to Scott, featuring two live albums—one from New York in 1978, the other from Paris in 1979 that is essentially the soundtrack to the *Let There Be Rock* film—a disc of outtakes, and a remastered version of *Back in Black*. For hardcore fans, this is something of a dream come true, since the live albums are stronger than any of the group's other live releases, with the possible exception *If You Want Blood, You've Got It*. The disc of alternate takes, outtakes, and stray live cuts offers no real revelations, but there are enough interesting moments to make it worthwhile. And while any AC/DC fan has *Back in Black*, it's nice hearing it in this context, because it shows that even if the band could carry on splendidly, they were still missing the insane, wild-man charisma of Bon Scott. Nowhere is that charisma better preserved—both through music and stories—than on *Bonfire*. —*Stephen Thomas Erlewine*

Stiff Upper Lip / Feb. 29, 2000 / East West ✦✦✦
Stiff Upper Lip, AC/DC's 15th studio album, may not reach the heights of *Back in Black* or *Highway to Hell*, but it delivers strongly and satisfyingly. It's the record that the highly-touted, Rick Rubin-produced *Ballbreaker* should have been: a simple, addictive, hard album, bursting with bold riffs and bolstered by a crunching, thrillingly visceral sound. Sure, there are absolutely no new ideas, but that's the point. AC/DC knows their strengths and they embrace them. And why shouldn't they? Nobody writes a better riff than the Young brothers; each song has a riff so catchy, it feels like you've heard it for years. Is there anything earth-shaking? Hardly, but it's largely terrific nonetheless, just because AC/DC are so good at what they do. It's simple music, to be sure, but it's unassumingly musical and, in a way rather smart. If making music like this was really that easy, why can't anybody else do it this well? Some bands are capable of knocking out one record like this—one, maybe two. AC/DC does it nearly every time out. They've never really stretched, yet that's why they have one of the most reliable catalogs in rock & roll. When you put on one of their records, you know what you're in for, and they always deliver. With *Stiff Upper Lip*, they're not at classic status, but they're still top-notch. This may not be the first AC/DC record for a collection, but once you're into their scene, it's a fine place to be. —*Stephen Thomas Erlewine*

Ace

f. Dec. 1972, Sheffield, Yorkshire, England, **db.** Jul. 1977
Pub Rock
Ace was one of the few pub rock groups to enjoy success on the pop charts, largely due to the warm, soulful vocals of Paul Carrack. While Carrack's voice certainly had crossover appeal—as he would later prove with his own records, as well as his work with Squeeze and Roxy Music—the band was also less devoted to the three-chord boogie and country-rock that marked most pub-rock bands, favoring soulful R&B. And while they did have hits, their time in the spotlight was brief, and they fell apart shortly after Carrack left for a solo career. After developing a small but dedicated following on the pub-rock circuit, Ace signed with Anchor Records, and recorded *Five-A-Side*. "How Long" was released as the first single, becoming a fluke hit in both the U.K. and the U.S. Ace released *Time for Another* in 1975, but it was generally ignored, especially since the popularity of pub-rock was declining rapidly. —*Stephen Thomas Erlewine*

Five-A-Side / 1974 / Anchor ✦✦✦✦✦
Five-A-Side, Ace's debut album, is notable for introducing the world to the soulful singing talent of Paul Carrack, especially on the hit "How Long," which went to number one on some charts in 1975. The band has a low-key style, frequently dominated by Carrack's piano and organ work, that is sometimes suggestive of Traffic and of the Tulsa country-rock sound of J.J. Cale, Delaney & Bonnie, and Leon Russell, although they never work up quite as much of a sweat as the last two. Already road-weary when they made this album, Ace, especially in Carrack's lyrics, comments extensively on the travails of being in a struggling rock & roll band. Even "How Long," which sounds like the lament of a lover betrayed, is really about somebody quitting the group. All of which makes the irony of the song being their sole hit all the more acute. —*William Ruhlmann*

Time for Another / Dec. 1975 / Anchor ✦✦✦
Although Ace emphasized its Englishness and pub rock origins by posing on the album cover in a pub, complete with dartboard and pints of beer in hand, their second album continued to bear the musical influence of America, specifically the Southwestern America

of Tulsa's soulful Shelter Records label and people like Leon Russell and J.J. Cale. Theirs was a low-key, percolating approach that would be taken to mass success a few years down the line by Dire Straits. But *Time for Another* lacked the chief ingredient that had made its predecessor, *Five-A-Side*, successful: a hit on the order of "How Long." Keyboard player and vocalist Paul Carrack made a couple of valiant attempts, notably on the side-openers "I Think It's Gonna Last" and "No Future in Your Eyes." But Ace was a group of equals in creative participation, if not in talent, and much of the album was given over to the undistinguished contributions of other band members. With this album, the band was on its way to being a one-hit wonder. —*William Ruhlmann*

No Strings / Jan. 1977 / Anchor ✦✦

● **Best of Ace** / 1988 / See For Miles ✦✦✦✦✦
Best of Ace is a smartly assembled, fourteen-track collection which draws from each of the band's albums. Ace is best remembered for the ultra-slick "How Long," but little of the collection bears resemblance to that hit. Instead, they're shown doing what they did best (and more often)—playing laidback, rootsy pub-rock. —*Chris Woodstra*

Ace of Base

f. 1990
Swedish Pop/Rock, Club/Dance, Euro-Dance, Euro-Pop, Adult Contemporary, Dance-Pop
The Swedish quartet Ace of Base became a phenomenally popular international act with their 1993 debut album, *The Sign*. Ace of Base's simple, melodic Euro-disco was equally popular on radio and in the clubs, earning the quartet three U.S. Top 10 singles—"All That She Wants," "Don't Turn Around," and "The Sign," which spent six weeks at number one. Within a year of their 1990 formation, the group signed with Mega Records and released their debut single, "Wheel of Fortune," in 1992. By that time, the quartet had joined forces with John Ballard, who produced their recordings and wrote the majority of their songs. "All That She Wants" was Ace of Base's first single in Europe and, thanks to heavy exposure on MTV, the song became a number one hit in ten different countries. It was released in America in the fall of 1993 and quickly went platinum, beginning a string of platinum Top 10 singles in the U.S. Released in the fall of 1993, Ace of Base's American debut album *The Sign* quickly sold nearly two million copies. The group released their second album, *The Bridge*, in the fall of 1995. Although it went platinum in its first six months of release, the record failed to duplicate the remarkable multi-platinum success of *The Sign*. —*Stephen Thomas Erlewine*

The Sign / Nov. 23, 1993 / Arista ✦✦✦✦
Ace of Base's strong point is not versatility—all of their hit singles have exactly the same beat. But that doesn't matter. On their debut album, *The Sign*, they managed to create a piece of melodic Euro-disco that was a huge hit all over the world, appealing to both dance clubs and pop radio. And with singles like "All That She Wants," "The Sign," and "Don't Turn Around," it's easy to see why they were hits—the beat is relentless and the hooks are incessantly catchy. —*Stephen Thomas Erlewine*

The Bridge / Nov. 21, 1995 / Arista ✦✦✦
Ace of Base's sequel to their multi-platinum debut *The Sign* sounds like the same record on the surface. There are the same bouncy Euro-pop beats, ingratiatingly catchy melodies, and shiny production. However, underneath that gloss is an improved sense of songwriting. Ace of Base still might not be innovators, but they don't need to be. Instead, they turn out tightly constructed pop songs that are better written than they appear—songs like the hit "Beautiful Life" would sound good in different arrangements or if they were performed acoustically. And the songs on *The Bridge* are, overall, better than the ones on *The Sign*. Ace of Base might not be able to replicate the phenomenal success of their debut, but they have managed to deliver an album that is just as satisfying. —*Stephen Thomas Erlewine*

● **Greatest Hits** / Apr. 18, 2000 / Arista ✦✦✦✦
Consistently written off as ABBA wannabes and subpar pop poseurs, Ace of Base actually wrote some of the best pop songs of the '90s. Though the vocals were never up to par with even the least accomplished singers and the production was often sparse, the hooks in most of their cuts are irresistible. From their stateside breakthrough hit "All That She Wants" and their biggest single, "The Sign," and through their Top 10 "Beautiful Life" and the remake of "Cruel Summer," this compilation covers the best of their material. But with the addition of the poetic "Everytime It Rains," the pretty "Lucky in Love," the '50s throwback "Always Have, Always Will," the acoustic "Life Is a Flower," and the young-at-heart "C'est la Vie Always 21," you can see that much of what didn't hit big in the U.S. was some of the band's best work. As often happens with pop acts, once they begin to grow as artists, their fan base shrivels, which is exactly what happened with Ace of Base. With this album, though, you can see that when they matured they actually hit their stride. —*Bryan Buss*

Johnny Ace

b. Jun. 9, 1929, Memphis, TN, **d.** Dec. 25, 1954, Houston, TX
Vocals, Piano / R&B
The senseless death of young pianist Johnny Ace while indulging in a round of Russian roulette backstage at Houston's City Auditorium on Christmas Day of 1954 tends to overshadow his relatively brief but illustrious recording career on Duke Records. That's a pity, for Ace's gentle, plaintive vocal balladry deserves reverence on its own merit, not because of the scandalous fallout resulting from his tragic demise. Signing with Memphis DJ David Mattis' fledgling Duke logo in 1952, Ace hit the top of the R&B charts his very first time out with the mellow ballad "My Song." From then on, he could do no musical wrong, racking up hit after hit for Duke in the same smooth, urbane style. "Cross My Heart," "The

Clock," "Saving My Love for You," "Please Forgive Me," and "Never Let Me Go" all dented the uppermost reaches of the charts. And then, with one fatal gunshot, all that talent was lost forever. Ace scored his biggest hit of all posthumously. His haunting "Pledging My Love" (cut with the Johnny Otis orchestra in support) remained atop *Billboard's* R&B lists for ten weeks in early 1955. *—Bill Dahl*

• **Johnny Ace Memorial Album** / 1974 / MCA ✦✦✦✦✦

It's downright bizarre that Ace's catalog hasn't enjoyed a fresh reissue in 40 years. This 12-song CD is the exact same package that Don Robey rushed out following the pianist's death, with all the velvety hits ("Pledging My Love," "My Song," "The Clock," "Never Let Me Go") and a mere two blistering rockers, "How Can You Be So Mean" and "Don't You Know." A more thorough examination of Ace's discography is definitely in order! *—Bill Dahl*

David Ackles

b. Feb. 20, 1937, Rock Island, IL, **d.** Mar. 2, 1999

Vocals / Singer/Songwriter

Even after his death from cancer in 1999, David Ackles continues to influence contemporary singer-songwriters with his combination of dark, desolate lyrics, emotionally wrenching songs and subtle, sonorous delivery. Singers like Elvis Costello have acknowledged a creative debt to him, and his albums, especially *American Gothic*, have become cult favorites.

Born on Feb. 20, 1937, he was working in vaudeville by age four and in the mid-'40s played a character named Tucky Worden in Columbia's Rusty the Dog film series. His costar was Dwayne Hickman, who would later go on to play Dobie Gillis on television.

He attended the University of Southern California and took a year to go to school in Edinburgh, where he studied literature. He eventually got a degree in film studies, though he was proficient in the theater, ballet and choreography. He held several odd jobs after school and was eventually hired as a songwriter by Elektra. He managed to parlay that assignment into a multi-record deal, and released a self-titled debut album in 1968. The album was met with considerable critical acclaim, but did not do well commercially. His follow-up, *Subway to the Country*, produced one of his most chilling songs, "Candy Man," which was about a war veteran exacting revenge by selling pornography to children. Bernie Taupin, lyricist for Elton John, helped Ackles produce what was to be his best album, *American Gothic*, in 1972. The album again won heaps of praise from critics and peers, but Elektra gave up on Ackles' commercial prospects and dropped him after the album's release. Columbia gave him a shot and he released *Five & Dime* in 1973, but they also failed to market him effectively and dropped him when the album failed to chart. Ackles gave up on solo albums and went to work in film and theater, eventually writing a musical, Sister Aimee, which was performed in Los Angeles in 1995. He moved to Tujunga, California where he taught songwriting and theater studies before his death on March 2, 1999. *—Stacia Proefrock*

The Road to Cairo / 1968 / Elektra ✦✦

David Ackles / 1968 / Elektra ✦✦

Subway to the Country / 1970 / Elektra ✦✦✦✦

While comparisons to Randy Newman are natural and, in places even valid, they fall short of the mark. David Ackles' music is much darker, already deeply entrenched in the American gothic his fourth album would be named after. While the post-Tin Pan Alley stylings of Newman are evident here, Ackles' inspiration is in the original texts and not his Cali counterparts. Other sides of Ackles come from John Stewart and the folk revival, and no less than Scott Walker's early work and Jacques Brel. *Subway to the Country* portends itself a rootsier record, but it is rooted only in the tradition of American song itself. From the bleak vaudevillian cabaret of "Main Street Saloon" to the shimmering string arrangements and chamber textures in "That's No Reason to Cry" to the surreal muted winds and brass in "Woman River," Ackles is like a Western Kurt Weill. His knowledge of song form and nuance is encyclopedic, and his command over his singing voice is total. He can rumble smooth, swinging blues in the lower register as he does on the latter track, or shift it into loopy swirls and theatrical splashes as he does on "Inmates of the Institution." Once one is an innovator of such dimension, one always has a restless creative soul, seeking to go ever-deeper levels in the well. *Subway to the Country* is not the classic that *American Gothic* is, but it remains a fine testament to Ackles' truly awesome poetic power as both a writer and a singer. *—Thom Jurek*

• **American Gothic** / 1972 / Elektra ✦✦✦✦✦

The years have only been kind to the album considered David Ackles' masterpiece when it was released. Ackles combined an early '70s singer-songwriter sensibility with a theater music background that placed him as much in the tradition of Brecht-Weill and Jacques Brel as Bob Dylan. Not only are his songs fully realized, dramatic statements, but Ackles proves himself a warm, accomplished singer. When this album got no higher than Number 167 in the charts, Ackles' fans were heartbroken. Decades later, *American Gothic* remains one of those great albums that never found its audience. It waits to be rediscovered. *—William Ruhlmann*

Five & Dime / 1973 / Columbia ✦✦✦✦

American Gothic, the predecessor to *Five & Dime*, was David Ackles' ambitious portrait of American life, in its broad scope and geography and diversity of style. *Five & Dime* is more a collection of miniatures, still drawn with Ackles' customary eye for detail and sung in his rich, knowing voice. Its pleasures are more subtle than those in the expansive *American Gothic*, but no less real. (And "Surf's Down," complete with harmonies by Dean Torrance of Jan & Dean, is the wickedest beach music parody since "Back In The U.S.S.R.") This is music of wit, feeling, and sophistication that should be heard by fans of American songcraft from Stephen Foster and Irving Berlin to Randy Newman. Criminally, it was also David Ackles' last album. *—William Ruhlmann*

The Action

f. 1965, **db.** 1967

Mod, Garage Rock, British Invasion, R&B, Soul

After the Beatles, the Action were the most impressive band signed to EMI by George Martin during the mid-'60s. That they never managed to chart a single in the space of two years with the label, even as lesser bands sold tens of thousands of records with seemingly no effort, is one of those great ironies of mid-'60s English rock & roll. The Action had a sound similar to the Small Faces but without as heavy an attack on their instruments or an outsized persona such as that of Steve Marriott to dominate their image. They were discovered by George Martin, who signed them to his newly founded AIR Productions in 1965 and got them a recording deal at Parlophone Records, where he'd formerly been the head of the label. The debut single, "Land of 1000 Dances" b/w "In My Lonely Room," and other early songs are irresistible dance numbers, performed with genuine flair and inspiration, not to mention an authentic white soul sound from vocalist Reggie King that was as credible as anything emanating from England at the time (or since). Late in 1967, still eager to pursue their new sound, the Action added keyboard player Ian Whitman to the lineup. Reggie King subsequently left the band to pursue a solo career, and Whitman took over the outfit that remained, rechristened Azoth. The band eventually transformed themselves into a pure psychedelic outfit, Mighty Baby, that had a sound far removed from that of the Action. *—Bruce Eder*

The Ultimate Action / 1981 / Edsel ✦✦✦✦✦

This collection is a slightly expanded version of an LP that first appeared in 1984. There are no notes—an unthinkable oversight today—but otherwise, this is one of the best pieces of British beat-style R&B available, a match for the best tracks off The Beatles' Second Album and any of the best R&B-style numbers by the early Who. The material isn't in chronological order, although that's not a huge problem for CD listeners, but it's heavily scrambled. The stuff stands on its own, in any case—"Harlem Shuffle," "Since I Lost My Baby," and "In My Lonely Room" are among the finest English R&B covers of the period, and even originals like "Never Ever" (written by Alan King, Reggie King, and Mike Evans and the group-composed "Twenty Fourth Hour" are fine pieces of songwriting, with attractive hooks and choruses, and good soulful performances. One fascinating discovery unearthed on this CD, amid hits that never were (like their cover of the Marvelettes' "I'll Keep On Holding On" and the brooding, modish "Wasn't It You,") is the group's cover of the Spector-Goffin-King classic "Just Once in My Life." In contrast to the Righteous Brothers' wall-of-sound approach, the five-piece band does it by themselves with no overdubbed help, and Reggie King and company are good enough singers to pull it off, despite a few awkward moments on the fade. The attempts at experimental, quasi-psychedelic material ("Shadows and Reflections") are nicely played and sung, but they lack the depth and urgency of the group's earlier material, and it's easy to understand EMI's misgivings over the direction the group was going in, based on this evidence. As an added attraction, the production by George Martin is also among the best work of his career in rock & roll, second only to his work with the Beatles. *—Bruce Eder & Richie Unterberger*

• **Action Packed** / Mar. 13, 2001 / Edsel ✦✦✦✦✦

Beginning in the fall of 1965 with their single "Land of 1000 Dances" b/w "In My Lonely Room," the Liverpool-based quintet the Action graced the world with some of the best R&B and soul ever to come out of a white British band, so utterly convincing and sung and played with such conviction that some listeners today can't believe they were white, much less English. They only got better with their next few singles, including "I'll Keep on Holding On," "Baby You've Got It" b/w "Since I Lost My Baby," and "Harlem Shuffle" (which wasn't even released until the 1980s), but somehow never made it to the charts. The 17 songs here overlap with the contents of the *Ultimate Action* CD, except that they've all been newly remastered in 24-bit sound from better sources, so the action on the drums is audible and the guitars, bass, and vocals are practically right in your lap (and they never sounded better, to boot). That new digital transfer, coupled with the extensive annotation and the array of group photographs, picture sleeves, advertising art, and original single labels all combine to make this CD an essential upgrade from the earlier release. Further, although it is a compilation of singles (and, thus, a bit unfair to stack up against individual albums by other bands), the music on *Action Packed* is every bit as essential, bracing, and enjoyable a listening experience as, say, *With the Beatles*, *Rolling Stones Now*, the Who's original U.K. *My Generation* album, or any of the other iconic music releases of the British Invasion. Even the one non-soul number here, "Shadows and Reflections," which reflected a change in direction for the group and closes the collection (and also surfaced on Rhino's *Nuggets II* box), is one of the catchier unknown pieces of British psychedelic pop you're ever likely to run into. *—Bruce Eder*

Bryan Adams

b. Nov. 5, 1959

Vocals, Guitar / Pop/Rock, Adult Contemporary, Album Rock, Arena Rock

Bryan Adams was one of the most popular mainstream rock & rollers to emerge in the '80s, producing a series of platinum albums and Top Ten hits. Adams wasn't an innovator on the level of Bruce Springsteen, or even John Cougar Mellencamp. He followed in their footsteps, smoothing out their rougher edges while retaining a down-to-earth earnestness in both his straightforward rock & roll and his husky voice. At the beginning of his career, he relied more on rock than pop, but as his career progressed, he became known for his ballads. But both his rockers and his slow numbers were the result of his craftsmanship, both as a writer and a performer—Adams never let anything obscure a good hook. —*Stephen Thomas Erlewine*

Bryan Adams / 1980 / A&M ✦✦

You Want It, You Got It / 1981 / A&M ✦✦✦
With its crystal-clear production, courtesy of Bob Clearmountain, *You Want It, You Got It* is state-of-the art nouveau rock & roll of the post-Springsteen era: the guitars rev up, the bass drum is deeper than a well, the vocals are nasal and punky. The songs don't have the craft or commitment of Adams' peers/competitors—Springsteen, Petty, Mellencamp, et al.—but you may not know it for the first few spins, just because the sound is so hot and infectious, and by then it may not matter. Actually, this is a much more enjoyable record in many respects than the rock & roll assembly-line products Adams constructed once he hit the arenas. As it was, with this one, he was on his way. All he did later was take this approach and make it slicker. —*William Ruhlmann*

Cuts Like a Knife / Jan. 1983 / A&M ✦✦✦✦✦
After the indifference which met his first album, Bryan Adams reportedly considered naming this sophomore release "Bryan Adams Hasn't Heard of You Either," but thankfully, the soon-to-be mega-star settled for the less offensive *Cuts Like a Knife* instead. Side one (for those of you who still remember vinyl sides) of this album is simply perfect. "The Only One," "This Time," and the title track are mid-paced melodic rockers with drop-dead choruses and hooks; they set the mold for most of Adams' finest and biggest hits. Though it rocks a little harder, "Take me Back" is just as radio-friendly thanks to its use of female back-up singers, and the fantastic "Straight Through the Heart" is Adams' first of many great ballads. Side two opens with a few misfires, but recovers soon enough thanks to the gutsy guitar of "Don't Leave Me Lonely" and the rather saccharine (but still good) ballad "The Best Was Yet to Come." Adams would finally achieve chart-topping perfection on his next release *Reckless*, but *Cuts Like a Knife* comes pretty close. —*Ed Rivadavia*

Reckless / 1984 / A&M ✦✦✦✦✦
Bryan Adams capitalized on the momentum of *Cuts Like a Knife* with 1984's *Reckless*, a virtually flawless collection of melodic hard rock which would dominate radio for years to come. "Run to You" was a brilliant lead-off single which remains one of Adams' best songs ever, but its success still pales in comparison to follow-up smashes such as "Summer of '69," "It's only Love," (a duet with Tina Turner), and the ballad to end all ballads, "Heaven." Although some songs haven't aged very well (especially the overtly cheesy "Kids Wanna Rock"), these weak links are easily eclipsed by further highlights such as the cool rock of "One Night Love Affair" and the irrepressible pop chorus of "Somebody." Sales figures may point to 1991's *Waking Up the Neighbors* as the peak of Bryan Adams career, but the songs from *Reckless* will most certainly prove to be his lasting legacy. —*Ed Rivadavia*

Into the Fire / Mar. 1987 / A&M ✦✦

Waking Up the Neighbours / Sep. 1991 / A&M ✦✦✦
After the disappointing *Into the Fire*, Adams returned to the top of the charts with *Waking Up the Neighbours*, thanks to the massive success of "(Everything I Do) I Do It for You." —*Stephen Thomas Erlewine*

● **So Far So Good** / Nov. 2, 1993 / A&M ✦✦✦✦✦
Throughout the 1980s and early '90s, few contemporary rock artists were able to come up with as many lighthearted, guilty pleasures as Bryan Adams. This is especially evident through *So Far So Good*, which neglects all album fillers and compiles many of his most noteworthy songs, from such rockers as "Summer of '69," "Run to You," and "Cuts Like a Knife" to the equally popular power ballads "Heaven" and "(Everything I Do) I Do It for You." Also included is the all-new "Please Forgive Me," one of his best power ballads yet. It's not quite a perfect compilation, however; in particular, his Top 20 hits "She's Only Happy When She's Dancin'" and "Thought I'd Died and Gone to Heaven" are overlooked. These are only minor flaws, though. There is no better introduction to Bryan Adams to date than *So Far So Good*. —*Barry Weber*

Live! Live! Live! / 1995 / A&M ✦✦

18 'til I Die / Jun. 1996 / A&M ✦✦

MTV Unplugged / Dec. 9, 1997 / A&M ✦✦✦
Only two years after delivering his first live set, Bryan Adams returned with his second, *Unplugged*. Of course, "unplugged" albums were in vogue in the '90s, but it has to be said that Adams arrived a little late in the game, several years after efforts by Eric Clapton and 10,000 Maniacs ruled the charts. Nevertheless, Adams' *Unplugged* is a strong effort, featuring stripped down versions of such staples as "Summer of '69," "Cuts Like a Knife" and "Heaven" that prove that he's a resourceful straightahead rocker with a knack for a tune. There's also a handful of surprises, like early cuts like "Fits Ya Good" and a few new songs, that keep the record interesting for dedicated fans, but the overall quality of the music makes the record one of his best efforts of the '90s. —*Stephen Thomas Erlewine*

On a Day Like Today / Oct. 27, 1998 / A&M ✦✦

Barry Adamson

b. Jun. 1, 1958
Producer, Vocals, Bass / Alternative Dance, Alternative Pop/Rock
Barry Adamson's work as a bassist for Magazine and Nick Cave's Bad Seeds gave little indication of the complex, cinematic works he has composed as a solo artist. After leaving the Bad Seeds in 1987, Adamson decided to follow the path of film composers like John Barry, Ennio Morricone, and Bernard Herrmann, whose work had intrigued him since childhood. His first full-length album, 1989's *Moss Side Story* (he had released one previous EP in 1988), was a *tour de force*, blending post-punk, industrial, spy guitar, and various classic movie composer quotes into a seamless 54-minute soundtrack to an omi-

nous film noir that didn't exist. This recording led to Adamson's work on soundtracks for actual films in the early '90s, including *Delusion*, *Gas Food Lodging*, and *Shuttle Cock*. Adamson also continued to compose quasi-cinematic recordings for imaginary films like 1996's *Oedipus Shmoedipus*, although none have matched the sustained excitement of *Moss Side Story*. *As Above, So Below* followed in 1998 and a best-of compilation titled *The Murky World of Barry Adamson* appeared a year after that. —*Richie Unterberger*

● **Moss Side Story** / 1989 / Mute ✦✦✦✦✦
Adamson's first full-length album is still unequivocally his best. Elements of rock, voices from news reports, blood-curdling wordless female vocals (courtesy of experimental/punk diva Diamanda Galas), lounge keyboards, and swirling funereal ambient music are interwoven on this taut and compelling, almost continuous imaginary "soundtrack." The result is a sinister and edgy soundscape that's as gripping as any black-and-white thriller. The CD adds three bonus cuts, including Adamson's updates of "The Man With The Golden Arm" and "Alfred Hitchcock Presents." —*Richie Unterberger*

Delusion / 1991 / Mute ✦✦

Soul Murder / 1992 / Mute ✦✦✦
Equally as ambitious as *Moss Side Story*, but this doesn't come off nearly as well. Apparently constructed to evoke similar underworld soundscapes, too much of this is built around simple, sparse (sometimes electronic) riffs. The production lacks force and density, and the pieces don't flow into each other with the cohesion that he's demonstrated in other work. Nifty bits of haunting orchestral ambience and lounge jazz keyboards remain, and it does hit a groove at times, especially with the goofy French pop song (with childish vocals) "Un Petit Miracle" and the brutal ska treatment of the James Bond theme. —*Richie Unterberger*

The Negro Inside Me / Oct. 19, 1993 / Mute ✦✦

Oedipus Schmoedipus / Aug. 7, 1996 / Mute ✦✦✦✦
After some releases with more of a pop, beat-heavy feel, Adamson moves back—sort of—into the land of noirish soundtrack. Unlike *Moss Side Story*, it's not really a soundtrack with repeated themes and motifs. A lot of pieces establish soundtrack-like moods, but the flow never builds up a momentum of its own. As individual soundscapes, though, the tracks (largely instrumental) are reasonably impressive, whether it's burlesque-type fare, a takeoff on Miles Davis, or lounge jazz. If noir is what you want, "It's Business As Usual" is especially creepy, with its neurotic answering machine messages nearly buried under waves of disquieting sounds; achieving a similar effect, in an entirely different manner, is "Vermillion Kisses," a fairytale narrative with a morbid ending. Nick Cave adds a guest vocal to (and co-writes) "The Sweetest Embrace"; Pulp's Jarvis Cocker can be heard (and co-writes) another cut. Adamson's skill in layering and devising unusual sound textures still qualifies him as one of experimental rock's more imaginative composers and producers. But on the more rock-oriented pieces, he's using too many of those damn beat-boxes for his own good. —*Richie Unterberger*

As Above, So Below / Jun. 23, 1998 / Mute ✦✦✦✦
Barry Adamson is playing quite the "jazz devil" on *As Above, So Below*. The album sees the dark noir guru taking a detour from the more experimental electronica of *Oedipus Schmoedipus* into a cool, brutal concept album of aggressive, ominous rock-jazz. It seems that a great deal of Nick Cave's cinematic themes have rubbed off on Adamson from his days as a Bad Seed. Where Cave deals mostly with vampiric goth ballads, Adamson creates his art under a moody, effective jazz noir cloud. Many of the songs shuffle about with a determined sense of cool, as Adamson utilizes deep crooning vocals; he often sounds remarkably like a more sane Nick Cave, especially on "Come Hell or High Water." Perhaps Adamson's work on David Lynch's *Lost Highway* soundtrack inspired the tales of dead detectives and shady women detailed on *As Above, So Below*. One can easily imagine these songs coming from a younger, *rocking*, and more sinister Angelo Badalamenti, a frequent Lynch collaborator. The album's high points include "Can't Get Loose," "Still I Rise," and "The Monkey Speaks His Mind." "Can't Get Loose" sees Adamson cooly cooing over keyboards reminiscent of New Order, with a fun, suave xylophone sound and a sample of "Can't Get Used to Losing You" by legendary songwriters Doc Pomus and Mort Shuman. The song operates under a pleasant, humorous atmosphere, while still displaying ample doses of Adamson's warped, dark vibes. "Still I Rise" is monumentally cool. Adamson sounds quite angry and defensive, sing-screaming "still I rise" repeatedly, alternating that mantra with verses of autobiographical, stream-of-consciousness lyrics. The final cry is as punishing and entertaining as it is crass. Barry Adamson has yet to release an album that isn't entirely compelling. *As Above, So Below* is a strong, winning mix of style, emotion, and rock-jazz noir power. It's a bold, satisfying vision from an artist who shows no fear in expressing the seedier sides of life. —*Tim DiGravina*

The Murky World of Barry Adamson / May 18, 1999 / Mute ✦✦✦✦
The Murky World of Barry Adamson collects the best of the former Bad Seed's solo recordings. Adamson's moody, filmic songs mix sex and menace with impenetrable cool, especially on "The Vibes Ain't Nothing but the Vibes" and "Something Wicked This Way Comes," both from his 1996 album *Oedipus Schmoedipus*. Along with selected tracks from every album from *Moss Side Story* to *As Above, So Below*, *The Murky World of Barry Adamson* also includes three previously unreleased tracks: "Walk the Last Mile," "Mitch & Andy" and "Saturn in the Summertime." *Murky World* is a delectable sampler of Adamson's dark musical talents. —*Heather Phares*

Add N to (X)

f. 1994, London, England
Electronica, Post-Rock/Experimental
Name-checking a diverse cast of progenitors including Varése, Xenakis, and Robert Moog

as well as Can and Stereolab, Add N to (X) are electro-historians of a sort, collectors of vintage synthesizer technology, and fierce propagators of the man-machine aesthetic (the cover of their second album features member Ann Shenton on the operating table with a synthesizer either being inserted or taken out of her organ cavity). The trio formed when Shenton met Barry Smith in 1993; both were fans of vintage synth and the proto-electronica crafted in the 1960s and '70s by such luminaries as Wendy Carlos, Pierre Henry and even Roxy Music. After becoming Add N to (X) one year later, Shenton and Smith recruited theremin expert Steven Claydon plus an organic rhythm section for their live show, consisting of Stereolab's Andy Ramsay on drums and Rob Hallam from the High Llamas. After the debut Add N to (X) album *Vero Electronics* was released in 1996 on Blow Up, the group toured America, where their propulsive live show earned more comparisons to Suicide than an ostensibly sympathetic group like Tortoise. *On the Wires of Our Nerves* appeared in 1998 and *Avant Hard* followed in April of 1999. The following year they released *Add Insult to Injury*, which saw the group move in a more accessible, pop direction. —*John Bush*

Vero Electronics / Jan. 29, 1996 / Blow Up ✦✦✦

On the Wires of Our Nerves / May 19, 1998 / Mute ✦✦✦✦

At this point in the trio's career, Add N to (X) isn't all that. They're good, but great? *On the Wires* answers that question with a convincing "maybe," raising another one along the way: what happens when a certain style of futurism finally becomes a retro style that can be slotted alongside everything from rockabilly to medieval folk chanting? Arguably Kraftwerk—one of Add N to (X)'s obvious mentors—were just as retro in their day, evoking in a quietly emotional way, an outdated 1920s/1930s vision of the future while also forecasting where forthcoming music would end up. To Add N to (X)'s further credit, they're not a one-note tribute band like Komputer or Kraftwelt, bringing in some of Krautrock's rougher, electronic side as well as early avant noisesters like Cabaret Voltaire. Add to that a great visual sense—the grotesque album cover is a wonderful blend of the sterile and visceral, its own sick joke—and there should be much more on this album than there is. But for all the hollow drum machine sounds (and real drumming, which underlays the best songs here), analog synth loops and tweaks, and odd Vocoder interjections that should make Add N to (X) a welcome alternative to Yet Another Rock Band, it feels like the trio recorded some jam sessions, thought them sufficient, and then left the studio. Praise doesn't belong to a band just for being there and using certain instruments—thankfully, though, the trio found a better way in its immediate future than what's on display in *On the Wires*. —*Ned Raggett*

● **Avant Hard** / Apr. 20, 1999 / Mute ✦✦✦✦✦

Add N to (X)'s third album, *Avant Hard*, combines the noisy, analog aesthetic of their previous works with an increasingly sophisticated, structured approach. Though the group's overdriven, menacing synth sound prevails on songs like "Robot New York" and "Buckminster Fuller," unexpected touches like the operatic vocals on "Fyuz" and the go-go guitars on "Skills" provide a welcome contrast and round out the band's sonic palette.

Avant Hard finds Add N to (X) expanding their emotional range as well. The album begins with theoretical pieces like the aptly named "Barry 7's Contraption" and segues into a brace of filmic songs like the horror-show creepiness of "Steve's Going to Teach Himself Who's Boss" to the robo-porn soundtrack that is "Metal Fingers in My Body." "Revenge of the Black Regent" and "Ann's Eveready Equestrian" take this trend toward drama and build it to near Wagnerian heights, blending synths, strings, choral voices, and sound effects into symphonies of urban decay. Finally, *Avant Hard* ends on a relatively gentle note, with a pair of songs—"Oh Yeah Oh No" and "Machine Is Bored With Love"—that explore Add N to (X)'s softer, even poignant side. "Machine" is based on samples from the early-'70s experimental band Egg, adding to a long list of musical pioneers—including Joe Meek, Suicide, Kraftwerk, and Bruce Haack—that the group borrows from and updates. With analog savvy and rock attitude, *Avant Hard* reveals itself as one of Add N to (X)'s finest moments. —*Heather Phares*

Add Insult to Injury / Oct. 17, 2000 / Mute ✦✦✦✦

Add N to (X)'s *Add Insult to Injury* should come with the disclaimer "no analog synths were hurt in the making of this album." The trio made an art of abusing their instruments on albums like 1999's brilliant *Avant Hard*. However, on their fourth full-length album they show a surprising streak of humanity toward their equipment, resulting in a curiously subdued, inhibited-sounding work. The division of labor on *Add Insult to Injury* is also curious. Ann Shenton, Steven Claydon, and the High Llamas' drummer Rob Allum wrote and performed eight of the album's songs, while Barry 7 wrote the other four. It gives the album a less-coherent feel; most of Shenton's and Claydon's songs, such as "You Must Create," put textures ahead of melody or structure, making them sound like cuts off of old synth reference albums. However, the fuzzed-out "Brothel Charge," the sleekly menacing "Kingdom of Shades," and "Hit for Cheese"—an S&M-tinged synth-punk duet between Shenton and a robot—are standouts. Meanwhile, Barry 7's tracks, which include the excellent "Monster Bobby," a stomping chant sung by soccer hooligan androids or a robotic Gary Glitter, and the streamlined, cute-as-an-iMac "Plug Me In," are more focused and accessible. "Incinerator No. 1" recalls *On the Wires of Our Nerves*' beautifully ugly noise, and "The Regent Is Dead" is both elegiac and martial, mixing a synth choir with theremins and a snare-driven beat. *Add Insult to Injury* still feels like a small step backward after *Avant Hard*'s synapse-frying creativity and energy, but it reaffirms that Add N to (X) are still a step ahead of most other vintage synth-based groups. Hopefully, they'll return to what they do best: sacrificing their keyboards in the name of art. —*Heather Phares*

Hasil Adkins

b. 1936, Madison, WV
Vocals, Guitar / Psychobilly, Honky Tonk, Rockabilly

A crazed rockabilly one-man band, Adkins has been recording in a tarpaper shack in the hills of West Virginia since the mid-'50s. The absolutely crudest and wildest of all rock & rollers, Hasil's lyrics stray as far from the standard '50s clichés as you can get. Songs about eating peanut butter on the moon, chopping girls' heads off and mounting them on his wall, and doing something called the "hunch" are typical lyrical fare for Adkins. Combining a three-octave voice that can go from sub-glottal Elvis moans to blood-curdling screams with an over-amplified guitar that sounds like a gigantic rubber band, there is nothing in pop music that sounds like Hasil Adkins, a true rock & roll primitive. —*Cub Koda*

● **Out to Hunch** / 1986 / Norton ✦✦✦✦

Hasil Adkins is a backwoods surrealist from rural West Virginia who spent most of the '50s, '60s, and '70s bashing ultra-crude rockabilly into an ancient reel-to-reel tape deck, one-man-band style (no overdubbing allowed—Adkins keeps the beat with bass drum pedals while laying down the melody on guitar and howling his lyrics in a single fevered take). Adkins' approach would be odd enough no matter what his songs were about, but a quick scan of his lyrics indicates this is where he really starts to drift into the Twilight Zone; he's recorded no fewer than three tunes about decapitation, "She Said" concerns an assignation with a woman who looked "like a dyin' can of that commodity meat," and "The Hunch" describes the nation's slowest rising new dance craze like so—"Now, if you ain't never seen nobody do the Hunch, you ain't never saw my woman! And I declare, son, you won't never see her! 'Cause I ain't got one!" Everybody clear on that? As you've no doubt gathered, *Out to Hunch* (compiled by Billy Miller from a decade's worth of home-recorded Adkins sessions, two of which were actually released as singles in the 1950s) doesn't sound a whole lot like anything else you've heard before, and if you're the sort of person who thinks Eric Clapton improves on Buddy Guy's guitar style, this probably won't be your bag. But if you believe that rock & roll is about passion and enthusiasm first and foremost, then Hasil Adkins has got to be one of the greatest rockers who ever walked the Earth—even the weirdest, crudest songs bubble with wired conviction, and odd as his style may be, Hasil rocks hard on every frantic cut of *Out to Hunch.* A true original and a thing of wonderment, *Out to Hunch* is a truly singular rock & roll experience; after listening to it, hot dogs will never seem quite the same again. —*Mark Deming*

Chicken Walk / 1986 / Buffalo Bop ✦✦✦✦✦
More crazed '50s and early '60s sides. (Import) —*Cub Koda*

The Wild Man / 1987 / Norton ✦✦✦
His '80s recordings, just as crazy. —*Cub Koda*

Peanut Butter Rock & Roll / 1990 / Norton ✦✦

Moon over Madison / 1990 / Norton ✦✦

Look at That Caveman Go!! / 1993 / Norton ✦✦✦
Seventeen careening, out-of-control live recordings by America's favorite rockabilly legend-lunatic. "She Goes like This" and "Devonna Rock" may be two of his wildest recordings ever, but the true highlight is a rockin' in the insane asylum version of George Jones' country classic "Today I Started Loving You Again." File under retro-alternative if the record store happened to be on the planet Mars. —*Cub Koda*

Achy Breaky Ha Ha Ha / 1994 / Norton ✦✦✦
The West Virginia wildman shows the other side of his talent, tackling a batch of early country standards and quirky originals in his usual one-man-band style. As far removed from modern country as you can get, Adkins originals like "Gonna Have Me a Yard Sale," "Song of Death," "Of Course Not," "Leaves of Autumn," and "Tomorrow I'll Still Be Loving You" sit alongside Bill Monroe's "I Hear a Sweet Voice Calling," Hank Williams' "You Win Again," and Johnny Cash's "I Still Miss Someone" for a roughcut set that's rife with high and lonesome charm. —*Cub Koda*

What the Hell Was I Thinking? / Feb. 24, 1998 / Epitaph ✦✦

Poultry in Motion: The Hasil Adkins Chicken Collection / Aug. 15, 2000 / Norton ✦✦✦✦
Every great songwriter has their great subject, and Hasil Adkins—rock legend, one-man band, and creator of America's slowest-rising new dance craze, "the Hunch"—is no exception. A perusal of Adkins' back catalog reveals that "the Haze" is a man who loves his chicken, and for this set the like-minded lunatics at Norton Records have combined six new recordings with highlights from Adkins' previous albums (and a few vintage unreleased cuts) to create *Poultry in Motion,* a collection of 15 songs about chicken (discussed both as barnyard friends and as part of a well-balanced diet). You get "Chicken Walk," its cousin "Chicken Twist," the manic "Chicken Hunch," no fewer than three takes of "Chicken Hop" (one with previously undocumented West Virginia R&B act the Dynamiters), the warped but soulful "Chicken Blues," and "Chicken on the Bone" in which Adkins repeatedly mentions McDonalds. As a concept album, this approaches a level of genius rarely witnessed since either *Tommy* by the Who or *We're in a Band* by the New Duncan Imperials, and it's encouraging to report that the new tunes are just as wild and wondrously incoherent as the stuff the Haze bashed out in the 1950s. Wild, primitive, and primal rock & roll that's tasty either baked or deep fried—just add beverages and you've got a meal! —*Mark Deming*

The Adverts

f. 1976, **db.** 1980
British Punk, Punk

With their raw, enthusiastic immaturity, the Adverts were a bright, though short-lived, light of the punk era, distinguished by the fact that their bassist, Gaye Advert, was one of the first female stars of punk rock. After they (barely) mastered one chord, the Adverts began playing at London's Roxy Club in 1976, where they quickly came to the attention of the Damned's guitarist Brian James. James offered the band an opening spot on the Damned's tour and directed them toward Stiff Records. Stiff released their self-deprecating debut single, "One Chord Wonders," in 1977, when the band could still barely play, but when they released their second single, the disturbingly funny "Gary Gilmore's Eyes," the group rocketed into the U.K. Top 20 in a storm of controversy. The Adverts' first album, *Crossing the Red Sea With the Adverts*, fulfilled the single's promise, but the second, 1979's *Cast of Thousands*, sounded like they poured all of their musical ideas into their first album; the group broke up the following year. —*Stephen Thomas Erlewine*

● **Crossing the Red Sea with the Adverts** / Mar. 1978 / Bright ✦✦✦✦✦
Some will argue eloquently that the Adverts' debut is the great overlooked U.K. punk record of the late '70s. From the moment they released their first single ("One Chord Wonders") up to and including the release of this album, the Adverts recorded great, arty, fast, and loud punk clamor rooted in anomie ("Bored Teenagers"), class consciousness ("Safety in Numbers"), and comic book horror ("Gary Gilmore's Eyes"). Led by the Rotten/Strummer-isms of frontman T.V. Smith, *Crossing the Red Sea* sounds as snotty, defiant, and liberating as it did in 1978. In fact, it sounds surprisingly relevant and more intelligent. An ignored masterpiece. —*John Dougan*

Cast of Thousands / Mar. 1980 / Anagram Punk ✦✦✦
Long considered the poor relation to the Adverts' crisper debut album, *Cast Of Thousands* is not nearly as wretched as some historians would have you believe. Even if some of T.V. Smith's attempts at expanding his songwriting come up short, there are the seeds of good things on the title-track and "Television's Over." Smith later lamented the fact that their second album saw the Adverts outgrow their audience—"We could hardly hear ourselves recording *Cast Of Thousands* over the sound of the critics sharpening their knives, but it still felt the right direction to go in." —*Alex Ogg*

The Punk Singles Collection / 1997 / Anagram Punk ✦✦✦✦✦
The Punk Singles Collection is a first-rate collection of all of the Adverts' late-'70s singles, including both the A-sides and B-sides. Although the group peaked with its first album, *Crossing the Red Sea*, and their subsequent singles were quite spotty, *The Punk Singles Collection* remains a worthwhile retrospective. Casual fans will still be better served with the debut, but dedicated fans will need the rare flipsides that are scattered throughout the disc. —*Stephen Thomas Erlewine*

The Best of the Adverts / Sep. 7, 1999 / Anagram Punk ✦✦✦✦

The Wonders Don't Care / Mar. 27, 2001 / Pilot ✦✦✦✦
The Adverts are generally regarded as second-stringers in the first wave of British punk, but while their work is rarely mentioned in the same breath as the Damned, the Clash, or the Buzzcocks, their best music has stood the test of time as well as any of their contemporaries. The group's first album, *Crossing the Red Sea With the Adverts*, and the classic single "Gary Gilmore's Eyes" are into-the-wind punk at its best, with energy to burn, sharp (if skeletal) tunes, and unusually thoughtful lyrics from frontman T.V. Smith. While the group's later work was less exciting, it also showed the Adverts were one of the first punk bands to acknowledge the limitations of the form and struggled to move past them, and if their ambition exceeded their reach, they still managed to write some good songs along the way. *The Wonders Don't Care* collects 17 songs the Adverts recorded for BBC Radio sessions between 1977 and 1979, and Smith's contention in the liner notes that the set allows listeners to "hear a band get born, grow up, get old and die, all in less than an hour" sums things up quite well, thank you. The first half of the album captures the band in their youthful and snarling period, and if bassist Gaye Advert and guitarist Howard Pickup don't display much virtuosity, they already learned what not to do, and Smith is in superb form; these sessions are a bit less polished than their records, but they're well-recorded and capture their energy with commendable accuracy. The later selections find the band slowing their tempos, writing more complex melodies, and (gulp) even adding a keyboard, but while the Adverts slipped as they attempted to reinvent themselves, Smith remained a strong singer and an intelligent, perceptive lyricist with plenty worth hearing. *Crossing the Red Sea* is easily the best Adverts album, but *The Wonders Don't Care* captures their sudden rise and brave fall as well as any set you can buy. —*Mark Deming*

Aerosmith

f. 1970, Boston, MA
Pop-Metal, Album Rock, Arena Rock, Heavy Metal, Pop/Rock, Hard Rock
Aerosmith was one of the most popular hard-rock bands of the '70s, setting the style and sound of hard rock and heavy metal for the next two decades with their raunchy, bluesy swagger. The Boston-based quintet—singer Steven Tyler, guitarists Joe Perry and Brad Whitford, bassist Tom Hamilton, and drummer Joey Kramer—found the middle ground between the menace of the Rolling Stones and the campy, sleazy flamboyance of the New York Dolls, developing a lean, dirty riff-oriented boogie that was loose and swinging and as hard as a diamond. In the meantime, they developed a prototype for power-ballads with "Dream On," a piano ballad that was orchestrated with strings and distorted guitars. Aerosmith's ability to pull off both ballads and rock & roll made them extremely popular during the mid-'70s, when they had a string of gold and platinum albums. By the early '80s, the group's audience had declined as the band fell prey to drug and alcohol abuse. However, their career was far from over—in the late '80s, Aerosmith pulled off one of the most remarkable comebacks in rock history, returning to the top of the charts with a group of albums that equalled, if not surpassed, the popularity of their '70s albums. —*Stephen Thomas Erlewine*

Aerosmith / Jan. 1973 / Columbia ✦✦✦
Over the years, Aerosmith has voiced dissatisfaction with its 1973 self-titled debut. While the songwriting may not be as exceptional as future releases, and Steven Tyler's singing style wasn't fully developed yet, the album succeeds on the band's raw, loose and bluesy performance. The now legendary quintet was unfairly labeled as a Stones/N.Y. Dolls rip-off at the time, but Aerosmith was more technically proficient at their instruments than the Dolls, and was much more hard rock-based than the Stones (i.e., Led Zeppelin, Yardbirds, etc.). *Aerosmith* spawned one of the first true rock ballads ever, the reflective "Dream On" (a hit single when re-released in 1976), while the rocking "Mama Kin" was one of the band's best early anthems, receiving further attention after Aero-disciples Guns N' Roses covered it on 1989's *G N R Lies*. Other tracks, such as "Make It," "Somebody," "One Way Street," "Write Me," and "Walking the Dog" serve as the perfect snapshot of the young band finding their foothold, while the oft-overlooked, long-and-winding storyteller, "Movin' Out," remains one of Aerosmith's all-time best. *Aerosmith* is one of their most underrated records. —*Greg Prato*

Get Your Wings / Mar. 1974 / Columbia ✦✦✦✦✦
Due to the commercial underachievement of Aerosmith's 1973 self-titled debut, the young band was nearly dropped by their record label. But a rigorous touring schedule helped strengthen their songwriting and tightened their playing even further, so after Columbia wisely decided to back the band again, the classic, *Get Your Wings*, was released. It didn't prove to be the sudden commercial breakthrough that Tyler and company hoped for, but it did go gold one year after it's release and set the stage perfectly for 1975's *Toys in the Attic*, which would propel Aerosmith into the rock & roll stratosphere. Comparing *Get Your Wings* to the 1973 debut is like night and day; it sounds almost like a completely different band—the playing is more aggressive, the songwriting succinct, and singer Steven Tyler had almost fully perfected his instantly recognizable yowl. But the sleaze and grit remained—"Same Old Song and Dance" combines a nasty blues groove with a tale of a drug deal gone bad, both "S.O.S. (Too Bad)" and "Lord of the Thighs" are straight-up rockers, and "Seasons of Wither" remains the band's most haunting ballad. But the best known song is their cover of "Train Kept A Rollin'," which would soon become a perennial showstopper in concert. *Get Your Wings* also marked the first time that producer Jack Douglas worked with the band; he would remain on the controls on nearly all of their future '70s hits. —*Greg Prato*

☆ **Toys in the Attic** / Apr. 1975 / Columbia ✦✦✦✦✦
After nearly getting off the ground with *Get Your Wings*, Aerosmith finally perfected their mix of Stonesy raunch and Zeppelin-esque riffing with their third album, *Toys in the Attic*. The success of the album derives from a combination of an increased sense of songwriting skills and purpose. Not only does Joe Perry turn out indelible riffs like "Walk This Way," "Toys in the Attic," and "Sweet Emotion," but Steven Tyler has fully embraced sleaziness as his artistic muse. Taking his cue from the old dirty blues "Big Ten Inch Record," Tyler writes with a gleeful impishness about sex throughout *Toys in the Attic*, whether it's the teenage heavy petting of "Walk This Way," the promiscuous "Sweet Emotion," or the double-entendres of "Uncle Salty" and "Adam's Apple." The rest of Aerosmith, led by Perry's dirty, exaggerated riffing, provide an appropriately greasy backing. Before *Toys in the Attic*, no other hard rock band sounded like this. Sure, Aerosmith cribbed heavily from the records of the Rolling Stones, New York Dolls, and Led Zeppelin, but they didn't have any of the menace of their influences, nor any of their mystique. Aerosmith was a gritty, street-wise hard rock band who played their blues as blooze and were in it for a good time; *Toys in the Attic* crystalizes that attitude. —*Stephen Thomas Erlewine*

★ **Rocks** / May 1976 / Columbia ✦✦✦✦✦
Few albums have been so appropriately named as Aerosmith's 1976 classic, *Rocks*. Despite hard drug use escalating among it's bandmembers, Aerosmith produced a superb follow-up to their masterwork, *Toys in the Attic*, nearly topping it in the process. Many Aero-fans will point to *Toys* as the band's quintessential album (it contained two radio/concert standards after all, "Walk This Way" and "Sweet Emotion"), but out of all their albums, *Rocks* did the best job of capturing Aerosmith at their most raw and rocking. Like it's predecessor, a pair of songs have become their most renowned—the menacing, hard-rock, cowboy-stomper "Back in the Saddle," as well as the downright viscous funk groove of "Last Child." Again, even the lesser-known tracks prove essential to the make up of the album, such as the stimulated "Rats in the Cellar" (a response of sorts to "Toys in the Attic"), the Stonesy "Combination," and the forgotten riff-rocker, "Get the Lead Out." Also included is the apocalyptic "Nobody's Fault," the up-and-coming rock star tale of "Lick and a Promise," and the album closing ballad, "Home Tonight." With *Rocks*, Aerosmith appeared to be indestructible, but this would not prove to be the case for long. —*Greg Prato*

Draw the Line / Dec. 1977 / Columbia ✦✦✦
Renting out an abandoned convent on the outskirts of New York City to record the follow-up to the hellacious *Rocks* may not have been the best idea, but 1977's *Draw the Line* still managed to be another down and dirty Aerosmith release. While it wasn't as awe inspiring as their last two albums—the members have said that the music suddenly got "cloudy" around this time (due to in-band fighting/ego-clashes, excessive living, etc.)–*Draw the Line* catches fire more times than not. Unlike their most recent album successes, the band shies away from studio experimentry and dabbling in different styles; instead they return to simple, straight-ahead, hard rock. The album-opening title track features a gloriously abrasive Joe Perry slide guitar riff and has been featured in concert ever since, while the punk-esque "Bright Light Fright" featured Perry's first ever lead vocal spot on an Aerosmith record. Other highlights include a re-working of the blues obscurity, "Milk Cow Blues," which Perry's pre-Aerosmith group, the Jam Band, played live, as well as "I Wanna Know Why," "Critical Mass," "Get It Up," "Kings and Queens," and

"Sight for Sore Eyes." *Draw the Line* would turn out to be the last true studio album from Aerosmith's original line-up for nearly a decade. *—Greg Prato*

Live Bootleg / Oct. 1978 / Columbia ✦✦

Night in the Ruts / Nov. 1979 / Columbia ✦

★ **Greatest Hits** / Oct. 1980 / Columbia ✦✦✦✦✦
Aerosmith's *Greatest Hits* remains one of the most popular and enduring best-of collections by any rock band, selling nearly ten million copies in the U.S. alone since it's release. But when it was issued in 1980, the band had just about reached its nadir. With original guitarist Joe Perry gone (and Brad Whitford soon to follow), Aerosmith had turned into a directionless, time-consuming ghost of its former self. Since there would be a three-year gap between 1979's *Night in the Ruts* and 1982's *Rock in a Hard Place, Greatest Hits* was assembled, more or less, to fill the void and buy the band some time. With the album clocking in at only 37-and a-half minutes, many Aero-classics are not included, such as what many consider the band's quintessential track, their cover of "Train Kept a Rollin'." The only poor selection is the forgettable "Remember (Walking in the Sand)," but nine out of ten are bonafide classics—"Dream On," "Same Old Song and Dance," "Sweet Emotion," "Walk this Way," "Last Child," "Back in the Saddle," and "Draw the Line." Also featured is their venomous cover of the Beatles' "Come Together," previously only available as a single and on the soundtrack to the 1978 movie, *Sgt. Pepper's Lonely Hearts Club Band.* For the casual fan, *Greatest Hits* will do the job, as well as its sister-album, 1988's *Gems.* *—Greg Prato*

Rock in a Hard Place / Aug. 1982 / Columbia ✦

Done with Mirrors / Nov. 1985 / Geffen ✦✦✦✦
Joe Perry returned to the fold in 1985, and the band turned out their finest record since *Rocks.* Unlike the records that preceded it, *Done with Mirrors* was powered by the same smart-assed lyrics and filthy guitars that formed the core of Aerosmith's best songs. It didn't receive the commercial or critical attention that *Permanent Vacation* did two years later, but *Done with Mirrors* is the better album; it marks the beginning of their remarkable comeback. *—Stephen Thomas Erlewine*

Classics Live / Apr. 1986 / Columbia ✦✦

Classics Live 2 / Jun. 1987 / Columbia ✦✦✦
When Aerosmith got wind that their then-former record label, Columbia, was going to release a follow-up to the lifeless *Classics Live,* the band wisely decided to get more involved this time around. The result is arguably the band's finest live album, even though it may be a bit short (not even 39 minutes in length). But the performances are vibrant and focused—almost all were taken from the reunited line-up's New Year's Eve, 1984 gig at the Orpheum Theater. The only criticism is that, again, the majority of the tracks were already released as live versions (on 1978's *Live Bootleg*), and only three make their in-concert debut on record. Still, positively smoking versions of "Back in the Saddle," "Walk this Way," "Same Old Song and Dance," "Last Child," "Draw the Line," and "Toys in the Attic" rock out like no other Aerosmith live recording. The album's undisputed highlight is a fantastic rendition of the autobiographical early nugget "Movin' Out," as well as the title track from the Joe Perry Project's 1980 debut, *Let the Music Do the Talking* (which was subsequently re-recorded for Aerosmith's *Done With Mirrors*). Although *Live Bootleg* may contain more songs, the more succinct *Classics Live II* succeeds with it's consistent, fiery performances. *—Greg Prato*

Permanent Vacation / Aug. 1987 / Geffen ✦✦✦✦
The much-ballyhooed reunion of the original Aerosmith lineup had pretty much fallen flat on its face after 1985's hit-and-miss *Done With Mirrors.* Realizing that the band simply couldn't do it alone, A&R guru John Kalodner capitalized on the runaway success of Run-D.M.C.'s cover of "Walk This Way" and decided to draft in the day's top hired hands, including knob-twiddler extraordinaire Bruce Fairbairn and career-revitalizing song doctors Desmond Child and Jim Vallance. Together, they would help craft *Permanent Vacation,* the album which would reinvent Aerosmith as '80s and '90s superstars. Yet, despite the mostly stellar songwriting, which makes it a strong effort overall, some of the album's nooks and crannies haven't aged all that well because of Fairbairn's overwrought production, featuring an exaggerated sleekness typical of most mid-'80s pop metal albums. Furthermore, Desmond Child's pedantic writing often compromises the timeliness of even the best material. On the other hand, pre-fab radio gems like "Rag Doll" and "Dude (Looks like a Lady)" remain largely unassailable from a "delivering the goods" perspective. But remember kids, this *is* Aerosmith, so that can only mean one thing: a guaranteed number of incredible tracks for any time and place. These include the earthy voodoo blues of "St. John" and the excellent hobo-harmonica fable of "Hangman Jury." And, although some of the remaining cuts lean to the filler side, both the awkwardly Caribbean title track and the cover of the Beatles' "I'm Down" are well executed. Finally, the crowd-pleasing schmaltz of "Angel" showcases the band at the peak of their power-ballad cheese. A valiant effort, this album proved to be the crucial catalyst in reintroducing Aerosmith to the masses, but if you're looking for an even better example of the band's renewed strength, check out *Pump* first. *—John Franck & Ed Rivadavia*

Gems / 1988 / Columbia ✦✦✦✦✦
With 1987's *Permanent Vacation* successfully restoring Aerosmith's reputation as one of hard rock's finest, Columbia Records (their first record company) decided the time was right to issue a follow-up of sorts to their 1980 compilation, *Greatest Hits.* The result, 1988's *Gems,* features almost all the tracks that were missing from the first collection, focusing more on their harder-rocking album cuts instead of the hits. Such favorites as their superb cover of "Train Kept a Rollin'" (a perennial concert showstopper) and the early classic "Mama Kin" are included, as well as tracks unfamiliar to the casual fan. Three selections are featured from their definitive album, *Rocks* ("Rats in the Cellar," "Lick and a Promise," and "Nobody's Fault"), plus other '70s highlights: "No Surprize," "Adam's Apple," "Round and Round," "Critical Mass," and "Lord of the Thighs." And a previously unreleased studio version of "Chip Away the Stone" will undoubtedly interest hardcore fans (only a live version from *Live Bootleg* had been issued before). Like the Stones and Zeppelin, Aerosmith's album cuts often eclipsed their more renowned material, making *Gems* an indispensable collection. *—Greg Prato*

Pump / Sep. 1989 / Geffen ✦✦✦✦✦
Where *Permanent Vacation* seemed a little overwhelmed by its pop concessions, *Pump* revels in them without ever losing sight of Aerosmith's dirty hard-rock core. Which doesn't mean the record is a sellout—"What It Takes" has more emotion and grit than any of their other power ballads; "Janie's Got a Gun" tackles more complex territory than most previous songs; and "The Other Side" and "Love in an Elevator" rock relentlessly, no matter how many horns and synths fight with the guitars. Such ambition and successful musical eclecticism make *Pump* rank with *Rocks* and *Toys in the Attic.* *—Stephen Thomas Erlewine*

Pandora's Box / Nov. 1991 / Columbia ✦✦

Get a Grip / Apr. 1993 / Geffen ✦✦✦
Coming on the heels of the commercially and artistically successful *Pump,* the fitfully entertaining *Get a Grip* pales against its predecessor's musical diversity. But it's not for lack of trying. In fact, Aerosmith tries too hard, making a stab at social commentary ("Livin' on the Edge") while keeping adolescent fans in their corner with their trademark raunch-rock ("Get a Grip" and "Eat the Rich"), as well as having radio-ready hit ballads ("Cryin'," "Amazing," and "Crazy"). The problem is, it's a studied performance—it sounds like what an Aerosmith album should sound like. Most of the album sounds good; it's just that there isn't much beneath the surface. *—Stephen Thomas Erlewine*

● **Big Ones** / Nov. 1, 1994 / Geffen ✦✦✦✦✦
Big Ones serves up the hits and nothing but the hits; Aerosmith's excellent debut for Geffen, *Done with Mirrors,* is conveniently overlooked. So what's left is some of the finest mainstream hard rock of the late '80s and early '90s—the fruits of one of the most remarkable comebacks in rock & roll history. Unfortunately, there's precious little of the classic Aerosmith raunch; in fact, the two new tracks are the hardest, slinkiest tracks here. Otherwise, the uptempo tracks bog down in overproduction ("Love in an Elevator"), and the frequently embarrassingly overwrought power ballads ("Angel" and "Crazy") dominate too much of the album. So what's left? The band's best stab at social commentary ("Janie's Got a Gun"), a sublime slinky throwaway ("Deuces Are Wild"), deliciously sleazy blues-rockers ("Rag Doll," "(Dude) Looks Like a Lady"), and their best ballads ("What It Takes" and "Cryin'"). *—Stephen Thomas Erlewine*

Box of Fire / Nov. 22, 1994 / Columbia ✦✦✦✦✦
For the serious Aerosmith fan looking to obtain all of the band's classic releases for Columbia, 1994's *Box of Fire* is a quintessential purchase. Included are all of the band's 12 releases for their original record company, as well as a five-track bonus disc that features previously unreleased/hard-to-find songs (an absolute highlight of which is a killer reading of "Rockin' Pneumonia and the Boogie Woogie Flu"). All of the albums have been remastered from the original source tapes using 20-bit technology, and the packaging is excellent—each CD booklet is chock-full of classic photos and memorabilia from each specific album's era. Such Aero masterpieces as 1974's *Get Your Wings,* 1975's *Toys in the Attic,* and 1976's *Rocks* have only improved with age; and by listening back to such releases as *Draw the Line* and *Night in the Ruts* (which were both panned by critics when first issued), you'll discover many forgotten classics. Although not all of the albums consist of original material (three live albums and two greatest-hits packages are included in the set), *Box of Fire* is highly recommended despite its steep price. *—Greg Prato*

Nine Lives / Mar. 18, 1997 / Columbia ✦✦✦
Aerosmith signed a multi-million-dollar contract with Columbia Records before they had completed their deal with Geffen, which meant that a lot was riding on their Columbia debut, *Nine Lives,* when it was finally delivered in 1997. During recording, the band nearly broke up, and they worked with a number of producers—including Glen Ballard, the man behind Alanis Morissette—before settling on Kevin Shirley, an in-house producer responsible for Silverchair and Journey. Perhaps that's the reason why *Nine Lives* sounds so calculated, as if it was assembled by a band trying to sound like Aerosmith. In a sense, it is—not one of the 13 songs was written without the assistance of professional songwriters. Of course, some of the best moments of *Pump* and *Permanent Vacation* were also written with professionals, but they had an appealing, slick surface that made them infectious. *Nine Lives,* in contrast, is over-labored, with Aerosmith making a conscious effort to sound hip and vibrant, which ironically simply makes them sound tired. Not only are the performances perfunctory, but the songs aren't catchy—no matter how hard it tries, "Falling in Love (Is Hard on the Knees)" never develops a hook, and it is not an exception. A handful of cuts approximate the raunchy appeal of prime Aerosmith, but *Nine Lives* is hardly the triumphant comeback it should have been. *—Stephen Thomas Erlewine*

A Little South of Sanity / Oct. 20, 1998 / Geffen ✦✦✦
Aerosmith signed with Columbia early in the '90s, before their contract with Geffen expired, and, as part of the deal, they owed a live album to Geffen—hence the appearance of *A Little South of Sanity,* a double-disc set culled from tapes from the *Get a Grip* and *Nine Lives* tours. Considering its origins, the record couldn't help but feel a little like the contractual obligation it is, but it's to Aerosmith's credit that it doesn't sound entirely tired. Not that it sounds vital—Steven Tyler's adolescent schtick sounds particularly embarrassing as he approaches his 50th birthday, and newer material like "Falling in Love (Is Hard on the Knees)" or even the hit "Amazing" pales in comparison to their '70s and

late-'80s classics. Still, Aerosmith developed into world-class showmen during the first Bush era, which is why *A Little South of Sanity* will be an entertaining romp for longtime fans; they're likely not to be disappointed by the slickness that runs rampant over the record, nor will they be dismayed by the predictable song selection, two criticisms that could be offered as proof that Aerosmith is past their prime, because it's all part of the show. *—Stephen Thomas Erlewine*

Just Push Play / Mar. 6, 2001 / Columbia ♦♦♦
Give Aerosmith credit for not only realizing something was wrong after *Nine Lives* relatively flat-lined, but deciding to do something about it. Ditching the outside producers who initially liberated but eventually straitjacketed them, Steve Tyler and Joe Perry seized control of the boards, working with the assistence of Mark Hudson and Marti Frederiksen. (Forever the Stones fanatics, Tyler and Perry dubbed this crew the Boneyard Boys, just like how Mick-n-Keef are the Glimmer Twins.) So, this isn't really a full-fledged band affair and Hudson and Frederiksen's fingerprints are all over the place, but that doesn't matter since the end result is tighter, savvier, and better than anything since *Pump.* It's still far from perfect, however, since it suffers from a surfeit of memorable material, and the group members' steadfast refusal to act their age results in a couple of embarrassing slips into stodginess (the "fuckin' A" chorus on the title track, a song improbably titled "Trip Hoppin'," or the ludicrous "Avant Garden"). These mean that the record doesn't come close to matching the twin comebacks of *Permanent Vacation* and *Pump*, but it's a sleek classicist hard rock record that sounds good—better than Aerosmith has sounded in nearly a decade, as a matter of fact, particularly when the group gets a hook as tuneful as that of "Jaded." Aerosmith sounds good enough on *Just Push Play* that it almost makes you forgive the Heavy Metal refugee on the front cover, a sexy robot illustration that looks far more out of date than the music sounds. *—Stephen Thomas Erlewine*

The Afghan Whigs

f. 1986, Hamilton, OH, **db.** 2001
Indie Rock, Alternative Pop/Rock
Evolving from a garage-punk band in the vein of the Replacements, Dinosaur Jr., and Mudhoney to a literate, pretentious, soul-inflected post-punk quartet, the Afghan Whigs were one of the most critically acclaimed alternative bands of the early '90s. Although the band never broke into the mainstream, they developed a dedicated cult following, primarily because of lead singer/songwriter Greg Dulli's tortured, angst-ridden tales of broken relationships and self-loathing. The Afghan Whigs were one of the few alternative bands around in the late '90s to acknowledge R&B, attempting to create a fusion of soul and post-punk. A 1988 debut with good word-of-mouth led to a record contract with the influential Seattle-based independent Sub Pop, and Afghan Wigs earned many positive reviews for their third album, 1992's *Congregation.* Signed to the major label Elektra, the band released *Gentlemen* one year later; "Debonair," the first single pulled from the album, received major play from MTV, and all of the reviews were positive. Nevertheless, the band wasn't able to ascend past cult status and the critical praise even engendered a backlash. An extended break during 1994 preceded the release of *Black Love* in 1996. Again, the album received positive reviews but the band failed to break out of their cult status. *1965*, their first effort for new label Columbia, followed two years later, but it would prove to be their last—the band called it quits in February of 2001, citing geographical separation. *—Stephen Thomas Erlewine*

Big Top Halloween / 1988 / Ultrasuede ♦♦

Up in It / 1990 / Sub Pop ♦♦♦
Though the Afghan Whigs were still about a year away from hitting the peak of their powers in the studio, their second album, 1990's *Up in It*, was a major improvement over their self-released debut, and it was their first recording to suggest that they would mature into one of the best American rock bands of the 1990s. As a songwriter, Greg Dulli was starting to really get in touch with his self-loathing, and "Retarded," "White Trash Party," and "I Know Your Little Secret" offer a powerful and sometimes disturbing look into one man's obsessions. Just as importantly, the band had finally learned to make the most of their musical muscle; Greg Dulli's nicotine-laced growl merged "heavy-alternative" bellow with a soul man's sense of phrasing, while the guitars of Dulli and Rick McCollum and the rhythm section of John Curley and Steve Earle managed to combine bruising power with a remarkable sense of drama and dynamics. While lots of bands riding the "grunge"/"alternative" bandwagon at the time owed an obvious debt to Led Zeppelin, the Afghan Whigs were one of the few that fully grasped not just their pomp and heaviosity, but their precision, their timing, and their understanding of R&B. While it pales in comparison to what the Whigs would achieve on *Congregation* and *Gentlemen*, *Up in It* made it clear the Afghan Whigs had truly arrived, and would not be ignored. *—Mark Deming*

Congregation / Aug. 1991 / Sub Pop ♦♦♦♦♦
The grunge era's most overlooked masterpiece, *Congregation* was the Afghan Whigs' breakthrough album, an incendiary and insidious set which bridges the gap between the noisy aggression of the band's early releases and the soulful swagger of their later work. Slipping with ominous ease into the sinister, self-obsessed lothario guise which would serve him so well from here on out, Greg Dulli announces his arrival as a truly magnetic presence—by turns predator ("Tonight") and prey ("I'm Her Slave"), he's the guy your parents always warned you about, delivering each syllable of his remarkable lyrics with equal measures of innuendo and venom. Equally startling is the Whigs' musical growth—while still unmistakably a member of the Sub Pop stable, there's a greater maturity and depth to their sinewy sound, with a newfound grasp of mood and nuance on tracks like the opening "Her Against Me" and "Let Me Lie to You"—the wah-wah guitar which dominates "Turn on the Water," meanwhile, offers the first taste of the funk ambitions to follow. It was hardly a surprise when the Whigs jumped to Elektra soon after—*Congregation* was clearly their ticket to the big leagues. *—Jason Ankeny*

Uptown Avondale / 1992 / Sub Pop ♦♦♦♦
The Afghan Whigs' final recording for Sub Pop, *Uptown Avondale* is anything but a contractual obligation—a five-track EP comprising four R&B covers and a remake of *Congregation*'s unlisted bonus track "Milez Iz Ded" (here retitled "The Rebirth of the Cool"), it's a soulful, scorching collection that captures the band at their gritty best. Quickly dispelling any lingering doubts that Greg Dulli's soul-man aspirations are anything but genuine, the disc's covers of chestnuts like Freda Payne's "Band of Gold" and the Supremes' "Come See About Me" are remarkable, remaining true to the music's R&B roots but infused with the Whigs' noise-punk energy—Dulli sings like a man possessed, rejuvenating this familiar material with both reverence and attitude. *—Jason Ankeny*

● **Gentlemen** / Oct. 5, 1993 / Elektra ♦♦♦♦♦
The Afghan Whigs' sound was growing larger by the release during the days on Sub Pop, so the fact that *Gentlemen* turned out the way it did wasn't all that surprising as a result ("cinematic" was certainly the word the band was aiming for, what with credits describing the recording process as being "shot on location" at Ardent Studios). While *Gentlemen* is no monolith, it is very much of a piece at the start. While "If I Were Going" opens things on a slightly moodier tip, it's the crunch of "Gentlemen," "Be Sweet," and "Debonair" that really stands out, each of which features a tightly wound R&B punch that rocks out as much as it grooves, if not more so. Dulli's lyrics immediately set about the task of emotional self-evisceration at the same time, with lines like "Ladies, let me tell you about myself—I got a dick for a brain" being among the calmer points. The album truly comes into its own with "When We Two Parted," though, as sad countryish guitars chime over a slow crawling rhythm and Dulli's quiet-then-anguished detailing of an exploding relationship. From there on in, things surge from strength to greater strength, sometimes due to the subtlest of touches—the string arrangement on "Fountain and Fairfax" or the unexpected, resigned lead vocal from Scrawl's Marcy Mays on "My Curse," for instance. Other times, it's all the much more up front, as "What Jail is Like," with its heartbroken-and-fierce combination of piano, feedback, and drive building to an explosive chorus. Dulli's blend of utter abnegation and masculine swagger may be a crutch, but when everything connects, as it does more often than not on *Gentlemen*, both he and his band are unstoppable. *—Ned Raggett*

What Jail Is Like / Aug. 9, 1994 / Elektra ♦♦

Black Love / Mar. 12, 1996 / Elektra ♦♦♦
Following the dense, psuedoliterary aspirations of *Gentlemen*, *Black Love* sounds nearly lighthearted. That doesn't mean it's a light record—lead singer/songwriter Greg Dulli has an overwhelming affection for the morose and the twisted. From the grinding guitars to the hardboiled lyrics, the Afghan Whigs revel in the dark side. The problem is, Dulli isn't a compelling enough melodicist to make the songs stick; furthermore, his lyrics frequently sound like posturing, as if they were learned from books and movies. When the Afghan Whigs are at their best, they create a soundscape that evokes the lyrical world Dulli tries so hard to conjure. Rooted in indie-guitar rock, the band blends in slight elements of early '70s soul and R&B, with an occasional country overtone. It reads better than it sounds—though they play with organs and attempt to land in a groove, but it doesn't amount to genuine, gritty soul. Instead, their funk experiments add another thick layer of grunge. Combined with the clanging guitars and the willfully bleak lyrics, the result is an album so lumbering and unmelodic that it can only be admired, not enjoyed. *—Stephen Thomas Erlewine*

1965 / Oct. 27, 1998 / Columbia ♦♦♦♦♦
With *1965*, the Afghan Whigs have finally made the gritty soul record just always out of their reach—seamlessly integrating the R&B aspirations which have textured the band's sound since the beginning, the music simmers with raw energy, its deep, dark grooves not so much white-boy as simply white-hot. Recorded in New Orleans, the album is plainly the product of its environment—sultry, sleazy and more than a little menacing; here more than ever, Greg Dulli is the frontman you love to hate, strutting and swaggering his way through standout tracks like "Something Hot," "Uptown Again," and "John the Baptist" with predatory aggression. (Who else would deliver a lyric like "I got the devil in me, girl" as though it were a pickup line?) Still, for all its cocksure arrogance, *1965* is neverthless a sincere tribute to the classic music recalled by the album's title—lyrics aside, even if Dulli did sell his soul, he's somehow managed to get it all back. *—Jason Ankeny*

Christina Aguilera

b. Dec. 18, 1980
Vocals / Teen Pop, Adult Contemporary, Dance-Pop
Teen pop diva Christina Aguilera was born December 18, 1980, in Staten Island, NY; the careers of her military father and musician mother ensured that the family traveled the globe before finally settling in Wexford, PA, where the youngster first began performing in area talent shows. At age eight, Aguilera appeared on the syndicated television series *Star Search*; four years later, she landed a regular role on Disney's *The New Mickey Mouse Club*, co-starring with future luminaries including Britney Spears, 'N Sync's JC Chasez and Justin Timberlake, and *Felicity*'s Keri Russell. Aguilera's first pop music success came in Japan thanks to "All I Wanna Do," a smash duet with Keizo Nakanishi; she returned to the U.S. in 1998 to record the song "Reflection" for the soundtrack of the animated film *Mulan*, that same week signing to RCA. Releasing her self-titled debut album the following year, Aguilera topped the pop charts with the single "Genie in a Bottle." *Christina Aguilera* sold over ten million copies worldwide in just under a year and turned its namesake into a superstar. She followed this success with performances at *the Super Bowl XXXIII Halftime Show* and for President Clinton and won a Best New Artist Grammy.

Just over a year after she released her debut album, Aguilera released *Mi Reflejo*, a collection of Spanish-language songs, as well as *My Kind of Christmas*, a holiday album. —*Jason Ankeny*

● **Christina Aguilera** / Aug. 24, 1999 / RCA ✦✦✦✦
Since Christina Aguilera is the third and last of *The New Mickey Mouse Club* alumni to hit the charts in the mid-'90s—following two members of 'N Sync and Britney Spears—it's easy for cynical observers to assume that she was the lesser of the three talents since she arrived last after everyone scaled the charts. That's not the case at all. If anything, Aguilera is the best of the three, blessed with a rich voice that's given the material it deserves. Her eponymous debut remains firmly within the teen-oriented dance-pop genre, but unlike Spears' album, this is done right. The songwriting is strong—the ballads are engaging, the dance numbers are catchy—the production is clean and uncluttered, letting Aguilera's voice take the foreground. Most impressively, she not only has charisma, she can actually sing, bringing conviction to these love and heartbreak songs. So, *Christina Aguilera* may be lightweight, but it's lightweight in the best possible sense—breezy, fun, engaging, and enjoyable on each repeated listen. Out of the deluge of teen-pop albums in 1999, this feels like the best of the lot. —*Stephen Thomas Erlewine*

Mi Reflejo / Sep. 12, 2000 / RCA International ✦✦✦
When Christina Aguilera's eponymous debut reached multi-platinum status in the summer of 1999, the charts were also ruled by the Latin pop explosion, headed by Ricky Martin. Since Aguilera had Venezuelan heritage, recording a Latin pop album was appropriate, even if she didn't know how to speak the language. Besides, a Latin album was an easy way to buy time for an artist waiting to produce an eagerly awaited sequel to a blockbuster album. So, she knocked out the record that became *Mi Reflejo* in 1999 and 2000, between tours and video shoots. She learned the words phonetically, but she already knew most of the melodies, since the bulk of the album was Spanish-language versions of songs on the debut album. In other words, it was a mirror image of the debut—her Spanish reflection, as it were. This results in an album that is just a little too familiar, even if it's classy and well-produced and spiked with a couple of new tunes that hold their own with the holdovers. Even so, it's hard to view *Mi Reflejo* as anything other than a bit of a pleasant holding pattern; it's enjoyable as it spins, but it doesn't add anything new to her music, since it's just the old music in new clothing. —*Stephen Thomas Erlewine*

My Kind of Christmas / Oct. 24, 2000 / RCA ✦✦✦
The second punch in a double whammy of stopgap releases in the fourth quarter of 2000, *My Kind of Christmas* appeared on the shelves two months after *Mi Reflejo*, Christina's Latin reworking of her debut album. *My Kind of Christmas* actually has more new material than *Mi Reflejo*, and Aguilera responds in kind, turning in passionate performances throughout the 11-song album. She can teeter on the edge of being *too* passionate, belting out when she should lay back, but the power of her voice, no matter how diva-esque she may be, remains remarkable; she needs to learn restraint, but she's clearly a better singer than her peers. Of course, *My Kind of Christmas* remains a holiday album, filled with covers of standards (from "Oh Holy Night" to "The Christmas Song" to "Merry Christmas, Baby") and a handful of obligatory new songs. None of the new songs are knockouts, but "Christmas Time" and "This Year" are pretty solid pieces of dance-pop, even if the marvelously titled "Xtina's Xmas" (easily the best name of any new holiday song of 2000) is a 90-second collage trifle that doesn't live up to its promise. But, hey—filler is part of a holiday record, and there's actually not too much of it here. Instead, it's pretty tight, entertaining seasonal dance-pop. It may not add too much to Christina's catalog, but it does suggest that she may not be a mere one-album wonder. —*Stephen Thomas Erlewine*

a-ha

f. 1982, Oslo, Norway
New Wave, Synth Pop

Pal Waaktaar and Magne Furuholmen formed a-ha in the early '80s. Morten Harket joined the duo, and they left for the now "legendary London flat" (so called because of its state of disrepair) to make it. By late 1983 they had achieved part of that goal by signing to WEA. "Take on Me" took three times to become a hit in the U.K., eventually hitting number two in November 1985. Going one better in the U.S. mainly due to the wide exposure of its stunning video on MTV, which fused animation with real-life action, their only further hit there was "The Sun Always Shines on T.V.," which became a U.K. number one single in early 1986 helping take the album *Hunting High and Low* to the Top Ten. Mostly an album of synth pop, the press were quick to dismiss them; however, there was more to a-ha in Waaktaar's writing and a matured effort, *Scoundrel Days*, which was released in October 1986. More focused, it had a stronger band feel thanks to live drumming displayed to great lengths on "The Swing of Things" and lead single "I've Been Losing You." After a world tour, a-ha supplied the soundtrack to the James Bond flick *The Living Daylights*. In 1990, a-ha were commended by the Everly Brothers for their rendition of "Crying in the Rain" from their fourth album, *East of the Sun, West of the Moon*, which was largely ignored in the U.K. 1993 heralded some much needed new blood in the U2 terrain of "Dark Is the Night" from the *Memorial Beach* album. Following the unfortunate lack of success following *Memorial Beach*, Furuholmen retreated into the art world while Waaktaar released the album *Mary Is Coming* with his new band, Savoy. —*Kelvin Hayes*

● **Hunting High and Low** / Jun. 1985 / Warner Brothers ✦✦✦✦
This is friendly synthesizer pop, fronted by the emotive, sometimes falsetto vocals of Morten Harket. But it was Harket's looks, as exhibited in the semi-animated video, that sent "Take on Me" to number one in the summer of 1985. The album also contains the follow-up, "The Sun Always Shines on T.V." (number 20). But so far, this million-selling

debut is the beginning and end of a-ha as legitimate record makers in the U.S. (In the U.K., in contrast, the album spawned four Top Ten hits, including the title track and "Train of Thought.") —*William Ruhlmann*

Scoundrel Days / 1986 / Warner Brothers ✦✦✦
While not quite as strong as the band's debut, *Scoundrel Days* is still a-ha succeeding as a marketed "pretty boy" band which can connect musically and lyrically as much as any musical sacred cow. The opening two songs alone make for one of the best one-two opening punches around: the tense edge of the title track, featuring one of Morten Harket's soaring vocals during the chorus and a crisp, pristine punch in the music, and "The Swing of Things," a moody, elegant number with a beautiful synth/guitar arrangement (plus some fine drumming courtesy of studio pro Michael Sturgis) and utterly lovelorn lyrical sentiments that balance on the edge of being overheated without quite going over. Although the rest of the disc never quite hits as high as the opening, it comes close more often than not. A definite downturn is the band's occasional attempts to try and prove themselves as a "real" band by rocking out, as on "I've Been Losing You"—there's really no need for it, and as a result they sound much more "fake," ironically enough. Other songs can perhaps only be explained by the need to translate lyrics—"We're Looking for the Whales" isn't an environmental anthem, and neither is "Cry Wolf," but both also don't really succeed in using nature as romantic metaphor. When a-ha are on, though, they're on—"October" snakes along on a cool bass/keyboard arrangement and a whispery vocal from Harket; "Maybe Maybe" is a quirky little pop number that's engagingly goofy; while "Soft Rains of April" captures the band at its most dramatic, with the string synths giving Harket a perfect bed to launch into a lovely vocal, concluding with a sudden, hushed whisper. The '80s may be long gone, but *Scoundrel Days* makes clear that not everything was bad back then. —*Ned Raggett*

Stay on These Roads / 1988 / Warner Brothers ✦✦

East of the Sun, West of the Moon / 1990 / Warner Brothers ✦✦✦
A small surprise, too quickly destined for the cut-out bins considering the way their career finally went after *Hunting High And Low*. This is a nicely crafted collection of songs, performed and sung beautifully, with lots of echoes and suggestions tucked into the music. While not an album one can discuss at length, it's an album that's a pleasure to listen to and one that deserves a better reception than the one, unfortunately, that it seems to have gotten. —*Steven McDonald*

Memorial Beach / Apr. 1992 / Warner Brothers ✦

Headlines and Deadlines: The Hits of a-ha / Sep. 22, 1998 / Wea International ✦✦✦✦
Norway's a-ha took "Take on Me" to the number one spot on Billboard's Top 40 in 1985, thanks to the award-winning animated video that accompanied it. Still, a-ha contributed rather accordingly to the '80s pop sound, drenching their music with bouncy riffs and employing the keyboard as the foundation to their colorful formula. *Headlines and Deadlines: The Hits of a-ha* assembles all of their singles together, a definite one-stop for all of their music. Combining ballads and radiant '80s pop, this set includes their most fervent offering in "The Sun Always Shines On T.V.," which hit number 20 in 1986 and originated from *Hunting High and Low*, the same album that included "Take on Me." After this album, the band's next couple of releases, *East of the Sun* and *Memorial Beach*, were total washouts, which makes this compilation all the more worthy. Other notables include remixed versions of "Hunting High and Low" and "You Are the One," as well as the theme song to *The Living Daylights*. Though comparisons to Duran Duran are difficult to avoid, a-ha did harbor some distinct qualities in their glossy sound, and quite a few of their songs still contain some redeeming factors, but are better appreciated when lined up in compilation form. —*Mike DeGagne*

Minor Earth Major Sky / Jun. 20, 2000 / Wea International ✦✦✦
A-ha's sixth studio CD (seventh if their greatest hits collection is included) came eight years after their previous album, *Memorial Beach*, and in that time it seems that a-ha have mellowed out. They do not seem to have concern about attracting the youth/dance market, but instead seem to be focusing in on how to make perfect middle-of-the-road pop songs with '90s technology. This is not a criticism, as it produces several fantastic songs, such as "Little Black Heart" and the wonderful "I Wish That I Cared." These, and many others, are full of catchy, beautiful melodies and Morten Harket's vocals are near perfect as usual—his voice has not lowered one octave since their debut. The one problem with this CD is the relative sameness to some of the music. The tempos do not change a great deal, and by the end the songs seem to run together. More variety would have been beneficial. However, in terms of production, this is as close to perfect as a CD can get, and the lyrics keep things interesting throughout. Overall, a good album, and one that fans will enjoy. —*Aaron Badgley*

Air

f. 1995, Paris, France
Ambient Pop, Electronica, Trip-Hop

More apt to cite stately rock paragons Burt Bacharach and Brian Wilson as their inspirations than Derrick May or Aphex Twin, the French duo Air gained inclusion into the late-'90s electronica surge due chiefly to the labels their recordings appeared on, not the actual music they produced. Their sound, a variant of the classic disco sound coaxed into a relaxing prozac vision of the late '70s, looked back to a variety of phenomena from the period—synthesizer maestros Tomita, Jean-Michel Jarre, and Vangelis, new wave music of the non-spikey variety, and obscure Italian film soundtracks. Despite gaining quick entrance into the dance community (through releases for Source and Mo' Wax), Air's 1998 debut album *Moon Safari* charted a light—well, airy—course along soundscapes composed with melody lines by Moog and Rhodes, not Roland and Yamaha. The presence of several female vocalists, an equipment list whose number of pieces stretched into the dozens, and a baroque tuba solo on one track; all of this conspired to make Air more of a happening in the living room than the dancefloor. *—John Bush*

★ **Moon Safari** / Jan. 19, 1998 / Astralwerks ✦✦✦✦✦
A cavalcade of analog synthesizers, organs, electric pianos, and processed voices populate *Moon Safari*, a thoroughly appealing, otherworldly debut album from Air. Where most of their dance contemporaries push the boundaries of trip-hop or jungle, Air blends Euro-dance with new wave. Any futuristic element on their album feels strangely outdated, since they're borrowed from the early '80s, which gives their music an odd, out-of-time feeling. The waves of gurgling synths beneath the spacious, colorful chords and melodies give the impression that the music is floating in space. For all the atmospherics and layers of synths, there's a distinct pop sense to *Moon Safari* that makes it accessible and damn near irresistible. *—Stephen Thomas Erlewine*

Premiers Symptomes [US] / Aug. 24, 1999 / Astralwerks ✦✦✦✦✦
It's usually just the collectors and obsessed fans that contend a band's first few singles are really their best work, far better than the material that ends up on their first album. With the French band Air, the collectors may just be right for once. *Premiers Symptomes*, a five-track EP boosted up to seven tracks for its eventual American issue on Astralwerks, features some of the most gorgeous moments in the duo's discography—no small task considering the gems included on their full-length debut, 1998's *Moon Safari*. Almost completely instrumental (except for the surprisingly smooth robot croon on "Le Soleil est Pres de Moi"), *Premiers Symptomes* offers a half-dozen tracks of beautiful, deliciously downtempo synth-pop. It's far more than just a compilation of substandard early material that works best for collectors, it takes its place right next to *Moon Safari* as another highlight of French electronica. *—John Bush*

The Virgin Suicides [Original Soundtrack] / Feb. 29, 2000 / Astralwerks ✦✦✦
Two years after the arrival of their debut album, the French twosome Air returned, not with a proper sophomore LP, but with *The Virgin Suicides*, a full soundtrack to the directing debut of Sophia Coppola. Only one track, "Playground Love," has vocals, and that comes from an outsider (Gordon Tracks) who sounds more like the Auteurs' Luke Haines than Beth Hirsch, the only real vocalist employed previously. The trademarked Air sound is for the most part unchanged; as on *Moon Safari*, producers Godin and Dunckel rely on contemplative electronic mood-music in a minor key, heavy on the analog synth and organ yet with plenty of traditional textures (guitar, brass, strings, live-sounding drums) in keeping with lounge music and space-pop from the 1960s and '70s. And though all the music here is as meticulously detailed as the tracks on *Moon Safari*, the soundtrack cultivates an atmosphere more in league with traditional scoring—instead of focusing on pop songs in an electronic context, Air constructed these tracks as mere soundbytes, simple themes with little embellishment on the basic ideas. Of course, that's perfectly in keeping with the secondary role soundtracks should play to truly serve the movies for which they're composed. Listeners eager for a second dose of the exquisite electronic pop found on *Moon Safari* will be pleased with much of *The Virgin Suicides*, but will probably have to wait until Air's proper follow-up to find more evidence of their greatness. *—John Bush*

10,000 Hz Legend / May 29, 2001 / Astralwerks ✦✦✦✦
Eager to prove their songwriting smarts and knowledge of traditionalist pop on their sophomore work, French band Air pulled back slightly from the milky synth pop of their 1998 debut, *Moon Safari*. *10,000 Hz Legend* is a darker work, just as contemplative and unhurried as its predecessor, but part of a gradual move from drifting, almost pastoral melancholia to a downright post-modern helplessness in league with Radiohead. Air are still tremendously effective producers, and have actually expanded their palate with a surprising array of pop instrumentation (acoustic guitars, flutes, pianos, a harmonica, harps, and many strings) to file alongside the countless trilling synthesizers and machine sequencers. The two lead-off tracks, "Electronic Performers" and "How Does It Make You Feel," are breathtaking productions that exploit the same robot-weariness tendencies that made "Sexy Boy" (from *Moon Safari*) an alternative hit. Still, those detached retro-vocoder treatments sound so much more passé in 2001 than when the duo first tried them out in 1996. Jason Falkner and Beck, a pair of equally hardworking slacker-pop icons, appear (respectively) on the next two tracks, the tongue-in-cheek single "Radio #1" and an excellent morning-after jam named "The Vagabond." Again, the production is stellar, but these find Air stranded between art rock and pop, caught in the trap of trying to make great pop music yet never sounding particularly studied or concerned about it. Falkner pops up again on "Lucky and Unhappy" and "People in the City," a pair of album standouts that subvert any pop inclinations with a raft of bridges and breakdowns among the layers of production. "Wonder Milky Bitch" is another precisely studied track, a haze of lunar-desert synth pop directly evocative of country-pop classicist Lee Hazlewood, and "Radian" brings Air back to the instrumental textures of their early work. Fans and involved listeners are definitely rewarded with increased dividends after multiple listens, but even they may wish for an album that harked back to the simpler days of the *Premiers Symptomes* EP and *Moon Safari*. *—John Bush*

Air Supply

f. 1976, Melbourne, Australia
Soft Rock, Adult Contemporary
With their heavily orchestrated, sweet ballads, the Australian soft-rock group Air Supply became a staple of early-'80s radio, scoring a string of seven straight Top Five singles. Air Supply, for most intents and purposes, was the duo of vocalists Russell Hitchcock and Graham Russell. The group's first worldwide album, *Lost in Love* was a major success in the U.S., selling over two million copies and spawning the hit singles "Lost in Love," "All Out of Love," and "Every Woman in the World." The following year they released their second album, *The One That You Love*. The title track became their only number one hit and it also featured two other Top Ten hits, "Here I Am (Just When I Thought I Was over You)" and "Sweet Dreams." From their 1983 *Greatest Hits* collection, the new single "Making Love Out of Nothing at All" spent two weeks at number two. It was clear by Air Supply's eponymous album from 1985 that their audience was shrinking. The group broke up after just one more album, though Hitchcock and Russell reunited in 1991 and released several albums during the decade as well as touring the oldies circuit. *—Stephen Thomas Erlewine*

Greatest Hits / 1988 / Arista ✦✦✦✦
Until Arista released *The Definitive Collection* in August 1999, 1988's *Greatest Hits* stood as the ultimate Air Supply compilation. It's easy to see why. Eleven of the group's big hits are here: "Lost in Love," "All Out of Love," "Every Woman in the World," "The One That You Love," "Here I Am," "Sweet Dreams," "Even the Nights Are Better," and "Making Love Out of Nothing at All." That's all that most Air Supply fans need, at least casual fans, but even the hardcore followers are sure to like having such a concentrated dose of hits in one package. Yes, *The Definitive Collection* remains more comprehensive, but for anyone who just wants the hits, with no excess fat, *Greatest Hits* is the right choice. *—Stephen Thomas Erlewine*

● **The Definitive Collection** / Aug. 24, 1999 / Arista ✦✦✦✦✦
The Definitive Collection more than lives up to its title's promise, delivering 18 tracks, including all of their Top 40 singles—"Lost in Love," "All Out of Love," "Every Woman in the World," "Here I Am (Just When I Thought I Was over You)," "Sweet Dreams," "Even the Nights Are Better," "Young Love," "Two Less Lonely People in the World," "Just As I Am"—plus the original Australian version of "Lost in Love." A pair of latter-day singles that didn't make the Top 40 are missing, but they're not missed, since what is here is prime Air Supply—the best songs they ever recorded. Granted, it won't convince any doubters, but this is the ideal collection for both dedicated and casual fans, while being perhaps the most listenable item in their catalog. *—Stephen Thomas Erlewine*

The Alarm

f. 1981, Rhyl, Wales, **db.** 1992
Alternative Pop/Rock
Comparisons to U2 have dogged Welsh quartet the Alarm throughout their career, but in light of the Alarm's socially conscious lyrics, melodic rock anthems, and gravitation toward a mainstream alternative sound over their career, perhaps the comparisons are justified. Lead singer and guitarist Mike Peters was actually inspired by U2's passion and commitment to form the group in 1981 with guitarist/vocalist David Sharp, bassist Eddie MacDonald, and drummer Nigel Twist. Their early sound was energetic and largely acoustic-based, while the group's stage look encompassed skintight leather pants, gaudy belts, and spiked hair. Their first of several U.K. hits was "Sixty Eight Guns," but didn't chart in America until 1987 with "Presence of Love," which reached number 77 and proved to be the extent of their U.S. singles chart success. By that point in their career, the group had adopted a more electric guitar-based sound and had gravitated more toward the mainstream, but since U2 had hit the big time, The Alarm seemed too much like a pale imitation. The band tried something different on 1989's *Change*, which featured more traditional Celtic influences and a guest appearance from the Welsh Symphony Orchestra, but it proved to be too little too late. The Alarm broke up early in the '90s, and Mike Peters embarked on a solo career. *—Steve Huey*

Declaration / 1984 / IRS ✦✦✦
The Alarm's first full-length album was, to a certain extent, a collection of the singles they had been releasing since October 1982: "Marching On," "The Stand," "Sixty Eight Guns" (number 17 U.K.), "Where Were You Hiding When the Storm Broke?" (number 22 U.K.) and "The Deceiver" (number 51 U.K.). As such, it had a strident, immediate appeal that was also somewhat relentless: The Alarm seemed to play every song as if it was the climax of their set. In the short term, that excited listeners, however; *Declaration* was a number six hit in England and broke through to the Top 50 in the U.S. In retrospect, it's more smoke than fire. *—William Ruhlmann*

Strength / 1985 / IRS ✦✦✦✦✦
In addition to an improved sense of musicality and dynamics, *Strength* featured The Alarm's finest group of songs, making it their single best studio album. *—Stephen Thomas Erlewine*

Eye of the Hurricane / 1987 / IRS ✦✦✦
This should have been the album that put The Alarm on the path to major stardom; instead, it marked the limits of their appeal. From the early fervor of their punk/acoustic debut, the group had evolved into more of a mainstream rock act without ever getting out from under the shadow of their mentors, U2. In fact, here, they sounded more like U2 than ever, and now that that group had ascended to superstardom, the comparison only hurt them. The signal hit here was "Rain In The Summertime," an overproduced leadoff track followed by "Rescue Me" and "Presence Of Love." All three tracks got AOR radio play in the U.S., so you couldn't say The Alarm wasn't getting exposure, especially when they were touring with Bob Dylan. However, they weren't getting through. *—William Ruhlmann*

Electric Folklore: Live / 1988 / IRS ✦✦

Change / 1989 / IRS ✦✦✦
Clearly, change was called for in The Alarm's career, and on their fourth album, the group achieved a tighter hard rock sound by turning to producer Tony Visconti. Their extensive roadwork and promotional efforts had opened doors for them at AOR and college radio, which played "Sold Me Down The River," "Devolution Workin' Man Blues," and "Love

Don't Come Easy." "River" even became The Alarm's biggest U.S. hit single, peaking at #50. But the album sold about the same as *Eye Of The Hurricane*, indicating that all the hard work had only enabled them to run in place. The problem remained the same: The Alarm had calmed down from its early martial style and turned into a competent mainstream rock band, but they still sounded too much like U2, and the rock riffs and throaty vocals still didn't add up to memorable songs. —*William Ruhlmann*

● **Standards** / Dec. 1990 / IRS ✦✦✦✦
During the early '80s, the Alarm were seen as rivals to U2—a Welsh variation of the passionate Dublin quartet, driven by the same righteous anger, anthemic hooks, and love for the Clash. They never quite matched their inspirations in terms of sales or critical respect, despite a series of acclaimed records that were minor sensations during the '80s. By the time the career retrospective *Standards* was released in late 1990, the band had already been somewhat forgotten. Listening to *Standards*, a thoroughly representative, basic collection of their singles and significant album tracks, confirms that the band were certainly not without talent or charms, but they suffered at the hands of state-of-the-art record production. They have a number of solid anthemic songs—"Sixty Eight Guns," "Marching On," "Spirit of '76," "Sold Me Down the River," among them—but it's hard to hear them as anything other than a product of their times, largely due to the glossy, shiny production. Such studio skills were evidently designed to make the band sound a bit like U2, but the band's music didn't have the jagged edges of U2—it was straight-ahead, driving rock, derived from the earnestness of folk-rock and the Clash's huge, rallying sound. This is not necessarily a bad thing, and it did produce some satisfying music, all of which is included here. But it ultimately produced music that was a sign of the times, not music that transcended it. The Alarm remain an interesting footnote because, ironically, while they strove to make music mean something in a slick commercial age, they were constantly plagued by overly slick productions—an irony only the '80s could produce, actually. —*Stephen Thomas Erlewine*

Raw / Apr. 1991 / IRS ✦✦

● **Best of the Alarm & Mike Peters** / 1998 / EMI ✦✦✦✦✦
The Best of the Alarm & Mike Peters is a generous collection, containing 16 of the Alarm's standards plus four solo cuts from their leader, Mike Peters. All of the group's hits and best album tracks are here, making this an excellent choice for either the curious or the casual fan. —*Stephen Thomas Erlewine*

Arthur Alexander

b. 1942, Florence, AL, d. Jun. 9, 1993, Nashville, TN
Vocals / Deep Soul, Southern Soul, Country-Soul, Soul
Arthur Alexander was one of the first true singing-songwriting stars of country-soul, a genre that wed Southern Black R&B singers to songs written in a country format and played basically by White musicians. Alexander's "You Better Move On" was the first hit to come out of Rick Hall's fledgling Muscle Shoals studio. His work was immediately appreciated by his peers in the business; those who have covered his tunes (self-penned or otherwise) read like a *Who's Who* from both sides of the Atlantic—"Anna" (Beatles); "Soldiers of Love" (Beatles and Marshall Crenshaw); "Burning Love" (Elvis Presley); "Set Me Free" (Joe Tex, Esther Phillips, Percy Sledge). The Rolling Stones' cover of "You Better Move On" led to valuable contacts for Rick Hall, and the resulting business enabled him to build the new FAME studio. It was the start of the whole Muscle Shoals sound, and Alexander's career was one of its cornerstones. He went on, after a brief retirement, to record for both Warner Brothers and Buddah. "Anna (Go to Him)," one of Alexander's best-known tunes, epitomizes the anguished, haunting tone of his music. From the onset, the heavily echoed piano and tortured vocal set a mood that is soulful, mysterious, a little spooky, and totally mesmerizing. His work is essential to any country-soul collection. —*Christine Ohlman*

Lonely Just Like Me / 1993 / Elektra/Nonesuch ✦✦✦✦
The final album from soul-country vocalist Arthur Alexander. It was like all his work—simple, unsophisticated, and sung with an earthy, direct intensity. This was part of the American Explorers series on Elektra/Nonesuch, and Alexander got some critical attention with his probing, often searing vocals. Unfortunately, he died just as this album was gaining some attention. —*Ron Wynn*

★ **The Ultimate Arthur Alexander** / Jun. 15, 1993 / Razor & Tie ✦✦✦✦✦
Alexander's songs are better known in versions by the Beatles, Elvis Presley, and the Rolling Stones, but no one recorded better versions than Alexander himself. *The Ultimate Arthur Alexander* truly lives up to its title, gathering together the best songs [including "Anna (Go to Him)," "You Better Move On," and "Soldiers of Love"] from Alexander's remarkably influential and underrated career. Absolutely essential for any R&B and soul collection. —*Stephen Thomas Erlewine*

Rainbow Road / Apr. 26, 1994 / Warner Archives ✦✦✦✦✦
Songwriter and vocalist Arthur Alexander was sorely neglected during his lifetime, despite possessing a stark, compelling voice and being among pop and soul's greatest storytellers. He remained on the outside, coming close but never attaining stardom. This CD features 15 fantastic songs, most from the great 1972 Warner Bros. album recorded in Memphis that Alexander thought would finally earn him that elusive smash. There are also some singles cut in Nashville as companion records to the Memphis session. The 15 tracks range from the hypnotic title cut and "In the Middle of It All" to the uptempo burners "You Got Me Knockin'" and "Burning Love." There's also a moving gospel number, "Thank God He Came." This disc is a wonderful tribute to an unjustly ignored artist. —*Ron Wynn*

The Monument Years / May 8, 2001 / Ace ✦✦✦
Between his most famous recordings in the first half of the 1960s, and his early-'70s al-

bum for Warner Brothers, Arthur Alexander kept sporadically active as a recording artist, putting out half a dozen singles on the Monument and Sound Stage 7 labels. None of these were hits, and as the original 45s are so hard to find, it remained a mysterious missing link in his career to most listeners. This CD rectifies that problem by collecting all of those singles, and adding 16 previously unreleased tracks that he cut in the last half of the 1960s and the early '70s. It's quite a useful service for fans, but it can't be denied that these performances aren't the high points of the fine soul singer/songwriter's career. The mix of soul, pop, and country forces at work in these sides is similar to those heard on Alexander's earlier efforts. However, the material, whether penned by Alexander or others, just isn't that outstanding, and sometimes sound like lesser reworkings of ideas and riffs he'd plied more effectively in prior days. When Alexander covers a well-known song like "Spanish Harlem" or "Cry Like a Baby," he adds little to it; when he tries to be uncharacteristically funny and risqué on "I Want to Marry You," it's embarrassing. On the later stuff, the pop influences become more prominent, usually to the disadvantage of the music. His distinctive brand of somber soul, with his reserved and sad, vulnerable vocals, does shine through to a large degree, and those that have enjoyed his other releases will find much to appreciate. But it should not be regarded as a first or second choice for the Alexander neophyte. —*Richie Unterberger*

Alice in Chains

f. 1987, Seattle, WA
Alternative Metal, Grunge, Heavy Metal, Alternative Pop/Rock
In many ways, Alice in Chains was the definitive heavy metal band of the early '90s. Drawing equally from the heavy riffing of post-Van Halen metal and the gloomy strains of post-punk, the band developed a bleak, nihilistic sound that balanced grinding hard rock with subtly textured acoustic numbers. They were hard enough for metal fans, yet their dark subject matter and punky attack placed them among the front ranks of the Seattle-based grunge bands. While this dichotomy helped the group soar to multi-platinum status with their second album, 1992's *Dirt*, it also divided them. Guitarist Jerry Cantrell always leaned toward the mainstream, while vocalist Layne Staley was fascinated with the seamy underground. Such tension drove the band towards stardom in their early years, but following *Dirt*, Alice in Chains suffered from near-crippling internal tensions that kept the band off the road for the remainder of the '90s, and, consequently, the group never quite fulfilled thier potential. —*Stephen Thomas Erlewine*

Facelift / Aug. 1990 / Columbia ✦✦✦
When Alice in Chains' debut album *Facelift* was released in 1990, about a year before Nirvana's *Nevermind*, the thriving Seattle scene barely registered on the national musical radar outside of underground circles (although Soundgarden's major-label debut, *Louder Than Love*, was also released that year and brought them a Grammy nomination). That started to change when MTV jumped all over the video for "Man in the Box," giving the group a crucial boost and helping to pave the way for grunge's popular explosion toward the end of 1991. Although their dominant influences—Black Sabbath, the Stooges—were hardly unique on the Seattle scene, Alice in Chains were arguably the most metallic of grunge bands, which gave them a definite appeal outside the underground; all the same, the group's sinister, brooding, suffocating sound resembled little else gaining wide exposure on the 1990 hard rock scene. Neither hedonistic nor especially technically accomplished, Alice in Chains' songs were mostly slow, oppressive dirges with a sense of melody that was undeniable, yet which crept along over the murky sludge of the band's instrumental attack in a way that hardly fit accepted notions of what made hard rock catchy and accessible. Although some parts of *Facelift* sink into turgid, ponderous bombast (particularly over the erratic second half), and the lyrics are sometimes immature, the overall effect is fresh, exciting, and powerful. While Alice in Chains would go on to do better and more consistent work, *Facelift* was one of the most important records in establishing an audience for grunge and alternative rock among hard rock and heavy metal listeners, and with its platinum sales certification, it also made Alice in Chains the first Seattle band to break through to a wider, less exclusively underground audience. —*Steve Huey*

Sap / Feb. 1992 / Columbia ✦✦✦✦
Upon its release, *Sap* was a revelation, a seemingly tossed-off EP of four mostly acoustic ballads (augmented with a goofy bonus track) that threw Alice in Chains' melodic gifts into stunning relief while exposing a gentler, more melancholy side of their sound, something that *Facelift* never even hinted at. The mood is still bleak, but not affectedly so, as was sometimes the case on *Facelift*. There's a newfound maturity in the subtlety and confessional introspection of the first four songs, whose somber beauty is unfortunately dispelled by the bonus track (in a different context, it might be idiotic fun, but it really doesn't fit here). Still, *Sap* served notice that there was a great deal more depth to Alice in Chains than their debut had let on, hinting at the potential that would be realized with *Dirt*. —*Steve Huey*

● **Dirt** / Oct. 1992 / Columbia ✦✦✦✦✦
Dirt is Alice in Chains' major artistic statement and the closest they ever came to recording a flat-out masterpiece. It's a primal, sickening howl from the depths of Layne Staley's heroin addiction, and one of the most harrowing concept albums ever recorded. Not every song on *Dirt* is explicitly about heroin, but Jerry Cantrell's solo-written contributions (nearly half the album) effectively maintain the thematic coherence—nearly every song is imbued with the morbidity, self-disgust, and/or resignation of a self-aware yet powerless addict. Cantrell's technically limited but inventive guitar work is by turns explosive, textured, and queasily disorienting, keeping the listener off balance with atonal riffs and off-kilter time signatures. Staley's stark confessional lyrics are similarly effective, and

consistently miserable. Sometimes he's just numb and apathetic, totally desensitized to the outside world; sometimes his self-justifications betray a shockingly casual amorality; his moments of self-recognition are permeated by despair and suicidal self-loathing. Even given its subject matter, *Dirt* is monstrously bleak, closely resembling the cracked, haunted landscape of its cover art. The album holds out little hope for its protagonists (aside from the much-needed survival story of "Rooster," a tribute to Cantrell's Vietnam-vet father), but in the end, it's redeemed by the honesty of its self-revelation and the sharp focus of its music. [Some versions of *Dirt* feature "Down in a Hole" as the next-to-last track rather than the fourth.] *—Steve Huey*

Jar of Flies / Jan. 25, 1994 / Columbia ✦✦✦✦
Written and recorded in about a week, *Jar of Flies* solidified Alice in Chains' somewhat bizarre pattern of alternating full-length hard rock albums with mostly acoustic, ballad-oriented EPs. That quirk aside, *Jar of Flies* is a low-key stunner, achingly gorgeous and harrowingly sorrowful all at once. In a way, it's a logical sequel to *Dirt*—despite the veneer of calm, the songs' voices still blame only themselves. But where *Dirt* found catharsis in its unrelenting darkness and depravity, *Jar of Flies* is about living with the consequences, full of deeply felt reflections on loneliness, self-imposed isolation, and lost human connections. The mood is still hopelessly bleak, but the poignant, introspective tone produces a sense of acceptance that's actually soothing, in a funereal sort of way. Jerry Cantrell's arrangements keep growing more detailed and layered; while there are a few noisy moments, most of *Jar of Flies* is bathed in a clean, shimmering ambience whose source is difficult to pin down, but is well served by Cantrell's varied guitar tones and even occasional string arrangements. And coming on the heels of *Dirt*, the restraint and subtlety of *Jar of Flies* are nothing short of revelatory—though it was written and recorded in about a week, it feels much more crafted and textured than *Sap*. Perhaps *Jar of Flies* would have gotten more credit if it had been a full-length album; as it stands, the EP is a leap forward and a major work in the Alice in Chains catalog. *—Steve Huey*

Alice in Chains / Nov. 21, 1995 / Columbia ✦✦✦
Dispelling rumors of their demise due to Layne Staley's heroin addiction, *Alice in Chains* is a sonically detailed effort that ranks as their best-produced record, and its best moments are easily some of their most mature music. *Alice in Chains* relies less on metallic riffs and more on melody and texturally varied arrangements than the group's previous full-length albums, finally integrating some of the more delicate acoustic moods of their EPs. The lyrics deal with familiar AIC subject matter: despair, misery, loneliness, and disappointment, but in a more understated fashion, and the lyrics take on more uplifting qualities of toughness and endurance, which were missing from much of their previous work. The consistent visceral impact *Alice in Chains* lacks in comparison to that previous work is partially made up for by the skilled production and songs like "Grind," "Brush Away," "Over Now," and the hit ballad "Heaven Beside You," which are among the band's best work. Still, in spite of its many virtues, it's hard not to feel a little frustrated with the record, as though, given those qualities, it should have turned out better than it did—there are some slow spots where the songs are undercrafted and not especially memorable, and those moments can make the band sound uncommitted and distracted. That, in turn, can make the defiance of songs like "Grind" ("you'd be well advised/not to plan my funeral 'fore the body dies") sound more like denial; just when Alice in Chains' music was finally beginning to emerge from the dark side, the intra-band problems became too much to bear and made *Alice in Chains* likely the last collection of new material the band will ever release. *—Steve Huey*

Unplugged / Jul. 1996 / Columbia ✦✦✦
Between the end of 1993 and a performance for *MTV Unplugged* in the spring of 1996, Alice in Chains performed no concerts—they didn't even support the release of their eponymous third album with a minor tour. There's a variety of reasons for their inactivity—primarily it's due to the health of certain members—but the lack of concerts made the *Unplugged* performance seem special. During the concert, Alice in Chains drew from their three albums and two EPs, offering new, more reflective arrangements for harder songs like "Would?" and virtually recreating the original versions of "Got Me Wrong" and "No Excuses." Throughout the album, the group sounds tight and professional—on the basis of this performance, it's hard to believe that they hadn't played together for nearly three years—but it doesn't offer anything that the albums don't already. The acoustic arrangements of the harder songs sound like novelties, and the rest sound like rehashes of their previous work, only without much energy. Again, it's a case of an *Unplugged* album that is designed to the band's core audience, which makes it a fairly entertaining effort that is essentially just an official bootleg. *—Stephen Thomas Erlewine*

Nothing Safe: Best of the Box / Jun. 29, 1999 / Columbia ✦✦✦✦
Nothing Safe: Best of the Box anticipated 1999's three-disc Alice in Chains box set, which covered the group's best songs and assorted rarities. Because *Nothing Safe* is ostensibly a sampler of the box, not the Alice in Chains back catalog, what at first glance looks like a comprehensive best-of is actually somewhat questionable. The package is not unattractive, since nearly all the hits are present in some form; also included are the new song "Get Born Again," and the better of the group's two contributions to the *Last Action Hero* soundtrack, "What the Hell Have I." The problem is that "present in *some* form" does not necessarily mean "original form." "Rooster" is included in a live version *not* present on the box, while a demo of "We Die Young" replaces the studio take, and the unplugged version of "Got Me Wrong" (which, granted, received more airplay) bumps the more effective arrangement from *Sap*. There's nothing really wrong with these versions of themselves; it's just that their selection seems designed to make this package incomplete, so that fans who want the original tracks will be forced to purchase three different original albums (and completists will *still* have to buy this for the exclusive version of "Rooster"). Fans who don't mind the substitutions will find this to be a strong introduction to the group—and it is a very impressive listen, making the case for Alice in Chains as one of the best metal bands of the '90s—but others will be frustrated by the crass marketing gimmicks marring what could have been a great, not merely good, best-of collection. *—Steve Huey*

Music Bank / Oct. 26, 1999 / Columbia ✦✦✦✦
Three studio albums, two EPs, one live album, and a few European B-sides seemingly is a scant body of work to provide the basis for a box set, but that proves not to be the case with *Music Bank*, a three-disc retrospective of Alice in Chains' decade-long career. In many ways, the very release of *Music Bank* and its single-disc distillation, *Nothing Safe*, is a roundabout admission that AIC is no longer an active proposition for any of its members. But even if the group makes a comeback sometime in the next century, the two compilations are good snapshots of an era when Alice in Chains was one of the best bands in metal. By its very nature, *Music Bank* is for the hardcore fan, since it spans three discs, but this is one box that gets it right. It does feature all the hits, but they're surrounded by so many rarities—including an abundance of demos, 12 previously unreleased cuts, live tracks, and alternate mixes and takes—that it never seems like a hits compilation. More impressively, *Music Bank* has a real narrative drive; it's easy to hear the band evolve, even if the set begins with the newly recorded "Get Born Again." True, the box set really isn't for casual fans—they should stick with *Nothing Safe* or the band's masterpiece, *Dirt*—but the dedicated will not be disappointed with this fine set, since it does deliver more rarities than expected. *—Stephen Thomas Erlewine*

Live / Dec. 5, 2000 / Columbia ✦✦✦
With Alice in Chains on hiatus by the turn of the 21st century (they strongly deny that they've broken up, however), Columbia Records issued several stop-gap releases to fill up the space—1999's greatest-hits collection *Nothing Safe* and the box set *Music Bank*, and a year later, their first true live collection, titled simply *Live*. Despite Alice in Chains' inability (or outright refusal) to launch a proper tour after 1994, fans lucky enough to have caught one of their early tours will attest that they were quite a powerful live act. Their detuned sound and tales from the darkside are even more sinister and gripping on the concert stage, as evidenced by this 14-track set. With a healthy helping of selections from their 1992 *tour de force*, *Dirt*, Alice in Chains lets it rip on such metallic standouts as "Dam That River," "Would," "Rooster," "Angry Chair," "Junkhead," and a "drunk and disorderly" version of *Dirt*'s title track. Also featured are the early classics "Man in the Box" and "Bleed the Freak," as well as a track that never appeared on any of their official studio albums, "Queen of the Rodeo." *Live* shows what a devastating live band Alice in Chains could be. *—Greg Prato*

Alice in Chains Greatest Hits / Jul. 24, 2001 / Columbia ✦✦✦
Greatest Hits is not, alas, the antidote to the botched *Nothing Safe: Best of the Box* compilation, but rather a lower-priced, ten-track sampler of Alice in Chains' career. The songs are mostly excellent and well-chosen but, unfortunately, there are simply too few of them. *Greatest Hits* will serve the needs of casual fans who just want ten of Alice in Chains' best songs on one disc without shelling out too much money, but there are too many other good moments in the group's back catalog to make this a good buy for anyone else. *—Steve Huey*

All About Eve

Dream Pop, Shoegazing, Goth Rock, Alternative Pop/Rock

All About Eve arose out of Britain's '80s goth rock scene with a unique, folk-rock-influenced take on the style. Former journalist and Gene Loves Jezebel bassist Julianne Regan was encouraged by members of the Mission U.K. to form her own band after singing background vocals on some of their material. She assembled former Aemotti Crii members Tim Bricheno (guitar) and Andy Cousin (bass), plus drummer Mark Price, and sprinkled her songs with references to hippiedom and white-magic mysticism. Their self-titled debut sold well in the U.K. in 1988 and produced the hit "Martha's Harbour." Following the release and tour of their difficult second record *Scarlet and Other Stories*, Bricheno left the group and subsequently joined Sisters of Mercy.

The band regrouped, with the Church mainstay Marty Willson-Piper taking over on guitar. The resulting record, *Touched by Jesus*, was met with a lukewarm reception, and the band decided on a stylistic change for their next LP. 1994's *Ultraviolet* got lost in the shuffle, and problems with how the record company percieved the band added to an already stressful situation. A short time later, All About Eve called it a day, with Julianne Regan going on to form Mice, work with Bernard Butler, start the atmospheric Jules et Jim project, and a regular day job.

When it seemed that the band would never be heard from again, old friends the Mission decided to start touring again, and asked Regan if she was interested in opening. This was enough to not only get the band back together but to start touring on their own. After the tour with the Mission, All About Eve embarked on what turned out to be two years worth of acoustic gigs, and in 2000 released the first collection of unplugged highlights, entitled *Fairy Light Nights*. *Fairy Light Nights, Vol. 2* and more acoustic shows appeared in 2001. *—Chris True & Steve Huey*

● **All About Eve** / 1988 / Mercury ✦✦✦✦
Even though All About Eve were immediately pegged as light goth-pop, their debut album is a unified piece of straightforward rock. The production may be a little clean, but the feeling is definitely there. Lush guitars and a solid rhythm section behind driving rockers ("Every Angel," "In the Meadow") and ballads ("Martha's Harbour," "Shelter From the Rain") give the album a majestic sound fused with dreamy wordplay. All About Eve had been one of the more accomplished acts to come out of the goth scene, and this debut is proof. *—Chris True*

Scarlet and Other Stories / 1989 / Mercury ✦✦✦
When All About Eve returned with the follow-up to their self-titled debut, the first

reactions seemed to include the word "difficult"; this is not far off the mark. Made under less than stable circumstances (lead singer Julianne Regan throwing furniture, for example), *Scarlet and Other Stories* is a varied affair, taking the best parts of the debut ("Tuesday's Child") and fusing them with new musical ideas ("Hard Spaniard"). The majestic opener "Road to Your Soul" is a shining moment for the band, and the slide blues-goth of "Blind Lemon Sam" is infectious. A balanced album recorded in unbalanced surroundings, *Scarlet and Other Stories* is one of All About Eve's brightest moments. —*Chris True*

Touched by Jesus / 1991 / Vertigo ✦✦✦
With the addition of Church guitarist Marty Wilson-Piper, All About Eve entered a new phase on *Touched by Jesus*. Julianne Regan's lyrics are a bit brighter and the music is less goth and more mainstream than previous releases. That is not to say that the songs aren't solid. They are, however, more intricately arranged, and the subject matter is a little more down to earth. *Touched by Jesus* is a mature step for All About Eve. As proof that the group wasn't interested in staying the same, the album was a well-timed growth spurt. —*Chris True*

Ultraviolet / 1992 / MCA ✦✦✦
While 1991's *Touched by Jesus* was an attempt to hit the mainstream, 1992's *Ultraviolet* was a shedding of the past for All About Eve. With the Church's Marty Wilson-Piper still in tow, Regan and crew made a conscious effort to enter the shoegazer/dream-pop sweepstakes on this release. And not unlike the Mission U.K.'s attempt to explore new territory, *Ultraviolet* was not received well by Eve fans. What is ironic about the whole thing is that the dreamy lyrics and sweeping melodies of *Ultraviolet* are very visible in the group's past catalogue. "Phased" and "Yesterday Goodbye" are great dream-pop tunes, and tracks like "Infrared," "I Don't Know," and "Some Finer Day" manage to meld old Eve with the new. *Ultraviolet* may have been a drastic change to some, but it held promise. Unfortunately, this was the band's last release—a premature end. —*Chris True*

Winter Words: Hits & Rarities / Jun. 30, 1998 / Polygram International ✦✦✦✦
A fairly good compilation, *Winter Words* features most of the singles that the band released during their short career. While the collection is buyable for the few B-sides thrown in for good measure ("Theft," in particular, is one of the best All About Eve tracks around, and makes this worth having), it's more "hits" than "rarities." —*Chris True*

Best of All About Eve / 1999 / Spectrum ✦✦✦
A one-disc collection of the band's pre-MCA singles, *Best Of* is a good place to start for the casual Eve fan. It runs in chronological order, and contains the non-album mix of "Flowers in Our Hair." Though it's worth picking up to hear the singles that helped fuel the British goth-pop scene in the late 1980s, a more extensive collection wouldn't hurt—especially one that covers both their indie and MCA days more thoroughly. —*Chris True*

Fairy Light Nights Vol. 2 / 2001 / www.candytree.com ✦✦✦
One of the more odd happenings of 2000-2001 was the sudden rebirth of bands that were big in the U.K. around a decade ago. The Mission, Wonder Stuff, and Ned's Atomic Dustbin had all regrouped and played highly successful shows. Close relative All About Eve joined in, not only touring electrically and acoustically, but releasing a two-volume set of highlights from the more intimate unplugged shows. Volume two of *Fairy Light Nights* is the stronger of the two in track selection, but it is just as enjoyable as the first. It's good to see them back, and hopefully there will be more to come in the near future. —*Chris True*

All Saints
f. 1993, London, England
Teen Pop, Adult Contemporary, Urban, House, Dance-Pop
Those unfamiliar with pop music would be forgiven for confusing All Saints with 1997's most hotly tipped music property, the Spice Girls. The four members of All Saints could stand for Spice Girls body doubles in a lineup: two brunettes, one blonde, and one of West Indian descent. While the Spice Girls have always been pure pop and barely musically functional, however, the members of All Saints are songwriters and music aficionados with a softer, more intelligent image less tied to their looks than their music.

The group came together in 1993 when Melanie Blatt and Shaznay Lewis came together to begin recording and writing at a studio on All Saints Road, in London's Ladbroke Grove. The duo hooked up with R&B vocalist Simone Rainford and released a single for ZTT Records in 1995, then parted ways with Rainford and were dumped by the label. Undeterred, Blatt and Lewis recruited native Canadian Nicole Appleton and later, her big sister Nathalie, to make All Saints a quartet.

With the help of friend Karl Gordon (formerly part of the British rap ensemble Outlaw Posse), All Saints recorded a demo of the song "I Know Where It's At." New manager John Benson signed the girls to London Records and connected them with top-flight producers Nellee Hooper (Massive Attack, Björk) and Cameron McVey (Neneh Cherry). Fully recorded, "I Know Where It's At" hit number four on the British charts and crossed over throughout Europe and Asia. By 1997, All Saints had reached the top spot with their second single "Never Ever." The quartet released their self-titled debut album in November 1997, and began to grow in America as well, hitting the Top 40 with "I Know Where It's At."—*John Bush*

● **All Saints** / Nov. 1997 / London ✦✦✦✦
As the first group of consequence to be saddled with the "new Spice Girls" tag, it would be reasonable to expect that All Saints would be cut-rate dance-pop without the weirdly magical charisma that made the Spices international phenomenons. It is true that All Saints lack the personality of the Spices, but they make up for that with musical skills. All four members have better voices than the Spices, and they all have a hand in writing at least one of the songs on their eponymous debut, with Shaznay taking the most writ-

ing credits. More importantly, they and their producers have a better sense of contemporary dance trends—there are real hip-hop and club rhythms throughout the record, and samples of Audio Two, the Rampage, and (especially) Steely Dan are fresh and inventive. But what really makes the record are the songs. The singles are the standouts, with the party-ready, Steely Dan-fueled "I Know Where It's At" and the extraordinary gospel-tinged "Never Ever" leading the way, but the covers are well-chosen (their take on "Under the Bridge" eclipses the Red Hot Chili Peppers', boasting a better arrangement and more convincing vocals) and the lesser songs are pleasantly melodic. Sure, there's some filler, but that should be expected on any dance-pop album. What counts is that the performances are fresh, the production is funky, and there are a handful of classic pop singles on the album, and you can't ask for much better than that from a dance-pop record, especially one from a group that almost beat the Spice Girls at their own game. —*Stephen Thomas Erlewine*

Saints & Sinners / Oct. 24, 2000 / London ✦✦✦
Whereas it took three albums for the Spice Girls to descend from unmatched cartoon pop to dreary two-step, All Saints got the job done in two. Except they substituted *Forever's* artless dodging with some sort of irksome middle-of-the-road, sub-salsa prancing about that's enough to cause worldwide Tiger Beat subscribers to torch themselves like Buddha monks. This is an album that's not afraid to title songs "Love Is Love"; an album that looks Gloria Estefan Latin pap in the face and gives it a big kiss on the lips. It's not that it's unpleasant hearing Shaznay, et al. careen off every chorus in those high-pitched coos, but for an unapologetic chart act there is an astonishing lack of tunes. It's unfortunate, since the swell of magical realism in "Pure Shores" is one of the finest, most spine-gushing pop moments of 2000. —*Dean Carlson*

Davie Allan
Guitar / Obscuro, Hot Rod, Surf
Providing the soundtrack to numerous biker and teen exploitation movies in the mid- and late '60s, Davie Allan & the Arrows bridged the surf and psychedelic eras. Their driving, basic instrumentals featured loads and loads of fuzz guitar, as well as generous dollops of tremolo bar waggling and wah-wah. The guitarist and his band first made their mark with the minor hit "Apache '65," a version of the Shadows/Jorgen Ingmann's instrumental classic "Apache." Hooking up with notorious exploitation movie producer Mike Curb, the Arrows provided the soundtracks to numerous B-movies on the Tower and Sidewalk labels; their greatest success, "Blues Theme" (from *The Wild Angels* starring Peter Fonda), made the Top 40 in 1967. When Curb abandoned racy movies for the Osmonds and purged MGM Records of their psychedelic acts, the Arrows' flight was over. —*Richie Unterberger*

● **King Fuzz** / 1990 / Fuzzwalk ✦✦✦✦✦
The only compilation of Allan's numerous '60s recordings, condensing the highlights of his 1965-67 soundtracks, albums, and B-sides into 15 songs. For all but specialists, "Blues Theme" is all you need. The guitar pyrotechnics are occasionally impressive, but the repetitive fuzz-psychedelic riffs are numbing over the course of an entire LP. —*Richie Unterberger*

Arrow Dynamic Sounds of Davie Allan & the Arrows / Sep. 21, 1999 / Total Energy ✦✦✦
Thirty-odd years after Davie Allan's "Blues Theme" gave him his only Top 40 hit, the fuzzmeister's still at it, his guitar skills undiminished. This nearly all-original set isn't really much different from those vintage '60s recordings, actually, except for the more modern production feel, particularly in the gunshot kick of the drums (which is not necessarily a great thing). The opening medley, stringing together a redone "Blues Theme" and "The Born Losers Theme," is probably a guaranteed crowd-pleaser for those who love Allan's biker soundtracks and want more of the same. And this disc *could* use more variety, like much instrumental rock could. But there are some tracks that show Allan capable of things other than ominous fuzz, like the impressive sustain lines of "Encounter," a hint of metallic boogie in "Fast & Loose," spy-rock ("James Bond Theme/Goldfinger"), and the country-blues of "Dakota." Overall, this is much like a modern Link Wray or Dick Dale album: not as good as the original classics, but not too dissimilar from them either (except that Wray and Dale are more imaginative players and composers). It's best when it's most melodically haunting, as on the standout "Peyote." —*Richie Unterberger*

The Allman Brothers Band
f. 1969, Macon, GA, **db.** 1982
Slide Guitar Blues, Album Rock, Boogie Rock, Southern Rock, Hard Rock, Blues-Rock
The story of the Allman Brothers Band is one of triumph, tragedy, redemption, dissolution, and a new redemption. Over nearly 30 years, they've gone from being America's single most influential band to a has-been group trading on past glories, to reach the 1990s as one of the most respected rock acts of their era. For the first half of the 1970s, the Allman Brothers Band was the most influential rock group in America, redefining rock music and its boundaries. The band's mix of blues, country, jazz, and even classical influences, and their powerful, extended onstage jamming altered the standards of concert performance—other groups were known for their onstage jamming, but when the Allman Brothers—guitarist Duane Allman, his singer/organist brother Gregg, guitarist Dickey Betts, bassist Berry Oakley, and drummers Butch Trucks and Jaimoe in their most celebrated incarnation—stretched a song out for 30 or 40 minutes, at their best they were exciting, never self-indulgent. They gave it all a distinctly Southern voice and, in the process, opened the way for a wave of '70s rock acts from south of the Mason-Dixon Line, including the Marshall Tucker Band, Lynyrd Skynyrd, and Blackfoot, whose music, at least

initially, celebrated their roots. And for a time, almost single-handedly, they also made Capricorn Records into a major independent label. *—Bruce Eder*

The Allman Brothers Band / 1969 / Polydor ✦✦✦✦✦
This might be the best debut album ever delivered by an American blues band, a bold, powerful, hard-edged, soulful essay in electric blues with a native Southern ambience. Some lingering elements of the psychedelic era then drawing to a close can be found in "Dreams," along with the template for the group's onstage workouts with "Whipping Post," and a solid cover of Muddy Waters' "Trouble No More." There isn't a bad song here, and only the fact that the group did even better the next time out keeps this from getting the highest possible rating. *—Bruce Eder*

☆ **Idlewild South** / 1970 / Polydor ✦✦✦✦✦
The best studio album in the group's history, electric blues with an acoustic texture, virtuoso lead, slide, and organ playing, and a killer selection of songs, including "Midnight Rider," "Revival," "Don't Keep Me Wonderin'," and "In Memory of Elizabeth Reed" in its embryonic studio version, which is pretty impressive even at a mere six minutes and change. They also do the best white cover of Willie Dixon's "Hoochie Coochie Man" anyone's ever likely to hear. *—Bruce Eder*

☆ **Live at Fillmore East** / Mar. 1971 / Polydor ✦✦✦✦✦
Whereas most great live rock albums are about energy, *Live at Fillmore East* is like a great live jazz session, where the pleasure comes from the musicians' interaction and playing. The great thing about that is, the original album that brought the Allmans so much acclaim is as notable for its clever studio editing as it is for its performances. Producer Tom Down skillfully trimmed some of the performances down to relatively concise running times (edits later restored on the double-disc set *The Fillmore Concerts*), at times condensing several performances into one track. Far from being a sacrilege, this tactic helps present the Allman's in their best light, since even if the music isn't necessarily concise (three tracks run over ten minutes, with two in the 20-minute range), it does showcase the group's terrific instrumental interplay, letting each member (but particularly guitarist Duane and keyboardist/vocalist Gregg) shine. Even after the release of the unedited concerts, this original double album (single CD) remains the pinnacle of the Allman's and Southern rock at its most elastic, bluesy, and jazzy. *—Stephen Thomas Erlewine*

★ **Eat a Peach** / 1972 / Polydor ✦✦✦✦✦
A tribute to the dearly departed Duane, *Eat a Peach* rambles through two albums, running through a side of new songs, recorded post-Duane, spending a full album on live cuts from the *Fillmore East* sessions, then offering a round of studio tracks Duane completed before his death. On the first side, they do suggest the mellowness of the Dickey Betts-led *Brothers and Sisters*, particularly on the lovely "Melissa," and this stands in direct contrast with the monumental live cuts that dominate the album. They're at the best on the punchier covers of "One Way Out" and "Trouble No More," both proof of the group's exceptional talents as a roadhouse blues-rock band, but Duane does get his needed showcase on "Mountain Jam," a sprawling 33-minute jam that may feature a lot of great playing, but is certainly a little hard for anyone outside of diehards to sit through. Apart from that cut, the record showcases the Allmans at their peak, and it's hard not to feel sad as the acoustic guitars of "Little Martha" conclude the record, since this tribute isn't just heartfelt, it offers proof of Duane Allman's immense talents and contribution to the band. *—Stephen Thomas Erlewine*

Brothers and Sisters / 1973 / Polydor ✦✦✦✦
The group's first new studio album in two years shows off a leaner, brand of musicianship, which, coupled with a pair of serious crowd-pleasers, "Ramblin' Man" and "Jessica," helped drive it to the top of the charts for a month and a half, and platinum record sales. This was the first album to feature the group's new lineup, with Chuck Leavell on keyboards and Lamar Williams on bass, as well as Dickey Betts' emergence as a singer alongside Gregg Allman. The tracks appear on the album in the order in which they were recorded, and the first three, up through "Ramblin' Man," feature Berry Oakley—their sound is rock hard and crisp. The subsequent songs with Williams have the bass buried in the mix, and an overall muddier sound. The interplay between Leavell and Betts is beautiful on some songs, and Betts' slide on "Pony Boy" is a dazzling showcase that surprised everybody. Despite its sales, *Brothers and Sisters* is not quite a classic album (although it was their best for the next 17 years), especially in the wake of the four that had appeared previously, but it served as a template for some killer stage performances, and it proved that the band could survive the deaths of two key members. Capricorn's 1997 reissue has a brighter sound than the older PolyGram CD, but the Mobile Fidelity audiophile disc has the best sound, a richer, broader tone. *—Bruce Eder*

☆ **Beginnings** / 1973 / Polydor ✦✦✦✦✦
This is where the group's CD release history gets complicated. *Beginnings* was originally put together by Atco as a double-LP to encourage new fans who'd missed them to buy the group's first two album, and proved so successful that it was kept in print on CD by Polydor when it acquired the group's catalog. Polydor's single-CD version of this double-LP, however, was substandard in audio quality, digitized from an LP production master, and their individual CDs of *The Allman Brothers Band* and *Idlewild South* were far superior. But when Capricorn got the library back in 1997, they remastered *Beginnings* along with the rest of the library, and the Capricorn version of this CD is one of the better bargains going *—Bruce Eder*

Win, Lose or Draw / 1975 / Polydor ✦✦

Wipe the Windows, Check the Oil, Dollar Gas / 1976 / Polydor ✦✦✦
This live album was released by Capricorn Records largely as a way of raising money in a hurry, but it fares surprisingly well musically. The 1973-74 Allman Brothers Band featured here is the one that most fans actually saw, since most listeners didn't discover them or get to their concerts until after the deaths of Duane Allman and Berry Oakley. *Wipe the Windows* isn't a landmark release like the Fillmore tapes—a collection of rock's greatest guitar albums could be complete without it. But no Allman Brothers Band fan should pass up *Wipe the Windows*, which is a most solid live album, and, in particular, a better representation of the songs off of *Brothers and Sisters* and *Win, Lose or Draw* than the original studio versions. "Southbound," "Ramblin' Man," "Jessica," and, to a lesser degree, "Wasted Words," come off exceptionally well. This second-generation band, with Dickey Betts as the sole lead guitar and Gregg Allman and Chuck Leavell sharing the keyboards, also performs a reconceived version of "In Memory of Elizabeth Reed"—they could never spark more fire than the version from the Fillmore, so they transform it into a moodier piece with more space for the keyboards to open up. Compiled from shows in New Orleans, San Francisco, Bakersfield, Oakland, and Watkins Glen (New York). *—Bruce Eder*

Enlightened Rogues / 1979 / Polydor ✦✦✦
The group's best studio album since *Brothers & Sisters* is a loud, brash, hard-rocking collection of consistently solid if not first-rate songs. The singing is some of the best since *Idlewild South*, and although they would do better once they brought in Warren Haynes, the dual guitar lineup of Dickey Betts and Dan Toler is a reminder of what the group had been missing since Duane Allman's death. The music isn't earth-shattering, but it is exciting through and through. *—Bruce Eder*

Reach for the Sky / 1980 / Razor & Tie ✦✦

Brothers of the Road / 1981 / Razor & Tie ✦✦

Dreams / Jun. 1989 / Polydor ✦✦✦✦✦
Spanning four discs and nearly 100 tracks, *Dreams* is one of those rare box sets that tells a story while delivering the definitive word on its subject. Its success has a lot to do with its status as Polygram/Bill Levinson's sequel to the acclaimed hit *Crossroads*, which summarized Eric Clapton's winding career perfectly. They follow the same approach here, gathering pre-Allman's recordings from the clan, including cuts by the Allman Joys, selecting the hits from the classic years, and adding stray cuts by solo projects to the mix. It's a smart move and it results in a terrific box that truly offers the definitive word on one of the longest-running dramas in Southern rock. Yes, the Allmans reunited rather successfully after this box, so none of that material is here, but it's not missed—this is the story of the band. *—Stephen Thomas Erlewine*

Seven Turns / Oct. 1990 / Epic ✦✦✦✦✦
The group's comeback album, their best blues-based outing since *Idlewild South*, and one that restored a lot of their reputation. With Tom Dowd running the session, and the group free to make the music they wanted to, they ended up producing this bold, rock-hard album, made up mostly of songs by Dickey Betts (with contributions by new keyboardman Johnny Neel and lead guitarist Warren Haynes), almost every one of them a winner. Apart from the rippling opening number, "Good Clean Fun," and which he co-authored, Gregg Allman's contribution is limited to singing and the organ, but the band seems more confident than ever, ripping through numbers like "Low Down Dirty Mean," "Shine It On," and "Let Me Ride" like they were inventing blues-rock here, and the Ornette Coleman-inspired "True Gravity" is their best instrumental since "Jessica." *—Bruce Eder*

Live at Ludlow Garage: 1970 / 1991 / Polydor ✦✦✦✦✦
Ninety-one minutes of the Allman Brothers Band in concert from a Cincinnati venue that they loved, nearly a year before their legendary Fillmore shows. The acoustics are good, though a little shaky—the tape was made at 7 1/2 ips, the bare minimum professional standard, which leaves more hiss than one might like, and a bit less clarity than a fully professional live album might show; on the other hand, the group's sound imparts its own punch and clarity, and it was done in stereo, and if not for the existence of the Fillmore tapes, and the fact that the albums they yielded sold a kajillion copies, this show might well have been released in the 1970s. It isn't as intense as the Fillmore shows, but it does capture the group as a little known working band with but a single album out and building a reputation—and with Dickey Betts yet to emerge as either a singer or composer, and their sound still being worked out ("Statesboro Blues" gets a startlingly subdued performance, anticipating the acoustic version of "In Memory of Elizabeth Reed" from the '90s recording *2nd Set*). They build their set on ambitious reinterpretations of songs by Blind Willie McTell, Muddy Waters ("Trouble In Mind"), John Lee Hooker ("Dimples"), and Willie Dixon, whose "Hoochie Coochie Man" is a soaring highlight of this two-disc set, in a version that makes every other white band's cover seem wimpy by comparison, climaxing with a searing, though somewhat disjointed 44-minute version of "Mountain Jam." *—Bruce Eder*

Shades of Two Worlds / Jul. 1991 / Epic ✦✦✦✦
The group's follow-up to their comeback album is a major step forward, with more mature songs, more improvisation than the group had featured in their work since the early 1970s, and more confidence than they'd shown since *Brothers and Sisters*. It's all here, from acoustic bottleneck playing ("Come On in My Kitchen") to jazz improvisation ("Kind of Bird"), with the most reflective songwriting ("Nobody Knows") in their history. *—Bruce Eder*

A Decade of Hits 1969-1979 / Oct. 1991 / Polydor ✦✦✦✦
The record industry's blatantly greedy ploy of remastering and "upgrading" CDs is shameful. The sonics are usually improved, but the CDs could have been mastered properly the first time. But then fans wouldn't buy the same titles twice. The Allman Brothers Band's indispensable compilation *A Decade of Hits 1969-1979* was reissued in 2000, just nine years after the original release. The remastered 2000 edition still features the same 16 songs, but the packaging and liner notes include an essay by Guitar World journalist Alan Paul, photos, and detailed recording credits. It would be easy to argue that individual albums like *Idlewild South*, *Live at Fillmore East*, *Eat a Peach*, or *Brothers and Sisters*

are more cohesive artistic statements, but no self-respecting rock & roll fan should be without a copy of *A Decade of Hits 1969-1979*, which includes the cream of those albums. It's impossible to go wrong with one CD featuring Gregg Allman's harrowing "Whipping Post" and gorgeous "Midnight Rider," Dickey Betts' soaring "Ramblin' Man," and the lovely instrumentals "Jessica" and "In Memory of Elizabeth Reed," let alone the blues covers "Statesboro Blues" and "One Way Out," which many people probably don't realize are covers because the band embodies them so much. Fans shouldn't have much of a problem recognizing the 2000 version. The cover featuring the band logo stitched on the denim jacket is still intact, but the white lettering is laid out a little differently on both the front and back covers. Plus, the shrink-wrap has an identifying sticker. Better still, just look at the copyright date. The first pressing's liner notes include a typographical error; there's a noticeable gap within the essay text where the *Enlightened Rogues* title is missing. —*Bret Adams*

An Evening with the Allman Brothers Band / Mar. 1992 / Epic ✦✦✦✦
A good live album, but not quite the worthy successor to the Fillmore shows in their various forms—the band is on form throughout this more than one-hour distillation of shows in Boston and New York from their 1992 tour, covering old and new repertory, but there are no surprises. The song lineup wastes some opportunities, however, and there isn't any serious new ground covered, which may be par for the course for a band in its 22nd year. On the up side, very much, the crispness of the recording helps one fully appreciate the power and articulation of the playing by everyone, but especially Dickey Betts and Warren Haynes. —*Bruce Eder*

The Fillmore Concerts / Oct. 20, 1992 / Polydor ✦✦✦✦✦
A good idea that worked out even better, with one small caveat. *The Fillmore Concerts* is made up of performances from the two Fillmore shows that originally comprised *Live at the Fillmore East* and the concert portions of *Eat a Peach*, plus one track ("One Way Out") from a Fillmore show from a couple of months later, the 16-track masters from each show transferred to digital and remixed by original producer Tom Dowd. The sound is sterling and the two hour-plus running time makes this a dream for fans of the band, as well as an improvement on the original releases of this material. It is also a slightly less honest release, where "In Memory of Elizabeth Reed" is concerned—Dowd edited the version here together from two different performances, first and second shows, the dividing line being where Duane Allman's solo comes in. Not that this is the only concert album where this kind of editing has been done, but the original *Live at the Fillmore* contained a single take of the song, and some purists may prefer that. Otherwise, this set runs circles around more than 99% of the guitar albums ever released, with breathtaking sound (which, unlike the similarly conceived but less effective *Derek and the Dominos Live at the Fillmore*, loses none of its bite), and most fans might as well start here. —*Bruce Eder*

Where It All Begins / May 3, 1994 / Epic ✦✦✦
After a year of personal and personnel problems, the group got back together to record this surprisingly consistent live-in-the-studio venture. It lacks the ambition and stretch of *Seven Turns* or *Shades of Two Worlds*, along with their peaks, but it is still a solidly consistent album, driven by some of the virtues of live spontaneity. Highlights include Gregg Allman's frank drug song "All Night Train," the Bo Diddley-beat-driven "No One to Run With," and the glorious dual guitar workout "Back Where It All Begins." —*Bruce Eder*

2nd Set / 1995 / Epic ✦✦✦✦✦
The Allman Brothers Band's fifth live release in 25 years, cut during 1994 in Raleigh, NC and at the Garden State Arts Center in New Jersey, is a high-water mark in their Epic Records catalog. If anything, they're even better here than they were on the earlier *Evening with the Allman Brothers Band*, the old material getting fresh new approaches— the band was *on* for both nights, and presented sets, including an acoustic version of "In Memory of Elizabeth Reed" and "Jessica" (which won a Grammy Award), that soared and flowed, especially Dickey Betts and Warren Haynes' guitars. What's more, the clarity of the recording and the volume at which it was recorded make this a most rewarding 70 minutes of live music on a purely technical level—you can practically hear the action on the guitars during the acoustic set. It won't replace *Live at the Fillmore* or the live portions of *Eat a Peach*, but it deserves a place on the shelf not very far from them. —*Bruce Eder*

Mycology: An Anthology / Jun. 9, 1998 / Epic ✦✦✦
Mycology: An Anthology collects highlights from the Allman Brothers' '90s recordings for Epic Records. Although these latter-day recordings didn't quite reach the heights of the group's '70s heyday, they were surprisingly strong and *Mycology* is the best way for the curious fan to discover that. By rounding up the best moments from *Seven Turns*, *Shades of Two Worlds*, *An Evening with the Allman Brothers Band* and *Where It All Begins*, the collection offers a good distillation of an underrated portion of the group's career, thereby making it of equal interest to casual and hardcore fans alike. —*Stephen Thomas Erlewine*

20th Century Masters—The Millennium Collection: The Best of The Allman Brothers Band / Jan. 25, 2000 / Polygram ✦✦✦
With the 1991 compilation *A Decade of Hits 1969-1979* still in print, you may ask why Polydor found it necessary to release *The Best of the Allman Brothers Band* as part of the Universal Music Group's 20th Century Masters/The Millennium Collection. After all, the new 11-track album shares nine selections with the earlier 16-track one. The simple answer is price: By purchasing *The Best of the Allman Brothers Band*, you get about 30 percent less music than you do on *A Decade of Hits*, and you pay one-third less. *The Best of the Allman Brothers Band* is a collection intended for the budget-conscious music lover who wants the cheapest possible album containing well-known Allman Brothers songs like "Ramblin' Man," "Crazy Love," and "Whipping Post" from their first ten years of recording. Of course, it remains true that a single-disc best-of is not the ideal way to appreciate the Allman Brothers—Polydor probably would be better advised to compile a

two-disc compilation for that purpose—but this set may serve to initiate new fans or satisfy older ones who stuck to AM Top 40 in the '70s without venturing over to the FM rock stations where the Allmans' extended jams were heard. —*William Ruhlmann*

Peakin' at the Beacon / Nov. 14, 2000 / Epic ✦✦✦
When Gregg Allman was asked why Dickey Betts was kicked out of the Allman Brothers Band in the spring of 2000, he is reported to have suggested the answer lay in the tapes from the group's two-week stand at the Beacon Theatre in New York. That makes it surprising that the Allmans would turn to those tapes to assemble their first new album release in 5 1/2 years, *Peakin' at the Beacon*. Happily, however, there is no evidence of Betts' alleged shortcomings on the disc, though it must be admitted that, since he is one of two lead guitarists (the other being Derek Trucks, making his recorded debut with the band), it isn't always easy to tell who is playing. There is plenty of guitar work, and it is up to the Allmans' usual standard. Following the instrumental opener, Gregg Allman sings lead on seven straight songs, all of which come from the band's first three studio albums. Betts finally appears as a vocalist on the ninth track, the 1990 folk-country tune "Seven Turns." Finally, there is a 27 1/2-minute version of the 1975 Betts instrumental "High Falls," a typical extended workout complete with jazzy interludes and a lengthy percussion section. The Allmans may not have been due for another live album (two of their last three releases being concert recordings), but the series of Beacon shows has become an annual event, and the disc serves as a souvenir from the March 2000 shows. Fans who attended those shows, or who just want to be reassured that the Allmans sound much the same as ever, may enjoy the album; less devoted listeners probably shouldn't bother. —*William Ruhlmann*

Gregg Allman

b. Dec. 8, 1947, Nashville, TN
Vocals, Keyboards, Piano, Guitar (Acoustic), Organ / Southern Rock, Blues-Rock, Album Rock

Gregg Allman's most visible contribution to rock music is as lead singer, organist, and songwriter within the Allman Brothers Band, founded by his brother Duane in 1969. He has never threatened to eclipse the band that carries his family name, but he has found occasional success and popularity with his solo work, which is distinctly different, more soulful, and less focused on high-wattage virtuosity. It was during the period that *Brothers and Sisters* was burning up the charts that Gregg Allman emerged as a solo artist with his first album, the critically well-received hit *Laid Back*, which put the softer, more serious, soul- and gospel-tinged side of his work in sharper focus. A tour followed, which yielded a live album that was also a success. This first period of solo popularity was interrupted by a combination of professional and personal conflicts; the Allman Brothers Band toured extensively and struggled to come up with a follow-up to *Brothers and Sisters*, and Gregg Allman began a relationship with Cher, the ex-wife and singing partner of Sonny Bono, which resulted in a tumultuous series of marriages and divorces for the two. Ironically, it was during this period, in 1977, that he delivered *Playin' Up a Storm*, a pop-soul effort that proved to be his most accomplished and successful album. Alas, this was to be the peak of his career away from the band. His next two albums, *I'm No Angel* and *Just Before the Bullets Fly*, released at the end of the 1980s, were quickly eclipsed by the re-formed and reinvigorated Allman Brothers Band's success on stage and on record. His 1997 release *Searchin' for Simplicity* and the double-CD anthology *One More Try* had none of the urgency or success of the band's activities. —*Bruce Eder*

Laid Back / 1973 / Polydor ✦✦✦✦✦
Recorded in the same year as the *Brothers and Sisters* album, this solo debut release is a beautiful amalgam of R&B, folk, and gospel sounds, with the best singing on any of Gregg Allman's solo releases. He covers his own "Midnight Rider" in a more mournful, dirge-like manner, and Jackson Browne's "These Days" gets its most touching and tragic-sounding rendition as well. Although Chuck Leavell and Jaimoe are here, there's very little that sounds like the Allman Brothers Band—prominent guitars, apart from a few licks by Tommy Talton (Cowboy, ex-We The People) are overlooked in favor of gospel-tinged organ and choruses behind Allman's soulful singing. —*Bruce Eder*

Tour / 1974 / Polygram ✦✦✦✦
Cut during his first solo tour, complete with an orchestra backing him, this CD (originally two LPs) is almost as good a musical showcase, complete with a honky-tonk arrangement of the Elvis hit "Feel So Bad" and a cover of "Turn On Your Love Light" spread among performances of stuff from *Laid Back* and the Allmans' repertory. —*Bruce Eder*

Playin' Up a Storm / 1977 / Razor & Tie ✦✦✦✦✦
In a way, *Playin' Up a Storm* doesn't really highlight Gregg Allman's strengths, since it's a little smoother and soul-inflected than his work with the Allman Brothers. Then again, that's not a problem; after all, why make a solo album that's exactly like your full-time gig? Consequently, *Playin' Up a Storm* is a well-made, expertly performed set of blues-rock, soul-pop, and straight-ahead rock & roll. There aren't any true classics here, but the thing that makes it one of Allman's best solo efforts is the terrific performances. Not only is he in fine voice, delivering each song with conviction, but his supporting band— featuring such luminaries as Dr. John and Bill Payne—is sterling. All the grooves are in the pocket, the sound is enticing, and the overall effect is just right. Not an earth-shattering record, but it will please true Allman fans. —*Stephen Thomas Erlewine*

I'm No Angel / 1986 / Epic ✦✦✦
Nearly ten years separate Gregg Allman's third and fourth solo albums (not counting *Allman & Woman*, which is quite a long stretch by anyone's standards). Of course, there were a number of reasons why Allman didn't release an album between 1977's *Playin' Up a Storm* and 1986's *I'm No Angel*—various substance addictions, bad marriage, disappearing bands. By 1986, he had pulled it all together and crafted *I'm No Angel*, an album

designed to be a comeback. After all, the title track alone was a statement of purpose, a declaration of his bad-boy ways. Since this album was released in the midst of the Reagan era, it's not only a little musically tame—slick surfaces and keyboards dominate—but the attitude is a little lax, too. On the title track, a song that justifiably became one of his signature tunes, the lyrics say "darn" instead of "damn," which is a little tame for someone like Allman. Still, what matters is the tune, and it's a corker—so much so that it overshadows many of the other cuts on the record. However, *I'm No Angel* is, by and large, a solid and thoroughly enjoyable set of songs. The main problem is the production, which is a bit too much of its time. However, that's an easy flaw to overlook, especially for hardcore fans, because Allman rarely delivered a solo album as solid as this. *—Stephen Thomas Erlewine*

Just Before the Bullets Fly / 1988 / Epic ✦✦

● **One More Try: An Anthology** / Sep. 23, 1997 / Polygram ✦✦✦✦✦
Although it may be a little too comprehensive for some tastes, *One More Try: An Anthology* is the definitive Gregg Allman collection. Spanning two discs and 34 songs, the collection touches upon every phase of his career. Of course, it concentrates on his solo career—all of his hits, key album tracks, and AOR staples are here—but it also contains a couple of Allman Brothers cuts for good measure. The end result is a weighty anthology that winds up as the final statement on Gregg Allman's career. *—Thom Owens*

Searching for Simplicity / Nov. 11, 1997 / 550 Music ✦✦✦
In his initial solo recordings, Gregg Allman tried for a more eclectic pop approach than the Southern blues-rock of his day job with the Allman Brothers Band. His later solo work, done during breaks in the Brothers' career, was much closer to the traditional ABB sound. On his first solo album since the Allmans' reformation in 1989, he again makes what is essentially an Allman Brothers Band record without the other members, except new guitarist Jack Pearson, whose Duane Allman/Dickey Betts-style slide work is all over the disc. Allman signals the same-but-different approach by opening the album with an "unplugged" version of the Allmans' signature song, "Whipping Post," and though he adds horns to some tracks for a more R&B feel, the rest of the album finds him growling through standard-issue blues-rock, some of the songs originals, some covers, among them an excellent version of "Dark End of the Street" and an arrangement of John Hiatt's "Memphis in the Meantime" that makes it sound like a Betts country-rocker. Recovering from personnel changes, the Allman Brothers Band didn't release an album in 1997; this record should help tide their fans over. *—William Ruhlmann*

Marc Almond

b. Jul. 9, 1959, Southport, England
Vocals / New Romantic, New Wave, Synth Pop, Dance-Pop
After disbanding Soft Cell, vocalist Marc Almond pursued a solo career that followed the same vaguely sleazy, electronic dance-pop his former group had made popular. Almond's strength was never his personality—his voice tends to waver around the notes instead of hitting them—it was the atmosphere he created with the synths and drum machines. Underneath all of the electronics and disco rhythms, Almond hearkened back to the days of cabaret singers, updating it with that sound for dance clubs of the '80s. Before he properly started a solo career, Marc Almond formed Marc and the Mambas. *"Untitled"* (1982), the group's first album, reflected a later career constant with several covers of Jacques Brel songs, learned from the records of Scott Walker. Almond formed a new backing group, the Willing Sinners, for 1984's *Vermin in Ermine* and 1985's *Stories of Johnny*, the latter spawning a British hit with the title song. In 1987, Almond finally released a true solo album, *Mother Fist . . . And Her Five Daughters*. *Stars We Are*, released the following year, was a brighter album that earned him a number one single "Something's Gotten Hold of My Heart," a duet with Gene Pitney Almond followed with a 1990 collection of Brel songs named *Jacques*. That same year, he released *Enchanted*, which was more successful than *Jacques*. In 1991, he released *The Tenement Symphony*, and in 1995, *Treasure Box* was released. *—Stephen Thomas Erlewine*

Untitled / 1982 / Some Bizarre ✦✦✦
For his debut solo album, *Untitled*, Marc Almond formed a hodgepodge band called the Mambas—the most prominent collaborators were Matt Johnson and Annie Hogan—and made a conscious departure from Soft Cell. There are some touches of synth-pop here and there, but for the most part the record is considerably more ambitious, covering torch songs, tortured balladry in the vein of Scott Walker, covers of the Velvet Underground and Syd Barrett, and straight pop. It doesn't ever add up to anything cohesive, but the parts are intriguing. *—Stephen Thomas Erlewine*

Torment & Toreros / 1983 / Some Bizarre ✦✦

Vermin in Ermine / 1984 / Some Bizarre ✦✦✦
With the wracked final days of Soft Cell behind him, Almond gleefully threw himself into a full-time solo career with a splash; while a chunk of bile still clearly remains—the portentous "Ugly Head" sounds as much personal therapy as it does grinding semi-big band blues—a much more musically upbeat angle dominates, especially on the lush, winning single "The Boy Who Came Back." Allied with producer Mike Hedges, already riding high from his work with the Cure and Siouxsie and the Banshees, and with a newly stable backing band, The Willing Sinners, featuring Hogan, McCarrick, and bassist Billy McGee at the core, Almond lets go over an interestingly varied palette of music, from the shimmering and sharp "Tenderness is a Weakness" to the percussion-heavy "Split Lip." Now freely continuing the classic Soft Cell lyrical vibe of passion in the city's darker, more secret corners—the titles "Shining Sinners" and "Gutter Hearts" almost say it all! Almond's in fine voice throughout. A lengthy release—the CD version runs a full 75 minutes with some extra B-sides attached—but a good one. *—Ned Raggett*

Stories of Johnny / 1985 / Some Bizarre ✦✦✦✦✦
Making his first label jump since signing to Mercury in the early Soft Cell days, *Stories* continues the drive towards a brighter commercial sound, with Hedges once again producing and the Sinners line-up in perfect sync and well-versed in everything from lush Eurodisco to nightclub jazz and smouldering ballads (add some extra credit for the solid work of album guest Martin Ditchum on "all kinds of percussion"!). The troika of brilliant singles from the album's first half makes the album a keeper alone: the tender title track (written about a young friend of Almond who OD'ed), a sassy remake of Mel Torme's "The House is Haunted," and "Love Letter," where electronics resurface to a degree not seen since Soft Cell's collapse. However, there's plenty of other fine delights throughout, such as the solid rocker "The Flesh is Willing" and the snarling "Contempt," not to mention "I Who Never," a soaring breakup number, and "My Candle Burns," another in the fine series of understatedly intense Almond love/obsession songs. Fans of Marc at his harsher will find this perhaps a bit too smooth at points, but as a balance of killer hooks, great music, and Almond's ever-improving singing, this is a winner through and through. *—Ned Raggett*

A Woman's Story / 1986 / Virgin ✦✦✦✦✦
Great screaming melodrama as Almond does his best to prove that he's the best possible cabaret performer that no one will put on a cabaret stage. Depending on the mood you happen to be in, this collection can either be taken seriously or as a tongue-in-cheek celebration of some great over-the-top material (which even applies to Peter Hammill's "Just Good Friends"). Almond's frenetic cover of "The Heel" alone should raise this mini-album to classic status. *—Steven McDonald*

Mother Fist and Her Five Daughters / 1987 / Some Bizarre ✦✦✦✦✦
Following up both *Stories* and his fine covers EP *A Woman's Story*, Almond took a turn for the more challenging on *Mother Fist*, to be rewarded with the loss of his contract and a search for a new label home. Quite why that should have happened is all the more surprising when upon listening it becomes clear that *Mother Fist* was and still is the best Almond album of original material to date. With Hedges once again producing and the Willing Sinners still producing instrumental magic—the great work of Hogan on keyboards, McCarrick on cello and accordion, and McGee on bass and orchestrations simply can't be overstated here—Almond created a generally sparer and more theatrical album that embraces classic European cabaret to wonderful effect, more so than any American or English "rock" album since Bowie's *Aladdin Sane* or Lou Reed's *Berlin*. The wonderful, cheeky swing of the opening title track—an unashamed, Truman Capote-inspired ode to masturbation—moves to the pulsing, piano-and-bass driven lover's lament "There is a Bed," followed by the supremely drugged out and sleazy "Saint Judy" (as in Garland), each track showcasing Almond with a different but equally accomplished vocal approach. *Mother Fist* keeps going from strength to strength as the album progresses, almost a series of short stories come to life exploring hustlers, burnt-out boxers, romantic dreams and desires; its centerpiece, the wonderful "Mr. Sad," shifts from a solo vocal with electric guitar to a full orchestral blast perfectly. All this and two great should-have-been hit singles, "Melancholy Rose" and the pulsing "Ruby Red," as well! An all-around triumph. *—Ned Raggett*

● **Singles: 1984-1987** / 1987 / Some Bizarre ✦✦✦✦
A classic "act leaves the label, repackage the singles" move, collecting every single from the *Vermin in Ermine* days through *Mother Fist*, with the one added bonus being the title track to his covers EP, an attractive version of the Judy Garland song "A Woman's Story." Not really necessary for the heavy-duty fan, but as an introduction to Almond's mid-to-late eighties work, it's fine enough. Still, the sole emphasis on his most commercial moments, lacking the context of his many striking album moments from that era, results in an unavoidably skewed picture of what he was up to at the time. *—Ned Raggett*

Stars We Are / 1988 / Capitol ✦✦✦✦✦
Another year and another label for Almond, along with a newly stripped down band, La Magia, with Willing Sinner vets Hogan, McGee, and Steve Humphreys on drums. Even more so than *Stories of Johnny*, this is Almond with an eye and ear on making a commercial record while still being himself, and the result is much better than expected. Bob Kraushaar's production feels much lighter and brighter in general than Mike Hedges' past efforts, and the songwriting often matches it—the sprightly opening title track, followed by the tenderly passionate "These My Dreams Are Yours, " makes for what has to be the most upbeat start to a Almond album yet! Similar moments crop up throughout the record, including "Bitter Sweet," with a killer sweeping chorus, the sparkling, slightly jazzy "The Very Last Pearl," which gives pulsing nightlife one of its best makeovers ever, and a triumphant, everything-and-the-kitchen-sink version of Gene Pitney's "Something's Gotten Hold of My Heart," replaced on later versions of the album with the UK-chart topping duet with Pitney himself. That said, it's still a Marc album through and through—the lighter songs still have his sweet purr in the vocals (and Hogan's keyboards and instrumental arrangements remain uniformly excellent), while moodier and expectedly dramatic numbers still turn up in abundance. The forceful duet with Nico, "Your Kisses Burn," calls to mind prime Lee and Nancy, with masses of strings to boot; elsewhere, "The Sensualist" acts as his clearest statement yet on the many erotic joys life has to offer. Perhaps most surprisingly of all, "Tears Run Rings," his most overtly political number to date, became a minor U.S. hit. *—Ned Raggett*

Jacques / 1989 / Some Bizarre ✦✦✦✦✦
Recorded on and off over three years, through all sorts of record company and band changes, and ultimately released independently when no major label would take a chance on it, perhaps the most striking thing about this labor of love is its general consistency. Much more than that, though, *Jacques* turns out to be one of the best single-artist tribute records yet recorded; certainly it was anything but a commercial cash-in, given

how its subject, French singer/songwriter Jacques Brel, had little more than a cult following in the English-speaking world, most notably through Scott Walker's various cover versions. Remaking two songs done earlier in his solo career, concert standby "If You Go Away" and "The Bulls," Almond adds on ten other songs, whose subject matter alone is testimony to Brel's abilities with lyrics both personal and political. The classic Willing Sinners line-up is mostly present throughout (Martin McCarrick's abilities with the accordion especially come to the fore here), with plenty of orchestral players as well, serving the Gallic cabaret/pop tunes well. The most striking performances include the worker's lament "The Lockman" and the astoundingly beautiful and lush "The Town Fell Asleep," certainly one his best-ever recordings. In the end, though, singling out songs from this remarkable album is nearly impossible; without any question, it's an out-and-out triumph. *—Ned Raggett*

Enchanted / 1990 / Capitol ✦

Memorabilia / 1991 / Mercury ✦✦✦✦

Memorabilia is a fine, but far from perfect, overview of Marc Almond's entire career, from Soft Cell to his solo recordings. Concentrating primarily on accessible, pop-oriented material, the collection overlooks some of his most ambitious material, but that makes the record a good introduction for the curious. However, they should be forewarned that Almond recut the vocals for three Soft Cell songs, including the hit "Tainted Love" and the title track, for this compilation, thereby lessening the value of the record in the eyes of most casual fans, since these are not the familiar versions. *—Stephen Thomas Erlewine*

Tenement Symphony / Oct. 29, 1991 / Sire ✦✦✦

Almond's newest label jump resulted in what looked like an ideal creation on paper—two songs produced and cowritten by the Grid, the techno duo featuring Marc's Soft Cell collaborator Dave Ball, three more songs worked on with sole surviving Willing Sinner/La Magia member, keyboardist/orchestrator Billy McGee, and a mini-song cycle, the Tenement Symphony itself, produced by uber-studio wizard Trevor Horn. But did it work? Much like *Enchanted*, there's a little too much of Almond getting lost in rote synthdisco for comfort at points. But there are enough pluses to outweigh the minuses—the opening "Meet Me in My Dream," one of the Grid collaborations, is a beautiful start, equal to "The Stars We Are," while the Symphony itself, though perhaps taking itself a bit too seriously as a conceit, has three solid singles to its credit—a completely over-the-top (but what else to expect from Trevor Horn?) version of Jacques Brel's "Jacky," the concluding "My Hand Over My Heart," another sweep of the heartstrings dance ballad, and the surprise U.K. hit single of the bunch, the gentle and (for Horn) understated "The Days of Pearly Spencer," another sixties cover given the Almond treatment to good effect. *—Ned Raggett*

Twelve Years of Tears / May 25, 1993 / Sire ✦✦✦✦✦

While Almond's tours during the early nineties had mostly consisted of performances backed only by the piano of Martin Watkins—both dramatic and admittedly cost-effective!—a lengthy mega-splash of a retrospective evening at London's Royal Albert Hall was staged in late 1992, consisting of three hours, costume changes galore, dancers, fireworks, the lot. *Twelve Years*, a full 75 minutes worth of highlights, does a mostly fantastic job of showcasing what on balance sounds like Almond's ultimate performance for all sides of his talented musical personality. Mostly, not totally—*Tenement*'s "Champagne" has Almond a bit more flat on the vocals than usual, while the *Enchanted* selections, though nice enough, just don't stand up well next to the other performances. And what performances those are! Besides full band versions of expected Soft Cell hits like "Bedsitter" and even "Tainted Love" itself, as well as solo smashes like "Something's Gotten Hold of My Heart" and "Jacky," Marc uses a featured section accompanied only by pianist Martin to sing two of *Mother Fist*'s best numbers, "Mr. Sad" and "There Is a Bed," a haunting, spare version of Soft Cell's lament "Youth," another solid version of Brel's "If You Go Away," and, to top it all off, a lovely, heartfelt version of Charles Aznavour's sympathetic, wry portrait of a transvestite, "What Makes a Man a Man." With an amazing eight-minute take of Soft Cell's break-up ballad "Say Hello Wave Goodbye" wrapping everything up with a full orchestra, back-up singers, guitars, and Marc singing at his bravura best, *Twelve Years* shines. *—Ned Raggett*

Absinthe: The French Album / 1996 / Thirsty Ear ✦✦✦

Initially recorded with some of the *Jacques* sessions but then completed in 1990 after the final break with long-time collaborator Hogan, *Absinthe* can't quite equal the brilliance of Almond's Brel tribute; as a loving overview and celebration of many other French songs that provided him inspiration, though, it's a more than fine release. Featuring pianist/arranger Martin Watkins, Marc's partner during his early nineties acoustic tours, on most of the tracks, the covers of such artists as Juliette Greco, Leo Ferre, Barbara and Charles Aznavour (plus new musical interpretations of poems by Sartre and Rimbaud) run from swinging nightclub fare, such as the wickedly enticing opener, "Undress Me," to emotional drama sessions of the most theatrical degree—and why not? It is Marc Almond! The sexual extremism of "The Slave" inevitably calls to mind the sensual darkness of the *Violent Silence* EP, as does "Incestuous Love." "A Man" grooves suavely and powerfully, while the spotlight-on-the-singer version of "Yesterday When I Was Young" closes out the collection well. In the end, more of a curiosity than *Jacques*, but an enjoyable one. *—Ned Raggett*

Fantastic Star / Feb. 1996 / Mercury ✦✦✦

Not so much a cohesive album as a collection of different sessions in both London and New York, featuring everyone from Soft Cell producer Mike Thorne to New York Dolls frontman David Johansen (on harmonica!) and Velvet Underground veteran John Cale (and Cale's solo sideman Chris Spedding to boot), *Fantastic Star* still showed enough of Marc at his magpie-like best that the album theoretically should have done a lot more—alas, no American release this time, and at home it undeservedly sank like a stone on the charts. The big change in the music comes from Marc's newest regular sideman and musical collaborator—none other than guitarist Neal X, previously only known for his work in Sigue Sigue Sputnik! *Star* experiments with a variety of styles and sounds, its strongest tracks being its singles: "Adored and Explored," a quick slice of techno rompery with Marc's signature marriage of sex and the city in the lyrics, "The Idol," a wry, synthed-up glam rock stomp about fame, "Child Star," a big dramatic weeper, and "Brilliant Creatures," very much the lyrical child of "Say Hello Wave Goodbye" but with a beautiful Hi-NRG pulse/synth shade to it. Not everything fully connects, and the generous length of the album makes it ultimately feel like it's gone on too long, but there's enough going on here to give an ear to. *—Ned Raggett*

Virgin's Tale / Apr. 21, 1998 / Thirsty Ear ✦✦✦

Appearing some years after Almond's departure from Virgin, this two-disc collection (sold as separate releases) covers the plentiful B-sides and non-album tracks from that era, with a brief but informative interview with Almond to explain some of the tunes present. While obviously not a cohesive release, both discs have plenty of worthy numbers, making it something more than a fan-only purchase; certainly hearing yet more of the classic Willing Sinners line-up becomes reason enough to investigate! The first disc is slightly stronger, with highlights including versions of "Stories of Johnny" and "Love Letter" done with the Westminster City Children's Choir, and "Blond Boy," a swinging and powerful number. For the real winners on the disc, though, listen to the tracks from the *Woman's Story* covers EP, aside from the otherwise-collected title song. Among them, the wonderfully bitchy Eartha Kitt number "The Heel," a dramatic version of Scott Walker's already theatrical "The Plague," and the quietly intense "For One Moment," a Lee Hazlewood song, stick in the mind. Perhaps the unexpected highlight, though, is Procol Harum's "A Salty Dog," turned into a breathtaking orchestrated blast of a performance. The second disc feels more iffy in comparison, but some distinct beauties reveal themselves. On the cover front, Almond salutes a clear musical ancestor, the Brecht/Weill team, with fine versions of "Surabaya Johnny" and especially a lengthy, piano-driven version of "Pirate Jenny." Other theatrical romps like "Gyp the Blood" and "Jackal Jackal" capture the ear, while the concluding number, "I'm Sick of You Tasting of Somebody Else," is a campy, relaxed zing. *—Ned Raggett*

Live at the Liverpool Philharmonic Hall, 1992 / Dec. 2000 / Blue Star Music ✦✦✦✦

In the early '90s, the majority of Almond's concert appearances were done as intimate affairs, with the singer accompanied only by a pianist, Martin Watkins. They swiftly achieved legend among his fan base and general notice outside of it for the performances' passion, Almond's astonishing vocal work, and Watkins' skill as a musical foil to Almond. While the *Twelve Years of Tears* live album featured a few songs with the Almond/Watkins pairing, a full recording of the duo's work had been unavailable officially until this welcome, long overdue release. Taken from a date in June 1992, the 16-song collection covers familiar and less-well-known material, the end result being one of the best torch-song recordings out there. Watkins' keyboard work is supple, flowing, intricate, matching Almond's vocal flights with skill. Consider the mid-song vocal break on "Stories of Johnny," where his higher notes play softly around Almond's own gentle repeating of the chorus without losing any of the song's energy. Almond himself is simply astonishing—if a case ever had to be made for his vocal abilities in and of themselves, this performance, focused as it is simply on vocals and piano, makes that case convincingly. Some of the many joys come from hearing material on the somewhat overheated *Enchanted* and *Tenement Symphony* albums get simpler and much more elegant performances. "Champagne" is a revelation, finally letting Almond's intriguing personal portrait breathe to its full, while performances of "Toreador in the Rain" and "Orpheus in Red Velvet" also are of note. Two total rarities surface, both among the album's best moments. "When I Was a Young Man," an old folk song performed off and on by Almond over the years, gets a strong delivery here, Watkins' piano and a bit of backing synth creating a mysterious, gloomy feeling. "Amnesia Nights," co-written by Almond and Watkins, combines glazed, slightly druggy electric piano with a grand, lovelorn lyric. *—Ned Raggett*

Stranger Things / Jul. 24, 2001 / XIII Bis ✦✦✦

For his follow-up to *Open All Night*, Marc Almond chose to work with a new partner, keyboardist and Iceland native Johann Johannson. A musical figure of some renown in his home country, with both his own projects Lhooq and Dip and his work with other acts, including the Hafler Trio, Johannson brought a very consciously cinematic touch to *Stranger Things*. Call it his own take on John Barry-touched trip-hop, though with generally less emphasis on rhythm and more on the dramatic strings, which he often arranged himself, though others assist in that role too. Almond himself, meanwhile, sounds in absolutely excellent voice—indeed, arguably he's at a technical peak, with little evidence of the emotional cracking that has often marked his work. Lyrically, his reflections on love and lust are some of his calmest—there's sparks at points, like on "Come Out," but little of his memorable turns of phrase. As a result, *Stranger Things* falls somewhere in the middle range of Almond albums—it's no disaster, by any means, but it's definitely an album rewarding repeated listenings rather than immediately connecting. Where *Open All Night* was dark, sly, and desperate, *Stranger Things*, a few songs aside like the brassy "Dancer" and "When It's Your Time," is dreamy, swoony, and much more subtly involving. Consider the orchestration on "Born to Cry," which turns a fine song into a really great one, a Shirley Bassey-sung spy movie theme for a new century. "Glorious," which opens and, in an instrumental reprise, closes the album, is the clear standout on the record, having something of the same sweep and inspiration of "Meet Me In My Dream" from *Tenement Symphony*. Other highlights include "Lights," another in Almond's long-running series of songs about the romance of urban landscapes at night, the glitch-techno tinged "Moonbathe Skin," and the both moody and pretty crawl of the brilliantly titled "Love In a Time of Science." *—Ned Raggett*

ALT

f. 1993

Celtic Rock, Adult Alternative Pop/Rock, Folk-Rock, Alternative Pop/Rock

ALT is a side project (and supergroup of sorts) consisting of Andy White, Liam O'Maonlai (Hothouse Flowers), and Tim Finn (ex-Split Enz)—the name comes from the first letters of each of their first names. In 1993, the three began writing together informally in Dublin—one of the songs, "Many's the Time (in Dublin)," appeared on Finn's 1993 album, *Before & After*. In June 1994, they reconvened in Finn's Melbourne-based Periscope Studios, where they recorded their debut album, *Altitude*. *Altitude* was released by EMI-Australia in 1995 and in the U.S. on Cooking Vinyl. —*Chris Woodstra*

Bootleg / 1995 / ALT Recordings ✦✦✦✦✦

This band-released official bootleg captures the group in an intimate live setting during their first tour of Australia and New Zealand. The band really can't be considered "tight" in the traditional musical sense, but that's not the point anyway—this is the work of a tight group of friends having fun with informal sing-alongs. In many ways, *Bootleg* is a stronger album than the proper release—wonderfully sloppy despite the fact that they know the songs better at this point, but probably capturing the spirit of the project better. Most of the songs from *Altitude* are performed, as well as "Many's the Time," the song from Tim Finn's *Before & After* documenting the band's formation, and the ever-charming Tim Finn's between-song stage banter is simply priceless. —*Chris Woodstra*

● **Altitude** / Oct. 24, 1995 / ALT/Cooking Vinyl ✦✦✦✦

Altitude represents the trio's drunken, post-pub jamming with the predictable result of an informal, at times sloppy, album filled with seemingly unfinished songs. While fans of any of the individual members may be put off by these qualities, there is a spirit to these sessions that not only overcomes the shortcomings in content but also gives the record a rare warmth and charm. —*Chris Woodstra*

Dave Alvin

b. 1955, Los Angeles, CA

Vocals, Guitar / Americana, Roots Rock, Singer/Songwriter

Former Blaster Dave Alvin has forged a singer-songwriter career since the band's official breakup in the late '80s. He also served as temporary guitarist for X, was a member of their acoustic side project the Knitters, and formed his own all-star band, the Pleasure Barons, which at times included Mojo Nixon, Rosie Flores, and Country Dick Montana. Alvin comes from a strictly California perspective—but not that of sun and fun; rather, he is a champion of the blue-collar man. Born in 1955 in Los Angeles, Alvin is a lifelong California resident and takes his inspiration from the state's inland-scapes and his own heart. He deftly juxtaposes the hard content with sprightly rockabilly and traditional music. His 1987 Epic debut, *Romeo's Escape*, showed the promise of his writing when Dwight Yoakam later covered his "Long White Cadillac," and X recorded "Fourth of July." That year, Alvin also handled soundtrack chores for Allison Anders' first feature film, *Border Radio*. *Blue Blvd* (1991, Hightone) took it further on down the dusty road, while *Museum of Heart* and *King of California* continued the thread of straight-ahead workingman's music from the Golden State. Country music also figures into the Alvin oeuvre, as he remains a devotee of Merle Haggard and Buck Owens; between records, he compiled an album of Haggard covers, *Tulare Dust*, in 1994. *Blackjack David* followed in 1998. *Public Domain: Songs from the Wild Land* arrived two years later. —*Denise Sullivan*

● **Romeo's Escape** / Dec. 1987 / Razor & Tie ✦✦✦✦✦

This is the quintessential California singer-songwriter album. Alvin comes out strong with "Fourth of July," "Long White Cadillac" (formerly recorded by the Blasters), along with "Every Night About This Time," and "Border Radio"—all standards in the contemporary canon. Aided by his friends and the best studio musicians available, there's nothing wrong with this record—a logical continuation of the Blasters' legacy and a stellar start on his solo career. —*Denise Sullivan*

Every Night About This Time / Dec. 1987 / Demon ✦✦✦✦✦

This is Dave Alvin's solo debut, which was released initially in the U.K., then picked up for U.S. release by Epic Records, which changed the album title to *Romeo's Escape*. —*William Ruhlmann*

Blue Blvd / Aug. 1991 / Hightone ✦✦✦

The only thing that mars this wonderful, rootsy singer-songwriter album is a heavy production hand and a drum sound attempting to give it a rock edge; consequently, some of the more beautiful songs like the title track suffer under the weight, but the final cut, "Dry River," is worth the price of the disc alone. Alvin's rock & roll pals come out to play—Dwight Yoakam, David Hidalgo, saxophonist Lee Allen—making the record essential for anyone interested in the state of California roots music in the early '90s. —*Denise Sullivan*

Museum of Heart / Sep. 20, 1993 / Hightone ✦✦✦

Alvin's vision falters slightly, as none of the songs here are as instantly likable or classic as on previous outings. Perhaps stunted by more than half of the songs being co-writes ("Between the Cracks" with Tom Russell), Alvin's normally clear and simple approach is muddled, but the instrumentation is flawless and his regular all-star cast (John Doe, Syd Straw, and Katy Moffatt) is present. —*Denise Sullivan*

King of California / May 1, 1994 / Hightone ✦✦✦✦

From the time The Blasters began making waves on the California rock scene, the standard line always was that Dave Alvin was the group's great songwriter and Phil Alvin was the great singer. And when Dave launched his solo career in 1987, he was frequently saddled with the criticism that he wasn't much of a vocalist compared to his brother.

While dozens of blues and roots rock performers have built solid careers without singing any better than Dave Alvin, it's true that on *Romeo's Escape* and *Blue Blvd* his rough, flinty voice lacked the natural grace and projection of Phil's work with The Blasters. But on 1994's *King of California*, Alvin recorded a few new songs alongside a stack of classics from his back catalog (and some well-chosen covers) with a small acoustic combo backing him up. Suddenly freed from having to shout over a high-powered rock band, Alvin proved on this release just how good of a vocalist he really was. While Alvin's natural instrument still shows certain limitations on *King of California*, when allowed to play with the nooks and crannies of his voice he reveals a subtle but dramatic sense of phrasing and a marvelous feel for the characters he created; he's still no Al Green, but as a musical storyteller he's mighty impressive. Of course, it helps that he has a bunch of superb songs to work with here, including "Barn Burning," "Fourth of July," "Border Radio," and "Little Honey," and that the great Greg Leisz is on hand to anchor the band, produce the sessions, and play marvelous slide guitar. While *King of California* was often lumped in with the then-fashionable unplugged craze, in retrospect it was the album where Dave Alvin's abilities as a performer began to catch up with his gifts as a songwriter, pointing the way for his later albums *Blackjack David* and *Public Domain*. —*Mark Deming*

Interstate City / Jul. 1996 / Hightone ✦✦✦✦

Recorded at the Continental Club in Austin, TX, with his backup band, the Guilty Men, *Interstate City* documents the nervy energy and gritty sound of Dave Alvin live in concert. Alvin tears through his back catalog with surprising gusto, touching on both the Blasters and his solo hits. Most enticing for fans, however, are the new songs he works into the set. Most of the newer numbers are on par with his finest material and they are delivered with an intoxicating rush. *Interstate City* is one of the rare live albums that actually improves on the original recordings. —*Thom Owens*

Blackjack David / Jun. 16, 1998 / Hightone ✦✦✦✦

Dave Alvin earned his crown as the King of California the hard way. A fourth-generation Californian, Alvin worked his way through various incarnations in order to arrive at this point. A long-standing monumental force in Los Angeles and California music, Alvin is essentially a blues player who writes and performs what he terms "American folk music." From Celtic and English folk tunes to early rock & roll, from classic blues and country & western to the Bakersfield Sound, Alvin knows his stuff. Gleaning from all the genres, Alvin sits firmly upon his throne, creating a brand of music that is intelligent, insightful, and broad in scope. At peace with his creative direction, *Blackjack David* picks up where *King of California* left off in 1994. More electric, *Blackjack David* almost rocks in places, as on "Abilene" and "New Highway." It ambles along nicely in other spots too. The title cut, a traditonal tune hundreds of years old, is given new life under the deft Alvin touch and a new arrangement. This effectively connects the past and the present in terms of Dave Alvin and his place in musical history. "1968," written with fellow "405 Freeway Boy" Chris Gaffney, reveals a country twist. As interesting as anything either of them have written individually, the Tom Russell co-write, "California Snow," is startling in its intensity. The final cut, "Tall Trees," is haunting and mysterious, displaying all of Alvin's power as a writer and communicator in a subtle fashion that demands attention. A Renaissance man, Dave Alvin continues to make and record music of integrity. —*Jana Pendragon*

Public Domain: Songs from the Wild Land / Aug. 15, 2000 / Hightone ✦✦✦✦✦

Drawing from the mother lode of traditional songs in the public domain, songwriter Dave Alvin brings an authentic voice and extraordinary understanding to his chosen tracks. Familiar songs from the folk canon like "Shenandoah" and "Walk Right In" are reworked by him and a full band with arrangements incorporating the roadhouse style they've honed from years of working together. He also unearthed lesser-known songs like "Mama, Ain't Long for Day" (perhaps credited to Blind Willie McTell), "Sign of Judgment," and "Railroad Bill," having learned versions from records he unearthed as a kid by obscure artists: from Will Bennett to Kid Prince Moore. This is the work of a scholar as well as a master craftsman. —*Denise Sullivan*

Amazing Blondel

f. 1969

Prog-Rock/Art Rock

One of England's most unusual rock outfits of the 1970s, Amazing Blondel was a trio whose members played instruments dating from medieval to Elizabethan times, and songs styled to those periods. Named for Richard the Lionhearted's legendary favorite minstrel, the trio of John David Gladwin, Terry Wincott, and Edward Baird recorded an eponymous album in 1970. Their first album was a collection of soft acoustic rock numbers that included one medieval-styled song that seemed to go over better than anything else, and that was the direction they aimed for in their future releases. The trio became known for playing upwards of 40 instruments on stage, though without backup musicians—each song was simply planned for no more than three instruments at any one time. Despite their reliance on acoustic instruments, the trio wasn't adverse to composing extended suites that ran up to 25 minutes, and while some of the music had a repetitive quality, the best of it played off of achingly beautiful melodies. *England*, released in 1972, was the high point for the trio and got them their heaviest airplay to date in America, if only modest sales. Reduced to a duo for their follow-up, 1973's *Blondel* marked the last of their "period" material. On subsequent albums, the group aimed for a harder, more contemporary sound vaguely resembling Steeleye Span. —*Bruce Eder*

Amazing Blondel / 1970 / Bell ✦✦

Evensong / 1970 / Island ✦✦✦

The trio's first fully realized album, a self-consciously archaic work built around medieval balladry and madrigals, and performed on period instruments. The group doesn't sound entirely at ease working in this style, but the crisp, folklike feel, and the timbre and singing have great charm. The strongest songs are those such as "Willowood," closest to the group members' own experiences and dealing with Kent, from which they all hailed. The 1996 Edsel CD reissue contains new notes by the original group members, and is very finely remastered. —*Bruce Eder*

Fantasia Lindum / 1971 / Island ✦✦✦✦✦
The concept album rears its head—and rears back about 500 years. While other progressive rock groups were doing album-length suites dealing with apocalyptic themes, Amazing Blondel were doing 20-minute long multi-part pieces ("fantasia" is the best classical music term) about Kent, England, and songs depicting idealized love between men and women, man and nature, and man and God. It all plays a little like the Strawbs' work of this same era without the sardonic edge, and is all achingly beautiful. The 1996 CD reissue is especially pleasing for eliminating the problem of surface noise that afflicted most copies of the original LP. —*Bruce Eder*

● **England** / 1972 / Island ✦✦✦✦✦
The best record ever made by the trio, a lyrical, gentle, yet ambitious expansion of their sound into a richer vein, with a wider range of instrumentation, some eerie mixes of medieval instruments and psychedelic effects, and a compelling beauty that makes this record linger long in the memory. The sound is very elegant, but this time out the group has timed and edited everything perfectly, so none of it overstays its welcome. Sort of the way the Moody Blues might've sounded circa the year 1500. —*Bruce Eder*

Blondel / 1973 / Edsel ✦✦✦
The group—reduced to a duo—in its swan song for Island Records. The album lacks the panache of their previous albums, although it also has a smoothness that makes each track a very easy listen, and the antique sensibilities are beginning to give away to more modern songwriting techniques. —*Bruce Eder*

Mulgrave Street / 1974 / DJM ✦✦

Inspiration / 1975 / DJM ✦✦✦
A further effort at rocking up the folky sound, and so successful at it that one had to wonder why stick with the name or the image at all? —*Bruce Eder*

Englishe Musicke / 1993 / Edsel ✦✦✦✦
Englishe Musicke is a 16-track collection which draws from the band's three prime-period albums—*Evensong* (1970), *Fantasia Lindum* (1971), and *England* (1972). Although most progressive rock doesn't translate well on collections due to its more album-oriented concept nature, *Englishe Musicke* shows Amazing Blondel's music in a fair light. The songs work well as self-contained pieces, and the real concept—the medieval sound—is kept consistent throughout, making this a nice career overview and a pretty good introduction, though the converted will undoubtedly need the albums in their entirety. —*Chris Woodstra*

Live Abroad / 1996 / H.T.D. ✦✦✦✦✦
Not only a beautiful record, but an amazing find some 24 years after the fact—a live Amazing Blondel album, 71 minutes of concert recordings made in Europe by the group during 1972 and 1973. All of the tracks were written by John David Gladwin, the composing mainstay of the group, making this a kind of live "best-of" album, comprised of the best songs off of the albums *England, Fantasia Lindum* (including the latter's 20-minute title track, in an astonishingly tight performance, better than the studio recording, marred only by some minor sound distortion toward the end), and *Evensong.* "Seascape," "Dolor Dolcis" (aka "Sweet Sorrow"), "Willowood," "Spring Air," and "Landscape" are among the highlights. The group acquits itself extremely well, with impeccable harmonies and gorgeous balance to the all-acoustic instruments that would've put most other English folk-rock groups to shame—moreover, on tracks such as "Willowood," the musicianship is quite overpowering, as Gladwin displays a virtuosity on the lute that, four centuries ago, would've made him a star in his local county. The sound is remarkably clean and the stereo separation gives a good sense of the intimacy of the performances, and the joking around on stage—especially the account of the sound of the crumhorn by Terry Wincott—presents a light side of the group that their albums seldom displayed adequately (the botched "Shepherd's Song" opening is also pretty funny, and the performance is beguilingly boisterous). —*Bruce Eder*

Restoration / 1997 / Castle ✦✦✦✦✦
The original trio's first album in a quarter of a century is a gem, a little more mellow than their classic early-'70s work but beautifully sung and played, and unlike a lot of other reunited bands of this era, it's just the three originals—no extra musicians to fill out the sound. The first song is in Latin, but it's so beautifully melodic that it's not a problem (yeah, like every rock & roll song has words that are understandable). The harmonies are as graceful as the old stuff, though they don't soar nearly as high, and the instrumentals are, if anything, more accessible and filled with better hooks than their older work. Easily the equal of their best '70s albums, and worth the wait. —*Bruce Eder*

The Amazing Rhythm Aces
f. 1974, Memphis, TN, **db.** 1981
Country-Rock
A mainstream country-rock band similar in execution (if not commercial success) to the Eagles, the Amazing Rhythm Aces issued *Stacked Deck,* their debut album, in 1975; it produced two significant crossover hits, "Third Rate Romance" and "Amazing Grace (Used to Be Her Favorite Song)," the group's lone Top Ten country single. A year later, the hit "The End Is Not in Sight (The Cowboy Tune)," from the LP *Too Stuffed to Jump,* won the Aces a Grammy for Country Vocal Performance by a Group. Efforts like 1977's *Toucan Do It Too* and 1978's *Burning the Ballroom Down* were met with critical ap-

proval, but sold poorly; the Aces released one final record, *How the Hell Do You Spell Rhythum,* before disbanding. After a hiatus of some 15 years, they reformed in 1994. —*Jason Ankeny*

☆ **Stacked Deck** / 1975 / Valley ✦✦✦✦✦
In contrast to such '70s country-rock outfits as the Eagles and Poco, whose members had passed through the West Coast folk-rock scene dominated by the Byrds, the Amazing Rhythm Aces were a Memphis-based band. Their debut album is an edgy effort, rooted in a purer Southern sound, and embracing a soulfulness that their West Coast rivals lacked. The country gospel tune "Life's Railway to Heaven," the funky "The 'Ella B'," the stomping "Hit the Nail on the Head," and the soulful "The Beautiful Lie" would never have been done in as raw, intense, or bracing a fashion by their rivals. Russell Smith brings a vocal performance to Charlie Rich's "Who Will the Next Fool Be" that sounds like he's channeling the ghost of Sam Cooke. And between those album highlights and the hits "Third Rate Romance" and "Amazing Grace (Used to Be Her Favorite Song)," the group works in a sweetly nostalgic piece called "King of the Cowboys," all about movie and television heroes. —*Bruce Eder*

Too Stuffed to Jump / 1976 / Valley ✦✦✦✦
The group's second album is only slightly less inventive than its first, still very countrified compared to most country-rock, and more soulful than most of the competition. The numbers range from rocking stompers like "Typical American Boy" to the lyrical "If I Just Know What to Say," with room in between for some fine western numbers ("The End Is Not in Sight," "Out of the Snow")—the former a Grammy-winning country tune, the latter a beautiful mandolin workout—and novelty songs ("A Little Italy Rag"). —*Bruce Eder*

Toucan Do It Too / 1977 / ABC ✦✦✦✦
The group's third album rocks a little harder and louder than its two predecessors, with particularly bracing guitar workouts from Barry Burton on "Living in a World Unknown" and "Who's Crying Now," but it still has room for some slow country-style ballads like "Last Letter Home" (which features some gorgeous mandolin from Burton), "Geneva's Lullaby," and the bluesy "Just Between You and Me and the Wall." And it ends with the hauntingly melodic yet crunchy rocker "You Can Do It Too," melding a brittle, lively guitar sound to beautiful harmonies. —*Bruce Eder*

Burning the Ballroom Down / 1978 / ABC ✦✦✦✦
The group's fourth album is amazingly consistent with its predecessors, the only change being a more memorable overall range of melodies (on both the rock songs and the more traditional numbers) running through most of the material. The highlights, in addition to the title cut—one of the best songs in the band's whole early output, and their most mainstream-sounding rock number—include the acoustic "Ashes of Love," which offers some of their best ever harmony singing, the country ballad "All That I Had Left (With You)," the cautionary tale "I Pity the Mother and the Father (When the Kids Move Away)," and the gospel number "The Spirit Walk." —*Bruce Eder*

★ **Stacked Deck/Too Stuffed to Jump** / Jul. 11, 2000 / Collectors' Choice Music ✦✦✦✦
The group's first two LPs assembled together on one CD from Collectors' Choice—there are no notes, but the original artwork is recreated with full music credits, and beautiful, state-of-the-art sound. The band's music has aged well, and although their master tapes evidently no longer reside with the ABC library (which is part of MCA-Universal), they haven't been lost track of either, to judge from the good results here. —*Bruce Eder*

Toucan Do It Too/Burning the Ballroom Down / Jul. 11, 2000 / Collectors' Choice Music ✦✦✦✦
The group's third and fourth albums assembled together, again with no annotation but excellent sound. In addition to being a fine showcase for the group overall, the CD gives a good account of Barry Burton's skills and development as a producer, and his ability to get some extraordinary sounds out of the group as singers as well as instrumentalists— "The Spirit Walk" by itself, which closes this disc, is one of the crowning achievements for the group and a stunning piece of white gospel music. —*Bruce Eder*

Ambrosia
f. 1971, Los Angeles, CA, **db.** 1982
Soft Rock, Prog-Rock/Art Rock
Los Angeles quartet Ambrosia, whose founding members included guitarist/vocalist David Pack, bassist/vocalist Joe Puerta, keyboardist Christopher North, and drummer Burleigh Drummond, fused symphonic art rock with a slickly produced pop sound. The group was discovered in 1971 by Los Angeles Philharmonic conductor Zubin Mehta, who featured Ambrosia as part of a so-called All-American Dream Concert. However, it took them four more years to get a record contract; *Ambrosia* was released in 1975 and spawned the chart singles "Holdin' on to Yesterday" and "Nice, Nice, Very Nice." The latter was based on Kurt Vonnegut Jr.'s *Cat's Cradle.* Ambrosia scored another hit in 1977 with a cover of the Beatles' "Magical Mystery Tour" from the film *All This and World War II,* which they also appeared in.

North left the group just before their biggest pop breakthrough in 1978 with the number three hit "How Much I Feel." Ambrosia followed this success in 1980 with another number three hit, "Biggest Part of Me," and the number 13 follow-up "You're the Only Woman." Their next album failed, ending their run of chart success, and the group broke up; individual members are still active as session musicians and vocalists, as well as producers. —*Steve Huey*

Ambrosia / 1975 / Warner Brothers ✦✦✦✦
Although they would become better known for smooth AOR ballads like "How Much I Feel," Ambrosia first made their name with this album of progressive rock with a pop music twist. Its songs skillfully blend strong melodic hooks and smooth vocal harmonies

with music of an almost symphonic density. Good examples of this crossbreeding are "Drink of Water," which sounds like the Beach Boys tackling a Pink Floyd space rock epic, and "Nice, Nice, Very Nice," which utilizes a combination of stately close-harmony vocals and dynamic instrumental breaks to put forth a clever lyric derived from a Kurt Vonnegut novel. The complexity of the music is further highlighted by its crystal-clear sonic landscape, mixed by Alan Parsons, which highlights unique touches like the use of a Russian balalaika ensemble and 300-year-old Javanese gongs on "Time Waits for No One." Despite this prog rock ambitiousness, the group is smart enough to avoid letting their instrumental chops take precedence over their music's melodic content: They keep their songs succinct and punchy (nothing extends over six-and-a-half minutes) and they infuse tunes like "Lover Arrive" and the radio favorite "Holdin' on to Yesterday" with a delicate sense of pop songcraft that makes the group's cinematic sound easy for listeners to assimilate. The end result is an album that is intricate enough to please prog rock addicts but catchy enough to win over a few pop fans in the process. Though Ambrosia would go on to score bigger hits later in their career, this is definitely their most cohesive and inspired album. —*Donald Guarisco*

Somewhere I've Never Travelled / 1976 / Warner Brothers ✦✦✦✦
After achieving moderate success with their self-titled debut, Ambrosia decided to up the ante by going for a bigger, more symphonic sound on this follow-up outing. To achieve this goal, they enlisted Alan Parsons, who mixed their first album, to produce and Andrew Powell (arranger for the Alan Parsons Project) to do full-blown orchestral arrangements on a number of the tracks. The resulting album lacks the careful fusion of pop and prog elements that characterized *Ambrosia*, with songs tending to fall into either progressive or soft rock categories. Just the same, it is a strong album with a number of sonically arresting moments. The finest songs are the most overtly progressive, the most dazzling being "Danse With Me, George," a tribute to Chopin that leads the listener through a bewildering array of styles (classical, jazz, and pop, to name just a few) in just under eight minutes. "Cowboy Star" is another knockout, bringing its tale of a city dweller who dreams of cowboy glory to life with a beautiful orchestral mid-section that is strongly reminiscent of Aaron Copland. None of the straightforward pop songs are as catchy or instantly memorable as "Holdin' on to Yesterday," but "Runnin' Away" presents an appealing blend of carefully arranged harmonies and acoustic sounds, and "We Need You Too" provides the album with a suitably stately finale by building from a piano-led solo ballad into a cascade of soaring strings and harmony vocals. All in all, *Somewhere I've Never Travelled* lacks the crossover appeal that made *Ambrosia* such a unique album but is still a worthwhile listen for progressive rock fans. —*Donald Guarisco*

Life Beyond L.A. / 1978 / Warner Brothers ✦✦✦
Ambrosia's third album (and first for Warner Bros.) is more commercial and less conceptual than their first two releases, *Somewhere I've Never Travelled* and the self-titled *Ambrosia*. The album opens effectively with the title track, which is about life, or the lack thereof, in Los Angeles. The better songs on this album, including the title track and the top ten single "How Much I Feel," were written and sung by lead vocalist/multi-instrumentalist David Pack. —*Tim Griggs*

One Eighty / 1980 / Warner Brothers ✦✦✦
When *Life Beyond L.A.* became their biggest hit to date on the strength of smooth AOR like "How Much I Feel," Ambrosia decided to continue in this direction on *One Eighty*. It became their most successful album but lacks the ambition or inspiration that infused their first two albums. The prog rock style that characterized the group's early work is almost completely gone: The only real progressive cut is "Kamikaze," which attempts to create a stylized blend of prog rock and traditional Japanese music but comes off as stilted and awkward. The rest of the album's songs are either pop/rock tunes or ballads. Rockers like "Ready" go for an ambitious blend of radio-friendly rock and new wave elements, but sound too forced to be convincing. The ballads are the album's redeeming feature. They are all lovingly crafted and boast strong, often complex melodies that keep them from getting too sappy or sentimental: "You're the Only Woman" is a keyboard-rich song that highlights Christopher North's soulful Hammond organ playing, and "Livin' on My Own" layers harmonies reminiscent of the Doobie Brothers over a jazzy tune driven by an intricate bass line. The album's finale, "Biggest Part of Me," is the best of these ballads. It combines rich Beach Boys-styled harmonies with a heartfelt lyric to create a rich slice of blue-eyed soul that gave the group a number two hit single. These classy ballads make *One Eighty* worth a listen for devoted Ambrosia fans, but the casual listener might want to seek these songs out on the group's *Anthology* album. —*Donald Guarisco*

Road Island / 1982 / Warner Brothers ✦✦✦
On their final album, Ambrosia forsakes the airbrushed AOR sounds that defined *Life Beyond L.A.* and *One Eighty* in favor of a strong, rock-oriented sound. They are aided in this aim by a gutsy production from James Guthrie (a producer better known for his work with groups like Judas Priest and Pink Floyd) that takes the group to a new level of sonic firepower. Songs like "For Starters" and "Still Not Satisfied" reverberate with a newfound sense of rock & roll muscle: The drums kick, the bass lines throb, and the guitars and Hammond organ wail with abandon. Even Ambrosia's trademark ballads benefit from their newly beefed-up sound: "Feelin' Alive Again" features the airy harmonies and delicate keyboard shadings expected from this style of song, but it also gains an added sense of dramatic weight from Burleigh Drummond's thick drumming and piercing, emotional guitar solos from David Pack. The group also revives their early progressive sound on "Ice Age," an impressive epic tune built on a militaristic drum pattern, heavy power chords, and Pink Floyd-styled sound effects. The end result is an album that harkens back to the blend of slick musicianship and prog rock imagination that characterized Ambrosia's early work. Despite receiving many good reviews, *Road Island* never achieved a notable level of success because, much like *Somewhere I've Never Travelled*, it lacks a standout

single that could have helped it cross over to mainstream pop fans. Just the same, it is an above-average album that is worthy of reappraisal by progressive rock fans and lovers of hard rock in general. —*Donald Guarisco*

● **Anthology** / May 20, 1997 / Warner Brothers ✦✦✦✦✦
For various legal reasons, no Ambrosia recordings were released on compact disc in America until 1997's *Anthology*, and while it's an imperfect collection, it does offer a reasonably thorough overview of the group's career. It only briefly touches on the band's early art-rock records, choosing to concentrate instead on their early-'80s soft-rock hits like "Biggest Part of Me," "You're the Only Woman," and "How Much I Feel." As a result, dedicated prog-rock fans will find this collection inadequate, but for most casual listeners, it will contain everything they need and then some, since the disc is padded with three new songs that are pleasant but unremarkable. —*Stephen Thomas Erlewine*

Amen Corner

f. Cardiff, Wales, **db.** 1969
British Psychedelia, Psychedelic Pop, Mod, British Invasion
The Amen Corner were a Welsh R&B-tinged pop band of the '60s featuring singer Andy Fairweather-Low, organist Blue Weaver, guitarist Neil Jones, bassist Clive Taylor, saxophonists Allen Jones and Mike Smith, and drummer Dennis Bryn. They scored the first of their six British chart hits with "Gin House" in the summer of 1967. "(If Paradise Is) Half as Nice" went to number one in early 1969. By then, Fairweather-Low had become a teenage heartthrob and the band had switched management and record companies, but they split up by the end of the year. —*William Ruhlmann*

Greatest Hits / 1977 / Immediate ✦✦✦✦
The Amen Corner managed to be on two different record labels, Deram and Immediate, during their brief existence and to score hits for both. Thus, neither label has enough to fill out a complete hits collection. This is Immediate's version, which does contain the chart-topping "(If Paradise Is) Half As Nice" and the Top 10 "Hello Susie." But the Deram hits, "Gin House Blues," "Bend Me, Shape Me," and "High In The Sky," are all represented here by live versions, and it's there you really get to hear the evidence of the group's teen appeal—the screams run right through the performances. The rest of the album contains the group's covers of songs like The Beatles' "Get Back" and the Band's "The Weight" and originals such as "Recess" that suggest their categorization as a kiddie band wasn't entirely unearned. The Amen Corner never made it in the U.S., but it's hard to understand why, given the band's chops and, especially, lead singer Andy Fairweather-Low's distinctively gravelly wail. —*William Ruhlmann*

● **If Paradise Was Half As Nice: The Immediate Anthology** / 2000 / Castle ✦✦✦✦
The 35 songs on this double-CD set represent the output of the Amen Corner on Immediate Records from 1968 through 1970. Listening to the 23 tracks on the first disc, one gets a good idea of the group's sound, and also why certain kinds of English pop/rock never transferred well to American shores. The Amen Corner were spirited (even frenzied) enough in their playing and singing, but they also came off as a very lightweight group, without a lot of depth—mostly that was true of their singles, but the singles were what defined them. "(If Paradise Is) Half As Nice" is a pleasant, catchy track, as are "Hello Susie" and most of the rest, but they all seem more like songs that are pleasant to hear, rather than to play. Still, there was a fair amount of talent in evidence. And then there is the second disc in this set, comprised of their concert album, *The National Welsh Coast Live Explosion Company*—and that's the highlight of this set. Turned loose on stage, the Amen Corner could put on a rousing show broken down evenly between American soul ("Baby Do the Philly Dog," "Shake a Tail Feather") and their established hits, including their pre-Immediate successes on Decca Records. They pound and stomp their way through the music that they love like nobody's business. This was (and is) the way to hear the Amen Corner, and if one can ignore a useless cover of "Penny Lane," it's a nearly perfect concert album; and if the overall recording quality isn't perfect, it is distinctly superior here to any prior CD and LP editions of this performance. The annotation is also very thorough, and nicely illustrated as well. —*Bruce Eder*

America

f. 1967, London, England
Pop/Rock, Soft Rock, Adult Contemporary
America was a light folk-rock act of the early '70s who had several Top Ten hits, including the number ones "A Horse with No Name" and "Sister Golden Hair." Formed around Dewey Bunnell, Dan Peak, and Gerry Beckley, the group landed a contract with a prominent promoter and opened for several major artists. America soon signed with Warner Bros. Records. Debut single "A Horse with No Name"—which strongly recalled the acoustic numbers of Neil Young—hit number three in the U.K. and number one in the U.S. Two straight Top Ten singles ("I Need You" and "Ventura Highway") followed, though the hits stopped coming fairly soon—they had only one minor Top 40 hit in 1973. One year later, *Holiday* returned America to the top of the charts, peaking at number three and launching the hit singles "Tin Man" and "Lonely People." "Sister Golden Hair," pulled from 1975's *Hearts*, became their second number one single. The group's audience began to decline in 1976, though they returned to the Top Ten in 1982 with "You Can Do Magic," an adult-contemporary pop number that featured synthesizers along with their trademark harmonies. After releasing *America in Concert* in the summer of 1985, the group continued to tour successfully into the '90s, resurfacing in 1998 with *Human Nature*. —*Stephen Thomas Erlewine*

● **History: Greatest Hits** / 1975 / Warner Brothers ✦✦✦✦✦
Mirroring the cover art depiction of America's dual life in England and the U.S., *History: Greatest Hits* perfectly spotlights both the polished and layered production of British stu-

dio legend George Martin and the West Coast tones of the band's folk-pop style. Featuring the group's many chart toppers from the first half of the '70s, this definitive roundup includes Neil Young-style acoustic sides like "Lonely People," the hippie MOR of "Muskrat Love," and breezy acid rock like "Sandman." And even though Martin didn't produce the entire lot of songs here, his sophisticated and mostly subtle way with strings, keyboards, and multi-track guitars is in evidence throughout. Adding to the fun are additional highlights like the updated surf cut "Sister Golden Hair" and ingenious McCartney-esque pop like "Only in Your Heart" and "Daisy Jane." An essential collection for fans who like their '70s folk with a pop sheen, loads of hooks, and top-drawer arrangements. *—Stephen Cook*

Encore: More Greatest Hits / Jul. 1991 / Rhino ✦✦✦✦✦
This follow-up to their *Greatest Hits* contains "The Border," "Right Before Your Eyes," "Today's the Day," and "You Can Do Magic." The rest of the tracks are album sides or previously unreleased material. *—AMG*

Highway: 30 Years of America / Jul. 18, 2000 / Rhino ✦✦✦✦✦
America may be best-known for "A Horse With No Name" but they had a number of hits right into 1982. These weren't just Top 100 hits, but songs that remained staples of soft rock and oldies stations for years: "I Need You," "Ventura Highway," "Tin Man," "Lonely People," "Sister Golden Hair," and "You Can Do Magic," all well-crafted, melodic, memorable gems. Rhino's three-disc box set *Highway: 30 Years of America* proves that much, but if that's all that it did, it wouldn't be recommended over a hits collection. To some, a single-disc collection still may be preferable (although no single-disc set has all the hits), yet this is an ideal box. *Highway* contains all the charting singles, selected album tracks, alternate mixes, single edits, and demos, but the key to its success is that it plays as smoothly as a well-sequenced studio album. The compilers did a terrific job, selecting nearly every noteworthy track from America's albums, so there is no discernable drop-off in quality until the very end of the collection when the demos and latter-day recordings are hauled out. This box reveals a band that may have been indebted to Crosby, Stills, Nash & Young and the Beatles, but still wound up developing their own voice, rising to the forefront of soft rock. As *Highway* moves from one well-constructed, charming cut to another, it's hard not to admire America's skill at crafting appealing pop tunes that were folky, but not folk-rock, soft but not shapeless, melodic and memorable. Make no mistake—America is decidedly uncool, yet anyone with a fondness for easy, melodic soft rock will certainly find much to treasure on this superb set. *—Stephen Thomas Erlewine*

American Analog Set

f. Austin, TX
Ambient Pop, Indie Rock
The Austin, Texas-based drone-pop quartet the American Analog Set evolved from the ashes of Dallas' Electric Company in 1994. After the Electric Company's demise, guitarist/vocalist Andrew Kenny, keyboardist Lisa Roschmann, and drummer Mark Smith reunited to cut a number of impromptu four-track recordings which ultimately led to their decision to re-form as a group; after the addition of bassist Lee Gillespie, the quartet renamed themselves the American Analog Set and soon played their first live performance. After just their second gig, the band earned a deal with the area label Emperor Jones (a subsidiary of Butthole Surfer King Coffey's label Trance Syndicate) and issued their debut single, "Diana Slowburner II." Their first full-length effort, the low-key *The Fun of Watching Fireworks*, followed in 1996; *From Our Living Room to Yours*, the group's superb sophomore effort, trailed a year later, as did the EP *Late One Sunday & the Following Morning*, released in conjunction with the Darla label's "Bliss Out" series. The third AmAnSet full-length album, *The Golden Band*, appeared in 1999. *—Jason Ankeny*

The Fun of Watching Fireworks / 1996 / Emperor Jones ✦✦✦✦✦
The American Analog Set's debut album is a hushed, evocative soundscape, an entrancing excursion into the realm of lo-fi dream-pop. Frontman Andrew Kenny's songs—typified by the aptly-titled opening cut "Diana Slowburner II"—are hypnotic and deceptively simple, constructed of little more than ringing guitars and gently insistent rhythms, with the steady, warm hum of a Farfisa coloring the music with a cosmic serenity; vocals creep in and out of the mix, rarely rising above a whisper. The cumulative effect is stunning: while the group owes a clear debt to artists like Galaxie 500 and Stereolab, theirs is nevertheless an original and unique voice—*The Fun of Watching Fireworks* is an experience in complete sonic immersion. *—Jason Ankeny*

• **From Our Living Room to Yours** / Jul. 8, 1997 / Emperor Jones ✦✦✦✦✦
The American Analog Set's wonderful second album delivers upon all the promise of their debut: From the spellbinding opener "Magnificent Seventies" onward, *From Our Living Room to Yours* weaves a sonic tapestry of remarkable intricacy and texture. Andrew Kenny's songs are more subtly dynamic here than on *The Fun of Watching Fireworks*, further exploring the strengths of his taut, austere compositions; vocals are at an even greater premium than before, translating as extended instrumental passages wherein the group's minimalist melodies achieve a trance-like power. Lisa Roschmann's Farfisa remains AmAnSet's greatest asset, limning tracks like "Using the Hope Diamond as a Doorstop" and "Where Have All the Good Boys Gone" with an energy and warmth which set the band far apart from the darker impulses of their Texas psych-rock contemporaries—*From Our Living Room to Yours* is truly a thing of beauty. *—Jason Ankeny*

The Golden Band / Jul. 6, 1999 / Emperor Jones ✦✦✦✦
The Golden Band reduces the American Analog Set's approach to its barest essentials—favoring shorter, more economical songs over the epics of past outings, the group's third album also strips away much of their cosmic veneer to reveal the human pulse which tethers Andrew Kenny's songs and keeps them from floating away. The effect is hardly less hypnotic than earlier AmAnSet efforts, but is simply more direct—while Kenny's hushed vocals and oblique lyrics still evoke first and foremost an eyes-wide-shut otherness, the record insinuates itself on the strength of a subtly expanded emotional palette which lends a haunting new dimension to the group's fragile beauty. And while songs like "Weather Report" and "A Schoolboy's Charm" still don't build toward any kind of conventional climax, they nevertheless boast a drama and tension all their own—ultimately, *The Golden Band*'s quiet power speaks volumes. *—Jason Ankeny*

Through the 1990s: Singles and Unreleased / May 22, 2001 / Emperor Jones ✦✦✦
The complexity and intricacy of the American Analog Set's albums betray their skills as a singles band—while it's highly doubtful any of their seven inches will ever threaten the top of the Billboard charts, their unique drone-pop tone poems translate to the single format with surprising effortlessness, their approach gaining in immediacy what it loses in scope. Borrowing its title from a lyric in *The Golden Band*'s "The Wait" (reprised here as a jingle for AmAnSet's favorite soft drink, "Dr. Pepper"), *Through the 90s: Singles and Unreleased* compiles 14 tracks scattered across the group's brief but so far brilliant career, spanning from their first single, 1996's "Diana Slowburner II," to 1999's "The Only Living Boy Around," arguably their catchiest moment to date. Although the disc is above all an exercise in completism—the alternate versions of cuts like "Magnificent Seventies," "On Our Way," and "It's All About Us" differ only superficially from their original LP versions—the clutch of uncollected material makes it an essential purchase for fans, although newcomers are advised to seek out *From Our Living Room to Yours* or *The Golden Band* first. *—Jason Ankeny*

Know by Heart / Sep. 4, 2001 / Tiger Style ✦✦✦

American Flyer

f. 1976, **db.** 1978
Country-Rock
American Flyer was a 1970s folk-rock quartet made up of former members of other groups: Craig Fuller was from Pure Prairie League, Eric Kaz had been a member of Blues Magoos, Steve Katz was in Blood, Sweat & Tears, and Doug Yule had played in The Velvet Underground. Together they charted with two albums on United Artists in the mid-'70s. *—William Ruhlmann*

• **American Flyer** / 1976 / United Artists ✦✦✦✦✦
American Flyer deserved better. Eric Kaz had written great love songs for Linda Ronstadt and Bonnie Raitt, and Craig Fuller was coming off his Top 40 hit "Amie" with Pure Prairie League. As it happened, Steve Katz's "Back In '57" turned out to be one of the album's highlights, but "Let Me Down Easy," by Kaz And Fuller, was a minor hit, and there was also Kaz's classic co-composition, "Love Has No Pride." But those were just the cream of an excellent set produced by George Martin. Add it all up, and it should have meant more than a chart peak in the lower reaches of the Top 100, an early indication that, for whatever reasons, American Flyer was not destined to become the next Crosby, Stills, Nash & Young. *—William Ruhlmann*

Spirit of a Woman / 1977 / United Artists ✦✦
Maybe there was only room for one really successful country-folk-rock group with good songs and strong harmonies in the mid-'70s, and the job had already been taken by The Eagles. Who knows? American Flyer's second and final album didn't have as many great songs as the debut, and some of them were swamped by strings, but it was a pleasant work, notably featuring a version of Eric Kaz's "I'm Blowin' Away," which Bonnie Raitt had covered a couple of years earlier. *—William Ruhlmann*

American Music Club

f. 1983, San Francisco, CA, **db.** 1995
Sadcore, Slowcore, Indie Rock, Alternative Pop/Rock
Although chosen for its deliberately nondescript qualities, in retrospect the name American Music Club was the perfect moniker for the lauded San Francisco-based band led by singer/songwriter Mark Eitzel: over the course of seven acclaimed albums, the group tied together the disparate strands of the American musical fabric—rock, folk, country, punk, even lounge schmaltz—into a remarkably distinct and riveting whole, creating a brilliant and cohesive body of work dappled by moments of haunting beauty and impenetrable darkness. Despite the skill and diversity of the other members, Eitzel quickly became the group's focal point: an evocative vocalist and gutter poet capable of composing songs of disquieting honesty and intensity, he was also frequently the band's worst enemy—a heavy drinker since the age of 16, AMC shows often disintegrated into surreal backdrops for Eitzel's alcoholic rants and self-destructive showmanship, and throughout the group's tumultuous career, his erratic behavior led him to briefly exit their ranks on numerous occasions. Still, Eitzel quelled his demons long enough for AMC to record their 1985 debut, *The Restless Stranger*. Later disowned by the group, the album does offer a rough outline of their increasingly eclectic sound, and firmly established Eitzel's worldview, a harrowing vision of life as seen through the bottom of a shot glass. American Music Club languished in obscurity until releasing their 1991 masterpiece, *Everclear*, which was released to phenomenal critical acclaim (and the usual negligible commercial interest). Still, the lavish praise heaped on the album finally made the major labels take notice, and a bidding war ensued. After months of negotiations, they signed with Reprise in the U.S. and Virgin throughout the rest of the world. When 1994's *San Francisco* failed to connect, American Music Club finally dissolved. *—Jason Ankeny*

The Restless Stranger / 1986 / Reprise ✦✦

Engine / 1987 / Reprise ✦✦✦
AMC's sophomore release marks a significant advancement over *The Restless Stranger*, and offers more than a few of the band's definitive moments. Much of the due credit goes

to producer Tom Mallon, who arranges the record with an intuitive grasp of the anatomical make-up of Mark Eitzel's burgeoning songcraft; the rest of the credit belongs to Eitzel himself, who offers up some of his first truly great compositions. Chief among them is "Outside This Bar," a chilling portrait of the hermetically-sealed comforts of the drinking life. *—Jason Ankeny*

California / 1988 / Frontier ♦♦♦♦
With the erratic *California*, Mark Eitzel's songwriting skills blossom into full maturity. From the pedal-steel inflected opener "Firefly" to the luminous "Western Sky," the best of his compositions reveal uncommon depth and emotional heft: "Somewhere" cuts with the savage humor of a master storyteller, while "Blue and Grey Shirt," a memoir of a friend's AIDS-related death, is simply devastating. A number of the cuts don't work at all—the muddy "Bad Liquor" is an indecipherable rant, while "Laughing Stock" is by-the-numbers melodrama—but those that do are nothing short of transcendent. *—Jason Ankeny*

United Kingdom / 1990 / Demon ♦♦♦♦♦
American Music Club's first indisputably great album, the import-only *United Kingdom*, is also the band's most spare and unsettling work. Originally conceived as a collection of site-specific songs (hence the opener, "Here They Roll Down," which samples the sounds of a freeway off-ramp), the LP instead cobbles together leftover material and live tracks which fuse together into a remarkably cohesive and balanced whole. Among the highlights: "Heaven in Your Hands" ranks firmly as one of Mark Eitzel's most beautiful and unguarded love songs, while the lounge-flavored "Hula Maiden" finds the singer at his most perversely comic; the solo acoustic "Never Mind" details an emotional free-fall, while on the lush "Dreamers of the Dream," Eitzel clings to one of the record's few rays of hope as though his life depended on it. *—Jason Ankeny*

● **Everclear** / Oct. 1991 / Alias ♦♦♦♦♦
Put simply, *Everclear* is AMC's masterpiece. Benefitting immensely from improved production values, the album crystallizes the band's often erratic vision into a unified, endlessly complex whole. While the arrangements are typically diffuse—"Crabwalk" is shambling rockabilly, "Royal Cafe" is sweet country-pop, and "Rise" is anthemic alterna-rock—there is a consistency of tone and a sense of place which runs through these songs that is absent from the band's other records. Similarly, Mark Eitzel's compositions achieve an uncommon emotional balance, never once slipping into pathos or melodrama; the atmospheric "Miracle on 8th Street" and "The Confidential Agent" offer cinema-verite evocations of relationships at the breaking point, while the brute force of alcoholic laments like "Sick of Food" or the funereal "Why Won't You Stay" is staggering—never before or since has this loser been quite so beautiful. *—Jason Ankeny*

Mercury / Mar. 1993 / Reprise ♦♦♦♦
Leave it to American Music Club to make their major-label bow with the most perversely idiosyncratic record in their catalog. Produced with eccentric panache by Mitchell Froom, *Mercury* spotlights the band at their darkest and most eclectic, favoring odd rhythms, bizarre effects, and extreme arrangements ranging from the synthetic lounge grandeur of the worshipful "Johnny Mathis' Feet" to the swirling sonic maelstrom of the fatalistic "Challenger." Under the cover of defense-mechanism titles like "What Godzilla Said to God When His Name Wasn't Found in the Book of Life," "If I Had a Hammer," and "The Hopes of Dreams of Heaven's 10,000 Whores," Mark Eitzel paints some of his bleakest portraits to date; even the most superficially upbeat tracks—"Keep Me Around," "Hollywood 4-5-92," "Over and Done"—are relentlessly grim at their core. A triumph of abject misery. *—Jason Ankeny*

San Francisco / Oct. 4, 1994 / Reprise ♦♦♦
Regrettably, with their final effort, *San Francisco*, American Music Club went out with a whimper, not a bang. An undeveloped, erratic collection of songs, the record suffers under the weight of overly slick, commercial arrangements and production which renders tracks like "It's Your Birthday," "Wish the World Away," and "Hello Amsterdam" as bland alterna-rock; only the effervescent "Can You Help Me?" manages to absorb and transcend its glossy pop veneer. Still, Mark Eitzel goes down swinging, conjuring a handful of haunting gems—the best cuts on *San Francisco*, from the luminous opener "Fearless" to the achingly tender "The Thorn in My Side Is Gone," are also the most simple; AMC never needed adornment, just a sympathetic ear. *—Jason Ankeny*

Amon Düül

f. 1968, Munich, Germany, **db.** 1981
Kraut Rock, Prog-Rock/Art Rock
One of the first active Krautrock units, Amon Düül grew out of a multi-media artist commune in Munich that mixed radical political criticism with a unique vision of free-form improvisation loosely tied to American psychedelia, at least compared to the avant-garde inclinations of other space-rock units like Tangerine Dream and Cluster. Such open-ended and non-musical origins made the later activity of the group quite confusing, as a group of (slightly) more musically inclined members branched out as Amon Düül II with 1969's *Phallus Dei*, while the original Amon Düül continued releasing albums, most of which had been recorded during a mammoth jam session by the entire conglomeration in 1968. Though Amon Düül ceased recording material by 1972, frequent reissues during the decade—and the resumption of the Amon Düül name by several Amon Düül II alumni in the 1980s—resulted in still more confusion. Listeners unfamiliar with the lineup of every Amon Düül-related release can content themselves with the fact that the main line of the group began with Amon Düül in the late '60s and moved to Amon Düül II for the 1970s recordings. *—John Bush*

Psychedelic Underground / 1969 / Repertoire ♦♦♦♦
Some albums just have the perfect name, and Amon Duul's debut nails that to a T. Obscure upon release and obscure even now, for all the cult appeal, *Underground* is music at its most experimental and relentlessly uncommercial, using late-'60s inspirations as a launching ground for what came to be described as Krautrock. Psych-folk was another common term, one which applies just fine to much of the music here, feeling like an enthusiastic medieval festival gone just out of control enough, and with electricity to boot. Taken from a jam session from the previous year, but treated with many studio effects that enhance the strangeness of the collection, *Underground* rocks to its own weird beat. Opening track "Ein Wunderhubsches Madchen Traumt von Sandosa" captures what sounds like a great experience for everyone involved, a 17-minute composition heavy on the drums and percussion, with a basic, chugging guitar riff in one channel and chanting, call-and-response vocals located throughout the mix. At one point the jam is faded out in favor of piano parts, train noises, and the like, only to be brought back in again just as strongly, before finally fading into the gentler "Kaskados Minnelied," a mix of acoustic and electric guitars, along with a stringed instrument of some sort, that favors drones as much as it does soft riffs. The tracks on the second side have the same understandable vibe, but some are sparer in comparison, as with the keening strummed guitar/vocal combination "Im Garten Sandosa" and "Mama Duul und Ihre Sauerkrautband spielt auf," which is mostly clattering percussion in one stereo channel! You could say the sound quality isn't the best, but given the year of recording and the prevelance of lo-fi production approaches in more recent years, it doesn't sound that bad at all. *—Ned Raggett*

Phallus Dei / 1969 / Repertoire ♦♦♦♦♦
"Kanaan" starts the album wonderfully, a melange of rumbling rock power, strings and sitars, Lothar Meid's almost Bowie-ish vocals with Renate Knaup's wordless chanting in the background, that's just as intoxicating many years after its first appearance as it was upon release. The slightly jazzy concluding minute avoids sounding forced, blending in beautifully with the song's general flow. "Dem Guten, Schoenen, Wahren" takes a truly wacked-out turn, with Meid's bizarre falsetto coming to the fore, swooping around the main melodies without regard for them in yelps and chants, while the music chugs along in what almost sounds like a beer-hall singalong at points, taking a more haunting, beautiful turn at others (the heavily produced violins are an especially spooky touch). "Luzifers Ghilom" brings out the psych-folk origins of the band a bit more with Shrat's bongos, while the rest of the band pulls off a nicely heroic rock piece that never sounds too inflated or stupid, with appropriately nutty vocal breaks and interjections along the way—the sublime and the ridiculous never sounded so good together. "Henriette Krotenschwanz" ends the first side with a brief choral military march (if you will). The title track takes up the remainder of the album, a complex piece which never loses a sense of fun while always staying musically compelling. After a quiet start, the opening minutes consist of a variety of drones and noises constantly brought up and down in the mix, leading to a full band performance that builds and skips along with restrained fuzz power. Everything builds to a sudden climax halfway through, where all the members play a series of melodies in unison, while drums pound in the background. After a quick violin solo, everything settles into a fine percussion jam, with the full band kicking in shortly thereafter. With Karrer's crazed vocals showing where Mark E. Smith got some good ideas from, *Phallus* gets the Düül II career off to a flying start. *—Ned Raggett*

Collapsing/Singvögel Rückwärts & Co. / 1970 / Metronome ♦♦♦
The second Amon Düül album bore marked similarities to the first for very good reason—it too consisted of tracks recorded at the 1968 jam session which ended up being the bulk of the group's released work. Instead of longer tracks, *Collapsing* instead consisted of snippets or songs that were the length of more conventional pop recordings, while sounding nothing like said recordings at all. The same sense of "instantaneous taping and damn the fidelity" is here as well, though at times things are much crisper than might be expected, as the piercing two-note guitar riff on "Booster" demonstrates. Though the album is also apparently credited to a mysterious outfit called *Singvögel Rückwärts*, of whom nothing appears to be known (a song is named after them, which actually has a clear introduction and plenty of post-production touches like backwards instruments and jarring edits), this sounds like Amon Düül straight up. Percussion here is even rougher than on *Psychedelic Underground*, feeling much more stripped-down and basic, while vocals are even more unintelligible or wordless (on "Bass, Gestrichen," only a low moaning is heard amongst the clatter, while the impossible-to-interpret grunts and wails on "Krawall" are weirdly fascinating). Evidence of later studio tweaking appears here as on *Underground*, with the muffled classical fanfare sampled to introduce "Tusch F. F." and the repeated vinyl skip-loop on "Lua-Lua-He" being two examples among several. "Nachrichten Aus Cannabistan" has one of the funnier such moments, when, 30 seconds in, the stomping rhythm is audibly slowed down as if a vinyl player were stopped, to be replaced by another drum pattern fading up in the mix. Very strange and interesting stuff, with a unique flavor to it that may never be recaptured. *—Ned Raggett*

Para Dieswärts Düül / 1970 / Ohr ♦♦♦
Surprisingly, the third Amon Düül album wasn't recorded at the jam session which produced the band's other major releases; even more surprisingly, *Para Dieswärts* sounded next to nothing like the other three. Out went the rough and ready drumming, stomping, and chanting; in went an extremely delicate sense of expansive songwriting, retaining the predilection for length (the shortest of the album's three songs was almost eight minutes long) but otherwise aiming at a new kind of tastefulness. This said, a completely radical reinvention this isn't; while the first track, the sidelong "Love Is Peace," has plenty of stuff none of the other albums did (intelligible lyrics in English no less, soft guitar melodies, low-key flutes, and more), that sense of simple rhythms and riffs repeated and slightly changed and altered over the course of the song predominates nonetheless. The song has a solid, sweet groove to it, becoming a sing-along in the chorus almost in spite of itself;

a slightly wigged-out midsection, with flange and echo, soon dissipates into acoustic fingerpicking and strumming rather than completely going nuts. "Snow Your Thirst and Open Your Mouth" approaches the other albums a bit more closely as well, in sounding like it could easily be a jam (the percussion especially sounds like a cousin to the freak-outs elsewhere), although it's far more restrained overall. "Paramechanische Welt" closes the record with a folky acoustic guitar, droning strings, and piano strum that moves along well, even without percussion until halfway through; it makes for a lovely conclusion to a surprising record. The CD reissue from 1997 adds on the tracks from the group's only 7" single; "Eternal Flow" is a minimal guitar melody with soft lead and backing vocals that's quite haunting, while "Paramechanical World" is a gentle stunner, with wistfully mournful singing and quietly emotional guitar music in a combination which Hood would rediscover nearly three decades later. *—Ned Raggett*

Yeti / 1970 / Repertoire ✦✦✦✦✦
The double-album *Yeti* defines the term *space rock* with a full-throttle voyage into the realms of supersonic guitars and keyboards. Highlights like the extended "Soap Shop Rock" suite, "She Came Through the Chimney," and "Archangels Thunderbird" fuse psychedelic and progressive elements to mind-blowing perfection. *—Archie Patterson*

● **Tanz der Lemminge** / Mar. 1971 / Mantra ✦✦✦✦✦
There aren't many double art-rock albums from the early '70s that have stood the test of time, but then again, there aren't many albums like *Tanz*, and there certainly aren't many groups like Amon Düül II. While exact agreement over which of their classic albums is the absolute standout may never be reached, in terms of ambition combined with both good musicianship and good humor, *Tanz*, the group's third album, is probably the best candidate still. The musical emphasis is more on expansive arrangements and a generally gentler, acoustic or soft electric vibe; the brain-melting guitar from *Yeti* isn't as prominent on *Tanz*, for example, aside from the odd freakout here and there. You will find lengthy songs divided up into various movements, but with titles like "Dehypnotized Toothpaste" and "Overheated Tiara," po-faced seriousness is left at the door. The music isn't always wacky per se, but knowing that the group can laugh at itself is a great benefit. The first three tracks each take up a side of vinyl on the original release, and all are quite marvelous. "Syntelman's March of the Roaring Seventies" works through a variety of acoustic parts, steering away from folksiness for a more abstract, almost playfully classical sense of space and arrangement, before concluding with a brief jam. "Restless Skylight-Transistor Child" is more fragmented, switching between aggressive (and aggressively weird) and subtle passages. One part features Meid and Knaup singing over an arrangement of guitars, synths, and mock choirs that's particularly fine, and quite trippy to boot. "Chamsin Soundtrack" exchanges variety for a slow sense of mystery and menace, with instruments weaving in and out of the mix while never losing the central feel of the song. Three briefer songs close out the record, a nice way to get in some quick grooves at the end. *—Ned Raggett*

Disaster / 1971 / BASF ✦✦✦✦
Like the first two albums, *Disaster* comes from the same 1968 jam session, which if nothing else shows that the phrase "burst of creativity" can have a very real equivalent. As with the previous two releases, the emphasis is on open-ended, percussion-heavy, choppy-guitared songs with random, often wordless chanting, with rough sound being the general order of the day. Compared to the other two, *Disaster* has a slightly more "live" feeling, with less evidence of later studio additions or tweaks. It's a touch calmer as well, though nowhere near as sweet as *Para Dieswärts Düül* turned out to be. Exactly how planned this release was is up to question—it appeared after the band had broken up, and its two-LP original format speaks of a serious clearing out of the vaults. Regardless, there are some definite winners here; *Disaster* could even be considered the logical conclusion of the band's "try anything and see what works" ethic. Opening song "Drum Things (Erschalgzuegtes)" is very much a classic lengthy jam in the style of *Psychedelic*'s "Ein Wunderhubsches," with what sound like fingerbells providing a notable percussion element along with the pounding drums, especially at the end. Numerous other longer tracks like "Somnium (Trauma)" (which ends with some great drum work) and "Chaoticolor (Entsext)" make up the bulk of the album's length, most settling on a key riff and grooving away on it just fine, with slight alterations appearing as each piece progresses. Some of the shorter numbers are as close as the group ever got to catchy pop; one sprightly number, a Beatles semi-revamp barely a minute long before petering out, has the perfect title "Yea Yea Yea (Zerbeatelt)." Unfairly trashed over the years, *Disaster* is just like the band that made it—wonderful, weird, and wiggy. *—Ned Raggett*

Carnival in Babylon / 1972 / Repertoire ✦✦✦
Amon Düül II's follow-up to their landmark double-LP set *Tanz der Lemminge* features a musical approach less experimental than previous recordings, but nonetheless distinctive and broad-reaching in its sphere of influences. The almost epic tack of the earlier works has been pared down here, but full-forward, guitar-heavy tracks like "C.I.D. in Uruk," "Ballad of the Shimmering Sands," and "Kronwinkl 12" use disparate folk and hard rock elements cannily. The band moves the music with a majestic sweep punctuated by the snaky guitar work of Chris Karrer and John Weinzierl. *—Nick Burton*

Wolf City / 1972 / A&M ✦✦✦✦
Amon Düül II's fifth studio album is a more conventional recording than most, though there's still a lot of the involved experimenting and dark undercurrent which sets the band apart from the mainstream, along with the off-kilter hooks and odd humor which saved them from being lumped alongside more serious (and less easy to take seriously) prog-rock outfits. After the lengthy explorations of *Tanz der Lemminge*, *Wolf City* seems targeted to an extent at a commercial English-speaking audience, perhaps reflective of their increased status in the United Kingdom, if not in America. Regardless, opening song "Surrounded by the Stars," the longest track on the album at just under eight minutes, is also one of the band's best, with strong vocals from Knaup, a dramatic building verse (complete with mock choir), an equally dramatic violin-accompanied instrumental break, and a catchy chorus leading to a fun little freakout. Knaup actually takes the lead vocals more often this time out and turns in some lovely performances, as on the beautiful, perhaps slightly precious "Green Bubble Raincoated Man," with a great full-band performance that grows from a nice restraint to a slam-bang, epic rockout. Meid gets his moments in as well, his sometimes straightforward, sometimes not-so-much vocals adding to the overall effect as before. The one full instrumental, "Wie Der Wind," is excellent, with guest Indian musicians adding extra instrumentation to an intoxicating, spacious performance. While *Wolf City* generally sounds like a tight band playing things live or near-live, there are some equally gripping moments clearly resulting from studio work, like the strange loop opening the title track (percussion, guitar?). Concluding with the groovy good-time "Sleepwalker's Timeless Bridge," including some fantastic e-bow guitar work, *Wolf City* works the balance between art and accessibility and does so with resounding success. *—Ned Raggett*

Viva La Trance / 1973 / Mantra ✦✦✦
Amon Düül II's extraordinary 1973 album finds the influential German art rock band working surprisingly well in a short song format while still stamping their music with their unique sound. "Fly United," "Trap," and "Ladies Mimikry" show diverse styles of pop and rock running happily into each other with memorably quirky results. The instrumentation here is as quirky as ever—perhaps even more than usual, with Chris Karrer's violin and sax playing now in the fore. The melodies are often shimmering. Unfortunately the band never again sustained the excellence displayed here after this album. *—Nick Burton*

Die Lösung / 1989 / Magnum ✦✦✦
This is one great album, and one needn't be familiar with a single note ever played by Amon Düül, Amon Düül II, or any other German progressive rock band to enjoy it; indeed, this is the kind of album that fans of the Doors might honestly be said to have been wishing for. Stylistically there's not a lot in common between the two groups apart from some highly melodic guitar, some of it blues-derived (the Groundhogs' Tony McPhee is on the album, so you knew there'd be blues in there somewhere), and swirling organ and synthesizer arabesques, but one does get the real sense of this being a performance piece for poet and band, mostly courtesy of Robert Calvert. The latter's lyrics are dense with meaning, some of it obscure but all of it intriguing, and the overall effect of it is like listening to a latter-day extension of the kind of work that the Doors aspired to in their best days, with maybe a freer use of keyboards and definitely more ambitious and effective jams. There's some question between the two co-leaders of this version of Amon Düül (which is really an offshoot of Amon Düül II) about whether this album should have been released, since Dave Anderson regards it as completed, and okayed its going out, but John Wienzierl didn't think of it as finished. In any case, it rocks very hard and, in most instances, very memorably, with a big sound that manages to embrace elements of progressive rock, psychedelia, and a good beat. *—Bruce Eder*

● **The Best of Amon Düül II 1969-1974** / Jan. 21, 1997 / Purple Pyramid ✦✦✦✦✦
The only side of the continually frustrating Cleopatra label that makes any sense at all, the reissue subsidiary Purple Pyramid continues its commitment to quality archival Krautrock with *The Best of Amon Düül II 1969-1974*, a collection that charts the best moments from the best period of one of the most fascinating (and often bewildering) German groups of the '70s. Included are tracks from several of Amon Düül II's best LPs: from *Yeti* comes "Soap Shop Rock" and "Pale Gallery," from *Tanz der Lemminge* comes "A Short Stop at the Transylvanian Brain-Surgery" and "Stumbling Over Melted Moonlight," and from *Wolf City* there's "Surrounded by the Stars," "Deutsch Nepal," and the title track. Though Amon Düül II's albums of the period are necessary for fans of the group, this makes not only a perfect introduction for new listeners but also a handy summation of what made the band great. *—John Bush*

The UA Years: 1969-1974 / Aug. 3, 1999 / Purple Pyramid ✦✦✦✦

Tori Amos

b. Aug. 22, 1963, Newton, NC
Vocals, Keyboards, Piano / Adult Alternative Pop/Rock, Alternative Pop/Rock, Singer/Songwriter
Tori Amos was one of several female singer/songwriters who combined the stark lyrical attack of alternative rock with a distinctly '70s musical approach. Her music falls between the orchestrated meditations of Kate Bush and the stripped-down poetics of Joni Mitchell. In addition to reviving the singer/songwriter traditions of the '70s, Amos revived the piano as a rock & roll instrument. With her 1992 album *Little Earthquakes*, Amos built a dedicated following that continued to expand with subsequent albums. The daughter of a methodist preacher, Amos began writing her own songs as a child and studied at Baltimore's Peabody Conservatory. After becoming infatuated by rock & roll, particularly the music of Led Zeppelin, she began performing in local bars and later moved to Los Angeles. Signed to Atlantic in 1987, Amos debuted with an uninspired pop-metal album called *Y Kant Tori Read*. By 1990, Amos had adopted a new approach, singing spare, haunting semiconfessional piano ballads. *Little Earthquakes*, Amos' first album as a singer/songwriter, was released in early 1992 and sold well in both the U.S. and the U.K. Her second album, *Under the Pink*, was a bigger hit and and launched the minor hit singles "God" and "Cornflake Girl." Two years later she released *Boys for Pele*, her most ambitious and difficult record to date. *From the choirgirl hotel* followed in 1998. *—Stephen Thomas Erlewine*

● **Little Earthquakes** / 1992 / Atlantic ✦✦✦✦✦
With her haunting solo debut *Little Earthquakes*, Tori Amos carved the template for the

female singer/songwriter movement of the '90s. Amos' delicate, prog-rock piano work and confessional, poetically quirky lyrics invited close emotional connection, giving her a fanatical cult following and setting the stage for the Lilith Fair legions. But *Little Earthquakes* is no mere style-setter or feminine stereotype—its intimacy is uncompromising, intense, and often far from comforting. Amos' musings on major personal issues—religion, relationships, gender, childhood—were just as likely to encompass rage, sarcasm, and defiant independence as pain or tenderness; sometimes, it all happened in the same song. The apex of that intimacy is the harrowing "Me and a Gun," where Amos strips away all the music, save for her own voice, and confronts the listener with the story of her own real-life rape; the free-associative lyrics come off as a heart-wrenching attempt to block out the ordeal. *Little Earthquakes* isn't always so stomach-churning, but it never seems less than deeply cathartic; it's the sound of a young woman (like the protagonist of "Silent All These Years") finally learning to use her own voice—sort of the musical equivalent of Mary Pipher's *Reviving Ophelia*. That's why Amos draws strength from her relentless vulnerability, and that's why the constantly shifting emotions of the material never seem illogical—Amos simply delights in the frankness of her own responses, whatever they might be. Though her subsequent albums were often very strong, Amos would never bare her soul quite so directly (or comprehensibly) as she did here, nor with such consistently focused results. *Little Earthquakes* is the most accessible work in Amos' catalog, and it's also the most influential and rewarding. *—Steve Huey*

Crucify / 1992 / Atlantic ✦✦✦
Crucify is a five-song EP that builds upon the success of *Little Earthquakes*. Most notable among the songs is her voice/piano reading of Nirvana's "Smells Like Teen Spirit," showing what a fine songwriter Kurt Cobain is; the title song (a different mix than the version on *Earthquakes*) and her versions of the Rolling Stones' "Angie" and Led Zeppelin's "Thank You" are equally noteworthy. *—Stephen Thomas Erlewine*

Under the Pink / Dec. 7, 1994 / Atlantic ✦✦✦✦✦
After sharing personal and emotional accounts on her stunning debut, *Little Earthquakes*, Tori Amos stirs those sensations up for an eclectic yet beautiful account of female security on *Under the Pink*. Being a woman, she's always in question of her actions, calling out and interrogating the opposite sex for her own pleasure. But it's not necessarily with a scolding tone. She's playful with her signature piano accompaniment, but allows for a twisted mess of guitars, violins, and bass loops, which are quite enigmatic like Kate Bush as well. "Baker Baker" and "Bells for Her" are aching with ballad-esque beauty, but the seething "The Waitress" sparks Amos' inner devil. She's quaint at first, but rages into a scalding vocal queen. It makes her even more a pioneer for female originality and independence. Singles such as "God" and "Cornflake Girl" are sultry and provocative, depicting that she's everything but shy. *Under the Pink* is typically melodic, but it contains a heavy desire. Amos is still breaking into something more definitive as both a woman and a singer/songwriter. The lyrical imagery is much more wide open, something that will become Amos' ever-changing swan song. *—MacKenzie Wilson*

Boys for Pele / Jan. 23, 1996 / Atlantic ✦✦✦
Highly ambitious, challenging, idiosyncratic, and confounding, *Boys for Pele* expands on the more experimental and progressive tendencies of *Under the Pink*. Amos frequently discards traditional song structures and employs wide-ranging, eclectic instrumentation in her music, while her lyrics seem to grow even more obscure, giving the album a very impressionistic feel. While there are certainly worthwhile moments, her experiments don't always work; some of the songs fail to stick, and it takes a few plays before many start to sink in. Ultimately, *Boys for Pele* is polarizing: Some Amos fans will only admire her more for taking the risks she does, while others may find to their disappointment that the intimacy and personal connection that helped Amos build her fan base are too difficult to detect. *—Steve Huey*

From the choirgirl hotel / May 5, 1998 / Atlantic ✦✦✦✦
Shortly before she began work on *From the choirgirl hotel*, Tori Amos suffered a miscarriage. While she was recording the album, she married her long-term boyfriend. As expected, both events cryptically wind their way into the album, which arguably has Amos' most personal lyrics since *Little Earthquakes*. The surprise is, *From the choirgirl hotel* is considerably more accessible than its immediate predecessor, *Boys for Pele*. Tori has opened up her sound by working live with a full band, bringing an immediacy to her sound that has never been heard before. Added to that are samples and drum loops, ballads supported by eerie, sweeping strings and heavy guitars—everything she played with on *Pele* have come to fruition here. All the while, she's kept the perversely cryptic, convoluted lyrics that have always marked her work, yet the lines that connect have more power and savage wit than ever. Besides, Amos' songs have an interior logic of their own. Until now, it seemed that she could only deliver them on her own, supported by her piano, a guitar, or strings. With *From the choirgirl hotel*, she proves that with a little aural experimentation and muscle, she's as potent and powerful as any modern rock artist. *—Stephen Thomas Erlewine*

To Venus and Back / Sep. 21, 1999 / Atlantic ✦✦✦
Originally intended as a rarities collection to tide fans over until she completed the follow-up to *From the choirgirl hotel*, the double-disc *To Venus and Back* mutated into something entirely different as Tori Amos worked on it. She experienced a sudden creative burst, writing 11 new songs. In light of these new tunes, she decided to devote the first disc of the collection to the fresh material, with the second dedicated to live material recorded during 1998. As such, it provides an interesting contrast. With *Choirgirl*, she decided to add muscle to her music by working with a full band, which naturally transformed her fragile, intimate songwriting into something weightier, or at least heavier. That much is evident from the live album, *Still Orbiting*, which puts many old favorites in a new light. The first disc, titled *Venus Orbiting*, proves that Amos is better in a more intimate setting. Ironically, the album was recorded with her touring band, but the arrangements aren't as showy as the live reworkings, and her songwriting is a bit more straightforward. That's not to say that she has changed direction or ironed out all her quirks—her lyrics remain almost impenetrably cryptic, her songs follow elastic, unpredictable structures—but she has returned to her strengths: namely, concentrating on ethereal, dream-like song-poems. She's still expanding her music, but letting it breathe naturally, resulting in her best, most cohesive record since *Under the Pink*. It's a bit of a shame that it's married to the live album, since that gives the impression that both discs are for hardcore fans. That's not the case at all—*Venus Orbiting* will likely win back fans that have strayed from the fold in the past few years. *—Stephen Thomas Erlewine*

Strange Little Girls / Sep. 18, 2001 / Atlantic ✦✦✦
Something that goes unspoken in the cult of Tori Amos is that she knows the value of press and that she knows how to exploit it. So, six albums into her career, and several years since she captured headlines, she released *Strange Little Girls*, a collection of covers intended to strike a dagger into the heart of how males view females in pop songs. To be honest, you wouldn't know that from listening to the record, but you might have an idea by looking at the four separate collector-oriented covers, and reading the reviews, previews, and interviews Tori did prior to and at the time of release. The only track that really feels that way is Eminem's "97 Bonnie and Clyde," where Amos heightens the tension by close-micing her vocals and reading with a hammy theatricalness that results in a cut about as chilling as the original, but without the context. After that, there really aren't many songs that sound like they're a female switch in perspective, apart from maybe the Stranglers' title track (which she does a nice job with), and it's very hard to tell what she's trying to say with these songs. Tori never tells us, either lyrically or through her musical arrangements. Her sexual politics are so poorly constructed, appearing almost nonexistent, that the music by default rises to the forefront and it almost meets the demands. Though there's a bit too much surface sheen, it's a solid record, yet it's not particularly distinctive. And while all that press may have given the impression that this is something new, something different—precisely what it was meant to do—it really is nothing more than another, pretty good Tori Amos record, only not quite as interesting because she didn't write the tunes. *—Stephen Thomas Erlewine*

The Amps

f. 1995, **db.** 1996
Indie Rock, Alternative Pop/Rock
After the overwhelming success of "Cannonball" and *Last Splash* took the Breeders by surprise—and led to their quick burnout—singer/songwriter/guitarist Kim Deal formed the Amps in 1994 as a way to release new material while the Breeders took a break. With her other group's drummer Jim MacPherson, Deal assembled a new band from members of other bands around her hometown of Dayton, OH, including Nathan Farley and Luis Lerma of the Tasties. Originally called Tammy & the Amps, the band sounded like a rougher, rawer version of the Breeder's skewed pop. The *Tipp City* EP heralded *Pacer*, their first and only album, which was released in late 1995. That year, the Amps toured with friends and like-minded acts such as Helium and Sonic Youth. The following year, Deal folded the Amps lineup into a new version of the Breeders—which also included *Pod*-era member Carrie Bradley—for a handful of California dates with Primus. As the Breeders' notoriously unstable lineup changed, all of the former Amps left the group within two years. *—Heather Phares*

● **Pacer** / Oct. 31, 1995 / 4AD/Elektra ✦✦✦✦✦
Initially, Kim Deal planned the Amps to be a solo project as she waited for her sister and fellow Breeder Kelly Deal to finish recovering from heroin addiction. Soon, the Amps flowered into a full-fledged band, recording material intended for both Kim's solo project and the third Breeders album. Recruiting drummer Jim MacPhearson and two local Dayton musicians, Deal recorded *Pacer* in the summer of 1995, releasing it in the fall. Appropriately, the album is raw, punky, and amateurish—it's lo-fi garage punk. Not only does Deal sound recharged by recording with a new band in such a rushed atmosphere, she contributes her most immediate and bracing songs since *Pod*, the first Breeders album. *Pacer* somewhat recalls the Pixies, but only in the sense that both bands rely on amateurish enthusiasm to rock, and both bands have an off-kilter sense of song-structure. In that sense, the Amps also take a great deal from Guided by Voices, who the Breeders covered on their 1994 *Head to Toe* EP. But the key to *Pacer* is its primative energy. From the brutally pounding "Empty Glasses" and the charmingly sleazy "Tipp City" to the sing-song pop of "Pacer" and the fractured melodic rock of "Hoverin" and "Breaking the Split Screen Barrier," *Pacer* is exciting, gut-level rock & roll. *—Stephen Thomas Erlewine*

... And You Will Know Us by the Trail of Dead

f. 1994
Indie Rock
Excellently named emo band ... And You Will Know Us by the Trail of Dead was formed in late 1994 by singers/guitarists/drummers Jason Reece and Conrad Keely, long-time friends who originally met in Hawaii before both settled in the perennial indie hotbed of Olympia, WA (where Reece fronted the notorious Mukilteo Fairies). Upon relocating together to Austin, TX, the duo played their first shows as You Will Know Us by the Trail of Dead, eventually adding both the conjunction and the ellipsis as well as recruiting guitarist Kevin Allen and bassist/sampler Neil Busch. After issuing a live cassette on the local Golden Hour label, the group—already legendary in indie circles for their anarchic concert sets—released their self-titled full-length debut on Trance Syndicate in early 1998. Following the label's collapse, T.O.D. moved to Merge to issue *Madonna* in the fall of 1999. *—Jason Ankeny*

● **. . . And You Will Know Us By the Trail of Dead** / Jan. 20, 1998 / Trance ◆◆◆◆
Labeled as "anti-musicians," named after a prayer to Mayan corn gods, and cause for press releases describing it as "set upon by rednecks," . . . And You Will Know Us By the Trail of Dead vies for that piece of scarred, post-punk real estate somewhere between the Who and chucking a whirring blender full of bolts straight into a jet engine. With this self-titled debut, the band will probably horrify the realtors. From moments of diversionary electronic tweaks to ones of shambolic, guitar-thrashed screeches (and sometimes both), the album realizes the importance of not trying to be important. The sound of bashing out unconventional "we hate something that we'll make sure to mumble" punk rock without parroting any one musical thing is what—if anything—ties these eight songs together. And for good reason. Few bands can sound like such a rightful mess. The band has been lumped in with fellow rock un-apologists Queens of the Stone Age and At the Drive-In, but this self-titled debut album is a caustic, fidgety yelp that almost belies its out-and-out intelligence. One of the band's news stories might have said it best: "The band defended themselves with their instruments, which are now destroyed." —*Dean Carlson*

Madonna / Oct. 19, 1999 / Merge ◆◆◆

Laurie Anderson (Laura Phillips Anderson)

b. Jun. 5, 1947, Chicago, IL
Vocals, Violin, Songwriter / Mixed Media, Experimental Rock, Experimental
After briefly entering the mainstream pop radar in 1981 with her lone hit "O Superman," Laurie Anderson enjoyed a public visibility greater than virtually any other avant-garde figure of her era. Her infrequent forays into rock aside, Anderson remained firmly grounded in performance art, her ambitious multimedia projects encompassing music, film, mime, visual projections, dance, and—most importantly—spoken and written language, the cornerstone of her work.
In her teens, she studied violin, and at 20 moved to NYC, earned an art history degree from Barnard College in 1969, and an M.F.A. in sculpture from Columbia University in 1972. She taught, then staged her first public performances in 1973. By 1976, Anderson was performing throughout North America and Europe. Based on the power of words and language, her work also emphasized visual imagery and cutting-edge technology. Anderson recorded "O Superman," for the tiny NY label 110 Records; at eleven minutes, built around electronic drones, with opaque half-spoken, half-sung lyrics, "O Superman" was a most unlikely hit. Nevertheless, it was a smash in Britain, reaching #2 on the pop charts in late 1981. Now signed to Warner Bros., Anderson issued *Big Science* (1982), a work drawn from the seven-hour multi-media performance *United States*. 1984's *Mister Heartbreak* was her most overtly pop-oriented work, included artists Peter Gabriel and Adrian Belew, and reached the American Top 100. That same year she also issued the complete *United States Live*, spread across a five-LP set. Her next project was concert film *Home of the Brave*, followed by the score for *Swimming to Cambodia*. The studio album, *Strange Angels*, came out in 1989. Anderson and boyfriend Lou Reed teamed with producer Brian Eno on *Bright Red* (1994), but she focused more on performing, including "The Nerve Bible" (1995) and "Songs and Stories from Moby Dick" (1999) tours. —*Jason Ankeny*

● **Big Science** / 1982 / Warner Brothers ◆◆◆◆◆
Big Science is essentially a chunk of the more elaborate and difficult four-part multi-media performance piece *United States*. But, that said, *Big Science* never sounds like a portion; it is in fact a meal in itself. The music is moody and minimalistic, and Anderson's wry observations are perspicacious, smartalecky, and, at times, laugh-out-loud funny. There have been numerous artists attempting work like this since *Big Science*; few, however, equal Anderson's panache. Not your average pop record. Oh yeah, "O Superman" is here in all its glory. —*John Dougan*

United States Live / 1984 / Warner Brothers ◆◆◆
Once her popularity seemed assured, Warner Bros. felt safe releasing this five-record set (since reissued on four CDs) comprising *United States'* entire four-and-a-half hours. It's not the first place I'd recommend going to hear Anderson's work, but for those so inclined it's well worth the effort. Although live performances of *United States* included film segments that ran during some of her monologues, *United States* is about communication and how we interpret and use language. It's a bit pretentious, a tad long-winded, and its size makes it unwieldy to listen to in one sitting, but this is an important work loaded with enough insight, wit, and humanity to make relistening and re-evaluating worthwhile. —*John Dougan*

Mister Heartbreak / 1984 / Warner Brothers ◆◆◆◆
A more pop-oriented record (there are songs here and musicians like Adrian Belew and Peter Gabriel), Anderson displays a functional singing voice that graces such wonderful songs as "Sharkey's Day" and "Excellent Birds" (a duet with Gabriel). More accessible than *Big Science*, but in some ways a record indicating that while she may not be a musician herself, Anderson certainly knows how to pick them, work with them, and challenge them. A thoroughly wonderful record. —*John Dougan*

Home of the Brave / 1986 / Warner Brothers ◆◆◆
The soundtrack to Anderson's film, containing both older songs, such as "Sharkey's Night," and new material, notably "Language Is A Virus." It suffers by being shortened for album length and missing the visual element, but is still enjoyable. —*William Ruhlmann*

Strange Angels / Oct. 1989 / Warner Brothers ◆◆◆◆◆
Purists may disagree, but I think *Strange Angels* is Anderson's most stunning work. It may be due to its nearly giddy selection of pop songs (including the supremely ecstatic "Babydoll"), but here Anderson sounds supremely confident—as a pop singer/songwriter. Rather than weighing down her songs with avant-gardisms, *Strange Angels* positively luxuriates in this conflation of the avant-garde and the popular. Hence, there is a relent-

less joyfulness that imbues this record, but never sacrifices intelligence one iota. A brilliantly conceived record, *Strange Angels* offers the best of both worlds to the benighted and aficionados. —*John Dougan*

Bright Red / Oct. 25, 1994 / Warner Brothers ◆◆◆

The Ugly One with the Jewels and Other Stories / Mar. 14, 1995 / Warner Brothers ◆◆◆◆
On her later albums, Laurie Anderson had moved from her earlier spoken word-plus-effects style to a more overtly musical approach, with less effective results. *The Ugly One with the Jewels*, a recording of a live performance of readings from her book *Stories from the Nerve Bible*, returned her to speaking instead of singing, and it was her best album since *Big Science*. The 18 stories reflected Anderson's extensive travels, including forays into the Third World and to convents, although she made Los Angeles and Houston sound just as exotic. In fact, telling her stories over sounds from birds, guitars, and electronic beeps, she seemed an anthropologist from another world, always finding the natives friendly but strange. And she didn't fail to recognize that she could appear just as odd to them: "The Ugly One with the Jewels" was a name used by one of her subjects to describe her. —*William Ruhlmann*

Talk Normal: The Laurie Anderson Anthology / Oct. 17, 2000 / Rhino ◆◆◆
Talk Normal: The Laurie Anderson Anthology gathers 35 career highlights that range from Anderson's most performance art-oriented material to her poppiest moments. Leading off with "O Superman (For Massenet)," her unlikely 1981 hit, the first disc pares down *Big Science*—itself a distillation of her four-hour piece *United States*—to its starkest and most hypnotic tracks, including "From the Air," "Born, Never Asked," and the title track. "Sharkey's Day," "Excellent Birds," and "Langue D'Amour," all from the more melodic, emotional *Mister Heartbreak*, close out disc one, along with more pieces from *United States*, including "Walk the Dog," "Cartoon Song," and "Lighting Out for the Territories." Similarly, the second disc picks highlights from the *Home of the Brave* soundtrack—"Smoke Rings" and "Language Is a Virus" chief among them—and includes six tracks from her most melodic, song-structured album, *Strange Angels*. "Coolsville," "The Day the Devil," and the title track work especially well outside of the album's context and mix nicely with *Bright Red* tracks like "Speak My Language" and "In Our Sleep." The anthology closes with a sampling of *The Ugly One with the Jewels*' vignettes, including "The Night Flight From Houston," "The Rotowhirl," and "The End of the World." Though the anthology distills Anderson's work so much that it tends to blur the character of her individual albums, *Talk Normal* still presents most of the nuances in Anderson's distant yet open, ironic yet emotional style. For new listeners who want a bigger, more representative picture of Anderson's work than *Big Science* provides, *Talk Normal* is a good starting point. —*Heather Phares*

Life on a String / Aug. 21, 2001 / Atlantic ◆◆◆

The Angels

f. 1961, Orange, NJ
Girl Group, Pop
The Angels' 1963 number one hit, "My Boyfriend's Back," is one of the half-dozen or so archetypal girl-group classics. Handclap beats, sassy vocals, slightly campy lyrics, and an arrangement paced by wailing horns and street-corner harmonies—it was a surefire hit and one that the group could never live up to, although they continued to record for some time. The Angels had actually been around for a while before "My Boyfriend's Back," making the Top 20 in 1961 with the ballad "'Till," and the Top 40 with a follow-up, "Cry Baby Cry." In 1963, they hooked up with the songwriting/production team of Feldman-Goldstein-Gottehrer, who penned and produced material more in line with the Spectorian "wall of sound" gracing the airwaves at the peak of the girl-group era. "My Boyfriend's Back" was originally cut as a demo that music publishers hoped to shop to the Shirelles, but it turned out so well that it was released as an Angels single. Surprisingly, they would never make the Top 20 again, although they had minor hits with "Thank You and Goodnight," "I Adore Him," and "Wow Wow Wee (He's the Boy for Me)." —*Richie Unterberger*

My Boyfriend's Back / 1963 / Collectables ◆◆◆◆
The Angels were a typical one-hit wonder girl group with a better than typical one hit. The title track is so familiar that it scarcely commands comment, but there's a big falloff in familiarity between that and too much else that the trio ever did. This 14-song collection features their two other chart hits, "Cry Baby Cry" and "Till," as well as a host of additional songs. "And the Angels Sing" has a pleasing mix of voices and bells, and their version of "Sentimental Journey" has a sweetly ethereal yet sultry quality about it and is highlighted by heavily trilled strings over the voices. Unfortunately, producer Gerry Granahan wasn't as creative with a lot of what else is here, and apart from the two early hits, and a relaxed rendition of "Cotton Fields," there's not a lot that stands out—"Thank You and Goodnight" does benefit from some soaring harmony singing, but that's about it. As a mid-priced collection, however, this may be all of the Angels that most interested parties require. —*Bruce Eder*

● **The Best of the Angels** / Jun. 18, 1996 / Polygram ◆◆◆◆◆
Twenty-one-song anthology of cuts from the early and mid-'60s, with all the hits, including the pre-"My Boyfriend's Back" charters "Till" and "Cry Baby Cry." Despite the spirited vocals, accomplished production, and occasional highlights like "Why Don't the Boy Leave Me Alone?," "World Without Love" (not the Lennon-McCartney song), the ska-flavored "Jamaica Joe," and the James Bond riffs of "Boy from Crosstown," nothing here lights up the room like "My Boyfriend's Back." It's certainly the best collection, though, for those who want to hear more from the group than what's available on various-artist oldies compilations. —*Richie Unterberger*

The Animals

f. 1964, Newcastle, England, **db.** 1968
British Blues, Psychedelic, British Invasion, Blues-Rock, Rock & Roll

One of the most important bands originating from England's R&B scene during the early '60s, the Animals were second only to the Rolling Stones in influence among R&B-based bands in the first wave of the British Invasion. A studio session in February 1964 yielded their Columbia debut single, "Baby Let Me Take You Home" (adapted from "Baby Let Me Follow You Down"). For years, it has been rumored incorrectly that the Animals got their next single, "House of the Rising Sun," from Bob Dylan's first album, but more recently it has been revealed that, like "Baby Let Me Take You Home," the song came to them courtesy of Josh White. In any event, the song—given a new guitar riff by Hilton Valentine and a soulful organ accompaniment devised by Alan Price—shot to the top of the U.K. and U.S. charts early that summer. This success yielded their first long-playing record, *The Animals*. Their third single, "I'm Crying," rose to number eight on the British charts. The group compiled an enviable record of Top Ten successes, including "Don't Let Me Be Misunderstood" and "We've Gotta Get Out of This Place," along with a second album, *Animal Tracks*. However, the group was growing increasingly unhappy with the material they were being given to record by manager Mickie Most. Not only were the majority of these songs much too commercial for their taste, but they represented a false image of the band, even if many were successful. "It's My Life," a number seven British hit and a similar smash in America, caused the Animals to terminate their association with Most and with EMI Records. They moved over to Decca/London Records and came up with a more forceful, powerful sound on their first album on the new label, *Animalisms*. Finally, in 1969, frontman Eric Burdon pulled the plug on the Animals. He hooked up with a Los Angeles-based group called War, and started a subsequent solo career that continues to this day. —*Bruce Eder*

The Animals (US) / 1964 / MGM ✦✦✦
Early blues-oriented material rounded out by a few more commercial tracks—this album is stronger than the British version, as it includes several more tracks off of their singles. —*Bruce Eder*

The Animals (UK) / 1964 / Columbia ✦✦

The Animals on Tour / 1965 / MGM ✦✦

In the Beginning / 1965 / Sundazed ✦✦✦
Recorded in December of 1963 at a live concert, this CD captures The Animals at their rawest and most animated on record, ripping ferociously through a bunch of standards (by Chuck Berry, James B. Odom, et al.), playing the crowd, and making snide comments about their London rivals the Rolling Stones, all with Sonny Boy Williamson II hanging somewhere around the stage. Sundazed has actually found the original master to this oft-bootlegged piece of rock/blues history. —*Bruce Eder*

Animal Tracks / 1965 / Columbia ✦✦✦✦✦
The band's second British album displays far more energy and dexterity than its predecessor. Originals such as "For Miss Caulker" are paired up with excellent covers like "Bright Lights Big City," "I Ain't Got You," and "Roadrunner," along with Ray Charles' "Hallelujah I Love Her So" and "I Believe to My Soul." Note: All tracks appearing on this album are available on EMI's *Complete Animals* double CD. —*Bruce Eder*

Animalization / 1966 / Polydor ✦✦✦✦✦
The best of the group's early albums, mostly sophisticated blues-based rock which, for the first time ever on a long-player, managed to capture the spontaneity of their live sound while also allowing them a chance to really stretch out in the studio. Around this time in the band's history, however, the albums get confusing: *Animalization*, released in September of 1966 by MGM in America, was simply the British *Animalisms* with three tracks missing, and four other songs ("Don't Bring Me Down," "Cheating," "Inside Looking Out," and "See See Rider") added. But MGM's *Animalism*, released two months later, consisted of tracks recorded in America during the original group's final U.S. tour that never saw the light of day in England. —*Bruce Eder*

Animalism / 1966 / MGM ✦✦✦
The last gasp of the original Animals, albeit with Barry Jenkins on the drums in place of John Steel and Dave Rowberry on the ivories in lieu of Alan Price. A superb collection of rock numbers, as advanced from the band's early classics as the Stones' *Aftermath* repertory was from "It's All Over Now." Loud, intense, well-focused, hard-rocking blues. —*Bruce Eder*

Animalisms / Jun. 1966 / Decca ✦✦✦✦✦
Very similar in lineup to the American *Animalization*, this is probably the group's best noncompilation album, with a finely developed R&B sound throughout and excellent playing, all yielding an incomparable collection of good, solid, bluesy, ballsy rock numbers, highlighted by "Gin House Blues" and "Don't Bring Me Down." —*Bruce Eder*

Winds of Change / 1967 / One Way ✦✦✦
This album marked the debut of Eric Burdon and the New Animals, a decidedly looser, more psychedelic outfit than any the blues-singing idol had previously been associated with. "San Franciscan Nights," "Paint It Black," and "Yes I'm Experienced" (Burdon's answer to Jimi Hendrix's "Are You Experienced?") were moody and pulsating, and also fiercely experimental—one can get a glimpse of this band at work in the D.A. Pennebaker movie *Monterey Pop*, doing "Paint It Black" on stage. It was a logical extension of the later work of the original Animals into the Summer of Love. —*Bruce Eder*

Eric Is Here / 1967 / One Way ✦✦

Every One of Us / 1968 / One Way ✦✦

The Twain Shall Meet / 1968 / One Way ✦✦✦

The Twain Shall Meet was a more lopsidedly experimental album—even its major hit, "Sky Pilot," a venture into anti-war politicking on an epic level, marked a new level of sophistication for the band, which played hard and became well known for their ability to jam on stage. —*Bruce Eder* ✦✦

Love Is / 1968 / One Way ✦✦

The Best of Eric Burdon & the Animals, Vol. 2 / 1969 / MGM ✦✦✦
Actually the third Animals hits LP to be released by MGM in the 1960s, this collection is the work of lead singer Eric Burdon with the backup group he assembled upon the breakup of the original Animals. The recordings all come from 1967 and 1968, Burdon's psychedelicized period, when he was penning praises of the Monterey Pop Festival ("Monterey," number 15) and San Francisco ("San Franciscan Nights," number nine). The only other Top 40 hit on the album was the antiwar epic "Sky Pilot" (number 15), in its full seven-and-a-half-minute glory. Burdon had come a long way from his Manchester roots and his blues records, and this was the last album in his second phase; in fact, the New Animals had split by the time it was released. —*William Ruhlmann*

Before We Were So Rudely Interrupted / 1976 / Repertoire ✦✦✦✦
Cut 11 years after the Animals' original lineup recorded their last LP and six years before their more well-remembered reunion tour, this oft-overlooked album is just short of a lost classic; it lacks the intensity of their 1983 studio effort, *Ark*, but it is more substantial musically than that album and fits in very neatly with their preceding work, as though they'd scarcely skipped a beat. Recorded under the auspices of the late Chas Chandler's Barn Productions, the album was highlighted by a dramatically bluesy rendition of "It's All Over Now, Baby Blue," boasting superb playing by Alan Price. Hilton Valentine's soaring guitar pyrotechnics light up "Fire on the Sun," perhaps the flashiest performance of his career for this most introspective of '60s British blues axemen, and "As the Crow Flies" has the group returning to its roots, as a dark, brooding rendition of the Jimmy Reed song that gives room for Chandler, Valentine, Price, and John Steel to show off their '60s-era blues chops in a more expansive form. After a promising start, the gospel number "Many Rivers to Cross" falls apart a bit, but "Just a Little Bit," with its rippling organ break, the group original "Riverside County," and the pounding finale, "The Fool," make the rest of side two eminently enjoyable, although, coming out in the midst of the punk and disco booms, the LP never had a chance to be heard by more than the most dedicated fans. The album was remastered and reissued on CD in the spring of 2000 by Repertoire Records. —*Bruce Eder*

Rip It to Shreds: Their Greatest Hits Live / 1984 / IRS ✦✦
A document of the group's 1983 reunion tour. They played better shows along this tour than the one they actually taped—some of the balances (especially on the guitars) are a little off, and the band's sound and overall performance are somewhat creaky and anemic at times, but it is a fair representation of a largely successful attempt at recapturing past glories. —*Bruce Eder*

Ark / 1983 / Castle ✦✦

★ **The Best of the Animals** / 1988 / ABKCO ✦✦✦✦✦
The original Animals' American hits, including "House of the Rising Sun," "Don't Let Me Be Misunderstood," "It's My Life," and "We Gotta Get Out of This Place," in a compilation originally released in 1965. The lineup of songs is strong, but the sound is indifferent—the British *Complete Animals* covers the same territory and a lot more to much greater effect, at only twice the cost with three times the music and infinitely superior sound and notes. —*Bruce Eder*

The EP Collection / 1989 / See For Miles ✦✦✦✦✦
This 20-track CD, running just under an hour, is a good bargain. The real value behind these *See For Miles* EP collections is that, particularly where British invasion bands are concerned, they allow the listener to truly track the group's progress and the real advancement of their sound. The Animals, in their years on EMI, only released two LPs but got out five EPs in the same period. This is prime material, a good balance between the group's blues and R&B influences on the one hand and producer Mickie Most's more pop-oriented leanings, and it shows just how powerful this band was, whatever kind of music they chose to play. Their key hits represented here, including "House of the Rising Sun," "Baby Let Me Take You Home," "Don't Let Me Be Misunderstood," and "We've Gotta Get Out of This Place," surrounded by very strong tracks which show the members gaining confidence and extending themselves musically, month by month. The only drawback for the more casual listener is the focus of the collection, which is limited to the band's stay on EMI, which lasted barely two years, if that, so later hits like "It's My Life" are not present. Everything here does appear on the label's *Complete Animals* double-CD set, but that's where the 1999 reissue of this disc is important—*The EP Collection* offers state of the art digital sound, better than that on EMI's late-'80s set, and it also easily runs circles around ABKCO Records' *Best of the Animals*. The instruments all have startling presence, and Eric Burdon's voice practically booms out on "We've Gotta Get Out of This Place." The notes are very informative as well, explaining how the formative Animals managed to cross paths with (and later diverge paths from) producer Mickie Most. —*Bruce Eder*

Inside Looking Out: The 1965-1966 Sessions / 1990 / Sequel ✦✦✦✦✦
Together with the double-CD *The Complete Animals*, *Inside Looking Out* forms a complete retrospective of the great British Invasion band. This 22-song compilation features all of the essential recordings cut by the group in 1965 and 1966 after they broke with their original producer Mickie Most, and before Eric Burdon dissolved the core of the original lineup to pursue solo stardom with an Animals group featuring entirely different musicians. These tracks were perhaps more soul-oriented than their previous recordings, but the group still burns on the hits "Inside Looking Out" and "Don't Bring Me

Down." Despite the absence of original keyboardist Alan Price, the group continued to showcase Burdon's passionate vocals and burning, vibrant organ (by Price's replacement Dave Rowberry) on both renowned and obscure R&B tunes, with an occasional original thrown in. Besides the entirety of their final British LP *Animalisms* (from 1966) and the above-mentioned singles, the CD includes the hits "Help Me Girl" and "See See Rider" (credited to "Eric Burdon and the Animals," these were possibly Burdon solo records). The four tracks from their first release, an independently released 1963 EP featuring primitive R&B standards, are small but noteworthy bonus cuts that close this collection. *—Richie Unterberger*

Roadrunners! / 1990 / Raven ♦♦♦
A 19-track collection of otherwise unavailable live performances from 1966-1968, taken from shows in Melbourne, Stockholm, London, and the '67 Monterey Pop Festival, as well as radio and television broadcasts. Most of this dates from the psychedelic version of the band, which will disappoint those who are primarily interested in the group's rock/R&B prime. It's quite a good relic, though, with rough and ready execution by both Burdon and the band, and some unusual R&B and psychedelic material alongside the versions of hits like "Inside Looking Out," "Monterey," "San Franciscan Nights," and "When I Was Young." Sound ranges from fair to very good. *—Richie Unterberger*

☆ **The Complete Animals** / Jul. 1990 / EMI ♦♦♦♦♦
The title is a bit of a misnomer; this double CD does include the complete sessions that the Animals recorded with producer Mickie Most in 1964 and 1965. The 40 songs capture the band at their peak, including most of their best and biggest hits: "House of the Rising Sun," "Don't Let Me Be Misunderstood," "Bring It on Home to Me," "We Gotta Get Out of This Place," "I'm Crying," "It's My Life," and "Boom Boom." Most of the rest of the tunes don't match the excellence of these smashes, though they're solid. The great majority of them are covers of vintage R&B/rock tunes by Chuck Berry, Fats Domino, and the like, which aren't quite as durable as reinterpretations from the same era by the Stones and Yardbirds. When they hit the mark, though, the Animals produced some great album tracks that have been mostly forgotten by time, such as "I'm Mad Again" (originally by John Lee Hooker), "Worried Life Blues," and "Bury My Body." After leaving Most, the group would maintain their peak for another year or so (this period is represented on the fine import collection *Inside Looking Out*) despite the departure of one of rock's all-time finest organists, Alan Price. This compilation has everything that Price recorded with the group, including four previously unreleased cuts and the non-LP Eric Burdon original on the B-side of "It's My Life," "I'm Gonna Change the World." *—Richie Unterberger*

The Best of Eric Burdon & the Animals, 1966-68 / 1991 / Polydor ♦♦♦
The best attempt so far to sort out the post-1966 Animals tracks, drawing from their English Decca and American MGM sides. The material is the best of their work from the post-British invasion era, remastered superbly and carefully organized, with informative and entertaining notes. *—Bruce Eder*

Paul Anka

b. Jul. 30, 1941, Ottawa, Ontario, Canada
Vocals / Brill Building Pop, Teen Idol, Pop
Paul Anka was one of the biggest teen idols of the late '50s, and a successful songwriter, music businessman, and recording artist well into the 1990s. After gaining an audition with ABC in 1957, his ode to a former babysitter, "Diana," hit number one on both sides of the Atlantic later that year and eventually sold a reported ten million copies. His biggest American hit however, was "Lonely Boy" from the 1959 film *Girls Town*. As the teen idol craze cooled off in the early '60s, Paul Anka moved to RCA, acquired the rights to his own ABC masters, made a fortune on reissues alone, and began moving toward a nightclub background (he was one of the first pop singers to do shows in Las Vegas). Anka also wrote the theme to *The Tonight Show* and the lyrics to Frank Sinatra's trademark "My Way," and also wrote Tom Jones' biggest hit, "She's a Lady." Although he had hit the Top 40 only once since 1963, Paul Anka stormed the number one slot in 1974 with "(You're) Having My Baby," a duet recorded with his singing protege, Odia Coates. Anka continued to chart into the early '80s, continuing his many casino and international appearances while recording sparingly but continually. *—John Bush*

● **30th Anniversary Collection** / Oct. 1989 / Rhino ♦♦♦♦♦
Not many artists can claim a 20-year run of hits, much less be credited with writing the majority of them as well, but Paul Anka can. Starting out as a sawed-off Canadian teen idol, he rocketed to the top of the charts with fare like "Diana," "Put Your Head on My Shoulder," "Lonely Boy," and "Puppy Love" before moving into the '70s with more adult fare like "(You're) Having My Baby," and "My Way." Pop enthusiasts will appreciate this package, even if rock & roll fans shun his work to the very end. *—Cub Koda*

The Essential RCA Recordings / Jun. 15, 1999 / Taragon ♦♦♦♦
Although he was emerging from his years as a teen idol, it is still debatable if Paul Anka could ever be refered to as a "rocker," hence the title of this compilation being a tad misleading. But if pop tunes with some guts to them is your cup of tea, these 19 tracks show off Anka's vocal and songwriting skills to good advantage on recordings from 1962 to 1968. Most interesting track: Anka's spin on his own "It Doesn't Matter Anymore," in a mode more and a bit differently melodic than the Buddy Holly version we're all used to hearing. *—Cub Koda*

Vegas Style: The Best of the Late RCA and Buddah Recordings / Oct. 24, 2000 / Taragon ♦♦♦♦
Taragon Records' second compilation of the recordings of Paul Anka, licensed from the vaults of BMG, picks up where its predecessor, 1999's *The Essential RCA Recordings*, left off. It is an equally intriguing, if necessarily less complete chronicle of a phase of Anka's career. In the period covered by the disc, 1968-1981, the singer had six record label affiliations, only three of which are represented here. They are: two stints on RCA Records, 1968-1970 and 1978-1981, and one on Buddah, 1971-1973. Two of the missing affiliations, a 1971 stay on Barnaby Records and one on Fame Records in 1973, each of which resulted in the release of a lone single, are insignificant. But Anka's 1974-1977 stay at United Artists Records was the site of a major comeback during which he scored four Top Ten singles including the chart-topper "(You're) Having My Baby" and two gold albums, so the omission of those recordings gives the present set something of a "before and after" feel. Nevertheless, there is much valuable work here. Taragon's title for this collection, *Vegas Style*, is actually a misnomer, since these recordings find Anka doing his best to meet the pop marketplace rather than retreating to the Vegas showrooms that were paying his bills. It is not a complete collection of his available singles from this period, but it gives a good sense of a talented artist trying to express himself in a commercial vein, circa the early and late '70s, even if the middle years during which he succeeded are not included. *—William Ruhlmann*

The Very Best of Paul Anka / Oct. 24, 2000 / RCA ♦♦♦
The Very Best of Paul Anka concentrates on his early RCA recordings, as well as the re-recorded, stereo versions of his first hits that he cut when he switched labels. The revamped versions of "Diana," "You Are My Destiny," "Put Your Head on My Shoulder," and "Puppy Love" are mixed with later singles like "A Steel Guitar and a Glass of Wine," "Remember Diana," "Eso Beso (That Kiss)," and "It Doesn't Matter Any More." Though it doesn't quite live up to its title, *The Very Best of Paul Anka* is still a decent and fairly comprehensive collection of his '60s sound. *—Heather Phares*

Adam Ant (Stuart Goddard)

b. Nov. 3, 1954, London, England
Vocals, Keyboards / Post-Punk, Pop/Rock, New Wave
One of the seminal figures of new wave, Adam Ant initially explored darkly angular, jagged post-punk with his group Adam and the Ants. After releasing their debut, *Dirk Wears White Sox*, in 1979, Malcolm McLaren became the group's manager, and after he convinced the group to revamp their style and sound, he lured the core of the band away to form Bow Wow Wow. Ant and his faithful guitarist/collaborator Marco Pirroni regrouped, carrying through on their newly revamped image. Dressing up in pirates outfits, streaking their faces with makeup, and using thunderous Burundi drumming as an anchor, they developed an infectious, silly, glam-speckled blend of pop and post-punk sensibilities. The group had enormous success in England with their second album, 1980's *Kings of the Wild Frontier*. Over the next few years, Adam and the Ants had several hits, such as "Ant Music" and "Stand and Deliver," and as their popularity grew, their sound got increasingly streamlined and pop-oriented, culminating in Adam Ant's first official solo album, 1982's *Friend or Foe*. This record proved to be his breakthrough to the American pop mainstream, thanks in large part to the clever videos for the title track and "Goody Two Shoes," which were heavily aired on MTV. With 1985's *Viva Le Rock*, the slickness outweighed the substance, and his sales dropped dramatically. Ant turned to acting, releasing his next album, *Manners & Physique*, in 1990, which faded away after a moderately successful single in "Room at the Top." As Ant again concentrated on acting, a new generation of bands, such as Nine Inch Nails and Elastica, built on his influence. During this revival, Ant released the understated 1995's *Wonderful*. It did respectable business, yet Ant again retreated from music until 2000's triple-disc retrospective, *Antbox*. *—Stephen Thomas Erlewine*

Dirk Wears White Sox / Dec. 1979 / Epic ♦♦♦♦♦
The original Ants line-up released only one LP, *Dirk Wears White Sox* for Do It in 1979. The album finds a young Adam Ant exploring the sometimes-awkward fusion of punk, glam, and minimalist post-punk with bizarre images and disturbing tales of alienation, sex, and brutality. And while the somewhat pretentious, overly-arty lyrics and inexperienced playing are a drawback, the album offers a fascinating look at the Ants' formative years, capturing a raw energy that would be sacrificed for more polish on subsequent releases. (At the height of Antmania, Adam Ant acquired the rights to the album, re-mixing it, dropping a few tracks, and adding a couple of early tracks for reissue in 1983 with a different cover for Epic. In 1995, Sony Music U.K. released a hybrid version for CD, restoring the cover art, original mixes, and the previously dropped tracks but retaining the additions and running order of the reissue. Epic chose to keep the re-mixed version for CD release in the U.S.) *—Chris Woodstra*

Kings of the Wild Frontier / 1980 / Epic ♦♦♦♦♦
Hooking up with Malcolm McLaren was a pivotal moment for Adam Ant, since the manager not only introduced Ant to the thundering, infectious Burundi drum beat that became his signature, he stole his band, too. Adam and the rest of the Ants had just worked up how to exploit the Burundi style when McLaren pirated the boys off to support Annabella Lwin in Bow Wow Wow—using the very same sound they had developed with Adam Ant. It was now a race to get that sound into the stores first, and Adam lucked out when he joined forces with guitarist Marco Pirroni. Adam and Marco knocked out a bunch of songs that retained some of the dark artiness of *Dirk Wears White Sox*, largely anchored by those enormous Burundi beats and given great, irresistible pop hooks—plus a flash sense of style, as the new Ants dressed up in something that looked like American Indians. It was a brilliant, gonzo move, and the resulting record, *Kings of the Wild Frontier*, is one of the great defining albums of its time. There's simply nothing else like it, nothing else that has the same bravado, the same swagger, the same gleeful self-aggrandizement and sense of camp. If image was all that they had, they would've remained a fad, but *Kings of the Wild Frontier* remains a terrific album because it not only has some tremendous songs—the title track and "Antmusic" are classic hits, while "Killer in the Home" and "Physical (You're So)" are every bit their equal—but because it fearlessly,

imperceptibly switches gears between giddy and ominous, providing nothing short of a thrill ride in its 13 songs. That's why it still sounds like nothing else years after its release. *—Stephen Thomas Erlewine*

Prince Charming / 1981 / Epic ✦✦✦
Kings of the Wild Frontier brought Adam and the Ants massive popularity in England, and it brought enormous pressure for Adam and guitarist Marco Pirroni to stand and deliver another slice of dynamite. The first single, the punchy horn-laden "Stand and Deliver," suggested that they were up to the task, but when *Prince Charming* appeared in late 1981, it was pretty much universally panned and it still stands as the weakest record from Ant's classic period. With its ridiculous song titles and cover photos, which suggest that the Ants were moving away from Native Americans and toward pirates, it's hard not to view it as a descent into camp, yet Adam claims in the liner notes for *Antbox* that he believes that *Prince Charming* is "a very serious record based on very classical, historical themes." That may be true on certain tracks, but it's hard to see where "Mile High Club," "S.E.X.," "Mowhok," and "Ant Rap" fit into that scheme, but he's right about the intent—this is a markedly different record than *Kings*, intentionally so. The group have not only moved on in image, they've also left behind their signature Burundi beats while upping the cinematic qualities inherent in their music. So, "5 Guns West" and "Mowhok" are given neo-spaghetti western backdrops, while eerie guitars, mariachi horns, and trilling vocals underpin "That Voodoo." There are a lot of little details like that to dwell on in the production—"Picasso Visita El Planeta de Los Simios" *sounds* absolutely terrific—but apart from "Scorpios," "Stand and Deliver," and the cheerfully ludicrous "Ant Rap," the songs just aren't there. *Kings* had style, sound, and songs, while *Prince Charming* simply has style and sound—which, in retrospect, isn't all that bad, but it's also not hard to see how it sparked a backlash at the time. *—Stephen Thomas Erlewine*

Friend or Foe / 1982 / Epic ✦✦✦✦
Adam Ant and Marco Pirroni ditched the rest of the Ants not long after the release of the widely derided *Prince Charming*, which provided them with the perfect opportunity for a new statement of purpose in the first Ant-less album, 1982's *Friend or Foe*. They had already begun moving away from Burundi beats and Indians on *Prince Charming*, but here they ditch any pretense at the underground, favoring big, glitzy glam pop. There's still residual artiness, of course, since Adam and Marco are post-modernists that love to paste together seemingly incongruous strands of pop culture in an attempt to craft something new. The difference is, they've wrapped this instinct in big, big production and cheerful, unabashed pop hooks, best heard on "Place in the Country" and the hits "Friend or Foe," "Desperate But Not Serious," and "Goody Two Shoes," the latter becoming Adam's biggest hit in the U.S. Since these are deliberate pop trifles, several critics laughed off Ant as a silly lightweight, but that's missing the point—these are intentionally tongue-in-cheek tunes, delivered with an excess of flair and good humor. Though *Friend or Foe* does lose momentum on the second side and the cover of the Doors' "Hello, I Love You" falls a little flat, this is good, giddy fun, one of Ant's best records and one of the best new wave albums. *—Stephen Thomas Erlewine*

Strip / Nov. 1983 / Epic ✦✦
With this album, Adam Ant's musical career began to hit the skids. He was still popular enough in the U.K. to squeeze out one more Top Ten hit with "Puss 'N Boots," but the album stopped at #20 after three straight Top Five hits. In the U.S., where Ant had peaked with his solo debut, *Friend Or Foe*, the year before, this one got only to a disastrous #65. And no wonder—the mixture of driving, danceable rock with humor that had made *Kings of the Wild Frontier*, *Prince Charming*, and even some of *Friend or Foe* enjoyable had given way to a lighter pop approach and outright camp, especially on the title track, a minor singles chart entry produced by Phil Collins. Somehow, Ant had lost his appeal, and fast. *—William Ruhlmann*

Vive Le Rock / 1985 / Epic ✦✦
Adam Ant adopted a '50s-style rock & roll sound for his third solo album, achieving a pastiche with some of the effervescence, but none of the definition (or popularity), of Elton John's "Crocodile Rock." Producer Tony Visconti tried to give him some of the plastic rock legitimacy of *Ziggy Stardust*-era David Bowie, but Ant was even goofier, and especially with his vocals smothered in harmony and echo and buried in the mix, he wasn't so much transformed into a rocker manque as rendered anonymous on his own record. The best track was the year-old U.K. Top 40 hit "Apollo 9," which had some of the manic energy of the Adam and the Ants hits. If the rest of the album had recreated its dizzy spirit, Ant might have made the comeback he needed with *Vive Le Rock*. Or maybe not—it's possible that his moment simply had passed. In any case, the album flopped on both sides of the Atlantic, Ant was dropped by his record label, and he didn't make another album for more than four years. (*Vive Le Rock* was reissued in 1996 with the added track "Mohair Locker Room Pin-Up Boys.") *—William Ruhlmann*

Manners & Physique / Feb. 1990 / MCA ✦✦

● **Antics in the Forbidden Zone** / Oct. 1990 / Epic ✦✦✦✦✦
The most comprehensive overview of the band. In 22 tracks, all of the hits are represented as well as key album cuts and a rare B-side, "Beat My Guest." An essential part of any new wave collection. *—Chris Woodstra*

Peel Sessions / Jul. 1, 1991 / Dutch East India ✦✦✦
A nice collection of recordings made for John Peel's radio show from 1978 to 1979. This is probably the best documentation of the early days of the band, combining live-in-the-studio versions of material from *Dirk Wears White Sox*, early singles, and previously unreleased tracks. Essential for hardcore fans. *—Chris Woodstra*

B-Side Babies! / Sep. 27, 1994 / Epic/Legacy ✦✦✦✦
Since Adam Ant once had a group called the B-Sides, it makes sense that his singles, both as lead singer of Adam and the Ants and as a solo, would have non-LP B-sides. And since Ant was a hit in the U.K. before he made it in America, and was always bigger in Britain, many of those B-sides appeared only on English singles. This is a collection of songs recorded between 1980 and 1985 that gave Ant a chance to try novelty approaches while the A-sides relentlessly beat out his trademark "Antmusic." In fact, songs like "Making History" do have that characteristic yodel and the Burundi-style drumming of Terry Miall and Merrick. But elsewhere, Ant tries different things, frequently light, slight things like "Juanito the Bandito." But fun was always one of his qualities, and it's here in abundance. *—William Ruhlmann*

Wonderful / Mar. 7, 1995 / Capitol ✦✦✦
Adam Ant recorded his first album in five years (and second in ten years) at Abbey Road Studio No. 2, where the Beatles recorded, and a Beatle sound wore off on the songs, which sounded like Beatle music of 1966-67, from the rhythmic cadences to the strummed acoustic guitars and backwards tape sounds. Ant was always better at image than music, whether he was mixing Native American and pirate gear or employing African-style drumming more for the look than the sound back in the Antmusic days. Since then, he hasn't had any musical compass, although he posed as a dance music frontman on 1990's *Manners & Physique*. Here he borrowed Madonna's photographer, Anton Corbijn, and her basic theme—sex-as-amusement/nourishment/salvation. He succeeded in sounding horny, but that didn't make him seductive. *—William Ruhlmann*

Antbox / Nov. 2000 / Epic ✦✦✦✦✦
There are some that will scoff at the very idea of a comprehensive, three-disc box set overview of Adam Ant's career, dismissing him as nothing more than a new wave fad. Let 'em laugh, since *Antbox* proves that he, along with trusty guitarist sidekick Marco Pirroni, was a post-punk heavyweight, adept at creating claustrophobic dark angular tunes and giddy glam revivals with equal vigor. *Antbox* gives room to both sides of the equation, and it's one of the rare boxes that succeeds precisely because of its rarities, which not only add depth and dimension, they fill in gaps in his history—particularly on the first disc, which is devoted entirely to pre-*Kings of the Wild Frontier* material, including demos, singles, BBC sessions, and rejected audition tapes for Decca. This is the cream of the crop of literally hundreds of unreleased songs from the *Dirk Wears White Sox* era and the amazing thing is, they more than hold their own with what actually made the cut. The high quality is maintained on the second disc, which contains all the blockbusters, sometimes duplicated in alternate versions which are interesting, not excessive. If the quality dips dramatically on the last disc, despite a few good unreleased cuts plus the absence of *Manners & Physique* (MCA/Universal wouldn't license the recordings), it still is the best way to listen to these years, and "Wonderful" remains a career-capping return to form. Yes, three discs is a bit much for most listeners, especially three discs filled with rarities, but this is the truest testament to Adam Ant's gifts as a musician. Any serious post-punk/new wave fan will find this a fascinating, revelatory set. *—Stephen Thomas Erlewine*

Complete Radio One Recordings / Jul. 17, 2001 / Strange Fruit ✦✦✦✦

Anthrax

f. Jun. 1981, New York, NY
Rap-Metal, Speed Metal, Heavy Metal, Thrash
Nearly as much as Metallica or Megadeth, Anthrax was responsible for the emergence of speed and thrash metal; combining the speed and fury of hardcore punk with the prominent guitars and vocals of heavy metal, they helped create a new subgenre of heavy metal on their early albums. Original guitarists Scott Ian and Dan Spitz were a formidable pair, spitting out lightning fast riffs and solos that never seemed masturbatory. Unlike Metallica or Megadeth, they had the good sense to temper their often serious music with a healthy dose of humor and realism. After their first album, *Fistful of Metal*, singer Joey Belladonna joined the lineup; he helped take the band further away from conventional metal clichés, and over the next five albums (with the exception of 1988's *State of Euphoria*, where the band sounded like they were in a creative strait-jacket), Anthrax arguably became the leaders of speed metal. As the '80s became the '90s, they also began to increase their experiments with hip-hop, culminating in a tour with Public Enemy in 1991 and a joint re-recording of PE's classic "Bring the Noise." *—Stephen Thomas Erlewine*

Fistful of Metal / 1984 / Megaforce ✦✦

Spreading the Disease / 1985 / Megaforce/Island ✦✦✦✦
Anthrax's first album with vocalist Joey Belladonna is a huge leap forward, featuring strongly rhythmic, pounding riffs and vocals that alternate between hardcore-type shouting and surprising amounts of melody. Two tracks left over from the Lilker days are here as well. The traditional metal lyrical fare is more original, while also introducing a penchant for paying tribute to favorite fictional characters and pop-culture artifacts ("Lone Justice" and "Medusa" are prime examples). One of Anthrax's best efforts. *—Steve Huey*

Among the Living / 1987 / Megaforce/Island ✦✦✦✦✦
Generally considered the band's best album, *Among the Living* broadened the scope of Anthrax's subject matter with socially conscious lyrics addressing prejudice, violence, drug abuse ["Efilnikufesin (N.F.L.)," a rip on John Belushi], and the hollowness of the music business, as well as a politically correct ode to the "Indians." However, the band refuses to take itself too seriously, also recording tributes to Stephen King and Judge Dredd. Musically, the band delivers a powerful, aggressive roar driven by impossibly fast riffing and the changing tempos and collectively shouted vocals of hardcore, especially on the classic "Caught in a Mosh." The brutal rhythm guitar work of Scott Ian and the explosive drumming of Charlie Benante relentlessly push the songs along while still maintaining a

solid groove, and more than make up for some lyrical awkwardness. *Among the Living* remains arguably Anthrax's foremost achievement. —*Steve Huey*

I'm the Man / 1987 / Megaforce/Island ✦✦✦✦
Genius. Pure genius. Way before Rage Against the Machine, before Run-DMC's collaboration with Aerosmith, and before their infamous collaboration with Public Enemy, Anthrax take the credit—or blame—for being the pioneers of merging rap and metal. Released in 1987, their now-classic *I'm the Man* is a funny tribute/parody/attempt at hip-hop that is not only pulled off successfully, but it's also the first release that showcases Anthrax's sense of humor—the latter of which was also a first for the genre of speed metal. There are also three live tracks—one of which being the title track—as well as a "mosh-able" version of Black Sabbath's "Sabbath Bloody Sabbath"—all of which are great but will probably be overlooked. Has it been mentioned that this EP is genius? —*Mike DaRonco*

State of Euphoria / 1988 / Megaforce/Island ✦✦✦
The proper follow-up to *Among the Living* was somewhat disappointing in its inconsistency. While there are some good moments—"Be All, End All" is one of the band's most melodic moments, and several other tracks catch fire—the best thing here is a cover of Trust's "Antisocial," and it doesn't bode well when covers outshine original material. The lyrics continue the self-consciously intellectual, P.C. approach begun on *Among the Living,* but about half of the album is surprisingly dull. —*Steve Huey*

Persistence of Time / Aug. 1990 / Megaforce/Island ✦✦✦✦
Persistence of Time rivals *Among the Living* as Anthrax's best album and might even be a clear-cut favorite if some of the songs had been trimmed a bit. The more cartoonish side of the band is missing here, trimmed in favor of a dark, uncompromising examination of society's dirty underbelly—nearly every song rails against hatred and prejudice, but without an excess of optimism. The standout track is, once again, a cover—Joe Jackson's "Got the Time"—but the rest of the album is strong enough to hold its own. This is the album for those who want Anthrax's serious side without any of the pop-culture references and tributes; others might miss those elements, particularly since there has always been a sort of clumsiness to some of the more intellectual lyrics. However, *Persistence of Time* is their most lyrically consistent album, and the music simply rages. —*Steve Huey*

Attack of the Killer B's / Jun. 1991 / Island ✦✦✦✦
Not just for devoted fans, this collection of B-sides, covers, rarities, and obscurities actually presents a surprisingly solid overview of the range and diversity of Anthrax's material in an engaging, entertaining manner. Listeners wanting to hear more of the band's sense of humor will be pleased with the bizarre "Milk (Ode to Billy)" (one of two S.O.D. songs redone here), the hilarious power-ballad satire "N.F.B.," and the anti-censorship tune "Startin' Up a Posse," which uses rather predictable tactics to make its point but has such a gleeful, idiotic bounce that it's difficult not to be amused anyway. Two live songs from *Persistence of Time* are included, capturing the band's serious side, and their various influences are documented through covers of Trust, Discharge, Kiss, and even surfrockers the Chantays. But the most important item here is the slamming (and highly influential) duet with Public Enemy on that group's classic "Bring the Noise," which paved the way for a host of other bands to mix the aggression and intensity of heavy metal with hip-hop. —*Steve Huey*

Sound of White Noise / May 1993 / Elektra ✦✦✦

Live—the Island Years / Apr. 5, 1994 / Island ✦✦✦

Stomp 442 / Oct. 24, 1995 / Elektra ✦✦

● **Return of the Killer A's: The Best of Anthrax** / Nov. 23, 1999 / Beyond ✦✦✦✦
Return of the Killer A's is a somewhat puzzling retrospective, its selections skewed heavily toward Anthrax's later years when their popularity was generally on the wane. Although this period did produce some quality material, Anthrax were also not the cutting-edge metal innovators they had once been; however, starting there may make it easier for newer listeners to understand Anthrax's lasting impact on alternative metal and rapmetal. About half the tracks are drawn from *Sound of White Noise* and *Volume 8: The Threat Is Real,* and there's at least one song (but rarely more) from each of the group's '80s albums, from *Spreading the Disease* on. Present, too, are the group's groundbreaking rap-metal fusions, 1987's "I'm the Man" and 1991's Public Enemy cover/collaboration "Bring the Noise"; there's also a newly recorded cover of the Temptation's "Ball of Confusion," which unites vocalists John Bush and Joey Belladonna. It seems odd that an Anthrax retrospective wouldn't include "Caught in a Mosh," "Black Lodge," "Be All, End All," "Belly of the Beast," "Keep It in the Family," or "Skeleton in the Closet," to name some of the most prominently missing items. But, on the plus side, the rough recent-to-early sequencing does help illustrate Anthrax's influence for relative newcomers, beginning with the most familiar sounds and backtracking to their roots; additionally, it provides more casual fans with most (but not all) of the highlights from their Bush-era albums. Still, *Return of the Killer A's* is far from definitive. —*Steve Huey*

Madhouse: The Very Best of Anthrax / Jun. 26, 2001 / Island ✦✦✦✦
Why the release of one Anthrax 'hits' collection (1999's *Return of the Killer A's*) so close to another (2001's *Madhouse: The Very Best of Anthrax*), you ask? Well, the answer's simple—the latest one is not the doing of the band, but their former label, Island. The 12-track set covers just the band's highlights from 1985's *Spreading the Disease* up to 1991's *Attack of the Killer B's.* Granted, there are quite a few thrash metal classics here ("A.I.R.," "I Am the Law," "Indians," "Antisocial," "Got the Time"), as well as some of the first ever rap-metal experiments ("I'm the Man," "Bring the Noise"), the latter almost single-handedly laying the groundwork for such future hit making '90s acts as Rage Against the Machine and Limp Bizkit. The earlier set *Return of the Killer A's* proves to be the better of

the two since it covers more ground, but if you're looking for a budget-priced collection that covers Anthrax's peak years, *Madhouse: The Very Best of Anthrax* manages to do the trick. —*Greg Prato*

Any Trouble

f. 1975, Manchester, England, **db.** Dec. 1984
Pub Rock, New Wave
Any Trouble was an underappreciated bright spot on Stiff Records, a label which had no shortage of talented artists. Bandleader Clive Gregson's appearance, hardened love songs, and vocal style may have led to comparisons to Elvis Costello, but they were no second-rate rip-off—each of their four albums revealed a songwriter of unique talent and a more-than-capable band to execute the songs. Manchester native Gregson formed the original band in 1975 as a folky trio; by 1976, Any Trouble was a four-piece rock group, speeding up their repertoire in response to the punk movement. They built a strong following playing the pub circuit and signed with Stiff Records by 1980. Any Trouble's first album, *Where Are All the Nice Girls?,* had all the makings of a new wave classic. It was met with some rave reviews, but failed to rack up the big sales that were expected of it. *Wheels in Motion* (1981), while certainly more accomplished, lacked the spark of the first album and simply didn't catch on in the U.K. Halfway through a small Stateside tour, the band heard by word-of-mouth that they had been dropped by Stiff and were left stranded in America. Eventually they found their way back, but the stress of the situation broke up the band temporarily. A new deal was arranged with EMI-America, and what was essentially a new band behind Gregson recorded *Any Trouble* in 1983. Again, the same story—the reviews were good, but the band's cult status didn't change. Gregson, knowing the band couldn't last much longer, decided to stretch out for *Wrong End of the Race,* a sprawling double album that allowed the band to show their diversity and influences. In December 1984, the band played their last gig and called it quits. Gregson went on to a distinguished, though still underappreciated, career both as a solo artist and as a collaborator with Christine Collister. —*Chris Woodstra*

● **Where Are All the Nice Girls?** / 1980 / Compass ✦✦✦✦✦
Where Are All the Nice Girls? is a pure pub/pop rock gem. Leading off with the infectious "Second Choice" (one of the great "should have been hits") and ending up with the unlikely ABBA cover "Name of the Game," Gregson and company run though 12 tunes, almost all obsessed with love gone wrong. A cult favorite. (In 1997, Compass Records reissued *Where Are All the Nice Girls?* on CD, dropping the ABBA cover in favor of adding the single "Yesterday's Love" and "Honolulu" (a track originally dropped from the U.S. edition).) —*Chris Woodstra*

Live at the Venue / 1981 / Line ✦✦✦✦✦
Originally released as a promo for radio, this live show from 1980 finds the band in its natural setting. Playing with higher energy than in the studio, this provides the best picture of the band at its peak. —*Chris Woodstra*

Wheels in Motion / Aug. 1981 / Stiff ✦✦✦
The playing on their sophomore effort is more sophisticated and the production is cleaner but it lacks some of the bite of the first album. Gregson's now-standard obsession makes an appearance on the album's highlight, "Trouble with Love." —*Chris Woodstra*

Any Trouble / 1983 / EMI ✦✦✦
The band's move from the Stiff label to EMI marked an attempt to crack the U.S. market with a mainstream radio-ready album, a new lineup, and another batch of well-crafted songs from Clive Gregson. Unfortunately overlooked at the time, material from this album continued to be a part of Gregson's solo sets in the '90s. —*Chris Woodstra*

Wrong End of the Race / 1984 / BGO ✦✦✦
Wrong End of the Race compiles unnecessary re-recordings of previously released songs, some new tracks, and a few interesting covers. Knowing that this would be their final album, Gregson attempted to assemble material that would show the band's diversity and their wide variety of influences. And while this does reveal some interesting sides to the band, ultimately, the exercise misses more often than it hits. —*Chris Woodstra*

The Apartments

Chamber Pop, Alternative Pop/Rock
A brisk Australian chamber pop group with echoes of Frenchman Serge Gainsbourg as well as Leonard Cohen and post-punk, the Apartments were formed early in the '80s by frontman and guitarist Peter Milton-Walsh, though the band's unhectic release schedule resulted in only three albums during their first dozen years. *The Evening Visits ...* was released in the Apartments' home country in 1985, and though it did only moderately well there, the album became a cult classic in France. Seven years after the debut, *Drift* followed with similar exposure, causing a French label to sign the group for third album *A Life Full of Farewells.* After re-releasing the first two LPs, plus *Fête Foraine* (which featured acoustic renditions of previous songs), the Apartments even gained American release on Twin/Tone Records. Their fourth proper album, *Apart,* was released in 2000. —*John Bush*

● **The Evening Visits ... And Stays for Years** / 1985 / Twin/Tone ✦✦✦✦✦
The Apartments' debut album *The Evening Visits ... And Stays for Years* is a gorgeous collection of folky jangle-pop spiked with country-rock and horn-laced pop. Frequently, the collection sounds under produced, but the songs themselves confirm that Peter Walsh, the brains behind the Apartments, is a graceful songwriter, capable of lovely melodies and affecting lyrics. —*Stephen Thomas Erlewine*

Drift / 1992 / Twin/Tone ✦✦✦
Drift features a heavier guitar sound than the albums that bookend it, but otherwise fits

right into the Apartments' whiskey-soaked, vaguely French universe. Frontman Peter Milton Walsh's obsessions—old hotels, deserted train stations, haunted women—are all present, and his songs as melancholy as ever, if less delicate this time out. With such gorgeous melodies and cinematic lyrics, though, it seems silly to complain—if the Apartments have settled into a groove, at least it's a good one. *Drift* does not reach the heights of 1995's *A Life Full of Farewells*, the Apartments' chamber-pop masterpiece. But fans of Tindersticks, Leonard Cohen, and Spain will find it rewarding all the same. *—Kristi Coulter*

A Life Full of Farewells / 1995 / Hot ✦✦✦

The first thing you notice on this disc is a muted trumpet playing a sad, midtempo refrain that echoes through the rest of the album and sets a mood that remains constant. All of the songs feature a shimmery, acoustic guitar-based sound and vague but attractive melodies; "End of Some Fear" comes close to rocking but never quite gets there, and everything else is slow, limpid, and regretful. Peter Walsh's voice is nice but unremarkable, and the lyrics seem to exist mostly to serve the songs' mood, not vice versa—frankly, you're not going to put this disc on to listen to the songs at all; you're going to put it on because you're in a particular mood. That said, there are some lyrics that will take you by surprise: lines like "You'll become my big excuse/The poison that I drink as I sink my teeth in you" are rather startling, particularly when sung in front of a sobbing steel guitar backdrop. There's nothing the matter with mood albums, anyway, and this really is a fine one. *—Rick Anderson*

Apart / May 23, 2000 / Hot ✦✦✦

Aphex Twin (Richard D. James)

b. Aug. 18, 1971

Producer / IDM, Drill'n'bass, Experimental Jungle, Experimental Techno, Electronica, Ambient Techno, Acid Techno, Trance, Techno

Exploring the experimental possibilities inherent in acid and ambience, the two major influences on home-listening techno during the late '80s, Richard D. James' recordings as Aphex Twin brought him more critical praise than any other electronic artist during the 1990s. Though his first major single "Didgeridoo" was a piece of acid thrash designed to tire dancers during his DJ sets, ambient stylists and critics later took him under their wing for *Selected Ambient Works 85-92*, a sublime touchstone in the field of ambient-techno. James' reaction to the exposure portrayed an artist unwilling to become either pigeonholed or categorizable. His second Aphex Twin album, *Selected Ambient Works, Vol. 2*, was so minimal as to be barely conscious—in what appeared to be an elaborate joke on the electronic community. Follow-ups showed James gradually returning to his hardcore and acid roots, even while his stated desire to crash the British Top Ten (and perform on *Top of the Pops*) resulted in a series of cartoonish pop songs whose twisted genius was near-masked by their many absurdities. His iconoclastic behavior surprisingly aligned with MTV audiences turned on to end-of-the-millennium nihilist-pop along the lines of Marilyn Manson and Nine Inch Nails. *—John Bush*

Analogue Bubblebath III / 1992 / EFA ✦✦✦

His first full-length release, this long out-of-print album features James's early brand of techno, indebted to acid and trance but still of a distorted quality all its own. No song titles are provided on the CD version (which comes in a slimline case with only a sticker on the front), but the LP version (enclosed in a brown paper bag) lists long decimals as the titles. *Analogue Bubblebath III* was re-released by Rephlex in late 1997, but again as a limited-edition issue. *—John Bush*

★ **Selected Ambient Works 85-92** / 1993 / Apollo ✦✦✦✦✦

Selected Ambient Works is a desperately sparse album: thin percussion and several haunted-synth lines are the only components on most songs, and Richard D. James added only one vocal sample on the entire album ("We are the music makers, and we are the dreamers of dreams"). Also, the sound quality is relatively poor; it was recorded direct to cassette tape and reportedly suffered a mangling job by a cat. All this belies the status of *Selected Ambient Works* as a watershed of ambient music. It reveals no influences and sounds unlike anything that preceded it, due in large part to the effects James managed to wrangle from his supply of home-manufactured contraptions. *—John Bush*

Selected Ambient Works, Vol. 2 / Mar. 8, 1994 / Sire ✦✦✦

Selected Ambient Works, Vol. 2 is a more difficult and challenging album than Aphex Twin's previous collection. The music is all texture; there are only the faintest traces of beats and forward movement. Instead, all of these untitled tracks are long, unsettling electronic soundscapes, alternately quiet and confrontational; although most of the music is rather subdued, it is never easy listening. While some listeners may find this double-disc album dull (both discs run over 70 minutes), many listeners will be intrigued and fascinated by the intricately detailed music of Aphex Twin. *—Stephen Thomas Erlewine*

Classics / 1995 / R&S ✦✦✦

Arguably Richard James' first full-length CD, comprised of various EP's from the early '90s when he was experimenting on his homemade electronic gear and cranking out material that surpassed the work his peers were putting out. Because of the nature of this re-release to CD, the tracks don't always flow from one to the next, but if you want a dense collection of his groundbreaking earlier work, this release will satisfy both the uninitiated and fans alike. Few others knew how to bend the rules of electronic music quite the way James does, and this skill bleeds into present day because he sets the standard for what is always on the horizon. He can turn an atonal collection of sounds into something that transcends the dancefloor, and therefore many of the pieces here require the listener's full attention. His imitable and straightforward track "Digeridoo" finally gets to CD not once but twice, both as the original recording and later as a live version recorded in Cornwall in 1990. Other standouts include "Isopropanol" and "Analogue Bubblebath 1," which are also available on the widely available EP *Analogue Bubblebath 1* by AFX (one of his many surnames). "Isopropanol" is ominous and relentless, but also hints at his playful side. Another standout is "Polynomial-C," which sounds like a dance-friendly version of the old *COSMOS* theme with the same steady rhythm of "Digeridoo." Also here are two early remixes of "We Have Arrived" (credited to "The Mover"), which hint at some of the type of blistering rearranging work he would later do for Nine Inch Nails. Collectors will revel in this disc, and others will simply wonder what just happened to them. Either way, it's worth adding to the shelf. *—Glen Swann*

I Care Because You Do / Apr. 25, 1995 / Sire ✦✦✦✦

James' most consistent work, *I Care Because You Do* fuses his earlier hardcore techno days with the smooth rhythm and atmosphere of his ambient work, often on the same song. "Ventolin" is one of the harshest singles ever recorded; the orchestrated closer "Next Heap With" is the highlight of the album. *—John Bush*

Richard D. James Album / Nov. 4, 1996 / Elektra ✦✦✦✦✦

Perhaps inspired by the experimental drum'n'bass being created by Squarepusher (a recent signee to his Rephlex label), Richard D. James' third major-label album as Aphex Twin was his first to work with jungle—though, to his credit, he had released the break-beat EP *Hangable Auto Bulb* almost a year earlier. Contemporaries Orbital and Underworld were beginning to incorporate moderate use of drum'n'bass in their work as well, but this album was more extreme than virtually all jungle being made at the time. The beats are jackhammer quick and even more jarring considering what is—for the most part—laid over the top: the same fragile, slow-moving melodies that characterized Aphex Twin's earlier ambient works. Most overtly disturbing is "Milkman," the first straight-ahead vocal track from Aphex Twin; the song is a child-like ode that gradually deteriorates into a bizarre fantasy concerning the milkman's wife. With all the Aphex Twin's curious idiosyncracies, though, *Richard D. James Album* is a very listenable record and a worthy follow-up to *I Care Because You Do.* (The American issue features the English EP "Girl/Boy.") *—John Bush*

Drukqs / Oct. 2001 / Warp/Sire ✦✦✦✦

Fiona Apple

b. 1977

Vocals / Adult Alternative Pop/Rock, Alternative Pop/Rock, Singer/Songwriter

Singer/songwriter Fiona Apple gained a recording contract in 1995 as one in a crop of mid-'90s female artists, but her confessional writing and throaty vocals made the teenager sound like much more than just the latest flavor. Born in 1977 in New York to singer Diana McAfee and actor Brandon Maggart, Fiona Apple began playing the piano at the age of eight and started composing her own songs just four years later, after the separation of her parents and her own brutal rape. After leaving high school at the age of 16, she journeyed to Los Angeles to see her father and make a demo tape of her songs. After several months of tape-passing, Sony Music signed Apple in 1995. After recording *Tidal* with producer Andrew Slater, she released the album in mid-1996 and began touring. Constant videoplay of the single "Shadowboxer" on both MTV and VH1 brought *Tidal* into the upper reaches of the album charts. The long-awaited *When the Pawn Hits the Conflicts He Thinks Like a King What He Knows Throws the Blows When He Goes to the Fight and He'll Win the Whole Thing 'Fore He Enters the Ring There's No Body to Batter When Your Mind Is Your Might So When You Go Solo, You Hold Your Own Hand and Remember That Depth Is the Greatest of Heights and if You Know Where You Stand, Then You Know Where to Land and if You Fall It Won't Matter, 'Cuz You'll Know That You're Right*—the album's full title—followed in 1999. *—John Bush*

Tidal / Jul. 23, 1996 / Clean Slate/Epic ✦✦✦✦

Fiona Apple demonstrates considerable talent on her debut album *Tidal*, but it is unformed, unfocused talent. Her voice is surprisingly rich and supple for a teenager, and her jazzy, sophisticated piano playing also belies her age. Given the right material, such talents could have flourished, but she has concentrated on her own compositions, which are nowhere near as impressive as her musicianship. Most of *Tidal* is comprised of confessional singer-songwriter material, and while they strive to say something deep and important, much of the lyrics settle for cliches. Apple does have a handful of impressive songs on *Tidal*, like the haunting "Shadowboxer" and "Sullen Girl," but the gap between her performing talents and songwriting skills is too large to make the album anything more than a promising, and very intriguing, debut. *—Stephen Thomas Erlewine*

● **When the Pawn Hits the Conflicts He Thinks Like a King . . .** / Nov. 9, 1999 / Clean Slate/Epic ✦✦✦✦✦

Fiona Apple may have been grouped in with the other female singer/songwriters who dominated the pop charts in 1996 and 1997, but she stood out by virtue of her grand ambitions and considerable musical sophistication. Even though her 1996 debut *Tidal* occasionally was hampered by naiveté, it showcased a gifted young artist in the process of finding her voice. Even so, the artistic leap between *Tidal* and its long-awaited 1999 sequel *When the Pawn Hits . . .* is startling. It's evident that not only have Apple's ambitions grown, so has her confidence—few artists would open themselves up to the ridicule that comes with having a 90-word poem function as the full title, but that captures the fearless feeling of the record. Apple doesn't break from the jazzy pop of *Tidal* on *Pawn*, choosing instead to refine her sound and then expand its horizons. Although there are echoes of everything from Nina Simone to Aimee Mann on the record, it's not easy to spot specific influences, because this is truly an individual work. As a songwriter, she balances her words and melodies skillfully, no longer sounding self-conscious as she crafts highly personal, slightly cryptic songs that never sound precocious or insular. With producer Jon Brion, she created the ideal arrangements for these idiosyncratic songs, finding a multi-layered sound that's simultaneously elegant and carnival-esque. As a result, *Pawn* is immediately grabbing, and instead of fading upon further plays, it reveals more with each listen, whether it's a lyrical turn of phrase or an unexpected twist in the arrangement; what's more, Apple has made it as rich emotionally as it is musically. That's quite a feat for any album, but it's doubly impressive since it is only the second effort by a musician who is only 22 years old. *—Stephen Thomas Erlewine*

The Apples in Stereo

f. 1993, Denver, CO

Indie Pop, Neo-Psychedelia, Indie Rock, Lo-Fi

Sunny pop band the Apples in Stereo was one of the leading lights of the Elephant 6 Recording Company collective, a coterie of like-minded, lo-fi indie groups—including the Olivia Tremor Control, Neutral Milk Hotel, and Secret Square—who shared musicians, ideas and sensibilities. They were led by singer/songwriter Robert Schneider, a native of the tiny town of Ruston, Louisiana, also home to Jeff Mangum (later of Neutral Milk Hotel) as well as William Cullen Hart and Bill Doss (who formed the Olivia Tremor Control). Throughout high school, the aspiring musicians—all influenced by the likes of the Beatles, the Zombies, Pink Floyd, and Sonic Youth—exchanged home recordings and played in each other's bands. After college, Schneider and Mangum relocated to Denver, Colorado, where Schneider struck up a friendship with fellow Beach Boys fan and bass player Jim McIntyre; after enlisting drummer Hilarie Sidney and guitarist Robert Parfitt, they formed the Apples, and issued their self-titled debut EP on the Elephant 6 label. To avoid confusion with other similarly-named bands, they officially became the Apples in Stereo for 1995's full-length debut *Fun Trick Noisemaker*. In 1996, Schneider produced the Olivia Tremor Control's *Music From the Unrealized Film Script "Dusk at Cubist Castle,"* and later in the year the Apples issued *Science Faire*, a collection of singles and rare material. The Apples in Stereo returned in the fall of 1997 with *Tone Soul Evolution*; shortly after its release, the band signed a distribution deal with Sire and the album was re-released in January of the following year. The excellent *Her Wallpaper Reverie* followed in the spring of 1999, and a year later the band returned with the equally wonderful *The Discovery of a World Inside the Moone*. The group also contributed a song to 2000's *Heroes & Villains: Music Inspired by the Powerpuff Girls*, and in 2001 they released the *Let's Go!* EP, which featured the track from *Heroes & Villains…* along with a cover of the Beach Boys classic of the same name. *—Jason Ankeny*

● **Fun Trick Noisemaker** / May 2, 1995 / spinART/Elephant 6 ✦✦✦✦✦

Childlike and effervescent, the debut album from the Apples (in Stereo) is a pure pop delight, a warm, fuzzy collection of chiming melodies and bubblegum attitudes. The songs—with their parade of references to GummiWorms, Saturday morning cartoons, Green Machines (the Big Wheel's bad-ass cousin), and the Phantom Zone—are wistfully nostalgic, but never naive or kitschy; a refeshingly simple and energetic collection of bright guitar-pop, *Fun Trick Noisemaker* more than lives up to its title. *—Jason Ankeny*

Science Faire / Sep. 1996 / spinART/Elephant 6 ✦✦✦

A collection of rarities cut between 1993 and 1995, *Science Faire* includes the group's 1993 debut seven-inch, recorded when they were simply the Apples, and features alternate versions of *Fun Trick Noisemaker*'s "Tidal Wave" and "Glowworm" along with gems like "Haley." *—Jason Ankeny*

Tone Soul Evolution / Sep. 30, 1997 / Sire ✦✦✦✦

Apples in Stereo have a problem. They appear to want to sound like the Beatles, only they want to add the Beach Boys into the mix. What comes across is a mixed bag of tunes that take a few listenings to get used to. Once you've allowed yourself to get over the sometimes lo-fi sound, *Tone Soul Evolution* comes across as an entertaining album with lots of special moments. A pleasant album. *—James Chrispell*

Her Wallpaper Reverie / Jun. 8, 1999 / spinART/Elephant 6 ✦✦✦✦✦

Her Wallpaper Reverie is the Apples in Stereo's finest effort to date—the band's most overtly psychedelic record, it's also their most experimental, achieving a near-perfect balance between candy-colored popcraft and musique concrete-influenced interludes. In a sense, the disc is a response to the grand ambitions of fellow Elephant 6-ers Olivia Tremor Control and their like-minded *Black Foliage* album, but the Apples' integration of Beatlesque melodies and experimental noises is much more seamless; not only are *Her Wallpaper Reverie*'s songs the best Robert Schneider's yet written, but they're produced with a new richness of detail—from the wonderfully Lennon-esque "Strawberryfire" to the Kinks-ish "Ruby," the music positively shimmers. *—Jason Ankeny*

The Discovery of a World Inside the Moone / Apr. 18, 2000 / spinART/Elephant 6 ✦✦✦✦

The Apples in Stereo's third full-length album is a return to their early-'60s Beatlesque sound—as opposed to the experimental, late-'60s Beatles trip on *Her Wallpaper Reverie*. This doesn't mean that *The Discovery of a World Inside the Moone* is a letdown full of derivative, overdone material—the Apples have further fine-tuned their sunny sound and remain defiantly jubilant on songs like "I Can't Believe," "The Rainbow," "All Right/Not Quite," "20 Cases Suggestive Of…," and "Go." The band relies on more backup vocals—as well as horns, beefed-up guitar, squiggly keyboards, and handclaps—which only add to the album's depth. Drummer Hilarie Sidney's stratospheric "20 Cases Suggestive Of…," a rollicking, melodic number that is equal parts melancholy and exuberance, is one of the best tracks on the album. Simplistic lyrics like "She don't like the way you look so she treats you like a crook" (from "Go") are contrasted with more poignant lines like "Once I cut my hand but the wound was not part of me/Now I'm a man there's a wound at the heart of me" (from "Stream Running Over")—and show that the band is turning toward more introspective ideas than they have on previous efforts. Not every song on *The Discovery of a World Inside the Moone* is an uptempo number: "Submarine Dream," "What Happened Then," "Stay Gold," and "The Afternoon" are somewhat cerebral and subdued tracks, and are well done even if they're not as immediately accessible as the other songs. Robert Schneider's lyrics are more emotional and personal here than on earlier releases, and the added intimacy, as well as the musical layers, make *The Discovery of a World Inside the Moone* an intricate, poignant lunar trip. *—Gina Boldman*

Sound Effects: 1995-2000 / Sep. 4, 2001 / spinART/Elephant 6 ✦✦✦✦

Aqua

f. 1996

Euro-Dance, Euro-Pop, Dance-Pop, Hi-NRG

Storming onto the international music scene in the fall of 1997, the Danish dance-pop outfit Aqua aroused controversy when Mattel filed a lawsuit against them for the sexual overtones inherent in their breakthrough hit "Barbie Girl." The roots of the quartet trace back to 1989, when Claus and Søren (both keyboards/drum machine) were working together on the soundtrack for a Danish film, *Fraekke Frida*. During this time they met future member Rene (rap/vocals), who introduced them to Norwegian singer Lene. The four soon formed the band Joyspeed, whose single "Itzy Bitzy" spent one week on the Swedish charts before vanishing. Disappointed with the song's lack of success, the group decided to reinvent themselves as Aqua (allegedly, this name was derived from a poster featuring an aquarium hanging in their rehearsal room). Soon after, they secured another record contract with the Danish label Universal Music, who released their first single, "Roses Are Red," in September 1996. The song stayed on the charts for two months, receiving a platinum record in the process. The follow-up, "My Oh My" (February 1997), went gold in only six days, becoming the fastest-selling Danish single of all time and paving the way for their breakthrough international hit "Barbie Girl." The band's first full-length album, *Aquarium*, was released in September 1997. *Aquarius* followed in early 2000. *—Jeremy Ulrey*

Aquarium / Sep. 9, 1997 / MCA ✦✦✦

"Barbie Girl" is one of those inexplicable pop culture phenomenons—a bouncy, slightly warped Euro-dance song that simultaneously sends up femininity and Barbie dolls. Mattel wasn't too amused, but the public was, making it a huge hit in Europe and America. Like many Euro-pop acts, Aqua isn't capable of delivering another song as insanely catchy as "Barbie Girl," but there's plenty of infectious filler that keeps the album moving along at a nice pace. *—Stephen Thomas Erlewine*

● **Aquarius** / Mar. 21, 2000 / MCA ✦✦✦✦

If ever there was a group that seemed destined for one-hit wonder status it was Aqua. Their huge 1997/1998 hit "Barbie Girl" was a cleverly designed piece of trifle, fueled by delirious Eurodisco beats and the helium-voiced Lene Grawford Nystrom, along with her comically gruff counterpart, Rene Dif. The song was giddy, silly fun, but it was hard to see how they could top it. Indeed, their debut, while entertaining, didn't show a lot of variety. So, it was easy to assume that their second album, *Aquarius*, would disappear upon its release in the spring of 2000. Well, that isn't really the case. Although they may never quite have a hit as large as "Barbie Girl"—particularly in America, where Europop acts are always seen as one-hit wonders (with the notable exception of ABBA)—*Aquarius* is superior to its predecessor in every way. Aqua never strays from their danceable Europop foundation, but they find remarkable variety within that framework. The hooks aren't always the same, the pace is varied and, most importantly, the production is bubbling with details. Each song is an individual creation, from the anthemic ballad "We Belong to the Sea" to the goofy country music parody "Freaky Friday." Every cut is blessed with its own vivid details—banjos, layered vocals, and the cinematic, sweeping strings of "Back From Mars"—thanks to chief producers and songwriters Søren Rasted and Claus Norreen. This is anything but a one-note album, even if Aqua's sonic signatures—the pounding disco beats, the high spirits, the big hooks, and the seemingly mismatched pair of Nystrom and Dif—remain the same. Certainly, *Aquarius* will not change anybody's mind about Aqua or Europop, but it stands as a high-water mark for the genre. *—Stephen Thomas Erlewine*

Arab Strap

f. Scotland

Indie Rock, Alternative Pop/Rock

The Scottish post-folk duo Arab Strap was formed in mid-1995 by vocalist Aidan Moffett and multi-instrumentalist Malcolm Middleton, longtime friends who after years of exchanging cassettes of their respective bands decided to finally begin collaborating together. Upon signing to the hip Chemikal Underground label, they issued their debut single, the stark, downcast "The First Big Weekend"; the song was a major critical hit, with Britain's Radio One declaring it the best record of the decade. In late 1996, Arab Strap issued their full-length debut, *The Week Never Starts Round Here*, followed a year later by the EP *The Girls of Summer*. In 1998, after scoring a hit with their remix of David Holmes' "Don't Die Just Yet," Arab Strap issued their second LP, *Philophobia*. *Elephant Shoe* followed in the summer of 2000 and *The Red Thread* was issued in early 2001. *—Jason Ankeny*

The Week Never Starts Round Here / 1997 / Chemikal Underground ✦✦✦

Philophobia / May 19, 1998 / Matador ✦✦✦

Hearing "Packs of Three" begin Arab Strap's second full album with a gentle electric guitar strum and crisp drum beat is one thing, hearing Moffat softly sing "It was the biggest cock you'd ever seen, but no one knows where that cock has been" is quite another. Put the two together and that's Arab Strap in a disturbing nutshell, once again. With a number of guest performers on keyboards, strings, and other instruments, Moffat and Middleton once again create a series of tense, melancholy, and emotionally eviscerating numbers. Given the album title, meaning "fear of love," it's no surprise that happy-go-lucky tunes aren't anywhere to be found, but then again, that was never the Arab Strap M.O. in the first place. Lyrics as naked, realistic, and ugly as the cover paintings abound, their acid impact again, carefully shaped by the moody arrangements and steady pace throughout. The Albini-tinged production familiar from *Week* recurs here, but the songs themselves feel perversely gentler on the one hand, more anthemic ("Soaps" being a good example) on the other. The ear Middleton has for astonishing, subtle touches—the soft reverb guitar loop ending "Here We Go," the combination of hum and crackle on "Islands," the piano/drum arrangement on "I Would've Liked Me a Lot"—proves its strength time and again on *Philophobia.* Moffat's lyrics are printed in the CD booklet, a useful touch given his varying delivery, but what needs to be heard often comes through all too clearly for comfort, unless one somehow has always had a flawless life when it comes to love, lust, and their foibles. When it comes to the guests, Alan Wylie's trumpet work on "The Night Before the Funeral" is quite lovely, while Adele Bethel duets excellently with Moffat on "Afterwards." *—Ned Raggett*

Singles / Feb. 21, 1999 / Bandai ♦♦♦

Elephant Shoe / Jun. 6, 2000 / Jetset ♦♦♦♦
If both *The Week Never Starts Round Here* and *Philophobia* were one-night stands put to music, *Elephant Shoe* turns out to be skeptical domestication. It is an album unmistakably touched by the vulnerability of being in love—or at least trying to love—as opposed to remembering, yearning for, or altogether avoiding it. Whereas the title of their previous album literally translated to "fear of falling in love," "elephant shoe" is a phrase uttered by Scottish youth afraid of saying "I love you," a way of implying the sentiment while deflecting its articulation. *Elephant Shoe*, in a sense, then, is Arab Strap's warped way of saying those three powerful little words. That doesn't hinder the typical brutal honesty of Aidan Moffat's lyrics. Even his most peaceful and content emotions are infused with hints of violence and misgiving. He is frequently scathing, spitting out ultimatums like "If you go/go for good," but such a breakup couplet suggests a long-term relationship in the first place. There are a fair share of cabaret-soaked moments—funereal soundscapes, mournful cello, lounge piano—but even in the face of Malcolm Middleton's beautifully forlorn electric guitar strumming, an underlying buoyancy is manifested in the use of punchy drum-machine rhythms on songs such as "Cherubs," "One Four Seven One," and "The Drinking Eye." The sex is no longer dirty, the guilt no longer flailing in the dark, and the misery no longer entirely hopeless. It is an emotional step forward that may not be an entirely convincing evolution for Arab Strap—and may, as is love's nature, prove short lived—but it is palpable, and considering their history, it is a courageous progression. *—Stanton Swihart*

Mad for Sadness / Jul. 4, 2000 / Jetset ♦♦♦♦
Arab Strap followed hot on the heels of *Elephant Shoe* (released domestically just a month before) with the stellar live recording *Mad for Sadness.* In many ways, the album differs little from their previous studio work. Aidan Moffat still mumbles bitingly frank—sometimes pathetic, sometimes agonizingly romantic—sentiments steeped in the dirty sweat of sex and regret and self-loathing. The music also betrays the same dozy lope, barely raising above its sloshed, inebriated din. On the other hand, Malcolm Middleton's moody musical constructions—sometimes punchy, sometimes hallucinatory and somnolent—positively glisten in the live setting, and serve due notice that the most important trait of the band is its sound. Even at its darkest and most melancholy, and even stripped of words, the music would shimmer with an insistent urgency that is part drone, part ambience. Eight of the ten songs on the album derive from their first two recordings. Arab Strap proves themselves capable of flawlessly replicating their spare grooves and slow burn on stage, and that further heightens the immediacy of *Mad for Sadness* beyond the level attained by their previous efforts. The excellent "Girls of Summer," with its smoldering electric guitar leads and chaotic shimmer, is the album's high point, and the closing mutant boy-girl duet, "Afterwords," is not far behind. But the music, in general, maintains a wonderful tension so completely that it is the most engulfing album the band has yet made. Each of Arab Strap's albums are worth owning because they are so uniformly compelling, but *Mad for Sadness* is perhaps the most representative album yet from the band. At the very least, it is not a bad first-purchase sampler for those who want to immerse themselves in the beautiful misery of the band's early days. *—Stanton Swihart*

● **The Red Thread** / Feb. 27, 2001 / Matador ♦♦♦♦
Scotland's answer to Walter Becker and Donald Fagen return for their fourth studio record in five years, offering ten more tracks of ribald slack that clock in at an hour. By now, the comparisons to any U.S. indie bands that preceded them seem silly—at no point did Aidan Moffat's tales of infidelity, fidelity, paranoia, and other degrees of romantic unease remotely resemble the bands that they were endlessly linked to. What becomes most evident now is that the comparisons were attributed to slow tempos and little else. It's not that Arab Strap have developed considerably since their first single. Their prolific output since then has been more about refinements than finding their own ground, because they've always been comfortable with their position. Moffat's tales fit somewhere between Pulp's Jarvis Cocker and the Afghan Whigs' Greg Dulli at their darkest, never really committing to either side but striking a sometimes clever but always blunt edge that neither would think to traipse upon. Anyone who has ever heard an Arab Strap song (*understood* might be a better term) will know what Moffat's talking about when he asks to be given something to wipe with on "Infrared." Shattering their previous best moment, "Love Detective" catches Moffat in a Woody Allen moment, as a paranoiac rummaging through a lover's "wee red cashbox" of memorabilia after she mistakenly leaves the key behind. Arab Strap's gradual refinements have hit a peak, but don't expect anything new. Slithery programmed beats, tingly guitars, plodding rhythms, and whispered/warbled sing-speak lead the way yet again, with occasional piano licks and strings thrown in for very good atmospheric measure. Just like Becker and Fagen, Moffat and Middleton stubbornly carry on with their unique wares and do so with excellence. Fittingly, both duos are named after sexual implements. *—Andy Kellman*

The Archies

f. 1968
Bubblegum
Not satisfied with his success with the Monkees, bubblegum pop manufacturer Don Kirshner formed this studio group based on the comic books and animated television show of the same name in the late '60s. Hiring an array of seasoned session musicians to support lead vocalists Ron Dante, Jeff Barry, and Ellie Greenwich, the Archies managed to produce several hits in the late '60s under the direction of Jeff Barry, including the massive hit single, "Sugar, Sugar." After a short spark of success, the group promptly vanished, leaving only nostalgic memories. *—Stephen Thomas Erlewine*

The Great Archies / 1998 / RCA ♦♦♦♦
The Great Archies is an 18-track collection that features all of the fabricated pop group's biggest hits, including the number one single "Sugar Sugar," and the Top 10 "Jingle Jangle," and "Bang-Shang-A-Lang." Though it is comprehensive, the album contains far more material than most fans could want—"Sugar Sugar" may be an infectious, guilty pleasure, but that doesn't mean re-writes of the song are enjoyable. Nevertheless, *The Great Archies* remains the definitive compilation. It is all the Archies you could ever need and more. *—Stephen Thomas Erlewine*

● **Absolutely the Best of the Archies** / May 22, 2001 / Varese ♦♦♦♦
Since nobody really remembers more than "Sugar, Sugar" from the Archies, it could be said that Varese's 16-track collection *Absolutely the Best* is more than most will need to hear from the Archies, but the fact of the matter is, if you're even considering purchasing an Archies collection, you'll be happy that there's this much material here. Furthermore, a lot of this is pretty damn good bubblegum, since much of it is written by Len Barry and Andy Kim, so it's well-crafted—and what isn't well-crafted is at least enjoyably dated. True, you have to be well into bubblegum to enjoy this—and, even then, there aren't any lost treasures—but if you are, this is a fun spin. *—Stephen Thomas Erlewine*

Argent

f. 1969, England, **db.** 1976
Album Rock, Pop/Rock, Prog-Rock/Art Rock
After the Zombies broke up, keyboardist/songwriter Rod Argent formed his own band in 1969, which incorporated more classical, jazz, and art rock influences in accordance with Argent's musical training. The group's other members were guitarist/songwriter Russ Ballard, bassist Jim Rodford, and drummer Bob Henrit. Argent's first two albums, *Argent* and *Ring of Hands*, received a fair amount of critical acclaim, but their real breakthrough came with 1972's *All Together Now*, which contained the Top Five smash "Hold Your Head Up"; *In Deep* produced a minor hit in "God Gave Rock & Roll to You," which was covered by Kiss in 1992. By 1974, Ballard had developed his songwriting talents enough to leave for a solo career (Three Dog Night had a Top Ten single in 1971 with his "Liar," from *Argent*), and was replaced by guitarist John Verity and string player John Grimaldi. Without Ballard, the group lost its focus and indulged its tendencies toward extended art rock passages and improvisational solos to somewhat excessive levels. Argent broke up in 1976; Rodford joined the Kinks, while Argent himself recorded several solo albums and became a record producer, working with Tanita Tikaram, among others. *—Steve Huey*

Argent / 1969 / BGO ♦♦♦
With hindsight, it seems as if the Zombies didn't so much come to a halt as split off into two different directions. Colin Blunstone would take the band's poppiest, sweetest elements; Argent would take the gutsier ones, and appropriate the intricate keyboard arrangements (naturally enough, as keyboardist Rod Argent was the leader of both Argent and the Zombies). Neither Blunstone nor Argent would approach the majesty of the Zombies' prime, but they'd offer some pretty fair approximations. And that's what you get on Argent's self-titled debut—a fair approximation of late-period Zombies, with a much heavier hard/progressive rock feel. There's nothing that's nearly as arresting as *Odessey And Oracle*, but it's not bad at all. Includes Russ Ballard's "Liar," the first Argent track to get heavy airplay in the U.S. *—Richie Unterberger*

All Together Now / 1972 / Epic ♦♦♦♦
Thanks to the hit single "Hold Your Head Up," *All Together Now* was Argent's most successful album, and in many ways, it's also their most consistent. Although it isn't quite as interesting as the debut, the band has perfected an anthemic rock that owes as much to hard rock and progressive rock, and cuts like "Be My Lover, Be My Friend," "I Am the Dance of Ages," and "Keep On Rollin'" will appeal to fans of "Hold Your Head Up," even if they lack the wild spark of *Argent.* *—Stephen Thomas Erlewine*

● **Anthology: The Best of Argent** / 1976 / Epic ♦♦♦♦♦
At eight tracks, *Anthology: The Best of Argent* might be a little skimpy, yet it includes all of the band's biggest hits and AOR staples, including "Hold Your Head Up," "Liar," "God Gave Rock & Roll to You," and a reworking of Rod Argent's Zombies hit "Time of the Season." *—Stephen Thomas Erlewine*

Joan Armatrading

b. Dec. 9, 1950, Basseterre, St. Kitts, West Indies
Vocals, Piano, Guitar / Adult Alternative Pop/Rock, Folk-Rock, Singer/Songwriter, Folk-Pop
Born on the island of St. Kitts, British singer/songwriter Joan Armatrading was her country's first Black woman to make commercial inroads into her chosen genre, spicing her take on folk with bits of soul and reggae, and has had a remarkably long, consistent career. Emigrating to England in 1958, Armatrading met lyricist Pam Nestor in a touring production of *Hair*, and the two began collaborating on material later featured on Armatrading's 1972 debut, *Whatever's for Us.* The two ended their partnership afterwards, and

Armatrading resurfaced in 1975 with *Back to the Night*. Featuring former members of Fairport Convention, *Joan Armatrading* catapulted the singer into the U.K. Top 20 and produced her only Top Ten single, "Love and Affection." Armatrading's subsequent albums sold well in the U.K. to her newly established fan base, but only respectably in the U.S., where it took her until 1980 to have a real hit (the all-electric *Me Myself I*). *The Key* also did quite well, but Armatrading remained largely a cult artist with a small but devoted following in America, never quite achieving the stardom she had in Britain. Armatrading has been successful enough to record regularly up through the mid-'90s and continues to tour. *—Steve Huey*

Whatever's for Us / 1972 / A&M ✦✦

Back to the Night / 1975 / A&M ✦✦✦
It was an unusually long time before A&M released a second album from Joan Armatrading, *Back to the Night*. Produced by Vinegar Joe guitarist Pete Gage (and featuring that band's Steve York on bass), the record is something of a transitional work between the singer/songwriter folk of her first album and the warmer melodies of her breakthrough eponymous effort. While it's not a markedly better record than *Whatever's for Us*, there are some appreciable differences. Most of the songs are written by Armatrading herself—only two are carryovers from her collaboration with lyricist Pam Nestor—which places the emphasis on matters of the heart. And it's on this record that glimpses of the greatness to come appear: the upbeat island feel of "Travel So Far," the powerfully intimate "Dry Land," and the inventive melodies of the title track. The Joni Mitchell comparisons still hold, but here Armatrading leans toward the jazzier side of that artist on tracks like "Come When You Need Me" and "Cool Blue Stole My Heart." Unlike her last producer, Pete Gage allows more of Ms. Armatrading to shine through. The backing musicians are again an accomplished lot, including members of Cat Stevens' band and a pre-Police Andy Summers, but there are no precious string arrangements. While this often gets lumped together with her last record, *Back to the Night* is a better bet to please fans of her subsequent work, though fans who pass on both won't be missing any essential hits. *—David Connolly*

Joan Armatrading / Sep. 1976 / A&M ✦✦✦✦✦
Joan Armatrading's eponymous third album is a charmer, almost single-handedly elevating her into the ranks of rock's leading female artists. Up to this point, Joan had shown that she had a lovely voice and an ear for interesting arrangements, but her work had been steeped in the folk idiom of the early '70s. Her third album changed all that, with producer Glyn Johns bringing in members of Gallagher & Lyle, Fairport Convention, and The Faces to punch up her folksy sound with elements of rock, country, and disco. The result is her most muscular music to date, with Joan adopting a swagger that showed her tales of unluckiness in love didn't have to have dire consequences ("Tall in the Saddle," "Water with the Wine"). Of course, it helped that the record featured her best material yet, delivered in a wonderfully expressive voice that can capture the shades between song and speech like a sweeter version of Ian Anderson. "Down to Zero" (which features pedal steel guitarist B.J. Cole) and "Love and Affection" are the album's most memorable tracks, the latter breaking into the U.K.'s Top 10 (the album itself made the U.K. Top 20). But what endears this record to fans is the quality of each song; it wouldn't be fair to call anything here filler. The artsy and eclectic "Like Fire," the beautiful ballad "Save Me," the ingratiating melodies of "Somebody Who Loves You" are just as likely to strike a chord with listeners as the better-known cuts. While Glyn Johns deserves credit for bringing Joan Armatrading's songs into a more flattering setting–it's not coincidental that the record feels like a polished version of *The Who By Numbers*–his real stroke of genius was letting the artist flower to her full potential. For many, this album remains the high point in her catalog. *—David Connolly*

Show Some Emotion / Oct. 1977 / A&M ✦✦✦
Retaining producer Glyn Johns and some of the same session players from her last record, *Show Some Emotion* repeated that album's chart success and included two more terrific singles in the same vein: "Show Some Emotion" and "Willow." However, the rest of the album sounds like outtakes from that effort. Gone is the smooth, honeyfied flow of *Joan Armatrading*; the lyrics seem to lack a sense of meter, the songs occasionally rely on pedestrian R&B arrangements to move them along, and the buoyant melodies are few and far between. Part of the problem stems from poor track placement–the vulnerable "Woncha Come on Home," which would have worked well at the end of side one or two, is an awful choice as the opening track. Placing the similar-sounding "Mama Mercy" and "Get in the Sun" next to each other suggests that Joan even had trouble coming up with filler, and waiting until the end of the album to unleash the energetic "Kissin' and a Huggin'" leaves the listener all charged up for nothing. While the title track and "Willow" are good enough to justify the album purchase alone, they're now available on any number of compilations. Without them, *Show Some Emotion* lacks any must-own material, although the aptly titled "Warm Love," "Kissin' and a Huggin'" and the compelling "Opportunity" are worth hearing. Overall, this feels like a step back after her last effort. The fine voice and smattering of rock, jazz, and island melodies place it as vintage Joan Armatrading, but the material is a cut below her better work. *—David Connolly*

To the Limit / Oct. 1978 / A&M ✦✦✦
She began to up the musical ante with a more rock-oriented approach, and her songs also took a more argumentative tone, especially in the critical "Barefoot and Pregnant." *—William Ruhlmann*

Steppin' Out / May 1979 / A&M ✦✦✦
In 1979, Armatrading's following in the U.S. was not big enough to justify the release of this concert album, although it was recorded in North America. It demonstrates her rapport with her fans and her effectiveness as a live performer and includes such favorites as "Love and Affection" and "You Rope You Tie Me." *—William Ruhlmann*

How Cruel / Nov. 1979 / A&M ✦✦✦
How Cruel is a four-song, one-sided, 12-inch EP released, according to the blurb on the cover, because the tunes were "so good they couldn't wait for an album!!!" (The title track had already appeared, albeit not in the U.S., on the live *Steppin' Out* album.) In fact, the songs are good, although the decision to release them probably had more to do with having something in the marketplace between the autumn 1978 release of *To the Limit* and the spring 1980 release of *Me Myself, I*. The best track is "How Cruel," a complaint about her career ("I had somebody say once I was way too black/And someone answers she's not black enough for me") with a terrific sax solo by Lon Price, although "He Wants Her," with a lazy reggae beat, also impresses. *—William Ruhlmann*

Me Myself, I / May 1980 / A&M ✦✦✦✦✦
On the trio of albums that made her reputation in 1976-1978, *Joan Armatrading*, *Show Some Emotion*, and *To the Limit*, Armatrading relied on the pristine production of Glyn Johns to underscore the sensitivity of her folk-based confessional songs. Here, on her first full-length album in two years, she turned to rock producer Richard Gottehrer and a session band that included Anton Fig, Chris Spedding, and members of the E Street Band, making her case for being a mainstream rocker. The songs were less serious, too, notably the title track, a U.K. hit. (The album's other British chart single was the ballad "All the Way from America," which was more in the style of her earlier work.) The result was the best selling album Armatrading has ever had in either the U.S. or U.K. *—William Ruhlmann*

Walk Under Ladders / Sep. 1981 / A&M ✦✦✦
Dominant keyboard lines and the characteristic fat percussion approach of producer Steve Lillywhite completed Armatrading's transformation from folky to new wave diva on this album. Still, it was songs like "The Weakness in Me" to which old fans responded, although the U.K. hits were "I'm Lucky" and "No Love." Another British Top Ten, the album was less successful in the U.S., consolidating Armatrading's expanded following without propelling her to major stardom. *—William Ruhlmann*

The Key / Mar. 1983 / A&M ✦✦✦
Many of the same musicians from *Walk Under Ladders* return for *The Key*, but gone are that album's warm island airs. Instead, producer Steve Lillywhite wraps—some might say smothers—Armatrading's voice in sophisticated synthesizers (courtesy of Larry Fast) and punchy rock arrangements that are enervating but less inviting than her earlier work. That more aggressive sound didn't come at the cost of commercial success, however, and both "(I Love It When You) Call Me Names" and "Drop the Pilot" (the latter produced by Val Garay) helped push *The Key* into the U.S. Top 40. Armatrading has always been an excellent communicator, and when given the spotlight—as on the otherworldly "I Love My Baby" or the sinister "The Dealer"—she is one of rock's more compelling female artists. Yet the decision to bring Tony Levin's bass up in the mix and find time for Adrian Belew's frenetic solos sells Armatrading's estimable talents short on some tracks. Thankfully, her humor and humanity rise above the arrangements at welcome intervals, notably with "Everybody Gotta Know," "What Do Boys Dream," and "Foolish Pride." Fans of her acoustic music may find *The Key* a little too aggressive for their tastes, but anyone open to modern rock should enjoy this album. *—David Connolly*

Track Record / Nov. 1983 / A&M ✦✦✦✦✦
Track Record was the first anthology of Joan Armatrading's '70s recordings to be assembled, and the 13-track collection remains an excellent sampler of her first eight albums, featuring such highlights as "Me Myself I," "Love and Affection," "Show Some Emotion," and her hit, "Drop the Pilot." *—Stephen Thomas Erlewine*

Secret Secrets / Feb. 1985 / A&M ✦✦✦
Mike Howlett, known for the dance-friendly, keyboard-dominated pop sheen of his productions for groups like A Flock of Seagulls and Berlin, gives a similar sound to Armatrading here (lots of echo on the vocals, lots of shimmering, horn-like synthesizer parts). It isn't really a good fit, though the record sold respectably and produced a minor U.K. chart hit in "Temptation." *—William Ruhlmann*

Sleight of Hand / May 1986 / A&M ✦✦

The Shouting Stage / Jul. 1988 / A&M ✦✦

Hearts and Flowers / Jun. 1990 / A&M ✦✦

Square the Circle / Jun. 23, 1992 / A&M ✦✦✦
Joan Armatrading, who has spent the better part of her career demanding greater commitment and fidelity from men than they seem willing to give her, turns the tables on her 13th album, abandoning herself to lust for "the wrong guy" and unfaithfulness to her beloved. The equation produces interesting, if not always successful, results, such as the characteristically convoluted "Can't Get Over (How I Broke Your Heart)," but makes a poor lead-in to the philosophical "If Women Ruled the World," which proves that sexism sounds just as lame-brained coming from a woman as it does coming from a man. "Not all men kill babies," Armatrading admits, which is certainly a relief to hear. But if women ruled the world, there would be "no more war, no more hate…no more sons dying young." This from a woman who lived under the Margaret Thatcher regime during the Falklands War. *—William Ruhlmann*

What's Inside / Oct. 10, 1995 / RCA ✦✦

● **Greatest Hits** / Jun. 18, 1996 / A&M ✦✦✦✦✦
Greatest Hits features all of Joan Armatrading's biggest hits and best-known tracks, including "Love and Affection," "Show Some Emotion," and "Rosie," as well as the previously unreleased live track, "Kissin' and a Huggin'." The disc is a thorough retrospective and functions as an excellent introduction to the introspective singer/songwriter. *—Thom Owens*

Love and Affection / 1997 / A&M ✦✦✦✦

Love and Affection is a 38-track, double-disc retrospective of Joan Armatrading's entire 20-year history with A&M, containing nearly all of her best material, from hit singles like "Show Some Emotion" and the title track to important album tracks. For casual fans wanting a more detailed and comprehensive compilation than a single-disc greatest hits collection, *Love and Affection* is an excellent summation of Armatrading's many strengths. — *Stephen Thomas Erlewine*

20th Century Masters—The Millennium Collection: The Best of Joan Armatrading / Aug. 29, 2000 / A&M ✦✦✦✦

The Joan Armatrading entry in Universal's discount-priced compilation series *20th Century Masters/The Millennium Collection* is a reduction of the 1996 *Greatest Hits* set, containing 12 of its predecessor's 19 tracks. Concentrating on the 1975-83 period of the singer-songwriter's career and culling tracks from six of her 13 studio albums for A&M Records (plus one song from an EP), the retrospective is faced with the challenge of integrating Armatrading's stylistic shifts during the period. Her 1970s albums, produced by Gus Dudgeon and Glyn Johns, were folk-pop efforts that brought her a fervent cult following, but in the '80s she turned to more rock-oriented producers Richard Gottehrer and Steve Lillywhite, and made records that reflected the influence of new wave music. Compilation producer Mike Ragogna deals with this by sequencing the material in roughly reverse chronological order, so that it begins with the hard-rocking numbers "Drop the Pilot" and "Me Myself I" and ends with the folkie ballads like "Willow" and "Love and Affection." In either style, Armatrading proves to be a versatile alto singer and an original, affecting songwriter, equally accomplished at sensitive tales of romantic conflict like "The Weakness in Me" and tongue-in-cheek satires like "I Love It When You Call Me Names," which starts out sounding like a first-person account of female masochism, only to turn out to be the ardent plea of a "short, short man" to his favorite dominatrix. ("It's their way of loving, not mine," the songwriter finally pipes up.) Although it contains some of Armatrading's best-known songs, the album is only a sampler. It may serve as a modestly priced way for neophytes to get a sense of her work, but those who are already fans will find it an inadequate summing up of her recording career. — *William Ruhlmann*

P.P. Arnold

b. 1946, Los Angeles, CA
Vocals / Uptown Soul, Soul

A soul vocalist who came from a family of gospel singers, Pat (P.P.) Arnold began singing as a four-year-old. She got her start backing Bobby Day before being invited to join the Ikettes, backing Ike and Tina Turner. Arnold toured with them in the '60s, including one stint with the Rolling Stones. Mick Jagger persuaded her to remain in London, and she later recorded for the Immediate label (then run by the Stones' manager Andrew Loog Oldham). Loog Oldham, Jagger, and Mike Hurst produced Arnold's debut LP, *The First Lady of Immediate*, in 1967, which included the single "The First Cut Is the Deepest," which was written by Cat Stevens and later popularized by Rod Stewart. Arnold also had moderate success with the singles "The Time Has Come," "(If You Think) You're Groovy," and "Angel in the Morning" in the late '60s, though they were hits in England and Europe rather than America. Arnold was part of the cast for the play *Catch My Soul* in 1969, and subsequently acted in the television shows *Fame* and *Knots Landing*, plus Andrew Lloyd Webber's *Starlight Express*. Arnold re-entered the music world in the mid-'80s. She sang lead on a Boy George song for the film *Electric Dreams* in 1984 while on 10 Records. She worked with Dexter Wansel and Loose Ends on the single "A Little Pain," which she recorded as Pat Arnold. She then had another English hit with the single "Burn It Up" on the Rhythm King label. The Beatmasters later produced her song "Dynamite." — *Ron Wynn*

● **P.P. Arnold Collection** / May 21, 1991 / Columbia ✦✦✦✦✦

Transplanted American R&B singer hits it big with achingly soulful ballads. A '60s curio and more, especially "The First Cut Is the Deepest." — *Bruce Eder*

● **The First Cut** / May 1998 / Castle ✦✦✦✦

Shortly after arriving in London, it wasn't long until the hip, young, beautiful singer Pat Arnold (who'd just quit the Ikettes) was approached by entrepreneur Loog Oldham to record for his fledgling Immediate label. Britain—its musical artists in particular—had been won over by the soulful black sounds of America. The up-tempo beat of Motown and Atlantic had increasingly been filling dancefloors, and even the Top 30; it was time for the one-time Tina Turner backup artist to stand up on her own. A wise move! Arnold's signing in late 1967 was perfect timing. *The First Cut* (originally released in 1998, now remastered and featuring two bonus tracks) pulls all of Arnold's Immediate material neatly together in one package—strangely, other than "The First Cut Is the Deepest" (1967) and "Angel of the Morning" (1968), few of these recordings dented the British Top 30. However, in retrospect, the perfect combination of husky-voiced American soul, U.K. mod beat, Bacharach-flavored balladry, and Oldham's obsession with the bombastic production techniques of his hero Phil Spector is a pleasure to hear and a wonderful hybrid. This material has a unique sound and feeling, which draws it apart from the "want to be" club soul acts that graced the nation throughout the period. From the ice-cold version of "The First Cut Is the Deepest" to the incredible Small Faces collaboration "(If You Think You're) Groovy," these 28 cuts of mid- to late '60s cross-pollination are a wonderful example of what happened when America and England met. — *Jon 'Mojo' Mills*

Arrested Development

f. 1988, Atlanta, GA, **db.** 1996
Southern Rap, Alternative Rap, Urban, Hip-Hop, Political Rap

One of the major success stories of 1992, Arrested Development was a progressive rap collective fusing soul, blues, hip-hop, and Sly and the Family Stone-influenced funk with political, socially conscious lyrics. The group was founded in the late '80s by rapper Speech and DJ Headliner, who decided to make the transition to a more positive, Afrocentric viewpoint after hearing Public Enemy. Arrested Development's debut album took its title from the amount of time it took the group to secure a record contract; *Three Years, Five Months and Two Days in the Life of…* produced the hit single "Tennessee," a strongly spiritual track that hit the Top Ten and sparked the album to sell over four million copies. Its two follow-ups, "People Everyday" (a rewrite of Sly's "Everyday People") and "Mr. Wendal" did likewise. Accolades poured in; Arrested Development won Grammys for Best Rap Album and Best New Artist, and were named *Rolling Stone's* Band of the Year. The group returned one year later with *Zingalamaduni*, which some reviews hailed as a major work, though overall response was more ambivalent. In 1996, contrary to Speech's earlier assertion that the group would be around for ten or twelve years, Arrested Development officially broke up. Speech went solo and recorded a debut album, which failed to make an impact. — *Steve Huey*

● **3 Years, 5 Months & 2 Days in the Life of …** / Mar. 24, 1992 / Chrysalis ✦✦✦✦✦

Arrested Development delivers an extremely witty and introspective work. Their speech in the arena of rap includes lyrical messages of hope, love, rain, politics, nature, religion, and evolution. The groups five members demonstrate their creative talents and ability to grab hold of and retain the listener. The record is strong and assertive throughout, with little space for weak spots, and is the perfect kind of release to reminisce back into the early 1990s with. An album of spontaneity and energy, Arrested Development leaves their mark as an influential rap/hip-hop act during the 1990s college scene and beyond. — *Shawn M. Haney*

Unplugged / Mar. 1993 / Chrysalis ✦✦

Zingalamaduni / Jun. 14, 1994 / Chrysalis ✦✦✦

Arrested Development's proper follow-up to their smash debut doesn't stray too far from the rootsy Southern hip-hop that made *3 Years* a hit, but it doesn't ignite as frequently as its predecessor. While its best tracks, like "Mister Landlord" and "Prasin," are the equal of "Mr. Wendal" or "People Everyday," there is no statement of purpose on the level of "Tennessee." The album is too unfocused to be as impressive as the debut, yet *Zingalamaduni* shows that the group is more than a one-hit wonder. — *Stephen Thomas Erlewine*

The Best of Arrested Development / Jun. 2, 1998 / EMI-Capitol Special Markets ✦✦✦✦

The Best of Arrested Development is part of EMI-Capitol Special Markets' excellent *Ten Best Series*, a budget-line series that features an artist's ten biggest hits in their original recorded versions. All of the group's seven charting R&B hits—"Tennessee," "People Everyday," "Revolution," "Mr. Wendal," "Natural," "Ease My Mind," and "United Front"—along with three album tracks, like "Fishin' 4 Religion" and "Give a Man a Fish," are here. Although the disc is not sequenced in chronological order, the very fact that all these hits are on one disc at such an affordable price makes *The Best of Arrested Development* a terrific choice for budget-minded casual fans. — *Stephen Thomas Erlewine*

Greatest Hits / Jul. 31, 2001 / EMI ✦✦✦✦

Released only in England/Europe, *Greatest Hits* rounds up pretty much anything that most Arrested Development fans could want from the band—which means that it leans pretty heavily on the first album, containing such hits as "Mr. Wendal" and "Tennessee," plus album cuts like "Fishin' 4 Religion" and the non-LP single "Revolution." There are also two unplugged cuts, which are OK, but the main problem with the collection is that the original version—or even the original single version—of "People Everyday" is not here, only the "Metamorphosis Radio Edit." This isn't enough to sink the collection, but it may be enough for some listeners to wait for a definitive anthology that contains all the original versions of the big hits. — *Stephen Thomas Erlewine*

The Art of Noise

f. Jan. 1984, London, England
Experimental Rock, New Wave, Synth Pop

Anne Dudley, Gary Lanagan, and J.J. Jeczalik were members of producer Trevor Horn's in-house studio band in the early '80s before they formed Art of Noise, a techno-pop group whose music was an amalgam of studio gimmickry, tape splicing, and synthesized beats. The Art of Noise took material from a variety of sources: hip-hop, rock, jazz, R&B, traditional pop, found sounds, and noise all worked their way into the group's distinctly postmodern soundscapes. The trio signed with Trevor Horn's ZTT label, releasing their first EP, *Into Battle with the Art of Noise*, in 1983. The following year, they released the full-length *(Who's Afraid Of?) The Art of Noise!*, which featured the hit single "Close (To the Edit)." 1986's *In Visible Silence* included the U.K. Top Ten hit "Peter Gunn," which featured Duane Eddy on guitar. *In No Sense? Nonsense!*, released in 1987, saw the band experimenting with orchestras and choirs, as well as horns and rock bands. *Below the Waste* (1990) captured the band experimenting with world music; it received a lukewarm critical and commercial reception. — *Stephen Thomas Erlewine*

Into Battle with the Art of Noise / 1983 / ZTT/Island ✦✦✦

☆ **(Who's Afraid Of?) The Art of Noise!** / 1984 / ZTT/Island ✦✦✦✦✦

Art of Noise's first full album consolidated the future shock of the earlier EPs and singles in one entertaining and often frightening and screwed-up package. Rarely has something aiming for modern pop status also sought to destroy and disturb so effectively. The most legendary song is still "Close (To the Edit)," benefiting not merely from the innovative video but from its strong funk groove and nutty sense of humor in the mostly lyric-less vocals, not to mention the "Hey!" vocal hook The Prodigy would sample for "Firestarter." Its close cousin, the title track, brilliantly blends a nagging bass synth, echoed drum, and percussion fills and constantly shifting vocal cut-ups, random noises, and strange melodies. They're just two highlights on this prescient release, though. Part of the thrill of *Who's Afraid* is the sense of juxtaposition and playing around, something still not very common in music and even less so in the pop music genre. The blunt political protest of "A Time for Fear (Who's Afraid)" and the more abstract "How to Kill," achieved via appropriate sampling, slams right up against the rough beat sonics and serene orchestration. If such material had appeared on Rephlex or even DHR in the mid- to late '90s, few would have been surprised. Things aren't all dour and gloomy, though; "Beat Box" captures heavy grooves from said source with quirky vocal bits and soft vibes. Patented Trevor Horn orchestral stabs surface throughout, while Anne Dudley's knack for gentler shadings and dramatic arrangements also comes through clearly, something that would surface ever more strongly in her freelance production career. The full ten-minute version of "Moments in Love" is perhaps her triumph here, a seemingly pretty instrumental turned increasingly strange. *—Ned Raggett*

In Visible Silence / 1986 / China/Chrysalis ✦✦✦
AON hit their stride with the release of this record, while showing their colors in the choices of material—while the usual offbeat AON elements were present, so was "Peter Gunn," with Duane Eddy guesting on guitar. Another AON hit, "Legs," was present, as was the original version of "Paranoimia," enhanced in its single versions by the addition of routines from Max Headroom performed by Matt Frewer, who would later play the digital ding-a-ling on a short-lived TV series. The Frewer versions replaced the original on some pressings, including the original CD, but the original version has since been restored, with both Frewer versions now confined to best-of collections. *—Steven McDonald*

Daft / 1987 / ZTT/Island ✦✦✦✦
The place for Art of Noise neophytes to start, *Daft* collects *(Who's Afraid Of?) The Art of Noise!* and *Into Battle with the Art of Noise*, along with two reworkings of "Moments in Love" from the original U.K. release of that song, to make a fantastic hour's worth of music. If anything, a single or two aside, *Daft* beats out the official *Best Of* compilation by a mile. Having aged superbly with time, AON's early works sound all the more advanced and of the moment, a testament especially to Trevor Horn's excellent production and Anne Dudley's gripping arrangements. Further entertainment comes from the liner notes, which aren't merely state-of-the-art 1984 album design but an apparently barbed attack on the further incarnation of the band from one Otto Flake. The exact seriousness of this is up to the reader. As for the "Moments in Love" versions, both are gentler and more elegant than the already lush original, and none the worse for that, though "(Three Fingers Of) Love" does have rather disconcerting sound effects added to it. *—Ned Raggett*

In No Sense? Nonsense! / 1987 / China/Chrysalis ✦✦✦✦
In No Sense? Nonsense! contains some of the Art of Noise's most compelling work. With this album, Anne Dudley and company expanded their new wave experiments to include more instrumental firepower. In addition to full rock band production (including electric guitars, drums, and synthesizers), this record makes use of brass band, orchestral, and choral music. The result is about as rich and complex as they ever got. *In No Sense? Nonsense!* is probably best known as the album that included their take on the theme from the '50s cop show *Dragnet*, used in the 1987 film version that starred Dan Akroyd and Tom Hanks. That track is certainly the most accessible on the record, but it somehow seems a little too punchy for the primary ambient pop surroundings. It might fit better on a different album. This record is more notable for tracks like "How Rapid?" and "Opus for Four" that engage in fanciful genre blending. At times, the sound almost begins to anticipate later ambient dance artists like Enigma and DJ Shadow. But the Art of Noise are aptly named and consequently limited. Their artful noise collage lacks the visceral impact afforded by those later bands. *In No Sense?* is more often interesting than beautiful. *—Evan Cater*

● **The Best of the Art of Noise** / 1988 / China/Polydor ✦✦✦✦✦
As an overview of Art of Noise's brief output, this best-of can't be beat, though it does inadvertently track their slide from forerunners to recyclers and cultural panderers. The 1-2-3 rush of "Beat Box," "Moments in Love," and "Close (To the Edit)" make this CD worth the money already—at the time of their release, these singles swiped electronic music back from America (by way of Germany) and cut the whole thing up with ridiculous samples (a car starting, the omnipresent orchestral hit) and enjoyable art school posturing. It was like Dada had invaded the charts, circa 1984. But soon, after their break with ZTT and joining China Records, it wasn't long until they were parodying themselves and trying to score pop hits with a recognizable "sound." Singles featured older pop stars trying to score a hit again (Duane Eddy on "Peter Gunn," Tom Jones on "Kiss"), current celebrities riding their own popularity wave (Max Headroom), or cover songs gussied up with a few more car starting sounds (the made-for-hire "Dragnet '88," used in the regrettable film remake). Only "Legs," which even then still borrows all its drum sounds from "Close (To the Edit)," sounds like a real follow up, and—no pun intended—can stand on its own feet. The vinyl version contains the (sometimes preferable) single mixes; the CD and cassette contain 12" remixes, good for the collector, bad on the patience. A similarly covered CD, only in pink (and released two years later), is also called *The Best Of* but focuses more on the group's album tracks. *—Ted Mills*

The Seduction of Claude Debussy / Jun. 15, 1999 / ZTT/Universal ✦✦

Ash

f. 1989, Ulster, Northern Ireland
Indie Pop, Punk-Pop, Britpop, Alternative Pop/Rock
Ireland's punk-pop trio Ash first formed in 1989 when childhood mates Tim Wheeler and Mark Hamilton got guitars for Christmas and established the metal act Vietnam. Nothing more than something for kicks, Vietnam switched to Ash in the early '90s as Wheeler (guitar/vocals), Hamilton (bass), and Rick "Rock" McMurray (drums) aimed to be something more serious. They shared a love for the raw British punk of the Buzzcocks and crafted their musical talents to take the Brit-pop scene by storm at the start of the decade. NME was swooning over these "teen punkers from Belfast" and by 1994 Ash had signed to Infectious Records. They weren't even out of high school before three singles hit the Top Five in the U.K. indie charts. A year later marked Ash's full-length debut with *1977* and a deal with Reprise Records in the U.S. Sharp guitar hooks and exact production work by Owen Morris gained the band the notoriety they'd been wishing for since childhood. They were headlining major festivals—T in the Park, Glastonbury, Roskilde, and Reading—and playing countless club dates across the globe. In fall 1997, female guitarist Charlotte Hatherly was added to the all-male lineup, a definite change for the band's sound and image. With the new bandmate and the end of their teenage years, Ash welcomed anything that came their way. The late '90s marked a maturation for Ash as a unit, as well as individually. Their sound played into heavier guitars while Wheeler's lyrical content experienced a much grittier shift. Their sophomore effort, *Nu-Clear Sounds* (1998), had Butch Vig at the mixing board and it wasn't necessarily their finest moment. NME turned on the band, criticizing Ash's new sound. Harsh words and reviews didn't distract Ash, however. *Free All Angels* followed in April 2001. *—MacKenzie Wilson*

Trailer / Oct. 1995 / Reprise ✦✦✦✦
Imagine classic punk maneuvers crossed with Nirvana and Dinosaur Jr. style leanings, goosed by a bolt of Mega City Four, and you've got this Irish trio's reference points. Such a blueprint sounds unimaginative on paper, but singer-guitarist Tim Wheeler's relentlessly catchy confections stand up to the Britpop vanguard's finest hours. Not surprisingly, then, the band's recorded debut emphasizes stripped-down velocity over finesse. Such priorities aren't surprising, since the band began racking up U.K. indie chart hits before graduating high school! (The original version of *Trailer* appeared in 1994, on Infectious Records.) Still, why quibble about Ash's influences, when the goods are so emphatically delivered? "Punk Boy" and "Jack Names The Planets" could give Green Day a run for its pop-punk roses, while grungier tracks like "Hulk Hogan Bubblebath" stay heavy, without losing their melody. "Day of the Triffids," which references the similarly-titled English thriller, points to the band's love of all things extraterrestrial. The standout track is "Petrol," a characteristically deft exercise in soft-loud, start-stop dynamics that points to the band's maturity—which included second guitarist Charlotte Hatherley, layered harmonies, greater tracking of guitars, and even orchestration, if required. More than a decade after they formed in their native Belfast, Ash's rugged individuality remains intact; here's where it all began. Heavy guitar devotees shouldn't miss this one. *—Ralph Heibutzki*

● **1977** / May 1996 / Infectious/Reprise ✦✦✦✦✦
Two-thirds of Ash were born in 1977, which means that their latter-day punk-pop isn't very catholic. Instead of sticking to the rigid rules of American punk-pop—which means you can't stretch the song past three minutes—Ash takes a cinematic approach to their songs, throwing in elements of power pop, glam, post-Nirvana grunge, and post-Oasis rock. It's a melting pot of pop styles, basically because the members of the band are so young, they haven't conformed to the standards of the indie and punk subcultures. Sure, Ash still uses loud guitars—they're all over *1977*—but they create a distinctive, melodic, and energetic sound that's equal parts heavy grunge and light pop. And while they may indulge in jamming a bit too much, they remain a pop band at heart, capable of turning out epic guitar-pop like "Goldfinger," pop-punk like "Kung Fu," and the lovely but loud "Girl from Mars" with equal flair. *—Stephen Thomas Erlewine*

Live at the Wireless / Feb. 1997 / Death Star ✦✦✦

Nu-Clear Sounds / Sep. 28, 1998 / DreamWorks ✦✦✦
While *Nu-Clear Sounds* lacks the immediate appeal of Ash's previous outing, *1977*, over the course of repeated listens it emerges as the group's most bracing effort to date; the opening maelstrom of "Projects" immediately sets the tone for the record's snarling approach—while there are a few gorgeously pensive moments, like the aptly titled "Folk Song," it's otherwise the raw, straightahead rock album the band's always threatened to make. The addition of second guitarist Charlotte Hatherley galvanizes Tim Wheeler's songs, giving them a dimension and scope they previously lacked—*Nu-Clear Sounds* is above all big and loud, but under its tumultuous surface lies Wheeler's most mature and poignant material yet, from the grippingly elegiac "Low Ebb" to the sweetly romantic "Aphrodite." Subtleties aside, however, *Nu-Clear Sounds* is first and foremost a rock & roll record, with all of the snotty swagger and attitude that the label implies—at a point in pop history at which old-fashioned noise and bombast are at their most unfashionable, Ash has bravely made an album that demands to be heard at maximum volume, and it's a glorious thing to behold. (*Nu-Clear Sounds* received an American release nearly a year after its initial British release. The U.S. version was decidedly different, containing one additional song—their theme for Danny Boyle's 1997 film *A Life Less Ordinary*—a reshuffled track sequence plus several songs given shiny, Americanized remixes by Butch Vig.) *—Jason Ankeny*

Free All Angels / Apr. 16, 2001 / Infectious ✦✦✦✦
Lurching out of disinterest, smelling of old curry and piss, this aging beast can't disguise its intentions. The sounds give it away. The scuttling. The screaming. A jet turbine belting out doo wop. It's the sound of teenagers starting to see premature strands of gray or beginning to feel the bulge of an alcohol gut. But if Ash has learned anything—especially in light of looking like wizened elders amidst all the latter-day King Adoras and JJ72s—it's knowing how ridiculous it is to be petrified of absolutely nothing. This, as it turns out, marks a new band under the same name, one which now likes to chomp at the bit of experienced immaturity. The grease-burn pop/punk of their debut has finally come to

speaking terms with the darker sulks of their follow-up, altering perception from a monstrous lost potential into something more resilient, smart, and human. At times, John Barry conducting the Buzzcocks; at others, EMF covering Petula Clark. *Nu-Clear Sounds* was a mid-adolescent crisis, this is the equivalent of facing the death of youth—laughing at the toothy smile, injecting beetles into its stale marrow—and living it up while you know from the bottom of your heart that you still have a chance to make things, the important things, completely and totally right. —*Dean Carlson*

Ashford & Simpson
f. 1964
Smooth Soul, Quiet Storm, Urban, Disco, Soul
Nickolas Ashford and Valerie Simpson have two careers, as songwriters and as performers, with the former seemingly more important than the latter until the mid-'80s. The two met in 1964 and scored their first songwriting hit in 1966 with Ray Charles' recording of their "Let's Go Get Stoned." After a period at Scepter Records, they moved to Motown, where they wrote hits for the duo of Marvin Gaye and Tammi Terrell ("Ain't Nothing Like the Real Thing," "You're All I Need to Get By"). When Diana Ross left the Supremes for a solo career, Ashford & Simpson wrote "Reach Out and Touch Somebody's Hand" for her. Their own performing career was launched in 1973 with *Keep It Comin'* on Motown and *Gimme Something Real* on Warner Bros. Their first success came in 1977 with the gold-selling *Send It*, which contained the Top Ten R&B hit "Don't Cost You Nothing." *Is It Still Good to Ya*, a second gold album, contained the number two R&B hit "It Seems to Hang On" in 1978. Their career saw a resurgence in 1984 with *Solid*, which went gold. —*William Ruhlmann*

Gimme Something Real / Oct. 1973 / Warner Brothers ✦✦

I Wanna Be Selfish / Jul. 1974 / Warner Brothers ✦✦✦

Come as You Are / Apr. 1976 / Warner Brothers ✦✦✦✦✦
One of Ashford & Simpson's best Warner Bros. albums, especially from a production standpoint. The mix between uptempo and slow, love songs and dance tunes, was perfect, and their interaction had been honed to the point where each anticipated the other. Simpson's soaring vocals and Ashford's less impressive but still strong support, plus their outstanding harmonizing, was at its peak. —*Ron Wynn*

So So Satisfied / Jan. 1977 / Warner Brothers ✦✦✦
The Ashford & Simpson sound has always been lush, sentimental, and soulful, yet subdued. That's the case on this '77 release. The title cut was a moderate hit, and, as always, the sweeping strings, lyrics, and production were first-rate. Ashford & Simpson albums can get extremely sappy, and at times this one did as well. But they're also usually superbly performed and constructed, and this was no exception. —*Ron Wynn*

Send It / Sep. 1977 / Warner Brothers ✦✦✦✦✦
Exuberant lead vocals, great teamwork, and excellent production made this '77 set a top entry in the *Ashford & Simpson* sweepstakes. They were at the top of their production and performance games in the late '70s, cranking out their own hits and also producing everyone in the R&B/soul world from Gladys Knight to themselves. —*Ron Wynn*

Is It Still Good to Ya / Aug. 1978 / Warner Brothers ✦✦✦✦✦
Having written many popular numbers for various artists over the years, the dynamic duo retain that same tradition for this project. The first release from this album was the midtempo "It Just Seems to Hang On." While each verse is conveyed in a soft texture, the chorus jumps with excitement and intrigue, as does the vamp. Prior to this album, the husband-and-wife team had just one prior R&B Top Ten hit ("Don't Cost You Nothing," #10 in 1978). This song had a stronger impact; it stayed on the charts for 17 weeks. But more importantly, it held the number two position on the Billboard R&B charts for five consecutive weeks. The title track was the follow-up single. With its mesmerizing intonation, Ashford & Simpson intensely deliver this classic R&B ballad with all the right ingredients. In spite of the beauty of the song, it only peaked at #12 on the charts in as many weeks. The final release was "Flashback." Not nearly as inviting as its predecessors, this disco number peaked at #70 after five weeks on the charts. Other notables are "Ain't It a Shame," "Get Up and Do Something," and "As Long As It Holds You." —*Craig Lytle*

Stay Free / Aug. 1979 / Warner Brothers ✦✦✦
The title track was spectacular, and the rest of the album was expertly produced, performed, and arranged. Ashford & Simpson dominated the '70s as few couples ever have in any era; they were the textbook blend of classic R&B energy and urban contemporary class and sophistication. Their best material was neither so generic that it lacked soul, nor so soulful that it couldn't attract a crossover audience. —*Ron Wynn*

A Musical Affair / Aug. 1980 / Warner Brothers ✦✦

Performance / Sep. 1981 / Warner Brothers ✦✦✦

Solid / Oct. 1984 / Warner Brothers ✦✦✦✦
Ashford & Simpson have always been the prime representatives in R&B of the joys of wedded bliss, and this extended valentine is their most consistent set as well as their biggest hit ever. —*William Ruhlmann*

● **Capitol Gold: The Best of Ashford & Simpson** / Jun. 21, 1993 / Capitol ✦✦✦✦✦
Ashford & Simpson scored 33 entries on the R&B singles charts between 1973 and 1990, all but one of them on Warner Bros. or Capitol. This compilation licenses the two biggest hits from the duo's tenure at Warner, "It Seems to Hang On" and "Found a Cure," both of which hit the Top Ten, and features the eight Capitol titles that made the R&B Top 40—"Street Corner," "Love It Away," "High-Rise," "Solid," "Outta the World," "Babies," "Count Your Blessings," and "I'll Be There for You." There are also six tracks culled from the five Capitol albums, bringing the disc's time to over 71 minutes. In other words, this is about

as comprehensive an overview of A&S's career as could be managed by one label on one disc. There are good biographical liner notes by compiler David Nathan. —*William Ruhlmann*

Gospel According to Ashford & Simpson / Oct. 29, 1996 / Capitol ✦✦✦✦
15-song sampler of their 1980s work, leaning far more heavily on tracks from the first half of the decade. Includes the hits "I'll Be There for You," "Count Your Blessings," "Street Opera," and "Solid," although one of their biggest, "Outta the World," is strangely absent. More than just about any other single-artist compilation you could name, this is a definitive representation of how mainstream soul often sounded in the 1980s. Which is to say, it often sounded more like adult contemporary pop than soul. —*Richie Unterberger*

The Best of Ashford & Simpson / Aug. 17, 1999 / EMI-Capitol Special Markets ✦✦✦
This compilation features Ashford & Simpson cuts from *Street Opera, High-Rise, Solid*, and *Real Love*, their four Capitol albums. Some but not all of the duo's best recordings are included—Ashford & Simpson were on the downslide at Capitol, their albums were no longer going gold as they had at Warner Brothers, and hits were hard to come by. The best of this lot includes the upbeat "Solid," where they sing about the joys of their long-lasting relationship, and "Street Corner." Ashford & Simpson fans should unapologetically love this, but casual fans might want to go with a more complete "best of" collection encompassing more of the duo's career. —*Andrew Hamilton*

Asia
f. Jan. 1981
Album Rock, Prog-Rock/Art Rock
When they appeared in the early '80s, Asia seemed to be a holdover from the '70s, when supergroups and self-important progressive rockers reigned supreme. Featuring members of such seminal art rock bands as King Crimson (John Wetton), Emerson, Lake & Palmer (Carl Palmer), and Yes (Steve Howe), as well as Geoff Downes from the Buggles, Asia did feature stretches of indulgent instrumentals on their records. However, they also could be surprisingly poppy, and that is what brought them to the top of the charts with their debut album, *Asia*, and its hit single, "Heat of the Moment." *Alpha*, their second album, also had a couple of hits ("Don't Cry" and "The Smile Has Left Your Eyes") but its follow-up, *Astra*, was a flop. The group disbanded in 1985, only to reunite in 1990 without John Wetton; John Payne took his place. After churning out a couple of new songs for a greatest hits collection, the band hit the road, including two sold-out dates in front of 20,000 fans in Moscow, of all places. Thereafter, they toured sporadically and released the albums *Aqua* (in 1992) and *Aria* (in 1994). —*Stephen Thomas Erlewine*

Asia / 1982 / Geffen ✦✦✦✦✦
This marriage of four players with impressive pedigrees proved to be the success story of 1982 when Asia's debut lodged itself at the top of the U.S. album charts for two months. The album spawned a massive number four single in "Heat of the Moment," a follow-up Top 20 hit in the sweeping "Only Time Will Tell," and a handful of other tracks that received heavy radio play despite going against the grain of the new-wave styling of the day. Produced by Mike Stone, *Asia*'s strengths were the powerful vocals of John Wetton, the nimble, classically tinged guitar work of Steve Howe, Geoff Downes' majestic keyboard playing, and anchoring the band, Carl Palmer's propulsive drumming. The lyrics are overwrought at moments, but there's no denying the epic grandeur of the music which provided some much-needed muscle to radio at the time, and did so with style. —*Tom Demalon*

Alpha / 1983 / Geffen ✦✦✦
The eagerly awaited follow-up to the supergroup's debut, *Alpha* landed with a resounding thud a year later. The album still managed to be a platinum selling Top Ten hit, as did the lead-off single "Don't Cry," but where *Asia* managed to make old sounds fresh, *Alpha* fails miserably. Nothing on *Alpha* packs the sheer sonic force of the band's debut. Instead, much of the record is lightweight both lyrically and musically, leaning heavier on keyboard-laden ballads like "The Smile Has Left Your Eyes," which managed to scrape into the Top 40, and "My Own Time (I'll Do What I Want)." The only real meat on the record comes during the last cut, "Open Your Eyes" (and only at the end of the song). Rumored creative differences, the album's lukewarm reception and flagging ticket sales for the ensuing tour led to lead singer John Wetton leaving the band before the year was out. *Alpha* is sorely disappointing, especially coming on the heels of a promising debut. —*Tom Demalon*

Astra / Nov. 1985 / Geffen ✦✦
Asia was always a bland, derivative excuse for a dinosaur rock band, but when their debut album came out in 1982 and sold three million copies, they seemed like a repudiation of the new wave movement, the pop music equivalent of the Reagan revolution in politics. Like Ronnie, however, Asia ran out of gas around mid-decade. True, they were still constructing keyboard-dominated, heroic-voiced arena pop, but suddenly nobody cared anymore, or at least not enough customers to vault them into the Top Ten, and for this kind of band, it's platinum or don't bother. So, first, guitarist Steve Howe took his marbles and went home to Yes, and then the rest of the band packed it in, too. They'd be back, of course, when the money was right. —*William Ruhlmann*

Then & Now / Aug. 1990 / Geffen ✦✦
Despite its sometimes bombastic nature, the debut record by '80s supergroup Asia was a strong collection of melodic, sweeping, muscular arena rock. The band's inability to duplicate that success is documented on *Then & Now*, a 1990 set designed to reintroduce the band to the pop market after a five-year absence. It collects several of the group's bigger singles ("Go" being absent) with new material (with "Voice of America" from 1985's *Astra* inexplicably grouped with the new). The quality declines noticeably from "Heat of the Moment" and "Only Time Will Tell," with the newer material being flaccid musically

and insipid lyrically. The exception being the anthemic "Days Like These," which nearly matches the band's strong debut material. In 2000, Interscope released *The Very Best of Asia: Heat of the Moment (1982-1990)*, which is a far better compilation of the band's best work, including all of their singles and three rare B-sides. —*Tom Demalon*

Aqua / 1992 / Rhino ◆◆

Aria / May 1994 / Mayhem ◆◆◆

Archives, Vol. 1 / Feb. 4, 1997 / Pavement ◆◆◆

● **The Very Best of Asia: Heat of the Moment (1982-1990)** / Jun. 6, 2000 / Interscope ◆◆◆◆
Why Asia was the recipient of so much venomous criticism from the so-called hip music press is baffling. Okay, the original supergroup's members, vocalist/bassist John Wetton, guitarist Steve Howe, keyboardist Geoff Downes, and drummer Carl Palmer, were veterans of reviled progressive rock acts like Yes and Emerson, Lake & Palmer, and perhaps the formation seemed cooked up by dollar-blinded record company brass and even the musicians themselves. But the fact is that Asia expertly combined stellar instrumental prowess with killer hooks and choruses—and, yeah, more than a little bombast—particularly on 1982's self-titled debut. What more could critics who allegedly value virtuoso musicianship and pop craftsmanship want? *The Very Best of Asia: Heat of the Moment (1982-1990)*, while not perfect, is superior to 1990's wretched, poorly conceived compilation *Then & Now* (which somehow considered 1985's "Voice of America" a "now" selection). It's a fine collection for casual fans of splendid hits like "Heat of the Moment," "Only Time Will Tell," "Don't Cry," and "The Smile Has Left Your Eyes." For diehards, it's essential for the three rare B-sides "Daylight," "Lying to Yourself," and "Ride Easy" and the detailed liner notes. Unfortunately, stellar *Asia* tracks "Sole Survivor" and "Here Comes the Feeling" are the choppily edited single versions. The powerful "The Heat Goes On" from 1983's *Alpha* showed the original quartet still had some magic, even if some other material on the album didn't. Krokus' Mandy Meyer replaced Howe on 1985's unjustly ignored *Astra*, which is best represented by the explosive rocker "Go." The oddly enjoyable *Then & Now* cut "Days Like These" features Toto guitarist Steve Lukather. —*Bret Adams*

Associates

f. 1979, **db.** 1991
Alternative Dance, New Romantic, Post-Punk, Alternative Pop/Rock
Formed in Edinburgh, Scotland in 1979, the Associates comprised vocalist Billy Mackenzie and multi-instrumentalist Alan Rankine. Built on an eclectic mix of influences and interests ranging from art-rock to glam and disco, the group debuted with a manic cover of David Bowie's "Boys Keep Swinging," which earned them a contract with Fiction Records. Their 1980 debut LP, *The Affectionate Punch*, was a critically-acclaimed work which expanded the duo's sound into both stark minimalism and melodramatic ballads, earning Mackenzie's powerful voice favorable comparisons to Scott Walker.

After jumping to the Situation Two label, the Associates released a series of singles which explored a continually diverse array of styles and textures. With 1982's "Party Fears Two," issued under their own Associates label imprint, the group finally hit the U.K. Top Ten, and the follow-up singles "Club Country" and "18 Carat Love Affair" both reached the Top 30. 1982's *Sulk* was the group's definitive statement, a fascinating blend of lush, New Romantic popcraft and dark, surreal cabaret stylings.

Following the LP's success, however, relations between Mackenzie and Rankine soured, and the latter left the group for a solo career, releasing the albums *The Day the World Became Her Age* (1986), *She Loves Me Not* (1987), and *The Big Picture Sucks* (1989). Undaunted, Mackenzie retained the Associates name and teamed with Martin Rushent to record an album which went unreleased, although a few of the tracks later emerged on 1985's *Perhaps*, fleshed out by keyboardist Howard Hughes and guitarist Steve Reid.

A long layoff followed, with another album, *The Glamour Chase*, recorded but rejected by label chiefs. In 1990, the Eurodisco-flavored *Wild and Lonely* emerged, and its lack of success effectively ended the Associates' story. In early 1997, while in the midst of preparing for a projected comeback, Mackenzie committed suicide. —*Jason Ankeny*

The Affectionate Punch / Aug. 1980 / Fiction ◆◆◆◆
In short order, Scotland's Associates placed themselves alongside Joy Division, Wire, and Magazine as part of the post-punk elite. Between their geographic location and the love-it-or-loathe it vocal acrobatics of Billy Mackenzie, the duo's ability to be widely regarded as such was hamstrung. Although their debut sounds slightly formative compared to their more art-damaged singles on Situation Two (compiled on *Fourth Drawer Down*) and their chart-blitzing gloss fest *Sulk*, *The Affectionate Punch* is a stellar record that speaks volumes of their singular voice in more ways than one. Ties to Bowie's late '70s phase are tangible vocally, as are the references to the likes of Roxy Music throughout the sexy rhythms and textures, especially Alan Rankine's Phil Manzanera-informed guitar playing. Mackenzie's football field-size vocal range is so fluid that he would have had to put forth a highly conscious effort to sound like an everyday male vocalist. And if you want to compare Mackenzie to other vocalists—scratch, make that *singers*—you might as well toss Billie Holiday into the mix. Rather bizarrely, each of the tracks on the record were laid down to a clicktrack; drums were the last thing added, giving them an unusual and *almost* inessential role when compared to the average rock record. At times they sound rudimentary, almost inessential to the whole. That's not to say rhythm is forsaken, because there are other elements making up for it—witness the thick snapping bass and jolting synth on "A Matter of Gender" or even Mackenzie's singing itself on "Even Dogs in the Wild." Glorious. Fiction remixed the album and re-released it in 1982, re-sequencing the same ten songs featured here. For vinyl hounds, the original sleeve depicts Rankine and Mackenzie as track stars. The remixed version features a headshot of Rankine.—*Andy Kellman*

● **Fourth Drawer Down** / Oct. 1981 / V2 ◆◆◆◆◆
Although the sleeve photos fittingly depict Billy Mackenzie and Alan Rankine immersed in a blue pool of seemingly chilly water, no set of images could bring the sound of the 1981 Situation Two singles collected on *Fourth Drawer Down* into full realization. Those who are familiar with Associates know this because of Mackenzie's operatically soulful voice, Rankine's wildly experimental production, and, when used, his atonal utilitarian guitar playing that seems like it's playing the multi-instrumentalist more than he's playing it. Just as there are Smiths fans who listen intently to Johnny Marr's guitar playing and attempt to block out Morrissey's flamboyance, there surely are numerous beings who tune out Mackenzie's crooning to hone in on Rankine's actions. Those who can appreciate both are in for a real feast, and those who prefer one over the other still have much to sink their teeth into. Cloistered noise fests like the aggressively doomy "Kitchen Person" still rattle the system as well as the best Siouxsie and the Banshees or Cure from the same era. "White Car in Germany," "A Girl Named Property," and "Q Quarters" glean from the three late '70s records David Bowie made with Brian Eno, adding further dementia and corrosion like a torturer would dash salt on an open wound. To wit, this still sounds great front to back; the ballsiness in juxtaposing the A-sides and B-sides demonstrates their depth. The U.K. wing of V2 thankfully made *Fourth Drawer Down* part of their 2000 reissue campaign, improving the sound and adding five extras, including other B-sides and unreleased tracks from the era. —*Andy Kellman*

Sulk / May 15, 1982 / Associates/WEA ◆◆◆◆◆
A jarring, difficult, but richly rewarding album, it's a classic of early '80s U.K. pop and is well worth seeking out in this original version. —*Steve Aldrich*

Perhaps / Feb. 9, 1985 / WEA ◆◆

Wild and Lonely / Mar. 24, 1990 / Circa ◆◆

Popera: The Singles Collection / Dec. 11, 1990 / Sire ◆◆◆◆
While it would be more accurate to call it "The '80s Singles Collection," given the continuing Associates and Billy Mackenzie story through much of the '90s, *Popera* does contain the major hits of the band's curious and wonderful career, along with many should-have-been chart toppers and some fine early obscurities. The result is the best single disc to start with for newcomers, though more hardcore fans will likely miss many of the fascinating tangents and album tracks that could not be included. That minor gripe aside, though, *Popera* lives up to its punnish name in spades. The first four tracks are unsurprisingly the big early '80s U.K. hits, as much controversial landmarks on the charts and via live TV performances as Soft Cell's similarly genre-busting smashes. "Partyfearstwo," elegant, romantic, and the biggest single of them all, "Club Country" and its barbed nightlife paranoia, the sparkling "18 Carat Love Affair," and the remake of Diana Ross' disco hit "Love Hangover" each burst forth with a unique energy and life. The tracks that follow never achieved those chart heights but came close at points, while artistically each was its own lovely universe, ranging from the cabaret morning blues of "Breakfast" and the sweet "Take Me to the Girl" to the giddy "Waiting for the Love Boat," included in two versions. The remake of Blondie's "Heart of Glass" is a touch perfunctory, but Mackenzie's swooning vocals as always save the day. Oddly, the earliest songs appear at the end, five independently released singles that serve to underscore the Associates' uniqueness in post-punk days, scratchy and dark guitar slamming up against bizarre melodies and keyboards. Through it all and all the lineup changes, Mackenzie's soaring, theatrical voice rings out like the unique gift it was, one of the most underrated instruments in modern pop of any stripe. —*Ned Raggett*

Double Hipness / 2000 / V2 ◆◆

The Association

f. 1965, Los Angeles, CA, **db.** 1973
Sunshine Pop, Baroque Pop, Pop
The Association was one of the more underrated groups to come out of the mid-to-late '60s. Creators of an enviable string of hits from 1966 through 1969, they got caught in a shift in popular culture and the unwritten criteria for significance in that field, and never recovered. The group's smooth harmonies and pop-oriented sound (which occasionally moved into psychedelia and, much more rarely, into a harder, almost garage-punk vein) made them regular occupants in the highest reaches of the pop charts for two years—their biggest hits, including "Along Comes Mary," "Cherish," "Windy," and "Never My Love," became instant staples of AM playlists, which was a respectable achievement for most musicians at the time. That same sound, along with their AM radio popularity, however, proved a liability as the music environment around them changed at the end of the decade. Additionally, their ensemble singing, essential to the group's sound and appeal, all but ensured that the individual members never emerged as personalities in their own right. The Association was as anonymous an outfit as their contemporaries the Grass Roots, in terms of any individual names or attributes, despite the fact that both groups generated immensely popular hits that millions of listeners embraced on a deeply personal level. —*Bruce Eder*

And Then . . . Along Comes the Association / 1966 / Valiant ◆◆◆◆◆
The group's debut album may be better listening today than it was in 1966, because it can be appreciated more—and it definitely deserves a better reputation than it has among folk-rock, psychedelic pop, and pop/rock enthusiasts. The album is usually neglected because of the Association's reputation as a soft rock outfit and the prominence of the hits "Cherish" and "Along Comes Mary," both of which are too poppy for most serious '60s archeologists. The original LP was one or two songs short of uniformly high-quality material, but that defect was compensated for by the better numbers and the production of the late Curt Boettcher. Admittedly one of Boettcher's softer creations, *And Then . . . Along Comes the Association* displayed the same creative use of stereo sound separation—the

interlocking instrumental and vocal parts divided in discreet two-channel sound—that was to characterize his work with groups like the Millennium and Sagittarius a little later in the decade. Indeed, *And Then…Along Comes the Association* was among the earliest American rock albums to make full creative use of stereo sound and to exploit it on behalf of a group. In those days, the stereo mix on a rock album was usually little more than an afterthought by the producer and engineer (most of whom hated rock & roll), but Boettcher appreciated just what he had here, with the six singers and instrumentalists in this band, and he spread their work out in front of the listener in vivid detail, giving each "voice" (human and instrumental) a close airing, yet meshing them together as well. (The 1999 Japanese reissue CD extended the running time to almost 50 minutes with the addition of five extra tracks.) —*Bruce Eder*

Renaissance / 1967 / Valiant ✦✦✦

Renaissance was a difficult album for the Association to record. Coming in the wake of a serious hit album (*And Then…Along Comes the Association*) and two huge hit singles ("Along Comes Mary," "Cherish") and at a time when the group was experiencing more bookings than its members had ever dreamed possible, *Renaissance* was rushed out under pressure from the band's label. Alas, *Renaissance* bore little resemblance to its predecessor. For starters, the Association had lost the services of producer Curt Boettcher, who was the architect of the earlier album's extraordinary sound. Additionally, *Renaissance* was comprised entirely of original material, much of which had been written while the group was touring. These songs were competent and showed some flashes of inspiration but, apart from "Come to Me," nothing here offered anything even remotely as catchy as either of the band's two previous singles.

With Association rhythm guitarist Jim Yester's brother Jerry Yester producing, *Renaissance* has a more stripped down, conventional folk-rock feel. Apart from lead guitarist Gary Alexander and wind player Terry Kirkman, none of the other members played on this album, but Alexander is a delight, mixing melodic folk-rock picking and strumming, throwing in a few high-energy licks on one or two numbers, and even using a koto for the album's single, "Pandora's Golden Heebie Jeebies." The latter, despite having a grotesque title when following up a single like "Cherish," is a prize piece of pop psychedelia, all gorgeous harmonies and spaced-out sensibilities backed by a bracing beat. *Renaissance* wasn't a bad album, but was a more routine, predictable recording than its predecessor and, without a hit single to help push sales, it never reached audiences in remotely the same numbers. —*Bruce Eder*

Insight Out / 1967 / Warner Brothers ✦✦✦

The Association's third album is not in a league with its debut, but *Insight Out* is an enjoyable folk/pop-rock album with a few digressions into garage punk, novelty tunes, and psychedelia, all displaying much of what the group did best. The harmonies and choruses are among the most beautifully textured singing in a rock outfit this side of the Beach Boys, while the playing is engaging. *Insight Out* was done somewhat in the shadow of Harper's Bizarre's experimental "Feelin' Groovy" single—the opening number, "Wasn't It a Bit Like Now," was an exercise in nostalgia similar to the later successful songs of Harper's Bizarre. "On a Quiet Night" and "We Love Us" are folk-rock ballads on which the group's harmonies are the highlight, while "When Love Comes to Me" is a breezy little mood piece that resembles a slightly more ornate cousin to Simon & Garfunkel's "Punky's Dilemma."

In that company, the number one single "Windy" (the presence of which helped drive up sales of this album) sounds almost heavy and hard-rocking. It and the accompanying single "Never My Love" (which was later a hit for the Fifth Dimension) are the strongest tracks here. The group's attempt at a harder, garage-band type sound on "Reputation" is passable, but this obviously wasn't what fans were buying the album to hear. The sunshine pop sound of "Happiness Is" and the radiant "Sometimes" were more to the point, and these are prime Association material, comprised of soaring harmonies and hook-laden guitar parts. The 1999 Japanese reissue features state-of-the-art sound, which is the right way to hear this material, with its delicate harmonies, and the harder-sounding mono single masters of "Windy" and "Never My Love" are thrown in as a bonus. —*Bruce Eder*

The Association's Greatest Hits / 1968 / Warner Brothers ✦✦✦✦✦

Beyond representing the best in '60s California pop, the Association blazed trails in album production and the folk-psychedelia genre. With the guidance of L.A. producers Bones Howe, Curt Boettcher, and Jerry Yester, the band deftly mixed airy harmonies, unobtrusive rhythm beats, and subtle "Age of Aquarius" accents from harpsichords, Farfisa organs, fuzz-box guitars, trumpets, and bongos—at times, the sophisticated blend was held together by L.A. session players. And while the group successfully expanded their harmonic horizons on "Requiem for the Masses," they also went a bit beyond their strengths with Jefferson Airplane-esque rockers like "Six Man Band." Luckily, the majority of this hits collection focuses on the band's dreamy combination of polished folk, limber vocal arrangements, and wide-screen instrumental backdrops. The summery program also includes chart-toppers like "Windy," "Cherish," "Along Comes Mary," and "Never My Love," along with progressive pop-and-harmony tracks like "No Fair at All," "Everything That Touches You," and "Time for Livin'." A great introduction to the band's prime work from the latter half of the '60s. —*Stephen Cook*

Birthday / 1968 / Warner Brothers ✦✦✦✦

This is a strong record. Vocally, the intricate harmonies shine, and there is a lyrical depth on some songs that challenge the group's reputation as a mere pop group. Granted, there are some light moments, such as the opening cut, "Come on In" (though the vocals do stand out on this cut). And "Toymaker" and "Hear in Here" show the vocal limitations of the lead singers. But "Like Always" does an excellent job of wryly commenting on the loss of a relationship, with the usual fine vocal interplay. "The Time It Is Today" mixes the political and personal in an effective way. And "Everything That Touches You" (their

final Top Ten) is one of their finest love songs, if not one of their best songs, period. The vocals are as intricate as the arrangement, and the sincerity of the lyrics is very apparent. Production by Bones Howe gives the record a very commercial, clean sound that fits well with the material presented. —*Michael Offord*

The Association / 1969 / Warner Brothers ✦✦

Stop Your Motor / Jul. 1971 / Warner Brothers ✦✦

Waterbeds in Trinidad! / 1972 / Columbia ✦

● **Songs That Made Them Famous** / 1986 / Pair ✦✦✦✦✦

Beyond the hits, all of which are included here ("Windy," "Cherish," "Along Comes Mary"), The Association made stunning orchestral folk-pop that still makes the listener feel good. —*Jeff Tamarkin*

The Association's Golden Heebie-Jeebies / 1987 / Edsel ✦✦

Rick Astley

b. Feb. 6, 1966, Warrington, England
Vocals / Adult Contemporary, Dance-Pop
With his rich, deep voice, Rick Astley became an overnight sensation in the late '80s with his well-crafted dance-pop. Astley was discovered by the producer Pete Waterman in 1985 singing in the English soul band FBI. After that, Waterman's production team—Stock, Aitken & Waterman—took Astley under their wing, writing and producing such impeccably crafted pop singles as "Never Gonna Give You Up" and "Together Forever." After two hugely successful albums in the U.S. and the U.K., Astley grew tired of being labeled Stock, Aitken & Waterman's "puppet" and severed his connections with the team; he resurfaced in 1991 with the soul-injected *Free*, which contained the Top Ten hit, "Cry for Help." —*Stephen Thomas Erlewine*

● **Whenever You Need Somebody** / 1987 / RCA ✦✦✦✦

In the '80s and '90s, England's dance-music team Stock, Aitken & Waterman was often accused of being too slick for its own good, and favoring style over substance. But the producers/songwriters (also known for their work with Dead or Alive and Samantha Fox) should definitely be proud of their work on fellow Briton Rick Astley's often captivating debut album, *Whenever You Need Somebody*. While the high-tech production is very '80s, Astley's soul/pop/dance music approach is very much a production of the '70s—sort of the Average White Band meets Philly soul/disco meets Tom Jones. The best dance music works both on and off the dance floor, and this certainly holds true on such slick yet gritty fare as "Together Forever," "Never Gonna Give You Up," and "Don't Say Goodbye." There are a few weak moments—the lackluster "No More Looking for Love" being a glaring example—but overall, this CD proved Astley to be a welcome addition to the British R&B scene. —*Alex Henderson*

Hold Me in Your Arms / 1988 / RCA ✦✦✦

Apart from "She Wants to Dance With Me," Astley's second album didn't have songs as strong as those on his debut. Most of the album was pleasant dance-pop filler, showing the weaknesses of the Stock, Aitken & Waterman production team. —*Stephen Thomas Erlewine*

Free / 1991 / RCA ✦✦

Body & Soul / Sep. 1993 / RCA ✦✦

At the Drive-In

Post-Grunge, Punk Revival, Indie Rock, Emo
Combining this trademark blend of emotional melodies and upbeat rhythm going at an unpredictable rate, At the Drive-In definitely stuck out of their hometown El Paso, TX. Formed in early 1994, it wasn't long after their first EP *Hell Paso* debuted, followed by a brief tour across the Lone Star State. With the secure line up including Cedric (vocals), Omar, Jim (guitar), Pall (bass) and Tony (drums), ATDI continued on with a second EP entitled *Alfaro Vive, Carajo* with a full-fledged tour of playing empty houses and clubs across the Western United States. A small gig in Los Angeles–with an audience only consisting of nine people–immediately got them the attention from Flipside Records, who put out their full-length *Acrobatic Tenement* in 1996. With their constant energy and a stubborn enthusiasm of continuing on, an audience started to develop courtesy of constant touring and word-of-mouth hype. Their 1997 follow-up EP *El Gran Orgo* was released with more of a melodic bite, but their musical depth and originality still remained. *In Casino Out* followed up in 1998, and 2000 saw the release of *Relationship of Command*. —*Mike DaRonco*

Acrobatic Tenement / Mar. 31, 1996 / Flipside ✦✦✦✦

Though *Acrobatic Tenement* may only be a blueprint for the band's later albums, it comes fully formed—and as forceful as a bullet to the head. Cedric Dixler's barked emotional ferocity is perfectly complemented by nimble dual guitars, while Pall's bass snakes in and out of the heady mix. The result is a lurching masterpiece of an album that threatens to explode—or implode—at any moment. Unlike most hardcore bands, At the Drive-In know the value of subtlety, a trick they use to create an elaborate punk/metal soundscape of rhythms and tempo shifts. Not that these guys don't rock; in fact, slowing down once in a while gives the harder sections even more intensity. This is great music in the tradition of the Stooges and Fugazi, and is reminiscent of both those bands at their best. Not just a great album of the post-everything '90s, but a true timeless masterpiece of oblique lyrical insights and furiously rocking good tunes. —*Ari Wiznitzer*

El Gran Orgo / Apr. 14, 1997 / One Foot ✦✦✦✦

At the Drive-In's *El Gran Orgo* EP fuses punk, hardcore, and emo on tracks like "Honest to a Fault" and "Give It a Name." The EP's original pressing sold out in three days, a testament to At the Drive-In's underground popularity. *—Heather Phares*

In Casino Out / Aug. 18, 1998 / Fearless ♦♦♦♦

Raw energy in both performance and music has not recently been captured by a band quite the way At the Drive-In does. Anyone who has experienced their live show knows just what this five-piece rock/punk/emo band from Texas are capable of. The music takes a lot from driving melodic punk riffs, meshed together with quieter interlocking note-picking. With the catchy and yet powerful music comes extremely forceful, heartfelt, and intense vocals that you can just feel the passion exploding from. Lyrics are often abstract and personal, but not too far gone. This is a must-have for just about anyone—if you buy it and aren't fully amazed, just go see them live and the album will take on an entirely new meaning for you. *—Blake Butler*

● **Relationship of Command** / Sep. 12, 2000 / Virgin ♦♦♦♦

Welcome to the breath-robbing, heart-pounding *Relationship of Command*, an album many have been waiting for with red-faced anticipation since their last EP, the brilliant *Vaya*. On this 11-track masterpiece, so full of adrenaline and swarming moods, ATDI has created one of the most infecting and mind-blowing rock albums in a long time. While most of the tracks are of the more aggressive edge, this is undeniably the band's most focused and well put together and, therefore, best all-around album yet. "Quarantined" and "Sleepwalk Capsules" alone make this album worth purchasing: This music is seamless and inspiring. Electronic movements meshed into "Enfilade" stretch the texture of the album further, into the unique backup vocals of Iggy Pop on "Rolodex Propaganda." Amidst all the rock, there is the undeniably unique edge about ATDI's sound, something that has permeated through their music from the *Hell Paso* 7". Beautiful vocals bursting passion in quirky, abstract, and often thrilling lyrics, youthful energy, driving melodies, and a sense of beyond-the-moment urgency. Moving from Relentless to Grand Royal, as well as to the notorious and mostly infamous producer Ross Robinson, has not killed the band's spirit or sound, as many loyal fans feared it would in the pattern of Jawbreaker, Jawbox, among others. If anything, it has allowed the band to push themselves to new limits, to fulfill what they have been working for relentlessly for so long. This is not a band that could ever be insincere. You can see it in their eyes and feel it in their music and work ethic. ATDI is one of the saviors of true emotional straight-up rock! *—Blake Butler*

Attila

f. 1969, **db.** 1970

Acid Rock, Hard Rock

Rising from the ashes of Billy Joel's Long Island-based rock & roll band, the Hassles, Attila was an embarrassingly discordant duo that also featured the Hassles' Jon Small. Described by Joel at the time as "psychedelic bullshit," their self-titled debut album came out in 1970. A critical and commercial disaster, it featured Joel on a heavily distorted B-3 organ, with an Attila the Hun theme that included Joel and Small's appearance on the cover dressed as Huns. The album's lack of success virtually guaranteed that there would not be another Attila project; the group's demise was also sealed when Joel began an affair with Small's wife, Elizabeth, whom he eventually married. *—Stacia Proefrock*

● **Attila** / 1970 / Back-Trac ♦

Many critics, fans, and college students have spent hours debating the serious question of what the worst album in the history of rock actually is. One listen to *Attila* would provide them with a definitive answer. *Attila* undoubtedly is the worst album released in the history of rock & roll—hell, the history of recorded music itself. There have been many bad ideas in rock, but none match the colossal stupidity of Attila. There's a reason why they're the only heavy rock organ-and-drums duo in the history of rock & roll—it's an atrocious combination. Organ and drum combos work well in jazz, because the musicians know how to balance the dynamics of the two instruments, but in this group of Huns, it becomes an unbearable, unholy noise. Billy Joel decided that the only way a keyboardist could compete with the guitarists popping up in Hendrix's wake was to rig his organ with piles of effects pedals, Leslie organs, distortion, and wah-wah—and use them all at once, while he yells, not sings, and Jon Small flails away haplessly at his drums. It's impossible to make out the riffs, since the organ just sounds like a wall of white noise, and there are no melodies, only shouting. Everything is turned to 11—because it's one louder than 10, innit?—and even when the group tries out a different, slower style, it still sounds the same, because the instrumentation, attack, and effects never change. By the end of the album, it feels as if a drill has punctured the center of your skull—it's that piercing, painful, and monotonous. Joel has gone on record describing the results as "psychedelic bullshit." Remove the word "psychedelic" and you have an accurate description of the album. (By the way, Joel and Small are dressed as Huns on the cover. For some reason, they're standing in a meat locker. It's as if the duo unconsciously knew they were creating the most ridiculous album package in rock & roll history.) *—Stephen Thomas Erlewine*

Rollin' Home / 1986 / Profile ♦

Rollin' Home is a retitled reissue of the *Attila* record. No matter what it's called, it's still a crappy album. *—Stephen Thomas Erlewine*

The Au Pairs

f. 1978, Birmingham, England, **db.** 1983

Post-Punk, New Wave

Blasting into the post-punk consciousness with a tremendous debut album, the Au Pairs, fronted by lesbian feminist Lesley Woods, played brittle, dissonant, guitar-based rock that shared political and musical kinship with the Mekons and (especially) the Gang of Four. The music was danceable, imbued with an almost petulant irony, and for a while, very hip and well-liked by critics. Unlike many bands of the moment, however, the Au Pairs (at least initially) backed it up with searing, confrontational songs celebrating sexuality from a woman's perspective. Also, they took swipes at the conservative political climate sweeping England after Margaret Thatcher's election as Prime Minister. Occasionally, Woods' commitments to sexual and social politics made her sound inflexible, doctrinaire, and hectoring (especially on their OK second album), but at first blush, the Au Pairs were a mighty intimidating proposition, able to take on so much and deliver great music in the process. After a desultory live album in 1983 (*Live in Berlin*), the band split up, and Woods and her bandmates have maintained a low profile. *—John Dougan*

● **Playing with a Different Sex** / 1981 / RPM ♦♦♦♦♦

Opening with the tongue-in-cheek "We're So Cool," the Au Pairs' debut record is a stunner, from Lesley Woods' scratchy guitar and declamatory vocals to lead guitarist Paul Foad's brittle soloing. This is an uncompromising, defiant record that asks no quarter; gender roles are turned upside down, hetero- and homosexual relationships put under a microscope, and theories about sex and sexuality turned upside down. Similarly, the tense political situation in Northern Ireland is harrowingly addressed in "Armagh," which details Tory-sanctioned torture and sexual abuse of wrongly imprisoned Irish women. An unfliching look at the world, *Playing with a Different Sex* is one of the great, and perhaps forgotten, post-punk records. The CD reissue on RPM adds eight significant bonus cuts from 1979-81 singles, which include different versions of tracks from the album and some songs which didn't make it onto the LP in any form. *—John Dougan*

Sense & Sensuality / 1982 / RPM ♦♦♦♦♦

On their second album, the Au Pairs were very much in tune with the growth pangs of the punk/new wave scene as a whole in the early 1980s. In stripping their music to a funkier, more rhythmic essence, and shifting the focus of their lyrics to the personal rather than the political, they lost some of the direct impact (and critical acclaim) of their debut. Musically, however, things were actually more interesting. The addition of horns and imaginative synthesizers allowed for more satisfying sonic diversity. The words were still confrontational, but more obscure in their intent. Although occasionally political (as in the blunt anti-Reagan screed "America"), they were far more concerned with questioning sex/relationship roles (as in "Sex Without Stress," "Intact," and "Instant Touch"). The record didn't get as much attention as their first LP, but it's just as much a touchstone of post-punk. The CD reissue adds six more pop-oriented bonus tracks (four from a BBC broadcast in 1983, and two from a 1983 demo) that were written for their never-completed third album. *—Richie Unterberger*

Live in Berlin / 1983 / AKA ♦♦♦

Recorded at a women's festival in Germany, *Live in Berlin* is an effective document of an economical, measured, and purposeful band, who were always well regarded for their live performances. The Au Pairs weren't the first feminist post-punk group on the block, but they were more accessible than the Slits and generally easier on the ear than the Poison Girls. Lesley Woods' voice dominates proceedings, as usual, and the set list includes most of the notable moments from the Au Pairs' limited catalogue. *—Alex Ogg*

Equal But Different—BBC Sessions 79-81 / 1994 / RPM ♦♦♦

Twenty tracks recorded for the BBC between 1979-1981, representing most of what the group performed on British radio. (Four other tracks from a 1983 session appear as bonus cuts on RPM's CD reissue of the *Sense & Sensuality* album.) It leans most heavily on the first LP and singles (in fact, versions of every single one of the debut album's tracks are here), though there are also a half-dozen songs from *Sense & Sensuality*. No big surprises, with the exception of a couple of otherwise unavailable items, "Ideal Woman" and "Monogamy." The latter tune is the set's clear highlight, as it represents the band's only foray (and quite a good one) into all-out, straightforward, guitar-heavy punk rock. Much of the rest is too monochromatic for the unconverted, but fans should like this. It's a better representation of their live prime than the *Live in Berlin* album, and with 79 minutes running time and meticulous liner notes, it offers terrific value. *—Richie Unterberger*

● **Shocks to the System: Very Best Of the Au Pairs** / Oct. 12, 1999 / Cherry Red ♦♦♦♦♦

Save yourself some money by not purchasing this compilation of the Au Pairs' best material. Instead, hunt down the RPM issues of their two proper albums, *Playing with a Different Sex* and *Sense & Sensuality*. Why? Because buying this Cherry Red compilation will only tell you that you need those two albums. Not only does *Shock to the System* fail to put anything new into circulation that wasn't included on the RPM issues, but the two proper albums feature more detailed liner notes, better graphics, and obviously more material between them. Honestly, the concept of releasing a best-of from a band with only two studio records to their credit is silly, especially when such a thing can't offer anything in the way of non-LP singles or stray compilation tracks. (Completists should be thankful, then, that this disc doesn't suck them in with one or two songs they don't have.) The tracks are well chosen and the material is solid—the Au Pairs were a fantastic post-punk band, after all—but this is catalog recycling at its worst. You're basically getting half of each of their albums; since they're both quite consistent throughout, investing a little time and just a little more money in tracking down the albums would be well worth it. *—Andy Kellman*

The Auteurs

f. 1992, London, England

Neo-Glam, Indie Rock, Britpop, Alternative Pop/Rock

When the Auteurs released their debut album in 1993, the British press linked them with the massively popular Suede as part of a "glam revival." While the band can blast out guitar-drenched rockers like Suede, the Auteurs come to life when they draw from the quiet side of such distinctively English guitar pop bands like the Kinks, the Smiths, and George Harrison. Luke Haines, the group's guitarist, vocalist, and songwriter, writes highly melodic pop songs that combine the airy melodies of Harrison with the cutting social observations of Davies; they're sharp, intelligent songs, full of humor and gorgeous melancholy, even when they're loud rockers. With their two albums, *New Wave* and *Now I'm a Cowboy*, they've earned a devoted cult in the U.K. without gathering much support in the United States. By the time the group released the Steve Albini-produced *After Murder Park* in early 1996, they had even lost most of their cult audience in the U.K.; accordingly, the album was a stiff, even on the indie charts. Before its release, Haines had dropped hints in interviews that the record may be the Auteurs' last; although six months later he released an album with his side project, Badder Meinhoff, a new Auteurs record, *How I Learned to Love the Bootboys*, appeared in 1999. —*Stephen Thomas Erlewine*

● **New Wave** / Mar. 1993 / Hut/Caroline ✦✦✦✦
The debut from the Auteurs hearkens back to the golden years of British pop. The auteur of the Auteurs, Luke Haines, is as acerbic and insightful about modern British life as Ray Davies, singing about marrying showgirls and the upper classes. Songs like "Junk Shop Clothes" and "Bailed Out" have a Merseybeat quality, while "Early Years" points the way to the group's angrier, harder sound. More than just pastiche artists, *New Wave* presents the Auteurs as a group with both wit and heart. —*Heather Phares*

Now I'm a Cowboy / May 31, 1994 / Virgin ✦✦✦✦
On the Auteurs' second album, the tunes are tighter, and the hooks and wit are even sharper than on the first. The band even rocks out (in a refined way, of course) on songs like "Lenny Valentino." Haines continues to write about the scheming rich and shabbily genteel, wrapping his words in loud guitars and sighing cellos. "New French Girlfriend" and "Chinese Bakery" are just two of the gems on *Now I'm a Cowboy*, proving that the Auteurs have plenty to say and a catchy way to say it. —*Heather Phares*

After Murder Park / Feb. 1996 / Hut ✦✦✦✦
The pairing of two curmudgeons like Luke Haines and Steve Albini in a studio seems like a marriage made in heaven to some, and the very thought triggers an instant headache to others. The Auteurs are unlike the typical downtrodden U.S. indie bands Albini works with, but they nonetheless walked out of Abbey Road Studios with their nastiest sounding record. That's probably what Haines wanted, and that's what he got. Grittier guitars and sharper drums don't get in the way of the more intricate arrangements that involve strings and a dash of horn every now and then. First single "Light Aircraft on Fire" is probably the most feisty Haines song yet, kicking down the doors with the opening line "When you cut your lover's slack, you'll get a fucking monster back." Haines' guitar lines sparkle during the chorus but dig like claws during the verses. Ace utility man James Banbury, in his usual Auteurs role as secret weapon, contributes threatening organ swells during the seething "New Brat in Town." *After Murder Park* serves the usual combo platter of growlers and barbed lullabies, but Haines definitely sounds more embittered than usual, quite possibly the result of watching too many of Albini's wildlife videos. He paints plenty of "sucks to be you" scenarios with sneering flair, exposing the corrupted side of humanity just as well as his engineer when he's on the other side of the glass. Not many fates could be worse than having Haines write a song with you as the subject, but listening to him air his insightful dirty laundry is an entirely unique experience. Pretentious and snotty as Haines might be, he's one of the sharpest tools in the shed. —*Andy Kellman*

How I Learned to Love the Bootboys / 1999 / Hut ✦✦✦✦✦
The most refined of England's bands manages to refine itself even further on their fourth disc. *How I Learned to Love the Bootboys* is Luke Haines' most immediate sounding release to date, and even though his claim that each of the record's 12 tracks are singles sounds a bit highfalutin, he's not far off. While each of the Auteurs' three prior LPs are equally arresting, there are points at which the mind tends to wander, but not here. Haines' familiar themes of Englishness, youth, and hooliganism remain, playing like another short movie. The cohesiveness of the record is no small feat, given the wide-ranging sounds and moods.
Opening bedroom tale "The Rubettes" features a delicate, Brill Building lullaby chorus while a repetitive staccato riff offplays the fragility. The title track's quiet chaos has Haines' whispered vocals buttressed by sirens, percolating electro bleeps, and a graceful dub bassline. "Your Gang Our Gang" relocates the fight scenes of *Grease* and *West Side Story* to the streets of London with equal doses of menace and tongue-in-cheek. Tough and joyful at the same time.
Haines and Pete Hofmann attain the band's best production yet. Haines' guitar has never sounded so fittingly sharp while avoiding abrasiveness. Even guitar guru Steve Albini couldn't coax such an ideal sound from his guitar. Haines' supporting cast punches in with some excellent work, providing all the necessary support for an excellent record. Surely the few who have stuck around since *New Wave* are being spoiled rotten by the Auteurs' remarkable consistency. —*Andy Kellman*

Frankie Avalon

b. Sep. 18, 1939, Philadelphia, PA
Vocals / Teen Idol, Pop
Frankie Avalon was the first of the manufactured teen idols, before Fabian and Bobby Rydell and the myriads of other pretenders to the throne who worked the turf with tight black pants and red, red sweaters to the fore while Elvis cooled his heels in Germany. In the late '50s and early '60s, post-Twist and pre-Beatles, these generally untalented pretty boys were the cardboard no-threat remnants of a post-Elvis age. But Avalon had a real musical background to go with the pretty boy looks. He broke into show business as a child prodigy trumpeter, and made a few early records for a subsidiary of RCA Victor. Later on, a local impresario became more impressed with his vocals than his trumpet playing and signed him. His third single, "Dede Dinah," became a Top Ten hit and with 1959's "Venus," Avalon placed his first number one. He gradually eased into more "adult"

fare, and though his chart domination ended in 1962, Avalon reinvented himself as a clean-cut surfer in a wildly successful batch of *Beach Party* movies with Annette Funicello that got him through the '60s in far better shape than most of his colleagues. Though he quit recording, he continued to perform and appeared on an oldies revival show with Bobby Rydell and Fabian into the 1990s. —*Cub Koda*

● **The Best of Frankie Avalon** / Apr. 11, 1995 / Varese Sarabande ✦✦✦✦
The definitive compilation: the original versions of 18 songs from 1958-1962, all but one of them a chart hit of some sort. Has all the Top Ten smashes and a bunch of minor post-1959 singles that found him swinging toward pop crooner material with barely any relation to rock & roll whatsoever. —*Richie Unterberger*

The EP Collection / Mar. 21, 2000 / See For Miles ✦✦✦✦
Another excellent entry in See for Miles' EP series, here's 28 of Avalon's sides for the Chancellor label pulled from various extended-play 45 albums issued in England, Sweden, and France. It's an interesting compendium of hits, B-sides, and album filler ranging from early rockers like "Dede Dinah" and "Gingerbread" to schmaltzy teen fare like "Why" and "Bobby Sox to Stockings." Although not a greatest hits package, it's pretty much all the Frankie Avalon you'll ever need for your collection. —*Cub Koda*

The Avengers

f. 1977, San Francisco, CA, **db.** 1982
American Punk, L.A. Punk, Post-Punk, Punk
The Avengers were a San Francisco-based hardcore punk rock group formed in 1977, featuring Penelope Houston (vocals), Greg Ingraham (guitar), Johnathan Postal (bass), and Danny Furious (drums). They had broken up by the time their only full-length album was released in 1983; the retrospective *Died for Your Sins* followed in 1999. —*William Ruhlmann*

● **Avengers** / 1983 / CD Presents ✦✦✦✦
Although it was released in 1983, this collection represents just about everything San Francisco's late, great Avengers recorded from 1977-78. By contemporary standards, it's by-the-book punk thrash: Greg Ingraham's guitar spews up hairball after hairball of distortion, while Penelope Houston snarls in her best impression of Johnny Rotten. However, contemporary standards diminish what great music this was and what a great band The Avengers were. Dozens of bands came in their wake, but few could recapture the excitement and ferocity of their sound. Houston, who re-emerged years later as a folk-rocker, is in full fury on these 14 tracks, especially the youth culture solidarity anthem "We Are the One" and the tale of desperation "Thin White Line." A few spins of this and you'll hear how The Avengers influenced everyone from Black Flag to X. Yes, they were that good. A forgotten classic. —*John Dougan*

The Average White Band

f. 1972, Scotland, **db.** 1982
Quiet Storm, Funk, Soul
Their self-effacing name to the contrary, Average White Band was anything but—one of the few white groups to cross the color line and achieve success and credibility playing funk, with their tight, fiery sound also belying their Scottish heritage, evoking American R&B hotbeds like Detroit, Memphis, and Philadelphia instead. Singer/bassist Alan Gorrie, guitarists Hamish Stuart and Onnie McIntyre, tenor saxophonist Malcolm Duncan, keyboardist/saxophonist Roger Ball, and drummer Robbie McIntosh comprised the original Average White Band lineup. After adopting the abbreviated moniker AWB, the band's 1974 sophomore effort topped the American pop charts with the instrumental "Pick Up the Pieces." The record's mammoth success was nevertheless tempered by the September 23, 1974 death of McIntosh, who died at a Hollywood party after overdosing on heroin.
Ex-Bloodstone drummer Steve Ferrone replaced McIntosh for AWB's third album, 1975's *Cut the Cake*, which scored a Top Ten hit with its title track as well as two other chart entries, "If I Ever Lose This Heaven" and "School Boy Crush." With 1976's *Soul Searching*, the group reclaimed the full Average White Band name, scoring their final Top 40 hit with "Queen of My Soul." After subsequent outings, including 1978's *Warner Communications*, 1979's *Feel No Fret*, and 1980's *Shine*, failed to recapture the energy of AWB's peak, the group dissolved in 1982, with Ferrone later joining Duran Duran and Stuart recording with Paul McCartney. Gorrie, Ball, and McIntyre reformed Average White Band in 1989, tapping vocalist Alex Ligertwood for their comeback effort *Aftershock*. Oft-sampled by hip-hop producers throughout the 1990s, the group continued touring prior to releasing *Soul Tattoo* in 1996. —*Jason Ankeny*

● **Pickin' Up the Pieces: The Best of Average White Band (1974-1980)** / Sep. 1, 1992 / Rhino ✦✦✦✦✦
Anyone who is seriously interested in '70s soul and funk should own at least three or four Average White Band albums. But if a person insists on allotting himself/herself only one AWB CD, this is the logical choice. All of the essential hits—everything from the sweaty funk of "Cut the Cake," "Pick Up the Pieces," and "School Boy Crush" to the unapologetically romantic "If I Ever Lose This Heaven" is included. Though most of the selections were recorded when AWB was still very much in its prime, a few were made after the Scottish band had peaked. "Let's Go Round Again" (1980) finds AWB taking a glossy pop/disco approach that's hardly in a class with its earlier triumphs, but is likable enough. Most of the selections, however, aren't simply decent; they're excellent. —*Alex Henderson*

David Axelrod

b. Apr. 17, 1936, Los Angeles, CA
Producer / Obscuro, Psychedelic Pop, Baroque Pop, Jazz-Funk
A Grammy award-winning producer for Capitol Records who helmed dozens of great

jazz, funk, and soul records during the 1960s and '70s (by everyone from Stan Kenton to Lou Rawls to the Electric Prunes to Cannonball Adderley), David Axelrod also forged a distinctive musical style while recording several of the most eccentric albums of the '70s. His sound, as immediately recognizable as it is sparse, combined cavernous, heavily mic'ed drums with baroque orchestration (just a step away from overblown) and ahead-of-his-time themes ranging from the environment to heightened mental awareness.

Born in Los Angeles in 1936, Axelrod learned about arrangement and production largely on his own. He began working as a staff producer for the cool jazz labels Specialty and Contemporary, and led a pair of 1959 LPs—*Free for All* by Frank Rosolino and *The Fox* by Harold Land—that developed an earthy response to the trademarked light, airy sound of West Coast jazz.

By the mid-'60s, Axelrod had grown famous in soul and jazz circles for his excellent site recording at concerts, including two of the finest live albums of the era, Lou Rawls' *Live!* and Cannonball Adderley's *Mercy, Mercy, Mercy! Live at "The Club."* Both artists tapped him for studio work as well, and Rawls especially benefited by scoring no less than five pop hits during 1966-67. Capitol rewarded one of its most successful producers just one year later, releasing Axelrod's solo debut, *Song of Innocence*. Based on the visionary, mystical poetry of William Blake (as was its follow-up *Songs of Experience*), the album sounded like nothing else from its era, with melodramatic strings tied to heavy, echoed breakbeats—often supplied by session-drummer supreme Earl Palmer. After *Songs of Experience*, Axelrod turned his attention to the growing plight of the environment with 1970's *Earth Rot*.

Even aside from his burgeoning solo career, Axelrod stayed busy as a producer during the '70s; he recorded several Cannonball Adderley LPs plus works by Gene Ammons and Joe Williams. After 1980's *Marchin'*, however, he took an extended hiatus from recording. Axelrod returned in 1993 with *Requiem: The Holocaust* on Capitol's Liberty subsidiary, and recorded a surprising tribute to roots music (*The Big Country*) two years later. After several big names in the dance community (including DJ Shadow) began sampling Axelrod grooves in the mid-'90s, Stateside released the retrospective *1968 to 1970: An Axelrod Anthology* in 1999. Album reissues appeared the following year, and Axelrod even recorded a remix of "Rabbit in the Headlights," originally by the DJ Shadow project UNKLE. *—John Bush*

Song of Innocence / 1968 / Ascension ♦♦♦♦♦
Producer, arranger, and engineer David Axelrod made his mark with Cannonball Adderley, Lou Rawls, and the Electric Prunes. No one, however, expected him to make his own records. Nonetheless, in 1968 his first concept work was issued under the EMI imprint. His inspiration was *Songs of Innocence*, English poet William Blake's watershed collection of poems; Axelrod set seven of them to music using a bevy of studio musicians and a lot of clout at the label. Using a rock orchestra, Axelrod created a suite that blended pop, rock, jazz, theater music, and R&B that has withstood the test of time. Perhaps the best known tune of this mystical mixture is the jazzed-out, slow groove of "Holy Thursday," with its bluesy bop piano lines and huger than huge string section playing a vamp from a Count Basie tune. Meanwhile, the rhythm section floats a steady, swinging rhythm to the guitars and brass who answer with dramatic harmonics centered around a complex yet elegant melodic, and the guitar itself screams overhead. It's a jazz boogaloo with classical overtones. And yes, it, and the rest of the album, sound as if it would be excessive and awful. This was visionary work in 1968, and withstands the test of time. Axelrod's psychedelia is implied; its compositional form and feeling that drive him to celebrate the wildness and folly of youth with celebration and verve. And as a result, the music here sounds fresh, free of cynicism and hipper-than-thou posturing, remaining new each time it is heard. *Song of Innocence* made critics turn their heads in its day, regarding it as a visionary curiosity piece; today it's simply a great, timeless work of pop art that continues to inspire over three decades after its initial release. *—Thom Jurek*

Songs of Experience / 1969 / Ascension ♦♦♦♦♦
After the modicum of success he'd experienced with his debut, *Song of Innocence*, set to William Blake's epic suite of poems, composer, arranger, and producer David Axelrod turned to the British poet's *Songs of Experience* for inspiration in creating his follow-up album. Using eight of Blake's poems, Axelrod composed a suite that was less rock in its aim and more pop- and jazz-oriented in places, but overall a more orchestral work. Texturizing a symphony with percussive elements and the use of British and Irish folk song, as well as the stylistic inventions of fellow arranger Gerald Wilson for effect, Axelrod created a sobering, and, in places, even melancholy collage of song and lyrical styles that slid rather than drove home its point: that experience is a good but bittersweet teacher. Axelrod's compositions are positively literary here, lush and varied, using as much space as they do sound for dramatic and dynamic effect. His complex use of the various colors the horn section was capable of producing allowed him to create new palettes for the rock instrumentation. The centerpiece of the album is "The Human Abstract"; other notables are the positively majestic "The Divine Image," and the pastoral sadness in "A Little Girl Lost." Axelrod's meditations were getting darker with the times in 1969, but they hadn't yet reached the horrific potential for darkness that they would on 1971's *Earth Rot*. In 1969, Axelrod was still a musical contemplative searching for a sound that best exemplified not only his feelings but also the heady text he sought to sonically illustrate. He succeeded in spades. *—Thom Jurek*

Heavy Axe / 1975 / Fantasy ♦♦

● **1968 to 1970: An Axelrod Anthology** / 1999 / Stateside ♦♦♦♦♦
Confounding dozens of vinyl-philes who'd paid hundreds of dollars for the original LPs, *1968 to 1970: An Axelrod Anthology* compiles 11 tracks from the first (and best) three albums released by David Axelrod, including the two-volume series devoted to William Blake (*Song of Innocence, Songs of Experience*) and the 1970 ecological nightmare, *Earth Rot*. Alongside those tracks are seven of Axelrod's best productions, for soul singers like Lou Rawls (the Buffalo Springfield's "For What It's Worth") and Letta as well as Cannonball Adderley and the psychedelic mystics known as the Electric Prunes. The solo Axelrod tracks are dreadfully spare, usually just cavernous drum pattern and occasional orchestral texture, but the songs have an odd power that grows over time. Overall, *1968 to 1970: An Axelrod Anthology* is quite preferrable to spending collectors' prices for the originals. *—John Bush*

The Axelrod Chronicles / May 30, 2000 / Fantasy ♦♦♦
The first half of this sixteen-track compilation is comprised of Axelrod's 1974 album *Heavy Axe* (which he arranged and conducted, without playing any instruments); the final eight tracks are cuts from 1973-74 that Axelrod produced and/or arranged on albums by Gene Ammons, Nat Adderley, Hampton Hawes, and Funk, Inc. Axelrod's reputation underwent an extraordinary reassessment in the late 1990s, with his instrumental albums and work as an arranger coming to be considered innovative and au courant by some tastemakers. Even taking into account that *Heavy Axe* is just one of many records bearing the Axelrod imprint, one has to wonder if the rehabilitation is in fact unwarranted inflation. It's run-of-the-mill, largely instrumental soul-jazz-funk, split between Axelrod originals and covers of tunes by Stevie Wonder, Carly Simon, Vince Guaraldi, and Cannonball Adderley. It would be eminently suitable for background soundtrack music for 1970s films and made-for-TV movies, and while some such efforts can be good, in this context, that is *not* meant as praise. Do you really want to hear a watery fusion cover of "You're So Vain," with Stephanie Spruill's straining soul vocals? You're welcome to it. Although about a couple of dozen musicians (including Adderley and Gene Ammons) take part in the string- and horn-drenched arrangements, really these aren't that creative. They sound more like quickly assembled, made-to-order filler music for video productions, the horns sometimes sounding rather like those of school marching bands, with touches of early '70s-style electric keyboards and wah-wahing funk-rock guitars. There's an orgiastic wordless female vocal on "Mucho Chupar," if that's your bag. As for the bonus cuts with assorted other artists, these are mostly pretty blah fusion, bearing the stamp of bloated, too-slick circa 1973-74 pop-jazz-rock production. Nat Adderley gets into moodily suave pop-soul vocals on "Quit It," which is about the best of the extras. *—Richie Unterberger*

David Axelrod / 2001 / Mo Wax ♦♦♦♦
After hiding out for six long years, receiving—and cashing—check after check from hip-hop DJs who sampled his material to various ends, the nefarious David Axelrod returns to the scene of his greatest glories, Capitol's Studio B, with a slew of his old musical gang in tow and wrestles a gem of an album from the jaws of antiquity. His first recording in six years is far from the storied excess of either 1993's *Requiem* or 1995's paean to country music, *The Big Country*. Instead, Axelrod has claimed seven songs from a recording begun for Reprise in 1969. It seems Axelrod had been tinkering about with the idea of writing an album based on Goethe's *Faust* for Reprise. His lead sheets had been written and the rhythm tracks were already recorded and put on acetates. For internal reasons at Warner Bros., the album never happened and the material was all but forgotten until Mo' Wax stepped in after hearing about the existence of the acetates. Seven of the nine tracks here come from those sessions. They have been reworked and adorned with orchestral textures. In addition there are two new tracks: "The Little Children," the album's opening salvo, is a collaboration between Axelrod and longtime co-producer H.P. Barnum and West Coast rapper MC Ras Kass; and the other, "Loved Boy," is a reunion between Axelrod and R&B singer Lou Rawls that closes the disc. "Loved Boy" is so heartbreakingly beautiful and moving that, along with the best performances in Rawls' career, it is one of the most personal and poetically honest songs in Axelrod's repertoire. To have it at all after such a fine piece of emotionally and aesthetically satisfying art has already been presented to listeners is a gift beyond the scope of any musician, critic, or music fan to assess. *—Thom Jurek*

Kevin Ayers

b. Aug. 16, 1945, Herne Bay, Kent, England
Vocals, Guitar, Bass / Canterbury Scene, British Psychedelia, Prog-Rock/Art Rock
Kevin Ayers is one of rock's oddest and more likable enigmas, even if often he's seemed not to operate at his highest potential. Perhaps that's because he's never seemed to have taken his music too seriously—one of his essential charms *and* most aggravating limitations. Since the late '60s, he's released many albums with a distinctly British sensibility, making ordinary lyrical subjects seem extraordinary with his rich low vocals, inventive wordplay, and bemused, relaxed attitude. Apt to flavor his songs with female backup choruses and exotic island rhythms, the singer/songwriter inspires the image of a sort of progressive-rock beach bum, writing about life's absurdities with a celebratory, relaxed detachment. Yet he is also one of progressive rock's more important (and more humane) innovators, helping to launch the Soft Machine as their original bassist, and working with noted European progressive musicians like Mike Oldfield, Lol Coxhill, and Steve Hillage. *—Richie Unterberger*

Joy of a Toy / Nov. 1969 / BGO ♦♦♦
As the Soft Machine's first bassist and original principal songwriter, Kevin Ayers was an overlooked force behind the group's groundbreaking recordings in 1967 and 1968. This, his solo debut, is so tossed-off and nonchalant that one gets the impression he wanted to take it easy after helping pilot the manic innovations of the Softs. Laissez-faire sloth has always been part of Ayers' persona, and this record's intermittent lazy charm helped establish it. That doesn't get around the fact, however, that this set of early progressive rock does not feature extremely strong material. Ayers' command of an assortment of

instruments is impressive, and his deep bass vocals and playful, almost goofy song-sketches are affecting, but they don't really stick with the listener. It's no accident that some of the tracks recall early Soft Machine: Robert Wyatt drums on most of the songs, and "Song for Insane Times" is virtually a bona fide Soft Machine performance, featuring actual backing from the group itself. A likable but slight album that is at its best when Ayers is at his folkiest. *—Richie Unterberger*

Shooting at the Moon / Mar. 1970 / BGO ✦✦
Ayers put together a progressive rock supergroup of sorts for his second album, including Lol Coxhill on sax, David Bedford on keyboards, and a 17-year-old Mike Oldfield on bass; all three musicians would go on to notable solo careers in progressive rock and experimental music. The success of this haphazard affair depends on your appetite for disjointed art rock. There's a not inconsiderable amount of challenging jams that owe a lot to avant-garde jazz and electronics. Ayers is better off when he sticks to his greatest strength: the sweet, folky ballads intoned in his unique bass voice, like "May I" and "The Oyster and the Flying Fish," though these eventually segue into discordant instrumental riffing. The title track is an update of an old song from the original Soft Machine repertoire that was performed more straightforwardly (and much more successfully) as "Jet-Propelled Photograph" on their 1967 demos (which have been reissued on numerous packages). *—Richie Unterberger*

Whatevershebringswesing / Jan. 1971 / BGO ✦✦✦✦✦
This album of songs about melancholy and solitude may, at first, seem like a disparate collection. After listening a few times, the essence of the song cycle becomes clear. The near-hit "Stranger in Blue Suede Shoes" and "Song from the Bottom of a Well" are among the standout tracks. *—Jim Powers*

Bananamour / May 1973 / BGO ✦✦✦
A solid, enjoyable collection of songs written from the point of view of Kevin Ayers' own particular brand of existentialism—self-conscious individualism sustained by plenty of wine. The American version of this album contains the near-hit "Caribbean Moon," as well as the Syd Barrett tribute "Oh Wot a Dream." *—Jim Powers*

Confessions of Dr. Dream / May 1974 / BGO ✦✦

Sweet Deceiver / Mar. 1975 / BGO ✦✦✦
One of Ayers' more mainstream efforts. Any album that has Elton John playing piano on a few tracks can't be too weird. That's not to say, though, that this is exactly mainstream in and of itself. Ayers continues to play his offhandedly charming miniatures, with occasional Caribbean rhythms and trademark droll, bemused lyrics. The problem is that while this has its charm while you're listening, little sticks or incites you to return. By this point in his career, Ayers was in danger of catching on a treadmill, restating his idiosyncratic concerns in familiar ways without amplifying them. *—Richie Unterberger*

Odd Ditties / 1976 / Harvest ✦✦✦✦✦
It is indeed an oddity that, for all the considerable ambition of his albums, this collection of singles and unreleased outtakes may be Ayers' most satisfying LP. Why? Perhaps because when he's constrained within the 45 format, he taps his strongest and most endearing qualities: easygoing, singalong melodies, droll, nonchalant (even non sequitur) lyrics, good-natured sotto voce vocals, even female backup harmonies. There's little trace of the inaccessible, difficult (usually instrumental) passages that occupy much of the space on his early albums. Spanning 1969 to 1973, this includes eight tracks that wound up on flop singles, as well as six outtakes from the albums he recorded during this period, though there were no obvious reasons for their exclusion (too pop oriented, perhaps?). These are, indeed, "odd ditties": catchy, with occasional Caribbean rhythms and French lyrics, but way too goofball to be taken to heart by a mass audience, at times sounding like a more together Syd Barrett. Needless to say, none of these nifty tunes were anything close to hits. But if they had been, the world would have been a better place. *—Richie Unterberger*

Yes We Have No Mañanas / Jul. 1976 / BGO ✦✦✦
Although the slick, nearly AOR-style production threatens to swamp the music on this album, the solid songwriting wins out in the end. Ayers has written several songs about achieving stardom; the pithy "Star" is a highlight. A cover of Marlene Dietrich's "Falling in Love with You" is this album's near-hit. *—Jim Powers*

Rainbow Takeaway / Apr. 1978 / BGO ✦✦
By the late '70s, Ayers was faced not only with the problem of increasingly redundant material, but also with the fact that the audience for his brand of weirdo progressive rock was shrinking precipitously, making him sound not just repetitious, but dated. There are still some good moments on this album—the chamber music arrangement of "Strange Song," the brief burst of singalong nonsense called "Hat Song." But it's one of his more faceless efforts, with anonymously laidback arrangements that are more prone to swirling keyboards than much of his previous output. And a song like "Beware of the Dog" is so meandering in its attempt to be likably weird that it's virtually meaningless. *—Richie Unterberger*

● **Kevin Ayers Collection** / 1983 / See For Miles ✦✦✦✦✦
This hour-long chronological sampling of Ayers' Harvest and Island discs features several rare single sides (like "Puis-Je?," the French version of "May I?") in addition to some of his best album cuts. With an extensive biographical essay in the liner notes, this is the ideal place to get acquainted with Ayers' work. *—Jim Powers*

Too Old to Die Young: BBC Live 1972-76 / Sep. 22, 1998 / Hux ✦✦✦
This double-CD contains three programs Ayers broadcast on the BBC from 1972 to 1976. A January 6, 1972 concert at the Paris Theatre in London takes up all of disc one, which is certainly the better half of this package, as it was almost a reunion of the Kevin Ayers & the Whole World lineup that had done *Shooting at the Moon* in 1970. Whole World-ers Mike Oldfield (guitar), Lol Coxhill (sax), and David Bedford (keyboards) are on hand to support Ayers, along with drummer Dave Dufort (who was not on *Shooting at the Moon*). Some singing accompanies the band, and orchestral arrangements also accent their playing on six of the nine songs. The material includes some of Ayers' strongest early material, such as "Lady Rachel," "May I," "Clarence in Wonderland," and "Why Are We Sleeping?" The combination of prog-rock and orchestration sometimes unexpectedly echoes Pink Floyd's *Atom Heart Mother*. On some parts of "Why Are We Sleeping?" you can hear Oldfield fooling around with ideas that would resurface on his own *Tubular Bells*. The sound is good but, unfortunately, the balance between the orchestral instruments and the rock ones is not always optimum, and the vocals are sometimes under-recorded. The second disc is divided between broadcasts from 1975 and 1976 (with Zoot Money on keyboards throughout). It isn't as inspired as the companion CD, either in terms of material or performance. As good-natured material interpreted nonchalantly, it falls between prog-rock and pub-rock, as odd as that combination sounds, highlighted by the Ayers staple "Stranger in Blue Suede Shoes." It *is* a worthwhile supplement to the Ayers library for his fans, particularly the first disc, as it shows dimensions to his arrangements that were not always evident on the studio recordings. *—Richie Unterberger*

Aztec Camera

f. 1980, Glasgow, Scotland
College Rock, New Wave, Alternative Pop/Rock
For most intents and purposes, Aztec Camera is Roddy Frame, a Scottish guitarist/vocalist/songwriter who throughout his career created sophisticated, lush, and nearly jazzy acoustic-oriented guitar pop, relying on gentle melodies and clever wordplay inspired by Elvis Costello. Aztec Camera released their debut album, *High Land, Hard Rain*, in 1983, winning significant critical praise for its well-crafted, multilayered pop. After releasing a stop-gap EP, *Oblivious*, the group's second full-length record, *Knife*, appeared in 1984. Produced by Mark Knopfler, the album was more polished and immediate than the debut, featuring horn arrangements and a slight R&B influence. Three years later, Roddy Frame returned with *Love*, a synthesized stab at pop-R&B, resulting in his greatest commercial success—the album launched four hit singles, including the Top Ten "Somewhere in My Heart." Two years later, Aztec Camera returned to a more guitar-oriented sound with *Stray*. It wasn't as commercially successful as *Love*, yet it was a hit with fans who missed the chiming hooks of Frame's early work. *Dreamland*, released in 1993, followed the same pattern as *Stray* and achieved about the same amount of commercial and critical success. *—Stephen Thomas Erlewine*

● **High Land, Hard Rain** / Jun. 1983 / Sire ✦✦✦✦✦
Some performers never make a bigger splash than with their first record, a situation which the Ramones and De La Soul know all too well. If that's the case, though, said musicians had better make sure that debut is a doozy. Aztec Camera, or more specifically, Roddy Frame, falls squarely into this scenario, because while he has doggedly plugged away ever since with a series of what are, at times, not bad releases, *High Land, Hard Rain* remains the lovely touchstone of Frame's career. Very much the contemporaries of such well-scrubbed Scottish guitar-pop confectionaries as Orange Juice, but with the best gumption and star quality of them all, Aztec Camera led off the album with "Oblivious," a minimasterpiece of acoustic guitar hooks, lightly funky rhythms, and swooning backing vocals. If nothing tops that on *High Land, Hard Rain*, most of the remaining songs come very close, while they also carefully avoid coming across like a series of general soundalikes. Frame's wry way around words of love (as well as his slightly nasal singing) drew comparisons to Elvis Costello, but Frame sounds far less burdened by expectations and more freely fun. References from Keats to Joe Strummer crop up (not to mention an inspired steal from Iggy's "Lust for Life" on "Queen's Tattoos"), but never overwhelm Frame's ruminations on romance, which are both sweet and sour. Musically, his capable band backs him with gusto, from the solo-into-full-band showstopper "The Bugle Sounds Again" to the heartstopping guitar work on "Lost Outside the Tunnel." Whether listeners want to investigate further from here is up to them, but *High Land, Hard Rain* itself is a flat-out must-have. *—Ned Raggett*

Knife / Sep. 1984 / Sire ✦✦✦
Aztec Camera's second album cuts back the ethereal atmosphere, revealing a stripped-down, vaguely R&B-influenced pop sense. *—Stephen Thomas Erlewine*

Aztec Camera / Mar. 1985 / Sire ✦✦

Love / Nov. 1987 / Sire ✦✦

Stray / Jun. 1990 / Sire ✦✦✦✦
A welcome comeback after the flaccid dance-pop of 1987's insipid *Love*, *Stray* is among Roddy Frame's most assured and diverse collections of songs. Unlike previous Aztec Camera albums, there's not one unifying style to the disc, and the variety makes *Stray* one of Frame's better collections. From the assured rocking pop of the singles "The Crying Scene" (the closest thing Aztec Camera ever got to an American hit single) and "Good Morning Britain" (a rousing collaboration with Mick Jones of the Clash and Big Audio Dynamite) to the cool, Chet Baker-ish cocktail jazz of "Over My Head," Frame covers the waterfront, but it's the quartet of songs that constitutes the second half of the album that impress the most. These four songs, "How It Is," "The Gentle Kind," "Notting Hill Blues," and the tender acoustic closer "Song For A Friend," are a loosely connected cycle mingling folk, soul, and pop in varying proportions. Starting with a bitterly cynical denunciation of modern society, the four songs move through sadness and resignation to a hopeful, sweet closure. Shorn of the pretentiousness that mars some of Frame's earlier lyrics—written, to be fair, while he was still in his mid-teens—the lyrics on *Stray* are the first that stand up to Frame's remarkable melodic sense. The simple, low-key production by Frame and Eric Calvi also retreats from the unfortunate excesses of both *Love* and its misbegotten Mark

Knopfler-produced predecessor, *Knife*. With the exception of Aztec Camera's 1983 debut *High Land Hard Rain*, this is Roddy Frame's best album. —*Stewart Mason*

Dreamland / May 25, 1993 / Sire ♦♦♦

Whoever got the idea of putting erstwhile lo-tech pop hero Roddy Frame in the studio with the legendarily hi-tech keyboardist/composer/producer Ryuichi Sakamoto ought to at least get credit for thinking outside the box. And if the experiment wasn't an unqualified success, well, that's what usually happens when you think outside the box. *Dreamland* is far from a failure; by this point in his career, Frame's pop craft is too instinctive to permit that. But Sakamoto does occasionally threaten to overwhelm the songs with his patented super-smooth production and studio fripperies (those strings! those backing vocals!), and in a few cases the songs themselves aren't structurally capable of supporting all that added weight. Several tracks, in particular the rather silly "Spanish Horses," will leave you thinking "Gosh, that was pretty. How did it go again?" And "Safe in Sorrow," a gorgeous pop/soul ballad, feels like it wants to go twice as fast as it does, but can't. All that said, there are some great moments here, including the aching "Let Your Love Decide" and the slightly creepy "Valium Summer"; fans of the Camera should like this album just fine. —*Rick Anderson*

Frestonia / Nov. 14, 1995 / Reprise ♦♦♦

Most of Aztec Camera's albums are similar to each other, featuring Roddy Frame's gently chiming guitars and laidback R&B. *Frestonia* is no exception to the rule. Throughout the album, Frame's meticulous production and sophisticated pop/R&B songwriting blends effortlessly together, providing a seamless sequence of songs. There may not be much to distinguish the songs from each other—or from previous Aztec Camera albums, for that matter—but that just means the album succeeds in sustaining a warm, engaging atmosphere. —*Stephen Thomas Erlewine*

B

The B-52's

f. Oct. 1976, Athens, GA, **db.** 1994
College Rock, Post-Punk, New Wave, Alternative Pop/Rock
The first of many acts to cement the college town of Athens, GA as a hotbed of alternative music, the B-52's took their name from the Southern slang for the mile-high bouffant wigs sported by singers Kate Pierson and Cindy Wilson, a look emblematic of the band's campy, thrift-store aesthetic. The group formed in the mid-1970s after a drunken evening at a Chinese restaurant; the band members had little or no previous musical experience, and performed most of their earliest shows with taped guitar and percussion accompaniment. After pressing up a few thousand copies of the single "Rock Lobster," the B-52's travelled to the famed Max's Kansas City club for their first paying gig. Subsequent appearances at CBGB's brought the group to the attention of the New York press, and in 1979, they issued their self-titled debut album, a collection of manic, bizarre, and eminently danceable songs which scored an underground club hit with a reworked version of "Rock Lobster." The following year, they issued *Wild Planet*, which reached the Top 20 on the U.S. album charts. 1989's *Cosmic Thing* was their most commercially successful effort to date—marked by club-friendly production from Don Was and Nile Rodgers, the album launched several hit singles, including the party smash "Love Shack," "Roam," and "Deadbeat Club." —*Jason Ankeny*

★ **The B-52's** / Jul. 1979 / Warner Brothers ✦✦✦✦✦
Even in the weird, quirky world of new wave and post-punk in the late '70s, the B-52's eponymous debut stood out as an original. Unabashed kitsch mavens at a time when their peers were either vulgar or stylish, the Athens quintet celebrated all the silliest aspects of pre-Beatles pop culture—bad hairdos, sci-fi nightmares, dance crazes, pastels, and anything else that sprung into their minds—to a skewed fusion of pop, surf, avant-garde, amateurish punk, and white funk. On paper, it sounds like a cerebral exercise, but it played like a party. The jerky, angular funk was irresistibly danceable, winning over listeners dubious of Kate Pierson and Cindy Wilson's high-pitched, shrill close harmonies and Fred Schneider's campy, flamboyant vocalizing, pitched halfway between singing and speaking. It's all great fun, but it wouldn't have resonated throughout the years if the group hadn't written such incredibly infectious, memorable tunes as "Planet Claire," "Dance This Mess Around," and, of course, their signature tune "Rock Lobster." These songs illustrated that the B-52's's adoration of camp culture wasn't simply affectation—it was a world view capable of turning out brilliant pop singles and, in turn, influencing mainstream pop culture. It's difficult to imagine the endless kitschy retro fads of the '80s and '90s without the B-52's pointing the way, but *The B-52's* isn't simply an historic artifact—it's a hell of a good time. —*Stephen Thomas Erlewine*

Wild Planet / Sep. 1980 / Warner Brothers ✦✦✦
Conventional wisdom has it that all the B-52's subsequent releases are highly inferior to their debut. While *Wild Planet* is not the rarefied wonder their first platter is, it's still darned good. The songs here are generally faster, tighter, and punchier than previously, though production values are not as wonderfully quirky and detailed; fewer songs here are as over-the-top crazy as the first album's "Rock Lobster" or "52 Girls." These formless selections continue to exhibit a cunning mix of girl-group, garage band, surf, and television theme song influences, all propelled along by an itchy dance beat. "Give Me Back My Man" allows Cindy Wilson a unique opportunity to croon a broad, expressive melodic line. Fred Schneider parades his inimitably nervous vocals on chucklesome ditties like "Quiche Lorraine" and "Strobe Light." The best songs here are "Private Idaho," a wonderfully jittery number that employs a variant on the famous melodic snippet from the *Twilight Zone* theme music, and "Devil in My Car," a delightfully loopy hoot that lays the craziness on very thickly. Performances and sound quality are fine. This album is well worth hearing and recommended. —*David Cleary*

Party Mix / Jul. 1981 / Warner Brothers ✦✦
Mesopotamia / Jan. 1982 / Warner Brothers ✦✦
Whammy! / Apr. 1983 / Warner Brothers ✦✦✦
Following the botched collaboration with David Byrne on *Mesopotamia*, the B-52's decided to craft their fourth album as a return to the pop-culture funk explosion of their debut. Smartly, they decided to not simply replicate the skewed Southern funk of that album, choosing to update their signature sound with drum machines and new wave synths. As a result, it now sounds a little forced and dated, but the best moments—"Legal Tender," "Whammy Kiss," "Butterbean," "Song for a Future Generation"—rank as B-52's classics, and the entire record is certainly entertaining, even with its faults. [*Whammy!* was originally released with a cover of Yoko Ono's "Don't Worry." When the time came to reissue the CD in 1989, the group ran into copyright troubles with Ono and the song was pulled, replaced by "Moon 83."] –*Stephen Thomas Erlewine*

Bouncing Off the Satellites / Sep. 1986 / Warner Brothers ✦✦
Cosmic Thing / Jun. 1989 / Reprise ✦✦✦✦
Many observers were prepared to write the B-52's off after the release of *Bouncing Off the Satellites*. Granted, the album was completed in the wake of Ricky Wilson's death, but the group appeared bereft of new musical ideas and were sounding rather stale. In other words, the last thing anyone expected was a first-class return to form, which is what they got with *Cosmic Thing*. Working with producers Don Was and Nile Rodgers, the B-52's updated their sound with shiny new surfaces and deep, funky grooves—it was the same basic pattern as before, only refurbished and contemporized. Just as importantly, they had their best set of songs since at least *Wild Planet*, possibly since their debut. "Cosmic Thing" and "Channel Z" were great uptempo rockers; "Roam" had a groovy beat blessed with a great Cindy Wilson vocal; and "Deadbeat Club" was one of their rare successful reflective numbers. Then there was "Love Shack," an irresistible dance number with delightfully silly lyrics and hooks as big as a whale that unbelievably gave the group a long-awaited Top Ten hit. The thing is, *Cosmic Thing* would already have been considered a triumphant return without its commercial success. The big sales were just the icing on the cake. —*Stephen Thomas Erlewine*

Best of the B-52's: Dance This Mess Around / 1990 / Island ✦✦✦✦
Released only in the U.K., Japan, and various parts of Europe in 1990, *The Best of the B-52's: Dance This Mess Around* was designed to capitalize on the unexpected success of *Cosmic Thing*. It's an excellent summation of the group's late '70s/early '80s heyday, featuring such staples as "Wig," "Give Me Back My Man," "Song for a Future Generation," "52 Girls," "Private Idaho," "Strobe Light," "Devil in My Car," "Planet Claire," and "Rock Lobster," as well as remixes of "Party Out of Bounds" and "Dance This Mess Around." Even though it ignores the group's most commercially successful period (because it was *released* during that era), it is arguably the best compilation of the group's work, since it has a focus and doesn't contain the chaff (namely, the new songs) that weighs down *Time Capsule*. Anyone looking for a far-reaching overview of the group's career should stick with *Time Capsule*, but *Dance This Mess Around* is a first-rate survey of the band's best (and most groundbreaking) years. —*Stephen Thomas Erlewine*

Party Mix/Mesopotamia / Feb. 1991 / Warner Brothers ✦✦
Good Stuff / Jun. 23, 1992 / Reprise ✦✦
● **Time Capsule** / May 26, 1998 / Warner Brothers ✦✦✦✦✦
Time Capsule is an excellent, 18-track collection that offers a comprehensive overview of the B-52's career, from their kitschy post-punk beginnings to their unexpected chart success in the early '90s. Along the way, all the big songs—"Planet Claire," "Rock Lobster," "Private Idaho," "Quiche Lorraine," "Summer of Love" (in its original mix), "Channel Z," "Deadbeat Club," "Love Shack," "Roam," "Good Stuff"—are here, making this an ideal choice for casual fans. For collectors, there are two new cuts ("Debbie," "Hallucinating Pluto") which are fine, but not particularly noteworthy outside of the fact they're only available on this disc. Then again, the very idea behind *Time Capsule* is to provide a concise introduction for the curious, and on that level, it works perfectly. —*Stephen Thomas Erlewine*

Babes in Toyland

f. 1987, Minneapolis, MN, **db.** 1997
Riot Grrrl, Grunge, Alternative Pop/Rock
Babes in Toyland is about as harsh as rock music gets—guitarist Kat Bjelland screams and thrashes her guitar to the gut-pounding, throttling beat of bassist Maureen Herman and drummer Lori Barbero. Over their two albums and two EPs, the all-female trio offers no escape from their strongly female-oriented, but not necessarily feminist, rock.
Bjelland formed Babes in Toyland in 1987 in Minneapolis, after playing around San Francisco for several years in various bands which featured, at various times, Jennifer Finch of L7 and Courtney Love of Hole. After releasing a single on Sub Pop's singles club, Babes in Toyland came to the attention of Sonic Youth, who took them on a tour of Europe. Soon, they recorded their abrasive debut, *Spanking Machine*, with producer Jack Endino; one more independent EP followed before they signed to Reprise. Between labels, original bassist Michelle Leon left the group.
Sonic Youth's Lee Ranaldo produced their second album, *Fontanelle*, which showed no signs of concession to a major label. In early 1993, the band broke up for several days before re-forming to record the *Painkillers* EP and hitting the road with Lollapalooza 1993.
Even though Lollapalooza offered the group a boost in public exposure, they chose not to capitalize on it; instead, it took them nearly two years before they released a new record, *Nemesisters*, in 1995. With Babes in Toyland on hiatus, Bjelland formed

Katastrophy Wife with husband Glen Mattson; in the spring of 2000, Reprise issued the Babes collection *Lived.* —*Stephen Thomas Erlewine*

Spanking Machine / 1990 / Twin/Tone ♦♦♦♦
Courtney Love was briefly a member of Babes in Toyland in the mid-'80s, and listening to the group's debut album, *Spanking Machine*, more than a decade after it first came out, one can't help but wonder who ended up borrowing from whom. In many ways, *Spanking Machine* sounds like the blueprint for the music Love would make during Hole's first incarnation—all jagged guitars, venomous spat-out vocals, pounding drums, and pit-of-the-stomach rage. But there's no arguing that Babes in Toyland got this sound on plastic first, and this writer would contend that *Spanking Machine* is a more compelling and emotionally powerful work than anything Hole has ever released. Kat Bjelland's songs pull no punches, but there's a purity and razor sharp honesty to songs like "Pain in My Heart" that communicate far more than just their obvious rage and pain, and the band's blunt, muscular attack doesn't obscure the fact their best songs rock hard, and with a rugged but genuine feel for melody and swing; "He's My Thing," "Fork Down Throat," and "Dust Cake Boy" manage to be violent, abrasive, and listenable all at the same time, a fairly remarkable accomplishment. As a guitarist, Bjelland can be best described as an inspired primitive, but with the first word receiving a bit more emphasis than the second, as she serves up shards of brittle noise that cohere into something quite eloquent, and bassist Michelle Leon and drummer Lori Barbero support her with sweaty, primal ferocity. Years before anyone had uttered the words "Riot Girl," Babes in Toyland were radically redefining what women in rock could sound like, and *Spanking Machine* has lost none of its transgressive power with the passing of time—which can hardly be said of, say, *Celebrity Skin.* —*Mark Deming*

To Mother / Jul. 1, 1991 / Twin/Tone ♦♦♦
An EP follow-up that's strong but not life-changing. —*John Dougan*

● **Fontanelle** / Aug. 11, 1992 / Reprise ♦♦♦♦
Babes in Toyland's most focused and powerful statement, *Fontanelle* was vaguely associated with grunge upon its release, and tossed in with the Pacific Northwest-centered riot grrrl movement after the fact. In truth, it lies somewhere in between, its raw punkish fury and metallic grind making it the spiritual kin of L7. *Fontanelle* isn't necessarily explicitly feminist, since the glorious noise of rock & roll is viewed as the ultimate empowerment. And that noise is all over *Fontanelle*—it's arguably the harshest, most abrasive recording to come out of any part of the riot grrrl camp. Like L7, Babes in Toyland are more about pure sound than songs, but the similarities end there. Instead of just grinding away on simple power chords, Kat Bjelland's distinctive guitar work is full of intentionally grating dissonance, which is complemented by the jittery rhythm section. Vocally, Bjelland can move from a faux little-girl coo to a bellowing snarl in the space of one line; put together, all of this imbues *Fontanelle* with a terrifically explosive tension. Fittingly, the closing track features nothing but Bjelland, her guitar, and the sound of breaking glass bottles. Measured by any standard, *Fontanelle* is a frighteningly primal record, one whose sheer ferocity Babes in Toyland never quite captured this convincingly anywhere else. —*Steve Huey*

Painkillers / Jun. 22, 1993 / Reprise ♦♦♦
Painkillers features four solid new tracks, one re-recording, and one track that is a brutal, 35-minute live performance of the *Fontanelle* album. It's a good introduction to the intense, loud punk rock of Babes in Toyland. —*AMG*

Nemesisters / May 9, 1995 / Reprise ♦♦

Devil / 2000 / Almafame Ltd. ♦♦♦

The Further Adventures of Babes in Toyland / Jun. 12, 2001 / Fuel 2000 ♦♦♦
What looks at first glance like something of a career overview from middle America's most beloved all-girl punk band is actually both something more and something less—an odds-and-ends collection of B-sides, live performances, and unreleased (some of them deservedly) songs and alternate versions. The heart of the program is a handful of songs recorded live during the 1993 Lollapalooza tour—these include "Handsome & Gretel," "Spun," and the notorious "Bruise Violet" (widely interpreted as a nasty put-down of the band's former friend Courtney Love). One of the album's best tracks, a brutal and charmingly amateurish rendition of "Ripe," was recorded live in Holland three years earlier. For curiosity seekers, there are cover versions of "We Are Family" and the kitsch classic "Calling Occupants of Interplanetary Craft," as well as a surprisingly straight-faced version of the disco classic "More, More, More," complete with horns. This is not a definitive Babes document, but fans will be sure to get a big kick out of it. —*Rick Anderson*

Baby Bird

f. 1995, Sheffield, Yorkshire, England
Indie Pop, Indie Rock, Lo-Fi, Singer/Songwriter

Baby Bird began as the alias of Steven Jones, a prolific British singer/songwriter who initiated his performing career as a member of the Dogs in Honey "anti-theater" troupe. After buying a four-track machine, he began making his first lo-fi home recordings; over the next several years, he wrote some 400 eclectic pop songs, ranging in content from surreal, comic narratives to intensely personal meditations.

At the urging of friends, Jones sent out Baby Bird tapes to record companies, but his music was roundly rejected; however, Chrysalis Music did offer a publishing deal which Jones accepted, applying his earnings towards financing a series of independently-released, limited-edition collections. The first disc of material culled from the vast Baby Bird archives, *I Was Born a Man*, appeared in 1995; within the course of a year, three other acclaimed albums—*Bad Shave, Fatherhood*, and *The Happiest Man Alive*—followed, and won Jones a contract with Echo Records.

Upon making the leap to a major label, Baby Bird mutated from a one-man project into a full band, as Jones assembled a backing group comprised of guitarist Luke Scott, bassist John Pedder, keyboardist Hugh Chadbourne, and drummer Rob Gregory. In its new incarnation, Baby Bird debuted in late 1996 with *Ugly Beautiful*, a lush, sparkling collection of re-recordings of favorite songs from Jones' back catalogue, all selected by fans by means of postcard ballots included in the first four albums.

In 1997, *Dying Happy* was assembled; issued in a limited pressing of 1000 copies, the disc compiled a number of previously unreleased songs that Jones had kicking around. *There's Something Going On* followed in 1998, and two years passed until the release of *Bugged*, Baby Bird's ninth full-length. —*Jason Ankeny*

I Was Born a Man / Jul. 1995 / Baby Bird ♦♦♦
For his first Baby Bird collection, *I Was Born a Man*, Stephen Jones assembled over 20 songs from his home recordings, thereby establishing his sound, style, and *modus operandi.* From the outset, Jones' records are devoted to mid-'80s British alternative rock—echoes of Echo & the Bunnymen, Robyn Hitchcock, and U2 can be heard throughout the album—yet they are delivered in an endearingly primitive fashion, due to the lo-fi constraints of his home portastudio. This works in his favor, as the poor songs sound like they were recorded for a lark, and the best songs shine through the hiss. Still, Jones' apparent lack of quality control can make the lengthy mess of *I Was Born a Man* a trying experience, even for listeners accustomed to sifting through Sebadoh records. —*Stephen Thomas Erlewine*

Bad Shave / Oct. 1995 / Baby Bird ♦♦♦♦
By tightening his quality control considerably, Stephen Jones makes a convincing case that he is a madly talented English eccentric with Baby Bird's second album, *Bad Shave.* About half of the album is devoted to full-fledged songs, several of which (including the title track) are genuinely eerie and haunting. The rest, of course, is comprised of lightweight material that sounds like Jones was indulging his warped sense of humor, but in this context, where they're balanced by more substantial songs, they have greater impact. Although it still is a little too obscure for its own good, *Bad Shave* is an intriguing listen, and one that suggests Jones' talent may be too big to stay in the bedroom. —*Stephen Thomas Erlewine*

● **Fatherhood** / Jan. 1996 / Baby Bird ♦♦♦♦♦
Unlike the other early Baby Bird releases, the songs which comprise *Fatherhood* actually stake out some thematic unity—in this case, of course, paternity. Sporting a rather disconcerting cover featuring a faux-pregnant Stephen Jones, *Fatherhood* is the strongest and most ambitious of the four initial collections of Baby Bird home recordings; from the Dylan-esque wordplay of "Bad Blood" to the psychedelia of "Aluminium Beach" to the surreal Franco-pop of the closer "May We," these are complex, mature songs which belie their primitive four-track origins. —*Jason Ankeny*

The Happiest Man Alive / Mar. 1996 / Baby Bird ♦♦
Baby Bird's *The Happiest Man Alive* is the fourth album Steven Jones has assembled from his home recordings in the span of just under a year. Given that fact, it shouldn't be entirely surprising that it is the weakest Baby Bird album to date. *The Happiest Man Alive* feels like outtakes from *Bad Shave* and *Fatherhood*, and in a way they are. Jones recorded some 600 songs in his home on a Casio and cheap guitar over the course of six years and began assembling his records from these very tapes in 1995. Though there are literally hundreds of songs left in his collection, *The Happiest Man Alive* suggests that he picked all the best tracks for his first three albums. Occasionally, he has buried a gem within his kitschy, melancholy camp-caberet, but the album is only of interest to fanatics and fetishists, willing to dig through everything Jones has recorded. —*Stephen Thomas Erlewine*

Ugly Beautiful / Oct. 1996 / Echo/Atlantic ♦♦♦♦♦
Moving to a major label and switching to a full backing band for *Ugly Beautiful* is both a positive and negative development for Baby Bird. In the positive sense, Steven Jones' songs—including a handful of tracks that were on his indie releases—are given a clarity they were lacking in the past, and the full-bodied arrangements reveal songs like "Good Night" and "You're Gorgeous" as effortlessly catchy pop singles. However, the sonic clarity and larger arrangements also reveal that Jones is neither as clever nor as strange as his lo-fi albums suggested. Indeed, he often sounds like he's stuck in 1985, replicating the quirky charms of Robyn Hitchcock and Echo & the Bunnymen, and he lacks the wit or the adventure of either artist. So, *Ugly Beautiful* often treads close to cutesy nostalgia, of all things, yet it's saved by the sporadic surfacing of his songcraft. Even in this radio-ready setting, "I Didn't Want to Wake You Up" has a disquieting power, and "You're Gorgeous" positively radiates with twisted sexuality. But the long, "ironic" jams and unfocused material that end the record suggest that instead of representing the first flowering of his full talent, *Ugly Beautiful* may be the peak of it. —*Stephen Thomas Erlewine*

Dying Happy / 1997 / Baby Bird ♦♦♦♦
Recorded at the same time as his first four collections of solo work, but not released until some months after *Ugly Beautiful* had finally come out, *Dying Happy* is another somewhat ragtag compilation of never-planned-for-public-listening material. Like the rest, though, it has more than its share of charms, thanks to Stephen Jones' seemingly effortless knack for hooks, and above all, the album's deep blue melancholia. While it's always been something that's cropped up in his work, there aren't any nutty asides like "Bad Jazz" or winsome songs like "Lemonade Baby" here. The emphasis instead is on late night, deep blue moods, with roots in everything from Massive Attack to electronic Krautrock. The opening number "Losing My Hair" is probably one of the most downbeat things he's recorded to date, with a gentle, sad electric guitar line and Jones' falsetto at its most extreme, detailing a desperate love lyric; it makes for a striking beginning, very much setting the tone for the collection. "Tomorrow's Gone" continues the feeling

admirably—an instrumental with buried synth tones and random radio samples that combines with a mixed-low operatic singer (if not Jones, then a great sample of someone). It progresses from there—percussion loops emphasize the moodier moments, and keyboard lines suggest shadows and a soft drift through dark dreams. Occasional scraps of lyrics surface with great effect, as on "TV," when Jones concludes the song with "Watch the window," a metaphor Thom Yorke would probably kill for. Not that Jones' sense of humor is entirely absent—labeling one particularly gripping instrumental "When Everyone Speaks English, the World Will Explode" and another with a perversely pretty music box melody "The Unemployable Rub Oil on Her Coffin" are nice touches. *—Ned Raggett*

● **Greatest Hits** / Aug. 26, 1997 / Baby Bird ✦✦✦✦✦
Of course, the title is ironic—irony is one of Stephen Jones/Baby Bird's fortes. It's ironic because the double-disc *Greatest Hits* doesn't contain "You're Gorgeous," the number two U.K. single that established his career. It's ironic because *Greatest Hits* is Baby Bird's first U.S. release, meaning that he hasn't had time to have any hits, let alone great ones. And it's ironic because the title actually does make some sense—it distills Baby Bird's five lo-fi, independent records (*I Was Born a Man, Bad Shave, Fatherhood, The Happiest Man Alive, Dying Happy*) to their essence, capturing all the highlights from each record. In a sense, it does for the American audience what those five albums did for the British: it establishes Baby Bird's name and sound by creating a low-key, underground buzz. However, it's even better than those records, since it cuts away the excesses and showcases Jones at his bizarre, moody best. Since his world is so insular, his songs sound better in their original, home-recorded versions—*Ugly Beautiful* was a bit too glossy to truly shine—and the best of these are included on *Greatest Hits*, a perfect introduction to the warped, occasionally enthralling world of Baby Bird. *—Stephen Thomas Erlewine*

There's Something Going On / Jul. 14, 1998 / Echo ✦✦✦✦
There's Something Going On is the least catchy of Stephen Jones' hi-fi Baby Bird albums. The only song suggesting the pop charm of "You're Gorgeous" is "If You'll Be Mine," a beautiful minor ballad. The album is almost unrelentingly dark and mysterious, in much the same manner as his earlier lo-fi productions. Indeed, two of the tracks here, "You Will Always Love Me" and "There's Something Going On," were recorded straight to four-track. Jones' voice echoes out of lyrical valleys that suggest he's quite disturbed when it comes to relationships and life in general. "Take Me Back" is a horrific tale of an obsessive relationship, with lyrics about eyeballs scratched with rusty nails and a creepy chant of "dead, dead, dead" *ad infinitum*. It's a conceit that starts with the very first track, "Bad Old Man," where Jones sings of wife-beaters and a drowning in a duck pond. Musically, the album is more of a lean toward the baroque than *Ugly Beautiful*. One might describe it as stark, disturbed chamber pop. Beautiful melodies appear quite majestically out of Jones' psychological studies. "It's Not Funny Anymore" is bittersweet and touching, with Jones reaching for the album's emotional core over weeping, organic keyboards. "There's Something Going On" is the tender conclusion, suggesting that Jones knows there's a better way of life than obsession and self-torture. *There's Something Going On* is definitely Baby Bird's most subtle album, and it's a fascinating listen from start to finish. *—Tim DiGravina*

Bugged / Aug. 8, 2000 / Echo/Roadrunner International ✦✦✦
"The F-Word" is the first sign that the album isn't a return to the optimistic joys of *Ugly Beautiful*. The song is a catchy, somewhat evil-sounding nursery rhyme telling how bad the f-word is; one has to wonder if Jones is singing about some word even more crude than the standard f-word because the track is such sinister good fun. This is, of course, the same man who sang some rather rude things about Father Christmas and Nintendo back in his early days of self-released songs. Even the sweeter numbers on *Bugged* have dark underpinnings. "Out of Sight" is elegant, pristine pop, but the lyrics speak of a kind of codependency not heard of since the Police's "Every Breath You Take." There are certainly pop charms galore on the album; it's just that things aren't as goodie-goodie as they were in the days of "You're Gorgeous," Baby Bird's big hit. Jones is now making music on his own terms, completely ignoring any drive to have another hit single. This means that lyrics can be as brutal as they are romantic. Compared to *There's Something Going On*, the songs on *Bugged* generally have more energy; at times, there's a rolling beat that might lead to some foot-tapping or subdued dancing. "All I Want Is Love" and "The Way You Are" are the closest things here to love ballads. It's a relatively thrilling and always interesting prospect that the songs are so fragile and pretty, yet the imagery constantly shifts back to blood, stinging bees, broken toes, and disease. Stephen Jones has proven himself to be an eccentric pop genius. *Bugged* is just another grand, intriguing feather in Baby Bird's hat. It's a statement of complete artistic control, which just happens to be filled with ten amazing songs. *—Tim DiGravina*

Babyface (Kenneth Edmonds)

b. Apr. 10, 1959, Indianapolis, IN
Producer, Vocals, Keyboards / Quiet Storm, Club/Dance, Adult Contemporary, Urban
With his friend Antonio Reid, Babyface formed a Cincinnati-based band, the Deele, in the early '80s. They were introduced by members of Midnight Star to Solar Records executive Dick Griffey, who put them to work producing music for Carrie Lucas, the Whispers, and Dynasty. Since then, they've produced hits for Sheena Easton, Pebbles, Paula Abdul, and others. During the '90s, Babyface's dominance has extended beyond the production arena and into the performing circle. A series of hit releases depicting him simultaneously as a vulnerable romantic and accomplished lover turned Babyface into arguably this decade's biggest urban male vocalist. *Tender Lover* crossed him over into pop territory and eventually sold more than two million copies, ending any doubts that Babyface would be a major solo star. The singles "Whip Appeal" and "It's No Crime" were Top Ten R&B and pop hits, and remain staples on urban radio. He followed that with *A Closer Look* in 1991, and *For the Cool in You* earned another platinum certification and ranked among 1993's biggest R&B/urban albums. Babyface hit his peak in 1995, as he produced hits for artists like Boyz II Men, Madonna, and Whitney Houston and coordinated the *Waiting to Exhale* soundtrack. *—Bil Carpenter*

Tender Lover / Jul. 1989 / Epic Associated/Solar ✦✦✦✦✦
Babyface's solo debut yielded the first number one R&B hit of the 1990s while establishing Edmonds as a major personality and performer. He wrote or co-wrote much of the material and even played several instruments. It was a combination of slick production and nicely sung sentimental tributes and heartache ballads. (The 2001 CD reissue adds historical liner notes and three bonus tracks: a "Dub L.A." version of "Tender Lover," a 12" version of "Whip Appeal," and a 12" version of "My Kinda Girl.")*—Ron Wynn*

Lovers / Sep. 1989 / Epic Associated/Solar ✦✦✦
On his second album, Babyface sings with just enough earnestness to be soulful and just enough sophistication and slickness to avoid sounding too much like a throwback. (The 2001 CD reissue adds historical liner notes and three bonus tracks: a "Free Style Mix" of "Mary Mack," a "Jazz Lover's Mix" of "Lovers," and a 12" version of "If We Try.") *—Ron Wynn*

A Closer Look / Nov. 19, 1991 / Solar/Epic ✦✦✦✦
Babyface has established himself as both a performing and production star in the '90s. His alternately innocent, hurt, and disillusioned vocals are this decade's equivalent of the soul/love songs of the '70s and '80s. He can sing sentimental material, tender tunes, or seem angry and confused. His lyrics get overly coy, but they've struck many responsive chords among women in particular. It's not soul, but it's what many who never heard Sam Cooke think it is. *—Ron Wynn*

For the Cool in You / Aug. 1993 / Epic Associated/Solar ✦✦✦✦
In late 1993 Babyface, who was at the top of his game as pop/R&B's hottest writer and producer, released his acclaimed solo album *For the Cool in You*. The album featured four hit singles, those being the title track, "Never Keeping Secrets," "And Our Feelings," and the song that went on to become his signature tune, "When Can I See You." In early 2001, the album was reissued with three bonus tracks, which do the album a great deal of service and widely expand its musical boundaries. "For the Cool in You" is served up with two additional mixes. One is the Quiet Storm Vocal Mix, which, as the name implies, is a laid-back, mellow quiet storm groove. The other is the album's closer, the Midnight Luv Instrumental Mix, which is a fine, mellow, jazzy way to close off the album. Finally, "When Can I See You" is served up with the Urban Soul Basement Mix, which is a dance-house version of the song. This version may displease some of the song's original fans (it was an acoustic ballad in its original inception), but ultimately serves to expand the musical boundaries of the album. For a record that was originally pop/R&B, the reissue is a jazzier offering that includes house music and makes for a surprisingly good listen from start to finish. Also included are beefed-up liner notes, which include all of the original liner notes' artwork. *—Jose Promis*

The Day / Oct. 29, 1996 / Epic Associated/Solar ✦✦✦✦✦
The Day was the first album Babyface released after being elevated into a virtually guaranteed hitmaker in the mid-'90s through his work with Whitney Houston, Boyz II Men, Madonna, and Mariah Carey, among many others. The album confirms his skill for subtle, inventive songwriting and accessible, polished yet soulful production. Babyface can straddle the line between hip-hop and traditional soul better than nearly any other artist, as evidenced by the hits he has orchestrated for other artists. On his own, he is still compelling—his voice is as smooth as silk, and nearly as seductive—but it doesn't quite have the force of personality as his greatest productions. Nevertheless, *The Day* qualifies as state-of-the-art mid-'90s soul, featuring a handful of terrific songs, and a lot of extremely pleasurable filler. [The 2001 CD reissue adds historical liner notes and three bonus tracks: remixes of "Everytime I Close My Eyes," "This Is For the Lover in You," and "Everytime I Feel the Groove," the last of which was previously unreleased and not found on the original album in any form.] *–Leo Stanley*

Kenny "Babyface" Edmonds & Manchild / Oct. 21, 1997 / Collectables ✦✦✦✦
Released in 1997, after Babyface became one of the most popular and successful producers in pop music, *Kenny "Babyface" Edmonds & Manchild* is a career-spanning compilation that covers all three albums by the '70s soul outfit. The group had only one hit—"Especially for You" in 1977—and, listening to this 17-track collection, it's easy to see why: they weren't very good. Manchild was certainly competent, and on a few songs Babyface suggests that he had the talent he eventually developed, but only diehard fans of the contemporary soul man—or fans of vocalist Reggie Griffin, who later launched a solo career—will need to explore this collection. *—Stephen Thomas Erlewine*

MTV Unplugged NYC 1997 / Nov. 25, 1997 / Epic ✦✦✦
Even though he's had several hits, Babyface is better-known as a producer and a songwriter than a performer, which may be the reason why he invited a number of musicians—including Stevie Wonder, Eric Clapton, and Jodeci's K-Ci and JoJo—to perform at the concert that resulted in *MTV Unplugged NYC 1997*. Babyface performs his solo hits and a selection of hits he has written for other artists, such as "Change the World" and "The End of the Road," delivering them all with a smooth authority that borders on slickness. And that slickness may alienate some listeners, preventing them from realizing how sturdy most of these songs are, or the suppleness of Babyface's voice. That fondness for MOR production and delivery has always been one of Babyface's primary weaknesses, surfacing even on a stripped-down live album such as this. Some fans will find this weakness excusable, but it's a little frustrating to hear that the live versions don't differ drastically from the studio cuts. It's interesting to hear him sing "The End of the Road," and since this contains many of his greatest hits, it may be of interest to some casual fans, but

on the whole, *MTV Unplugged* is a disappointingly modest effort. —*Stephen Thomas Erlewine*

● **A Collection of His Greatest Hits** / Nov. 14, 2000 / Epic ✦✦✦✦

As can be expected with a Babyface retrospective, the songs are top notch and the production is excellent. At his peak in the mid-'90s, Babyface was arguably the American music industry's hottest producer/songwriter. He also established himself as a top-rate balladeer, as evidenced by the songs on this selection. "Everytime I Close My Eyes," "Never Keeping Secrets," and "When Can I See You" are quintessential slow jam Babyface. His up-tempo numbers, such as "It's No Crime" and the Shalamar cover, "This Is for the Lover in You," are just as engaging. However, despite the inclusion of some of his best ballads and up-tempo hits, this album suffers from several glaring omissions, and leaves one hoping for a more complete product, or at least a second volume to complement what's lacking in this one. Glaring omissions include two hits from his *Tender Lover* album, those being "My Kinda Girl" and the title track. Incidentally, both those songs were remixed (and greatly improved) when released as singles, so their inclusion on this hits package would have been a huge bonus for the singer's fans. Other omissions include his hit duet with Pebbles, "Love Makes Things Happen," his hit duet with Toni Braxton, "Give U My Heart," early singles "Mary Mack" and "Lovers," later singles "And Our Feelings" and "Rock Bottom," as well as his hard-to-find duet with Lisa Stansfield, "Dream Away," and his Top Ten hit with protégé Jon B., "Someone to Love." Omitting those songs in favor of non-hit album tracks such as "Soon as I Get Home" seems a tad bewildering. For completists, this collection is thoroughly lacking, but for the casual listener, it's a pleasure nonetheless. As a final note, two new songs are included, "When Men Grow Old" and "Reason for Breathing," as well as a live, unplugged version of a hit he wrote for Eric Clapton, "Change the World." —*Jose Promis*

Face2Face / Sep. 11, 2001 / Arista ✦✦✦✦

The Babys

f. 1976, London, England, **db.** 1981
Album Rock, Arena Rock, Pop/Rock

The Babys generated extensive hype upon formation in 1976 as one of mainstream pop/rock's brightest hopes for the future. While competent, their music never broke away from its Raspberries-meets-AOR style and developed its own distinctive sound. The group consisted of vocalist/bassist John Waite, guitarist Wally Stocker, former Spontaneous Combustion and Strider drummer Tony Brock, and keyboardist/guitarist Mike Corby, who was replaced by Jonathan Cain in 1978; bassist Ricky Phillips also joined later on. Overshadowed by the punk and new wave movement in their native U.K., the band concentrated on the American market and did score two Top 20 singles with "Isn't It Time" and "Every Time I Think of You." By 1981, the Babys' future didn't look so bright anymore and the group disbanded, with Stocker joining Air Supply's road band. Waite went solo and finally broke through on the charts in 1984 with the number one smash "Missing You," while Cain joined Journey; the two later reunited in the AOR supergroup Bad English. —*Steve Huey*

● **Anthology [Expanded]** / Jan. 25, 2000 / Capitol ✦✦✦

Thank goodness for the 2000 remastered and expanded version of the Babys' *Anthology* because it rights a terrible wrong. The sound quality of the original version was absolutely horrible—flat, muddy, and lifeless. This vastly improved 17-song, 24-bit digitally remastered edition brings out the punch in their underrated brand of power pop and rock. Vocalist/bassist John Waite is quoted in Brad Elliott's liner notes as saying the Babys were a better band than they were given credit for, and he's right. Arguably part of the problem was that in the late 1970s and early 1980s the band didn't fit well between the punk and new wave movements. Nevertheless, the Babys had a smart grasp of how to blend a variety of pop and rock influences into tightly arranged, catchy songs with bursts of horns and female background vocals, and renowned producers like Bob Ezrin, Ron Nevison, and Keith Olsen guided these recordings. The Babys' biggest hits are obviously included: "Isn't It Time," "Every Time I Think of You," "Head First," "Back on My Feet Again," and "Midnight Rendezvous." These glorious highlights only tell part of the story. 2000's *Anthology* also smartly adds "Silver Dreams" (the only charted single not included on the original version), album cuts, and a revelatory live track. "Looking for Love (Live)" shows that the band could shed the studio veneer and cut loose on stage, as proven by Waite's strong singing and lead guitarist Wally Stocker's unleashed riffing. "Head Above the Waves" is a relaxed acoustic-guitar ballad. "I Love How You Love Me" shows traces of a doo wop groove. The only drawback here is the substandard liner notes. Despite a thorough discography, there are no individual album or producer credits. It's also unclear which lineup cut "Looking for Love (Live)." —*Bret Adams*

Burt Bacharach

b. May 12, 1928, Kansas City, MO
Producer, Composer, Arranger, Strings, Songwriter, Piano / Baroque Pop, Film Music, Brill Building Pop, Pop

With a hit-single track record spanning four decades, Burt Bacharach became one of the most important composers of popular music in the 20th century, almost equal to such classic tunesmiths as George Gershwin or Irving Berlin. His sophisticated yet breezy productions borrowed from cool jazz, soul, Brazilian bossa-nova, and traditional pop to virtually define and undoubtedly transcend the staid forms of Brill Building adult-pop during the 1960s. His first hit came from Marty Robbins in late 1957 when Robbins took "The Story of My Life" to the American Top 20 and the number one spot in England. The single was also notable for its co-composer, Hal David, who became Bacharach's songwriting partner and collaborated on most of his big hits. By late 1962, Bacharach and David be-

gan focusing most of their composing energy on singer Dionne Warwick, who was the recipient of 15 Top 40 singles from 1962 to 1968 (including the Top Tens "Anyone Who Had a Heart," "Walk on By," "I Say a Little Prayer," and "Do You Know the Way to San Jose?") The duo also remained dominant in England, where Frankie Vaughan, Cilla Black, Sandie Shaw, the Walker Brothers, and Herb Alpert all hit number one with Bacharach/David compositions. If their schedule wasn't busy enough throughout the '60s, the songwriters contributed film scores for *What's New Pussycat?, Alfie, Casino Royale* and *Butch Cassidy and the Sundance Kid.* Bacharach and David began working on the musical *Promises, Promises* in the late '60s; it won a Tony and a Grammy Award (for cast album) during a popular three-year Broadway run. At the beginning of the '70s, three of his closest partners—Hal David, Dionne Warwick, and his second wife Angie Dickinson—left him. Bacharach's next hit was over a decade in coming; finally in 1981, he collaborated with Christopher Cross, Carole Bayer Sager, and Peter Allen on the Oscar-winning "Arthur's Theme." Once Bacharach resumed composing he began to hit, and 1986 was one of his finest years, with two American number ones: "That's What Friends Are For" and "On My Own." By the mid-1990s, many alternative bands began name-checking the hit-maker as an influence, and a three-disc retrospective of his compositions was released by Rhino in 1998. That same year he collaborated with Elvis Costello on the acclaimed *Painted from Memory,* and was celebrated at an all-star concert at Radio City Music Hall which later formed the basis for the LP *One Amazing Night.* —*John Bush*

★ **The Look of Love: The Burt Bacharach Collection** / Nov. 3, 1998 / Rhino ✦✦✦✦✦

While this three-CD, 75-song box set only has a half-dozen tracks actually credited to Burt Bacharach, it's certainly the best representation of his music likely to ever be assembled. Spanning the late '50s to a 1996 duet with Elvis Costello, this is the cream of his work as a composer (and, frequently, producer), properly concentrating mostly on the 1960s hit versions of his songs (usually, though not always, co-written with Hal David) by Dionne Warwick, Gene Pitney, Jackie DeShannon, Dusty Springfield, the Drifters, Chuck Jackson, and many others. Classics like "Baby It's You," "Walk on By," "What the World Needs Now Is Love," and "Wishin' and Hopin'" are here, of course. What really makes this exceptional by box set standards, however, is the deft intermingling of familiar smash hits with interesting minor hits and rarities. Thankfully only a little of his sub-par work from the '80s is included. Aficionados may find some things to carp about, particularly the absence of some small hits (quantity and licensing would have made it difficult to bring *everything* together) and the track choice when several singers made worthy versions: sometimes the big hit is used, sometimes it's a rare original version, sometimes it's a rare rendition that was neither the original nor the biggest hit. Certainly there's more Bacharach-David worth hearing; the first places to start after getting through this are vintage Dionne Warwick compilations. For a rich but manageable anthology of his best work, though, it could hardly be bettered, enhanced by nearly 100 pages of liner notes and track annotations. —*Richie Unterberger*

● **The Very Best of Burt Bacharach** / Mar. 6, 2001 / Rhino ✦✦✦✦✦

Like Rhino's exquisite three-disc *The Look of Love,* this set does not concentrate on proper Burt Bacharach recordings. Instead, it contains versions of Bacharach's greatest songs, usually the greatest versions—or cuts that are damn close to the greatest versions. And, really, that's what makes it magical, since Bacharach wasn't the best interpreter of his material—vocalists like Dionne Warwick, Sandie Shaw, Gene Pitney, Dusty Springfield, and the Shirelles were. This doesn't contain every one of his great songs or recordings, and it does run out of steam toward the end, when "That's What Friends Are For" rears its ugly head, but there are no other single-disc collections that offer such a succinct, accurate overview of Bacharach at his best, as a melodicist and songwriter. *The Very Best of* starts to flow with "Baby It's You," and then runs through such indelible classics as "(There's) Always Something There to Remind Me" by Sandie Shaw, "Walk on By" by Dionne Warwick, "What the World Needs Now Is Love" by Jackie DeShannon, and "Raindrops Keep Falling on My Head" by B.J. Thomas, among many, many others. Yes, it's possible to point out songs that should have been here, but what's here is nearly impeccable (though the last three songs, with the possible exception of Christopher Cross' "Arthur's Theme," should have been replaced by better songs from the '60s). There is no better, succinct introduction to the glories of Burt Bacharach than this. —*Stephen Thomas Erlewine*

Bachman-Turner Overdrive

f. 1972, Winnipeg, Canada, **db.** 1979
Album Rock, Boogie Rock, Arena Rock, Hard Rock

Following his 1970 departure from the Guess Who, guitarist Randy Bachman recorded a solo album (*Axe*) before forming Bachman-Turner Overdrive in 1972. Originally called Brave Belt, the metal group was comprised of singer/guitarist Bachman, fellow Guess Who alum Chad Allan, bassist C.F. "Fred" Turner, and Randy's brother, drummer Robbie; after a pair of LPs (*Brave Belt I* and *Brave Belt II*), Allan was replaced by another Bachman brother, guitarist Tim, and in homage to the trucker's magazine *Overdrive,* the unit became BTO. While their self-titled 1973 debut caused little impact in the U.S. or the band's native Canada, *Bachman-Turner Overdrive II* was a smash, netting a hit single with the anthemic "Takin' Care of Business." 1974's *Not Fragile* was a chart-topping success, and notched a number one single with "You Ain't Seen Nothing Yet." After two more albums—*Four Wheel Drive* and *Head On,* both issued in 1975—Randy Bachman left the group for a solo career. —*Jason Ankeny*

The Anthology / Jul. 20, 1993 / PolyGram ✦✦✦✦

Two discs, 31 tracks—that's a lotta Bachman-Turner Overdrive even for some die-hard fans—but that's what *Anthology* offers, complete with remastered sound, liner notes, and a handful of rarities, including the previously unreleased "Stayed Awake All Night" and four "quad mixes." These rarities aren't enticing for anybody but hardcore followers and, really, most listeners will be better served by *Greatest Hits*, which contains all the radio hits. Here, those are surrounded by album tracks, ranging from pedestrian to pretty good, actually. BTO doesn't really have any hidden gems, per se, yet there's enough good stuff here to satisfy fans of the big hits who want to hear a little bit more. That doesn't mean it's perfect, or even consistently entertaining, but it does prove that there's more than just the hits to BTO. —*Stephen Thomas Erlewine*

● **The Best of B.T.O. (Remastered Hits)** / May 19, 1998 / Mercury ✦✦✦✦
Best of B.T.O. (Remastered Hits) is essentially a remastered version of the 1976 compilation *Best of B.T.O. (So Far)*, augmented by three bonus tracks: "Four Wheel Drive," "Free Wheelin'," and "Down to the Line," which was previously only available as a single. The sound is better than on the initial issue, and the album remains an effective summary of BTO's career, the perfect choice for anyone looking for just one album from the hard-rocking Canadians. —*Stephen Thomas Erlewine*

20th Century Masters—The Millennium Collection: The Best of Bachman-Turner Overdrive / Sep. 26, 2000 / MCA ✦✦✦✦
The Millennium Collection: The Best of Bachman-Turner Overdrive gathers 12 of the group's anthemic hits, including the staples "Let It Ride," "You Ain't Seen Nothing Yet," and "Takin' Care of Business." "Blue Collar," "Shotgun Rider," and "Lookin' Out for #1" are some of the other highlights of this adequate collection; though it doesn't offer any surprises, it does bring most of BTO's career highlights. —*Heather Phares*

Backstreet Boys
f. 1992
Teen Pop, Euro-Dance, Euro-Pop, Adult Contemporary, Dance-Pop
Paradoxical in many ways, the Backstreet Boys were white Americans that sang a hybrid of R&B and dance-pop and found their first success in Europe and Canada. While their 1996 debut album made the Top 10 in nearly every European country, it took another two years for them to succeed in the U.S.

The group featured cousins and Lexington, KY natives Kevin Richardson and Brian Littrell, who sang doo-wop and new-jack R&B at local events, and Orlando, FL residents Howie Dorough and A.J. McLean, who met each other—and the fifth Backstreeter, transplanted New Yorker Nick Carter—through TV and theater auditions. When Richardson moved to Orlando, he met the trio through one of his Disney World co-workers. The four formed a group, naming themselves after an Orlando flea market; they invited Littrell to make the band a quintet.

Record producer Louis J. Pearlman found them managers Donna and Johnny Wright, who invited A&R reps to see the Boys perform; Jive Records signed the group in 1994. In late 1995, the Backstreet Boys released their eponymous debut in continental Europe, where it spent several weeks near the top of the charts and featured the international hits "We've Got It Goin' On" and "I'll Never Break Your Heart." Success also greeted the album's 1996 Canadian and U.K. releases; however hits eluded them in the U.S. until the release of the American version of *Backstreet Boys*. A mix of their singles with tracks from their album *Backstreet's Back*, it sold over 13 million copies and featured platinum-selling singles like "Quit Playin' Games (With My Heart)," and "Everybody (Backstreet's Back.)" Despite setbacks in 1998 like their royalties lawsuits against Pearlman and their other managers, the Boys persevered; Pearlman remained their manager and they worked on their follow-up album, *Millennium*. It debuted at #1 in the summer of 1999, selling over a million copies its first week and ended up with sales of over 12 million. Later that year they released a *Christmas Album* and issued *Black & Blue* in fall 2000. —*Stephen Thomas Erlewine*

Backstreet Boys / 1996 / Jive ✦✦✦✦
The Backstreet Boys' eponymous debut album was released in America nearly a full year after its original European release, and the wait proved to be a blessing in disguise. In that year, light dance-pop—such as the Spice Girls and Hanson—returned to the top of the American charts, paving the way for the frothy pleasures of *Backstreet Boys*. Like those groups, the Backstreet Boys divide their time between catchy, uptempo dance numbers and syrupy ballads, and they are as reliant on their personality as they are their talent. As a result, there are a couple of slow spots on the record, but each of the singles, plus a handful of album tracks, are potent combinations of professional hooks and personal charm that make *Backstreet Boys* a thoroughly enjoyable affair. —*Stephen Thomas Erlewine*

● **Millennium** / May 18, 1999 / Jive ✦✦✦✦
Backstreet Boys finally broke (and broke big) in America during 1998, as if by design. They had been Euro sensations for a couple of years, but it wasn't until *Backstreet's Back* was unleashed in the U.S. in 1997 that they had a presence in the States, and it was no small presence, either—after selling over ten million copies, the album remained in the Top 40 on the eve of the release of its sequel, *Millennium*. And sequel is the appropriate word—*Millennium* has no pretense of being anything other than an album for the moment, delivering more of everything that made *Backstreet's Back* a blockbuster. There's a familiar blend of ballads and dance-pop, a similar shiny production, a reliance on the Boys' charisma that brings to mind the debut. If *Millennium* were anything other than big, glossy mainstream pop, such calculation may be a little unseemly, but in this context, it can be rather fun. True, the album doesn't pack as much punch as its predecessor—there's a number of good songs, but more filler than before, and the Backstreet sound isn't as fresh as it was the first time around—but it does deliver what fans want: more of the same. And since there are singles as infectious as "I Want It That Way" and a handful of good ballads, that will be enough to satisfy anyone craving more, more, more. —*Stephen Thomas Erlewine*

Black & Blue / Nov. 21, 2000 / Jive ✦✦✦

When 'N Sync usurped the Backstreet Boys' record of number of albums sold in a single week early in 2000, it had to hurt the Backstreets, since it was played in the press as if they had lost the teen pop throne. By the time the group released their third album, *Black & Blue*, Thanksgiving week 2000, 'N Sync was still popular, but the arc of *No Strings Attached* illustrated that they were weak where the Backstreets were strong—namely, they couldn't really deliver the seductive mid-tempo pop tunes and ballads that were the backbone of the Boys' crossover success. Songs like "Shape of My Heart," which flows as gracefully as "I Want It That Way," prove that the Backstreet Boys do teen pop ballads better than anyone, but what's interesting about *Black & Blue* is how aggressively they protect their territory. Of course, it's relative protection, since they, like 'N Sync and Britney Spears, work with Max Martin, the man behind the biggest hits by all three artists. Consequently, it's not a coincidence that "Get Another Boyfriend" is a dead ringer for "It's Gonna Be Me" crossed with "Baby One More Time," but what gives *Black & Blue* character is that it's clear that the Backstreets want to remain kings of their world. So, the ballads are smoother than ever, and their dance numbers hit harder, all in an attempt to keep their throne. It works, even if it takes a couple spins before the singles stand out, since the Backstreets' material and voices are stronger than that of their peers, adding up to state of the art teen-pop. —*Stephen Thomas Erlewine*

Bad Brains
f. 1979, Washington, D.C., db. 1995
Hardcore Punk, Alternative Pop/Rock, American Underground
By melding punk with reggae, Bad Brains became one of the definitive American hardcore punk groups of the early '80s. Although the group released only a handful of records during their peak, including the legendary cassette-only debut *Bad Brains*, they developed a dedicated following, many of whom would later form their own hardcore and alternative bands. Inspired by both the amateurish rage of the Sex Pistols and the political reggae of Bob Marley, guitarist Dr. Know formed Bad Brains in 1979. Realizing that the lines between punk and reggae were already blurred in the U.K., he set out to replicate that situation in the U.S., recruiting several similarly minded musicians—vocalist H.R., bassist Darryl Aaron Jenifer, and drummer Earl Hudson—to prove his point. Poor distribution and erratic touring prevented the band from breaking out of the hardcore scene until their third album *I Against I* appeared in 1986 on SST. In the wake of the alternative rock boom of the early '90s, Bad Brains moved to the major label Epic in 1993 for *Rise*, though the album failed and the group was dropped. Maverick Records signed Bad Brains two years later for the band's next album, *God of Love*, though it also performed poorly. —*Stephen Thomas Erlewine*

Bad Brains / Feb. 1982 / ROIR ✦✦✦✦✦
For fans of hardcore, many would agree that the holy-grail of the genre is the Bad Brains' self-titled album, originally released back in 1982 as a cassette-only release on ROIR. Although it was available on CD on the now-defunct In Effect label in the late '80s (then titled *Attitude: The ROIR Sessions* with a different album cover), it's been remastered and re-released (on ROIR) with it's original cover, as well as an untitled bonus track added at the end. The ensuing years after its initial release haven't dulled the album's fury and rage in the least, and it's still impressive how the band can switch gears from red-hot hardcore to cool reggae dubs in the blink of an eye. All the classics are here: "Sailin' On," "Banned In D.C.," "Pay To Cum," "Right Brigade," as well as one of their strongest reggae tunes, "I Luv I Jah." The back of the album boasts a quote from the Beastie Boys' Adam Yauch, which sums up the proceedings simply, "the best punk/hardcore album of all time." —*Greg Prato*

Rock for Light / 1983 / Caroline ✦✦✦✦
After the tinny sound quality of the band's debut, the second Bad Brains album came as a real blast of sonic fresh air. Producer Ric Ocasek is largely responsible, but the increased tightness and focus are also a function of maturation. This band was a weird bundle of contradictions from day one: black, Rastafarian instrumental virtuosos playing hard-core punk, formerly the exclusive domain of white, aggressively atheist musical amateurs. That last contradiction would come to full musical flower on *I Against I*, but *Rock for Light* shows the band at the height of its punk energy. "P.M.A.," "Joshua's Song," and "Coptic Times" are typical examples of Bad Brains' unique blend of punk velocity and Rasta ideology. When they suddenly swing into mellow reggae (on "I and I Survive," "The Meek," "Rally 'Round Jah Throne," and the dubwise instrumental "Jam") the effect is like some kind of pleasant musical whiplash. The 1990 CD reissue of this album was remixed by Ocasek and bassist Darryl Jennifer, and it includes several bonus tracks. —*Rick Anderson*

● **I Against I** / 1986 / SST ✦✦✦✦✦
This album was for Bad Brains what *London Calling* was for the Clash—the band's first fully mature work, one which successfully brought together all of its diverse influences while at the same time showcasing a singular vision. Also like *London Calling*, it was to be the band's masterpiece, in the original sense of that term—a creative pinnacle which they would not reach again. The album opens with the title track, a blistering and musically exhilarating deploration of violence, and then moves directly into "House of Suffering," teasily the most complex and yet viscerally compelling song the band ever produced. Singer H.R. digs deep into his bag of voices and pulls them all out, one by one: the frightening nasal falsetto that was his signature in the band's hardcore days, an almost bel canto baritone, and a declamatory speed-rap chatter that spews lyrics with the mechanical precision of a machine gun. He positively croons on the surprisingly melodic "Secret 77" and "Let Me Help." But his voice isn't even the best thing happening here. It's the incredibly tight, funky, and tonally rich interplay between guitarist Dr. Know, bassist Darryl Jenifer, and drummer Earl Hudson that gives this album its deeply satisfying

texture. The stop/start rhythms of "Secret 77" and "Sacred Love," the gorgeous guitar hook on "She's Calling You," Dr. Know's completely counterintuitive ability to meld the raw directness of hardcore punk with an almost supernatural virtuosity without sacrificing the power of either approach—this is music-making of an order not usually seen in rock & roll. *—Rick Anderson*

Live / 1988 / SST ♦♦♦
Compiled from a series of 1987 concerts, *Live* captures Bad Brains at the height of their onstage prowess. It is necessary listening for hardcore fans. *—Stephen Thomas Erlewine*

Attitude: The ROIR Sessions / 1989 / Ineffect ♦♦♦♦♦
Technically, the album sounds terrible. Musically, it's mostly serious thrash punk from 1982, with the odd spot of reggae thrown in. The lyrics are all but incomprehensible, most of the songs are under two minutes in length, and the experience could be likened to spending a day inside a concrete mixer on high speed. Yet, the experience is actually rather entertaining, if you're in the mood for some serious high-speed noise. This album was produced for cassette-only label ROIR, combining two of label-owner Neil Cooper's areas of interest. The tape, in fact, has become one of ROIR's best-sellers, and the CD has followed suit. Basically, it's a short course in thrash—the first five numbers are essentially sequenced back to back with each other, so you get blasted from the opening chord right through to the first reggae number without having a chance to stop. The only time things clear up enough to hear what anyone's singing is on the reggae numbers. And they're pretty good at those, too. All in all, this is not likely to be everyone's cup of tea. It is, however, fun—if you're in the mood—as well as being a great document of one of the louder, faster, harder alternative moments in music history. *—Steven McDonald*

Quickness / Sep. 1989 / Caroline ♦♦♦
This is an interesting, if not entirely successful detour into funk-metal for the band that pioneered Rastafarian hard-core punk. Everything is slowed down here, and the sonic textures have thickened considerably. Drummer Earl Hudson delivers both ponderous, stomping metal rhythms and funked-up grooves, while Dr. Know gets to show off his chops a bit more than he has in the past. The religious messages have, if anything, gotten more mystical and less coherent—song titles like "Soul Craft," "Voyage into Infinity," and "Messengers" give you an idea of what to expect. "Don't Blow Bubbles" may or may not be a slightly homophobic cautionary tale for the age of AIDS, and "Sheba" appears to be a paean to King Solomon's wife (a perennial favorite subject for reggae musicians). As on *I Against I*, reggae is given short shrift on this album. In fact, the only reggae rhythm to be found at all is on "The Prophet's Eye," an awkward tune that feels tacked onto the album's end. Fans will defend it, and *Quickness* is by no means a failure, but it's also far from being Bad Brains' best work. *—Rick Anderson*

Youth Are Getting Restless: Live in Amsterdam / May 1990 / Caroline ♦♦♦
Youth Are Getting Restless repeats some of the same material from *Live*, albeit in different versions. The album was culled from the same tour as *Live*, but it captures a blistering concert from Amsterdam instead of compiling various performances. Consequently, it's a tighter and more exciting album, their best live record. *—Stephen Thomas Erlewine*

Rise / Aug. 1993 / Epic ♦♦

God of Love / May 23, 1995 / Maverick ♦♦

Black Dots / 1996 / Caroline ♦♦

Omega Sessions / Nov. 11, 1997 / Victory ♦♦♦♦
There has never been a hardcore punk band better than Bad Brains. This despite the fact that they broke all three of the basic hardcore rules by being virtuosos, reggae musicians, and black. H.R. sang in about eight different voices, sometimes using three or four of them in a single song; bassist Darryl Jenifer had a jazz player's chops wedded to a reggae player's taste; drummer Earl Hudson could move from one-drop skank to 300 bpm thrash at half a moment's notice and never drop a beat; and Dr. Know had obviously never been told how punk rock was supposed to transcend guitar heroism, because his guitar heroics were all over the place even as he laid down the hardcore law with vinegary, genre-perfect atonal power chord riffs. Others may have done it more authentically, but nobody ever did it better. Comprising five previously unreleased studio demos better known in later, more polished versions, the 15-minute *Omega Sessions* EP contains at least one real shocker: It turns out that the complex and electrifying "I Against I," which was formally released on the band's third album and which had always seemed like the pinnacle of their mature songcraft, was apparently a fully realized composition as early as 1980, when these tracks were recorded. The other entries are less surprising: ragged-but-right renditions of "Attitude" and "At the Movies," as well as the archetypal (some would say hackneyed) Rasta reggae of "I Luv I Jah" and the adolescent lover's reggae of "Stay Close to Me." All in all, only *Rock for Light* stands as a more essential document of this group's early years. *—Rick Anderson*

Bad Company

f. 1973, England
Album Rock, Arena Rock, Hard Rock, Blues-Rock
Formed in 1973, the British hard-rock outfit Bad Company was a supergroup comprised of ex-King Crimson bassist Boz Burrell, former Mott the Hoople guitarist Mick Ralphs, and singer Paul Rodgers and drummer Simon Kirke, both onetime members of Free. Powered by Rodgers' muscular vocals and Ralphs' blues-based guitar work, Bad Company was the first group signed to Led Zeppelin's vanity label Swan Song; their eponymously titled 1974 debut was an international hit which topped the U.S. album charts and scored a number one single with "Can't Get Enough of Your Love." *Straight Shooter*, issued the following year, was another major success, notching the hit "Feel Like Makin' Love," while 1976's *Run with the Pack* was Bad Company's third consecutive million-selling record. After 1977's *Burnin' Sky*, the group recorded 1979's *Desolation Angels*, which embellished their sound with synthesizers and strings; a three-year hiatus followed before the release of *Rough Diamonds*, the group's final LP in its original incarnation. *—Jason Ankeny*

Bad Company / Jun. 1974 / Swan Song ♦♦♦♦♦
Bad Company's 1974 self-titled release stands as one of the most important and accomplished debut hard rock albums from the '70s. Though hardly visionary, it was one of the most successful steps in the continuing evolution of rock & roll, riding on the coattails of achievement from artists like the Eagles and Crosby, Stills, Nash and Young. From the simple electric guitar lick on "Can't Get Enough" to the haunting bass line in "Bad Company" and the fast beats of "Movin' On," *Bad Company* exemplified raw rock & roll at its best. Erupting out of an experimental period created by the likes of Pink Floyd, Bad Company signified a return to more primal, stripped-down rock & roll. Even while labelmates Led Zeppelin's *Houses of the Holy* and *IV* featured highly acclaimed, colorful album artwork, *Bad Company*'s austere black and white record cover stood out in stark contrast. Six years later, AC/DC used the same idea on their smash *Back in Black*. Throughout the 35-minute album, Paul Rodgers' mesmerizing and gritty vocals hardly vary in tonal quality, offering a perfect complement to Mick Ralphs' blues-based guitar work. Several songs include three-chord verses offset by unembellished, distorted choruses, filled rich with Rodgers' cries. *Bad Company* is an essential addition to the rock & roll library; clearly influential to '70s and '80s hard rock bands like Tom Petty, Lynyrd Skynyrd, and Boston. *—Gautam Baksi*

Straight Shooter / Apr. 1975 / Swan Song ♦♦♦
One year after Bad Company's multi-platinum self-titled debut, the British band returned to London to record a follow-up. Utilizing material written earlier in 1973, vocalist and songwriter Paul Rodgers wrote two acoustic-based rock ballads that would live on forever in the annals of great rock history. "Shooting Star" and the Grammy-winning "Feel Like Makin' Love" helped *Straight Shooter* rise quickly through the charts to reach Billboard's number three spot both in the U.S. and U.K. However, critically and commercially the album never achieved the tremendous success of its predecessor, largely due to the lack of strong follow-up singles and supporting tracks. Simon Kirke stepped out from behind the drum-set to help produce and write "Anna" and "Weep No More," two slower and less aggressive ballads indicative of the overall diminishing quality of the album. Following the release of *Straight Shooter*, Bad Company headlined their first North American tour. *—Gautam Baksi*

Run with the Pack / Jan. 1976 / Swan Song ♦♦
By this, their third album, it was becoming increasingly clear that Bad Company's music was a formula, and an unusually restrictive one. (They did try adding strings on the title track, which is one of the rewrites of the song "Bad Company.") With the band touring the world and momentum on their side, *Run with the Pack* shot up the charts, too, but it didn't get quite as high or stay quite as long as its predecessors, mostly because of the lack of really memorable material—the biggest single was a cover of the Coasters' hit "Young Blood." *—William Ruhlmann*

Burnin' Sky / Mar. 1977 / Swan Song ♦♦♦
The string finally ran out for Bad Company with its fourth album. Their approach was so simple that it almost inevitably became formulaic, and although Mick Ralphs continued to screech with his sparse guitar leads and Paul Rodgers continued to present his lust in a soulful voice—well, we had heard it several times. By its fourth album, Bad Company was getting sloppy around the edges, but the real reason this was the first Bad Company to miss the Top Ten in the U.S. and the U.K. is that there was no hit single. Clearly, it was time to try something new. *—William Ruhlmann*

Desolation Angels / Mar. 1979 / Swan Song ♦♦♦
After a couple of mediocre efforts, *Desolation Angels* marked a return to form for Bad Company. It was also the band's last consistent album, powered by "Rock & Roll Fantasy" and "Gone, Gone, Gone." *—Stephen Thomas Erlewine*

Rough Diamonds / Aug. 1982 / Swan Song ♦♦

● **10 from 6** / Dec. 1985 / Swan Song/Atlantic ♦♦♦♦♦
10 from 6 means ten songs from six albums—namely, Bad Company's first six records, all of which were big hits on album-rock radio. This brief yet very effective collection gathers all of the group's best-known songs ("Can't Get Enough," "Feel Like Makin' Love," "Shooting Star," "Bad Company," "Rock & Roll Fantasy," "Ready for Love") in one place. Although most album-oriented hard-rock acts are better heard on the original albums, Bad Company's records tended to be more uneven than those of their peers, making *10 from 6* a valuable collection for the group's casual fans, who will want to bypass the cluttered studio albums and just get the cream of the crop. *—Stephen Thomas Erlewine*

Dangerous Age / Aug. 1988 / Atco ♦♦♦
Bad Company launched a major comeback in 1988 with *Dangerous Age*. It wasn't the original lineup, lacking Paul Rodgers, but Mick Ralphs was still on board, and he could still turn out some pretty solid numbers, like the title track and "One Night." The album also suffers from a slick, late '80s AOR production, but compared to some of the albums that came later, *Dangerous Age* was satisfying. *—Stephen Thomas Erlewine*

Holy Water / Jun. 1990 / Atco ♦♦♦
Bad Company's last platinum album, *Holy Water* was a formulaic, yet reasonably engaging, collection of AOR hard rock. Although the only original members on *Holy Water* are guitarist Mick Ralphs and drummer Simon Kirke, the band does a fair job of approximating the sound of classic Bad Company while adding enough elements of '80s pop metal to make the record appealing to teenagers that grew up on power ballads. And the band does turn in a first-rate power ballad with "If You Needed Somebody," which

rose all the way to number 16 on the charts. Surprisingly, that was one of three hits from the album—"Holy Water" and "Walk Through Fire" also received a fair amount of airplay. What that success signals is not a creative rebirth for Bad Company, but that the group knew how to follow a formula very well. *Holy Water* hasn't aged as well as their orginal hit albums—instead of the clean, ballsy attack of *Bad Company* and *Straight Shooter*, it's awash in echo and synths—but it is a finely-crafted, big-budget record of the late '80s and early '90s. It's just as indicative of its era as *Bad Company* is. —*Stephen Thomas Erlewine*

Here Comes Trouble / Sep. 1992 / Atco ◆◆◆
Down to a trio of Mick Ralphs, Simon Kirke, and Brian Howe, the-band-that-calls-itself Bad Company relied on studio musicians to fill out the sound and Howe and producer Terry Thomas to write most of the material on this anonymous-sounding fourth album at the second edition of the group. Even those willing to tolerate Ralphs/Kirke/Howe calling itself "Bad Company" didn't show much interest, so that they fell off from the platinum showing of 1990's *Holy Water* to much more modest sales this time around, despite the chart singles "How About That" (#38) and "This Could Be The One" (#87). —*William Ruhlmann*

Company of Strangers / 1995 / East West ◆◆

Stories Told & Untold / Oct. 15, 1996 / East West ◆◆

Original Bad Company Anthology / Mar. 23, 1999 / Elektra ◆◆◆◆
Somehow or other, Bad Company got lumped in with other '70s rock dinosaurs. In a way they were—not because their music was excessive or dated, but because when Bad Company walked the earth, the ground shook. Featuring the voice of Paul Rodgers, one of rock's greatest singers, the thoroughly excellent *Original Bad Company Anthology* re-establishes Bad Company as a force in the music world. The 33-song, two-CD set contains all the classic songs that made the band a top-selling recording and concert attraction, as well as four brand new songs and six B-sides and outtakes. The new songs are (surprise!) awesome. All four tracks (two by Mick Ralphs, two by Paul Rodgers) sound like they could be on the band's classic early albums. The first single, "Hey Hey," is a blustery rocker; "Tracking Down a Runaway," a totally exhilarating number, sounds like a future hit. The rarities include "Easy on My Soul," a remade Free song from the *Straight Shooter* sessions—complete with Paul Rodgers' signature piano—that blows the Free version out of the water, and might just be the best track Bad Company has ever done. Other highlights include "Superstar Woman," a soulful outtake from the first LP sessions, and "Smokin' 45" from the *Burnin' Sky* sessions. "Little Miss Fortune," with its cool lyrics and groove, is a former B-side finally seeing the light of day in the CD age. The set draws from all of their albums, emphasizing the first two, but the band even found two good tracks from the utterly pathetic *Rough Diamonds*; if those songs are good you can be sure the rest kick some serious butt as well. —*Geoff Ginsberg*

Bad English

f. U.S.A.
Album Rock, Hair Metal, Hard Rock
In the late '80s, ex-Journey guitarist Neal Schon teamed up with ex-Babys vocalist John Waite and other arena rock veterans to form Bad English. One of the last supergroups of the decade, they made power ballads like there was no tomorrow, and they did it better than most because Waite could carry a tune and Schon created the power ballad prototype during his years in Journey. In late 1989/early 1990, the group scored two huge hit singles—"When I See You Smile" and "Price of Love"—and were big draws in concert. However, the follow-up album, *Backlash*, experienced one of massive proportions, failing to have even one Top 40 hit. The band called it quits soon after its release. —*Stephen Thomas Erlewine*

● **Bad English** / Jun. 1989 / Epic ◆◆◆◆
Amid some tailor-made power ballads lurks some decent hard rock. —*Dan Heilman*

Backlash / Aug. 1991 / Epic ◆◆

Bad Manners

f. 1979, U.K.
Ska Revival, New Wave
Bad Manners, composed of vocalist Buster Bloodvessel (born Douglas Trendle), Louis Cook (guitar), David Farren (bass), Martin Stewart (keyboards), Brian Tuitti (drums), Gus Herman (trumpet), Chris Kane (saxophone), and Andrew Marson (saxophone), were one of the many bands to take their inspiration from the Specials and the ska revival movement in England in the late '70s. They quickly became the novelty favorites of the fad through their bald, enormous bodied frontman's silly onstage antics, earning early exposure through 2-Tone Records package tours and an appearance in the live documentary *Dance Craze*. In the early '80s, they managed several U.K. hits including "Ne-Ne Na-Na Na-Na Nu-Nu," "Lip Up Fatty," "Special Brew," and "Can Can." By the mid-'80s, the ska craze was over and the band retired temporarily after the release of 1985's *Mental Notes* only to return in 1989 with *Return of the Ugly*, remaining a live attraction despite a lack of recent hits. By the mid-'90s a third wave of ska-revival renewed interest in the band. *Eat the Beat* was relased in 1996 and *Uneasy Listening* followed in 1997 as well as several collections from the band's peak years. —*Chris Woodstra*

● **Klass** / 1983 / MCA ◆◆◆◆
This is the most representative collection of the band's fun version of ska/bluebeat. All of their British hits are covered including the endlessly catchy "Ne-Ne Na-Na Na-Na Nu-Nu." —*Chris Woodstra*

Collection / Mar. 10, 1998 / Cleopatra ◆◆

Rare & Fatty / Feb. 9, 1999 / Moon ◆◆◆
Bad Manners is the only 2-Tone band left–the only group from the original British ska

revival that never broke up, never stopped touring, and never stopped making great music. *Rare & Fatty* is a collection of previously unreleased demos, outtakes, and remixes, most (but not all) of them recorded fairly terribly but all of them infused with that gleeful, good-natured yobbishness that informs every Bad Manners record. Included are a fine version of the classic rock steady instrumental "Double Barrel," and a remix of the epochal "That'll Do Nicely" and a song called "Paranoid" that has nothing to do with Black Sabbath. There's also a weird and wonderful reggae tune called "Are You Monster," a weird and ... well, just weird reggae instrumental called "Elizabethan Reggae," and ten more. A must for fans, but newcomers might want to start with something a bit more well-produced. —*Rick Anderson*

Bad Religion

f. 1980, Los Angeles, CA
L.A. Punk, Hardcore Punk, Alternative Pop/Rock, Punk, American Underground
Out of all of the Southern Californian hardcore punk bands of the early '80s, Bad Religion stayed around the longest. For over a decade, they retained their underground credibility without turning out a series of indistinguishable records that all sounded the same. Instead, the band refined their attack, adding inflections of psychedelia, heavy metal, and hard rock along the way, as well as a considerable dose of melody. Between their 1982 debut and their first major-label record, 1993's *Recipe for Hate*, Bad Religion stayed vital in the hardcore community by tightening their musical execution and keeping their lyrics complex and righteously angry. Formed around guitarist Brett Gurewitz and vocalist Greg Graffin, Bad Religion debuted with 1983's *Into the Unknown*, released on Gurewitz's label Epitaph. After a lengthy hiatus, *Suffer* followed in 1988 and re-established the group as prominent players in the American hardcore scene. By the time of 1993's *Recipe for Hate*, alternative rock had become such a mainstream commodity that the group signed to Atlantic. The label re-released *Recipe for Hate*, then new album *Stranger Than Fiction*, the album that proved to be Gurewitz's last (his label's unexpected hit, the Offspring's *Smash*, caused Gurewitz to spend more time on business matters). Bad Religion followed with *The Gray Race* in 1996, and *No Substance* two years later. In summer 2000, Gurewitz rejoined the lineup. —*Stephen Thomas Erlewine*

Into the Unknown / 1983 / Epitaph ◆◆◆◆◆
At a time when most L.A. bands were playing extremely fast, stripped-down rock, Bad Religion released this chunk of '70s-styled hard rock that anticipated the '70s revival by about a decade. It's a bit off-putting at first blush, mainly because the tempos are slower and more deliberate, and because of the use of swirling organs and pianos. But it's a terrific record that was perhaps more daring than anyone realized at the time of its release. An extremely influential and interesting record, one that any fan of hard rock should own. —*John Dougan*

Suffer / 1988 / Epitaph ◆◆◆◆◆
Featuring a reunited version of the original band, *Suffer* is a fast, stripped-down, blazing record that relentlessly tears through its songs. In terms of sheer sonic intensity, *Suffer* is their best record yet, even if it is lacking in musical diversity. —*Stephen Thomas Erlewine*

No Control / Dec. 1989 / Epitaph ◆◆◆◆◆
No Control is even more uncompromising than *Suffer*, except that this time, Bad Religion concentrated more on songwriting and melody, making the album their most impressive straight hardcore effort. —*Stephen Thomas Erlewine*

80-85 / 1990 / Epitaph ◆◆◆
A tremendous collection of early Bad Religion that covers most of their hardcore and early post-hardcore period, including their debut record, *How Could Hell Be Any Worse*. Graffin's snarl is prominently displayed, and the band rages through this anthology's 28 tracks, which includes three takes of their signature theme "Bad Religion." Lots of tracks are suffused with a quasi-liberal, populist message (e.g., "Politics," "World War III," and "Oligarchy") and are more lyrically sophisticated than one might assume. An excellent introduction. —*John Dougan*

Against the Grain / 1990 / Epitaph ◆◆◆◆
After reuniting in 1988, Bad Religion went on a recording binge that saw the release of three records in two years. All are good, with *No Control* hands-down the best of the three. What's crucial at this point in their career is that the band was concerned with simply being a good rock band and less concerned with being aging punks. As a result the music doesn't sound retrograde or tossed-off, and Graffin, Gurewitz, and Co. never come off like a pathetic bunch of middle-age punks desperately attempting to sound young. This music takes maturity head-on and deals with it in a way that gets to the roots of living in society as opposed to dying before you get old—the former being much tougher than the latter. But, even from the start Bad Religion's music was never about taking the easy way out, and these three releases are a testament to that attitude. —*John Dougan*

Generator / Mar. 13, 1992 / Epitaph ◆◆◆
Generator demonstrates an improved sense of melody from Greg Graffin, which doesn't mean Bad Religion has abandoned their blistering hardcore inclinations. Instead, the band has managed to incorporate melody within the framework, adding an increased depth to their already provocative songs. —*Stephen Thomas Erlewine*

Recipe for Hate / Sep. 21, 1993 / Epitaph ◆◆◆
Although it doesn't sound all that different from what X was doing ten years ago (and fairly close to the music they were making, too), the seminal L.A. punk rockers gained a larger audience with *Recipe for Hate*. Featuring guest spots from Eddie Vedder and Johnette Napolitano from Concrete Blonde, *Recipe for Hate* features a smoother version of punk. All of the trademark anger and guitars are still present, but some of the

melodies, harmonies, and riffs lean toward mainstream rock & roll. Fortunately, this all works in Bad Religion's favor—their music is more accessible, but it doesn't lack integrity. *—Stephen Thomas Erlewine*

Stranger Than Fiction / Aug. 30, 1994 / Atlantic ✦✦✦
Paced by the terrific single "21st Century Digital Boy," and an equally terrific video, Bad Religion's biggest selling record to date comes a decade and a half after they decided to enter the rock & roll sweepstakes. Few bands sound this good this far into a career and it's a tribute to the talent of this quintet that they sound this good this far on. As expected, the production values have increased considerably since the days of *How Could Hell...*, and this record comfortably fits in both hard rock and alternative rock formats, but that's not a knock against Bad Religion. More than anything, it's a compliment. *—John Dougan*

• **All Ages** / Nov. 7, 1995 / Epitaph ✦✦✦✦✦
A best-of collection from Bad Religion's latter-period Epitaph years, *All Ages* has a pretty good selection of the standout tracks from their 1988 to 1992 period (*Suffer* to *Generator*) with just a couple of songs predating 1985 (including a live version of "Fuck Armageddon... This Is Hell"). It's a consistently fine, often exhilarating selection, boasting such enduring tracks as "Flat Earth Society," "21st Century Digital Boy," and others. The title, incidentally, is a salute to the Southern Californian hardcore scene's determination to play venues where alcohol was not on sale (and thus allow entry to under-21s). Alongside the *80-85* compilation, it provides a comprehensive introduction to one of the few hardcore bands with the legs to take relevance and social critique into a second decade of existence. *—Alex Ogg*

The Gray Race / Feb. 27, 1996 / Atlantic ✦✦

No Substance / May 5, 1998 / Atlantic ✦✦✦
Granted, the title *No Substance* is clearly intended as a put-on, yet there's more than a kernel of truth to it as well—with each successive release, Bad Religion seems more and more to be simply going through the motions, bludgeoning listeners with a streamlined punk attack which carries increasingly little weight. Tracks like "The Biggest Killer in American History," "Sowing the Seeds of Utopia," and "The State of the End of the Millennium Address" are the same kind of populist polemics which dominate every Bad Religion record, and that's the problem—the group recycles the same ideas (political and musical) over and over again, to the point of their songs lacking any kind of real impact; there's no doubting Bad Religion's passion, but at this point in the game that's about all that's keeping them going. *—Jason Ankeny*

The New America / May 9, 2000 / Atlantic ✦✦✦✦
Todd Rundgren may seem like an odd choice of producer for Bad Religion, but as *The New America* illustrates, it was an inspired, even necessary, one for the veteran Californian punkers. Bad Religion painted themselves into a corner in the late '90s, adhering to the literate, hard-driving punk that marked their indie releases. That may have kept them pure, but as they grew older, they wound up repeating many of their musical ideas, while losing some of their focus. Rundgren blends his talents as a pop maverick and a vital hard rock producer on *The New America*, pushing Bad Religion to strengthen their melodies and hooks without losing their edge. Of course, if the record was just production, it would fall flat, but Bad Religion seems eager to embrace the challenge of making their tightest, tuneful record yet. Maybe some longtime fans will cringe at the big, powerful sound, the backing harmonies, or the catchy melodies, but these were all present on previous Bad Religion releases—here, they're just presented with more focus. The focus, the careful production, and the group's solid, well-constructed songs result in one of the group's strongest records, while illustrating that the group can indeed grow old gracefully. And that's the most remarkable thing about *The New America*—it is clearly the work of a band that's been around for nearly 20 years, but the experience hasn't worn them down, it's strengthened them. They've stayed true to their original vision while expanding its boundaries, which is something many veteran bands, regardless of genre, just can't do. Some credit may go to Rundgren, but the achievement really is Bad Religion's, not his. *—Stephen Thomas Erlewine*

Badfinger

f. 1968, England, **db.** 1983
Album Rock, Pop/Rock, Power Pop, Soft Rock

There are few bands in the annals of rock music as star-crossed in their history as Badfinger. Pegged as one of the most promising British groups of the late '60s, and the one world-class talent ever signed to the Beatles' Apple Records label that remained with the label, Badfinger enjoyed the kind of success in England and America that most other bands could only envy—and a string of memorable hit singles, "Come and Get It," "No Matter What," "Day After Day," and "Baby Blue"—yet saw almost no reward from that success. Instead, four years of hit singles and international tours precipitated the suicide of its two creative members and legal proceedings that left lawyers as the only ones enriched by the group's work. Originally known as the Iveys and comprised of Pete Ham, Joey Molland, Tom Evans, and Mike Gibbins, Badfinger earned a Top Ten hit in Britain and America with the Paul McCartney composition "Come and Get It." In 1970, they released their debut, *Magic Christian Music*, and *No Dice*, the latter yielding an original song ("Without You") that was turned into a monster worldwide hit by Harry Nilsson. One year later, *Straight Up* produced two huge singles, "Day After Day" and "Baby Blue," plus an FM hit in the form of "Name of the Game." Their final Apple album, entitled *Ass*, was released in 1973, just as the label was nearing the end of its existence as a viable company. Badfinger's debut for Warner Bros., 1974's *Wish You Were Here*, should have been a triumphant comeback for the group, though financial troubles necessitated its withdrawal just weeks after release. The group was dropped from their Warner Bros. contract in 1975, and later that year, Pete Ham hanged himself. Though 1979's *Airwaves* and 1981's *Say No More* tried to revive the Badfinger name, the suicide of Tom Evans in 1983 ended the band's career. *—Bruce Eder*

Magic Christian Music / Feb. 16, 1970 / Capitol ✦✦✦
If Badfinger's debut album *Magic Christian Music* sounds patchy, there's a reason why: It was assembled from three different sources. Although the title suggests that the record is a soundtrack to *The Magic Christian* it isn't. It's a hodgepodge, containing the group's three contributions to the film, six highlights from the band's pre-Badfinger album *Maybe Tomorrow* (released when they were known as the Iveys), an alternate take from *Maybe Tomorrow*, and four new songs. It's little wonder that it doesn't hold together, winding up as a document of Badfinger's unharnessed potential. Since their breakthrough hit "Come and Get It" was written by Paul McCartney, Badfinger was dogged by comparisons to the Beatles but they were hardly copyists. Elements of the Hollies, the Kinks, and very mild psychedelia are discernable throughout *Magic Christian Music*, all part of the band's search for their own voice. Apart from the lovely pop tune "Dear Angie" and Tom Evans' stately, yearning "Maybe Tomorrow," the Iveys numbers aren't particularly distinguished pop but they are, by and large, pleasant period pieces. On the newer material, Badfinger sounds stronger and their craftsmanship surfaces. Pete Ham emerges as a fine songsmith, with the convincing rocker "Midnight Sun" and the gentle "Walk Out in the Rain." Still, the true standouts among the newer songs are "Crimson Ship" and "Carry on Till Tomorrow," both co-written by Ham and Evans. They're two sides of the same coin—dreamy post-psych pop tunes driven by strong hooks and harmonies. They might not always deliver on that promise on *Magic Christian Music*, but with its appealing melodies, lite psychedelic flourishes and, yes, Beatlesque harmonies, it's an enjoyable artifact of its time. *—Stephen Thomas Erlewine*

No Dice / Nov. 9, 1970 / Capitol ✦✦✦✦✦
Badfinger's second album *No Dice* kicks off with "I Can't Take It," a rocker that signaled even if Badfinger still played pop and sang ballads, they considered themselves a rock band. What gave Badfinger character is they blended their desire to rock with their sensitive side instead of compartmentalizing. Even when they rock on *No Dice*, it's never earthy, like, say, the Stones. Badfinger's very sensibility and sound is modeled after the early British Invasion, where bands sang catchy, concise love songs. Yet there's a worldliness to their music absent from that of their forefathers, partially because Badfinger styled themselves as classicists, adapting the sound of their idols and striving to create a similar body of work. *No Dice* bears this out, boasting old-fashioned rockers, catchy pop tunes, and acoustic ballads. On the surface, there's nothing special about such a well-crafted, sharply-produced, straight-ahead pop record, but the pleasure of a power-pop album is in the craft. *No Dice* is not without flaws—a byproduct of an all-writing, all-singing band is that some songs don't measure up—but it does achieve the right balance of craft, fun, and emotion, due in no small part to Pete Ham's songwriting. Ham dominates the record, providing note-perfect openers and closers, along with the centerpiece singles "No Matter What" and "Without You," the latter a yearning, painful ballad co-written with Tom Evans. Collaborating with new guitarist Joey Molland, Evans wrote two other excellent songs ("I Don't Mind," "Better Days"), while Molland's own "Love Me Do" chugs along with nice momentum. Still, the heart of the album lies in Ham's work.. He proves that songcraft is what separates great power-pop from good, and it's what makes *No Dice* a superb pop record. *—Stephen Thomas Erlewine*

Straight Up / Dec. 13, 1971 / Capitol ✦✦✦✦✦
Straight Up winds up somewhat less dynamic than *No Dice*, largely because that record alternated its rockers, pop tunes, and ballads. Here, everything is at a similar level, as the ballads are made grander and the rockers have their melodic side emphasized. Consequently, the record sounds more unified than *No Dice*, which had a bit of a split personality. Todd Rundgren's warm, detailed production makes each songwriter sound as if he was on the same page, although the bonus tracks—revealing the abandoned original Geoff Emerick productions—prove that the distinctive voices on *No Dice* were still present. Frankly, the increased production is for the best, since Badfinger sounds best when there's as much craft in the production as there is in the writing. Here, there's absolutely no filler and everybody is in top form. Pete Ham's "Baby Blue" is textbook power-pop—irresistibly catchy fuzz riffs and sighing melodies—and with its Harrison-esque slide guitars, "Day After Day" is so gorgeous it practically aches. "Perfection" is an unheralded gem, while "Name of the Game" and "Take It All" are note-perfect pop ballads. Tom Evans isn't as prolific here, but the one-two punch of "Money" and "Flying" is the closest *Straight Up* gets to *Abbey Road*, and "It's Over" is a fine closer. Still, what holds the record together is Joey Molland's emergence as a songwriter. His work on *No Dice* is enjoyable, but here, he comes into his own with a set of well-constructed songs. This fine songwriting, combined with sharp performances and exquisite studio craft, make *Straight Up* one of the cornerstones of power-pop, a record that proved that it was possible to make classic guitar-pop after its golden era had passed. *—Stephen Thomas Erlewine*

Ass / Nov. 26, 1973 / Apple ✦✦✦
Badfinger produced the sessions for the *Straight Up* sequel themselves, abandoning its lush production for a live, hard-rocking sound. Apple wasn't keen on the record, insisting that it be remixed, then, once it was remixed, refusing to release it, so the band jumped ship to Warner Bros. in the fall of 1973. Just after Badfinger released their debut single for the label and were prepping a new album, Apple sprung *Ass* on the world. As it happened, it would be the last record Apple would release, so it was barely given any support by the label and made little impression on the sales charts. Still, it certainly hurt the band, since its heavier rock alienated some pop fans and its chart belly-flop tainted plans for a triumphant return on Warner. Truth is, *Ass* probably should have remained on Apple's shelves. Their eponymous Warner debut, which appeared just months after *Ass*, feels

more like the sequel to *Straight Up* than this. Where that album is an unabashed pop record, *Ass* is the sound of a pop band rocking out rather clumsily. That's not to say it's without its moments, since Pete Ham's "Timeless" and "Apple of My Eye" (a hurt but lovely kiss-off to their label) are pretty good. But, by and large, *Ass* is a misguided effort, heavy on stumbling rockers and mediocre songs. It may be tempting to lay some of the blame at Joey Molland's feet, since he wrote half of the album, but that's too easy. Badfinger were in a transitional phase and chances are, *Ass* would have stiffed if Ham had written half of the record. It wasn't fated to be a great album, and it wound up being the weakest thing the original band cut. *—Stephen Thomas Erlewine*

Badfinger / Feb. 1974 / Warner Brothers ✦✦✦
In many ways, *Badfinger* is a continuation of *Straight Up*—an unabashed, concise pop album—but there's one important difference: Todd Rundgren was a taskmaster on *Straight Up*. He may have not jelled with the band, but he brought out their best. Chris Thomas didn't work the same way, although he's equally skilled in the studio, and he made a state-of-the-art pop record, which meant that they didn't necessarily play to the band's strengths. Instead, they tried a little bit of everything, with everybody throwing in a song or two, all in hopes that something would click on the radio. As a result, *Badfinger* is a bit of a mess. Some moments work quite well—Pete Ham scores with "Lonely You" and "Song for a Lost Friend" (sounding a bit like Ray Davies on the latter), along with his collaboration with Tom Evans, "Shine On," while Joey Molland's "Love Is Easy" has a pleasing pop hook, and his "Andy Norris" rocks harder and more convincingly than anything they'd yet recorded. But they're surrounded with failed experiments and songs that, for one reason or another, just don't click. Sometimes, the fault is the production. For instance, Ham's "Matted Spam" is pretty catchy, even with its terrible title, but the faux-soul arrangement doesn't fly. Similarly, Mike Gibbons' "My Heart Goes Out" sinks in its own neo-folkie pretensions, and Molland's brooding "Give It Up" flails under then-contemporary AOR cliches. On the whole, *Badfinger* is a stronger record than its immediate predecessor, since it plays to their pop strengths, but there are enough missed opportunities and forgettable moments to make it worthwhile only for truly dedicated fans. The rest can make do with the selections on *Shine On* or *The Best of Badfinger, Vol. 2*. *—Stephen Thomas Erlewine*

Wish You Were Here / Nov. 1974 / Warner Brothers ✦✦✦✦
Wish You Were Here is a glistening, powerful rock record that stays true to power-pop while sounding as contemporary as any mainstream rock band of the mid-'70s. It was the kind of record that could have been a hit, but due to a series of legal and managerial entanglements, it was pulled from stores before it had a chance to find its audience. Despite its relative obscurity, most diehard Badfinger fans maintain that the group shines brilliantly on *Wish You Were Here* and they're correct. For one, it's easily the most cohesive album the group ever recorded—a nice by-product of working with one talented producer (in this case, Chris Thomas) for an entire album instead of piecing a record together. Also, it showcases each band member at a peak of songwriting. As the band's most prolific and gifted composer, Ham naturally has the strongest presence, and while each of his songs stands as proof that he was a consummate pop craftsman—particularly the elegant "Dennis," the hard-hitting "Just a Chance," and the *Abbey Road*-esque "Meanwhile Back at the Ranch." Joey Molland has a strong showing with the stately ballad "Love Time" and "Should I Smoke," his complement to "Ranch." What is surprising is that Mike Gibbins' two contributions are of the same caliber, as is Tom Evans' electric-piano laden "King of the Load," since they were in a bit of a slump prior to this album. Thomas ties the record together with a clean, professional production that keeps the rockers energetic without losing their melodic edge, while preventing the sentimental numbers from seeming syrupy. All of this results in a classy, catchy pop record, possibly the best Badfinger ever released. It could have been a hit, too, but we'll never know. *—Stephen Thomas Erlewine*

Airwaves / Mar. 1979 / Elektra ✦✦
Using the magic of overdubbing and a complement of star studio musicians, Tom Evans and Joey Molland take a respectable shot at recreating the three-part harmonies and pop sheen of the early '70s Badfinger. "I Want to Get Back," Evans sings on the title track, and you would, too, if you had been reduced to manual labor after hobnobbing with the Beatles. Like early Badfinger, much of this evokes their old mentors, especially "Love Is Gonna Come At Last" (number 69), their first singles chart hit in seven years. Often, however, the material is only pedestrian, and although this album actually did a little better commercially than the group's two Warner Bros. albums of 1974, it didn't make for a real comeback. *—William Ruhlmann*

Say No More / 1981 / Real Music ✦✦
Badfinger lists itself as a quintet on this album, including longtime members Joey Molland and Tom Evans, plus keyboard player Tony Kaye, drummer Richard Bryans, and guitar player Glenn Sherba. Certainly, they sound more like a band on this record than they did on its predecessor, *Airwaves*, which was basically a Molland-Evans duo album, but that is not an improvement. They tend to rock out more here, downplaying the more folkish and melodic pop tendencies in their music. Sometimes, as on "Because I Love You," they sound like the Raspberries trying to sound like the Beatles. The hit, such as it was, was "Hold On" (number 56), a shadow of former glories, and although this album charted briefly, it only confirmed that Badfinger was no longer a record seller. *—William Ruhlmann*

The Best of Badfinger, Vol. 2 / 1989 / Rhino ✦✦✦
Released in 1989 when the post-Apple albums were hard to come by, Rhino's *The Best of Badfinger, Vol. 2* does an excellent job of summarizing the last three Pete Ham albums [*Badfinger*, *Wish You Were Here*, and the unreleased (until 2000) *Head First*], adding a couple of selections from *Airwaves* for good measure. Fanatics can complain about missing tracks (and, at a certain stage, most Badfinger fans were fanatics by their very nature), yet this hits most of the high points, offering proof that the group remained viable—in some ways getting better—until the end. *Wish You Were Here* remains essential, and Capitol's 2000 *The Very Best of Badfinger* is the best overall compilation, yet as a sampler of the group's latter days, this is hard to beat. *—Stephen Thomas Erlewine*

Come and Get It: The Best of Badfinger / Apr. 1995 / Apple ✦✦✦✦✦

● **The Very Best of Badfinger** / Sep. 12, 2000 / Capitol ✦✦✦✦✦
The difference between 2000's *The Very Best of Badfinger* and 1995's *Come and Get It: The Best of Badfinger* is a simple one—the 1995 collection concentrated on the group's Apple recordings, where the 2000 collection runs all the way until 1974's *Wish You Were Here*, the band's final album with Pete Ham. Not only does the collection benefit from the expanded timeline, but it has a sharp selection of songs from the classic Apple years—yes, "Flying" is absent and *Ass* is bypassed (perhaps understandably so), but "We're for the Dark" is a more than welcome addition. The 19 tracks may not be in chronological order, but the sequencing packs a real punch and, in this context, the best of the Warner material more than holds its own with the Apple cuts. Inevitably, there are some fan favorites missing, but apart from "Flying," all the classics are here and this compilation is unquestionably the most thorough (and arguably the best) overview of Badfinger's entire career yet assembled. *—Stephen Thomas Erlewine*

Head First / Nov. 14, 2000 / Artisan/Snapper Music Group ✦✦✦✦
Badfinger completed their best album in 1975, then had it pulled from the shelves in a haze of managerial misdeals and contractual screw-ups. They were good soldiers, at least for a while, heading into the studio (without Joey Molland, who bailed at the last minute) to bash out another album for Warner, completing it in two weeks. Warner rejected the effort, lead songwriter Pete Ham committed suicide not long afterward, and the album sat in the vaults until late 2000, when Artisan/Snapper released *Head First* as a double-disc set (the second disc consisting of demos and outtakes). *Head First* confirms that Badfinger had settled into a groove with *Wish You Were Here*, finding an effective middle ground between their pop gifts and hard rock inclinations, with both Ham and Tom Evans contributing equally strong works. That they're equally embittered to the music industry (three of the songs deal directly with their business troubles) is no surprise, yet they manage to make it tough, melodic, and remarkably sympathetic. There are no songs that shine as brilliantly, when isolated, as those on its immediate predecessors, but *Head First* works as a cohesive album, holding together better than any Badfinger record outside of *Wish You Were Here*. It's not likely that it would have changed their destiny any if it had been released in 1975, yet it certainly wouldn't have been an embarrassment, and it's now a welcome addition to their catalog; it provides a sense of closure. *—Stephen Thomas Erlewine*

Badly Drawn Boy

Vocals, Guitar / Indie Pop, Adult Alternative Pop/Rock
Belying his status as a narcoleptic slacker icon, Badly Drawn Boy proved himself a tireless pop songwriter, with arrangements that reflect a great deal of creativity. Born Damon Gough, he began recording after meeting the like-minded Andy Votel at a Manchester nightclub. The pair formed the Twisted Nerve label, and Gough debuted as Badly Drawn Boy with an EP and several singles. The recordings dovetailed nicely with the experimentalist pop fringe of artists like Scott 4 and the Beta Band, and the attendant media hype allowed him to guest alongside Thom Yorke, Richard Ashcroft, and Mike D on 1997's celebrity-filled U.N.K.L.E. LP *Psyence Fiction*. His 1999 single "Once Around the Bend" grazed the British charts, while XL Recordings signed the pop auteur and released his debut album, *The Hour of Bewilderbeast*, in 2000. Just before its American release, the album earned another round of critical praise with Britain's vaunted Mercury Prize for Best Album. December 2000 brought the birth of his daughter. *—John Bush*

● **The Hour of Bewilderbeast** / Jun. 26, 2000 / Twisted Nerve/XL Recordings ✦✦✦✦✦
What has the field of lo-fi slacker pop come to when faced by an LP as ambitious and entertaining as Badly Drawn Boy's *The Hour of Bewilderbeast*? Despite all attempts to sabotage his songwriting and production with innumerable experimental tidbits, songs within a song, and (seemingly) tossed-off arrangements, Damon Gough has to face the fact that he wrote and produced over a dozen excellent songs of baroque folk-pop for his album debut, and the many gems can't help but shine through all the self-indulgence. The sprightly orchestration for cello and trumpet (Gough's own) that begin the album are eventually taken over by the sparse guitar pickings and wistful folky sunshine of "The Shining," which veers into the skewed slide guitar and ominous tone of "Everybody's Stalking." Gough rarely pauses for breath (even when he's doing a ballad) or follows any traditional sense of album flow, but after a listen or two *The Hour of Bewilderbeast* is revealed as a shambling masterpiece of a pop album. Most of these songs are Gough's entirely (he plays as many as eight instruments), with occasional help from friends like Twisted Nerve co-labelhead Andy Votel and assorted drummers for accompaniment. His songwriting is great, but Gough's twisted sense of humor helps the album shine as well, as on "Fall in a River" where the down-a-lazy-river feel carries through to the point where not just Gough but the entire production is submerged with a splash and attendant warping of the sound. *The Hour of Bewilderbeast* surely isn't a traditional pop album, but a continually beguiling trip through lo-fi post-modern folk that draws as much from Harry Nilsson as Beck. *—John Bush*

Erykah Badu (Erykah Wright)

b. Feb. 26, 1972
Vocals / Contemporary R&B, Alternative Rap, Adult Alternative Pop/Rock, Urban, Hip-Hop
She grew up listening to '70s soul and '80s hip-hop, but Erykah Badu drew more

comparisons to Billie Holiday upon her breakout in 1997, after the release of her first album, *Baduizm*. The grooves and production on the album are bass-heavy R&B, but Badu's langurous, occasionally tortured vocals and delicate phrasing immediately removed her from the legion of cookie-cutter female R&B singers. A singer/songwriter responsible for all but one of the songs on *Baduizm*, the first single "On & On" became a number one R&B hit in early 1997, and the LP followed it to the top of the R&B album charts by March. Opening for R&B acts as well as rap's Wu-Tang Clan, Badu stopped just short of number one on the pop album charts in April. Her *Live* album followed later in the year *—John Bush*

● **Baduizm** / Feb. 11, 1997 / Kedar/Universal ♦♦♦♦
Erykah Badu's debut album, *Baduizm*, is an astonishing display of vocal virtuosity and musical vision. Badu has fashioned a variation of urban soul that is utterly modern yet thoroughly rooted in tradition. There are elements of Billie Holiday, blues, soul, and hip-hop in *Baduizm*, and she seamlessly fuses them together, creating music that is wise beyond her years. That doesn't mean that the album is flawless. Like many debut artists, Badu's reach occasionally exceeds her grasp, and several of the songs are a little too similar, but that doesn't prevent *Baduizm* from being a remarkable and refreshing debut. *—Leo Stanley*

Live / Nov. 18, 1997 / Kedar/Universal ♦♦♦
Conventional wisdom dictates that an artist should not release a live album as their second record, especially if it follows the debut by a matter of months. However, Erykah Badu is not a conventional artist and *Live* is not a conventional live album. While her debut, *Baduizm*, earned strong reviews and healthy sales, her concerts became equally popular and she became known as a powerhouse live performer. *Live* solidifies that reputation, delivering soulful, gritty versions of cuts from *Baduizm*, a few covers, and the spectacular new single, "Tyrone." Not only does it illustrate the depths of Badu's talents, but *Live* is as strong and captivating as *Baduizm*. *—Leo Stanley*

Mama's Gun / Oct. 31, 2000 / Kedar/Universal ♦♦♦♦
Since the arrival of Erykah Badu onto the nu soul scene back in 1997 with *Baduizm*, commercial music has stood up and taken notice with an onslaught of similar artists reaching comparable peaks of mainstream success. After taking some time off for introspection and to raise her son, Badu returns with *Mama's Gun*, which is a turning point for her in many ways. Gone are the cryptic "Baduizms" that glossed all over her first release, replaced with a more honestly raw Badu singing directly from her heart rather than her head. Sonically, Badu wades out into adventurous territories as well. From the Jimi Hendrix-inspired opening number to the closing ten-minute song suite, she develops fresh aspects of her sound, employing artists such as legendary jazz vibraphonist Roy Ayers, jazz trumpeter Roy Hargrove, Stephen Marley, and Roots drummer ?uestlove; she sought after producer Jay Dee as well. The results are consistently tasteful, which only helps to prove once again that Badu is miles ahead of the rest. *—Rob Theakston*

Joan Baez

b. Jan. 9, 1941, Staten Island, NY
Vocals, Guitar / Folk Revival, Contemporary Folk, Folk-Rock, Singer/Songwriter, Traditional Folk, Political Folk
The most accomplished interpretive folksinger of the 1960s, Joan Baez has influenced nearly every aspect of popular music in a career still going strong after more than 35 years. Baez is possessed of a once-in-a-lifetime soprano, which, since the late '50s, she has put in the service of folk and pop music as well as a variety of political causes Baez first gained recognition at the 1959 Newport Folk Festival, then cut her 1960 self-titled debut album for Vanguard Records. It was made up of 13 traditional songs given near-definitive treatment. A moderate success on release, the album took off after the breakthrough of *Joan Baez, Vol. 2* (Sep. 1961), and both albums became huge hits, as did her third album, *Joan Baez in Concert*. From 1962 to 1964, Baez was the popular face of folk music, headlining festivals and concert tours and singing at political events, including the August 1963 March on Washington. During this period, she began to champion the work of folk songwriter Bob Dylan, and gradually her repertoire moved from traditional material toward the socially conscious work of the emerging generation of '60s artists like him. Like other popular folk performers, Baez was affected by the changes in popular music wrought by the appearance of the Beatles in the U.S. in 1964 and Dylan's introduction of folk-rock in 1965, and she began to augment her simple acoustic guitar backing with other instruments. Baez continued to experiment in the late '60s, releasing *Baptism—A Journey Through Our Time* (Jun. 1968), in which she recited poetry, and *Any Day Now* (Dec. 1968), a double album of Dylan songs done with country backing, which went gold. Baez switched record-label affiliation to A&M Records with *Come from the Shadows* (May 1972), which moved her in a more pop direction. *—William Ruhlmann*

☆ **Joan Baez** / 1960 / Vanguard ♦♦♦♦♦
At the time of its release, Joan Baez's debut album was something of a revelation. The folk music revival was beginning to gather steam, stoked on the popular side by artists such as the Kingston Trio and the Easy Riders, as well as up-and-coming ensembles such as the Highwaymen, and on the more intense and serious side by the Weavers. The female singers on the scene were mostly old-time, veteran activist types like Ronnie Gilbert and Malvina Reynolds, who was in her 60s. And then along comes this album, by a 19-year-old who looked more like the kind of coed every mother dreamt her son would come home with, displaying a voice from heaven, a soprano so pure and beguiling that the mere act of listening to her—forget what she was singing—was a pleasure. Baez's first album, made up primarily of traditional songs (including a startling version of "House of the Rising Sun"), was beguiling enough to woo even conservative-leaning listeners. Accompanied by the Weavers' Fred Hellerman and a pair of session singers, Baez gives a fine account of the most reserved and least confrontational aspects of the folk revival, presenting a brace of traditional songs (most notably "East Virginia" and "Mary Hamilton") with an urgency and sincerity that makes the listener feel as though they were being sung for the first time, and opening with a song that was to become her signature piece for many years, "Silver Dagger." The recording was notable at the time for its purity of sound, but like a lot of Vanguard releases from this period reissued in the 1980s, it could do with a fresh remastering on the CD, which is not quite up to modern standards. *—Bruce Eder*

Joan Baez, Vol. 2 / 1961 / Vanguard ♦♦♦♦
Joan Baez's second album, recorded when she was 20 years old, is a hearty helping of folk masterpieces that give ample evidence to exactly how she was established as a leader of the contemporary folk scene of the day. The material chosen is truly exceptional, from the beautifully stark British ballad "The Trees They Do Grow High" to the tragic tales of death and lost love in "Engine 143" and "Banks of the Ohio," which recall the Carter Family in presentation as much as spirit. Without a doubt, Baez's version of "Pal of Mine" is every bit as vibrant as when the Carters recorded it, though here given a more bluegrass sound by the banjo and backup vocal accompaniment of the Greenbriar Boys. The traditional Christmas tune "The Cherry Tree Carol" is presented perfectly by Baez's gorgeous arrangement. Baez is a true master of her craft, and though she hasn't always made the best choices for material, the 14 interpretations here are as timeless as the songs themselves. Similar to Bob Dylan's self-titled debut, this is an album that all fans of traditional folk music should seek out. [In August of 2001, *Joan Baez, Vol. 2* was reissued in an audiophile remastered edition, with new annotation and containing three additional songs from the same sessions—all are a match for anything on the original album, and "I Once Loved a Boy" and "The Longest Train I Ever Saw" count among the saddest, most emotionally enveloping songs of Baez's early career.] *–Matt Fink & Bruce Eder*

Joan Baez in Concert, Pt. 1 / 1963 / Vanguard ♦♦♦♦
Joan Baez's early performances weren't so much folk concerts as virtuoso recitals, each one a major event. So pure and striking was the singer's falsetto, that she elevated whatever material she chose to perform, and at the time she enjoyed near universal acclaim. This first of two live LPs, derived from performances on various campuses from 1962 and 1963, offers many of the same virtues as the two studio albums that preceded it, with added immediacy and spontaneity. Her playing and singing was like nothing else heard on the folk circuit at the time, and coupled with sympathetic audiences—one of which joins in gently on "Danger Waters"—the resulting album is just about as good as Baez's early output got. The material, including "Black Is the Color of My True Love's Hair," "The House Carpenter," "Lady Mary," "What Have They Done to the Rain," and "Kumbaya," is presented in extraordinary renditions, some very unexpected—Woody Guthrie's "Pretty Boy Floyd," done in a soaring, operatic-like manner, is worlds removed from any other version. The CD transfer is also very clean, and the booklet reprints the original LP's jacket notes. *—Bruce Eder*

Joan Baez in Concert, Pt. 2 / 1963 / Vanguard ♦♦♦

Five / 1964 / Vanguard ♦♦♦

Farewell, Angelina / 1965 / Vanguard ♦♦♦

Noël / 1966 / Vanguard ♦♦♦♦♦
An album of stately beauty, Baez's pure, soaring soprano is accompanied by a consort of recorders and viols, lute, harpsichord, baroque organ, winds, strings, and percussion. Her rendition of the "Coventry Carol" is stirring, and Baez pours her heart into "The Carol of the Birds." Considering Baez's politics, one would never know she recorded this album in the Vietnam War era. The 2001 CD reissue on Vanguard adds liner notes by arranger Peter Schickele, and seven previously unreleased bonus tracks. All the additional tracks are, as is the original album, Christmas-related. Two are instrumental, and one is a French version of "Away in a Manger," which appears on an English version on the original album. *—Dennis MacDonald*

Joan / 1967 / Vanguard ♦♦♦
Ornate, heavily orchestrated versions of other people's songs. Over-produced, but quite beautiful. *—Bruce Eder*

Any Day Now / 1968 / Vanguard ♦♦♦
Any Day Now is an all-Dylan album which includes a definitive performance of "Love Is Just a Four-Letter Word." *– William Ruhlmann*

One Day at a Time / 1970 / Vanguard ♦♦♦♦
One Day at a Time finds Joan Baez beginning to modernize her repertoire. The clear soprano voice that wowed Woodstock still finds time to add the folk/protest tunes such as "Joe Hill" and her own "A Song for David" while covering the Stones' "No Expectations," Delaney and Bonnie's "Ghetto," and the title track, written by Willie Nelson. Recorded in Nashville at Bradley's Barn, this was one more step toward commercial success in Baez's career. Satisfying. *—James Chrispell*

● **The First Ten Years** / 1970 / Vanguard ♦♦♦♦♦
The First Ten Years is an excellent overview of Joan Baez's first decade of recording, balancing her work as an interpreter of both traditional and contemporary folk songs. There may be a few fan favorites missing, but all the essentials are here, making it an excellent introduction for the novice. *—Stephen Thomas Erlewine*

Blessed Are… / 1971 / Vanguard ♦♦♦♦
With *Blessed Are…*, Joan Baez found herself with a hit single on the charts. That song, a cover of Robbie Robertson's "The Night They Drove Old Dixie Down," is just one of the many surprises on *Blessed Are…* Once again using some of Nashville's finest pickers and songwriters, Baez runs the gamut of such influences as the Beatles, the Rolling Stones, Mickey Newberry, Jesse Winchester, Stevie Wonder and, of course, herself, while sound-

ing nothing more than like Joan Baez always has. Great music, and a lot of it, too, for when it was released on vinyl, it was a double album with a special 7" single included. Altogether, 22 tracks of some of Joan's finest. —*James Chrispell*

Carry It On / 1971 / Vanguard ✦✦✦
A soundtrack interspersing acoustic live performances with politically oriented dialog, much of which is spoken by her then-husband, draft resister David Harris. It's certainly one of the most minor entries of her Vanguard catalog. The dialogue is distracting, and the music reasonable but uneven, as Baez offers interpretations of songs by Gram Parsons, Bob Dylan, Tom Paxton, Edwin Hawkins, Leonard Cohen, and "We Shall Overcome." Her cover of Aretha Franklin's "Do Right Woman, Do Right Man," however, was not a good idea. —*Richie Unterberger*

Come from the Shadows / 1972 / A&M ✦✦✦
After recording for the folk label Vanguard for more than a decade, Baez moved to A&M. On this label debut, she maintained her interest in country music, recording in Nashville with some of the city's session aces. She also continued to dedicate herself to radical politics, from her set opener "Prison Trilogy," which pledged, "We're gonna raze the prisons to the ground," to the closer, John Lennon's "Imagine." In between were her call on Bob Dylan to return to protest music ("To Bobby") and her sister Mimi Farina's touching tribute to Janis Joplin, "In the Quiet Morning." —*William Ruhlmann*

Where Are You Now, My Son? / 1973 / A&M ✦✦✦
This isn't only not the place to start listening to Joan Baez, it's the album that separates the true fans from the, um, fellow travelers. Side 2 is taken up by the title song, a musical account of Baez's trip to Hanoi over Christmas of 1972, complete with the sound of U.S. bombs falling on the city. Side 1, on the other hand, contains one of Baez's best original songs, "A Young Gypsy," and two by her sister, "Mary Call" and "Best of Friends." —*William Ruhlmann*

★ Diamonds & Rust / 1975 / A&M ✦✦✦✦✦
With the Vietnam War winding down, Joan Baez, who had devoted one side of her last album to her trip to Hanoi, delivered the kind of commercial album A&M Records must have wanted when it signed her three years earlier. But she did it on her own terms, putting together a session band of contemporary jazz veterans like Larry Carlton, Wilton Felder, and Joe Sample, and mixing a wise selection from the work of current singer-songwriters like Jackson Browne and John Prine with pop covers of Stevie Wonder and the Allman Brothers Band, and an unusually high complement of her own writing. A&M, no doubt recalling the success of her cover of the Band's "The Night They Drove Old Dixie Down," released her version of the Allmans' "Blue Sky" as a single, and it got halfway up the charts. But the real hit was the title track, a self-penned masterpiece on the singer's favorite subject, her relationship with Bob Dylan. Outdoing the current crop of confessional singer/songwriters at soul baring, Baez sang to Dylan, reminiscing about her '60s love affair with him intensely, affectionately, and unsentimentally. It was her finest moment as a songwriter and one of her finest performances, period, and when A&M finally released it on 45, it made the Top 40, propelling the album to gold status. But those who bought the disc for "Diamonds & Rust" also got to hear "Winds of the Old Days," in which Baez forgave Dylan for abandoning the protest movement, as well as the jazzy "Children and All That Jazz," a delightful song about motherhood, and the wordless vocals of "Dida," a duet with Joni Mitchell accompanied by Mitchell's backup band, Tom Scott and the L.A. Express. The cover songs were typically accomplished, making this the strongest album of Baez's post-folk career. —*William Ruhlmann*

From Every Stage / 1976 / A&M ✦✦✦✦
Recorded on the *Diamonds & Rust* tour, *From Every Stage* is a satisfying portrait of Joan doing what she does best. Performing selections from every stage of her career, this live release is a testament to Baez's long and illustrious career. Divided into acoustic and electric sets, highlights include "Blowin' in the Wind," "The Night They Drove Old Dixie Down," and "Diamonds & Rust." Faithful to her ideals, Joan Baez is here at one of the peaks of her long career. —*James Chrispell*

Joan Baez in Concert / 1976 / Vanguard ✦✦✦
A vibrant concert recording with a radiant sound, humor, and topicality. —*Bruce Eder*

The Best of Joan Baez [A&M] / 1977 / A&M ✦✦✦✦✦
A&M's 1977 collection *The Best of Joan Baez* doesn't chronicle her most influential work, but that doesn't mean it's not without merit. Far from it, actually. This is a concise recapping of her poppier recordings for A&M, which includes such classic Baez moments as her original "Diamonds & Rust" and a definitive reading of Robbie Robertson's "The Night They Drove Old Dixie Down." The rest of the album splits the difference between covers (including Stevie Wonder's lovely "I Never Dreamed You'd Leave in Summer" and Dylan's "Simple Twist of Fate") and originals, providing an entertaining, enlightening encapsulation of her '70s recordings. —*Stephen Thomas Erlewine*

Honest Lullaby / 1979 / Portrait ✦✦✦
On her second album for CBS's Portrait label (and her last new album issued in the U.S. for eight years), Baez was given a full-scale pop-rock production by veteran Barry Beckett and the studio band in Muscle Shoals, AL. The result, on songs that range from "Let Your Love Flow" to "Before the Deluge," is accessible but not particularly memorable '70s-style pop. If you always wanted to know what the words to "No Woman, No Cry" are, however, this is the place to find out. —*William Ruhlmann*

Very Early Joan Baez / 1983 / Vanguard ✦✦✦✦
This Vanguard release is a heartwarmingly intimate look at Joan Baez during her most influential period (1960-1963). The album's 22 tracks are all live, performed before audiences held in silent and rapt attention in packed concert halls. The singer's trademark politically tinged folk songs are charmingly blended with a few pop interpretations like the

Jerry Ragovoy early soul classic "She's a Trouble Maker" and a fun version of the Diamonds' "Little Darlin'," revealing a rarely seen lighthearted side of the activist. Baez's voice never sounded better than during this era, and her live performances resonate with a confident honesty.

The only detractions of this CD are in the production: the whole album is mixed very quietly (requiring the listener to crank up the volume) but the applause between songs seems brashly loud. The other nitpick is that, for some reason, the album's engineer fades Baez's voice from left to right within the songs; this isn't a tremendous problem but listening on headphones to the sound bobbing back and forth can create a feeling of seasickness. However, these minor flaws should not discourage anyone from picking up *Very Early Joan Baez*, a shining example of the bridge from the traditional Weavers/Kingston Trio folk singing of the fifties and the youthful fire of the political folk of the '60s. —*Zac Johnson*

Live in Europe '83: Children of the Eighties / 1983 / Ariola ✦✦✦✦✦
Recently / 1988 / Gold Castle ✦✦✦✦✦
Baez returned to U.S. record shops with a vengeance here, delivering her interpretations of songs by Dire Straits, Johnny Clegg, U2, and Peter Gabriel, performers whose political consciousness had been formed by listening to old Joan Baez albums. And on the title track, a stunning original, she boldly answered ex-husband David Harris' downbeat memoir of the '60s, *Dreams Die Hard*, as well as other '80s revisionists. —*William Ruhlmann*

Play Me Backwards / 1992 / Virgin ✦✦✦
Rare, Live & Classic [Box] / Sep. 1993 / Vanguard ✦✦✦✦✦
Spanning three discs, the box set *Rare, Live & Classic* is an odd mix of Baez's best-known songs and rarities. For the hardcore collector, there are plenty of interesting items here, including previously unreleased duets with Bob Dylan, Donovan, Bill Wood, and Jeffrey Shurtleff, but for the casual fan, there's too much material; they would be better off with her original albums or single-disc compilations. —*Stephen Thomas Erlewine*

Greatest Hits / May 7, 1996 / A&M ✦✦✦✦✦
Greatest Hits is a reasonably comprehensive collection of Joan Baez's best-known songs, concentrating mainly on her crossover hits. Although it misses several fine items, the compilation remains an effective introduction for the curious listener. —*Stephen Thomas Erlewine*

Best of Joan Baez [Vanguard] / Sep. 30, 1997 / Vanguard ✦✦✦
Vanguard's *Best of Joan Baez* is a solid, if brief, collection that features a handful of her best-known songs—"The Night They Drove Old Dixie Down," "There But for Fortune," "I Am a Poor Wayfaring Stranger," "Joe Hill," "Silver Dagger," "Pack up Your Sorrows," "We Shall Overcome"—but it leaves just as many off the disc. It's a serviceable, but hardly definitive, introduction to her career, and there are far better collections on the marketplace. —*Stephen Thomas Erlewine*

Vanguard Sessions: Baez Sings Dylan / Jun. 9, 1998 / Vanguard ✦✦✦✦
Culling 15 tracks from her 1968 release of *Any Day Now* and adding five tracks taken from her releases of the early '60s, *Vanguard Sessions: Baez Sings Dylan* is a wonderful example of Joan Baez's ability to transcend the work of other songwriters. Though it could be said that the genius of Dylan's songcraft can occasionally be obscured by the understated starkness of his presentation, Baez's use of slightly countrified arrangements to compliment her powerful vocals succeeds in recasting these classics in a slightly prettier package. Baez takes few liberties, so most tracks don't count as surprises, though a bluesy a cappella rendition of "Tears of Rage" and a funky, soulful "Dear Landlord" nearly qualify as such. More than anything, Baez's renditions make the listener realize just how incredibly nuanced Dylan's delivery can be. Though standards like "You Ain't Goin' Nowhere," "It Ain't Me Babe," and "I Shall Be Released" are covered, just as many tracks are of a lesser-known variety, such as "Walkin' Down the Line," "Love Is Just a Four-Letter Word," and "Walls of Red Wing." Of course, bringing out the genius in Dylan's work isn't exactly akin to pulling teeth, but the timeless quality of Baez's thoughtful renditions more than does the work justice. —*Matt Fink*

Bailter Space
f. 1987, Christchurch, New Zealand
New Zealand Rock, Indie Rock, Alternative Pop/Rock
Led by former Gordons guitarist Alister Parker, noise-rock unit Bailter Space emerged from Christchurch, New Zealand in 1987. Originally joined by former Clean and Great Unwashed drummer Hamish Kilgour, Pin Group alum Ross Humphries on bass, and Glenda Bills on drums, the group issued their debut EP, *Nelsh Bailter Space*, on the famed Flying Nun label later that year; both Humphries and Bills departed soon after, resulting in the addition of former Gordons bassist John Halvorsen in time to record the 1988 full-length *Tanker*. A tour followed, but when the Clean re-formed, Kilgour joined them on a permanent basis; his replacement in Bailter Space was Brent McLachlan, also the drummer in the Gordons. Despite the restoration of the Gordons' core roster, however, Bailter Space was a clearly distinct entity, their sound more dense and imposing than in their previous incarnation; the trio resurfaced in 1990 with *Thermos*, mounting a tour of the Northern Hemisphere the following year. An EP, *The Aim*, appeared in 1992, and in 1993 Bailter Space released *Robot World*, their most acclaimed outing to date. Their prolific output continued in 1994 with *Vortura*; *Wammo* followed in 1995, although a brief hiatus preceded the release of *Solar.3* and *Capsul*. —*Jason Ankeny*

Tanker / 1988 / Flying Nun ✦✦✦✦✦
Stripping the lineup down to just Kilgour on drums and old Gordons mate Halvorsen on bass, Parker and a revamped Bailter Space cooked up a full-length debut much closer in

spirit to what '90s audiences were familiar with, while simultaneously distancing themselves from the ghost of the Gordons. The nervy, aggressive edge of the Gordons is still there, but now it's tempered by a slightly less aggressive approach. The downbeat guitar chiming and squalling feedback of "Glass" and "The 'W' Song" give a good sense of this, as do Parker's vocals, which are buried deep in the mix on these tracks. "Your Invisible Life" has a great push to it and features a particularly inspired performance from Parker. "The Today Song" achieves almost inspirational heights in its own way, while "Grader Spader" fuses the spirit of old and new quite effectively, and was understandably chosen as a single. Parker continues to sing in his new, tenderer way, while the band kicks up a catchy storm. The trio work well together, and a few songs sound like they grew out of particularly productive jam sessions. The punchy instrumental "Titan"—which features Parker and Halvorsen exchanging moody, ringing chords and notes before building into a false climax and an astonishing return—and the equally fine title track are probably the best songs on the album for that reason alone. —*Ned Raggett*

Thermos / 1990 / Flying Nun ✦✦✦
Starting with the alternately tender and driving "Fish Eye," *Thermos* finds Bailter Space coming fully into their own. McLachlan, having engineered *Tanker*, takes over for Kilgour on this record, restoring the original Gordons lineup. Rather than indulging in simple nostalgia, though, the threesome expand on the strengths of their previous releases to create possibly their best album yet—under either name. Parker's equally bitter and emotional lyrics touch on many different areas of life, while his newfound singing powers impress; he'll never be mistaken for a soul wailer, but he brings a careful passion to his range like few others can. Musically, the trio continue with the same blend of accessibility and aggression as before, striking a near-perfect balance between the two. "Fused" is Bailter Space at their considerable best, with the digital ring of Parker's guitar and the crisp rhythm work of Halvorsen and McLachlan creating a powerful, moody roll as Parker half whispers the vague threat of the lyrics. "Zero Return" both lulls and kicks, and the band fires up an explosive climax. The Gordons' roots aren't entirely forgotten over the course of the album: "The State" captures the declamatory feel of many of their cuts, while still sounding more like the current band than the old one. "Hard Wired" is more aggressive, but in an abstract fashion—much like *154*-era Wire—featuring echoed vocals looped throughout the mix. Parker's sense of personal politics is as fiery as before: "Ad Man" rides a great McLachlan drum line that could almost be a tribute to glam rock, as Parker cautiously regards the titular figure in question. Powerful and beautiful, *Thermos* is flat-out great. —*Ned Raggett*

● **The Aim** / 1992 / Matador ✦✦✦✦✦
Bailter Space's first American release is also one of its strongest, a near-perfect four-song slice of original material that shows why the band's hype was so well deserved. Concentrating the strengths of *Thermos* and adding a few new touches, like the hushed whispers on the title track, the trio show their ability to rock both tenderly and loudly, but in ways that never sound like the typical connotations of either description. The title track is actually the least memorable of the four, with Parker sounding a bit lazy on the vocals. "We Know" is something else again, with its heavily processed vocals and crunching melody. "Shine" is simply gorgeous, featuring a beautiful background melody, another fantastic Parker love lyric, and understated vocal passion. The kicking thrash of "Unseen" wraps it up, with all three musicians going off, while sticking to that steady beat that's served them so well over the years. —*Ned Raggett*

Robot World / 1993 / Matador ✦✦✦
Hot on the heels of *The Aim*, *Robot World* elevated Bailter Space to even more fascinating levels, their winning combination of arty edge and wistful flow honed even more thoroughly than before. "Begin" not only starts the album but captures the trio's increasingly fascinating touch, with lyrics half heard in the feedback and crunch. It's more gently abstract, exchanging overload for a more stripped down, yet equally produced, power. Sometimes other hints of MBV's massively influential reinterpretations of rock do surface, as on the brief "Fascination," which sounds almost like a cross between Kevin Shields and Xpressway-style lo-fi experimentalism. Hints of the latter also surface on "EIP," with its buried percussion and strange clattering. But all in all, this is Bailter Space steering its own fine path. "Be On Time" is a cousin to *The Aim*'s "We Know," but with a slightly different melody in the nearly incomprehensible verse. Sometimes the band retreats from their often elegant compositions: "Get Lost" is almost a punk-style thrash, at least at the beginning, though the mixed-down vocals and alternately ugly/beautiful guitars readily identify it as a Bailter Space track. When it cuts into a slightly slower pace a couple of minutes in, it suddenly assumes an even greater power and beauty, achieving once again that perfect synthesis of the two sides of the band. —*Ned Raggett*

Vortura / May 20, 1994 / Matador ✦✦✦✦
Bailter Space open up *Vortura* with something far fiercer than their usual combination of fire and ice. Defying expectations sometimes backfires, but "Projects" is a massive, brawling monster of a track, on which Parker rages about people stuck living in ghettos while others "in high places" live comfortably. Overall, it's one of Bailter Space's best efforts ever—a call to arms that works on all fronts. "Process Paid," featuring a ranted verse and softly sung chorus over a propulsive trance-rock track, recalls the general sound of *Robot World*. From there on, it's business as usual for the trio, who do what they do best over the course of these 11 songs. The first single, "X," is another definite high point for the band—a confidently anthemic charge that brings to mind Echo & the Bunnymen and various shoegaze bands, but without sounding like either. Some songs are slightly tweaked from the basic Bailter Space sound, such as "I.C.Y.," which is much more stripped down than many of the band's songs, and "Reactor," which consists mainly of Halvorsen's bass, McLachlan's generally buried percussion and pulses, and Parker's guitar filling in shades and sounds instead of crunching through a lead riff. Generally, though, it's pretty

much typical Bailter Space, and while it may lack the sense of freshness and achievement of *Robot World*, *Vortura* still serves up the goods. Halvorsen and McLachlan make for a great rhythm section, as always, while Parker's guitar playing and evocative, if often cryptic, lyrics and singing remain sure and true. —*Ned Raggett*

Wammo / 1995 / Matador ✦✦✦

Capsul / Jul. 13, 1997 / Turnbuckle ✦✦✦✦

Solar.3 / Mar. 30, 1999 / Turnbuckle ✦✦✦

Anita Baker

b. Jan. 26, 1958, Toledo, OH
Vocals / Quiet Storm, Adult Contemporary, Urban
Anita Baker's strong, sensual alto helped her break down the doors in the middle of the '80s. More than any other singer, she defined quiet storm—smooth, romantic soul for adults. Baker's music is sophisticated without being cold, romantic without being saccharine; besides soul, her singing has roots in jazz and classic pop, bringing a refined romanticism to her music. Although her 1983 debut, *The Songstress*, disappeared upon its release, her 1986 album, *Rapture*, was a modern classic that ushered in a new era of urban contemporary and modern pop singing. None of her following records were quite as good, but her singing remains impressive on each album and she was one of the most popular urban/adult contemporary singers of the '80s and '90s. —*Stephen Thomas Erlewine*

The Songstress / Jun. 1983 / Elektra ✦✦✦✦✦
Trends in African-American music changed considerably between Anita Baker's first taste of national exposure in 1979 (when she was a member of Detroit soul band Chapter 8 and sang lead on the hit ballad "I Just Wanna Be Your Girl") and her debut solo album, *The Songstress*, in 1983. While 1979's Black music charts were full of large funk bands, standup vocal harmony groups, and disco divas, rappers and techno-funksters like the System were very much in vogue in 1983. Instead of following trends, Baker excelled by doing what she does best: gospel-influenced, '70s-type soul/pop with jazz overtones. *The Songstress*, released by the small Beverly Glen label and reissued by Elektra in 1991, wasn't the mega-hit her next album, *Rapture*, would be. But the Sarah Vaughan-influenced singer began to build a following with such honest, heartfelt ballads and "slow jams" as "No More Tears," "You're the Best Thing Yet," and the caressing "Angel." A sweaty taste of gospel-drenched funk, the invigorating "Squeeze Me" is atypical of the ballad-oriented Baker—although she definitely shines at this faster tempo. Indeed, Baker's solo career was off to a most impressive start with *The Songstress*. For those who savored *Rapture* and *Givin' You the Best That I Got*, *The Songstress* is also essential listening. —*Alex Henderson*

● **Rapture** / Mar. 1986 / Elektra ✦✦✦✦✦
Though Anita Baker got some airplay out of *The Songstress*, that promising solo debut didn't bring her financial security. In fact, Baker was earning her living as a legal secretary in her native Detroit when she signed with Elektra in the mid-'80s. Elektra gave her a strong promotional push, and the equally superb *Rapture* became the megahit that *The Songstress* should have been. To its credit, Elektra made her a major star by focusing on Baker's strong point—romantic but gospel-influenced R&B/pop ballads and "slow jams," sometimes with jazz overtones—and letting her be true to herself. *Rapture* gave Baker one moving hit after another, including "Sweet Love," "Caught Up in the Rapture," "Same Ole Love," and "No One in This World." Praising Baker in a 1986 interview, veteran R&B critic Steve Ivory asserted, "To me, singers like Anita Baker and Frankie Beverly define what R&B or soul music is all about." Indeed, *Rapture*'s tremendous success made it clear that there was still a sizeable market for adult-oriented, more traditional R&B singing. —*Alex Henderson*

Givin' You the Best That I Got / Oct. 1988 / Elektra ✦✦✦✦
The sizeable following that Baker acquired with *Rapture* proved quite receptive to the only slightly less appealing *Givin' You the Best That I Got*—an album that's quite similar to its predecessors. Though not quite on a par with *The Songstress* or *Rapture*, *Best* is far superior to most of 1988's uninspired R&B releases. Instead of tampering with *Rapture*'s consistently romantic and mellow soul/pop approach, Elektra brought back that album's producer, Michael J. Powell, and kept her at the top of the charts with such sleek yet earthy fare as "Just Because" (whose harmonies bring to mind producers Jimmy Jam & Terry Lewis, but lack the hip-hop elements they're quick to employ), "Priceless," the haunting "Good Love," and the title song. Much of Baker's music has contained jazz overtones, but on the Brazilian-influenced, slightly bossa nova-ish "Good Enough," Sarah Vaughan's influence becomes even more apparent—and indicates that she is making a tremendous mistake by not recording outright jazz. —*Alex Henderson*

Compositions / Jun. 1990 / Elektra ✦✦✦
On *Rapture* and *Givin' You the Best That I Got*, Baker embraced a blend of technology and "real instruments"—a definite contrast to the completely high-tech approach of so much '80s and '90s R&B. But on *Compositions*, producer Michael J. Powell moved even closer to a '70s-like approach to R&B—recording Baker's vocals live in the studio, employing a live rhythm section and avoiding drum machines altogether. What stayed the same was the type of material. Once again, Baker rejects hip-hop, techno-funk, new jack swing, and other '80s/'90s Black music styles in favor of a consistently relaxed soul/pop mood. Though there's a lot to admire here—including "No One to Blame," "Soul Inspiration," and "Whatever It Takes," a song Baker wrote with Gerald Levert and Marc Gordon of Levert—Baker's approach was beginning to sound like a formula in 1990. Clearly blessed with a magnificent range and lots of soul, Baker needs to experiment and take more risks. And one way to go just might be jazz. The torchy and captivating "Lonely"

shows that she has the ability to record a first-rate jazz album (if Elektra would okay such a project for her). Imagine Baker backed by James Moody, Tom Harrell, Chick Corea, Ray Brown, and Grady Tate! —*Alex Henderson*

Rhythm of Love / Sep. 13, 1994 / Elektra ✦✦✦

As the 1990s progressed, Anita Baker was sounding more and more contrived. One hoped that someone with so appealing a voice would challenge herself and try something different—perhaps recording more standards or exploring straight-ahead jazz (which she's obviously quite capable of doing). But instead of gambling with inspiration and risking a decline in sales, Baker tends to play it safe and offers a disc that often sounds like formula at work. Though *Rhythm of Love* is a generally decent album and even contains a few gems (including the dusky "Wrong Man," the torchy "Sometimes I Wonder Why," and heartfelt interpretations of "My Funny Valentine" and "The Look of Love"), Baker is capable of a lot more. The diva gives the impression that she desperately needs to follow Natalie Cole's lead and get away from catering to radio. —*Alex Henderson*

George Baker

b. Dec. 9, 1944, Netherlands
Vocals, Trumpet / Euro-Pop, Soft Rock

George Baker is Johannes Bouwens from Holland, a singer, guitarist, and keyboard player. As the leader of the five-member George Baker Selection, he was part of the "Dutch invasion" of 1970, when such groups as the Tee Set and the Shocking Blue also had U.S. hits. The Baker Selection scored with "Little Green Bag" (#21 pop) and "Dear Ann" (#93 pop), then disappeared for five years, returning with a third, final hit, "Una Paloma Blanca" (#1 easy listening, #26 pop, #33 country) in 1975. —*William Ruhlmann*

● **Little Green Bag** / 1970 / Colossus ✦✦✦✦

He had a hit with the title song, but for most latter-day pop listeners, the George Baker Selection is known for that song because it provided an oddly appropriate opening salvo for Quentin Tarantino's classic *Reservoir Dogs*. For most listeners of the early '70s and the early '90s, the best way to hear the GBS is to just listen to those three minutes of magic, but if you find that song endlessly listenable, *Little Green Bag* is a pretty fun listen. And it's a bit weirder than expected too, displaying a bizarre Europop vibe that keeps it interesting decades after its original release. No, there's nothing here that's nearly as good as the title track, but as an artifact, it has its merits. —*Stephen Thomas Erlewine*

LaVern Baker

b. Nov. 11, 1929, Chicago, IL, **d.** Mar. 10, 1997, New York, NY [Manhattan]
Vocals / Jump Blues, R&B

LaVern Baker was one of the sexiest divas gracing the mid-'50s rock & roll circuit, boasting a brashly seductive vocal delivery tailor-made for belting the catchy novelties "Tweedlee Dee," "Bop-Ting-A-Ling," and "Tra La La" for Atlantic Records during rock's first wave of prominence. Baker made her recording debut with RCA Victor in 1949 and signed to Atlantic four years later, debuting with the incendiary "Soul on Fire." The coy, Latin-tempoed "Tweedlee Dee" was a smash in 1955 on the R&B and pop charts, and her follow-ups "Bop-Ting-A-Ling," "Play It Fair," "Still," and the rocking "Jim Dandy" all vaulted into the R&B Top Ten over the next couple of years. She also hit big in 1958 with the ballad "I Cried a Tear," adopted a pseudosanctified bellow for the rousing Leiber & Stoller-penned gospel sendup "Saved" in 1960, and cut a Bessie Smith tribute album before leaving Atlantic in 1964. A brief stop at Brunswick Records preceded a late-'60s jaunt to entertain the troops in Vietnam. Baker became seriously ill after the trip and was hospitalized, eventually settling far out of the limelight in the Philippines for over 20 years. She finally returned in 1988, starring in the Broadway musical *Black & Blue* and making a nice comeback disc for DRG (*Woke Up This Mornin'*). She died in 1997. —*Bill Dahl*

Sings Bessie Smith / Jan. 27, 1958 / Atlantic ✦✦✦✦

This is an album that should not have worked. LaVern Baker (a fine R&B singer) was joined by all-stars from mainstream jazz (including trumpeter Buck Clayton, trombonist Vic Dickenson, tenor-saxophonist Paul Quinichette, and pianist Nat Pierce) for twelve songs associated with the great '20s blues singer Bessie Smith. Despite the potentially conflicting styles, this project is quite successful and often exciting. The arrangements by Phil Moore, Nat Pierce, and Ernie Wilkins do not attempt to re-create the original recordings; Baker sings in her own style (rather than trying to emulate Bessie Smith), and the hot solos work well with her vocals. —*Scott Yanow*

★ **Soul on Fire: The Best of LaVern Baker** / 1991 / Rhino/Atlantic ✦✦✦✦✦

The cream of this vivacious 1950s R&B belter's Atlantic catalog comprises this 20-track hits collection. Includes Baker's bouncy "Tweedlee Dee," and the storming rockers "Jim Dandy" and "Bop-Ting-a-Ling," the pseudo-gospel raveup "Saved," and Baker's torchy blues ballads "Soul on Fire" and "I Cried a Tear." She imparts "See See Rider" with a lighthearted reading that contrasts starkly with Chuck Willis' Atlantic smash of a few years before. —*Bill Dahl*

Blues Side of Rock & Roll / 1993 / Star Club ✦✦✦✦✦

This import may be of slightly dubious origins (sounds like everything was dubbed from vinyl, though the sound quality is quite acceptable), but it delves a lot deeper into LaVern Baker's Atlantic discography (26 cuts) and picks up a few essential sides ignored by Atlantic's own CD: "Tra La La," "Voodoo Voodoo," "Hey Memphis" (Baker's sequel to Elvis' "Little Sister"), and a hellacious version of "He's a Real Gone Guy" sporting a vicious King Curtis sax break. —*Bill Dahl*

Mickey Baker

b. Oct. 15, 1925, Louisville, KY
Guitar / East Coast Blues, Rock & Roll, R&B

Of all the guitarists who helped transform rhythm & blues into rock & roll, Mickey Baker is one of the very most important, ranking almost on the level of Chuck Berry and Bo Diddley. The reason he isn't nearly as well known as those legends is that a great deal of his work wasn't issued under his own name, but as a backing guitarist for many R&B and rock & roll musicians. Baker originally aspired to be a jazz musician, but turned to calypso, mambo, and then R&B, where the most work could be found. In the early and mid-'50s, he did countless sessions for Atlantic, King, RCA, Decca, and OKeh, playing on such classics as the Drifters' "Money Honey" and "Such a Night," Joe Turner's "Shake Rattle & Roll," Ruth Brown's "Mama, He Treats Your Daughter Mean," and Big Maybelle's "Whole Lot of Shakin' Going On." He also released a few singles under his own name, and made a Latin jazz-tinged solo album, *Guitar Mambo*. Baker's best work, though, was recorded as half of the duo Mickey & Sylvia. Their hit "Love Is Strange," as well as several other unknown but nearly equally strong tracks, featured Baker's keening, bluesy guitar riffs, which were gutsier and more piercing than most anything else around in the late '50s. Mickey & Sylvia split in the late '50s (though they recorded off and on until the middle of the next decade), and Baker recorded his best solo album, the all-instrumental *The Wildest Guitar*. In 1961, he took the male spoken part (usually assumed to be Ike Turner) on Ike & Tina Turner's first hit, "It's Gonna Work Out Fine." Shortly afterwards he moved to France, making a few hard-to-find solo records and working with a lot of French pop and rock performers, including Ronnie Bird, the best '60s French rock singer. He's recorded only sporadically since the mid-'60s. —*Richie Unterberger*

The Wildest Guitar / 1959 / Atlantic ✦✦✦✦✦

Despite Baker's well-deserved reputation as one of the most influential guitar players of early rock & roll, *The Wildest Guitar* was one of the few chances he really got to strut his stuff as a solo artist. This entirely instrumental set features keening, sharp bluesy riffs in much the same distinctive style that gained him fame on "Love Is Strange" and other tunes with Mickey & Sylvia. The choice of material, though, is a bit surprising, favoring some surprisingly cornball standards: "Third Man Theme," "Autumn Leaves," "Lullaby Of The Leaves," and Cole Porter's "Night And Day." Baker (who also arranged the album) manages to invest all of these with a snazzy R&B feel and biting solos. And he does actually write four of the twelve tunes himself, on which he fashions the kind of straightforward R&B that one would be more likely to expect. This is a pretty good showcase to hear Baker's unadorned virtuosity. But he's really better appreciated within the context of stronger material, either as half of Mickey & Sylvia or on the innumerable '50s R&B cuts (many on Atlantic) that feature his session work. —*Richie Unterberger*

● **Rock with a Sock** / Jun. 28, 1994 / Bear Family ✦✦✦✦

This 28-cut single disc covers several early and mid-'50s tracks with Baker finding creative ways to perform on period-piece rock and R&B/novelty material. His playing is uniformly impressive, even when fitting into less-than-outstanding productions and compositions. There are five Mickey And Sylvia tracks that conclude the session; they range from the interesting "Hello Stranger" to the odd "Woe, Woe Is Me," but really take away from the disc's purpose—to showcase Mickey Baker the player and demonstrate why he has such a sterling reputation among guitar fans and musicians. —*Ron Wynn*

Hank Ballard

b. Nov. 18, 1936, Detroit, MI
Vocals, Leader, Songwriter / R&B

Though born in Detroit, Ballard moved down to Alabama at an early age, to stay with relations after his father died. He was back in Detroit by the age of 15, forming a doo wop group called the Royals one year later. He signed to King Records in early 1953. Mid-size chart hits followed, and the group's name was changed to the Midnighters to avoid confusion with labelmates the Five Royales when "Work with Me Annie" became a national hit. Banned because of "explicit" lyrics, the song spawned a flurry of answer records (some by Ballard himself), most of them hitting the R&B charts as well. The hits kept coming throughout the early '60s, but the flipside of one of them became a national hit when Chubby Checker re-recorded "The Twist," spawning a national craze. Ballard's best records are informed by gospel-style harmonies and gritty guitar work, usually played by Alonzo Tucker. —*Cub Koda*

★ **Sexy Ways: The Best of Hank Ballard & the Midnighters** / Nov. 16, 1993 / Rhino ✦✦✦✦✦

Hank Ballard & the Midnighters were the 2 Live Crew of the early '50s, burning up the airwaves and black jukeboxes with lascivious-for-the-time period tunes like "Work with Me Annie," "Annie Had a Baby," and the title track. Although Ballard would go on to write dance hits, including the original version of "The Twist," the Midnighters at their best ("Open Up the Back Door") were Black doo wop at the end of a dark alley. Forget all previous compilations of these guys, this is the one you want. —*Cub Koda*

The EP Collection ... Plus / Sep. 12, 2000 / See For Miles ✦✦✦✦

See for Miles' *EP Collection*, like most of the series, is a greatest-hits collection from Hank Ballard containing almost all of his biggest hits, plus a bunch of notable B-sides and covers. There are a few nifty rarities here, but also a couple of obscurities that aren't all that interesting (the instrumental "The Big Frog"), and just because there are a generous 24 tracks doesn't necessarily mean that this is preferable to tighter collections. All the same, it's a fine collection of Ballard's best recordings and, while Rhino's set may be preferable, you'll still understand Ballard's greatness if you get this instead. —*Stephen Thomas Erlewine*

Dancin' and Twistin' / Oct. 31, 2000 / Ace ✦✦✦
Since Ballard & the Midnighters remain most known for their mid-'50s R&B/early rock & roll hits, it has sometimes been overlooked that they actually reached their crossover pop peak in the early '60s. In 1960 and 1961, they had seven Top 40 hits in the pop charts, and two Top Ten hits with "Finger Poppin' Time" and "Let's Go, Let's Go, Let's Go." All of those hits are on this 24-song anthology, which is devoted almost exclusively to Ballard's 1960s output. Ballard's original version of "The Twist," recorded in 1958 (and a Top Thirty hit in 1960, although Chubby Checker's cover went to #1), is here, and its success laid the foundation for an endless series of dance records over the next few years. "The Coffee Grind," "The Continental Walk," "The Switch-A-Roo," "It's Twistin' Time," "Good Twistin' Tonight," "Do You Know How to Twist?," even "The Float": all are on board. (And how could one resist calling "The Float" a dance bound to be dead on the water, even if it did make #10 R&B?) Ballard may have been more earthy, more funky, and more authentic in every way than Chubby Checker, but in this era he was really pursuing a similar formula: twist and dance records, the themes recycled ad infinitum. And it must be conceded that the formula, in Ballard's hands, wears out its welcome when the singles are heard bang right after each other. It's competent dance rock bridging 1950s R&B and early soul, without nearly enough variation or innovation to sustain interest. Really, "Finger Poppin' Time," "Let's Go, Let's Go, Let's Go," and "The Twist" are all you need to hear from this era, and you can probably find them on various-artists anthologies without breaking too heavy a sweat. *—Richie Unterberger*

Afrika Bambaataa (Kevin Donovan)

b. Apr. 10, 1960, New York City, NY [South Bronx]
DJ, Producer, Vocals / Old School Rap, Electro, Club/Dance, Urban, Hip-Hop
A seminal Bronx DJ during the '70s, Afrika Bambaataa ascended to godfather status with "Planet Rock," the 1982 hip-hop classic which blended the beats of hip-hop with techno-pop futurism inspired by German pioneers Kraftwerk. Even before he began recording in 1980, Bambaataa was hip-hop's foremost DJ, an organizer and promoter of the large block parties during the mid-to-late-'70s which presaged the rise of rap. After the success of "Planet Rock," he recorded electro-oriented rap only sparingly, concentrating instead on fusion—exemplified by his singles with ex-Sex Pistol John Lydon and fellow godfather James Brown. Bambaataa had moved to the background by the late '80s (as far as hip-hop was concerned), but the rise of his Zulu Nation collective—including De La Soul, Queen Latifah, A Tribe Called Quest, and the Jungle Brothers—found him once more being tipped as one of rap's founding fathers. *—John Bush*

Planet Rock—The Album / 1986 / Tommy Boy ✦✦✦✦✦
All the important early 12-inchers from 1982-1984 are here, including "Planet Rock" and "Looking for the Perfect Beat," plus three previously unreleased tracks recorded with Soulsonic Force. *—John Floyd*

Beware (The Funk Is Everywhere) / 1986 / Tommy Boy ✦✦✦✦

The Light / 1988 / EMI America ✦✦

1990-2000: The Decade of Darkness / Jun. 1991 / EMI America ✦✦✦

★ **Looking for the Perfect Beat: 1980-1985** / Mar. 20, 2001 / Tommy Boy ✦✦✦✦✦
As a major architect of early hip-hop, Afrika Bambaataa is perhaps more deserving of a respectable compilation treatment than anyone. And while his considerable influence has largely been brushed aside by a rap world that sadly ignores far too many of its innovators, *Looking for the Perfect Beat* may help to change that. Whatever your opinion on the shelf life of his music, Bambaataa was an innovator of the highest order. While many rappers would be content to sample and name check James Brown ad nauseam, Bambaataa collaborated with the Godfather of Soul himself on the sharp "Unity Part 1 (The Third Coming)". The amazing double-punch of "Planet Rock" and "Looking for the Perfect Beat" serve as the centerpiece of this disc, while "Zulu Nation Throwdown" sits as a perfect opening track, in its time initiating a back-to-roots aesthetic that was years ahead of the Afrocentric rap explosion of the late '80s. *Looking for the Perfect Beat* also nicely augments the résumé of producer Arthur Baker, a trailblazing dance remixer of the early '80s. Sadly missing are any significant liner notes or photographs. Also available as a limited edition two-LP set. *—John Duffy*

Banana Splits

f. 1967
Bubblegum
To a pre-teen generation for whom the concept of "free love" equaled unlimited hugs from mom and the notion of "getting high" meant nothing more than a breakfast cereal-induced sugar coma, the Banana Splits marked the apotheosis of such staples of late-'60s culture as psychedelia, pop art, and, of course, music. Like the Archies and Josie & the Pussycats, the band was essentially nothing more than a marketing front for a collective of faceless studio musicians; unlike their peers, however, in their own unique way the Banana Splits represented the acid culture's subtle encroachment into mainstream children's entertainment. By employing the kinds of camera techniques, surreal set designs, and hallucinatory images more commonly associated with the era's underground film-making, their television series brought the lessons of the Summer of Love to Saturday mornings; not unlike the similarly subversive (and, not coincidentally, similarly structured) *Pee-Wee's Playhouse* two decades later, *The Banana Splits* freed children's minds as it captured their imaginations, and its lasting influence has proven remarkable. Essentially, the Banana Splits concept was like the Monkees once removed; clearly modeled on the exuberance and slapstick comedy of the Beatles' film *A Hard Day's Night*, the show also borrowed heavily from the bright, psychedelic image the Fab Four sported on the cover of *Sgt. Pepper's Lonely Hearts Club Band*. Like both the Beatles and the Monkees, the Splits were a four-piece pop band, and like the Monkees (and the Beatles in *Help!*), they even lived together in the same mod digs. Unlike their human predecessors, however, the Banana Splits were bizarre, anthropomorphic animals. In total, some 23 bubblegum tunes were produced for the show. *—Jason Ankeny*

● **We're the Banana Splits** / 1985 / Decca ✦✦✦✦✦
We're the Banana Splits collects a dozen ace performances from the first season of the band's Saturday morning series. In addition to the oft-covered theme tune "The Tra-La-La Song"—offered here in a longer version than heard over the opening credits—the set includes the buoyant "(You're the) Lovin' End" and "Gonna Find Me a Cave." *—Jason Ankeny*

Bananarama

f. 1981, London, England
Pop/Rock, New Wave, Dance-Pop
The most successful British girl-group in pop history, Bananarama formed in London in late 1981 and comprised Keren Woodward, Sarah Dallin, and Siobhan Fahey. After the group backed Fun Boy Three on the single "It Ain't What You Do, It's the Way You Do It," the Three returned the favor for 1982's "He Was Really Sayin' Somethin'," a cover of the 1965 Velvelettes song that was the first of Bananarama's 26 U.K. chart smashes. While their initial hits, including "Shy Boy," "Na Na Hey Hey (Kiss Him Goodbye)" and "Cruel Summer" (their first U.S. smash) were roundly dismissed as fluffy pop fare, the success of 1984's rape-themed release "Robert DeNiro's Waiting" convinced the group to tackle more serious topics; however, the follow-up single, "Rough Justice"—a song protesting political tensions in Northern Ireland—bombed, and the trio's career stalled. In 1986, Bananarama's fortunes improved considerably when they joined forces with the production team of Stock, Aitken, and Waterman, who produced the album *Wow!*; the group's most successful outing to date, the LP's cover of the Shocking Blue's "Venus" was an international chart-topper, and both "Love in the First Degree" and "I Heard a Rumour" were major hits as well. *—Jason Ankeny*

Deep Sea Skiving / Mar. 1983 / London ✦✦✦✦✦
Bananarama's first album is by far their best. Before they fell in with the lucrative but often boring Stock, Aitken, and Waterman assembly line starting with 1986's *True Confessions*, Siobhan Fahey, Sarah Dallin, and Keren Woodward were unashamedly poppy, but they had enough artistic credibility to create a debut album that, barring a couple of small missteps, actually works as an album instead of a collection of singles with some filler. (They were even hip enough for their first single to be produced by ex-Sex Pistol Paul Cook.) Of course, the singles are terrific. There are four British chart hits in these 11 songs, and every one of them still sounds terrific, where later hits like "I Can't Help It" are terribly dated. The slinky "Shy Boy" and a rattling cover of the Marvelettes' "He Was Really Sayin' Somethin'" (co-starring the trio's early mentors, Fun Boy Three) are classic girl group songs updated for the '80s, every bit as credible as any mid-level Spector or Motown singles. That Cook-produced debut single, "Aie a Mwana" (oddly left off the album's first U.S. edition), now sounds mostly like a curio of the brief tropical craze that hit the U.K. in 1981/1982, but "Cheers Then" is a heartbreaker, an absolutely lovely lost-love song that's possibly the best thing Bananarama ever did and certainly one of the top singles to come out of Great Britain in 1982. Surprisingly, though, *Deep Sea Skiving* has some album tracks that are the equal of the singles. It's Bananarama's finest album by far, and an underappreciated pop gem of its era. *—Stewart Mason*

Bananarama / May 1984 / London ✦✦✦
The group adopted a more glamorous fashion style for this album, which finally brought them U.S. success with the Top Ten "Cruel Summer." Also included "Robert De Niro's Waiting." *—William Ruhlmann*

True Confessions / Jul. 1986 / Razor & Tie ✦✦✦✦
After becoming one of the biggest girl groups in U.K. pop music history, and after scoring a top ten U.S. hit with "Cruel Summer", Bananarama reached the commercial pinnacle of their career with their third album *True Confessions*. This album also marked an artistic change of pace for the trio because they began to utilize super hit producers Stock, Aitken, and Waterman, who helped them turn the 1970 rock hit "Venus" into an unstoppable, unforgettable dance smash. In fact, their version was so huge that it became their only U.S. number one hit. The rest of the album, however, is a little darker than one might expect, with heavy lyrics and themes permeating the songs. Other highlights include the second single "More Than Physical" which was also produced by Stock, Aitken, and Waterman, the moody third single "Trick of the Night," the saucy "Hooked on Love," the dance-pop of "Promised Land," and the seductive "Dance with a Stranger." To some, *True Confessions* was a departure of sorts from the post-punk, new-wave girl group sound which made Bananarama so essential to early 1980s British alterna-pop music. To others, it represents a shift to platinum success (which continued with their follow-up album *Wow!*), and this album, along with the hit "Venus," are prime examples of classic 1980s dance/pop music. *—Jose F. Promis*

● **Greatest Hits Collection** / Nov. 1988 / London ✦✦✦✦✦
Theoretically, this should be a note-perfect example of commercial '80s pop music at its best. But it isn't. Half of this album is actually pretty great, though—particularly the early Bananarama hits. The Fun Boy Three-produced "He Was Really Sayin' Somethin'" throws that band's quirky avant-funk underneath the threesome's harmonizing; the cover of "Aie a Mwana" shows off some slightly unexpected Afrobeat chops over a brisk arrangement; while "Shy Boy" takes a more mainstream approach, but without losing its understated sass. The American hits "Robert De Niro's Waiting" and "Cruel Summer" show how the trio could balance chart aspirations with atypical singing or subject matter. When it comes to the multi-national smashes produced by Stock, Aitken and Waterman, though,

it's not quite a case of the emperor having no clothes as much as a case of SAW being a one-trick pony. The reworking of Shocking Blue's "Venus" was a well-deserved success, taking the off-kilter pop/rock of the original and giving it a sparkling dance undercarriage. "I Heard a Rumour" isn't bad either, with a catchy chorus and a similar synth sheen. Unfortunately, the rest of the SAW-overseen selections do both the band and producers a major disservice, all being pallid and boring revamps of those two songs. If they ever felt defensive about the critical slams they received, the fact remains that at this point in the band's career there wasn't much to shout about. A new version of the Beatles' "Help!" at least provided them with a song that was more distinct than most of the late-'80s hash they received, but it wasn't as compelling a reworking as the others. —*Ned Raggett*

Pop Life / May 1991 / London ✦✦

Ultra Violet / Jan. 23, 1996 / ZYX ✦✦

The Band

f. 1967, Toronto, Ontario, Canada, **db.** Nov. 1976
Album Rock, Folk-Rock, Country-Rock, Rock & Roll
The Band were arguably the most important North American rock band of the late '60s, leading a retreat from psychedelia and a return to roots music, blending folk, country, blues, and rock & roll into a warm, freewheeling sound. The Band first coalesced as rockabilly wildman Ronnie Hawkins' supporting band in the early '60s. In 1965, they were hired as Bob Dylan's backing band for his 1965/66 tour. Drummer Levon Helm left shortly afterward, yet it was an artistically productive relationship, extending to a series of sessions recorded in Woodstock after the tour's completion—recordings that became known as the Basement Tapes. Around this time, Helm returned to the group and they signed to Capitol, releasing their debut, *Music from Big Pink*, in summer 1968. It sent shockwaves throughout rock, earning praise in the underground press and the respect of peers. Their second album, *The Band*, appearing in 1969, was their commercial breakthrough, reaching the Top 10. As their sales increased, the spotlight shifted to guitarist/songwriter Robbie Robertson, causing tensions within the group that escalated during the Todd Rundgren-produced sessions for *Stage Fright*. Their fourth album, 1971's *Cahoots*, was poorly received and failed to crack the Top 20. The Band took a bit of a break in 1972, releasing the double-live *Rock of Ages*, then a covers album, 1973's *Moondog Matinee*. They supported Dylan on his 1973 *Planet Waves* LP and its supporting tour, which was captured on *Before the Flood*. *Northern Lights–Southern Cross*, the Band's first album of new material in four years, appeared in 1975. One final studio album, 1977's *Islands*, was turned out, before they called it a day, commemorating their final concert with a triple-album set and Martin Scorsese documentary called *The Last Waltz*. The Band minus Robertson reunited occasionally in the '80s until pianist Richard Manuel took his own life in 1986. Helm, bassist Rick Danko, and organist Garth Hudson assembled a new Band in 1993, releasing *Jericho*, followed by 1996's *High on the Hog*. The Band continued to work until Danko's death in 1999. —*Stephen Thomas Erlewine*

☆ **Music from Big Pink** / Jul. 1, 1968 / Capitol ✦✦✦✦✦
None of the Band's previous work gave much of a clue about how they would sound when they released their first album in July 1968. As it was, *Music from Big Pink* came as a surprise. At first blush, the group seemed to affect the sound of a loose jam session, alternating emphasis on different instruments, while the lead and harmony vocals passed back and forth as if the singers were making up their blend on the spot. In retrospect, especially as the lyrics sank in, the arrangements seemed far more considered and crafted to support a group of songs that took family, faith, and rural life as their subjects and proceeded to imbue their values with uncertainty. Some songs took on the theme of declining institutions less clearly than others, but the points were made musically as much as lyrically. Tenor Richard Manuel's haunting, lonely voice gave the album much of its frightening aspect, while Rick Danko and Levon Helm's rough-hewn styles reinforced the songs' rustic fervor. The dominant instrument was Garth Hudson's often icy and majestic organ, while Robbie Robertson's unusual guitar work further destabilized the sound. The result was an album that reflected the turmoil of the late '60s in a way that emphasized the tragedy inherent in the conflicts. *Music from Big Pink* came off as a shockingly divergent musical statement only a year after the ornate productions of *Sgt. Pepper*, and initially attracted attention because of the three songs Bob Dylan had either written or co-written. Soon, however, as "The Weight" became a minor singles chart entry, the album and the group made their own impact, influencing a movement toward roots styles and country elements in rock. Over time, *Music From Big Pink* came to be regarded as a watershed work in the history of rock, one that introduced new tones and approaches to the constantly evolving genre. —*William Ruhlmann*

★ **The Band** / Sep. 22, 1969 / Capitol ✦✦✦✦✦
The Band's first album, *Music from Big Pink*, seemed to come out of nowhere, with its ramshackle musical blend and songs of rural tragedy. *The Band*, the group's second album, was a more deliberate and even more accomplished effort, partially because the players had become a more cohesive unit and partially because guitarist Robbie Robertson had taken over the songwriting, writing or co-writing all 12 songs. Though a Canadian, Robertson focused on a series of American archetypes from the union worker in "King Harvest (Has Surely Come)" and the retired sailor in "Rockin' Chair" to, most famously, the Confederate Civil War observer Virgil Cane in "The Night They Drove Old Dixie Down." The album effectively mixed the kind of mournful songs that had dominated *Music from Big Pink*, here including "Whispering Pines" and "When You Awake" (both co-written and sung by haunting tenor Richard Manuel), with rollicking uptempo numbers like "Rag Mama Rag" and "Up on Cripple Creek" (both sung by Levon Helm and released as singles, with "Up on Cripple Creek" making the Top 40). As had been true

of the first album, it was the Band's sound that stood out the most, from Helm's (and occasionally Manuel's) propulsive drumming to Robertson's distinctive guitar fills and the endlessly inventive keyboard textures of Garth Hudson, all topped by the rough, expressive singing of Manuel, Helm, and Rick Danko that mixed leads with harmonies. The arrangements were simultaneously loose and assured, giving the songs a timeless appeal, while the lyrics continued to paint portraits of 19th century rural life (especially Southern life, as references to Tennessee and Virginia made clear), its sometimes less savory aspects treated with warmth and humor. The 2000 CD reissue featured seven bonus tracks. —*William Ruhlmann*

Stage Fright / Aug. 17, 1970 / Capitol ✦✦✦✦
Stage Fright, the Band's third album, sounded on its surface like the group's first two releases, *Music from Big Pink* and *The Band*, employing the same dense arrangements, with their mixture of a deep bottom formed by drummer Levon Helm and bassist Rick Danko, penetrating guitar work by Robbie Robertson, and the varied keyboard work of pianist Richard Manuel and organist Garth Hudson, with Helm, Danko, and Manuel's vocals on top. But the songs this time around were far more personal, and, despite a nominal complacency, quite troubling. Only "All La Glory," Robertson's song about the birth of his daughter, was fully positive. "Strawberry Wine" and "Sleeping" were celebrations of indolence, while "Time to Kill," as its title implied, revealed boredom while claiming romantic contentment. Several of the album's later songs seemed to be metaphors for trouble the group was encountering, with "The W.S. Walcott Medicine Show" commenting on the falseness of show business, "Daniel and the Sacred Harp" worrying about a loss of integrity, and the title song talking about the pitfalls of fortune and fame. "The Shape I'm In" was perhaps the album's most blatant statement of panic. The Band was widely acclaimed after its first two albums; *Stage Fright* seemed to be the group's alarmed response, which made it their most nakedly confessional. It was certainly different from their previous work, which had tended toward story songs set in earlier times, but it was hardly less compelling for that. The 2000 expanded edition was the first CD reissue containing the mixes that had been used on the original LP. —*William Ruhlmann*

Cahoots / Sep. 15, 1971 / Capitol ✦✦✦
In comparison to its predecessors, *Cahoots*, the Band's fourth album, may be characterized as an essentially minor effort that nevertheless contains a few small pleasures. These pleasures begin with the leadoff track "Life Is a Carnival," a song that continues the theme of *Stage Fright* by emphasizing the false nature of show business and its impact on reality. The song features a lively Dixieland horn chart courtesy of Allen Toussaint. "When I Paint My Masterpiece," a Bob Dylan song making its recorded debut here as the second selection, is another welcome track, buoyed by mandolin and accordion in a charming arrangement appropriate to its tale of an odd trip to Europe. "4% Pantomime" is a duet between the Band's Richard Manuel and Van Morrison that is entertaining to hear, even if the song itself is slight. Unfortunately, that just about completes the list of the album's attractions. Annotator Rob Bowman claims that the overriding theme of the songs is "extinction and the sadness that accompanies the passing of things that once were held to be of great value"; actually, there is no overriding theme to the minor songs written by Robbie Robertson. Several of the songs' lyrics come across as half-baked film scenarios, but they fail to be evocative, and they are paired to music lacking in structure. The failure is solely in the writing; the Band sounds as good as ever playing the songs, with singers Manuel, Levon Helm, and Rick Danko all performing effectively and primary instrumentalist Garth Hudson filling in the arrangements cleverly. It's just that the material is not strong enough, particularly in comparison to the three impressive albums the Band had released previously. By adding four good bonus tracks, the 2000 reissue significantly strengthens the collection. —*William Ruhlmann*

Rock of Ages / Aug. 15, 1972 / Capitol ✦✦✦✦✦
Recorded on New Year's Eve 1971/1972, this was the Band's last gig for a year and a half. Allen Toussaint was brought in again to write horn arrangements for many of their classics. The results were inspired. Highlights are many, but of particular note are a cover of Marvin Gaye's "Baby Don't Do It" and a live recording of a track that had earlier been relegated to B-side status only, "Get Up Jake." —*Rob Bowman*

Moondog Matinee / Oct. 15, 1973 / Capitol ✦✦
The Band essentially went back to being the Hawks of the late '50s and early '60s on this album of cover tunes. They demonstrated considerable expertise on their versions of rock & roll and R&B standards like Clarence "Frogman" Henry's "Ain't Got No Home," Chuck Berry's "The Promised Land," and Fats Domino's "I'm Ready," but of course that didn't do much to satisfy the audience they had established with their original material and that, two years after the disappointing *Cahoots*, was waiting for something in the same league with their first three albums. —*William Ruhlmann*

Northern Lights–Southern Cross / Nov. 1, 1975 / Capitol ✦✦✦✦
The first studio album of Band originals in four years, in many respects *Northern Lights–Southern Cross* was viewed as a comeback. It also can be seen as a swan song. The album was the Band's finest since their self-titled sophomore effort. Totaling eight songs in all, on this album the Band explores new timbres, utilizing for the first time 24 tracks and what was (then) new synthesizer technology. "Acadian Driftwood" stands out as one of Robertson's finest compositions, the equal to anything else the Band ever recorded. —*Rob Bowman*

The Best of the Band / Jul. 15, 1976 / Capitol ✦✦✦✦✦
With this album, Capitol Records began the inevitable process of repackaging the music of the Band, which the company would do at increasing length without solving the fundamental problem that the Band, despite the quality of their individual songs, was not a singles act and was hard to summarize in a compilation. That said, for the real neophyte, this single-disc, 11-song album may be as good as anything. It contains the Band's two

most famous songs, "The Weight" and "The Night They Drove Old Dixie Down," as well as the group's only Top 30 hit, "Up on Cripple Creek," and such songs as "Tears of Rage" and "Stage Fright" that they probably played at nearly every show they performed. It's true that if you really want to understand the Band, you have to hear all of *Music from Big Pink* and *The Band*. But if you just want a snapshot, here it is. — *William Ruhlmann*

Islands / Mar. 15, 1977 / Capitol ✦✦
Theoretically, even though the Band had given up touring as of Thanksgiving 1976, they were going to keep making records, and *Islands* was the first album released in the new era. Only it wasn't; it was the album they scraped together to complete their ten-LP contract with Capitol Records and the last new full-length album the original five members ever made. The playing, as ever, was impeccable, and the record had its moments, notably a Richard Manuel vocal on the chestnut "Georgia on My Mind" that had been released as a single in 1976 to boost Georgia governor Jimmy Carter's successful run for the presidency. But the songwriting quality was mediocre, and the Band had set such a standard for itself in that department that *Islands* couldn't help suffering enormously in comparison. — *William Ruhlmann*

Anthology / 1978 / Capitol ✦✦✦
Deciding 1976's *The Best of the Band* wasn't enough (or wanting to have a product out to compete with *The Last Waltz*), Capitol released the two-LP *Anthology*, a skimpy 20-track, two-LP set with liner notes by rock critic Robert Palmer. It's more complete than *The Best of the Band*, but shares the same problem—that the Band is best appreciated on their full-length albums rather than on any compilation. — *William Ruhlmann*

The Last Waltz / Apr. 1978 / Warner Brothers ✦✦✦✦
As a film, *The Last Waltz* was a triumph—one of the first (and still one of the few) rock concert documentaries that was directed by a filmmaker who understood both the look and the sound of rock & roll, and executed with enough technical craft to capture all the nooks and crannies of a great live show. But as an album, the soundtrack to *The Last Waltz* had to compete with the Band's earlier live album, *Rock of Ages*, with which it bears a certain superficial resemblance—both found the group trying to create something grander than the standard issue live double, and both featured the group beefed up by additional musicians. While *Rock of Ages* found the Band swinging along with the help of a horn section arranged by Allen Toussaint, *The Last Waltz* boasts a horn section (using Toussaint's earlier arrangements on a few cuts) *and* more than a baker's dozen guest stars, ranging from old cohorts Ronnie Hawkins and Bob Dylan to contemporaries Joni Mitchell, Neil Young, and Van Morrison. The Band are in fine if not exceptional form here; on most cuts, they don't sound quite as fiery as they did on *Rock of Ages*, though their performances are never less than expert, and the high points are dazzling, especially an impassioned version of "It Makes No Difference," and blazing readings of "Up on Cripple Creek" and "The Night They Drove Old Dixie Down." Ultimately, it's the Band's "special guests" who really make this set stand out. It could be argued that you're better off watching *The Last Waltz* on video than listening to it on CD, but either way it's a show well worth checking out. — *Mark Deming*

To Kingdom Come / Sep. 1989 / Capitol ✦✦✦✦✦
Released in the fall of 1989, *To Kingdom Come* is a double-disc set that purports to be "The Definitive Collection" and, in a sense, it does provide a good overview of the band's career. Over the course of 31 songs, the collection works its way through the hits and album tracks, adding such rarities as "Get Up Jake," "Back to Memphis," and "Lovin' You Is Sweeter Than Ever," even if it never touches on *The Basement Tapes*. All the predictable items are here and the album tracks are well-chosen, and it is a good representation of the band, worth the time of listeners who want a smartly assembled anthology. The 2000 *Greatest Hits* gets the edge for casual fans, since it has 20 tracks on one disc, yet this remains worthwhile for listeners who want a fairly comprehensive, thorough anthology. — *Stephen Thomas Erlewine*

Jericho / Nov. 2, 1993 / Pyramid/Rhino ✦✦✦
A full seventeen years after *The Last Waltz*, the Band re-formed without Robbie Robertson or the late Richard Manuel and recorded *Jericho*. Far from being an embarrassment, *Jericho* is their strongest record since *Northern Lights–Southern Cross* and arguably their best since *Stage Fright*. Without Robertson, the Band relies on a variety of sources for their material (including Bob Dylan, Bruce Springsteen, and Jules Shear) and prove that they can interpret nearly any song well. Musically, the Band can still juggle rock, folk, blues, and country effortlessly, producing a rootsy sound distinctly their own. It sounds like the heyday of the group, which is more than can be said of either of Robertson's solo albums. — *Stephen Thomas Erlewine*

Across the Great Divide / Nov. 15, 1994 / Capitol ✦✦✦
Capitol's 1989 Band compilation *To Kingdom Come* was subtitled "The Definitive Collection," so what is this? Well, the other one was only a two-disc set, and this is a three-disc set. As the CD reissue/box set boom goes on, record companies have taken to redoing acts they've already done once, so even though the Band has one classy CD anthology (and a few tacky ones), Capitol gives us another. In this case, they've divided it into two discs' worth of the greatest hits, followed by a disc of rarities (some not so rare) and unreleased tracks that includes pre-Band recordings by the Hawks, collaborations with Bob Dylan, live tracks from the Woodstock and Watkins Glen festivals, and the like. All of which pushes this set up a price point or two from the earlier one without adding anything substantial to the story. — *William Ruhlmann*

Live at Watkins Glen / Apr. 4, 1995 / Capitol ✦✦

High on the Hog / Feb. 27, 1996 / Rhino ✦✦

Jubilation / 1998 / River North ✦✦✦
Jubilation, the tenth studio album by the Band, showcases a group that has aged better

than the finest port wine. Yes, although the voices have aged noticeably (particularly in the cases of Rick Danko and Levon Helm), this fact only makes the record more charming. The songwriting is still spiritual and evocative, and all of the tunes are peppered with a Grant Wood-ish plain-spoken sensibility that are at once familiar and instantly engaging.

The group (Danko, Helm, and resident keyboard genius Garth Hudson) are augmented by Richard Bell (keyboards), Randy Ciarlante (drums, vocals), and Jim Weider (guitar). The odd thing is that this version of the group has probably been together as long as the original Band. Guest appearances by Eric Clapton and John Hiatt are nice additions, but are not reasons to buy this album, as it holds up quite well on its own merits. — *Matthew Greenwald*

The Best of the Band, Vol. 2 / Oct. 5, 1999 / Rhino ✦✦✦
The name of the album is *The Best of the Band, Vol. 2*, the label is Rhino, the lauded reissue specialist—it would be easy to assume that the collection would fill in gaps left by Capitol's fine 1976 sampler, *The Best of the Band*. That train of logic forgets an important point. The Band, minus Robbie Robertson, reunited in 1993 and recorded *Jericho*, which was the first of three new albums by the group. *Jericho* and its successor, *High on the Hog*, happened to be released by Pyramid, Rhino's new music label; the third, 1998's *Jubilation*, appeared on River North. These three albums provide the basis for *The Best of the Band, Vol. 2*. Even hardcore fans would admit that these comeback albums did not match the original records, yet they could justifiably argue that the music wasn't bad, even quite good at times. And it was—none of the three albums were perfect, but they had strong moments, most of which are collected here. That's not to say this music is for everybody, or even for fans of the Band's prime years, since it does have the feel of a reunion and is a bit nostalgic-minded. However, it is a good summary of the Band's reunion, and listeners willing to take a chance may be surprised how strong they sound on "Atlantic City" and "Blind Willie McTell" or how loose they are on "Youngblood," the set's sole unreleased track. — *Stephen Thomas Erlewine*

Greatest Hits / Sep. 26, 2000 / Capitol ✦✦✦✦✦
The Band was a very album-oriented group, and only had two Top 40 hit singles. So one could argue that a single-disc greatest hits compilation, or best-of anthology as this might more properly be called, is not the optimum way to dig into their repertoire. But if you're limiting yourself to one Band collection and your budget or patience does not stretch for the two-CD *To Kingdom Come* set, this 18-song program hits all the famous buttons, including "The Weight," "Chest Fever," "Up on Cripple Creek," "The Night They Drove Old Dixie Down," "The Shape I'm In," "Stage Fright," and "When I Paint My Masterpiece." Naturally, it leans most heavily on their first two albums, which supply four songs each. Good, lengthy liner notes by Rob Bowman are a nice bonus, considering that single-disc career-spanning overviews often dispense with such frills. Strange, though, that "Don't Do It," their one Top 40 hit single other than "Up on Cripple Creek," isn't here; in fact, there's nothing from their live *Rock of Ages*. — *Richie Unterberger*

Band of Susans

f. 1986, U.S.A., **db.** 1996
Post-Punk, Alternative Pop/Rock, Experimental Rock, American Underground
Favoring chaotic squalls of guitar noise and avant textures over the dynamics of conventional songcraft, the New York-based Band of Susans formed in 1986 around the core duo of singers/songwriters Robert Poss and Susan Stenger, longtime friends who reunited only after pursuing dramatically different musical paths: while Poss became a fixture on the NYC punk scene in the Clash-inspired Tot Rocket before joing Rhys Chatham's guitar ensemble, Stenger relocated to Prague, where she studied the theories of John Cage. Originally, Band of Susans featured Poss on lead guitar and Stenger on bass, rounded out by guitarists Susan Tallman and Susan Lyall (hence the outfit's name) and drummer Ron Spitzer; four months after forming, they issued their debut EP, *Blessing and Curse*.

In 1988, Band of Susans released their first full-length album, *Hope Against Hope*; both Tallman and Lyall departed soon after, and were replaced by Page Hamilton (a former student of Glenn Branca, a frequent Susans reference point) and Karen Haglof. After 1989's *Love Agenda*, Hamilton too left the group to found Helmet; he was replaced by Mark Lonergan, and following Haglof's exit, Anne Husick stepped in for 1991's *The Word and the Flesh*, which employed a more focused attack, typified by a lesser emphasis on reverb and feedback, to arrive at a more accessible sound.

Without the usual attendant line-up changes, Band of Susans issued 1993's dense, droning *Veil*, followed two years later by *Here Comes Success*, a uniformly strong collection of lengthy pieces including the instrumental "In the Eye of the Beholder (Song for Rhys)," a tribute to Poss' mentor. In mid-1996, Band of Susans dissolved, although Stenger and Poss continued working with Wire's Bruce Gilbert in the trio GilbertPossStenger in addition to mounting other projects. — *Jason Ankeny*

Hope Against Hope / 1988 / Blast First ✦✦✦
Drawing on the influence of the early-'80s New York downtown art rock scene, Band of Susans' three guitarists construct a thundering wall of guitar worthy of the Jesus and Mary Chain minus distortion. While sharing some of the same influences (Glenn Branca, Rhys Chatham) as Sonic Youth, the Susans' guitar structures never stray into the dissonant territory staked out by Thurston Moore and company. The result is a more melodic creature, unfortunately lacking in character. While the loud wash of guitar is intriguing and sometimes engaging, it too often seems a bit directionless, without a great deal of dynamics or thrust. Part of the problem rests with a rhythm section that is no more than solid, which also goes for Poss' singing. There are moments, however, that scream with promise, such as the title track (reworked from the debut EP), which is notably tighter and more propulsive than most of the other tracks, the rumble of ringing guitars thundering

out of the speakers. "All the Wrong Reasons" is another winner, taking a slower, bittersweet tact that meshes the three guitars in a tender ballad featuring a dreamy, somnambulant pulse consistent with the slower Velvet Underground work. While the elements are there, Band of Susans hasn't got the flavor quite right yet. *—Chris Parker*

Love Agenda / 1989 / Blast First ✦✦✦✦
While Page Hamilton's work on guitar here is often referenced in stories about Helmet, the fact is that Band of Susans is very much Poss and Stenger's band, and the at-times grotesquely grinding feel of Hamilton's later work is thankfully missing in favor of the more intricate while still powerful music here. The group's second full album is one of those creations of its time which ages well rather than just sounding dated. Though you can easily imagine the band in its particular late-eighties New York context right from the first track, "The Pursuit of Happiness," from the squalling guitars and Poss' just a little bit like Thurston Moore at points vocals, the fact is that this album just plain kicks out the jams, art that is blessedly unafraid to rock. "It's Locked Away" is a killer example of this, centered around a great riff that has much more of an angular, drony sound to it than anything else, but is wedded to a full-on crunch that also has a great groove (one of the Susans' many instrumental secret weapons) to it as well. Poss, who produced the record, mixes his vocals, as well Stenger's occasional backing efforts, fairly deep into the mix throughout the record; rather than being annoying or pointlessly obscure, it just feels right, a good way of letting his voice be another instrument to carry the songs. Perhaps to reference that fact, "Thorn in My Side" and "Sin Embargo" are both instrumentals, and are as great numbers as any of the rest on the album. The CD version contains the band's noted cover of the Rolling Stones' "Child of the Moon," which in its guitar-overdriven way pretty much beats out the entire remake of *Exile on Main Street* that Pussy Galore did. *—Ned Raggett*

The Word and the Flesh / 1991 / Restless ✦✦✦✦✦
Despite featuring their third pair of guitarists in as many albums (Love Agenda's Page Hamilton departed to form Helmet), Band of Susans deliver their most assured, accessible album. The guitars operate as interlocking pieces of a larger puzzle, while bassist Susan Stenger floats below, providing structure without being chained to the beat. The sound alternates between haunting and crushing, and the guitars are finally consistently corralled into the dramatic service of the song. The clean, nearly reverb-less guitar sound leaves plenty of room to hear the guitars' idiosyncratic directions while maintaining a nearly opaque wall of sound. Most rewarding are the moments when the band breaks loose from their throbbing chords to deliver a crunchy punch to the solar plexus, such as on "Plot Twist" and "Silver Lining." Mostly, though, the effect is of rich lattices of guitar and intermingling swells, lifting and propelling the songs through an omnipresent guitar drone. Bassist Stenger's throaty vocals add a moody counterpoint to the guitars' pitched screech and anchor the album's opening two tracks, not incidentally two of the better compositions on the disc. The album closes with a nod to Robert Poss' mentor, Rhys Chatham, with a cover of Chatham's hypnotic, slow-building fugue "Guitar Trio." *—Chris Parker*

Now / 1992 / Restless ✦✦

Veil / 1993 / Restless ✦✦✦✦✦
The fourth full-length album from Band of Susans is their most assured to date. Perhaps not as immediately compelling as *The Word and the Flesh*, the band members are nonetheless at the top of their game, expanding the margins of their sound. Whereas the last album was focused on songcraft, here the compositions reign. The band is no longer content to let the guitars drone with feral ferocity, instead exploring greater use of dynamics, dissonance, and interplay. Far more experimental in approach than their previous albums, the rewards are revealed with repeated listening as the complexity of the songs' interior structures becomes more transparent. For example, "Mood Swings" begins with a lean-to of stereo call-and-return guitar lines before the throbbing bass and drums come in with the foundation and the song swells, becoming a storm with flashes of guitar audible within the squall. At the break, the guitars drop out, and after several measures of choppy rhythm, the storm returns. This intermingling of intermittent sounds and effects is made even more effective by expanding the palette beyond a melodic crush of guitar to include individual dissonant and minor chords that bring all three guitars into bas-relief. The lyrics are often lost, like a lone figure in a field beneath a thundering, searing cloud of sound, with only the refrain echoing softly. This is no great loss, as the sheer muscular musical virtuosity of this album requires few words. *—Chris Parker*

● **Wired for Sound** / 1995 / Blast First ✦✦✦✦
Wired for Sound is a great introduction to the Band of Susans, conveniently wrapping up the New York group's 1986 to 1993 output. In fact, it could be argued that an average admirer of the band would only need this and their excellent swan song, *Here Comes Success*, to get a full picture. Although most of the material is excellent, the sometimes tuneless din can grow tiresome pretty quickly; the collection works best in small doses. Moody textures are the rule for the Susans, and when they leave second gear, they're at their best ("Trash Train," "Hope Against Hope"). Neatly divided between "songs with words" on the first disc and "songs without words" on the second, *Wired for Sound* will likely please any Sonic Youth or Television fan. *—Andy Kellman*

Here Comes Success / 1995 / World Service ✦✦✦✦
Though their prior records were all respectable, Band of Susans saved a knockout punch for their swan song, *Here Comes Success*. A solid collection of lengthy guitar workouts, it's not the best record to get a quick fix from (the nine tracks average seven minutes in length). *Success* certainly demands close attention, but that's easy to give, thanks to its thick hypnotics. "Hell Bent" is the Susans' absolute zenith, an entrancing ice-jolt that unfolds and coils in superb dynamic fashion. When bassist Susan Stenger drops to a one-note bass line, it speaks just as loud as a lengthy lead solo. "Pardon My French" features some Stonesy riffing and some dead-on societal commentary from Robert Poss: "The voice of god is Charlton Heston/He's told the FBI they should have me arrested/Bullets will fly but he'll never get the message/That people with guns can never be trusted." At 64 minutes, *Success* might test one's attention, but it's the Susans at their catchiest and most exciting. *—Andy Kellman*

The Bangles

f. 1981, Los Angeles, CA
Jangle Pop, Paisley Underground, Pop/Rock, New Wave
The all singing/all performing four-woman Bangles formed in 1981 and sprung from the L.A. Paisley Underground scene. Later they traded their garage band roots for a slick, heavily-produced pop sound that turned them into one of the most successful chart groups of either gender during the '80s. Sisters Debbi and Vicki Peterson (drums and bass, respectively) and singer/guitarist Susanna Hoffs formed the group, and released an EP on IRS before signing to Columbia. For their second album, 1985's *Different Light*, the band was aided by Prince with his song "Manic Monday," which charted at number two and paved the way for the follow-up smash, "Walk Like an Egyptian," which went to number one and sent the album to the top of the charts. Their next single, a cover of Simon and Garfunkel's "Hazy Shade of Winter," from the *Less Than Zero* soundtrack, reached number one in 1987. The follow-up album *Everything* spawned another number one, "Eternal Flame," in 1988. One year later, the band broke up. Hoffs recorded two solo albums after the band's break-up, *When You're A Boy* in 1991 and a self-titled record in 1996. *—Denise Sullivan*

Bangles / Jun. 1982 / Faulty ✦✦✦✦✦
The Bangles' debut EP is the perfect example of what was going on in L.A.'s Paisley Underground during the early '80s. Singer Susanna Hoffs literally growls her way through "The Real World," a tight, up-tempo pop song in the tradition of Love. The guitars ring out and the layered, three-part harmonies recall the Mamas and Papas and the Beatles. The Bangles later proved to be a garage band made good, but this early version produced arguably their best work and proves beyond a shadow of a doubt that they were never a girl group creation but an entirely rocking, working band, schooled in the best traditions of '60s rock. *—Denise Sullivan*

All Over the Place / May 1984 / Columbia ✦✦✦✦
The Bangles' major label debut is an essential album in the band's catalog. Guitarist and vocalist Vicki Peterson penned most of the '60s and early '70s guitar-rock songs, like the mini-hit "Hero Takes a Fall" (it was rumored the hero in the title was Dream Syndicate's Steve Wynn). The record also includes covers of the obscure Merry Go Round hit "Live" and ex-Soft Boy Kimberley Rew's "Going Down to Liverpool." The band was polished a bit by producer David Kahne and the release capitalized on the pretty, all-girl-group angle rather than the band's actual raw talent, which might otherwise have been too rough and retro for radio at the time. Nonetheless, the band retained enough of the original spunk that made them appealing in the first place. *—Denise Sullivan*

Different Light / Jan. 1986 / Columbia ✦✦✦
The band's second album went to number one on the strength of the first single, "Manic Monday," written especially for the band by Prince, and its follow-up, "Walk Like an Egyptian," penned by '80s hit-making giant Liam Sternberg. Though even more polished than the debut, *Different Light* is a testament to the mid-'80s sound, replete with synthesizers (Mitchell Froom assisted); even on Jules Shear's magnificent "If She Knew What She Wants" and Alex Chilton's standard "September Gurls," the band's vocal strengths shine through the gloss, and their pop sensibilities are not completely lost. *—Denise Sullivan*

Everything / Oct. 1988 / Columbia ✦✦
The band really turned up the glamour meter for *Everything*, but the success of *Different Light* would have been hard for anyone to top. Yet again enlisting the aid of professional songwriters along the lines of Billy Steinberg and Tom Kelly, the band's original guitar-rock intent suffered at the hands of over-the-top song structures and production. Teaming the Bangles with such odd pairings as metal guitarist Vinnie Vincent and future Jane's Addiction/Red Hot Chili Peppers guitarist Dave Navarro was a very misguided concept. Although the record yielded the number one hit "Eternal Flame" and another hit, "In Your Room," the group imploded a year later under the weight of diminished expectations and artistic differences. At that point, they could afford to retire. *—Denise Sullivan*

● **Greatest Hits** / May 1990 / Columbia ✦✦✦✦✦
Weighing in at 14 tracks, *Greatest Hits* is a good, basic collection of the Bangles' biggest singles, containing all the hits, including the previously non-LP "Hazy Shade of Winter," plus a couple of album tracks and, for the dedicated, a new cover of the Grass Roots' "Where Were You When I Needed You." It may be easy to carp about fine album tracks from *All Over the Place* and *Different Light* that should have been included, yet this is a fine sampler/introduction that might not necessarily capture the Bangles' best—in this context, their ties to the Paisley Underground and college rock seem nonexistent—but still finds them as masters of irresistible pop singles. *—Stephen Thomas Erlewine*

The Bar-Kays

f. 1966, Memphis, TN
Instrumental Rock, Funk, Soul
Even though four group founders were killed in a 1967 plane crash along with Otis Redding, the Bar-Kays came back to reign as one of the top R&B outfits of the '70s. The original Bar-Kays were a Memphis instrumental combo that scored an R&B hit in 1967 on Volt with the rousing "Soul Finger." Guitarist Jimmy King, organist Ronnie Caldwell, drummer Carl Cunningham, and saxist Phalon Jones perished with Redding, leaving

trumpeter Ben Cauley and bassist James Alexander to re-form the group. After honing their chops with session work at Stax, the new Bar-Kays kicked off a long string of R&B smashes in 1976 with "Shake Your Rump to the Funk" on Mercury. —*Bill Dahl*

● **The Best of the Bar-Kays [Stax]** / 1988 / Stax ✦✦✦✦✦
Stax's *The Best of the Bar-Kays* inexplicably leaves off "Soul Finger," as well as "Knuckle-head" and "Give Everybody Some," concentrating instead on the group's early-'70s incarnation as a funk band. Although it is missing their soul instrumentals from the late '60s, the compilation remains a good overview of their early-'70s work for Stax/Volt, featuring such songs as "Montego Bay," "Humpin'," "A.J. the Housefly" and the Top Ten R&B hit "Son of Shaft." —*Stephen Thomas Erlewine*

The Best of the Bar-Kays [Mercury] / May 18, 1993 / Mercury ✦✦✦✦✦
When the Bar-Kays joined Mercury Records in 1976, they shifted musical styles slightly, veering away from the goofy yet funky soul instrumentals that defined their Stax days and concentrating on loose, wild funk driven by fat bass lines and whining synthesizers. Mercury's *The Best of the Bar-Kays* captures the majority of the highlights from their '70s recordings for the label. Over the course of 16 tracks, the compilation features the majority of their Top Ten R&B hits—including "Shake Your Rump to the Funk," "Too Hot to Stop," "Move Your Boogie Body" and "Hit and Run"—as well as several fine album tracks like "Freakshow on the Dance Floor," "Shut the Funk Up" and "Sexomatic," which illustrate the depth of the group's musical skills. —*Stephen Thomas Erlewine*

The Best of Bar-Kays, Vol. 2 / May 21, 1996 / Mercury ✦✦✦
Another scoop of mid-'70s-mid-'80s material from the Mercury era, for those with an interest in the band's slicker phase. It's pretty formulaic, but does include several R&B hits, such as "Spellbound," "Do It," "Boogie Body Land," "Let's Have Some Fun," "Dirty Dancer," "Your Place or Mine," "Sexomatic," and "She Talks to Me with Her Body," whose thematic concerns can be easily gleaned from the titles. —*Richie Unterberger*

The Ballads Collection / May 19, 1998 / Mercury/Chronicles ✦✦✦
The Ballads Collection contains 12 slow jams and seductive ballads from the Bar-Kays. James Alexander has helped compile the album, which means it features both surefire hits like "Flying High on Your Love" and album tracks. That very diversity makes it a worthwhile addition to the group's catalog, and the record should please anyone looking for a romantic Bar-Kays album. —*Stephen Thomas Erlewine*

The Barbarians
f. 1964, **db.** 1966
Garage Rock
With their appearances on the *Nuggets* compilation and *The T.A.M.I. Show*, the Barbarians are one of the best-remembered garage bands of the '60s. Not that it's easy to forget the sight of a one-handed drummer, complete with hook, driving his band through a garage punk number in the company of the day's biggest British Invasion, soul, and surf stars. Moulty was hardly self-conscious about his handicap; on the tiny hit single immortalized on *Nuggets* (titled, logically enough, "Moulty"), he tells the story of the triumph over his loss in no uncertain melodramatic terms. The band also managed a somewhat bigger hit single, the British Invasion-inspired novelty "Are You a Boy or Are You a Girl." —*Richie Unterberger*

● **Are You a Boy or Are You a Girl?** / Nov. 1965 / One Way ✦✦✦
While the Barbarians live up to a lot of people's vision of the classic garage band imagewise, their album is disappointing and thin-sounding. The material, none of which was penned by the group, is average and doesn't even rock terribly hard. "Are You a Boy or Are You a Girl" is here, but much of the rest of the songs are overdone standards ("House of the Rising Sun" is especially lame). "What the New Breed Say" is an okay anthem of rebellion, and "I'll Keep on Seeing You" is a modestly touching ballad. However, as eight of the 12 songs are covers and four tunes are supplied to them by songwriters not in the band, the album does not reflect much in the way of an original vision. The 2000 Sundazed reissue adds three important bonus tracks: "Moulty" and, at long last, both sides of their rare 1964 single on Joy, "Hey Little Bird"/"You've Got to Understand." "Hey Little Bird," the song they performed on their *T.A.M.I. Show* appearance, is easily their best track, although the studio version isn't as ferocious as their rendition on film. —*Richie Unterberger*

Barclay James Harvest
f. Sep. 1966, Oldham, England
British Folk-Rock, Folk-Rock, Prog-Rock/Art Rock
Barclay James Harvest was, for many years, one of the most hard-luck outfits in progressive rock. A quartet of solid rock musicians with a knack for writing hook-laden songs built on pretty melodies, they harmonized like the Beatles and wrote extended songs with more of a beat than the Moody Blues. In 1970, they released their first album, *Barclay James Harvest*, which included several of the early songs and displayed the group's strengths: filled with strong harmony singing, aggressive electric guitar, and swelling Mellotron parts, it set the pattern for their subsequent releases. They were signed to EMI at the same time as Pink Floyd, and both bands moved over to the company's progressive rock-oriented Harvest imprint at the same time, yet somehow, they never managed to connect with the public for a major hit in England, much less America. Later in 1973, the band signed with Polydor, and their fortunes began turning around, though only very gradually. Their first album for the new label, *Everyone Is Everybody Else*, seemed promising: it was a more powerful and coherent work than the group had ever released for EMI, with Lees' guitar dominating on songs like "Paper Wings" and "For No One." The album failed to chart, however, as did the single "Poor Boy Blues," with its gorgeous harmonies. It seemed at first as though BJH was locked once again into a cycle of failure.

Finally, in late 1974, their double album *Barclay James Harvest Live* broke through to the public. In 1977, they released *Gone to Earth*, their most accomplished album to date, and by the end of the year the group found themselves playing to arena-sized audiences. —*Bruce Eder*

Barclay James Harvest / Jun. 1970 / Sire ✦✦✦✦✦

Once Again / 1971 / Sire ✦✦✦
The band's follow-up still finds it working very much in the vein of orchestral rock, largely driven by Stuart "Woolly" Wolstenholme's keyboards and the presence of the London Symphony Orchestra. The reach of the music exceeds the grasp of the lyrics, though—they lack the cold oracularity of Peter Sinfield or the allusive cleverness of Peter Gabriel. Still, there's some fine compositions here. "She Said" turns upon a keening opening Mellotron riff to develop into a slow-four dirge. "Song for Dying" shows off the band's fine ability at vocal harmonies, while the later concert standard, "Mocking Bird," shows a dramatic evolution from pensive acoustic guitar to a full-blown orchestral attack. —*Paul Collins*

● **Barclay James Harvest & Other Short Stories** / 1972 / Sire ✦✦✦✦✦
In a shift from the weighty *Once Again*, this album saw John Lees emerge as an effective counterweight to the band's tendency toward morose progressive rock. His "Harry's Song" is built around a muscular piano part by erstwhile bassist Les Holroyd, and closes with gorgeous repeating harmonies. "Blue Johns Blues" takes the aggression up a notch with a crashing chorus and some wonderfully stinging slide guitar. Wolstenholme's keyboards and the use of somber orchestral arrangements still typify most of the compositions, though, and they shine on the uplifting "Someone There You Know." —*Paul Collins*

Baby James Harvest / 1972 / Harvest ✦✦✦✦✦

Everyone Is Everybody Else / Jun. 1974 / Polydor ✦✦

Octoberon / 1976 / Polydor ✦✦✦
With Wolstenholme's keyboards pushed back in the mix, and strangely missing the harmonies that enriched their earlier work, *Octoberon* is something of a departure for the band. While Wolstenholme's stately "Ra" shows a dabbling in mysticism and the soaring sound of their previous work, most of the album is a strangely glum affair. John Lees adopts a pub rock sound in his compositions, although "May Day" manages to veer unexpectedly into a glorious choral and organ arrangement. "Polk Street Rag", despite its name, is a slick rocker about a sordid X-rated movie house in San Francisco. There's a black humor throughout, as in this brutally funny line from "Suicide?": "Heard a voice shouting 'Don't jump, please for God's sake let me move my car.'" Not up to the level of their best work, but worth a listen for fans. —*Paul Collins*

Gone to Earth / 1977 / Polydor ✦✦✦✦✦
The group's best album, featuring some of their most effective hard rock and their best tunes. John Lees' soaring, poetic "Hymn" became a major part of their stage act, but is still pretty powerful in its studio version, and Les Holroyd's "Hard Hearted Woman" also turned into a concert favorite. The real highlight, however, is John Lees' "Poor Man's Moody Blues," which manages to outdo the other band at their own game. [British import] —*Bruce Eder*

Live Tapes / 1978 / Polydor ✦✦

The Harvest Years / Jun. 7, 1991 / EMI ✦✦✦✦
A double CD consisting of more than 30 songs culled from BJH's first six Harvest albums. In addition to excellent sound (the stuff has been treated with Sonic Solutions' "No Noise" process), this set also includes oddities for the hardcore collectors, such as lost quadraphonic mixes on various early-'70s tracks. At $30, it's the comprehensive collection to get on their Harvest material, but also maybe a bit of overkill for the casual fan. [British import] —*Bruce Eder*

The Best of Barclay James Harvest / 1996 / EMI ✦✦✦✦✦
The title of this compilation might at first glance cause serious Barclay James Harvest fans to ignore it in favor of individual albums, but this is hardly a greatest hits set. While a few classics, like "Mocking Bird" and "Medicine Man," are thrown in, this is primarily a collection of lesser known singles and B-sides, several of which never made it onto the albums. For some cuts, this makes sense—it's hard to see how the strutting "Rock & Roll Woman" would fit in with the repertoire of a band better known at that time for lugging around the 60-piece orchestra that drenches concluding track "Moonwater." But each piece stands up well, from the groovy flashback of clavinet and Leslie-distorted vocals in "Good Love Child" to the Crosby, Stills, Nash & Young-influenced choruses of the driving "Child of Man." Well worth a look for the fan in need of a few rare tracks. —*Paul Collins*

Bardo Pond
f. 1993, Philadelphia, PA
Dream Pop, Space Rock, Indie Rock
The leading light of the Psychedelphia scene, Bardo Pond comprised singer/flautist Isobel Sollenberger, guitarist brothers Michael and John Gibbons, bassist Clint Takeda, and drummer Joe Culver. After issuing a handful of singles on the Compulsive label, the group delivered their full-length debut *Bufo Alvarius Amen 29:15*—so named in honor of a Colorado River-area toad famed for its hallucinogenic secretions—on Drunken Fish in 1995. *Big Laughing Jym*, a collection of outtakes and home recordings, followed later that same year before Bardo Pond signed to Matador for 1996's *Amanita*. *Lapsed* appeared a year later, and in 1999 Bardo Pond returned with *Set and Setting*. *Dilate* arrived in early 2001. —*Jason Ankeny*

Bufo Alvarius Amen 29:15 / Mar. 1, 1995 / Drunken Fish ✦✦✦✦
It starts with feedback, hum, and fuzz, then a heavy guitar riff emerging from the murk—

arguably Bardo Pond in a nutshell. Then again, enough other bands do the same thing, so why should the Pond get singled out? It's hard to pin down an exact reason, but whatever "it" is that a band needs to connect, they've got it. The slow, stony pace that "Adhesive" establishes for *Bufo Alvarius Amen 29:15* continues through the album's remaining tracks, but in such a way that Bardo Pond rapidly become their own band and not merely the sum of their influences. There's something about the combination of lo-fi crunch, post-shoegaze bliss-out, stoner Quaalude head-nodding, and Loop/Spacemen 3-inspired drone that's truly unique. Standout moments abound: "Back Porch" has a series of instrumental breaks with brief, beautiful guitar lines, while on the soft jangle of "On a Side Street," various solos unfold slowly but surely in the background as lowly sung lyrics amble about. "Capillary River" has some astonishing, transcendent soloing in the middle of the song, building up to a brilliant final verse as Gibbons' vocals are lost in feedback and haze. The low-key shuffle/drone "Absence" is a good showcase for Sollenberger's singing—sweeter and clearer here than might be expected. The CD version includes what might be the ultimate head-trip of them all, at least for this particular album: the 30-minute "Amen." The central part of the song is a fairly simple chord progression repeated again and again, but it's the various touches throughout the number—the extra drones, watery deep reverb on the bass, and slow overall rhythm—that make it the understated monster it is. *—Ned Raggett*

Big Laughing Jym / Oct. 30, 1995 / Compulsiv ♦♦♦

Amanita / Apr. 1996 / Matador ♦♦♦♦♦
Not changing all that much but whipping up just as compelling a mix of drone, volume, and blissout as before, on *Amanita* the now officially-a-quintet Pond cranked the amps, switched on the pedals, and let fly with 11 monster songs. After a four-minute series of guitar feedback and fuzz, "Limerick" fully kicks in the album with a slow, stoned groove that's as big as one could want it to be, with Sollenberger's echoed vocals emerging out of somewhere while the slow shuffled beat builds higher and higher. Effortlessly combining psychedelic inspirations from Pink Floyd's original explorations to the more modern reachings into the beyond by My Bloody Valentine and Main, it's a simply stunning way to begin an equally stunning album. Many of the songs take a generally quieter approach before fully turning on the riff action. Two good examples are "Tantric Porno," where things are more understatedly shuffled before pumping up the volume and riff-out in the midsection, and the similarly paced "Yellow Turban," with its slow, downward crawl and wonderful guitar from the Gibbons brothers, alternately watery, weird, loud, and crumbling. Another song of note in this vein is the floating "Rumination," sounding not dissimilar at points to the crystalline melancholy also explored by labelmate and future collaborator Roy Montgomery. Otherwise, it's tune-up and zone-out to the max. "The High Frequency," for instance, steps away from lyrical meaning by burying what sounds like a random selection of spoken word snippets deep in the mix, just letting that wash of sound do what it does. Final number "RM" lets Sollenberger more clearly contribute her flute to the proceedings, while in general, whipping a last conclusive blast of sound to close out an astonishing and inspiring album. *—Ned Raggett*

High Frequencies / Apr. 9, 1996 / Matador ♦♦♦

Lapsed / Oct. 21, 1997 / Matador ♦♦♦♦♦
With each successive album, Bardo Pond continues to reshape and refine their monolithic sound, drawing ever closer to the oxymoronic ideal of controlled chaos that their brand of supreme noise seems to promise. *Lapsed* doesn't reach that holy grail, but it takes the group to a new level regardless, expanding into new dimensions of cacophony while sharpening the focus of their music to reflect an increasing emphasis on shape and form; the tension between the melodies of songs like "Pick My Brain," "Flux" and the epic closer "Aldrin" and the feverish blasts of noise which ultimately erupt from them is electrifying. The achievement of *Lapsed* is that for the first time, it's possible not merely to get lost in Bardo Pond's music, but to let it actually lead you somewhere as well—certainly a trip well worth taking. *—Jason Ankeny*

Set and Setting / Aug. 10, 1999 / Matador ♦♦♦
The broken-down blues of Bardo Pond might just alter the world. The cilia-pulling strains of *Set and Setting* become utterly more infectious with each new spin. It's as though Bardo Pond is tugging the earth into their psychedelic orbit without anyone's knowledge or consent. The band is at their most effective on instrumental cuts like "Datura" and the violin-based "Cross Current." Here, sounds get their most stretched out and visual. On the whole, *Set and Setting* is another cohesive step forward, a slow parade of seductive experimentation and noise that crawls on rock's foundation and doesn't care what anyone thinks. This description could also apply to some of Sonic Youth's better music. Imagine then, Sonic Youth strewn across the desert on blotter acid; *Set and Setting* probably sounds something like that. *—Matthew Kantor*

Vol. II / 2001 / [self released] ♦♦♦
Like its similarly titled predecessor, *Vol. II* was first sold on the road, in this case during the band's amazing tour with Mogwai in late spring 2001. As with *Vol. I*, *Vol. II* consists of outtakes and improvisational experiments recorded at the band's Lemur House rehearsal/base of operations in Philadelphia. Those who are fond of the group's sheer power live will likely find this release to their taste, though they should be warned that this is, after all, stuff Bardo Pond initially didn't think would go down easy on the real albums. Unlike some of the near white noise work on the first collection, though, *Vol. II* generally focuses on Bardo Pond's driftier, mellower side, occasionally calling to mind some of the stoned work from their Hash Jar Tempo collaboration with Roy Montgomery. "Precious Metal" begins the collection on a fairly even keel; a low-volume, slow-paced number with Sollenberger's vocals floating in and out of intelligibility. "Took the One" will appeal to those who loved *Set and Setting*'s combination of Sollenberger beat poetry and atonal, off-kilter feel, squawking sax (or the equivalent) the wild card on this particular number. The possibly more-than-one-recording, possibly not, "Montanasacra" is more or less the central piece of the collection, a 15-minute long zone-out in the finest Bardo Pond style. There's no flute on evidence, or vocals, but otherwise it's all of the band getting in there, starting out as a quieter sort of exploration before pouring it on. It's not quite the same impact as being at a Bardo Pond show, but it's as good a stand-in as any. "How's Annie?" is almost as long and easily as strung out, but makes its point in a much more low-key fashion, with a near-silent ambient midsection that's defined practically by a mere ghost of feedback if nothing else. *—Ned Raggett*

● **Dilate** / Apr. 24, 2001 / Matador ♦♦♦♦♦
On its sixth album, *Dilate*, Bardo Pond cuts through the dense, smoky haze of *Set and Setting* and *Lapsed* to deliver its most refined collection to date. Even the title's drug reference (the band's first three releases were named after various mind-altering toads and mushrooms) is subtler, yet more evocative. Bardo Pond's roaring guitars, trippy flutes, and pummeling drums are all still in place, but now the group uses them sparingly instead of in heroic doses. Indeed, the album's best moments mix equally vast amounts of noise and space, giving *Dilate* an appropriately expansive feel. Isobel Sollenberger's double-tracked vocals take the lead on "Sunrise" and "Inside," a pair of spacy epics that hover around the edges of pop before veering into guitar maelstroms. The album also celebrates the prettier, emotional side of Bardo Pond's music, which the group has often obscured with clouds of distortion. A melancholy beauty permeates the string-driven instrumental "Two Planes" as well as rolling, folk-meets-fuzz ballads like "Aphasia" and "Favorite Uncle." These songs and *Dilate's* centerpiece, "Despite the Roar" (which shimmers like heat distortion before exploding into a trippy climax after five and half minutes), suggest vulnerability in a gauzy, abstract way that's more affecting than directly stating it. But the album also indulges Bardo Pond's interest in textures, as the Eastern-inspired motifs of "Swig" and subtle guitar washes and backward snares of "Hum" prove. However, it wouldn't be a Bardo Pond album without some glorious guitar excesses, and *Dilate* delivers with the heavy, wittily named "Lb.," a kinetic piece of stoner rock more in keeping with the group's two previous efforts. And though it's over 11 minutes long, the album closer "Ganges" manages to keep its mix of crunchy riffs and droning strings inventive throughout. Likewise, *Dilate* proves that the members of Bardo Pond keep finding ways to reinvent their sound, surpassing themselves each time they do. *—Heather Phares*

Barenaked Ladies

f. 1990
Adult Alternative Pop/Rock, Post-Grunge, Alternative Pop/Rock
Barenaked Ladies is a pop quintet from Toronto founded by Ed Robertson (guitar, vocals) and Steven Page (guitar, vocals) in 1988. Completing the band are Tyler Stewart (drums) and brothers Jim (bass) and Andrew Creeggan (keyboards). They released a successful independent EP, *Be My Yoko Ono*, in 1990 and their debut album, *Gordon*, was a substantial hit in Canada in 1992. Their second album, *Maybe You Should Drive*, was released in 1994; *Born on a Pirate Ship* followed two years later, promoted by the group's appearance on the popular drama *Beverly Hills 90210*. Barenaked Ladies resurfaced in 1998 with *Stunt*, also co-headlining that year's H.O.R.D.E. tour. 2000 saw the release of *Maroon*, which was produced by Don Was. *—William Ruhlmann*

● **Gordon** / Mar. 1992 / Reprise ♦♦♦♦
Gordon contains re-recordings of key tracks from their Indy cassette that outsold many, a "big star" major-label release in Canada, and that cemented BNL's witty, gosh-darn reputation: "Brian Wilson," "If I Had A Million Dollars," and "Be My Yoko Ono." New numbers "Box Set"—poking fun at music industry excess—and "New Kid (On The Block)"—poking fun at different music industry excess—carry on the tradition. But... surprise surprise... the group has decided it doesn't want to be typecast as a cute, cuddly, novelty-tune act. *Gordon* also contains several serious moments, notably "The Flag"'s metaphor for abusive relationships, and the poignant, "it's tough growing up in a complicated world" ballad "What A Good Boy." *—Roch Parisien*

Maybe You Should Drive / 1994 / Sire/Reprise ♦♦♦
Barenaked Ladies are a little less interested in the quirky and comic on their second album, perhaps recognizing that They Might Be Giants have that niche covered. Instead, though, they are showing their sensitive folk-pop roots, which makes them winning, if a little wet. (XTC, anyone?) But one thing they aren't is "alternative," a matter dealt with in the chorus of the song "Alternative Girlfriend," when they sing, "There's nothing left that won't cross over." Well put, and present company included. *—William Ruhlmann*

Born on a Pirate Ship / Mar. 19, 1996 / Reprise ♦♦♦
Canada's multi-platinum group of humorists comes marching across the border with their latest bunch of songs. It could be said that Barenaked Ladies are North America's answer to England's XTC, judging from their wry sense of humor and sly twist of a phrase. Including such takes on life as "The Old Apartment," the really XTCish "I Know" and "Straw Hat and Old Dirty Hank" which touches on fan mania, *Born on a Pirate Ship* is such good listening you won't want to stop. *—James Chrispell*

Rock Spectacle / Nov. 19, 1996 / Reprise ♦♦♦
Rock Spectacle is a live album from the Barenaked Ladies, capturing most of the band's best-known songs in their best possible setting—the stage, where their musical jokes sit well with their funny story and quirky sense of humor. Granted, the album isn't going to convert anyone into a fan, but for dedicated followers, *Rock Spectacle* is the next best thing to being there. *—Stephen Thomas Erlewine*

Stunt / Jul. 7, 1998 / Reprise ♦♦♦♦
By trying to mask their smart-assed humor in a big pop production, the Barenaked Ladies attempt to set themselves up for the big crossover that they nearly achieved with such past singles as "Be My Yoko Ono" and "Brian Wilson." Nothing on *Stunt*, the group's

fourth studio album, is so clearly jokey (although "Alcohol" comes close), but they still rely on clever satire. That may irritate some listeners who would otherwise be won over by the group's increased musical skill. Never before has the band been able to pull off so many different styles, from jangly pop and alt-country to loungey bossa nova, so well. Musically, it could convince the doubters who have written off Barenaked Ladies as novelty pranksters, but the lyrics still will stand in the way of trad-rockers predisposed to this style of music. Of course, listeners who are a little less uptight will find *Stunt* to be a fine collegiate party record and one of the best albums the Barenaked Ladies have released. —*Stephen Thomas Erlewine*

Maroon / Sep. 12, 2000 / Reprise ✦✦✦

Canada's favorite musical comics the Barenaked Ladies didn't get distressed by the mainstream success of their fifth album, 1998's *Stunt*. The single "One Week" catapulted the five-piece into the homes of *TRL* diehards and their self-defined cheeky pop sound captured pop music at its finest. They had only been crafting their freewheeling musical perfection since their inception in the late '80s, so the Barenaked Ladies were about due. Two years later, the boys joined forces with producer Don Was (Bob Dylan, Bonnie Raitt, Iggy Pop, Rolling Stones) and delivered yet another merry-making batch of pop songs on *Maroon*. Ed Robertson and Steven Page split vocal duties and their sparkling honesty of musicianship and friendship once again makes for a spherical delight of humor and grandeur.

Barenaked Ladies might not have been distracted by their previous accolades, but *Maroon* hints at the band's hesitation to refrain from repetition. The lyrical rhymes are typically amusing and the musicianship is colorful and quirky, but first single "Pinch Me" doesn't feel entirely comfortable. A conservative BNL listener would be able to catch the trickling acoustics and thumping bass lines, but its head-bopping, toe-tapping excitement is hauntingly similar. But never despair, *Maroon* does indicate the band's impeccable musical brightness and playful creativity, specifically on songs such as "Falling for the First Time" and "Conventioneers." They toy around with adult responsibility and the fear of conflict with such attractive wit, and the messages are right on. And aside from being intelligently impressive, they twist and turn inside their musical sauciness to pluck at jaunty Americana sounds ("Baby Seat") and frilly bossa nova ("Sell, Sell, Sell"). Barenaked Ladies mold blushing harmonies with loopy guitar hooks— *Maroon* is simply charming. It's not outstanding, but the Barenaked Ladies do keep their self-defined whimsicality top-notch. —*MacKenzie Wilson*

Bark Psychosis

f. 1986, Snaresbrook, England, **db.** 1994

Experimental Ambient, Post-Rock/Experimental, Experimental

Despite a relatively small recorded output and little media recognition, Bark Psychosis were one of the most innovative artists of their era. The British quartet evolved by leaps and bounds, moving from moody, lush pop to ambient soundscapes to taut, atmospheric experimental music; their work was so revolutionary, and so impossible to define, that noted critic Simon Reynolds even found it necessary to invent a new sub-genre—"post-rock"—simply to categorize their vision. Founded in 1986, the band recorded several singles and EPs before entering the studio in 1992 to begin work on *Hex*, their long-awaited full-length debut. In sum, the LP took over a year to complete, forcing the group to the brink of emotional and financial collapse. Even as *Hex* appeared to massive critical acclaim—Reynolds' review of the album marked the first mention of the post-rock label, a tag later attached to similarly-uncategorizable bands like Tortoise—Bark Psychosis was essentially dissolved. After a farewell appearance at Russia's Electronic Music Festival, the group officially disbanded; two posthumous retrospectives, 1994's *Independency* and 1997's *Game Over*, were their final full-length releases. In the wake of Bark Psychosis' demise, vocalist Graham Sutton plunged fully into the realm of drum'n'bass, recording under the name Boymerang. —*Jason Ankeny*

★ **Hex** / 1994 / Caroline ✦✦✦✦✦

A masterpiece of unrivalled beauty and complexity, Bark Psychosis' *Hex* channels the experimentation of the group's prior singles into a more controlled setting; a series of atmospheric set pieces, the songs find a common ground between accepted musical formulas and avant innovation—at first glance, tracks like "Big Shot" and "Eyes & Smiles" appear tightly structured, yet they avoid the dynamics of conventional songcraft like choruses and solos with remarkable dexterity. Similarly, both "The Loom" and "Fingerspit" are too melodic and finely-honed to pass as mere ambient soundscapes, leaving the record best ascribed to a force not unlike alchemy—*Hex* begins with base musical materials, but transforms them into something mysterious, haunting, and breathtakingly visionary. —*Jason Ankeny*

Independency / Jul. 1994 / 3rd Stone ✦✦✦✦✦

Collecting a series of singles first issued between 1989 and 1992, *Independency* charts Bark Psychosis' extraordinary period of evolution prior to the creation of their lone studio LP, *Hex*. Opening with the delicate "I Know," the set grows by leaps and bounds, expanding in complexity and innovation over the course of tracks like "Manman" and "Tooled Up" before culminating in the 21-minute improvisational ambient opus "Scum," perhaps the band's definitive moment. An invaluable document. —*Jason Ankeny*

Game Over / Aug. 5, 1997 / Third Stone ✦✦✦✦

Game Over is a schizophrenic epitaph to Bark Psychosis' too-short career, collecting a handful of non-LP tracks (including the single "Blue," the previously unreleased "Murder City," a live "Pendulum Man" and a cover of Wire's "Three Girl Rhumba") along with a number of cuts from both the *Hex* LP and the *Independency* compilation. While not the place for new fans to begin, the set is essential for completists, and does include some of

the group's finest moments, including "A Street Scene" and the epic "Scum." —*Jason Ankeny*

Syd Barrett

b. Jan. 6, 1946, Cambridge, England

Vocals, Guitar / British Psychedelia, Psychedelic, Prog-Rock/Art Rock

Like a supernova, Roger "Syd" Barrett burned briefly and brightly, leaving an indelible mark upon psychedelic and progressive rock as the founder and original singer, songwriter, and lead guitarist of Pink Floyd. He was responsible for most of their brilliant first album, 1967's *The Piper at the Gates of Dawn*, but left and/or was fired from the band in early 1968 after his erratic behavior had made him too difficult to deal with; Pink Floyd never recaptured the playful humor and mad energy of their work with Barrett. After a period of hibernation, he re-emerged in 1970 with a pair of albums, *The Madcap Laughs* and *Barrett*, which featured considerable support from his former bandmates. Barrett's eccentric humor, sly wordplay, and infectious melodies range from brilliant to chaotic on his solo work. Lacking the taut power of his recordings with the Floyd in 1967, they nevertheless remain fascinating and moving glimpses into a creative psyche gone awry after (it is theorized) too much fame and too many drugs too early. With increasing psychological problems, Barrett withdrew into near-total reclusion after these albums. He never released any more material, and these days rarely appears in public, let alone to play music. —*Richie Unterberger*

● **The Madcap Laughs** / Jan. 3, 1970 / Capitol ✦✦✦✦✦

Wisely, *The Madcap Laughs* doesn't even try to sound like a consistent record. Half the album was recorded by Barrett's former bandmates Roger Waters and Dave Gilmour, and the other half by Harvest Records head Malcolm Jones. Surprisingly, Jones' tracks are song for song much stronger than the more-lauded Floyd entries. The opening "Terrapin" seems to go on three times as long as its five-minute length, creating a hypnotic effect through Barrett's simple, repetitive guitar figure and stream-of-consciousness lyrics. Like many of the "band" tracks, "Here I Go" is a Barrett solo performance with overdubs by Mike Ratledge, Hugh Hopper, and Robert Wyatt of the Soft Machine; the combination doesn't always particularly work, as the Softs' jazzy, improvisational style is hemmed in by having to follow Barrett's predetermined lead, so on several tracks, like "No Good Trying," they content themselves with simply making weird noises in the background. The solo tracks are what made the album's reputation, though, particularly the horrifying "Dark Globe," a first-person portrait of schizophrenia that's seemingly the most self-aware song this normally whimsical songwriter ever created. Honestly, however, the other solo tracks are the album's weakest tracks, with the exception of the plain gorgeous "Golden Hair," a musical setting of a James Joyce poem that's simply spellbinding. The album falls apart with the appalling "Feel." Frankly, the inclusion of false starts and studio chatter, not to mention some simply horrible off-key singing by Barrett, makes this already marginal track feel disgustingly exploitative. But for that misstep, however, *The Madcap Laughs* is a surprisingly effective record that holds up better than its "ooh, lookit the scary crazy person" reputation suggests. —*Stewart Mason*

Barrett / Nov. 1970 / Capitol ✦✦✦

On his second solo album, Barrett was joined by Humble Pie drummer Jerry Shirley and Pink Floyd members Rick Wright (organ) and Dave Gilmour (guitar). Gilmour and Wright acted as producers as well. Instrumentally, the result is a bit fuller and smoother than the first album, although it's since been revealed that Gilmour and Wright embellished these songs as best they could without much involvement from Barrett, who was often unable or unwilling to perfect his performance. The songs, however, are just as fractured as on his debut, if not more so. "Baby Lemonade," "Gigolo Aunt," and the nursery rhyming "Effervescing Elephant" rank among his peppiest and best-loved tunes. Elsewhere, the tone is darker and more meandering. It was regarded as something of a charming but unfocused throwaway at the time of its release, but Barrett's singularly whimsical and unsettling vision holds up well. —*Richie Unterberger*

Peel Sessions / 1987 / Dutch East India ✦✦

Opel / Apr. 1989 / Capitol ✦✦✦

For several years, the existence of "lost" material by Barrett had been speculated on by the singer's vociferous cult, fueled by numerous patchy bootlegs of intriguing outtakes. The release of *Opel* lived up to, and perhaps exceeded, fans' expectations. With 14 tracks spanning 1968 to 1970, including six alternate takes and eight songs that had never been officially released in any form, it is equally as essential as his two 1970 LPs. The tone is very much in keeping with his pair of solo albums; ragged, predominantly acoustic, melodic, and teetering on the edge of dementia. At the same time, it's charming and lyrically pungent, with Barrett's inimitable sense of childlike whimsy. The production is generally more minimal than on his other albums, even bare-bones at times, but if anything, this adds to the music's stark power. Highlights are the lengthy brooding title track, the multi-layered swirl of "Swan Lee," the alternate take of "Dark Globe" (with much better, more restrained vocals than the previous version), and the exuberant, infectious "Milky Way." Meticulous liner notes and excellent sound complete this lovingly archival package. —*Richie Unterberger*

Octopus: The Best of Syd Barrett / May 29, 1992 / Cleopatra ✦✦✦

A well-chosen, 14-track, single-disc compilation of Barrett's solo work, presumably discount-priced and aimed at the casual listener. But Barrett is such a specialized taste and has such a small body of work that one wonders why Cema Special Markets (a division of EMI) would bother. —*William Ruhlmann*

Crazy Diamond / Apr. 19, 1994 / Harvest/EMI ✦✦✦✦✦

A three-CD box set that enshrines Barrett's complete recorded legacy as a solo artist. Besides including his two 1970 albums, this collection includes the 1989 compilation of unreleased material, *Opel*. The chief attraction of this set for Barrett fans is no less than 19 previously unreleased alternate takes from throughout his quite brief solo career. All of those alternate takes, it's important to note, are alternate versions of songs that appear on the three previously available albums; no entirely unheard compositions were unearthed. Nonetheless, these alternate takes are more interesting listening than you might expect, for a couple of reasons. First, Barrett was so mercurial (and occasionally unfocused) in the studio that it was difficult to get him to play a song the same way twice. Second, the alternate takes are usually starker and more acoustic in nature than the official versions; they're not better, but have interesting different slants. With some of the songs repeated two, three, or even four times, this is definitely for the hardcore fan. But it's a beautifully produced document, with a meticulously detailed booklet, of a uniquely primitive visionary, and has many moments of charming and chilling power. It includes everything salvageable that he produced, with the exception of the *Peel Sessions*. It doesn't match his work with the original Pink Floyd, but the music continues to influence and be emulated (most notably by Robyn Hitchcock), though never equaled. *—Richie Unterberger*

Wouldn't You Miss Me: The Best of Syd Barrett / Mar. 27, 2001 / Harvest/EMI ♦♦♦♦
You know the situation is getting desperate when a compilation recycles material from an *outtakes* collection released a decade prior. Such is the case with *Wouldn't You Miss Me: The Best of Syd Barrett*, a package that basically combines the best of Barrett's two proper albums, *The Madcap Laughs* and *Barrett*, with a number of previously issued outtakes and a straggler from producer and Pink Floyd band mate David Gilmour's vaults ("Bob Dylan's Blues"). But to be perfectly fair, the now-recycled outtakes release in question, 1989's *Opel*, was a rare instance where such a release lived up to the quality of the artist's proper studio albums. And it's not as if Syd Barrett's two proper albums, *The Madcap Laughs* and *Barrett*, feature such a glossy, professional sheen that the average ear would need to tell the difference between the painstakingly crafted and the whimsically patched together. Barrett wasn't exactly Jeff Lynne, was he? So in this most bizarre situation, it makes a fair amount of sense to consider some of the *Opel* material to be worthy of inclusion on a best of.

If you're keeping score at home, here's how the track distribution works out: seven songs come from *The Madcap Laughs*, nine are from *Barrett*, four are from *Opel*. That leaves enough space for the early "Bob Dylan's Blues," a decent song that serves as a flimsy ruse to rope completists into buying the disc, as well as a previously available Peel Session version of "Two of a Kind." All in all, it is a fine introduction to Barrett's solo material, but does someone who released two proper studio albums *really* need an "introduction" to their work? Longtime fans might want to exercise some restraint, especially since those still-unissued outtakes are being released water torture style. *—Andy Kellman*

Barry & The Remains

f. 1964, **db.** 1966
Frat Rock, Garage Rock, Rock & Roll
A strong contender for the finest overlooked American band of the mid-'60s, the Remains (led by Barry Tashian) were the most notable Boston group of the era. But they never broke out nationally, despite signing to Epic and copping an opening slot on the Beatles' final American tour in 1966. Sometimes described as a garage band, that designation isn't at all accurate; the Remains shared the same British Invasion influences as many American teen acts, but had a lot of professional finesse to their straight-ahead attack and sharp songwriting, sometimes sounding like a fusion of the Beatles and the Zombies with their energetic harmonies and guitar-electric keyboard blend.

Four fine singles for Epic found little action outside of the Northeast. Frustrated by the disparity they perceived between their studio work and their furious live show, they cut an audition tape for Capitol, although no offer from the label was forthcoming (the session was issued for collectors many years later). An uneven but solid debut album for Epic was released near the end of 1966, but by that time the Remains were breaking up, dispirited by the stalemate in which their career seemed to have been mired. Remains drummer N.D. Smart II played with Gram Parsons and Emmylou Harris; Tashian also played with Harris, and today is a Nashville-based country-folk musician, often recording as a duo with his wife, Holly. *—Richie Unterberger*

Live in Boston / 1984 / Eva ♦♦
This live-in-the-studio demo was accorded raves by the few collectors who managed to hear it before its appearance on this LP. Although Remains leader Barry Tashian had said that it captures the band's prowess better than their studio material, in the event it's a disappointment. Six of the seven songs are cover versions of very well-known rock hits—"Johnny B. Goode," "I'm A Man," "All Day and All of the Night," "Hang on Sloopy," "Like a Rolling Stone"—competently done, but hardly revelatory, as the Remains' chief strength was their excellent songwriting. The version of the original tune "Why Do I Cry" is indeed fine and powerful, but the Remains' legacy is best heard on the excellent, nearly all-original *The Remains* collection on Epic. *—Richie Unterberger*

● **The Remains [Epic/Legacy]** / Jan. 29, 1991 / Epic/Legacy ♦♦♦♦♦
Most 1960s garage rock obsessives collect singles rather than albums for a good reason: While plenty of snarling teenagers could come up with two decent songs at a stretch, a precious few seemed able to brainstorm a dozen tunes without reaching to the bottom of the barrel or resorting to covers of other people's hits. But there were exceptions to this rule, among them the Sonics, the Litter, and, especially, the Remains, who never enjoyed much success on the national charts but were fabled heroes in their home town of Boston. The Remains' 1966 album for Epic is a classic, packed with great songs from singer/guitarist Barry Tashian, bassist Vern Miller, and pianist Bill Briggs, and boasting exciting, fiery performances, and if the full firepower of their legendary live shows didn't always come through on tape, even the album's weakest moments made clear the Remains were tougher, smarter, and tighter than the vast majority of their competition. When Epic/Legacy reissued the album in 1991 (with the band's name augmented to Barry & the Remains), they added a handful of non-LP singles and unreleased tracks and gave the album a crisp digital remix, and against all odds, Epic actually improved a masterpiece. If the old analog version sounds harder and dirtier (a good thing for garage rock), the CD allows you to hear more of the details, and nearly every one of the 21 cuts on board is killer stuff (their cover of Don Covay's "Mercy, Mercy, Mercy" shows them beating the Rolling Stones at their own game, and after you've heard "Don't Look Back," you'll always wonder why it wasn't a Top Ten hit). *The Remains* is mid-'60s American rock & roll at it's best, and you don't have to own any paisley clothing to enjoy it. *—Mark Deming*

Session with the Remains / Feb. 27, 1996 / Sundazed ♦♦♦
The first official release of their '66 live-in-the-studio Capitol demo, in considerably better sound quality than when it appeared on a French import of dubious legality. This has a very high reputation in collector circles, but in my opinion it is not the Remains at their best, principally because they record only one original ("Why Do I Cry"). The rest of the seven demos are high-energy run-throughs of typical live standards of the era, like "Hang on Sloopy," "I'm a Man," and "Johnny B. Goode." The CD is fleshed out with five previously unreleased demos of group originals (different versions of all of these appear on the Epic reissue), and a previously unknown demo of "Walkin' the Dog." Most listeners will be satisfied with Epic's excellent Remains retrospective, but this is a useful supplement for collectors who want a little more. *—Richie Unterberger*

Len Barry (Leonard Borisoff)

b. Jun. 12, 1942, Philadelphia, PA
Vocals
Blue-eyed soul vocalist Len Barry paced several hits of the early '60s, both as a member of Dovells and as a solo act. Born in Philadelphia in 1942, he debuted on wax as the vocalist for the 1958 single "Mope-Itty Mope," as recorded by the Boss-Tones. He formed the group that became Dovells in 1957, and sang along on their Top Ten hits "The Bristol Stomp" and "You Can't Sit Down." Barry quit the group in late 1963 though, and soon signed with Decca as a solo act. The single "1-2-3" became a big hit in 1965, and just missed topping the charts. Amidst quickly changing times, however, Barry hit the Top 40 just twice more, with the early 1966 follow-ups "Like a Baby" and "Somewhere" (the latter from *West Side Story*). He continued performing his entertaining stage act, and later moved into production as well. *—John Bush*

● **The Very Best of Len Barry** / 1995 / Taragon ♦♦♦♦
Ex-Dovells' lead singer Len Barry carved a prolific solo career via hits like "1-2-3" and "Like a Baby," both included among the 11 songs. The CD starts badly with "Introduction to Len Barry" where Barry mouths about how hard it is to get a hit record, etc. He sticks to singing on the rest in a penny candy sweet first tenor that moles into your membrane, a voice you never forget once you heard it, á la Frankie Valli, Smokey Robinson, et al. Notables include "Somewhere" sung to a marching beat that Barry steps right along with, and the Barry, Kenny Gamble, Leon Huff collaboration "Struck It Rich," which makes you pine for more by the threesome. At under ten bucks, this brief overview of Barry's solo career will fit most budgets. *—Andrew Hamilton*

Dave Bartholomew

b. Dec. 24, 1920, Edgard, LA
Vocals, Trumpet, Songwriter / New Orleans R&B, Rock & Roll, R&B
Dave Bartholomew is the multi-talented figure behind a majority of classic New Orleans R&B of the '50s and the self-proclaimed inventor of the "Big Beat." Bartholomew has over 4,000 songs in his enormous catalog and is responsible for arranging and producing timeless records by Shirley & Lee, Lloyd Price, Smiley Lewis, and especially Fats Domino. Bartholomew was born in Edgard, LA, on December 24, 1920. His first instruments were tuba and trumpet. He fronted several bands in the Crescent City before being drafted into the army. His military time brought scoring and arranging experience which came in handy following World War II. After his stint in the service, Bartholomew returned to New Orleans and put together a group of musicians that would comprise the bedrock of R&B in the city, including saxophonists Alvin "Red" Tyler, Lee Allen, and drummer Earl Palmer. This became the band that backed up the majority of solo talent traveling through New Orleans. Bartholomew led his first studio session under his own name in 1947 for Deluxe, but the label went out of business shortly thereafter and the sessions went unnoticed. In 1949, Bartholomew met Lew Chudd who was forming a new label, Imperial Records. Chudd hired Bartholomew as house arranger, bandleader, and talent scout, and he immediately started cranking out numerous hits through the '50s for Fats Domino, Shirley & Lee, Smiley Lewis, Earl King, Chris Kenner, Tommy Ridgely, Frankie Ford, Robert Parker, and a host of others. Bartholomew stayed with Imperial until the hits dried up in the mid-'60s, followed by short stays at Trumpet, Mercury, and his own Broadmoor label. In the '70s and '80s, he took various behind-the-scenes musical jobs while living off his many song royalties and formed a Dixieland jazz band that continues to play around the Crescent City. The '90s found Bartholomew being inducted into the Rock & Roll Hall of Fame in 1991 and releasing two discs: *Dave Bartholomew and the Maryland Jazz Band* in 1995 and *New Orleans Big Beat* three years later. *—Al Campbell*

In the Alley / 1991 / Charly ♦♦♦♦
Dave Bartholomew is best known for producing and arranging classic New Orleans R&B sides from the '50s, especially for Fats Domino. It's curious that success eluded him on sessions released under his own name. Recorded between 1949 and 1952, the jump blues tracks on *In the Alley* were originally released on Deluxe and King, separate from

Bartholomew's work with the Imperial label. King signed Bartholomew as a name artist, and ten of this compilation's 20 tracks find him backed up by the Todd Rhodes Orchestra. The remaining tracks are credited to the Dave Bartholomew Orchestra and feature some of the greatest Crescent City R&B session men from the period, including drummer Earl Palmer, bassist Frank Fields, and pianist Salvador Doucette. Six of the titles, including the excellent "Basin Street Breakdown," are previously unissued takes. Also included is the original song for which Bartholomew is most widely known, though again not for his version of it: "My Ding-A-Ling," which became a huge hit for Chuck Berry in 1972. Bartholomew was more of a Louis Jordan-style vocalist than a Joe Turner blues shouter, and that influence is prevalent throughout this disc. While this is a highly recommended set, there are a few clunkers here and there, including a strained and soulless "Stormy Weather" and the lengthy call-and-response vamp "Lawdy Lawdy Lord, Pt. 1 and 2," which would have been sufficient concluding with part one. *—Al Campbell*

★ **The Spirit of New Orleans: The Genius of Dave Bartholomew** / 1993 / EMI ✦✦✦✦✦

A two-disc set featuring 50 tracks and several different artists (including Fats Domino, Smiley Lewis, T-Bone Walker, Shirley and Lee, and Earl King), *The Spirit of New Orleans* effectively conveys Bartholomew's groundbreaking achievements in R&B and rock & roll. *—Stephen Thomas Erlewine*

Basement Jaxx

f. 1994, London, England

Progressive House, Club/Dance, House, British Garage, Electronica

The production duo of Simon Ratcliffe and Felix Buxton released several of Britain's most respected and enjoyable progressive house anthems of the '90s from their base in South London. Before they met (at a Thames riverboat party organized by Buxton), Ratcliffe grooved to the deep Latin funk of War and George Duke while Buxton was turned on to Chicago house. The pair formed Atlantic Jaxx Records in 1994, and were undoubtedly honored to count among fans of their first release none other than DJ legend and Basement Jaxx influence Tony Humphries, who played "Da Underground" from the EP on his New York mixshow consistently during 1994-95. For their second release, Ratcliffe and Buxton recruited vocalist Corrina Josephs, who later became practically a member of the team herself.

The 1995 single "Samba Magic" was picked up for distribution by Virgin, and in time, Basement Jaxx was drawing praise as one of the top house production units, from all corners of the American and British house community. The pair spent much of 1996 working on remixes (for the Pet Shop Boys, Roger Sanchez, and Lil' Mo Yin Yang among others), then released a third Basement Jaxx EP. One track from the EP, "Flylife," became a Top 20 hit in England after being re-released by Multiply in mid-1997, and the single proved one of the most popular anthems of the year on the worldwide club-scene. Late that year, Ratcliffe and Buxton released a compilation of their most crucial Atlantic Jaxx sides. After being courted by several major labels, Basement Jaxx signed to the independent XL Recordings (also home to the Prodigy) and readied their debut full-length *Remedy* for a 1999 release. Second album *Rooty* followed two years later, the outgrowth of the duo's similarly named club night. *—John Bush*

★ **Remedy** / Aug. 3, 1999 / XL Recordings/Astralwerks ✦✦✦✦✦

The duo's long-awaited debut album is one of the most assured, propulsive full-lengths the dance world had seen since Daft Punk's *Homework*. A set of incredibly diverse tracks, *Remedy* is indebted to the raw American house of Todd Terry and Masters at Work, and even shares the NuYoricans' penchant for Latin vibes (especially on the horn-driven "Bingo Bango" and the opener, "Rendez-Vu," which trades a bit of salsa wiggle with infectious vocoderized disco). True, Ratcliffe and Buxton do sound more like an American production team than a pair of Brixton boys would—they get props (and vocal appearances) from several of the best American house producers out there including DJ Sneak, Erick Morillo, and Benji Candelario. And "U Can't Stop Me" is an R&B production that could probably have gotten airplay in major rap markets across the U.S. Elsewhere, Buxton and Ratcliffe chew up and spit out mutated versions of hip-hop, ragga, Latin, R&B, soul, and garage—the varied sound that defined the worldwide house scene of the late '90s. *—John Bush*

Rooty / Jun. 26, 2001 / Astralwerks ✦✦✦✦✦

Sophomore album blues from a pair of producers who just want to party all night and make a few tracks during the day? Not a chance. Two years of globetrotting as house superstars fortunately hasn't dulled the keen blade of Basement Jaxx's production style. So raw you can't believe they spent over an hour per track, so perfect you're glad they stopped noodling about long before most producers would, and so poppy they should get picked up by commercial radio in America as well as the rest of the world, *Rooty* is the second straight triumph from a pair of producer/DJs who look set to carry the torch for dancefloor electronica in the years to come. Though it's missing the genre-spanning flair and red-line energy that made 1999's *Remedy* the best dance album of the '90s, *Rooty* comes very close. It's much funkier than *Remedy*, much closer to commercial pop, and much more sensuous, with several tracks of moaning, juiced-up funk from the Prince playbook. The opener "Romeo" is groovy and luscious enough to be the next single from Destiny's Child (with a tad more vocal histrionics), and almost every track features vocalists who sound less like professional singers (or flavor-of-the-month robots) and more like they've been tapped as finalists at a posh karaoke bar. Add a little filtered disco ("Jus 1 Kiss"), a track of rowdy New York house (the Gary Numan-sampling "Where's Your Head At," with background shouting from Erick Morillo and Junior Sanchez), bleepy acid house ("Crazy Girl"), and some P-Funked-up house ("Breakaway") and the result is a stunning, diverse album that's not only an immediate winner but a great album down the line as well. You can take the boys out of Brixton, but you just can't take Brixton out of the boys. *—John Bush*

The Basement Wall

f. 1963, **db.** 1968

Garage Rock

One of the more pop-oriented '60s garage bands, this Baton Rouge, LA, group had a big regional hit with "Never Existed" in 1967. Their sound contained elements of Texas punk, the bouncing Farfisa organ style of the Five Americans, and British Invasion harmonies. Likeable if not terribly significant, they disbanded in 1968 and much of their unreleased material was issued in the mid-'80s. *—Richie Unterberger*

● **Incredible Sound Of . . .** / 1985 / Cicadelic ✦✦✦

The Basement Wall hailed from Louisiana and was formed in 1966. The band recorded one album in 1966 for a small regional U.S. label, that despite limited distribution, won over a large following across the nation. The band combined the sounds of the Beatles, Zombies, and Association to form a unique psychedelic pop sound that was becoming popular with the underground music fans. The New Breed hailed from California and despite the surf movement of the area, decided to explore a psychedelic and garage sound. The band recorded a number of singles for various labels before recording an album entitled *Want Ad Reader*. The album contained and was named after the band's biggest hit, the title track. With no label support for the album it was never released and the New Breed evolved into Glad and recorded one album for ABC records before breaking up in 1969. Band members went on to become part of such notable '70s acts as Redwing, Poco, and the Eagles. This single CD release compiles all of the two band's recorded output including rare singles and the unreleased album. *—Keith Pettipas*

There Goes the Neighborhood, Vol. 2 / 1993 / Collectables ✦✦✦

A top '60s garage band captured in primitive stereo, in concert for more than an hour, from part of a show (the rest is on Collectables' *Texas Punk Vol. 8* and part of *Acid Visions, Part 3*). As is typical on tapes of this era, the miking is haywire, with the vocals under-recorded, the guitars a little too prominent in spots, and the drummer mostly sounding like he's playing old cardboard boxes. The material is weighted heavily toward covers of then popular hits, including "Kicks," "Him or Me," "I Had a Dream," "Windy," "Along Comes Mary," "Let's Spend the Night Together" (introduced as "the most controversial tune in the nation," which gives us a rough idea of the date of this show—early 1967), "In the Midnight Hour," "Summer In the City," and "Brown-Eyed Girl." The band doesn't add much new to these songs, just gives pretty intense interpretations of "The Letter," "We Ain't Got Nothin' Yet," "Ticket to Ride," "We Gotta Get Out of This Place," and "Let's Spend the Night Together"; and it's interesting to hear how the Beatles' "Eleanor Rigby" and "Rain" sound as covered by a garage band (the cheesy organ and rhythm guitars subbing for the strings on "Eleanor Rigby" is pretty cool)—the audience obviously appreciated the familiar repertory. This isn't a fully memorable musical document, although it does show the neophyte what most of these legendary garage bands did to make a living between the times they were trying to evolve their own sound in the studio. *—Bruce Eder*

Fontella Bass

b. Jul. 3, 1940, St. Louis, MO

Vocals, Piano / Chicago Soul, Pop-Soul, Northern Soul, Soul

An explosive gospel and soul singer, Fontella Bass is the daughter of the great vocalist Martha Bass and sister of David Peaston, as well as ex-wife of Art Ensemble of Chicago trumpeter Lester Bowie. But none of that family history means as much as her own skills, which include a tremendous voice, great range, and distinctive delivery. Bass first sang in several church choirs but later moved into R&B, singing in Oliver Sain's band and working with Little Milton in the early '60s. Bass teamed with Bobby McClure for two duets on Checker in 1965. "Don't Mess Up a Good Thing" reached number five on the R&B charts and inched into the pop Top 30, while "You'll Miss Me When I'm Gone" got into the R&B Top 30. Bass' debut single as a solo act was her greatest: "Rescue Me" topped the R&B charts for a month, peaked at number four on the pop charts, and was among the era's finest soul singles. The follow-up, "Recovery," was better than it has been credited, and reached number 13. Bass never again attained soul stardom, but has remained busy in the ensuing years. She later sang with Bowie's group, the Art Ensemble of Chicago, and was also part of the gospel group From the Root to the Source. *—Ron Wynn*

Free / 1972 / Varese ✦✦✦

An expanded version of her 1972 Paula album *Now That I Found a Good Thing*, Fontella Bass' *Free* adds a new version of her classic "Rescue Me" along with four B-sides: "It Sure Is Good," "I'm Leaving the Choice to You," "Home Wrecker," and "It's Hard to Get Back In." Bass wrote most of the songs included here herself—along with a few collaborative efforts with her then-husband Lester Bowie—and all the tracks showcase her dynamic, dramatic approach to soul. *—Heather Phares*

● **Rescued: The Best of Fontella Bass** / Mar. 10, 1992 / Chess/MCA ✦✦✦✦✦

"Rescue Me" might have been her only big hit, but Fontella Bass was a terrific gospel-influenced soul vocalist who cut several great sides for Checker/Chess Records in the mid-'60s. They might not have gotten the attention they deserved when they were released, but they have held up very well over the years. *Rescued: The Best of Fontella Bass* collects sixteen of her finest tracks, including "Rescue Me," three duets with Bobby McClure, and a previously unreleased song; it makes a convincing case that she should have had more hit singles than she did. *—Stephen Thomas Erlewine*

The Bats

f. 1982, Christchurch, New Zealand
College Rock, New Zealand Rock, Alternative Pop/Rock

Yet another outgrowth of the seminal Clean, the Bats were an institution on the New Zealand music scene, their melancholy jangle-pop sound and infectious melodies consistently defining the kiwi-rock aesthetic at its very best. The Bats were formed in Christchurch in 1982 by ex-Clean bassist Robert Scott, ex-Toy Love bassist Paul Kean, singer/multi-instrumentalist Kaye Woodward, and drummer Malcolm Grant; with Scott adopting lead vocal and guitar duties as well as serving as the group's chief songwriter, they issued their debut *By Night* in 1984, the first in a series of EPs which also included 1985's *"And Here Is 'Music for the Fireside'!"* and 1986's *Made Up in Blue*. (All three were subsequently collected as *Compiletely Bats*.)

The Bats finally released a full-length album, the stunning *Daddy's Highway*, in 1987; soon after the group went on hiatus, with Scott participating in a Clean reunion tour and Woodward giving birth. The quartet came back together in 1990 to release *The Law of Things*, another critical favorite which received almost no commercial interest. *Fear of God* appeared in 1991, and two years later the Bats resurfaced with *Silverbeet*; an intermittent series of EPs (including *Live at WFMU* and *Spill the Beans*, the latter recorded with Superchunk frontman Mac McCaughan on guitar) followed as Scott again focused much of his energies on another Clean reunion, but in 1995 the group returned with a new LP, *Couchmaster*. —*Jason Ankeny*

Compiletely Bats / 1987 / Communion ✦✦✦✦
Compiletely Bats collects the band's early output, including some non-LP rarities. —*Chris Woodstra*

● **Daddy's Highway** / 1987 / Mammoth ✦✦✦✦✦
The Bats' first full album continues the early promise of their EPs and, with only the slightest deviations and changes since, established their sound for just about everything that followed. Scott and company may not be the most willfully experimental of musicians, but when they're on—more often the case than not—their lovely, melancholic songs simply hit the spot. Woodward forms the perfect singing partner for Scott, while guest violinist Alastair Galbraith brings his talent to the fore as he has for so many other New Zealand bands. "Treason" makes for a good start to the album, but the real standout on *Daddy's Highway* is the surging "North by North." Featuring a fantastic Galbraith violin solo, it gives the band the opportunity to show its sometime hidden strengths for more energetic, nervous material. Scott's vocal performance is one of his best, and the quick, on-edge pace seems to get even more so as the song continues. Quieter songs unsurprisingly abound as well, from the understated sweetness of "Sir Queen" to the gentle keyboard-touched "Candidate." "Tragedy" is one of the best in this vein, ending in a disturbing low drone (or at least as much of a drone as the generally quick-length songs by the Bats allow for). Though *Daddy's Highway* suffers a touch from the same problem that affects all Bats releases—an increasing sameness, especially towards album's end—it's still a great full album debut. —*Ned Raggett*

The Law of Things / 1990 / Mammoth ✦✦✦✦
Returning from his Clean reunion, Scott and company reunited for *The Law of Things*, showing once again that the Bats will likely forever remain the Bats. As always, they retain just enough subtle touches and changes to prevent complete repetition while still staying focused on the post-punk/folky/jangly/wistful sound that defines their work from start to finish. Opening cut "The Other Side of You" demonstrates that nicely thanks to what sounds like a piano buried in the mix, though it could easily be a guitar played just so as well. With the usual Scott/Woodward vocal blend on the chorus and a sweetly giddy pace tinged a touch by melancholia, it's another lovely Bats winner. Other strong songs include the chugging "Yawn Vibes," with one of the band's most memorable musical and lyrical hooks, the slow-building edge of "Nine Days" and the surprisingly muscular pound (and Alastair Galbraith's reappearance on violin) of "Ten to One." As always, calmer cuts like "Mastery" and the declaration of love "Cliff Edge" surface amid the brisker efforts, effortlessly combining melody, wistful vibes, and the low-key heart-to-heart feeling of so much of Scott's work. Closing cut "Smoking Her Wings" is the best of them all, making for a mysterious and moody way to close out *The Law of Things*. Of all the Bats' albums, though, *Law of Things* is perhaps the least successful; no Bats release is anything like terrible, but the unavoidable criticism that the group sticks to one particular sound and style is especially understandable here. Enough twists and turns, always the group's saving grace, help ensure that such isn't entirely the case, but those wanting to take the plunge into full Bats worship should start elsewhere. —*Ned Raggett*

Fear of God / 1991 / Mammoth ✦✦✦
When the band switched to a new American label, Mammoth, little else changed in the world of the Bats, with Scott again leading his musicians through a set of songs that, on the face of it, seem like just more indie rock but often achieve quietly spectacular heights. "Boogey Man" begins *Fear* on a perfectly Bats note—ringing guitar, Scott's straightforward singing with Woodward on counterpoint vocals, a medium-speed pace, and understated but sharp detailing of emotions and thoughts. It's that lyrical element which so often distinguishes the Bats from other acts, combining images that are just cutting enough to make a listener stop and think rather than simply sing along, easy as that is to do. "Dancing as the Boat Goes Down," with guest performances on viola, "You Know We Shouldn't," an invocation of secrets and feelings best kept unspoken, and the slightly more rocking title track are three more of the highlights in that area. The slight musical differences between each song won't likely be everyone's cup of tea—the Bats do have a formula and they rarely if ever deviate from it here. Even allowing for the fact that the songs tend to blend into one another, the fine balance between musical joy and lyrical

concern still works well. What changes there are here from their musical norm bring out the band's strengths all that much more. Highlights include the stripped-down break in "Straight Image," the acoustic guitar/accordion beginning of "Looming Past," and the serene flow of "Watch the Walls," with its subtle drum start, serene string/guitar combination, and generally slower pace. —*Ned Raggett*

Silverbeet / 1993 / Mammoth ✦✦✦
Yet another Bats album—on the one hand that can sound like an insult, but when it comes to simply doing a fine job on album after album, with a set but still captivating sound, the Bats nail it here as they have always done before. It certainly doesn't hurt that *Silverbeet* begins with two of the band's best songs ever: "Courage," a restrained surge of inspiring music that, unsurprisingly, backs a slightly doubting, questioning lyric on love and life, and "Sighting the Sound," with a killer chorus sung by Scott and Woodward together. After that, things settle into that no-surprises-no-disappointments groove that characterizes all of the Bats' albums; everyone's just fine at what they do, catchy melodies are plentiful, and occasional tweaks and touches keep things from being too completely soundalike, such as the addition of slightly droning keyboards on "Slow Alight." Though sometimes the similarities keep songs from standing out as they should, every so often something will connect a little more readily. A great example is "Green," commemorating the environmental group Greenpeace and the underhanded assault on its Rainbow Warrior flagship by France in a New Zealand harbor, an attack not fully prosecuted by the Kiwi government. With a simple but powerful chorus and some quiet, fiery guitar work, it's a protest song that feels far less soppy than most wannabe social anthems. They may be spiritual cousins of the Ramones in terms of not really changing over the moons, but the Bats know their collective strengths and play to them well—something most bands can't manage. —*Ned Raggett*

Spill the Beans / Jul. 12, 1994 / Mammoth ✦✦✦
An EP bridging the Bats' most significant period of artistic growth—between 1993's *Silverbeet* and 1995's *Couchmaster*—*Spill The Beans* was recorded in Raleigh, North Carolina, with Mac McCaughan of Superchunk providing additional guitar. Of the five songs, the standouts are the title-track, the alt-guitar rocker "Under the Law" and the semi-acoustic "Give Into the Sands." —*Alex Ogg*

Couchmaster / Oct. 24, 1995 / Mammoth ✦✦✦
Breaking just enough from the formula but never losing that inspired gift for softer melody and doubting lyrics, *Couchmaster* lets the Bats finally move from being simply a very good group with inspired moments to a great band, flat out. Part of it could be ascribed to the brief, fragmentary tunes that crop up throughout the album, serving as brief transitions from song to song. Other times it's the newer space in the recordings, the alternation between quieter and louder points (but not the rapidly clichéd loud/soft/loud approach that Nirvana popularized, happily). Whatever the source or reasons for the change, though, it works in spades. "Afternoon in Bed," the first full song on the record, kicks things off excellently. It's easily the Bats' best song since "North by North," Scott's reflective lyric on puzzling out another's statements accompanied with a perfectly balanced build and retreat in the music, not to mention some low-key but strong soloing. From there on in, the Bats steer away from doing "just another Bats song"; they play around with the arrangements, lower or raise voices in the mix, and try different rhythms or elements. Standouts include the slow chug of guitars in "Around You Like Snow," the frazzled background electric scrapes and wails on the wonderful "Chain Home Low," and even the first turn of Woodward on a lead vocal on "Shoeshine." Scott's still wistful, still questioning lyrics are as strong as ever, and the band sounds newly energized; they're willing to go that extra step, and it shows. —*Ned Raggett*

Bauhaus

f. 1978, Northampton, Northamptonshire, England, **db.** 1987
Post-Punk, Goth Rock, Alternative Pop/Rock

Bauhaus are the founding fathers of goth-rock, creating a minimalistic, overbearingly gloomy style of post-punk rock driven by jagged guitar chords and cold, distant synthesizers. Throughout their brief career, the band explored all the variations on their bleak musical ideas, adding elements of glam rock, experimental electronic rock, funk, and heavy metal. While their following never expanded beyond a cult, they kept that cult alive well into the '90s. Guitarist/vocalist Daniel Ash, bassist/vocalist David J, and drummer Kevin Haskins had played together before forming Bauhaus in Northampton, England with vocalist Peter Murphy. In August 1979, the group released their debut single "Bela Lugosi's Dead;" although it did not make the pop charts, it became the de facto goth-rock anthem, staying in the U.K. independent charts for years. In October 1980, following a couple more singles, they released their debut album, *In the Flat Field*, whose success led to their first hits on the pop charts the following year. 1981's *Mask* revealed a more ambitious musical direction; elements of metal and electronic textures made the music more accessible without abandoning its dark, foreboding core, and it was a commercial success. In the fall of 1982, the group had a number 15 hit with their version of David Bowie's "Ziggy Stardust." The success of the single propelled their third album, *The Sky's Gone Out*, to number four. Peter Murphy contracted pneumonia at the beginning of 1983, which prevented him from participating in the recording sessions for Bauhaus' fourth album, *Burning from the Inside*. Consequently, the record featured substantial contributions from Daniel Ash and David J, who both pursued more personal and atmospheric directions; the album was another hit. In July, Bauhaus split up. Murphy pursued a solo career; Ash, Haskins, and J formed the successful Love and Rockets in 1985 after a proposed Bauhaus reunion fell apart. More than a decade later, Bauhaus re-formed for a full-blown tour in 1998; the two-disc *Gotham* documented the reunited group's performance in New York. —*Stephen Thomas Erlewine*

In the Flat Field / Oct. 1980 / 4AD/Beggars Banquet ✦✦✦✦

Few debut albums ever arrived so nearly perfectly formed; that *In the Flat Field* practically single-handedly invented what remains for many as the stereotype of goth music—wracked, at times spindly vocals about despair and desolation of many kinds, sung over mysterious and moody music—demonstrates the *sui generis* power of both the band and its work. This said, perhaps the best thing about the album isn't what it's supposed to sound like, but what it actually does—an awesomely powerful, glam-inspired rock band firing on all fours, capable of restraint and complete overdrive both, fronted by a charismatic, storming frontman. Starting with the challenging angst of "Double Dare," with shattering guitar over a curious but fierce stop-start rhythm while Murphy rages ever more strongly over the top, *In the Flat Field* contains a wide variety of inspirations and ideas. The astonishingly precise rhythm section of David J and Haskins pulls off a variety of jaw-dropping performances, including the high-paced tension of the title track and the brooding crawl from "Spy in the Cab." Ash, much like his longtime hero Mick Ronson, turns out to be a master of turning relatively simple guitar parts into apocalyptic explosions, from the background fills on "St. Vitus Dance" to the brutal descending chords of "Stigmata Martyr." Murphy, meanwhile, channels as much Iggy Pop as he does Bowie, proving to be no simple copyist of either, able to both maniacally sing-shout and take a somewhat lighter touch throughout. Concluding with the seven-minute "Nerves," an aptly titled piece that alternates between understated energy and unleashed power toward a dramatic ending, *In the Flat Field* started off Bauhaus' album career with a near-perfect bang. —*Ned Raggett*

Mask / Oct. 1981 / Beggars Banquet ✦✦✦✦

Managing the sometimes hard-to-negotiate trick of expanding their sound while retaining all the qualities which got them attention to begin with, on *Mask* the members of Bauhaus consciously stretched themselves into newer areas of music and performance, resulting in an album that was arguably even better than the band's almost flawless debut. More familiar sides of the band were apparent from the get-go; opening number "Hair of the Dog," one of the band's best songs, starts with a double-tracked squalling guitar solo before turning into a stomping, surging flow, carefully paced by sudden silences and equally sudden returns to the music, while Murphy details cases of mental addictions in pithy phrases. The energy wasn't all just explosive angst and despair, though; the one-two punches of "Kick in the Eye" and "In Fear of Fear" have as much hip-shaking groove and upbeat swing to them as portentous gloom (Ash's sax skronk on the latter, as well as on the similarly sharp "Dancing," is a particularly nice touch). Elsewhere, numerous flashes of the band's quirky sense of humor—something often missed by both fanatical followers and negative critics both—make an appearance; perhaps most amusing is the dry spoken-word lyric beginning "Of Lillies and Remains," as David J details a goofily grotesque situation as much Edward Gorey as Edgar Allen Poe. Add to that three of the most dramatic things the band ever recorded—the charging, keyboard-accompanied "The Passion of Lovers," the slow, dark fairy-tale-gone-wrong "Hollow Hills," and the wracked, trudging title track, where the sudden appearance of an acoustic guitar turns a great song into a near-perfect blend of ugliness and sheer beauty—and the end result was a perfect trouncing of the sophomore-slump myth. —*Ned Raggett*

Press the Eject and Give Me the Tape / 1982 / Atlantic ✦✦✦

Just two albums into their career, Bauhaus' repertoire consisted of plenty of standards and fan favorites. Despite the punk world's disdain for live albums (because of their association with arena rock), the group issued an 11-track collection recorded in London, Liverpool, Manchester, and Paris. Though Peter Murphy's stage theatrics and the dark atmosphere of a Bauhaus live date are obviously lost on the translation to record, the band are electrifying on standards such as "In the Flat Field," "Bela Lugosi Is Dead," "Kick in the Eye," "Stigmata Martyr," and "Dark Entries." The more obscure songs, including "Rose Garden Funeral of Sores" and "The Man with X-Ray Eyes," also come off well. Though these tracks aren't quite subsitutes for their studio versions, fans of the band will love to hear them playing in their prime. [A Beggars Banquet CD reissue added six additional live tracks.] —*John Bush*

The Sky's Gone Out / Oct. 1982 / A&M ✦✦✦

More fragmented in origin than it might appear on first glance—the leadoff track, a phenomenal, nuclear-strength rip through Brian Eno's "Third Uncle," featuring some fantastic soloing from Ash, came from a BBC radio session performance—*The Sky's Gone Out* was caught between the expectations of an audience now thoroughly embracing the incipient goth genre, with all the built-in limitations such expectations often provide, and a band which wanted to please them while still following its own muse. On balance it's quite a fine album, but unlike *Mask* it misses the infusion of a more positive energy, and simply doesn't gel as perfectly, more notable for individual songs than as a whole. Old, pre-recording-career songs like the strong but already dated "In the Night" were revived and balanced against experiments and attempts to further develop the band's sound, ultimately making *The Sky's Gone Out* feel more like a compilation than anything else. Piece by piece, though, the songs still often showed Bauhaus in excelsis. Ash's elegant, haunting acoustic guitar work received two great showcases—"Silent Hedges," adding a more familiar electric explosion to a fine Murphy performance detailing a desperate mental collapse, and "All We Ever Wanted Was Everything," a sympathetic, nostalgic reflection on dreams of the past, again matched by a perfectly balanced Murphy vocal. Other standouts include the brooding lope of "Swing the Heartache," with a skeletal rhythm matched against some of Ash's best guitar work, and "Spirit," a live standout inspired by the performance vibe the band received from its fans. —*Ned Raggett*

Burning from the Inside / Jul. 1983 / A&M ✦✦✦

If *The Sky's Gone Out* felt like a collection of various recordings, *Burning from the Inside* really was, due in large part to outside events—Murphy had fallen victim to a life-threatening illness, so the rest of the band began recording without him, which more than any-

thing else foreshadowed both Bauhaus' breakup and the trio's future work as Love and Rockets. As a result, two songs ended up on the album, the piano-led cinematic moodiness of "Who Killed Mr. Moonlight" and the sweet acoustic drive of "Slice of Life," with David J and Ash on lead vocals respectively. Furthermore, more songs from the earliest days of the band were dug up to provide material, the most notable and successful being the dub-inflected, heavily dramatic "She's in Parties," using filmmaking as a metaphor for romance and life, with Murphy's excellent lead balanced against a near-whispering chorus from the other two singers. The end result of all this was an album that was good in spots but not as strong throughout as it could be, while betraying the other performing and writing strains that would soon cause the band to call it a day. As before, though, when the band members were on, they were on with a vengeance, such as the medieval folk dance "King Volcano" and the starkly beautiful "Kingdom's Coming." The ten-minute title track takes a good idea and stretches it out a little too long, but the concluding track "Hope" follows it with a life-affirming, inspirational vibe that serves as much as a farewell for Bauhaus' audience as anything else. While imperfect, *Burning from the Inside* has much more to recommend it than many other albums. —*Ned Raggett*

1979-1983: Volume One / 1986 / Beggars Banquet ✦✦✦✦✦

If all single-artist compilations were like this, the world would be a much better place—while lacking liner notes, or even specific references as to what songs come from where, *Volume One*, drawing mostly from *In the Flat Field* and *Mask* does a frankly smashing job at capturing the many early high points of Bauhaus' recording career. No real obscurities appear—singles tracks like "Dark Entries" and "Terror Couple Kill Colonel" had been available on EP and would soon be reissued with the *Field* CD—while the version of "Bela Lugosi's Dead" in fact was the live take from the *Press the Eject* album. As an overview, though, it's just flat-out great, covering many of the band's different facets, from aggressive thrash ("Double Dare," "In the Flat Field," "Hair of the Dog") to mysterious, arty shades ("A God in an Alcove," "Spy in the Cab," "Mask") and more. While one could argue over including other worthwhile tracks—the nutty humor of "Of Lillies and Remains" would have demonstrated the band's reach even more—*Volume One* remains as near perfect a starting place for a neophyte listener as any. —*Ned Raggett*

1979-1983: Volume Two / 1986 / Beggars Banquet ✦✦✦✦

Understandably complementing *Volume One*, *Two* is as similarly bereft of any sort of packaging notes as its predecessor, but is also as successful at pulling together many of Bauhaus' best moments from its later career into one knock-your-socks-off release. More *Mask* numbers crop up here—two funk-heavy groovers ("In Fear of Fear" and "Kick in the Eye"), counterpointed by the slow, haunting "Hollow Hills." *The Sky's Gone Out* is cherry-picked for some of its best moments, including "Swing the Heartache" and "All We Ever Wanted Was Everything," though the version of "Spirit" is the less effective single re-recording rather than the dramatic album take. Rather tellingly, only three songs from *Burning from the Inside* are included—"She's in Parties," the David J-sung "Who Killed Mr. Moonlight," and the Daniel Ash number "Slice of Life." Added to all of this are the peerless covers of "Ziggy Stardust" and "Third Uncle," a couple of ringers from earlier in the band's career ("Satori" and "Crowds"), stand-alone singles "Lagartija Nick" and "The Sanity Assassin," and one honest-to-goodness rarity, "Paranoia Paranoia," a radical dub reworking of "Silent Hedges" that's just as good as the original in its own unique way. In all, a great overview of the latter years of a great band, at least in its original career. —*Ned Raggett*

Swing the Heartache: The BBC Sessions / Jul. 1989 / Beggars Banquet ✦✦✦

Whether it was the immediacy of recording or some other unexplainable element, Bauhaus always thrived when doing British radio appearances, with no less than five of the 18 tracks collected here seeing official release by the band on singles or albums during its first lifetime. That one of these was Bauhaus' biggest-ever British hit, the completely and perfectly over-the-top rendition of Bowie's "Ziggy Stardust," is further testimony to the band's success at the Beeb. The five show appearances here, including both John Peel sessions and guest spots with other DJs, make for an excellent sampling of the band in many different guises, from obscure rarities to redone versions of some of Bauhaus' most successful songs. The first six tracks cover *In the Flat Field*-era material, including a slightly more laid-back version of T. Rex's "Telegram Sam" and an energetic thrash through "A God in an Alcove," as well as the powerful take of "Double Dare" which was used to begin *Field*. The midsection covers a lot of ground, from the familiar takes on "Ziggy" and Eno's "Third Uncle" used on singles and albums to the quirky, film-dialogue-sampling drama of "Party of the First Part," not to mention an otherwise unavailable song, the funky, percussion-heavy "Poison Pen," never successfully recorded by the band elsewhere. Another rarity pops up among the final tracks—of all things, the Strangeloves' legendary Nuggets-compiled garage-rocker "Night Time," given a great bouncy reading here. Add to that some sharp takes on the lengthy title track and "She's in Parties," not to mention a version of "The Three Shadows Pt. 2" that's notably more successful than the recording on *The Sky's Gone Out*, and *Swing* is an unparalleled success, a collection that will interest and satisfy newcomers as much as longtime band fanatics. —*Ned Raggett*

● **Crackle** / Jul. 7, 1998 / Beggars Banquet ✦✦✦✦✦

To celebrate their twentieth anniversary, Bauhaus reunited for a tour and released the *Crackle* compilation in the U.S. The band initially claimed that *Crackle* was an American edition of *1979-1983: Vol. 2*, which was never released in the U.S., but less than half of the songs appear on both collections. Which means, of course, that *Crackle* shouldn't be viewed as a compilation for collectors—instead, it's an excellent single-disc overview of the group's brief career, containing all of their essential songs, from "In the Flat Field" and "Bela Lugosi's Dead" to "Ziggy Stardust" and "Burning from the Inside." Hardcore fans may wish there was something special about the comp—the only thing new is the perfectly adequate remastering—but it's nice that there's finally a thorough single-disc retrospective of the groundbreaking goth quartet. —*Stephen Thomas Erlewine*

Gotham / Nov. 9, 1999 / Metropolis ✦✦✦✦✦
After years of fruitless wishing on the part of Bauhaus fans worldwide, while Peter Murphy pursued a solo career and the remaining three members scored their own successes with various solo and group efforts, the announcement of a reunion tour caught nearly everyone by surprise. By the time the punningly titled *Gotham* was recorded at, indeed, a New York City concert, the reunited band was ripping through their sets with an energy and sense of drama which most late-'90s acts would have given their eyeteeth for. Despite a set list generally devoid of surprises, the old live fire evident on *Press the Eject and Give Me the Tape* was easily reconjured here, with vicious takes on "In the Flat Field," "Kick in the Eye" and "Ziggy Stardust" some of the many highlights. Murphy is in fine voice throughout, subtly altering some lyrics to project his more positive, spiritual outlook on life while losing none of the original impact; Ash, David J, and Haskins, well seasoned by their nearly two decades worth of playing experience together, are never content to simply be Murphy's backing band in turn. The foursome tackle quieter numbers with grace and restraint as well, including a marvelous "Hollow Hills" and a new cover version, a take on Dead Can Dance's "Severance," given a stately, majestic performance and a deeply affecting Murphy vocal (a studio version appears at the end of the album). As the signal for Bauhaus' unexpected rebirth, *Gotham* is both a fine souvenir for fans and a great reminder of just how wonderful the band was and is. —*Ned Raggett*

Bay City Rollers

f. 1967, Edinburgh, Scotland, db. 1978
Pop/Rock, Power Pop
The Bay City Rollers were a Scottish pop/rock band of the '70s with a strong following among teenage girls. Adopting their name again by pointing at random to a spot on a map of the United States and hitting Bay City, MI, their first hit was a cover of the Gentrys' "Keep on Dancing," which reached number nine in the U.K. in September 1971. After flopping with three singles, they finally hit the Top Ten again in February 1974 with a cover of the Shangri-Las' "Remember (Walking in the Sand)." At this point, the Rollers became a teen sensation in Great Britain, with their good looks and tartan knickers, and they scored a series of Top Ten U.K. hits over the next two and a half years: "Shang-a-Lang," "Summerlove Sensation," "All of Me Loves All of You," "Bye Bye Baby" (a cover of the Four Seasons hit that went to number one), "Give a Little Love" (another number one), "Love Me Like I Love You," and "I Only Want to Be with You" (a cover of the Dusty Springfield hit). Their albums *Rollin'* and *Once Upon a Star* topped the charts as well. They scored their first U.S. hit with "Saturday Night," which reached number one in January 1976. It was followed by the Top Ten hits "Money Honey" and "You Made Me Believe in Magic." —*William Ruhlmann*

Greatest Hits / Nov. 1977 / Arista ✦✦✦✦
The Bay City Rollers never got their fair shake as a "legitimate" band, and this ten-track, no-frills collection proves it. It collects only their biggest, most overexposed hits, but when removed from the hype, the Rollers' music has an enduring innocence and charm with enough catchy hooks and pure pop melodies to compete with other power-pop bands of the era. —*Chris Woodstra*

● **The Definitive Collection** / Feb. 8, 2000 / Arista ✦✦✦✦
This very straightforward selection is based almost exclusively on the Bay City Rollers' British and American singles file. It opens, of course, with "Saturday Night"—in U.S. terms, their most memorable release—but thereafter adheres to strict and joyful chronology. The original hit version of "Keep On Dancing," featuring founding vocalist Nobby Clarke, sets the ball rolling with lovable exuberance; two years later, "Remember" finds Les McKeown installed at the front, Bill Martin and Phil Coulter entrenched in the writers' seat, and the Rollers themselves preparing to assume world domination. With hindsight, it seems staggering that the quintet's heyday was so brief. As early as "Money Honey," the first cracks are beginning to show, and, though their American breakthrough at least postponed the day of judgment, by the time Ian Mitchell replaced original guitarist Alan Longmuir, in time for the *Dedication* album, the entire edifice was teetering. The inclusions from that period are uniformly, and deceptively, elegant: "Love Me Like I Love You," "I Only Want to Be with You," "Dedication," "Rock & Roll Love Letter," and "Yesterday's Hero" mark the apogee of the Rollers as both a creative and a commercial force. But Mitchell's sudden retirement finally sent the whole shebang over and, as *The Definitive Collection* approaches its close, the entire affair takes on a very different complexion. Four final singles pass by with barely a hummable note between them and, though this album closes by turning back a few years, to the title track from the all-powerful *Wouldn't You Like It* album, the damage has already been done. Wouldn't you like it? Not anymore. —*Dave Thompson*

The Beach Boys

f. 1961, Hawthorne, CA
Sunshine Pop, Psychedelic Pop, Pop/Rock, Surf, Psychedelic, Pop, Rock & Roll
The Beach Boys are the most successful and important American band of the rock era. They were formed in 1961 in Hawthorne, CA, around the three Wilson brothers: Brian, Dennis, and Carl. Additional members were Mike Love, the Wilsons' cousin, and Al Jardine. From the start, the focus of the group's music was Brian Wilson, who combined a fascination with vocal harmony in the Four Freshmen mold with a love of Chuck Berry-derived rock & roll. Added to that was the subject matter of middle-class teenage life in Southern California—surfing, cars, and girls. The result was massive popular success for the group during the first half of the 1960s, starting with their first chart entry, "Surfin',"

in 1962. Soon, Brian Wilson, who was composing nearly all of the material, had taken over production of the group's records as well. Given the accelerated recording schedule of the day, it was an awesome task when coupled with his onstage performing duties. The strain of all that work caught up with Brian Wilson, however, and at the end of 1964, he retired from onstage work with the Beach Boys, retaining his composing and producing duties. The group eventually settled on Bruce Johnston as his replacement. Such recordings as "California Girls" gave evidence of the expansion of Brian Wilson's musical imagination, which found him taking longer to make records that were more ambitious than the group's early teen anthems. 1966's *Pet Sounds* LP was universally hailed as one of the greatest rock albums of all time; Wilson trumped it with the #1 gold single "Good Vibrations." By this point, he was being hailed as a genius in the media, as he prepared a new album tentatively titled *Smile*. The album never appeared, however. A single, "Heroes and Villains," offered tantalizing clues to what would become a legendary unheard, unfinished masterpiece. But Brian Wilson, whether because of the pressure to top himself and compete with the Beatles and others, internal disagreements within the group, psychological problems, or drug abuse, ceded leadership of the Beach Boys, and their next album, *Smiley Smile* (September 1967), was produced by the group as a whole. The Beach Boys returned to prominence in the mid-'70s on a wave of nostalgia and a potent concert act that focused on their early hits. —*William Ruhlmann*

Surfin' Safari / Oct. 29, 1962 / Capitol ✦✦

Surfin' U.S.A. / Mar. 25, 1963 / Capitol ✦✦✦✦
The real breakthrough, as Brian Wilson asserts himself in the studio as both songwriter and arranger on a set of material that was much stronger than *Surfin' Safari*. Besides the hit title track and its popular drag-racing flip side ("Shut Down"), this has a lovely, heartbreaking ballad ("Lonely Sea") and a couple of strong Brian Wilson originals ("The Noble Surfer" and "Farmer's Daughter"). There are also a surprisingly high quotient of instrumentals (five) that demonstrate that, before session musicians took over most of the parts, the Beach Boys could play respectably gutsy surf rock as a self-contained unit. Indeed, the album as a whole is the best they would make, prior to the late '60s, as a band that played most of their instruments, rather than as a vehicle for Brian Wilson's ideas. The LP was a huge hit, vital to launching surf music as a national craze, and one of the few truly strong records to be recorded by a self-contained American rock band prior to the British Invasion. A 1990 Capitol CD combines this and *Surfin' Safari* onto one disc, with the addition of three rare bonus cuts from the same era. —*Richie Unterberger*

Surfer Girl / Sep. 23, 1963 / Capitol ✦✦✦
Capitol pushed the Beach Boys for too much material in too short a time for the group to maintain as much quality control as would have been desirable. Consequently, most of their pre-1965 albums contain a high degree of filler, and thus stack up poorly next to those of such contemporaries as the Beatles, who were able to maintain high standards on almost all of their tracks. *Surfer Girl* does have some great tunes, including the title song, the hot rod ditty "Little Deuce Coupe," and "Catch a Wave" (which could have been a substantial hit single on its own merits). Most significant of all is the gorgeous ballad "In My Room," which anticipated future Beach Boys releases both in its sophisticated production (strings, organ, dense harmonies) and its personal, solipsistic lyrics. The rest is surprisingly mediocre filler, especially as at this point they were restricting their lyrical themes to beach culture almost exclusively; "Your Summer Dream," with its unusual harmonies, is about the most interesting of the obscure tracks. If you're not a dedicated Beach Boys fan, though, you should pass, as you can find the first-rate tracks on best-of anthologies. A 1990 Capitol CD combines this and *Shut Down, Vol. 2* onto one disc, adding the 45 version of "Fun, Fun, Fun," a German version of "In My Room," and the previously unreleased Brian Wilson composition "I Do." —*Richie Unterberger*

Little Deuce Coupe / Oct. 21, 1963 / Capitol ✦✦

Shut Down, Vol. 2 / Mar. 23, 1964 / Capitol ✦✦✦
Another erratic early album from the Beach Boys; few other rock LPs have such a wide gap between the best and worst material. On the good side, you have absolute classics in the Chuck Berry-ish "Fun, Fun, Fun," and its superb B-side, "Don't Worry Baby," one of the most advanced pop productions of 1964 with its breathtaking harmonies and unusual lyric. "The Warmth of the Sun" is one of the most melodic (and melancholic) ballads they ever recorded, and "Why Do Fools Fall in Love" is one of their best oldies covers. Yet the rest reduces the oceanic scale of the classics to dishwater, whether they're throwaway hot rod tunes and instrumentals, innocuous high school romantic ditties, or a soulless cover of "Louie Louie." When this album hit the racks in early 1964, the Beatles were proving that you could make LPs that were all killer, no filler; the Beach Boys would soon be forced to up their ante. A 1990 Capitol CD combines this and *Surfer Girl* into one disc, adding the 45 version of "Fun, Fun, Fun," a German version of "In My Room," and the previously unreleased Brian Wilson composition "I Do." —*Richie Unterberger*

All Summer Long / Jul. 13, 1964 / Capitol ✦✦✦
The best pre-1965 Beach Boys album featured their brilliant #1 single "I Get Around," as well as other standout cuts in the beautifully sad "Wendy," "Little Honda" (one of their best hot rod tunes, covered by the Hondells for a hit), and their remake of the late-'50s doo-wop classic "Hushabye." The nostalgic "All Summer Long," another great production, seemed (whether intentionally or not) like a sort of farewell to the frivolous California beach culture that had supplied the lyrical grist for most of their music up to this point, with a longing, regretful chorus that was totally at odds with the bouncy arrangement. Other relatively little-known treasures are the sumptuous ballad "Girls on the Beach," with some of their best early harmonizing, and "Don't Back Down," with uncommonly anxious lyrics. You can't give a high rating, however, to an album that also contained such disposable filler as the "Our Favorite Recording Sessions" comedy bit and "Do You Remember?," and a "let's-pay-tribute-to-rock's-early-days" number with a shit-eating grin

wide enough to qualify as an oldies radio ID jingle. A 1990 Capitol CD combines this and *Little Deuce Coupe* onto one disc, adding the 45 version of "Be True to Your School," alternate takes of "Little Honda" and "Don't Back Down," and the previously unreleased "All Dressed Up for School." *—Richie Unterberger*

Beach Boys Concert / Oct. 19, 1964 / Capitol ♦♦♦

Recorded live in Sacramento in 1964, the Beach Boys run through several of their big early hits and a bunch of covers that hadn't made it to record. The screaming, while not at a *Beatles at Hollywood Bowl* level, is loud enough to present a real problem as far as sonic clarity, especially given that the instruments aren't recorded too well either. Even more crucially, the Beach Boys simply didn't play nearly as well onstage as on record, at least at this concert; the arrangements are thin and the playing and singing are ragged, though the group is enthusiastic. None of this stopped it from becoming one of their biggest sellers; in fact, it topped the charts for four weeks, at the height of the British Invasion. It's also of interest in that it has several covers that they didn't release as studio recordings in the '60s, including "Johnny B. Goode," Jan & Dean's "The Little Old Lady from Pasadena," the dorky "Long Tall Texan," "Monster Mash," the Four Freshmen's "Graduation Day," and the Rivingtons' goofy doo-wop raveup, "Papa-Oom-Mow-Mow." Everyone other than major Beach Boys fans, however, should give it a miss. A 1990 Capitol CD combines this and *Live in London* (1968 live material that has also, confusingly, been issued as *Beach Boys '69*) onto one disc, adding previously unreleased live versions of "Don't Worry Baby" (from 1964) and "Heroes and Villains" (from 1967). *—Richie Unterberger*

The Beach Boys Today! / Mar. 8, 1965 / Capitol ♦♦♦♦♦

Brian Wilson's retirement from performing to concentrate on studio recording and production reaped immediate dividends with *Today!*, the first Beach Boys album that is strong almost from start to finish. "Dance, Dance, Dance" and "Do You Wanna Dance" were upbeat hits with Spector-influenced arrangements, but Wilson began to deal with more sophisticated themes on another smash 45, "When I Grow Up," on which these eternal teenagers looked forward to the advancing years with fear and uncertainty. Surf/hot rod/beach themes were permanently retired in favor of late adolescent-early adult romance on this album, which included such decent outings in this vein as "She Knows Me Too Well," "Kiss Me Baby," and "In the Back of My Mind." The true gem is "Please Let Me Wonder," one of the group's most delicate mid-'60s works, with heartbreaking melodies and harmonies. Be aware that the version of "Help Me, Rhonda" found here is an inferior, earlier, and slower rendition; the familiar hit single take was included on their next album, *Summer Days (And Summer Nights!!)*. A 1990 Capitol CD combines this and *Summer Days (And Summer Nights!!)* onto one disc, adding alternate takes of "Dance, Dance, Dance," "I'm So Young," and "Let Him Run Wild," as well as a previously unreleased studio version of "Graduation Day." Most significantly, it also adds the non-LP single from late 1965, "The Little Girl I Once Knew," which looked forward to *Pet Sounds* in its studio experimentation and lyrical themes. *—Richie Unterberger*

Summer Days (And Summer Nights!!) / Jul. 5, 1965 / Capitol ♦♦♦♦

Summer Days (And Summer Nights!!) was a bit of a regression from the success of *Today*, lapsing back into that distressing division between first-rate cuts and lightweight also-rans that characterized their pre-1965 albums. The difference is that the very best tracks were operating on a more sophisicated level than the 1962-1964 classics. "Help Me, Rhonda" was a number one single and would be their last Top 40 exercise in sheer fun for a while. More impressive was "California Girls," with its symphonic arrangement, glorious harmonies, and archetypal statement of Californian lifestyle. On the other hand, subpar efforts like "Amusement Park U.S.A." and "Salt Lake City," throwbacks to the emptyheaded summer filler of previous days, will necessitate that the CD remote button remains close at hand. The covers of "The Girl From New York City" and "Then I Kissed Her" are well done but don't break new ground. Yet a couple of cuts are among their most essential LP-only efforts. "Let Him Run Wild" is a soulful ballad with a great Brian Wilson falsetto vocal. "Girl Don't Tell Me," with its gorgeous melody, fine lead vocal debut from Carl Wilson, and subtle depiction of romantic rejection and disappointment, may be *the* best obscure pre-*Pet Sounds* Beach Boys track. A 1990 Capitol CD combines this and *The Beach Boys Today!* onto one disc, adding alternate takes of "Dance, Dance, Dance," "I'm So Young," and "Let Him Run Wild," as well as a previously unreleased studio version of "Graduation Day." Most significantly, it also adds the non-LP single from late 1965, "The Little Girl I Once Knew," which looked forward to *Pet Sounds* in its studio experimentation and lyrical themes. *—Richie Unterberger*

Beach Boys Party! / Nov. 8, 1965 / Capitol ♦♦♦♦

Capitol, which had already released ten Beach Boys albums in three years, was bugging the group for product that it could release in time for the 1965 Christmas season. To buy time while Brian Wilson began conceiving the *Pet Sounds* masterpiece, the group issued a set of covers, mostly of the '50s rock and R&B they had listened to as schoolboys. Packaged as if it had been recorded at an actual party, it was in fact recorded in the studio, with friends and romantic partners adding sounds and vocals to create an informal atmosphere. With the exception of a bass guitar, all the instruments were acoustic; the acoustic guitar-and-bongo arrangements, in fact, give this a hootenanny campfire feel. In recent years, this album has gone up a few notches in critical esteem, praised for its loose, casual feel and insight into the group's influences. Realisically, though, its present-day appeal lies mostly with dedicated fans of the group, as fun and engaging as it is. Others will find the material shopworn in places, and the presentation too corny. It does have the massive hit "Barbara Ann," which actually features Dean Torrence (of Jan & Dean) on much of the lead vocals; other highlights include "Mountain of Love," an unexpected version of "The Times They Are a-Changin'," and *three* Beatles covers. A 1990 Capitol CD combines this and *Stack-O-Tracks* onto one disc, adding three previously unreleased backing tracks to the *Stack-O-Tracks* half of the program. *—Richie Unterberger*

☆ **Pet Sounds** / May 16, 1966 / Capitol ♦♦♦♦♦

The best Beach Boys album, and one of the best of the 1960s. The group here reached a whole new level in terms of both composition and production, layering tracks upon tracks of vocals and instruments to create a richly symphonic sound. Conventional keyboards and guitars were combined with exotic touches of orchestrated strings, bicycle bells, buzzing organs, harpsichords, flutes, the theremin, Hawaiian-sounding string instruments, Coca-Cola cans, barking dogs, and more. It wouldn't have been a classic without great songs, and this has some of the group's most stunning melodies, as well as lyrical themes that evoke both the intensity of newly born love affairs and the disappointment of failed romance (add in some general statements about loss of innocence and modern-day confusion as well). The spiritual quality of the material is enhanced by some of the most gorgeous upper-register male vocals (especially by Brian and Carl Wilson) ever heard on a rock record. "Wouldn't It Be Nice," "God Only Knows," "Caroline No," and "Sloop John B" are the well-known hits, but equally worthy are such cuts as "You Still Believe in Me," "Don't Talk," "I Know There's an Answer," and "I Just Wasn't Made for These Times." It's often said that this is more of a Brian Wilson album than a Beach Boys recording (session musicians played most of the parts), but it should be noted that the harmonies are pure Beach Boys (and some of their best). Massively influential upon its release (although it was a relatively low seller compared to their previous LPs), it immediately vaunted the band into the top level of rock innovators among the intelligentsia. The 1990 CD reissue added a few interesting but inessential outtakes, and a 1999 reissue added a new stereo version of the entire album to the original mono program. *—Richie Unterberger*

Smile [Not Released] / May 1967 / Capitol ♦♦♦

In 1966, Brian Wilson began work on the *Smile* LP, which was intended as the ultimate pop/progressive/psychedelic record. Many vocal and instrumental tracks were recorded, but the project was abandoned in 1967 due to accumulated pressures from Wilson's family, fellow Beach Boys, and the record company, combined with Wilson's own fragile and sensitive ego. In the ensuing years, *Smile* was accorded status as the most legendary unreleased album of all time, although the record was, in fact, never close to being finished. Many, though by no means all, of the tracks in progress were bootlegged in the 1980s; many, though by no means all, of these, in turn, finally surfaced on Capitol's *Good Vibrations* box set. Several bootlegs of the *Smile* sessions are still easily available, most featuring tracks which still haven't been officially released, or alternate takes and mixes of ones that did surface. A lot of these are interesting, to say the least, including the "Fire" part of the legendary "Elements" suite, the downright avant-garde "George Fell Into His French Horn," and extended snippets of "Good Vibrations" and "Heroes and Villains" as works in progress. There are numerous exquisitely beautiful passages, great ensemble singing, and brilliant orchestral pop instrumentation to be found on these outtakes, but the fact is that Wilson somehow lacked the discipline needed to combine them into a pop masterpiece that was both brilliant and commercial. Search for the double-CD compilation versions of these outtakes, which, though expensive, are more thorough than the various single-disc versions available. In 1999, the bootleg label Vigotone released an expansive four-disc set of *Smile* sessions, the fourth disc of which functions as Vigotone's best guess at an LP running order. *—Richie Unterberger*

Smiley Smile / Sep. 18, 1967 / Capitol ♦♦♦♦

After the much-discussed, uncompleted *Smile* project—which was supposed to take the innovations of *Pet Sounds* to even grander heights—collapsed, the Beach Boys released *Smiley Smile* in its place. (To clarify much confusion: *Smiley Smile* is an entirely different piece of work than *Smile* would have been, although some material that ended up on *Smiley Smile* would have most likely been used on *Smile*. Also, much of *Smiley Smile* was in fact recorded *after* the *Smile* sessions had ceased.) For fans expecting something along the lines of *Sgt. Pepper* (and there were many of them), *Smile* was a major disappointment, replacing psychedelic experimentation with spare, eccentric miniatures. Heard now, outside of such unrealistic expectations, it's a rather nifty, if rather slight, effort that's plenty weird—in fact, often downright goofy—despite Brian Wilson's retreat from both avant-pop and active leadership of the group. "Wind Chimes," "Wonderful," "Vegetables," and much of the rest is low-key psychedelic quirkiness, with abundant fine harmonies and unusual arrangements. The standouts, nonetheless, were two recent hit singles in which Brian Wilson's ambitions were still intact: the inscrutable mini-opera "Heroes and Villains," and the #1 hit "Good Vibrations," one of the few occasions where the group managed to be recklessly experimental and massively commercial at the same time. A 1990 Capitol CD combines this and *Wild Honey* onto one disc, adding previously unreleased in-progress versions of "Good Vibrations" and "Heroes and Villains," the a cappella B-side "You're Welcome," a 1967 version of "Their Hearts Were Full of Spring," and an excellent outtake, "Can't Wait Too Long." *—Richie Unterberger*

Wild Honey / Dec. 18, 1967 / Capitol ♦♦♦♦

After the *Smile* sessions shut down, the Beach Boys became much more of a *band* than they had been in the mid-'60s. They began playing most of their own instruments on record for the first time since 1963, and Brian Wilson was no longer nearly as dominant a production mastermind. The problem was, as Wilson increasingly withdrew from a leadership role (and, subsequently, from the real world altogether), the Beach Boys were revealed as a group that, although capable of producing some fine and interesting music, were no longer innovators on the level of the Beatles and other figureheads. *Wild Honey* had a looser, funkier feel than any previous Beach Boys effort, at times approaching a kind of bleached-out white soul. The resulting music was often quite pleasant, for the great harmonies if nothing else, but the material and arrangements were quite simply thinner than they had been for a long time. The record does feature a nice Top Twenty hit in "Darlin'" (even if it was a rewrite of a song that had been composed four years earlier, and recorded by Sharon Marie). The small hit single "Wild Honey," with its seductive Theremin lines, was also a highlight, and "Here Comes the Night" (a group original, not the Them hit) also had a lot of appeal. But much of the rest was pleasing but inessential. A 1990 Capitol CD combines this and *Smiley Smile* onto one disc, adding previously unreleased in-progress versions of "Good Vibrations" and "Heroes and Villains," the a cappella B-side "You're Welcome," a 1967 version of "Their Hearts Were Full of Spring," and an excellent outtake, "Can't Wait Too Long." *—Richie Unterberger*

Friends / Jun. 24, 1968 / Capitol ♦♦♦
Released when Cream and Jimi Hendrix were at their apex, the low-key pleasantries of *Friends* seemed downright irrelevant in mid-1968. Today it sounds better, but it's certainly one of the group's more minor efforts, as the members started to divide the songwriting more or less evenly among themselves, rather than letting Brian Wilson provide most of the material. The title track was a charming, if innocuous, minor hit. The bossa nova "Busy Doin' Nothin'" was a subtly subversive piece of rock Muzak, though hindsight reveals a rather worrisome indolencey in the lyrics, as penned by Wilson, who was starting to withdraw into his own world. The production and harmonies remained pleasantly idiosyncratic, but there was little substance at the heart of most of the songs. The irony was that *Smile* had collapsed, in part, because some of the Beach Boys felt that Wilson's increasingly avant-garde leanings would lose their pop audience; yet by the time of *Friends*, the Beach Boys had done a pretty good job of losing most of their audience by retreating to a less experimental, more group-based approach. A 1990 Capitol CD combines this and *20/20* onto one disc, adding five bonus tracks also cut in the late '60s, highlighted by the minor hit "Break Away," Dennis Wilson's oddly spacy "Celebrate the News," and a cover of "Walk on By." *—Richie Unterberger*

Stack-O-Tracks / Aug. 1968 / Capitol ♦♦
One of the oddest albums released by a major rock group in the '60s, *Stack-O-Tracks* consisted of instrumental backing tracks to 15 of their more famous songs, stripped of their vocals to encourage karaoke-like singalongs. It's an indication of how low the Beach Boys' commercial stock had fallen at Capitol that the label was desperate enough to put out the kind of release that usually only surfaces via bootleg. It's thus of interest mostly to collectors and Beach Boys scholars who want to dig a little deeper into the instrumental tracks than they can otherwise (although on some of the tunes, you can hear some faint remnants of the vocal lines bleeding in). A 1990 Capitol CD combines this and *The Beach Boys Party!* onto one disc, adding three previously unreleased backing tracks (of "Help Me Rhonda," "California Girls," and "Our Car Club") to the *Stack-O-Tracks* half of the program. *—Richie Unterberger*

20/20 / Feb. 3, 1969 / Capitol ♦♦♦
20/20 was not a proper album, being compiled from singles and leftovers in order to fulfill contractual obligations to Capitol. Nonetheless, it's one of their better post-*Pet Sounds* records, with a couple of good medium-sized late-'60s hit singles, "Do It Again" and "I Can Hear Music," that were fun retro sort of exercises. "Time to Get Alone," with its unusually shifting, jazzy melody, was one of Brian Wilson's last outstanding compositions. "Never Learn Not to Love" is far more notorious, not for the music (which is average), but for the fact that it was, according to some sources, composed by Charles Manson (although the song is credited to Dennis Wilson). The highlights, however, were a couple of *Smile*-session era tunes, especially "Cabinessence," a suite-like collaboration between Brian Wilson and Van Dyke Parks that gives some idea of the complex directions that were being explored during that ill-fated project. Therein lay the group's dilemma: as hard as they were trying to establish their identity as an integrated band in the late '60s, their new recordings were overshadowed by the bits and pieces of *Smile* that emerged at the time. A 1990 Capitol CD combines this and *Friends* onto one disc, adding five bonus tracks also cut in the late '60s, highlighted by the minor hit "Break Away," Dennis Wilson's oddly spacy "Celebrate the News," and a cover of "Walk on By." *—Richie Unterberger*

Sunflower / Aug. 21, 1970 / Caribou ♦♦♦♦♦
After Reprise rejected what was to be their debut album for the label, the Beach Boys reentered the studio to begin work on what would become a largely different set of songs. The results signaled a creative rebirth for the band, a return to the beautiful harmonies and orchestral productions of their classic mid-'60s material. Though the songwriting didn't quite reach the high quality of "California Girls" or "God Only Knows," *Sunflower* showed the Beach Boys truly working as a band, and doing so better than they ever had in the past (or would in the future). Many of the songs were co-compositions, and the undeniable songwriting and performance talents of Dennis Wilson and Bruce Johnston were finally allowed to flourish: Dennis contributed "Slip on Through," "Forever," and "Got to Know the Woman," while Bruce wrote "Deirdre" and "Tears in the Morning." After a succession of spare, unadorned lead vocals on rock-oriented albums like *Wild Honey* and *20/20*, *Sunflower* returned the Beach Boys to gorgeous vocal harmonies on the tracks "Add Some Music to Your Day," "Cool, Cool Water," and "This Whole World." And the arrangements, tight and inventive, showed Brian Wilson once again back near the top of his game (though the production is credited to the entire band). *Sunflower* is also a remarkably cohesive album, something not seen from the Beach Boys since *Pet Sounds*. As with that album, *Sunflower* earned critical raves in Britain but was virtually ignored in America. *—John Bush*

Surf's Up / Aug. 30, 1971 / Caribou ♦♦♦♦
The Beach Boys' catalog is littered with forgotten 1970s LPs that barely scraped the charts upon release but matured into solid fan favorites despite—and occasionally, because of—their many and varied eccentricities. *Surf's Up* could well be the most definitive, beginning with the cloying "Don't Go Near the Water" and ending a bare half-hour later with the baroque majesty of the title track (originally written in 1966). The LP is a virtual laundry list of each uncommon intricacy that made the Beach Boys' forgotten decade such a bittersweet thrill—the fluffy yet endearing pop (od)ditties of Brian Wilson, quasi-mystical white-boy soul from brother Carl, and the downright laughable songwriting on tracks charting Mike Love's devotion to Buddhism and Al Jardine's social/environmental concerns.

Those songs are enjoyable enough, but the last three tracks are what make *Surf's Up* such a masterpiece. The first, "A Day in the Life of a Tree," is simultaneously one of Brian's most deeply touching *and* bizarre compositions; he is the narrator and object of the song (though not the vocalist; co-writer Jack Rieley lends a hand), lamenting his long life amidst the pollution and grime of a city park while the somber tones of a pipe organ build atmosphere. The second, "Til I Die," isn't the love song the title suggests; it's a haunting, fatalistic piece of pop surrealism that appeared to signal Brian's retirement from active life. The album closer, "Surf's Up," is a masterpiece of baroque psychedelia, probably the most compelling track from the *Smile* period. Carl gives a soulful performance despite the surreal wordplay, and Brian's coda is one of the most stirring moments in his catalog. Wrapped up in a mess of contradictions, *Surf's Up* defined the Beach Boys' tumultuous career better than any other album. *—John Bush*

Carl and the Passions–So Tough / May 15, 1972 / Brother ♦♦♦
With the addition of drummer Ricky Fataar and guitarist Blondie Chaplin to the lineup, the Beach Boys entered a period of surprisingly earthy arrangements, obviously based on what they'd been hearing on cooler outlets like FM radio and AOR. Kicking off with the rough Carl Wilson rocker "You Need a Mess of Help to Stand Alone," *Carl and the Passions—So Tough* cycles through all manner of roots-based rock; Fataar and Chaplin lead the band through a bluesy number ("Here She Comes") and a country song complete with steel guitar ("Hold on Dear Brother"), while Mike Love exercises his spiritual side on the gospel-inspired "He Came Down." The songwriting was neither as solid as 1970's *Sunflower* nor as idiosyncratic as 1971's *Surf's Up* though, and the few fans left from the '60s were undoubtedly turned off—if not by the weak songs, then certainly by the muddy sound. Still, there are a few moments of beauty: Brian's "Marcella" is a midtempo gem, and side two ends with three excellent ballads, "All This Is That," "Make It Good," and "Cuddle Up" (the latter two featuring heart-wrenching performances by Dennis). *—John Bush*

Holland / Jan. 8, 1973 / Caribou ♦♦♦
The surprisingly weak result of a concerted effort by both band and label to push the Beach Boys back into the Top 40 (they succeeded, barely), *Holland* continued the muddy sound of *Carl and the Passions—So Tough*. The highlights here—Carl's "The Trader," Brian's "Sail on Sailor" and "Funky Pretty"—are marginally better than their immediate predecessors, though "Leavin' This Town" (from recent addition Blondie Chaplin) is rather tiresome. Also, Al Jardine and Mike Love's three-part "California Saga" shows the effects of their environmentalist spirituality left to bake in the sun a few minutes too long (though the conclusion, "California," is a solid return to the harmony-laden sun-and-surf '60s). Dennis' sole lead-vocal contribution, "Only With You," is yet another tender ballad given an excellent reading by the most underutilized member of the group. *—John Bush*

The Beach Boys in Concert / Nov. 19, 1973 / Caribou ♦♦♦
With virtually no audience presence on this live album, it's a good deal less exciting than either of their Capitol live recordings. But some of the concert renditions ("Don't Worry Baby") are superior to the studio originals, and the record as a whole is consistently rewarding. A farewell to the band's third golden era, with a big sound and an excellent cross-section of songs. *—Bruce Eder*

☆ **Endless Summer** / Jun. 24, 1974 / Capitol ♦♦♦♦♦
This was the album by which millions of sons of late baby boomers (and sons and daughters of the early ones) first really discovered the Beach Boys, beyond hearing the occasional oldie on the radio. It was the summer of 1974, and the Beach Boys were still trying to get themselves back on track commercially after a seven-year commercial dry spell, when this double LP of their 1963-66 material (all but one cut pre-dating *Pet Sounds*) came along and did the job. *Endless Summer*, which was assembled in consultation with Mike Love, soared to number one and charted high over two subsequent summers (spending three years on the charts, the longest of any of the group's albums), and attracted the enthusiastic attention of millions of listeners too young to have bought their singles back when. The programming was a little thin, not even running an hour total, spread among two LPs, but most of the group's best loved singles were represented—no notes, not a word of historical context, just a great collection of songs that proved irresistible to many shoppers. The packaging was nigh perfect, a simple, celebratory sun-lit graphic that spoke volumes about the music. Although it's been supplanted by other compilations (including the British *20 Golden Greats*), on LP and CD alike, *Endless Summer* was a sentimental favorite for many listeners, sufficient to justify not only a standard CD release but a re-sourced, re-compiled audiophile disc as well from DCC Records. *—Bruce Eder*

Spirit of America / Apr. 14, 1975 / Capitol ♦♦♦
A followup to *Endless Summer*, much weaker in content (except for the inclusion of "Breakaway"), but its near-repeat success helped put the group back in the spotlight. *—Bruce Eder*

15 Big Ones / Jul. 5, 1976 / Caribou ♦♦♦
Thanks to the surprising success of the compilation *Endless Summer*, the Beach Boys entered the studio in 1975 for the first time in almost three years. The album that followed, *15 Big Ones*, balanced covers of rock and doo-wop standards with seven new Beach Boys songs (including five Brian Wilson compositions). Most of the covers are mistakes, part of a misguided attempt by the aging Beach Boys to recapture the energy of their youth.

The "contemporary" production techniques and overly polished sound do nothing for these oldies, and effectively sap them of any energy they might once have had. And the choices—including Chuck Berry's "Rock & Roll Music," the Dixie Cups' "Chapel of Love," Fats Domino's "Blueberry Hill," Freddy Cannon's "Palisades Park"—are simply too well known to be reworked effectively, by anyone. The only one that succeeds is the closer, the lesser-known Righteous Brothers hit "Just Once in My Life," given an emotional reading by Carl and Brian. Of the band originals, the good-time standard "It's OK" and the quirky, endearing "Had to Phone Ya" are excellent, reminiscent of Brian's odd popsongs on late-'60s albums like *Friends* and *20/20*. Most of the other originals are quite inferior though, including the silly history-of-music salute "That Same Song," Al Jardine's "Susie Cincinnati," and the meditation primer "TM Song." *—John Bush*

Beach Boys '69 (Beach Boys Live in London) / Nov. 15, 1976 / Caribou ✦✦

Love You / Apr. 11, 1977 / Caribou ✦✦✦✦
Judging by the title and the quilted design on the cover, *Love You* would appear to be an album of ballads or romantic tracks, maybe '70s remakes of "Surfer Girl" or "In My Room." But from the brutal synthesizer stabs and Carl Wilson's throaty yell, "Harrahhh!," on the opening track, it's clear this is no ordinary Beach Boys LP. Besides several hard-charging pop songs ("Honkin' Down the Highway," "Roller Skating Child," "Let Us Go on This Way"), there are a couple of baffling but ultimately endearing tracks whose titles ("Johnny Carson," "Solar System," "Ding Dang") are good indicators of the amateurish lyrics and subject matter.

What makes *Love You* one of the best Beach Boys LPs of the 1970s, though, is the return to an uncommonly Brian Wilson sense of romantic naivete and "adult child" wonder at the world. "The Night Was So Young," "I'll Bet He's Nice," and "Let's Put Our Hearts Together" form a suite during the middle of side two that rivals *Pet Sounds* for breadth of emotional attachment. Originally slated to be a Brian Wilson solo album (titled *Brian Loves You*), it shows the aging genius with many of his pop smarts intact, his wildly eccentric lifestyle tweaking his sense of songcraft in an intriguing direction. *—John Bush*

M.I.U. Album / Sep. 25, 1978 / Caribou ✦✦
Recorded at the Maharishi International University in Fairfield, Iowa, *M.I.U. Album* was the first album to carry Alan Jardine's name as producer. (Notoriously unsteady at the time, Brian Wilson was listed as executive producer.) Unfortunately, the mainstream late-'70s production techniques are predictable and frequently cloying. *M.I.U. Album* also included several of the worst Beach Boys songs ever to make it to vinyl—up to that point, of course. Though a few of them are partially saved by great harmony vocals, "Belles of Paris," "Winds of Change," and "Match Point of Our Love" (the latter complete with embarrassing tennis metaphors) are close to unlistenable. Still, the group's covers of rock & roll standards ("Come Go with Me," "Wontcha Come Out Tonight") work better than they did on 1975's *15 Big Ones*. Of the originals, "She's Got Rhythm" and "Hey Little Tomboy" are oddly entertaining, and a few tracks ("Kona Coast," "Pitter Patter") enable the group to exercise some gorgeous vocal harmonies. Compared with what had come before, *M.I.U. Album* was a pathetic attempt at musicmaking; compared with what was to come however, this was a highlight. *—John Bush*

L.A. (Light Album) / Mar. 16, 1979 / Caribou ✦✦
The Beach Boys' last album of the '70s, *L.A. (Light Album)*, leads off with "Good Timin'," a midtempo number with excellent harmonies and a charming laidback vibe. Unfortunately, there's nothing else of that caliber here (the song actually dated from 1974), and the Beach Boys ended the decade by releasing the worst album of their career. True, there are a few solid spots for Carl and Dennis Wilson, including the quasi-duet "Baby Blue" and several songs originally intended for Dennis' unfinished second solo album, *Bamboo*. But songs like Al Jardine's "Lady Lynda" (a tribute to his wife), Mike Love's "Sumahama" (a Japanese fantasy), and Brian Wilson's bizarre run through one of his favorite nursery rhymes ("Shortenin' Bread") would never have made it onto vinyl five years before, much less ten. The real shock for fans, however, comes at the beginning of side two, with a reworked version of "Here Comes the Night" (originally on 1967's *Wild Honey*). Easily the most idiosyncratic production ever attempted by the group, "Here Comes the Night" tried to get the Beach Boys onto the charts by latching on to the already fading disco movement—if the Bee Gees could do it, why couldn't they?—with an 11-minute disco single complete with thumping beat and a few digital effects. Though the single never charted, the production (by Bruce Johnston and longtime West Coast producer Curt Becher) was surprisingly well done. And the group's excellent harmonies and Carl's over-the-top vocal made "Here Comes the Night" a natural for disco audiences. Besides the occasional pleasing eccentricity, however, *L.A. (Light Album)* was yet another oddball attempt to push the Beach Boys into the contemporary mainstream despite their many songwriting and production flaws. *—John Bush*

Keepin' the Summer Alive / Mar. 17, 1980 / Caribou ✦

The Beach Boys / Jun. 1985 / Sessions ✦✦
The Beach Boys' first all-new studio album in five years (and last for seven years) is a concerted attempt to regain old glories, which it did to an extent, selling better than any record since *15 Big Ones* (1976) and spinning off the Top 40 single "Getcha Back" and the chart entry "It's Gettin' Late." But despite the production sheen provided by Steve Levine (of Culture Club fame), this is another competent but uninspired effort. *—William Ruhlmann*

Still Cruisin' / Aug. 1989 / Capitol ✦✦

Lost and Found! (1961-62) / 1991 / DCC ✦✦

Summer in Paradise / Aug. 3, 1992 / Brother ✦

☆ **Good Vibrations: Thirty Years of the Beach Boys** / Jun. 21, 1993 / Capitol ✦✦✦✦✦
A five-CD box set, containing a whopping 142 tracks and covering the group's entire career, that manages to feel like too much and not enough at the same time. True, all of the key hits and most of their finest album tracks are here. The group's decline after 1966—and very sharp decline after 1970—is inescapable, and even though most of the material here is from the 1960s, the fourth disc especially (spanning the early 1970s to the late 1980s) is very rough sailing indeed. It's true that about 50 of these tracks are previously unreleased, but be warned that many of them are demos, backing tracks, and alternate versions of well-known songs that aren't a great deal different from the officially released versions. Also, some of the unreleased "tracks" are radio spots. That's not to say that these rare items aren't interesting for the fan; they are. It's just that it's too overwhelming a package for the non-fanatic, and a rather expensive, spotty one for the devoted fan (who will undoubtedly already have at least half the contents). By far, the most interesting unreleased tracks date from the legendary *Smile* sessions (nearly an album's worth). Never actually completed, they aren't quite the masterpiece that some have claimed, but are extremely interesting, often beautiful excursions into psychedelic production and songwriting that often resemble sound paintings more than songs. Comes with a 60-page booklet by Beach Boy historian David Leaf. *—Richie Unterberger*

20 Good Vibrations: The Greatest Hits / Apr. 4, 1995 / Capitol ✦✦✦
Amazingly, given the number of Beach Boys compilations, there has yet to be a one-disc anthology presenting their biggest singles from "Surfin' Safari," which hit the Top Ten on some charts in 1962, to "Kokomo," a number one hit in 1988. This album attempts to fill that gap. It includes those two, as well as such chart-toppers as "Surfin' U.S.A.," "I Get Around," "Barbara Ann," and "Good Vibrations." But it fails in its mission in a number of respects. For one thing, it's only 49 minutes long—another 25 minutes of hits could have been included. For another, the choices are somewhat idiosyncratic. "Catch a Wave" was never a single, much less a hit, but it's here, while "When I Grow Up (To Be a Man)," a Top Ten single, is not. All the tracks except "Kokomo" are Capitol recordings from 1962 to 1966, which means later hits on other labels, notably the Top Ten "Rock & Roll Music" (1976), are missing. And in a couple of instances, the hit versions are not included: "Be True to Your School" and "Help Me, Rhonda" are significantly different album tracks, not the original singles. Finally, the sequencing is not chronological, which makes the group's stylistic changes confusing. All in all, this is not the ideal hits collection, and unless you're a big fan of "Kokomo" who happens not to own the *Cocktail* soundtrack, you'd be better off sticking to one or both of the *Absolute Best* collections or *Endless Summer*. *– William Ruhlmann*

Stars & Stripes, Vol. 1 / Aug. 20, 1996 / River North ✦

The Pet Sounds Sessions / Nov. 4, 1997 / Capitol ✦✦✦
There's little arguing that *Pet Sounds* is one of the greatest albums in rock & roll, and its cult, if anything, has only grown in the 30 years since its intial release. Part of the fascination with *Pet Sounds* lies in its detailed, multi-layered arrangements, in which all the parts blend together into a symphonic whole. The richness of the music is one of the reasons hardcore fans have desired a set like *The Pet Sounds Sessions*, a four-disc box that presents an abundance of working mixes, alternate takes, instrumental tracks and rarities, as well as the first true stereo mix of the album. Certainly, a set this exacting is only of interest to serious fans, and even they might find the endless succession of work tracks tedious. Nevertheless, there's something fascinating about hearing the album broken down to its individual parts; after hearing horn lines, vocals, and percussion tracks out of their original context, the scope and originality of Brian Wilson's vision becomes all the more impressive. (Make no mistake about it, *Pet Sounds* is entirely Wilson's project, despite what Mike Love states in his self-serving liner notes.) The original mono mix of *Pet Sounds* (included here in a minature, cardboard record sleeve) remains the best way to appreciate Wilson's gifts, but for fans already convinced of his genius, *The Pet Sounds Sessions* is a fascinating, educational listen, even if it's not necessarily indispensable. *—Stephen Thomas Erlewine*

Endless Harmony / Aug. 11, 1998 / Capitol ✦✦✦✦
This is a maddening collection, at once one of the most fascinating and frustrating compilations of the Beach Boys' work ever issued. On one level, it seems to be the group's answer to the Beatles' *Anthology* discs, consisting of unissued songs, home and studio demos, live tracks cutting across more than 15 years, early versions of material later issued in substantially altered form, and stereo mixes of material previously only available in mono. It all sounds tantalizing, and individually many of the tracks are—but it doesn't hold together as a collection. It's difficult to imagine that many people attracted by the live medley of surfing tunes from 1966 will get excited about the alternate mix of 1971's "Til I Die," fine as that song is, or the 1972 live version of Carl Wilson's "Long Promised Road." The grouping may work for viewers of the television special *Endless Harmony: The Story of the Beach Boys*, to which this is the soundtrack, but for everyone else, it will just seem as though a bunch of outtakes and oddities were tossed into a hat and assembled together. Having said that, it should be added that the material is gorgeous, song by song. Just maybe, however, it's time for Capitol to put together a definitive collection of live middle/late-1960s Beach Boys performances, instead of spreading those tracks around, as well as an authoritative live 1970s set, a CD of new stereo mixes, etc. The problem with this CD is that there's no hook—nothing to explain in its name or packaging what it is or what it offers, and that is sad, because it's not only a worthwhile addition to any collection, but an okay place to begin developing a deeper appreciation of the band. *—Bruce Eder*

★ **Greatest Hits, Vol. 1** / Sep. 21, 1999 / Capitol ✦✦✦✦✦
With the *Absolute Best* collections out of print at the end of the '90s and the *20 Good Vibrations: The Greatest Hits* missing about as many great singles as it included, Capitol's release of two generous Beach Boys *Greatest Hits* discs in 1999 was welcome. Unfortunately, they got it only half-right. Since the Beach Boys had too many hits to fit onto one

20-track collection, it made sense to have two separate 20-track discs, but the dividing line is arbitrary. For three quarters, *Greatest Hits, Vol. 1* appears to be a straight chronological trawl through the hits, beginning with "Surfin' Safari" and running through "Barbara Ann." Upon close inspection, a number of major songs—"Surfin'," "Shut Down," "In My Room," "Don't Worry Baby"—are missing, yet that portion of the album plays very well. The last five songs are a bit problematic. True, there's a good selection of *Pet Sounds*-era highlights, but the late '60s and '70s are skipped in favor of "Kokomo," which has never sounded more out of place than it does here. Of course, to some casual fans, this will seem like nitpicking since *Greatest Hits, Vol. 1* does have the lion's share of the Beach Boys' popular material, and it is nice to have these songs on one disc, even if "Do It Again," "Caroline No," and "Heroes and Villains" are missing, along with the previously mentioned cuts. What is here qualifies as a top-notch introduction, yet it's hard not to wish that the two *Greatest Hits* were chronological, with *Vol. 1* ending before *Pet Sounds* and the second volume tying up the remaining Capitol recordings. —*Stephen Thomas Erlewine*

☆ **Greatest Hits, Vol. 2** / Sep. 21, 1999 / Capitol ♦♦♦♦♦
Since Capitol's two-volume 1999 *Greatest Hits* only seemed to be chronological—they followed a rough timeline, but *Vol. 1* had many curious omissions from the early years, yet it basically stopped after *Pet Sounds*—there were many early hits that should have fit on the first volume that were saved for the second. In other words, if you were wondering where "In My Room," "Warmth of the Sun," "Don't Worry Baby," "All Summer Long," "Wendy," "Little Honda," "When I Grow up to Be a Man," and "Caroline No" all were, the answer is, they're here on the first half of *Vol. 2* ("Surfin'" is still curiously absent from these collections). The second half of the disc rounds up highlights from the Beach Boys' late-'60s recordings for Capitol—"Heroes and Villains," "Wild Honey," "Darlin'," "Friends," "Do It Again," "I Can Hear Music"—stopping when they switched to Reprise in 1970. Combined with *Vol. 1*, this offers an excellent portrait of the Beach Boys as a singles band, which was always their strength in the '60s. It would have been nice if the two volumes complemented each other chronologically, yet they still work very well together; as they stand, they're the best available collection of the Beach Boys' hits. —*Stephen Thomas Erlewine*

Greatest Hits, Vol. 3: Best of the Brother Years / Feb. 1, 2000 / Capitol ♦♦♦♦
Long out of print but often treasured by collectors and particularly obsessive fans, the Beach Boys' work from the '70s and early '80s also enjoyed a growing cachet with music cognoscenti during the '90s. Finally, in 2000, Capitol reissued the group's later catalog on a series of two-fers. *Greatest Hits, Vol. 3: Best of the Brother Years* preceded the reissues with a 20-track overview of the years 1970 through 1986, from the first Brother single ("Add Some Music to Your Day") to the last ("California Dreamin'"). Besides the inclusion of '70s classics like "Surf's Up" and "Til I Die," there are a few engaging Brian Wilson rockers ("Honkin' Down the Highway," "Good Timin'") and the many classic R&B standards ("Rock & Roll Music," "Peggy Sue," "Come Go With Me") pointing the way to the county-fair oldies act the Beach Boys were soon to become. On the whole, the track selection is solid but rather unappealing: the *Greatest Hits, Vol. 3* may have taken a lot of singles from the Brother years, but it didn't take all of the best songs. And the short shrift given to Dennis Wilson is *very* disappointing. The tender ballads Dennis delivered at the end of albums like *Carl and the Passions—So Tough* and *Holland* were excellent, and among the most affecting work of the Beach Boys' career. For listeners curious about the quality of the '70s years, this probably isn't the best compilation: the group just wasn't a singles act anymore, and the most entertaining Beach Boys albums of the decade—*Sunflower, Surf's Up, The Beach Boys Love You*—are best heard in their entireties. —*John Bush*

Surfin' / Apr. 4, 2000 / Varèse ♦♦♦
It is the rare major recording act who hasn't cut a session early in their career for some small label, whose owner licenses the tracks over and over, diluting the catalog's value. For the Beach Boys, it's the handful of recordings they made for music publisher Hite Morgan in 1961-62. These skeletons in the closet often helped the artists early on; the Beach Boys certainly owe a lot to Morgan of Guild Music, who took them into a professional recording studio to cut "Surfin'," which went on to become their first chart single. A few months later, he took them in again to cut their first versions of "Surfin' Safari" and "Surfer Girl." Morgan naturally retained rights to these early recordings (which also included several other numbers, demos, and outtakes), and over the years they were licensed for a dizzying number of albums, usually with some miscellaneous tracks by other artists added, since there weren't enough finished masters to make up a full-length album. The best collection is DCC's 1991 CD *Lost & Found 1961-1962*, which is extensively annotated and contains many previously unreleased outtakes. If that's a bit too thorough, Varèse Sarabande's *Surfin'* may make for a more listenable alternative. Running a brief 32 minutes, *Surfin'* is a nicely arranged collection of rarities that never pretends to be anything more than what it is. The Beach Boys recordings are rudimentary, but identifiable, and the group's fans should have at least one version of this material in their collections (given its proliferation, they probably already do). This one at least can be recommended as a reasonable selection of Beach Boys juvenilia. —*William Ruhlmann*

Hawthorne, CA / May 22, 2001 / Capitol ♦♦♦
Ever wanted to hear the Beach Boys' 1965 album track "Salt Lake City" in stereo instead of mono, or maybe an a cappella version of "Can't Wait Too Long," which the band recorded in 1967 but never released until it was tacked onto a 1990 reissue? If so, then you're undoubtedly one of the more obsessive Beach Boys fans out there, and *Hawthorne, CA* was produced with you—and only a scant few others—in mind. More akin to an audio scrapbook or musical documentary than a true rarities compilation, this two-disc set is packed with over two exhausting hours of session excerpts, alternate versions, backing

tracks (à la *Stack-O-Tracks*), and a handful of stereo remixes. It's also interspersed with dialogue from bandmembers, a process that only enhances the already fragmentary nature of a collection like this. The only genuinely new songs are "Lonely Days," an artifact from the *Wild Honey* era, and Dennis Wilson's "A Time to Live in Dreams" from 1968. Still, almost every track has never been released previously, and fans of the band's lost masterpiece *Smile* will find several tracks of intriguing material, including revealing stereo versions of "Heroes and Villains" and "Vegetables." Also included is a considerable excerpt from the original tapes of the Beach Boys' first garage session (for the "Surfin'" single), complete with Dennis' wacky mic testing and threats from various bandmates that they'll get popped in the nose if they laugh during another take. *Hawthorne, CA* proves two things over and over again—with every a cappella mix, it proves the Beach Boys were one of the most amazing harmonists of the rock era, and with several of the newly stereo versions, listeners can hear what a good stereo remix can do to even the most lackluster songs, like 1970s "Cotton Fields (The Cotton Song)"—itself a misguided attempt to duplicate the success of 1966's "Sloop John B." A bounty of intriguing songs for the collector and true-believer fan, but far from necessary for disinterested listeners. —*John Bush*

Beachwood Sparks

f. 1998
Indie Pop, Alternative Country-Rock
Los Angeles-based cosmic country-pop combo the Beachwood Sparks was formed in mid-1998 by onetime Strictly Ballroom singer/guitarist Chris Gunst, slide guitarist/keyboardist Dave Scher, ex-Further bassist Brent Rademaker, and Lilys drummer Aaron Sperske. Inspired by the pioneering country-rock efforts of West Coast legends like the Byrds, the Flying Burrito Brothers, and Buffalo Springfield, the group issued acclaimed singles for Bomp! ("Desert Skies") and Sub Pop ("Midsummer Daydream") prior to the spring 2000 release of their superb self-titled debut LP. —*Jason Ankeny*

Beachwood Sparks / Mar. 21, 2000 / Sub Pop ♦♦♦♦
The Beachwood Sparks are space cowboys—although their self-titled Sub Pop debut most closely recalls the sound of vintage Laurel Canyon country-rock, its shimmering twang-pop melodies and gorgeous harmonies bask in a kind of interstellar psychedelia which lends the album an otherworldly glow. The hypnotically dreamlike instrumental passages which wind their way through luminous country-pop moments like "Sister Rose," "Something I Don't Recognize" and "Old Sea Miner" completely transform the album's chemical makeup. Rooted in the earth but reaching for the stars, the group realizes Gram Parsons' "Cosmic American music" aesthetic in its truest sense. —*Jason Ankeny*

● **Once We Were Trees** / Oct. 9, 2001 / Sub Pop ♦♦♦♦♦
Throughout *Once We Were Trees*, the sophomore release from the Beachwood Sparks on Sub Pop Records, the SoCal indie cowboys deliver an album completely displaying musical, songwriting, and repertory growth from their critically acclaimed self-titled debut. Previously, the Beachwood Sparks were labeled a retro extension of the late-'60s country-rock icons Buffalo Springfield and the Flying Burrito Brothers. On *Once We Were Trees*, the Beachwood Sparks prove themselves as one of the most exciting subgenre leaders in the current indie rock world. The mid-tempo groove of "The Sun Surrounds Me" illustrates the songwriting growth the Sparks have achieved in the last three years, followed by the somewhat campy yet cool "You Take the Gold," which reverts to a simple carefree singalong melody and guitar-driven hook. One notable track is a revamped version of the adult contemporary Sade hit "By Your Side," which stands as the album's "must listen" track. —*Matt Reasor*

The Beacon Street Union

f. 1966, Boston, MA, db. 1969
Psychedelic
The Beacon Street Union was a '60s rock band from Boston comprised of John Wright (vocals), Paul Tartachny (guitar, vocals), Robert Rhodes (keyboards), Wayne Ulaky (bass, vocals), and Richard Weisburg (drums) who moved to New York in 1967 and got caught up in MGM Records' "Bosstown Sound" promotion—the company tried, unsuccessfully, to promote an invented Boston music scene to rival the real one in San Francisco at the time. Like other bands used in the promotion, the Beacon Street Union suffered from the hype, and though they made two charting albums, they never had much of a chance to succeed. —*William Ruhlmann*

The Eyes of the Beacon Street Union / Feb. 1968 / MGM ♦♦♦♦

The Clown Died in Marvin Gardens / Aug. 1968 / MGM ♦♦♦♦
The Clown Died in Marvin Gardens is an original statement by a Boston group which was musically superior to Eden's Children and Ultimate Spinach, but not as focused as the Remains, the Hallucinations with Peter Wolf, or the emerging J. Geils Band. Where national groups like the Peanut Butter Conspiracy may have been misguided and sputtered with no direction, vocalist John Lincoln Wright developed into a first-rate songwriter and country singer with purpose. Hearing his work on highly experimental tunes like the title track or the impressionistic "May I Light Your Cigarette?" is true culture shock. "The Clown's Overture" seems pointless, yet "Angus of Aberdeen" is inspired and a bright spot in the morass that was the "Bosstown Sound." The rave-up version of "Blue Suede Shoes" is great, the guitar funneled through effects and brimming with excitement. Therein lies the problem with this album, and this group. The most structured piece is a Carl Perkins cover while "A Not Very August Afternoon" feels like a song wanting to belong to some hippy movie that was never made. Where the Chocolate Watchband rocked with authority, the Beacon Street Union are feeling their way through the times, the business, and their music. Producer Wes Farrell should have nudged them into a more

commercial direction and brought more accessible material to their attention. Wright is a major talent and had he the right direction this early in his career, who knows what kind of chart action he could have enjoyed. The tragedy of *The Clown Died in Marvin Gardens* is that it could have been so much more. *—Joe Viglione*

● **The Eyes of the Beacon Street Union/The Clown Died in Marvin Gardens** / 1998 / See For Miles ♦♦♦♦

The Bears

f. 1987, **db.** 1988

Power Pop, Alternative Pop/Rock

The Bears were formed in 1987 when noted guitarist Adrian Belew, desiring a break from his solo career, recruited several friends, all former members of the Raisins, to record pop songs in the style of XTC and Squeeze. The Bears marked a major upturn in Belew's musical accessibility and gave him the opportunity to hone his compositional skills and musical focus. After two albums, he returned to his solo career, writing oddball pop songs in largely the same style and finding greater success in the alternative market. The three remaining Bears continued as a trio called the Psychodots. *—Steve Huey*

● **The Bears** / 1987 / Primitive Man ♦♦♦♦♦

The debut album from the Bears is a solid slice of great guitar-driven pop tunes. Although Adrian Belew was seen nominally as the frontman, this was truly a band; four friends who had known each other for years, playing for pure joy. Songwriting duties were shared, with each member contributing at least one track, and they also wrote several together as a team. The tunes are tight, smart pop gems, distinguished from so many other bands by the wild antics of Belew's guitar. Although he doesn't have the immediately identifiable tone of Belew, Rob Fetters is no slouch on guitar himself, and their playing styles complement each other nicely. Belew and Fetters share the lead vocal duties, and their vocal harmonizing is up to the standards set by Lennon and McCartney. The rich upright electric bass of Bob Nyswonger and the crisp drumming of Chris Arduser anchor the band perfectly, as Belew and Fetters sing and play their hearts out. You can tell that this was a band that really enjoyed playing together (especially in a live setting), and that comes across loud and clear, even on a recording. *—Sean Westergaard*

Rise and Shine / Apr. 1988 / Primitive Man ♦♦

The guitar experimentation of Adrian Belew and Rob Fetters is top-notch on this record, but the material itself is not. Belew and his backing group of Toledo, Ohio-based musicians tend to sound like many other bands. On the first track, "Aches and Pains," the Bears literally break out all the bells and whistles, as those items are incorporated into what seems to be a second-rate Squeeze song. Belew and Fetters do manage to polish up some of the rough spots, however, on songs like "Robobo's Beef," which transforms a distorted electric guitar into what sounds like an electric violin helmed by Jean-Luc Ponty's evil twin brother. The album doesn't lack diversity, as heard on tracks ranging from lullabyes ("Little Blue River") to fusion worldbeat ("Rabbit Manor"), but it does lack fully developed writing. The record is a mixed palette with bits of music that could have made up a beautiful canvas if they were carefully thought out. *—Stephen Howell*

Beastie Boys

f. 1979, New York, NY

Old School Rap, Alternative Rap, Hardcore Punk, Alternative Pop/Rock, Hip-Hop, Golden Age

As the first White rap group of any importance, the Beastie Boys received the scorn of critics and strident hip-hop musicians, who accused them of cultural pirating, especially since they began as a hardcore punk group in 1981. But the Beasties weren't pirating—they treated rap as part of a post-punk musical underground, where the do-it-yourself aesthetics of hip-hop and punk weren't that far apart. Of course, the exaggerated B-boy and frat boy parodies of their unexpected hit debut album *Licensed to Ill* didn't help their cause. For much of the mid-'80s, the Beastie Boys were considered as macho clowns, and while their ambitious, Dust Brothers-produced second album *Paul's Boutique* dismissed that theory, it was ignored by both the public and the press at the time. In retrospect, it was one of the first albums to predict the genre-bending, self-referential pop kaleidoscope of '90s pop. The Beasties refined their eclectic approach with 1992's *Check Your Head*, where they played their own instruments. *Check Your Head* brought the Beasties back to the top of the charts, and within a few years, they were considered one of the most influential and ambitious groups of the '90s, cultivating a musical community not only through their music, but with their record label Grand Royal and their magazine of the same name. *—Stephen Thomas Erlewine*

☆ **Licensed to Ill** / 1986 / Def Jam ♦♦♦♦♦

The impact of this album in 1987 was about as subtle as a brick through a window. It was the first #1 hip-hop album, selling four million copies, and the first album from a White rap group. From the opening kick of John Bonham's drums (taken from "When the Levee Breaks"), the Beasties proceed to steal from every record they can get their hands on and rhyme about an absurd array of macho fantasies. Sure, it's obnoxious—but it's an act, and an insanely humorous one at that; no other rappers brag about being thrown out of White Castle, drinking Budweiser, or having "more rhymes than Phyllis Diller." Even if some of it sounds dated today, the sheer force of the music and the whiny rhymes still make this worth hearing. *—Stephen Thomas Erlewine*

★ **Paul's Boutique** / Jul. 1989 / Capitol ♦♦♦♦♦

Endlessly complex and relentlessly innovative, *Paul's Boutique* is the Beastie Boys' masterpiece. It's very dense, with samples from nearly every genre of music and clever, literate, absurd lyrics dropping references from Jack Kerouac to *Dragnet*; *Paul's Boutique* is a virtual catalog of pop culture, deeply rooted in the 1970s. As rappers, the Beasties have grown immeasurably, writing lyrics that are both smart-assed and smart. Musically, the album is much richer than *Licensed to Ill*, covering everything from funk and pop to country and hip-hop, with several layers of samples and beats on each track. *Paul's Boutique* is a brilliant, visionary album, and hasn't aged a day since its release. *—Stephen Thomas Erlewine*

☆ **Check Your Head** / Apr. 21, 1992 / Grand Royal/Capitol ♦♦♦♦♦

Check Your Head returned the Beastie Boys to the spotlight, although in the most unlikely manner possible. Refashioning themselves as a loose and gritty groove band, the Beasties picked up their instruments again and made an album of dirty Stax and New Orleans funk, tripped-out reggae, hard hip-hop, blistering hardcore punk, and scores of pop culture references and jokes. In its own way, *Check Your Head* is as trailblazing as *Paul's Boutique*; with its inspired amateurishness, it acknowledges no boundaries or limitations, creating a post-post-punk world where Eddie Harris, Bob Dylan, Cheap Trick, Groove Holmes, Spoonie Gee, and Biz Markie exist together as one music. And, strange as it may sound, it works. *—Stephen Thomas Erlewine*

Some Old Bullshit / Feb. 8, 1994 / Grand Royal/Capitol ♦♦

Ill Communication / May 23, 1994 / Grand Royal/Capitol ♦♦♦♦

More of a refinement and restatement of *Check Your Head* than a bold departure, *Ill Communication* still finds the Beastie Boys in prime form, adding more elements of jazz to their dense, surrealistic sound. From the scores of wah-wah guitars to the short hardcore punk songs, *Ill Communication* is firmly entrenched in '70s worship without ever once sounding like it's recycled. It may offer the same thing as *Check Your Head*, but *Ill Communication* never sounds formulaic or tired. *—Stephen Thomas Erlewine*

Aglio E Olio / Nov. 13, 1995 / Grand Royal ♦♦

The In Sound from Way Out! / Apr. 2, 1996 / Grand Royal/Capitol ♦♦♦

Originally released through the Beasties' French fan club, *The In Sound from Way Out* is a collection of the group's funky instrumentals from *Check Your Head* and *Ill Communication*, with a couple of new tracks thrown in. The Beasties have a flair for loose, gritty funk and soul-jazz and the stuttering, greasy keyboards of Money Mark give the music an extra edge—he helps make the music sound as authentic as anything from the early '70s. Fans of the band's dynamic wordplay might find *The In Sound from Way Out* a disappointment, but anyone that grooved on the wildly eclectic fusions of *Check Your Head* and *Ill Communication* will find the album endlessly enjoyable. *—Stephen Thomas Erlewine*

Hello Nasty / Jul. 14, 1998 / Grand Royal/Capitol ♦♦♦♦♦

Hello Nasty, the Beastie Boys' fifth album, is a head-spinning listen loaded with analog synthesizers, old drum machines, call-and-response vocals, freestyle rhyming, futuristic sound effects, and virtuoso turntable scratching. The Beasties have long been notorious for their dense, multi-layered explosions, but *Hello Nasty* is their first record to build on the multi-ethnic junk culture breakthrough of *Check Your Head*, instead of merely replicating it. Moving from electro-funk breakdowns to Latin-soul jams to spacey pop, *Hello Nasty* covers as much ground as *Check Your Head* or *Ill Communication*, but the flow is natural, like *Paul's Boutique*, even if the finish is retro-stylized. Hiring DJ Mixmaster Mike (one of the Invisibl Skratch Piklz) turned out to be a masterstroke; he and the Beasties created a sound that strongly recalls the spare electronic funk of the early '80s, but spiked with the samples and post-modern absurdist wit that have become their trademarks. On the surface, the sonic collages of *Hello Nasty* don't appear as dense as *Paul's Boutique*, nor is there a single as grabbing as "Sabotage," but given time, little details emerge, and each song forms its own identity. A few stray from the course, and the ending is a little anticlimactic, but that doesn't erase the riches of *Hello Nasty*—the old-school kick of "Super Disco Breakin'" and "The Move"; Adam Yauch's crooning on "I Don't Know"; Lee "Scratch" Perry's cameo; and the recurring video game samples, to name just a few. The sonic adventures alone make the album noteworthy, but what makes it remarkable is how it looks to the future by looking to the past. There's no question that *Hello Nasty* is saturated in old-school sounds and styles, but by reviving the future-shock rock of the early '80s, the Beasties have shrewdly set themselves up for the new millennium. *—Stephen Thomas Erlewine*

The Sounds of Science / Nov. 23, 1999 / Grand Royal/Capitol ♦♦♦♦

At the close of the '90s, the Beastie Boys had only released five albums, which may not seem like enough music to provide the foundation for a double-disc retrospective. But between 1981 and 1999, they released countless B-sides, non-LP singles, and EPs, resulting in a sprawling discography ripe for a compilation. So, in 1999, the Beasties released the two-disc compilation *The Sounds of Science*, which covers every incarnation of the band from *Pollywog Stew* to *Hello Nasty*. Inevitably, some well-known songs are missing—only three cuts from *Licensed to Ill* are here, and their breakthrough single "Rock Hard" had to be pulled when AC/DC refused permission for a sample. Ultimately, that doesn't matter, since the set captures the spirit of the Beasties so well. Usually, compilations that don't follow chronological order are a little muddled, but *The Sounds of Science* benefits from its jumbled sequencing, since it emphasizes the band's astonishing musical reach and consistency. After all, every album since *Paul's Boutique* has followed a similarly unpredictable pattern, as the group moved from hip-hop to punk to funk to jazz. What's remarkable about *The Sounds of Science* is that it has all the obvious suspects, but since they're rubbing singles with album tracks and B-sides like "Skills to Pay the Bills," two outtakes from the abandoned country album, alternate versions of "Jimmy James" and "Three MC's and One DJ," Fatboy Slim's brilliant remix of "Body Movin'," goofs like the Biz Markie-sung cover of "Benny and the Jets," and the excellent new single "Alive," it all sounds fresh. There's much more than hits here, but *The Sounds of Science* achieves something most anthologies don't: it summarizes the attitude and spirit of the band, while offering some new revelations even for dedicated fans. —*Stephen Thomas Erlewine*

Beat Farmers

f. 1983, San Diego, CA, **db.** Nov. 11, 1995
Cowpunk, Jangle Pop, Roots Rock
The Beat Farmers enjoyed a cult following throughout the 1980s and early 1990s until the untimely passing of lead singer/drummer/guitarist Country Dick Montana in November 1995. He was just 40, and he collapsed of a massive heart attack at the Long Horn, a bar in Whistler, British Columbia. Montana, a former record store owner, and past president of the Kinks Preservation Society fan club, formed the Beat Farmers in San Diego in 1983, influenced on the one hand by country and blues music, but on the other by the first wave of punk-rock bands to come out of Los Angeles. The group began to latch on to a following at San Diego and Los Angeles-area clubs, satisfying a need for roots-based rock & roll before most people even knew the need existed. By March 1984, they were signed to Rhino Records for a one-off deal, and with a $4,000 budget, recorded *Tales of the New West*, their debut. The group's album *Pursuit of Happiness* spurred the single "Make It Last" which got airplay on more than 40 country western stations. But once country radio programmers had a chance to hear the rest of the album, they quickly dropped the single, since many of them felt the rest of the album was too rock & roll oriented. —*Richard Skelly*

Tales of the New West / May 1985 / Rhino ✦✦✦✦
Hailing from San Diego, the Beat Farmers burst on the California music scene like a locomotive in the mid-1980s with amazing live shows. Their powerful combination of rock & roll, country, blues, and folk styles—performed exquisitely tight—was truly a wonder to behold. This, their first album, accurately captured the band's live intensity. Along with some glorious covers, notably "There She Goes Again" (Lou Reed) and "Never Goin' Back" (John Stewart), the band could write quite well too, with Paul Kamanski's "Bigger Stones" being the best example. This album is an extremely good snapshot of post-punk California rock & roll. —*Matthew Greenwald*

Van Go / Jun. 1986 / Curb ✦✦✦
With the original band personnel intact, the second Beat Farmers album, *Van Go*, continues the group's approach as a down and dirty country-rock band. Lead singer/guitarist/songwriter Jerry Raney comes up with some great originals, such as "Deceiver" and "Gun Sale Down at the Church," that are delivered in the Farmers' sweaty, alcohol-drenched sound. There is also an amazing cover of Neil Young's "Powderfinger," which sounds like it was written for the band, and it's easily one of the album's highlights. Drummer/vocalist and part-time frontman Country Dick Montana continues on with his skewed version of Johnny Cash with an excellent version of "Big Ugly Wheels." All of this proves that a change to a major label didn't diminish the band's style or appeal. —*Matthew Greenwald*

Pursuit of Happiness / Aug. 1987 / Curb ✦✦✦
The final studio album for the Beat Farmers saw a change in the lineup. Second guitarist/vocalist Buddy Blue was replaced by Joey Harris, who had sung on the group's two previous albums. Harris proves to be a more than competent singer and guitarist, and also shares lead vocals with Jerry Raney on some new songs. "Ridin'" is one of the finer songs on the record, fitting in easily with the band's country-rock, bar-room style. An excellent Paul Kamanski original titled "Hollywood Hills" opens the album, and it's one of the finest tracks the group ever recorded. Raney comes up with a few good originals such as "King of the World," but the cracks in the foundation are evident. It's an excellent album in the end, but there is evidence of some alienation (in terms of band identity) in the grooves. —*Matthew Greenwald*

Poor and Famous / 1989 / Curb ✦✦

● **Loud and Plowed and ... LIVE!!** / May 1990 / Curb ✦✦✦✦✦
Loud and Plowed and...LIVE!! is a "best of live" collection that shows the band at the height of their powers in their best environment. Since none of their studio albums were able to completely capture the raw energy and fun of the Beat Farmers, this remains the definitive document of their career and is the best place to start. —*Chris Woodstra*

● **The Best of the Beat Farmers** / May 2, 1995 / Curb ✦✦✦✦
The Best of the Beat Farmers is a skimpy, 10-track survey of the band's career that covers their best known songs. For those who just need a taste, the album works well as a basic introduction. Liner notes would have been nice. —*Chris Woodstra*

Manifold / Oct. 1995 / Sector 2 ✦✦

Beat Happening

f. 1982, Olympia, WA
Twee Pop, Indie Rock, Alternative Pop/Rock, American Underground
Beat Happening was among the truly seminal and influential American bands of the post-punk era, a paragon of pop minimalism, rebellious innocence, and indie defiance. The linchpin of the Olympia, Washington-based International Pop Underground, members Calvin (Johnson), Heather (Lewis), and Bret (Lunsford) expressed simple truths and simple emotions with simple music, favoring off-key, tuneless vocals and three-chord primitivism over slick, processed packaging; implicit in their work was also a rejection of major-label trappings, as the group steadfastly remained with K Records, Calvin's self-owned imprint and a model of D.I.Y. indie success. After several EPs and many shows around Olympia, Beat Happening's 1985 eponymous full-length debut brought the trio their first widespread exposure, as well as a number of comparisons to the burgeoning British twee-pop scene spearheaded by the Pastels. With the release of 1991's *Dreamy*, the group's influence on the indie community and the blossoming cuddle-core movement became increasingly pronounced. The sublime *You Turn Me On* followed, but the band spent much of the decade in limbo as Calvin focused on his Dub Narcotic Sound System project as well as the Halo Benders. Despite their absence from the stage and the studio, the trio maintained that they had not disbanded, and reportedly continued practicing on a monthly basis. —*Jason Ankeny*

Beat Happening / 1985 / K ✦✦✦
Beat Happening can't be given credit for *creating* the indie-pop genre, but they certainly gave it life in America. This, their first album, is indie-pop in its purest form: fuzzy bedroom recordings of simplistic, cutesy songs, with intentionally innocent and juvenile lyrics, which Calvin Johnson belts out with one of the most endearingly bad voices in music history. Their later albums sport better songwriting and are more listenable from a production standpoint, but *Beat Happening* is as twee and charming as this type of music can get. *1985-85*, its CD reissue (with a few live songs and early recordings added), is for *devoted* indie-pop fans only. —*Nitsuh Abebe*

Jamboree / 1988 / K/Sub Pop ✦✦✦✦✦
Co-produced by Steve Fisk and the Screaming Trees' Mark Lanegan and Gary Lee Conner, Beat Happening's brief, brilliant sophomore effort significantly expands the trio's horizons without sacrificing any of their naive charm. Sporting a fuller, more intricate sound and stronger songs than their debut, *Jamboree* crystallizes the trio's love-rock aesthetic in its embryonic stages; veering sharply from the idyllic drones of the perennial "Indian Summer" to the poignant crush-pop of "Cat Walk" to the indie-party classic "Midnight A Go-Go," each cut is a marvel of innocence and ingenuity. —*Jason Ankeny*

Black Candy / 1989 / K/Sub Pop ✦✦✦
As evidenced by its title, *Black Candy* is Beat Happening's darkest, most deliriously ominous album; clearly influenced by the Cramps, the record is dominated by Calvin Johnson's coffin-creak vocals, with Heather Lewis' breathy sweetness rarely in earshot to lighten the mood. A less developed batch of compositions than the previous *Jamboree*, it strives to evoke the mood of a grade-Z teen horror flick soundtrack, with faux-creepy songs ("Pajama Party in a Haunted Hive," "Gravedigger Blues," "Bonfire") and primal, drum-dominated production; less eclectic and nuanced than the trio's other LPs, *Black Candy* quickly grows tiresome, although the oft-covered highlight "Cast a Shadow" is a treat. —*Jason Ankeny*

1983-85 / 1990 / K ✦✦✦✦
1983-85 compiles 27 early Beat Happening tracks, spanning the trio's eponymous debut LP, the *Three Tea Breakfast* EP, a handful of compilation appearances, singles, and a wealth of unreleased material. A portrait of the group at their most primitive, the fidelity is often poor, but the kinetic energy of the early sessions is palpable, and the wide-eyed charm of gems like "Look Around," "Foggy Eyes," "fourteen" and the classic "Bad Seeds" is undeniable. —*Jason Ankeny*

Dreamy / 1991 / K/Sub Pop ✦✦✦✦✦
A stunning return to form, *Dreamy* reprises the dark aggression of the preceding *Black Candy*, but brings to the table a significantly stronger and more assured collection of songs. Measuring Calvin Johnson's increasingly menacing lead turns with Heather Lewis' more wistful contributions, the album strikes a careful balance between maturity and naivete; for all of their ragged minimalism, tracks like "Collide," "Revolution Come and Gone" and "Me Untamed" are remarkably sophisticated and assured. And in addition to the newfound sexiness of cuts like "Nancy Sin" and "Red Head Walking," there's also a renewed sense of emotional urgency—Heather's beguiling "Fortune Cookie Prize" is one of the group's most buoyant love songs, while the mournful "Cry for a Shadow" exposes the tenderness beneath Calvin's tough-guy veneer. —*Jason Ankeny*

● **You Turn Me On** / Oct. 2, 1992 / K/Sub Pop ✦✦✦✦✦
Beat Happening's (possibly) final LP is also their best: concluding the emotional and musical progression begun with the minimalist innocence of their earliest work, *You Turn Me On* is a mature record of tremendous breadth and complexity. Where once the trio's songs were brief and bouncy, the nine tracks here are epic (several top out at over six minutes) and ambitious; produced in part by ex-Young Marble Giant Stuart Moxham (an obvious influence), the record's full, deep sound belies its bare-bones performances—"Teenage Caveman" sports booming, primal drums perfectly suited to its title, while the propulsive "Noise" manufactures the illusion of a bassline where none ever existed. The most democratic record in an output founded on egalitarian ideals, *You Turn Me On* offers Heather Lewis' strongest songs ever—her hypnotic nine-minute "Godsend" is the LP's heart and soul—and she and Calvin Johnson even trade verses on the closing "Bury the Hammer." As for Calvin himself, his solo contributions are exceptional—the spartan opener "Tiger Trap" is an evocative heartbreaker, and the title track is a fire-breathing corker. A masterpiece. —*Jason Ankeny*

The Beatles

f. 1960, Liverpool, England, **db.** 1970
British Psychedelia, Pop/Rock, Folk-Rock, Merseybeat, Psychedelic, British Invasion, Rock & Roll, Pop
The Beatles were the most popular and influential rock act of all time, but their significance cannot solely be measured in sales records (as impressive as those are). John Lennon, Paul McCartney, George Harrison, and Ringo Starr synthesized all that was good about early rock & roll, and changed it into something original and even more exciting. They established the prototype for the self-contained rock group that wrote and performed their own material. As composers, their craft and melodic inventiveness were second to none, and key to the evolution of rock from its blues/R&B-based forms into a style that was far more eclectic, but equally visceral. As singers, both Lennon and

McCartney were among the best and most expressive vocalists in rock; the group's harmonies were intricate and exhilarating. As performers, they were exciting and photogenic; when they retreated into the studio, they were instrumental in pioneering advanced techniques and multi-layered arrangements. They were also the first British rock group to achieve worldwide prominence, launching a British Invasion that made rock truly an international phenomenon. With their unmatched songwriting savvy, brash guitar-oriented attack, and wildly enthusiastic vocals, they were the embodiment of the youthful flair of their generation, ready to dispense with post-war austerity and claim a culture of their own. The Beatles were also unsurpassed in their eclecticism, willing to borrow from blues, popular standards, gospel, folk, or whatever seemed suitable for their musical vision. Producer George Martin was the perfect foil for the group, refining their ideas without tinkering with their essence. During the last half of their career, he was indispensable for his ability to translate their concepts into arrangements that required complex orchestration, innovative applications of recording technology, and an ever-widening array of instruments. Just as crucially, the Beatles were never ones to stand still and milk formulas. All of their albums and singles would show remarkable artistic progression (though never at the expense of a damn catchy tune). *—Richie Unterberger*

☆ **Please Please Me** / Mar. 22, 1963 / Capitol ✦✦✦✦✦

Once "Please Please Me" rocketed to number one, the Beatles rushed to deliver a debut album, bashing out *Please Please Me* in a day. Decades after its release, the album still sounds fresh, precisely because of its intense origins. As the songs rush past, it's easy to get wrapped up in the sound of the record itself without realizing how the album effectively summarizes the band's eclectic influences. Naturally, the influences shine through their covers, all of which are unconventional and illustrate the group's superior taste. There's a love of girl groups, vocal harmonies, sophisticated popcraft, schmaltz, R&B, and hard-driving rock & roll, which is enough to make *Please Please Me* impressive, but what makes it astonishing is how these elements converge in the originals. "I Saw Here Standing There" is one of their best rockers, yet it has surprising harmonies and melodic progressions. "Misery" and "There's a Place" grow out of the girl group tradition without being tied to it. A few of their originals, such as "Do You Want to Know a Secret" and the pleasantly light "PS I Love You," have dated slightly, but endearingly so, since they're infused with cheerful innocence and enthusiasm. And there is an innocence to *Please Please Me*. The Beatles may have played notoriously rough dives in Hamburg, but the only way you could tell that on their first album was how the constant gigging turned the group into a tight, professional band that could run through their set list at the drop of a hat with boundless energy. It's no surprise that Lennon had shouted himself hoarse by the end of the session, barely getting through "Twist and Shout," the most famous single-take in rock history. He simply got caught up in the music, just like generations of listeners did. *—Stephen Thomas Erlewine*

☆ **With the Beatles** / Nov. 22, 1963 / Capitol ✦✦✦✦✦

With the Beatles is a sequel of the highest order—one that betters the original by developing its own tone and adding depth. While it may share several similarities with its predecessor—there is an equal ratio of covers-to-originals, a familiar blend of girl group, Motown, R&B, pop, and rock, and a show tune that interrupts the flow of the album—*With the Beatles* is a better record that not only rocks harder, it's considerably more sophisticated. They could deliver rock & roll straight ("I Wanna Be Your Man") or twist it around with a little Latin lilt ("Little Child," one of their most underrated early rockers); Lennon and McCartney wrote sweet ballads (the achingly gorgeous "All I've Got to Do") and sprightly pop/rockers ("All My Loving") with equal aplomb; and propulsive rockers ("It Won't Be Long") were as richly melodic as slower songs ("Not a Second Time"). Even George Harrison's first recorded song, "Don't Bother Me," is a standout, with its wonderfully foreboding minor-key melody. Since the Beatles covered so much ground with their originals, their covers pale slightly in comparison, particularly since they rely on familiar hits (only "Devil in Her Heart" qualifies as a forgotten gem). But for every "Roll Over Beethoven," a surprisingly stiff reading of the Chuck Berry standard, there is a sublime moment, such as Lennon's soaring interpretation of "You Really Got a Hold on Me," and the group always turns in thoroughly enjoyable performances. Still, the heart of *With the Beatles* lies not in the covers, but the originals, where it was clear that, even at this early stage, the Beatles were rapidly maturing and changing, turning into expert craftsmen and musical innovators. *—Stephen Thomas Erlewine*

☆ **A Hard Day's Night** / Jul. 10, 1964 / Capitol ✦✦✦✦✦

A Hard Day's Night not only was the *de facto* soundtrack for their movie, not only was it filled with nothing but Lennon-McCartney originals, but it found the Beatles truly coming into their own as a band. All of the disparate influences on their first two albums had coalesced into a bright, joyous, original sound, filled with ringing guitars and irresistible melodies. *A Hard Day's Night* is where the Beatles became mythical, but this is the sound of Beatlemania in all of its giddy glory. Decades after its original release, its punchy blend of propulsive rhythms, jangly guitars, and infectious, singalong melodies is remarkably fresh. There's something intrinsically exciting in the *sound* of the album itself, something to keep the record vital years after it was recorded. Even more impressive are the songs themselves. Not only are the melodies forceful and memorable, but Lennon and McCartney have found a number of variations to their basic Merseybeat style, from the brash "Can't Buy Me Love" and "Any Time at All" through the gentle "If I Fell" to the tough folk-rock of "I'll Cry Instead." It's possible to hear both songwriters develop their own distinctive voices on the album, but, overall, *A Hard Day's Night* stands as a testament to their collaborative powers—never again did they write together so well or so easily, choosing to pursue their own routes. John and Paul must have known how strong the material is—they threw the pleasant trifle "I'm Happy Just to Dance with You" to George and didn't give anything to Ringo to sing. That may have been a little selfish, but it hardly hurts the album, since everything on the record is performed with genuine glee and excitement. It's the pinnacle of their early years. *—Stephen Thomas Erlewine*

☆ **Beatles for Sale** / Dec. 4, 1964 / Capitol ✦✦✦✦✦

It was inevitable that the constant grind of touring, writing, promoting, and recording would grate on the Beatles, but the weariness of *Beatles for Sale* comes as something of a shock. Only five months before, the group released the joyous *A Hard Day's Night*. Now, they sound beaten, worn, and, in Lennon's case, bitter and self-loathing. His opening trilogy ("No Reply," "I'm a Loser," "Baby's in Black") is the darkest sequence on any Beatles record, setting the tone for the album. Moments of joy pop up now and again, mainly in the forms of covers and the dynamic "Eight Days a Week," but the very presence of six covers after the triumphant all-original *A Hard Day's Night* feels like an admission of defeat or at least a regression. (It doesn't help that Lennon's cover of his beloved obscurity "Mr. Moonlight" winds up as arguably the worst thing the group ever recorded.) Beneath those surface suspicions, however, there are some important changes on *Beatles for Sale*, most notably Lennon's discovery of Bob Dylan and folk-rock. The opening three songs, along with "I Don't Want to Spoil the Party," are implicitly confessional and all quite bleak, which is a new development. This spirit winds up overshadowing McCartney's cheery "I'll Follow the Sun" or the thundering covers of "Rock & Roll Music," "Honey Don't," and "Kansas City/Hey, Hey, Hey Hey," and the weariness creeps up in unexpected places—"Every Little Thing," "What You're Doing," even George's cover of Carl Perkins' "Everybody's Trying to Be My Baby"—leaving the impression that Beatlemania may have been fun but now the group is exhausted. That exhaustion results in the group's most uneven album, but its best moments find them moving from Merseybeat to the sophisticated pop/rock they developed in mid-career. *—Stephen Thomas Erlewine*

☆ **Help!** / Aug. 6, 1965 / Capitol ✦✦✦✦✦

Considering that *Help!* functions as the Beatles' fifth album and as the soundtrack to their second film—while filming, they continued to release non-LP singles on a regular basis—it's not entirely surprising that it still has some of the weariness of *Beatles for Sale*. Again, they pad the album with covers, but the Bakersfield bounce of "Act Naturally" adds new flavor (along with an ideal showcase for Ringo's amiable vocals) and "Dizzy Miss Lizzie" gives John an opportunity to flex his rock & roll muscle. George is writing again and if his two contributions don't touch Lennon and McCartney's originals, they hold their own against much of their British pop peers. Since Lennon wrote *a third* more songs than McCartney, it's easy to forgive a pair of minor numbers ("It's Only Love," "Tell Me What You See"), especially since they're overshadowed by four great songs. His Dylan infatuation holds strong, particularly on the plaintive "You've Got to Hide Your Love Away" and the title track, where the brash arrangement disguises Lennon's desperation. Driven by an indelible 12-string guitar, "Ticket to Ride" is another masterpiece and "You're Going to Lose That Girl" is the kind of song McCartney effortlessly tosses off—which he does, with the jaunty "The Night Before" and "Another Girl," two very fine tunes that simply update his melodic signature. He did much better with "I've Just Seen a Face," an irresistible folk-rock gem, and "Yesterday," a simple, beautiful ballad whose arrangement—an acoustic guitar supported by a string quartet—and composition suggested much more sophisticated and adventurous musical territory, which the group immediately began exploring with *Rubber Soul*. *—Stephen Thomas Erlewine*

☆ **Rubber Soul** / Dec. 3, 1965 / Capitol ✦✦✦✦✦

While the Beatles still largely stuck to love songs on *Rubber Soul*, the lyrics represented a quantum leap in terms of thoughtfulness, maturity, and complex ambiguities. Musically, too, it was a substantial leap forward, with intricate folk-rock arrangements that reflected the increasing influence of Dylan and the Byrds. The group and George Martin were also beginning to expand the conventional instrumental parameters of the rock group, using a sitar on "Norwegian Wood," and Greek-like guitar lines on "Michelle" and "Girl," fuzz bass on "Think for Yourself," and a piano made to sound like a harpsichord on the instrumental break of "In My Life." While John and Paul were beginning to carve separate songwriting identities at this point, the album is full of great tunes, from "Norwegian Wood" and "Michelle" to "Girl," "I'm Looking Through You," "You Won't See Me," "Drive My Car," and "Nowhere Man" (the last of which was the first Beatle song to move beyond romantic themes entirely). George Harrison was also developing into a fine songwriter with his two contributions, "Think for Yourself" and the Byrdsish "If I Needed Someone." *—Richie Unterberger*

☆ **Revolver** / Aug. 5, 1966 / Capitol ✦✦✦✦✦

All the rules fell by the wayside with *Revolver*, as the Beatles began exploring new sonic territory, lyrical subjects, and styles of composition. It wasn't just Lennon and McCartney, either—Harrison staked out his own dark territory with the tightly wound, cynical rocker "Taxman"; the jaunty yet dissonant "I Want to Tell You"; and "Love You To," George's first and best foray into Indian music. Such explorations were bold, yet they were eclipsed by Lennon's trippy kaleidoscopes of sound. His most straightforward number was "Doctor Robert," an ode to his dealer, and things just got stranger from there, as he buried "And Your Bird Can Sing" in a maze of multi-tracked guitars, gave Ringo a charmingly hallucinogenic slice of childhood whimsy in "Yellow Submarine," and then capped it off with a triptych of bad trips: the spiraling "She Said She Said"; the crawling, druggy "I'm Only Sleeping"; and "Tomorrow Never Knows," a pure nightmare where John sang portions of the *Tibetan Book of the Dead* into a suspended microphone over Ringo's thundering, menacing drumbeats and layers of overdubbed, phased guitars and tape loops. McCartney's experiments were formal, as he tried on every pop style from chamber pop to soul, and when placed alongside Lennon and Harrison's outright experimentations, McCartney's songcraft becomes all the more impressive. The biggest miracle of *Revolver* may be that the Beatles covered so much new stylistic ground and executed it perfectly on one record, or it may be that all of it holds together perfectly. Either way, its daring sonic adventures and consistently stunning songcraft set the standard for what pop/rock could achieve. Even after *Sgt. Pepper, Revolver* stands as the ultimate modern pop album and it's still as emulated as it was upon its original release. *—Stephen Thomas Erlewine*

☆ **Sgt. Pepper's Lonely Hearts Club Band** / Jun. 1, 1967 / Capitol ✦✦✦✦✦
With *Revolver*, the Beatles made the Great Leap Forward, reaching a previously unheard-of level of sophistication and fearless experimentation. *Sgt. Pepper*, in many ways, refines that breakthrough, as the Beatles consciously synthesized such disparate influences as psychedelia, art-song, classical music, rock & roll, and music hall, often in the course of one song. Not once does the diversity seem forced—the genius of the record is how the vaudevillian "When I'm 64" seems like a logical extension of "Within You Without You" and how it provides a gateway to the chiming guitars of "Lovely Rita." There's no discounting the individual contributions of each member or their producer George Martin, but the preponderance of whimsy and self-conscious art gives the impression that Paul McCartney is the leader of the Lonely Hearts Club Band. He dominates the album in terms of compositions, setting the tone for the album with his unabashed melodicism and deviously clever arrangements. In comparison, Lennon's contributions seem fewer, and a couple of them are a little slight but his major statements are stunning. "With a Little Help from My Friends" is the ideal Ringo tune, a rolling, friendly pop song that hides genuine Lennon anguish, ala "Help!"; "Lucy in the Sky with Diamonds" remains one of the touchstones of British psychedelia; and he's the mastermind behind the bulk of "A Day in the Life," a haunting number that skillfuly blends Lennon's verse and chorus with McCartney's bridge. It's possible to argue that there are better Beatles albums, yet no album is as historically important as this. After *Sgt. Pepper*, there were no rules to follow—rock and pop bands could try anything, for better or worse. Ironically, few tried to achieve the sweeping, all-encompassing embrace of music as the Beatles did here. *—Stephen Thomas Erlewine*

☆ **Magical Mystery Tour** / Nov. 27, 1967 / Capitol ✦✦✦✦✦
The U.S. version of the soundtrack for their ill-fated British television special embellished the six songs that were found on the British *Magical Mystery Tour* double EP with five other cuts from their 1967 singles. (The CD version of the record has now been standardized worldwide as the 11 tracks found on the American version.) The psychedelic sound is very much in the vein of *Sgt. Pepper*, and even spacier in parts (especially the sound collages of "I Am the Walrus"). Unlike *Sgt. Pepper*, there's no vague overall conceptual/thematic unity to the material, which has made *Magical Mystery Tour* suffer slightly in comparison. Still, the music is mostly great, and "Penny Lane," "Strawberry Fields Forever," "All You Need Is Love," and "Hello Goodbye" were all huge, glorious, and innovative singles. The ballad "The Fool on the Hill," though only a part of the *Magical Mystery Tour* soundtrack, is also one of the most popular Beatles tunes from the era. *—Richie Unterberger*

☆ **The Beatles [White Album]** / Nov. 22, 1968 / Capitol ✦✦✦✦✦
Each song on the sprawling double album *The Beatles* is an entity to itself, as the band touches on anything and everything they can. This makes for a frustratingly scattershot record or a singularly gripping musical experience, depending on your view, but what makes the *White Album* interesting is its mess. Never before had a rock record been so self-reflective, or so ironic; the Beach Boys send-up "Back in the USSR" and the British blooze parody "Yer Blues" are delivered straight-faced, so it's never clear if these are affectionate tributes or wicked satires. Lennon turns in two of his best ballads with "Dear Prudence" and "Julia"; scours the Abbey Road vaults for the musique concrete collage "Revolution 9"; pours on the schmaltz for Ringo's closing number, "Good Night"; celebrates the Beatles cult with "Glass Onion"; and, with "Cry Baby Cry," rivals Syd Barrett. McCartney doesn't reach quite as far, yet his songs are stunning—the music-hall romp "Honey Pie," the mock country of "Rocky Raccoon," the ska-inflected "Ob-La-Di, Ob-La-Da" and the proto-metal roar of "Helter Skelter." Clearly, the Beatles' two main songwriting forces were no longer on the same page, but neither were George and Ringo. Harrison still had just two songs per LP, but it's clear from "While My Guitar Gently Weeps," the canned soul of "Savoy Truffle," the haunting "Long Long Long," and even the silly "Piggies" that he had developed into a songwriter who deserved wider exposure. And Ringo turns in a delight with his first original, the lumbering country-carnival stomp "Don't Pass Me By." None of it sounds like it was meant to share album space together, but somehow *The Beatles* creates its own style and sound through its mess. *—Stephen Thomas Erlewine*

Yellow Submarine / Jan. 13, 1969 / Capitol ✦✦✦
The only Beatles album that could really be classified as inessential, mostly because it wasn't really a proper album at all, but a soundtrack that only utilized four new Beatles songs. (The rest of the album was filled out with "Yellow Submarine," "All You Need Is Love," and a George Martin score that held little appeal to rock listeners.) What's more, the four new tracks were little more than pleasant throwaways that had been recorded during 1967 and early 1968. These aren't all that bad; "All Together Now" is a kiddieish singalong, "Hey Bulldog" has some mild Lennon nastiness, and Harrison's "It's All Too Much" is highlighted by some tidal waves of feedback guitar. It would have been far better value if it had been released as a four-song EP (an idea the Beatles even considered at one point, with the addition of a bonus track in "Across the Universe," but ultimately discarded). *—Richie Unterberger*

☆ **Abbey Road** / Sep. 26, 1969 / Capitol ✦✦✦✦✦
The last Beatles album to be recorded (although *Let It Be* was the last to be released), *Abbey Road* was a fitting swan song for the group, echoing some of the faux-conceptual forms of *Sgt. Pepper*, but featuring stronger compositions and more rock-oriented ensemble work. The group were still pushing forward in all facets of their art, whether devising some of the greatest harmonies to be heard on any rock record (especially on "Because"), constructing a medley of songs/vignettes that covered much of side two, adding subtle touches of Moog synthesizer, or crafting furious guitar-heavy rock ("The End," "I Want You (She's So Heavy)," "Come Together"). George Harrison also blossomed into a major songwriter, contributing the buoyant "Here Comes the Sun" and the supremely melodic ballad "Something," the latter of which became the first Harrison-penned Beatles hit. Whether *Abbey Road* is the Beatles' best work is debatable, but it's certainly the most immaculately produced (with the possible exception of *Sgt. Pepper*) and most tightly constructed. *—Richie Unterberger*

In the Beginning: The Early Tapes / May 4, 1970 / Polydor ✦✦
Before beginning their recording career, the Beatles recorded a few tracks in Hamburg in 1961 as the backing group for British singer Tony Sheridan. Reissued in countless different packages around the globe after the Beatles became famous, this should in no way be considered their first album; not only were their skills rudimentary, but Sheridan takes all but one of the lead vocals on this set of fairly tame covers of popular and early rock standards. Several tracks are of interest: "Ain't She Sweet," with a lead vocal by John Lennon, was a small American hit single in 1964; the driving instrumental "Cry for a Shadow" was written by Lennon and George Harrison; and "My Bonnie," with Paul McCartney's shouts clearly audible in the background, was responsible for bringing the group to the attention of Brian Epstein. *—Richie Unterberger*

☆ **Let It Be** / May 8, 1970 / Capitol ✦✦✦✦✦
The only Beatles album to occasion negative, even hostile reviews, there are few other rock records as controversial as *Let It Be*. First off, several facts need to be explained: Although released in May 1970, this was *not* their final album, but largely recorded in early 1969, way before *Abbey Road*. Phil Spector was enlisted in early 1970 to do some post-production mixing and overdubs, but he did *not* work with the band as a unit. And, although his use of strings has generated much criticism, by and large he left the original performances to stand as is: only "The Long and Winding Road" and (to a lesser degree) "Across the Universe" and "I Me Mine" get the wall-of-sound treatment. The main problem was that the material wasn't uniformly strong, and that the Beatles themselves were in fairly lousy moods due to intergroup tension. All that said, the album is on the whole underrated, even discounting the fact that a substandard Beatles record is better than almost any other group's best work. McCartney in particular offers several gems: the gospelish "Let It Be," which has some of his best lyrics; "Get Back," one of his hardest rockers; and the melodic "The Long and Winding Road," ruined by Spector's heavy-handed overdubs. The folky "Two of Us," with John and Paul harmonizing together, was also a highlight. Most of the rest of the material, by contrast, was going through the motions to some degree, although there are some good moments of straight hard rock in "I've Got a Feeling" and "Dig a Pony." As flawed and bumpy as it is, it's an album well-worth having, as when the Beatles were in top form here, they were as good as ever. *—Richie Unterberger*

1962-1966 / Apr. 2, 1973 / Capitol ✦✦✦✦✦
Assembling a compilation of the Beatles is a difficult task, not only because they had an enormous number of hits, but also because singles didn't tell the full story; many of their album tracks were as important as the singles, if not more so. The double-album *1962-1966*, commonly called the *"Red Album,"* does the job surprisingly well, hitting most of the group's major early hits and adding important album tracks like "You've Got to Hide Your Love Away," "Drive My Car," "Norwegian Wood" and "In My Life." Naturally, there are many great songs missing from the 26-track *1962-1966*, and perhaps it would have made more sense to include the *Revolver* cuts on its companion volume, *1967-1970*, yet the *Red Album* captures the essence of the Beatles' pre-*Sgt. Pepper* records. *—Stephen Thomas Erlewine*

1967-1970 / Apr. 2, 1973 / Capitol ✦✦✦✦✦
Picking up where *1962-1966* left off, the double-album compilation *1967-1970*, commonly called the *"Blue Album,"* covers the Beatles' later records, from *Sgt. Pepper* through *Let It Be*. Like the *Red Album*, the *Blue Album* contains a mixture of hits, including singles like "Lady Madonna," "Hey Jude" and "Revolution" that were never included on an LP, plus important album tracks like "Lucy in the Sky with Diamonds," "A Day in the Life," "While My Guitar Gently Weeps" and "Come Together." Like its predecessor, *1967-1970* misses several great songs, but the compilation nevertheless does capture the essence of the Beatles' later recordings. *—Stephen Thomas Erlewine*

Live at the Hollywood Bowl / May 4, 1977 / Capitol ✦✦✦
Previously unreleased live performances culled from shows at the Hollywood Bowl in 1964 and 1965. The screaming never stops, but the group's musical talent and personal charm shine through. *—William Ruhlmann*

Live! At the Star-Club in Hamburg, Germany / Jun. 13, 1977 / Lingasong ✦✦
The historical interest of this album is considerable: the Beatles, on the precipice of fame, playing their last Hamburg club show on December 31, 1962 (contrary to the 1961 date given on some liner notes). The problem, from a latter-day perspective, was that the Beatles didn't play all that well, and, more importantly, the sound is not up to par in the least, as it was captured on a primitive portable recorder. That said, it's interesting to hear the Beatles as they were in their club days, with a set list (almost exclusively covers) of early rock & roll tunes, several of which never made their way onto any official Beatle release. Their primal energy does come through, despite the missed notes and faint vocals. The U.S. and European versions of this double album differ slightly, and the album has been reissued, in its entirety and in piecemeal excerpts, numerous times since it first appeared. *—Richie Unterberger*

☆ **Past Masters, Vol. 1** / Mar. 7, 1988 / Capitol ✦✦✦✦✦
When Capitol decided to release the original British editions of the Beatles' albums

instead of the bastardized American versions, they were left with a bit of a quandary. Since the Beatles had an enormous number of non-LP singles, some of their greatest hits—from "I Want to Hold Your Hand" through "Hey Jude"—would not be included on disc if Capitol simply served up straight reissues. They had two options: They could add the singles as bonus tracks to the appropriate CDs, or they could release a compilation of all the non-LP tracks. It should come as no surprise that they chose the latter. In fact, they took it one further, issuing two separate compilations of non-LP tracks, which is fairly appropriate since the Beatles released far more singles and EPs in the first two years of their recording career than they did in the last five. *Past Masters, Vol. 1* covers those first two years and, to be fair, there are some cuts that are unnecessary for anyone outside of the hardcore—only a handful of people will be able to spot the difference in the alternate "Love Me Do," while German versions of "I Want to Hold Your Hand" and "She Loves You" aren't even good for a chuckle. Still, the sheer number of astounding singles makes this essential, even with its faults. These 17 songs capture the exuberance of Beatlemania while confirming their talents as pop craftsmen ("This Boy," "Yes It Is") and proving that they could rock really, really hard ("I Feel Fine," "She's a Woman," the peerless "I'm Down"). Apart from the cuts that are merely rarities, this is a near-perfect compilation that captures the energy and spirit of the Beatles' early years. *—Stephen Thomas Erlewine*

☆ **Past Masters, Vol. 2** / Mar. 7, 1988 / Capitol ♦♦♦♦♦

Picking up in 1965 where *Past Masters, Vol. 1* left off, *Past Masters, Vol. 2* collects the 15 non-LP tracks that the Beatles released in the last five years of their career (not counting the singles that were released on *Magical Mystery Tour*). If *Vol. 2* is more eclectic than its predecessor, it isn't quite as thematically consistent, but it does hit greater highs with a greater frequency. Indeed, some of the greatest singles in pop history are here: "Day Tripper," "We Can Work It Out," "Paperback Writer," "Rain," "Lady Madonna," "Hey Jude," "Revolution," "Don't Let Me Down" and "The Ballad of John and Yoko." All of the aforementioned are staples in the Lennon/McCartney canon and while George Harrison's two contributions aren't as familiar, "The Inner Light" is arguably his best Indian excursion and "Old Brown Shoe" is a charmingly jaunty tune that points toward his solo career. In the middle of all this, single versions of "Get Back" and "Let It Be" appear (the former is stiffer than the LP version, the latter is better than its counterpart), along with the alternate (and superior) "Across the Universe" and the silly yet strangely irresistible "You Know My Name (Look Up the Number)." Overall, the compilation feels a little disjointed, mainly because it covers so much ground so quickly, but that takes nothing away from the quality of the music, since many of these songs rank among the best, most inventive recordings of the pop-rock era. *—Stephen Thomas Erlewine*

Live at the BBC / Dec. 1994 / Apple/Capitol ♦♦♦♦♦

From 1962 to 1965, the Beatles made 52 appearances on the BBC, recording live-in-the-studio performances of both their official releases and several dozen songs that they never issued on disc. This magnificent two-disc compilation features 56 of these tracks, including 29 covers of early rock, R&B, soul, and pop tunes that never appeared on their official releases, as well as the Lennon-McCartney original "I'll Be on My Way," which they gave in 1963 to Billy J. Kramer rather than record it themselves. These performances are nothing less than electrifying, especially the previously unavailable covers, which feature quite a few versions of classics by Chuck Berry, Little Richard, Carl Perkins, and Elvis Presley. There are also off-the-beaten-path tunes by the Everly Brothers and Buddy Holly, on down to obscurities by the Jodimars, Chan Romero (a marvelous "Hippy Hippy Shake"), Eddie Fontaine, and Ann-Margret. The greatest gem is probably their fabulous version of Arthur Alexander's "Soldier of Love," which (like several of the tracks) would have easily qualified as a highlight of their early releases if they had issued it officially. Restored from existing tapes of various quality, the sound is mostly very good and never less than listenable. Unfortunately, they weren't able to include every single rarity that the Beatles recorded for the BBC; the absence of Carl Perkins' "Lend Me Your Comb," which has circulated on bootlegs in a high-fidelity version, is especially mystifying. Minor quibbles aside, these performances, available on bootlegs for years, compose the major missing chapter in the Beatles' legacy, and it's great to have them easily obtainable in a first-rate package. *—Richie Unterberger*

Anthology 1 / Nov. 21, 1995 / Apple/Capitol ♦♦♦

The first in a series of three double-CD sets of previously unreleased and rare Beatles material, released in conjunction with the mammoth *Anthology* video documentary. This covers the late '50s to the end of 1964, mixing studio outtakes, live performances, primitive recordings from the Quarrymen/Silver Beatles days, excerpts from the famous 1962 Decca audition, the most notable 1961 Tony Sheridan-era recordings, and brief spoken bits from interviews. Although this material is undeniably of vast historical importance, it can't be placed in the same company as the Beatles' proper albums, in either cohesion or quality. While the studio outtakes (many never even heard on bootleg) are the most enticing items, these are almost exclusively alternate versions of songs they placed on their official releases (the most notable exceptions being the 1964 R&B cover "Leave My Kitten Alone," the 1962 demo "How Do You Do It," and the unimpressive 1964 Harrison original "You Know What to Do"). Sometimes the differences are quite interesting (a much more electric-oriented version of "And I Love Her," for example), but the alternates also illustrate how the group were virtually unerring in selecting the best arrangement and take of their songs for the final versions. The pre-1962 items are sometimes taken from private rehearsal tapes of primitive fidelity and are really of archival value only. One could go on at great length about the many curiosities and finds unearthed by this compilation, but for most general consumers, two observations may suffice. It does not stand up to the Beatles' fully conceived albums (even *Live at the BBC*), but the Beatles' scraps and leavings are more interesting than over 95 percent of other performers' best work. By that standard, this must be judged a worthwhile collection, especially (but not solely) for dedicated Beatles fans. *—Richie Unterberger*

Anthology 2 / Mar. 19, 1996 / Apple/Capitol ♦♦♦

As expected, the second installment of the *Anthology* series reflects the Beatles' increasing use of the studio-as-laboratory during their "middle years." Some live material from 1965 to 1966 appears on the first disc, and the second "reunion" single ("Real Love") leads off the set. But the emphasis is upon alternate takes from early 1965 to early 1968, during which time the group rapidly evolved from post-Merseybeat through folk-rock to psychedelia. As with the first volume, this is nearly always interesting but perhaps thinner on revelations than some might expect. The *Help!*-era outtakes "If You've Got Troubles" and "That Means a Lot" are on the light side but very fun, especially the latter, which Paul and the group perform much better than P.J. Proby (who covered the song shortly afterward). Some of the alternate takes are extremely different and excellent performances on their own merits: the funkier version of "I'm Looking Through You" and the less mellow arrangement of "Norwegian Wood," a wall-of-drugs reverb for "Tomorrow Never Knows," a very Byrds-like approach to "And Your Bird Can Sing" (with giggle-laden vocals), and an acoustic demo of "Fool on the Hill." The earlier, much more acoustic version of "Strawberry Fields Forever" is the most notable gem. On the other hand, much of the material differs from the official cuts in fairly minute gradations and will be of greater interest to scholars than general listeners (although discoveries like a different solo on "Penny Lane" are fascinating). The seven live tracks on disc one, from the waning days of Beatlemania, are better than many would have assumed, showing the group still capable of generating heat onstage. *—Richie Unterberger*

Anthology 3 / Oct. 29, 1996 / Apple/Capitol ♦♦♦♦

The final installment of the *Anthology* series has two discs of previously unreleased material from the *White Album* era through the group's demise in early 1970. In terms of sheer listenability, this may be the strongest volume of the three, if only because it focuses almost solely upon studio recordings, rather than mixing live concerts/broadcasts and outtakes. Also, by this time the Beatles had perfected their approach to recording, meaning that even the early/alternate versions of many of their cuts were often of outstanding quality. There's some prime stuff here: "unplugged" *White Album* demos from mid-'68, radically different versions of "While My Guitar Gently Weeps" and "Helter Skelter," a stringless "The Long and Winding Road," three beautifully sung and played Harrison solo demos from early 1969, and several songs the Beatles never released, like "All Things Must Pass," "Not Guilty," "Teddy Boy," "Come and Get It," and "Junk." Not everything here is so great that the casual consumer will be fascinated, of course. As on previous *Anthology* sets, some of these alternates are only very slightly different from the official versions; the oldies covers from the *Let It Be* era are off-the-cuff jams that aren't up to the group's usual level of brilliance. It's still a fascinating collection, both for the insight it affords us into the group's creative process at the end of their career, and for the considerable excellence of the music itself. *—Richie Unterberger*

● **The Beatles One** / Nov. 14, 2000 / Apple/Capitol ♦♦♦♦♦

Apparently, there was a gap in the Beatles' catalog, after all—all the big hits weren't on one tidy, single-disc compilation. It's not the kind of gap you'd necessarily notice—it's kind of like realizing you don't have a pair of navy blue dress socks—but it was a gap all the same, so the group released *Beatles 1* late in 2000, coinciding with the publication of their official autobiography, the puzzlingly titled *Anthology*. The idea behind this compilation is to have all the number one singles the Beatles had, either in the U.K. or U.S., on one disc, and that's pretty much what this generous 27-track collection is. It's easy, nay necessary, to quibble with a couple of the judgment calls—look, "Please Please Me" should be here instead of "From Me to You," and it's unforgivable to bypass "Strawberry Fields Forever" (kick out "Yellow Submarine" or "Eleanor Rigby")—but there's still no question that this is all great music, and there is a bit of a rush hearing all these dazzling songs follow one after another. If there's any complaint, it's that even if it's nice to have something like this, it's not really essential. There's really no reason for anyone that owns all the records to get this too—if you've lived happily without the red or blue albums, you'll live without this. But, if you give this to any six- or seven-year-old, they'll be pop fans, even fanatics, for life. And that's reason enough for it to exist. *—Stephen Thomas Erlewine*

The Beau Brummels

f. 1964, San Francisco, CA, **db.** 1968

Folk-Rock, Pop, Country-Rock

While they only had two big hits, the Beau Brummels were one of the most important and underrated American groups of the 1960s. They were the first U.S. unit of any sort to successfully respond to the British Invasion. They were arguably the first folk-rock group, even predating the Byrds, and also anticipated some key elements of the San Francisco psychedelic sound with their soaring harmonies and exuberant melodies. Before they finally reached the end of the string, they were also among the first bands to record country-rock in the late '60s. After signing to the Autumn label in 1964, they made the Top 20 right off the bat with "Laugh, Laugh," and hit the Top Ten with "Just a Little." The Beau Brummels made a couple of fine albums in 1965, dominated by strong original material and featuring the band's ringing guitars and multipart, mournful harmonies. The band was losing ground commercially though, partially because Autumn lacked promotional muscle. The label was sold in 1966 to Warner, who made the lunkheaded move of forcing the band to record an entire album of Top 40 covers—ignoring the fact that original material was one of the Brummels' primary fortes. Regrouping as a trio, the group recorded a more experimental album in 1967, *Triangle*. Their last Warner LP, *Bradley's Barn*, found the group branching into country-rock, a year or so before it became trendy. *—Richie Unterberger*

Introducing the Beau Brummels / Apr. 1965 / Sundazed ✦✦✦✦✦
A much stronger debut than the norm for the era. Ten of the 12 cuts are Ron Elliott originals, including the hits "Laugh Laugh," "Still in Love with You Baby," and "Just a Little." The hard-rocking numbers are the weakest, but "Stick Like Glue" and "I Would Be Happy" are fine Beatlesque numbers, and "They'll Make You Cry" is a first-rate moody folk-rocker. The CD reissue adds two bonus tracks, a demo of "Just a Little" and the single "Good Time Music." *—Richie Unterberger*

The Beau Brummels, Vol. 2 / Aug. 1965 / Sundazed ✦✦✦
No big hits on this album, but it's the best album by the Brummels' first lineup. The 12 original songs feature several fine Ron Elliott harmony folk-rockers that stand up well to the Byrds' material from the same era, including "I Want You," "You Tell Me Why," "Sad Little Girl," and the Byrds imitation "Don't Talk to Strangers." The CD reissue adds bonus alternate versions of "Woman" and "When It Comes to Your Love." *—Richie Unterberger*

Beau Brummels '66 / Jul. 1966 / Warner Brothers ✦✦

Triangle / Jul. 1967 / Warner Brothers ✦✦✦✦
The jewel in the Beau Brummels' crown, *Triangle* was an unexpected departure from the band's earlier hit-making formula—and demonstrated Ron Elliott's growing maturation as a songwriter. All the band's signature styles (folk, country swing, and Brit-pop) are still heard in the mix, but the tunes here assume an added aura of mysticism. Buried commercially by the likes of *Sgt. Pepper*, *Triangle* shared its premise of songs loosely united by a common theme—in this case, a ruminative dream cycle (though to call *Triangle* a concept album might be overstating the case). The exquisite "Magic Hollow," graced by Van Dyke Parks' delicate harpsichord, was surely the LP's highlight. Plucked as a single, it barely dented the charts, yet remains one of the most beautiful tunes in the entire Brummels canon. The album's first five songs—"Are You Happy," "Only Dreaming Now," "Painter of Women," "Keeper of Time," and "It Won't Get Better"—form a surprisingly coherent and cohesive whole despite marked differences. "Dreaming"'s accordion transports the listener to Paris' Montmartre, while "Painter" suggests the shifting sands of the Middle East. Elliott's lyric imagery in these tunes and a third track—"The Wolf of Velvet Fortune"—is particularly striking, and Sal Valentino's richly expressive voice elevates all three to sublime heights. Too long ignored by rock cognoscenti, *Triangle* is (all hyperbole aside) a fine album which deserves to be heard by a wider audience. Though out of print in the U.S. since its original release, import CD reissues are available in both Germany and Japan. *—Stansted Montfichet*

Bradley's Barn / Oct. 1968 / Edsel ✦✦✦✦
After taking the Beau Brummels to the pop/folk psychedelic edge, producer Lenny Waronker took the band to Nashville, literally. Possibly influenced by the Byrds *Sweetheart* experiments, the group (now down to just Sal Valentino on vocals and Ron Elliott on guitars) wedded with Nashville's finest, including guitarist Jerry Reed and drummer Kenneth A. Buttrey, both veterans of Dylan's Nashville sessions. These players were not just good musicians, but *smart* musicians, easily embellishing the Elliott/Valentino duo as if they had been playing with the two for years, not days. The resulting masterpiece, no doubt due to the awesome Brummels original songs (especially "Cherokee Girl," "Turn Around," and "Deep Water"), is a virtual tapestry in country and rock. *—Matthew Greenwald*

The Beau Brummels / Apr. 1975 / Warner Brothers ✦✦✦✦
Revisiting their country & western roots, surviving Brummels Ron Elliott and Sal Valentino joined forces with a host of ace session men at Owen Bradley's Nashville studios in 1968 and cut a clutch of tunes which included some of their finest work to date. From these sessions came "Deep Water" and the similarly constructed "Turn Around"—each a solid 24-carat gold specimen of a new musical hybrid: country-rock. Both tracks are distinguished by stellar Dobro guitar work (the instrument's distinctive twang is heard on several other cuts as well). Valentino's lush voice, alternately playful and plaintive, is on this LP at its absolute peak. Valentino's effortless readings of "Jessica" and "An Added Attraction (Come and See Me)" could charm birds out of trees, and his persuasive handling of the smoke-filled bar ballad "Love Can Fall a Long Way Down" should make a believer out of anyone who ever doubted his vocal gift. Like its predecessor, *Triangle*, *Bradley's Barn* failed to attract the attention that it so richly deserved, though many critics gave it high marks. The more accessible and mainstream of the two, *Bradley's Barn* ranks right up there with the Byrds' *Sweetheart of the Rodeo*, the International Submarine Band's *Safe at Home*, and the freshman efforts of Gene Clark, Steve Young, and the Flying Burrito Brothers as a milestone of early country-rock. Fans of the genre would do well to seek out its German or Japanese CD reissue. *—Stansted Montfichet*

From the Vaults / 1982 / Rhino ✦✦✦✦✦
A very solid collection of rare or previously unreleased material from the group's mid-'60s prime. Mostly Ron Elliott originals, they're easily up to the standard of the ones that made it onto their first two LPs, with "Gentle Wondering Ways," "She Loves Me," "She Sends Me," and "Love Is Just a Game" being standouts. Achingly tuneful folk-rock, it also includes an alternate, slower version of "Sad Little Girl," the silly dance-rock confection "The Jerk," and a few cuts that hint at the country-rock direction they would take in the late '60s. While over half of the cuts were finally issued on the *Autumn of Their Years* CD in 1994, a few of the better ones (notably "Gentle Wondering Ways," "Lonely Man," and the alternate "Sad Little Girl") were not. Perhaps they'll find their way onto the boxed set that Sundazed is planning, but if not, this is a worthwhile pickup, and one that is a more consistent and solid sampler of their rarities than the more extensive *Autumn of Their Years*. *—Richie Unterberger*

● **The Best of the Beau Brummels: Golden Archive Series** / 1987 / Rhino ✦✦✦✦✦
Probably the best (and best-sounding) anthology covering their golden years, although it lacks their brilliant, later country-based work at its best. *—Bruce Eder*

Autumn of Their Years / 1994 / Big Beat ✦✦✦
These underrated folk-rock pioneers cut a great number of unreleased outtakes/demos during their mid-'60s prime that didn't make it onto the albums they released for the tiny Autumn label during that period. Fourteen of those songs were released in the early 1980s by Rhino on the fine *From the Vaults* album. *Autumn of Their Years* reprises ten of those tunes and adds 16 previously unreleased cuts for a grand total of 26, all of which are group originals. There are a lot of fine moments here, but it's actually a bit much for all but hardcore fans. First off, the best cuts—ones like "She Sends Me," "Dream On," and "Love is Just a Game," which display their supremely haunting folk-rock melodicism and minor-key harmonies—were already available on *From the Vaults*. The 16 newly found demos aren't as good, production-wise (several are acoustic sketches) or material-wise. Earlier demos of their hits "Laugh Laugh," "Just a Little," and "Still in Love with You Baby" are interesting in comparison to the originals, but not as good. And some strong cuts from *From the Vaults* are inexplicably omitted. Of the new vault finds, the highlight is "Tomorrow Is Another Day," an acoustic ballad showcasing Sal Valentino's rich and moving vocals. *—Richie Unterberger*

San Fran Sessions / Jun. 11, 1996 / Sundazed ✦✦✦
Be clear from the git-go: this three-CD, 60-song set, which consists *solely* of rarities, demos, alternate takes, and unissued performances from 1964-66, should only be acquired by serious fans of the band. It's not the place to start, and most listeners would be better served by picking up a greatest hits disc or the original Autumn albums. If you do love the band, though, it's an excellent journey through the back waters of their early repertoire. The Brummels rarely wrote or recorded anything lousy, and this presents interesting, substantially different versions of officially released songs like "Laugh, Laugh" and "Just a Little"; and quite a few demos that have never before seen the light. The beautifully sad harmonies and glittering guitar arrangements are usually present, and the compositions—even the totally unissued ones—are usually quite strong. From a historical viewpoint, it's interesting in that it presents a lot of previously unheard Sal Valentino-penned tunes (Ron Elliott wrote most of the songs that ended up on official releases). The sound is superb, as are the liner notes. *—Richie Unterberger*

The Beautiful South

f. 1989, Hull, England
Adult Alternative Pop/Rock, Pop/Rock, Alternative Pop/Rock
Following the disbandment of the British indie-pop group the Housemartins in 1989, vocalist Paul Heaton and drummer David Hemmingway formed the Beautiful South. Where their previous group relied on jazzy guitars and witty, wry lyrics, the Beautiful South boasted a more sophisticated, jazzy pop sound, layered with keyboards, R&B-inflected female backing vocals and, occasionally, light orchestrations. The group's relaxed, catchy songs often contradicted the sarcastic, cyncial thrust of the lyrics. Nevertheless, the band's pleasant arrangements often tempered whatever bitterness there was in Heaton's lyrics, and that's part of the reason why the Beautiful South became quite popular within its native Britain during the '90s. Though the group never found a niche in America—by the middle of the decade, their records weren't even being released in the U.S.—their string of melodic jazz-pop singles made them one of the most successful, if one of the least flashy, bands in Britain. Their popularity was confirmed by the astonishing success of their 1994 singles compilation, *Carry on Up the Charts*, which became one of the biggest-selling albums in British history. *—Stephen Thomas Erlewine*

Welcome to the Beautiful South / Oct. 1989 / Go! Discs ✦✦✦✦✦
The difference between the catchy light pop that constitutes the Beautiful South's music and the bitter, pessimistic lyrics innocently sung by Paul Heaton is so great it constitutes a kind of malevolent seduction. But that's the point. Released in the U.S. in January 1990. *—William Ruhlmann*

Choke / Nov. 1990 / Go! Discs ✦✦✦
The Beautiful South's second album conceals its bitter, mean cynicism in layers of lush, jazz-tinged pop, making all of the bile go down easily. *—Stephen Thomas Erlewine*

0898 / Apr. 1992 / Go! Discs ✦✦✦
There are no big poses or walls of crunchy guitars on *0898*. Instead, the group—which includes three lead vocalists—deals in fragile melodies and harmonies, soulful but low-key instrumentation, and lyrics full of subtle social commentary and humor. In North America, where mainstream audiences have been well trained to salivate to very obvious musical bells, the Beautiful South may be too clever for its own good. At times, the group even couches itself in the guise of a smooth lounge act, rebelling against current trends by having something to say while not making a racket about it. Producer John Kelly (Peter Gabriel) has contributed an incisive and full-bodied production to *0898*, a great improvement over the rather thin sound of the group's previous *Choke*. *—Roch Parisien*

Miaow / 1994 / Go! Discs ✦✦✦
The Beautiful South expanded upon the sound of *0898* with *Miaow*, another expertly crafted set of sophisticated, jazzy pop. Even with the addition of new vocalist Jacqueline Abbot, the band has not changed much between the two albums and what is different is subtle—the arrangements are more intricate and the melodies are more graceful. Though the album is slightly uneven, much of the music is excellent, highlighted by "Prettiest Eyes" and a cover of Fred Neil's "Everybody's Talkin'." *—Stephen Thomas Erlewine*

● **Carry on Up the Charts: The Best of the Beautiful South** / Oct. 9, 1995 / Go! Discs ✦✦✦✦✦
Carry on Up the Charts: The Best of the Beautiful South was the surprise British hit of

1994, going quintuple platinum five times between its late fall release and the summer of 1995. The success was surprising, because while the band had been modestly popular, their last few albums were sliding down the charts. However, their hits collection, *Carry on Up the Charts*, flew to number one and stayed there for weeks. It's nothing more than all their singles, yet compiled together they make the most convincing case for the Beautiful South's sly, cynical sophisticated pop. *Carry on Up the Charts* was finally released in the United States in the fall of 1995. *—Stephen Thomas Erlewine*

Blue Is the Colour / Nov. 5, 1996 / Ark 21 ♦♦♦♦

"Don't marry her... fuck me." Light, dreamy pop that includes lines like this may knock the listener over. An added feature is the various ways vocal duties are shared by Jacqueline Abbot, Dave Hemingway, and Paul Heaton. Finely produced, it should be noted that the knob-twiddler here was Jon Kelly (Bob Dylan, Paul McCartney, Tori Amos, Kate Bush). Beautiful South reminds one of the blunt simplicity of some of the Ann Magnuson-sung Bongwater, but much more accessible. Dulcet harmonies with casual bar talk rewritten as poetry. "Have fun/And if you can't have fun/Have someone else's fun." The songs here transform spite and hurt into tuneful gems. "The whole place is pickled/The people are pickles for sure/And no one knows if they've done more here/Than they would do in a jar." Yes, yes, yes. Next time your significant other does you significant pain, just put *Blue Is the Colour* on for a few spins. It will be more healing than a public drunk and save you any day-after embarrassment. *—Thomas Schulte*

Quench / Oct. 1998 / Mercury ♦♦♦

In what has become a familiar pattern, *Quench*, the Beautiful South's sixth regular album release (not counting the singles compilation *Carry on Up the Charts*), entered the British charts at number one in October 1998, following the number two success of its single, "Perfect 10," while in the U.S. its release was delayed until July 1999, when it made no commercial impression at all. As usual, Paul Heaton and his comrades take a jaundiced look at the world while crooning melodically over pop, rock, and cocktail jazz tracks. The CD booklet contains only one photograph, an out-of-focus shot of a barroom, and as the album's title implies, *Quench* is awash in alcohol. Its most telling self-portrait may be "Look What I Found in My Beer," in which Heaton views his musical career as his salvation from alcoholism and self-loathing. "Look what I found in the mic," he sings, "An end to screwed-up drinking and a Paul I actually like." But he often uses metaphors to get across his viewpoint, notably on such songs as 'The Slide," "The Table," and "Window Shopping for Blinds." Singer Jacqueline Abbott serves as his foil and expands the dramatic possibilities, especially on the album-closing "Your Father and I," in which parents tell conflicting stories about a child's conception and birth, only to conclude, "Your father and I won't tell the truth." If the Beautiful South's early work mixed biting sarcasm with pop riffs, *Quench* finds the group playing in less of a pop style, while Heaton's lyrics have become more bitter and self-pitying, but no less witty. Still, American recognition continues to seem unlikely for a writer who likes to make puns involving Peter Lorre and a lorry (that's a truck to us Yankees). *—William Ruhlmann*

Painting It Red / Oct. 31, 2000 / Ark 21 ♦♦♦

The Beautiful South once again run aground with diminishing sales, bungled CD pressings, and—probably the most troubling—the reported departure of longtime vocalist Jacqueline Abbott. Still, the band had always managed to sound unflinchingly upbeat amidst bleak situations in the past, and *Painting It Red* comes off, in some ways, grinning more like an unsuspecting teenager than ever before. The band's staples of lyrical chicanery and mid-'80s inbred folk-pop are still lurking about apologizing to no one. Which might strike longtime listeners with the force of wet asparagus (what with predictably Heaton-esque lines like "Don't feel ever sorry for the dicks" or the kind of overproduced jangle this side of Orange Juice and Tears for Fears mud-wrestling for five hours, it's arguable the template has run its course), but—nevertheless—it can strike others of a band mastering their own roots. It's a challenge the album poses now and again. Single "Closer Than Most" is instantly likable, yet wouldn't be so out of step with *Welcome to the Beautiful South*. "You Can Call Me Leisure," a saucy, subtle duet rolling around on a bed of prancing pianos, is about as antagonistic to the band's discography as Menswear's "Daydreamer" is to Wire. But there's definitely something here that makes it hard to hate. This is a path much taken that still somehow promises rewards after ten years of traveling. Odd even while surrounded by new rumors of imminent breakup. If this marks the South's final statement, then so be it—at least they went out with a blast of delusional air. *—Dean Carlson*

Be-Bop Deluxe

f. 1972, England, **db.** 1978

Album Rock, Prog-Rock/Art Rock

Be-Bop Deluxe was a '70s British rock group led by guitarist Bill Nelson (born on December 18, 1948, Wakefield, Yorkshire, England) who veered between glam rock, pop, and heavy metal, with lots of demonstrations of Nelson's guitar prowess. After recording with Gentle Revolution and on his own, Nelson put together the first lineup of Be-Bop Deluxe in 1972: Ian Parkin (guitar), Robert Bryan (bass), and Nicholas Chatterton-Dew (drums). But after the release of the first album, *Axe Victim*, Nelson sacked the band. The second album, *Futurama*, featured Nelson with a rhythm section of bassist Charles Tumahai and drummer Simon Fox. Keyboard player Andrew Clark joined for the third album, *Sunburst Finish*, which contained the U.K. chart single "Ships in the Night." Be-Bop Deluxe released a fourth album, *Modern Music*; a concert recording, *Live! In the Air Age*, that became their only U.K. Top Ten hit; and a fifth studio album, *Drastic Plastic*, before Nelson folded the enterprise, briefly tried another group, Red Noise, and went solo again in 1979. Since then he has recorded prolifically, if experimentally, and handled occasional production jobs. *—William Ruhlmann*

Axe Victim / 1974 / Harvest ♦♦♦

When Be-Bop Deluxe's first album was released during the glam-rock wave in 1974, and the band (then comprising Bill Nelson and Ian Parkin on guitars, Robert Bryan on bass, and Nicholas Chatterton-Dew on drums) turned up on the back of the record cover in heavy makeup, it was viewed as being in the David Bowie mold, which certainly took in Nelson's thin but confident tenor vocals and the uptempo rock approach, and even ballads like "Adventures In A Yorkshire Landscape" that sounded a lot like Bowie's "Rock & Roll Suicide." But it was already obvious that Nelson was an unusually lyrical guitarslinger, and in fact the tunes often took a backseat to his sometimes jazzy, sometimes metallish excursions. He was, as he sang, "an axe victim," but at the same time, Be-Bop Deluxe's musical identity was uncertain. *—William Ruhlmann*

Futurama / Jul. 1975 / Harvest ♦♦

Sunburst Finish / Jan. 1976 / Harvest ♦♦♦♦♦

Adding keyboard player Andrew Clark to make Be-Bop Deluxe a quartet, Bill Nelson finally found a balance between his virtuosic guitar playing and the demands of pop songwriting. The arrangements were still busy, but the humor of Nelson's music was on display as never before, and the songs frequently were catchy. For the first time, it began to seem that the group had a future beyond serving as a foundation for Nelson's splashy guitar work, as Be-Bop Deluxe charted in the U.S. and the U.K. and even scored a Top 25 British hit with "Ships in The Night." *—William Ruhlmann*

Modern Music / Sep. 1976 / Harvest ♦♦♦

Things had changed for Be-Bop Deluxe by the time of its fourth album. The band that turned up in glam-rock regalia on its 1974 debut, *Axe Victim*, was in suit and tie on the cover of *Modern Music* in 1976. Inside, the band's transformation into a sophisticated pop group seemed complete. Arrangements were still ornate, but the songs were dominated by their highly imagistic lyrics, and as often as not, Nelson was borrowing ideas from the Beatles. It didn't quite work, despite pleasant numbers such as "Orphans of Babylon" and "Kiss of Light," perhaps because a true pop sensibility requires a gift for simplicity that Nelson has never exhibited. The album charted high in England and made the Top 100 in the U.S., but it was Be-Bop's peak, not its breakthrough. *—William Ruhlmann*

Drastic Plastic / Feb. 1978 / Harvest ♦♦♦

Guitarist/leader Bill Nelson has always had his head in a space that's defined by the 1950s World's Fair idea of the future—a world of monorails and strange machines. This is particularly evident here, with Nelson's affection for Japan competing for space with paeans to electrical communication. At times charming and even romantic, at other times outré, *Drastic Plastic* marked the end of the band and hinted at Nelson's musical experiments to come. *—Steven McDonald*

Singles A's & B's / 1981 / See For Miles ♦♦♦♦♦

A collection of eight A-sides and seven B-sides (one B-side, "Lights," was used twice, first for the withdrawn "Between the Worlds" and then for "Maid In Heaven"). This particular collection is an excellent way to get a quick introduction to Be-Bop Deluxe, the band that helped turn Bill Nelson into a British guitar hero. There's a small suggestion of glam-rock in the first single, but this was soon eschewed in favor of a proto-new wave attitude. The B-sides, by the way, are equally as interesting as the A-sides of these singles—of particular note is "Shine," which would later turn up in an extended instrumental version on *Live! In the Air Age*. *—Steven McDonald*

Raiding the Divine Archive: The Best of Be-Bop Deluxe / Aug. 1990 / Capitol ♦♦♦♦

Be-Bop Deluxe strived on the guitar manipulation of Bill Nelson and were regarded as one of the greatest art rock groups ever to form. Aside from arranging and writing most of the music and lyrics, Nelson could sculpt his guitar playing to form experimental, irregular, and unaccustomed notes and phrases, encompassing themes of the future and science fiction in many of the group's songs. *Raiding the Divine Archives* is a hearty compilation of tracks taken from the bulk of Be-Bop Deluxe's catalog. Representing their innovative debut release, *Axe Victim*, 1975's *Futurama*, and the dazzling *Drastic Plastic* album from 1978 among others, this assortment offers a defined overview of this band's incomparable and imaginative music. Nelson's creativity bursts through the seams on the weirdly entertaining "Jet Silver & the Dolls of Venus," complete with its *Barbarella*-ish entendres. "Ships in the Night," with a robust saxophone solo from Nelson's brother Ian is one of this band's best singles from 1976's *Sunburst Finish*, and tunes like "Sister Seagull" and "Life in the Air Age" are testimony to Be-Bop's intriguing musical craft. The four bonus tracks contain metaphysical musical rudiments as well, especially the nightmarish "Sleep That Burns" that deals with the concept of hell during a dream. These bonus tracks are only available on the compact disc version of this collection and are not included in album or cassette form, but they do round out a definitive and beguiling array of songs from this extraordinary band. *—Mike DeGagne*

● **Life in the Air Age** / 1997 / EMI ♦♦♦♦♦

Life in the Air Age—a play on the title of one of the band's live albums—is a double-disc set covering Be-Bop Deluxe's entire career, culling highlights from each record (although the booklet doesn't tell which track came from which album). Be-Bop Deluxe was an album-oriented band, but *Life in the Air Age* nevertheless encapsulates the group's appeal and achievements, making it useful for casual fans. *—Stephen Thomas Erlewine*

Beck (Beck Hansen)

b. Jul. 8, 1970, Los Angeles, CA

Vocals, Guitar / Experimental Rock, Alternative Dance, Indie Rock, Lo-Fi, Club/Dance, Alternative Pop/Rock, Singer/Songwriter

With his portastudio, keyboard, drum machine, and guitar, singer/songwriter Beck (born Beck Hansen) created music that celebrated the junk culture of the '90s. Beck's music drew from hip-hop, folk, experimental rock, psychedelia, pop, and rock & roll, recycling everything into a colorful, messy, and willfully diverse brand of postmodern rock, filled with warped, satiric imagery and clumsy poetry. With all of his rootless eclecticism, Beck is distinctly a product of the '90s; all of his influences were processed through television and records, not real-life experiences. But that trashy, disposable quality is what makes his music unique.

Beck came to national attention in early 1994, when his folky hip-hop single "Loser" began to receive airplay on alternative rock stations across America. "Loser" was originally released independently on a Californian label in late 1993. The single became a club hit and quickly spread to underground and alternative radio stations. Beck became the center of a major-label bidding war; he eventually signed with DGC Records. Beck released his debut album, *Mellow Gold*, in early 1994. *Mellow Gold* received rave reviews and became a gold record as "Loser" climbed into the Top Ten. Beck's contract with DGC allowed him to release records that he and the company deemed as uncommercial on indie labels. Consequently, the singer/songwriter released two new records by the summer of 1994, which were both recorded roughly around the same time as *Mellow Gold*. *Stereopathetic Soul Manure* was a noisy, more experimental album than his debut and was released on Flipside Records. *One Foot in the Grave* accentuated his folk roots and was released on K Records. Neither album sold on the level of *Mellow Gold*, but they sold respectably.

As he prepared his second album for DGC, Beck toured with Lollapalooza Five in the summer of 1995. Beck's second major-label album, *Odelay*, finally appeared in the summer of 1996; it was released to overwhelmingly positive reviews. Throughout 1996, word-of-mouth began to spread on *Odelay*, and earned Album of the Year status from most major critics' polls and, even more surprisingly, it received several Grammy Nominations, including Album of the Year. Originally slated for release on indie label Bong Load, *Mutations* instead became *Odelay*'s "unofficial" follow-up when it was released on DGC in the autumn of 1998; the soul-influenced *Midnite Vultures* followed a year later. *—Stephen Thomas Erlewine*

☆ **Mellow Gold** / Mar. 1994 / DGC ♦♦♦♦♦

From its kaleidoscopic array of junk-culture musical styles to its assured, surrealistic wordplay, Beck's debut album *Mellow Gold* is a stunner. Throughout the record, Beck plays as if there are no divisions between musical genres, freely blending rock, rap, folk, psychedelia, and country. Although his inspired sense of humor occasionally plays like he's a smirking, irony-addled hipster, his music is never kitschy, and his wordplay is constantly inspired. Since *Mellow Gold* was pieced together from home-recorded tapes, it lacks a coherent production, functioning more as a stylistic sampler: there are the stoner raps of "Loser" and "Beercan," the urban folk of "Pay No Mind (Snoozer)," the mock-industrial onslaught of "Motherf—er," the garagey "F—in With My Head," the trancy acoustic "Blackhole," and the gently sardonic folk-rock of "Nitemare Hippy Girl." It's a dizzying demonstration of musical skills, yet it's all tied together by a simple yet clever sense of songcraft and a truly original lyrical viewpoint, one that's basic yet as colorful as free verse. By blending boundaries so thoroughly and intoxicatingly, *Mellow Gold* established a new vein of alternative rock, one that was fueled by ideas instead of attitude. *—Stephen Thomas Erlewine*

Stereopathetic Soul Manure / Apr. 1994 / Flipside ♦♦

Within months of the release of *Mellow Gold*, Beck released his second album, *Stereopathetic Soul Manure*, a schizophrenic collection of lo-fi recordings from between 1988 and 1993. Much of the music on the album draws from the noisy, experimental post-punk of Sonic Youth and the dirty, primitive junk rock of Pussy Galore; his absurdist sense of humor surfaces only rarely, and only in the guise of such sophomoric cuts as "Jagermeister Pie" and "Satan Gave Me a Taco," while his sense of songcraft is inaudible. Essentially, the record was both a palate cleanser, one designed to scare away the "Loser" fans, and a bid for indie credibility, since the music on *Stereopathetic* is equally as uncompromising and as unlistenable as Sonic Youth or their many imitators at their most extreme. *—Stephen Thomas Erlewine*

One Foot in the Grave / Aug. 1994 / K ♦♦♦♦

One Foot in the Grave appeared not long after the noisy freak-out of *Stereopathetic Soulmanure*, and its quiet, folky textures couldn't be more different than its predecessor, or the genre-bending *Mellow Gold*, for that matter. Recorded before *Mellow Gold*, the record showcases Beck as a post-modern folkie, and the results are revelatory. Stripped of the intoxicating production that dominated *Mellow Gold*, Beck's songs prove to be wonderful, vibrant tunes, teeming with emotion, haunting wordplay, and simple, memorable melodies. It's alternately haunting and jubilant, and Calvin Johnson's occasional harmonies lend the record an intimate warmth. It's a gentle record, and its collection of small gems are every bit as impressive as the songs on *Mellow Gold* or its 1996 follow-up, *Odelay*. *—Stephen Thomas Erlewine*

★ **Odelay** / Jun. 18, 1996 / DGC ♦♦♦♦♦

Beck's debut, *Mellow Gold*, was a glorious sampler of different musical styles, careening from lo-fi hip-hop to folk, moving back through garage rock and arty noise. It was an impressive album, but the parts didn't necessarily stick together. The two albums that followed within months of *Mellow Gold—Stereopathetic Soul Manure* and *One Foot in the Grave*—were specialist releases that disproved the idea that Beck was simply a one-hit wonder. But *Odelay*, the much-delayed proper follow-up to *Mellow Gold*, proves the depth and scope of his talents. *Odelay* fuses the disparate strands of Beck's music—folk, country, hip-hop, rock & roll, blues, jazz, easy listening, rap, pop—into one dense sonic collage. Songs frequently morph from one genre to another, seemingly unrelated genre—bursts of noise give way to country songs with hip-hop beats, easy listening melodies transform into a weird fusion of pop, jazz, and cinematic strings; it's genre-defying music that refuses to see boundaries. All of the songs on *Odelay* are rooted in simple forms—whether it's blues ("Devil's Haircut"), country ("Lord Only Knows," "Sissyneck"), soul ("Hotwax"), folk ("Ramshackle"), or rap ("High 5 (Rock the Catskills)," "Where It's At")—but they twist the conventions of the genre. "Where It's At" is peppered with soul, jazz, funk, and rap references, while "Novacane" slams from indie rock to funk and back to white noise. With the aid of the Dust Brothers, Beck has created a dense, endlessly intriguing album overflowing with ideas. Furthermore, it's an album that completely ignores the static, nihilistic trends of the American alternative/independent underground, creating a fluid, creative, and startlingly original work. *—Stephen Thomas Erlewine*

Mutations / Nov. 3, 1998 / DGC/Bong Load ♦♦♦♦

According to party line, neither Beck nor Geffen ever intended *Mutations* to be considered as the official follow-up to *Odelay*, his Grammy-winning breakthrough. It was more like *One Foot in the Grave*, designed to be an off-kilter, subdued collection of acoustic-based songs pitched halfway between psychedelic country-blues and lo-fi folk. The presence of producer Nigel Godrich, the man who helmed Radiohead's acclaimed *OK Computer*, makes such claims dubious. Godrich is not a slick producer, but he's no Calvin Johnson, either, and *Mutations* has an appropriately clean, trippy feel. There's little question that with the blues, country, psych, bossa nova, and folk that comprise it, *Mutations* was never meant to be a commercial endeavor—there's no floor-shaker like "Where It's At," and it doesn't trade in the junk culture that brought *Odelay* to life. Recording with his touring band—marking the first time he has entered the studio with a live band—does result in a different sound, but it's not so much a departure as it is a side road that is going in the same direction. None of the songs explore new territory, but they're rich, lyrically and musically. There's an off-the-cuff wit to the songwriting, especially on "Cancelled Check" and "Bottle of Blues," and the performances are natural, relaxed, and laid-back, without ever sounding complacent. In fact, one of the nifty tricks of *Mutations* is how it sounds simple upon the first listen, then reveals more psychedelic layers upon each play. Beck is not only a startling songwriter—his best songs are simultaneously modern and timeless—he is a sharp record maker, crafting albums that sound distinct and original, no matter how much they may borrow. In its own quiet, organic way, *Mutations* confirms this as much as either *Mellow Gold* or *Odelay*. *—Stephen Thomas Erlewine*

Golden Feelings / 1999 / Sonic Enemy ♦♦♦

Before *Mellow Gold* and even before *A Western Harvest Field By Moonlight*, there was *Golden Feelings*, an extremely limited-edition, cassette-only collection of songs. Re-released in 1999 by Sonic Enemy, this 17-track collection documents Beck's first officially released, self-recorded, full-length album of four-track noodlings and documents his genius in embryo. Like *Stereopathetic Soul Manure*, *Golden Feelings* features muddy production values, an array of taped TV and music blurbs, and entertaining between-track dialogues and noises. The opening cut "The Fucked Up Blues" is a fine early example of Beck's surrealist blues; some songs, such as "Magic Station Wagon," which sounds like two broken guitars being plucked violently over and over for some sort of percussive effect, are more interesting than listenable. The folkish "No Money No Honey"—which also appeared on *Stereopathetic Soul Manure*, sung by a homeless man Beck recruited—appears here in a more developed version and features what must be one of the loudest, most distorted acoustic guitar tracks ever recorded. The primitive Velvet Underground-meets-Jon Spencer Blues Explosion garage rock of "Schmoozer," as well as the humorous folk narrative of "Heartland Feeling," are some of his strongest songs to date. Dark, haunting ballads like "Super Golden Black Sunchild," the country-blues of "Gettin' Home," and an early attempt at funk on "People Gettin' Busy" round out a very eclectic set. An early, even more distorted version of *Mellow Gold*'s "Mutherfukka" is also included. Overall, *Golden Feelings* is an extremely interesting, entertaining, and humorous document that proves that from the start Beck had his heart set on making experimentation his only gimmick. *—Matt Fink*

Midnite Vultures / Nov. 16, 1999 / DGC ♦♦♦

By calling the muted psychedelic folk-rock, blues, and tropicalia of *Mutations* a stopgap, Beck set expectations for *Midnight Vultures* unreasonably high. Ironically, *Midnite Vultures* doesn't feel like a sequel to *Odelay*—it's a genre exercise, like *Mutations*. This time, Beck delves into soul, funk, and hip-hop, touching on everything from Stax/Volt to No Limit but using Prince as his home base. He's eschewed samples, more or less, but not the aesthetic. Even when a song is reminiscent of a particular style, it's assembled in strange, exciting ways. As it kicks off with "Sexx Laws," it's hard not to get caught up in the rush, and "Nicotine & Gravy" carries on the vibe expertly, as does the party jam "Mixed Bizness" and the full-on electro workout "Get Real Paid," an intoxicating number that sounds like a *Black Album* reject. So far, so good—the songs are tight, catchy, and memorable, the production dense. Then comes "Hollywood Freaks." The self-conscious gangsta goof is singularly irritating, not least because of Beck's affected voice. It's the first on *Midnite Vultures* to feel like a parody, and it's such an awkward, misguided shift in tone that it colors the rest of the album. Tributes now sound like send-ups, allusions that once seemed affectionate feel snide, and the whole thing comes off as a little jive. Musically, *Midnite Vultures* is filled with wonderful little quirks, but these are undercut by the sneaking suspicion that for all the ingenuity, it's just a hipster joke. Humor has always been a big part of Beck's music, but it was gloriously absurd, never elitist. Here, it's delivered with a smug smirk, undercutting whatever joy the music generates. *—Stephen Thomas Erlewine*

B Side Collection: Stray Blues / May 9, 2000 / Geffen International ♦♦♦♦

Beck's Japanese eight-song B-sides collection *Stray Blues* is a short but sweet reminder of all the different sounds and styles he's capable of embodying and combining. It's especially refreshing after the somewhat forced, funk-soul-brotha vibe of *Midnite Vultures* to hear reflective, stoner-folk epics like "Totally Confused" (which features three-quarters of That Dog on violin and backing vocals), "Brother," and "Feather in Your Cap" next to noisy workouts like "Lemonade," the deadpan hipster-hop of "Clock," and a surprisingly straight mariachi version of "Burro." His groovy, *Odelay*-style pastiche is in full effect on the '60s pop send-up "Electric Music and the Summer People" and the rambling, ultra-psychedelic cover of Skip Spence's "Halo of Gold," which originally appeared on the Spence tribute *More Oar*. Impressively, most of these songs were recorded years apart from each other and with different musicians, but *Stray Blues* holds together nearly as well as any of Beck's proper albums, proving that he's at his best when he's at his most eclectic. The album's Japanese-only release (and corresponding priceyness) is frustrating because *Stray Blues* deserves to be heard by more people than just die-hard fans (who may already own most of this material anyway). Not only is this collection a reminder of Beck's impressive diversity but of how necessary a domestic B-sides collection is to his discography. *—Heather Phares*

Jeff Beck

b. Jun. 24, 1944, Wallington, Surrey, England

Leader, Guitar (Electric), Guitar, Bass / Album Rock, Guitar Virtuoso, British Blues, Fusion, Hard Rock, Blues-Rock, Rock & Roll

While he was as innovative as Jimmy Page, as tasteful as Eric Clapton, and nearly as visionary as Jimi Hendrix, Jeff Beck never achieved the same commercial success as any of his contemporaries, primarily because of the haphazard way he approached his career. After Rod Stewart left the Jeff Beck Group, Beck never worked with a charismatic lead singer who could have helped sell his music to a wide audience. Furthermore, he was simply too idiosyncratic, moving from heavy metal to jazz-fusion within a blink of an eye. All the while, Beck retained the respect of fellow guitarists, who found his reclusiveness all the more alluring.

Jeff Beck began his musical career as the Yardbirds' lead guitarist, following the departure of Eric Clapton. He stayed with the band for nearly two years, then formed the Jeff Beck Group in 1967 with a lineup including vocalist Rod Stewart and bassist Ron Wood. With their crushingly loud reworkings of blues songs and vocal/guitar interplay, 1968's *Truth* and 1969's *Beck-Ola* became early templates for heavy metal. After Stewart and Wood left to join the Faces in 1970, Beck recorded two more albums with a new version of the group before releasing a lone LP as the head of a power trio including former Vanilla Fudge members Tim Bogert (bass) and Carmine Appice (drums). He moved from hard rock to jazz-rock with 1975's *Blow by Blow* and 1976's *Wired*, but recorded only three studio albums during the next 15 years. (One of which, the slick 1985 LP *Flash*, featured Beck's only hit single, "People Get Ready.") In 1993, he recorded the Gene Vincent tribute *Crazy Legs*, but then remained quiet for over five years before resurfacing in 1999 with *Who Else!* *—Stephen Thomas Erlewine*

☆ **Truth** / Aug. 1968 / Epic ✦✦✦✦✦

Despite being the premiere of heavy metal, Jeff Beck's *Truth* has never quite carried its reputation the way the early albums by Led Zeppelin did, or even Cream's two most popular LPs, mostly as a result of the erratic nature of the guitarist's subsequent work. Time has muted some of its daring, radical nature, elements of which were appropriated by practically every metal band (and most arena rock bands) that followed. *Truth* was almost as groundbreaking and influential a record as the first Beatles, Rolling Stones, or Who albums. Its attributes weren't all new—Cream and Jimi Hendrix had been moving in similar directions—but the combination was: the wailing, heart-stoppingly dramatic vocalizing by Rod Stewart, the thunderous rhythm section of Ron Wood's bass and Mickey Waller's drums, and Beck's blistering lead guitar, which sounds like his amp is turned up to 13 and ready to short out. Beck opens the proceedings in a strikingly bold manner, using his old Yardbirds hit "Shapes of Things" as a jumping-off point, deliberately rebuilding the song from the ground up so it sounds closer to Howlin' Wolf. There are lots of unexpected moments on this record: a bone-pounding version of Willie Dixon's "You Shook Me"; a version of Jerome Kern's "Ol' Man River" done as a slow electric blues; a brief plunge into folk territory with a solo acoustic guitar version of "Greensleeves" (which was intended as filler but audiences loved); the progressive blues of "Beck's Bolero"; the extended live "Blues Deluxe"; and "I Ain't Superstitious," a blazing reworking of another Willie Dixon song. It was a triumph—a number 15 album in America, astoundingly good for a band that had been utterly unknown in the U.S. just six months earlier—and a very improbable success. *—Bruce Eder*

Beck-Ola / Jun. 1969 / Epic ✦✦✦✦✦

When it was originally released in June 1969, *Beck-Ola*, the Jeff Beck Group's second album, featured a famous sleeve note on its back cover: "Today, with all the hard competition in the music business, it's almost impossible to come up with anything totally original. So we haven't. However, this disc was made with the accent on heavy music. So sit back and listen and try and decide if you can find a small place in your heads for it." Beck was reacting to the success of peers and competitors like Cream and Led Zeppelin here, bands that had been all over the charts with a hard rock sound soon to be dubbed heavy metal, and indeed, his sound employs much the same brand of "heavy music" as theirs, with deliberate rhythms anchoring the beat, over which the guitar solos fiercely and the lead singer emotes. But he was also preparing listeners for the weakness of the material on an album that sounds somewhat thrown together. Two songs are rehauls of Elvis Presley standards ("All Shook Up" and "Jailhouse Rock") and one is an instrumental interlude contributed by pianist Nicky Hopkins, promoted from sideman to group member, with the rest being band-written songs that serve basically as platforms for Beck's improvisations. But that doesn't detract from the album's overall quality, due both to the guitar work and the distinctive vocals of Rod Stewart, and *Beck-Ola* easily could have been the album to establish the Jeff Beck Group as the equal of the other heavy bands of the day. Unfortunately, a series of misfortunes occurred. Beck canceled out of a scheduled appearance at Woodstock; he was in a car accident that sidelined him for over a year; and Stewart and bass player Ron Wood decamped to join Faces, breaking up the group. Nevertheless, *Beck-Ola* stands as a prime example of late-'60s British blues-rock and one of Beck's best records. [Epic Records remastered the album and reissued it on CD on July 4, 2000.] *—William Ruhlmann*

Rough and Ready / Oct. 1971 / Epic ✦✦✦

Recouping after a car crash and faced with the loss of Rod Stewart and Ron Wood, Jeff Beck redefined what the Jeff Beck Group was about, deciding to tone down the bluesy bombast, adding keyboardist Max Middleton for a jazz edge, then having Bob Tench sing to give it an overblown early-'70s AOR edge. As expected, these two sides are in conflict and Tench can be a little overbearing, but there are moments here that bring out the best in Beck. Namely, these are the times when the group ventures into extended, funk-inflected, reflective jazzy instrumental sections. These are the moments that point the way toward the success of *Blow by Blow*, yet this remains an unabashed rock record of its time, and it falls prey to many of its era's excesses, particularly lack of focus. Still, there are moments that are as fine as anything Beck played here. *—Stephen Thomas Erlewine*

Jeff Beck Group / Apr. 1972 / Epic ✦✦✦

Continuing with the same group lineup as on *Rough and Ready*, *Jeff Beck Group* was slagged off by critics for Steve Cropper's admittedly lazy production. However, several of the songs hold up masterfully, including the skronky "Ice Cream Cakes," the superlative redo of Don Nix's "Going Down," and the beautifully sad and wistful instrumental, "Definitely Maybe." Beware of early, poor-sounding versions. *—Tom Graves*

Blow by Blow / Mar. 1975 / Epic ✦✦✦✦✦

When Jeff Beck announced that he was working on an all-instrumental album, few but his legion of guitar fans could have predicted the far-reaching impact of this pivotal jazz-rock fusion album. Teamed with the Beatles' ex-producer George Martin, Beck single-handedly created a new subtext for rock & roll. With his virtuosity and taste at an all-time peak, Beck let loose with such unforgettable tracks as the Roy Buchanan-inspired "Cause We've Ended as Lovers" and the percolating "Freeway Jam." This is one of rock's great instrumental works. *—Tom Graves*

Wired / May 1976 / Epic ✦✦✦✦✦

Nearly *Blow by Blow*'s equal, although Beck doesn't venture any further musically. Charles Mingus' "Goodbye Pork Pie Hat" is worth the price alone. [Available on Mobile Fidelity's Ultradisc] *—Tom Graves*

Jeff Beck with the Jan Hammer Group Live / Mar. 1977 / Epic ✦✦

There & Back / Jun. 1980 / Epic ✦✦✦

Jeff Beck's first new studio album in four years found him moving from old keyboard partner Jan Hammer (three tracks) to new one Tony Hymas (five), which turned out to be the difference between competition and support. Hence, the second side of this instrumental album is more engaging and less of a funk-fusion extravaganza than most of the first. If it were anybody else, you'd say that this was a transitional album, but this was the only studio album Beck released between 1976 and 1985, which makes it more like an unexpected Christmas letter from an old friend: "Everything's fine, still playing guitar." *—William Ruhlmann*

Flash / Jul. 1985 / Epic ✦✦✦

Produced by Nile Rodgers and Arthur Baker, *Flash* is Beck's surprisingly successful stab at a pop album, featuring a fine performance with Rod Stewart on "People Get Ready." *—Stephen Thomas Erlewine*

Jeff Beck's Guitar Shop / Oct. 1989 / Epic ✦✦✦✦

"Guitar Shop" represents guitar hero Jeff Beck's return to the scene following his 1985 Pop/Rock-based recording, *Flash* an outing that featured his one time lead vocalist, Rod Stewart. Essentially, this 1989 release provides Beck's ardent admirers with a power packed outing, brimming with memorable melodies, drummer Terry Bozzio's often blistering rock drumming, and keyboardist Tony Hymas' effective synth textures. Here, Beck surges onward in altogether stunning fashion via his quirky lead lines, sweet-tempered slide guitar work, disfigured extended notes, and deterministic mode of execution. With "Behind The Veil," the band delves into a reggae groove, featuring Beck's lower register thematic statements and well-placed notes. Otherwise, the ensemble tackles the blues and hard-rock motifs amid Beck's crunching chord clusters, animated lines, and soaring heavenward soloing on the lovely and somewhat ethereal ballad titled "Two Rivers." Simply put, this is a wonderfully produced effort and a significant entry into the artist's extensive recorded legacy. *—Glenn Astarita*

Beckology / Nov. 19, 1991 / Epic/Legacy ✦✦✦✦✦

Jeff Beck is a genius, arguably the greatest rock guitarist of his generation (and, yes, that includes Hendrix), but never has such a gifted musician had such a spotty discography. Beck did some of his best work on his solo albums, yet he only cut a few terrific albums, with the rest of the albums being remarkably uneven. Often, he had inspired work as a sideman or as part of a band, such as the Yardbirds. This means that even the dedicated fans have had to sort through a lot of dreck, not to mention the casual fans that wanted a way to explore his vast, at times, confusing discography. The triple-disc box set *Beckology* performs its duty exceedingly well, drawing a history from his earliest recordings with his first band, the Tridents, right up to 1989's *Jeff Beck's Guitar Shop*. Some great moments are missing (there always are on a box), but it's impossible to argue with what's here, which not only offers everything essential he recorded, but winds up summarizing his career brilliantly. This is the one necessary Beck album, the one that makes the case that he is indeed a genius. *—Stephen Thomas Erlewine*

Frankie's House / Jan. 5, 1992 / Epic ✦✦

Crazy Legs / Jun. 29, 1993 / Epic ✦✦

● **The Best of Beck [Epic]** / Aug. 15, 1995 / Epic ✦✦✦✦✦
Basically this record exists because the record company wanted to have some product on the shelf while Beck was touring. The 14 tracks do contain some of his most often-played (by radio, at any rate) recordings, including "Shapes of Things," "Plynth," and "Beck's Bolero" from the original Jeff Beck Group days in the late '60s, and the vocoder showcase "She's a Woman" and fusion landmark "Freeway Jam" from *Blow by Blow*. It may do for casual listeners who only want one Beck CD, although more serious fans would be better off with the *Beckology* box. *—Richie Unterberger*

Who Else! / Mar. 16, 1999 / Epic ✦✦✦✦
Jeff Beck has never shied away from following trends, at least as far as the musical styles he uses to back up his signature guitar sound. Back in 1969, in a sleeve note on *Beck-Ola*, he noted that he hadn't come up with "anything totally original," and instead made an album "with the accent on heavy music" at a time when the "heavy music" of the Jimi Hendrix Experience and Led Zeppelin was all the rage. In 1975, at the height of the jazz fusion movement, he made a jazz fusion album, and a good one, too. In both cases, however, the fashionable genres only provided a contemporary-sounding context in which his playing could flourish. If anyone has ever needed to be inspired to work, it's this recluse. So on his first regular studio album of new material in ten years, Beck, on at least a few tracks, solos over heavily percussive techno tracks reminiscent of Prodigy. But whether he's piercing such a rhythmic wall, rearranging the blues on the live "Blast from the East," or floating over an ambient soundscape on "Angel (Footsteps)," it's the same old Beck, with his stinging and sustained single-note melodies, his harmonics, his contrasting tones, his drive. And the man who played "Greensleeves" straight on *Truth* in 1968 is the same one who is faithful to the Irish air "Declan" here. Older fans who haven't been spending time at raves in recent years may want to program their CDs to avoid the electronica, but they should at least give those tunes a listen—are they any heavier than the "heavy music" of 1969? *—William Ruhlmann*

You Had It Coming / Feb. 6, 2001 / Sony ✦✦✦
Jeff Beck returns two years after the ten-years-in-the-making *Who Else?*, and *You Had It Coming* isn't surprising just for its rapidity, but for its music. From the moment the electronicized, post-rave beats of "Earthquake" kick off the record, it's clear that Beck isn't content to stay in place—he's trying to adapt to the modern world. To a certain extent, this isn't an entirely new phenomenon, since each of his records is clearly, inextricably of its time, from the crunching metal of *Truth* through the breezy jazz fusion of *Blow by Blow*, to the modernized album rock of *Guitar Shop*. This is just another side of that, as Beck works with electronic music, both noisy and new age introspective. It's a bit clever, actually, since Beck's playing has always been otherworldly, dipping, bending, and sounding like anything other than a normal guitar. The problem is, when he's surrounded by lockstep, processed beats and gurgling synths, his guitar doesn't leap to the forefront and capture attention the way it does on his best recordings. Still, there's something to be said for the effort, because even if it doesn't sound like a Beck record, it isn't a bad record, and it's certainly a helluva lot more successful than Clapton's similar forays into these waters. Besides, knowing that he knocked this out so quickly makes it a little endearing. *—Stephen Thomas Erlewine*

Best of Jeff Beck [Columbia Import] / Columbia ✦✦

The Bee Gees

f. 1958, Brisbane, Australia
Psychedelic Pop, Pop/Rock, Soft Rock, Adult Contemporary, Disco
No popular music act of the 1960s, 1970s, 1980s, and 1990s experienced more ups and downs in their popularity than the Bee Gees, or drew more of a varied audience. Beginning in the mid-to-late '60s as a kind of Beatles-lite ensemble, Barry Gibb and his fraternal twin brothers Robin and Maurice quickly developed as songwriters in their own right and perfected a strange mix of progressive-pop music. "New York Mining Disaster 1941," released in 1967, made the Top 20 in England and America, and established the pattern of the group's work for the next several years. "Massachusetts" was a chart-topper in England and, after a temporary break-up, 1970's "Lonely Days" became the group's first number one hit in America. Then, after hitting a trough in their popularity in the early '70s, the Bee Gees reinvented themselves with a heavily Americanized, R&B-flavored sound that emphasized high harmonies and funk rhythms. "Jive Talkin'" became their second American number one in 1975, and two years later, the group's soundtrack of a forthcoming movie called *Saturday Night Fever* led to three chart-topping hits: "Stayin' Alive," "How Deep Is Your Love," and "Night Fever." It didn't last, nor did the Bee Gees' second wave of success. The group may have helped contribute to the end of the party with their own excesses, in particular their contribution to a multi-million dollar film called *Sergeant Pepper's Lonely Hearts Club Band*, "inspired" (if that's the word) by the Beatles' album and songs. The youngest Gibb brother, Andy Gibb, had emerged as a star in his own right late in the 1970s and he fell even harder when the decade ended, eventually losing his life in 1988 at the end of a downward personal spiral. The Bee Gees were virtually invisible for most of the mid-'80s as recording artists, though 1987's *ESP* received a good reception around the world and the title track of 1989's *One* even generated a Top Ten U.S. single. Their induction into the Rock & Roll Hall of Fame in 1997 led to the release of *Still Waters*, and in 1998, they issued the second live album in their history, cut at their first concert appearance in ten years. *—Bruce Eder*

Bee Gees 1st / Jul. 1967 / Polydor ✦✦✦
The debut long-player by the Bee Gees may shock anyone who only remembers them for their mid- to late-'70s disco mega-hits, or their quirky early-'70s romantic balladry. Up until 1966, they'd shown a penchant for melodic songs and rich, high harmonies, in the process becoming Australia's answer to the Everly Brothers. When the brothers arrived in London late in 1966, however, they proved quick studies in absorbing and assimilating progressive pop and rock sounds around them. In one fell swoop, they became competitors to the likes of veteran rock bands such as the Hollies and the Tremeloes, and their debut long-player is more of a rock album than the group usually got credit for generating. Parts of it do sound very much like the Beatles circa *Revolver*, but there was far more to their sound than that. The three hits off of *Bee Gees 1st*, "To Love Somebody," "New York Mining Disaster 1941" and "Holiday," were gorgeous but relatively somber, thus giving *Bee Gees 1st* a melancholy cast, but much of the rest is relatively upbeat psychedelic pop. "In My Own Time" may echo elements of "Dr. Robert" and "Taxman," but it's difficult to dislike a song with such delicious rhythm guitars and a great beat, coupled to the trio's soaring harmonies; "Every Christian Lion Hearted Man Will Show You" was closer in spirit to the Moody Blues of this era, opening with a Gregorian chant backed by a Mellotron, before breaking into a strangely spaced-out, psychedelic main song body. Robin Gibb's lead vocals veered toward the melodramatic and poignant, and the orchestra did dress up some of the songs a little sweetly, yet overall the group presented themselves as a proficient rock ensemble who'd filled their debut album with a full set of solid, refreshingly original songs. *—Bruce Eder*

Horizontal / Jan. 1968 / Polydor ✦✦✦
The group's second album, cut late in 1967 amid their first major British success, is less focused than their first, but also presents a more majestic sound than its predecessor. The opening track, "World," is a poignant, even somber yet gorgeous ballad filled with clever lyrics, and highlighted by a quavering Mellotron accompaniment, a very close grand piano sound (anticipating elements of the *Odessa* album), and twangy fuzz-tone guitar. "And the Sun Will Shine" is an even more serious, regretful ballad that is bearable because it is also prettier than "World." The enigmatically titled "Lemons Never Forget" breaks up the mood with a harder rocking sound, just the group without any orchestra, dominated by a pounding piano and volume-pedal guitar. The most interesting aspect of "Really and Sincerely"—a song that descends into an even more emotionally melodramatic mood than "And the Sun Will Shine"—is its opening, which contains a musical phrase that seems to anticipate the group's disco-era "Nights on Broadway." "Birdie Told Me" is another tale of lost love that offers the variety of some leaner and tasteful electric guitar accompaniment. Side two of the original LP was more upbeat, opening with the group's catchy chart-topping British hit, "Massachusetts," followed by the cheerful "Harry Braff." "The Earnest of Being George" and "The Change Is Made" are attempts at a harder rock sound, featuring heavy guitar on both and an attempt at bluesy feel on the latter, while the title track is a trippy psychedelic number that closes the album on an upbeat note. *—Bruce Eder*

Idea / Aug. 1968 / Polydor ✦✦✦
The Bee Gees' third album is something of a departure, with more of a rocking sound and with the orchestra (apart from a few well-placed harp arpeggios) somewhat less prominent in the sound mix than on their first two LPs. The two hits, "I've Gotta Get a Message to You" and "I Started a Joke," are very much of a piece with their earlier work, but on "Kitty Can," "Indian Gin and Whisky Dry," and "Such a Shame" (the latter written by the group's then lead guitarist, Vince Melouney), among other cuts, they sound much more like a working band with a cohesive group sound, rather than a harmony vocal group with accompaniment. Their writing still has a tendency toward the dramatic and the melodramatic, which would manifest itself prominently again on their next album, *Odessa*, six months later, but here the group seemed to be trying for a somewhat less moody, dark-toned overall sound, and some less surreal lyrical conceits, though "Kilburn Towers" (despite some pop-jazz inflections) and "Swan Song," as well as "I Started a Joke," retain elements of fantasy and profundity. *—Bruce Eder*

Odessa / Jan. 1969 / Polydor ✦✦✦✦✦
The group members may disagree for personal reasons, but *Odessa* is easily the best and most enduring Bee Gees album of the 1960s. It was also their most improbable success, owing to the conflicts behind its making. The record started out as a concept album, to be called "Masterpeace" and then "The American Opera," but musical differences between Barry Gibb and Robin Gibb that would split the trio in two also forced the abandonment of the underlying concept. Instead, it became a double LP—largely at the behest of their manager and the record labels; oddly enough, given that the group didn't plan on doing something that ambitious, *Odessa* is one of perhaps three double albums of the entire decade (the others being *Blonde on Blonde* and *The Beatles*) that don't seem stretched, and the group's most densely orchestrated album as well. Yet, amid the progressive rock sounds of the title track and ethereal ballads such as "Melody Fair" and "Lamplight" were country-flavored tunes like "Marlery Purt Drive" and the vaguely Dylan-esque bluegrass number "Give Your Best," delicate pop ballads like "First of May," and strange, off-beat rock numbers like "Edison" and "Whisper Whisper," interspersed with three heavily orchestrated instrumentals. The myriad sounds and textures made *Odessa* the most complex and challenging album in the group's history, and if one accepts the notion of the Bee Gees as successors to the Beatles, then *Odessa* was arguably their *Sgt. Pepper* album. Ironically, the making of *Odessa* was to herald a split between the Gibb brothers that would leave the group sidelined for most of the next 18 months, and was the last to be heard from them as a trio for two years. *—Bruce Eder*

★ **The Best of the Bee Gees, Vol. 1** / Jun. 1969 / Polydor ✦✦✦✦✦
If anyone needs conclusive proof that the brothers Gibb weren't always the chest-medallion-flashing kings of mainstream disco or, since about 1980 on, meaningless AOR washouts, the nearly 40-minute collection of the Bee Gees' earliest hits will suffice in spades. At their (perhaps, in hindsight) surprising best, the threesome, along with capable

if generally unremarkable rhythm section members Melouney and Colin Peterson, created a slew of tender, affecting, and quite lovely hits. While the Stones/proto-metal crowd of the time probably thought them unbearably wimpy, their songwriting acumen, combined with their harmonies, fine production by Robert Stigwood, and ace orchestral/band arrangements by Bill Shephard, holds up astonishingly well. For all that the band clearly was often following the lead of the more elaborate Beatles songs of the same time—consider the watery piano line opening "Words" as one example of many—the Bee Gees didn't so much ape as they did come up with their own flavor. Considering that everyone from Catherine ("Every Christian Lion Hearted Man Will Show You") and Jimmy Somerville ("To Love Somebody") to Low ("I Started a Joke") and Jose Feliciano ("I've Gotta Get a Message to You") has covered something from this collection is testimony to the songs' continuing influence. Other times the connections to the future are subtler but still present—"I Can't See Nobody," sonically and lyrically, has the same deep blue/string-backed feeling as Verve's "History." Sometimes the line between emotion and deep schmaltz is pretty fine, admittedly. However, when Robin's lead vocal on "I Started a Joke" hits the high notes while his brothers add soft backup as the music swells, it's just one example of many why the Bee Gees deserved their long overdue induction into the Rock & Roll Hall of Fame. *—Ned Raggett*

Cucumber Castle / Apr. 1970 / Polydor ♦♦♦

An overlooked work in the Brothers Gibb catalog, *Cucumber Castle* is an excellent album that plays to the Bee Gees' strengths of melody, arrangement, and craftsmanship. Though at times one may miss the distinctive trembling vocals of Robin Gibb (the brothers had split up at this point), Barry and Maurice carry on with 12 cuts that continue in the tradition of their distinctive pop sound. Orchestral arrangements and Mellotrons abound, and the sound tends toward full productions, especially in "Then You Left Me" and "I Lay Down and Die." One can also hear country influences ("Sweetheart"), gospel ("Bury Me Down by the River"), and light jazz ("My Thing"). What sets this album above others is that there is not a bad cut on the album, and Barry's vocals are particularly strong and heartfelt. Although most of the cuts deal with the usual subject of love and particularly love lost, superb eye for detail in the arrangements of the songs give them added life. Adding a few songs with classic singalong melodies ("Sweetheart" and "Don't Forget to Remember") certainly doesn't hurt the cause. All in all, this is a fine album that cements the Brothers Gibb's reputation as superior pop songwriters and craftsmen. *—Michael I. Ofjord*

2 Years On / Jan. 1971 / Polydor ♦♦♦♦

The Bee Gees split apart in the wake of a dispute regarding the single to be released from their album *Odessa*, spent a year with Barry and Maurice Gibb recording together (and doing a television special) while Robin Gibb cut music on his own, and fighting a lawsuit in which their ex-drummer tried to claim the name "the Bee Gees." Finally, they regrouped with *2 Years On* and surprised everyone with their biggest selling single to date, "Lonely Days," and a surprisingly hard-edged accompanying album, on which the supposed Beatles influences of their earlier days were pushed aside (it also didn't hurt that the Beatles were now history). The music is somewhat less fey and more progressive here, and at times they sound like a lighter-weight version of the Moody Blues of the same era, with sharper vocals. The surprises on this album, apart from the overall tone and quality, include the sprightly title track, which was one of the first Bee Gees songs to feature surreal lyrics that weren't downbeat, and "Back Home," with the loudest guitar ever heard on a Bee Gees record. The quality of the recording itself was also improved over their earlier releases, with a much wider range and less compression, and between that and the song selection, the Bee Gees suddenly found themselves right back in the thick of popular music, and as close to the cutting edge of pop/rock as they'd ever been. *—Bruce Eder*

Trafalgar / Sep. 1971 / Polydor ♦♦♦♦

The Bee Gees had entered the early '70s with a roaring success in the guise of "Lonely Days" and its accompanying album, which established their sound as a softer pop variant on the Moody Blues' brand of progressive rock. *Trafalgar*, which followed, carried the process further on what was their longest single LP release, clocking in at 47 minutes. The music all sounded meaningful, much of it displaying the same kind of faux-grandeur that the Moody Blues affected on their music of this era, the core group (playing pretty hard) accompanied by either Mellotron-generated orchestra or the real thing, with the group's soaring harmonies and Robin Gibb's quavaring lead vocals all over the place. As with *2 Years On*'s "Man for All Seasons," there was also one title ("Lion in Winter," featuring a startling falsetto performance) lifted from a recently popular film and play having to do with English history. It was all very beautifully produced and, propelled into record-store racks by the presence of "How Can You Mend a Broken Heart," the group's first No. 1 single, *Trafalgar* shipped very well initially. Nothing else on the record was remotely as memorable as the single, however, and its sales were limited. *Trafalgar* was also the handsomest and most elaborately designed of their albums, its cover reprinting Pocock's painting "The Battle of Trafalgar" and the interior gatefold containing a shot of the brothers enacting the scene of the death of Lord Nelson. It all imparted the sense of a concept album, though nothing in the music said so, except perhaps the finale, "Walking Back to Waterloo." Despite the hit single, the album showed the limits of the Bee Gees' talents as songwriters and of their appeal as album artists. *—Bruce Eder*

To Whom It May Concern / 1972 / Polydor ♦♦♦

The next to last of the Bee Gee's "old-style" albums is one of their most fully realized works, with pleasing and memorable songs from beginning to end, and for a change this time, it's the single ("Run to Me"), rather than the surrounding tracks, that suffers from predictability. Another in a string of haunting ballads, it has a more plaintive, whining quality, and less of an ethereal feel than its predecessor, "How Can You Mend a Broken Heart"—not that "Run to Me" isn't a lovely song, but it was possible to tire of hearing it on the radio faster than their prior singles. By contrast, the album's other tracks are all intensely melodic and varied enough in tempo and texture to make for very satisfying listening, "You Know It's for You" calling to mind Paul McCartney at his most accessible; the group plunges into relatively hard rock, with a heavy guitar sound, on "Bad Bad Dreams," and a country-ish sound on "Road to Alaska," before returning to a kind of post-psychedelic mode in "Sweet Song of Summer." The Bee Gees were pushing their credibility as a cohesive band more than ever, emphasizing Barry Gibb and Maurice Gibb's contributions to their instrumental sound and retaining guitarist Alan Kendall, who had debuted with them on the *Trafalgar* album and who would play with them for the next two decades. As it turned out, *To Whom It May Concern* was also the commercial swan song for the trio in this phase of their career, and the last of their albums to be released by Atlantic Records in the United States, something of an artistic peak before a period of massive change in their sound and future. *—Bruce Eder*

Life in a Tin Can / Jan. 1973 / Polydor ♦♦

The Bee Gees moved their base of operations from England to America, specifically to Los Angeles, in the early '70s, and *Life in a Tin Can* was the result of their first recording sessions out there. This was the album that heralded the group's collapsing fortunes. It seemed to break no new ground for the group, made up of tuneful if not always memorable material. Even some of the better tunes, like "Living in Chicago," ran too long for their own good, and many fans felt like they'd begun to have heard it all before. And for the first time in a long time, the Bee Gees' knack for devising hit singles to drive an album's sales failed them—"Saw a New Morning" was just not exciting or particularly memorable and was overlooked by most listeners despite the group's hitting the talk-show circuit very heavily promoting it, and the rest of the album lacked the sense of emotional urgency that had characterized their best work up to this time. *—Bruce Eder*

The Best of the Bee Gees, Vol. 2 / Jul. 1973 / Polydor ♦♦♦♦♦

This volume spans from 1970-1973. Although the hits aren't as abundant as *The Best of the Bee Gees, Vol. 1*, there is still plenty of strong material on this edition. The hits include "Run to Me," "Lonely Days," and "How Can You Mend A Broken Heart," but some of the best songs are among the non-hits, including "Morning Of My Life," "Man for All Seasons," and "Let There Be Love." Prior to the disco years, the Bee Gees were excellent songwriters, composing some of the finest introspective and soul searching songs of the late sixties and early seventies. As this volume features material from the brothers' brief breakup, there is also some weaker material, such as the reggae-tinged "I.O.I.O," the country ballad "Don't Forget To Remember," and Robin Gibb's solo single "Saved by the Bell," which was a huge hit in Britain. However, despite these mediocre tracks, the album is still a worthwhile addition to a collection of some of the best pop music of its era. *—Jim Powers*

Mr. Natural / May 1974 / Polydor ♦♦♦♦

Their previous album having scarcely made a ripple, and now hitless for two years, the Bee Gees went for a new sound in the hands of producer Arif Mardin. The result was *Mr. Natural*, the sultriest and most soulful record they had ever delivered up to that time. Shedding their pop sensibilities here and singing in a freer, more soulful idiom (with a strong Philadelphia soul influence) on songs such as "Throw A Penny," and with a funky beat backing them up on a lot of this record, the group is scarcely recognizable in relation to their previous work—*Mr. Natural* was the liveliest, most invigorating body of music to come from the group since their debut, but it also had moments of extraordinary sensuality, most notably "Charade" and "Had A Lot of Love Last Night." In between those two bookends were the beginnings of the sound that would reach maturity on *Main Course*, the *Saturday Night Fever* soundtrack, and *Children of the World*. Most of it is extraordinarily lively and upbeat, which was also a major change for the group; there are still some ballads here in their old style, such as "Down the Road" (which includes the extensive use of a Mellotron), but even these have a subtlety and freshness that had been lacking in the group's work since their debut. The main virtue throughout is, of course, the singing, which is some of the finest that all three Gibb brothers had ever turned in on a single LP up to that time, mated to some of their loveliest and liveliest songs up to that time. *Mr. Natural* generated no hits, but it was their best original album since *Odessa* (though also very different from that progressive-oriented double LP), and the Polygram CD reissue is one of the more successful in the label's digital remasterings of the group's sound. *—Bruce Eder*

Main Course / May 1975 / Polydor ♦♦♦♦♦

It may sound silly to call the 12th album by a group with an eight-year string of gold records behind them a "breakthrough," but that's what *Main Course* was. The group's first disco album—and, for many white listeners, the first disco album they ever purchased—*Main Course* marked a huge change in the Bee Gees' sound. The group's earlier LPs, steeped in a dense romantic balladry, were beautifully crafted but too serious for anyone but hardcore fans. *Main Course* had a few ballads, such as "Songbird" and "Country Lanes," but the writing was simpler, and the rest of it was made up of catchy dance tunes (heavily influenced by the Philadelphia-based soul music of the period), in which the beat and the texture of the voices and instruments took precedence over the words. The combination proved irresistible, and *Main Course*—driven by the singles "Jive Talkin'," "Nights on Broadway," and "Fanny (Be Tender With My Love)"—attracted millions of new listeners. It also repelled fans of the group's earlier style, which was a bit ironic. Years later, *Main Course* holds up as well as anything the group ever did, and with killer album cuts like "Wind of Change" (featuring a superb Joe Farrell tenor sax solo) and "Edge of the Universe" all over it, demands as much attention as any hits compilation by the group. *—Bruce Eder*

Children of the World / Sep. 1976 / Polydor ♦♦♦♦

The Bee Gees' second R&B album, *Children of the World* had the advantage of being written and recorded while the group was riding a string of Top Ten singles and the biggest wave of public adulation in their history off of the *Main Course* album. The group felt emboldened, but were also hamstrung by the absence of producer Arif Mardin, whose services were no longer available to them now that RSO Records had severed its ties to Atlantic Records. So they produced it themselves, all six band members doing their best to emulate what Mardin would have had them do, with assistance from Albhy Galuten and Karl Richardson. The result still sounds a lot like Mardin's production from the previous album, and the group was in very good form—stretching out not only on disco numbers like "You Should Be Dancing" but also delivering beautiful soul ballads such as "You Stepped Into My Life" and "Love So Right" on side one, while side two featured a last look back at the older, more romantic Bee Gees sound. The album was also somewhat experimental in its way, making more use of synthesizers in a pop music setting than had ever been heard on a mainstream, commercial long-player before—not all of it works, because the technology wasn't quite perfected yet, but "Boogie Child," "Love Me," and "The Way It Was," as well as the title-track, were quite daring on a production level in their time, for a group shooting for millions of sales. Overall, the album isn't quite as beguiling as *Main Course*, which was a liberating experiment from start-to-finish. *Children of the World* is beautifully sung, but the group's sound changed here as well, Barry Gibb's falsetto now dominating the vocals, with Robin and Maurice Gibb moved out of center-stage. But it's still one of the most enjoyably light-hearted albums in the group's history, and the dance numbers provided a fore-taste of their work on the *Saturday Night Fever* soundtrack. *—Bruce Eder*

The Bee Gees Gold, Vol. 1 / Oct. 1976 / Polydor ✦✦✦✦✦

The Bee Gees Gold, Vol. 1 compiles the group's biggest singles from their first five years of hit records, beginning with 1967's "New York Mining Disaster 1941" and ending with 1971's "How Can You Mend a Broken Heart." Although the compilation isn't presented in chronological order, it does contains all of their biggest hits ("To Love Somebody," "Holiday," "Lonely Days," "I've Got to Get a Message to You," "I Started a Joke"), making it a fine overview of the group's first heyday. *—Stephen Thomas Erlewine*

☆ **Saturday Night Fever** / Nov. 1977 / RSO ✦✦✦✦✦

One of the biggest-selling albums of all time, this double-disc soundtrack features the Bee Gees hits "Stayin' Alive," "Night Fever," and "How Deep Is Your Love"; Yvonne Elliman's "If I Can't Have You"; and a selection of popular disco hits by Tavares, K.C. & the Sunshine Band, and others. This wasn't only the soundtrack to a film, it was the soundtrack to an era. That era is over, but it's evoked by the music. *—William Ruhlmann*

1963-1966: Birth of Brilliance / 1978 / Festival ✦✦✦✦✦

Thirty-two song double CD presents much of the best material from the domestic Excelsior compilations of their early years, as well as some songs (some of which are pretty good) that don't appear on those sets. Because of its better sound, this collection has the edge as the best compilation of their early work, though it's hard to find. *—Richie Unterberger*

Spirits Having Flown / Jan. 1979 / Polydor ✦✦✦✦✦

How does one follow up a phenomenal success? Well, that was the question the Bee Gees faced after their contributions catapulted them into the disco stratosphere. It appeared they could do no wrong, writing hits not only for themselves, but for many others as well. However, *Spirits Having Flown*, while a solid effort, did not catch fire with the public. This time out, there were no memorable hooks to grab the listener, or even the dancer. Who knows? Perhaps they tried too hard. The tracks "Too Much Heaven," "Tragedy" and "Love You Inside and Out" were all number one hits, but the public didn't bite the way they had before. Good music, but a bit dated. Reminders of polyester jumpsuits abound. *—James Chrispell*

● **Greatest** / Oct. 1979 / Polydor ✦✦✦✦✦

Greatest is a double-album, 20-song retrospective of the Bee Gees' late '70s hits. All of the band's biggest disco-era hits—"Jive Talkin'," "Nights on Broadway," "Fanny (Be Tender with My Love)," "You Should Be Dancing," "Love So Right," "How Deep Is Your Love," "Stayin' Alive," "Night Fever," "Too Much Heaven," "Tragedy," "Love You Inside Out"—are included, as well as several fine album tracks and the group's version of Andy Gibb's "(Our Love) Don't Throw It All Away." Although it's a little too long for some casual fans, it remains an excellent overview of the Bee Gees' most commercially successful era. *—Stephen Thomas Erlewine*

Living Eyes / 1981 / RSO ✦✦✦

Staying Alive / Jun. 1983 / RSO ✦✦✦

This sequel to *Saturday Night Fever* lacked the box office clout of the original, and the soundtrack album was likewise a disappointing seller, but it actually contains some of the better Bee Gees work of the '80s, notably the sad ballad "Someone Belonging to Someone." *—William Ruhlmann*

E.S.P. / Sep. 1987 / Warner Brothers ✦✦

One / Jul. 25, 1989 / Warner Brothers ✦✦✦

The Bee Gees made a commercial comeback outside the U.S. with 1987's *E.S.P.* and its single, "You Win Again." *One*, on the other hand, had an improved chart showing in the U.S., while sales fell off elsewhere. The Bee Gees are remarkable pop craftsmen—"It's My Neighborhood" is a canny, if blatant, rewrite of Michael Jackson's "Beat It," for example, and it only reminds you that Jackson's falsetto whoops owe something to Barry Gibb. And, say what you will, "One" and "House of Shame" are convincing pop music. ("One" was a Top Ten comeback hit that topped soft-rock radio playlists.) This stuff works as pop for the same reason "I've Gotta Get a Message to You" and "You Should Be Dancing" did: the melodies are catchy, the hooks are deathless, and the vocals convey emotion over meaning. It may be weightless, but it's polished. *—William Ruhlmann*

Tales from the Brothers Gibb / Oct. 1990 / Polydor ✦✦✦✦

Although the Bee Gees were a singles band, and consequently their hits compilations were frequently more consistent than their actual albums, the four-disc box set *Tales from the Brothers Gibb* is an example of a wasted opportunity. While all of the big hits are featured over the course of 71 tracks, the set is unevenly balanced, featuring more latter-day material than their generally more interesting early recordings. Also, it doesn't choose particularly well from the group's albums, overlooking several key tracks in favor of bland cuts from '80s records, and the rarities, including several live tracks and a demo of "E.S.P.," aren't of much worth. Consequently, *Tales from the Brothers Gibb* neither appeals to the collector, who will have the bulk of this material, nor the casual fan, since it contains too much mediocre material for them to sift through. *—Stephen Thomas Erlewine*

High Civilization / Apr. 1991 / Warner Brothers ✦✦

Size Isn't Everything / Nov. 1993 / Polydor ✦✦✦

These guys are persistent and they work hard for the money, carefully cloning current fashion. You can just hear them saying, "We did disco, we can do hip-hop," and you can hear them try on "Paying the Price of Love," with its heavy percussion track. But it wasn't their approximation of the Compton beat that got them (just barely) back in the pop charts, it was the hook, which wasn't all that different from "Massachusetts." *—William Ruhlmann*

To Be or Not to Be / Dec. 12, 1995 / Thunderbolt ✦✦✦

A 26-track, single-disc collection culled from the Bee Gees' mid-'60s recordings as Australian pop stars mimicking the styles and sound of the British Invasion, *To Be or Not to Be* has many of the best songs from their early career, but it isn't the most comprehensive collection available. Nevertheless, it is a solid sampler and it only has four songs less than the definitive double-disc compilation, *1963-1966: Birth of Brilliance*. *—Stephen Thomas Erlewine*

Still Waters / May 6, 1997 / Polydor ✦✦✦

As if they finally realized that they couldn't quite compete with contemporary musical fashions any more, the Bee Gees moved firmly into "mature" territory with *Still Waters*. However, they are canny enough to realize that they shouldn't abandon the frothy disco that made them superstars in the late '70s—they should merely temper it with measured rhythms and tasteful melodies. Consequently, nothing on *Still Waters* is infectious, but it is pleasant, and while only a handful of singles stand out—"I Could Not Love You More" is a sweet ballad—it is still a fine, professional effort from these consummate professionals. *—Stephen Thomas Erlewine*

Brilliant from Birth / Apr. 27, 1999 / Festival ✦✦✦

At last, a comprehensive collection of everything the group recorded in their "Australian years," from 1963 to 1966, before their move to England and rapid ascent to international stardom. These two CDs—an entirely different package from the similarly titled, but much shorter, compilation *1963-1966: Birth of Brilliance*—include 63 songs, some of which are quite familiar to Bee Gees fans via numerous reissues, but some of which were hard to find outside of Australia, or indeed anywhere. Actually, this turns out to be a mixed blessing, since the rarer tracks are usually way less interesting than the numerous fine Beatlesque ones (such as "Peace of Mind," "Wine and Women," "I Want Home," "All of My Life") that have been pretty easy to acquire on U.S. repackages. There are, for instance, a bunch of fairly horrible MOR pop and country covers, presumably dating from circa 1963. Although it has sometimes been claimed that the Bee Gees sounded like the Beatles by coincidence because they grew up in Manchester, on the basis of this evidence, it seems unquestionable that they deliberately revamped their sound into a Fab Four vein after the Beatles became huge. There are some cool rarities like the moody, folk-rockish "Lonely Winter" and good quality TV broadcasts of Beatles, Lovin' Spoonful, and Dave Clark Five covers (their take on the DC5's "Can't You See That She's Mine" is surprisingly good). It's also good to have comprehensive (and typo-filled) liner notes covering the Australian period, but the utter lack of specific recording/release dates and sources for any of the tracks is exasperating. *—Richie Unterberger*

Bees Make Honey

f. 1972, **db.** 1974

Pub Rock

Bees Make Honey, one of the most fondly regarded of the U.K. pub rock explosion's originators, was founded on the remains of one of Ireland's most popular show bands, the Alpine Seven. That band's leader, string bassist Barry Richardson, moved to London in the late '60s. Fellow Alpine Seven members Ruan O'Lochlainn, Deke O'Brien, and Mick Molloy soon joined him in England and, with the lineup completed by American-born drummer Bob Cee, the unnamed quintet settled into a residency alongside Eggs Over Easy at the Tally Ho pub in North London. They officially became Bees Make Honey in January 1972. Under the inventive aegis of manager Dave Robinson, the band graduated to other venues on the fast-exploding pub rock circuit; Robinson also oversaw their first recordings, cut at Rockfield Studios in Monmouthshire during 1972. By 1973, Bees Make Honey was widely regarded as the most likely band on the entire scene to make the transition into the big time; they attracted enthusiastic press coverage across the media spectrum and, by summer, the group had signed with EMI. Their first single, "Knee Trembler," followed, but even as the band prepared their debut album, fall's superlative *Music Every Night*, the original quintet began to splinter. Bees Make Honey cut a second album for EMI, only for the label to reject it and drop the group from the roster. A move to the DJM label proved similarly disastrous, with another album's worth of material cut and then shelved. By fall 1974, Bees Make Honey had broken up, with Richardson going on to his own Barry Richardson Band. *—Dave Thompson*

- **Music Every Night** / 1973 / EMI ♦♦♦♦♦
Bees Make Honey / 1977 / Charly ♦♦♦

Adrian Belew

b. Kentucky

Producer, Vocals, Guitar (Electric), Guitar / Album Rock, Experimental Rock, Guitar Virtuoso, Jazz-Rock, Pop/Rock, Prog-Rock/Art Rock

Over the course of his career, Adrian Belew has lent his left-of-center guitar playing to the jazz-rock dementia of Frank Zappa (*Sheik Yerbouti*), the off-kilter funk of *Remain in Light*-era Talking Heads (as well as spinoff group the Tom Tom Club), the sonic explorations of David Bowie's *Lodger*, and the extended, guitar-dominated progressive rock of early-'80s King Crimson (i.e., *Three of a Perfect Pair*). As well as contributing session work to rock's avant-garde for many years, Belew has also pursued a wide-ranging solo career. His early releases tended to reflect the styles of those groups he had previously worked with. In 1987, Belew took a break from experimental rock and formed the Bears with former members of the Raisins and revealed his pop sensibilities that were obscured up to that point. Belew departed the Bears after two albums and returned to his solo career refreshed, recording several albums of XTC and Squeeze-influenced pop similar to the Bears and showing more focus than his previous solo output. Belew worked with Bowie on *Young Lions* prior to serving as the musical director for Bowie's *Sound + Vision* tour, and offered his own Beatles pastiche on *Inner Revolution*. In 1995, a year after guesting on Nine Inch Nails' *The Downward Spiral*, Belew rejoined Robert Fripp in a new edition of King Crimson for the album *Thrak*. Two years later, Belew returned with a pair of solo albums, *The Guitar as Orchestra* and *Op Zop Too Wah*. *Coming Attractions* followed in early 2000. —*Steve Huey*

Lone Rhino / Jul. 1982 / Island ♦♦♦
The first solo album from monster alternative guitarist Belew comes in the middle of Robert Fripp's early-'80s reformulation of King Crimson, so it's no surprise that many a Crimson-esque herky-jerky guitar run and melody line pops up among Belew's other trademark sound, that of the animal-turned-guitar wail. Songs similarly explore Belew's fascination with raw animal nature: "Big Electric Cat" (the album's obvious single) is exactly that, howling five-stringed felines over a propulsive Afro-funk beat, and "Animal Grace" is its less frazzled companion. But Belew can also be gentle, exploring guitar synth ambience on "Naive Guitar" and even performing a duet with his four-year-old daughter Audie Belew on "The Final Rhino." —*Ted Mills*

Twang Bar King / Sep. 1983 / Island ♦♦

Desire Caught by the Tail / 1986 / Island ♦♦♦

Mr. Music Head / Apr. 1989 / Atlantic ♦♦♦
On *Mr. Music Head*, guitar virtuoso Adrian Belew serves up a pure pop-sounding album, and does a satisfying job to boot. He puts his guitar to good use, at times sounding experimental, but only doing so to add color to his three-minute tunes. On "Oh Daddy," his daughter Audie shares the singing on this light, cheery little number. With "Bad Days," the piano is the main instrument, projecting Belew's emotions quite fittingly. Belew's fondness for animal rights is the main theme behind "Hot Zoo," and "Cruelty to Animals" is an assortment of animal noises heard amongst background instrumentation, reminding listeners that he hasn't abandoned his avant-garde style completely. While Belew's voice isn't really his largest asset, it's not unlistenable, and along with the multitude of instruments used on every track, each song carries its own persona. Past work with the Talking Heads can be heard from start to finish, showing up by way of certain staccato rhythms and well-constructed melodies. Hearing Adrian Belew in a pop sense is surprisingly enjoyable, even if he can't leave his experimental string bending behind entirely. —*Mike DeGagne*

Young Lions / May 1990 / Atlantic ♦♦♦
Young Lions is as solid an album as Adrian Belew had put out in some time, including his work with the Bears. Apparently, the relative chart success he had with his last effort fueled the desire for another single, and no less a luminary than former employer David Bowie was brought in to write and duet with Belew on "Pretty Pink Rose" (they even did a video to support it). While that song and "Gunman" (the pair's second collaboration on the album) are little more than a reprise of Bowie's work with Tin Machine, they clearly relieve Belew from having to scrap together all the material himself. Leaning on a not-too-distant King Crimson standard, "Heartbeat," and the Traveling Wilburys' "Not Alone Anymore" leaves Belew holding the bag for an even half-dozen originals, which reduces the filler ratio that plagued some of his earlier efforts. From the energetic opener, "Young Lions," to the Motown-inspired "Looking for a U.F.O.," Belew comes up with some off-center pop/rock songs that hold up under inspection. His work with the Bears had smoothed out the guitarist's rough edges, but on his own, Belew is more nimble and quirky, as "Men in Helicopters" and "Small World" demonstrate. Like *Mr. Music Head* before it, *Young Lions* presents Belew's assets in a very palatable package. Despite the lack of a real standout single, Belew's one-man performance on *Young Lions* is worth hearing. —*David Connolly*

Desire of the Rhino King / 1991 / Island ♦♦♦
Desire of the Rhino King is a compilation of songs from Belew's three albums, *Lone Rhino*, *Twang Bar King*, and *Desire Caught by the Tail*. This generous, 20-track album epitomizes Adrian Belew in all his avant garde glory, complete with information about all three albums written by Belew himself. A good feel for his experimental guitar playing, his work with feedback, and his use of tape loops all converge on this album, creating an excellent overview of this talented artist. Belew's guitar work is at its best on "Big Electric Cat" and "Hot Sun." He shows that he can be compassionate on "The Man in the Moon," a song about the death of his father. The first eight tracks from *Lone Rhino* include abrupt sax playing from Bill Janssen and numerous other effects, adding to the brightness. Tracks nine to 16 are from *Twang Bar King* and are the leanest part of the album, since Belew seems to go off on a rip-roaring tangent and the looseness causes the tunes to slightly unravel. The last five tracks are taken from *Desire Caught by the Tail*, and this is where Belew glistens. Inspired by Pablo Picasso, he paints his music on an invisible canvas creating some unique and imaginative sounds. A great cross section of Adrian Belew is experienced on this album, and is digitally remastered as well. —*Mike DeGagne*

- **Inner Revolution** / Feb. 1992 / Atlantic ♦♦♦♦♦
Belew uses his well-developed one-man-band and state-of-the-studio abilities to produce a Beatle pastiche record that ranks with the best of such Fab Four idolators as Todd Rundgren, the Raspberries, and ELO, and that's no mean feat. He can sing (almost) like John Lennon and play guitar like George Harrison. His sturdy songwriting makes this much more than just a successful genre exercise. —*William Ruhlmann*

Here / 1994 / Plan 9/Caroline ♦♦♦
Adrian Belew is one of the world's most underrated guitarists, and his unique talents truly deserve more attention. He's played guitar with Frank Zappa and David Bowie, and also handled lead vocal duties with King Crimson. On his 1994 solo release *Here*, Belew not only wrote all of the material himself (co-writing one with Ross Rice), he also played every single instrument and served as the album's producer. His vocal style is quite similar to David Byrne, while his guitar style cannot be compared to anyone—it's completely unpredictable and off the wall. The album's biggest surprise is the calm, psychedelic track "Fly," with a stark arrangement (voice, acoustic guitar, and an effect here and there) only intensifying the song's spacious, haunting feel. The album's upbeat opener, "May 1, 1990," finds Belew telling about a date on which "something changed inside me," while "Never Enough" is a warped rocker in classic Belew style (on which he makes his guitar sound like a violin). *Here* is a good representation of present-day Belew, but as his longtime fans know, it's not by any means a permanent direction. —*Greg Prato*

The Guitar as Orchestra / 1997 / Discipline ♦♦

Op Zop Too Wah / 1997 / Passenger ♦♦♦
Op Zop Too Wah is a typically idiosyncratic and entertaining effort from Adrian Belew, demonstrating equal amounts of unparalleled guitar virtuosity and maddeningly pedestrian songcraft. Occasionally, Belew hits upon thrilling compromises between the two extremes, but just as often he meanders, missing his targets as frequently as he hits them. Nevertheless, the mediocre material is redeemed for his dedicated fans by his stellar guitar skills and the wide variety of sounds he can coax out of his instrument. —*Stephen Thomas Erlewine*

BelewPrints / 1998 / Adrian Belew Presents ♦♦♦

Salad Days / 1998 / Thirsty Ear ♦♦♦♦

Coming Attractions / 2000 / Thirsty Ear ♦♦♦
Adrian Belew is easily one of rock's most prolific guitarists. He's lent his six-string talents to such notables as David Bowie, Frank Zappa, the Talking Heads, and Nine Inch Nails; played with King Crimson and the Bears; performed as a solo artist; produced bands like Jars of Clay; and wrote songs for others (such as Mariah Carey's "Daydream Interlude"). In 2000, Belew had several projects in the working stages—a new solo album, a new Bears album, a live acoustic album titled *This Is a Pencil*, a new King Crimson album, and a box set titled *Dust*. Tasters from all of these projects (save Crimson) plus a few odds and ends were included on *Coming Attractions*, as well as a couple of live acoustic tracks (the latter sounding similar to hit last Thirsty Ear release, *Salad Days*). From his upcoming solo album, the track "Inner Man" is perhaps Belew's heaviest rock track yet, while the pop perfection of "117 Valley Drive" (from the Bears release) is reminiscent of Belew's last couple of solo releases (*Here*, *Op Zop Too Wah*). Other highlights include the two live acoustic tracks "Inner Revolution" and "Time Waits," which highlight Belew's underrated vocal talents in addition to his superb guitar skills, as well as a solo demo titled "People," which previously appeared as a fully realized version on King Crimson's *Thrak*. —*Greg Prato*

Bell Biv DeVoe

f. 1988

New Jack Swing, Urban, Hip-Hop

Bell Biv DeVoe was hatched in the minds of its members, New Edition's Ricky Bell, Michael Bivins, and Ronnie DeVoe, upon the departure of lead singer Bobby Brown in 1986. But it wasn't until after the group completed its supporting tour for the album *Heart Break* in 1988 that the trio gave in to the urgings of *Heart Break* producers Jimmy Jam and Terry Lewis and decided to chart its own course. Bell Biv DeVoe's debut album was quite unlike anything in New Edition's repertoire: The beats were funkier, the lyrics and vocals were sexier, and the overall sound had a harder, hip-hop-tinged edge. The album's title track, "Poison," became a number three smash, and it was followed by the equally successful "Do Me!" The album itself went on to sell over three million copies and was followed by a remix album the next year. Meanwhile, Bivins took some time off to assemble the so-called East Coast Family, discovering and producing debut albums for another Bad Creation and Boyz II Men. *Hootie Mack*, Bell Biv DeVoe's second proper album, was released in 1993, but didn't make as much of an impact. In 1996, all three members of Bell Biv DeVoe participated in a reunion of the New Edition. —*Steve Huey*

Poison / Mar. 1990 / MCA ♦♦♦♦
With so many faceless, soundalike albums having come out of the "new jack swing" hybrid in the late '80s and early- to mid-'90s, it's important to give credit to the form's more

creative and imaginative figures. Along with Guy and Bobby Brown, Bell Biv DeVoe (a New Edition spinoff trio comprised of Ricky Bell, Michael Bivens and Ronnie DeVoe) delivered some of "new jack swings'" most worthwhile material. A hard-edged, tough-minded blend of R&B/funk and hip-hop, *Poison* was (like Brown's *Don't Be Cruel*) a radical departure from the Jackson 5-influenced "bubble gum soul" New Edition was originally known for. Defined by their urgency, rawness, and vitality, "Poison," "B.B.D. (I Thought It Was Me)?," "She's Dope!" and "Do Me!" are considered "new jack swing" classics and are indeed among the best the style has to offer. Taking a break from the CD's overall aggression, BBD moves closer to New Edition's sound with the decent, though far from outstanding, ballads "When Will I See You Again" and "I Do Need You." While other "new jacks" were content to simply emulate Guy, the distinctive BBD deserves applause for daring to stake out its own territory. —*Alex Henderson*

Hootie Mack / Jun. 1993 / MCA ✦✦✦
Hootie Mack not only keeps the same energetic vibe that made *Poison* a hit, but expands upon that base, adding a more street-oriented production that, at its best, is more sexy and funky than their debut. Unfortunately, the high points on this album aren't as numerous as those on *Poison*; not only that, but the good songs didn't receive much airplay, causing the album to drop off the charts quickly. —*Stephen Thomas Erlewine*

● **The Best of Bell Biv DeVoe** / Sep. 26, 2000 / MCA ✦✦✦✦
The Best of Bell Biv DeVoe gathers 13 of the group's biggest hits, including "Poison," "B.B.D. (I Thought It Was Me)?," "Something in Your Eyes," and "Do Me!" "Gangsta," "Hootie Mack," "Ghetto Booty," and "She's Dope!" showcase Bell Biv DeVoe's salaciousness and sentimentality, as well as the hip-hop-inspired beats that sparked the new jack sound. Remixes of "Ain't Nuttin' Changed," "Poison," and "Do Me!" round out this collection of highlights from one of the style's pioneering and most distinctive trios. —*Heather Phares*

Archie Bell

b. Sep. 1, 1944, Henderson, TX
Vocals, Songwriter / Philly Soul, Disco, Soul
Few groups offered good-time soul music as danceable and high-spirited as Archie Bell & the Drells. The singer (from Houston, as he was eager to proclaim in the middle of some of his up-tempo hits) had a left-field number one smash with the limb-loosening "Tighten Up," which took off right after Bell was drafted. In 1968, Bell (who was able to fit in some recording and performing duties until his stint in the army was over) teamed with emerging Philadelphia soul mavens Kenneth Gamble and Leon Huff, who produced and wrote his material over the next couple years. With sophisticated arrangements and punchy horn charts, dance hits like "I Can't Stop Dancing," "(There's Gonna Be A) Showdown," and "Do the Choo Choo" were instrumental in establishing the sound of Philadelphia as an artistic force. After a fallow period in the early '70s, Bell reunited with Gamble and Huff on the Philadelphia International label for a run of successful, disco-fied dance-soul in the mid-'70s. —*Richie Unterberger*

● **Tightening It Up: The Best of Archie Bell & the Drells** / Aug. 16, 1994 / Rhino ✦✦✦✦✦
It could be assumed that Archie Bell & the Drells essentially did the same thing over and over again, since "Tighten Up" almost consigns them to the level of one-hit wonders, but that's not an accurate assessment of their gifts. True, they often followed the same stylish, sunny, utterly infectious sound, but there was a lot more depth and variety there, as Rhino's terrific 20-track collection *Tightening It Up: The Best of Archie Bell & the Drells* illustrates. What it reveals to those that weren't paying close attention is that the group was one of the first great Philly soul outfits, recording a number of Gamble & Huff's early songs and providing a training ground for the seminal duo. Though the hits didn't come fast and furious, like they would later, they, Bell & the Drells, created some wonderful singles, highlighted by "(There's Gonna Be A) Showdown" and "A World Without Music." There's plenty of other terrific moments throughout this collection, which proves that Bell & the Drells were far more than a one-hit wonder—they were one of the great underappreciated soul outfits of their time. —*Stephen Thomas Erlewine*

Chris Bell

b. Jan. 12, 1951, Memphis, TN, d. Dec. 27, 1978, Memphis, TN
Vocals, Guitar / Power Pop, Singer/Songwriter
Chris Bell was one of the unsung heroes of American pop music; despite a life marked by tragedy and a career crippled by commercial indifference, the singer/songwriter's slim body of recorded work proved massively influential on the generations of indie rockers who emerged in his wake. With high-school friend Alex Chilton, Bell formed Big Star, whose debut album, 1972's *#1 Record*, eventually earned mythic status as an underground classic (though it was deemed a commercial failure at the time of release). Crushed, Bell became suicidal and left the band. Though he continued working on music, his depression worsened; to help revitalize his career, his brother David led him to France, where a batch of demos were cut for a planned album (the songs were mixed with Beatles engineer Geoff Emerick). The completed tracks were roundly rejected however, and Bell soon dropped out of music. In 1977 however, the remarkable single "I Am the Cosmos" was issued on the tiny Car label; its positive reception spurred him to form a new band. But in late 1978, Bell was killed in a car crash. Over the course of the following decade, the legendary stature of Big Star continued to grow exponentially, and finally, Bell's long-unreleased demos were released as *I Am the Cosmos*. —*Jason Ankeny*

I Am the Cosmos / Feb. 21, 1992 / Rykodisc ✦✦✦✦✦
Unreleased for over 15 years, *I Am the Cosmos* is nevertheless an enduring testament to the brilliance of Chris Bell; lyrically poignant and melodically stunning, this lone solo album is proof positive of his underappreciated pop mastery. While cuts like "Get Away,"

"I Got Kinda Lost" and "Fight at the Table" recall the glowing, energetic power-pop of Bell's earlier work, the majority of the songs on *I Am the Cosmos* are more reflective and deeply personal; the title track is a harrowingly schizophrenic tale of romantic despair, while other cuts like the lurching "Better Save Yourself" and the lovely "Look Up" are infused with a spiritual power largely missing from his Big Star material. The album's highlight, "You and Your Sister"—which features backing vocals from none other than Bell's Big Star mate Alex Chilton—is simply one of the great unknown love songs in the pop canon, a luminous and fragile ballad almost otherworldly in its beauty. —*Jason Ankeny*

William Bell (William Yarborough)

b. Jul. 16, 1939, Memphis, TN
Vocals, Piano / Northern Soul, Soul
A principal architect of the Stax-Volt sound, singer/composer William Bell remains best known for his classic "You Don't Miss Your Water," one of the quintessential soul records to emerge from the Memphis scene. Born William Yarborough on July 16, 1939, he cut his teeth backing Rufus Thomas, and in 1957 recorded his first sides as a member of the Del Rios. After joining the Stax staff as a writer, in 1961 Bell made his solo debut with the self-penned "You Don't Miss Your Water," an archetypal slice of country-soul and one of the label's first big hits. A two-year armed forces stint effectively derailed his career, however, and he did not release his first full-length album, *The Soul of a Bell*, until 1967, generating a Top 20 hit with the single "Everybody Loves a Winner"; that same year, Albert King also scored with another classic Bell composition, the oft-covered "Born Under a Bad Sign."
Bell's next solo hit, 1968's "A Tribute to a King," was a poignant farewell to the late Otis Redding; the R&B Top Ten hit "I Forgot to Be Your Lover" soon followed, and a series of duets with Judy Clay, most notably "Private Number," also earned airplay. In 1969 he relocated to Atlanta and set up his own label, Peachtree; the hits dried up as the next decade opened, but in 1977 Bell capped a major comeback with "Trying to Love Two," which topped the R&B charts. In 1985 he founded another label, Wilbe, and issued *Passion*, which found its most receptive audiences in the U.K. (although "I Don't Want to Wake Up Feeling Guilty," a duet with Janice Bullock, was a minor U.S. hit). In addition to subsequent LPs including 1989's *On a Roll* and 1992's *Bedtime Stories*, in 1987 Bell was inducted into the Georgia Music Hall of Fame, that same year receiving the Rhythm & Blues Foundation's R&B Pioneer Award. —*Jason Ankeny*

The Soul of a Bell / 1967 / Stax ✦✦✦✦✦
William Bell's history illustrates just how singles-oriented soul was in the 1960s. Though he'd enjoyed a hit in 1961 with "You Don't Miss Your Water," it wasn't until 1967 that Stax finally released his first album, the magnificent *The Soul of a Bell*. From that classic and Bell's moderate hits "Never Like This Before" and "Everybody Loves A Winner" to heartfelt versions of "Do Right Woman, Do Right Man" and "I've Been Loving You Too Long," everything on this album (reissued on CD in 1991) illustrates the gospel-drenched richness of Southern soul. Meanwhile, the influence of Motown and the Four Tops is hard to miss on the riveting single "Eloise (Hang On In There)," which should have been a major hit, but surprisingly, never even charted. —*Alex Henderson*

Duets / 1968 / Stax ✦✦✦
In the late '60s, Bell recorded a number of male/female duets with partners Judy Clay, Carla Thomas, and Mavis Staples; the ones with Clay were the most successful, "Private Number" and "My Baby Specializes" becoming modest R&B hits. All of his duet projects are assembled here, along with three solo sides that he cut in the 1970s. It's not among Bell's most striking work, but it's decent pop/soul, closer to Motown in feel than a lot of Stax material. I don't know what the deal is, but the version of "My Baby Specializes" here, though credited to Bell and Clay, only seems to feature Clay, unless that's Bell adding an odd backup grunt here and there. —*Richie Unterberger*

Phases of Reality / 1973 / Stax ✦✦✦
Many of Stax's releases in its final years were dull soul. But by the standards of the era, Bell's second-to-last Stax LP was an above-average affair that was more diverse than many such efforts of the time. The three songs he co-wrote with guitarist Horace Shipp Jr. were socially conscious tunes in a different bag than the straightforward romantic odes Bell usually purveyed. "Save Us" was indebted to Marvin Gaye's *What's Going On* era, with a Philly-influenced funk-soul groove, and "Fifty Dollar Habit" was, of course, about drug use. Elsewhere, Bell stuck mostly to love songs, self-penned and otherwise, getting into a pre-disco lope on the title track, sweet soul balladry on "What I Don't Know Won't Hurt Me" and "If You Really Love Him," and light reggae-influenced rhythms on "Lonely for Your Love." [The album is now available as part of a reissue that combines *Phases of Reality* and Bell's final Stax LP, 1974's *Relating*, onto a single CD.] –*Richie Unterberger*

● **The Best of William Bell** / 1988 / Stax ✦✦✦✦✦
The Best of William Bell focuses on the singer's output from 1968-1974, covering the albums *Duets*, *Bound to Happen*, *Wow...*, *Phases of Reality*, and *Relating*. While his 1967 debut *The Soul of a Bell*, may be his finest album, this collection compiles many of the highlights that followed, including his exquisite 1968 single "I Forgot to Be Your Lover." That same year, Bell cut a satisfactory set of *Duets* (1968) with Judy Clay, Carla Thomas, and Mavis Staples, three of which are featured here. By 1969, however, Bell was singing with increased confidence and, while the arrangements retained all the grand gestures of old, they seemed tougher somehow. That year, Bell released *Bound to Happen* (1969), displaying a harder edge on the funky "Born Under a Bad Sign." The material on *Wow...* (1971) benefited as well with female backing singers, solid drumming, and a host of strings framing fine vocal performances on "All for the Love of a Woman" and "Till My Back Ain't Got No Bone." Add the hit "I Forgot to Be Your Lover" and you have one of Bell's finest album sets. Further changes surfaced in 1973, Bell adopting the cinematic

funk stylings of Curtis Mayfield's *Superfly* on the pleading "Save Us." All of the material mentioned above is included on this Stax set. Still, no Bell Best Of can be complete without his reading of the Otis Redding classic "I've Been Loving You Too Long" or Moman & Penn's "Do Right Woman, Do Right Man," let alone the singer's best loved number: his very own "You Don't Miss Your Water." In lieu of the perfect William Bell package however, this disc serves him well, demonstrating both the breadth of his vocal powers and his stylistic range. *—Nathan Bush*

A Little Something Extra / 1992 / Stax ♦♦♦
A fine collection of Stax outtakes from the 1960s, *A Little Something Extra* features several tracks, including his smoldering version of "Will You Love Me Tomorrow?," that rival his original singles. *—Stephen Thomas Erlewine*

Greatest Hits, Vol. 2 / 1995 / Ichiban ♦♦♦♦
William Bell's gentlemanly, deep soul sound, like fine wine, gets better with age. The 11 cuts include re-recordings of some of his Stax Records hits. His marvelous duet with Judy Clay, "Private Number," remains a crown jewel in his discography, and the new version is just as playful. Bell proves he still has strong pipes on the stately "I Need Your Love So Bad," and his tribute to the late Otis Redding, "A Tribute to a King," is as significant now as it was in the '60s. "Easy Coming Out" and "Everybody Loves a Winner" are two excellent examples of R&B. And the forewarning message in "You Don't Miss Your Water," Bell's signature song, still rings true. A good CD from an overlooked soul singer. *—Andrew Hamilton*

Wow . . . /Bound to Happen / Apr. 1, 1997 / Stax ♦♦♦♦♦
In 1997, Fantasy combined two of William Bell's classic Stax albums, *Wow . . .* and *Bound to Happen*, on a single CD. The albums found the soul man in two notably different settings. The last Bell album that was produced by organist Booker T. Jones, *Bound to Happen* is a Memphis-oriented treasure boasting a number of songs that should have been major hits but weren't, including the sweaty "All God's Children Got Soul" and a magnificent remake of Albert King's "Born Under a Bad Sign." And under Jones, Bell shows us how well Sly & the Family Stone's "Everyday People" works in a Memphis soul setting. *Wow . . .*, meanwhile, marked the first time Bell didn't record in Memphis. Instead, he recorded in Muscle Shoals, Alabama under Stax's Al Bell and went for a consistently sleeker sound and more of a Northern soul orientation. *Wow . . .* isn't quite as strong as *Bound to Happen*, but it does have its share of impressive material, including "Penny for Your Thoughts" and the hit "I Forgot to Be Your Lover." As it turned out, that sleeker approach would be a primary direction for Bell in the 1970s. *—Alex Henderson*

Phases of Reality/Relating / 1999 / Stax ♦♦♦
This CD reissue combines Bell's final two Stax albums, 1973's *Phases of Reality* and *Relating*, in one disc. Many Stax releases in the label's final years were dull soul. But by the standards of the era, *Phases of Reality* was an above-average affair that was more diverse than many such efforts of the time. The three songs Bell co-wrote with guitarist Horace Shipp Jr. were socially conscious tunes in a different bag than the straightforward, romantic odes Bell usually purveyed. "Save Us" is indebted to Marvin Gaye's *What's Going On* era, with a Philly-influenced funk-soul groove, and "Fifty Dollar Habit" is, of course, about drug use. Elsewhere Bell sticks mostly to love songs, self-penned and otherwise, getting into a pre-disco lope on the title track, a style of sweet soul balladry on "What I Don't Know Won't Hurt Me" and "If You Really Love Him," and some light reggae-influenced rhythms on "Lonely for Your Love." Other than a couple of bright spots, *Relating* is blandly sentimental mid-'70s sweet soul. It has more of an Al Green-Hi Records influence, partially due in all probability to the contribution of horn arrangements and backup vocals by musicians that were also involved in Hi sessions. There is also co-production by Booker T. & the MG's drummer Al Jackson Jr., who was doing a lot of work for Hi at the time. There are a few singles that hit low on the R&B charts—"I've Got to Go on Without You," "Lovin' on Borrowed Time," and "Gettin' What You Want (Losin' What You Got)." None particularly deserved to do better, though "Gettin' What You Want" is a decent midtempo ballad. Actually the star cut is "Nobody Walks Away From Love Unhurt," with its pin-prick, bluesy guitar licks. *—Richie Unterberger*

Belle & Sebastian

f. 1995, Glasgow, Scotland
Indie Pop, Twee Pop, Chamber Pop, Alternative Pop/Rock
A band named for a French children's television series about a boy and his dog would almost have to be precious, and Glasgow's Belle & Sebastian certainly is—but in the good way; they make gorgeous, delicate melodies sound full-bodied. Their penchant for whimsical, unsettling lyrical details mirrors their quirky approach to being a band, which includes publicity photos with fake band members and performances in odd venues like homes, church halls, and libraries. Belle & Sebastian's idiosyncratic career isn't surprising, given the group's unusual beginnings. Vocalist/guitarist Stuart Murdoch formed the band as the final project for a music business course at his university. He chose band members by instinct at a local cafe in late 1995, eventually assembling Sarah Martin (violin), Stevie Jackson (guitar), Chris Geddes (keyboards), Stuart David (bass), Richard Colburn (drums), and Isobel Campbell (cello). All of them agreed that the band was to stay on a small scale; they even assumed they would release two albums and break up. But in May 1996 their self-released debut album *Tigermilk* became a sensation, earning terrific word of mouth even though only 1000 copies of the LP were released. Six months later, *If You're Feeling Sinister* earned the band widespread critical acclaim and a large cult following in the U.K. Some of this buzz reached the U.S., where *If You're Feeling Sinister* was released by the EMI subsidiary Enclave just before it closed shop. The band's cult continued to build in 1997 helped by three EPs—*Dog on Wheels*, *Lazy Line Painter Jane*, and *3, 6, 9 Seconds of Light . . .*—all of which were well-received by critics and indie fans alike. By the year's end, the group finalized an American deal with Matador Records, who issued *The Boy with the Arab Strap* in 1998 and re-released *Tigermilk* in 1999. After completing 2000's *Fold Your Hands Child, You Walk Like a Peasant*, Stuart David left the group for his solo project, Looper. *—Stephen Thomas Erlewine*

Tigermilk / May 1996 / Matador ♦♦♦♦
Belle & Sebastian's first album, *Tigermilk*, was initially pressed in a quantity of 1000 on their own label, Electric Honey Recordings. The record was intended to be the end result of Stuart Murdoch's music business school course, but it became an unexpected word-of-mouth sensation in England, and the LP quickly disappeared from shops. As a result, once the group's second album, *If You're Feeling Sinister*, became a hit, there were no copies of *Tigermilk* available for newly converted fans and it remained unheard by the majority of the group's audience. Those that have heard it say it is quite similar stylistically to *If You're Feeling Sinister* and the songs match that record's high standard. *Tigermilk* was re-released in 1999 to the delight of the often cultish fans of Belle & Sebastian. *—Stephen Thomas Erlewine*

● **If You're Feeling Sinister** / Nov. 18, 1996 / Matador ♦♦♦♦♦
Belle & Sebastian's second record was, for all intents and purposes, really its first, since their debut in 1997 was not heard outside of privileged inner circles, due to its status as a self-released pseudo-class project. And it really did have quite a bit of an impact upon its release in 1997, largely because during the first half of the '90s, the whimsy and preciousness that had been an integral part of alternative music was suppressed by grunge. Whimsy and preciousness is an integral part of *If You're Feeling Sinister*, along with clever wit and gentle, intricate arrangements—a wonderful blend of the Smiths and Simon & Garfunkel, to be reductive. Even if it's firmly within the college, bed-sit tradition, and is unabashedly retrogressive, that gives *Sinister* a special, timeless character that's enhanced by Stuart Murdoch's wonderful, lively songwriting. Blessed with an impish sense of humor, a sly turn of phrase, and an alluringly fey voice, he gives this record a real sense of backbone, in that its humor is far more biting than the music appears and the music is far more substantial that it initially seems. *Sinister* plays like a great forgotten album, couched in '80s indie, '90s attitude, and '60s folk-pop—it's beautifully out of time and even if other Belle & Sebastian albums sound like it, this is where they achieved a sense of grace. *—Stephen Thomas Erlewine*

The Boy with the Arab Strap / Sep. 8, 1998 / Matador ♦♦♦♦♦
Belle & Sebastian quietly built a dedicated following after the release of their second album, *If You're Feeling Sinister*, as word of mouth spread from indie kids to record collectors to store clerks to critics. By the end of 1997, the Scottish septet had developed a following every bit as passionate as the Smiths at their peak, which is only appropriate since leader Stuart Murdoch is as wittily literate as Morrissey. *If You're Feeling Sinister* proved this, as did the three excellent EPs that followed, increasing expectations for *The Boy with the Arab Strap*. Even if the album doesn't match the peerless *If You're Feeling Sinister* or break new ground for Belle & Sebastian, it's not a sophomore slump. From the Motown stomp of "Dirty Dream No. 2" to the Paul Simon shuffle of the title track, there is more musical texture on *Boy* than *Sinister*, but much of this was already explored on the EPs, which means *Arab Strap* essentially consolidates the group's talents. Murdoch recedes from the spotlight on occasion, letting Steve Jackson deliver two music-biz spiels and giving Isobel Campbell space to shine with the lilting "Is It Wicked Not to Care." All three songs are highlights, but Murdoch's songs still attract the most attention. His vicious wit, often overlooked in favor of his poetic narratives, surfaces on the title track, while "It Could Have Been a Brilliant Career" summarizes his effortless gift for elegant melancholia. Such small, precious gems are what Belle & Sebastian are all about, and *The Boy with the Arab Strap* offers another round of timeless, endlessly fascinating pop-folk treasures. *—Stephen Thomas Erlewine*

Fold Your Hands Child, You Walk Like a Peasant / Jun. 5, 2000 / Matador ♦♦♦
When Belle & Sebastian cancelled several dates on their 1998 North American tour after cellist Isobel Campbell fell ill, many fans cried foul; couldn't the rest of the group have gone on without her? Of course not—Belle & Sebastian is a band in the most democratic sense of the word, a point reinforced by *Fold Your Hands Child, You Walk Like a Peasant*, their fourth and most ambitiously eclectic album to date. Nominal frontman Stuart Murdoch recedes into the background even more than on *The Boy with the Arab Strap*, allowing bandmates like Campbell and Stevie Jackson to take on a greater share of the writing and vocal duties. Also like its predecessor, *Fold Your Hands Child* opts for a subtle, intimate palette that reveals its charms only in its own sweet time. It may be too subtle for its own good; even after repeated listens it fails to connect on any meaningful level. The record has many intriguing ideas (like the delicate "Beyond the Sunrise," which evokes the classic duets of Nancy Sinatra and Lee Hazlewood, and the vaguely rootsy "The Wrong Girl"), but few of the concepts seem fully developed. For better or worse, *Fold Your Hands Child*'s best moments are those which hew most closely to the classic Belle & Sebastian sound—i.e., Stuart Murdoch songs. Though there's little advancement in his contributions, they capture the band's past glories. The radiant "Woman's Realm" is a dead ringer for *The Boy with the Arab Strap*'s title cut, while "The Model" retreads so much lyrical and musical ground it could be a self-parody. Still, the album provokes an intriguing question: Belle & Sebastian may be a band, not Stuart Murdoch's solo project, but is that a good thing? *—Jason Ankeny*

Belly

f. 1992, Boston, MA, **db.** 1996
Dream Pop, Indie Rock, Alternative Pop/Rock
Following several years in the Throwing Muses, as well as a brief detour in the Breeders in 1990, Tanya Donelly formed her own band, Belly, in 1992. With Belly, Donelly ex-

panded her dreamy pop hooks into more concise, catchy songs, as well as harder-edged rock. The band's 1993 debut, *Star*, became one of the first beneficiaries of the commercialization of alternative rock; it rode to gold status within its first year of release, as "Feed the Tree" made headway on mainstream pop radio. Despite their strong start, Belly never became genuine stars, and once their 1995 followup *King* bombed, Donelly disbanded the group. Tanya Donelly (vocals, guitar) broke away from the Throwing Muses in late 1991, forming Belly with fellow ex-Muse Fred Abong (bass), drummer Chris Gorman, and his guitarist brother Tom. Donelly hired Pixies producer Gil Norton to work on the group's debut EP, *Slow Dust*, which confirmed that her dream-pop sensibilities had more hooks than many of her peers. *Slow Dust* reached number one on the British indie charts in early 1992, and two other EPs followed that year, generating strong word of mouth. Belly's debut album, *Star*, was released in February of 1993 to strong reviews, and its first single, "Feed the Tree," reached the U.K. Top 40, helping the album enter the British charts at number two. Shortly afterward, the single became a crossover hit in the U.S. The band added Gail Greenwood as bassist—Abong left the band during the recording of *Star*—that spring, and spent the remainder of 1993 on tour, helping send the album to gold status in America.

During 1994, Belly recorded their second album with classic rock producer Glyn Johns. The resulting record, *King*, was more rock-oriented than its predecessor, partially because of Johns' work and partially because of Greenwood, who was a harder rocker than Donelly. *King* was expected to be Belly's breakthrough into the mainstream, yet was greeted with mixed reviews upon its spring release and quickly fell off the charts. In the wake of its failure, Donelly disbanded Belly in 1996, releasing her first solo EP, *Sliding and Diving*, at the end of the year. Greenwood joined L7 by the end of the year. —*Stephen Thomas Erlewine*

● **Star** / Feb. 1993 / Sire/Reprise ✦✦✦✦✦
Tanya Donelly's songwriting began to blossom on the Throwing Muses' *The Real Ramona*, and Belly's debut *Star* is where it reaches fruition. Using the trancy harmonies of dream-pop as a foundation, Donelly expands the genre's boundaries, trimming away its pretensions and incorporating a flair for sweet, concise pop hooks and folk-rock inflections. She also spikes her airy melodies with disarmingly disturbing lyrics. Images of betrayal and death float throughout the album, but what hits home initially—and what stays after the album is finished—are the hooks, whether it's the rolling sing-along of "Gepetto," the surging "Slow Dog," the melancholy "Stay" or the cool, detached sexiness of "Feed the Tree." Occasionally, Donelly suffers from preciousness or unformed ideas, yet *Star* remains an enchanting debut. —*Stephen Thomas Erlewine*

King / Feb. 14, 1995 / Sire/Reprise ✦✦✦
By developing a flair for tight, melodic hooks on *Star*, Tanya Donelly unexpectedly achieved the crossover success with Belly that eluded her with the Throwing Muses and Breeders. Evidently inspired by such success and eager to prove that Belly was a full-fledged band, not just a solo project, Donelly and company made a bid for stardom with their second album, *King*. Veteran producer Glyn Johns gives the band an appealingly punchy sheen, and with the assistance of Tom Gorman and new bassist Gail Greenwood, Donelly cuts away her remaining arty preciousness, concentrating solely on big pop songs. While some fans will miss the occasional detour into spacy dream-pop, Belly's makeover is quite convincing, and the cloaked stardom of "Super-Connected," the quirky hooks of "Now They'll Sleep" and the epic ballad of "Judas My Heart" are neglected gems of post-alternative modern rock. Ironically, such shiny hooks didn't make Belly stars—it lost them their original fan base, and by the time the record was released in 1995, modern rock radio was concentrating solely on harder guitar rock, so *King* was overlooked and the band broke up shortly afterward. The album and the group deserved a better fate. —*Stephen Thomas Erlewine*

Pat Benatar

b. Jan. 10, 1953, Brooklyn, NY
Vocals / Album Rock, Arena Rock, Pop/Rock, Hard Rock
Pat Benatar's polished mainstream pop/rock made her one of the more popular female vocalists of the early '80s. Although she came on like an arena rocker with her power chords, tough sexuality, and powerful vocals, her music was straight pop/rock underneath all the bluster. Benatar signed with Chrysalis Records in 1979, releasing her debut album, *In the Heat of the Night*, that same year. The record launched her string of hit singles with the number 23 "Heartbreaker." Featuring the Top Ten hit "Hit Me with Your Best Shot," Benatar's second album, 1980's *Crimes of Passion* was a greater success, selling over four million copies and winning the Grammy for Best Female Rock Vocal Performance. Her third album, *Precious Time* (1981), reached number one on the album charts; a single from the album called "Fire and Ice" won Benatar another Grammy. Benatar released a live album, *Live from Earth*, in 1983; it contained one of her biggest hits, "Love Is a Battlefield." Although 1984's *Tropico* contained her biggest hit "We Belong" (number five), the album was her lowest-charting to date. "Invincible" (1985), taken from *The Legend of Billie Jean* soundtrack, was her last Top Ten hit. Even though it included the hit single "Sex as a Weapon," Benatar's *Seven the Hard Way* (1985) became her first album not to go platinum—it didn't even go gold. —*Stephen Thomas Erlewine*

In the Heat of the Night / Sep. 1979 / Chrysalis ✦✦✦✦
Pat Benatar's debut album takes the tough-but-tender sensibility of Chrissie Hynde and gives it the arena rock treatment, with a splash of new wave. Which isn't a bad thing; in fact, many consider this to be Benatar's best album. Guitarist (and husband) Neil Geraldo never fails to supply just the right amount of guitar heroism to make the songs rock convincingly and accessibly. "Heartbreaker" has become an AOR classic (and a sort of "an-

gry woman" anthem), and the cover of John Cougar's "I Need a Lover" may even outdo the original. —*Andy Hinds*

Crimes of Passion / Aug. 1980 / Chrysalis ✦✦✦✦✦
The success of Pat Benatar's debut single "Heartbreaker" made it evident that listeners longed to hear the Long Islander rock out more often. Instead of stressing new wave-ish material as she generally did on *In the Heat of the Night*, Benatar cranked up the electric guitars the second time around and delivered the loudest, most aggressively rockin' album of her career. Both artistically and commercially, this change of direction paid off handsomely. In 1980, women who rocked forcefully were the exception instead of the rule, and Benatar was among the enjoyable exceptions. From "Out of Touch" to the celebrated "Hit Me with Your Best Shot," *Crimes of Passion* is a gritty hard rock gem that is as fun as it is loud. One song that definitely isn't escapist, however, is "Hell Is for Children"—a commentary on child abuse that is downright chilling. —*Alex Henderson*

Precious Time / Jul. 1981 / Chrysalis ✦✦✦
Pat Benatar's third album *Precious Time* was her only number one record, yet it wasn't as consistent as her previous two albums. While it follows the same polished arena rock formula of *In the Heat of the Night* and *Crimes of Passion*, *Precious Time* only takes off on the singles "Fire and Ice" and "Promises in the Dark," which exploit Benatar's powerful voice and her band's sleek variation on hard rock. —*Stephen Thomas Erlewine*

Get Nervous / Nov. 1982 / Chrysalis ✦✦✦
In interviews, Pat Benatar made it clear that she had no desire to be stereotyped as a hard rocker—often adding that she preferred new wave's melodic keyboards over hard rock and metal's crunching guitars. Indeed, *Get Nervous* was the most melodic album she'd done since *In the Heat of the Night*. This isn't to say that *Get Nervous* was a return to new wave-ish leanings; in fact, songs like "Anxiety (Get Nervous)," "The Victim," and "Silent Partners" are intense, forceful jewels that rock aggressively. But at the same time, the album's pop elements and strong emphasis on melody leave no doubt that the last thing on Benatar's mind was recording another *Crimes of Passion*. —*Alex Henderson*

Live from Earth / Oct. 1983 / Chrysalis ✦✦

Tropico / Nov. 1984 / Chrysalis ✦✦✦

Seven the Hard Way / Nov. 1985 / Chrysalis ✦✦✦
Seven the Hard Way continues the slick pop approach of *Tropico* and is benefitted by a wealth of songs written by professional songwriters. At this point, Benatar and her band weren't coming up with material as catchy or memorable as "Invincible" and "Sex as a Weapon," so the presence of the pro songwriters was a blessing, not a curse. —*Stephen Thomas Erlewine*

Wide Awake in Dreamland / Jun. 1988 / Chrysalis ✦✦✦

● **Best Shots** / Nov. 1989 / Chrysalis ✦✦✦✦✦
Several compilations have appeared in the years since it first hit the shelves, but *Best Shots* remains the finest Pat Benatar collection yet assembled, largely because it is the most concise. True, there may be a few lesser hits missing in favor of a couple newly recorded songs—"Sex as a Weapon," "Treat Me Right," "I Need a Lover," "Promises in the Dark," "Little Too Late" and "Looking for a Stranger" all could have made the cut instead of "Painted Desert" and "Outlaw Blues"—but the remainder of the disc is nearly flawless, delivering arena-rock staples such as "Hit Me with Your Best Shot," "Fire and Ice," "Heartbreaker," "We Belong," "Invincible" and "All Fired Up" one after another. It may not be perfect, but it delivers enough thrills to make it all worthwhile. —*Stephen Thomas Erlewine*

True Love / Apr. 1991 / Chrysalis ✦✦

Gravity's Rainbow / Jun. 1, 1993 / Chrysalis ✦✦

All Fired Up: The Very Best of Pat Benatar / 1994 / Chrysalis ✦✦✦✦✦
All Fired Up: The Very Best of Pat Benatar is an excellent two-disc compilation of one of rock & roll's first ladies. Her previous hit collection, *Best Shots*, was too brief (and is now outdated), and 1999's *Synchronistic Wanderings* is a little too much for the casual (or even devoted) fan—this set is just right. All of Pat Benatar's charted singles are included, as are some of her key album tracks (unfortunately, "Precious Time" is the only glaring omission). Disc one includes the singer's earlier, more straightforward rock hits, from her first single, "I Need a Lover," to classics like "Hit Me with Your Best Shot," "Fire and Ice," "Promises in the Dark," "Shadows in the Night," "Little Too Late," and the single edit of "Love Is a Battlefield." Disc two includes her mid-'80s, more pop-leaning hits, as well as several songs from her post-commercial success period, including "We Belong," "Invincible," "Sex as a Weapon," "All Fired Up," the blues tracks "Payin' the Cost to Be the Boss" and "True Love," and later singles such as the overlooked "Everybody Lay Down" and "Somebody's Baby." This collection also includes excellent cover and interior art and a wonderful booklet with great photos, pictures of all her singles and albums, and release dates. For those unfamiliar with Benatar's work, this is an excellent introduction, and a great hits package for the fans. —*Jose F. Promis*

16 Classic Performances / Jul. 9, 1996 / EMI ✦✦✦✦✦
If you're serious about your Benatar, you'll probably aim for the two-CD *All Fired Up* anthology. This 16-track single-disc compilation has many of her biggest hits (with some notable ones, like "Treat Me Right," omitted), and previously unreleased live versions of "Helter Skelter" and "Hit Me with Your Best Shot" from the early '80s. —*Richie Unterberger*

Synchronistic Wanderings / Oct. 5, 1999 / Chrysalis/Capitol ✦✦✦
Pat Benatar was certainly one of the best arena rockers of the early '80s. Not only did she sell albums, but she made records that sounded great on the radio—"Heartbreaker," "Hit Me with Your Best Shot," "Shadows of the Night," "I Need a Lover," "Love Is a Battlefield,"

"We Belong," "Invincible," "Sex as a Weapon," even the latter-day "All Fired Up." Enough hits for a really good hits collection, which she has several of in her catalog; however, not enough for a three-disc box set, which is what *Synchronistic Wanderings* is. That's not to say that all Benatar had to offer were hit singles, since she did have some good album tracks, or that she shouldn't have a collection of rarities and unreleased material, since some of the demos, live tracks, and unreleased cuts aren't bad, and certainly of interest to fans. Problem is, this doesn't work in an exhaustive, multi-disc retrospective where the hits dry up at the end of the second disc. That means that it's a little difficult for anyone other than hardcore fans to make it through the entire collection. Diehard Benatar aficionados would be better served by a single-disc rarities collection, which, by the way, is the most interesting part of this set. *Synchronistic Wanderings* does give a comprehensive overview of Benatar's career, concentrating as much on the detours and sideroads as on the well-known paths, but that turns out to be a journey that's a little too exhausting for anyone that isn't already familiar with the general route. *—Stephen Thomas Erlewine*

Brook Benton (Benjamin Franklin Peay)

b. Sep. 19, 1931, Camden, SC, **d.** Apr. 9, 1988, New York, NY
Vocals / R&B, Soul

Silky smooth: that was Brook Benton's byword from his first record to his very last, as the singer parlayed his rich baritone pipes into seven #1 R&B hits and eight Top Ten items. Stints on the gospel circuit preceded Benton's first secular session for Okeh in 1953, but his career didn't begin to take off until he teamed with writer/producer Clyde Otis. Benton cowrote and sang hundreds of demos for other artists before frequent collaborator Otis signed his friend to Mercury; together they pioneered a lush, violin-studded variation on the standard R&B sound, which beautifully showcased Benton's intimate vocals.

Benton crashed the top spot on the R&B charts in early 1959 with his moving "It's Just a Matter of Time," then rapidly encored with three more R&B chart-toppers—"Thank You Pretty Baby," "So Many Ways," and "Kiddio." Pairing with Mercury labelmate Dinah Washington, their delightful repartee on "Baby (You've Got What It Takes)" and "A Rockin' Good Way" paced the R&B lists in 1960.

The early '60s were a prolific period for Benton, but he left Mercury a few years later and bounced between labels before reemerging with the atmospheric Tony Joe White ballad "Rainy Night in Georgia" on Cotillion in 1970. Benton later made a halfhearted attempt to cash in on the disco craze, but his hitmaking reign was at an end long before his death in 1988. *—Bill Dahl*

40 Greatest Hits / 1989 / Mercury ✦✦✦✦✦
Everything you need to know about Benton's bluesy, sexy pop music is included here, in the duets with Dinah Washington. *—Hank Davis*

● **Endlessly: The Best of Brook Benton** / Jun. 16, 1998 / Rhino ✦✦✦✦✦
Twelve years after they released *Anthology*, arguably the definitive career-spanning Brook Benton collection, Rhino adapted the compilation for CD, releasing *Endlessly: The Best of Brook Benton*. *Endlessly* features three tracks less than *Anthology*, yet it doesn't suffer—it remains a nearly flawless overview of Benton's career, featuring all of his big hits plus many terrific lesser-known singles. Every one of his great singles—from "It's Just a Matter of Time," "Baby (You've Got What It Takes)" and "Kiddio" to "The Boll Weevil Song" and "Rainy Night in Georgia"—are here, in a more concise and accessible form than Mercury's double-disc *40 Greatest Hits*. That double-disc set remains an ideal choice for collectors, but less dedicated fans will find *Endlessly* to be essential. *—Stephen Thomas Erlewine*

20th Century Masters—The Millennium Collection: The Best of Brook Benton / Aug. 29, 2000 / Mercury ✦✦✦✦
20th Century Masters–The Millennium Collection: The Best of Brook Benton gathers a dozen of the singer/songwriter's greatest hits, including "It's Just a Matter of Time," "Fools Rush In," "The Boll Weevil Song," and his duets with Dinah Washington, "Baby (You've Got What It Takes)" and "A Rockin' Good Way (To Mess Around and Fall in Love)." "Kiddio" and "Endlessly" are two more of the many highlights of this collection, which certainly isn't the most comprehensive Brook retrospective available but is nevertheless a delightful introduction to his best known work. *—Heather Phares*

The Essential Vik and RCA Victor Recordings / Jan. 30, 2001 / Taragon ✦✦✦
Brook Benton's *Essential Vik and RCA Victor Recordings* collects some of his best moments from his work on both of those labels, including "Break Her Heart," "If You Only Knew," "Your Love Alone," and "Only Your Love." Much of the collection dates to the mid-'60s, and tracks such as "Mother Nature, Father Time" and "Too Much Good Lovin' (No Good for Me)" trace the evolution of Benton's smooth, lush sound during that time. Though this period of his career didn't generate as many hits as his earlier or later years, *Essential Vik and RCA Victor Recordings* proves that this era is just as enjoyable as his more famous work. *—Heather Phares*

Berlin

f. 1982, Los Angeles, CA, **db.** 1987
New Wave, Adult Contemporary

This Los Angeles-based synth-pop group, founded by bassist John Crawford, singer Terri Nunn, and keyboard player David Diamond, made its first national impression with the provocative single "Sex (I'm A...)" from the gold-selling debut EP *Pleasure Victim* in 1982. The group was filled out by guitarist Rick Olsen, keyboard player Matt Reid, and drummer Rob Brill. Berlin's first full-length LP was the gold *Love Life* in 1984. In 1985, the group was pared down to a trio of Crawford, Nunn, and Brill. Berlin topped the charts in 1986 with the single "Take My Breath Away," the love theme from the Tom Cruise movie *Top Gun*. Nunn left for a solo career in 1987, and Crawford and Brill teamed up in the Big F. In 1999, the band reunited to record some new studio material and also performed a concert, which, along with the new songs, was released as 2000's *Berlin Live: Sacred & Profane*. *—William Ruhlmann*

Pleasure Victim / 1982 / Geffen ✦✦✦✦

Love Life / 1984 / Geffen ✦✦✦

Count Three and Pray / 1986 / Geffen ✦✦✦✦
A major change of direction for Berlin, *Count Three and Pray* was an artistic triumph but a commercial disappointment. After making a name for itself playing very European-sounding synth-pop, the L.A. trio recruited producer Bob Ezrin (known for his work with Alice Cooper and others) and unveiled a more hard-edged, guitar-oriented sound. From the rockin' "Trash" (which features none other than Ted Nugent—the last person one would expect to work with Berlin!) to the ballad "Pink and Velvet" (a tale of two heroin addicts' romance that is as poignant as it is disturbing), *Count Three and Pray* leaves no doubt just how much lead singer Terri Nunn and her colleagues were enjoying this radical change. But sadly, record buyers weren't ready for it. Despite the inclusion of the hauntingly pretty number one hit "Take My Breath Away" (included in the film *Top Gun*) the album didn't sell nearly as well as *Pleasure Victim* or *Love Life*. Geffen was bitterly disappointed, and Berlin soon broke up. *—Alex Henderson*

● **The Best of Berlin 1979-1988** / 1989 / Geffen ✦✦✦✦
Berlin's electro-pop sound is salvaged only by the enduring and assertive voice of Terri Nunn, which is why *The Best Of Berlin* is the most preferable place to hear this Los Angeles-based group's music. The synth-soaked punch of "No More Words" from 1984's *Love Life* album and the week-long number one ballad "Take My Breath Away" from the film *Top Gun* are the album's high points, while the other tracks are made up of clean and bright techno pop-rock with heavy emphasis stemming from three different keyboard players that were employed throughout the band's career. Berlin's eighties poignancy provided some rather palatable music, even if the charts didn't say so. Songs like "For All Tomorrow's Lies" and "Blowin' Sky High" could compete with anything Soft Cell or A Flock Of Seagulls spouted at the time, and the range of Nunn's vocals elevated most of Berlin's efforts above the norm of the run-of-mill synthesizer glitz, but only marginally. A compressed lineup of their most accomplished material is definitely the best way in which to enjoy Berlin, avoiding all the inessentials that crept through their albums. *—Mike DeGagne*

Chuck Berry (Charles Edward Anderson Berry)

b. Oct. 18, 1926, St. Louis, MO
Vocals, Leader, Guitar (Electric), Songwriter, Guitar / Rock & Roll

Of all the early breakthrough rock & roll artists, none is more important to the development of the music than Chuck Berry. He is its greatest songwriter, the main shaper of its instrumental voice, one of its greatest guitarists and one of its greatest performers. Quite simply, without him, there would be no Beatles, Rolling Stones, Beach Boys, Bob Dylan, nor a myriad others. There would be no standard "Chuck Berry guitar intro," the instrument's clarion call to get the joint rockin' in any setting. The clippety clop rhythms of rockabilly would not have been mainstreamed into the now standard 4/4 rock & roll beat. There would be no obsessive wordplay by modern-day tunesmiths; in fact, the whole history (and artistic level) of rock & roll songwriting would have been much poorer without him. Like Brian Wilson said, he wrote "all of the great songs and came up with all the rock & roll beats." Those who do not claim him as a seminal influence or profess a liking for his music and showmanship show their ignorance of rock's development as well as his place as the music's first great creator. Elvis may have fueled rock & roll's imagery, but Chuck Berry was its heartbeat and original mindset. *—Cub Koda*

After School Session / 1958 / Chess ✦✦✦✦✦
While Chuck Berry's first album, *After School Session*, featured only one hit single, the Top Ten "School Day," several of the songs became rock & roll standards, including "Too Much Monkey Business," "No Money Down," and "Brown Eyed Handsome Man." *After School Session* also featured a couple of stylistic variations, including the calypso-flavored "Havana Moon" and the straight blues of "Wee Wee Hours." *—Stephen Thomas Erlewine*

One Dozen Berrys / 1958 / Chess ✦✦✦✦✦
Just in case MCA's latest Chuck Berry anthology isn't sufficiently diverting, this CD from England's Beat Goes on Records, containing remastered versions of his second and fifth LPs, is a good place to start looking further into his Chess Records history. Apart from their intrinsic musical merits, between them, these albums—his first two LP releases in England—provided the British bands of the early '60s a big chunk of their repertory, the Rolling Stones alone pulling no less than three of their early songs from *Juke Box Hits*. The charted hits—"Sweet Little Sixteen," "Reelin' & Rockin'," "Rock & Roll Music"—speak for themselves, but there's a lot more music to enjoy here that usually doesn't make it onto any compilations: "Oh Baby Doll," a brash, stomping account of teenage life and romance that has somehow been overlooked for 40-some years; the instrumentals "Rocking at the Philharmonic," "Ingo," "Low Feeling," and "Guitar Boogie" (the source for the Yardbirds' "Jeff's Boogie"); the slow blues numbers "How You've Changed," "Sweet Sixteen," "Away From You," and "Stop and Listen"; the high-wattage Elmore James-inspired "Run Around"; the rollicking hillbilly flavored "It Don't Take but a Few Minutes"; "I'm Talking About You," a rocked-up adaptation of a Memphis Minnie number; the cocky Tampa Red adaptation "Don't You Lie to Me"; and his pounding rendition of the Nat "King" Cole hit "(Get Your Kicks On) Route 66." Not everything worked, such as the attempts to turn Berry into a crooner aimed at the teen market on "Diploma for Two" and "The Way It Was Before," although "Little Star" is pretty in a rough-hewn way. The remastering brings out all kinds of nuances in Berry's playing and also the bass and

drums that were only suggested in earlier editions of these albums, but the clarity doesn't detract from the punch of the finished recordings. —*Bruce Eder*

☆ **Chuck Berry Is on Top** / 1959 / Chess ✦✦✦✦✦
If you had to sweat all of Chuck Berry's early albums on Chess (and some, but not all, of his subsequent greatest-hits packages), this would be the one to own. The song lineup is exemplary, cobbling together classics like "Maybellene," "Carol," "Sweet Little Rock & Roller," "Little Queenie," "Roll Over Beethoven," "Around and Around," "Johnny B. Goode" and "Almost Grown." With the addition of the Latin-flavored "Hey Pedro," the steel guitar workout "Blues for Hawaiians," "Anthony Boy" and "Jo Jo Gunne," this serves as almost a mini-greatest hits package in and of itself. While this may be merely a collection of singles and album ballast (as were most rock & roll LPs of the 1950s and early '60s), it ends up being the most perfectly realized of Chuck Berry's career. —*Cub Koda*

Rockin' at the Hops / 1960 / Chess ✦✦✦
The two classic cuts that bookend this album should be enough to attract the uninitiated—Berry at his best wrote danceable little "vest-pocket" screenplays dealing with teen life, of which "Bye Bye Johnny" and "Let It Rock" were two of his best; but because they've been so heavily anthologized, those two cuts don't have the pulling power here that they would have had 40-some years back. So get this record for everything else that's on it—*Rockin' at the Hops* not only has no filler, but it's chock full of records that show off a bluesy side of Berry's output that was never fully appreciated at the time. His version of Big Maceo's "Worried Life Blues" shows how good a bluesman Berry might've been had he been more the Muddy Waters-type player and singer that Chess had been looking for; "Down the Road a Piece," a song written by Don Raye (of "Boogie Woogie Bugle Boy" fame), is a lost Berry single that could've rated right up there with "Roll Over Beethoven," except that its roadhouse ambience and story line were more mature than a lot of kids might've embraced in 1959; and Walter Brown's "Confessin' the Blues" and "Driftin' Blues" fit into the same category, Berry the adult bluesman rather than the teen-oriented teaser. "Childhood Sweetheart" is a sequel to "Wee Wee Hours," Berry's very first blues side, lifting a fragment or two from Elmore James' "Dust My Broom" for its guitar break. "Too Pooped to Pop" and "Betty Jean," by contrast, are a pair of enjoyably upbeat rock & roll numbers, each featuring uncharacteristic elements, a sax solo on the former, and a male chorus on the latter; in between them is "Mad Lad," an instrumental that presents Berry drifting into what would later be defined as a surf guitar mode—a quicker tempo would have done it (and does anyone want to bet that a young Carl Wilson didn't wear out a copy or two listening to this track?). —*Bruce Eder*

New Juke Box Hits / 1961 / Chess ✦✦✦
Chuck Berry's fifth Chess Records album, *New Juke Box Hits*, was recorded and released in the midst of the legal difficulties that would put him in jail the following year. That distraction seems to have kept him from composing top-flight material, while the attendant publicity adversely affected his record sales, such that the album contained no hits. The included single was "I'm Talking About You," later successfully recorded by the Rolling Stones, and the album also contained "The Thirteen Question Method" and "Don't You Lie to Me," worthy minor entries in the Berry canon. Elsewhere, Berry filled out the record covering others' hits—Nat "King" Cole's "Route 66," B.B. King's "Sweet Sixteen," Little Richard's "Rip It Up." The result is a good rock & roll set, but not in the same league with Berry's earlier albums. —*William Ruhlmann*

☆ **St. Louis to Liverpool** / 1964 / Chess ✦✦✦✦✦
This album puts the lie to the popular myth that Chuck Berry's music started to fade away around the same time that the Beatles, the Rolling Stones, et al. emerged covering his stuff. His songwriting is as strong here as ever—side one is packed with now-familiar fare like "Little Marie" (a sequel to "Memphis, Tennessee"), "No Particular Place to Go," "Promised Land," and "You Never Can Tell," but even filler tracks like "Our Little Rendezvous" and "You Two" are among Berry's better album numbers, the latter showing off the slightly softer pop/R&B side to his music that many listeners forget about. Side two includes a bunch of tracks, including the hard-rocking "Go Bobby Soxer" and the even better "Brenda Lee," the slow blues "Things I Used to Do" (with a killer guitar break), and the instrumentals "Liverpool Drive" and "Night Beat," one fast and the other slow, that never get reissued or compiled anywhere. The sound on the 1984 reissue LP is excellent, and it's a lot easier to find than an original album. —*Bruce Eder*

Chuck Berry's Golden Hits / 1967 / Mercury ✦

The London Sessions / 1972 / Chess ✦✦✦
One-half of this album is a studio recording featuring Ian McLagan and Kenny Jones of the Faces. The other half is a live recording from the Lancaster Arts Festival in Coventry, England, featuring performances of "My Ding-a-Ling" and "Reelin' and Rockin'" that, in edited form, became the first hit singles for Chuck Berry in many years. ("My Ding-a-Ling" went gold and hit #1.) This gold-selling, Top Ten album represents Berry's commercial, if not artistic, peak. —*William Ruhlmann*

★ **The Great Twenty-Eight** / 1982 / Chess ✦✦✦✦✦
This is the place to start listening to Chuck Berry. *The Great Twenty-Eight* was a two-LP, single CD compilation that emerged during the early '80s, amid a brief period in which the Chess catalog was in the hands of the Sugar Hill label, a disco-oriented outfit that later lost the catalog to MCA. It has proved to be one of the most enduring of all compilations of Berry's work. Up until the release of this disc, every attempt at a compilation had either been too sketchy (the 1964 *Greatest Hits* album on Chess) or too demanding for the casual listener (the three *Golden Decade* double-LP sets), and this was the first set to find a happy medium between convenience and thoroughness. Veteran listeners will love this CD even if they learn little from it, while neophytes will want to play it to death. All of the cuts come from Berry's first nine years in music, including all of the major singles as well as relatively minor hits such as "Come On" (which was more significant in the history of rock & roll in its cover version performed by the Rolling Stones as their debut release). The sound is decent throughout (surprisingly, except for "Come On," which has some considerable noise), although it is considerably outclassed by the most recent round of remasterings. In the decades since its release, there have been more comprehensive collections of Berry's work, but this is the best single disc, if one can overlook the relatively lo-fi digital sound. —*Bruce Eder*

Rock & Roll Rarities / 1986 / Chess ✦✦✦✦✦
On this follow-up to *The Great Twenty-Eight*, the songs are familiar, but the versions are not. Delving into the Chess Records archives, producer Steve Hoffman has come up with 20 tracks, many in unreleased or unusual versions. Some are demos, some are stereo recordings of songs usually heard in mono. Hoffman has remixed many of them, bringing up the '50s and '60s sound quality to near-'80s standard. Start with *The Great Twenty-Eight*, but come to this collection for interesting new ways to hear the old Berry favorites. —*William Ruhlmann*

More Rock & Roll Rarities from the Golden Era of Chess Records / Aug. 1986 / Chess ✦✦✦
This second volume of producer Steve Hoffman's discoveries in the Chess Records vaults features some less prominent Chuck Berry tunes, again in the form of demos, unreleased alternate takes, and stereo remixes. We are getting into collector territory here, but there are still some enjoyable examples of the Berry repertoire. —*William Ruhlmann*

Hail! Hail! Rock & Roll / 1987 / MCA ✦✦✦
This is the soundtrack to a documentary film chronicling a concert held to celebrate Chuck Berry's 60th birthday. The band was led by Keith Richards and featured Berry's regular pianist, Johnnie Johnson, Richards' regular pianist, Chuck Leavell, Rolling Stones sax player Bobby Keys, bassist Joey Spampinato from NRBQ, and drummer Steve Jordan from Richards' solo band. The guests included Robert Cray, Linda Ronstadt, Eric Clapton, Julian Lennon, and Etta James. Berry was ragged-voiced but enthusiastic, the band had spirit, and the guests, even if they were sometimes unlikely, were sincere. The best way to hear Berry's music is to obtain the original recordings, of course, but as a souvenir of the Taylor Hackford film, this is an enjoyable romp through the catalog. —*William Ruhlmann*

☆ **The Chess Box** / 1988 / Chess ✦✦✦✦✦
Over the course of three compact discs, *The Chess Box* contains all the highlights from Chuck Berry's career, including all of the hit singles. In addition to the familar items, which are all included here, there are numerous tracks that are lesser-known but equally as good. That's particularly true on the stellar first two discs, where album tracks, B-sides, and forgotten singles like "Downbound Train," "Drifting Heart," "Havana Moon," "Betty Jean," "Bye Bye Johnny," "Down the Road a Piece," and "The Thirteen Question Method" get equal space with "Maybellene," "Thirty Days," "No Money Down," "Roll Over Beethoven," "Too Much Monkey Business," "Brown Eyed Handsome Man," "School Day," "Rock & Roll Music," "Sweet Little Sixteen," "Johnny B. Goode," and "Carol." Toward the end of the set, the quality of the material begins to sag a bit, but there are still forgotten gems like "Tulane" that prove that Berry's songwriting hadn't completely dried up. *The Great Twenty Eight* remains the definitive hits collection, but *The Chess Box* is an absolutely essential item for any serious fan, either of Chuck Berry or rock & roll. —*Stephen Thomas Erlewine*

Missing Berries / Jul. 1990 / Chess ✦✦✦
The third and final collection of Chuck Berry rarities from the Chess Records vaults, *Missing Berries* concentrates on Berry's blues recordings, which were never quite as captivating as his rock & roll, yet they're fascinating for devoted fans. —*Stephen Thomas Erlewine*

★ **His Best, Vol. 1** / Mar. 25, 1997 / Chess ✦✦✦✦✦
Strictly focusing on his single tracks in a chronological manner, this first of two volumes in MCA's Chess 50th Anniversary collection hits all the high spots of Chuck's career up to 1958. It also serves as the first compilation to really showcase Berry's development as a songwriter over the first three years of his massive crossover success, including the seldom-anthologized "Downbound Train" (perhaps the darkest and most demonic ditty he ever recorded) juxtaposed against his car songs ("Maybellene," "You Can't Catch Me"), his calculated and carefully crafted instant classics for the 1950s teenage market ("Reelin' and Rockin'," "Sweet Little Sixteen," "School Day") and his celebrations of the music itself ("Rock & Roll Music," "Johnny B. Goode," "Roll Over Beethoven"). There's a ton of great music here (with a second companion volume to complete the picture) and for a big chunk of what makes Chuck Berry perhaps rock & roll's original triple-threat package (singer, songwriter, and its first guitar hero), there's much here to tip the scales in its favor to recommend this volume as a first-time purchase. Note: This collection and its companion volume now take the place of the single disc *The Great Twenty Eight*, which is now out of print. —*Cub Koda*

☆ **His Best, Vol. 2** / May 20, 1997 / Chess ✦✦✦✦✦
Picking up where the first volume left off, *His Best, Vol. 2* runs through Chuck Berry's best-known singles in 1958 with "Sweet Little Rock & Roller" and runs through 1972, when he inexplicably had his first number one record with "My Ding-a-Ling." In addition to hits like "Let It Rock," "Little Queenie," "Almost Grown," "Nadine," "No Particular Place to Go," "You Never Can Tell," and "Promised Land," there are lesser-known gems like "Jo Jo Gunne," making it more than just a rote greatest-hits collection. No matter how good the two-part *His Best* series is—and for fans that don't want to spring for *The Chess Box*, it's the best way to assemble a reasonably comprehensive Chuck collection—it's still a shame that Chess decided to delete the flawless single-disc compilation *The Great Twenty-Eight* in favor of this series. —*Stephen Thomas Erlewine*

The Latest & the Greatest/You Never Can Tell / 1998 / BGO ✦✦✦✦

The value of this two-on-one CD from England's Beat Goes On Records is greater than the sum of its parts—most of the important tracks here can be found on either the Chuck Berry box or one of the individual MCA-Chess CDs, but they sound infinitely better here, in new late-'90s transfers, than they do on MCA's mid-'80s digital editions. And "good" in this case means they're clean but mean, crisp but raunchy, not like the over-cleaned up versions off of the Chess Box's first disc. The notes are a bit vague as far as the origins of the two LPs are concerned—they were patchwork creations from recent singles and old U.S. album tracks, done specifically for the British market by Pye Records—but the sound makes up for those shortcomings. —*Bruce Eder*

★ **Anthology** / Jun. 27, 2000 / Chess ✦✦✦✦✦

Falling squarely between the 71-track triple-disc *Chess Box* and numerous single-album distillations of Chuck Berry's hits, most notably *The Great Twenty-Eight*, is this 2000-released, chronologically compiled double-disc set. Its 50 tunes include all of Berry's seminal Chess hits plus key album tracks like "Beautiful Delilah," "Jo Jo Gunne," and "Jaguar & Thunderbird" that were influential but never cracked the charts. The 20-page booklet features a fascinating, extensive essay that provides crucial insights into Berry's work as well as rare pictures and track-by-track personnel listing. Since virtually all of Berry's essential work was done for the Chess label, now part of the Universal empire, there's no reason to decry the lack of anything from Berry's Mercury years, even though those tracks are now owned by the same company and could have been included, especially tacked onto disc two that times out at a relatively conservative 64 minutes. But with a lineup like this, who's complaining? Berry is the undisputed father of rock & roll and his music, much of it blues based and in a few cases like "Havana Moon" even Caribbean inspired, remains timeless as well as inspirational decades after it was recorded. The joys of discovering forgotten, relatively obscure cuts like "Come On" or "I'm Talking About You," both of which are easily on par with any of his more popular hits, is one of life's little bonuses. Berry's lyrics remain intriguingly descriptive, and the remastered sound brings these songs alive with every instrument, especially Willie Dixon's dynamic, jazzy stand-up bass clearly defined. The savvy track selection makes this a better, more consistent listen than the bulky box and stands as the best introduction to one of the most significant pop musicians of 20th century music and the single most important rock & roller ever. —*Hal Horowitz*

Richard Berry

b. Apr. 11, 1935, Extension, LA, **d.** Jan. 23, 1997
Vocals / Rock & Roll, R&B

If for no other reason than that he was the original writer and performer of "Louie Louie," Richard Berry holds a permanent place of honor in the history of rock & roll. Beyond that, though, Berry was an important if secondary figure of the early- and mid-'50s Los Angeles R&B scene. As a teenager, with the Flairs and as a solo act, Berry recorded quite a few singles that demonstrated his versatilty with ballads, novelty songs, and even Little Richard-styled numbers. He originally recorded "Louie Louie" in 1956; the record was a regional hit in several West Coast cities, but no more than that. Berry's recording career petered out in the late '50s, though he remained an active performer. In the early '60s, several Northwest bands seized upon "Louie Louie" as cover material, scoring sizable regional hits; finally, in 1963, the Kingsmen broke the song nationally, reaching number two. In the decades since then, "Louie Louie" became one of the most oft-covered rock standards of all time; there are probably well over 1000 versions by now. —*Richie Unterberger*

● **Get Out of the Car** / 1982 / Flair ✦✦✦✦✦

20 songs from the mid-'50s, both solo and with the Flairs. Berry wrote or co-wrote most of the tunes, which are solid if somewhat generic R&B on the verge of rock & roll, occasionally treading into doo-wop territory. He's most memorable on the uptempo, comic jiving numbers, with a sardonic and sassy tone that pointed the way for the Coasters. This doesn't have "Louie Louie" or any of the late-'50s material he recorded for the Flip label, which is available on the hard-to-find Swedish import *Louie Louie*. —*Richie Unterberger*

The Beta Band

f. 1997, Edinburgh, Scotland
Experimental Dub, Electronica, Neo-Electro, Indie Rock, Trip-Hop

Their sound veering from post-grunge balladry to funk and ambient breakbeat to Madchester acid-house, the Beta Band emerged on the British scene as (nominally) a pop group with few similarities to any other act going. Formed around three friends originally from Edinburgh—vocalist Stephen Mason, drummer Robin Jones, and DJ/sampler John Maclean—the group later added bassist Richard Greentree. Scant months after forming, the Beta Band gained a formidable ally in gaining exposure: manager Brian Cannon, the designer responsible for virtually every Oasis sleeve released to that point. The group's first EP, 1997's *Champion Versions*, featured mixing by the Verve's Nick McCabe. Two additional EPs followed in early 1998, *The Patty Patty Sound* and *Los Amigos del Beta Bandidos*. After collecting all three EPs on an album, the Beta Band began recording for their proper debut, a self-titled effort released in 1999. While prepping for the release of their sophomore effort, *Hot Shots II* in summer 2001, the Beta Band scored the opening slot on Radiohead's monumental summer tour of the United States. —*John Bush*

● **The 3 E.P.'s** / Sep. 28, 1998 / Astralwerks ✦✦✦✦✦

This grouping of the Beta Band's first recordings—three EPs, four tracks each—is a collection of practically indescribable songs. In fact, many of the tracks are only nominally pop songs; the group ranges from Kraut and avant-rock musings to heavy funk and hip-hop without the feeling of force that it's being done for the sake of critics. —*John Bush*

The Beta Band / Jun. 15, 1999 / Astralwerks ✦✦✦✦

Though dismissed by the group themselves as "fucking awful" and "the worst record made this year," the Beta Band's self-titled album otherwise defies simple criticism—seemingly infinite in its sonic complexities, it's an album of remarkable density and detail, a brashly schizophrenic freak-out which weaves its way throughout the history of rock & roll. Pop, blues, folk, psychedelia, hip-hop—they're all here, sometimes even colliding within the same song; the disc somehow sounds almost completely different with each successive listen, consistently revealing new layers and possibilities. It all constantly runs the risk of collapsing into complete self-indulgence, but in its way the Beta Band's genius is their wanton disregard for niceties like verses, choruses, and melodies; rejecting musical theory in favor of the chaos theory, the album's neither a masterpiece nor a mess, but both. —*Jason Ankeny*

Hot Shots II / Jun. 26, 2001 / Astralwerks/Regal ✦✦✦✦✦

Following an LP that was slagged by even the group themselves before release, the Beta Band got down to business for their second proper record. While their self-titled debut reveled in a near-blinding collage of samples, synthpads, noise, and obtuse figures, for *Hot Shots II* the group took a much different path. Many of the tracks are (comparatively) quiet songs, the productions pared down to minimal proportions and focused on slow, darkly descending chords. The band's methods are innovative as before, but now they've taken on the challenge of saying more with less—with fewer production fragments to obscure the songs, they're left to survive on their own. During the opener "Squares," a minute passes before the song even begins to make sense; a few glimpses of beats and basslines are the only accompaniment to Stephen Mason's chanted vocals, until the chorus sweeps in to reveal a tight, beautiful trip-hop-with-strings production. "Gone" does well with just bass, piano, and background vocals from the band. Elsewhere, the Beta Band rely on spare bits—stuttered acoustic-guitar samples, whining melodica, regal horns in the background—to get their point across, but aren't afraid to rock out either. While the songwriting certainly isn't direct, it's much less consciously unscrutable compared to the madcap toss-offs spread over *The Beta Band*. Understandably suspicious when the group promised an even better record their second time out, listeners have the proof with *Hot Shots II*. —*John Bush*

Bettie Serveert

f. 1990, Amsterdam, The Netherlands
Indie Pop, Twee Pop, Indie Rock, Alternative Pop/Rock

Comprised of vocalist/guitarist Carol van Dijk, guitarist Peter Visser, bassist Herman Bunskoeke, and drummer Berend Dubbe, the Dutch guitar pop quartet Bettie Serveert released their debut album, *Palomine*, in 1992. Bettie Serveert has jangly hooks and sweet melodies to spare, yet the group can rock as hard as the Pretenders. Featuring the radio hits "Kid's Allright" and "Tom Boy," *Palomine* made the band alternative rock stars. The group's second album, *Lamprey*, was released in 1995 to favorable reviews, as was 1997's *Dust Bunnies*. The live *Plays Venus in Furs and Other Velvet Underground Songs* followed in 1998. —*Stephen Thomas Erlewine*

● **Palomine** / 1992 / Matador ✦✦✦✦✦

Bettie Serveert's charm, as established from the get-go on their debut album, wasn't any kind of new radicalism but the members' way around well-known rock styles to unexpected effect. Everything from third album Velvet Underground and Neil Young's furious electric heights to the Wedding Present's bruised romanticism (the production especially calls to mind some of Steve Albini's work for that band) has an echo here. What makes it all connect isn't simply the considerable abilities of the group, especially guitarists Visser and van Dijk, but van Dijk's strong singing and lyrics both. Combining both a low-key sass and a slightly distanced, concerned tone, her voice cuts directly through the arrangements, the most upfront thing in the mix. Comparisons aren't easy to make; early Chrissie Hynde makes a certain amount of sense, but van Dijk is no clone. As for her subject matter, small details of everyday life, especially concerns of identity and dealing with others, form the basis of her sharp, sometimes painfully close to the heart images. "Brain-Tag," with her plaintive refrain "Have I ever laid my hands on you before?" and "Healthy Sick" are two of the standouts on that level. When she stops to let the music fully take over, the transition is often perfect—"Kid's Allright" is a good example, the instrumental breaks carrying the forceful feel of the words into the nonverbal. "Tom Boy," the surprise U.S. minor radio hit from the album, shows the quartet's mix of skills quite nicely. A mid-paced but lovely number with a descending chord riff à la T. Rex (if not as glammy otherwise) and van Dijk's multi-tracked vocals claiming the term for herself, "because only a tom boy could rise above it," make *Palomine* a quietly addictive number from this fine album. —*Ned Raggett*

Lamprey / Jan. 24, 1995 / Matador ✦✦

Dust Bunnies / Mar. 25, 1997 / Matador/Capitol ✦✦✦

While *Dust Bunnies* is a tighter, more melodic album than Bettie Serveert's flawed second record *Lamprey*, it doesn't necessarily return to the band the heights of *Palomine*. Musically, *Dust Bunnies* is no different than its two predecessors, and the group's lack of development is a little bit eerie—it's one thing to have a distinctive sound and quite another to make two albums that sound like outtakes from your debut. Instead of developing or refining their sound, Bettie Serveert stay within their self-imposed boundaries, crafting small, simple jangle-pop songs that never rock too hard or sound too soft. Occasionally, as on "Co-Coward" and "Sugar the Pill," they create wonderful pop gems, but too often the music never is anything more than pleasant. —*Stephen Thomas Erlewine*

Plays Venus in Furs and Other Velvet Underground Songs / Aug. 18, 1998 / Brinkman ✦✦✦

Tackling a touchstone like the Velvet Underground invites comparisons that aren't flattering. Carol van Dijk's bassy alto lacks the sweetness and knowing naivete that Nico brings to her tracks ("Sunday Morning," "Stephanie Says" are tackled), nor does she quite nail Reed's dark, understated swagger. The playing is pretty reverential, and the band seems hesitant to put their own stamp on the songs. In the end, Bettie Serveert sounds too much like a competent bar cover band and doesn't add enough to the musical sensibility to be anything else. At the same time, it's understood that it'd be hard to improve on the Velvets, especially after these songs have been so imprinted on the consciousness after years of loving homage that served as the basis for large swaths of alternative rock. The band does do a better job with the longer, free-flowing, less pop pieces ("Euopean Son," "Black Angel's Death Song," and "Venus in Furs"), accurately capturing the dark hypnotic tones, thanks to Peter Visser's smoldering guitar work which complements van Dijk's own smoky vocals. Indeed, the band begins to hit their stride about midway into the live set, roaring through the rocking rave "I Can't Stand It" on to "Rock & Roll," and the letter-perfect, appropriate closer "Afterhours." —*Chris Parker*

Private Suit / Jul. 18, 2000 / Hidden Agenda ✦✦✦✦
Bettie Serveert's classic 1992 debut *Palomine* was ultimately a bit too perfect—the band effectively left themselves no margin for error, and subsequent efforts had nowhere to go but down, each record doomed to suffer by comparison. *Private Suit*, Bettie Serveert's fourth studio outing, is a considerable return to form in the sense that so many years later, both artist and listener alike finally understand that what's past is past—when Carol Van Dijk wails "So don't worry about me/'cause you can't please everyone" on the disc's bewitching title track, it's clear that the group is finally back to making music solely on their own terms; and ironically enough, *Private Suit* comes closer to recapturing the brilliance of *Palomine* than any other Bettie Serveert record, by implicitly acknowledging that a return to former glories is an unreachable ideal. Credit much of the album's dusky allure to the atmospheric production of John Parish, which lends a shadowy beauty, revealing new layers of subtlety lurking underneath the band's ragged guitar-pop approach; the focal point is still van Dijk's searing vocals, which harness the extremes of both pride and desperation to devastating effect. Welcome back. —*Jason Ankeny*

Beulah

f. 1994
Indie Pop, Indie Rock, Lo-Fi
San Francisco's entry into the ever-expanding Elephant 6 indie-pop collective, Beulah originally comprised the duo of Miles Kurosky and Bill Swan; after debuting in 1997 with the EP *A Small Cattle Drive in a Snow Storm*, Anne Mellinger signed on to record the full-length *Handsome Western States*, released late that same year. In the spring of 1999, Beulah—now consisting of Kurosky, Swan, Steve LaFolette, Pat Noel, Steve St. Cin, Bill Evans, and Ana Pitchon—returned with the excellent *When Your Heartstrings Break*. —*Jason Ankeny*

Handsome Western States / 1997 / Elephant 6 ✦✦✦
Possibly due to the surreal combination of day traders and hippies, the San Francisco area has always stood fast as one of the more peculiar bases of music. Which helps explain how Beulah—while valiantly trying to tempt that XTC or Beach Boys muse—ends up sounding like an exasperated Pavement. If nothing else, this low-budget affair demonstrates a blustery education in guitar pop with a mostly shallow well of styles. The angular, bopping "I've Been Broken (I've Been Fixed)" pun-fest, the "She Don't Use Jelly" appropriation in "Dig the Subatomic Holdout #2," or the lo-fi pseudo-pop of "Disco: The Secretaries Blues" certainly disguise any individualistic merit just yet. Apart from glimmers of true choruses ("Queen of the Populists"), there are especially few instances of attention-grabbing toils either. One can't imagine San Francisco's ghosts of Spent Poets past approving of such little progression. Which is probably why *Handsome Western States* sounds like a demo-level holding pattern for the band as they seemingly wait to finally land a good tune. In fact, despite what the chronology of their discography might claim, Beulah's debut album has yet to be recorded. —*Dean Carlson*

● **When Your Heartstrings Break** / Mar. 9, 1999 / Sugar Free ✦✦✦✦✦
Beulah's sophomore record is another irresistible addition to the Elephant 6 canon—artfully texturing its infectious guitar-pop melodies with lush strings, woodwinds, and horns (courtesy of no less than 18 guest musicians), *When Your Heartstrings Break* delivers fully on the promise of the group's debut *Handsome Western States*. What sets Beulah apart from their E6 peers is a straightforward pop sensibility that dreamier, more spaced-out counterparts like the Olivia Tremor Control or Elf Power lack—for all of their flourishes, the 11 tracks which comprise *When Your Heartstrings Break* are at their core simple love songs; under their ironic surface, Miles Kurosky's lyrics possess a disarming sweetness which perfectly complements his buoyant melodies. Highly recommended. —*Jason Ankeny*

The Coast Is Never Clear / Sep. 11, 2001 / Velocette ✦✦✦✦✦

Big Audio Dynamite

f. 1984, London, England
College Rock, Alternative Dance, Alternative Pop/Rock
After Mick Jones was fired from the Clash in 1983, he formed Big Audio Dynamite (B.A.D.) one year later with video artist Don Letts (effects and vocals), Greg Roberts (drums), Dan Donovan (keyboards), and Leo "E-Zee Kill" Williams (bass). B.A.D. debuted on record with the single "The Bottom Line" in September 1985. The group followed the more experimental funk elements of the Clash's *Combat Rock*, adding samplers, dance tracks, and found sounds to Jones' concise pop songwriting. Jones suffered from a near-fatal bout of pneumonia in 1988, but bounced back with 1989's *Megatop Phoenix*. After that record, the band split apart at the end of 1989. Jones added Gary Stonadge (bass/vo-

cals), Chris Kavanagh (drums/vocals), and Nick Hawkins (guitar/vocals) to form Big Audio Dynamite II, while Letts, Williams, and Roberts formed Screaming Target and Donovan joined the Sisters of Mercy. Releasing *The Globe*, the first full-length album with the new lineup, in 1991, B.A.D. II experienced their greatest success with the American Top 40 hit single "Rush." In 1994, the band's name was truncated to Big Audio, and the album *Higher Power* was released.

After *Higher Power*, Big Audio parted ways with Epic Records, signing with Radioactive in early 1995 and releasing *F-Punk* later that year. —*Stephen Thomas Erlewine and William Ruhlmann*

This Is Big Audio Dynamite / Oct. 1985 / Columbia ✦✦✦
Since Mick Jones was the more melodic, pop force in The Clash, it was a surprise that the band he formed after being kicked out of that group was such an unusual mix of synthesized drumming and spoken-word tape inserts, although beneath all the gimmicky sounds (and perhaps accentuated by them) were Jones's often winning songs, among which were the U.K. Top 40 hits "E = MC²" and "Medicine Show." —*William Ruhlmann*

No. 10, Upping St. / Oct. 1986 / Columbia ✦✦✦✦
Temporarily reuniting with his former Clash partner Joe Strummer (who co-produced this album and co-wrote five songs), Mick Jones expands on the formula of the debut with Big Audio Dynamite's second album. *No. 10 Upping Street* features better songs that meld samples, found sounds, dance rhythms, and elements of hip-hop more completely and effectively than those on the first record. "C'mon Every Beatbox" and "V. Thirteen" made the U.K. singles chart. "Badrock City," added to the album after its initial release, made the U.S. R&B singles chart. —*Stephen Thomas Erlewine and William Ruhlmann*

Tighten Up, Vol. 88 / Jun. 1988 / Columbia ✦✦

Megatop Phoenix / Sep. 1989 / Columbia ✦✦✦
On *Megatop Phoenix*, Jones delves even further into a dance-influenced, cut-and-paste approach to pop music that manages to capture all of the inventiveness of late-'80s dance music without losing sight of the melodies that have always been his strength. —*Stephen Thomas Erlewine*

The Globe / Aug. 1991 / Columbia ✦✦✦✦
Although the second incarnation of Big Audio Dynamite doesn't sound all that different from the first, Mick Jones's songwriting and concepts are reinvigorated on *The Globe*, making it one of the best B.A.D. albums. It also ranked as their most commercially successful in the U.S., where "Rush" hit the Top 40, with the title track also charting. —*Stephen Thomas Erlewine*

Higher Power / Nov. 8, 1994 / Columbia ✦✦

F-Punk / Jun. 20, 1995 / Radioactive ✦✦

● **Planet BAD: Greatest Hits** / Sep. 12, 1995 / Columbia ✦✦✦✦✦
Big Audio Dynamite's albums have always been fairly inconsistent affairs, which makes *Greatest Hits* such a worthwhile purchase. Collecting 15 songs from their six albums at Columbia, when they were alternately called B.A.D. and B.A.D. II, the album contains hits like "The Globe" and "Rush," as well as album tracks and college radio hits. —*Stephen Thomas Erlewine*

Super Hits / May 4, 1999 / Columbia/Legacy ✦✦✦
Like many conceptual bands, Big Audio Dynamite were primarily an album-based group, turning out records that had a consistent sound and theme. The problem was, Mick Jones had too many ideas. Each B.A.D. record was teeming with intriguing sounds that only made sense on a handful of tracks—in other words, they were an album band most listenable in small doses. That made them easier to anthologize than the average album-rock band, as the enjoyable hits collection *Planet BAD* proved. *Super Hits*, a budget-line comp that concentrates on their Columbia recordings, is nearly as entertaining as the full-fledged hits package, since it contains nearly all of their biggest hits, including "The Bottom Line," "C'Mon Every Beatbox," "Rush," "E = MC²," "Contact," "Medicine Show," and "The Globe"—everything except "Free," really. Hardcore fans will naturally prefer the full-fledged albums, and some will like the more extensive hits package, but this *Super Hits* will satisfy the needs of most casual listeners, especially those on a budget. —*Stephen Thomas Erlewine*

Big Black

f. 1982, Evanston, IL, **db.** 1988
Noise-Rock, Indie Rock, Post-Punk, Alternative Pop/Rock, American Underground
Proudly and self-consciously abrasive, Big Black's music is polarizing; either you think that Steve Albini's relentlessly thin, metallic, emotionless guitar grind and distorted vocals is an uncompromising work of art or you think it's self-indulgent crap. The band's clinical noise and grotesque, often misogynist, lyrics easily made them the most extreme, nihilistic band in the American underground in the mid-'80s. None of their recordings show much of a musical progression; instead, the band gets harder, noisier, and nastier on each subsequent record. Although Big Black's lifespan was short, Albini's influence on the American independent music scene of the late '80s and '90s has been substantial. After Big Black's breakup he formed the equally uncompromising Rapeman, but Albini's real influence has been through his numerous productions. Over the years he has produced literally hundreds of bands; most of them are justifiably unknown, but some are quite famous—including the Pixies, the Breeders, Urge Overkill, PJ Harvey, and Nirvana. Many young bands of the '90s have embraced his signature guitar grind, as well as his strident punk-rock ethics, as a reaction to alternative music's move into the mainstream. —*Stephen Thomas Erlewine*

Atomizer / 1986 / Touch & Go ✦✦✦✦✦
After countless rock and neo-industrial outfits attempted to one-up each other's levels of

extremity over the years, *Atomizer* holds up extremely well. It's not every day that one hears a song considering self-immolation as "just something to do" or another that tackles the case of an alleged parent-child molestation ring from the viewpoint of the offender. Instrumentally, *Atomizer* is a wailing behemoth of assaultive Roland beats, Steve Albini and Santiago Durango's clanging and whirring guitars, and new member Dave Riley's lumberjack bass. Their musical invention went a couple steps further, most obviously on the warped-beyond-recognition guitars of "Passing Complexion" and "Kerosene." The latter is undeniably Big Black's brightest/bleakest moment, an epically roaming track that features an instantly memorable guitar intro, completely incapable of being accurately described by vocal imitation or physical gesture. It's also Albini at his most plainspoken and bleak: "Stare at the wall/Stare at each other and wait 'til we die." It's Big Black's "Light My Fire," literally. "Bad Houses" tops Killing Joke in affecting moodiness, serving as a perhaps unintentional reply to John Mellencamp's "Pink Houses." Both Albini and Mellencamp were commenting on the Midwest, so why not? Other points of interest include the demented, storming menace of "Fists of Love" and a live version of "Cables" that features an extended guitar wobbly from Albini. The record remains as horrifying as the day it was recorded. [*Atomizer* was released on CD as part of *The Rich Man's Eight Track Tape.* The mediocre, largely instrumental "Strange Things" was removed from the digital version. Touch & Go kept the original record in print on vinyl.] *–Andy Kellman*

The Hammer Party / 1986 / Touch & Go ✦✦✦✦

Initially a pairing of Big Black's first two EPs, *Lungs* and *Bulldozer, The Hammer Party* first found release through Homestead on vinyl and CD. When Touch & Go bought out the band's material, they reissued it, adding the band's third EP, *Racer-X.* Those seeking a quick introduction to the early-'80s post-punk combo who welded industrial's nihilism to the angularities of Gang of Four, Killing Joke, and the Pop Group and the sheer claustrophobic terror and mayhem of Suicide should look no further. Though containing later material, *The Rich Man's Eight Track Tape* is actually the best place to go for a first dose of Big Black. The earlier stuff found here isn't up to snuff when compared to *Atomizer* and *Songs About Fucking,* but it's still remarkably riveting. *–Andy Kellman*

● **The Rich Man's Eight Track Tape** / 1987 / Touch & Go ✦✦✦✦✦

An indispensable compilation, *The Rich Man's Eight Track Tape* combines Big Black's monumental *Atomizer* LP with the following *Headache* EP and "Heartbeat" three-song single. While *Atomizer* undoubtedly remains one of the standout records of the mid-'80s underground scene, the *Headache* EP (released a year following) doesn't belong on the same playing field, although it's fine in its own right. Had *Headache* been released prior to *Atomizer,* it would probably be held in higher regard. Obviously not a fan of the compact disc medium, Steve Albini goes to great lengths in the packaging and on the disc itself to encourage the consumer to scratch, fingerprint, and eat off of the CD. He also reminds the listener that the format taking the title was state-of-the-art in the early '70s. Regardless of the medium and its supposed limitations, *The Rich Man's Eight Track Tape* is worth seeking out. *–Andy Kellman*

Songs About Fucking / 1987 / Touch & Go ✦✦✦✦✦

Ever notice how rock bands tend to keep things interesting for themselves by pointlessly dragging out their songs and introducing awkward conceptual threads? Also, how many bands veil their subject matter in euphemisms to avoid being taken literally, to stay safe, or—better yet—to be "mysterious?" Big Black's final LP does the diametric opposite of both. Not only do the 14 songs here whip by with only one exceeding the three-minute mark, but each one is incisive enough to render a razor as effective as a butter knife. And, how could a title be more direct? The only band that had courage enough to be this direct was Spinal Tap, and that was for a song, not an album title. (Clue: it was a ballad in the saddest of keys).

Songs About Fucking brought about a definite sharpening of the band's sound. Steve Albini's mangled screaming is at its most bileful, his and Santiago Durango's guitars don't meander, and the rhythm section of Dave Riley and Roland is more taut than prior. Ugly characters line up in the songs like early arrivals at a monster truck rally. Most significantly, there's the murderer in "Fish Fry." Who else but Steve Albini could paint the picture of a man hosing out his truck after chucking a dead body from it into a nearby pond? His use of the first person can be misleading, but it's a necessary perspective for effect. Big Black left with more of a kling klang than a bang, bowing out with a reverent cover of Kraftwerk's "The Model." To sum up: yowl, ching, thump-thump-screech. [The CD version adds the B-side of "The Model," a swell cover of Cheap Trick's "He's a Whore."] *–Andy Kellman*

The Big Bopper (Jiles Perry Richardson)

b. Oct. 24, 1930, Sabine Pass, TX, **d.** Feb. 3, 1959, Clear Lake, IA

Vocals / Rock & Roll

Legendary as one of the three rock greats to die in the tragic 1959 Clear Lake, IA, plane crash that also claimed the lives of Buddy Holly and Ritchie Valens, the Big Bopper (born Jiles Perry Richardson) had just established himself as a rock hitmaker with the rollicking "Chantilly Lace." Born in the heart of Texas, Richardson grew up in Beaumont and changed his first name to Jape. He broke into show biz as a DJ over KTRM radio, where he coined the nickname "The Big Bopper." He began recording for Mercury in 1957, his animated baritone scaling pop playlists the next year with "Chantilly Lace"—easily his top seller—and the equally raucous novelty "Big Bopper's Wedding." Richardson wrote "White Lightning," a huge country hit for George Jones, and Johnny Preston's number one smash "Running Bear." *–Bill Dahl*

● **Hellooo Baby!: Best of the Big Bopper, 1954-1959** / 1989 / Rhino ✦✦✦✦✦

Hellooo Baby!: Best of the Big Bopper, 1954-1959 is a single-CD compilation of the Bopper's finest, including "Chantilly Lace," "Little Red Riding Hood," and "Big Bopper's Wedding." It's wild and fun. *–Cub Koda*

Big Brother & The Holding Company

f. 1965, San Francisco, CA, **db.** 1972

Album Rock, Acid Rock, Psychedelic, Blues-Rock

Big Brother are primarily remembered as the group that gave Janis Joplin her start. There's no denying both that Joplin was by far the band's most striking asset, and that Big Brother would never have made a significant impression if they hadn't been fortunate enough to add her to their lineup shortly after forming. But Big Brother also occupy a significant place in the history of San Francisco psychedelic rock, as one of the bands that best captured the era's loosest, reckless, and indulgent qualities in its high-energy mutations of blues and folk-rock. Soon after Joplin joined the lineup in mid-1966, it became evident to both band and audience that Joplin's fiery wail—mature and emotionally wrenching, even at that early stage—had to be spotlighted to make Big Brother a contender.

The band's legendary performance at 1967's Monterey Pop Festival catapulted themselves into national attention, though an ill-advised contract with the tiny Mainstream label forced them to record one album before accepting any of the major-label bids rolling in. After signing with Columbia, the one Big Brother album that featured Joplin, *Cheap Thrills,* went to number one when it was released. By the end of 1968 though, Joplin had decided to go solo, a move that totally knocked the wind out of the band's sails. Although they did re-form for a while in the early '70s with different singers (indeed, they continue to perform in watered-down variations today), nothing would ever be the same. *–Richie Unterberger*

Big Brother & the Holding Company / 1967 / Columbia ✦✦✦

Big Brother's debut album was not recorded under optimum circumstances. The sessions were too rushed, and the sound thinner than the band would have liked, especially given how much more powerful some of the material (such as "Down on Me") would sound in later concerts. Still, it's not the useless throwaway some critics have portrayed it as, and it decently conveys the band's loose, sometimes reckless blend of blues, folk-rock, and psychedelia. Janis Joplin sings with soulful intensity on "Down on Me" and "Call on Me"; Peter Albin's "Light Is Faster Than Sound" is good wacked-out early Haight-Ashbury psychedelic rock; and the rock cover of Moondog's "All Is Loneliness" is spookily imaginative. The 1999 CD reissue adds the worthy single "Coo Coo"/"The Last Time" (good Eastern-influenced guitar work on the former, a good hurt hard rock vocal from Joplin on the latter) and previously unreleased alternate takes of "Call on Me" and "Bye, Bye Baby." *–Richie Unterberger*

★ **Cheap Thrills** / Aug. 1968 / Columbia ✦✦✦✦✦

Cheap Thrills, the major-label debut of Janis Joplin, was one of the most eagerly anticipated, and one of the most successful, albums of 1968. Joplin and Big Brother had earned extensive press notice ever since they played the Monterey Pop Festival in June 1967, but their only recorded work was a poorly produced, self-titled Mainstream album, and they spent a year getting out of their contract with Mainstream in order to sign with Columbia while demand built. When *Cheap Thrills* appeared in August 1968, it shot into the charts, reaching number one and going gold within a couple of months, and "Piece of My Heart" became a Top 40 hit. Joplin, with her ear- (and vocal cord-)shredding voice, was the obvious standout. Nobody had ever heard singing as emotional, as desperate, as determined, as loud as Joplin's, and *Cheap Thrills* was her greatest moment. Big Brother's backup, typical of the guitar-dominated sound of San Francisco psychedelia, made up in enthusiasm what it lacked in precision. But everybody knew who the real star was, and Joplin played her last gig with Big Brother while the album was still on top of the charts. Neither she nor the band would ever equal it. Heard today, *Cheap Thrills* is a musical time capsule and remains a showcase for one of rock's most distinctive singers. The 1999 CD reissue adds the previously unreleased outtakes "Roadblock" and "Flower in the Sun" from the *Cheap Thrills* sessions, along with previously unreleased live March 1968 versions of "Catch Me Daddy" and "Magic of Love." *–William Ruhlmann*

Be a Brother / Oct. 1970 / Columbia ✦✦

Cheaper Thrills / Apr. 1984 / Acadia ✦✦

Live at Winterland '68 / 1998 / Columbia/Legacy ✦✦✦

Recorded live in San Francisco on April 12 and April 13, this set is a snapshot of the band—with fine sound—reaching the peak of their form. All of the well-known songs from their first two albums are present: "Ball and Chain," "Down on Me," "Piece of My Heart," "Summertime," "Combination of the Two," and "Light Is Faster Than Sound," for starters. There isn't a single song that isn't available in some form on either the *Janis* box or the *Farewell Song* compilation, though. Also, these versions aren't remarkably different or better than the familiar ones, although they tend to run longer, particularly on the seven-minute "Light Is Faster Than Sound" and the ten-minute "Ball and Chain." A treat for fans to hear, with a 24-page booklet that has lots of comments from the band. *–Richie Unterberger*

Big Country

f. 1981, Dunfermline, Scotland

Pop/Rock, New Wave

With their ringing, bagpipe-like guitars and the anthemic songs of frontman Stuart Adamson, Scotland's Big Country emerged as one of the most distinctive and promising new rock bands of the early '80s, scoring a major hit with their debut album, *The Crossing;* though the group's critical and commercial fortunes dimmed in the years to follow, they nevertheless outlasted virtually all of their contemporaries, releasing new material into the next century. The England-born Adamson formed Big Country in mid-1981 following his exit from the Scottish punk quartet the Skids, enlisting childhood friend Bruce Watson on second guitar; Clive Parker and brothers Pete and Alan Wishart completed the original lineup, but were soon replaced by bassist Tony Butler and drummer Mark Brzezicki. Signing to Polygram's Mercury imprint, the band issued its debut single, "Harvest Home," in the fall of 1982; a series of opening dates on the Jam's farewell tour increased Big Country's visibility exponentially, and the follow-up, "Fields of Fire," cracked the U.K. Top Ten. *The Crossing* appeared in 1983, its passionate, idealistic approach and Celtic-inspired arrangements far removed from the prevailing new wave mentality of the moment; the album not only went platinum at home but went gold in America as well, its success spurred by the Top 20 pop hit "In a Big Country." Critics raved, and in early 1984 Big Country returned to the British Top Ten with the single "Wonderland." Their second album, *Steeltown*, entered the charts at number one, but despite good reviews there were already rumblings that all of the band's material sounded much the same; charges against 1986's *The Seer* did little to rectify (although the single "Look Away" was their biggest hit yet). *—Jason Ankeny*

The Crossing / Aug. 1983 / Mercury ✦✦✦✦
With producer Steve Lillywhite at the helm, Scotland's Big Country managed to deliver earnest, socially conscious arena anthems in a similar vein to U2 and The Alarm. The twist was their trademark bagpipe sound, achieved through the use of E-Bow. The unique sound of "In a Big Country" garnered the band considerable attention and a Top 20 single in the U.S. *The Crossing*, however, is an album whose richness goes beyond the single. The more subdued "Chance" is more sparse and its personal lyrics are every bit as heartfelt as the more populist-inclined anthems like the wonderful "The Storm" or the thundering "Fields of Fire." The lyrics are straightforward and, despite the grand themes of many of the tracks, manage to steer clear of being overly pretentious. While this album earned the band a gold record, Big Country's sound and image (reinforced by the members' tartan, checked shirts) resulted in them being tagged a novelty and they never duplicated their initial success in America. *—Tom Demalon*

Steeltown / Nov. 1984 / Mercury ✦✦✦
Big Country came out of one of the less dominant parts of the United Kingdom with an anthemic sound and vaguely revolutionary-sounding lyrics to captivate the British listening public and at least interest Americans. Big Country continued their winning ways at home with this, its second album, which topped the charts and produced three Top 40 hits—"East of Eden," "Where the Rose is Sown," and "Just a Shadow." But in the U.S., the album was perceived as proving that the band's sound, guitars-as-bagpipes, courtesy of the E-Bow, was a one-time novelty, while Stuart Adamson's lyrics, full of British socialist working-class fervor, seemed jingoistic and pretentious. Nevertheless, much of the music, as on the first album, made for stirring rock & roll. *—William Ruhlmann*

The Seer / Jul. 1986 / Mercury ✦✦

Peace in Our Time / Sep. 1988 / Reprise ✦✦

The Buffalo Skinners / Sep. 14, 1993 / Fox ✦✦✦

● **The Best of Big Country** / Feb. 22, 1994 / Mercury ✦✦✦✦
Big Country made big music—maybe not according to the definitions of Mike Scott, but certainly big in the sense of post-U2 anthemic college rock. They had one big hit—the glorious "In a Big Country," where the ebows chimed like bagpipes and the chorus surged with a barely constrained urgency. Big Country never hit those heights again, either artistically or commercially, but they did write a number of fine, big anthems, all of which are collected on Mercury's *The Best of Big Country*. Since it weighs in at 17 tracks, this may try the attention span of anyone but the devoted, yet this still works as a fine summary of their strengths while pointing out why they might not have gone much further. *—Stephen Thomas Erlewine*

Why the Long Face / Jun. 5, 1995 / Transatlantic ✦✦

Driving To Damascus / 1999 / Pinnacle ✦✦✦✦✦

20th Century Masters—The Millennium Collection: The Best of Big Country / Apr. 10, 2001 / Mercury ✦✦✦
The selections on the mid-priced *20th Century Masters: The Millennium Collection: The Best of big Country* are mostly duplicates of *The Best of Big Country*, but there are a couple tracks not on that more extensive compilation, including a rare Jimmy Iovine remix of "All Fall Together." The fact that Big Country was a one-hit wonder in the U.S. makes this release's audience somewhat uncertain; chances are that if you're interested enough in Big Country to purchase a best-of compilation, you'll want the more generous one. But *The Millennium Collection* does feature all of Big Country's big British hits, and it may be a worthy alternative for those who will be satisfied with a brief overview of the band's career. *—Steve Huey*

Big Daddy Kane (Antonio Hardy)

b. Brooklyn, NY
Rap, Vocals / Pop-Rap, Hardcore Rap, Hip-Hop, Golden Age
Brooklyn-ite Big Daddy Kane (born Antonio Hardy, KANE is an acronym for King Asiatic Nobody's Equal) has nicely been able to balance his image as the ultimate hipster with the requisite solemnity and air of indignation and anger necessary to creditably deliver messages of Afrocentric awareness and Muslim reverence. He's done alternately inspirational, prophetical, ridiculous, and scandalous raps over his career, and has also managed to include duets with the maestro of love Barry White and legendary comedian Rudy Ray Moore, aka Dolemite, who laid waste to Kane in a dozens (insult-swapping) classic.

Big Daddy Kane has been a high-profile figure the past couple of years. Not only has he appeared in such films as *Posse* and *Gunmen*, but he also posed in Madonna's controversial photo book *Sex*, and issued a defiant disc *Looks Like a Job for Big Daddy Kane* that offered no apologies for past actions and ridiculed unnamed individuals he claimed were fronting as gangsters. After 1994's *Daddy's Home*, he was absent from the studio for four years prior to releasing *Veteranz Day*. *—Ron Wynn*

● **The Very Best of Big Daddy Kane** / Mar. 6, 2001 / Rhino ✦✦✦✦✦
In the winter of 1988, Kane announced his arrival on his first 12" single, "Raw"; the rest was hip-hop history. Beats from producers like Marley Marl and Prince Paul with his legendary DJ Mister Cee provided the sonic canvas for Kane to flex his ample rhyme prowess. This Warner Archives collection encapsulates Kane's early perfection on "Raw," "Ain't No Half Steppin," "Just Rhymin' With Biz," and "Word to the Motherland," all taken from arguably one of the best hip-hop albums to date, *Long Live the Kane*. While Kane's second album, *It's a Big Daddy Thing*, was initially met with some consternation, since then the album has realized its power and import. From *Big Daddy Thing*, the compilation features the seminal "Smooth Operator," "Warm It Up, Kane," and the rare "Wrath of Kane," but misses the boat by leaving off the irresistible "Pimpin' Ain't Easy." The compilation is also remiss in its selections from Kane's later work on *A Taste of Chocolate* and *Looks Like a Job for Big Daddy*. Kane's propensity toward the occasional rap ballad or new jack swing was never his strong suit, but this album captures these weaker moments with the somewhat horrendous "I Get the Job Done" and the reprehensible "Very Special." The very best of Kane is certainly his groundbreaking late-'80s joints, but the Kane canon here is thoroughly incomplete. While Kane's later work is a dice roll for quality, another volume in this series is needed to feature latter-day jewels like "Taste of Chocolate Exit," "How U Get a Record Deal," "Show & Prove," and "In the PJ's." A more appropriate title for the album: "Kane's Very Best and Some of His Mediocre." *—Michael Di Bella*

Big Star

f. 1971, Memphis, TN, **db.** 1975
Proto-Punk, Pop/Rock, Power Pop
The quintessential American power pop band, Big Star remains one of the most mythic and influential cult acts in all of rock & roll. Originally led by the singing and songwriting duo of Alex Chilton and Chris Bell, the Memphis-based group fused the strongest elements of the British Invasion era—the melodic invention of the Beatles, the whiplash guitars of the Who, and the radiant harmonies of the Byrds—into a ramshackle but poignantly beautiful sound which recaptured the spirit of pop's past even as it pointed the way toward the music's future. Although creative tensions, haphazard distribution, and marketplace indifference conspired to ensure Big Star's brief existence and commercial failure, the group's three studio albums nevertheless remain unqualified classics, and their impact on subsequent generations of indie bands on both sides of the Atlantic is surpassed only by that of the Velvet Underground.

Big Star came together in 1971, with Chilton (the onetime Box Tops vocalist) and Bell plus bassist Andy Hummel and drummer Jody Stephens. After a brilliant debut, 1972's *#1 Record*, Bell and Chilton began butting heads over Big Star's direction. In 1972 Bell finally left the band—his subsequent attempts to mount a solo career proved largely fruitless, with only a spectacular solo single, "I Am the Cosmos," receiving official release prior to his untimely death in a 1978 car crash. Big Star temporarily disbanded but returned with 1974's *Radio City*, a record that remains their masterpiece. Sessions for a planned third album proved disastrous, and then Big Star was no more. After finally earning release overseas in 1978, the third Big Star album earned a significant cult following, and countless alternative rock bands cited the band's enormous influence in the years to follow. In 1993, Chilton and Stephens appeared at a reunion gig that was captured on the *Columbia* live disc, although no new studio recordings were forthcoming. *—Jason Ankeny*

#1 Record / 1972 / Ardent ✦✦✦✦✦
The problem with coming in late on an artwork lauded as "influential" is that you've probably encountered the work it influenced first, so its truly innovative qualities are lost. Thus, if you are hearing Big Star's debut album for the first time decades after its release (as, inevitably, most people must), you may be reminded of Tom Petty and the Heartbreakers or R.E.M., who came after—that is, if you don't think of the Byrds and the Beatles, circa 1965. What was remarkable about *#1 Record* in 1972 was that nobody except Big Star (and maybe Badfinger and the Raspberries) wanted to sound like this—simple, light pop with sweet harmonies and jangly guitars. Since then, dozens of bands have rediscovered those pleasures. But in a way, that's an advantage because, whatever freshness is lost across the years, Big Star's craft is only confirmed. These are sturdy songs, feelingly performed, and once you get beyond the style to the content, you'll still be impressed. *—William Ruhlmann*

Radio City / 1974 / Ardent ✦✦✦✦✦
Largely lacking co-leader Chris Bell, Big Star's second album also lacked something of the pop sweetness (especially the harmonies) of *#1 Record*. What it possessed was Alex Chilton's urgency (sometimes desperation) on songs that made his case as a genuine rock & roll eccentric. If *#1 Record* had a certain pop perfection that brought everything together, *Radio City* was the sound of everything falling apart, which proved at least as compelling. *—William Ruhlmann*

☆ **Third/Sister Lovers** / 1978 / Rykodisc ✦✦✦✦✦
A shambling wreck of an album, Big Star's *Third/Sister Lovers* ranks among the most harrowing experiences in pop music; impassioned, erratic, and stark, it's the slow, sinking sound of a band falling apart. Recorded with their label, Stax, poised on the verge of bankruptcy, the album finds Alex Chilton at the end of his rope, sabotaging his own music long before it can ever reach the wrecking crew of poor distribution, indifferent marketing, and disinterested pop radio; his songs are haphazardly brilliant, a head-on colli-

sion between inspiration and frustration. The album is a kind of self-fulfilling prophecy, each song smacking of utter defeat and desperation; the result is either one of the most vividly emotional experiences in pop music or a completely wasted opportunity, and while the truth probably lies somewhere in between, there's no denying *Third*'s magnetic pull—it's like an undertow. Although previously issued on a variety of different labels, Rykodisc's 1992 release is the definitive edition of this unfinished masterpiece, its 19 tracks most closely appoximating the original planned running order while restoring the music's intended impact; in addition to unearthing a blistering cover of the Kinks' "At the End of the Day" and a haunting rendition of Nat King Cole's "Nature Boy," it also appends the disturbing "Dream Lover," which distills the album's messiest themes into less than four minutes of psychic torment. *—Jason Ankeny*

Big Star Live / Feb. 21, 1992 / Rykodisc ♦♦♦

Recorded in the wake of the release of *Radio City, Big Star Live* documents a freewheeling radio date originally broadcast in 1974. Spotlighting the strongest material from the group's first two LPs, the mood is both lighthearted and world-weary, the attitude of a band fully cognizant of the fact that the music they're creating is exceptional, yet dumbfounded by their almost complete lack of commercial success. A cover of Loudon Wainwright's "Motel Blues" is wholly indicative of Alex Chilton's mindset at this point in the game; already a battle-scarred veteran of the music industry, his frustration is palpable, lending even greater urgency to remarkable songs like "September Gurls," "The Ballad of El Goodo," "O My Soul" and "Thirteen." While certainly not the best starting point for new fans, *Big Star Live* is essential stuff for the converted. *—Jason Ankeny*

★ **#1 Record/Radio City** / Jun. 10, 1992 / Fantasy ♦♦♦♦♦

A two-fer combining Big Star's first and second albums, *#1 Record/Radio City* remains a definitive document of early-'70s American power pop and a virtual blueprint for much of the finest alternative rock that came after it. The lone Big Star record to merit the full participation of founder Chris Bell, the brightly produced *#1 Record* splits the songwriting credits evenly between him and Alex Chilton (in the tradition of Lennon-McCartney). But from the beginning, the group is tearing apart at the seams: Bell and Chilton's relationship seems less a working partnership than a battle of wills, and each possesses his own distinctive vision. The purist, Bell crafts electrifying and melodic classic pop like "Feel" and "In the Street," while Chilton, the malcontent, pens luminous, melancholy ballads like "The Ballad of El Goodo" and "Thirteen." Ultimately, their tension makes *#1 Record* brilliant. However, *Radio City* shifts gears dramatically: Bell is largely absent (though he guests, uncredited, on a few tracks, including the wonderful "Back of a Car"), allowing Chilton's darker impulses free reign. From the raucous opener "O My Soul" onward, the new Big Star is noisier, edgier, and even more potent. Erratic mixing, spotty production, shaky performances—by all rights, *Radio City* should be a failure, yet Chilton is at his best when poised on the brink of disaster, and the songs hang together seemingly on faith and conviction alone. Each track recalls pop's glory days, from the Kinks-ish snarl of "Mod Lang" to the Byrds-like guitar glow that adorns "Way Out West." The much-celebrated "September Gurls" is indeed a classic—everything right and good about pop music distilled down to three minutes of pure genius. *—Jason Ankeny*

Columbia: Live at Missouri University / Sep. 14, 1993 / Zoo/Volcano ♦♦

Nobody Can Dance / Mar. 16, 1999 / Norton ♦♦♦

A mix of early rehearsal tapes and a board tape from an early 1971 live show featuring a rare performance of "The Letter" makes this an official bootleg (band approved) worth adding to the collection after you've scored all the essentials. The rehearsals feature John Lightman on bass (no Chris Bell involvement in these performances), but Chilton's guitar cuts like a knife and his singing is inspired and that's half the joy in a great Big Star cut, anyway. The live show emanates from Memphis' Overton Park Band Shell and also demonstrates the band (and Chilton in particular) involved and turning in a rock & roll show well worth documenting and issuing nearly some 30 years later. Between the live stuff and the studio demos, there are two versions apiece of "September Gurls," "O My Soul," "You Get What You Deserve" and "Mod Lang" aboard in this 15-track collection, but even alternate versions of demos and alternate takes are worth the excavation when it comes to this cult group of cult groups. As solid a collection of leftovers as you're likely to find out there. *—Cub Koda*

Bikini Kill

f. Oct. 1990, **db.** Apr. 13, 1998

Riot Grrrl, Indie Rock, Alternative Pop/Rock

The point band of the early-'90s Riot Grrrl movement, Olympia, WA's Bikini Kill exploded onto the male-dominated indie rock scene by fusing the visceral power of punk with the impassioned ideals of feminism. Calling for "Revolution Girl Style Now," the group's fiercely polemical and anthemic music helped give rise to a newly-empowered generation of women in rock, presaging the dominance female artists would enjoy throughout the decade. Led by singer/songwriter Kathleen Hanna, a former stripper, the group laced their incendiary live performances with aggressive political stances which challenged the accepted hierarchy of the underground music community; slam dancers were forced to mosh at the fringes of the stage so that women could remain at the front of the crowd, for example, and female audience members were often invited to take control of the microphone to openly discuss issues of sexual abuse and misconduct. In 1991, Bikini Kill issued its first recording, *Revolution Girl Style Now,* before signing with the aggressively independent Olympia-based label Kill Rock Stars. In 1992, the band issued *Yeah, Yeah, Yeah,* a split 12-inch released with the British group Huggy Bear's *Our Troubled Youth* on its flipside; a subsequent U.K. tour with Huggy Bear in early 1993 raised the visibility of the Riot Grrrl groundswell to unprecedented heights, and the movement became the focus of many media outlets on both sides of the Atlantic. Bikini Kill quietly disbanded in early 1998. *—Jason Ankeny*

The CD Version of the First Two Records / 1992 / Kill Rock Stars ♦♦♦

The group's first two scabrous LPs combined into one CD release. Hanna's lyrics and singing are equally caustic, creating explosive songs like "Feels Blind" and the amusingly titled "Suck My Left One." This group has anger and intelligence on its side. *—Heather Phares*

● **Pussywhipped** / 1994 / Kill Rock Stars ♦♦♦♦♦

A more experimental follow-up from these punk rock furies. While there's still lots of vitriol, the songs are more varied and even catchy. "Rebel Girl" is a manifesto just waiting to be discovered, and the rest of the album sees the band occasionally adding fun to their recipe for punk chaos. A good starting point. *—Heather Phares*

Reject All American / Apr. 5, 1996 / Kill Rock Stars ♦♦♦

Bikini Kill delivered their second album just a little bit too late. By the time *Reject All American* hit the stores in 1996, the media's fascination with riot grrrl had passed, leaving the band the province of a small cult. Of course, they prefer it that way, but the insularity of their audience and their message is reflected in the music. *Reject All American* has the requisite raw production, blistering three-chord riffs, and Kathleen Hanna's gut-churning screams, but the result isn't necessarily entirely effective. The problem is the band is preaching to a converted audience—and their music doesn't have enough hooks to effectively sell their message. There are some good songs on the album, and on the whole it's a tighter album than their debut, but it doesn't capture the moment the way *Pussywhipped* did, and Bikini Kill are all about immediacy. Therefore, *Reject All American* is sort of irrelevant. *—Stephen Thomas Erlewine*

The Singles / May 26, 1998 / Kill Rock Stars ♦♦♦♦♦

The Singles is not a Bikini Kill career overview, but rather a compilation of three 45 rpm-only releases recorded for Kill Rock Stars in between 1994's *Pussywhipped* and 1996's *Reject All American.* All told, this material is some of the band's most accessible, highlighted by the three songs from the Joan Jett-produced "New Radio" single; one is yet another re-recording of "Rebel Girl," which is justified by a driving, kinetic energy that makes the version on *Pussywhipped* sound tame and plodding by comparison. There's no noisy, murky meandering at all, and the brighter production and melodic hooks pack a wallop—so even if *Pussywhipped* remains Bikini Kill's most crucial statement, *The Singles* might actually be a better place to get acquainted with them. *—Steve Huey*

Billie

Club/Dance, Dance-Pop

At the scant age of 15, Swindon native Billie Piper (b. Sept. 22, 1982) was catapulted to stardom in England when her debut single, "Because We Want To," entered the British charts at number one in 1998. Piper began her career by entering talent contests at a very young age, eventually winning a scholarship to the Sylvia Young Theatre School (which also produced the likes of the Spice Girls' Emma Bunton, as well as three members of All Saints). She appeared as an extra in several movies, including *Evita,* and landed a job as a model in an ad campaign for the female-teen-oriented pop magazine Smash Hits. An executive at Virgin Records liked the attitude that Billie projected in the advertisements, and signed her to a contract.

A promotional blitz of TV performances prefaced the release of "Because We Want To," providing the massive publicity necessary for the single to debut at number one. Billie became the first female solo artist to accomplish that feat in Britain, and she was also the youngest female artist to score a British number one single since Helen Shapiro in 1961. Further hits followed in "Girlfriend" and "She Wants You." In 1999, Billie's first full-length album appeared under the title of *Honey to the B,* also the title of her fourth British single; the album was released in the U.S. with a rejigged running order in May 1999, and "She Wants You" issued as her first American single. *—Steve Huey*

Honey to the B / May 18, 1999 / Virgin ♦♦♦

British-born Billie Piper brings her chart-topping pop to the States with the release of her debut full-length album *Honey to the B.* The first ever British female with a number one debut on the U.K. pop chart, Piper's first album captures her youthful energy and exuberance with upbeat dance-pop tunes like "She Wants You" and "Because We Want To." *—Heather Phares*

The Birds

f. 1964, Yiewsley, London, England, **db.** 1967

Freakbeat, British Psychedelia, Mod, British Blues, British Invasion

The Birds were one of the hard-luck outfits in the annals of '60s British rock. By reputation, they were one of the top R&B-based outfits in England during the mid-'60s, with a sound as hard and appealing as the Who, the Yardbirds, or the Small Faces. In contrast to a lot of other acts that never charted a hit, the Birds are remembered slightly by some serious fans, and are mentioned in several history books—but for entirely the wrong reasons. The Birds are remembered for the fact that Ron Wood got his start in the band before moving on to bigger things with the Faces and the Rolling Stones; and that they shared a name, albeit spelled differently, with an American band of considerable prominence. Nobody knows a lot about their music, however, which, on record, consisted of fewer than a dozen songs. The Birds were one of the better bands of their era, as evidenced by the large following they built up from their live performances, playing a hard, loud brand of R&B, with polished vocals and a forceful, crunchy guitar sound. They weren't far removed from the Small Faces or the Who in sound, and perhaps they might've fared better, or had a longer run at success, if they hadn't been signed to a label that already had the Small Faces and the Rolling Stones under contract. The name confusion probably killed whatever chance they had of cracking the English charts, as well as eclipsing their musical virtues for posterity. *—Bruce Eder*

These Birds Are Dangerous / 1985 / Edsel/Nest ♦♦♦♦

A six-song, 12-inch EP that gathers both sides of their first three singles (the fourth single couldn't be licensed). Echoes of the Stones, Pretty Things, and Who abound on these tracks, which rock out but don't establish an identifiable or original style. Includes three Ron Wood originals, as well as covers of Eddie Holland's "Leaving Here" (also part of the Who's repertoire at the time), Marvin Gaye's "No Good Without You," and Bo Diddley's "You Don't Love Me." The excellent liner notes refer, frustratingly, to several other unissued sides that could not be obtained for release on this collection. Their fourth single, an unexceptional effort released under the name Bird's Birds, can be found on the obscure compilation reissue *Nowhere Men*. *—Richie Unterberger*

● **Collectors' Guide to Rare British Birds** / 1999 / Deram ♦♦♦♦♦

This is an astonishingly lively and exciting collection, coming from a band that scarcely sold any records in their own time and are known today for their name and their line-up, but not their music. The stuff here is as crunchy and grinding as the early Who material, and if the band's own songwriting isn't as distinctive, the style of the performing is more appealing. The songs range from some hot Ron Wood originals ("You're On My Mind," "Next In Line," "That's All I Need") to covers of obscure Motown songs and Pete Townshend material. Think of the Kinks from "Long Tall Sally," the Yardbirds from "A Certain Girl," or the Who from "The Good's Gone" and that's the dominant sound here–curiously, their cover of Townshend's "Run Run Run" starts out as though it's going to turn into "My Generation." Ali MacKenzie sounded like a punkier Roger Daltrey, and Ron Wood's playing was a delightful compendium of rhythm fills and angular blues licks that must've been devastating on stage. There's also an unlisted bonus track on the CD–at the risk of spoiling the surprise, it's their number from The Deadly Bees, which seems not to have survived as a formal, free-standing studio master. *—Bruce Eder*

The Birthday Party

f. 1977, Melbourne, Australia, **db.** 1983

No Wave, Post-Punk

The Birthday Party was one of the darkest and most challenging post-punk groups to emerge in the early '80s, creating bleak and noisy soundscapes that provided the perfect setting for vocalist Nick Cave's difficult, disturbing stories of religion, violence, and perversity. Under the direction of Cave and guitarist Rowland S. Howard, the band tore through reams of blues and rockabilly licks, spitting out hellacious feedback and noise at an unrelenting pace. As the band's career progressed, Cave's vision got darker and their songs alternated between dirges to blistering sonic assaults. Originally, the Australian band was called the Boys Next Door; after moving to London and switching their name to the deceptively benign Birthday Party, the group's demented, knotty post-punk began to gel. Cave had the most successful solo career, recording a series of albums in the '80s and '90s that maintained his status as a popular cult figure. *—Stephen Thomas Erlewine*

Prayers on Fire / 1981 / Buddha ♦♦♦♦

It should come as no surprise that there is an album in Nick Cave's oeuvre called *Prayers on Fire*; a fascination with the dark, (self-)destructive side of religion is more than evident in his later work with the Bad Seeds. While there might not be any of the explicit Biblical imagery on *Prayers on Fire* that Cave would later ejaculate, the title of the album is apt, and its aptness is revealed almost immediately. The lyrics for "Figure of Fun" aren't even printed in the booklet; instead, merely "obsessive, deadpan, moribund, seasick, etc." And perhaps that best sums up *Prayers on Fire*'s graveyard poetry. The rest of the album is a subterranean labyrinth full of "sand and soot and dust and dirt," peopled by bizarre characters like Nick the Stripper and King Ink, and replete with images of murder, decay, blood, and Kafka-esque insects. Then, of course, there's Cave himself, the literate ghoul with an impressive vocal range who just stepped out of a B horror flick, trying to parry the intensity of the music like an Iggy Pop wasted on goth pills. But be careful not to overlook his subtle sense of humor and his awareness of the camp. With Mick Harvey being the only future Bad Seed on hand (Anita Lane also contributed one set of lyrics), the music here foreshadows Cave's later work without quite resembling it (with the exception of his first album). Though present on most of the tracks, the moody piano that would dominate much of Cave's solo work is never really prominent here. Instead it's the squiggles of Rowland Howard's guitar dodging the blows of the furious rhythm section that distinguishes the Birthday Party. Oppressive and unrelenting, *Prayers on Fire* is highly recommended for those aspiring to advanced states of dementia. *—Greg Maurer*

Junkyard / 1982 / Buddha ♦♦♦

The Party's second and final full studio album, also the final release with the five-person lineup, was perhaps its scuzzy masterpiece, its art/psych/blues/punk fusion taken to at times outrageous heights. Right from its start, nobody held back on anything, Cave's now-demonic vocals in full roar while the rest of the players revamped rhythm & blues and funk into a blood-soaked cabaret exorcism. Nearly every tune is a Party classic one way or another, from the opening slow, sexy grind of "She's Hit," Cave's freaked tale of death and destruction matched by clattering percussion and a perversely crisp guitar from Howard, to the ending title track's crawl toward a last gruesome ending. Tips of the hat to literary influences surface at points, notably "Hamlet (Pow, Pow, Pow)," though the protagonist isn't so much the indecisive tragic figure of Shakespeare as a Romeo-quoting criminal on the loose. The ultimate Party song sits smack dab at the center—"Big-Jesus-Trash-Can," a hilarious and blasphemous blues/jazz show tune with some great brass from Harvey to top it all off. Guest performers crop up at points; future Bad Seed Barry Adamson plays bass on "Kiss Me Black," while Anita Lane contributes two sets of lyrics if not her direct vocals. Later CD versions included three extra tracks. "Blast Off" and "Release the Bats" were originally issued as a single; both seethe with rage and fire in spades. The latter is at once powerful and a bit of a tongue-in-cheek goth goof, with Cave serving up lines like "Don't tell me that it doesn't hurt/A hundred fluttering in your skirt." The other bonus, a second version of the album's "Dead Joe" recorded in London, is if anything even more frenetically gone than the original, a car crash sample punctuating the lyrical reference to same all the more. *—Ned Raggett*

Drunk on the Pope's Blood/The Agony Is the Ecstasy [EP] / 1982 / 4AD ♦♦♦

An extremely harrowing live EP, with Lydia Lunch. *—John Dougan*

Hee-Haw / 1988 / Buddha ♦♦♦

The initial tracks on *Hee-Haw* come from two of their earliest proper Birthday Party singles, "Mr. Clarinet" and "The Friend Catcher." Three other tracks included on the 1980 self-titled American-only compilation, the squealing sax and raunch of "Hats on Wrong," the slightly more straightforward punch and thrash of "Guilt Parade," and "Riddle House," surface as well. All showcase the violent, thrashing energy of the Party of legend perfectly; even the organ on "Mr. Clarinet" sounds like it's being strangled as much as being played. Cave may be in utterly hyperdramatic mode throughout, spitting out barks on "Happy Birthday" and braying out the title call on the slow, brilliant burn of "The Friend Catcher," but the band aren't holding back either; Howard's spindly, aggro guitar work complements Calvert's drum punch nicely, balancing nerves and body slam, while Pew and Harvey flesh out everything else in the same spirit. Things aren't quite on the level of sheer sonic pain of later releases, but with the help of engineer Tony Cohen, who brings out the overall performances well, the fivesome is already well on its curious way. The last five songs come from the original *Hee-Haw* EP, which was also the final Boys Next Door release. While not quite as frazzled as what the group would soon fully mutate into, the tracks do have a more pushing, discordant air than the earlier Boys tracks, Cave still hesitant at points but starting to let go a bit elsewhere. "Faint Heart" has a great breakdown into random vocal mumblings and instrumental nuttiness, especially on piano, while "The Hair Shirt" especially is already the Birthday Party in anything but name. *—Ned Raggett*

Mutiny/The Bad Seed / 1989 / Buddha ♦♦♦♦

Collecting the two EPs onto one disc, this release also includes two rough mixes from the *Mutiny* sessions as a bonus. "The Six Strings That Drew Blood," also later recorded by Cave's Bad Seeds, is a quick brawler like many a past Party classic, Cave hitting a strangled falsetto at points as the group rips along. "Pleasure Avalanche" works on the slow grind trip; Cave husks his vocals over a nicely creepy arrangement from the rest, calling for the titular situation in question with increasing desperation. *—Ned Raggett*

● **Hits** / Oct. 13, 1992 / 4AD ♦♦♦♦♦

As an album title, *Hits* is an intentionally ironic misnomer for one of Australia's most influential rock bands of the late '70s and early '80s. Having "hits" was the furthest thing from the Birthday Party's collective mind over the course of five tumultuous years that followed the group's move to England from Down Under; the members reviled anything that hinted at mainstream acceptance. Ten years on, the intensity of this music is still frightening. It's a dense, mutant hybrid that evolved from punk, progressive rock, funk, and improvisational jazz, without directly owning up to any of these base materials. Vocalist Nick Cave (who has gone on to an equally creative solo career) didn't just sing about society's dark, depraved underbelly, he lived the experience right there on disc and on stage. *—Roch Parisien*

Live, 1981-1982 / Apr. 20, 1999 / 4AD ♦♦♦♦

Though various live releases had emerged over the course of the band's existence, no full-length capturing of the Party's particular bacchanalia approved by the group had officially emerged until this release. Stitching together tracks from a London date in 1981 and a German show in 1982 (plus a ringer cut from Athens, Greece—a version of the Stooges' "Funhouse" with Jim Thirwell aka Foetus on sax)), *Live* threatens at all points to leap from the speakers and throttle innocent bystanders. Clear sound on the first ten songs, all from the London date, makes resistance even harder. Given the sometimes (though intentionally) unclear or unexpected mixing of Party songs in studio, hearing everything via in-your-face stun methods brings out the abilities of the band all the more, especially Pew and his vicious bass work. Songs like "The Dim Locator" and "King Ink" cut all the more closer to the bone as a result. "Nick the Stripper," amazingly, is even more viciously sleazy than the original, which is saying something and a half; Cave sounds like he's summoning his voice from his shoes on up. The German date's sound is only slightly less thorough than the London's, and the performances no less wired. "Big-Jesus-Trash-Can" thrashes around like there's no tomorrow, Pew's bass again shooting through the mix, while "The Friend Catcher" seethes with a creepy, frigid energy. Harvey takes over on drums for the last two German tracks and the "Funhouse" cover, but even down to four people the band still generates more noise and activity than most other acts could hope to achieve. Definite bonus points have to go to Cave for his occasional, softly spoken between-song asides—"Thank you, I love your haircuts as well." *—Ned Raggett*

Bis

f. 1994

Indie Pop, Indie Rock, Britpop

Taking inspiration from the amateurish antics of Huggy Bear and then acting like they were seven years old, Bis were one of the strangest phenomenons of late-'90s British indie rock. Comprised of keyboardist/vocalist Manda Rin, guitarist Sci-Fi Steven, and his younger brother John Disco (guitar), Bis formed in Giffnock, Scotland, in late 1994. All three had been friends since their early childhood, but they didn't form a band until they finished high school. In addition to writing music, they also published the fanzines Funky Spunk and Paper Bullets. Aggressively primitive and defiantly childish, Bis claimed to be at the forefront of "the Teen-C Revolution," which apparently translated as young adults wishing they were still in elementary school. Inspired by the Nation of Ulysses, Huggy Bear, Blur, and the "cutie" indie movement of Sarah Records, the group crossed D.I.Y. aesthetics with the incessant bounce of new wave dance-pop. Bursting out from nowhere in early 1996, Bis became the first unsigned band to appear on *Top of the Pops*, and over the first six months they became a sensation within the British music press. But just as quickly as they rose to prominence the backlash began, and by the end of the year, only a handful of supporters remained in the U.K. However, Bis had won fans in the Beastie Boys, who signed them to Grand Royal Records, positioning the band to join the ranks of the international pop underground, where the message was just, if not more, important than the music. *—Stephen Thomas Erlewine*

This Is Teen-C Power! / Dec. 10, 1996 / Grand Royal ♦♦♦♦
A six-song compilation of early singles by the Glasgow-based teenage trio Bis, *This Is Teen-C Power!* is both the group's U.S. debut and the best distillation of their anarchic early style. Singer Manda Rin's voice is at its most uncontrolled here, yelping and squalling like a younger and hyper-caffeinated Nina Hagen, while brothers John Disco and Sci-Fi Steven create noisy punk-dance-indie thrash out of beats, samples, and noisy guitars. It's a mildy uneven collection; "School Disco" and "Burn the Suit" are nothing special, but the anthemic, sloganeering "Teen-C Power!" and "Kandy Pop" or the sneering "Kill Yr Boyfriend" and (especially) "This Is Fake D.I.Y." are among the best tracks Bis have ever done. The follow-up full-length *The New Transistor Heroes* showed that this rather restrictive style has a somewhat limited utility, but *This Is Teen-C Power!* shows off the best of Bis' early incarnation. *—Stewart Mason*

● **The New Transistor Heroes** / Apr. 7, 1997 / Wiiija ♦♦♦♦
Delivered a full year after the hype on Bis had peaked, the band's debut album *The New Transistor Heroes* is, perhaps inevitably, a mixed bag. Part of the band's initial appeal was the unexpected impact of their shouty, amateurish yet melodic, keyboard-driven dilution of riot grrrl, intercut with new wave pop—it was immediate and infectious. Spread out over the course of a full-length album, the music becomes less appealing, as does the group's championing of candy, kids, and D.I.Y. By the second side, the whole thing becomes a little too insular for comfort, and its charm has waned, but taken in small doses, *The New Transistor Heroes* is punky fun. *—Stephen Thomas Erlewine*

Intendo / Aug. 11, 1998 / Grand Royal ♦♦♦
Released to appease fans anxiously awaiting the follow-up to *The New Transistor Heroes*, *Intendo*'s blend of demos and B-sides is surprisingly short on throwaways. Bis doesn't break any new ground here, turning out more takes on neo-'80s pop complete with layman's drum machines, cheesy keyboards, and innocently ranting choruses that showcase their school spirit. But their gift for a golden melody can't be argued, as "Famous" proves when lead cheerleader Manda Rin lets her vocals, laced with attitude and cutie-pie theatrics, cast an air of optimistic whimsy that makes even the hollow demo take sound radio friendly. If anything, the abbreviated length of this collection hits harder at times than the whole of the slightly long-winded *Heroes*, making their nostalgic dance formula easier to swallow. *—Jason Kaufman*

Social Dancing / Aug. 10, 1999 / Capitol ♦♦♦♦
As Bis' career progressed, their music changed, ever so slightly. (Somehow, the word "mature" seems singularly inappropriate as far as this trio is concerned.) The D.I.Y.-punk influences faded into the background, as their kandy-colored, trashy new wave-dance roots took hold. Simultaneously, their calls for Teen-C power rescinded, leaving them without any message, genuine or manufactured, outside of pop music and fun (or something along those lines). Nevertheless, when it came time to record their second album *Social Dancing*, Bis teamed with producer Andy Gill, best known as part of the socialist post-punk band, Gang of Four. Following their transformation from underground activists to Casio-driven bubblegum practitioners, Bis turned into the kind of band that would have been in direct opposition to Gang of Four in the early '80s—all the more ironic, since Gill's production makes *Social Dancing* sound uncannily like a period piece. That turns out to be a blessing, since his shiny retro sounds make the album go down, even when the trio's kiddie choruses deteriorate from charming to annoying. Consequently, the record is more cohesive than their debut, but it never feels relevant—and at one point, that's what Bis were all about. Arriving at the tail-end of Brit-pop, their first EPs seemed fresh, original, part of a new zeitgeist. But since that zeitgeist was all about youth—and the fact that Bis were teenagers pining for the golden age of elementary school—sealed the fate on the trio; they were of the moment in 1996, and when that year was gone, they would never again sound hip or relevant. To their credit, they figured out how to move on, entrenching themselves within new wave, and they have made an album that's pretty entertaining. But that triumph is compromised somewhat by the fact that the album ultimately sounds as good and is as substantive as a Haysi Fantayzee record. *—Stephen Thomas Erlewine*

Return to Central / Sep. 18, 2001 / Spin Art ♦♦♦♦
Glasgow's Bis tweak their indie pop quirkiness on their fourth album, *Return to Central*, and it's a desirable and funkadelic feel-good mix of Bis' signature disco hooks and thick pop beats. Surely their most ambitious release, Bis shrug off their post-pubescent punk-pop snarlings and kiddie chants found on *The New Transistor Heroes* and *Intendo* and make *Return to Central* a vibrant twist in their Teen-C Revolution. Manda Rin tames her little girl rants for something sassy, tossing all criticism aside to transcend into electronic bliss. She and Bis cohorts John Disco and Sci-Fi Steve frolic with new wave synth breaks, and let their fondness for Talk Talk, New Order, and Can be known. "What Are You Afraid Of" and "Silver Spoon" splice heavy techno-pop with Rin's vocalic glossy flare; however, Sci-Fi Steven's and Disco's riveting guitars on "Chicago" shimmy into Bis' finest moment on "A Portrait From Space," a loopy celestial soundscape of floating orchestration kicked off with old-school Nintendo samples, yet it's the dream pop guitar work that sets up Bis' new rock cleverness. Bis isn't consumed with angst for the music follower, for they'd rather spiral into club land in their own musical mystery. *Return to Central* allows Bis to relish in their fun and self-indulgence without them being regarded as snotty indie punks. A sophistication is cast, spawning Bis' bold move from "Kandy Pop." *—MacKenzie Wilson*

Elvin Bishop

b. Oct. 21, 1942, Glendale, CA
Vocals, Guitar / Modern Electric Chicago Blues, Southern Rock, Blues-Rock, Modern Electric Blues, Album Rock
Elvin Bishop was already playing blues guitar when he left Tulsa, OK, to go to the University of Chicago in 1960. There he hooked up with harmonica player Paul Butterfield, and they founded The Paul Butterfield Blues Band, for which Bishop served as guitarist from 1965 to 1968. Going off on his own, he was signed to promoter Bill Graham's Fillmore label. In 1974, he moved to Phil Walden's Capricorn Records, home of the Southern rock movement of the early '70s. In 1976, he scored a gold-selling Top Ten pop hit with "Fooled Around and Fell in Love." He spent most of the '80s out of the limelight, but then was signed to Bruce Iglauer's independent blues label, Alligator, for which he recorded into the '90s. *—William Ruhlmann*

The Best of Elvin Bishop: Tulsa Shuffle / 1969-1972 / Epic/Legacy ♦♦♦♦♦
In his first manifestation as a band leader (1969-1972), Elvin Bishop lived in Marin County, California, and performed under the auspices of promoter Bill Graham. Not surprisingly, the three albums he cut in that period fit into the soul-blues-rock style of post-psychedelic San Francisco, even to the point of featuring an extended instrumental, "Hogbottom," on which Bishop takes Carlos Santana's place fronting the Santana percussion section. This 18-track compilation selects from the albums *The Elvin Bishop Group*, *Feel It!*, and *Rock My Soul*, effectively summarizing this phase in Bishop's career. The only thing wrong with it is that it would be easy to make the mistake of thinking that it covers all of his solo career rather than only the first four years, especially because there have now been four different albums released with the title *The Best of Elvin Bishop*. *—William Ruhlmann*

● **Sure Feels Good: The Best of Elvin Bishop** / 1970-1972 / Polydor ♦♦♦♦♦
A fine collection of the blues-rock guitarist's best moments, which covers more material than the earlier compilation, *Best of Elvin Bishop/Crabshaw Rising*. *—Stephen Thomas Erlewine*

Stephen Bishop

b. Nov. 14, 1951, San Diego, CA
Vocals, Guitar / Soft Rock, Adult Contemporary
Stephen Bishop's light pop style garnered him a small amount of success as a solo artist in the late '70s and a greater reputation as a quality songwriter. After his first group, the Weeds, disbanded following high school, Bishop spent the next seven years looking for a recording contract and was finally discovered by Art Garfunkel in 1976. Bishop had worked in a publishing house, where he wrote songs for Chaka Khan, the Four Tops, and Barbra Streisand. His debut album, *Careless*, was nominated for a Grammy and produced several chart singles, including "On and On." Guest performers on the album included Garfunkel, Khan, Gary Brooker, Steve Cropper, and Phil Collins, who later recorded Bishop material on his *Face Value* album. Bishop achieved his greatest visibility as a composer of movie themes, contributing to *Animal House*, *Roadie*, *Tootsie*, *The China Syndrome*, *Unfaithfully Yours*, and a number one duet for Phil Collins and Marilyn Martin from *White Nights*, "Separate Lives." Bishop also appeared in *The Blues Brothers* and *Kentucky Fried Movie*. *—Steve Huey*

On & On: The Hits of Stephen Bishop / 1994 / MCA ♦♦♦♦♦
Soft rock specialist Stephen Bishop contributed handily to some of the late-'70s' most insipid ballads, but they always contained a little bit of elegance and passion in one form or another. *The Hits of Stephen Bishop* captures 18 of his best tracks, conveniently comprising both his soundtrack work and his charted singles. Bishop supplied the film *Tootsie* with the emotional "It Might Be You," which peaked at number 25 on Billboard in 1983. His soundtrack work also included the genuine sounding "Only Love" from *Arthur*, as well as the theme from *China Syndrome* entitled "Somewhere In-Between." Outside of his soundtrack work, "On and On" was his highest charting single and is by far his most moving, reaching number 11 in 1977. His delicate vocal approach is what makes the other tracks on this compilation creditable, but taking his frail form of mush pop at face value should be implemented all the while. Songs like "Little Italy" and "Losing Myself in You" harbor some appeal, and Eric Clapton's guitar work with Chaka Khan's background vocals make "Save It for a Rainy Day" that much more worthwhile. This hits package is all that is required in order to enjoy Bishop's overly sentimental offerings. *—Mike DeGagne*

Biz Markie (Marcel Hall)

b. Apr. 8, 1964, Harlem, NY
Vocals / Comedy Rap, Pop-Rap, East Coast Rap, Golden Age
Biz Markie's inclination toward juvenile humor and his fondness for goofy, tuneless, half-sung choruses camouflaged his true talents as a freestyle rhymer. The Biz may not have been able to translate his wild rhyming talents to tape, but what he did record was worthwhile in its own way. With his silly humor and inventive, sample-laden productions, he proved that hip-hop could be funny and melodic, without sacrificing its street credibility. His distinctive style made his second album, *The Biz Never Sleeps*, a gold hit and its single "Just a Friend" into a Top 10 pop single. While its success made Biz Markie a semi-star, it

also cursed him. Not only was he consigned as a novelty act, but it brought enough attention that Gilbert O'Sullivan sued him over the unauthorized sample of "Alone Again (Naturally)" on Biz's 1991 album, *I Need a Haircut*. The lawsuit severely cut into Markie's career and 1993's *All Samples Cleared* was the last record he released during the '90s. However, his reputation was restored somewhat in the mid-'90s, as the Beastie Boys championed him and other alternative-rap groups showed some debt to his wild, careening music. *—Stephen Thomas Erlewine*

★ **The Best of Cold Chillin'** / Oct. 17, 2000 / Landspeed ♦♦♦♦♦
Much more than just the clown prince of hip-hop during the late '80s and early '90s, Biz Markie was one of the golden age's most talented, distinctive, and inventive rappers whether he was talking about his skills on the mic ("Nobody Beats the Biz") or his favorite brand of spaghetti sauce ("Biz Is Goin' Off"). And like the other acts on the Cold Chillin' label, he benefited from one of the era's greatest producers, Marley Marl. Led by Marl's raw, drum-heavy tracks and great scratching, *The Best of Cold Chillin'* is a definitive look back for rap fans, gathering 17 tracks from the Biz's four LPs for the label and wisely balancing trademark hits like "Just a Friend" and "Vapors" with rare, early material like the solo human-beatbox number "One Two." The compilation also focuses heavily on his first two albums, with tracks from 1988's seminal *Goin' Off* and the following year's breakout *The Biz Never Sleeps*. *—John Bush*

Björk (Björk Gumundsdóttir)

b. Nov. 21, 1965, Reykjavik, Iceland
Vocals, Keyboards / Electronica, Alternative Dance, Trip-Hop, Club/Dance, Alternative Pop/Rock

Björk first came to prominence as one of the lead vocalists of the avant-pop Icelandic sextet the Sugarcubes, but when she launched a solo career after the group's 1992 demise, she quickly eclipsed her old band's popularity. Instead of following in the Sugarcubes' arty guitar-rock pretentions, Björk immersed herself in dance and club culture, working with many of the biggest names in the genre, including Nellee Hooper, Underworld, and Tricky. *Debut*, her first solo effort (except for an Icelandic-only smash released when she was just eleven years old) not only established her new artistic direction, but it became an international hit, making her one of the '90s most unlikely stars. The first result of her partnership with Hooper was "Human Behaviour," which became a Top 40 hit in the U.K., setting the stage for the surprising number three debut of the full-length album, *Debut*. Throughout 1993, Björk had hit U.K. singles—including "Venus as a Boy" and "Big Time Sensuality"—as well as modern rock radio hits in the U.S., and in both countries, she earned rave reviews. "Army of Me," the first single from Björk's forthcoming album, was released as a teaser single in the spring of 1995; it debuted at number 10 in the U.K. and became a moderate alternative rock hit in the U.S. *Post*, her second album, was released in June of 1995 to positive reviews and yielded the British hit singles "Isobel," "It's Oh So Quiet" and "Hyperballad." Late in 1996, Björk released *Telegram*, an album comprised of radical remixes of the entire *Post* album, in the U.K.; *Telegram* was released in America in January 1997. *Homogenic*, her most experimental studio effort to date, followed later that same year. *—Stephen Thomas Erlewine*

Gling Glo / 1990 / One Little Indian ♦♦♦
Björk's elastic, somersaulting voice is right at home delivering these traditional Icelandic and jazz tunes. Happy songs performed by Björk with the Icelandic jazz group, Gudmundur Ingólfssonar Trio, really showcase her voice, and reveal how her unique singing style shares some common ground with scatting. The trio consists of pianist Gudmundar Ingólfsson (who, contrary to popular rumor is not Björk's father), Gudmundur Steingrímsson on drums, and Thórdur Högnason on bass. Björk performed with this trio a few times before they recorded *Gling Glo*, and everyone must've had a good time, because the album captures the group moving through a mixture of jazz numbers and Icelandic songs with a free and easy feel. When *Gling Glo* was first released in 1990 on the Smekkleysa (Bad Taste) label, it went platinum, becoming the label's best seller. The first 14 songs are from this original issue, while the last two tracks (and the only songs sung in English— "Ruby Baby," and "I Can't Help Loving That Man") are drawn from a rehearsal recording made a year prior to the album. *—Joslyn Layne*

★ **Debut** / Jul. 1993 / Elektra ♦♦♦♦♦
Freed from the Sugarcubes' confines, Björk takes her voice and creativity to new heights on *Debut*, her first work after the group's breakup. With producer Nellee Hooper's help, she moves in an elegantly playful, dance-inspired direction, crafting highly individual, emotional electronic pop songs like the shivery, idealistic "One Day" and the bittersweet "Violently Happy." Despite the album's swift stylistic shifts, each of *Debut*'s tracks are distinctively Björk. "Human Behaviour"'s dramatic percussion provides a perfect showcase for her wide-ranging voice; "Aeroplane" casts her as a yearning lover against a lush, exotica-inspired backdrop; and the spare, poignant "Anchor Song" uses just her voice and a brass section to capture the loneliness of the sea. Though *Debut* is just as arty as anything she recorded with the Sugarcubes, the album's club-oriented tracks provide an exciting contrast to the rest of the album's delicate atmosphere. Björk's playful energy ignites dance-pop-like "Big Time Sensuality," and turns the genre on its head with "There's More to Life Than This." Recorded live at the Milk Bar Toilets, it captures the dancefloor's sweaty, claustrophobic groove, but her impish voice gives it an almost alien feel. But the album's romantic moments may be its most striking; "Venus as a Boy" fairly swoons with twinkly vibes and lush strings, and Björk's vocals and lyrics—"His wicked sense of humor/suggests exciting sex"—are sweet and just the slightest bit naughty. With harpist Corki Hale, she completely reinvents "Like Someone in Love," making it one of her own ballads. Possibly her prettiest work, Björk's horizons expanded on her other releases, but the album still sounds fresh, which is even more impressive considering electronic music's whiplash-speed innovations. *Debut* not only announced Bjork's remarkable talent, it suggested she had even more to offer. *—Heather Phares*

Post / Jun. 13, 1995 / Elektra ♦♦♦♦♦
After *Debut*'s success, the pressure was on Björk to surpass that album's creative, tantalizing electronic pop. She more than delivered with 1995's *Post*; from the menacing, industrial-tinged opener "Army of Me," it's clear that this album is not simply *Debut* redux. The songs—especially the epic, modern fairy tale "Isobel"—production, and arrangements all aim for, and accomplish, more. *Post* also features *Debut* producer Nellee Hooper, 808 State's Graham Massey, Howie B., and Tricky, who help Björk incorporate a spectrum of electronic and orchestral styles into songs like "Hyperballad," which sounds like a love song penned by Aphex Twin. Meanwhile, the bristling beats on the volatile, sensual "Enjoy" and the fragile, weightless ballad "Possibly Maybe" nod to trip-hop without being overwhelmed by it. As on *Debut*, Björk finds new ways of expressing timeworn emotions like love, lust, and yearning in abstractly precise lyrics like "Since you went away/I'm wearing lipstick again/I suck my tongue in remembrance of you," from "Possibly Maybe." But *Post*'s emotional peaks and valleys are more extreme than *Debut*'s. "I Miss You"'s exuberance is so animated, it makes perfect sense that *Ren & Stimpy*'s John Kricfalusi directed the song's video. Likewise, "It's Oh So Quiet"—which eventually led to Björk's award-winning turn as Selma in *Dancer in the Dark*—is so cartoonishly vibrant, it could have been arranged by Warner Bros. musical director Carl Stalling. Yet Björk sounds equally comfortable with an understated string section on "You've Been Flirting Again." "Headphones" ends the album on an experimental, hypnotic note, layering Björk's vocals over and over till they circle each other atop a bubbling, minimal beat. The work of a constantly changing artist, *Post* proves that as Björk moves toward more ambitious, complex music, she always surpasses herself. *—Heather Phares*

Telegram / Jan. 14, 1997 / Elektra ♦♦♦♦
In theory, *Telegram* is a remixed album of all the songs from *Post*, but the arrangements are so different, it might as well be another record entirely. Björk has re-recorded several of her vocals, handing the original backing tracks to a variety of producers and musicians—everyone from Dillinja to the Brodsky Quartet. While *Telegram* provides some of the most challenging listening yet heard on a Björk album, it is essentially because the new arrangements are radical—in terms of electronic dance music, the actual music and remixes are far from radical. Still, *Telegram* works as an excellent introduction to techno for alternative-pop fans unsure of where to begin exploring. *—Stephen Thomas Erlewine*

☆ **Homogenic** / Sep. 22, 1997 / Elektra ♦♦♦♦♦
By the late '90s, Björk's playful, unique worldview and singular voice became as confining as they were defining. With its surprising starkness and darkness, 1997's *Homogenic* shatters her "Icelandic pixie" image. Possibly inspired by her failed relationship with drum'n'bass kingpin Goldie, Björk sheds her more precious aspects, displaying more emotional depth than even her best previous work indicated. Her collaborators—LFO's Mark Bell, Mark "Spike" Stent, and *Post* contributor Howie B.—help make this album not only her most emotionally brave work, but her most sonically adventurous as well. A seamless fusion of chilly strings (courtesy of the Icelandic String Octet), stuttering, abstract beats, and unique touches like accordion and glass harmonica, *Homogenic* alternates between dark, uncompromising songs such as the icy opener "Hunter" and more soothing fare like the gently percolating "All Neon Like." The noisy, four-on-the-floor catharsis of "Pluto" and the raw vocals and abstract beats of "5 Years" and "Immature" reveal surprising amounts of anger, pain, and strength in the face of heartache. "I dare you to take me on," Björk challenges her lover in "5 Years," and wonders on "Immature," "How could I be so immature/To think he would replace/The missing elements in me?" "Bachelorette," a sweeping, brooding cousin to *Post*'s "Isobel," is possibly *Homogenic*'s saddest, most beautiful moment, giving filmic grandeur to a stormy relationship. Björk lets a little hope shine through on "Joga," a moving song dedicated to her homeland and her best friend, and the reassuring finale "All Is Full of Love." "Alarm Call"'s uplifting dance-pop seems out of place with the rest of the album but, as its title implies, *Homogenic* is her most holistic work. While it might not represent every side of Björk's music, *Homogenic* displays some of her most impressive heights. *—Heather Phares*

Selmasongs: Music from the Motion Picture Soundtrack Dancer in the Dark / Sep. 19, 2000 / Elektra ♦♦♦♦
Selmasongs: Music From the Motion Picture Soundtrack Dancer in the Dark is, and is not, a Björk album. While it's filled with rampant creativity, startling emotional leaps, and breathtaking vocals and arrangements, it isn't as playful as her other albums, even 1997's relatively dark *Homogenic*. Instead, it presents Björk as Selma, her character from Lars VonTrier's *Dancer in the Dark*: a Czech factory worker who is going blind but finds hope and refuge in the musicals she watches at the cinema. (VonTrier wanted to work with Björk after seeing Spike Jonze's musical-inspired video for "It's Oh So Quiet.") She acts through the music she composed, performed, and produced with conductor/arranger Vincent Mendoza and her longtime collaborators Mark "Spike" Stent and Mark Bell. Selma's unsinkable optimism and tragic end are telegraphed through songs like the irrepressible, cartoonish "Cvalda" to the sad, starry lullaby "Scatterheart." *Selmasongs*' best tracks are poignant, inventive expressions of Björk's talent and Selma's daydreams and suffering. "In the Musicals" shows how easy it is for Selma to slip into one of her Technicolor reveries: "There is always someone to catch me," Björk sighs as clouds of strings, harps, and xylophones rise up to meet her. "New World" reprises the simultaneously hopeful and ominous melody of "Overture," adding striking vocals and shuffling, industrial beats that reflect Selma's life in the factory as well as Björk's distinctive style. *Selmasongs* also succeeds as a soundtrack, sketching in details of Selma's story. "I've Seen It All," a duet with Thom Yorke, captures her stunted romance with a co-worker, while the tense "107 Steps" takes the listener to her journey's end. Intimate and theatrical, innovative and tied to

tradition, *Selmasongs* paints a portrait of a woman losing her sight, but it maintains Björk's unique vision. *—Heather Phares*

Vespertine / Aug. 28, 2001 / Elektra ✦✦✦✦✦

After cathartic statements like *Homogenic*, the role of Selma in *Dancer in the Dark*, and the film's somber companion piece *Selmasongs*, it's not surprising that Björk's first album in four years is less emotionally wrenching. But *Vespertine* isn't so much a departure from her previous work as a culmination of the musical distance she's traveled: within songs like the subtly sensual "Hidden Place" and "Undo" are traces of *Debut* and *Post*'s gentle loveliness, as well as *Homogenic* and *Selmasongs*' reflective, searching moments. Described by Björk as "... about being on your own in your house with your laptop and whispering for a year and just writing a very peaceful song that tiptoes," *Vespertine*'s vocals seldom rise above a whisper, the rhythms mimic heartbeats and breathing and a pristine, music-box delicacy unites the album into a deceptively fragile, hypnotic whole. Even relatively immediate, accessible songs, such as "It's Not Up to You," "Pagan Poetry" and "Unison" share a spacious serenity with the album's quietest moments. Indeed, the most intimate songs are among the most varied, from the seductively alien "Cocoon" to the dark, obsessive "An Echo, A Stain" to the fairytale-like instrumental "Frosti." The beauty of *Vespertine*'s subtlety may be lost on Björk fans demanding another leap like the one she made between *Post* and *Homogenic*, but like the rest of the album, its innovations are intimate and intricate. Collaborators like Matmos–who, along with their own *A Chance to Cut is a Chance to Cure*, now appear on two of 2001's best works–contribute appropriately restrained beats crafted from shuffled cards, cracking ice, and the snap-crackle-pop of Rice Krispies; harpist Zeena Parkins' melodic and rhythmic playing adds to the post-modernly angelic air. An album singing the praises of peace and quiet, *Vespertine* isn't merely lovely; it proves that in Björk's hands, intimacy can be just as compelling as louder emotions. *—Heather Phares*

Black Box Recorder

f. 1998, England

Alternative Pop/Rock

Black Box Recorder combined the talents of Auteurs main man Luke Haines, former Jesus and Mary Chain member John Moore, and vocalist Sarah Nixey. Like the Auteurs, Black Box Recorder's songs commented on the state of English affairs, both social and personal, often using character sketches that exposed the less-than-pleasant with sharp frankness and masterful simplicity. Coming together in 1998 as Haines kept his primary vehicle operable, the trio introduced themselves with their first single ("Child Psychology") being banned from U.K. radio for the charming line "Life is unfair/Kill yourself or get over it"—most likely a direct response to the "woah is me" trends of the British pop charts.

The full-length *England Made Me* followed later in the year, establishing Moore and Haines as a songwriting team that excelled at getting its points across with the least amount of instrumentation necessary. Raw and minimal but still perversely pop, Nixey's detached and fragile-yet-rich voice (usually kept up front in the mix) provided the ideal characteristics for their songs. Imagine a sober, somber, dub-influenced version of the Velvet Underground with an elegantly smooth Nico singing on top.

Jumping ship from Chrysalis to Nude for 2000's *The Facts of Life*, the first single from the album surprisingly went Top 20, providing Haines with the highest chart position of his career. Despite this, Haines made no bones about his disdain of Nude within a week of the chart placement, feeling that they dropped the ball after being handed it on a silver platter. Artistically, *The Facts of Life* was another success for the trio and an excellent extension of *England Made Me*. 2001 saw the release of *The Worst of Black Box Recorder*, a collection of the trio's B-sides. *—Andy Kellman*

England Made Me / 1998 / Chrysalis ✦✦✦

With its gentle acoustic-electric guitar mix, metronomic drum beats, and Sarah Nixey's lovely breathy vocals, *England Made Me* does not seem on the surface to be a sardonic comment on anything, but rather an exquisite, even upbeat, bit of pop. The more one digs, however, the more one unburies. Black Box Recorder is harshly critical of life in England, the bland, dull mundanities of daily living as well as the stale political world, and their debut album touches on issues ranging from teenage sex and single mothers to repressive family life and wife swapping. Such topics are seemingly impossible to weave into listenable pop music, but the songs that multi-instrumentalists Luke Haines and John Moore write are cleanly stylized in a way that conceals the raw-nerved lives their characters exist in but are also reflective of the internalization of such relentless barrenness. External appearances often belie the reality, the gnawing discomfort in the gut. Black Box Recorder seemingly approaches its subjects without judgment; the band, though, does not shy away from cynicism. Many of the songs on *England Made Me* are, at least lyrically, severe, naked reminders of a bloodless existence. Even when Black Box Recorder do inject a bit of pop cheerfulness into the music, it is seemingly done ironically. Each song sounds sparse because it is infused with a spatial quality that suggests beneath it all there is only emptiness, and nothing good comes from emptiness. In "Child Psychology" Nixey repeats the couplet "Life is unfair/Kill yourself or get over it" like a mantra. One gets the feeling that the way Black Box Recorder gets over it is through their music, which can make *England Made Me* a suffocating listen if experienced in more than short spurts. *—Stanton Swihart*

● **The Facts of Life** / May 1, 2000 / Nude ✦✦✦✦✦

You take the good, you take the Badalamenti—anyone who thinks *The Facts of Life* includes half-baked songs without meat is missing the point. Would you consider dumping a bucket of lime green paint on that new marble countertop in your kitchen nook? Didn't think so. That's pretty much what you'd be doing to Black Box Recorder's second LP if you feel the tunes need more substance. Half-baked? Not in the least; *The Facts of Life* is a fresh wedge of sourdough (dourdough?), just as simple but more tasty. Luke Haines and John Moore get the most mileage possible out of their sparse, noir-tinged melancholia, rarely needing extraneous things like overdubs or distortion for the sake of it. Sarah Nixey increases her stock as a worthy Bond siren, less kitschy and more swaggerly than that other Sarah. Like the finest charms of songs by the other Sarah's St. Etienne, "Weekend" carries its weight as a gorgeous, slightly upbeat pop song. You want catchy simplicity? Try a chorus of "Friday night/Saturday morning," with Haines' hypnotically shimmering guitar spirals to add accent. Flashes of Haines' tasteful glam jones run rampant in "Straight Life," which slyly references Roxy Music in a number of ways. The play on Roxy Music's "Street Life" is apparent in the title, as well as having lyrical nods to Roxy's "In Every Dream Home a Heartache." Seemingly embracing middle class Englishness while simultaneously rejecting it, Nixey ponders escaping transient lifestyles while grimacing at the thought of home repairs. Black Box Recorder is a master of the simple, effective melody (as are Haines' Auteurs). Also, not too many vocalists possess Nixey's ridiculous skill at making sheer boredom sound so affecting. If David Lynch should ever film a TV series in England, here are the soundtrack composers. "Hey folks, have you seen Angelo Badalamenti and Julee Cruise?" Sorry mate, we dropped them off at Big Ed's Gas Farm. They're in a bag, wrapped in plastic. *—Andy Kellman*

The Worst of Black Box Recorder / Aug. 21, 2001 / Jetset ✦✦✦✦

Hip hip hooray. Maybe someone up there likes us after all. *The Worst of Black Box Recorder* is a rare instance where restraint in buying a band's singles has paid off. Compiling all the B-sides from Black Box Recorder's first four singles (two of which were two-parters), a handful of studio extras that were included on the U.S. versions of *England Made Me* and *The Facts of Life*—including the stinging "Lord Lucan Is Missing," a take on Rod McKuen's-via-Jacques Brel's "Seasons in the Sun," the Bowie-worthy "Start As You Mean to Go On," and the equally spiky "Brutality"—and also throwing in the band's videos for the A-sides ("The Facts of Life," "Child Psychology," "The Art of Driving," and "England Made Me"), the whole package adds up to an LP that's just as worthy of your hard-earned scratch as the trio's two proper studio albums. Outside of the obvious space/time constraint, it's hard to imagine how most of the songs weren't able to find a way on the original incarnations of *England Made Me* or *The Facts of Life*. There isn't a weak moment to be found here, not even on the remixes; both the Chocolate Layers' (Pulp's Steve Mackey and Jarvis Cocker) mix of "The Facts of Life" and BBR's own versioning of "Uptown Top Ranking" don't fail to impress. If that's not enough to rope you in, the disc concludes in perfect fa-fa-fa-fa-fashion with an ultra sultry cover of the Thin White Duke's "Rock & Roll Suicide"; if you close your eyes tight enough, you can envision vocalist Sarah Nixey working her magic onstage for the drunken patrons of the Roadhouse, clad in a funny leather hat. *—Andy Kellman*

The Black Crowes

f. 1984, Atlanta, GA

Jam Bands, American Trad Rock, Southern Rock, Hard Rock

At the time of their 1990 debut, the kind of rock & roll the Black Crowes specialize in was out of style. Only Guns & Roses came close to approximating a vintage Stones-style raunch, but they were too angry and jagged to pull it off completely. The Black Crowes replicated that Stonesy swagger and Faces boogie perfectly. Vocalist Chris Robinson appropriated the sound and style of vintage Rod Stewart while guitarist Rich Robinson fused Keith Richards' lean attack with Ron Wood's messy rhythmic sense. At their best, the Black Crowes echo classic rock without slavishly imitating their influences. "Jealous Again," the first single from their 1990 debut *Shake Your Money Maker*, was a moderate hit but it was the band's cover of Otis Redding's "Hard to Handle" that made the group a multi-platinum success. The acoustic ballad "She Talks to Angels" became their second Top 40 hit in the spring of 1991. The Black Crowes delivered their second album, *The Southern Harmony and Musical Companion*, in the spring of 1992. It entered the charts at number one, but it didn't have as many hit singles as the debut; none of the singles cracked the Top 40 and only "Remedy" and "Thorn in My Pride" made the Top 100. *Amorica* debuted in the Top Ten, but none of the singles from the album made the charts; even though the record went gold, it slipped off the charts in early 1995. *—Stephen Thomas Erlewine*

Shake Your Money Maker / Jan. 1990 / American ✦✦✦✦

The Black Crowes' debut album, *Shake Your Money Maker*, may borrow heavily from the bluesy hard-rock grooves of the Rolling Stones and Faces (plus a bit of classic soul), but the band gets away with it due to sharp songwriting and an ear for strong riffs and chorus melodies, not to mention the gritty, muscular rhythm guitar of Rich Robinson and brother Chris's appropriate vocal swagger. Unlike their later records, the Crowes don't really stretch out and jam that much on *Money Maker*, but that helps distill their virtues into a handful of memorable singles ("Jealous Again," "She Talks to Angels," a cover of Otis Redding's "Hard to Handle"), and most of the album tracks maintain an equally high standard. *Shake Your Money Maker* may not be stunningly original, but it doesn't need to be; it's the most concise demonstration of the fact that the Black Crowes are a great, classic rock & roll band. *—Steve Huey*

The Southern Harmony and Musical Companion / May 12, 1992 / American ✦✦✦✦✦

The addition of the more technically gifted guitarist Marc Ford and a full-time organist gives the Black Crowes room to stretch out on *The Southern Harmony and Musical Companion*, perhaps the band's finest moment. Using Rich Robinson's descending chord progressions as a base, the band grooves its way through a remarkably fresh-sounding collection of Faces-like rockers and ballads, tearing into the material with flair and confidence and really coming into its own as a top-notch rock & roll outfit. But while the focus is undeniably on the band's musical chemistry, *Southern Harmony* also boasts a strong collection of songs, striking a perfect balance between the concise *Shake Your Money Maker* and their later, more jam-oriented records. While there aren't as many obvious singles as on their debut album, *The Southern Harmony and Musical Companion* is the best expression of the Crowes' ability to take a classic, tried-and-true sound and make it their own. *—Steve Huey*

Amorica / Nov. 1, 1994 / American ♦♦♦♦♦

On *Amorica*, the Black Crowes finally come into their own, taking their cue from the most relaxed, groove-oriented tracks on their previous album. While the album contains no immediately obvious singles, the songs are the best the band has ever written, stretching out into a hard, jam-oriented, funky blues-rock. The Black Crowes' influences are still discernable—no band celebrates the glory days of rock culture quite as enthusiastically—but they use the music of the Stones, the Faces, and Little Feat much the same way the Stones used the music of Chuck Berry: it's a starting point that leads the band into a new direction, incorporating different musical genres and making the music original. That sense of reinterpretation is what keeps *Amorica* fresh. *—Stephen Thomas Erlewine*

Three Snakes & One Charm / Jul. 23, 1996 / American ♦♦♦

With *Amorica*, the Black Crowes began developing a distinctive sound, shading their Stonesy Southern boogie with a variety of rootsy and psychedelic overtones. But where *Amorica* was rich with kaleidescopic colors, *Three Snakes & One Charm* is stripped down and direct. Sure, it has a punchy, muscular sound that is, if anything, more eclectic than its predecessor, but the production is distressingly monotonous and the songs lack strong hooks. Even with its faults, *Three Snakes & One Charm* is a winning album, mainly because the Black Crowes' musicianship continues to deepen—the musical fusions and eclecticism are seamless, particularly from lead guitarist Rich Robinson. Their musicianship would be even more impressive if the songs were equal in quality. *—Stephen Thomas Erlewine*

By Your Side / Jan. 12, 1999 / American ♦♦♦♦

Between *Shake Your Money Maker* and *Three Snakes & One Charm*, the Black Crowes evolved from a muscular, Stonesy hard rock outfit to full-fledged modern-day Southern rockers, drawing from a wealth of blues, country, folk, and rock styles to create a sprawling, fluid sound that was simultaneously traditional and distinctive. The problem was, their loose-limbed grooves tended to connect better in concert than on record, especially since they were sacrificing songs for the sake of sound, which in turn was decreasing their audience. Aware of the situation, the Crowes went back to their roots with *By Your Side*. Armed with a string of concise, energetic rockers, the Crowes hit harder than they have since their debut, yet they retain the sonic detail that reared its head on *Amorica*, adding pianos, choirs, and scores of other flourishes throughout the record. It's a back-to-basics set performed with all of the knowledge they have gained over the years, and the result is a thoroughly enjoyable record, their most satisfying and accessible effort since *The Southern Harmony and Musical Companion*. Not that it's necessarily in that league—it lacks the parade of great songs that elevate that album above all their other records—but it does find the Crowes in lean fighting form for the first time in years, proving that they're possibly the best straight-ahead rock & roll band of the '90s. *—Stephen Thomas Erlewine*

● **Greatest Hits 1990-1999: A Tribute to a Work in Progress** / Jun. 20, 2000 / American/Columbia ♦♦♦♦♦

At the end of the decade, the Black Crowes parted ways with American/Columbia, which made sense for both parties. The band didn't sell records like they used to, and they preferred to be independent anyway. It wasn't an entirely amicable parting—the label wouldn't let the band record old songs for an independently released live album—but as the last album in the contract, the compilation *Greatest Hits 1990-1999: A Tribute to a Work in Progress*, is a nice addition to the catalog anyway. Basically, the album has every song a casual fan would want ("Jealous Again," "Twice As Hard," "Hard to Handle," "She Talks to Angels," "Remedy," "Sting Me," "Wiser Time," "A Conspiracy," "Kickin' My Heart Around") and is a nice listen for the hardcore. There are several great songs missing and there's perhaps a little bit too much of *By Your Side* here, but the only glaring omission is "Sometimes Salvation"; so, in other words, it's pretty close to a perfect compilation of that first decade. Gathered like this, the Black Crowes' finest songs are all the more impressive. The band not only sounds tight, but they sound diverse, able to handle full-throttle barroom ravers as easily as folk ballads, soulful vamps, blues, and laid-back Southern rock. Even more impressive, it's easy to see what good songwriters the brothers Robinson are. Yes, they're classicists, cribbing from the Stones and Allman Brothers and everything in between, but they know how to put it all together, write good hooks, and deliver them expertly. *Greatest Hits* is proof of that, and it's some of the best pure hard rock since the golden age of album rock. *—Stephen Thomas Erlewine*

Lions / May 8, 2001 / V2 ♦♦♦

If the Black Crowes are anything, they are survivors, weathering years of popularity and disdain, before emerging at the end of the '90s as a rarity—a real, road-weathered rock & roll band, in the classic sense. And it wasn't just that they played classic rock—they stayed out on the road constantly, bashing out albums when they weren't fighting record labels. By the dawn of the new millennium, there weren't many bands like that out on the market, and it was a mixed blessing—it meant that they had an ugly breakup with their long-time label, American, but it also meant that there really wasn't anybody else for Jimmy Page to turn to when he wanted to tour in 1999. These two events inform *Lions*, their first album for V2 records, and their most idiosyncratic album since 1994's neglected gem, *Amorica*. Like that record, this is more about the music and the texture than the songs, which is disconcerting for anybody looking for the knockout songwriting of their first two records. Here, the songs can seem incomplete, as if they got the sound of the track down, but not the structure. Still, this is a powerful, textured hard rock record that covers a lot of ground, surging from powerful riffs to gospel choruses and funkier-than-expected riffs. There are few bands of their time that could sound so versatile within the confines of hard rock, and if this doesn't really deliver memorable songs, tracks do jell on repeated plays, and the Black Crowes' kaleidoscopic vision of rock's history is reason enough to listen to this record—even if you're left with a nagging suspicion that this could have been a knockout with some real songs in tow. *—Stephen Thomas Erlewine*

Black Flag

f. 1977, Los Angeles, CA, **db.** 1986

American Punk, L.A. Punk, Hardcore Punk, American Underground

In many ways, Black Flag were the definitive Los Angeles hardcore punk band. Although their music flirted with heavy metal and experimental noise and jazz more than that of most hardcore bands, they defined the image and the aesthetic. Through their ceaseless touring, the band cultivated the American underground punk scene—every year, Black Flag played in every area of the U.S., influencing countless numbers of bands. Although their recording career was hampered by a draining lawsuit, which was followed by a seemingly endless stream of independently released records, the band was unquestionably one of the most infuential American post-punk bands. A full decade and a half before the fusion of punk and metal became popular, Black Flag created a ferocious, edgy, and ironic amalgam of underground aesthetics and gut-pounding metal. Their lyrics alluded to social criticism and a political viewpoint, but it was all conveyed as seething, cynical angst, which was occasionally very funny. Furthermore, Black Flag demonstrated an affection for bohemia—both in terms of musical experimentation and a fondness for poetry—that reiterated the band's underground roots and prevented it from becoming nothing but a heavy metal group. And it didn't matter who was in the band—throughout the years, the lineup changed numerous times—because the Black Flag name and four-bar logo became punk institutions. *—Stephen Thomas Erlewine*

★ **Damaged** / 1981 / SST ♦♦♦♦♦

Perhaps the best album to emerge from the quagmire that was early-'80s California hardcore punk, the visceral, intensely physical presence of this record has yet to be equaled, although many bands have tried. Although Black Flag had been recording for three years prior to this release, the fact that Henry Rollins was now their lead singer made all the difference. His furious bellow and barely contained ferocity was the missing piece the band needed to become great. Also, guitarist/mastermind Greg Ginn wrote a slew of great songs for this record that, while suffused with the usual punk conceits (alienation, boredom, disenfranchisement), were capable of making one laugh out loud, especially the proto-slacker satire "TV Party." Extremely controversial when it was released, *Damaged* endured the slings and arrows of outrageous criticism (some reacted as though this record alone would cause the fall of America's youth) to become and remain an important document of its time. *—John Dougan*

Everything Went Black / 1983 / SST ♦♦♦

When it was first released in 1983, Black Flag was in the middle of a backbreaking legal dispute with Unicorn Records. As a result of litigation, the band was prevented from using the Black Flag name on any records. Hence the original packaging for this album, which listed only the names of individual band members on the cover (this was rectified on subsequent issues). It's a double album (on vinyl) compilation of previously released material and outtakes—though the European edition features a wholly different running order. The material, dating from 1978 to 1981, is excellent in places, average in others. However, only obsessives need track it down—as signified by the inclusion of two versions of several songs (including stalwarts "Damaged" and "Police Story"). The fourth side of the original vinyl issue also included a sequence of radio spots discussing forthcoming Black Flag gigs, which is entertaining stuff, but it's more useful as a historical document than a listening experience. *—Alex Ogg*

Family Man / 1984 / SST ♦♦♦

Black Flag's most experimental album, *Family Man* features one LP side of spoken-word performances from Henry Rollins and another of instrumental music from the late-Flag lineup of Greg Ginn (guitar), Kira (bass), and Bill Stevenson (drums). Although occasionally chilling in its intensity, the spoken-word material, much like the between-song recitations of fellow Californian Jim Morrison (with whom Rollins sometimes shares a vocal similarity here) on the live Doors albums, mostly sounds juvenile and dated after the fact. That said, *Family Man*'s spoken word tracks, along with Jello Biafra's recordings with the Dead Kennedys, can largely be credited with bringing "alternative" spoken word to a larger audience who were either unaware of, or could not relate to, the Patti Smith/downtown New York scene. Unlike the solo Rollins tracks, the instrumental music is still challenging and vibrant. Although sounding at times like a high school garage band attempting to perform Rush covers, Ginn and company play with a sense of desperation and punk rock fury that makes much of the music positively electrifying. Similar in spirit to the less poppy tracks on Hüsker Dü's contemporary *Zen Arcade*, side two of *Family Man* is characterized by its emotional purity. Greg Ginn reveals himself as a refreshingly and brilliantly free improviser and his playing should serve as an inspiration and lesson to later "punk" bands who value technical proficiency over rockin' out. Overall, *Family Man* is an essential, if atypical, part of the Black Flag canon and should appeal to fans of Sun Ra, Ornette Coleman, or the New York "noise" scene as well. *—Pemberton Roach*

The First Four Years / 1984 / SST ♦♦♦

The best collection of pre-Rollins-era Black Flag. Much of *The First Four Years* finds the band in developmental mode, but the sonic anarchy and political vituperation met head-on more than once, creating a ferociously good time. Not simply for completists, this is an important recording of the then-burgeoning L.A. hardcore scene. *—John Dougan*

Live '84 / 1984 / SST ♦♦

Keeping up with their furious pace came *Live '84*, a cassette-only release of a standard (for them anyway) Black Flag gig. Opening up with an eight-and-a-half minute hardcore/punk/jazz instrumental "The Process of Weeding Out" (which came from an earlier Black Flag instrumental EP of the same title), it was abundantly clear that Black Flag was no longer just another punk band; as much as they loved to kick out the jams, they also loved destroying the audience's preconceived notions of how punk bands were supposed to behave. Running at 70 minutes, this is a terrific live recording of Black Flag at their performing peak. *—John Dougan*

My War / 1984 / SST ✦✦

After a rancorous three-year legal battle with their label Unicorn which prevented them from releasing any new material, Black Flag binged in the mid-'80s, releasing a flurry of records that had even the most devoted fans scrambling to keep up. They did, however, start this period somewhat inauspiciously with *My War*, a pretentious mess of a record with a totally worthless second side. Featuring three tracks of slower-than-Black Sabbath muck with Rollins howling like a caged animal, it was self-indulgence masquerading as inspiration and about as much fun as wading through a tarpit. Side one, however, was quite good, with the title tracks especially intimidating. *—John Dougan*

Slip it In / 1984 / SST ✦✦✦

Slip It In followed *My War* almost immediately, and while a bit better (fewer mega-volume angst drones), the band still wanders a bit, experimenting with expanding the breadth of hardcore into a newer hard rock/punk sound. This is especially true of Greg Ginn's guitar playing, which was becoming increasingly avant-garde and exciting. Rather than simply coughing up one cliched solo after another, he wandered harmolodically up and down the fretboard as a jazz player like Blood Ulmer would, making the material more interesting than what most Black Flag-influenced bands were playing. *—John Dougan*

In My Head / 1985 / SST ✦✦✦✦✦

Hot on the heels of the live record came *Loose Nut* and *In My Head* which showed significant improvement over *My War* and *Slip It In*. Rollins and Ginn were exploring by-now standard lyrical themes: hate, paranoia, loneliness, anomie, and violence, but framing them around music that was demanding, powerful, and exciting. *In My Head* is the slightly better of the two, primarily because it's a little edgier and uncontrolled, but at this juncture, Black Flag was making some of the best contemporary rock music extant. *—John Dougan*

Loose Nut / 1985 / SST ✦✦✦

One of three LPs released by Black Flag in 1985, *Loose Nut* suffers from its creators' rampant profligacy. Too much of the record is under-rehearsed and under-ripe, yet when the group hits its stride, as on Rollins's brutal "This Is Good," it's hard to deny the group's trademark, adrenaline-rush appeal. Other highlights include "Annihilate This Week" and "Bastard in Love." *—Alex Ogg*

Who's Got the 101/2? / 1986 / SST ✦✦✦✦✦

Black Flag's second live album, recorded at a 1985 Portland show with the Kira/Martinez rhythm section, is about what you'd expect the late period of the band to sound like live. A couple of older songs crop up—"Slip It In" and "Gimmie Gimmie Gimmie" are transformed into a great fifteen-minute medley with Rollins getting in some audience-baiting that explains the album title—but mostly this is from *Loose Nut*, its songs sounding generally better here than on that release. Rollins is in typically fiery form throughout; whatever dissatisfactions with the band he spoke of in future years evidently didn't keep him from forgetting how to put on a show. It's interesting to realize how much of the vaunted Rollins attitude comes from singing lyrics written mostly by Ginn, but the singer definitely makes those words his own regardless. Certainly his generally terse spoken-word bits practically drip with the man's essence—talking about "Annihilate": "This is a song about killing yourself to live." Ginn's blend of straight-ahead punk riffage and ponderous if still exciting open-ended sludge tones and soloing matches Rollins just fine, while Kira and Martinez do their job well enough. Kira adds some deadpan backing vocals at points as well. Strong numbers include "Bastard in Love," given a tight performance and an almost sweet touch of guitar jangle at points, and smoking takes on "The Best One Yet" and their inimitable version of "Louie, Louie." The CD version is the one to get, with a further half-hour of music from the show than on the vinyl version. *—Ned Raggett*

Wasted . . . Again / 1987 / SST ✦✦✦✦✦

Wasted . . . Again is a posthumous release that is an essential career summation. For those hearing the ear-searing sounds of early-'80s SoCal hardcore punk for the first time, *Wasted . . . Again* is an essential purchase. *—John Dougan*

Black Grape

f. 1993, Manchester, England, **db.** Jul. 1998

British Rap, Alternative Dance, Britpop, Alternative Pop/Rock

After the Happy Mondays disbanded in 1992, most observers would have guessed that the group's leader, vocalist Shaun Ryder, would succumb to the myriad drug addictions that hastened the breakup. But Ryder recouped his strengths and came back with a new band, Black Grape. Black Grape was embraced by both the British public and press, making Shaun Ryder one of the more unexpected comebacks in rock & roll history. Ryder formed the group with ex-Happy Monday Bez (dancer, percussion) in 1993 and began recording demos only weeks after the implosion of the Happy Mondays. Black Grape's debut album, *It's Great When You're Straight . . . Yeah*, was recorded over a period of seven weeks in late 1994 and early 1995, by which time Ryder had recruited a number of musicians and rappers; after it was completed, the band signed with Radioactive Records. The group's first single, "Reverend Black Grape," entered the Top Ten upon its release, and the album entered the U.K. charts at number one in August of 1995. "In the Name of the Father" and "Kelly's Heroes" followed "Reverend Black Grape" into the Top 20 later in 1995. Toward the end of the year, rapper Kermit suffered a severe case of septicemia, a form of blood poisoning caused by bad water he drank while in Mexico; although he came close to death—bits of his heart and liver were flaking off—he had recovered by the following spring, though not in time for the band's U.S. tour. Prior to the tour, Bez left the band due to financial disagreements with the record company. During the spring and summer of 1996, the single "Fat Neck" and the football anthem "England's Irie"—recorded with Smiths guitarist Johnny Marr and Clash singer Joe Strummer, respectively—both became Top Ten hits. The album *Stupid, Stupid, Stupid*, followed in 1997, but due in part to the revolving-door membership, Black Grape disbanded in the summer of 1998, after which Ryder reunited Happy Mondays. *—Stephen Thomas Erlewine*

● **It's Great When You're Straight . . . Yeah** / Oct. 10, 1995 / Radioactive ✦✦✦✦✦

When the Happy Mondays fell apart in 1992, most observers assumed that Shaun Ryder would never recover from his numerous drug addictions. No one could have ever predicted that he would return to the top of the charts three years later, relatively fit and healthy, with a new band that fulfilled all of the promises of his old group. Black Grape is what the Happy Mondays always were, only better. Leaving behind the stiff musicianship that plagued even the best Mondays records, Black Grape's debut *It's Great When You're Straight . . . Yeah* is a surreal, funky, profane, and perversely joyous album, overflowing with casual eclecticism and giddy humor. Working with a band that is looser and grittier than the Mondays, Ryder sounds reinvigorated, creating bizarre rhymes that tie together junk culture, drug lingo, literary references, and utter nonsense. Ryder's lyrics have always been free-wheelingly impenetrable, but now he's working with Kermit, a rapper that is the equal of his skills. Even better, the music has deep grooves and catchy pop hooks that come straight out of left field. From the blaring harmonica of the triumphant "Reverend Black Grape" and the trippy sitars of "In the Name of the Father" to the seedy, rolling "Shake Your Money" and the stinging guitars of "Tramazi Parti," *It's Great* is filled with music that goes in unconventional directions without ever sounding forced. Not only is *It's Great When You're Straight* a triumphant return for Shaun Ryder and his sidekick Bez, it's the first album they have ever recorded that justifies all of the hype. *—Stephen Thomas Erlewine*

Stupid, Stupid, Stupid, / Nov. 1997 / Radioactive ✦✦✦

Arriving out of nowhere, Black Grape's debut, *It's Great When You're Straight . . . Yeah*, was a complete surprise, a post-acid house party record that delivered on all of the Happy Mondays' promise. It was a kinetic, exciting record that disregarded boundaries between rap, house, rock, soul, and pop—it was the culmination of what Shaun Ryder began with *Pills N Thrills N Bellyaches*. *It's Great* was greeted warmly by critics and fans, which meant that the group's second album, *Stupid, Stupid, Stupid*, was eagerly anticipated. Perhaps nothing could live up to the expectations of hardcore fans, but *Stupid, Stupid, Stupid*, fails to deliver in a variety of ways. Essentially, it plays like *It's Great*, part two, only without its predecessor's infectious beats, mammoth hooks, and surreal humor. There's a heavier soul influence this time around ("Lonely" is a straight cover of Frederick Knight's 1972 hit "I've Been Lonely for So Long"), but it doesn't sit well with Ryder's thuggish rasp, and that's one of the problems about the album—the vocals and the music don't match. Apart from the dynamite opening trilogy of "Get Higher," "Squeaky," and "Marbles," Ryder and Kermit don't sound integrated with the music; they sound as if they're rapping over pre-existing backing tracks, which aren't as funky or inventive as those from *It's Great*. Perhaps *Stupid, Stupid, Stupid* would sound intoxicating if you're intoxicated, but such stimulation shouldn't be necessary—the music should be intoxicating enough on its own. *—Stephen Thomas Erlewine*

Black Oak Arkansas

f. 1970, Black Oak, AR

Boogie Rock, Southern Rock, Hard Rock, Arena Rock, Album Rock

Southern rock veterans Black Oak Arkansas never quite achieved the level of success enjoyed by contemporaries like Lynyrd Skynyrd and the Allman Brothers, but have remained a cult band thanks to their raw, primitive energy and the testosterone-fueled antics of lead vocalist/showman James "Big Jim Dandy" Mangrum. Named for Mangrum's hometown, Black Oak Arkansas dates back to the mid-'60s, when a group of young, long-haired misfits headed by Mangrum, unable to find work, turned to rock & roll. The band secured a deal with Atlantic after several trips to Los Angeles and released its self-titled debut in 1971. While it wasn't a hit, the band toured extensively, building a reputation as a raw, incendiary live act that made up for occasional musical deficiencies with energy and the explicit sexuality of Mangrum, who flaunted his body at every opportunity and became known for such antics as miming sex with the washboard he used for musical accompaniment. Black Oak Arkansas eventually built up a solid following through incessant touring and enjoyed a run of ten charting albums between 1971 and 1976. The band also found itself with a Top 30 single in their raunchy cover of a LaVern Baker R&B hit called "Jim Dandy to the Rescue," which became Mangrum's signature song. When album sales dried up, Mangrum re-formed the band with more musically skilled veteran players and continued to tour, although the group's glory days were past. *—Steve Huey*

● **Hot & Nasty: The Best of Black Oak Arkansas** / 1993 / Rhino ✦✦✦✦✦

Although Lynyrd Skynyrd and the Allman Brothers Band remain better known today, Black Oak Arkansas was once an important group in the southern rock scene. This generous compilation provides a solid thumbnail sketch of the group's career, including all their hits and radio favorites plus a generous assortment of album tracks. Black Oak Arkansas were often criticized by the music press for their cartoonish hillbilly image (especially frontman Jim Dandy Mangrum's strangled vocal style), but *Hot & Nasty: The Best of Black Oak Arkansas* reveals that the group's tunes hold up pretty well: their big hit "Jim

Dandy" remains a tub-thumping slice of country rock and "Keep the Faith" mines similar territory to an equally listenable effect. The group also shows off a surprising funkiness on tracks like "Mutants of the Monster," presented here in a smoking, wah-wah guitar-drenched live version, and "Hot and Nasty," which has a hard-grooving drum beat that's begging to be sampled by a hip-hop group. Other tracks show off the group's chops on country sounds: "When Electricity Came To Arkansas" starts off with a convincing, old-fashioned hoedown (complete with washboard) before moving into its hard-rock portion and "Everybody Wants To See Heaven (Nobody Wants To Die)" is a solid slice of country philosophy driven home by an effective bluegrass-style acoustic arrangement. The listener's tolerance for this music will most likely depend on what they think of Jim Dandy Mangrum's vocals, but anyone who enjoys the heavier side of country rock will most likely find something to enjoy on this entertaining, one-of-a-kind disc. *—Donald A. Guarisco*

Black Sabbath

f. 1969, Birmingham, England
Album Rock, British Metal, Heavy Metal
No other band has come closer to embodying heavy metal than Black Sabbath. Over the years, their lineup may have changed, but their music hasn't—it has remained the same loud, methodical guitar-based heavy rock that it was in the early '70s. Their slow, sludgy attack was part design and part accident. Because of an accident that cut the tips of his fingers, Tony Iommi played with strings that were slightly slack—the lower tuning made his mammoth riffs sound heavier. Bassist Geezer Butler's lyrics reveled in black magic, fantasy, drugs, mental illness, and the occult, but never sex; Ozzy Osbourne sang them in a flat, almost tuneless, banshee wail. Taken together, the primitive musicianship, bad poetry, obsessive fantasy world, crawling tempos, and overpowering volume simultaneously represents everything good and bad about heavy metal. Of course, after Black Sabbath hit their peak, they stuck around way too long. Each of their first six albums had, at the very least, something to recommend them. Osbourne hung around for two more records before jumping ship for good. After former Rainbow lead vocalist Ronnie James Dio replaced him in 1979, band members kept shifting throughout the '80s, with Iommi the only original remaining throughout. With Butler rejoining in 1991, Black Sabbath continued to lurch forward (sometimes with Osbourne back in the fold), oblivious of the criticism and declining record sales. *—Stephen Thomas Erlewine*

Black Sabbath / May 1970 / Warner Brothers ♦♦♦♦♦
Black Sabbath's debut album is given over to lengthy songs and suite-like pieces where individual songs blur together and riffs pound away one after another, frequently under extended jams. There isn't much variety in tempo, mood, or the band's simple, blues-derived musical vocabulary, but that's not the point; Sabbath's slowed-down, murky guitar rock bludgeons the listener in an almost hallucinatory fashion, reveling in its own dazed, druggy state of consciousness. Songs like the apocalyptic title track, "N.I.B.," and "The Wizard" make their obsessions with evil and black magic seem like more than just stereotypical heavy metal posturing because of the dim, suffocating musical atmosphere the band frames them in. This blueprint would be refined and occasionally elaborated upon over the band's next few albums, but there are plenty of metal classics already here. *—Steve Huey*

★ **Paranoid** / Jan. 1971 / Warner Brothers ♦♦♦♦♦
Paranoid was not only Black Sabbath's most popular record (it was a number one smash in the U.K., and "Paranoid" and "Iron Man" both scraped the U.S. charts despite virtually nonexistent radio play), it also stands as one of the greatest and most influential heavy metal albums of all time. *Paranoid* refined Black Sabbath's signature sound—crushingly loud, minor-key dirges loosely based on heavy blues-rock—and applied it to a newly consistent set of songs with utterly memorable riffs, most of which now rank as all-time metal classics. Where the extended, multi-sectioned songs on the debut sometimes felt like aimless jams, their counterparts on *Paranoid* have been given focus and direction, lending an epic drama to now-standards like "War Pigs" and "Iron Man" (which sports one of the most immediately identifiable riffs in metal history). The subject matter is unrelentingly, obsessively dark, covering both supernatural/sci-fi horrors and the real-life traumas of death, war, nuclear annihilation, mental illness, drug hallucinations, and narcotic abuse. Yet Sabbath makes it totally convincing, thanks to the crawling, muddled bleakness and bad-trip depression evoked so frighteningly well by their music. Even the qualities that made critics deplore the album (and the group) for years increase the overall effect—the technical simplicity of Ozzy Osbourne's vocals and Tony Iommi's lead guitar vocabulary; the spots when the lyrics sink into melodrama or awkwardness; the lack of subtlety and the infrequent dynamic contrast. Everything adds up to more than the sum of its parts, as though the anxieties behind the music simply demanded that the band achieve catharsis by steamrolling everything in its path, including its own limitations. Monolithic and primally powerful, *Paranoid* defined the sound and style of heavy metal more than any other record in rock history. *—Steve Huey*

☆ **Master of Reality** / Aug. 1971 / Warner Brothers ♦♦♦♦♦
With *Paranoid*, Black Sabbath perfected the formula for their lumbering heavy metal. On its followup, *Master of Reality*, the group merely repeated the formula, setting the stage for a career of recycling the same sounds and riffs. But on *Master of Reality* Sabbath still were fresh and had a seemingly endless supply of crushingly heavy riffs to bludgeon their audiences into sweet, willing oblivion. If the album is a showcase for anyone, it is Tony Iommi, who keeps the album afloat with a series of slow, loud riffs, the best of which—"Sweet Leaf" and "Children of the Grave" among them—rank among his finest playing. Taken in tandem with the more consistent *Paranoid*, *Master of Reality* forms the core of Sabbath's canon. There are a few stray necessary tracks scattered throughout the group's other early '70s albums, but *Master of Reality* is the last time they delivered a consistent album and its influence can be heard throughout the generations of heavy metal bands that followed. *—Stephen Thomas Erlewine*

Black Sabbath, Vol. 4 / Sep. 1972 / Warner Brothers ♦♦♦♦♦
Vol. 4 is just a cut below its two undisputedly classic predecessors, as it begins to run out of steam—and memorable riffs—toward the end. However, it finds Sabbath beginning to experiment successfully with its trademark sound on tracks like the ambitious, psychedelic-tinged, multi-part "Wheels of Confusion," the concise, textured "Tomorrow's Dream," and the orchestrated piano ballad "Changes" (even if the latter's lyrics cross the line into triteness). But the classic Sabbath sound is still very much in evidence; the crushing "Supernaut" is one of the heaviest tracks the band ever recorded. *—Steve Huey*

Sabbath, Bloody Sabbath / Dec. 1973 / Warner Brothers ♦♦♦♦♦
With 1973's *Sabbath, Bloody Sabbath* (their fifth masterpiece in four years), Black Sabbath made a concerted effort to raise their creative stakes and dispensed unprecedented attention to the album's production, arrangements, and even the cover artwork. While faithful to the band's signature compositional style and sound, brilliant songs such as the title track, "A National Acrobat," and "Killing Yourself to Live" also displayed a newfound sense of finesse and maturity. The introduction of keyboards and synthesizers, on the other hand, meets with mixed results. Erstwhile Yes keyboard wizard Rick Wakeman makes a positive contribution to "Sabbra Cadabra," but "Who are You" definitely suffers from synth overkill. Still, "Spiral Architect" benefits from its tasteful background orchestration, and the gentle "Fluff" is the first truly memorable solo instrumental from guitarist Tony Iommi, whose previous attempts often seemed pointless and haphazard. Simply put, this album is essential to any heavy metal collection. *—Ed Rivadavia*

Sabotage / Aug. 1975 / Warner Brothers ♦♦♦♦♦
Heavy metal gods Black Sabbath's impeccable recording legacy finally began to unravel with 1975's *Sabotage*, which attempted to continue the evolution begun with 1973's *Sabbath, Bloody Sabbath*, but somewhat lacked its focus. The plodding rhythm of "Hole in the Sky" and the guitar interlude that is "Don't Start (Too Late)" merely serve as tasters for the album's tour de force, "Symptom of the Universe," arguably Sabbath's last great classic, despite its rather pointless acoustic outro. The group treads familiar but compelling ground with "Thrill of It All" and the multipart epics "The Writ" and "Megalomania," but problems emerge when they attempt to stretch creatively. While they were largely successful with the experiments on *Sabbath, Bloody Sabbath*, the band goes so far overboard on the peculiar "Supertzar" (basically an instrumental overlayed with wordless, chorused vocals), and the obvious hit single fiasco "Am I Going Insane (Radio)" that the result is virtually unrecognizable as Black Sabbath. Unfortunately, subsequent efforts would see the band continue this reckless attempt to evolve at the expense of their original identity. *—Ed Rivadavia*

We Sold Our Soul for Rock & Roll / Feb. 1976 / Warner Brothers ♦♦♦♦♦
We Sold Our Soul for Rock & Roll is a good single-disc collection of many—but not all—of Black Sabbath's best tracks from the Ozzy Osbourne era, drawing about half of its material from the group's first two albums, *Black Sabbath* and *Paranoid*. That makes it ideal for the fan who only wants one Black Sabbath disc, but those who want to dig deeper should be advised that all six LPs from the Osbourne period contain high-quality items not present here, especially the underrepresented *Master of Reality* and *Vol. 4*. Still, there's no quibbling with what is here. *—Steve Huey*

Technical Ecstasy / Oct. 1976 / Warner Brothers ♦♦

Never Say Die! / Oct. 1978 / Warner Brothers ♦♦

Heaven and Hell / May 1980 / Warner Brothers ♦♦♦♦♦
Many had left Black Sabbath for dead at the dawn of the '80s, and with good reason—the band's last few albums were not even close to their early classics, and original singer Ozzy Osbourne had just split from the band. But the Sabs had found a worthy replacement in former Elf and Rainbow singer Ronnie James Dio, and bounced back to issue their finest album since the early '70s, 1980's *Heaven and Hell*. The band sounds reborn and re-energized throughout. Several tracks easily rank among Sabbath's all-time best, such as the vicious album opener, "Neon Knights," the moody, mid-paced epic "Children of the Sea," and the title track, which features one of Tony Iommi 's best guitar riffs. With *Heaven and Hell*, Black Sabbath were obviously back in business. Unfortunately, the Dio-led version of the band would only record one more studio album before splitting up (although Dio would return briefly in the early '90s). One of Sabbath's finest records. *—Greg Prato*

Mob Rules / Nov. 1981 / Warner Brothers ♦♦♦♦
1981's *Mob Rules* was the second Black Sabbath album to feature vertically challenged singer Ronnie James Dio, whose powerful pipes and dungeons and dragons lyrics initially seemed like the perfect replacement for the recently departed and wildly popular Ozzy Osbourne. In fact, all the ingredients which had made their first outing, *Heaven and Hell*, so successful are re-utilized on this album, including legendary metal producer Martin Birch (Deep Purple, Whitesnake, etc.) and supporting keyboard player Geoff Nichols. And while it lacks some of its predecessor's inspired songwriting, *Mob Rules* was given a much punchier, in your face mix by Birch, who seemed re-energized after his recent work on the New Wave of British Heavy Metal upstarts Iron Maiden's *Killers* album. Essentially, *Mob Rules* is a magnificent record, with the only serious problem being the sequencing of the material, which mirrors *Heaven and Hell*'s almost to a tee. In that light, one can't help but compare otherwise compelling tracks like "Turn Up the Night" and "Voodoo" to their more impressive *Heaven and Hell* counterparts, "Neon Knights" and "Children of the Sea." This unhappy streak is finally snapped by the unconventional "E5150," a synthesizer-driven instrumental conceived for the animated motion picture *Heavy Metal*. Then, the unbelievably heavy, seven-minute epic "The Sign of the Southern Cross" delivers one of the album's best moments before unleashing the roaring title track. Side

two is less consistent, hiding the awesome "Falling off the Edge of the World" (perhaps the most overlooked secret gem to come from the Dio lineup) amongst rather average tracks like "Slipping Away" and "Over and Over." Over the next year, the shit would quite literally hit the fan for Black Sabbath, and Dio's exit would mark *Mob Rules* as the last widely respected studio release of the band's storied career. *—Ed Rivadavia*

Live Evil / Dec. 1982 / Vertigo ✦✦

Born Again / Oct. 1983 / Warner Brothers ✦

Seventh Star / Jan. 1986 / Warner Brothers ✦✦✦
An often misunderstood and underrated album, 1986's *Seventh Star* was never intended to be a Black Sabbath release, as the band had effectively broken up following their disastrous 1984 tour. Instead, it was originally conceived by guitarist Tony Iommi as his first solo project, but record company pressure forced him to use his old band's name at the last minute. With this in mind, one can better appreciate both the record's un-Sabbath-like songwriting and the participation of journeyman singer Glenn Hughes. Hughes' incredibly powerful and soulful vocal style was certainly inept for classic Black Sabbath material (a fact that would spell his departure during the subsequent tour), but here it positively shines, especially on ballads such as "In Memory" and the gorgeous "No Stranger to Love." Iommi's riffs and solos are also much more inspired than in recent years, and other highlights include the fiery "In for the Kill," the brooding title track, and the amazingly catchy "Danger Zone." *—Ed Rivadavia*

The Eternal Idol / Dec. 1987 / Warner Brothers ✦✦✦
After years of playing musical chairs with various singers during the early '80s, Black Sabbath guitarist Tony Iommi finally found a dependable frontman with unknown Tony Martin, who made his debut on 1987's underrated *The Eternal Idol*. Despite a slight resemblance to former singer Ronnie James Dio, Martin's powerful voice added new fire to songs like "Hard Life to Love," "Glory Ride," and "Born to Lose," which also feature some of Iommi's heaviest riffs in years. The ever-reliable Geoff Nicholls adds impeccable supporting keyboards throughout, but most notably on "Ancient Warrior" and the fantastically gloomy title track. Finally, even the most skeptical of Sabbath fans will be amazed at the undeniably brilliant riffing of massive opener "The Shining." *—Ed Rivadavia*

Headless Cross / Apr. 1989 / IRS ✦✦✦✦
By the late '80s everyone had pretty much given up on Black Sabbath... and why not? Guitarist Tony Iommi was the only remaining original member and the band had seen an outrageous number of musicians and frontmen (six overall) slip through its ranks since Ozzy Osbourne's departure. So it was quite a shock when singer Tony Martin returned for a second go-round on 1989's pleasantly surprising *Headless Cross*. The album also benefited from the arrival of journeyman Cozy Powell—one of the few drummers who's sound is instantly recognizable. Arguably the finest non-Ozzy or Dio Black Sabbath album (along with 87's *The Eternal Idol*), *Headless Cross* is certainly the most consistent. Its songs place all emphasis on the almighty riff (from whence all rivers flow), with the drums, bass, keyboards, and voice playing only a supporting role. Morbid monsterpieces, such as the title track and "Kill in the Spirit World," possess massive power chords, but still manage to flow seamlessly into the more radio-friendly, yet still incredibly heavy material like "Devil and Daughter" and "Black Moon." For sheer malevolent power, "When Death Calls" is one of Iommi's most stunning compositions ever, while "Nightwing" flips the coin by introducing beautiful acoustic playing and, daringly said, highly poetic lyrics. For those who feel the need to stray from the Osbourne and Dio classics, there can be no better place to start. *—Ed Rivadavia*

Under Wheels of Confusion: 1970-1987 / Nov. 6, 1996 / Essential/Castle ✦✦✦✦
An unwieldly four-disc, 52-track box set, *Under Wheels of Confusion: 1970-1987* nevertheless contains the bulk of Sabbath's best work, dipping considerably in quality during the second half of the set, when Ozzy Osbourne left the group and was replaced by Ronnie James Dio. Even though all of the stone-cold classics are here, as are all of Dio's best tracks, Sabbath remains best appreciated through their original albums, which capture the essence of the metal giants much better than this box. *—Stephen Thomas Erlewine*

Reunion / Oct. 20, 1998 / Epic ✦✦✦
Though it was conceived as a mere cash-in for the long-awaited return of the original Black Sabbath, 1998's *Reunion* is as close to an official live album as the band has had in their historic 30-year career. 1980's *Live at Last* was released without their permission, and 1982's *Live Evil* featured then-singer Ronnie James Dio. With this in mind, the band must be commended on the excellent quality of the recordings, which include their most enduring classics ("War Pigs," "Paranoid," "Iron Man"), as well as a few surprises ("Dirty Women," "Behind the Wall of Sleep"), and were culled from a series of concerts in their native Birmingham in December 1997. The real key to this album, however, is the band's ability to avoid the most common pitfall of live recordings: speeding up the songs. This patience is crucial, since such Sabbath staples as "Sweet Leaf," "Black Sabbath," and "Snowblind" owe much of their unique personality and somber atmospherics to the band's trademark "snail's pace." "Children of the Grave" proves itself once again as one of the band's most dependable live favorites, and the massive riffs of "Into the Void" are simply timeless. The two brand new studio tracks are another treat for long-time fans, and while "Selling My Soul" is rather mundane, "Psycho Man" is absolutely incredible thanks to its slow intro and raging final riff. *—Ed Rivadavia*

Black Sheep

f. 1990, New York, NY [The Bronx]
East Coast Rap, Alternative Rap, Hip-Hop
Bronx rapper Andre "Dres" Titus and William "Mista Lawnge" McLean scored a big hit with their debut, *A Wolf in Sheep's Clothing*, for Mercury in 1991. The disc went gold, with the single "The Choice Is Yours" scoring on the R&B charts and getting extensive pop exposure as well. The follow-up, *Non-Fiction*, had less of an impact, and the group did not again resurface until 1999's *Which Side R/U On*. *—Ron Wynn*

● **A Wolf in Sheep's Clothing** / 1991 / Mercury ✦✦✦✦✦
Bronx rappers Black Sheep scored with the single "The Choice Is Yours," a song featuring the catch phrase "you can get with this or you can get with that." But while this hit and "Strobelite Honey" were more satirical, the album also included the biting "Black With N.V. (No Vision)" and "To Whom It May Concern," message tracks that harshly criticized successful blacks who turned their backs on the inner city. *—Ron Wynn*

Non-Fiction / 1994 / Mercury ✦✦✦
The follow-up to 1992's massive debut, *Non-Fiction* is a troubled sophomore album; it has a few good moments, but it can't compare to the raw immediacy of *A Wolf in Sheep's Clothing*. Dres' raps are just as solid, but the mostly R&B-influenced backing is flat and unexciting. "Without A Doubt," however, is as house-rockin' a cut as any on the debut. *—John Bush*

Cilla Black

b. May 27, 1943, Liverpool, England
Vocals / Girl Group, British Invasion, Pop
Who was the second biggest selling music star to come out of Liverpool after the Beatles? It wasn't Gerry & the Pacemakers or Billy J. Kramer & the Dakotas, nor was it the Searchers. It was Cilla Black, a one-time coat-check girl from the Cavern Club who was still learning to sing with confidence, forget developing a technique, just about the time that the Beatles were cutting their first EMI record. Black holds a unique position in the history of pop music, and the British Invasion. As Brian Epstein's discovery and protégée, she was the first and only important female performer to emerge from Liverpool in the heyday of the British beat boom. Black was a non-distinct female persona—virtually a tabula rasa, with a "girl next door" look—onto whom the sexually ambiguous Epstein could project his ideas of style and beauty. Neither was she a natural singer, or performer. She did try hard, however, and with the right look and presentation, and the right song and producer, had a chance for success. All of those things Epstein secured for her, either directly or in the guise of George Martin at Parlophone Records. In conjunction with Epstein's management and Martin's production skills, she became a formidable ballad singer, her hits lasting longer than any Epstein clients other than the Beatles. And she became one of the most beloved pop/rock performers in England during the late '60s and 1970s, and one of the country's most popular television stars. *—Bruce Eder*

● **Best of Cilla** / Nov. 1968 / Parlophone ✦✦✦✦✦
By the fall of 1968, Cilla Black had scored 14 chart entries in the U.K., of which eight had hit the Top Ten and two had gone to number one. This 14-track British compilation contains 11 of those songs, including all but one of the Top Tens. Her singles began with "Love of the Loved," and a Beatles cast-off in their Merseybeat style, but she really hit her stride copying Dionne Warwick on "Anyone Who Had a Heart," and went on to score all her hits in a melodramatic ballad style, with lots of strings and heartbreak. She is thus in a category with contemporaries like Dusty Springfield and Lulu, but unlike them, she never showed much taste for rock or blues, moving instead unerringly to the middle of the road. As a result, today she seems not much more than a footnote in the history of The Beatles. *—William Ruhlmann*

The Abbey Road Decade 1963-1973 / 1997 / EMI Zonophone ✦✦✦✦✦
Three CDs and 65 songs is probably more Cilla Black than most of us want to own. At least, that was this reviewer's impression when he first spotted this collection; as it turns out, however, Black's output is far superior to the limited reputation she carries in the U.S.A., where she charted but a handful of songs. The material features all of Black's hits, all of her important B-sides and album tracks; also, disc three is made up entirely of rarities, including some surprising demos like "Step Inside Love" from 1968 with Paul McCartney accompanying her on acoustic guitar—it's almost good enough to have been released, which also proves that McCartney could have been a top session player if he hadn't made it in any other area. There's also Black's original rehearsal cut of "A Shot of Rhythm and Blues," a full-blown, Cavern-style Merseybeat performance with a band; a surviving Dick James Music acetate of Black's cover of "Fever," accompanied by Gerry & the Pacemakers; plus her unissued versions of "Heatwave" and "Shotgun," both among the best records she ever made, and closing with her mid-1970s cover of Phil Ochs' "Changes." All of the relevant tracks that weren't originally released in stereo have been remixed that way, and a good job done of it, too. The surprise for most casual listeners will come from the non-hits—even with her original vocal limitations, which she quickly overcame, Black had a distinctive sound that made her work eminently enjoyable and even impressive. Coupled with some good arrangements and George Martin's crisp production, her music holds up astonishingly well. And Black, as she gained confidence, displays a surprisingly soulful approach on songs such as "He Won't Ask Me" and "You've Lost That Loving Feeling." *—Bruce Eder*

● **The Best of the EMI Years** / Jun. 30, 1998 / EMI ✦✦✦✦
Among the many recording artists who rode to fame on the Beatles' bandwagon, Cilla Black—the singing hat-check girl at Liverpool's Cavern Club—was truly one with enduring talent. It's hard to find anything more reminiscent of swinging '60s London than "Love of the Loved," a Paul McCartney tune and Cilla's debut single (1963). Two McCartney follow-ups, "It's for You" and "Step Inside Love," utilized Cilla's high-powered, slightly nasal delivery as the key element in a highly successful formula—luring listeners with a softly bewitching intro, then knocking 'em dead with a full-tilt chorus. A generous selection of cabaret ballads appear on this release, many of which were big hits back in Britain. Among these are the Bacharach-David tunes "Alfie," "Make It Easy On

Yourself" and "What the World Needs Now Is Love," though Cilla's renditions are somehow less convincing than Dionne Warwick's. Still, if you're a fan—for completeness' sake anyway—this is the Cilla CD to own. —*Stansted Montfichet*

The Essential Cilla Black 1963-1978 / Oct. 5, 1999 / EMI ✦✦✦✦✦

35th Anniversary Collection / Mar. 27, 2001 / EMI ✦✦✦✦

Best of Cilla Black / Apr. 3, 2001 / EMI ✦✦✦✦

Frank Black

b. 1965, Long Beach, CA

Vocals, Guitar / Indie Rock, Alternative Pop/Rock

Inverting his stage name from Black Francis to Frank Black, the former Pixies lead singer/songwriter embarked on a solo career after he broke up the band in early 1993; actually, he began recording his solo album *before* he told the band the news. Working with former Pere Ubu member Eric Drew Feldman, Black occasionally heads into the ferocious post-punk guitar territory that marked such landmark albums as *Surfer Rosa* and *Doolittle*, but more frequently he plays up his considerably underrated melodic side. His self-titled 1993 debut album was an adventurous sketchbook of pop styles ranging from surf rock to heavy metal, from Beatlesque pop to new wave. Black's second album, 1994's *Teenager of the Year*, was a sprawling and diverse album that amplified all the best points of *Frank Black*. He released his first album for American and Sony, the hard-rocking *The Cult of Ray*, in January 1996. It hardly found the wide audience Black had hoped for, selling considerably less than his two previous efforts. —*Stephen Thomas Erlewine*

Frank Black / Mar. 9, 1993 / 4AD/Elektra ✦✦✦✦✦

Underneath their noise and weirdness, the Pixies had a thorough knowledge of rock history, spanning '50s and '60s' surf-rock, '70s punk's menacing energy, and '80s college rock's quirkiness. After dismantling the band, Black Francis inverted his name, collaborated with Captain Beefheart/Pere Ubu sideman Eric Drew Feldman, and let his inner rock historian loose on *Frank Black*. Much of the album nods at Black's inspirations, but his own gifts still shine through. The chugging Iggy Pop homage "Ten Percenter" borrows the Stooges' primitive grind, while the arty, dissonant UFO convention tale "Parry the Wind High, Low" recalls Bowie's Berlin era. However, "I Heard Ramona Sing"—a Ramones tribute—is an airy, jangly pop number that sounds nothing like its subject; the Beach Boys' "Hang On To Your Ego" gets a new wave makeover with crunchy guitars and shiny keyboards. Despite his efforts to escape the Pixies' sound, many of *Frank Black*'s songs would have fit on *Trompe Le Monde*. "Los Angeles" builds on that album's spacy, metallic feel; with its thrashy choruses and dreamy coda, it almost caricatures the Pixies' extreme dynamics. However, whimsical vignettes like "Brackish Boy" and "Two Spaces" sound more like They Might Be Giants—one of Black's favorite groups—than his old band, while softer songs like "Adda Lee" and "Every Time I Go Around Here" reveal more emotional depth. *Frank Black* also boasts an unabashedly big, polished sound; keyboards and brass embellish "Places Named After Numbers" and the epic surf-rock instrumental "Tossed." Just a few years later, new wave-inspired punk-pop bands like Weezer, the Rentals, and even No Doubt ruled alternative rock, proving that even if his solo career wasn't as influential as his Pixies years, Frank Black was still ahead of his time. —*Heather Phares*

● **Teenager of the Year** / May 24, 1994 / 4AD/Elektra ✦✦✦✦✦

A sprawling double album, Frank Black's *Teenager of the Year* builds on the clever, carefully crafted pop he forged on his solo debut and moves even farther away from the Pixies' sound. It feels like the album Black wanted to make since *Bossanova*: "Whatever Happened To Pong?" and "Thalassocracy" are a one-two blast of energetic fun, but the tight songwriting and detailed arrangements on the strummy "Headache" and gentle, piano-driven "Sir Rockaby" are more interesting. Despite its 22-song length, most of *Teenager of the Year*'s tracks are keepers; the first nine rank among Black's catchiest songs with or without the Pixies. "I Want to Live on an Abstract Plain" and "The Vanishing Spies" mix sweet straightforward melodies with spacy keyboards, and Black delivers a creative love song in "Speedy Marie"; the first letter of each line in the song's second half spells out his girlfriend's name. The driving, anthemic "Freedom Rock" is one of the album's more ambitious tracks, along with the catchy, educational "Ole Mulholland," a musical history lesson about William Mulholland, the developer and planner of Los Angeles' municipal water system. *Teenager*'s beginning is so consistent, it's not surprising that its second half isn't quite as essential, but it's still interesting. The spacy, ska-tinged "Fiddle Riddle," the cryptic "Superabound" and the sprightly final track "Pie in the Sky"—which sounds strangely like a punk version of Gary U.S. Bonds' hit "A Quarter to Three"—all add to the album's individuality. Even less-developed songs like "Fazer Eyes" and "The Hostest with the Mostest" are still worthwhile. Though his later albums took a sparer, simpler approach, *Teenager of the Year*'s ambition and quirkiness begin Black's evolution into a cult artist who makes the music he wants to, regardless of whether or not it's fashionable. —*Heather Phares*

The Cult of Ray / Jan. 30, 1996 / American ✦✦✦

Frank Black has never had a problem with being weird; when he led the Pixies to the outer limits of pop music in the '80s, he pioneered mixing bizarre lyrics about science fiction, sex, and religion with loud guitars. In its own way, his third solo album *The Cult of Ray* is his strangest album yet; it flirts with the ordinary. His previous solo albums sound liberated in their wideband weirdness, and flashes of Black's usual eccentricity pop up on songs like "The Marsist," "Men in Black," and "The Creature," but for the most part this album is strangely straightforward. There are three songs about moshing on *The Cult of Ray*, each employing the same tired, chugging, punk guitars that lesser artists have made their bread and butter for years. Even the ballads, such as "I Don't Want to Hurt You (Every Single Time)," sound watered-down and forced compared to some of the unique and personal love songs he's created over the years with the Pixies and on his own. While *The Cult of Ray* isn't a disaster, it's certainly a disappointment. —*Heather Phares*

Frank Black & the Catholics / May 1998 / spinART ✦✦✦

Never trust an artist's opinion on his own recordings. Frank Black calls *Frank Black & the Catholics* the "best recording I ever made," ignoring a decade worth of great, innovative indie rock. A better assessment may be: *Frank Black & the Catholics* is the most direct record he's ever made. If you just want garage punk, stripped of all the odd time signatures, subverted chord progressions, cryptic lyrics, and sonic experimentation that marked his first two albums, as well as his work with the Pixies, this album may satisfy your needs. Then again, all those "frills" were part of the reason Black was such a respected and influential artist, and without them he sounds disturbingly conventional. Fortunately, *The Catholics* doesn't trade in the sub-metal clichés that plagued *The Cult of Ray*, concentrating on straight-ahead garage punk. There are some good hooks on the songs and the performances have some real energy, but all the songs wind up blending into each other by the end of the record. On the whole, it's a step forward from *The Cult of Ray*, but it still feels like a retreat from his entire body of work. —*Stephen Thomas Erlewine*

Pistolero / Mar. 23, 1999 / What Are? ✦✦✦

After the creative nadir of *The Cult of Ray* and *Frank Black & the Catholics'* disappointingly straightforward punk-pop, Frank Black's fifth solo album *Pistolero* is something of a return to form. Though he still opts for a stripped-down production style, his songwriting is both more natural and more intriguing on clever, driving pop songs like "Skeleton Man" and "I Love Your Brain," an off-kilter rocker that lives up to its title. Once again, Black's poppier songs are his most creative, as "Billy Radcliffe," a bouncy, melancholy elegy to the first boy born in space, and the shimmery, whimsical "85 Weeks" prove. *Pistolero*'s rock songs range from the menacing "I Switched You"—which also boasts some refreshingly ferocious vocals from Black—to monotonous punk-pop like "I Want Rock & Roll," "I Think I'm Starting to Lose It," and "Smoke Up," all of which recall the most tedious moments of *The Cult of Ray* and *Frank Black & the Catholics*. Black's ambitious, subversive style of old tries to resurface on the epic "So Hard to Make Things Out," the vibrant "Western Star," and the tightly written "Tiny Heart," but *Pistolero*'s back-to-basics production gives the songs a simplistic, bar band feel that doesn't do them justice. However, the strangely Stones-ish ballad "You're Such a Wire" and the earnest "Bad Harmony" actually benefit from the album's no-frills sound, and "So. Bay" somehow combines surfy guitars and extreme dynamics without sounding like the Pixies. It's a frustratingly inconsistent album, but it revives the interesting qualities of Frank Black's earlier albums without rehashing them. Though a more imaginative production would have suited it better, *Pistolero* suggests that Black's best work may not be behind him. —*Heather Phares*

Dog in the Sand / Jan. 30, 2001 / What Are? ✦✦✦✦

Now that he's released more albums as a solo artist than with the Pixies, Frank Black seems comfortable with his place in alternative rock's history. Instead of avoiding the anachronistic tendencies of his old band and his first two solo albums, on *Dog in the Sand*, he embraces them. A happy marriage of his recent work's directness and the whimsical rock of *Frank Black* and *Teenager of the Year*, the album also features the return of Eric Drew Feldman and Joey Santiago. His most interesting work since *Teenager of the Year*, *Dog in the Sand* sounds like a slightly slower, rootsier version of that album. "Blast Off"'s angular riffs and surreal lyrics ("I'm in a Beckett trance / From all that chemical") recall Black's heyday, mixed with the rougher, spontaneous feel of his Catholics work, as does the epic "Robert Onion," which sounds like a distant cousin to *Teenager*'s "Freedom Rock." The Stones-y "Hermaphroditos" is one of Black's most convincing rockers in years, and features some great, Black Francis-style lyrics: "Forget your yin / And go fuck your yang." If they were faster, spaghetti-western ballads like "Bullet" and "Llano Del Rio"—a song about California's first Socialist collective—would fit on *Doolittle*. But *Dog in the Sand* expands on Black's past triumphs instead of rehashing them. "I'll Be Blue" and "St. Francis Dam Disaster" prove that his ballads keep growing more genuine and emotional; rootsy pop songs like "Stupid Me" and "If It Takes All Night" feature pedal steel, banjo, and understated keyboards. Though it's likely that the most influential years of Black's career are in the past, *Dog in the Sand* makes it clear that not all of his best work is. —*Heather Phares*

Blackfoot

f. 1972, Jacksonville, FL, **db.** 1995

Southern Rock, Hard Rock, Blues-Rock

Blackfoot were contemporaries of Lynyrd Skynyrd, and tried for years to make it as a Southern rock band, although they finally succeeded as a hard rock outfit, in the manner of AC/DC and the Scorpions. They racked up a hit album (*Strikes*) and a pair of successful singles ("Train, Train," "Highway Song") in the late 1970s and early 1980s, before they became lost in the post-MTV era of visually oriented bands.

The group started out as a quartet: singer/guitarist Rickey Medlocke, the grandson of bluegrass musician Shorty Medlocke, who wrote "Train, Train"; drummer/singer Jakson Spires, bassist/singer Greg T. Walker, and lead guitarist Charlie Hargrett. They were signed to Island Records in 1975, evidently as that label's resident Southern rockers, but moved to Epic Records the following year. Neither relationship was successful, but in 1979, after moving to Atco, their first album for the new label, *Strikes*, hit a responsive chord—the group spent the next few years on Atco, racking up impressive sales with the follow-ups *Tomcattin'* and *Marauder*.

In the mid-1980s, the group added ex-Uriah Heep keyboardman Ken Hensley in order to bring a new side to their sound. The group's fortunes declined amid the advent of MTV and the growth in importance of rock video promotional clips, as well as the influence of sounds from Europe and Australia, and they never recovered, despite efforts to adapt their sound and image. Hensley was replaced near the end of their history, but Blackfoot (who took their name from the Native American tribe, part of Medlocke's heritage) had broken up by 1984, before the new lineup recorded. Medlocke revived the name in 1990 with a new backing group. —*Bruce Eder*

● **Rattlesnake Rock & Roll: The Best of Blackfoot** / 1994 / Rhino ◆◆◆◆◆

Southern rock's last great gasp is spelled out on this 18-track compilation. Wisely leaving off anything from the weak albums (*No Reservations, Siogo, Vertical Smiles* and *Rick Medlocke and Blackfoot*) and cherry-picking from the rest of their output, this slims the group's best down to a nice solid chunk of heavy twin Southern-rock guitars, macho lyrics, and thundering drumbeats. While some naysayers will point to the group's "Highway Song" as being little more than a spirited "Free Bird" knockoff, the guitar interplay between Medlocke and Charlie Hargrett is well worth the listen. Other highlights include "Train Train," "Left Turn on a Red Light" and a cover of Free's "Wishing Well." Another special bonus is three tracks from *Highway Song—Blackfoot Live*, a U.K.-only release that clearly illustrates what a potent live combination the original quartet truly was. —*Cub Koda*

Blackstreet

f. 1992, db. 1999

New Jack Swing, Club/Dance, Urban, Hip-Hop

Teddy Riley, one of the most innovative and successful R&B producers of the '80s and '90s, formed Blackstreet in 1994 with Chauncey Hannibal, Levi Little, and David Hollister. Under Riley's direction, Blackstreet's smooth fusion of pop, R&B, and hip-hop became an across-the-board hit upon its release. *Another Level*, featuring the monster hit "No Diggity," followed in 1996, and in 1999 the group returned with *Finally*. —*Stephen Thomas Erlewine*

Blackstreet / 1994 / Interscope ◆◆◆

Teddy Riley is an impeccable craftsman and genius of sorts, not to mention a trendsetter. In releasing so much product, however, his music can also occasionally descend into a pedestrian, formulaic version of new jack swing, the production style he himself invented, fine-tuned, and perfected. That pitfall plays out intermittently on Blackstreet's debut album. Some of the music and vocal harmonies blend together or sound like new jack retreads, and a handful of the songs are so commercially savvy and obviously directed toward the mainstream public that it is hard to wholly enjoy them. Some of the songs, too, are less than fully formed, consisting of just a single melody or groove that exists for the sole purpose of moving feet and/or giving the quartet an excuse to harmonize. More often, however, Blackstreet hits the spot with a sleek and inventive progression on the new jack template, sharpening and filling out the sound that Guy made famous. Riley makes sure the beats are hip-hop savvy and the bass is booming, and then slathers squealing synthesizer lines all over them. Frankly, he is not technically a fantastic singer, at least in comparison to his three harmonizing mates, but his voice has such a distinctive character that it has always been entirely ingratiating, making up in expressiveness for any lack in range or virtuosity. The songs on which he takes lead invariably stand out the most and tend to be the most appealing cuts. The glue on the album, though, is the tight four-part harmony singing of Blackstreet, and it leads to some brilliantly catchy R&B tracks, songs that easily stood out in the mid-'90s urban soul crowd. —*Stanton Swihart*

● **Another Level** / Sep. 9, 1996 / Interscope ◆◆◆◆

Powered by the massive hit single "No Diggity," *Another Level* is arguably the finest album created by Teddy Riley, the leader of Blackstreet. Riley has masterminded an album that blends street-level rhythms with urban soul and pop crossover potential, adding two new members—Eric Williams and Mark Middleton—to the lineup in order to position Blackstreet as an heir to the classic R&B vocal group tradition. The realignment works, since the group sounds fuller and more eclectic with the two added voices. But the key to the success of *Another Level* is Riley's songwriting, which is by and large catchy and inventive, whether he is writing ballads or party jams. *Another Level* sags a bit halfway through—it's hard to sustain interest for a nearly 70 minute album—but it has enough strong moments to make it an enjoyable listen. —*Stephen Thomas Erlewine*

Finally / Mar. 23, 1999 / Interscope ◆◆◆

The title is a not-so-subtle admission that it took a little longer than expected for Blackstreet's third album to hit the shelves. Delays are commonplace in pop music, but they're not welcome, since part of the game is capitalizing on recent successes—in this case, that would have been "No Diggity," a Teddy Riley masterpiece that broke Blackstreet big. *Finally* didn't arrive quickly enough to expand on that success, but it feels as if it could have followed shortly after *Another Level*, since Riley doesn't really expand their sound that much on the third record. That's not to say it isn't enjoyable, since Riley knows how to make infectious funk and seductive ballads. He also knows that cameos sell a record, and he's loaded this disc with appearances from celebrities like Stevie Wonder and Janet Jackson. It's fun to hear the guests appear, but it takes away from Blackstreet somewhat, especially since the guests are the only noteworthy things on a few cuts. Nevertheless, there's no discounting Riley's skills, and he delivers some dynamic grooves and soothing slow jams throughout the record. They're not radically different from those on *Another Level*, but in a way, they don't need to be. At their best, Riley and Blackstreet are among the best '90s new jack soul has to offer, and there's just enough of the group at their best on *Finally* to make it worth the wait. —*Stephen Thomas Erlewine*

Otis Blackwell

b. 1931, Brooklyn, NY

Songwriter, Piano / East Coast Blues, Urban Blues, Rock & Roll, R&B

Few 1950s rock & roll tunesmiths were as prolifically talented as Otis Blackwell. His immortal compositions include Little Willie John's "Fever," Elvis Presley's "Don't Be Cruel" and "All Shook Up," Jerry Lee Lewis's "Great Balls of Fire" and "Breathless," and Jimmy Jones's "Handy Man" (just for starters). Though he often collaborated with various partners on the thriving '50s New York R&B scene (Winfield Scott, Eddie Cooley, and Jack Hammer, to name three), Blackwell's songwriting style is as identifiable as that of Willie Dixon or Jerry Leiber & Mike Stoller. He helped formulate the musical vocabulary of rock & roll when the genre was barely breathing on its own. —*Bill Dahl*

● **Otis Blackwell 1953-55** / 1953-Feb. 9, 1955 / Flyright ◆◆◆◆◆

The British Flyright logo has neatly compiled all 17 known titles that Blackwell cut for Jay-Dee, including "Daddy Rollin' Stone," and the equally ominous "On That Power Line," and four sides with a killer New York combo featuring tenor sax wailer Sam "The Man" Taylor and guitarist Mickey Baker. —*Bill Dahl*

All Shook Up / Oct. 14, 1976-Oct. 27, 1976 / Shanachie ◆◆◆◆

Blackwell's "comeback" album, originally cut in 1976 for Herb Abramson's Inner City label, is a successful effort at reclaiming the songs of his that made people like Elvis, Jerry Lee Lewis ("Great Balls of Fire," "Breathless"), Dee Clark ("Hey Little Girl"), et al. famous. For some listeners this album won't offer any real revelation, alas—the backings seem a little too smooth (one suspects that the original demos on "Fever," "All Shook Up," etc., had some rough edges that made them more interesting). They're all played well, however, and Blackwell's singing is impeccable. Anyone else might be accused of mimicking Elvis's style on "All Shook Up" and related numbers, except that history tells us different, and the performances are genuine and honest. Blackwell shows off a surprisingly wide range, most notably on the lullaby "Sleep Is Just Around the Corner" and the ballad "Clinging to a Dream," all of which makes this far more than just an Elvis Presley-related curio. Also included is Blackwell's credible rendition of "Searchin'," a song authored by his contemporary rivals Leiber and Stoller. —*Bruce Eder*

Hal Blaine (Harold Simon Belsky)

b. Feb. 5, 1929, Holyoke, MA

Drums, Percussion / Rock & Roll

Hal Blaine was the busiest recording session drummer in Los Angeles in the 1960s and 1970s, playing the drums on—by his count—tens of thousands of recordings, from the Wall of Sound productions of Phil Spector to Brian Wilson's productions of the Beach Boys, and including most of the pop/rock performers in Los Angeles in the '60s, as well as such notables as Elvis Presley and Frank Sinatra. Blaine published a book of his memories, *Hal Blaine and the Wrecking Crew*, in 1990. —*William Ruhlmann*

● **Drums! Drums! A Go Go** / 1966 / Varese Sarabande ◆◆◆◆◆

The real way to gain an appreciation for Blaine's Hall-of-Fame-caliber abilities is to hear him as a session man, and not on his occasional recordings as a solo artist. This instrumental album is something of a novelty rather than a serious attempt to build solo credentials. It consists almost entirely of cover versions of well-known rock hits from the late 1950s through the mid-1960s, with live "party" noises dubbed on to simulate a concert recording (although it was cut in the studio). Still, it's better than might be expected considering its frivolity, with a bunch of top fellow Hollywood session musicians providing pretty energetic support, particularly in the surf-ish guitars. Producers P.F. Sloan and Steve Barri take the writing credits for "Drums a Go Go," although in fact it's built around the main riff of the Kinks' "All Day and All of the Night." The CD reissue adds three bonus tracks from the 1967 album *Have Fun!! Play Drums!!*, as well as the 1966 non-LP single "Bang Bang Rhythm." —*Richie Unterberger*

Blake Babies

f. 1986, Boston, MA, db. 1991

Jangle Pop, Indie Rock, Alternative Pop/Rock

While Blake Babies made several engaging records in the late '80s and early '90s, they never broke out of the collegiate rock circles where they were adored. It wasn't until 1992 that their leader, Juliana Hatfield, began getting recognition as a songwriter in more mainstream publications, but that was after the group was broken up. Over their four albums, Hatfield's songwriting and thin, girlish singing improved drastically as the band's post-R.E.M. alternative pop grew more muscular, branching out into both punkier and folkier territories on each record. By the time of their last full-length album, 1990's *Sunburn*, guitarist John Strohm was emerging as an impressive songwriter in his own right. After a final EP in 1991, the band split, with Hatfield emerging as an alternative superstar and Strohm and drummer Freda Love forming the acclaimed guitar pop band Antenna.

In 2000 the Blake Babies came out of a ten-year retirement to record a new album, *God Bless the Blake Babies*. The album was released March 6, 2001, on Rounder Records. Drummer Freda Love conceived the comeback, talking the other two original members into a reunion. She was rewarded with having her first Blake Babies composition "Nothing Ever Happens" be the first single. Older and better musicians, this version of the band sacrifices the charm of the amateur indie pop for a smarter, crafted sound that works as a natural progression of the band. The side projects and solo careers shaped the individual members into hardened veterans of the music industry, and their experiences give their new material a depth that their earlier work lacked. Spring of 2001 saw the band hit the road playing old haunts like Chapel Hill, NC's Cat's Cradle and new versions of the 9:30 Club in Washington, DC, and the Knitting Factory in New York City to receptive audiences. John Strohm called it the best the Blake Babies ever sounded.—*Stephen Thomas Erlewine & Chris Lawrence*

Nicely, Nicely / 1987 / Hollywood ✦✦✦✦
The Blake Babies' debut album, released on their own record label. —*William Ruhlmann*

Earwig / 1989 / Hollywood ✦✦✦✦✦
On their first full-length album, the Blake Babies' knack for melodic, chiming guitar-pop became evident, with songs like "Outta My Head" and "Take Your Head Off My Shoulder" leading a pack of fine original numbers. —*Stephen Thomas Erlewine*

Sunburn / 1990 / Hollywood ✦✦✦✦✦
Juliana Hatfield, John Strohm, and Freda Love (puckishly billed here as Freda Boner) create a literate, emotionally direct brand of catchy, melodic pop based on the post-punk jangle pop of the '80s, but with a slightly tougher edge, particularly in Strohm's guitar sound. For the first time, Strohm contributes two solo writing credits on which he sings lead, the disturbing "Girl in a Box" and the anthemic "Train," which somehow manages to quote both "Mystery Train" and "I Melt With You." However, *Sunburn* is primarily the album on which Juliana Hatfield's songwriting prowess first flourishes, and it's possibly her finest collection of songs. Kicking off with the one-two punch of the tart kiss-off "I'm Not Your Mother" and the aching "Out There," the finest song of the Blake Babies' career, the album continues through ten more punchy guitar pop songs with lyrics filled with Hatfield's trademark combination of innocence, brashness, wit, and moments of extreme self-doubt. "I'll Take Anything" and "Kiss and Make Up" are early examples of the kind of disarming emotional vulnerability further explored on the more controversial songs of Hatfield's early solo career. "Watch Me Now, I'm Calling," though, has to be the most emotionally masochistic song of Hatfield's entire career, expressing romantic dependency in disturbingly graphic images of physical self-mutilation, which become all the more powerful and discomfiting given Hatfield's perfectly matter-of-fact delivery. Gary Smith's production keeps things simple without sounding like the songs are unfinished or underarranged, and Strohm, Hatfield, and Love have the casually impressive interplay of a band that knows it's making the best record of its career. —*Stewart Mason*

● **Innocence and Experience** / Sep. 28, 1993 / Hollywood ✦✦✦✦✦
Featuring songs from all of their albums as well as a couple of rare tracks, *Innocence and Experience* is a fine collection of the Blake Babies' best work; it's a fine introduction to their ringing, R.E.M.-style guitar-pop. —*Stephen Thomas Erlewine*

God Bless the Blake Babies / Mar. 6, 2001 / Rounder ✦✦✦
The Blake Babies are back, melodic hooks and great songs in tow. Even if you aren't familiar with their previous work, both individually and collectively, you can jump right in with this one because *God Bless the Blake Babies* is as welcome as the title implies. Juliana Hatfield and crew open the jangle pop gates with "Disappear." You'd almost think it was a happy song, until you listen closely—"What I wouldn't do: go back to '92 and erase the moment I met you and make you disappear." That's a kiss-off of the highest order. Hatfield shares the songwriting chores fairly equally with guitarist John Strohm, with drummer Freda Love Smith chiming in for two tunes and guest bassist/vocalist Evan Dando for one. Strohm even steps up to the center mic for his "Picture Perfect" and "Invisible World." The former is a great track, a loving ode to balance out the sentiment of "Disappear" and "What Did I Do." "She's my favorite shade of blue" goes a long way to counteract that erasing you business. Then it's Smith's turn in the spotlight for "When I See His Face," which has a slightly more alternative feel than most of the other tunes. Drugs seem to be a recurring theme. Witness "Baby Gets High," "Until I Almost Died," and "Brain Damage." Life can't be all roses and sunshine. They are rock stars, after all. The beauty of the Blake Babies is that it all *sounds* like roses and sunshine. Bless them, indeed. —*Kelly McCartney*

The Blasters

f. 1979, Los Angeles, CA
College Rock, Roots Rock, Rock & Roll
The all-American roots music band, the Blasters were principally brothers Dave and Phil Alvin, whose first-hand experience with blues masters shaped their sound and turned them both into contemporary singer-songwriters whose interest in roots rock has never waned. Their musical education involved hanging out with musicians like Lee Allen, Marcus Johnson, and T-Bone Walker, all of whom tipped the band to the ways of blues and R&B. Ironically, by the time they were ready to work in Los Angeles clubs, the punk rock explosion was in full swing, and they found an audience for their rough and ready sound among the punks, particularly fans of X with whom they frequently shared the bill. *American Music* (1980) was a collection of roots covers and originals. Amazingly, their self-titled 1981 album reached number 36 on the charts. Less focused on rockabilly revivalism, Dave Alvin had become the band's chief cook and songwriter, and *Hard Line* in 1985 was even more polished. The band called it a day after that, but continue to perform live. —*Denise Sullivan*

American Music / 1980 / Hightone ✦✦✦✦✦
Right from the beginning, with Dave Alvin's title song, the Blasters made their statement, that basic rock & roll was as contemporary in 1980 as it had been in the mid-1950s. The other 12 tracks, which mixed Dave and Phil Alvin originals with covers like "I Wish You Would" and "Never No More Blues," reiterated the opening remark, re-creating the feel of a biker bar after a couple of tall ones. Actually, the Blasters didn't have much to say beyond this record, of which only a couple of thousand copies were pressed, but they went on to a few years with Warner Bros. After 17 years, the debut was released on CD with six bonus tracks, all covers, and that statement seemed just as valid as it had at first. —*William Ruhlmann*

The Blasters / 1981 / Slash ✦✦✦✦✦
You might have thought the Blasters had been in suspended animation for 25 years when their major-label debut turned up in late 1981 sounding for all the world like something cut in the Sun Studios in Memphis in 1956. Dave Alvin knew all the licks and his brother Phil had the R&B/country wail down. Best of all, you couldn't tell the oldies from Dave's newly written classics. Welcome to the birth of rock & roll, all over again. —*William Ruhlmann*

Over There [Live] / Oct. 1982 / Slash ✦✦✦
On this six-song EP, recorded May 22, 1982, at the Venue in London, the Blasters take on such '50s rock & roll classics as Jerry Lee Lewis's "High School Confidential" and Little Richard's "Keep a-Knockin'." The band's fidelity to their influences does not dampen their enthusiasm—they may be looking back, but they're bringing the old sound back to life. Maybe the best way to experience this band was live, not on record, at least in their early days, and this recording catches them at a fiery peak. —*William Ruhlmann*

Non Fiction / 1983 / Slash ✦✦✦✦
An album of originals by Dave Alvin, accompanied by the expanded lineup that included Steve Berlin and Lee Allen on sax, this is prime-time vintage Blasters. Opening with the crowd-pleasing love song "Red Rose," moving through "Barefoot Rock" (no doubt inspired by Jimmy McCracklin's "Georgia Slop," later covered by Los Lobos), on to one of Alvin's finest hours of songwriting with "Long White Cadillac" (made famous by Dwight Yoakam), and winding down with "Boomtown," the Blasters are effective at retracing and reflecting the concerns of the common man and woman—a celebration of Americana, careful never to wallow in nostalgia. —*Denise Sullivan*

Hard Line / 1985 / Slash ✦✦

● **The Blasters Collection** / Mar. 12, 1991 / Slash ✦✦✦✦✦
The Slash years are compiled here, along with three previously unreleased tracks, forming the perfect overview of the Blasters' short recording career devoted to blues, country, and R&B. From the outset of their career, from "Marie Marie" to "Border Radio," it was clear Dave Alvin would be a songwriter to be reckoned with—one for the ages. Tracing his development through "Long White Cadillac" (later recorded by Dwight Yoakam), "Trouble Bound" (with the Jordanaires on vocals), and the hard country of "Dark Night," brother Phil Alvin brings the necessary heart, soul, and authenticity to the work, and the band is a master of their form. Few work or rock harder. —*Denise Sullivan*

Mary J. Blige

b. Jan. 11, 1971, New York, NY [The Bronx]
Vocals / Contemporary R&B, Club/Dance, Urban, Hip-Hop
Crowned the new "Queen of Hip-Hop Soul," Mary J. Blige enjoyed a breakout year in 1992 with *What's the 411?* Such singles as "Reminisce" and "Real Love" thrust the Atlanta-born singer into the spotlight at age 21. She was raised in Yonkers and performed in local groups before making her debut for the Uptown label. The album went platinum, and a remixed version was later issued. The single "Reminisce" had a second life when it was reworked and re-done in a rap version by the duo of Pete Rock and C.L. Smooth. After 1994's *My Life*, she released *Share My World* in 1997. *The Tour* appeared a year later, and in 1999 she returned with *Mary*. —*Ron Wynn*

● **What's the 411?** / 1992 / MCA ✦✦✦✦✦
Mary J. Blige's debut album, *What's the 411?*, was a revolution in disguise. Like her new jack predecessors, Blige combined R&B with hip-hop, but unlike Guy and Bobby Brown, her music was more seductive and sly. More importantly, she sounds grittier and more real than most new jack swingers or female R&B vocalists. Blige can slip between singing and rapping with ease, which is partially the reason why *What's the 411?* is so successful. It doesn't hurt that her collaborators, from Grand Puba to Sean "Puffy" Combs, help construct backing tracks that are both melodic, relentlessly funky, and sexy. —*Stephen Thomas Erlewine*

My Life / 1994 / MCA ✦✦✦✦
Perhaps the single finest moment in Sean "Puffy" Combs' musical career has been the production on this, Mary J. Blige's second proper album. The production is not exactly original, and there is evidence here of him borrowing wholesale from other songs. The melodic sources this time around, though, are so expertly incorporated into the music that they never seem to be intrusions, instead playing like inspired dialogues with soulsters from the past, connecting past legacies with a new one. This certainly isn't your parents' (or grandparents') soul. But it is some of the finest modern soul of the '90s, backing away to a certain extent from the hip-hop/soul consolidation that Blige introduced on her debut album. The hip-hop part of the combination takes a few steps into the background, allowing Blige's tortured soul to carry the album completely, and it does so with heartwrenching authority. *My Life* is, from beginning to end, a brilliant, wistful individual plea of desire. Blige took a huge leap in artistry by penning almost everything herself (the major exception being Norman Whitfield's "I'm Going Down") in collaboration with co-producers Combs and multi-instrumentalist Chucky Thompson, and everything seems to leap directly from her gut. Blige's strain is sleekly modern and urban, and the grit in it comes from being streetwise and thoroughly realistic about the travails of life. *My Life*, nevertheless, emanates from some deep, dark place where both sadness and happiness cohabitate and turn into one single, beautiful sorrow. —*Stanton Swihart*

Share My World / Apr. 22, 1997 / MCA ✦✦✦✦
The hype that surrounded Mary J. Blige in the beginning was simply ridiculous. When *What's the 411?* was released in 1992, she was exalted as "the new Chaka Khan"—a definite exaggeration, considering how uneven that debut album was. But Blige did show promise, and by the time she recorded her third album, *Share My World*, she had

developed into a fairly convincing soul/urban singer. Her strongest and most confident effort up to that point, *Share* had much more character, personality, and honesty than most of the assembly line fare dominating urban radio in 1997. For all their slickness, emotive cuts like "Get to Know You Better," "Love Is All We Need," and "Keep Your Head" left no doubt that Blige was indeed a singer of depth and substance. Although high tech, the production of everyone from R. Kelly (with whom she duets on the inviting "It's On") and Babyface to Jimmy Jam and Terry Lewis doesn't come across as forced or robotic, but, in fact, is impressively organic. With *Share My World*, Blige definitely arrived. —*Alex Henderson*

The Tour / Jul. 28, 1998 / MCA ✦✦✦

The hype that surrounded Mary J. Blige in 1992 was definitely excessive, and those who exalted her as the "new Chaka Khan" did both Khan and Blige an unforgivable disservice (few could live up to such a title). But as the 1990s progressed, Blige really did evolve into one of the decade's most appealing R&B vocalists, and she's in good to excellent form on *The Tour*, which was recorded on her *Share My World* Tour of 1997-98. The very fact that a live urban contemporary album came out in the late 1990s was quite surprising; after all, R&B had become so technology-driven and studio-oriented that few R&B artists even bothered to make live albums anymore. But Blige was an exception, and she proves herself capable of taking it to the stage on passionate versions of such hits as "My Life," "Mary Jane (All Night Long)," "Reminisce" and "Mary's Joint." Blige could have done without the male band member who tries to function as her onstage cheerleader, but even so, this is an impressive release that her followers will want. —*Alex Henderson*

Mary / Aug. 17, 1999 / MCA ✦✦✦✦

Perhaps it was inevitable that Mary J. Blige would mature, toning down the raunchier elements of her persona that have been evident since her debut, while repositioning herself as a classicist soul singer. Even so, the sheer classiness of *Mary*, her fourth album, may come as a bit of a surprise. Blige made a conscious effort to create an album that recalled the classic dawning days of quiet storm yet worked as a unified, cohesive album. That meant that the more overt hip-hop elements have been subdued in favor of '70s soul. There's still grit in the music, but it's been glossed over with a polished production, and she now favors sophisticated songs, including material from such writers as Stevie Wonder, Bacharach & David, Lauryn Hill, and Elton John & Bernie Taupin. Some of these writers were collaborators and others contributed songs outright, but the amazing thing about the end result belongs to nobody else but Blige. It's different, to be sure, but still her—and it's a rewarding, engaging way to mature. Blige's voice is richer and her skills have deepened, and her new songs, while not as streetwise, are worthy of her talents. Consequently, *Mary* is a thoroughly winning album. —*Stephen Thomas Erlewine*

No More Drama / Aug. 28, 2001 / MCA ✦✦✦✦

Mary J. Blige came a long way since 1992's breakthrough *What's the 411?*, and that's made very clear on *No More Drama*. The singer/songwriter blossomed into an all-out R&B diva—with a hip-hop edge—full of soul and command. Her songs on this recording exude the wisdom of a woman who's seen it all and has found her center. And she will no longer tolerate drama, pettiness, and overall bullshit. In 2001's crop of R&B singers, Blige's voice is truly inimitable. It's husky, strong, soulful, and full of maturity. Make no mistake, though: This lady can still flow like no one's business; just check out the bouncy album opener, "Love." In fact, many of the record's cuts are standout moments. For instance, only Blige has the balls to write and pull off a song called "PMS," a soulful and bluesy number that describes, in detail, this condition inherent to the female experience. And while she also explores themes of love, Blige's disc is essentially a journey through her personal evolution and spirituality. The final cut, "Testimony," best summarizes the album's theme: finding what's real in life. And for Blige, that's self-love and God. To her credit, Blige has a killer instinct for penning lyrics that people can relate to and creating gritty, thick, and soul-infused R&B fare. (She does get some help on this disc from such R&B and hip-hop heavyweights as Missy Elliot, Jimmy Jam, and Terry Lewis, among others.) Her music is more than heard, it is felt, and audiences would be hard-pressed to not surrender to her groove. Interestingly, many of Blige's peers sing about drama, but not this artist, not anymore. —*Liana Jonas*

Blind Faith

f. May 1969, England, **db.** Nov. 1969
Album Rock, British Blues, Hard Rock, Blues-Rock

Blind Faith was either the culmination of a decade's efforts by three legendary musicians, or a disaster of monumental proportions, symbolizing everything that had gone wrong with the business of rock at the close of the '60s. They generated some great songs and sold hundreds of thousands of concert tickets and perhaps a million more albums, all in under seven months together. The initial spark for Blind Faith came from ex-Cream guitarist Eric Clapton and ex-Traffic leader Steve Winwood, who began jamming together in early 1969. The notion of forming a band took a more immediate turn when Cream drummer Ginger Baker sat in, even though Clapton was not looking forward to the expectations that their link up would engender. By the time tours were booked (with millions of dollars promised), the group was known as Blind Faith, a slyly cynical reference to the fact that they'd barely had any time to work out songs. Despite being under-rehearsed, all the quartet had to do to please the crowds was show up, and riots ensued at several American venues. By the time the tour ended in late August, the self-titled album—which ran into controversy over its cover, a topless pre-pubescent girl—had been out for almost a month, and had already sold more than half a million copies in America alone. There was very good music on *Blind Faith*, but there wasn't a lot of it—six songs didn't constitute a repertory. The band had left its members a bit shell shocked, and by October, it became official that there would be no second Blind Faith album. Blind Faith's

short life span made them a symbol of the tail end of the '60s: too much too soon in that overheated environment, even for the prodigious talents and personalities involved, resulting in a quick burnout. —*Bruce Eder*

● **Blind Faith** / Jul. 1969 / Polydor ✦✦✦✦

Blind Faith's first and last album, more than 30 years old and counting, remains one of the jewels of the Eric Clapton, Steve Winwood, and Ginger Baker catalogs, despite the crash-and-burn history of the band itself, which scarcely lasted six months. As much a follow-up to Traffic's self-titled second album as it is to Cream's final output, it merges the soulful blues of the former with the heavy riffing and outsized song lengths of the latter for a very compelling sound unique to this band. Not all of it works—between the virtuoso electric blues of "Had to Cry Today," the acoustic-textured "Can't Find My Way Home," the soaring "Presence of the Lord" (Eric Clapton's one contribution here as a songwriter, and the first great song he ever authored) and "Sea of Joy," the band doesn't do much with the Buddy Holly song "Well All Right"; and Ginger Baker's "Do What You Like" was a little weak to take up 15 minutes of space on an LP that might have been better used for a shorter drum solo and more songs. Unfortunately, the group was never *that* together as a band and evidently had just the 42 minutes of new music here ready to tour behind. —*Bruce Eder*

Blind Melon

f. 1989, **db.** 1999
American Trad Rock, Alternative Pop/Rock

Whereas most up-and-coming alternative bands of the early '90s borrowed from the leaders of the pack (Nirvana, Soundgarden, Nine Inch Nails), Blind Melon was an exception to the rule—their roots lay in classic rock (Lynyrd Skynyrd, Grateful Dead, Led Zeppelin). And while a promising career lay ahead of them, tragedy would ultimately end the band abruptly. The group came together in 1989 in Los Angeles, although all their respective members had migrated there from other U.S. locales. The complete opposite of all the glossed-up glam metal that was permeating the Sunset Strip at the time, the quintet used a refreshing back-to-basics approach, both musically and visually (giving off a heavy retro vibe early on). With a high profile appearance on MTV's 120 Minutes Tour in spring 1992, a buzz began to emerge. The band had gone into the studio earlier in the year, and although the sessions were completed by the springtime, their self-titled debut didn't see the light of day until September 1992. For the remainder of the year and the early part of 1993, the quintet toured nonstop. Although several videos/singles came and went without much MTV/radio fanfare, the Samuel Bayer-directed clip for their upbeat ditty "No Rain" became a smash—catapulting the single and the album to the top of the charts. Recording sessions began in fall 1994 for their sophomore effort, with renowned producer Andy Wallace behind the boards. The dark and challenging *Soup* was a true diamond in the rough, but the album was savagely bashed by fickle critics everywhere, which in turn led to a cool reception. Concerned but anxious to get back on tour, the band hit the road once again. On October 21, 1995, vocalist Shannon Hoon was found dead on the tour bus from an apparent drug overdose. —*Greg Prato*

● **Blind Melon** / Sep. 14, 1992 / Capitol ✦✦✦✦

Managing to be equally mellow and introspective as well as rough and rocking, Blind Melon's 1992 self-titled debut remains one of the most pure sounding rock albums of recent times—completely devoid of '90s production tricks. While the group was never the toast of the critics, their self-titled '92 debut has held up incredibly well over time—resembling a true rock classic. For reasons unknown, the late Shannon Hoon was, unfairly, usually the brunt of reviewer's criticisms, yet his angelic voice and talent for penning lyrics that examined the ups and downs of everyday life were an integral part of Blind Melon's sound, as well as the band's supreme jamming interplay. The most renowned song remains the uplifting hit, "No Rain," but the whole album is superb—the homesick rocker "Tones of Home," the desperate "I Wonder," the epic album closer, "Time," and the gentle acoustic strum of "Change," which included lyrics that turned out to be sadly prophetic for Hoon. Other highlights are a song inspired by the homeless ("Paper Scratcher"), "Sleepyhouse," which describes the feeling of isolation the band felt recording the debut in a secluded residence, and the retro (yet refreshing) sounds of "Soak the Sin" and "Dear Ol' Dad." Although the album started out slow sales-wise, constant touring and the success of "No Rain" one year after the debut's initial release proved to be Blind Melon's breakthrough success, eventually almost topping the charts and going multi-platinum. —*Greg Prato*

Soup / 1995 / Capitol ✦✦✦

Most '90s rock bands that enjoyed massive breakthrough success with their debut album seemed to follow it up with an effort similarly styled to its predecessor, hence guaranteeing repeat success. This proved not to be the case with Blind Melon. It appeared as though the band rejected the jovial spirit of "No Rain" and focused on much darker material for their follow-up, *Soup*. While it did not match the commercial success of the debut, *Soup* proved to be a challenging, gripping record that is just as strong and perhaps even more rewarding. Shannon Hoon was in the throes of drug addiction (which would prove fatal only two months after the album's release), and his experience at a drug detox is clearly detailed in the Zep-groover, "2x4." Hoon's lyrics often examine his growing sense of mortality, as evidenced in "The Duke," "St. Andrew's Fall" and "Car Seat," while "New Life" shows Hoon hoping that the birth of his baby daughter will put his life back on track. The country-tinged "Skinned" is written from the standpoint of notorious killer, Ed Gein, the anthemic rocker, "Galaxie," appears to deal with a troubled relationship, and "Vernie" is a tribute to his grandmother. Some of the tracks prove hopeful ("Walk"), while others are steeped in despair ("Toes Across the Floor," "Wilt"). *Soup* deserved to be another big hit, but due to MTV and radio's abrupt abandonment of the band, harsh reviews from close-minded critics, and worst of all, Hoon's untimely death mid-tour, all hopes of the album receiving the attention it deserved were extinguished. *Soup* is one of the most underrated and overlooked great rock albums of the '90s. *—Greg Prato*

Nico / 1996 / Capitol ♦♦

blink-182

f. Poway, CA

Punk-Pop, Post-Grunge, Punk Revival, Alternative Pop/Rock

The new-school punk trio blink-182 was formed near San Diego, California around guitarist/vocalist Tom Delonge, bassist Mark Hoppus, and drummer Scott Raynor. Originally known as simply blink, the band debuted in 1993 with a self-released EP, *Fly Swatter*. After releasing the album *Buddha* in 1994, the trio signed to Grilled Cheese/Cargo and released *Cheshire Cat* the following year. The threat of a lawsuit from a similarly named Irish band forced them to change their name to blink-182, but the group earned a higher profile touring the world with Pennywise and NOFX on the 1996–97 Warped Tour, plus appearing on innumerable skate/surf/snowboarding videos. The third blink-182 LP, *Dude Ranch*, was released in 1997. *Dude Ranch* expanded the group's audience and won the attention of major labels. blink-182 wound up signing with MCA, who released the band's fourth album, *Enema of the State*, in the summer of 1999. Travis Barker, formerly with the Aquabats, later replaced Raynor. After selling over four million copies of *Enema of the State*, the trio played on with the limited edition release *The Mark, Tom, and Travis Show (The Enema Strikes Back)* in fall 2000. The album featured the band's radio hits on a live setting intertwined with their quirky sense of humor as well as the new song "Man Overboard." *Take Off Your Pants and Jacket*, issued in spring 2001, saw the band return to their SoCal punk rock roots. *—John Bush*

Buddha / 1994 / Kung Fu ♦♦♦

blink-182's first full-length album *Buddah* may be a little generic, but it's nevertheless a solid skate-punk record that illustrates the group's flair for speedy, catchy hooks and irreverent humor. There are a few weak cuts, but on the whole, it's a promising debut. *—Stephen Thomas Erlewine*

Cheshire Cat / 1995 / Cargo/Grilled Cheese ♦♦♦

Looking back, it's possible to see the roots of blink-182's tuneful frat punk on *Cheshire Cat*, but the fact of the matter is, this isn't as good an album as the ones that came later. That doesn't mean it's bad, since it skates by on its impish pranks and brash musicality, but the group is rather scattershot here, hitting the target as often as they miss it. There's enough here to dig into if you're a fan, but you have to be a fan to appreciate it. *—Stephen Thomas Erlewine*

● **Dude Ranch** / Jun. 17, 1997 / Cargo/Grilled Cheese ♦♦♦♦

On their second album, *Dude Ranch*, blink-182 follows in the same path as their debut, turning out 15 tracks of juvenile, adrenaline-fueled punk-pop. Some listeners will find their potty humor ("Dick Lips") somewhat irritating, but the group has written some surprisingly catchy hooks, which might win over skeptics. The songwriting is still a little uneven, but overall, *Dude Ranch* is an improvement over their first album, *Cheshire Cat*. *—Stephen Thomas Erlewine*

Enema of the State / Jun. 1, 1999 / MCA ♦♦♦♦

If the title *Enema of the State* didn't give it away, it should be clear from songs like "Dumpweed," "What's My Age Again?," and "Dysentery Gary" that moving to a major label isn't a sign of maturity for blink-182. "Dammit (Growing Up)," the first single from their third album, *Dude Ranch*, brought them a wider audience and the attention of major labels, which was just too tempting to resist. They signed with MCA, but the only sign that *Enema of the State* is a major-label effort is the somewhat cleaner production and the fact that they could afford porn superstar Janine—all decked out as (surprise!) an enema nurse—for the album cover. Of course, the lovely Janine is as much an indication as "Going Away to College," a catchy little number that pretty much repeats the narrative of "Dammit": blink-182 is not growing up, no way, no how, nowhere. And that's fine, because few of their peers are quite as blissfully stupid and effortlessly catchy as them. Sure, they might not show the emotional depth of Green Day, but they have good tunes and deliver them in a speedy, punchy fashion. *Enema of the State* isn't going to change anyone's life—unless it's the first time a 13-year-old boy has seen Janine—and it will likely irritate old codgers, but it's a fun record that's better than the average neo-punk release. *—Stephen Thomas Erlewine*

The Mark, Tom and Travis Show (The Enema Strikes Back) / Nov. 7, 2000 / MCA ♦♦♦

Power punk funny guys blink-182 capture their witty stage presence on the limited-edition release *The Mark, Tom and Travis Show (The Enema Strikes Back)*. Celebrating the quick success of their major-label debut, 1999's *Enema of the State*, *The Mark, Tom and Travis Show* showcases playful live cuts and previously unreleased tracks and, in keeping with blink-182's punk revivalism, the album is only available from the time of release to January 2001. *The Mark, Tom and Travis Show* is indeed a real rock show and catches blink-182's shameless personalities and childlike giggling about oral sex, dog semen, and masturbation. But that's what makes blink-182 popular: the band's ability to not care about anything is a carefree look for the pop kids buying its records. The band members' immaturity is harmless and fans love it. The quick guitar riffs and swirling percussion are intact, and guitarist Tom Delonge's hyperactive retaliations against the audience are merely an act for the sake of being cool. Delonge and bassist Mark Hoppus are even funnier with their on-stage brotherly love affair. It's high-speed energy at it's finest, probably the cheekiest punk rock stake since Green Day's "Longview." And in the midst of teen pop mediocrity and post-grunge rollickers, it's good to see a band such as blink-182 enjoying its time on top of the world. *—MacKenzie Wilson*

Take Off Your Pants and Jacket / Jun. 12, 2001 / MCA ♦♦♦♦

Not too much has changed since you last left blink-182. You might hear the same snap, crackle, and pop that the trio has prided themselves on for almost ten years. There's even the continual cabbage patch screech of Tom Delonge and support for rampant teen angst. But five albums later, these San Diego natives grab their rosy-cheek punkadelics and add a bit more of a flamboyant, passionate maturation on *Take Off Your Pants and Jacket*. When *Enema of the State* leaped onto the charts in 1999, the lyrical direction was 90 percent party-boy mentality, leaving little room for traces of a growth spurt. And while the continual back-drip of tracks from *Enema*... remains, the fresh plethora of tunes from these rambunctious Toys-R-Us rockers have more purpose than ever. With a fight for your right joviality that's often irresistible, songs like "Anthem, Pt. 2" and "Stay Together for the Kids" house an indomitable school-kid voice where a surging vapor of knock-out speed chords meet wrecking-ball percussion. The meanings are bucketed and spilled with lines like "If we're fucked up/you're to blame" ("Anthem, Pt. 2"). "First Date" and "Roller Coaster" are only a couple of their tunes that act as therapy for post-pubescent dilemma, also present on previous efforts like *Enema*... and *Dude Ranch*. Each song about the rotten girlfriend or unhip parent speaks loud and often to the 2000 MTV generation. Nevertheless, the dumped-in-the-amusement-park tone and lyrical progression are sharp if not entertaining. *Take Off Your Pants*... is one of their finest works to date, with almost every track sporting a commanding articulation and new-school punk sounds. They've definitely put a big-time notch in the win column. *—Darren Ratner*

Blonde Redhead

f. 1993

Indie Rock

Blonde Redhead's noisy, dissonant guitars, alternate tunings, and quiet, stilted lyrics have often been compared to early Sonic Youth. After randomly meeting at an Italian restaurant in New York, Japanese art students Kazu Makino and Maki Takahashi and Italian twin brothers Simone and Amedeo Pace formed the band in 1993. The name was taken from a song by the '80s no-wave band DNA. With Makino and Amedeo on guitars and vocals, Simone on drums, and Takahashi on bass, the band's chaotic, artistic rock caught the attention of Sonic Youth drummer Steve Shelley, who produced and released the band's debut album, *Blonde Redhead*, on his Smells Like Records label. Shortly after the album's release, Takahashi left the band. The remaining members continued as a trio, releasing a second album in 1995 on Shelley's label, titled *La Mia Vita Violenta*.

For their 1997 release *Fake Can Be Just as Good*, recorded on Touch and Go, the trio was joined by guest bass player Vern from Unwound. By 1998, the band eliminated bass and scaled back to guitars, drums, and vocals for *In an Expression of the Inexpressible*. *Melody of Certain Damaged Lemons* and the *Melodie Citronique* EP followed two years later. *—Tracy Frey*

Blonde Redhead / Jan. 19, 1995 / Smells Like ♦♦♦

Recalling the no wave movement of the late '70s, the self-titled debut of New York City's Blonde Redhead is a glorious piece of dense, art-damaged noise, with songs that move from drifting melodicism to raging aural assaults in the course of a few measures. Taking their cues most directly from Sonic Youth (Steve Shelley produced the album), Blonde Redhead revel in noise and create vast sonic landscapes out of which songs naturally emerge. The focus here tends to be on atmospherics, and yet there is never the feeling of utter chaos; instead, the album functions like a work of controlled mayhem, referencing a wide range of musical approaches. The opening track, "I Don't Want U," starts off like jazz-rock, building momentum until it erupts in a blast of indie rock noise, anchored throughout by a steadily rolling bass line. "Snippet"'s quite-loud-quiet dynamics are offset by the driving rock of "Mama Cita," and the album's closer, "Girl Boy," comes across like delirious dream pop. The entire album is drenched in dense, multilayered feedback, with a rhythm section that works to keep the guitars in control, underpinning the attack. Blonde Redhead have created a great record, especially for fans of experimental rock: difficult, noisy, and exhilarating. *—Brandon Gentry*

La Mia Vita Violenta / Sep. 4, 1995 / Smells Like ♦♦♦

With their second release, *La Mia Vita Violenta*, Blonde Redhead maintain their organically low-fi aesthetic and continue to prove themselves as one of indie rock's real triumphs. Even after the departure of guitarist Maki Takahashi, they still make more noise with three people than most bands could make with ten. Guitars tear into the songs—pointed, direct, and tough—while the vocals of Kazu Makino and Amedeo Pace weave tightly into drummer Simone Pace's impeccably precise backing. Timing is everything, and Blonde Redhead certainly have it. They're dirty when they need to be and crystal-clear when the situation calls for it. Never angry, the trio play hard and fast to the point where the instruments seem to play themselves with the deftest of precision. The production is so skillful that even with the most Spartan of recording gear, guitars end up sounding synthetic, in that painting-looks-like-a-photograph kind of way. And the volatile changes—from sweet acoustic strums to drilling power chords—make this album a whirl of unexpected surprises. *La Mia Vita Violenta* is math rock without the nerdiness and art rock without the pretentiousness. *—Ken Taylor*

Fake Can Be Just as Good / Mar. 11, 1997 / Touch and Go ♦♦♦

Fake Can Be Just as Good is the third album from the no-wave influenced Blonde Redhead. The album's constant nervous tension and dissonance evoke a sense of foreboding. It's almost as if the album were made specifically to convey anxiety because every song is saturated with it. The songs are rich with noise and texture and punctuated by staccato lyrical delivery. The album's first track, "Kazuality," has a strong bass line that compliments Amedeo Pace's hard vocal phrases to give the song a great sense of urgency. The band's other singer, Kazu Makino, has a high-pitched, shrill voice that is interesting but at times can be irritating and whiny. "Oh James" is a nice blend of both voices. Again, a strong bass line underscores the desperation of Makino's piercing vocals. Pace's smoother voice brings an intermittent calm although the guitars continually suggest chaos. "Futurism vs. Passeism," which closes the album, is an inspired, moody instrumental that carries the band's dissonance and tension to the very end. *—Tracy Frey*

● **In an Expression of the Inexpressible** / Sep. 8, 1998 / Touch and Go ✦✦✦✦
The oft-used comparison to Sonic Youth doesn't really hold a lot of water, as Blonde Redhead's music has always been a bit less swirling, more spontaneous, and rougher around the edges. Further differentiating them from Sonic Youth is their bass-less approach. *In an Expression of the Inexpressible*, their fourth release, is as uncompromising as *Fake Can Be Just as Good* and *La Mia Vita Violenta*, but this time Blonde Redhead wanted to be produced by someone outside the band. The sound is fuller and more polished, and in the capable hands of producers John Goodmanson and Guy Picciotto (of Fugazi fame), they've never sounded quite as good. Still, Kazu Makino's high-pitched, Björk-ish vocals can get irritating at times, and the two guitars never quite reach a compelling level of interplay. Blonde Redhead, who sometimes are too clever for their own good, could, in fact, learn a great deal from Sonic Youth, since most of the tracks never come across with much urgency. *—Matthew Hilburn*

Melody of Certain Damaged Lemons / Jun. 6, 2000 / Touch and Go ✦✦✦✦
For a record produced by Guy Picciotto (Fugazi, Rites of Spring), *Melody of Certain Damaged Lemons* is a surprisingly quiet affair. Rarely do the cuts on Blonde Redhead's 2000 release get much louder than an electric guitar. With their fifth record, Blonde Redhead finally emerges from the shadows of Sonic Youth's post-punk legacy by avoiding the expected detunings, distortions, and shrillness of the genre. The three-piece band manages to create a record that is subtle, tuneful, and sublime. On "Loved Despite of Great Faults," instrumentation mainly consists of acoustic guitar, piano, and percussion rather than an assault of power chords, yet the mood of the song is just as effective. While the record may be quieter, it still manages to move in several different directions. "This Is Not" tips its hat to Ric Ocasek with a new wave-inspired piece while the opening cut, "Equally Damaged," and "Ballad of Lemons" suggest an influence from Danny Elfman. *Melody of Certain Damaged Lemons* may not accurately reflect the full body of Blonde Redhead's work, yet it presents an easy place to start. *—Yancey Strickler*

Blondie

f. Aug. 1974, New York, NY, **db.** Oct. 1982
American Punk, New York Punk, Club/Dance, Pop/Rock, New Wave, Punk
Blondie was the most commercially successful band to emerge from the much vaunted punk/new wave movement of the late '70s. Formed by singer Deborah Harry and guitarist Chris Stein, the group released a self-titled album in 1976, then signed to Chrysalis for their second album, *Plastic Letters*. Blondie broke commercially in the U.K. in 1978, when their singles "Denis" and "(I'm Always Touched by Your) Presence, Dear" became Top Ten hits. Third album *Parallel Lines* broke them worldwide, with the disco-influenced "Heart of Glass" hitting #1 in both the U.K. and the U.S. Two more transatlantic chart toppers ("Call Me" and "The Tide Is High") followed in 1980, though the band began breaking apart one year later, helped along by Harry's gold-selling solo album, *KooKoo*. *The Hunter*, Blondie's sixth and last new album, was a commercial disappointment. At the same time, Stein became seriously ill with the genetic disease pemphigus. As a result, Blondie broke up in October 1982, with Deborah Harry launching a part-time solo career while caring for Stein, who eventually recovered. In 1998, the original line-up reunited to tour Europe, their first series of dates in 16 years; a new LP, *No Exit*, followed early the next year. *—William Ruhlmann*

Blondie / Dec. 1976 / Chrysalis ✦✦✦✦✦
If new wave was about reconfiguring and re-contextualizing simple pop/rock forms of the '50s and '60s in new, ironic, and aggressive ways, then Blondie, which took the girl group style of the early and mid-'60s and added a '70s archness, fit right in. True punksters may have deplored the group early on (they never had the hip cachet of Talking Heads or even the Ramones), but Blondie's secret weapon, which was deployed increasingly over their career, was a canny pop straddle—they sent the music up and celebrated it at the same time. So, for instance, songs like "X Offender" (their first single) and "In the Flesh" (their first hit, in Australia) had the tough-girl-with-a-tender-heart tone of the Shangri-Las (Brill Building songwriter Ellie Greenwich even sang backup on the latter), while going one step too far into hard-edged decadence—that is, if you chose to see that. The whole point was that you could take Blondie either way. *—William Ruhlmann*

Plastic Letters / Oct. 1977 / Chrysalis ✦✦✦✦✦
Blondie's second album was a less distinctive version of its first, matching the first record's bright, sharp production (courtesy of Richard Gottehrer), but marking a fall-off in songwriting. The two best tracks—both U.K. hits—were "Denis," a remake of an oldie, and "(I'm Always Touched by Your) Presence, Dear," written by departed bass player Gary Valentine, and that didn't bode well. Nevertheless, those songs were enough to assure the album's British success and to make some noise in the U.S. But Blondie would take a distinctly different approach next time out. *—William Ruhlmann*

☆ **Parallel Lines** / Sep. 1978 / Chrysalis ✦✦✦✦✦
Blondie turned to British pop producer Mike Chapman for their third album, on which they abandoned any pretensions to new wave legitimacy (just in time, given the decline of the new wave) and emerged as a pure pop band. But it wasn't just Chapman that made *Parallel Lines* Blondie's best album; it was the band's own songwriting, including Deborah Harry, Chris Stein, and James Destri's "Picture This," and Harry and Stein's "Heart of Glass," and Harry and new bass player Nigel Harrison's "One Way or Another," plus two contributions from non-band-member Jack Lee, "Will Anything Happen?" and "Hanging on the Telephone." That was enough to give Blondie a #1 on both sides of the Atlantic with "Heart of Glass" and three more U.K. hits, but what impresses is the album's depth and consistency—album tracks like "Fade Away and Radiate" and "Just Go Away" are as impressive as the songs pulled for singles. The result is state-of-the-art pop-rock circa 1978, with Harry's tough-girl glamour setting the pattern that would be exploited over the next decade by a host of successors led by Madonna. *—William Ruhlmann*

Eat to the Beat / Oct. 1979 / Chrysalis ✦✦✦✦✦
Just as Blondie's second album, *Plastic Letters*, was a pale imitation of their debut, *Blondie*, *Eat to the Beat*, their fourth album, was a secondhand version of their breakthrough third album, *Parallel Lines*: one step forward, half a step back. There was an attempt, on such songs as "The Hardest Part" and "Atomic," to recreate the rock-disco fusion of the group's one major U.S. hit, "Heart of Glass," without similar success, and elsewhere, the band just tried to cover too many stylistic bases. The British, who had long since been converted, made *Eat to the Beat* another chart-topper, but in the U.S., which still saw Blondie as a slightly comic one-hit wonder, the album was greeted for what it was—slick corporate rock without the tangy flavor that had made *Parallel Lines* such ear candy. *—William Ruhlmann*

Autoamerican / Nov. 1980 / Chrysalis ✦✦✦
The basic Blondie sextet was augmented, or replaced, by a dozen session musicians for the group's fifth album, *Autoamerican*, on which they continued to expand their stylistic range, with greater success, at least on certain tracks, than they had on *Eat to the Beat*. The rap pastiche "Rapture" and the Caribbean-flavored "The Tide Is High" both went to #1 on the singles charts, but they are the only memorable tracks on an album that leads off with a string-filled instrumental and also finds Deborah Harry crooning ersatz '20s pop on "Here's Looking at You" and tackling Broadway show music in a cover of "Follow Me" from *Camelot*. What a mess. *—William Ruhlmann*

★ **The Best of Blondie** / 1981 / Chrysalis ✦✦✦✦✦
Although Blondie made several first-rate albums, most of their best songs were released as singles, which makes *The Best of Blondie* an essential collection. *The Best of Blondie* glosses over their punk roots—very little from the first album, apart from the vicious "Rip Her to Shreds" and the seductive "In the Flesh"—but the band's pop hits are among the finest of their era and encapsulate all of the virtues of new wave. Apart from genuine chart hits like "Heart of Glass," "One Way or Another," "Dreaming," "Call Me," "Atomic," "The Tide Is High," and "Rapture," *The Best of Blondie* picks up several of the group's best album tracks, like "(I'm Always Touched by Your) Presence, Dear" and "Hanging on the Telephone." *The Best of Blondie* isn't all you need to know, but it is an excellent introduction to one of the best new wave bands. *—Stephen Thomas Erlewine*

The Hunter / Jul. 1982 / Chrysalis ✦✦
Autoamerican was Blondie's last real album, after which the band collapsed in legal problems and solo aspirations. *The Hunter* was only made because they still owed Chrysalis an album on their contract, and it sounds like the obligatory record it was. "Island of Lost Souls" (the album's only U.S. singles chart entry) was a try at remaking "The Tide Is High," and "The Beast" tried to recreate at least the rap section of "Rapture." Elsewhere, Deborah Harry and Co. scraped the bottom of their songwriting barrel for an incomprehensible science fiction epic ("Dragonfly") and other second-rate material. *—William Ruhlmann*

Blonde & Beyond / Nov. 16, 1993 / Chrysalis ✦✦✦
Most new wave bands tended to have short flashes of brilliance. Not Blondie. They were a great singles band, but they weren't limited to that—they also made strong albums and, as the rarities collection *Blonde & Beyond* illustrates, they had a lot of terrific material that never made it on the official records. Like most odds-and-ends collections, *Blonde & Beyond* is a little scattershot, which is only appropriate for a compilation comprised of demos, B-sides, live tracks, and foreign-language versions of familiar hits. Still, the treasures make the digging worthwhile, since the keepers here—including early versions of "Denis" and "X Offender," "Poets Problem," "Underground Girl" and a live version of "Bang a Gong (Get It On)"—rank among the group's very best efforts and are certainly worth the time of any true fan. *—Stephen Thomas Erlewine*

The Platinum Collection / Nov. 1, 1994 / Chrysalis ✦✦✦✦✦
The Platinum Collection reigns as Blondie's finest compilation, outshining *The Best of Blondie* in overall quality and quantity. This fine retrospective covers every U.S. and U.K. A- and B-side on two discs while adding unreleased material and club remixes as bonuses at the finale. Opening with the poppy, yet venomous, first U.K. single, "X Offender," disc one reveals Blondie's liveliest and most ambitious efforts as they merge their punk, reggae, and roots rock influences into what would soon be considered new wave. While Blondie is generally known for their charting singles, the spectacular B-sides/album tracks, including the dazzling space rocker "Fade Away and Radiate" and the punk/synth pop hybrid "Contact in Red Square," are equally essential. Disc two recalls some of the band's most accessible singles including "The Tide Is High," "Call Me," and "Rapture," which became the first Top Ten single to contain a rap vocal. Despite the excellent material represented so far, the second half unfortunately fails to sustain the momentum. Marked by selections from Blondie's 1982 swan song *The Hunter*, four 1975 demos, and two 1994 remixes, the rest of the disc suffers from poor sequencing and inferior selections. The terrible, unnecessary remixes of "Atomic" and "Rapture" and ho-hum demos would only appeal to collectors. Nonetheless, the demo "Once I Had a Love" would eventually receive a disco makeover and evolve into the international chart-topper "Heart of Glass" three years later. Ultimately, fans may prefer the distinguished single edits for "Heart of Glass" and "The Tide Is High" over the album versions, and yet despite all revealed shortcomings, *The Platinum Collection* provides more music per dollar spent compared to other Blondie releases. In addition, the compilation's colorful liner notes in-

clude insightful song commentary by most of Blondie, single and album information, and a descriptive family tree. *—Jacob N. Lunders*

No Exit / Feb. 23, 1999 / Beyond ✦✦✦
Once you've cherished Blondie you never really go back, even if for half of your life you must cherish them out of forgiveness, or just plain heartfelt concern. Debbie Harry loves to make curious decisions about her music, and it's always important to listen to her work carefully and several times (while trying to keep her performance in Jon Waters' *Hairspray* either firmly in, or out, of your mind as you do). In the old days, Harry and her guys covered terrific old blues and trippy, backwater pieces, popped up and pretty, punkified, otherwise unremarkable rock tunes, and flat out treated us to a show, whether live or Memorex. *No Exit* is a gritty downtown incarnation that almost sounds like a cutting room castaway, filled with raw and abject moments and digressions that suggest an improvised, irrelevant feel. The talkative "Screaming Skin" is a lyrically confused, stream of consciousness piece that sounds as if it was written on a paper bag on the subway—and some of us really like this stuff! But some of the instrumental tracks have the veneer of an afterthought, particularly in the percussion department. Miss Debbie is always at her rockin' finest when futzing with the blues (and country, really), which she does on most of the latter half of the disc like the consummate, crazy pro that she is. If nothing else, *No Exit* is a testament to authentic rock & roll durability, and, well, the abiding "wow" that is Debbie Harry. *—Becky Byrkit*

Blood, Sweat & Tears

f. 1967, New York, NY
Album Rock, Jazz-Rock, Pop/Rock, Psychedelic
For a brief period at the end of the '60s and the start of the '70s, Blood, Sweat & Tears, which fused a rock & roll rhythm section to a horn section, held out the promise of a jazz-rock fusion that could storm the pop charts. The eight-piece band signed to Columbia Records and released their debut album *Child Is Father to the Man* in February 1968. Singer David Clayton-Thomas was added for BS&T's self-titled second album, released in January 1969. It was a runaway hit, spawning three gold-selling Top Ten singles, "You've Made Me So Very Happy," "Spinning Wheel," and "And When I Die," selling three million copies and winning the Grammy Award for Album of the Year. It was also their highwater mark, as BS&T increasingly became a backup group for Clayton-Thomas. Nevertheless, the third album, *Blood, Sweat & Tears 3* (1970), and the fourth, *Blood, Sweat & Tears 4* (1971), were substantial hits. Clayton-Thomas went solo in early 1972, but returned in 1974. Numerous other personnel changes took place, as the group's commercial fortunes gradually declined. *—William Ruhlmann*

Child Is Father to the Man / Feb. 1968 / Columbia/Legacy ✦✦✦✦✦
This is keyboard player/singer/arranger Al Kooper's finest work, an album on which he moves the folk-blues-rock amalgamation of the Blues Project into even wider pastures, taking in classical and jazz elements (including strings and horns), all without losing the pop essence that makes the hybrid work. This is one of the great albums of the eclectic post-*Sgt. Pepper* era of the late '60s, a time when you could borrow styles from Greenwich Village contemporary folk to San Francisco acid rock and mix them into what seemed to have the potential to become a new American musical form. It's Kooper's bluesy songs, such as "I Love You More Than You'll Ever Know" and "I Can't Quit Her," and his singing that are the primary focus, but the album is an aural delight; listen to the way the bass guitar interacts with the horns on "My Days Are Numbered" or the charming arrangement and Steve Katz' vocal on Tim Buckley's "Morning Glory." Then Kooper sings Harry Nilsson's "Without Her" over a delicate, jazzy backing with flügelhorn/alto saxophone interplay by Randy Brecker and Fred Lipsius. This is the sound of a group of virtuosos enjoying themselves in the newly open possibilities of pop music. Maybe it couldn't have lasted; anyway, it didn't. [Columbia/Legacy's 1994 gold Mastersound edition reissue, and the 2000 regular-line Columbia/Legacy reissue, add three bonus tracks from their November 1967 audition: the instrumental "Refugee From Yuhupitz" and alternate versions of "I Love You More Than You'll Ever Know" and "The Modern Adventures of Plato, Diogenes and Freud."] *–William Ruhlmann*

Blood, Sweat & Tears / Jan. 1969 / Columbia/Legacy ✦✦✦✦✦
The difference between this album and the group's preceding long-player, *Child Is Father to the Man*, is the difference between a monumental seller and a record that was "merely" a huge critical success. Arguably, the Blood, Sweat & Tears that made this self-titled second album—consisting of five of the eight original members and four newcomers, including singer David Clayton-Thomas—was really a different group from the one that made *Child Is Father to the Man*, which was done largely under the direction of singer/songwriter/keyboard player/arranger Al Kooper. They had certain similarities to the original: the musical mixture of classical, jazz, and rock elements was still apparent, and the interplay between the horns and the keyboards was still occurring, even if those instruments were being played by different people. Kooper was even still present as an arranger on two tracks, notably the initial hit "You've Made Me So Very Happy." But the second BS&T, under the aegis of producer James William Guercio, was a less adventurous unit, and, as fronted by Clayton-Thomas, a far more commercial one. Not only did the album contain three songs that neared the top of the charts as singles—"Happy," "Spinning Wheel," and "And When I Die"—but the whole album, including an arrangement of "God Bless the Child" and the radical rewrite of Traffic's "Smiling Phases," was wonderfully accessible. It was a repertoire to build a career on, and they did exactly that, although they never came close to equaling this album. *—William Ruhlmann & Bruce Eder*

Blood, Sweat & Tears 3 / Jun. 1970 / Columbia ✦✦✦
Blood, Sweat & Tears had a hard act to follow in recording their third album. Nevertheless, BS&T constructed a convincing, if not quite as impressive, companion to their previous hit. David Clayton-Thomas remained an enthusiastic blues shouter, and the band still managed to put together lively arrangements, especially on the Top 40 hits "Hi-De-Ho" and "Lucretia Mac Evil." Elsewhere, they recreated the previous album's jazzing up of Laura Nyro ("He's a Runner") and Traffic ("40,000 Headmen"), although their pretentiousness, on the extended "Symphony/Sympathy for the Devil," and their tendency to borrow other artists' better-known material (James Taylor's "Fire and Rain") rather than generating more of their own, were warning signs for the future. In the meantime, *BS&T 3* was another chart-topping gold hit. *—William Ruhlmann*

Blood, Sweat & Tears 4 / Jun. 1971 / Columbia ✦✦

Blood, Sweat & Tears' Greatest Hits / Feb. 1972 / Columbia ✦✦✦✦✦
Sometimes, a greatest-hits set is timed perfectly to gather together a group's most successful and familiar performances just at the point when that group has passed the point of their maximum exposure to the public, but before the public memory has had a chance to fade. That was the case when Columbia Records assembled this compilation for release in early 1972. At that point, Blood, Sweat & Tears had released four albums and scored six Top 40 hits, each of which is heard here. But lead singer David Clayton-Thomas had just quit the group, so that the unit that recorded songs like "You've Made Me So Very Happy" was not working together anymore. And even when Clayton-Thomas returned, the band would continue to decline commercially. As such, BS&T's *Greatest Hits* captures the band's peak in 11 selections—seven singles chart entries, plus two album tracks from the celebrated debut album when Al Kooper helmed the group, and two more from the Grammy-winning multi-platinum second album. Using the short singles edits of songs like "And When I Die" emphasizes their radio-ready punch over the more extended suitelike arrangements on the albums, but this selection gains in focus what it lacks in ambition. For the millions who learned to love BS&T in 1969 when they were all over AM radio, this is the ideal selection of their most accessible material. [A later CD reissue of *Blood, Sweat & Tears' Greatest Hits* replaced each singles edit with the original full-length version.] *–William Ruhlmann*

What Goes Up: The Best of Blood, Sweat & Tears / Nov. 7, 1995 / Columbia ✦✦✦✦
Blood, Sweat & Tears' 11-track *Greatest Hits* album, released in February 1972, contained all of the group's six Top 40 singles, plus notable tracks from its two best albums, *Child Is Father to the Man* and *Blood, Sweat & Tears*. Almost 24 years later came this 32-track, 138 1/2-minute, double-CD expansion, much of it extraneous. Where *Greatest Hits* contained the single edits of songs like "You've Made Me So Very Happy" and "And When I Die," here "all titles are original album versions," as the back cover noted, which means the jazzy interludes, frequently having nothing to do with the rest of the song, remained. There were a couple of unreleased tracks, and otherwise the bloated running time was filled out by, for example, four tracks from the 1972 stiff *New Blood*, which didn't even feature singer David Clayton-Thomas. Legacy would have better served consumers by either expanding the original 41-minute *Greatest Hits* to proper CD length with a few bonus tracks or reissuing the first two albums in a double-disc set, again with a few bonus tracks to fill up the time. This compilation did not enhance the band's reputation. And the error-filled liner notes are less than worthless. *—William Ruhlmann*

● **Blood, Sweat & Tears' Greatest Hits [Remastered]** / Feb. 23, 1999 / Columbia ✦✦✦✦✦
While no substitute for the remastered version of the *Child Is Father to the Man* album or the Mobile Fidelity version of *Blood, Sweat & Tears*, this disc is a good idea since it has remastered versions of tracks from the later, non-upgraded albums. Columbia/Legacy went back and recompiled this multimillion selling album (previously available as a fairly lackluster 40-minute, 11-song CD), adding two songs ("So Long Dixie" and "More and More") that were previously available only on singles from 1972 and 1968, respectively, and upgrading the sound. It's more compact and much less pricey than the double-CD *What Goes Up: The Best of Blood, Sweat & Tears*. Using the single edits—as on the old CD edition and the original LP—would have made it perfect, but the producers chose to use the extended album versions instead. To serious fans, it's still sort of Blood, Sweat & Tears-lite, but at least the tracks now sport state-of-the-art sound—hard, upfront bass and drums, horns that pour out of the speakers, and close and intimate singing from David Clayton-Thomas (or, on two tracks here, Al Kooper and Steve Katz). The new release also recreates the packaging of the original LP, with reviewers' quotes across the band's prime years (1968-1972) and a time-line history, as well as release and production information on each song. The two additional numbers and the use of the LP cuts bring the running time up to 48 minutes. *—Bruce Eder*

Bobby Bloom

d. Feb. 28, 1974
Vocals / Pop-Soul, Blue-Eyed Soul, Bubblegum, Pop/Rock
Remembered most for his sweet, bubbly 1970 album, *Montego Bay*, Bobby Bloom also played a role as a songwriter and entrepreneur connected to the Kama Sutra/Buddah group of labels. He did engineering work for a number of artists including Louis Jordan and Shuggie Otis. He formed a producing/songwriting partnership with Jeff Barry what included working on a late Monkees album. Early solo projects include *Love Don't Let Me Down* and *Count on Me*, but his break came with *Montego Bay*. All of the recordings that followed it employed its successful formula of pop, calypso, and rock. They include *Heavy Makes You Happy* and the *Bobby Bloom Album*, which was produced by Barry. Toward the end of his life, Bloom suffered from depression and was killed in an accidental shooting on February 28, 1974. *—Stacia Proefrock*

● **Where Are We Going** / 2000 / BMG International ✦✦✦

Michael Bloomfield

b. Jul. 28, 1943, Chicago, IL, **d.** Feb. 15, 1981, San Francisco, CA
Vocals, Keyboards, Guitar / Modern Electric Chicago Blues, Blues-Rock, Electric Chicago Blues

Michael Bloomfield was one of the first white players who got right into the Chicago blues scene and could actually play the music. As lead guitar for the Butterfield Blues Band, he exerted a powerful influence with far-reaching effect on young rock guitarists. He almost single-handedly pioneered the extended guitar solo, introducing many Western ears to the sounds of the Far East with his sitar-inspired solos. The Butterfield Blues Band album *East-West* (and the lovely title cut) broke new ground in the progressive rock scene—psychedelic rock was born. Bloomfield also backed Bob Dylan in his move into electric-land on *Highway 61 Revisited*, one of the landmarks of modern rock music. He went on to record albums with his own band, Electric Flag, and with others (*Super Session* w/Al Kooper). These later efforts saw only limited success. He was best at blues, and those first two Butterfield albums marked a high point. Part of Bloomfield's enormous influence on younger rock guitar players was due to his very outgoing and generous spirit. Bloomfield was one of those rare performers who cared as much for sharing his vision with others as he did for the music he loved. —*Michael Erlewine*

Don't Say That I Ain't Your Man / 1964-1969 / Columbia/Legacy ✦✦✦✦✦
15 tracks covering the pioneering blues-rock guitarist's '60s work, which was by far his best and most influential. Bloomfield worked with a bunch of bands during the decade, and the compilation flits rather hurriedly from his contributions to the Paul Butterfield Blues Band and Electric Flag to his collaborations with Al Kooper and some late-'60s solo tracks (none of his groundbreaking mid-'60s work with Dylan is here). Collectors will be interested in the first five songs, which date from previously unreleased sessions produced by John Hammond in late 1964 and early 1965. Featuring Charlie Musselwhite on harmonica, this pre-Butterfield Blues Band outfit plays convincingly, but the material is standard-issue, and Bloomfield's vocals are thin and weak (they didn't improve much over time). As befits Bloomfield's considerable but erratic talent, this is an interesting but erratic compilation; seek out the first two Paul Butterfield albums for a more cohesive showcase of his skills. —*Richie Unterberger*

● **Super Session** / 1968 / Columbia ✦✦✦✦✦
Al Kooper was the mastermind behind this appropriately named album, one side of which features his "spontaneous" studio collaboration with Mike Bloomfield and the other a session with Stephen Stills. The recordings have an off-the-cuff energy that displays the inventiveness of the two guitarists to best advantage. The best-selling recording of Bloomfield's career, it inspired the follow-up *The Live Adventures of Mike Bloomfield and Al Kooper.* —*Jeff Tamarkin*

Live at Bill Graham's Fillmore West / 1969 / Columbia ✦✦✦✦✦
This session from early 1969 featured Nick Gravenites, Mark Naftalin, John Kahn, and Snooky Flowers (among others), with cameos from Taj Mahal and Jesse Ed Davis, but it's clear from the opening notes who the real star is. Over the years, Bloomfield's titanic solos on "Blues on a Westside" have dwarfed the rest of the album in my memory, but the truth is his playing just burns across every track. [More of Michael's great guitar work from these shows is on Nick Gravenites' *My Labors* on Columbia.] —*Cary Wolfson*

The Live Adventures of Mike Bloomfield and Al Kooper / 1969 / Columbia ✦✦

It's Not Killing Me / 1969 / Columbia ✦✦

Triumvirate / 1973 / Columbia ✦✦✦
In 1973 someone at Columbia evidently decided to try and recoup some of the investment the label had made in Bloomfield and John Hammond—they were thrown into a recording studio along with Dr. John, who had recently scored a hit with "Right Place, Wrong Time." It probably sounded like a good idea at the time, but the results were uninspired. Pass by this CD and pick up any one of their solo recordings instead. —*Jan Mark Wolkin*

Try It Before You Buy It / 1975 / One Way ✦✦

Live at the Old Waldorf / 1976 / Columbia/Legacy ✦✦✦✦
If you've never really experienced Mike Bloomfield just letting loose and playing ripping and inspired guitar, this is a darn good starting point. Recorded live in 1976 and 1977 by producer Norman Dayron at the Old Waldorf nightclub on Bloomfield's home turf in San Francisco with a hand-picked band, the results are startling to say the least. Bloomfield plays with assurance and authority throughout, exploring new ideas with each new chorus from his guitar, arguably at his best since his early Butterfield/Dylan days. He plays a lot of slide guitar here, too, and tracks like "Bad Luck Baby," "The Sky Is Crying," "Dancin' Fool" and "Buried Alive In the Blues" showcase his mighty talents with the bottleneck, taking the lessons learned first hand from Robert Nighthawk to places new and wild. Bloomfield was never much of a singer, and everybody from old pal Nick Gravenites to bassist Roger Troy to drummer Bob Jones end up handling all the vocals on this disc. But one listen to the "Blues Medley" that kicks off the proceedings is reason enough to know why Bloomfield's reputation on his chosen instrument ranks up there with the greats. Consider this disc validation of that rep. —*Cub Koda*

Best of Michael Bloomfield / 1978-1980 / Takoma ✦✦✦✦
By the time the majority of these 12 songs from various solo projects were recorded, Bloomfield was already well established as America's first official guitar slinger of the baby boomer generation. The selections on this CD come from the later stages of his career, and as such are a marvelous showcase for his wide-ranging versatility. They run the gamut from Mississippi John Hurt-style fingerpicking ("Frankie and Johnny"), Scrapper Blackwell acoustic style flat-picking, and Lonnie Johnson slide playing (with "Mr. Johnson and Mr. Dunn," "Effinona Rag," "See That My Grave Is Kept Clean" featuring him on

acoustic slide, piano, accordion, and tipple, and two duets with Little Brother Montgomery, "Pleading Blues" and "Michigan Water Blues") to the red-hot electric solo work he's best noted for. Other highlights include "Between the Hard Place and the Ground" and a stray track with the Woody Herman big band, "Hitch-Hike On the Possum Trot Line." —*Cub Koda*

Between the Hard Place and the Ground [Takoma] / 1979 / Takoma ✦✦✦✦

Living in the Fast Lane / 1980 / AJK ✦✦✦
Michael Bloomfield was a pioneer in blues-rock, one of the performers who found a way to maintain his own sound while paying tribute to the blues greats that created the music he idolized. The 10 tracks presented on *Living in the Fast Lane* weren't as vital as his earlier material, but were done with the same intensity and passion that marked all his numbers. They were backed on several cuts by Duke Tito and the Marin Country Playboys, while on "When I Get Home," The Singers of The Church of God In Christ joined lead vocalist Roger Troy for a rousing, spirit-filled performance that was the album's high point. —*Ron Wynn*

Blossom Toes

f. 1965, **db.** 1969
British Psychedelia, Psychedelic

They never had any commercial success in the U.K. or the U.S., but Blossom Toes was one of the more interesting British psychedelic groups of the late '60s. Starting as the Ingoes, just another of thousands of British R&B/beat bands of the mid-'60s, the group hooked up with legendary impresario Giorgio Gomelsky (early mentor of the Stones and manager of the Yardbirds and Soft Machine, among others) in 1966. Gomelsky changed their name and put them on his Marmalade label. Their 1967 debut LP was miles away from R&B, reflecting an extremely British whimsy and skilled, idiosyncratic songwriting more in line with Ray Davies. After some personnel changes, the group released their second (and final) album a couple years later. Another extremely accomplished work, it was markedly different in character than their first effort, showing a far more sober tone and heavier, guitar-oriented approach. The group broke up at the end of the decade; members Brian Godding and Brian Belshaw formed the equally obscure B.B. Blunder, and Godding became active on the fringes of the British experimental rock scene. —*Richie Unterberger*

We Are Ever So Clean / 1967 / Marmalade ✦✦✦✦✦
Imagine the late-'60s Kinks crossed with a touch of the absurdist British wit of the Bonzo Dog Band, and you have an idea of the droll charm of Blossom Toes' debut album. Songwriters Brian Godding and Jim Cregan were the chief architects of the Toes' whimsical and melodic vision, which conjured images of a sun-drenched Summer of Love, London style. With its references to royal parks, tea time, watchmakers, intrepid balloon makers, "Mrs. Murphy's Budgerigar," and the like, it's a distinctly British brand of whimsy. It has since been revealed that session men performed a lot of these orchestral arrangements, which embellished the band's sparkling harmonies and (semi-buried) guitars. But the cello, brass, flute, and tinkling piano have a delicate beauty that serves as an effective counterpoint. The group sings and plays as though they have wide grins on their faces, and the result is one of the happiest, most underappreciated relics of British psychedelia. —*Richie Unterberger*

If Only for a Moment / 1969 / Marmalade ✦✦✦✦✦
Brian Godding and Jim Cregan were still Blossom Toes' chief songwriters on their second album, but the LP stands in bold contrast to their debut in sound and attitude. Having scuttled the orchestras and developed their chops in the two-year interlude, the record bears the influence of heavy California psychedelia and Captain Beefheart with its intricate, interwoven guitar lines and occasional gruff dissonance. The more serious instrumental approach spills over to the lyrics, which are somber and at times even gloomy, occasionally reflecting the social turbulence of the late '60s, with their uncertain tenor and references to ominous "peace loving men" and "love bombs." Far less uplifting than their debut, the weighty approach is leavened by the close harmonies and sparkling guitar interplay. While not as memorable as the first album, it's above-average late-'60s psychedelia that almost acts as the downer flipside to the stoned, happy-face ambience of their early work. —*Richie Unterberger*

● **Collection** / 1988 / Decal ✦✦✦✦✦
The definitive anthology, packaging most of *We Are Ever So Clean* and the entirety of *If Only for a Moment*. Unfortunately, a couple minor tracks from the first LP were omitted for space reasons, but as compensation it includes the non-LP 1968 single "Postcard"/"Everyone's Leaving Me Now," which is quite similar in mood to the *Ever So Clean* songs. The double album includes an exhaustive history of the group by John Platt. —*Richie Unterberger*

New Day: Blossom Toes '70 / 1989 / Decal ✦✦✦
Originally titled *Workers Playtime*, this album was attributed to B.B. Blunder when it was first released in 1971. It appears under the Blossom Toes discography because it was reissued, confusingly, as *New Day* in 1989 by Decal, who attributed the LP not to B.B. Blunder, but to "Blossom Toes '70 (formerly B.B. Blunder)." Featuring ex-Blossom Toes Brian Godding, Brian Belshaw, and Kevin Westlake, B.B. Blunder's sole outing had some nice typically thick circa 1970 British rock guitars, and some bits of promising melodies buried in the mix. Overall, though, one gets the impression that the group went into the studio before getting the songs into shape—there's a lot of meandering, and the songs either don't say much or never get to the point. Mick Taylor makes a little-known cameo appearance on bottleneck guitar on "New Day." —*Richie Unterberger*

Kurtis Blow

b. Aug. 9, 1959, New York, NY
Vocals, Keyboards / Old School Rap, Hip-Hop
No discussion of early hip-hop would be complete without some mention of Kurtis Blow, whose cocky, flamboyant, in-your-face brand of old-school rapping made him an inspiration to Run D.M.C., Whodini, and many other MCs who emerged in the early '80s. Born in New York on August 9, 1959, Blow grew up in Harlem and was rapping in Charles Gallery (a Harlem club) as early as 1976. In 1977 and 1978, the MC's frequent club appearances earned him a small inner-city cult following in Harlem and the South Bronx. But it wasn't until 1979 that Blow enjoyed his first taste of national exposure. That year, he signed with Mercury (Blow was the first rapper to record for a major label) and provided his debut single, "Christmas Rappin'." The song did OK nationally, but not as well as Blow's second single, "The Breaks," a 1980 gem that went to number four on Billboard's R&B singles chart and was certified gold by the RIAA. It was also in 1980 that Blow recorded his self-titled debut album, which was the first rap album to come out on a major label. Several other Mercury LPs followed, including *Deuce* in 1981, *Tough* in 1982, and *Ego Trip* in 1984. By 1984, Blow's rapping style was sounding dated; nonetheless, he had gone down in history as one of hip-hop's most influential pioneers. Blow, who turned 40 in 1999, wasn't as visible in the 1990s, although he hosted a hip-hop radio show on L.A.'s KPWR-FM (Power 106) and wrote the liner notes for Rhino's 1997 series Kurtis Blow Presents the History of Rap. *—Alex Henderson*

★ **The Best of Kurtis Blow** / Jun. 7, 1994 / Mercury ✦✦✦✦✦
While he made many groundbreaking singles, Kurtis Blow was never a consistent album artist, making this best-of collection his definitive artistic statement. Throughout the early '80s, Blow helped define what rap could do, and these tracks confirm his status as one of hip-hop's legendary acts. *—Stephen Thomas Erlewine*

Blue Cheer

f. 1967, San Francisco, CA, **db.** 1972
Acid Rock, Heavy Metal, Psychedelic, Hard Rock
San Francisco-based Blue Cheer was what, in the late '60s, they used to call a "power trio": Dickie Peterson (b. 1948, Grand Forks, ND) (bass, vocals), Paul Whaley (drums), and Leigh Stephens (guitar). They played what later was called heavy metal, and when they debuted in January 1968 with the album *Vincebus Eruptum* and a Top 40 cover of Eddie Cochran's hit "Summertime Blues," they sounded louder and more extreme than anything that had come before them. As it turned out, they were a precursor of much that would come after. Unfortunately, Blue Cheer itself didn't get much chance to profit from its prescience. Shortly after its breakthrough, the group was wracked by personnel changes. Leigh Stephens was replaced by Randy Holden after the release of the second album, *Outsideinside* (August 1968). Holden left during the recording of the third album, and Bruce Stephens (b. 1946) (vocals, guitar), and Ralph Burns Kellogg (keyboards) joined to finish *New! Improved! Blue Cheer* (March 1969). Then Whaley quit and was replaced by Norman Mayell (b. 1942, Chicago), leaving Peterson as the only original member. Bruce Stephens quit during the recording of the fourth album, *Blue Cheer* (December, 1969), and Gary L. Yoder joined to complete it. Peterson, Kellogg, Mayell, and Yoder then made *The Original Human Being* (September 1970), and *Oh! Pleasant Hope* (April, 1971) before Blue Cheer broke up. Dickie Peterson reorganized a new version of the group in 1979, and in 1985, Peterson, Whaley, and guitarist Tony Ranier released a new Blue Cheer album, *The Beast Is Back...* *—William Ruhlmann*

● **Vincebus Eruptum** / Jan. 1968 / Polygram ✦✦✦✦✦
Had "Summertime Blues" not gone Top 15 in the spring of 1968, Blue Cheer might not have had the opportunity to unleash their expression over numerous albums through multiple personnel changes. *Vincebus Eruptum* sports a serious silver/off-purple cover wrapped around the punk-metal fury. Leigh Stephens is nowhere near Hendrix, Beck, Clapton, or Jimmy Page, the skill of a Yardbird replaced by a thud of bass/drums/low-end guitar. Vocalist Dickie Peterson takes almost six minutes on Allison's "Parchment Farm" to talk about shooting his arm, shooting his wife, picking cotton, and having sex. Definitely more risqué than Grand Funk Railroad's "T.N.U.C.," Abe "Voco" Kesh's production is almost nonexistent. They certainly influenced the way Grand Funk would take the power trio; you can hear in Peterson's voice that tonal quality Mark Farner had to employ as well to get the lyrics over the morass of sound. *Vincebus Eruptum* is a dark power trio recording with punk attitude exploring blues through heavy metal. That a later version of the band would go on to produce "I'm the Light," a spacy cosmic anthem as delicate as Grand Funk's "Closer to Home," says a lot about the musical journey initiated by *Vincebus Eruptum*. The album is an underappreciated classic with "Rock Me Baby" leaning more toward Ten Years After than Steppenwolf, without Alvin Lee's technical expertise. Guitar that quivers and roars with a heavy dependence on rhythm à la the Who, Blue Cheer knows that attitude is as important as musicianship in rock, and they exploit that virtue for all it is worth here. *—Joe Viglione*

Outsideinside / Aug. 1968 / Polygram ✦✦✦✦
There's a swagger and aggression to Blue Cheer's power blues that can be traced through the decades of heavy metal and the post-metal mutations of hard music. The second of only two Blue Cheer recordings featuring the classic lineup of Leigh Stephens on guitar, Dickie Peterson on bass and lead vocals, and Paul Whaley playing drums, *Outsideinside*, along with its predecessor, *Vincebus Eruptum*, ranks among the most underappreciated hard rock collections ever. Blue Cheer's second, more refined offering stands as a testament to the power-for-its-own-sake mentality that helped forge '70s hard rock out of the blues, psychedelia, and energetic rock & roll. Whaley's hyper drumming sounds almost punk during a frantic rework of the Rolling Stone's "Satisfaction" and the instrumental "Magnolia Caboose Babyfinger." This was quite an accomplishment considering that *Outsideinside* was released a full year before either the Stooges' debut or MC5's *Kick Out the Jams*. Stephens' fuzzed-out guitar solos shift and weave through each of *Outsideinside*'s nine tracks, but the guitars work best as rhythmic support of Peterson's vocals on the standout tracks "Just a Little Bit" and "Come and Get It." Unfortunately, Blue Cheer simply did not possess the virtuosity to fight through the record's more ambitious moments; when the San Francisco trio tries to cop Hendrix in "Sun Cycle," the music sputters and loses focus. In true metal tradition, critics have generally ignored Blue Cheer's vast musical influence except for the most derivative of bands. Meanwhile, artists like Smashing Pumpkins, Mudhoney, and the Melvins have consistently covered the group both live and in the studio. Anyone interested in the history of hard music will want to familiarize themselves with this exceptional, innovative release. *—Vincent Jeffries*

Good Times Are So Hard to Find: The History of Blue Cheer / Oct. 1990 / Mercury ✦✦✦✦
Blue Cheer's massive contribution to the early evolution of American heavy metal exists entirely on their first two 1968 releases, *Vincebus Eruptum* and *Outsideinside*. While those initial releases charted admirably, critics largely ignored the band's loud, bluesy, psychedelic-tinged hard rock. The touchy-feely summer of love lasted a lot longer than three months and building heavy metal momentum in the States was a difficult affair. There resulted some lineup shifts, minor stylistic excursions, brief creative flourishes, more lineup changes, solo projects, half retirement, and reunion retreads. Some decent songs were recorded during that long descent and fortunately many of them were picked to grace the track list of *Good Times Are So Hard to Find*. Chief among them is the title cut and "Pilot" from 1970's *Original Human Being*. Other tracks from the group's eponymous release and 1971's *Oh! Pleasant Hope* have a boogie-down and MOR feel respectively that, while competent, contains hardly any of the group's original fire. Of course there are a few 1968 classics like the splendid "Out of Focus," "Parchment Farm," and the band's first (and only) big hit "Summertime Blues." Fans of '70s rock in its many forms might enjoy this 1990 retrospective, but metal historians need not worry about anything beyond Blue Cheer's first two offerings. *—Vincent Jeffries*

The Blue Nile

f. 1981, Glasgow, Scotland
College Rock, Sophisti-Pop, Dream Pop, Adult Alternative Pop/Rock
The Scottish folk-ambient band the Blue Nile has enjoyed a mystique contrived by its inaccessibility and the infrequency of its recordings, but it has also made a series of critically acclaimed discs. The group was formed by three Glasgow natives who had graduated from university there: singer/songwriter/guitarist Paul Buchanan, bassist Robert Bell, and keyboardist Paul Joseph Moore. (Engineer Callum Malcolm and drummer Nigel Thomas have worked with the trio consistently, to the point of being considered secondary band members.) (*The Blue Nile* is the title of Alan Moorehead's 1962 sequel to *The White Nile*, the two books making up a history of the Nile River.) They recorded their own single, "I Love This Life," which was distributed by Robert Stigwood's RSO Records just before the company closed its doors. They were then signed by Linn Products, which released their debut album, *A Walk Across the Rooftops*, in 1984. (A&M handled it in the U.S.) Since the company was small and the band did not tour, the album took some time to find its audience, though it briefly reached the U.K. charts and led to high expectations for a second album. This came in 1989 with *Hats*, which reached the British Top 20, throwing off three chart singles, "The Downtown Lights," "Headlights on the Parade," and "Saturday Night." The album also made the lower reaches of the American charts as the Blue Nile embarked on its first tour, a 30-date journey taking place in the British Isles and the U.S. In the ensuing years, the band members switched record labels, signing to Warner Bros., and contributed to recordings by Robbie Robertson and Julian Lennon. They finally emerged with their third album, *Peace at Last*, in June 1996. Another critically acclaimed release, it placed in the U.K. Top 20, but failed to chart in the U.S. *—William Ruhlmann*

A Walk Across the Rooftops / May 1984 / A&M ✦✦✦✦
The Blue Nile's debut LP is an oblique, supremely enigmatic work which immediately establishes the Glaswegian trio as a force to be reckoned with; while *A Walk Across the Rooftops* doesn't iron all the wrinkles out of the group's spaciously atmospheric sound, its thoughtful and original use of electronic textures nevertheless makes for compelling listening, an experience furthered by Paul Buchanan's keen sense of compositional dynamics on such highlights as "Tinseltown in the Rain" and "Stay." *—Jason Ankeny*

● **Hats** / Oct. 1989 / A&M ✦✦✦✦✦
Five long years in the making, the Blue Nile's stellar *Hats* was well worth the wait; sweeping and majestic, it's a triumph of personal vision over the cold, remote calculations of technology. While created almost solely without benefit of live instruments, it is nevertheless an immensely warm and human album; Paul Buchanan's plaintive vocals and poignant songs are uncommonly moving, and his deployment of lush synth washes and electronic percussion is never gratuitous, each song instead crafted with painterly precision. Impressionistic and shimmering, tracks like "The Downtown Lights" and "From a Late Night Train" are perfectly evocative of their titles: Rich in romantic atmosphere and detail, they conjure a nocturnal fantasy world lit by neon and shrouded in fog, leaving *Hats* an intensely cinematic experience as well as a masterpiece of musical obsession. *—Jason Ankeny*

Peace at Last / Jun. 1996 / Warner Brothers ✦✦✦
The members of the Blue Nile seem to have taken seriously all those articles and reviews about what audiophiles and technicians they are, and this time around they've spent a half-dozen years concocting an album that sounds like they made at least some of it in

their living rooms rather than their space-age studio. They achieve the appearance of simplicity and humanity by foregrounding either an acoustic guitar or piano on most tracks, by restraining other instrumentation, by making their synthesizers sound like strings most of the time, and by using real strings on occasion. All of which makes for appropriate settings for Paul Buchanan's songs of domestic contentment. "Happiness," "Sentimental Man," "Holy Love": the titles tell the story, though they don't reveal the underlying fear that it will all go bust. ("Now that I've found peace at last," Buchanan sings to open up the album, "Tell me, Jesus, will it last?") Nor do they explain why a guy who keeps insisting that he's happy sounds so mournful. Buchanan belongs to the Bono/Peter Gabriel school of throaty emotiveness, in which sudden, arbitrary ascensions toward the falsetto signal fits of otherwise unacknowledged passion (or maybe just a sneeze coming on). In Buchanan, the singing style and the loose structure of the songs make his protestations of tranquility unconvincing. That may be what he intends, especially since they lend an implied depth to what is the Blue Nile's lightest effort yet. — *William Ruhlmann*

Blue Öyster Cult

f. 1967, Long Island, NY
Album Rock, Arena Rock, Heavy Metal, Hard Rock
Blue Öyster Cult was the thinking man's heavy-metal group. Put together on a college campus by a couple of rock critics, it maintained a close relationship with a series of literary figures (often in the fields of science fiction and horror), while turning out some of the more listenable metal music of the early and mid '70s. Formed by Sandy Pearlman and Richard Meltzer with guitarist Donald "Buck Dharma" Roeser, the group later added vocalist Eric Bloom and released two albums (one as Soft White Underbelly, another as Oaxaca) before debuting as Blue Öyster Cult in 1972. Their fourth studio album, *Agents of Fortune*, included the Top 40 hit single "(Don't Fear) the Reaper" (featured in the classic John Carpenter horror film *Halloween*). The group continued recording albums popular with hard rock audiences during the late '70s before a series of lineup changes curtailed their career during the '80s. After being dropped from Columbia in 1988, BÖC scored the movie *Bad Channels* in 1992 and, two years later, released an album of rerecorded favorites (*Cult Classic*), in connection with the use of their music in the TV miniseries of horror novelist Stephen King's *The Stand*. — *William Ruhlmann*

Blue Öyster Cult / Jan. 1972 / Columbia/Legacy ✦✦✦✦✦
Blue Öyster Cult's debut album provided the missing link between the heavy, blues-based rock of the late '60s and the bombastic heavy metal of the '70s and beyond. You could hear major influences like Steppenwolf, with its melodic, aggressive rock, the Rolling Stones (post-1965), and even boogie bands like Canned Heat in their sound. But BÖC streamlined the approach, picked up the tempo, overlaid the guitars, brought the rhythm section up in the mix, and de-emphasized the blues, giving the music a machinelike propulsion. Manager/co-producer Sandy Pearlman (who co-wrote five songs) and lyricist Richard Meltzer (who co-wrote two) may have seen the group as a vehicle for their "clever" (in fact, pretentious) lyrics, but in fact lead vocalist Eric Bloom was the weakest element in the band, and you couldn't make out much of what he had to say over guitarist Donald "Buck Dharma" Roeser's furious power chording. What you could seemed to express some sort of mythology—or demonology; future metal bands would fill their songs with just such half-baked philosophies. *Blue Öyster Cult* was not quite full-fledged heavy metal: the production was too compressed, the playing too light and energetic. But it was the sound of something new and different in the world of hard rock. [The 2001 CD reissue on Columbia/Legacy adds four previously unreleased demos from 1969, when they were known as Soft White Underbelly, including a cover of Bobby Freeman's "Betty Lou's Got a New Pair of Shoes."] — *William Ruhlmann*

Tyranny and Mutation / Feb. 1973 / Columbia/Legacy ✦✦✦✦✦
Co-producers Murray Krugman and Sandy Pearlman achieved a far sharper, more spacious production on Blue Öyster Cult's second album than they had in the cramped sound of its first, twinning, for instance, the high, ringing tone of Donald Roeser's lead guitar to Albert Bouchard's cymbals or Alan Lanier's keyboards and adding echo to give presence to Eric Bloom's still barely (or not quite) discernable vocals. In a sense, it's remarkable that albums like this have been categorized as heavy metal: despite the fullness of the aural attack, the fast tempos and raunchy sound give it much more the feel of old rockabilly or punk-rock-to-come. [The 2001 CD reissue on Columbia/Legacy adds four bonus tracks: a live version of "Cities on Flame with Rock & Roll" (previously available on the promo-only *Bootleg EP*); a previously unissued studio version of "Buck's Boogie" recorded during the *Tyranny and Mutation* sessions; and previously unreleased live 1974 versions of "Screaming Diz-busters" and "OD'd on Life Itself."] — *William Ruhlmann*

Secret Treaties / Apr. 1974 / Columbia/Legacy ✦✦✦
If Blue Öyster Cult's first two albums had established its particular brand of high-energy hard rock and murky, if melodramatic, lyrical world view, *Secret Treaties* took a generic approach to that persona. The riffs (many recycled) ruled, and the same sort of imagery—titles like "Career of Evil," "Flaming Telepaths," and "Astronomy"—suggested that BÖC was rocking in place rather than moving forward. Maybe all that suggested a consistency of theme, especially in Sandy Pearlman and Richard Meltzer's mythology for the group, but it sounded dangerously like repetition; they'd said and done these things better on their debut. BÖC would take more than two years to make their next studio album. [The 2001 CD reissue on Columbia/Legacy adds five bonus tracks: the B-side cover of "Born to Be Wild," the single version of "Career of Evil," and three previously unreleased outtakes from the *Secret Treaties* sessions.] — *William Ruhlmann*

On Your Feet or on Your Knees / Feb. 1975 / Columbia ✦✦
Blue Öyster Cult's first live album was also its first to peak inside the Top 40, which is more of an indication of the audience the group was building up through extensive tour-

ing than of its quality. Songs that had a tight, concentrated impact on studio albums got elongated here, and that impact was dissipated. And the song selection left a great deal to be desired if this were to be a fitting summation of the band's career so far. By its 1974 tour, BÖC had dropped some classics from its first album, and the less impressive material from the third album was no substitute. — *William Ruhlmann*

Agents of Fortune / May 1976 / Columbia/Legacy ✦✦✦✦✦
Nothing Blue Öyster Cult had produced previously prepared listeners for its infectious mid-tempo hit, "(Don't Fear) the Reaper," which propelled it into a higher commercial orbit and caused (or reflected) a change in the balance of power in the group. The song was written by guitarist Donald "Buck Dharma" Roeser and was an indication that the band was now largely doing its own songwriting; co-producer Sandy Pearlman earned only one co-writing credit on the record, while drummer Albert Bouchard had five. Poetess Patti Smith, meanwhile, not only co-wrote two tracks, but also performed on one, "The Revenge of Vera Gemini." The result was a record much more in a pop-rock vein than the vaunted metal of the first three albums and BÖC's biggest hit ever. [The 2001 CD reissue on Columbia/Legacy adds four previously unreleased bonus tracks: the original version of "Fire of Unknown Origin" (recorded for the album but not used); a demo of "(Don't Fear) the Reaper"; a demo of "Dance the Night Away," not recorded for release by the band, but covered and issued by Jim Carroll; and the demo "Sally," a song which makes its first appearance here in any form.] — *William Ruhlmann*

Spectres / Oct. 1977 / Columbia ✦✦✦
On the all-important follow-up to its commercial breakthrough with *Agents of Fortune*, Blue Öyster Cult introduced some enjoyable additions to its repertoire in "Godzilla" and "R.U. Ready 2 Rock," but did not come up with a song as memorable as "(Don't Fear) the Reaper," despite trying the same formula with "Fireworks" and "Nosferatu." Instead of consolidating its success, the group seemed to be, as one of the better songs had it, "Goin' Through the Motions," seemingly unable to follow through on the pop aspirations of the previous album and unwilling to retreat to the metal pretensions of its early records. Talk about being caught between a rock and a hard place—just when Blue Öyster Cult should have been conquering, they seemed ready to retreat. — *William Ruhlmann*

Some Enchanted Evening / Sep. 1978 / Columbia ✦✦

Mirrors / Jun. 1979 / Columbia ✦✦✦
Blue Öyster Cult tried a new producer on *Mirrors*, replacing longtime mentor Sandy Pearlman with Tom Werman, a CBS staffer who had worked with Cheap Trick and Ted Nugent. The result is an album that tried to straddle pop and hard rock just as those acts did, emphasizing choral vocals (plus female backup) and a sharp, trebly sound. But this approach appeared to displease longtime metal-oriented fans without attracting new ones: "In Thee" became a minor singles-chart entry, but the album broke BÖC's string of five gold or platinum albums in a row. The real reason simply may have been that the songs weren't distinctive enough. Much of this was generic hard rock that could have been made by any one of a dozen '70s arena bands. — *William Ruhlmann*

Cultosaurus Erectus / Jun. 1980 / Columbia ✦✦✦
Signing on with Deep Purple/Black Sabbath producer Martin Birch, Blue Öyster Cult made more of a guitar-heavy hard-rock album in *Cultosaurus Erectus*, after flirting with pop ever since the success of *Agents of Fortune*. (They also promoted this album by going out on a co-headlining tour with Sabbath.) Gone are the female backup singers, the pop hooks, the songs based on keyboard structures, and they are replaced by lots of guitar solos and a beefed-up rhythm section. But the band still was not generating strong enough material to compete with their concert repertoire, so they found themselves in the bind of being a strong touring act unable to translate that success into record sales. — *William Ruhlmann*

Fire of Unknown Origin / Jun. 1981 / Columbia ✦✦✦✦
Just when Blue Öyster Cult was nearly written off after a series of mediocre albums, the band came roaring back with *Fire of Unknown Origin*, their best record in five years, on which they found the appropriate mixture of metal, rock, and pop that had eluded them since "(Don't Fear) the Reaper." With Sandy Pearlman, Richard Meltzer, and Patti Smith, among others, back in the writing credits, the Cult sounded like they'd been listening hard to their first two albums and *Agents of Fortune* for inspiration. Images of fire, darkness, and war were everywhere, the guitar riffs were inventive, and the melodies compelling. There was a new hit single in the Top 40, "Burnin' for You," but the overall song quality was unusually high. Somehow, BÖC had recaptured the trashy gothic appeal of its best work, and the result was a gold-selling album that seemed to put the band's career back on track. — *William Ruhlmann*

Extraterrestrial Live / Apr. 1982 / Columbia ✦✦✦
Of Blue Öyster Cult's three live albums, this is the one to own. The two-record set, partially recorded on BÖC's home base of Long Island, contains the band's biggest hits, "(Don't Fear) the Reaper" (making its second live appearance) and "Burnin' for You," as well as longtime concert favorites like "Cities on Flame," "The Red and the Black," and "Godzilla." But it isn't just the superior song selection that gives this album the nod over *On Your Feet or on Your Knees* and *Some Enchanted Evening*; BÖC had regained its momentum in 1981 with *Fire of Unknown Origin*, and this album demonstrated their renewed spirit in the forum in which they were most comfortable—live work. In the absence of a good compilation of studio work, *Extraterrestrial Live* is the best overview of BÖC available. — *William Ruhlmann*

The Revolution by Night / Oct. 1983 / Columbia ✦✦

Club Ninja / Jan. 1986 / Koch International ✦✦

Career of Evil: The Metal Years / 1987 / Columbia ✦✦

Imaginos / Jul. 1988 / Columbia ✦✦✦

Cult Classic / Jun. 14, 1994 / Herald ✦✦

Workshop of the Telescopes / Sep. 26, 1995 / Columbia/Legacy ✦✦✦✦✦

Blue Öyster Cult was long in need of a thorough career retrospective, and this is it. Thirty-two tracks filling up two discs with a total running time of 154:46, *Workshop of the Telescopes* traces BÖC through 14 years as the kings of lite metal, 1972-1986. Actually, as annotator Arthur Levy notes, there are at least two phases in that era. The first, running through 1974, includes the classic first two albums, *Blue Öyster Cult* and *Tyranny and Mutation*, when BÖC was one of the few acts in those pre-punk days bucking the trend toward soft rock without indulging in the more grotesque aspects of heavy metal. This material takes up disc one. Disc two leads off with "(Don't Fear) the Reaper," which launched the second phase of the band's career, when it sought to balance its hard rocking approach (heard especially in concert) with pop accessibility. Since this period was marked by uneven material, it is ripe for compiling, and the selection here is good. (We could have used a bit more from *Agents of Fortune*, but that's a quibble.) On the whole, *Workshop of the Telescopes* lives up to Levy's description of it as "the ultimate BÖC anthology." It's about time. —*William Ruhlmann*

● **Don't Fear The Reaper: The Best Of Blue Öyster Cult** / Feb. 8, 2000 / Columbia/Legacy ✦✦✦✦✦

With 16 cuts spanning 1971-83, this is a briefer, single-disc counterpart to the 1995 double-CD *Workshop of the Telescopes* compilation. This has taken care—perhaps too much care—to draw evenly from all of their first nine studio albums, with one or two songs from each (except for *Spectres*, which is represented by three). The early years are a little underrepresented, with just a tune apiece from *Blue Öyster Cult* and *Tyranny and Mutation*. For listeners on a tight budget, this might be satisfactory, but otherwise it's a considerably inferior value to the much more comprehensive *Workshop of the Telescopes*. —*Richie Unterberger*

The Blue Ridge Rangers

f. 1973, United States, **db.** 1973

Roots Rock, Rock & Roll

The Blue Ridge Rangers were never a band. In fact, it was never more than one person: Creedence Clearwater Revival heart and soul John Fogerty. With acrimony over the breakup of Creedence (or more to the point, the jettisoning of rhythm players Stu Cook and Doug Clifford) still fresh, Fogerty released what is ostensibly his first solo album, notable for being an all-covers country/gospel record and for Fogerty's impression of Todd Rundgren by playing all the instruments, overdubbing all the vocals, producing—everything but selling it door-to-door. The point(s) of submerging his identity (Fogerty's face is nowhere on the jacket cover) was to put some distance between himself and the Creedence legacy he wore like an albatross, pay homage to the American vernacular music he loved, and, rather inconspicuously (except for that distinctive voice), announce himself as a solo performer. Oddly enough, life as a solo artist (compounded by lengthy litigation against former Fantasy Records chair Saul Zaentz) didn't seem to agree with Fogerty, and his extremely limited production (a total of four records in 22 years), while not helping him in terms of sales, did, ironically, cement his reputation as an American rock icon. —*John Dougan*

The Blue Ridge Rangers / 1973 / Fantasy ✦✦✦

With wonderfully chosen songs like "Hearts of Stone" and George Jones's classic country weeper "She Thinks I Still Care," Fogerty's solo debut has held up well over the last two decades. It isn't the most supple or technically proficient one-man recording of all time, but it's a wonderfully engaging record; upbeat, unpretentious, and loaded with good songs. Fogerty's rigid, no-frills drumming took a lot of heat for being mechanical, but no one has ever explained to my satisfaction how Fogerty's abilities on the trap kit are significantly different from Creedence's Doug Clifford. In retrospect, this was a tremendously risky record to make; country music in the early '70s was regarded as the domain of right-wing, rock & roll-hating Nashville traditionalists, and it was reasonable to assume that fans (even staunch ones) wouldn't take kindly to this genre switch. While it wasn't a huge success, it was in no way a disaster, and perhaps more importantly, served as a much-needed rock & roll history lesson. —*John Dougan*

Blue Rodeo

f. 1985

Heartland Rock, Americana, Alternative Country-Rock, Folk-Rock

Blue Rodeo's style has drawn comparisons to a number of pop and rock icons, including the Beatles, Buffalo Springfield, the Band, and Bob Dylan. Formed in Toronto, Blue Rodeo is led by the songwriting team of vocalists/guitarists Jim Cuddy and Greg Keelor, and also features bassist Bazil Donovan, drummer Glenn Milchem, and keyboardist Bob Wiseman, who also plays harmonica and accordion. Their debut album, 1987's *Outskirts*, showcased the group's harmonies and musical interplay in a classic, rootsy folk-rock style. The punchier *Diamond Mine* (1989) covered more lyrical ground, bringing a bit of social commentary into Blue Rodeo's tales of loss and heartbreak, but the recording site (an empty hall in Toronto) dulled the songs' impact somewhat. In 1990, Wiseman recorded his own solo album, *Bob Wiseman Sings Wrench Tuttle: In Her Dreams*. Producer Pete Anderson (Michelle Shocked, Dwight Yoakam) accentuated the group's vocal harmonies on the following year's *Casino*, which was well-received. Even higher praise was reserved for *Lost Together*, which synthesized the previous albums' stylistic changes into a cohesive whole. Wiseman left soon after the album's release, and was replaced on keyboards by James Gray. Also, Kim Deschamps joined the group on pedal steel. Blue

Rodeo continued innovating throughout the '90s, releasing three more studio albums during the decade. *The Days in Between* followed in mid-2000. —*Steve Huey*

Outskirts / 1987 / Discovery ✦✦✦

Outskirts is a highly likeable debut featuring mid-tempo country rockers fleshed out by tasteful use of organ in the arrangements—a subtle touch that, along with the sheer quality of the material, distinguished Blue Rodeo from the hordes of other Gram Parsons devotees in the mid-'80s. —*Chris Woodstra*

Diamond Mine / 1989 / Discovery ✦✦✦

Diamond Mine is a considerably more quiet affair. Beginning with the very Dylan-esque "God and Country," a darker, introverted mood is set by their minimalist approach and slow tempos. —*Chris Woodstra*

● **Casino** / 1991 / Discovery ✦✦✦✦

Casino is a more pop-oriented album. They seem to have finally established their fine blend of harmonies and laidback country-rock à la the Band and Bob Dylan. Produced by Pete Anderson (Dwight Yoakam, Michelle Shocked). —*Chris Woodstra*

Lost Together / Aug. 4, 1992 / Discovery ✦✦✦✦

Lost Together is easily the best Blue Rodeo album to date. Hit the random button on the disc player and no matter where the laser touches down, you're assured a worthwhile listening experience. Blue Rodeo have built a fortress on the foundation of their previous three outings. The straight pop song "Flying" and ballads "Already Gone" and the epic title track offer added depth and maturity without rehashing previous successes. "Willin' Fool" and "Angels" tackle the progressive elements of Blue Rodeo's second album *Diamond Mine* and sharpen them to a manic, cutting edge. "Fools Like You" spits out a defense of native rights, Greg Keelor doing his best outraged-Bob Dylan impression. —*Roch Parisien*

Five Days in July / Sep. 27, 1994 / Discovery ✦✦✦✦

While the members of Blue Rodeo are stars in their native Canada, the roots-based band remains a brilliant, well-kept secret south of the border. Blue Rodeo's fifth album *Five Days in July* didn't heighten the band's profile, but it is another stellar entry into the sextet's catalog. The group continues to experiment with longer mood pieces like the sparse, gentle (save for some fierce, almost dissonant guitar from Greg Keelor) title track. Lead singer Jim Cuddy's warm vocals add to the compelling, emotional thrust of songs like the infectious "It Hasn't Hit Me Yet," the heartbreakingly honest "Bad Timing" (with some breathtaking harmonies between Cuddy and Keelor), and the plaintive "English Bay." Sarah McLachlan lends some vocals (and piano) to a couple tracks, including the solemn "Dark Angel." *Five Days in July* builds on Blue Rodeo's wonderful blend of melodic rock and Americana, while continuing to push out around the edges, and it does so in spectacular fashion. —*Tom Demalon*

Nowhere to Here / Sep. 5, 1995 / Discovery ✦✦✦✦

Blue Rodeo continues to experiment on this release. Opening and closing with expansive mood pieces, it takes a little bit of listening to get into this album. But sandwiched in between lies the real meat of this record. Bluesy ballads such as "Sky" and "Train" are balanced by upbeat poptunes like "What You Want" and "Better Off as We Are." The rockin' Beatles-esque "Get Through to You" shows them in top form. Every song here tends to evoke the pictoral majesty of the Canadian countryside while never sounding hokey. Once you let these tunes seep into your psyche, you'll find there isn't a bum tune in the bunch. Fantastic! —*James Chrispell*

Tremolo / Jul. 15, 1997 / Discovery ✦✦✦

The songs on *Tremolo* were deliberately sprung on the entire group on the day of recording, in order to ensure spontaneity—they spent a day working on each song, but not becoming overly familiar with any of it, in order to keep a fresh edge to their performances. And for the most part, it worked—the result is a technically polished album that retains a good deal of jam-type spontaneity, and can rank up there with the very best work of Poco; indeed, this is sort of the studio analog to that group's most popular early-'70s album, *Deliverin'*, achieving similar results in the reverse manner. The sounds range from genial acoustic folk-rock ("Moon and Tree") to more reflective singer/songwriter-type pieces like "Falling Down Blue" to bluesier songs like "Fallen from Grace" and harder, heavier numbers like "No Miracle, No Dazzle," which could pass for Buffalo Springfield on a good day. Other numbers aren't quite as strong, and a few, like "Disappear," run a little too long for their own good; but then there are songs like "It Could Happen to You," with its dazzling word-play and wonderfully fluid guitar work which, in an alternate universe, would have been the greatest song ever written by Richie Furay. And "Brother Andre's Heart" bears a startling—but not unpleasant or excessive—resemblance to "Wild Horses" as the Flying Burrito Brothers did the song. One must conclude, a triumphant album. —*Bruce Eder*

Just Like a Vacation / 1999 / WEA ✦✦✦

The Days in Between / Jan. 11, 2000 / WEA ✦✦✦

The Blue Things

f. 1964, **db.** 1967

Folk-Rock, Garage Rock

Along with the Remains, the Blue Things are serious contenders for the title of the Great Lost Mid-'60s American Band. The Kansas group was extremely popular in the Midwest and Texas, but remained unknown on a national level, despite a deal with RCA. Piloted by the songwriting of singer and guitarist Val Stecklein, the group often sounded like a cross between the Byrds and the Beau Brummels with their melodic, energetic, guitar-oriented folk-rock and haunting harmonies. The group's sole album (*Listen & See*, 1966) and several singles chart a rapid growth from British Invasion-like material with a heavy

Searchers and Buddy Holly influence to full-blown psychedelic efforts with careening guitars, organ, and backward effects. Quite innovative for the time, these 1966 psychedelic singles met with no more than regional success. The group's impetus was derailed by the departure of Stecklein at the end of 1966, although they struggled on for a bit. Stecklein went to California and recorded a disappointing MOR folk album for Dot in the late '60s that reprised some of his Blue Things songs. *—Richie Unterberger*

Listen & See / 1966 / RCA ♦♦♦♦♦
One of the most underappreciated albums of the '60s. Composed of Val Stoecklein originals and well-chosen covers, the group synthesized the Beatles and Dylanesque folk-rock with a skill similar to the Byrds. Ringing 12-string and acoustic guitars, melodic harmonies, passionate vocals, and strong material abound on this nearly forgotten near-classic. *—Richie Unterberger*

The Blue Things Story, Vol. 1 (1964-1965) / 1987 / Cicadelic ♦♦♦
This collection of 1964 and 1965 demos, coupled with some rare early singles, shows the band at its most British Invasion-influenced. It has quite a few fine Beatlesesque harmony rockers by Stocklein, along with some nifty covers. There's a marked difference between the 1964 and 1965 demos, which show the band shifting from British Invasion emulation to a more mature and far more folk-rock-influenced direction. *—Richie Unterberger*

The Blue Things Story, Vol. 2 (1965-1966) / 1987 / Cicadelic ♦♦♦♦
Basically a repackage of *Listen & See*, with a couple of the less impressive cover songs deleted. In their place are four fine previously unreleased demos, two of which feature the entire band, two of which are performed by Stocklein alone on acoustic guitar. The epic ballad "Desert Wind" is a special standout among the previously unreleased cuts. *—Richie Unterberger*

The Blue Things Story, Vol. 3 (1966) / 1987 / Cicadelic ♦♦♦
Wraps up their legacy with all of their groundbreaking, non-LP 1966 single sides—"Orange Rooftop of Your Mind," "One Hour Cleaners," and "You Can Live in Our Tree." It also has half a dozen 1966 demos (several acoustic), some of which are early versions of songs that ended up on *Listen & See*. The package is rounded out by a few impressive 1967 cuts from the post-Stocklein lineup, consisting of a couple of unreleased originals by other band members and their astounding psychedelic fuzz-guitar rearrangement of "Twist and Shout." *—Richie Unterberger*

● **The Blue Things** / 2001 / Rewind ♦♦♦♦♦
This self-titled CD reissue is basically a reissue of their only album (from 1966), which has been known both as *Listen & See* and *The Blue Things*, bolstered by the significant addition of all six songs from their three non-LP 1966-1967 RCA singles. All of this material, except the final 1967 single (recorded after the departure of Val Stecklein), has been reissued in some form on other releases. This edition, however, has a big advantage over other reissues in that it was remastered from the RCA tapes, also adding extensive, excellent historical liner notes. As for the 1966 album that forms the backbone of this disc, it's still one of the finest overlooked folk-rock records of the 1960s, combining some of the best elements of the Byrds and Beau Brummels in its mid-tempo electric-acoustic arrangements. The 1966 psychedelic single tracks "Orange Rooftop of Your Mind," "One Hour Cleaners," and "You Can Live in Our Tree" are also fine cuts that show the band progressing at a furious rate, with psychologically complex lyrics and unusual fuzz and violin-ish distorted guitar textures. The final single ("Somebody Help Me"/"Yes, My Friend"), though, was a pretty lame offering considering the quality of the band's prior RCA efforts. *—Richie Unterberger*

The Blues Brothers

Retro-Soul, Soul

Whether celebrated as a sincere tribute or derided as a tongue-in-cheek put-on, the Blues Brothers—Joliet Jake and his silent brother Elwood—was among the most popular groups of the late '70s; what started as a skit on the hit NBC television sketch comedy series *Saturday Night Live* quickly snowballed to become a true phenomenon, complete with hit records, a sold-out concert tour, and even a feature film. Clad in vintage black suits, narrow ties, fedoras, and omnipresent wrap-around sunglasses, the Blues Brothers delivered spirited renditions of classic soul hits in the tradition of the signature Stax-Volt sound; purists may still cringe, but if nothing else the group deserves credit for introducing any number of soul and blues classics to a new generation of listeners while also allowing some of the most gifted session men in the business a chance to shine on stage and screen. In reality, vocalist Jake and harpist Elwood were music lovers John Belushi and Dan Aykroyd, two of *SNL's* brightest stars who created their respective aliases in early 1976 to warm up crowds before performances of the hit series. The Blues Brothers made their national TV debut with Belushi and Aykroyd outfitted in the bee costumes they often wore for another sketch, performing (naturally enough) Slim Harpo's "I'm a King Bee," and in the months to follow they grew in popularity, releasing a series of hit albums and starring in a 1980 film prior to Belushi's 1982 death from an accidental drug overdose. *—Jason Ankeny*

Briefcase Full of Blues / Dec. 1978 / Atlantic ♦♦♦♦
"The Blues Brothers" began as an affectionate joke-cum-tribute to R&B music, and taken in that spirit it retained its entertainment value, even after this live album topped the charts, sold two million copies, and produced hit singles in "Rubber Biscuit" and "Soul Man." The guardians of popular music have always been entirely too reverent and humorless, however, and it wasn't long before they were leveling charges of rip-off against the Brothers and complaining that John Belushi couldn't sing as well as Otis Redding. So what? No one seems to have noticed that Belushi was as obsessive about citing his sources as Frank Sinatra is about naming his arrangers—you'd have thought those critics would have appreciated the footnotes. The beneficiaries of Belushi's encomiums didn't mind the increased exposure or the renewed royalty checks ("I suggest you buy as many blues albums as you can," Belushi told the audience), and even today, what comes across in these performances is the sincerity of feeling—that and some tasty playing from a top-notch band. *—William Ruhlmann*

Blues Brothers [Original Soundtrack] / Jun. 1980 / Atlantic ♦♦♦
Comic actors John Belushi and Dan Aykroyd received a lot of flak for their Blues Brothers shtick—mostly for the albums, not 1980's beloved classic film. But they should be given credit for exposing many people—including this reviewer—to the music of blues and R&B veterans. *The Blues Brothers* soundtrack was released on Atlantic Records. On the surface this doesn't seem unusual, since the Blues Brothers' Atlantic debut, *Briefcase Full of Blues*, was a number one album; but the movie was released by Universal, and its parent company, MCA, passed on the soundtrack. The rollicking remake of the Spencer Davis Group's "Gimme Some Lovin'" was a hit, featuring an arrangement notable for the horn section that replaces Steve Winwood's rumbling organ work. Ray Charles has a good time with "Shake a Tail Feather," and he's helped out by Jake and Elwood Blues (Belushi and Aykroyd, respectively). The cover of Solomon Burke's "Everybody Needs Somebody to Love" is a lot of fun, thanks to the great overall rhythm and Elwood's lightning-fast stage rap, while James Brown and the Reverend James Cleveland Choir provide a blast of gospel music on "Old Landmark." Aretha Franklin's "Think" is explosive, and Cab Calloway's "Minnie the Moocher" is slyly irresistible. Charles, Brown, Franklin, and Calloway all have small roles in the film, yet so does John Lee Hooker, but he's not represented here. *—Bret Adams*

The Best of the Blues Brothers / Dec. 1981 / Atlantic ♦♦♦
A solid collection, this includes the hits "Rubber Biscuit," "Soul Man," and "Gimme Some Lovin'," plus music from *The Blues Brothers* movie soundtrack. *—AMG*

● **The Definitive Collection** / 1992 / Atlantic ♦♦♦♦
Definitive, not in the sense that it contains everything that the Blues Brothers recorded, but definitive in the sense that it contains everything anybody would want to hear from the Blues Brothers. And that means anything from *Briefcase Full of Blues* or anything from *The Blues Brothers* soundtrack that anyone could want to hear, all of the hits and anthems that made the group a baby boomer favorite. No, these may not hold a candle to the originals, but they're spirited and fun, and they'll certainly introduce listeners to an amazing amount of good music. *—Stephen Thomas Erlewine*

The Blues Brothers Complete / May 2, 2000 / Wea International ♦♦♦♦
The title of *The Blues Brothers Complete* pretty much says it all; the double-disc, 35-track collection contains everything Jake and Elwood Blues recorded during the peak of their career. The catch is that the compilation was only released by EastWest/Atlantic's Australian division, therefore, it's hard to find outside of Australia. But, for hardcore fans, it's worth tracking down since it has every track from *Briefcase Full of Blues*, the soundtrack to *The Blues Brothers* (including the selections sung by Cab Calloway, James Brown, and Aretha Franklin), and *Made in America*, plus "I Ain't Got You," which was only on *The Best of the Blues Brothers*, and "From the Bottom," which was the B-side of the "Soul Man" single. In other words, it's everything. Some may laugh that anyone would want the complete works of the Blues Brothers who were often considered a joke (especially by blues purists), but in hindsight, these recordings don't sound bad at all. How could they when Belushi and Aykroyd were backed by a world-class studio band. And, a lot can be said for enthusiasm. No, Belushi wasn't the greatest vocalist, and neither was his brother, but he had true love and passion for this music, which translates in his performances. The result may not match the original recordings they strove to replicate, but they're fun and they undoubtedly introduced many listeners to the original artists. Strangely, that's the reason why they hold up fairly well; they were labors of love and that love is apparent throughout the recordings, from the truly impeccable song selection (they did have good taste) to the enthusiastic performances. *—Stephen Thomas Erlewine*

Blues Magoos

f. 1964, New York, NY [The Bronx], **db.** 1969
Garage Rock, Psychedelic

A Bronx-based quintet, denizens of the Greenwich Village club scene, and originally known by the *tres*-psychedelic moniker the Bloos Magoos (yikes!), the Blues Magoos made their mark in 1967 with a rousing, full-throttle, sub-literate, psychedelic garage rock single, "(We Ain't Got) Nothin' Yet." It wasn't a spacy, pretentious song, nor did it contain vague attempts at hippie-era mysticism, but was rather the kind of simple, direct, infectious rock & roll you could imagine five guys from the Bronx making. With a snotty lead vocal from keyboardist Ralph Scala and some wild-eyed guitar playing courtesy of then-16-year-old Emil "Peppy" Theilheim, America made the Magoos' debut single a Top Ten hit, sending it to number five in January 1967. With this impetus, the band used all the trappings of marketable psychedelia to promote their second album, *Psychedelic Lollipop*, which, despite the title's obvious pandering, was a fairly cool chunk of psych-garage rock: trebly, crappy-sounding guitars, a whiny Farfisa organ, yelled vocals, and a rhythm section that shelved nuance for thudding simplicity. But as the psychedelic era gave way to the hippie era's extended raga-rock proclivities, by 1969, the Magoos seemed anachronistic. Amazingly, they released a third album, with an equally idiotic title, *Electric Comic Book*, that wasn't nearly as bad as it sounds. The original Magoos split up in 1969, but Theilheim couldn't resist beating a dead horse and led a mediocre blues-rock version of the band into 1972. *—John Dougan*

● **Kaleidescopic Compendium: The Best of the Blues Magoos** / May 5, 1992 / Mercury ♦♦♦♦
The Blues Magoos were one of the most underrated U.S. bands of the late '60s, known almost exclusively for their one irresistible hit "(We Ain't Got) Nothing Yet," which charted

at #5 in July 1967. *Kaleidescopic Compendium: The Best Of The Blues Magoos* confirms the group's depth. The disc compiles a generous 23 tracks from their first three albums and a brace of single sides. The group's psychedelia holds up better than most from the period. Andy Sandoval's four-page history of the group is concise, complete, and entertaining. —*Roch Parisien*

Psychedelic Lollipop/Electric Comic Book / Jul. 27, 1999 / Collectables ✦✦✦✦

The Blues Project

f. 1965, New York, NY, db. 1972, New York, NY
Folk-Rock, Blues-Rock, Modern Electric Blues
One of the first album-oriented, "underground" groups in the United States, the Blues Project offered an electric brew of rock, blues, folk, pop, and even some jazz, classical, and psychedelia during their brief heyday in the mid-'60s. It's not quite accurate to categorize them as a blues-rock group, although they did plenty of that kind of material; they were more like a Jewish-American equivalent to British bands like the Yardbirds, who used a blues and R&B base to explore any music that interested them. Erratic songwriting talent and a lack of a truly outstanding vocalist prevented them from rising to the front line of '60s bands, but they recorded plenty of interesting material over the course of their first three albums, before the departure of their most creative members took its toll. —*Richie Unterberger*

Live at the Cafe Au-Go-Go / May 1966 / Verve/Forecast ✦✦✦
Although Tommy Flanders (who'd already left the band by the time this debut hit the streets) is credited as sole vocalist, four of the then-sextet's members sang; in fact, Danny Kalb handles as many leads as Flanders (four each), Steve Katz takes center stage on Donovan's "Catch the Wind," and Al Kooper is featured on "I Want to Be Your Driver." The band could be lowdown when appropriate (Kalb's reading of "Jelly, Jelly"), high energy (Muddy Waters' "Goin' Down Louisiana" sounds closer to Chuck Berry or Bo Diddley), and unabashedly eclectic (tossing in Donovan or Eric Andersen with no apologies). Kalb's moody take on "Alberta" is transcendent, and the up-tempo arrangement of "Spoonful" is surprisingly effective. —*Dan Forte*

Projections from the Past / Sep. 1, 1966 / Hablabel ✦✦✦
A double album of dubious legality, but fairly easy availability. This captures the Blues Project's best lineup—Kooper, Katz, Kalb, Kulberg, and Blumenfeld—live at the Matrix club in San Francisco on September 1, 1966. If there's any revelation to be had from these fair-quality tapes, it's that there's not much of a revelation at all. The group performs a lot of the stronger material from their first and second albums in versions very close to the records. They shine brightest on the more adventurous material with jazz and folk tangents, like "Steve's Song," "Flute Thing," "Catch the Wind," and "Cheryl's Going Home." Most of the rest is competent but not especially brilliant white-boy blues renditions of numbers like "Hoochie Coochie Man," "You Can't Catch Me," and "You Can't Judge a Book By the Cover"; the swaggering "Shake That Baby" is about the best of these. Essential only for serious collectors. Be warned that there are a few (not many) clumsy edits, and that the entire fourth side is simply tracks lifted from their *Live at Town Hall* LP. —*Richie Unterberger*

Projections / Nov. 1966 / Verve/Forecast ✦✦✦✦✦
Produced by Tom Wilson (Dylan, Zappa), the Blues Project's second effort was their finest hour. In less than a year the enthusiastic live band had matured into a seasoned studio ensemble. Steve Katz's features are lightweight folk but Al Kooper reworks two gospel themes ("Wake Me, Shake Me," "I Can't Keep from Crying") into ambitious blues-rock compositions, and Danny Kalb proves he's no mere folkie on extended versions of "Two Trains Running" and "Caress Me Baby." Bassist Andy Kulberg switches to flute and Kalb gets psychedelic on the jazzy "Flute Thing," penned by Kooper. —*Dan Forte*

The Best of the Blues Project [Rhino] / 1966-1967 / Rhino ✦✦✦✦✦
With the exception of a live version of "Flute Thing" from the Blues Project's 1973 reunion concert included only on the CD version, this compilation is culled entirely from the albums *Live at the Cafe Au-Go-Go*, *Projections*, and *The Blues Project Live at Town Hall*, all recorded and released in the period 1966-1967. Just as those individual albums do, it confirms the acclaim accorded the Blues Project at the time. The group's sophistication and ability to create a hybrid of musical styles keeps the music from sounding dated. In fact, this music not only stands as among the best of its time, but it continues to appeal where much of the music made simultaneously fails to escape its era. [Not to be confused with *No Time Like the Right Time—The Best of the Blues Project*, Verve Forecast FTS 3077 (1969 07), which is an earlier compilation with a different selection of songs.] —*William Ruhlmann*

The Blues Project Live at Town Hall / Sep. 1967 / One Way ✦✦✦
Released just after Al Kooper left the band, one imagines that neither he nor the other members of the group were pleased with this LP. According to Kooper, it was a pastiche of studio outtakes and a few live performances, and only one of the songs was actually recorded at New York City's Town Hall. Anyway, this has a meandering, ten-minute "Flute Thing" and decent live versions of "Wake Me, Shake Me" and "I Can't Keep from Crying" which, despite a somewhat rawer feel, are not necessary supplements to the fine studio takes. "Where There's Smoke, There's Fire" and the great "No Time Like the Right Time" had already been released as singles; to hear them without canned applause, you only need to turn to Rhino's first-rate *The Best of the Blues Project* instead. That compilation also contains the other cut of note on this album, an outtake-sounding cover of Patrick Sky's "Love Will Endure." —*Richie Unterberger*

No Time Like the Right Time—The Best of the Blues Project [Forecast] / Jul. 1969 / Verve/Forecast ✦✦✦✦

No Time Like the Right Time—The Best of the Blues Project is the best anthology of the band ever likely to be done. It encompasses their wealth of high points in better sound than ever. —*Bruce Eder*

Original Blues Project Reunion in Central Park / 1973 / One Way ✦✦✦
Considering that the original lineup had broken up six years earlier, this ranks as one of the most artistically successful reunions in blues or rock. If there were any ego problems, they don't show; typically Kalb and Kooper shine, but all five are playing as a team. Most important, the members seem to respect their own past—and re-create it with spontaneity and energy. —*Dan Forte*

● **Anthology** / Jan. 28, 1997 / Polydor/Chronicles ✦✦✦✦✦
The most complete Blues Project collection ever assembled, the two-disc *Anthology* compiles 36 tracks taken from their three albums on Verve and their two records on Capitol as well as rare singles, previously unreleased songs and alternate versions, and material from solo projects. —*Jason Ankeny*

Blues Traveler

f. 1988
Jam Bands, American Trad Rock, Pop/Rock, Blues-Rock
A New York-based blues-rock quartet formed in 1988 by singer/harmonica player John Popper, guitarist Chan Kinchla, bassist Bobby Sheehan, and drummer Brendan Hill. Blues Traveler was part of a revival of the extended jamming style of '60s and '70s groups like the Grateful Dead and Led Zeppelin. Signed to A&M, they released their first album, *Blues Traveler*, in May 1990 and followed it with *Travelers & Thieves* in September 1991. Popper was in a serious car accident in 1992, leaving him unable to perform for a number of months. Fortunately, he recovered, yet he still had to perform in a wheelchair for a period of time. In April 1993, Blues Traveler released its third album, *Save His Soul*, which became its first to make the Top 100. Blues Traveler's aptly named fourth album, *Four*, released in September 1994, at first looked like a sales disappointment, but it rebounded in 1995 when "Run-Around," a single taken from it, became the group's first chart hit. "Run-Around" became one of the biggest singles of 1995, spending nearly a full year on the charts and sending *Four* into quintuple platinum status.

As the group prepared the follow-up to *Four*, Blues Traveler released the live double-album *Live From the Fall* in the summer of 1996. The group returned in the summer of 1997 with its fifth studio album, *Straight on Till Morning*. After completing his 1999 debut solo effort *Zygote*, Popper—who'd been experiencing chest pains for months—was forced to undergo an angioplasty; weeks later, tragedy struck on August 20, 1999, when Sheehan was found dead in his New Orleans home. He was just 31 years old. The new millennium saw a newly charged Blues Traveler, and their sixth record, *Bridge*, appeared in April 2001. —*William Ruhlmann*

● **Blues Traveler** / May 1990 / A&M ✦✦✦✦
Blues Traveler's loose jam structures on basic blues riffs mark them as a band in the tradition of such predecessors as the Grateful Dead. Unlike that communal effort, however, this group has a distinct focal point in virtuoso harmonica player and vocalist John Popper, who keeps things from meandering too much. —*William Ruhlmann*

Travelers & Thieves / Sep. 1991 / A&M ✦✦✦
"I have my moments," John Popper declares, and many of them, as harmonica player, singer, and lyricist are here, on an album that finds Blues Traveler stretching out much as they do onstage. Popper is a man with a lot on his mind, but when he reaches "The Best Part," his verbosity approaches a Walt Whitman-like exuberance, and guitarist Chan Kinchla is right with him, contributing sweet fills here, Pete Townshend-style strumming there. And as for the rhythm work of bassist Bobby Sheehan and drummer Brendan Hill, as Popper says, "It's all in the groove." —*William Ruhlmann*

Save His Soul / Apr. 1993 / A&M ✦✦✦
Led by the guttural vocals and incisive harmonica of imposing frontman John Popper, *Save His Soul* is a savory package that dresses obvious influences in a fresh suit of clothes. While six and 12 strings rule, the true inspiration here is Popper's delivery on harmonica and other wind instruments, which spits in machine-gun-rapid fire or carries a piercing, emotive melody line with equal ease. Having restrained themselves for most of *Save His Soul*, Blues Traveler close with the seven-minute opus "Fledgling," flowing from epic, orchestral ballad mode to angst-ridden wall-of-noise. —*Roch Parisien*

Four / Sep. 13, 1994 / A&M ✦✦✦✦
Lacking the rootsier edge of *Save His Soul*, *Four* finds Blues Traveler retreating to their standard blues-boogie formula, with mixed results. Of course, there are some fine songs here—including their breakthrough hit single "Run-Around"—but too often the band sounds like they're coasting. *Four* is a solid record, but it shows signs that the band's formula may be wearing thin. —*Stephen Thomas Erlewine*

Live from the Fall / Jul. 1996 / A&M ✦✦✦✦✦
Like any jam-oriented band, Blues Traveler has a reputation for being better in concert than they are in the studio. Therefore, it would make sense that the double-disc *Live from the Fall* would be the ideal Blues Traveler album, since it allows the band to stretch out and demonstrate their true talents. In a sense, that is true. The two discs—which were recorded in the fall of 1995, as the band was supporting the surprise success of *Four*—do give the band room to improvise, and they exploit the extra space for all of its worth. Initially, Blues Traveler wanted to release without track indexes, so the listener could hear how each song flowed into the next. And the album does sound like that—like a never-ending medley, where melodic themes pop in and out of the long solos. Occasionally, they detour into covers (War's "Low Rider," John Lennon's "Imagine"), but they mainly weave a tapestry of their own material, including rarities like the B-side "Regarding Steven" and

the unreleased "Closing Down the Park." For fans of pop hits like "Run-Around" and "Hook," this can be a little irritating, but for those who have been with the band since the beginning, *Live from the Fall* is a priceless document—more than any other album, this showcases what Blues Traveler is about. *—Stephen Thomas Erlewine*

Straight on Till Morning / Jul. 1, 1997 / A&M ♦♦♦♦
The commercial success of *Four* was a mixed blessing for Blues Traveler. It did give them a wider audience, but it also put them in the delicate position of pleasing their new, hook-happy fans while retaining their hardcore, jam-oriented cult following. They skillfully manage to do just that on *Straight on Till Morning*, the bluesy, ambitious follow-up to *Four*. On the whole, *Straight on Till Morning* is a tougher album than any of its predecessors, boasting a gritty sound and several full-on jams. But the key to the album is its length and its sprawling collection of songs, which find Blues Traveler trying anything from country-rock to jangling pop/rock. They manage to be simultaneously succinct and eclectic, and they occasionally throw in a good pop hook or two. Blues Traveler is still too loose to be a true pop/rock band, and John Popper would still benefit from a sense of meter, but *Straight on Till Morning* is the first studio record that captures the essence of the band. *—Stephen Thomas Erlewine*

Bridge / Apr. 2001 / Interscope ♦♦♦♦
Blues Traveler went through a lot after their sequel to *Four*, *Straight on Till Morning*, stiffed in 1997. John Popper went through a severe health scare after cutting a schizophrenic solo album and, not long afterward, bassist Bob Sheehan died from a drug overdose. Reeling on both the personal and professional fronts, they took some time off, resurfacing mid-way through 2001 with *Bridge*, the album they should have released as the sequel to *Four*. This cuts back significantly on winding jams, upping the ante with tight songs and performances, a clean muscular production, and a lack of vocal histrionics from Popper. Melodically, they've rarely been stronger, and there's a sense of peace and maturity to the record that's appealing, especially since it's weighted with an undercurrent of loss and experience. This doesn't surface all that often, yet it's enough to provide a substantive center to one of the group's strongest records. They may not be in the public spotlight anymore, but the return to relative anonymity, along with the decade of experience underneath their belt, has mellowed and enriched their music, and while this may not be a record that will win new fans, it's certainly one that satisfies anyone that's taken the journey with them. *—Stephen Thomas Erlewine*

The Bluetones

f. 1994, Hounslow, England
Indie Pop, British Trad Rock, Britpop
The Bluetones filled the gap that the Stone Roses left behind, providing graceful but muscular guitar pop with slightly psychedelic overtones. The band appeared during the waning days of Brit-pop, which guaranteed them a considerable amount of press coverage that helped their debut album rocket to the top of the charts upon its release in early 1996.

Originally called the Bottlegarden, the Bluetones formed in Hounslow, England in 1994. The group consisted of guitarist Adam Devlin, drummer Ed Chester, vocalist Mark Morris, and his brother Scott, who played bass. All of the members had previously played in local bands before forming the Bluetones. During 1995, the group released two singles, "Are You Blue or Are You Blind?" and "Bluetonic," on their Superior Quality Recordings label, which received positive reviews in the British music weeklies. By the fall of 1995, they were being touted as the next big thing in Brit-pop, since their sound fell halfway between the Stone Roses and Oasis. Early in 1996, the group released "Slight Return" which shot to number two a month before their debut album, *Expecting to Fly*, was released. *Expecting to Fly* was greeted with mixed reviews, but it debuted at number one on the British charts and became a sizable hit. Despite their British success, the group had trouble breaking in America. Furthermore, they were the subject of a quick backlash, as many critics believed the group embodied the conservatism of Brit-pop—the non-LP single "Marblehead Johnson" was welcomed cooly upon its fall release, and it only dented the charts. During early 1997, the Bluetones began working on their second album, *Return to the Last Chance Saloon*; *Science & Nature* followed in mid-2000. *—Stephen Thomas Erlewine*

● **Expecting to Fly** / Jan. 31, 1996 / A&M ♦♦♦♦♦
If anything, the Bluetones' debut album *Expecting to Fly* is too accomplished. Like their idols, the Stone Roses, the band has made a first album that is assured, low-key, and subtly charming. Unlike the Roses, they haven't made a consistently engaging album, but that isn't a major flaw, given the abundant hooks and melodies on *Expecting to Fly*. Lacking the dance inclinations of the Stone Roses, the Bluetones instead concentrate on perfectly-crafted guitar-pop songs, occasionally stretching out into long jams, like the opener "Talking to Clarry," which is too close to "Breaking into Heaven" for comfort. Nevertheless, when the band kicks into a small, hook-laden song like the chiming, infectious "Bluetonic," they are at their peak. Most of the album has gems like "Bluetonic," whether it's the wonderful "Slight Return" or the liquid riffs of "Things Change," but the record could have used more sonic variety. Where their pre-album singles had several lovely acoustic numbers, there is an over-reliance on loud, fuzzy—but certainly not heavy—guitars that gives the album an unfortunate sameness. However, that feeling begins to fade away as each of the song's melodies come into focus with repeated listens. *—Stephen Thomas Erlewine*

Return to the Last Chance Saloon / 1998 / A&M ♦♦♦♦
Stylistically, *Return to the Last Chance Saloon* isn't a drastic change from the Bluetones' debut *Expecting to Fly*. The major problem with the debut, however, was that there was little musical variety, and the album seemed to drag at times. Luckily, on their sophomore effort, the Bluetones have added some much-needed tempo changes to the mix, making this album a more consistently engaging listen than their debut. They still have massive, Stone Roses-style riffs, but they also have tossed in a few acoustic numbers and an instrumental. Many of the songs here have an obsession with the American Wild West, especially "Ames" and the opening medley of "Tone Blooze" and "Unpainted Arizona." Still, the band's sound is deeply rooted in British pop—and that is what dominates the majority of this disc. The real highlight is the soaring "Hey Jude" soundalike, "If:" with a galloping bassline and ultimately memorable chorus, this is possibly the band's best song. There's more, though—"4 Day Weekend" is more aggressive than anything on the debut, and the trashy blues tune "Sleazy Bed Track" are two more excellent cuts on this accomplished effort. While it was never released in the U.S., this is an essential purchase for fans. *—Jason Damas*

Science & Nature / May 30, 2000 / Mercury ♦♦♦
After the American-country-rock-meets-the-Stone-Roses sound of the Bluetones' sophomore release *Return to the Last Chance Saloon*, press on the band indicated they were up for a change in image and sound. Most suggested that the band's new sound was somewhat influenced by new wave, a seemingly bizarre and somewhat intriguing suggestion. What was produced, however, was considerably different. One track, the excellent paranoid rocker "Mudslide," which is complete with a new wavey keyboard hook, did sound like articles had hinted, but the rest of the disc was, well, more Bluetones. On every Bluetones release, they seem to get close to creating an excellent and truly memorable album, and then they end up coming up just short because something about their music just doesn't quite seem right. That is exactly what plagues *Science & Nature* from start to finish. There are excellent moments, such as the country-influenced single "Autophilia (How I Learned to Stop Worrying and Love My Car)," but much of the album is composed of pleasant, but unspectacular, material similar to what made up the first two Bluetones albums. Granted, the material is much more concise and there is a bit more of a pop leaning, but at its heart, *Science & Nature* is pure Bluetones from start to finish. *—Jason Damas*

Blur

f. 1989, Colchester, England
Indie Pop, Alternative Dance, Britpop, Pop/Rock, Alternative Pop/Rock
Initially, Blur were one of the multitude of British bands that appeared in the wake of the Stone Roses, mining the same swirling, psuedo-psychedelic guitar-pop, only with louder guitars. Following an image makeover in the mid-'90s, the group emerged as the most popular band in the U.K., establishing themselves as the heir to the English guitar-pop tradition of the Kinks, the Small Faces, the Who, the Jam, Madness, and the Smiths. In the process, the group broke down the doors for a new generation of guitar bands that became labelled as Brit-pop. With Damon Albarn's wry lyrics and the group's mastery of British pop tradition, Blur were the leaders of Brit-pop, but they quickly became confined by the movement; since they were its biggest band, they nearly died when the movement itself died. Through some reinvention, Blur reclaimed their position as an art-pop band in the late '90s by incorporating indie-rock and lo-fi influences, which finally gave them their elusive American success in 1997. But the band's legacy remained in Britain, where they helped revitalize guitar-pop by skillfully updating the country's pop traditions and bringing it into the '90s. *—Stephen Thomas Erlewine*

Leisure / Aug. 27, 1991 / Food/SBK ♦♦♦
"She's So High" and "There's No Other Way" were auspicious debut singles, alternately trancy and melodic, suggesting how shoegazing and baggy beats could be incorporated into pop song structures. Both songs suggested that Blur was capable of a striking debut album, but *Leisure* wasn't it. Mired by directionless soundscapes and incomplete songwriting, *Leisure* was nevertheless full of promise. Whenever the group tread close to the warped psychedelia of Syd Barrett, their compositions sprang to life, and "Sing" was an eerie, entrancing minor-key drone reminiscent of the Velvet Underground's "Venus in Furs." Those moments, however, were few and far between on *Leisure*, since much of the record was devoted to either naïve pop like "Bang" or washes of feedback and effects. From *Leisure*, it appeared that Blur was only capable of a pair of fine singles, which is what made the complete reinvention of *Modern Life Is Rubbish* such a surprise. [For the American release of *Leisure*, SBK Records lopped off one of the album's best songs, "Sing," and shuffled the running order for no apparent reason other than having "She's So High" and "There's No Other Way" appear first.] *–Stephen Thomas Erlewine*

Modern Life Is Rubbish / May 10, 1993 / Food/SBK ♦♦♦♦♦
As a response to the dominance of grunge in the U.K. and their own decreasing profile in their homeland—and also as a response to Suede's sudden popularity—Blur reinvented themselves with their second album, *Modern Life Is Rubbish*, abandoning the shoegazing and baggy influences that dominated *Leisure* for traditional pop. On the surface, *Modern Life* may appear to be an homage to the Kinks, David Bowie, the Beatles, and Syd Barrett, yet it isn't a restatement, it's a revitalization. Blur use British guitar-pop from the Beatles to My Bloody Valentine as a foundation, spinning off tales of contemporary despair. If Damon Albarn wasn't such a clever songwriter, both lyrically and melodically, *Modern Life* could have sunk under its own pretensions, and the latter half does drag slightly. However, the record teems with life, since Blur refuse to treat their classicist songs as museum pieces. Graham Coxon's guitar tears each song open, either with unpredictable melodic lines or layers of translucent, hypnotic effects, and his work creates great tension with Alex James' kinetic bass. And that provides Albarn a vibrant background for his social satires and cutting commentary. But the reason *Modern Life Is Rubbish* is such a dynamic record and ushered in a new era of British pop is that nearly every song is carefully constructed and boasts a killer melody, from the stately "For Tomorrow" and the punky "Advert" to the vaudeville stomp of "Sunday Sunday" and the neo-psychedelic "Chemical World." Even with its flaws, it's a record of considerable vision and ex-

citement. [The American version of *Modern Life Is Rubbish* substitutes the demo version of "Chemical World" for the studio version on the British edition. It also adds the superb single "Pop Scene" before the final song, "Resigned."] *—Stephen Thomas Erlewine*

★ **Parklife** / Apr. 25, 1994 / Food/SBK ♦♦♦♦♦
Modern Life Is Rubbish established Blur as the heir to the archly British pop of the Kinks, Small Faces, and the Jam, but its follow-up *Parklife* revealed the depth of that transformation. Relying more heavily on Ray Davies' seriocomic social commentary, as well as new wave, *Parklife* runs through the entire history of post-British Invasion Brit-pop in the course of 16 songs, touching on psychedelia, synth-pop, disco, punk, and musichall along the way. Damon Albarn intended these songs to form a sketch of British life in the mid-'90s, and it's startling how close he came to his goal; not only did the bouncy, disco-fied "Girls & Boys" and singalong chant "Parklife" become anthems in the U.K., but they inaugurated a new era of Brit-pop and lad culture, where British youth celebrated their country and traditions. The legions of jangly, melodic bands that followed in the wake of *Parklife* revealed how much more complex Blur's vision was. Not only was their music precisely detailed—sound effects and brilliant guitar lines pop up all over the record—but the melodies elegantly interweaved with the chords, as in the graceful, heartbreaking "Badhead." Surprisingly, Albarn, for all of his cold, dispassionate wit, demonstrates compassion that gives these songs three dimensions, as on the pathos-laden "End of a Century," the melancholy Walker Brothers tribute "To the End," and the swirling, epic closer "This Is a Low." For all of its celebration of tradition, *Parklife* is a thoroughly modern record in that it bends genres and is self-referential (the mod anthem of the title track is voiced by none other than Phil Daniels, the star of *Quadrophenia*). And, by tying the past and the present together, Blur articulated the mid-'90s zeitgeist and produced an epoch-defining record. *—Stephen Thomas Erlewine*

The Great Escape / Sep. 11, 1995 / Food/Virgin ♦♦♦♦♦
In the simplest terms, *The Great Escape* is the flipside of *Parklife*. Where Blur's breakthrough album was a celebration of the working class, drawing on British pop from the '60s and reaching through the '80s, *The Great Escape* concentrates on the suburbs, featuring a cast of characters all trying to cope with the numbing pressures of modern life. Consequently, it's darker than *Parklife*, even if the melancholia is hidden underneath the crisp production and catchy melodies. Even the bright, infectious numbers on *The Great Escape* have gloomy subtexts, whether it's the disillusioned millionaire of "Country House," and the sycophant of "Charmless Man," or the bleak loneliness of "Globe Alone" and "Entertain Me." Naturally, the slower numbers are even more despairing, with the acoustic "Best Days," the lush, sweeping strings of "The Universal" and the stark, moving electronic ballad "Yuko and Hiro" ranking as the most affecting work Blur has ever recorded. However, none of this makes *The Great Escape* a burden or a difficult album. The music bristles with invention throughout, as Blur delves deeper into experimentation with synthesizers, horns, and strings; guitarist Graham Coxon twists out unusual chords and lead lines, and Damon Albarn spits out unexpected lyrical couplets filled with wit and venemous intelligence in each song. But Blur's most remarkable accomplishment is that it can reference the past—the Scott Walker homage of "The Universal," the Terry Hall/Fun Boy Three cop on "Top Man," the skittish, XTC-flavored pop of "It Could Be You," and Albarn's devotion to Ray Davies—while still moving forward, creating a vibrant, invigorating record. *—Stephen Thomas Erlewine*

Blur / Feb. 10, 1997 / Food/Virgin ♦♦♦♦♦
The Great Escape, for all of its many virtues, painted Blur into a corner and there was only one way out—to abandon the Brit-pop that they had instigated by bringing the weird strands that always floated through their music to the surface. *Blur* may superficially appear to be a break from tradition, but it is a logical progression, highlighting the band's rich eclecticism and sense of songcraft. Certainly, they are trying for new sonic territory, bringing in shards of white noise, gurgling electronics, raw guitars, and druggy psychedelia, but these are just extensions of previously hidden elements of Blur's music. What makes it exceptional is how hard the band tries to reinvent themselves within their own framework, and the level of which they succeed. "Beetlebum" runs through the *White Album* in the space of five minutes; "M.O.R." reinterprets Berlin-era Bowie; "You're So Great," despite the corny title, is affecting lo-fi from Graham Coxon; "Country Sad Ballad Man" is bizarrely affecting, strangled lo-fi psychedelia; "Death of a Party" is an affecting resignation; "On Your Own" is an incredible slice of singalong pop spiked with winding, fluid guitar and synth eruptions; while "Look Inside America" cleverly subverts the traditional Blur song, complete with strings. And "Essex Dogs" is a six-minute slab of free verse and rattling guitar noise. *Blur* might be self-consciously eclectic, but Blur is at their best when they are trying to live up to their own pretensions, because Damon Albarn's exceptional sense of songcraft and the band's knack for detailed arrangements that flesh out the song to its fullest. There might be dark overtones to the record, but the band sounds positively joyous, not only in making noise but wreaking havoc with the expectations of their audience and critics. *—Stephen Thomas Erlewine*

13 / Mar. 15, 1999 / Food/Virgin ♦♦♦♦
Blur's penitence for Brit-pop continues with the aptly named *13*, which deals with star-crossed situations like personal and professional breakups with Damon Albarn's long-time girlfriend, Justine Frischmann of Elastica, and the group's longtime producer, Stephen Street. Building on *Blur*'s un-pop experiments, the group's ambitions to expand their musical and emotional horizons result in a half-baked baker's dozen of songs, featuring some of their most creative peaks and self-indulgent valleys. Albarn has been criticized for lacking depth in his songwriting, but his ballads remain some of Blur's best moments. When Albarn and crew risk some honesty, *13* shines: on "Tender," Albarn is battered and frail, urged by a lush gospel choir to "get through it." His confiding continues on "1992," which alludes to the beginning—and ending—of his relationship with Frischmann. On "No Distance Left to Run," one of *13*'s most moving moments, Albarn addresses post-breakup ambivalence, sighing, "I hope you're with someone who makes you feel safe while you sleep." While these songs reflect Albarn's romantic chaos, "Mellow Song," "Caramel," and "Trimm Trabb" express day-to-day desperation. Musically, the saddest songs on *13* are also the clearest, mixing electronic and acoustic elements in sleek but heartfelt harmony. However, "B.L.U.R.E.M.I." is a by-the-numbers rave-up, and the blustery "Swamp Song" and "Bugman" nick Blur's old punky glam pop style but sound misplaced here. "Trailerpark" veers in yet another direction, a too-trendy trip-hop rip-off that emphasizes the band's musical fog, proving that William Orbit's kitchen-sink production doesn't serve the songs'—or the band's—best interests. *13*'s strange, frustrating combination of expert musicianship and self-indulgence reveals the sound of a band trying to find itself. With some closer editing, this could have been the emotionally deep, sonically wide album Blur yearns to make. *—Heather Phares*

The Best of Blur / Nov. 21, 2000 / Food/Virgin ♦♦♦♦
It's boring to point out omissions on hits compilations, especially when a collection is as generous as the 18-track *The Best of Blur*, but let's do it anyway. *The Best of Blur* largely bypasses the group's key album, *Modern Life Is Rubbish*, the record that invented Brit-pop, skewing in favor of the self-consciously "experimental" *13*, which, for all of its attributes, wasn't a singles album. Plus, the group continues to punish the British record-buying public by not including the brilliant "Pop Scene" (to beat a dead horse, the single that invented Brit-pop), since nobody bought it at the time. So, without "Pop Scene," "Chemical World" or "Sunday Sunday," a crucial chapter of Blur's history is missing from *The Best of Blur*—the chapter where they essentially *became* Blur. It's to their immense credit that the album doesn't *feel* like it's missing anything, since these singles (plus one album track) are dazzling on their own. Of course, the trick is that the record isn't assembled chronologically. Instead, it flows like a set list, complete with the set closer "This Is a Low" followed by a two-song encore that ends with the new song (the good, not great, "Music Is My Radar"), which not only gives it a momentum of its own, but draws attention to the songs themselves. And "dazzling" isn't hyperbole—based on these 18 songs, Blur isn't just the best pop band of the '90s, with greater range and depth than their peers, they rank among the best pop bands of all time. *The Best of Blur* illustrates that, even as it misses some of their best moments—omissions that prevent it from being the flat-out classic it should be. Even so, it's pretty damn terrific, particularly for the unconverted. *—Stephen Thomas Erlewine*

Bob & Earl

R&B, Soul

Bob & Earl had already recorded under a myriad of pseudonyms during their careers before they were a duo; both "Bob"s (the first was Bobby Byrd, aka Bobby Day, and his replacement was Bobby Relf) and "Earl" (Earl Nelson) were key players in L.A.'s doo wop and R&B vocal scene in the mid- to late '50s. Their vocal interplay presaged Stax Records' Sam & Dave. The duo recorded several singles for various L.A.-based labels, but their lone hit was "Harlem Shuffle," a dance number punctuated by trumpet blasts and echo-laden percussion. Arranged by a young Barry White, who played piano, "Harlem Shuffle" was originally released in the U.S. on the Marc label in 1963. It climbed into the low end of the American Top Forty in 1964 before slipping off the charts. However, the duo failed to follow up with any additional hits and soon were splitting for solo careers. Nelson began recording solo tracks under a bunch of aliases, but his biggest success was as Jackie Lee, for another popular R&B dance cut in 1965, "The Duck," for the Mirwood label. Relf waxed singles under the names Bobby Garrett and Bobby Valentino. "Harlem Shuffle" was re-released in 1969, and became a Top Ten U.K. hit (number seven pop). Since its 1963 debut, the song has seen numerous cover versions, including those by the Righteous Brothers, Edgar Winter, Wayne Cochran, and the Rolling Stones, who revived it in 1986 for their *Dirty Work* LP. In 1968, the song appeared on blue-eyed soul singer Danny Wagner's album, *The Kindred Soul of Danny Wagner*; Barry White produced the album. *—Bryan Thomas*

● **Harlem Shuffle** / 1966 / Sue ♦♦♦♦♦
Bob & Earl were Bobby Relf and Earl Nelson. Relf replaced Nelson's former partner Bobby Byrd, who worked with him in James Brown's Famous Flames. That duo cut songs for various labels, but hadn't clicked as an act. The new Bob & Earl struck gold with this single, which made it to the Top 50 when it was issued in 1963. *—Ron Wynn*

Bob & Earl / 1969 / Crestview ♦♦♦
A curious album that has the feel of a thrown-together exploitation LP—there's no indication of when the tracks were recorded, although an educated guess would put the era in the mid-'60s. It's serviceable period soul with a slight uptown production feel, but not outstanding. The version of "Harlem Shuffle" here is *not* the original, but an instrumental rendition with a faster tempo and fuzz guitars. *—Richie Unterberger*

The BoDeans

f. 1984, Waukesha, WI
Heartland Rock, Roots Rock

The BoDeans are a rock & roll band formed in Waukesha, Wisconsin, by singer/songwriters/guitarists Sammy Llanas and Kurt Neumann, who had played together since high school, along with a rhythm section of bassist Bob Griffin and drummer Guy Hoffman. The quartet signed to Slash Records (manufactured and distributed by Warner Bros.) and released its first album, the critically well-accepted *Love & Hope & Sex & Dreams* (the title comes from a line in the Rolling Stones song "Shattered") in 1986. *Outside Looking In* (1987), produced by Talking Head and Wisconsin native Jerry Harrison, saw the band reduced to a trio with the departure of Hoffman. It broke into the Top 100 best-sellers, as the BoDeans toured with U2, appeared on Robbie Robertson's self-titled debut solo album, and were named "Best New Band" in *Rolling Stone* magazine. By the time of the release of the third album, *Home* (1989), Michael Ramos (keyboards) and Danny Gayol (drums) had joined. This lineup stayed intact for the release of *Black and White* (1991), but the BoDeans were drummerless again as of the release of *Go Slow Down* (1993). Following the release of the 1995 live double-album *Joe Dirt Car*, the BoDeans returned in 1996 with *Blend*. Around the time of *Blend*'s release, "Closer to Free," a song taken from *Go Slow Down*, became a hit, thanks to its exposure as the theme song for the popular television show, *Party of Five*. *—William Ruhlmann*

● **Love & Hope & Sex & Dreams** / May 1986 / Slash/Warner Bros. ✦✦✦✦✦
When the BoDeans appeared with their first album, *Love & Hope & Sex & Dreams*, in 1986, they immediately were filed under "roots rock" (a popular term of the day) because of the Western twang in their guitars, their bouncy beat, and their simple, neo-rockabilly approach to songwriting, not to mention the production of T-Bone Burnett. They led off the album with "She's a Runaway," a song of spousal abuse and revenge that indicated a higher social consciousness than much of the rest of the album, which was typified by "Misery," in which the singer laments that his girlfriend sleeps around. At their best, on "She's a Runaway," "Fadeaway," and "Angels," the BoDeans came up with infectious riffs and made maximum use of the sweet-and-sour vocal interaction between the conventional voice of Kurt Neumann and Sammy Llanas' distinctive nasal whine. Much of the album was slight, but there was enough of an individual sound to the better material to think of the BoDeans as a band of considerable promise. *—William Ruhlmann*

Outside Looking In / Sep. 1987 / Slash/Reprise ✦✦

Home / Jul. 27, 1989 / Slash/Reprise ✦✦✦
The BoDeans toured as opening act to U2 while promoting their second album, and their third album, *Home*, contained at least four songs with guitar work that seemed to have been copied from the fingers of U2's the Edge. Elsewhere, the BoDeans seemed to be seeking to escape their roots-rock tag by turning out one genre exercise after another—country & western on "Beaujolais," '60s Motown R&B on "When the Love Is Good," '50s rock & roll on "Good Work" and "Sylvia." The only times when the band sounded like itself were when Sammy Llanas got to do one of his story songs, such as "No One" or "Far Far Away from My Heart," but those sounded more like Llanas solo efforts than group works. Things had changed for this band over three albums: initially, they sounded so stylebound that you wondered if any growth was possible, but with this album they were charging off in half a dozen directions at once. *—William Ruhlmann*

Black and White / Apr. 26, 1991 / Slash/Reprise ✦✦✦
After moderate sales on their first three albums threatened to forever classify them as an alternative band, the BoDeans started tackling bigger themes on *Black and White*, produced by Prince-sideman David Z. The band hardly sounds like the roots-oriented band of their previous efforts, and Sam Llanas and Kurt Neumann sound more ambitious as songwriters. So "Black, White and Blood Red" is about more than race, the same way the anthemic "Naked" is about more than sex, the same way the hooky "Good Things" is about more than some guy who can't meet a girl. *Black and White* is about using individual problems as analogies to social ones. It's also about loneliness and hardship. It also didn't sell that much better (if any) than the first albums. *—Brian Mansfield*

Go Slow Down / Oct. 12, 1993 / Slash/Reprise ✦✦✦✦✦
The BoDeans made their best album since their debut by returning to the basic folk and rock elements that had always worked best for them. On their most acoustic outing, they also rediscovered themselves as songwriters, pursuing subjects unusually close at hand, whether sex, suicide, or the frustrations of the music business. No matter what the topic, they sounded like they meant it, and for once their eclecticism worked for them, providing them with a bagful of styles to evoke without overdoing it. *Go Slow Down* may have been the statement of a band that had been through a lot and reached a point of emotional exhaustion, but the BoDeans used their experience to craft their most deeply felt and satisfying music. Two and a half years after the abum's release, its leadoff track, "Closer to Free," became a hit after being made the theme song of the *Party of Five* TV series. *—William Ruhlmann*

Joe Dirt Car / Aug. 8, 1995 / Slash/Reprise ✦✦✦
Kurt and Sammy BoDean sing like slightly tarnished angels. You haven't heard harmonies this pure and unaffected since the Everly Brothers, and that's no exaggeration. Sure, their lyrics run to bathetic claptrap like "Say About Love" ("Some say love is just a freaky trip/That's what they say/Say about love"), but for every line like those there's a gem of hokey brilliance like "Idaho" (despite its recycled tag line) or the yearning "Lookin' for Me Somewhere." Kurt is a nifty guitar player with more taste than originality (which is also true of James Burton, bear in mind). Sammy has a sharp tenor voice that covers a spectrum of two or three emotions but wrings each of them dry. This is an album with clear limitations, certainly—two hours' worth of non-stop catharsis is too much for almost anybody—but it's still well worth your attention. *—Rick Anderson*

Blend / Nov. 5, 1996 / Slash/Reprise ✦✦✦
The tunes are achingly, unrelentingly lovely; the guitars jangle and shimmer charmingly; the chord progressions move from catharsis to catharsis. Sam Llanas and Kurt Neumann's voices blend like angels in a choir. Sometimes the effect is subtle—like when they sing about a woman who will "Sit on the front porch, watch the sun go down/Holding hands with her newborn baby." It's a sweet image, but one undermined by the fact that it's pretty hard to picture a woman holding hands with a newborn. Sometimes the effect is more abrasive—like when they sing "Sometimes she snores, sometimes she breathes on me/So I push her away so tenderly" or "When two hearts feel they could be as one/Ya just superglue 'em down until the fear is done." It's not hard to discern the good intentions here, but it takes some effort to ignore the clumsy, and sometimes downright

gross, realization of them. However, at times the formula works; "Can't Stop Thinking" is an unbeatable hopeless-guy-in-love anthem, and "Hurt By Love" finds Llanas telling his baby that "All those wishing stars/Hang out where you are" as an acoustic guitar jingles and twinkles merrily behind him. "Hurt By Love" is what the BoDeans are trying for throughout this whole album, but they only get there once or twice. *—Rick Anderson*

Curt Boettcher

Vocals / Sunshine Pop, Psychedelic Pop, Baroque Pop, Soft Rock, Psychedelic, Pop
Producer and composer Curt Boettcher was among the principal architects of the sunshine pop sound of the mid-1960s, his harmony-laden, melody-rich approach gracing the Top Ten hits of the Association as well as his own projects including Sagittarius and the Millennium. Born and raised in Wisconsin, he began his career as a folksinger, co-founding the GoldeBriars in 1962; the group's self-titled debut album appeared on Epic two years later. Although the GoldeBriars' complex harmonies anticipated the style of Boettcher's subsequent work, the foursome dissolved after a second LP, *Straight Ahead*; he then turned to studio work, in 1966 arranging the Association's breakthrough hit "Along Comes Mary." The chart-topping "Cherish" followed, and Boettcher also produced the band's debut album *And Then...Along Comes the Association*; however, the collaboration soon ended, and in between producing material for Tommy Roe, Boettcher turned his focus to his own group the Ballroom, recording a long-unreleased LP which finally saw release three decades later on Rev-Ola under the title *Preparing for the Millennium*. Boettcher then signed on with producer Gary Usher's studio supergroup Sagittarius—1967's *Present Tense* also featured contributions from the Beach Boys' Bruce Johnston and Glen Campbell, the latter assuming lead vocals on the classic "My World Fell Down." While recording *Present Tense*, Boettcher formed the Millennium, which issued its sole album *Begin*—the product of what was then the most costly recording session in the history of Columbia Records—in 1968. After the record's commercial failure, he returned to studio work, but in 1973 issued a solo album, *There's an Innocent Face*. In the process of contributing productions and session vocals to a handful of late-'70s Beach Boys releases, Boettcher changed his name to the more phonetic "Becher"; he died in 1987. *—Jason Ankeny*

Misty Mirage / Oct. 2000 / Together ✦✦✦✦✦
Following their collaboration on the first Sagittarius album, Curt Boettcher and Gary Usher set up shop with their own Together label, before Boettcher and friends formed the Millennium and recorded their landmark 1968 album. When the band disintegrated, Boettcher began his own experimental sessions with the possible intention of putting out a solo album on Together. By that point, the label's distributor was already beginning to falter, but not before Boettcher spent a considerable amount of time in the studio laying down the basic tracks, which ultimately went unreleased until this exceptional Poptones archival release collected those sessions, including demos, outtakes, instrumental versions, and even a few commercial spots. Boettcher had already placed many of the songs on *Misty Mirage* elsewhere in the two or three preceding years. But these recordings do not have the dreamy luminescence that marks much of his previous oeuvre. This is partly due to a less complex production and partly because songs like the title track, only a year or so removed from Sagittarius and the Millennium, had already relinquished some of their guileless innocence and taken on a patina of maturity and experience. This is transitional music, and shows Boettcher trying on different timbres and textures and frequently scaling back on the production, whether purposefully or because the recordings were left unfinished. If it is the former, with the benefit of hindsight one can place *Misty Mirage* alongside records like the *White Album*, *Wild Honey*, and *John Wesley Harding*—an example of a former production prodigy returning to the basics. Regardless, it is a blessing that this music has finally found its way to the public, both to round out and extend Boettcher's already considerable legacy. A fascinating listening experience. *—Stanton Swihart*

Tommy Bolin

b. 1951, Sioux City, IA, **d.** Dec. 4, 1976, Miami, FL
Vocals, Keyboards, Guitar / Guitar Virtuoso, Heavy Metal, Fusion, Hard Rock
A versatile guitarist, Tommy Bolin has graced several artists with his jazz fusion and hard rock chops. Bolin began his musical career as a member of Lonnie Mack's backing band, leaving to form the band Zephyr in 1968. Zephyr's first album reached the Top 50, but when the follow-up stiffed, Bolin left to form the jazz-rock group Energy with flute player Jeremy Steig. Through Steig, Bolin met Billy Cobham and guested on his *Spectrum*. Having achieved a measure of recognition, Bolin was invited to become the lead guitarist of the James Gang, since Joe Walsh's replacement, Domenic Troiano, had recently departed. Bolin stuck around for the *Bang* and *Miami* albums and then took a job in Deep Purple as Ritchie Blackmore's replacement in 1975, playing on *Come Taste the Band*. When Deep Purple showed signs of breaking up later in the year, Bolin went solo, formed a backing band, and recorded the albums *Teaser* and 1976's *Private Eyes*. In December of 1976, Bolin was found dead in a Miami hotel room of a drug overdose. *—Steve Huey*

Teaser / 1975 / Columbia ✦✦✦✦✦
After performing in a variety of bands since the late '60s, Bolin finally released his first solo album in 1975. *Teaser* is an impressive display of the guitarist's prowess and range, and is a natural progression from the previous Bolin-dominated James Gang albums *Bang* and *Miami* and his work with drummer Billy Cobham. The album features heavy doses of jazz-rock fusion (furthered by guests Jan Hammer, Dave Sanborn, and Michael Walden) in the instrumentals "Homeward Strut" and "Marching Powder," and straight-ahead rock in tracks like "The Grind." Bolin was always equally adept at subtleties, and the ballad "Dreamer" and the exotic "Savannah Woman" (with percussion from Phil Collins) represent this stylistic range here. Overshadowed historically by his guitar dy-

namics, Bolin's understated yet strong vocals are another selling point. *Teaser* is a stronger album than its one successor, the uneven *Private Eyes*, and survives as Bolin's signature work. *—Rob Caldwell*

● **Private Eyes** / 1976 / Columbia ✦✦✦✦✦
After the breakup of Deep Purple in 1976, guitarist Tommy Bolin wasted little time beginning work on his second solo album, *Private Eyes*. While it was more of a conventional rock album than its predecessor, *Teaser* (which served primarily as a showcase for his guitar skills and contained several jazz/rock instrumentals), it was not as potent. The performances aren't as inspired as those on *Teaser* or even those on Bolin's lone album with Deep Purple, *Come Taste the Band*, although there a few highlights could be found. The nine-minute rocker "Post Toastee" merges a long jam section with lyrics concerning the dangers of drug addiction, while "Shake the Devil" is similar stylistically. But Bolin wasn't simply a hard-rocker; he was extremely talented with other kinds of music: the quiet, acoustic-based compositions "Hello, Again" and "Gypsy Soul," and the heartbroken ballad "Sweet Burgundy." With his solo career starting to take shape (after the album's release, he opened for some of rock's biggest names: Peter Frampton, Jeff Beck, Rush, ZZ Top, etc.), Bolin's life was tragically cut short at the end of the year due to a drug overdose in Miami, FL. *—Greg Prato*

The Ultimate: The Best of Tommy Bolin / Sep. 1989 / Geffen ✦✦✦
Although guitarist Tommy Bolin died well before his time, he left a wide variety of scattered recordings behind (as both a session musician and permanent member of several rock bands). One of the more versatile guitarists of all-time, Bolin touched upon many different styles—Janis Joplin-style blues rock, heavy metal, jazz fusion, and serene ballads, which are all on display on 1989's 2-CD boxset, *The Ultimate*. In addition to the music, the set comes with a large, gorgeous booklet chock full of pictures, plus a very detailed and informative biography. Disc 1 chronicles Bolin's early years, and while it contains several standouts (the amazing instrumental "Quadrant 4" with Billy Cobham, The James Gang's "Alexis" and "Standing In the Rain," etc.), the selections by his first band, Zephyr, and as a hired hand with a Zep-clone band called Moxy, have not aged well. Disc 2 proves to be more consistent, including tracks with jazz drummer Alphonse Mouzon ("Golden Rainbows," "Nitrogyclerin"), as part of Deep Purple's final '70s line-up ("Gettin' Tighter," "Owed To G"), and as a solo artist ("Dreamer," "Teaser," "Sweet Burgundy," "Shake the Devil," etc.). Although the set was out-of-print by the late '90s, *The Ultimate* serves as a solid introduction to the talents of the great Tommy Bolin. *—Greg Prato*

Michael Bolton (Michael Bolotin)

b. Feb. 26, 1954, New Haven, CT
Vocals / Adult Contemporary
Singer/songwriter Michael Bolton had an extensive, though not very successful, career under his real name, Michael Bolotin, before emerging in the mid-'80s as a major soft-rock balladeer. He first turned up on RCA Records in the mid-'70s, then later became the lead singer in Blackjack, a heavy-metal band. In 1983, he changed his name to Michael Bolton, signed to Columbia Records as a solo act, and relaunched his career.

Michael Bolton was released in April 1983 and made the Top 100 bestsellers. His real breakthrough began with his third album, *The Hunger*, released in September 1987. On this album, Bolton abandoned the more hard-rock aspects of his style to concentrate on blue-eyed soul singing. *Soul Provider*, released in July 1989, turned Bolton into a superstar, reaching the Top Ten, selling four million copies, spawning five Top 40 singles, and earning him a Grammy. *Time, Love & Tenderness*, released in April 1991, was even more successful, hitting #1, selling six million copies, and featuring four Top 40 hits, including "Love Is a Wonderful Thing" (later the subject of a successful plagiarism suit brought against Bolton by the Isley Brothers.)

Bolton won another Grammy Award in 1992 for "When a Man Loves a Woman." Bolton's next album of original material, *The One Thing*, came in November 1993. It hit the Top Ten and sold three million copies. *All That Matters*, his first album of new material since *The One Thing*, came in the fall of 1997. Instead of continuing his success, it was a surprise flop. Its lack of success didn't stop Bolton from turning his attention to *My Secret Passion*, a collection of opera and arias that he released in January 1998. By classical standards, the album was a hit, and the record received a great deal of press and surprisingly good reviews. *—William Ruhlmann*

Michael Bolton / Apr. 1983 / Columbia ✦✦✦

Everybody's Crazy / 1985 / Columbia ✦

The Hunger / Sep. 1987 / Columbia ✦✦✦

Soul Provider / Jul. 1989 / Columbia ✦✦✦✦
Michael Bolton is no fool, and when he broke through to platinum sales with *The Hunger*, nobody had to tell him to record a follow-up devoted to more of the same. Bolton produced most of the record himself, and he teamed with the cream of the era's romantic rock ballad writers, people like Diane Warren (who gets five co-credits here) and Desmond Child, while the R&B copy this time was Ray Charles' version of "Georgia on My Mind." He also reclaimed "How Am I Supposed to Live Without You" from Laura Branigan. The result was five Top 40 hits and millions of albums sold. Maybe Bolton wasn't the king of the hockey rinks, but his voice was now stoking the romantic fires in bedrooms across America, which is nice work if you can get it. *—William Ruhlmann*

Time, Love & Tenderness / Apr. 1991 / Columbia ✦✦✦✦
Michael Bolton cloned his approach from *Soul Provider* on its follow-up, *Time, Love & Tenderness*, and sold as many records for his trouble. (That's six million copies.) His key collaborator once again was Diane Warren, who applied her goldplated gift for writing contemporary love songs to six tunes, among them the hits "Time, Love & Tenderness" and "Missing You Now" (which featured saxmeister Kenny G). The obligatory R&B carbon copy was Percy Sledge's "When a Man Loves a Woman," which hit number one. The only unusual songs came at the beginning and the end. The album led off with "Love Is a Wonderful Thing" (a Top Ten hit), a song in standard '60s R&B mode that would be the subject of a plagiarism suit from the Isley Brothers, and it concluded with "Steel Bars," co-written by Bolton and . . . Bob Dylan? That's what it said, and if the song wasn't one of Dylan's best, it at least indicated that Bolton might have possibilities that had so far gone unnoticed. *—William Ruhlmann*

Timeless: The Classics / Sep. 1992 / Columbia ✦✦✦
It's hard to resist the notion that Michael Bolton, who took considerable flak in the press for storming the charts with copycat reproductions of '60s soul hits felt "suddenly compelled," as he put it here in a sleeve note, to devote an entire album to cover songs after publicly confronting his critics at the Grammy Awards ceremony in February 1992. There's not much you can do with "Yesterday" or "White Christmas" at this point. On the other hand, as with his previous R&B appropriations, versions of songs like the Four Tops' "Reach Out I'll Be There" and Sam and Dave's "Hold On, I'm Comin'" only succeeded in confirming Bolton's inferiority to his predecessors. *—William Ruhlmann*

The Artistry of Michael Bolotin / Mar. 1993 / RCA ✦✦

The One Thing / Nov. 1993 / Columbia ✦✦✦

● **Greatest Hits 1985-1995** / Sep. 19, 1995 / Columbia ✦✦✦✦
Although he has always been a favorite target of rock critics, Michael Bolton amassed a large number of hit singles in the late '80s and early '90s, including seven Top Ten hits and two number one singles ("How Am I Supposed to Live Without You" and "When a Man Loves a Woman"). With the notable exception of "Love Is a Wonderful Thing," all of his big hits are collected on *Greatest Hits 1985-1995*, as well as a handful of new tracks that aren't quite as successful as the older hits. Nevertheless, *Greatest Hits 1985-1995* is the one definitive Michael Bolton album. *—Stephen Thomas Erlewine*

All That Matters / Nov. 11, 1997 / Columbia ✦✦✦

My Secret Passion / Jan. 20, 1998 / Columbia ✦✦✦

Timeless: The Classics, Vol. 2 / Nov. 16, 1999 / Columbia ✦✦✦
For his second collection of pop standard covers, Michael Bolton doesn't really change his course of action, choosing to sing the songs everybody knows ("Sexual Healing," "Tired of Being Alone," "Let's Stay Together," "Try a Little Tenderness," "(What A) Wonderful World," "A Whiter Shade of Pale," etc., etc.). There are two surprises here, Bobby Caldwell's "What You Won't Do for Love" and Bob Dylan's "Like a Rolling Stone," but they're done up in the same adult contemporary arrangements as everything else on the record. So, *Timeless: The Classics, Vol. 2* delivers exactly what you expect: predictable songs, as done by Michael Bolton. In one sense, that makes it stronger than some Bolton albums, since the material is all good, but it also highlights the fact that he isn't as subtle or nuanced a singer as his idols, even though he's grown more powerful over the years. Still, by 1999, that was hardly a revelation, and it seems churlish to complain about Bolton's singing or the predictability of the material, since that all comes as no surprise. Thus, that leaves *Timeless: The Classics, Vol. 2* as a solid Bolton album. No revelations, no surprises—just pure Bolton. *—Stephen Thomas Erlewine*

Love Songs / Feb. 6, 2001 / Columbia ✦✦✦✦
Though Michael Bolton's *Love Songs* isn't tremendously different than his *Greatest Hits 1985-1995*—his popular body of work is virtually nothing but love songs—this collection will probably please his biggest fans. Gathering smash hits from 1987 to 1997, the album includes "Soul Provider," "Said I Loved You . . . But I Lied," "How Am I Supposed to Live Without You," "Missing You Now," and "When a Man Loves a Woman." Though it's not quite as definitive as *Greatest Hits 1985-1995*, anyone looking to own just one Michael Bolton album wouldn't go wrong with this one, either. *—Heather Phares*

Bon Jovi

f. 1983, Sayreville, NJ
Pop-Metal, Album Rock, Arena Rock, Hair Metal, Heavy Metal, Pop/Rock, Hard Rock
Few bands embodied the era of pop-metal like Bon Jovi. By merging Def Leppard's loud but tuneful metal with Bruce Springsteen's working-class sensibilities, the New Jersey-based quintet developed an ingratiatingly melodic and professional variation of hard-rock—one that appealed as much to teenagers as to housewives. Bon Jovi skillfully employed professional songwriters to give their songs, especially their power ballads, an appropriately commercial sheen, inaugurating a trend that dominated mainstream hard rock and metal for the next decade. They also made simple performance videos that emphasized lead singer Jon Bon Jovi's photogenic good looks, and these clips helped propel 1986's *Slippery When Wet* and 1988's *New Jersey* into multi-platinum status around the world. Both records were criticized for being more pop than metal, as well as being targeted toward teenyboppers, yet the group managed to subtly change their image in the early '90s, moving away from metal and concentrating on straightforward arena-rock and big ballads. The shift in style worked, and Bon Jovi were the only American pop-metal band of the '80s to retain a sizable audience in the '90s. *—Stephen Thomas Erlewine*

Bon Jovi / Jan. 1984 / Mercury ✦✦✦
From the opener, "Runaway," which rode to glory on Bruce Springsteen's E Street Bandmate Roy Bittan's distinctive keyboard riff, to the sweaty arena rock of "Get Ready," which closes the album, Bon Jovi's debut is an often-overlooked minor gem from the heyday of hair metal. The songs may be simple and the writing prone to all the clichés of the form, but the album boasts a pretty consistent hard rock attack, passionate playing, and a keen sense of melody. The prominence David Bryan's (he was David Rashbaum on the cred-

its) keyboards get on this record is an indicator, perhaps, that Bon Jovi had more than a passing interest in the pop market, which was then dominated by new wave and synth pop. Mixing Journey-like '70s rock ("She Don't Know Me") with shout-along stadium anthems ("Love Lies"), *Bon Jovi* showcases a hot young band who is hungry for the big time, doing what they did best. It may not be the most noteworthy of debuts, but *Bon Jovi* has a contagious sense of energy and an endearing romanticism that mark it as a classic in its own right. *—Leslie Mathew*

7800 Fahrenheit / Apr. 1985 / Mercury ♦♦♦

The band's 1985 sophomore effort was slammed by critics upon release, but showed considerable growth in songwriting and playing. It was their first gold record and their last album before entering superstardom with the follow-up, *Slippery When Wet*. Highlights include "In and Out of Love" and "Hardest Part of the Night." *—David Jehnzen*

Slippery When Wet / Aug. 1986 / Mercury ♦♦♦♦♦

It is probably true that Bon Jovi's breakthrough success with *Slippery When Wet*, their third album, had more to do with lead singer Jon Bon Jovi's mop of curls and winning smile than with anything in the grooves of the record. Nevertheless, the album contained competent contemporary pop/rock, from its Eddie Van Halen-inspired guitar solos to the singer's enthusiastic, husky wail (which owed a lot to Bruce Springsteen). Jon Bon Jovi, guitarist Richie Sambora, and songwriter-for-hire Desmond Child had little more on their minds than girls and rock-as-mythology (even the working-class anthem "Livin' on a Prayer" featured a character who was forced to hock his "six string"), but that may only mean they had identified their audience—young white adolescent males—and were targeting it accurately. *—William Ruhlmann*

New Jersey / Sep. 1988 / Mercury ♦♦♦♦♦

Bon Jovi had perfected a formula for hard pop/rock by the time of this album, concentrating on sing-along choruses sung over and over again, frequently by a rough, extensively overdubbed chorus, producing an effect not unlike what these songs sounded like in the arenas and stadiums where they were most often heard. The lyrics had that typical pop twist—although they nominally expressed romantic commitment, sentiments such as "Lay Your Hands on Me" and "I'll Be There for You" worked equally well as a means for the band and its audience to reaffirm their affection for each other. The only thing that marred the perfection of this communion was Jon Bon Jovi's continuing obsession with a certain predecessor from his home state; at times, he seemed to be trying to recreate *Born to Run* using cheaper materials. *—William Ruhlmann*

Keep the Faith / Nov. 1992 / Mercury ♦♦♦

After being missing in action for nearly four years, Bon Jovi returns with *Keep the Faith*, an update on their trademark pop-metal sound. Because the rules had changed since *New Jersey*, the band knew they had to shake things up a bit. Bon Jovi wants to be taken seriously this time around—hence, epics like the ten-minute "Dry County" and stabs at significance like "Fear" (plus the new short haircuts). Most of these grand statements fall flat, but there are songs here ("Bed of Roses," "Keep the Faith") that nearly match the glory days. *—Stephen Thomas Erlewine*

● **Cross Road** / Oct. 4, 1994 / Mercury ♦♦♦♦♦

While Bon Jovi always managed to stick a couple of killer album tracks on their records, their main strength has always been singles. *Cross Road* collects all of their biggest hits, adding a couple of new songs and Jon Bon Jovi's solo hit, "Blaze of Glory," for good measure. Even the band's detractors may not be able to resist the constant flow of big guitars, big hooks, and sweet melodies that pour out on *Cross Road*. After all, this is what state-of-the-art mainstream hard rock was all about in the late '80s. *—Stephen Thomas Erlewine*

These Days / 1995 / Mercury ♦♦♦

With *These Days*, Bon Jovi firmly established themselves as an adult contemporary act. They still have their fair share of rockers, but they seem half-hearted and incomplete. Instead, the band sounds the most comfortable with love ballads and working class anthems, from hits "This Ain't a Love Song" and "Lie to Me" to the acoustic "Diamond Ring." In fact, as the years go by, Bon Jovi gets musically stronger. Not only are their best songs stronger now, their playing is more accomplished. Keeping these improvements in mind, it's no surprise that the group was one of the few pop-metal bands to sustain a career in the mid-'90s. *—Stephen Thomas Erlewine*

Crush / Jun. 13, 2000 / Island ♦♦♦♦

Even if it was classified as pop-metal, Bon Jovi never really was much of a metal band, relying on big, catchy melodies and not guitar riffs to make their songs memorable. That's why, in 2000, they're able to make an album like *Crush*, which strays far enough into pop/rock to actually stand a chance of getting airplay (which it did, with the hit lead single "It's My Life"). The guitar crunch on the uptempo numbers keeps Bon Jovi from becoming a full-fledged pop/rock band, but in addition to the typical hard rockers, there are nods to heartland rock, Bryan Adams-style adult contemporary balladry ("Thank You for Loving Me"), the Beatles (the surprisingly effective "Say It Isn't So"), and even British glam à la T. Rex or David Bowie ("Captain Crash and the Beauty Queen From Mars"). Occasionally, it sounds like the band is attempting to cover as many bases as possible for multi-format appeal, but for the most part, the variety—coupled with the consistently polished songcraft—makes for a surprisingly listenable album. The production is a little more electronic-tinged, but not obtrusively high-tech, so the band doesn't come off as desperate to sound contemporary. Aside from a couple of missteps (the soppy, aforementioned "Thank You for Loving Me" and the mawkish posturing of "Save the World"), *Crush* is a solidly crafted mainstream rock record that's much better than most might expect. Even if *Crush* is more measured than Bon Jovi's early work, "Just Older" sums up the band's acceptance of their status nicely: "The skin I'm in is all right with me/It's not old, just older." *—Steve Huey*

One Wild Night: Live 1985–2001 / May 22, 2001 / Uptown/Universal ♦♦♦♦

Die-hard Bon Jovi fans will swear on their sacred *Slippery When Wet* albums that Bon Jovi is by far one of the best rock bands to sing (or scream) along to, no matter where you are—in the car, on the road, or in your room, crooning into your hairbrush or anything you can get your hands on. *One Wild Night: Live 1985–2001* is the perfect album for fans and newcomers alike, as it features a plentiful bounty of the band's biggest hits and most-screamable tunes. Set against the backdrop of the roars and accolades of its adoring fans at concerts across the world, the songs on this live album become even bigger hits that blast right out of your speakers, making you feel like you're part of the action. The opening track, "It's My Life," starts the *Wild Night* album off right, with Jon Bon Jovi singing what could be considered the band's credo—"It's my life/It's now or never/I ain't gonna live forever"—as the band rocks on around him. The classic Bon Jovi tune "Livin' on a Prayer" may be addictive enough for you to hurt your vocal chords, but Jovi pulls off the 1986 tune seemingly without effort, working the crowd into a frenzy. The album also features a live recording of the band's popular ballad, "Something to Believe In," from its show in Japan and one of the band's coolest bad songs ever, "Wanted Dead or Alive." *—Kerry L. Smith*

Graham Bond (Graham John Clifton Bond)

b. Oct. 28, 1937, Romford, Essex, England, **d.** May 8, 1974, London, England
Vocals, Saxophone, Organ / British Blues, British Invasion, Blues-Rock

An important, underappreciated figure of early British R&B, Graham Bond is known in the U.S., if at all, for heading the group that Jack Bruce and Ginger Baker played in before they joined Cream. He met Bruce and Baker in 1962 after joining Alexis Koerner's Blues Incorporated, and the trio formed their own band one year later, with Bond on the Hammond organ, as well as handling the lion's share of the vocals. In its prime, the Graham Bond Organization played rhythm and blues with a strong jazzy flavor, emphasizing Bond's demonic organ and gruff vocals. The band performed imaginative covers and fairly strong original material, and Bond was also perhaps the very first rock musician to record with the Mellotron synthesizer. Hit singles, though, were necessary for British bands to thrive in the mid-'60s, and Bond's group began to fall apart in 1966, when Bruce and Baker formed Cream with Eric Clapton. After struggling on with the Organization for a few years, he moved to the U.S. in the late '60s to record a few albums, then moved back to Britain to form the band Holy Magick. Bond's demise was more tragic than most: he developed serious drug and alcohol problems, and committed suicide by throwing himself into the path of a London Underground train in 1974. *—Richie Unterberger*

● **The Sound of 65** / Mar. 1965 / Edsel ♦♦♦♦♦

Although the Organization's first album was recorded a mere year or two before Cream's debut, it bears little resemblance to Cream's pioneering hard blues-rock. Instead, it's taut British R&B with a considerable jazz influence. That influence comes not so much from the rhythm section as saxophonist Dick Heckstall-Smith and lead singer/organist Bond himself. This LP is not as exciting or rock-oriented as those of contemporaries like the Rolling Stones or John Mayall, but is respectably gritty, mostly original material, with an occasionally nasty edge. There are some obscure treasures of the British R&B explosion to be found here, including the original version of "Train Time" (later performed by Cream), the thrilling bass runs on "Baby Be Good to Me," and the group's hardboiled re-arrangements of such traditional standards as "Wade in the Water" and "Early in the Morning." Even their blatant stab at commercialism (the ballad "Tammy") has its charm. *—Richie Unterberger*

There's a Bond Between Us / Nov. 1965 / Edsel ♦♦♦♦♦

Bond's second album stakes out similar territory as his debut in a more polished but slightly less exciting fashion. Some of the covers are a bit routine and hackneyed, and the original material isn't quite as strong (or frequent) as on the first effort. On a few tunes, the group expands from rave-ups to mellower, jazzier ballads that retain an R&B base. Highlights include the early Jack Bruce composition "Hear Me Calling Your Name" (to which he also contributes a fine lead vocal) and the excellent Bond tune "Walkin' in the Park," which holds up to the best early British R&B numbers. The album is also notable for being one of the very first rock LPs to feature the Mellotron, which Bond uses subtly and well. *—Richie Unterberger*

Graham Bond Organization / 1984 / Charly ♦♦

Sound of 65/There's a Bond Between Us / Dec. 14, 1999 / BGO ♦♦♦♦♦

In England during the years 1957-1962, jazz and blues used to intermix freely, especially among younger blues enthusiasts and more open-minded jazzmen—by 1963, most of the former had gone off to form bands with guitars at the forefront of their sound, while the latter kept some jazz elements in their work. The Graham Bond Organization represented the jazzier side of the British blues boom, less charismatic and sexually provocative than blues-rock bands like the Stones or the Yardbirds, but no less potent a product of the same inspiration, sax and organ being much more prominent in their sound. Indeed, Bond's playing on the organ as represented on this CD is the distant antecedent to Keith Emerson's more ambitious keyboard excursions of three to four years later, without the incessant copping of classical riffs. The playing and singing (by Bond and a young Jack Bruce) are curiously soulful, and when Ginger Baker takes a solo on "Oh Baby," it's a beautiful, powerful, even lyrical experience (as drum solos go), and one of those bold, transcendent, virtuoso moments, akin to Brian Jones' harmonica solo on the Stones' version of "Hi Heel Sneakers." The band was more exciting on stage, as the evidence of their one surviving early live performance indicates, but they were worth hearing on record as well. In a universe that was fair and idealized, this CD and the two albums contained on it would rank right up there in sales with anything (including the *Bluesbreakers with Eric Clapton* album) that John Mayall ever released, and Bond also proves himself a more fervent and exciting figure here than Mayall ever seemed on his records. —*Bruce Eder*

Holy Magick/We Put Our Magick on You / Mar. 21, 2000 / BGO ✦✦

Gary "U.S." Bonds

b. Jun. 6, 1939, Jacksonville, FL
Vocals / Rock & Roll, R&B

After moving to the Norfolk, VA, area in the mid-'50s, young Gary Anderson began plying his vocal wares, first in church, later with a local group called the Turks. When he was not yet 21, he was approached by local record producer Frank Guida to join his tiny Legrand label. Guida changed Anderson's name to U.S. Bonds, hoping the first release would get extra airplay by disc jockeys mistaking it for a public-service announcement. The result was the classic "New Orleans," combining rock-combo raunch with impassioned, scorched soul-singing that set the stage for all that would follow. Guida double-and triple-tracked Bonds' voice, and the resulting murky production gave all the hits (including "Quarter to Three," "School Is Out," and "Dear Lady Twist") a party-in-outer-space quality all their own. Though he has kept recording, making a couple of excellent solo albums in the early '80s with the help of Bruce Springsteen, Bonds is best seen today dotting the landscape of oldies shows the world over, singing the songs that made him famous. —*Cub Koda*

Dedication / Apr. 1981 / Razor & Tie ✦✦✦

Bruce Springsteen played guitar, sang a duet, wrote three songs, and co-produced and co-arranged four on Gary U.S. Bonds' comeback album, recorded 20 years after his heyday. Springsteen also lent his backup group, The E Street Band, while E Street guitarist Miami Steve (Van Zandt) also contributed a song and produced the bulk of the record. The result, naturally, sounds like a Bruce Springsteen and the E Street Band album with lead vocals by Gary U.S. Bonds. Bonds' elastic tenor, heard in much greater clarity than it ever was in his early years, has just enough grit to be soulful, and he puts across the pop-soul tunes Springsteen and Van Zandt have constructed for him effectively. He also tackles the Beatles' "It's Only Love" and Bob Dylan's "From a Buick 6," and sings Jackson Browne's "The Pretender" as if the lyric was devoid of irony. It's an enjoyable album that does nothing to change the notion that Bonds as a recording artist essentially conforms himself to the intentions of his producer, whether that's Frank Guida, Jerry Williams, Jr., or Bruce Springsteen. —*William Ruhlmann*

On the Line / Jun. 1982 / Razor & Tie ✦✦✦

On the Line, Gary U.S. Bonds' second comeback album under the sponsorship of Bruce Springsteen, was even more of a Springsteen record than its predecessor. This time, Springsteen wrote seven of the 11 songs, co-produced all of them with Miami Steve (Van Zandt) and again lent the E Street Band for the sessions. While there were no Springsteen masterpieces here, the rock & roll revival style of the material, similar to that on *Dedication*, made it, in effect, the follow-up to Springsteen's *The River* album, albeit with a different vocalist. And that vocalist was, if anything, more expressive than the author—on a song like "Out of Work," one of Springsteen's blue-collar anthems, Bonds sang with the conviction of a journeyman who knows what work is and what it's like not to have it. —*William Ruhlmann*

The School of Rock & Roll: Best of Gary U.S. Bonds / Apr. 1990 / Rhino ✦✦✦✦✦

In the early '60s, nobody made noisier, crazier sounding rock & roll party records than U.S. Bonds, with records rife with massive amounts of echo and good times galore. The crudeness of Frank Guida's production techniques is undeniable; overdub upon overdub are lopped on top of each other until the original band track is buried under a muck of tape hiss and echo, a swirling pool of party noise that is unabated. Why Guida and Bonds were so successful with this formula, milking it for all it was commercially worth, is here to be investigated on this single-disc 18-track collection. The big hits are here: "Quarter to Three," "New Orleans," "School Is In," "School Is Out" (although the last two are missing the spoken intros that graced the original singles), "Dear Lady Twist," "Twist Twist Senora," and "Not Me." But curiously left out are several powerful tracks, most notably "Trip to the Moon," to make room for lesser tracks from later in Bonds's career. This is still the best overview available though, until somebody does a better retrospective or decides to reissue the original Legrand album. —*Cub Koda*

● **The Very Best of Gary "U.S." Bonds: Original Legrand Masters** / Aug. 11, 1998 / Varese ✦✦✦✦✦

The title to this 16-track collection has more than its share of quirks and wrinkles. 14 tracks are duplicated with Rhino's 1990's *Best of Gary U.S. Bonds*, making it a negligible buy for anyone who already owns the latter compilation. All the chart hits are here, including "New Orleans," "Quarter to Three," "School Is Out" (again with the original intro clipped off, same as the Rhino comp), "School Is In," "Twist Twist Senora," and "Dear Lady Twist." New to this collection are the inclusion of "Gettin' a Groove," "Copy Cat," and "I Dig This Station." The latter two items grazed the bottom of the charts, hence their inclusion, but leaving off strong album and single material like "Trip to the Moon," "I Know Why Dreamers Cry," "Mixed Up Faculty" and "Cecelia" to make room for the second go round of non-charters like "Take Me Back to New Orleans," "Having So Much Fun," "Where Did the Naughty Little Girl Go," and "I Want To Holler (But the Town's Too Small)" makes this a less than stellar supplement to the Rhino package. But it's a decent alternative, leaving a half of a compilation's worth of material between the two best-of's. —*Cub Koda*

Boney M.

f. 1976, Germany
Euro-Dance, Disco

Although they never had much success in America, the Euro-disco group Boney M. was a European phenomenon during the '70s. After German record producer Frank Farian recorded the single "Baby Do You Wanna Bump?," he created Boney M. to support the song, bringing in four West Indian vocalists who had been working as session singers in Germany—Marcia Barrett, Liz Mitchell, Maizie Williams, and Bobby Farrell. "Daddy Cool" reached the U.K. Top Ten in 1977, followed by a remake of Bobby Hebb's "Sunny." "Ma Baker" just missed the U.K. number one spot, and "Belfast" hit the Top Ten in December. In 1978, Boney M. was at the height of its popularity with "Rivers of Babylon," which became the second-biggest selling single in U.K. chart history. It also was Boney M's only U.S. Top 40 hit. Boney M's album *Nightflight to Venus* also topped the U.K. charts, as did *Oceans of Fantasy*. Their music continues to sell well in Europe, with a compilation hitting the U.K. Top Ten in 1994. Farian went on to create the late-'80s dance sensation Milli Vanilli. —*Stephen Thomas Erlewine*

● **The Magic of Boney M. [20 Hits]** / 1980 / Musicrama ✦✦✦✦✦

Boney M's top Euro-disco creations—songs that ruled the continent for a while in the mid-'70s—are compiled on this singularly pleasing singles collection. —*Stephen Thomas Erlewine*

The Bongos

f. 1980, **db.** 1986
Jangle Pop, Power Pop

Hoboken's Bongos—founded as a trio consisting of Richard Barone (guitar, vocals), Rob Norris (bass), and Frank Giannini (drums, vocals)—made no pretense of being anything other than a pop band; fortunately, they were a good pop band, covering guitar pop from the Byrds to T. Rex, all of it pulled together by Barone's original songs. Although he was the focal point, the other members were by no means peripheral; after their first full-length album, *Drums Along the Hudson* (1982), James Mastro joined and contributed some stellar hooks. After releasing a series of singles and an EP on tiny Fetish Records in 1980 and 1981, the Bongos signed to independent PVC Records. *Drums Along the Hudson* compiled all their previously released tracks. They then moved up to major label RCA and released the five-song *Numbers with Wings* EP (1983) and the album *Beat Hotel* (1985), before leaving RCA and splitting up. (Later, *Drums Along the Hudson* and a two-fer of *Numbers with Wings* and *Beat Hotel* were reissued on CD by Razor & Tie.) At their best, the Bongos made some irresistible guitar pop. —*William Ruhlmann*

Drums Along the Hudson / 1982 / Razor & Tie ✦✦✦

Richard Barone's brief lyrics frequently lack clarity, but he sings them earnestly, and the trio plays irresistibly catchy, guitar-based pop music. Heard from the perspective of the following decade, both the playing and the lyrics sound remarkably prescient (this band could clean up in the alternative market today), although at the time they sounded noticeably retro. (*Drums Along the Hudson* compiles all the tracks on the U.K. EP *Time and the River*, along with the Bongos' previously released singles.). —*William Ruhlmann*

Numbers with Wings / 1983 / RCA ✦✦✦✦✦

This five-song EP (now available, along with *Beat Hotel*, on a single CD) marks several upgrades in the Bongos' career. They have added second guitarist James Mastro, moved up to RCA Records, and brought in producer Richard Gottehrer. Gottehrer, who has a sharp sense of rock & roll dynamics (listen to his work on the Angels' "My Boyfriend's Back"), is a felicitous choice, and the added instrumentation (and no doubt better-budgeted recording and mixing) allows the Bongos to better realize their pop sound. As a result, songs like "Numbers with Wings," with its echoed vocals and full sound, have the kind of epic sweep Richard Barone's compositions have always suggested without achieving before. Not that the band has become overblown—just fulfilled. —*William Ruhlmann*

Beat Hotel / 1985 / RCA ✦✦✦

Beat Hotel is, in a sense, the Bongos' only "real" album; *Drums Along the Hudson*, its predecessor, was a compilation of previously released single and EP tracks. As such, *Beat Hotel* is a more unified effort than the earlier LP, but lacks the urgent immediacy that all those singles tracks gave it. Richard Barone makes extensive use of a guitar synthesizer to fill out the band's sound, although it's still the normal guitar licks that dominate the music. Barone also sings engagingly, filling his songs with catchy hooks, even though on the lyric sheet it's hard to figure out what he's talking about. It's a shame that *Beat Hotel*, which seems like a transitional album, proved to be the Bongos' final effort—they remain a promising group that never had a chance to reach their potential. —*William Ruhlmann*

● **Beat Hotel/Numbers with Wings** / Jul. 24, 1992 / Razor & Tie ✦✦✦✦✦

This two-fer CD handily compiles the Bongos' two releases for RCA on one compact disc. 1983's *Numbers with Wings*, the group's major-label debut, found them expanding into a four-piece with the addition of guitarist James Mastro. While the production on *Numbers with Wings* is far slicker than anything on *Drums Along the Hudson*, and the songs lack the physical punch of such previous Bongos classics as "In the Congo" or "Three Wise Men," the EP's five cuts are as clever and tuneful as anything they ever recorded and proved they could smooth out the rough edges of their early work and still retain their unique sonic personality. "Tiger Nights" and "Barbarella," in particular, gain a lot from the band's newly polished approach. Sadly, *Beat Hotel*, the band's last album, is a severe disappointment; producer John Jansen made the quirky Bongos sound like a typical radio-friendly "new wave" band of the period, and while the group performs with genuine enthusiasm, the quality of the songwriting was not up to their previous standards.

With the exception of "A Story (Written in the Sky)" and "Splinters," there's little on *Beat Hotel* that suggests the inspiration and inventiveness of the Bongos best work; while EPs are usually tacked onto CD reissues of albums as a bonus, *Numbers with Wings* is the item worth owning here, and *Beat Hotel* is just along for the ride. —*Mark Deming*

Bongwater

f. 1985, USA, db. 1992

Experimental Rock, Indie Rock, Alternative Pop/Rock, American Underground

As much a performance art troupe as a band, Bongwater was the brainchild of guitarist (Mark) Kramer—chief of the Shimmy-Disc label and a former member of Shockabilly—and actress Ann Magnuson, best known to mainstream audiences for her role in the ABC sitcom *Anything But Love* as well as the feature film *Making Mr. Right*. Kramer and Magnuson first met at her downtown New York nightspot Club 57, where he engineered the sound for her performances with the all-female percussion group Pulsalamma; after forming Bongwater in 1985, the duo enlisted avant-garde guitarist Fred Frith to record their 1987 EP debut *Breaking No New Ground*, a crazed neo-psychedelic set typified by Magnuson's surreal narratives, often inspired by her dreams about major celebrities and fellow downtown NYC denizens.

After garnering a reputation for their anarchic live sets, Bongwater re-entered Kramer's Noise New York studios with ex-Phantom Tollbooth guitarist Dave Rick and former Shockabilly drummer David Licht to record 1988's sprawling two-LP opus *Double Bummer*, a wildly experimental collection peppered by bizarro-world covers of Gary Glitter's "Rock & Roll Pt. 2" and Led Zeppelin's "Dazed and Confused" (retitled "Dazed and Chinese" and sung in Mandarin) as well as media satires like "Decadent Iranian Country Club" and "David Bowie Wants Ideas." The follow-up, *Too Much Sleep*—a collection of lo-fi recordings mottled with dialogue fragments, sampled answering machine messages, and television soundbites—appeared in 1989.

With 1991's *The Power of Pussy*, Bongwater parodied sex in all its forms; a European tour with rhythm guitarist Dogbowl in tow followed, but Kramer and Magnuson's complex relationship soon began to unravel, and after one final record, 1992's *The Big Sell-Out*, the duo parted both personally and professionally. The dissolution of the partnership was acrimonious, and resulted in a protracted legal battle which ultimately resulted in Shimmy-Disc's bankruptcy; Magnuson, meanwhile, mounted a solo career, issuing *The Luv Show* on Geffen in 1995. —*Jason Ankeny*

● **Double Bummer** / 1988 / Shimmy-Disc ✦✦✦✦✦

Beginning an album career with an utterly schizophrenic double album that ran the gamut from reinterpretations of Led Zeppelin songs with Chinese lyrics to such zingily titled rants as "David Bowie Wants Ideas" might not seem like the most sane approach. Then again, Bongwater were one insane group. Kramer and Magnuson's screwy take on art rock á la Henry Cow or early Faust is fairly overwhelming, though perhaps this is the whole point. With the help of Kramer's fellow Shockabilly vet David Licht on drums and King Missile guitarist Dave Rick, not to mention free jazz legend Don Cherry on a cut or two, the duo cranks up the overall weirdness factor, whether quiet or loud, to great effect. One definite carryover from Kramer and Licht's Shockabilly days is a fondness for tweaked reinterpretations of older tunes. Gary Glitter's "Rock & Roll, Pt. 2," Michael Nesmith's "Just May Be the One," and the Beatles' "Love You Too" and "Rain" are among some of the victims, at points rendered unrecognizable. Johnny Cash's "There You Go," however, gets a lovely, straightforward take. The musicians' overall abilities are quite impressive; given all the recording took place at Kramer's hole-in-the-wall studio, everything sounds pretty sharp throughout, and the use of various multi-tracking and production tricks fills out *Double Bummer* very well. Magnuson, though, steals the show with both her strong singing and witty, nutty spoken word pieces. "Decadent Iranian Country Club" recounts a dream set at such a location—"pre-Ayatollah," she carefully notes—with a sweetly off semi-whisper over an increasingly queasy guitar arrangement. As for the Bowie number, she details receiving a form letter from the Thin White Duke accidentally inviting her to contribute to a new album before meeting David Byrne out of nowhere and drinking perfume, the band doing a weird-ass psych jam behind it all. The CD version includes a three-song epilogue, the *Breaking No New Ground* EP, and a single featuring covers of Roky Erickson's "You Don't Love Me Yet" and the Monkees' "The Porpoise Song." —*Ned Raggett*

Too Much Sleep / 1989 / Shimmy-Disc ✦✦✦

Helped by first album vets Rick and French horn player Coby Batty, Magnuson and Kramer whip up another set of sometimes squalling, sometimes weirdly pretty, but always just off-balance enough songs on *Too Much Sleep*. Covers again surface here, though generally done more in a spirit of appreciation rather than destruction. Two of Bongwater's witty art rock forebears Slapp Happy and the Soft Machine get the nod with fine takes on, respectively, "The Drum" (complete with a lyrical alteration or two to match Bongwater's name) and "Why Are We Sleeping." Meanwhile, American roots also get acknowledged with a nice run through the 13th Floor Elevators' "Splash 1." Fun though these are, though, it's the originals which deservedly take center stage, mixing often thick, fuzzy production, quirky pop, psychedelic strangeness, and especially Magnuson's singing and speaking abilities. Her spoken word pieces really come to the fore here, more than once resulting in overlapping recitations thanks to the joys of multi-tracking. "The Bad Review" takes a pan from Rolling Stone as a launching point for a surreal tale, while "Then the Babies Return" puts together a strange recollection of family with strange synth-pop backing. Even when the lyrics sometimes head out to realms of the curious, the music is often captivating. The title track is a great example of the group's musical chops, an at once soothing and strange vocal performance matched by Batty's French horn, seaside noises, and guitar playing and production that won't surprise anyone familiar with Kramer's work producing Galaxie 500. A number of songs feature joint

Kramer/Magnuson vocal takes, which often manages the neat trick of making things sound like a folky campfire sing-along in a radically different context. A special note should be given to the nutty album cover, done in a chunky end-of-the-'60s lettering that seems perfectly appropriate for, say, an early Black Sabbath opening act. —*Ned Raggett*

The Power of Pussy / 1991 / Shimmy-Disc ✦✦✦

Kicking off with the great title track, a slow-chugging anthem with a sharp Magnuson lead and lyric, along with guest vocals from none other than the B-52s' Fred Schneider, *Pussy* pumps up Magnuson's vicious, intelligent feminism to an even higher level than before. From the barbed "What If…" and "Women Tied Up in Knots" to her incredible spoken word "What Kind of Man Reads Playboy" and more, she's on a very artistic rampage. Style, performance, sass, and rage combine brilliantly throughout. In general, Bongwater, with Licht back on drums in place of *Sleep*'s rhythm boxes, continue as before, incorporating a more creepy sweetness at points. "Great Radio" is a standout, the group performing a slow, drony, and druggy piece with gentle power, while other songs like "I Need a New Tape" mix up the zoned psychedelic hush of past albums once again. Covers again crop up, both quite striking. The Weavers' folk standard "Kisses Sweeter Than Wine" gets a lovely, haunting take, with guest banjo from roots music legend Peter Stampfel, while Dudley Moore's hilariously dismissive "Bedazzled," from the mid-'60s film of the same name, is tailor-made for a crackerjack Magnuson spotlight vocal. Throughout *Pussy*, pop culture is roasted over a slow fire in a multitude of ways. "Nick Cave Dolls," besides concluding with Magnuson's breathy, delicious whine about wanting one of said items, slips in everything from references to Hollywood and Dorothy Stratten to some of the notorious profane tapes of Buddy Rich abusing his band. The absolute hands-down winner comes right at the end, the lengthy "Folk Song." Tackling everything from wannabe rebels to corporate and political idiocy from the top on down—not to mention a ripping dissection of then-recent hit-movie *Pretty Woman* that spares absolutely nobody—Magnuson is in excelsis throughout. —*Ned Raggett*

The Big Sell-Out / 1992 / Shimmy-Disc ✦✦✦✦✦

What turned out to be Bongwater's last album before the acrimonious end of the personal and professional Magnuson/Kramer partnership was a sellout only in the sense of the slick cover art and presentation, tongues firmly in cheek. Otherwise, the blend of folk, shadowy psych weirdness, and satiric spoken word and lyrical jabs against the state of the world, specifically America, run as rampant as always. Rick was replaced on second guitar by Raymond Hudson, but this made little general difference to Bongwater's overall approach and Kramer's distinct production style. The title track is one of their best, some lovely guitar drones and singing bringing out the weird, gentle melancholy of the song. Magnuson as always has a great time with her inspired monologues. "What's Big in England Now?" has her in sassy Noo Yawk voice talking about everything from pudgy editors at Rolling Stone to Lenny Kravitz talking about mushy peas. "Celebrity Compass" is even sharper, her depiction of a teenager at a Led Zeppelin party wondering, "Which one will take me away to live with him in his castle in England?," at once hilarious and just a little unsettling. Kramer's hero rock guitar in the background makes all the more sense. There are a couple of interesting deviations from the norm: "Free Love Messes Up My Life" keeps the duet singing prominent throughout, but the arrangement and general groove is very '60s/easy listening, some years before the big cult hype for that sound kicked in. "Flop Sweats," meanwhile, transforms Bongwater into a heavy blues/hard rock group, at least up until Magnuson starts talking about a performance artist who has merchandised and licensed her name with frightening efficiency. A lovely cover of Fred Neil's "Everybody's Talking," with additional ruminations from Magnuson, concludes this intriguing album. —*Ned Raggett*

Box of Bongwater / Oct. 20, 1998 / Shimmy-Disc ✦✦✦✦

The Bonzo Dog Band

f. 1965, Goldsmith's College, Lewisham, London, db. 1970

British Psychedelia, Psychedelic Pop, Song Parody, Comedy Rock, Psychedelic

Besides, perhaps, the Mothers of Invention (with whom they were sometimes compared), the Bonzo Dog Band was the most successful group to combine rock music and comedy. Starting off as the Bonzo Dog Dada Band, then becoming the Bonzo Dog Doo-Dah Band, and then finally just the Bonzo Dog Band, the group was started by British art college students in the mid-'60s. Initially they were inclined toward trad-jazz and vaudevillian routines, but by the time of their 1967 debut album, they were leaning further in pop and rock directions. Paul McCartney (under the pseudonym Apollo C. Vermouth) produced their single "I'm the Urban Spaceman," which reached the British Top Five in 1968. The Bonzos really hit their stride with their second and third albums, which found them adding elements of psychedelia to their already absurdist mix of pop, cabaret, and Dada. The Bonzos could be side-splitting, but their records also hold up well because they were also capable musicians and songwriters, paced by Neil Innes and Viv Stanshall. —*Richie Unterberger*

Gorilla / Oct. 1967 / BGO ✦✦✦

Gorilla was the 1967 debut album by the Bonzo Dog Doo-Dah Band, who would thereafter drop the Doo-Dah from their name and establish themselves as the greatest satirical British pop band of all time. Their first effort is far more tentative and tamer than their second and third albums, when they hit their stride by expanding their musical and topical recklessness. The Bonzos, after all, did not begin as a rock band, or even a pop band, but as a somewhat vaudevillian comedy outfit that owed a great deal to British music-hall traditions. This album may be low-key, but that's not to say it doesn't retain a good deal of charm. The humor is extremely dry, subtle, and British, leaning more toward their trad-jazz roots than the churning London pop-rock scene. It nonetheless includes a few great moments: the deadpan jazz vamp "The Intro and the Outro" (wherein a smarmy

MC introduces a bevy of historical figures in a show band, including Adolf Hitler on vibes), the film-noir satire "Mickey's Son and Daughter," and their vicious send-up of "The Sound of Music." It's not recommended as a starting point, but those who already appreciate these wonderful British eccentrics will find this an enjoyable document of the band's more restrained roots. *—Richie Unterberger*

The Doughnuts in Grannys Greenhouse / Dec. 1968 / Edsel ✦✦✦✦✦
Taking the "Doo Dah" out of their name for this 1968 LP, the Bonzos' second album was probably their best. Although they were hardly a rock or pop group in the traditional sense, the Bonzos couldn't help absorbing some of the vibes of British psychedelia, and the heady ambience of the era is reflected in the recklessly diverse and outrageous material. Almost all of the songs were penned by the two top dogs, Viv Stanshall and Neil Innes, who deflate British blues, psychedelia, and other pop, jazz, and musichall styles with priceless wit. Star tracks on this saxophone-heavy album include the doo wop ode to a spacegirl ("Beautiful Zelda"), "Trouser Press" (which gave the late American underground rock magazine its name), the droll series of poker-faced spoken sketches on "Rhinocratic Oaths" (certainly an influence on Monty Python), and the boozy "My Pink Half of the Drainpipe," which ranks as one of the most ridiculous and hysterical songs released by a pop group of any era. *—Richie Unterberger*

Urban Spaceman / Jun. 9, 1969 / One Way ✦✦✦
The band's second release, while perhaps not as delightful as their debut disc *Gorilla*, is still an enormously worthy listen. Songs here are still wonderfully bizarre and funny, clearly hinting at such over-the-top parody-minded acts as Monty Python's Flying Circus, R. Stevie Moore, and They Might Be Giants. There are no covers here as there were on their prior album, but many well-recognized styles are successfully burlesqued on this record. "Trouser Press" is an intentionally wimpy soul takeoff. The brief "Kama Sutra" is a funny parody of the Jimmy Jones hit "Handy Man." "Rockalizer," which savages psychedelic-era Beatles and related bands, is also a plausible precursor in spots for Blood, Sweat, & Tears' "Spinning Wheel." Television background music provides some of the inspiration for "Rhinocratic Oaths." "We are Normal" begins as a fragmented nonsense number redolent of free jazz and collage-style tape pieces and morphs into a fast garage-psychedelic rock song. "Hello Mabel" hearkens back to the smooth days of Rudy Vallee. "Can Blue Men Sing the Whites?" spoofs 1960s electric blues numbers. "Postcard" is primarily a lounge mood-music selection. And "My Pink Half of the Drain" betrays a cornucopia of influences, including vaudeville and urbane French movie music. Note that the Bonzos album entitled *The Doughnuts in Granny's Greenhouse* is for all practical purposes the same release as this one, lacking only the track "I'm the Urban Spaceman." *—David Cleary*

Tadpoles / Aug. 1, 1969 / One Way ✦✦✦
The Bonzos' third album is a bit of a retreat from the cosmic anything-goes atmosphere of their second LP (*Doughnuts in Granny's Greenhouse*), slanted much more heavily toward their vaudevillian trad-jazz roots. Perhaps that's because Viv Stanshall and Neil Innes, who dominated the second album, contribute only three tunes here. Still, it's never less than entertaining and has some stellar moments, like the psychedelic African safari of "Ali Baba's Camel," the skit "Shirt" (another clear forerunner of Monty Python), and the British hit single "I'm the Urban Spaceman," produced by Paul McCartney. *—Richie Unterberger*

Keynsham / Oct. 1969 / One Way ✦✦
The delightfully clever humor of the Bonzo Dog Band's prior releases almost totally eludes the group on this record. Songs here still parody familiar styles, but generally do so in a leaden and unengaging manner. A number of the selections here burlesque the late Beatles, Buffalo Springfield, and similar bands (see the songs "You Done My Brain In," "Quiet Talks and Summer Walks," "The Bride Stripped Bare by 'Bachelors,'" and "What Do You Do?" for examples). "We Were Wrong" is derived from 1950s doo wop (without the full vocal harmony to pull it off), "Mr. Slaters' Parrot" [sic] shows clear Spike Jones influences, "Sport (The Odd Boy)" is a faux-baroque period selection, and "Look at Me, I'm Wonderful" lampoons lounge singers. Unfortunately, a number of these selections are poorly paced; certain songs, such as "Busted" and "Mr. Slaters' Parrot," are either too long or too repetitive to maintain listener interest. Lyrics and performances are bland and pedestrian by past group standards, and a noticeable lack of enthusiasm permeates this disc. This weak release is only recommended to completists. *—David Cleary*

Let's Make Up & Be Friendly / Apr. 1972 / One Way ✦✦

● **History of the Bonzos** / May 24, 1974 / BGO ✦✦✦✦✦
This compilation was released as a double-LP set in 1974 and is the best Bonzos compilation (and there have been quite a few). Running an hour and 42 minutes and containing 35 tracks that span the Bonzos' five albums and some of their solo work, the album effectively presents their offbeat humor and diverse musical styles, from the 1920s music-hall pop and jazz of their early period to the more rock-oriented material they made later on. The humor is absurd and whimsical rather than laugh-out-loud funny—maybe a video compilation would be the best way to appreciate them—but you can definitely hear the makings of British comedy in the Monty Python mold here. *—William Ruhlmann*

Unpeeled / 1995 / Strange Fruit ✦✦✦
These BBC sessions from 1967-69 were titled *Unpeeled* since all but one track were recorded for John Peel's Top Gear radio show. Most of the songs are from the Bonzos' first four albums, including some of their more renowned numbers ("I'm the Urban Spaceman," "Canyons of Your Mind," "Can Blue Men Sing the Whites?") and some of rather faint renown (several tracks from *Keynsham*). For the most part these aren't too different from the studio versions, though there are memorable highlights here and there, like the raunchier vocal of "Do the Trouser Press" and Legs Larry Smith's showcase "Look at Me I'm Wonderful." Only a couple cuts didn't make it onto any of their studio recordings: the throwaway "Give Peace a Chance" parody "Give Booze a Chance," and the variety program satire "The Craig Torso Show." The latter's actually a pretty good piece, with brief but riotous takes on the Beatles' "With a Little Help From My Friends," the Diamonds' "Little Darlin'," and Frank Ifield's "I Remember You," and justly inane patter from the master of ceremonies linking the anarchic musical snippets. Note that the Strange Fruit EP *The Peel Sessions* has two 1969 BBC tracks ("We're Going to Bring It On Home" and "Sofa Head") that don't turn up on either *Unpeeled* or in studio versions on any of their five proper albums. *—Richie Unterberger*

Cornology / Jun. 30, 1998 / EMI ✦✦✦✦✦
Four-CD box including all five of their albums and various non-LP singles, rarities, and solo efforts. Of most interest to anyone who's enough of a Bonzo nut to invest in this, naturally, are the rare items, which comprise about half of the third disc (which also includes the *Let's Make Up and Be Friendly* album). There are the two 1966 singles for Parlophone, predating their first album, which find them at their most 1920s vaudevillian-influenced (even on the cover of "Alley Oop"). "Mr. Apollo" appears in its German version (which actually isn't German, except for a spoken passage by Vivian Stanshall), and its non-LP B-side, "Ready Mades," is a gentle folky tune that sounds like a *Keynsham* outtake. There's also one early solo item apiece from Vivian Stanshall (his 1970 single "Labio-Dental Fricative," on which Eric Clapton plays), Neil Innes (his 1974 single "Re-Cycled Vinyl Blues"), and Roger Ruskin Spear's "Trouser Freak" (from his 1971 EP). As an extra incentive, there are also lengthy historical liner notes. For all its length, however, it doesn't have everything by the Bonzos: BBC sessions are on *Unpeeled*, outtakes and rehearsals on *Anthropology*, and the 1966 outtake "On Her Doorstep Last Night" is on the *By Jingo It's... British Rubbish* compilation. *—Richie Unterberger*

Anthropology / Apr. 20, 1999 / Voiceprint ✦✦✦
Although the (very brief) liner notes say this is a compilation of rehearsals and demos from 1967-1968, those dates must be at least a little off, since "Give Booze a Chance" is a parody of "Give Peace a Chance," which was not released until 1969. Anyway, the 30-track disc will be of value to serious Bonzo fans, as the sound is good to excellent and the material offers glimpses of works in progress, alternate versions, and some wholly unreleased songs. Since most of this consists of not-terribly-different versions of tunes that are on Bonzo albums, however, it couldn't be recommended to the less enamored with gusto. As for some of the prime otherwise unavailable numbers, there are Viv Stanshall's doo wop parody "Mr. Hyde in Me," Neil Innes' silly piano ballad "Boiled Ham Rhumba" (a John Lennon parody perhaps?), and the oom-pah-time vaudevillian goof "Little Sir Echo." Some of the numbers have only been heard in BBC versions previously ("Give Booze a Chance," "Sofa Head"); at the other extreme, there are also renditions of some of their best-known (and best) songs, like "I'm the Urban Spaceman," "Canyons of Your Mind," and "The Equestrian Statue." *—Richie Unterberger*

The Boo Radleys

f. 1988, Liverpool, England, **db.** Feb. 1, 1999
Indie Pop, Dream Pop, Britpop, Shoegazing, Alternative Pop/Rock
Initially wannabe shoegazers, the English dream-pop group the Boo Radleys developed a dedicated cult following in the early '90s before edging into the mainstream a few years later. Formed in Liverpool in 1988, the Boo Radleys consisted of guitarist/songwriter Martin Carr, vocalist/guitarist Sice, bassist Timothy Brown, and drummer Steve Hewitt. They released their debut *Ichabod and I*, on a local independent label in 1990; Rob Cieka replaced Hewitt after the record's release. British disc jockey John Peel's support helped the band sign with Rough Trade Records, who released the 1991 EP *Every Heaven*, which was a minor U.K. chart success. Soon after, Rough Trade folded and the Boo Radleys moved to Creation Records, releasing *Everything's Alright Forever* in 1992. Columbia released the album in the U.S., but it didn't gain much attention. In England, it received favorable reviews and the group began building a fan base. Topping several Best-of-the-Year lists, including *Melody Maker*'s, 1993's *Giant Steps* was a critical success in England and sold respectably. In America, the record launched the minor alternative-rock hit "Lazarus" and led to a second-stage spot on Lollapalooza '94.

1995's Britpop-influenced *Wake Up!* was the band's commercial breakthrough, debuting at number one. The bright, brassy single "Wake Up Boo" entered in the Top Ten and stayed on the charts until the early summer, preventing the follow-up single "Find the Answer Within" from charting higher than the Top 30. Columbia did little to promote *Wake Up!* when they released it in America in the fall of 1995; they dropped the band in early 1996.

The Boo Radleys returned that fall with *C'Mon Kids*, a self-consciously arty album designed to shake off the band's newfound pop fans. It worked—the album debuted in the Top 10 but soon fell off the charts, despite overwhelmingly positive reviews. Early in 1997, the band finalized an American contract with Mercury, and *C'Mon Kids* was released in March, a half a year after its initial British release. *Kingsize* followed in late 1998, though the group officially broke up just months later. *—Stephen Thomas Erlewine*

Ichabod & I / Jul. 1990 / Action ✦✦

Everything's Alright Forever / Aug. 1992 / Creation/Columbia ✦✦✦
Happily settled on Creation Records—their understandable spiritual home, given the My Bloody Valentine connection—on their second album, the Boos create a fine but limited ode to the icons of fuzzpedals, melancholy and hooks. At the time of release, *Forever* seemed little more than yet another blissout-by-numbers, but looking back on it there's more here than on first blush. Still, *Forever* is more an anticipatory release, signaling the great leaps forward to come rather than standing on its own. Carr in particular is still

clearly enthralled by Kevin Shields' groundbreaking guitar work, with queasy riffs and shadings plentiful throughout. Producer Ed Buller does a solid job in tweaking the then-standard Boo sound, capturing the group's straightforward rock side and its experimental tendencies with inventive, lush arrangements. Check out "Lazy Day," a brief but effective number where Carr's nuclear-strength guitars are interrupted by sudden shifts to vocals and acoustic strumming with a rapid, breathless pace. Sice is the group's secret weapon; his sweet, choirboy vocals add gentleness and serenity to the proceedings, particularly "Does This Hurt?," the album's most memorable number. Based on a fine all-around band performance and Carr's gorgeous feedback shimmers and skyward solos, Sice's heavenly singing provides the perfect hook at the center of it all. Other high points include the opening "Spainard," with a lovely performance heightened by guest trumpet from Kick Horns member Roddy Lorimer. *Forever* lives up to its title well enough: everything's alright, but not yet truly astounding. *—Ned Raggett*

Giant Steps / Aug. 31, 1993 / Creation/Columbia ♦♦♦♦♦
Titling an album after John Coltrane's masterpiece may well seem the height of pretension, but heck, it never stopped the Replacements from a similar move vis-a-vis the Rolling Stones. As it is, the title is perfectly justified—Carr, a Coltrane aficionado among many other things, here finally leads his band from the promising to the truly inspired. With the inventive, groundbreaking *Lazarus* EP as a touchstone (the title track is included here in an unfortunately abbreviated form), the Boos self-produce themselves to new heights. The genius of the Boos definitely lies in their ability to adapt many a different touch and make it their own, taking what are often straightforward, hooky pop songs and turning them into something more, an ability *Giant Steps* shows in spades. The old fuzz blast is here, but less beholden to the likes of My Bloody Valentine, instead drawing on Carr's wide-ranging tastes (Beach Boys, psych-pop, Human League/New Order-inspired arrangements) to reach different, individual conclusions. From the near free-noise wash of "Run My Way Runway" to the soaring pop blast of "Barney (... and Me)," a poignant, nostalgiac lyric backed by a thrilling overall performance, the band does little wrong. Brown and Cjeka effectively incorporate dub/reggae rhythms, as "Lazarus" itself showed they could do, blending in loping, funky skank to "Upon 7th and Fairchild" and the fantastic "Butterfly McQueen." Carr's guitar work is much more distinctly his own throughout the album, with often volcanic, inspired soloing adding a huge, echoed sound to many of the songs. A number of guest performers help, notably Steve Kitchen on brass; his trumpet and flugelhorn parts and flourishes add jazzy touches throughout, at times reminiscent of Miles Davis' work on *Sketches of Spain*. *—Ned Raggett*

● **Wake Up!** / Sep. 12, 1995 / Creation/Columbia ♦♦♦♦♦
With their third album, the Boo Radleys abandoned the overt noise that obscured the pop sensibilities of their early work and scaled back the ambitions of *Giant Steps*. The result is *Wake Up!*, a glorious, brightly colored gem of a pop record. From the Beach Boy harmonies and trumpet fanfares of the opening "Wake Up Boo!" to the closing epic, McCartney-styled ballad "Wilder," the group winds through many styles of British pop. Much of the darkness—both musically and lyrically—of their previous music has been lifted; in its place is a sterling piece of pure pop, with all the big choruses, bright melodies, and simple hooks that word implies. *Giant Steps* had elements of this grand pop, yet it tried too hard. *Wake Up!* doesn't try for as much, and in doing so, it achieves more, both musically and commercially—upon the release of the album and the "Wake Up Boo!" single, the Boos became genuine Top Ten pop stars in England. The Boo Radleys were always a band with ambitions. The only difference with *Wake Up!* is that they finally fulfilled them. *—Stephen Thomas Erlewine*

C'mon Kids / Sep. 9, 1996 / Creation/Mercury ♦♦♦♦
Wake Up! brought the Boo Radleys pop success that they weren't sure what to do with. After embracing the album's number one success, the group eventually recoiled from the spotlight and Martin Carr wrote *C'mon Kids* as a direct response to the group's celebrity status in the U.K. Simply put, *C'mon Kids* is an attempt to scare away any of the fellow travelers who welcomed the sunny-sounding pop of *Wake Up!* It's a gnarled, twisted and disorted album, as dense as *Giant Steps* and as loud as the Boos' early EPs. And, if you can make it through the murky guitars, fragments of songs, altered vocals and tape effects, there's a number of melodies and creatively crafted songs that make the album nearly as rewarding as *Giant Steps* or *Wake Up!* However, it takes time to get into *C'mon Kids*, though. At first, it's disarming to hear Sice scream his vocals and the Boos play heavy riffs. After a while the melodies begin to reveal themselves, as do the clever song structures and inversions of the band's psychedelic hooks and folk tendecies. *C'mon Kids* might not be as accessible as even *Giant Steps* but it displays a feverish sense of purpose and a perverse willfullness to refashion their sound that makes it an easy album to admire, if not love. *—Stephen Thomas Erlewine*

Kingsize / Oct. 1998 / Creation ♦♦

Boogie Down Productions

f. 1986, Brooklyn, NY, **db.** 1993
Hardcore Rap, East Coast Rap, Gangsta Rap, Hip-Hop, Political Rap, Golden Age
Formed in 1986 by Laurence Krisna Parker and Scott Sterling, Boogie Down Productions quickly became one of the most influential and important hip-hop groups. Parker adopted the name KRS-One (an acronym for Knowledge Reigns Supreme Over Almost Every One) and Sterling became DJ Scott LaRock. They released an independent single, "Crack Attack," in 1986. BDP's groundbreaking 1987 debut, *Criminal Minded*, full of blunt, matter-of-fact tales of life on the mean streets, was a prototype for gangsta-rap. As the album was building to a massive underground success, LaRock was shot to death in the South Bronx as he tried to settle an argument. Instead of calling it quits, KRS-One continued BDP with *By All Means Necessary* the following year. KRS-One began calling himself "the Teacher," promoting self-awareness and education in his rhymes. It became evident that KRS-One had taken his role as the Teacher too far on 1990's *Edutainment*, where most tracks were lectures pasted over lackluster beats. KRS-One obliterated all concerns that he sold out on 1992's *Sex and Violence*, where he sounds angrier and stronger than he has in years. The following year, KRS-One released his first solo album, *Return of the Boom Bap*, which was even better; many hip-hop critics equated it with the seminal *By All Means Necessary*. But by early 1994, it had already dropped off the R&B and hip-hop charts. *—Stephen Thomas Erlewine*

★ **Criminal Minded** / 1987 / Landspeed ♦♦♦♦♦
Boogie Down Productions' 1987 debut was a watershed release in an art form poised for mass consumption. South Bronx natives KRS-One and Scott LaRock combined to form not only a signature and celebrated hip-hop group, but a social and political movement; using hip-hop as the medium, BDP gave disenfranchised inner-city citizens a voice. The album's cover and title suggest that *Criminal Minded* glorifies violence. However, this was a ploy to appeal to the reality faced by inner-city youth: self-preservation through sometimes violent means. It was a gateway to BDP's true message: self-knowledge, empowerment, and peace. DJ/producer Scott LaRock sadly became a martyr for that cause, gunned down soon after the album was released after trying to settle an argument. The legacy of BDP was left to KRS-One, the poet, scholar, teacher, and B-boy who became a hip-hop immortal from the moment he clicked on the mic and his voice rang out on the opening cut, "Poetry." On "South Bronx," KRS lays claim to the true genealogy of hip-hop, stating in true battle fashion that hip-hop's Plymouth Rock is located in his South Bronx stomping grounds. "The Bridge Is Over" is further affirmation, the definitive salvo in the Bronx vs. Queens feud and an answer to MC Shan's "The Bridge." The production on *Criminal Minded* is pure, stripped-down, skeletal brilliance. *Criminal Minded* was one of the first rap albums to utilize rock & roll and pop samples and elements; "Dope Beat" uses an AC/DC guitar riff, the a cappella opening of the title cut paraphrases the Beatles' "Hey Jude," and the bridge portion of "The Bridge Is Over" embodies Billy Joel's "It's Still Rock n' Roll to Me." *Criminal Minded* is a classic hip-hop album, a manifesto that outlines the essence of the art form. *—Michael Di Bella*

☆ **By All Means Necessary** / 1988 / Jive/Novus ♦♦♦♦♦
When his partner Scott LaRock was murdered in the Bronx in 1987, KRS-One seriously considered discontinuing Boogie Down Productions. But thankfully, the thought-provoking MC decided to keep the group going, and delivered one of 1988's finest rap albums with *By All Means Necessary*. Social and political commentary, long KRS's forte, abounds here—ranging from the anti-drug song "Illegal Business" to "Stop the Violence," a heartfelt condemnation of violence in hip-hop circles, to the humorous yet hard-hitting call for safe sex, "Jimmy." In fact, "Stop the Violence" became a rallying cry for KRS, who passsionately spoke out against Black-on-Black crime when he founded the Stop the Violence Movement. A superb follow-up to BDP's debut album, *Criminal Minded*, *Necessary* made it abundantly clear that as great a loss as LaRock's death was, KRS could be artistically triumphant on his own. Indeed, it turned out to be one of many excellent post-LaRock BDP albums. *—Alex Henderson*

Ghetto Music: The Blueprint of Hip Hop / Jun. 1989 / Jive/Novus ♦♦♦♦♦
With Boogie Down Productions' third album, *Ghetto Music: The Blueprint of Hip Hop*, KRS-One offered additional proof that he had evolved into one of rap's most intelligent voices. When other MCs were content to simply brag about their microphone skills, KRS focused on his strong point: hard-hitting social and political commentary. KRS is angry, but he's also lucid and thoughtful. From police abuse to obsessive materialism, he denounces injustice without becoming an extremist. In the 1990s, fusing rap and reggae isn't out of the ordinary; but such arresting gems as "Bo! Bo! Bo!" and "Jah Rulez" underscore the fact that KRS was among those combining the two before it became so fashionable. *—Alex Henderson*

Edutainment / Jul. 1990 / Jive/Novus ♦♦♦
KRS-One's artistic winning streak continued with *Edutainment*, Boogie Down Productions' fourth album. True to form, he focuses on Black history and speaks out on homelessness, racism, police excesses, and materialism with clarity and insight. KRS was often compared to Public Enemy leader Chuck D because of his consistently socio-political focus, but there's no mistaking the fact that his unique mixture of Black nationalism, Eastern religion (both Hinduism and Buddhism), and Rastafarian philosophy is very much his own. From a commercial standpoint, he had become a little too intellectual and wasn't selling as many albums as many in rap's gangster school. But from an artistic perspective, *Edutainment* is as commendable as it is riveting. *—Alex Henderson*

Live Hardcore Worldwide / Mar. 12, 1991 / Jive/Novus ♦♦♦

Sex and Violence / Feb. 25, 1992 / Jive/Novus ♦♦♦

Booker T. & the MG's

f. 1962, Memphis, TN, **db.** 1971
Southern Soul, Instrumental Rock, R&B, Soul
As the house band at Stax Records in Memphis, Booker T. & the MG's may have been the single greatest factor in the lasting value of that label's soul music—not to mention Southern soul as a whole. Their tight, impeccable grooves can be heard on classic hits by Otis Redding, Wilson Pickett, Carla Thomas, Albert King, and Sam & Dave, just to name the very most prominent examples. For that reason alone, they would deserve their spot in rock & roll's hall of fame. But in addition to their formidable skills as a house band, on their own they were one of the top instrumental outfits of the rock era, cutting classics like "Green Onions," "Time Is Tight," and "Hang 'em High." The anchors of the Booker T. sound were Steve Cropper, whose slicing, economic riffs influenced tons of other guitar

players, and Booker T. Jones himself, who provided much of the groove with his floating organ lines. In 1960, Jones started working as a session man for Stax; there he met Cropper, who had been in the Mar-Keys, whose 1961 instrumental hit "Last Night" laid out the protoype for much of the MG's (and indeed Memphis soul's) sound with its organ-sax-guitar combo. The band's first and biggest hit, "Green Onions" (number three, 1962), came about by accident. Jamming in the studio while fruitlessly waiting for Billy Lee Riley to show up for a session, they came up with a classic minor-key, bluesy soul instrumental, distinguished by its nervous organ bounce and ferocious bursts of guitar. For the next five years, they'd have trouble recapturing its commercial success, though the standard of their records remained fairly high, and Stax's dependence upon them as the house band ensured a decent living. In the late '60s, the MG's really hit their stride with "Hip Hug-Her," "Groovin'," "Soul-Limbo," "Hang 'em High," and "Time Is Tight," all of which were Top 40 charters between 1967 and 1969. *—Richie Unterberger*

Green Onions / Oct. 1962 / Atlantic ♦♦♦♦♦
There's not a note or a nuance out of place anywhere on this record, which was 35 of the most exciting minutes of instrumental music in any category that one could purchase in 1962 (and it's no slouch four decades out, either). "I Got a Woman" is the single best indicator of how superb this record is and this band was—listening to this track, it's easy to forget that the song ever had lyrics or ever needed them, Booker T. Jones' organ and Steve Cropper's guitar serving as more-than-adequate substitutes for any singer. Their version of "Twist and Shout" is every bit as satisfying. Even "Mo' Onions," an effort to repeat the success of "Green Onions," doesn't repeat anything from the earlier track except the tempo, and Jones and Cropper both come up with fresh sounds within the same framework.

"Behave Yourself" is a beautifully wrought piece of organ-based blues that gives Jones a chance to show off some surprisingly nimble-fingered playing, while "Stranger on the Shore" is transformed into a piece of prime soul music in the group's hands. "Lonely Avenue" is another showcase for Jones' keyboard dexterity, and then there's the group's cover of Smokey Robinson's "One Who Really Loves You," with a ravishing lead performance by Jones on organ and Cropper's guitar handling the choruses. Just when it seems like the album has turned in all of the surprises in repertory that it could reasonably deliver, it ends with "Comin' Home Baby," a killer jazz piece on which Steve Cropper gets to shine, his guitar suddenly animated around Jones' playing, his quietly trilled notes at the crescendo some of the most elegant guitar heard on an R&B record up to that time. *—Bruce Eder*

Soul Dressing / 1965 / Atlantic ♦♦♦
Assembled mostly from (non-hit) 1963-65 singles, this is solid stuff, but a notch below their peak collections. The best tracks ("Soul Dressing," "Tic-Tac-Toe," "Can't Be Still") are usually included on their best-of anthologies, but "Plum Nellie," featuring some ferocious, cutting-edge solos by Cropper and Jones, is an overlooked highlight. *—Richie Unterberger*

☆ **The Best of Booker T. & the MG's [Atlantic]** / Nov. 1968 / Atlantic ♦♦♦♦♦
The Stax Records catalog ended up partially in the hands of Atlantic Records and partially with Fantasy Records, and the dividing point is 1968. That's why there are two Booker T. & the MG's hits compilations. This one, *The Best Of...*, presents the material owned by Atlantic. There are 12 tracks, covering the group's popular instrumental hits from "Green Onions" in the summer of 1962 to "Groovin'" in the summer of 1967. Booker T. & the MG's scored some of their biggest hits, including "Hang 'em High" and "Time Is Tight," in 1968-1969, and for those you will have to look to the Stax/Fantasy *Greatest Hits*, originally released in October 1970. Just to be confusing, in 1991 Fantasy released an album called *The Best Of* that again contains only the later material. [Rhino's *Very Best Of* finally combined the two eras.] *–William Ruhlmann*

The Best of Booker T. & the MG's [Stax] / 1986 / Stax ♦♦♦
Somewhat confusingly, this disc is titled identically to a CD on Atlantic that concentrates on their earlier material. This 17-cut disc draws from 1967-1971, and includes three of their four Top 20 pop hits: "Soul Limbo," "Hang 'em High," and "Time Is Tight." This perhaps lacks a bit of the edge of their mid-'60s recordings, concentrating on loping, relaxed grooves more than biting, incisive chops. The standard remains pretty high, though, with the interplay between Steve Cropper's guitar, Booker T. Jones' organ, and the rhythm section never less than telepathic. Most of the material is original, but even on the covers of period pop hits—including unlikely versions of "Something," "Eleanor Rigby," and "Mrs. Robinson"—the group is soulful and tight. This is perhaps better music for background and party listening than anything else, but within those confines it's quite good. *—Richie Unterberger*

★ **The Very Best of Booker T. & the MG's** / Jun. 21, 1994 / Rhino ♦♦♦♦♦
This 16-song CD, clocking in at 46 minutes, is the second-best, and the handiest and most easily affordable, compilation available on Booker T. & the MG's. It's not remotely as comprehensive as Fantasy Records' three-CD set (although this disc does have two tracks, "Booker-Loo" and "Slum Baby," that don't appear on the triple-CD set) but is more comprehensive and better representative of their work (and offers better sound) than either Fantasy's single-disc best-of or the old Atlantic Records' best-of compilation. The collection does jump around a bit across history in the course of covering the years 1963-1971, bouncing between late-'60s singles and album tracks and odd early/middle-'60s tracks. "Booker-Loo," one of the pieces unique to this set, features some very crunchy rhythm guitar and flamboyant organ work in its intro, before Steve Cropper takes center stage with an unusually flashy lead guitar solo spot. "Slum Baby," from three years later, features a much smoother and funkier sound. "Slim Jenkins' Place" shows off Booker T. Jones' piano skills as well as his organ playing, and all of it is marked by virtuoso playing. The collection also makes a strong case for the band's members as composers—hits like "Hang 'Em High" come off beautifully, especially in the crisply remastered version presented here, which brings out every nuance in the organ and guitar-dominated rendition of Dominic Frontiere's theme from the Clint Eastwood movie of that name. But originals like the majestic, soaring "Time Is Tight" and the lyrical, playful "Soul-Limbo" are great pieces of pop-soul composition as well, and stand up just as well to repeated listening. Buy the triple-disc set if it's in your budget, but at less than one-third of the cost, this collection shouldn't be dismissed for its compactness and range. *—Bruce Eder*

Time Is Tight / Oct. 6, 1998 / Stax ♦♦♦♦♦
A three-CD, 65-song box set that includes all their hits from 1962 through 1971, in addition to numerous LP tracks and failed singles; the third disc is devoted entirely to previously unreleased live material (most from 1992-94) and rarities. Greatest-hits compilations will serve the needs of all but intense Booker T. and Stax fans. However, if you really dig their instrumental sound, this is a fine package. It might skip an odd worthy track from their catalog, but basically has just about everything deserving of attention, concentrating more on their original compositions than their covers. Some of the more obscure selections, like their jazzy 1967 LP cut "Pigmy" and their inventive 1969 cover of "Lady Madonna," are overlooked standouts. A number of sides here, like "Burnt Biscuits," "Fannie Mae," "Sunday Sermon," "MG Party," and the moody, dignified "Meditation," were never on album before. Other oddities fans will want to know about is a live medley of James Brown material from 1968, Albert King doing "Born Under a Bad Sign" with them live (also from 1968), a hit 1965 single ("Hole in the Wall") released under the name "the Packers," and "Booker's Theme," which was only available on the 1969 Stax various-artists sampler *Soul Explosion*. The 1992-94 live cuts (all previously unreleased), with various drummers in place of the late Al Jackson, show the band in decent though not amazing form, including a ten-minute jam on "Time Is Tight" and a version of "(Sittin' On) The Dock of the Bay" with Neil Young on vocals. The booklet contains extensive liner notes by Stax Records authority Rob Bowman. *—Richie Unterberger*

The Boomtown Rats

f. 1975, Dun Laoghaire, Ireland, **db.** 1986
New Wave, Punk
The Boomtown Rats were an Irish rock band that scored a series of British hits between 1977 and 1980 and were led by singer Bob Geldof, who organized the Ethiopian relief efforts Band Aid and Live Aid. After moving from Ireland to London in late 1976, the group became associated with punk rock and released their debut single, "Lookin' After No. 1." It was the first of nine straight singles to make the U.K. Top 15. The Boomtown Rats' second album, 1978's *A Tonic for the Troops*, featured a number one hit in "Rat Trap" and spawned an American contract with Columbia Records. "I Don't Like Mondays" became their second straight British number one (and their only U.S. chart entry), though the band slipped from the charts soon after. Shades of the end came in 1983, when Columbia rejected the Boomtown Rats' sixth album *In the Long Grass* (eventually released by Ensign). One year later, Geldof formed the star-studded Band Aid group to record his song "Do They Know It's Christmas?" for Ethiopian relief, resulting in the biggest selling single in U.K. history. He then organized the two Live Aid concerts. Despite a belated U.S. release of *In the Long Grass*, the Boomtown Rats folded soon after and Geldof launched a solo career. *— William Ruhlmann*

The Boomtown Rats / Sep. 1977 / Mercury ♦♦♦
Anyone who heard the Boomtown Rats' debut single, "Lookin' After No. 1," with its rapid drum beat, slashing guitars, and aggressive singing about impatience with the dole queue, would think of the group as a particularly tight, standard punk rock band on the London scene in 1977. The Rats' debut album also featured the leering "Mary of the Fourth Form," their second single, but the rest of the album revealed more traditional rock influences. "Joey's on the Street Again" sounded like the sort of street opera Bruce Springsteen was aiming for on *The Wild, the Innocent & the E Street Shuffle*. "I Can Make It If You Can" was the sort of ballad the Rolling Stones favored in the mid-'70s. Overall, there were enough power chords and snotty sentiments to justify the punk tag, but it was already clear that the Rats aspired to the mainstream. *— William Ruhlmann*

Tonic for the Troops / Jun. 1978 / Columbia ♦♦♦
Bob Geldof had revealed a taste for the seamy side of things in his lyrics for the Boomtown Rats' first album. On their second record, he fantasized about being Hitler in the person of the Leader of the Pack ("I Never Loved Eva Braun"), romanticized tropical suicide ("Living In An Island"), and identified with a certain wealthy recluse ("Me And Howard Hughes"). The band retained a punk energy on the album's U.K. hit singles, "Like Clockwork," "She's So Modern," and "Rat Trap" (another of Geldof's Springsteen homages), but musical identity was still a song-by-song affair. [In the U.S., Columbia replaced "Can't Stop" and "(Watch Out For) The Normal People" with "Mary Of The 4th Form" and "Joey's On The Street Again" from the first album.] *— William Ruhlmann*

The Fine Art of Surfacing / Oct. 1979 / Columbia ♦♦♦
The Boomtown Rats had achieved a peak of band interplay by their third album, leading inevitably to such developments as the use of strings, while lyricist/singer Bob Geldof had taken on an acerbic social consciousness about the pressures of modern life as his major subject. But this didn't always add up to strong songwriting. When it did, on the singles "Someone's Looking at You" and especially "I Don't Like Mondays," the Boomtown Rats could be compelling—Geldof's lyrics seemed acute instead of obvious, the band arrangements seemed crisp and clever rather than gimmicky. But that didn't happen often enough to make *The Fine Art of Surfacing* a consistent success. *— William Ruhlmann*

Mondo Bongo / Feb. 1981 / Columbia ♦♦
On their fourth album, the Boomtown Rats submitted to ambitiousness, with singer Bob Geldof attempting to assume the mantle of Bob Dylan, the Beatles, and the Rolling Stones, while the band tried to keep up with musical fashions in Britain. The combina-

tion led to such oddities as a ska-beat rewrite of the Stones' "Under My Thumb" and a couple of side-opening mambos. The band was at its best when it returned to the pop music that was its core on such songs as the Buddy Holly-ish "Don't Talk to Me" and especially the danceable "Up All Night," but they were buried on the second side of an uneven collection that made the Rats' sense of direction seem uncertain. *—William Ruhlmann*

V Deep / Apr. 1982 / Columbia ✦✦

On their fifth album and reduced to a quintet, the Boomtown Rats moved closer to Caribbean rhythms, employing a percussionist and upping the bass guitar in the mix. They even had Dennis Bovell do a dub mix of "House on Fire" and included it at the end of the album. Meanwhile, Bob Geldof's lyrics indicated an increasingly embattled sensibility; he noted in a song called "The Bitter End" that "It isn't too far." Unfortunately, nothing here matched the catchy, daring work on the Rats' first three albums, and even in England their star was beginning to fade. In America, Columbia Records at first declined to release the album, opting for a four-track EP, then allowed it to escape in September 1982, when it failed to chart. *—William Ruhlmann*

In the Long Grass / May 1985 / Columbia ✦✦✦

The Boomtown Rats' sixth album was very much a return to the pop/rock style of their first two albums: 4/4 beats, prominent rock guitar lines, urgent vocals. But as the desperate lyrics (titles include "Drag Me Down" and "Hard Times") implied, the record was more a last hurrah than a new beginning. Upon its 1984 release on Mercury Records in the U.K., it did spawn a couple of minor British chart singles, but it missed the LP chart, a major decline for a band that had enjoyed Top Ten success at its height. In America, Columbia Records rejected the album, and only released it a year later to try to cash in on Bob Geldof's fame in connection with his organization of Live Aid. *—William Ruhlmann*

● **Great Songs of Indifference: The Best of Bob Geldof & the Boomtown Rats** / Apr. 22, 1997 / Columbia/Legacy ✦✦✦✦✦

Great Songs of Indifference: The Best of Bob Geldof & the Boomtown Rats is the first comprehensive collection compiled on not only the Boomtown Rats, but also Bob Geldof's solo career. All of the group's biggest hits, including "I Don't Like Mondays," "Looking After Number One" and "Banana Republic," are here, as are a handful of solo tracks; while those aren't as strong as the Rats cuts, they neverthless sum up Geldof's post-Boomtown career quite effectively. In other words, it's a definitive retrospective. *—Stephen Thomas Erlewine*

Pat Boone (Charles Eugene Patrick Boone)

b. Jun. 1, 1934, Jacksonville, FL

Vocals / Teen Idol

In the years immediately prior to the British Invasion, only one performer rivaled the chart dominance of Elvis Presley, and that was Pat Boone. With his trademark white buck shoes, perfectly combed hair and gleaming smile, Boone was the very essence of wholesome American values, and at a time when the rise of rock & roll was viewed as a sign of the apocalypse, he made the music appear safe and non-threatening, earning some 38 Top 40 hits in the process. It's fitting that his achievements rank closest to those of Presley; after all, both claimed the sound of the black R&B culture for their own, in the process straddling both sides of the color line and popularizing a form of music which otherwise might never have gained widespread acceptance. Of course, while Elvis—with his flashy suits, swiveling hips and suggestive leer—remained persona non grata throughout many corners of mainstream America, Boone was embraced by teens and parents alike; his music polished rock's rough edges away, making songs like "Tutti Frutti" and "Ain't That a Shame" palatable to white audiences raised on the soothing pop traditions of a vanishing era. *—Jason Ankeny*

● **Pat Boone's Greatest Hits** / Aug. 1962 / MCA ✦✦✦✦✦

Including 18 of his highest charting hits for the Dot label in the '50s and early '60s, this is easily the best basic Boone collection. It doesn't include his hit covers of "At My Front Door" and Little Richard's "Long Tall Sally" and "Tutti Frutti," which is perhaps just as well for all concerned. *—Richie Unterberger*

Jivin' Pat / Feb. 1986 / Bear Family ✦✦✦✦✦

All of Boone's rockers—cover versions of Fats Domino, Little Richard, et al.—are included with a revealing set of liner notes. You won't find these elsewhere unless you have an enormous singles collection. *—Hank Davis*

More Greatest Hits / Oct. 25, 1994 / Varese Sarabande ✦✦✦

Contains 17 of Pat Boone's later and lesser chart hits. *—William Ruhlmann*

Fifties: Complete / Aug. 5, 1997 / Bear Family ✦✦✦✦✦

This 12-CD box set containing 347 songs—Pat Boone's entire 1950s recorded output, including over 80 previously unissued tracks—deserves an honest, open-minded, and thorough examination. Listeners may like or dislike Pat Boone's early R&B hits—"Two Hearts," "Ain't That a Shame," "Tutti Frutti," etc.—but it is important to remember that those songs comprise but a very small part of his 1950s recorded output and demonstrate one side only of his amazing versatility. Certainly on any voluminous, comprehensive collection, not all the tracks are going to be gems, and this anthology contains a few that don't shine so brightly. However, the vast majority of material here has so very much to recommend it. "Exquisite" and "impeccable" are adjectives that do not exaggerate Boone's unaffected, natural, and totally wholehearted way with a song. Whether it's "Stardust," "Begin the Beguine," "Cheek to Cheek," "Yes Indeed," "St. Louis Blues," "More Than You Know"—these and countless others are all done to perfection. The accolades that came Pat Boone's way during the '50s included critical acclaim and raves from Sinatra, Crosby, Como, and many other contemporaries and critics alike. In an August 1957 interview with Red Robinson in Vancouver, BC, Elvis Presley said of Pat Boone, "the finest voice in music today." That all by itself says a lot. This box set has the potential of opening a lot of new eyes and maybe some closed eyes as well. *—Arthur Rowe*

20th Century Masters—The Millennium Collection: The Best of Pat Boone / Dec. 5, 2000 / MCA ✦✦✦✦

The title of this collection seems to suggest that the new millennium is cause for a re-examination of Boone's musical contributions. And that may be the case, if only to remember that he rivaled the chart dominance of Elvis Presley during the early years of rock-and-roll, and that whereas Elvis popularized the stylings of unrecognized black artists, Boone "protected" suburban America from black R&B performers by offering tamer versions of their hits. As evidence, this collection offers his stilted, ultra-velvety takes on Fats Domino's "Ain't That a Shame," the Flamingos' "I'll Be Home," and Ivory Joe Hunter's "I Almost Lost My Mind," all of which provided hits for Pat. (Strangely absent, however, is his version of Little Richard's "Tutti Frutti.) To his credit, Boone was somehow able to extricate any sense of sexuality or danger from rock-and-roll—no mean feat. Nevertheless, one can't dismiss the fact that Boone was a first-class pop crooner, and that when he wasn't committing offenses against rock & roll, he was rivaling the talents of Dean Martin and Eddie Fisher on such well-suited tracks as "Friendly Persuasion (Thee I Love)." *—Erik Hage*

Boredoms

Noise, Experimental Rock, Noise-Rock

With the support of Sonic Youth and Nirvana behind them, Boredoms released a major-label album in 1993, which may be the most impressive thing about this almost unlistenable band. For several years, Boredoms have been the leaders of Japan's wave of noise bands inspired by Sonic Youth's early records and other artists from that scene. What separates Boredoms from early Sonic Youth is songs—Boredoms don't have any. And they don't care if they do, either. Instead, records like 1994's *Chocolate Synthesizer* and 1996's *Super Roots, Vol. 6* get by on sheer willpower and stacks of effects pedals and amplifiers. *Vision Creation Newsun* followed with more noisy quirkiness in early 2001. Unless one has an extreme amount of patience or enjoys listening to the sounds of heavy machinery, chances are they won't be able to tolerate Boredoms. Which is exactly what they want, by the way. *—Stephen Thomas Erlewine*

Soul Discharge / 1990 / Shimmy-Disc ✦✦✦✦✦

For American and European audiences, Boremania began with this album. Released on the then hyperhip Shimmy-Disc, *Soul Discharge* turned out to be the calling card for a whole host of Japanese noise/psychedelic bands to make the leap from noteriety at home to cult status worldwide. Time hasn't dulled the impact of the album, as astonishing then as it is now. Playing what the liner notes describe (with a nod to George Clinton), as "psychoalphadiscobetaudioaquadoloop sound," *Soul* beggars easy description, taking the band's previous work to an even more compelling level of insanity. The Butthole Surfers were always the easiest point of comparison, but even that doesn't fully capture what's at play. Tempo shifts occur as a matter of course, lyrics are flat-out unintelligible in no matter what language they're sung, or rather screamed, and guitars seem to randomly trip, sprawl, and vomit over each other as roiling and rolling drums drive the whole thing along (Human Rich Vox Y and No. 1 Y, aka Yoshimi, make for a killer dual-percussionist team). Simply put, it's wonderful. The bandmembers' sense of humor and sheer fun predominate more than anything else, taking sonics most thrash metal bands would kill for and making them the equivalent of a sugar/caffeine high. Definitely one of the funnier moments occurs when "52 Boredom (Club Mix)" begins almost exactly like a B-52s' song, and then freaks out completely within seconds. Another strength of the band is how they sneak in catchy bits amidst weirdness, like the almost straightforward, hip-shaking break in "Sun, Gun, Run" or the heavy-duty riff in "TV Scorpion." Adding the squealing insanities of Yamatsuka Eye and P-We YY results in something that even Captain Beefheart might never have been able to create. *—Ned Raggett*

Wow 2 / Oct. 1992 / Avant ✦✦✦✦

Released on Avant, run by Yamatsuka Eye's Naked City bandmate John Zorn, and recorded by him with help from Martin Bisi, *Wow 2* surfaced around the same time that *Pop Tatari* made its initial Japanese bow on Warner Bros. Saying the first album is more experimental and uncommercial than the second is pushing it—it's not like the Boredoms were going to release catchy pop ditties all of a sudden. Rather, *Wow 2* is just another wiggy slice of what makes the Boredoms' sound such a great, unpredictable experience. If anything, this release is actually more straightforward than *Pop Tatari*. The overall sound of the album feels a bit hollow; there's a lot of echo at points, especially noticeable on the scraps of unaccompanied vocals. Still, it's presumably intentional, as is the feeling that everything was recorded in single takes without overdubbing. Eye is the predominant vocalist throughout, and compared to the near Bomb Squad levels of musical interplay on *Soul Discharge*, the songs here are blunter and much more direct, with crunching lead riffs quite obvious at points. Various flute and sax noises crop up in the usual tumult of sound; whether it's Zorn having fun is left unclear in the liner notes, but it's equally likely that the Boredoms simply tackle wind instruments the same way they do electric: with gusto. "Pop Can" deserves mention for its remarkably restrained feel, with an ominous call-and-response feel to it; even when things start freaking out a bit, the plodding drum/bass combination keeps grinding along while the guitar plays a few high notes rather than launching into more slabs of feedback. The spacy guitar on "Rydeen!!" also sounds great—a nice indication of the semi-prog sense that creeps further into their music on later releases. *—Ned Raggett*

● **Pop Tatari** / 1993 / Reprise ✦✦✦✦✦

Appearing in America after an initial Japanese release, and with a revamped track listing and song titles to boot ("Bocabola" is called that here only because somebody somewhere was worried about what a certain soft drink company might think of the original title), *Pop Tatari* definitely holds the crown as being one of the strangest things to surface under a major label's auspices. Even the Butthole Surfers' major label debut that year looked straightforward in comparison. Starting off with "Noise Ramones," which consists solely of various high-pitched tones like those of the Emergency Broadcast System, *Tatari* contains some nearly conventional bits. Yet even the semi-lounge smoothness of "Nice B-O-R-E Guy Boyoyo Touch" collapses just enough, while elsewhere the screaming lunacy of fullthrottle Boremania rampages unchecked. Songs shudder to stops, launch into roaring mania and deathstomp rattle, and crunch more quickly and unexpectedly than those of just about anybody else—no real change there, then! Add dashes of heavy funk mania ("Bo Go" would do early Funkadelic proud) along with whatever logic operates inside the band members' skulls, and the result is more cockeyed genius. Yamatsuka Eye rants above the whole mess like a man possessed, trading off with other band members in ways that practically redefine call and response. Singling out all the highlights would take forever, but "Bore Now Bore" feels like a mid-'60s frug played by berserk aliens, with some random electronics to boot, while a cover of the old Peggy Lee standard "Fever," retitled "Heeba," keeps the central riff but abandons just about everything else; the lyrics sound like they're slurred through cotton and various thrashy instrumental breaks. Concluding with the multigenre purée of "Cory & the Mandara Suicide Pyramid Action or Gas Satori," *Tatari* kicks out the jams eight different ways at once. —*Ned Raggett*

Chocolate Synthesizer / 1994 / Reprise ✦✦✦

Super Roots / 1994 / Reprise ✦✦✦

Onanie Bomb Meets Sex Pistols / Nov. 22, 1994 / Reprise ✦✦✦
Collecting the contents of the band's first two Japanese releases, *Onanie Bomb* shows that, from the start, the Boredoms were interested in musical chaos of a most unique degree. Rough but not lo-fi, *Onanie* rips, stomps, and explodes all over the place in several directions at once. Purists might object to calling some of what is whipped up "songs," but the goofy insanity in the death-march-meets-squalling-cartoon-voices of "We Never Sleep," and even the song titles which reach beyond over the top, like "Lick'n Cock Boatpeople" and "Anal Eater," could only be resisted by the stodgiest of souls. For all the extreme noise at play, what's evident on *Onanie* is the sheer sense of fun, much like the Boredoms' early inspirations, the Butthole Surfers. Thus, "Bite My Bollocks" sounds like a '50s strut and stroll revisited after several apocalypses—a party where everyone has lost any sense of trying to be cool; where everyone wants to not merely burn down the house, but smash it to atoms. More than a few sounds wouldn't seem out of place on some of Yoko Ono's early albums, but there's something just a little more gone about tracks like the hyperspeed thrash of "No Core Punk" and "Melt Down Boogie"; they aren't so much stretching the boundaries of rock as they are torpedoing them and tossing the bits around in the air. One track ends with extended burp noises that eventually fade into semi-nothingness; another seems to consist of feedback noises recorded in a sheet metal factory and interspersed with wails and sudden attempts at solos. Topping off all of that with album art indicating that the performers play such instruments as "bicyclesynth," "tennis," and "kick & hit & shot," and clearly, the Boredoms aren't catering to "normalville"—nobody is in Kansas anymore. —*Ned Raggett*

Super Roots, Vol. 6 / Aug. 20, 1996 / Reprise ✦✦
Super Roots, Vol. 7 / 1998 / Warner Brothers Japan ✦✦✦✦
The seventh volume of the Boredoms' between-album *Super Roots* project is one of the Japanese band's finest releases, and possibly its most accessible. The lengthy original track "7" is a radically expanded instrumental cover of the Mekons' "Where Were You" with two remixes serving as bookends. Though a 34-minute EP based around a single brief punk song seems ridiculous, Boredoms pull it off with widely varying sounds and textures. The original track begins by following the structure of the anthemic Mekons song closely, then slides into hypnotic motorik rock inspired by Neu! before abruptly shifting into Stooges-style thrash, and then fading out on woozy, downcast note. The two remixes are comparatively tame but no less interesting, with gurgling electronics and slow, choppy beats. Because they are blended seamlessly with the original track, this EP has the feel of one long piece. Fold in some of Eye's most successful tape manipulation experiments and you have a high-water mark for this consistently inventive band. —*Mark Richardson*

Super Ae / Oct. 20, 1998 / Birdman ✦✦✦
Surfacing again with an American release after a couple years of absence, the Boredoms showed themselves to still be truly a unique proposition with *Super Ae*. Taking some more of the prog/Kraut influences that crept into earlier efforts while still firing up the amps all around, Eye and his cohorts (forming a core quintet this time around) once again become the most out-there band in the world. "Super You" is a simply fantastic way to start, with initial whizzing stereo-to-stereo sounds leading into a wonderful collection of slow, ponderous death rock riffs that sound like all the Black Sabbath and Metallica wannabes of the world gathered to create one massive opening fanfare via guitars. Logically the Boredoms spike the punch by interrupting things with sped-up tape sounds and pitch changes, making the proceedings all the more fun. From there, *Super Ae* continues along to something close to a concept album; each track feels like a perfect lead in to the rest, while the whole sense is of one long, mantra-like piece, faster or slower as the band feels like it. The big change is that the volume is not so much used to stun as it is to maintain a general atmosphere while the rhythm section cranks along in semi-motorik style, a bit like Can with some even freer spirits at play. Not everything is total destruction in the Boredoms scheme of things, admittedly—"Super Coming" has some hilarious cartoony vocals from all participants. "Super Are" begins with a serene keyboard performance and chanting background vocals before turning into a psych/acid folk drum/singing jam session á la Amon Düül or fellow countrymen Ghost. Needless to say, though, the amps and

monster sludge kick in soon enough, and quite well at that! "Super Good," the album closer, also has a nicely calm way about it. —*Ned Raggett*

Soul Discharge: 1999 / Apr. 4, 2000 / Wea International ✦✦✦

Vision Creation Newsun / Feb. 6, 2001 / Warner Brothers Japan ✦✦✦
Vision Creation Newsun finds Boredoms moving even further away from the random noise that marked their early output and settling into a loose, jam-oriented aesthetic. The first two tracks (no song titles here, only symbols) find Boredoms further investigating pounding tribal rock with propulsive drumming, energetic guitar work, and vocal chants. The overall feel bears some similarity to *Super Ae*, with tracks that draw from Krautrock and psychedelia, but *Vision Creation Newsun* adds a folk element, including softer instrumental textures like hand percussion, lengthy cymbal washes, and acoustic guitars. Some passages even flirt with new age, as they weave bird songs and the sound of falling water into the mix. These delicate touches aptly demonstrate the sonic range of Boredoms, but some of these meandering pieces can get tedious. Still, the highlights are many. Guitarist Yama-Motor is the star here, and most of *Vision Creation Newsun*'s best moments come from his hypnotic style and deep bag of effects. He is equally at home with the Spacemen 3-style feedback shriek of the second track as he is with the minimalist acoustic work that dominates the latter half of the album. The dual percussion of Yoshimi and ATR is also powerful, but when songs break into long drum solos, Boredoms will lose their more punk-oriented fans. This is not the left-field triumph that *Super Ae* was, but it's a strong album nonetheless. —*Mark Richardson*

Boss Hog

Indie Rock, Alternative Pop/Rock
All-star NYC blues-punk combo Boss Hog was helmed by the husband-and-wife team of singer Cristina Martinez and singer/guitarist Jon Spencer, who previously teamed in the legendary cult band Pussy Galore. The duo formed Boss Hog to fill a last-minute cancellation at the famed CBGB's, earning instant notoriety when Martinez performed their debut show au naturel; guitarists Jerry Teel and Kurt Wolf, bassist Pete Shore, and drummer Charlie Ondras completed the line-up for 1989's cassette-only *Drinkin', Lechin', and Lyin'*. In the wake of 1990's *Cold Hands*, Spencer formed the Blues Explosion, forcing Boss Hog on the backburner; by the time the group returned in 1993 with *Girl +*, only Martinez and Spencer remained from the original lineup, with ex-Swan Jens Jürgensen assuming bass duties and Hollis Queens joining on drums. The record's success in indie circles resulted in a deal with major label Geffen which yielded a self-titled 1995 LP; little was heard from Boss Hog throughout the remainder of the decade (although Spencer and Martinez had a baby), but in early 2000 the group finally resurfaced with *Whiteout*, featuring ex-Goats keyboardist Mark Boyce. —*Jason Ankeny*

Drinkin' Lechin' & Lyin' / 1989 / Amphetamine Reptile ✦✦✦

Cold Hands / 1990 / Amphetamine Reptile ✦✦

Boss Hog / Oct. 10, 1995 / DGC ✦✦✦
While Jon Spencer spent much of his time in Pussy Galore trying to destroy rock & roll as fans know it, by the time he got the Jon Spencer Blues Explosion rolling, he'd come to the belated conclusion that old-school rock and R&B could be pretty cool after all, and since the history of Boss Hog—one of Spencer's seemingly infinite number of side projects—overlaps with Pussy Galore, you get to witness this transformation over the course of their recording career. While Boss Hog's first album was a nearly unlistenable morass of aural sludge, six years later, their self-titled major-label debut turns out to be a very solid album in the same rootsy grit-rock vein as the Blues Explosion's best work. If anything, Christina Martinez, Spencer's partner in crime (and spouse), is a stronger vocal presence on this record, if only because she hasn't developed quite as elaborate a *shtick* as Spencer—she just belts it out in a sturdy blues-punk style, unlike Spencer's often amusing but sometimes irritating collection of blues and rockabilly affectations. Boss Hog also display a far greater willingness to get funky than JSBX; they're not ready to face the Meters in a battle of "on the one," but the best cuts here boast a more sensuous feel for groove than the prime suspects have shown in the past. In short, *Boss Hog* shows that somewhere down the line Spencer and Martinez learned the importance of getting a groove on, and though that groove is rough, noisy, and ill-tempered, you can still dance to it. —*Mark Deming*

● **Whiteout** / Feb. 22, 2000 / In The Red ✦✦✦✦
It's difficult to consider Boss Hog without invoking the name of Jon Spencer. Not only is the Blues Explosion leader a member of Boss Hog, but he's also married to Boss Hog leader Christina Martinez, so his overwrought post-modern downtown, white-boy bluesfunk is always lurking just around the corner. To her credit, on *Whiteout* Martinez keeps the dude at bay by taking the aesthetic helm (taking bass player Jens Jurgensen, drummer Hollis Queens, and keyboardist Mark Boyce along for the ride, too). The ten cuts that comprise this, Boss Hog's sixth album, are obviously her vessel. Don't be fooled by the dreamy atmospherics, the sultry vocal ruminations, or the awkwardly funky new romantic synth beats; she's painting the picture of garage punk and new wave girl groups as refracted through a 21st century looking glass. So, while it's occasionally as cheesy as Human League or as awkwardly skittish as the Rezillos, *Whiteout* ultimately finds Boss Hog able to manipulate the best of these associations to its benefit and remain as smoldering and funky as a hot NYC August night. And, while past recorded excursions have been hit or miss scattered affairs, *Whiteout* is a cohesive sonic effort that manages to keep its sneer without resorting to too many of Spencer's goofball faux-Elvis machismo antics. Christina Martinez has broken the indie rock rules again. —*Chris Handyside*

Boston

f. 1971, Boston, MA

Album Rock, Arena Rock, Pop/Rock, Hard Rock

The arena-rock group behind one of the fastest-selling debut albums in history, Boston was essentially the vehicle of studio wizard Tom Scholz. A rock fan and songwriter even while earning a master's degree at MIT, he joined a local band led by guitarist Barry Goudreau and constructed his own 12-track recording studio in his basement. Along with vocalist Brad Delp, bassist Fran Sheehan and drummer John "Sib" Hashian, the group—now dubbed Boston—earned a contract with Epic. The 1976 release of *Boston* (consisting largely of Scholz's original basement tapes) spawned three hit singles ("More Than a Feeling," "Long Time" and "Peace of My Mind"), shot immediately to the top of the charts, and became the best-selling pop debut in history. Scholz spent over two years working on the follow-up, 1978's number one hit *Don't Look Back*. The third Boston album, *Third Stage*, didn't appear until 1986, at which time only Scholz and Delp remained. During the '80s, Scholz was sued by Goudreau, who alleged that Scholz had damaged his solo career (they settled out-of-court) and Epic, who claimed Boston had reneged on their contract by taking so long between releases (he won). When the band resurfaced again in 1994 with *Walk On*, Scholz was the lone remaining member; Delp and Goudreau had reunited in 1992 as RTZ, releasing the album *Return to Zero*. In addition to his fame as a musician, Scholz also found success as an inventor and businessman. *—Jason Ankeny*

● **Boston** / Sep. 1976 / Epic ✦✦✦✦✦

Boston is one of the best-selling albums of all time, and deservedly so. Because of the rise of disco and punk, FM rock radio seemed all but dead until the rise of acts like Boston, Tom Petty, and Bruce Springsteen. Nearly every song on Boston's debut album can still be heard on classic rock radio today due to the strong vocals of Brad Delp and unique guitar sound of Tom Scholz. Tom Scholz, who wrote most of the songs, was a studio wizard and used self-designed equipment such as 12-track recording devices to come up with an anthemic "arena rock" sound before the term was even coined. The sound was hard rock, but the layered melodies and harmonics reveal the work of a master craftsman. While much has been written about the sound of the album, the lyrics are often overlooked. There are songs about their rise from a bar band ("Rock & Roll Band") as well as fond remembrances of summers gone by ("More Than a Feeling"). *Boston* is essential for any fan of classic rock, and the album marks the re-emergence of the genre in the 1970s. *—Vik Iyengar*

Don't Look Back / Aug. 1978 / Epic ✦✦✦✦

The follow-up to Boston's mega-hit first album, *Boston*, *Don't Look Back* took two long years to complete. It is hard to figure out why it took so long because it is almost exactly the same as their debut. The guitars still sound like they are being fed through computers and stacked into great walls of sound by robots. Lead singer Brad Delp still sounds like he is ripping his throat out. The harmony vocals still sound like a choir of androids warbling angelically. Most importantly, the songs are overflowing with hooks, there are plenty of riffs to air guitar to, and the songs stick in your head like dirt on a dog. The main difference lies in the semi-melancholy tone of the record. *Boston* was a nonstop block rockin' record but one look at the song titles lets you know that *Don't Look Back* is a little less upbeat: "A Man I'll Never Be," "Used to Bad News," "It Ain't Easy." These songs reveal a reflective side that was nowhere to be found on *Boston*. Not to say the record doesn't rock because it does mightily. "Don't Look Back" has a killer riff that's very similar to the timeless riff in "More Than a Feeling." "Party" is a storming rocker much like "Smokin'." *Don't Look Back* is basically *Boston*, Pt. 2, but don't let that put you off because even though the band was treading water they were treading it like Esther Williams. This record is better than 95 percent of the AOR records released in the 1970s. *—Tim Sendra*

Third Stage / Oct. 1986 / MCA ✦✦✦

After rushing their second album *Don't Look Back*, Boston took eight years to complete the album *Third Stage*. The long delay is even more surprising considering that their sound didn't change at all; even though only songwriter/guitarist Tom Scholz and vocalist Brad Delp remained from the original lineup, they were the ones responsible for Boston's sound. As such, it is difficult to avoid comparisons with their landmark debut. *Third Stage* has some strong moments, especially the number one hit "Amanda" where the band blends acoustic and electric guitars to complement the layered vocals. However, the songs are not as strong as those on their debut, and the album is marred by the presence of instrumental fillers and an attempt to cling to a theme of "journey through life's third stage." Thus, rather than focusing on universal topics such as the exuberance and uncertainties associated with youth, the mature lyrics are lost on most of their young rock audience. Given the time between albums and the changes in the pop landscape, it was a little disappointing to find Boston stuck in the same sound. The album still sounds great when it works on all cylinders ("We're Ready," "Cool the Engines"), but the album is not filled with enough satisfying moments. This may be nostalgic pop rock of the '80s, but casual listeners should start with their debut. *—Vik Iyengar*

Walk On / Jun. 7, 1994 / MCA ✦✦

Boston's long-awaited fourth album—this time it took Tom Scholz a full seven years to complete—failed to capture the attention of most AOR fans and became the group's first record to not spawn a hit single. Perhaps the reason was AOR and classic-rock stations began losing their audiences in 1992; more likely, it was because Scholz's legendary perfectionism didn't yield the same results it did in the past. Although the production is certainly state of the art and is overflowing with detail, there aren't any memorable songs or hooks to justify such extravagence. On the surface, the record sounds fine, but there is no substance beneath the layers of gloss. *—Stephen Thomas Erlewine*

Greatest Hits / Jun. 3, 1997 / Epic ✦✦✦✦

Since Tom Scholz is such a slow worker, there were only four Boston albums between the group's 1976 debut and this *Greatest Hits* collection in 1997. That may mean that there isn't much music to compile, as the reliance on their biggest-selling album *Boston* suggests, but that doesn't matter for most casual fans, since *Greatest Hits* gathers all of their best songs, from "More than a Feeling" to "Amanda," on one compact disc. For the collector, the record isn't quite as appealing, even if it contains three new songs as bait. Given that the likelihood of another Boston album in the 20th century seems slim at the time of *Greatest Hits*' 1997 release, these three songs could be the only new tracks fans hear for years, and they simply don't deliver the melodic punch or guitar crunch that distinguishes the group's best work. It's nice to hear original vocalist Brad Delp on "Higher Power," but "Tell Me" is slight, and an instrumental version of "The Star Spangled Banner" is nearly an insult. So, for the devoted, *Greatest Hits* is a mixed bag, but for less dedicated listeners, it may be all the Boston they need. *—Stephen Thomas Erlewine*

Bourgeois Tagg

f. 1984, Sacramento, CA

Pop/Rock, Soft Rock, Adult Contemporary, Album Rock

Brent Bourgeois began performing in Dallas clubs at the age of 13. After graduating from high school he moved with his friend Larry Tagg to Sacramento, California, forming the pop group Bourgeois Tagg in 1984. A duo by name, the band also included drummer Rick Walter and guitarist Lyle Workman. They released a self-titled debut album in 1986, which produced the hit single "Mutual Surrender (What a Wonderful World)." The following year they released their second album, *Yoyo*, which was produced by Todd Rundgren, and had another hit, "I Don't Mind at All," which reached the top 40. The band appeared to have a bright future, but Bourgeois became addicted to drugs and alcohol. When fellow musician and drinking buddy Charlie Peacock began going to church, Bourgeois followed and became a Christian. Conflicts that were brewing in the band became exacerbated by Bourgeois' trend toward Christian lyrics and they split. Tagg eventually released two solo albums, both on Damian, *With a Skeleton Crew* in 1995 and *Rover* in 1997. Bourgeois worked as a producer and solo artist within the CCM scene, and continues to produce new work. *—Stacia Proefrock*

Bourgeois Tagg / 1986 / Island ✦✦✦

Smart debut release from Los Angeles-based band combines Beatlesque influences with quirky new wave sensibility. Members Brent Bourgeois and Larry Tagg share lead vocal duties; while Tagg's vocals are pleasing but generic, Bourgeois lends his deep, somewhat spooky delivery to most of the tracks on *Bourgeois Tagg*. The funky "Mutual Surrender" became a minor hit single in 1986; like most of the tunes on *Bourgeois Tagg*, "Mutual Surrender" is odd, catchy, and undeniably pleasing. "Changed" boasts amusing but off-putting lyrics ("I had a lover that won't love me back/So I put her in a cement sack"), the trippy "Perfect Life" is insanely melodic, and "Dying to Be Free" is a surprising ballad about geriatric suicide, certainly an uncommon subject in a pop song.

Bourgeois Tagg was not a hit, but the album is just as good as anything by similar sounding but far more successful '80s bands like Duran Duran. Bourgeois Tagg released one more album (1987's Todd Rundgren-produced *YoYo*) before disbanding; Brent Bourgeois and Larry Tagg eventually began solo careers, both with little success. *—William Cooper*

● **Yoyo** / 1987 / Island ✦✦✦✦✦

Produced by Todd Rundgren, this contains the hit single "I Don't Mind at All" and the flawless "Waiting for the Worm to Turn." *—Dan Heilman*

Bow Street Runners

f. 1969

Psychedelic

Sounding like a blend of Jefferson Airplane and the Doors, Bow Street Runners was a Fayetteville, North Carolina-based psychedelic band who released one eponymous album in limited quantities on B.T. Puppy Records in 1970. While the group was ignored at the time, *Bow Street Runners* became a collectible item among psychedelic aficionados during the '80s and '90s, leading to its 1996 reissue by Sundazed Records. *—Stephen Thomas Erlewine*

● **The Bow Street Runners** / 1970 / Sundazed ✦✦✦✦

Using the trippy, folky rock of Jefferson Airplane and eerie, organ-driven soundscapes as a foundation, the Bow Street Runners may not have many original ideas in their head, but that's part of their appeal. Their lone, eponymous album is filled with attempts at hippie mysticism and menacing, swirling fuzzy psychedelia, yet the group has neither the inclination or the talent to turn it into something original. Nevertheless, the group is somewhat distinctive in the ways its attempts fail—"Spunky Monkey" is an aimless and slightly ridiculous blues jam, "Eating from a Plastic Hand" has a silly, ominous minor-key melody and, best of all, "Watch" sounds like Ringo Starr fronting the Doors. It doesn't make for good or provocative music, but as a late-'60s artifact, it's fascinating. *—Stephen Thomas Erlewine*

Bow Wow Wow

f. 1980, London, England, **db.** 1983

New Wave

Bow Wow Wow was a quartet organized by U.K. manager Malcolm McLaren (best known as the mastermind behind the Sex Pistols) at the start of the '80s. McLaren matched the trio of musicians who had constituted Adam Ant's Ants—Matthew Ashman (b. 1962) on guitar, Leigh Gorman (b. 1961) on bass, and David Barbarossa (b. 1961) on drums—with teenage singer Annabella Lwin (b. Oct. 31, 1965), retaining the earlier group's African-derived drum sound. In 1983, Lwin quit the group for a solo career, and the remaining three changed their name to the Chiefs of Relief. Both Lwin and the Chiefs issued their own albums. In 1995, Ashman passed away due to diabetes. Headed by Lwin and Gorman, a reformed Bow Wow Wow resurfaced in 1998 with *Wild in the U.S.A.*, which featured both remixes and concert performances from the reunion tour; guitarist Dave Calhoun and drummer Eshan Khadaroo filled the other slots. —*William Ruhlmann*

See Jungle! See Jungle! Go Join Your Gang, Yeah, City All Over! Go Ape Crazy! / 1981 / One Way ✦✦✦

Malcolm McLaren, of Sex Pistols' fame, made teenager Annabella Lwin the centerpiece of his next creation. Backing her with members of Adam & the Ants, they were dubbed Bow Wow Wow and released *See Jungle! See Jungle!* in 1981. The focus was on style and the music was a mix of dance and new wave always with a heavy nod toward percussion. The results are mixed and you sometimes have the feeling that you are hearing the same song repeated. However, it's difficult not to find yourself drumming your fingers to the frantic beats. Lwin makes sure that we never forget that she's only 15, either through her vocal delivery or her outright declarations (as on "Chihuahua"). The band also serves up an interesting spaghetti Western instrumental on "Orang-outang" and everything falls into place on "Go Wild in the Country," with Lwin's uninhibited shrieks touting the merits of getting away from it all. —*Tom Demalon*

I Want Candy / 1982 / RCA ✦✦✦✦

For many in America, "I Want Candy" was their first introduction to young Annabella Lwin and the band Bow Wow Wow. The song, a cover of a Strangeloves' hit, barely scraped the Top 50, but became an enduring new wave classic. The song gave its name to the band's 1982 release, which was mainly a compilation, but included a couple new cuts produced by Kenny Laguna (Joan Jett & the Blackhearts). The Laguna-produced tracks find Lwin sounding more self-assured and slightly less frantic in her vocal delivery. "Louis Quatorze," with its theme of falling for the bad boy, has an instantly catchy chorus that is matched by the stuck-in-your-brain "Baby, Oh No." Of course, no Bow Wow Wow album would be complete without the obligatory come-hither insinuations from Lwin, which appear on "Cowboy." With solid new songs, some of the better old ones and the hit that made them one-hit wonders, *I Want Candy* is an enjoyable romp that doesn't overstay its welcome. —*Tom Demalon*

When the Going Gets Tough, The Tough Get Going / 1983 / One Way ✦✦✦

Producer Mike Chapman, who had recently worked with Pat Benatar and Blondie, came on board for Bow Wow Wow's *When the Going Gets Tough...* set. Perhaps it's Chapman's involvement that finds lead singer Annabella Lwin sounding a bit like Debbie Harry at times. This 1983 album was also the first that had no writers from outside the band contributing. *When the Going Gets Tough...* is a well-polished, well-executed effort that holds some surprises mainly in the fact that there is more diversity than prior Bow Wow Wow records. Chapman adds a gloss to the ballads "Lonesome Tonight" and the dreamy "Love Me," with Lwin toning down her usual frantic delivery. "The Man Mountain" sounds like an old, folk song. And, there's also the straight-ahead, playful pop that you'd expect from the band on the ultra-hooky single "Do You Wanna Hold Me" and "Tommy Tucker," which begins as a nursery rhyme and concludes with a quasi-football chant. —*Tom Demalon*

Girl Bites Dog / Sep. 21, 1993 / EMI ✦✦✦✦✦

A CD reissue of their first cassette-only release. Featuring a 15-year-old Annabella Lwin singing songs with sex-obsessed themes backed by a driving tribal beat, *Girl Bites Dog* gives a representative view of a band with limited scope. Though it sounds a bit dated today, new wave fanatics will find this newly expanded version essential, especially for the unreleased rarities, B-sides, and extensive discography information. —*Chris Woodstra*

● **The Best of Bow Wow Wow** / Oct. 29, 1996 / RCA ✦✦✦✦✦

The Best of Bow Wow Wow is a thorough overview of Malcolm McLaren's manufactured new wave pop group, featuring all the highlights of the group's albums and EPs—including, of course, "I Want Candy," but also "Go Wild in the Country," "W.O.R.K." and "Do You Want to Hold Me"—as well as the previously unreleased "Where's My Snake." Since the group didn't make consistent albums, *The Best of Bow Wow Wow* is the best way to listen to the band, since it features every one of their worthwhile tracks, plus good liner notes. —*Stephen Thomas Erlewine*

David Bowie (David Robert Jones)

b. Jan. 8, 1947, Brixton, England

Vocals, Saxophone, Keyboards, Guitar / Experimental Rock, Blue-Eyed Soul, Proto-Punk, Pop/Rock, Glam Rock, Prog-Rock/Art Rock, Hard Rock

The cliche about David Bowie says he's a musical chameleon, adapting himself according to fashion and trends. While such a criticism is too glib, there's no denying that Bowie demonstrated remarkable skill for perceiving musical trends at his peak in the '70s. After spending several years in the late '60s as a mod and as an all-around music-hall entertainer, Bowie reinvented himself as a hippie singer/songwriter. Prior to his breakthrough in 1972, he recorded a proto-metal record and a pop-rock album, eventually redefining glam-rock with his ambiguously sexy Ziggy Stardust persona. Ziggy made Bowie an international star, yet he wasn't content to continue to churn out glitter-rock. By the mid-'70s, he developed an effete, sophisticated version of Philly soul that he dubbed "plastic soul," which eventually morphed into the eerie avant-pop of 1976's *Station to Station*. Shortly afterward, he relocated to Berlin, where he recorded three experimental electronic albums with Brian Eno. At the dawn of the '80s, Bowie was still at the height of his powers, yet following his blockbuster dance-pop album *Let's Dance* in 1983, he slowly sank into mediocrity before salvaging his career in the early '90s. Even when he was out of fashion in the '80s and '90s, it was clear that Bowie was one of the most influential musicians in rock, for better and for worse. Each one of his phases in the '70s

sparked a number of subgenres, including punk, new wave, goth-rock, the New Romantics, and electronica. Few rockers ever had such lasting impact. —*Stephen Thomas Erlewine*

David Bowie / 1967 / Deram ✦✦✦

Rebound's *David Bowie* is essentially a straight-up reissue of the endlessly reissued *David Bowie (Love You Till Tuesday)* album. There are no bonus tracks, since Mercury had just issued the extensive 27-track *The Deram Anthology* in 1997, which contained all of Bowie's recordings for the label. This is just the album itself, containing such cult classics as "Uncle Arthur," "Rubber Band," "Sell Me a Coat," "Love You Till Tuesday," "Come and Buy My Toys," "Join the Gang" and "Please Mr. Gravedigger." Curious fans looking for a taste of these Anthony Newley-esque music hall shenanigans may be tempted by the budget price on this disc, but any fan truly interested in this material should spring for the full *Deram Anthology*, since it not only contains his best song of this era ("London Boys"), it also contains the notorious "Laughing Gnome," plus such unsung vaudevillian novelties as "The Gospel According to Tony Day" and an early take of "Space Oddity." If you're gonna dip your toe in water this cold, you'd be better off diving headfirst into the deep end. —*Stephen Thomas Erlewine*

Space Oddity / 1969 / Virgin ✦✦✦

Originally released as *Man of Words/Man of Music*, *Space Oddity* was David Bowie's first successful reinvention of himself. Abandoning both the mod and Anthony Newley fascinations that marked his earlier recordings, Bowie delves into a lightly psychedelic folk-rock, exemplified by the album's soaring title track. Bowie actually attempts a variety of styles on *Space Oddity*, as if he were trying to find the ones that suited him best. As such, the record isn't very cohesive, but it is charming, especially in light of his later records. Nevertheless, only "Wild Eyed Boy From Freecloud" and "Memory of a Free Festival" rank as Bowie classics, and even those lack the hooks or purpose of "Space Oddity." —*Stephen Thomas Erlewine*

The Man Who Sold the World / 1970 / Virgin ✦✦✦✦✦

Even though it contained no hits, *The Man Who Sold the World*, for most intents and purposes, is the beginning of David Bowie's classic period. Working with guitarist Mick Ronson and producer Tony Visconti for the first time, Bowie developed a tight, twisted heavy guitar rock that appears simple on the surface, but sounds more gnarled upon each listen. The mix is off-center, with the fuzz-bass dominating the compressed, razor-thin guitars and Bowie's strangled, affected voice. The sound of *The Man Who Sold the World* is odd, but the music is bizarre itself, with Bowie's bizarre, paranoid futuristic tales melded to Ronson's riffing and the band's relentless attack. Musically, there isn't much innovation on *The Man Who Sold the World*—it is almost all hard blues-rock or psychedelic folk-rock—but there's an unsettling edge to the band's performance, which makes the record one of Bowie's best albums. [Rykodisc's 1990 CD reissue includes four bonus tracks, including the previously unreleased "Lightning Frightening," and the single "Holy Holy," and both sides of the 1971 "Arnold Corns" single, "Moonage Daydream" and "Hang on to Yourself," which are early and inferior versions of songs that would later appear on *Ziggy Stardust*.] —*Stephen Thomas Erlewine*

☆ **The Rise & Fall of Ziggy Stardust** / 1972 / Virgin ✦✦✦✦✦

Borrowing heavily from Marc Bolan's glam rock and the future shock of *A Clockwork Orange*, David Bowie reached back to the heavy rock of *The Man Who Sold the World* for *The Rise & Fall of Ziggy Stardust and the Spiders From Mars*. Constructed as a loose concept album about an androgynous alien rock star named Ziggy Stardust, the story falls apart quickly, yet Bowie's fractured, paranoid lyrics are evocative of a decadent, decaying future, and the music echoes an apocalyptic, nuclear dread. Fleshing out the off-kilter metallic mix with fatter guitars, genuine pop songs, string sections, keyboards, and a cinematic flourish, *Ziggy Stardust* is a glitzy array of riffs, hooks, melodrama, and style and the logical culmination of glam. Mick Ronson plays with a maverick flair that invigorates rockers like "Suffragette City," "Moonage Daydream," and "Hang Onto Yourself," while "Lady Stardust," "Five Years," and "Rock & Roll Suicide" have a grand sense of staged drama previously unheard of in rock & roll. And that self-conscious sense of theater is part of the reason why *Ziggy Stardust* sounds so foreign. Bowie succeeds not in spite of his pretensions but because of them, and *Ziggy Stardust*—familiar in structure, but alien in performance—is the first time his vision and execution met in such a grand, sweeping fashion. —*Stephen Thomas Erlewine*

☆ **Hunky Dory** / 1972 / Virgin ✦✦✦✦✦

After the freakish hard rock of *The Man Who Sold the World*, David Bowie returned to singer/songwriter territory on *Hunky Dory*. Not only did the album boast more folky songs ("Song for Bob Dylan," "The Bewlay Brothers"), but he again flirted with Anthony Newley-esque dancehall music ("Kooks," "Fill Your Heart"), seemingly leaving heavy metal behind. As a result, *Hunky Dory* is a kaleidoscopic array of pop styles, tied together only by Bowie's sense of vision: a sweeping, cinematic mélange of high and low art, ambiguous sexuality, kitsch, and class. Mick Ronson's guitar is pushed to the back, leaving Rick Wakeman's cabaret piano to dominate the sound of the album. The subdued support accentuates the depth of Bowie's material, whether it's the revamped Tin Pan Alley of "Changes," the Neil Young homage "Quicksand," the soaring "Life on Mars?," the rolling, vaguely homosexual anthem "Oh! You Pretty Things," or the dark acoustic rocker "Andy Warhol." On the surface, such a wide range of styles and sounds would make an album incoherent, but Bowie's improved songwriting and determined sense of style instead made *Hunky Dory* a touchstone for reinterpreting pop's traditions into fresh, post-modern pop music. —*Stephen Thomas Erlewine*

Aladdin Sane / 1973 / Virgin ✦✦✦✦✦

Ziggy Stardust wrote the blueprint for Bowie's hard-rocking glam, and *Aladdin Sane* essentially follows the pattern, for both better and worse. A lighter affair than *Ziggy*

Stardust, Aladdin Sane is actually a stranger album than its predecessor, buoyed by bizarre lounge-jazz flourishes from pianist Mick Garson and a handful of winding, vaguely experimental songs. Bowie abandons his futuristic obsessions to concentrate on the detached cool of New York and London hipsters, as on the compressed rockers "Watch That Man," "Cracked Actor," and "The Jean Genie." Bowie follows the hard stuff with the jazzy, dissonant sprawls of "Lady Grinning Soul," "Aladdin Sane," and "Time," all of which manage to be both campy and avant-garde simultaneously, while the sweepingly cinematic "Drive-In Saturday" is a soaring fusion of sci-fi doo wop and melodramatic teenage glam. He lets his paranoia slip through in the clenched rhythms of "Panic in Detroit," as well as on his oddly clueless cover of "Let's Spend the Night Together." For all the pleasures on *Aladdin Sane*, there's no distinctive sound or theme to make the album cohesive; it's Bowie riding the wake of *Ziggy Stardust*, which means there's a wealth of classic material here, but not enough focus to make the album itself a classic. —*Stephen Thomas Erlewine*

Pin-Ups / 1973 / Virgin ✦✦✦
Perhaps the covers album *Pin-Ups* was conceived as a breather, a way for Bowie and the Spiders from Mars to regroup admist the hysteria of the *Ziggy Stardust* mania, or perhaps it was meant as a genuine tribute to Bowie's influences. Either way, *Pin-Ups* was the first sign that the Ziggy persona was running out of energy. The album isn't bad—in fact, it's an energetic, infectious collection of relatively obscure British rock & roll, R&B and mod anthems—but the timing of a covers album was odd, suggesting that Bowie was running out of ideas. On its own, *Pin-Ups* is quite enjoyable, especially since the selections are fairly arcane. Bowie relies primarily on songs that never were hits outside America—even the Kinks, the Who, Yardbirds and Pink Floyd songs were relatively obscure—which makes the record fascinating. Bowie and the Spiders make songs by the Pretty Things ("Rosalyn," "Don't Bring Me Down"), the Merseys ("Sorrow"), and the Easybeats ("Friday On My Mind") tough and nervy, occasionally surpassing the original versions in terms of attitude. So, if *Pin-Ups* isn't a major entry in Bowie's catalog, it is fun, even though it's a rather undistinguished final effort from the Spiders from Mars. —*Stephen Thomas Erlewine*

Images 1966-1967 / 1973 / London ✦✦✦
This double album is becoming hard to find, which is unfortunate, as it's easily the most comprehensive collection of Bowie's 1966-67 work for Deram. The 21 tracks include the entirety of his 1967 debut album, plus seven stray songs from singles and sessions that were unreleased at the time. Possibly because it wasn't heard by many listeners until it was reissued in the early '70s during Bowie's ascent to stardom, this material has been unfairly maligned. Critics and fans of *Ziggy Stardust* were shocked to discover an all-around entertainer seemingly bent upon becoming the new Anthony Newley. Indeed, much of his work from this era was overbearingly cloying and saccharine, both in the West End matinee aspirations of the lyrics and the unabashedly theatrical orchestration, which bore hardly any resemblance to good old rock & roll whatsoever. One of these, "Laughing Gnome" (featuring Chipmunk-like backup vocals), would cause Bowie considerable embarrassment when it was reissued—and became a hit—in Britain in 1973. The less idiotically cheerful efforts, though, show definite signs of an idiosyncratic talent: the odd character sketches, the fleeting references to transvestites and mysticism, even the occasional London swinging pop number ("Let Me Sleep Beside You"). The best track, "London Boys" (a 1966 single), is a neglected classic look at the downer side of the mod experience, and is the best of his many obscure pre-*Space Oddity* recordings. —*Richie Unterberger*

David Live / 1974 / Rykodisc ✦✦
The supporting tour for *Diamond Dogs* was supposed to be a theatrical extravaganza, yet as he headed out on the road, David Bowie became infatuated with Philly soul and changed his entire approach to reflect his new interest, as well as his backing band in the process. As a result, the double-album *David Live* captures Bowie in transition, as he moves from glam-rock to plastic soul. The set list draws heavily from *Ziggy Stardust*-era songs, yet a few surprises, like a stilted cover of "Knock on Wood" and an inspired version of "All the Young Dudes," a song Bowie gave Mott the Hoople. Since Bowie's attempts at soul are a little awkward at this stage, *David Live* is primarily of interest as a historical document, yet there's enough good material to make it worthwhile for fanatics. —*Stephen Thomas Erlewine*

Diamond Dogs / 1974 / Virgin ✦✦✦
David Bowie fired the Spiders from Mars shortly after the release of *Pin-Ups*, but he didn't completely leave the Ziggy Stardust persona behind. *Diamond Dogs* suffers precisely because of this—he doesn't know *how* to move forward. Originally conceived as a concept album based on George Orwell's *1984*, *Diamond Dogs* evolved into another one of Bowie's paranoid future nightmares. Throughout the album, there are hints that he's tired with the Ziggy formula, particularly in the disco underpinning of "Candidate" and his cut-and-paste lyrics. However, it's not enough to make *Diamond Dogs* a step forward, and without Mick Ronson to lead the band, the rockers are too stiff to make an impact. Ironically, the one exception is one of Bowie's very best songs—the tight, sexy "Rebel Rebel." The song doesn't have much to do with the theme, and the ones he does throw in to further the story, usually fall flat. *Diamond Dogs* isn't a total waste, with "1984," "Candidate" and "Diamond Dogs" all offering some sort of pleasure, but it is the first record since *Space Oddity* where Bowie's reach exceeds his grasp. —*Stephen Thomas Erlewine*

Young Americans / 1975 / Virgin ✦✦✦
Bowie had dropped hints during the *Diamond Dogs* tour that he was moving toward R&B, but the full-blown blue-eyed soul of *Young Americans* came as a shock. Surrounding himself with first-rate sessionmen, Bowie comes up with a set of songs that approximate the sound of Phillie-soul and disco, yet remain detached from their inspirations;

even at his most passionate, Bowie sounds like a commentator, as if the entire album was a genre exercise. Nevertheless, the distance doesn't hurt the album—it gives the record its own distinctive flavor, and its plastic, robotic soul helped inform generations of synthetic British soul. What does hurt the record is a lack of strong songwriting. "Young Americans" is a masterpiece, and "Fame" had a beat funky enough that James Brown ripped it off, but only a handful of cuts ("Win," "Fascination," "Somebody Up There Likes Me") come close to matching their quality. As a result, *Young Americans* is more enjoyable as a stylistic adventure, than as a substantive record. [The 1991 CD has three bonus tracks, including the terrific outtake "Who Can I Be Now?"] —*Stephen Thomas Erlewine*

Station to Station / 1976 / Virgin ✦✦✦✦✦
Taking the detached plastic soul of *Young Americans* to an elegant, robotic extreme, *Station to Station* is a transitional album that creates its own distinctive style. Abandoning any pretense of being a soulman, yet keeping rhythmic elements of soul, Bowie positions himself as a cold, clinical crooner and explores a variety of styles. Everything from epic ballads and disco to synthesized avant-pop is present on *Station to Station*, but what ties it together is Bowie's cocaine-induced paranoia and detached musical persona. At its heart, *Station to Station* is an avant-garde, art rock album, most explicitly on "TVC15" and the epic sprawl of the title track, but also on the cool crooning of "Wild Is the Wind" and "Word on a Wing," as well as the disco stylings of "Golden Years." It's not an easy album to warm to, but its epic structure and clinical sound were an impressive, individualistic achievement, as well as a style that would prove enormously influential on post-punk. —*Stephen Thomas Erlewine*

☆ **Low** / 1977 / Virgin ✦✦✦✦✦
Following through with the avant-garde inclinations of *Station to Station*, yet explicitly breaking with Bowie's past, *Low* is a dense, challenging album that confirmed Bowie's place at rock's cutting edge. Driven by dissonant synthesizers and electronics, *Low* is divided between brief, angular songs and atmospheric instrumentals. Throughout the record's first half, the guitars are jagged and the synthesizers drone with a menacing robotic pulse, while Bowie's vocals are unnaturally layered and overdubbed. During the instrumental half, the electronics turn cool, which is a relief after the intensity of the preceding avant-pop. Half the credit for *Low*'s success goes to Brian Eno, who explored similar ambient territory on his own releases. Eno functioned as a conduit for Bowie's ideas, and in turn Bowie made the experimentalism of not only Eno, but of the German synth group Kraftwerk and the post-punk group Wire, respectable, if not quite mainstream. Though a handful of the vocal pieces on *Low* are accessible—"Sound and Vision" has a shimmering guitar hook, and "Be My Wife" subverts soul structure in a surprisingly catchy fashion—the record is defiantly experimental and dense with detail, providing a new direction for the avant-garde in rock & roll. —*Stephen Thomas Erlewine*

☆ **Heroes** / 1977 / Virgin ✦✦✦✦✦
Repeating the formula of *Low*'s half-vocal/half-instrumental structure, *Heroes* develops and strengthens the sonic innovations Bowie and Eno explored on their first collaboration. The vocal songs are fuller, boasting harder rhythms and deeper layers of sound. Much of the harder-edged sound of *Heroes* is due to Robert Fripp's guitar, which provides a muscular foundation for the electronics, especially on the relatively conventional rock songs. Similarly, the instrumentals on *Heroes* are more detailed, this time showing a more explicit debt to German synth-pop and European experimental rock & roll. Essentially, the difference between *Low* and *Heroes* lies in the details, but the record is equally challenging and groundbreaking. [The CD reissue includes the previously unreleased instrumental "Abdulmajid" and a remix of "Joe the Lion."] —*Stephen Thomas Erlewine*

Stage / 1978 / Rykodisc ✦✦✦
Stage was David Bowie's second live double album, documenting his supporting tour for *Heroes*. Supported by a band that featured guitarists Adrian Belew and Carlos Alomar, Bowie doesn't recast his earlier work in a new light—the songs from *Ziggy Stardust* essentially remain the same, as do the selections from *Station to Station*—but they are infused with a new avant-garde spirit which comes to the forefront during the songs from *Low* and *Heroes*. Though the newer material isn't arranged in a different manner than the studio versions—and they lack some of the studio trickery which made the originals so thrilling—the live versions do illustrate that much of the innovation of the Bowie-Eno collaborations lay in their subversion of conventional song structure. That said, *Stage* doesn't offer enough revelations to make it necessary for anyone but hardcore Bowie fanatics. —*Stephen Thomas Erlewine*

Lodger / 1979 / Virgin ✦✦✦✦✦
On the surface, *Lodger* is the most accessible of the three Berlin-era records Bowie made with Brian Eno, simply because there are no instrumentals and there are a handful of concise pop songs. Nevertheless, *Lodger* is still gnarled and twisted avant-pop; what makes it different is how it incorporates such experimental tendencies into genuine songs, something that *Low* and *Heroes* purposely avoided. "D.J.," "Look Back in Anger," and "Boys Keep Swinging" have strong melodic hooks which are subverted and strengthened by the layered, dissonant productions, while the remainder of the record is divided between similarly effective avant-pop and ambient instrumentals. *Lodger* has an edgier, more minimalistic bent than its two predecessors, which makes it more accessible for rock fans, as well as giving it a more immediate, emotional impact. It might not stretch the boundaries of rock like *Low* and *Heroes*, but it arguably utilizes those ideas in a more effective fashion. —*Stephen Thomas Erlewine*

☆ **Scary Monsters (And Super Creeps)** / 1980 / Virgin ✦✦✦✦✦
Bowie returns to relatively conventional rock & roll with *Scary Monsters*, an album that effectively acts as an encapsulation of all his '70s experiments. Reworking glam rock themes with avant-garde synth flourishes, and reversing the process as well, Bowie creates dense but accessible music throughout *Scary Monsters*. Though it doesn't have the

vision of his other classic records, it wasn't designed to break new ground—it was created as the culmination of Bowie's experimental genre-shifting of the '70s. As a result, *Scary Monsters* is Bowie's last great album. While the music isn't far removed from the post-punk of the early '80s, it does sound fresh, hip, and contemporary, which is something Bowie lost over the course of the '80s. [Rykodisc's 1992 reissue includes re-recorded versions of "Space Oddity" and "Panic in Detroit," the Japanese single "Crystal Japan," and the British single "Alabama Song."] *—Stephen Thomas Erlewine*

Let's Dance / 1983 / Virgin ✦✦✦

After summing up his maverick tendencies on *Scary Monsters*, David Bowie aimed for the mainstream *Let's Dance*. Hiring Chic bassist Nile Rodgers as a co-producer, Bowie created a stylish, synthesized post-disco dance music that was equally informed by classic soul and the emerging New Romantic subgenre of New Wave, which was ironically heavily inspired by Bowie himself. *Let's Dance* comes tearing out of the date, propulsed by the skittering "Modern Love," the seductively menacing "China Girl" and the brittle funk of the title track. All three songs became international hits, and for good reason—they are catchy, accessible pop songs that have just enough of an alien edge to make them distinctive. However, that careful balance is quickly thrown off by a succession of pleasant but unremarkable plastic soul workouts. "Cat People" and a cover of Metro's "Criminal World" are relatively strong songs, but the remainder of the album indicates that Bowie was entering a songwriting slump. However, the three hits were enough to make the album a massive hit, and their power hasn't diminished over the years, even if the rest of the record sounds like an artifact. *—Stephen Thomas Erlewine*

Love You Til Tuesday / 1984 / Deram ✦✦

The bulk of this reissue comes from the soundtrack to Bowie's little-seen short film of the same name. Completed in early 1969, it was shelved until its re-release on video in 1984. While several of the songs had already been released by Bowie in the U.K. on Deram, this LP has some slightly different versions. The title track and "When I Live My Dream" are represented by their 45 single takes, not the more familiar album ones; "Sell Me a Coat" has added vocals by John Hutchinson and Hermione Fatheringale, who played with Bowie in his short-lived group Feathers. The previously unreleased "Ching-A-Ling" and "When I'm Five" are in keeping with the fey, fairy-tale, childlike ambience of much of his 1967 material. The version of "Space Oddity" also features Hutchinson and Fatheringale, and is faster and less effective than the eventual hit single version. Rounding out the collection are some of the more well-known numbers from his Anthony Newley period (especially the notorious "Laughing Gnome"), and his 1964 debut single "Liza Jane," an out-and-out R&B number in the Stones/Pretty Things style. A scattershot anthology that is pretty much for collectors only, focusing on his uncharacteristically showtune-like 1967 period; that era is more definitively documented on the double album *Images*. *—Richie Unterberger*

Tonight / 1984 / Virgin ✦✦

On the basis of *Tonight*, it appears that David Bowie didn't have a clear idea of how to follow the platinum success of *Let's Dance*. Instead of breaking away from the stylized pop of "Let's Dance" and "China Girl," Bowie delivers another record in the same style. Apart from the single "Blue Jean," none of the material equals the songs on *Let's Dance*, but that didn't stop *Tonight* from becoming another platinum success. Nevertheless, the record stands as one of the weakest albums Bowie ever recorded. *—Stephen Thomas Erlewine*

Never Let Me Down / 1987 / Virgin ✦✦

Bowie broke away from the mainstream pop of *Tonight* with 1987's *Never Let Me Down*, turning out a jumbled mix of loud guitar rockers and art-rock experiments, like the failed "Glass Spider." While it's not as consistent as *Tonight*, it's far more interesting, with the John Lennon homage of the title track being one of his most underrated songs. *—Stephen Thomas Erlewine*

Sound + Vision [Box] / Sep. 1989 / Rykodisc ✦✦✦✦✦

Sound + Vision is a triple-disc box set designed to introduce Rykodisc's extensive reissue program of David Bowie's RCA albums. As a result, it has a number of idiosyncrasies that prevent it from becoming a definitive box set. Conceptually, the set was intended to showcase Rykodisc's remastering expertise, as well as the rarities lying in the vaults. Consequently, the song selection is targeted toward hardcore Bowie fans, ignoring such hits as "Jean Genie," "Starman," "Golden Years," and "Fame," among many others. However, there is an abundance of terrific rare material, including the demo for "Space Oddity," the *Man Who Sold the World* outtake "London Bye Ta-Ta," an alternate "John, I'm Only Dancing," the soulful *Young Americans* outtake "After Today," and a single version of "Rebel Rebel," which arguably is better than the more familiar version. However, such rarities and unpredictable selections ("Red Sails" but not "DJ" from *Lodger*, live versions of "Sufragette City," "Station to Station," and "Breaking Glass") mean that the set is neither a good introduction or compliment to *Changesbowie*. Instead, it's a good, if frustrating, curio piece for collectors. [The initial pressings of *Sound + Vision* included a bonus disc which contained a CD-video of "Ashes to Ashes," as well as three live tracks. It was replaced in 1995 with a CD-ROM of the same material.] *—Stephen Thomas Erlewine*

★ **Changesbowie** / Mar. 1990 / Rykodisc ✦✦✦✦✦

Changesbowie is a CD greatest hits collection that revamps the original *Changesonebowie* by adding selections from Bowie's late '70s and early '80s albums. Consequently, it functions as a definitive single-disc introduction to David Bowie, featuring all of his major hits from "Space Oddity," "Changes," "Ziggy Stardust," "Jean Genie" and "Rebel Rebel" to "Heroes," "Ashes to Ashes," "Let's Dance," "Modern Love" and "Blue Jean." One complaint: it wasn't necessary to substitute the "Fame '90" remix for the original to hook completists, since it is inferior and was already issued as a separate single. *—Stephen Thomas Erlewine*

Early On (1964-1966) / 1991 / Rhino ✦✦

Before landing his first commercial success with 1969's "Space Oddity," David Bowie released a number of flop records in a variety of styles. He first emerged in the mid-1960s as a mod following the paths of The Who, Kinks, and Rolling Stones. The 17-cut CD *Early On (1964-66)* is by far the most comprehensive anthology of his first works, gathering all six of his first singles and adding five previously unreleased demos from 1965. Fans of Bowie's famous work may be nonplussed by this material, in which the singer shifts from sub-Stones R&B to Who/Kinkish power chords to trendy Swinging London pop in search of his own style. He didn't establish his own identity on these fairly derivative recordings, but that's not to say they aren't without their enjoyable aspects. The 1965 single "You've Got A Habit Of Leaving" has some fierce Who-styled feedback, "Can't Help Thinking About Me" is an uneasily introspective number that foreshadows his later lyrics, and the acoustic demos find him groping closer toward a more familiar and distinctive vocal style. Several of the tunes on this collection were produced by the legendary Shel Talmy, who also handled sessions for The Who and Kinks in the mid-'60s. *—Richie Unterberger*

Black Tie White Noise / Oct. 1993 / Virgin ✦✦✦

A fitfully successful comeback effort by Bowie, *Black Tie White Noise* works best when he subtly tries to update his sound. When he duets with Al B. Sure! on the title track and does a tepid remake of Cream's "I Feel Free," the modernization of soul and glam sounds forced, which never happens on the house beats of "Jump They Say" or the moving reworking of Morrissey's "I Know It's Gonna Happen Someday." Unfortunately, the good songs—and the best material here is easily his best since *Scary Monsters*—are obscured by the filler and ill-conceived dance experimentations. Had it been trimmed by five or six songs, the album could indeed have brought him back to the top of the charts. *—Stephen Thomas Erlewine*

☆ **Singles: 1969-1993** / Nov. 16, 1993 / Rykodisc ✦✦✦✦✦

Taking *Changesbowie* one step further, *Singles 1969-1993* collects all of David Bowie's biggest hits while picking up such overlooked gems as "Drive-In Saturday" and "Loving the Alien." The comprehensiveness and quality of the songs make *Singles* the best Bowie compilation available; fans will be pleased with the inclusion of the complete lyrics to all of the songs on this two-disc set. *—Stephen Thomas Erlewine*

Rarest One Bowie / 1995 / Trident ✦✦

Santa Monica '72 / Mar. 28, 1995 / Golden Years ✦✦✦

Recorded from Bowie's first live American broadcast, this October 20, 1972 concert is a good choice for those who found themselves left cold by the awkward soul and the absence of Mick Ronson on *David Live*. Coming on the heels of the release of *Ziggy Stardust*, Bowie is captured here at the height of his creative powers. He gives a nod to the influence of Lou Reed with a fine "Waiting For The Man," and the live renditions of "Jean Genie" and "Rock & Roll Suicide" surpass the studio versions, thanks in no small part to the inimitable Mick Ronson. "Life on Mars?" and other tunes off *Hunky Dory* can be a bit disappointing, though, without original keyboardist Rick Wakeman, who was now busy becoming a star with Yes. But this is only a minor qualm; the Spiders band is wonderfully aggressive, all the more because live performance was perhaps the true home for its glam theatrics. *—Paul Collins*

Outside / Sep. 26, 1995 / Virgin ✦✦✦

David Bowie has seemed like an artist without direction ever since the success of *Let's Dance*, switching styles and genres with a speed that made him appear nervous, not innovative. Recorded with his former collaborator Brian Eno, *Outside* was intended to return some luster to his rapidly tarnishing reputation. Instead of faux-soul or mainstream pop—or even dissonant hard rock, for that matter—Bowie concentrates on the atmospheric, disturbing electronic soundscapes of his late-'70s "Berlin" trilogy (*Low, Heroes,* and *Lodger*), adding slight, but detectable, elements of industrial, grunge, and ambient techno. Bowie also raised the stakes by making *Outside* the first in a series of concept albums about mystery, murder, art, and cyberspace. Everything that would have made *Outside* a triumphant comeback seemed to be in place, but the album is severely flawed. Not only is the story poorly developed and confusing, but the album is simply too long. Throughout the record, good ideas bubble to the surface, yet are never fully explored, and the sheer bulk of the album means that the good songs—"Hallo Spaceboy," "Strangers When We Meet," "The Hearts Filthy Lesson"—are buried underneath the weight of the mediocre material. Furthermore, nothing on the album is a departure from Bowie's late-'70s records; when he does experiment with newer musical forms or write about futuristic technology, he seems unsure of himself. That said, *Outside* is Bowie's most satisfying and adventurous album since *Let's Dance*. It's clear that he's trying once again, and when he does hit his mark, he remains a brilliant artist. *—Stephen Thomas Erlewine*

The Buddha of Suburbia / Oct. 24, 1995 / Virgin ✦✦✦

It was probably David Bowie's record-company affiliation difficulties that kept this 1993 soundtrack to a British TV miniseries from being released in the U.S. until 1995, when it was slipped out in the wake of his new album, *Outside*. That's too bad, because *The Buddah of Suburbia* is an often engaging collection of songs and instrumental passages that recalls many previous Bowie albums, including such disparate efforts as *The Man Who Sold the World, Aladdin Sane,* and *Low*. It's not a major effort by any means, but in another context songs like "Strangers When We Meet" easily could become Bowie favorites. *—William Ruhlmann*

The Deram Anthology 1966-1968 / 1997 / Deram ✦✦✦✦

In 1973, at the height of David Bowie's *Ziggy*-shaped excess, a small, smirking skeleton came creeping out of his closet, paused to adjust its merry pointy hat, then rocketed to number eight on the U.K. chart. It was, of course, "The Laughing Gnome," a reminder of his days directionlessly drifting through the '60s, and a cause for ribald amusement wherever it played. Initial intentions for this compilation included a second disc packed with outtakes and oddities; these plans were abandoned at Bowie's own request (the bootleg *The Forgotten Songs of David Robert Jones* celebrates his demands), and *Anthology* suffers accordingly. Of its 27 tracks, a mere handful can be missing from even a disinterested Bowie collection. Everything else has now been repackaged so many times that even fresh remastering at first seems academic. And then you play the album. And then you play "The Laughing Gnome." It's not difficult to understand why this work was doomed to commercial failure. He was, at this time, targeting most of his energy directly into the heart of the hip easy listening intelligentsia—without pausing to wonder whether that crowd actually existed. Of course it didn't, and Bowie was doomed before he got started. Today, excellent liner notes and a top-notch remastering job do not disguise the sheer unconventionality of this material. Even now, with his subsequent reputation as a musical chameleon firmly a part of his legend, "Silly Boy Blue," "Maid of Bond Street," and "There Is a Happy Land" remain disconcerting members of his canon. *—Dave Thompson*

Earthling / Feb. 11, 1997 / Virgin ♦♦♦
Jumping on the post-grunge industrial bandwagon with *Outside* didn't successfully rejuvenate David Bowie's credibility or sales, so he switched his allegiance to techno and jungle for the follow-up, *Earthling.* While jungle is a more appropriate fit than industrial, the resulting music is nearly as awkward. Though he often gets the sound of jungle right, the record frequently sounds as if the beats were simply grafted on top of pre-existing songs. Never are the songs broken open by a new form, they are fairly conventional Bowie songs with fancy production. Fortunately, Bowie sounds rejuvenated by this new form, and songs like "Little Wonder" and "Seven Years in Tibet" are far stronger than the bulk of *Outside.* Still, the record falls short of its goals, and it doesn't offer enough intrigue or innovations to make *Earthling* anything more than an admirable effort. *—Stephen Thomas Erlewine*

● **Best of David Bowie: 1969-1974** / Oct. 7, 1997 / Virgin ♦♦♦♦
Early in 1997, David Bowie sold the rights to his RCA catalog to EMI, and the first release to appear under the new agreement was *The Best of 1969-1974,* which was part of EMI's limited-edition 100th Birthday series. Instead of playing it straight, the 20-track set offers both the predictable classics—"The Jean Genie," "Space Oddity," "Starman," "Drive In Saturday," "Ziggy Stardust," "Suffragette City," "Changes," "Sorrow," "The Man Who Sold the World"—and relative obscurities, like the B-side "Velvet Goldmine," Bowie's version of "All the Young Dudes" and alternate takes of "John, I'm Only Dancing" and "The Prettiest Star." There are also album tracks like "Oh! You Pretty Things" and "Life on Mars" that have become classics, making *The Best of 1969-1974* an impressive, reasonably thorough overview of Bowie's glam years. *—Stephen Thomas Erlewine*

● **Best of David Bowie: 1974-1979** / Apr. 1998 / Virgin ♦♦♦♦
Picking up where EMI's first compilation, *The Best of David Bowie: 1969-74,* left off, *The Best of David Bowie: 1974-79* is an excellent 18-track overview of what are arguably Bowie's most creative years. During these five years, he moved from the stylized "Plastic Soul" of *Young Americans* to the cold, synthesized Berlin collaborations with Brian Eno, turning out some classic singles along the way ("Sound and Vision," "Golden Years," "Fame," "Young Americans," "TVC 15," "DJ," "Boys Keep Swinging," "Heroes"). Those hits, along with some strong album tracks, the discofied "John I'm Only Dancing (Again)" and the rarity "It's Hard to Be a Saint in the City," are all here. Unfortunately, the compilation wasn't sequenced in chronological order—although his range is impressive, it's even more astonishing when it's placed in the proper sequence. Nevertheless, *The Best of David Bowie: 1974-79* is a good summation of those five years and a nice companion piece to its predecessor, even if the double-disc *Singles* set or the concise *Changesbowie* are better career overviews. [Although *The Best of David Bowie: 1969-74* was released initially in the U.S., then in the U.K., this volume was released in Britain and not in America.] *—Stephen Thomas Erlewine*

Hours / Oct. 5, 1999 / Virgin ♦♦♦
Since David Bowie spent the '90s jumping from style to style, it comes as a shock that *Hours,* his final album of the decade, is a relatively straightforward affair. Not only that, but it feels unlike anything else in his catalog. Bowie's music has always been a product of artifice, intelligence, and synthesis. *Hours* is a relaxed, natural departure from this method. Arriving after two labored albums, the shift in tone is quite refreshing. "Thursday's Child," the album's engaging mid-tempo opener, is a good indication of what lays ahead. It feels like classic Bowie, yet recalls no specific era of his career. For the first time, Bowie has absorbed all the disparate strands of his music, from *Hunky Dory* through *Earthling.* That doesn't mean *Hours* is on par with his earlier masterworks; it never attempts to be that bold. What it does mean is that it's the first album where he has accepted his past and is willing to use it as a foundation for new music. That's the reason why *Hours* feels open, even organic—he's no longer self-conscious, either about living up to his past or creating a new future. It's a welcome change, and it produces some fine music, particularly on the first half of the record, which is filled with such subdued, subtly winning songs as "Something in the Air," "Survive," and "Seven." Toward the end of the album, Bowie branches into harder material, which isn't quite as successful as the first half of the album, yet shares a similar sensibility. And that's what's appealing about *Hours*—it may not be one of Bowie's classics, but it's the work of a masterful musician who has begun to enjoy his craft again and isn't afraid to let things develop naturally. *—Stephen Thomas Erlewine*

Bowie at the Beeb: The Best of the BBC Radio Sessions / Sep. 26, 2000 / Virgin ♦♦♦♦♦
Some collectors might complain that the double-disc *Bowie at the Beeb,* the first official collection of David Bowie's BBC Radio sessions, isn't complete, yet they likely have bootlegs of this material. All other fans are in for a real treat. Spanning from 1968 to 1972, these recordings find Bowie, if not in his prime, at least at a peak, as he developed from a swinging Carnaby Street pop crooner to swaggering glam rock star. *Bowie at the Beeb* makes this era come alive. Opening with the lovely, florid "In the Heat of the Morning," the sessions spend time with David the Dandy before he delves into his dramatic heavy rock of the early '70s. That's where guitarist Mick Ronson made his public debut with Bowie at the session that comprises the middle of disc one. This is lean, powerful, terrific music, not as pummeling as *The Man Who Sold the World,* but it's slightly overshadowed by the session that concludes the first disc. It contains the bulk of rarities here, including the never-released "Looking for a Friend," a rollicking cover of Chuck Berry's "Almost Grown," a version of "It Ain't Easy" where Bowie trades verses with Geoffery Alexander and George Underwood, and a performance of the exquisite "Bombers." After a pair of songs by just Bowie and Ronson, the second disc finds the Spiders of Mars forming and quickly hitting its stride. Since this disc is largely devoted to recordings from 1972, it's a bit more consistent than the first, and it results in a live Spiders album better than any yet officially released. This may not be revelatory, yet this set is filled with wonderful music that deepens appreciation of Bowie's first great blast of creativity. Any true fan needs it in their collection. *—Stephen Thomas Erlewine*

The Box Tops

f. 1966, Memphis, TN, **db.** Feb. 1970
Sunshine Pop, Blue-Eyed Soul, Pop
If you forget about the Rascals and the Righteous Brothers, the Memphis-based Box Tops are the finest blue-eyed soul group. Lead singer (and former Big Star honcho) Alex Chilton had a tough, swaggering voice that belied his teenage years, sounding at times as if he were in a cutting match with the young Steve Winwood. Producers Chips Moman and Dan Penn surrounded Chilton with a crack American studio band, giving the music more muscle and deep funk than you'll ever find in "Mary Mary."

Instead of knocking off pimply, lightweight teen-fodder, the Box Tops managed to add another link in the Memphis soul chain, mixing blues, Beatlesque pop, and the sound of Stax, Hi, and Goldwax. And unlike the Monkees, the Box Tops benefited from top-notch material: Dan Penn and Spooner Oldham's "Cry Like a Baby" and "I Met Her in Church"; Wayne Thompson's "The Letter" and "Soul Deep"; and the occasional Chilton-penned nugget, such as "I Must Be the Devil." The group's heyday was brief—two years, tops—but their music remains a staple on oldies stations and has retained its vitality for over two decades. *—John Floyd*

The Letter/Neon Rainbow / 1967 / Sundazed ♦♦♦
It has since been revealed that most of the music on the Box Tops' records—with the exception of (ironically) "The Letter"—was done by session men. Even as early as the first album, this method cut both ways. It ensured a Southern soul professionalism that the young band likely couldn't have conjured on their own, but also worked against the development of a solid group identity, particularly as Alex Chilton was allowed to record very little of his own material. In fact, there are no Chilton songs on this debut, a spotty affair showing every indication of having been assembled very quickly in the wake of "The Letter" soaring to number one. Although "The Letter" author Wayne Carson Thompson and the Dan Penn-Spooner Oldham team wrote most of the songs, their blue-eyed soul compositions are surprisingly journeyman, with nothing nearly as outstanding as "The Letter," save maybe the follow-up hit "Neon Rainbow." Chilton's vocals are strong and, for the most part, as gritty as those on "The Letter." Has there every been another case in pop history when a teenager sounded like a wizened adult at the outset of his career, but his voice became higher and more youthful in subsequent years? The 2000 Sundazed reissue adds four bonus tracks: the mono single versions of "The Letter" and "Neon Rainbow," the routine non-LP 45 track "Turn on a Dream," and the previously unreleased "Georgia Farm Boy." The last of these, a plaintive country-soul tune, is credited to "Newbury," presumably Mickey Newbury (the liner notes don't give a first name or initial). *—Richie Unterberger*

Cry Like a Baby / 1968 / Sundazed ♦♦♦
Searching for a hit to follow up the widely successful "The Letter," and at the end of their creative rope, in a burst of inspiration, songwriters Dan Penn and Spooner Oldham came up with the title track to this album within hours of the scheduled recording session. The song, a perfect slice of blue-eyed soul, subsequently became a hit for the Alex Chilton-fronted Box Tops. The rest of the album builds off of "Cry Like a Baby," but with less success. Songs like "The Trouble With Sam" and "Weeping Analeah" foreshadow the British Invasion style that Chilton would employ with Big Star, but the melody lines and instrumentation lack the gritty authenticity found on *The Letter.* And the normally outstanding writing team of Penn and Oldham, responsible for such soul classics as "Do Right Woman" and "A Woman Left Lonely," seem to have softened up their approach in order to make the Box Tops sound more pop. All in all, with the exception of "Cry Like a Baby," an album that could've potentially contained some real gems just doesn't. The 2000 Sundazed reissue adds five bonus tracks: the mono 45 version of "Cry Like a Baby," three non-LP songs from singles, and the previously unreleased "Take Me to Your Heart." *—Steve Kurutz*

Non-Stop / 1968 / Sundazed ♦♦♦
The Box Tops—or more precisely Alex Chilton and producer Dan Penn—were treading water on the third album to be churned out under the group's name in less than a year. The usual blue-eyed soul dominates the program, without anything on the order of "Cry Like a Baby" or "The Letter," although with "I Met Her in Church," Penn and songwriting partner Spooner Oldham were probably trying for something on that level. Sometimes the moods are a bit on the bluesy side ("Choo Choo Train," "Rock Me Baby"), at others on a gentler and poppier one ("Rollin' in My Sleep"). For the first time Chilton had the opportunity to write an LP track, and with "I Can Dig It," he brought out his most gravelly

voice for an average midtempo soul belter. That's nothing compared with "Yesterday Where's My Mind," in which he sounds like he's trying to out-gravel the most sandpaper-voiced white singer of the era, Tim Rose; in fact, the track bears more than a passing similarity to "Morning Dew," one of the songs Rose interpreted on his debut album. "Sandman," a luscious ballad by the composer of "The Letter," Wayne Carson Thompson, is the most interesting little-known cut. Overall, though, this, like all of the Box Tops' albums, is a middling product with its share of filler. [The 2000 reissue on Sundazed adds five bonus tracks: two of them mono single versions (of "Choo Choo Train" and "I Met Her in Church"), the others from non-LP 45s. Those non-LP items include a Randy Newman cover ("Let Me Go") on which Chilton sounds like Paul Jones of Manfred Mann, and another of Chilton's earliest self-penned numbers, the soul-pop ballad "Since I Been Gone."] *—Richie Unterberger*

Dimensions / 1969 / Sundazed ♦♦♦
There were mild signs of artistic progression and evolution on the Box Tops' final album. For the first time, Dan Penn was not involved in the record (as either producer or songwriter), and Alex Chilton was allowed no less than three original compositions. A couple of these clearly hinted at an original songwriting voice. "I Must Be the Devil" was a wrenching, grind-it-out blues/soul ballad worthy of the mid-'60s Animals, and "(The) Happy Song" was an uncharacteristic (for the Box Tops) wistful Dylanesque tune (Dylan's "I Shall Be Released" was covered elsewhere on the LP). Closing the record was a pointless, nine-minute "Rock Me Baby," which the group had already recorded (in a much shorter version) on *Nonstop*. The rest of the album consisted mostly of the journeyman soul-pop that people had come to expect from Box Tops long-players, though "Soul Deep" (by the composer of "The Letter," Wayne Carson Thompson) gave the group their last big hit. The 2000 Sundazed reissue has five bonus tracks, including the mono single versions of "Soul Deep" and "Sweet Cream Ladies, Forward March," as well as two non-LP cuts from 45s, "King's Highway" and the Chilton-penned "I See Only Sunshine." There's also a previously unissued cut, "Lay Your Shine on Me." *—Richie Unterberger*

● **The Best of the Box Tops: Soul Deep** / Oct. 1, 1996 / Arista ♦♦♦♦♦
This compilation boasts "20-bit digital mastering from the original master tapes," if that matters to you. Audiophile considerations aside, it's the best anthology of the group, the 18 songs including all of the hits and their best LP-only tracks. Their credentials as the best pop-oriented blue-eyed soul group fly high, with occasional glimpses of something rootsier, especially the bluesy, Chilton-penned "I Must Be the Devil," which has one of his grittiest vocals. Another high-caliber Chilton original, "(The) Happy Song," affords a glimpse of his lighter, poppier aspirations. *—Richie Unterberger*

Boyz II Men

f. 1988, Philadelphia, PA
New Jack Swing, Club/Dance, Adult Contemporary, Urban
Under the guidance of Michael Bivins of Bell Biv Devoe, the four-man vocal group Boyz II Men became a pop sensation in 1992. Although they call their music "hip-hop doo wop," there's very little traditional doo wop in it. Instead, they bring the sound of '60s and early-'70s R&B vocal groups into the '90s, adding a little new jack swing to that timeless sound. Their 1991 debut, *Cooleyhighharmony*, featured a massive hit single, "Motownphilly," which exemplifies the best of their dance work. Their second single, a ballad called "It's So Hard to Say Goodbye," was an even bigger hit; its success paved the way for "The End of the Road" (taken from the *Boomerang* soundtrack), the group's follow-up single, which broke Elvis Presley's record for the most weeks spent at number one. After releasing a Christmas album in 1993, Boyz II Men went to work on their second album, which appeared in the fall of 1994. *II* proved to be even more successful than its predecessor, selling over seven million copies by summer of 1995 and spawning the record-breaking hit "I'll Make Love to You." *Evolution* followed in 1997 and their long-awaited fourth album *Nathan Michael Shawn Wanya* was issued three years later. *—Stephen Thomas Erlewine*

Cooleyhighharmony / Apr. 30, 1991 / Motown ♦♦♦♦♦
Boyz II Men's retro sound dominated the 1991 pop and R&B marketplaces, with their singles "It's So Hard to Say Goodbye to Yesterday" and "Motownphilly" hitting the Top Ten on both charts. The album eventually sold over five million copies and put Boyz II Men at the forefront of a movement returning the emphasis in Black popular music to vocal harmonies and a cappella interaction. *—Ron Wynn*

● **II** / Aug. 30, 1994 / Motown ♦♦♦♦♦
With their second album, Boyz II Men assured their place at the top of the charts, as well as history. "I'll Make Love to You," the album's first single, stayed on the top of the charts for over two months, only to be unseated by "On Bended Knee," the album's second single. Not surprisingly, *II* is a carefully constructed crowd pleaser, accentuating all of the finest moments from their hit debut. While there are some high-energy dance tracks, the album's main strength is its slower numbers, where the group's vocals soar. *—Stephen Thomas Erlewine*

Evolution / Sep. 23, 1997 / Motown ♦♦♦
Evolution is supposed to capture Boyz II Men in full maturity, but it sounds surprisingly similar to their blockbuster, *II*. Like that album, *Evolution* relies on ballads, downplaying the group's dance-pop side. There are still several uptempo numbers on the record, but it's clear that the group and their producers were more concerned with smooth ballads like "4 Seasons of Loneliness" and "A Song for Mama," which they deliver with typical grace. However, Boyz II Men's signature sound is beginning to sound like a formula, especially since the group fails to offer any new twists on their trademark hip-hop doo-wop. There's enough strong material on *Evolution* to satisfy Boyz II Men's large fan base, but they will truly need to evolve on their fourth album in order to stay viable. *—Stephen Thomas Erlewine*

Nathan Michael Shawn Wanya / Sep. 12, 2000 / Universal ♦♦♦♦
Even if Boyz II Men's third album *Evolution* didn't rival *II* in terms of commercial clout, the group was still inescapable. Every male urban vocal group that reached the pop and R&B charts were clearly indebted to the quartet's stylish blend of old-school harmony, post-Aretha hyper-vocalizing, and lite hip-hop beats. The group returned to action in the fall of 2000 with *Nathan Michael Shawn Wanya*, a nearly eponymous title for their first full-fledged adult album. And, as adults, they've made sure they're responsible for their own music—at least one member (usually all) has songwriting credits for all but two of the album's 14 songs, and the group is credited with all but four of the album's productions. Usually, when a popular group seizes control of their reins in such a dramatic fashion, the result is muddled to say the least, but a remarkable thing happens here—the group succeeds. True, they don't expand on the formula they developed on *II*, but they do fulfill the expectations that album set. There are no unexpected twists or turns, just the standard lush ballads and swinging hip-hop soul, but it delivers both sonically *and* substantively. Not every cut on the record is a standout, but even the average cuts are pleasant, and the best of the batch are either seductive or effortlessly danceable. Also, the group is beginning to cut back on their vocal histrionics, resulting in a record that is truly their most mature yet. It might not be their best—it doesn't have the powerhouse singles of *II*—but Boyz II Men make up for it by demonstrating that they can do much of this on their own, and still sound like the standard-bearers for urban soul. *—Stephen Thomas Erlewine*

Billy Bragg

b. Dec. 20, 1957, Barking, Essex, England
Vocals, Guitar / College Rock, Alternative Folk, British Folk, Alternative Pop/Rock, Singer/Songwriter, Urban Folk, Anti-Folk
Finding inspiration in the righteous anger of punk rock and the socially conscious folk tradition of Woody Guthrie and Bob Dylan, Billy Bragg was the leading figure of the anti-folk movement of the '80s. For most of the decade, Bragg bashed out songs alone on his electric guitar, singing about politics and love. While his lyrics were bitingly intelligent and clever, they were also warm and humane, filled with detail and wit. Even though his lyrics were carefully considered, Bragg never neglected to write melodies for songs that were strong and memorable. His first LP, 1984's *Brewing Up with Billy Bragg*, climbed to number 16 in the charts and Bragg soon became a minor celebrity in Britain, appearing at leftist political rallies, strikes, and benefits across the country. Featuring some subtle instrumental additions of piano and horns, 1986's *Talking to the Taxman About Poetry* reached the UK Top Ten. The singer recorded with a full band for the first time on 1988's *Workers Playtime* and three years later, again worked with a full band to record his most pop-oriented and accessible set of songs, *Don't Try This at Home* (featuring the hit single, "Sexuality"). Bragg took several years off but returned in 1996 with *William Bloke*. In 1998, he teamed with the American alternative country band Wilco to record *Mermaid Avenue*, a collection of performances based on unreleased songs originally written by Woody Guthrie. *—Stephen Thomas Erlewine*

Life's a Riot With Spy Vs Spy [EP] / 1983 / Go! Discs/Utility ♦♦♦♦♦
It is likely that non-fans will have encountered the tracks on *Life's a Riot* on the re-packaged *Back to Basics* CD (which also included 1984's *Brewing Up With Billy Bragg* EP). However, it is useful to discuss this debut in its historical context, for on release in 1983 nobody had encountered anyone like Billy Bragg before. A gruff Woody Guthrie for the post-punk generation, Bragg's heavy Essex accent moderated a singing voice that was anything but operatic. Yet the singer's strident, passionate non-singing provided the perfect conduit for a suite of lyrics that matched polemic with romantic observation. Another important factor in that equation was his technique as a guitarist—both extraordinarily resourceful and highly rhythmic. Bragg's underrated musicianship was perfect for songs such as "A New England," the album's cornerstone lovelorn track (and Bragg's calling card for many years to come). Sometimes, as on "The Milkman of Human Kindness," the artist succumbs to mawkish sentimentality, but his sheer conviction and empathy with his characters (who seem to be self-analogous) wins through, particularly on the affecting "The Man in the Iron Mask." *—Alex Ogg*

Brewing Up / 1984 / Go! Discs ♦♦♦♦♦
Bragg's first full album delivers another clutch of memorable, clever songs. Here the rudimentary voice and electric guitar arrangements prevalent in *Life's a Riot With Spy Vs. Spy* are refined and sweetened by occasional use of overdubbed vocals ("Love Gets Dangerous"), organ ("A Lover Sings"), and trumpet ("The Saturday Boy"); this last selection is a jaunty mid-tempo number about unrequited love that makes reference to the Delfonics' "La-La Means I Love You." Occasional 1950s influences surface on this album, most notably Bo Diddley in the jittery "This Guitar Says Sorry" and Chuck Berry in the bouncy "From a Vauxhall Velox" (which has the classic couplet "Some people say love is blind/But I just think that it's a bit short-sighted"). In addition to songs about relationships, there are also pointedly critical numbers that deal with social/political issues; examples include "It Says Here" (a ringing gruff tune that lampoons the press) and "Island of No Return" (a gripping and angry antiwar song). This excellent release has been supplanted by *Back to Basics*, which combines this album with *Life's a Riot* and *Between the Wars* into a single entity. *—David Cleary*

Between the Wars / 1985 / Go! Discs ♦♦♦♦♦
Billy Bragg's earliest releases suggest a no-frills Cockney version of Bob Dylan with electric guitar substituted for acoustic. This particular platter combines his first and third albums into one release, side one repeating *Life's a Riot With Spy Vs. Spy* and the flip side

reprising the EP *Between the Wars*. While there are some topically critical songs on the opening side such as "To Have and to Have Not," most of the tracks here deal with personal relationships. "A New England" borrows the racing guitar strum from "Little Honda" and weds it to unsentimental lyrics about love. "The Man in the Iron Mask" is a spare, slow ballad describing a masochist's acceptance of a bad marriage. "The Milkman of Human Kindness" has unusually warm lyrics and a surprisingly expressive melodic line atypical of Bragg's output. Side two is unabashedly left-wing political. The title track is a mid-tempo folk song-like number telling the story of a worker willing to look the other way for a government that will take care of him "from cradle to grave" and then finds that his faith is misplaced. There are also two covers, a forthright and sonorous song about an unsuccessful 1649 squatters' rebellion entitled "The World Turned Upside Down" and "Which Side Are You On," a union rallying song given in clipped, angry fashion. This raw, wonderfully effective record has now been superseded by *Back to Basics*, which combines this release with *Brewing Up* into one essential album. —*David Cleary*

Talking with the Taxman About Poetry / 1986 / Go! Discs/Elektra ✦✦✦✦✦
The cover to Billy Bragg's *Talking With The Taxman About Poetry* features the subtitle "the *difficult* third album," and while it's obviously meant as a joke, there's also a certain truth to the statement—after two EP's and a full album that only rarely featured anything other than Billy Bragg's voice and electric guitar, *Talking With The Taxman* found him and producers John Porter and Kenny Jones trying to add a bit of polish to Bragg's stark sound without losing either the charm of his performances or the power of his political statements. While nearly all the tracks on *Talking With The Taxman* feature Bragg alongside other musicians (among them Johnny Marr and Kirsty MacColl), the arrangements are purposefully spare, and ultimately they sweeten the songs without getting in the way of Bragg's homey melodies or passionate lyrics. However, as a songwriter, Billy's heart was stronger than his head on this album; while *Talking With The Taxman* features several of his best love songs (such as "The Marriage," "Greetings To The New Brunette," and "Wishing The Days Away") and some superb character studies ("Levi Stubbs' Tears" and "The Passion"), the political numbers are unexpectedly strident and obvious, especially the clumsy "Ideology" and "Help Save The Youth Of America." *Talking With The Taxman About Poetry* proved that Billy Bragg could take his music in a new direction and still hold on to the qualities that made his songs so special; too bad his political instincts were not as keen as his musical ones at the time. —*Mark Deming*

• **Back to Basics** / 1987 / Go! Discs/Elektra ✦✦✦✦✦
After Elektra signed Billy Bragg to his first major-label deal and released *Talking With the Taxman About Poetry* in 1986, the label decided to do a clean-up job on his back catalog and compiled *Back to Basics*, which combined the material from Bragg's first three records, *Life's a Riot With Spy Vs Spy, Brewing Up With Billy Bragg*, and *Between the Wars*, into one two-record set (now available on a single CD). The first seven cuts, from the *Life's a Riot* EP, are Bragg as his most basic; recorded in an afternoon with no overdubs, the audio is rough and Billy's electric guitar often threatens to drown out his voice, but the performances are game, and Bragg was already writing top-notch songs like "A New England" and "The Milkman of Human Kindness." The next 11 songs were originally released on Bragg's first LP, *Brewing Up With Billy Bragg*, while the sound is still spare and stark, the engineering is a good bit cleaner than on *Life's a Riot*, and Billy fleshed out his one-man-with-a-guitar approach to include the occasional vocal and/or guitar overdub, and even guest musicians on two tracks. *Back to Basics* closes with three somber political numbers that first surfaced on Bragg's *Between the Wars* EP, released when tensions over trade union strikes in the U.K. were at their height—one original ("Between the Wars") and two vintage labor anthems. While the tone is downbeat, the performances are strong and compassionate. While *Back to Basics* fudges a bit with the sequence of the original material, it's still a strong collection of some of Bragg's most engaging work, and it's a lot easier (and cheaper) to find than the original out of print LPs. —*Mark Deming*

Help Save the Youth of America E.P.: Live & Dubious / 1988 / Go! Discs/Elektra ✦✦✦

Workers Playtime / 1988 / Go! Discs/Elektra ✦✦✦
Bragg's first attempt at working with a full band could be better—most of the songs are mopey and depressing, and some of his socialist manifestos are tiresome and dogmatic. Still, cuts like "She's Got a New Spell," "Must I Paint You a Picture," and "Little Time Bomb" are excellent, and "Waiting for the Great Leap Forward" is a humble and humorous explanation of Bragg's motives and intentions, both political and emotional. —*John Floyd*

The Internationale / Jun. 1990 / Utility/Elektra ✦✦

Don't Try This at Home / Sep. 17, 1991 / Go! Discs/Elektra ✦✦✦✦✦
After dipping his toes in the notion of using backing musicians on *Talking With The Taxman About Poetry*, Billy Bragg finally dove in head first with *Worker's Playtime*, but *Don't Try It At Home* was where Bragg first began to sound completely comfortable with the notion of a full band. With Johnny Marr (who helped produce two tracks), Peter Buck, Michael Stipe, and Kirsty MacColl on hand to give the sessions a taste of starpower, *Don't Try This At Home* sounds full but uncluttered; the arrangements (most complete with—gasp!—drums) flesh out Bragg's melodies, giving them greater strength in the process, and Billy's craggy scouse vocals wrap around the melodies with significantly more flexibility than on previous recordings. With the exception of the rabble rousing "Accident Waiting To Happen" and "North Sea Bubble," and the witty "Sexuality," most of *Don't Try This At Home* finds Billy Bragg in a contemplative mood; the political tunes are subtle (and don't hector), such as the mournful "Rumours Of War," and the songs about love tend to examine the less hopeful side of relationships, like "Mother Of The Bride" and the lovely "You Woke Up My Neighborhood." But there's also an understated wit to many of the songs, especially the well-drawn "God's Footballer," and Bragg approached the work

of other songwriters to splendid effect on Fred Neil's "Dolphins and Sid Griffin's "Everywhere." *Don't Try This At Home* isn't the sort of album that announces itself loudly, but slip into its understated textures and you'll discover one of Billy Bragg's warmest and most thoughtful albums. —*Mark Deming*

The Peel Sessions / May 1992 / Strange Fruit ✦✦✦
Because Bragg started his career as a solo act, these live-in-the-studio radio transcriptions don't offer anything you can't find on *Back to Basics*. But fanatics will enjoy the occasional lyric deviations, and "A13 Trunk Road to the Sea" (a rewrite of "Route 66" with British directions) is a keeper. —*John Floyd*

William Bloke / Sep. 9, 1996 / Elektra ✦✦✦
Despite taking five years off to marry and have a son (named Jack, of course), which should've given him plenty of time to write, Bragg gives listeners half an album of "B" material. Four of the lesser songs regress to Bragg's mid-'80s beginnings, when he bellowed like a foghorn in a thick cockney accent over a scratchy guitar. "From Red to Blue," "Brickbat," "Northern Industrial Town," and especially his setting of Rudyard Kipling's fiery "A Pict Song" to music revisit *Spy Vs. Spy, Brewing Up*, and *Talking to the Taxman About Poetry*, ignoring the stylistic advances he's shown since (except for clearer singing). However, even those rough days bore close listening thanks to Bragg's lyrical wit, conviction, and knack for punky hooks. Likewise, *William Bloke's* other tracks fall short of his best but remain hugely entertaining and thought-provoking. "Goalhanger" is a hilarious, clever roasting of conniving, manipulating jerks who use others set to a ska beat and an organ out of Henry Mancini's "Baby Elephant Walk." "Sugardaddy" is a similar lighthearted soul homage that barely obfuscates Bragg's long-standing, wrathful contempt for capitalism's caste system and greed. "The Space Race Is Over" and "The 14th of February" recall the more tender moments of *Don't Try This*, as does the bemused yet hopeful "King James Version." Better, "Everybody Loves You Babe" is a piano and vocal delight, turning a torch love song on its ear, while the single "Upbeat" echoes *Don't Try This'* highs: the barking brass, insistent Motown choruses, and Bragg's soul-searching about socialism when so many of his old compadres have sold out like Jerry Rubins all add up to a gripping single from an LP that reminds listeners that the well-missed Bragg is super valuable, even when firing flowers instead of bullets. —*Jack Rabid, The Big Takeover*

Mermaid Avenue / Jun. 23, 1998 / Elektra ✦✦✦✦
During the spring of 1995, Woody Guthrie's daughter Nora contacted British urban folk troubadour Billy Bragg about writing music for a selection of completed Guthrie lyrics. This was no minor task—Guthrie left behind over a thousand sets of complete lyrics written between 1939 and 1967 that had no music other than a vague stylistic notation. Bragg chose a number of songs to finish, as did Jeff Tweedy of the alt-country band Wilco (often with bandmate Jay Bennett). Nora Guthrie impressed a common goal upon them: Rather than recreating Guthrie tunes, they should write as if they were collaborating with Woody, creating new, vital music for the lyrics. Both artists completed more songs than could fit on *Mermaid Avenue*, which is neatly split between Bragg and Wilco, with Bragg taking lead on eight of the 15 songs. The results are almost entirely a delight, mainly because all involved are faithful to Guthrie's rowdy spirit—it's a reverent project that knows how to have fun. There are many minor, irresistible gems scattered throughout the album, and most of them come from Bragg. Where Wilco's fine contributions sound inextricably tied to the '90s, both for better and for worse, Bragg's music sounds contemporary while capturing Guthrie's folk traditions. That's not to say Wilco's contributions are failures—it's just hard to imagine Guthrie singing the plaintive "California Stars" or the plodding "Christ for President," neither of which quite fit the lyrics. Nevertheless, their hearts are in the right place; more often than not, they come close to the target, and their joyous playing invigorates *Mermaid Avenue*. The blend of Bragg's traditionalist sensibility and Wilco's contemporary style ultimately illustrates that Guthrie's words, ideals, and aesthetics remain alive in the '90s. It's a remarkable record that deserves a sequel. —*Stephen Thomas Erlewine*

Reaching to the Converted / Aug. 31, 1999 / Rhino ✦✦✦✦
Rhino's *Reaching to the Converted* collects 17 non-LP cuts Billy Bragg released between 1985 and 1997, including singles, B-sides, and compilation album contributions, along with the previously unreleased "Shirley," a 1992 re-recording of "Greetings to the New Brunette," which features Johnny Marr. Some hardcore fans will have nearly all of the material presented here, yet they'll still want this collection, not only because it provides a bunch of rarities in a simple package, but because it is a thoroughly engaging and entertaining listen. —*Stephen Thomas Erlewine*

Mermaid Avenue, Vol. 2 / May 30, 2000 / Elektra ✦✦✦
Like many sequels, *Mermaid Avenue, Vol. 2* isn't the equal of its predecessor—that felt fully realized, where this feels a little patchwork—yet it is still satisfying on many levels. As on the first, the Billy Bragg-written and sung music is the most convincing since he captures the cadences and spirit of Guthrie's music. They sound like classic, weathered folk songs whereas Wilco's numbers are modern inventions, splicing music that is clearly theirs with Guthrie's words. The chasm between the two artists was apparent on the first, but it's more evident this time around, largely due to the fact that several of Wilco's songs were recorded without Bragg after the release of *Mermaid Avenue*. This gives the record a strangely disjointed feel that isn't helped by the guest appearances by Natalie Merchant on "I Was Born" and Corey Harris whose vocals overpower "Aginst th' Law." Since Bragg and Wilco are pursuing slightly different directions in the first place, the guest artists only add to the patchwork quality of the record. Still, even with its weaknesses, there are plenty of worthwhile things here from both sides of the spectrum. If Wilco occasionally is a little too somber or introspective, they do have moments where everything aligns perfectly. But, as on the first, it's the Bragg-led numbers that truly catch fire, feeling every bit

as warm, funny, and vibrant as Guthrie's best work. His contributions go a long way to making *Mermaid Avenue, Vol. 2* a pleasing sequel. —*Stephen Thomas Erlewine*

Braid

f. 1993, Champaign-Urbana, IL, **db.** 1999
Emo, Indie Rock, Alternative Pop/Rock

In a search to find others interested in trading videos of live shows, drummer/singer Bob Nanna, of Friction, placed a classified ad in Maximum Rock & Roll and met drummer Roy Ewing, of Champaign-Urbana, IL, in 1993. That fall, Bob, a freshman at the University of Illinois in Champaign-Urbana, started hanging out with Roy, who played in Lowercase N. Bob's friend guitarist Pete Havranek, of 42 Loads and Inkadink, wanted to play with someone new, so Roy volunteered. Bob became their singer and guitarist, Jay Ryan joined them on bass, and Braid was born.

Shortly after, Jay left the band and went on to play with Hubcap and Dianogah. Todd Bell, who had played with Roy in Lowercase N, replaced Jay on bass. Kate Reuss was recruited to sing. Braid played their first show December 10, 1993, in Danville, IL. Kate left the band after the second show.

After this, Braid went through some drastic changes. Bob's other band, Friction, broke up for good, which meant that Braid was no longer a side project. Chris Broach joined as singer. Pete left the band in August 1994, and Chris took over on guitar. A week later Braid recorded the *Rainsnowmatch* 7-inch, which was released in December 1994 on Enclave Records. Braid's debut album *Frankie Welfare Boy Age Five* was released in June 1995 on Divot Records.

In March 1997, Roy left the band. Damon Atkinson, of Figurehead, joined Braid's spring tour and became the band's drummer. Two years later, in August 1999, Braid disbanded; the posthumous *Lucky to Be Alive* followed in the spring of 2000. —*Tracy Frey*

Frankie Welfare Boy Age Five / Jun. 1995 / Divot ◆◆◆

Documentation of the elementary school years of one of the more popular indie-label acts who flout an aggressively poppy rock sound. Across 26 tracks, each one named using a different letter of the alphabet, Braid meticulously defines, in somewhat course means, a smattering of the different textures and movements they would later follow on their more popular *Age of Octeen* and *Frame & Canvas*. Jangly energetic bursts of melodic punk styles in more excess than you can handle. Despite the many moments that lag or lack focus, there are many moments encrusted here that make this album a necessity for most Braid fans. —*Blake Butler*

The Age of Octeen / 1996 / Mud ◆◆◆◆

Braid's second full-length, *The Age of Octeen*, exudes a passion and roughness reminiscent of high school. From the boyish shouted/sung vocals to the straightforward, punk-influenced guitars to the lyrics dealing with failed relationships and memories, the album has an unpolished, garage-band energy. Although the album has that raw quality, there isn't a weak track on it. The first track, "My Baby Smokes," starts with quiet, mumbled lyrics, rolling drums, and understated guitars before bursting into wailing vocals backed by a wall of sound. "American Typewriter" is a little more complex with its tight, staccato drumming and quick guitar riffs. "Chandelier Swing" and "Autobiography" close the album on a quieter, more thoughtful note. Overall, *The Age of Octeen* is a solid effort that manages to capture the abandon and freedom of being 19. —*Tracy Frey*

● **Frame & Canvas** / Apr. 7, 1998 / Polyvinyl ◆◆◆◆

The latest release from these poppy math-rock emo veterans. Braid puts together very technical pop melodies, often with time changes and beautiful interlocking melodic guitar parts, fused together with yelled/sung boyish vocals. *Frame and Canvas* proves to be one of their best efforts—by the end of the first song, "The New Nathan Detroits," you know you will be humming these melodies in your head for at least the next few days. The album continues to mature throughout, providing a sense of heartbreak and sentimentality on amazing tracks like "A Dozen Roses" and "Breathe In." If you are looking for emo-pop with overflowing energy and highly skilled composition, this is for you. —*Blake Butler*

Please Drive Faster / 1999 / Polyvinyl ◆◆◆

The thinking man's version of the Promise Ring has called it quits, and what better way to say goodbye than to add yet another single to their already massive discography? *Please Drive Faster* continues in the Braid tradition of choppy emo pop that remains at a midtempo speed. And with their melodic formula of complex riffs that graduated from the school of Cap 'n Jazz, Braid can be remembered as indie legends who quit while they were at the peak of their career. —*Mike DaRonco*

Lucky to Be Alive / Mar. 21, 2000 / Glue Factory ◆◆◆

Movie Music, Vol. 1 / Mar. 28, 2000 / Polyvinyl ◆◆◆

Movie Music, Vol. 2 / Mar. 28, 2000 / Polyvinyl ◆◆◆

Brainiac

f. 1992, Dayton, OH, **db.** 1997
Experimental Rock, Indie Rock, Alternative Pop/Rock

Well after the death of new wave, Brainiac formed in 1992 with a sound that perfectly epitomized the uptight, herky-jerky tension of the early-'80s movement, as well as its warped sense of song structure and electronic breakdown. The band came together in Dayton, Ohio, originally the basement experiments of vocalist/keyboard player Tim Taylor and bassist Juan Monasterio. After recruiting guitarist Michelle Bodine and drummer Tyler Trent, Brainiac began playing around the Midwest and hooked up with Limited Potential Records, which released the single "Super Duper Seven" in September 1992. After another single, a split with Bratmobile on Dayton's 12X12 label, Brainiac signed with

Grass Records. The group's debut album *Smack Bunny Baby*, produced by Girls Against Boys' Eli Janney, appeared in mid-1993. During 1994, Brainiac replaced Bodine with guitarist John Schmersal and released their second album, *Bonsai Superstar*. After a tour on Lollapalooza's second stage, a performance in Chicago impressed the indie-label heavyweight Touch & Go, which signed the band and issued their third album, *Hissing Prigs in Static Couture*, in early 1996.

Brainiac released an EP, *Electro Shock for President*, in April 1997, prior to entering the studio to record their fourth album. Over the course of 1996-97, their profile had grown, and there were rumors that major labels like DreamWorks were interested in signing them after the new album was completed. As the group was recording during the summer, Tim Taylor was tragically killed in a one-car accident, driving home from the studio. —*John Bush*

Smack Bunny Baby / Jul. 1993 / Grass ◆◆◆◆

This 1993 album shows the band relying less on the sonic experimentation that marked their later work, than on pure punk exuberance. Tracks like "Ride" and "Draag" seethe with a manic fury that creates a pervading sense of tension and urgency throughout the album. Also, the band's pop sensibilities shine through the hectic clatter of the title track and "Martian Dance Invasion," on which guitarist Michelle Bodine assumes vocal duties. On these tracks and others are indications of the frantic cacophony that would be further developed on Brainiac's later albums. —*Brian Christopher Egan*

Bonsai Superstar / Nov. 1994 / Grass ◆◆◆

Whereas *Smack Bunny Baby* had shown Brainiac to be a band that was still developing, *Bonsai Superstar* is an astounding blast of cohesive madness. The band finds its voice and vision and moves light years ahead of their peers (as well as where they had been musically only a year earlier). From the opening moments of "Hot Metal Dobermans," it is apparent that listeners are in the hands of an assured, ambitious group of musicians—including the newly arrived John Schmersal on guitar. The music is far more adventurous than on the previous album, incorporating more raw noise and sound effects, and even constructing "Fucking with the Altimeter" around a series of spoken samples. But lead singer Tim Taylor is the star of this show—his combination of a Betty Boop falsetto and an Elvis-style croon on "Flypaper" is mesmerizing, and his explosive strut through "Sexual Frustration" exudes pure star power. *Bonsai Superstar* captures a band that was ahead of their time and still moving forward. —*Brian Christopher Egan*

● **Hissing Prigs in Static Couture** / Mar. 26, 1996 / Touch & Go ◆◆◆◆◆

On their final full-length album, Brainiac move further into the unchartered territory that they explored on *Bonsai Superstar*, and perhaps because of that, the album seems initially less exciting. However, while they take a somewhat smaller creative step between these two albums than between *Bonsai Superstar* and *Smack Bunny Baby*, *Hissing Prigs in Static Couture* nonetheless offers up a fascinating dose of space-age sound bites, falsetto vocals and chant-along choruses. The opening four tracks are astounding, especially "Pussyfootin'" and the loopy "This Little Piggy." The middle of the album drags a bit, but it comes to a blistering conclusion with "Nothing Ever Changes" (recorded by Steve Albini) and "I Am a Cracked Machine." —*Brian Christopher Egan*

Electro-Shock for President / Apr. 1, 1997 / Touch & Go ◆◆◆

Brainiac's last release, *Electro Shock for President*, underlines the tragedy of Tim Taylor's untimely death; the EP's six songs find the group in the middle of a creative renaissance, moving away from their crazed, guitars-and-Moogs sound toward a colder, increasingly electronic, yet equally distinctive style. "Fresh New Eyes"' ping-ponging synths and static-burst percussion introduce this darker, more ominous Brainiac sound, while "Flash Ram" upgrades their skronky punk into cybernetic thrash, complete with robotic singing. Similarly, "Mr. Fingers" fuses the choppy noisebursts of *Hissing Prigs in Static Couture* with the EP's buzz-and-bleep aesthetic. Tracks like "Fashion 500" and "Turnover" are even more surprising, discarding much of the group's strategically chaotic noise for tense, implosive synths and muffled vocals. Though it was intended as a teaser for their fourth album, *Electro Shock for President* remains one of Brainiac's most interesting efforts, reflecting their ever-evolving style, which embraced electronica, new wave, and even industrial elements, as well as pop, punk, and noise. The EP's only flaw is that it—like Brainiac's career—ends all too quickly, reinforcing the incomplete feeling that surrounds the group's sad, abrupt end. —*Heather Phares*

The Brand New Heavies

f. 1985, London, England
Alternative Rap, Alternative Dance, Club/Dance, Acid Jazz, Urban, House, Hip-Hop

Pioneers of the London acid-jazz scene, the Brand New Heavies translated their love for the funk grooves of the 1970s into a sophisticated sound which carried the torch for classic soul in an era dominated by hip-hop. The Brand New Heavies were originally an instrumental unit inspired by the James Brown and Meters records its members heard while clubbing the "rare groove" scene in vogue at the moment; the trio soon began recording their own music, gaining enormous exposure when their demo tracks were spun at the influential Cat in the Hat Club. Eventually adding a brass section, the Brand New Heavies built a cult following throughout the London club circuit, surviving the shift which saw the rare groove scene fade in the wake of acid house. After signing with the fledgling indie label Acid Jazz, their self-titled LP appeared in 1990 to strong critical acclaim, resulting in a licensing deal with the American company Delicious Vinyl. After scoring at home with "Dream Come True" and "Stay This Way," the single "Never Stop" soon landed on the American R&B charts, with the Heavies the first British group to accomplish such a feat with a debut single since Soul II Soul several years earlier. —*Jason Ankeny*

● **Trunk Funk Classics: 1991-2000** / Oct. 17, 2000 / Rhino ◆◆◆◆

Trunk Funk Classics: 1991-2000 is the first Brand New Heavies best-of available domestically in the U.S. Not to be confused with the similarly titled British release *Trunk Funk: Best of the Brand New Heavies*, the American version doesn't feature all of the group's U.K. chart singles ("Midnight at the Oasis" and "You Are the Universe" are missing), but it does give more airtime to the Heavies' collaborations with American rappers, including Main Source, the Pharcyde, Mos Def, and Q-Tip. There's also a newly recorded track, "Finish What You Started," which temporarily reunites the group with longtime vocalist N'Dea Davenport; wisely, it's also the 1991-1994 Davenport era that's most heavily drawn upon for the collection. It may not be *entirely* comprehensive, but *Trunk Funk Classics* does cover the essence of the Brand New Heavies, and just as importantly, it's a consistently infectious listen. —*Steve Huey*

Brandy

b. Feb. 11, 1979, McComb, Mississippi

Vocals / Club/Dance, Urban

Though still in her teens, singer Brandy was among the biggest and brightest new stars to emerge during the 1990s—a multimedia sensation, she was a success not only on the pop and R&B charts, but also on television. Born in McComb, Missouri in 1979, Brandy Norwood was raised in California, first attracting attention singing with area youth groups. From there she moved on to a series of television award shows and specials, and later co-starred in the short-lived ABC sitcom *Thea*. Brandy's self-titled debut LP appeared in 1994, launching a series of hits, among them "I Wanna Be Down," "Baby" and "Brokenhearted"; by now a major star, she returned a year later with the blockbuster "Sittin' Up in My Room," a cut from the soundtrack to the film *Waiting to Exhale*. "Missing You," from the soundtrack to 1996's *Set It Off*, was also a hit, but instead of immediately releasing a follow-up LP, Brandy returned to acting, starring in the acclaimed UPN sitcom *Moesha* and also appearing in the title role of the 1997 Disney telefilm *Cinderella*, one of the biggest success stories of the television season. Her long-awaited sophomore album, *Never Say Never*, was finally issued in mid-1998. —*Jason Ankeny*

● **Brandy** / Sept. 27, 1994 / Atlantic ◆◆◆◆

This teenage R&B singer hit the Top Ten late in 1994 with "I Wanna Be Down," a representative track from her solid debut album. Brandy knows her way around a hip-hop beat, layering tender-tough vocals over spare arrangements like a lower-key Janet Jackson or a more stripped-down Mary J. Blige. Good songs and crisp production make Brandy a moody, moving success. —*Eddie Huffman*

Never Say Never / Jun. 9, 1998 / Atlantic ◆◆◆◆

Shortly after the release of her eponymous debut in 1995, Brandy became a star. Not only did the album sell well, but she starred on UPN's *Moesha* and Disney's made-for-TV *Cinderella*, all before she released her second album, *Never Say Never*, in 1998. Needless to say, there was much more riding on the second record than the debut and, fortunately, she follows through with *Never Say Never*, delivering an album that rivals her first. Brandy wisely decides to find a middle ground between Mariah Carey and Mary J. Blige—it's adult contemporary with a slight streetwise edge. As with most adult contemporary albums, the record is bogged down by some filler, but Brandy's delivery has improved and her subdued vocals can make mediocre material sound convincing. Still, what makes *Never Say Never* a winning record are quality songs and production. The smooth Monica duet "The Boy Is Mine" and the tripped-out "Top of the World" (which features a rap from Mase) are two examples of what Brandy can achieve when everything's in the right place, and they help make *Never Say Never* a better, more adventurous record than her debut. —*Stephen Thomas Erlewine*

Laura Branigan

b. Jul. 3, 1957, Brewster, NY

Vocals / Pop/Rock, Adult Contemporary, Dance-Pop

Laura Branigan is a singer and, increasingly, an actress from Brewster, New York, who first gained notice when she became a backup singer for Leonard Cohen in 1977. Branigan achieved considerable popular success in the early '80s by applying her big, powerful voice to translated versions of Eurodisco hits. She was less successful with subsequent recordings in the second half of the '80s, though by then she had begun to appear on television and in films. —*William Ruhlmann*

● **The Best of Branigan** / 1995 / Atlantic ◆◆◆◆

The woefully underrated Laura Branigan's first stateside greatest-hits package has every one of her hits and some of her best tracks that didn't make a dent on the charts. From her breakthrough signature song "Gloria" all the way through to her last Top 40 appearance with "The Power of Love," Branigan's powerhouse voice and career are fairly represented here. Beyond the joy of hearing some of the forgotten hits like "Solitaire," "The Lucky One," and "Spanish Eddie," you can hear how her underutilized voice can bring life to productions that aren't necessarily on its par. She is remarkably understated on the subtly over the top "Over You," while her dramatic appeal is used to its fullest on "How Can I Help You Say Goodbye?" and "Ti Amo." Though her career never had the type of trajectory Celine Dion did, her voice is just as strong and just as full. With cuts like the playful "Is There Anybody Here but Me?," a faithful remake of Donna Summer's "Dim All the Lights," and the pop ballad "Show Me Heaven," you can hear how her voice matured in fullness and timbre and how maturity brought her music and her talent to a new level in the latter portion of her career, though it didn't help bring back the sales she initially enjoyed. —*Bryan Buss*

Toni Braxton

b. Oct. 7, 1967

Vocals / Contemporary R&B, Adult Contemporary, Urban

Toni Braxton made her vocal debut with the single "Love Shoulda Brought You Home" from the *Boomerang* soundtrack. She issued her first full album in 1993, and it soared to the top of both the pop and R&B charts. Braxton eventually earned two Grammy and two Soul Train awards, saw her self-titled release go platinum, and also reaped both critical and commercial plaudits for such singles as "Love Shoulda Brought You Home" and "Just Another Sad Love Song." In the summer of 1996, Braxton released her second album, *Secrets*, which entered the charts at number two and produced the number one single, "You're Makin' Me High." *Heat* followed in the spring of 2000. —*Ron Wynn*

● **Toni Braxton** / Jul. 1993 / La Face ◆◆◆◆◆

Toni Braxton is both an elegant and earthy songstress, nicely balancing those seemingly divergent sentiments on her self-titled debut disc. Braxton's husky, enticing voice sounds hypnotic on "Breathe Again," dismayed on "Another Sad Love Song" and disillusioned on "Love Shoulda Brought You Home." But she's never out of control, indignant or so anguished and hurt that she fails to retain her dignity. It's a sign of how great the Babyface/L.A. Reid production team was that they didn't settle for a defining mood; they presented Braxton with enough diverse emotional settings to hold the interest of urban contemporary males and females. —*Ron Wynn*

Secrets / Jun. 18, 1996 / La Face ◆◆◆◆◆

Toni Braxton's second album, *Secrets*, follows through on the promise of her eponymous debut. Like her first album, the majority of *Secrets* was co-produced by Babyface and his partner L.A. Reid, while the material is divided between songs written by outside songwriters like R. Kelly, Tony Rich, and Diane Warren and originals by Braxton and Babyface. Braxton and Babyface's collaborations are the highlights of the album, combining rich melodies and gorgeous choruses with subtle, clever lyrics that are never laced with clichés. Nearly equalling the original numbers are contributions by Tony Rich ("Come On Over Here") and R. Kelly ("I Don't Want To"); with these tracks, both musicians demonstrate why they are considered two of the top songwriters in '90s R&B and soul. *Secrets* does have a couple of weak moments. The numbers produced by David Foster are too predictable in their slick commercial appeal, but Braxton manages to infuse the songs with life and passion that elevates them beyond their generic confines. And her vocal talent is what unites *Secrets* and makes it into a first-rate contemporary R&B collection. Braxton is a singer who can cross over into the smooth confines of adult contemporary radio without losing or betraying the soul that lies at the foundation of her music, and her talent burns at its brightest on *Secrets*. —*Stephen Thomas Erlewine*

The Heat / Apr. 25, 2000 / La Face ◆◆◆◆

Toni Braxton went through a lot in the years separating her star-making *Toni* and her 2000 comeback *The Heat*. Yes, she became a star, but she also went through a painful bankruptcy that delayed her sequel for years. Fortunately, you wouldn't be able to tell that there was so much behind-the-scenes drama from *The Heat*—it's a confident, assured, sexy effort that reaffirms Braxton's status as one of the finest contemporary mainstream soul singers. She may not be as street-smart as Mary J. Blige, nor does she push the boundaries of the genre the way TLC does, but she has a full, rich voice that instantly lends her songs a sense of maturity and sensuality, especially since she never, ever oversings or misjudges her material. And, while that material can occasionally be a little generic, much of *The Heat* is built on solid ballads and smoldering, midtempo dance numbers. Producers as diverse as Babyface, Rodney Jerkins, Daryl Simmons, Teddy Bishop, and David Foster are responsible for various tracks on the album, which is typical for a big-budget, superstar release like this, but rarely are the tracks quite as consistent and cohesive as they are here. The skittering beats of "He Wasn't Man Enough" and "Gimme Some" are every bit as effective as the simmering title track or ballads "I'm Still Breathing" and "Spanish Guitar"—or "Just Be a Man About It," an instant classic telephone break-up song, with Dr. Dre playing the wayward lover breaking the news to Ms. Braxton. True, *The Heat* slightly runs out of momentum toward the end, but there aren't many dull spots on the record—it's all stylish, sultry, seductive, appealing urban contemporary soul that confirms Braxton's prodigious talents. —*Stephen Thomas Erlewine*

Bread

f. 1968, Los Angeles, CA, **db.** 1977

Soft Rock

Bread was one of the most popular pop groups of the early '70s, earning a string of well-crafted, melodic soft-rock singles, all of which were written by keyboardist/vocalist David Gates. Gates met guitarist/vocalist James Griffin in 1968, and recorded a self-titled debut for Elektra by the end of the year. Their second album, *On the Waters*, established Bread as hit-makers with the number one single "Make It with You" and the Top Ten hit "It Don't Matter to Me" (actually taken from *Bread*). In 1971, *Manna* launched another Top Ten single with "If," but the group then hit with "Baby I'm-A Want You," which peaked at number three. At the beginning of 1973, Bread disbanded after a songwriting dispute between Gates and Griffin, but reunited three years later with one last Top Ten hit, "Lost Without Your Love." After Griffin left in 1977, Gates assembled a new version of Bread, leading to a lawsuit over the name that wasn't resolved until 1984. Both pursued solo careers, with Gates gaining the upper hand courtesy of a Top 20 hit, 1978's "Goodbye Girl." —*Stephen Thomas Erlewine*

Bread / 1969 / Rhino ◆◆◆◆◆

Bread is seen as nothing but a wimp-pop band—an impression which is justified, but it wipes out the fact that the group was quite good and rather slyly diverse in its early days, particularly on its debut, *Bread*. This is effectively the birth of Californian soft rock, as

David Gates and compatriots blend the folk-rock of the Byrds and Buffalo Springfield with a distinctly British melodicism and a streak of sentimentality borrowed from McCartney. The result is a modest little gem, with more strange turns than you'd expect from their reputation—including soaring falsettos, spiraling melodies, rough guitars, and, best of all, a set of tightly-written, appealing songs. Only "It Don't Matter Me," which became a hit *after* the second album, ranks among their best-known material, but each of the songs illustrates the exceptional craftsmanship of not just Gates, but Robb Royer and James Griffin. As such, this may not seem like the record for casual fans, if judged just on the track listing, but it will convince the pop fans that may have been doubters. *—Stephen Thomas Erlewine*

On the Waters / 1970 / Rhino ✦✦✦✦
Bread broke big with their second album, thanks to David Gates' sentimental soft pop classic, "Make It With You"—the song that set the standard for sensitive mellow pop ballads for the '70s and for years to come. Its pull is strong, but it's a bit misleading, since the group hardly just turns out a series of these lovely, luxurious pop tunes throughout the record. In fact, with the considerable assistance of Robb Royer and James Griffin, the group actually rocks it harder than Crosby Stills & Nash (if not CSNY, true enough), and they continue to show that the diversity and range of material they demonstrated on their debut was no fluke. If anything, "Make It With You" doesn't set the pace for the rest of the record, since even the softer moments, such as "Look What You've Done," isn't as lushly mellow as that—there is more coloring through the guitars, and the songwriting has more edge and melody than that. Of course, this is hardly a hard rock record, but it's a first-class Californian pop record, one that is as blissful as a sunset when it lays back, and as incandescent as a day at the beach when the tempo is sprightly. *—Stephen Thomas Erlewine*

Manna / 1971 / Rhino ✦✦✦✦✦
Bread's third album, *Manna*, isn't so much a step forward as it is a consolidation of strengths, as the group sharpens their skills and carves out their own identities. It's clear that the rift between David Gates and Robb Royer & James Griffin is beginning to take shape, as the album is evenly divided between Gates tunes and Royer/Griffin compositions. This benefits the album, since it spurs each member to greater heights, and they even tend to sequence the record in ways that support that sentiment—Gates' "Let Your Love Go," complete with its rockin' harpsichords, is followed by the hard-driving verses of "Take Comfort," which, admittedly, is tempered by a dreamy chorus. And while some of the rougher edges present on *Bread* or *On the Waters* are sanded down slightly, they're still there, providing good contrast to such soft pop landmarks as "If." Yet, this is a record that is laid-back and even tempered, which isn't a bad thing—it results in a fine listen, especially since the group's songwriting remains at the high standard instituted on that first Bread album. *—Stephen Thomas Erlewine*

Baby I'm—A Want You / 1972 / Elektra ✦✦✦✦✦
The group's best album, showcasing its soft and hard sides (yes, Bread had a hard side) at their respective peaks. "Mother Freedom," with its crunchy James Griffin guitar solo, and the superb soft-rocker "Baby I'm-A Want You" made a brilliant opening which the rest of the album had a hard time matching. The songs range from wistful sentimentality ("Diary") to spirited protest ("This Isn't What the Government," a poor man's "Taxman" with an anti-war slant). The high points outnumber the flat spots, and the playing is very polished (with unexpected hard-rock flourishes on "Dream Lady"), but this is still a '70s period piece. Reissued in 1996. *—Bruce Eder*

Anthology / 1985 / Elektra ✦✦✦✦✦
This is the definitive collection for these soft rock giants of the early '70s. Contained within are all of their hits, plus some delectable gems unknown to those familiar with Bread only from the radio. This set begins with "Make It with You," which hit the number one spot in 1970, and ends with the group's last Top Ten hit, "Lost Without Your Love" from their reunion album of 1977. Other Top Ten hits include "If," "Baby I'm-a Want You," "Everything I Own," "It Don't Matter to Me," and "Guitar Man," which reached number 11. The popular songs have held up well, but perhaps the most interesting cuts here are the lesser-known ones, like "Dismal Day," "Down on My Knees" and "The Last Time." David Gates and company had quite a run, and this anthology shows why. *—Jim Newsom*

Retrospective / Jul. 1996 / Rhino ✦✦✦✦✦
Retrospective is the definitive compilation of Bread, perhaps the definitive soft-rock group of the '70s. If anything, it may be too comprehensive for most listeners. Covering the entire course of Bread's career, plus selected highlights from David Gates in the late '70s and early '80s, the compilation spans two very full compact discs. For those who want more than the hits but are unwilling to delve into individual albums, the collection is ideal. Listeners who want the hits might find the album tracks a little tedious. Then again, the presence of Gates' solo hits like "The Goodbye Girl" is enticing for even casual fans, since he lacks a solo compilation and there are no sets that cover both his solo career and Bread. Since *Retrospective* does cover all the Bread hits plus solid obscurities and Gates' solo highlights, it does qualify as the definitive collection. In fact, it's hard to imagine how another set could be as thorough as this. *—Stephen Thomas Erlewine*

● **The Best of Bread** / Jun. 19, 2001 / Rhino ✦✦✦✦✦
Rhino's 2001 collection *The Best of Bread* is the definitive single-disc collection of Bread's hits, spanning 20 tracks and all of the group's hits, including lesser-known hits that didn't reach the heights of "Make It With You," "Everything I Own," "If" or "Baby I'm a Want You." Though this isn't as comprehensive as Rhino's previous double-disc set—which means it doesn't contain the David Gates solo cuts that *Retrospective* does—it still provides most casual listeners with all the Bread they'd need, in a highly listenable fashion, too. *—Stephen Thomas Erlewine*

The Breeders

f. 1988, Dayton, OH
Indie Rock, Alternative Pop/Rock
One of alternative rock's most promising—and frustrating—groups, the Breeders began as a way for Pixies' bassist Kim Deal and Throwing Muses' guitarist Tanya Donelly to escape their second-banana status. After Donelly left to form Belly, the group achieved massive success with the hit "Cannonball," but the group seemed stuck in limbo during the late '90s, playing a handful of dates and releasing even fewer songs. Deal, Donelly, Perfect Disaster's Josephine Wiggs and Slint's Britt Walford played on 1990's *Pod*, their critically acclaimed debut album. Donelly left after 1992's *Safari* EP and was replaced by Kim's sister Kelley; the EP also featured drummer Jim MacPherson, who was billed as "Mike Hunt." In 1993, the Pixies split and the Breeders released *Last Splash*, which featured the breakthrough single "Cannonball." *Last Splash* earned platinum sales and the band played 1994's Lollapalooza, but as quickly they became stars, the Breeders went on hiatus, exhausted by their sudden fame and extensive touring. Late in 1994, Kelley was arrested for drug possession and went to a Minnesota rehab clinic. Wiggs formed the Josephine Wiggs Experience and Kim returned to Dayton with MacPherson and formed the Amps. After rehab, Kelley formed the Kelley Deal 6000, and Kim played and recorded under the Breeders name again. Kelley rejoined the band in 1998; the only song to surface from their sessions was a cover of 3 Degrees' "Collage," which appeared on *The Mod Squad* soundtrack. In 2000, the Deals recorded with Steve Albini and played a secret show in Los Angeles. A new Breeders record was expected sometime in 2001 but seemed unlikely, given the group's unpredictable history. *—Stephen Thomas Erlewine & Heather Phares*

● **Pod** / 1990 / 4AD/Elektra ✦✦✦✦✦
On their 1990 debut album *Pod*, the Breeders—led by the Pixies' Kim Deal and Throwing Muses' Tanya Donelly—prove that they have more potential, and more fun, than the average side project. In fact, thanks to the album's creative songwriting, immediate production (courtesy of *Surfer Rosa* producer Steve Albini), and clever arrangements, *Pod* is a fresher and more successful work than the Pixies' *Bossanova* and the Muses' *Hunkpapa*, their main projects' releases from around that time. Though the album doesn't feature as many of Donelly's contributions as was originally planned—which was part of the reason she formed Belly a few years later—songs like "Iris" and "Lime House" blend the best of the Pixies' elliptical punk and the Muses' angular pop. *Pod* reaffirms what a distinctive songwriter Deal is, and how much the Pixies missed out on by not including more of her material on their albums. With their unusual subjects—"Hellbound" is about a living abortion—and quirky-but-direct sound, songs like "Opened" and "When I Was a Painter" could have easily fit on *Doolittle* or *Bossanova*. But the spare, sensual "Doe," "Fortunately Gone," and "Only in Threes" are more lighthearted and good-natured than the work of Deal's other band, pointing the way to the sexy, clever alternative pop she'd craft on *Last Splash*. A vibrantly creative debut, *Pod* remains the Breeders' most genuine moment. *—Heather Phares*

Safari / 1992 / 4AD/Elektra ✦✦✦
There are only four songs, but the Breeders continue to improve, growing more muscular and melodic. All of the songs here, especially "Do You Love Me Now" and a cover of the Who's "So Sad About Us," rival the best on *Pod*. *—Stephen Thomas Erlewine*

Last Splash / Aug. 31, 1993 / 4AD/Elektra ✦✦✦✦
Thanks to good timing and some great singles, the Breeders' second album, *Last Splash*, turned them into the alternative rock stars that Kim Deal's former band, the Pixies, always seemed on the verge of becoming. Building on *Safari's* driving, polished sound, *Last Splash* is half-brilliant singles and half-unfinished, uninspired ideas. When it's good, it's very, very good: "Cannonball"'s instantly catchy collage of bouncy bass, rhythmic stops and starts, and singsong vocals; the sweetly sexy "Divine Hammer"; and swaggering "Saints" are among the Breeders' finest moments, and deserved all of the airplay they received. And the charming country-pop of "Drivin' on 9," "I Just Wanna Get Along"'s spiky punk-pop, and the bittersweet "Invisible Man" proved *Last Splash* had a bit of depth. But underdeveloped snippets such as "Roi" and "No Aloha" drag down the album's momentum; likewise, the band tries to stretch their range on the rambling, cryptic "Mad Lucas" and "Hag," but neither quite comes together as a full-fledged song. Though instrumentals such as "S.O.S." and "Flipside" showcase the Breeders' chops and some nifty production tricks, they feel like filler; worst of all, *Last Splash* features an inferior, plodding new version of *Safari's* soaring "Do You Love Me Now" that emphasizes the album's unevenness. One of the definitive alternative rock albums of the '90s, *Last Splash* is equally inspired and infuriating; that it was the Breeders' last album of that decade makes it even more frustrating. *—Heather Phares*

Brewer & Shipley

f. 1967, Los Angeles, CA, **db.** 1978
Jesus Rock, Folk-Rock, Folk-Pop
California duo Mike Brewer and Tom Shipley began their careers separately on the 1960s Los Angeles folk club circuit before teaming up to write and perform together. Their song "Keeper of the Seven Keys" was recorded by H.P. Lovecraft and also appeared on their 1968 debut, *Down in L.A.* Their second album, *Weeds*, featured guest appearances by Jerry Garcia, Mike Bloomfield, and Nicky Hopkins. In 1971, the duo scored a surprise Top Ten hit with "One Toke Over the Line," in spite of radio bans owing to the song's marijuana-oriented lyrics. Following this success, Brewer and Shipley moved to rural Missouri, but their appeal dwindled, and the partnership was dissolved in 1979. Brewer recorded the solo album *Beauty Lies* in 1983. At the request of a Kansas City radio station, Brewer & Shipley reunited for a concert in 1989 and began touring occasionally. In

1995, the duo released their first album in almost 20 years, *Shanghai. Heartland* followed two years later. *—Steve Huey*

- **One Toke Over the Line: The Best of Brewer & Shipley** / Aug. 7, 2001 / Buddha ✦✦✦✦
Brewer & Shipley were more than a one-hit wonder, turning out some enjoyable folk-pop reminiscent of their big smash, "One Toke Over the Line." All the same, they probably don't need an exhaustive retrospective, and Buddha's *One Toke Over the Line: The Best of Brewer & Shipley* does an admirable job of distilling the B&S catalog to its finest moments and keeping it interesting for those who love the title hit and want to dig deeper. There will certainly be devotees who want to dig even deeper but, for many listeners, this will satiate their needs. *—Stephen Thomas Erlewine*

The Brian Jonestown Massacre

f. 1990, San Francisco, CA

Garage Rock Revival, Neo-Psychedelia, Indie Rock, Rock & Roll

Named in tribute to the legendary Rolling Stones guitarist and his influence in introducing Eastern culture and music into the world of Western rock & roll, the Brian Jonestown Massacre formed in San Francisco, California in 1990. Some 40 different members passed through the group's ranks over the next half of the decade, but throughout their focal point remained singer/guitarist Anton Newcombe, who along with bassist Matt Hollywood, guitarist Dean Taylor, organist Mara Regal, accordionist Dawn Thomas, drummer Brian Glaze and Spokesman for the Revolution Joel Gion recorded the Massacre's 1995 shoegazer-influenced debut LP *Methodrone*. A collection of early recordings, *Spacegirl and Other Favorites*, followed on the band's own Tangible label in early 1996, and was the first of four Brian Jonestown Massacre LPs to appear that year; next up was the brilliant *Their Satanic Majesties' Second Request*, a full-blown homage to the Stones' glorious psychedelic-era excesses. Recorded live in the studio, the grittier *Take It From the Man!* found the band exploring even broader territory; finally, the year ended with the release of *Thank God for Mental Illness*, a showcase for strong country and blues leanings. In 1997, the BJM—now consisting of Newcombe, Hollywood, Gion, Taylor, guitarists Jeff Davies and Peter Hayes, and drummer Brad Artley—resurfaced with *Give It Back!* Upon signing to TVT, they released *Strung Out in Heaven* the following year; an EP, *Bringing It All Back Home Again*, appeared on the Which label in 1999. *—Jason Ankeny*

Methodrone / 1995 / Bomp ✦✦✦
While Brian Jonestown Massacre have since become known for their wasted Stones take on music (in any number of permutations), when the debut album *Methodrone* finally surfaced after months of delay (to the point where a side project album by ImaJinary Friends actually came out first), there was an easy, one-word reaction: shoegazers. Redolent with the spirit of such high priests of effects and delay as Loop, Spaceman 3, and My Bloody Valentine, not to mention a fair dollop of the Jesus and Mary Chain (sample song titles: "That Girl Suicide," "Hyperventilation," "She's Gone"), *Methodrone* clearly is the sum of its influences. Thankfully BJM does a very solid job with them throughout the album's course of over 70 minutes. Anton Newcombe favors breathy, sighing vocals over post-Jagger drawls, understandably ("Crushed" is as perfect an example of American Anglo singing as it gets), while the seven other rotating bandmembers whip up a good amount of machine-like chugging and rave-up bliss as they go. Part of the reason why it all works so well is Newcombe's impressive abilities to actually perform rather than pose. "Wisdom," for instance, isn't very complex, but it successfully creates a psychedelic haze. While assembled from a variety of different sessions and about seven different engineers, *Methodrone* feels like a unified collection. Newcombe is due further credit for ensuring that his own particular (if second-hand) vision is carried throughout. The album closes on a spectacular high, with the wafting feedback prettiness of "Outback" followed by the majestic drone of "She's Gone," armed with a stunning guitar line, then wrapping up with an untitled bonus track that assuredly builds to a strong end with quirky touches. Though the band never returned to this sound in full, Newcombe and BJM as a whole have nothing to be ashamed of here. *—Ned Raggett*

Spacegirl and Other Favorites / 1996 / Tangible ✦✦✦

Their Satanic Majesties' Second Request / Jun. 18, 1996 / Tangible ✦✦✦✦✦
Truth in advertising: the Brian Jonestown Massacre's sophomore album does, as promised, spring forth from the Rolling Stones' long-underrated 1967 masterpiece *Their Satanic Majesties Request*, copping not only Mick and Keith's leering bad-boy attitude but also their their rock-and-roll-circus spirit. Opening with the brilliant "All Around You (Intro)," a tongue-in-cheek guide to the mind-altering journey ahead, the record is a kaleidoscopic, drug-fueled freakout—like the Stones' namesake album, *Second Request* is painted by Eastern drones and psychedelic tangents, each track bubbling with dozens of sound effects including sitars, mellotrons, farfisas, didgeridoos, tablas, congas, and glockenspiels. Travelling through the past, darkly, the Massacre arrives on the other side unscathed; their music is too rich to be merely retro, and too knowing to be merely slavish—the Stones themselves haven't made a record this strong or entertaining in years. *—Jason Ankeny*

- **Take It from the Man!** / 1996 / Bomp ✦✦✦✦✦
The Brian Jonestown Massacre's obsession with the Rolling Stones continues unabated on the brilliant *Take It from the Man!*; where the group resurrected psychedelic-era excesses on the previous *Their Satanic Majesties' Second Request*, here they jump further back in time to the Stones' mid-'60s period, with even more superlative results. From the opening "Vacuum Boots" onward, *Take It from the Man!* is gritty, swaggering R&B-influenced rock, delivered with remarkable assurance and attitude; singer Anton Newcombe is half madman and half shaman, and he commands each delirious moment with absolute mastery, emerging not so much a disciple of Mick Jagger but as a serious threat to the throne. Tracks like "Who?," "(David Bowie I Love You) Since I Was Six" and the epic finale "Straight Up and Down" are simply amazing, evoking rock's golden age without ever disintegrating into slavish devotion—clearly, the BJM is a group which believes in killing their idols, and their intensity begs the question: just who is the World's Greatest Rock & Roll Band again? *—Jason Ankeny*

Thank God for Mental Illness / Oct. 25, 1996 / Bomp ✦✦✦✦
At the risk of further belaboring a rather obvious point, with *Thank God for Mental Illness*, their third collection of absolutely stunning music in less than a year, the Brian Jonestown Massacre parallels the prolific and effortless brilliance of the Rolling Stones at their fevered late-1960s peak; the sheer scope of their achievements is stunning—rarely are bands quite so productive, or quite so consistently amazing. *Thank God* is the BJM's down-and-dirty country-blues outing, all 13-odd tracks supposedly recorded on a single July day at a cost of just $17.36; while it lacks the blistering immediacy of their previous material, the album swaggers and struts with all of the group's usual attitude intact, coming complete with a loose, offhanded feel perfectly accenting the overall atmosphere of debauchery—"Too Crazy to Care," "Sound of Confusion" and "Talk Minus Action Equals Shit" aren't just song titles, they're words the band lives by. *—Jason Ankeny*

Give It Back / Aug. 26, 1997 / Bomp ✦✦✦✦
With a name like this, it's pretty clear these guys have '60s on the brain, but as revivalist-type bands go, they're definitely above average. They could use more editing, though; this is their sixth album in about two years, and while no one complains about short value with a running time of 55 minutes, about half of this is run-of-the-mill pseudo-'60s garage/psych with too many indulgent guitar breaks. They get a lot more interesting when they slow things down to a wasted quasi-junkie folk-rock mode, similar in spirit to Nikki Sudden or early-'70s Stones. The spooky "The Devil," which sounds like a Satanic cousin to a Stones track like "Heart of Stone," is a standout in this regard; "Malela" (a close facsimile of the Chocolate Watch Band) and "Salaam" show them to be one of the few '90s bands capable of intelligent use of sitars in a rock context; and "(You Better Love Me) Before I Am Gone," for a change of pace, is a goofy (and not very good) homage to Lee Hazlewood and Nancy Sinatra's duet style. Inspired song title: "Their Satanic Majesties' Second Request." *—Richie Unterberger*

Strung Out in Heaven / Jun. 23, 1998 / TVT ✦✦✦✦
It's with typical perversity that the Brian Jonestown Massacre makes the leap from the indie ghetto into the majors with their least immediate, most restrained record to date; given time to sink in, however, *Strung Out in Heaven* proves as engaging as their past efforts, with a focus and cohesiveness often lacking from their more visceral work. Settling into a blissfully psychedelic drift, the album opts not for the Stones-inspired raunch of before but for Byrds-like guitars, muffled drums and pulsating Hammond organ lines, all topped off by Anton Newcombe's half-stoned, half-shamanic vocals; thanks to standout tracks like "Going to Hell," "Wasting Away" and "Maybe Tomorrow," the cumulative impact makes for the BJM's most mature outing yet, evoking a kind of narcotic euphoria perfectly in keeping with the album's title. *—Jason Ankeny*

Brick

f. 1972, Atlanta, GA, **db.** 1981

Disco, Funk

Brick was an Atlanta band that created a successful merger of funk and jazz in the '70s they called "dazz." Brick's roster included lead vocalist/saxophonist/flutist Jimmy Brown, guitarist/bassist/vocalist Regi Hargis Hickman, lead singer Ray Ransom, who doubled as a bassist/keyboardist/percussionist, and Eddie Irons, who did lead vocals and played drums and keyboards. They recorded "Music Matic" for Main Street in 1976, before signing to the CBS-distributed label Bang. Their first Bang single, "Dazz," topped the R&B charts and was number three pop in 1976, and they continued on Bang until 1982. Brick scored two more huge hits in 1977, "Dusic" and "Ain't Gonna' Hurt Nobody," each with a chunky, propulsive beat and catchy, light pop-jazz refrain. Their last Top Ten R&B hit was "Sweat (Til You Get Wet)" in 1981. *—Ron Wynn*

- **The Best of Brick** / Jun. 13, 1995 / Epic/Bang ✦✦✦✦✦
The Best of Brick is a fine compilation featuring all of the funk band's biggest hits, including the Top Ten R&B hits "Dazz," "Dusic," "Ain't Gonna' Hurt Nobody" and "Sweat (Til You Get Wet)." *—Stephen Thomas Erlewine*

Edie Brickell

b. Mar. 10, 1966, Oak Cliff, TX

Vocals / College Rock, Adult Alternative Pop/Rock, Jangle Pop, Alternative Pop/Rock

Edie Brickell was born in 1966 in the Oak Cliff section of Dallas. She attended Southern Methodist University for a year and a half before drinking up enough courage in a bar one night in 1985 to get up on stage with a local band, the New Bohemians. She joined the band and wrote songs over the next year as the band changed and evolved. They finally settled on the personnel of Brad Houser (bass), Kenny Withrow (guitar), and Matt Chamberlain (drums), before taking off for Rockfield Studios in Wales to record their debut album.

That album, *Shooting Rubberbands at the Stars*, revealed Brickell to be a songwriter with a unique perspective and a singer with an intimate, conversational style. The album was hailed by critics and became a massive hit, selling over a million copies and producing the Top Ten hit "What I Am."

After the disappointing performance of their follow-up album, *Ghost of a Dog*, the New Bohemians disbanded. Brickell married Paul Simon and the couple had a child. After several years of remaining artistically quiet, Brickell released her first solo album in late summer 1994. *—William Ruhlmann*

- **Shooting Rubberbands at the Stars** / 1989 / Geffen ✦✦✦✦✦
As debut albums by young bands go, *Shooting Rubberbands at the Stars* is nearly

flawless. With a slight southern twinge in her voice, the 23-year-old Brickell churned out brilliant lyrics and captivating vocal performances, backed by the solid and innovative players that comprised the original *New Bos*—Kenny Withrow, Brad Houser, John Bush, and Brandon Aly. Twisting words like putty, Brickell wraps herself up in phrases and melodic lines with layers of meaning not easily grasped at first listen. Her simple observations offer deep contemplations for the willing disciples of her musical philosophies. The catchy breakthrough hit "What I Am" is the perfect example: "I'm not aware of too many things/I know what I know, if you know what I mean." Zen and the art of songwriting. On other fronts, Brickell's fascination with actress Edie Sedgwick turned itself into "Little Miss S.," while strained friendships inspired "Circle." Every song on this record hits its mark and is worthy of special attention. How well does "Nothing" capture the frustration of a non-communicative partner? Very well, indeed. Then there's "The Wheel," "She," and "Air of December." Highlights, one and all. Rather than an overblown big rock finish, *Shooting Rubberbands at the Stars* closes with a solo acoustic performance of "I Do," a quiet plea for a partner who's equal and true, complete and steady; yet another testimony to the simplicity and thoughtfulness that this album and this band offer. "What I Am" did more than kick off a record, it jump started a career amidst the clamor of the late '80s folk-rock scene. Along with 10,000 Maniacs, Tracy Chapman, and others, Edie Brickell & New Bohemians took their place in the spotlight, basking in every second of their 15 minutes of fame. *—Kelly McCartney*

Ghost of a Dog / 1990 / Geffen ♦♦♦♦
Folk-rockers Edie Brickell & New Bohemians returned in 1990 with *Ghost of a Dog*, the follow-up to their extremely successful debut, *Shooting Rubberbands at the Stars*. Once again, the musicianship and instrumentation are supremely appropriate, right down to the guest accordion licks that set the playful mood for "Carmelito." Top that with thoughtful, thought-provoking lyrics and memorable melodies and you have a great second record on the New Bos resume. Brickell has a way with phrases unlike most other songwriters. She finds the similarity in differences and uses it to her advantage, spinning webs with words entangled in unique rhymes and patterns. The opening lines are a perfect example: "If a child lives with money, he learns to spend his time/If a child lives with crazy, he goes out of his mind." This record is full of such cleverness. And as bouncy and whimsical as some of the songs are, such as "Woyaho," "Oak Cliff Bra," and "Carmelito," things get downright poignant, if not serious, on "He Said," "10,000 Angels," and "This Eye." However exquisite Brickell is as a songwriter and vocalist, enough can't be said of the guys who support her musically. Kenny Withrow, Wes Burt-Martin, Brad Houser, John Bush, and Matt Chamberlain are wonderfully creative musicians, and the cohesiveness of their sound is exciting to hear. These guys know what it means to play together, each giving his all without stepping on anyone's toes. *Ghost of a Dog* is definitely a record to own if you love the music that came out of the early '90s folk-rock scene. Along with the efforts of bands like 10,000 Maniacs, it stands the test of time and can be enjoyed over the years. But, sadly, it marks the second and last release from this band. *—Kelly McCartney*

Picture Perfect Morning / Aug. 16, 1994 / Geffen ♦♦

Brinsley Schwarz

f. Oct. 1969, England, **db.** 1975
Pub Rock, Country-Rock, Rock & Roll
Pub rock, the English roots-rock movement of the early '70s, would never have earned a cult following if it wasn't for Brinsley Schwarz. Initially, Brinsley Schwarz was a rambling, neo-psychedelic folk-rock band, who borrowed heavily from Crosby, Stills & Nash and the Grateful Dead. Following a disastrous publicity stunt to promote their debut album, the band went into seclusion outside of London and developed a laid-back, rootsy sound inspired by Eggs Over Easy, an American band who had been playing a mixture of originals and covers in English pubs. Following their conversion to pub rock, the Brinsleys ditched their pretensions of stardom and became a down-to-earth, self-effacing rock & roll band. Between 1971 and 1974, Brinsley Schwarz toured England innumerable times, playing pubs across the country. Along the way, they established a circuit for similar bands like Dr. Feelgood and Ducks Deluxe to follow. Though the group was nominally guitarist Brinsley Schwarz's band, bassist/lead vocalist Nick Lowe provided the bulk of the group's songs. Lowe developed a distinctive songwriting voice—conversational, melodic, off-beat, and funny—and the band was infused with his skewed sense of humor. Despite strong reviews and a dedicated fan base, the Brinsleys never managed to escape cult status, yet they influenced a legion of other artists, creating an underground, back-to-basics movement that laid the foundation for punk rock. *—Stephen Thomas Erlewine*

Brinsley Schwarz / 1970 / One Way ♦♦♦
Brinsley Schwarz's eponymous debut is the stuff of rock legend because it is the punch line to a great story. It arrived after a disastrous publicity blitz, where the band's management arranged for prominent British journalists to cross the ocean to hear the Brinsleys' showcase performance at the Fillmore East. In a series of mishaps that would shame Spinal Tap, the band arrived in New York hours before their show and the journalists, who dipped heavily into the courtesy bar when their plane nearly crashed, arrived minutes before the concert. The press was underwhelmed to say the least and savaged the band and the record. Listening to *Brinsley Schwarz*, it's easy to see why they weren't turned on by the Brinsleys: this is a bizarre, naïve blend of Crosby, Stills & Nash, Dylan & the Band, and Buffalo Springfield, with a heavy dose of early Yes. It's filled with awkward steps and bad judgments, fueled by the group's romanticized view of Californian hippies. Consequently, it's hard not to cringe or chuckle by their hippie affectations, whether it's the lyrics ("she was my lady/had no plans to make her my wife") or the a cappella folk-rock harmonies that come out of nowhere on "Lady Constant" (it doesn't help that they sing "colored serpent coiled around your waist") or the bongo solo that ends "Shining Brightly." But, amidst all this hippie posturing, there are some weird touches, like the multi-octave chromatic guitar break on "Hymn to Me" or the heavy prog jam of "What Do You Suggest?" and "Ballad of a Has-Been Beauty Queen" that illustrate how English the Brinsleys still were at this stage. All of this adds up to a debut that's decidedly uneven and unsure, but in retrospect, it's easy for sympathetic listeners to be charmed by their eccentricities. *—Stephen Thomas Erlewine*

Despite It All / 1970 / Liberty ♦♦♦
Brinsley Schwarz was hit hard by the terrible performance of their debut, so they rented a communal house and concentrated on becoming a real, organic band. They also recorded a second album swiftly, releasing *Despite It All* by the end of 1970. As soon as the folksy, fiddle-driven "Country Girl" amiably ambles out of the gates, the difference between the two records is apparent. They tried this kind of rootsy country-rock before, but it sounded awkward. Here, it rings true, not just because the songwriting is stronger, but because the band knows what they're doing, adding real grit and passion to the performances. *Despite It All* benefits from this looser playing, and for a while, it sounds like the group accomplished everything it wanted to do, since the first three songs are all early Nick Lowe masterpieces—"Country Girl," the fine ballad "The Slow One" and the flat-out terrific "Funk Angel," which is the first real flowering of his gifts as a pop tunesmith and sly humorist. After this, the record doesn't go off the rails, but it slowly loses its momentum, deteriorating to pleasant aping of CSN and Band plus the prog-inflected jams that were the bane of their debut. Some of this works—"Love Song" is a sweet tune, "Ebury Down" has a campfire charm—but when it ends with the drawn-out "Old Jarrow" (which does boast the timeless question "why don't you financially back her?" in its refrain) it's clear that the group is still in the process of finding of its voice. Their stumbles are brought into perspective by those three wonderful songs that begin the album, which not only make the record, but prove that the group does indeed have greatness in them. *—Stephen Thomas Erlewine*

Silver Pistol / 1972 / Edsel ♦♦♦♦♦
Silver Pistol isn't the definitive pub rock album, but it is the first great record to surface from the scene. Like much of the first wave of pub rock, *Silver Pistol* is quiet, laid-back and low-key—with its warm, rustic sound and a gentleness that infuses even the rockers, this is the closest to the Band that the Brinsleys got. There are some major differences, most of them coming from Nick Lowe. That's not to denigrate new guitarist/songwriter Ian Gomm, since his four numbers (particularly "Dry Land" and "Range War") reveal a fine songwriter with a keen sense of melody and a knack for synthesizing country, rock, and folk into something distinctive, but Lowe really hits his stride with this record. This is in to some degree due to the influence of Jim Ford, a renegade American roots-rocker who Brinsley Schwarz backed on an unreleased and subsequently lost 1971 album. The group covers two of his songs, "Niki Hoeke Speedway" and "Ju Ju Man," on *Silver Pistol*, and these numbers reveal the appealingly off-kilter sense of humor and pop hooks that would form the foundation of Lowe's style. Those sensibilities are just beginning to creep into his songwriting on *Silver Pistol*, on the Beatles-meets-Band "Unknown Number," the lovely "Nightingale," the wonderful pop tune "The Last Time I Was Fooled," and the epic "Silver Pistol." His other two songs are sturdy country-rock numbers a notch below Gomm's best on the record, but still very good, and it all adds up to an endearing low-key roots rock album that doesn't just find Brinsley Schwarz coming into their own, it stands as one of the most appealing records of its kind. *—Stephen Thomas Erlewine*

☆ **Nervous on the Road** / 1972 / United Artists ♦♦♦♦♦
Silver Pistol wrote the blueprint for Brinsley Schwarz's pub rock, but *Nervous on the Road* perfected their sound, becoming the definitive pub rock band in the process. *Nervous on the Road* has a fuller, more detailed production than its predecessor, as well as a looser feeling—even with the smooth production, it sounds like the band was captured on a good night at the Tally Ho. But what really makes the record is its excellent selection of songs, almost all of which are written by Nick Lowe. "Happy Doing What We're Doing," "Surrender to the Rhythm," and "Nervous on the Road" are all great rock & roll songs about rock & roll, spiked with an off-kilter sense of humor. "Don't Lose Your Grip on Love" is Lowe's first great ballad, while Ian Gomm's "It's Been So Long" is one of his best songs. And the covers of "I Like It Like That" and "Home In My Hand" are wonderful pub-rockers, and help give the album the feeling of an excellent concert. Nevertheless, what makes *Nervous on the Road* such a fine record is the combination of empathatic performances, unpredictable songwriting and a charming unpretentiousness, all of which help make the album one of the great forgotten rock & roll records. *—Stephen Thomas Erlewine*

Please Don't Ever Change / 1973 / Edsel ♦♦♦♦
Released in 1973 as Brinsley Schwarz were busy touring and recording the followup to *Nervous on the Road*, *Please Don't Ever Change* is a collection of singles, live cuts and radio sessions from the early '70s. The odds-and-sods nature of the record actually works in its favor, since it accentuates the group's ramshackle nature. Sure, there's a fair amount of filler on the record—their ill-advised reggae excursion "The Version (Hypocrite)" is simply mystifying—but unevenness was part of the Brinsley's charm, and the simply enjoyable cuts make the best tracks feel like classics. And some of them are definitive Brinsley cuts. "I Worry ('bout You Baby)" is a revamped R&B number, the live "Home in My Hand" speeds along with a relentless energy, the cover of Goffin/King's "Don't Ever Change" indicates Nick Lowe's latent pop roots, "Down in Mexico" is a hysterical travelogue and "Play That Fast Thing (One More Time)" is among the classic pub rock singles, distilling the essence of pub rock into one piledriving song. *—Stephen Thomas Erlewine*

New Favourites of Brinsley Schwarz / 1974 / United Artists ♦♦♦♦♦
With their final album, Brinsley Schwarz turn in their most pop-oriented record, filled

with infectious gems like "The Ugly Things," "Trying to Live My Life Without You," and "(What's So Funny 'bout) Peace, Love and Understanding." Lowe's songs were the best he had ever written and show that his ambitions were beginning to conflict with those of the rest of the band. Nevertheless, there isn't a weak song or uninspired performance on *New Favourites*, making it an excellent farewell album. —*Stephen Thomas Erlewine*

Original Golden Greats / 1974 / United Artists ✦✦✦
Released after *Silver Pistol*, and featuring the non-LP singles "(It's Gonna Be A) Bring Down" and "Run Rudolph Run," the 12-track compilation *Original Golden Greats* does a good job of summarizing Brinsley Schwarz's career to date. As such, it's a little laid-back and a little indebted to Californian country-rock, but it does show Nick Lowe's songwriting skills shining brightly, particularly on "Country Girl," "Funk Angel," "Happy Doing What We're Doing," and "Don't Lose Your Grip on Love." Since it covers only the early years, it isn't an extensive compilation, but it's not a bad sampler at all. —*Stephen Thomas Erlewine*

★ **Nervous on the Road/The New Favourites of Brinsley Schwarz** / 1975 / BGO ✦✦✦✦
Two of Brinsley Schwarz's finest albums, *Nervous on the Road* and *The New Favorites of Brinsley Schwarz*, have been combined on one compact disc. *Nervous on the Road* is the definitive pub rock album, featuring such defining songs as "Happy Doing What We're Doing," "Play That Fast Thing One More Time," and "Home in My Hand." *The New Favorites* is a more polished, commercial collection that points toward Nick Lowe's solo career, but it also has such classic cuts as "(What's So Funny 'bout) Peace, Love and Understanding," "The Ugly Things," and "Down in the Dive." —*Stephen Thomas Erlewine*

15 Thoughts of Brinsley Schwarz / 1978 / United Artists ✦✦✦✦
Released at the end of the band's career, *15 Thoughts of Brinsley Schwarz* has a few questionable oversights and inclusions, and it does take a couple of detours, but it contains the bulk of the group's best-known songs. Yes, some highlights are missing, and it does overlap with *Original Golden Greats*, but it's a stronger overall collection than its predecessor, capturing the Brinsleys at their best. [It was made even stronger in 2000, when BGO combined *15 Thoughts* and *Golden Greats* as a two-fer.] —*Stephen Thomas Erlewine*

☆ **Surrender to the Rhythm** / 1991 / EMI ✦✦✦✦✦
The 20-track compilation *Surrender to the Rhythm* is an excellent retrospective of Brinsley Schwarz's career. The compilation is culled from each of the group's albums, touching lightly on their earlier records and drawing heavily from *Silver Pistol*, *Nervous on the Road*, and *The New Favourites*, which is appropriate, since they were the stronger records. Although *Nervous on the Road* remains a necessary album, *Surrender to the Rhythm* compiles nearly every one of the Brinsleys' greatest tracks, including "Country Girl," "Ju Ju Man," "Down in Mexico," "Play That Fast Thing (One More Time)," "Happy Doing What We're Doing," "Don't Lose Your Grip on Love," "The Ugly Things," a ripping live version of "Home in My Hand," and the original version of Nick Lowe's classic "(What's So Funny 'Bout) Peace, Love and Understanding." *Surrender to the Rhythm* offers convincing evidence that Brinsley Schwarz is one of the great underrated bands of the early '70s, while essentially summing up the spirit of pub rock. —*Stephen Thomas Erlewine*

Brinsley Schwarz/Despite It All / 1994 / BGO ✦✦✦
BGO's two-fer of Brinsley Schwarz's first two albums offers more liner notes than the two-fer available on One Way, and its cover artwork is different, offering miniatures of the two album covers instead of a blown-up version of the debut. Musically, it's nearly the same, with the sole exception being that *Despite It All* runs before *Brinsley Schwarz*. So, it's a tradeoff—if you want historical accuracy without documentation, pick One Way; if you want the notes, pick BGO. —*Stephen Thomas Erlewine*

Hen's Teeth / May 5, 1998 / Edsel ✦✦✦
Hen's Teeth is a bit of a godsend for longtime Brinsley Schwarz collectors, gathering all of the group's non-LP singles—including the first singles released when the band was a Swinging London pop combo called Kippington Lodge—plus singles the group released under aliases. As the Hitters, they released the reggae single "Hypocrite," complete with the dub "Version" on the flip. As the Knees and Limelight, they released 45s of Beatles covers. All this is interesting, fun trivia, but the true meat of the collection lies in the Kippington Lodge material and the official non-LP Brinsley tunes. Kippington Lodge may not be earth-shattering and the band is quite derivative, borrowing heavily from psychedelic British pop, in particular the Beatles and early Yes. This isn't bad, but it is silly, whether it's the cascading psychedelia of "Lady on a Bicycle," the exhortation to have a "peace-off" on "Tomorrow Today," or the Vanilla Fudge-styled, bombastic soul cover of "In My Life." All artifacts, of course, but they're pretty engaging artifacts all the same, and the last Kippington song, "I Can See Her Face," is notable as Nick Lowe's first recorded song. The Brinsley material stands the test of time, finding the group at its very poppiest, whether turning out spirited covers of Naomi Neville's "I've Cried My Last Tear" and Tommy Roe's stomping "Everybody," or on originals, divided equally between Lowe, Ian Gomm, and co-compositions between the two. These four songs—"(It's Gonna Be a) Bring Down," "I Like You, I Don't Love You," "There's a Cloud in My Heart," and "I Got the Real Thing"—are shiny, glittering pop, finding the group exercising its mainstream melodic muscle. The songs didn't land the band any hits, but they stand as terrific little gems that offer a nice conclusion to this terrific, necessary compilation. —*Stephen Thomas Erlewine*

Original Golden Greats/15 Thoughts of Brinsley Schwarz / May 17, 2000 / BGO ✦✦✦✦✦
Cleverly, BGO decided to consolidate the two originally-released compilations *Original Golden Greats* and *15 Thoughts of Brinsley Schwarz* onto one disc, eliminating any over-

lap between the two collections. There are still some terrific songs missing, but it does have the otherwise difficult to find "Run Rudolph Run," and since *Surrender to the Rhythm* is out of print, this 20-song collection is the best available summary of the group's career. —*Stephen Thomas Erlewine*

Bronski Beat

f. 1983, London, England, db. 1991
New Wave, Synth Pop, Dance-Pop, Hi-NRG
A synth-pop trio from London, everything that made Bronski Beat interesting, and at times compelling, came primarily from the larynx of Glasgow-born vocalist Jimmy Somerville. Possessing a soaring tenor voice that frequently exploded into falsetto, Somerville was a rare singer, capable of imbuing even the most rote dance songs with near-palpable heartache and layers of emotional turmoil. Openly gay, Somerville and the Bronskis, despite the rock world's implicit homophobia, became cover darlings of the British music press in 1984 after the U.K. success of their first two singles, "Why" and "Smalltown Boy." From that point on, Bronski Beat seemed poised to rule the pop world (at least in England), releasing a superb cover of the Donna Summer disco hit "I Feel Love" and a remarkable debut album, 1984's *The Age of Consent*. It was only a year later that Somerville announced he was leaving Bronski Beat to form the more explicitly left-wing Communards. There were more Bronski Beat recordings, but even fanatics would agree that the band lost everything when it lost Somerville. —*John Dougan*

● **The Age of Consent** / 1984 / London ✦✦✦✦
To say this is a great album of dance-oriented synth-pop music is to sell it extremely short; this is simply a great album, period. Somerville's soaring tenor may take some getting used to, but the songs, many of them dealing with homophobia and alienation (none more eloquently than "Smalltown Boy") are compelling vignettes about the vagaries of life as a gay man. Cynics predisposed to dismissing entire genres of music based on trendiness or a limited appeal ("dance music is for dancing, not listening") miss the point in lumping this in with more mindless forays into techno or neo-disco. As the Pet Shop Boys (the world's greatest disco band) proved a few years later, you can have substantive content and wrap it up in a compelling, visceral, dance-oriented package. Few bands understood this better, or earlier, than Bronski Beat. —*John Dougan*

Hundreds & Thousands / 1985 / London ✦✦✦

Truthdare Doubledare / 1986 / London ✦✦✦

The Brothers Johnson

f. 1975, Los Angeles, CA
Pop/Rock, Funk, Soul
Led by guitarist/vocalist George Johnson and bassist/vocalist Louis Johnson, in 1973 the Brothers Johnson were hired by Quincy Jones to play on his LP *Mellow Madness*; Jones also recorded four of their songs, including "Is It Love That We're Missing?" and "Just a Taste of Me." Jones also took them on a Japanese tour, then produced their debut LP, *Look Out for Number 1*, after they signed with A&M, which was also his label at the time (1976). They scored a number-one R&B and number-three pop hit with "I'll Be Good to You," and enjoyed R&B chart toppers in 1977 and 1980 respectively with "Strawberry Letter 23" and "Stomp!," while sustaining a consistent hit presence via such songs as "Get the Funk Out Ma Face" and "Runnin' for Your Lovin." The Brothers earned platinum records for *Look Out for Number 1* and *Right on Time*. The group produced its single "The Real Thing" in 1981. It reached number 11 on the R&B charts, and the Brothers had another hit with "Welcome to the Club" in 1982. —*Ron Wynn*

● **Greatest Hits** / Jun. 18, 1996 / A&M ✦✦✦✦
Greatest Hits contains all of the Brothers Johnson's biggest singles, including the gold singles "I'll Be Good to You" and "Strawberry Letter 23." In addition to all the familiar hits, there are some lesser-known singles that are nearly as good, making this single-disc compilation the definitive retrospective. —*Stephen Thomas Erlewine*

20th Century Masters—The Millennium Collection: The Best of the Brothers Johnson / Sep. 26, 2000 / A&M ✦✦✦✦
The Millennium Collection: The Best of the Brothers Johnson features 13 of the duo's '70s and '80s hits, including "Get the Funk out Ma Face," "Strawberry Letter 23," "Ain't We Funkin' Now," and "I'll Be Good to You." "Is It Love That We're Missin'" from Quincy Jones' *Mellow Madness*, "Light Up the Night," and "Runnin' for Your Lovin'" are some of the other singles and tracks included on this decent, if not extensive, retrospective. —*Heather Phares*

Edgar Broughton

b. Oct. 24, 1947
Vocals, Keyboards, Guitar / Hard Rock, Blues-Rock
Formed in Warwick, England, the Edgar Broughton Band arrived on the London underground music scene in 1968. Led by the Broughton brothers, vocalist/guitarist Edgar and drummer Steve, and fleshed out by bassist Arthur Grant and guitarist Victor Unitt (who also briefly served with the Pretty Things), they soon signed with the Harvest label, and issued their debut *Wasa Wasa*—a collection of underground electric blues jams anchored by Edgar's Captain Beefheart-like vocals—in late 1969.
The Edgar Broughton Band returned in 1970 with *Sing Brother Sing*, which reached the U.K. Top 20 and spawned a pair of minor hit singles, "Out Demons Out" and "Apache Drop-Out" (a fusion of Beefheart's "Dropout Boogie" and the Shadows' "Apache"). The group seemed poised for a major commercial breakthrough, but as their brand of heavy rock was flourishing thanks to groups like Black Sabbath and Deep Purple, the Broughton Band made an about-face, and their music became considerably more quiet

and politically-charged. Their chart momentum stalled, and a 1971 self-titled effort failed to catch on.

After both 1972's *Inside Out* and 1973's *Oora* met a similar fate, the group left Harvest for NEMS. Legal wrangles locked them out of the studio for a number of months, but they finally resurfaced in 1975—minus Unitt, who'd been replaced by guitarist John Thomas—with *Bandages*. A brief break-up followed, but in 1978 they returned with *Live Hits Harder*. By the release of 1979's *Parlez Vous English?*, the group had expanded to a six-piece, and was now going under the name the Broughtons. The record was their last, but they continued on, eventually returning to the Edgar Broughton Band moniker and touring throughout the 1980s and 1990s. —*Jason Ankeny*

Wasa Wasa / 1969 / BGO ✦✦✦✦

● **Sing Brother Sing** / 1970 / Harvest ✦✦✦✦✦

Edgar Broughton Band / 1971 / Repertoire ✦✦✦✦

Inside Out / 1972 / Harvest ✦✦✦

Oora / 1973 / Bang On ✦✦✦

Arthur Brown

b. Jun. 24, 1944, Whitby, Yorkshire, England
Vocals / British Psychedelia, Psychedelic
One of the most electrifying one-shot artists of the '60s, British singer Arthur Brown briefly set the charts alight in 1968, as well as thrilling audiences with his theatrical performances, which saw him wearing helmets of fire and outlandish costumes. His debut album was surely one of the most left-field commercial successes of the late '60s, if not of rock history. In addition to topping the British charts (and reaching number two in the U.S.) with his brilliantly demonic single "Fire," the self-proclaimed god of hellfire actually scored a Top Ten LP with his 1968 debut. Unveiling Brown's demented, fire-obsessed lyrical visions and swooping, theatrical vocals, it showcased his band's manic, agitated psychedelic sound, which was anchored by incendiary drumming, Pete Townshend's production, and an organist who could be best described as Jimmy Smith on acid. Brown's original band broke up in early 1969; in the early '70s he released several albums with Kingdom Come, which saw him pursuing a maddeningly obscure and less exciting brand of art rock. He recorded off and on after, with an additional flash of fame springing from his role as a priest in the film *Tommy*. —*Richie Unterberger*

● **The Crazy World of Arthur Brown** / 1968 / Polydor ✦✦✦✦✦
Though a bit over-the-top, this album was still powerful and surprisingly melodic, and managed to be quite bluesy and soulful even as the band overhauled chestnuts by James Brown and Screamin' Jay Hawkins. "Spontaneous Apple Creation" is a willfully histrionic, atonal song that gives Captain Beefheart a run for his money. Though this one-shot was not (and perhaps could not ever) be repeated, it remains an exhilaratingly reckless slice of psychedelia. The CD reissue includes both mono and stereo versions of five of the songs. Although the mono mixes lack the full-bodied power of the stereo ones, they're marked by some interesting differences, especially in the brief spoken and instrumental links between tracks. —*Richie Unterberger*

Strangelands / 1988 / Reckless ✦✦

Bobby Brown

b. Feb. 5, 1969, Boston, MA
Vocals / New Jack Swing, Club/Dance, Urban, Dance-Pop
At the end of the '80s, former New Edition member Bobby Brown made the album that made new jack swing a dominant force not only on the urban charts, but on the pop charts as well. Brown's first album, *King of the Stage*, wasn't that remarkable but 1988's *Don't Be Cruel* is the definitive new jack album, thanks to L.A. Reid's and Babyface's massive production and songs, including the hits "Don't Be Cruel," "Every Little Step," and "Roni." While recording the follow-up album, Brown married pop star Whitney Houston and they had a child; their marriage has been plagued with tabloid-fueled rumors. In 1992, Brown released *Bobby*, a follow-up record that didn't have the commercial success of *Don't Be Cruel*, mainly because it lacked the focused songs and production that made that album such a huge success. —*Stephen Thomas Erlewine*

King of Stage / 1987 / MCA ✦✦✦
Bobby Brown's style was still fairly close to that of his comrades in New Edition when he recorded his first solo effort, *King of Stage*—an album giving little indication of the hard-edged, aggressive "new jack swing" that was only two years away on *Don't Be Cruel*. While comparisons to his subsequent work are inevitable, *Stage* is a generally decent, though not breathtaking, album that stands on its own merit—and one that proves that there was indeed life outside of New Edition for the singer/rapper. Although Cameo leader Larry Blackmon, who serves as producer on "Girl Next Door," "Spending Time" and "Baby I Wanna Tell You Something," brings an undeniably Cameo-ish element to these high-tech funk smokers, Brown's individuality comes through loud and clear. But as enjoyable as the Blackmon-produced tracks are, top honors must go to "Seventeen"— a riveting account of a teenage mother who turns to drugs and prostitution—and the unapologetically sentimental, '70s-like soul ballad "Girlfriend." Brown sounds like he's going through the motions on the Rick James-ish "Your Tender Romance" and the lackluster ballad "Spending Time," but thankfully, *Stage* has more strengths than weaknesses. —*Alex Henderson*

Don't Be Cruel / 1988 / MCA ✦✦✦✦
Don't Be Cruel was to Bobby Brown what *Control* was to Janet Jackson—a tougher, more aggressive project that shed his "bubble gum" image altogether and brought him to a new artistic and commercial plateau. With "My Prerogative" and the title song, Brown became

a leader of "new-jack swing"—a forceful, high-tech blend of traditional soul singing and rap/hip-hop that's also associated with Guy and Brown's New Edition colleagues, Bell Biv DeVoe. Brown had been a strong advocate of rap since his days with New Edition, and on *Cruel*, he did even more rapping than before. But for all the tough-mindedness he exhibited on his "new-jack" hits, the charismatic Bostonian hadn't lost his love of sentimental, old-fashioned R&B romanticism—and he definitely excels in that area on his hits "Every Little Step," "Roni" and "Rock Wit' Cha." Much of *Cruel* was produced by the ubiquitous production/songwriting duo L.A. & Babyface, who've often been accused (and rightly so) of taking a formulaic, cookie-cutter approach to R&B. But here, their work is never less than inspired. —*Alex Henderson*

Dance! . . . Ya Know It! / 1990 / MCA ✦✦

Bobby / 1992 / MCA ✦✦✦
Brown's follow-up to the groundbreaking *Don't Be Cruel* isn't as innovative or consistent as his previous album, but that doesn't mean it's without any charms; the singles "Humpin' Around," "Good Enough," and "Get Away" are strong and memorable, which almost makes the abundance of filler forgivable. —*Stephen Thomas Erlewine*

● **Greatest Hits** / Sep. 26, 2000 / MCA ✦✦✦✦
Although the bulk of Bobby Brown's most important work is featured on *Don't Be Cruel*, he was a fairly consistent singles artist throughout most of his solo career (that is, when he actually recorded). *Greatest Hits* doesn't feature anything from 1997's lackluster *Forever*, but that's entirely forgivable; the 14 tracks that are here include an amazing 11 Top Ten R&B hits, six of which went to number one, and eight of which also reached the pop Top Ten. Brown's hit duets with Glenn Medeiros ("She Ain't Worth It") and wife Whitney Houston ("Something in Common") are also included, although there's nothing from his first or second go-rounds with New Edition. However, there doesn't need to be—the body of work presented on *Greatest Hits*, while not completely uniform in style or production, is arguably the catchiest urban pop-soul of its time. There are a few silky ballads, but Brown's real bread and butter is slamming, up-tempo new jack dance-pop. On those numbers, Brown is the total urban contemporary package, able to stick with the melody, improvise around it, or throw in credible raps that complement the hard-hitting hip-hop-derived beats. He may not be a technical master, but Brown's understanding of how to construct a tight, catchy single makes *Greatest Hits* an essential purchase for even the most casual fans of late-'80s/early-'90s R&B. —*Steve Huey*

James Brown

b. May 3, 1933, Macon, GA
Vocals, Leader, Arranger, Piano, Organ / Blaxploitation, R&B, Funk, Soul
Soul Brother Number One, the Godfather of Soul, the Hardest Working Man in Show Business, Mr. Dynamite—those are mighty titles, but no one can question that James Brown has earned them more than any other performer. Other singers were more popular, others were equally skilled, but no other African-American musician has been so influential on the course of popular music in the past several decades. And no other musician, pop or otherwise, put on a more exciting, exhilarating stage show—Brown's performances are marvels of athletic stamina and split-second timing. Through the gospel-impassioned fury of his vocals and the complex polyrhythms of his beats, Brown was a crucial midwife in not just one, but two revolutions in American Black music. He was one of the figures most responsible for turning R&B into soul; he was, most would agree, *the* figure most responsible for turning soul music into the funk of the late '60s and early '70s. Since the mid-'70s, he's done little more than tread water artistically; his financial and drug problems eventually got him a controversial prison sentence. Yet in a sense his music is now more influential than ever, as his voice and rhythms are sampled on innumerable rap and hip-hop recordings, and critics have belatedly hailed his innovations as among the most important in all of rock or soul. —*Richie Unterberger*

Please, Please, Please / 1959 / Polydor ✦✦✦
Though James Brown and His Famous Flames had scored an R&B Top 10 hit in 1956 with "Please, Please, Please," Brown's next nine singles for Federal Records flopped until "Try Me," his third single of 1958, scored. That was when King Records (Federal's parent label) assembled this, Brown's debut album, out of some of those singles sessions. You can hear the sound of a group and its enthusiastic singer looking for a hit, sometimes in the rock & roll of "Chonnie-On-Chon" (1957) or the 1956 B-side "I Feel That Old Feeling Coming On," sometimes by remaking "Please, Please, Please" under another name, such as "I Don't Know" (1956), sometimes by tackling Coasters-like novelty material such as "That Dood It" (1958), sometimes by aping the smooth Sam Cooke, as on the 1958 B-side "That's When I Lost My Heart," and once by rewriting "My Bonnie (Lies Over The Ocean)" as the 1958 B-side "Baby Cries Over The Ocean." Only the two hits were really memorable, but the album presented the sound of a major star-to-be in search of his sound. —*William Ruhlmann*

Think / 1960 / Polydor ✦✦✦
James' third album (his first for King), gets a straight-up reissue on compact disc, right down to the booklet featuring both original covers on either side—a nice touch. This is 1960 James Brown, moving from King's Federal subsidiary to the parent label with the hits "Bewildered," "If You Want Me," "You've Got the Power," "I'll Go Crazy," "Baby You're Right" (co-written with Joe Tex), and "I'll Never, Never Let You Go." Although Brown's albums would soon be interchangeable, the same cuts reappearing again and again, this is one of his better efforts as well as a pivotal point in his career. —*Cub Koda*

★ **Live at the Apollo [1963]** / Jan. 1963 / Polydor ✦✦✦✦✦
An astonishing record of James and the Flames tearing the roof off the sucker at the mecca of R&B theatres, New York's Apollo. When King Records owner Syd Nathan refused to fund the recording, thinking it commercial folly, Brown single-mindedly pro-

ceeded anyway, paying for it out of his own pocket. He had been out on the road night after night for a while, and he knew that the magic that was part and parcel of a James Brown show was something no record had ever caught. Hit follows hit without a pause—"I'll Go Crazy," "Try Me," "Think," "Please Please Please," "I Don't Mind," "Night Train," and more. The affirmative screams and cries of the audience are something you've never experienced unless you've seen the Brown Revue in a Black theater. If you have, I need not say more; if you haven't, suffice to say that this should be one of the very first records you ever own. *—Rob Bowman*

Live at the Apollo [1968] / Aug. 1968 / Polydor ✦✦✦✦✦
As a whole, this double album is pretty erratic—there are a bunch of torchy R&B ballads that were somewhat anachronistic in light of the explosive funk innovations Brown was unleashing in the studio during this time, and some of those funk hits are reprised here in super-brief versions that seem to cut off before they have a chance to get started. On the other hand, some of it is as essential as anything else Brown ever recorded. In particular, the 20-minute medley of "Let Yourself Go/There Was a Time/I Feel All Right/Cold Sweat" is a magnificent, seamless ball of energy, a landmark performance in the evolution of soul and funk. Other highlights are "Bring It Up" and an 11-minute "It's a Man's, Man's, Man's World." *—Richie Unterberger*

Say It Loud, I'm Black and I'm Proud / Mar. 1969 / Polydor ✦✦✦
Although historical evaluations of Brown's work during the last half of the '60s tend to focus on the innovative funk of his biggest hit singles, his repertoire—both live and on record—in fact remained pretty versatile. Like his other '60s studio albums, *Say It Loud* is more R&B/pop-conscious than a lot of listeners would expect, mixing the funky monsters "Say It Loud I'm Black and I'm Proud" and "Licking Stick" with soul ballads. It's a notch above similar albums from earlier in the decade, however, in that the slow numbers are usually gritty slow burns that eschew syrupy orchestration. Reissued on CD in 1996, it includes a couple of minor hits ("Goodbye My Love" and "I Guess I'll Have to Cry, Cry, Cry") that don't turn up on the *Star Time* box set. Reissued on CD in 1996. *—Richie Unterberger*

Sex Machine / Aug. 1970 / Polydor ✦✦✦✦✦
A double live outing from Brown's seminal 1970 J.B.'s lineup, including Bootsy Collins, Clyde Stubblefield, Fred Wesley, Maceo Parker, Bobby Byrd, and many more. While it's a cut below *Love Power Peace* in documenting this lineup live, Brown and his band still smoke, tearing into extended versions of funk classics like "Sex Machine" (nearly eleven minutes), "Brother Rapp," "Give It Up Or Turnit-a Loose," and "Mother Popcorn," plus a healthy quotient of earlier soul material sprinkled in between. *—Steve Huey*

Hot Pants / Aug. 1971 / Polydor ✦✦✦
Brown left his label King after 12 successful if not always peaceful years. *Hot Pants* is his first effort for Polydor. With signing to a bigger outfit, Brown would no doubt get more of a budget, better presentation, and, most importantly, artistic freedom. The original set of the J.B.'s with Bootsy Collins dissolved, and Brown and his newer band had only been together for a few months. Although the original J.B.'s were more rock-based and fiery, *Hot Pants* proves that the reformed band was more ductile. It was at this point where trombonist Fred Wesley became the bandleader and the band became even more efficient than the earlier group. The leisurely "Blues and Pants" has a great bass pattern from Fred Thomas and Wesley's sly horn charts. "Can't Stand It" is a busier take on the 1968 hit "I Can't Stand Myself." The most recognizable track is the title song. The version here is less potent. The early '90s CD reissue of *Hot Pants* features the complete take of "Escape-ism," which clocks in at 19-plus minutes. While that might be cause for alarm for some, it is truly instructive. The track goes to the bridge, stays there, and has great studio chatter between Brown and his band and solos from Wesley and saxophonist St. Clair Pinckey. This album features only four tracks and is basically Brown getting acquainted with his new band, but the camaraderie makes it worth listening to. *—Jason Elias*

Revolution of the Mind / Dec. 1971 / Polydor ✦✦✦
Subtitled "Recorded Live At The Apollo, Vol. III," *Revolution Of The Mind* presents a 1971 James Brown concert performance, which means the set list is given over largely to the singles Brown had released over the previous couple of years, including "Give It Up Or Turnit A Loose," "Super Bad," and "Make It Funky," all of them groove tunes with chanted slogans for lyrics, plus a medley of slightly less recent hits and the occasional real oldie, such as "Try Me." Brown concentrates on communicating with his audience, generating female screams, for example, when he comes out against dieting "'cause the more you got, the more I want." On the one hand, this can be considered indulgent—Brown spends the nearly 13 minutes of "Make It Funky" introducing the band by asking each member where he's from—on the other hand, the aural evidence suggests it went over better in the theater than it does in your living room. That wasn't true of the first *Live At The Apollo*, though. [Initially released as a double-LP, *Revolution Of The Mind* was reissued on CD in 1993.] *–William Ruhlmann*

There It Is / Jun. 1972 / Polydor ✦✦✦✦✦
Brown's Polydor debut, *Hot Pants*, was nothing more than the inferior remake of the title track baited with a batch of half-baked vamps. *There It Is*, his second Polydor studio album, was a marked improvement. Not that he put much into this one either. This 1972 effort collected five of his best early-'70s tracks and mixed in minimal filler. "Talking Loud and Saying Nothing" and "There It Is (Parts 1 and 2)," with its bebop style horns, were both innovative and hard driving to a fault. The hilarious "I'm a Greedy Man," with its hypnotic bass and help from Bobby Byrd, has Brown firing off such witticisms as "I'm a greedy man/yes I are" and "Taking care of my business/now run tell that." Brown wasn't all fun and games on this one. "King Heroin," an eerie, laid-back jazz offering, has him reciting chilling poetry about the ills of the drug. "Public Enemy #1 (Pt. 1)" attempts to re-create the same message. By "Public Enemy #2 (Pt. 2)" he is doing nothing but connecting the same dots and screaming himself hoarse to little effect. Although by this point Brown was best known for his dance tracks, he still had a way with a ballad. "Who am I," a song that had been kicking around his oeuvre for aeons, gets a strong arrangement and has Brown giving an impassioned performance. Like many of his '70s albums, *There It Is* was out of circulation for close to 20 years until it was reissued on CD in the mid-'90s. It's well worth picking up. *—Jason Elias*

Get on the Good Foot / Nov. 1972 / Polydor ✦✦✦✦
In an era where Brown went on to make three studio doubles, *Get on the Good Foot* was the first. This 1972 album finds Brown having great chemistry with both his newer J.B.'s and the New York session players. The title track is particularly stunning. "Get on the Good Foot" was so off-the-cuff and nonpareil, he couldn't have replicated the formula even if he wanted to. "I Got a Bag of My Own," on the other hand, sounds forced and synthetic. Although Brown was known for his new product, this album has him recycling some of his King singles. Doing so-so remakes of "Cold Sweat" and "Ain't It a Groove" could be taken as an attempt for Brown to ease some of his old catalog to his new label. It was a nice try, but you should stick with the originals. Not surprisingly, *Get on the Good Foot* does have its share of throwaway cuts. "Recitation By Hank Ballard" is a spoken word effort with Ballard extolling his buddy's virtues as well as giving unsolicited advice about the perils of showbiz. "Dirty Harri," a lukewarm instrumental, goes nowhere fast for all of its six-plus minutes. The 1995 CD reissue offered a track that was previously available only on the international release. The warm "I Know It's True" hearkens back to Brown's '60s-ballad style as he turns in a genuinely affecting performance. Although *Get on the Good Foot* only managed to yield two hits, the album is one of his more varied and fun efforts. *—Jason Elias*

Black Caesar / Feb. 1973 / Polydor ✦✦✦
A classic early '70s soundtrack by James Brown. The film *Black Caesar* was prototype "blaxploitation" fodder, but Brown's soundtrack both defined the urban nightmare the film was trying to depict and garnered him a hit single in "Down and Out in New York City." *—Ron Wynn*

Slaughter's Big Rip-Off / Jul. 1973 / Polydor ✦✦✦
1973 was an extremely busy year for Brown. Not only did he continue to release two-plus albums a year, he was producing and writing for the J.B.'s, plus other acts. During the early '70s Brown was still doing great work, but not much of it shows up here. This is the follow-up to the successful soundtrack, *Black Caesar*. But while that effort found Brown engaged enough to offer great tracks, particularly, "The Boss" and "Down and Out In New York City," this one finds him preoccupied. The swaggering and slick title track kicks things off here. "Trying to Get Over" and "Big Strong" both fall into the traps of bad movie music. As an album of Brown doing chase themes seems horrifying, *Slaughter's Big Rip Off* does offer more. Throughout this effort he recycles some of his classic tracks. The oddly titled "Happy for the Poor" is actually a Latinized version of the J.B.'s 1971 single, "Gimme Some More." He goes back even further for his own 1970 classic, "Brother Rapp," which makes an appearance and has the "live" crowd removed. While it's unclear why he would resort to such odd song choices, he had one more shocker in store. "Sexy, Sexy, Sexy" uses the exact backing track from his 1967 hit "Money Won't Change You," with new vocals and lyrics on top. The sad part is that it works too well. While *Slaughter's Big Rip Off* proved that he wasn't going to be a soundtrack innovator, the idea of Brown in film scoring business has its own appeal. *—Jason Elias*

The Payback / Dec. 1973 / Polydor ✦✦✦✦✦
A superb funk album by James Brown, one of his '70s masterpieces. The title cut, with its jutting horn charts, lyric hooks, repeated phrases, and striding bass line was extremely influential, while Brown's trademark screams on the breaks, and the breaks themselves, were later sampled ad infinitum by various hip-hop groups. *—Ron Wynn*

Hell / Jul. 1974 / Polydor ✦✦✦✦✦
Brown's early '70s run of classic singles and good to great albums is still impressive. *Hell* was the double album released a year after the gold selling *The Payback*. To some, the title might put this effort in the realm of kitsch, but in many ways *Hell* was one of Brown's strongest albums. The album was the pinnacle of his work as the Minister of the Super New New Heavy Funk. From the tough and nimble Latin rhythms of "Coldblooded," and "Sayin' It and Doin' It" to the title track, all are prime pre-disco Brown. "My Thang" is probably as hard and unrelenting as he got without spontaneously combusting. The biggest surprise of *Hell* is that no matter how odd the song choices seemed, practically everything worked, excluding a few key songs of course. Both "When the Saints Go Marching In" and "Stormy Monday" don't belong in James Brown's catalogue, let alone the same album. Ballad wise, Brown fares better. "These Foolish Things Remind Me of You" has him getting all warm and fuzzy as he inexplicably throws in a "I'm hurt, I'm hurt" for good measure. That song, as well as the weepers "A Man Has to Go to the Cross Road Before He Finds Himself" and "Sometime," were produced by David Matthews who could always get good ragged yet poised vocals from Brown. Although Brown did roll snake eyes on all of side three, he did leave *Hell* on a good note. "Papa Don't Take No Mess" is laid-back, funky jazz that's worth each of its 13-plus minutes. Despite a few detours, *Hell* is worth listening to. *—Jason Elias*

Roots of a Revolution / 1984 / Polydor ✦✦✦✦✦
A double-CD retrospective of 1956-1964 recordings that charts Brown's progress from doo wop and Little Richard-influenced R&B to the verge of his groundbreaking mid-'60s funk. It doesn't include his biggest hits of the era (which are found on *Star Time*), but these are by and large equally exciting. Many fine overlooked R&B hits and B-sides are included like "Shout and Shimmy," "I've Got Money," the gospel-influenced "Oh Baby Don't You Weep," and "Maybe the Last Time," which inspired the Rolling Stones' "The Last Time." *—Richie Unterberger*

In the Jungle Groove / 1986 / Polydor ✦✦✦✦✦
In the Jungle Groove was one of the first (and still one of the best) collections of James Brown's transitional and hard-hitting soul/funk workouts from 1969-1971. While the first few numbers here feature Brown sidemen who were in on his mid-'60s hits, the majority feature the original JBs outfit that helped the singer forge several extended and funk-defining sides during 1970. Faced with a walkout by his old band, Brown partially formed the J.B.'s out of the New Dapps from Cincinnati, taking aboard brothers Phelps "Catfish" Collins on guitar and William "Bootsy" Collins on bass; many of those ex-band members, namely drummer Clyde Stubblefield, guitarist Clair St. Pinckney, and trombonist Fred Wesley, would eventually return to flesh out the J.B.'s lineup. The one constant was vocalist and organist Bobby Byrd, who had been with Brown since the singer's start in 1956. The incredible grooves Bootsy Collins and Stubblefield laid down here would become manna for hip-hop DJs over 15 years later, with the album's "Funky Drummer (Bonus Beat Reprise)" becoming one of the supreme breakbeats of all time. Filling out the collection are the very soulful pre-J.B.'s tracks "It's a Brand New Day" (tenor saxophonist Maceo Parker's only appearance on the disc) and the original "Funky Drummer," as well as the post-Bootsy cut "Hot Pants (She's Got to Use What She's Got to Get What She Wants)." All the numbers here are as in the pocket as you will ever hear in soul and funk. And while many of these tracks are found on various packages like Polydor's *Funk Power* and *Foundations of Funk, In the Jungle Groove* has the upper hand with its unequaled coverage of Brown's transformation from soul brother number one to funk originator. *—Stephen Cook*

James Brown's Funky People / 1986 / Polydor ✦✦✦✦
Technically speaking, this is not a James Brown album; it is a various artists compilation culled from the People Records label, which Brown ran during the early '70s. But the songs were all produced, arranged, and written by Brown (sometimes in collaboration with others), and the artists represented—the J.B.'s, Lyn Collins, Fred Wesley, and Maceo and the Macks—all were members of Brown's backup band. In fact, Brown also performs on several of the tracks. Hence, the material is not far removed from the funk music Brown was recording under his own name at the same time. A number of the songs were R&B hits, and though they constitute a minor part of the Brown catalog, they remain enjoyable. *—William Ruhlmann*

James Brown's Funky People, Pt. 2 / Feb. 1988 / Polydor ✦✦✦✦
The second volume of material compiled from Brown's People Records label isn't quite as strong as the first, as it reaches for more obscurities—but those obscurities can be interesting, especially Brown's collaboration with Hank Ballard on "From the Love Side." Again, Brown wrote (or co-wrote), arranged, and produced much of the material, appearing on vocals several times, and the J.B.'s are featured heavily, whether as a unit or with individual members stepping out as solo acts. The highlights are Bobby Byrd's two 1971 R&B hits, "I Know You Got Soul" and "Hot Pants—I'm Coming, Coming, I'm Coming"; also featured are Marva Whitney, Lyn Collins, and Fred Wesley, among others. *—Steve Huey*

Messing with the Blues / 1991 / Polydor ✦✦✦
Although he is most famous for his innovations in soul and funk music, James Brown never lost sight of his blues and R&B roots. His albums often placed surprisingly rootsy covers of old chestnuts alongside his groundbreaking polyrhythmic workouts. This double CD compiles thirty of the bluesiest items from his vast recorded legacy. Cut between 1957 and 1985, most of the tracks actually date from the '60s; many of these, in turn, were laid down in the early part of the decade, when J.B. was gradually evolving from his more conventional beginnings. The artists whose songs are covered here read like a *Who's Who* of R&B pioneers: Louis Jordan, Roy Brown, Memphis Slim, Ivory Joe Hunter, Fats Domino, Chuck Willis, Little Willie John, Billy Ward, Guitar Slim, and Bobby Bland. It's quite an instructive insight into Brown's not-always-visible roots. It would be fair to say that this does not rank among his most exciting material, finding him in a smoother and more conventional style than his most innovative work. It is nonetheless always entertaining and accomplished, with Brown's love for this material shining through strongly in his committed interpretations. Especially intriguing are an 11-minute cover of Chuck Willis' "Don't Deceive Me" and a two-part, blues-based rap vamp from the early '70s, "Like It Is, Like It Was (The Blues)." The disc includes several unreleased cuts, alternate takes, and unedited versions of previously released songs. *—Richie Unterberger*

☆ **Star Time** / Jun. 1991 / Polydor ✦✦✦✦✦
One of the great box sets of all time; over four CDs, Brown's recorded legacy is traced from "Please Please Please" in 1956 through his 1984 duet with Afrika Bambaataa, "Unity Pt. 1." With 71 tracks in all, the set places the #1 R&B artist ever in his proper perspective as the prime progenitor of funk, one of the architects of soul, and the Godfather of Rap. To have done any one of these things would have been a bid for immortality; having done all three makes him a god. Four CDs at once is virtually too rich for one sitting. The well-written liner notes provide three different perspectives on Brown's career. A cornerstone of any great collection. *—Rob Bowman*

★ **20 All-Time Greatest Hits!** / Oct. 1991 / Polydor ✦✦✦✦✦
A first-rate greatest-hits package that covers the essential soul singles and some of the funk-period material as well. While the finest James Brown package is the boxed set, if you're not going to get that, you wouldn't be far wrong getting this one instead. *—Ron Wynn*

The Greatest Hits of the Fourth Decade / Apr. 14, 1992 / Scotti Bros. ✦✦✦
Collecting Brown's 1980s hits that didn't make it onto *Star Time, Greatest Hits of the Fourth Decade* shows that the period was not among his most creatively fertile, even with the monster hit "Living in America." Still, the disc does pick the best tracks from a dry spell, making it a nice supplement to the box set. *—Stephen Thomas Erlewine*

Love Power Peace / Jun. 23, 1992 / Polydor ✦✦✦✦✦
James Brown with the then newly-formed J.B.'s—the maestro's second great band, including Bootsy Collins, Phelps Collins, Jabo Starks, Bobby Byrd, and Fred Wesley. *Live at the Apollo* had caught James Brown, the '50s gospel/rhythm and blues singer; *Love Power Peace* captures James the funkster. In the early '70s Brown turned up the funk, recording such litanies for Black America as "Ain't It Funky Now," "Sex Machine," "Give It Up or Turn It Loose," "Super Bad," "Get Up, Get Into It, Get Involved," and "Soul Power." They're all here, along with revved-up, white-hot versions of the early- and middle-period classics. Brown had planned to release this as a triple album in 1971. When several band members left shortly after it was recorded, Brown switched from King to Polydor Records, leading him to scrap it and record a new studio album instead. In 1992, Polygram decided to make the recording available for the first time. *—Rob Bowman*

Soul Pride: The Instrumentals (1960-69) / Mar. 23, 1993 / Polydor ✦✦✦✦✦
Everyone knows how hot James Brown's bands were, but not everyone's aware that he and his sidemen recorded lots of instrumental sides in the '60s. Originally scattered haphazardly over many out-of-print singles and albums, *Soul Pride* brings together the best of this work into one cohesive and chronological package. These cuts are nearly equal in power to J.B.'s vocal performances. Not only does the band cook on most of these insinuating vamps, but you can also hear the evolution of the man's sound from gritty R&B to tight-as-a-drum soul to free-form funk. Soul Brother #1 himself plays organ and adds unpredictable shouts and screams on most of these tracks. But the chief stars are sidemen like Maceo Parker, Fred Wesley, and Pee Wee Ellis, who broke new ground with their compulsive counterpoint riffs. This fiery two-disc, 36-track box set contains over two hours of music, as well as a few non-LP B-sides and previously unreleased tracks. *—Richie Unterberger*

☆ **Foundations of Funk: A Brand New Bag,1964-1969** / Mar. 19, 1996 / Polydor ✦✦✦✦✦
There are several worthy James Brown compilations. But this is the one, more than any other, that presents his most fertile and innovative soul and funk material. From 1964's "Out of Sight" through 1969's "Mother Popcorn," this was Brown at the apex of his creativity, turning soul into funk in the mid-'60s, then pushing the rhythm even more to the forefront. Most of his hit singles from this five-year explosion of white heat are on this 27-track, two-CD set, including "Out of Sight," "Papa's Got a Brand New Bag," "I Got You (I Feel Good)," "Say It Loud—I'm Black and I'm Proud," and "Cold Sweat." There are some minor omissions that could be questioned (the absence of the studio version of "Bring It Up," for instance), and big James Brown fans will already have the lion's share of tracks, on the *Star Time* box and other releases. It does, however, contain minor but significant bonuses: an alternate take of "Cold Sweat," a previously unreleased live medley of "Out of Sight" and "Bring It Up," and a previously unreleased live version of "Licking Stick—Licking Stick." There are also longer versions of "I Don't Want Nobody to Give Me Nothing" (ten minutes!), "I Got the Feelin'," "The Popcorn," and "Brother Rapp" that were edited when they were prepared for official release. *—Richie Unterberger*

Funk Power 1970: A Brand New Thang / Jun. 4, 1996 / Polydor ✦✦✦✦✦
The period during which Brown was backed by the original J.B.'s (with Bootsy and Catfish Collins) was extremely brief, lasting only a year. But it was also an extremely important and influential phase of Brown's career, when he moved from soul-funk to hard funk, stretching out the grooves and putting more stress on the bottom than ever before. This 78-minute disc is the cream of his recordings from the Bootsy Collins era. The nine tracks (the tenth is a brief public-service annoncement) include some of his core funk workouts—"Get Up I Feel Like Being a Sex Machine" (two versions), "Super Bad," "Give It Up or Turn It Loose," "Talkin' Loud and Sayin' Nothing," "Get Up, Get Into It, Get Involved," and "Soul Power." It's not for those who find Brown's funk phase too monotonous, and indeed the grooves do get a bit similar when experienced all at once. But it's unquestionably the best of Brown's '70s recordings, and indeed some of the hardest funk ever waxed by anyone at any time. As a bonus, the CD has previously unreleased complete versions of "Soul Power" (12 minutes) and "Talkin' Loud and Sayin' Nothing" (14 minutes), as well as a previously unreleased version of "There Was a Time." *—Richie Unterberger*

Make It Funky—The Big Payback: 1971-1975 / Jul. 23, 1996 / Polydor ✦✦✦✦✦
While the first half of the 1970s saw Brown's sales and art start to slowly decline, at their best he and the J.B.'s remained capable of generating a lot of heat. Record-wise it was a very erratic period, especially on his albums, which makes this two-and-a-half-hour double-disc compilation of his best material from the era especially welcome. Besides his biggest hits from the time ("Make It Funky," "Get on the Good Foot," "The Payback," "Funky President"), it has a number of high-charting R&B 45s that didn't make it onto the *Star Time* box. Familiar hits are sometimes presented in their full unedited mega-versions (12 minutes of "Make It Funky," 14 of "Papa Don't Take No Mess"), and there are also a few previously unreleased outtakes and alternate versions. It's only a disappointment relative to the towering accomplishments of his 1960s and early-'70s classics. On its own terms, it's excellent funk, if rather homogenous taken all at once, with occasional departures from the formula, like "Down and Out in New York City," with its poppy woodwinds. *—Richie Unterberger*

★ **JB40: 40th Anniversary Collection** / Oct. 8, 1996 / Polydor ✦✦✦✦✦
Brown's catalog was in a shambles for years, but the CD age has reversed the situation to such an extent that you now have a wide variety of greatest-hits options to choose from. On the whole, this might be the best buy, cramming 40 of his biggest hit singles from 1956-1979 onto two discs. It's perhaps a little too weighted toward the '70s (which comprise all of disc two), and some decent moderate-size hits are omitted, like "Oh Baby Don't You Weep," "Bring It Up," and "Get It Together." But it does have the core classics.

If you don't want to spring for the *Star Time* box, but want more than a single-disc collection, this is the one to have. *—Richie Unterberger*

Dead on the Heavy Funk / May 12, 1998 / Polydor ✦✦✦

The last in Polydor's series of double-disc James Brown anthologies, *Dead on the Heavy Funk 1975-83*, is inarguably the weakest. By the late '70s, all the great musicians that populated J.B.'s band had left, leaving him with a competent band that largely recycled old funk and tried its hand at disco. Most of their records were uneven, yet every once in a while they brought it all together and worked a good groove, even if they tended to let it go on a bit too long. *Dead on the Heavy Funk* has all those moments, as well as some less successful moments, extended mixes, previously unreleased takes and live cuts, plus the independent single "Bring It On... Bring it On." It's an effective summary of these eight years, containing all of the good moments without disguising Brown's artistic decline. For hardcore fans, it's worth exploring, but most listeners—especially ones who loved his groundbreaking '60s funk—will be satisfied by the sampling of this material on the classic box set *Star Time*. *—Stephen Thomas Erlewine*

Maxine Brown

b. Apr. 27, 1932, Kingstree, SC

Vocals / Uptown Soul, Pop-Soul, R&B, Soul

Although she never had many hits, Maxine Brown was one of the most underrated soul and R&B vocalists of the '60s, releasing a series of singles with only a couple of songs-managing to become either pop or R&B hits. Despite her lack of hits, Brown is acknowledged as one of the finest R&B vocalists of her time, capable of delivering soul, jazz and pop with equal aplomb. In 1960, she signed with the small Normar label, who released the smooth soul ballad "All in My Mind" late in the year. The single became a hit, climbing to number two on the R&B charts,and it was quickly followed by "Funny," which peaked at number three. Brown was poised to become a star, and she moved to ABC-Paramount in 1962, but she left the label within a year, without scoring any hits. She signed to the New York-based, uptown soul label Wand in 1963. Brown recorded her best work at Wand, having a string of moderate hits for the label over the next three years. Among these were "Oh No Not My Baby," "It's Gonna Be Alright" and the Chuck Jackson duets "Something You Got," "Hold On I'm Coming," and "Daddy's Home." Part of the reason Brown didn't receive much exposure is that the label focused much of their attention on Dionne Warwick, leaving Maxine to toil in semi-obscurity. *—Stephen Thomas Erlewine*

● **Oh No Not My Baby: The Best of Maxine Brown** / 1990 / Kent ✦✦✦✦✦

This 28-song CD is undoubtedly the best compilation of this underrated soul singer's work, featuring many of her '60s singles and several tunes from the era that were unreleased until the '80s. This disc draws from her recordings for the Wand label between 1963 and 1967, when Brown was at her artistic peak. Of course the hit title track is a highlight, but there are no clunkers in this excellent collection of overlooked '60s pop-soul, featuring the New York "uptown" production that also graced the records of fellow Wand/Scepter artists like Dionne Warwick and Chuck Jackson. Brown was one of the most versatile soul divas of the '60s, showing the influence of Brill Building pop, girl groups, Motown, and even Stax soul and supper-club ballads. As with a similar artist like Betty Everett, this versaility has worked against her in some ways. Neither full-fledged pop nor unabashedly soul, her work cannot be easily pigeonholed into a certain soul genre, and has cost her the respect that some purists reserve for "deep" soul singers. But her work holds up well. Collectors should be aware that this disc doesn't include any of the records she cut in the early '60s before joining Wand; the version of her 1961 Top 20 hit "All in My Mind" here is from a live 1964 release, not the original single. *—Richie Unterberger*

● **Greatest Hits** / 1995 / Tomato ✦✦✦✦✦

This 23-track best-of has a lot of overlap with the British import *Oh No Not My Baby*; both cover her mid-'60s period with Wand, and each has some songs not on the other. There's not a crucial difference between the pair, but the nod probably goes to the import, which has more songs and better sound. In its favor, this compilation includes five of her duets with Chuck Jackson, none of which are on the other CD (although the duets don't rank among her best material). It also has a studio version of "All in My Mind," rather than the live one on the British anthology. *—Richie Unterberger*

Something You Got: The Best of Chuck Jackson & Maxine Brown / 1996 / Soul Classics/Ichiban ✦✦✦

All 20 of the duet tracks that Brown and Chuck Jackson recorded for the Wand label between 1965 and 1967 are here, comprising the entirety of their two albums for the company. It's reasonable pop/soul, but not nearly as memorable as the best male-female soul duets of the era (like the ones by Marvin Gaye and various Motown partners, or by Otis Redding and Carla Thomas). Highlights are the early compositions by the Jo Armstead-Nick Ashford-Valerie Simpson team, including a version of "Let's Go Get Stoned" that was recorded (though not released) before Ray Charles' more famous hit rendition. *—Richie Unterberger*

Spotlight on Maxine Brown/Greatest Hits / Aug. 29, 2000 / Kent ✦✦✦✦

A confusing release that seems to have tried to both sweep up rarities for the completist and offer something approximating a greatest-hits package, the result being, of course, that everyone's a bit unsatisfied. Basically, the idea was to combine all the songs from her 1965 LP *Spotlight* (actually largely a collection of 1963-65 singles) and her 1967 LP *Greatest Hits* (which duplicated five tracks from *Spotlight*) onto one CD, adding eight rare bonus tracks. Those additional cuts are taken from non-LP mid-'60s recordings and a couple of previously unissued items. There are two problems with that concept. The first is that no less than 15 of the 28 tracks also appear on another Kent release, the fine anthology *Oh No Not My Baby: The Best of Maxine Brown*, which many of the people considering buying any Brown reissue are likely to have already. The second is that this CD actually does not include "All in My Mind" and "Funny," which—if the cover art of *Greatest Hits*, complete with track listing, reproduced on the cover of this two-fer is to be believed—were on the original 1967 *Greatest Hits* LP. That's an uncommon gaffe for Ace/Kent to make, but from all appearances that's what happened. Now, certainly this is still a fine pop-soul disc from one of the best pop-soul vocalists. Of the material on *Spotlight On/Greatest Hits* not on that other Kent collection, it ranges from good—the bluesy "You Upset My Soul," an odd cover of the Beatles' "We Can Work It Out," the brassy 1966 single "Anything You Do Is Alright," a nice interpretation of the pop standard "When I Fall in Love"—to unmemorable. *—Richie Unterberger*

Roy Brown

b. Sep. 10, 1925, New Orleans, LA, **d.** May 25, 1981, San Fernando, CA

Vocals, Leader, Songwriter, Piano / Jump Blues, West Coast Blues, R&B

When you draw up a short list of the R&B pioneers who exerted a primary influence on the development of rock & roll, respectfully place singer Roy Brown's name near its very top. His seminal 1947 DeLuxe Records waxing of "Good Rockin' Tonight" was immediately ridden to the peak of the R&B charts by shouter Wynonie Harris and subsequently covered by Elvis Presley, Ricky Nelson, Jerry Lee Lewis, and many more early rock icons (even Pat Boone!). In addition, Brown's melismatically pleading, gospel-steeped delivery impacted the vocal styles of B.B. King, Bobby Bland, and Little Richard (among a plethora of important singers). Clearly, Roy Brown was an innovator—and from 1948-1951, an R&B star whose wild output directly presaged rock's rise. Though Harris' version of "Good Rockin' Tonight" beat him out for top chart honors, Brown didn't have to wait long to dominate the R&B lists himself. He scored 15 hits from 1948 to 1951 for DeLuxe, ranging from emotionally wracked crying blues to party-time rockers. Strangely, his sales slumped badly during the early '50s, even though his output for Cincinnati's King label rates among his hottest. He briefly rejuvenated his commercial fortunes in 1957 with the single "Let the Four Winds Blow," recorded at Imperial. Inactive during much of the '60s, he'd begun to rebuild his long-lost momentum during the '70s when he died of a heart attack in 1981, his role as a crucial link between postwar R&B and rock's initial rise still underappreciated by the masses. *—Bill Dahl*

★ **Good Rocking Tonight: The Best of Roy Brown** / 1947-1957 / Rhino ✦✦✦✦✦

An unassailable 18-cut cross-section of the monstrously popular and influential New Orleans jump blues shouter's sides for DeLuxe, King, and Imperial labels that spans 1947-57 and takes in his seminal "Good Rocking Tonight" (where it all began!), "Rockin' at Midnight," "Boogie at Midnight," and "Love Don't Love Nobody"; the almost unbearably tortured "Hard Luck Blues," and the unbelievably raunchy two-parter "Butcher Pete." Looking for the origins of rock? Here they are! *—Bill Dahl*

Mighty Mighty Man! / 1953-1959 / Ace ✦✦✦✦✦

Another British import that really delivers the rocking goods! This time zeroing in on Brown's 1953-59 King sides exclusively, the 22-cut CD shows that Brown actually picked up his tempos to meet rock's rise head on. The clever sequel "Ain't No Rocking No More," "Black Diamond," "Gal from Kokomo," and "Shake 'Em Up Baby" rate with his hottest rockers, with great support from a crew of Crescent City stalwarts. *—Bill Dahl*

The Complete Imperial Recordings / Sep. 27, 1956-Mar. 6, 1958 / Capitol ✦✦✦

In the mid-'50s Brown, like many other early R&B pioneers, was a bit lost at sea amid the rock & roll explosion. From 1956 to 1958, he recorded these 20 tracks for Imperial under the direction of legendary New Orleans R&B producer Dave Bartholomew. Brown and Bartholomew were attempting to update Brown's jump blues/R&B hybrid with a lot of Fats Domino-type Crescent City influence on these sides. The results weren't bad, but with Bartholomew co-writing most of the tunes and using local musicians like saxophonist Lee Allen, Brown sounded more like a journeyman New Orleans R&B singer than an innovative, bluesy forefather of rock & roll. There were a couple of commercial successes; his cover of Buddy Knox's "Party Doll" made the R&B Top 20, and "Let the Four Winds Blow" actually made the pop Top 40, although Fats Domino would have much greater success with the same song when he covered it a few years later. Diluted by occasional pop and rock influences, as well as a substandard variation of "Good Rockin' Tonight," this compilation shouldn't be the first Brown on your shelf. But for those who want to go a little further, it's packaged very well, with thorough liner notes and seven previously unissued cuts. *—Richie Unterberger*

Ruth Brown

b. Jan. 12, 1928, Portsmouth, VA

Vocals / Jump Blues, R&B

They called Atlantic Records "the house that Ruth built" during the 1950s, and they weren't referring to the Sultan of Swat. Ruth Brown's regal hitmaking reign from 1949 to the close of the '50s helped tremendously to establish the New York label's predominance in the R&B field. After performing with bandleaders including Lucky Millinder, she signed to the fledgling Atlantic label in 1948 and found a hit with her first single, the torch ballad "So Long."

Brown's seductive vocal delivery shone incandescently on her Atlantic smashes "Teardrops in My Eyes," "I'll Wait for You," "I Know," "5-10-15 Hours," the seminal "(Mama) He Treats Your Daughter Mean," "Oh What a Dream" and "Mambo Baby." After an even two dozen R&B chart appearances for Atlantic that ended in 1960, Brown faded from view. After raising her two sons and working a nine-to-five job, Brown began to rebuild her musical career in the mid-'70s. There were more records for Fantasy, notably 1991's jumping *Fine and Mellow*. Her pipes are mellowed but not frayed by the ensuing decades that have seen her rise to stardom not once, but twice. *—Bill Dahl*

Sweet Baby of Mine (1949-1956) / Apr. 6, 1949-Mar. 2, 1956 / Route 66 ♦♦♦♦♦
Excellent collection covering blues and R&B songs Brown did prior to becoming a huge hit artist for Atlantic in the late '50s. These were R&B gems, but such artists as Patti Page and Georgia Gibbs were covering them for the white market and Brown was locked out until 1957. But she enjoyed 11 Top 10 R&B hits, which are contained on this anthology. *—Ron Wynn*

★ **The Best of Ruth Brown** / May 25, 1949-May 1959 / Rhino ♦♦♦♦♦
For those who want a cheaper and more concise collection of her best Atlantic cuts than the two-CD *Miss Rhythm*, this superb 23-track CD has the cream of her '50s work, including no less than 19 Top Ten R&B singles. Charting her evolution from her jazzy debut, "So Long," through jump blues and early rock'n'roll, it also adds a bonus of two previously unissued live cuts from 1959. *—Richie Unterberger*

☆ **Miss Rhythm (Greatest Hits and More)** / May 25, 1949-Aug. 30, 1960 / Rhino/Atlantic ♦♦♦♦♦
Before Aretha Franklin was exalted as the Queen of Soul, Ruth Brown was dubbed "Miss Rhythm"—and with good reason. A gritty, aggressive belter with an impressive range and a powerhouse of a voice, Brown was the top female R&B singer of the early-to-mid-'50s, and would directly or indirectly have an influence on such greats as Etta James and LaVern Baker. A two-CD set ranging from Brown's early hits to engaging obscurities and rarities, *Miss Rhythm* offers a fine overview of her Atlantic years. Early hits like "Mama, He Treats Your Daughter Mean," "Teardrops from My Eyes," "Mambo Baby" and "5-10-15 Hours" point to the fact that a lot of early R&B was essentially blues at a fast tempo. The set also reminds us of early R&B's connection to jazz—in fact, classics like 1949's "So Long" (her first single) and "Have a Good Time" are examples of first-class torch singing. There are numerous Brown albums that are well worth acquiring, but for those interested in exploring her early music for the first time, *Miss Rhythm* is an excellent place to start. *—Alex Henderson*

Jackson Browne

b. Oct. 9, 1948, Heidelberg, Germany
Vocals, Keyboards, Piano, Guitar / Pop/Rock, Folk-Rock, Soft Rock, Singer/Songwriter
In many ways, Jackson Browne was the quintessential sensitive Californian singer-songwriter of the early '70s. Only Joni Mitchell and James Taylor ranked alongside him in terms of influence, but neither artist tapped into the post-'60s zeitgeist like Browne. While the majority of his classic '70s work was unflinchingly personal, it nevertheless provided a touchstone for a generation of maturing baby boomers coming to terms with adulthood. Not only did his introspective, literate lyrics strike a nerve, but his laid-back folk-rock set the template for much of the music to come out of California during the '70s. With his first four albums, Browne built a loyal following that helped him break into the mainstream with 1976's *The Pretender*. During the late '70s and early '80s, he was at the height of his popularity, as each of his albums charted in the Top 10. Midway through the '80s, Browne made a series of political protest records which caused his audience to gradually shrink, but when he returned to introspective songwriting with 1993's *I'm Alive*, he made a modest comeback. *—Stephen Thomas Erlewine*

☆ **Jackson Browne** / Jan. 1972 / Asylum ♦♦♦♦♦
An auspicious debut that doesn't sound like a debut: although only 23, Browne had kicked around the music business for several years and developed an unusual use of language, studiedly casual yet full of striking imagery, and a post-apocalyptic viewpoint to go with it. He sang with a calm certainty over spare, discretely placed backup that highlighted the songs and always seemed about to disappear. In song after song, Browne described the world as a desert in need of moisture: in "Doctor My Eyes," the album's most propulsive song and a Top Ten hit, he sang, "Doctor, my eyes/Cannot see the sky/Is this the prize/For having learned how not to cry?" If Browne's outlook was cautious, its expression was original. His conditional optimism seemed to reflect hard experience, and in the early 1970s, a lot of his listeners shared that perspective. Like any great artist, Browne articulated the tenor of his times. But the album has long since come to seem a timeless collection of reflective ballads touching on still-difficult subjects—suicide (explicitly), depression and drug use (probably), spiritual uncertainty and desperate hope—all in calm, reasoned tones, and all with an amazingly eloquent sense of language. *Jackson Browne*'s greater triumph is that, having perfectly expressed its times, it transcended them as well. *—William Ruhlmann*

For Everyman / Oct. 1973 / Asylum ♦♦♦♦♦
Jackson Browne faced the nearly insurmountable task of following a masterpiece in making his second album. Having cherry-picked years of songwriting the first time around, he turned to some of his secondary older material, which was still better than most people's best and, ironically, more accessible—notably such songs as "These Days," which had been covered six times already, dating back to Nico's *Chelsea Girl* album in 1967, and "Take It Easy," a co-composition with the Eagles' Glenn Frey, which had been a Top 40 hit for the group in 1972. Browne unsuccessfully looked for another hit single with the uptempo "Red Neck Friend," reminisced about meeting his wife and starting a family in the coy "Ready or Not," and, at the end, finally came up with a new song to rank with those on the first album in the philosophical title track, which reportedly was his more positive reply to Crosby, Stills, Nash & Young's "Wooden Ships." (David Crosby sang harmony.) Musically, the album was still restrained, but not as austere as *Jackson Browne*, as the singer had hooked up with multi-instrumentalist David Lindley, who would introduce interesting textures to his music on a variety of stringed instruments for the next several years. All of which is to say that *For Everyman* was a less consistent collection than Browne's debut album. But Browne's songwriting ability remained impressive. *—William Ruhlmann*

★ **Late for the Sky** / Sep. 1974 / Asylum ♦♦♦♦♦
On his third album, Jackson Browne returned to the themes of his debut record (love, loss, identity, apocalypse), and, amazingly, delved even deeper into them. "For a Dancer," and a meditation on death like the first album's "Song for Adam," is a more eloquent eulogy; "Farther On" extends the "moving on" point of "Looking Into You"; "Before the Deluge" is a glimpse beyond the apocalypse evoked on "My Opening Farewell" and the second album's "For Everyman." If Browne had seemed to question everything in his first records, here he even questioned himself. "For me some words come easy, but I know that they don't mean that much," he sang on the opening track, "Late for the Sky," and added in "Farther On," "I'm not sure what I'm trying to say." Yet his seeming uncertainty and self-doubt reflected the size and complexity of the problems he was addressing in these songs, and few had ever explored such territory, much less mapped it so well. "The Late Show," the album's thematic center, doubted but ultimately affirmed the nature of relationships, while by the end, "After the Deluge," if "only a few survived," the human race continued nonetheless. It was a lot to put into a pop music album, but Browne stretched the limits of what could be found in what he called "the beauty in songs," just as Bob Dylan had a decade before. *—William Ruhlmann*

The Pretender / Nov. 1976 / Asylum ♦♦♦
On *The Pretender*, Jackson Browne took a step back from the precipice so well defined on his first three albums, but doing so didn't seem to make him feel any better. Employing a real producer, Jon Landau, for the first time, Browne made what sounded like a real contemporary rock record, but this made his songs less effective; the ersatz Mexican arrangement of "Linda Paloma" and the bouncy second half of "Daddy's Tune," with its horn charts and guitar solo, undercut the lyrics. The man who had delved so deeply into life's abyss on his earlier albums was in search of escape this time around, whether by crying ("Here Come Those Tears Again"), sleeping ("Sleep's Dark and Silent Gate"), or making peace with estranged love ones ("The Only Child," "Daddy's Tune"). None of it worked, however, and when Browne came to the final track—traditionally the place on his albums where he summed up his current philosophical stance—he delivered "The Pretender," a cynical, sarcastic treatise on moneygrubbing and the shallow life of the suburbs. Primarily inner directed, the song's defeatist tone demands rejection, but it is also a quintessential statement of its time, the post-Watergate '70s; dire as that might be, you had to admire that kind of honesty, even as it made you wince. *—William Ruhlmann*

Running on Empty / 1977 / Asylum ♦♦♦
Having acknowledged a certain creative desperation on *The Pretender*, Jackson Browne lowered his sights (and raised his commercial appeal) considerably with *Running on Empty*, which was more a concept album about the road than an actual live album, even though its songs were sometimes recorded on stage (and sometimes on the bus or in the hotel). Although unlike most live albums, it consisted of previously unrecorded songs, Browne had less creative participation on this album than on any he ever made, solely composing only two songs, co-writing four others, and covering another four. And he had less to say—the title song and leadoff track neatly conjoined his artistic and escapist themes. Figuratively and creatively, he was out of gas, but like "the pretender," still had to make a living. The songs covered all aspects of touring, from Danny O'Keefe's "The Road," which detailed romantic encounters, and "Rosie" (co-written by Browne and his manager Donald Miller), in which a soundman pays tribute to auto-eroticism, to, well, "Cocaine," to the travails of being a roadie ("The Load-Out"). Audience noises, humorous asides, loose playing—they were all part of a rough-around-the-edges musical evocation of the rock & roll touring life. It was not what fans had come to expect from Browne, of course, but the disaffected were more than outnumbered by the newly converted. (It didn't hurt that "Running on Empty" and "The Load-Out"/"Stay" both became Top 40 hits.) As a result, Jackson Browne's least ambitious, but perhaps most accessible, album ironically became his biggest seller. But it is not characteristic of his other work: for many, it will be the only Browne album they will want to own, just as others always will regard it disdainfully as "Jackson Browne Lite." *—William Ruhlmann*

Hold Out / 1980 / Asylum ♦♦
If Jackson Browne had convincingly lowered the bar set by his first three albums on his fourth and fifth ones, his sixth, *Hold Out*, found him once again seeking some measure of satisfaction, albeit in reduced circumstances. His songs were less philosophical, but they were also more personal. In "Of Missing Persons," he once again took on a eulogy as his subject, but unlike "Song to Adam" or "For a Dancer," there the song was directed to his late friend's daughter and encouraged her recovery: it was more a song for the living than for the dead. Newly aware of the world around him ("Boulevard"), he was also newly sensitive to others, notably on the mutual dependency song "Call It A Loan." But the personal tone sometimes made him less sure-footed as a performer; "Hold On Hold Out," the traditional big, long, last song on the album, was awkwardly, not winningly intimate, just as the attention-grabbing lead-off track, "Disco Apocalypse," was merely foolish instead of whatever it may have been intended to be (satire? drama?). If Browne was still trying to write himself out of the cul-de-sac he had created for himself early on, *Hold Out* represented an earnest attempt that nevertheless fell short. *—William Ruhlmann*

Lawyers in Love / 1983 / Asylum ♦♦
Jackson Browne's messages had always seemed so important that one tended to overlook the sheer songwriting craft that went into his work, craft that was apparent, for example, on his 1982 single "Somebody's Baby," which became his biggest hit ever (and which appears on none of his albums, only being available on the soundtrack to *Fast Times at Ridgemont High*), and on songs like "Downtown," a street-life portrait on his seventh album, *Lawyers in Love*. The craft seemed all the more important because Browne was so intent on turning his back on the conundrums that had obsessed him in the past. On "Cut it Away," he sang of his desire to remove his "desperate heart" (a phrase he had used

before), to rid himself of "this crazy longing for something more/This question that I don't have the answer for." In place of such ambitions, Browne substituted the beginnings of social concern ("Say It Isn't True") and, most imaginatively, a humorous look at contemporary trash culture in the title track, one of the more exhilaratingly silly moments in Browne's generally dour catalog. But the craft, and the familiar tightness of Browne's veteran studio/live band, couldn't hide the essentially retread nature of much of this material. — *William Ruhlmann*

Lives in the Balance / 1986 / Asylum ✦✦✦
Usually among the most introspective of songwriters, Jackson Browne cast his gaze on the world outside on *Lives in the Balance* and did not like what he saw. Beginning with "For America," he lamented his previous indifference to social issues—"I went on speaking of the future/While other people fought and bled"—but immediately tried to make up for lost time. The album's context, of course, was five years of Ronald Reagan's presidency, with what the Left saw as an indifference to the plight of the poor at home and a dangerously aggressive policy against insurgent movements in the Central American countries of El Salvador and Nicaragua they feared would lead to a Vietnam-like war. Without naming those places, Browne wrote and sang passionately against poverty in the songs "Soldier of Plenty" and "Lawless Avenues" and against war in "For America," "Lives in the Balance," and "Till I Go Down." Elsewhere, his more familiar themes of romantic ("In the Shape of a Heart") and philosophical ("Black and White") disillusionment also made appearances. But, from its hard rock sound and forceful singing to its frankly agitprop lyrics, "For America" remained primarily a political statement, and if Browne sounded more involved in his music than he had in some time, the specificity of its approach inevitably limited its appeal and its long-term significance. — *William Ruhlmann*

World in Motion / Jun. 1989 / Elektra ✦✦
Jackson Browne continued amassing a repertoire best suited to an Amnesty International benefit on his second highly politicized album, *World In Motion*. War, homelessness, and Oliver North (though not by name) were condemned; freedom, truth, and Nelson Mandela were praised. Now and then, Browne drew parallels between the personal and the political, notably in the double-edged "Anything Can Happen," but for the most part he sermonized, frequently adopting the generalized terms and reasoning that sermons usually employ. Except for the gloomy viewpoint, it was hard to recognize the Jackson Browne of his first few albums amid all the commentary, and even if you agreed with his overall political stance, that was disappointing. — *William Ruhlmann*

I'm Alive / Oct. 1993 / Elektra ✦✦✦
Jackson Browne abandoned politics for the war between the sexes on *I'm Alive*. "I have no problem with this crooked world," he sang; ". . . My problem is you." The album detailed the ups and downs of a relationship, starting with the defiant post-breakup title track and then doubling back to describe irritation ("My Problem Is You"), devotion ("Everywhere I Go," "I'll Do Anything"), increasing tension ("Miles Away," "Too Many Angels"), separation ("Take This Rain," "Two of Me, Two of You"), forgiveness ("Sky Blue and Black"), and finally acceptance ("All Good Things"). Longtime fans welcomed the album as a return in style to the days of *Late for the Sky*, but a closer model might have been *Hold Out*, a complementary album concerned with the flowering of an affair rather than the withering of one, since Browne eschewed the greater philosophical implications of romance and, falling back on stock imagery (angels, rain), failed to achieve an originality of expression. Just as, in *Hold Out*, one wasn't so much inspired as informed that Browne had found love, on *I'm Alive*, one wasn't so much moved as told that he'd lost it. While it was good news that he wasn't tilting at windmills anymore, Browne did not make a full comeback with the album, despite a couple of well-constructed songs. — *William Ruhlmann*

Looking East / Feb. 1996 / Elektra ✦✦✦
Jackson Browne begins his most Los Angeles-oriented album standing in the Pacific Ocean "Looking East" across the country and, as usual, doing so without much approval, but with a persistent hope. After reflecting on his youth in "The Barricades of Heaven," he compares the rich and poor in "Some Bridges" and takes time out to watch a little television in "Information Wars," before considering romance in "I'm the Cat," "Culver Moon," and "Baby How Long" and childhood in "Nino." He then decides he would like to be "Alive in the World," as opposed to inside his head or "behind some wall," and declares of that world, "It Is One." Thus, we are taken on another of Jackson Browne's tours, which manages to travel to outer and inner space without leaving the county of Los Angeles. After 24 years of record-making, he remains puzzled by the same personal and philosophical issues, and he approaches them in the same way, alternately hopeful and pessimistic, but more often than not ending up determined to persevere. He now uses fewer words, such that the songs sometimes seem no more than sketches, and he continues to set them to loping rock rhythms played against slabs of ringing guitar with traces of world music. Here, he co-credits eight of the ten songs to his backup musicians, yet the haunting, longline melodies remain familiar from his earlier work. But then, *Looking East* is a highly referential work from an artist who started where most end and has been earnestly seeking the right direction ever since. *Looking East* finds him in his own backyard, still searching. — *William Ruhlmann*

The Next Voice You Hear: The Best of Jackson Browne / Sep. 23, 1997 / Elektra ✦✦✦
Theoretically, assembling a Jackson Browne greatest-hits collection would be easy, but *The Next Voice You Hear: The Best of Jackson Browne* proves that isn't necessarily the case. Boasting 13 tracks, plus two new songs, *The Next Voice You Hear* contains some of Browne's biggest hits—"Doctor My Eyes," "Running on Empty," "Somebody's Baby," "Tender is the Night"—but it leaves just as many off, including "Rock Me on the Water," "Here Come Those Tears Again," "Stay," "Boulevard," "Lawyers in Love" and "For America." Of course, singles only told half the story with Browne, and many of his greatest

songs were only available as album tracks. Therefore, it makes sense that album cuts like "These Days," "Late for Sky," and "The Pretender" are present, but there are still a number of equally good, if not better, cuts that are left off. As a result, *The Next Voice You Hear* is merely adequate for casual Browne fans, but it's nowhere near definitive. — *Stephen Thomas Erlewine*

Brownsville Station

f. 1969, Ann Arbor, MI, **db.** 1979
Detroit Rock, Boogie Rock, Hard Rock, Rock & Roll
A Detroit-area rock & roll band formed in 1969 by guitarist Cub Koda. Original members also included Mike Lutz (guitar), T.J. Cronley (drums), and Tony Driggins (bass). Initially influenced by Chuck Berry, Bo Diddley, Jerry Lee Lewis, and other '50s rockers, their early albums included inspired covers and genre-faithful originals, all presented in Marshall stack, double-bass-drum bigness. Far more effective as a live act (with Koda's onstage banter influencing everyone from J. Geils' Peter Wolf to Alice Cooper), the group finally hit paydirt in late 1973 with their number-three hit, the Koda-penned "Smokin' in the Boys' Room." After disbanding the group in 1979, Koda went on to a career as a solo recording artist (see separate entry) and as a journalist for several music magazines. — *Stephen Thomas Erlewine*

No B.S. / 1970 / Warner Brothers ✦✦✦✦✦
Their debut album, featuring pedal-to-the-metal renditions of "Road Runner," "Rumble," and "Be Bop Confidential." — *Stephen Thomas Erlewine*

Brownsville Station [Palladium] / 1971 / Palladium ✦✦✦✦

A Night on the Town / 1972 / Big Tree ✦✦✦

Yeah! / 1973 / Big Tree ✦✦✦✦✦
With ten great songs, *Yeah!* is an album that lives up to its name—quite possibly the only fully realized LP the band ever made. Eight covers, all given the treatment, and two originals—one of which sold two million copies. *Yeah!* is the quintessential "nice little record"—it won't take up a lot of your time, and it's got a very friendly vibe to it. The cover songs span a wide variety of musical styles, which isn't that surprising, considering that guitarist/vocalist Cub Koda has a deep knowledge of music history. From Hoyt Axton's "Lightning Bar Blues" to then-unknown Jimmy Cliff's "Let Your Yeah Be Yeah" to Lou Reed's "Sweet Jane," the band pumps out all of its songs in a chugging, lighthearted manner that ends up being nothing but fun. Lead vocals were previously the exclusive domain of bassist Michael Lutz, but Koda emerges as a singer as well; Lutz may have been the more prototypical rock singer, but it was Koda's sleazy, nasal snarl that worked to perfection on the classic hit single "Smokin' In the Boys Room." While the success of "Smokin" opened a lot of doors for the band, it also pigeonholed them in such a way as to render them almost un-arrestable only a couple of years later. Between their wild onstage antics and the fact that the follow-up album, *School Punks*, was a blatant attempt at cashing in, the band lost a lot of the credibility they had earned by playing straightahead rock & roll. Although Brownsville Station would never again capture the magic here, *Yeah!* easily stands the test of time—it's truly delightful. — *Geoff Ginsberg*

School Punks / 1974 / Big Tree ✦✦✦

Motor City Connection / 1975 / Big Tree ✦✦

Brownsville Station [Private Stock] / 1977 / Private Stock ✦✦✦
Their next-to-last album, featuring the cult favorite "The Martian Boogie." — *Stephen Thomas Erlewine*

Air Special / 1980 / Epic ✦✦

● **Smoking in the Boys' Room: The Best of Brownsville Station** / Dec. 14, 1993 / Rhino ✦✦✦✦✦
A roaring romp through the Brownsville Station's back pages compiled by Cub Koda himself, *Smokin' in the Boys' Room* makes a convincing case that these Ann Arbor, Michigan garage punks were one of the most underrated rock & roll bands of the 1970s. — *Stephen Thomas Erlewine*

B.T. Express

f. 1973, Brooklyn, NY, **db.** 1981
Disco, Funk
This funk-disco group was formed by Jeff Lane in Brooklyn during the '70s. They started in 1972 as the King Davis House Rockers, and later were called the Brooklyn Trucking Express. The roster consisted of saxophonist/vocalist Bill Risbrook, percussionist Dennis Rowe, guitarist Rick Thompson, saxophonist/flutist Carlos Ward, keyboardist Michael Jones (Kashif), lead guitarist/vocalist Wesley Hall, drummer Leslie Ming, bassist, organist and vocalist Louis Risbrook, and vocalist Barbara Joyce Lomas. Their debut LP *Do it Till You're Satisfied* had two number one R&B and Top Ten pop hits in the title cut and "Express." Subsequent LPs yielded two more R&B Top Ten singles, "Give It What You Got/Peace Pipe" in 1975 and "Can't Stop Groovin' Now, Wanna Do It Some More" in 1976. After 1977's "Shout It Out," which cracked the R&B Top 20 (number 12), the group slumped with the album *Shout!* They were off the charts until 1980. They made a slight comeback that year with *B.T. Express 1980*, though only the single "Give Up the Funk (Let's Dance)" made it into the Top 30 (number 24). They later recorded for Record Shack, Earthtone, and King Davis, but couldn't duplicate their earlier success. Kashif scored hits as a producer, performer, and composer in the '80s. — *Ron Wynn*

● **The Best of B.T. Express** / May 27, 1997 / Rhino ✦✦✦
Although B.T. Express didn't have that many major radio hits, the New Yorkers' extremely danceable funk reigned supreme in the clubs (especially Black clubs). "Do It (Til You're Satisfied)," "Peace Pipe," "Shout It Out" and "Express" are among the handful of jams on

this engaging 15-song CD that were actually sizable hits on Black radio; most of the other songs, however, don't fit that description. But play this collection for anyone who deejayed in a Black club in the 1970s, and chances are they'll know most of the material. Express, a major influence on East Coast units like the Brass Construction and Mass Production, was very much a party band, and addictive album tracks like "This House Is Smokin'" and "Once You Get It" found their way to club turntables without ever coming out as singles. Although pleasant enough, a cover of Burt Bacharach & Hal David's "Close To You" shows that ballads were never the Express' strong point (which is truly ironic, given that one of its members, Kashif, would become known as a top R&B love man in the 1980s). And the 1980 recordings "Stretch" and "Does It Feel Good" are pretty generic, but on the whole, this disc is something funksters should savor. *—Alex Henderson*

Bubble Puppy

f. Austin, TX

Psychedelic

Though typically overshadowed by International Artists labelmates the 13th Floor Elevators, Bubble Puppy enjoyed arguably the greatest commercial success of all the Texas psychedelic bands, scoring a Top 20 pop hit with "Hot Smoke & Sasafrass." The roots of the group lie in the Corpus Christi-based Bad Seeds, a trio comprising singer/guitarist Rod Prince, bassist Roy Cox, and drummer Clayton Pulley (later replaced by David Fore); with the 1967 addition of guitarist Todd Potter, the foursome changed their name to Willowdale Handcar, finally settling on Bubble Puppy a year later. Their raw, garage-psych sound soon landed the group a deal with the famed Texas label International Artists, which issued Bubble Puppy's debut LP, *A Gathering of Promises*, in 1969; despite the runaway success of "Hot Smoke & Sasafrass," subsequent singles including "If I Had a Reason," "Days of Our Time," and "What Do You See?" stiffed, prompting the quartet to change its name to Demian. A self-titled effort followed in 1971 on ABC/Dunhill, but when the single "Face the Crowd" garnered little attention, the band dissolved. In 1977 Prince and Potter teamed under the name Sirius, recruiting bassist George Rarey and drummer Mark Evans to record 1979's *Sirius Rising*; in 1987, the original Bubble Puppy lineup reunited, drawing influence from the latter-day Texas rock of ZZ Top for their comeback LP, *Wheels Go Round*. Cox subsequently fronted the BluesKnights. *—Jason Ankeny*

A Gathering of Promises / 1969 / International Artist ♦♦♦

Unpretentious psychedelic punk from one of the more accessible bands hatched by Texas' International Artists label. The most striking aspect is the fast and fluid guitar work, closer in spirit to Bobby Fuller than some of the more solo-happy guitar gods of the day. "Hot Smoke and Sasafrass" was the surprise hit off the album, although most of the other songs continue in the same vein, with harmonies reminiscent of some of the better Haight-Ashbury bands. *—Peter Kurtz*

Roy Buchanan

b. Sep. 23, 1939, Ozark, AL, **d.** Aug. 14, 1988, Fairfax, VA

Vocals, Guitar / Blues-Rock, Modern Electric Blues

Buchanan's reputation as a hot-shot guitarist extends back to the beginnings of rock & roll itself. On the road and recording with Dale Hawkins by his teens, Buchanan became the law of the land around the Washington, D.C., area by the mid-to-late '60s. His use of the Fender Telecaster, using high harmonic squeals in place of feedback and distortion, was part and parcel of rock guitar's vocabulary by the early '70s. A reluctant superstar, Buchanan later became more unfocused as his career waned, but his unique stylings remain etched into his best records.

Sadly, when Buchanan seemed on the verge of a comeback in 1988, he hung himself in a police cell after he was arrested for public intoxication. He left behind a number of records which testify that he was a consummate guitarist, capable of tones and techniques that other guitarists only dream of. *—Cub Koda*

When a Guitar Plays the Blues / Jul. 1985 / Alligator ♦♦♦

Roy Buchanan was always one of the most respected guitarists in his field, ever since the '70s. However, he hit a rough patch in the early '80s, falling out of favor and finding record contracts hard to find. He made a startling comeback in 1985 with *When a Guitar Plays the Blues*, his first record for Alligator Records. Though the record still suffers the slightly antiseptic formula of Alligator Records, Buchanan shines throughout, making it clear why this brought him back to the spotlight in 1985. *—Stephen Thomas Erlewine*

● **Sweet Dreams: The Anthology** / Sep. 22, 1992 / Polydor/Chronicles ♦♦♦♦♦

Over two CDs, *Sweet Dreams* collects the finest moments from Buchanan's '70s albums, including nine unreleased tracks; as a career retrospective, it's the finest collection available. *—Stephen Thomas Erlewine*

Guitar on Fire: The Atlantic Sessions / Apr. 20, 1993 / Rhino ♦♦♦

Rhino's *Guitar on Fire: The Atlantic Sessions* is a terrific 16-track overview of Buchanan's Atlantic recordings, containing nearly all of the material he cut for the label. This may not capture Buchanan at his very best, but it's a near-peak, and anyone that wants to delve into this portion of his career is advised to pick this up. *—Stephen Thomas Erlewine*

Deluxe Edition / Jan. 30, 2001 / Alligator ♦♦♦♦♦

The third non-crossed licensed anthology from the master guitarist focuses on his three-album stint at Chicago's blues-based Alligator Records. The artist considered the music he made during his 1985-1987 association with the label the most honest of his career. Since he received complete creative control on these discs, his 1988 suicide, a short year after *Hot Wires*—one of Roy Buchanan's best albums ever—was released, makes his untimely death even more shocking. With its 16 tracks—two previously unreleased—almost evenly divided between instrumentals and (predominantly) guest vocals shared by Otis Clay, Delbert McClinton, and Johnny Sayles, this is not only a terrific overview of the musician's astounding guitar virtuosity, but a sad coda to a short yet intense career that never broke him through to a wide audience. With a completely unique guitar style that effortlessly shifted from a crying moan (as in the opening bars) to his cover of Otis Redding's "These Arms of Mine" to a raging howl Buchanan effectively covered all the blues-soul-rock bases with passion, integrity, and class. Although the guitarist's material was often subpar on his two previous labels, the music he recorded during these three years was top-notch, and consistently throbbed with his trademarked rugged, steely tone. There's none of the gospel and low-key country he often dipped into during his Polydor years, yet the essence of those genres is imbedded in his blues and R&B work here. This Alligator *Deluxe Edition* features rare photos, adequate track information, and a heartfelt remembrance penned by label boss Bruce Iglauer. At 61 minutes, only its playing time is questionable. Still, for those who need a concise compilation of Roy Buchanan's phenomenal skills with no filler, this handy disc fits the bill. *—Hal Horowitz*

Lindsey Buckingham

b. Oct. 3, 1948, Palo Alto, CA

Producer, Vocals, Guitar (Electric), Guitar / Pop/Rock

Before he joined Fleetwood Mac, Lindsey Buckingham was sketching out his brand of Brian Wilson-influenced pop with Stevie Nicks in the folky duo Buckingham Nicks. Mick Fleetwood invited the duo to join his band in late 1974. After Buckingham joined, the band's pop tendencies flowered under his direction. Not only did he provide the group with some brilliant, surprisingly dark pop songs, he sharpened the other members' songs with his production, arrangements, and breathtaking guitar playing. Buckingham left the band after their 1987 album, *Tango in the Night*, to concentrate on his solo work.

While Buckingham's solo albums are deceptively simple and calm on the surface, there are complex arrangements and emotions beneath the smooth production. None of them have sold anything approaching the level of *Rumours*—or even *Tango in the Night*—yet they are rich, layered pop albums; his first solo record, *Law & Order*, had a hit single with "Trouble." *—Stephen Thomas Erlewine*

Buckingham Nicks / 1973 / Polydor ♦♦♦

While it will be hard to find, this lone album cut by a young and ambitious (and still romantically attached) Stevie Nicks and Lindsey Buckingham a short two years before joining Fleetwood Mac is well worth digging out for your turntable. There are a few CD versions floating around, but they were no doubt burned from vinyl copies anyway, so don't be fooled. With the Mac's highly lucrative 1997 reunion there was serious talk of a re-release, but apparently it was just talk. Considering what the duo was to later accomplish, *Buckingham Nicks* is an engaging listen and served as a proving ground of sorts for both artists' songwriting chops and for Buckingham's skills as an emerging studio craftsman. It was a good enough resumé for Fleetwood Mac, who re-recorded the beautifully cerebral "Crystal" when the duo joined them for 1975's self-titled comeback album. The high-octane rockabilly of "Don't Let Me Down Again" became a staple of the band's concert sets well into the 1980s. Crisp, ringing acoustic guitars and a bottom-heavy rhythm section (using the talents of Waddy Watchel, Jim Keltner, and Jerry Scheff) framed the pair's songs in a sound something akin to FM-ready folk-rock. Lesser known tracks like the glistening opener, "Crying in the Night," from Nicks and Buckingham's lonely-guy lament, "Without a Leg to Stand On," are on a par with their later mega hits. At the same time, the misogyny of Buckingham's "Lola, My Love" is a real eye-roller and the orchestral overtones of "Frozen Love" show that the two were over reaching themselves just a bit. *Buckingham-Nicks* was a stiff however and the couple had lost their deal with Polydor. But 1975, of course, proved to be one of their better years. *—John Duffy*

Law and Order / Oct. 1981 / Asylum ♦♦♦♦♦

Lindsey Buckingham's talents as guitarist, arranger, and producer were particularly well suited to Fleetwood Mac, a band in which he was only one among three songwriters whose material complemented each other's. As a solo artist, Buckingham retains his strengths, but he encounters a form-over-substance problem. The seven songs he wrote for his debut album come across as sketches, musical pieces for which he has constructed interesting guitar riffs and the occasional sonic effect, plus a lyric tag—"Trouble," "That's How We Do It in L.A." But they have not been fleshed out into full-fledged songs, perhaps because Buckingham hasn't much interest in lyrics, or because he declines to use more than one or two of his ideas per tune. On the eclectic choice of covers ("September Song," "A Satisfied Mind"), Buckingham at least has fully composed and written pieces to work with, but he embalms them in his production techniques. As such, *Law and Order* comes off as a high-quality demo of largely unfinished material. [Nevertheless, "Trouble" became a Top Ten single.] *—William Ruhlmann*

Go Insane / Jul. 1984 / Warner ♦♦♦

Lindsey Buckingham's second album, like his first, *Law and Order*, was a triumph of studio wizardry over songwriting craft. Buckingham's work was ear-catching, but once he'd gotten your attention with some gimmicky sound effect or busy arrangement, he had very little to tell you. The exception was the album's most ambitious piece, the closing track, "D.W. Suite," on which Buckingham, always strongly influenced by the Beach Boys, took on what sounded like an elaborate tribute to Beach Boy Dennis Wilson, who died while the album was being made. The title track, which also had massed choral sounds (all made by Buckingham) reminiscent of a Fleetwood Mac track, became a Top 40 hit, but the album lacked the accessibility to make it more than a moderate seller, and at least at this point it appeared that Buckingham's solo albums were going to serve as laboratory experiments in which he tried out new musical ideas before bringing them to greater popular attention through Fleetwood Mac. *—William Ruhlmann*

- **Out of the Cradle** / Jun. 16, 1992 / Reprise ♦♦♦♦♦

Lindsey Buckingham quit Fleetwood Mac after the release of their *Tango in the Night* album in 1987 and spent the subsequent five years working on his first post-Mac solo album, *Out of the Cradle*. Perhaps because he was now focused on his solo career, Buckingham reined in the experimental style of his first two albums, producing more conventional, accessible material, much of it similar to his later work with Fleetwood Mac. The inventiveness this time was heard largely in Buckingham's electro-acoustic guitar style, which combined the power of a rock guitarist with the delicacy and precision of a classical nylon-string player. Perhaps the biggest difference from his previous solo work, however, was that Buckingham actually wrote a group of songs that were about something, not just riffs full of aural tricks. Unfortunately, Buckingham had never fully established himself in the public mind as a separate entity apart from Fleetwood Mac, so taking eight years between solo albums made *Out of the Cradle* a tough sell. Which means that, although this is his most listenable solo album, not many people heard it. *—William Ruhlmann*

The Buckinghams

f. 1966, Chicago, IL, **db.** 1970

Sunshine Pop, Pop

If everyone on the northwest side of Chicago who claims to have hung out with the Buckinghams during their heyday had faithfully bought all their releases, the rock group might have sold more records than the Beatles.

Popular attractions while still in high school, the quintet changed its name from the Pulsations to the Buckinghams to reflect the British Invasion craze and signed with Chicago's USA Records in 1966. Backing Dennis Tufano's buoyant lead vocals with prominent harmonies and punchy soul-styled brass, the group came across the wistful "Kind of a Drag," and in short order, the Buckinghams had a million-selling pop chart-topper on their hands. They quickly graduated to recording for Columbia.

As long as songwriter Jim Holvay supplied more material of the same high quality as "Kind of a Drag," the Buckinghams were sitting pretty. Holvay cowrote "Don't You Care," "Hey Baby (They're Playing Our Song)," and the pseudo-psychedelic "Susan," and they all proved to be major hits for the band. The group's R&B roots surfaced on a vocal adaptation of Cannonball Adderley's jazz standard "Mercy, Mercy, Mercy," their second-biggest hit.

But the Buckinghams' fortunes soon changed drastically—one of the top-selling rock groups of 1967, they managed only one hit after early 1968, and by 1970 the group was kaput. Two original members, guitarist Carl Giammarese and bassist Nick Fortuna, have since revived the Buckinghams for oldies tours. *—Bill Dahl*

- **Mercy, Mercy, Mercy** / Aug. 27, 1991 / Columbia ♦♦♦♦♦

Although they never had a hit album, the Buckinghams sold more records in 1967 than any American group other than the Monkees. This collection includes every Buckinghams song you'd want to hear, and more. The disc opens with "Kind of a Drag," the number one single in the U.S. in February '67. The band's other pop hits are here as well: "Don't You Care," "Hey Baby (They're Playing Our Song)," "Susan," and the group's vocal take on Cannonball Adderley's jazz classic, "Mercy, Mercy, Mercy," which reached number five in August. As 1967 ended, so did the band's string of hits. Except for the minor hit "Back in Love Again" from the spring of '68, the band disappeared into oblivion. However, *Mercy, Mercy, Mercy* includes other worthwhile tracks steeped in the happy production style of the hits. "Where Did You Come From" and "It's a Beautiful Day (For Lovin')" are pleasant, optimistic-sounding pop confections, while "Difference of Opinion" and "You" show the Buckinghams attempting to move beyond their singles-band image in their final recording sessions in 1969. *—Jim Newsom*

Jeff Buckley

b. Nov. 17, 1966, Orange County, CA, **d.** May 29, 1997

Vocals, Guitar, Organ / Adult Alternative Pop/Rock, Alternative Pop/Rock, Singer/Songwriter

Since he was the son of cult songwriter Tim Buckley, Jeff Buckley faced more expectations and pre-conceived notions than most singer/songwriters. Perhaps it wasn't surprising that Buckley's music was related to his father's by only the thinnest of margins. His voice was grand and sweeping, which fit with the mock-operatic grandeur of his Van Morrison-meets-Led Zeppelin music. Buckley first surfaced in Gods & Monsters with the experimental guitarist Gary Lucas; the band became a hip name, yet their life-span was short. Buckley began a solo career playing clubs and coffeehouses, building up a considerable following. Soon, he signed a record deal with Columbia Records, releasing the *Live at Sin-e* EP in November of 1993. It received good reviews, yet they didn't compare to the raves Buckley's full-length debut, 1994's *Grace*, received. A long hiatus followed as Buckley worked on material for his follow-up effort, provisionally titled *My Sweetheart, the Drunk*. He finally began work on the record in Memphis during the late spring of 1997; tragically, that May 29, he drowned in the Mississippi River. A collection of unreleased recordings, *Sketches (For My Sweetheart the Drunk)*, appeared in 1998. *—Stephen Thomas Erlewine*

Live at Sin-E [EP] / 1993 / Columbia ♦♦♦

Jeff Buckley resented being called a folk singer, but he made his name playing solo acoustic sets like this one on the New York coffee circuit. Sony released this live EP before his first fully produced rock album, *Grace*, perhaps to attract attention to the raw power of Buckley's greatest gift, his voice. These four songs certainly accomplished that end. Buckley hurdled seemingly unreachable octaves, suspends notes for what seems like minutes, and belted out his falsetto without a scintilla of restraint. That's a positive inasmuch as it allowed him to show off his considerable talent; it's a negative when it *sounded* like he was showing off. But his ten-minute cover of Van Morrison's "The Way Young Lovers Do" is a tour de force of strumming and scatting, and his acoustic "Eternal Life" has an electricity that is paradoxically lacking on the plugged-in album version. *—Darryl Cater*

- **Grace** / Aug. 23, 1994 / Columbia ♦♦♦♦♦

Jeff Buckley was many things, but humble wasn't one of them. *Grace* is an audacious debut album, filled with sweeping choruses, bombastic arrangements, searching lyrics and, above all, the richly textured voice of Buckley himself, which resembled a cross between Robert Plant, Van Morrison, and his father Tim. And that's a fair starting point for his music: *Grace* sounds like a Led Zeppelin album written by an ambitious folkie with a fondness for lounge jazz. At his best—the soaring title track, "Last Goodbye," and the mournful "Lover, You Should've Come Over"—Buckley's grasp met his reach with startling results; at its worst, *Grace* is merely promising. *—Stephen Thomas Erlewine*

Live from the Bataclan / 1996 / Columbia ♦♦

Sketches (For My Sweetheart the Drunk) / May 26, 1998 / Columbia ♦♦♦♦

Jeff Buckley was a mess of contradictions: a perfectionist who believed in spontaneity, a man who was at once humble and vain, a musician who shunned his father's tumultuous legacy while creating one of his own. These are some of the reasons why he took his time writing and recording the material for his second album, laboring over many songs for months at a time. Given such painstaking methods, it shouldn't have been a surprise that recording was an equally fastidious process. Buckley recorded enough material for an album with producer Tom Verlaine, but deciding that the results weren't quite right, he scrapped them and moved to Memphis to record the album again. He reworked a few songs as home demos as he prepared to cut the album, but it was never made—Buckley died in a tragic drowning accident before entering the studio. As a way to enlarge his legacy, his mother and record label rounded up the majority of the existing unreleased recordings, releasing them as the double-disc set *Sketches (For My Sweetheart the Drunk)*. Excepting a few awkward moments and middle-eights, it's hard to see why Buckley rejected the Verlaine productions that make up disc one. The material isn't necessarily a progression from *Grace*; it's more like a stripped-down, edgier take on the sweeping, jazz-tinged goth folk-rock that made the first album so distinctive. Neither the nearly finished first disc nor the homemade demos and re-recordings on the second disc offer any revelations, but that's not necessarily a disappointment. *Sketches* adds several wonderful songs to his catalog, offering further proof of his immense talent. And that, of course, is what makes the album as sad as it is exciting. *—Stephen Thomas Erlewine*

Mystery White Boy / May 9, 2000 / Columbia ♦♦♦

It's hard to judge Jeff Buckley's live collection *Mystery White Boy: Live '95-'96* without thinking of what might have been, without realizing that he never fulfilled the extent of his potential. If that sounds harsh, it's not meant to be—it's more of an acknowledgment of the tragedy of his premature death. After all, *Mystery White Boy* simply wouldn't exist if Buckley was alive when it was released in the spring of 2000. That wasn't the case with *Sketches for My Sweetheart the Drunk*, the first posthumous release of his unreleased recordings. Those tapes were the foundation of what would have become his second album; the tapes that formed *Mystery White Boy* were DAT recordings of his supporting tour for *Grace* (which the album was named after), many of which weren't intended for release at any time. Once Buckley unexpectedly passed away, they became a core part of his legacy, particularly because his concerts were notoriously unpredictable and thrilling, sometimes transcendent (at least according to partisan fans). *Mystery White Boy* doesn't quite convey that sense of majesty, largely due to the uneven sound quality and the fact that it's a compilation, thereby lacking the ebb and flow of a real live show. Buckley's mother Mary Guibert claims in the liner notes that the compilation worked better than any individual concert, and she may well be right, since the album has a consistency that a full concert may not have. Still, it's hard not to slightly miss the dramatic rhythm of a real show. Even so, *Mystery White Boy* is a valuable document, since it does prove that Buckley could transcend time and place with a live show. That might only be of interest to hardcore fans, but they'll still thrill to this, all the same. *—Stephen Thomas Erlewine*

Tim Buckley

b. Feb. 14, 1947, Washington, D.C., **d.** Jun. 29, 1975, Santa Monica, CA

Vocals, Guitar / Jazz-Rock, Folk-Jazz, Folk-Rock, Singer/Songwriter

One of the great rock vocalists of the 1960s, Tim Buckley drew from folk, psychedelic rock, and progressive jazz to create a considerable body of adventurous work in his brief lifetime. His multi-octave range was capable of not just astonishing power, but great emotional expressiveness, swooping from sorrowful tenderness to anguished wailing. His restless quest for new territory worked against him commercially: By the time his fans had hooked into his latest album, he was onto something else entirely, both live and in the studio. In this sense he recalled artists such as Miles Davis and David Bowie, who were so eager to look forward and change that they confused and even angered listeners who wanted more stylistic consistency. However, his eclecticism has also ensured a durable fascination with his work that has engendered a growing posthumous cult for his music, often with listeners who were too young (or not around) to appreciate his music while he was active. *—Richie Unterberger*

- **Tim Buckley** / 1966 / Asylum ♦♦♦♦♦

Buckley's 1966 debut was the most straightforward and folk-rock-oriented of his albums. The material has a lyrical and melodic sophistication that was astounding for a 19-year-old. The pretty, almost precious songs are complemented by appropriately baroque, psychedelic-tinged production. If there was a record that exemplified the '60s Elektra folk-rock sound, this may have been it, featuring production by Elektra owner Jac Holzman and Doors producer Paul Rothchild, Love and Doors engineer Bruce Botnick, and string arrangements by Jack Nitzsche. That's not to diminish the contributions of the band, which included his longtime lead guitarist Lee Underwood and Van Dyke Parks on keyboards. Buckley was still firmly in the singer-songwriter camp on this album, showing only brief flashes of the experimental vocal flights, angst-ridden lyrics, and soul influences that would characterize much of his later work. It's not his most adventurous outing, but it's one of his most accessible, and retains a fragile beauty. *—Richie Unterberger*

Goodbye & Hello / 1967 / Asylum ✦✦✦✦✦
Often cited as the ultimate Tim Buckley statement, *Goodbye and Hello* is indeed a fabulous album, but it's merely one side of Tim Buckley's enormous talent. Recorded in the middle of 1967 (in the afterglow of *Sgt. Pepper*), this album is clearly inspired by *Pepper's* exploratory spirit. More often than not, this helps to bring Buckley's awesome musical vision home, but occasionally falters. Not that the album is overrated (it's not), it's just that it is only one side of Buckley. The finest songs on the album were written by him alone, particularly "Once I Was" and "Pleasant Street." Buoyed by Jerry Yester's excellent production, these tracks are easily among the finest example of Buckley's psychedelic/folk vision. A few tracks, namely the title cut and "No Man Can Find the War," were co-written by poet Larry Beckett. While Beckett's lyrics are undoubtedly literate and evocative, they occasionally tend to be too heavy-handed for Buckley. However, this is a minor criticism of an excellent and revolutionary album that was a quantum leap for both Tim Buckley and the audience. *—Matthew Greenwald*

Dream Letter: Live in London / Jul. 1968 / Rhino/Bizarre ✦✦✦✦✦
This, like so many Enigma releases, was literally a dream project, and carries a lot of energy and love with it in the music and the performance. Recorded in London in 1968, when Buckley was just beginning to be really successful and had yet to move out of his folk-oriented phase. The band he's working with here is simple—Buckley's voice and fairly simple guitar; Lee Underwood providing subtle, almost jazz-like electric accompaniment; Pentangle's Danny Thompson sitting in on bass (with a minimum of rehearsal); and vibraphone player David Friedman. There's an assortment of songs from the three albums Buckley had released up to then, plus a couple that would turn up on later albums, and six songs that he never released in any form. This album, however, was released for the first time in 1989, and what you get is the complete concert—no cuts, no edits, no rearranging. It's difficult to believe that the tape was made in 1968—there's almost no noise, the music seems perfectly recorded, and the ambience is breathtaking. Buckley's voice is right up front, hovering over the acoustic guitar, clear as a bell. The instruments are carefully separated, clean, and glitch free. Musically, it's a spirited affair. Buckley is a beautiful singer, and had a broad selection of excellent, often breathtaking, songs. Even when the songs are a bit of a mish-mash, as happens with the unfortunately over-energetic "Who Do You Love" (one of the unreleased songs), you're caught by the vocal pyrotechnics he displays—he can be seductive, and he can be a shouter, and he's always very, very good. If you're at all interested in Buckley, or in various hybrids of folk music, then this album is a must. *—Steven McDonald*

Blue Afternoon / 1969 / Rhino/Bizarre ✦✦✦✦✦
On these alternately dark and romantic ballads with a brooding intensity, Buckley's fine vocal and acoustic guitar work is backed up capably by Lee Underwood (guitar, piano), David Friedman (vibes), John Miller (bass), and Jimmy Madison (drums). Songs include "Chase the Blues Away," "Cafe," "So Lonely," "Blue Melody," and "The Train." *—Roundup Newsletter*

Happy Sad / 1969 / Asylum ✦✦✦✦✦
Easily Tim Buckley's most underrated album, *Happy Sad* was another departure for the eclectic Southern California-based singer/songwriter. After the success of the widely acclaimed *Goodbye and Hello*, Buckley mellowed enough to explore his jazz roots. Sounding like Fred Neil's Capitol-era albums, Buckley and his small, acoustic-based ensemble weave elegant, minimalist tapestries around the six Buckley originals. The effect is completely mesmerizing. On "Buzzin' Fly" and "Strange Feelin'," you are slowly drawn into Buckley's intoxicating vision. The extended opus in the middle of the record, "Love from Room 109," is an intense, complex composition. Lovingly underproduced by Jerry Yester and Zal Yanovsky, this is one of the finest records of the late '60s. *—Matthew Greenwald*

Lorca / 1970 / Asylum ✦✦✦
Buckley stunned and, to a rare degree, alienated fans with the dissonant, at times wearying, avant-garde exercises in vocal gymnastics that took up the entire first side of this LP. Side two was far more accessible, though Buckley's fusion of folk instrumentation with jazzy improvisation on extended compositions continued to take him further away from his folk-rock roots. *—Richie Unterberger*

Starsailor / 1970 / Rhino/Bizarre ✦✦✦✦✦
After his beginnings as a gentle, melodic baroque folk-rocker, Buckley gradually evolved into a downright experimental singer/songwriter who explored both jazz and avant-garde territory. *Starsailor* is the culmination of his experimentation and alienated far more listeners than it exhilarated upon its release in 1970. Buckley had already begun to delve into jazz fusion on late-'60s records like *Happy Sad*, and explored some fairly "out" acrobatic, quasi-operatic vocals on his final Elektra LP, *Lorca*. With former Mother of Invention Bunk Gardner augmenting Buckley's group on sax and alto flute, Buckley applies vocal gymnastics to a set of material that's as avant-garde in its songwriting as its execution. At his most anguished (which is often on this album), he sounds as if his liver is being torn out—slowly. Almost as if to prove he can still deliver a mellow buzz, he throws in a couple of pleasant jazz-pop cuts, including the odd, jaunty French tune "Moulin Rouge." Surrealistic lyrics, heavy on landscape imagery like rivers, skies, suns, and jungle fires, top off a record that isn't for everybody, or even for every Buckley fan, but endures as one of the most uncompromising statements ever made by a singer/songwriter. *—Richie Unterberger*

Greetings from L.A. / 1972 / Rhino/Bizarre ✦✦✦✦
Stepping back from the swooping avant-garde touches of *Starsailor* for a fairly greasy, funky, honky tonk set of songs, the opening lines of *Greetings from L.A.* set the tone: "I went down to the meat rack tavern/And I found myself a big ol' healthy girl." Sassy backing vocalists, honking sax, and more add to the atmosphere, while Tim Buckley himself blends his vocal acrobatics with touches not unfamiliar to fans of Mick Jagger or Jim Morrison. The studio band backing him up might not be the equal to, say, War, but in their own way they do the business; extra touches like the string arrangement on "Sweet Surrender" help all the more. The argument that this was all somehow a compromise or sellout doesn't seem to entirely wash. While no doubt there were commercial pressures at play, given Buckley's constant change from album to album it seems like he simply found something else to try, which he did with gusto. "Get On Top," one of his best numbers, certainly doesn't sound like something aimed for the charts. The music may have a solid groove to it (Kevin Kelly's organ is worth a mention), but Buckley's frank lyrics and improv scatting both show it as him following his own muse. *—Ned Raggett*

Sefronia / 1973 / Manifesto ✦✦

Look at the Fool / 1974 / Manifesto ✦

Peel Sessions / Jul. 1, 1991 / Strange Fruit ✦✦

Live at the Troubadour 1969 / Mar. 22, 1994 / Rhino/Bizarre ✦✦✦
A previously unreleased, recently unearthed recording that catches Buckley at the time he began to incorporate jazz-influenced vocal improvisation and dense, impressionistic lyrics into his recordings. Backed by a small combo, it features loose numbers with blood-curdling vocal scatting and instrumental jamming. The nine tracks on this 78-minute disc are mostly drawn from his *Lorca* and *Blue Afternoon* albums and include two previously unavailable songs. *—Richie Unterberger*

Honeyman / Nov. 1995 / Manifesto ✦✦✦
A previously unreleased live 1973 radio broadcast, in excellent sound, that offers a valuable supplement to Buckley's often disappointing final albums. Buckley's last LPs were marred by unsympathetic L.A. production, and this presents the material with much sparser, focused, and appropriate arrangements. As the songs originate mostly from the *Sefronia* and *Greetings from L.A.* records (although a couple of songs from the '60s do appear), this couldn't be placed among his best work, or even among his best live albums (*Dream Letter* and *Troubadour 1969* are both considerably better). Buckley's vocals are great, though, and if the tunes are sometimes too funky for their own good, this is generally good stuff, especially his riveting interpretation of Fred Neil's "Dolphins," which is probably worth the price of admission alone for Buckley fans. *—Richie Unterberger*

Works in Progress / 1999 / Rhino Handmade ✦✦✦
Previously unreleased 1968 sessions (with the exception of an instrumental track from 1967) that, for the most part, are a missing link between his second and third albums, *Goodbye and Hello* and *Happy Sad*. The process through which *Happy Sad* evolved was not a smooth one, entailing a few tracks in New York in March 1968 and more unused sessions in the summer of 1968 in L.A., producing a good deal of material that lay in vaults until it was accidentally discovered in the 1990s. The four tracks from the New York sessions are a bit demo-ish, featuring just Buckley and his acoustic guitar, Lee Underwood's electric guitar, and an unidentified acoustic bassist (probably Jimmy Bond). Nevertheless, these have a lovely sincerity, particularly the lilting "Danang," which would later form a part of "Love From Room 109 at the Islander" on *Happy Sad*. There were also different takes of *Happy Sad*'s "Sing a Song for You" and "Buzzin' Fly," and a sparse version of "Song to the Siren," recorded in a more strained, elaborate manner on *Starsailor*. On most of the L.A. tracks, Buckley is joined by the *Happy Sad* band on a mixture of alternate versions and songs that would surface on post-*Happy Sad* releases. With most of the other alternates, the feel is somewhat more tentative than on the versions listeners are used to. It's interesting to hear the two unfinished tunes titled "Ashbury Park Version 2," which would be the foundation of the first movement of "Love From Room 109 at the Islander," especially as some of them are graced by delicate harp that didn't get used in the final arrangement. This complex assortment of material, it must be noted, is not collector ephemera: it's gorgeously melodic music that is both historically important and emotionally powerful on its own terms. *—Richie Unterberger*

Once I Was / 1999 / Varese ✦✦✦
All but one of these eight songs from 1968 and 1974 are from the BBC. Five of the tracks were recorded in April 1968 for the John Peel show, and previously released by Strange Fruit as the *Peel Sessions* CD. These feature Tim Buckley at his most melodic and intimate. As on his posthumously issued 1968 concert recording *Dream Letter*, the instrumentation is sparser than on his Elektra albums. On these sessions, he was backed only by long-time guitarist Lee Underwood and percussionist Carter Collins. This quintet of tunes features songs from his second and third albums, as well as a couple of cuts that didn't make it onto records in the '60s, highlighted by a ten-minute medley of "Hallucinations" and "Troubadour." There are also a couple of less vital cuts—"Dolphins" and "Honey Man"—from a May 1974 broadcast. Ending the disc is a previously unreleased, live 12-minute version of "I Don't Need It to Rain," recorded in Copenhagen in October 1968 with Underwood on guitar, Nils Henning on double bass, and David Friedman on vibes. It's a reasonable, jazzy number in sync with the mood of *Blue Afternoon* and *Dream Letter*, but the fidelity, from a tape "found in a box of disintegrating reel-to-reels at Tim's home," is muffled; a higher-energy and higher-fi version is on *Live at the Troubadour 1969*. *—Richie Unterberger*

Morning Glory: The Tim Buckley Anthology / Mar. 20, 2001 / Rhino ✦✦✦✦
Buckley whizzed through a bunch of different styles in his approximately decade-long career, and was always an album-oriented artist. That makes the assembly of a best-of col-

lection a difficult task to fulfill without omitting much of the context of what made the singer special. Still, *Morning Glory* does a pretty good job of touching upon highlights of his work, aided by the generous running time, with two CDs and 33 songs that add up to about two-and-a-half hours of music. It does concentrate on his most accessible tunes, drawing most heavily from his earliest albums and shorter songs, pitching in four tracks from late-'60s live recordings that were not released until long after his death. There is nothing at all, in fact, from his least commercial effort, 1970's *Lorca* (although "I Had a Talk With My Woman" is identified as coming from *Lorca* in the track list, it in fact is taken from *Live at the Troubadour 1969*). As is proper, his final albums, in which both his material and voice were in decline, are lightly represented. There's just one previously unreleased track, though it's a goodie: the legendary solo version of "Song to the Siren" that Buckley performed on an episode of *The Monkees*, with a much sparer arrangement than was used when it was included on 1970's *Starsailor*, as well as a different lyric. *—Richie Unterberger*

The Dream Belongs to Me: Rarities & Unreleased 1968-1973 / May 8, 2001 / Manifesto ♦♦♦♦

The folks at Manifesto have done an excellent job in keeping the music of Tim Buckley on the market over the past ten years, even going so far as to release three highly revealing new discs of live recordings. Nicely bookending Buckley's most productive years, *The Dream Belongs to Me* continued that streak. Split between two 1968 demo sessions and a similar tracking date from 1973, the music contained illustrates that quite a lot had happened to Buckley in the intervening years, both personally and musically. Included from the March and June 1968 tapes, previously released on an Internet-only offer, are working versions (and arguably better in some respects) of "Song to the Siren," "Buzzin' Fly," and the superior "Sing a Song for You," tunes that would see official release in much more developed form on mid-period Buckley albums like *Happy Sad*, *Starsailor*, and *Blue Afternoon*. From February 1973 came tunes of a much different pedigree. Gone was much of the wistful folksiness that marked Buckley's early tunes and the jazzy experimentation of his mid-career records, replaced by obviously concerted effort to make more commercial music. Working versions of four songs from the album *Sefronia* are augmented by never-before-heard tunes "Falling Timber" and "The Dream Belongs to Me." While these tunes are interesting enough (even with a wildly phased guitar effect that gets a tad annoying), it is depressing to hear Buckley forcing himself to resolve the eclectic exploration he wished to continue with the pop-oriented material his record company was strong-arming him into doing at the time. The fact that his final album was titled *Look at the Fool* (self-directed no doubt) speaks volumes. *—John Duffy*

Richard Buckner

b. 1967

Vocals, Guitar / Americana, Alternative Country, Country-Folk, Singer/Songwriter

A husky-voiced country/folk singer-songwriter very much in the mold of the Lubbock, TX school of mavericks, including Butch Hancock, Terry Allen, and Jimmie Dale Gilmore. Richard Buckner is actually based in San Francisco, but the Lubbock connection is no accident. His debut album *Bloomed* was recorded in Lubbock, for one thing, with producer Lloyd Maines, who has also worked with Hancock, Allen, Joe Ely, and Uncle Tupelo. Buckner's principal following, however, is not with the country audience, but the alternative rock one. Like Allen and Hancock, the guitarist's work is based in rootsy country traditions, but his lyrics are far too personal and ambitious for those who think of country music as virtually synonymous with Nashville. So, like those Lubbock musicians, he tends to appeal to open-minded rock fans, or adventurous general music fans, more than country ones. Appearing on a small Texas independent label, his album won good critical notices, and his signing to a major company for 1997's acclaimed *Devotion + Doubt* probably means that both rock and country listeners will be much more widely exposed to him in the future. *Since* followed in 1998 and *The Hill*, an interpretation of Edgar Lee Masters' *Spoon River Anthology*, was issued two years later. *—Richie Unterberger*

Bloomed / 1994 / Dejadics ♦♦♦

Buckner's debut is an accomplished but subdued affair with hardly a trace of rock in sight. The emphasis is on his rich-but-weary vocals and sober tales of romance and restlessness, with dignified Texas prairie backup by such esteemed regionals as Lloyd Maines (who produced) and Ponty Bon. Very much in the vein of Butch Hancock, but much more ordinary at this point, without the eccentricity and boisterousness that characterizes much of Hancock and fellow Lubbockite Terry Allen's work. [The 1999 reissue of *Bloomed* contains five previously unreleased bonus tracks.] *–Richie Unterberger*

● **Devotion + Doubt** / Mar. 11, 1997 / MCA ♦♦♦♦

Buckner's second album of cross-country folk is an exploration of love's paranoia and its resulting desperation and hopelessness. Stemming from the singer-songwriter's divorce, the 13 songs on *Devotion + Doubt* reflect and, to a lesser degree, celebrate both his newfound independence and loneliness. His road-weary voice (often calmed to a whisper here), coupled with the sparing strums of his acoustic guitar, strikes a point of intimacy within the songs, giving the best of them ("Pull," "4am") the feeling that they were reluctantly cribbed from personal diary entries. But Buckner never sounds defeated on *Devotion + Doubt*, only a bit haunted, as if he's convinced himself—based on past attempts at love and their eventual failures—that he's destined to make the same mistakes again and again, no matter how hard he tries to make the relationships work. *—Michael Gallucci*

Since / Aug. 11, 1998 / MCA ♦♦♦

Richard Buckner's follow-up to his 1997 divorce odyssey *Devotion + Doubt* is a more upbeat affair, with questions of faith and being tossed into the electric mix. Moving from contemplative singer-songwriter treks ("Once") to blurry guitar rave-ups ("Believer"), *Since* is the picking-up-and-getting-on antidote to *Devotion + Doubt's* downer trip. Buckner still seems troubled by life's little hang-ups, but instead of falling into an acoustic-drenched funk, he rages against his blues with his guitar. That doesn't mean *Since* isn't without its distressing moments; there are plenty of hushed and fragile songs here that recall the breaking tone of his previous two albums. Yet, for all of the creeping positivity going on within the grooves, Buckner sounds more weary than ever, his already delicate voice cracking under the pressure as he trudges his way through his own brand of electric folk music. *—Michael Gallucci*

The Hill / Oct. 3, 2000 / Overcoat ♦♦♦

Edgar Lee Masters' *Spoon River Anthology*, a series of poems originally published in serial form in 1914-1915, provided the subject matter for nomadic troubadour Richard Buckner's 2000 release *The Hill*. In the poems, the dead in an Illinois graveyard relay details from their lives in matter-of-factly haunting tones. When originally published, Masters' believable characters tore away at the strict moral facade of small-town life through their tales of adultery, casual murder, and morphine addiction. Who better than Buckner to interpret these lost souls' voices in his growling, plaintive murmur, accompanied most often by sparse acoustic guitar and stark accompaniment. Through this earthy channeler, the names from ragged gravestones almost float in front of the listener while hollowed eyes reveal the details of their own deaths.

Unfortunately, while the subject matter and the musician are an ideal match, the album as a whole falls short of Buckner's famous heartfelt intimacy and inventive songwriting. Fans who have come to appreciate his snapshot imagery and dark wordplay may be disappointed at this interpretation of someone else's work, as appropriate as it may be. The 18 individual poems are recorded as one continuous 34-minute track, making it difficult to tell when one woman's childbirth death travels into another man's drunken despair, and the warm acoustic guitar, mandolin, and violin are on occasion jarringly interrupted by misplaced electronic sweeps and buzzes. Still, the haunting charm of "Oscar Hummel" and "Emily Sparks" show the familiar passion and honesty the singer is known for. Buckner continues to distance himself from the limiting country-folk label with increasingly ambitious projects, all of which are interesting but some of which fail to fully utilize his talents. *—Zac Johnson*

Buffalo Daughter

Shibuya-Kei, Indie Rock, Alternative Pop/Rock

Japanese sonic collagists Buffalo Daughter formed in 1993, comprising vocalists/multi-instrumentalists SuGar Yoshinaga and Yumiko Ohno along with turntablist Moog Yamamoto. Cutting-and-pasting sounds ranging from funk to lounge-pop to avant-noise, the trio debuted the following year with the LP *Shaggy Headdressers*, followed in 1995 by *Amoeba Soundsystem*; with the 1996 seven-inch *Legend of the Yellow Buffalo*, they made their American debut, signing to Grand Royal. The full-length *Captain Vapour Athletes* followed later that same year, and in 1997 Grand Royal issued *Socks, Drugs & Rock & Roll*, a collection of material remixed by the likes of Alec Empire, Money Mark and U.N.K.L.E. Buffalo Daughter returned in 1998 with *New Rock*, and another remix collection, *WXBD*, appeared a year later. *—Jason Ankeny*

Captain Vapour Athletes / Aug. 26, 1996 / Grand Royal ♦♦♦♦

The Japanese trio Buffalo Daughter spent their early career contributing to everything from commericals to video games and soundtracks overseas. Their American debut honors that cut-and-paste past with a combination of songs from two earlier EPs and new tracks that display their mobile mentality. Daughter manages to blend abrupt breakbeat snippets, rough guitar work, sugary synth-pop and lazy-day harmonies, often seconds apart in the same song. While their dependence on complex samples and retro electronics helps add a certain edge, some of the best moments on *Captain Vapour Athletes* come from the simple, shy and naked harmonies of Yumiko Ohno. Buffalo Daughter's desire to get experimental can stop a song dead in its tracks, like the dreary techno of "Baby Amoebae Goes South" or "Vapour Action Forever." But when all elements click, like the new wave robotics of "Cold Summer" or the sublimely droning 10-minute epic "LI303VE," a near-rhapsody of downtown funk and scratching, they prove themselves to be one of the more innovative and adventurous indie rock imports operating today. *—Jason Kaufman*

● **New Rock** / Mar. 10, 1998 / Grand Royal ♦♦♦♦

Buffalo Daughter's 1998 album, *New Rock*, finds the group balancing their talents for sample-friendly pastiche pop with a simpler, more direct sound. The title track introduces this concept, opening the album with a straightforward guitar-and-drum foundation topped with spacy, distorted vocals. "Super Blooper," "Sky High" and the lovely "Jellyfish Blues" continue the trend, pairing stripped-down, guitar-prominent arrangements with the group's innovative production techniques. But Buffalo Daughter's too-much-is-never-enough sonic approach resurfaces on songs like "Rhythm and Basement," "Great Five Lakes" and "Autobacs," which feature the funky synths and samples the group is so fond of, and sound collages like "No Tokyo" and "Airport Rock" showcase BD's kitchen sink recording style. With as much simple as there is sample, *New Rock* shows progression and restraint. *—Heather Phares*

Great Five Lakes / 1999 / Cardinal ♦♦♦

Japan's Buffalo Daughter has had fun at our happy expense since 1993, seeping into our delicate collective consciousness with Listerine commercials, video games, soundtracks and film scores, CD ROMs and other alternative musical techno media. Two previous BD albums on Japan's Cardinal Records, *Shaggy Headdressers* and *Amoeba Soundsystem* (released in '94 and '95, respectively), heralded the band's emergence as something other than an attitudinal gaggle of oddballs, although the music that SuGar, Yumiko and Moog make is still a far cry from what we have come to expect from a traditional "band." The title track on *New Rock* demonstrates their movie-music influence with the air of a credits sequence, revisited with "Super Blooper" later on down the disc. "Rhythm and Basement" reintroduces a funky balance of electronic and simpler sounds reminiscent of their previous *Captain Velour Athletes* projects. The breezy "Great Five Five Lakes" reassures you that the kids will be all right only until the album blossoms into its realized strange self with "Socks, Drugs, and Rock N Roll," "No New Rock," and "Autobacs." The Daughters have been accurately—and favorably—compared to the Slits, the Flying Lizards, Kraftwerk and even a riff or two as hardwired into all our heads from the Beatles transcendental *White Album*, which is all good news for the weird BD and their happy, weirder-yet fans. *—Becky Byrkit*

Buffalo Springfield

f. 1966, Los Angeles, CA, **db.** 1968
Folk-Rock, Country-Rock, Rock & Roll

Apart from the Byrds, no other American band had as great an impact on folk-rock and country-rock—really, the entire Californian rock sound—than Buffalo Springfield. The group's formation is the stuff of legend: driving on Sunset Boulevard in Los Angeles, Stephen Stills and Richie Furay spotted a hearse that Stills was sure belonged to Neil Young, a Canadian he had crossed paths with earlier. Indeed it was, and with the addition of fellow hearse passenger and Canadian Bruce Palmer on bass and ex-Dillard Dewey Martin on drums, the cluster of ex-folkies determined, as the Byrds had just done, to become a rock & roll band. Buffalo Springfield wasn't together long—they were an active outfit for just under two years, between 1967 and 1968 —but every one of their three albums was noteworthy. Their debut, including their sole big hit (Stills' "For What It's Worth"), established them as the best folk-rock band in the land barring the Byrds, though the Springfield were a bit more folk and country oriented. *Again*, their second album found the group expanding their folk-rock base into tough hard rock and psychedelic orchestration, resulting in their best record. Not long after *Again*, the group began to splinter, calling it a day in 1968 but leaving behind a rich, influential body of work. *—Richie Unterberger & Stephen Thomas Erlewine*

Buffalo Springfield / 1967 / Atco ♦♦♦♦
The band themselves were displeased with this record, feeling that the production did not capture their onstage energy and excitement. Yet to most ears, this debut sounds pretty great, featuring some of their most melodic and accomplished songwriting and harmonies, delivered with a hard-rocking punch. "For What It's Worth" was the hit single, but there are several other equally stunning treasures. Stills' "Go and Say Goodbye" was a pioneering country-rock fusion; his "Sit Down I Think I Love You" was the band at their poppiest and most early Beatlesque; and his "Everybody's Wrong" and "Pay the Price" were tough rockers. Although Neil Young has only two lead vocals on the record (Richie Furay sang three other Young compositions), he's already a songwriter of great talent and enigmatic lyricism, particularly on "Nowadays Clancy Can't Even Sing," "Out of My Mind," and "Flying on the Ground is Wrong." The entire album bursts with thrilling guitar and vocal interplay, with a bright exuberance that would tone down considerably by their second record. A 1997 CD reissue presents both mono and stereo mixes of the album, and includes "Baby Don't Scold Me" (which was on the first pressing of the record, but soon replaced by "For What It's Worth"). *—Richie Unterberger*

☆ **Buffalo Springfield Again** / 1967 / Atco ♦♦♦♦♦
Due in part to personnel problems which saw Bruce Palmer and Neil Young in and out of the group, Buffalo Springfield's second album did not have as unified an approach as their debut. Yet it doesn't suffer for that in the least—indeed, the group continued to make major strides in both their songwriting and arranging, and this record stands as their greatest triumph. Stills' "Bluebird" and "Rock & Roll Woman" were masterful folk-rockers that should have been big hits (although they did manage to become small ones); his lesser-known contributions "Hung Upside Down" and the jazz-flavored "Everdays" were also first-rate. Young contributed the Rolling Stones-derived "Mr. Soul," as well as the brilliant "Expecting to Fly" and "Broken Arrow," both of which employed lush psychedelic textures and brooding, surrealistic lyrics that stretched rock conventions to their breaking point. Furay (who had not written any of the songs on the debut) takes tentative songwriting steps with three compositions, although only "A Child's Claim to Fame," with its memorable dobro hooks by James Burton, meets the standards of the material by Stills and Young; the cut also anticipates the country-rock direction of Furay's post-Springfield band, Poco. Although a slightly uneven record that did not feature the entire band on several cuts, the high points were so high and plentiful that its classic status cannot be denied. *—Richie Unterberger*

Last Time Around / 1968 / Atco ♦♦♦
The internal dissension that was already eating away at the group's dynamic on their second album came home to roost on their third and final effort. This was in some sense a Buffalo Springfield album in name but not in spirit, as the songwriters sometimes did not even play on cuts written by other members of the band. Young's relatively slight contribution was a particularly tough blow. He wrote only two of the songs (though he did help Furay write "It's So Hard to Wait"), both of which were outstanding: the plaintive "I Am a Child" and the bittersweet "On the Way Home" (sung by Furay, not Young, on the record). The rest of the ride was bumpier: Stills' material in particular was not as strong as it had been on the first two LPs, though the lovely Latin-flavored "Pretty Girl Why," with its gorgeous guitar work, is one of the group's best songs. Furay was developing into a quality songwriter with the orchestrated "The Hour of Not Quite Rain" and his best Springfield contribution, the beautiful ballad "Kind Woman," which became one of the first country-rock standards. But it was a case of not enough, too late, not only for Furay, but for the group as a whole. *—Richie Unterberger*

★ **The Best of Buffalo Springfield . . . Retrospective** / 1969 / Atco ♦♦♦♦♦
Best of Buffalo Springfield . . . Retrospective may not be definitive, but it's a good, basic overview of the group's career, containing most of the group's biggest hits and signature songs. Yes, several worthy album cuts are missing, but as a sampler, this works quite well, offering a nice introduction to the group. *—Stephen Thomas Erlewine*

Box Set / Jul. 17, 2001 / Rhino ♦♦♦♦♦
The plainly named *Box Set*—that's the actual title—contains four CDs by a band that made only three albums in its brief lifetime. It goes without saying that this has a lot of great music, and is an essential purchase for fans of this phenomenal 1960s folk-rock-psychedelic band, containing no less than 36 previously unreleased demos, outtakes, and previously unissued mixes. It's the unreleased stuff that holds the most interest, especially since even on their outtakes, Buffalo Springfield were often superb. The sound is very good, and on the rarities, notably superior to bootlegs (such as the famous *Stampede*) on which some of the songs have previously surfaced. The 82-page booklet, primarily comprised of vintage clippings, is nice too. At the same time, this box—which, other than the last disc, sequences the material in the chronological order it was recorded—is not all it could have been. First of all, for some reason, this does *not* have everything the band ever released. Secondly, first-rate songs from *Last Time Around* are represented by different demos and remixes, though it would have been easily possible to include the official final versions too. Worst of all, disc four is comprised solely of all the material from the group's brilliant first two albums—which would not be cause for criticism, except that identical versions of every one of them (except for "Mr. Soul" and "Baby Don't Scold Me") also appear at some point in the course of the preceding three discs. This could have been one of the greatest rock box sets of all time, if only a saner approach to presenting the band's complete official albums, and more rarities, in one place had been employed. *—Richie Unterberger*

Buffalo Tom

f. 1986, Boston, MA
Adult Alternative Pop/Rock, Alternative Pop/Rock

When they released their first album in 1989, the Boston-based trio Buffalo Tom was written off as Dinosaur Jr. junior. Admittedly, their debut was in debt to J Mascis' thundering guitar and folk-tinged songs and it didn't help that Mascis produced the record, either. Over time, Buffalo Tom stripped away their grungier influences and developed into a straight-ahead rock group of the early '90s, capable of throttling rockers and beautiful ballads.

Comprised of guitarist/vocalist Bill Janovitz, bassist/vocalist Chris Colbourn, and drummer Tom Maginnis, Buffalo Tom began to develop their own style with their second album, 1990's *Birdbrain*, which featured a noticeable improvement in songwriting. In 1992, Buffalo Tom released *Let Me Come Over*, a gritty set of driving rock and achingly melancholy ballads; several of its tracks became alternative radio staples, including the gorgeous ballad "Taillights Fade." Despite an increased amount of critical praise and some radio airplay, the album didn't sell. The follow-up, 1993's *Big Red Letter Day*, featured a more polished, radio-ready production, but the album received only a small push from radio and MTV. "Soda Jerk," the first single from the album, became a minor alternative radio and MTV hit. After a year-long tour, the group returned in the summer of 1995 with *Sleepy Eyed*, a return to the more direct sound of *Let Me Come Over*. *Smitten* followed in 1998, and two years later the best-of, *Asides From Buffalo Tom*, arrived. *—Stephen Thomas Erlewine*

Buffalo Tom / 1989 / Beggars Banquet ♦♦♦
All these years later, it's hard to blame anyone for calling Buffalo Tom "Dinosaur Jr." after their self-titled debut album was released; even if J. Mascis hadn't produced the sessions (and played lead guitar on one track), the band's approach at this point—big sludgy neo-grunge guitar mauling, with a busy rhythm section bashing away behind it all trying to keep up—was similar enough to what Mascis and company were serving up at the time that comparison was inevitable. But from the jump, it was obvious that Bill Janovitz was a stronger and more emphatic vocalist than Mascis ever was, and if he still had a lot to learn as a songwriter, "Sunflower Suit" and "Impossible" offered evidence that Janovitz had a knack for crafting hooky melodies that were clearly visible under the sheets of noisy guitar (which he could mangle nearly as well as Mascis himself). Some bands offer up everything they have on their first album, and some bands just get started; *Buffalo Tom* indicates that this band was clearly in the latter category, but if they had a way to go in the originality sweepstakes, there was no arguing they had plenty of talent and potential. *—Mark Deming*

Birdbrain / Nov. 1990 / Beggars Banquet ♦♦♦
From the first notes of Buffalo Tom's second album, *Birdbrain*, it was clear the band had done more than their share of growing up since their self-titled debut which had come out the year before. The title cut leaps out of the gate with a tight snap that leaves anything on the first album in the dust; drummer Tom Maginnis and bassist Chris Colbourn sound far tighter and more unified as a rhythm section, and guitarist and vocalist Bill Janovitz reveals a taut, slashing authority that was quite a change from the sloppy, sometimes meandering sound he'd summoned up his first time at bat. Just as roadwork had firmed up Buffalo Tom's sound, their songwriting was also steadily improving; the ultra-catchy "Birdbrain" sounded like it could have been a hit single in some alternate universe, while "Guy Who Is Me" and "Crawl" indicated they were learning to work better with trickier structures, and "Enemy" and "Skeleton Key" prove they could slow down effectively and communicate something other than a rant. While the band were still working the last vestiges of their clear Dinosaur Jr. influence at this point (J. Mascis was in the producer's chair once again for this set), *Birdbrain* made it clear Buffalo Tom were far more than just Dino Jr.'s little brother band. The CD adds a nice acoustic cover of

"Heaven" by The Psychedelic Furs as a bonus—yet another touch you would never have expected judging from their debut. *—Mark Deming*

Let Me Come Over / Mar. 10, 1992 / Beggars Banquet ♦♦♦♦♦
While *Birdbrain* was a marked improvement over Buffalo Tom's self-titled debut album, *Let Me Come Over* was truly the great leap forward for the band, sounding richer, more imaginative, and more emotionally powerful than anything they'd attempted in the past. Guitarist Bill Janovitz, bassist Chris Colbourn and drummer Tom Maginnis individually displayed a greater command of their respective instruments, and collectively their interplay was certainly more confident and intricate, having traded in the muddy clamor of their first recordings for a more layered sound (complete with overdubbed acoustic guitars) that was clean, vibrant and compelling. (Producers Paul Kolderie and Sean Slade certainly helped, bringing a clearer and better focused sound to these sessions than J. Mascis drew from the band.) And while Buffalo Tom were shouting less on *Let Me Come Over*, they seemed to have a lot more to say; there's a heart and soul to the lovelorn "Taillights Fade" and the yearning "Velvet Roof" that digs a good bit deeper than their previous work (and is also a lot easier to sort through), while even hard rockers such as "Stymied" and "Saving Grace" reflect a new maturity and seriousness of purpose. In fact, if *Let Me Come Over* has a flaw, it's that Buffalo Tom seem to display a bit less *joie de vivre* than one might have expected, though after gaining this much in the way of both skills and smarts, you can't blame them for wanting to show them off a bit. *—Mark Deming*

Big Red Letter Day / Nov. 2, 1993 / Beggars Banquet ♦♦♦♦
Buffalo Tom proved that their palate was a lot broader and their reach a lot farther than anyone might have expected on *Let Me Come Over*, and while the following year's *Big Red Letter Day* didn't show the same sort of growth, it also proved the band hadn't forgotten any of their tricks along the way. *Big Red Letter Day* sounds a bit poppier than it's immediate predecessor, though that seems largely a function of the production by the Robb Brothers, which features a bit more body and a significant amount more gloss than the leaner, cleaner tone of *Let Me Come Over*, and to these ears the strong, infectious melodies of the songs (and the tight ensemble playing by the group) hold up well to such treatment. And while the palpable angst of *Let Me Come Over* was obviously sincere but a wee bit samey by the end of that album, *Big Red Letter Day* cuts back on the rueful self-examination just a bit, and the hopefulness of "Dry Land" and "Anything That Way" was a welcome touch from a band that often had a hard time embracing their happiness. Unlike their last two albums, *Big Red Letter Day* didn't display much in the way of unexpected new sides to Buffalo Tom—it just found them doing what they do very well indeed, and anyone who loves the band will enjoy this record. *—Mark Deming*

Sleepy Eyed / Jul. 11, 1995 / East West ♦♦♦
Put *Sleepy Eyed* in your CD player, hit play, and prepare to be amazed—"Tangerine," the lead-off cut, signals the brief but welcome return of "Dinosaur Jr." with two-and-three-quarters minutes of charging neo-grunge guitars and galloping drums, the likes of which you haven't heard from this band since *Birdbrain*. But, of course, Buffalo Tom sound a lot tighter, stronger, and more confident when they dig into the big shaggy dog rock than they did five years previous, and while they never get quite as rollicking as "Tangerine" again on *Sleepy Eyed*, cut for cut it's a far more direct and straightforward rock album than anything they'd managed since their creative breakthrough on *Let Me Come Over*. To some listeners, *Sleepy Eyed* might sound like a regression, moving back into noisy power trio mode after the more polished surfaces and intricate arrangements of *Let Me Come Over* and *Big Red Letter Day*, but play *Sleepy Eyed* back to back with *Birdbrain* and you'll be pleasantly surprised by the differences. *Sleepy Eyed* decisively proves Buffalo Tom write better hooks and better melodies, write smarter lyrics, and even rock harder than when they were still trying to find their way out from under J. Mascis's shadow, and they sound like they're having a great time just turning up the amps and letting rip, especially Bill Janovitz, whose rock-dude guitar outros are a hoot (and this is one band who I cannot begrudge for enjoying themselves every once in a while). On *Sleepy Eyed*, Buffalo Tom go back to the old neighborhood and show everybody how much bigger and stronger they've become—it's sorta like a high school reunion, but louder and a lot more fun. *—Mark Deming*

Smitten / Sep. 29, 1998 / Beggars Banquet/Polydor ♦♦
The perennial bridesmaids of the modern rock scene, Buffalo Tom have been flirting with mainstream success since 1992's critically acclaimed album, "Let Me Come Over." Unfortunately, though *Smitten* may please devoted fans, it will do little to give them the breakthrough they have long deserved. In many ways the record follows the pattern started with *Let Me Come Over* and its follow-up, *Big Red Letter Day*—namely, alternating between a rough around the edges, feedback laden sound and a more polished studio sounding album. Whereas their last release, *Sleepy Eyed* drew on the fuzz of *Let Me Come Over*, *Smitten*, like *Big Red Letter Day*, has the mark of a "studio" album. Granted, Buffalo Tom being Buffalo Tom, studio care doesn't equal a schmaltzy Celine Dion record, but the sampled guitar loops of "Knot in It," the strings of "Scottish Windows," the horns of "White Paint Morning" and the piano and organ sprinkled throughout the album show that Buffalo Tom is trying to expand their sonic palate. Janovitz's trademark power ballads blossom wonderfully with the extra treatment and "Wiser" and "Scottish Windows" are among his best compositions. Yet, as good as a Buffalo Tom song can be, it is frustrating to hear that, in spite of the added production there always remains a certain formulaic predictability to the songs that even they can't break away from. The good news is that, unlike most current bands, Buffalo Tom have a distinct sound. The bad news is that, with many of their records sounding similar, it's easy to opt for the familiar territory of the classic *Let Me Come Over*, the album that pioneered their style. *—Steve Kurutz*

● **Asides from Buffalo Tom** / Aug. 22, 2000 / Beggars Banquet ♦♦♦♦♦
Buffalo Tom began life as a trio of pre-grunge, neo-psychedelic guitar maulers owing a heavy debt to Dinosaur Jr. (though one might argue that on *Birdbrain* they actually beat J. Mascis at his own game), but over the next dozen years they matured into a considerably more dynamic and intelligent band, capable of generating crunching rockers or acoustic ballads with equal precision, all of which possessed heart, soul, and a compassionate intelligence. *Asides from Buffalo Tom* compiles most of the band's best-known songs, including the top sides of their singles, radio emphasis tracks, a few fan favorites, and a cover of the Jam's "Going Underground" from a 1999 tribute album. While the album isn't sequenced chronologically, which would have made a greater case for their growth over time, it does a superb job of capturing the many sides of their musical personality, and it is both a fine summation of their first 11 years as a recording act and great introduction to one of the better bands to rise from the alt-rock scene in the 1990s. *Asides from Buffalo Tom* also features excellent and enlightening liner notes from the three members of the band, Bill Janovitz, Chris Colbourn, and Tom Maginnis. *—Mark Deming*

Jimmy Buffett

b. Dec. 25, 1946, Pascogoula, MS
Vocals, Guitar / Pop/Rock, Singer/Songwriter, Country-Rock
Singer/songwriter Jimmy Buffett has translated his easy-going Gulf Coast persona into more than just a successful recording career—he has expanded into clothing, nightclubs, and literature. But the basis of his business empire is undeniably music. After recording in Nashville during the early '70s, Buffett moved to Key West, Florida, where he gradually evolved the beach bum character and tropical folk-rock style that would endear him to millions. Signed to ABC-Dunhill, Buffett achieved notoriety but not much else with his second album, 1973's *White Sport Coat & A Pink Crustacean*, which featured a song called, "Why Don't We Get Drunk" ("... and screw?," goes the chorus). It took the 1977 Top Ten song "Margaritaville" and the album in which it was featured, *Changes in Latitudes, Changes in Attitudes*, to capture his tropical worldview and, for a while, turn him into a pop star. By the '80s, a steadily growing core of Sun Belt fans he dubbed "Parrotheads" began making his concerts into successful, Mardi Gras-like affairs. His recording career, meanwhile, languished, though a hits compilation, a 1990 live album and a 1992 box-set retrospective were quite successful. Buffett finally returned to the studio for 1994's *Fruitcakes*; the album became one of his fastest-selling records. It was followed in 1995 by *Barometer Soup* and *Banana Wind* in 1996. After a short-lived Broadway venture, he returned in 1999 with *Beach House on the Moon*. *— William Ruhlmann*

Down to Earth / 1970 / Varese ♦♦

A White Sport Coat & A Pink Crustacean / Jun. 1973 / MCA ♦♦♦
Buffett was beginning to put in place his folk/rock/country sound and his laid-back, humorous, hedonistic persona with this album, which features later concert favorites like "Why Don't We Get Drunk (and Screw)" and "Grapefruit—Juicy Fruit." *—William Ruhlmann*

Living & Dying in 3/4 Time / Feb. 1974 / MCA ♦♦♦
Jimmy Buffett was already on the second edition of his Coral Reefer Band by the time his third album rolled around. He had also firmly established his Gulf Coast beach-bum/poet persona, but he hadn't written a classic song until "Come Monday," which put him, and the album, on the map. *— William Ruhlmann*

A-1-A / Dec. 1974 / MCA ♦♦♦
Before Jimmy Buffett became a novelist, entrepreneur, and founder of a business empire, he was a prolific singer/songwriter and a great storyteller. In the song "Migration," which chronicles his failed first marriage and his subsequent move to Florida, he sings "I got a Caribbean soul I can barely control and some Texas hidden here in my heart." This perfectly describes the music of Jimmy Buffett, who incorporates steel drums, harmonica, and slide guitar to tell stories about life by the sea. While many of the songs for which he is famous involve a life of leisure told with a keen sense of humor, Buffett is more thoughtful than your average beachcomber. In fact, the best moments on this album are the slower tunes such as "A Pirate Looks at Forty" where a reflective Buffett looks back at his lifelong love of the ocean and his place in the universe. *A-1-A* may be Buffett's most autobiographical album, as he sings about making music on his own terms in the opening up-tempo "Makin' Music for Money" and tells stories of his idyllic childhood in "Life Is Just a Tire Swing." As with most of Buffett's work, his stories convey the importance of enjoying life, living free, and doing as you please. This is one of Jimmy Buffett's classic '70s albums that established his persona, and it is a perfect introduction to his music. *— Vik Iyengar*

Rancho Deluxe / 1975 / Rykodisc ♦♦♦

High Cumberland Jubilee (1972) / 1976 / Varese ♦♦

Havana Daydreamin' / Jan. 1976 / MCA ♦♦♦♦♦
Buffett's best overall collection of songs yet bears the influence of Steve Goodman, who wrote "This Hotel Room" and cowrote "Woman Goin' Crazy on Caroline Street." But a personal favorite is Buffett's own "My Head Hurts, My Feet Stink, and I Don't Love Jesus." *— William Ruhlmann*

Changes in Latitudes, Changes in Attitudes / Jan. 1977 / MCA ♦♦♦♦♦
Buffett's biggest-selling regular release contains his biggest hit single, "Margaritaville." It's also a peak in terms of songwriting, both for the artist himself and in his covers of the work of Steve Goodman and Jesse Winchester, among others. Funny, wistful, and celebratory, the album is the definitive statement of Buffett's worldview. *—William Ruhlmann*

Son of a Son of a Sailor / Mar. 1978 / MCA ♦♦♦♦♦

If this album was a slight step down from its predecessor, it was almost equally successful commercially, and it contained its share of terrific material, notably the uptempo hit "Cheeseburger in Paradise" and one of Buffett's older songs, "Livingston Saturday Night." —*William Ruhlmann*

You Had to Be There / Oct. 1978 / MCA ✦✦

Volcano / Aug. 1979 / MCA ✦✦

Coconut Telegraph / Feb. 1981 / MCA ✦✦

Somewhere over China / Jan. 1982 / MCA ✦✦

One Particular Harbour / Sep. 1983 / MCA ✦✦

Riddles in the Sand / Sep. 1984 / MCA ✦✦

Last Mango in Paris / Jun. 1985 / MCA ✦✦✦
Buffett's rapid recording schedule tended to outrun his muse in the late '70s and early '80s, resulting in some uneven albums with occasional good songs. This time he came up with a far more consistent collection, including three entries on the country charts: "Gypsies in the Palace," "If the Phone Doesn't Ring, It's Me," and "Please Bypass This Heart." —*William Ruhlmann*

● **Songs You Know By Heart** / Oct. 1985 / MCA ✦✦✦✦✦
Combining aloof humor with a laid-back, devil-may-care island attitude, Jimmy Buffet sang songs about alcohol consumption, lazing around in the sun, and the freedom of not having to work for a living. *Songs You Know By Heart* is a solid offering of Buffet's greatest hits, pulling together his truly strongest material and avoiding the unnecessary filler that appears on his albums. His claim to fame, "Margaritaville," is the jewel in the crown here, which still harbors that tropical feel thanks to its Caribbean-styled rhythm and relaxed flow. "Come Monday" picks up where "Margaritaville" leaves off, only this ballad plays out with subdued sincerity and has Buffet sounding strangely serious, and romantic. Most of the songs from Buffet are centered around his frolicking lifestyle, like the comical "Cheeseburger in Paradise" or the naughtiness of "Why Don't We Get Drunk," an ode to his party-filled outlook on life. Buffet's voice shines on the clever "Changes in Latitudes, Changes in Attitudes," which again spotlights his love of living without concern, especially in someplace warm. The catchy and whimsical "Fins" is lifted by a contagious pace with a smart chorus and serves as one of the highlights of this collection. As a compilation, this bunch of Jimmy Buffet's most famous tunes contains just the right amount of tracks. Any less would be inconsistent and any more would be deemed as overkill. —*Mike DeGagne*

Floridays / Jun. 1986 / MCA ✦✦

Hot Water / Jun. 1988 / MCA ✦✦

Off to See the Lizard / Jun. 1989 / MCA ✦✦

Feeding Frenzy / Oct. 1990 / MCA ✦✦

Boats, Beaches, Bars & Ballads / May 1992 / MCA ✦✦✦✦✦
Most listeners will be satisfied with the excellent Jimmy Buffett summary *Songs You Know By Heart*, but anyone that wants to dig deeper should bypass the albums (there are several that are first-rate, yet many are spotty) and pick up the four-disc, 72-track box set, *Boats, Beaches, Bars & Ballads*. Assembled thematically, with each disc devoted to one of the words in the title, this rounds up not just every Buffett hit, but pretty much every one of his noteworthy album tracks, plus a couple of rarities and unreleased cuts. For some, this much Buffett may cause sunstroke, yet this proves that he had some fine moments that weren't singles, and even those that aren't Parrotheads will be impressed by the consistency of his music—if you like Jimmy, he usually delivers what you like. —*Stephen Thomas Erlewine*

Before the Beach / May 25, 1993 / MCA ✦✦

Fruitcakes / May 24, 1994 / MCA ✦✦

Barometer Soup / Aug. 1, 1995 / Margaritaville/MCA ✦✦

Banana Wind / Jun. 1996 / Margaritaville/MCA ✦✦✦

The Buggles
f. 1979, England, **db.** 1980
New Wave, Synth Pop
As the answer to the trivia question "What was the first act ever played on MTV?," the Buggles assured their place in pop music history. Vocalist and bassist Trevor Horn and keyboardist Geoff Downes formed the electro-pop duo in England in 1979 after meeting two years prior as session musicians. Their first single, "Video Killed the Radio Star," hit number one in the U.K. in late 1979; when MTV went on the air in 1981, the prophetically-titled record's video was the first ever broadcast on the fledgling cable network.

Although the Buggles enjoyed three more British hits—"The Plastic Age," "Clean Clean" and "Elstree"—both Horn and Downes were more interested in production than performing; in 1980, they helmed Yes' *Drama*, and later joined the group as replacements for Rick Wakeman and Jon Anderson. After Yes' break-up, Downes signed on with Asia, while Horn formed ZTT Records and produced hits for the likes of Frankie Goes to Hollywood and ABC. —*Jason Ankeny*

● **The Age of Plastic** / 1980 / Island ✦✦✦✦✦
The fun, quirky single "Video Killed the Radio Star" garnered The Buggles international attention in 1980, but it was just one of *The Age of Plastic*'s fascinating, futuristic visions. From the title track's opening strains, Trevor Horn and Geoff Downes transform your living room into a world of *Jetson*-like proportions. It's a world, though, where technology is seen for what it is—full of both promise and frightening implications. On "I Love You

Miss Robot," a metaphorical love affair with a robot explores modern man's relationship to, and dependence on, technology. "Kid Dynamo"'s spirited tempo, biting lyrics, and menacing vocal track questions the loss of imagination plaguing the mass media age. For the most part, *The Age of Plastic* is a fun record that doesn't need to be taken too seriously, though a subtle sense of loss is woven throughout. Variety is the constant and tracks vary from the giddy "Video," to the dark and pulsating "Johnny on the Monorail." The vision here is so beautifully articulated that the superb musicianship and production wizardry is easily overlooked. Paradoxically, Horn and Downes employed electronic devices (which were considered new and cutting edge in the late seventies) to create an album which, at times, spoke eloquently about their drawbacks. With *The Age of Plastic*, Horn and Downes stamped an indelible image in the collective pop psyche. What is equally impressive is the sound of this disc given its analog origins and 1980-release date. While hiss can be heard in some of the quieter passages, it would be difficult to find a record from this era that sounds half as good. Pop rarely reaches these heights. —*Jeri Montesano*

Adventures in Modern Recording / Feb. 1982 / EMI ✦✦✦✦
It wasn't surprising that the Buggles' second release, *Adventures in Modern Recording*, didn't meet the expectations that 1980's internationally successful *The Age of Plastic* set. Both Horn and Downes had been working on several outside projects, including Yes' 1980 release *Drama*, which severely limited their time, and for the most part, *Adventures* was a Trevor Horn solo project; Geoff Downes only appears on three tracks. However, many of the criticisms leveled against this outing were unfounded and there is still much to like; several songs, such as the infectious title track, equal *The Age of Plastic*. Both "Adventures in Modern Recording" and "Inner City," with its lush arrangement and engrossing melody, show off Horn's remarkable production savvy. Horn and Downes collaborations like the sultry "Vermillion Sands" and "I Am a Camera"—a melancholy, stripped-down version of "Into the Lens," which appeared on *Drama*—are top-notch. Meanwhile, "Lenny" is a shot of adrenaline that could have fit nicely on *Drama* as well; actually, a good portion of that album is as much a Buggles recording as anything you'll find here, so to consider *Adventures* the second Buggles release would be unfair. Instead, *Adventures* and *Drama* should be seen as a collective statement. Buggles fans should look for the Japanese import of *Adventures in Modern Recording* (Flavour TFCK-87577), which has been remastered and includes unreleased tracks like the bubbly "Fade Away" and the unusual "Blue Nylon," and a 12" mix of "I Am a Camera." Both of the Buggles albums still sound fresh, especially compared to the '90s unimaginative pop. The only disappointment here is that it is unlikely there will be further adventures for the Buggles. —*Jeri Montesano*

Built to Spill
f. 1992, Boise, ID
Indie Rock, Alternative Pop/Rock
Built to Spill hail from the unlikely town of Boise, Idaho. Vocalist/guitarist Doug (sometimes Dug) Martsch's songs sound far out too, mixing Neil Young's plaintive yearning with offbeat melodies and lyrics. Martsch released three albums with the Treepeople before forming Built to Spill. The band's debut album, *Ultimate Alternative Wavers*, was released by C/Z in 1993. Replacing drummer Ralf was bassist Brett Nelson's former Butterfly Train bandmate, drummer Andy Capps, joining for their second album *There's Nothing Wrong with Love*, which appeared in 1994 on the Up! label. After a split EP with Caustic Resin (also on Up!), Built to Spill signed with Warner Brothers and issued 1997's *Perfect from Now On*; *Keep It Like a Secret* followed two years later and a live album was released in 2000. Martsch has also collaborated on a series of albums with Beat Happening's Calvin Johnson as the Halo Benders. —*John Bush*

Ultimate Alternative Wavers / 1993 / C/Z ✦✦✦

The Normal Years / 1993 / K ✦✦✦
This collection strings together Built to Spill's loose ends: outtakes from each of the band's first two albums, three independently released singles, and two tracks recorded for compilations. Given bandleader Doug Martsch's penchant for exquisite production and extensive arranging on his later albums, this mix-and-match release is certainly the least desirable full-length the band has released. The sound is sparse, and Martsch is still learning the intricacies of his craft. But the innocence in songs like "Girl" and "Joyride" is an aural treat, and *The Normal Years* works as a good illustration of Built to Spill's humble beginnings. —*Troy Carpenter*

There's Nothing Wrong with Love / 1994 / Up ✦✦✦✦✦
Beneath the wacky guitar fooling and somewhat nasal vocals, Built to Spill write great love songs, whether its bouncy pop or fragile melodies. Strings are used to good effect on three songs, and vocal harmonies make this disc an all-around winner. —*John Bush*

Perfect from Now On / Jan. 28, 1997 / Warner Brothers ✦✦✦✦✦
Not many groups would take a major label contract as a cue to put out an album where the shortest song is still a radio-unfriendly five minutes in length. For that listeners can thank their stars that Built to Spill isn't like many groups and Martsch not like many artists. *Perfect From Now On* manages the amazing trick of being the band's best album to that point, Martsch and company using the opportunities for larger budgets and distribution to create an album at once inspiring and quietly emotional, not the easiest combination to pull off. With drummer Scott Plouf and bassist Nelson as the other core performers, plus second guitarist Brett Netson and cellist John McMahon as key guests, the result was astounding all around. The length of the songs allow the band to create uniquely post-everything mantras, blending psych trances and drones, post-punk airiness and flow, and Martsch's affecting, tender singing and lyrics into a whole. Martsch's high tones and the guitar passion here helped fuel further comparisons to Neil Young—to pick

out one moment, consider the closing minutes of "I Would Hurt a Fly," feedback peeling out over the rhythm and strings—but the Boise musician is his own man through and through. Selecting standout moments from such a solid disc almost defeats the purpose, but many examples still deserve further notice. "Stop the Show" builds to a dramatic, but not in the least bit hammy, shift from a roaring wash to a quick, clipped pace; Martsch's vocals and further sudden tempo switches are the icing on the cake. "Velvet Waltz" indeed plays at that musical pace, McMahon's playing and Martsch's heartbreaking, lovely lyrics and singing the core of an incredible song. "Untrustable/Part 2 (About Someone Else)" concludes a simply fantastic record. *—Ned Raggett*

• **Keep It Like a Secret** / Feb. 2, 1999 / Warner Brothers ✦✦✦✦✦
Perhaps realizing that their time on a major label was likely limited, Built to Spill made a gutsy choice for *Keep It Like a Secret*, their second album for Warner Brothers. They embraced the sounds of a big studio and focused their sound without sacrificing their fractured indie-rock aesthetic. In a sense, this is Built to Spill's pop album: every song is direct and clean, without the long, cerebral jamming that characterized their earlier albums. That's not to say that the album is compromised—the songwriting may be streamlined, but Doug Martsch now packs all of his twists, turns and detours into dense, three-minute blasts. This approach, combined with the shiny sonic textures, makes *Keep It Like a Secret* the most immediate and, yes, accessible Built to Spill record, but they steadfastly open their music and breathe up the way, say, Pavement did on *Crooked Rain, Crooked Rain* or *Brighten the Corners*. Built to Spill still demand that the listener meet them on their own terms—these just happen to be the easiest terms to understand in their catalog. *—Stephen Thomas Erlewine*

Live / Apr. 18, 2000 / Warner Brothers ✦✦✦✦
Although the sensibility did show up on most of their studio recordings, Built to Spill was long renowned for their ability to stretch out in concert, where the balance between two of their most dominant influences—noisy, electric Neil Young and noisy, angular Pavement-esque pop—tilted decidedly toward the former's extended jams. In fact, *Live*'s defining performance is a 20-minute cover of Young's "Cortez the Killer," on which Doug Martsch's vocal *and* guitar work bear an amazingly accurate similarity to Young, almost to the point of flat-out imitation. Yet somehow, the performance doesn't feel derivative—it seems more like Martsch is staking out long-coveted territory and one-upping his way into something very much his own, making the expanded length of the already epic song absolutely necessary. It's a powerful, majestic performance that makes the preceding songs seem like a perfect buildup, and it also has the effect of dwarfing the extremely good performances that follow it. The exception, of course, is another 20-minute jam that closes the album, this time the Built to Spill original "Broken Chairs," which essentially underlines the point made with "Cortez." As for the non-epic songs, there are five other well-chosen Built to Spill originals, plus terrific versions of the Halo Benders' "Virginia Reel Around the Fountain" (actually a Martsch side project) and Love as Laughter's "Singing Sores Make Perfect Swords." What's more, the sound quality is excellent, even crystalline (for a concert recording). It's as definitive a concert document of the band as we're likely to get, and it's close to being essential listening even for fans who aren't keen on live albums. *—Steve Huey*

Ancient Melodies of the Future / Jul. 10, 2001 / Warner Brothers ✦✦✦✦
With *Ancient Melodies of the Future*, Built to Spill expands on the big sound that they crafted with *Keep It Like a Secret*. Like their Northwestern peers Modest Mouse, Built to Spill anachronistically creates indie rock that can be played in arenas. "In Your Mind," with its Far Eastern guitar lines and thumping beat, beautifully updates "Tomorrow Never Knows" for the guitar rock set. "Alarmed" spirals into a satisfying guitar and keyboard noise jam, while "Trimmed and Burning" brings a dark "Sunday Bloody Sunday"-era U2 grandiosity to the band's usual jangle pop. "Happiness" is like a speeding car—it has the intensity, rush, and twanging swagger of an automobile race. The following song, "Don't Try," unleashes a full-on assault of melancholy guitar whine in a validation of life and experience where Doug Martsch repeats matter of factly "and everyone goes on and on." The album closes with "The Weather," a shimmering love song that begins with a resonant acoustic guitar. The narrator describes being "outside in the cool night, and the stars gravitate towards you." These few lyrics are a fitting description of Built to Spill, a band that goes on and on, always changing, always moving forward, but somehow always staying the same—familiar and comforting—as they carry the ancient melodies of personal histories, theirs and yours, into the future. *—Charles Spano*

Sandy Bull

b. 1941, New York, NY, **d.** Apr. 11, 2001
Guitar / Contemporary Folk, Folk-Rock, World Fusion
Long before Ry Cooder, Leo Kottke, Richard Thompson, and others were impressing us with their ability to hop from genre to genre, Sandy Bull glided from classical and jazz to ethnic music and rock & roll with grace and verve on his first two albums. Accompanied on his first two albums by renowned jazz drummer Billy Higgins, Bull produced some of the first extended instrumental compositions for guitar that incorporated elements of folk, jazz, and Indian and Arabic-influenced dronish modes. Not "rock" by any stretch of the imagination, it's nevertheless easy to see that it could have had an influence on the rock musicians who began incorporating eclectic and Middle Eastern sensibilities into their music a few years later. After his debut, Bull expanded his arsenal from the acoustic guitar and banjo to include oud, bass, and electric guitar. After his second album, however, his recordings were less focused and less impressive. In the 1970s, he dropped out of music altogether due to drug problems, although he began recording again in the late '80s. On April 11, 2001, Sandy Bull died of lung cancer at his home just outside of Nashville. *—Richie Unterberger*

Fantasias for Guitar & Banjo / Aug. 1963 / Vanguard ✦✦✦
Sandy Bull should be a household name, as he was a true musical visionary who was clearly ahead of his time. This, his first album, is a truly auspicious debut. Blending Eastern, gospel, folk, and blues styles (and that's just a start), he gave a musical preview of what were to become commonplace forms (in rock and pop music) several years ahead of their time. This album could also be accurately described as one of the very first psychedelic records. The album is primarily Bull alone, aided only by jazz drummer Billy Higgins. The side-long "Blend" is a virtual travelogue of styles done in a then revolutionary modal tuning. The second half of the record features several cuts of different styles. Bull performs the gospel classic "Little Maggie" superbly on banjo, his first instrument. His electric guitar proves excellent as well on "Gospel Tune," an original done very well in the Pop Staples, tremolo-laden style. Bull didn't make another record for a couple of years after this, but with such an incredible debut, it took the audience at least that much time to catch up. *—Matthew Greenwald*

• **Inventions for Guitar & Banjo** / 1964 / Vanguard ✦✦✦✦✦
On his second and best album, Bull added more instruments and a bit of electricity. The centerpiece of the record is "Blend II." Like "Blend" from his first album, it is a melange (somewhat more electric in tone) of folk, jazz, and the Middle East, this time 24 minutes' worth. Also included on this 54-minute LP are two versions (electric and acoustic) of a Bach passage, a composition from the 14th century (Guillaume de Machaut's "Triple Ballade"), and Luiz Bonfa's "Manha de Carnival." A heavily reverbed (with drums), extended version of Chuck Berry's "Memphis, Tennessee" closes the set with an unexpected blast of rock & roll. *—Richie Unterberger*

E Pluribus Unum / 1968 / Vanguard ✦✦

Re-Inventions: The Best of the Vanguard Years / Jan. 26, 1999 / Vanguard ✦✦✦✦
Sandy Bull's technical skills have always been correlated with his vision. As a guitarist, he could often slip into repetitive drags of both time and space; but as a musical theorist, those crawls into other dimensions were often fascinating excursions that were years ahead of their time. *Re-Inventions: Best of the Vanguard Years* gathers eight songs from three of the four albums Bull recorded for Vanguard for a decade beginning in 1963. It's Bull's most productive and exciting period, and this splendidly assembled compilation serves it well. His mastery of the acoustic and electric guitar, bass, banjo and oud is prominently on display here. And on his most sublime track, the 21-minute "Blend," Bull constructs a psychedelic folk song that meanders through several glorious fields before slamming into an open crevice for a rejoicing journey home. It's a straight take, with no overdubs or edits, and it's Bull—with drummer Billy Higgins—at his most poetic and timeless. *—Michael Gallucci*

Sonny Burgess

b. May 28, 1931, Newport, AR
Vocals, Guitar / Rockabilly
Sonny Burgess is one of the wildest rockers to record for the legendary Sun label in Memphis. He and his band the Pacers came out of Newport, Arkansas, with a hard-rocking style that, unlike that of most rockabillies, owed little to nothing in the way of a stylistic debt to country music. With his red-dyed hair, matching stage suit and guitar, and wild stage performances, Burgess and the Pacers made mincemeat of the competition on many of the early-'50s rock & roll package tours. Though his Sun releases never brought him much in the way of commercial success, his recordings nonetheless remain landmarks of the early rockabilly style. Currently touring and recording with other Memphis alumni in the Sun Rhythm Section, the rockin' flame that is Sonny Burgess refuses to be snuffed out. *—Cub Koda*

We Wanna Boogie / 1990 / Rounder ✦✦✦✦✦
If you want a fairly definitive compilation of the Sun material by this minor rockabilly figure, but don't want to go the whole nine yards for the expensive import double CD on Bear Family, this domestic anthology is a recommended alternative. The 13 tracks contain six sides from his '50s singles (including the most noted, "Red Headed Woman" and "My Bucket's Got a Hole in It"), and seven other cuts from the '50s that were unissued at the time. *—Richie Unterberger*

The Classic Recordings 1956-1959 / Jul. 1991 / Bear Family ✦✦✦✦✦
Sonny's complete output for Sun spread over two CDs. Wild and crazed, featuring Burgess' spitfire guitar and booming vocals and the relentless drive of the Pacers in support. *—Cub Koda*

• **Hittin' that Jug: Best of Sonny Burgess** / Jun. 20, 1995 / AVI ✦✦✦✦✦
Sonny Burgess is one of the most enduring wildmen of the '50s Sun Records rockabilly scene, and a half-century later his classic "We Wanna Boogie" is still about as exciting as a record can be. *Hittin' That Jug!* is a 26-track collection of Sun recordings, including several alternate takes. Burgess offered fun and excitement with his unique, horn-driven rockabilly sound and bluegrass-inflected vocals, but not a lot of variety. Consequently, casual listeners may opt for a well-packed anthology such as this, rather than Bear Family's two-disc set of Burgess' complete Sun recordings. *—Greg Adams*

Sonny Burgess / Jun. 18, 1996 / Rounder ✦✦✦✦
If trying to bring back an old artist from the '50s is an idea that seldom merits results that exceed you can't go home again or worse, here is an album that proves it *can* be done and done right. Producer Gary Tallent keeps Burgess focused with the lead vocal and blistering lead guitar duties squarely on his shoulders, gives him a pile of great songs from the likes of Radney Foster, Fred James, Dave Alvin, Steve Forbert and Springsteen to interpret, then frames it all with a backing band that's the essence of drive and simplicity. The spotlight stays on Burgess throughout, just letting him do what he does best.

While it all sounds simple enough, it seldom if ever happens on these kind of affairs, making the achievement of this record all that more astounding. A modern rockabilly classic, this also features a wonderful guest appearance turn by Scotty Moore and the Jordanaires on Henry Gross' "Bigger than Elvis." The tray card on this reads, "Sonny Burgess has still got it." Believe it. *—Cub Koda*

Solomon Burke

b. 1936, Philadelphia, PA

Vocals / Deep Soul, Southern Soul, Soul, Country-Soul

While Solomon Burke never made a major impact upon the pop audience—he never, in fact, had a Top Twenty hit—he was an important early soul pioneer. On his 1960s singles for Atlantic, he brought a country influence into R&B with emotional phrasing and intricately constructed, melodic ballads and mid-tempo songs. At the same time, he was surrounded with sophisticated "uptown" arrangements, and provided with much of his material, by his producers, particularly Bert Berns. The combination of gospel, pop, country, and production polish was basic to the recipe of early soul. While Burke wasn't the only one pursuing this path, not many others did so as successfully. He began recording gospel and R&B sides for Apollo in the mid-to-late '50s, and was molded into a more secular direction when he signed with Atlantic in the 1960s. Burke had a wealth of high-charting R&B hits in the early half of the '60s, which crossed over to the pop listings in a mild fashion as well. "Just out of Reach," "Cry to Me," "If You Need Me," "Got to Get You off My Mind," "Tonight's the Night," and "Goodbye Baby (Baby Goodbye)" were the most successful. He left Atlantic in the late '60s, and spent the next decade hopping between various labels, getting his biggest hit with a cover of Creedence Clearwater Revival's "Proud Mary" in 1969. *—Richie Unterberger*

★ **The Very Best of Solomon Burke** / Feb. 3, 1998 / Rhino ♦♦♦♦♦

The Very Best of Solomon Burke is an excellent 16-track collection that features his biggest hits from 1961-1968, including "Just Out of Reach (Of My Two Open Arms)," "Cry to Me," "Down in the Valley," "I'm Hanging Up My Heart for You," "If You Need Me," "You're Good for Me," "Goodbye Baby (Baby Goodbye)," and "Everybody Needs Somebody to Love." All of his best-known songs in their hit versions are available on this concise, affordable disc, not always in strict release order but still an education in and of themselves—the tracks all come from the first generation original single masters, many of which were remixed or even shunted aside in favor of re-recorded versions for his albums during the 1960s, including his greatest-hits and best-of collections. The producers spent the time to track down those long-unused and forgotten originals for this, their first authentic representation on CD. Additionally, the 16th song is a true diamond among the R&B treasures here—the June 1968 single "Soul Meeting" cut by the Soul Clan, which consisted of Burke, Arthur Conley, Don Covay, Ben E. King, and Joe Tex, the super-session product of a short-lived experiment in raising money for the black community. This is the only appearance of this Don Covay-authored track on CD, and makes this release essential even for those who already own the 1992 double-CD set *Home In Your Heart*. *—Stephen Thomas Erlewine & Bruce Eder*

Proud Mary: The Bell Sessions / Jul. 18, 2000 / Sundazed ♦♦♦

This is a somewhat spruced-up version of Burke's 1969 *Proud Mary* album, containing all of the songs from that LP, and adding seven bonus cuts from 1969-70 singles and outtakes. Burke kept pace with changing soul and rock trends fairly well on *Proud Mary*, which has a funkier, bluesier deep soul feel than his more famous early- and mid-1960s Atlantic material. That feel didn't come about by total accident, of course; the record was recorded at Muscle Shoals, where he could sing with the area's esteemed session musicians, rather than the uptown New York players he'd worked with at Atlantic. There's a bit of a sense of Burke following the crowd rather than blazing his own path, and the song selection is a bit unimaginative (not that this was an unusual happenstance on soul albums). Still, even those are given respectable readings, and Burke also tackles a couple of songs Dan Penn co-penned, in addition to waxing one of his own, "How Big a Fool (Can a Fool Be)," which has that thin electric sitar-guitar hybrid sound peculiar to some pop-soul discs of the era. The bonus tracks are pretty interesting, including previously unissued covers of Bob Dylan's "The Mighty Quinn" and Sam Cooke's "Change Is Gonna Come," along with some non-LP singles that showed Burke absorbing (as he had on the *Proud Mary* album) some contemporary rock influences. His own "The Generation of Revelations," a 1969 single, made some fashionable lyrical bows to the counterculture; an odd 1970 single matched a post-Elvis Presley cover of "In the Ghetto" with the gospel rock of "God Knows I Love You," written by the unusual songwriting team of Delaney Bramlett and "In the Ghetto" composer Mac Davis. *—Richie Unterberger*

T-Bone Burnett

b. Jan. 18, 1945, St. Louis, MO

Producer, Vocals, Guitar / College Rock, Heartland Rock, Roots Rock, Singer/Songwriter

Despite critical acclaim as a performer, the rootsy singer-songwriter T-Bone Burnett earned his greatest renown as a producer, helming recording sessions for acts ranging from Roy Orbison and Elvis Costello to Counting Crows and Sam Phillips. After high school, Burnett opened his own recording studio in Fort Worth and he relocated to Los Angeles in the early '70s, producing sessions for Glen Clark and Delbert McClinton. He recorded his own debut album, *The B-52 Band and the Fabulous Skylarks*, in 1972 and toured with Bob Dylan's Rolling Thunder Revue tour during the mid-'70s. Burnett also recorded three albums as the Alpha Band (with Rolling Thunder alumni Dave Mansfield and Steve Soles), then resurfaced as a solo act during the '80s. Still, commercial success eluded him, so he continued working as a producer, overseeing highly regarded records by Los Lobos, Marshall Crenshaw and the BoDeans. Burnett also began producing for the successful Christian pop singer Leslie Phillips (later known by her nickname Sam), and the two later wed. Though Burnett continued his solo career with albums in 1988 and 1992, he remained one of the most prolific and distinctive producers of his day, crafting successes like Costello's *Spike*, Counting Crows' *August and Everything After*, the Wallflowers' *Bringing Down the Horse* and Gillian Welch's *Revival*. *—Jason Ankeny*

Truth Decay / 1980 / Demon ♦♦♦♦♦

T-Bone Burnett released *Truth Decay* for John Fahey's Takoma Records, his first solo effort since 1972. Burnett delivers a collection of parables, tales, and personal struggles propelled by his strong beliefs and some captivating roots rock. "Quicksand," with a rhythm reminiscent of "Ring of Fire," opens the proceedings with a word of caution, and from there Burnett takes you through scenes of international affairs, betrayal, pure and untamed love, need, greed, and resolution. Songs such as "Talk Talk Talk Talk Talk," "Boomerang," and "Love at First Sight" couple sophisticated lyrical content with the simplest of materials (rockabilly, blues, folk, and country), as does the album's best cut, the bare-bones "House of Mirrors," a spoken, state-of-the-times parable in which the protagonist's fate is summed up in a wonderful historical reference. This, along with his passion and reverence for the music—as well as a willingness to subvert it if necessary—keeps him from coming across as retro or revivalist. Aside from the more complex material here, Burnett also proves to be equally adept at a more direct lyrical approach. Whereas in the past he would tend to lean toward the abstract, much of *Truth Decay*, with songs such as "Come Home," "Power of Love," and "Tears Tears Tears," owe as much to the eloquent simplicity of Hank Williams, Buddy Holly, and Willie Dixon as it does to Dylan. Removed from the big label, budget, and expectations of the Alpha Band, T-Bone Burnett produced a modest, passionate gem. *—Brett Hartenbach*

Trap Door [EP] / 1982 / Warner Brothers ♦♦♦♦♦

Following a short stint with Takoma Records, T-Bone Burnett moved back into the majors with a 1982 release for Warner Bros., the six-song EP *Trap Door*. Whereas his previous record, *Truth Decay*, had the feel of an early Sam Phillips recording for Sun Records, Trap Door is filled with tight, radiant folk-rock. Fronting the same basic lineup (Davids-Mansfield, Miner, and Kemper), Burnett adorns this batch of provocative tunes with shimmering guitar hooks, crafty rhythms, and an astute sense of detail and subtlety to create some of the most irresistible pop of his career (check out his terrific cover of the Marilyn Monroe standard "Diamonds Are a Girl's Best Friend"). "Hold on Tight," a message of love and mercy, is pure '60s pop, while "I Wish You Could've Seen Her Dance" opens with what could be a lyrical update of "I Saw Her Standing There" and then proceeds to recollect a conversation with a beautiful dancer set to a propulsive, shifting rhythm and an engaging melody. The title track closes the record with a half-spoken array of life's contradictions before an infectious chorus diverts your attention, only to arrive at the stark warning, "Watch out for the trap door." Intelligent and compelling, *Trap Door* is well worth hunting down. *—Brett Hartenbach*

Proof Through the Night / 1983 / Warner Brothers ♦♦♦♦

Proof Through the Night, T-Bone Burnett's first, and last, full-length release for Warner Brothers, is an ambitious take on the state of the union and times, personified by various fallen characters. To some, his persistent morality may come across as being a bit cold or even self-righteous, but further investigation reveals an underlying empathy for the individuals, even if a cynicism for the times in which they live is expressed. And if Burnett may seem tough, don't think he excludes himself from the same scrutiny. In cuts such as "Pressure" and the record's best song, "Shut It Tight," he sees himself as "... just an ordinary man," struggling with the same sort of questions, temptations and contradictions as, for instance, those of the protagonist in the record's centerpiece, "The Sixties." Musically, he serves his tales of "beautiful, wealthy, young divorcees," fallen women and victims of times where we "keep all the bad, destroy all the good," on a bed of vibrant, guitar driven rock & roll and folk, even lacing spoken parables such as "Fatally Beautiful," "The Sixties" and "Hefner and Disney" with subtle hooks, enticing nuances and choruses. Like T-Bone Burnett's other Warner Brothers release, *Trap Door*, *Proof Through the Night* is smart, tight, insightful and, unfortunately, not yet available on CD. Guests include Pete Townsend, Mick Ronson, Richard Thompson, the Williams Brothers and Ry Cooder. *—Brett Hartenbach*

Behind the Trap Door / 1984 / Demon ♦♦♦

Behind the Trap Door, T-Bone Burnett's fourth recording (his second EP) since the breakup of the Alpha Band, is a varied collection of material that includes collaborations with Bono, Bob Neuwirth and Richard Thompson. The record, with its stripped down and decidedly uncommercial sound, along with the inclusion of a soundtrack instrumental and a cut recorded prior to 1980's *Truth Decay* sessions, has the feel of a career filler for Burnett (he was between major labels). This by no means suggests that *Behind the Trap Door* is without its charms. The opener, "Strange Combination," is pure T-Bone Burnett, with its impressionistic, spoken lyric over a chunky acoustic guitar and clanging percussion. "Amnesia and Jealousy" and "The Law of Average" are infectious acoustic pop while the winsome instrumental "Welcome Home Mr. Lewis," written with Richard Thompson, closes the record nicely. Fans of Burnett's work will find pleasures throughout *Behind the Trap Door*, although it's by no means an essential piece of his catalogue. *—Brett Hartenbach*

T-Bone Burnett / 1986 / Dot ♦♦♦

Released as a one-off project for MCA's briefly revived country subsidiary Dot Records, T-Bone Burnett's self-titled fourth album is the most austere and uncluttered project he's released to date, quite a switch from the high-concept folk-pop of his best-known work. Recorded and mixed live to two track in four days, *T-Bone Burnett* is subtle but strong, with a warm, natural acoustic sound that's gentle but surprisingly full-bodied, and the production is the perfect match for the songs, especially on the beautiful "River of Love," which is among Burnett's finest moments on record. Backed by a superb acoustic band (including David Hidalgo, Jerry Douglas, Byron Berline, and Jerry Scheff), Burnett's vocals are in superb form here, and while the album is a bit short on top-shelf T-Bone originals (half the album's songs are either covers or collaborations), what is here is compelling and listenable. *T-Bone Burnett* in many ways sounds like a casual project sandwiched between Burnett's "real" albums, but one listen confirms it's still the work of a major talent. —*Mark Deming*

The Talking Animals / 1988 / Acadia ✦✦✦
Following a brief brush with country music, T-Bone Burnett's seventh solo release, *The Talking Animals*, continues the studio rock he began in 1983 with *Proof Through the Night*. Burnett once again starts with basic rock, pop and folk roots, which he wastes no time in subverting, adding assorted twists along the way. Along with co-producer and guitarist David Rhodes, he colors a foundation of steady rhythms driven by drummer Mickey Curry and bassist Tony Levin with affected and atmospheric guitars, as well as Mitchell Froom's various keyboards. One exception is the Van Dyke Parks-arranged "Image," with its swirling strings and one verse repeated in four different languages by Burnett and three guest vocalists (Cait O'Riordan, Ruben Blades and Ludmila). Here he sheds the bounds of the standard pop song format to create a piece that seems to have sprung from a Weill-Brecht musical. Lyrically, *The Talking Animals*, like his best work, can be scathing, searching and surreal. Burnett explores uncertainty, longing, fear, lust, fantasy, greed, and eventually justice and mercy in his quest for "The Wild Truth" (the title of one of the album's best tracks). Often criticized for preaching, Burnett seems to ask as much of himself as he does of the cast of characters here, even allowing one of them to denounce him in the wonderful final cut, "The Strange Case of Frank Cash and the Morning Paper" (although it's T-Bone Burnett who gets the last word). Even with a few less than stellar songs, *The Talking Animals* is a strong, inspired record. Bono, Peter Case and Tonio K each co-write with Burnett, as well as lending support on vocals. —*Brett Hartenbach*

● **The Criminal Under My Own Hat** / Jul. 14, 1992 / Columbia ✦✦✦✦
On 1992's *The Criminal Under My Own Hat*, T-Bone Burnett seemed to be searching for a middle ground between his previous two albums, the bright, angular pop-rock of *The Talking Animals* and the spare, acoustic introspection of *T-Bone Burnett*. On this album, though, Burnett was willing to let these two sides of his musical personality display a greater influence upon one another; the acoustic numbers are more passionate and fuller-sounding than on his previous efforts (often buoyed by Jerry Douglas on dobro and Mark O'Connor on violin), and the rockers have been peeled back a bit, giving the individual musicians a bit more room to move and letting the inner workings of the songs show. The operative philosophy appears to have been to allow the songs to shine though without excess gingerbread, and that's just what the material demanded; as always, Burnett's songs reveal his obsessions with the human failings of pride, fear, and greed, and he's willing to point the finger at himself as often as he finds shortcomings in others (though he saves his greatest wrath for the corrupt politicians and media savvy preachers attacked on "I Can Explain Everything," in which he suggests a little selective beheading might be a good idea—as Burnett puts it, "the French knew how to lynch"). But unless his subjects happen to be George Bush or Jimmy Swaggart, Burnett finds room for compassion in nearly all of these songs, once again proving he's one of the few avowed Christians in pop music who seems to understand how tricky the nature of sin and forgiveness can be. Thoughtful, often witty, and boasting a stellar cast of fine musicians, *The Criminal Under My Own Hat* was easily T-Bone Burnett's strongest album since *Proof Through The Night*, and a rare pleasure for thinking music fans. —*Mark Deming*

Johnny Burnette

b. Mar. 28, 1934, Memphis, TN, **d.** Aug. 1, 1964, Clear Lake, CA
Vocals, Songwriter, Guitar / Rockabilly
A contemporary of Elvis Presley in the Memphis scene of the mid-'50s, Burnette played a similar brand of fiery, spare wildman rockabilly. With his brother Dorsey (on bass) and guitarist Paul Burlison forming his Rock & Roll Trio, he recorded a clutch of singles for Decca in 1956 and 1957 that achieved nothing more than regional success. Featuring the groundbreaking fuzzy tone of Burlison's guitar, Johnny's energetic vocals, and Dorsey's slapping bass, these recordings—highlighted by the first rock & roll version of "Train Kept a-Rollin'"—compare well to the classic Sun rockabilly of the same era. The trio disbanded in 1957, and Johnny found pop success as a teen idol in the early '60s with hits like "You're Sixteen" and "Dreamin'." Burnette died in a boating accident in 1964. His brother, Dorsey, achieved modest success as a solo act in the early '60s, and Burlison recently resurfaced as a member of the Sun Rhythm Section. —*Richie Unterberger*

● **Rockabilly Boogie** / 1989 / Bear Family ✦✦✦✦✦
All of the Johnny Burnette Trio's primal rockabilly records, including the blazing "Train Kept A-Rollin'," are collected on this single-disc compilation. The alternate takes might border on overkill, but the original takes remain powerful years after they were recorded. —*Stephen Thomas Erlewine*

The Best of Johnny Burnette: You're Sixteen / 1992 / EMI America ✦✦✦✦
Burnette's best pop-oriented recordings are featured on this collection, including the classic "You're Sixteen." —*Stephen Thomas Erlewine*

Rock & Roll Trio/Tear It Up / Jan. 23, 1996 / BGO ✦✦✦✦✦
This two-fer assembles Johnny Burnette's 1956 debut LP along with the later *Tear It Up*, which offers highlights including "Train Kept a-Rollin'," "Rock Therapy," and "Honey Hush." —*Richie Unterberger*

Rock & Roll Tonight / 1999 / Hydra ✦✦✦
Rock & Roll Tonight is a German import collection of odds and ends that pairs Johnny and Dorsey Burnette. Sources include television performances, demos, and studio recordings, the latter of which are dubbed from vinyl. Some of the original vinyl records repre-

sented are extremely rare, such as "We're Having a Party," only 50 or so copies of which were pressed as an invitation to a friend's party. "Green Grass of Texas," released under the pseudonym The Texans, was a (barely) charting single. The 32-page full-color booklet and detailed notes are chock full of esoteric information for die-hard fans who will be the only ones dedicated enough to track down this collection. —*Greg Adams*

● **Dreamin': Very Best Of** / Jul. 27, 1999 / Collectables ✦✦✦✦✦
Collectables' *Dreamin': Very Best Of* does something many Johnny Burnette collections do not—captures both the sweet teen dreams of "Dreamin'" and "You're Sixteen" and the wildman rockabilly of "The Train Kept a Rollin'." True, the collection leans a bit too much on the former in expense of the latter, but this is one of the rare CD collections to feature both sides of Burnette's personality and to do it quite well. —*Stephen Thomas Erlewine*

Burning Airlines

f. 1997, Washington, DC
Indie Rock, Post-Punk, Alternative Pop/Rock
Almost immediately following the April 1997 breakup of Jawbox, J. Robbins (guitars/vocals) began writing and playing with ex-Wool and former Government Issue bandmate Peter Moffett (drums). One day, the bassist couldn't make it to practice, so Robbins convinced the other Jawbox guitarist and vocalist Bill Barbot to slide into the role. By the end of 1998, Burning Airlines (named after a Brian Eno song) had their debut single and a split release with Braid in the bins of mom-and-pop record shops.

The band took enough "time off" from a hectic touring schedule to record *Mission: Control!*, released in early 1999. As with the remainder of the band's major works, it was released by DeSoto, the label run by former Jawbox bassist Kim Coletta and spouse Barbot. Featuring arrangements that were sharper and scaled back from those of Jawbox, the record held the spirit of early XTC and the Pixies, along with retaining the Mission of Burma and Gang of Four-influenced foundation of Jawbox. Robbins also made a concerted effort to make his songwriting more direct, no longer writing in code or cut-and-paste snippets.

As the band set out to hit the road in support of the well-received record, Barbot decided that his responsibilities as an adult were too numerous to allow for the dusting off of his passport. Friend and Jawbox touring aide Mike Harbin was brought in, seamlessly fitting into the band as they toured for 18 months, traversing the United States as well as Japan, Europe, and Canada.

Since Robbins had become an in-demand producer throughout the last few years, the trio wasn't able to visit the recording studio until mid-2000. Throughout the following six months, they recorded the fuller-sounding *Identikit*, which hit the shelves in May 2001. Just before the release of the record, the band became a quartet, adding the keyboard and guitar skills of D.C.-scene vet Ben Pape, which enabled Robbins to be less of a juggling act on stage. —*Andy Kellman*

● **Mission: Control!** / Feb. 23, 1999 / DeSoto ✦✦✦✦
After Jawbox's amicable split in 1997, frontman J. Robbins and guitarist Bill Barbot teamed up with ex-Government Issue drummer, Pete Moffett, to form Burning Airlines, with Barbot switching from guitar to bass duties. *Mission: Control!* the band's debut album, brilliantly channels Robbins' pop sensibilities through muscular hardcore riffs with insistent, rhythmic foundations. With its seamless, dynamic shifts, thick riffs and killer melody, "3 Sisters" epitomizes the transition away from Jawbox's clipped, angular post-punk and onto a much more open-ended playing field. Barbot's bass work is a big surprise; Jawbox bassist Kim Coletta always rattled off cool melodies, but Barbot has a sharper and more intuitive sense of placement. His rubber-band lines do the dirty work on the slick "Wheaton Calling," and tug on Robbins' riffs like a magnet in "Pacific 231." Jawbox's music had begun to incorporate a greater range of moods by its final album, and Burning Airlines finds Robbins' melodies highly effective in a variety of settings: insanely catchy punk-pop ("Pacific 231"), furious Nirvana-esque rock ("Sweet Deals on Surgery") and head-spinning opener, ("Carnival") and arty dissonance ("I Sold Myself In," the intelligently weird "Crowned"). "Scissoring" is the album's standout cut, with its wicked harmonic riff, bad-ass bassline and thrashy second-half. With rarely a dull or unoriginal moment, *Mission: Control!* is a very promising start to life after Jawbox. —*Jonathan Cohen*

Identikit / May 8, 2001 / DeSoto ✦✦✦
It's not quite a Hall without Oates situation, but there's a significant element missing on *Identikit*. That would be the departed Bill Barbot, J. Robbins' partner in noise for the prior decade. It was his tight and jumpy McCartney-style bass that helped make *Mission: Control!* such a spectacular successor to the final Jawbox record. And when Barbot joined the band after their debut LP, he forged an immediate bond with Robbins as second guitarist and vocalist. You could always bank on the two providing riveting dialogue of the instrumental and vocal varieties. The negative sentiment shouldn't come at the expense of replacement Mike Harbin, who packs his own wallop. Robbins is more than a formidable force as the lone lyricist and guitarist, but he's either spread himself too thin or is too cognizant of Barbot's absence. While it's impossible to pick out substandard moments, it's equally challenging to pick highlights. That said, it remains a solid record, despite not being entirely remarkable. Hardly any progression is made from the debut, sounding more like the post-hardcore of latter-day Jawbox than the "XTC on steroids" of the first BA outing. New percussive devices and group harmonies require an attentive ear to catch, doing little to alter the band's sound. The melodicism of the debut gets placed on the back burner here, generally kept to the periphery. Robbins' guitar leads tend to stick to the skillful bash-'em-out nature that he perfected years ago, all but shelving the choppy staccatos used so well on the prior record. Ultimately, the only sore point of *Identikit* is its stubbornness to cut the cord from oft-traveled territory. The closing tracks—which seem

more like bonuses than part of the album—suggest an increasing glut of ideas up their sleeves. Let 'em out! —*Andy Kellman*

Tony Burrows

Vocals / AM Pop, Bubblegum, Pop

Though Burrows never had a hit under his own name, he holds the unusual honor (you can look it up in the *Guiness Book of Records*) of having four records in the British Top Ten at once—all under different names. The British session vocalist sang Edison Lighthouse's "Love Grows (Where My Rosemary Goes)," White Plains' "My Baby Loves Lovin'," the Pipkins' ridiculous "Gimme Dat Ding," and the Brotherhood of Man's "United We Stand," all of which were big hits in both the US and UK in 1970. With his high range and pleasantly anonymous-yet-versatile pipes, Burrows was an ideal tool for songwriters looking to craft bubblegum or light pop/rock for the AM airwaves—they were looking for hit songs, not for hit artists, and what did it matter to most consumers that the "groups" didn't really exist? Burrows continued to lend his voice out for hire throughout the '70s, entering the Top Ten again in 1974 with his lead on First Class' Beach Boys tribute, "Beach Baby." —*Richie Unterberger*

● **Love Grows (Where My Rosemary Goes): The Voice of Tony Burrows** / Aug. 27, 1996 / Varese ✦✦✦✦✦

Not a Tony Burrows album proper, but an 18-song compilation of records that he sang lead on from 1969 through 1985 (mostly from the first half of the 1970s), for Edison Lighthouse, First Class, White Plains, the Brotherhood of Man, the Pipkins, the Flowerpot Men, and others. All the big hits are here ("Love Grows," "Gimme Dat Ding," "My Baby Loves Lovin'," "United We Stand," "Beach Baby"), as well as quite a few misses. It's candy-floss early '70s pop of the most disposable variety, many of the flops being pale Beach Boys imitations. —*Richie Unterberger*

Bush

f. 1992

Post-Grunge, Grunge, Alternative Pop/Rock

Led by guitarist/vocalist Gavin Rossdale, Bush became the first post-Nirvana British band to hit it big in America. Of course, they became a hit by playing by the grunge rules—they had loud guitars, guttural vocals, stop-start rhythms, and extreme dynamics. Bush landed an American record deal before they had a British label; *Sixteen Stone*, their debut album, was released in late 1994 by Interscope Records. By the end of December, Bush's "Everything Zen" video had landed in MTV's Buzz Bin and the album began to take off; by spring of 1995, the record had gone gold, despite a stack of bad reviews. Over the course of 1995, *Sixteen Stone* became a major hit in the US, with "Little Things" reaching number four on the modern rock charts in the spring; later that year "Comedown" and "Glycerine" both reached number one on the modern rock charts, as well as crossing over into the pop Top 40. Despite their success, Bush received scathing reviews from the press and many alternative-rock insiders, who believed the group was manufactured. To counter such charges, the band asked Steve Albini—notorious for his abrasive productions for not only Pixies, Nirvana and PJ Harvey, but also countless indie bands—to helm their second album, *Razorblade Suitcase*. —*Stephen Thomas Erlewine*

● **Sixteen Stone** / Dec. 5, 1994 / Trauma/Interscope ✦✦✦✦

Bush's grunge-by-the-numbers is certainly well produced. Under the guidance of Clive Langer and Alan Winstanley—the kings of early-'80s British pop—Bush turns in an album that follows all the rules and sounds of American hard rock, specifically Nirvana and Pearl Jam. Their songwriting isn't original, nor is it particularly catchy. What makes "Everything Zen" and "Little Things" memorable is the exact reproduction of all of Nirvana's trademarks, only with a more professional execution—in other words, all the guitars keep rhythm perfectly and Gavin doesn't shred his throat when he sings, he projects from his diaphragm. As far as pop craftmanship goes, it's actually quite impressive. It would be even more so if they had songs to accompany their sounds. —*Stephen Thomas Erlewine*

Razorblade Suitcase / Nov. 19, 1996 / Trauma/Interscope ✦✦✦

Bush was criticized from most quarters of the music press for sounding too much like Nirvana on their debut album, *Sixteen Stone*, so in order to shed all of the comparisons ... well, they hired producer Steve Albini (Nirvana, Pixies, PJ Harvey) and proceeded to record their own version of Nirvana's dark, difficult *In Utero*. Actually, *Razorblade Suitcase*, Bush's second album, cribs heavily from two of Albini's best productions, *In Utero* and Pixies' *Surfer Rosa*—they even hired Vaughn Oliver, the designer behind *Surfer Rosa*, to do the artwork. Of course, relying so much on their idols only brings out Bush's weakness. Granted, Albini has helped make the band sound tougher, simply by stripping away the layers of effects and concentrating on a hard, driving rhythm and stop-start dynamics. The problem is Gavin Rossdale has not come up with any hooks, which means while *Razorblade Suitcase* is more pleasing and visceral on the surface, it offers no hooks to make it memorable, unlike the hit singles from *Sixteen Stone*. —*Stephen Thomas Erlewine*

The Science of Things / Oct. 26, 1999 / Trauma/Interscope ✦✦✦

For their third album *The Science of Things*, Bush returned to Clive Langer and Alan Winstanley, the Madness producers who helmed *Sixteen Stone*, but along the way, they fell out with the duo. Rossdale claimed the two were only credited on the album for legal reasons, and that the real work was done by the band with engineer Tom Elmhirst, which is probably true, since it's slicker than *Razorblade Suitcase* but doesn't glisten like *Stone*. *Science* is carefully crafted and sequenced, flowing nicely from hard rockers to power ballads, but little of it catches hold. It plays better than the disjointed *Razorblade Suitcase* due to studiocraft, since the measured, detailed production fleshes out songs held together by a bare minimum of hooks and melodies. Without hooks, Bush's earnestness is unavoidable. Rossdale's emotive, gut-wrenching vocals and the band's hard, heavy delivery are all this record has to offer and the mystery is, why the music has such little impact, either as emotional catharsis (which it was intended to be, if the tenor of the performances and Rossdale's interviews are to be believed) or as catchy commercial hard rock (which is what the best moments of their first two records were). In an effort to develop their own voice and to be taken seriously, Bush has left behind their natural strengths—a knack for melodic hooks and riffs. They're undoubtedly sincere and have delivered a professional record, but once *The Science of Things* is finished it fades away, since it has neither the emotional nor musical substance to make a lasting impact. —*Stephen Thomas Erlewine*

Kate Bush

b. Jul. 30, 1958, Bexleyheath, Kent, England

Vocals, Keyboards, Piano / College Rock, Prog-Rock/Art Rock, Alternative Pop/Rock

One of the most successful and popular solo female acts of the past 20 years to come out of England, Kate Bush is also one of the most unusual, with her keening vocals and unusually literate and complex body of songs. By the time Bush was 16, she had signed to EMI Records, though the company made the decision to bring her along slowly. In 1977, her debut single "Wuthering Heights" rose to number one on the British charts. By the beginning of the 1980s, Bush was established as one of the most challenging and eccentric artists ever to have achieved success in rock music, with a range of sounds and interests that constantly challenged listeners. Her third album *Never for Ever* hit number one, as did her fifth, *Hounds of Love*. The latter remained on top for a full month, and soon after, the single "Running Up That Hill" gave Bush her long-awaited American breakthrough, reaching number 30 on *Billboard's* charts. In October of 1989, Bush's first new album in almost four years, *The Sensual World*, reached the British number two spot. Bush's next album, *The Red Shoes* (1993), debuted in the American Top 30, the first time one of her albums had ever charted that high. —*Bruce Eder*

The Kick Inside / Feb. 17, 1978 / EMI America ✦✦✦✦✦

Bush's first album is her most unabashedly romantic, the sound of an impressionable and highly precocious teenage singer/songwriter spreading her wings for the first time. "Wuthering Heights" was a monster hit everywhere in the world except America, and it's still an impressive debut nearly 20 years later, but Bush would do better work than this. —*Bruce Eder*

Lionheart / Nov. 13, 1978 / EMI America ✦✦✦

Bush's second album was something of a disappointment, lacking the depth and certainty of direction of her debut. The title track is an enigmatic paean to her mother country, "Wow" is a strong vocal workout but somewhat on the obscure side, and the rest is enjoyable and teasing but nowhere near what Bush is capable of. —*Bruce Eder*

Never for Ever / Sep. 8, 1980 / EMI America ✦✦✦

Kate Bush returned to form on her third album, which is steeped in images of violence and anger ("Babooshka," "The Wedding List") but also includes fascinating references to classical music ("Delius"). Very finely produced as well. —*Bruce Eder*

The Dreaming / Sep. 13, 1982 / EMI America ✦✦

Four albums into her burgeoning career, Kate Bush's *The Dreaming* is a theatrical, and abstract piece of work, as well as Bush's first effort in the production seat. She throws herself in head first, incorporating various vocal loops, sometimes campy, but always romantic and inquisitive of emotion. She's angry and pensive throughout the entire album, typically poetic while pushing around the notions of a male-dominated world. However, Kate Bush is a daydreamer. Unfortunately, *The Dreaming*, with all it's intricate mystical beauty, isn't fully embraced compared to her later work. Album opener "Sat In Your Lap" is a frightening slight on individual intellect with a booming chorus echoing over throbbing percussion and a butchered brass section. "Leave It Open" is goth-like with Bush's dark brooding, which is a suspending scale of vocalic laments, but it's the vivacious and moody "Get Out of My House" that truly brings Bush's many talents for art and music to the forefront. It prances with dripping piano drops and gritty guitar, and the violent rage felt as she screams "Slamming," sparking a fury similar to what Tori Amos ignited during her inception throughout the 1990s. Not one to be in fear of fear, *The Dreaming* is one of Kate Bush's underrated achievements in depicting her own visions of love, relationships, and role play, not to mention a brilliant predecessor to the charming beauty of 1985's *Hounds of Love*. —*MacKenzie Wilson*

Hounds of Love / 1985 / EMI America ✦✦✦✦✦

Bush's strongest album to date marked her breakthrough into the American charts, and yielded a set of dazzling videos. The material ranges from the sensual ("Hounds of Love," "Running Up That Hill"—the latter one of the most sensual recordings ever made) to the mystical ("Hello Earth," "The Morning Fog"). This was also the first album produced by Bush entirely at her own home studio, and the results are spellbinding, the layered instruments recalling the Beatles at the most ornate, but also displaying an exquisite timbral range, bringing out the richness of the individual instruments. Note: The British edition of this and Bush's earlier albums all have significantly better sound than their American editions and are worth finding as imports. [In 1997, as a part of EMI's 100th Anniversary, *Hounds of Love* was reissued, augmented with a bunch of rare singles, B-sides, outtakes etc. from the same period.] —*Bruce Eder*

● **The Whole Story** / Nov. 10, 1986 / EMI America ✦✦✦✦✦

Bush's first best-of is an excellent compilation/overview, encompassing all her best-known songs (including "Wuthering Heights" with an improved, re-recorded vocal track) up through the major tracks off of *Hounds of Love* and her follow-up single, the haunting and dramatic "Experiment IV." —*Bruce Eder*

The Sensual World / Oct. 1989 / Columbia ♦♦♦♦♦

The enchanting songstress Kate Bush reflects the most heavenly views of love on the aptly titled *The Sensual World*. Her most intimate, yet most charming effort since *Hounds of Love*, Bush is unafraid to be a temptress, vocally and lyrically. She's a romantic, frolicking over lust and love, but also a lover of life and its spirituality. The album's title track exudes the most sensually abrasive side of Bush, but she is also one to remain emotionally intact with her heart and head. The majority of *The Sensual World* beams with a carefree spirit of strength and independence. "Love and Danger," which features blistering riffs by Bush's mentor and cohort David Gilmour, thrives on self-analysis—how typically cathartic of Bush. Michael Nyman's delicate string arrangements allow the melodic "Reaching Out" to simply arrive, freely floating with Bush's lush vocalic declaration—"Reaching out for the Star/Reaching out for the Star that explodes"—for she's always searching for a common peace, a commonality to make comfort. What makes Kate Bush so intriguing is her look toward the future—she appears to look beyond what's present and find a peculiar celestial atmosphere in which human beings do exist. She's conscious of technology on "Deeper Understanding" and of a greater life on the glam-rock experimental "Rocket's Tail (For Rocket)," yet she's still intrinsic to the reality of an individual's heart. "Between a Man and a Woman" depicts pressure and heartbreak, but it's the beauty of "This Woman's Work" that makes *The Sensual World* the outstanding piece of work that it is. She possesses maternal warmth that's surely inviting, and it's something that's made her one of the most prolific female singer/songwriters to emerge during the 1980s. She's never belonged to a core scene. Bush's intelligence, both as an artist and as a woman, undoubtedly casts her in a league of her own. *—MacKenzie Wilson*

This Woman's Work (1978-1990) / 1990 / EMI ♦♦♦♦♦

Excellent box collecting all of Bush's work, including obscure B-sides, odd mixes, and other rarities in one place. The notes are skimpy, and some people who already own some of her individual CDs will be unhappy having to duplicate their purchases, but the rarities are fascinating, and because this set is from England, it uses the superior British masters on the 1978-1985 albums. [British import] *–Bruce Eder*

The Red Shoes / Nov. 2, 1993 / Columbia ♦♦

The album is a continuation of Bush's multi-layered and multiple musical pursuits and interests. If not her strongest work—a number of songs sound okay without being particularly stellar, especially given Bush's past heights—*Red Shoes* is still an enjoyable listen with a number of diversions. The guest performer list is worthy of note alone, ranging from Procol Harum keyboardist Gary Brooker and Eric Clapton to Prince, but this is very much a Kate Bush album straight up as opposed to a collaborative work like, say, Santana's *Supernatural*. Opening song "Rubberband Girl" is actually one of her strongest singles in years, a big and punchy song served well with a horn section, though slightly let down by the stiff percussion. "Eat the Music," another smart choice for a single, mixes calypso and other Caribbean musical touches with a great, classically Bush lyric mixing up sexuality, romance, and various earthy food-based metaphors. Another highlight of Bush's frank embrace of the lustier side of life is "The Song of Solomon," a celebratory piece about the Bible's openly erotic piece. Those who prefer her predominantly piano and vocal pieces will enjoy "Moments of Pleasure" with a strong string arrangement courtesy of Michael Kamen. Other standouts include "Why Should I Love You?" with Prince creating a very Prince-like arrangement and backing chorus for Bush (and doing quite well at that) and the concluding "You're the One," with Brooker laying down some of his trademark Hammond organ sound for the slow piece. *—Ned Raggett*

Bernard Butler

Guitar / Adult Alternative Pop/Rock, Britpop, Alternative Pop/Rock, Hard Rock, Singer/Songwriter

Hailed by some critics as the greatest guitarist of his generation, Bernard Butler shied away from the ramifications of that statement, abandoning the Brit-pop pioneers Suede at the height of their career in 1994 to pursue his own muse. And, much like his idol Johnny Marr, Butler's solo career was anything but predictable, as he flipped between session work, a duo with David McAlmont and eventually a recording career as a solo singer/songwriter. Butler rose to prominence with Suede, the British indie band who fused glam crunch with the songcraft and exaggerated angst of the Smiths. Upon the release of their 1992 debut single, "The Drowners," Suede were hailed by many corners of the British music press as the best band in Britain. In many ways, they lived up to the hype, as their eponymous 1993 debut broke sales records and kick-started the indie rock revolution that became Brit-pop. In August 1994, he decided he had enough and he left the band. Early in 1995, he hooked up with cult soul singer David McAlmont. It was unclear whether the teaming was permanent or temporary, but that summer they released two singles, "Yes" and "You Do," which were modest successes. By the fall, the duo had split up acrimoniously, with a compilation album, *The Sound of McAlmont-Butler*, being released early in 1996. For much of that year, he worked as a sideman. He then signed with Creation and began work on his first album, playing nearly all the instruments himself. Released in the fall of 1997, his first single "Stay" indicated that he was going in a more subdued direction than Suede. Those suspicions were confirmed by his full-length debut *People Move On*, a folk-tinged singer/songwriter album released to generally positive reviews in the spring of 1998. *—Stephen Thomas Erlewine*

People Move On / Apr. 14, 1998 / Creation/Columbia ♦♦♦

People Move On suffers from a problem common to solo albums—now that the artist is freed from the confines of his group, he is compelled to show that he can do it all on his own. Since Bernard Butler has always traded in major statements, this flaw hurts him less than others, but it still prevents *People Move On* from being the tour de force it was intended to be. Part of the problem is Butler's thin, wispy voice, which often sounds like it's straining to hit the notes. On the gentle acoustic numbers, it can be convincing, but it hardly sells the sweeping, cinematic songs. "Woman I Know," "You Just Know," "Not Alone" and "Stay" are so busy they barely make sense. All the overdubbed backing vocals, keyboards and guitars sound disassociated from each other, adding up to awkward attempts at grand statements that fall flat. He's much better at the quieter moments, such as "You've Got What It Takes" and "You Light the Fire." These moments of introspection are what give *People Move On* weight, and what make it a promising solo debut. *—Stephen Thomas Erlewine*

● **Friends and Lovers** / Feb. 1, 2000 / Creation/Columbia ♦♦♦♦

For his second album, *Friends & Lovers*, Bernard Butler trimmed away the folkier elements of his debut—ironically, those were highlights on *People Move On*—returning to the sweeping, glam-inflected pop-rock that provided the impetus for Suede. He may have a grander vision and a larger palette, yet he has greater focus this time. *Friends & Lovers* opens majestically with its title track, surging forward with an anthemic, post-Bowie chorus and subdued psychedelic strings. Butler uses this template throughout the record, delivering songs that blend late-'60s and '70s rock conventions and clichés in unpredictable ways, never once resorting to irony or pastiche. Butler is a craftsman, laboring on the structure of his songs, the flow of the arrangement, and the sonic texture of the production, resulting in an abundance of great guitar playing and some wonderful harmonies and keyboards, all woven together in a stylish, seamless sonic tapestry. This technique may be sonically resplendent, but it's not without pitfalls. Each track has dazzling moments, yet few stand apart from the pack, largely because, as a frontman, Butler doesn't sell them. His thin voice tends to fade into the mix, becoming part of the wall of sound; consequently, *Friends & Lovers* gracefully rolls in, then washes away without leaving a lasting impression. This may sound churlish, but this music is crying out for a larger-than-life personality, a vocalist on the level of Brett Anderson. *Friends & Lovers* must be enjoyed as the work of a meticulous, talented, craftsman, a musician who loves to slowly build his record, track by track, and there's a lot to enjoy on that level, even if it leaves you with a nagging feeling that it could have been something more. *—Stephen Thomas Erlewine*

Jerry Butler

b. Dec. 8, 1939, Sunflower, MS

Vocals / Chicago Soul, Uptown Soul, Pop-Soul, Northern Soul, R&B, Soul

Jerry Butler's career spans four decades; he's recorded more than 50 albums and his voice is one of the most distinguished voices in all of music. As soulful as ever, yet smooth as ice, his nickname "The Iceman" epitomizes his demeanor—and sound. Butler scored his first hit with the Impressions in 1958 with the timeless ballad "For Your Precious Love." That same year he began his solo career. Butler had his first hit as a solo artist with "He Will Break Your Heart." The single popped to the top of the charts at number one and stayed there for seven consecutive weeks. In 1961 Butler bounced back with two top ten singles: "Find Another Girl" and "I'm a Telling You." In 1967 Butler signed with Mercury and teamed up with the production duo of Kenny Gamble and Leon Huff. His work with these two master producers and songwriters resulted in some classic recordings, including the outstanding album *Ice Man Cometh*. The album featured one superb track after another, including the number one singles "Hey, Western Union Man" and "Only the Strong Survive." Always known for being a crooner, "Hey, Western Union Man" revealed to many that Butler was more than capable of singing uptempo songs. In 1971 Gamble and Huff formed their own label and subsequently Butler formed a creative workshop to help provide material for his forthcoming albums. He continued his hit-making tradition with "Ain't Understanding Mellow," a classic soul-ballad duet with Brenda Lee Eager that peaked at number three on the Billboard R&B charts. The timeless single remains a Quiet Storm jewel. "(I'm Just Thinking About) Cooling Out" was his last top 20 hit. *—Craig Lytle*

★ **The Best of Jerry Butler** / 1987 / Rhino ♦♦♦♦♦

The primary value of this 14-song collection is that it includes material from both the Vee-Jay and Mercury eras. Butler fans are much better advised to get the compilations that cover his output for each label in much greater depth (*The Ice Man* for Vee-Jay, *Iceman: The Mercury Years* for Mercury). For the casual fan, though, it might be the best buy, as it's the only best-of spanning both labels, and includes all of his biggest hits. *—Richie Unterberger*

☆ **Iceman: The Mercury Years** / Feb. 4, 1992 / Mercury ♦♦♦♦♦

A glorious 44-song double-disc set, it collects Butler's best Mercury sides, with several previously unreleased songs and alternate mixes. The liner notes are crummy, though. *—John Floyd*

20th Century Masters—The Millennium Collection: The Best of Jerry Butler / Oct. 17, 2000 / Mercury ♦♦♦♦

The Best of Jerry Butler: The Millennium Collection collects 11 of the soul singer's definitive hits, including "Only the Strong Survive," "Hey, Western Union Man," "One Night Affair," "I Dig You Baby," and his duet with Brenda Lee Eager, "Ain't Understanding Mellow." A new essay about Butler and new remastering add to this collection's worth; though it may not be the most comprehensive Butler retrospective available, it's still a good introduction to his career highlights. *—Heather Phares*

The Sweetest Soul / Feb. 9, 2001 / RPM ♦♦♦♦

This is a very good British anthology covering Butler's Vee-Jay era, the 26 tracks including all of his major solo hits with the label in the first half of the 1960s: "He Will Break Your Heart," "Moon River," "Find Another Girl," "I'm a Telling You," "Make It Easy on Yourself," and "Need to Belong." There's also the bonus of his big 1958 hit with the Impressions, "For Your Precious Love," although his huge 1964 duet smash with Betty

Everett, "Let It Be Me," is absent. It's not just a recycling of the material found on the most comprehensive U.S. retrospective of Butler's Vee-Jay period, *The Iceman*; almost half of these songs are not found on the American counterpart. That's an important distinction, since some of the cuts only on *The Sweetest Soul* are notable, such as the fine 1964 ballad "Giving Up on Love," and a few songs that Curtis Mayfield wrote or co-wrote. Unfortunately the original release dates are not given for all of the songs in the track listings and liner notes, and some of the non-hit tracks are much less memorable than Butler's best efforts for Vee-Jay. But these are the only small reservations that apply to this quality early soul disc. *—Richie Unterberger*

Paul Butterfield

b. Dec. 17, 1942, Chicago, IL, **d.** May 4, 1987, Hollywood, CA

Vocals, Leader, Harmonica, Guitar, Flute / Modern Electric Chicago Blues, Harmonica Blues, Blues-Rock, Electric Chicago Blues, Chicago Blues, Electric Harmonica Blues

The first two Paul Butterfield Blues Band albums are essential from an historical perspective. While *East-West*, the second album, with its Eastern influence and extended solos set the tone for psychedelic rockers, it was that incredible first album that alerted the music scene as to what was coming. Although it has been perhaps over-emphasized in recent years, it is important to point out that the release of *The Paul Butterfield Blues Band* on Elektra in 1965, had a huge effect on the White music culture of the time. Used to hearing blues covered by groups like the Rolling Stones, that first album had an enormous impact on young (and primarily White) rock players. Here is no deferential imitation of Black music by Whites, but a racially-mixed hard-driving blues album that, in a word, rocked. It was a signal to White players to stop making respectful tributes to Black music, and just play it. In a flash the image of blues as old-time music was gone. Modern Chicago-style urban blues was out of the closet and introduced to mainstream White audiences, who loved it. Fueled by guitarist Michael Bloomfield's infatuation with Eastern music and Indian ragas at the time and aided by Billy Davenport's jazz-driven sophistication on drums, there arose in the group a new music form that was to greatly affect rock music—the extended solo. There is little question that here is the root of psychedelic (acid) rock—a genuine fusion between East and West. Those first two albums served as a wakeup call to an entire generation of White would-be blues musicians. Speaking as one who was on the scene, that first Butterfield album stopped us in our tracks and we were never the same afterward. It changed our lives. *—Michael Erlewine*

An Offer You Can't Refuse / 1963 / M.I.L. Multimedia ♦♦♦

An album released on the Red Lightnin' label in 1972 consisting of one side of Big Walter Horton and the other side with very early Paul Butterfield (1963) (See: Big Walter Horton). Contains six tracks with Butterfield, Smokey Smothers on guitar, Jerome Arnold on bass, and Sam Lay on drums. This was recorded at Big Johns, the North side Chicago club where the Butterfield Band first played in 1963—some two years before the material on the first Paul Butterfield Blues Band album, which was released in 1965. The six tracks include two instrumentals, "Got My Mojo Working" and the Butterfield-authored tune "Loaded." Although this is very early Butterfield, the harp playing is excellent and already in his own unique style. The singing is a little rough and heavy sounding. Butterfield fans will want to find this rare vinyl for musical and historical reasons. *—Michael Erlewine*

The Original Lost Elektra Sessions / Dec. 1964 / Rhino ♦♦♦♦♦

All but one of these 19 tracks were recorded in December, 1964, as Butterfield's projected first LP; the results were scrapped and replaced by their official self-titled debut, cut a few months later. With both Bloomfield and Bishop already in tow, these sessions rank among the earliest blues-rock ever laid down. Extremely similar in feel to the first album, it's perhaps a bit rawer in production and performance, but not appreciably worse or different than what ended up on the actual debut LP. Dedicated primarily to electric Chicago blues standards, Butterfield fans will find this well worth acquiring, as most of the selections were never officially recorded by the first lineup (although different renditions of five tracks showed up on the first album and the *What's Shakin'* compilation). *—Richie Unterberger*

☆ **Paul Butterfield Blues Band** / 1965 / Elektra ♦♦♦♦♦

Butterfield's unique amplified harmonica style is already present on this classic first album—a wakeup call for a generation of young White players used to hearing blues filtered through covers by groups like the Rolling Stones or as a part of music history. Here was a racially mixed group of brilliant young players that rocked—an historic album. Great guitar from Michael Bloomfield and Elvin Bishop. With Mark Naftalin (organ), Jerome Arnold (bass), and Sam Lay (drums). *—Michael Erlewine*

★ **East-West** / 1966 / Elektra ♦♦♦♦♦

The second Butterfield album had an even greater effect on music history, paving the way for experimentation that is still being explored today. This came in the form of an extended blues-rock solo (some 13 minutes)—a real fusion of jazz and blues inspired by the Indian raga. This ground-breaking instrumental was the first of its kind and marks the root from which the acid rock tradition emerged. *—Jeff Tarmarkin and Michael Erlewine*

East-West Live / 1966-1967 / Winner ♦♦♦♦

The tune "East-West" from the second Butterfield Blues Band album of the same name made music history. It is arguably the first extended rock solo, a fusing of blues-rock with Eastern scales and tone. Here is the root of psychedelic—acid rock. Now, thanks to Mark Naftalin (the original Butterfield keyboardist), we have three live recordings of "East-West" recorded in 1966-1967 that capture the origin and development of this classic tune. The first example (some 12 minutes) was taped prior to the edited studio version; the second (16 minutes) and third (28 minutes) were recorded after the album cut. There is some great music (and music history) here. *—Michael Erlewine*

The Resurrection of Pigboy Crabshaw / 1967 / Elektra ♦♦♦♦♦

In his third album, Butterfield adds a horn section and the direction of the group has started to veer away from straight Chicago-style blues toward a sound more influenced by R&B. By this time, Bloomfield has left the group and Elvin Bishop (aka Pigboy Crabshaw) takes over on lead guitar. A lot of great tunes here, like "Driftin' and Driftin." *—Michael Erlewine*

Strawberry Jam / 1996 / Winner ♦♦♦

These nine cuts are from various live performances of the Paul Butterfield Blues Band during their heyday in the middle-to-late '60s. This album was put together by Mark Naftalin, who played keyboards on those first few incredible Butterfield albums. Don't look for the clearest sound (it's adequate) because these are live tunes recorded at clubs, often with minimal equipment. It is the music that is in focus here—a window into that incredible band at a time when they were hot. Those of us who were on the scene at the time know that, although the original Butterfield albums are great, the band was a total knockout when heard live. Featuring Butterfield's harmonica, here are glimpses into that time and music. Most of the tunes have appeared elsewhere, but the extended instrumental "Strawberry Jam" (written by Naftalin) is unique to this album—worth hearing. It features great guitar by Elvin Bishop. *—Michael Erlewine*

An Anthology—The Elektra Years / Oct. 28, 1997 / Elektra ♦♦♦♦♦

An Anthology—The Elektra Years is a double-disc, 33-song set that offers a comprehensive overview of Paul Butterfield's eight years with the label. His first two albums, *Paul Butterfield Blues Band* and *East-West*, were seminal, groundbreaking records that blurred the boundaries between blues, jazz and rock, suggesting everything from blues-rock to psychedelia. They were stunning achievements which proved to be difficult to match, but Butterfield's remaining albums for the label all had a few good cuts. *An Anthology* does a nice job of rounding up those highlights, picking the best moments from uneven records; consequently, it's quite a valuble package for listeners who simply want a sampling from those later albums instead of purchasing them individually. Butterfield's first two albums remain necessary listens in their own right, but this set offers an excellent summary of his entire stint with Elektra. *—Stephen Thomas Erlewine*

The Butthole Surfers

f. 1982, San Antonio, TX

College Rock, Experimental Rock, Noise-Rock, Alternative Pop/Rock, American Underground

Arguably the most infamously named band in the annals of popular music—for years, radio found their moniker unspeakable, and the press deemed it unprintable—the Butthole Surfers long reigned among the most twisted and depraved acts ever to bubble up from the American underground. Masters of calculated outrage, the group fused the sicko antics of shock-rock with a distinct and chaotic mishmash of avant-garde, hardcore and Texas psychedelia which seemed destined to guarantee the Buttholes little more than a lifetime of cultdom. Yet, by the mid-'90s, they were left-field Top 40 hitmakers, success perhaps their ultimate subversion of mainstream ideals. Gibby Haynes and Paul Leary founded the band and in 1981 signed to Alternative Tentacles for their hallucinatory eponymous debut. The Surfers' lineup stabilized with the 1983 addition of drummers King Coffey and Theresa Nervosa and a move to the Chicago-based indie Touch and Go precipitated a turn towards even greater thematic offensiveness, as evidenced by 1985's *Psychic... Powerless... Another Man's Sac*. Following a series of late-'80s albums, they remained uncharacteristically silent until 1991's uneven *Pioughd*, recorded for the Rough Trade label. One year later, the group signed with major label Capitol, which released 1993's *Independent Worm Saloon*. The Butthole Surfers returned in 1996 with *Electriclarryland*, scoring a major chart hit with the trip-hop-flavored "Pepper." *—Jason Ankeny*

Brown Reason to Live [EP] / 1983 / Alternative Tentacles ♦♦♦♦

Live PCPPEP / 1984 / Alternative Tentacles ♦♦♦

Psychic... Powerless... Another Man's Sac / 1985 / Latino Bugger Veil ♦♦♦♦

The Surfers' Touch and Go debut remains their highlight for many fans, an inspired blast of ugly noise, knowing idiocy, drugged-out insanity and some backhanded surprises. Haynes is still relatively interpretable here; the vocal distortions are only on a few songs, like the opening "Concubine," and what one can't quite understand one can still sense. The band's self-production brings out the mighty rumbles of drummers Coffey and Nervosa and Leary's avant-junkyard guitar work with clarity and a big, thick punch. Leary begins with screwy blues and gentle strums, then cranks up the amps and lets fly. The band also officially recorded their semi-theme song "Butthole Surfer," after which they were accidentally named; the bizarro backing vocals and sudden sped-up shifts at the end are just part of the oddities on display. "Negro Observer" is one of the most straightforward, calmest songs of the bunch, and even that's saying something, with Haynes going off about the title characters—described as aliens coming to "count heads in singles bars"—like a barely stable street crazy, insane laughter and all. When it comes to full-on craziness, though, nothing beats the obscene "Lady Sniff," which sounds like an amped-up blues act fronted by a 100-year-old man, and the hallucinatory "Mexican Caravan," with Haynes raving about "that heroin BROWN!" The nods to rock history are subtle but present, from the Black Sabbath-quoting (specifically "Children of the Grave") opening rhythm of "Dum Dum" to the fried Tex/Mex-ranting of "Gary Floyd," written about the legendary Dicks bandleader. However, the Surfers' crazy blend is completely distinctive, taking punk and the inspiration of their acid-addled Texas forebears to new heights. *—Ned Raggett*

Cream Corn from the Socket of Davis / 1985 / Touch & Go ♦♦♦

The title makes about as much sense as anything in the Surfers' universe, so hey, why complain? This four-song slice of surferdom has one of the group's most well-known numbers, "Moving to Florida." It's actually one of the more atypical songs from the band, consisting of little more than a brisk blues/rockabilly run with heavy echo alternating with a cappella weirdness from Gibby Haynes muttering about things like "toilet training with Chairman Mao." Occasional screaming outbursts (vocally and musically) keep the variety up. "Comb" is a slow cruncher with the patented Haynes vocal distortion and weirdness in full effect; Paul Leary really goes to town with treatments on his guitar, foreshadowing the screwier work to come, while the whole thing ends with fart and piss sounds (of course). "To Parter" has Haynes talking about selling Quaaludes to monkeys and the like over an at-times pretty Morricone-gone-psych arrangement, while "Toronados" ends things with a goofy romp and rant. *—Ned Raggett*

Rembrandt Pussyhorse / 1986 / Latino Bugger Veil ♦♦♦♦
Everything seems to start almost normally on *Pussyhorse* with "Creep in the Cellar," even with the rather gone violin line—Haynes is intelligible, the piano part is quiet serene. Then again, Haynes is talking about the creep in question doing things like taking off his skin, so clearly all is still at least somewhat tweaked in Surferland. The rest of the album makes that pretty clear; if not quite as strong as *Psychic... Powerless*, *Pussyhorse* is still a strong slice of homegrown art/psychedelia gone to a murky hell. Gentler songs like "Sea Ferring" still have a distinct queasiness to them, its sea chanty feeling undercut by the nagging bass line and Haynes' yelps. When the group goes totally nuts, as on a drum-blasting, squiggly voiced cover of the Guess Who's "American Woman" that makes the later Lenny Kravitz version seem like the redundant slice of nostalgia it is, no prisoners are taken. "Perry" is another definite nutter, with Haynes or somebody talking about this and that to his "baby" over a slow, organ-heavy groove. This said, the trick about *Pussyhorse*, and arguably why it's slightly lesser than *Psychic... Powerless*, is its overall subtlety in comparison. Things are more dark and gloomy throughout, downright gothic, even, with the organ start and whispery lyrics of "Strangers Die Everyday" being a good example. Leary keeps his playing low and strange throughout, fitting in with new bassist Pinkus rather well as a result. Get past the slight surprise of not always hearing the Surfers going near-all out most of the time, though, and *Pussyhorse* is still mighty fine, whether talking about the drony guitar weirdness opening "Whirling Hall of Knives" or the echo-treated reprise of "In the Cellar." CD versions of *Pussyhorse* conveniently include the *Cream Corn From the Socket of Davis* EP. *—Ned Raggett*

● **Locust Abortion Technician** / 1987 / Latino Bugger Veil ♦♦♦♦♦
The aural equivalent of a nightmarish acid trip and arguably the band's best album (or worst, depending on your point of view), *Locust Abortion Technician* tops the psychedelic, artsy sonic experimentation of *Rembrandt Pussyhorse* while keeping one foot planted firmly in the gutter. The record veers from heavy Sabbath sludge (even parodying that band on "Sweat Loaf") to grungy noise-rock to progressive guitar and tape effects to almost folky numbers in one big, gloriously schizophrenic mess. Gibby Haynes debuts his "Gibbytronix" vocal effects unit here as well. *—Steve Huey*

Hairway to Steven / 1988 / Latino Bugger Veil ♦♦♦♦♦
The final album for the Surfers' legendary run on Touch and Go got a reception probably not even the band figured on—lead reviews in major music magazines, increasingly higher profiles, and more. As it is, though, *Hairway* is actually a touch lazy in comparison to the previous releases, sometimes sounding almost all too normal. When it connects, though, *Steven* works wonders, whether continuing in the punk/psychedelic fusion vein of the past or exploring a gentler, tuneful side. The lengthy opener "Jimi" is the album's high note, and as one might guess from the title it's something of a tribute to Hendrix—at least, if "Third Stone From the Sun" sounded like it was recorded in a sewer tunnel and was even more gone than it already was. Haynes' alternately deep and hyper-high-pitched vocals work perfectly against Leary's searing, crazed guitar noises, while the Pinkus/Coffey rhythm section lays down a massive beat. Everything concludes with deceptive peacefulness: acoustic guitar, tweeting birds, sounds of bowling, and the like. Other highlights include "I Saw an X-Ray of a Girl Passing Gas," a relatively straightforward, mostly acoustic-plus-rhythm section number sung clearly (!) by Haynes, and the mock live recording "John E. Smokes," with Haynes often sounding like a rural preacher gone mad. The humming guitar buzz of "Backass" and the quick blast of "Fart Song" concludes *Steven* with vim. As a final note, the song titles themselves can't be found anywhere on the release—instead, and quite notoriously, a series of cartoon drawings stand in for them. Some are fairly calm, but most show things like nude women displaying their butts and rabbits taking dumps on deer. Juvenile? Of course, but the Butthole Surfers never pretended to be nice and sweet. *—Ned Raggett*

Double Live / 1989 / Touch & Go ♦♦

Pioughd / 1991 / Capitol ♦♦

Independent Worm Saloon / Mar. 23, 1993 / Capitol ♦♦♦
After *Pioughd*'s semi-misfire and Rough Trade's subsequent collapse, the Surfers were in a surprising position. Not only were they courted and signed to Capitol thanks to the Nirvana-led alternative explosion, they also got high-profile arranger and Led Zeppelin legend John Paul Jones to produce the new album. When *Saloon* surfaced in early 1993, some accused the band of basically cloning Haynes' memorable collaboration with Ministry, "Jesus Built My Hot Rod," for the entire album. It's true that "Some Dispute Over T-Shirt Sales," simply takes the lyrics from that number and grafts it onto a quick rip from the band, but *Saloon* is far from a clone of Ministry or anything else. More energetic than the straggling *Pioughd* and benefiting from Jones' brilliant ear and tight, crisp arrangements, *Saloon* starts with the fierce "Who Was In My Room Last Night?"; from there, the Surfers tear through hilarious and strong numbers. Creating radio-friendly unit shifters was clearly the last thing on the band's mind, as numbers like "The Annoying Song," with Haynes sounding like what a radar dish would do if it could sing, and the wittily solemn acoustic ditty "The Ballad of Naked Man" demonstrate. The Surfers' taste for rude grostequerie surfaces throughout—the foul "Chewin' George Lucas' Chocolate," the series of vomit sounds that conclude the record after "Clean It Up"'s heavy trudge and the extremely disturbing artwork are just a few examples. Combined with numerous examples of Surfer-mania at its finest—the dipsomaniacal rager "Alcohol," the electric country hoedown "You Don't Know Me" and more—and *Saloon* is that rarest of records, a major-label debut that surpasses the indie release preceding it. *—Ned Raggett*

Hole Truth . . . And Nothing Butt / Mar. 27, 1995 / Trance Syndicate ♦♦♦

Electriclarryland / Apr. 1996 / Capitol ♦♦♦
On *Electriclarryland*, their second major-label album, the Butthole Surfers continue the streamlined direction they began with *Independent Worm Saloon*, which basically means it's a loud guitar rock album. Even though there's potential for the record to become unnecessarily generic, it's to the Buttholes' credit that they still have the desire to throw enough bizarre wrenches into the machinery to keep most of their diehard audience satiated. Certainly, *Electriclarryland* will sound way too tame for fans of *Locust Abortion Technican* and *Hairway to Steven*, and they're right, to a certain extent. For listeners accustomed to their unhinged, perverse '80s recordings, there is nothing on this guitar-heavy record to please them. But *Electriclarryland* is a logical maturation for the band. It's odd to think of the Buttholes maturing, but that is the case with this album. They have a couple of jangly pop numbers that appear to be played relatively straight and the heavier numbers have a piledriving inevitability that make them memorable. In short, *Electriclarryland* rocks and it rocks hard, with enough energy for bands half of the Buttholes' age. And underneath the seemingly normal surface, the Buttholes have thrown in enough jokes and have twisted around enough clichés to prove that the band may mature, but they'll never really grow up. *—Stephen Thomas Erlewine*

After the Astronaut / Apr. 7, 1998 / Capitol ♦♦

Weird Revolution / Aug. 28, 2001 / Hollywood ♦♦♦♦

The Buzzcocks

f. 1975, Manchester, England
British Punk, Punk
With their crisp melodies, driving guitars, and guitarist Pete Shelley's biting lyrics, the Buzzcocks were one of the best, most influential punk bands. Inspired by the Sex Pistols' energy, the Buzzcocks didn't copy the Pistols' angry political stance; they brought that intense, brilliant energy to the three-minute pop song. Shelly's alternately funny and anguished lyrics about adolescence and love were some of the best of his era, and their melodies and hooks were pointed and memorable. Their punk-pop proved to be enormously influential, with echoes of their music being apparent in everyone from Hüsker Dü to Nirvana.

Shelley and Howard Devoto formed the Buzzcocks in Manchester in early 1976, adding bassist Steve Diggle and drummer John Maher. In January 1977, the group released their debut EP, *Spiral Scratch*, the first independently released record of the punk era. Shortly after its release, Devoto quit the group; he later formed Magazine. Following Devoto's departure, Shelley became lead vocalist. The Buzzcocks signed with United Artists September 1977, releasing their debut single, "Orgasm Addict," a month later. Their first album, *Another Music in a Different Kitchen* appeared in March 1978; the second, *Love Bites*, arrived six months later. Their rapid recording and performing schedules had effects on the group, and their third album, 1979's *A Different Kind of Tension*, displayed some signs of wear and tear. EMI bought out UA in 1980 and the new label prevented the Buzzcocks from recording their fourth album until the compilation *Singles Going Steady* was released in the U.K. Shelley decided to break up the band instead of fight the label. In 1989, the group re-formed and toured the United States. By 1990, the reunion had become permanent, albeit with a new lineup of Shelley, Diggle, bassist Tony Barber, and drummer Phil Barker; this incarnation debuted on 1993's *Trade Test Transmission*. Throughout the rest of the '90s, the Buzzcocks continued to tour and record at a steady pace. *—Stephen Thomas Erlewine*

Time's Up / 1977 / Mute ♦♦♦
A fascinating semi-legitimate release of all the studio work the Howard Devoto-fronted band recorded in Manchester in October 1976. This is an expensive disc that only clocks in at 24 minutes, but it's 24 pretty great minutes. Some of the material (e.g., the cover of Captain Beefheart's "I Love You, You Big Dummy") Devoto took with him to Magazine, but the rest of the material is prime Buzzcocks: "Orgasm Addict," "Breakdown," and "Boredom" to name but a few. With Devoto singing lead, the band sound a bit more Sex Pistols-ish (something that would change when Shelley took over singing lead), and, therefore, a tad more ominous. Difficult to find but well worth the effort. *—John Dougan*

Spiral Scratch / Jan. 29, 1977 / Mute ♦♦♦♦♦
The Buzzcocks' self-financed debut is every bit as important as the Sex Pistols' "Anarchy in the UK" in the establishment of the U.K. punk scene. And playing those two cultural artifacts back to back two decades later, it is the Pistols' effort which sounds more like the museum piece. *Spiral Scratch*'s hand-pressed, blurry black-and-white sleeve housed four tracks—each one a uniquely compelling experience, marrying raw, youthful zest with belligerent intelligence. The EP's release achieved several things at once. It opened up the independent scene, making D.I.Y. labels the natural springboard for aspiring musicians. It gave the punk scene a second regional base in Manchester, and it expanded punk's vocabulary beyond the outright nihilism evinced by London bands. And, even at this stage, the band's musicianship was a joy to behold, particularly the uninhibited drumming of John Maher. This was also, bootlegs apart, the only chance to hear Howard Devoto front the band before he left to form Magazine. For more of the same, check out the *Time's*

Up album, a classic bootleg of the group's early days which has seen official release. —*Alex Ogg*

Another Music in a Different Kitchen / 1978 / United Artists ✦✦✦
General judgment holds the Buzzcocks' peerless singles, the definition of punk-pop at its finest, as the best expression of their work. However, while the singles showcased one particular side of the band, albums like the group's long-playing debut *Another Music* showcased the foursome's other influences, sometimes brilliantly. The big secret is Shelley's worship of Krautrock's obsessive focus on repetition and rhythm, which transforms what would be "simply" basic punk songs into at-times monstrous epics. The ghost of Can particular hovers even on some of the shorter songs—unsurprising, given Shelley's worship of that band's guitarist Michael Karoli. "Moving Away From the Pulsebeat" is the best instance of this, with a rumbling Maher rhythm supporting some trancelike guitar lines. As for the sheer rush of pop craziness, *Another Music* is simply crammed with stellar examples. Lead-off track "Fast Cars" starts with the opening of *Spiral Scratch*'s "Boredom"'s intentionally hilarious two-note solo intact, before ripping into a slightly bemusing critique of the objects in question. Most of the similar tracks on the album may be more distinct for their speed, but Shelley in particular always seems to sneak in at least one astonishing line per song, sometimes on his own and sometimes thanks to Devoto via older cowritten tunes redone for the record. One favorite standout: "All this slurping and sucking—it's putting me off my food!" on "You Tear Me Up." Top all this off with any number of perfect moments—the guitar work during the breaks on "Love Battery," the energizing yet nervous coda of "Fiction Romance," the soaring angst throughout "I Don't Mind —and *Another Music* flat out succeeds. —*Ned Raggett*

Love Bites / Sep. 22, 1978 / United Artists ✦✦✦
More musically accomplished, more obsessively self-questioning, and with equally energetic yet sometimes gloomy performances, *Love Bites* finds the Buzzcocks coming into their own. With Devoto and his influence now fully worked out of the band's system, Shelley is the clearly predominant voice, with the exception of Diggle's first lead vocal on an album track, the semi-acoustic, perversely sprightly "Love is Lies." Though the song received even further acclaim on *Singles Going Steady*, "Ever Fallen in Love," for many the band's signature song, appears here. With its note-perfect blend of romance gone wrong, a weirdly catchy, treated lead guitar line, and Shelley's wounded singing deserves its instant classic status, but it's only one of many highlights. The opening "Real World" is one of the band's strongest: a chunky, forceful yet crisp band performance leads into a strong Shelley lyric about unrequited love and life. "Nostalgia"'s strikingly mature, inventive lyrics about where one's life can lead, and the sometimes charging, sometimes quietly tense, heartbroken "Nothing Left" are two other standouts. The group's well-seasoned abilities, the members' increasing reach and Martin Rushent's excellent production make *Love Bites* shine. The Garvey/Maher rhythm section is especially fine; Maher's fills and similar small but significant touches take the music to an even higher level. His undisputed highlight is the terribly underrated concluding instrumental "Late for the Train." Originally done for a John Peel radio session and rerecorded with even more a dramatic sweep here, it gives the group's motorik/Krautrock new power. Not far behind it is "E.S.P.," a strong rock burn that only fades out at the end very slowly and subtly. —*Ned Raggett*

★ **Singles Going Steady** / Sep. 1979 / IRS ✦✦✦✦
If *Never Mind the Bollocks* and *London Calling* are held up as punk masterpieces, then there's no question that *Singles Going Steady* belongs alongside them. In fact, the slew of astonishing seven-inches collected on *Steady* and their influence on future musicians—punk or otherwise—sometimes even betters more famous efforts. The title and artwork alone (the latter itself partially inspired by the Beatles' *Let it Be*) have been parodied or referred to by Halo of Flies and Don Caballero, which titled its own singles comp *Singles Breaking Up*. As for the music, anybody who ever combined full-blast rock, catchy melodies and romantic and social anxieties owes something to what the classic quartet did here. The deservedly well-known masterpiece "Ever Fallen in Love" appears along with *Love Bites*' "Just Lust," but the remaining tracks originally appeared only as individual A and B-sides, making this collection all the more essential. The earlier numbers showcase a band bursting with energy and wicked humor—the tongue-in-cheek "Orgasm Addict," details the adventures of a sex freak with a ridiculous fake orgasm vocal break to boot. However, the slightly more serious but no less frenetic singles are equally enthralling. "What Do I Get?" with its pained cry about lacking love, the deeply cynical "Everybody's Happy Nowadays" and Diggle's roaring "Harmony in My Head" are just three highlights on an album made of them. The final songs show the band incorporating their more adventuresome side into their singles, as with the slower, very Can-inspired "Why Can't I Touch It?," the semi-jokey stop-start thrash "Noise Annoys," and the Murphy's Law worries of "Something's Gone Wrong Again." —*Ned Raggett*

A Different Kind of Tension / Sept. 1979 / IRS ✦✦✦
The final album of the Buzzcocks' first phase of existence is the most fragmented of the three, with increasingly ambitious songs fighting for time with tracks that sound much like the group's earliest efforts. Said songs are often quite good, like the opening "Paradise" or the great romantic angst of "You Say You Don't Love Me," but one can sense the band working to avoid the trap the Ramones fell into by simply offering up yet more soundalikes. Diggle makes a definite mark on this album, as on the slow crawl then fast thrash "Sitting Round at Home," a highlight of *Tension* that also features his electronically distorted vocals. "Mad Mad Judy" is a slightly more straightforward blitz, but with energy to spare and a spacious feel (credit again to producer Rushent). As the album closes, the sense of slight schizophrenia resolves itself as the group embraces all-out experimentation, producing some of the Buzzcocks' all-time best songs. "Hollow Inside" shows the band's knack for disguising scalpel-sharp sentiments with seeming simplicity,

and the title track's contradictory slogans/demands, disturbing robot vocals, and nagging beat and melody up the ante even further. "I Believe" concludes things (aside from the fake found-sound snippet "Radio Nine") on the highest possible note. Shelley's slightly bemused recitation of all the things he believes in is suddenly interrupted by the line "There is no love in this world anymore," turned and electronically distorted into an obsessive, anthemic mantra as the band charges along with him up and out. An invigorating blast of, indeed, tension and angst, it alone makes *Tension* worth investigating. —*Ned Raggett*

Parts 1, 2, 3 / Feb. 1981 / IRS ✦✦✦

Lest We Forget / 1988 / ROIR ✦✦

Many Parts / 1988 / Restless Retro ✦✦✦
This collection is a bit of a ringer, surfacing only as part of the *Product* box set, but it is handy nonetheless, compiling the remaining tracks recorded by the band during its first lifetime along with a previously unreleased eight-song concert snippet. The title refers to the original *Parts 1, 2, 3* compilation of the band's final six singles, which appear here in the order of original release. "Are Everything" is a standout, featuring full string orchestration, the first and only time the group tried that, and quite successfully, too. "Strange Thing" is another winner, with a sharp speaker-to-speaker guitar arrangement and a weird, sheet-metal sounding main melody, while the horn-driven "What Do You Know?" is a bit off the mark but still has the unique touch of Shelley aiming for a soul falsetto. Diggle's brisk "Why She's a Girl From the Chainstore" is a fine number with an attractive mid-song break, but more impressive is his sweetly soaring, synth-touched "Running Free," with Shelley on a good counterpoint backing vocal. As for the concert, it's a crisp and clean document of the band's on-stage abilities, generally favoring the more direct crunch-and-bash side of their existence than the more fragile or nervy elements, musically if not lyrically. Two old *Spiral Scratch*/Devoto-era nuggets, "Breakdown" and "Time's Up," get enthusiastic blasts here, Shelley easily equaling Devoto's original singing. The remaining tracks range from some of their legendary singles—the fun "Noise Annoys" and a fine one-two punch of "What Do I Get?" and "Whatever Happened To?"— and equally strong album monsters like "Fiction Romance" and "Moving Away from the Pulsebeat." Shelley's amusingly lackadaisical countdowns for a number of the songs are an extra bonus. Closing everything out is the jaunty rarity "I Look Alone," originally appearing only on a multi-band compilation. —*Ned Raggett*

Product / 1989 / Restless ✦✦✦✦✦
Probably the first punk-era box set, *Product* is an almost-complete collection of the Buzzcocks' original 1976-1980 incarnation. It's only almost complete because it doesn't contain their debut indie EP, *Spiral Scratch*, the legendary bootleg *Time's Up!*, or their songs from the *Live at the Roxy, London WC2* compilation. By removing the Buzzcocks' earliest and punkiest songs, *Product* skews the group's history somewhat, presenting them as more of a power pop group than the DIY punk pioneers they were in the very beginning. (Needless to say, this also erases Howard Devoto from the group's history almost entirely.) On the other hand, it's impossible to argue with this music. The Buzzcocks were arguably the best of the first wave of U.K. punk bands (only the Clash could touch them in terms of musical quality, and they weren't nearly as consistent) and listening to this three-CD set, it's immediately apparent that they were never ones to be bound by punk orthodoxy. There's no empty nihilism in these songs; even the dark, alienated stuff is based in heartfelt emotion. There's a really big difference between the posturing of "Holidays in the Sun" and the reality of "Ever Fallen in Love." The set includes all four of the group's original albums—*Another Music in a Different Kitchen, Love Bites, A Different Kind of Tension,* and the near-perfect 45 compilation *Singles Going Steady*—along with the 1980 singles that had later been collected on the EP *Parts 1, 2, 3*, a previously unheard track ("I Look Alone," slated to be the group's last single but never released), and a fiery eight-song, 24-minute live set recorded at the Lyceum in 1977. The hefty booklet contains a long and fascinating history of the group written by Jon Savage that stands as the most complete and detailed account of the group's often confusing life. Despite its flaws and omissions, *Product* is a stellar repackaging and an essential document for all fans of British punk. —*Stewart Mason*

Operators Manual / Nov. 12, 1991 / IRS ✦✦✦✦✦
Did The Buzzcocks invent pop-punk? Probably not. Did they perfect it? You bet. Marrying glorious pop melodies, the chainsaw roar of a downstroked guitar, and the furious angst of a million confused teenagers, The Buzzcocks played punk rock that was physical, passionate, and emotionally compelling, but also joyously listenable (and danceable) in a way The Damned and The Clash could never dream of being. If the Buzzcocks Mk. 1 (1976-1981) ever made a bad record, they've done a splendid job of keeping it a secret; all three of the group's original albums are brilliant, and *Singles Going Steady* (which collects the A and B sides of their first eight 45's) is as perfect a compilation album as you're ever likely to encounter. But if you're looking for a single disc package that covers the history of the band's first era, *Operators Manual* is just what you've been needing; it features 11 of *Singles Going Steady*'s 16 tracks (including all the A sides), and adds fourteen superb songs from the group's three albums. And unlike *Singles, Operators Manual* features material from *A Different Kind of Tension,* and while The Buzzcocks were brilliant right out of the box, "You Say You Don't Love Me" and "I Don't Know What To Do With My Life" revealed a surprising maturity, and "I Believe" found Pete Shelley going past the perfect pop song into a moving (and heartbreaking) statement of purpose. *Operators Manual* is hardly everything you'd ever need from The Buzzcocks, but if you're looking for an introduction to their remarkable body of work, you could hardly do better. —*Mark Deming*

Entertaining Friends / Nov. 3, 1992 / IRS ✦✦✦
Entertaining Friends is from a Hammersmith Odeon show in London in 1979 and is

mostly good, but not transcendent. Although, to be fair, the band gets better as the set progresses. *—John Dougan*

A Different Kind of Tension/Parts 1, 2, 3 / 1993 / IRS ✦✦✦✦✦
Even at the end of their career, the Buzzcocks were recording an amazing array of ferocious pop songs. Their last album, *A Different Kind of Tension*, featured some of Pete Shelley's best songs, including some of the most personal material he has ever written. *Parts 1, 2, 3* collect the band's last three singles, which are all quite impressive. *—Stephen Thomas Erlewine*

Trade Test Transmission / Jun. 2, 1993 / Caroline ✦✦✦
Surfacing a couple of years after the band's unexpected resurrection but after the departure of bassist Garvey and drummer Maher, who were content to continue their other lines of work, *Trade Test Transmissions* is at once a fine, celebratory album and something of a disappointment. On the one hand, hearing the Shelley/Diggle partnership fully reestablished is fantastic enough; both singers sound just fine, and their guitar abilities are no less powerful than in the group's original heyday. New bassist Barber and drummer Barker do their jobs quite well enough. If not as distinctly powerful as the original Garvey/Maher section—the subtle, inventive side of Maher's work is especially hard to replace—they approach the songs with energy and don't let anything down. For all this, though, there's a sense of unfulfilled promise through *Trade*. It specifically surfaces in the way that Shelley and Diggle want to draw more on the strictly listener-friendly touch of the band's original days while generally ignoring the more adventuresome side that surfaced in songs like "Late for the Train," "Why Can't I Touch It?," and "I Believe." It's not quite pandering per se, but it's almost too easy an approach for a band that so clearly transcended the punk/pop formula as much as it perfected it. This aside, *Trade* is definitely enjoyable on its own terms, with a number of songs—"Innocent," "Smile," the Diggle-penned and sung "Isolation," and "Alive Tonight"—near equal to many moments on *Singles Going Steady*. "Palm of Your Hand" is a fun scream, an "Orgasm Addict" updated for the '90s that celebrates the joys of mutual masturbation. As a bonus, the American version includes two tracks from the *Do It* single, including the tough-rocking title cut, along with "Inside," a Diggle-composed number. *—Ned Raggett*

Love Bites/Another Music in a Different Kitchen / Feb. 22, 1994 / IRS ✦✦✦✦✦
While the Buzzcocks' singles captured the band's energetic, tightly wound pop style perfectly, the band experimented a bit more with song structures on their full-length albums. Many of the album tracks were in the vein of their classic singles, but the band also played some twisted, draining instrumental sections that were almost as impressive as their concise pop songs. Of their first two albums, the debut *Another Music in a Different Kitchen* is the stronger record, but *Love Bites* is only a shade weaker. *—Stephen Thomas Erlewine*

French / Jan. 23, 1996 / IRS ✦✦

All Set / Apr. 1996 / IRS ✦✦✦

Modern / Sep. 7, 1999 / Go Kart ✦✦✦

The Byrds

f. 1964, Los Angeles, CA, **db.** 1973
Folk-Rock, Psychedelic, Country-Rock
Although they only attained the huge success of the Beatles, Rolling Stones, and the Beach Boys for a short time in the mid-'60s, time has judged the Byrds to be nearly as influential as those groups in the long run. They were not solely responsible for devising folk-rock, but they were certainly more responsible than any other single act (Dylan included) for melding the innovations and energy of the British Invasion with the best lyrical and musical elements of contemporary folk music. The jangling, 12-string guitar sound of leader Roger McGuinn's Rickenbacker was permanently absorbed into the vocabulary of rock. They also played a vital role in pioneering psychedelic rock and country-rock, the unifying element being their angelic harmonies and restless eclecticism. Often described in their early days as a hybrid of Dylan and the Beatles, the Byrds in turn influenced Dylan and the Beatles almost as much as Bob and the Fab Four had influenced the Byrds. The Byrds' innovations have echoed nearly as strongly through subsequent generations, in the work of Tom Petty, R.E.M., and innumerable alternative bands of the post-punk era that feature those jangling guitars and dense harmonies.*—Richie Unterberger*

☆ **Mr. Tambourine Man** / 1965 / Columbia/Legacy ✦✦✦✦✦
One of the greatest debuts in the history of rock, *Mr. Tambourine Man* was nothing less than a significant step in the evolution of rock & roll itself, demonstrating that intelligent lyrical content could be wedded to compelling electric guitar riffs and a solid backbeat. It was also the album that was most responsible for establishing folk-rock as a popular phenomenon, its most alluring traits being McGuinn's immediately distinctive 12-string Rickenbacker jangle and the band's beautiful harmonies. The material was uniformly strong, whether they were interpreting Dylan (on the title cut and three other songs, including the hit single "All I Really Want to Do"), Pete Seeger ("The Bells of Rhymney"), or Jackie DeShannon ("Don't Doubt Yourself, Babe"). The originals were lyrically less challenging, but equally powerful musically, especially Gene Clark's "I Knew I'd Want You," "I'll Feel a Whole Lot Better," and "Here Without You"; "It's No Use" showed a tougher, harder-rocking side and a guitar solo with hints of psychedelia. The CD reissue adds six less impressive (but still satisfying) bonus tracks and alternate takes from the same era. *—Richie Unterberger*

Turn! Turn! Turn! / Dec. 12, 1965 / Columbia/Legacy ✦✦✦✦✦
The group's second album was only a disappointment in comparison with *Mr. Tambourine Man*. They couldn't maintain such a level of consistent magnificence, and the follow-up was not quite as powerful or impressive. It was still quite good, however, particularly the ringing number one title cut, a classic on par with the "Mr. Tambourine Man" single. Elsewhere they concentrated more on original material, Gene Clark in particular offering some strong compositions with "Set You Free This Time," "The World Turns All Around Her," and "If You're Gone." A couple more Dylan covers were included as well, and "Satisfied Mind" was their first foray into country-rock, a direction they would explore in much greater depth throughout the rest of the '60s. The CD adds seven decent alternate takes and bonus tracks, the most interesting being a version of Dylan's "It's All Over Now, Baby Blue," and an enigmatic Gene Clark song, "The Day Walk (Never Before)." *—Richie Unterberger*

Fifth Dimension / Jul. 18, 1966 / Columbia/Legacy ✦✦✦✦✦
Although *Fifth Dimension* was wildly uneven, its high points were as innovative as any rock music being recorded in 1966. Immaculate folk-rock was still present in their superb arrangements of the traditional songs "Wild Mountain Thyme" and "John Riley." For the originals, they devised some of the first and best psychedelic rock, often drawing from the influence of Indian raga in the guitar arrangements. "Eight Miles High," with its astral lyrics, pumping bass line, and fractured guitar solo, was a Top 20 hit, and one of the greatest singles of the '60s. The minor hit title track and the country-rock-tinged "Mr. Spaceman" are among their best songs; "I See You" has great 12-string psychedelic guitar solos; and "I Come and Stand at Every Door" is an unusual and moving update of a traditional rock tune, with new lyrics pleading for peace in the nuclear age. At the same time, the R&B instrumental "Captain Soul" was a throwaway, "Hey Joe" not nearly as good as the versions by the Leaves or Jimi Hendrix, and "What's Happening?!?!" the earliest example of David Crosby's disagreeably vapid hippie ethos. These weak spots keep *Fifth Dimension* from attaining truly classic status. The CD reissue has six notable bonus tracks, including the single version of the early psychedelic cut "Why" (the B-side to "Eight Miles High"), a significantly different alternate take of "Eight Miles High," "I Know My Rider" (with some fine McGuinn 12-string workouts), and a much jazzier, faster instrumental version of "John Riley." *—Richie Unterberger*

☆ **Younger than Yesterday** / 1967 / Columbia/Legacy ✦✦✦✦✦
Younger than Yesterday was somewhat overlooked at the time of its release during an intensely competitive era that found the Byrds on a commercial downslide. However, time has shown it to be the most durable of the Byrds' albums, with the exception of *Mr. Tambourine Man*. Crosby, McGuinn, and especially Hillman come into their own as songwriters on an eclectic but focused set blending folk-rock, psychedelia, and early country-rock. The sardonic "So You Want to Be a Rock & Roll Star" was a terrific single; "My Back Pages," also a small hit, was the last of their classic Dylan covers; "Thoughts and Words," the flower-power anthem "Renaissance Fair," "Have You Seen Her Face," and the bluegrass-tinged "Time Between" are all among their best songs. The jazzy "Everybody's Been Burned" may be David Crosby's best composition, although his "Mind Gardens" is one of his most excessive. The CD reissue has six bonus tracks, including the fine Crosby-penned single "Lady Friend" and notably different alternate versions of "Mind Gardens" and "My Back Pages." *—Richie Unterberger*

The Notorious Byrd Brothers / Jan. 3, 1968 / Columbia/Legacy ✦✦✦✦✦
The recording sessions for the Byrds' fifth album were conducted in the midst of internal turmoil that found them reduced to a duo by the time the record was completed. That wasn't evident from listening to the results, which showed the group continuing to expand the parameters of their eclecticism, while retaining their hallmark guitar jangle and harmonies. With assistance from producer Gary Usher, they took more chances in the studio, enhancing the spacy quality of tracks like "Natural Harmony" and Goffin-King's "Wasn't Born to Follow" with electronic phasing. Washes of Moog synthesizer formed the eerie backdrop for "Space Odyssey," and the songs were craftily and unobtrusively linked with segues and fades. But the Byrds did not bury the essential strengths of their tunes in effects: "Goin' Back" (also written by Goffin-King) was a magnificent and melodic cover, with the expected tasteful 12-string guitar runs, that should have been a big hit. "Tribal Gathering" has some of the band's most effervescent harmonies; "Draft Morning" is a subtle and effective reflection of the horrors of the Vietnam War; and "Old John Robertson" looks forward to the country-rock that would soon dominate their repertoire. The CD reissue adds six bonus tracks, including different versions of "Goin' Back" and "Draft Morning," a few instrumentals, and David Crosby's controversial "Triad"; unlisted on the sleeve is a rehearsal outtake which captures comically vitriolic arguments among the band. *—Richie Unterberger*

★ **Sweetheart of the Rodeo** / Aug. 1968 / Columbia/Legacy ✦✦✦✦✦
The Byrds' *Sweetheart of the Rodeo* was not the first important country-rock album (Gram Parsons managed that feat with The International Submarine Band's debut *Safe at Home*), and The Byrds were hardly strangers to country music, dipping their toes in the twangy stuff as early as their second album. But no major band had gone so deep into the sound and feeling of classic country (without parody or condescension) as The Byrds did on *Sweetheart*; at a time when most rock fans viewed country as a musical "L'il Abner" routine, The Byrds dared to declare that C&W could be hip, cool, and heartfelt. Though Gram Parsons had joined the band as a pianist and lead guitarist, his deep love of C&W soon took hold, and Roger McGuinn and Chris Hillman followed his lead; significantly, the only two original songs on the album were both written by Parsons (the achingly beautiful "Hickory Wind" and "One Hundred Years From Now"), while on the rest of the set classic tunes by Merle Haggard, The Louvin Brothers, and Woody Guthrie were sandwiched between a pair of twanged-up Bob Dylan compositions. While many cite this as more of a Gram Parsons album than a Byrds set, given the strong country influence of McGuinn and Hillman's later work, it's obvious Parsons didn't impose a style upon this band so much as he tapped into a sound that was already there, waiting to be released. If The Byrds didn't do country-rock first, they did it brilliantly, and few albums

in the style are as beautiful and emotionally effecting as this. Columbia's 1997 CD reissue of the album improves on the masterpiece by adding eight strong bonus tracks, including four cuts with Gram Parsons singing lead trimmed from the original release for legal reasons. *—Mark Deming*

Preflyte / 1969 / Bumble ♦♦♦
A blip in the Byrds' discography that could easily be missed, as all of the songs from these pre-*Mr. Tambourine Man* sessions are also found on the much more widely available *In the Beginning*. Byrds fans really need to track this down, though, because six of the 11 cuts are actually entirely different versions than the ones that appear on *In the Beginning*, and in some cases the differences are substantial. "You Showed Me," in particular, appears here in a bare-bones, almost acoustic version with a heart-wrenching Gene Clark vocal; this is the sound of the Byrds at their very birth in the nest. It's a matter of taste, but to my ears the takes of "She Has a Way" and "Here Without You" on *Preflyte* are clearly superior to the ones used on *In the Beginning*, though the arrangements are very similar. Originally released on the small Together label, this was reissued on Columbia a few years later; the Columbia pressing is much easier to find, can still be easily (and affordably) found in used stores, and has enough otherwise unavailable quality material to make the search worth the effort. *—Richie Unterberger*

Dr. Byrds & Mr. Hyde / 1969 / Columbia/Legacy ♦♦♦
Chris Hillman, Gram Parsons, and Kevin Kelley all left The Byrds in wake of the release of *Sweetheart of the Rodeo*, leaving Roger McGuinn to assemble a new band from scratch. *Dr. Byrds & Mr. Hyde*, the first album with McGuinn as unquestioned leader (and sole founding member), was an interesting but uneven set that saw him attempting to bring together the psych-tinged rock of the group's early period with the pure country that Parsons had brought to *Sweetheart*. The new line-up on this album was as strong as any the band would ever have, with guitarist Clarence White sounding revelatory whenever he opens up, and Gene Parsons and John York comprising a strong and sympathetic rhythm section. But while everyone on board was a great musician, they don't always sound like a band just yet, and the strain to come up with new material seems to have let them down; McGuinn contributes a few strong originals (especially "King Apathy III" and "Drug Store Truck Drivin' Man," the latter written with Parsons before his departure from the group), but the two songs he penned for the movie *Candy* are just short of disastrous, and the closing medley of "My Back Pages" and "Baby What You Want Me to Do" sounds like padding. *Dr. Byrds & Mr. Hyde* proved there was still life left in The Byrds, but also suggested that they hadn't gotten back to full speed yet. *—Mark Deming*

The Ballad of Easy Rider / Feb. 1969 / Columbia/Legacy ♦♦♦♦
If *Dr. Byrds and Mr. Hyde* found Roger McGuinn having to recreate The Byrds after massive personnel turnovers (and not having an easy time of it), *Ballad of Easy Rider* was the album where the new lineup really hit its stride. Gracefully moving back and forth between serene folk rock (the title cut, still one of McGuinn's most beautiful melodies), surehanded rock & roll ("Jesus Is Just All Right"), heartfelt country-rock ("Oil In My Lamp" and "Tulsa County"), and even a dash of R&B (the unexpectedly funky "Fido," which even features a percussion solo), *Ballad of Easy Rider* sounds confident and committed where *Dr. Byrds and Mr. Hyde* often seemed tentative. The band sounds tight, self-assured, and fully in touch with the music's emotional palate, and Clarence White's guitar work is truly a pleasure to hear (if Roger McGuinn's fabled 12-string work seems to take a back seat to White's superb string bends, it is doubtful that any but the most fanatical fans would think to object). While not generally regarded as one of the group's major works, in retrospect this release stands alongside *Untitled* as the finest work of The Byrds' final period. *—Mark Deming*

Live at the Fillmore West February 1969 / Feb. 1969 / Columbia/Legacy ♦♦♦
Recorded by Columbia engineers in February 1969, this is an early show by the first Byrds lineup to feature only one original member: founding member Roger McGuinn and Clarence White on guitars, John York on bass, and Gene Parsons on drums. Despite the recent departures of Chris Hillman and Gram Parsons for the Flying Burrito Brothers, the sound and repertoire are still very much in the Byrds' country-rock phase, many of the 16 tracks coming from the *Sweetheart of the Rodeo* and *Dr. Byrds & Mr. Hyde* albums. The big mid-'60s hits are revisited in a medley, and a few other songs first recorded in the pre-White days—"So You Want to Be a Rock & Roll Star" and "Chimes of Freedom" among them—also show up. There are also covers of Merle Haggard and Buck Owens tunes that would *not* show up on Byrds albums. It's a pleasant, but not outstanding, set, probably of most interest to those who enjoy White's guitar playing. He and McGuinn work pretty well together here, but the timing of the band as a whole is sometimes tenuous, and the vocal harmonies are not as full as those of other Byrds configurations. *—Richie Unterberger*

Untitled / 1970 / Columbia/Legacy ♦♦♦♦
This two-CD set contains the Byrds' 1970 *Untitled* album (originally a double LP) on disc one, and 14 previously unissued alternate versions, studio recordings, and live performances on disc two. This was not the Byrds' most exciting era, but a lot of extra material existed, and *Untitled* was going to be reissued either way. *Untitled* itself was one of the Byrds' better late efforts, with an album of live material (built around updates of their most famous tunes) sharing space with uneven new studio recordings in the expected country/folk-rock mode, highlighted by "Chestnut Mare" and "Just a Season." Listeners will be most interested in this expanded reissue for the disc of previously unreleased stuff, which is not remarkable, but is okay for those who enjoyed *Untitled*. There are alternate studio versions of two songs from *Untitled*'s studio portion ("Yesterday's Train" and a more jangly "All the Things"); a studio alternate of "Kathleen's Song," without the orchestration that would be added when it was redone for *Byrdmaniax*; a studio version of "Lover of the Bayou" (done live on *Untitled*); the instrumental "White's Lightning Pt. 2"; and Lowell George's "Willin'" (different from the version that appears on the Byrds' box set). Then you get eight previously unavailable 1970 live recordings, much in the style of what's heard on the live part of *Untitled*, and including such favorites as "It's Alright Ma (I'm Only Bleeding)," "Ballad of Easy Rider," "My Back Pages," and "Jesus Is Just Alright." An unindexed bonus track, an a cappella studio rendition of "Amazing Grace," ends the set. *—Richie Unterberger*

Byrdmaniax / 1971 / Columbia/Legacy ♦♦
As legend has it, the Byrds wrapped up the basic tracks for *Byrdmaniax* in early 1971 and then hit the road for a concert tour, leaving producers Terry Melcher and Chris Hinshaw to polish the final mix. Melcher and Hinshaw then proceeded to add copious overdubs to what the group had set down, drowning the songs in a swampy morass of keyboards, horns, strings, and massed background singers in the misguided hope of making the album sound more "commercial" (even Clarence White's superb lead guitar often gets lost in the murk). The shame of it is that the aural gingerbread managed to spoil what might have been one of the Byrds' better albums; it's hard to imagine what Skip Battin's goofy "Citizen Kane" or Roger McGuinn's witty "I Wanna Grow Up to Be a Politician" were intended to sound like originally, but "I Trust" and "Kathleen's Song" are lovely if you can listen past the overproduction, and "Green Apple Quick Step" gives White and Gene Parsons plenty of room to show off their old-time country chops. Not an awful album, but *Byrdmaniax* is hardly the pleasure it could have been in the hands of a more tasteful production team. The 1999 CD reissue adds three bonus tracks, including an un-overdubbed alternate take of "Pale Blue" that indicates how the album was originally intended to sound. *—Mark Deming*

Farther Along / 1972 / Columbia/Legacy ♦♦♦
One thing the Byrds had in common with most of their fans was that they weren't especially happy with the absurd overproduction that had been inflicted upon *Byrdmaniax* in their absence. As a response, the group quickly cut *Farther Along* in 1971, producing the sessions themselves and getting the album into stores a mere six months after its predecessor. It's certainly a significant improvement, but something short of a triumphant return; the band sounds a bit tired in spots, as if they were starting to run out of gas—which quickly proved to be the case as the Byrds split up a few months after the album's release. However, Roger McGuinn and Clarence White were nothing if not professionals, and if *Farther Along* doesn't always sound inspired, it's never less than well-played, really connecting when the group can get their enthusiasm up; the tough rockin' "Tiffany Queen" and the pensive "Bugler" are the late-period Byrds at the top of their game, and "Bristol Steam Convention Blues" features some superb bluegrass picking from White. This is hardly the rousing conclusion the Byrds' story that some fans might have hoped for, but it's a strong and well-crafted set from a band that inarguably gave it their all right up to the finish line. *—Mark Deming*

The Byrds [1973] / 1973 / Asylum ♦♦
In 1972, Roger McGuinn's final version of the Byrds unceremoniously broke up, but the following year the group briefly reunited—surprisingly enough, with the classic original lineup of McGuinn, Gene Clark, Michael Clarke, David Crosby, and Chris Hillman. However, if most of the participants meant for this to be anything more than a one-shot get-together, you couldn't tell from listening to the resulting album; *Byrds* never sounds much like a Byrds album, with McGuinn's chiming 12-string guitar and the group's striking harmonies (the Byrds' twin aural calling cards) largely absent, and much of the original material (especially David Crosby's) sounding like cast-offs from their other projects. And what sort of a Byrds album features two Neil Young covers and not a single Bob Dylan tune? In all fairness, *Byrds* has its moments: Gene Clark's "Full Circle" and "Changing Heart" are great songs from the group's least-appreciated member, and McGuinn's "Born to Rock & Roll" is a top-notch rock anthem. But for the most part, *Byrds* sounds like a competent but unexciting country-rock band going through their paces, rather than the work of one of the best and most innovative American bands of the 1960s. *—Mark Deming*

In the Beginning / 1988 / Rhino ♦♦♦
Before signing to Columbia Records, the Byrds made hours of rehearsal and demo tapes as they perfected their blend of folk and rock. The *Preflyte* album, released in the late '60s, presented nearly a dozen of those cuts. This CD takes the bulk of that LP and embellishes it with alternate takes and previously unreleased tracks. Discography-wise, this 17-song disc is a real tongue-twister. Five of the 11 *Preflyte* tracks reappear in the exact same version, along with six alternate takes of *Preflyte* cuts. There are also alternate takes of both sides of their 1964 Elektra single (released as the Beefeaters), the primitive acoustic demo "The Only Girl I Adore" (previously available only on an obscure Elektra compilation), a previously unissued early version of "It's No Use" (later on their first LP), and the previously totally unreleased original "Tomorrow Is a Long Ways Away," in both electric and acoustic versions. Amidst the collector details, one shouldn't lose sight of the fact that the music is excellent, though more tentative and less polished than their "official" Columbia work. The harmonies are angelic and the melodies beautiful. Though this is more derivative of the early Beatles than their later Dylan-influenced folk-rock, one can hear the group's unsurpassed crystalline blend of guitars and voices approaching full bloom. With the exception of an early version of "Mr. Tambourine Man," all the cuts are originals, most of which are fine and never appeared on their later albums; there are many good, otherwise unavailable Gene Clark songs in particular. Minor complaint: Some of the alternate takes here are inferior to those on the original *Preflyte* album. *—Richie Unterberger*

Never Before / 1989 / Murray Hill ♦♦♦
This 17-song compilation of alternate takes, unreleased songs, and assorted oddities from the Byrds' mid-'60s prime is a necessary purchase for their many fanatics, but a bit choppy and insubstantial in places. The highlights are many: a rough but endearing previously

unreleased cover of Dylan's "It's All Over Now, Baby Blue"; an alternate take of "Eight Miles High" that is quite different (though not as good) as the hit version; a couple pretty David Crosby ballads (including "Triad," later covered by the Jefferson Airplane); a cover of the traditional folk tune "I Know You Rider" with scintillating 12-string guitar solos from Roger McGuinn; "Why," the raga-rock B-side of "Eight Miles High" (both the original 45 version and an alternate take are included); and the non-LP B-side of "Turn, Turn, Turn," "She Don't Care About Time" (written by Gene Clark). A couple of instrumental jams show McGuinn at his most recklessly experimental; "Flight 713" is a taut, almost jazzy piece, while the synthesizer burps of "Moog Raga" give an insight into the electronic direction the group might have pursued if Gram Parsons hadn't joined the band. On the down side, some of the outtakes were clearly throwaways, and the stereo version of their first single was hardly a coveted item. The 1968 B-side "Lady Friend," one of Crosby's best compositions, is ruined by a ham-fisted drum track overdubbed in the 1980s (it was restored to its original version on the box set). A ragtag collection, yes, but there are plenty of stellar moments, and this CD (together with *In the Beginning*) rounds up virtually everything from the group's classic period that didn't appear on their first five albums. —*Richie Unterberger*

☆ **The Byrds [Box Set]** / Oct. 1990 / Columbia/ Legacy ✦✦✦✦✦
The value of the four-disc box set *The Byrds* as a rarities set has diminished somewhat, as much of the truly rare items later appeared on Columbia/Legacy's excellent reissues as bonus tracks, but this set remains a good overview of the group's career. Although the remastering and rarities are prominent enough to draw in the hardcore, the main strength of this compilation is that it tells the story exceedingly well, capturing the scope of their career. Very few (if any) great songs are missing, and if it dwells a little bit too long on the fourth disc, such is the nature of box sets. The rest of the record is remarkably well-balanced, containing all their hits and key album tracks, making it a nice, thorough retrospective. —*Stephen Thomas Erlewine*

20 Essential Tracks from the Boxed Set: 1965-90 / 1991 / Columbia/Legacy ✦✦✦
For those who don't want to invest the time or money in the full four-disc *The Byrds*, *20 Essential Tracks* is a decent sampler of the Byrds' better tracks throughout the years. If the collection has any faults, it's that only 12 of the 20 tracks come from the quintessential 1965 to 1968 period, and selections from the country-rock classic *Sweetheart of the Rodeo* have been omitted entirely. Instead, unnecessary tracks such as "I Wanna Grow Up to Be a Politician" and a few more obscure songs like the Beach Boy-esque "Lady Friend" are included. The low point of the collection is the inclusion of box-set-only tracks like "Paths of Victory," "Love That Never Dies," and a maudlin "From a Distance"—while interesting, these cuts are definitely not essential. Still, as greatest hits compilations go, this one does a fairly good job of showing quite a few different sides of the entire Byrds body of work. —*Matt Fink*

Full Flyte (1965-1970) / Aug. 21, 1998 / Raven ✦✦✦✦
Raven's *Full Flyte (1965-1970)* is a first-rate single-disc compilation of the Byrds' prime years. Weighing in at a generous 27 tracks, the disc contains all of the major and most of the minor hit singles, plus many key album tracks and non-hit singles such as "Feel a Whole Lot Better," "Chimes of Freedom," "She Don't Care About Time," "Renaissance Fair," "Everybody's Been Burned," "Goin' Back," "Hickory Wind," "You're Still on My Mind," and "Chestnut Mare." Although there have been single-disc sets that have had better remastering, few rival this in terms of sheer selection. For many fans, Sony/Legacy's expanded *Greatest Hits* will still be the first price, since it is a little tighter and a lot easier to find, but anyone that purchases this will have an excellent capsule history of the Byrds' prime. —*Stephen Thomas Erlewine*

Byrd Parts / Sep. 15, 1998 / Raven ✦✦✦✦✦
Some of those involved with Columbia's Byrds box urged the producers to use tracks by the Jet Set, the Beefeaters, the pre-Byrds David Crosby, and the Hillmen; instead, they chose to weigh it down with a lot of later, Skip Battin-era tracks. So Raven Records has done the job instead, gathering together the major pre-Byrds and early Byrds-related tracks in one place: David Crosby's bluesy "Willie Gene" and "Come Back Baby"; the pre-Byrds Jet Set trio's Beatles-esque "The Only Girl I Adore" (complete with "yeah-yeah"'s) from the *Early L.A.* album; the Hillmen's bluegrass version of Dylan's "When the Ship Comes In"; and the Byrds/Beefeaters' "It Won't Be Wrong" from Elektra. But the producers haven't stopped with obvious stuff like that. They've also included David Hemmings' rendition of Gene Clark's "Backstreet Mirror" from the all-but-forgotten Jim Dickson-produced, Byrds-backed *David Hemmings Happens*; Jackie DeShannon's previously unissued demo recording of "Splendor in the Grass," backed by the Byrds; the Fred Neil-Gram Parsons "Ya Don't Miss Your Water" off of Neil's 1971 *Other Side of This Life* album; the International Submarine Band's lost Columbia single; rare single cuts by Dillard & Clark; and tracks by Clarence White, Skip Battin, Gene Parsons, and McGuinn, Clark & Hillman. Hemmings' "Anathea," even with his non-singing out in front, manages to achieve a trippy decadence through the Byrds playing and Dickson's production. Most of the rest gets far afield of the original Byrds, although "Ya Don't Miss Your Water" has a dark, brooding, ominous feel that makes it well worth owning, the Doug Dillard-Gene Clark stuff is always welcome, and the early International Submarine Band songs sound a lot more Beatles-esque (and punkier) than anything on their subsequent *Safe at Home* album. —*Bruce Eder*

★ **Greatest Hits [Expanded Edition]** / Mar. 30, 1999 / Columbia/Legacy ✦✦✦✦✦
Without question, the Byrds were one of the great bands of the '60s and one of the few American bands of their time to continually turn out inventive, compelling albums. As they were recording a series of fine records, they released a number of classic singles that defined their era. *The Byrds' Greatest Hits* does an excellent job of chronicling the peak years of their popularity before they went country-rock on 1968's *Sweetheart of the Rodeo*. Columbia/Legacy's expanded 1999 reissue added the three minor hits missing from the original collection, which means that *Greatest Hits* now contains all of the group's hit singles—from 1965's "Mr. Tambourine Man" to 1967's "Have You Seen Her Face." That's an impressive collection indeed, and it also includes "All I Really Want to Do," "Turn! Turn! Turn! (To Everything There Is a Season)," "It Won't Be Wrong," "Set You Free this Time," "Eight Miles High," "5D (Fifth Dimension)," "Mr. Spaceman," "So You Want to Be a Rock & Roll Star" and "My Back Pages." Yes, some great songs were left behind on the albums, but important cuts like "I'll Feel a Whole Lot Better," "The Bells of Rhymney" and "Chimes of Freedom" are included, making this pretty close to a definitive single-disc summary of the Byrds' prime. —*Stephen Thomas Erlewine*

David Byrne

b. May 14, 1952, Dumbarton, Scotland
Producer, Vocals, Guitar / Experimental Rock, Alternative Pop/Rock, Worldbeat
Best known for his groundbreaking tenure fronting the new wave group Talking Heads, David Byrne's solo work, while not as successful, was no less adventurous, encroaching upon such diverse media as world music, filmmaking, and performance art. During a band sabbatical in 1981, Byrne teamed with Brian Eno, the producer of much of the Heads' work, for the collaborative effort *My Life in the Bush of Ghosts*, a complex, evocative album which fused electronic music with Third World percussion and hypnotic vocal effects. That same year, Byrne also began exploring theatre. In 1986, Byrne wrote, starred in, and directed the feature film *True Stories*. He also wrote and produced the majority of music for the film's score in addition to performing his usual duties for that year's Talking Heads LP, also named *True Stories*. In 1988, in tandem with Ryuichi Sakamoto and Cong Su, he won an Academy Award for his musical work on Bernardo Bertolucci's historical epic *The Last Emperor*. Also in 1988, Byrne's fascination with world music, a longtime influence on his herky-jerky performance style as well as the Talking Heads' complex polyrhythms, inspired him to form his own record label, Luaka Bop, to give widespread American release to global music. In 1989, he resurfaced with *Rei Momo*, a collection inspired by Latin rhythms, and also directed the documentary *Ile Aiye* (The House of Life), which focused on the rituals of Yoruban dance music. 1992's *Uh-Oh* marked Byrne's return to more conventional rock performance, a direction continued on a self-titled effort issued in 1994. —*Jason Ankeny*

The Catherine Wheel / Dec. 1981 / Luaka Bop ✦✦✦
This is Byrne's score for a Broadway dance production choreographed and directed by Twyla Tharp. Its sound—with herky-jerky rhythms and unusual sounds, along with Byrne's own vocals and odd lyrics on many songs—will be familiar to Talking Heads fans. —*William Ruhlmann*

Music for "The Knee Plays" / May 1985 / ECM ✦✦✦
For David Byrne, this was one of the last times he would write in the hyper-objective style that marked his work with Talking Heads up through *Remain in Light* and some of *Speaking in Tongues*. The occasion, the chance to write interludes—or "knee plays"—for a large scale Robert Wilson opera, *The Civil Wars*, called on this kind of approach, Wilson being as detached as Byrne. Musically, Byrne was strangely influenced by hearing the Dirty Dozen Brass Band, and created these brass-led marches that sound like an art school has landed on Bourbon Street, though in places it is also reminiscent of a sunnier patch of the territory staked out in *The Catherine Wheel*, his other dance score. In the mix, Byrne stirs in some traditional gospel tunes, arranged to match the iconoclastic style. Byrne's words, performed in his dry, ever-so-slightly amused style, are acutely observed and/or humorously naïve slices of American life—anthropological tomfoolery. The wry aphorism-led "In the Future" ("In the future, water will be expensive"; "In the future, we will not have time for leisure activities") is the album highlight, and a perfect end to this experiment. —*Ted Mills*

● **Rei Momo** / Oct. 1989 / Luaka Bop/Sire ✦✦✦✦✦
On his first full-fledged solo album, Byrne indulges his fascination with Latin and South American musical styles, employing a variety of native musicians but mixing up the sounds to suit his own distinctly non-purist vision and singing over the tracks the same kind of witty, oddball lyrics found on Talking Heads albums. [When released, the cassette version contained three more tracks than the LP.] —*William Ruhlmann*

The Forest / Jun. 1991 / Luaka Bop/Warner Brothers ✦✦

Uh-Oh / Mar. 1992 / Luaka Bop/Warner Brothers ✦✦✦
Uh-Oh was only David Byrne's second pop-oriented solo album and his first to be released after the formal end of Talking Heads. Though informed by his various investigations into world music, the album was a natural successor to the Talking Heads records, relying on involved percussion tracks topped by Byrne's quirky singing and lyrics. By this point, disaffected fans may have grown accustomed to the idea that a David Byrne solo album could contain anything from an extended flirtation with Latin styles (*Rei Momo*) to an eclectic instrumental score (*The Forest*), to name only his most recent solo projects. Maybe Byrne and his record label failed to get out the message that he was back to making Heads-style pop-rock (he didn't organize a tour until the album had come and gone on the charts), but *Uh-Oh* never reached its potential audience. Talking Heads fans should give it a listen. —*William Ruhlmann*

David Byrne / May 24, 1994 / Luaka Bop/Warner Brothers ✦✦

Feelings / Jun. 17, 1997 / Luaka Bop/Warner Brothers ✦✦✦
Attempting to inject some adventure into his multicultural, worldbeat-inflected avant-pop, David Byrne dabbled with trip-hop and drum'n'bass on *Feelings*. These tracks, including a collaboration with Morcheeba, are essentially window dressing, a way to distract attention from Byrne's lack of new ideas. The songs that work best on *Feelings*, like

"Miss America," are reminiscent of the percolating, Latin-tinged *Rei Momo*; when Byrne tries to sound contemporary, he simply seems out of touch. Still, *Feelings* is stronger and more adventurous than *David Byrne*, even if it never quite fulfills its ambitions. —*Stephen Thomas Erlewine*

Look into the Eyeball / May 8, 2001 / Virgin ♦♦♦

It goes without saying that any David Byrne solo release will be all over the sonic map, and true to form, *Look Into the Eyeball* provides a pancultural stew of musical styles, exotic rhythms, and international guest stars. But what separates *Eyeball* from Byrne's previous offering, the only-fitfully successful *Feelings*, is a renewed emphasis on lush, natural sounds and consistent production. Nearly every track boasts strings and/or horns, and the textures go a long way in unifying Byrne's insistent genre-hopping. Tracks such as "Smile," "The Revolution," "The Accident," and "Everyone's in Love With You" best demonstrate his new approach: Spare melodies are layered atop subtle, percolating rhythms and then filled in with evocative string arrangements. Better yet, Byrne's two collaborations with legendary Philly soul producer Thom Bell—the buoyant "Like Humans Do" and "Neighborhood"—blend in effortlessly with the other material. Of course, old habits die hard: "U.B. Jesus" and "The Great Intoxication" are at once too slick and too simple, with muddled messages both musically and lyrically. (It doesn't help that the latter track features a cringe-inducing, self-referential "Who disco? Who techno? Who hip-hop? Who bebop?..." shout-out.) The remainder of the album vacillates between pleasant Talking Heads-ish pop ("Walk on Water") and accomplished if out-of-place forays into the Latin avant-garde ("Desconocido Soy"). It's hard to fault Byrne—who produces an album every three or four years—for packing as much as he can into one release. So it's best to view *Look Into the Eyeball* for what it is: an entertaining assimilation of the sundry artists and sounds he's gotten into since his last trip into the studio. —*Michael Hastings*

C+C Music Factory

f. 1990, New York, NY, **db.** 1994
Club/Dance, House, Dance-Pop

C+C Music Factory wasn't really a group—it was the product of Robert Clivillés and David Cole, two pop-savvy dance producers. In 1990, Clivillés and Cole hired all the singers and created all the tracks for *Gonna Make You Sweat*, C+C Music Factory's first album. While it was prepackaged, it wasn't necessarily faceless; in Freedom Williams, the producers had a solid, if not original or distinctive, rapper. What was really important to the success of the album was how Clivillés and Cole assembled the tracks, melding hip-hop and club sensibilities to mindlessly catchy pop songs. The three hit singles—"Gonna Make You Sweat (Everybody Dance Now)," "Here We Go," "Things That Make You Go Hmmmm…"—were very good pop singles, and all of them were massive hits in early 1991.

After their moment in the sun, Williams left for an unsuccessful solo career and Clivillés and Cole released *Greatest Remixes, Vol. 1*, a collection of their work with C+C Music Factory as well as other artists; the album had a hit single with their re-recording of U2's "Pride."

C+C Music Factory released their second album, *Anything Goes!*, in the summer of 1994; it was a moderate hit, spending nine weeks on the charts. Unfortunately, it was the last album the duo ever made—David Cole died of spinal meningitis in early 1995. —*Stephen Thomas Erlewine*

● **Gonna Make You Sweat** / 1990 / Columbia ✦✦✦✦

All their hit hip-hop-pop singles are here—"Gonna Make You Sweat (Everybody Dance Now)," "Here We Go," and "Things That Make You Go Hmmm…" —*Bil Carpenter*

Anything Goes! / 1994 / Columbia ✦✦✦

C+C Music Factory's first album was an enormous hit, filled with infectious bubblegum dance-pop singles. It was music of the moment, and by the time *Anything Goes* was released, the moment had passed. Clivillés And Cole's production was just as skilled, and several of the hooks on *Anything Goes* were strong, but the music was too dated to fit into the pop landscape of the mid-'90s. —*Stephen Thomas Erlewine*

Ultimate / Oct. 3, 1995 / Columbia ✦✦✦

Ultimate doesn't quite live up to its billing as the definitive C+C Music Factory collection, simply because the group's biggest hits—"Gonna Make You Sweat (Everybody Dance Now)," "Here We Go," "Things That Make You Go Hmmmm…"—are all included in remixed form. While it does offer a representative overview of the duo's career, most fans would have been better served by an official greatest hits collection. —*Stephen Thomas Erlewine*

● **Super Hits** / Feb. 15, 2000 / Columbia/Legacy ✦✦✦✦

"Perhaps next time a C+C compilation will be executed properly…." —*Stephen Thomas Erlewine, from his review of the 1996 C+C Music Factory collection* In the Groove.

When I wrote those words, I was a little exasperated. Sony had released two C+C Music Factory compilations within two years, neither of which did its job properly. It's an easy job: Take the hit versions of the handful of C+C Music Factory hits and put them on one disc. Neither *Ultimate* nor *In the Groove* did that. Instead, they included remixed versions of the singles. These were pleasant enough, but anyone who knew these songs from the radio was bound to be disappointed. Those disappointed fans should be somewhat satiated by the budget-line release Super Hits. Of the three C+C Music Factory comps, it comes the closest to fulfilling those basic objectives, since it has the hit versions of "Gonna Make You Sweat (Everybody Dance Now)," "Here We Go," and "Things That Make You Go Hmmmm…," plus two tracks from the first (and best) album: "A Groove of Love (What's This Word Called Love?)" and "Just a Touch of Love." However, instead of including such second-tier hits as "A Deeper Love," "Pride (In the Name of Love)," and "Keep It Comin'," it throws in selections from the forgotten second album. One of those, "Do You Wanna Get Funk," was a minor hit, but the rest are expendable (especially the "C+C Music Factory MTV Medley" tacked onto the end). Perhaps the compilers decided that "A Deeper Love" and "Pride" weren't worthy candidates because they technically were Clivilles & Cole tracks, not C+C Music Factory hits, but that's just splitting hairs—they should have been here, since without them, the disc feels like a reshuffled *Gonna Make You Sweat* with bonus tracks. However, *Super Hits* is cheaper than the full-length album, which may be enough for most casual fans…even if they may wonder where "Pride" is. —*Stephen Thomas Erlewine*

The C.A. Quintet

Psychedelic, Acid Rock
Virtually no one outside Minneapolis heard of the C.A. Quintet during their late-'60s hey-

day. It was their fortune (or curse) to actually reach a considerably bigger international audience when their album was reissued in the '80s. Starting as a rather conventional pop-soul/garage band, their one and only album, *Trip Thru Hell* (1968), was a worthy slice of dark psychedelia. With spooky organ and the occasional trumpet of singer/songwriter Ken Erwin, the group's murky and macabre vision—dotted with trips through hell, cold spiders, Colorado mornings, and the like—was genuinely original and chilling. *Trip Thru Hell* only sold 700-800 copies when it was first issued, but after gaining status among hardcore '60s psychedelic collectors, it was reissued in 1983. The group also released a few non-LP singles in 1967 and 1968, most in a much poppier vein. —*Richie Unterberger*

● **Trip Thru Hell** / 1968 / Sundazed ✦✦✦✦

There's not much to compare this album to, even in the weird musical climate of 1968—there are echoes of Country Joe & The Fish and the Doors, perhaps, in the mysterioso organ and morbid imagery. Not that Ken Erwin was in the same league as Jim Morrison, or even Country Joe, as a songwriter. But (with the exception of the brassy good-time cut "Underground Music"), psychedelia was very rarely this dementedly gloomy. Occasional pealing bells and curdling screams (to say nothing of the Boschlike cover art) add to the foggy underworld menace. Reissued without authorization in Europe in the 1980s, the 1995 domestic CD is a first-class job: the 12 bonus cuts gather some rare non-LP singles, alternate takes, and previously unreleased songs, and the liner notes feature extensive interviews with Ken Erwin and engineer Steve Longman. —*Richie Unterberger*

Cabaret Voltaire

f. 1974, Sheffield, Yorkshire, England
Experimental Rock, Post-Punk, Techno, Acid House, Electronic, Industrial
Though they're one of the most important groups in the history of industrial and electronic music, Cabaret Voltaire are sometimes forgotten in the style's timeline—perhaps because they continued recording long after other luminaries (Throbbing Gristle, Suicide, Chrome) called it quits. Also related to the fact is that CV rarely stayed in one place for long, instead moving quickly from free-form experimentalism through arty white-boy funk and on to house music in the late '80s and electronica the following decade. The band, formed by guitarist Richard H. Kirk, bassist Stephen Mallinder and tape manipulator Chris Watson, were influenced by the Dadaist movement (whence came their name) and as such, came closer to performance art than music during many of their early performances. After several years of recording with no contract, the group signed to the newly formed Rough Trade label in 1978 and began releasing records that alternated punk-influenced chargers with more experimental pieces incorporating tape loops and sampled effects.

Following Watson's departure, the remaining duo inaugurated a new contract with Some Bizzare/Virgin in 1983 by shifting their sound, away from raging industro-funk and towards a more danceable form. The singles "Sensoria" and "James Brown" hit the indie charts during 1984, and Cabaret Voltaire moved to EMI/Parlophone in 1986 for *The Code*. Two years later, the band traveled to Chicago to record *Groovy, Laidback & Nasty* with Marshall Jefferson, one of the mavericks in the new house sound blowing up in the British charts. After another break of several years, the new-electronica label Instinct released a trio of CV LPs during 1993-94, after which the band's future appeared cloudy. Kirk continued his solo career (recording as Electronic Eye, Sandoz and himself) while Mallinder moved to Australia. —*John Bush*

Mix-Up / 1979 / Mute ✦✦

The Voice of America / 1981 / Mute ✦✦

Red Mecca / 1981 / Mute ✦✦✦✦✦

Cabaret Voltaire's first consistent record, *Red Mecca* offers a highly stylized revision of Judas Priest's "Touch of Evil" set to a dark, dense electronic landscape. —*Stephen Thomas Erlewine*

● **2 X 45** / 1982 / Mute ✦✦✦✦✦

Collecting two separate sessions, one with Watson and one without (the former also with guest drummer Alan Fish of fellow Sheffield experimentalists Hula), *2 x 45* shows the Cabs now well on their way to the perversely upbeat yet ominous funk of their early eighties days. A song like "Breathe Deep" may have things like Kirk's sax and clarinet lines over the stripped-down polyrhythms of Fish and Mallinder, yet the way Mallinder husks the vocals and the claustrophobic feel of the recording don't entirely lend themselves to just going ahead and tearing the roof off the sucker. It's a careful balance the Cabs maintain, but it does work more often than not, while the influence on later industrial-affiliated acts is readily apparent. Watson's work in the band at this point isn't as noticeable as before, but the drop-in samples on "Yashar" of intense voices asking where all the people on earth are hiding give a sense of where he still turns up. The second session, with Nort and Eric Random on drums, guitar and percussion, is a touch murkier at points but only just. "War of Nerves (T.E.S.)" may start with a tape of a guy talking about tortures involving rats and have Mallinder's distorted, demonic vocals in full effect, but the crisp rhythm punch is still predominant. "Wait and Shuffle" is even, dare it be said, perkier, with a brisk, reggae-touched drum/bass combination and some sprightly keyboards playing around with the sax wails and further found-sound oddities. The lengthy "Get Out of My Face" concludes the session and release on perhaps the quirkiest note yet. Mallinder's cryptic sloganeering peppers things throughout, but it's Kirk's intriguing guitar and the relentless but still somehow fun rhythm push which defines the song best of all. *—Ned Raggett*

Johnny YesNo / 1983 / Mute ✦✦

The Crackdown / 1983 / Virgin ✦✦✦✦✦
One of Cabaret Voltaire's strongest albums, *The Crackdown* features the band working a number of menacing electronic textures into a basic dance/funk rhythm; the result is one of their most distinctive, challenging records. *—Stephen Thomas Erlewine*

Micro-Phonies / 1984 / Virgin ✦✦✦
Following neatly after *The Crackdown*'s aggressive art/funk/electro combination, *Micro-Phonies* shows the duo taking that combination to a stronger level. Having invented the shadowy, murkier side of industrial/noise experimentation, here the Cabs made their equally justified claim at fully kickstarting the beat-heavy crunch such labels as Wax Trax! would pursue shortly thereafter. DAF and the On-U Sound collective deserve as much notice for this, but the Cabs' relatively higher profile in the English/American cultural scheme made them the harbringers as much as anyone. Flood's sympathetic coproduction with the band is another feather in his cap, and the album sounds just as strong even today as upon its release. *Micro-Phonies*' most noted tracks are the appropriately funky, horn-heavy "James Brown" and the gripping "Sensoria," which makes for a brilliant album closer, nervous-tension synth signals and a spare but compelling guitar line over another strong beat combination. Subtler moments abound as well, a nice combination of the Cabs' initially understated approach and the greater opportunities available to them in the album's recording. "The Operative" is an unheralded highlight of the release, Mallinder's low-key speak/singing sidling along the crisp but not overpowering rhythm, controlled funk bass and guitar and touches of dub melodica sneaking through the mix. Other hints of the dub influences that the band have always embraced crop up on songs like (unsurprisingly) "Digital Rasta." Throughout the album Mallinder submerges his vocals into the music rather than calling overt attention to them, the reverse of what a lot of later industrial acts would do (often to their detriment). It's a sharp continuation of the Cabs' similar practice from many earlier numbers, here used in a newer musical style. The CD version of *Micro-Phonies* includes the fine 12" mixes for "Sensoria" and "Blue Heat," a welcome bonus. *—Ned Raggett*

Drinking Gasoline / 1985 / Caroline ✦✦✦

The Covenant, the Sword and the Arm of the Lord / 1985 / Some Bizarre ✦✦✦

Code / 1987 / Manhattan ✦✦✦✦
1987's *Code*, co-produced by On-U Sound mastermind Adrian Sherwood, finds Cabaret Voltaire at their loosest and most accessible. Though its subject matter remains dark and paranoid, in sound *Code* is the closest thing CV ever made to a party record. Aided perhaps by Sherwood's rhythmic expertise, it achieved a genuine mechanistic funkiness reminiscent of late-'70s Kraftwerk. That didn't necessarily endear it, of course, to fans of the Cabs' harsher, more challenging material. Many of them dismissed *Code* as lightweight, but the rest of us can find much to enjoy here. "Sex, Money, Freaks" answers the eternal question, What would it sound like if Roger Troutman of Zapp joined Cabaret Voltaire? "Trouble (Won't Stop)" dips one toe into the blues, with harmonica making a surprising appearance and Bill Nelson providing atmospheric guitar. *Code*'s most memorable song, though, is "Here to Go," a hook-laden and bass-heavy concoction that offers the paradoxical advice, "Sharpen up, relax/ Lighten up, get serious/ Stick with it, sit back/ Live with it, commit yourself." *—Bill Cassel*

The Golden Moments of Cabaret Voltaire / 1987 / Rough Trade ✦✦✦✦✦
A solid collection of Cabaret Voltaire's earliest recordings, which features some of the noisiest and bleakest music they have ever recorded. *—Stephen Thomas Erlewine*

8 Crépuscule Tracks / 1988 / Positive ✦✦✦

Groovy, Laidback & Nasty / 1990 / Parlophone ✦✦✦

The Living Legends / Jul. 1990 / Mute ✦✦✦✦✦
If one needs a starting place to discover how an obscure trio of Sheffield sound experimentalists became one of the founders of industrial/EBM music, not to mention a whole range of artists interested in pushing the boundaries of recorded sound, *The Living Legends* is it. Conveniently collecting the series of singles the classic trio line-up released on Rough Trade Records, *Legends* makes for astonishing listening even today, alien now as it was then, and perhaps even more so. Compiled in more or less chronological order with a few exceptions, the tracks range from the quietly mysterious to astonishing, in-your-face sonics. The earliest single, "Do the Mussolini," and its various B-sides initially cast the band as gloomy, dour figures interested in fooling around with tape machines, rhythm boxes and a sense of echo that always made them sound like they were recording in the deep bowels of the earth. The Velvet Underground's "Here She Comes Now" gets an intriguing revamp here, Kirk's guitar buzzing the main riff in the background. After that, things really kick in with the groundbreaking "Nag Nag Nag," brilliantly co-produced by Rough Trade boss Geoff Travis and Red Krayola bandleader Mayo Thompson. Mallinder's abstract aggression as his electronically treated voice roars the title line is breathtaking enough, but the combination of heavily treated guitar and keyboard noise over the basic but effective rhythm pulse adds to the fantastic effect. Many other standouts follow from here, including the lengthy drone/groove of "Walls of Jerico" and the near-clinical push of "Second Too Late," with a gripping duet between a distanced Mallinder vocal and an upfront, vocodered and dead sounding voice. The sense of how the Cabs used everything from the more chaotic end of Krautrock to dub techniques surfaces throughout, capturing the sense of how they at once synthesized past approaches and created new ones. *—Ned Raggett*

Listen Up with Cabaret Voltaire / Sep. 1990 / Mute ✦✦✦✦
Given the band's constant outpouring of work in its late seventies/early eighties days via both singles and albums, it's no surprise that enough unreleased or compilation-only material could be brought together to form a two CD collection. What's a bit more surprising is the quality throughout *Listen Up*, but then again, given the Cabs' abilities in general, it's not too unexpected. The sources for the previously released numbers range from fanzine flexidiscs to John Giorno's *Clean, But It Just Looks Dirty* video compilation, neatly situating the band's wide appeal among any number of undergrounds. The two initial tracks, from a very early Factory Records sampler EP, both rank high as masterpieces of ominous threat. "Baader Meinhof" begins with a German speaker, presumably discussing the terrorist group in question, before Mallinder's heavily distorted voice talks over a combination of ambient drift and unnerving noises. "Sex in Secret" introduces a low rhythm box rumble and slightly more clear lyrics, but the heavy echo throughout combined with another combination of gentle and grating sonics marks it once again as Cabaret Voltaire material. Other strong rarities include the lengthy "Loosen the Clamp," with one of the band's most "industrial" rhythm attacks, and "Trust In the Lord," with one of Mallinder's strongest and clearest vocals over brusque music. When it comes to the numerous unreleased tracks, amid more tentative or less focused material some gems come forth, many showcasing the band's increasing focus on in-your-face electrofunk. "This Is Our Religion" is notable for its Latin/funk rhythm touches, however treated or given a traditional Cabs touch, while "Why" perfectly captures the incipient EBM sound that early Front 242 would use as the basis for their own work. Mallinder's almost passionate vocals are an interesting touch, at least when not fed through the Vocoder. The packaging contains more examples of the band's early cut-up art. *—Ned Raggett*

Plasticity / Oct. 20, 1993 / Instinct ✦✦✦

The Cadets

f. Los Angeles, CA, **db.** 1958

Doo Wop, R&B

This West Coast group used two names for recording sessions. They called themselves the Jacks when doing dates for Modern and the Cadets on RPM. They began as a gospel group during the late '40s in Los Angeles. Ted Taylor, Aaron Collins, Lloyd McCraw, and Will Jones were the original lineup, and the Cadets were among the more popular bands doing R&B covers. The Cadets' lone hit was "Stranded in the Jungle," which they recorded for Modern as the Jacks in 1956. It peaked at number eight R&B and number 15 pop. Davis and Collins would later join the Flares in 1961, while Taylor would enjoy solo success as a blues, soul, and gospel vocalist. Jones joined the Coasters in 1958 and remained there for over a decade. Collins' sisters, Betty and Rose, also recorded for Modern/RPM as the Teen Queens. *—Ron Wynn*

● **Stranded in the Jungle** / 1994 / Ace ✦✦✦✦
Recording frequently as the Jacks, the Cadets produced some of the greatest doo wop rockers of the '50s, many of which are featured here as companions to 1956's huge novelty hit, "Stranded in the Jungle." Blessed with one of doo wop's most distinctive vocalists in Dub Jones, the disc also features many of the Cadets' best covers, including Nappy Brown's "Don't Be Angry" and an English version of the French cabaret hit "Hands Across the Table." Some great originals include the sweaty "Baby Ya Know" and "Let's Rock & Roll," one of the era's awesome lost anthems. *—Jim Smith*

The Cadillacs

f. 1953, Harlem, NY, **db.** 1962

Doo Wop

Equally adept at polished ballads or torrid rockers, the Cadillacs were one of New York's top doo wop groups. The Harlem quintet signed with Josie in 1954 and debuted with the beautiful "Gloria," but with Earl Carroll's prominent energetic lead vocals, the Cadillacs became known for humorous jump material and hot choreography after "Speedoo" hit big for them in 1956. Tapping into the novelty R&B market pioneered by the Coasters, the Cadillacs cut a load of great rockers during the late '50s, such as "Peek-a-Boo" and "Please, Mr. Johnson," and performed in the quickie flick *Go, Johnny, Go!* in 1959. Carroll left to join the Coasters in 1958 but the group persevered, eventually signing with Mercury. Carroll has re-formed the Cadillacs in recent years. *—Bill Dahl*

★ **The Best of the Cadillacs** / 1990 / Rhino ✦✦✦✦✦
Although completists will have to have the multi-disc set on Collectables, for the rest of their listeners, this seldom championed but nonetheless superlative single-disc compilation will more than fill the bill. At 18 tracks, a few collectors' favorites are understandably absent ("Wishing Well," "Jaywalkin'"), but *all* of the major and minor hits are well aboard, clearly showcasing the groups' ability to tackle everything from beautiful ballads ("Gloria," "The Girl I Love") to jump numbers ("Speedo," "My Girl Friend") to Coaster-style novelties ("Peek-a-Boo," "Please, Mr. Johnson") and do it all with style, grace, and choreography that *burned*. Covering their stint with Josie Records from 1954 to 1960 in a straight chronological fashion with excellent liner notes from John Neilson, this particular compilation offers great value for the bread and should be one of your very first stops in assembling a definitive doo wop collection. The Cadillacs were one of the first and one

of the very best, and here's where you go to dig their basic message before proceeding further. —*Cub Koda*

The Complete Josie Sessions / 1995 / Bear Family ✦✦✦✦✦
This box is really the CD descendant of Murray Hill Records' early-'80s-era LP set, which included lots of outtakes. It seems like complete and absolute overkill to put out four CDs on a vocal quintet that only ever charted two songs ("Speedoo," "Peek-A-Boo") nationally, and, yet…it works. But, if you like '50s R&B, doo wop music, or generally just good singing, there's so much here to listen to that will delight you that the package suddenly seems reasonable. The Cadillacs' secret was the sheer variety of their music—they started out working in a slow romantic vein, and eventually hit it big with one of the fastest-rocking vocal numbers of the period, but they also sang blues (with solid backing, including some fine guitar work) like "(That's) All I Need." Their last sides are still finely sung, but aren't romantic—rather, they began moving toward comedic and satiric pieces such as "Please Mr. Johnson" and "Jaywalker." The diversity is entertaining in itself, and the only real objection that one could have is the presence of different versions of the same songs. Even these are very interesting, such as the slower alternate version of "Speedoo," which would never have been a hit but does reveal more about the song itself. The sessionography is also a big help in sorting out precisely who was in the group at any given moment after their early sides. —*Bruce Eder*

John Cafferty

b. Narragansett, RI
Vocals, Guitar / Bar Band, Heartland Rock, Rock & Roll
Arguably the quintessential one-shot band of all time, Cafferty and Co. (who, back in the early '70s, were simply a hack New England bar band) had their 15 minutes of fame courtesy of a ridiculously overwrought 1983 film called *Eddie and the Cruisers* (starring the ridiculously overwrought Michael Pare), which dealt with the suspicious death of a fictional singer/songwriter, modeled on a conflation of Bob Dylan and Bruce Springsteen, who had made the transition from smart rock & roller to serious artist. Seems as though Eddie had recorded a "brilliant" but unreleased album that fused Chuck Berry-style rock & roll with French Symbolist poetry (all this in 1963!). A record way ahead of its time, the master tapes of *The Dark Side* (ooh, now that's a heavy title) went missing, right around the time of Eddie's "death." Needing a band to supply music for the film, the producers used the Springsteenish-sounding Cafferty and his clock-punching backup band. With the Springsteenish single "On the Dark Side" leading the way, Cafferty led, arguably, the most anonymous band with a hit record in the history of rock & roll. With the movie doing reasonably well in theaters and extremely well on video, sales of Cafferty's album (which, ironically, had been out for months before the band's involvement with the film and barely caused a murmur) skyrocketed. But, as the movie faded from the public consciousness, so did Cafferty's lousy, cynical imitation of Springsteen. —*John Dougan*

● **Eddie & the Cruisers [Original Soundtrack]** / 1983 / RCA ✦✦✦✦✦
There was a year's delay before this film, which concerns the mysterious death of a fictional '60s rock star, took off via video and cable TV; but when it did, the soundtrack album, featuring such songs as "On the Dark Side" and "Tender Years," by John Cafferty And The Beaver Brown Band, took off with it. To most, the music sounded like Bruce Springsteen clones, but it was appealing nonetheless. —*William Ruhlmann*

Tough All Over / 1985 / Scotti Brothers ✦✦✦
On the strength of the double platinum soundtrack to *Eddie and the Cruisers*, John Cafferty And The Beaver Brown Band were able to record *Tough All Over*, an album of their original songs, and release it under their own name. Released in the summer of 1985 at the tail-end of Eddie-mania, the record managed to spawn hard-rocking Top 40 hits, "C-I-T-Y" and "Tough All Over," which strongly recalled Springsteen, much like the rest of Cafferty's songs. Besides the two hits, *Tough All Over* lacked material that ranked with the best of the *Eddie and the Cruisers* soundtrack. Nevertheless, the album stayed on the charts for an impressive 32 weeks. —*Stephen Thomas Erlewine*

Roadhouse / 1988 / Scotti Bros. ✦✦

Eddie & The Cruisers 2: Eddie Lives! / 1989 / Scotti Bros. ✦✦
The soundtrack to the sequel for *Eddie & the Cruisers* follows the basic blueprint of John Cafferty's songs for the first film—they're all high energy, pounding three-chord rock & roll. However, Cafferty wasn't able to come up with a batch of songs as good as "The Dark Side," which leaves the soundtrack as bland and predictable as the movie it was supporting. —*Stephen Thomas Erlewine*

Eddie & The Cruisers: The Unreleased Tapes / Oct. 22, 1991 / Scotti Bros. ✦✦
Since Eddie & the Cruisers were a fictional band to begin with, the idea of a collection of unreleased material is sort of ridiculous. Of course, these are unreleased and new recordings by John Cafferty & The Beaver Brown Band, the group that provided all of the music for the semi-legendary *Eddie & the Cruisers*. Most of Cafferty's best songs appeared on the soundtrack to the film, which is also the place he experienced his greatest success. Most of the songs here sound like leftovers, but they are performed with conviction by The Beaver Brown Band. They might not have been much more than a bar band, but they were a good bar band. —*Stephen Thomas Erlewine*

Cake

f. 1994
Post-Grunge, Alternative Pop/Rock
Cake's all-purpose eclectic rock appeared nationwide in 1995, when Capricorn released their debut album *Motorcade of Generosity*. The Sacramento-based band originally included guitarist Greg Brown, bassist Victor Damiani, trumpeter Vince Di Fiore, vocalist and guitarist John McCrea, and drummer Todd Roper. In 1996, Cake scored their first ra-

dio hit with "The Distance," which eventually pushed its accompanying album *Fashion Nugget* to platinum sales status. Consisting of McCrea, Di Fiore, Roper, guitarist Xan McCurdy and bassist Gabe Nelson, Cake toured in support of their third album *Prolonging the Magic* two years later, notching the hit "Never There." In the spring of 2000, the band jumped ship to Columbia, and their former label Capricorn immediately set about preparing a greatest-hits collection, which was released later that fall. —*John Bush*

Motorcade of Generosity / 1994 / Capricorn ✦✦

● **Fashion Nugget** / Sep. 17, 1996 / Capricorn ✦✦✦
Sounding like a suburban, melodic white-funk-injected version of King Missile's performance art/standup comedy, "The Distance" became a novelty hit in the fall of 1996, sending Cake's second album *Fashion Nugget* to platinum status. Certainly, "The Distance" was the only reason *Fashion Nugget* went platinum, because the remainder of the album is too collegiate and arcane for mainstream music tastes. It isn't because it's obscure or intellectual—it's because the band is smirking. An "ironic" cover of Gloria Gaynor's "I Will Survive" is the key to the album, sending the signal that Cake consider themselves above *everyone* else, and nothing is too insignificant to make fun of. And that wouldn't necessarily have been a problem if they had the wit or musical skills which would make their music either funny or listenable. Instead, they wallow in sophomoric jokes which rely on self-consciously elaborate wordplay. Occasionally, their blend of collegiate musical styles—funk, hip-hop, alternative rock—makes the music easy to digest in small doses, such as "The Distance," but it isn't varied enough to prevent the album from becoming tedious. —*Stephen Thomas Erlewine*

Prolonging the Magic / Oct. 6, 1998 / Capricorn ✦✦✦
Supposedly their attempt to make a smugness- and irony-free album, Cake's third release does hold back the barbs a bit more than usual. And the strain shows. In these guys' hands, love songs without smirks and pop tunes straight-up come out forced. So, they often fall back into familiar territory: post-modern takes on post-modern life. Flipping between earnest alt-rock rhythms and jittery, funky jazz that somehow manages to whitewash both styles, *Prolonging the Magic* works best when Cake lay on the irony extra heavy, or when they make their sober ambitions mesh slightly with the type of smart-ass pop they've based a career on (like the formulaic "Never There"). At least they seem to realize their place in the alt-rock universe as a novelty band with chops, counteracting the genre's overwhelming seriousness with a light dose of heavy-handed yuks. —*Michael Gallucci*

Comfort Eagle / Jul. 24, 2001 / Columbia ✦✦✦
While so many rock bands try to reinvent themselves with every new album, Cake has made a name for itself by sticking to its brand of smirking funk-pop. Blending jazz, rockabilly, experimental rock, and a little less country than usual, *Comfort Eagle*, the band's first album since leaving Capricorn Records for Columbia, carries on the Cake tradition of offbeat humor and catchy melodies. While some fans may be waiting for its sound to evolve, singer/songwriter John McCrea and company seem content to reign over their quirky little corner of the popular music landscape. "Opera Singer" and the first single, "Short Skirt/Long Jacket," follow in the footsteps of Cake's previous hits, but are no less enjoyable because of it. "Shadow Stabbing" is one of the most straightforward rock songs the band has ever recorded, with McCrea forgoing his usual half-spoken vocals for an almost irony-free delivery. While it is still unmistakably Cake, it would sound right at home on a Cars album. The rest of the album is by the numbers Cake, which is comforting and slightly disappointing at the same time. The group has certainly perfected its sound, and one can understand why it would be hesitant to turn its back on its extremely distinctive style, but with *Comfort Eagle* Cake comes dangerously close to simply remaking its previous release, *Prolonging the Magic*. While new fans might enjoy *Comfort Eagle* on its own merits, Cake followers may feel as though they've bought the same album twice. However, both albums are strong enough that they probably won't mind. —*Mark Vanderhoff*

J.J. Cale

b. Dec. 5, 1938, Oklahoma City, OK
Vocals, Guitar / Singer/Songwriter, Blues-Rock
Notorious for his laidback, rootsy style, J.J. Cale (b. Jean Jacques Cale) is best known for writing "After Midnight" and "Cocaine," songs that Eric Clapton later made into hits. But Cale's influence wasn't only through songwriting; his distinctly loping sense of rhythm and shuffling boogie became the blueprint for the adult-oriented roots-rock of Clapton and Mark Knopfler, among others. Cale's refusal to vary the sound of his music over the course of his career caused some critics to label him as a one-trick pony, but he managed to build a dedicated cult following with his sporadically released recordings.

Raised in Tulsa, OK, Cale arrived in Los Angeles in 1964. After a short stint with Delaney and Bonnie he began a solo career in 1965, cutting the first version of "After Midnight," which would become his most famous song. Cale returned to Tulsa in 1967. Within a year, he had recorded a set of demos which led to a deal with the fledgling Shelter Records in 1969. The following year, Eric Clapton recorded "After Midnight," taking it to the American Top 20. In December of 1971, Cale released his debut album, *Naturally* which was followed by *Really* in 1972. *Okie*, his third album, appeared in 1974. Two years later, he released *Troubadour*, which yielded "Cocaine," a song that Clapton later covered. Following 1979's *Number Five*, he signed with MCA, where he released only one album, 1981's *Shades*. The next year, he moved to Mercury Records, releasing *Grasshopper*, which was followed by *#8* in 1983. The album became his first not to chart. After its release, Cale left Mercury and entered a long period of seclusion, reappearing in late 1990 with *Travel Log*. He released *Number 10* in 1992, an album that failed to chart but re-established his status as a cult artist. He moved to Virgin in 1994, releasing *Close to You* the same year; it was followed by *Guitar Man* in 1996. —*Stephen Thomas Erlewine*

Naturally / Dec. 1971 / Mercury ✦✦✦
J.J. Cale's debut album, *Naturally*, was recorded after Eric Clapton made "After Midnight" a huge success. Instead of following Slowhand's cue and constructing a slick blues-rock album, Cale recruited a number of his Oklahoma friends and made a laid-back country-rock record that firmly established his distinctive, relaxed style. Cale included a new version of "After Midnight" on the album, but the true meat of the record lay in songs like "Crazy Mama," which became a hit single, and "Call Me the Breeze," which Lynyrd Skynyrd later covered. On these songs and many others on *Naturally*, Cale effortlessly captured a lazy, rolling boogie that contradicted all the commercial styles of boogie, blues and country rock at the time. Where his contemporaries concentrated on solos, Cale worked the song and its rhythm, and the result was a pleasant, engaging album that was in no danger of raising anybody's temperature. —*Thom Owens*

Really / Dec. 1972 / Mercury ✦✦✦
Cale's guitar work manages to be both understated and intense here. The same is true of his seemingly offhand singing, which finds him drawling lines like "You get your gun, I'll get mine" with disarming casualness. But he has trouble coming up with original material as strong as that on his debut, and for some, his approach will be too casual; there are many times, when the band is percolating along and Cale is muttering into the microphone, that the music seems to be all background and no foreground. You may find yourself waiting for a payoff that never comes. —*William Ruhlmann*

Okie / May 1974 / Mercury ✦✦✦
Cale moves toward country and gospel on some songs here, but since those are two of his primary influences, the movement is slight. And longtime producer Audie Ashworth attempts to place more emphasis on Cale's vocals on some songs by double-tracking them and pushing them up in the mix. But much of this is still low-key and bluesy in what was becoming Cale's patented style. —*William Ruhlmann*

Troubadour / Sep. 1976 / Mercury ✦✦✦✦✦
Producer Audie Ashworth introduced some different instruments, notably vibes and what sound like horns (although none are credited), for a slightly altered sound here. But Cale's albums are so steeped in his introspective style that they become interchangeable. If you like one of them, chances are you'll want to have them all. This one is notable for introducing "Cocaine," which Eric Clapton covered on his *Slowhand* album a year later. —*William Ruhlmann*

5 / Aug. 1979 / Mercury ✦✦
As Cale's influence on others expanded, he just continued to turn out the occasional album of bluesy, minor-key tunes. This one was even sparer than usual, with the artist handling bass as well as guitar on many tracks. Listened to today, it sounds so much like a Dire Straits album, it's scary. [Mark Knopfler & Co. had appeared in 1978, seven years after Cale.] —*William Ruhlmann*

Shades / Feb. 1981 / Mercury ✦✦

Grasshopper / Mar. 1982 / Mercury ✦✦

8 / 1983 / Mercury ✦✦

Special Edition / 1984 / Mercury ✦✦✦✦✦
Sinuous rhythms, conversational singing, and, most of all, intricate, bluesy guitar playing characterize Cale's performances of his own songs. This compilation, covering 11 years of recording, includes the songs Eric Clapton, who borrowed heavily from Cale's style in his 1970s solo work, made famous: "After Midnight" and "Cocaine." —*William Ruhlmann*

Travel Log / Feb. 1990 / Silvertone ✦✦✦✦✦
Cale's first album in six years finds him taking a more aggressive stance in terms of tempos and playing, although he remains a man with a profound sense of the groove and, especially as a singer, a minimalist. But as he says, "Shuffle or die." —*William Ruhlmann*

10 / Nov. 10, 1992 / Silvertone ✦✦✦

Closer to You / Aug. 23, 1994 / Virgin ✦✦

Guitar Man / Jun. 25, 1996 / Virgin ✦✦✦

Anyway the Wind Blows: The Anthology / Jun. 17, 1997 / Mercury ✦✦✦✦✦
Although it is a little too extensive for casual fans, the double-disc, 50-track *Anyway the Wind Blows—The Anthology* is a definitive retrospective of J.J. Cale's career, featuring all the highlights from his career. Cale's albums often sounded similar, but they were remarkably uneven in terms of quality, which is what makes *Anyway the Wind Blows* essential for both neophytes and collectors. Not only is it a perfect introduction, containing such essentials as "Cocaine," "Call Me the Breeze" and "After Midnight," but it is one of his most consistently listenable and enjoyable discs. —*Stephen Thomas Erlewine*

● **The Very Best of J.J. Cale** / Jun. 9, 1998 / Mercury ✦✦✦✦
The Very Best of J.J. Cale is an excellent single-disc collection of the music from one of the most influential singer-songwriters that emerged out of America during the 1970s. Just as Townes Van Zandt and Guy Clark define Texas songwriting, Cale is the epitome of the Oklahoma writers. Although most people know him as the writer of Eric Clapton's hit "Cocaine," Cale constantly offered up other quality material that could only be defined by his vocal style, which can accurately be described as "reclining in the groove." Popular tunes such as "Call Me the Breeze," "Hey Baby" and "Crazy Mama" have a deceptively laid-back intensity that to a large degree influenced such rockers as Lowell George of Little Feat and the previously mentioned Clapton. Cale's guitar work proved to be influential as well (again on Clapton), but also popular swamp-rockers such as Delaney Bramlett. The

Very Best of J.J. Cale offers a comprehensive collection from Cale's early-'70s recordings in Nashville, to Muscle Shoals in Alabama, to his later work in Hollywood. If you're going to explore Cale's groove, this is the place to start. —*Matthew Greenwald*

John Cale

b. Mar. 9, 1942, Garnant, South Wales
Vocals, Viola, Keyboards, Harpsichord, Piano, Guitar, Bass, Organ / Experimental Rock, Proto-Punk, Experimental, Prog-Rock/Art Rock

While John Cale is one of the most famous and, in his own way, influential underground rock musicians, he is also one of the hardest to pin down stylistically. Much has been made of his schooling in classical and avant-garde music, yet much of what he's recorded has been decidedly song-oriented, dovetailing close to the mainstream at times. Terming him a forefather of punk and new wave isn't exactly accurate either. Those investigating his work for the first time under that premise may be surprised at how consciously accessible much of his output is, at times approaching (but not quite attaining) a fairly "normal" rock sound. There is always a tension between the experimental and the accessible in Cale's solo recordings, meaning that he usually finds himself (not unwillingly) caught between the cracks: too weird for commercial success, and yet not really weird or daring enough to place him among the top rank of rock's innovators. Any assessment of Cale's solo contributions also tends to be overshadowed by his other considerable achievements. Before launching his solo career, he was, with Lou Reed, a primary creative force behind the Velvet Underground, as bassist, viola player, keyboardist, and occasional co-songwriter (the exact nature of his compositional contributions is still a matter of heated debate among the group). He was without question one of the most influential producers of pre-punk, punk, and new wave, overseeing important recordings by the Stooges, Nico, Patti Smith, the Modern Lovers, and Squeeze. Ultimately he may be better remembered for his work in the Velvets, and as a producer, than for his own large discography. —*Richie Unterberger*

Vintage Violence / Mar. 25, 1970 / Columbia/Legacy ✦✦✦✦✦
John Cale had the strongest avant-garde credentials of anyone in the Velvet Underground, but he was also the Velvet whose solo career was the least strongly defined by his work with the band, and his first solo album, *Vintage Violence*, certainly bears this out. While the banshee howls of Cale's viola and the percussive stab of his keyboard parts were his signature sounds on *The Velvet Underground and Nico* and *White Light/White Heat*, Cale's first solo album, 1970's *Vintage Violence*, was a startlingly user-friendly piece of mature, intelligent pop whose great failing may have been being a shade too sophisticated for radio. Cale's work with the Velvets was purposefully rough and aurally challenging, but *Vintage Violence* is buffed to a smooth, satin finish, with Cale and his group sounding witty on tunes like "Adelaide" and "Cleo," pensive on "Amsterdam," and lushly orchestrated on "Big White Cloud." (Cale also gets a lot of production value out of his backing group, credited as "Penguin" but actually members of Garland Jeffreys' band, Grinder's Switch.) And anyone expecting the fevered psychosis that Cale let loose on later albums like *Fear* and *Sabotage/Live* is in for a surprise; Cale has rarely sounded this well-adjusted on record, though his lyrical voice is usually a bit too cryptic to stand up to a literal interpretation of his words. If Cale wanted to clear out a separate and distinct path for his solo career, he certainly did that with *Vintage Violence*, though it turned out to be only one of many roads he would follow in the future. [The 2001 CD reissue adds two bonus tracks: a previously unreleased alternate version of "Fairweather Friend," and the previously unreleased "Wall."] —*Mark Deming*

Church of Anthrax / Feb. 10, 1971 / Columbia ✦✦✦
Cale and Terry Riley produce a dense instrumental sound equal parts jazz, rock, and contemporary classical on this album. (There is also one vocal track, sung by Adam Miller.) A bit too busy to be called "minimalist," a bit too intense to be called "ambient," it is sometimes reminiscent of the fusion style later pioneered by the likes of Miles Davis and Frank Zappa. Not easy listening by any means, but rewarding. —*William Ruhlmann*

The Academy in Peril / Jul. 19, 1972 / Reprise ✦✦

Paris 1919 / Mar. 1973 / Reprise ✦✦✦✦
One of John Cale's very finest solo efforts, *Paris 1919* is also among his most accessible records, one which grows in depth and resonance with each successive listen. A consciously literary work—the songs even bear titles like "Child's Christmas in Wales," "Macbeth" and "Graham Greene"—*Paris 1919* is close in spirit to a collection of short stories; the songs are richly poetic, enigmatic period pieces strongly evocative of their time and place. Chris Thomas' production is appropriately lush and sweeping, with many tracks set to orchestral accompaniment; indeed, there's little here to suggest either Cale's noisy, abrasive past or the chaos about to resurface in his subsequent work—for better or worse, his music never achieved a similar beauty again. —*Jason Ankeny*

Fear / Oct. 1, 1974 / Island ✦✦✦✦
Right from the start, Cale makes it clear he's not messing around on *Fear*. If his solo career before then had been a series of intriguing stylistic experiments, here he meshes it with an ear for his own brand of pop and rock, accessible while still clearly being himself through and through. Getting musical support from various Roxy Music veterans like Brian Eno, Phil Manzanera, and Andy Mackay didn't hurt at all, and all the assorted performers do a great job carrying out Cale's vision. He himself sounds confident, sharp, and incisive throughout; his playing on both various keyboards and guitar equally spot-on. The almost title track "Fear Is a Man's Best Friend," starting with focused, steady piano into a full band performance before ending on a ragged, psychotic note, makes for as solid a statement of artistic purpose for Cale and the album as any. There's everything from slightly (but not completely) lugubrious ballads to bright, sparkling numbers—"Ship of Fools" alone is a treasure; its steady, sweet pace and beautiful chorus simply to die for.

Cale's own bent for trying things out isn't forgotten on the album, with his voice recorded in different ways (sometimes with hollow echo, other times much more direct) and musically touching on everything from early reggae to, on "The Man Who Couldn't Afford to Orgy," a delightful Beach Boys pastiche. As for sheer intensity, little can top "Gun," the equal of Eno's own burning blast "Third Uncle" when it comes to lengthy, focused obsession translated into music and lyrics. Having earlier experimented with his own version of country & western, "Buffalo Ballet" finds him creating something close to meta-country: stately piano and backing singing mixing with gentle twang. It practically invents Nick Cave's late solo career all on its own. *—Ned Raggett*

Slow Dazzle / Mar. 25, 1975 / Island ✦✦✦✦✦
Recording again with Phil Manzanera, along with noted journeyman guitarist Chris Spedding, Cale kept up the focus and amazing music on *Slow Dazzle*, easily the equal of *Fear* in terms of overall quality. With Brian Eno again helping out on synth work, *Slow Dazzle* comes across as a little more fried and unsettling than earlier work. Even the warm, epic lift of the chorus of "Mr. Wilson," very much a tribute to the Beach Boys' main man and one of the best he's ever received, is surrounded by strings and piano both lovely and paranoid. The more accurate tone of the record can be found in such numbers as "Dirty Ass Rock & Roll," an intelligent, sly demolition of the lifestyle done to a glam-touched chug topped off with brass and backing singers, and even more dramatically with "Heartbreak Hotel." One of the most amazing cover versions ever, and arguably the best Elvis Presley revamp in existence, the slower pace, freaked-out Eno synth arrangement and above all else Cale's chilling delivery make it a masterpiece. Then there's "Guts," which deserves notice for its low-key but still sharp feedback snarl and steady, cool rhythm, but perhaps has its best moment with Cale's gasped, killer starting lyric: "The bugger in the short sleeves fucked my wife." For all of the stronger rock power, Cale's obviously not out to be pigeonholed, thus the calmer swing of many other numbers, like the great '50s rock tribute "Darling I Need You," featuring great guest sax from Andy Mackay, and the quick, almost sprightly "Ski Patrol." In terms of his own performance, Cale's voice again sounds marvelous, balanced perfectly between roughness and trained control, while his piano skills similarly find the connection between straightforward melodies and technical skill. *—Ned Raggett*

Helen of Troy / Nov. 14, 1975 / Island ✦✦✦✦✦
The supporting crew on Cale's final Island album makes for a lineup that could never have happened again—at least, in terms of future results, imagining, among others, Cale, Chris Spedding, Brian Eno, and Phil Collins once more in the same room together seems totally unlikely. Regardless of the oddity, Cale once again led a great ensemble band (Spedding now having fully taken over from Manzanera on guitar) through another set of great, inspiring songs. Whoever is putting in the guitar solos, Spedding or Cale, sometimes misfires, sometimes succeeds brilliantly—consider opening song "My Maria," where the earlier efforts are intrusive but the concluding parts a perfect addition to the building smack of the song. Cale's songs generally tend towards the uneasy throughout, his sometimes strained but never forced singing, high volume at points, making the most of the material. The atmosphere of the album as a whole is perhaps the most band-oriented of the three Island records, with further arrangements sounding like additions more than intrinsic parts of the songs. It's not a criticism, though, more an interesting experiment with often strong results, like the strident horns and heavily treated noise on the title track. "I Keep a Close Watch" is the secret emotional sucker punch on *Helen of Troy*—Cale long harbored a sadly unfulfilled dream that Frank Sinatra might cover it, and there's little doubt why. Taking the opening line from Johnny Cash's "I Walk the Line" as inspiration, with a much different thematic intent, it's an unabashedly romantic number with a great string and horn arrangement. There are, again, gentler moments that call to mind earlier tributes to the Beach Boys here and there, such as "China Sea," along with a great rendition of Jonathan Richman's "Pablo Picasso." Overall, *Helen of Troy* finds Cale at his edgiest, with fascinating results. *—Ned Raggett*

Guts / 1977 / Mango ✦✦✦✦
Guts is a compilation album selecting the best from Cale's three Island releases of 1974-1975: *Fear, Slow Dazzle*, and *Helen Of Troy*. *—William Ruhlmann*

Sabotage/Live / Dec. 1979 / Diesel Motor ✦✦✦
By 1979, Cale was leading a hard rock band (and wearing a hardhat onstage), and this live album, recorded in June at New York club CBGBs, finds him angrily churning out songs like "Mercenaries (Ready for War)" and the title track, in which be declares, "Military intelligence isn't what it used to be." Was it ever? *—William Ruhlmann*

Honi Soit / Mar. 10, 1981 / A&M ✦✦✦
The rise of the punk/new wave scene finally provided John Cale with a context in which he didn't seem *that* much more eccentric than the other musicians surrounding him, and after reintroducing himself to the new audience with 1979's purposefully aggressive *Sabotage/Live*, recorded onstage at CBGB and filled with bleak rants about global militarization, he released *Honi Soit*, his first studio album in six years. *Honi Soit* was considerably more polished and stylistically eclectic than *Sabotage/Live*, but Cale had hardly shaken off the intense paranoia and foreboding echoes that dominated the previous album, and if anything the cleaner surfaces of Mike Thorne's production and the efficient, no-nonsense support of Cale's road band of the moment brought the album's psychodrama to a finer point; *Honi Soit* rivals *Fear* as the most lividly uncomfortable album in Cale's catalog, and that's saying something. While there are a few moments of relief—the languid "Riverbank," and the pop melodies of "Dead Or Alive" and "Magic & Lies"—more typical are the battlefield nightmare "Wilson Joliet," the bemused espionage of "Strange Times In Casablanca," and the paramilitary ranting of "Russian Roulette." Probably most telling is "Magic & Lies," which starts out with an upbeat keyboard pattern Barry Manilow would envy, and ends in a barrage of crashing drums and swooping bass swells that closes the album like a lid slamming shut on a coffin; here even Cale's token upbeat numbers wouldn't escape his overpowering sense of dread, and on *Honi Soit* there is no corner sunny enough to escape the shadow of World War III. *—Mark Deming*

Music for a New Society / Aug. 1982 / Rhino ✦✦✦✦✦
The aural chaos and intense paranoia of John Cale's "comeback" albums *Sabotage/Live* and *Honi Soit* seemingly left Cale with very few places left to go, short of setting back issues of Soldier Of Fortune to music. 1982's *Music For A New Society* was, from a musical standpoint, a remarkable about-face, sounding calm, spare and spectral where his last few albums has been all rant and rage; the arrangements were dominated by Cale's open, languid keyboard patterns, and there was far more aural "white space" in their framings than he had permitted himself since *The Academy In Peril*. But beyond the cool, reserved exteriors of *Music For A New Society*, one finds a handful of stories of terribly damaged lives; on close inspection, the ethereal opening cut "Taking Your Life In Your Hands" turns out to be the story of a mother gone on a killing spree, while "Sanities," "Thoughtless Kind," and "Damn Life" are full of dashed hopes and painful emotional betrayals. If the approach to the material is a good bit different than what most fans had been used to from Cale, the results were, if anything, among the most compelling music of his career; the open spaces of the arrangements are at once ambient and melodically compelling, and the songs have an emotional resonance that communicates on a deeper and more emotional level than the political hectoring of *Sabotage* or *Honi Soit*, intelligent as they may have been. Spare, understated, and perhaps a masterpiece. *—Mark Deming*

Caribbean Sunset / Jan. 1984 / Mango ✦✦

Comes Alive / Sep. 1984 / Mango ✦✦

Artificial Intelligence / Sep. 6, 1985 / Beggars Banquet ✦✦

Words for the Dying / Sep. 1989 / Opal ✦✦✦

Songs for Drella / 1990 / Sire ✦✦✦✦✦
Lou Reed and John Cale's tribute to Andy Warhol brings out the best in both of them. It's a spare collection, the only instruments being Reed's guitar and Cale's keyboards and viola. The songs trace Warhol's life in a witty, conversational way that evokes his spirit far better than any biographical work of the artist yet attempted. *—William Ruhlmann*

Even Cowgirls Get the Blues / Sep. 10, 1991 / ROIR ✦✦

Fragments of a Rainy Season / Sep. 25, 1992 / Hannibal ✦✦✦✦
It's hard to imagine John Cale on MTV, but if he appeared on *Unplugged*, the result probably would sound like this. Alone, Cale accompanies himself on acoustic piano and guitar, playing a retrospective set of some of his best and most accessible music. The emphasis is on his more contemplative material, such as the early *Paris 1919* album, his later *Words for the Dying*, which features the poetry of Dylan Thomas set to music, and other notable Cale ballads. He does throw in some rock & roll fervor and some of his noisy avant-garde effects on numbers like "Guts," but for the most part this is a John Cale who, while intense, is quiet and dignified. *— William Ruhlmann*

● **Seducing Down the Door** / Jul. 5, 1994 / Rhino ✦✦✦✦✦
The range of John Cale's work can be shocking: It's hard to believe that the piano duets with minimalist composer Terry Riley on *Church of Anthrax*, the lush orchestral pop of *Paris 1919*, and the raucous, dissonant guitar rock of "Gun" and the rest of *Fear* are all the work of the same man, much less that they were all released within a four-year span. This well-chosen 38-track, 2 1/2-hour double-CD/cassette anthology does nothing to reconcile the apparent musical contradictions in Cale's classical-to-punk sensibility, but it does bring coherence and consolidation to a recording career that, spread across a multitude of labels and plagued by popular indifference, has been difficult to grasp as a whole. *— William Ruhlmannn*

The Island Years / Jul. 1996 / Island ✦✦✦✦✦
This double CD combines all three of his mid-'70s Island albums (*Fear, Slow Dazzle*, and *Helen of Troy*) into one package, with the addition of some interesting bonus tracks: outtakes from *Slow Dazzle* and *Helen of Troy*, the B-side "Sylvia Said," "Leaving It Up to You" (which only appeared on early copies of *Helen of Troy* before "Coral Moon" took its place), and "Mary Lou" (from the 1977 *Guts* compilation). This was undeniably one of Cale's most fertile periods. There is also no other body of work from the mid-'70s with such a confluence of listenable FM radio-ready tunes and sneaky, at times subversive experimentation, its eclecticism encompassing art rock, macabre recitations, and Beach Boy pastiches. *—Richie Unterberger*

Walking on Locusts / Sep. 24, 1996 / Hannibal ✦✦✦

Eat/Kiss: Music for the Films of Andy Warhol / Jun. 10, 1997 / Hannibal ✦✦✦

Dance Music / 1998 / Detour ✦✦✦

● **Close Watch: An Introduction to John Cale** / Apr. 20, 1999 / Island ✦✦✦✦✦
Tidily packaged and generously annotated, this 16-track compilation offers a glimpse inside the aural laboratory wherein John Cale has relentlessly labored to reconcile the low (rock) and high (avant-garde/classical) musical aesthetics over the course of his lengthy post-Velvets solo career.

Although the integrity of the quest (not to mention Cale's impeccable pedigree) has to be admired, the end result has been an artistic chimera of innocuous curios (his cabaret noir retake on Elvis Presley's "Heartbreak Hotel"), inspired hybrids (the viola-driven, Beatlesque musings of "Paris 1919," "A Child's Christmas in Wales"), and torpid failures ("Close Watch," "Cable Hogue").

Within the Cale methodology, there is no pop convention that can't be gleefully sabotaged with some well-placed harmonic and/or lyrical dissonance; an approach that too often mistakes non-conformity for originality, ultimately producing music that lumbers under the weight of it's own schizophrenic conceits. Listeners already enamored of Cale's baleful voice and peculiar brand of recombinant songcraft will probably want to opt for the more comprehensive *Island Years* or *Seducing Down the Door* anthologies, but for the more casual listener this is probably all you'll ever need. *—Andrew Vance*

Calexico

f. Tucson, AZ

Americana, Indie Rock, Alternative Pop/Rock

Calexico, a Tucson collective of musicians focused around Joey Burns and John Convertino, forged an eclectic identity through their exploration of Southwestern culture. Composer Ennio Morricone's spaghetti westerns as well as Portuguese fado, Afro-Peruvian music, and '50s and '60s jazz, country, and surf music all factored into the group's music. Calexico formed after Burns met Convertino in Los Angeles in 1990. At the time, Convertino was playing with Howe Gelb's experimental rock group Giant Sand. Burns joined the group as their upright bassist for a European tour. Burns and Convertino found their voice as a duo during a break from work with Giant Sand. They moved to Tucson in 1994 and worked with neo-lounge combo Friends of Dean Martinez. They started to play marimba, cello, accordion, and vibraphone in addition to their usual work on bass, guitar, and drums. After a split with Friends of Dean Martinez founder Bill Elm in 1996, the duo began to get session work with Barbara Manning, Richard Buckner, Victoria Williams, Michael Hurley, Bill Janovitz, Vic Chesnutt, and Lisa Germano. The duo experimented on their own with their new instruments in a home recording studio in 1996, releasing their debut CD, *Spoke*, on Germany's Haus Musik Records. After signing with Quarterstick/Touch and Go Records in Chicago, they released *The Black Light* in 1998 and *The Hot Rail* in 2000. For their 2001 EP, *Even My Sure Things Fall Through*, Calexico enlisted the support of longtime members Martin Wenk, Volker Zander, and Jacob Valenzuela, as well as members of Mariachi Luz de Luna. In effect, the EP was a collection of outtakes from the group's 2000 CD release, *The Hot Rail*, as well as B-sides, remixes, and previously unreleased material from their European label, City Slang. *—Robert Hicks*

Spoke / Aug. 12, 1997 / Quarterstick ✦✦✦

The back cover photo of *Spoke* is a furrowing farm machine. When I see such machinery working, clouds of birds follow to eat up the disturbed insects. Calexico snatches up the bits of Americana turned out by a rototilling of the national music psyche. The nineteen resultant tracks can be insect small (0:28 to 3:54) and erratic in flight. The tracks are lo-fi songs suggested and themes follow without concern for what preceded. One bit is held up by guitar, another by accordion, then one by vibes. A bit of desert dust sprinkled throughout may be the only constant theme—a Santa Fe rummage sale of sounds. *Spoke* is very intriguing and well-worth exploring. *—Thomas Schulte*

● **The Black Light** / May 19, 1998 / Quarterstick ✦✦✦✦✦

Deeper and richer than their debut *Spoke*, Calexico's second album expands upon the sun-baked, cinematic sound of before with the addition of Latin jazz rhythms, mariachi trumpets and pedal steel; in and of themselves, the group's songs are not exactly compelling, but they're produced with such a fine sense of texture and atmosphere that *The Black Light* still makes for intriguing listening. *—Jason Ankeny*

Hot Rail / May 9, 2000 / Quarterstick ✦✦✦

Continuing the Tijuana Brass meets Giant Sand and Ennio Morricone in a dark neuvo-waveo spaghetti Western approach they've gradually refined over the past two albums, multi-instrumentalists John Convertino and Joey Burns keep exploring terrain they've uniquely staked out. While not as cinematic, sprawling, and impressive as 1998's *The Black Light*, the duo create vivid soundscapes as dry, hot, and shimmering as the weather of their Tucson, Arizona home. Although they subtly expand their palette in all sorts of interesting ways, the spooky, late-'70s Miles Davis feel they inject into the nearly eight-minute "Fade" through jazzy drums, spacy vibes, and ominous cello works best. The songs, especially the appropriately named atmospheric instrumentals "Untitled II" and "Untitled III" tend to meander, but the duo keeps peeling back more layers and different instruments to pull the listener's interest. "Sonic Wind" and "Ballad of Cable Hogue" are as succinct, melodic, and tight as they've ever been, and Joey Burns' yearning, whisper of a voice suits this evocative music perfectly. This could easily turn into schtick, though, and it's to the duo's credit that they not only take themselves seriously, but don't pummel their weirdness into the ground. Instead, they push and knead the already elastic boundaries of a genre they've practically created, in jazzy, bluesy, and experimental directions that indicate they have a rich future ahead of them. *Hot Rail* isn't a great album; it's far too spotty and inconsistent musically. But it's an important one because it proves Calexico isn't content to remain stuck in an intriguing but limiting rut and is willing to explore new sonic directions while maintaining a distinctive identity and vision. *—Hal Horowitz*

Even My Sure Things Fall Through / May 22, 2001 / Quarterstick ✦✦✦

On *Even My Sure Things Fall Through*, Tucson's Calexico compiles eight European B-sides, remixes, covers, and other unreleased tracks, as well as three CD-ROM videos. Such albums often come off as hastily compiled and shoddily sequenced, but Calexico's attempt at a rarities release is surprisingly coherent. From the as-yet-unreleased opener, "Sonic Wind (Instrumental Mix)," to the elegantly lush remake of American Music Club's "Chanel No. 5," the 45-plus minute EP manages to wonderfully showcase the band's deserted desert songs, Tex-Mex music and arid roots-rock. And while diehards may more fully appreciate having these hard-to-find titles all on one domestically released album, *Even My Sure Things Fall Through* should prove to be a mini-treasure trove for new Calexico fans as well. *—Jimmy Draper*

The Call

f. 1980, **db.** 1990

New Wave, Alternative Pop/Rock, College Rock

Led by vocalist and songwriter Michael Been, California's the Call mixed the fire and social awareness of the Clash with the passion and big, anthemic sound of early U2, plus a healthy dose of Christian mysticism. The band also included guitarist Tom Ferrier, bassist Greg Freeman (replaced by keyboardist Jim Goodwin in 1984), and drummer Scott Musick. The group broke through in 1983 with the minor hit "The Walls Came Down" from *Modern Romans*; later LPs *Reconciled* and *Let the Day Begin* were also moderately successful. However, the Call never quite achieved the transcendence they were aiming for and broke up; Been compiled the band's best tracks on *The Walls Came Down: Best of the Mercury Years*. *—Steve Huey*

The Call / 1982 / Mercury ✦✦

Modern Romans / 1983 / Mercury ✦✦✦

Scene Beyond Dreams / 1984 / Mercury ✦✦✦

Reconciled / 1986 / Elektra ✦✦✦✦

Though none of the singles from The Call's *Reconciled* made a dent on the pop charts, the anthemic march "I Still Believe" and the galloping "Everywhere I Go" (with backup vocals by Jim Kerr and Peter Gabriel) both received significant AOR and college radio airplay. It significantly raised the profile of the quartet and their earnest, U2-like brand of rock. It is easy to apply spiritual overtones to the socially conscious lyrics, but the words are malleable enough to be mainstream and only on occasion become heavy handed ("Blood Red (America)"). Robbie Robertson plays guitar on the thundering stomp "The Morning" and the song itself has the same vibe as the band's later hit "Let the Day Begin." Some of the keyboards sound a bit dated, but, overall, *Reconciled* is enjoyable and established the band as one of the better purveyors of '80s "big music." *—Tom Demalon*

Into the Woods / 1987 / Elektra ✦✦✦

Coming off the success of the previous year's *Reconciled*, the Call returned in 1987 with *Into the Woods*. The slow-building "I Don't Wanna" is a bit ragged at moments but reaches an impressive sonic swell and Michael Been's vocals are passionate as always. "In the River"'s tone is forlorn, but backed by a solid, smoldering melody and gospel background vocals. A tumbling, percussive beat drives "It Could've Been Mean," a rumination on fate that is simple, yet effective. "Day or Night" probably comes the closest to best capturing the band's usual anthemic style. Much of *In the Woods* has a darker, more serious feel to it. The somber, introspective nature of the lyrics and the lack of a track with a hook as memorable as the radio hits from *Reconciled* undoubtedly doomed a further commercial breakthrough. However, *Into the Woods* is a worthy and challenging artistic follow-up. *—Tom Demalon*

Let the Day Begin / May 1989 / MCA ✦✦✦✦

After losing some commercial ground with 1987's *Into the Woods*, the California quartet quickly regained it as the title track to The Call's 1989 release became the band's biggest crossover hit. With its insistent bassline and driving guitars, "Let the Day Begin" was a rousing track that was a memorable introduction to the band's fifth album. The album consists of some of The Call's strongest material and the undercurrent of optimism and big arena rock hooks results in it being their best bid for wider success. Unfortunately, nothing else clicked at radio like "Let the Day Begin." However, songs like keyboard-driven "Surrender," the vibrant "When," the blues stomp of "For Love" (with Harry Dean Stanton adding harmonica), and the moody vibe of "Jealousy" are just a few of the highlights of a consistently solid and enjoyable record. *—Tom Demalon*

Red Moon / Aug. 1990 / MCA ✦✦✦✦

After the big sounding (even by their standards) *Let the Day Begin*, The Call returned three years later with *Red Moon*, an intimate-sounding, organic record, particularly the use of rich organ passages in many songs. Admirer Bono makes a guest appearance on the warm, gospel-tinged "What's Happened to You," which edges the group toward Band territory. The gentle, dreamy title song is one of the loveliest songs the band has ever done. As usual, songs like "You Were There" (driven by keyboardist Jim Goodwin's saxophone playing) and the chugging "What a Day" feature Michael Been's always literate, socially conscious lyrics. Other standout tracks include the twangy, shuffling "A Swim in the Ocean" and the punchy "Like You've Never Been Loved" (with T-Bone Burnett on backing vocals). With its lovely textures and melodic songs, *Red Moon* is start to finish the most fully realized and finest work. The group would disband following this album and not work together again for nearly a decade. *—Tom Demalon*

● **The Walls Came Down: The Best of the Mercury Years** / Jun. 11, 1991 / Mercury ✦✦✦✦✦

The Walls Came Down: The Best of the Mercury Years is a generous overview of the Call's peak years, containing 18 tracks from their days at Mercury. That means, of course, that it has everything most listeners could want, including the title track and many other college-radio big music anthems of the '80s. The music may have dated somewhat, along with the message, and it is missing the non-Mercury hit "Let the Day Begin" but this still summarizes the Call's strengths and weaknesses better than any other collection could hope. *—Stephen Thomas Erlewine*

● **The Best of the Call** / Jul. 8, 1997 / Warner Resound ✦✦✦✦✦

The Best of the Call compiles all of the hits and best-known songs from the group's career, adding a couple of solo tracks from their leader, Michael Been, as well as two new tracks by the band, which feature contributions from Bruce Cockburn and Jim Keltner. It's a near-definitive collection, and for the casual fan, it contains all the Call they'll need. *—Thom Owens*

20th Century Masters—The Millennium Collection: The Best of the Call / Oct. 31, 2000 / Hip-O ✦✦✦✦

The Walls Come Down may offer more songs, beating this by six songs, but *20th Century Masters* may satisfy the tastes of the group's casual followers somewhat better, since it includes "Let the Day Begin" (Al Gore's 2000 campaign theme, incidentally) along with "The Walls Come Down" and "Surrender," among other Call anthems. Michael Been's songwriting remains admirably strident, but the Call probably remains best heard in concentrated form for anyone other than the converted—so this is the place for most listeners to go. —*Stephen Thomas Erlewine*

Camel

f. 1972

Prog-Rock/Art Rock

Camel never achieved the mass popularity of fellow British progressive-rock bands like the Alan Parsons Project, but they cultivated a dedicated cult following. Over the course of their career, Camel experienced numerous changes, but throughout the years, Andrew Latimer remained the leader of the band. Their breakthrough album was their third, 1975's *The Snow Goose*, which climbed into the British Top 30. The band's English audience declined with 1976's *Moonmadness*, but the album was more successful in America, reaching number 118—the highest chart position the band ever attained in the US. Camel suffered from the shift in popular taste after the emergence of punk rock—*I Can See Your House from Here* received less attention than any of the band's releases since their debut. Camel's 1982 album, *The Single Factor*, was a slicker, more accessible affair than previous Camel records, but it failed to chart. By the mid-'80s, Camel entered a long period of hibernation that lasted until the early '90s. By the time Camel recorded their next album (1991's *Dust and Dreams*), the band was, for most intents and purposes, simply Andrew Latimer and a handful of session musicians. In early 1996, Camel released *Harbour of Tears*. —*Stephen Thomas Erlewine*

Camel / 1973 / Camel ✦✦

Camel was still finding their signature sound on its eponymous debut album. At this point, Peter Bardens and his grand, sweeping organ dominate the group's sound and Andrew Latimer sounds tentative on occasion. Furthermore, the music fluctuates uncertainly between arty improvisations, jazz-inflected rhythms and uninspired rock numbers. There are hints of promise scattered throughout the album, yet the record never gels into something special. —*Daevid Jehnzen*

Mirage / 1974 / Deram ✦✦✦

With their second album *Mirage*, Camel begins to develop their own distinctive sound, highlighted by the group's liquid, intricate rhythms and the wonderful, unpredictable instrumental exchanges by keyboardist Peter Bardens and guitarist Andy Latimer. Camel also distinguishes itself from its prog-rock peers with the multi-part suite "Lady Fantasy," which suggests the more complex directions they would take a few albums down the line. Also, Latimer's graceful flute playing distinguishes several songs on the record, including "Supertwister," and it's clear that he has a more supple technique than such contemporaries as Ian Anderson. Camel is still ironing out some quirks in their sound on *Mirage*, but it's evident that they are coming into their own. —*Daevid Jehnzen*

The Snow Goose / 1975 / Deram ✦✦✦

Camel's classic period started with *The Snow Goose*, an instrumental concept album based on a novella by Paul Gallico. Although there are no lyrics on the album—two songs feature wordless vocals—the music follows the emotional arc of the novella's story, which is about a lonely man named Rhayader who helps nurse a wounded snow goose back to health with the help of a young girl called Fritha he recently befriended. Once the goose is healed, it is set free, but Fritha no longer visits the man because the goose is gone. Later, Rhayader is killed during a battle as he defends his village from intruders. The goose returned during the battle, and it is then named La Princesse Perdue, symbolizing the hopes that can still survive even during the evils of war. With such a complex fable to tell, it is no surprise that Camel keeps their improvisational tendencies reigned in, deciding to concentrate on surging, intricate soundscapes that telegraph the emotion of the piece without a single word. And even though *The Snow Goose* is an instrumental album, it is far more accessible than some of Camel's later work, since it relies on beautiful sonic textures instead of musical experimentation. —*Stephen Thomas Erlewine*

Moonmadness / 1976 / Passport ✦✦✦

Abandoning the lovely soundscapes of *Snow Goose*, Camel delved into layered guitar and synthesizers similar to those of Pink Floyd's *Wish You Were Here* on the impressive *Moonmadness*. Part of the reason behind the shift in musical direction was the label's insistence that Camel venture into more commercial territory after the experimental *Snow Goose*, and it is true that the music on *Moonmadness* is more akin to traditional English progressive rock, even though it does occasionally dip into jazz-fusion territory with syncopated rhythms and shimmering keyboards. Furthermore, the songs are little more concise and accessible than those of its predecessor. That doesn't mean Camel has abandoned art. *Moonmadness* is indeed a concept album, based loosely on the personalities of each member—"Chord Change" is Peter Bardens, "Air Born" is Andy Latimer, "Lunar Sea" is Andy Ward and "Another Night" is Doug Ferguson. Certainly, it's a concept that is considerably less defined than that of *The Snow Goose*, and the music isn't quite as challenging, yet that doesn't mean that *Moonmadness* is devoid of pleasure. In fact, with its long stretches of atmospheric instrumentals and spacy solos, it's quite rewarding. —*Daevid Jehnzen*

Rain Dances / 1977 / Deram ✦✦✦✦✦

Rain Dances, Camel's fifth release, offers the most consistent and representative package in their saga. This is the band at its best. The addition of Caravan-cofounder Richard

Sinclair proves profitable, as do a few colorist touches by Brian Eno on "Elke." Mel Collins' woodwinds are among the highlights, especially on "Tell Me" and the title track. From beginning to end, this project flows gracefully. —*Matthew Plichta*

Breathless / 1978 / Deram ✦✦✦✦✦

With *Rain Dances*, Camel began exploring shorter, more concise songs, but it wasn't until its follow-up *Breathless* that they truly made a stab at writing pop songs. Although they didn't completely abandon improvisatory prog-rock—there are several fine, jazzy interludes—most of the record is comprised of shorter songs, designed for radio play. While the group didn't quite achieve that goal, *Breathless* is nevertheless a more accessible record than Camel's other albums, which tend to focus on instrumentals. Here, they try to be a straightforward prog-rock band, and while the results are occasionally a little muddled, it is on the whole surprisingly successful. —*Daevid Jehnzen*

● **I Can See Your House from Here** / 1979 / Deram ✦✦✦✦✦

Although not an honest representation of the band's character, this is undoubtedly their most popular work. The one-time addition of American Kit Watkins produces some fine keyboard lead work. Rupert Hine's resourceful production and appearances by Phil Collins and Mel Collins round out this strong import release. "Survival" and "Who We Are" feature some fine orchestrations, and guitarist Latimer delivers some exceptional lead work on the album's closer, "Ice." —*Matthew Plichta*

Nude / 1981 / Decca ✦✦✦✦

A new, larger version of Camel debuted on *Nude*, a concept album about a Japanese soldier stranded on a deserted island during World War II, and stayed there, oblivious to the outside world, for 29 years. More ambitious than the preceding *I Can See Your House from Here*, *Nude* is in many ways just as impressive. Although it's a less accessible effort, it has a number of quite intriguing passages, particularly since it boasts heavier improvisation, orchestration and even some worldbeat influences. It's not as spacey as Camel's earlier progressive-rock records, yet it is quite atmospheric, creating its own entrancing world. —*Daevid Jehnzen*

The Single Factor / 1982 / Deram ✦✦

Stationary Traveller / 1984 / Decca ✦✦✦

Although *Stationary Traveller* is a concept album, it musically falls into line with its predecessor *The Single Factor*, which found Camel trying to refashion themselves as the Alan Parsons Project. Where *The Single Factor* suffered from Camel's attempts to write pop hooks, *Stationary Traveller* finds the band breaking down the barriers, opening up their relatively concise songs with long, atmospheric instrumental passages. The album's lyrics, which were written by Susan Hoover, is about the divided Berlin and its political, emotional and physical divides. Often, the lyrics and music—which work as individual entities—don't quite work together, since they follow different emotional directions, yet the record remains a worthwhile listen, especially since it features Andy Latimer on pan flute. —*Daevid Jehnzen*

Compact Compilation / 1986 / Rhino ✦✦✦✦

Rhino's *A Compact Compilation* is a surprisingly thorough collection of highlights from Camel's '70s albums, hitting most of the group's highlights including "Lady Fantasy," "Rhayader Goes to Town," "Lunar Sea," "Metrognome" and "Rain Dances." Although Camel's music makes more sense on the original concept albums and the sound quality of *A Compact Compilation* could have been better, it remains a good introduction for neophytes. —*Daevid Jehnzen*

Dust and Dreams / 1991 / Camel ✦✦✦✦

As with *Nude* and *The Snow Goose*, Camel continues refining their concept album approach, here based on Steinbeck's *The Grapes of Wrath*. Latimer maintains a symphony-like coherence throughout, with subtle character-based themes. Guest vocalist Mae McKenna has a hand in "Rose of Sharon," a gem of lyrical and musical depth. This recent album was produced and packaged by Latimer himself and may be harder to find than their others. [Available from Camel Productions, PO Box 4876, Mtn. View, CA 94040.] —*Matthew Plichta*

● **Echoes: The Retrospective** / Jul. 20, 1993 / Deram/Chronicles ✦✦✦✦✦

This English quartet of progressive rock is known for their thorough but imaginative style of music, as well as their use of numerous synthesizers and sequencers. Nearly every song they perform consists of intricate harmonic passages and rich, melodic sweeps, with vocals used every once in a while. *Echoes* is a comprehensive two-disc set that takes all of their best work and lays it out over an hour and a half. Camel's talents are bewildering, combining accordion, flute, mini-Moog synthesizers, and saxophones throughout their music to instill a genuine progressive sound. The tracks, spanning 20 years, include songs from *Mirage*, *Snow Goose*, *Rain Dances*, and *Stationary Traveller*, just to name a few, and while an incredible 11 albums are represented here, not one track strays from the essence of the group. Appearances by Brian Eno on "Elke" and Phil Collins on "Ice" just add spark to the already amazing tracks. Andrew Latimer, who sings on a few of the tracks, as well as plays guitar and keys, is a stunning musician and proves it on "Never Let Go" and "Rhayder Goes to Town." Lovers of synthesizer and other keyboard machinery will drool over Peter Bardens' detailed playing on "Lunar Sea" and on "Skylines," saturating them both with electrical magic. No other set captures the lifeblood of this prog band quite like *Echoes*. —*Mike DeGagne*

Harbour of Tears / Jan. 20, 1996 / Camel ✦✦

On the Road 1981 / Jun. 10, 1997 / Camel ✦✦✦

Rajaz / Oct. 21, 1999 / Camel ✦✦✦

Cameo

f. 1974, New York, NY

Quiet Storm, Urban, Funk

Over the years, Cameo has reflected the numerous changes in the world of funk. When they started in 1974, they frequently toured with Parliament and Funkadelic, which is a clue to how their sound was styled. Even though they were in the hard funk vein of George Clinton's classic outfits, they were not copycats. As the '70s became the '80s, they started to play around with their sound slightly. In 1984, they found a successful style—the synth-powered title track to their album *She's Strange*. But that only hinted at what was to come. With 1986's *Word Up*, Cameo recorded a funk classic—bass-driven and synth heavy, the album was the sound of the mid-'80s. "Word Up" was also the song that broke them into the mainstream, reaching the Top Ten on the pop charts; thankfully, the album didn't have just one good song, it had a whole album's worth. *Word Up* proved to be the pinnacle of Cameo's career. Although the group kept recording and touring into the '90s, their style became a bit formulaic, as synthesizers and robotic funk took precedence over songs in their later records. By the mid-'90s, Cameo was, for most intents and purposes, finished as a recording phenomenon, yet could still tour successfully. *—Stephen Thomas Erlewine*

● **The Best of Cameo** / May 18, 1993 / Casablanca ✦✦✦✦✦

Larry Blackmon and his Cameo mates ruled funk's domain for over a decade. Cameo evolved from its origins as a horn-based and dominated ensemble into a synthesizer-oriented group that still featured sturdy bass lines and exuberant vocals, but was in tune with urban and black America's new sensibility. These 14 selections range from the formative cuts "Rigor Mortis," "Shake Your Pants," and "It's Over" to the definitive "Word Up," "Candy," and "Back and Forth." Blackmon's alternately sneering, defiant, and aggressive vocals were the constant from Cameo's beginnings in the 1970s to their emergence as funk's reigning champions in the 1980s. *—Ron Wynn*

20th Century Masters—The Millennium Collection: The Best of Cameo / Feb. 6, 2001 / Mercury ✦✦✦✦

Cameo's volume of Universal's *20th Century Masters* series is first-rate, containing most of the cuts a casual fan needs, including all their biggest pop crossover hits: "She's Strange," "Word Up," "Candy," and "Back and Forth." There may be several singles missing and it's not nearly as far-reaching as the *Best Of* compilations, but for anyone looking for a concise hits collection, this is a nice choice. *—Stephen Thomas Erlewine*

Camper Van Beethoven

f. 1983, Santa Cruz, CA, **db.** 1990

College Rock, Jangle Pop, Indie Rock, Alternative Pop/Rock, American Underground

At the time of their 1985 debut, Camper Van Beethoven's merging of punk, folk, ska and world musics was truly a revelation. Self-described as "surrealist absurdist folk," the band was formed by singer-songwriter David Lowery, with his dry humor and valley-boy voice (sometimes confused for a faux English accent), and boyhood friends Chris Molla and Chris Pedersen. The 1985 re-release of their debut *Telephone Free Landslide Victory* did well with critics, and on their second album, *II & III*, they went for a purer indie-rock sound with touches of country. The band deftly switched modes from punk to ska to rock on alternate takes, and the eponymous third album continued the thread. For their Virgin Records debut, subsequent with the label's US re-launch in 1988, the band took a more serious tack for *Our Beloved Revolutionary Sweetheart*. For *Key Lime Pie*, the band's final release in 1989, they took it as far as it could go. Pedersen's side-project Monks of Doom soon turned into a full-time job, while Lowery later formed Cracker. *—Denise Sullivan*

● **Telephone Free Landslide Victory** / 1985 / IRS ✦✦✦✦✦

They say "never say never," but it's still extremely unlikely something so goofily low-key, inventive, and fun will ever achieve cult status so quickly again, especially in terms of musical range on display. Not simply a rock group but not anything else, Camper Van Beethoven pulled off a series of entertaining fusions throughout its debut record, as the opening song "Border Ska" indicates by name alone. Eastern European folk, tropical grooves, post-punk atmospherics, country laid-back good times, psych/garage band aesthetics, lyrics about Mao, Greece, and more—a lot of stuff went into the Santa Cruz band's brew, and most of it came up trumps on *Telephone*. Lowery's lead vocals aren't much like what his more famous work in Cracker would indicate, being more speak-singing through shaggy dog stories (even one about Lassie) of all stripes. Hearing his tale of woe on "Wasted"—"I was a punker, and I had a Mohawk/I was so gnarly and I drove my dad's car"—delivered in a "yeah dude" tone of voice is pretty darn funny. Segel's keyboards and violins color the arrangements with a fun touch, while rhythm team Krummenacher and then recently departed drummer Anthony Guess try out nearly everything at least once. The production is eminently suited for the proceedings, sounding a bit like the thick, fuzzy flow of many Shimmy-Disc releases but with just enough of a crisp edge. When it comes to humor, it's everywhere—for instance, the plaintively sung chorus of "Where the Hell Is Bill?," not to mention the various speculative answers ("Maybe he went to get a Vespa scooter"). Or, of course, the song that kick-started the band's reputation, "Take the Skinheads Bowling," two and a half minutes of chiming, goofy nonsense with references to Jah and incomplete rhymes. *—Ned Raggett*

II & III / Jan. 1986 / IRS ✦✦✦

Admittedly, it's understandable to see why CVB's sense of humor rubbed some people the wrong way. Titling a second album *II & III* and sprinkling it with songs titled "ZZ Top Goes to Egypt" and "No Kruggerands for David" sounds more like a parody of rock rather than rock itself. That never stopped Pavement, though, and on *II & III*, CVB sounds as inventive and unexpectedly inspired as before, mashing its influences together into a delightful brew. However, this time the band sounds a touch more straightforward; new member Chris Pederson's drumming sounds stronger, providing a good pace throughout and pumping up the energy on "Down And Out." Wigginess abounds musically and lyrically—"Cowboys from Hollywood" sounds like an amped-up honky-tonk, and following it with the on-the-level country of "Sad Lovers Waltz" fits whatever master plan there was. Lowery doesn't sing lead as much this time out; he's still the primary singer, but often is accompanied by most of the rest of the band as well. But as always, Segel is the wild card with violin and nutty keyboards ahoy. There's some refreshing iconoclasm at play—years before Sonic Youth became 'the legendary Sonic Youth,' CVB took that group's "I Love Her All the Time" and transformed its New York art angst into a kick-up-your-heels bit of yee-haw ska. It's worth hearing for Lowery and company's vocal drawls alone. The album concludes with the hilarious "No More Bullshit," mixing wanky solos with repetitive punk-rock slogans and strange comments–"Elvis Presley died! And no one knows why!" *—Ned Raggett*

Camper Van Beethoven / Aug. 1986 / IRS ✦✦✦

CVB's self-titled third album generally differs little from *II & III*, continuing the blend of wistfully weird lyrics, any number of musical touches from all over the map and good-time vibes. The opening "Good Guys & Bad Guys" proves that much, with reggae, folk, country and more stewed together as Lowery plaintively sings about lawyers and the people in Russia and the like. From there on in it's another collection of generally short and generally fun ditties, but with a few more tweaks here and there. The bandmembers definitely have more fun with the studio this time out, thus a lot of tape manipulation and semi-psychedelic oddities sprinkled around the album. Something of a Led Zeppelin fascination seems to crop up throughout, perhaps not too surprising considering that band's similar fondness for many musical influences and Jimmy Page's more acoustic numbers. Lowery drawls "Has anyone seen the bridge?" on "Joe Stalin's Cadillac," the following song is "Five Sticks," while later on in the album one gets "Stairway to Heavan (sic)," most definitely not a remake of the referenced song in question. Not to say there aren't reinterpretations here: an obscure sixties track, "Lulu Land," lets CVB fool around with a bit of twinkly jauntiness, while early Pink Floyd gets the band treatment with an impressive, strong version of "Interstellar Overdrive." Then there's the catchy pop salute to a certain Mr. Garcia of the Grateful Dead, "We Saw Jerry's Daughter," the sitars and kicks on "Still Wishing to Course," the concluding 90-second long "Shut Us Down" and more to fill out this album's corners well. *—Ned Raggett*

Our Beloved Revolutionary Sweetheart / 1988 / Virgin ✦✦✦✦✦

With Lowery's by-now more sharply sung words up front and Segel's multi-instrumental abilities helping to lead the way, the quintet came up trumps more often than not. "Eye of Fatima (pt. 2)," for instance, could have easily fit in on most of the group's earlier records at the start. Even so, the addition of some screaming Lisher guitar solos on top of the measured reggae/hard rock/folk stew cooked up didn't feel anything like, say, Eddie Van Halen's drop-in on "Beat It." Distinctly nonrock tempos and touches run merrily rampant as always, as a listen to the fiddle, dub and brass revamp of the traditional number "O Death" demonstrates. However, the fivesome can pump it up when needed—the group's appreciation of Led Zeppelin certainly hasn't dimmed any, based on the majestic stomp of "Waka." When CVB aim to create something possibly more radio-friendly, the members pull it off in their own way rather than anyone else's. Thus, the almost anthemic "She Divines Water," with some great Segel violin work, or the gentler groove of "One of These Days." Add in multitudes of other joys like the fun romp "My Path Belated" and Bruce Licher's clever cover art—at one point you see Bob Dylan looking towards a Turkish music combo in another photo with resignation—and once again CVB create an enjoyable, not-easily-pegged down listening experience. *—Ned Raggett*

Key Lime Pie / Sep. 1989 / Virgin ✦✦✦✦✦

Our Beloved Revolutionary Sweetheart closed with Lowery singing about how "Life Is Grand" in pointed response to "those of you who have appointed yourselves to expect us to say something darker." So when *Key Lime Pie* came out, its moodier music and imagery, not to mention that soon after the fact the band fell apart on the tour for the album, led more than one person to think those darker times had finally arrived. As it is, the group had already gone through one major shake-up between the two albums—founding member Segel had taken a powder to concentrate on other efforts, with Morgan Fichter brought in as a replacement violinist. Her abilities were certainly praiseworthy, as the album-starting instrumental "Opening Theme" shows quite well. However, it's definitely not the same band that did *Telephone Free Landslide Victory* a mere four years previous—things are more straightforwardly rock here most of the time, perhaps not too surprising in light of Lowery's subsequent work in Cracker. As it is, though, it's excellently conceived rock, with space, moodiness, and more to spare. Consider "Jack Ruby," with its wordless backing vocals, tense rhythms, and thick soloing, or "Laundromat" and its steady but unnerving crunch. It's not all potential melancholia, though—"June" in particular is an underrated number, celebrating the early summer with sweetness and love (at least up to the increasingly stranger ending). Lowery's singing is his best yet, perhaps a little less prone to wackiness but an emergent, distinct voice all the same, and certainly prone to sing a quirky lyric or two still. The oddest thing of all was that the band actually gained a little mainstream attention on MTV and radio via a cover of Status Quo's psych-era nugget "Pictures of Matchstick Men." *—Ned Raggett*

Camper Vantiquities / Mar. 23, 1993 / IRS ✦✦✦

A collection of B-sides, rarities and the entire EP *Vampire Can Mating Oven* (an anagram of the band's moniker), the disc is essential for the Camper completist, but the songs "Never Go Back" and "Seven Languages" are beauties in their own right and the covers of the Kinks' "I'm Not Like Everybody Else" and Ringo Starr's "Photograph" are a perfect fit for the band who excelled at everything odd and unexpected during their too-brief stay in the late '80s. *—Denise Sullivan*

Camper Van Beethoven Is Dead: Long Live Camper Van Beethoven / Jun. 6, 2000 / Pitch A Tent ♦♦♦♦
Falling somewhere between a reunion LP and an odds-and-sods compilation, *Camper Van Beethoven Is Dead: Long Live Camper Van Beethoven* is an appropriately bizarre record by any measure; a crazy-quilt of live tracks, unreleased cuts, demos, and rarities all newly edited and manipulated in late 1999 by founding members David Lowery, Victor Krummenacher, and Jonathan Segel, the album goes out of its way to do seemingly everything but summarize the band's history. The finale, "We're All Wasted and We're Wasting All Your Time"—a backwards reading of the classic "Take the Skinheads Bowling" complete with new vocals—perfectly encapsulates CVB's deconstructionist approach to their own legacy, an irreverence wholly in keeping with the band's original spirit. It's impossible to know where the vintage material ends and the latter-day studio trickery begins. Old songs made new and vice versa, the album isn't a retrospective but a resurrection. *—Jason Ankeny*

Can

f. 1968, Cologne, Germany, **db.** 1978
Experimental Rock, Kraut Rock, Experimental, Prog-Rock/Art Rock, Electronic
Always at least three steps ahead of contemporary popular music, Can was the leading avant-garde rock group of the '70s. From their very beginning, their music didn't conform to any commonly held notions about rock & roll—not even those of the countercultures. Inspired more by 20th century classical music than Chuck Berry, their closest contemporaries were Frank Zappa or possibly the Velvet Underground. Yet their music was more serious and inaccessible than either of those artists. Instead of recording tight pop songs or satire, Can experimented with noise, synthesizers, nontraditional music, cut-and-paste techniques, and, most importantly, electronic music; each album marked a significant step forward from the previous album, investigating new territories that other rock bands weren't interested in exploring. When the band split in 1978 following the success of the album *Flow Motion* and the hit "I Want More," they left behind a body of work that has proven surprisingly groundbreaking; echoes of Can's music can be heard in Public Image Limited, the Fall, and Einsturzende Neubauten, among others. As with much aggressive and challenging experimental music, Can's music can be difficult to appreciate, yet their albums offer some of the best experimental rock ever recorded. *—Stephen Thomas Erlewine*

Monster Movie / 1969 / Mute ♦♦♦♦♦
Can's debut is the only full-length, proper release to feature original vocalist Malcolm Mooney, whose free-form ranting is matched by a raw, aggressive dynamic unlike anything else in the group's canon; driving, dissonant songs like the extraordinary "Father Cannot Yell" and "Outside My Door" even owe a rather surprising debt to psychedelia and garage rock. More indicative of things to come is the closer "Yoo Doo Right," a 20-minute epic built on the kinds of hypnotic motifs and minimal rhythms which quickly became Can trademarks. *—Jason Ankeny*

Soundtracks / 1970 / Mute ♦♦♦
Malcolm Mooney passes the baton to Damo Suzuki for *Soundtracks*, a collection of film music featuring contributions from both vocalists. The dichotomy between the two singers is readily apparent: Suzuki's odd, strangulated vocals fit far more comfortably into the group's increasingly intricate and subtle sound, allowing for greater variation than that allowed by Mooney's stream-of-consciousness discourse. *—Jason Ankeny*

Tago Mago / 1971 / Mute ♦♦♦♦♦
With the band in full artistic flower and Suzuki's sometimes moody, sometimes frenetic speak/sing/shrieking in full effect, Can released not merely one of the best Krautrock albums of all time, but one of the best albums ever, period. *Tago Mago* is that rarity of the early '70s, a double album without a wasted note, ranging from sweetly gentle float to full-on monster grooves. "Paperhouse" starts things brilliantly, beginning with a low-key chime and beat, before amping up into a rumbling roll in the midsection, then calming down again before one last blast. Both "Mushroom" and "Oh Yeah," the latter with Schmidt filling out the quicker pace with nicely spooky keyboards, continue the fine vibe. After that, though, come the huge highlights—three long examples of Can at its absolute best. "Halleluwah"—featuring the Liebezeit/Czukay rhythm section pounding out a monster trance/funk beat; Karoli's and Schmidt's always impressive fills and leads; and Suzuki's slow-building ranting above everything—is 19 minutes of pure genius. The near-rhythmless flow of "Aumgn" is equally mind-blowing, with swaths of sound from all the members floating from speaker to speaker in an ever-evolving wash, leading up to a final jam. "Peking O" continues that same sort of feeling, but with a touch more focus, throwing in everything from Chinese-inspired melodies and jazzy piano breaks to cheap organ rhythm boxes and near babbling from Suzuki along the way. "Bring Me Coffee or Tea" wraps things up as a fine, fun little coda to a landmark record. *—Ned Raggett*

☆ **Ege Bamyasi** / 1972 / Mute ♦♦♦♦♦
The follow-up to *Tago Mago* is only lesser in terms of being shorter; otherwise the Can collective delivers its expected musical recombination act with the usual power and ability. Liebezeit, at once minimalist and utterly funky, provides another base of key beat action for everyone to go off on—from the buried, lengthy solos by Karoli on "Pinch" to the rhythm box/keyboard action on "Spoon." The latter song, which closes the album, is particularly fine, its sound hinting at an influence on everything from early Ultravox songs like "Hiroshima Mon Amour" to the hollower rhythms on many of Gary Numan's first efforts. Liebezeit and Czukay's groove on "One More Night," calling to mind a particularly cool nightclub at the end of the evening, shows that Stereolab didn't just take the brain-melting crunch side of Can as inspiration. The longest track, "Soup," lets the band take off on another one of its trademark lengthy rhythm explorations, though not without some tweaks to the expected sound. About four minutes in, nearly everything drops away, with Schmidt and Liebezeit doing the most prominent work; after that, it shifts into some wonderfully grating and crumbling keyboards combined with Suzuki's strange pronouncements, before ending with a series of random interjections from all the members. Playfulness abounds as much as skill: Slide whistles trade off with Suzuki on "Pinch"; squiggly keyboards end "Vitamin C"; and rollicking guitar highlights "I'm So Green." The underrated and equally intriguing sense of drift that the band brings to its recordings continues as always. "Sing Swan Song" is particularly fine, a gentle float with Schmidt's keyboards and Czukay's bass taking the fore to support Suzuki's sing-song vocal. *—Ned Raggett*

Future Days / 1973 / Mute ♦♦♦♦♦
Damo Suzuki's final effort is Can's most atmospheric and beautiful record, a spartan collection of lengthy, jazz-like compositions recorded with minimal vocal contributions. Employing keyboard washes to create a breezy, almost oceanic feel (indeed, two of the tracks are titled "Spray" and "Bel Air"), the mix buries Suzuki's voice to elevate drummer Jaki Liebezeit's complex rhythms to the foreground; despite the deceptive tranquility of its surface, *Future Days* is an intense work, bubbling with radical ideas and concepts. *—Jason Ankeny*

Soon Over Babaluma / 1974 / Mute ♦♦♦♦
With Suzuki departed, vocal responsibilities were now split between Karoli and Schmidt. Wisely, neither try to clone Mooney or Suzuki, instead aiming for their own low-key way around things. The guitarist half speaks/half whispers his lines on the opening groover, "Dizzy Dizzy," while on "Come Sta, La Luna" Schmidt uses a higher pitch that is mostly buried in the background. Czukay sounds like he's throwing in some odd movie samples on that particular track, though perhaps it's just heavy flanging on Schmidt's vocals. Karoli's guitar achieves near-flamenco levels on the song, an attractive development that matches up nicely with the slightly lighter and jazzier rhythms the band comes up with on tracks like "Splash." Also, his violin work—uncredited on earlier releases—is a bit more prominent here. Musically, if things are a touch less intense on *Babaluma*, the sense of a band perfectly living in each other's musical pocket and able to react on a dime hasn't changed at all. "Chain Reaction," the longest track on the album, shows that the combination of lengthy jam and slight relaxation actually can go together rather well. After an initial four minutes of quicker pulsing and rhythm (which sounds partly machine provided), things downshift into a slower vocal section before firing up again; Karoli's blistering guitar work at this point is striking to behold. "Chain Reaction" bleeds into *Babaluma*'s final song, "Quantum Physics," a more ominous piece with Czukay's bass closer to the fore, shaded by Schmidt's work and sometimes accompanied by Liebezeit. It makes for a nicely mysterious conclusion to the album. *—Ned Raggett*

Landed / 1975 / Mute ♦♦

Flow Motion / 1976 / Mute ♦♦

Unlimited Edition / 1976 / Mute ♦♦♦
Expanding the original *Limited Edition* release to a full double-LP/single-CD set, *Unlimited* is very much a dog's breakfast—albeit a highly entertaining one—of previously unreleased performances. Suzuki and Mooney take the spotlight on some songs, while on others the key foursome go at it in their usual way. A number of songs are mere snippets, like the vaguely tribal-sounding "Blue Bag," while one tune, the 20-minute "Cutaway," from 1969, is a sprawling pastiche of oddities. (Keep an ear out for the very formal request to keep modulations in frequency with other bandmembers!) Five cuts are listed as part of the band's continuing *Ethnological Forgery Series*, on which they recreate or interpret a variety of world musics through their own vision. The majority of songs come from 1968-1971—manna from heaven for those interested in the band's roots. Many cuts show off the varying abilities of the players. Leibezeit plays wind instruments on five separate cuts, while Schmidt is credited with "schizophone" on the Mooney-sung funk-soul of "The Empress and the Ukraine King." Though a few tracks are seemingly here to fill space, a lot of what's present easily stands up on its own, and with the band's legend as well. The opening cut, "Gomorrha," recorded after Suzuki's departure, is quite fine, an understated but still epic piece with lovely keyboards from Schmidt and intoxicating Karoli guitar. On the Suzuki-era cut "I'm Too Leise," Leibezeit's medieval flutes and light percussion add to a half-folk/half-something-else vibe. Mooney gets an interesting moment of glory with "Mother Upduff," a spoken-word tale of tourists in Europe that turns increasingly strange after the encounter with the octopus. *—Ned Raggett*

Saw Delight / 1977 / Mute ♦♦♦

Can / 1979 / Mute ♦♦

Cannibalism 1 / 1980 / Mute ♦♦♦♦♦
Given the cohesion of the group's studio albums, Can's songs work surprisingly well in compilation form, as evidenced by *Cannibalism 1*, a collection of tracks taken from the first six years of the group's existence. Covering ground from 1969's *Monster Movie* to 1974's *Soon Over Babaluma* (although nothing from 1973's superb *Future Days* makes the cut), the sampler compiles many of the group's high points (including "Father Cannot Yell," "She Brings the Rain," "Mushroom," and "Soup"), and offers a thorough overview of Can's eclectic musical history to date, even if the abridged versions of cuts like "Mother Sky," "Aumgn," and "Halleluhwah" don't measure up to the full-length renditions featured on the original albums. *—Jason Ankeny*

Delay . . . 1968 / 1981 / Mute ♦♦♦
Although recorded in the late '60s, the material included on *Delay 1968* did not appear commercially until 1981. A collection of cuts featuring early vocalist Malcolm Mooney,

these seven songs are among the very first Can ever recorded; while nowhere near as intricate or assured as the group's later work, the visceral energy of tracks like the deranged "Uphill" and "Butterfly" is undeniable. —*Jason Ankeny*

Cannibalism 2 / 1990 / Mute ✦✦✦✦

Cannibalism 3 / 1990 / Mute ✦✦✦
A compilation drawn from the solo releases of various Can members (though it would seem that percussionist Jaki Leibezeit has made his way onto the majority of them) between 1979 and 1991. Curious musical moments keep company with band works, as well as departing for musical territory far divergent from anything known to fans of the band. Fascinating selections that many will find tempting them to acquire full albums. —*Steven McDonald*

● **Anthology 1968-1993** / 1995 / Mute ✦✦✦✦✦
For listeners daunted by the band's long and winding discography, *Anthology 1968-1993* presents short-form highlights like "Spoon," "Future Days," "Moonshake," "She Brings the Rain" and 25 others. Yes, the albums are better places to hear all of these tracks, and there's a typically Cannish disregard for chronology or narrative (i.e., don't hope for liner notes), but this double-disc set is an excellent introduction to the band's 25-year career. —*Keith Farley*

Can Box / May 18, 1999 / Mute ✦✦✦✦✦
Mute celebrated Can's 30th Birthday with the release of the *Can Box*. Formed in Cologne, Germany, in 1968, the feckless sound experimenters went on to reach the lofty cult and seminal status of bands like the Velvet Underground and Mothers of Invention. The three-item box contains a double CD of live music recorded from 1971-1977, a book of history, interviews, reviews, and photos, as well as a video of a 1972 concert and a previously unreleased documentary made in 1988 and 1997. The CD is compiled from cassettes and other non-professional fan recordings with professional sound processing and mastering applied. Four of the pieces are extemporaneous jams that have as heretofore not seen the light of day. The tome proves to be of just such rare and personal content. The concert was a free event attended by over 10,000 when Can had placed "Spoon" (available on the *Box* album) into the number one chart position. The footage was made with help from Wim Wenders' film editor Peter Przygodda. While this attention brought the group to do a small German tour where each member presented a solo project, there were no plans for a reunion. —*Tom Schulte*

Can Box Music (Live 1971-77) / Nov. 2, 1999 / Mute ✦✦✦✦
Can Box Music: Live 1971-1977 gathers the live material from the limited-edition *Can Box* set that was released in the U.K. earlier in 1999. The album collects six years' worth of live recordings by Can's friend Andy Hall and features nine of the group's transcendent, abrasive compositions, which stretch over two discs. Early works like *Monster Movie*'s "Yoo Doo Right" and mid- to late-period songs like *Soon Over Babaluma*'s "Dizzy Dizzy" and *Flow Motion*'s "Cascade Waltz" are all well represented. More importantly for Can fans, however, are the four "instantaneous compositions": "Jynx," "Fizz," "Kata Kong," and the appropriately named, nearly 40-minute-long "Colchester Finale," which ended their 1972 University of Essex performance. *Can Box Music: Live 1971-1977* is a hypnotic collection and a must for fans, especially since it has been liberated from limited-edition status. —*Heather Phares*

Canned Heat

f. 1966, Los Angeles, CA
Boogie Rock, Blues-Rock, Modern Electric Blues
A hard-luck blues band of the '60s, Canned Heat was founded by blues historians and record collectors Alan Wilson and Bob Hite. They seemed to be on the right track and played all the right festivals (including Monterey and Woodstock, making it very prominently into the documentaries about both) but somehow never found a lasting audience. Canned Heat's debut album—released shortly after their appearance at Monterey—was every bit as deep into the roots of the blues as any other combo of the time mining similar turf, with the exception of the original Paul Butterfield band. Hite was nicknamed "The Bear" and stalked the stage in the time-honored tradition of Howlin' Wolf and other large-proportioned bluesmen. Wilson was an extraordinary harmonica player, with a fat tone and great vibrato. His work on guitar, especially in open tunings, gave the band a depth and texture that most other rhythm players could only aspire to. Canned Heat's breakthrough moment occurred with the release of their second album, establishing them with hippie ballroom audiences as the "kings of the boogie." After two big chart hits with "Goin' up the Country" and an explosive version of Wilbert Harrison's "Let's Work Together," Wilson died under mysterious (probably drug-related) circumstances in 1970, and Hite carried on with various reconstituted versions of the band until his death just before a show in 1981, from a heart seizure. —*Cub Koda & Bruce Eder*

● **The Best of Canned Heat** / 1972 / EMI America ✦✦✦✦✦
All of Canned Heat's best tracks and biggest hits ("Goin' up the Country," "On the Road Again") are included on this single-disc collection. —*Stephen Thomas Erlewine*

On the Road / 1989 / EMI ✦✦✦✦
On the Road is a compilation concentrating entirely on Canned Heat's earliest recordings, hitting all the highlights ("On the Road Again," "Goin' up the Country") from their biggest albums and offering most casual fans a definitive—if not a little too comprehensive—overview. —*Stephen Thomas Erlewine*

Uncanned! The Best of Canned Heat / May 17, 1994 / EMI America ✦✦✦✦✦
Uncanned! The Best of Canned Heat is exactly what it claims to be—the definitive portrait of the blues-soaked hippie boogie band. Spreading 41 tracks (including numerous rarities, alternate takes, and Levi commercials) over two CDs, the set is perfect for the

hardcore Canned Heat collector. For casual fans, the collection simply contains too much music; they would be better served by the single-disc collection, *The Best of Canned Heat*. —*Stephen Thomas Erlewine*

Canned Heat 1967-1976: The Boogie House Tapes / Jun. 27, 2000 / Ruf ✦✦✦
This double disc assembled by drummer Fido de la Parra, the only remaining member of the original '60s band, and Canned Heat collector Walter de Paduwa is a compilation of some previously "lost" studio and live performances of the indefatigable boogie band. While hardcore fans will rejoice hearing the great Alan Wilson, who appears on roughly half of these tracks, in his prime, it's still a very mixed bag. Guitarists Harvey Mandel and Henry Vestine are featured prominently, as is vocalist Bob "the Bear" Hite who, along with drummer de la Parra, is the only constant band member across these two CDs. Many of these tunes were never intended for release, and as such they are subpar blues workouts that might have been fun at the time but lay lifeless on album. Still, there are some stunning moments, mostly provided by bird-voiced Wilson, that make this worth the bargain price. Sound quality ranges from just above bootleg to fairly good, sometimes wavering in the same tune, and the skimpy liner notes are barely adequate. Although the information is useful, it's split between pages, forcing the reader to flip back and forth to see who is playing on which track and where the performance was originally recorded. Clearly this is *not* the place for a Canned Heat novice to begin, and even more established fans might find its few gems slim pickings among the unfocused, extended, you-had-to-be-there tracks. It's an intermittently interesting, warts-and-all document of a blues band with good intentions that had some inspired moments, but this inconsistent collection does not show them at their best. —*Hal Horowitz*

Freddy Cannon

b. Dec. 4, 1940, Lynn, MA
Vocals / Rock & Roll
No one would claim that Freddy Cannon was one of the great early rock & roll singers. His throaty rasp rated much higher for enthusiasm than impressive chops, and his 17 hit singles were often repetitious variations of his most successful tunes: "Tallahassee Lassie," "Way Down Yonder in New Orleans" and "Palisades Park." Yet he did his own small part to keep the rock & roll spirit burning in the late '50s and early '60s, a time at which it sometimes seemed in danger of being extinguished. He was an unabashed rock & roller, for one thing, even when he was fed ancient Tin Pan Alley standards to retool for teenagers. And he was not one to let the lack of top-notch skills stand in the way of putting his heart into his vocals for all he was worth. His enthusiasm is infectious, though much of his material cannot be rescued by enthusiasm alone. Sometimes categorized as a teen idol, he was in fact too raw to fit comfortably into that mold (not to mention not quite good-looking enough). As ludicrous as it sounds, he was something of an early prototype of rock & roller as Everyman, where spirit and fun counted more than conventional skill. —*Richie Unterberger*

● **The Best of Freddy "Boom Boom" Cannon** / Nov. 21, 1995 / Rhino ✦✦✦✦✦
The definitive collection. Twenty tracks, 17 of them Top 100 singles, including "Tallahassee Lassie," "Way Down Yonder in New Orleans," "Palisades Park," "Abigail Beecher," and "Action," as well as a rare 1958 single by Spindrift. The other selections really aren't up to the level of the best hits, despite occasional raw detours like "Buzz Buzz A-Diddle-It" and the odd novelty "If You Were a Rock and Roll Record," with the immortal line, "If you were a rock and roll record, I know they'd sell a million of you." —*Richie Unterberger*

EP Collection / Aug. 11, 1999 / See For Miles ✦✦✦✦
See for Miles' *EP Collection* is something more than an average greatest hits collection, since it contains the songs that made the flipside of British EPs—which means these are B-sides, covers and album tracks, which will likely not be of interest to anybody that already isn't a Freddy Cannon fan. If you are so, this is pretty fun, especially for collectors that are looking for some of the relative rarities here. If you're not a collector, but are pretty dedicated, this has its charms, since it gives a good idea what Cannon's records sounded like at the time. Rhino and Varese's collections remain the best bet for most fans, but if you'd like a hits collection with quirks, this is a good choice. —*Stephen Thomas Erlewine*

Palisades Park: The Very Best of Freddy Cannon: 1959-1963 / May 2, 2000 / Varese ✦✦✦✦

The Capitols

f. Jan. 1966, Detroit, MI
Pop-Soul, Soul
The energetic Detroit-based Capitols capitalized on mid-'60s R&B dance fever with one of the most memorable entries of the genre, "Cool Jerk." Successful local producer Ollie McLaughlin signed the trio—lead singer Sam George, Donald Norman (who wrote most of the group's material under his real surname of Storball), and Richard Mitchell—to his Karen logo, and the irresistible "Cool Jerk" made them an overnight sensation. After a couple more chart entries later that year, the trio faded quickly. George was murdered on March 17, 1982. —*Bill Dahl*

● **Golden Classics** / Apr. 1990 / Collectables ✦✦✦✦✦
Dance-oriented mid-'60s Detroit soul, this features the notable classic "Cool Jerk." —*Bill Dahl*

The Capris

f. 1957, Ozone Park, NY
Doo Wop
The only major Capris hit, the romantic "There's a Moon Out Tonight," is a New York

street-corner harmony classic. Doo wop was back in fashion by 1961, and it was no longer limited to R&B aggregations. Led by Nick Santo (born Nick Santamaria in 1941), the Capris named themselves after the Isle of Capri in Italy. The Queens, NY, natives originally cut "There's a Moon Out Tonight" for the obscure Planet imprint in 1958, but when the song was reissued on Lost Nite (and eventually on Old Town) it became a national smash its second time around in early 1961. After many moons out of the spotlight, the Capris came back triumphantly in 1981 with an album on Ambient Sound and an appearance on the PBS-TV series "Soundstage." *—Bill Dahl*

● **The Very Best of the Capris: There's a Moon Out Tonight** / Jan. 25, 2000 / Collectables ♦♦♦♦
The Capris were known for the wonderful "There's a Moon Out Tonight," one of the great doo wop songs of all time, a song so lovely and delicate that it remains the standard for love songs. They never had another song as good as that—few bands do—but they had a number of fine romantic doo wop ballads, all collected on Collectables' *The Very Best of the Capris: There's a Moon Out Tonight*. Be warned—this is still the province of dedicated doo wop fans, since there really aren't any cuts that could legitimately be called lost treasures, but for those who love the sound and the Capris in particular, this delivers some nice tunes. *—Stephen Thomas Erlewine*

Captain & Tennille

f. 1973
Soft Rock, Adult Contemporary
Vibrant, relentlessly upbeat harmonies made Captain (born Daryl Dragon, Aug. 27, 1942) & Tennille (born Toni Tennille, May 8, 1943) stars during the latter half of the '70s. Dragon, dubbed the "Captain" because of his distinctive headgear, had played keyboards with the Beach Boys prior to teaming with his wife. Their first hit on A&M, the buoyant "Love Will Keep Us Together," was a million-selling chart-topper in 1975, and a reissue of their 1974 single "The Way I Want to Touch You" also went gold. The couple hung three more gold records in their den in 1976—"Lonely Night (Angel Face)," "Shop Around," and Willis Alan Ramsey's "Muskrat Love"—and that was enough for ABC-TV to install them as hosts of their own variety program. "Do That to Me One More Time" was the last #1 item for the pair in 1979. *—Bill Dahl*

● **Captain & Tennille's Greatest Hits** / 1977 / A&M ♦♦♦♦
A solid collection of all of their mid-'70s hits. *—Stephen Thomas Erlewine*

● **Ultimate Collection: The Complete Hits** / May 22, 2001 / Hip-O ♦♦♦♦♦
Hip-O's *Ultimate Collection: The Complete Hits* will likely be too much music for most audiences, simply because most listeners don't remember much more than "Love Will Keep Us Together," "Muskrat Love" and "Do That To Me One More Time" from Captain & Tennille. They actually had many more hits than that—11 more, four of which hit the Top Ten, actually (for the record, they are "The Way I Want to Touch You," "Lonely Night (Angel Face)," "Shop Around" and "You Never Done It Like That"). All of them are here, along with several other singles and album tracks on this generous 22-track collection. To be frank, Captain & Tennille weren't quite varied or deep enough to make this collection not lose steam toward the middle, but the highlights—the three Neil Sedaka-penned tunes ("Love Will Keep Us Together," "Lonely Night (Angel Face)," "You Never Done It Like That," plus "Do That to Me One More Time"—are all very good, standing proudly amongst soft-rock hits of the time. Still, all of these can be better heard on a more concise collection, since a shorter running time makes Captain & Tennille sound like more consistent hitmakers. Although some listeners will prefer to have this more thorough overview, the number of tracks on *Ultimate Collection* reveals that the duo could only occasionally put it across the plate. *—Stephen Thomas Erlewine*

Captain Beefheart (Don Van Vliet)

b. Jan. 15, 1941, Glendale, CA
Vocals, Keyboards, Harmonica, Guitar / Experimental Rock, Proto-Punk, Experimental, Psychedelic, Prog-Rock/Art Rock, Blues-Rock
Born Don Van Vliet, Captain Beefheart was one of modern music's true innovators. The owner of a remarkable four-and-one-half octave vocal range, he employed idiosyncratic rhythms, absurdist lyrics and an unholy alliance of free jazz, Delta blues, latter-day classical music and rock & roll to create a singular body of work virtually unrivalled in its daring and fluid creativity. While he never came even remotely close to mainstream success, Beefheart's impact was incalculable, and his fingerprints were all over punk, New Wave and post-rock. In their original incarnation, Captain Beefheart and His Magic Band were a blues-rock outfit which became staples of the teen-dance circuit; they quickly signed to A&M Records, where the success of the single "Diddy Wah Diddy" earned them the opportunity to record a full-length album. Label president Jerry Moss rejected the completed record as "too negative," however, and a crushed Beefheart went into seclusion. After producer Bob Krasnow radically remixed 1968's hallucinatory *Strictly Personal* without Beefheart's approval, he again retired. At the same time, however, longtime friend Frank Zappa formed his own Straight Records, and he soon approached Van Vliet with the promise of complete creative control; a deal was struck, and after writing 28 songs in a nine-hour frenzy, Beefheart recorded the seminal 1969 double album *Trout Mask Replica*. After 1982's *Ice Cream for Crow*, Van Vliet again retired from music, this time for good; he returned to the desert, took up residence in a trailer and focused on painting. In 1985, he mounted the first major exhibit of his work, done in an abstract, primitive style reminiscent of Francis Bacon. Like his music, his art won wide acclaim, and some of his paintings sold for as much as $25,000. In the 1990s Van Vliet dropped completely from sight when he fell prey to multiple sclerosis. *—Jason Ankeny*

☆ **Safe as Milk** / 1967 / Buddha ♦♦♦♦♦
Beefheart's first proper studio album is a much more accessible, pop-inflected brand of blues-rock than the efforts that followed in the late '60s—which isn't to say that it's exactly normal and straightforward. Featuring Ry Cooder on guitar, this is blues-rock gone slightly askew, with jagged, fractured rhythms, soulful, twisting vocals from Van Vliet, and more doo wop, soul, straight blues, and folk-rock influences than he would employ on his more avant-garde outings. "Zig Zag Wanderer," "Call on Me," and "Yellow Brick Road" are some of his most enduring and riff-driven songs, although there's plenty of weirdness on tracks like "Electricity" and "Abba Zaba." [Buddha's 1999 reissue of *Safe as Milk* contained restored artwork and seven bonus tracks.] *—Richie Unterberger*

☆ **Trout Mask Replica** / 1969 / Reprise ♦♦♦♦♦
Trout Mask Replica is Captain Beefheart's masterpiece, a fascinating, stunningly imaginative work that still sounds like little else in the rock & roll canon. Given total creative control by producer and friend Frank Zappa, Beefheart and his Magic Band rehearsed the material for this 28-song double album for over a year, wedding minimalistic R&B, blues, and garage rock to free jazz and avant-garde experimentalism. Atonal, sometimes singsong melodies; jagged, intricately constructed dual-guitar parts; stuttering, complicated rhythmic interaction—all of these elements float out seemingly at random, often without completely interlocking, while Beefheart groans his surrealist poetry in a throaty Howlin' Wolf growl. The disjointedness is perhaps partly unintentional—reportedly, Beefheart's refusal to wear headphones while recording his vocals caused him to sing in time with studio reverberations, not the actual backing tracks—but by all accounts, the music and arrangements were carefully scripted and notated by the Captain, which makes the results even more remarkable. As one might expect from music so complex and, to many ears, inaccessible, the influence of *Trout Mask Replica* was felt more in spirit than in direct copycatting, as a catalyst rather than a literal musical starting point. However, its inspiring reimagining of what was possible in a rock context laid the groundwork for countless future experiments in rock surrealism, especially during the punk/new wave era. *—Steve Huey*

Lick My Decals Off, Baby / 1970 / Bizarre/Straight ♦♦♦♦♦
Produced by Captain Beefheart himself, *Lick My Decals Off, Baby* was a further refining and exploration of the musical ideas posited on *Trout Mask Replica*. As such, the imaginative fervor of *Trout Mask* is toned down somewhat, but in its place is an increased self-assurance; the tone of *Decals* is also a bit darker, examining environmental issues in some songs rather than simply concentrating on surreal wordplay. Whatever the differences, the jagged, complex rhythms and guitar interplay continue to amaze. Those wanting to dig deeper after the essential *Trout Mask Replica* are advised to begin doing so here (be warned: *Decals* has tended to flutter in and out of print). *—Steve Huey*

Mirror Man / 1970 / Castle ♦♦♦
Released by Buddah in the wake of critical acclaim for *Trout Mask Replica* and *Lick My Decals Off, Baby*, *Mirror Man* contained only four songs, over 50 minutes of extended bluesy jamming recorded live in Los Angeles in 1965 (according to the cover; some think it may be later). While it doesn't match its two predecessors' inventiveness, the Magic Band is a highly skilled outfit, and the lack of tight structure makes the album unique in Beefheart's oeuvre. *—Steve Huey*

The Spotlight Kid / 1972 / Reprise ♦♦♦♦
On *Spotlight* Beefheart took over full production duties. Rather than returning to the artistic aggro of *Trout Mask/Decals* days, *Spotlight* takes things lower and looser, with a lot of typical Beefheart fun crawling around in weird, strange ways. Consider the ominous opening cut "I'm Gonna Booglarize You Baby"—it isn't just the title and Beefheart's breathy growl, but Rockette Morton's purring bass, Zoot Horn Rollo's snarling guitar, Ed Marimba's brisk fade on the cymbals again and again, and more. The overall atmosphere is definitely relaxed and fun, maybe one step up from a jam. Marimba's vibes and other percussion work—including, of course, the marimba itself—stand out quite a bit here as a result, perhaps, brought out from behind the drums and the more straightforward work on *Clear Spot*. Consider "When It Blows Its Stacks," with its unexpected breaks into more playful parts, or "Alice in Blunderland"'s admittedly more aimless approach, but vibing along well nonetheless. Sometimes things do sound maybe just a little too blasé, but Beefheart at his worst still has something more than most groups at their best. *Spotlight* does have one stone-cold Beefheart classic—"Grow Fins," an understated number with fine harmonica and a brilliant lyric about getting so tired of his woman that the best option is to take to the sea and fall in love with a mermaid. Another song, though, does have an all-time great title—"There Ain't No Santa Claus on the Evenin' Stage." Definite fun touch—the cover photo of Beefheart looking great in a classic Nudie suit, outlined in yellow light to boot. *—Ned Raggett*

Clear Spot / 1972 / Reprise ♦♦♦♦
Producer Ted Templeman was a bit of a surprising choice given his firmly mainstream production credits, with the Doobie Brothers already under his belt and Van Halen lurking in the near future. As it turned out, such a combination led to a better-working fusion than might be expected, making one wonder why in the world *Clear Spot* wasn't more of a commercial success than it was. The sound is great throughout, and the feeling is of the coolest bar-band in town, not to mention one that could eat all the patrons for breakfast if it felt like it. Fans of the fully all-out side of Beefheart might find the end result not fully up to snuff as a result, but those less concerned with pushing back all borders all the time will enjoy his unexpected blend of everything tempered with a new accessibility. "Nowadays a Woman's Got to Hit a Man," besides having a brilliant title, shows the balance perfectly—Van Vliet serves up his rough asides with all his expected wit and sass, while the Magic Band trade off notes here and there just so. At the same time, the track is strong blues-rock that doesn't pander, with a particularly fierce solo thanks to Zoot Horn Rollo. "My Head Is My Only House Unless It Rains" is a great love song, the softer

arrangement saved from being too off by Beefheart's delivery. Other winners include the title track, a sharp combination of an off-kilter arrangement for a straightforward melody, the great shaggy-dog story of "Golden Birdies," and "Big Eyed Beans from Venus," a fantastically strange piece of aggression. *—Ned Raggett*

Bluejeans & Moonbeams / 1974 / Blue Plate ✦✦

Unconditionally Guaranteed / 1974 / Blue Plate ✦✦

Shiny Beast (Bat Chain Puller) / Jan. 1978 / Bizarre/Straight ✦✦✦✦✦
So titled because the original album, simply titled *Bat Chain Puller*, had to be ditched and rerecorded after a legal tuzzle involving Frank Zappa's manager, *Shiny Beast* turned out to be manna from heaven for those feeling Beefheart had lost his way on his two Mercury albums. Then again, what else could be assumed with a song titled "Tropical Hot Dog Night" that sounds like what happened when Beefheart encountered Miami disco and decided to make something of it? When it comes to singing, though, he's still the atypical growler, snarler and more of lore, conjuring up more wonderfully odd lyrical stories than can easily be measured, while the album as a whole gets steadily more and more bent. "You Know You're a Man" is at once straightforward and incredibly weird when it comes to love and gender, while other standouts include "Bat Chain Puller," a steady chugger that feels like a goofy death march, and the nervy freak of "Owed T'Alex." As for the Magic Band in general, keyboardist Eric Drew Feldman, guitarists Jeff Tepper and Richard Redus and drummer Robert Williams lay down the business with appropriately gone aplomb, as a listen to "Suction Prints" will demonstrate. *—Ned Raggett*

Doc at the Radar Station / 1980 / Blue Plate ✦✦✦✦✦
Generally acclaimed as the strongest album of his comeback, and by some as his best since *Trout Mask Replica, Doc at the Radar Station* had a tough, lean sound owing partly to the virtuosic new version of the Magic Band (featuring future Pixies sideman Eric Drew Feldman, New York downtown-scene guitarist Gary Lucas, and a returning John "Drumbo" French, among others) and partly to the clear, stripped-down production, which augmented the Captain's basic dual-guitar interplay and jumpy rhythms with extra percussion instruments and touches of *Shiny Beast*'s synths and trombones. Many of the songs on *Doc* either reworked or fully developed unused material composed around the time of the creatively fertile *Trout Mask* sessions, which adds to the spirited performances. Even if the Captain's voice isn't quite what it once was, *Doc at the Radar Station* is an excellent, focused consolidation of Beefheart's past and then-present. *—Steve Huey*

Ice Cream for Crow / 1982 / Blue Plate ✦✦✦✦✦
With yet one final Magic Band lineup in place, featuring Richard Snyder on bass and Cliff Martinez on drums alongside returning vets Tepper and Lucas, Beefheart put the final touch on his recording career to date with *Crow*. It's a last entertaining blast of wigginess from one of the few truly independent artists in late 20th century pop music, with humor, skill, and style all still intact (as even the song titles like "Semi-Multicoloured Caucasian" and "Cardboard Cutout Sundown" show). With the Magic Band turning out more choppy rhythms, unexpected guitar lines, and outré arrangements, Beefheart lets everything run wild as always, with successful results. Sometimes he sounds less like the blues shouter of lore and more of a spoken word artist with an attitude, thus the stuttering flow of "The Host the Ghost the Most Holy." "Hey Garland, I Dig Your Tweed Coat" is even more entertainingly outrageous, Beefheart's addictive if near impenetrable ramble about tobacco juice and straw hats and more backed by an insanely great arrangement. Magic Band members each get chances to shine one way or another—"Evening Bell" in particular demonstrates why Lucas went on to later solo renown, a complex, suddenly shifting solo instrumental that sits somewhere between background music and head-scratching "how did he do that?" intrigue. *—Ned Raggett*

Legendary A&M Sessions / 1984 / A&M ✦✦✦
Before gaining a cult with his avant-garde excursions in the late '60s, Captain Beefheart wielded a much more traditional sort of blues-rock. That's not to say that these two obscure mid-'60s A&M singles (packaged together on this five-song EP, which adds a previously unreleased track from the same era) aren't well worth hearing. The Captain's Howlin' Wolf-like growl led a tough outfit that ranked among the best early American blues-rock groups, and among the few that could reasonably emulate the Rolling Stones' toughness. Produced, unbelievably enough, by future Bread leader David Gates, this reissue includes their regional hit cover of Bo Diddley's "Diddy Wah Diddy." The best track, though, is "Moonchild," their shameless derivation of Howlin' Wolf's "Smokestack Lightning." Featuring wailing harmonica, stomping riffs and adventurous, quasi-psychedelic production, it was actually written by Gates himself. To think that the same man was also responsible for "If" and "Baby I'm A-Want You" blows the mind. *—Richie Unterberger*

The Mirror Man Sessions / Jun. 1, 1999 / Buddha ✦✦✦
The Mirror Man Sessions features the complete remastered contents of *Mirror Man*, albeit in a resequenced running order, and fills out the rest of the CD with a number of bonus tracks taken from additional recordings, both finished and unfinished, made around the same time for what would have been a *double* album titled *It Comes to You in a Plain Brown Wrapper*. As a listening experience, the package will appeal more to those who value the instrumental Beefheart; the *Mirror Man* album is, of course, essentially a 50-plus-minute jam session, containing as it does only four songs, and the bonus tracks—many of which appeared on the One Way label's reissue of *Safe as Milk*—mostly consist of jams and instrumentals which push the boundaries of conventional blues-rock, with a Beefheart vocal tossed in here and there. Some may miss Beefheart's surreal poetry, gruff vocals, and/or free jazz influence, while others may find it fascinating to hear the Magic Band simply letting go and cutting loose. *—Steve Huey*

● **The Dust Blows Forward: An Anthology** / Aug. 17, 1999 / Rhino ✦✦✦✦✦
Leaving alone the obvious condition that Captain Beefheart's numerous experimental albums aren't as prime for a "best of" treatment as the discographies of most artists are, this is a pretty good overview of career highlights. The two CDs span his 1966 "Diddy Wah Diddy" single to his final album (1982's *Ice Cream for Crow*), each disc weighing in at about 75 minutes. With so much material to draw from (not even counting that mammoth five-CD box set of unreleased stuff), there will be inevitable disagreements among fans as to which songs were selected; there are seven from *Clear Spot*, for instance, but only two from *Safe as Milk*. Every period is sampled, however, and his weakest albums (*Unconditionally Guaranteed* and *Bluejeans & Moonbeams*) are judiciously represented by just one cut each. A few rarities do crop up, including a quite good and bluesy previously unreleased *Clear Spot* outtake ("Little Scratch"), "Hard Workin' Man" (from the soundtrack to *Blue Collar*), and the 1982 instrumental B-side "Light Reflected off the Oceands [sic] of the Moon." There are also little detours from Beefheart's albums for two tracks from 1966 singles and two collaborations with Frank Zappa from Zappa's *Bongo Fury*. It's not for the collector, but it's a decent package for someone who wants to get familiar with the Captain or doesn't need more than a few of his regular albums. Comprehensive notes in a 60-page booklet offer a good straightforward cruise through his oft-confusing history and shifting Magic Band personnel. *—Richie Unterberger*

Grow Fins: Rarities (1965-1982) / 1999 / Revenant ✦✦✦
An unprecedented project in the rock field: a five-CD box set of unreleased material by a cult artist that never had anything close to a chart hit. Of course Captain Beefheart is the ultimate cult artist, and one with a following so rabid (if limited) that the compilation has a wider audience than many would anticipate. Despite the impressive chronological span and variety of demos, live performances, backing tracks, and outtakes, be cautioned that this is *not* a best-of or ad hoc career overview. A good deal of the tracks (some of which have long been available on bootleg) are of slightly substandard or low fidelity, and Beefheart's most significant work is ultimately contained on his numerous official releases. However, this is an important addition to his catalog, and one that many of his fanatics will find essential, though it won't do much to convert the casual fan due to the difficult nature of much of the material. Disc one, with live cuts and demos from 1966-67 that include a few songs recorded on *Safe as Milk*, is certainly the most interesting and accessible of the quintet. Disc two is more shambling and experimental, with its assortment of 1968 live performances. Disc three is for the hardcore: home-recorded (though in okay fidelity) run-throughs of *Trout Mask Replica* material from 1969, without vocals. Disc four is for the harder core: 12 more minutes of *Trout Mask* home sessions, plus enhanced-CD live performance footage from 1968-73. CD five is an interesting, erratic assortment of live, radio, demo, and work tape material from 1969-82, fidelity varying from good to poor. The liner notes are exceptionally detailed, with many first-hand quotes by band members and much historical narrative by frequent Magic Band drummer John French. *—Richie Unterberger*

Caravan

f. 1968, England, **db.** 1983
Canterbury Scene, Prog-Rock/Art Rock, Jazz-Rock, Album Rock
Along with the Soft Machine, Caravan was one of two eccentric, distinctively British art rock bands to grow out of Canterbury's Wilde Flowers. Caravan itself was founded in 1968 by guitarist/vocalist Pye Hastings, keyboardist Dave Sinclair, bassist/vocalist Richard Sinclair, and drummer Richard Coughlan. The band immediately set itself off from the rest of the art rock pack with its gentle melodies, complicated improvisational passages, and British folk-influenced arrangements sometimes featuring strings and woodwinds. Caravan received a fair amount of critical acclaim for its early work, particularly 1971's *In the Land of Grey and Pink*. The first of many personnel changes followed that album when David Sinclair joined Matching Mole and was replaced by former Delivery member Steve Miller for *Waterloo Lily*. Richard Sinclair left after that album and David returned for *For Girls Who Grow Plump in the Night* and *Caravan and the New Symphonia*. *Cunning Stunts* (1975) came out of left field to become Caravan's only charting album in the U.S., but critics and fans found that the group's charm had evaporated into an obsession with technical perfection. Hastings fronted the group into the '80s, and their last album, 1983's *Back to Front*, featured all the original members. The group has performed occasionally since then and played several London club dates in 1991 with several former members of Camel. *—Steve Huey*

Caravan / 1968 / Verve ✦✦✦✦✦
Caravan's debut album is an underrated gem in this Canterbury band's catalog, its warmest and most psychedelic offering. Incidentally, *Caravan* is the first album on Verve Records by an English artist. Following the Soft Machine's breakoff in 1967 from the Wilde Flowers, the wellspring group of Canterbury rock, the remaining members rehearsed for a year before re-emerging as Caravan. The band's debut album features "Place of My Own," a staple in its repertoire for years to come, as well as the sentimental but not sappy "Love Song With Flute," featuring a one-take flute solo by Caravan leader Pye Hastings's brother Jimmy. Other highlights include the majestic, Traffic-inspired "Ride," the dreamy "Magic Man," and the epic "Where but for Caravan Would I." Organist Dave Sinclair is probably the best keyboardist of all the Canterbury groups, and he is given ample room to shine. Some of Caravan's best vocal harmonizing also adds to the appeal of this record. *—Jim Powers*

If I Could Do It All Over Again I'd Do It All Over You / 1970 / Decca ✦✦✦✦
Caravan followed up their eponymous debut with the cryptically titled *If I Could Do It All Over Again I'd Do It All Over You* in the fall of 1970. The album has been reissued with remastered sound, copious bonus material, and an expanded liner notes booklet containing memorabilia as well as an historical essay. *If I Could Do It All Over Again*

contains significant progressions over the first album. These include the intricacy with which compositions are sculpted around some of the finest instrumental improvisation in British rock at the time—or arguably since. Caravan's uncanny ability to create a montage that effortlessly maneuvers through acoustic folk and electric progressive rock is best exemplified on the "With an Ear to the Ground" suite. The extended instrumental passages weave in and out of each other, creating a hypnotic and otherwise psychedelic soundscape that would become a trademark of the European progressive rock movement. Another epic, "For Richard" quickly found solid standing as the Caravan live performance closer for decades after first appearing on this album. Juxtaposed against these pieces are several shorter works, which in essence clear the palette for the longer ones. The title track, as well as "Hello, Hello" are perfect examples of how Caravan was able to one-up many of their progressive contemporaries, creating shorter and more accessible songs for radio airplay—resulting in a guest appearance on BBC TV's *Top of the Pops* program. The remastered disc contains four bonus tracks: "A Day in the Life of Maurice Haylett"—which first appeared on the *Where, but for Caravan Would I* CD compilation—as well as three demos for tracks found on the *If I Could Do It All Over Again* album. *—Lindsay Planer*

In the Land of Grey and Pink / 1971 / Decca ✦✦✦✦✦
In the Land of Grey and Pink is considered by many to be a pinnacle release from Caravan. The album contains an undeniable and decidedly European sense of humor and charm. In addition, this would mark the end of the band's premiere lineup. Co-founder David Sinclair would leave Caravan to form Matching Mole with Soft Machine drummer and vocalist Robert Wyatt in August of '71. As a group effort, *In the Land of Grey and Pink* displays all the ethereal brilliance Caravan created on their previous pair of 12" outings. Their blending of jazz and folk instrumentation and improvisational styles hints at Traffic and Family, as displayed on "Winter Wine," as well as the organ and sax driven instrumental introduction to "Nine Feet Underground." These contrast the decidedly aggressive sounds concurrent with albums from King Crimson or Soft Machine. In fact, beginning with the album's title, there seems to be pastoral qualities and motifs throughout. Another reason enthusiasts rank this album among their favorites is the group dynamic which has rarely sounded more singular or cohesive. Richard Sinclair's lyrics are of particular note, especially the middle-earth imagery used on "Winter Wine" or the enduring whimsy of "Golf Girl." The remastered version of this album includes previously unissued demos/alternate versions of both tracks under the titles: "It's Likely to Have a Name Next Week" and "Group Girl," respectively. The remastered disc also includes "I Don't Know Its Name (Alias the Word)" and "Aristocracy," two pieces that were completed, but shelved in deference to the time limitations imposed during the days of wine and vinyl. The latter composition would be reworked and released on Caravan's next album, *Waterloo Lily*. The 12-page liner notes booklet includes expanded graphics, memorabilia, and an essay penned specifically for the reissue. *—Lindsay Planer*

Waterloo Lily / 1972 / Decca ✦✦✦
Before the recording of *Waterloo Lily*, David Sinclair departed Caravan to join forces with Soft Machine skinsman Robert Wyatt and form Matching Mole. With the subsequent arrival of former Delivery member Steve Miller and an overwhelming jazz influence, the edgier progressive rock and folk elements that were so prevalent on their previous albums is somewhat repressed. The band's performance level did not suffer in the transition. In fact, the addition of Miller only punctuates Caravan's previously honed improvisational skills. Beginning with *Waterloo Lily*'s leadoff title track, there is a sound more akin to the jazzier efforts of Traffic. Miller's "Nothing At All" incorporates the jazz-fusion even farther as the long instrumental introduction more than hints at Steely Dan circa *Katy Lied*. The up-tempo staccato bop featuring Miller's electric piano accents, when juxtaposed with Pye Hastings' liquid-toned electric guitar could easily be mistaken for that of Walter Becker and Donald Fagan. The remainder of the album centres on a couple of pieces that evoke the sound and spirit of the previous Caravan outings. Most reminiscent of the classic sound is Hastings' epic "The Love In Your Eye suite". The track recalls the laid-back intensity and phenomenal improvisational synergy of earlier tracks such as "For Richard" and "Where, But For Caravan Would I," while wisely incorporating Miller's formidable jazz chops to give the instrumental sections sustained substance throughout. The remastered CD offers three additional compositions circa the *Waterloo Lily* sessions. "Pye's June Thing" and "Ferdinand" are two Hastings' acoustic demos. A considerably more complete "Looking Left, Looking Right" is a treasured recovery from the vaults. Originally vaulted due to the time limitations of vinyl, this track, along with "Pye's Loop"—which acts as a coda to "Looking Left ..." mark their debut release here. *—Lindsay Planer*

● **For Girls Who Grow Plump in the Night** / 1973 / Decca ✦✦✦✦✦
After the musical uncertainty of *Waterloo Lily*, Caravan returned with their most inspired recording since *In the Land of the Grey and Pink*. The splendidly titled *For Girls Who Grow Plump in the Night* is several steps ahead in terms of fresh musical ideas that wholly incorporate the band's trademark humor within the otherwise serious and challenging sonic structures. Two of the more dominant reasons for the change in Caravan's sound were the return of keyboardist Dave Sinclair and the addition of violist Peter Geoffrey Richardson. Die-hard fans gladly welcomed Sinclair back, however, Richardson was met with heckles from enthusiasts during live appearances. They were soon silenced as his place on *For Girls Who Grow Plump in the Night* easily ranks among Caravan's watershed moments. There are perhaps none better than the mesmerizing counterpoint melodies he weaves during the "L'Auberge Du Sanglier" suite. While not completely abandoning their jazz leanings, *For Girls Who Grow Plump In The Night* is considerably focused back into the rock genre. Ironically, the album also features some rather elaborate orchestration. In context, it is quite effective in creating emphasis—especially on the leadoff track "Memory Lain, Hugh," as well as the dreamy mid-tempo "The Dog, The Dog, He's At It Again." The remastered CD also includes five additional tracks. The first four are demos featuring the band without orchestra and with some notable differences, such as the distinct lead guitar opening to "Memory Lain, Hugh." "Derek's Long Thing" is another instrumental piece penned by keyboardist Derek Austin—one of the two transitional Caravan members chosen to replace Steve Miller. A must-own for inclined parties. *—Lindsay Planer*

Caravan & the New Symphonia / 1974 / Decca ✦✦✦✦
The newly mined creative energies that guided *For Girls Who Grow Plump in the Night* continued into the *Caravan & the New Symphonia* project. Fusing with a 39-piece orchestra is a daring move that pays off. The remastered CD includes over a half an hour of unissued material from Caravan, with and without the New Symphonia, during the same October 28, 1973 Theatre Royal concert. Subtitled "The Complete Concert," this performance captures Caravan at a creative zenith. The newly restored program commences with a brief introduction from BBC Radio's Alan Black. The band then presents three from *For Girls Who Grow Plump in the Night*: "Memory Lain, Hugh"/"Headloss" suite, "The Dog, the Dog, He's at It Again," and "Hoedown." This mini-set sparkles with the frenetic energy that a live audience will often provide. The intense interaction during the waning moments of "The Dog, the Dog, He's at It Again" allow Caravan to reach a whole different stratum. The second set features the orchestra with the band and commences with "Introduction," an orchestrated piece which leads into the very delicate preface of "The Love in Your Eye." The synergies truly begin to flow as the band weaves in and out of the orchestra. Pye Hastings composed two new pieces specifically for this recording: "Mirror for the Day" and the brilliant "Virgin on the Ridiculous"; the latter became a performance standard for Caravan. The remainder of the set features some of their most formidable performance numbers, including an emotive "For Richard." The newly restored encore, "A Hunting We Shall Go" is stunning in it's scope and perfectly encapsulates what *Caravan & the New Symphonia* is really all about: allowing good music and good musicians the chance to be mutually superior. *—Lindsay Planer*

Cunning Stunts / 1975 / Repertoire ✦✦✦

Blind Dog at St. Dunstans / 1976 / Repertoire ✦✦

Show of Our Lives / 1981 / Decca ✦
This release is not for enthusiasts whose primary criteria include those of sonic quality or program continuity. In fact, bootlegs containing much of the same material as *Show of Our Lives* circulate from a higher quality source. Primarily owing to the legal ambiguity that governs European broadcast recordings, discs such as this continue to skulk into the marketplace stymieing curious consumers. While the performances highlighted on this volume are quite good, most tracks fade up several seconds in, rendering them incomplete. Another flagrant display of questionable sonic mastering appears during a noisy vinyl transcription of "Love to Love You." Additionally, "Memory Lain, Hugh" and "Headloss"—which are usually presented as a unified suite—are separated here by the album's title track. Beyond the sonic foibles, however, are otherwise solid performances by the classic Caravan lineup. Included are the rare "Love Song Without Flute," from Caravan's eponymously titled 1968 debut, and the humorously titled "And I Wish I Were Stoned" and "If I Had to Do It All Over Again, I'd Do It All Over You," both from the album of the latter's name. Other notable works include unique renderings of "Golf Girl," as well as an epic "For Richard." As the liner notes fail to identify source recordings, the supposition is that the material on *Show of Our Lives* originated as radio broadcasts of varying quality. Indeed, there are striking similarities between this release and the two Caravan sanctioned editions of their BBC Radio appearances—*Songs for Oblivion Fishermen* and *Ether Way*. Additionally, the two legit releases boast infinitely better sound and comprehensive track listings. *—Lindsay Planer*

Back to Front / 1983 / Kingdom ✦✦✦

● **Canterbury Tales: The Best of Caravan** / Feb. 22, 1994 / Decca/Chronicles ✦✦✦✦✦
Canterbury Tales is a generous two-disc helping of this great progressive-rock band's first seven albums. The compilation draws most heavily from the albums *If I Could Do It All Over Again…*, *In the Land of Grey and Pink*, *For Girls Who Grow Plump in the Night*, and *Caravan and the New Symphonia*. There are also selections from *Cunning Stunts*, *Waterloo Lily*, and *Caravan*. A good balance is struck between Caravan's shorter single-length pop songs and its more extended suites. The liner notes feature an informative biographical and discographical essay and lots of photographs and credits. The remastering is excellent. *—Jim Powers*

The Battle of Hastings / 1995 / Castle Music America ✦✦✦✦
Listening to this beautifully melodic, midtempo album by Caravan is a bit like stepping inside of a time-warp. The group sounds astonishingly good vocally, and Pye Hastings' songwriting skills are as fine as (and maybe finer than) ever, as though they've scarcely skipped a beat from their 1970s heyday. Released in 1995, *The Battle of Hastings* might have put them on the U.S. charts, at least if an edited version of the hook-laden and memorable "Liar" had been released as an accompanying single—indeed, this is the record that might've broken the band in America. It's a little late for that now, but time shouldn't prevent anyone from taking in the sweet, folk-like melodies and the rich harmonies. The playing is a curious mix of sharp attacks on mostly acoustic instruments punctuated with lead electric guitar that manages to be both sinewy and elegant (except where it's delightfully understated, as on most of "It's Not Real"), juxtaposed with Jimmy Hastings's richly melodic sax playing. Everything on this record works well, even the editing—not a note is wasted, as though this were 1970 or so and the band is still competing at the forefront of art-rock and progressive rock circles. One important reason why this music works so well is that there is no pretentiousness about it. The band doesn't try to be heavy or

profoundly serious; nor do they try to force rock music to carry ideas it was never meant to carry. Additionally, there's no slackness here, just wonderfully inventive composition and performance, all wrapped together in a gloriously elegant sound. *—Bruce Eder*

Where But For Caravan Would I? / Jul. 31, 2000 / Decca ♦♦♦
This double-disc European import offers something for both the Caravan novice, as well as the hardcore fan. One of the highlights of this collection is the radically improved sound. Nowhere is this more evident than on the opening quartet of tracks—originally on the band's short-lived self-titled album. *Where But For Caravan Would I?* presents these songs in their original glorious monophonic form for the first time since their original, albeit brief, appearance on MGM/Verve in 1968. Additionally, there are several tracks making their debut release on this compilation. "A Day in the Life of Maurice Haylett" for instance, although it was recorded between the band's debut and their second release—*If I Could Do It All Over Again, I'd Do It All Over You. In The Land of Grey and Pink,* Caravan's third LP, gets royal treatment with four of the album's five tracks presented here. "Golf Girl" and "Love to Love You" have been remixed and augmented beyond their previous fade out. The results are uniformly remarkable. The remainder of the set accurately compiles highlights from *For Girls Who Grow Plump in the Night, Cunning Stunts,* and *Caravan & the New Symphonia.* The track "Stuck in a Hole" from *Cunning Stunts* is presented here in its 45 rpm version. All said, *Where But For Caravan Would I?* is a great collection. The liner notes booklet contains many rare photos and memorabilia from band member Pye Hastings. *—Lindsay Planer*

The Cardigans

f. 1992, Jonkoping, Sweden
Swedish Pop/Rock, Indie Pop, Ambient Pop, Twee Pop, Adult Alternative Pop/Rock, Alternative Pop/Rock
One of the most pleasing pop groups of the '90s, the Cardigans' sugary confections would grow annoying very quickly if they weren't backed by great musicianship and clever arrangements. The band's 1995 breakout album *Life* reflected the Cardigans at their most saccharine—the sunny disposition of vocalist Nina Persson being the major argument in favor—and critics inserted the group into the space-age pop revivalist camp. The Cardigans later proved that they were more difficult to pigeonhole, however. They released their debut album *Emmerdale* in May 1994. The single "Rise & Shine" became a hit on Swedish radio soon after the release of the LP, and a readers poll in Sweden's *Slitz* magazine voted *Emmerdale* the best album of 1994. A satirical response to their moody debut, *Life* showed the band at their most upbeat, including an angelic picture of Nina in an ice-skating outfit for the cover. Released in March 1995, the album eventually sold one and a half million copies worldwide and became especially popular in Japan, where it achieved platinum status. American major labels began to notice the attention, and Mercury signed them soon after. *First Band on the Moon,* released in September 1996, deemphasized the pure pop in favor of abstract arrangements and some rather violent themes. Nevertheless, the infectious single "Lovefool" became a radio hit by early 1997. *—John Bush*

Emmerdale / 1994 / Minty Fresh ♦♦♦
Though the sky is sunny on the cover, *Emmerdale* is quite a melancholy affair. First song "Sick & Tired" (the single) hints that all is not well in the Cardigans' camp, and later songs ("Black Letter Day," "After All . . . ," "Cloudy Sky") also capture a depressed mood which conflicts with the mostly upbeat and positive arrangements. Of course, all but two of the original songs were written by a converted metal fan, bassist Magnus Sveningsson. In keeping with that fact, the cover of "Sabbath Bloody Sabbath" shouldn't surprise anyone, though its clever arrangement and the touching vocals of Nina Persson—even though she's throwing around Ozzy Osbourne lyrics—render the song practically unrecognizable. In the end, the battle between positive arrangements and melancholy lyrics creates a wistful mood that suits the Cardigans well. *—John Bush*

● **Life** / 1995 / Minty Fresh ♦♦♦♦♦
With tongue firmly in cheek, the Cardigans decided to play up the candyfloss arrangements of their debut for second album *Life.* Where *Emmerdale* studied an introverted melancholy, *Life* is undiminished in both its independent-minded exuberance ("Hey! Get Out of My Way") and zest to enjoy life with others ("Daddy's Car," "Gordon's Gardenparty"). The incredible production and quality of arrangement from the debut is here also, even more strikingly crisp and spot-on. (Over 50 instruments were used on the 14 songs included on the Minty Fresh American release.) Though the Cardigans planned *Life* as something of a joke, it became one of the finest pop albums of the '90s. *—John Bush*

First Band on the Moon / Sep. 17, 1996 / Mercury ♦♦♦♦♦
For listeners who had caught up with the Cardigans on their breakout album *Life,* the group's third album was a confusing pastiche which included several conventional pop songs, but also added tracks with left-field arrangements and some (comparatively) disturbing lyrics. In reality, however, the group had simply returned to the mood and feel of their debut album. On *Emmerdale,* the melancholy was personal and solitary in nature, but here depression is focused on unfaithful lovers—in both the songs which vocalist Nina Persson helped out with lyrics and those written by the rest of the band ("Choke," "Step on Me," "The Great Divide"). Even the single "Lovefool" is a depressing lament of unrequited affection, and the presence of another Black Sabbath cover ("Iron Man") certainly isn't an immediate upper. Still, *First Band on the Moon* is saved by the Cardigans' core strengths: Persson's vocals and Svensson's arrangements. *—John Bush*

Gran Turismo / Nov. 3, 1998 / Mercury ♦♦♦
With "Lovefool," the Cardigans catipulted from a cult favorite to an international phenomenon. Instead of being happy with their success, they fretted about their artistic credibility, concerned that they were seen as merely a light pop band instead of an ironic pop band. This is usually a danger sign for any young band, since it results in a self-conscious departure from form—and that is exactly what *Gran Turismo,* the followup to *First Band on the Moon,* is. There are still elements of the group's appealing melodic style, but they have trimmed away their sense of humor and style, adding vague electronica experiments and mildly distorted guitars in their wake. Truth be told, there were always hints of despair beneath the Cardigans' shiny surface, but they often sound as if they're trying too hard to be serious throughout this labored, self-conscious album. Since the band has talent, there are not only hints of past glory, there are suggestions where the group intended to go, but too often *Gran Turismo* sounds like diluted Garbage, not new school Cardigans. It may simply be a transitional album, but it's a dispiriting listen, nevertheless. *—Stephen Thomas Erlewine*

Cardinal

f. 1994, **db.** 1995
Indie Pop, Chamber Pop, Alternative Pop/Rock
Cardinal was a one-off project from singers/songwriters Richard Davies and Eric Matthews. The duo came together in 1994 following ex-Moles frontman Davies' relocation from his native Australia to the U.S.; he wrote and sang all but one of the songs that comprised Cardinal's self-titled debut, while the Oregon-born Matthews arranged the compositions, layering them with ornate strings, horns and pianos inspired by the lush, baroque sounds of late-'60s pop. While *Cardinal* was released to great acclaim, internal strife quickly split the duo apart, and both Davies and Matthews embarked on solo careers. *—Jason Ankeny*

● **Cardinal** / 1994 / Flydaddy ♦♦♦♦♦
The sole album from the Davies/Matthews pairing has already achieved something close to legend status in a few short years, at least among those taken by the fusion of guitar pop with orchestrations. But is it any good? Getting beyond the fact that the combination isn't that groundbreaking to begin with—everyone from the Left Banke to Burt Bacharach had already tried something similar 30 years previous, for a start—*Cardinal* is still definitely enjoyable while not, in fact, being greater than the sum of its parts. While Matthews is a brilliant arranger, playing everything from harpsichord to trumpet and marimba, it's Davies' songs that carry the day, which a cursory review of Matthews' solo work versus Davies' makes clear. Regardless, together the two did achieve unexpectedly sharp heights. The recruited backing band, including, of all people, drummer/co-producer Thee Slayer Hippy from Portland punk legends Poison Idea, keeps everything moving well enough, while the two chief figures happily eschew the prevailing grunge fallout of 1994 for something else entirely. Davies' quietly impassioned, slightly dry singing avoids both whispery vagueness and trying to sweat too much, perfectly matched by Matthews' fun, killer interpretations. Matthews gets moments of slightly lugubrious and breathy lead singing at points, most notably on his own solo composition "Dream Figure," while the duet with Davies on "You're Lost Me There" is enjoyably low-key and mysterious. While Davies' lyrics are generally clever enough, they're also easy to avoid concentrating on in favor of the experience as a whole. Full-on cult appeal arrives in the form of "Singing to the Sunshine," a cut from the self-titled album by the late '60s group Mortimer. Other strong numbers include the clever time signature shifts throughout "Tough Guy Tactics" and the closing drama of "Silver Machines." *—Ned Raggett*

Mariah Carey

b. Mar. 27, 1970, New York, NY
Vocals / Club/Dance, Adult Contemporary, Urban, Dance-Pop
The best-selling female performer of the 1990s, Mariah Carey rose to superstardom on the strength of her stunning five-octave voice; an elastic talent who moved easily from glossy ballads to hip-hop-inspired dance-pop, she earned frequent comparison to rivals Whitney Houston and Celine Dion, but did them both one better by composing all of her own material. Signed to Columbia before she turned 20, Carey found a chart-topping smash with her self-titled debut album, launching no less than four number one singles—"Vision of Love," "Love Takes Time," "Someday" and "I Don't Wanna Cry." Expectations were high for Carey's follow-up, 1991's *Emotions.* The album did not disappoint, as the title track reached number one—a record fifth consecutive chart-topper. Carey's next release was 1992's *MTV Unplugged* EP, which generated a number one cover of the Jackson 5's "I'll Be There." Her third full-length effort, *Music Box,* was her best selling record to date. Two more singles, "Dreamlover" and "Hero," reached the top spot on the charts. 1995's *Daydream* reflected a new artistic maturity; the singles "Fantasy" and "One Sweet Day" both hit the top of the charts (the latter for 16 weeks). Carey returned in 1997 with *Butterfly,* another staggering success and her most hip-hop-flavored recording to date. *—Jason Ankeny*

Mariah Carey / May 1990 / Columbia ♦♦♦
This extremely impressive debut is replete with smooth-sounding ballads and uplifting dance/R&B cuts. Carey convincingly seizes many opportunities to display her incredible vocal range on such memorable tracks as the popular "Vision of Love" (featured during her television debut on *The Arsenio Hall Show,* an appearance noted by many as her formal introduction to stardom), the energetic "Someday," and the moody sounds of the hidden treasure "Vanishing." With this collection of songs acting as a springboard for future successes, Carey establishes a strong standard of comparison for other breakthrough artists of this genre. *—Ashley S. Battel*

Emotions / Sep. 1991 / Columbia ♦♦♦
A strong follow-up to Carey's self-titled debut album, *Emotions* puts to rest any concern of a "sophomore jinx." The same mix of dance/R&B/ballads that gave Carey's debut such tremendous auditory appeal can be found with equal strength on this release, indicating

that placing firm belief in the notion of "Why fool with success?" may, in fact, have its merits. Most notably, the gospel influences of "If It's Over" (with music co-written by Carole King), the yearning cries for a lost love in "Can't Let Go," and the catchy, upbeat title track, all serve to send the listener on a musical journey filled with varying emotions. However, the one emotion that prevails upon completion of the album is definitely a positive one—satisfaction! *—Ashley S. Battel*

MTV Unplugged [EP] / Mar. 1992 / Columbia ♦♦♦
This live performance is the perfect peak into the life of rising pop/soul vocal sensation Mariah Carey at a youthful and innocent age in an intimate acoustic setting. Throughout this performance recorded live for MTV's *Unplugged*, Carey is quite electric and charismatic within her vocal presence and succeeds in enlightening the already engaged audience from the get-go. The audience certainly feels the warmth and sincerity of Carey lyrical messages of longing, loss, friendships and love. Mariah's supporting cast of gifted group musicians back her up with soulful melodiousness, spontaneity and enriching percussion. Gradually, the power and esteem of these tales lift to new heights and remain at a peak with the breathtaking, moment-making performance of "I'll Be There," a charming song first cut by the Jackson five. All and all, this is an inspiring event, though still simple for the listener to catch those musical places that need to be polished. "Can't Let Go," Carey's radio single for the album makes it as the seventh and final track, though the cameras are shut off for the *Unplugged* episode. Certainly, this is a record of hope, virtue and the possibilities of newfound love. *—Shawn M. Haney*

Music Box / Sep. 1993 / Columbia ♦♦♦♦
Mariah Carey has been stung by critical charges that she's all vocal bombast and no subtlety, soul or shading. Her solution was to make an album in which her celebrated octave-leaping voice would be downplayed and she could demonstrate her ability to sing softly and coolly. Well, she was partly successful; she trimmed the volume on *Music Box*. Unfortunately, she also cut the energy level; Carey sounds detached on several selections. She scored a couple of huge hits, "Hero" and "Dreamlover," where she did inject some personality and intensity into the leads. Most other times, Carey blended into the background and let the tracks guide her, instead of pushing and exploding through them. It was wise for Carey to display other elements of her approach, but sometimes excessive spirit is preferable to an absence of passion. *—Ron Wynn*

Daydream / Oct. 3, 1995 / Columbia ♦♦♦♦♦
Mariah Carey certainly knows how to construct an album. Positioning herself directly between urban R&B with tracks like "Fantasy" and adult contemporary with songs like "One Sweet Day," a duet with Boyz II Men, Carey appeals to both audiences equally because of the sheer amount of craft and hard work she puts into her albums. *Daydream* is her best record to date, featuring a consistently strong selection of songs and a remarkably impassioned performance by Carey. A few of the songs are second-rate—particularly the cover of Journey's "Open Arms"—but *Daydream* demonstrates that Carey continues to perfect her craft and that she has earned her status as an R&B/pop diva. *—Stephen Thomas Erlewine*

Butterfly / Sep. 16, 1997 / Columbia ♦♦♦♦
Upon its release, *Butterfly* was interpreted as Mariah Carey's declaration of independence from her ex-husband (and label president) Tommy Mottola, and to a certain extent, that's true. *Butterfly* is peppered with allusions to her troubled marriage and her newfound freedom, and the music is supposed to be in tune with contemporary urban sounds instead of adult contemporary radio. Nevertheless, it feels like a Mariah Carey album, which means that it's a collection of hit singles surrounded by classy filler. What is surprising about *Butterfly* is the lack of uptempo dance-pop. Apart from the Puffy Combs-produced "Honey," *Butterfly* is devoted to ballads, and while they are all well-crafted, many of them blend together upon initial listening. Subsequent plays reveal that Carey's vocals are sultrier and more controlled than ever, and that helps "Butterfly," "Break Down," "Babydoll" and the Prince cover "The Beautiful Ones" rank among her best; also, the ballads do have a stronger urban feel than before. Even though *Butterfly* doesn't have as many strong singles as *Daydream*, it's one of her best records, illustrating that Carey is continuing to improve and refine her music, which makes her a rarity among her '90s peers. *—Stephen Thomas Erlewine*

● **#1's** / Nov. 17, 1998 / Columbia ♦♦♦♦♦
Protest as she may—and she does, claiming in the liner notes that *#1's* is "not a greatest hits album! It's too soon, I haven't been recording long enough for that!"—it's hard to view *#1's*, Mariah Carey's first compilation, as anything other than a greatest-hits album. Carey was fortunate enough to have nearly every single she released top the pop charts. Between 1990's "Vision of Love" and 1998's "My All," all but four commercially released singles ("Anytime You Need a Friend," "Can't Let Go," "Make It Happen," "Without You") hit number one, with only a handful of radio-only singles ("Butterfly," "Breakdown") making the airwaves, not the charts. That leaves 12 big hits on *#1's*, all number ones. Since Carey's singles always dominated her albums, it comes as no surprise that *#1's* is her best, most consistent album, filled with songs that represent state-of-the-art '90s adult contemporary and pop-oriented urban soul. That said, it isn't a perfect overview—a couple of good singles are missing because of the self-imposed "#1 rule"; plus, the Ol' Dirty Bastard mix of "Fantasy" is strong, but fans familiar with the radio single will be disappointed that the chorus is completely missing on this version. The album is also padded with a personal favorite (her Brian McKnight duet "Whenever You Call," taken from *Butterfly*) and three new songs—the Jermaine Dupri-produced "Sweetheart," the Whitney Houston duet "When You Believe" (taken from *The Prince of Egypt* soundtrack), and "I Still Believe," a remake of a Brenda K. Starr tune—which are all fine, but not particularly memorable. Still, that's hardly enough to bring down a thoroughly entertaining compilation that will stand as her best record until the "official" hits collection is released. *—Stephen Thomas Erlewine*

Rainbow / Nov. 2, 1999 / Columbia ♦♦♦
Mariah Carey claims *Rainbow*, her first album since divorcing Tommy Mottola, "chronicles my emotional roller coaster ride of the past year," but less subjective listeners could be forgiven for viewing it as simply another Mariah Carey album. After all, all the elements are in place—the crossover dance hits, the ballads, the cameos, the hip producers, the weird cover choice from the early '80s. But dig a little deeper, and her words ring true. *Rainbow* is the first Carey album where she's written personal lyrics, and allusions to her separation from Mottola are evident throughout the album, even if it doesn't really amount to the "story" she mentions in the liner notes. As appropriate for any introspective album, it's a bit ballad heavy, which makes *Rainbow* seem a little samey. Yet that's not the only reason the record has a weird sense of déjà vu, since this follows the same formula as its two predecessors, distinguished primarily by her newfound fondness for flashing flesh. That repetition isn't necessarily a problem, since she does formula very well, managing to appeal to both housewives as well as B-boys. *Rainbow* proves that she can still pull off that difficult balancing act, but it's hard not to be a little disappointed that she'd didn't shake the music up a little bit more—after all, it would have been a more effective album if the heartbreak, sorrow, and joy that bubbles underneath the music were brought to the surface. *—Stephen Thomas Erlewine*

Eric Carmen

b. Aug. 11, 1949, Cleveland, OH
Vocals, Keyboards, Piano / Pop/Rock, Soft Rock, Adult Contemporary
Eric Carmen was the lead vocalist and songwriter of the Raspberries, an early-'70s band heavily influenced by mid-'60s pop, especially the Beatles. For his 1975 self-titled debut album, Carmen looked even farther into the past, to the early 20th century. His two hit singles, the heavily produced ballads "All by Myself" and "Never Gonna Fall in Love Again," were based on pieces by Russian classical composer Serge Rachmaninoff. The rest of the album and Carmen's subsequent, less commercially successful albums were a pastiche of classic pop styles. Carmen didn't enjoy a big commercial success again until 1987's "Hungry Eyes," from the *Dirty Dancing* concert tour. *—Kenneth M. Cassidy*

Eric Carmen / 1975 / Geffen ♦♦♦
Carmen achieved far greater success with his debut solo album than he ever had with his old group, The Raspberries. In part this was because, freed from the restrictions of leading a rock band, he could indulge his taste in big, lush ballads. That's what he did here, especially on the album's three Top 40 hits, one of which, "All by Myself," was a gold-selling #2 hit. *—William Ruhlmann*

● **Definitive Collection** / Jun. 17, 1997 / Arista ♦♦♦♦♦
The Definitive Collection lives up to its title. Over the course of a single disc, the compilation features all of Eric Carmen's best-known songs and biggest hits, from the pair of Raspberries hits ("Go All the Way," "Overnight Sensation (Hit Record)") to such mainstream pop singles as "All By Myself" and "Hungry Eyes." While the Raspberries albums are worthwhile listening in their own right, Carmen's solo records were often wildly uneven. *The Definitive Collection* distills all of the best songs from his spotty albums, making it essential for both casual listeners and Raspberries fans who want a sampler of the songwriter's solo career. *—Stephen Thomas Erlewine*

Kim Carnes

b. Jul. 20, 1945, Los Angeles, CA
Vocals / Pop/Rock, Soft Rock, Adult Contemporary
The raspy-voiced singer's atmospheric #1 smash, "Bette Davis Eyes," was cowritten by Jackie DeShannon. Carnes was once a member of the New Christy Minstrels with Kenny Rogers, who gave her welcome exposure in 1980 with their duet "Don't Fall in Love with a Dreamer." Later that year, a Carnes cover of the Miracles' "More Love" was a smash. She scored numerous pop hits throughout the decade and experimented with country in 1988. *—Bill Dahl*

● **Gypsy Honeymoon: Best of Kim Carnes** / 1993 / EMI America ♦♦♦♦♦
Drawing heavily on her early-'80s peak, when she spent nine weeks at number one with "Bette Davis Eyes," *Gypsy Honeymoon: The Best of Kim Carnes* may not be a definitive collection, but it nevertheless is a first-rate one, containing the majority of her best-known songs. There's "Bette Davis Eyes," plus "Don't Fall in Love With a Dreamer," "More Love," "Mistaken Identity," and "Crazy in the Night (Barking at Airplanes)." While "Draw of the Cards" and "Voyeur" should have been here, this still winds up being a fairly satisfying collection for most casual fans. *—Stephen Thomas Erlewine*

Mistaken Identity Collection / Mar. 23, 1999 / Razor & Tie ♦♦♦♦
Kim Carnes formed her style on the folk-rock circuit, where a dulcet, technical pop voice is not required. Her husky, full voice signifies early '80s radio and is still unforgettable. The sixteen-song collection starts with her 1981 single "Bette Davis Eyes." This song initiated a string of hits that kept her on the world's charts through 1986. Included here is a duet with Kenny Rogers, another gravel-voiced legend. This is a sparse, piano-introduced ballad from Rogers' 1980 *Gideon*, a concept album on a modern cowboy. Basically, this collection is an album reissue with six bonus tracks. The *Mistaken Identity* (1981) album contributes the first ten tracks of bouncy synth-pop, such as its title track and "Don't Call It Love." Other songs, like the acoustic guitar-led "When I'm Away From You," the hard rock "Break the Rules Tonite (Out of School)," and the piano and mandolin lament "My Old Pals" expose different facets of this pop talent. Kim Carnes drew on resources of country and folk to bring grace and individuality to the '80s charts. *—Tom Schulte*

The Carpenters

f. 1968, New Haven, CT, **db.** 1983

Soft Rock, Pop

With their light, airy melodies and meticulously crafted, clean arrangements, the Carpenters stood in direct contrast with the excessive, gaudy pop/rock of the '70s, yet they became one of the most popular artists of the decade, scoring 12 Top Ten hits, including three number one singles. Karen Carpenter's calm, pretty voice was the most distinctive element of their music, settling in perfectly amidst the precise, lush arrangements provided by her brother Richard. The duo's sound drew more from pre-rock pop than rock & roll, but that didn't prevent the Carpenters from appealing to a variety of audiences, particularly Top 40, easy listening and adult contemporary. While their popularity declined during the latter half of the '70s, they remained one of the most distinctive and recognizable acts of the decade produced.

Offering, the Carpenters' first album, was released in November 1969 but failed to make a big impression. However, the Carpenters' fortunes changed with their second single, a version of Burt Bacharach and Hal David's "(They Long to Be) Close to You," which became the group's first number one, spending four weeks on the top of the U.S. charts. "Close to You" became an international hit, beginning a five-year period where the duo was one of the most popular recording acts in the world. During that period the Carpenters won two Grammy Awards, including Best New Artist of 1970, and had an impressive string of Top Ten hits, including "Rainy Days and Mondays," "Superstar," "Hurting Each Other," "Goodbye to Love," "Yesterday Once More," and "Top of the World." After 1975's number four hit "Only Yesterday," the group's popularity began to decline. On February 4, 1983, Karen was found unconscious at her parents' home in New Haven; she died in the hospital that morning from a cardiac arrest, which was caused by a long battle with anorexia. *—Stephen Thomas Erlewine*

Offering [Ticket to Ride] / 1969 / A&M ✦✦✦

The duo's first album, cut in 1969, amid the breakdown of America's social contract, the coming apart of the Beatles, the final flowering (and wilting) of the youth rebellion of the prior four years, and generally several seasons in hell. And in the middle of all of that, Karen and Richard Carpenter issued a finely crafted record that sometimes sounded like Spanky & Our Gang ("Your Wonderful Parade") and at other times like art-song—among the latter pieces, "Someday" is overproduced and overdramatic but also very beautiful, and a superb showcase for Karen Carpenter. "All I Can Do" is the most solid reminder of their origins as part of a light jazz trio called Spectrum, a pleasing vocal workout that might have been well covered by the Manhattan Transfer. Their version of "Get Together" is about as convincing as a version by the Cowsills would have been, but it's balanced by Richard Carpenter's slow ballad arrangement of "Ticket to Ride," an unexpected and beguiling (if too upbeat) cover of Neil Young's "Nowadays Clancy Can't Even Sing," and a couple of superb originals, "Eve" and "All of My Life." *—Bruce Eder*

Close to You / Aug. 1970 / A&M ✦✦✦✦

Hurriedly put together in the wake of the success of the title song, and containing the follow-up hit "We've Only Just Begun," this is a surprisingly strong album, and not just for those hits. Richard Carpenter's originals "Maybe It's You" and "Crescent Noon" are superb showcases for Karen Carpenter's developing talent, the latter a superbly atmospheric, hauntingly beautiful art-song of the kind that Judy Collins was doing well at the time, and gorgeously arranged. There's also a Swingle Singers-style number, "Mr. Guder," showing off their paired vocal talents and more of Richard Carpenter's arranging talents. Karen Carpenter's singing on "Reason to Believe" isn't so much somber as it is passionate, as she emphasizes the melancholy component in the song more than most versions. Their version of "Help" lacks the inventiveness of "Ticket to Ride," although it has some pleasing vocal flourishes. The finale, "Another Song," tries hard for a serious rock sound, especially in Karen's animated drumming, but it's her voice that stands out. Released amid the political turmoil of 1970, in the wake of the Cambodian incursion, Kent State, and the conservative backlash against the anti-war forces, there was no way that the rock press or the most politically active listeners were going to appreciate this record, but the fact that it had two huge hit singles and earned a gold record award raised their ire against the Carpenters, a problem that would dog the duo for most of their careers. But the public bought, and kept on buying. *—Bruce Eder*

The Carpenters / May 1971 / A&M ✦✦✦

This is where the duo began running a little short of material for albums, having raided many of the song catalogs with which they were most familiar on their two previous LPs—although it didn't seem it to anyone at the time except Richard Carpenter, since there were three hit singles present: "For All We Know," the huge selling "Superstar" (done on the first take because it was a little uncertain how comfortable Karen Carpenter would be with the sexually suggestive lyrics to the Leon Russell song) and "Rainy Days and Mondays." They ensured the popularity of the long-player and the unusual jacket design, like an invitation with a decorative picture of the duo (like a graduation photo), seemed to go over well with older listeners while not repelling teens, which is lost in the transformation to CD packaging. In retrospect, *Carpenters* is a very MOR album—"Superstar" aside, its influences are more pop than rock, and any of the duo's original interest in jazz is long-gone as well. The Burt Bacharach-Hal David medley, in particular, was distinctly more appealing to the over-30 set than to teenage listeners, and "Saturday" made them few new friends. *—Bruce Eder*

A Song for You / Jun. 1972 / A&M ✦✦✦✦✦

Up to the release of *A Song for You*, the Carpenters' success had seemed an awesome if somewhat fluky phenomenon, built on prodigious talent, some beautifully crafted pop sensibilities, and a very fortunate choice of singles—their albums *Close to You* and *Carpenters*, though they were top sellers, both seemed just a bit thrown together. Then came *A Song for You*, a seemingly unified concept album written and recorded during a frantic period of concert activity, and brimming with lovely musical ideas even more lovingly executed, laced with good humor, and enough hits of its own to have established any artist's career on its own. And even in between the hits, the album was built on material that could have made a whole career for anyone. The duo's version of a then-new Carole King song, "It's Going to Take Some Time," not only became a hit single but helped them in the "cool" department, Carole King being about the hottest musical personality there was at that particular time. One song, "Top of the World," which Richard Carpenter had only visualized as album track, became an unexpected hit single and one of the most popular songs of the decade. The high point of their recording career, *A Song for You* marked the last time that their music (and the only occasion that one of their albums) would be accepted in the rock world on its own terms, without the duo's squeaky-clean image and sound, and middle-class dorkiness becoming a drag on their sales and image. *A Song for You* has been released several times on CD, the best of which by far is the 1999 A&M remastering with new notes and full lyrics. *—Bruce Eder*

Now & Then / May 1973 / A&M ✦✦✦

It was with the release of *Now and Then* that the Carpenters lost any pretense of being even dorky-cool . The album jacket was a giveaway, depicting them in a car in front of a suburban home. The problem also laid in the relentlessly cheerful childrens' chorus on "Sing," which seemed to come out of every public music outlet that spring and summer; the silly version of "Jambalaya" on side one; and the oldies medley on the second side, which at least predated *Happy Days*' going on the air but still botched its job, mixing Karen Carpenter's haunting rendition of "Johnny Angel" and her spirited version of "One Fine Day" (anticipating her white-bread but effective version of "Beechwood 4-5789") with filler like "Fun Fun Fun" and "Deadman's Curve," all interspersed with Tony Peluso doing his best (i.e., worst) imitation of an obnoxious disc jockey. Whatever the reason, from the moment of the release of *Now and Then*, anyone under 30 buying a Carpenters album would have *good* reason to go to a neighborhood where no one knew them to make the purchase, and hide it from their friends. The pity is that the medley paled next to its framing song, the wistful "Yesterday Once More," the last really memorable song that the duo introduced, which summed up in four minutes all of the emotions and sensations that the medley took 15 to deliver. And that song was botched in its album edit, which, instead of giving it an ending, made it part of the medley, with an annoying segue into the latter. *—Bruce Eder*

● **The Singles (1969-1973)** / Nov. 1973 / A&M ✦✦✦✦✦

There's a certain inherent sadness listening to this concise 12-song collection of the duo's early hits, especially as it opens with "We've Only Just Begun," with its hopeful, dreamy lyrics—for it was never supposed to be definitive, just the first of at least two such collections. But changes in the public's taste and a slackening (though never a disappearance) of hits for the duo, and Karen Carpenter's death in 1983, made this the first and only real mass choice for a Carpenters' collection. Ten of the duo's dozen Top Ten hits are present, from "Close to You" to "Top of the World," with their gorgeous and original slow ballad interpretation of "Ticket to Ride" and their cover of Carole King's "It's Going to Take Some Time" thrown in to offer a slightly wider perspective. Listening to this material, it's easy to accuse the Carpenters of being hopelessly retro even in their own time—bear in mind that "We've Only Just Begun" and "Superstar" being contemporaneous with the Allman Brothers' *At the Fillmore* and *Eat a Peach* and you get the idea. But the lush melodies brought out in Richard Carpenter's arrangements and Karen's singing are justification in themselves—additionally, the 1999 reissue in A&M's "Remastered Classics" series (#82839-3601-2) has a closer, toughened but warmer sound; yes, the strings are brighter, to the point of glistening, but the rhythm section (Joe Osborn on bass, Hal Blaine on drums) has more impact as well. Moreover, the full original notes from the insert are now included, explaining how each song came to be discovered and recorded. *—Bruce Eder*

Horizon / Jun. 1975 / A&M ✦✦

A Kind of Hush / Jun. 1976 / A&M ✦✦✦

The formula behind the Carpenters' albums was starting to get fairly routine—a hit single and an oldie or two (which sometimes was the single) surrounded by some well-produced soft pop/rock, driven by electric piano, strings, and a guitar solo or two cropping up. "There's a Kind of a Hush" and "Breaking Up Is Hard to Do" are the two most memorable tracks on this pleasant, well-sung and well-played, but basically bland, album. There are virtues here—"You" has a good guitar solo by Tony Peluso, and the vocals on "Sandy" are radiant, but this record was where the real rot began to set into the Carpenters' fortunes, in terms of remaining connected to rock. Instead of covering Leon Russell's or Carole King's contemporary material, they're doing songs like "Can't Smile Without You"—the latter is very sweetly sung by Karen Carpenter, and gets a lyrical but spare arrangement from Richard Carpenter, but they needed something more credible to the under-30 audience (and especially material that, if not attractive to guys in that age range, at least wouldn't make them self-conscious about listening to it with their girlfriends) on this album, and it wasn't here. If you close your eyes, it's possible to imagine the Captain & Tennille, not to mention Debbie Boone, taking lessons from this release, although Karen Carpenter's voice was still beyond comparison with any of them. *—Bruce Eder*

Passage / Oct. 1977 / A&M ✦✦

The Passage is surprisingly ambitious, almost experimental by the standards of the Carpenters—there are no Richard Carpenter-authored songs, a first for the duo, and what is here seems an almost conscious effort to sound different from their prior work. That includes the ornate versions of "Don't Cry for Me Argentina" and "Calling Occupants of Interplanetary Craft," both arranged by Peter Knight (best known for his work with the Moody Blues on *Days of Future Passed*). The *Evita* song, which comes complete with its surrounding musical material, is so much more elaborate than anything else on the album that it seems completely out of place. Richard evidently had what he felt were good reasons for choosing to record Klaatu's piece of space rock ersatz, and it is hard not to luxuriate in Karen Carpenter's enunciation of the lyrics, but overall "Calling Occupants of Interplanetary Craft" is one of those '70s records that is truly embarrassing to be caught listening to today, a pop culture Jimmy Carter-era artifact on a par with pet rocks. The album also has its unusually playful side, represented by the country number "Sweet, Sweet Smile" and the Calypso piece "Man Smart, Woman Smarter," although the latter doesn't work at all and neither track would ever find a place even on a "volume three" of the best of the Carpenters. Much more memorable was "All You Get From Love Is a Love Song," which also had more of a beat than one was accustomed to in the duo's music, and the dark, melancholy-tinged "Two Sides." The effort was admirable even if most of the results aren't memorable or essential. *—Bruce Eder*

Made in America / Jun. 1981 / A&M ♦♦♦

The duo's final album, released after their two-year break from work, a period in which Karen Carpenter attempted a solo album and when Richard was incapacitated due to a drug problem, is very much a comeback effort, with a fair amount of energy on most of it, newly radiant arrangements ("The Wedding Song," etc.), one cute oldie cover ("Beechwood 4-5789," which was made into a video), and the best new songs they'd had since the mid '70s ("Those Good Old Dreams," "Touch Me When We're Dancing"). The latter song, in particular, marked a breakthrough to a new sound and a new sensuality in Karen's image as a singer, and could have led to a new beginning for all concerned, and the album as a whole was more energetic and memorable than anything they'd done since *A Song for You*. Unfortunately, the singer was already suffering from worsening effects of the psychological disorder that would kill her less than two years after the release of this album—"The Wedding Song," in particular, seems now like an unintentionally poignant bookend on the other end of her life and career from "We've Only Just Begun." The 1999 CD release, as part of Polygram's *Remastered Classics* series, has especially bright sound, and also reprints all lyrics. *—Bruce Eder*

Yesterday Once More / May 1985 / A&M ♦♦♦♦♦

This double-CD set was probably too much of the Carpenters for the average fan, but just the same, it touches bases that *The Singles* misses, and it is rewarding. The 1998 remastering (catalog number 31454 1000-2) is doubly attractive, as a mid-priced item with 24-bit remastered sound and new notes by Paul Grein. The 28 songs, totaling more than 110 minutes of music, still have a few holes, like their cover of "Beechwood 4-5789" and the deeply atmospheric "Crescent Noon," but every one of their albums is represented from *Ticket to Ride* on up. The remastering makes all of the difference in the enjoyment of the songs, presenting Karen Carpenter's voice and Richard Carpenter's arrangements in close, rich detail and intimacy; it all makes the care that was put into the original performances completely worth the effort. The duo's music never sounded less like recordings and more like performances, a fact—brought home by the crystalline tones of Joe Osborn's bass—that may distress those who merely want to relive their memories of hearing these songs on the radio. There will also be a few worthwhile surprises even for the casual listener, including the melodic dance number "(Want You) Back in My Life Again" from their final album and the rhapsodic "I Just Fall in Love Again" from *Passage*. This set is a decent compromise between the superficiality of *The Singles* and the deep but awkward construction of the four-CD boxed set, made more valuable by the remastering, which renders its sound superior to that of the same material on the box. *—Bruce Eder*

From the Top / 1991 / A&M ♦♦♦♦♦

The Carpenters' box set retrospective *From the Top* is a 67-track, four-CD set running under 3 1/2 hours (which means it could have fit on three CDs) that traces Richard and Karen Carpenter's musical efforts from the formation of the Richard Carpenter Trio in 1965 to Karen's final recording session in April 1982. This is Richard's compilation; he introduces it and writes a track-by-track commentary, and has also done a lot of refurbishing, remixing 40 tracks and providing "additional recording" on many. The set proceeds chronologically, and most of the 20 previously unreleased tracks date from the '60s, as the group's emerging sound can be traced in demos. The Carpenters' hitmaking period of 1970-75 is extensively covered from the last quarter of the first disc to the start of the third, with most of their big hits included, though Richard excludes a few without comment. Also included are many album tracks that sometimes match the quality of the singles. Richard includes a couple of the Carpenters' singles from the second half of the '70s, and devotes the rest of the third disc and most of the fourth to excerpts from stray projects—Christmas albums, TV specials, Karen's solo album (which Richard carefully notes went unreleased "at Karen's behest"). As such, there is necessarily a fall-off in the set's quality. But by sequencing the songs chronologically, choosing only the ones he wants, and remaking them to his satisfaction, Richard is telling his version of the Carpenters' story, chronicling his band's rise and fall, which occurred in artistic and commercial terms well before his sister's death. *—William Ruhlmann*

Love Songs / Mar. 24, 1998 / A&M ♦♦♦♦

There may be too many Carpenters compilations on the market—there are certainly enough to confuse the average neophyte—but *Love Songs* is a welcome addition to the clutter, since it offers 20 of the duo's very best love songs, including "We've Only Just Begun" and "Top of the World." Anyone looking for a collection of the duo's romantic songs should definitely consider this fine collection, even it does leave off some of their poppier, rock-inflected material. *—Stephen Thomas Erlewine*

● **Singles (1969-1981)** / May 23, 2000 / A&M ♦♦♦♦♦

Singles (1969-1981) expands the popular *Singles (1969-1973)* album with more of the group's later hits, such as "Please Mr. Postman," "Only Yesterday," "Touch Me When We're Dancing," and "I Won't Last a Day Without You." "(They Long to Be) Close to You," "We've Only Just Begun," "Superstar," and other '70s hits are still here, making this collection a comprehensive gathering of all of their charting singles and definitive album tracks. *—Heather Phares*

James Carr

b. Jun. 13, 1942, Memphis, TN

Vocals, Sax (Tenor) / Deep Soul, Southern Soul, Soul

Considered to be among the very greatest of "deep" Southern male soul singers, James Carr's succession of R&B hits on the Memphis Goldwax label were all gems of "country" soul, that wonderful '60s marriage of Southern Black R&B vocalists with songs written in a country format and played mostly by White musicians. Carr's dark, gospel-inflected style, marked by a subtle, rich voice that is almost frightening in its intensity and range, has been compared to that of Otis Redding and Percy Sledge; many reviewers would class him above even these formidable peers. "At the Dark End of the Street," the first songwriting collaboration between Dan Penn and Chips Moman, is Carr's undisputed masterpiece. Also recorded by Aretha Franklin, Clarence Carter, Linda Ronstadt, and Ry Cooder, it is the quintessential country-soul take on adulterous love.

Carr's career initially was short; Goldwax ceased operation in 1969, and Carr cut only one other single for Atlantic in 1971; however, he has recently emerged from retirement with a new album on Goldwax. His work stands at the apex of '60s soul—with Aretha, Otis, Percy, and Wilson—essential stuff! *—Christine Ohlman*

● **The Essential James Carr** / Feb. 21, 1995 / Razor & Tie ♦♦♦♦♦

When the soul era of the mid-'60s was in full bloom, for a period of three years James Carr was the maker of some of its mightiest music. His warm, soulful voice could make the reading of virtually anything he touched (even his version here of the Bee Gees' "To Love Somebody") a transcendent event. He is also the mystery man of the genre, unlettered and imbued with an almost childlike innocence, disappearing for a decade after these recordings were made with charges of mental instability cropping up whenever his name is mentioned. But music this special doesn't come without a price and certainly Carr paid that price, not unlike the gospel singers who influenced him who sometimes sang themselves to death right on stage. But the music will always win out, because personal problems aside, the music James Carr made is as deep as Southern soul music gets, on an equal par with the best of a Sam Cooke or an Otis Redding. Tracks like "You've Got My Mind Messed Up," "Pouring Water on a Drowning Man" and his masterpiece, "The Dark End of the Street" are all justifiable classics of the genre, and this 20-track collection is where you go to get the big picture on an artist who deserves a much wider hearing. *—Cub Koda*

Paul Carrack

b. Apr. 22, 1951, Sheffield, Yorkshire, England

Vocals, Keyboards, Piano / Blue-Eyed Soul, Pop/Rock, Soft Rock, Adult Contemporary

Paul Carrack was pop music's ultimate journeyman. A vocalist and keyboardist who enjoyed considerable success over the course of his lengthy career while in the service of bands ranging from Ace to Squeeze to Mike + the Mechanics, his finest work often came at the expense of his own identity as a performer; indeed, of the many big hits on which the unassuming singer was prominently featured, only one, 1987's "Don't Shed a Tear," bore his own name. He first hit the charts after writing and singing Ace's debut single "How Long," a number three hit in the US during 1975. After the group disbanded in 1977, Carrack resurfaced in Roxy Music before releasing his solo debut, 1980's *Nightbird*. He next joined Squeeze, assuming lead vocal duties on the hit "Tempted." Once again, he attempted to forge a solo career with the 1982 LP *Suburban Voodoo*, and cracked the US Top 40 with "I Need You." In 1985 he joined Genesis' Mike Rutherford in his side project Mike + the Mechanics, singing on the hits "Silent Running" and "All I Need Is a Miracle." Subsequently, his third solo album *One Good Reason* proved to be by far his most popular effort to date, with the single "Don't Shed a Tear" reaching the Top Ten. After his 1989 solo LP *Groove Approved*, Carrack split time between Mike + the Mechanics and Squeeze during the '90s. The solo album *Blue Views* appeared in 1996, followed in 1997 by *Beautiful World*. *—Jason Ankeny*

The Nightbird / 1980 / Vertigo ♦♦♦

Suburban Voodoo / Aug. 1982 / Epic ♦♦♦

With *Suburban Voodoo*, Paul Carrack re-launched his solo career following a successful stint with Squeeze that produced a hit with his lead vocal on "Tempted." By this point, Carrack was playing with Nick Lowe, who produced *Suburban Voodoo*, and the album sounds very much like a Lowe album with Carrack singing. That's all to the good, though, since Carrack's supple voice is well suited to Lowe's updated '60s rock & roll style. Carrack scored his first solo Top 40 hit with "I Need You," but that was one of the slighter tracks on an unusually tuneful album. *—William Ruhlmann*

When You Walk in the Room / 1987 / Chrysalis ♦♦

One Good Reason / Nov. 1987 / Chrysalis ♦♦

One Good Reason verified that Paul Carrack was a much better musician surrounded by others than he was by himself. Carrack's presence with Roxy Music, Squeeze, Nick Lowe and Mike + The Mechanics was easily felt, and his beginnings with the seventies band Ace gave him his first crack at singing lead, which spawned their biggest hit in "How Long" back in 1975. 1987's *One Good Reason* reveals Carrack's song writing prowess more than it does his ability to perform. The album's highlight, the #9 hit "Don't Shed A Tear" is bolstered by its subtle, laid back groove with a start-and-stop tempo which comes across as unique to a certain extent, but from this point on Carrack's songs seem to fade into a light pop mist. "One Good Reason" managed to crack the Top 30 as the album's follow up, but lacks the charisma of its predecessor. The songs are well written, lyrically, but they're dispensed rather half-heartedly from a musical standpoint, with Tim Renwick's guitar playing accentuating things from time to time. It's apparent in tracks like "Fire With Fire" and "Give Me A Chance" that Paul Carrack has reached the point of pop pedestrianism, on this album anyway. Carrack's 1989 effort entitled *Groove Approved* refreshingly wakes things up a bit. — *Mike DeGagne*

Groove Approved / Oct. 1989 / Chrysalis ✦✦✦
After pulling four singles off 1987's *One Good Reason*, Paul Carrack looked to be on the verge of finally establishing himself as a solo star. Instead, he stumbled with the follow-up, *Groove Approved*, a solid, workman-like collection that featured only one Top 40 number in "I Live By The Groove." One suspects that this had less to do with the album's real commercial potential than with upheavals in the record company, which was being sold by its founders to EMI during this period. Yet, afterward, Carrack went back to working with Squeeze and Mike + the Mechanics, putting his solo career on hold. — *William Ruhlmann*

● **Collection: Twenty-One Good Reasons** / Jan. 25, 1994 / Chrysalis ✦✦✦✦
Containing not only his solo hits, but also the ones that he sang for Ace ("How Long"), Squeeze ("Tempted"), and Mike + the Mechanics ("Silent Running" and "The Living Years"), as well as two songs with Carlene Carter, *Twenty-One Good Reasons: The Paul Carrack Collection* is the one Carrack disc to own. — *Stephen Thomas Erlewine*

Blue Views / Jan. 1996 / IRS/EMI ✦✦✦
After spending eight years working with Mike + the Mechanics, among other bands and side projects, Paul Carrack returned in 1996 with *Blue Views*. Because Carrack's side projects since the mid-'80s have all been variations on slick but soulful pop-rock, it's not a surprise that *Blue Views* sounds like it could have been released in 1991. That's not necessarily a bad thing, since Carrack's vocals are terrific and the sound is appealingly polished. The material is a bit too spotty to make it a triumphant comeback, but the best moments, including a version of the Eagles' "Love Will Keep Us Alive," are solid adult contemporary pop. — *Stephen Thomas Erlewine*

Beautiful World / 1997 / Ark ✦✦✦
While it lacks a standout on the lines of "Don't Shed a Tear," *Beautiful World* is a thoroughly enjoyable collection of polished, mature pop-soul that is another fine addition to Paul Carrack's catalog. — *Stephen Thomas Erlewine*

Satisfy My Soul / Sep. 12, 2000 / Compass ✦✦✦
With *Satisfy My Soul*, Carrack crafted another collection of melodic pop songs. Though some of the material is weak, his distinctive vocal gifts make even the most mediocre song worth hearing. There is certainly no shortage of catchy tunes on *Satisfy My Soul*. Both "My Kind" and the funky "Better Than Nothing" rank as some of Paul Carrack's best material, and "Inspire Me" is a dead ringer for '80s-era Hall & Oates. *Satisfy My Soul* also includes collaborations with Carrack's former bandmates Chris Difford (Squeeze) and Mike Rutherford (Genesis, Mike + the Mechanics). The title track (written with Difford) is a tuneful, upbeat ballad that sounds similar to Sam Cooke, and "Running Out of Time" (with Rutherford) is an edgy, soulful rocker. Carrack, who also produced, should be commended for his straightforward approach on *Satisfy My Soul*. Instead of resorting to pretentious production techniques and overblown arrangements in an attempt to sound contemporary, Carrack keeps things simple, wisely allowing his vocals to take center stage. While the melodies remain strong for the most part, some of the material suffers from trite lyrics. However, Carrack more than compensates for the clichés with his superb vocal performances; he sounds just as good here as he did on "Tempted" almost 20 years earlier. Carrack has proven for decades he is a true pop craftsman. *Satisfy My Soul* is further evidence of his ability to remain an engaging, solid performer, even when the music business is dominated by fads and marketing gimmicks. — *William Cooper*

Joe "King" Carrasco

Vocals, Guitar / New Wave, Tex-Mex
Texas native Joe "King" Carrasco has devoted his career to re-creating the Tex-Mex, Farfisa organ rock & roll sound of such '60s groups as the Sir Douglas Quintet and Sam the Sham & the Pharoahs. After playing in a succession of bands around Texas in the late '60s and early '70s, Carrasco founded his band El Molino in 1976 and recorded *Tex-Mex Rock-Roll* in 1978. (The album was reissued by ROIR in 1989.) By 1979 he had formed the Crowns and was calling his music "nuevo wavo," playing especially in New Wave, where he appeared on stage in a cape and crown. He was signed to the U.K. Stiff label and Joe Boyd's Hannibal label in the U.S., and released *Joe "King" Carrasco and the Crowns* in 1980. By 1982 he had moved up to major label MCA for *Synapse Gap*, followed by *Party Weekend* (1983). These missed the charts, however, and although Carrasco has recorded since, turning increasingly political meanwhile, his work has been harder to find. *Bandido Rock* (1987) on Rounder was credited to Joe "King" Carrasco Y Las Coronas. — *William Ruhlmann*

Joe "King" Carrasco and El Molino / 1978 / Big Beat ✦✦✦
This UK release is a reissue of *Joe "King" Carrasco and El Molino*, originally released in a limited edition by Texas label Lisa Records in 1978. The album was reissued in the US under the title *Tex-Mex Rock-Roll* by ROIR in 1989. — *William Ruhlmann*

Joe "King" Carrasco and the Crowns / Nov. 1980 / Hannibal ✦✦✦
At a time when the New York club scene was dominated by the remnants of punk and quirky power pop of Devo and the B-52s, Joe "King" Carrasco, whose music complemented those styles, constituted comic relief. He would sweep on in his crown and cape and play Farfisa organ-based mid-'60s-style Tex-Mex rock & roll. Carrasco was a delightful club act, but inevitably, that didn't translate adequately to vinyl. Nevertheless, this, his first national release, made a brave attempt, and even if you couldn't have Joe jumping on your table at home, a song like "Caca de Vaca" was bound to raise a smile. [This al-

bum was released originally by Stiff Records in the U.K. with a slightly different track listing.] — *William Ruhlmann*

Synapse Gap / 1982 / MCA ✦✦✦✦✦
Joe "King" Carrasco's Crowns boasted a beefed-up sound on their major label debut, which leaned more toward guitar rock with a loud rhythm section than earlier, cheesier Tex-Mex efforts. That did not constitute an improvement necessarily, though it probably was intended to broaden Carrasco's appeal. For the most part, this didn't lessen the band's effervescence, though the reggae tune was a bit trendy (it even featured harmonies by Michael Jackson!) and the overall impression was of an artist closer to the mainstream than the border. — *William Ruhlmann*

Party Weekend / 1983 / MCA ✦✦✦

Tales from the Crypt / 1984 / ROIR ✦✦

Bordertown / 1984 / Big Beat ✦✦

Bandido Rock / Aug. 1987 / Rounder ✦✦

● **Anthology** / Mar. 21, 1995 / One Way ✦✦✦✦✦
This is an 18-track compilation drawn from Joe "King" Carrasco's two MCA albums *Synapse Gap (Mundo Total)* (1982) and *Party Weekend* (1983). — *William Ruhlmann*

The Cars

f. 1976, Boston, MA, **db.** 1988
Album Rock, Pop/Rock, New Wave
Blondie may have had a string of number one hits and Talking Heads may have won the hearts of the critics, but the Cars were the most successful American New Wave band to emerge in the late '70s. With their sleek, mechanical pop-rock, the band racked up a string of platinum albums and Top 40 singles that made them one of the most popular American rock & roll bands of the late '70s and early '80s. While they were more commercially-oriented than their New York peers, the Cars were nevertheless inspired by proto-punk, garage rock and bubblegum pop. The difference was in packaging. Where their peers were as equally inspired by art as music, the Cars were strictly a rock & roll band, and while their music occasionally sounded clipped and distant, they had enough attitude to crossover to album rock radio, which is where they made their name. Nevertheless, the Cars remained a New Wave band, picking up cues from the Velvet Underground, David Bowie and Roxy Music. Ric Ocasek and Ben Orr's vocals uncannily recalled Lou Reed's dead-pan delivery, while the band's insistent, rhythmic pulse was reminiscent of Berline-era Iggy Pop. Furthermore, the group followed Roxy Music's lead and had artist Alberto Vargas design sexy illustrations of pinups for their record sleeves. These airbrushed drawings were the group's primary visual attraction until 1984, when the group made a series of striking videos to accompany the singles from *Heartbeat City*. The videos for "You Might Think," "Magic," and "Drive" became MTV staples, sending the Cars to near-superstar status. Instead of following through with their success, the Cars slowly faded away, quietly breaking up after releasing one final album in 1987. — *Stephen Thomas Erlewine*

The Cars / May 1978 / Elektra ✦✦✦✦✦
The Cars' 1978 self-titled debut, issued on the Elektra label, is a genuine rock masterpiece. The band jokingly referred to the album as their "true greatest-hits album," but it's no exaggeration—all nine tracks are new wave/rock classics, still in rotation on rock radio. Whereas most bands of the late '70s embraced either punk/new wave or hard rock, the Cars were one of the first bands to do the unthinkable—merge the two styles together. Add to it bandleader/songwriter Ric Ocasek's supreme pop sensibilities, and you had an album that appealed to new wavers, rockers, and Top 40 fans. One of the most popular new wave songs ever, "Just What I Needed," is an obvious highlight, as are such familiar hits as "Good Times Roll," "My Best Friend's Girl," and "You're All I've Got Tonight." But like most consummate rock albums, the lesser-known compositions are just as exhilarating—"Don't Cha Stop," "Bye Bye Love," "All Mixed Up," and "Moving In Stereo," the latter featured as an instrumental during a steamy scene in the popular movie *Fast Times at Ridgemont High*. With flawless performances, songwriting, and production (courtesy of Queen alumni Roy Thomas Baker), the Cars' debut remains one of rock's all-time classics. — *Greg Prato*

Candy-O / Jun. 1979 / Elektra ✦✦✦
Since the Cars had created a perfect album with their 1978 self-titled debut, it would be nearly impossible to top it. Instead of laboring long and hard over a follow-up like many '70s bands did after a huge commercial success, the band cranked out their sophomore effort, *Candy-O*, (Elektra) almost exactly one year later from the first LP. And while the album was not as stellar as its predecessor was, it did contain several classics, resulting in another smash album that solidified the band's standing as one of the most promising new bands of the late '70s. The first single, the Top 20 anthem "Let's Go," proves to be the best track, but plenty of other standouts can be found as well. The title track remains one of the band's best rockers, while the gentle "It's All I Can Do" also deserved to be a hit. The band pays tribute to T. Rex on "Dangerous Type" (the main guitar riff resembles "Bang a Gong"), rocks out on "Got a Lot on My Head" and "Night Spots," shows their softer side on "Since I Held You," and embraces modern pop on "Double Life" and "Lust for Kicks." Their second strong release in a row, *Candy-O* proved that the Cars were not one-hit wonders, like so many other bands from the same era. — *Greg Prato*

Panorama / Aug. 1980 / Elektra ✦✦

Shake It Up / Nov. 1981 / Elektra ✦✦✦
By augmenting their sound with more synthesizers, electronics, and drum machines, the Cars' fourth release, *Shake It Up* (1981, Elektra), helped bridge their hard rock-based early work (1978's *The Cars*) with the futuristic-pop direction of 1984's *Heartbeat City*. The

band's sound may have been evolving with each succeeding album, but Ric Ocasek was still writing compelling new wave compositions despite all the change, many of which would ultimately become rock & roll standards. The up-tempo title track remains a party favorite to this day (reaching number four on the singles charts), while the melancholic "Since You're Gone" remains one of Ocasek's best-ever tales of heartbreak. Intriguing videos were made for both songs, officially introducing the band to the MTV/video age. Like it's predecessor, 1980's *Panorama*, filler is present ("This Could Be Love," "Maybe Baby"), but many lesser-known album tracks prove to be highlights: the almost entirely synth-oriented tracks "Think It Over" and "A Dream Away," the rocking "Cruiser," plus the more pop-oriented "I'm Not the One" and "Victim of Love." Although *Shake It Up* was another resounding commercial success, their next album would be the one that made the Cars one of rock's quintessential acts of the '80s. *—Greg Prato*

Heartbeat City / Mar. 1984 / Elektra ✦✦✦✦✦
MTV had become a major marketing tool by 1984, and the Cars were one of the first bands to use the new video medium to their advantage. The band's fifth album, *Heartbeat City* (Elektra), spawned several imaginative and memorable videos, which translated into massive chart and commercial success, making it one of the biggest releases of the year. Produced by hitmaker John "Mutt" Lange (AC/DC, Def Leppard), the album included two Top Ten singles—the ballad "Drive" and the charismatic "You Might Think," plus an additional two that landed in the Top 20—the summer anthem "Magic," and the eccentric "Hello Again." But it didn't just stop there, plenty of other tracks could have been hits as well, such as the sparse rocker "It's Not the Night" and the breezy pop of "Looking for Love." Other highlights included the ethereal title track, the melodic rocker "Stranger Eyes," and the moderately paced love song "Why Can't I Have You." Although the Cars experienced their greatest success yet with *Heartbeat City*, it would unfortunately not last for long—after just one more studio album (1987's spotty *Door to Door*), the band split up. *—Greg Prato*

● **Greatest Hits** / Oct. 1985 / Elektra ✦✦✦✦✦
The Cars were responsible for some of rock's most recognizable radio hits by the mid '80s, so when the band took an extended break after their successful tour for *Heartbeat City*, 1985's *Greatest Hits* (Elektra) was assembled. Mixed in with the familiar selections was a brand new track, the playful "Tonight She Comes" (which became a Top Ten hit), as well as a remix of the overlooked "Shake It Up" ballad, "I'm Not the One." And while most of the expected hits are represented ("Just What I Needed," "Let's Go," "Drive," "Shake It Up," etc.), some of the selections prove questionable—why was the title track from *Heartbeat City* (an unsuccessful single) included instead of the 1984 Top 20 hit "Hello Again"? Other missing radio staples include "You're All I've Got Tonight," "It's All I Can Do," and the title track from *Candy-O*, which would have made the collection definitive (all are included on the more extensive *Just What I Needed: Cars Anthology* from 1995). But for the casual fan, *Greatest Hits* will do the trick. *—Greg Prato*

Door to Door / Aug. 1987 / Elektra ✦

Just What I Needed: The Cars Anthology / Nov. 7, 1995 / Rhino ✦✦✦✦✦
While casual admirers of the Cars can stick with their 1985 *Greatest Hits* collection, more serious fans should go right to the more thorough two-CD set, *The Cars Anthology: Just What I Needed*. Whereas *Greatest Hits* stuck more or less with their singles, *The Cars Anthology* contains strong album cuts, non-album B-sides, demos and unreleased takes, as well as all the expected hits (and a 27-page booklet crammed with rare photos and the band's bio). Just about every rock fan is long familiar with such tracks as "Just What I Needed," "Shake It Up," "Magic" and "Let's Go" (to name a few), but the collection's main attraction is its abundance of unfamiliar material. Such previously-released album tracks as "Dangerous Type," "Gimme Some Slack" and "Cruiser" are highlights, as are the rarities "Cool Fool" (one of their hardest rocking tracks ever), "That's It," a cover of Iggy Pop's "Funtime" and a pair of album-closing early demos ("Leave or Stay" and "Ta Ta Wayo Wayo"). At nearly two and a half hours long, *The Cars Anthology: Just What I Needed* is the ultimate Cars collection, which only confirms their standing as one of the finest bands of the new wave era. *—Greg Prato*

The Cars [Deluxe Edition] / Apr. 20, 1999 / Rhino ✦✦✦✦
Back in 1996, Rhino Records had plans for a Cars rarities disc entitled *Prototypes*, which was to include their entire first album in demo form, as well as other rarities from all eras of the band. And even though *Ice* magazine ran a story on it and a track listing was set, the album never saw the light of day for reasons unknown. Three years later, Rhino reconsidered (helped by a fan write-in campaign), and issued a similarly assembled package, *The Cars: Deluxe Edition*. A two-CD set, it contains their classic 1978 self-titled debut in its entirety (an album you just can't hear enough), while the second disc presents the complete album in demo form, with an additional five early demos of previously unreleased compositions tacked on at the end. Diehard fans will have a feast with disc two, the demos for such radio standards as "My Best Friend's Girl," "Just What I Needed," "You're All I've Got Tonight," and "Bye Bye Love" capture the songs in their rawest form—akin to what they must have sounded like back in the band's club days. Out of the five unissued songs, two are instant classics (the amiable "Wake Me Up" and the red-hot rocker "Hotel Queenie"), while "They Won't See You" proves interesting, despite an underdeveloped chorus—which is forgivable, since these are demos, after all. [Note: since a demo version of "Good Times Roll" couldn't be found, a live take from 1978 is used on disc two.] *—Greg Prato*

Lori Carson

Vocals, Guitar (Electric), Guitar (Acoustic) / Alternative Pop/Rock, Singer/Songwriter
Although Lori Carson's name may not automatically come to mind when discussing the best singer-songwriters of the late '90s, it doesn't mean that she isn't deserving of such accolades. Although she has received much critical acclaim and acquired many fans along the way, her talents have unfortunately gone unrecognized (hopefully this will soon change in the Lilith Fair-friendly late '90s). Beginning with her debut in 1990, *Shelter*, Carson was predicted to be a major recording force by the likes of Time and Rolling Stone. But instead of following the path laid down by her debut, which she wasn't entirely happy with, she put her solo career on hold and joined friend Anton Fier in the Golden Palominos. Appearing on two of their albums, 1993's *This Is How It Feels* and 1994's *Pure*, Lori turned out to be an important addition and integral member of the band.

Returning to solo work in 1995, she released her gentle sophomore effort, *Where It Goes*, on Restless Records, with Fier handling production chores. Again she received praise from *Rolling Stone*, as well as *Entertainment Weekly*, *Details*, and other publications. It was also during 1995 that Lori began getting involved in composing for movies, as she co-wrote "Fall In the Light" for the motion picture *Strange Days* with writer Graeme Revell, and contributed "You Won't Fall" (from *Where It Goes*) to the movie *Stealing Beauty*. Her most stripped-down album yet, *Everything I Touch Runs Wild*, was released in 1997, again to rave reviews, as Carson spent the rest of the year touring the world. *Stars* followed in 1999. *—Greg Prato*

Shelter / Apr. 24, 1990 / Geffen ✦✦✦
Lori Carson's 1990 debut showcases her charmingly imperfect soprano voice, but otherwise only hints at the adventurous work she would later produce. Most of what's here is pleasant but unremarkable folk-pop in the Edie Brickell mold, with the glossy production smoothing out the vocal eccentricities that make Carson's later albums so moving. "Pretty Girls" and the heartfelt title track are highlights, while a duet with Gregg Allman on "Imagine Love" seems like an awkward stab at an adult-contemporary hit. *Shelter* is not an embarrassment in the *Y Kant Tori Read* vein; it's simply a tentative album from an artist still finding her feet. *—Kristi Coulter*

Where It Goes / 1995 / Restless ✦✦✦✦
Well, she's not exactly a household name, but she's known in hip circles as the latest in a long and distinguished line of singers for downtown supergroup the Golden Palominos. And true to New York tradition, she's not about to sound cheerful or anything like that. The most obvious stylistic referent is Counting Crows, believe it or not—lots of studied and solipsistic sadness that gets by on irresistible tunefulness just before it starts irritating you. In fact, Carson's "Down Here" (the lead track on her debut album) sounds suspiciously like a rewrite of the Crows' "Round Here" (the lead track on their debut album). Song titles like "Twisting My Words" and "Fell Into the Loneliness" pretty much tell you what to expect, but when Carson wraps her lovely voice around a lyric as affecting as that in "You Won't Fall," the effect is irresistible. In fact, throughout the album it's her light, effortless delivery and her winning melodicism that consistently keep the music's head above water, and even though she has a few moments of off-putting preciousness (at certain points sounding almost like Lisa Germano at her worst), there is simply no arguing with the transcendent grace of songs like "Down Here" and "Anyday." *—Rick Anderson*

● **Everything I Touch Runs Wild** / Mar. 25, 1997 / Restless ✦✦✦✦
On her third solo effort, *Everything I Touch Runs Wild*, the underrated singer/songwriter Lori Carson offers her barest, most personal compositions yet. One reason for this direction was due in part to the album being recorded entirely in her apartment, as well as Carson producing it herself. By combining her soothing, gentle vocals with an acoustic backing, the results are often both irresistibly sweet and engaging. Her voice can be compared at times to Sarah McLachlan's, especially on the album's opener, "Something's Got Me" (which is also present in an album-closing "original version"). Simplicity and economy are stressed throughout, with the instruments (piano, clean guitar, accordion, etc.) leaving plenty of room to be filled by Lori's vocals, such as the track "Make a Little Luck." The picture of a calm winter landscape is painted convincingly on "Snow Come Down," while "Fade" creates a feeling of melancholia. Included on initial pressings of *Everything I Touch Runs Wild* is a bonus second disc of remixes, which contains radical electronic makeovers of "Something's Got Me" (three separate versions) and "I Saw the Light." *—Greg Prato*

Stars / Sep. 28, 1999 / Restless ✦✦✦
Lori Carson's fourth album *Stars* may not be as consistently compelling as its immediate predecessor, the sublime *Everything I Touch Runs Wild*, but that's not to say that it's a bad record. It's quite good, actually, and her songcraft continues to improve; it's subtle, yet sturdy work. The main problem is that the production doesn't pull the listener into the album, but Carson's songs and performance are passionate enough that they become quite gripping once you get past the surface. *—Stephen Thomas Erlewine*

Clarence Carter

b. Jan. 14, 1936, Montgomery, AL
Vocals, Leader, Keyboards, Guitar / Deep Soul, Southern Soul, Soul
A blind soul singer whose numerous hits of the late '60s and early '70s epitomized the Muscle Shoals rhythm & blues sound, Carter hit the big time with his Atlantic single "Patches" (1970) and won a lasting place in the annals of Southern soul with others like "Slip Away" and "Too Weak to Fight." In 1981 Carter broke out of a dry spell with the Venture album *Let's Burn*, featuring a track called "Workin' (On a Love Building)," which set the theme for much of what was to follow: robust, lascivious lovemaking boasts. More recent tracks such as his salacious reworking of Tampa Red's "Love Me with a Feeling" and the jukebox favorite "Strokin'" (too risque for some radio stations) further solidified the carnal Carter image. Still primarily a soul/R&B singer, Carter has incorporated more hard blues elements in his music recently than in the Muscle Shoals days, despite his new and unblues-minded penchant for playing and programming all the instruments on his albums. *—Jim O'Neal*

● **Snatchin' It Back** / 1992 / Rhino ✦✦✦✦✦

Snatchin' It Back—The Best of Clarence Carter is a great compilation, spotlighting Carter's stellar guitar work and trademark vocals on classics like "Slip Away," "Too Weak to Fight," and "Lookin' for a Fox." His great "Tell Daddy" (covered by Etta James as "Tell Mama") is included. Dave Marsh contributes the liner notes. Soul music at its funky best, and the compilation to own if you're a Carter fan. *—Christine Ohlman*

Neko Case

b. Sep. 8, 1970, Alexandria, VA

Americana, Adult Alternative Pop/Rock, Alternative Country-Rock, Indie Rock, Alternative Pop/Rock

Singer/songwriter Neko Case first rose to prominence as a drummer in the punk-pop unit Maow before enjoying concurrent success as an alternative country-rocker. Born in 1970 in Alexandria, Virginia, Case later relocated to Vancouver, British Columbia to study art; there she joined Maow, which signed to the Mint Records label to issue their debut LP *The Unforgiving Sounds of Maow*. Pursuing her longtime love of country music, Case also signed on with the roots-rock group the Weasles before mounting her own solo project; assembling a backing band dubbed the Boyfriends—comprised of members of the Softies, Zumpano, and Shadowy Men on a Shadowy Planet—she soon began work on her debut LP *The Virginian*, released on Mint in 1997. *Furnace Room Lullaby* followed in early 2000. *—Jason Ankeny*

The Virginian / Jul. 29, 1997 / Bloodshot ✦✦✦✦

Neko Case's solo debut is a delightful collection of heartfelt originals and vibrant covers ranging from traditional country fare (Ernest Tubb's "Thanks a Lot," Loretta Lynn's "Somebody Led Me Away") to more eclectic material (Scott Walker's "Duchess"); the highlight is a rip-snorting rendition of the Everly Brothers' "Bowling Green," a duet with Zumpano's Carl Newman. *—Jason Ankeny*

● **Furnace Room Lullaby** / 2000 / Bloodshot ✦✦✦✦✦

It would be easy to call Neko Case alt-country's answer to k.d. lang; after all, they're both from Canada, both came into country music through artier pursuits, and both blend trad-style twang with a modernist lyrical perspective. But Case also has a couple more important things in common with lang—she has a superb voice that's as big as all outdoors, and there's nothing at all ironic about her love for the luxurious sadness of classic country & western. Case fronts a dramatically revamped line-up of Boyfriends on her second solo album, *Furnace Room Lullaby*, and it's even stronger and more impressive than her fine debut set, *The Virginian*. Case co-wrote all of the album's 12 songs, and the material strikes a more deeply personal note this time out, from the busted romance of "Set Out Running" and "We've Never Met" to the road-weary and unsentimental nostalgia of "Thrice All American" and "South Tacoma Way" (not many artists could put a lump in your throat at the notion of a Wal-Mart replacing the old downtown, but Case does it here). Case's vocals are superb from front to back, as smooth and fiery as good brandy, and her revolving circle of musicians (including Ron Sexsmith and Kelly Hogan on backing vocals) are subtle and beautifully evocative, balancing sorrow and good times with an easy grace. Dozens of rock artists have wrung cheap laughs from the sound and feel of classic country, but Neko Case understands the honest emotions and working-class poetry Loretta Lynn and Dolly Parton brought to their best music, and if her own take on such things is a bit different, *Furnace Room Lullaby* makes clear how deeply she cares for this music, and confirms her status as one of alt-country's strongest artists. *—Mark Deming*

Peter Case

b. Apr. 5, 1954

Vocals, Harmonica, Guitar / College Rock, Contemporary Folk, New Wave, Singer/Songwriter

After disbanding the Los Angeles new wave/power-pop group the Plimsouls, Peter Case launched a career as an important American singer/songwriter, specializing in the flat-pick guitar style and semi-autobiographical stories of drifters delivered in narrative style. As a teenager he took to the troubadour's life, playing coffeehouses and busking. He was discovered on the streets of San Francisco in 1976 by songwriter Jack Lee, with whom he collaborated in the Nerves, a short-lived but influential power-pop act. After the Plimsouls found success with the power-pop standard "A Million Miles Away," they called it quits and Case debuted with *Peter Case* for Geffen in 1986, helping to launch the so-called "unplugged" movement. In 1989, he released *The Man With the Blue Post-Modern Fragmented Neo-Traditionalist Guitar*; in a *Rolling Stone* interview that year, Bruce Springsteen cited Case as the songwriter he was listening to most at the time. For 1992's *Six-Pack of Love*, Case chucked the folk aesthetic for something more rock-oriented, but the collection flopped, as did his liaison with Geffen. Meanwhile, 1993's *Peter Case Sings Like Hell* earned him a new recording contract with Vanguard in 1995 and Case came on strong for *Torn Again*, his best set of spare songs about lonesome losers since *Blue Guitar*. *—Denise Sullivan*

Peter Case / 1986 / Geffen ✦✦✦✦

This solo debut by former Plimsouls leader Peter Case shows the singer's rootsier side off quite well. Produced by T-Bone Burnett and Mitchell Froom, the primarily acoustic songs are adeptly arranged and filled with great melodies. Case has a reputation for being a bit too clever at times and on occasion the album's lyrics can be a bit obtuse, but overall songs like the Van Dyke Parks-arranged "Small Town Spree" and the harmonica-driven "Old Blue Car" rock with an immediacy that hits the listener where it should, in the gut rather than between the ears. *—Steve Kurutz*

The Man with the Blue Post Modern Fragmented Neo-Traditionalist Guitar / Apr. 11, 1989 / Geffen ✦✦✦✦✦

As more musicians started to catch the wave of the return to roots and acoustic music, Case had already delivered one gem, and this follow-up was the crowning jewel on his king-of-neo-folk crown. Again, a host of name musicians like David Hidalgo, Ry Cooder and Benmont Tench were pulled in to work out Case's songs; the story of "Poor Old Tom," the love song "Two Angels," and the semi-autobiographical "Entella Hotel" are timeless pieces by a songwriter experiencing an artistic peak. *—Denise Sullivan*

Six-Pack of Love / Mar. 1992 / Geffen ✦✦✦

A failed attempt at expanding his folk roots and augmenting it with the tricky production of Mitchell Froom, Case's simple songs were lost in the morass. A number of songs were co-written with legendary artists whom Case admires (Billy Swan, John Prine) but don't stand up against the sheer force of Case's voice and Froom's inexplicable arrangements. Nonetheless, "Beyond the Blues" by Case, Tom Russell and Bob Neuwirth and the jaunty tragedy (!) "Never Coming Home" make the record worth owning. *—Denise Sullivan*

Sings Like Hell / 1993 / Vanguard ✦✦✦✦

After a tumultuous tenure with a giant label, Case took the time to regroup and reassess his roots on *Sings Like Hell*, a set of unaccompanied traditional and modern folk songs delivered in Case's forthright manner, completely in step with the trend toward mainstream rock reclaiming roots music. The perfect introduction to traditional American music for rock fans; folk and blues fans will also appreciate the richness in Case's delivery. His reading of "Lakes of Pontchartrain" is one for the books. *—Denise Sullivan*

● **Torn Again** / Apr. 25, 1995 / Vanguard ✦✦✦✦✦

Case returns to the form he perfected on his second album and again turns to producers Larry Hirsch and J. Steven Soles for a collection of rock and folk songs—and first album of original material in three years. The tone of the pop song "Baltimore" recalls his Plimsouls sound, while "Anything" and "Breaking the Chain" are gentler, metaphorical songs with a folk-rock base. More heartfelt and less hardened, Case sings for the grown-ups. *—Denise Sullivan*

Full Service No Waiting / Feb. 17, 1998 / Vanguard ✦✦✦✦

Case doesn't get much better than this—the stories are refined, if that's possible, and his voice is stronger and clearer with age. He excels at the self-proclaimed semi-autobiographical numbers, whether on the bittersweet "On the Way Downtown," a lament like "Drunkard's Harmony" or the career retrospective "Still Playin'." With such a strong debut, follow-up and mid-career resurrection, the question still remains: when will Case achieve the recognition he deserves as one of his generation's finest songwriters? *—Denise Sullivan*

Flying Saucer Blues / Apr. 18, 2000 / Vanguard ✦✦✦✦

Never one to rely on formula, Case mixes his brand of incisive folk-rock with some simpatico musical styles for his seventh solo album, a sort of companion to its predecessor, *Full Service No Waiting*. Using a folk-rock base for songs like "Paradise Etc." and "Black Dirt & Clay," Case continues to ponder his past in song—from East Coast kid to California musician and seeker. Aiding the new dimension are a folk-blues boogie with horns, "Cool Drink O' Water," and a smoky cabaret number, "Lost in Your Eyes." An old-fashioned Mexican folk melody moves the spiritually directed "Cold Trail Blues"; there's only one of his signature long narrative pieces ("Two Heroes"). For the second time running, producer Andrew Williams guides a slight departure and successful collaboration. *—Denise Sullivan*

Thank You St. Jude / 2001 / Travelin' Light ✦✦✦✦✦

Fans of Case's captivating live shows have asked for this 13-song collection for years: It features rearranged acoustic versions of some of his most memorable songs, recorded in the stripped-down format in which he customarily bangs them out on the road hundreds of nights a year. Recorded in three afternoon sessions and accompanied only by a fiddle, Case reels and rocks through "Ice Water" from his self-titled debut album, a host of titles ("Put Down the Gun," "Two Angels," "Entella Hotel," and others) from his watershed acoustic music record, *Blue Guitar*, and various covers like the wailing Sleepy John Estes song "Someday Blues" and the previously unrecorded rocker "One More Mile." Without a doubt, Case is at the top of his form in the vocal department, with his voice reaching further than it ever did during his already-impressive younger days in the Plimsouls. This disc is an essential part of the Case catalog—a document of the state of the acoustic rock nation he had a hand in reviving in the mid-'80s and a testament to the evolution and staying power of his compositions. At the same time, new fans, particularly of acoustic folk, will find this a good introduction to the rich catalog of one of the most hardworking and consistently innovative songwriters in the hard-rockin' folk section. *—Denise Sullivan*

Cashman & West

Singer/Songwriter

Though best known for producing the classic hits of singer/songwriter Jim Croce, the team of Terry Cashman and Tommy West also enjoyed successful performing and composing careers in their own right. In 1964 Cashman joined the promotions staff of ABC Records; there he eventually teamed with songwriter Gene Pistilli. In time the duo joined forces with fellow tunesmith Tommy West. As Cashman, Pistilli & West, the threesome recorded a series of singles and a pair of LPs, 1967's *Bound to Happen* and the following year's *For Love of Ivy*, to little notice. Meanwhile, at West's urging, Capitol signed his old friend Croce and wife Ingrid to a record deal; Cashman, Pistilli & West also produced the resulting LP, 1969's *Approaching Day*, but when the record failed to generate much interest, the Croces were dropped from their contract. Soon after, Pistilli dissolved the partnership to join the Manhattan Transfer; Cashman and West continued as a duo, recording as Morning Mist before issuing 1972's *A Song or Two* under their given names and scoring a Top 30 hit with "American City Suite." When Croce signed to ABC in 1972, Cashman and West resumed production duties, and as the album *You Don't Mess Around With Jim* launched a pair of hit singles, "Operator" and the title cut, they divided their time between their own career (issuing *Moondog Serenade* in 1973) and Croce's (helming *Life and Times* and *I Got a Name*). In the wake of Croce's tragic death in a September 20, 1973, plane crash, Cashman and West issued one more LP, *Lifesong*, before ending their recording partnership, although in 1975 they founded their own label—also dubbed Lifesong—scoring a Top Ten hit the following year with Henry Gross' "Shannon." *—Jason Ankeny*

- **The AM FM Blues: Their Very Best** / 1993 / Razor & Tie ♦♦♦♦

American City Suite: The Very Best Of Cashman & West / Oct. 12, 1999 / Taragon ♦♦♦♦

Shaun Cassidy

b. Sep. 27, 1958, Los Angeles, CA
Vocals / Teen Idol, Bubblegum, Pop/Rock

A major teen idol of the late 1970s, actor/singer Shaun Cassidy rocketed to fame both on the pop charts and on television, much as his half-brother David Cassidy had done earlier in the decade. The son of actors Jack Cassidy and Shirley Jones, he was born in Hollywood on September 27, 1959 and formed his first band at the age of 11. After signing with Mike Curb's division of Warner Bros. in 1975, Cassidy issued his 1976 debut single "Morning Girl," which became a major European hit and made the singer the subject of considerable fan adulation and teen-magazine scrutiny. The follow-up, a cover of Eric Carmen's "That's Rock & Roll," was also a success abroad, especially in Australia.

Cassidy's first American release followed in early 1977: a cover of the Crystals' 1963 classic "Da Do Ron Ron," it immediately hit number one, and overnight he became a heartthrob in his native land as well as internationally. Cassidy's fame increased with the 1977 premiere of *The Hardy Boys Mysteries*, a weekly TV series based on the popular teen detective novels, and his self-titled debut LP went platinum. "That's Rock & Roll" was also reissued for American audiences, and went gold. The 1977 follow-up *Born Late* was another success, spawning the Top Ten hit "Hey Deanie."

Cassidy's fame proved short-lived, however; 1978's *Under Wraps* struggled to crack the Top 40, and 1979's *Room Service* failed to even chart. With 1980's *Wasp*, he recruited producer Todd Rundgren in an attempt to make a serious rock album, performing material from the likes of David Bowie, Pete Townshend and David Byrne; however, the LP stiffed, and Cassidy's recording career was essentially finished. Television became his primary focus, and he starred in the 1980 series *Breaking Away*, followed several years later by a stint on the soap opera *General Hospital*. After starring with David Cassidy and Petula Clark in Broadway's *Blood Brothers* in 1993, he returned to television as the creator and producer of the 1995 program *American Gothic*. *—Jason Ankeny*

- **Greatest Hits** / May 1993 / Curb ♦♦♦♦♦

Curb's 12-track *Greatest Hits* contains all of Shaun Cassidy's biggest hits, including "Da Doo Ron Ron," "That's Rock & Roll," "Hey Deanie" and "Do You Believe in Magic." While the minor hit "Our Night" is omitted, the remainder of the collection is devoted to entertainingly lightweight originals from Cassidy ("Hard Love," "Teen Dream," "Break for the Street") and covers of the Who's "So Sad About Us" and Ian Hunter's "Once Bitten, Twice Shy," making it a representative and enjoyable overview of Cassidy's brief run as a teen idol. *—Stephen Thomas Erlewine*

Cast

f. 1993
British Trad Rock, Britpop

As one of the most traditional guitar bands to emerge during the Brit-pop era of the mid-'90s, Cast has weathered negative criticism from certain quarters of the media, who labeled them as mere revivalists. But the criticism didn't prevent Cast from becoming a very, very popular band within Britain following the success of Oasis and Blur. Led by vocalist/guitarist John Power, Cast carved out a sound that was heavily indebted to the British Invasion of the early '60s, yet it was infused with a mystical, pseudo-hippie lyrical sensibility, which Power expanded upon in all of his interviews. What really made Cast into a success was Power's gift for simple, classic pop hooks, as demonstrated on the hit singles "Fine Time," "Alright," and "Walkaway."

The roots of Cast lay in the La's, the seminal late-'80s British guitar pop combo led by Lee Mavers. John Power was the bassist in the La's from their inception in the mid-'80s to the early '90s, when the band had a major British hit with their eponymous debut album. Following the supporting tour for the record, the La's were scheduled to record a second album, yet it soon became clear that Mavers was not only not going to write a batch of new songs any time soon, but he wasn't going to allow Power to contribute his own material. Power left the band, forming Cast with guitarist Liam Tyson, bassist Peter Wilkinson, and drummer Keith O'Neill early in 1994.

Cast received their first big break when Elvis Costello had the group open for him on his summer 1994 U.K. tour. By the end of 1994, Cast had signed a record contract with Polydor Records, and began recording with John Leckie (XTC, Stone Roses). "Finetime," Cast's debut single, reached number 17 on the pop charts in the spring, followed by another hit single, "Alright," in the summer. *All Change*, the band's debut, was released in October of 1995, debuting in the British Top Ten.

Over the course of 1996, Cast's audience continued to grow, as *All Change* worked its way toward platinum status, and the band toured America several times, gaining a cult audience. In the fall, the band released the single "Flying," their first new recording since their debut. The single entered the British charts at number four. Cast's second album, *Mother Nature Calls*, was released in the spring of 1997. *—Stephen Thomas Erlewine*

- **All Change** / Oct. 1995 / Polydor ♦♦♦♦

Cast's *All Change* serves as the perfect antidote to the inner rage fueling much American alternative rock—it would be hard to imagine a more gloriously upbeat backbeat of a guitar pop record, one that appeals to the eternal adolescent in each of us. The group's pedigree derives from good stock, founder John Power having served time with another fine Mersey combo the La's. But Cast transcends the hackneyed expectations of its environment, structure, and genetics through sheer, relentless quality of songcraft and performance. No sooner has one wide-eyed, hook-infested injection stormed the synapses demanding total capitulation than another of equal potency lines up to take its place. Cast vocals recall Small Faces-era Steve Marriott fused, in places, to Suede's Brett Anderson. There's a soft-psych feel to several tracks (try "Sandstorm") that calls to mind "Pictures of Matchstick Men"-era Status Quo; Cast has clearly assimilated several volumes of Bam Caruso's *Rubble* and A.I.P.'s *Electric Sugarcube Flashbacks* series, without sacrificing its power-Mod backbone. Production is brittle and uncluttered. On the lyrics front, all is positively cheery, anthemic stuff about truth, honor, living well, having fun and getting the girl, delivered exuberantly enough to strip away several coats of accumulated cynicism and almost make you believe it's possible. Two favorites are the shifting falsetto angst anthem "Tell It Like It Is" and the ballad "Walk Away"—a clue to how Mott the Hoople's "Roll Away the Stone" would have come out recorded in 1967. *—Roch Parisien*

Mother Nature Calls / Apr. 14, 1997 / Polydor ♦♦♦

If Cast's debut album *All Change* was trad-rock at its most joyous, their second album *Mother Nature Calls* is considerably more problematic. Electing to expand their sound slightly instead of replicating *All Change*, Cast paints itself into a corner. They haven't abandoned the traditional Brit-pop stylings of their debut, but they've strengthened it with a tougher sound and neo-hippie mysticism that manifests itself not only in John Power's dippy lyrics, but also in trippy instrumental sections. In theory, this is a way out of the trad-rock straitjacket, but in practice it falls flat. The main problem is that Power's melodies aren't nearly as sharp or memorable as they were on the debut; this immediately brings attention toward his lyrics, which are naive and often embarassingly simplistic. Cast also doesn't have enough charisma to save the songs with energetic, distinctive performances when they're flailing. These problems become all the more evident when they do get it right, such as on the shimmering "Guiding Star," the punchy "She Sun Shines" and the heart-tugging "I'm So Lonely (Calling You Back)," and they have the same sparkling joy that made *All Change* a delight. But that's a rarity on *Mother Nature Calls*. When the tunes and attitude are there, such weaknesses are easy to overlook, but since Cast comes up deficient on both counts, *Mother Nature Calls* is simply a dull listen. *—Stephen Thomas Erlewine*

Magic Hour / May 1999 / Polydor ♦♦♦

Magic Hour is a slight step up from Cast's sophomore release *Mother Nature Calls*. Opening with the rousing, party-ready anthem "Beat Mama" (which is, surprisingly, accentuated with a breakbeat), at least half of this album is a return to the more hard-rocking roots of their debut LP *All Change*. The best songs here recall classic hard rock bands like AC/DC and the Who—Cast offer the same loud, arena-ready guitar anthems. The catch, however, is that many of the ballads feel like filler. With the sole exception of the string-laden title-track, most of the slow songs merely serve as breaks between the louder, more uptempo numbers, and fail to make much of an impression on their own. Still, *Magic Hour* is an improvement in quality and proves that Cast is not simply a one-hit wonder. *—Jason Damas*

The Castaways

f. 1962, Minneapolis, MN
Garage Rock

Best remembered for their garage-rock perennial "Liar Liar," the Castaways formed in 1962 around the nucleus of guitarist Roy Hensley, bassist Dick Roby and drummer Denny Craswell; originally founded simply to perform at a fraternity party, the group proved such a smashing success that it remained an ongoing concern, expanding to a quintet with the subsequent additions of lead guitarist Bob Folschow and keyboardist Jim Donna. The Castaways' lone hit, "Liar Liar" was written by Donna and released on the Soma label in 1965, reaching the number 12 slot on the U.S. charts on the strength of its inimitable echo-drenched vocals and wheezing keyboards. A series of follow-up efforts flopped, however, and despite an appearance in the 1967 film *It's a Bikini World*, the Castaways' career ground to a halt, although the band often performed live in the decades to follow. *—Jason Ankeny*

- **Liar Liar: The Best of the Castaways** / Sep. 28, 1999 / Plum ♦♦♦♦

One of the great one-hit wonders of the mid-'60s, the Castaways were a Minneapolis group with a catchy, garage sound best exemplified by their lone national hit, "Liar Liar." This 22-track anthology takes listeners through the band's entire history, right up to the present time, including a "Liar Liar 2000" remake. Along the way, the band goes through the customary stylistic changes (from garage to Beatles cops to soul to psychedelia) in search of that elusive second hit that most bands go through, trying new styles to fit the changing times until coming full circle back to their original sound. Great notes on the band's history and the new cuts brings a nice sense of closure to the package. *—Cub Koda*

Jimmy Castor

b. Jun. 1943, New York, NY
Vocals, Saxophone / Funk

A master of novelty/disco funk, saxophonist Jimmy Castor started as a doo wop singer in

New York. He wrote and recorded "I Promise to Remember" for Wing With the Juniors in 1956, a group whose roster included Al Casey, Jr., Orton Graves, and Johnny Williams. Castor replaced Frankie Lymon in the Teenagers in 1957 before switching to sax in 1960. He appeared on several soul-jazz and Afro-Latin sessions and had a solo hit with "Hey Leroy, Your Mama's Callin' You" on Smash in 1966. Castor also played sax on Dave "Baby" Cortez's hit "Rinky Dink." He formed the Jimmy Castor Bunch in 1972 and signed with RCA. Their first release, *It's Just Begun*, launched Castor's next phase with the song "Troglodyte (Cave Man)." It was a Top Ten R&B and pop smash. Castor continued the trend in 1975 with "The Bertha Butt Boogie" and later recorded "E-Man Boogie," "King Kong," "Bom Bom," and "Amazon." The Castor band included keyboardist/trumpeter Gerry Thomas, bassist Doug Gibson, guitarist Harry Jensen, conga player Lenny Fridle, Jr., and drummer Bobby Manigault. Thomas left the band to join the Fatback band. Castor recorded as a solo performer from 1976 until 1988. He had one of his bigger hits in many years with a 1988 revival of "Love Makes a Woman," which paired him with disco diva Joyce Sims. Castor had his own label, Long Distance, in the '80s. —*Ron Wynn*

● **Everything Man: The Best of the Jimmy Castor Bunch** / Nov. 21, 1995 / Rhino ✦✦✦✦
Some music is just so immediately full of the groove and desire to dance that anyone who doesn't or can't must be dead, if still breathing. Jimmy Castor is a master of same, and if the slightly overheated claims in the knowledgeable and appreciative liner notes for this excellent compilation making him second only to James Brown might be a bit much in cold print, the music is its own best argument for his quality. Starting with his great Latin/soul hit "Hey Leroy, Your Mama's Callin' You" and concluding with an item from his doo wop days in the '50s, "I Promise to Remember," *Everything Man* covers whole eras of American popular music with style and skill. The two numbers that sealed his fame and reputation into the hip-hop era are unsurprisingly here: the Latin funk monster "It's Just Begun," with one of the deepest bass lines in creation and a fantastic mid-song percussion breakdown, and "Troglodyte," with its freakish, wigged-out spoken word intro. Bertha Butt of the Butt Sisters makes her first legendary appearance here, while the snarling guitar and grunting bass perfectly match Castor's rasped, hilarious shaggy dog tale about caveman love. Those are just two highlights of a well-chosen and brilliantly mastered set, with many guest appearances from Bertha and Leroy both (the deep grunt of "Bertha Butt Boogie," "The Return of Leroy, Pt. 1," and so forth). Castor's penchant for bizarro covers is discussed but not included among the cuts—presumably all for the better, given selections like "You Light Up My Life"—but his sharp take on Redbone's "Maggie" does make the grade. Other great cuts include the vocal tradeoffs on "Potential" between Castor and his bandmembers, the monster stomp and shake of "Supersound," and the upbeat, salsa-tinged "Bom Bom." —*Ned Raggett*

Cat Power

Vocals, Guitar, Piano / Sadcore, Indie Rock, Singer/Songwriter
Cat Power was the alias of Chan Marshall, a Southern-bred singer/songwriter whose father Charlie was an itinerant pianist. After dropping out of high school, Marshall found herself in New York; performing under the name Cat Power, she was booked as the opening act for Liz Phair, where she met Sonic Youth drummer Steve Shelley and Two Dollar Guitar's Tim Foljahn, who agreed to become her backing band. Following the release of 1995's *Dear Sir* and 1996's *Myra Lee*—both recorded on the same day—Cat Power signed to Matador for 1996's *What Would the Community Think?*, which won acclaim for Marshall's unsettling, emotional songs and cathartic vocals. The superb *Moon Pix* followed two years later, and in the spring of 2000 Cat Power resurfaced with *The Covers Record*. —*Jason Ankeny*

Dear Sir / Oct. 1995 / Plain ✦✦✦
Cat Power's first full-length album, *Dear Sir*, spotlights Chan Marshall's demanding but rewarding songwriting. Her distinctive blend of blues, country, folk and punk creates songs like the dark, noisy "Itchyhead" and "Rockets," which mixes tension and hope, and tops it with Marshall's earnest, expressive vocals. Though the album needs the listener's complete attention, *Dear Sir* more than keeps it with nine of Marshall's searching meditations on life. —*Heather Phares*

Myra Lee / Mar. 1996 / Smells Like Records ✦✦✦✦
The 1996 album *Myra Lee* presents a more diverse and fully developed version of Cat Power's music, ranging from the winding, acoustic menace of "Enough" to the sinewy rock of "We All Die." Introspective epics like "Great Expectations," "Faces" and "Wealthy Man" use churning tempos and spiraling guitars to convey Marshall's melancholy musical vision, but gentler songs like the trembling cover of Hank Williams' "Still in Love" and originals like "Top Expert" and "Ice Water" are parts of the picture as well, adding warmth and roundness to the album. As always, Marshall's yearning voice lends extra emotion to her songs, whether it's her clear, soaring vocals on the new version of "Rockets" or her distant, half-heard moans on the final track "Not What You Want," which sounds genuine to the point of eavesdropping. This raw, overheard sound infuses *Myra Lee* with a sonic honesty that matches the album's heartfelt songwriting. —*Heather Phares*

What Would the Community Think / Sep. 10, 1996 / Matador ✦✦✦✦
What Would the Community Think was the second album Chan Marshall released in 1996, but its richness suggests a longer period of evolution. From the first warm notes of "In This Hole," it's clear that Marshall's voice—as a singer and a songwriter—is not only stronger and more focused, but more empathetic as well. Where her previous works were dense and cathartic, *What Would the Community Think* gives her voice and lyrics space to unfurl and involve the listener; the title track alone holds an album's worth of eloquence in Marshall's hushed, clear vocals, backed by guitar, feedback and an eerie, echoing piano. Fortunately, that leaves Marshall 11 other tracks with which to forge a fine

balance between angular, angst-ridden punk and her gentler, folk-country tendencies. Different combinations of these extremes make Cat Power's sound more diverse but also more cohesive. Tense, tight songs like "Good Clean Fun" and "Nude as the News" retain the reflective, thoughtful nature of quieter numbers like "King Rides By" and "Water and Air," which turn the power of the album's louder moments into slow-building, implosive tension. Two of *What Would the Community Think*'s finest moments, "They Tell Me" and "Taking People," are unabashedly blues and country-inflected, revealing Marshall not just as a cathartic vocalist, but as a true soul singer. Similarly, her covers of Peter Jefferies' "Fate of the Human Carbine" and Smog's "Bathysphere" show off Marshall's ability to make any song a Cat Power song. An intimate, personal album, *What Would the Community Think* makes imperfection beautiful and turns vulnerability into musical strength. —*Heather Phares*

● **Moon Pix** / Sep. 22, 1998 / Matador ✦✦✦✦✦
Cat Power's 1998 album *Moon Pix* continues Chan Marshall's transformation from an indie rock Cassandra into a reflective, accomplished singer/songwriter. Where her previous works were an urgent, aching mix of punk, folk, and blues, *Moon Pix* is truly soul(ful) music: warm, reflective, complex, and cohesive.

For this album, Marshall moved the recording sessions for the album to Australia, and switched her rhythm section to the Dirty Three's Mick Turner and Jim White; the lineup changes add new depth and light to her compelling, intricate guitar work and gently insistent vocals. From the backwards drum loop on "American Flag" (borrowed from the Beastie Boys' "Paul Revere") to the fluttering, smoky flutes on "He Turns Down" to the double-tracked vocals and crashing thunderstorms of "Say," *Moon Pix*'s expressive arrangements mirror the songs' fine emotional shadings. Marshall is sunny on the quietly hopeful "You May Know Him," hypnotic and seductive on "Cross Bones Style," and poignant on "Colors & the Kids," where she sings, "It's so hard to go into the city/Because you want to say hi, hello, I love you to everybody." As natural and refined as a pearl, *Moon Pix* is a collection of fragile yet strong songs that reveal Marshall's unique, personal songwriting talents in their full glory. —*Heather Phares*

The Covers Record / Mar. 21, 2000 / Matador ✦✦✦
On the *The Covers Record*, Chan Marshall continues her evolution into a remarkably expressive interpreter of songs; her earlier covers of Pavement's "We Dance" and Smog's "Bathysphere" are among her most distinctive performances. This collection includes songs originally by Bob Dylan, the Rolling Stones, the Velvet Underground, Moby Grape, Michael Hurley, and Anonymous. Marshall's sparest album yet, *The Covers Record* uses guitar and piano as the only foils for her malleable, emotional voice. These tools are more than enough to turn the Stones' anthem "(I Can't Get No) Satisfaction" into a bluesy, slinky version emphasizing the song's tension and frustration as much as its jaded sexiness, and "Kingston Town" from a reggae standard into a hymnal reflection. Marshall's gentle version of Hurley's "Sweedeedee" and plaintive reading of the Velvets' "I Found a Reason" recall the quietest, most spiritual moments from *Moon Pix*. This culminates on the cover of her own "In This Hole" from *What Would the Community Think*, one of the most drastic revisions, its soft pianos and serene vocals replace the original's turbulent anguish, reflecting her changing musical path. Marshall explores many emotional directions, from her yearning version of Moby Grape's "Naked If I Want To" to her brooding sensuality on "Wild Is the Wind," to her down-home optimism on Bob Dylan's "Paths of Victory." "Salty Dog"'s lilting melody and humorous lyrics bring out Marshall's Georgia twang, while her version of Smog's "Red Apples" shows off her voice's sensual lows and keening highs. The joyous cover of "Sea of Love" (originally by Phil Phillips) brings this accomplished, heartfelt *Covers Record* to a very happy end. —*Heather Phares*

Catatonia

f. 1991, Wales
Indie Pop, Post-Grunge, Indie Rock, Britpop, Alternative Pop/Rock
The most traditional pop band of all the Welsh bands to emerge in the post-Brit-pop days of the mid-'90s, Catatonia reworked the sound of jangling late-'80s alternative rock with the punchy, amateurish indie-rock attack. Comprised of vocalist Cerys Matthews, guitarist/vocalist Mark Roberts, guitarist Owen, bassist Paul Jones and drummer Aled Richards, Catatonia formed in Cardiff, Wales in the early '90s. Matthews and Roberts used to busk together in Cardiff before officially forming the band.

Catatonia released its first EP, *For Tinkerbell*, in 1993. At the time, the band featured Matthews, Roberts, Jones, drummer Dafydd Ieuan and keyboardist C. Pegg. The same line-up recorded *Hooked*, which was released the following year. After the release of *Hooked*, both Pegg and Ieuan left the band; Dafydd went on to join Super Furry Animals. Replacing Ieuan with Aled Richards, the group released "Sweet Catatonia" in late 1995 and then added in Owen as a second guitarist. Early in 1996, "You've Got a Lot to Answer For" became the band's first charting single, appearing at number 35 on the British charts. A full-length album, *Way Beyond Blue*, followed in September, and it was greeted with positive reviews, peaking at number 40 on the charts. Catatonia returned in 1998 with their second album, *International Velvet*, a British smash which hit the top of the charts and stayed there for several weeks thanks to the hit singles "I Am the Mob" and "Mulder and Scully." *Equally Cursed and Blessed* followed in the spring of 2000. —*Stephen Thomas Erlewine*

The Sublime Magic of Catatonia / Feb. 1996 / Nursery ✦✦✦✦
The Sublime Magic of Catatonia is the group's first, independent album, and while it's a little rough around the edges, it is a ragged collection of terrific pop, highlighted by "Bleed," "Whale," "Hooked" and "Fall Beside Her." —*Stephen Thomas Erlewine*

● **Way Beyond Blue** / Sep. 30, 1996 / Blanco Y Negro ✦✦✦✦✦
Catatonia's major-label debut *Way Beyond Blue* is an infectious set of jangle-pop, injected

with the punkish attitude of indie-rock. The guitars ring as if they were recorded in the late '80s, but it has a muscular backbone, and vocalist Cerys Matthews has a tough edge to her voice, which never makes the music sound weak. And a good majority of the songs—from "Sweet Catatonia" and "You've Got A Lot To Answer For" to "Painful" and "Way Beyond Blue"—are excellent, shimmering pop gems, making it an impressive debut. —*Stephen Thomas Erlewine*

Equally Cursed & Blessed / Mar. 28, 2000 / Atlantic ◆◆◆◆

Equally Cursed and Blessed is another breath of fresh pop air from Catatonia. Cerys Matthews' distinctive vocal roars and whispers are in full force throughout these tracks, and the blend of songs on this release surpasses all of Catatonia's prior collections. The first single, the weeping "Dead From the Waist Down" features a full string section, and the magnificent "Karaoke Queen" is backed by a disco beat and razor-sharp guitar hooks. Pure pop like "She's a Millionaire" helps color the album on the brighter side, while the dark, brooding "Bulimic Beats" adds depth. Closing the album is the excellent "Dazed, Beautiful, and Bruised" where Matthews sends off an abusive former lover. *Equally Cursed and Blessed* could easily be Catatonia's chance to break into the United States, because with music like this, you simply can't go wrong. —*Jason Damas*

Paper Scissors Stone / Aug. 6, 2001 / Blanco Y Negro ◆◆

Catherine Wheel

f. Apr. 1990, Great Yarmouth, England
Shoegazing, Alternative Pop/Rock

By using their influences as a mere launching pad and consistently developing their many strengths, Catherine Wheel was able to outlast all of their early peers. The band from East Anglia fit snugly with the remainder of bands that the British press eventually labeled as shoegazers with their initial singles and first album, *Ferment*. The cinematic *Chrome* followed in 1993, toughening the band's sound and providing increased exposure on U.S. alternative radio through "Crank." As always, extensive touring ensued and the band's heavier edge on stage was captured on 1995's *Happy Days*, which hardcore fans dismissed for being too flat-out rock for their tastes. Neo-metal single "Waydown" was the radio staple in the U.S., giving the band more exposure than ever. Meanwhile, Catherine Wheel had been stockpiling spectacular B-sides that only rabid collectors and those who would listen to their tales of depleted wallets knew about. To provide a stop-gap between albums, *Like Cats and Dogs* was released in 1996, which only contained a small fraction of those extras. Ingeniously, those that were selected were sequenced in a manner that resembled a regular studio album; the immediacy and experimentalism of the hodgepodge made for the band's best full-length in the eyes of several fans. Peeling back from the aural onslaught of *Happy Days*, they exposed more of their atmospheric knack on 1997's *Adam and Eve*, which was designed specifically to play as a single piece. The transitional *Wishville*, released in 2000, saw the band weather creative blockage, a label shift and a lineup change. The always tuneful Catherine Wheel survived by refusing to repeat themselves and remaining accessible to their constantly swelling fanbase by touring like dogs. They might not have reached the level of popularity that they aimed for, but their career was one that most bands would commit felonies to experience. —*Andy Kellman*

Ferment / Jun. 9, 1992 / Fontana ◆◆◆◆◆

Centered around re-recorded versions of four songs from the band's two Wilde Club singles and the seven minute lovelorn "Black Metallic"—which was referred to as the "Like a Hurricane" of the '90s—the deeply rich *Ferment* firmly established Catherine Wheel amongst the shoegaze contingent of the early '90s. The band would proceed to denounce the shoegaze tag, but it was a fitting one, at least with everything they released prior to 1993's harder edged *Chrome*. Along with bands like Lush, Ride, and Slowdive, Catherine Wheel buried their sing-along melodies in wafts of distortion and blurry production values. Rob Dickinson had yet to find comfort as a lead singer, so his somewhat fey and dazed emoting blended perfectly with Tim Friese-Greene's comfy production. A fair amount of the bands thrown into the same category as Catherine Wheel were criticized for lacking knowledge of their instruments, but a couple listens to *Ferment* should prove that they were hardly amateurish. The employment of numerous guitar pedals didn't serve as a smoke-and-mirrors ruse, and Friese-Greene knew enough to allow room for bassist Dave Hawes and drummer Neil Sims to flex their able muscles. Dickinson and lead guitarist Brian Futter were immensely skilled and complementary to each other from the band's inception; certainly they were one of the most unrecognized guitar duos of their stylistic brethren. Like all fine debuts, *Ferment* is varied emotionally, ranging from lust ("I Want to Touch You") to bliss ("Shallow" and "Salt"). It's a record that makes you want to crawl inside its sleeve and remain. It's as welcoming as it is insular and sheltered. —*Andy Kellman*

● **Chrome** / Jul. 20, 1993 / Fontana ◆◆◆◆◆

The biggest change in Catherine Wheel's sound, whether from Gil Norton's production or the decision of the band as a whole, is in *Chrome*'s general aggressiveness: not brutish, but definitely more in your face, even as Dickinson's lyrics and singing call to mind emotional calamities and internal collapses as much as exultation. The edges are a touch sharper, the sound bursts from the speakers, and Futter in particular earns his deserved guitar god reputation, peeling off powerful rhythms and brilliant, non-wanky solos in profusion. "I Confess" is a great example of how the two work well together, Dickinson taking advantage of a quieter passage to softly sing, "Took too many drugs, popped too many pills" before a massive, charging crash back into the song. Other strong numbers include the snarling title track, one of the band's angriest and most passionate, and the anthemic up-and-out surge of "Ursa Major Space Station," named after a guitar pedal and yet anything but cold technical ability. The real ringer is at the end, the poppy burst of "Show Me Mary," which slightly hints at where *Happy Days* would end up. When it comes

to the absolute highlight, though, it's "Pain." While it has similar loud/soft dynamics as "Black Metallic," the shifts are crisper and the deep ache conveyed by the lyrics all that much more powerful. Add on some simply stunning guitar in the mid-song break, and it's another example of the Wheel's abilities. —*Ned Raggett*

Happy Days / May 1995 / Fontana/Mercury ◆◆◆

A good percentage of Catherine Wheel's fans might have chucked *Happy Days* out of their players after the unleashing of Rob Dickinson's David Coverdale-like "oooh" during the brain bash of "God Inside My Head." In the event that the listener had the open-mindedness required to tackle the lengthy record in whole, they would have heard more *Headbanger's Ball* vocalisms, wanky guitar solos, and some lyrical passages that would lead admirers of *Ferment* and *Chrome* to wonder what happened. "Grow my hair long and strange/I'll be a walking mountain range?" What the? Although the onslaught of pounding, throbbing hard rock prevails throughout the course of *Happy Days*, there are moments of respite. "Heal" tugs the heartstrings, summing up the record's theme of combating cynicism and coming to grips with adulthood. (The line "Everyone needs someone to live by" comes straight from Talk Talk.) The smoldering eight-minute "Eat My Dust" is unfortunately buried half way through the record. It's easy to get lost in the web of dazzling atmospherics. But more than anything, the greatest challenge of *Happy Days* is wading through it. At 14 songs and 58 minutes, it's not necessarily bloated for records of its time, but with the tug of war between cocksure heaviness and grandiose pop, it's a chore to get through. It's only four minutes longer than *Chrome*, but it feels like it doubles it in length. The band seems like they lowered themselves to make a play for the U.S. alternative charts, but they undeniably sound full of fire. The record undeniably misses the imagination of their previous conquests, and it ultimately sounds like a lesser band. Metal health *will* drive you mad. —*Andy Kellman*

Like Cats and Dogs / Sep. 9, 1996 / Mercury ◆◆◆◆

Like Cats and Dogs is a somewhat puzzling but still masterful hodgepodge that pieces together roughly one-fourth of Catherine Wheel's load of B-sides, adding a few studio outtakes. Rather than continuing the band's upward scale into harder material, *Cats and Dogs* scales it back to showcase the atmospheric, somber side of the band. Oddly enough, the record all but ignores the blinding number of excellent *Ferment*-era extras, which, when put together, would make for a recording nearly as solid as their debut. Roughly half of the tracks come from *Chrome*'s singles/EPs. The minimalism and immediacy of some of the tracks favorably bring to mind the last days of Talk Talk, most notably *Laughing Stock*. It's no small coincidence that Catherine Wheel have been working with Talk Talk's Tim Friese-Greene since their early days. The delicate "Girl Stand Still" is the House of Love's "Love in a Car" times two, finishing with a noisy climax. The band's walloping fireworks aren't completely forsaken, however. "High Heels" stomps and seethes, with Rob Dickinson sounding like a crazed self-doubter nearing the brink of losing it. "Tongue Twisted" weaves Dickinson and Brian Futter's guitars into a double helix of paranoia and claustrophobia. "Harder Than I Am," is one of their most jarring, soul-bearing songs, nailed with a beautiful sing-along chorus. *Like Cats and Dogs* may have frustrated many of the band's admirers who hadn't shelled out the cash for the band's numerous multi-format, limited edition singles, as this does nothing to appease the completist. It does expose some relatively hidden sides of one of the most range-roaming rock bands of the '90s. —*Andy Kellman*

Adam and Eve / Jul. 29, 1997 / Mercury ◆◆◆◆

With Catherine Wheel's records getting heavier, harder, and more bloated in succession, it came as great relief that their fourth proper record would provide a change. From the opening atonal plink of Brian Futter's guitar on "Future Boy," it is apparent that they're focusing more than ever on the use of sublime atmospherics, an arrow in the band's quiver that had only been exposed briefly during prior outings on their full-lengths and largely shelved for use as B-sides until then. Prior comparisons to Pink Floyd didn't make a great deal of sense, but here they did. The solemn, dusky edge to the likes of "Future Boy" and "Ma Solituda" recalls parts of *Wish You Were Here* and *Animals*, although leaning toward pop and removing most strains of gargoyle rock. Furthermore, when was the last time a song was closed off with the sound of a car door being slammed?

The references don't end there. The constant, repetitive drum pattern from Neil Sims that forms the basis of the ten-times gorgeous "Thunderbird" is lifted from Talk Talk's "After the Flood." Much more than a batch of smart references, *Adam and Eve* is a cold splash of water in the face of the pessimistic and cynical. Even in the most melancholy of *Adam and Eve*'s songs, there's an uplifting quality that carries throughout, extracting most of the emotional detritus that seeped through the band's earlier work. Not everything is windswept atmospherics, either. The romping "Delicious" catches Rob Dickinson at his most randy, imagining he's Bruce Lee and Michael Caine. "Broken Nose" and "Satellite" are dynamic, muscular modern rock at its finest. Anyone finding that some of this material errs on the side of sappiness or boldness really needs more sunshine in their life. —*Andy Kellman*

Wishville / May 2000 / Columbia ◆◆

Nick Cave (Nicholas Edward Cave)

b. Sep. 22, 1957, Wangaratta, Victoria, Australia
Vocals, Piano, Organ / Post-Punk, Alternative Pop/Rock, Singer/Songwriter

After goth pioneers the Birthday Party called it quits in 1983, singer/songwriter Nick Cave assembled the Bad Seeds, a post-punk supergroup featuring former Birthday Party guitarist Mick Harvey on drums, ex-Magazine bassist Barry Adamson, and Einsturzende Neubauten guitarist Blixa Bargeld. With the Bad Seeds, Cave continued to explore his obsessions with religion, death, love, America, and violence with a bizarre, sometimes self-consciously eclectic hybrid of blues, gospel, rock, and arty post-punk, although in a more subdued fashion than his work with the Birthday Party. Cave also allowed his literary aspirations to come to the forefront; the lyrics are narrative prose, heavy on literary allusions and myth-making and taking some inspiration from Leonard Cohen. Cave's gloomy lyrics, dark musical arrangements, and deep baritone voice recall the albums of Scott Walker, who also obsessed over death and love with a frightening passion. However, Cave brings a hefty amount of post-punk experimentalism to Walker's epic dark pop. *—Stephen Thomas Erlewine & Steve Huey*

From Her to Eternity / 1984 / Mute/Elektra ✦✦✦✦✦
Nick Cave launched his solo career in style with *From Her to Eternity,* an accomplished album mixing the frenzy and power of his Birthday Party days with a dank, moody atmosphere that showed he was not interested in simply continuing what the older group had done. To be sure, Mick Harvey joined him from the Party days, as ever playing a variety of instruments, while one-time Party guest Blixa Bargeld now became a permanent Cave partner, splitting his time between the Bad Seeds and Einsturzende Neubaten ever since. The group took wing with a harrowing version of Leonard Cohen's "Avalanche," Cave's wracked, buried tones suiting the Canadian legend's words perfectly, and never looked back. *From Her to Eternity* is crammed with any number of doom-laden songs, with Cave the understandable center of attention, his commanding vocals turning the blues and rural music into theatrical exhibitionism unmatched since Jim Morrison stalked stages. Songs like "Cabin Fever," with its steadily paced drumming and relentless piano line, and the more restrained and moody "The Moon Is in the Gutter" sound like cabarets in hell. "In the Ghetto," already perfectly suited to such a treatment, shows the underlying sense of beauty that defines the Seeds as much as drama. Even though it's a Presley cover, the sense of Scott Walker's influence isn't far away at all. The title track is and remains a Bad Seeds classic, played at shows up through the present, a tense piano/organ beginning then accompanied by the edgy build of the band, pounding drums, stabbing feedback and keyboard parts and more. *—Ned Raggett*

The Firstborn Is Dead / 1985 / Mute ✦✦✦✦
The blues had long been a potent undercurrent in the Birthday Party's music, so it wasn't all that surprising that Nick Cave embraced the sound and feeling of rural blues on his second album with the Bad Seeds, *The Firstborn Is Dead.* What was startling was how well Cave and his bandmates—Barry Adamson, Mick Harvey, and Blixa Bargeld—were able to absorb and honor the influences of artists like Skip James and Charley Patton while creating a sound that was unmistakably their own. The moody obsessions of rural blues—trains, floods, imprisonment, sin, fear, and death—seemed made to order for Cave, and he was able to tap into the doomy iconography of this music with potent emotional force; on "Tupelo," he makes a sweeping and disturbing epic of the rain-swept night when Elvis Presley was born, and "Knocking on Joe" is a tale of life on the work gang that communicates the pain of the spirit as clearly as the ache of the body. Also, the blues helped transform Cave's music as well as his lyrics; the brutal sonic pummel of the Birthday Party here gave way to a more subtle and dynamic approach that still made effective use of dissonance and bare-wired electric guitar noise while proving the balance of loud and soft only made each side deeper and more resonant. (The stark, barely there guitar and drums of "Blind Lemon Jefferson" are as startling and malignantly fascinating as anything in the Birthday Party's catalog.) *The Firstborn Is Dead* proved Nick Cave's musical palate was significantly broader than his debut album suggested and pointed to a path (channeling the sounds and emotions of American roots music) he would return to on many of his albums that followed. *—Mark Deming*

Kicking Against the Pricks / 1986 / Mute/Elektra ✦✦✦✦
Besides being noteworthy as an astonishingly good all-covers album, *Kicking Against the Pricks* is notable for the arrival of a new key member for the Seeds, drummer Thomas Wydler. Besides being a fine percussionist, able to perform at both the explosive and restrained levels Cave requires, Wydler also allowed Harvey to concentrate on adding guitar and keyboards live as well as in the studio, a notable bonus. Race reappears briefly to add some guitar while former Birthday Party cohorts Rowland Howard and Tracy Pew guest as well, the latter on some of his last tracks before his untimely death. The selection of songs is quite impressive, ranging from old standards like "Long Black Veil" to everything from John Lee Hooker's "I'm Gonna Kill That Woman" and Gene Pitney's pop aria "Something's Gotten Hold of My Heart." Matching the range of material, the Seeds are well on their way to becoming the rock/cabaret/blues showband of Cave's dreams, able to conjure up haunting, winsome atmospheres ("Sleeping Annaleah") as much as higher-volume takes (Roy Orbison's "Running Scared," the Velvet Underground's "All Tomorrow's Parties"). The version of Leadbelly's "Black Betty" is particularly grand, Harvey's drumming driving the track with ominous power. This said, often holding everything back is the key, as the creepout build of "Hey Joe" demonstrates. Even more striking is how Cave's own vocals rebut the charges that all he ever does is overdramatize everything he sings—consider the husky, purring delivery on Johnny Cash's "The Singer." Other winners include a masterful version of Jimmy Webb's "By the Time I Get to Phoenix" and the stately, album-closing "The Carnival Is Over," originally a mid-'60s hit for the Seekers. *—Ned Raggett*

Your Funeral . . . My Trial / 1986 / Mute/Elektra ✦✦✦
Reduced to a quartet for the most part, with Adamson joining Cave, Bargeld, Harvey and Wydler on only a couple of tracks, the Seeds turn from the interpretive triumph of *Kicking Against the Pricks* to another strong high, the mostly-original *Your Funeral . . . My Trial.* The one cover is a sharp, unsurprisingly dramatic version of Tim Rose's "Long Time Man." As for the rest of the album, *Trial* shows the Seeds working as, again, a remarkably accomplished and varied act, ever available and ready to explore a wide range of musics distilled into Cave's often dark, always passionate vision. Arguably Cave and company have by now so clearly established their overall style that *Your Funeral . . . My Trial* is much more a refinement of the past than anything else, but so good is their work that resistance is near impossible. If anything, the brooding power of the Seeds is more restrained than ever, suggesting destructive endings and overwhelming love without directly playing it. Songs like "Jacks Shadow" and the gentler but still melancholy moods of "Sad Waters," detailing a riverside scene between a couple, are simply grand. The opening title track sets the mood well, Cave handling not merely vocals but Hammond organ, adding a strangely sweet air to the late-night atmosphere of the piece. "The Carny" is a definite highlight, the cracked music-box/carnival accompaniment courtesy of Harvey utterly appropriate for Cave's tale of a circus gone horribly wrong in ways Edward Gorey would appreciate. "Hard On for Love," as the title pretty clearly gives away, is at once sensual and blunt right down to the lyrics, Biblical references and all, as the feverish music rises in a tide of emotion. *—Ned Raggett*

Tender Prey / 1988 / Mute ✦✦✦✦✦
With guitarist/keyboardist Roland Wolf and Cramps/Gun Club veteran Kid Congo Powers on guitar added to the ranks, along with guest appearances from old member Race, the Seeds reached 1988 with their strongest album yet, the insanely powerful, gripping *Tender Prey.* Rather than simply redoing what they'd already done, Cave and company took their striking musical fusions to deeper and higher levels all around, with fantastic consequences. The album boldly starts out with an undisputed Cave masterpiece—"The Mercy Seat," a chilling self-portrait of a prisoner about to be executed that compares the electric chair with the throne of God. Queasy strings from a Gini Ball-led trio and Harvey's spectral piano snake through a rising roar of electric sound—a common musical approach from many earlier Seeds songs, but never so gutwrenching as here. Cave's own performance is the perfect icing on the cake, commanding and powerful, excellently capturing the blend of crazed fear and righteousness in the lyrics. Matching that high point turns out to be impossible for anything else on *Tender Prey,* but more than enough highlights take a bow that demonstrate the album's general quality. "Deanna" is another great blast from the Seeds, a garage rock style rave-up that lyrically is everything *Natural Born Killers* tried to be, but failed at—killing sprees, Cadillacs and carrying out the work of the Lord, however atypically. The echoing, gentle-yet-rough sonics on the Blind Willie Johnson-inspired "City of Refuge" and the gentler drama of "Sugar Sugar Sugar" also do well in keeping the energy level up. On the quieter side, Cave indulges his penchant for gloomy piano-led ballads throughout, and quite well at that, with such songs as "Watching Alice," "Mercy" and the end-of-the-evening singalong "New Morning." "Sunday's Slave" has a beautifully brooding feeling to it thanks to the combination of acoustic guitar and piano, making it a bit of a cousin of Scott Walker's "Seventh Seal." *—Ned Raggett*

The Good Son / Oct. 1990 / Mute ✦✦✦
Losing Wolf, aside from the final reprise of "Lucy," but otherwise making no changes in the line-up, the Seeds followed up *Tender Prey* with the equally brilliant but generally calmer *Good Son.* At the time of its release there were more than a few comments that Cave had somehow softened or sold out, given how he was more intent on exploring his dark, cabaret pop stylings than his thrashy, explosive side. This not only ignored the constant examples of such quieter material all the way back to *From Her to Eternity,* but Cave's own constant threads of lyrical darkness, whether in terms of romance or something all the more distressing. This said, the softly crooning group vocals and sweet strings on the opening "Foi Na Cruz" certainly would catch some off guard. The title track itself captured the overall mood of the album, a retelling of the Bible's prodigal son story from the other son, the one who stayed at home and did what he was meant to do. The elegant, reflective "Lucy" and the staccato then sweeping "Lament" are two further high points, but the flat-out winners come dead center. "The Weeping Song," a magnificent duet between Cave and Bargeld, starts out sounding a bit like Gene Pitney's "Something's Gotta Hold of My Heart," which the Seeds covered on *Pricks,* before shading into its own powerful, blasted drama. "The Ship Song," meanwhile, equals if not overtakes the Scott Walker ballads Cave so clearly is inspired by, a soaring, tearjerking declaration of intense love that's simply amazing. *—Ned Raggett*

Henry's Dream / May 12, 1992 / Mute ✦✦✦✦
Continuing the creative roll of *Tender Prey* and *The Good Son, Henry's Dream* showed the band in fierce and fine fettle once more. The biggest change was with the choice of producer—David Briggs, famed for his work on some of Neil Young's strongest albums. While Cave later thought the experiment didn't work as well as he might have hoped, Briggs does a fine enough job, perhaps not letting the group's full intensity through but still capturing a live feel nonetheless. Cave himself offers up another series of striking, compelling lyrics again exploring love, lust and death. Here, though, some of his images are the strongest he's yet delivered, especially with the near apocalyptic "Papa Won't Leave You, Henry," which begins the album brilliantly as the narrator lurches through a landscape of storms, brothels and urban decay. Equally powerful, if slower and calmer, is *Dream*'s lead single, "Straight to You," with Cave delivering a forceful declaration of love. It's the near equal of "The Ship Song," the same sense of beautiful sweep running free. Other numbers like "Brother, My Cup is Empty" and "I Had a Dream, Joe" showcase the Seeds' peerless abilities at fusing older styles with noisy aggression and tension. The former is especially strong, almost dripping with soft then loud musical drama. The quieter numbers aren't to be ignored, though, such as the string-laden "Christina the Astonishing" and especially "Loom of the Land." One of Cave's best songs ever, his portrait of a nighttime walk with a lover is Romantic with a capital R, with a sweet passion that matches the soothing performance from the Seeds, topped off with a particularly fine chorus. *—Ned Raggett*

Live Seeds / Sep. 28, 1993 / Mute ✦✦✦✦
Exactly what it says it is, and quite good at that—some fans consider many of the songs

on *Live* to be superior to their studio equivalents, testament to its overall quality. Recorded at various spots on the *Henry's Dream* tour and originally sold with a small picture book documenting said tour, *Live* features the same sextet that performed on *Dream* bringing the noise with commanding authority. Cave himself is unsurprisingly in excelsis, his declamatory and quieter sides both showcased with skill. Harvey and Bargeld's guitar exploits, sometimes snarling with fire and other times strumming with deceptive calm, lead the charge from the rest, with the Wydler and Casey rhythm section ratcheting up the intensity and Savage's piano and organ work shading everything out. Three of the thirteen songs are from *Dream*, with the rest drawn from throughout Cave's solo career, including a dramatic version of "From Her to Eternity" that takes the 1987 re-recording as its start and gets an even more punishing makeover. Few cuts differ drastically from the more familiar album versions, but generally everything is crisper, at times much more brusque, perhaps exchanging texture for force. The opening performance of "The Mercy Seat" doesn't achieve the melodramatic power of the *Tender Prey* performance, but still makes for a fiery start, Cave's lyric of dues-paying via death delivered with the appropriate power. The *Dream* cuts arguably have the most difference from the studio takes, given a more punchy approach all around, especially on "Brother, My Cup is Empty." Other highlights include the beautiful passion of "The Ship Song," its tear-jerking appeal fully intact, and the doom-laden "The Weeping Song," Bargeld and Cave's duet once again a striking fusion of voices. An end-of-the-night singalong take on "New Morning" concludes this striking record, definitely one of Cave's best. *—Ned Raggett*

Let Love In / Apr. 19, 1994 / Mute ♦♦♦♦♦
Keeping the same line-up from *Henry's Dream*, Nick Cave and company turn in yet another winner with *Let Love In*. Compared to *Henry's Dream*, *Let Love In* is something of a more produced effort—longtime Cave boardsman Tony Cohen oversees things, and from the first track, one can hear the subtle arrangements and carefully constructed performances. Love, unsurprisingly, takes center stage of the album. Besides concluding with a second part to "Do You Love Me?," two of its stronger cuts are the (almost) title track "I Let Love In," and "Loverman," an even creepier depiction of lust's throttling power so gripping that Metallica ended up covering it. On the full-on explosive front, "Jangling Jack" sounds like it wants to do nothing but destroy sound systems, strange noises and overmodulations ripping throughout the song. The Seeds can always turn in almost deceptively peaceful performances as well, of course—standouts here are "Nobody's Baby Now," with a particularly lovely guitar/piano line, and the brooding drama of "Ain't Gonna Rain Anymore." The highlight of the album, though, has little to do with love and everything to do with the group's abilities at music noir. "Red Right Hand" depicts a nightmarish figure emerging on "the edge of town," maybe a criminal and maybe something more demonic. Cave's vicious lyric combines fear and black humor perfectly, while the Seeds' performance redefines "cinematic," a disturbing organ figure leading the subtle but crisp arrangement and Harvey's addition of a sharp bell ratcheting up the feeling of doom and judgment. *—Ned Raggett*

Murder Ballads / Feb. 1996 / Mute/Reprise ♦♦♦
In some ways, *Murder Ballads* is the record Nick Cave has been waiting to make for his entire career. Death and violence have always haunted his music, even when he wasn't explicitly singing about the subject. On *Murder Ballads*, he sings about nothing but death in the most grusome, shocking fashion. Divided between originals and covers, the record is awash in both morbid humor and sobering horror, as the Bad Seeds provide an appropriate backdrop for the carnage, alternating between blues, country, and lounge-jazz. Opening the affair is "Song for Joy," a tale from a father who has witnessed his family's death at the hands of serial killer. It is the most disturbing number on the record, lacking any of the gallows humor that balances out the other songs. Cave's duets with Kylie Minogue ("Where the Wild Roses Grow") and PJ Harvey ("Henry Lee") are intriguing, but the true *tours de force* of the album are "Stagger Lee" and "O'Malley's Bar." Working from an obscure, vulgar variation on "Stagger Lee," Cave increases the sordidness of the song, making Stagger an utterly unredeemable character. The original "O'Malley's Bar" is even stronger, as he spins a bizarrely funny epic of one man's slaughter of an entire bar. During "O'Malley's Bar," Cave and the Bad Seeds are at the height of their powers and the performances rank among the best they have ever recorded. *—Stephen Thomas Erlewine*

The Boatman's Call / Mar. 4, 1997 / Mute/Reprise ♦♦♦♦♦
Murder Ballads brought Nick Cave's morbidity to near-parodic levels, which makes the disarmingly frank and introspective songs of *The Boatman's Call* all the more startling. A song cycle equally inspired by Cave's failed romantic affairs and religious doubts, *The Boatman's Call* captures him at his most honest and despairing—while he retains a fascination for Gothic, Biblical imagery, it has little of the grand theatricality and self-conscious poetics that made his albums emotionally distant in the past. This time, there's no posturing, either from Cave or the Bad Seeds. The music is direct, yet it has many textures, from blues to jazz, which offers a revealing and sympathetic bed for Cave's best, most affecting songs. *The Boatman's Call* is one of his finest albums and arguably the masterpiece he has been promising throughout his career. *—Stephen Thomas Erlewine*

● **The Best of Nick Cave & the Bad Seeds** / May 26, 1998 / Mute/Reprise ♦♦♦♦♦
Nick Cave is unquestionably an album artist. Each of his records has a specific mood and theme, standing as an individual work. That said, his albums also have been notoriously uneven. Sometimes, as on *From Her to Eternity* or *The Boatman's Call*, he has delivered near-masterpieces, while on other albums, only a handful of songs have hit the mark accurately, which is why *The Best of Nick Cave* is a welcome addition to his catalog. Granted, the title is a bit odd (it's better than "Greatest Hits," however), but the compilation itself is as good as it could possibly be. All the major songs—"Red Right Hand," "Straight to You," "Nobody's Baby Now," "Into My Arms," "Do You Love Me?," "Henry Lee," "Where the Wild Roses Grow," "From Her to Eternity"—are on this 16-track collection, along with several strong album cuts. Some hardcore fans will find a couple of favorites missing, and the disc should have been sequenced in chronological order, but *The Best of Nick Cave and the Bad Seeds* is nevertheless a terrific single-disc overview of his rewarding, occasionally inaccessible work with the Bad Seeds; it's ideal for both the curious and the casual fan. [Collectors will be interested in the initial British pressings of *The Best of Nick Cave & the Bad Seeds*, which contained a bonus disc, *Live at the Royal Albert Hall*. The bonus live album was recorded in May of 1997 and contains such songs as "Lime Tree Arbour," "Stranger Than Kindness," "The Weeping Song," "Red Right Hand" and "Where the Wild Roses Grow."] *—Stephen Thomas Erlewine*

No More Shall We Part / Apr. 10, 2001 / Reprise ♦♦♦♦♦
No More Shall We Part ended a four-year silence from Nick Cave & the Bad Seeds. A best-of was issued in 2000, but no new material had appeared since 1997's landmark album *The Boatman's Call*. With that record Cave had finally delivered what everyone knew he was capable of: an entire album of deeply tragic and beautiful love songs without irony, sarcasm, or violent resolution. It appears that *The Boatman's Call* altered the manner in which Cave writes songs, and the Bad Seeds illustrate them. Here, two musical directors—the ubiquitous Mick Harvey and Dirty Three violinist Warren Ellis—craft a sonic atmosphere whose textures deepen and widen Cave's most profound and beautiful lyrics to date. Lyrically, and as a vocalist, Cave has undergone a startling, profound metamorphosis. Gone is the angry, humorous cynic whose venom and bile touched even his lighter moments. His deep taunting ambivalence about Jesus Christ and Christianity in general is gone, vanished into a maturity that ponders spiritual things contemplatively. Over these 12 tracks, Cave has taken the broken heart—so openly exhibited on *The Boatman's Call*—and elevated it to the place where he has learned to live with, and speak from it as both an artist and a human being. There is powerful emotion here, spiritual, psychological, and romantic, without a hint of the sentimentality that would make it false. As both a singer and a songwriter, his work has been transformed into something so full of depth, color, and dimension that there is simply no one except his mentors working on this level in popular music. *—Thom Jurek*

Celibate Rifles

f. 1982

Aussie Rock, Alternative Pop/Rock

Playing stripped-down, loud and fast, Ramones-inspired guitar rock, the Celibate Rifles were one of the earliest Australian punk bands to emerge during the post-Radio Birdman/Saints era. Taking their cues from these Aussie bands, along with American hard rock of the Stooges, MC5 and Blue Oyster Cult, the Rifles exploded out of the gates in 1982 with records fueled by high-speed guitars, wah-wah-strangulated solos, and cartoonish, tongue-in-cheek lyrics.

It didn't take long for the Rifles to develop a following on their home continent, though outside they were virtually unknown. The lengthy compilation EP *Quintessentially Yours* changed things slightly in 1985, though the band's seeming disinterest in touring America didn't help matters. As they continued recording and maturing, the band were unafraid to take risks with their tried and true loud-and-fast sound. Soon, acoustic guitars entered the mix, tempos slowed, pianos tinkled in the background, and vocal harmonies were added. Another development was the increased politicization and social consciousness of their material.

By 1989, lead vocalist Damien Lovelock had released a solo album and the time between Rifles releases seemed to grow longer. In late 1994, the Rifles stormed back with *Spaceman in a Satin Suit*, an exhilarating return to form. They may be a grizzled bunch of punk rockers, but there's nothing the Celibate Rifles couldn't teach young rock bands. *—John Dougan*

The Celibate Rifles / 1984 / Hot ♦♦♦♦
Australia's Celibate Rifles, the band that almost single handedly carried the torch of Detroit rock & roll into the '90s (and beyond?), have done the unthinkable: they've released an acoustic disc. Actually, it's not fully acoustic, but rather "on the quiet," as the title suggests. Here we have our heroes redoing eight of their older numbers, and four electric cover versions of Australian rock songs. Of the older songs, "Netherworld," and "Sentinel" are two of the band's dark and moody jam numbers, which are even spookier in this dense acoustic setting, not to mention (OK I'm mentioning them) the classics, "Jesus on TV," and the rarely performed "Electric Snake River." Of the covers, particularly notable are the Lipstick Killers' "Hindu Gods of Love," an underground hit from 1979 which got released stateside by Bomp records. The Rifles turn up the juice and these last few songs could have been called on the loud. Also, "Boys (What Did The Detective Say)," by the Sports (remember them?), rocks furiously. As on all Rifles' recordings, the playing throughout the disc is exemplary. The turbo acoustic guitars of Kent Steedman and Dave Morris mesh with Damien Lovelock's monotone and highly literate lyrics to create something a bit different, but yet, the same. In other words, even though the Celibate Rifles are known for their shit-hot playing, energy and insight, this lacks only the volume—not the thunder. *—Geoff Ginsberg*

The Turgid Miasma of Existence / 1986 / Hot ♦♦♦♦♦
The first recording of new Celibate Rifles material to be released in America. Now fully incorporating acoustic guitars, cellos, zithers, and bass clarinets (!) into the mix, this record is more eclectic than your average Rifles release, but amazingly, there are no false moments, bad songs, or failed experiments. From the opening salvo of "Bill Bonney Regrets" through the hair-raising "Conflict of Instinct" to the sarcastically funny closing track "New Mistakes," this is a simply wonderful record that will sound refreshingly direct

and engaging another 15 years from now. Lovelock's lyrics are especially wonderful, running the gamut from terse imagism to comedic tomfoolery to polemical broadsides. The album is dedicated to James Darroch, the original Rifles bass player who left in 1984 to form the great, little-known Eastern Dark (one very good EP, *Long Live the New Flesh*). Darroch died in a car accident while *Miasma* was being recorded. —*John Dougan*

Mina Mina Mina / 1986 / What Goes On ✦✦✦
Much of the earliest material recorded by the Rifles (covering the years 1982-1984) is difficult to find in its original form, but these two records do an excellent job of anthologizing those heady post-Birdman/Saints days. Mostly speedy (guitars, guitars, and more guitars!) and poppy, there are some hilarious songs ("Let's Get Married"), some that show a strong '70s influence ("God Squad"), and some that indicate the band's growing maturity ("Back in the Red"). Although they would make better records, the exuberance and excitement of this music, as well as its power, hasn't diminished a bit since the day it was recorded. —*John Dougan*

Kiss Kiss Bang Bang / 1987 / What Goes On ✦✦✦
Live, loud and fast. Turn it up to 11. Added bonus: the definitive version of Radio Birdman's supercharged Aussie punk anthem, "Burn My Eye." —*John Dougan*

● **Roman Beach Party** / 1987 / What Goes On ✦✦✦✦✦
This record was bound to be the LP that broke the Rifles with the college radio crowd (pre-alternative rock) in America. It was more direct and hard-hitting than *Miasma*, but it didn't sacrifice smarts, nor did it pander to a punk rock crowd that was evolving into a neo-heavy metal crowd. It was around the time of this LP that MTV's early alternative rock show *The Cutting Edge* (hosted by Fleshtones lead singer Peter Zaremba) had the Rifles play live. Of course they were last, and that meant staying up until the wee hours of the morning, but if you did, you saw a ripsnorting version of *Roman Beach Party*'s opening track, the anti-televangelism ode "Jesus on T.V." Unfortunately, this appearance didn't translate into huge record sales, and those who missed out on *Roman Beach Party* ignored one of the classiest hard rock records of the '80s. —*John Dougan*

Blind Ear / 1989 / True Tone-EMI ✦✦✦✦✦
The best Celibate Rifles recording? Yes, but only on the days it's not *Roman Beach Party*, or maybe *Mina Mina Mina*. Along with being the only album in Australian rock history to contain two songs about the troubles in Northern Ireland ("Sean O'Farrell" and "Belfast"), *Blind Ear* continues the Rifles' maturation process from snarling young punks to snarling adult punks. Sounding at times like the Stones (and that's meant as a compliment), the Rifles—now nearly a decade into their career—were recording some of their best songs. For proof, listen to the two aforementioned songs, along with their critique of yuppiedom ("Wonderful Life") and the closing track, "O Salvation." Another record that should have been huge. —*John Dougan*

Spaceman in a Satin Suit / 1994 / Hot ✦✦✦✦✦
Starting off with one of the hardest, fastest, ecstatic bursts of rock they've ever recorded ("Spirits"), *Spaceman* is a resounding assertion that this band's career is far from over. In fact, this record wipes the floor with nearly every note issued by the endless succession of post-Nirvana, MTV-approved alternative rock bands. Like the Ramones (and perhaps Motorhead), the Rifles seem to get better with age, and for all of us punks way past 30, that's life-affirming news. —*John Dougan*

Chad & Jeremy

f. 1964, London, England, **db.** 1969
Sunshine Pop, British Invasion, Pop
The American success of the folkish duo of Chad Stuart (b. Dec. 10, 1943, Durham, England) and Jeremy Clyde (b. Mar. 22, 1944, Buckinghamshire, England) pointed up the impact of the British Invasion led by the Beatles in February 1964. Chad & Jeremy charted only once in their native country, but their single "Yesterday's Gone," released in May 1964, was the first of 11 U.S. chart hits they achieved through 1966. The biggest of these, and their only Top Ten, was "A Summer Song" (July 1964). Adopting a lighter approach than many of their Mersey Beat contemporaries, Chad & Jeremy focused on pop revivals such as "Willow, Weep for Me" and songs from Broadway shows, such as "I Have Dreamed" from *Carousel*, both Top 40 hits for them. Having moved to Hollywood, they were frequent television guests, both on music shows such as "Hullabaloo" and series like "Batman." Their commercial progress was complicated after 1965, when they signed to Columbia Records, while Capitol Records continued to issue their earlier recordings (previously issued on the World Artists label), such that they were forced to compete with themselves. They recorded the musically ambitious *Of Cabbages and Kings* (September 1967) in the wake of the Beatles' *Sgt. Pepper's Lonely Hearts Club Band*. They broke up after the commercial failure of its equally ambitious follow-up, *The Ark* (September 1968). Jeremy Clyde established himself as a British stage actor. The duo reunited for a new album in 1983; *Of Cabbages & Kings* was re-released in 1999. —*William Ruhlmann*

Distant Shores / Aug. 15, 1966 / Columbia ✦✦✦

Of Cabbages & Kings / Sep. 1967 / M.I.L Multimedia ✦✦✦
Of Cabbages and Kings was Chad & Jeremy's attempt to remake themselves in a more exotic, progressive/psychedelic mode, taking the rock-as-art implications of *Sgt. Pepper* to a high-concept conclusion. The duo's melodic gifts tend to clash with the sometimes overambitious material—one full side of the original LP was taken up with the five-movement "Progress Suite"—in a fashion that some listeners will find unfulfilling, and others will find fascinating. —*Steve Huey*

● **Very Best of Chad & Jeremy** / Mar. 7, 2000 / Varese ✦✦✦✦✦
Although this 18-song best-of duplicates much of what was on the best previous Chad & Jeremy CD compilation (One Way's *The Best of Chad & Jeremy*), this release is definitely

the superior option. Its most crucial edge is the inclusion of four songs from 1965-1966 Columbia singles, as the One Way disc was limited to the material they released on World Artists. In addition, the Varese Sarabande anthology has comprehensive liner notes, songwriting credits, and original release date info, whereas the One Way disc had none of those things at all. This CD still concentrates on the World Artists sides from 1964-1965, including all of the hit singles. Some of the inessential covers of hits and standards from the One Way compilation are axed, but decent original tunes like "My How the Time Goes By" are retained. The four Columbia sides include the three Top 40 hits "Before and After" and "I Don't Wanna Lose You Baby" (both written by Van McCoy), and "Distant Shores" (by future Chicago and Blood, Sweat & Tears producer James Guercio). Oddest of all, though, is the 1966 single "Teenage Failure," a satirical folk-rocker in which writer Jeremy Clyde does a middling parody of protest singers in the sub-Bob Dylan mold. As British Invasion duos performing folk music with a folk-rock tinge go, Peter & Gordon definitely still have the edge; nonetheless, Chad & Jeremy make for pleasant if undemanding listening. Speaking of which, a photo of the somewhat similar-looking Peter & Gordon was apparently mistaken for Chad & Jeremy and snuck past quality control into page three of these liner notes (with no accompanying label to indicate that it was *not* Chad & Jeremy), unless this was an inside joke on someone's part. —*Richie Unterberger*

The Chairmen of the Board

f. 1969, Detroit, MI, **db.** 1976
Pop-Soul, Soul
Best-known for the stuttering hit single "Give Me Just a Little More Time," the Chairmen of the Board were one of the smoothest and most popular soul acts to emerge from Detroit in the early '70s. Although their time at the top of the R&B charts was brief—their first Top 10 arrived in 1970, their last in 1973—they recorded a handful of '70s soul classics, all distinguished by the high, trembling vocals of General Norman Johnson, who also wrote the bulk of the group's material. Formed by Johnson after he signed to the fledgling Invictus label of former Motown producers and songwriters Holland-Dozier-Holland, the Chairmen of the Board found an instant hit with their debut single "Give Me Just a Little More Time," which reached number three on the pop charts. Though they managed only one more major hit on the pop charts ("Pay to the Piper"), Johnson's songs became hits for the likes of Clarence Carter ("Patches"), Freda Payne ("Bring the Boys Home") and Honey Cone, who had no less than three hits—"Want Ads," "Stick Up," "One Monkey Don't Stop No Show"—with his compositions. After a temporary break-up in 1971, the Chairmen of the Board continued touring and releasing albums until 1976, when they disbanded (with each member releasing solo albums). Johnson and group-member Danny Woods reunited as the Chairmen in the early '80s and regularly toured the Southeast to much success. —*Stephen Thomas Erlewine*

● **Greatest Hits** / Jan. 9, 1992 / Fantasy ✦✦✦✦✦
When hit songwriters/producers Holland-Dozier-Holland left Motown Records and founded Hot Wax/Invictus, there was plenty of cause for optimism. And, to be sure, the labels had their share of Motown-ish "uptown soul" hits courtesy of the Honey Cone, 100 Proof (Aged in Soul), Freda Payne and Laura Lee. Another one of the company's strong points was the Chairmen of the Board, a vocal harmony group that, like the Four Tops at Motown, could be gritty and sweet at the same time. Lead singer General Norman Johnson, in fact, had a Levi Stubbs-like quality. Though not quite on a par with HDH's work with the Tops, enjoyably Detroit-sounding hits like "Dangling on a String," "Give Me Just a Little More Time" and "Pay to the Piper" showed that the team's knack for finding memorable, hook-laden soul/pop hadn't gone away. The group gets away from its Four Tops-influenced approach on the arresting "Try My Love on for Size" and the surprisingly bluesy "Chairman of the Board," a moderate hit. Unfortunately, the Chairmen's success—like that of Hot Wax/Invictus—was short-lived. —*Alex Henderson*

The Challengers

f. 1963, Los Angeles, CA
Surf, Instrumental Rock
One of the most popular of the early Southern Californian surf bands, the Challengers were formed by drummer Richard Belvy after he left the Belairs, who had recorded one of the very first surf singles, "Mr. Moto." Their debut LP, *Surfbeat* (early 1963), was one of the very first all-instrumental surf albums and sold 200,000 copies, an astronomical number for a regional act. Recording several albums over the next couple of years, most of their repertoire consisted of covers of popular rock and surf tunes; undeniably exciting at the time, their lack of originality can make their work generic to wade through. The moody "K-39," also available on surf compilations, is their most famous cut. —*Richie Unterberger*

The Challengers on the Move / 1963 / Sundazed ✦✦✦

Surfbeat / 1963 / Sundazed ✦✦✦✦✦

Lloyd Thaxton Goes Surfing with the Challengers / 1963 / Sundazed ✦✦✦

● **K-39** / 1964 / Sundazed ✦✦✦✦✦
Their first four LPs are quite similar to each other overall, but if you have to choose one, the nod would go to the last of the quartet. Featuring the title track (their most famous performance), it also has hot versions of "Telstar" and "Mark Of Zorro," and three bonus cuts of their competent forays into vocal hot rod music. —*Richie Unterberger*

Killer Surf: The Best Of The Challengers / 1994 / GNP Crescendo ✦✦✦
Clocking in at 30 tracks, this is a top-heavy collection of surf sides the Challengers cut for the GNP/Crescendo label. As the group never really had a hit, this is arguably all the Challengers you might ever need for the collection. But it *is* grade-A surf music,

extremely well played with various session ringers like Hal Blaine, Jim Keltner, Steve Douglas, and Paul Johnson brought in on various numbers. —*Cub Koda*

Tidal Wave! / Sep. 29, 1995 / Sundazed ✦✦✦

It's rare that a minor band such as The Challengers rates a package of the sort of alternate takes and rarities that you'll find on a Rolling Stones bootleg. That's what this 18-track compilation is, though. Half are alternate takes, five songs were previously unissued in any form, and three come from their rare 1965 LP, *Surf's Up*. This doesn't offer any radical redefinition of The Challengers' oeuvre, but it certainly doesn't suffer in comparison with their official vintage albums. In fact, you're about as well off with this compilation as any of their proper full-length recordings, and some tracks do burn, such as "Satan's Theme" and "Moovin' & Groovin." Sound quality is excellent. —*Richie Unterberger*

The Chambers Brothers

f. 1954, Lee County, MS, **db.** 1972
Psychedelic, Soul
Like their West Coast contemporaries Sly and the Family Stone, the Chambers Brothers shattered racial and musical divides to forge an incendiary fusion of funk, gospel, blues, and psychedelia which reached its apex with the perennial 1968 song "Time Has Come Today." The Chambers siblings—bassist George, guitarist Willie, harpist Lester, and guitarist Joe, all of whom contributed vocals—were born and raised in Lee County, MS; the products of an impoverished sharecropping family, the brothers first polished their vocal harmonies in the choir of their Baptist church, a collaboration which ended after George was drafted into the army in 1952. Following his discharge he relocated to Los Angeles, where the other Chambers brothers soon settled as well; the foursome began performing gospel and folk throughout Southern California in 1954, but remained virtually unknown until appearing in New York City in 1965. The addition of white drummer Brian Keenan not only made the Chambers Brothers an interracial group, but pushed their music closer to rock & roll; a well-received appearance at the Newport Folk Festival further enhanced their growing reputation, and they soon recorded their debut LP, *People Get Ready*.

As the Chambers Brothers toured rock clubs (including the famed Fillmore in San Francisco) and R&B venues (most notably the Apollo Theatre) alike, their music increasingly embraced elements of both; after recording 1968's *Shout!* for the Vault label, the group signed to Columbia to issue *Time Has Come Today*, scoring a major pop hit with the title track, an 11-minute psychedelic soul epic in its original album incarnation. The follow-up, *A New Time—A New Day*, yielded another Top 40 hit, a cover of the Otis Redding's classic "I Can't Turn You Loose," but subsequent efforts including 1969's *Love, Peace and Happiness* and 1970's *Live at Fillmore East* failed to maintain the commercial momentum. Upon completing 1972's *Oh My God!*, the Chambers Brothers disbanded, only to reunite two years later for *Unbonded. Right Move* appeared in 1975, and although no new studio records were forthcoming, the group regularly performed live in the decades to follow, with the brothers also pursuing individual projects; the Chambers Family Choir, a gospel group including the siblings' own children, remained a priority as well. —*Jason Ankeny*

The Time Has Come / Nov. 1967 / Columbia/Legacy ✦✦✦✦✦

Love, Peace & Happiness / Dec. 1969 / GNP Crescendo ✦✦✦

● **Time Has Come: The Best of the Chambers Brothers** / Oct. 15, 1996 / Columbia/Legacy ✦✦✦✦✦

As the Chambers Brothers' albums could be erratic and/or excessive, this 16-track best-of, covering their 1966-70 prime, is a most welcome distillation of their career highlights. Focusing mostly on their late-'60s singles (some of them non-LP), it also includes a live rendition of "Wade in the Water" and a rejected, even more psychedelicized, 1966 version of their signature tune, "Time Has Come Today." By concentrating on the band's most economic and soulful outings, this disc is the most effective compilation of their gospel-soul-psychedelia. —*Richie Unterberger*

The Chameleons UK

f. 1981, Middleton, Manchester, England, **db.** 1986
Dream Pop, Post-Punk, Alternative Pop/Rock
The atmospheric pop band the Chameleons formed in Manchester, England in 1981 from the ashes of a number of local groups: vocalist/bassist Mark Burgess began with the Cliches, guitarists Reg Smithies and Dave Fielding arrived from the Years, and drummer John Lever (who quickly replaced founding member Brian Schofield) originated with the Politicians. After establishing themselves with a series of high-profile BBC sessions, the Chameleons signed to Epic and debuted with the EP *Nostalgia*, a tense, moody set produced by Steve Lillywhite which featured the single "In Shreds."

The quartet was soon released from their contract with Epic, but then signed to Statik, and they returned in 1983 with their first full-length effort, *Script of the Bridge. What Does Anything Mean? Basically* followed in 1985, and with it came a new reliance on stylish production; following its release, the Chameleons signed to Geffen and emerged the following year with *Strange Times.* The dark, complex record proved to be the group's finale, however, when they split following the sudden death of manager Tony Fletcher; while Burgess and Lever continued on in the Sun and the Moon, Smithies and Fielding later reunited in the Reegs. —*Jason Ankeny*

Script of the Bridge / 1983 / Statik ✦✦✦✦✦

With two years, numerous radio sessions and incessant gigging under their belts since their debut single "In Shreds," the Chameleons came to the studio determined to make a great first album with *Script*. To say they succeeded would be like saying Shakespeare did pretty well with that one *Hamlet* play of his. *Script* remains a high-water mark of what can generally be called "post-punk music," an hour's worth of one amazing song

after another, practically a greatest hits record on its own: the John Lennon tribute "Here Today," "Monkeyland," "Pleasure and Pain," "Paper Tigers," "As High As You Can Go," the breathtaking closer "View From a Hill." Starting with the passionate fire of "Don't Fall," *Script* showcases how truly inventive, unique and distinctly modern rock & roll could exist, instead of relentlessly rehashing the past to little effect. The scalpel-sharp interplay between the musicians is a sheer wonder to behold, the Fielding/Smithies guitar team provoke nothing but superlatives throughout, and Lever and Burgess make a perfect rhythm section—while the crisp production of Colin Richardson and the band adds delicate synthlines and shadings, courtesy of early touring keyboardist Alistair Lewthwaite, and just the right amount of reverb and effects on the guitars. Add to that the words of Burgess, one of the few lyricists out there who can tackle Big Issues while retaining a human, personal touch, and it all just adds up perfectly. The best one-two punch comes from "Second Skin," a complex, beautifully arranged and played reflection on the meaning of music and fandom, and "Up the Down Escalator," an at once harrowing and thrilling anti-nuclear/mainstream politics slam. An important note: avoid at all costs the original US vinyl issue on MCA, which not only switches the song order but removes a full third of the songs. —*Ned Raggett*

What Does Anything Mean? Basically / 1985 / Statik ✦✦✦✦✦

Easily the high point of the Chameleons' fascination with digital delays, pedals and making the studio an instrument, the band's second album still is seen by many a fan as being just a little too lost in the production to have the same impact as *Script* did, despite equally excellent songs. The decision must ultimately be the listener's, but in the end the production argument is much more a quibble than a condemnation—no matter how you look at it, *What* proved to be that rarity of sophomore albums, something that at once made the band all the more unique in its sound while avoiding a repetition of earlier work. Ironically, the first track, "Silence, Sea and Sky," turned out to be the least Chameleons-like track ever, being only a two-minute synth intro piece played by Burgess and Fielding. But with the gentle intro to the absolutely wonderful "Perfumed Garden," lyrically one of Burgess' best nostalgic pieces, it rapidly becomes clear exactly which band is doing this. The empathetic fire that infused Burgess' words for songs like "Singing Rule Britannia (While the Walls Close In)," a poetic attack on the Thatcher government, finds itself matched as always by brilliant playing all around. Lever's command of the drums continues to impress, and Fielding and Smithies remain guitarists par excellence; the searing, sky-bound solo on "Return of the Roughnecks" alone is a treasure. The sublime combination of the rushing "Looking Inwardly" and the soaring, blasting rip "One Flesh," leading into a relaxed instrumental coda, anchors the second side, while "P.S. Goodbye" provides a lovely, melancholic conclusion to an astounding record. CD copies include the 1981 "In Shreds/Nostalgia" single as bonus tracks. —*Ned Raggett*

● **Strange Times** / 1986 / Geffen ✦✦✦✦✦

If there was a should-have-been year in the Chameleons' history, 1986 would clearly be it, and *Strange Times* demonstrates that on every track, practically in every note. Signed to a huge label, with production help from the Dave Allen/Mark Saunders team which worked on the Cure's brilliant series of late-'80s records (here providing a more balanced sound between guitar effects and direct punch than appeared on *What*), the Chameleons delivered an album that should have been the step to a more above-board existence on radio and beyond. Right from the start, a stunning upward spiral of a guitar riff which begins the unnerving character study "Mad Jack," the band members mix their skills, experience, and songwriting ability perfectly and take everything to an even higher level. The first half continues with three more stunners: "Caution," "Tears," and "Soul in Isolation." And just when you think it couldn't get any better: "Swamp Thing," the definitive Chameleons song, complex, building, tense, epic, perfectly played, and with one of Burgess' most poetic, personal lyrics. It just keeps going from there, the second half covering everything from more sweeping tunes ("Time," "In Answer") to bare-bones melancholy ("In Answer," "I'll Remember"). From back to front, *Strange Times* could never have enough praise. [U.K. versions of *Strange Times* on CD and LP came with a second disc of bonus tracks; when the album was reissued on CD in the U.S. in 1995, the bonus tracks were simply added to the album proper, without adding an extra disc.] —*Ned Raggett*

The Fan & the Bellows / 1988 / Caroline ✦✦✦

Mark Burgess has gone on record describing this collection's subtitle, "A Collection of Classic Early Recordings," as more than slightly misleading; understandable, since it first surfaced as an attempt to cash in on the Chameleons after their break-up by their first label. Even so, the various tracks here, including singles, demos and tracks otherwise nowhere else available, mostly from 1981 (half of which were produced by Steve Lillywhite with his trademark punch), offer a better view into the Chameleons' early days than might be guessed. The legendary debut single's tracks, "In Shreds" and "Nostalgia," the latter featured in two versions, already capture the mix of brawling post-punk drive and melancholic reflection that would only flower further on future releases. Similar combinations appears elsewhere on "Turn to the Vices" and "Everyday I'm Crucified"—one of the few uses of the Jesus Christ pose lyrical gambit in rock that actually works! The title track itself is a stunner, one of Burgess' best shouts into the void meshing with the vicious power of Fielding and Smithies' guitars perfectly. Add to that such songs as an early version of "Less than Human" and the gentle, semi-ambient curiosity "Prisoners of the Sun," featuring the same obscure movie sample which leads off the later tune "Don't Fall," and while it's not as classic as the subtitle claims, there's more here than many other bands could ever offer. —*Ned Raggett*

Tripping Dogs / 1990 / Glass Pyramid ✦✦✦

Recorded during rehearsals in 1985. —*Steve Aldrich*

Peel Sessions / 1990 / Dutch East India ✦✦✦✦

A constant subject of debate among Chameleons fans has been and remains whether or not their three studio albums, for all their brilliance, were nonetheless overproduced, with Smithies and Fielding especially lost in reams of digital delay. For those who believe so, *Peel Sessions* clearly came as a godsend, but even if a listener doesn't care either way, the benefits of capturing near-live sessions of such amazing performers with high-end studio sound is reason enough to give an ear. Covering sessions from 1981, 1983 and 1984, the song selection mixes selections from the first two albums plus a few rarities—the earliest session, featuring original drummer Brian Schofield (solid, but nowhere as inventive as Lever proved to be later), contains fine versions of "The Fan and the Bellows" and "Things I Wish I'd Said," not to mention a brisk "Looking Inwardly," not officially recorded until four years later! Takes on *Script* classics like "Second Skin" and "Don't Fall" are more than welcome, but the standouts have to be the many numbers from *What*, such as "Return of the Roughnecks," "One Flesh" and "Perfumed Garden," here given a bite and drive that amazes. The closing track, "P.S. Goodbye," has a beautiful alternate beginning that, while simple enough, gives the song a totally different feel from the album version—more proof that even in the smallest of ways the Chameleons were truly one of a kind. *—Ned Raggett*

Return of the Roughnecks: The Best of Chameleons UK / Jun. 30, 1998 / Dead Dead Good ♦♦♦♦

Why even bother with a best-of? After all, with brilliance running rampant throughout the course of the Chameleons' discography, which includes myriad radio session and live releases, it's a monster task to whittle a fair representation onto one CD. The track selection is excellent, though no compilation is likely to be seen as completely accurate from the judgment of one Chams fan to another. But since best-ofs are meant for beginners, this is a moot point. Avoiding the risk of making a fractured compilation, *Return of the Roughnecks* flows extremely well, and each of their LPs are represented quite evenly: five songs are from *Script of the Bridge*, three are from *What Does Anything Mean*, and four are off *Strange Times* (both sides of the "In Shreds"/"Nostalgia" single are included as well). Beginners certainly won't be disappointed in this. I can almost guarantee that you'll be wanting to snap up nearly anything with the Chameleons' name on it after a couple plays. The already committed likely own this already, unless they don't know of its existence—Chameleons fans are usually rabid completists. Packaged lovingly with the involvement of the band, it's made to please the familiar as well. Some copies include their swan song, the *Tony Fletcher Walked on Water* EP, as a second disc. If given a choice between the single and double disc set, go with the double—regardless of price difference. *—Andy Kellman*

The Champs

f. 1957, Los Angeles, CA

Frat Rock, Instrumental Rock, Rock & Roll

An instrumental quintet formed in Los Angeles in 1957, the Champs comprised Challenge Records executive Dave Burgess (born Lancaster, CA) (guitar) and session players Buddy Bruce (guitar), Chuck Rio (born Daniel Flores, Rankin, TX) (saxophone), Cliff Hills (bass), and Gene Alden (born Cisco, TX) (drums). This lineup recorded Rio's "Tequila" as a B-side to Burgess's "Train to Nowhere." "Tequila" topped the charts in 1958. The Champs essentially were a one-hit wonder, though they recorded a few more singles in the same Latin dance style and kept going until the mid-'60s. The group's lineup was fluid, and later members included Glen Campbell as well as Jimmy Seals and Dash Crofts, who formed the successful '70s duo Seals and Crofts. *—William Ruhlmann*

Tequila: The Very Best of the Champs / 1997 / Music Club ♦♦♦♦

A budget-priced but bountiful—18 tracks—collection of the group's best. All of their chart hits are aboard ("El Rancho Rock," "Chariot Rock," "Tequila Twist," "Midnighter," "Too Much Tequila," "Limbo Rock," and an especially crisp transfer of the title track), a fact all the more amazing since the group is generally misrepresented as a one-hit wonder. The Champs may have only worked a small, select piece of rock instrumental turf, but it remains theirs to this day. This single-disc compilation is a one-stop buy, containing just about everything you'll need on this seminal rock & roll combo. *—AMG*

● **25 All-Time Greatest Recordings** / Jun. 27, 2000 / Varese ♦♦♦♦

As solid an overview of everything the various incarnations of the Champs ever recorded as you're likely to find. This one features all the hits with a great smattering of important album cuts, featuring late-model versions of the band turning in solid versions of bandstand staples like "Honky Tonk," "Night Train," "Last Night," and "Raunchy." If you're looking to round up the hits, this one fills the bill as well as giving a nice overview to the album side of the band's output. Liner notes by AMG's own Cub Koda. *—Elmer Valo*

James Chance

Vocals, Sax (Alto) / No Wave, New Wave

One of the central figures of the No Wave movement of the late '70s, James Chance and the Contortions formed in New York City in 1977. They were led by vocalist/saxophonist Chance, a Milwaukee native (born James Sigfried) who also answered to the alias James White. After relocating to the Big Apple to play free jazz, he fell in with the city's avant-garde community; upon adopting the surname Chance and acquiring a wardrobe of outrageously loud suits, Chance formed the Contortions, an abrasively chaotic funk-noise outfit featuring organist Adele Bertei, guitarists Pat Place and Jody Harris, and drummer Don Christiansen.

After winning acclaim and notoriety for their wild, often combative live shows (the aggressive, nihilistic Chance often picked fistfights with audience members), the Contortions entered the studio with producer Brian Eno to record four tracks for the *No New York* compilation. After cutting enough material for an LP, 1979's *Buy the Contortions*, the group crashed along with the No Wave scene; as James White, Chance soon resurfaced fronting the Blacks, a bizarre disco outfit comprised of most of the Contortions alumni, albeit with the notable exception of Bertei. *—Jason Ankeny*

● **Buy the Contortions** / 1979 / ZE ♦♦♦♦♦

A wacky fusion of off-kilter rock and the Ornette Coleman-influenced saxophonist Chance. Lots of fun, but it's for special tastes. Includes "Contort Yourself" and "I Don't Want to Be Happy." *—Michael G. Nastos*

Off White / 1979 / ZE ♦♦♦

Soul Exorcism / 1991 / ROIR ♦♦♦♦♦

Recorded in June of 1980, *Soul Exorcism* proves that jazz, funk, experimental, and new wave make quite an intoxicating mix when perfected. James Chance sums up the proceedings perfectly in the liner notes, where he states that the music perfectly reveals the essence and soul of New York City (even though it was recorded in Rotterdam). Backed up by a stellar backing band, which Chance himself calls one of the most volatile units he's worked with, the Contortions simply shine. Like most other Contortions recordings, cacophony rears its head from time to time, but that's what the band uses to paint different moods and textures... it's not used haphazardly. The whole album is inspired from beginning to end, and features such great tracks as "I Danced with a Zombie," "Exorcise the Funk," and a pair of interesting covers—Michael Jackson's "Don't Stop 'Til You Get Enough" and James Brown's "King Heroin." *—Greg Prato*

Lost Chance / Oct. 1995 / ROIR ♦♦♦♦

Picking up where their previous ROIR live release left off (the excellent *Soul Exorcism*), James Chance & the Contortions offer another collection of their cutting-edge musical blend. Recorded live in Chicago back in September of 1981, *Lost Chance* may be a tad more visceral than their previous in-concert recording, but the over-the-top performances never get in the way of the music. And although the album contains traces of jazz and new wave, *Lost Chance* is highly recommended to funk connoisseurs—the Contortions may have been the most underrated funketeers to ever hit the stage. Out of the album's nine tracks, three are James Brown covers ("Super Bad," "I Got You," and "King Heroin"), which would surely bring a smile to the Godfather of Soul's face. And although the whole band wails throughout, bassist Colin Wade proves to be outstanding, playing some of the most fluid and funky basslines ever committed to tape. Highlights are many, but tops would have to be "Sax Maniac," "White Cannibal," and "Hell on Earth." *—Greg Prato*

White Cannibal / Sep. 12, 2000 / ROIR ♦♦♦♦

Originally released as a ROIR cassette-only, these brutal, yet danceable, live tracks were recorded in New York at the Peppermint Lounge and the '80s Club in 1980 and '81. James Chance and the Contortions mixed punk, free jazz, and funk that has yet to be matched, epitomizing the seedy underbelly of the New York no wave scene of the period. Unlike certain Lydia Lunch performance art projects of the time, Chance provides a timeless attack by combining screeching alto sax and vocal rants with a relentless disco beat. Ornette Coleman and Ronald Shannon Jackson guitarist Bern Nix and trombonist Joseph Bowie (brother of Lester) bring jazz credentials to this late edition of the Contortions while the background vocals of the Discolitas provide the sleazy stage pageantry Chance championed. The sound quality is not great, but that only adds to the original highly charged haze under which it was made. Three of the seven tracks are covers, "That Old Black Magic" and two from James Brown, "I Got You" and "King Heroin." *—Al Campbell*

Gene Chandler (Eugene Dixon)

b. Jul. 6, 1937, Chicago, IL

Vocals / Brown-Eyed Soul, Chicago Soul, Pop-Soul, Northern Soul, Soul, Uptown Soul

Chandler is remembered by the rock & roll audience almost solely for the classic novelty and doo wop-tinged soul ballad "Duke of Earl"; the unforgettable opening chant of the title leading the way, the song was a number one hit in 1962. He's esteemed by soul fans as one of the leading exponents of the '60s Chicago soul scene, along with Curtis Mayfield and Jerry Butler. Born Eugene Dixon, he was a member of the doo wop group the Dukays and "Duke of Earl" was actually a Dukays recording; Dixon was renamed Gene Chandler and the single bore his credit as a solo singer. Chandler never approached the massive pop success of that chart-topper (although he occasionally entered the Top 20), but he was a big star with the R&B audience with straightforward mid-tempo and ballad soul numbers in the mid-'60s, many of which were written by Curtis Mayfield and produced by Carl Davis. Chandler's success became more fitful after Mayfield stopped penning material for him, although he enjoyed some late-'60s hits and had a monster pop and soul smash in 1970 with "Groovy Situation." His last successes were the far less distinguished disco- and dance-influenced R&B hits "Get Down" (1978) and "Does She Have a Friend?" (1980). *—Richie Unterberger*

Just Be True / 1964 / Collectables ♦♦♦

Led by the title track, Gene Chandler's biggest hit of the '60s after "Duke of Earl," *Just Be True* is a set of period soul tracks including "You Threw a Lucky Punch" (an answer record to Mary Wells' "You Beat Me to the Punch") and the lame "Duke of Earl" knockoff "Walk On With the Duke." Chandler's wonderful voice raises all this material to a level unimagined by any but the half-dozen best soul singers out there. The Collectables reissue includes four bonus tracks. *—John Bush*

● **Nothing Can Stop Me: Gene Chandler's Greatest Hits** / Aug. 30, 1994 / Varese Sarabande ♦♦♦♦♦

This 20-track CD is the only collection that has all of his most popular recordings, from "Duke of Earl" through his soul hits for Constellation, Vee Jay, Checker, Mercury, and Chi-Sound, spanning 1962 to 1980 (all but three tracks were released before 1968). Some fans might prefer *The Duke of Earl*, which focuses on his Vee Jay years, but this has a much wider breadth, and includes "Groovy Situation." Curtis Mayfield wrote eight of the songs, although they frankly don't fully measure up to the Chicago soul he was writing for his own group, the Impressions, at the time. *—Richie Unterberger*

The Soul of Gene Chandler / Jun. 18, 1996 / Brunswick ♦♦♦♦
A collection of Gene's Brunswick sides, 20 tracks of lively productions by producer Carl Davis. None of these sides made an impact on the pop chart and did only fair on the R&B chart, which is perplexing. Tunes like "Good Times," the romping, confident "Nothing Can Stop Me," his duet with Barbara Acklin "From the Teacher to the Preacher," "Fool For You," and the soulful "Here Comes the Tears" should have been much bigger. This is not definitive Chandler, but the 20 tracks are a good helping of some of his better recordings that were victimized by poor promotion. *—Andrew Hamilton*

Duke of Soul: The Brunswick Years / Oct. 27, 1998 / Diablo ♦♦♦♦♦
Edsel's 20-track summation of Gene Chandler's short career at Brunswick Records (1966 through 1969) hits all of the obvious high points: "Nothing Can Stop Me," "(Gonna Be) Good Times," "Here Comes the Tears," "There Was a Time," "Those Were the Good Old Days," "Cowboys to Girls," and "You Can't Hurt Me No More." Perhaps wisely, the compilers completely bypassed his inferior final album for Brunswick, *The Two Sides of Gene Chandler.* Though there's still a lot of quality material from the period for which space didn't allow, *Duke of Soul: The Brunswick Years* is an excellent study of one of the most underrated soul singers of the '60s. [Since the two-disc set—*The Brunswick Years 1966-69*, also known as *The Girl Don't Care/There Was a Time/Two Sides of Gene Chandler*—includes all three of Chandler's original Brunswick LPs, and can be found at a relatively inexpensive price, some listeners may find it worthwhile to bypass this greatest-hits volume and spring for the complete set instead.] *–John Bush*

The Brunswick Years: 1966-1969 / Oct. 26, 1999 / West Side ♦♦♦♦♦
Give this high marks for definitiveness—it's the most comprehensive assemblage of Gene Chandler's Brunswick sides ever, and includes six duets with Barbara Acklin all on two shiny, durable compact discs. Chandler's solo sides represent three complete albums fattened with a few singles that didn't make it to an LP. The Acklin duets are the best from their album together. High notes include "Nothing Can Stop Me," "I'm Just a Fool for You," "Here Come the Tears," "Good Times," "The Girl Don't Care," and remakes of James Brown's "There Was a Time," and the Intruders' "Cowboys to Girls." This is the best of the many compilations of Chandler's Brunswick sides on the market. *—Andrew Hamilton*

The Best of Gene Chandler: The Duke of Earl / Oct. 17, 2000 / Collectables ♦♦♦♦
Early Gene Chandler sides, many recorded with the Dukays, including the immortal "Duke of Earl." Feature tracks include "Walk on With the Duke," which was a total bust although it is interesting in retrospect, as it was the answer to "Duke of Earl"; the original studio cut of "Rainbow"; the stark and magnificent "Man's Temptation"; an answer to Mary Wells' "You Beat Me to the Punch" via "You Threw a Lucky Punch"; a remake of the Temptations' "Check Yourself," where Chandler outdoes Paul Williams who led the original; and a whole slew of Dukays tracks when Chandler toiled with them. *—Andrew Hamilton*

Bruce Channel

b. Nov. 28, 1940, Jacksonville, TX
Vocals / Rock & Roll
Bruce Channel's "Hey Baby"—a classic one-shot, number one hit from 1962—is one of the many records proving that, during a period in which rock has sometimes been characterized as near death, the form was continuing to evolve in unexpected and delightful ways. An irresistible mid-tempo shuffle from the first few bars of homespun harmonica (played by Delbert McClinton), it was a seemingly effortless blend of rock, blues, country, and Cajun beats, featuring Channel's lazy, drawling vocals and an instantly catchy tune. It was perhaps too much of a natural—Channel could never recapture the organic spontaneity of the track, failing to re-enter the Top 40 despite many attempts.

The Texan had written "Hey Baby" around 1959 with his friend Margaret Cobb, and had already been performing the tune for a couple of years before recording it amidst a series of demos for Fort Worth producer Major Bill Smith. First released locally on Smith's label, it was picked up for national distribution by Smash. Channel would continue to write most of his own material (sometimes in collaboration with Cobb) for a series of moderately enjoyable follow-ups that echoed the riffs of "Hey Baby" too closely.

McClinton played his immediately identifiable harmonica on several of these, and made his own contribution to rock history in 1962, when he was touring as a member of Channel's band in Britain. On one of their shows, they were supported by a then-unknown Liverpool group, the Beatles, who had yet to cut their first record. John Lennon was smitten by McClinton's style of playing, and picked up some pointers that he put to use on the Beatles' very first single, "Love Me Do"; in fact, McClinton's influence can be easily detected in Lennon's harmonica playing on many early Beatles tracks from 1962 and 1963.

Channel did get another Top 20 hit in Britain in 1968, "Keep On," which was written by Wayne Carson Thompson (famous for penning the Box Tops' "The Letter"). Nothing else clicked in a big way on either side of the ocean, and by the late '70s he was working in Nashville as a songwriter. *—Richie Unterberger*

● **Hey! Baby** / Apr. 24, 1995 / Collectables ♦♦♦♦
Here's Bruce's original Smash album, recorded hot on the heels of the title hit, along with the bonus of the follow-up single, "Number One Man." The album filler all features Delbert McClinton's harmonica, which added the signature sparkle to "Hey! Baby" (the track that made John Lennon want to pick up a harp), with credible renditions of "Baby, It's You," "Chantilly Lace," Jivin' Gene's "Breakin' Up Is Hard to Do," "Ain't Got No Home," Roy Orbison's "Dream Baby," and Elvis' "Love Me," probably all staples of his then-current stage act. For a quickie album, this is a marvelously cohesive-sounding effort, and a nice souvenir of early-'60s Texas rock & roll/pop. *—Cub Koda*

The Chantays

f. 1962, Santa Ana, CA
Surf, Instrumental Rock
In 1963, this teenage group from Santa Ana, CA, had one of the biggest and best instrumental surf hits, "Pipeline." Competent players who went heavy on the rumbling bass, ghostly reverb, and electric keyboards, they were very much a one-shot act; their repertoire was crowded with rock & roll covers and "Pipeline" sound-alikes, and none of their follow-up singles charted. *—Richie Unterberger*

Pipeline / 1963 / Varese Sarabande ♦♦♦♦♦
A CD reissue of their 1963 debut album, with the addition of "Pipeline"'s B-side and both sides of the non-LP flop follow-up single. Mostly it's lesser variations of the "Pipeline" formula, including one instrumental penned by Tony Asher, Brian Wilson's writing partner for much of the *Pet Sounds* album. It doesn't include the single "Beyond," which can be found on the surf volume of Rhino/*Guitar Player*'s *Legends of Guitar* series. *—Richie Unterberger*

● **Two Sides of the Chantays/Pipeline** / 1990 / Dot ♦♦♦♦
Two Chantays albums on one CD, comprising much of the surf band's early '60s repertory. The "Move It" that opens the disc is not the Cliff Richard song but a slower, raunchier number with vocal choruses carrying a lot of the melody. "Maybe Baby" is the Buddy Holly song, however, and the group does a decent job of singing it. Unfortunately, not a lot of what else is here is exactly first-rate material—"It Never Works Out for Me" is a tuneless bore, and much of the rest is similarly uninteresting, and generally vocals were not this band's strong point, based on the evidence here. "Beyond" is a follow-up to "Pipeline" with a similar opening, and it is far and away the best track off of that album. The *Pipeline* album includes several attempts to emulate that hit, repeating its introduction and mimicking passages, but without much of the vitality or excitement of "Pipeline." The best parts of the album are the band's instrumental cover of Del Shannon's "Runaway," which is a tense, exciting workout for the entire band—and that goes double for lead guitarist Bob Spickard and pianist Bob Marshall, and "Blunderbus," an almost bluesy number that, if not for the piano, could almost pass for a Yardbirds demo. "El Conquistador" gives Spickard a chance to play an electric version of Spanish guitar. The sound is excellent, perhaps too good in the sense of being almost too clean—surf music was supposed to have its loud, aggressive edge, like early rock & roll, and Steve Hoffmann's domestic remasterings of the Chantays' releases for DCC have that hard edge. *—Bruce Eder*

The Chantels

f. 1956, New York, NY [The Bronx], **db.** 1970
Girl Group, Doo Wop, R&B, Harmony Vocal Group
One of the very first girl groups, the Chantels are best-known for their 1957 hit "Maybe." Between 1957 and 1963, the trio racked up a number of hit singles, but none of them was ever as popular as "Maybe," which came to be regarded as one of the definitive singles of the genre. All five members of the Chantels met as children, and sang in the choir of a Bronx-area school. Arlene Smith, the leader of the quintet, wrote all of the group's early material including their second single, "Maybe." A smash hit, it peaked at number two on the R&B charts and number 15 on the pop charts in early 1958. Two hit singles—"Every Night (I Pray)" and "I Love You So"—followed on End Records, but the label dropped them soon after. In 1961, the Chantels signed with Carlton Records, where they had two minor pop hits: "Look in My Eyes" and "Well, I Told You." Carlton dropped the group the following year and the band moved to Ludix, where they had a minor hit with "Eternally" in the spring of 1963. Though the Chantels officially disbanded in 1970, Arlene Smith later re-formed the group with a new lineup and continued to lead various incarnations into the '90s. *—Stephen Thomas Erlewine*

● **The Best of the Chantels** / May 1990 / Rhino ♦♦♦♦♦
The Chantels were rock & roll's first great female group. This 18-track best-of gathers all of their important recordings for George Goldner's End label, along with some rarities amongst the hits. In addition to the smashes "Maybe," "He's Gone," and "Every Night," the set also includes their work with Richard Barrett and their one-off single backing Willie Wilson, issued as the Tunemasters. An interesting chapter of the distaff side of rock & roll history. *—Cub Koda*

The Look in My Eyes: The Best of Carlton & Ludix Years / Oct. 21, 1997 / Collectables ♦♦♦
The Chantels' story is usually told in terms of Arlene Smith's involvement with the group, and little is said of their work after her departure, following their being dropped by End Records. This disc covers their lesser-known but equally beguiling early 1960s sides for the Carlton and Ludix labels, when their lead singer was Annette Smith. The material is palpably different from the classic Chantels' sound, mostly because the early '60s weren't the late '50s—R&B had grown more sophisticated, a shift reflected in producer Richard Barrett's use of string arrangements on "Look in My Eyes" and its even prettier B-side, "Glad to Be Back," which heralded a new Chantels sound. Even the hard-rocking "Well I Told You" features a tasteful and effective use of an orchestra, buried very deep in the mix but just audible enough to add extra color to the up-tempo piece. The reconstituted Chantels kept their string going for close to another year, getting serious radio play on "Here It Comes Again" and cutting perhaps their prettiest vocal performance in George Gershwin's "Summertime," when Carlton Records ran into financial trouble, and they were forced to jump to Ludix, where they succeeded again with the single "Eternally." The later

Barrett-composed songs are upbeat dance numbers that anticipate the sound that he would later perfect with the Three Degrees. The Chantels were, by the middle of the decade, one of the more sophisticated female R&B outfits of their era. That's the side profiled here, and it's worth hearing, even if it isn't quite the groundbreaking work of the original group. The CD is nicely programmed. *—Bruce Eder*

We Are the Chantels/There's Our Song Again / Jun. 9, 1998 / West Side ♦♦♦♦
This combines the first two Chantels albums recorded for End Records between 1957 and 1961. The track listing for the group's first album consists of little more than both sides of the first six singles the girls recorded for the label. As such, it's almost a greatest-hits package, as it includes "Maybe," "Every Night" and "I Love You So," all very big hits for the group. Their second album, *There's Our Song Again*, was issued in 1962 and completes the package, featuring "I," "Believe Me (My Angel)" and tracks from their two extended play (EP) 45s released in front of this album. The transfers are clear and crisp, and the cover art depicts the rare original "plantation girls" cover to their first album. *—Cub Koda*

Harry Chapin

b. Dec. 7, 1942, Greenwich Village, NY, **d.** Jul. 16, 1981, Jericho, NY
Vocals, Guitar / Folk-Rock, Soft Rock, Singer/Songwriter
Harry Chapin's career as a popular singer/songwriter was cut short by an auto accident in 1981, yet he left behind a series of recordings that his fans continue to treasure well over a decade after his death. Accused of over-sentimentalizing his subjects and attaching heavy-handed morals to his socially aware story-songs, Chapin was never a critically acclaimed singer/songwriter. Nevertheless, he earned a devoted audience during the '70s, through his music and his charity work as a social activist.

After pursuing a career as a documentary filmmaker, Chapin switched gears and recruited a backing band through an ad in the *Village Voice*. The group began performing in various clubs around New York and the singer/songwriter was soon signed to Elektra records.

Heads and Tails, Chapin's first album, was released in the summer of 1972 and became a success thanks to the hit single "Taxi," which soon became the songwriter's signature tune. After recording *Verities and Balderdash* in 1974, Chapin began work on his musical *The Night that Made America Famous*. While he was working on the musical, *Verities and Balderdash* became his biggest hit, peaking at number four on the U.S. charts and becoming a gold record.

The Night that Made America Famous opened on February 26, 1975 and earned two Tony nominations. That spring, the singer/songwriter also co-founded World Hunger Year, a charity designed to raise money to fight international famine.

Greatest Stories—Live, a double album released in the spring of 1976, became the singer/songwriter's second gold album. In 1980, he signed with Boardwalk records, releasing *Sequel* that fall; the title track of the album was a sequel to his first hit single, "Taxi," and became his last Top 40 hit.

On July 16, 1981, Chapin was killed in an auto accident near Jericho, New York. A memorial fund was established in his name following his death, supporting a variety of social causes that were close to his heart. *—Stephen Thomas Erlewine*

● **Anthology of Harry Chapin** / 1985 / Elektra ♦♦♦♦♦
Anthology of Harry Chapin is a fine 11-track collection that contains the cream of the inconsistent singer-songwriter's career, including "Taxi," "Sunday Morning Sunshine," "She Is Always Seventeen," "WOLD," "I Wanna Learn a Love Song," "Better Place to Be" and "Cat's in the Cradle." *—Stephen Thomas Erlewine*

Story of a Life: The Harry Chapin Box / Oct. 19, 1999 / Rhino ♦♦♦♦
Harry Chapin was always a bit of a polarizing figure, attracting many dedicated fans but never earning much critical respect. Rhino's comprehensive three-disc box set *Story of a Life* doesn't really offer an opportunity for re-evaluation, nor does it even try to win over doubters. Instead, it tells a thorough history of Chapin's career, not missing a single hit or major song along the way. There are some rarities scattered throughout the set, mostly live tracks, but also the Chapin Brothers' 1966 single "Someone Keeps Callin' My Name." However, the box shouldn't be seen as a treasure trove of unreleased material; instead, it's a journey through Chapin's career, providing an exhaustively detailed travelogue. Really, it contains too much material for anyone but the die-hard fan. But that's where *Story of a Life* is a success—it's a loving tribute to Chapin, made with the cooperation of his estate and designed for his loving fans. It works quite well on that level, even if it's far too much for the average fan who just likes "Taxi" and "Cat's in the Cradle." *—Stephen Thomas Erlewine*

Tracy Chapman

b. Mar. 20, 1964, Cleveland, OH
Vocals, Guitar / College Rock, Alternative Folk, Contemporary Folk, Adult Alternative Pop/Rock, Singer/Songwriter
Tracy Chapman helped restore singer-songwriters to the spotlight in the '80s. The multi-platinum success of Chapman's eponymous 1988 debut was unexpected, and it had lasting impact. Although Chapman was working from the same confessional singer-songwriter foundation that had been popularized in the '70s, her songs were fresh and powerful, driven by simple melodies and affecting lyrics. At the time of her first album, there were only a handful of artists performing such a style successfully, and her success ushered in a new era of singer-songwriters that lasted well into the '90s. Furthermore, her album helped usher in the era of political correctness—along with 10,000 Maniacs and R.E.M., Chapman's liberal politics proved enormously influential on American college campuses in the late '80s. Of course, such implications meant that Chapman's subsequent recordings were greeted with mixed reactions, but after several years out of the spotlight, she managed to make a very successful comeback in 1996 with her fourth album, *New Beginning*, thanks to the Top Ten single "Give Me One Reason." *—Stephen Thomas Erlewine*

★ **Tracy Chapman** / 1988 / Elektra ♦♦♦♦♦
Arriving with little fanfare in the spring of 1988, Tracy Chapman's eponymous debut album became one of the key records of the Bush era, providing a touchstone for the entire PC movement while reviving the singer/songwriter tradition. And *Tracy Chapman* is firmly within the classic singer/songwriter tradition, sounding for all the world as if it was recorded in the early '70s—that is, if all you paid attention to were the sonics, since Chapman's songs are clearly a result of the Reagan revolution. Even the love songs and laments are underscored by a realized vision of trickle-down modern life—listen to the lyrical details of "Fast Car" for proof. Chapman's impassioned liberal activism and emotional resonance enlivens her music, breathing life into her songs even when the production is a little bit too clean. Still, the juxtaposition of contemporary themes and classic production precisely is what makes the album distinctive—it brings the traditions into the present. At the time, it revitalized traditional folk ideals of social activism and the like, kickstarting the PC revolution in the process, but if those were its only merits, *Tracy Chapman* would sound dated. The record continues to sound fresh because Chapman's writing is so keenly observed and her strong, gutsy singing makes each song sound intimate and immediate. *—Stephen Thomas Erlewine*

Crossroads / Sep. 1989 / Elektra ♦♦♦
Tracy Chapman's self-titled debut album of 1988 was an incredibly tough act to follow, but the folk-rocker delivered an inspired sophomore effort with *Crossroads*. While it falls short of the excellence of her stunning debut, *Crossroads* is a heartfelt, honest offering that's well worth obtaining. Dedicated to South African freedom fighter Nelson Mandela, the anthemic "Freedom Now" is one of Chapman's best protest songs. Equally compelling is "Subcity," a lament for the poor, disenfranchised underclass that stands on the outside of the American Dream looking in. Much of the time, however, Chapman isn't going for immediacy—introspective and subtle, songs like "Bridges," "Be Careful of My Heart" and "All That You Have is Your Soul" require at least several listenings in order to be fully appreciated. *—Alex Henderson*

Matters of the Heart / Apr. 28, 1992 / Elektra ♦♦
Less bold and angry than her previous work, Chapman paces *Matters of the Heart* over an acoustic course that touches equally on personal vignettes and social commentary. With her fluid, rapid-fire delivery, Chapman takes aim at society and lands several direct hits devoid of self-righteousness: songs about the downtrodden ("Bang Bang Bang"), feminism ("Woman's Work"), and freedom ("I Used to Be a Sailor"). The album's centerpiece is "If These Are the Things," a subtle, passionate masterpiece about coming to grips with innocence lost. A couple of songs suffer from too much sweetening in the studio, diluting the impact of Chapman's potent lyrics. The extraneous bells and whistles dressing up "Dreaming on a World" provide the most obvious example of a trend Chapman would do well to avoid in the future. *—Roch Parisien*

New Beginning / Nov. 14, 1995 / Elektra ♦♦♦
One might assume that the difference between Tracy Chapman's third album, which spent less than three months in the charts and failed to go gold after her first two albums had sold in the millions, and her fourth, which restored her to substantial commercial success, was the album's hit single, "Give Me One Reason." In fact, after a disappointing start, *New Beginning* turned around and started selling a few months after its release and before the single took off. It went gold the week that "Give Me One Reason" hit the charts. Of course, having a hit single helps, too, but since "Give Me One Reason" is a nearly generic blues song that isn't particularly characteristic of Chapman or of the album, it may have brought in an audience that didn't get what it expected. Though she has added a backup band, Chapman continues to take a simple musical approach that focuses attention on her voice and to sing lyrics that alternate between intimate emotional portraits and broad political generalizations that seem more felt than deeply thought out. Three songs here, "Heaven's Here on Earth," "The Rape of the World," and the title cut, are about the state of the whole world, which is viewed in either excessively sunny or gloomy terms. As such, Chapman's relationship songs, though they too can be a little vague, register more powerfully because they are so personal. As the title suggests, Chapman is adopting a more open and hopeful posture in both her feelings and her politics on *New Beginning*, and while the surprise success of "Give Me One Reason" is heartening from a career perspective, that's the real news here. *—William Ruhlmann*

Telling Stories / Feb. 15, 2000 / Elektra ♦♦♦
Forget that Tracy Chapman's fourth album shares a title with the Charlatans [UK]'s fifth album (and sole masterpiece) *Telling Stories*—as far any fan knows, Chapman probably isn't even aware of the Madchester group's existence. Instead, it should be viewed as what it is—the sequel to *New Beginning*, the album that reaffirmed Chapman's status as a fine singer/songwriter to a wide audience. That record became a hit thanks to a bluesy, hooky cut called "Give Me One Reason." *Telling Stories*, as the title suggests, leans toward narratives, but not necessarily in the conventional sense of the term. There are no story songs, in the way that "Fast Car" was a story. Instead, they are emotional, poetic snapshots—sort of like the musical equivalent of a dense, impressionistic short story. Chapman's songs on *Telling Stories* may not be as packed with detail as, say, Raymond Carver's work, but they certainly have a way of creating impressionistic lyrics, making short lines mean a lot. Also, the last album taught her a valuable lesson: her lyrics can be rich, but her compositions won't work collectively as a record if she doesn't craft melodic songs and warm productions. That's exactly what she delivers on *Telling Stories*. Some may think she does this to a fault—it's easy to coast on the sound of the record without

digging into the lyrics—but the end result is basically the same: a strong, appealing collection of sturdy, tuneful, and evocative songs. This album may not sparkle with genius, as her debut did, nor is it as direct as its predecessor, but it's a strong, solid record that maintains Chapman's reputation as a reliably intriguing and substantive singer/songwriter. *—Stephen Thomas Erlewine*

Chapterhouse

f. 1988, Reading, Berkshire, England

Noise Pop, Dream Pop, Space Rock, Shoegazing, Alternative Pop/Rock

After initially being lumped in with the acid-rock revival scene, Chapterhouse was pegged as one of the British "shoegazer" groups of the early '90s, along with Lush, Moose, and Slowdive. They formed in Reading in 1987 with Andrew Sherriff (guitar, vocals), Simon Rowe (guitar), Ashley Bates (drums), and Jon Curtis (bass; replaced by Russell Barrett early on). The group got its start supporting Spacemen 3 before releasing several well-received singles featuring the group's trademark distorted pop melodies. *—Steve Huey*

● **Whirlpool** / 1991 / Dedicated ♦♦♦♦

Victim of a double-whammy—caught in the already building backlash to the shoegazer scene at home and completely ignored in the States, as was just about anything else British, once *Nevermind* and *Ten* hit the charts Chapterhouse's album debut could have, and should have, won a bigger name for itself. At once more dance-flirting and garage-punky than most recordings by other My Bloody Valentine obsessives that emerged in the early nineties, though suffering the same underplaying in the vocal department, *Whirlpool* builds nicely on the three earlier EP releases with a similar sense of "what the hey—if it works, try it." As an album, it doesn't per se connect as a unified piece—the final track listing comes from a variety of recording sessions with a large number of producers and remixers, including Robin Guthrie, Stephen Hague, John Fryer and Ralph Jezzard. As a collection of mostly killer tracks, though, this is mighty fine. "Breather" kicks it off with a rushing shudder that mixes its acoustic and electric guitars well, while "Pearl" throws in trancey beats, John Bonham samples, and some fine art-glazed feedback riffs to create as perfect a nugget of the era as any. "Falling Down" has similar heavy-groove action to it, Madchester as played by Loop. Other highlights are more strictly rocky, like the slow build/rave-up/freakout/repeat "Autosleeper" and "April," with a big guitar wash up and out through the length of the song. A gentler version of early track "Something More" closes the album well; the overall effect is strong promise for whatever would come next. *—Ned Raggett*

Blood Music / Oct. 1993 / Dedicated ♦♦♦

Even more out of sync with the prevailing trends upon its release—Suede had hit the UK and Britpop's incipient reign was under way, while the USA still wanted its rock as manly grunge straight up—*Blood Music* at once wasn't quite the best follow-up in the world and yet worked much better as an album than *Whirlpool*, which given that it was constructed from almost as many different sessions as the first album ranks as even more of a surprise. The band's increasingly schizophrenic tastes reflected themselves in the music from the start, as opener "Don't Look Now" started with a swirling bit of techno/psychedelia, punctuated by a guitar riff shortly afterward. Songwise, things were not quite as distinct this time around; singles "We Are the Beautiful" and "She's a Vision" felt a little too much like pale copies of earlier stompers like "Pearl," though admittedly the vocals were a bit more upfront. Taken as a whole, however, somehow the album holds together well—everything flows just right throughout, shifting from the peppier semi-dance of "Everytime" to the chillier, slightly emptier "Deli," from the more rocked-up nuggets like "Greater Power" to the calm, floaty ending "Love Forever." It wasn't enough in the end to ensure the success of the album or the continuation of the band, but *Blood Music* still has enough going for it to suggest Chapterhouse might have gone on to greater things next time through. Differing bonus discs appeared on UK and US versions—the former consisted of a full remix of the album by techno duo Global Communication, while the latter included a couple of remixes from other acts, a sweet little number called "Frost," and the awesome "Picnic," a fifteen-minute ambient/rock piece that arguably was their best ever number. *—Ned Raggett*

Rownderbowt / 1996 / Dedicated ♦♦♦♦

Possibly one of the more unexpected "greatest hits"/archival releases ever, *Rownderbowt* is a surprise just by existing. Not many bands who only released two albums and a handful of singles to general public indifference would end up being the beneficiary of record company largess in getting a double-packed-to-the-max CD release, with plenty of rarities and unreleased tracks to boot. Whether the fanbase just proved more rabid than anyone expected or if Dedicated felt that a few more units shifted couldn't hurt, *Rownderbowt* turns out to be that rarest of beasts, a career overview for unfamiliar listeners equally appealing to the longtime supporter. The first disc covers the "hits," for lack of a better word—plenty of tracks from both studio albums, including all single A-sides (including their brilliant non-album cut "Mesmerised"), plus a generous amount of B-sides, including solid songs like the early rocker "Sixteen Years," their not-bad cover of the Beatles' "Rain," and the low-key "In My Arms." (This said, a little more room could have been made for such B-side joys as "Come Heaven" and "Precious One," but who said life was perfect?) The second disc mostly covers the hitherto unavailable goodies, including a good throb through Spacemen 3's "Losing Touch With My Mind," six demos of mostly fine tunes that never reached a final version, and one or two other random tracks. Also included: two remixes, the *Blood Music* bonus epic "Picnic," and the nuttiest thing Chapterhouse ever did, "Die Die Die," an over the top Stoogefest primal punk rant initially only available with the vinyl version of *Whirlpool* that single-handedly demolishes the bloodless shoegazer image the bandmembers had. *—Ned Raggett*

The Charlatans

f. 1966, **db.** 1970

Folk-Rock, Psychedelic

No relation to the British alternative rock band, the Charlatans, this San Francisco group has been widely credited as starting the Haight/Ashbury psychedelic scene. In retrospect, their contribution was more of a social one, planting seeds of a rock counterculture with their unconventional, at times outrageous dress and attitudes. While they occasionally delved into guitar distortion and fractured, stoned songwriting, the Charlatans' music was rooted in good-time jug-band blues, not psychedelic freakouts. That's not to say their records didn't have a low-key, easygoing charm, although they didn't match the innovations of the Jefferson Airplane and other peers. Cutting demos for a couple labels in 1966, most of the material they recorded at this time was unissued, and the commercial explosion of San Francisco rock passed them by. The band eventually did release a nationally distributed album in the late '60s, by which time personnel changes had diluted some of the crazy energy of the original lineup, although the LP has its engaging moments. *—Richie Unterberger*

The Charlatans / 1969 / One Way ♦♦♦

The word is that this album failed to capture the group's essence, but it has its share of good stuff. Their good-timey sound is balanced by an engaging sincerity and folky, melodic compositions reminiscent of very early Jefferson Airplane, although there are a couple ho-hum jug-band tunes. But the production and performances are too complacent and tame, lacking the spaced-out recklessness of the San Francisco scene that groups like the Airplane captured so well on record. *—Richie Unterberger*

Alabama Bound / 1970 / Eva ♦♦♦♦

Mid-1966 demos, recorded by Lovin' Spoonful producer Erik Jacobsen. Featuring blues, good-time music, and tentative psychedelia, it doesn't sound as crazy as one might have thought, but remains the only glimpse into the band at their most original during their early days. Also includes a live, ten-minute 1969 recording of the title track. *—Richie Unterberger*

First Album/Alabama Bound / Feb. 1996 / ROIR ♦♦♦♦♦

Eva Records' 24-song CD reissue of its two former LPs has far better sound than either of the vinyl discs. The material is enhanced, and the best of it (like the live "Alabama Bound") is indispensable. The notes are still rather sketchy, but this is still a worthwhile acquisition. *—Bruce Eder*

● **The Amazing Charlatans** / Sep. 17, 1996 / Big Beat ♦♦♦♦♦

After almost 30 years, there's finally a definitive document of one of the first San Francisco psychedelic groups—or, at least, as definitive a document as surviving tapes allow. This compilation assembles 23 tracks from their demos for the Kama Sutra and Autumn labels, as well as a couple of later sessions recorded at San Francisco area studios. Much of this material has been bootlegged previously, on both vinyl and tape, but here it appears in its best fidelity to date by far. Those expecting psychedelic fireworks will be surprised. There's some acid-soaked folk-rock here (most notably "We're Not on the Same Trip" and "I Saw Her," the two best cuts), but on the whole it's much more of a travelog of roots music, with White blues, jugband, folk, country, and music hall influences much more to the fore. Sure the Charlatans never really got the opportunity to flex their muscles in the studio, but it's also true that they didn't possess either the songwriting or instrumental chops to rival the Jefferson Airplane or Moby Grape. If you gear your expectations to the appropriate level, there's plenty of good-time mid-to-late-'60s Bay Area rock to savor here. Big Beat's meticulous packaging and programming also ensures that an important chapter in psychedelic/San Francisco music has been properly presented for the first time. *—Richie Unterberger*

The Ones Who Started It All . . . / 2000 / Shark ♦

Beware of this bootleg-type collection of mid-'60s material; almost all of it shows up, in much better fidelity, on the official *Amazing Charlatans* compilation on Ace, which also has about twice as many tracks. The sleeve doesn't tell you so, but the one song that is not included on the Ace retrospective, "Styrofoam," is not even a Charlatans song, but an early '70s cut by Loose Gravel (which included Charlatans member Mike Wilhelm). *—Richie Unterberger*

Charlatans UK

f. 1989, Manchester, England

Madchester, British Trad Rock, Britpop, Alternative Pop/Rock

For many years, the Charlatans [U.K.] were perceived as the also-rans of Madchester, the group that didn't capture the zeitgeist like the Stone Roses or the band that failed to match the mad genre-bending of the Happy Mondays. Of course, they were more traditional than either of their peers. Working from a Stonesy foundation, the Charlatans added dance-oriented rhythms and layers of swirling organs straight out of '60s psychedelia. At first, the Charlatans had great promise, and their initial singles—including "The Only One I Know"—were hits, but as Madchester and "baggy" faded away, the group began to look like relics. It was commonly assumed that their third album, 1994's *Up to Our Hips*, was the end of the line. However, the Charlatans made a remarkable comeback in 1995 with their eponymous fourth album, which found them embracing not only the flourishing Brit-pop movement, but also underground dance and techno, as well as their mainstay of classic rock. *The Charlatans* debuted at number one, and the group was hailed as survivors. Unfortunately, few knew how literal that term was—as the band was recording its follow-up album in 1996, organist Rob Collins, who had defined the band's sound, died in a car crash. The Charlatans decided to continue as a quartet, and their subsequent album, *Tellin' Stories*, debuted at number one upon its 1997 release, suggesting that they had become one of the great British journeyman bands of the '90s. —*Stephen Thomas Erlewine*

Some Friendly / 1990 / Beggars Banquet ♦♦♦♦
Emerging out of semi-nowhere—well, Norwich—the Charlatans UK were saddled with a name that lent itself to jibes about their quality, perceived bandwagon jumping and the burden of being a one-hit wonder with "The Only One I Know." Then *Some Friendly*, the group's debut, planted itself at the top of the UK charts; while the rest of the '90s were up-and-down for the band, this album set the band on its way. Drawing on Blunt's background in mod and psych outfits, Collins' outrageously funky keyboards and Burgess' unexpected star quality—even if his voice wasn't the strongest—*Some Friendly* is just that, a friendly and fun vibe. Some of the lyrics betray Burgess' sharp-tongued punk background—"You're Not Very Well," the opener, expresses anything but sunny sentiments—but otherwise *Some Friendly* delivers everything from '60s beat groove to Madchester bagginess with verve. True, the group was still following in the Roses/Mondays slipstream—"Fool's Gold" was the blueprint for much of the album—but the individual delights of the slow trance "Opportunity," "Polar Bear"'s upfront rhythms and "Flower"'s slightly ominous funk all show the band's abilities well. "The Only One I Know" remains the best-known cut, Blunt's crisp bass and Collins' Deep Purple-inspired keyboards providing its charge. But *Some Friendly*'s hidden masterpiece comes at the very end—"Sproston Green," a monster jam based on Collins' supreme keyboard work, with Burgess' soaring lyric matching the massive surge of the music. It remains the concluding number of the band's sets to this day for good reason. —*Ned Raggett*

Between 10th and 11th / Apr. 14, 1992 / Beggars Banquet ♦♦♦♦
A few songs aside, the Charlatans generally regard this release as their least successful album, considering it was recorded at a personal and professional crossroads (Baker's departure, Rob Collins' conviction, and so forth). Criticism within and without settled on Flood's production style as well, his crisp, technically sharp abilities seem to go against the band's natural flow. In hindsight, though, *Between* is much stronger than its reputation, with many fans proclaiming it their favorite. It's partly due to Burgess' more up-front vocals—his singing is still some of the calmest one will ever hear at the front of such a band, but his performance maintains *Some Friendly*'s loose flow while sounding more compelling. Similarly, Blunt's bass sounds stronger and Rob Collins' keyboards stand out more, either shading or leading the songs perfectly. "Weirdo," the album's lead single and strongest point, has a brilliant lead organ break from Collins and series of great funk stabs that became his strongest performance ever. Equally fine is the electric piano start to "Tremolo Song," leading to a deep Blunt bass and sassy flow of a song. Brookes and Mark Collins also fill out their parts equally well, with Flood's production strengthening and creating excellent arrangements for everyone as a whole. His numerous touches are really something, from the sudden shift to buried/flanged production on "Ignition" to "Subtitle"'s atmospheric mixing and burbling bass. Other highlights include the string-laden charge of "Can't Even Be Bothered" and the concluding "No One (Not Even the Rain)." —*Ned Raggett*

Up to Our Hips / Mar. 22, 1994 / Beggars Banquet ♦♦♦♦
Having experienced initial fame and its retreat, the Charlatans (perhaps somewhat self-consciously) set out to create a series of classic-rock-inspired albums, fusing everything from Dylan and the Stones to whatever else caught their fancy. *Up to Our Hips*, the first result, was produced by Steve Hillage, who made a career ranging from wacked-out hippie ramblings in Gong to the clean, inspired synth/Krautrock surge suffusing his production for Simple Minds. One thing he contributed to the Charlatans was more active percussion. While Flood didn't hide the drums on *Between*, on "Come In Number 21" Brookes' work feels strong and punchy for the first time. While production was a touch more straightforward than on *Between*, Hillage otherwise let the Charlatans be the Charlatans; where changes are apparent, it's more in the name of atmosphere than attention-getting, especially on the echoed, rumbling funk instrumental "Feel Flows" (excellent Blunt bass and Rob Collins clavinet on this one). The band stretches with the lovely, acoustic stomp "Autograph"; Mark Collins' guitar work was, increasingly, a larger part of the band's sound than Rob Collins' Hammond, but both worked well together. The laid-back lead single "Can't Get Out of Bed"'s lazy *Exile on Main Street* vibe and the equally groovy "Patrol" and "Jesus Hairdo" showcased both of their work to good effect, especially on the breaks between chorus and verse. Rob Collins certainly still has his moments—witness the opening build to the title track, another great effort with Blunt. Burgess sounds his strongest yet; while his singing still lurks in the mix more than anything else, he never disappears entirely. —*Ned Raggett*

The Charlatans [UK] / Sep. 12, 1995 / Beggars Banquet ♦♦♦♦
The Charlatans demonstrated signs of a revival on *Up to Our Hips*, yet that record in no way suggested the full-fledged return to form of *The Charlatans [UK]*, the group's most ambitious, focused and successful album. The group hasn't changed its sonic approach, yet their music has deepened, incorporating heavy dance elements without losing their core sound. Occasionally, the album relies too heavily on trippy dance instrumentals, but those are funkier and wilder than ever before, and they fit neatly next to the group's Stonesy pop, which is consistently catchy this time around. *The Charlatans [UK]* illustrates how a working rock & roll band can balance between traditional rock and modern, post-acid house music, and the results are frequently glorious. —*Stephen Thomas Erlewine*

Tellin' Stories / Apr. 21, 1997 / MCA ♦♦♦♦♦
The Charlatans made a surprising comeback in 1995, turning in an eponymous album that earned them their best reviews and sales ever. *Tellin' Stories*, the follow-up to *The Charlatans*, should have been triumphant, but tragedy struck midway through its recording, when keyboardist Rob Collins was killed in a car accident. Collins was an integral

part of the band's lineup, creating a distinctive, swirling, neo-psychedelic sound, and it seemed unlikely that the band could carry on without him, much less record a record as earthy and warm as *Tellin' Stories*. Primal Scream's Martin Duffy volunteered to help the band complete the album, which was bascially written before Collins' death, and that might explain why there are no overt references to his absence anywhere on the album. Instead, *Tellin' Stories* is another collection of classicist rock & roll spiked with dance beats, much like any other Charlatans album. Where its predecessor was more informed by mechanicized beats, the rhythms are more organic, which perfectly suits the rolling "North Country Boy," the sweeping "One to Another" and the heart-tugging "How Can You Leave Us?" And, like any other Charlatans album, it doesn't quite hold together, falling apart with instrumentals and ill-conceived songs toward the end. On the whole, however, *Tellin' Stories* is more consistent than their earlier records, and the best songs showcase the band at their strongest, which is quite an achievement considering the traumas the Charlatans underwent during its recording. More than anything, that's a fitting salute to Rob Collins. —*Stephen Thomas Erlewine*

● **Melting Pot** / Jun. 9, 1998 / Beggars Banquet ♦♦♦♦♦
When the Charlatans emerged with "The Only One I Know" in 1991, there were countless bands similar to them, but they immediately catapulted to the forefront of the Madchester scene, standing alongside such icons as the Stone Roses and the Happy Mondays. They had such success because they not only could ride the groove, like so many Madchester bands, but they could also write great songs, drawing partially from the '60s-saturated Roses and the Rolling Stones. These were the gifts that made them among the greatest British survivors of their time, rolling through tragedy and stylistic changes to amass a terrific little body of work—one that was modern enough to play in clubs (they were the first rock band to embrace the Chemical Brothers, after all) but classicist enough to stand the test of time. Occasionally, they could pull all this together throughout the course of a proper album—particularly on 1995's *The Charlatans* and 1997's masterpiece, *Tellin' Stories*—but usually they shined their brightest on singles. And this means that the 1998 singles compilation *Melting Pot* shines bright among their catalog, making a strong argument for their talents. Over the course of 17 songs (including such nominal rarities as the US Version of "Sproston Green" and the Chemical's mix of "Patrol"), the singles unfurl at an intoxicating pace; some get by only on texture, but there are more than enough where the sound and song merge brilliant, highlighted by the lazy Jaggerisms of "Can't Get Out of Bed," the raucous "Jesus Hairdo," "Just Lookin'," the hard dark funk of "One to Another," the blissful "North Country Boy" and, of course, "The Only One I Know," a record that transcends its baggy times to stand as a pop classic. And if this doesn't necessarily prove that they shine like geniuses, *Melting Pot* does prove they were a damn fine band, whose best moments hold their own alongside bigger stars from either side of the ocean. —*Stephen Thomas Erlewine*

Us and Us Only / Oct. 19, 1999 / MCA ♦♦♦♦
Us and Us Only picks up where *Tellin' Stories* left off and twists that album's virtues around. Where that record was essentially a stripped-down, straight-ahead collection, *Us and Us Only* dresses up the band's continually impressive songcraft in a moody atmosphere, borrowed in equal parts from *Blonde on Blonde*, Beggars Banquet, and the Chemical Brothers. The album unfolds in a haze of keyboards and subdued beats, and this murky veil never really lifts throughout the record, even as harmonics and acoustic guitars break through the mist every once and a while. Consequently, the album can initially seem a little amorphous, albeit intriguingly amorphous, filled with deep grooves and tantalizing sonic textures. Repeated plays reveal that *Us and Us Only* is merely a step below their previous high point of *Tellin' Stories*. If nothing is as immediately grabbing as "North Country Boy" or "One to Another," that's not a problem, since nearly every song works its charms with subtle grace and considerable muscle. "Forever" soon reveals itself as a minor masterpiece of swirling menace and swagger, while the Dylan inflections of "A House Is Not a Home" and "My Beautiful Friend" seem natural instead of grandstanding. Soon, it becomes apparent that, unlike most of their trad rock contemporaries, the Charlatans figured out how to make their music sound both timeless and modern by quietly adding influences and changing their attack each time around, while remaining true to their core sound, much like the Stones did in their prime. The Charlatans may not be as innovative or as song-oriented as the Stones, but after a decade of recording, they're turning out to be nearly as consistent as the Stones were at the same point in their career, which is no small accomplishment. —*Stephen Thomas Erlewine*

Wonderland / Sep. 11, 2001 / MCA ♦♦♦
Seven albums in, and the Charlatans haven't so much settled into a groove as they've settled into a style. They long ago carved out a niche between classic British rock and post-Madchester British dance, and that's what made their music seem fresh for several different generations—they represented whatever you wanted to see within their distinctly British blend. In that sense, they are indeed proving themselves to be like the Stones, who subtly incorporated modern trends into the sound, sometimes so seamlessly you didn't realize they were branching out. The Charlatans work from the same template, gradually expanding their sonic texture in terms of modern dance trends, without ever abandoning their rock base. They occasionally emphasize one side over another—*Us and Us Only* played to the rock side of the fence, while *Wonderland* is very heavy on groove and texture, a move that's strangely emphasized by Tim Burgess' unexpected reliance on a falsetto. This can mean that the songs fade into the background, but that often seems like an intentional move, since it happens so frequently throughout a record where the surface remains stylish and sleek. Still, that means there's not a whole lot to hold onto, although certain songs start to emerge upon repeated listens—"You're So Pretty—We're So Pretty" seduces with its minor-key swagger, "Love Is the Key" rocks convincingly, "I Just Can't Get Over Losing You" swings nicely. Even so, this winds up as simply a good, solid

Charlatans record, despite the efforts to jazz things up with a heavier dancefloor quotient. That may seem like a slight, but a solid Charlatans record still satisfies, and can't quite be taken for granted just yet. *—Stephen Thomas Erlewine*

Ray Charles

b. Sep. 23, 1930, Albany, GA

Vocals, Leader, Piano / Pop-Soul, Country-Soul, Jazz Blues, Urban Blues, Piano Blues, R&B, Soul

Ray Charles was the musician most responsible for developing soul music. Singers like Sam Cooke and Jackie Wilson also did a great deal to pioneer the form, but Charles did even more to devise a new form of Black pop by merging '50s R&B with gospel-powered vocals, adding plenty of flavor from contemporary jazz, blues, and (in the '60s) country. Then there is his singing—his style is among the most emotional and easily identifiable of any 20th-century performer, up there with the likes of Elvis and Billie Holiday. He's also a superb keyboard player, arranger, and bandleader. The brilliance of his 1950s and 1960s work, however, can't obscure the fact that he's made few classic tracks since the mid-'60s, though he's recorded often and tours to this day. Blind since the age of six (from glaucoma), by the late '40s he was recording in a smooth pop/R&B style derivative of Nat "King" Cole and Charles Brown. He got his first Top Ten R&B hit with "Baby, Let Me Hold Your Hand" in 1951. It was at Atlantic Records that Ray truly found his voice with "I Got a Woman," a number two R&B hit in 1955. This is the song most frequently singled out as his pivotal performance, on which Charles first truly let go with his unmistakable gospelish moan, backed by a tight, bouncy horn-driven arrangement. Throughout the '50s, Charles ran off a series of R&B hits that, although they weren't called "soul" at the time, did a lot to pave the way for soul by presenting a form of R&B that was sophisticated without sacrificing any emotional grit. "This Little Girl of Mine," "Drown in My Own Tears," "Hallelujah I Love Her So," "Lonely Avenue," and "The Right Time" were all big hits. But Charles didn't really capture the pop audience until "What'd I Say," which caught the fervor of the church with its pleading vocals, as well as the spirit of rock & roll with its classic electric piano line. It was his first Top Ten pop hit, and one of his final Atlantic singles, as he left the label at the end of the '50s for ABC. One of the chief attractions of the ABC deal for Charles was a much greater degree of artistic control of his recordings. He put it to good use on early-'60s hits like "Unchain My Heart" and "Hit the Road Jack," which solidified his pop stardom with only a modicum of polish attached to the R&B he had perfected at Atlantic. In 1962, he surprised the pop world by turning his attention to country & western music, topping the charts with the "I Can't Stop Loving You" single, and making a hugely popular album (in an era in which R&B/soul LPs rarely scored high on the charts) with *Modern Sounds in Country and Western Music*. *—Richie Unterberger*

Genius & Soul: The 50th Anniversary Collection / Feb. 1949-1993 / Rhino ✦✦✦✦✦
As the first comprehensive, multi-label box set assembled on Ray Charles, the five-disc, 101-song *Genius & Soul: The 50th Anniversary Collection* is an extensive overview of one of the greatest musicians of the 20th century. Charles produced a body of work so rich and diverse that even five CDs only scratches the surface of his accomplishments. None of his instrumentals are on *Genius & Soul*, nor are his jazz and traditional pop efforts spotlighted. Instead, the box traces the evolution of his career, as he moves from an R&B pioneer to a mainstream pop crooner to a country-pop vocalist to a contemporary soul singer. Charles was a gripping, captivating vocalist, capable of making even bland music sound vital, but the fact is, his '70s and '80s recordings pale in comparison to his seminal '50s and '60s sides. Which means that the set becomes less compelling as it reaches the fifth disc, but the first three and a half discs are filled with timeless music that remains exciting, vital and altogether wondrous. *—Stephen Thomas Erlewine*

The Early Years / 1949-1952 / Tomato ✦✦✦
In the late '40s and early '50s, Charles recorded several dozen sides for the Swingtime/Downbeat label, 30 of which are presented here. As has been noted many times by critics, these usually found Charles in a Nat "King" Cole swing-blues groove that was much smoother than the gritty R&B/soul he'd record for Atlantic in the later '50s; the influence of urban blues balladeer Charles Brown is also evident. Some critical essays, in fact, may lead you to believe that this work is trivial, but while it's undeniably derivative, it's enjoyable on its own terms, and not without strong hints of the searing soulfulness that was to come. Some of the selections are delivered with such refined polish that it doesn't even sound like Charles. But on the more anguished and fast-tempoed cuts in particular, you can hear him starting to arrive at the phrasing and emotion that would flower in the mid-'50s. Unfortunately, like most Tomato reissues, the sound is substandard; even assuming that the master tapes can't be located, a better job was probably possible, and a couple of cuts even duplicate skips from the vinyl. Exact dates and songwriting credits are also missing, although Pete Welding's essay does at least discuss the material on the discs in some detail, unlike many of Tomato's liner notes. *—Richie Unterberger*

The Birth of a Legend / 1949-1952 / Valley Vue ✦✦✦✦✦
Of all the countless compilations that have been stitched together of Ray Charles' early sides for Jack Lauderdale's Swing Time Records, this two-disc box is the only CD package that treats these enormously important works with the reverent respect that they deserve (meaning decent mono sound quality instead of murky electronic reprocessed stereo dubbed from vinyl, cogent liner notes, and full discographical annotation). This is where the genius began, imitating Charles Brown at the very start (1949) and sounding like nobody but Brother Ray by 1952 (when he defected to Atlantic and hit the real big time). Forty-one tracks in all. *—Bill Dahl*

Blues + Jazz / May 26, 1950-Jun. 26, 1959 / Rhino/Atlantic ✦✦✦✦✦
Another easy access point for Charles' seminal Atlantic catalog. This two-disc set is evenly split between his bluesiest sides on the first disc and a selection of his greatest jazz sides on disc two (gorgeously showcasing the sax work of David "Fathead" Newman on several pieces). Charles was a masterful blues purveyor; his "I Believe to My Soul" is simultaneously invested with heartbreak and humor, while the earlier "Sinner's Prayer," "The Sun's Gonna Shine Again," and the gospel-based "A Fool for You" emanate both hope and deep pain. *—Bill Dahl*

☆ **The Birth of Soul** / 1951-1959 / Atlantic ✦✦✦✦✦
The title isn't just hype—this absolutely essential three-disc box is where soul music first took shape and soared, courtesy of Ray Charles' church-soaked pipes and bedrock piano work. Brother Ray's formula for inventing the genre was disarmingly simple: he brought gospel intensity to the R&B world with his seminal "I Got a Woman," "Hallelujah I Love Her So," "Leave My Woman Alone," "You Be My Baby," and the primal 1959 call-and-response classic "What'd I Say." There's plenty of brilliant blues content within these 53 historic sides: Charles' mournful "Losing Hand," "Feelin' Sad," "Hard Times," and "Blackjack" ooze after-hours desperation. No blues collection should be without this boxed set, which comes with well-researched notes by Robert Palmer, a nicely illustrated accompanying booklet, and discographical info aplenty. *—Bill Dahl*

★ **The Best of Atlantic** / 1951-1961 / Rhino ✦✦✦✦✦
The 20-track compilation (only 12 tracks on cassette) *The Best of Atlantic* compiles all of Ray Charles' Top Ten R&B hits for Atlantic Records, from "I've Got A Woman" and "This Little Girl of Mine" to "Drown in My Own Tears," "Halleujah I Love Her So," "Lonely Avenue," "(Night Time Is) The Right Time," and "What'd I Say (Part 1)." In addition to the big hits, there are minor hits that nevertheless showcase Charles at his peak, like "Swanee River Rock" and "Just for a Thrill." For fans that only want the hits and don't want to invest in the splendid three-disc set *The Birth of Soul*, *The Best of Atlantic* is an essential purchase. *—Stephen Thomas Erlewine*

The Great Ray Charles / 1956 / Atlantic ✦✦✦
This set is rather unusual, for it is strictly instrumental, allowing Ray Charles a rare opportunity to be a jazz-oriented pianist. Two selections are with a trio (bassist Oscar Pettiford joins Charles on "Black Coffee"), while the other six are with a septet taken from his big band of the period. Key among the sidemen are David Newman (soloing on both tenor and alto) and trumpeter Joseph Bridgewater; highlights include Quincy Jones' "The Ray," "My Melancholy Baby," "Doodlin'," and "Undecided." Ray Charles should have recorded in this setting more often in his later years. *—Scott Yanow*

The Genius After Hours / 1956 / Rhino ✦✦✦✦✦
Taken from the same three sessions as *The Great Ray Charles* but not duplicating any of the performances, this set casts Charles as a jazz-oriented pianist in an instrumental setting. Brother Ray has five numbers with a trio (three songs have Oscar Pettiford on bass) and jams on three other tunes ("Hornful Soul," "Ain't Misbehavin" and "Joy Ride") with a septet arranged by Quincy Jones; solo space is given to David "Fathead" Newman on tenor and alto and trumpeter Joseph Bridgewater. Fine music, definitely a change of pace for Ray Charles. *—Scott Yanow*

The Genius Hits the Road / 1956-1972 / Rhino ✦✦✦
In keeping with his jazz/pop crossover ambitions, Charles decided to record a concept album of sorts with a dozen songs devoted to various parts of the U.S.—"Alabamy Bound," "Georgia On My Mind," "Moonlight in Vermont," "California, Here I Come," "Blue Hawaii," etc. The crossover vibe is further heightened by the brassy big-band arrangements, and material from the likes of Al Jolson and Hoagy Carmichael. It sounds a bit corny now, with an in-your-face gung-ho cheer. But it did what Charles wanted it to do, reaching the Top Ten of the album charts, and spinning off a big hit with "Georgia On My Mind." The 1997 CD reissue on Rhino adds seven bonus tracks from 1956-1972 that also had a travel/geographic theme, and the best of these are actually the highlights of the record, most notably "Hit the Road Jack," "Lonely Avenue," and his cover of Hank Snow's "I'm Movin' On." *—Richie Unterberger*

Ray Charles at Newport / Jul. 5, 1958 / Atlantic ✦✦✦✦✦
For his appearance at the Newport Jazz Festival on July 5, 1958, Charles pulled out all the stops, performing raucous versions of "The Right Time," "I Got a Woman," and "Talkin' 'bout You." [This album was reissued in 1973 as a two-record set, packaged with *Ray Charles in Person* under the title *Ray Charles Live* (Atlantic SD 2-503).] *—William Ruhlmann*

The Genius of Ray Charles / 1959 / Atlantic ✦✦✦✦✦
Some players from Ray Charles' big band are joined by many ringers from the Count Basie and Duke Ellington bands for the first half of this program, featuring Charles belting out six songs arranged by Quincy Jones. "Let the Good Times Roll" and "Deed I Do" are highlights, and there are solos by tenorman David "Fathead" Newman, trumpeter Marcus Belgrave and (on "Two Years of Torture") tenor Paul Gonsalves. The remaining six numbers are ballads, with Charles backed by a string orchestra arranged by Ralph Burns (including "Come Rain or Come Shine" and "Don't Let the Sun Catch You Cryin'"). Ray Charles' voice is heard throughout in peak form, giving soul to even the veteran standards. *—Scott Yanow*

Genius + Soul = Jazz/My Kind of Jazz / Dec. 26, 1960-1970 / Rhino ✦✦✦✦✦
Single-disc CD reissue combines two of Charles' more jazz-oriented outings, though *Genius + Soul* (from 1961) enjoys a much more sterling reputation than the comparatively obscure *My Kind of Jazz* (1970). Question: if genius plus soul equals jazz, does that mean genius minus soul equals fusion? *—Richie Unterberger*

Ray Charles and Betty Carter / Jun. 13, 1961-1966 / ABC/Paramount ✦✦✦✦
This pairing of two totally idiosyncratic vocalists acquired legendary status over the decades in which it had been out of print. But the proof is in the listening, and frankly it

doesn't represent either artist's best work. There is certainly a powerful, often sexy rapport between the two—Charles in his sweet balladeering mode, Carter with her uniquely keening, drifting high register—and they definitely create sparks in the justly famous rendition of "Baby, It's Cold Outside." The main problem is in Marty Paich's string/choir arrangements, which too often cross over the line into treacle, whereas his charts for big band are far more listenable. Moreover, Charles' sweetness can get a bit cloying too, although some of the old grit emerges on "Takes Two To Tango." On the CD reissue—remixed by Charles himself—Dunhill adds the great, rare B-side to the "Unchain My Heart" single, "But On The Other Hand Baby," and two excellent if unrelated album cuts, "I Never See Maggie Alone" (1964) and "I Like To Hear It Sometime" (1966). *—Richard S. Ginell*

The Genius Sings the Blues / Oct. 1961 / Atlantic ✦✦✦✦✦
Down-home, anguished laments and moody ballads were turned into triumphs by Ray Charles. He sang these songs with the same conviction, passion, and energy that made his country and soul vocals so majestic. This has not as of yet turned up in the reissue bins, but is probably headed in that direction. *—Ron Wynn*

Modern Sounds in Country & Western Music / 1961-1962 / Rhino ✦✦✦✦✦
Less modern for its country-R&B blend (Elvis Presley & company did it in 1955) and lushly produced C&W tone (the Nashville sound cropped up in the late '50s) than for its place as a high-profile crossover hit, *Modern Sounds in Country and Western* fit right in with Ray Charles' expansive musical ways while on the Atlantic label in the '50s. In need of even more room to explore, Charles signed with ABC-Paramount and eventually took full advantage of his contract's "full artistic freedom clause" with this collection of revamped country classics. Covering a period from 1939 to the early '60s, the 12 tracks here touch on old-timey fare (Floyd Tillman's "It Makes No Difference to Me Now"), honky tonk (three Hank Williams songs), and early countrypolitan (Don Gibson's "I Can't Stop Loving You"). Along with a Top Ten go at Eddy Arnold's "You Don't Know Me," the Gibson cover helped the album remain at the top of the pop charts for nearly three months and brought Charles international fame. Above a mix of swinging big band charts by Gerald Wilson and strings and choir backdrops from Marty Paich, Charles' intones the sleepy-blue nuances of country crooners while still giving the songs a needed kick with his gospel outbursts. No pedal-steel or fiddles here, just a fine store of inimitable interpretations. *—Stephen Cook*

Greatest Hits, Vol. 1 / 1961-1965 / DCC ✦✦✦✦✦
The first of two DCC compilations to collect the best of Brother Ray's 1960s stint at ABC-Paramount Records, when he flew off in a dozen different stylistic directions. Included on this 20-track disc are Charles' immortal rendering of "Georgia on My Mind," and the sinuously bluesy "Unchain My Heart," the Latin-beat instrumental "One Mint Julep," personalized remakes of the country standards "Born to Lose," "Your Cheating Heart," and "Crying Time," and his exultant rendition of the soulful "Let's Go Get Stoned." *—Bill Dahl*

Greatest Hits, Vol. 2 / 1961-1965 / DCC ✦✦✦✦✦
More seminal performances from the '60s ABC catalog of the Genius (DCC split the classics evenly between the two discs, making both of them indispensable). His beloved "Hit the Road Jack" (one of several Percy Mayfield copyrights dotting Charles' repertoire), the daring country crossover "I Can't Stop Loving You," an electric-piano powered "Sticks and Stones," a wise "Them That Got," and a wonderfully mellow "At the Club" rank with the 20-song disc's standouts (though versions of the Beatles' "Yesterday" and the corny "Look What They Done to My Song, Ma" end the set on a bummer note). *—Bill Dahl*

☆ **Modern Sounds in Country & Western, Vol. 2** / 1962 / Rhino ✦✦✦✦✦
Charles' second installment of *Modern Sounds in Country and Western Music* is every bit as essential as the first, containing stellar interpretations of "Your Cheatin' Heart" and "You Are My Sunshine." *—Stephen Thomas Erlewine*

Ingredients in a Recipe for Soul / Jul. 1963 / ABC ✦✦✦✦
Although it was a big commercial success, reaching number two on the LP charts, this record would typify the erratic nature of much of Charles' '60s output. It's too eclectic for its own good, really, encompassing pop standards, lowdown blues, Mel Torme songs, and after-hours ballads. The high points are very high—"Busted," his hit reworking of a composition by country songwriter Harlan Howard, is jazzy and tough, and one of his best early-'60s singles. And the low points are pretty low, especially when he adds the snow-white backup vocals of the Jack Halloran Singers to "Over the Rainbow" and "Ol' Man River." A number of the remaining cuts are pretty respectable, like the tight big-band arrangement of "Ol' Man Time" and the ominously urbane "Where Can I Go?" In 1997, it was paired with the 1964 LP *Have a Smile with Me* on a two-for-one CD reissue on Rhino, with the addition of historical liner notes. *—Richie Unterberger*

Ingredients in a Recipe for Soul/Have a Smile with Me / 1963-1964 / Rhino ✦✦✦
A two-for-one pairing of albums from 1963 (*Ingredients in a Recipe for Soul*) and 1964 (*Have a Smile with Me*), with the addition of historical liner notes. Neither rate among his better albums—both are inconsistent mixtures of hard-edged jazz/pop/soul and mainstream pop standards. Each, though, has some fine cuts, notably the Top Ten hit "Busted" (on *Recipe*) and a jazzy cover of Hank Williams' "Move It On Over" (on *Have a Smile With Me*). The CD also adds two bonus tracks: both parts of the orchestral pop "Without a Song" single from 1965. *—Richie Unterberger*

Sweet & Sour Tears / Mar. 1964 / Rhino ✦✦✦
One of a series of ultra-loose concept albums Charles cut in the '60s, this one dedicated entirely to songs with titles or lyrical references to crying and tears. It's an excuse for Ray to choose his usual varied menu of upbeat jumpers, slow countrified weepers, and proudly saccharine pop standards. The production, as one might fear, also tends to the lachrymose side on the slow tunes, with the thick strings and backup vocals straight out of TV variety shows. One is almost tempted to think that Charles was toying with audience expectations by mixing unabashedly sentimental slow tunes with the far more bluesy, satisfying, and upbeat numbers, such as "Don't Cry, Baby" and "Baby, Don't You Cry," as well as his surprisingly brassy, punchy treatment of "Cry Me a River." These outings have always played much better with critics than the gloppy pop tunes, and for good reason—they are much better. The Rhino CD reissue adds seven bonus tracks from throughout his early career (1956-71) that also tapped into the "crying" motif. These threaten to steal the show from the *Sweet & Sour Tears* album it's supposedly embellishing, including the Bacharach-David penned 1964 single "I Wake Up Crying," the smoldering 1966 album track "No Use Crying," and the 1956 R&B chart-topper "Drown in My Own Tears," next to which much of the rest of the program sounds positively hokey. *—Richie Unterberger*

Genius After Hours/Great Ray Charles / Jul. 7, 1987 / Rhino/Atlantic ✦✦✦
A pair of Ray Charles masterpieces. These spotlight his instrumental and jazz side. They were recorded in the late '50s, and Charles' band at the time included Hank Crawford, Fathead Newman, and Buster Cooper, with Charles doubling on keyboards and alto sax. Quincy Jones was providing the arrangements as well. Some spectacular combo material, showing the links between blues and jazz. *—Ron Wynn*

Anthology / 1989 / Rhino ✦✦✦✦✦
Perhaps the best single CD collection of Ray Charles' '60s and '70s ABC-Paramount material. They've also been issued on two separate anthologies, but for someone who only wants the essential items, this disc has them all over its 20 tracks. *—Ron Wynn*

Soul Brothers/Soul Meeting / 1989 / Atlantic ✦✦✦✦✦
This brings together all of the extant takes recorded for two albums that Milt Jackson made with Ray Charles for Atlantic in 1957 and 1958. With Oscar Pettiford, Connie Kay, and Kenny Burrell in the various lineups, this is bluesy jazz in a laid-back manner; it surprised many hardcore R&B fans when these albums were originally issued. Jackson moves from vibes to piano, and even guitar (on "Bag's Guitar Blues"), while Ray jumps between piano and alto sax on these sessions. A rare glimpse of Charles' jazz soul coming up for air. *—Cub Koda*

Complete Country & Western Recordings 1959-1986 / Oct. 27, 1998 / Rhino ✦✦✦✦
Ray Charles' explorations into country music were no mere dalliance. They have their genesis in "I'm Movin' On," the last record he made for Atlantic before moving on to ABC Paramount in 1960. But it was with the enormously successful *Modern Sounds in Country & Western* series of albums in 1962 (and the career making single "I Can't Stop Lovin' You") that made their mark, crossing over genre boundaries that were unthinkable at the time. An African-American doing hillbilly music was not a first, nor were uptown arrangements of hillbilly songs, but here was the Genius of Soul validating the music of the white working class, plain and simple. He was putting his own spin to it (hence the *Modern Sounds*), not merely a black voice singing Gene Autry songs, investing them with pain, emotion, and sorrow. It was an unprecedented achievement, both commercially and artistically, and now—decades later—it's viewed as just another genre-bender in the grand Ray Charles tradition. But this 92-track, four-CD box set is the first to gather them all in one place and view it as a consistent piece of work spread over a career as a stylist that's second to none. The first disc combines both volumes of the *Modern Sounds* albums; the rest of the anthology moves through singles, various returns to the concept over the years, and stray tracks from his later stretch at Columbia to spice it all up. This multi-disc set contains some very special music, nicely packaged—a moment in American music well worth investigating. *—Cub Koda*

The Very Best of Ray Charles / Mar. 14, 2000 / Rhino ✦✦✦✦
This 16-track budget package hits all the high notes of Brother Ray's rise to greatness. Starting in the '50s with classic Atlantic sides like "I've Got a Woman," "Hallelujah I Love Her So," "Night Time (Is the Right Time)," and "What'd I Say," the set also includes his landmark ABC country sides of the '60s ("I Can't Stop Loving You," "Georgia on My Mind"), finishing up with a duet with Willie Nelson on "Seven Spanish Angels." A perfect introduction to an American musical treasure. *—Cub Koda*

Chavez

f. 1993, New York, NY
Math Rock, Indie Rock
The angular indie rock unit Chavez was led by singer/guitarist Matt Sweeney, the former frontman of New Jersey's Skunk. Following the group's demise, Sweeney joined the New York band Wider, which included onetime Live Skull drummer James Lo; when Wider dissolved in 1992, Sweeney began playing with ex-Bullet Lavolta guitarist Clay Tarver. Lo joined not long after, and with bassist Davey Hoskins, Chavez cut its first demo recordings in late 1993. Following Hoskins' exit and the recruitment of bassist Scott Masciarelli, the band made its live debut; soon, the anthemic 1994 debut single "Repeat the Ending" and a reputation for stunning live sets made Chavez a hot commodity on the New York club scene. Their acclaimed debut *Gone Glimmering* and the follow-up EP *Pentagram Ring* appeared in 1995; the full-length *Ride the Fader* followed a year later. *—Jason Ankeny*

Gone Glimmering / May 18, 1995 / Matador ✦✦✦✦
Despite the group's tendency to meander, Chavez's *Gone Glimmering* is an impressive debut, finding the group marrying complex, grinding riffs to cerebral melodies and hooks. *—Stephen Thomas Erlewine*

● **Ride the Fader** / Nov. 5, 1996 / Matador ✦✦✦✦
Working from the basic foundation they established on *Gone Glimmering*, Chavez spins off into new territories on their second album, *Ride the Fader*. Equal parts post-hardcore

punk and prog-metal, Chavez's music is intellectual guitar rock—riffs are fractured and self-consciously asymmetrical, winding in on themselves and then turning inside out. What prevents *Ride the Fader* from becoming a tedious, pompous exercise in experimental rock is visceral directness, combined with detail. Chavez is a powerful, muscular band, capable of giving their densely packed songs a startling immediacy. *—Stephen Thomas Erlewine*

Cheap Trick

f. 1975, Rockford, IL

Album Rock, Arena Rock, Pop/Rock, Power Pop, New Wave, Hard Rock

Combining a love for British guitar-pop songcraft with crunching power chords and a flair for the absurd, Cheap Trick provided the necessary links between '60s pop, heavy metal, and punk. The band's early albums were filled with highly melodic, well-written songs that drew equally from the crafted pop of the Beatles, the sonic assault of the Who, and the tongue-in-cheek musical eclecticism and humor of the Move. Their sound provided a blueprint for both power-pop and arena rock, plus influenced alternative and heavy-metal bands of the '80s and '90s.

Although beloved by fans and acclaimed in some quarters, Cheap Trick's first three albums, didn't reach anything larger than a cult audience in the late '70s. These same recordings made them virtual superstars in Japan, something the band realized when they toured the country in 1978. They recorded their sold-out shows at Budokan Arena, and the album, *At Budokan,* appeared after 1978's *Heaven Tonight* made headway on the pop charts. *At Budokan* turned into a smash, reaching number four, staying on the charts for over year, giving them their first Top 10 hit with "I Want You to Want Me" and eventually selling over three million copies. *Dream Police,* their fourth album, followed it into the Top 10. Following the recording of 1980's George Martin-produced *All Shook Up,* Petersson left the group. *All Shook Up* performed respectably, as did 1982's *One on One,* yet they soon hit a commercial slump that lasted over five years. Petersson rejoined the band in 1988, as the band began work on *Lap of Luxury.* Thanks to the number one power ballad "The Flame," the album was a genuine comeback, reaching the Top 20. Its follow-up, *Busted,* stalled on the charts. During the '90s, they never had a hit, yet they were held in high regard by a new generation of rockers who embraced the group's early records. Toward the end of the decade, the group released two acclaimed independent records—1997's *Cheap Trick* plus the 1999 live LP, *Music For Hangovers.* *—Stephen Thomas Erlewine*

☆ **Cheap Trick [1977]** / 1977 / Epic/Legacy ✦✦✦✦✦

Cheap Trick's eponymous debut is an explosion fusion of Beatlesesque melodic hooks, Who-styled power, and a twisted sense of humor partially borrowed from the Move. But that only begins to scratch the surface of what makes *Cheap Trick* a dynamic record. Guitarist Rick Nielsen has a powerful sense of dynamics and arrangments, which gives the music an extra kick, but he also can write exceptionally melodic and subversive songs. Nothing on *Cheap Trick* is quite what it seems. While the songs have hooks and attitude that arena-rock was sorely lacking in the late '70s, they are also informed by a bizarre sensibility, whether it's the driving "He's a Whore," the dreamy "Mandocello," or the thumping Gary Glitter perversion "ELO Kiddies." "The Ballad of TV Violence" is about mass murder, while "Daddy Should Have Stayed in High School" concerns pedophiles. All of it is told with a sense of humor, but it doesn't come off as cheap or smirking because of the group's hard-rocking drive and Robin Zander's pop-idol vocals. Even "Oh, Candy," apparently a love song on first listen, is an affecting tribute to a friend who committed suicide. In short, Cheap Trick revels in taboo subjects with abandon, devoting themselves to the power of the hook, as well as sheer volume and gut-wrenching rock & roll—though the record was more musically accomplished than punk rock, it shared the same aesthetic. The combination of off-kilter humor, bizarre subjects and blissful power-pop made *Cheap Trick* one of the defining albums of its era, as well as one of the most influential. *—Stephen Thomas Erlewine*

In Color / 1977 / Epic/Legacy ✦✦✦✦✦

Though Cheap Trick's second album *In Color (And In Black and White)* draws from the same stockpile of Midwestern barroom favorites as their debut album, it was produced by Tom Werman, who had the band strip away their raw attack and replace it with a shiny, radio-ready sound. Consequently, *In Color* doesn't have the visceral attack of its predecessor, but it still has the same sensibility and a similar set of spectacular songs. From the druggy psychedelia of "Downed" and the bubblegum sing-a-long "I Want You to Want Me" to the "California Girls" homage of "Southern Girls," the album has the same encyclopedic knowledge of rock & roll, as well as the good sense to subvert it with a perverse sense of humor. Portions of the album haven't dated well, simply due to the glossy production, but the songs and music on *In Color* are as splendid as the debut. *—Stephen Thomas Erlewine*

☆ **Heaven Tonight** / 1978 / Epic/Legacy ✦✦✦✦✦

Heaven Tonight, like *In Color,* was produced by Tom Werman, but the difference between the two records is substantial. Where *In Color* often sounded emasculated, *Heaven Tonight* regains the powerful, arena-ready punch of *Cheap Trick,* but crosses it with a clever radio-friendly production that relies both on synthesizers and studio effects. Even with the fairly slick production, Cheap Trick sounds ferocious throughout the album, slamming heavy metal, power-pop and hard rock together in a humongous sound. "Surrender," the definitive Cheap Trick song, opens the album with a tale about a kid whose parents are hipper than himself, and the remainder of the record is a rollercoaster ride, peaking with the sneering "Auf Wiedersehen," the dreamily psychedelic title track, the roaring rocker "On Top of the World," the high-stepping, tongue-in-cheek "How Are You" and the pulverizing cover of the Move's "California Man." *Heaven Tonight* is the culmination of the group's dizzying early career, summing up the strengths of their first two albums, their live show and their talent for inverting pop conventions. They were never quite as consistently thrilling on record ever again. *—Stephen Thomas Erlewine*

★ **Live at Budokan** / Feb. 1979 / Epic ✦✦✦✦✦

While their records were entertaining and full of skillful pop, it wasn't until *Live at Budokan* that Cheap Trick's vision truly gelled. Many of these songs, like "I Want You to Want Me" and "Big Eyes," were pleasant in their original form, but seemed more like sketches compared to the roaring versions on this album. With their ear-shatteringly loud guitars and sweet melodies, Cheap Trick unwittingly paved the way for much of the hard-rock of the next decade, as well as a surprising amount of alternative rock of the 1990s, and it was *Live at Budokan* that captured the band in all of its power. *—Stephen Thomas Erlewine*

Dream Police / Oct. 1979 / Epic ✦✦✦✦✦

At the Budokan unexpectedly made Cheap Trick stars, largely because "I Want You to Want Me" had a tougher sound than its original studio incarnation. Perversely—and most things Cheap Trick have done are somehow perverse—the band decided *not* to continue with the direct, stripped-down sound of *Live at Budokan,* which would have been a return to their debut. Instead, the group went for their biggest, most elaborate production to date, taking the synthesized flourishes of *Heaven Tonight* to extremes. While it kept the group in the charts, it lessened the impact of the music. Underneath the gloss, there are a number of songs that rank among Cheap Trick's finest, particularly the paranoid title track, the epic rocker "Gonna Raise Hell," the tough "I Know What I Want," the simpy pop of "Voices" and the closer "Need Your Love." Still, *Dream Police* feels like a let-down in comparison to its predecessors, even though it would later feel like one of the group's last high-water marks. *—Stephen Thomas Erlewine*

All Shook Up / 1980 / Epic ✦✦

Found All the Parts / 1980 / Epic ✦✦✦

This EP consists of four cuts that hadn't found their way onto Cheap Trick's releases as of yet. Of note is their version of the Beatles' "Day Tripper." A nostalgic bit of history. *—James Chrispell*

One on One / 1982 / Epic ✦✦✦

Tom Petersson left the group after the muddled *All Shook Up,* which was another sign that Cheap Trick was entering a confused period. *One on One,* the first record the group recorded with his replacement Jon Brant, confirms that suspicion. Though it has two fine singles with the power ballad "If You Want My Love" and the lewd rocker "She's Tight," both songs fall short compared to their old standards. Still, they sound like gems compared to the remaining album. Though *One on One* is nowhere near as ambitious as *All Shook Up,* the songwriting is forced and stilted, lacking not only imagination, but also hooks. A couple of cuts—"Lookin' Out for Number One" and "Love's Got a Hold On Me"—work as standard-issue arena-rockers, but by and large, *One on One* is another disappointment. *—Stephen Thomas Erlewine*

Next Position Please / 1983 / Epic ✦✦✦

Perhaps sensing something was going wrong, Cheap Trick hired superstar producer Todd Rundgren for *Next Position Please.* Rundgren helped the band return to the appealing pop-rock of their *In Color* days, albiet stamping it with his heavy-handed production. However, Cheap Trick do benefit from Rundgren's control, since it gives them a sense of focus lacking on *All Shook Up* and *One on One.* Though the record was hampered somewhat by Epic's insistence of adding a bad cover of the Motors' terrific "Dancin' the Night Away" and the lightweight "You Say Jump," *Next Position Please* is effectively a return to form for Cheap Trick, boasting their most consistent set of songs since *Heaven Tonight.* "I Can't Take It," "Borderline," "Younger Girls," "Heaven's Falling" and "Invaders of the Heart" may not quite reach the heights of the first three albums, but they come within shooting distance, making *Next Position Please* Cheap Trick's last satisfying record. *—Stephen Thomas Erlewine*

Standing on the Edge / 1985 / Epic ✦✦

The Doctor / 1986 / Epic ✦

Lap of Luxury / 1988 / Epic ✦✦✦

Cheap Trick's comeback album is by no means a return to the creativity and vitality of their glory days. But even though *Lap of Luxury* is largely formulaic, the band's strongest collection of material in some time fills that late-'80s pop/metal formula quite well. Combining grandly romantic power ballads ("Ghost Town") with catchy hard rockers ("Never Had a Lot to Lose"), *Lap of Luxury* consistently delivers strong hooks and well-crafted songs, proving that Cheap Trick was still capable of outdoing many of the bands they helped inspire. The album produced two Top Five singles in a cover of Elvis Presley's "Don't Be Cruel" and the band's first number one hit, "The Flame." *—Steve Huey*

Busted / Jun. 1990 / Epic ✦✦

Greatest Hits / 1991 / Epic ✦✦✦✦✦

The greatest failing of *Greatest Hits* is the fact that much of Cheap Trick's best material didn't come near the charts. "I Want You to Want Me," "Surrender," and "Dream Police," either climbed the charts or scraped them, as did the fine singles "Ain't That a Shame," "Voices," "If You Want My Love," and "She's Tight," but many of their stone-cold classics—including "He's a Whore," "Oh, Candy," "Downed," "Southern Girls," "Auf Wiedersehen"—weren't successes. What were successes were pleasant arena-rockers and power ballads like "Tonight It's You," "The Flame," and "Don't Be Cruel," and that's what forms the basis of *Greatest Hits,* along with an extraneous new rendition of the Beatles' "Magical Mystery Tour." Casual fans who only want the hits will be satiated by this collection, but the album misses the point of Cheap Trick, and thereby doesn't work as either an introduction or retrospective. *—Stephen Thomas Erlewine*

Budokan II / Feb. 1994 / Epic ♦♦♦♦♦
Budokan II is exactly what it says it is—the sequel to Cheap Trick's career-making *Live at Budokan*. Picking up where its predecessor left off (the tracks even begin at number 11), the record contains all of the band's classics—"ELO Kiddies," "Southern Girls," "California Man," "Downed," "How Are You," "On Top of the World," "Oh Caroline," "Auf Wiedershen," "Speak Now or Forever Hold Your Piece"—that didn't make the first record. While the performances aren't quite as tight as *At Budokan*—possibly because they weren't doctored as heavily in the studio—the record is nevertheless a muscular, energetic set of definitive power-pop and will please not only diehard fans of Cheap Trick, but casual fans attracted by *Live At Budokan*. *—Stephen Thomas Erlewine*

Woke up with a Monster / Mar. 22, 1994 / Warner Brothers ♦♦♦
The title track is a nice little radio-ready chunk of fun, but it has this thing about getting repetitive too damn quickly, after which it starts getting annoying, despite the catchy stuff that's going on. Other than that, this is a lumpy bit of mediocre rock & roll that's mainly annoying because it had tons of potential, little of which is realized. Everybody sounds like they're going through the motions, and Robin Zander keeps sounding too much like Mick Jagger. *—Steven McDonald*

Sex, America, Cheap Trick / Aug. 1996 / Epic/Legacy ♦♦♦
Sex, America, Cheap Trick is a classic example of a botched box set. Spanning four discs and 64 songs, the box contains nearly all of the group's hit singles and an amazing amount of rarities—a grand total of 30 outtakes, live tracks, demos, single versions, soundtrack songs, and B-sides. Despite all of the abundance of material, there are still a lot of essential items missing, as well as several odd inclusions. Many of the group's biggest hits and concert staples are present, but Cheap Trick classics like "He's a Whore," "Downed," "Come On, Come On," "Taxman, Mr. Thief," "California Man," and several others are inexplicably absent. Furthermore, the final two discs bog down with slick radio-ready pop, even though they rescue all the highlights from the band's decidedly uneven '80s recordings. Still, the rarities—particularly single versions of early tracks like "Oh, Candy" and "Southern Girls," demos like "Fan Club," and a ripping live set—are usually worthy, even if they might have been better showcased on a double-disc rarities set. *—Stephen Thomas Erlewine*

Cheap Trick [1997] / Apr. 29, 1997 / Red Ant ♦♦♦
Titled *Cheap Trick* like the group's debut album presumably because the record represents a new beginning, *Cheap Trick* is indeed their most powerful, direct and melodic album in years, and certainly their heaviest since their late '70s heyday. Stripping away all of the glossy, big-budget excesses of their late-'80s and early-'90s major-label releases, Cheap Trick keep their sound to the basics—loud guitars, crunching chords and sweet melodies. Certainly the unvarnished sound helps the record sound immediate, but the real key to the success of *Cheap Trick* is the reinvigorated songwriting. All of the songs are written by the band themselves, with only a couple of cuts featuring outside songwriters, and the result is a tight, melodic set of hard rockers and ballads. Not everything on the album is first-rate—the forced opener "Anytime" is almost a fatal misstep—and a couple of songs are simply pleasant, but there are more terrific moments—"Hard to Tell," "You Let a Lotta People Down," "Say Good Bye," "It All Comes Back to You"—than there have been on any Cheap Trick record in years. It's a fine, distinguished comeback, and one that suggests that the group could continue making records just as good for several more years. *—Stephen Thomas Erlewine*

Cheap Trick at Budokan: The Complete Concert / Apr. 21, 1998 / Epic/Legacy ♦♦♦♦♦
At Budokan was the pivotal album for Cheap Trick, the one that made them stars. The louder, harder-rocking versions of such Rick Nielsen classics as "I Want You to Want Me" and "Come On, Come On" connected with a wide audience in a way the studio recordings didn't and the record consequently became a smash. Given its enduring popularity, it wasn't surprising that Epic and Cheap Trick celebrated its 20th anniversary by releasing *The Complete Concert*, a double-disc set that contains all of the 19 songs the band had performed. Much of this material was released on *Budokan II*, but this set restores all the music to its original running order, making it an entirely unique album in its own right. There's no question that the music is terrific and it certainly is interesting to hear all of this the way it was actually performed, but *The Complete Concert* doesn't have the punch of the original album, which hit hard at only 10 tracks. The length of this set might make it frustrating for some fans, but any hardcore Trick fan will need this comprehensive, detailed document of the band's most celebrated concert. *—Stephen Thomas Erlewine*

Music for Hangovers / Jun. 15, 1999 / Cheap Trick Unlimited ♦♦♦♦
Cheap Trick celebrated their 25th anniversary in the best way possible. In a handful of major cities, the band did a brief residency, performing one of their classic first three albums in its entirety on three separate nights. And for their stay at Cabaret Metro in their hometown Chicago, they added a fourth night, where they ran through *Live at Budokan*. *Music for Hangovers* collects 14 highlights from their stand at the Metro, including selections from the encores, where they dipped into songs from *Dream Police*, *One on One*, and *Next Position Please*. In this context, the music is stripped of the novelty—after all, it's not every day that a band decides to run through a classic album, in its original running order—and left to stand on its own merits. Astonishingly, the record rivals the legendary *Live at Budokan* and, at times, sounds harder and rocks harder than that album. They may be doing oldies, but their hearts are in it, and the results are giddily entertaining. There are no new arrangements or anything unexpected (even the cameos from Billy Corgan and D'arcy of the Smashing Pumpkins fit seamlessly into the band's sound), just tight, exciting versions of classics, from hit singles ("Dream Police," "I Want You to Want Me," "Surrender") to cult favorites ("How Are You?," "Madocello," "Oh Caroline"). *Music for Hangovers* proves that getting older is not necessarily a death knell for a rock band, since Cheap Trick sounds as good as ever throughout the record. A welcome surprise from a great band. *—Stephen Thomas Erlewine*

Authorized Greatest Hits / Aug. 29, 2000 / Epic/Legacy ♦♦♦♦
This is an "authorized" greatest hits collection in the sense that the band picked the selections themselves. It's preferable to the 1991 *Greatest Hits* comp for its slightly greater length (16 songs) and better choice of material; the single version of "Southern Girls" makes it on this time around, for instance. Still, like that other album with "Greatest Hits" in the title, it misses a number of rockers that fans might rate among their best work. The only previously unreleased item is a live 1988 performance of "The Flame"; a live version of "I Can't Take It" and their rendition of "That 70's Song (In the Street)," the latter famed for its use as a television theme, are the only tracks recorded after 1990. *—Richie Unterberger*

Silver / Feb. 27, 2001 / Cheap Trick Unlimited ♦♦♦♦♦
On August 28, 1999, power pop masters Cheap Trick played a special show for fans at Davis Park in their hometown of Rockford, IL, to salute their 25th anniversary as a band together. The show included several musical celebrities making cameo appearances (as well as relatives of Cheap Trick band members) and the inclusion of the Rockford Symphony Orchestra String Quartet on several tracks, while the 29-song set list dipped deep into the band's catalog—including at least one song from every album of their career thus far. The evening's proceedings have been captured on the 2001 double-disc *Silver*, the band's second live release in two years. All of the expected fan faves are included—"Ain't That a Shame," "I Want You to Want Me," "Surrender," "Dream Police"—but longtime fans will go straight to the set's abundance of more uncommon material. Standouts include two standards of early MTV ("If You Want My Love" and "She's Tight"), the Big Star tribute "That 70s Song," the forgotten 1979 Beatles-esque power ballad "Voices," a song that two members of CT cut with John Lennon back in 1980 ("I'm Losin' You"), the jamfest "Gonna Raise Hell," plus tracks sung by other members—"World's Greatest Lover" (Rick Nielsen) and "I Know What I Want" (Tom Petersson). Also featured are guest appearances by big-name fans Billy Corgan ("Just Got Back"), Slash ("You're All Talk"), and Art Alexakis ("Day Tripper"). Although it lacks the punch of their 1979 classic *Live at Budokan* (widely regarded as one of the greatest live rock albums of all-time), *Silver* shows that the band is still having fun on stage 25 years later. *—Greg Prato*

Chubby Checker (Ernest Evans)

b. Oct. 3, 1941, Philadelphia, PA
Vocals / Rock & Roll, R&B
Chubby Checker was the unrivaled king of the rock & roll dance craze; although most of the dances his records promoted—the Pony, the Fly and the Hucklebuck, to cite just three—have long since faded into obscurity, his most famous hit, "The Twist," remains the yardstick against which all subsequent dancefloor phenomena are measured. Signed to Philadelphia's Cameo-Parkway in 1959, he recorded a number of minor novelty hits before 1960's "The Twist" (a cover of a 1958 Hank Ballard & the Midnighters B-side) rocketed to number one in 1960 and again in 1961. After "The Twist" first made Checker a superstar, he returned to the top in 1961 with "Do the Pony"; that same year, he also reached the Top Ten with "Let's Twist Again," which assured the dance's passage from novelty to institution. In addition to 1961's "The Fly," Checker's other Top Ten hits included three 1962 smashes—"Slow Twistin'," "Limbo Rock" and "Popeye the Hitchhiker." In total, Checker notched 32 chart hits before the bubble burst in 1966. From the 1970s onward, he was a staple of oldies revival tours. In 1988, Checker returned to the Top 40 for the first time in a quarter century when he appeared on the Fat Boys' rap rendition of "The Twist." *—Jason Ankeny*

● **Chubby Checker's Greatest Hits** / Nov. 1972 / London ♦♦♦♦♦
In 1972, when nostalgia for late-'50s and early-'60s rock & roll was bringing Chuck Berry and others back into the charts, Allen Klein's ABKCO Records obtained the rights to reissue Chubby Checker's Cameo-Parkway singles on this 15-track hits LP. Checker actually had many more hits than just "The Twist" and "Let's Twist Again," and this LP presents his other dance tunes—"Pony Time," "The Fly," "Limbo Rock"—and several of his later, less successful singles when he was trying to branch out into a sort of Harry Belafonte-style folk approach. But the heart of the collection is still the early-'60s dance tunes, which demonstrate that, while Checker was not a great rocker, he still, like Freddy Cannon and Gary U.S. Bonds, was one of the people keeping the flame of rock & roll flickering between the time Buddy Holly's plane went down in Iowa and the day the Beatles flew in from London. [Released on LP, this album is long out of print, and it is listed as Checker's "pick" album because, as of 1995, there is no in-print album containing his original hits.] *- William Ruhlmann*

The Chemical Brothers

f. 1989, Manchester, England
Big Beat, Funky Breaks, Electronica, Trip-Hop, Club/Dance
The act with the first arena-sized sound in the electronica movement, the Chemical Brothers united such varying influences as Public Enemy, Cabaret Voltaire and My Bloody Valentine to create a dance-rock-rap fusion which rivalled the best old-school DJs on their own terms—keeping a crowd of people on the floor by working through any number of groove-oriented styles featuring unmissable samples, from familiar guitar riffs to vocal tags to various sound effects. And when the duo (Tom Rowlands and Ed Simons) decided to supplement their DJ careers by turning their bedrooms into recording studios, they pioneered a style of music (later termed big beat) remarkable for its lack of energy-loss

from the dancefloor to the radio. Chemical Brothers albums were less collections of songs and more hour-long journeys, chock full of deep bomb-studded beats, percussive breakdowns and effects borrowed from a host of sources. All in all, the duo proved one of the few exceptions to the rule that intelligent dance music could never be bombastic or truly satisying to the seasoned rock fan; it's hardly surprising that they were one of the few dance acts to enjoy simultaneous success in the British/American mainstream and in critical quarters. *—John Bush*

☆ **Exit Planet Dust** / Aug. 15, 1995 / Astralwerks ♦♦♦♦♦
The former Dust Brothers make oblique reference to litigation averted on their debut full-length. The Brothers' sound is big on bombast, replete with screeching guitar samples and lots of sirens and screaming divas. A breakthrough album of sorts, *Exit* was, upon its release, one of the few European post-techno albums to make any sort of headway into the stateside market. *—Sean Cooper*

★ **Dig Your Own Hole** / Apr. 7, 1997 / Astralwerks ♦♦♦♦♦
Taking the swirling eclecticism of their post-techno debut, *Exit Planet Dust*, to the extreme, the Chemical Brothers blow all stylistic boundaries down with their second album, *Dig Your Own Hole*. Bigger, bolder, and more adventurous than *Exit Planet Dust*, *Dig Your Own Hole* opens with the slamming cacophony of "Block Rockin' Beats," where hip-hop meets hardcore techno, complete with a Schoolly D sample and an elastic bass riff. Everything is going on at once in "Block Rockin' Beats," and it sets the pace for the rest of the record, where songs and styles blur into a continuous kaleidoscope of sound. It rocks hard enough for the pop audience, but it doesn't compromise either the Chemicals' sound or the adventurous, futuristic spirit of electronica—even "Setting Sun," with its sly homages to the Beatles' "Tomorrow Never Knows" and Noel Gallagher's twisting, catchy melody, doesn't sound like retro psychedelia; it sounds vibrant, unexpected, and utterly contemporary. There are no distinctions between different styles, and the Chemicals sound as if they're having fun, building *Dig Your Own Hole* from fragments of the past, distorting the rhythms and samples, and pushing it forward with an intoxicating rush of synthesizers, electronics, and layered drum machines. The Chemical Brothers might not push forward into self-consciously arty territories like some of their electronic peers, but they have more style and focus, constructing a blindingly innovative and relentlessly propulsive album that's an exhilarating listen—one that sounds positively new but utterly inviting at the same time. *—Stephen Thomas Erlewine*

Brothers Gonna Work It Out / Sep. 22, 1998 / Astralwerks ♦♦♦
To buy time after the success of *Dig Your Own Hole*, the Chemical Brothers released their first DJ mix album, *Brothers Gonna Work It Out*. *Dig Your Own Hole* was one of the handful of electronica albums to find a wide audience in both the U.K. and the U.S., largely because of its gigantic, straight-ahead beats. Whether by design or not, it was electronic music that could reach a wide audience because it was about what all rock or pop music is about at its core—rhythm. To their credit, the Chemicals viewed themselves as part of a continuum, not as ambassadors of techno, which is presumably why they used their elevated profile to showcase a style of music unfamiliar to a mass audience with songs unfamiliar to a mass audience. That might lead to the preconception that *Brothers Gonna Work It Out* is a chore or an educational lesson, which couldn't be further from the truth. *Brothers Gonna Work It Out* is a rush, pure and simple. Using their own songs, plus a huge selection of other records and remixes, they've created a relentless, frequently exciting record that pushes forth on the momentum of unpredictable juxtapositions and big, big beats. During the course of the 70-minute disc, the Brothers spin everything—Willie Hutch, Meat Beat Manifesto, Spiritualized, Renegade Soundwave, Manic Street Preachers—which only emphasizes how they've created their own identity through piecing together remnants of pop and DJ culture, from forgotten favorites to cult classics. Artistically, it doesn't quite match their pair of studio efforts, but it's a nice stopgap for fans awaiting their third full-length album. *—Stephen Thomas Erlewine*

Surrender / Jun. 22, 1999 / Astralwerks ♦♦♦♦
By the time of the Chemical Brothers' third album, *Surrender*, the big-beat phenomenon they had done much to engender was more apt to be heard on a soft-drink commercial than the world's hipper dancefloors. And with the growing omnipresence of big-beat's simplistic party vibes threatening to cave in the entire scene, Tom and Ed came to grips with what is—compared to their previous work—a house record. The pounding four-on-the-floor thump of tracks like "Music:Response," "Got Glint" and the duo's take on KLF-style stadium house for the single "Hey Boy Hey Girl" signals that this is a transition record for the Chemical Brothers.

The irony here is that even considering the changes, *Surrender* still feels very similar to its predecessors. The focus on wave-of-sound production, bucketfuls of old-school vocal samples, and various sirens and beatbox effects sound like they were lifted wholesale from their previous albums. And while a few of the vocal tracks focus on new collaborations, they're along the same lines, making it tough to spot the differences from past albums. Sure, the Chemical Brothers do this type of music very well; it's just that *Surrender* isn't quite the change of direction they'd been aiming for—it's simply the *same* great album they'd made two years earlier. *—John Bush*

Cher (Cherilyn Sarkasian LaPier)

b. May 20, 1946, El Centro, CA

Vocals / Girl Group, Pop/Rock, Folk-Rock, Soft Rock, Pop, Adult Contemporary, Dance-Pop

Cher has had three careers that place her indelibly in the public consciousness, and two have been in association with her then-husband, composer/producer/singer Salvatore "Sonny" Bono. She charted major hit records in the 1960s and 1970s, working in idioms ranging from early '60s girl group-style ballads to Jackie Deshannon folk-influenced pop, to adult pop in the manner of later Dusty Springfield. She also embarked on an acting career, initially in the late 1960s in association with her work as part of Sonny and Cher but later on her own, which led to a series of increasingly polished and compelling performances in *Silkwood*, *Mask* and *Moonstruck*, for which she won the Academy Award(tm) for Best Actress. Since the mid-1970s, Cher has been known more for her acting than for her music, although she has continued to record for numerous labels, including Columbia, and in 1998 scored an international chart-topping smash with the club-friendly single "Believe." *—Bruce Eder*

The Best of the Casablanca Years / Apr. 1996 / Casablanca/Chronicles ♦♦
Cher's *The Best of the Casablanca Years* collects all of her hit singles from the late '70s, and there weren't that many. Only three singles charted in the Top 100 and only one—the number eight "Take Me Home"—cracked the Top 40. So, the rest of the collection is padded with album tracks, making the disc into a mammoth, 17-track compilation. Nearly everything she released on the label is included and it all sounds similar—it's all insistent, mildly catchy disco. During this era, Cher didn't work with particularly gifted producers or songwriters, which meant her disco tracks were undistinguished. Occasionally, such as "Take Me Home," she had a strong song, but she was more likely to cut a wealth of mediocre material, throwing in a few genuinely embarassing tracks along the way. And that means *The Best of the Casablanca Years* is an artifact of the late '70s that is only of use for dedicated Cher fans. It's a well-produced and thorough collection, but no one but the most devoted fan needs to own this music *—Stephen Thomas Erlewine*

Bittersweet: Love Songs Collection / Jan. 26, 1999 / MCA ♦♦♦
Subtitled *The Love Songs Collection*, this collection promotes the idea of Cher as torch ballad singer, a notion not as far-fetched as one would imagine. Taken from five different albums recorded during her '70s stay at the MCA and Kapp labels, this states a strong case for the lung power of Cher's vocal range, as well as her taste for challenging and off-the-beaten-path material. Her *Bittersweet White Light* album from 1973 (her first with a full orchestra) is here in its entirety, along with selections from *Foxy Lady*, *Dark Lady*, *Half Breed* and *Gypsys, Tramps & Thieves*, all from Sonny & Cher's second wave of popularity and many featuring Sonny Bono at the production helm. Highlights include nice readings of "By Myself," "I Got It Bad and That Ain't Good," "Am I Blue," "How Long Has This Been Going On," "More Than You Know," "The Man That Got Away" and "What'll I Do." Cher as torch singer? If you can suspend belief for the time it takes to pop this one in the player and listen, you're in for a very pleasant surprise. *—Cub Koda*

Bang Bang: The Early Years / May 18, 1999 / Capitol ♦♦♦
Released in the spring of 1999, *Bang Bang: The Early Years* arrived at the perfect time. After years in exile—she hadn't had a hit single or movie in over five years—Cher returned to the spotlight in early 1998 under tragic circumstances, delivering a moving eulogy at Sonny Bono's funeral. It served as a reminder to a mass audience that she was alive and well, and within a year, she had a huge hit single with "Believe" and a hit movie with *Tea with Mussolini*. All in all, it was the perfect opportunity for a collection that spotlighted her recordings for Imperial from the mid-'60s. There had been many compilations focusing on her duets with Sonny, but *Bang Bang* was the first in many years to focus directly on her solo recordings, and at a generous 18 tracks, it ranks among the best of its kind ever assembled. All seven of her charting singles for Imperial—"All I Really Want to Do," "Where Do You Go," "Bang Bang (My Baby Shot Me Down)," "Alfie," "Behind the Door," "Hey Joe," "You Better Sit Down Kids"—are here, along with most of the B-sides and selected album tracks. There may be a personal favorite or two missing, but overall this is as close as it comes to a definitive collection of Cher's early solo recordings. Overall, the songs aren't quite as strong as those she recorded with Sonny, but it's still very good indeed. *—Stephen Thomas Erlewine*

20th Century Masters—The Millennium Collection: The Best of Cher / Jan. 25, 2000 / MCA ♦♦♦
You might have thought that, since the 1998 merger of MCA and PolyGram, creating Universal Music, brought the hits Cher scored in the 1970s and '80s for Kapp, MCA, Casablanca, and Geffen under one roof, the next time they got around to doing a best-of they would combine all those catalogs. No such luck. In the wake of Cher's 1999 comeback with "Believe," Geffen issued its own comp, *If I Could Turn Back Time: Cher's Greatest Hits*. So, when MCA came to compile *The Best of Cher* as part of the midline-priced 20th Century Masters/The Millennium Collection series, they simply took the 1974 MCA *Greatest Hits* album, stripped off two B-sides, and added the 1979 Casablanca disco hit "Take Me Home" and the 1971 Sonny & Cher hit "All I Ever Need Is You." The result is an improvement on the still-in-print and also discount-priced *Greatest Hits* that really should be called "The Best of Cher in the '70s." But, with the '80s hits on the Geffen set and Cher's '60s hits belonging to Warner EMI, anyone looking for a comprehensive single-disc compilation on the artist remains frustrated. *—William Ruhlmann*

● **The Way of Love: The Cher Collection** / Nov. 21, 2000 / MCA ♦♦♦♦♦
This collection is a good attempt at bringing together Cher's more popular recordings from the mid-'60s to her Casablanca years in the late '70s, and the results are almost a total success. Most of her U.S. Top 40 hits are included (save for "Where Do You Go" and "Alfie"), as well as a few tracks with Sonny ("All I Ever Need Is You," "When You Say Love," live versions of "I Got You Babe" and "The Beat Goes On," and the campy "A Cowboy's Work Is Never Done"). The bulk of the material comes from her albums *Gypsys, Tramps & Thieves*, *Foxy Lady*, *Bittersweet White Light*, *Half Breed*, and *Dark Lady*, as well as a few rarities, including "Classified 1A," which, at the time of its release, was deemed un-American and shelved away. This collection showcases Cher not only as a rock, pop and, folk star, but also as an interpreter of standards ("What'll I Do"), as well as contemporary hits (her covers of the Bee Gees' "How Can You Mend a Broken Heart" and Paul McCartney's "My Love" are quite notable). This set also includes her signature smashes,

ranging from "Bang Bang," "The Way of Love," "Half Breed," "Dark Lady," and "Gypsys, Tramps & Thieves" to her 1979 disco hit "Take Me Home." Unfortunately, however, "Take Me Home" is the sole representative of her stint with Casablanca. Had they included its two follow-ups, "Hell on Wheels" and "Wasn't It Good," as well as "Alfie" and "Where Do You Go," this collection would have been absolutely definitive. It does, however, stand as a more-than-adequate representation of the singer's work from that period, and with its excellent song selection, liner notes, and photographs, provides a fantastic look back at this singer's amazing career. *—Jose Promis*

Neneh Cherry

b. Mar. 10, 1964, Stockholm, Sweden

Vocals / Pop-Rap, Alternative Rap, Alternative Dance, Club/Dance, Urban, Dance-Pop

The stepdaughter of jazz trailblazer Don Cherry, vocalist Neneh Cherry forged her own groundbreaking blend of pop, dance and hip-hop which presaged the emergence of both alternative rap and trip-hop. Cherry dropped out of school at age 14, and in 1980 she relocated to London to sing with the punk group the Cherries. Following brief flings with the Slits and the Nails, she joined the experimental funk outfit Rip Rig + Panic. When the band broke up, Cherry remained with one of the spin-off groups, Float Up CP, and led them through one album, 1986's *Kill Me in the Morning.* After attracting some notice singing back-up on the The's "Slow Train to Dawn" single, she became romantically and professionally involved with composer and musician Cameron McVey, who, under the alias Booga Bear, wrote much of the material that would comprise Cherry's 1989 debut LP *Raw Like Sushi.* One song McVey did not write was "Buffalo Stance," the album's breakthrough single; originally tossed off as a B-side by the mid-Eighties pop group Morgan McVey, Cherry's cover was an international smash which neatly summarized the album's eclectic fusion of pop smarts and hip-hop energy. While 1992's *Homebrew* was not as commercially successful as its predecessor, Cherry returned to the charts in 1994 duetting with Youssou N'Dour on the global hit "Seven Seconds." *—Jason Ankeny*

● **Raw Like Sushi** / May 1989 / Virgin ✦✦✦✦✦

Those arguing that the most individualistic R&B and dance music of the late '80s and early to mid-'90s came out of Britain could point to Neneh Cherry's unconventional *Raw Like Sushi* as a shining example. An unorthodox and brilliantly daring blend of R&B, rap, pop, and dance music, *Sushi* enjoyed little exposure on America's conservative, urban, contemporary radio formats, but was a definite underground hit. Full of personality, the singer/rapper is as thought-provoking as she is witty and humorous when addressing relationships and taking aim at less-than-kosher behavior of males and females alike. Macho homeboys and Casanovas take a pounding on "So Here I Come" and the hit "Buffalo Stance," while women who are shallow, cold-hearted, or materialistic get lambasted on "Phoney Ladies," "Heart," and "Inna City Mamma." Cherry's idealism comes through loud and clear on "The Next Generation," a plea to take responsibility for one's sexual actions and give children the respect and attention they deserve. *—Alex Henderson*

Homebrew / Oct. 27, 1992 / Virgin ✦✦✦✦✦

Neneh Cherry doesn't get into the studio nearly often enough. Three years passed before the British singer/rapper came out with a second album. Thankfully, she more than lived up to the tremendous promise of *Raw Like Sushi* on the equally magnificent and risk-taking *Homebrew.* Cherry shows no signs of the dreaded sophomore slump—everything on the CD is a gem. She triumphs with a seamless and unorthodox blend of hip-hop, R&B, dance music, and pop, and on "Money Love" and "Trout," the presence of R.E.M.'s Michael Stipe brings rock to the eclectic mix. As humorous as Cherry can be, her reflections on relationships and social issues are often quite pointed. While "Money Love" decries the evils of materialism, the moving "I Ain't Gone Under Yet" describes an inner-city woman's determination not to be brought down by the poverty and drugs that surround her. And "Twisted" is about keeping yourself sane in a world gone insane. Unfortunately, *Homebrew* wasn't the commercial breakthrough Cherry was more than deserving of. *—Alex Henderson*

Man / 1996 / Hut ✦✦✦

Neneh Cherry, the critically acclaimed singer/songwriter and rapstress who burst onto the scene in 1989 with the mega-hit "Buffalo Stance," did not even see the release of her third album, *Man,* in the United States. This set differs from her previous efforts in that there is absolutely no rap to be found anywhere on the disc, and all of the songs are slow-burning, mid-tempo alt-rock numbers, as opposed to anything remotely resembling dance or rap (though there are some hip-hop styled beats). There are really no immediate hits on this album, although it includes the international chart-topping duet with Youssou N'Dour, "7 Seconds," as well as several other highlights, including "Woman," "Hornbeam," and "Everything." Also included here is a tribute cover she recorded of Marvin Gaye's "Trouble Man." The album is a high-quality collection of alt-rock womens' anthems, at times bluesy, at times folksy, and much more akin to her previous rock-leaning effort *Homebrew* than her breakthrough *Raw Like Sushi.* The songs have an organic, earthy feel, in tune with the Lilith Fair alternative-style musical movement going on at the time. A good deal of alterna-sexual references are found, especially considering some of the song titles (first single "Kootchi" and "Beastiality," to mention two). A solid album, but definitely not very commercial. Still, it should have been given a chance in the U.S. market, especially given her previous track record. *—Jose Promis*

Vic Chesnutt

b. 1965

Vocals, Guitar / Alternative Pop/Rock, Singer/Songwriter, Urban Folk

Though Michael Stipe had been a fan of Vic Chesnutt since the late '80s, producing his first two full-lengths, it took the *Sweet Relief Two* tribute album to make a star of him in mid-1996. The album featured artists such as Madonna, Hootie & the Blowfish, Smashing Pumpkins and R.E.M. covering the songs of Chesnutt, a paraplegic who was injured in a car accident when he was 18. The singer/songwriter began playing contemporary acoustic folk around Athens, GA soon after his injury. A show at the 40 Watt Club brought him to the attention of Stipe, who helped with production on 1990's *Little* and 1991's *West of Rome,* both on Texas Hotel Records. A documentary video of Chesnutt's life called *Speed Racer* was produced and directed by Peter Sillen in 1991, and has aired on PBS. Chesnutt's third album *Drunk* followed in late 1993, but the release of his fourth album was delayed by Chesnutt's membership in Brute, a project with members of Widespread Panic including David A. Schools, Michael Houser, Todd Nance, John Hermann, Johnny Hickman, David Lowery and John Keane. After *Sweet Relief Two* was released in July 1996, Capitol signed Chesnutt and released *About to Choke,* his major-label debut, in the fall of that year. *The Salesman and Bernadette* followed in 1998 on Capricorn and featured Lambchop as his backing band. The record's poor sales led him to be dropped by that label, but Chesnutt continued to record, cutting an album with Kelly and Nikki Keneipp called *Roses for the Butt of All Our Merriment* that was issued in 2000. That same year, he teamed up with longtime friend and admirer Kristin Hersh for a series of U.S. tour dates. The following year, Chesnutt issued *Left to His Own Devices,* a collection of rarities, outtakes, and demos. *—John Bush*

Little / 1990 / Texas Hotel ✦✦✦

West of Rome / 1991 / Texas Hotel ✦✦✦✦✦

Vic Chesnutt is a very unique, peculiar personality and songwriter who shares the company of folks like Kristin Hersh, Mary Margaret O'Hara, Victoria Williams, Howe Gelb, and Benjamin Smoke. He's a charter member of that pantheon of brilliant songwriters and performers who are all defined by singularity, but are not ruled by quirk and never allow themselves to fall into self-parody. All play a skewed, refracted version of Americana that is haunting, funny, poignant, and occasionally mystical, usually all at once. *West of Rome* is a spare, skeletal record that's inhabited by all of the aforementioned qualities, is beautiful in its simplicity and finds strength in imperfection. Chesnutt's craggy voice, classical guitar, and outrageous imagination are his tools, and his performances were faithfully preserved by Scott Stuckey's resonant living room production. After a few spins, listening to Chesnutt and company sound like they're playing in your living room, the record begins to sound familiar; it's nooks and crannies, cracks and crevices start to feel homey and comfortable, like an old house or an old friend. There's a humble magic that *West of Rome* perpetuates that is ultimately the most enchanting thing about it—it offers a gentle reminder of things that are far too often taken for granted to those who care to listen. *—Bryan Carroll*

● **Drunk** / 1993 / Caroline ✦✦✦✦✦

On his third, and maybe most conceptually complete, album, Vic Chesnutt emerges as that rare kind of artist who can see right into the living room of small-town America. *Drunk* opens with one of Chesnutt's more overtly hook-oriented songs, the punchy "Sleeping Man," which also appears later in the album as a slightly twangier reprise, and is a fine commentary on the insatiable hunger for human spectacle that plagues American culture. "One of Many" is a bleak tale of murder and execution that finds Chesnutt truly at the top of his game lyrically and melodically. A fine example of Chesnutt's songcraft is the plaintive narrative "When I Ran Off and Left Her," which is indicative of his style in that its laid-back delivery masks a certain amount of tension and paranoia. A consistent theme on *Drunk,* as well as in Chesnutt's other work, is transition—whether escaping or just moving—to someplace else. Very few artists can communicate these kinds of themes as eloquently and as uniquely as Chesnutt, and *Drunk* is a fine example of how he can turn seemingly self-absorbed songs into something strangely universal. The distorted, guttural title cut and the bouncy "Super Tuesday" offer further proof of Chesnutt's impressive ability to evoke different moods. In the end, it is probably that ability which makes his genius the most readily apparent. *—Matt Fink*

Is the Actor Happy / May 23, 1995 / Caroline ✦✦✦✦✦

Probably as good an album as Chesnutt has made. *Is the Actor Happy?* remains as definite verification of his standing as one of the most relevant songwriters of the '90s. Pristine production that insures that not a note is wasted or out of place, it provides the perfect vehicle for Chesnutt's slice-of-life short stories. At times more accessible than the average Chesnutt record with instantly engaging tracks like "Gravity of the Situation," "Onion Soup" and "Guilty By Association" (featuring Michael Stipe), it is still not by any means a light-hearted affair. The album is a beautiful testament to Chesnutt's unique voice and the adversity that he's been through. Heartbreakingly delicate folk rock arrangements are followed by crashing guitar crescendos as the perfect vehicles for taking Chesnutt's songs to places very few songwriters have been or can go. *—Matt Fink*

About to Choke / Nov. 12, 1996 / Capitol ✦✦✦✦

About to Choke appeared only a few months after the Vic Chesnutt tribute album *Sweet Relief II,* which meant that it received more attention in the media than most of his other records. However, it's likely that it would have been put into the spotlight anyway, since it is another exceptional set of songs, delivered with a gritty vulnerability that makes his music so affecting. Chesnutt's music is a little more textured and full-bodied on *About to Choke* than his previous albums, yet that adds depth and maturity to his music, which also means its one of his most accessible efforts. *—Thom Owens*

The Salesman and Bernadette / Nov. 10, 1998 / Polygram ✦✦✦✦

Sounding more upbeat and a whole lot more soulful than on previous outings, Chesnutt has invited the Dixie-fried experimental group Lambchop along with his wife Tina into the studio for his sixth album, a concept about a traveling salesman. The result sounds less like his usual doleful, sometimes baleful, Southern Gothic self and is perhaps his best recording to date. Chesnutt's is a vulnerable voice, and though he can project frailty, his m.o. isn't pity-making; in fact, he's quite humorous. "Duty Free" sounds like a New Orleans funeral march. The Lambchop horn section apes the Tijuana Brass to a hip-hop beat on "Replenished." "Maiden" has a sweet melody, driven by vibes and a very subtle horn line. "Until the Led" has the spunk and spirit of R.E.M.'s "Can't Get There From Here" and "So. Central Rain"; Chesnutt draws on that keening vocal quality that probably appealed to his early mentor, Michael Stipe, in the first place. But even R.E.M. in all their new experimentation would never have let the horns run to the border like they do here. The best thing of all is that Chesnutt's "new direction" still has a warm, organic and homespun quality—the very things that are missing on recent recordings by his Athens, GA brothers. *—Denise Sullivan*

Merriment / May 30, 2000 / Backburner ✦✦✦✦

Chesnutt's seventh album is a collaboration with Jack Logan associates Kelly Keneipp and Nikki Keneipp (Logan himself plays bass on one track). The Keneipps wrote all of the music; Chesnutt supplied the lyrics and some guitar; and the Keneipps played most of the other instruments. It still sounds very much like a Vic Chesnutt record. It's his rich, melancholy voice that dominates the tracks and his odd, brooding, enigmatic lyrics that set the tone. In the stately melodicism of the material, and the way Chesnutt has with wrenching soulful vocal nuances, you're sometimes reminded of two British singer/songwriters that might seem likely unlikely comparisons: Robert Wyatt and Elvis Costello. He's goofier and folkier than Wyatt, and nonetheless not as pop as Costello, but the similarities are there (though certainly these are to Costello's most reflective side rather than his power pop stuff). Piano is the prevalent instrument on many of the slow to mid-tempo arrangements, although there are occasional deviations from the usual, as in the angry, slashing guitars on "Preponderance." Chesnutt's words are often oblique, and sometimes inscrutable. It's a good thing he's a good vocalist, because the overall mood—of dignified struggle and a man winding maze-like through life's difficulties and absurdities—is established much more by the turns and twists of the vocals than it is by the words alone. This is a fairly impressive effort, and the Keneipps are sympathetic collaborators, but if one important criticism must be voiced, it's that the consistently sluggish pace gets a little enervating by the end of the disc. It's suitable for reflective moods, but downbeat enough to get you verging on a stupor by the close. *—Richie Unterberger*

Left to His Own Devices / Apr. 24, 2001 / spinART ✦✦✦✦

A collection of demos and outtakes recorded on four-track cassette, *Left to His Own Devices* is Vic Chesnutt's strongest and most memorable album since *Is the Actor Happy*—not so surprising maybe given that Chesnutt's strength has always been the distinctive personality he brings to his songs rather than musical embellishments that come later. Herein lie classic Chesnutt lines like "your mother's being poked by some bloke in the Bahamas" (the chorus to "Wounded Prince," an ode to the "richest boy in the world") and "history is a daisy chain of lies" (from "Distortion"), lyrics that might sound trite, melodramatic, or just plain goofy coming from a less able tunesmith. But Chesnutt's laid-back delivery, his self-consciousness to the point of not being self-conscious, and his way of deceptively weaving a personal mythology out of his quirky images, make it easy to succumb to his spell. As might be expected, the instrumentation on *Devices* is simply Chesnutt's voice and acoustic guitar on most tracks, although on a few songs he breaks out a sampler ("Caper") or an electric guitar (the aforementioned "Distortion"). One interesting sonic feature on *Devices* is the way Chesnutt harmonizes with himself using multiple lead vocal tracks, sounding at times like a lo-fi, Southern Cat Stevens. *—Jason Nickey*

The Chi-Lites

f. 1959, Chicago, IL, **db.** 1983

Smooth Soul, Chicago Soul, Soul

One of the most popular smooth soul groups of the early '70s didn't hail from Philadelphia or Memphis, the two cities known for sweet, string-laden soul. Instead, the Chi-Lites were from Chicago, a town better-known for its gritty urban blues and driving R&B. Led by vocalist Eugene Record, the Chi-Lites had a lush, creamy sound distinguished by their four-part harmonies and layered productions. During the early '70s, they racked up 11 Top 10 R&B singles, ranging from the romantic ballads "Have You Seen Her" and "Oh Girl" to protest songs like "(For God's Sake) Give More Power to the People" and "There Will Never Be Any Peace (Until God Is Seated at The Conference Table)." All the songs featured Record's warm, pleading tenor and falsetto, and the majority of the group's hits were written by Record, often in collaboration with other songwriters like Barbara Acklin. *—Stephen Thomas Erlewine*

★ **Greatest Hits [Brunswick]** / 1972 / Brunswick ✦✦✦✦✦

The Chi-Lites were one of the most influential and skilled vocal groups of the late '60s to the mid-'70s. Producer and lead singer Eugene Record always crafted interesting tracks that made the group stand out in a genre that was full of competition. *Greatest Hits* assembles 16 of their best 1969-1972 tracks. Early songs, "I Like Your Lovin'" and "Are You My Woman," still are a little cluttered and unfocused. This package proves that Record more than caught on. The well-produced "(For God's Sake) Give More Power to the People" accurately depicts the problems of early '70s America without being preachy. The astute "We're Are Neighbors" is a production gem with its blaring horns and fuzz/acid guitar. As polemic tracks began to play out, the Chi-Lites began to concentrate more on ballads. Classics "Oh Girl" and "Have You Seen Her" both have retained their melancholy strength and lyrical prowess. Perhaps the most interesting thing about *Greatest Hits* is the breadth of their work. From the not too bright protagonist of the "I'm Ready If I Don't Get to Go" to the unintentionally hilarious "Living in the Footsteps of Another Man," the group simply covered more lyrical ground than most of their contemporaries. *Greatest Hits* also includes the Chi-Lites and Record's most ambitious work. The dreary yet skilled "Coldest Days of My Life" certainly attains the sense of loneliness and isolation that Record often covered in his work. Other anthologies covering their work certainly came after this 1972 set, but *Greatest Hits* may be most desired by their fans. *—Jason Elias*

☆ **Greatest Hits [Rhino]** / 1992 / Rhino ✦✦✦✦✦

All of the Chi-Lites' best songs and biggest hits—including "Oh Girl," "(For God's Sake) Give More Power to the People" and "Stoned Out of My Mind"—are collected on the definitive single-disc retrospective *Greatest Hits*. *—Stephen Thomas Erlewine*

Greatest Hits, Vol. 2 / Oct. 15, 1996 / Rhino ✦✦✦

Greatest Hits, Vol. 2 picks up where Rhino's first volume of Chi-Lites' *Greatest Hits* left off, compiling all of the group's lesser-known R&B hit singles. The compilation contains recordings that the group made between 1968 and 1981 for the record labels Dakar, Brunswick, Mercury, and Chi-Sound. Though there are a few gems on the record—including "I Like Your Lovin' (Do You Like Mine)," "A Lonely Man," and "You Got to Be the One"—the material on *Greatest Hits, Vol. 2* by and large pales to the songs on the first collection, yet fans of the group's smooth soul sound will find several cuts to treasure on this album. *—Stephen Thomas Erlewine*

Chic

f. 1977, New York, NY

Disco, Funk, Dance-Pop

Chic was the best and most influential disco band of the latter half of the '70s, earning hits with both their own records and the outside productions of co-leaders Nile Rodgers and Bernard Edwards. Atlantic picked up their demo for "Dance Dance Dance" in late 1977 after a series of rejections from other record labels; the single sold a million copies in one month, catapulting Chic into the forefront of the disco scene. Chic's biggest hits—"Le Freak" (number one), "I Want Your Love" (number seven), and "Good Times" (number one)—came in 1978-1979, and as disco started to fade, so did the group's popularity. Still, Chic's influence was apparent throughout the '80s; "Good Times" alone spawned Queen's hit "Another One Bites the Dust" (a complete rip-off), and Sugarhill Gang used the record as the foundation for "Rapper's Delight," arguably the first rap single. Rodgers was one of the most successful producers of the early '80s, scoring hits with David Bowie's *Let's Dance*, Madonna's *Like a Virgin*, and Mick Jagger's solo debut, *She's the Boss*. Chic re-formed in 1992, but failed to recapture the fire of its glory days. *—Stephen Thomas Erlewine*

Dance Dance Dance: Best of Chic / Nov. 5, 1991 / Atlantic ✦✦✦✦✦

You think disco was nothing more than assembly line funk and freeze-dried beats? Then you need to step into the crisp grooves and walloping boogie found on this stunning collection of Chic's '70s recordings. Such hits as "Good Times," "Dance Dance Dance," and "Le Freak" used the stylistic innovations of James Brown and Sly Stone as a blueprint for a new era of funk. Bernard Edwards' bass lines are so provocative they seem to talk, while Nile Rodgers' skeletal guitar runs hark back to Steve Cropper's slashing style. Sure, the songs don't say much. Sure, the dance mixes collected here ramble on after about six minutes. But once you step into these grooves—grooves that influenced an entire generation of artists from David Byrne to Prince—you will realize that these were indeed good times. *—John Floyd*

The Best of Chic, Vol. 2 / Nov. 10, 1992 / Rhino ✦✦✦✦✦

Filling out the gaps left by the first volume, *Best of Chic—Vol. 2* proves with its collection of album tracks and singles that Chic was not merely a great disco band, but was a great band, period. *—Stephen Thomas Erlewine*

★ **The Very Best of Chic** / Mar. 14, 2000 / Rhino ✦✦✦✦✦

To the rock critics who dismissed Chic's music as disposable and mindless back in the late '70s: it might seem like a stretch to say that Nile Rogers and Bernard Edwards had as great an impact as Gamble & Huff, George Clinton, and the folks at Stax Records. But in fact, Chic's music *was* that influential—and its disco/funk/soul innovations would be having an impact long after the '70s ended. From Madonna, Change, and Queen, to Duran Duran, Soul II Soul, and ABC—new wave, hip-hop, house, European Hi-NRG, Latin freestyle, and acid jazz—you could write a book about all the artists who have been influenced by Chic. This collection, which came out in 2000 and spans 1977-1982, is full of grooves that prove to be anything but disposable. Most of Chic's essential hits are provided, including "Good Times," "Le Freak," "Dance, Dance, Dance," "I Want Your Love," and "Everybody Dance." Less than essential, but still likable and decent, are early '80s recordings such as "Rebels Are We" from *Real People*, and "Stage Fright" from *Take It Off*. By 1980, Chic wasn't having as many hits and was feeling the sting of the death-to-disco movement. But disco never really died—it simply changed its name to dance music and evolved into such forms as Hi-NRG, Latin freestyle and house. When that happened, Chic's long-lasting influence was impossible to miss—you could say that Chic's influence lasted a lot longer than Chic itself. For those who need a concise introduction to Chic's legacy and want to hear some of R&B's most influential grooves, *The Very Best of Chic* is highly recommended. *—Alex Henderson*

Chicago

f. Feb. 15, 1967, Chicago, IL

Jazz-Rock, Pop/Rock, Soft Rock, Adult Contemporary

Chicago is second only to the Beach Boys as the most successful American rock band of all time. The group formed officially on February 15, 1967, in the city from which it eventually would take its name. The band members intended to launch a rock group with a fully integrated horn section (a novel idea at the time); initially, they did without a bass player, but in December 1967, bassist/vocalist Peter Cetera joined from rival band the Exceptions. Under the guidance of manager/producer James William Guercio, who initially named them Chicago Transit Authority (the name was shortened after the real C.T.A.

objected), the group moved to Los Angeles and signed to Columbia Records, recording its debut album, *Chicago Transit Authority*, in 1969. It sold over two million copies and spawned four chart singles, beginning a string of massive hits that lasted to the end of the decade, with each album cover sporting a variation on the Chicago logo and a sequential title with a roman numeral. Chicago's music was a mixture of styles, from hard rock to light pop, incorporating elements of jazz and classical, but after Cetera's "If You Leave Me Now" became a gold-selling #1 hit in 1976, the group became more identified with romantic ballads than anything else. Chicago went into decline after a split with Guercio in 1977, but rebounded in 1982 with "Hard to Say I'm Sorry" and the million-selling *Chicago 16*, and was able to sustain its renewed popularity despite Cetera's departure for a solo career in 1985. After several years of hits, Chicago's popularity began to decline in the early '90s, as the group retired to the oldies circuit. — *William Ruhlmann*

Chicago Transit Authority / Apr. 1969 / Chicago ✦✦✦✦
The first rock & roll band to integrate a horn section into its sound successfully, Chicago Transit Authority (later Chicago), fresh from years on the Midwest bar circuit, demonstrated a wide versatility on its debut album. The band seemed capable of playing everything from lounge music to hard rock, and here it mixed ballad material with gritty funk and psychedelic guitar, often on the same song. This time capsule of the varying strands of popular music in the late '60s features the hits "Does Anybody Really Know What Time It Is?," "Beginnings," and "Questions 67 and 68." — *William Ruhlmann*

Chicago II / Jan. 1970 / Chicago ✦✦✦✦
With its second double album (now on one CD), Chicago became even more ambitious and even more successful, mounting the extended "Suite for a Girl in Buchannon," from which were excerpted the hit singles "Make Me Smile" and "Color My World." "25 or 6 to 4" is also featured on this album. — *William Ruhlmann*

Chicago III / Jan. 1971 / Chicago ✦✦

At Carnegie Hall, Vols. 1-4 (Chicago IV) / Oct. 1971 / Chicago ✦
Carnegie Hall may be prestigious, but it has never been a good rock venue, and Chicago seems intimidated on this four-LP (three-CD) set, recreating material from its first three albums. Completists should note the inclusion of the anti-Nixon "A Song For Richard And His Friends," not previously available. — *William Ruhlmann*

Live in Japan 1972 / 1972 / Chicago ✦✦✦✦
This double-CD set, *not* the "legendary" triple-CD (four-LP) Carnegie Hall concert, is the one to get to hear what Chicago sounded like in their classic early period. In contrast to the Carnegie Hall show, where the band emphasized its precision to the point of deadening any excitement that might have been generated, here Chicago sounds upbeat and lively, bent on giving a good, exciting show and not on capturing a perfect performance. There are moments, as on the crescendo of "Dialogue," where the spirit outstrips the cleanness of the performance, but the group is so tight and forceful that one lets them slide by; at other times, as on "Beginnings," they're so smooth and lithe in their extension of the piece that one just wants to bask in it; and then they switch gears to the rougher, harder "Mississippi Delta City Blues," and make that work too. The whole performance is good, with a steady stream of worthwhile high points. The repertory runs up through "Saturday in the Park" and "Dialogue," and includes the core of their albums up through *Chicago V* (including the notorious "Song for Richard Nixon and His Friends"). The recording is so close that one hears every bass note and guitar lick, and feels practically in the bells of the trumpets, trombones, etc., and the mix is vivid and spacious. It shows what an embarrassment of riches Columbia was faced with in the group's output that they never issued this performance in America, favoring the more hyped but far less entertaining and exciting Carnegie Hall show—it was only Chicago's buying back of their catalog in the mid-1990s that got *Live In Japan* released in the U.S., more than 20 years after its first appearance in Japan. The only complaint about the CD is that they didn't reprint the information from the original LP jacket inside with the lyrics, so one has to squint at a miniature reproduction of the jacket to read the credits properly. — *Bruce Eder*

Chicago V / Jul. 1972 / Chicago ✦✦✦
The group's avant-garde roots are explored on the set-opening "A Hit by Varese," while the album also includes the autobiographical "Alma Mater" and the hits "Saturday in the Park" and "Dialogue." — *William Ruhlmann*

Chicago VI / Jun. 1973 / Chicago ✦✦✦
Chicago demonstrates all its strength here, turning in one of its great ballads in "Just You 'N' Me" and one of its great rockers in "Feelin' Stronger Every Day." Elsewhere, the group takes on its negative reviews in "Critics' Choice" and acknowledges the impact of L.A. stardom on a bunch of Midwestern kids in "Something in This City Changes People." — *William Ruhlmann*

Chicago VII / Mar. 1974 / Chicago ✦✦
Originally intended as a jazz-oriented record, Chicago's first double studio album since *Chicago III* (now on one CD) is an ambitious but ultimately uneven affair, buttressed by the hit singles "(I've Been) Searchin' So Long," "Call On Me," and "Wishing You Were Here." — *William Ruhlmann*

Chicago VIII / Mar. 1975 / Chicago ✦✦
Chicago keyboardist Robert Lamm had been the band's main songwriter to this point, and although he contributed four of the ten songs here, only his "Harry Truman" was memorable. The album's biggest hit was James Pankow's "Old Days," but little else stands out. — *William Ruhlmann*

● **Greatest Hits (Chicago IX)** / Nov. 1975 / Chicago ✦✦✦✦✦
The biggest hits of Chicago's first five years of recording, including "Just You 'N' Me," "Feelin' Stronger Every Day," "Wishing You Were Here," "Call On Me," and "(I've Been) Searchin' So Long." — *William Ruhlmann*

Chicago X / Jun. 1976 / Chicago ✦✦

Chicago XI / Sep. 1977 / Chicago ✦✦
On its last album to be produced by James William Guercio and to feature guitarist Terry Kath, Chicago turns in another competent but unremarkable effort. Peter Cetera's "Baby, What a Big Surprise" is his follow-up to "If You Leave Me Now," Robert Lamm continues to wax political on "Policeman" and "Vote for Me," and "Take Me Back to Chicago" accurately expresses an exhausted band's sentiments at this point. — *William Ruhlmann*

Hot Streets / Sep. 1978 / Chicago ✦✦

Chicago 13 / Aug. 1979 / Chicago ✦

Chicago XIV / Jul. 1980 / Chicago ✦

Chicago's Greatest Hits, Vol. 2 / 1981 / Chicago ✦✦✦
This album chronicles Chicago's gradual transformation in the second half of the '70s into a group that produced big ballads, usually sung by Peter Cetera. And here they are, starting with "If You Leave Me Now" and continuing with "Baby, What a Big Surprise" and the nostalgic "Old Days." — *William Ruhlmann*

If You Leave Me Now / 1982 / Chicago ✦✦

Chicago 16 / Jun. 1982 / Full Moon/Warner Brothers ✦✦
With its back to the wall, Chicago switched record labels, dropped Donnie Dacus in favor of Bill Champlin (of the Sons of Champlin), brought in producer David Foster as new Svengali, and went back to power ballads. And it all worked, at least commercially. "Hard to Say I'm Sorry" was the summer ballad of 1982, the album went Top Ten, and Chicago was back in business, albeit with far more limited musical goals than it had had at the beginning. — *William Ruhlmann*

Chicago 17 / May 1984 / Full Moon/Warner Brothers ✦✦✦
With sales of four million, this is the biggest-selling regular studio album Chicago has made. That's what happens when you really go for the ballads: "Stay the Night," "Hard Habit to Break," "You're the Inspiration," and "Along Comes a Woman" all fit into that category; all featured Peter Cetera, and all made the Top 40. Not surprisingly, Cetera decamped soon after. — *William Ruhlmann*

Chicago 18 / Sep. 1986 / Full Moon/Warner Brothers ✦✦
It is an article of faith in corporate lore that everyone is expendable, and Chicago Music, Inc., responded to the departure of Peter Cetera by hiring another blonde, bass-playing tenor with sex appeal in the person of Jason Scheff. Some people were fooled, especially by the power ballad "Will You Still Love Me?," but others weren't (the album stopped at gold), and longtime fans were dismayed at the re-recording of "25 or 6 To 4." — *William Ruhlmann*

Chicago 19 / Jun. 1988 / Full Moon/Reprise ✦✦
This album contained four Top Ten hits, "I Don't Wanna Live Without Your Love," "Look Away" (which hit #1), "You're Not Alone," and "What Kind of Man Would I Be?," yet did not reach the Top 10 on the album list, definite proof that Chicago was reaching an easy-listening (or "Adult Contemporary") radio audience but missing the rock audience. It paid the bills, though. — *William Ruhlmann*

Greatest Hits: 1982-1989 / Nov. 1989 / Full Moon/Reprise ✦✦✦✦
Chicago returned from a career dip in 1982 with "Hard to Say I'm Sorry" and continued to hit with power ballads, among them "Hard Habit to Break" and "You're the Inspiration," all sung by Peter Cetera. But the streak continued after Cetera departed in 1985, as Jason Scheff stepped in and Chicago went on to score hits like "Will You Still Love Me?," "I Don't Wanna Live Without Your Love," and "Look Away," which are all heard here. — *William Ruhlmann*

Group Portrait / 1991 / Chicago ✦✦✦✦✦
Weighing in at four discs and 63 songs, *Group Portrait* offers an excellent, comprehensive overview of Chicago's prime period. Be forewarned: this does not dip into the group's early-'80s hits or post-Peter Cetera recordings, choosing to end the story before their 1982 comeback. Although this music is missed, this isn't a fatal flaw, since instead of telling the band's story, this box sketches a portrait of the group at their creative peak. And it works very well indeed. Chicago most certainly made albums, yet those albums, no matter if they were intended conceptually, really played better as a series of moments. This collects those moments, whether they're hits or album tracks, spotlighting Chicago at their very best. Is it for everybody? No, since most casual listeners will be content with the fine hits collections, and some hardcore fans will still swear by the albums—yet for the audience that wants all of prime '70s Chicago in one set, this box set couldn't be better. — *Stephen Thomas Erlewine*

Twenty 1 / Jan. 1991 / Full Moon/Warner Brothers ✦✦

Night and Day: Big-Band / May 23, 1995 / Giant ✦✦

The Heart of Chicago 1967-1997 / Apr. 22, 1997 / Warner Brothers ✦✦✦
Heart of Chicago 1967-1997 is a cheap way to celebrate Chicago's 30th anniversary. Featuring 13 arbitrarily picked hits from throughout the band's career—from "Saturday in the Park" and "Does Anybody Really Know What Time It Is" to "If You Leave Me Now," "You're the Inspiration," "Hard to Say I'm Sorry," and "Look Away"—adding two new tracks, the Lenny Kravitz-produced "The Only One" and "Here in My Heart," which was co-written by Glen Ballard and James Newton Howard. Although Chicago has enlisted heavy hitters for the new tracks, both fall flat. And as a thorough hits collection, *Heart of Chicago 1967-1997* is unsuccessful as well, since it omits such hits as "25 or 6 to 4" and "Baby, What a Big Surprise," yet it works well as sampler for casual fans, since it has only the biggest hits. — *Stephen Thomas Erlewine*

Chickasaw Mudd Puppies

f. 1989, **db.** 1992
Jangle Pop, Roots Rock, Alternative Pop/Rock

A primitive swamp-rock duo comprised of Ben Reynolds (vocals, electric guitar, percussion) and Brant Slay (vocals, harmonica, washboard), the Chickasaw Mudd Puppies were proteges of R.E.M.'s Michael Stipe, a fellow Athens, Georgia resident who teamed with John Keane to co-produce their 1990 debut *White Dirt*. Chicago blues legend Willie Dixon split production chores with Stipe for 1991's *8 Track Stomp*, after which the duo called it quits; Reynolds later resurfaced as a solo artist. —*Jason Ankeny*

White Dirt / 1990 / Wing ♦♦♦♦

Calling the Chickasaw Mudd Puppies both roots-rock and alternative rock may seem like a contradiction, but both terms would be appropriate in describing *White Dirt*. This unorthodox band, which enjoyed a small cult following, has a delightfully bluesy, Louisiana-influenced swamp boogie foundation that owes a strong debt to Creedence Clearwater Revival. But Brant Slay's eccentric vocals (which sometimes bring to mind Primus' goofy Les Claypool) aren't what you'd expect from a roots band. This isn't to say that the Mudd Puppies have actually been influenced by Primus' dissonant funk-metal—the instrumentation is a lot closer to what you'd expect from a blues-rock band in Baton Rouge. But if any songs have even come close to bridging the gap between Claypool's vocal style and the sounds of the swamp, they would have to be "Ponky Knot," "Frogmore" and "Raven." The Puppies' adventurous spirit serves them consistently well on a CD that is as quirky as it is captivating. —*Alex Henderson*

● **8 Track Stomp** / 1991 / Wing ♦♦♦♦♦

The Chiffons

f. 1960, New York, NY [The Bronx], **db.** 1972
Brill Building Pop, Girl Group, Pop

One of the best early-'60s New York girl groups, combining sassiness and innocence on several of the style's greatest classics. The Chiffons had some singles under their belt when they reached number one with "He's So Fine," whose classic "doo-lang, doo-lang" riff was appropriated by George Harrison in 1970 for his own chart-topper, "My Sweet Lord" (Harrison was subsequently ordered to pay substantial damages to the original publishers, though he always claimed the resemblance was unintentional). Their follow-up, Goffin-King's "One Fine Day," was just as good, featuring killer piano riffs from King herself. Actually cut as a Little Eva track, the Chiffons' vocal was substituted, resulting in a Top Five hit. There were a couple other memorable hits—"I Have a Boyfriend" and the Motown-influenced "Sweet Talkin' Guy"—and interesting misfires like the Martha & the Vandellas-inspired "The Real Thing," as well as some singles issued under an alter ego, the Four Pennies. The group recorded quite a bit of material during the '60s, much of it derivative. —*Richie Unterberger*

Greatest Recordings / 1990 / Ace ♦♦♦♦♦

A generous collection that not only features their greatest hits, but many forgotten songs that are surprisingly good. —*Stephen Thomas Erlewine*

● **16 Golden Classics** / Apr. 18, 1990 / Collectables ♦♦♦♦♦

Jane Child

b. Toronto, Ontario, Canada
Vocals / Club/Dance, Dance-Pop

Born into a musical family in Toronto, Jane Child took violin lessons from her father and voice lessons from her mother. Rock wasn't allowed in her home, but she did listen to an R&B station from nearby Buffalo, NY, and had hopes of starting a band. Child dropped out of the Royal Conservatory of Music to join a rock band in Toronto. Signed to Warner Music in 1988 on the strength of just a demo tape, Jane Child released her first single, "Don't Wanna Fall in Love," in 1990. Her self-titled debut album appeared that same year and *Here and There* followed in 1993. —*John Bush*

● **Jane Child** / 1989 / Warner Brothers ♦♦♦♦♦

Jane Child's debut album was a pleasant excursion into synthesized dance-pop that was distinguished by the ingratiatingly catchy single, "Don't Wanna Fall in Love." A handful of other songs on the album—including the minor hit "Welcome to the Real World"—demonstrated Child's skills as a pop craftswoman, but just as many fell flat. —*Stephen Thomas Erlewine*

Here Not There / 1993 / Warner Brothers ♦♦

Billy Childish (Stephen Hamper)

b. 1958, Chatham, England
Vocals / Garage Rock Revival, Indie Rock, Alternative Pop/Rock

Few performers in rock history have been as ferociously prolific as Billy Childish. In fact, a complete discography of his work as a solo performer and with his various bands would take up quite a few pages. A singer, songwriter, artist, poet, critic, fanzine editor, and guitarist who suffers from severe dyslexia, he's a punk-inspired Renaissance man. However, you may have never heard of him, or heard one of the over 50 recordings he's made either solo or with one of his many bands (Pop Rivets, the Milkshakes, Thee Mighty Caesars, the Delmonas, Thee Headcoats and the Natural Born Lovers), *or* read his over 40 books of poetry and assorted scribblings. Surprisingly, Childish has been recording since 1979, playing a rough-and-tumble, punk-inspired approximation of what is normally called garage rock. Not one for elaborate production techniques, the consistent element of Childish's music is that all of it sounds as though it was recorded and mixed in about an hour. He values immediacy and intensity and frequently seems itching to move on to

to the next song, or, more specifically, the next band. A truly primitive talent (due to his learning disability, he has had little formal education) who, a la Jad and David Fair of Half Japanese, eschews technical ability for pure emotion, Childish occupies an artistic role somewhere between mad genius and bratty goofball. Unfailingly sure of himself and his vision, his music is as honest and emotionally direct as one is likely to hear. Unfortunately, he also lacks the discipline of self-editing, and as a result, some of his lesser work rambles incoherently or simply sounds so similar as to be uninteresting. Years after his first single, "Fun in the U.K." (a tongue-in-cheek send-up of the Sex Pistols' "Anarchy in the U.K."), Childish is still producing material at an amazing rate, epitomizing the endurance and drive of an artist who in many ways is the archetypal rock outsider. —*John Dougan*

Play: Capt'n Calypso's Hoodoo Party / 1988 / Hangman ♦♦♦♦

Assembling a coterie of friends and players as the Blackhands—notably including a trumpeter, one Dave—Childish turned in a loose and lively romp through originals and covers both, yet one more collection of rough and tumble wiggery from the man. Recorded at a single date—and perhaps in fact recorded at a party, but who can say?—*Hoodoo* is the sound of folks playing for their own enjoyment and having a fun time while they're at it. It's not quite rock, not exactly calypso, definitely not lounge, and not really big band jazz, but somehow the Blackhands make it all sound like a fusion of same, like a record dropped somewhere out of the thirties or the late forties into the present. Childish sends his vocals through some light effects, or maybe it's just the mike, giving it a mid-century scratchiness. His banjo takes the basic lead, but Dave's trumpet provides the flair, and even if it's not always note-perfect, that's hardly the point. Vocals from Ludella and Kyra provide nice contrast, sometimes taking lead and sometimes pairing up with Childish in duets, while Seamus on accordion adds more fills and fun to it all. Everything kicks off with the old standard "Rum and Coca-Cola," delivered with an infectious glee—the punchy drums from Richard add to the entertainment. Other oldies include the calypso number "Underneath the Mango Tree," as featured in *Dr. No*, "I Love Paris (in the Springtime)" and the Champs' legendary instrumental "Tequila." The one song sure to do in any punk-rock purists lurking about is "Anarchy in the UK"—yep, the Sex Pistols anthem, given a hilarious and energetic run-through. Hearing Childish play the opening riff on banjo is reason enough to give an ear. —*Ned Raggett*

● **I Am the Billy Childish** / 1991 / Sub Pop ♦♦♦♦♦

There is simply too much Billy Childish music available (good, bad and indifferent) to examine here in great detail. Fortunately, America's super-hip indie label Sub Pop released this superb two-CD anthology that gets to the heart of Childish's aesthetic, offering an extremely strong selection of material that covers a nearly 14-year period. Subtitled *50 Songs from 50 Records*, you will get a taste of nearly all of Childish's bands and hear "Fun in the U.K.," which he recorded with his short-lived Pop Rivets. Fans of idiosyncratic singer/songwriters like Kevin Coyne and Jonathan Richman may find themselves immediately enamored of Childish's defiantly different approach to rock & roll. If that's the case, the liner information in this set provides a solid discographical overview of Childish's work from the late '70s up to the early '90s. Buyer alert: this set was originally limited to 1,500 copies; it's a mystery as to how many are still for sale. —*John Dougan*

Made with a Passion: Kitchen Demo's / Sep. 24, 1996 / Sympathy for the Record Industry ♦♦♦♦

One would think that Childish couldn't get any more control over the recording of his material than he does, doggedly pursuing the punk route music to its logical conclusions. However, as he says in the liner notes to this entertaining collection, "I've made 80 LPs without a producer, but still there's always a manipulation going on, a dressing up (or dressing down) of the sound … (*Passion*) sets out to please no one … I like it." Taken from his demo recordings in his kitchen from 1990 to 1996, *Passion* is what it is, no treatment for tape hiss or apologies made for off notes or intrusions. Unlike the painful earnestness of lo-fi, though, this just sounds like Childish being himself instead of fitting any kind of scene, and all the better for that. The first track, "A to Z of Your Hart," starts with a separate collage of random poetry reading from what sounds like a young girl, a drum fill and general laughs from all assembled—po-faced seriousness left at the door, thanks. Similar bursts of randomness crop up throughout, whether it sounds like bits from a Lenny Bruce routine or older English pop songs or full band blasts fuzzily ripping along. The songs themselves, most often performed on acoustic guitar, capture the Childish view of life nicely—ranting against the assholes of the world in his distinct voice and accent, from a uniquely English point of view but in a way that anyone can empathize with. One of the funniest cuts is "Art or Arse?," where Childish ponders the ways of everyone from Kurt Schwitters to Damien Hurst. The young Zanna contributes some readings of Childish's poetry as well, a nice balance –"Judging Them All to Hell" and "The Naked Poet" are particularly sharp. —*Ned Raggett*

Chilli Willi & The Red Hot Peppers

f. 1971, **db.** Feb. 1975
Pub Rock, Rock & Roll, Country-Rock

Chilli Willi and the Red Hot Peppers were one of the main British pub rock groups of the early '70s, playing a laid-back yet rocking mixture of rock & roll, R&B, country and folk. The band has its origins in a folk-rock duo formed by ex-Junior's Blues Band members, Martin Stone (vocals, guitar, mandolin) and Phil "Snakefinger" Lithman (vocals, guitar, piano, lap steel, fiddle). Lithman moved to San Francisco in the late '60s, leaving Stone to play with Savoy Brown and Mighty Baby. The duo reunited in the early '70s, recording *Kings of Robot Rhythm* with vocalist Jo-Ann Kelly and various members of Brinsley Schwarz. *Kings* was released in 1972; that same year, the duo expanded to a band, adding Paul "Dice Man" Bailey (guitar, banjo, saxophone), Paul Riley (bass), and drummer Pete Thomas. During the next two years, Chilli Willi and the Red Hot Peppers became a popular live act in Britain. The full band released *Bongos Over Balham* in 1974, yet the record sold poorly and the band split in February 1975. Thomas became the drummer for Elvis Costello's backing band, the Attractions, Riley played with Graham Parker, Bailey formed Bontemps Roulez, and Stone played with the Pink Fairies before quitting the music business. Lithman moved back to San Francisco where he began to work with his former associates, the Residents, under the name Snakefinger. *—Stephen Thomas Erlewine*

Kings of the Robot Rhythm / 1972 / Revelations ♦♦♦

● **Bongos over Balham** / 1974 / Mooncrest ♦♦♦♦♦

I'll Be Home / Oct. 12, 1999 / Proper ♦♦♦♦

Chilliwack

f. 1970, Canada

Album Rock, Arena Rock, Pop/Rock, Soft Rock

Formed in Vancouver as the Classics and later the Collectors, Bill Henderson (guitar, vocals), Claire Lawrence (keyboards, sax), Glenn Miller (bass), Ross Turney (drums) and Howie Vickers (vocals) recorded several singles from 1967 to 1970, but changed their name to Chilliwack after Vickers and Miller left the group. The band had several Canadian hits in the 1970s and early '80s, from their 13 albums: *Chilliwack* (1970; for Parrot), *Chilliwack* (1971; for A&M), *Music for a Quiet Time* (1972), *All over You* (1973), *Riding High* (1974), *Rockerbox* (1976), *Dreams, Dreams, Dreams* (1976), *Lights from the Valley* (1978), *Breakdown in Paradise* (1979), *Wanna Be a Star* (1981), *Opus X* (1982), *Segue* (1983) and *Look In, Look Out* (1984). Brian Macleod (keyboards, sax) and Howard Froese (guitar) joined in 1977. *—John Bush*

Wanna Be a Star / 1981 / Millennium ♦♦♦♦♦

● **Greatest Hits** / 1994 / CBS ♦♦♦♦♦

Chilliwack's sound harnesses a smooth, semi-hard rock feel that is spotlighted by Bill Henderson's fly-away vocals, on top of some light keyboard work sprinkled in the background. With nine albums under their belt, this greatest-hits album fuses all of their best songs in one place and makes for a truly solid package. Their biggest hit, "My Girl (Gone Gone Gone)" is one of the most enjoyable tunes here, along with the beautiful "I Believe" and the lonely sounding "Fly at Night." The pace is sped up a bit on songs like "Don't Stop" and "Whatcha Gonna Do," helping to balance out the lighter material. Henderson's voice is pleasing to the ear and is the soul of this group. Some of the lesser-known tracks on this album, like "Rain-O" and "Getting Better," hold their own, and round out a sincerely delightful collection. *—Mike DeGagne*

The Chills

f. Oct. 1980, Dunedin, New Zealand

College Rock, New Zealand Rock, Alternative Pop/Rock

The Chills were one of New Zealand's best and most popular bands of the '80s, making a small but consistent series of chiming, hook-laden guitar pop. Both the songs and the arrangements were constructed with interweaving guitar hooks and vocal harmonies, creating a pretty, almost lush, sound that never falls into cloying sentimentality. Throughout their existence, the band's personnel changed frequently—there were more than ten different lineups—with the only constant member being guitarist Martin Phillipps, the band's founder. In 1982, the Chills signed with Flying Nun and released much material (collected on 1986's *Kaleidoscope World*) before issuing their proper debut, 1987's *Brave Words*. *Submarine Bells*, released in 1990, became their first record for an American major label. The album was well received by critics and college radio, yet it failed to break the band into the mainstream in either America or Britain. Two years later, they released *Soft Bomb*, which suffered the same fate as *Submarine Bells*. The following year, Martin Phillipps broke up the Chills again, yet the group reconvened in 1996 to release *Sunburnt*. *—Stephen Thomas Erlewine*

● **Kaleidoscope World** / 1986 / Homestead ♦♦♦♦♦

Kaleidoscope World is the Chills' essential document, although it's not an album, but a collection of tracks from early and mid-'80s EPs, singles, and compilation cuts. Perhaps that's not surprising: the Chills are more skilled at crafting interesting odds and sods than sustaining interest over the course of an album, where their somewhat monochrome approach tends to drag things down. The influence of Syd Barrett/early Pink Floyd is stronger on these early tracks than it would be on subsequent releases, both on the easy-going singalong numbers and the more experimental outings. The highlight (of both the album and the Chills' career) is their New Zealand hit single, the haunting "Pink Frost." *—Richie Unterberger*

Brave Words / 1987 / Homestead ♦♦♦

The band's first proper album (years after making their recording debut) was something of a disappointment, both in terms of production and material. The sound is too blurry and homogenous, and the songs aren't distinctive enough to surmount that obstacle, although they strive to attain the group's typically foggy, vaguely psychedelic atmosphere. *—Richie Unterberger*

Submarine Bells / Feb. 1990 / Slash ♦♦♦♦

On a major label for the first time, Phillipps crafted a lovely record indeed, a mere thirty-six minutes and not a second wasted. Lead-off track and single "Heavenly Pop Hit" remains the most famous track and deservedly so—over a rapturous keyboard/rhythm combination, Phillipps sings just that, an inspiring lyric with a soaring chorus, aided by additional backing vocals from guest Donna Savage. From there it's one high point after another, never losing the sense of elegance and drive that characterizes the band's work. Phillipps' at-once strong and amiably regular-guy vocals and astonishingly intelligent but never overly obtuse lyrics are both wonders, while Andrew Todd's excellent keyboard work provides both energy and lovely shading. Add to that a fine rhythm section in bassist Justin Harwood and drummer James Stephenson, and it's no wonder this version of the Chills succeeds as it does. One fantastic example of their work together is "Singing In My Sleep," with Phillipps giving heavy tremolo treatment to his guitar as everyone else creates something that's not too far from Neu!'s motorik throb, in a gentler pop vein. More such Krautrock-inspired chug has plenty of echoes on *Bells*, following in the same vein as "I Love My Leather Jacket"—check out the brisk delivery on "The Oncoming Day" or the skipping intensity of "Dead Web." Otherwise, there are hints of the gentle folky/medieval touches they enjoy on "I SOAR" and "Don't Be—Memory" and more straightforward rocking out on the sharp "Familiarity Breeds Contempt," where Phillipps' New Zealand burr comes through with intensity. The title track, with serene orchestration filling out the grand arrangement, is a note-perfect way to conclude such a fantastic release. *—Ned Raggett*

Soft Bomb / Jun. 30, 1992 / Slash ♦♦♦

Going through yet another line-up revamp—Phillipps is the only one remaining from the *Submarine Bells* performers—the Chills approached what turned out to be the final album as simply the Chills (instead of "Martin Phillipps and...") in an unsettled state. Former bassist Terry Moore rejoined, dB's legend Peter Holsapple was drafted to provide additional guitars and keyboards, while Van Dyke Parks provided unnerving orchestration for one track, "Water Wolves," but Phillipps remained dead center as always. The result was okay, but not as distinctly Chills as before—the near-perfect fusion and extension of earlier styles on *Bells* became more of a grab-bag, with a few awkward stabs at proto-adult album alternative airplay. Other tunes range from brawling (and overproduced?) rockers to the series of tracks called "Soft Bomb" scattered throughout the album like commercial breaks. More quirky numbers include the drunk music hall band arrangement on "There Is No Harm in Trying" and "Song for Randy Newman Etc.," an odd homage to the musician obliquely addressing artistic struggles over a nice piano melody. Opener "The Male Monster From the Id" shows Phillipps' smart way with words hasn't changed at all, but the music isn't the strongest he's done, signaling the album's sometimes-on sometimes-off nature. The chorus of "Background Affair," an airy, inspiring float with the music, or the clever opening of the first "Soft Bomb": "If you'd asked me at a concert standing by the Clean/ I'd have said I'm OK, and this is what I mean" are among the "on" highlights. Further high points include the lovely "Halo Fading," and the slightly bluesy, ominous late-night vibe of "Entertainer." *—Ned Raggett*

Heavenly Pop Hits / 1995 / Flying Nun ♦♦♦♦

Supplanting the earlier *Kaleidoscope World* as a singles overview of the band, from early days to cuts from *Soft Bomb*, *Heavenly* is a great starting point for any Chills newcomer. The opening three songs alone make this a winner—the title track, a shimmering pop gem, "I Love My Leather Jacket," a poppy Velvet Underground/Krautrockin' salute to deceased drummer Martyn Bull, and "Doledrums," a perverse celebration of collecting unemployment and killing time with a neat clock-chime opening. From there on in its one great highlight after another, sprightliness and beauty tinged with melancholy and gloom in equal amounts, not to mention the quick, brisk surge that colored so many of their tracks ("Oncoming Day," "Never Never Go" and the charging "Look For the Good in Others," presented in a remixed form). "Pink Frost," probably the band's most famous number, is unsurprisingly featured, but that's merely the tip of the iceberg, especially when it comes to the earlier songs like "Kaleidoscope World" itself and "Rolling Moon." Concluding with later winners like "Part Past Part Fiction" and "Male Monster From the Id," *Heavenly Pop Hits* is, indeed, just that. *—Ned Raggett*

Sunburnt / Oct. 8, 1996 / Flying Nun ♦♦♦♦

Secret Box: Chills Rarities 1980-2000 / 2001 / Definitive ♦♦♦♦♦

It's the motherlode for fans of New Zealand pop: a three-disc set of rarities and unreleased songs by the Chills, arguably the finest kiwi rockers ever. Literally dozens of songs were written and performed by the Chills in the '80s, but until now, they've never been available to anyone who wasn't lucky enough to see them perform at the time. The first of these three discs consists of 23 of these never-otherwise-recorded gems, presented in roughly chronological order with widely varying levels of fidelity. The first third of the second disc covers live tracks from the mid-'80s, as Martin Phillipps' song structures were becoming twistier and he was starting to perfect the tumbling logorrhea that would become the lyrical trademark of later Chills albums. The middle third collects three 1985-1988 radio sessions in full, featuring early versions of songs that would later appear on *Brave Words*, 1990's *Submarine Bells*, and 1992's *Soft Bomb*. Early demos of other songs from those later albums also appear on the last third of this disc; in nearly every case, the demo is superior to the over-produced album versions. The final disc is subtitled "Singular Booty," and although it largely consists of previously released material, it's every bit as essential as the first two discs. These B-sides and compilation tracks are not mere throwaways, but excellent, well-constructed pop songs in their own right. At 83 tracks spread over nearly four hours, *Secret Box* is undoubtedly for fans only, but the near total lack of filler, or even substandard songs, is testament to Phillipps' remarkable, underappreciated talent. *—Stewart Mason*

Alex Chilton

b. Dec. 28, 1950, Memphis, TN

Vocals, Guitar / College Rock, Roots Rock, Rock & Roll

In a business that reinvents itself at every turn, Alex Chilton has managed to survive for three decades with a three-fold career as well—his early recordings with the Box Tops, the three albums he did with Big Star in the mid-'70s and the spate of cool, but chaotic, solo albums he's recorded since then. To some, he's a classic hit-maker from the '60s. To others, he's a genius British-style pop musician and songwriter. To yet another audience, he's a doomed and despairing artist who spent several years battling the bottle, delivering anarchistic records and performances while thumbing his nose at all pretenses of stardom, a quirky iconoclast whose influence has spawned the likes of the Replacements and Teenage Fanclub. With the Box Tops, he cut "The Letter," a record that sounded White enough to go number one on the pop charts and yet Black enough to track on R&B stations, too. Chilton was still in his teens, but armed with a strong conception of how pop and R&B vocals should be handled. The hits kept coming, with "Cry like a Baby," "Soul Deep" and "Sweet Cream Ladies" all showing visible chart action. After a few errant solo sessions, Chilton next found himself in Big Star with singer/guitarist Chris Bell. Their blend of ethereal harmonies, quirky lyrics and Beatlesque song structure appeared to be radio-friendly, but distribution for their label, Ardent Records, spelled disaster. Around 1976, Chilton started producing a wild cross-section of solo outings for various foreign and American independent labels, all featuring his love for obscure material, barbed-wire guitar playing, howling feedback and bands who sounded barely familiar with the material. *—Cub Koda*

Bach's Bottom / 1975 / Razor & Tie ♦♦♦
Recorded during one of Chilton's more chaotic periods, *Bach's Bottom* is an interesting document of misguided talent. It's not so much the music as it is the sense of what is going on around the music that makes this 1975 outing fascinating. Chilton's dismemberment of "Free Again," "Take Me Home and Make Me Like It," the Beatles' "I'm So Tired," and "Jesus Christ" are pretty funny, while his great self-productions of "Bangkok" and the Seeds' "Can't Seem to Make You Mine" reveal his penchant for making something special happen at times when everything seems to be falling apart. *—AMG*

Like Flies on Sherbert / 1979 / Peabody ♦
On the strength of his Big Star releases from the early 1970s and a host of live performances he gave during the latter half of the 1970s, Alex Chilton had rightly become a rock connoisseur's darling and an inspiration to independent-label bands throughout the United States. Despite all this favorable attention, he would not return to the studio until 1980. Sadly, this release is a dreadful disappointment. Production values are among the worst this reviewer has ever heard: sound quality is terrible, instrumental balances are careless and haphazard, and some selections even begin with recording start-up sound. Chilton's false-start vocal on "Boogie Shoes" is simply left in without correction. Many of the songs here stop dead or fall apart rather than ending properly. Instrumental playing is universally slipshod and boorish, and vocals are sloppy and lackluster. A cover of the Lonnie Mack hit "I've Had It" contains vocals that, without exaggeration, sound like a group of tavern inebriates trying to sing. An attempt to burlesque Elvis Presley's vocal excesses in "Girl after Girl" misfires badly. A few of Chilton's songs here, such as "My Rival" and "Hook or Crook," aren't bad in their own right and would have been listenable had they been performed and produced better. Regrettably, this album cannot be recomended under any circumstances. *—David Cleary*

Live in London / 1982 / Varese ♦♦

Black List / 1990 / New Rose ♦♦♦
This album continues to successfully mine the retro-music lodestone found in *High Priest*, *Feudalist Tarts*, and similar releases of this period. Half the songs here are blues numbers of differing stripes: "Jailbait" is an irresistibly rocking song featuring prominent organ and baritone saxophone that has humorous, worldly lyrics in praise of the speaker's underaged sweetie; "Baby Baby Baby" is a fine down-and-dirty slow-tempo selection with rudimentary verses; Furry Lewis' "I Will Turn Your Money Green" is an enjoyably lazy, loping number. Other styles are showcased as well. The Chilton original "Guantanamerika" is a smooth, almost jazz-lounge-oriented ditty with ironic lyrics. A cover of "Nice and Easy Does It" reveals a fine song given as a sophisticated crooner's tune. There's also a bouncy, faithful cover of the 1960s surf-style car classic "Little GTO," on which Chilton plays all the instruments and sings all the vocals. Sound quality is top-notch. Performances are first-rate, with as always excellent solo work from guitarist Chilton and saxophonist Jim Spake; Chilton's singing is a bit strained on the high notes on "Little GTO," but is otherwise fine. This excellent release is strongly recommended. *—David Cleary*

• **19 Years: A Collection** / Feb. 1991 / Rhino ♦♦♦♦
Collecting tracks from, indeed, 19 years of Chilton's career, *19 Years* remains the best place to get a sampling of his widely varied work. Big Star is represented (perhaps a bit too strongly) by five tracks from *3rd/Sister Lovers*, which at that time had not been rereleased in America by Rykodisc, including such masterpieces of desolation as "Kanga Roo" and "Holocaust." Otherwise, this is Chilton solo getting the focus, starting with "Free Again," an infectious country-rock cut from his then unreleased debut album away from the Box Tops, *1970*, and concluding with cuts from his 1987 release *High Priest*. Even Chilton's fans admit to—or perhaps can't easily take or understand—his almost willful stylistic jumps and sidesteps, making a full encapsulation of his interests and detours impossible, but *19 Years* comes pretty close. Both sides of his one-off single from 1977, "Bangkok"/"Can't Seem to Make You Mine," make the grade, the former being one of the better punk-influenced tunes by older musicians out there. If the sound is more quavering Marc Bolan meets rockabilly, why not? The latter serves up a Seeds cover with folk-rocky panache and more than a few strange noises. Ragged tracks from *Like Flies on Sherbert* capture the half-engaging, half-troubling points of his late-'70s life, while cuts from the *Feudalist Tarts* and *No Sex* EPs show him exploring his rootsier, New Orleans-tinged side with low-key fire. The addition of a Troggs cover, "With a Girl Like You," from a French compilation gives *19 Years* a nice little bonus. Detailed liner notes from Darcy Sullivan trace the strange course of his career, not shying away from acknowledging periods where his drinking and other problems disrupted any kind of regular career flow, while the remastering and presentation is up to Rhino's usual standard. *—Ned Raggett*

Cliches / Feb. 11, 1994 / Ardent ♦♦♦
While Alex Chilton has shown a certain disinclination toward songwriting since his "comeback" with *Feudalist Tarts* in 1985, *Cliches* is his first solo project without a single original tune. Instead, Chilton, accompanied only by his acoustic guitar, croons ten romantic standards from the '40s and '50s, along with two instrumentals (one of which is a slimmed-down version of a Bach guitar piece). Anyone hoping to hear Chilton rock out (or serve up a pop confection like "September Gurls") is advised not to bother, but on its own terms, *Cliches* is a very enjoyable listen. While Chilton's approach to the vintage R&B tunes that have become his stock in trade is cloaked in so many layers of irony it's hard to tell if he likes the songs or not, on this material his delivery is warm, easygoing, and straightforward, and he seems to genuinely enjoy himself in a way he hasn't on record since the first Big Star album. Despite the occasional rough moment in his vocals and guitar playing (doubtless attributable to the fact this was recorded in a single evening), *Cliches* is a pleasant reminder of just how good a singer Alex Chilton can be when he cares about what he's doing. *—Mark Deming*

Feudalist Tarts/No Sex / May 1, 1994 / Razor & Tie ♦♦♦♦♦
Since Alex Chilton seems to have had trouble coming up with an LP's worth of tunes at one time since re-emerging as an active performer in the 1980s, he's released a number of EPs, and this CD reissue pairs up two of his best. 1985's *Feudalist Tarts* was Chilton's first studio release since 1979; after spending most of the 1970s as one of the few rock acts from the Deep South who displayed almost no visible R&B influence, Chilton belatedly embraced the pleasures of vintage soul music after moving to New Orleans and giving up alcohol, and *Feudalist Tarts* is dominated by covers of Slim Harpo's "Ti Ni Nee Ni Noo" and Carla Thomas's "B-A-B-Y," with bare-wired originals like "Lost My Job" along for good measure. Cut in a single day, *Feudalist Tarts* is a bit rough around the edges, but Chilton's guitar playing is solid, and the band of veteran Southern studio players give Chilton as good as he gets (if not better). The following year, Chilton released the three-song *No Sex* 12"; the title tune is the best song he's written since Big Star's breakup, a witty but ominous meditation on the consequences of the AIDS pandemic (which, given his reputation as a ladies' man, has doubtless been a matter of great concern to Chilton). *Feudalist Tarts* and *No Sex* don't do much to fill out a CD together—their combined length is less than 33 minutes—but they are two of the most solid records of Chilton's mid-'80s "comeback" period. *—Mark Deming*

High Priest/Black List / May 1, 1994 / Razor & Tie ♦♦♦
1987's *High Priest* was Alex Chilton's first full-length studio album since the fascinatingly disastrous *Like Flies on Sherbert* in 1979. While it certainly wasn't the return to pure-pop form some fans were hoping for from the former leader of Big Star, it at least showed Chilton to be in firm command of his faculties again, and fronting a solid band of Memphis/New Orleans studio heavyweights. *High Priest* boasted only four original songs from Chilton, the best being the mildly sleazy "Thing for You" (though the just-plain-weird "Dalai Lama" has a certain perverse charm), but he dug up a handful of worthwhile covers, including the good-and-greasy "Make a Little Love" and a fine, obscure Carole King number, "Let Me Get Close to You." While Chilton's vocals betray a certain inscrutable irony, he's in fine voice throughout, and his wildly underrated guitar work is very much in evidence. *Black List*, a six-song EP Chilton released in 1989, is featured on this CD release as a bonus; it works on the same level as *High Priest*, only with six songs instead of 12. It does include that modern rarity, a noteworthy original Alex Chilton song ("Guantanamerika," a witty meditation on right-wing politics and Tammy Faye Bakker) and a solid version of the R&B chestnut "I Will Turn Your Money Green." In addition, Razor and Tie have dug up unreleased tunes from the sessions for each record that, for a change, are actually worth hearing; "Magnetic Field," a leftover from *Black List*, is a frantic old-school rocker written by Chilton, while his superb cover of Charlie Rich's "Lonely Weekends" is an outtake from *High Priest* that's better than most of what made the cut. *—Mark Deming*

A Man Called Destruction / Sep. 12, 1995 / Ardent ♦♦♦
Since the mid-'80s, all Alex Chilton albums are basically interchangeable. Chilton and his bar band get together and knock off a handful of mediocre new songs and several (mostly obscure) R&B and rock & roll oldies. Now that Chilton is more or less sober, his pitch is a bit better, yet there isn't anything particularly special about *A Man Called Destruction*, other than the delightfully corny "What's Your Sign?," where Alex sings the horoscope in an attempt to pick up a girl. It's the best thing here, and he didn't write it. *—Stephen Thomas Erlewine*

1970 / Apr. 1996 / Ardent ♦♦♦
1970 comprises the sessions that would have formed Alex Chilton's first solo album. As the title suggests, Chilton recorded these songs after he left the Box Tops but right before he joined Big Star—appropriately, the music sounds caught between the Box Tops' blue-eyed soul and Big Star's jangly power-pop. In that respect, it has more in common with his numerous solo recordings than either of his bands. And like his solo records, *1970* is wildly uneven and lacks focus. It careens between charming tributes to R&B and pop (a medley of the Archies' "Sugar, Sugar" and James Brown's "There Was a Time"), and his originals, which only hint at the heights he would reach with Big Star. If *1970* does anything, it illustrates that Chilton needs a strong collaborative force like Chris Bell to bring out the best in his music. *—Stephen Thomas Erlewine*

Set / Feb. 22, 2000 / Bar/None ♦♦♦

The Chocolate Watchband

f. 1965, Los Altos, California, **db.** 1968
Garage Rock, Psychedelic
The Chocolate Watchband never charted a record nationally. Indeed, ask most casual

1960s rock fans about them and you'll probably get little more than a blank stare. Most will remember their AVI Records labelmates the Standells more clearly, because they actually managed to chart a few singles. Alas, the Watchband had the disadvantage of being a punkier band than the Standells, and suffering continual lineup changes. The Chocolate Watchband was a mod-outfitted garage punk unit par excellence, their sound founded on English-style R&B with a special fixation on the Rolling Stones at their most sneering. After hooking up with producer Ed Cobb, a former member of the 1950s vocal ensemble the Four Preps, the group released *No Way Out* in mid-1967, though the Watchband had already begun breaking up. A new incarnation carried them through 1967, though the band's existence as a viable performing unit were all but over. The group's producers had other ideas, however, releasing two more albums (*The Inner Mystique, One Step Beyond*) in 1968 & 1969, sporting the band's name but not too much else associated with the group. That would probably have been the end of the group's story, but in the early '80s, record buyers and, more particularly, young musicians discovered the Watchband. A set of Australian reissues of the group's albums quickly found a market in America and Europe. Thus, it was no surprise when, in 1994, Sundazed Records reissued the complete Watchband catalog on compact disc. *—Bruce Eder*

No Way Out / 1967 / Sundazed ✦✦✦
Possibly the best garage-punk album ever to make it out the door from a major label in the '60s, despite the presence of some non-Watchband tracks. "Are You Gonna Be There (At the Love-In)" is worth the price of admission, and "Let's Talk About Girls" makes an unforgettable opening track. Reissued on Sundazed for CD, and worth owning in that form, as an original on vinyl might set you back $100 or more. *—Bruce Eder*

The Inner Mystique / 1968 / Sundazed ✦✦✦
The group's second album, like its first, features too many tracks that really aren't the Watchband, but this time some of it even works. Side one of the original long-player consisted mostly of a bunch of psychedelic studio noodling courtesy of musicians hired by the producer, but even among these, "In the Past" is a bejeweled psychedelic treasure that ought to be in any collection. The rest is pure garage-punk, raw and undiluted, including savage covers of the Kinks' "I'm Not Like Everybody Else" and Bob Dylan's "It's All Over Now, Baby Blue," and "Medication," rendered here in a version superior in its lustful decadence to the original by their labelmates the Standells. Reissued in unbelievably good sound, with bonus tracks, on Sundazed Records in the '90s. *—Bruce Eder*

One Step Beyond / 1969 / Sundazed ✦✦✦
A last-gasp effort at milking some money out of the band's name is a fairly weak album, seldom above fair-to-mediocre musically, except for lead singer David Aguilar's "Don't Need Your Lovin'," rounded out by some killer bonus tracks ("Sitting There Standing," etc.). The notes are a brilliant finish to the Watchband saga, tying up a pile of loose ends. *—Bruce Eder*

● **The Best of the Chocolate Watchband** / 1983 / Rhino ✦✦✦✦✦
The first CD-era collection of this hard-luck band's work was also the best compilation of the band's work, but it was a good idea done a little too early. The sound is deficient compared with Rhino's usual standard, and the notes were later outdone by Sundazed Records' reissue of the band's complete catalog. It's still a good starter, however, if one can find it. *—Bruce Eder*

The Choir

f. 1965, Cleveland, OH
Garage Rock, Power Pop
Stars in their Cleveland hometown, unknown elsewhere (except for the minor national hit "It's Cold Outside"), the Choir played an accomplished, if a bit anachronistic, British Invasion-influenced pop/rock in the late '60s. The Mersey-mod hybrid "It's Cold Outside" went to number one in Cleveland in 1967. The group was then picked up by Roulette, but a couple of subsequent singles were subject to inappropriate material and over-production, and stiffed. Obscure and unissued material by the Choir is beginning to appear on CD, and reveals them branching out from power-pop to encompass progressive sounds as they changed personnel in the late '60s. Members of the group later played in the Raspberries, and the Choir is still fondly remembered in Cleveland for their strong and melodic original material. *—Richie Unterberger*

The Choir / 1987 / Green Light ✦✦✦
Nine songs from an early 1969 session that found the band moving from the more basic British mod-inspired rock of their earlier recordings into more sophisticated songwriting that also embraced psychedelic and soul influences. Four of these songs were eventually issued on Sundazed's *Choir Practice* CD; the remaining five, however, were not, which makes a copy of this cassette-only release desirable for serious collectors. These five songs are in the main acceptably gutsy pop-rockers that were probably too progressive for the Top 40 audiences of their time, yet not progressive enough for the rock underground. The long, keyboard-dominated instrumental "Foreric" (in the vein of the Blues Project's "Flute Thing") and the vaudevillian rock of "Mummer Band" show more diverse edges of the band's repertoire; "Have I No Love to Offer" is a wrenching, piano-dominated ballad worthy of the early Bee Gees. Sound quality is good. *—Richie Unterberger*

● **Choir Practice** / 1994 / Sundazed ✦✦✦✦✦
This 18-song CD is the first official compilation of their work that covers their entire career, from 1966 to 1969. As the group cut only a few singles during their lifetime, most of this is previously unissued, culled from their generous vault of demos. Much anticipated by 1960s collectors, it's frankly a bit of a disappointment, despite a fair number of highlights. The Americanized mod-Merseybeat of "It's Cold Outside" is delightful; other originals like "I'd Rather You Leave Me" and "Don't Change Your Mind" show similarly irresistible harmony vocals, crafting a catchy '60s pop-rock sound that avoids sappiness. The final tracks, cut in 1969 after several personnel changes, have slightly updated progressive rock influences, but retain a core of smart pop-rock hooks. Some of the demos, though, are a bit weak, particularly the soul-rockish ones from 1968. Most crucially, though, it fails to include a number of fine previously available tracks, like the version of the beautiful ballad "Treeberry" that was briefly available on a Bomp EP (the sketchy acoustic demo here pales by comparison), and several moody numbers from the 1969 lineup (also available for a time on a cassette-only reissue in the 1980s). The crunchy Stones-ish B-side of "It's Cold Outside," "I'm Going Home," is also inexplicably missing. Perhaps this is because the compilers made every effort to include material from the original master tapes and couldn't locate the masters for those tracks. It's still not a bad compilation for '60s collectors, but it could have been better. *—Richie Unterberger*

Lou Christie

b. Feb. 19, 1943, Glen Willard, PA
Vocals / Bubblegum, Pop
While Lou Christie's shrieking falsetto was among the most distinctive voices in all of pop music, he was also one of the first solo performers of the rock era to compose his own material, generating some of the biggest and most memorable hits of the mid-1960s. Born Lugee Alfredo Giovanni Sacco in Glen Willard, Pennsylvania on February 19, 1943, he won a scholarship to Moon Township High School as a teen; there he studied music and vocal technique, later joining a group dubbed the Classics. Between 1959 and 1962, in collaboration with a variety of Pittsburgh-area bands, he cut a series of records for small local labels, adopting the stage name Lou Christie along the way. Eventually he made the acquaintance of Twyla Herbert, a classically trained musician and self-proclaimed mystic some 20 years his senior; they became songwriting partners, and in 1962 penned "The Gypsy Cried," which he recorded on two-track in his garage. The single became a local phenomenon, and was eventually licensed for national release by the Roulette label, peaking at number 24 on the pop charts in 1963.

After relocating to New York and landing session work as a backing vocalist, Christie wrote and recorded a follow-up, "Two Faces Have I"; it landed in the Top Ten, but shortly after its release he began a two-year stint in the Army. He returned to action in 1966, picking up right where he left off with his biggest hit yet—the lush, chart-topping "Lightnin' Strikes." Christie's next smash, 1966's "Rhapsody in the Rain," was notorious for being among the more sexually explicit efforts of the period. After brief stays with Colpix and Columbia, he next moved to the Buddah label, scoring one last Top Ten hit in 1969 with "I'm Gonna Make You Mine." Drug problems plagued Christie during the early 1970s, and after getting clean at a London rehab clinic, he dropped out of music, working variously as a ranch hand, offshore oil driller and carnival barker; by the 1980s, he was making the occasional appearance on oldies package tours, and in 1997 issued *Pledging My Love*, his first new material in over a quarter-century. *—Jason Ankeny*

● **Enlightnin'ment: The Best of Lou Christie** / 1991 / Rhino ✦✦✦✦✦
This solid collection contains "Lightnin' Strikes," "Two Faces Have I," and others. *—Dan Heilman*

Glory River: The Buddah Years, 1968-1972 / 1992 / Sequel ✦✦✦✦
Although he is best known for scoring hits like "Lightning Strikes" and "Rhapsody in the Rain" during the mid-1960s, Lou Christie continued to record long after that time and a valuable chunk of his recording legacy is captured on *Glory River: The Buddah Years 1968-1972*. Only a handful of the songs contained in this compilation achieved chart success (the most notable hit being "I'm Gonna Make You Mine"), but the other songs are much more than just failed pop-chart fodder. Christie wrote much of his own material, so the songs presented here have a much more personal touch and tend to be more adventurous than a lot of pop music being produced around this time. For instance, early songs like "Genesis and the Third Verse" and "Rake Up the Leaves" combine the Frankie Valli-like blue-eyed soul that characterized Christie's sound with psychedelic touches like fuzz guitar and Beatles-ish trumpet obligatos. As the songs move into the 1970s, a few of the selections tread water (an interesting but unnecessary cover of "Tell Her") but the majority of the songs continue to fascinate with their mixture of strong pop hooks and off-beat elements: "She Sold Me Magic" and "Indian Lady" both mix catchy harmonies, pseudo-psychedelic arrangements, and lyrics that tackle love from an intriguingly mystical standpoint. However, the highlight of *Glory River: The Buddah Years 1968-1972* is the generous array of tracks that it includes from Christie's legendary lost album, *Paint America Love*. Songs like "Wood River" and "Lighthouse" represent a spellbinding creative peak for the artist: their combination of personal lyrical concerns like peace and ecology, strong pop songcraft, and adventurous spirit result in accessible yet totally personalized pop music to create Lou Christie's answer to *What's Going On* and *Pet Sounds*. In the end, *Glory River: The Buddah Years* may be a little too eccentric for the casual listener, but is an important document of an underrated artist whose uniquely personal brand of pop music remains as fascinating as ever. *—Donald A. Guarisco*

The Complete Co & Ce/Roulette Recordings / Jun. 30, 1998 / Taragon ✦✦✦✦✦
Although he had made some good, and interesting, doo-wop records around his native Pittsburgh, this 21-track collection is where the career of Lou Christie begins in earnest. Still working out of Pittsburgh with his collaborator/mentor Twyla Herbert, the majority of these sides have a homegrown, small-label session feel to them, even if they were almost all simultaneously issued for national consumption on the Roulette imprint. Christie's otherworldly falsetto wails on the two big hits here ("The Gypsy Cried" and "Two Faces Have I"), which need no introduction, but his trademarked sound is equally at home and just as fine on B-sides and album filler like "Red Sails In the Sunset," "Tears On My Pillow," "Tonight I Fell In Love" and "When You Dance." The previously unreleased version of the rocker "Money" yields a quirky take to the standard, but everything on here

is vintage and prime Lou Christie, a true song stylist who just happened to also write a solid third of the material compiled here. An important, but often neglected, chapter in rock & roll's history that deserves a wider hearing. *—Cub Koda*

Beyond the Blue Horizon / Nov. 3, 1998 / Varese ♦♦♦♦
Originally issued in 1973 on the Three Brothers label as *Lou Christie*, this is Lou's first dabble into doing something that could get play on a country radio station. The big hit, of course, is the title tune, now a soundtrack mainstay of *Rain Man, Dutch, A Home of Our Own* and cable TV's Travel Channel. But Christie's interpretations of Tony Romeo's original material (in addition to producing and arranging everything, eight of the 14 tunes on here are Romeo's, who also wrote "I'm Gonna Make You Mine" for Lou) brings spark to songs like "Saddle the Wind," "Blue Canadian Rocky Dream," "Sunbeam" and "Morning Rider." In addition to the ten original album sides, bonus tracks—all previously unreleased—include Christie and longtime collaborator Twyla Herbert's "Little Bit of God," "Wheel of Fortune," and a pair of tunes written by Romeo, "Two Little Clouds Passing By" and "There'll Never Be (A We Like You and Me)." Another hidden gem in the highly underrated career of Lou Christie. *—Cub Koda*

Lou Christie/Lou Christie Strikes Again / Jun. 22, 1999 / Collectables ♦♦♦
Lou's first two albums, originally released on Roulette and Colpix, reissued on one compact disc. Lou's debut album features all his early hits ("Two Faces Have I," "The Gypsy Cried") and some nice covers of old doo-wop favorites like "Tears On My Pillow" and "Stay," while the Colpix album was more early material rushed out to cash in on Christie hitting the charts with "Lightning Strikes," a track not included here. *—Cub Koda*

Chumbawamba

f. 1984, England
Indie Rock, Post-Punk, Alternative Pop/Rock
Formed in a squat in Leeds, England, in 1984, the anarchist pop group Chumbawamba was a most unlikely mainstream success story; after more than a decade in relative obscurity, much of it spent attacking the very notion of stardom, they signed to a major label in 1997, quickly scoring a major international hit with the riotous single "Tubthumping." Chumbawamba originally comprised former Men in a Suitcase frontman Dunst, onetime Ow My Hair's on Fire drummer Alice Nutter and computer technician Lou Watts. After recording a song for a compilation album, they teamed with Harry Hamer and Mavis Dillon—members of one of the LP's other contributors, the Passion Killers—and the Chumbawamba lineup was complete. The band quickly became a thorn in the side of British conservatives, mounting a series of benefit concerts for a variety of anti-Thatcherite causes and campaigns; before long, they were also the subject of frequent police raids. Released at the height of Live Aid-era goodwill, Chumbawamba's debut LP, *Pictures of Starving Children Sell Records: Starvation, Charity and Rock & Roll—Lies and Tradition*, appeared in 1986, brutally attacking the principles of media limelight and career-boosting they perceived at the heart of the charitable event. All appeared to be business as usual until it was announced that Chumbawamba had signed to EMI; their 1997 major-label debut, *Tubthumper*, became a smash, propelled by the infectious "Tubthumping," a Top Ten hit in the U.S. and throughout Europe. A second single, "Amnesia," was also a success. Their newfound popularity also allowed the group to bring their anarchist message to a new audience. *—Jason Ankeny*

Pictures of Starving Children Sell Records / 1986 / Agit Prop ♦♦♦♦♦
Long before a song about relentless alcohol consumption ("Tubthumping") made them the toast of sports stadia worldwide, a rather different Chumbawamba stalked the toilet venues of England's counter-culture. In 1986, as the rock world congratulated itself on its new, enlightened attitude to world poverty following Band Aid, a refusenik group of Leeds anarchists pointed out some of the inconsistencies behind the arguments. On the aptly-titled *Pictures of Starving Children Sell Records*, Freddie Mercury, Cliff Richard and Paul McCartney are ridiculed for their patronizing hypocrisy ("How To Get Your Band On Television"). Other targets included apartheid, multinationals and cultural imperialism. The group's pervasive lyrics were augmented by music varying from punk thrash to folk and jazz. This was a sophisticated approach entirely divorced from their fellow travellers (who contented themselves with sloganeering and three-chord bluster). For an album that adopted Crass' admirable but po-faced concerns about commercial exploitation of the planet and its inhabitants, the results were surprisingly listenable, and also extremely entertaining—an "inconsistent, over-wordy dog-bark pop record" according to its authors when it was reissued on CD in 1991 (alongside *Never Mind The Ballots* as *First 2*) *–Alex Ogg*

Slap! / 1990 / Agit Prop ♦♦♦♦
Unabashedly political, *Slap!* refers to the Bader-Meinhof Gang, Bernadette Devlin and the Irish troubles, Tiananmen Square and the 1956 Hungarian uprising (which receives the studiously ironic "That's How Grateful We Are," about the destruction of a statue of Stalin). The politics are salted into an entertaining mix of beats and hooks that make the whole album easy to digest. Entertaining music designed to make the listener think—not a bad deal. *—Steven McDonald*

First 2 LP's / 1991 / Agit-Prop ♦♦♦
Completists can find some excellent material on this compilation, notably first album *Pictures of Starving Children Sell Records* in its entirety, but it's hardly a comprehensive overview of the band's early days. Long before the release of that album, Chumbawamba had been minor celebrities on the DIY tape-trading circuit—it's a shame nothing survives from those old C-90s. It would have been nice, for example, to listen once again to their pseudonymous outing as Skin Disease—a spoof of the Oi movement recorded in 1982 and featuring the lyric "I'm Thick" repeated 64 times. Also missing is the superb debut single, "Revolution" (featuring a copy of John Lennon's "Imagine" being ripped from a turntable and smashed in two). However, there is plenty to fill out the grooves here—with the inclusion of the group's *Never Mind The Ballots* follow-up. While less immediately arresting, polemical tracts such as "Always Tell the Voter what the Voter Wants to Hear" and "The Candidates Find Common Ground" have their moments. *—Alex Ogg*

Showbusiness! / 1995 / One Little Indian ♦♦♦
Reservations about this album do not concern Chumbawamba's status as an excellent live prospect, especially in their formative days. But to truly appreciate the group's carnival of anti-authoritarian bonhomie, you require the visual aids. In their early shows this was achieved via a series of sketches, including the ritual burning of tabloid newspapers. Later, Danbert Nobacon's propensity for cross-dressing and Alice Nutter's devil-may-care dancing provided panoramic stimulus for the eye. *Showbusiness*, taken from a show at Leeds' Duchess of York Club in 1994, remains a well-packaged collection of live songs with decent sound—the sleevenotes provide an exhaustive (and funny) history of the group, and the performance itself features Harry's father Jimmy Echo providing karaoke backing vocals. But there are better starting points for those wishing to explore the band beyond "Tubthumping." The album was issued in America as the *For A Free Humanity: For Anarchy* double CD—a coupling of *Showbusiness* alongside Noam Chomsky's *Capital Rules*. *—Alex Ogg*

Swingin' with Raymond / Jan. 1996 / One Little Indian ♦♦♦

● **Tubthumper** / Sep. 23, 1997 / Republic/Universal ♦♦♦♦♦
Chumbawamba had been kicking around the British indie scene for years, releasing nine albums before *Tubthumper* unexpectedly brought the band to the top of the charts not only in England, but around the world. The difference between *Tubthumper* and the rest of Chumbawamba's catalog lay in "Tubthumping," a giddily infectious blend of big dance beats, pop hooks and football chants. It's a standout single, one that finds the group at their catchiest, and there isn't anything quite as good on the remainder of *Tubthumper*, an album that finds the group downplaying their notorious political radicalism in favor of pop and dance. Still, there's a handful of cuts scattered throughout the record that make the album worthwhile, and there's no denying that "Tubthumping" is a hit single unlike any other. It's one of the least likely hit singles ever, and that alone makes the record distinctive. *—Stephen Thomas Erlewine*

Anarchy / Jun. 30, 1998 / EMI ♦♦♦

What You See Is What You Get / Apr. 4, 2000 / Republic/Universal ♦♦♦♦
Nearly everyone that was seduced by Chumbawamba's irresistible "Tubthumping" wasn't aware that the band had not only kicked around for over decade, but that they were politically active, social satirists with a penchant for anarchy, both in their politics and music. Of course, nobody would be able to discern that from "Tubtumping," since its send-up of lads shouting "lager, lager, lager" was so accurate that it appealed to the very audience it was spoofing. Still, it was a terrific pop single, and it broke down the doors for the group in America. If America was amused by Chumbawamba and their antics, the band was even more amused, even befuddled, by the U.S.—so much so that they decided to make *What You See Is What You Get*, their sequel to *Tubthumping*, a snapshot of their view of the land of excess. Consisting of 22 songs in under 48 minutes, *WYSIWYG* is as fast and furious and saturated with pop culture—just like life at the end of the 20th century. Every song moves so fast that the album initially seems a bit like a blur, albeit a tuneful, clever blur. The very brevity of the tracks guarantees that there isn't a track here as chart-friendly as Chumbawamba's fluke hit, but there are plenty of melodies and catchy hooks here—they just happen to be pieced together like a collage with a bunch of sound samples, found sounds, snippets of television, spoken words, drum loops, and the like. *WYSIWYG* may cover too much ground and be too sprawling for tubthumpers, but it's pretty smart and tuneful and often funny. It'll inevitably sound dated, possibly just two years after its release, but it's a pretty fun snapshot of the end of the American century. *—Stephen Thomas Erlewine*

The Church

f. 1980, Sydney, Australia
College Rock, Neo-Psychedelia, Alternative Pop/Rock
Best known for the shimmering "Under the Milky Way," their lone Top 40 hit, the Australian band the Church combined the jangling guitar-pop of '60s icons like the Byrds with the opaque wordplay of frontman Steve Kilbey to create a lush, melancholy brand of neo-psychedelia rich in texture and melody. Their 1981 debut *Of Skin and Heart* was an evocative collection highlighted by the ringing "The Unguarded Moment," a major success down under; the group resurfaced in 1982 with *The Blurred Crusade*, a stunning effort featuring mature standouts like "Almost With You" and "When You Were Mine." After moving to Arista, the Church teamed with famed session guitarists Danny Kortchmar and Waddy Wachtel to record 1988's *Starfish*, their most artistically and commercially successful effort to date. Highlighted by "Under the Milky Way," the album also featured the minor hits "Reptile" and "Spark," a marvelous pop blast penned by guitarist Marty Willson-Piper. The follow-up, 1990's *Gold Afternoon Fix*, failed to repeat the success of its predecessor as the single "Metropolis" garnered only minor airplay. *—Jason Ankeny*

Of Skins and Heart / 1981 / Arista ♦♦♦♦♦
On their debut, *Of Skin and Heart*, the Church play a straightforward pop/rock firmly rooted in new wave, though owing no small debt to '60s pop. Edgier and more direct than their later work, it also ranks among their finest for that very reason. None of the excesses and ambitions that would sometimes get out of hand on later releases are present, though much of the band's basic formula was laid down—Steve Kilbey's cool, detached vocals and slightly surrealistic lyrics combined with some outstanding pop hooks, nice harmonies, and layers of ringing guitar. The classic "Unguarded Moment" (arguably one of the greatest singles of the '80s) overshadows much of the material on the album, but there is really

no shortage of great songs here. [The album was originally released in the U.S. as *The Church* with some tracks dropped in favor of three tracks from singles released around the same time. In 1988, Arista released *Of Skin and Heart* on CD in its original form with the added tracks from *The Church* tacked on to the end.] *–Chris Woodstra*

The Blurred Crusade / 1982 / Arista ✦✦✦✦✦

After such a fine debut as *Of Skins and Heart*, creating a follow-up might have been a burden for the Church—and maybe it was, but the end result was well worth it. Perhaps even better than their first, *Blurred Crusade* captures what for many remains the classic early Church sound, blending both the various strains of '60s inspiration and postpunk drive detected from the start with an even more elegant melancholy. Musically, both Willson-Piper and Koppes are just fantastic, their combination of guitar playing running the range from sparkling post-Byrds chime to sharp power. If the group doesn't fully explode here as much as later albums would demonstrate, especially on *Heyday*, that perhaps can be laid at producer Bob Clearmountain's feet. Consider the slow but steady build up of "When You Were Mine," guitar lines and notes setting the scene before fully kicking into the main riff and the clever but not forced production on the vocals on some of the middle verses. Add on the fantastic solo about four minutes in, and this is great rock music, period, deeply impressive coming on a sophomore album. Highlights are plentiful throughout *Blurred*, but the best numbers are perhaps the opening "Almost With You," a note-perfect combination of hooks and downbeat but not morose atmosphere, and the lengthy, powerful "You Took." Willson-Piper's lead vocal number "Field of Mars" and the brief, concluding "Don't Look Back" are further songs of note. *—Ned Raggett*

Seance / 1983 / Arista ✦✦✦

The cover may have looked like something of a goth record of the era, though then again not many goths would have used pink as the dominant color of an album. On this, the band's third full album, the band consolidated the advances of *Blurred Crusade* well; if *Seance* isn't as immediately striking as the first two albums, it still has its share of winners, starting with the opening "Fly." Its string-synth touched, stripped-down arrangement almost sounded like something from the Chameleons' quieter moments, but the following "One Day" returned the Church to more familiar ringing-yet-forceful guitar territory. One very curious thing about this song and many of the others on the album has to with the drumming—while Ploog very much remains the key credited drummer, here and on many other cuts nearly everything sounds produced by a particularly muffled drum machine. Whether or not one was used, the result is at once stiff and more than a little underwhelming, making what should be stronger songs sound more run of the mill than they are. Even the otherwise excellent remastering of the early catalog when the albums were reissued on Arista can't save some of the problems. Aside from this major flaw, *Séance* keeps at the understated guitar groove that the Church rapidly made its own, containing marvelous songs like "Disappear?" and the nicely paced "Electric Lash." Experimenting with keyboards more provides some nice results, as the Kilbey-and-synth introduction to the lovely "It's No Reason" shows. Meanwhile, the interplay between Willson-Piper, Koppes, and Kilbey on their respective instruments remains strong, with many noted strong points: the dramatic, tense build of "Travel By Thought," the low-key combination on "Electric" bursting into keyboard-touched life on its choruses, and the quick, punchy "Dropping Names." *—Ned Raggett*

Remote Luxury / 1984 / Arista ✦✦✦✦

Collecting the contents of two separate EPs into a full-length album for American purposes, *Remote Luxury* actually makes for a reasonable release, avoiding the miserable drum sound that plagued *Séance*. The band are hardly so groansome, mixing the light synth touches evident on *Séance* with a tight, sharp postpunk groove. While the comparisons to bands like R.E.M. were sometimes stretched a bit, there's no denying the similar love of brisk, economic velocity which crops up on many of these songs, including the steady beat of "Violet Town" and the crisp flow on "Into My Hands." "No Explanation" perhaps fits the R.E.M. likeness best after a brief instrumental beginning, a shimmering, strummed gem with a great main melody. Kilbey again handles the vocals with his usual mix of low-key singing and sometimes clever, sometimes obscure lyrics, while the band as a whole keep things moving. Willson-Piper, who handles lead vocals for "10,000 Miles" and "Volumes," and Koppes by now show their excellent guitar abilities almost at every turn, their avoidance of pointless flash in favor of compelling hooks and a little extra shading when needed always coming through. "A Month of Sundays" and "Shadow Cabinet" are just two highlights of their abilities, beautiful and hummable all at once. An interesting if slightly atypical effort on the disc is "Maybe These Boys," with a relentless keyboard hook that almost sounds like a military fanfare leading into the full band performance, though with further keyboards still prominent. Kilbey's vocals are eventually contrasted with a Vocodered treatment of the same words, making for a strange, unsettling ending. *—Ned Raggett*

Heyday / 1986 / Arista ✦✦✦✦✦

Whether it was the assistance of Peter Walsh on production, a decision to bear down and see what could be done, or some further combination of that and other factors, the Church came up with its best release since *The Blurred Crusade* with the powerful *Heyday*. Not changing anything in the basic Church sound but presenting both a brilliant slew of songs and some fantastic performances, the quartet created a flat-out fantastic record. The first side alone almost reads like a greatest-hits collection, with one highlight following hard on the other. "Myrrh," leading things off with a careful build up to the main part of the song much like "When You Were Mine," has a strange chorus that almost shouldn't work but does. It's only two lines long and sung in harmony by the full band, all while Willson-Piper and Koppes' guitars keep things moving. "Tristesse" begins with a playful guitar line before shifting into another mid-paced, just dreamy enough effort. "Already Yesterday," with a fine, low-key backing choir, the dramatic "Columbus" and the gentle, string-touched instrumental "Happy Hunting Ground" continue the mood, one lovely moment after another. The second side kicks off with a barnstormer, "Tantalized," easily the band's most aggressive and upfront song since its earliest days. With horns and bells adding to the rushed feel, Kilbey delivers quickly sung verses and staccato choruses, the music continuing to soar along as Willson-Piper and Koppes turn in brilliant guitar work. Add to that further horn and string orchestrations on songs like the wistful "Youth Worshipper" and "Night of Light," and *Heyday* is a total success. *—Ned Raggett*

Starfish / 1988 / Arista ✦✦✦✦✦

Signing to Arista might have seemed an unusual move to start with, getting produced by L.A. studio types like Waddy Wachtel even more so. But for the Church the rewards were great—if sometimes too clean around the corners in comparison to the song-for-song masterpiece *Heyday*, *Starfish* set up the band's well-deserved breakthrough in the States. The reason was "Under the Milky Way," still one of the most haunting and elegant songs ever to make the Top 40. As Kilbey details a lyric of emotional distance and atmosphere, the band executes a quietly beautiful—and as is so often the case with the Church, astonishingly well-arranged—song, with mock bagpipes swirling through the mix for extra effect. That wasn't the only strong point on an album with more than a few; the lead-off track "Destination" was as strong an album opener as "Myrrh," if slower paced and much more mysterious, piano blending through the song's steady pace. The rest of the first side has its share of highlights, such as the quietly threatening edge of "Blood Money" and the confident, restrained charge of "North, South, East and West." Willson-Piper gets to lead off the second side with "Spark," a vicious, tight rocker that captures some of the best '60s rock edge and gives it a smart update. Equally strong is Kilbey's "Reptile," with an appropriately snaky guitar line and rhythm punch offset against weirdly soothing keyboards. Koppes has an okay vocal to his credit on "A New Season," but the stronger tracks are Kilbey's other contributions, the strong guitar waltz of "Antenna" (with great guest mandolin from David Lindley) and the closing charge (and very Church-like title) of "Hotel Womb." Performances throughout are at the least fine and at the most fantastic. *—Ned Raggett*

Hindsight / 1988 / EMI ✦✦✦✦

This two-disc collection is a perfect introduction to the Church for new fans, given all the many singles collected from *Of Skins and Heart* up through *Heyday*, along with an album cut or two. As an overview of the band's evolution from catchy postpunk pop to its own thrilling musical recipe, along with some amusing liner notes from Kilbey song per song, it's a definite winner. But hardcore fans will want this collection as well for an even stronger reason—the inclusion of many B-sides not collected anywhere else. Ranging from the randomly goofy to the sublime, they give a great peek into the band's diversions and experiments over its first few years. A clutch of B-sides from the *Blurred Crusade* era helps close out the first disc, including the thrashy, semi-surf touched "Fraulein," with some neat vocals (background) supporting Kilbey, and the slightly cinematic instrumental "The Golden Dawn," strings and/or keyboards helping out along the way. The rarities on the second disc are also an intriguingly mixed bag, starting with the *Sing-Songs* EP cut "The Night is Very Soft," a mysterious, slightly strange number. "Autumn Soon" has Koppes doing a quick but atmospheric sitar/guitar melody, though fighting through a slightly murky mix, while Koppes himself takes the quietly moody (and more than slightly echoed) lead vocals on "As You Will," a smart and brisk number. Willson-Piper gets a vocal lead himself with "The View," while the rarities wrap up with "Trance Ending," a nice blend of Middle Eastern percussion, vaguely Spanish guitar and sweet synthesizer. *—Ned Raggett*

Gold Afternoon Fix / Feb. 1990 / Arista ✦✦✦

Gold Afternoon Fix should have been a consolidation of the band's increased commercial profile and cachet after "Under the Milky Way," heightened by the welcome reissue of the band's first five albums. Unfortunately, the Church's original choice for producer—John Paul Jones, who likely would have helped oversee a total masterpiece—was rejected, leading to another session with Wachtel. This time the balance between accessibility and art didn't succeed as planned. The end result is an album that's sometimes fantastic, sometimes merely there. Some of the singles didn't help things any—the first, "Metropolis," is one of the band's more subtle rockers, with a catchy chorus and some fine guitar, especially at the end, but not immediate first-listen success. The first track on the album as a whole is a different matter—"Pharoah" is a dramatic start, with the slow builds so favored by the band given a decidedly threatening, ominous twist. After that things move between hit and miss, but there's enough character coming through to ensure a pleasant listen. "Monday Morning" lightly repeats the waltz-time feel of *Starfish*'s "Antenna," while "Russian Autumn Heart," Willson-Piper's vocal lead on the album, is a crisp rocker with the guitarist delivering things in his trademark ragged-but-right fashion. Other general highlights include "Disappointment" and the gentle "Laughing," but "Grind" is the other main keeper on *Fix*, a slow destructive burn of a song that matches the opening menace of "Pharoah" with a measured downward slide. *—Ned Raggett*

Priest = Aura / Mar. 10, 1992 / Arista ✦✦✦✦

Probably the most obscure album title yet from the Church, and definitely one of the least likely to provide a catchy radio single, but with this defiant reclaiming of their own destiny after the mess of *Gold Afternoon Fix*, the Church came up with its best album to date. If not as gloriously catchy as *Heyday*, *Priest = Aura* shows the Church fully in charge of creating evocative, poetic and gripping music with a distinctly unsettling edge. Part of the strength of *Priest = Aura* is its excellent sequencing, organized from start to finish. The opening song, "Aura," finds the band coming in after an atmospheric synth start, Kilbey's sly lyric equally applicable to the band's recent situation and standing as a cryptic invocation of strange experiences away from home. "Ripple," which immediately follows, was the lead single, its soothing chorus floating above a strong, shadowy undertow of music below. With that as a start, everything continues up until the album's wrenching conclusion, starting with the dramatic, unnerving music hall chant of "The Disillusionist." After a brief break with "Old Flame," "Chaos" kicks in, a nearly ten-minute invocation of the title subject. Willson-Piper and Koppes rarely have sounded so powerful, while the final song, "Film," doesn't provide much further comfort. In between these two extremes, many other great songs—"Swan Lake," with its portrait of a hellish home, the gentle dance-groove of "Feel," "Kings" and its epic U2-done-right feel and more—fill out this astonishing album. *—Ned Raggett*

Sometime Anywhere / May 24, 1994 / Arista ✦✦✦✦
The departure of Koppes reduced the Church down to a core duo of Kilbey and Willson-Piper, though on the bright side the drum slot was finally permanently filled by Tim Powles, whose excellent playing easily matched up to Ploog's best work, if not bettering it. His skill at producing and mixing, which would later prove crucial, isn't used here, but he's still off to a fine start. Best thought of as a collection of experiments and new songwriting approaches than a cohesive release like *Priest = Aura, Sometime Anywhere* still hits the spot more times than not, showing that the key vision of Kilbey and Willson-Piper remains strong. Kilbey's quietly compelling visions and singing remain at the heart of the group, his bass playing is as fine as ever, while Willson-Piper's guitar work contains all the fire and edge one would expect. Atmospheres, as always, are key to the Church sound, with some extremely textured and lovely keyboard sounds and buried samples adding to the mysterious flow of many of the songs. The songs that employ dance rhythms, like the murky, distorted hip-hop punch of "Lost My Touch" and Willson-Piper's charging vocal standout "Angelica," don't have the weak, johnny-come-lately feeling that bedevils rock artists dabbling around. It's not their forte, just something to work with to see what happens, and more often than not it turns out very well. Other numbers like the slow build of "My Little Problem" and the delicate then crunching, Willson-Piper-sung "Fly Home," meanwhile, shows the band still in fine overall form. *—Ned Raggett*

Magician Among the Spirits / 1996 / Griffin Music ✦✦✦✦
Arista dropped them but the Church soldiered on—Tim Powles fully joined in the songwriting process a number of times, while Peter Koppes guested on various cuts after his absence from *Sometime Anywhere.* Violinist Linda Neil also appeared along with other guests from that record, with *Magician Among the Spirits* being the attractive end result. If the band was still a touch fragmented, *Magician* shows them well on the road to becoming a fully tight unit once again, with a number of interesting diversions along the way. Sonically, things followed in the vein of *Sometime* to a large extent, trying out different approaches and backing, often exploring more spacious, sometimes very late-night, relaxed arrangements. This underlays the key Church elements of mysterious, attractive, but always slightly melancholic songs, resulting in a fine blend of past and present. Steve Kilbey perhaps gets lost from time to time lyrically—the opening track, "Welcome," is one of his least successful, naming what seems like a random list of celebrities and noted figures past and present. Frankly, his at-times cryptic poetry would be a much better choice. That and other slight stumblings aside, *Magician* hits some great high points. "Comedown" was unsurprisingly selected to be a single, its orchestrated surge recalling prime T. Rex mixed with the typically dark-but-sweet guitar chime of the band. The well-titled "Grandiose" and beautifully blue "The Further Adventures of the Time Being" are wonderful, while Marty Willson-Piper and Koppes unsurprisingly once again do some fine work on guitar, as songs like "Ladyboy" and the quieter title track show. Powles' drumming is revelatory, capable of both straight-ahead rock surge and more complex, subtle work informed by other traditions—consider his work on the lovely "Romany Caravan," which also gives Neil a chance to shine on her instrument. The original version of *Magician* has since been overtaken by *Magician Among the Spirits & Some,* which adds some B-sides from that time as welcome bonuses. *—Ned Raggett*

Quick Smoke at Spot's / 1996 / Mushroom ✦✦✦
Conveniently collecting all the various B-sides from the *Starfish* and *Gold Afternoon Fix* singles, *Quick Smoke* is a godsend to the hardcore Church fan, acting as a useful adjunct to *Hindsight* without also being a greatest hits/singles overview. Steve Kilbey's liner notes this time out don't study everything song by song, but are instead a witty pondering on the nature of liner notes in the first place, so those wanting knowledge on where every song comes from will have to look elsewhere. As for the music, the by-definition fragmented collection still contains a number of true winners. Most follow in the general Church vein, but as tracks often recorded away from the LA-based production team that handled the parent albums, they often show a nice contrast in sound. Many use drum machines for percussion, possibly for convenience but likely also foreshadowing Richard Ploog's eventual departure. Lead-off track "Texas Moon" is actually one of the band's strongest songs, a powerful, energetic number with great work from Marty Willson-Piper and Peter Koppes on complex, shimmering guitar riffs, while Kilbey and Ploog create a strong, varied rhythm punch. Buried harmonica and Kilbey's strong singing make for the icing on the cake. "Much Too Much" is another strong rocker, with a fine chorus and rough, immediate feel, while "You Got Off Light" and "Hunter" also give the band a chance to get out some feedback crunch and belting performances, though Kilbey as always sings in his deceptively calm, attractive way. An amusing touch in "Anna Miranda" is the use of a line from "Under the Milky Way" from time to time, dropped in and then moved on from. Generally, the collection tends toward such louder, more driving tracks, but there are quieter moments scattered throughout. "Forgotten Reign" has a fair amount going on, but the pace is measured, led by a single guitar chime over an acoustic/electric blend, while "Ride Into the Sunset" benefits from additional string-synth orchestration. *—Ned Raggett*

Hologram of Baal / 1998 / Thirsty Ear ✦✦✦

A Box of Birds / Aug. 24, 1999 / Thirsty Ear ✦✦✦
Covers albums could be seen as the last refuge of a dying band, but that's a cynical reading of the situation. At their best, covers albums can be fun and even revealing, as the band stretches out and plays with their favorite songs. Such is the case with the Church's *A Box of Birds.* Their roots have always been evident—they were fans of '60s psychedelia, plus bits of '70s album rock and prog-rock and post-punk. Not surprisingly, that's what's heard on *A Box of Birds,* but they've been very clever about their choices; only Mott the Hoople's "All the Young Dudes," Hawkwind's "Silver Machine" and Neil Young's "Cortez the Killer" are covered regularly by other bands. The remainder of the songs—ranging from the Beatles' "It's All too Much" and the Monkees' "The Porpoise Song" to Kevin Ayers' "Decadence," Television's "Friction," Ultravox's "Hiroshima Mon Amour" and Iggy Pop's "The Endless Sea"—aren't obvious choices, which give the record considerable character. The Church don't really reinvent these songs, choosing to remain faithful to the tenor of the original while retaining their own signature sound. The end result may not be revelatory, like the best covers albums, but it is fun, and the band sounds like they're having fun, too. After all, fun is the main reason you'd quote Eddy Grant's "Electric Avenue" and the Pretty Things' "Sorrow" in the coda of "It's All Too Much." *—Stephen Thomas Erlewine*

• **Under the Milky Way: The Best of the Church** / Sep. 28, 1999 / Buddha ✦✦✦✦✦
Buddha's *Under the Milky Way: Best of the Church* is a terrific, comprehensive anthology, tracing their career from their 1981 debut *Of Skin and Heart* to 1994's *Sometime Anywhere.* Some hardcore fans may notice some personal favorites missing, but all their best-known songs—"The Unguarded Moment," "Tear it All Away," "Month of Sundays," "Myrrh," "Under the Milky Way," "Reptile," "Metropolis," "Ripple"—are here, along with an excellent, representative sampling of album tracks. It's an ideal record for casual fans, along with being a great introduction for the curious and neophytes. *—Stephen Thomas Erlewine*

Cibo Matto

f. 1994, New York, NY
Shibuya-Kei, Alternative Dance, Indie Rock, Trip-Hop, Alternative Pop/Rock
A Japanese-born duo relocated to New York and christened with an Italian band name, Cibo Matto's music mirrored the melting-pot aesthetics of their origins, resulting in a heady brew of funk samples, hip-hop rhythms, tape loops and fractured pop melodies all topped off by surreal narratives sung in a combination of French and broken English. Cibo Matto comprised vocalist Miho Hatori and keyboardist/sampler Yuka Honda, a pair of expatriate Japanese women who arrived in the U.S. independently. After meeting in 1994, they first teamed in the Boredoms-inspired noise outfit Leitoh Lychee (translated as "frozen lychee nut"); after that band's breakup, the duo formed Cibo Matto, Italian for "food madness" (their love of culinary delights quickly becoming the stuff of legend). After a pair of acclaimed 1995 independent singles, "Birthday Cake" and "Know Your Chicken," Cibo Matto signed to Warner Bros., surfacing in 1996 with *Viva! La Woman,* a delirious, stunningly inventive record celebrating love, food, and love of food. The EP *Super Relax* followed in 1997; bassist Sean Lennon, percussionist Duma Love and drummer Timo Ellis were installed as full-time members for the follow-up, 1999's *Stereotype A.* *—Jason Ankeny*

Cibo Matto [EP] / 1996 / El Diablo ✦✦✦
This five-track EP assembles the early independent singles which first earned Cibo Matto notice in hipster circles, in some cases offering radically different renditions of material which later resurfaced on the *Viva! La Woman* album. The most startling is "Know Your Chicken," which appears in a wonderfully scuzzy rendition heavily influenced by the Jon Spencer Blues Explosion (whose Russell Simins sits in on drums); the real treat, however, is a wonderfully loopy cover of Soundgarden's "Black Hole Sun," rearranged like a lounge favorite and sung in French. *—Jason Ankeny*

• **Viva! La Woman** / Jan. 16, 1996 / Warner Brothers ✦✦✦✦✦
Fresh and funky, female and Japanese, the trip-hop/rap duo Cibo Matto has been the recipient of a lot of hype. Fortunately, it's well-founded; all trendiness aside, *Viva! La Woman* is an innovative and catchy mix of eclectic samples and stream-of-consciousness lyrics. The likes of Paul Weller, Ennio Morricone, and Duke Ellington combine with observations like "My weight is three hundred pounds/my favorite is beef jerky" (from "Beef Jerky") and "Shut up and eat! You know my love is sweet!" from ("Birthday Cake") in a fun and refreshing way. The tone of the album varies with each song; on tracks like "Sugar Water" and "Artichoke," Cibo Matto plays it spooky and ethereal, while "Birthday Cake" and the single "Know Your Chicken" find them as a couple of cryptic Beastie Girls, tossing off wacky non sequiturs over found soundscapes. Cibo Matto cooks up a tasty appetizer of their talent with *Viva! La Woman.* Like their tongue-in-cheek cover of "The Candy Man," Cibo Matto makes everything they bake satisfying and delicious. A diverse and entertaining album, *Viva! La Woman* leaves the listener hungry for more of their crazy food for thought. *—Heather Phares*

Super Relax / Jan. 28, 1997 / Warner Brothers ✦✦✦✦
Granted, the four separate versions of *Viva! La Woman's* sublime "Sugar Water" are unnecessary, but the rest of the material on Cibo Matto's follow-up EP *Super Relax* is superb. No longer relying solely on Yuka Honda's slice-and-dice samples, the duo's sound is considerably more organic this time out; "Spoon" locks into an infectious groove worthy of Luscious Jackson, while the live "BBQ" is breathlessly manic. The highlights, however, are the two covers: the first, a rendition of Antonio Carlos Jobim's "Aguas de Marco" (also found on the benefit LP *Red Hot and Latin*) opens up a vast new global playground of exotic textures and rhythms for the group to romp around in, while their exemplary take on the Stones' "Sing This All Together" proves Honda and vocalist Miho Hatori are equally capable of tackling straightforward rock & roll. *—Jason Ankeny*

Stereo Type A / Jun. 8, 1999 / Warner Brothers ♦♦♦
Cibo Matto's eagerly anticipated second album, *Stereo Type A*, reflects growth and change in the band's lineup and sound. Joining the core duo of Yuka Honda and Miho Hatori are new band member Sean Lennon and guests like Arto Lindsay, Caetano Veloso, Sebastian Steinberg of Soul Coughing, and John Medeski and Billy Martin of Medeski, Martin & Wood. The new additions reflect the changing sound of Cibo Matto: Relying less on samples and more on their latent funk and jazz elements, *Stereotype A* sounds like summer in New York—eclectic, hot, and funky. Hatori's vocals are her most fluid and assured yet, and Honda's harmonies, particularly on "Moonchild," add a dreamy undercurrent to the sound. Though the hip-hop of "Sci-Fi Wasabi" and filmic quality of "Spoon" (which originally appeared on the *Super Relax* EP) hearken back to old-school Cibo Matto, *Stereotype A*'s overall sound is more direct and less fanciful than of their debut album *Viva! La Woman*. Tracks like "Clouds" and "Morning" reflect a nice fusion of the group's old and new sounds, while the brassy "Speechless" and thrash metal of "Blue Train" round out a delightfully sunny collection from this diverse group. *—Heather Phares*

Ciccone Youth

f. 1988
Alternative Pop/Rock, American Underground
More of a good-natured prank than an actual band, Ciccone Youth was a short-lived vehicle in which indie underground noisemakers Sonic Youth further explored their obsession with popular culture. In the mid-'80s, the members of Sonic Youth (especially Thurston Moore and Kim Gordon) made no secret of their fascination with Madonna; they were known to discuss her life and career in interviews, and the album *EVOL* listed "Madonna, Sean, and I" as an alternate title for the closing tune "Expressway to Yr. Skull." At the peak of their Madonna frenzy, the band decided to record a tribute single to the Material Girl; on the A-side, Sonic Youth performed a dark, ominous version of "Into the Groove" (dubbed "Into the Groovey") that sounds slow, until samples from Madonna's original recording confirm it's being played at the same tempo as the upbeat original. The flip-side featured former Minutemen bassist and fellow Madonna enthusiast Mike Watt on a jacked-up rock version of "Burnin' Up," with former Black Flag leader Greg Ginn contributing a bracingly discordant guitar solo; it was one of Watt's first musical projects following the Minutemen's collapse after the death of D. Boon. Released by Watt's New Alliance label under the name Ciccone Youth (in honor of Madonna's surname), the single became an underground success, and a widespread (but unconfirmed) rumor had it that Madonna herself persuaded Warner Bros. not to take legal action against the record for unauthorized use of her sampled voice. The single's success led to a Ciccone Youth album, *The Whitey Album* (referring to Sonic Youth's often-threatened intention to record an album in which they covered *The Beatles* in its entirety), but Watt's participation was limited to his original four-track demo for "Burnin' Up" and the disc featured no new Madonna interpretations from Sonic Youth, though Kim Gordon did offer up an intriguingly strange karaoke version of Robert Palmer's "Addicted to Love." The rest of the album was for the most part devoted to playful noise experiments, and by the end of 1986, Watt and Sonic Youth had seemingly retired the Ciccone Youth banner; there were no further recordings, and they never performed live using the name. *—Mark Deming*

The Whitey Album / 1988 / Capitol ♦♦♦♦
On its initial release, this album was treated like a collaboration between Minutemen bass virtuoso Mike Watt and punk rock revolutionaries Sonic Youth. This would have been a perfect match, with two enormous talents coming together for an entire album. But in reality it is far stranger than that: a highly experimental tribute to Madonna performed by Sonic Youth with the exception of one song which is entirely played by Mike Watt without any other musicians accompanying him. The DGC re-release features a cleaner sound and the original packaging from the 1988 SST version, along with liner notes written by Watt explaining his small role in the project. His song, a cover of Madonna's "Burnin' Up," is a smooth, groovy home recording that showcases his rich voice. Sonic Youth take a shot at "Into the Groove" (renamed "Into the Groovey") and manage to mold a fantastic dirge out of the original. Thurston Moore's lazy vocals pair up with Madonna's sampled voice seamlessly, and the low-quality production only adds to the homegrown feel. Besides Kim Gordon's karaoke remake of "Addicted to Love," little else on this album resembles a normal song. Edgy noise experiments and heavy sound manipulation make these songs more than interesting, and the emphasis on dance rhythms keeps things from getting too unlistenable. Although the song order is questionable (after the first song there is a minute of silence), this album is incredibly fun and experimental. Although it was only a side project, the intense creativity of this time in Sonic Youth's career spills out all over this album, making it a rare treat for fans. *—Bradley Torreano*

Cinderella

f. 1985, Pennsylvania
Pop-Metal, Hair Metal, Heavy Metal, Hard Rock
When Cinderella released their debut album, *Night Songs*, in 1986, they were packaged like a second-rate Bon Jovi imitation, which isn't surprising since Jon Bon Jovi was responsible for bringing the band to Mercury Records. Although the record wasn't bad, it was standard lite metal without much distinction, apart from lead guitarist/vocalist Tom Keifer's exaggerated Steven Tyler howl. With their second album, 1988's *Long Cold Winter*, they began to open up their sound slightly, bringing more blues and Rolling Stones influences to their hard rock. That approach reached its apex with their third album, 1990's *Heartbreak Station*, which swaggers defiantly, appropriating Stones and Aerosmith licks as if they had thought of the whole thing first. It didn't sell as much as *Long Cold Winter* did, which might be the reason why the band kept a low profile until late 1994. Either that or the drastically changed hard rock marketplace of the early '90s is what kept the band from releasing their fourth album until then. When *Still Climbing* did come out, the band was met with disinterest and resistance at MTV and radio. *—Stephen Thomas Erlewine*

Night Songs / 1986 / Mercury ♦♦♦
Featuring a minor guest appearance by Jon Bon Jovi, Cinderella's debut album, *Night Songs*, positions the band as a second-tier pop-metal outfit, with a mix of ballads ("Nobody's Fool") and rockers ("Somebody Save Me") one might find on an album by any similar '80s band with a high-pitched vocalist. It's not bad, just generic; the band does hint at the potential they would fulfill on later albums, but little of Cinderella's own personality shows through at this point. *—Steve Huey*

Long Cold Winter / 1988 / Mercury ♦♦♦♦
Long Cold Winter is a transition album for Cinderella, mixing pop-metal tunes with better hooks than those on *Night Songs* with a newfound penchant for gritty blues-rock *a la* the Stones or Aerosmith. The ballads, the grandiose "Don't Know What You Got (Till It's Gone)" and the excellent, lower-key "Coming Home," are what made the album Cinderella's most commercially successful, but the effective combination of pop hooks and tough, swaggering rock & roll on songs like "Gypsy Road" and "Fallin' Apart at the Seams" prevents the album from becoming simply a vehicle for hit singles and keeps it interesting. Not all of the songs are memorable, but most of them are. *—Steve Huey*

Heartbreak Station / 1990 / Mercury ♦♦♦♦
After successful albums that effectively followed contemporary hard-rock trends, Cinderella reached back into The Stones and Aerosmith songbooks and created a sneering, raunchy hard-rock album that was artistically their finest moment, even if it didn't reach the same commercial heights as its predecessors. But the sales figures don't matter (it *only* sold a million copies); *Heartbreak Station* shows that Cinderella has more genuine rock & roll grit than most of the metal bands of the late '80s. *—Stephen Thomas Erlewine*

Still Climbing / Nov. 8, 1994 / Mercury ♦♦♦♦
Cinderella returned from their self-imposed exile in late 1994 with *Still Climbing*, a gritty record that shows them building upon the bluesy hard rock of *Gypsy Road*. Arguably, it boasts a more consistent song selection and tougher sound than *Gypsy*, yet radio and MTV were resistant to the band's classical good-times-and-hard-rockin' attitude and the record disappeared soon after its release. *—Stephen Thomas Erlewine*

● **Looking Back** / May 20, 1997 / Mercury ♦♦♦♦
Looking Back is a comprehensive collection of Cinderella's entire career, featuring all of their hits—"Nobody's Fool," "Don't Know What You Got (Till It's Gone)," "The Last Mile," "Coming Home," "Gypsy Road," "Shelter Me"—plus highlights from their inconsistent records, and the previously unreleased "War Stories." The compilation doesn't overlook nearly any of their best songs, and it's hard to imagine that a more thorough retrospective than *Looking Back* could ever be assembled. *—Stephen Thomas Erlewine*

20th Century Masters—The Millennium Collection: The Very Best of Cinderella / Aug. 15, 2000 / Mercury ♦♦♦♦
The Millennium Collection: The Very Best of Cinderella gathers highlights from the hair metal group's body of work, including "Nobody's Fool," "Shake Me," "Don't Know What You've Got Till It's Gone," "Coming Home," and "The Last Mile." Choice album tracks, radio favorites, and their hit from the *Wayne's World* soundtrack, "Hot and Bothered," make up the rest of this overview. While it's not as extensive as *Looking Back* or *Bad Attitude*, *The Very Best of Cinderella* is a concise, affordable hits collection from one of the most popular hard rock bands from the late '80s. *—Heather Phares*

The Circle Jerks

f. 1979, Los Angeles, CA
American Punk, L.A. Punk, Heavy Metal, Hardcore Punk
One of the leading lights on the L.A. hardcore scene of the early '80s, the Circle Jerks were formed after Black Flag vocalist Keith Morris left that group after their *Nervous Breakdown* EP and hooked up with former Redd Kross guitarist Greg Hetson. The band's early lineup was rounded out by bassist Roger (Dowding) Rogerson and drummer Lucky Lehrer. The Jerks developed a stellar live reputation among the skateboarding and slam dancing crowds and released their debut album, *Group Sex*, in 1980. A year later, they were featured in the L.A. punk documentary *The Decline of Western Civilization* and appeared on the soundtrack. The albums *Wild in the Streets* and *Golden Shower of Hits* continued in much the same loud, fast, tastelessly funny vein, and the latter included a medley of AM radio hits like "Along Comes Mary," "Afternoon Delight," "Having My Baby," and "Love Will Keep Us Together" done Circle Jerks style.

The Circle Jerks' later albums pursued more of a heavy metal direction and featured the rhythm section of Zander Schloss and Keith Clark. In spite of attracting little attention outside their core following, they continued to perform live, releasing an anthology of concert performances titled *Gig* in 1992. The Circle Jerks pulled off one of 1995's more memorable publicity stunts when they recorded a version of the Soft Boys' "I Wanna Destroy You" on their major-label debut, *Oddities, Abnormalities and Curiosities*, with a lead vocal by former teen queen Debbie Gibson; Gibson later made crowd-surfing cameo appearances to perform the song live at several Jerks gigs. *—Steve Huey*

Group Sex / 1980 / Epitaph ♦♦♦♦
Keith Morris once described his brief tenure as Black Flag's lead singer by saying, "I was the Tasmanian devil, the court jester; I was the dog on the chain who was let out of the cage." So it made sense that after the beer-swilling frontman decided to move on, he would form a band even less subtle and more obnoxious than Black Flag (who represented punk rock at its most brutal in 1979). *Group Sex*, the first "album" from Morris'

group the Circle Jerks, barrels through 14 songs in just under 16 minutes, and pretty much defined the state of the art in SoCal hardcore, circa 1980: raging minor-chord guitar bashing (courtesy of Greg Hetson, later in Bad Religion), speedy drumming (Lucky Lehrer punctuates his manic four-four stomp with short, frantic rolls whenever possible), and a bassist (Roger Rogerson) trying to keep up with it all while Morris bellows about sex ("I Just Want Some Skank"), drugs ("Wasted"), politics ("Paid Vacation"), the idle rich ("Beverly Hills"), and his own post-teenage rage ("World Up My Ass"). Some of it's funny, some of it seems to be serious, and it's all one not-so-long blast of raging energy. As such things go, it's tight, reasonably well played, the songs kinda sorta have hooks, and Keith Morris is a pretty good frontman, but if you're looking for nuance, you're pretty much out of luck. Then again, if you were *looking* for nuance in a Circle Jerks album, you've obviously been misinformed as to how this punk rock stuff works. The CD reissue of *Group Sex* pads out the running time by repeating the album after the last cut is done; I'll leave it to others to decide if these really count as "bonus tracks." —*Mark Deming*

Wild in the Streets / 1982 / Epitaph ✦✦✦
Wild in the Streets doesn't have the wild, appealingly offensive mixture of crude lyrics and frenetic riffs that made the Circle Jerks' debut *Group Sex* a minor hardcore classic, but there are enough tracks that nearly make the mark—including a tongue-in-cheek cover of "Put A Little Love in Your Heart" and the title track, which is a version of the theme song to the '60s teen exploitation flick of the same name—to make it worthwhile for Orange County punk fanatics. —*Stephen Thomas Erlewine*

● **Golden Shower of Hits** / 1983 / Rhino ✦✦✦✦
Everything you love about legendary Californian punkers the Circle Jerks is gloriously displayed on *Golden Shower of Hits*. Obnoxious humor (Keith Morris' vocals, the album cover), disjointed guitars courtesy of Greg Hetson, and sloppy yet excited rhythm work (bassist Roger Rogerson and drummer John Ingram) all add up to perhaps the ultimate punk rock party. The band never excelled in subtlety, as evidenced in the song titles "When the Shit Hits the Fan" and "Parade of the Horribles," but the Jerks were one of the first bands to play lightning fast, yet still memorable punk (the 41-second classic "In Your Eyes"). Included is *Golden Shower*'s title track medley, which upset longtime fans for the covers (albeit very tongue-in-cheek) of such middle-of-the-road schlock as "Close to You," "Afternoon Delight," and "Love Will Keep Us Together." But all the faves are here—"Under the Gun," "Bad Words," "coup d'etat," and "Product of My Environment," among a host of others. *Golden Shower of Hits* is the ultimate introduction to this one-of-a-kind band. —*Greg Prato*

Wonderful / 1985 / Combat/Relativity ✦✦

VI / 1987 / Combat/Relativity ✦✦✦
This strong album is one of the band's best. Tempos here are slowed down from that of standard hardcore; as a result, the songs here inhabit the uneasy netherworld between punk and heavy metal traversed most successfully by the Stooges and the Dictators. Only Keith Morris' raspy, growling vocals retain the band's tie with classic hardcore. Songwriting is still inconsistent, but there are a surprisingly large number of strong selections here, and all are performed with fiery energy. Highlights include "Casualty Vampire," "I Don't," and the top-notch "Beat Me Senseless." There's also a rushed and raw cover of the Creedence Clearwater Revival chestnut "Fortunate Son." This platter is well worth hearing. —*David Cleary*

Oddities, Abnormalities and Curiosities / Jun. 1995 / Mercury ✦✦✦
Legendary L.A. hardcore punk band The Circle Jerks change their approach a bit on their major label debut *Oddities, Abnormalities and Curiosities*. The album contains 12 songs that lean more towards a punk inspired hard rock approach than their earlier hardcore sound. The tracks on this effort are also longer than many of their earlier recordings, compared to their early classic "In Your Eyes" which runs all of 46 seconds, "Sinking Ship" at 3 minutes and 48 seconds is practically an epic. This may be a change of pace, but it isn't necessarily a bad thing. This set still displays plenty of the trademarks that make The Circle Jerks so endearing, including Keith Morris' distinct howling vocal style, Greg Hetson's great guitar work and their unmistakable sense of humor. Nowhere on this album, or possibly in the band's entire career, has their sense of humor been so prominently on display than on their cover of The Soft Boys "I Wanna Destroy You" which features guest vocals by none other than former teen queen Debbie Gibson. This collaboration is not only brilliant but it could only be pulled off by The Circle Jerks. "22," "Teenage Electric" and "Fable," are straightforward rockers that set the tone for rest of the album. Although the mainstream sound and more polished production may alienate a few early fans who are looking for something more hardcore, this is an excellent hard rock album with few weak spots along the way. —*Paul Tinelli*

Eric Clapton (Eric Patrick Clapp)

b. Mar. 30, 1945, Ripley, England
Vocals, Guitar (Electric), Guitar / Album Rock, British Blues, Pop/Rock, Adult Contemporary, Hard Rock, Blues-Rock
By the time Eric Clapton launched his solo career with the release of his self-titled debut album in mid-1970, he was long established as one of the world's major rock stars due to his group affiliations—the Yardbirds, John Mayall's Bluesbreakers, Cream, and Blind Faith—affiliations that had demonstrated his claim to being the best rock guitarist of his generation. That it took Clapton so long to go out on his own, however, was evidence of a degree of reticence unusual for one of his stature. And his debut album, though it spawned the Top 40 hit "After Midnight," was typical of his self-effacing approach: It was, in effect, an album by the group he had lately been featured in, Delaney & Bonnie & Friends. Clapton did not launch a sustained solo career until July 1974, when he released *461 Ocean Boulevard*, which topped the charts and spawned the #1 single "I Shot the

Sheriff." The persona Clapton established over the next decade was less that of guitar hero than arena rock star with a weakness for ballads. *Slowhand* (November 1977), which featured both the powerful "Cocaine" (written by J.J. Cale, who had also written "After Midnight") and the hit singles "Lay Down Sally" and "Wonderful Tonight," was a million-seller, and its follow-ups were all big sellers. Clapton's popularity waned somewhat in the first half of the '80s, but he was buoyed up by the release of the boxed set retrospective *Crossroads* (April 1988), which seemed to remind his fans of how great he was. On March 20, 1991, Clapton's four-year-old son was killed in a fall. While he mourned, he prepared a movie soundtrack, *Rush* (January 1992). The soundtrack featured a song written for his son, "Tears in Heaven," that became a massive hit single. In March 1992, Clapton recorded a concert for *MTV Unplugged* that, when released on an album in August, became his biggest-selling record ever. Two years later, Clapton returned with a blues album, *From the Cradle*, which became one of his most successful albums, both commerically and critically. —*William Ruhlmann*

Eric Clapton / Jul. 1970 / Polydor ✦✦✦✦✦
Eric Clapton's eponymous solo debut was recorded after he completed a tour with Delaney & Bonnie. Clapton used the core of the duo's backing band and co-wrote the majority of the songs with Delaney Bramlett—accordingly, *Eric Clapton* sounds more laid-back and straightforward than any of the guitarist's previous recordings. There are still elements of blues and rock & roll, but they're hidden beneath layers of gospel, R&B, country, and pop flourishes. And the pop element of the record is the strongest of the album's many elements—"Blues Power" isn't a blues song and only "Let It Rain," the album's closer, features extended solos. Throughout the album, Clapton turns out concise solos that de-emphasize his status as guitar god, even when they display astonishing musicality and technique. That is both a good and a bad thing—it's encouraging to hear him grow and become a more fully rounded musician, but too often the album needs the spark that some long guitar solos would have given it. In short, it needs a little more of Clapton's personality. —*Stephen Thomas Erlewine*

461 Ocean Boulevard / Jul. 1974 / Polydor ✦✦✦✦✦
461 Ocean Boulevard is Eric Clapton's second studio solo album, arriving after his side project of Derek & the Dominos and a long struggle with heroin addiction. Although there are some new reggae influences, the album doesn't sound all that different from the rock, pop, blues, country, and R&B amalgam of *Eric Clapton*. However, *461 Ocean Boulevard* is a tighter, more focused outing that enables Clapton to stretch out instrumentally. Furthermore, the pop concessions on the album—the sleek production, the concise running times—don't detract from the rootsy origins of the material, whether it's Johnny Otis' "Willie and the Hand Jive," the traditional blues "Motherless Children," Bob Marley's "I Shot the Sheriff," or Clapton's emotional originals, "Let It Grow" and "Better Make It Through Today" (the latter included only on several reissues of the album). With its relaxed, friendly atmosphere and strong bluesy roots, *461 Ocean Boulevard* set the template for Clapton's '70s albums. Though he tried hard to make an album exactly like it, he never quite managed to replicate its charms. —*Stephen Thomas Erlewine*

There's One in Every Crowd / Mar. 1975 / Polydor ✦✦

E.C. Was Here / Aug. 1975 / Polydor ✦✦✦
Since Eric Clapton and his longtime fans have always thought of him primarily as a bluesman, it is curious that this live album, which is devoted to extended guitar solos on blues standards like "Have You Ever Loved a Woman," "Rambling on My Mind," and "Further on up the Road," didn't become a massive hit. Maybe it was that the once reclusive Clapton was now spitting out new albums every six months, but *E.C. Was Here* did not achieve the renown it deserved upon release, and Clapton, who had been reluctant to put out a straight blues album to begin with, didn't try anything similar again for almost 20 years, instead making sure to keep his records within a pop framework that usually diluted their effectiveness. In its CD reissue, with "Drifting Blues" extended out to its full 11 minutes, the album is even more impressive. —*William Ruhlmann*

No Reason to Cry / Aug. 1976 / Polydor ✦✦✦
When he gave a speech inducting the Band into the Rock & Roll Hall of Fame, Eric Clapton said that after he heard their debut album, *Music from Big Pink*, he wanted to join the group, the fact that they already had a guitarist in Robbie Robertson notwithstanding. In the winter of 1975-1976, when he cut *No Reason to Cry* at the Band's Shangri-la Studio in Malibu, California, he came as close as he ever would to realizing that desire. Clapton is a musical chameleon; though some of *No Reason to Cry* is identifiable as the kind of pop/rock Clapton had been making since the start of his solo career (the best of it being "Hello Old Friend," which became his first Top 40 single in two years), the most memorable music on the album occurs when Clapton is collaborating with members of the Band and other guests. He duets with Band bassist Rick Danko on Danko's "All Our Past Times," and with Bob Dylan on Dylan's "Sign Language," as Robertson's distinctive lead guitar is heard rather than Clapton's. As a result, the album is a good purchase for fans of Bob Dylan and the Band, but not necessarily for those of Eric Clapton. [The CD reissue adds a bonus track, "Last Night," which is a traditional 12-bar blues song credited to Clapton.] —*William Ruhlmann*

Slowhand / Nov. 1977 / Polydor ✦✦✦✦✦
After the guest-star-drenched *No Reason to Cry* failed to make much of an impact commerically, Eric Clapton returned to using his own band for *Slowhand*. The difference is substantial—where *No Reason to Cry* struggled hard to find the right tone, *Slowhand* opens with the relaxed, bluesy shuffle of J.J. Cale's "Cocaine" and sustains it throughout the course of the album. Alternating between straight blues ("Mean Old Frisco"), country ("Lay Down Sally"), mainstream rock ("Cocaine," "The Core"), and pop ("Wonderful Tonight"), *Slowhand* doesn't sound schizophrenic because of the band's grasp of the material. This is laid-back virtuosity—although Clapton and his band are never flashy, their

playing is masterful and assured. That assurance and the album's eclectic material make *Slowhand* rank with *461 Ocean Boulevard* as Eric Clapton's best albums. *—Stephen Thomas Erlewine*

Backless / Nov. 1978 / Polydor ♦♦♦
Having made his best album since *461 Ocean Boulevard* with *Slowhand*, Eric Clapton followed with *Backless*, which took the same authoritative, no-nonsense approach. If it wasn't quite the masterpiece, or the sales monster, that *Slowhand* had been, this probably was because of that usual Clapton problem—material. Once again, he returned to those Oklahoma hills for another song from J.J. Cale, but "I'll Make Love to You Anytime" wasn't quite up to "Cocaine" or "After Midnight." Bob Dylan contributed two songs, but you could see why he hadn't saved them for his own album, and Clapton's own writing contributions were mediocre. Clapton did earn a Top Ten hit with Richard Feldman and Roger Linn's understated pop shuffle "Promises," but it was not one of his more memorable recordings. Of course, Clapton's blues playing on the lone obligatory blues cut, "Early in the Morning" (presented in its full eight-minute version on the CD reissue), was stellar. [*Backless* was his last album to feature the backup group that had been with him since 1974.] *—William Ruhlmann*

Just One Night / Apr. 1980 / Polydor ♦♦♦♦♦
Although Eric Clapton has released a bevy of live albums, none of them have ever quite captured the guitarist's raw energy and dazzling virtuosity. The double-live album *Just One Night* may have gotten closer to that elusive goal than most of its predecessors, but it is still lacking in many ways. The most notable difference between *Just One Night* and Clapton's other live albums is his backing band. Led by guitarist Albert Lee, the group is a collective of accomplished professionals that have managed to keep some grit in their playing. They help push Clapton along, forcing him to spit out crackling solos throughout the album. However, the performances aren't consistent on *Just One Night*—there are plenty of dynamic moments like "Double Trouble" and "Rambling on My Mind," but they are weighed down by pedestrian renditions of songs like "All Our Past Times." Nevertheless, more than any other Clapton live album, *Just One Night* suggests the guitarist's in-concert potential. It's just too bad that the recording didn't occur on a night when he *did* fulfill all of that potential. *—Stephen Thomas Erlewine*

Another Ticket / Feb. 1981 / Polydor ♦♦♦
Now, here's a star-crossed album. Polydor rejected the first version of it, produced by Glyn Johns, and Eric Clapton was forced to cut it all over again with Tom Dowd. Then, a few dates into a US promotional tour coinciding with its release, Clapton collapsed and was found to be near death from ulcers due to his alcoholism. Finally, it turned out to be the final record of his 15-year association with Polydor, which therefore had no reason to promote it. Nevertheless, the album made the Top Ten, went gold, and spawned a Top Ten single in "I Can't Stand It." And the rest of it wasn't too shabby, either. The first and last Clapton studio album to feature his all-British band of the early '80s, it gave considerable prominence to second guitarist Albert Lee and especially to keyboard player/singer Gary Brooker (formerly leader of Procol Harum), and they gave it more of a blues-rock feel than the country-funk brewed up by the Tulsa shuffle crew Clapton had used throughout the 1970s. Best of all, Clapton had taken the time to write some songs—he's credited on six of the nine selections—and tunes such as the title track and "I Can't Stand It" held up well. This wasn't great Clapton, but it was good, and it deserved more recognition than conditions allowed it at the time. *—William Ruhlmann*

Time Pieces: Best of Eric Clapton / May 1982 / Polydor ♦♦♦♦♦
Time Pieces is a good single-disc collection of Eric Clapton's solo hits—including "I Shot the Sheriff," "After Midnight," "Wonderful Tonight," Derek & the Dominos' "Layla," and "Cocaine"—that has since been supplanted by the more thorough *The Cream of Eric Clapton*, which combines his solo work with selections of his Cream and Blind Faith work. Nevertheless, the compilation still provides a good introduction for neophyte Clapton fans, especially those that just want copies of his '70s hits. *—Stephen Thomas Erlewine*

Money and Cigarettes / Feb. 1983 / Warner ♦♦♦
Money and Cigarettes marked several important turning points in Eric Clapton's recording career. It was his debut release on his own Duck imprint within Warner Bros.' Reprise Records subsidiary. It was also the first album he made after coming to terms with his drinking problem by giving up alcohol. Newly focused and having written a batch of new songs, he became dissatisfied with his longtime band and fired them, with the exception of second guitarist Albert Lee. In their place, he hired session pros like Stax Records veteran bassist Donald "Duck" Dunn and Muscle Shoals drummer Roger Hawkins, also bringing in guest guitarist Ry Cooder. His new songs reflected on his changed condition, with "Ain't Going Down," a thinly veiled musical rewrite of the Jimi Hendrix arrangement of "All Along the Watchtower," serving as a statement of purpose that declared, "I've still got something left to say." "The Shape You're In" was a criticism of his wife for her alcoholism that concluded, "I'm just telling you baby 'cause I've been there myself," while the lengthy acoustic ballad "Pretty Girl" and "Man in Love" reaffirmed his feelings for her. The album's single was the relatively slight pop tune "I've Got a Rock & Roll Heart," but Clapton's many blues fans must have been most pleased with the covers of Sleepy John Estes' "Everybody Oughta Make a Change" (significantly placed as the album's leadoff track), Albert King's "Crosscut Saw," and Johnny Otis' "Crazy Country Hop." For all the changes and the high-powered sidemen, though, *Money and Cigarettes* ended up being just an average effort from Clapton, which his audience seems to have sensed since, despite the Top 20 placement for the single, it became his first album in more than six years to miss the Top Ten and fail to go gold. *—William Ruhlmann*

Time Pieces, Vol. 2: Live in the '70s / 1985 / Polydor ♦♦♦
Neither a career retrospective nor a rarities collection, *Time Pieces II: Live in the '70s* is an odd record. Featuring a selection of material recorded in concert at various points in the '70s, the album never gives an accurate impression of Clapton's progression as a guitarist—it's sequenced haphazardly, with tracks falling outside of strict chronological order. Nevertheless, there are a number of fine performances here, especially on album tracks like "Tulsa Time" and "If I Don't Be There by Morning," as well as the extended solos of "Rambling on My Mind." Diehard fans will find things of interest on *Time Pieces II*, but the album can be safely ignored by most listeners. *—Stephen Thomas Erlewine*

Behind the Sun / Mar. 1985 / Warner ♦♦♦
Clapton's career was in decline in the early '80s when he switched record labels from Polydor to Warner Bros. and his debut Warner album, *Money and Cigarettes*, became his first to fall below gold-record status in more than six years. As a result, Warner looked critically at his follow-up, the Phil Collins-produced *Behind the Sun*, in the fall of 1984 and rejected the first version submitted, insisting that he record several new songs written by Jerry Williams, backed by Los Angeles session players under the auspices of company producers Lenny Waronker and Ted Templeman. Warner then emphasized the new tracks, releasing two of them, "Forever Man" (which reached the Top 40) and "See What Love Can Do," as singles. The resulting album, not surprisingly, was somewhat schizophrenic, though the company may have been correct in thinking that the album as a whole was competent without being very exciting. The added tracks were not bad, but they were not the surefire hits they were supposed to be. As usual, there was some effective guitar soloing (notably on "Same Old Blues"), but despite the tinkering, *Behind the Sun* was not one of Clapton's better albums. [It went gold after nearly two years in release.] *—William Ruhlmann*

August / Nov. 1986 / Warner ♦♦
Eric Clapton adopted a new, tougher, hard R&B approach on *August*, employing a stripped-down band featuring keyboard player Greg Phillinganes, bassist Nathan East, and drummer/producer Phil Collins, plus, on several tracks, a horn section and, on a couple of tracks, backup vocals by Tina Turner, and performing songs written by old Motown hand Lamont Dozier, among others. The excellent, but incongruous, leadoff track, however, was "It's in the Way That You Use It," which Clapton and Robbie Robertson had written for Robertson's score to the film *The Color of Money*. Elsewhere, Clapton sang and played fiercely on songs like "Tearing Us Apart," "Run," and "Miss You," all of which earned AOR radio play. That radio support may have helped the album to achieve gold status in less than six months, Clapton's best commercial showing since 1981's *Another Ticket*, despite the album's failure to generate a hit single. The title commemorates the birth in August 1986 of Clapton's son Conor. [The CD version of the album contains the bonus track "Grand Illusion."] *—William Ruhlmann*

☆ **Crossroads** / Apr. 1988 / Polydor ♦♦♦♦♦
A four-disc box set spanning Eric Clapton's entire career—running from the Yardbirds to his '80s solo recordings—*Crossroads* not only revitalized Clapton's commerical standing, but it established the rock & roll multi-disc box set retrospective as a commercially viable proposition. Bob Dylan's *Biograph* was successful two years before the release of *Crossroads*, but Clapton's set was a bonafide blockbuster. And it's easy to see why. *Crossroads* manages to sum up Clapton's career succinctly and thoroughly, touching upon all of his hits and adding a bevy of first-rate unreleased material (most notably selections from the scrapped second Derek & the Dominos album). Although not all of his greatest performances are included on the set—none of his work as a session musician or guest artist is included, for instance—every truly essential item he recorded is present on these four discs. No other Clapton album accurately explains why the guitarist was so influential, or demonstrates exactly what he accomplished. *—Stephen Thomas Erlewine*

Journeyman / Nov. 1989 / Reprise ♦♦♦♦♦
For most of the '80s, Eric Clapton seemed rather lost, uncertain of whether he should return to his blues roots or pander to AOR radio. By the mid-'80s, he appeared to have made the decision to revamp himself as a glossy mainstream rocker, working with synthesizers and drum machines. Instead of expanding his audience, it only reduced it. Then came the career retrospective *Crossroads*, which helped revitalize his career, not only commercially, but also creatively, as *Journeyman*—the first album he recorded after the success of *Crossroads*—proved. Although *Journeyman* still suffers from an overly slick production, Clapton sounds more convincing than he has since the early '70s. Not only is his guitar playing muscular and forceful, his singing is soulful and gritty. Furthermore, the songwriting is consistently strong, alternating between fine mainstream rock originals ("Pretending") and covers ("Before You Accuse Me," "Hound Dog"). Like any of Clapton's best albums, there is no grandstanding to be found on *Journeyman*—it's simply a laid-back and thoroughly engaging display of Clapton's virtuosity. On the whole, it's the best studio album he's released since *Slowhand*. *—Stephen Thomas Erlewine*

24 Nights / Oct. 8, 1991 / Reprise ♦♦♦
Eric Clapton, who had not released a live album since 1980, had several good reasons to release one in the early '90s. For one thing, his spare backup band of keyboardist Greg Phillinganes, bassist Nathan East, and drummer Steve Ferrone, was his best live unit ever, and its powerful live versions of Cream classics like "White Room" and "Sunshine of Your Love" deserved to be documented. For another, since 1987, Clapton had been playing an annual series of concerts at the Royal Albert Hall in London, putting together various special shows—blues nights, orchestral nights, etc. *24 Nights*, a double album, was culled from two years of such shows, 1990 and 1991, and it demonstrated the breadth of Clapton's work, from his hot regular band to assemblages of bluesmen like Buddy Guy and Robert Cray to examples of his soundtrack work with an orchestra led by Michael Kamen. The result was an album that came across as a lavishly constructed retrospective and a testament to Clapton's musical stature. But it made little impact upon release (though it quickly went gold), perhaps because events overcame it—three months later, Clapton's elegy for his baby son, "Tears In Heaven," was all over the radio, and a few

months after that he was redefining himself on *MTV Unplugged*—a live show as austere as *24 Nights* was grand. Still, it would be hard to find a more thorough demonstration of Clapton's abilities than the one presented here. *—William Ruhlmann*

Unplugged / Aug. 18, 1992 / Reprise ♦♦♦♦♦
Clapton's *Unplugged* was responsible for making acoustic-based music, and *Unplugged* albums in particular, a hot trend in the early '90s. Clapton's concert was not only one of the finest *Unplugged* episodes, but was also some of the finest music he had recorded in years. Instead of the slick productions that tainted his '80s albums, the music was straightforward and direct, alternating between his pop numbers and traditional blues songs. The result was some of the most genuine, heartfelt music the guitarist has ever committed to tape. And some of his most popular—the album sold over seven million copies in the U.S. and won several Grammies. *—Stephen Thomas Erlewine*

From the Cradle / Sep. 13, 1994 / Reprise ♦♦♦♦♦
For years, fans craved an all-blues album from Clapton; he waited until 1994 to deliver *From the Cradle.* The album manages to recreate the ambience of postwar electric blues, right down to the bottomless thump of the rhythm section. If it wasn't for Clapton's labored vocals, everything would be perfect. As long as he plays his guitar, he can't fail—his solos are white-hot and evocative, original and captivating. When he sings, Clapton loses that sense of originality, choosing to mimic the vocals of the original recordings. At times, his overemotive singing is painful; he doesn't have the strength to pull off Howlin' Wolf's growl or the confidence to replicate Muddy Waters' assured phrasing. Yet, whenever he plays, it's easier to forget his vocal shortcomings. Even with its faults, *From the Cradle* is one of Clapton's finest moments. *—Stephen Thomas Erlewine*

● **The Cream of Clapton** / Mar. 7, 1995 / Polydor/Chronicles ♦♦♦♦♦
Eric Clapton was contracted to Polydor Records from 1966 to 1981, first as a member of Cream, then Blind Faith, and later as a solo artist and as the leader of Derek and the Dominos. This 19-track, 79-minute disc surveys his career, presenting an excellent selection from the period, including the Cream hits "Sunshine of Your Love," "White Room," and "Crossroads"; "Presence of the Lord," Clapton's finest moment with Blind Faith; "Bell Bottom Blues" and "Layla" from Derek and the Dominos; and 11 songs from Clapton's solo work, among them the hits "I Shot The Sheriff," "Promises," and "I Can't Stand It." The selection is thus broader and better than that found on 1982's *Time Pieces* collection, and with excellent sound and liner notes by Clapton biographer Ray Coleman, *The Cream of Clapton* stands as the single-disc best-of to own for Clapton's greatest recordings. [Not to be confused with the popular 1987 Polydor (U.K.) compilation *The Cream of Eric Clapton,* which has since been retitled *The Best of Eric Clapton.*] *—William Ruhlmann*

Eric Clapton's Rainbow Concert [Expanded] / Jul. 25, 1995 / Polydor/Chronicles ♦♦♦
In these days of CD expansion, it is not unusual for a record company to reissue an old album with a bonus track or two. This reconstruction of the January 13, 1973, comeback concert by Eric Clapton is something else again, however. The original six-track LP ran less than 27 minutes; the new 14-track CD runs almost 74 minutes. The eight additions—"Layla," "Blues Power," "Bottle of Red Wine," "Bell Bottom Blues," "Tell the Truth," "Key to the Highway," "Let It Rain," and "Crossroads"—make the disc an effective recapitulation of Clapton's career over the previous seven years, including his solo work and his appearances with John Mayall's Bluesbreakers, Cream, and Derek and the Dominos. Despite the addiction that had kept him largely homebound for almost two years, Clapton played well, though the all-star backup band was as ragged as it was spirited. The loose feel of the evening was brought out in the stage announcements, many by Pete Townshend, who even mentioned a social disease just before introducing "Presence of the Lord." This still isn't a great Eric Clapton show, but it has been transformed from a historical curiosity to a historical document. *—William Ruhlmann*

Crossroads 2: Live in the Seventies / Apr. 2, 1996 / Polydor Chronicles ♦♦♦
Crossroads was a box set that appealed to both beginners and fanatics. *Crossroads 2 (Live in the Seventies)* only appeals to fanatics. Spanning four discs and consisting almost entirely of live material (there are a handful of studio outtakes), this is music that will only enthrall completists and archivists. For those listeners, there is a wealth of fascinating, compelling performances here, as well as a fair share of mediocre, uninspired tracks. The key word for the entire album is detail—it is an album for studying the intricacies of Clapton's playing and how it evolved. For example, it's easy to hear the differences and progressions between the four versions of Robert Johnson's "Rambling on My Mind." And it is Clapton that evolves, not his supporting band—although they are proficient, they are hardly exciting. However, their static, professional support provides a nice bed to chart Slowhand's growth over the course of the decade, simply because he is always the focal point. *Crossroads 2* may only be for a collector, but for those collectors, it is a treasure, even if some of the tracks are fool's gold. *—Stephen Thomas Erlewine*

Pilgrim / Mar. 10, 1998 / Reprise ♦♦

Clapton Chronicles: Best of 1981-1999 / Oct. 12, 1999 / Reprise ♦♦♦♦
Clapton Chronicles ignores Clapton's 1983 Reprise debut, *Money and Cigarettes* (which sounded more like an RSO album, anyway), starting with the pair of Phil Collins-produced mid-'80s albums, *Behind the Sun* and *August.* Though these had a pop sheen, they were album-rock holdovers. Clapton didn't get the balance between hard rock and commercial gloss right until 1989's *Journeyman,* whose featured songs—"Before You Accuse Me," "Bad Love," and "Pretending"—form the heart of this compilation. *Journeyman* was overshadowed by the phenomenal success of "Tears in Heaven" and 1992's *Unplugged.* Not only did *Unplugged* go platinum ten times, it established a new public image—classy, stylish, and substantial. That's the image that prevails on *Clapton Chronicles.* His triple-platinum blues album *From the Cradle* is written out of the picture, with songs from movie soundtracks taking its place. Apart from the Babyface-produced "Change the World," these tunes are a little too self-conscious and subdued, as are selections from 1998's *Pilgrim.* However, this deliberate move to paint Clapton's '80s and '90s recordings as adult-contemporary fare is accurate. Clapton's musical journey from 1985 to 1999 was taken mostly in the middle of the road, and *Clapton Chronicles* certainly captures that journey, missing no major hits from the late '80s and '90s. Whether it's a necessary addition to a Clapton collection is a matter of taste. It's certainly an excellent compliment to *Unplugged* and *Time Pieces,* his two most popular and pop-oriented albums, but that might not be what every fan wants. *—Stephen Thomas Erlewine*

Riding with the King / Jun. 13, 2000 / Reprise ♦♦♦♦
The potential for a collaboration between B.B. King and Eric Clapton is enormous, of course, and the real questions concern how it is organized and executed. This first recorded pairing between the 74-year-old King and the 55-year-old Clapton was put together in the most obvious way: Clapton arranged the session using many of his regular musicians, picked the songs, and co-produced with his partner Simon Climie. That ought to mean that King would be a virtual guest star rather than earning a co-billing, but because of Clapton's respect for his elder, it nearly works the other way around. The set list includes lots of King specialties—"Ten Long Years," "Three O'Clock Blues," "Days of Old," "When My Heart Beats Like a Hammer"—as well as standards like "Hold on I'm Coming" and "Come Rain or Come Shine," with some specially written and appropriate recent material thrown in, so King has reason to be comfortable without being complacent. The real danger is that Clapton will defer too much; though he can be inspired by a competing guitarist such as Duane Allman, he has sometimes tended to lean too heavily on accompanists such as Albert Lee and Mark Knopfler when working with them in concert. That danger is partially realized; as its title indicates, *Riding With the King* is more about King than it is about Clapton. But the two players turn out to have sufficiently complementary, if distinct, styles so that Clapton's supportive role fills out and surrounds King's stinging single-string playing. (It's also worth noting that there are usually another two or three guitarists on each track.) The result is an effective, if never really stunning, work. *—William Ruhlmann*

Reptile / Mar. 13, 2001 / Reprise ♦♦♦
Reptile seems conceived as an album to address all the disparate audiences Clapton has assembled over the years. His core audience may think of him as the premier blues guitarist of his generation, but especially as a solo artist, he has also sought a broader pop identity, and in the 1990s, with the hits "Tears in Heaven" and "Change the World," he achieved it. The fans he earned then will recognize the largely acoustic sound of such songs as "Believe in Life," "Second Nature," and "Modern Girl." But those who think of Clapton as the guy who plays "Cocaine" will be pleased with his cover of another J.J. Cale song, "Travelin' Light," and by the time the album was in record stores mainstream rock radio had already found "Superman Inside," which sounds like many of his mid-tempo rock hits of the '80s. This diversity is continued on less familiar material, especially the many interesting cover songs. Somebody, perhaps the artist himself, had been busy looking for old chestnuts, since *Reptile* contains a wide variety of them. Still, *Reptile* looks like an album that started out to be more ambitious than it ended up being. There may be a song here for each of the artist's constituencies (and, more important to its commercial impact, for every major radio format except talk and country), but as a whole the album doesn't add up to the statement Clapton seems to have been hoping to make. *—William Ruhlmann*

The Dave Clark Five

f. 1961, Tottenham, London, England, **db.** 1970
British Invasion
For a very brief time in 1964, it seemed that the biggest challenger to the Beatles phenomenon was the Dave Clark Five. The quintet had the fortune to knock "I Want to Hold Your Hand" off the top of the British charts with "Glad All Over," and were championed (for about 15 minutes) by the British press as the Beatles' most serious threat. They were the first British Invasion band to break in a big way in the States after the Beatles, though the Rolling Stones and others quickly supplanted the DC5 as the Fab Four's most serious rivals. The Dave Clark Five reached the Top 40 seventeen times between 1964 and 1967 with memorable hits like "Glad All Over," "Bits and Pieces," "Because," and a remake of Bobby Day's "Over and Over," as well as making more appearances on *The Ed Sullivan Show* than any other English act. The DC5 were distinguished from their British contemporaries by their larger-than-life production, Clark's loud stomping drum sound, and Mike Smith's leathery vocals. Though accused by detractors of lacking finesse and hipness, they had a solid ear for melodies and harmonies, and wrote much of their early material, the best of which has endured quite well, although their albums were fairly weak. *—Rick Clark & Richie Unterberger*

● **History of the Dave Clark Five** / Aug. 3, 1993 / Hollywood ♦♦♦♦♦
For many years, the Dave Clark Five were one of the few major groups of the 1960s whose work was unavailable on compact disc. This two-disc, 50-track reissue not only rectifies that situation but arguably includes more than all but devoted fans will want to hear. All of the band's mammoth mid-'60s hits —"Glad All Over," "Bits and Pieces," "Because," "Catch Us If You Can," "Any Way You Want It," and others—are included, and while they don't rival the work of British Invasion heavyweights like the Beatles, Stones, and Kinks, they still burst with exuberant melodies, harmonies, and dense production. This compilation also features worthy lesser-known hits like "Try Too Hard" and "Everybody Knows," as well as obscure but commendable beat ballads and raveups from their B-sides and albums. Nonetheless, there is a fair amount of filler, and their post-1966 work is undistinguished by either artistic growth or the hooks and heavy beat of their early material. But at their peak, the DC5 captured the joie de vivre of the British Invasion with a

lasting power that cannot be dismissed. This reissue includes a comprehensive booklet featuring recollections from Dave Clark himself. *—Richie Unterberger*

Dee Clark

b. Nov. 7, 1938, Blythesville, AR, **d.** Dec. 7, 1990, Smyrna, GA

Vocals / R&B, Soul

Dee Clark was a solid R&B vocalist who had some huge hits in the late '50s and early '60s. The Arkansas-born singer moved to Chicago as a child and was in the Hambone Kids with Sammy McGrier and Ronny Strong. They recorded for Okeh in 1952; the next year Clark sang with the Goldentones. This group later became the Kool Gents, then recorded as the Delegates for Vee-Jay in 1956. Clark went solo in 1957 and in 1958 enjoyed his first smash with "Nobody for You," an Abner release that reached number three R&B and just missed the Top 20 on the pop charts. He continued a string of R&B winners with "Just Keep It Up," "Hey Little Girl," and "How About That" for Abner in 1959 and 1960. Clark teamed with guitarist Phil Upchurch to write "Raindrops" in 1961, his signature tune. The song peaked at number three R&B and number two pop, and was his last major hit. Clark continued performing through the '60s, '70s, and '80s, but never again was a factor, though "Raindrops" remains a staple on oldies radio. *—Ron Wynn*

● **Rain Drops** / 1994 / Vee-Jay ♦♦♦♦♦

Dee Clark was one of the most adaptable R&B vocalists of the '50s and early '60s, as this 25-song reissue shows. He did songs in a Little Richard mode, an Afro-Latin setting, and also performed ballads, novelty tunes ("Kangaroo Hop"), and covers ("Cupid"). Clark's gem was "Raindrops," a song with enough drama, hooks, and appeal to nearly top both the pop and R&B charts. It was his biggest hit, but not his only fine number. There are many cuts, such as "Nobody but You," "What Kind of Fool," and the newly issued "Bring Back My Heart," that equal or even top the tune that made him famous. *—Ron Wynn*

Golden Classics / Nov. 5, 1996 / Collectables ♦♦♦♦

Not exactly a greatest-hits package, but an interesting blend of three of Dee's biggest hits on Vee-Jay (a nice stereo mix of "Raindrops" kicks things off) with a generous helping of his later sides for Constellation. These sides capture Clark moving toward a proto-soul style, with tracks like "Crossfire Time," "I'm Going Home," "Warm Summer Breezes," and "Heartbreak" showing the depth of Clark's vocal range on ballads, soul grinders, and jazz-tinged material. Lots of great Vee-Jay sides MIA on this, but a nice companion once you track the earlier sides down. *—Cub Koda*

Take Care of Business / Aug. 11, 1998 / West Side ♦♦♦

Subtitled "The Constellation Masters, 1963-1966," this picks up the second phase of Clark's solo career after his hit-making days at Vee-Jay. These sides find him moving in a more soulful direction, making hard Southern and Motown-inflected soul with the best of them on "Crossfire Time," "I'm Going Home," "Come Closer" and "That's My Girl." Although material like "Heartbreak," "I Ain't Gonna Be a Fool," "Warm Summer Breezes," and "I Don't Need (Nobody Like You)" were top-flight, Clark couldn't score a hit during his three years with Constellation chronicled here. But the lack of hits still yields a 17-track feast of brand-name mid-'60s Chicago soul music, played and sung with a professional flair that's unmistakably Dee Clark. Other highlights include "T.C.B.," "She's My Baby," "Hot Potato" and a live two-part workout on "Nobody But You" that makes a fitting closer to this set. *—Cub Koda*

Gene Clark (Harold Eugene Clark)

b. Nov. 17, 1944, Tipton, MO, **d.** May 24, 1991, Sherman Oaks, CA

Vocals, Songwriter, Guitar / Folk-Rock, Singer/Songwriter, Country-Rock, Progressive Bluegrass

Very few musicians had as much influence in creating new styles of music as Gene Clark. As co-founder of the Byrds, he helped pioneer what was to become known as folk-rock. Clark and Bob Dylan were the most prolific songwriters of the genre. After leaving the group, he and banjoist Doug Dillard invented newgrass, a progressive blend of traditional bluegrass instrumentation augmented by electronics, drums, piano and even harpsichord. The fusion of country and rock on Clark's first solo album predated the Byrds' *Sweetheart of the Rodeo* by nearly two years and the first Flying Burrito Brothers album by three years. A member of the New Christy Minstrels as early as 1962, Clark later moved to Los Angeles and formed the Byrds though he left the group in 1966 to pursue a solo career on *Gene Clark with the Gosdin Brothers* in 1967. The following year *The Fantastic Expedition of Dillard and Clark* heralded the dawning of newgrass. Two solo albums followed, *White Light* and *Roadmaster* (the latter featured the original Byrds on two tracks and foreshadowed a brief Byrds reformation). Clark recorded two more solo albums in the '70s, then joined Roger McGuinn and Chris Hillman for two albums as McGuinn, Clark and Hillman. He died in 1991, just a few short months after he and the Byrds were inducted into the Rock & Roll Hall of Fame. *—Dan Pavlides*

Gene Clark with the Gosdin Brothers / 1967 / Edsel ♦♦♦♦

The first album that Gene Clark released after his departure from the Byrds followed very closely on the model of his earlier efforts on the Byrds' first two albums. His backing musicians included ex-bandmates Chris Hillman and Michael Clarke, as well as future Byrd Clarence White and Clark collaborator Doug Dillard; not to mention the Gosdin brothers, whose harmonies resembled a rockier Everly Brothers and brought the sound very close to the Byrds'. The album contains a number of fine pop-oriented tunes and stellar folk-rock/country-rock numbers (a year before the Byrds' *Sweetheart of the Rodeo*, which employed both White and Dillard) and established Gene Clark as a major songwriter, rivaling his old band and often coming close to the fabness of the Beatles. Still, despite such solid songs and backing musicians, *Gene Clark With the Gosdin Brothers* failed to make much of an impact, perhaps due to its being released in the same week as the Byrds' *Younger Than Yesterday*, itself a *tour de force* that cemented their influence. However, in the realm of Clark's recorded output, this album stands as the one of the best, if not the best, example of how powerful a singer, writer, and bandleader Gene Clark was. *—Alex Stimmel*

Echoes / 1967 / Columbia/Legacy ♦♦♦♦♦

This is Gene Clark's debut album, *Gene Clark With the Gosdin Brothers*. The Byrds comparison is really unavoidable: it's both Clark's best solo work, and not coincidentally, the one which resembles The Byrds most strongly. Indeed, this could easily pass for a somewhat less-than-average vintage Byrds album, with actual Byrds Chris Hillman and Michael Clarke forming the rhythm section, and Vern and Rex Gosdin on guitar (hence the title). To be brutal, it doesn't measure up to Clark's best songs from his Byrds days, but it's fairly strong, melodic '60s folk-rock nonetheless, perhaps with a bit of a more countrified, laidback, generic feel. "So You Say You Lost Your Baby," "Echoes," and especially "Tried So Hard" are standouts. The CD adds three interesting previously unreleased outtakes from the era, as well as six of the best early Byrds songs graced by Clark's songwriting and vocals. *—Richie Unterberger*

Gene Clark / 1969 / Together ♦♦♦♦

American Flyer / 1971 / MediaArts ♦♦

White Light / 1972 / A&M ♦♦♦♦♦

Easily one of Gene Clark's finest outings ever. This, his first solo album for A&M (after the wonderfully ahead of its time Dillard & Clark), was an album that should have put Gene Clark in the same league as Neil Young. Aside from Clark's incredible eight originals (as well as a great cover of "Tears of Rage"), one reason this record succeeds is the pairing of Clark and producer/guitarist Jesse Ed Davis. Davis' guitar accompaniment has all of the subtlety of Robbie Robertson, and he framed the songs perfectly, especially the expansive set closer, "1975." As for the songs themselves, Clark rarely bettered himself. "Spanish Guitar" is easily one of Clark's most intense and arresting compositions, with lines like "from deep in my soul to my brain to a Spanish guitar..."; it's no wonder Bob Dylan claims that he wished he'd written the song. The whole album, frankly, is that good, and is a must for anyone interested in the most criminally underrated singer/songwriter of his era. *—Matthew Greenwald*

Roadmaster / 1972 / Demon ♦♦♦♦♦

Gene Clark, record business equals bad news. Case in point, this album. Or masterpiece, you could say. After two brilliant Dillard & Clark albums, A&M signed Clark to a solo deal. Okay, fair enough—so far. In 1972, he delivered perhaps the finest album of his career, *Gene Clark*, (also known as *White Light*). Excellent reviews in all the top magazines, including Rolling Stone. Guess what? Almost zero sales. Now, here's the follow up, almost—if not more—brilliant. Released only in Holland. Aside from containing some of Clark's finest tracks like "In a Misty Morning" and "Full Circle Song," this record contains two gems recorded with the willing participation of the other original Byrds. "One in a Hundred" and "She's the Kind of Girl" are so good that they would have easily stood out on *The Byrds* box set, had McGuinn elected to include them. Oh well, the music is still here—an example of an artist who couldn't quite get in on with commerce. What a disaster. The man should be mentioned in the same breath as Neil Young. *Roadmaster* is one of the many reasons why. *—Matthew Greenwald*

No Other / 1974 / Line ♦♦♦

This album is easily Gene Clark's most misunderstood and strangest project that he ever involved himself with. By turns described as Clark's "*Sgt. Pepper*," and "one of the greatest albums of the '70s" to "largely un-listenable in certain places..." well, you get the idea. With a monumental budget at Asylum Records, and Thomas Jefferson Kaye in the producers chair, it was one wild ride, and that is certainly reflected in the grooves. Clark's songwriting rarely needed more than a four-piece backing band at any stage of his career. Granted Leon Russell used strings and horns on the epic *Echoes* album to great effect, but these arrangements are just over the top, and Clark's songs and vocals are clearly weak under the weight. And there are some fine songs. "No Other" is a wondrous composition, showing Clark exploring the metaphysical. "Lady of the North" (co-written by Doug Dillard) is a beautiful song, and fortunately escaped Kaye's overindulgence with a fine, restrained arrangement by Richard Greene. Overall though, it's indulgent and the *sound* of the record says more about the '70s than the songs do. You can almost *taste* the cocaine. *—Matthew Greenwald*

Two Sides to Every Story / 1977 / RSO ♦♦

Firebyrd / 1987 / Takoma ♦♦♦

Gene Clark's post-Byrds solo career was as frought with false starts, and unmet promises as his two years with the Byrds were filled with fame, fulfillment, and recognition. *Firebyrd* was an artistic triumph and a commercial disaster—released to rave reviews and an enthusiastic response, as one of the finest solo projects ever to come from an ex-Byrd, it was killed by poor distribution (demand in Europe, especially Germany and Italy, where fan interest in Clark and the Byrds was very high, resulted in high premiums being paid for used copies). "Rain Song," "Rodeo Rider," and "Something About You" were some of Clark's best songs in years, and his covers of two old Byrds numbers, "Mr. Tambourine Man" and "Feel A Whole Lot Better," are perfectly credible reinterpretations, and he even does justice to Gordon Lightfoot's "If You Could Read My Mind." Not a "lost Byrds album" by any means, but a must-own for any serious Byrds fan. (see *This Byrd Has Flown*) *—Bruce Eder*

So Rebellious a Lover / 1987 / Razor & Tie ♦♦♦♦

An exquisite pairing of talent, the duo of Carla Olson and Gene Clark apparently came out of casual living room sessions while Clark was preparing for another project. The feeling of spontaneity and closeness of spirit engulfs all of the cuts here. Olson's strident and powerful vocals mesh beautifully with Clark's slightly world-weary, soulful performances. As for the material, both songwriters obviously put their best foot forward here. Olson's "The Drifter" and "Are We Still Making Love" are excellent country/folk outings. Clark contributes one of his finest later compositions, "Gypsy Rider," a multi-leveled song that can easily be viewed as autobiographical. Excellent support is provided by an array of backing musicians, especially Stephen McCarthy (lap steel and dobro) and guest Chris Hillman (mandolin). Chemistry is the operative word here. The only sad thing was that this was to be the only studio effort by the duo, as Gene passed away only two years after its release. This record is important not only for what it is, but what it could have become. *—Matthew Greenwald*

Silhouetted in Light / 1992 / Edsel ✦✦✦

This Byrd Has Flown / Oct. 1995 / Edsel ✦✦✦✦✦
This Byrd Has Flown is an expanded British import CD of *Firebyrd*, with extra tracks added from later recording sessions. The songs add a considerable amount to the original album: "C'est La Bonne Rue" is a hot little rocker, and "All I Want" is one of Clark's most poignant and impassioned love songs, and by itself is worth the price of the album. The notes by drummer/singer/composer Andy Kandanes add considerably to the information about the circumstances behind the recording of *Firebyrd* and Clark's later career, up until his death in May of 1991. *—Bruce Eder*

American Dreamer / Feb. 11, 1997 / Raven ✦✦✦✦✦
Kudos to Australia's Raven for assembling this fine 24-track overview of Gene's most fertile period. Included are three Clark-penned Byrds stunners, two of the best from his first solo album, six from the Dillard and Clark albums (the Velvet Crush-covered "Why Not Your Baby" is unfortunately overlooked), a Flying Burritos-backed gem, two ersatz Byrds-reunion cuts from *Road Master*, a whopping six from *White Light*, "Full Circle" from the otherwise tepid 1973 Byrds reunion, and two selections from *No Other* (though not the This Mortal Coil-covered "Strength of Strings"). An interesting early mix of "Full Circle" is included as a bonus. For the uninitiated, this is a great place to start, but even a fanatic will be pleased by the inclusion of the hard-to-find *White Light* cuts and Sid Griffin's fannish liner notes. *—Michael Ribas*

● **Flying High** / 1998 / A&M ✦✦✦✦✦
When someone mentions the Byrds in conversation, the names of McGuinn, Crosby, and maybe Hillman pop up, but hardly anyone mentions Gene Clark, the Byrds' first original songwriter and lead singer until a fear of flying caused him to leave the band and strike out on his own. With *Flying High*, all of that should be put to rest, because the spotlight is finally on Clark and his many contributions to both rock and country. Starting with Byrds cuts like "Feel a Whole Lot Better" and "She Don't Care About Time," this two-disc set moves through Clark's early solo career into his fine collaboration with Doug Dillard on to more mature solo work while attempting to reunite the Byrds on "One In a Million" and "She's the Kind of Girl," which never quite got off the ground. Added here are some otherwise unreleased cuts, such as "Winter In," "That's Alright By Me" and Dylan's "I Pity the Poor Immigrant," which show that Clark had more talent than was released to the public in his lifetime. And while disc two does have waning interest and fewer cuts, it does show that Clark never gave up on trying to restart his career, even if the chips appeared to be down; of special note is his sensitive cover of Phil Ochs' "Changes." Compiled and re-produced for disc by Sid Griffin, *Flying High* is a fine spotlight on an underappreciated artist. With liner notes by Griffin and Chris Hillman, this has just about everything one needs to know about Gene Clark. *—James Chrispell*

Petula Clark

b. Nov. 15, 1932, Epsom, England
Vocals / Sunshine Pop, British Invasion, Pop
The most commercially successful female singer in British chart history, Petula Clark embarked on a stage career at the age of seven, began hosting her own radio show four years later and made her film debut soon after. By the dawn of the 1950s she was a superstar throughout the UK, with a Top 20 single by 1954 and her first chart-topper, "Sailor," in 1960. Riding the wave of the British Invasion, Clark was finally able to penetrate the US market in 1964 with the Grammy-winning "Downtown," the first single by a British woman ever to reach number one on the American pop charts. It was also the first in a series of American Top Ten hits (most written and arranged by Tony Hatch) which also included "I Know a Place," "I Couldn't Live Without Your Love" and the number one smash "My Love." In addition to hosting her own BBC series, she also starred in the 1968 NBC television special *Petula*. As the 1960s drew to a close, Clark's commercial stature slipped. In 1968 she revived her film career by starring in *Finian's Rainbow*, followed a year later by *Goodbye, Mr. Chips*. In later years Clark focused primarily on international touring and her stage career. *—Jason Ankeny*

The Greatest Hits of Petula Clark / 1986 / GNP ✦✦✦✦
This import collection is much crisper and more vibrant-sounding than the domestic releases. All the major US hits are here, plus some British and European chart successes never heard in the US. *—Bruce Eder*

The Pye Years / 1995 / RPM ✦✦✦
Two of Clark's mid-'60s British albums, *Petula Clark Sings the International Hits* (1965) and *This Is My Song* (1967), combined onto one CD, with three B-sides from the time added as bonus tracks. *International Hits*, as the title implies, is devoted to covers of standards and then-popular hit songs. Often that spells snoozefest, but it's more interesting than you might think, mainly because of the MOR-meets-Swinging London ear candy of Tony Hatch's production. A few of these songs, like "I (Who Have Nothing)," are actually pretty dynamic interpretations, and "You Can't Keep Me From Loving You" in particular is a performance on par with her mid-'60s hits. *This Is My Song*, although it includes the hits "Don't Sleep in the Subway" and "This Is My Song," is considerably duller, with less imaginative arrangements. The highlights are actually Clark's own compositions, like "Resist" (another obscurity with hit potential) and the anti-war "On the Path of Glory." The three B-sides will interest serious Pet fans, including a couple other self-penned items and a brassy number, "High," co-written by Lee Hazlewood and Billy Strange. *—Richie Unterberger*

The Classic Collection / Mar. 23, 1999 / Pulse/Castle ✦✦✦✦✦
Four-CD, 80-song box set of Clark's '60s material contains all of her big U.S. and U.K. hits, numerous singles that were only hits in other countries (usually France), and a bunch of interesting covers, B-sides, and LP tracks, some quite rare. If you're enough of a fan to want more than what you'll find on the usual thorough hits anthology, but not enough of a fan to want everything she ever did, this is perfect. It's got all of the classics, serviceable (although not terribly extensive) liner notes, and a host of interesting items that aren't well-known. These include a 1963 version of "Please Please Me" (sung in French) that was most likely one of the very first Lennon-McCartney covers; a French-sung cover of "Nobody I Know," the Lennon-McCartney tune never done by the Beatles, although Peter & Gordon had a hit with it; the original versions of "I Will Follow Him" (in English and French), covered for a chart-topper by Little Peggy March in the U.S.; yet another French-sung British Invasion cover, of the Kinks' "Well Respected Man," that was a hit in Canada; and "You're the One" (covered for a hit by the Vogues in the States). Best of all is the mid-'60s B-side "Heart" (covered by the Remains in America), a Clark original that's her hardest-rocking cut, and proof that she could muster the energy to sing rock & roll convincingly on occasion. *—Richie Unterberger*

● **Downtown: The Greatest Hits of Petula Clark** / Oct. 12, 1999 / Buddha ✦✦✦✦✦
Although it's a little skimpy at 12 tracks—especially compared with GNP's import *The Greatest Hits of Petula Clark*, which features 16 cuts—Buddha's *Downtown: The Greatest Hits of Petula Clark* is nevertheless an excellent, concise chronicle of her peak hit-making years. All of her American Top Ten hits are here—"Downtown," "I Know a Place," "My Love," "I Couldn't Live Without Your Love," "This Is My Song," "Don't Sleep in the Subway"—plus the majority of her Top 40 singles, including "You'd Better Come Home," "A Sign of the Times," "Colour My World," "Kiss Me Goodbye," and "Who Am I?" They've all been perfectly remastered, sounding clean and vibrant, yet still of their era. All of this makes *Downtown* an ideal choice for most fans, especially casual listeners. It may not be as comprehensive as some collections, but it's concise, delivering everything you need in terrific sound. *—Stephen Thomas Erlewine*

Anthology: Downtown to Sunset Boulevard / Feb. 15, 2000 / Uptown/Universal ✦✦✦✦✦
Here's a two-disc set of every last great Petula Clark side you'll need for a collection. Truly an anthology, this includes all of the hits and rarities that make up an artist's career, taking it right through to present time 2000. It's all big-band pop appended with strident rock & roll beats; the best songs are immediately recognizable and immensely hummable. Clark wrote her own notes for the inside booklet, commenting on each of the 41 songs included. As the best bang for your buck, this is the one to get. *—Cub Koda*

The Clash

f. 1976, London, England, **db.** 1986
British Punk, Hard Rock, Punk
The Sex Pistols may have been the first British punk rock band, but the Clash were the definitive British punk rockers. Where the Pistols were nihilistic, the Clash were fiery and idealistic, charged with righteousness and a leftist political ideology. From the outset, the band was more musically adventurous, expanding their hard rock & roll with reggae, dub, and rap rockabilly among other roots musics. Furthermore, they were blessed with two exceptional songwriters in Joe Strummer and Mick Jones, each with a distinctive voice and style. The Clash copped heavily from classic outlaw imagery, positioning themselves as rebels with a cause. As a result, they won a passionately devoted following on both sides of the Atlantic. While they became rock & roll heroes in the UK, second only to the Jam in terms of popularity, it took the Clash several years to break into the American market and when they finally did in 1982, they imploded several months later. Though the Clash never became the superstars they always threatened to become, they restored passion and protest to rock & roll. For a while, they really did seem like "the only band that mattered." *—Stephen Thomas Erlewine*

☆ **The Clash [UK]** / Apr. 8, 1977 / Epic ✦✦✦✦✦

Give 'em Enough Rope / Nov. 10, 1978 / Epic ✦✦✦✦✦
For their second album, the Clash worked with the American hard rock producer Sandy Pearlman, best-known for his work with Blue Öyster Cult and the Dictators. The teaming was quite controversial within the punk community, and the sound of *Give 'Em Enough Rope* is considerably cleaner, yet the more direct sound hardly tamed the Clash. While the record doesn't burn with the same intense, amateurish energy of *The Clash*, it does have a big, forceful sound that is nearly as powerful. What keeps *Give 'Em Enough Rope* from being a classic is its slightly inconsistent material. Many of the songs are outright classics, particularly the first half of the record ("Safe European Home," "English Civil War," "Tommy Gun," "Julie's in the Drug Squad") and "Stay Free," but the group loses some momentum toward the end of the record. Even with such flaws, *Give 'Em Enough Rope* ranks as one of the strongest albums of punk era. [In 2000 Columbia/Legacy reissued and remastered *Give 'Em Enough Rope*.] *—Stephen Thomas Erlewine*

☆ **The Clash [US]** / Jul. 1979 / Epic ✦✦✦✦✦
Never Mind the Bollocks may have appeared revolutionary, but the Clash's eponymous debut album was pure, unadultarated rage and fury, fueled by passion for both rock &

roll and revolution. Though the cliché about punk rock was that the bands couldn't play, the key to the Clash is that although they gave that illusion, they really could play—*hard.* The charging, relentless rhythms, primitive three-chord rockers, and the poor sound quality give the album a nervy, vital energy. Joe Strummer's slurred wails perfectly compliment the edgy rock, while Mick Jones' clearer singing and charged guitar breaks make his numbers righteously anthemic. Even at this early stage, the Clash were experimenting with reggae, most notably on the Junior Murvin cover "Police and Thieves" and the extraordinary "White Man in Hammersmith Palais," which was one of five tracks added to the American edition of *The Clash.* "Deny," "Protex Blue," "Cheat," and "48 Hours" were removed from the British edition and replaced for the U.S. release with the British-only singles "Complete Control," "White Man in Hammersmith Palais," "Clash City Rockers," "I Fought the Law," and "Jail Guitar Doors," all of which were stronger than the items they replaced. Though the sequencing and selection were slightly different, the core of the album remained the same, and each song retained its power individually. In 2000, Columbia/Legacy re-issued and re-mastered the album to include the UK songs. Few punk songs expressed anger quite as bracingly as "White Riot," "I'm So Bored With the U.S.A.," "Career Opportunities," and "London's Burning," and their power is all the more incredible today. Rock & roll is rarely as edgy, invigorating, and sonically revolutionary as *The Clash.* —*Stephen Thomas Erlewine*

★ **London Calling** / Dec. 14, 1979 / Epic ✦✦✦✦✦
Give 'Em Enough Rope, for all of its many attributes, was essentially a holding pattern for the Clash, but the double album *London Calling* is a remarkable leap forward, incorporating the punk aesthetic into rock & roll mythology and roots music. Before, the Clash had experimented with reggae, but that was no preparation for the dizzying array of styles on *London Calling.* There's punk and reggae, but there's also rockabilly, ska, New Orleans R&B, pop, lounge jazz, and hard rock; and while the record isn't tied together by a specific theme, its eclecticism and anthemic punk function as a rallying call. While many of the songs—particularly "London Calling," "Spanish Bombs," and "The Guns of Brixton"—are explicitly political, by acknowledging no boundaries the music itself is political and revolutionary. But it is also invigorating, rocking harder and with more purpose than most albums, let alone double albums. Over the course of the record, Strummer and Jones (and Paul Simonon, who wrote "The Guns of Brixton") explore their familiar themes of working-class rebellion and anti-establishment rants, but they also tie them in to old rock & roll traditions and myths, whether it's rockabilly greasers or "Stagger Lee," as well as mavericks like doomed actor Montgomery Clift. The result is a stunning statement of purpose and one of the greatest rock & roll albums ever recorded. [In 2000 Columbia/Legacy reissued and remastered *London Calling.*] —*Stephen Thomas Erlewine*

Sandinista! / Dec. 12, 1980 / Epic ✦✦
The Clash sounded like they could do anything on *London Calling.* For its triple-album followup, *Sandinista!,* they tried do *everything,* adding dub, rap, gospel and even children's choruses to the punk, reggae, R&B and roots-rock they already were playing. Instead of presenting a band with a far-reaching vision, like *London Calling* did, *Sandinista!* plays as a messy, confused jumble, which means that its numerous virtues are easy to ignore. Amid all the dub experiments, backward tracks, unfinished songs and instrumentals, there's a number of classic Clash songs which rank among their best, including "Police on My Back," "The Call-Up," "Somebody Got Murdered," "Charlie Don't Surf," "Hitsville U.K.," and "Lightning Strikes (Not Once, But Twice)," yet it's difficult for anyone but the most dedicated listeners to find them. A few of the failed ideas were worth exploring, but even more—like the children's choir version of "Career Opportunities" or the Terry Doggs song "Lose This Skin"—weren't even worth pursuing. As the cliche says, there's a great single album within these three records, and those songs make *Sandinista!* worthwhile. Nevertheless, its sloppy attack is disheartening after the tour-de-force of *London Calling* and the focused agression of *The Clash.* [In 2000 Columbia/Legacy reissued, remastered, and restored the artwork for *Sandinista!*] —*Stephen Thomas Erlewine*

Combat Rock / May 14, 1982 / Epic ✦✦✦
On the surface of things, *Combat Rock* appears to be a retreat from the sprawling stylistic explorations of *London Calling* and *Sandinista!* The pounding arena-rock of "Should I Stay or Should I Go?" makes the Clash sound like an arena rock band, and much of the album boasts a muscular, heavy sound courtesy of producer Glyn Johns. But things aren't quite that simple. *Combat Rock* contains heavy flirtations with rap, funk and reggae, and it even has a cameo by poet Allen Ginsberg—if this album is, as it has often been claimed, the Clash's sell-out effort, it's a very strange way to sell-out. Even with the infectious, dance-inflected New Wave pop of "Rock the Casbah" leading the way, there aren't many overt attempts at crossover success, mainly because the group is tearing in two separate directions. Mick Jones wants the Clash to inherit the Who's righteous arena rock stance and Joe Strummer wants to forge ahead into Black music. The result is an album that is nearly as inconsistent as *Sandinista!,* even though its finest moments—"Should I Stay or Should I Go," "Rock the Casbah," "Straight to Hell"—illustrate why the Clash were able to reach a larger audience than ever before with the record. [In 2000 Columbia/Legacy reissued and remastered *Combat Rock.*] —*Stephen Thomas Erlewine*

Cut the Crap / 1985 / Epic/Legacy ✦✦
Hoping to keep the Clash as a raw punk phenomenon, Joe Strummer and Paul Simonon kicked Mick Jones out of the band following the success of *Combat Rock,* hiring three unknowns to replace him for *Cut the Crap.* As the title suggests, the group attempts to get back to its roots by sticking to short, fast, hard punk songs. Unfortunately, they sound like a parody of a classic punk band—with the exception of the surprisingly nervy "This Is England," this is all formulaic, tired punk rock that doesn't have the agression or purpose of early Clash records, let alone the hardcore punk that the new band was now competing with. It's a sad end to one of the greatest rock & roll bands, not even offering much of interest for the dedicated fans. [In 2000 Columbia/Legacy reissued and remastered *Cut the Crap.*] —*Stephen Thomas Erlewine*

Story of the Clash, Vol. 1 / Mar. 1988 / Epic/Legacy ✦✦✦✦
In some ways, the double-disc, 28-track compilation *The Story of the Clash, Vol. 1* does its job quite well—if the job is indeed presenting a relatively thorough overview for casual fans. The great majority of the band's hits and signature tunes are here, including album tracks and such non-LP singles as "Bank Robber," "Armagideon Time," and "Capital Radio," albeit in non-chronological order. While there may be many worthy tunes missing, nothing here is undeserving of inclusion, and its expansive method of operation works in its favor, since it hints at the richness of the Clash's music. After all, it's no great loss to have such official singles as "Hitsville U.K." missing, since there are some extraordinary album tracks included. Still, the compilation is a little problematic. Not because the music isn't great—it's so great that the rather bewildering sequencing does nothing to dilute its power—but because it's hard to tell who needs this compilation, apart from complete neophytes. Granted, in 1988, it marked the first CD release of this music, but since the appearance of *The Singles, Super Black Market Clash,* and the comprehensive box set *Clash on Broadway,* no diehard need own it, unless they need the otherwise unavailable edits of such songs as "The Magnificent Seven" that are included here in lieu of the full-length originals. For novices, it's not a bad introduction at all, but it's sort of like a set of training wheels on a bicycle. Still, as training wheels go, it's about the best Clash compilation out there, since it draws a fuller picture than *The Singles* and is more manageable than *Clash on Broadway.* Of course, jumping in with *The Clash* or *London Calling* is just as effective an introduction. —*Stephen Thomas Erlewine*

The Singles / 1991 / Epic/Legacy ✦✦✦✦
The Singles is exactly what the title says—a collection of the Clash's U.K. single A-sides. This approach can hardly result in a definitive compilation, since the Clash's albums were such cohesive, important works in their own right, and even more erratic LPs like *Sandinista!* and *Combat Rock* had their share of fine album tracks. Nevertheless, the collection does have some value, particularly for more casual fans who don't want to spend the time or money sifting through those uneven albums. And because the best way to hear the Clash is on their original albums, *The Singles* can also be useful for fans who already own those albums and don't want to purchase the three-disc *Clash on Broadway,* thereby duplicating a good portion of their collection. *The Singles* does illustrate the progression of the Clash's music from raw, energetic punk to eclectic dabblings in rockabilly, reggae, and dance-rock (even if it doesn't do so as seamlessly as *London Calling*), and so far, it is the only single-disc Clash comp to feature the original version of the non-LP single "Bankrobber" (the one on *Super Black Market Clash* is a dub version with most of the lyrics missing). So, the utility of *The Singles* all depends on how deeply you want to dig into the Clash, and how much tolerance you have for duplication in the compilations necessary for supplementing the original albums (if your tolerance is high, stick with the more thorough *Clash on Broadway*). —*Steve Huey*

Clash on Broadway / Nov. 19, 1991 / Epic/Legacy ✦✦✦✦✦
Clash on Broadway is a fine triple-disc, 63-song box set covering the Clash's entire career. Although there are very few rarities, it does include all of the band's important songs, including cuts that were only available on EPs, singles and B-sides. As a result, it's a useful box set even for dedicated fans, presenting their evolution in a logical fashion. Nevertheless, compilations don't always suit the Clash well, because *The Clash* and *London Calling* were powerful individual works in their own right, and hearing them cut up in this fashion alters their impact. Even so, for anyone looking for one set illustrating why the Clash were a great, important and influential band, *Clash On Broadway* explains exactly why. —*Stephen Thomas Erlewine*

Super Black Market Clash / 1994 / Epic/Legacy ✦✦✦✦
An expanded version of the *Black Market Clash* EP, *Super Black Market Clash* adds assorted singles and remixes to the original recording. A couple of tracks aren't that interesting, but the majority of the disc is splendid, featuring some of the band's best, but unfortunately overlooked tracks, including "Armagideon Time," "The Prisoner," "Gates of the West," and "Capital Radio One." —*Stephen Thomas Erlewine*

Classics IV

f. Jacksonville, FL
Sunshine Pop
The Classics IV were actually a quintet comprised of several top studio musicians: lead vocalist Dennis Yost, guitarist/songwriter James Cobb, guitarist Wally Eaton, bassist Joe Wilson, and drummer Kim Venable. Prior to joining together as a group, the five had played on recordings for Tommy Roe, Billy Joe Royal, and the Tams, all groups discovered by Bill Lowery. Lowery was instrumental in getting Classics IV a record deal upon their 1967 move from Jacksonville to Atlanta, and the group's commercially viable brand of soft rock produced three Top Five hits in "Spooky," "Stormy," and "Traces." All of the group's hits were written by Cobb and producer Buddy Buie. Yost was eventually billed ahead of the group in an attempt to make him a recognizable star, but the move failed to ignite much interest, and Cobb left the group in 1970 to form the Atlanta Rhythm Section with Buie and Wilson's replacement, Dean Daughtry. —*Steve Huey*

● **The Very Best of the Classics IV** / 1988 / EMI America ✦✦✦✦✦
A no-frills CD reissue of what was already a pretty frills-free vinyl anthology from the '70s, *The Very Best of the Classics IV* is not geared for the obsessive fan of Dennis Yost and crew, even assuming such people exist. The sound is serviceable, the liner notes nonexistent, and the skimpy 26-and-a-half-minute running time is just barely on the right side of a gyp. On the other hand, for the casual fan who just wants decent-sounding

versions of "Spooky," "Traces," and "Stormy"—this Atlanta-based group's three mellow blue-eyed soul hits—this is an inexpensive way to do just that. The other seven tracks contain no hidden gems, but they're perfectly serviceable, even the cover of Bobby Hebb's maudlin "Sunny." —*Stewart Mason*

Judy Clay

b. St. Paul, NC
Vocals / R&B, Soul
A talented journeywoman soul singer, Judy Clay (born Judy Lee) joined the Drinkard Singers gospel group (who also included Cissy Houston) in the late '50s. Like many singers who started with gospel, she moved to soul in the '60s, releasing a string of non-hit singles for the Ember and Scepter labels that are esteemed by British Northern soul fans today; she also sang backup vocals for soul singers like Wilson Pickett and Solomon Burke. In the late '60s, she briefly teamed with Billy Vera to form what may have been the first interracial recording duo, recording an album and a couple minor hit singles, "Storybook Children" and "Country Girl-City Man (Just Across the Line)." Her other recordings with Stax and Atlantic in the late '60s (which included a 1969 session at Muscle Shoals Sound) produced a hit R&B duet with William Bell, "Private Number," and a minor hit solo single, "Greatest Love." She continued to work as a backup vocalist in the '70s with Aretha Franklin and Ray Charles, among others. Struck with a brain tumor in 1979, she returned to gospel music shortly after her recovery. —*Richie Unterberger*

● **Featuring Storybook Children & Greatest Love** / 1995 / Ichiban/Soul Classics ◆◆◆◆◆
11 of these 19 tracks are actually taken from her duet recordings with Billy Vera, including "Storybook Children" and "Country Girl-City Man (Just Across The Line)," most of the 1968 *Storybook Children* LP, and the 1969 non-LP single "Reaching For The Moon"/"Tell It Like It Is." The CD also has eight songs that Clay recorded on her own for Atlantic and Stax in the late '60s (most at the Muscle Shoals Sound Studio) which are generally more impressive than her duets with Vera, sporting a much earthier soul sound. Six of those solo tracks are from singles never available on album; two were previously unreleased. —*Richie Unterberger*

Otis Clay

b. Feb. 11, 1942, Waxhaw, MS
Vocals, Leader / Memphis Soul, Southern Soul, Soul-Blues, R&B, Soul
Otis Clay made most of his best-known records in Memphis during the early '70s, but he's still universally hailed as Chicago's deep-soul king. In a city filled to overflowing with legendary blues artists, Clay has become the proud standard-bearer for Chicago's enduring soul tradition.

Like so many of his contemporaries, Clay's intense vocal style reflects a gospel background. He made the secular jump in 1965, signing with Chicago's One-derful Records and issuing a series of gospel-tinged soul records that were a lot grittier than the customary Windy City soul sound. Clay inaugurated Atlantic's Cotillion subsidiary in 1968 with a supercharged cover of the Sir Douglas Quintet's "She's About a Mover," produced by Rick Hall in Muscle Shoals shortly before the singer joined forces with Hi Records boss Willie Mitchell. With the relentlessly driving Hi Rhythm Section in tow, Clay waxed his biggest seller in 1972, "Trying to Live My Life without You," later covered very successfully by Bob Seger.

Although Clay's tenure on Hi may have been his most commercially potent, he's steadily recorded and gigged ever since. He is a genuine hero in Japan, where he's recorded two sizzling live albums filled with the churning grooves, punchy horns, and searing vocals that inevitably characterize the best deep soul—no matter where it's recorded. —*Bill Dahl*

The Best of Otis Clay: The Hi Records Years / Jul. 23, 1996 / Hi/The Right Stuff ◆◆◆◆◆
Best of the Hi Records Years is an excellent collection of Otis Clay's early-'70s heyday, featuring such songs as "If I Could Reach Out" and the classic "Trying to Live My Life Without You." Although these recordings aren't quite as gritty as his singles for One-derful! and Cotillion Records, the tight Hi rhythm section keeps things at a steady, sexy groove, so they are nevertheless excellent and deeply soulful and are arguably his best work, making this compilation an essential addition to any comprehensive '70s soul collection. —*Stephen Thomas Erlewine*

● **The Complete Otis Clay On Hi Records** / Mar. 7, 2000 / Hi ◆◆◆◆◆

The Clean

f. 1978
College Rock, New Zealand Rock, Post-Punk, Alternative Pop/Rock, Indie Rock
The Clean were one of the most influential New Zealand bands of the post-punk era. The band formed in the town of Dunedin in 1978, when Hamish Kilgour (drums) and his brother David (guitar) recruited David's school friend, guitarist Peter Gutteridge. Soon afterward, they opened for New Zealand punk rockers Enemy. The Clean were one of the first bands in the country to play original material. They carved out a distinctive, noisy but melodic sound, distinguished by David's screeching, distorted guitar. When the Kilgour brothers decided in 1979 to relocate the band to Auckland, Gutteridge had already left the lineup. The Clean played with a rotating bassist before David quit the band and moved back to Dunedin. Once he was back home, he was introduced to bassist Robert Scott and the two started playing together; news of his brother's new musical relationship prompted Hamish to move back to Dunedin and begin the Clean again. In early 1980, the group began playing around town in earnest. In early 1981, a fan named Roger Shepherd began Flying Nun Records to release a single by the Clean, "Tally Ho!" With its jagged guitar, sweet melody and persistent organ, "Tally Ho!" reached number 19 on the

charts. In November, the *Boodle Boodle Boodle* EP was released; it surprised every observer by climbing to number four on the New Zealand charts. *Boodle* and the 1982 EP *Great Sounds Great* captured the quirky sides of the Clean's sound, since they did not have the technology to replicate the band's roaring live sound. Later in 1982, the group released their loudest single yet, "Getting Older." Soon after its release, the Clean disbanded, reuniting in 1988 and again in 1994. —*Stephen Thomas Erlewine*

Oddities / 1983 / Flying Nun ◆◆◆
Definitely somewhere in the shadowy side of New Zealand rock, but all the more charming for it—*Oddities* is a nutshell. As the name makes clear enough, this collection, expanded for its CD release over a decade after first surfacing as a "super lo-fi cassette," to quote the liner notes, captures random and fun efforts from the trio not on regular releases. Exactly what comes from where is utterly unclear—the packaging only acknowledges a general recording range of 1980 to 1982 "on a Revox B77 2 track," and that's about that. Taken as a whole, though, it's a fuzzy and wiggy collection of catchy tunes caught somewhere between punk energy, pop hooks, arty touches and echoing murkiness (the latter possibly coming from the fact the Revox came courtesy of the Dead C, masters of echoing murkiness). The Kilgours and Scott kick up what must have been a fairly overwhelming din in the actual recording process, even if the nature of the end result prevents the full crunch from coming through. The general production values actually make a number of tracks sound like the Jesus and Mary Chain's earliest efforts, but with a generally sweeter taste all around (the collapsing din of "Mudchucker Blues" being a notable exception). The gems are scattered throughout, but they can be fine ones. An alternate take of "Getting Older" is the first truly great one of the bunch, a four and a half minute winner with the right sense of hooks, just enough melancholia amidst the fun (David Kilgour's guitar work is particularly great) and lines like "Why don't you do yourself in?" A number of songs have a lighter acoustic touch, but still sound like they're bubbling up through the depths, as "End of My Dream," the amusing lament "David Bowie" and the wistful but warning "Inside Out." —*Ned Raggett*

● **Compilation** / 1986 / Homestead ◆◆◆◆◆
Compilation offers a nearly complete overview of the Clean's legendary early recordings, including the classic "Tally Ho!" single and highlights from their two EPs (*Boodle Boodle* from 1981 and 1982's *Great Sounds*), as well as six live bonus tracks (on the CD version only). —*Chris Woodstra*

Oddities 2 / 1988 / Flying Nun ◆◆◆

Vehicle / 1990 / Rough Trade ◆◆◆

Modern Rock / Oct. 10, 1995 / Summershine ◆◆◆
While part of the Clean's undeniable charm is its overall familiarity—every new album, when it appears, feeling like another pleasant greeting from an old friend—it's a familiarity that doesn't breed contempt. The archly titled *Modern Rock*, slyly digging at the tag often applied to the band's music in earlier years, a "college rock," finds the trio merrily making its way through fourteen gently rocking, gently chiming originals. Though recorded over only ten days, the combined experience and ability of the three members allowed them to whip up a fairly elaborate set of songs, as indicated by some of the intriguing arrangements. The spacey echo on the keyboards for "Outside the Cage" and spectral backing vocals on "Something I Need" are two highlights among many. There's also a pleasant low fuzz at points bespeaking both the continuing influence of the Velvet Underground and New Zealand's vaunted tape subculture that seems just right for the proceedings. Hearing Scott's vocals on a slightly different tip than his work in the Bats is especially a treat—after the series of eternally sparkling jangle-rock he's made his own, hearing more consciously experimental touches behind his voice makes a fine contrast. The Kilgours continue in their own particular veins, with everyone trading around vocals in a fairly even split. Those familiar with the band mostly through "Tally Ho!" or the other earlier work will find this version of the Clean—generally calmer in many areas, downright reflective or melancholic in more—an intriguing change. The members have matured, but in such a way as not to sound like typically sleepy midlife crises come to life. —*Ned Raggett*

Unknown Country / Nov. 5, 1996 / Flying Nun ◆◆

Getaway / Aug. 21, 2001 / Merge ◆◆◆

Cleaners from Venus

f. 1980
College Rock, Alternative Pop/Rock
The most extensive of singer-songwriter Martin Newell's various projects, Cleaners from Venus recorded some of the finest—and most neglected—British pop/rock of the 1980s. Its failure to find a wider audience is due at least in part to its unconventional method of distribution. After a short, bitter experience in the music business recording for a large label, Newell retreated to his home studio in the beginning of the 1980s, determined not to have to play by the usual compromising music business rules. As the chief of Cleaners from Venus, he and cohorts recorded and distributed several albums on their own.

Newell's main partner in the early days of Cleaners from Venus was drummer Lol Elliott. By the mid-'80s Martin had hooked up with the more conventionally skilled pianist Giles Smith, and the Cleaners' recording techniques had improved to the level of "real" records. One result was the glorious *Living with Victoria Grey* tape, with uniformly strong songs that usually reflected pastoral English life with affectionate irony. Another result of their increasing success and popularity were deals to produce for record labels, including RCA in Germany. By the end of the 1980s, Newell had discontinued the Cleaners from Venus and founded a new, very similar project called Brotherhood of Lizards. In the 1990s, Newell established a solo career on indie labels that found him carrying on the Cleaners tradition of thinking pure pop in an undiluted manner. There have been a couple of Cleaners compilations, but unfortunately much of the group's best work is heard on their privately produced cassettes, which can be hard to find. *—Richie Unterberger*

Blow Away Your Troubles / 1981 / (no label) ♦♦
The only Cleaners project where the home production values are a serious impediment to pleasurable listening. There's lots of muffle, and too much bottom, on these 1980-81 efforts, "recorded on a hand-cranked, mud-cooled, reel-to-reel, sound-on-sound tape recorder" (from the sleeve note). As a *songwriter,* however, Newell was already a talent of some distinction. It's too bad these weren't recorded better, but Newell fans will appreciate the melodic strength of much of the material. "Marilyn on a Train," in particular, is about as achingly tuneful as anything he's come up with in his whole career. *—Richie Unterberger*

On Any Normal Monday / 1982 / (no label) ♦♦♦
Because the fidelity here is rather primitive compared to his later tapes and records, it's likely that only serious Newell/Cleaners fans will want to get this deep into his discography. If (only slightly) funky production values don't bother you (or actually please you), you shouldn't be disappointed with this. The songs are there, and that's the important thing. Nicely catchy, interesting compositions, sung with a sense of humor, especially "Be An Idiot Popstar" (a David Byrne satire, perhaps?) and the lounge-pop satire "A Fool Like You." *—Richie Unterberger*

In the Golden Autumn / 1983 / (no label) ♦♦♦♦♦
Martin Newell—working on this particular project with Martin Chapman and Paul Ripley-Thomas—really began to hit his stride on this tape, which was filled to the gills with fetching melodies and odd, evocative lyrics, like Syd Barrett with a far stronger hold on reality. The limitations of home recording technology are sometimes a drawback, particularly in the boxy quality of the percussion. Yet it's also a good illustration of how imaginative home recording auteurs can be, especially in the tinkly pianos, hauntingly echoing guitar jangles, and the mysterious ways the guitars and voices are often altered via various effects. It's tied together with his unique mix of cheery optimism and longing regret/nostalgia. *—Richie Unterberger*

Under Wartime Conditions / 1984 / Acid Tapes ♦♦♦
Actually this was first issued as a tape in 1984, and then on vinyl in 1986. It's not the most outstanding of their efforts, but it's a reasonably solid survey of their combination of savvy pop melodies with idiosyncratically English weirdness. "Song for Syd Barrett" isn't the only thing here reminiscent of Television Personalities, but Newell crafts a more diverse sound, using touches of glockenspiel, drum machine, sleighbells, and even a saucepan to embellish the guitar-rock core. *—Richie Unterberger*

● **Living with Victoria Grey** / 1986 / (no label) ♦♦♦♦♦
One of the lost treasures of '80s rock, this is a rousingly melodic set of jangly guitar tunes reflecting the charms and foibles of modern-day England, with zany sound bites à la Monty Python linking the tracks. "Ilya Kuryakin Looked at Me" and the gorgeous, acoustic "Clara Bow" illustrate Newell's knack for paying homage to past heroes with a curious sense of loss and ambiguity. "Victoria Grey," on the other hand, is anthemic guitar power pop at its best; "Pearl" (written by XTC's Andy Partridge) is an a cappella meeting of the Turtles and the Beach Boys. The best album that Cleaners From Venus ever did. *—Richie Unterberger*

Going to England / 1987 / Ammunition ♦♦
A major disappointment, even though this contains some of Newell's strongest songwriting. Many of these songs were first released on the superb *Living with Victoria Grey* cassette; subjected to antiseptic production in studios with bigger budgets, the impact of the songs is neutered. There are few other clearer examples of the heart of a group's vision being torn out by over-professionalism. The material's heard to much better effect on the *Living with Victoria Grey* tape, which will unfortunately be hard to locate (though hardly any more so than this import LP). *—Richie Unterberger*

Town and Country / 1988 / RCA ♦♦♦♦♦
A big improvement on *Going to England.* The sound is still somewhat cleaned up from what you'll hear on Cleaners' cassettes, but not so much so that it gets in the way of the songs. Some of Newell's most jubilant ("Let's Get Married") and gleefully silly ("I Was a Teenage Idiot Dancer") writing is here; "The Beat Generation and Me" is one of the best examples of his ability to write about the icons of the past with bittersweet nostalgia that steers clear of revivalism. Giles Smith proves to be a songwriter of merit as well on his two compositions, particularly the dainty "Felicity." *—Richie Unterberger*

Number 13 / Jun. 1990 / Man at the Off License ♦♦♦♦♦
No surprises here, just the well-constructed, deviously quirky pop-rock that one came to expect from Cleaners From Venus. Everything here was written and played in a bedroom on an eight-track machine by "the Psychedelic Gardener" (i.e., Martin Newell). It's probably one of Cleaners' most straightforward releases, but also one of their most accomplished, with a few songs that would be re-recorded for Newell's solo album, *The Greatest Living Englishman.* *—Richie Unterberger*

Climax Blues Band

f. 1969, Stafford, England
Pop/Rock, Soft Rock, Blues-Rock
Led by Colin Cooper, the former frontman of the R&B unit the Hipster Image, the Stafford, England-based Climax Chicago Blues Band was one of the leading lights of the late-1960s blues boom. A sextet also comprised of guitarists Derek Holt and Peter Haycock, keyboardist Arthur Wood, bassist Richard Jones and drummer George Newsome, the group debuted in 1969 with a self-titled effort recalling the work of John Mayall.

Prior to the release of 1969's *Plays On,* Jones left the group, prompting Holt to move to bass. In 1970 the Climax Chicago Blues Band moved to the Harvest label, at the same time shifting towards a more rock-oriented sound on the LP *A Lot of Bottle.* Around the release of 1971's *Tightly Knit,* Newsome was replaced by drummer John Holt; upon Wood's exit in the wake of 1972's *Rich Man,* the unit decided to continue on as a quartet, also dropping the "Chicago" portion of their name to avoid confusion with the American band of the same name.

In 1974 the Climax Blues Band issued *FM Live,* a document of a New York radio concert. 1975's *Stamp* was their commercial breakthrough, and 1976's *Gold Plated* fared even better, spurred on by the success of the hit "Couldn't Get It Right." However, the rise of punk effectively stopped the group in their tracks, although they continued recording prolifically well into the 1980s; after 1988's *Drastic Steps,* the Climax Blues Band was silent for a number of years, but resurfaced in 1994 with *Blues From the Attic.* *—Jason Ankeny*

● **Couldn't Get It Right** / 1987 / See For Miles ♦♦♦♦♦
Couldn't Get It Right contains all of the Climax Blues Band's big hits from 1974 on, which means that it bypasses their earliest material—which was the closest they ever came to the blues. But it does contain all their big hits, from the title track to "Running Out of Time," making it a near-definitive retrospective. *—Stephen Thomas Erlewine*

25 Years 1968-1993 / 1994 / Repertoire ♦♦♦♦♦
Most casual fans know the Climax Blues Band through "Couldn't Get It Right" and "I Love You," a pair of slick pop and soft rock hits from the late '70s and early '80s. Anyone who heard those two hits probably was puzzled by the "Blues" in the group's name, since they were in no way bluesy. But, as shown by the double-disc, 32-track set *25 Years,* they started out as a British blues band in the late '60s. Unfortunately, they just weren't very good, slogging through the same three chords without much inspiration for nearly ten years. That decade is represented on the first disc, and while the group does show signs of improvement over those 16 songs, the music is still unbelievably dull (and, in the case of "Shoot Her If She Runs," offensive). By the late '70s, the band was in desperate need of a hit, so they changed their tune, incorporating pop, disco, and soft rock. "Couldn't Get It Right" was an excellent song, far catchier than any of their early blues tunes, and it deservedly became a Top Ten hit. The group subsequently tried to replicate its success, but they couldn't get it right until 1981, when the appealingly schmaltzy "I Love You" almost went Top Ten. Afterward, they played soft rock until they broke down and returned to the blues, with only a handful of memorable songs along the way. *25 Years* is a little tedious to anyone who just wants the hits, but, unfortunately, it's the only readily available compilation from the group. It will suit anyone who really wants to dig into the Climax Blues Band, since it accurately sketches the progression of their career, but it doesn't have enough good music to warrant such an extensive compilation. *—Stephen Thomas Erlewine*

Clinic

f. 1997
Indie Rock, Post-Punk
Liverpool's art punk four-piece Clinic formed in 1997 out of the ashes of Ade Blackburn and Hartley's previous band, Pure Morning. The duo added Brian Campbell and Carl Turney to the fold and released the thrashy debut single *IPC Sub-Editors Dictate Our Youth* on the group's own Aladdin's Cave of Golf label; it reached number nine in John Peel's Festive 50 singles roundup that year. 1998 saw the release of equally well-received singles like "Cement Mixer" and "Monkey on My Back," which also showcased Clinic's blend of chugging, Velvet Underground-style guitars, icy, Suicide-esque keyboards and drum machines, and Blackburn's acidic, Lennon-esque vocals. In 1999, the band signed to Domino Records and released "The Second Line." Clinic began a flurry of activity in 2000, releasing their first album, *Internal Wrangler,* and the singles "The Return of Evil Bill" and "Distortions," appearing at Scott Walker's Meltdown and All Tomorrow's Parties festivals, and touring with Radiohead. *—Heather Phares*

Clinic / Mar. 1999 / Domino ♦♦♦
Clinic's self-titled EP collection gathers all of the Liverpool group's early singles, which they released on their own Aladdin's Cave of Golf imprint. On their very first EP, 1997's *I.P.C. Subeditors Dictate Our Youth*—which, ironically enough, was named a Single of the Week by NME— Clinic's signature sound arrived fully formed: dramatic drums courtesy of Phil Spector, taut, chugging guitars and creepy, creaky organs. A-sides like "Monkey on Your Back" and "Cement Mixer" display Clinic's (relatively) pop side, but it's on the collection's B-sides where the group stretches their range. From Ade Blackburn's spooky yet sensual wail on "Porno" to thrashy numbers like "D.P." and "D.T." to "Evil Bill"'s scratch & surf guitar workout, *Clinic* displays the band's expertise at using a few sounds in a wide variety of ways. Though it's just nine songs long, the album is a must-have for fans missing these now hard to find EPs, or for anyone craving more Clinic after hearing *Internal Wrangler.* *—Heather Phares*

● **Internal Wrangler** / May 2, 2000 / Domino ♦♦♦♦
Clinic's long-awaited debut album *Internal Wrangler* fleshes out the sound the group crafted on their self-released EPs, and it also adds a few new twists. Though eerie, punk-tinged songs like "The Return of Evil Bill" and the title track sound like they could have appeared on the band's first singles, *Internal Wrangler*'s best songs concentrate on the experimental yet accessible sides of Clinic's sound. "The Second Line"'s darkly catchy throb, the aptly named "2nd Foot Stomp"'s organ-driven pulse, and "Voodoo Wop"'s blend of surf and Krautrock are a logical progression from Clinic's roots, but ballads like the "Pale Blue Eyes"-esque "Distortions" and the late-night calm of "Goodnight Georgie" are a leap

into new territory for the band. Though some of the thrashier songs like "C.Q." and "T.K." and a bottom-heavy song sequence detract from the album's flow, *Internal Wrangler* is still a strong debut from one of England's most promising and distinctive indie bands. —*Heather Phares*

George Clinton

b. Jul. 22, 1940, Kannapolis, NC

Producer, Vocals, Keyboards, Synthesizer / Urban, Funk

The mastermind of the Parliament/Funkadelic collective during the 1970s, George Clinton broke up both bands by 1981 and began recording solo albums, occasionally performing live with his former bandmates as the P-Funk All-Stars. Clinton became interested in doo wop while living in New Jersey during the early '50s. He formed the Parliaments in 1955, based out of a barbershop back-room where he straightened hair. The group had a small R&B hit during 1967, but Clinton began to mastermind the Parliaments' activities two years later. Recording both as Parliament and Funkadelic, the group revolutionized R&B during the '70s, twisting soul music into funk by adding influences from several late-'60s acid heroes: Jimi Hendrix, Frank Zappa, and Sly Stone. The Parliament/Funkadelic machine ruled black music during the '70s, capturing over 40 R&B hit singles (including three number ones) and recording three platinum albums. His first solo album, 1982's *Computer Games*, contained the Top 20 R&B hit "Loopzilla." Several months later, the title track from Clinton's *Atomic Dog* EP hit #1 on the R&B charts; it stayed at the top spot for four weeks. During the latter half of the '80s Clinton's reputation as a true forefather of rock was disintegrating; by the end of the decade, however, a generation of rappers reared on P-Funk were beginning to name-check him. —*John Bush*

● **Computer Games** / Nov. 5, 1982 / Capitol ✦✦✦✦✦

In the late '70s George Clinton helmed a massive empire bound to eventually decline—which it did, in a rather ugly manner. Once he finally distanced himself in the early '80s from the massive kinetic force that was Parliament/Funkadelic and signed a solo contract with Capitol, he suddenly seemed rejuvenated in terms of creativity and enthusiasm. This freewheeling disposition comes across clearly on *Computer Games*, his first solo album. Of course, calling this a true solo album isn't exactly true, since Bootsy, Gary Shider, and Walter "Junie" Morrison all play a role in the album's success. Still, you get the sense that Clinton is firmly in control of this album, something you can't honestly say about the latter-day Parliament and Funkadelic records, and this sense makes the album quite revealing. Above anything, Clinton turns here to the early-'80s vogue for synthesizers and drum machines that would later become staples of hip-hop and techno production. This fetish for new studio technology still in its primitive stage gives the album a slightly stiff feeling, as the humans are replaced by machines, a very different style of funk. It's this proto-techno funk that colors the album's better moments, particularly "Atomic Dog," "Loopzilla," and the title track. If you're expecting the freewheeling style of his earlier work, you may be disappointed by the confined feeling of Clinton's '80s work. Ultimately, this album ends up being by far the best of Clinton's solo career, with nearly every song having its own character and its own strengths, while latter albums struggled to come up with anything as inventive or effective. Furthermore, no successive album has anything remotely as catchy as "Atomic Dog," a song that Clinton himself could never duplicate no matter how hard he tried on his next three albums. —*Jason Birchmeier*

You Shouldn't-Nuf Bit Fish / Dec. 1983 / Capitol ✦✦✦

When George Clinton rebounded with *Computer Games*, an album met with unanimous acclaim, it seemed as if his already long-winded career was about to enter a new era of inspired creativity. *You Shouldn't-Nuf Bit Fish* surfaced a year later in 1983, though, and whatever momentum Clinton had garnered quickly dissipated. From the Pedro Bell artwork to the ensemble of contributors to the early-'80s synth-drum aesthetic, *You Shouldn't-Nuf Bit Fish* seemed a fitting follow-up upon initial inspection, though there was one glaring difference between the two albums—quality. *Computer Games* had been stacked with great songs; *You Shouldn't-Nuf Bit Fish* clearly wasn't. It's hard to pinpoint exactly what makes the songs of lesser quality: Clumsy attempts at rapping, a lack of effective hooks, awkward attempts to make primitive drum machines funky, a brief running length, and just plain bad songwriting all figure into the album's failure as an adequate follow-up, with none being any worse than the other. "Nubian Nut" stands as Clinton's first attempt at rapping, a truly jarring moment best forgotten. In fact, only "Quickie" is worth bothering with here, a Walter "Junie" Morrison song carried largely by Andre Williams' great guitar riff. Overall, the songs on this album are just plain bad. It's that simple, leaving one to ask the inevitable question: What happened? Well, the answer may lie in Bell's cryptic artwork, where an enigmatic statement alludes to the fact that this album is comprised of leftovers from the *Computer Games* sessions. Whether or not this is indeed the case, *You Shouldn't-Nuf Bit Fish* marked a turning point in Clinton's briefly ignited solo career, a turn toward quick oblivion. —*Jason Birchmeier*

Some of My Best Jokes Are Friends / Jul. 1985 / Capitol ✦✦✦

With technology having taken over R&B in a major way by the mid-'80s, George Clinton made a point of "updating" his P-Funk by being much more high tech and using keyboards, drum machines, and sequencers extensively. On his third "solo album," *Some of My Best Jokes Are Friends*, Clinton even recruits Britain's very technology-oriented new waver Thomas Dolby to help with the production on a few cuts. *Jokes* is far from his best effort, and sometimes comes across as forced and unnatural. But the CD definitely has its strong points, including the addictive "Bodyguard," the eerie "Bangladesh," and the antiwar protest songs "Bullet Proof" and "Thrashin'." With Parliament and Funkadelic, Clinton often had fun making strong social and political statements in a subliminal fashion—this time, however, he's much more direct. Despite its strengths, *Jokes* is an album

that only Clinton's most devoted followers should invest in—those exploring his innovations for the first time would do much better to purchase one of his classic Parliament or Funkadelic albums of the '70s (or, for that matter, his first "solo album" *Computer Games*). —*Alex Henderson*

R&B Skeletons in the Closet / Apr. 1986 / Capitol ✦✦✦✦✦

A definite improvement over the uneven *Some of My Best Jokes Are Friends*, the considerably more focused and confident *R&B Skeletons in the Closet* is one of George Clinton's strongest solo efforts. The P-Funkster continues using technology extensively, but this time, his blend of technology and "real instruments" sounds much more natural. Though not quite in a class with Parliament classics like *Mothership Connection* or *Funkentelechy Vs. the Placebo Syndrome* or Funkadelic treasures ranging from *Cosmic Slop* to *Uncle Jam Wants You*, *Skeletons* is a superb collection that's well worth acquiring. The CD kicks into high gear with the wildly infectious "Hey Good Lookin'" and maintains that high level of excitement on such driving, sweaty funk treasures as "Do Fries Go With That Shake?" and the appropriately titled "Intense" and the title song. Clinton's eccentricity and outrageous sense of humor serve him well on "Electric Pygmies" and "Mix-Master Suite," an unorthodox, quirky, and cinematic ode to hip-hop drawing on everything from jazz to classical music to Western movies. Many of Clinton's longtime associates are on hand to help make this album the artistic success it is, including saxman Maceo Parker, trombonist Fred Wesley, and the ever-amusing Bootsy Collins. —*Alex Henderson*

The Cinderella Theory / Aug. 1989 / Paisley Park ✦✦✦

On his first album for Prince's Paisley Park record label, George Clinton's willingness to experiment with samplers and hip-hop (including guest appearances by such artists as Chuck D and Flavor Flav of Public Enemy) resulted in a slightly inconsistent record, but it has more than enough truly fine songs to make *The Cinderella Theory* rank among his best solo albums. —*Stephen Thomas Erlewine*

Hey Man, Smell My Finger / Oct. 1993 / Paisley Park ✦✦✦✦

Hey Man, Smell My Finger is everything a great George Clinton album should be—conceptually disjointed, overlong, silly, sloppy, and funky as hell. Thankfully, the music here is his best since *Computer Games*, and the album proves just how responsible he is for much of the music of the 1990s, as the irresistible single "Paint the White House Black" illustrates with its numerous cameos. —*Stephen Thomas Erlewine*

T.A.P.O.A.F.O.M. (The Awesome Power of a Fully Operational Mothership) / Jun. 1996 / 550 Music/Epic ✦✦

Greatest Funkin' Hits / Oct. 29, 1996 / Capitol ✦✦✦

Greatest Funkin' Hits has something of a misleading title. It implies that all of George Clinton's biggest solo hits, in their original forms, are featured on this compilation. Instead, *Greatest Funkin' Hits* takes Clinton's best-known songs—not just solo hits like "Atomic Dog" and "Do Fries Go With That Shake," but also Parliament/Funkadelic songs like "Flashlight," "Mothership Connection," "Knee Deep" and "Bop Gun"—and presents them in remixed forms. Sometimes, the remixes are good—Coolio's take on "Atomic Dog" is fun, and Ice Cube's appearance on "Bop Gun (One Nation)" is terrific—but often, the remixes are perfunctory and uninspired, making the album a tedious listening experience. Most importantly, it should not be considered in any way as a greatest-hits album—it's simply another in a long line of pointless Clinton-associated remix albums. —*Leo Stanley*

Greatest Hits / May 9, 2000 / Right Stuff/Capitol ✦✦✦✦

George Clinton's solo output of the 1980s and 1990s wasn't as consistent as his work with Parliament/Funkadelic in the 1970s—nonetheless, the P-Funk innovator has had his share of inspired moments as a solo artist, and some of his best solo recordings are united on this collection. Released in 2000, *Greatest Hits* spans 1976-1986 and draws on such solo albums as *Computer Games*, *You Shouldn't-Nuf Bit Fish*, *Some of My Best Jokes Are Friends*, and *R&B Skeletons in the Closet*. The oldest recording is the bonus track, a live Parliament/Funkadelic medley of "Let's Take It to the Stage" and "Do That Stuff" from a 1976 Houston show; most of the selections, however, come from Clinton's Capitol solo albums of 1982-1986. Not surprisingly, the CD opens with "Atomic Dog," Clinton's best-known and most essential solo hit. And Right Stuff's other choices are also wise ones, including "Do Fries Go With That Shake?," "Cool Joe," "Loopzilla," "Hey Good Lookin'," and the quirky rap item "Nubian Nut." *Greatest Hits* isn't the last word on George Clinton's solo career, but if you need a concise introduction to the funkmeister's Capitol efforts of the 1980s, it's the logical place to go. —*Alex Henderson*

The Clique

f. Texas

AM Pop, Sunshine Pop, Bubblegum

The Clique had a medium hit in late 1969 with "Sugar on Sunday," a cover of a song from Tommy James' *Crimson and Clover* album, and a smaller hit with "I'll Hold Out My Hand," a song from their sole album. Emphasizing harmonies and carefully arranged light pop-rock tunes with horns, they were part of the scene that's now known as L.A. sunshine pop, except that they fell closer to bubblegum than some other acts in the genre. Like several such acts of the time, they were less a self-contained group than a vehicle for producer/songwriter Gary Zekley, who co-wrote much of their material with Mitchell Bottler and used session musicians on most of their tracks. If other such singer/producers in California at the time (like Gary Usher and Curt Boettcher) emulated the lightest aspects of The Beach Boys, then Zekley and the Clique were lighter still, sometimes sounding a little like the Monkees or bubblegum groups of the time like the Cuff Links, and at gutsier moments like Tommy James (who produced a couple of Clique cuts). As it turned out, however, the Clique are not remembered today for "Sugar on Sunday," but for its B-side,

"Superman." Out of the ordinary for the Clique in its cool paisley moodiness and forceful guitar strumming, it was covered in 1986 by R.E.M. on *Life's Rich Pageant*; their version has become far more famous than the original. The Clique's album was reissued on CD by Varese Sarabande, with bonus tracks. —*Richie Unterberger*

● **The Clique** / 1969 / Varese ◆◆◆◆◆

The Clique is a group seldom remembered today, all the more surprising because they spawned no less than four hit singles in their truncated career. Produced on various outings by pop impresario Gary Zekley (Yellow Balloon, Grass Roots) and Tommy James, their hits "Sugar On Sunday," "I'll Hold Out My Hand" and the original version of "Superman" are all aboard, along with the rest of their lone original album from 1970. This CD reissue also features six bonus tracks (including "I'm Alive," "Memphis," "Shadow of Your Love" and "Southbound Wind") that also anthologizes their two other hits that James produced, "Sparkle and Shine" and the single version of "Superman," which R.E.M. covered in 1986. —*Cub Koda*

The Clovers

f. 1946, Washington, D.C.
Doo Wop, R&B

One of the earliest doo wop vocal groups, formed in the late '40s in Washington, DC. Original members were Buddy Bailey, Matthew McQuater, Hal Lucas, and Harold Winley. Bobby Mitchell replaced Bailey by the time the group was signed to the fledgling Atlantic label in 1950. The Clovers racked up 13 Top Ten R&B hits between 1951 to 1954, all showcasing their solid harmonies and unerring rhythmic verve.

Before the early '50s, most non-gospel Black vocal groups were in the smooth pop vein of the Inkspots and Mills Brothers. Then the Clovers burst on the scene in 1951 with "Don't You Know I Love You," and things would never be the same.

Under the influence of Atlantic Records' Ahmet Ertegun (who wrote and produced most of their early songs), the Clovers combined quartet harmony, the big dance beat of the R&B jump bands, and the rawer sounds of urban blues into an exciting new blend that caught on with the young Black audience and put them consistently at the top of the R&B charts in the early '50s.

Going beyond this, just as their contemporary B.B. King was doing for blues, lead singers Buddy Bailey and later Charlie White brought a gospel influence to Ertegun's bluesy R&B songs—helping to lay the foundation for the soul music to come. —*George Bedard & Cub Koda*

☆ **Down in the Alley: The Best of the Clovers** / Oct. 1, 1991 / Rhino/Atlantic ◆◆◆◆◆

This 21-song compilation covers the six-year history of one of history's most important R&B groups at Atlantic Records. All of the Clovers' charting singles are represented (albeit not in release order), along with notes indicating their chart history. For the uninitiated, this is where rhythm & blues started as a popular phenomenon, from a group that was incredibly consistent for its six years on the label. The material is representative of rhythm & blues as it sounded at its point of origin, and at its most well-defined and powerful, an unerring jump band beat melded with elements of urban blues and superb quartet singing, all of which were a new musical phenomenon when the Clovers brought it to the charts in 1951. Moreover, one hears the basis in these early tracks for Atlantic's subsequent move into R&B vocals with the Drifters and the Coasters, the sound of these early sides highlighted by very powerful sax and electric guitar accompaniment and the stomping beat one would expect out of a roadhouse band. From "Don't You Know I Love You" through "Ting-A-Ling," "Crawlin'," "Hey, Miss Fannie," and "Lovey Dovey," right into the middle of the decade, this CD moves from one jewel-like R&B-cum-rock & roll classic to the next, and the only complaint that one could reasonably have is that there isn't a complete compilation of the Clovers' work on Atlantic, from Rhino, Collectables, or Sequel. —*Bruce Eder*

Love Potion No. 9 / the Best of the Clovers / 1991 / EMI America ◆◆◆◆◆

The Best of the Clovers—Love Potion No. 9 features their later sides for United Artists including the classic title track. —*Cub Koda*

★ **Very Best of the Clovers** / Feb. 3, 1998 / Rhino ◆◆◆◆◆

The Very Best of the Clovers is an excellent 16-track collection that features their biggest hits from 1951-1959, including "Don't You Know I Love You," "Fool, Fool, Fool," "One Mint Julep," "Ting-A-Ling," "I Played the Fool," "Hey, Miss Fannie," "Good Lovin'," "Lovey Dovey," "Little Mama," "Your Cash Ain't Nothin' But Trash," "Blue Velvet," "Devil or Angel" and "Love Potion No. 9." All of the group's best-known songs in their hit versions are available on this concise, affordable disc, which makes for an ideal introduction to this legendary R&B group. —*Stephen Thomas Erlewine*

The Coasters

f. Feb. 1956, Los Angeles, CA, db. 1972
Doo Wop, Rock & Roll, R&B

Possibly the most popular doo wop group of the '50s, the Coasters started on the West Coast as the Robins, scoring hits under the writing-and-production helm of Jerry Leiber and Mike Stoller. When Atlantic signed Leiber and Stoller as a production team, the group split into two factions; the core of the group became the Coasters and moved to New York to record, while the Robins continued on the West Coast to diminishing acclaim. The Coasters' hits, some of the most finely crafted, well written, and hilarious in the genre, continued throughout the rest of the decade. The sly leads of Carl Gardner and bass singing by Will "Dub" Jones defined their sound through numerous personnel changes. When their time on the charts came to an end a number of "Coasters" groups suddenly proliferated (much like the Drifters), many of them still dotting the landscape of a million oldies shows and still singing those classic songs. —*Cub Koda*

☆ **50 Coastin' Classics: Anthology** / Nov. 24, 1992 / Rhino ◆◆◆◆◆

Although it may well be too much for the casual fan, this double CD is easily the best Coasters retrospective ever assembled. Besides featuring every one of their hits, it also contains nine strong tunes cut in the mid-'50s by the Robins, who evolved into the Coasters after some personnel changes. As for the enticing obscurities, "Three Cool Cats" and "Besame Mucho" were cut by the Beatles on unreleased recordings in the early '60s, and "Ain't That Just like Me" would be a small hit for the Searchers. "Down in Mexico" and "Brazil" are cool R&B/Latin melodramas, and "Shoppin' for Clothes," "What About Us," and "That Is Rock & Roll" are half-forgotten vignettes of youthful independence that stack up against the best songs of Jerry Leiber and Mike Stoller, who wrote most of the group's material. Indeed, there's little difference in quality between the hits and the B-sides on this comp, either in the group's matchless ensemble R&B/comedy vocals or Leiber/Stoller's witty songwriting. The accompanying booklet features comments on most of the tracks by Leiber and Stoller themselves. —*Richie Unterberger*

★ **The Very Best of the Coasters** / 1993 / Rhino ◆◆◆◆◆

The Coasters were the 1950s' (and early rock's) dominant novelty/comic R&B ensemble, benefiting from Jerry Leiber and Mike Stoller's lyrical wit and inspired production. They weren't simply proficient clowns; the Coasters were a skilled vocal unit whose talents were utilized on slice-of-life narratives, prophetic youth manifestos, and even an occasional teen anthem, as well as the prototype humorous vehicles "Yakety Yak" and "Poison Ivy." Although Rhino has already given them the deluxe two-disc treatment, consumers who either don't want that much Coasters material or prefer only the hits are nicely served by this 18-track anthology. It contains every major release, plus valuable lesser-known selections such as "Shoppin' for Clothes" and "What About Us." —*Ron Wynn*

Eddie Cochran

b. Oct. 3, 1938, Albert Lea, Minnesota, d. Apr. 17, 1960, Wiltshire, England
Vocals, Guitar (Electric), Drums, Guitar, Bass / Rockabilly, Rock & Roll

Somehow, time has not accorded Eddie Cochran quite the same respect as other early rockabilly pioneers like Buddy Holly, or even Ricky Nelson or Gene Vincent. This is partially attributable to his very brief lifespan as a star: he only had a couple of big hits before dying in a car crash during a British tour in 1960. He was in the same league as the best rockabilly stars, though, with a brash, fat guitar sound that helped lay the groundwork for the power chord. He was also a good songwriter and singer, celebrating the joys of teenage life—the parties, the music, the adolescent rebellion—with an economic wit that bore some similarities to Chuck Berry. Cochran was more lighthearted and less ironic than Berry, though, and if his work was less consistent and not as penetrating, it was almost always exuberant. Cochran had his first Top 20 hit in early 1957, "Sittin' in the Balcony," with an echo-chambered vocal reminiscent of Elvis. That single was written by John D. Loudermilk, but Eddie would write much of his material, including his only Top Ten hit, "Summertime Blues." A definitive teenage anthem with hints of the overt protest that would seep into rock music in the 1960s, it was also a technical tour de force for the time: Cochran overdubbed himself on guitar to create an especially thick sound. That, disappointingly, was the extent of Cochran's major commercial success in the U.S. "C'mon Everybody," a chugging rocker that was almost as good as "Summertime Blues," made the Top 40 in 1959, and also gave Eddie his first British Top Tenner. —*Richie Unterberger*

Portrait of a Legend / 1985 / Rockstar ◆◆◆

Fine-looking and fine-sounding collection of unreleased stereo versions and alternate takes, this is nonetheless unnecessary for all but Cochran completists. In the spirit of numerous Beatles bootlegs (though this LP is quite official), these are in the main studio recordings with small (sometimes minute) differences in the mixing, or stereo versions which are not easy to come by on official releases, although mono versions of the exact same takes are plentiful. There are plenty of fine songs here ("Weekend," "Summertime Blues," "C'mon Everybody," "Three Steps to Heaven"), but they're better heard both in their more common versions, and in the context of a coherent anthology. And if you need to settle for just one version of "Summertime Blues" or "C'mon Everybody," why spring for the "Summertime Blues" *without* the echoed vocal, or "C'mon Everybody" *missing* a guitar overdub? —*Richie Unterberger*

The Early Years / 1988 / Ace ◆◆◆

Compilation of 16 tracks from the mid-'50s, most or all dating from before Cochran's breakthrough to national recognition with "Twenty-Flight Rock." Some were recorded when Eddie was half of the Cochran Brothers, with (the unrelated) Hank Cochran; there are also tracks credited to Jerry Capehart and Albert Stone, which Eddie most likely had a prominent role on, as session man or producer (the liner notes are resolutely unhelpful on providing exact details). Most of this is pretty solid rockabilly, not much below the standards of Cochran's best releases. There are also a couple of hot instrumentals, and ballad-type numbers on which Eddie employs a husky, echoed Elvisoid delivery. A decent release, but assembled in a scattershot fashion. Also, if you're interested enough in Cochran to want to track this down, you may well also be interested enough in him to spring for a box set, and most or all of these are also contained on whatever box set you manage to locate. —*Richie Unterberger*

Box Set / 1988 / Liberty ◆◆◆

This six-LP import—which still, somehow, manages to not include every track Cochran recorded—is excessive for the non-fanatic. Nevertheless, it does include quite a few obscure, interesting pre-fame performances from the mid-'50s (some as part of the Cochran Brothers). Other bonuses include a live 1960 British TV broadcast, an album's worth of sessions and his work as a producer, and entire sides of instrumentals and stereo versions, as well as a 32-page booklet. *—Richie Unterberger*

Legendary Masters / Jan. 29, 1990 / EMI America ✦✦✦✦✦
EMI did a bit of adjusting to their excellent 1971 Eddie Cochran collection for CD release in 1990, and that wasn't necessarily a bad idea—losing a few of the lesser tracks on that slightly overstuffed two-LP set wouldn't have hurt the disc in the least. While that album's most obvious filler got the axe, so did a few obscurities that added a lot of flavor to a superb collection (especially Cochran's early country-influenced material), and adding "Drive-In Show" and "Three Steps To Heaven" hardly make up for deleting the guitar showcase "Eddie's Blues" or the Everly Brothers-style pop tune "Opportunity." And shame on whoever decided to scrap Lenny Kaye's brilliant liner notes from the LP edition! But if you want most of Eddie Cochran's best stuff on one disc, this set more than fits the bill, and the truth is if you hadn't heard the earlier version of this compilation, you'd never know what you were missing. The *Legendary Masters* CD is all choice cuts and no filler, and a fine introduction from one of the finest artists of the first rock & roll era—if you don't know Eddie's music, this will get you started right, and if you know and love his work, you'll find this disc a joy from start to finish—it's as good a cure for the "Summertime Blues" as you'll ever find. *—Mark Deming*

Singin' to My Baby/Never To Be / Feb. 23, 1993 / Capitol ✦✦✦✦✦
Two original albums on one compact disc, with only two hits between the two—"Sittin' in the Balcony" and "Twenty Flight Rock." But for devoted fans of Eddie Cochran, this lovingly packaged CD is worth their time, even if some of the material is slightly weak. *Singin' to My Baby* concentrates on ballad material; the posthumously released *Never To Be Forgotten* has more rockers. *—Stephen Thomas Erlewine*

★ **Somethin' Else: The Fine Lookin' Hits of Eddie Cochran** / Feb. 24, 1998 / Razor & Tie ✦✦✦✦✦
Eddie Cochran hasn't been unaccounted for in the reissue sweepstakes since the rockabilly revival of the late 1970s/early '80s—quite the contrary. His greatest hits have been around the block a few times, and his voluminous amount of session work has all resurfaced on myriads of foreign collector labels. This 1998 best-of on Razor & Tie duplicates 15 of the 20 tracks on EMI's *Legendary Masters Series* compilation from 1990. Hits *are* hits, after all, and Cochran's best is hardly open to debate. What distinguishes this package is the inclusion of "Tired and Sleepy" from the Cochran Brothers, an early swipe at "Long Tall Sally," the instrumental "Guybo," "Cherished Memories" and the almost pop-folk "Boll Weevil." Great liner notes from Colin Escott and top-flight sound also make this disc highly recommended. If you're looking to start your Eddie Cochran collection, this makes an excellent first purchase. *—Cub Koda*

Bruce Cockburn

b. May 27, 1945, Pembroke, Ontario, Canada
Vocals, Guitar, Dulcimer / Contemporary Folk, Singer/Songwriter
Immensely popular in his native Canada, singer/songwriter Bruce Cockburn has found only cult success south of the border, in spite of a rich, varied body of work and considerable critical nods. He has won numerous Juno Awards and has kept the quality control on most of his albums at a high level. Cockburn's first decade of work (1970-1979) is largely literate, singer/songwriter folk-rock, often with a strong Christian tone and mystical, devotional lyrics. In 1979, Cockburn had his only major U.S. single, "Wondering Where the Lions Are," which peaked at number 21. The accompanying album, *Dancing in the Dragon's Jaw*, saw him augmenting his music with worldbeat rhythms, an approach he would continue over his next few albums. Cockburn toned down his Christian viewpoint for much of the 1980s, partially as a way of disconnecting himself from the American religious right, which he found antithetical to his own spiritual beliefs, and partially to concentrate on more humanitarian, political subject matter. In 1984 Cockburn produced an AOR hit, "If I Had a Rocket Launcher," whose accompanying video depicted conditions in war-torn Central America and gained a fair amount of MTV play. Cockburn's later 1980s work took on a more streamlined rock sound, and his political agenda was weighted towards environmental concerns, as well as oppression. In the 1990s, Cockburn has returned to a more introspective feel recalling his earlier work. *—Steve Huey*

Bruce Cockburn / 1970 / Columbia ✦✦

High Winds White Sky / 1971 / Columbia ✦✦

Sunwheel Dance / 1972 / Columbia ✦✦

Night Vision / 1973 / Columbia ✦✦

Salt, Sun and Time / 1974 / Columbia ✦✦✦
After coming across with a band, Bruce Cockburn pulled back and came up with an album that recalls his first release. That's not to say that the sound is folky, it's not. There's a much more complex feel to what's here, especially the instrumental title track which shows a strong John Martyn influence. And while the songs are complex in texture and feel, they aren't hard to get into. In fact, this album grows on you the more you play it. Truly something that has endured. *—James Chrispell*

Joy Will Find a Way / 1975 / Columbia ✦✦✦
Though it will appeal to the converted, *Joy Will Find a Way*, Bruce Cockburn's sixth album, won't do much to garner support outside of these circles. As always, Cockburn is never less than literate, and his guitar is consistently impressive throughout (check out the instrumental "Skylarking"), but there remains the tendency to become overwrought lyrically, as well as to get bogged down musically in the sort of folkish repetition that can be more tiresome than entrancing. Still, like his previous efforts, *Joy Will Find a Way* contains the usual handful of scattered gems that keep the faithful coming back. His songwriting and acoustic guitar are once again at the center of economical, tasteful production, which, though grounded in folk, suggest touches of jazz, pop, and world music—all of which are reflected in the feel of much of the material. Songs such as "A Long-Time-Love Song" and "January in the Halifax Airport Lounge," with its jazz-inflected electric piano, are warm and charming meditations on love, while "Joy Will Find a Way (A Song About Dying)" is built around a hypnotic, Indonesian-inspired arrangement, and "Burn" (the only real social statement here) is a moderately effective indictment of U.S. foreign policy, wrapped in island-flavored, folk-pop. Though he hadn't quite hit his stride at this point, this is the best of Bruce Cockburn's first half-dozen albums. *—Brett Hartenbach*

In the Falling Dark / 1976 / Columbia ✦✦✦✦
With every album he released during the first half of the '70s, Bruce Cockburn continued to evolve and show signs of greatness, and with his seventh, *In the Falling Dark*, he makes good on these promises. As a whole, this record trumps anything that its predecessors had to offer, almost to the point where it's difficult to imagine that it followed the release of *Joy Will Find a Way* by only a year. The sound that was merely suggested on his previous recordings is fully realized here: check out the flute and trumpet interplay on the jazz inflected instrumental "Giftbearer," the hypnotic "I'm Gonna Fly Someday" with its irresistible flute, horn, and voice line, and Fred Stone's flügelhorn on "Silver Wheels." Furthermore, the songwriting is without a doubt his most consistent; "Lord of the Starfields" and the evocative title track are the pinnacle of his Christian mysticism, whereas the aforementioned "Silver Wheels" is one of his keenest social observations to date. There's still the occasional slide into the sort of hippie-ish sentiments that have plagued his recordings from time to time, but even at its most mawkish, there's a sweetness and warmth to the material. His first U.S. release since 1972, *In the Falling Dark* may not have made Bruce Cockburn a household name, but it did mark his emergence as an important artist. *—Brett Hartenbach*

Circles in the Stream / 1977 / True North ✦✦✦
Released shortly after the transitional *In the Falling Dark*, *Circles in the Stream* seemed to serve as the final chapter in Bruce Cockburn's promising, yet inconsistent early career. Recorded live in Toronto, the record brings together some of Cockburn's best songs from this period, including the beautiful meditation "All the Diamonds in the World," the bluesy "Mama Just Wants to Barrelhouse All Night Long," and "Lord of the Starfields" from his previous release. And while there isn't anything drastically different here, many of the tracks are more assured and fully realized than their studio counterparts, with Cockburn's guitar and voice front and center—solo or backed by subtle bass, percussion, and piano or marimba. There are also a scattering of new tunes that mix nicely with the older material, with the Native American tribute "Red Brother, Red Sister" and the instrumental "Deer Dancing Round a Broken Mirror" the true standouts. Strong performances and a good selection of songs help *Circles in the Stream* succeed not only as a good live album, but also as a decent retrospective of Cockburn's first seven years. *—Brett Hartenbach*

Further Adventures of Bruce Cockburn / 1978 / True North ✦✦✦
Further Adventures Of, though it may contain Bruce Cockburn's usual mix of beautifully intricate acoustic work and pastoral mysticism, along with the occasional touches of anger and irony, continues the growth that was so evident on his last studio outing *In the Falling Dark*. And while it may lack anything quite as powerful as "Lord of the Starfields" or the title song from that record, the use of his electric guitar, which is at the forefront on a couple of tracks, brings a bit more of an edge to the proceedings. Lyrically, his odes to God and nature can still at times be as soft as his social relevance can be heavy-handed, but cuts such as the joyful "Rainfall," the bilingual "Pernons La Mer," and the Eastern meditation "Nanzen Ji" get by on their sheer beauty, while "A Montreal Song" and the pensive "Outside a Broken Phone Booth With Money in My Hand" are sharp and effective. The latter, with its lyrical urgency and effected electric guitar, shows a toughness in his songwriting, as well as the direction of his sound, both of which would become even more prevalent in the coming years. Like much of Cockburn's earlier output, *Further Adventures Of*, though not a major work in his catalog, shows flashes of brilliance among some fairly ordinary material that's distinguished only by his excellent guitar. Beyond this, it serves as another steppingstone to what would be the most impressive period of his career—including the gorgeous *Dancing in the Dragon's Jaws* (1979) and his stunning work of the early '80s—and is worth a listen. *—Brett Hartenbach*

Dancing in the Dragon's Jaws / 1979 / Columbia ✦✦✦✦
After nearly a decade spent in relative obscurity outside of his native Canada, Bruce Cockburn finally made a dent in the US market with the Top 40 hit "Wondering Where the Lions Are" from 1979's *Dancing in the Dragon's Jaws*. The album continues the jazz-inflected folk he had been pursuing on his past several releases, but with a heavier emphasis on the worldbeat rhythms that would play a larger part in his music in the years to come. This album is the gentler side of Bruce Cockburn, beautiful and searching, with his acoustic guitar once again at the forefront; his intricate, yet melodic patterns the perfect backdrop for his poetic ruminations on spirituality and nature. From the opener, "Creation Dream," his vision of the Earth's genesis to the meditative "No Footprints" Cockburn is overcome by the wonderment of God's work. Even amidst the "concrete vortex" and "people looking ill-at-ease," there's a sense of peace and overwhelming faith that runs throughout. Only "Incandescent Blue" (coincidentally the only song written outside of Canada) exhibits the kind of urban tension and consciousness that would become so evident in his work throughout the next decade; although he still finds a sort of respite in the chorus with its "white birds… [soaring] away free." *Dancing in the Dragon's Jaws*, though it can't match the sheer power of his next few releases, may be his most beautiful record, as well as an excellent culmination of his '70s work. *—Brett Hartenbach*

● **Humans** / Nov. 1980 / Columbia ✦✦✦✦✦
Bruce Cockburn asks, "You see the extremes, of what humans can be?" in "Rumours of

Glory," which works as an excellent summation of *Humans*, his 11th album. Between the opener "Grim Travellers" and the beautifully contemplative final track "The Rose Above the Sky," he examines these "extremes" not only in others, but also in himself. Along the way, Cockburn attempts to make sense of his own spirituality and faith in a world of imperialism, greed, urban violence, and even his own divorce. However, he questions himself as thoroughly as he does the world around him. Although he'd often touched on social issues in the past, he'd never dealt with them quite so acutely, or on such a grand scale as he does here. Cockburn also seemed to understand that the U.S. Top 40 success of "Wondering Where the Lions Are" from the previous year, though a pleasant surprise, was somewhat of a fluke, and continued to progress without necessarily trying to duplicate the feat. There's a toughness here, both musically and lyrically, at which he had merely hinted before. More than any of his prior releases, *Humans* is able to convey, not only the love and mercy of his Christian beliefs, but also the anger and frustration of trying to live in a world of "gutless arrogance and rage…" where people are treated as if they were "…so many cattle." In the late '70s, Cockburn's music began to change and grow to a great degree, and with *Humans* it reaches fruition and remains one of the most important recordings in his extensive catalog. —*Brett Hartenbach*

Inner City Front / 1981 / Columbia ✦✦✦✦
Inner City Front continues the urban toughness that moved to the forefront on Bruce Cockburn's previous release, *Humans*. Furthermore, like that record, there's an uneasiness that runs throughout, from the jazz-tinged opener, "You Pay Your Money and You Take Your Chance," to the disquieting "Loner," which closes the album. Even a love song like "Wanna Go Walking," one of the most straightforward rockers he's ever recorded, reflects the weight of the outside world. Only the jazzy instrumental "Radio Shoes" and the joyful "And We Dance" remain free of this underlying tension. Musically, moody synths, violin, and woodwinds on *Inner City Front* underscore the dark, reflective nature of the material, which like its predecessor, deals with the "paradox and contrast" in the human condition, from personal relationships to world affairs. Also, for the second consecutive recording, Cockburn eschews the folkier, acoustic leanings of his '70s work and places both feet squarely into the jazz and worldbeat rock that dominated the majority of *Humans*. One track, "The Strong One," is even given a slow, brooding, techno treatment. Since the release of *In the Falling Dark*, Cockburn was gaining creative momentum with each release, and *Inner City Front* continues that trend. —*Brett Hartenbach*

The Trouble with Normal / 1983 / Columbia ✦✦✦✦
Like his two previous efforts in the '80s, *The Trouble With Normal* places Bruce Cockburn yet another step further from his days as Canada's resident mystic folky. And while he had touched on similar musical themes on earlier recordings, the eclectic blend of folk, rock, and world music here is much more defined and realized. The use of synths, electric guitar, violin, and Chapman Stick, along with the occasional keyboard and drum sequences, complement the weighty, ominous nature of his lyrical concerns, which seem to paint a picture of a world, though teetering on the edge, still filled with beauty ("Hoop Dancer"), hope ("Put Our Hearts Together"), and contentment ("Waiting for the Moon to Show"). Amidst the "chaos" and "fashionable fascism," Cockburn's message, though cloaked in frustration and cynicism, and not nearly as overt as it has been in the past, is still one of faith and love. There is the tendency to get heavy-handed at times, but still, *The Trouble With Normal* contains some of Cockburn's most beautifully imagistic writing to date and is another strong effort. The U.S. release contains an alternate, yet inferior take of the title track, which makes the Canadian (True North) version preferable. —*Brett Hartenbach*

Stealing Fire / 1984 / Columbia ✦✦✦✦✦
After visiting Central America, Bruce Cockburn recorded *Stealing Fire*, part of which passionately and eloquently details what he'd seen while in Nicaragua and Guatemala. With the opening track, the terse rocker "Lovers in a Dangerous Time," Cockburn conveys both a sense of urgency and uncertainty. There's a brief calm as the second half begins, before a triad of songs written about his time spent in Central America brings the record to a sober conclusion. These three tunes, which, like the majority of the album, sport a tight, worldbeat, folk and rock flavor, are the true highlights of *Stealing Fire*, and Cockburn at his very best. The first, "Nicaragua," is part observation, part commentary, and part tribute to the Sandinista-led revolution in that country. "If I Had a Rocket Launcher" follows, and is arguably Cockburn's most powerful merging of personal and political feelings. Written after witnessing Guatemalan refugees being chased across the border by gun-wielding helicopters, "Rocket Launcher" evokes not only the pain and suffering of the people, but the conflict between Cockburn's pacifist leanings, and the vengeful anger and hatred incited by such a horrific sight. The Nicaraguan, road-inspired "Dust and Diesel" closes the record with a portrait of a country whose daily contrast of beauty and violence is summed up by the images of people who are proud, hopeful, passionate, afraid, and tired. *Stealing Fire*, despite a few less than compelling tracks, is the work of an artist at his peak. It also contains some of the most intensely significant material by a singer/songwriter in the 1980s. —*Brett Hartenbach*

World of Wonders / 1986 / Columbia ✦✦✦
It's doubtful that there are many major-label performers who share Bruce Cockburn's knowledge of global politics and events, and few, if any, have the ability and/or conviction to convey it so eloquently over the majority of an album. The aptly titled *World of Wonders*, his 14th studio release, does just that, expanding the worldview of its predecessor *Stealing Fire*. Whereas that record's best moments centered around his time in Central America, *World of Wonders* takes you across the globe, through Berlin, Chile, parts of the Caribbean, and North America. Along the way, Cockburn, who has always been intrigued by life's contradictions, is both "dazzled…at this world of wonders" and troubled, "…when life isn't so sweet." Musically and lyrically, though, he's always been

known for his serious bent; Cockburn can be as warm and inviting as he can be haunting or ominous. But while there are moments that will appeal to even the unconverted, there are times when the casual listener may feel a bit overwhelmed by his intense poetry or put off by the overt political leanings of much of the album. Still, how many artists could write a song decrying the evils of the International Monetary Fund ("Call It Democracy"), complete with expletive, and make it spirited enough to be released as a single, or pen a love song ("See How I Miss You") that contains references to "secret police" and reading a "psychopath's" magazine? Bruce Cockburn is a complex artist writing about complex times, and *World of Wonders* does a good job of capturing that. —*Brett Hartenbach*

Rumours of Glory / 1986 / Plane ✦✦✦
One of three Bruce Cockburn "best of" collections released in the 1980s—including *Resume* (1981) and *Waiting for a Miracle (Singles 1970-1987)* (1987)—*Rumours of Glory* concentrates primarily on his work of the late '70s and early '80s. There's some definite overlap in the track selections of the three, though one cut, "Yanqui Go Home" (presumably added as an enticement to fans), is only available here. Although it stops short of the excellent *Stealing Fire* (1984), only including material through 1983's *The Trouble With Normal*, *Rumours of Glory* still draws from the bulk of what is easily the best period of Cockburn's career. It also does a nice job of highlighting the various sides of Bruce Cockburn, from political ("Trouble With Normal," "Grim Travellers") to personal ("Wanna Go Walking," "Coldest Night of the Year") to mystical ("Lord of the Starfields," "Rumours of Glory"), as well as showing him equally at home with folk, rock, or world-influenced music. Though hardly comprehensive, *Rumours of Glory* is a good, single-disc assemblage of 14 tunes from an artist working at the top of his game. —*Brett Hartenbach*

● **Waiting for a Miracle (Singles 1970-1987)** / Jan. 1987 / Gold Castle ✦✦✦✦
Waiting for a Miracle, with two discs spanning 17 years and 22 songs, is the third and by far most comprehensive of three Bruce Cockburn retrospectives released in a six-year period. Still, because it's centered around his Canadian singles, it lacks the sort of impact a best-of collection should have from someone such as Cockburn, who could never be mistaken for a "singles" artist. On the other hand, if you're looking for an overview of his career, *Waiting for a Miracle*, which also has a sprinkling of new songs and alternate takes to lure fans, isn't a bad place to start. The chronological order of the tracks makes it easy to see the progression of his career, from mystic folky, to outspoken, left-wing, worldbeat rocker. It also shows Cockburn's growth as both a writer and performer, although the choices included here from his early records are good ones. *Waiting for a Miracle* may not be a perfect representation of Cockburn's work, but until something better comes along, it will have to do. —*Brett Hartenbach*

Big Circumstance / 1989 / Columbia ✦✦✦
This was Cockburn's first release of new material in three years. It was a move away from the somewhat dated, overblown sound of his previous *World of Wonders*, toward a leaner, more guitar-dominated sound. Budgeting for album art seemed to be a little low, but luckily the collection of songs was of consistent high quality. As with most Cockburn albums, this is a mix of socially conscious, spiritual, and reflective songs. Cockburn had spent time in Nepal in 1987 and what he saw there found its way into some songs, including "Tibetan Side of Town" and "Understanding Nothing." Time spent in Germany soon after the Chernobyl nuclear disaster in the Soviet Union inspired "Radium Rain," while deforestation of the globe inspired "If a Tree Falls," the first single from the album. Cockburn is equally at home writing about matters of the heart, though his lyrics take a much more unconventional turn in "Don't Feel Your Touch," with lines such as "the night grows sharp and hollow as a junkie's craving vein" and "the night grows clear and empty as a lake of acid rain." Elsewhere on the album, in "Gospel of Bondage" he takes pains to differentiate himself from right-wing Christianity and express his different view of the faith. Unusually for Cockburn, he ends the album on a slightly humorous (albeit dark humor) note with "Anything Can Happen," a look at the temporariness of life, where "anything can happen" at any time "to put out the light." —*Rob Caldwell*

Live / Jun. 1990 / Gold Castle ✦✦✦✦
Recorded in Toronto in the summer of 1989, *Live* is a good collection of Bruce Cockburn's music, presented in a stripped-down setting. Fronting a tight three-piece unit, which sounds bigger thanks to Fergus Marsh's stick, Michael Sloski's eloquent drumming and his own fingerstyle guitar work, Cockburn delivers a nice overview of his career, dating back as far as the record's opener "Silver Wheels" from 1976. Amidst his usual elements of spirituality and state-of-the-world messages, there's also a lightness and even a sense of humor that is rarely, if ever, seen in his studio work. His choice to close with "Always Look on the Bright Side of Life" from the crucifixion scene in Monty Python's *Life of Brian* is both funny and inspired, while "Rumours of Glory," with it's playful harmonica, gains a joyful bounce, and his lone Top 40 U.S. hit "Wondering Where the Lions Are" becomes a crowd-pleasing singalong. Elsewhere Cockburn gives a new look to old tunes, whether it's solo performances of "After the Rain" and "Call It Democracy," the stark power of the bodhran, vocal rendition of "Stolen Land," or the more palatable, jumping blues treatment of "Maybe the Poet." Even though there are no songs, with the exception of "Always Look on the Bright Side of Life," that are not available elsewhere, there's enough personality in these live versions to recommend the record on its own merit, and not just as a souvenir of a successful tour. —*Brett Hartenbach*

Nothing but a Burning Light / Nov. 5, 1991 / Columbia ✦✦✦
Nothing but a Burning Light, Bruce Cockburn's first release for Columbia, teams him with producer T-Bone Burnett, whose singer/songwriter background and spiritual leanings, seemed to be a perfect match. Throughout, Burnett's production is understated, allowing Cockburn's voice, guitar, and songs to lead the way over a solid foundation of bass, drums, and tasteful organ by Booker T. Jones. This sort of sympathetic production brings

out the best in Cockburn and his material, which is consistently strong. Songs such as "Kit Carson," "Mighty Trucks of Midnight," and "Indian Wars" continue the weightier concerns of his work of the past decade, but the majority of the record takes on a more personal, introspective tone. "One of the Best Ones" and "Great Big Love" are winning affirmations of love and life, while the retelling of the nativity, "Cry of a Tiny Babe," is as beautiful and moving a contemporary Christmas song as you're likely to hear. Cockburn also decides to include a rare cover, his excellent reading of the Blind Willie Johnson gospel-blues "Soul of a Man," which fits nicely in the whole of the album. Though it may lack the immediate power, *Nothing but a Burning Light* is Bruce Cockburn's best since his 1984 release *Stealing Fire*. Jackson Browne and Sam Phillips guest on backing vocals. *—Brett Hartenbach*

Dart to the Heart / Mar. 1, 1994 / Columbia ✦✦✦
Even more than its predecessor, the aptly titled *Dart to the Heart* eschews the heavier, more political tendencies that had become synonymous with Bruce Cockburn's music for more than a decade, returning to a more personal, introspective side. The opening track, "Listen for the Laugh," a horn-driven rocker that wouldn't have been out of place on many of his recordings during the '80s, and the almost joyful finality of "Tie Me at the Crossroads," bookend what is primarily more subdued material, including the tender second track, "All the Ways I Want You," which more suitably sets the tone for the album. And though it may not possess the intensity or power of his early-'80s output, *Dart to the Heart* comes with nearly a quarter century of experience behind it, bringing an insight, depth, and maturity to Cockburn's ventures into love and the mystic. Still, there's just enough outrage and frustration to keep things interesting. Musically, T-Bone Burnett's sympathetic production tastefully and engagingly frames the songs, placing Cockburn's vocals and characteristically superb guitar at center stage. Those who may have found his overtly political, worldbeat and jazz-inflected rock a bit strident in the past should find his approach here more inviting. And while he may have revisited this familiar ground from time to time throughout his career, *Dart to the Heart* is a convincing reminder of a gentler, more reflective Bruce Cockburn. *—Brett Hartenbach*

The Charity of Night / Feb. 4, 1997 / Rykodisc ✦✦

Breakfast in New Orleans Dinner in Timbuktu / Sep. 14, 1999 / Rykodisc ✦✦✦
Breakfast in New Orleans Dinner in Timbuktu is Bruce Cockburn's 20th studio album. Lyrically, Cockburn doesn't stray from the impressionist poetic lyrics that he's honed over the years, nor does he stray from his favored topics: travelogs, including those drawn from his trips to Third World nations that emphasize his social concerns; reflections on the dynamics of relationships between men and women; and a spiritual mysticism rooted in Christianity. Musically, too, there's a consistency to his folk-jazz-rock amalgam. The album features the vocal contributions of a rotating cast of three women who appear throughout the album. Jonell Mosser sings on two songs, including the single "Last Night of the World." Margo Timmins of Cowboy Junkies lends her breathy pipes to two songs: the sultry "Mango" and a cover of the Fats Domino nugget "Blueberry Hill" that turns up the "rock" and de-emphasizes the "roll." Most important, Lucinda Williams appears on four tracks. The standout track on the album is "Isn't That What Friends Are For." This tender song of friendship is made more poignant by Williams' voice, which always manages to convey a deep sense of hurt. While the lyrics are sure to be enjoyed by those who are willing to listen and think, fans of Cockburn's guitar playing won't be disappointed, either.

There are two instrumental pieces, both band efforts, which feature Cockburn's acoustic guitar. "Down to the Delta" is an up-tempo tune, while "Deep Lake" is a quiet, more reflective piece that is close to the impressionistic style of Michael Hedges—except, of course, that Cockburn has been playing this sort of thing since 1971's *High Winds White Sky*. *—Martin Monkman*

Joe Cocker

b. May 20, 1944, Sheffield, Yorkshire, England
Vocals / Pop/Rock, Soft Rock, Adult Contemporary, Blues-Rock

After starting out as an unsuccessful pop singer, Joe Cocker found his niche singing rock and soul in the pubs of England with his superb backing group, the Grease Band. He hit #1 in the UK in November 1968 with his version of the Beatles' "A Little Help from My Friends." His career really took off after he sang that song at the Woodstock festival in August 1969. A second British hit came with a version of Leon Russell's "Delta Lady" in the fall of 1969 (by then, Russell was Cocker's musical director) and both of his albums, *With a Little Help from My Friends* and *Joe Cocker!*, went gold in America. In 1970, his cover of the Box Tops' hit "The Letter" became his first US Top Ten. Cocker's first peak of success came when Russell organized the "Mad Dogs & Englishmen" tour of 1970, featuring Cocker and over 40 others, and resulting in a third gold album and a concert film. Subsequent efforts were less popular, and problems with alcohol (both on stage and off) reduced Cocker's once-powerful voice to a croaking rasp. But he returned to the US Top Ten with the romantic ballad "You Are So Beautiful" in 1975 and topped the charts in a duet with Jennifer Warnes on "Up Where We Belong," the theme from the 1982 film *An Officer and a Gentleman*. He has survived, still charting into the '90s, albeit with less frequency than he did in the '70s and '80s. *—Cub Koda & William Ruhlmann*

With a Little Help from My Friends / Apr. 1969 / A&M ✦✦✦✦✦
The album that foisted Joe Cocker on an unsuspecting public is full of tasteful, raucous covers, Cocker's trademark hysterical vocals, and outstanding studio backing by pros like Jimmy Page and Steve Winwood. *—Tom Graves*

Joe Cocker / Oct. 1969 / A&M ✦✦✦✦
Joe Cocker's first three A&M albums form the bedrock of a career that spans over three decades. While Cocker certainly wasn't always in top form during this stretch—thanks in no small part to

alcohol problems and questionable comeback moves in the '80s and '90s—his early records did inform the classic pub rock sound later credited to proto-punk figures like Graham Parker and Brinsley Schwarz. On those early records, Cocker mixed elements of late-'60s English blues revival recordings (John Mayall, et al.) with the more contemporary sounds of soul and pop; a sound fused in no small part by producer and arranger Leon Russell, whose gumbo mix figures prominently on this eponymous release and the infamous *Mad Dogs & Englishmen* live set. Russell's sophisticated swamp blues aesthetic is felt directly with versions of his gospel ballad "Hello, Little Friend" and Beatles-inspired bit of New Orleans pop—and one of Cocker's biggest hits—"Delta Lady." Following up on the huge success of an earlier cover of "With a Little Help From My Friends," Cocker mines more Beatles gold with very respectable renditions of "She Came in Through the Bathroom Window" and "Something." And rounding out this impressive set are equally astute takes on Dylan's "Dear Landlord," Leonard Cohen's "Bird on the Wire," and John Sebastian's "Darling Be Home Soon." Throughout, Cocker gets superb support from his regular backing group of the time, the Grease Band. A fine introduction to the singer's classic, late-'60s and early-'70s period. *—Stephen Cook*

Mad Dogs & Englishmen / Aug. 1970 / A&M ✦✦✦✦✦
A superb document of Cocker's high-energy 1970 tour, it included about a zillion musicians and hangers-on. All the goods are here, and many consider this Cocker's last great moment. *—Tom Graves*

I Can Stand a Little Rain / Aug. 1974 / A&M ✦✦✦
With *I Can Stand a Little Rain*, Joe Cocker returned to interpreting songs instead of essaying his original songs. As usual, there are a couple of highlights, but a couple of awkward choices prevent the album from being as effective as *Joe Cocker!* or *Mad Dogs & Englishmen*. *—Stephen Thomas Erlewine*

Jamaica Say You Will / Aug. 1975 / A&M ✦✦

Stingray / Apr. 1976 / A&M ✦✦✦
Recorded in Jamaica, *Stingray* was an attempt to meld Joe's raspy vocals with reggae music. It was an experiment which had mixed results. Using crack New York session men instead of Jamaicans somewhat defeated the purpose, but did work well in off-setting the reggaefied tunes. Joe turns in a fine vocal performance throughout and shines on such covers as "A Song For You" and Bob Dylan's "The Man In Me." *Stingray* is full of gems worth seeking out. *—James Chrispell*

Luxury You Can Afford / Aug. 1978 / A&M ✦✦✦

Space Captain / 1982 / Cube ✦✦✦

Sheffield Steel / Jun. 1982 / Island ✦✦✦

Civilized Man / May 1984 / Capitol ✦✦

Unchain My Heart / Oct. 1987 / Capitol ✦✦

One Night of Sin / Aug. 1989 / Capitol ✦✦

Live! / May 1990 / Capitol ✦✦✦

Night Calls / Jul. 6, 1992 / Capitol ✦✦✦
Cocker's rep has always been as a superb interpreter of other people's material. For *Night Calls*, the Sheffield native peaks with the opening track—a memory-engraving rendition of the Bryan Adams/Diane Warren-penned "Feels Like Forever." It's the higher profile songs that ultimately develop on *Night Calls*. Cocker eventually works up a lather toward the end of "You've Got to Hide Your Love Away," but it never reaches the standard of other Beatles classics in his repertoire ("With a Little Help from My Friends," "She Came in Through the Bathroom Window"). The biggest let-down is the lack of commitment projected on Elton John's "Don't Let the Sun Go Down On Me." Still, even slumming Cocker sounds more real and soulful than, say, Michael Bolton in his wildest dreams. *—Roch Parisien*

The Best of Joe Cocker / Mar. 16, 1993 / Capitol ✦✦✦✦✦
Although his Capitol material wasn't as consistent as his A&M work, this compilation successfully distills the highlights, including the splendid "When the Night Comes," onto a single CD. *—Stephen Thomas Erlewine*

Have a Little Faith / Sep. 8, 1994 / 550 Music/Epic ✦✦✦

Long Voyage Home / Nov. 21, 1995 / A&M ✦✦✦✦✦
Long Voyage Home: The Silver Anniversary Collection is nearly the definitive Joe Cocker anthology, covering his recording career from the late '60s to the mid-'90s, featuring material from all the labels he recorded for—A&M, Elektra, Island, and Capitol. After an early single from 1964 (a version of the Beatles' "I'll Cry Instead"), the set skips ahead to his late-'60s recordings with his Mad Dogs & Englishmen troupe. From there, the collection doesn't miss many of Cocker's greatest hits or favorite album tracks. In addition to the familiar tracks, there are a handful of unreleased cuts that are tantalizing for the collector; casual fans will find them of marginal interest. *—Stephen Thomas Erlewine*

● **The Anthology** / Aug. 17, 1999 / A&M ✦✦✦✦✦
A&M's double-disc *Anthology* may be too much for casual fans that just want the hits, but anyone else will find this exhaustive 37-track chronicle of Joe Cocker's prime years definitive. The first disc concentrates on his first three albums, buttressed by a rare 1964 single of the Beatles' "I'll Cry Instead" and his 1970 non-LP single "The Letter"/"Space Captain." Disc two features highlights of all the albums he recorded between 1972 and 1982, selecting not only hits, but key album tracks. The end result is a collection that is concise and definitive. It may be missing such latter day hits as "When the Night Comes" and doesn't cover as much ground as the box set *Long Voyage Home*, but anyone looking for a comprehensive collection of Cocker's classic recordings will be satisfied by *Anthology*. *—Stephen Thomas Erlewine*

Super Hits / Feb. 15, 2000 / 550/Legacy ✦✦✦

Joe Cocker didn't have any hits while he was recording for Sony's 550 Music, so it's a little disingenuous to call this ten-track collection *Super Hits*. Technically, there's only one hit here, "You Are So Beautiful," and that wasn't cut for 550 in the '90s—it was released on A&M in 1975. Similarly, the other song here that's even close to a hit is a cover of Randy Newman's "You Can Leave Your Hat On," which never charted—it just became a popular strip-club favorite after its appearance in *9 1/2 Weeks*. So, what does that make *Super Hits*? Actually, something that's not that bad: Neglected as they were, the 550 recordings were well produced and as entertaining as anything he made in the late '80s. But they probably won't appeal to casual fans (who are most likely to pick up a budget-line collection like this), and hardcore fans will want to stick with *Have a Little Faith* and *Organic*, the two records he released on 550. —*Stephen Thomas Erlewine*

20th Century Masters—The Millennium Collection: The Best of Joe Cocker / Jun. 6, 2000 / A&M ✦✦✦

Another one-stop shop from Universal's *20th Century Masters Millennium Collection*, here's all the Joe Cocker you need in one packed-with-hits single-disc collection. Kicking off with "Feelin' Alright," "With a Little Help From My Friends," and "Delta Lady," the set also includes his later hits like "You Are So Beautiful" and his duet with Jennifer Warnes, "Up Where We Belong." This may only clock in at 11 tracks, but it's a very potent little package and highly recommended as the perfect starter set. —*Cub Koda*

Cocteau Twins

f. 1979, Grangemouth, Scotland, **db.** 1997
Ambient Pop, Dream Pop, Post-Punk, Alternative Pop/Rock
A group whose distinctly ethereal and gossamer sound virtually defined the enigmatic image of their record label 4AD, the Cocteau Twins were originally formed by guitarist Robin Guthrie and bassist Will Heggie and later rounded out by Guthrie's girlfriend Elizabeth Fraser, an utterly unique performer whose swooping, operatic vocals relied less on any recognizable language than on the subjective sounds and textures of verbalized emotions. In 1982, the trio signed to 4AD and debuted with *Garlands*, which offered an embryonic taste of their rapidly-developing, atmospheric sound, crafted around Guthrie's creative use of distorted guitars, tape loops and echo boxes and anchored in Heggie's rhythmic bass as well as an omnipresent Roland 808 drum machine. Shortly after the release of the *Peppermint Pig* EP, Heggie left the group, and Guthrie and Fraser cut 1983's *Head Over Heels* as a duo; nonetheless, the album largely perfected the Cocteaus' gauzy formula, and established the foundation from which the group would continue to work for the duration of its career. In late 1983, bassist Simon Raymonde joined the band to record the EP *The Spangle Maker*. After 1990's *Heaven or Las Vegas*, the Cocteaus severed their long-standing relationship with 4AD; notably, the album also found Fraser's vocals offering the occasional comprehensible turn of phrase, a trend continued on 1993's *Four-Calendar Cafe*. —*Jason Ankeny*

Garlands / Jun. 1982 / 4AD ✦✦

Head Over Heels / Aug. 1983 / 4AD ✦✦✦✦✦

Losing original member Heggie might at first have seemed a troubling blow, but in fact it allowed the duo of Fraser and Guthrie to transcend the darkened one-note gloom of *Garlands* with *Head Over Heels*. The album introduces a variety of different shadings and approaches to the incipient Cocteaus sound, pointing the band towards the exultant, elegant beauty of later releases. Opening number "When Mama Was Moth" demonstrates the new musical range nicely; Fraser's singing is much more upfront, while Guthrie creates a bewitching mix of dark guitar notes and sparkling keyboard tones, with percussion echoing in the background. Other songs, like the sax-accompanied "Five Ten Fiftyfold" and "The Tinderbox (Of a Heart)" reflect the more elaborate musical melancholy of the group, while still other cuts are downright sprightly. "Multifoiled" in particular is a charm, a jazzily-arranged number that lets Fraser do a bit of scatting (a perfect avenue for her lyrical approach!), while "In the Gold Dust Rush" mixes acoustic guitar drama into Fraser's swooping singing. Perhaps the two strongest numbers of all are: "Sugar Hiccup," mixing the mock choir effect the band would use elsewhere with both a lovely guitar line and singing; and "Musette and Drums," a massive, powerful collision of Guthrie's guitar at its loudest and most powerful and Fraser's singing at its most intense. —*Ned Raggett*

● **Treasure** / Oct. 1984 / 4AD ✦✦✦✦✦

The opening two numbers are simply flawless, starting with "Ivo," where gently strummed guitar and low bass support Fraser's singing; then suddenly added, astonishing chimes and steady percussion build up to a jaw-dropping Guthrie guitar solo. Topping that would be hard for anyone, but in "Lorelei," the Twins do it, with an introductory, breathtaking guitar surge leading into one of Fraser's best vocals, compelling in both its heavenly and earthly tones and rolls. Not a word may be understandable, but it isn't necessary, while the music, driven on by a pounding rhythm, is as perfect a justification of digital delay pedals and the like as can be found. As *Treasure* continues, the accomplished variety is what stands out the most, whether it be the gentle, futuristic-medieval pluckings on "Beatrix," the understated moody washes and Fraser whispers on "Otterley," the upbeat guitar lines of "Aloysius," or the slightly jazzy touches on "Pandora." The concluding number ends the record on the peak with which it began. "Donimo" starts with a mysterious mix of mock choir sounds, ambient echoes and noises, and Fraser's careful singing before finally exploding into one last heavenly wash of powerful sound; Guthrie's guitar, Raymonde's steady bass, and drum machine smashes provide the perfect bed for Fraser's final, exultant vocals. *Treasure* lives up to its title and then some as a thorough and complete triumph. —*Ned Raggett*

The Pink Opaque / Nov. 1985 / 4AD ✦✦✦✦✦

After having built up a considerable reputation in the U.K. and Europe, the Cocteaus first fully reached America via this compilation, cherry-picking some of the group's finest moments for this trans-Atlantic co-release between home label 4AD and then-stateside label Relativity. None of the ten tracks had been released in America before, but whoever assembled the release knew exactly what they were doing in terms of whetting appetites. The only absolute rarity on the disc was "Millimillenary," originally turning up on a compilation tape given away by New Musical Express. It's a fine number, recorded soon after Raymonde joined the group—a good mix of the Cocteaus' instrumental lushness and Fraser's vocal acrobatics. The version of *Garlands*' "Wax and Wane" included here is slightly remixed and arguably even better than the original, bringing out everything a little more clearly and powerfully. A sage decision was the inclusion of all three tracks from the *Pearly-Dewdrops' Drops* EP; as flawless as that was, all deserved inclusion, while beginning the compilation with "The Spangle Maker" was also inspired. Other cuts include "Hitherto," "From the Flagstones," "Lorelei," and the then-recent single "Aikea-Guinea." Concluding with the similarly album-ending "Musette and Drums" from *Head Over Heels*, *The Pink Opaque* is a lovely taster for anyone wanting to discover the peerless early years of the Cocteaus. —*Ned Raggett*

The Moon & the Melodies / 1986 / 4AD ✦✦✦

The Moon and the Melodies is a collaboration between the Cocteau Twins and keyboardist/composer Harold Budd that fits soundly between the stylistic signatures of the two, both of whom make organic music that relies heavily on electronics. Budd's use of spacious treated piano and keyboard sounds (influenced by a previous collaborator, Brian Eno) combine with the Cocteau Twins' shimmering waves of guitars and Elizabeth Fraser's layered wordless vocals to create what amounts to a soundtrack to a dream about sleeping, with saxophones courtesy of Richard Thomas (of the now defunct Dif Juz) breathing further life into the music. Too bland to be the best introduction to the music of either, but a welcome addition to the collection of fans of both. —*Peter Stepek*

Victorialand / Apr. 1986 / 4AD ✦✦✦

With Raymonde taking a break to work on the second This Mortal Coil album, Fraser and Guthrie made up the Cocteaus for the first full-length follow-up to *Treasure*. Rather than trying for a full-band approach, Fraser and Guthrie instead created a much more simply beautiful effort, with a relaxed air to it. Rhythms are subtler, with bass and drum machine often totally eschewed in favor of Guthrie's delicate guitar filigrees and lush, produced textures. Fraser is, as always, in wonderfully fine voice; her words are quite indecipherable, but the feelings are no less strong for it. "Lazy Calm" starts things perfectly, as deep, heavily-treated guitar strums combine with a heavy flange and guest saxophone from Dif Juz member Richard Thomas. Other songs sparkle with a lovely vivaciousness. Far from being stereotypical arty music to sit around and be gloomy to, two pieces especially shine with a gentle energy: "Fluffy Tufts," with its many-layered ringing strings and Fraser's overdubbed vocals; and the joyful "Little Spacey," with a soft rhythm underlying more sheer electric loveliness. Guthrie adds heavy reverb and overdubbed lines to create the Cocteaus' wash on such songs as "Throughout the Dark Months of April and May" and "Feet Like Fins," the latter again featuring Thomas, this time on tablas. For all the sweet beauty of *Victorialand*, things end on a quietly dramatic note, but a dramatic one nonetheless. "The Thinner the Air" starts with treated piano and rather spooky guitar leads—the mysterious soloing is especially wonderful—while Fraser then sings with a slightly haunted feeling, concluding with slightly nervous wails. It's an unexpected but effective touch for this fine record. —*Ned Raggett*

Blue Bell Knoll / Oct. 1988 / 4AD ✦✦✦

The first Cocteaus album to feature a full-band lineup since *Treasure* was also their first full studio record released in America, resulting from the group's stateside deal with Capitol. Much to longtime fans' surprise, the Twins in fact were much more content with Capitol than 4AD, hinting at their eventual full departure from that label. This was all well and good, but the trio's new inspiration didn't fully translate into their work, unfortunately. While *Blue Bell Knoll* has some striking moments that are pure Cocteaus at their best—the opening title track is especially lovely with a keyboard loop leading into Fraser's ever-wonderful vocals, a light rhythm, and a great final Guthrie solo—it's still the band's least noteworthy release since *Garlands*. The feeling throughout is of a group interested in dressing up older approaches that have served them well, but aren't as distinct; the quite-lush arrangements by Guthrie are fine but the songs are a touch more pedestrian. *Blue Bell Knoll* has enough initial steam, however, to ensure that there are reasons to listen, happily. "Athol-Brose" has the inspirational feel that the Twins can easily create. "Carolyn's Fingers," the clear album standout, is perhaps the strongest individual Cocteau song since "Aikea-Guinea," with Fraser singing against herself over a rough, hip-hop-inspired rhythm while Guthrie peels off a fantastic main guitar melody and Raymonde contributes some supple bass work. After that amazing opening, things slowly but surely slide back a bit; most of the rest sounds okay enough to listen to, but the heartgripping intensity that defines the Twins at their best isn't present. —*Ned Raggett*

Heaven or Las Vegas / Sep. 1990 / 4AD ✦✦✦✦✦

Deciding to scale back the overly pretty sound on *Blue Bell Knoll* while experimenting with more accessibility—the Twins ended up creating their best album since *Treasure*. From the start, *Heaven...* is simply fantastic: on "Cherry-Coloured Funk," Guthrie's inimitable guitar work chimes leading a low-key but forceful rhythm, while Raymonde's grand bass work fleshes it out. Fraser simply captivates; her vocals are the clearest, most direct they've ever been, purring with energy and life. Many songs have longer openings and closings; rather than crashing fully into a song and then quickly ending, instead the trio carefully builds up and eases back. These songs are still quite focused, though, almost sounding like they were recorded live instead of being assembled in the studio. Due credit has to be given to the Cocteaus' drum programming; years of working with the machines translated into the detailed work here, right down to the fills. "Fifty-Fifty Clown," starting with an ominous bass throb, turns into a lovely showcase for Fraser's singing and Guthrie's more restrained playing. But the Twins don't completely turn their back on *Knoll*'s sound; "Iceblink Luck," has the same lush feeling and a newfound energy—the instrumental break is almost a rave-up!—and everything pulses to a fine conclusion. There are many moments of sheer Cocteaus beauty and power, including the title track, with its great chorus, and two spotlight Guthrie solos: "Fotzepolitic," a powerful number building to a rushing conclusion, and the album-ending "Frou Frou Foxes in Midsummer Fires." Possessing the same climactic sense of drama past disc-closers as "Donimo" and "The Thinner the Air," it's a perfect way to end a near-perfect album. *—Ned Raggett*

Four-Calendar Cafe / Nov. 1993 / Capitol ♦♦♦

The Cocteau Twins' first release following their exodus from the 4AD stable, *Four-Calendar Cafe* is also, tellingly, their most earthbound effort; as with *Heaven or Las Vegas*, the emphasis here is on substance as much as style—"Evangeline," "Bluebeard" and "Know Who You Are at Every Age" continue the trio's advance into more accessible melodic and lyrical ground without sacrificing even an ounce of their trademark ethereality. *—Jason Ankeny*

Milk & Kisses / Mar. 1996 / Capitol ♦♦♦

Throughout the '80s, Cocteau Twins created some of the most beautiful and innovative music of the decade. Liz Fraser's uncanny, gossamer voice and Robin Guthrie's shimmery guitar work both garnered acclaim and inspired bands. *Milk and Kisses* finds the band in a comfortable rut; they've created, and now perfected, a style of music so distinctive that there seems to be little recent creative growth. The result is a beautiful, lush, but somewhat dated and unengaging sounding album that tends to wash over the listener without making any real impact. It is, however, everything that a Cocteau Twins album promises; hypnotic, dreamy, awash in ethereal voices, and delicate, liquid guitars. "Tishbite" in particular delivers an accessible dream pop sound that sounds nice while it's playing but fails to have anything really memorable about it, a problem that plagues most of *Milk and Kisses*. "Half-Gifts," "Rilkean Heart," and "Treasure Hiding" have an airy, otherwordly prettiness to them—but that's about it. Necessary for Cocteau Twins diehards and potentially interesting to those that have never heard the band before, *Milk and Kisses* says nothing, but says it beautifully. *—Heather Phares*

BBC Sessions / Oct. 12, 1999 / Rykodisc ♦♦♦♦

Cocteau Twins have always been a love 'em-or-hate 'em kind of band—to some, Elizabeth Fraser's cool, chirpy warble, the shimmering multi-layered guitars and bass of Simon Raymonde and Robin Guthrie, and the affectless electronic percussion that always accompanies them combine to approximate the music of the spheres. To others, it's all frosting and no cake. This two-disc compilation of live and radio studio recordings (some of which are previously unreleased) probably won't change anyone's mind either way, but if there was ever any doubt of Fraser's vocal virtuosity, that doubt can be laid to rest now: imagine a cross between Emmylou Harris (without any twang) and Sinéad O'Connor (with discipline). The program proceeds chronologically, from the relatively tuneless "Wax and Wane" and "Garlands" through "Ivo" and "Otterley" (two luscious melodies from the band's aptly titled *Treasure*) and several almost equally pretty tracks from 1996. At their best, no one can match Cocteau Twins for sheer, swooning, inscrutable elegance, and they're frequently at their best on this fine collection. *—Rick Anderson*

Stars and Topsoil / 2000 / 4AD ♦♦♦♦♦

Stars and Topsoil collects some of the Cocteau Twins' better-known 4AD material, which ends at 1990, before they departed for Fontana in the U.K. and Capitol in the U.S. This wasn't distributed in the States, the country where it would be most useful. Outside of college radio support, the Cocteaus really had to be sought out in the '80s; in the U.K., they were a higher profile act. With that in mind, *Stars and Topsoil* would be best suited for the uninitiated non-Brit. More of a barometer than anything else, its effect will either lead to the buyer obtaining the remainder of the band's catalog or nothing more. You'll consider them music of the gods or precious art wank. Though they never really repeated themselves, they held a set of characteristics throughout their discography that either stunned or repelled.

Before, there never really was a definitive first place to go with the Cocteaus, and there still isn't. An era spanning seven LPs of studio material and nine singles is a good load to pick from, and the track listing of *Stars and Topsoil* is just one of hundreds a fan could come up with in terms of representation. You could get a just as good sampling by putting their discs in a changer, hitting "shuffle," and listening for an hour. The disc is just as quality as most other Cocteaus releases, though missing the feel of a proper studio album. For the disciples, the things you gain from the purchase are the artwork and remastered versions of the tracks, certainly a signal of the inevitable remaster/remodel campaign that looms ahead. *—Andy Kellman*

Codeine

f. 1989

Slowcore, Indie Rock, Alternative Pop/Rock, Sadcore

The early-'90s New York trio Codeine is one of the founders of the slowcore scene that includes groups like Bedhead, American Analog Set, and Low. Taking audible inspiration from the third Velvet Underground album and scene pioneers Galaxie 500 but adding a more aggressive tone and slowing the tempos down even further, Codeine sounded almost entirely unique at the time. However, their style was immediately adopted by a number of other new bands, some of which do the tense and glacial thing even better. Codeine was formed in 1989 by bassist/singer Stephen Immerwahr, guitarist John Engle, and drummer Chris Brokaw. Their demo, a tortured version of the Pete Ham/Tom Evans classic "Without You" that stretches the four-minute song out to nine, got the band signed to Glitterhouse Records in Europe and Sub Pop in the U.S. the following year. Their debut album, *Frigid Stars*, was released by Glitterhouse in late 1990 and Sub Pop in the spring of 1991 to generally positive reviews. A lengthy EP, *Barely Real*, came out in 1992. Although the record varies Codeine's sound a bit with piano by ex-Squirrel Bait member turned art-rocker David Grubbs (Codeine had toured Europe with Grubbs' instrumental group Bastro) and a noise guitar freakout by Bitch Magnet leader Jon Fine, plus a cover of MX-80 Sound's "Promise of Love," *Barely Real* is basically a continuation of the style perfected on *Frigid Stars*. A single produced by Grubbs, "Tom," was released in the fall of 1993, followed by the full-length *The White Birch* in April 1994. Slightly more melodic than the earlier albums but just as languorously paced, *The White Birch* is probably the group's best record. After an extensive U.S. tour, the trio split amicably to work on other projects. *—Stewart Mason*

Frigid Stars / Aug. 1990 / Sub Pop ♦♦♦♦♦

The cover sets the mood well—a negative black and white shot of some stars, looking even more haunting as a result. As for the album, the tone isn't simply being cold or unemotional, but simply gripped by a deep black mood, where everything seems on the verge of suddenly going wrong or collapsing. There's actually a cryptic warmth in the slow tempos and feedback produced from the deliberate strumming and chords from John Engle and Chris Brokaw's guitars. It isn't the narcotic hush of Low—there's actually a little more relative energy than that!—or sludgy stoner rock a la Black Sabbath, but something else entirely. Bassist Stephen Immerwahr's vocals lend to that feeling, softly ruminative, sometimes straining, but never sounding self-important or whining (though sometimes the lyrics are creepily macabre—check out the start of "Cave-In"). If one lets oneself go for the album's general feel, then it all flows together to make a touching, surprising experience, but those seeking variety aren't likely to be happy. It avoids sounding repetitious by virtue of the dynamics—treat the entire album as an extended mood piece, and it works well. Engle's lead guitar work throws in enough heartbreakingly strong moments to help—the sudden low swoop on "Pickup Song" is a standout, while the dark, forbidding drones on "Second Chance" are truly chilling. An interesting cover surfaces a few songs in—"New Year's," cowritten by Bitch Magnet singer Sooyoung Park but not recorded by him until the first Seam album, *Headsparks*, two years later. Codeine here sound a touch cleaner than elsewhere on *Frigid Stars*, where the guitars can really sprawl when needed, but Brokaw's drumming and Immerwahr's great delivery mark it out as their version instead of merely a straightforward remake. *—Ned Raggett*

● **Barely Real** / 1992 / Sub Pop ♦♦♦♦♦

A six-song EP that appeared between the two albums proper, without sharing any songs with either, *Barely Real* essentially extends the same musical and lyrical spirit of *Frigid Stars*, with a couple of slight but intriguing changes woven in. Admittedly, that won't be apparent on the first song, "Realize," which fully confirms that Codeine's combination of deliberate pace and electric guitar playing both, along with softly sung rumination courtesy of Immerwahr, is pretty much its compositional mode rather than affectation. Those put off by earlier Codeine won't want to continue; those taken by its way of doing things will happily embrace it. From there *Barely Real* makes its careful way over about twenty-five minutes, with some guest performers popping up to leaven things. One Jon Fine adds "noisy guitar" to the mix on "Jr.," with a quick stuttering main riff to its credit, while David Grubbs contributes both piano and arrangement for "W." It's a highlight of *Barely Real*, essentially a Grubbs solo performance, but still sounding exactly like something Codeine would write. Other high points include the echo and burying in the mix of Immerwahr's voice on "Hard to Find" and the slightly surprising conclusion, a cover of MX-80 Sound's "Promise of Love" done in a bit of a late-night jazz club style with more typical Codeine interjections towards the end. *—Ned Raggett*

The White Birch / Apr. 4, 1994 / Sub Pop ♦♦♦

The final Codeine release, *The White Birch*, finds the band stretching out more beyond its usual style here and there, while still pretty much sounding like it always has. It's not quite a case of "heard one, heard them all," but at points it's hard to see how they would have continued without completely repeating themselves. There is a slight change in the lineup, with Douglas Scharin replacing Chris Brokaw, at that time fully involved with Come, on drums, while David Grubbs once again guests, playing guitar on "Tom" and "Wird." He's not fully noticeable on either track per se, but his playing doesn't take away anything from the overall mood or performance either. John Engle's own lead guitar work now often has a stronger, stentorian sense of playing than before, in part resulting from the greater sense of space in a number of songs. While there was a relative calm on moments of *Frigid Stars*, here there's even more of it—not quite relaxed, but allowing more stripped-down moments to come in along with the thicker roil of cuts like "Vacancy" and the searing, compressed snarl on "Washed Up." The opening cut "Sea" captures that well, especially given that Stephen Immerwahr's vocals are as lost and murky in the mix as they've ever been. Other moments betray what sounds like a Slint touch here and there—not surprising given the Louisville connection via Grubbs and others (indeed, Louisville as a whole is specifically thanked in the credits). Scharin, meanwhile, throws in a couple of extra fills and subtle touches along the way, though whether this results from what he brings to the band or just a change in style from the band as a whole is not immediately apparent. Ending with the soft contemplation of "Smoking Room," *White Birch* sees out Codeine's career on a strong enough note. *—Ned Raggett*

Leonard Cohen

b. Sep. 21, 1934, Montreal, Quebec, Canada

Vocals, Guitar / Folk-Rock, Singer/Songwriter

One of the most interesting and enduring, if not the most successful singer-songwriters of the late 1960s, Leonard Cohen has retained a substantial following for more than 30 years, along with the attention of critics who long since ceased worrying about new works by most of his contemporaries. Cohen was born nearly a decade earlier than the Beatles or the Rolling Stones, and a year before Elvis Presley, but his personal, social and intellectual background couldn't be more different from *any* rock stars of any generation, nor can he be easily compared even with any members of the generation of folksingers that came of age in the 1960s—he didn't start performing or recording until he was in his mid-'30s, after he had already written several books. As an established novelist and poet, his literary accomplishments far exceed those of Bob Dylan, though as a performer, his rather monotone voice is less appealing than Dylan's singing. *—Bruce Eder*

★ **The Songs of Leonard Cohen** / 1968 / Columbia ♦♦♦♦♦

A breathtaking and perfect debut, *Songs of Leonard Cohen* marked the emergence of one of the most enduring, unique and brilliant voices in popular music. Led off by the gorgeous "Suzanne," previously a hit for both Judy Collins and Noel Harrison, the album is an exposed nerve, a Fellini-esque parade of losers, victims and fallen angels. Brittle and unforgiving, tracks like "So Long, Marianne," "Winter Lady" and "Sisters of Mercy" are unflinchingly honest and desolate; the subdued beauty of the songs' spartan backdrop only adds to their force—Cohen takes acoustic folk, for so long a musical expression of empowerment and hope, and bleeds it dry of all its redemptive qualities. A masterpiece of perversity and pain. *—Jason Ankeny*

Songs from a Room / 1969 / Columbia ♦♦♦♦♦

Somehow even darker and more melancholy than *Songs of Leonard Cohen, Songs From a Room* is an emotionally claustrophobic set produced with austere beauty by Bob Johnston. The arrangements are eerily spare, heightening the impact of Cohen's weary vocals; the intermittent and idiosyncratic appearance of a Jew's harp only adds to the record's overwhelming sense of disorientation. While not as uniformly strong as its predecessor, *Songs From a Room* does contain a number of Cohen's finest compositions, including "Bird on the Wire," "Lady Midnight" and "Story of Isaac." *—Jason Ankeny*

Songs of Love and Hate / 1971 / Columbia ♦♦♦♦♦

Songs of Love and Hate is one of Leonard Cohen's most emotionally intense albums—which, given the nature of Cohen's body of work, is no small statement. While the title *Songs of Love and Hate* sums up the album's themes accurately enough, it's hardly as simple as that description might lead you to expect—in these eight songs, "love" encompasses the physical ("Last Year's Man"), the emotional ("Famous Blue Raincoat"), and the spiritual ("Joan of Arc"), and the contempt in songs like "Dress Rehearsal Rag" and "Avalanche" is the sort of venom that can only come from someone who once cared very deeply. The sound of the album is clean and uncluttered, and for the most part the music stays out of the way of the lyrics, which dominate the songs. Thankfully, Cohen had grown noticeably as a singer since his first two albums, and if he hardly boasts a range to rival Roy Orbison here, he is able to bring out the subtleties of "Joan of Arc" and "Famous Blue Raincoat" in a way his previous work would not have led you to expect. And while Bob Johnston's production is spare, it's spare with a purpose, letting Cohen's voice and guitar tell their stories and using other musicians for intelligent, emotionally resonant punctuation (Paul Buckmaster's unobtrusive string arrangements and the use of a children's chorus are especially inspired). And *Songs of Love and Hate* captured Cohen in one of his finest hours as a songwriter, and the best selections (especially "Famous Blue Raincoat," "Joan of Arc," and "Love Calls You by Your Name") rank with the most satisfying work of his career. If *Songs of Love and Hate* isn't Cohen's best album, it comes close enough to be essential to anyone interested in his work. *—Mark Deming*

New Skin for the Old Ceremony / 1974 / Columbia ♦♦♦♦♦

Leonard Cohen was a poet long before he decided to pick up a guitar. Despite singing in a dry baritone over spare arrangements, Cohen is a gifted lyricist who captivates the listener. *New Skin for the Old Ceremony* may be Leonard Cohen's most musical album, as he is accompanied by violas, mandolins, banjos, and percussion that give his music more texture than usual. The fact that Cohen does more real singing on this album can be seen as both a blessing and a curse—while his voice sounds more strained, the songs are delivered with more passion than usual. Furthermore, he has background vocalists including Janis Ian that add significantly to create a fuller sound. It is no surprise, however, that he generally uses simple song structures to draw attention to the words ("Who By Fire"). The lyrics are filled with abstract yet vivid images, and the album primarily uses the metaphor of love and relationships as battlegrounds ("There Is a War," "Field Commander Cohen"). Cohen is clearly singing from the heart, and he chronicles his relationship with Janis Joplin in "Chelsea Hotel No. 2." This is one of his best albums, although new listeners should start with *Songs of Leonard Cohen. — Vik Iyengar*

☆ **The Best of Leonard Cohen** / 1975 / Columbia ♦♦♦♦♦

The Best of Leonard Cohen samples 12 of the many highlights from the singer's first four studio LPs. With a heavy emphasis on the debut *Songs of Leonard Cohen* and its follow-up *Songs From a Room,* the set includes such masterpieces as "Suzanne," "So Long, Marianne" and "Bird on the Wire," as well as later efforts including "Chelsea Hotel" and "Famous Blue Raincoat." *—Jason Ankeny*

Death of a Ladies' Man / 1977 / Columbia ♦♦

While not the unmitigated disaster conventional wisdom holds it to be, *Death of a Ladies' Man* remains one of Leonard Cohen's least successful efforts. In a 180-degree turn from the spare, muted settings of most of Cohen's work, the record is produced by Phil Spector, whose trademark Wall of Sound swallows the singer whole; Cohen's songs are up to snuff, and Spector's vision remains as awe-striking as ever, but the two artists are simply incompatible—apart from a few bright spots ("True Love Leaves No Traces," "Paper Thin Hotel"), *Death of a Ladies' Man* is an ambitious failure. *—Jason Ankeny*

Recent Songs / 1979 / Columbia ♦♦♦♦

The first thing Leonard Cohen's music fans noticed about his sixth new studio album, given the typically open-ended title *Recent Songs,* was that, musically, it marked a return to the gypsy folk sound of his early records after the incongruous arrangements Phil Spector imposed on its predecessor, *Death of a Ladies' Man,* only two years earlier. There were subtle musical developments, particularly a flavor of the American Southwest, courtesy of the band Passenger, which played on several tracks, but the acoustic guitars and violin recalled classic Cohen. Fans of the artist's poetry noticed something else. His writing had become increasingly bitter and angry during the 1970s in the books *The Energy of Slaves* and *Death of a Ladies' Man* as well as in his lyrics, but there was a new equanimity in these *Recent Songs* that began with the welcoming introduction of "The Guests." All was not suddenly well, of course, but "the open-hearted many" outnumbered "the broken-hearted few." Cohen's usual mixture of religious and sexual imagery in the songs was elegant and evocative rather than painful. If he was conscious of the sacrifices he had made in vain in "Came So Far for Beauty," he was nevertheless able to make a sincere plea to a woman in "The Window," mixing it with a prayer to "gentle this soul." The album was full of references to absence and dislocation, but Cohen deliberately countered them with humor. The cover of "The Lost Canadian (Un Canadient Errant)" was enlivened by a mariachi arrangement, and the album ended with "Ballad of the Absent Mare," an allegory about a cowboy's search for a horse that ended with the suggestion that the pursuit was only a romantic game. Though often abstract, *Recent Songs* suggested Cohen had regained a certain equilibrium after a long dark period. *—William Ruhlmann*

Various Positions / 1985 / Columbia ♦♦♦

Recorded with vocalist Jennifer Warnes (who later cut the album *Famous Blue Raincoat,* a collection of Cohen compositions), *Various Positions* is a stunning return to form—Cohen's strongest work since *New Skin for the Old Ceremony.* Cryptic and spartan, the set continues in the eclectic vein of recent efforts, but with greater clarity and focus, resulting in an intriguingly diffuse collection ranging from the Serge Gainsbourg-esque pop of "Dance Me to the End of Love" to the boozy, country-inflected "The Captain." *—Jason Ankeny*

I'm Your Man / 1988 / Columbia ♦♦♦♦♦

A stunningly sophisticated leap into modern musical textures, *I'm Your Man* re-establishes Leonard Cohen's mastery. Against a backdrop of keyboards and propulsive rhythms, Cohen surveys the global landscape with a precise, unflinching eye: the opening "First We Take Manhattan" is an ominous fantasy of commercial success bundled in crypto-fascist imagery, while the remarkable "Everybody Knows" is a cynical catalog of the landmines littering the surface of love in the age of AIDS. *—Jason Ankeny*

The Future / Nov. 10, 1992 / Columbia ♦♦♦

As with most every Leonard Cohen album, a new record means a new means of musical exploration. With *The Future,* Cohen adds chiming synthesizers and eerie orchestrations to his brooding anthems about life's darker half. One of the last of Cohen's full-length albums, *The Future* is definitely one of the most direct. More notable tracks include "The Future" and "Anthem," both of which were featured on the *Natural Born Killers* soundtrack. Closer to spoken word poetry set to music than simply songs, the entire album is one long manifesto calling all to challenge the concepts of righteousness and despair in our modern world. Regardless of the music behind the man, Cohen still manages to bring to *The Future* what he brought to his earlier recordings: one man against the world with nothing but a gruff voice and a cause. *—Christopher Fielder*

Cohen Live / Jun. 28, 1994 / Columbia ♦♦♦

More Best of Leonard Cohen / Oct. 7, 1997 / Columbia ♦♦♦♦♦

This second compilation covers Leonard Cohen's career from 1984 to the present (skipping over both *Death of a Ladies' Man,* which is understandable, and *Recent Songs,* which is more questionable). Cohen did not have any hits during this period, though a few songs, notably "Everybody Knows" and "Tower of Song," became well enough known to be essential choices. Otherwise, Cohen's craftsmanship makes a choice from among his work difficult. This set chooses four of the eight songs from the celebrated *I'm Your Man* album (and more might have been included) and four from its less successful follow-up, *The Future.* One track, "Dance Me to the End of Love," comes from *Various Positions,* with another of that album's songs, "Hallelujah," included in a live version. There is also a live version of the Cohen standard "Suzanne," and there are two previously unreleased songs, the typically funny and erotic "Never Any Good" and the minute-long disembodied recitation "The Great Event." It's easy to note important omissions—"Came So Far for Beauty," "If It Be Your Will," and "First We Take Manhattan" are perhaps the most missed—but what's here chronicles both the continuance of Cohen's talent as a songwriter and the improvement in his deepened voice and record-making abilities in the second half of his career. *— William Ruhlmann*

Field Commander Cohen: Tour of 1979 / Oct. 9, 2001 / Columbia ♦♦♦

As he'd firmly established himself as a poet and novelist years before he made his first album, Leonard Cohen is often regarded less as a musician than as a writer who happens to sing. But his songs have always displayed a subtle but mesmerizing melodic sense that dovetails gracefully with his lyrics, and though his craggy voice has its limits, no one else interprets Cohen's songs with his degree of intelligence and quiet passion. In 1979, after the release of his album *Recent Songs,* Cohen set out on an international concert tour accompanied by members of the jazz-rock group Passenger; *Field Commander Cohen* was compiled from recordings of the 1979 tour, and it presents an especially strong argument for Cohen's gifts as a musician. Cohen's voice had gained a great deal of strength and nuance since the dates preserved on 1973's *Live Songs,* and the smoky rasp that began to scar his vocals on *I'm Your Man* had yet to set in; this may well be Cohen's best set of recorded performances as a singer, and having Jennifer Warnes and Sharon Robinson on hand as duet partners is especially rich icing on the cake. While the musicians take care to never intrude upon the songs, they play beautifully, with remarkable taste and skill. While it falls short of the stark emotional force of *Songs of Leonard Cohen* or *Songs of Love and Hate, Field Commander Cohen* makes clear that Cohen writes songs, not literature accompanied by incidental music, and here these 12 songs possess a passionate, aching beauty that's a wonder to behold; this is easily the best Cohen live recording to emerge to date. —*Mark Deming*

Coil

f. 1983, London, England
Experimental, Ambient, Electronic, Industrial
Initially established in 1983 as a solo outlet for vocalist and percussionist John Balance, the experimental sonic manipulation unit Coil became a full-fledged concern a year later following the arrival of keyboardist/programmer Peter Christopherson, a founder of Psychic TV as well as a member of Throbbing Gristle. After debuting with the 17-minute single "How to Destroy Angels," the duo recruited the aid of Possession's Stephen Thrower, J.G. "Foetus" Thirlwell, and Gavin Friday to record their full-length 1984 bow, *Scatology*, an intense, primal work of sculpted industrial noise thematically devoted to the concepts of alchemy and transmutation. Following 1986's *Nightmare Culture* Christopherson and Balance invited Stephen Thrower to join the group in a full-time capacity. As a trio, they recorded 1986's *Horse Rotorvator*, an LP introducing classical, jazz, and Middle Eastern textures into the mix, as well as the EP *The Anal Staircase*. After 1987's *Unreleased Themes From 'Hellraiser'*—a collection of atmospheric Gothic instrumentals commissioned for, but ultimately cut from, the Clive Barker horror film—Coil issued 1987's *Gold Is the Metal (With the Broadest Shoulders)*, a remixed history of the group's first several years of work. 1990's *Unnatural History*, another career overview, effectively ended the first phase of the band's career; when Coil resurfaced a year later with *Love's Secret Domain*, their music reflected the strong influence of the acid house culture. Another long layoff brought on by financial difficulties ended in 1995, when the group signed to Nine Inch Nails frontman Trent Reznor's label nothing to release *Backwards*. Additionally, they recorded the LP *Worship the Glitch*, issued under the name ELpH, and in 1996 cut *A Thousand Lights in a Darkened Room* as Black Light District, the first in an ongoing series of "Black Light District" releases. —*Jason Ankeny*

Scatology [Some Bizarre] / 1984 / Some Bizarre ✦✦✦

Horse Rotorvator / 1986 / Some Bizarre ✦✦✦✦✦
The title *Horse Rotorvator* is explained in the liner notes as a device large enough to "plough up the waiting world," created from the bones of the horses of the Four Horsemen of the Apocalypse. The Bay City Rollers this isn't. On the group's second full album, Coil continue the refinement of brute noise and creepily serene arrangements into a truly modern psychedelia, from tribal drumming and death march guitars to disturbing samples and marching band samples and back. Balance shares the same haggard, mystic vocal delivery common to fellow explorers of the edge like David Tibet and Edward Ka-Spel, but he has his own blasted and burnt touch to it all. His lyrical subjects range from emotional extremism of many kinds to blunt, often homoerotic imagery (matched at points in the artwork and packaging) and meditations on death. As a result the cover of Leonard Cohen's "Who by Fire" isn't as surprising as one might think. Past guest Marc Almond appears again on the track with backing vocals, as well as adding them to "Slur," which is composed of an unsettling mix of harmonica, bells, percussion and whatever else can be imagined. Other guests include Almond's then-musical partner Billy McGee, adding a haunting, sometimes grating, string arrangement to "Ostia," which is about the murder of radical Italian filmmaker Pasolini, and Clint Ruin, aka Foetus, adding his typically warped brass touches to "Circles of Mania." Paul Vaughan narrates the lyrics on "The Golden Section," creating a stunning piece that in its combination of demonic imagery and sweeping, cinematic arrangements holds a common ground with In the Nursery. All the guests help contribute to the album's overall effect, but this is Coil's own vision above all else, eschewing easy cliches on all fronts to create unnerving, never easily digested invocations of musical power. —*Ned Raggett*

Gold Is the Metal / 1987 / Threshold House ✦✦✦✦✦

● **Love's Secret Domain** / 1991 / Wax Trax ✦✦✦✦✦
Though Coil's Balance and Christopherson were inspired by the acid-house revolution of the late '80s, their drug-inspired "dance" album isn't quite as indebted to the style as the contemporary work of Psychic TV. The influence comes through mostly in the deranged effects and vaguely surreal air, though several tracks do increase the rhythmic wattage. For the most part, the duo retained the gothic synth-pop of *Horse Rotorvator*, but with a special emphasis on stuttered cut-and-paste sections rather than organic instruments and environmental sublimation. —*John Bush*

Stolen and Contaminated Songs / Dec. 11, 1992 / Threshold House ✦✦✦✦

The Angelic Conversation / 1994 / Threshold House ✦✦✦

Worship the Glitch / 1995 / Eskaton ✦✦✦✦
Officially, this is released by ELpH vs. Coil, which only makes sense since ELpH is in fact Coil, the name having been adopted for work where unplanned results come out of the musical equipment in use—a technological collaborative effort, one can say. Whatever the exact origins, the results are even more on the edge than many Coil pieces, eschewing formal song structures for exploratory efforts in sampling and instrumental rhythm. Having previously released three singles under the moniker, Coil went ahead with the full album in 1995, another interesting twist in their involved discography. Beginning and ending with murky pieces featuring the voice of Leah Hersig, wife of longtime Coil touchstone Aleister Crowley, *Worship the Glitch* profiles the use of random chance and possible mistakes right from the title. The exact membership is unclear—presumably it's Peter Christophersen and John Balance at heart as always—but whoever participated, the emphasis on machine-created sounds and results is prominent. Anyone expecting

glitch/laptop techno à la Kid 606 won't find that here, but there certainly is much use of heavily distorted and treated sound throughout, which will sound awfully familiar. The overall combination of tweaked instrumentation and weird, flat atmospheres, especially in the strange use of echo, clearly had an influence on the IDM crowd in later years. An intriguing homage to an earlier gay lit figure surfaces with "The Halliwell Hammers," three versions of which are scattered throughout the record. Kenneth Halliwell was the ex-lover of noted playwright Joe Orton, who in a final fit killed him with hammer blows to the head before killing himself. For all the violence this would imply, the songs themselves are weird, jittery numbers in keeping with the album as a whole, with odd string or pseudo-string loops and mournful bell tones. —*Ned Raggett*

Black Light District: A Thousand Lights in a Darkened Room / 1996 / Eskaton ✦✦✦
The Coil project Black Light District debuted with an album of broad, minimalistic textures and beatless ambience. Though the vibes are similar to the duo's past work, there are no vocals and few beats; what remains is the restless exploration of sound which Coil have always made a prime concern. —*John Bush*

Tribe / 1997 / Threshold House ✦✦✦

Time Machines / 1998 / Eskaton ✦✦✦✦
Although *Time Machines* wasn't precisely credited to Coil, upon its arrival in early 1998 the CD was the first full-length of new material Balance, Christophersen, et al., released in nearly seven years. An hour-long meditation on drone ostensibly inspired by the psychophenomenological properties of hallucinogenic drugs, *Time Machines* is constructed entirely from cycling, oscillating synth tones, and continues in the vein of shapeless experimentalism established with *Black Light District* and *Worship the Glitch*. Enjoyable, if a mite limited in scope. —*Sean Cooper*

Music to Play in the Dark, Vol. 2 / 2000 / Chalice ✦✦✦
Two types of records usually have the highest potential for embarrassment: "comedy" records and "scary" records. Unlike an awful pub rock mistake or a tuneless ambient workout, there seems to be nothing more obnoxious than listening to a record that tries—and fails—to be either funny or frightening. Coil's *Music to Play in the Dark, Vol. 2* takes the latter stab into forbidding, blood-velvet territory and consistently bungles it up. "Ether" ends with a magnificently processed, sincerely unsettling chant, but it takes almost 11 minutes of "cats + piano" melodies to get there. Elsewhere, opener "Something" takes a deeply effective, goth Gaia heartbeat and polishes it with cartoonish "menacing" swooshes and sirens that probably could be found on a two-buck "Boo! Halloween Hits!" supermarket CD. The sincerity of Coil should not be undervalued—as work here and in the past can easily attest to—it's the failure to harmonize it with a minimalist instinct that gets in the way. Because no matter how much somebody tries to tell you a joke or scare you, only the gifted can do it without sounding like a moron. —*Dean Carlson*

Cold Chisel

f. 1973, Australia, db. 1983
Hard Rock
Cold Chisel is the classic Australian "pub rock band," playing a tough breed of rock and blues inspired by '70s bands like Free, Deep Purple, and Led Zeppelin but characterized by the storytelling skills of their main songwriter, Don Walker, whose personal influences came from Bob Dylan. They came together in Adelaide during September 1973 on the initiative of guitarist/singer Ian Moss. At the start of 1977 the band resettled in Sydney hoping to land the record contract that had alluded them. In the era of Fleetwood Mac, ELO, and the Eagles, Cold Chisel's sound was not deemed commercial. However WEA Records took the chance and the first self-titled album was released in April 1978. Between 1978 and 1983 Cold Chisel ruled as Australia's most popular band on record and stage. Disillusionment set in when the band's music failed to find favor in America, adding to the internal tensions created by various members' songwriting ambitions and singer Jimmy Barnes' volatile personality. On innumerable occasions throughout the band's life he had quit the band and rejoined. But now, after ten years together Cold Chisel decided to call it quits with a farewell tour ending at the Sydney Entertainment Centre in December 1983. Barnes immediately launched an incredibly successful solo career, accumulating seven Australian number one albums. Guitarist Ian Moss took five years off before releasing a number one album of his own, reuniting him with the songs of Don Walker. The band sold over three million records in Australia alone, two thirds of that number after their bitter break-up. —*Ed Nimmervoll*

● **The Best of Cold Chisel** / Jun. 30, 1998 / WEA ✦✦✦✦✦
Cold Chisel started life as just another pub rock band, but it finished as one of Australia's all-time greatest acts. This disc provides the perfect retrospective of one of the seminal Australian acts of the early '80s.

Cold Chisel was a band that was able to rock hard, but it also showed a deceptive depth and perceptiveness in their lyrics. They managed to record songs that covered not only a range of styles but a full range of emotions, from the bitter "You Got Nothing I Want" to the tender "Choir Girl." They wrote tales of drunken excesses ("Cheap Wine") and re-signed sadnesses ("Flame Trees"), and their superb ode to a returned Vietnam War veteran, "Khe Sanh," is a song that will forever epitomize this period of Australian music.

While the drug and alcohol excesses of Cold Chisel and their lead singer Jimmy Barnes are the stuff of legend, their music never suffered for it. These songs are classics, and to have them all collected here makes this disc nothing short of sublime. —*Jonathan Lewis*

Coldplay

f. 1998
Indie Pop, Indie Rock, Britpop
The Brit-rock quartet Coldplay are Chris Martin (vocals), Jon Buckland (guitar), Will

Champion (drums), and Guy Berryman (bass). Forming at the University College of London in early 1998, Coldplay were heart-rending like Travis, passionate like Jeff Buckley, and as fresh as Oasis when they first burst onto the scene in 1994. Coldplay independently released *The Safety EP* in 1998, with the *Brothers and Sisters EP* being picked up by Fierce Panda and released a year later. Both releases saw only 500 pressings. Their sweet melodies and swooning lyrics landed Coldplay a UK deal with Parlophone in April 1999, and the limited edition five-track *The Blue Room* EP followed that fall. With endearing nods from the media, the dream-pop foursome were hailed as the next Travis thanks to their simplistic acoustics and charming personas. Two more EPs, *Shiver* and *Yellow*, arrived in spring 2000. Their full-length debut *Parachutes*, which earned the band a Mercury Music Prize nomination, was released in the UK shortly thereafter. In November 2000, *Parachutes* saw a US release with Nettwerk; a month later "Yellow" was chosen as the theme song for all promo spots for ABC. The well-received hype surrounding the band continued throughout 2001 as well, taking on three Brit Awards nominations and a sold-out ten-date tour of the U.S. in February. *—MacKenzie Wilson*

Parachutes / Jul. 10, 2000 / Parlophone ✦✦✦✦
The London foursome Coldplay are constant critic's darlings in the band's native U.K., showcasing melodic pop in a slew of EP releases and constant live shows since the spark of the new millennium. Not as heavy as Radiohead or snobbish as Oasis, Coldplay is a band of young musicians who are still honing their sweet harmonies on the debut release *Parachutes*. Combining bits of distorted guitar riffs and swishing percussion, *Parachutes* is a delightful introduction and also quickly indicates the reason why this album earned Coldplay a Mercury Music Prize nomination in fall 2000. Frontman Chris Martin's lyrical wordplay is feministic in the manner of Geneva's Andrew Montgomery, but far more withered. The imagery captured on *Parachutes* is exquisitely dark and artistically abrasive, and the entire composition is tractable thanks to gauzy acoustics and airy percussion. Coldplay's indie rock inclinations are also obvious, especially on songs such as "Don't Panic" and "Shiver," but it's the dream pop soundscapes captured on "High Speed" and "We Never Change" that illustrate the band's dynamic passion. This basic pop is surely a refreshing effort in the face of big productions like the Spice Girls and Westlife. *Parachutes* deserves the accolades it has received because it follows the general rule when introducing decent pop songs: keep the emotion genuine and real. And Coldplay has done that without hesitation. *—MacKenzie Wilson*

Lloyd Cole

b. Jan. 31, 1961, Buxton, England
Vocals, Guitar / College Rock, Alternative Pop/Rock, Singer/Songwriter, Adult Alternative Pop/Rock
Through both his lauded work fronting the Commotions and his more eclectic solo efforts, Lloyd Cole established himself as one of the most articulate and acute songwriters of the postpunk era. The uncommon quality of Cole's writing earned the Commotions a contract with British Polydor in 1984, and they debuted with *Rattlesnakes*, a wry, heartfelt record of jangling guitar pop heralded by the shimmering single "Perfect Skin," which reached the U.K. Top 30. 1985's *Easy Pieces* was a slicker effort that included the singles "Lost Weekend" and "Brand New Friend," both of which earned significant airplay on alternative radio outlets. Following the release of 1987's *Mainstream*, Cole disbanded the Commotions and moved to New York City to establish himself as a solo performer. His eponymously-titled 1990 solo debut continued much in the vein of his work with the Commotions, but 1991's *Don't Get Weird on Me, Babe* marked a major artistic shift, as the entire second half of the album explored lush, string-sweetened cabaret music. Commercial success continued to elude Cole, however, and it took 1993's *Bad Vibes*—a diverse effort touching upon psychedelia and electronics—a year to find U.S. distribution. By the time of 1995's *Love Story*, his sound had come full circle, with a return to the more minimalist, folk-rock inspired work of the Commotions. *—Jason Ankeny*

Rattlesnakes / Oct. 1984 / Capitol ✦✦✦✦✦
One of the finest debuts of the '80s and possibly the defining album of the whole U.K. indie jangle scene that also included Prefab Sprout, Aztec Camera, and dozens of other bands, Lloyd Cole and the Commotions' *Rattlesnakes* is a college rock masterpiece of smart, ironic lyrics and sympathetic folk-rock-based melodies. The Glasgow-based band has a level of interplay remarkable in a group that had been playing for less than two years, and for all the attention given to Cole's hyper-literate lyrics, the album's finest moments are things like the slinky interludes between the wry verses on the Renata Adler-inspired "Speedboat" and Clark's glorious extended solo at the end of the album's finest song, "Forest Fire." Originally released in the U.S. by Geffen but reissued on CD as part of Capitol's acquisition of the Commotions in 1988, *Rattlesnakes* consists of ten perfect, or close to it, pop songs in just a hair under 36 minutes. Kicking off with the group's first U.K. single, the impossibly wordy, stream-of-consciousness "Perfect Skin," the album is basically a series of verbal snapshots of love gone wrong among the overeducated and underemployed. Cole's low-pitched and surprisingly soulful—for a philosophy student from the University of Glasgow, anyway—voice flits between earnestness, compassion, and arch derision ("Must you tell me all your secrets when it's hard enough to love you knowing nothing?"), while his lyrics sketch incisive character studies filled with smart and funny one-liners, near-obsessive name-dropping, and references to enough novels and movies for a semester-long pop culture class. In less skilled hands, this would all be unbearably pretentious, but Cole's sly sense of humor and self-mocking wit keep things on the right side of ambitious. *—Stewart Mason*

Easy Pieces / Nov. 1985 / Capitol ✦✦✦
Producers Clive Langer and Alan Winstanley, as is their wont, created a shimmering pop surface for Lloyd Cole & the Commotions' second album, sweetening the tracks with string and brass countermelodies and emphasizing the chiming highs of the guitar and keyboards for an attractive sound that echoed the earnestness of British bands like the Hollies and Herman's Hermits, circa 1966. It was, of course, like sugar coating cyanide capsules, given Lloyd Cole's pleasantly sung lyrics, which detailed philosophical disillusionment, romantic discord, and, yes, at least attempted suicide. In the U.K., *Easy Pieces* was a Top Ten hit. But although the album saw something like a proper release in the U.S. and the Commotions toured extensively, no American breakthrough materialized. *—William Ruhlmann*

Mainstream / Sep. 1987 / Capitol ✦✦

● **1984-1989** / Jun. 1989 / Capitol ✦✦✦✦✦
The lush, facile simplicity of Lloyd Cole's music is brimmed with cushioned harmonies and soft-spoken choruses, and more often than not deals with the complexity of love. Accompanied by the bright jangle of guitar that's hitched to palatable pop tempos, his work with backup band the Commotions produced a number of melody-ridden songs that are best accessed on *1984-1989*, a collection of their finest material. Not unlike Orange Juice or the Blue Nile, Cole's music used polished instrumentation behind elements of subdued '80s Euro-pop, best exemplified in songs like "Perfect Skin" and "You Will Never Be No Good." As an enduring and enjoyable compilation, *1984-1989* really does gather the cream of their music, and each song relinquishes a clean, robust sound. Some of the more beautiful tracks include the friendly candor of "Are You Ready to Be Heartbroken?" or the irregularity between the lines of "Jennifer She Said." "Brand New Friend" glimmers with Cole's vocal resilience, as does the pristine bounce of "Lost Weekend." All three of Lloyd Cole & the Commotions' albums contribute songs to this best-of, with the stronger pieces coming from 1984's *Rattlesnakes*. Cole's music strays from sounding contrived or overlapped and sports comparisons to the Beautiful South in that they share the same lyrical wit and appeal. Relatively unknown in North America, Lloyd Cole & the Commotions contributed to some of the finest music to ever hover with pop ease, and this compilation lines up his best work all in one place. *—Mike DeGagne*

Lloyd Cole / Feb. 1990 / Capitol ✦✦✦
In the two and a half years following the release of *Mainstream*, Lloyd Cole signed to Capitol Records in the U.S., split from the Commotions, and moved to New York. For his first solo album, he assembled a team consisting of two New York band veterans—drummer/co-producer Fred Maher and guitarist Robert Quine, both of whom had played in Richard Hell's Voidoids and Lou Reed's backup group—plus bassist Matthew Sweet and Commotions keyboard player Blair Cowan. As a result, *Lloyd Cole* boasts a tougher, harder sound than the Commotions' records. Cole's vocals, meanwhile, have become more direct and less stylized. Cole's lyrics are also less adorned, and he has lightened up somewhat. Much of *Lloyd Cole* is musically astringent in a way Cole hasn't managed previously, even if the album is far less ambitious than his first two records. *—William Ruhlmann*

Don't Get Weird on Me Babe / Sep. 16, 1991 / Capitol ✦✦✦✦
Lloyd Cole's second solo album, 1991's *Don't Get Weird on Me, Babe*, was about a half-decade ahead of its time. If it had come out in 1996, after Richard Davies' Cardinal project, the High Llamas' *Gideon Gaye*, and the new belief in indie circles that *Pet Sounds* and Burt Bacharach were musical icons worthy of veneration, this would have slotted right in. In the year bracketed by My Bloody Valentine's *Loveless* and Nirvana's *Nevermind*, *Don't Get Weird on Me, Babe* (title courtesy of Raymond Carver) was considered a self-indulgent oddity. In retrospect, however, it's clearly one of Lloyd Cole's finest works. The album is divided into two distinct parts. One (the first half in the U.S., the second half everywhere else) is more of Cole's trademark literate, jangly guitar pop, featuring the sterling "Tell Your Sister" and the uncharacteristically rocking "She's a Girl and I'm a Man," the closest Cole ever came to an American hit single. This side features a core band of Fred Maher (who co-produced) on drums, Matthew Sweet on bass, and Robert Quine on drums. That trio also appears on the other half of the album, but that set of six songs is dominated by a full orchestra arranged and conducted by Paul Buckmaster. Buckmaster's dramatic orchestrations add an entirely new dimension to the darker-edged songs without drowning them in Mantovani-style glop. In fact, the arrangements are rather low-key, especially on the haunting, hushed "Margo's Waltz," a gorgeous song with a jazzy bass part by Leland Sklar, subtle vibes, breathy female backing vocals, and almost subliminal brushed drums. Strongly reminiscent of Bacharach's most restrained '60s work—especially during ex-Commotion Blair Cowan's lovely Hammond B3 solos—"Margo's Waltz" is among the three or four best songs Cole has ever written. However, it's only one of many highlights on this exceptional, underrated album. *—Stewart Mason*

Bad Vibes / Oct. 1993 / Rykodisc ✦✦✦
Bad Vibes, Lloyd Cole's sixth new studio album, marks a big change in terms of sound. Producer Adam Peters and mixer Bob Clearmountain have tried to recreate the experimental days of the mid-'60s, employing a wide variety of studio gimmicks. But if *Bad Vibes* is Lloyd Cole's most produced record, it also is his earthiest. The singer's voice is recorded (sometimes with echo or double-tracking) especially high in the mix, and his singing is as stylized as it was on his first two albums, though in a different way. Here, he affects a sardonic, disengaged tone. All of this makes *Bad Vibes* Cole's most varied and most ambitious album, but far from his best. The odd sound stage and attitude are anything but accessible, and Cole himself has rarely been as vitriolic. [The U.S. Rykodisc version contains two bonus tracks, "For the Pleasure of Your Company" and "4 M.B.," not contained on the Fantana version.] *—William Ruhlmann*

Love Story / Oct. 3, 1995 / Rykodisc ✦✦✦
It stands to reason that a Lloyd Cole album called *Love Story* would not have a happy beginning or middle, much less ending. Actually, though, it does start out happy, "Trigger

Happy," that is, and later on, Cole is "Happy for You," in which he sings, "If you love him, you should leave me." In between, things get no sunnier, as Cole and his characters drink and despair, but carry on. That determination is very much part of Cole's negative world view: "Everybody knows this is nowhere," he says, to coin a phrase, "but you've gotta be there." (Except, one supposes, for Lucy, who jumps from the 39th floor in the rollicking "Let's Get Lost.") Typically, Cole couches these sentiments in melodic folk-rock, such that, with the volume low and just following the attractive lilt of his voice, a listener might find this a a far more soothing piece of music than it turns out to be on closer examination. — *William Ruhlmann*

The Negatives / Nov. 14, 2000 / What Are? ✦✦✦✦
This moody yet self-deprecating singer/songwriter's album will be nothing new to fans that have followed the long arc of Lloyd Cole's career. One listen to "What's Wrong With This Picture"—which offers the sentiment "'Smile,' she said, 'If you want I'll look the other way/Til you regain your melancholy disposition or until you get over yourself'" over a bright guitar figure—places longtime fans on familiar ground. Cole's uncanny melodic ear is also still in place. What is new, however, is his return to fronting a full-time band after spending his post-Commotions years (they split in 1988) as a fairly singular figure. *The Negatives* includes such talent as Jill Sobule ("I Kissed a Girl") and one-time Dambuilder Dave Derby, and the merry-band-of-thieves ethic seems to lend some levity to the proceedings. "Tried to Rock" casts a wry eye on Cole's early solo days (circa his 1990 self-titled solo debut), when the onetime arch '80s intellectual/singer (a la Morrissey) moved to New York, grew his hair, and embraced general debauchery. "I did not fail to see what it takes to rock/Is that which I have not," sings Cole in highly un-rock, grammatical fashion over a ponderous rock-ballad beat. The album opener, "Past Imperfect," also serves up some retrospection, offering lyrical references to Cole's "Brand New Friend" and "Lost Weekend" (as well as Leonard Cohen's "Chelsea Hotel" with "Why was my head in the unmade bed?"). Cole, at age 40, seems comfortable with himself and his career—quirks, blemishes, and all—and one would be hard pressed to find any of his U.K. '80s contemporaries making such a strong, winningly melodic album...if they're still making albums at all. — *Erik Hage*

Paula Cole

Vocals, Piano / Adult Alternative Pop/Rock, Singer/Songwriter
Paula Cole was one of the many female singer-songwriters that rose to prominence in the mid-'90s in the wake of alternative's commercial breakthrough. Drawing heavily from the ethereal, pretty sound of Sarah McLachlan and Tori Amos, Cole created songs that relied equally on dreamy melodies and poetic, introspective lyrics. Her first big break arrived when Peter Gabriel invited her to perform on his 1992-93 world tour. Shortly afterward, she signed to Imago Records, where she released her debut album, *Harbinger*, in 1994. Within a year of the album's release, Imago went out of business, which prevented the record from getting exposure on radio and in the press. In 1995, she signed to Warner Brothers, who reissued *Harbinger* in the fall of that year. Cole returned with her second album, *This Fire*, in October of 1996. The album and its accompanying single, "Where Have All the Cowboys Gone?," became word-of-mouth hits, breaking through into the mainstream in the spring of 1997. That summer, Cole participated in the first Lilith Fair, a traveling festival Sarah McLachlan designed to showcase female artists. In 1998, Cole won the Grammy for Best New Artist, despite the fact that she released her debut album in 1994 and therefore was technically ineligible. — *Stephen Thomas Erlewine*

Harbinger / 1994 / Imago ✦✦✦
Paula Cole wanted to produce her debut 14 track opus herself, but was "led by the hand" of her record company toward quietly unsung genius Kevin Killen. *Harbinger* opens with the remorseful yet poppy "Happy Home" and the acoustic breeze of "I Am So Ordinary." Cole is strong melodically and vocally, soaring high and low. She also plays it correctly by producing her most commercially minded work first before diversifying. Signs of what's to come are evident on Kate Bush-like "Watch the Woman's Hands," "Dear Gertrude," and "She Can't Feel Anything Anymore." More upbeat is the driving "Saturn Girl," and her backing band is sharp on "Chairoscuro." "Bethlehem" laments Cole's hatred of her small town upbringing while "Garden of Eden" and "The Ladder" echo her spiritual interest. — *Kelvin Hayes*

● **This Fire** / Oct. 15, 1996 / Imago ✦✦✦✦
Paula Cole's songwriting and musical skills sharpened considerably on her second album, *This Fire*. Occasionally, she flirts a little too closely with Sarah McLachlan territory, but Cole has developed her own, subtly mature style, equally informed by textured electronics, light worldbeat influences and soul-baring lyrics. "Where Have All the Cowboys Gone" may epitomize the sound of the album, but it only scratches the surface of what *This Fire* has to offer. — *Stephen Thomas Erlewine*

Amen / Sep. 28, 1999 / Imago/Warner Brothers ✦✦✦✦
Thanks to Paula Cole's appearance on the first Lilith Fair and "Where Have All the Cowboys Gone?," *This Fire* didn't really take off until nearly a year after its 1996 release; plus, its closer "I Don't Want to Wait" became nearly omnipresent in 1998. So, the gap between *This Fire* and its sequel, *Amen*, didn't feel all that long, but a cursory listen to *Amen* reveals that Cole matured considerably during those three years. *Amen* is the work of a professional record-maker, someone who not only knows how to craft a song, but knows how to craft sound. It's certainly in the same vein as *This Fire*, yet tighter and subtler, and fits right into adult alternative pop radio circa 1999. She may tread uncomfortably close to the smooth, sweetly cloying pop of Sarah McLachlan, but Cole somehow became convinced that she was a soul singer. So, the pretty music is underpinned with light hip-hop rhythms or R&B chord progressions, while she pours out passion through her voice and lyrics. She may get carried away with self-righteous naïveté and clichéd liberal dogma,

but such impassioned beliefs give *Amen* greater weight, grit, and character than the average adult alternative pop album. Also, she saves most of her lyrical excess through strong, assured singing that's soulful but not overdone (the exception is when she dips into rap on "Rhythm of Life," which is positively embarrassing, especially when she's supported by scratching). Despite the occasional sophomoric lyric, Cole never sounds as strident as she occasionally did on *This Fire*, and the entire album is clearly the work of an artist who is more assured than ever before. Musically, that results in a stronger album than its predecessor, even if it lacks singles as grabbing or memorable as "Cowboys" or "Wait." — *Stephen Thomas Erlewine*

Collective Soul

f. 1992
American Trad Rock, Post-Grunge, Alternative Pop/Rock, Hard Rock
With their catchy, melodic pop/rock and mildly distorted but warm guitar tone, Collective Soul leapt out of Stockbridge, GA, to the top of the 1990s AOR world. Vocalist/guitarist/songwriter Ed Roland, whose parents prohibited listening to music, originally founded the band in the mid-'80s after dropping out of the Berklee School of Music due to lack of funds and getting a job in a 24-track recording studio. The band drew no interest whatsoever from any label, and a disheartened Roland called it quits in 1992 to put together a songwriter's demo in hopes of finding work. A demo of "Shine" caught the attention of several radio stations and eventually Atlantic Records, and Roland hastily put together a new version of Collective Soul with his brother Dean on guitar, Ross Childress on lead guitar, Will Turpin on bass, and original drummer Shane Evans. "Shine" became an AOR smash and was an inescapable hit on MTV and radio during the spring and summer of 1994; it helped the band's debut album, *Hints, Allegations and Things Left Unsaid*, sell over a million copies by the end of the year. Their self-titled follow-up was released in 1995 and spawned the radio hits "Gel," "December," and "The World I Know." *Disciplined Breakdown*, Collective Soul's third album, was released in March 1997; *Dosage* followed two years later and *Blender* was issued in fall 2000. — *Steve Huey*

Hints Allegations and Things Left Unsaid / Mar. 22, 1994 / Atlantic ✦✦✦
Collective Soul never claimed it was an alt-rock band, but it arrived with the debut *Hints Allegations and Things Left Unsaid* when anything with guitars was marketed as anti-establishment, underground rock. In retrospect, it's sort of hard to see how this record, with its loving debts to Southern rock and AOR anthems, ever shared airplay on modern rock radio stations and *120 Minutes*, but that's just the way things were in the heady days of 1994. Ironically, Collective Soul succeeded where cult heroes Urge Overkill couldn't—making late-'70s arena rock popular. Urge, of course, was a band of hardcore ironists, where the members of Collective Soul were dogged traditionalists, which sells better with a mainstream audience, and that's part of the reason why this debut was a hit. The other reason is that the band hits the riff jackpot a couple of times here: "Wasting Time" and "Love Lifted Me" are strong classicist rock, but "Shine" is a tremendous guilty pleasure, built on a guitar riff so indelible you swear it's stolen, blessed by a sighing melody that makes this a fine album-rock single that would have sounded as good in '74 as it did in '94. This is the song that signaled that the group had the skills and smarts to be a first-rate singles band, even if the rest of the record vacillates between pleasant and forgettable filler. — *Stephen Thomas Erlewine*

● **Collective Soul** / Mar. 14, 1995 / Atlantic ✦✦✦✦
It would not have been surprising if Collective Soul had become a one-hit wonder. Straddling a line between '80s arena rock and jangling, '90s alternative pop, their debut was a pleasant affair that became a multi-platinum smash. They don't tamper much with that sound on *Collective Soul*, but the results are every bit as enjoyable due to the engaging melodies that lead singer Ed Roland and company seem to create at will. The hits included the infectious "Gel," sarcastic, mid-tempo "December," and the lovely, soaring ballad "The World I Know." However, most everything else works just as well, from the churning "Where the River Flows" to the gospel-tinged "Reunion." While not exactly ground-breaking, *Collective Soul* delivers the goods with a dozen, hook-laden songs for which they were awarded another multi-platinum outing. — *Tom Demalon*

Disciplined Breakdown / Mar. 11, 1997 / Atlantic ✦✦✦✦
Disciplined Breakdown has to be one of only a handful of records inspired by a songwriter's breakup with his manager, but despite its origins, the album is another smartly assembled arena-rock collection from Collective Soul. Ed Roland knows how to co-opt contemporary alternative-rock trends and re-fashion them into hard-rocking anthems, as evidenced by the first single "Precious Declaration." He still has a problem coming up with a consistent set of songs, but *Disciplined Breakdown* is nearly as slickly entertaining as Collective Soul's eponymous second album, and its best moments indicate that Roland is beginning to develop a distinctive hard-rock style of his own. — *Stephen Thomas Erlewine*

Dosage / Feb. 9, 1999 / Atlantic ✦✦✦
After the disappointing sales of *Disciplined Breakdown*, Collective Soul made a move back to the sound that was so successful on their self-titled sophomore effort. *Dosage* is a step backwards into familiar territory, and it invites mixed results. While the singles "Run" and "Heavy" are two of the band's biggest hits in years, much of this album seems to sound slightly more tired than Collective Soul's recent efforts. Collective Soul has always been best when performing a mix of ballads and harder material, and *Dosage* holds true to that formula, although the ballads (which are not quite as strong as the ballads on previous albums) rule this album. Kicking off with the upbeat "Tremble for My Beloved" and "Heavy," the album quickly slows down and fails to reignite. Only a few of the ballads (among them the hit "Run" from the film, *Varsity Blues*, and the mid-tempo "No More, No Less") manage to leave any lasting impression, and the majority of the uptempo

rockers seem like filler. This doesn't mean that *Dosage* is a weak effort, though, as there is still more than enough here to please fans. Ed Roland continues to grow as a songwriter, and *Dosage* is another successful set of radio-friendly pop/rock that, while far from radical, is a worthwhile listen. *—Jason Damas*

Blender / Oct. 10, 2000 / Atlantic ✦✦

● **7even Year Itch: Collective Soul Greatest Hits 1994-2001** / Sep. 18, 2001 / Atlantic ✦✦✦✦
Collective Soul had just enough good singles to make you think that a collection, such as *7even Year Itch: Greatest Hits 1994-2001*, would be a great guilty pleasure for all of those that hummed along to "Shine" even as they bought Nine Inch Nails and Alice in Chains discs. And it is true that there are some very good songs here, such as the assured "Shine," the tempered power ballad "December" and the terrific Urge Overkill rip "Gel," perhaps not their biggest hit but arguably their finest moment. These, of course, are all on *7even Year Itch* but there aren't quite enough other cuts in this 13-track collection to convince the doubters (the non-chronlogical sequencing doesn't really help matters, either). But even if this collection doesn't make the case for being a great populist, critically-shunned band (Stone Temple Pilots hold that title for the '90s), it still does summarize Collective Soul's career well, and will be of interest to the casual listeners who enjoyed certain songs on the radio during the headly post-grunge days of the second half of the '90s. *—Stephen Thomas Erlewine*

The Collins Kids

f. 1954, California, **db.** 1962
Rockabilly
By the time Lawrence (b. 1944) and Lawrencine (b. 1942) Collins were eleven and thirteen, respectively, they were already tearing it up on country package shows, recording for Columbia Records, and performing on national TV almost weekly. Older sister Lorrie held up the cowgirl fringe-rustling-against-nylons teenage-sensuality department; kid brother Larry was a bundle of hyperkinetic energy, bopping all over the place while laying down exciting, twangy guitar breaks learned firsthand from the "King of Double-necked Mosrite," Joe Maphis. The Collins' recordings as time went on veered from mawkish brother/sister country-style duets to white-hot rockabilly, and they were just reaching their peak when Lorrie eloped, effectively breaking up the act. Revered by rockabilly collectors the world over, their filmed television appearances and recordings are testimony to the fact that the Collins Kids weren't just "good for their age," they were just plain good, period. *—Cub Koda*

● **Introducing Larry and Lorrie** / 1958 / Columbia ✦✦✦✦✦
For those who don't want to spring for the lengthy and expensive Bear Family box, this is an excellent distillation of 12 of their best late-'50s rockabilly sides. "Hoy Hoy," "Whistle Bait," "Mercy," "Just Because," and "Party," rank among the most smokin' rockabilly sides ever waxed. *—Richie Unterberger*

Television Party / 1989 / TV ✦✦✦
14 lo-fi songs from vintage television broadcasts, on a label of questionable legitimacy. There's a 31-song compilation of this stuff on a 1993 Krazy Kat album; hold out for that one instead. *—Richie Unterberger*

Hop, Skip and Jump / Aug. 1991 / Bear Family ✦✦✦✦✦
The Collins Kids were a brother-and-sister act that got real good real young and made it out of their native Oklahoma, settling out in California where they landed a radio/TV hookup with Tex Ritter's *Town Hall Party* out of Compton. Older sister Lorrie handled the teenage-sensuality department with nylons rustling against cowgirl fringe, while little brother Larry was a hot-as-a-firecracker bundle of energy, bopping all over the place while laying down excitable, twangy guitar breaks learned first-hand from another *Town Hall Party* regular, the King of the double-neck Mosrite, Joe Maphis. With all that in mind, what we have here is another excellent CD box set from Bear Family, two discs with booklet in an album-size format. Everything's here; from the great early sides like "Beetle Bug Bop," "The Cuckoo Rock," "I'm in My Teens" and "The Rockaway Rock" to the rockabilly classics "Just Because," "Hoy Hoy," "Mercy," "Sweet Talk," and "Party," through the Maphis/Collins guitar instrumentals to Larry and Lorrie's solo sides from the end of the trail. Joe Maphis' great guitar is sprayed all over the place and the master tape transfer is as clear as you expect stuff out of the Columbia vaults produced by Don Law to be. A booklet crammed full of great live photos and excellent liners by Colin Escott round out the package. *—Cub Koda*

Rockin' on T.V. / 1993 / Krazy Kat ✦✦✦✦
Larry and Lorrie, the Collins Kids, were a live act to be savored. In their early days, they were cute without being cloying, highly energetic without being annoying. As they moved into their teens by the late '50s, Larry had developed into a phenomenal guitarist while Lorrie had bloomed into a beautiful teenager with a voice that could belt out both rock & roll and sensual ballads. The recordings contained on this CD stem from live television appearances on the *Town Hall Party* television show, culled mostly from shows in February and May of 1959 and January 1960. Tex Ritter and Jay Stewart were the hosts of this West Coast version of the *Grand Ole Opry*, and some of their introductions and interview chat has been left on between numbers. Larry and Lorrie were the nominal rock & roll act on the show; their appearances would always give a show a quick shot of much-needed energy between the staid and traditional country acts, and that energy and youthful passion literally leaps off this disc. The Kids clock in with aces-up versions of "Kokomo," "Hoy Hoy," "Hot Rod," "Chantilly Lace," a blistering "Way Down Yonder in New Orleans," and "Dance to the Bop," while Larry and Joe Maphis' duets on "Feisty," "Under the Double Eagle," "Wildcat," and "Hurricane" are guitar showcases with the accent on show. Lorrie's sultry voice is heard to great effect on "Waiting Just for You," an original they never got around to recording. Perhaps the most intriguing tunes here are a trio of Buddy Holly numbers ("That'll Be the Day," "Peggy Sue," and "Oh Boy!") rearranged to fit Larry and Lorrie, in completely different keys and with completely different guitar breaks than the original versions. There's not a lot of Collins Kids material available and this collection makes a wonderful addition to their small but rocking discography. *—Cub Koda*

Rockin'est / Feb. 11, 1998 / Bear Family ✦✦✦✦✦
If Larry and Lorrie, the Collins Kids, were denied their rightful place at the hit-making table during the 1950s, then the music some 40 years later poises them as the very energetic embodiment of ground-floor rockabilly music. Lorrie's sexy vocals and Larry's twangy guitar breaks fused to his hyperkinetic little-brother stance makes for some pretty exciting music on this collection; performances like "Hoy Hoy," "I'm in My Teens," "Whistle Bait," "Party," "Hot Rod" and the flame-throwing "Mercy" show the kids at their rocking best. The collection is also sprinkled with their country big sister/cute but pesky little brother novelties ("Make Him Behave," "Hush Money") and early country-approved rockers ("Shortnin' Bread Rock," "Beetle Bug Bop") to give a more complete picture of the duo's recorded oeuvre. If springing for their deluxe box set is too much for your wallet to handle, then this 22-track single-disc collection is absolutely the way to go. *—Cub Koda*

Bootsy Collins

b. Oct. 26, 1951, Cincinnati, OH
Vocals, Bass / Funk
Bootsy (born William Collins) is a funk/R&B bassist/singer/bandleader. He formed his first group, the Pacesetters, in 1968, featuring Phelps "Catfish" Collins (his brother) (guitar), Frankie "Kash" Waddy (drums), and Philippe Wynne. From 1969 to 1971, the group functioned as James Brown's backup band and was dubbed the JB's. In 1972, Bootsy joined George Clinton's Parliament/Funkadelic. He launched Bootsy's Rubber Band as a spin-off of P-Funk in 1976, the band including his brother Phelps, Waddy, Joel "Razor Sharp" Johnson (keyboards), Gary "Mudd-Bone" Cooper (drums), and Robert "P-Nut" Johnson (vocals), along with "the Horny Horns." (He was sometimes billed alone as Bootsy, and sometimes as William "Bootsy" Collins.)

Signing to Warner Bros. Records, he enjoyed the first of his 15 R&B singles chart entries in 1976 with "Stretchin' Out (In a Rubber Band)." His most successful singles were "The Pinocchio Theory" (1977) and the chart-topping "Bootzilla" (1978). He also released six albums on Warners through 1982, including the gold-sellers *Ahh... The Name Is Bootsy Baby!* (1977) and *Bootsy? Player of the Year* (1978), then took a six-year recording hiatus and returned on Columbia in 1988 with the appropriately named *What's Bootsy Doin'?* In 1989, Bootsy was a member of The Bootzilla Orchestra on Malcolm McLaren's album *Waltz Dancing*. In 1990, Bootsy was a featured guitarist and bassist with the dance music trio Deee-Lite. Bootsy's New Rubber Band released *Blasters of the Universe* on August 2, 1994. *Straight Outta P University* followed four years later. *—William Ruhlmann*

● **Back in the Day: The Best of Bootsy** / Aug. 9, 1994 / Warner Brothers ✦✦✦✦✦
This one-disc collection could easily be a two-disc or more if one wanted to include every last highlight from Collins' up-down-all-around career—his work with James Brown alone is beyond the bomb—but when it comes to solo work, this is as perfect a place to start as any. Drawing mostly on the albums done with the active help of George Clinton in the late '70s, *Back in the Day* is a model for what a good compilation should be. Sound is excellent throughout, while full details on who plays what and where, along with where everything came from in the first place, all appear in exhaustive detail. The liner notes, meanwhile, come from longtime funk road manager (Brown, Prince, plenty of others) Alan Leeds, explaining every step of Collins' wonderful story. Collins himself gets in a great concluding bit of thanks and message that's a joy to read, and needless to say the photos of him in his sunglassed late-'70s star-bass-guitar glory abound. And the music? "Bootzilla," "Stretchin' Out (In a Rubber Band)," and "Pinocchio Theory" are just three jam masterpieces of many. A couple of fine rarities flesh things out; "What So Never the Dance," recorded in 1971 when Collins' band was still known as the House Guests, is a great slice of greasy, JBs-tinged funk. "Body Slam!" shows him getting to grips with electro nicely, while "Scenery," originally a B-side ballad, has him doing his loveman-goes-nuts deal at the end. A fierce 1976-era live take on "Psychoticbumpschool," with the Horny Horns in full blow, wraps up this fantastic collection. *—Ned Raggett*

● **Glory B da' Funk's on Me!: The Bootsy Collins Anthology** / Jun. 5, 2001 / Rhino ✦✦✦✦✦
Bootsy Collins has rightfully received accolades as funk's second officer (after George Clinton—and it should be third after James Brown and Clinton). For decades he has been sampled by nearly every rapper, and virtually created the bass sound that made the Red Hot Chili Peppers a household name and that created a career for Les Claypool. Yet, his most influential sound emanated not from his tenure with James Brown or P-Funk, but his own Rubber Band, and for years that wooly, wild, and surreal unit had never been properly anthologized. Rhino, in their usual thorough, crazy fashion, directed the folks at the Warner archives and created a massive, drop-the-bomb two-disc set that sets the record straight. This may not be no disco but it sho' 'nuff is some mean foolin' around. Sorry. Got carried away. This collection is every bit as necessary as the Funkadelic singles compilation, Parliament's *Chronicles and First Thangs* collection, and the James Brown *20 Greatest Hits* comp. This is the shit that got kickin' and keeps on tickin' over 30 years after the original bomb was dropped. *—Thom Jurek*

Edwyn Collins

b. Aug. 23, 1959, Edinburgh, Scotland
Vocals, Guitar / Indie Pop, Alternative Pop/Rock
Best known for leading Glasgow's pop revivalists Orange Juice and his international solo

hit "A Girl Like You," singer Edwyn Collins' career ranged from hit singles to extended periods without a record deal. He formed the Nu-Sonics in 1976, which resurfaced three years later as Orange Juice. The band's devoted cult following earned them little commercial success: by the early 1980s, Collins was the only remaining founding member. After a self-titled 1984 release failed to chart, Orange Juice disbanded; Collins was freed from his contract with the group's label, Polydor.

Though a solo career seemed imminent, Collins' reputation as a stubborn perfectionist made getting a contract difficult. In 1986, after a pair of sold-out London performances, Creation's Alan McGee signed him to the label's subsidiary Elevation. The singles "Don't Shilly Shally" (produced by Cocteau Twin Robin Guthrie) and "My Beloved Girl" followed, but didn't chart. Elevation folded in 1987, and after Collins and McGee had a falling out, the singer was again left without a contract.

Later that year, Collins recorded at a small German studio run by devoted Orange Juice fans. Cut with the aid of producer Dennis Bovell and Aztec Camera frontman Roddy Frame, the resulting LP *Hope and Despair* was eventually released by the Demon label in 1989. The album—a brooding, ambitious collection spotlighting Collins' smooth, soulful baritone—did well on the independent charts, and Collins returned to the studio to record 1990's spartan *Hellbent on Compromise.* Demon dropped him when the LP failed to repeat its predecessor's success; another long sabbatical followed.

After spending the early '90s producing sessions for artists like longtime pal Paul Quinn, A House and the Frank & Walters, Collins signed with the tiny UK indie Setanta and recorded 1994's *Gorgeous George,* a scathing, shimmering set highlighted by the single "A Girl Like You." A massive hit throughout Europe and the U.S., the song was Collins' first big single since Orange Juice's 1983 smash "Rip It Up." In 1997, he returned with *I'm Not Following You,* another strong—if not quite as commercially successful—album. —*Jason Ankeny*

Hope and Despair / 1989 / Demon ✦✦✦✦✦

Collins's post-Orange Juice debut album has the familiar trappings of one of Glasgow's most celebrated songwriters—a man whose main fallbacks seem to be lovelorn pessimism and cynicism toward the entertainment industry. Still, when you prepare the same feast as lovingly as Collins does, you'll never be short of house guests. The songwriting craft here is as keenly evident as you'd expect, with reggae hero Dennis Bovell (previously a member of Orange Juice's inner circle) providing production help and bass. Aztec Camera's Roddy Frame also contributes guitar. Highlights include "The Beginning of the End," which is downcast even by Collins' world-weary standards, as the artist treads carefully through everything from blue-eyed pop to rustic country in his resolutely sure-footed manner. —*Alex Ogg*

Hellbent on Compromise / 1990 / Demon ✦✦✦

Following the demise of Orange Juice, the solo Edwyn Collins took some time to build a commercial platform—at least, he did in his native Britain. Fans of his wistful yet terse songwriting were mainly scattered around central Europe, but his debut effort, 1989's *Hope and Despair* won a series of glowing reviews. Sadly, he largely squandered those good impressions with this follow-up, which too often lacks the strength of arrangement to carry through Collins' lyrical ideas and projects. "You Poor Deluded Fool" and "What's the Big Idea?" would certainly have benefited from a proper band setting, instead of the largely predictable studio keyboards that dominate. The cover of Smokey Robinson's "My Girl Has Gone" does no one any favors either. The campaign for real songwriting, to paraphrase a later Collins' track, would have to wait until his next album for a second significant, by-election victory. —*Alex Ogg*

● **Gorgeous George** / 1994 / Bar/None ✦✦✦✦✦

Edwyn Collins made a remarkable and unexpected comeback with *Gorgeous George,* and it's not hard to see why. The album represents a consolidation of Collins' skills as a songwriter, demonstrating both his vicious wit and his effortless melodicism. Working with former Sex Pistols drummer Paul Cook and bassist Claire Kenny, he develops the hardest-hitting musical attack of his career, but it's also surprisingly versatile, capable not only of glam-rock, but also jangle-pop, folk-rock and blue-eyed soul. And while Collins can occasionally be accused of lyrical sniping—the attack on Guns & Roses in "North of Heaven" is simply silly—there's no denying that when his words and music hit the same target, such as on the darkly catchy Iggy Pop tribute "A Girl Like You," the results are wonderfully cerebral pop music. —*Stephen Thomas Erlewine*

I'm Not Following You / Oct. 21, 1997 / Epic ✦✦✦

Having found himself back in the commercial limelight with *Gorgeous George,* Collins followed it up with the equally—possibly even more—delightful *I'm Not Following You.* Trademark wit blended with passion intact and with key sideplayers drummer Paul Cook and bassist Clare Kenny helping out among many others—including a wonderfully scabrous vocal cameo by Mark E. Smith on the very disco "Seventies Night"—Collins tries all sorts of different things and more often than not comes up with the goods. "The Magic Piper (Of Love)" was the understandable lead single, catchy and with more than a little bite to it, drawing from finger-snapping hep-lounge Vegas sources and his own fun lyrics: "My girlfriend she got blotto/Half cut in Santa's grotto/It turns out he's a dirty old man." Add to that some just right flute and a clever brass sample that suddenly turns into an orchestrated sample from the Velvet Underground, and the man still has it. It's one of many joys throughout, with Collins showing a musical heterodoxy that would probably stupefy most other bands or acts. "Seventies Night," for example, is followed up by the sweet orchestration and quick acoustic fingerpicking of "No One Waved Goodbye," a regretful look at a relationship in pieces. There's full-on feedback and pounding drums, there's sly, compressed production touching quirky keyboards and Euro/cabaret arrangements, and even the self-explanatory Hammond-tinged "Country Rock." The hint of wistful nostalgia is often matched by the lyrics, with asides like "I'm going back to my old

school/Cause to tell you the truth/All those songs of my youth/Move this old fool." Not many musicians so readily and easily allow for the hints of the passage of time. Leave it to Collins to find a number of ways to do just that. —*Ned Raggett*

Judy Collins

b. May 1, 1939, Seattle, WA
Vocals, Keyboards, Guitar / Folk Revival, Folk-Rock, Singer/Songwriter

Judy Collins was one of the major interpretive folksingers of the '60s. She released her first album, *A Maid of Constant Sorrow,* in 1961 when she was 22. That album and its follow-up, *The Golden Apples of the Sun,* consisted of traditional folk material, with Collins's pure, sweet soprano accompanied by her acoustic guitar playing. By the time of *Judy Collins #3,* she had begun to turn to contemporary material and to add other musicians. Collins' musical horizons were expanded further by 1966 and the release of *In My Life,* which added theater music to her repertoire and introduced her audience to the writing of Leonard Cohen; it was one of her six albums to go gold. Her first gold-seller, however, was 1967's *Wildflowers,* which contained her hit version of "Both Sides Now" by the then-little-known songwriter Joni Mitchell. By the '70s, Collins had come to be identified as much as an art song singer as a folksinger and had also begun to make a mark with her original compositions. Her best-known performances cover a wide stylistic range: the traditional gospel song "Amazing Grace," the Stephen Sondheim Broadway ballad "Send in the Clowns," and such songs of her own as "My Father" and "Born to the Breed." —*William Ruhlmann*

Maid of Constant Sorrow / 1961 / Elektra ✦✦✦

Collins's talent is to sing these traditional chestnuts, even at the time, without the prissiness of so many female folk singers. Her phrasing has enough strength to stand up to the "Prickile Bush" and give in to "Wild Mountain Thyme." —*Richard Meyer*

Golden Apples of the Sun / 1962 / Elektra ✦✦✦

Collins takes on such diverse repertoire as Gary Davis' "Twelve Gates to the City," "Crow on the Cradle" and her setting of "Golden Apples of the Sun." —*Richard Meyer*

Judy Collins #3 / 1963 / Elektra ✦✦✦

Having established herself as one of the foremost interpreters of traditional material, Collins did the same for contemporary folk songwriters on this album, which mixed standards with pristine covers of compositions by Dylan, Bob Gibson, Pete Seeger, Ewan MacColl, and Shel Silverstein. With Jim (Roger) McGuinn arranging and playing second guitar and banjo, this album, which included a fine version of Seeger's "Turn! Turn! Turn!," had a clear (if overlooked) influence on the folk-rock he pioneered with The Byrds a couple years later. —*Richie Unterberger*

Judy Collins' Concert / 1964 / Elektra ✦✦✦

On this live set recorded at Town Hall in New York in 1964, Collins stirs up the audience with a rich mixture of traditional and contemporary covers, including Billy Ed Wheeler's "Coal Tattoo" and Paxton's "Ramblin' Boy." —*Richard Meyer*

Fifth Album / 1965 / Elektra ✦✦✦✦✦

Collins took a major stride forward with this fine, consistent album, tailoring both her material and arrangements to reflect contemporary changes shaking folk and folk-rock. Features stellar interpretations of songs by several major '60s songwriters (Dylan, Eric Andersen, Phil Ochs, Gordon Lightfoot, Malvina Reynolds, Richard Farina), and first-rate accompaniment by some of the day's finest folk and folk-rock musicians, including Eric Weissberg, Bill Lee, Danny Kalb, John Sebastian, and Richard Farina (although no drums are present). —*Richie Unterberger*

In My Life / 1966 / Elektra ✦✦✦✦✦

Collins, who by this point has moved from the acoustic renderings of traditional folk ballads to more extensive instrumentation and the work of contemporary folk writers, takes another step here, turning to tasteful string arrangements by Joshua Rifkin and adding theater music from *Threepenny Opera* and *Marat/Sade* to the Bob Dylan covers. She also starts covering Leonard Cohen ("Suzanne," "Dress Rehearsal Rag"). —*William Ruhlmann*

Wildflowers / 1967 / Elektra ✦✦✦

Soothing. Unique. Natural. These are clear adjectives used best when describing the style and grace of Judy Collins and her album, *Wildflowers.* Her blend of folk and meditative music paints a tapestry of soft, nurturing colors that transcends the mind of the listener and seeks one's soul. Much of the material feels uplifting and full of spirit, or even spiritual to some degree. Yet other parts of the record can be viewed and felt as sad and morose, which gives the record some dexterity and variety among its ability to appeal toward contrasting moods. Collins makes a well-earned statement in her original tunes, "Since You Asked," "Sky Fell" and "Albatross" that deep, meditative and subtle can be effective within the realms of music as an art form. She is certainly artistic with her approach, staying away from the cliche folk, pop music that flooded much of the '60s radio-friendly airwaves. Collins also includes her favorite melodies from the songbooks of Joni Mitchell and Leonard Cohen. This can benefit one as a pleasant listen, easy to sooth the mind and body, and release the burdens of everyday stress in today's society. —*Shawn M. Haney*

Who Knows Where the Time Goes / 1968 / Elektra ✦✦✦

Rock and country leanings are found on this album featuring guitarists James Burton and Stephen Stills. Includes the hit "Someday Soon" and Collins' own brilliant "My Father." —*William Ruhlmann*

Recollections: The Best of Judy Collins / 1969 / Elektra ✦✦✦✦

Collins sings "Tomorrow Is a Long Time," "Early Mornin' Rain" and "Winter Sky." This is a best-of compilation. —*Richard Meyer*

Whales & Nightingales / 1970 / Elektra ♦♦♦
Judy Collins found herself in the top forty with her adaptation of "Amazing Grace." *Whales & Nightingales* is full of good songs ranging from Bob Dylan's "Time Passes Slowly" to songs by Jacques Brel and also Pete Seeger. Judy also had a hit with her adaptation of the song "Farewell To Tarwathie" which she sang over the accompaniments of Humpback Whales. It opened new doors for her and folk music in general. *—James Chrispell*

Living / 1971 / Elektra ♦♦♦
A much more contemporary record than her previous releases, *Living* shows Judy Collins stretching out, although sometimes, this could be said to show her stretching a little too far. Contains her versions of Ian Tyson's "Four Strong Winds," Leonard Cohen's "Famous Blue Raincoat" and Joni Mitchell's "Chelsea Morning." However, it also shows that while she interprets songs well, her version of Bob Dylan's "Just Like Tom Thumb's Blues" lets one see that not all songs are fitted well into the Collins style. *—James Chrispell*

● **Colors of the Day: The Best of Judy Collins** / 1972 / Elektra ♦♦♦♦♦
An excellent collection of some of the best tracks from Judy Collins' early Elektra albums, *Colors of the Day* will both entertain and leave you wanting more. Lovingly programmed (it leads off with her excellent country-pop hit, "Someday Soon," an Ian Tyson classic), this is Collins at her finest. Earlier explorations into folk-pop ("Both Sides Now"), British folk ("Sunny Goodge Street," "In My Life") and gospel ("Amazing Grace") clearly show her eclecticism. Some of the record's finest moments are from her exquisite 1968 album, *Who Know's Where the Time Goes* (such as that album's title track and the aforementioned "Someday Soon"). This anthology brings the "best of" collection to a new art form. *—Matthew Greenwald*

True Stories and Other Dreams / 1973 / Elektra ♦♦♦
Collins at her most political, saluting Che Guevara, among others. Elaborately produced and well sung. *—Bruce Eder*

Judith / 1975 / Elektra ♦♦♦
A soaring collection of songs from the Depression, '70s Broadway ("Send in the Clowns"), and modern C&W. *—Bruce Eder & William Ruhlmann*

Bread and Roses / 1976 / Elektra ♦♦

Hard Times for Lovers / 1979 / Elektra ♦♦

Book-of-the-Month Records Box Set / 1981 / Warner Special Products ♦♦♦♦♦
There's no widely distributed Judy Collins box set (as of 1997), but collectors may want to be aware of this four-LP box that Warner Special Products put together for the Book-of-the-Month club in 1981. Drawing from 13 albums, it includes much of her best '60s and '70s material, with LP sides devoted to "Beginnings," "Songs of Leonard Cohen," "Contemporary Songwriters," "Love Songs," "Protest and Prayer," and "Her Own Songs." It still manages to miss some of her best tracks—most notably, her cover of Richard Farina's "Hard Lovin' Loser," one of her best '60s rock performances. There's a booklet too, but the photos and essays aren't anything special. *—Richie Unterberger*

Fires of Eden / Sep. 1990 / Columbia ♦♦♦♦
Fires of Eden marked Judy Collins' debut on Columbia Records, and she seemed to rise to the occasion with her best overall body of new material in more than a decade. Not everything on this album is memorable, but what is, is intensely so, beginning with the opening cut, "The Blizzard," a seven-minute epic that rates alongside any of Collins' most beautiful work from her classic years on Elektra. The words and music combine to form a screenplay in miniature, and the transitions between standard lyric and conversational passages in the lyric only add to the complexity of this long, flowing, lyrical piece. Her version of "The Air That I Breathe" is pretty enough, even if it won't make anyone forget the Hollies' recording, but a lot of the new songs have a special power. The title track offers an alluring vocal performance of a surprisingly impassioned lyric, while "Home Before Dark" presents her in a more ethereal mode. The production and instrumentation are the fullest heard on one of Collins' records since her transition from folk music to art song on the *Wildflowers* album, which makes the best of the melodies here come alive in rich and robust fashion. *—Bruce Eder*

Live at Newport, 1959-1966 / Oct. 25, 1994 / Vanguard ♦♦♦
A 13-song compilation of material recorded at the 1959, 1963, 1964, and 1966 Newport Folk Festivals; it would have been nice if they'd been able to document what year each song was recorded. In any case, it does reflect Collins' artistic growth during this period, from an interpreter of strictly traditional fare to more contemporary material by Bob Dylan, Richard Farina, and others. Highlights include her versions of "Turn, Turn, Turn," "Blowin' In the Wind," "Hey, Nelly Nelly," "Get Together," "Hard Lovin' Loser," and "The Great Silkie," which has the same melody the Byrds used for "I Come and Stand at Every Door" on their *Fifth Dimension* album. All of the songs are previously unreleased, except "The Greenland Whale Fisheries," a duet with Theodore Bikel; on some tracks, Collins is accompanied on upright bass by Bill Lee, and on second guitar by Steve Mandell or Eric Weissberg. With good sound, a nice if not essential addition to the Collins catalog. *—Richie Unterberger*

Forever: An Anthology / Oct. 28, 1997 / Elektra ♦♦♦♦♦
Forever: An Anthology is a good but flawed double-disc overview of Judy Collins' long, prolific and productive career at Elektra/Asylum Records. Over the course of 35 tracks, nearly all of Collins' best-known songs are showcased ("Someday Soon," "Who Knows Where the Time Goes," "Send in the Clowns," "Both Sides Now," "Hard Lovin' Loser," "Amazing Grace"). Scattered throughout the collection are four new songs—including, inexplicably, a re-recorded version of "Chelsea Morning"—that may not live up to the quality of her classic songs, but still are quite strong. It might have been more appealing if the songs were sequenced in chronological order, and if "Chelsea Morning" was present in its original version, but *Forever: An Anthology* remains an ideal compilation for the serious Collins fan. *—Stephen Thomas Erlewine*

Classic Broadway / Sep. 21, 1999 / Madacy ♦♦♦

● **The Very Best of Judy Collins** / Aug. 21, 2001 / Rhino ♦♦♦♦♦
Rhino's *The Very Best of Judy Collins* may miss some of her finest songs, and it doesn't provide a comprehensive overview of her career, but it is nevertheless an excellent summary of her work for Elektra Records, spanning from her third album in 1964 to 1975's *Judith*. These were her most popular and accessible recordings, and they're presented handsomely in this collection, with a reminiscence from Collins and notes by Gillian G. Gaar. Yes, there may be some cuts that fans will miss, along with tracks from her first two records, but this is a generous 16-track collection that provides an excellent summary of most of her finest work. *—Stephen Thomas Erlewine*

Phil Collins

b. Jan. 31, 1951, Chiswick, London, England
Vocals, Drums, Percussion / Pop/Rock, Soft Rock, Adult Contemporary
Phil Collins' ascent to the status of one of the most successful pop and adult-contemporary singers of the '80s and beyond was probably as much of a surprise to him as it was to many others. Balding and diminutive, Collins was almost 30 years old when his first solo single, "In the Air Tonight," became a #2 hit in his native U.K. (the song was a Top 20 hit in the U.S.). Between 1984 and 1990, Collins had a string of 13 straight U.S. Top Ten hits. He got his first break in music at the end of his teens, when he was chosen to be a replacement drummer in the British art-rock band Genesis in 1970. When frontman Peter Gabriel abruptly left in 1974, Genesis auditioned 400 singers without success, then decided to let Collins have a go. The result was a gradual simplifying of Genesis' sound and an increasing focus on Collins's expressive, throaty voice. Collins made his debut solo album *Face Value* in 1981, which turned out to be a bigger hit than any Genesis album. It concentrated on Collins' voice, often in stark, haunting contexts such as the piano-and-drum dirge "In the Air Tonight." During the '80s, Collins balanced his continuing solo work with Genesis with enormous success. *—William Ruhlmann*

Face Value / 1981 / Atlantic ♦♦♦♦♦
Collins proves himself a passionate singer (and distinctive drummer) with a gift for both deeply felt ballads and snarling rockers. His debut album transformed him from the frontman of Genesis to a solo star who happened to be in Genesis, too. Contains "In the Air Tonight" and "I Missed Again." *—William Ruhlmann*

Hello, I Must Be Going / 1982 / Atlantic ♦♦♦
As his hit cover of "You Can't Hurry Love" demonstrates, Collins began to inject his highly melodic pop songwriting with more soul and R&B influences on his second solo album. While some of the material was successful, much of it showed that he was still coming to grips with how to incorporate R&B techniques into his style; in retrospect, *Hello, I Must Be Going* laid the groundwork for his breakthrough album, *No Jacket Required*. *—Stephen Thomas Erlewine*

No Jacket Required / 1985 / Atlantic ♦♦♦♦♦
From ballads like the #1 "One More Night" to uptempo funk like the #1 "Sussudio," another tour de force in what was by now one of the most identifiable styles in pop music. The 1985 Grammy winner for Album of the Year. *—William Ruhlmann*

But Seriously / Nov. 1989 / Atlantic ♦♦♦
This chart-topping fourth album contains "Another Day in Paradise," "I Wish It Would Rain Down," "Do You Remember?," and "Something Happened on the Way to Heaven," all Top Five hits. *—William Ruhlmann*

Serious Hits . . . Live! / 1990 / Atlantic ♦♦♦

Both Sides / Nov. 9, 1993 / Atlantic ♦♦♦
Returning to the stark, melancholy sounds of *Face Value*, Phil Collins delivers a personal album with *Both Sides* in more than one sense of the word. Collins played all of the instruments on *Both Sides*, and the songs are troubled, haunting tales of regret, romance, and society. Although Collins has not lost his flair for melody, the songs are edgier than most of his recent work. Some fans might not go along with Collins on this dark ride, but *Both Sides* is one of his most artistically satisfying albums. *—Stephen Thomas Erlewine*

Dance into the Light / Oct. 22, 1996 / Atlantic ♦♦♦

● **Hits** / Oct. 6, 1998 / Atlantic ♦♦♦♦♦
If *Hits* seems a little inadequate, even though it weighs in at 16 tracks, that's because Phil Collins had such a long, productive run. Also, to casual listeners (and possibly even some fans), it's hard to tell which singles are by Genesis and which ones are solo cuts. So, it's almost a certainty that listeners will find something missing from this disc—and not just because Genesis cuts are absent, but because there's not enough space to fit all of Collins' solo hits, especially since the compilers decided to include a couple of lesser, latter-day hits at the expense of some earlier, bigger ones, while adding his non-LP cover of Cyndi Lauper's "True Colors" to entice hardcore fans. Thus, there are only 13 hits, which means some other big hits and good songs are absent—"I Missed Again," "I Don't Care Anymore," "Don't Lose My Number," "Do You Remember?" are all MIA. A few of these omissions are quite regrettable, but in the end, *Hits* is nevertheless a representative and pretty entertaining collection. The sequencing is not chronological, so it doesn't develop a nice flow (although "Take Me Home" is admittedly the ideal closer), but the chief strength of this collection is that it puts all of the big hits—including "Easy Lover," "Against All Odds," "In the Air Tonight," "Sussudio," "One More Night" and "Separate Lives"—in one place. No, it's not perfect—and it's hard not to wish that it was—but *Hits* still contains the majority of Collins' solo smashes, and that alone makes it a nice addition to his catalog. *—Stephen Thomas Erlewine*

A Hot Night in Paris / Jul. 27, 1999 / Atlantic ✦✦✦

The Colourfield

f. 1983, Manchester, England, **db.** 1987

New Wave

By the summer of 1983, the Fun Boy Three were peaking in popularity and Terry Hall disbanded the group. Hooking up with ex-Swinging Cats members Toby Lyons and Karl Shale, Hall moved to Manchester and formed the Colourfield, a more lush and melodic outfit than the Fun Boy Three. In January of 1984, the band released their first single, "The Colourfield," which just missed the Top 40. It was followed later that summer with "Take," which didn't even come close to the Top 40. The Colourfield had its first hit in January of 1985, when "Thinking of You" reached number 12. It was followed by "Castles in the Air," another failed single that preceded the release of their debut album, *Virgins and Philistines*, by just a few weeks. Like the band's singles, *Virgins and Philistines* failed to gain a large audience for the Colourfield. The band released a second album, *Deception*, in the spring of 1987. During the sessions, Lyons left the band, leaving Hall to finish the album by himself; to complete the album, Hall hired Raquel Welch's band. *—Stephen Thomas Erlewine*

● **Virgins & Philistines** / Jan. 1985 / Chrysalis ✦✦✦✦✦

A good mix of folk and rock comes from this band led by Terry Hall (ex-Specials, Fun Boy Three). Hall is an interesting if somewhat gloomy writer. *—Kenneth M. Cassidy*

The Colour Field / 1986 / Chrysalis ✦✦✦

Deception / Apr. 1987 / Chrysalis ✦✦

Ray Columbus & The Invaders

f. 1964, **db.** 1966

One of the best New Zealand groups of the '60s, and the first to successfully react to the changes wrought by the British Invasion. Starting out as a fairly accomplished outfit in the mold of Cliff Richard & the Shadows, though rawer, the group hit the top of the charts in both New Zealand and Australia with "She's a Mod" in 1964. A cover of an obscure British beat single by the equally obscure Senators, it took obvious inspiration from "She Loves You" with its "yeah-yeah" chorus, but it was a strong harmony rocker that was one of the biggest singles of the '60s in Australia. Although their biggest hit was quite Beatlesque, most of the group's repertoire (much of it self-penned) was in a decidedly more pronounced R&B direction. The Invaders would have most likely ground ashore had they actually made a determined effort to invade the U.S. or U.K. markets, but they were a decent outfit that stood way above most other Kiwi acts in 1964. The group managed a few more New Zealand hits, but couldn't crack Australia in as big a way again before splitting in 1966. Ray Columbus actually tried to crack the States as a solo artist for a year or two, recording the collectable psychedelic "Kick Me" single with a California group, the Art Collection. *—Richie Unterberger*

● **Anthology** / 1981 / Epic ✦✦✦✦✦

16-track compilation includes all of their key singles: "She's A Mod" and the N.Z. hits "C'-Mon And Swim," "Now You Shake," "Till We Kissed," and "Yo Yo." According to the liner notes, The Yardbirds' management considered having the band cover the moody, bluesy "Now You Shake" as a single in early 1966. Also includes a live version of "She's A Mod" and their 1963 take on "I Wanna Be Your Man," which was one of the first overseas Beatle covers. *—Richie Unterberger*

Greatest Numbers / 2000 / Ascension ✦✦✦✦

With 30 songs, this is about twice as long as the only other Columbus anthology that has been at all available to international consumers (Epic's 1981 vinyl collection *Anthology*). Being twice as long, however, does not necessarily mean twice as good. The songs here that were not included on *Anthology* are largely run-of-the-mill, whether they're shopworn covers like "Shakin' All Over" and "Poison Ivy," Shadows-type instrumentals, or less familiar tunes. As it contains 12 of the 16 songs on *Anthology*, and as none of the other 18 tracks are as good as the best of the *Anthology* cuts, you're not missing much if you just stick with the 1981 compilation (which is admittedly much harder to find than it was in the 1980s). As another strike against this package, there are no liner notes or songwriting credits, though it does have a discography. *—Richie Unterberger*

Shawn Colvin

b. Jan. 10, 1956, Vermillion, SD

Vocals, Guitar / Contemporary Folk, Adult Alternative Pop/Rock, Singer/Songwriter

Shawn Colvin is one of the bright spots of the so-called "new folk movement" that began in the late '80s. And though she grew out of the somewhat limited "woman with a guitar" school, she has managed to keep the form fresh with a diverse approach, avoiding the clichéd sentiments and all-too-often formulaic arrangements that have plagued the genre. In less than a decade of recording, Colvin has emerged as a songcraftsman with plenty of pop smarts, which has earned her a broad and loyal following. She played in several bands while growing up, and began building a following on New York's singer/songwriter scene after moving there in 1983. Her work appeared in *Fast Folk Magazine*, and she got her first break in 1987 singing backup on Suzanne Vega's hit "Luka." A live tape sold at gigs gained her a contract with Columbia, and Colvin's major-label debut *Steady On* won the Grammy for Best Contemporary Folk Recording. Her 1992 follow-up, the more pop-oriented *Fat City*, earned her considerable critical praise and a growing crossover audience. The single "I Don't Know Why" became a big adult contemporary hit. Colvin's 1996 album *A Few Small Repairs* slowly became a hit over the course of 1997, thanks to strong word of mouth and the single "Sunny Came Home," which won a Grammy for Song of the Year. *—Chris Woodstra*

Steady On / Oct. 1989 / Columbia ✦✦✦✦✦

Sonically, *Steady On* is a triumph, with its emotional intimacy captured with smooth precision. Vocally, Colvin's tender, sometimes whisper-like performances are astonishing and haunting, provocative and seductive all at once. Then there are the songs that flow so effortlessly into one another that to remove even one would seemingly upset the entire balance of the cosmos as we know it. The sly Colvin adeptly plays with words, beats, phrasing, and rhymes, focusing not just on the meaning, but also the feel and rhythm of the lyrics to great effect. Having once claimed that she tends to write about the "positive side of the painful experience," this album proves her point, for even if you do listen amidst gray skies and drizzles, you will be soothed to the point of contentment. The opening strains of the wistful title track set the mood and ease you into Colvin's head and heart, as you embark on this journey with her to discover countless souls and their heretofore untold truths. On a album full of great songs, "Shotgun Down the Avalanche" still stands as one of her finest compositions, with its metaphoric imagery of riding an out-of-control emotional tide as one would cascade helplessly down a mountain of snow. The requisite troubadour-on-the-road tune, "Ricochet in Time," is made ever more poignant by Colvin's sleepy vocal track, bringing home the weariness that is a very large part of being an artist on tour. *Steady On* is a must have for anyone who loves acoustic music created in the grand tradition of Joni Mitchell and James Taylor, two legends Colvin now counts as contemporaries. *—Kelly McCartney*

Fat City / Oct. 1992 / Columbia ✦✦✦✦

For her second album, Shawn Colvin took a temporary break from longtime collaborator and producer John Leventhal, teaming up instead with Larry Klein. And while the strongest songs—"Tennessee," "Climb On (A Back That's Strong)" and "Object of My Desire"—are Colvin/Leventhal collaborations, credit should be given to Klein, who incorporated a glossy, more dynamic production and top-notch session players for a stronger and more accessible album. In addition to turning in a strong batch of songs, Colvin shows much more diversity, tackling everything from rootsy rockers to more sensitive folk ballads with equally passionate delivery. "I Don't Know Why" (the first song she wrote) and "Round of Blues" both found considerable success in adult contemporary radio formats, adding to her growing fan base. *—Chris Woodstra*

Cover Girl / Aug. 23, 1994 / Columbia ✦✦

When Shawn Colvin first turned up playing Greenwich Village folk clubs in the early 1980s, she used to perform a variety of cover songs, often taking rock recordings and reimagining them for her girl-with-guitar format. When Colvin began recording in the late '80s, however, she concentrated on her own original material. *Cover Girl* brings her interpretive abilities back into focus. Songs like the Police's "Every Little Thing [He] Does Is Magic" and Talking Heads' "This Must Be the Place (Naive Melody)" are the most radical reworkings here, but not the best, perhaps because they depend on their original productions. Colvin is more successful in choosing classic but not well-known songs already in the folk idiom—Greg Brown's "One Cool Remove," Willis Alan Ramsey's "Satin Sheets," and Rolly Solley's "Killing the Blues." A fan from the old Village days can only lament that she didn't choose to include her version of Dire Straits' "Romeo and Juliet." *—William Ruhlmann*

Live '88 / Oct. 1995 / Plump ✦✦✦✦✦

It's a folkie tradition and an economic boon to carry with you tapes to sell at your gigs, and before Shawn Colvin released her first Columbia Records album, *Steady On*, she used to sell a tape made at an April 1988 show in Somerville, Massachusetts, containing acoustic versions of songs that later turned up on her Columbia releases—"Diamond in the Rough," "Shotgun Down the Avalanche," "I Don't Know Why," and "Knowing What I Know Now," among others. In the studios, such songs acquired arrangements and other instrumentation, which may have made them more commercial, but didn't improve them. Now, Colvin's management has launched Plump Records and released her live tape (with a couple of additions), though her contract with Columbia is still in effect. And guess what? It's still her best recording. *—William Ruhlmann*

● **A Few Small Repairs** / Oct. 1, 1996 / Columbia ✦✦✦✦✦

A Few Small Repairs, the proper follow-up to *Fat City*, was recorded on the heels of Colvin's divorce. And while the album is certainly a response, she avoids the obvious clichés in dealing with the aftermath, revealing instead the complex thought processes and complete range of human emotion, from anger, sadness, confusion, yearning, and disillusionment to resolve and recovery. Colvin has always been a songwriter of note, but with *A Few Small Repairs*, she reaches new heights, painting haunting vivid images that address not only relationships but also life in general with great insight. The subject matter predictably gives a generally dark mood to the album, but musically, the album is both diverse and irresistibly catchy. The album marks a reunion with former collaborator/producer John Leventhal, and the two have found a perfect blend between words, music, and tasteful, organic arrangements for Colvin's finest effort to date. *—Chris Woodstra*

Holiday Songs and Lullabies / Oct. 27, 1998 / Columbia ✦✦✦

Shawn Colvin's seasonal album is in effect a musical adaptation of the children's book *Lullabies & Night Songs*, which, like the CD, features illustrations by Maurice Sendak. As such, it includes mostly traditional tunes, along with some Christmas standards such as "Silent Night" and "Christmas Time Is Here," and several Alec Wilder compositions and arrangements, among them settings of lyrics by Robert Louis Stevenson and Rudyard Kipling. Often employing a string quartet, Colvin turns in calm but deeply felt performances of the songs for a set appropriate for putting the children to sleep on Christmas Eve. *—William Ruhlmann*

Whole New You / Mar. 27, 2001 / Columbia ✦✦✦✦

Whole New You is an appropriate title for Shawn Colvin's fourth studio album of new material, her first in four and a half years. Much happened in the interim. Within all this change, however, there are certain constants. She continues to collaborate with writer, producer, and multi-instrumentalist John Leventhal, who continues to come up with imaginative musical tracks clearly informed by mid-'60s pop sensibilities. The title track (and first single), for example, is distinctly Beatlesque, with twangy guitar and George Martin-style spare string arrangement. The arrangements are full of such echoes, but they remain echoes; Leventhal weaves instruments and effects together evocatively, but not overtly. In a sense, the album's 11 tracks make up one elliptical song in which the narrator thinks about the choices she has made recently with a sense that those choices are irrevocable. For the most part, she doesn't mind that, it seems, but she's certainly aware of it. Amid the various references to steadfastness and the allusions to childhood, there is little passion, but plenty of clear-headed acceptance. This is an album about marriage and family, not love, at least not the kind of romantic love that most pop songs are concerned with. *Whole New You* may not contain a song that will spark sales and awards the way "Sunny Came Home" did, but anyone who, like the artist herself, has come to the safe harbor of family life (even with its many challenges) after a long, uncertain voyage through personal relationships and life experiences will appreciate Colvin's ruminations on the subject. —*William Ruhlmann*

Come
f. 1990, Boston, MA
Indie Rock, Alternative Pop/Rock
The dark and dissonant blues-rock band Come formed in Boston, Massachusetts in 1990. The group was led by singer/guitarist Thalia Zedek—a recovering heroin addict and veteran of the indie-rock scene whose career included tenures fronting Live Skull, Uzi, the Dangerous Birds and White Women—and guitarist Chris Brokaw, also the drummer for Codeine. Fleshed out by a pair of Athens, Georgia refugees—former Kilkenny Cats bassist Sean O'Brien and onetime Bar-B-Q Killers drummer Arthur Johnson—Come spent its first year of existence improvising and jamming together before recording "Car," a single for the Sub Pop label which made them one of the most highly-touted new acts on the underground scene.

After signing to Matador, Come recorded their superbly atmospheric 1992 debut *Eleven: Eleven* in less than eight days; in 1994, they resurfaced with both an EP, *The Wrong Side*, and a full-length album, *Don't Ask Don't Tell*. After the band backed Steve Wynn on his solo album *Melting in the Dark*, both O'Brien and Johnson exited in 1995, leaving Zedek and Brokaw to record 1996's *Near Life Experience* with two different rhythm batteries; while Tortoise's Bundy K. Brown and the Jesus Lizard's Mac McNeilly backed the duo on half of the tracks, Rodan alumni Tara Jane O'Neil and Kevin Coultas provided support on the rest. The excellent *Gently, Down the Stream* followed in early 1998. —*Jason Ankeny*

Eleven: Eleven / 1992 / Matador ✦✦✦
One couldn't throw a brick around rock critics and college rock types in 1992 without hitting somebody who would talk about how Come was the new incarnation of the blues, often loudly and at great length. As in other cases where good bands were overburdened by hype, this both set up the quartet with impossible-to-realize expectations (Come plays anything but straight blues purism or revival à la Alligator Records) and wrote out Zedek's own unique artistic skills from the equation. To be sure, the CD version includes both sides of the "Fast Piss Blues" single, the flip being the Rolling Stones' own "I Got the Blues." But it's the Stones and acts like Patti Smith and Black Sabbath, not to mention the confrontation of no wave and other punk-inspired acts, that provide more of a touchstone to what's going on than Robert Johnson. It's a uniquely sludgy, electric, and strong fusion of sounds and styles, combining extreme angst and commanding power. Zedek's often twangy singing is both harsh and cool, the sound of someone burnt out but not crushed, and her guitar work suggests something more of bruised majesty—consider the steady, despairing flow of "Brand New Vein"—than anything else. Her introduction to "Submerge" may be "Now we sing so softly," but her voice cuts through the dark chime of the music even while talking about sinking to the bottom as things fire up even more. With Brokaw contributing equally strong feedback blasts (and vocals on the searing "Sad Eyes") and a sometimes lumbering but still good enough rhythm section rounding things out, Come takes things directly to a listener on *Eleven: Eleven* with fine results. Other good numbers include the lengthy drive of "Off to One Side" and the concluding surge of "Orbit," confronting demons with a roar. —*Ned Raggett*

● **Don't Ask Don't Tell** / Oct. 1994 / Matador ✦✦✦✦✦
Marginally brighter than their oppressive debut *Eleven: Eleven*, Come's second album is pretty heavy sledding regardless. Although the core duo of singing guitarists Thalia Zedek and Chris Brokaw has pure art punk credentials (Zedek in Boston's Dangerous Birds and Uzi, Brokaw in New York slowcore pioneers Codeine), Come is basically an exceptionally intense blues-rock band. They aren't simply lifting old Chess Records riffs in the manner of the dull and overrated Jon Spencer Blues Explosion, though; their music is basically a neurotic '90s urban take on the roots of the blues: guitar music as catharsis. Zedek's lead vocals have the sensuous drawl of a blues mama, but her lyrics are expressions of alienation, pain, and general pissed-offness that are more than matched by the dual lead guitars, which play intertwining lines that bounce off of each other at unexpected angles. The combination of those two elements and the extended song lengths—nearly half of the ten songs are over six minutes—makes *Don't Ask Don't Tell* a particularly intense and emotional experience. —*Stewart Mason*

Near Life Experience / May 21, 1996 / Matador ✦✦✦✦
Come's *Near Life Experience* covers both old territory for the band as well as heading in new, exciting directions. Singers/guitarists Thalia Zedek and Chris Brokaw weathered

the departure of the band's original rhythm section a year ago, to be replaced by 11 different musicians for the recording of this album, including bassists and drummers from groups like the Jesus Lizard, Retsin, Tortoise and Rachel's. Whoever's playing on the tracks, it's clear from the opening of "Hurricane" that Come is a re-energized, even more powerful band than they used to be, and that *Near Life Experience* is their most concise and affecting release yet. Come's trademark bluesy-punk sound is still apparent on songs like "Hurricane" and "Bitten," but the group stretches in different directions with gentle ballads like "Weak As the Moon" and "Slow Eyed." Zedek's voice is as gravelly and emotive as ever, and with the different song styles on *Near Life Experience*, has even more room to express itself. Brokaw also sings lead (a first) on two of the album's more accessible tracks, the single "Secret Number" and "Shoot Me First." Though it's only eight tracks long, Come pack more musical experiences into *Near Life Experience* than most groups do in an entire discography. —*Heather Phares*

Gently, Down the Stream / Feb. 10, 1998 / Matador ✦✦✦✦
Come's music has always been a bit difficult to come to terms with, but it rewards repeated listens immensely. Nowhere is that more true than on their fourth album, *Gently, Down the Stream*. Although it's a lengthy, dark album, it's arguably their most accessible, since the rage that flowed throughout *Don't Ask Don't Tell* and *Near Life Experience* has turned into a resigned bitterness, and that means there aren't as many all-out sonic assaults. Instead, the guitars intertwine perfectly, creating cathartic, sometimes atonal, sometimes bluesy sheets of sound. Similarly, the individual songs of Thalia Zedek and Chris Brokaw are woven together seamlessly throughout the album, making this Come's most band-oriented effort to date. It's not as immediately bracing as *Don't Ask Don't Tell*, but it's worth the extra effort to deal with Come's ambitious, difficult music. —*Stephen Thomas Erlewine*

Commander Cody
b. Jul. 19, 1944, Ann Arbor, MI
Western Swing Revival, Country-Rock, Rock & Roll
Commander Cody and the Lost Planet Airmen were equally adept at stripped-down basic rock & roll, R&B, and gritty country-rock. Commander Cody's country-rock rocked harder than the Eagles or Poco—essentially, the group was a bar band. Much like English pub rock bands like Brinsley Schwarz and Ducks Deluxe, Commander Cody resisted the overblown and bombastic trends of early-'70s rock, preferring a basic, no-frills approach. Commander Cody and the Lost Planet Airmen never had the impact of the British pub rockers, yet their straightforward energy gave their records a distinguishing drive; they could play country, western swing, rockabilly, and R&B, and it all sounded convincing. In 1972, the group scored a fluke Top Ten hit with "Hot Rod Lincoln," taken from their first album, *Lost in the Ozone*. Commander Cody was never able to capitalize on the single's success, partially because their albums never completely captured their live energy. —*Stephen Thomas Erlewine*

Lost in the Ozone / 1971 / MCA ✦✦✦
This is the monumental debut by one of insurgent country's pioneer bands. Playing with electric instruments, including the all important steel and fiddle, and a good dose of irreverence allowed the band to adhere to their own agenda. This first release was only a taste of the things to come. A combination of original tunes and some dusty covers, Cody & His Airmen were at the head of a parade that continued on through the '90s. Songs by Billy C. Farlow like "Daddy's Gonna Treat You Right" and the ever-popular "Lost in the Ozone" were instant hits with the country-rock and hippie crowds. But, the rednecks loved them, too, and this was an amazing social phenomenon. Cody, whose real name is George Frayne, partnered with Farlow on a number of songs from this first collection that still pack a wallop. "Wine Do Yer Stuff" and the tearful "Seeds and Stems (Again)" left no doubt where these boys were coming from. A strong honky tonk album that swings, *Lost in the Ozone* is a viable recording. Cover tunes performed with energy and humor won crowds over everywhere. "Hot Rod Lincoln" is still played on outlaw country radio stations, as is "20 Flight Rock," a boogie number that lets everything hang out. With not a single cut wasted, this is one of the buried gems of modern country music that displays guitarman Bill Kirchen at his wildest and Bruce Barlow, Lance Dickerson, Andy Stein, John Tichy, Bobby Black, West Virginia Creeper, Farlow, and Commander Cody comin' out of the shoot ready to change the world for the better. —*Jana Pendragon*

Hot Licks, Cold Steel & Truckers' Favorites / 1972 / MCA ✦✦✦
Again, a groundbreaking release from the wildest band in country music (during the '70s). This time around they are honoring the American trucker. A part of society few see into, the music that keeps the big rigs running is something else again. With originals and some oldies, the Commander and his band make a big sound that is still reverberating through time. With their own trucker tunes, "Truck Stop Rock" and "Semi Truck," leading the way, this LP includes some classics like "Looking' at the World Through a Windshield," "Mama Hated Diesels," and the granddaddy of the bunch, "Truck Drivin' Man," a performance hit for Rick Nelson and the New Riders of the Purple Sage as well. Other high-powered covers include Little Richard's "Tutti Frutti" done up in a way no one will forget. The Cajun "Diggy Liggy Lo" is given a workout as is "Rip It Up," and the Commander's class-A performance of "It Should've Been Me" leaves no doubt as to the punch this outfit gives to everything they do. From the band comes "Cravin' Your Love," "Watch My .38," and "Kentucky Hills of Tennessee." Again, every cut counts. As with *Lost in the Ozone*, this is top-flight music in every regard that shows another side to this great band. —*Jana Pendragon*

Country Casanova / 1973 / MCA ✦✦✦
A studio effort, this didn't reflect their live prowess but was still a good time. —*Jeff Tamarkin*

Live From Deep in the Heart of Texas / 1974 / MCA ✦✦✦✦✦
This is Commander Cody & His Lost Planet Airmen at their best, live on stage and out on the road with the New Riders of the Purple Sage. What a bill and what a grand time for a live album. This is how it really was—wild, loud and fun. Again they intersperse their own songs with old favorites. "Armadillo Stomp" was penned for this event, and a woolly version of "Down to Seeds and Stems Again Blues" has the crowd on its feet. Their "Oh Momma Momma" and "Too Much Fun" become legendary during this performance. But, it is their reworking of Buck Owens' "Crying Time" that makes them such a wonderful country band. Johnny Horton's "I'm Comin' Home" is also masterful as is their take on a favorite cowboy tune, "Sunset on the Sage." "Mean Woman Blues" is another highlight. As for the Commander, his wanton style is perfectly at home when he takes the Leiber-Stoller tune, "Riot in Cell Block #9" and makes it his own vehicle for a musical theatrical performance. Every cut is perfection, every cut is substantial. This 1973 performance, captured here for posterity, is evidence enough to suggest that Commander Cody & His Lost Planet Airmen were one fine honky tonk band, perhaps one of the finest. *—Jana Pendragon*

Commander Cody & His Lost Planet Airmen / 1975 / Warner Brothers ✦✦✦

We've Got a Live One Here / 1976 / Warner Brothers ✦✦✦✦✦
This is really the final hurrah for the band in spite of the fact that there were more recordings to follow. This is a two-record set from their 1976 tour of Europe with most of the original members still on board. After this tour, George Frayne, aka Commander Cody, broke up the band which now included Norton Buffalo. While this live recording is just as powerful as the preceding, *Live From Deep in the Heart of Texas*, it is obvious that some of their fire is burning mighty low. Still, this bunch always did their best work on stage and they never failed to satisfy. Full of old standards, some new favorites and plenty of wattage to make it all work just right, the stand out tunes here are the Commander Cody classics like "Seeds and Stems," "Too Much Fun" and "Lost in the Ozone." Other numbers that bring back the good old days include the Airmen's version of "Milkcow Blues" and "San Antonio Rose." Trucker songs, big with the Continental crowd, are "Semi Truck," "Lookin' at the World Through a Windshield" and "18 Wheels." Other numbers of note are "One of Those Nights," written by Farlow, Frayne and Kirchen, as well as the Commander's send ups of "Smoke! Smoke! Smoke!," "Riot in Cell Block #9" and "Hot Rod Lincoln." Always extraordinary, the era of Commander Cody & His Lost Planet Airmen was a special moment in time that created a place for hipsters, cosmic cowboys, rednecks and the working class to all come together and enjoy some real American music. Never will there be another band like this one or recordings like the ones they made between 1971 and 1976. They ended this project with "Lost in the Ozone," bringing the band and its audience full circle. *—Jana Pendragon*

Sleazy Roadside Stories / 1988 / Relix ✦✦✦

Aces High / 1990 / Relix ✦✦✦

● **Too Much Fun: Best of Commander Cody** / Oct. 1990 / MCA ✦✦✦✦✦
Not only could they play the hell out of their instruments, but C.C. and his Lost Planet Airmen were a virtual melting pot of American music—country, R&B, rockabilly, Western swing. And always too much fun. *—Jeff Tamarkin*

The Best of Commander Cody & His Lost Planet Airmen / Aug. 8, 1995 / Relix ✦✦✦✦✦
This brings together 14 of the group's biggest successes in one collection. Commander Cody and His Lost Planet Airmen were one of the very first country-rock groups, with guitarist Bill Kirchen who later moved on to a successful solo career of his own. Although much of the material consists of retreads of old and sometimes obscure country standards, the group handles the material with a tongue-in-cheek attitude, tempering that with a heartfelt understanding of it at the same time. A marvelous document of one of the more unique groups of the '70s. *—Cub Koda*

The Very Best of Commander Cody & the Lost Planet Airmen / Feb. 11, 1999 / See For Miles ✦✦✦✦✦

The Commodores

f. 1967, Tuskegee, AL
Quiet Storm, Urban, Funk, Soul
Formed by a group of friends from Tuskeegee Institute in Alabama, the Commodores were one of the top bands during their long tenure at Motown. Known for such hits as "Just to Be Close to You," "Easy," "Brickhouse," to name a few, the group is credited with seven number one songs and a host of other top ten numbers on the Billboard charts. They also have a vast music catalog that has generated more than 50 albums, and the recordings continue to be in demand. Initially formed to simply play music as a pastime and to meet girls, the line-up consisted of William King (trumpet), Thomas McClary (guitar), Ronald LaPread (bass), Walter "Clyde" Orange (drums), Lionel Richie (saxophone) and Milan Williams (keyboards). After attaining regional success performing, the band moved to New York City, where gigs at Smalls led to being invited to tour with the Jackson 5. That tour ultimately solidified a deal with Motown which would last until the mid-'80s. In 1982, Lionel Richie left the band and the group courted the talents of tenor J.D. Nicholas (formerly of Heatwave) and would go on to release its biggest hit, "Nightshift" in 1985. Soon after, however, the group left Motown and signed with Polydor, producing their final top ten hit, "Goin' to the Bank," before the end of the year. *—Craig Lytle*

Machine Gun / Jul. 1974 / Motown ✦✦✦
Before the Commodores started having major adult contemporary hits like "Three Times a Lady," "Easy," and "Still," they were happy to be a full-time funk/soul band. The Southerners became increasingly pop-minded in the late '70s, but when their debut album, *Machine Gun*, came out in 1974, their music was unapologetically gritty. This was, without question, a very promising debut—Lionel Richie and his allies really hit the ground running on sweaty funk items like "Young Girls Are My Weakness," "The Bump," "Gonna Blow Your Mind," and the single "I Feel Sanctified." These songs aren't funk-pop or sophisticated funk—they're hardcore funk. What you *won't* find on *Machine Gun* are a lot of sentimental love ballads. In the late '70s, the Commodores became as famous for their ballads as they were for their funk and dance material, but believe it or not, there are no ballads to be found on this consistently funky, mostly up-tempo debut. As much as this LP has going for it, *Machine Gun* isn't the Commodores' best or most essential album. *Machine Gun* is rewarding, but their subsequent albums *Caught in the Act* (1975), *Movin' On* (1975), and *Hot on the Tracks* (1976) are even stronger. *—Alex Henderson*

Caught in the Act / Feb. 1975 / Motown ✦✦✦✦✦
The sophomore slump wasn't a problem for the Commodores. The band's first album, *Machine Gun*, was quite promising, but its sophomore album, *Caught in the Act*, is even stronger. This superb 1975 LP, which the Commodores produced and arranged with James Carmichael, is more diverse than its mostly up-tempo predecessor. There are plenty of up-tempo funk gems; anyone with a taste for hard, sweaty 1970s funk won't be disappointed by "Look What You've Done to Me," "Wide Open," or the hit "Slippery When Wet," which soared to number one on Billboard's R&B singles chart and urges unfaithful husbands to give up their adulterous ways. But *Caught in the Act*, unlike *Machine Gun*, doesn't neglect slower material; "You Don't Know That I Know" and "This Is Your Life" are first-rate soul ballads. Excellent from start to finish, *Caught in the Act* is among the Commodores' finest albums. *—Alex Henderson*

Movin' On / Oct. 1975 / Motown ✦✦✦✦✦
R&B purists have often argued that the Commodores did their most essential work before 1977. It was in 1977 that they crossed over to the pop/adult contemporary audience in a major way with "Easy," and subsequent hits like 1978's "Three Times a Lady" and 1979's "Still" (both of which reached number one on Billboard's pop singles charts) certainly weren't the work of R&B snobs. Of course, Lionel Richie never claimed to be an R&B purist, although it is safe to say that the Commodores were still a hardcore funk/soul band when their third album, *Movin' On*, came out in 1975. From an R&B standpoint (as opposed to a pop or adult contemporary standpoint), this is one of their most essential releases. Those who love hard, gutsy 1970s funk can't go wrong with horn-powered gems like "Mary, Mary," "(Can I) Get a Witness," "Gimme My Mule," and "Hold On"; however, the song that *Movin' On* is best remembered for is the laid-back, gospel-drenched hit "Sweet Love." Written by Richie, "Sweet Love" is one of those secular soul tunes that isn't really gospel but borders on it; when Richie belts out the lyrics, "You got to keep on searching/harder/day by day," you feel like you're in the front row during an AME church service. And even though *Movin' On* is an LP that R&B purists rave about (rightly so), you can't say that it was ignored by pop audiences—"Sweet Love" was a number two R&B hit, but it also reached number five on Billboard's pop singles chart. *—Alex Henderson*

Hot on the Tracks / Jun. 1976 / Motown ✦✦✦✦✦
1976's *Hot on the Tracks* was the Commodores' fourth album, and it was also the last album they recorded before becoming a major crossover act. From 1977 on, the Commodores were as big among pop and adult contemporary audiences as they were with R&B audiences. That isn't to say that pop fans ignored them before 1977; "Just to Be Close to You," the single that *Hot on the Tracks* is best known for, reached number seven on Billboard's pop singles chart as well as number one on its R&B singles chart. The album itself made it to number one on Billboard's R&B albums chart, while climbing to number 12 on its pop albums chart. Nonetheless, this is an R&B record first and foremost, and the Commodores never sound like they're going out of their way to be pop. R&B purists should have no problem with "Just to Be Close to You," which is very much a soul ballad and doesn't have the adult contemporary appeal of subsequent hits like "Three Times a Lady," "Easy," and "Still." Nor should they have any problem with hardcore funk treasures such as "Fancy Dancer" (a number nine R&B hit), "Come Inside," "Let's Get Started," and the quirky "Quick Draw." For those who prefer the Commodores' hardcore funk and soul over their crossover material, *Hot on the Tracks* is recommended without hesitation. *—Alex Henderson*

Commodores / Mar. 1977 / Motown ✦✦✦✦
The Commodores' early years were spent on the Southern funk circuit, where their energetic, catchy tunes and keyboard-oriented funk made them both a college and a radio staple. They scored seminal hits with "Brick House" and "Slippery When Wet," although it became apparent quite early that lead vocalist Lionel Richie also had a bright future as a solo balladeer, with such tunes as "Easy" signaling his future on adult contemporary and Quiet Storm/urban contemporary radio. This collection highlights early uptempo and ballad hits. *—Ron Wynn*

Natural High / May 1978 / Motown ✦✦✦
The Commodores' sixth studio album, *Natural High*, is best known for the ballad "Three Times a Lady," which became a staple of adult contemporary radio and reached number one on both the pop and R&B charts. "Three Times a Lady" was their first number one pop hit, and Lionel Richie was being recognized as a major crossover star. Not everyone liked "Three Times a Lady"—some people found the song to be much too sappy, and R&B purists argued that the Commodores were watering their music down. But even if "Three Times a Lady" isn't your cup of tea, *Natural High* still has a lot to offer R&B fans. "X-Rated Movie," "Such a Woman," and "I Like What You Do" are exhilarating examples of hardcore funk, and those who appreciate artists like Heatwave and the Brothers Johnson will find a lot to admire about "Fire Girl" and "Flying High" (both of which are sleek examples of the sophisticated funk style). Meanwhile, "Say Yeah" (featuring Richie) is a first-rate R&B slow jam. Whatever your opinion of "Three Times a Lady"—whether you love it or

hate it—the fact is that *Natural High* has more plusses than minuses and was a generally respectable, if imperfect, addition to the Commodores' catalog. —*Alex Henderson*

Midnight Magic / Jul. 1979 / Motown ✦✦✦

Heroes / Jun. 1980 / Motown ✦✦✦

In the Pocket / Jun. 1981 / Motown ✦✦✦

Nightshift / Jan. 1985 / Motown ✦✦✦

The Commodores made one final stab at regaining R&B glory when Lionel Richie and producer/arranger James Anthony Carmichael both left in the mid-'80s. J.D. Nicholas became their lead singer, and Dennis Lambert assumed production duties. They rebounded temporarily when "Nightshift" leaped out of an otherwise ordinary album to become a Grammy-winning R&B and pop smash. It stayed atop the R&B charts for a month and peaked at #3 pop. Unfortunately, it was also the end for Thomas McClary, who left the group once the album had run its course. It was their next-to-last hit and basically the end for the band, although they continued for a couple more years. —*Ron Wynn*

● **Ultimate Collection** / Mar. 25, 1997 / Motown ✦✦✦✦

The various stages of the Commodores' tenure on Motown are summarized on the excellent *Ultimate Collection*, which features 13 Top Ten hits including the monumental "Brick House," "Machine Gun," "Slippery When Wet," "Sweet Love," "Just to Be Close to You," "Fancy Dancer," "Easy," "Too Hot Ta Trot," "Three Times a Lady," "Still," "Lady (You Bring Me Up)" and "Nightshift." —*Jason Ankeny*

20th Century Masters—The Millennium Collection: The Best of The Commodores / Nov. 23, 1999 / Motown ✦✦✦

The Millennium Collection: The Best of the Commodores collects 11 of their Motown hits, including their first hit, the instrumental "Machine Gun," as well as classics like "Brick House," "Three Times a Lady," "Easy," and "Nightshift." A concise journey through the group's brand of Southern funk and romantic ballads. —*Heather Phares*

Anthology / Sep. 25, 2001 / Motown ✦✦✦✦

The Communards

f. 1985, db. 1988
Alternative Dance, Club/Dance, Post-Punk, Dance-Pop

Following his exit from Bronski Beat in early 1985, falsetto vocalist Jimmy Somerville formed the neo-disco duo the Communards with classically-trained pianist Richard Coles; originally dubbed the Committee, they ran afoul of another group using the same name, and adopted the Communards title in tribute to a group of 19th-century French Republicans. The duo bowed in late 1985 with the Top 30 U.K. hit "You Are My World," the first of some 30-odd singles and EPs released during their relatively brief lifespan; a self-titled debut LP followed in 1986, as did the Communards' chart-topping remake of the Thelma Houston classic "Don't Leave Me This Way." In December 1986, "So Cold the Night" hit the U.K. Top Ten and the following year they issued the Stephen Hague-produced *Red*, which featured their smash cover of Gloria Gaynor's "Never Can Say Goodbye." Despite their success, the Communards disbanded in 1988, and Somerville began a solo career. —*Jason Ankeny*

Communards / 1986 / London ✦✦✦✦

Despite the inability of the music to live up to the high standards of Jimmy Somerville's ridiculously skilled falsetto voice, the Communards' first album achieved platinum status in several countries. Somerville's spirited duet with Sarah-Jane Morris on a cover of Thelma Houston's "Don't Leave Me This Way" helped push the record into the Top Ten on the U.K. charts, and a decent blend of other dancefloor fillers with Richard Coles-centric piano ballads lends variety for the ears that can't take a full album's worth of dance music. Both "Breadline Britain" and "Reprise" continue Somerville's activist ideals; the latter has to be one of the sharpest dissections of Margaret Thatcher. Compared to the following *Red*, much of the duo's self-titled debut sounds flat, lacking punch—all the more surprising from a Mike Thorne (Wire, Marc Almond) production. [The remastered version adds a lengthy mix of "Don't Leave Me This Way."] —*Andy Kellman*

● **Red** / 1987 / London ✦✦✦✦✦

Opting to have Pet Shop Boys and New Order producer Stephen Hague lend his skills to half of their second record proved to be a smart move for Jimmy Somerville and Richard Coles. *Red* tops their respectable debut in nearly every aspect. Increasingly melodic, increasingly polished, and increasingly tight, the front-to-back strong album is a defining Euro-dance record of the latter half of the '80s. The re-working this record is based around is Gloria Gaynor's version of "Never Can Say Goodbye," which stands apart from any other recorded rendition thanks to Somerville's distinct vocals. Again, the poppy disco is broken up by the occasional piano workout, and Somerville continues to bounce around with differing lyrical subjects, including the gripping "For a Friend," written for an AIDS victim close to him and Coles. The two other singles from the record, "Tomorrow" and "There's More to Love Than Boy Meets Girl," are stronger than anything on the debut. —*Andy Kellman*

Heaven / 1994 / London ✦✦✦

The Comsat Angels

f. 1978, Sheffield, England, db. 1995
New Romantic, Post-Punk, Alternative Pop/Rock, Synth Pop

Erroneously regarded as a synth-pop band—or worse yet—as "that group that had the song in that one scene of *Real Genius*," the Comsat Angels were actually amongst the cream of the early-'80s post-punk and new wave flock. Their first three albums were every bit on par with the best of the era. Frequently darker but less dramatic than Joy Division, their early material featured haunting (*not* goth) atmospherics and moody lyrics,

supplanted by economic instrumental interplay that never sounded jumbled. After this early period that spawned three marvelous LPs, the band fell prey to commercial and legal pressures for several years. In the early '90s they surprisingly re-emerged as a bang-up rock band, a return to their original spirit and drive. At this point, the Comsats finally realized that their efforts at pleasing others—whether it be label heads or consumers—had been fruitless. They inked a deal with RPM/Thunderbird in the U.K. and Caroline in the States, releasing *My Mind's Eye* in 1992. Harking back to their early days, while throwing on more layers of guitar, the album was an undeniable success artistically. Unsurprisingly, it was met with commercial indifference and spotty critical praise. The band issued *The Glamour* in 1995, their heaviest effort. Donning more obvious guitar riffs and hooks than ever, it made for a fine post-grunge record, without losing the necessary presence of nifty keyboard swells. The Comsats opted to retire soon after, bowing out in fine fashion. —*Andy Kellman*

Waiting for a Miracle / 1980 / Polydor ✦✦✦✦✦

One of the finest debuts of the golden age of post-punk, *Waiting for a Miracle* is an inelastic tension ball of paranoia, romantic strife, and alienation. Even at the Comsats' most bouncy, there's a sense of cloistered, impending peril. The cover photo of a desolate nighttime motorway encapsulates perfectly the tone of the album. Never to the extreme level of self-parody or doom for doom's sake, Stephen Fellows sounds like a raw nerve throughout standouts like "Postcard" and "Monkey Pilot." In the latter, Fellows declares, "Sometimes I feel out of control." In the former, he's stifled by a stagnant relationship: "I don't think you're listening/I think I'll tell you again." Each of the ten tracks is equally strong; some take two plays to sink into, and others might take dozens. The Comsats create such an un-forced web of despair that it's impossible not to be rattled. Much of this is due to Fellows' voice—while many vocalists of the era used their multi-octave vocal acrobatics to the point of dramatizing the most trivial of things, his soulful, common man singing resonates penetratingly despite his lack of range. His limitations aren't crippling, and he never steps outside of it—no over-emoting. The instrumentation is complex but minimal. Andy Peake's creepy, circumfluent keyboards add swirling accents here and provide a lead there; Fellows' ringing, arpeggiated guitars dart in and out, like U2's Edge without ego; bassist Kevin Bacon rumbles economically—each note of his is an important one; Mik Glaisher's complex, rolling toms thud and rattle with sophisticated ease. [RPM's 1995 reissue lovingly remasters the album to pristine quality, with detailed liner notes and three B-sides appended.] —*Andy Kellman*

● **Sleep No More** / 1981 / Polydor ✦✦✦✦✦

The Comsats' well-titled second LP has the strange effect of placing you on an emotional glacier in your birthday suit. More striking in this situation would be discovering that the normally teeth-chattering conditions have no effect on you, as you feel perfectly warm and cozy. All the while, you feel watched. If such a state as "chillingly inviting" was previously impossible or not easy to comprehend on vinyl, the Comsats plunge the depths here. Much of what made their debut so remarkable remains intact, but there are slight improvements. What they established with *Waiting for a Miracle* is only streamlined to a slightly higher standard. Their haunting atmospherics crystallize, especially on the hypnotically swirling title-track—Mik Glaisher's incisively relentless kick/tom combination (recorded in a lift shaft for a densely echoed effect) provides foreground as Andy Peake's keyboards and Stephen Fellows' guitar combine for an unholy haze warp. And overall, the material is a little more direct, if only detectable after plenty of listens. Fellows sounds downright dejected and furious in "Diagram" and "Goat of the West," and if his level of paranoia wasn't high enough on the debut, you can practically visualize hunched shoulders and carefully darting eyes throughout the thumping "Be Brave." Hints at the increasingly atmospheric spare sound the band would take on *Fiction* is foreshadowed on "Restless," a lushly beautiful bed of echoing guitar and gently plodding percussion. Glaisher's *huge* drums are the standout of the album. Not overwhelming in a brutish Zeppelin sense, his accents instead hit like unexpected blows to the belly. Every bit as dark as Joy Division's *Closer*, the Comsats have a way of crafting their menace by hovering above, as opposed to JD's more guttural manner via endless sheets of dark gray. Another near-flawless gem. —*Andy Kellman*

Fiction / 1982 / Polydor ✦✦✦✦

Fiction closes out a trilogy of year-to-year-to-year brilliance. Quite a feat to release three solid albums in successive years, with no sense of rushed nature or cut-rate quality. Even more pared down instrumentally than its predecessors, *Fiction* shows signs of the band lightening up somewhat, actually having flashes of positive outlook. "After the Rain" explicitly demonstrates that notion, signaled with Eastern-sounding mallets that lend a levitational quality, somewhat like sprightly fallout from Japan's *Tin Drum*. Though a different direction from the band, it avoids cheesy new age-isms. True, this slight emotional shift might lend itself to a more commercial-sounding record that can't be denied. Kevin Bacon's bass sounds a bit rubbery from time to time and the songwriting isn't *quite* as strong (hokey on "Birdman"). However, what made their first two releases so different and bizarre from the rest of the pack remains in the majority. "More," much like earlier skeletal workouts, relies on simple kick drum cluster-thumps and sparkling interplay between keyboard and guitar—has there ever been a more dazzling and complementary guitar/keyboard combo as Stephen Fellows and Andy Peake? And becoming par for the course for the band, the second side is just as strong as the first, even picking up steam at the very end. "Don't Look Now," likely inspired by the movie of the same name, features stacked walls of guitar shimmers. The mutant keyboards on "What Else" add to the disorienting melancholy of Fellows' subject: "You feel caught up in the circumstances/don't take it out on me." [RPM's 1995 reissue dolls it up nicely, again with bonus B-sides, though not as strong as their earlier extras. Liner notes abound yet again, with loads of press clippings and biographical info.] —*Andy Kellman*

Enz / 1982 / Polydor ◆◆◆◆

The Comsat Angels weren't big in Japan, but they developed a dedicated following in Holland, which was where *Enz* found release in 1982. Existing then as a great summation of B-sides and highlights, it has since been rendered obsolete by RPM's reissue of the band's first three studio albums—their golden age. Non-album stunners like "(Do the) Empty House," "Eye of the Lens," and "Home is the Range" stick out most prominently. It was never issued on CD, but for completists, the LP is worth hunting down for witty liner notes and spiffy artwork, which certainly beat the garish graphics of 1983's *Land. —Andy Kellman*

Land / 1983 / Connoisseur ◆◆◆

After three remarkable records and a new label, the Comsat Angels decided to tinker with their formula. They had the critical approval, but they were intent to win public approval. Bringing in Mike Howlett (producer of Berlin, OMD, and Flock of Seagulls), the band threw caution to the wind and let him do what he pleased with the band's already commercial-leaning material. They didn't just sacrifice much of their trademark tension, atmosphere, and paranoia. Mik Glaisher's inventive drums are painfully missing in action for much of the proceedings; studio wizardry cuts up his playing for incidental use. Andy Peake's keyboards are transformed from mood mechanism to central character, which means Stephen Fellows' guitar gets lost in the shuffle. As far as synth-pop records are considered, *Land* is fine—it still carries its own mood. For the high standard of such skilled musicians, enabling their work to be manipulated by outside sources results in a less-inspired record. Lodged beneath the gadgetry and shelved chemistry is a decent batch of songs, some of Fellows' most vocally melodic. The first side is solid, including a remake of their near-hit "Independence Day." The second side's "Nature Trails" matches earlier songs like "More" and "After the Rain" in gentle beauty. Truly, the only thing that sounds genuinely bad is "Mister Memory," thanks to an obstructive synth vamp that sounds like a ColecoVision video game sound effect. [Connoisseur's 2001 reissue does wonders for the record, which was previously unavailable on CD. Full in sound and package, fans of the earlier records might want to consider picking it up. It also includes a number of OK bonus tracks.] —*Andy Kellman*

7 Day Weekend / 1985 / Jive/Novus ◆◆

Chasing Shadows / 1986 / Island ◆◆◆

Less concerned with attaining hits, *Chasing Shadows* is a return to form and an attempt to just make a good record. It's also the result of an association with Robert Palmer, a fan who executive produced the record. Despite dated production and material that doesn't match the band's first three records, the members refer to it as their fourth record. (So they essentially disown both *Land* and *7 Day Weekend*.) That's because there's focus on the music, not allowing any room for outside concerns. Since the late-'80s production values sounded dated within a few years of release, the songs that hold up best are the ones with the most basic arrangements. "The Cutting Edge," "Carried Away," and "Pray for Rain" offer the best moments, and they're also the most quiet and most simplistic. Andy Peake plays plaintive piano for most of the record, instead of his usual synth stylings and frosty atmospherics. Other songs like the driving opener "The Thing That Counts" and "Under the Influence" are almost heavy, probably their closest to flat-out rock to date. One thing that *Chasing Shadows* suffers from is an almost cold, clinical feel. Even with the band's most dejected early material, there was a sense of warmth that is missing on approximately half of the record. As a benefit, it does sound much more like the Comsat Angels than *7 Day Weekend*. Definitely not amongst the band's best, but a point of curiosity nonetheless. —*Andy Kellman*

Time Considered as a Helix of Semi-Precious Stones / 1992 / RPM ◆◆◆◆◆

Time Considered, a collection of BBC Sessions from 1979-1984, is an excellent introduction to the genius of the Comsat Angels' early work. Not only is the track selection nearly flawless, but the quality of the recordings on most songs is such that the band views them as better than the originals. A sparse, slightly faster rendition of "Independence Day," along with a take on "JuJu Money" appear from their first session with John Peel from 1979. It was Peel who got the ball rolling for the Comsats. The band sent him a copy of their *Red Planet* EP, and he became an early and vocal supporter. He ended up having the Comsats in the studio four times between 1979 and 1981. Another Peel session from January of 1981 yields the strongest material; each of the five tracks top their original renditions. Most notable is "At Sea," which transforms a decent B-side into a monstrous opener on the disc. Mik Glaisher's drums are completely devastating. "Be Brave" is far more powerful than its *Sleep No More* version, with Kevin Bacon's bass propelling the song more than before, and the amped intensity of Stephen Fellows' vocals lead to its superiority over the original. Anything off the Sheffield band's first three records is masterful, and for what it's worth, a session from the Kid Jensen Show yields stronger versions of songs from 1983's synthpop letdown *Land.* Also notable is *Time Considered's* version of the Rolling Stones' "Citadel," their only recorded cover. —*Andy Kellman*

My Mind's Eye / 1992 / Caroline ◆◆◆◆◆

After a failed record as Dream Command, the Comsat Angels were running dangerously close to diluting the excellence of their first three albums. By the early '90s, the group's battles with label and legal forces had snowballed into a daunting mass capable of ending the life of most bands. It would have been perfectly understandable if the Comsats called it quits at this point. They had been around for a decade and had produced four straight albums that, while decent, failed to reach the level of their first three. Prior to the release of 1992's *My Mind's Eye*, it seemed like a bad move for the band to carry on. It didn't take much convincing for the harshest cynic to realize that *My Mind's Eye* was a complete rebirth for the band. Sounding little like the group that made the gutless *Fire on the Moon*, *My Mind's Eye* could have rated on a blindfold test as a fiery new group only *influenced* by the spirit of early Comsat Angels. Had the Comsats shrouded this

record in mystery under a different alias, it might have received more of the attention it deserved. Instead, a few critics picked up on it and wrote highly of it; otherwise, who's interested in an old band who had one chart hit eight years prior? How many of the original fans are still paying attention? Surprisingly, *My Mind's Eye* is undeniably muscular in sections but welcomes back the subtle atmospherics that made records like *Sleep No More* so addictively haunting. For the time it was released, the record stood shoulder-to-shoulder with albums by young'uns like Catherine Wheel and Swervedriver. Moody, lush, and every bit as intensely consuming, the record has a cinematic edge the band wasn't able to capture at any previous point. File under "unexpected treasure." —*Andy Kellman*

The Glamour / 1995 / Thunderbird ◆◆◆

My Mind's Eye was an undeniable artistic triumph for the Comsat Angels, so it was impressive for them to return a couple years later with a just-as-intense follow-up that offered a slight change of pace. Not many bands continue to grow well over a decade into their career; 1995's *The Glamour* is proof of a band doing such a rare thing. The loss of bassist Kevin Bacon was the first change in the band's lineup since forming. Replacement Terry Todd and additional guitarist Simon Anderson bring a heavy rockist edge to their elders, most exemplary on the title track. Like approximately half of the record, the song features thick, near-grunge riffing. What separates the record from the vast number of angst-ridden grunge bands is the ever-present atmospherics and noise mongering from keyboardist Andy Peake, along with Stephen Fellows' detached cool, both of which are placed perfectly in the mix. No deep-throat yowling and over-emoting here. It might be a less personal record than *My Mind's Eye*, but it sounds like a band having a blast, something the band's earlier works never really demonstrated. (Don't miss Fellows' incidental "rock" grunting, an odd development that seems humorous when considering his usual emotional turmoil.) With 13 songs that combine for over an hour's length, there's obviously some stretching out here that the band previously avoided. Prior to *The Glamour*, the Comsats tended to keep things to four minutes or less, but a couple songs here weigh in between six and eight minutes. Some songs might have been better left to the cutting room floor, but two-thirds of the record is extremely strong. Beginning marvelously and ending well in their career, their fifth best record would end up being their last. —*Andy Kellman*

From Beyond 2: 1987-1995 / Jun. 13, 2000 / Cherry Red ◆◆◆

Oddly released first as the second volume of an anthology (at the time of release, Cherry Red was waiting for the rights of the band's earlier material), the Stephen Fellows-selected tracks for *From Beyond 2* include some of the band's better outings and previously unissued recordings. Bizarrely, it also adds some of the members' post-Comsats works, which range from iffy to decent. As an attempt to introduce diehards to the members' new (and very different) projects, it works nicely. But one would think that the space would be better suited for more later period highlights. The latter half of the Comsats' career wasn't their best, but it ended with two excellent LPs. One gripe with *From Beyond 2* would be the lack of representation of those records, as this hardly demonstrates their strengths. A faithful cover of the Soft Boys' "I Wanna Destroy You" is the highlight of the rarities, making the disc worth the purchase on its own. The Comsats had seemingly few touchstones and rarely covered anyone. No recording date for the track is given, but judging from the sound of it, it came before the band added Terry Todd and Simon Anderson to their lineup. Fellows' vocals don't quite have the sneer that Robyn Hitchcock had, but the multi-tracked chorus snipes and roaring guitars make up for it. Excellently packaged, *From Beyond 2* contains excellent historical liner notes, as well as song commentary by Fellows. Putting this together couldn't have been an easy task, but Fellows balances the selections nicely to provide interest for the initiated and uninitiated. —*Andy Kellman*

Con Funk Shun

f. 1972, Memphis, TN, **db.** 1988

Quiet Storm, Funk

First formed as a backing band, Con Funk Shun became one of the premiere party-funk bands of its time and turned in the early '80s to R&B ballads. After recording an album for Crankshaft Productions, the band signed to Mercury and hit the charts with "Ffun," written as a tribute to the R&B/funk band Brick. Con Funk Shun found much success at Mercury; for a ten-year span, they released one hit after another and were a popular concert attraction. It was not until the early eighties that Con Funk Shun began receiving national notoriety for its ballads. The septet's last album with Mercury was without their longtime musical center, vocalist Felton Pilate. Pilate was responsible for much of the production and songwriting; he departed the group in 1986 due to business differences with the record company and became a successful producer. Pilate eventually became the musical force behind MC Hammer, contributing his skills as producer, arranger, co-writer, engineer and vocalist. Melvin Carter, a frequent collaborator of Con Funk Shun, joined the group upon Pilate's exit. That same year, the group's other main vocalist, Michael Cooper, departed and emerged as a solo artist, continuing a tradition of chart-topping success. Though Con Funk Shun disbanded after their last album with Mercury, they reunited in the '90s and performed at oldies festivals. —*Craig Lytle*

● **The Best of Con Funk Shun** / 1993 / Mercury ◆◆◆◆

Con Funk Shun's brand of funk was polished with spirited horns, titillating guitar rhythms and ear-pleasing vocals. These 17 tracks encompass the group's tenure at Mercury beginning with their first charted single "Sho' Feels Good to Me," and also including six Top Ten singles, three Top 20 singles and a horde of Top 30 hits. Of the many gems found on this compilation album, two that never charted are "Love's Train" and "All Up to You," both Quiet Storm classics. Also included in this package are liner notes by Harry Weinger, chronicling the reign of funk the self-contained septet had on the music industry. All numbers feature the lead vocals of Felton Pilate and Michael Cooper. —*Craig Lytle*

The Best of Con Funk Shun, Vol. 2 / May 21, 1996 / Mercury ♦♦♦
A mix of LP cuts and moderate-to-big R&B hits, the most famous of those being the novelty "Electric Lady," and "Too Tight" (presented here in an extended version). *—Richie Unterberger*

Ballads Collection / May 19, 1998 / Mercury ♦♦♦♦
Michael Cooper and Felton Pilate compiled *The Ballads Collection*, a selection of 12 romantic numbers the group have recorded over the years. The collection not only features singles like "Love's Train" and "Baby I'm Hooked (Right Into Your Love)," it also has album tracks, making it an ideal choice for any listener looking for a romantic Con Funk Shun collection. *—Stephen Thomas Erlewine*

Concrete Blonde

f. 1982, Los Angeles, CA, **db.** 1995
College Rock, Alternative Pop/Rock
Concrete Blonde grew out of the Los Angeles post-punk club circuit that produced bands like X, Wall of Voodoo, and the Go-Go's, but it wasn't until 1987 that the band even recorded its first album. The group was founded by singer/songwriter/bassist Johnette Napolitano and guitarist Jim Mankey, who initially called themselves Dream 6 and released an EP. Their insistence on complete artistic control was offputting to the major labels who took notice, however, and it wasn't until 1987 that the group signed to I.R.S. and changed its name to Concrete Blonde at the suggestion of labelmate Michael Stipe. Concrete Blonde's self-titled debut album betrayed the influence of the Pretenders, while 1989's *Free* was a tighter showcase for Napolitano's developing songwriting and produced a college radio hit with "God Is a Bullet." The morose, textured *Bloodletting*, a more accomplished record than both of its predecessors, broke the band to a wider audience with the left-field Top 20 hit "Joey," the tale of a love affair ended by alcoholism. *Mexican Moon* reflected Napolitano's interest in Hispanic music and culture, but Concrete Blonde's commercial fortunes had declined since *Bloodletting*, and Napolitano broke up the band. *—Steve Huey*

Concrete Blonde / 1987 / IRS ♦♦

Free / Apr. 1989 / IRS ♦♦♦
Concrete Blonde beefed up their lineup by adding a second guitarist, Alan Block, for 1989's *Free*. Like their self-titled debut release, the L.A.-based band focuses on the dark side of modern life, but they also intersperse a few lighter songs into the mix with good results. *Free* also found the band producing themselves. The grinding guitars and lead singer Johnette Napolitano's passionate vocals made the searing "God Is a Bullet" a college radio hit. "Roses Grow" is an interesting track with Napolitano making barstool observations over a metallic drumbeat. It is the lighter moments on the album that really shine, though, like the gentle warmth of the optimistic "Sun" and "Happy Birthday," a jangly pop rocker. The band also takes a stab at Thin Lizzy's "It's Only Money." *Free* shows a considerable amount of growth in both the songwriting and playing of their debut and makes it a worthwhile follow-up. *—Tom Demalon*

Bloodletting / May 1990 / IRS ♦♦♦♦♦
Though the sudden embrace of the trappings of goth culture via Anne Rice was a bit odd, given Napolitano's long-standing fascination with both Catholic and Mexican imagery (and the elements of sex and death prevalent in both) it wasn't too strange. Her songwriting and singing focus remains much more roots-oriented, as the opening strut/stroll of "Bloodletting (The Vampire Song)" makes clear. Not that she and the band can't kick out the jams as well—immediately following that is "The Sky is a Poisonous Garden," a punk-speed thrash with deliciously decadent imagery to boot. The most well known song was "Joey," which actually got some top 40 airplay; while it has a certain catchiness to it, ultimately it comes off as a less successful Heart song from the same era, which is saying something. Far more successful is nearly everything else on the album, from the dark chime of "Caroline," addressing a departed friend, to the soothing "Lullabye," which far from being a mere kiddie tune is a great love song with some fantastic guitar from Mankey. R.E.M.'s Peter Buck adds mandolin to "Darkening of the Light," which adds to the song's mysterious, haunting edge, while "I Don't Need a Hero" is barely there, the softest of music accompanying Napolitano's lyric. Her singing throughout *Bloodletting* is passionate and catchy, with a deep throaty ache on many cuts. Everything wraps up with a version of Andy Prieboy's "Tomorrow, Wendy." Having done a duet with him on his own recording of the song, she takes full lead here, delivering a bravura performance of the bitter, heartbreaking lyric. *—Ned Raggett*

Walking in London / Mar. 1992 / IRS ♦♦♦
Concrete Blonde followed up their gold record *Bloodletting*, containing the left-field hit "Joey," with this 1992 release. *Walking in London*, the band's fourth album, was produced by the band along with Chris Tsangarides and includes guest musicians Tom Petersson of Cheap Trick on bass and Wall of Voodoo's Andy Prieboy on vocals. Johnette Napolitano is in fine voice on *Walking in London* and the playing is as inspired as ever with original drummer Harry Rushakoff rejoining the band. However, the album reprises many themes from earlier albums with less satisfying results such as the vignette on urban life, "City Screaming." That said, there are some inspired moments. The leadoff track and single, "Ghost of a Texas Ladies' Man," is a hyperkinetic ghost story with eerie vocals and alterna-twang guitar. Both "Someday" and "Long Time Ago" are both slices of bright, singalong pop with an alternative bent. They also succeed on the gorgeous ballad "Les Ceours Jumeaux." Accordion adds to the romantic feel created by the lush background vocals and bilingual lyrics. Overall, a good record but not nearly as pleasing as its breakthrough predecessor. *—Tom Demalon*

Mexican Moon / Oct. 19, 1993 / IRS ♦♦♦♦
After the demise of their original label, I.R.S., Concrete Blonde released *Mexican Moon* on Capitol in the fall of 1993. The band, once again, produced themselves with Sean Freehill, and Paul Thompson returned to the fold on drums after sitting out *Walking in London* due to immigration problems.

The album is a striking marriage of Johnette Napolitano's dark, lyrical imagery and the band's alternative-tinged pop sensibilities making it, perhaps, their most fully realized effort. "Jenny I Read" kicks things off with the tale of a chance encounter of a fallen, reclusive starlet. Guitarist James Mankey shows versatility playing acoustic and Spanish guitar on the dreamy title track and the wah-wah effects of the brooding "Jesus Forgive Me (For the Things I'm About to Say)." "Heal It Up" was the unsuccessful single but is a bracing number with a ferocious vocal performance by Napolitano. Despite the inspired playing, intelligent and insightful lyrics, and the crisp production, *Mexican Moon* failed to expand the group's audience and would prove to be their last release before breaking up. *—Tom Demalon*

Still in Hollywood / Nov. 1, 1994 / IRS ♦♦♦
With their brief moment of commercial success having long since faded, Concrete Blonde had essentially split by the time this collection was released. For fans, it's a well-conceived treat, gathering together many of the band's non-album tracks (although most had been available as B-sides). There's really not a track that won't be a delight to the band's devoted following. There are a handful of well-chosen cover songs. Leonard Cohen's "Everybody Knows" is given a suitably ominous treatment and there is a beautiful, heartfelt take on the Cheap Trick ballad "Mandocello." Early college radio hit "God Is a Bullet" appears as a brutal live version (with some searing guitar work from James Mankey). The band's punk roots show on another live track, "The Sky Is a Poisonous Garden," and the chilling "Tomorrow, Wendy" retains its potency in a sparse, stripped-down version, showing off Johnette Napalitano's compelling vocal abilities. The B-side originals are consistently good, with the swaggering, loner lyrics and Mankey's spidery, twang guitar making "100 Games of Solitaire" especially noteworthy. The liner notes are concise, but informative, and *Still in Hollywood* is a well-done packaging of work that reinforces Concrete Blonde as a very talented creative unit. *—Tom Demalon*

● **Recollection: The Best of Concrete Blonde** / Feb. 20, 1996 / IRS ♦♦♦♦♦
Despite their obvious ambition, Concrete Blonde rarely made consistent albums, which is why the 18-track *Recollection: The Best Of* is welcome. Collecting all of the group's high points, not just singles like "Joey," "Still in Hollywood," "Ghost of a Texas Ladies Man," "Walking in London" and "Heal It Up," but also album tracks like "Tomorrow, Wendy," "Scene of a Perfect Crime," "Bloodletting" and "Mexican Moon." Although it would have been nice if *Recollection* was presented in chronological order instead of in the jumbled mess that constitutes its final sequencing, it remains an excellent overview of Concrete Blonde's career. *—Stephen Thomas Erlewine*

Concrete Blonde Y Los Illegals / May 5, 1997 / Ark 21 ♦♦♦

Arthur Conley

b. Jan. 4, 1946, Atlanta, GA
Vocals, Horn / Deep Soul, Southern Soul, Soul
A protégé of Otis Redding and, like Redding, a musical disciple of Sam Cooke, Conley co-wrote (with Redding) and sang "Sweet Soul Music," one of the true anthems of the '60s. Based on Cooke's "Yeah, Man," the record was sweet and hot at the same time, with a readily identifiable horn intro and lyrics that immortalized the soul stars of the day. Conley, although signed to Atco, toured overseas with the Stax/Volt Revue and later joined the Soul Clan with Atlantic label-mates Wilson Pickett, Solomon Burke, Don Covay, Ben E. King, and Joe Tex. He has lived in Holland for a number of years, where he has appeared on television and radio programs and runs an independent record label. *—Christine Ohlman*

● **Sweet Soul Music: The Best of Arthur Conley** / 1995 / Soul Classics/Ichiban ♦♦♦♦♦
Conley was ultimately a minor soul performer, but he made his share of decent records. Aside from "Sweet Soul Music," most of them have been inaccessible until this 22-song compilation of '65-'70 material. There's no getting around the fact that "Sweet Soul Music" towers above his other efforts, but Conley was a decent exponent of Southern soul. This includes all seven of his chart singles, cuts from several albums, and half a dozen songs from non-LP singles. Conley sometimes sounded like a watered-down Otis Redding (particularly in his latter years), and some of his later singles were trendy and slight (like "Aunt Dora's Love Soul Shack" and the cover of "Ob-La-Di, Ob-La-Da"). There are some good unheralded performances here, though, particularly on the pre-"Sweet Soul Music" singles; Conley emotes more heavily than would be his wont in later times, aided by material supplied by ace songwriters Dan Penn and Spooner Oldham. *—Richie Unterberger*

The Connells

f. 1984, Raleigh, NC
College Rock, Jangle Pop, Alternative Pop/Rock
The Raleigh, North Carolina-based jangle-pop outfit the Connells formed in the spring of 1984. Fronted by guitarist Mike Connell and his bassist brother David, the first incarnation of the group also featured vocalist Doug McMillan and drummer John Schultz, who was soon replaced by former Johnny Quest percussionist Peele Wimberley. In late 1984 the quartet recorded a four-song demo; after one of the tracks, "Darker Days," was selected to appear on the North Carolina compilation *More Mondo*, the Connells' ranks expanded with the addition of singer/guitarist George Huntley, who made his debut on a March 1985 session co-produced by Don Dixon.

With the help of the band's friend Ed Morgan, the resulting demo made its way to the offices of the British label Demon, which agreed to fund the recording of enough additional tracks to complete a full-length LP. *Darker Days* was released in Europe by Demon in 1985, and when Morgan returned to the U.S., he formed his own label, Black Park, to issue the album domestically. After the low-budget videos for the tracks "Seven" and "Hats Off" garnered MTV airplay, the Connells won a contract with the TVT label prior to entering producer Mitch Easter's Drive-In Studios to record 1987's brooding, more assured *Boylan Heights*, which featured the superb single "Scotty's Lament."

The edgier *Fun and Games* followed in 1989, and a year later the group resurfaced with *One Simple Word*, scoring an alternative radio hit with the single "Stone Cold Yesterday." After a three-year tour which saw the Connells add keyboardist Steve Potak to their lineup in 1991, they finally returned to the studio to begin work on 1993's *Ring*, highlighted by the single "Slackjawed," as well as "74-75," a major hit throughout Europe. After another three-year hiatus, the Connells issued 1996's *Weird Food and Devastation*, released concurrently with Huntley's solo debut *brain junk*. The group returned in 1998 with *Still Life*. —*Jason Ankeny*

Darker Days / 1985 / TVT ✦✦✦

● **Boylan Heights** / 1987 / TVT ✦✦✦✦✦
Their second album shows a great improvement over its predecessor. With help from producer Mitch Easter, the band effectively combines Southern jangly guitars with Celtic influences. One of the more distinctive, though generally overlooked college rock albums of the late-'80s. —*Chris Woodstra*

Fun & Games / 1989 / TVT ✦✦

One Simple Word / 1990 / TVT ✦✦✦✦✦
In the course of four albums, The Connells have evolved their own style within the jangling guitar-rock sound so prevalent in alternative bands of the '80s. Mainly it's been a matter of writing more distinctive songs and having them sung by guitarist George Huntley so they sink in. This is their first album to cross over from the category of "promising" to the beginnings of a fulfillment of that promise. —*William Ruhlmann*

Ring / 1993 / TVT ✦✦✦✦
After scoring a college radio hit with "Stone Cold Yesterday" from 1990's *One Simple Word*, the Connells followed up with their strongest effort to date, the radio-ready *Ring*. While muddy production and underdeveloped songs occasionally plagued their earlier releases, *Ring* is an album aimed squarely at the mainstream, and is a clear attempt to pick up on fans of R.E.M., alt-country like Uncle Tupelo, and rootsy power pop like Marshall Crenshaw. The album's first single, a lilting and seemingly unassuming acoustic ballad entitled "'74-'75" became an unexpected smash hit in Europe, topping the pop charts in many countries across the continent. The song was equally indebted to acoustic-based roots rock as it was to Celtic music (as witnessed in the ornate backing vocals) and was one of the band's most successful concoctions. Subsequent singles, such as the poppy "Slackjawed" and the nostalgic "New Boy" (which sounds like it was written as musical accompaniment to a James Thurber story) each managed to garner some alternative radio attention as well. The album tracks were equally as strong, especially the tense "Carry My Picture," a stark portrait of a vindictive relationship. *Ring* established the Connells as the forerunners in the group of jangle pop bands that had previously lived largely in the shadow of R.E.M. and helped the band become a moderate commercial success. While time has not been kind to the band or this album, the Connells clearly held some influence. In 2000, Fran Healy of the British guitar pop band Travis admitted that his band's 1999 hit "Writing to Reach You" was written while listening to "'74-'75" on the radio, and was, in effect, a bit of a rip-off. The songs sound unmistakably similar, and it's enough proof that the Connells deserve much more credit for their contributions to guitar-based pop than they have previously been given. —*Jason Damas*

Weird Food & Devastation / Aug. 20, 1996 / TVT ✦✦✦
Weird Food & Devastation follows the pattern of the Connells' previous album, *Ring*, by adding harder-edged guitars to their ringing guitar pop. The Connells aren't able to come up with a set of memorable songs for *Weird Food*, but the album nevertheless remains a pleasurable listen, especially for fans of Southern jangle-pop (R.E.M., Let's Active) or melodic alternative rock in the vein of Buffalo Tom. —*Thom Owens*

Still Life / May 12, 1998 / TVT ✦✦✦

The Contours
f. 1958, Detroit, MI
Frat Rock, Motown, R&B, Soul
One of Berry Gordy's earliest discoveries at Motown, the hard-rocking Contours cultivated a new generation of fans when their "Do You Love Me" was featured in the 1987 hit movie *Dirty Dancing*. Led by gravelly-voiced Billy Gordon, the quintet scored an R&B chart-topper in 1962 with the rollicking "Do You Love Me" on Gordy's label, then smoothed out their sound just a bit for the mid-'60s soul classics "First I Look at the Purse" and "Just a Little Misunderstanding." Dennis Edwards, who joined the group well after "Do You Love Me," was recruited to replace David Ruffin as lead of the Temptations in 1968. —*Bill Dahl*

Do You Love Me / 1962 / Motown ✦✦✦
The first LP released on Gordy Records is also the Contours' first and only regular album release on Motown; a later collection also titled *Do You Love Me* was a greatest-hits compilation. This is worth a few bucks if you can find a copy. Three cuts were released on the Motown label before they were switched to Gordy ("The Stretch," "Funny," and "Whole Lotta Woman"); all stiffed. On Gordy, the group enjoyed their biggest hit the first time out in "Do You Love Me." "You Better Get In Line," a slick dance number, died as the flip of "Shake Sherrie." A lively "You Must Be Love" has Billy Gordon swapping leads with Joe Billingslea. "Shake Sherrie" has a looping beat, a wandering baritone sax, and incredulous vocals from Gordon, Billingslea, Sylvester Potts, Billy Hoggs, and Hubert Johnson.

The rest suffer from a lack of identity; neither the group nor Motown had defined their sound when these were cut. —*Andrew Hamilton*

● **The Very Best of the Contours** / Mar. 23, 1999 / Motown ✦✦✦✦
The first CD best-of compilation for the Contours actually takes the exact same ten tracks that were available on the *Do You Love Me* album and adds five more, most of which are of secondary interest. Regardless, it's a decent overview of a minor but good Motown act. "Do You Love Me" will always be their calling card, but "Shake Sherry," "First I Look at the Purse," "It Must Be Love" and "Can You Do It" are well worth hearing for anyone who wants to hear the Motown sound at its rawest and most raucous. Smokey Robinson's "That Day When She Needed Me" and the 1961 doo wop single "Funny" show an unexpectedly mellow side of the group. The 1966-67 sides, "Just a Little Misunderstanding" and "It's So Hard Being a Loser" find them being steered toward a slicker, Temptations-like direction; indeed, future Temp, Dennis Edwards, sings lead on the latter cut. —*Richie Unterberger*

Ry Cooder
b. Mar. 15, 1947, Los Angeles, CA
Slide Guitar, Vocals, Mandolin, Guitar / Slide Guitar Blues, Cuban Pop, Contemporary Blues, Roots Rock, Worldbeat, Ethnic Fusion, Country-Rock, Blues-Rock, Modern Electric Blues, Album Rock, Film Music, Instrumental Rock, Original Score
Whether serving as a session musician, solo artist, or soundtrack composer, Ry Cooder's chameleon-like fretted instrument virtuosity, songwriting, and choices of material encompass an incredibly eclectic range of North American musical styles, including rock & roll, blues, reggae, Tex-Mex, Hawaiian, Dixieland jazz, country, folk, R&B, gospel, and vaudeville. The 16-year-old Cooder began his career in 1963 in a blues band with Jackie DeShannon and then formed the short-lived Rising Sons in 1965 with Taj Mahal and Spirit drummer Ed Cassidy. During his subsequent career as a session musician, Cooder's trademark slide guitar work graced the recordings of such artists as Captain Beefheart, Randy Newman, Little Feat, Van Dyke Parks, the Rolling Stones and Gordon Lightfoot. Cooder made his debut as a solo artist in 1970; the follow-up, *Into the Purple Valley*, introduced longtime cohorts Jim Keltner on drums and Jim Dickinson on bass, and it and *Boomer's Story* largely repeated and refined the syncopated style and mood of the first. In 1974, Cooder produced what is generally regarded as his best album, *Paradise and Lunch*; its follow-up, *Chicken Skin Music*, showcased a potent blend of Tex-Mex, Hawaiian, gospel, and soul music, and featured contributions from Flaco Jimenez and Gabby Pahinui. In 1979, *Bop till You Drop* was the first major-label album to be recorded digitally. In the early '80s, Cooder began to augment his solo output with extensive soundtrack work. —*Steve Huey*

Ry Cooder / 1970 / Reprise ✦✦✦
His debut serves as a neat prototype, with its Sleepy John Estes and Woody Guthrie covers. It also introduces a most talented musician in its leader. But it's still a prototype; the best was yet to come. —*Jeff Tamarkin*

Into the Purple Valley / 1971 / Reprise ✦✦✦✦✦
First there are no other credits for musicians; because of his reputation for honesty in music, I will assume that he plays all the instruments, including the ones with no strings. He is known as a virtuoso on almost every stringed instrument and on this CD he demonstrates this ability on a wide variety of instruments. The main focus of the music here is on the era of the Dust Bowl, and what was happening in America at the time, socially and musically. Songs by Woody Guthrie, Leadbelly, and a variety of other people show Ry's encyclopedic knowledge of the music of this time, combined with an instinctive feel for the songs. "Phenomenal" is the descriptive word to describe his playing, whether it is on guitar, Hawaiian "slack key" guitar, mandolin, or more arcane instruments he has found. This is a must for those who love instrumental virtuosity, authentic reworkings of an era, or just plain good music. —*Bob Gottlieb*

Boomer's Story / 1972 / Reprise ✦✦✦✦✦
Largely laidback and bluesy, this album features a number of paeans to an America long lost. —*Jeff Tamarkin*

● **Paradise & Lunch** / 1974 / Reprise ✦✦✦✦✦
Working with an intriguing collection of veteran musicians, the master musician and archivist turns in a stunning set of timeless remakes and new compositions. —*Jeff Tamarkin*

Chicken Skin Music / 1976 / Reprise ✦✦✦✦✦
Hawaiian traditional music meets Leadbelly and Ben E. King on Cooder's gospelization of rock & soul. —*Jeff Tamarkin*

Showtime / 1976 / Reprise ✦✦✦
Recorded live in 1976, Cooder cooks and struts his stuff on this grand tour of his abilities. The great Flaco Jimenez is on accordion. —*Jeff Tamarkin*

Jazz / 1978 / Reprise ✦✦✦
A tribute to Dixieland, with a stopover at the blues hotel. Joseph Byrd's arrangements on tunes by Bix Beiderbecke, Joseph Spence, et al., are inspired. —*Jeff Tamarkin*

Bop Till You Drop / 1979 / Reprise ✦✦

The Long Riders / 1980 / Reprise ✦✦✦
Ry Cooder's soundtrack for *The Long Riders* received a top-notch treatment from Warner Bros. (Japan), who not only did an excellent remastering job, but backed it up with English lyrics to the songs, notes, and a Japanese insert. Cooder was in fine form with this score, using original material, unusual and anachronistic instruments (saz, tamboura, electric guitar), and elements of traditional songs from the Civil War period. As a result,

the album can be appreciated as a unique entity, away from the film—and bonded to the film, the music provides grace and power to the onscreen events. —*Steven McDonald*

Borderline / 1980 / Reprise ✦

The Slide Area / 1982 / Reprise ✦✦✦

Crossroads / 1986 / Reprise ✦✦✦
The ersatz blues story of the film gives Ry Cooder leeway to turn in an impressive blues-derived soundtrack featuring Sonny Terry along with his usual collaborators Van Dyke Parks, Jim Keltner, Nathan East, and others. But it's Cooder's guitar playing that highlights the album. —*William Ruhlmann*

Get Rhythm / 1987 / Reprise ✦✦✦

A Meeting by the River / 1993 / Waterlily Acoustics ✦✦✦✦✦
A Meeting by the River can best be described as a spontaneous outpouring of music, unhindered by convention or form, brought into being by musicians so supremely capable that the music is never labored, the technique of their craft always subservient to the final product. Cooder and Bhatt are genuine masters of the guitar and mohan vina, respectively. The latter, an instrument created by Bhatt himself, is a sort of hybrid between a guitar and a vichitra vina, and is played with a metal slide. This fact is just one of the many things that connect Bhatt's playing to Cooder's, who plays nothing but bottleneck guitar here. The voices of the two instruments blend marvelously, first alternating melodic statements, then doing so together, each dancing around the other, playing cat and mouse, probing, answering, reflecting. *A Meeting by the River* is one of those few cross-genre albums in which the listener never feels for a second that there is some kind of fusion going on; one does not hear the component parts so much as the integrated whole. However, one can theoretically separate guitar from vina, America from India, the Mississippi from the Ganges. Once this is done, the resulting music makes more sense than ever before, the combination of two traditions of stringed instruments that use slides to produce sound and value improvisation and voice-like phrasing. The splendor of the music is aided in its transmission by the fact that this album is masterfully recorded; each instrument is clear, distinct, and three-dimensional sounding. *A Meeting by the River* is a must-own, a thing of pure, unadulterated beauty. —*Daniel Gioffre*

Music by Ry Cooder / Jul. 11, 1995 / Reprise ✦✦✦✦✦
Since he's a limited vocalist with erratic songwriting skills, one could justifiably argue that the soundtrack medium is the best vehicle for Cooder's talents, allowing him to construct eclectic, chiefly instrumental pieces drawing upon all sorts of roots music and ethnic flavors (often, but not always, employing his excellent blues and slide guitar). This two-CD, 34-song compilation gathers excerpts from eleven of the soundtracks he worked on between 1980 and 1993 (three of the cuts, from the 1981 film *Southern Comfort*, are previously unreleased). As few listeners (even Cooder fans) are dedicated enough to go to the trouble of finding all of his individual soundtracks, this is a good distillation of many of his more notable contributions in this idiom, although it inevitably leaves out some fine moments. Still, it's well programmed and evocative, often conjuring visions of ghostly landscapes and funky border towns. —*Richie Unterberger*

Sam Cooke (Sam Cook)

b. Jan. 22, 1931, Clarksdale, MS, **d.** Dec. 11, 1964, Los Angeles, CA
Vocals / R&B, Soul

A performer whose sophisticated, crystalline vocal delivery and alchemical fusion of pop and gospel laid the foundations for the rise of modern soul music, Sam Cooke was a singer of remarkable spiritual resonance, a supreme talent whose vision transcended all barriers of race and faith. A champion of creative rights who wrote much of his own material and even established his own business empire to better realize his far-reaching musical ambitions, Cooke was also a champion of civil rights who utilized his stature as a performer to break down the color lines separating blacks from whites; a major crossover success, his brilliant career was tragically brief, but his shadow looms large over the generations of artists who emerged in his wake. As a teen, Cooke became a member of the gospel group the Highway QCs, and in 1950, he joined the Soul Stirrers. 1957's "You Send Me," a majestic soul confection which sold some two million copies, made him a secular pop star. A series of hits—most of them light romantic ballads and novelty tunes—followed over the next two years, most notably the Top 40 hits "Wonderful World," "Only Sixteen" and "Everybody Likes to Cha Cha." As the 1960s dawned, Cooke began taking an active interest in the music business, founding his own independent label, SAR; upon his arrival at RCA, his music adopted a grittier, more gospel-influenced feel, and his gifts reached their full potential as he reeled off a string of early 1960s hits ranging from the bluesy "Sad Mood" to the gospel-pop of "Bring It on Home to Me," through to the smooth soul of "Another Saturday Night" and the buoyant R&B of "Twisting the Night Away." As his reputation as a performer grew, Cooke established fervent fan bases in both the pop and R&B markets, and eventually he graduated from the so-called "chitlin' circuit" of black-owned venues to Las Vegas casino stages and white nightclubs, emerging as a crossover superstar. Cooke was murdered on December 11, 1964; "A Change Is Gonna Come," a posthumous 1965 smash, was his epitaph—a thoughtful, spiritually charged assessment of the then-current state of American race relations, it presaged the ascendent civil rights movement with remarkable clarity. —*Jason Ankeny*

Night Beat / Aug. 1963 / ABKCO ✦✦✦✦✦
Intense, spiraling uptempo numbers, gripping ballads, and simply marvelous performances by a legend who sadly wouldn't be around much longer. Originally released in August 1963, *Night Beat* [RCA 2709] was reissued on CD on June 6, 1995 [ABKCO 1124]. —*Ron Wynn*

Sam Cooke at the Copa / Oct. 1964 / ABKCO ✦✦✦
Cooke's classic live album is a mixed bag—he was playing to a White supper-club audience and altered his sound accordingly, favoring ballads and folk songs over most of his celebrated classic soul numbers. The voice is there, and the style, but he never does cut loose completely, and the backing band is too clean. —*Bruce Eder*

Two Sides of Sam Cooke / 1970 / Specialty ✦✦✦✦✦
This 12-song release, a straight-up reissue of the original vinyl album from 1970, splits its time between Cooke's early gospel sides as a member of the Soul Stirrers ("The Last Mile of the Way," "Were You There," "Touch the Hem of His Garment") and his early attempts at crossing over into pop music, including "Lovable," which was originally issued under the name of Dale Cooke to avoid upsetting his gospel fans. A major highlight is "Jesus Gave Me Water," Sam's first recording, done when he was 19 years old. Top-notch liner notes from Barret Hansen (aka Dr. Demento) make this a great little package well worth checking out. —*Cub Koda*

The Legendary Sam Cooke / 1974 / Candlelite Music/RCA Special Products ✦✦✦✦✦
Usually it's best to steer way clear of these sort of budget packages, but this is an exception, primarily because Cooke's catalog has been handled so poorly. This triple album has 30 songs from Cooke's RCA peak, including all the big smashes, and quite a few big and small hits ("Little Red Rooster," "Good News," "Sugar Dumplin'," "Sad Mood," "That's It, I Quit, I'm Movin' On") that don't appear on the only decent Cooke anthology currently in print (*The Man and His Music*). That makes it a decent pickup if you find a cheap used copy, but the real solution would be to have RCA finally get its act together and give the man the multi-disc retrospective he deserves. —*Richie Unterberger*

☆ **Live at the Harlem Square Club** / Jun. 1985 / RCA ✦✦✦✦✦
Long believed lost, this live album—rejected for release in 1963 by Cooke's managers, who wanted to broaden his appeal to White listeners—captures Cooke playing to a largely Black crowd, and it couldn't be more different from his *At the Copa* live album. A hot, sweaty performance, with Cooke and a proper band luxuriating in his most soulful material in its most wrenching and impassioned form. —*Bruce Eder*

★ **The Man and His Music** / Feb. 1986 / RCA ✦✦✦✦✦
The ultimate Sam Cooke collection, and really the only one worth owning, covering his post-1957 career from his pop music breakthrough ("You Send Me") to his final impassioned soul statement, "A Change Is Gonna Come" (which is included in its seldom-heard uncut version). Few stones are left unturned, the sound is clean and sharp, and the tragedy of Cooke's early death is recalled with each play of this collection. —*Bruce Eder*

His Earliest Recordings / 1991 / Specialty ✦✦✦✦✦
A superb collection of 25 of the earliest recordings made by Sam Cooke, including "Touch the Hem of His Garment." —*Stephen Thomas Erlewine*

The SAR Records Story / 1994 / ABKCO ✦✦✦✦✦
Sam Cooke's SAR Records Story is a double-disc set presenting material recorded for the legendary soul singer's own SAR label from 1959-1965, much of it produced by Cooke himself and including a few of his rough, unreleased demos. The first disc covers the label's religious side, with a multitude of cuts from Cooke's former group the Soul Stirrers (now with Jimmie Outler on lead vocals), plus a generous helping of songs by R.H. Harris & His Gospel Paraders and the Womack Brothers. The second disc covers essentially the same gospel-derived soul territory but with a secular bent, featuring future stars Bobby Womack (with the Valentinos), Billy Preston, and Johnnie Taylor, plus L.C. Cooke, Johnnie Morisette, the Simms Twins, and Mel Carter. All in all, it's an excellent look at a lesser-known portion of Cooke's career, and there's some great, underappreciated music to boot. —*Steve Huey*

The Rhythm and the Blues / Oct. 24, 1995 / RCA ✦✦✦✦
From the title, you might infer that this 20-track compilation—taken from early-'60s sessions, and principally composed of LP-only cuts—aims to showcase Cooke's most soulful side. That's true to some degree, but this isn't his funkiest stuff; for that, look to *Live at the Harlem Square Club 1963*, or even his most uptempo singles. Most of this is in fact suave pop/R&B, the emphasis sometimes falling on the pop, with lightly swinging, jazzy arrangements and some orchestration. Cooke didn't write most of the material here, and while "Little Red Rooster" (a hit single) represents the earthiest extreme that the CD touches upon, there are also quite a few songs that were originally performed by jazz/popsters from the '20s, '30s, and '40s. Certainly these are decent offerings; Cooke's a great singer and interpreter, and the arrangements are smooth without being overdone. But it's neither Cooke at his very best (the hits compilation *Man and His Music* is much better) or his grittiest (that honor belongs to *Harlem Square*). It does restore much of his better obscure material to wide availability and is recommended to those who have the above-mentioned albums and want more Cooke, although the 1963 LP *Night Beat* (reissued on CD in 1995) is a bluesier and better one to check out first. —*Richie Unterberger*

★ **Greatest Hits** / Feb. 24, 1998 / RCA ✦✦✦✦✦
Although it isn't as sublime as the definitive *The Man and His Music*, *Greatest Hits* still does a good job of rounding up the majority of Sam Cooke's biggest pop hits. Ironically, it doesn't have enough gospel or R&B cuts, skipping over such essentials as "Touch the Hem of His Garment," "Ain't That Good News" and "A Change Is Gonna Come" in favor of such pop hits as "Sugar Dumpling." However, it has just enough songs that aren't on *The Man and His Music* to make it worth exploring for fans who haven't been able to hear some of this material before, since some of these songs have been out of print for years. Nevertheless, the curious and the novice should be aware that this is not a good introduction to Sam Cooke, because it doesn't provide a full portrait of his career and it overlooks too many necessary songs. —*Stephen Thomas Erlewine*

☆ **The Man Who Invented Soul [Box Set]** / Sep. 26, 2000 / RCA ✦✦✦✦✦
This set is near essential to fans of Sam Cooke, despite the fact that it contains none of his gospel recordings for Specialty Records or any of the work from the final year of his

career (owned by ABKCO Records). Scattered every few minutes across this four-disc collection are reminders of just how far ahead of all existing musical forms Cooke was, creating sounds that stretched the definitions of song genres as they were understood and created completely new categories. Indeed, he was so successful that it's easy to underestimate the impact and importance of many of his early triumphs. "You Send Me," which opens this set, may seem today like the safest, tamest pop music, but in 1957 it was a genre-bending single, a new kind of R&B/pop music hybrid and one that quietly shook the foundations of the music business when it hit number one.

Disc one offers a fresh appreciation of the best of the early Keen Records sides, drawing on the best of nearly two years of singles and the strongest of Cooke's LP tracks in the best account to date of his early career in popular music. Disc two begins Cooke's RCA years, and the quality of his singles, which clearly and easily bridge the gap between genres, races, and generations, improves dramatically. The development of Cooke's writing and singing and his growing confidence and range culminate with disc four, which encompasses the *Night Beat* album and Cooke's live performance from the Harlem Square Club. The sound is extraordinary throughout, expansive, rich-textured, and vividly detailed; a choice earlier CD release, *The Man and His Music*, by comparison, sounds thin and tinny. —*Bruce Eder*

The Cookies

f. 1953, Brooklyn, NY, **db.** 1963
Brill Building Pop, Girl Group
The forerunner of Ray Charles' Raelettes, the original Cookies were Margie Hendrix, Ethel "Earl-Jean" McCrea, and Pat Lyles. They recorded for Lamp (Aladdin) in 1954 and Jesse Stone brought them to Atlantic in 1955. They recorded three sessions under The Cookies banner and scored a Top Ten R&B hit with "In Paradise" in 1956. The group also backed Joe Turner and Chuck Willis on their hit recordings in 1956 before being absorbed into the Charles empire and becoming The Raelettes. Almost six years later, a new trio emerged as the Cookies on Dimension, with only McCrea from the first group in its lineup. They did backup vocals for Neil Sedaka, Little Eva, and Carole King, while scoring two Top Ten R&B, one Top Ten, and one Top 20 pop hit in 1962 and 1963. "Don't Say Nothin' Bad (About My Baby)" was their biggest, peaking at number three R&B (number seven pop) in 1963. "Girls Grow up Faster than Boys" was their final chart outing in November 1963. —*Ron Wynn*

Don't Say Nothin' Bad about the Cookies / 1991 / Teenager ✦✦✦✦
This import compilation includes the hits "Chains" and "Don't Say Nothin' Bad About My Baby," and is jammed with obscure Goffin-King tunes. The problem is, most of them aren't anywhere nearly as good as the two hits the team penned for the Cookies or their work with other girl groups. It does include the obscure gem "Girls Grow Up Faster Than Boys," a sassy cut that's as good as the hits. —*Richie Unterberger*

● **Complete Cookies** / 1994 / Sequel ✦✦✦✦
Apparently, Gerry Goffin and Carole King saddled the Cookies with songs they couldn't place on other artists. Maybe they should have called them "the Dumpies." Occasionally magic occurred, as it did on "Chains," and their signature song "Don't Say Nothing Bad About My Baby." But others like "Girls Grow Up Faster Than Boys," "Randy," and "They're Jealous Of Me," are less than memorable. A remake of the Drifters' "On Broadway," is one of few substantive songs on the CD, but if you're a fan of the Cookies, Goffin & King, or the Brill Buildings' songwriters, you'll find this CD essential; if not, this disc isn't for you. It's a piece of nostalgia, definitive, but it's not for everyone. —*Andrew Hamilton*

Coolio

b. Aug. 1, 1963
Vocals / Pop-Rap, West Coast Rap, Hip-Hop
Coolio (born Artis Ivey) is a native of Compton, CA, yet his variation of the P-Funk-inspired rap of Dr. Dre is calmer, less violent and funnier. Recorded with his DJ Bryan "Wino" Dobbs, Coolio's 1994 debut album, *It Takes a Thief* was a smash hit, selling over a million records and featuring the number three single, "Fantastic Voyage." His second record, 1995's *Gangsta's Paradise*, was an even bigger hit, thanks to the title track, which was the biggest rap single of the year. *My Soul* followed in 1997. —*Stephen Thomas Erlewine*

It Takes a Thief / Jul. 19, 1994 / Tommy Boy ✦✦✦✦
Just when it looked like rap would completely succumb to the violent hyperbole and mean-spirited "realness" of gangsta rap, new blood entered the scene in 1994 to nudge the genre back toward friendlier turf. That new blood included Nas, Craig Mack, and Coolio, whose *It Takes a Thief* starts with the easy-rolling funk of Lakeside's "Fantastic Voyage" and goes from there, infusing rap with a much-needed sense of humor and the promise of good times. While Coolio is no simp—"County Line" playfully explores the hassles of welfare, while some tracks dip into gangsta territory—he manages to make rap a cool, inclusive journey. —*Eddie Huffman*

● **Gangsta's Paradise** / Nov. 21, 1995 / Tommy Boy ✦✦✦✦✦
Most of Coolio's hit debut *It Takes a Thief* was fairly upbeat material, but the appearance of the stark single "Gangsta's Paradise" in the summer of 1995 signaled a change in the rapper's music. Driven by an ominously deep bass line and slashing strings, the creeping, threatening funk of "Gangsta's Paradise" was the most chilling thing Coolio had recorded to date, but the menace didn't come at the expense of his considerable talent for immediate, catchy hooks. Consequently, the single shot to the top of the charts and hovered in the Top Ten for many weeks. The album followed shortly afterwards, and it didn't fail to deliver on the promise of the single. Not only did Coolio expand his sound, but his songwriting skills improved, as *Gangsta's Paradise* has very few weak moments. Alternating

between slow, funky grooves and elastic, party-ready anthems, *Gangsta's Paradise* is proof that Coolio is one of the most exciting and interesting hip-hop artists of the mid-'90s. —*Stephen Thomas Erlewine*

My Soul / Aug. 26, 1997 / Tommy Boy ✦✦✦✦
Coolio's third album, *My Soul*, follows the same formula as its two predecessors, which isn't necessarily a bad thing. Where others have failed as pop-rappers, Coolio succeeds because of his love of melody, message, and funky beats. *My Soul* lacks anything as monolithic as "Gangsta's Paradise," yet it has a more elaborate production, boasting obscure samples, violins, sound bites and guitars. It also is remarkably consistent, delivering very few subpar cuts over the course of the album. That would be enough to distinguish it from the ranks of overstuffed gangsta rappers, but what makes *My Soul* another winner is how Coolio is unafraid to be both serious and funny, catchy and funky. It's a small, subtle difference, but it's what makes *My Soul* a thoroughly enjoyable record, no matter if you're going out or staying in. —*Stephen Thomas Erlewine*

Fantastic Voyage: The Greatest Hits / Jul. 17, 2001 / Tommy Boy ✦✦✦✦✦
Over the course of three albums in the 1990s, Coolio took West Coast hip-hop even farther into the mainstream than Dr. Dre. Even though he nearly succumbed to the perils of the streets in his youth, Coolio's take on the '70s funk-obsessed L.A. sound was usually far more good-humored than the menacing Death Row crew. His gangsta roots could play to the hardcore faithful, but he also snagged plenty of younger listeners with his fun-loving party music and genial (if profane) comic persona. (In fact, it's difficult to imagine Puff Daddy becoming an across-the-board pop star without Coolio first sparking that younger audience's interest in hip-hop.) Coolio's broad appeal, combined with a knack for finding (often borrowing) memorable hooks, helped make him one of the best pop-rap artists of the '90s, as demonstrated by *Fantastic Voyage: The Greatest Hits*. It's a straightforward 13-track collection centered around Coolio's signature party anthems—"Fantastic Voyage," "Too Hot," "1, 2, 3, 4 (Sumpin' New)"—plus his moody masterpiece, "Gangsta's Paradise," and one previously unissued track, "Aw Here It Goes" (a theme for the Nickelodeon comedy series *Kenan & Kel*). Yet the lesser-known tracks are often pretty catchy themselves, proving that Coolio's talents extend beyond the handful of irresistible singles for which he's primarily known. Even if nothing else quite matches the heights of those few classics, *Fantastic Voyage: The Greatest Hits* is still an infectious, consistently entertaining listen. —*Steve Huey*

Alice Cooper

b. Feb. 4, 1948, Detroit, MI
Vocals, Leader / Heavy Metal, Hard Rock
Originally, there was a band called Alice Cooper led by a singer named Vincent Damon Furnier. Under his direction, Alice Cooper pioneered a grandly theatrical and violent brand of heavy metal that was designed to shock. Drawing equally from horror movies, vaudeville, heavy metal, and garage rock, the group created a stage show that featured electric chairs, guillotines, fake blood, and huge boa constrictors, all coordinated by the heavily made-up Furnier. By that time, Furnier had adopted the name for his androgynous onstage personality. While the visuals were extremely important to the group's impact, the band's music was nearly as distinctive. Driven by raw, simple riffs and melodies that derived from '60s guitar pop as well as showtunes, it was rock & roll at its most basic and catchy, even when the band ventured into psychedelia and art rock. After the original group broke up and Furnier began a solo career as Alice Cooper, his actual music lost most of its theatrical flourishes, becoming straightforward heavy metal, yet his stage show retained all of the trademark props that made him the king of shock rock. —*Stephen Thomas Erlewine*

Pretties for You / 1969 / Bizarre ✦✦✦
Alice Cooper's debut album had none of his legendary grotesque hard rock; instead, *Pretties for You* was an earnest, but flawed, stab at psychedelia which occasionally caught fire. —*Stephen Thomas Erlewine*

Love It to Death / Jan. 1971 / Warner Brothers ✦✦✦✦✦
Alice Cooper's third album, 1971's *Love It to Death*, can be pinpointed as the release when everything began to come together for the band. Their first couple of albums (*Pretties for You* and *Easy Action*) were both largely psychedelic/acid-rock affairs, and bore little comparison to the band's eventual rip-roaring, teenage-anthem direction. The main reason for the quintet's change was that the eventually legendary producer Bob Ezrin was on board for the first time, and helped the Coopers focus their songwriting and sound, while they also perfected their trashy, violent, and theatrical stage show and image. One of the band's most instantly identifiable anthems, "I'm Eighteen," was what made the album a hit, as well as another classic, "Is It My Body." But like Alice Cooper's other albums from the early '70s, it was an incredibly consistent listen from beginning to end. The garage rocker "Caught in a Dream," as well as the ass-kicking "Long Way to Go," and a pair of epics—the Doors-esque "Black Juju" and the eerie "Ballad of Dwight Fry"—showed that Alice was easily in league with other high-energy Detroit bands of the era (MC5, Stooges). *Love It to Death* was the first of a string of classic releases from the original Alice Cooper group. —*Greg Prato*

Killer / Feb. 1971 / Warner Brothers ✦✦✦✦✦
Alice Cooper wasted little time following up the breakthrough success of 1971's *Love It to Death* with another album released the same year, *Killer*. Again, producer Bob Ezrin was on board, and helps the group solidify their heavy rock (yet wide-ranging) style even further. The band's stage show dealt with the macabre, and such disturbing tracks as "Dead Babies" and the title track fit in perfectly. Other songs were even more exceptional, such as the perennial-barnstorming concert standard "Under My Wheels," the melodic yet

gritty "Be My Lover," and the tribute to their fallen friend Jim Morrison, "Desperado." The long and winding "Halo of Flies" correctly hinted that the band would be tackling more complex song structures on future albums, while "You Drive Me Nervous" and "Yeah, Yeah, Yeah" showed that Alice Cooper hadn't completely abandoned their early garage-rock direction. With *Killer*, they became one of the world's top rock bands and concert attractions; it rewarded them as being among the most notorious and misunderstood entertainers, thoroughly despised by grown-ups. *—Greg Prato*

School's Out / 1972 / Warner Brothers ✦✦✦✦✦
1972's *School's Out* catapulted Alice Cooper into the hard rock stratosphere, largely due to its timeless, all-time classic title track. But while the song became Alice's highest charting single ever (reaching number seven on the U.S. charts) and recalled the brash, three-and-a-half-minute garage rock of yore, the majority of the album signaled a more complex compositional directional for the band. Unlike Cooper's previous classic, early-'70s releases (*Love It to Death, Killer*) which contained several instantly identifiable hard-rock classics, *School's Out* appeared to be a concept album, and aside from the aforementioned title track anthem, few of the other tracks have ever popped up in concert. That's not to say they weren't still strong and memorable; while such cuts as "Gutter Cat vs. the Jets/Street Fight," "My Stars," and "Grande Finale" came off like mini-epics with a slightly progressive edge, Alice Cooper still managed to maintain their raw, unrefined punk edges, regardless. Other highlights included the rowdy "Public Animal #9," the mid-paced "Luney Tune," and the sinister, cabaret-esque "Blue Turk." *—Greg Prato*

Billion Dollar Babies / 1973 / Warner Brothers ✦✦✦✦✦
With 1973's *Billion Dollar Babies*, Alice Cooper refined the raw grit of their earlier work in favor of a slightly more polished sound (courtesy of super-producer Bob Ezrin), resulting in a mega-hit album that reached the top of the U.S. album charts. Song for song, *Billion Dollar Babies* is probably the original Alice Cooper group's finest and strongest. Such tracks as "Hello Hooray," the lethal stomp of the title track, the defiant "Elected" (a re-write of an earlier song, "Reflected"), and the poison-laced pop candy of "No More Mr. Nice Guy" remain among Cooper's greatest achievements. Also included are a pair of perennial concert standards—the disturbing necrophilia ditty "I Love the Dead" and the chilling macabre of "Sick Things"—as well as such strong, lesser-known selections as "Raped and Freezin'," "Unfinished Sweet," and perhaps Cooper's most overlooked gem, "Generation Landslide." Nothing seemed like it could stop this great hard-rock band from overtaking the universe, but tensions between the members behind the scenes would force the stellar original A.C. band to split up after just one more album. Not only is *Billion Dollar Babies* one of Alice Cooper's very best; it remains one of rock's all-time, quintessential classics. *—Greg Prato*

★ **Alice Cooper's Greatest Hits** / 1974 / Warner Brothers ✦✦✦✦✦
With the future of the original Alice Cooper band in doubt by mid-1974 (they would soon break up for good with Alice going solo), Warner Bros. decided to issue a best-of compilation entitled *Greatest Hits*. If you're a newcomer to Alice, this 12-track compilation is a must-hear—all the selections are exceptional. While many have chosen to focus primarily on Cooper's theatrics over the years, the original band members were indeed supreme rock songwriters; such anthems as "I'm Eighteen," "Under My Wheels," "School's Out," and "No More Mr. Nice Guy" are unquestionably among the finest hard rock tracks of all time. And the other selections prove to be just as strong—"Is It My Body," "Desperado," "Be My Lover," "Elected," "Billion Dollar Babies," and "Muscle of Love" are all outstanding as well. The only criticism of the original release is that the collection overlooked the band's key album tracks never issued as singles, but the 2000 Rhino reissue corrected this with an expanded track listing. *—Greg Prato*

Welcome to My Nightmare / 1975 / Atlantic ✦✦✦✦✦
With the 1974 disintegration of the original Alice Cooper group, Alice was free to launch a solo career. He wisely decided to re-enlist the services of Bob Ezrin for his solo debut, 1975's *Welcome to My Nightmare*, which was a concept album tied into the storyline of the highly theatrical concert tour he launched soon after the album's release. While the music lost most of the gritty edge of the original AC lineup, *Welcome to My Nightmare* remains Alice's best solo effort—while some tracks stray from his expected hard rock direction, there's plenty of fist-pumping rock to go around. The disco-flavored, album-opening title track would be reworked on the stage as more of a hard rock tune, while "Some Folks" dips into cabaret territory, and "Only Women Bleed" is a sensitive ballad which became a Top Ten hit. But the rockers serve as the album's foundation—"Devil's Food," "The Black Widow," "Department of Youth," and "Cold Ethyl" are all standouts, as is the more tranquil yet eerie epic "Steven." Despite this promising start to Cooper's solo career, the majority of his subsequent releases were often not as focused and of varying quality. *—Greg Prato*

Alice Cooper Goes to Hell / 1976 / Warner Brothers ✦✦
Following the success of his first solo album, *Welcome to My Nightmare*, Alice Cooper followed it up with another concept album, 1976's *Goes to Hell*, similar in style to its predecessor. Again, longtime Alice producer Bob Ezrin was on board, and while there are a few highlights, *Goes to Hell* signaled an Alice era where he pretty much forsook the raw garage rock of his early days (*Killer, School's Out*) in favor of polished studio glitz. That said, the title track is worthy of any headbanger's time (and remains one of Cooper's most overlooked rock tunes), while "I Never Cry" was another Alice ballad that found a place near the top of the charts. Other highlights include such tracks as the disco-rock-boogie of "You Gotta Dance" and the laid-back yet sinister funk groove of "I'm the Coolest." Elsewhere, the musical experiments aren't as successful—the old-time sounds of "Give the Kid a Break," "I'm Always Chasing Rainbows," and the album-closing "Going Home" are about as far removed from the expected hard-rocking AC direction as you can get. And while the rocker "Wish You Were Here" would become a late-'70s concert standard for the Coop, the original studio version lacks the firepower the song achieved on the stage. Alice was supposed to follow-up the album's release with another highly theatrical stageshow (following the cue of his first solo tour in 1975), but an illness squashed the tour altogether. Despite its missteps, the gold-certified *Goes to Hell* would prove to be Alice's most commercially successful solo album for quite some time. *—Greg Prato*

Alice Cooper Show / Dec. 1977 / Warner Brothers ✦✦

From the Inside / 1978 / Metal Blade ✦✦

Constrictor / 1986 / MCA ✦✦✦

Raise Your Fist and Yell / 1987 / MCA ✦✦✦

Trash / Jul. 1989 / Epic ✦✦✦✦✦
Alice Cooper hadn't had a hugely successful album in over a decade when, in 1989, he teamed up with Bon Jovi producer Desmond Child for *Trash*—a highly slick and commercial, yet edgy, pop/metal effort that temporarily restored him to the charts in a big way. Fueled by the irresistible hit single "Poison," the album temporarily gave back to Cooper the type of visibility he deserved. There's nothing shocking here, and Cooper's ability to generate controversy had long since faded. But while the escapist *Trash*—which was clearly aimed at the Motley Crue/Guns N Roses crowd.—may not be the most challenging album of Cooper's career and isn't in a class with *School's Out* or *Billion Dollar Babies*, it's fun and quite enjoyable. And it was great to see the long-neglected Cooper on MTV next to so many of the '80s rockers he had influenced. *—Alex Henderson*

Hey Stoopid / Jul. 2, 1991 / Epic ✦✦✦
Unfortunately, the return to the high end of the charts that Alice Cooper enjoyed with 1989's *Trash* was short-lived. On his similar follow-up—another slick pop-metal effort—Cooper no longer had the input of hit producer/songwriter Desmond Child and worked with Peter Collins instead. The result is an album that, although generally enjoyable and far from bad, isn't essential. The CD's more memorable offerings include the clever and amusing "Feed My Frankenstein," the dramatic "Love's a Loading Gun" and the inspired title song—which admonishes rockers not to self-destruct. But despite its strong points, *Hey Stoopid* is for only Cooper's more devoted followers. *—Alex Henderson*

The Last Temptation / Jul. 1994 / Epic ✦✦✦✦
Though Alice Cooper's 1989 comeback gave him his first hit album in over a decade, the *Trash* record left some diehard fans disappointed, as did 1991's *Hey Stoopid*. Many listeners felt that Cooper had sold himself short, now completely focusing on sleazy sexual anthems, making him just another face in the heavy metal crowd. By the time *The Last Temptation* was released in 1994, the hair band fad that had fueled Cooper's return was dead, and Cooper was obviously aware of its downfall—the album sounds almost nothing like its two predecessors. Instead of relating to such albums as Motley Crue's *Dr. Feelgood*, *Last Temptation* seems more similar to Ozzy Osbourne's *No More Tears*. Thematically, the record returns to mostly conceptual songs, such as "Nothing's Free," "You're My Temptation," and "Cleansed by Fire." Though the album still has a few goofy interruptions, such anthems as "Lost in America" nonetheless boast more originality than anything off of *Hey Stoopid* or *Trash*. Far surpassing anything Cooper recorded in almost 20 years, *The Last Temptation* is unquestionably some of his best work. *—Barry Weber*

Classicks / Aug. 22, 1995 / Epic ✦✦✦
1995's *Classicks* is another in a long line of Alice Cooper best-of compilations, and it includes both live and studio material. Featured are such late-'80s and early-'90s favorites as "Poison," "Hey Stoopid," "House of Fire," and a great duet with Soundgarden's Chris Cornell, "Stolen Prayer," among others. While the live material is advertised as being issued officially for the first time on CD, it turns out that it comprises nothing more than the exact versions lifted from Alice's 1989 home video *Alice Cooper Trashes the World*. Still, you can never go wrong with *any* version of such early-'70s anthems as "Under My Wheels," "Billion Dollar Babies," "I'm Eighteen," "No More Mr. Nice Guy," "School's Out," and the ballad "Only Women Bleed." While the album's title may be a bit misleading (only six of the 14 tracks are true classics), and while it isn't in the same league as 1974's *Greatest Hits*, hardcore Cooper fans will find a decent collection in *Classicks*. [Note—the Japanese version of *Classicks* includes an extra bonus track, the rare B-side "It Rained All Night."] *—Greg Prato*

● **The Life & Crimes of Alice Cooper** / Apr. 20, 1999 / Rhino ✦✦✦✦
What made Alice Cooper a star? Sure, he had a tight, exciting band and some great songs that were as good as hard rock got in the early '70s, but he distinguished himself as a showman. By bringing shameless theatricality to rock & roll, he separated himself from the pack and became a superstar—the kind of person who is known for being himself more than for his achievements. This trajectory and the melodrama that inspired it are evident on the generous four-disc box set *The Life & Crimes of Alice Cooper*. Most box sets play like a sober history lesson, but this one plays like a grand epic, filled with love, lust, blood, and guts. Witness the humble beginnings of Vincent Furnier, as he leads an Arizona garage rock band called the Spiders through some credible, fuzzed-out Yardbirds-styled rock & roll! See how the Spiders transform into Nazz, then to the Alice Cooper Band! Gasp as Furnier becomes shock-rocker Alice Cooper! Thrill to Alice's biggest hits—every cut from *Alice Cooper's Greatest Hits* is here, some in their original single incarnations, all impeccably remastered! Wonder what went wrong as disc three begins to unfurl, and Alice Cooper the star cannibalizes the band, making such bizarre choices as recording with the Bee Gees from the *Sgt. Pepper* movie! Then, as soon as you figure Alice is down for the count, see his glorious resurrection as a hair metal godfather! It's no wonder that listening to all four discs in a row is exhausting—this is a rock & roll Horatio Alger story. And thank God for that, since that narrative drive makes *The Life & Crimes of Alice Cooper* one of the truly satisfying and definitive box sets of the late '90s. *—Stephen Thomas Erlewine*

★ **The Best of Alice Cooper** / Jan. 16, 2001 / Rhino ♦♦♦♦♦
Rhino's *The Best of Alice Cooper* presents a more concise alternative to 1999's mammoth, four-disc set *The Life & Crimes of Alice Cooper.* Like the box set, this album delivers digitally remastered versions of 22 of Cooper's best-known rock anthems, including "Eighteen," "School's Out," "Billion Dollar Babies," "Poison," and "Welcome to My Nightmare." Just thorough enough to please both casual fans and diehards, *The Best of Alice Cooper* is the most complete retrospective available on one disc. *—Heather Phares*

Cop Shoot Cop

f. 1987
Indie Rock, Alternative Pop/Rock, American Underground
Starting with their intentionally confrontational (and controversial) name, New York City's Cop Shoot Cop are descended from the darker impulses of the early-'80s "no-wave" movement that produced noisy, disagreeable, anti-social, but often very intriguing bands such as Mars, DNA, and Teenage Jesus & the Jerks. As with those combos, the Cops eschew the impulse of pop altogether, preferring a rumbling, clattering, deafening, metallic sound that focuses on the band's two-bass, no-guitar attack. The song narratives tend towards simplistic doom-and-gloom observations that "life sucks, man"—a point they often belabor. But when this bummer-rock clicks, it's oddly compelling, if slightly intimidating stuff, crammed to the gills with the standard litany of contemporary urban angst: anomie, alienation, and boredom. Add to this the odd meters, the yelling (he never describes it as singing) by low-end bassist Natz, and forays into pure noise, and what you end up with is an anti-rock style that, despite its repetitive tendencies, is furious, frightening and powerful. Oddly, despite the inherent anti-commerciality of their music, as well as the band's disdain for corporate-controlled major labels, they did land a contract with Interscope Records (home of Helmet), part of the Atlantic family. Despite the more accessible sound of their recent records, Cop Shoot Cop remain an acquired taste, even for those who like their rock edgy and uncompromising. *—John Dougan*

Consumer Revolt / 1990 / Big Cat ♦♦♦♦
Employing two basses and no guitar, Cop Shoot Cop's debut album proper (following the 1988 EP *Headkick Facsimile*) sets out the band's agenda—an overpowering wash of staccato riffs and obtuse samples married to harrowing narratives. Though placing them amid the burgeoning industrial music scene, Cop Shoot Cop's aesthetic shares something with New York's No Wave explosion of the late '70s. There is light at the end of their bleak tunnel of nihilism—even a kind of urban romanticism. And, like fellow travellers Big Black, Cop Shoot Cop recognize the importance of hooks, which resonate throughout their best songs. Initially issued on a tiny Long Island indie, it was later picked up by UK-based label Big Cat. The two longest tracks, "Burn Your Bridges" and album-closer "Eggs For Rib" are the highlights. *—Alex Ogg*

White Noise / 1991 / Big Cat ♦♦♦

Suck City / Nov. 19, 1992 / Interscope ♦♦♦♦
The Lower East Side avant garde-industrialists made their major label debut with this four-track EP in 1992. It's as if they can sense the majors panic-buying in the wake of Nirvana—alongside the Jesus Lizard, they are certainly the most unlikely bunch ever to take their seats on the back of the major label gravy train. On the title-track, they show how their heads have not been turned—indeed, the predictions of their own mortality are as chilling as they are funny ("We'll be history by 34/There's always the reunion tour . . . "). You've got to love a band with such a shrewd sense of perspective. *—Alex Ogg*

• **Ask Questions Later** / Mar. 30, 1993 / Interscope ♦♦♦♦♦
The band's full album debut on Interscope resulted in a surprise alt-radio hit in "$10 Bill." It's definitely Cop Shoot Cop at its most accessible while still being abrasive—the guest horn section continues the jazz-via-Foetus connection, while Puleo's impressive drumming and Tod A's piercing whistle set the initial tone nicely. A pity Tod A's lyric is one of his most pedestrian—unless one really gets off on the idea about how money equals murder—but his delivery is as fierce as always. As for the album as a whole, the foursome sounds resolutely unchanged by becoming part of the major-label machine; having already disposed of that contradiction on *Suck City* ("Nowhere" reappears from that EP), they cranked the amps further and let fly. About the only across-the-board change would be slightly clearer singing from Tod A, but given how the band values getting its message across, this hardly compromises the group's art. Musically, Filer is given even more room to breathe with his array of random, disturbing samples, hot-fusing electronic/industrial keyboards and the continual air of imminent destruction that past albums showed. "Surprise, Surprise" makes for a fantastic, corrosive beginning, trashing American society left, right, and center, while "Furnace," dedicated to a deceased friend, crackles with angst and fire. "Room 429" shows a subtler sense of aggression sneaking in, with an almost elegiac chorus and gripping midsection where the band slowly builds to an explosion behind Tod A's almost whispered singing. Guest appearances throughout lend even more artistic edge to the proceedings—besides the "$10 Bill" appearance, the three-member Motherhead Horns (including David Ouimet, future Tod A collaborator in Firewater) take a bow on "Got No Soul." April Chung's violin on "Cut to the Chase," meanwhile, adds a distinctly Eastern European folk vibe to the fierce clang. *—Ned Raggett*

Release / Sep. 13, 1994 / Interscope ♦♦♦

Julian Cope

b. Oct. 21, 1957, Deri, Mid Glamorgan, Wales
Vocals, Guitar, Organ / Post-Punk, Alternative Pop/Rock
Midway through the recording of the Teardrop Explodes' third album, leader Julian Cope decided to go solo and dissolved the band. Cope's reputation as a rock eccentric was already well established, and following his solo debut, *World Shut Your Mouth,* many believed he was downright deranged. The music strongly echoed the garage rock of Roky Erickson and the psychedelia of Syd Barrett, two of rock's most notorious LSD addicts, while Cope himself intentionally slashed his stomach with a broken microphone and gave interviews advocating the use of hallucinogens during his supporting tour. In 1986, Cope scored a surprise U.K. Top 20 hit with a re-recorded version of "World Shut Your Mouth," and Island attempted to introduce the singer to U.S. audiences with the *Julian Cope* EP. Cope followed his success with *Saint Julian* in 1987, his first album since recovering from his earlier mental difficulties. *Peggy Suicide* set a tone for much of Cope's subsequent work; it was an ambitious concept album addressing political, environmental, and spiritual issues in Cope's own idiosyncratic, sometimes confusing way. *—Steve Huey*

World Shut Your Mouth / 1984 / Mercury ♦♦♦
Retreating from the collapse of the Teardrop Explodes to his hometown of Tamworth, Cope produced his first solo effort with help from producer Steve Lovell on guitar and fellow Teardrop Gary Dwyer on drums. The result is a surprisingly vibrant, rich album that shows Cope easily moving on from his group days while retaining his unique powerful and natural gifts for singing and songwriting. If there's something about the sound of *World* that suggests its early-'80s recording dates—Dwyer's drums sound like Steve Lillywhite's been after them at points!—Cope's own particular, heavily psych-into-pop-inspired goals aren't lost in it. Some of his songs are so inspired that one just has to wonder how in the world they didn't end up as hits somewhere. "An Elegant Chaos" is a great example, an at-once cryptic and fascinating lyric peppered with just enough knowing irony ("Here comes the part where I break down and cry") and a synth-string-touched crunch given a breezy pace. Top it off with Cope's singing and the result is simply genius. Two songs from the final Teardrops sessions, "Metranil Vavin," an homage to a Russian poet, and "Pussyface" get enthusiastic run-throughs here. "Metranil Vavin" in particular is a kick, shifting from garagey crunch and energy to a show tune chorus at the drop of a hat, while sitar from Lovell and concluding oboe from Kate St. John, who plays on many other cuts, add even more pastoral trippiness. Further strong cuts include "Kolly Kibber's Birthday," with a fast rhythm machine and keyboard drones leading the way; the quirky string/brass surge of "Sunshine Playroom"; and the upbeat "Greatness and Perfection." Throughout *World,* Cope demonstrates why he's one of the best, most unaffected singers in rock around, his vocals carrying sweep and passion without sounding like he's trying to impress himself or others. *—Ned Raggett*

Fried / 1984 / Mercury ♦♦♦
In contrast to the crisp, clean sound of *World, Fried* often sounds rougher, a bit more shut in. Combine that with Cope's generally successful attempts to project an image of barely stable sanity, helped in large part by the notorious wearing-nothing-but-a-turtle-shell cover photos, and the idea of *Fried* as his album of crazed musical collapse understandably is a strong one. However, *World* producer Steve Lovell once again handles things here, along with playing guitar, while even more importantly, key Cope collaborator Donald Ross Skinner, a young musician from Cope's hometown, makes his debut. Kate St. John again contributes cor anglais throughout, adding a haunting atmosphere on many cuts. If anything, the album shows that Cope may be completely musical tripping out as he chooses but he knows exactly what he's doing throughout. Certainly the first cut, "Reynard the Fox," shows him balancing inspiration and arrangement perfectly—one of his strongest, catchiest choruses eventually bleeds into a freaked-out spoken word bit followed by a total rave-up. Other songs range from further on-the-edge efforts—the frenetic "O King of Chaos" and more generally weird "Sunspots"—to gentler, wistful numbers like "Laughing Boy" and "Search Party" that effectively capture a rural psych feeling akin to XTC's own work at the same time. In all, *Fried* shows Cope at his dramatic best—he's not disintegrating by inches, but he knows how to project that impression with vigor and skill, all while sounding like himself most of all. He gets in a hilarious slam along the way—"Bill Drummond Said" trashes, by means of an energetic enough folk/rock combination, his former manager from Teardrop Explodes days. Drummond got his revenge years later—while most well-known for his work in the KLF, his solo album *The Man* featured a ditty called "Julian Cope Is Dead." *—Ned Raggett*

Julian Cope / 1986 / Island ♦♦♦

Saint Julian / Mar. 1987 / Island ♦♦♦
A switch to Island Records resulted in the best possible start—not merely a generally fine album but a simply fantastic hit U.K. single, "World Shut Your Mouth." Nothing to do with the record of the same name but definitely possessing much of the same energy, it's a great slice of modern rock, with a crisp arrangement and punchy performance from Cope and his band. Skinner and *Fried* drummer Chris Whitten reappear, while bassist James Eller and keyboardist Double DeHarrison fill out the lineup. Kate St. John once again adds cor anglais here and there, one of her best moments being the bright charge of the title track. Together they tackle a set of songs notably less insular than much of the *Fried* material, with full-on performances to match. One song shows that best of all—"Shot Down," which originally appeared on *Fried* and here becomes a swaggering, pounding rocker with keyboards adding to the impact. More than ever before in his solo career, Cope sounds like he's performing songs meant to be heard live, as the charging "Trampoline" and "Spacehopper" show. There's an almost finger-snapping, swinging vibe to a number of the performances that recall Teardrop Explodes days without trying to simply re-create that sound—he's not trying to revisit the past, there's no need. A few numbers sound a bit too cold and crisp to work entirely—"Planet Ride" is arena soul/rock that sounds like something Robert Palmer would have done around the same time, lyrics aside. A couple of other moments like that crop up, but with the balance skewed more to joys like Cope's in-your-face vocal on "Pulsar" and the lengthy final track "A Crack in the Clouds," *Saint Julian* is another winner. *—Ned Raggett*

My Nation Underground / Oct. 1988 / Island ✦✦✦✦✦
Recruiting another key sideman, percussionist Rooster Cosby, Cope approached an album that, by the end of recording, he was on the verge of disowning. Inspired moments aside, one can understand why: *My Nation Underground* has just about everything going for it (good sound, neat cover, some sharp songs) except for Cope's own vision. That he rebounded from this with three far more individual efforts—the semi-official *Skellington* and *Droolian*, and the masterful *Peggy Suicide*—makes all that much more sense when giving *My Nation Underground* an ear. The high points that are here are actually quite fine—though he professed to hate the results, his rushed run-through of the cheese classic "5 O'Clock World," spliced with a bit from "I Know a Place," is a kicky, fun way to start the album. "Charlotte Anne," meanwhile, manages the odd trick of sounding like a snaky Peter Gabriel track circa his third album plus just enough fillips and touches to make it a Cope song, especially with his mid-song spoken word bit. Most of the time, though, Cope, Skinner, DeHarrison, and company sound like they're fulfilling a record company brief to make a saleable commercial alternative album, late-'80s style. Ron Fair's production touches tended towards the anonymously clichéd, pushing forward *Saint Julian*'s one big problem and making it more consistent throughout. The title track is a good example of something which should be right going terribly wrong—the squelchy synths and arrangement almost drown Cope's idiosyncratic lyric, while the backing chorus sounds unfortunately like the type of pseudo-funky thing to be expected from contemporaneous Steve Winwood or Eric Clapton. Even the cover of the old Shadows of Knight nugget "Someone Like Me" falls a bit victim to this, despite the very Teardrops-like horn arrangement. *—Ned Raggett*

Skellington / 1989 / CopeCo/Zippo ✦✦✦✦
Near the end of the '80s, according to his second autobiography, *Repossessed*, Cope was signed up to produce another band who, due to health reasons, cancelled a pre-booked, three-day studio session. With time and technology available, Cope seized the chance, called in his band (Skinner, DeHarrison, and Cosby), and, on the sly, recorded the half-hour long *Skellington*, which he released via the Zippo label much to Island's consternation. Very much conceived as an initial riposte to what he considered the failure of *My Nation Underground*, *Skellington* lets Cope call the shots on a sometimes fragmentary and goofy but often fascinating example of his quick mind at work. Though he does sound like he's straining for material at points—one number, "Robert Mitchum," is a totally archival piece written with Ian McCulloch before the Teardrop Explodes days—clearly he's not aiming for deathless art, but a good, righteous blast of inspiration. Allegedly recorded and mixed in the order in which the songs appear, *Skellington* shows Cope's voice in much better form than the sometimes indifferent mixing on *My Nation* would indicate. His voice is often lower and richer than on many previous outings, making for a great contrast to the past while foreshadowing much of the approach on *Peggy Suicide*, as does the organic flow of the music. The band keeps up with Cope like a charm, not minding the ragged edges—the sheer vibe alone beats out everything back to *Fried*, if not earlier. Murky horn arrangements and the generally acoustic-led songs drew comparisons to similarly fractured recordings like Syd Barrett's solo work and Skip Spence's *Oar*. Even with a quick, wired song called "Out of My Mind on Dope and Speed" and the concluding high-pitched semi-wail of "Commin' Soon," *Skellington* is less minds losing sanity than Cope and company unwinding to generally fun effect. *—Ned Raggett*

Droolian / 1990 / MoFoCo-Zippo ✦✦✦✦
Even more of an odd one-off than *Skellington*, *Droolian* is another 30-minute collection of random fun from the Cope files, in this case taken from a Skinner-produced session in Liverpool. Like *Skellington*, it was also released via the Zippo label as an end runaround of Island, but under even more curious circumstances. The album was designed to raise funds for psych legend Roky Erickson, then facing jail time in Texas, so it was in fact only released in that state with a bold "FREE ROKY ERICKSON" logo on the back cover. One further similarity with *Skellington* is that *Droolian* clearly foreshadows Cope's imminent masterpiece *Peggy Suicide*—one of that album's best moments, the epic "Safesurfer," appears here in a shorter, murkier edit that still has much of the intensity of the later take. Another song, "Commin' Down," actually reappears from *Skellington* in a rougher take here. Cope's quirky liner notes, mixing the silly and serious as he so often does, talk about most of the contents of *Droolian*. It ranges from the hair gel and Carl Jung letter that inspired the sweet, slightly Suicide/Spacemen 3 sounding keyboard drone and twinkle of "Jellypop Perky Jean" to his intentionally rough semi-country-blues tribute to deceased Echo and the Bunnymen drummer Pete DeFreitas, "Louis 14th." The demo-level sound of much of the album—all percussion comes from drum machines, light keyboards fill out the arrangements—suits the casual, relaxed atmosphere, but Cope himself is again in excelsis, his strong singing and speaking parts exactly what the doctor ordered. There's whispery, low-key moodiness on "Look After Your Leathers," a barbed, hilarious spoken word number with music rip into the myth of the Artiste, there's a recounting of a strange spiritual experience on "... Atonement of Wasp," and much goodness in between. *—Ned Raggett*

Peggy Suicide / Mar. 1991 / Island ✦✦✦✦✦
Casting the ill-advised attempts at too-clean modern rock from his late-'80s days firmly aside and fulfilling the promise of *Skellington* and *Droolian*, Cope on *Peggy Suicide* produced his best album to date, overtopping even his Teardrop Explodes efforts. Showing a greater musical breadth and range than ever before, from funk to noise collage—and more importantly, not sounding like a dilettante at any step of the way—Cope and his now seasoned backing band, with drummer J.D. Hassinger in and De Harrison out, surge from strength to strength. Ostensibly conceived as a concept album regarding potential ecological and social collapse, Cope wisely seeks to set moods rather than create a straitjacketed story line. As a result, *Peggy Suicide* can be enjoyed both as an overall statement and as a collection of individual songs; its sequencing is excellent to boot, moving from song to song as if it was always meant to be that way. Cope's voice is a revelation—for those not having heard the hard-to-find *Skellington* and *Droolian*, his conversational asides, bold but not full-of-itself singing, and equally tender, softer takes when the material demands it must have seemed like a complete turnaround from the restrained *My Nation Underground* cuts. He handles all the guitar as well, with Skinner concentrating on bass and keyboards; guest Michael "Moon-Eye" Watts does some fine fretbending as well, including an amazing performance on the awesome "Safesurfer," a lengthy meditation on AIDS and its consequences. Picking out only some highlights does the album as a whole a disservice, but besides offering up an instant catchy pop single, "Beautiful Love," Cope handles everything from the minimal moods of "Promised Land" and experimentation of "Western Front 1992 CE" to the frenetic "Hanging Out and Hung Up on the Line" and commanding "Drive, She Said." An absolute, stone-cold rock classic, full stop. *—Ned Raggett*

● **Floored Genius: The Best, Vol. 1 (1979-1991)** / Oct. 20, 1992 / Island ✦✦✦✦✦
A convenient enough stopgap release that turned up in between *Peggy Suicide* and *Jehovahkill*, the pun-titled *Floored Genius* provides a fine one-stop spot for those new to Cope's work, starting with Teardrop Explodes hits and going all the way up to *Peggy Suicide*'s "Safesurfer." Total die-hards won't need it, as no unreleased tracks surface, but those unable to find *Skellington* or *Droolian* will appreciate the appearance of, respectively, the nicely crazed "Out of My Mind on Dope & Speed" and the sweetly silly "Jellypop Perky Jean." Otherwise it's key singles and notable album cuts over Cope's higher profile career, showing how the precocious genius who came up with such instantly catchy pop hits like "Reward" and "Passionate Friend" became an even more distinct, individual artist as he went. One of the most striking things about Cope is how he at once incorporates any range of '60s and '70s influences, high profile or obscure, and is able to turn them all into his own sound, high on life (and other things, no doubt) and bursting with creative energy. Even his supposedly lost years documented on *World Shut Your Mouth* and *Fried* find him hitting new heights, as "Reynard the Fox" and "An Elegant Chaos" show. Extensive liner notes from his longtime friend and confidant Mick Houghton give a nicely off-kilter history of the man and his work, while a selection of photos, press clips and other ephemera help trace the path further. Those intrigued by the antiquarian side of Cope's life will appreciate the artistic map of his hometown, Tamworth, with reference to the various album covers and promo shots taken there over time. *Peggy Suicide* remains Cope's best standalone album, but *Floored Genius* is crucial at showing the heights of his work. *—Ned Raggett*

Jehovahkill / Dec. 8, 1992 / Island ✦✦

Head On / 1994 / Ma-Gog ✦✦✦✦

Floored Genius: The Best, Vol. 2 (1983-1991) / Feb. 21, 1994 / Dutch East ✦✦✦✦✦
Released some months after the first *Floored Genius* and sharing its basic artwork and design concept—even though it was released on a completely different label—*Floored Genius 2* is a wonderful collection of recordings Cope did for the BBC in between his earliest solo days in 1983 and *Peggy Suicide*'s release in 1991. Mick Houghton, who did the liner notes for the other *Floored Genius*, does the same job here, detailing the various sessions and songs with an appreciative eye. As he indicates, most of the sessions date from his semi-reclusive years in the early '80s, so the collection skews heavily towards the many gems found on *World Shut Your Mouth* and *Fried*, along with their relevant singles and B-sides. These generally consist solely of Cope, a guitar and a keyboard/rhythm machine, resulting in stripped down renditions that benefit from warm, glowing production and often gentle but understatedly strong singing from the man himself. Opening cuts "The Greatness and Perfection of Love" and "Head Hang Low" are revelations, Cope using what he has to create excellent renditions that sound like they should soundtrack a magical, rural English sunset. A variety of rarities crop up throughout, including "Hey High Class Butcher" and the more than slightly wacky "24A Velocity Crescent," both of which would later become B-sides. Brief but sharp rips through "O King of Chaos" and "Reynard the Fox" show Cope's more demonstrative side is hardly asleep either. Later tracks include longtime collaborators and musical allies helping out, including Skinner, Moon-Eye Watts, Rooster Cosby, and even his brother Joss on keyboards at points. The *Peggy Suicide*-era cuts are as worthy as the album in question, including a massive "soul medley" blending the Funkadelic classic "Free Your Mind and Your Ass Will Follow" and the Mothers of Invention's "Are You Hung Up?" with Cope's own freakout "Hung Up and Hanging Out to Dry." *—Ned Raggett*

Autogeddon / Aug. 9, 1994 / American ✦✦

20 Mothers / Oct. 31, 1995 / Echo ✦✦✦✦✦
Returning to a full CD's worth of material, Cope on *20 Mothers* creates 20 songs, covering a wide variety of topics as opposed to the general concept records from his then-recent past. Everything from reestablishing contact with his estranged brother Joss ("Wheelbarrow Man") to vegetarianism, bandmates, his mother-in-law, and even Kurt Cobain get touched on, as discussed in his entertaining liner notes. It's a bit of a fractured record as a result, but no less interesting for it, containing the range of *Peggy Suicide* without sounding like a revamp of it. Moon-Eye is the main guitarist in place of Skinner, who only contributes a bit of Omnichord here and there, while Thighpaulsandra is a full part of the band, contributing synths, piano, and string arrangements (which crop up throughout the album and are quite exquisite). Cosby provides his excellent drumming as always, while old bassist James Eller and producer Ed Stasium turn up for "Try, Try, Try." This lovely ballad-into-energy number was the lead single, providing Cope with one last U.K. Top 40 hit before fully turning his back on the charts and major labels. Often his singing on *20 Mothers* is a bit strained in comparison to earlier albums, whether it's the production, his throat, or just the way he wants to do things is unclear, but it's a touch

disconcerting on first blush. Musically, the same rough but right feeling on *Autogeddon* prevails, with plenty of detours into tribal psych, feedback madness, even quirky synth-pop; if anything, the overall sound is a bit thicker in points than the at-times hollower recordings on the earlier record. An amusing cover note is that the front picture is, indeed, 20 mothers, with Cope's legendary-in-her-own-right wife Dorian second from the right in the front row, while Cope is pictured with his daughters Albany and Avalon on the back. —*Ned Raggett*

Interpreter / 1996 / Cooking Vinyl ✦✦✦✦
What turned out to be the last Cope solo album (at least under his own name) of the '90s, before he embarked on a series of other musical projects along with continuing his archaeological research, was another wiggy, involved collection of musical highs. If anything can be said about Cope's activity in the mid-'90s, it's that he sounds like a man on a mission, but determined to have fun as he goes. Certainly the opening track is one of his most upbeat and fun ever, "I Come From Another Planet, Baby." His vocal similarity to David Bowie is a bit surprising, but he's obviously having delicious fun singing the lyrics in an exaggeratedly "English" style. Thighpaulsandra once again helps produce, arrange, and perform, creating a string-laden, full-bodied sound for the entire album, while Cosby turns in some of his best drumming ever. About ten other guests pop up throughout, and the result is an adventurous, fun romp, with the atmosphere often recalling such lush and beautiful Cope numbers as "An Elegant Chaos." Sometimes it gets completely nutty: "s.p.a.c.e.r.o.c.k. with me" takes its cue from the likes of Amon Düül II, with guest singer Lynn Davies contributing what Cope himself calls "outrageous Diva vocals." Cope's message is far from lost; two of his sharpest slams turn up next to each other halfway through. The gloriously garage trashy "Cheap New-Age Fix," as one can guess from the title, seems to slyly slam wannabe poseurs taking away from his rather more intense focus on heathen studies and environmentalism in many forms. The glammy epic "The Battle for the Trees," meanwhile, celebrates an organized protest against development near the English town of Newbury that occurred shortly before the album's recording. The elaborate packaging and artwork contain everything from a "mythological mind map" of Cope's surroundings in the Marlborough Downs to any number of righteous political and social quotes. —*Ned Raggett*

The Followers of Saint Julian / 1997 / Island Masters ✦✦✦
The cleverly titled *Followers* is a boon for hardcore Cope fanatics, collecting a wide range of B-sides, rarities, and random tracks from his early Island Records days. Nearly everything has something to do with the *Saint Julian* album and the accompanying tours, thus its title. While more casual Cope followers won't need it, those especially interested in Cope's completely gone side of his music will consider this manna. In contrast to the sometimes too clean parts of *Saint Julian* itself, Cope here goes all out in several different directions at once, foreshadowing the wide range of approaches that would define his work in the '90s. Opening cut "Transporting," a "World Shut Your Mouth" B-side, is as chaotic as one could hope for, with squalling noises, a completely weird mix that keeps changing, and general production goofiness abounding. "Transporting" reappears in another version later, with a variety of interview snippets scattered throughout the mix—there are a couple of wonderfully awkward moments preserved. The calmer demo tracks "Mock Turtle" and the weirdly stentorian "Warwick the Kingmaker" show him in gently ruminative mode, creating winsome music without sounding overly precious. Another demo-level track, or so it sounds—"Almost Beautiful Child (I & II)"—has him flexing instrumental muscles with a piano-led number accompanied by the odd moan or two. A few remixes surface on *Followers*—while some are fairly anonymous, "World Shut Your Mouth" gets a work-over courtesy of D.C. go-go legends Trouble Funk. They leave a fair chunk of the song exactly as is, but have some fun stripping things down to bass and drums here and there. Two covers—solid run-throughs of the 13th Floor Elevators' "Levitation" and Pere Ubu's "Non-Alignment Pact"—and good live versions of *Saint Julian*'s "Pulsar" and "Shot Down" help to fill out the corners. —*Ned Raggett*

Rite² / 1997 / Head Heritage ✦✦✦✦
Available only by mail order, *Rite²* is one of Julian Cope's most consistent works. Instead of leaping to and fro between undeniably catchy synth-pop and fractured end-of-the-century prog, Cope sticks to the prog and comes out better for it. The full-length album contains only four tracks, and each charts the same cosmic blueprint of deep Kraut grooves and half-chanted, half-sung vocals. The third track, "D-c.o.m.p.o.s.e.r.," is 20 minutes of stark sequencer trance in the grand Tangerine Dream manner, and the closing "The Ringed Hills of Ver" restates the theme with help from guitar and organ. —*John Bush*

Cornelius (Keigo Oyamada)

b. Jan. 27, 1969, Setagaya-ku, Tokyo, Japan
Producer / Shibuya-Kei, Indie Rock, Alternative Pop/Rock
Japanese pop-noise savant Cornelius was born Keigo Oyamada in 1971; a self-taught guitarist inspired early on by Kiss and Black Sabbath, his musical alias was later chosen as an homage to the film series *Planet of the Apes*. A product of the same Shibuya-kei bubblegum scene that also gave rise to Pizzicato Five, Cornelius debuted in 1993 with the EP *Holydays in the Sun*, the first release from his own Trattoria label. He became a national teen idol in the wake of the release of 1994's full-length *The First Question Award* and a year later he issued the album *69/96*, followed in 1996 by the remix LP *96/69*. 1997's *Fantasma* was his creative and commercial breakthrough, a kaleidoscopic, genre-hopping joyride through contemporary musical history which became Cornelius' first American release when it was reissued by Matador a year later. Another pair of remix collections, *CM* and *FM*, followed in 1999. —*Jason Ankeny*

69/96 / Jun. 9, 1995 / Trattoria ✦✦✦✦
Western critics often compare Cornelius (Keigo Oyamada) to Beck. If so, *69/96* is his *Ode-*

lay, a gigantic leap from his debut only a year or two before—and this was a year before Beck even released "Where It's At." Using a drum kit seemingly stolen from "When the Levee Breaks," but re-skinned with sandpaper, and vocals that come at the listener as if from some distant planet, Oyamada drops the earnest rock of his earlier work and seriously bugs out, delivering a varied plate of rock, breakbeats, and pop that samples unashamedly from the '80s, ditching the cultural context, and cleaning out your prejudiced ears in the process. Strong tracks are "Heavy Metal Thunder," a library of AC/DC and Queen riffs learned by a Martian, "How Do You Feel?"—penned by Yasuharu Konishi of Pizzicato Five—a psychedelic disco where sitar meets turntable, and "Moon Walk," where the drums come out in full force. And "Brand New Season" is as sweet a hula lullaby as they get. Western fans who know the follow-up, *Fantasma*, will find much to appreciate here. A centerpiece of Shibuya-kei that no comprehensive survey of that movement should be without. —*Ted Mills*

96/69 / Sep. 6, 1995 / Trattoria ✦✦

● **Fantasma** / 1997 / Matador ✦✦✦✦✦
Cornelius fits right in with the Beastie Boys' Grand Royal aesthetic. He sees no difference between pop and avant-garde, high culture and lowbrow trash—he throws it all together, coming up with completely unexpected combinations. The thrill of hearing hip-hop loops morph into sheets of My Bloody Valentine guitar noise, then into sweet Beach Boys harmonies, is what makes his American debut *Fantasma* such a wonder. It's easy to write Cornelius off as a Japanese Beck, particularly since his pop songcraft is as impressive as the busy, multi-layered production, but it's a little patronizing. Cornelius is operating on his own terms, equally influenced by sunny pop ("Chapter 8—Seashore and Horizon," boasting harmonies by Apples in Stereo), garagey hard rock, and kitsch (the cartoonish "Magoo Opening"). He assembles the parts in unpredictable ways—the hard beats of "Mic Check" suddenly give way to floating acoustics; "Chapter 8" literally has a tape recorder stopping and starting the different parts—which is why *Fantasma* is so intoxicating. It is one of those rare records where you can't tell what's going to happen next, and it leaves you hungry for more. —*Stephen Thomas Erlewine*

Cornershop

f. 1992, London, England
Alternative Dance, Indie Rock, Alternative Pop/Rock
Cornershop is a London-based quintet who mixes noisy alternative rock sounds with musical influences drawn from lead vocalist/songwriter Tjinder Singh's Punjabi culture. The rest of the band consists of guitarists Ben Ayres and Avtar Singh, sitarist/keyboardist Anthony Saffery, drummer Nick Simms, and percussionist Pete Hall. The group became known in England for its anti-racist politics, an issue at the forefront of Singh's consciousness owing to British maltreatment of Indians in their society. In response to singer Morrissey's experimentation with skinhead imagery, Cornershop burned pictures of him at gigs and at a press conference. Most of the British media dismissed it as a publicity stunt, since the group's musical skills at the time were amateurish at best, if excitingly ragged. A bit more technical polish eventually helped attract the attention of ex-Talking Heads singer David Byrne, who signed the group to his Luaka Bop label in 1995, set up a recording session with poet Allen Ginsberg, and released their acclaimed second album, *Woman's Gotta Have It*. The excellent *When I Was Born for the 7th Time*, highlighted by the hit single "Brimful of Asha" (a tribute to Indian singer Asha Bhosle) followed in 1997. —*Steve Huey*

Hold on It Hurts / Jan. 23, 1995 / Merge ✦✦✦
Although Cornershop's first album rings with some of the fevered scrappiness prominent in U.S. indie bands of the early '90s (like Unrest), it's also a throwback to leftist post-punk groups of the late '70s (Gang of Four, Au Pairs). Spiking their songs with social commentary and balancing it out with an infectious sense of playfulness, the spirit and passion overrides the obvious amateurism that the band makes no attempt to hide. They're having fun, they have something to say, they love disco beats just as much as they love atonal shards of guitar and traditional Indian instrumentation. It all makes for a bold, exciting mix, even if it's sloppy and lacking direction every now and then. It also sounded little like anything else released at the time. The American version of the album, released in 1995 on Merge, adds the band's *Lock, Stock and Double Barrel* EP from 1993. "England's Dreaming," taking its name from Jon Savage's book on punk rock, is one of their strongest songs overall. —*Andy Kellman*

Woman's Gotta Have It / 1995 / Luaka Bop/Warner Bros. ✦✦✦✦
Tjinder Singh's Cornershop has created the perfect hybrid of Western indie rock and swirling Eastern traditional music: Hindi-pop. It's not like what the Beatles did with sitars nor is it classifiable as worldbeat: Cornershop is unique. "Jullandar Shere" opens and closes the album on an Eastern note but with a hip-hop twist. It's an adventure in lo-fi noise pop with the drone of tamboura, native percussion, and processed vocal sung in Punjabi providing the rhythm. "Hong Kong Book of Kung Fu" conveys indignation through its angry guitar and spit-sung lyrics. "Call All Destroyer" has Singh leading on funky bass like old-school political rockers Gang of Four. The anti-melodies are similar to stock indie rock, but the sonic dissonance created on dholki, harmonium, and flute separates Cornershop from the pack as they reclaim a racial stereotype (that every Asian in Great Britain tends a corner shop) while creating their very own roots music with a message. —*Denise Sullivan*

● **When I Was Born for the 7th Time** / Sep. 8, 1997 / Luaka Bop/Warner Bros. ✦✦✦✦✦
When I Was Born for the 7th Time is a remarkable leap forward for Cornershop, the place where the group blends all of their diverse influences into a seamless whole. Cornershop uses Indian music as a foundation, finding its droning repetition similar to the trancier elements of electronica, the cut-and-paste collages of hip-hop, and the skeletal melodi-

cism of indie pop. Tying all of these strands together, the band creates a multicultural music that is utterly modern; it is conscious of its heritage, but instead of being enslaved to tradition, it pushes into the future and finds a common ground between different cultures and musics. Like *Woman's Gotta Have It*, large portions of *When I Was Born for the 7th Time* are devoted to hypnotic instrumentals, but the music here is funkier and fully realized. Cornershop hits an appealing compromise between detailed arrangements and lo-fi technology. There may be cheap keyboards and drum machines scattered throughout the album, but they are used as sonic texturing, similar to the turntables, synthesizers, samplers, sitars, and guitars that drive the instrumentals punctuating the full-fledged songs. When it chooses, Cornershop can write hooky, immediate pop songs—"Sleep on the Left Side" and "Brimful of Asha" are wonderful pop singles, and "Good to Be on the Road Back Home" is an impressive, country-tinged tale—but what makes *When I Was Born for the 7th Time* such a rich, intoxicating listen is that it balances these melodic tendencies with deceptively complex arrangements, chants, drones, electronic instrumentals, and funky rhythms, resulting in an album that becomes better with each listen. *—Stephen Thomas Erlewine*

The Corrs

f. 1991

Celtic Fusion, Adult Alternative Pop/Rock, Celtic Pop

Comprising three sisters and one brother of the Corr family—vocalist Andrea, drummer Caroline, violinist Sharon and guitarist/keyboard player Jim—the Corrs blend the music of their Irish background with contemporary pop/rock and occasional use of synthesizers. The quartet formed in 1991, and was confined to regional popularity in Ireland until 1994, when the American ambassador to the country invited the Corrs to perform at the 1994 World Cup in Boston. The attraction led to a support slot on Celine Dion's 1996 tour, which the group joined just after an appearance at that year's Olympic Games in Atlanta. The Corrs' debut album *Forgiven, Not Forgotten* (released on Lava/Atlantic in America) became internationally popular, but nowhere more so than their homeland, where the LP's four-times-platinum status made it one of the most popular debuts by an Irish group. *Talk on Corners* followed in 1998, and was reissued in expanded form early the following year. Andrea Corr, who had made a small appearance in the 1991 film *The Commitments*, returned to acting five years later with a role in *Evita*. The group returned to the studio and produced a fourth album in 2000, *In Blue*. *—John Bush*

• **Forgiven, Not Forgotten** / 1996 / East West ♦♦♦♦

The appropriately named Corrs are an Irish pop group consisting of Andrea Corr on lead vocals and tin whistle; Caroline Corr on drums, bodhran, and vocals; Jim Corr on keyboards, guitar, and vocals; and Sharon Corr on violin and vocals. The traditional Irish instruments like the bodhran and tin whistle add a twist to the pop melodies of tracks like the title track and "The Right Time," where they are allowed some solo time. The Irish musical background of the band members is most obviously heard in Sharon Corr's violin work, used here more like a traditional Irish fiddle than a true classical violin. There are glimpses of the Corrs' skill as instrumentalists on tracks like "Erin Shore," the introduction on the album. There are a few of these instrumentals placed throughout the album, but unfortunately, none are much longer than two minutes. The focus is on the adult contemporary mid-tempo songs. The Corrs are more reminiscent of vocal pop group Wilson Phillips than traditional Irish bands like the Chieftains. *—Susan Cruickshank*

Talk on Corners / 1998 / East West ♦♦♦♦

Songs on the Corrs' *Talk on Corners* fly inoffensively past the window like scenery on a drive through the countryside, with two pretty singers at the wheel. This essentially Irish sister act (with Corr group Andrea, Caroline and Sharon on vocals, drums and violin, respectively, and brother Jim on guitar and keyboards) legitimately bring to mind comparisons with another family-based girl group, Wilson Phillips, particularly since the impulses and instincts are truly pop and not so much alt-traditional Celtic (as they are often cited to be). This timely record documents a high-riding point for the Corrs by re-releasing newly mixed versions of "What Can I Do?" and "So Young," both highly compressed digital productions featuring their trademark glass voices and barely discernible acoustic musical instruments. Also on the record: "Queen of Hollywood," "Runaway," "No Good for Me" and their huge international hit ballad "I Never Loved You Anyway." The best and most spirited Celtic cut is "Little Wing," deliciously resting on the contributions of the dropping-by Chieftains. Each and every cut sounds wired for radio play; unlike the less Americanized, riskier Cranberries, the Corrs should enjoy a career as nicely sustained as some of the girls' best musical notes. *—Becky Byrkit*

In Blue / Sep. 12, 2000 / Atlantic ♦♦♦

A very straightforward release from the Corrs, who spend the majority of this outing in full-blown pop mode, with the Celtic elements mostly being relegated to the backgrounds of several songs. The one exception is the closing instrumental, "Rebel Heart," which stirs itself up full-bloodily to provide the album with an anthem. *In Blue* is a bright, peppy set that bears more than a few comparisons to the work of bands such as the Bangles and Fanny, though the Corrs have an additional advantage in that Caroline Corr is an impressively muscular drummer. The CD includes a HyperCD section with a video for "Breathless" and various web links. *—Steven McDonald*

Dave "Baby" Cortez (David Cortez Clowney)

b. Aug. 13, 1938, Detroit, MI

Piano, Organ / Instrumental Rock, Soul

Though hardly a soulful, bluesy master like Jimmy Smith or dashing experimentalist like Larry Young, organist Dave "Baby" Cortez made his mark in the '50s,'60s, and '70s as a capable, often clever soloist and pop instrumentalist. His flair for catchy melodies, riffs, and hooks resulted in a number one pop and number five R&B hit with "The Happy Organ" in 1959. Cortez had another double winner in 1962 with "Rinky Dink," this one peaking at number nine R&B and number ten pop. Before his instrumental success, Cortez recorded for Ember as David Clowney in 1956, and was in The Pearls from 1955 to 1957. He landed one other song on the R&B Top 50, "Someone Has Taken Your Place," in 1973 for All Platinum. His other songs were recorded for Clock and Chess. There has been no domestic reissue of Cortez's songs, but there are import anthologies available. *—Ron Wynn*

• **Golden Hits** / 1964 / London ♦♦♦♦♦

Happy Organs Wild Guitars & Piano Shuffles / Mar. 1, 1994 / Ace ♦♦♦

Presented here are 25 songs recorded by Cortez, mostly or entirely, for Clock between 1958 and 1961—mostly or entirely, because although each track is grouped into a "New York 1958-1961" discography, a couple of them are given the dates 1965 on the CD track listing; the three dated 1993 are presumably unreleased outtakes from the era (although they are not precisely identified as such). The real question is: do you need to hear anything else besides his number one hit (and this album's opener) "The Happy Organ"? For almost everyone, the answer is no. The other songs are average R&B-based rockers, sometimes given a lift above similar generic instrumental fare from the era by Cortez's zippy organ and some sharp guitar (much or all of which was probably played by Jimmy Spruill, who did the guitar solo on "The Happy Organ"). The majority is instrumental, with Cortez occasionally adding vocals that are either perfunctory, or that fall within the ordinary, early Black vocal group style (as on "Love Me as I Love You"). Otherwise, this is for instrumental rock fans only, although Cortez deserves credit for popularizing the organ as a rock instrument. The moody reading of "Summertime" isn't bad, and when he and the band get a little less restrained on "Tootsie," it seems possible that he could have influenced the sound of 1960s soul-rockers who used the organ, like Booker T. & the MG's. Cortez's low-charting, soundalike follow-up to "The Happy Organ," "The Whistling Organ," is included, but his only other big hit, "Rinky Dink" (1962), is not, as it was done for Chess. *—Richie Unterberger*

3 on 1: Organ Shindig/Tweetie Pie/In Orbit / Nov. 1995 / Sequel ♦♦

Cosmic Rough Riders

f. 1998, Glasgow, Scotland

Folk-Rock, Soft Rock, Country-Rock

Singer/songwriters Daniel Wylie and Stephen Fleming met while volunteering in the community recording studio of Castlemilk, Glasgow. In time, Fleming became the studio's manager and chief engineer. Each time Wylie recorded there, Fleming would end up playing with him during the sessions, so in 1998 the duo finally forged a partnership by forming Cosmic Rough Riders, with Wylie on lead vocals and Fleming on electric guitar. Gradually the lineup was filled out by Gary Cuthbert (acoustic guitar), Mark Brown (drums), and James Clifford (bass), and the band developed a sound unabashedly influenced by the California rock sound of the 1970s. They released their first album, *Deliverance*, in 1999 on their own Raft Records to widespread critical acclaim, quickly selling out an initial pressing of 2,000 and developing a small cult following in the process. They followed that debut with the self-produced *Panorama* (also released on Raft) in March 2000. The album earned raves from established British publications such as Q, NME, and Mojo, and mimicked the debut by selling out its first pressing of 3,000. Both albums were distributed by Shell Shock Distribution, and both also earned a place in Virgin's *Encyclopaedia of the Greatest Albums of All Time*. In May 2000, Cosmic Rough Riders began playing live and touring for the first time in their career and simultaneously began discussions about future plans with several interested record and publishing companies. *—Stanton Swihart*

• **Deliverance** / Jun. 1999 / Raft ♦♦♦♦♦

Daniel Wylie and Stephen Fleming certainly wear their collective influences on their sleeves, but that doesn't have to be a criticism, and in the case of their striking, out-of-nowhere debut album, it is an entirely captivating trait. As curious as it is to imagine a couple Glaswegian fellows calling on the same musical gods as California bands such as the Byrds, CSNY, and the Eagles did 30 years before them, Cosmic Rough Riders accomplished just that on *Deliverance*, a recording so engrossing that any criticisms or charges of imitation that could be leveled at it are immediately rendered irrelevant. Full of glassily plucked acoustic guitars crisp with rural, sun-baked charm and angelic chorale harmonies that Crosby, Stills, and Nash themselves would be hard-pressed to match, it is as much Hollywood Hills as it is Scotland Highlands, but that does nothing to obscure the brilliant luster the album exudes. Wylie and Fleming spin a love of the drowsy late-'60s and early-'70s Laurel Canyon vibe into pure country-pop gold. "Emily Darling" would have been one of the best songs of 1971, the country melody morphing midway through into a long, jazzy coda complete with the same gorgeous wordless vocals that David Crosby once used to achieve mystical perfection. What makes the song such a phenomenal accomplishment—and it is a sentiment that holds for the album as a whole—is that it also happens to be one of the best songs of 1999. Wylie and Fleming reinvent Golden State riffs with ease, a modern extension of both the sound and the spirit of their influences rather than a direct throwback. *—Stanton Swihart*

Panorama / Mar. 2000 / Raft ♦♦♦♦♦

Deliverance was content to find a groove and ride it for all it was worth, but Daniel Wylie and Stephen Fleming just happened to find a fabulous groove, steeped in the laid-back ease of '70s California folk and country-rock. *Panorama*, however, shows considerably more variation—both in influences and in sound—and the result is an impossibly dynamic masterpiece, irresistible and breathtaking in its accomplishment. As striking as the debut was, *Panorama* is a far more stunning achievement. Some of the same sonic touches remain. Light-as-air vintage Byrds harmonies bloom throughout, as do chiming guitars straight out of *Mr. Tambourine Man*, while Jayhawks harmonies buoy the wonderful country ballad "Afterglow." But gone for the most part are the overt country-rock inflections and in their place are even more resonant touches of rural psychedelia and a sound dense with strummed acoustic guitars and tangibly cosmic undertones. California is still an unseen Mecca for the duo, but even when they do reference familiar elements from its rock and pop past—the surf-insistent Beach Boys harmonizing that opens "Value of Life," for instance, or the expansive hungover quality of the opening "Revolution (In the Summertime)"—they place them in contexts so far removed from the original intent that it creates an entirely new dynamic. As on their previous album, though, it is too easy to simply use allusions to get at the essence of what makes Cosmic Rough Riders such a phenomenal band. *Panorama* on its own terms is an album of sweeping scope and poignancy, mindful of the heritage that it continues, but so brilliantly executed that it feels like a quantum leap into uncharted waters, full of genuinely glorious moments of epiphany. *—Stanton Swihart*

Enjoy the Melodic Sunshine / Nov. 6, 2000 / Poptones ♦♦♦♦
The third album from the Cosmic Rough Riders in just over a year is the band's first album not released independently and its first to get the royal treatment courtesy of outstanding neophyte British label Poptones. So it is understandable that *Enjoy the Melodic Sunshine* includes a healthy portion of songs from the Rough Riders' first two musical forays, especially the previous album *Panorama*. In fact, with no less than nine of *Panorama*'s 14 songs present, *Enjoy the Melodic Sunshine* could almost be seen as a repackaged version of that album. Three tracks from the band's debut, *Deliverance*, are also revisited, two of which are vastly improved upon (although they were pretty sensational in their original incarnations as well). A few more songs from that first album could easily have been included, but then this really isn't meant to be a compilation, although it functions as such to a certain degree. Rather, *Enjoy the Melodic Sunshine* can be considered as an EP of new recordings extended to full-length by the addition of some (but certainly not all) of the better songs from *Panorama*. The result is a record that displays, perhaps better than either of the Cosmic Rough Riders' first two albums, the immense talents of the duo at the core of the band. For those listeners who know and love the previous albums, *Enjoy the Melodic Sunshine* might seem slightly less cohesive; the different song sequence, particularly where songs from the flawless *Panorama* are concerned, can be a bit jarring to hear at first. But before long, the logic and bolstered strength of the new sequence take hold. Regardless, every song—old, new, and re-recorded alike—is an unequivocally brilliant example of folk-rock songwriting at its peak, as good as anything by the Byrds. *—Stanton Swihart*

Elvis Costello (Declan Patrick McManus)

b. Aug. 25, 1955, Liverpool, England
Vocals, Keyboards, Guitar / College Rock, British Punk, Adult Alternative Pop/Rock, Pub Rock, New Wave, Singer/Songwriter
Elvis Costello emerged from the punk explosion of 1977, soon proving that he was a singer/songwriter and musician of extraordinary talent. Throughout his career, musical eclecticism has distinguished Costello's records as much as his fiercely literate lyrics, confirming his place as one of the best singer-songwriters to emerge since Bob Dylan.

Costello began his career toiling away in folk clubs and leading a pub-rock group called Flip City. Still performing under his given name Declan McManus, he took his demo tapes to the fledgling British independent Stiff Records. Impressed with what they heard, they signed him, encouraging him to change his name to Elvis Costello. His Nick Lowe-produced debut *My Aim is True* appeared in 1977 to great critical acclaim. That year, he assembled the Attractions, who were showcased to great effect on the scathing *This Year's Model*, which became a British Top 10 hit. Costello began to diversify on 1979's *Armed Forces*, a glimmering pop record that gave him his American breakthrough. Despite some press controversies, he continued his momentum with the soul-influenced sound of 1980's *Get Happy* and 1981's *Trust*. Costello stretched with 1981's *Almost Blue*, a country album produced by Nashville legend Billy Sherrill. He followed in 1982 with the lush, ambitious *Imperial Bedroom;* although it was highly acclaimed, it stalled on the charts. Costello then tried for a hit with the streamlined *Punch the Clock*, a moderate success followed by the tired *Goodbye Cruel World*. He bounced back with a pair of masterpieces in 1986, the Americana album *King of America* and the tough *Blood and Chocolate*. He then signed with Warner, put the Attractions on hiatus and took three years off. He returned in 1989 with *Spike*, a wildly eclectic affair that gave him a hit with "Veronica," yet signaled how erratic his Warner years would be. Throughout the '90s, Costello worked consistently, trying something new each time out, whether it was avant-pop, classical chamber pop or a reunion with the Attractions, appealing only to his cult. In 1998, he began his time at Mercury with *Painted from Memory*, a collaboration with Burt Bacharach that earned his strongest reviews and sales in years, even if it failed to turn into a genuine hit. *—Stephen Thomas Erlewine*

★ **My Aim Is True** / Aug. 1977 / Rykodisc ♦♦♦♦♦
Elvis Costello was as much a pub-rocker as he was a punk-rocker and nowhere is that more evident than on his debut, *My Aim Is True*. It's not just that Clover, a San Franciscan rock outfit led by Huey Lewis (absent here), back him here, not the Attractions, it's that his sensibility is borrowed from the pile-driving rock & roll and folksy introspection of pub-rockers like Brinsley Schwarz, adding touches of cult singer/songwriters like Randy Newman and David Ackles. Then, there's the infusion of pure nastiness and cynical humor, which is pure Costello. That blend of classicist sensibilities and cleverness make this collection of shiny roots rock a punk record—it informs his nervy performances and his prickly songs. Of all classic punk debuts, this remains perhaps the most idiosyncratic because it's not cathartic in sound, only in spirit. Which, of course, meant that it could play to a broader audience, and Linda Ronstadt did indeed cover the standout ballad "Alison." Still, there's no mistaking this for anything other than a punk record, and it's a terrific one at that, since even if he buries his singer/songwriter inclinations, they shine through as brightly as his cheerfully mean humor and immense musical skill; he sounds as comfortable with a '50s knockoff like "No Dancing" as he does on the reggae-inflected "Less Than Zero." Costello went on to more ambitious territory fairly quickly, but *My Aim Is True* is a phenomenal debut, capturing a songwriter and musician whose words were as rich and clever as his music. [Ryko/Demon's 1993 reissue contained several bonus tracks, including the country B-sides "Radio Sweetheart" and "Stranger in the House," plus demos of his first group, Flip City.] *—Stephen Thomas Erlewine*

☆ **This Year's Model** / Jul. 1978 / Rykodisc ♦♦♦♦♦
Where *My Aim Is True* implied punk rock with its lyrics and stripped-down production, *This Year's Model* sounds like punk. Not that Costello's songwriting has changed—*This Year's Model* is comprised largely of leftovers from *My Aim Is True* and songs written on the road. It's the music that changed. After releasing *My Aim Is True*, Costello assembled a backing band called the Attractions, which were considerably tougher and wilder than Clover, who played on his debut. The Attractions were a rock & roll band, which gives *This Year's Model* a reckless, careening feel. It's nervous, amphetamine-fueled, nearly paranoid music—the group sounds like they're spinning out of control as soon as they crash in on the brief opener, "No Action," and they never get completely back on track, even on the slower numbers. Costello and the Attractions speed through *This Year's Model* at a blinding pace, which gives his songs—which were already meaner than the set on *My Aim Is True*—a nastier edge. "Lipstick Vogue," "Pump It Up," and "(I Don't Want to Go To) Chelsea" are all underscored with sexual menace, while "Night Rally" touches on a bizarre fascination with fascism that would blossom on his next album, *Armed Forces*. Even the songs that sound relatively lighthearted—"Hand in Hand," "Little Triggers," "Lip Service," "Living in Paradise"—are all edgy, thanks to Costello's breathless vocals, Steve Nieve's carnival-esque organ riffs, and Nick Lowe's bare-bones production. Of course, the songs on *This Year's Model* are typically catchy and help the vicious sentiments sink into your skin, but the most remarkable thing about the album is the sound—Costello and the Attractions never rocked this hard, or this vengefully, ever again. *—Stephen Thomas Erlewine*

☆ **Armed Forces** / 1979 / Rykodisc ♦♦♦♦♦
After releasing and touring the intense *This Year's Model*, Elvis Costello quickly returned to the studio with the Attractions to record his third album, *Armed Forces*. In contrast to the stripped-down pop and rock of his first two albums, *Armed Forces* boasted a detailed and textured pop production, but it was hardly lavish. However, the more spacious arrangements—complete with ringing pianos, echoing reverb, layered guitars, and harmonies—accent Costello's melodies, making the record more accessible than his first two albums. Perversely, while the sound of Costello's music was becoming more open and welcoming, his songs became more insular and paranoid, even though he cloaked his emotions well. Many of the songs on *Armed Forces* use politics as a metaphor for personal relationships, particularly fascism, which explains its working title, *Emotional Fascism*. Occasionally, the lyrics are forced, but the music never is—the album demonstrates the depth of Costello's compositional talents and how he can move from the hook-laden pop of "Accidents Will Happen" to the paranoid "Goon Squad" with ease. Some of the songs, like the light reggae of "Two Little Hitlers" and the impassioned "Party Girl," build on his strengths, while others like the layered "Oliver's Army" take Costello into new territories. It's a dense but accessible pop record and ranks as his third masterpiece in a row. *—Stephen Thomas Erlewine*

☆ **Get Happy!!** / 1980 / Rykodisc ♦♦♦♦♦
Get Happy was born as much from sincere love for soul as it was for Costello's desire to distance himself from an unfortunate verbal faux-pas where he insulted Ray Charles in an attempt to get Stephen Stills' goat. Either way, it resulted in a 20-song blue-eyed soul tour-de-force, where Elvis doesn't just want to prove his love, he wants to prove his knowledge. So, he tries everything, starting with Motown and Northern Soul, then touching on smooth uptown ballads and gritty southern soul, even finding common ground between the two by recasting Sam & Dave's "I Can't Stand Up (For Falling Down)" as a careening stomper. What's remarkable is that this approach dovetails with the pop carnival essayed by *Armed Forces*, standing as a full-fledged Costello record instead of a genre exercise. As it furiously flits through 20 songs, Costello's cynicisms, rage, humor and misanthropic sensibility gel remarkably well. Some songs may not quite hit their target, but that's part of the album's charm—it moves so fast, its lesser songs rush by on the way to such full-fledged masterpieces as "New Amsterdam," "High Fidelity" and "Riot Act." *Get Happy* bursts with energy and invention, standing as a testament to how Costello, the pop encyclopedia, can reinvent the past in his own image. [The Ryko/Demon reissue contains no less than 10 bonus tracks, including such Costello essentials as "Girls Talk," "So Young," "Getting Mighty Crowded," "Hoover Factory," "Dr. Luther's Assistant" and "Just a Memory," written for Dusty Springfield.] *—Stephen Thomas Erlewine*

☆ **Trust** / Feb. 1981 / Rykodisc ♦♦♦♦♦
Following the frenzied pop-soul of *Get Happy*, Elvis Costello & the Attractions quickly returned to the studio and recorded *Trust*, their most ambitious and eclectic album to date. As if he was proving his stylistic diversity and his sophistication after the concentrated genre experiment of *Get Happy*, Costello assembled *Trust* as a stylistic tour-de-force, packing the record with a wild array of material. "Clubland" has jazzy flourishes, "Lovers' Walk" rolls to a Bo Diddley beat, "Luxembourg" is rockabilly-redux, "Watch Your Step" is soul-pop, "From a Whisper to a Scream" rocks as hard as anything since *This Year's Model*, "Shot With His Own Gun" is Tin Pan Alley pop, "Different Finger" is the first country song he put on an official album. And that's not even counting highlights like "New

Lace Sleeves" and "White Knuckles," which essentially stick to Costello's signature pop but offer more complex arrangements and musicianship than before. In fact, both "complexity" and "sophistication" are keywords to the success of *Trust*—without delving into the minutely textured arrangements that would dominate his next pop album, *Imperial Bedroom*—Costello & the Attractions demonstrate their musical skill and savvy by essentially sticking to the direct sound of their four-piece band. In the process, they recorded arguably their most impressive album, one that demonstrates all sides of Costello's songwriting and performing personality without succumbing to pretentiousness. —*Stephen Thomas Erlewine*

Almost Blue / Nov. 1981 / Rykodisc ✦✦✦

Costello's "country record" is usually written off as a vanity project, but *Almost Blue* is quite a bit more than that. It's one of the most entertaining cover records in rock & roll, simply because of its enthusiasm. The album begins with a roaring version of Hank Williams' "Why Don't You Love Me" and doesn't stop. Costello sings with conviction on the tear-jerking ballads, as well as barn burners like "Tonight the Bottle Let Me Down." It's clear that Costello knows this music, and it's also clear who he learned it from—Gram Parsons. Costello covers Parsons' "Hot Burrito No. 1" and "How Much I Lied," and all of the music on *Almost Blue* recalls Parsons' taste for hardcore honky-tonk and weepy ballads. It's to Costello's credit that he made a record relying on emotion to pay tribute. —*Stephen Thomas Erlewine*

☆ **Imperial Bedroom** / Jul. 1982 / Rykodisc ✦✦✦✦✦

Having gotten country out of his system with *Almost Blue*, Elvis Costello returned to pop music with *Imperial Bedroom*—and it was *pop* in the classic, Tin Pan Alley sense. Costello chose to hire Geoff Emerick, who engineered all of the Beatles' most ambitious records, to produce *Imperial Bedroom*, which indicates what it sounds like—it's traditional pop with a post-*Sgt. Pepper* production. Essentially, the songs on *Imperial Bedroom* are an extension of Costello's jazz and pop infatuations on *Trust*. Costello's music is complex and intricate, yet it flows so smoothly, it's easy to miss the bitter, brutal lyrics. The interweaving layers of "Beyond Belief" and the whirlwind intro are the most overtly dark sounds on the record, with most of the album given over to the orchestrated, melancholy torch songs and pop singles. Never once do Costello and the Attractions deliver a rock & roll song—the album is all about sonic detail, from the accordion on "The Long Honeymoon" to the lilting strings on "Town Cryer." Of course, the detail and the ornate arrangements immediately peg *Imperial Bedroom* as Costello's most ambitious album, but that doesn't mean it's his absolute masterpiece. *Imperial Bedroom* remains one of Costello's essential records because it is the culmination of his ambitions and desires—it's where he proves that he can play with the big boys, both as a songwriter and a record-maker. It may not have been a commercial blockbuster, but it certainly earned the respect of legions of musicians and critics who would have previously disdained such a punk rocker. And, perhaps, that's also the reason that he abandoned this immaculately crafted style of work on his next album, *Punch the Clock*. —*Stephen Thomas Erlewine*

Punch the Clock / 1983 / Rykodisc ✦✦✦

Perhaps frustrated by the lack of commercial success *Imperial Bedroom* encountered, Elvis Costello enlisted British hitmakers Clive Langer and Alan Winstanley to produce its followup, *Punch the Clock*. The difference between the two records is immediately noticeable. *Punch the Clock* has a slick, glossy surface, complete with layered synthesizers, horns, studio effects and the backup vocals of Afrodiziak. The approach isn't necessarily a misguided one, since Costello is as much a pop musician as he is a singer/songwriter and many of the best moments on the record—"Everyday I Write the Book," "Let Them All Talk"—work well as shiny pop singles. However, the problem with *Punch the Clock* is that Costello is entering a fallow songwriting period; it is his least consistent of original songs to date. The best moments, the anti-war ballad "Shipbuilding" and the eerie pseudo-rap "Pills and Soap," are as articulate and effective as any of his past work, but frequently Costello falls short of meeting his standards, particularly when he's trying to write a song in the style of his older songs. Nevertheless, the sheen of the Langer & Winstanley production makes *Punch the Clock* a pleasurable listen. Costello's uneven writing means that only portions of the album are memorable. —*Stephen Thomas Erlewine*

Goodbye Cruel World / 1984 / Rykodisc ✦✦

During the making of *Goodbye Cruel World*, Costello was undergoing a multitude of personal problems, including a divorce, that resulted in a number of poor production decisions and ill-conceived, unformed songs. Like *Punch the Clock*, *Goodbye Cruel World* was produced by Clive Langer and Alan Winstanley, the top British hit makers of the '80s. Consequently, most of the record suffers from a stiff, synthesized production that instantly dates the record. In some cases—like the duet with Daryl Hall, "The Only Flame in Town," and the cover of the lost Hi R&B gem "I Wanna Be Loved"—the songs benefit from the shiny, streamlined production but it obscures the merits of the finest songs on the album. "Room with No Number," "The Comedians," "Sour Milk-Cow Blues," and "Peace in Our Time" all cry out for a simple, stripped-down presentation, but they're weighted down with stylized sounds and trendy synthesizers; however, once the sound of the album settles in, the strength of these songs is apparent. The remainder of *Goodbye Cruel World* isn't as memorable, primarily because Costello's uninspired vocals and the Attractions' muted performances fail to make the weaker songs musically compelling. —*Stephen Thomas Erlewine*

King of America / Jan. 1986 / Rykodisc ✦✦✦✦✦

Stripping away much of the excess that cluttered *Punch the Clock* and *Goodbye Cruel World*, Elvis Costello returned to his folk-rock and pub-rock roots with *King of America*, creating one of his most affecting and personal records. Costello literally took the album as a return to roots, billing himself by his given name Declan MacManus and replacing

the Attractions with a bunch of L.A. session men (although his old band appears on one cut), who give the album a rootsy but sleek veneer which sounds remarkably charged after the polished affectations of his Langer/Winstanley productions. And not only does the music sound alive, but so do his songs, arguably his best overall set since *Trust*. Working inside the limits of country, folk and blues, Costello writes literate, introspective tales of loss, heartbreak and America that are surprisingly moving—he rarely got better than "Brilliant Mistake," "Glitter Gulch," "American Without Tears," "Big Light" and "Indoor Fireworks." What separates *King of America* from the underrated *Almost Blue* is that Costello's country now sounds lived-in and worn, bringing a new emotional depth to the music, and that helps make it one of his masterpieces. —*Stephen Thomas Erlewine*

Blood & Chocolate / Feb. 1986 / Rykodisc ✦✦✦✦

Costello returned to the Attractions as quickly as he abandoned them, hiring the band and old producer Nick Lowe to record *Blood & Chocolate*, his second record in the span of one year. Where *King of America* was a stripped-down, roots-rock affair, *Blood & Chocolate* is a return to the harder rock of *This Year's Model*. Occasionally, there are hints of country and folk, but the majority of the album is straight-ahead rock & roll—the opener, "Uncomplicated," only has two chords. The main difference between the reunion and the Attractions' earlier work is the tone—*This Year's Model* was tense and out-of-control, where *Blood & Chocolate* is controlled viciousness. "Tokyo Storm Warning," "I Hope You're Happy Now" and "I Want You" are the nastiest songs he has ever recorded, both lyrically and musically—Costello snarls the lyrics and the Attractions bash out the chords. *Blood & Chocolate* doesn't retain that high-level of energy throughout the record and loses momentum toward the end of the album. Still, it's a lively and frequently compelling reunion, even if it is a rather mean-spirited one. —*Stephen Thomas Erlewine*

Out of Our Idiot / 1987 / Demon ✦✦✦

Following in the tradition of *Taking Liberties* and *Ten Bloody Marys & Ten How's Your Fathers*, *Out of Our Idiot* compiles 21 rarities Elvis Costello released during the early and mid-'80s, usually under pseudonyms. Many of these songs are collaborations—"Seven Day Weekend" is a rollicking duet with Jimmy Cliff, Elvis sings "Baby It's You" with Nick Lowe; Costello and T-Bone Burnett form the Coward Brothers—hence the album's billing as a "various artists" record, which is indicative of its freewheeling, goofy humor. Even with a cover of Richard Thompson's harrowing "Withered and Died," *Out of Our Idiot* is pure fun, and it's not just for collectors. Costello's throwaways are frequently excellent, whether it's covers (Yoko Ono's "Walking on Thin Ice," Smokey Robinson's "From Head to Toe," "So Young"), genre exercises, jokes or full-fledged songs. Most of the songs on *Out of Our Idiot* were later included as bonus tracks in the Demon/Rykodisc reissue series, but this remains the only place "Little Goody Two Shoes" (a working version of "Inch By Inch") is available. Besides, it's a great listen in its own right. —*Stephen Thomas Erlewine*

Girls Girls Girls / 1989 / Columbia ✦✦✦

Elvis Costello assembled this compilation himself. It is highly idiosyncratic, not the least of its peculiarities being that the CD and cassette versions differ considerably. Costello describes a vague concept in his notes, but the collection of songs (47 on the CDs, 51 on the cassettes) seems a jumble. At least he demonstrates that songs from different periods work well together. A large part of Costello's oeuvre, including some of his best work, is represented. —*William Ruhlmann*

Spike / 1989 / Warner Brothers ✦✦

Following a pair of near-masterpieces in 1986, Elvis Costello went into semi-seclusion, separating from the Attractions (once again) and Columbia records, emerging three years later on Warner Brothers with *Spike*. Mockingly billing himself as "the Beloved Entertainer" on the album's front cover, there's nevertheless a real sense of showbiz pizzazz here, as he tries on a little bit of everything. You like Costello, the soul singer? Try "Deep Dark Truthful Mirror," recorded with the Dirty Dozen Brass Band. Costello the pop sophisticate? How about the torch song "Baby Plays Around" or "God's Comic," a tune that mocks Andrew Lloyd Webber, while aching to eclipse him. The angry young man? There's "Tramp the Dirt Down," perhaps the nastiest anti-Thatcher song ever waxed. Costello, the witty wordsmith? Well, there's "Pads, Paws and Claws," a rockabilly tune overflowing with labored puns. Costello, the gifted pure pop tunesmith? There's plenty of that here, from "This Town" with Roger McGuinn and Paul McCartney and the lovely "Veronica," a tune co-written with McCartney that became one of his biggest hits. So, there's a lot here—everything except focus, actually. And Costello certainly likes to indulge himself here, throwing in the awkward "Chewing Gum" and the instrumental "Stalin Malone" for good measure. There are some moments that work quite well, but there's nothing connecting them, and if anything, he's trying way too hard—and, for all of the overarching ambition of his early-'80s recordings, that criticism never applied before. Certainly, there are cuts for cultists to enjoy, but *Spike*'s sprawl works against it, resulting in a maddeningly diffuse listen. —*Stephen Thomas Erlewine*

Mighty Like a Rose / May 14, 1991 / Warner Brothers ✦✦

If *Spike* seemed frustratingly incoherent, it's nothing compared to *Mighty Like a Rose*, a deliberately dense, difficult record that is easily the most impenetrable Elvis Costello ever cut. With producers Mitchell Froom and Kevin Killen, Costello made a record with no easy entrances, even if the sparkling Beach Boys-esque "The Other Side of Summer" and the lovely "So Like Candy" would have been accessible with different production. And, certainly, production is the most notable thing about this record. Filled with clattering production, spongy bass, cardboard guitars, studio white noise, and layers upon layers of tracks, there's so much going on that it's hard to get to the core of the songs. Not that Costello makes it any easier for the listener, either, since only a few songs (the aforementioned pair, plus "All Grown Up" and "Playboy to a Man") don't seem self-satisfied in their own construction. And his performances are nearly as affected as the songs, as he over-sings (albeit for effect) and contributes to the muddy wall of sound. Yes, this is "interesting," but it takes many plays before you realize all those "interesting" effects lead nowhere—only to the strangest record Costello ever cut (and that's not a compliment, unfortunately). *—Stephen Thomas Erlewine*

The Juliet Letters / Jan. 19, 1993 / Warner Brothers ♦♦♦
Looking back on it, it's remarkable that Warner didn't sue Elvis Costello for making deliberately noncommercial, non-representative records, the way Geffen did with Neil Young in the '80s. After all, it's not just that he made a record as anti-pop as *Mighty Like a Rose*, it's that he followed it with a full-fledged classical album, *The Juliet Letters*—"a song sequence for string quartet and voice," recorded with the Brodsky Quartet. It's inspired by a Verona professor who responded to letters addressed to Juliet, of *Romeo and Juliet* fame, too. Given this history, it's little wonder that the record didn't storm the charts, but it is remarkable that Warner, even with their reputation for being an artist's label, decided to release it, since this just doesn't fit anywhere—not within pop (especially in the grunge-saturated 1993) and not within classical, either. Of course, that's precisely what's interesting about the record, and if interesting didn't signify any rewards with *Mighty*, it does here. This is a distinctive, unusual affair that, at its best, effectively marries chamber music with Beatlesque art pop. And there are a number of moments that work remarkably well on the record, such as "I Almost Had a Weakness" and "Jacksons, Monk and Rowe." True, these are the songs closest to straight-ahead Costello songs, yet they're still nice, small gems, and even if the rest of the record can be a little arch and awkward, it's not hard to admire what Costello and the Brodskys set out to do. And that's the problem with the record—it's easy to intellectualize, even appreciate, what it intends to be, but it's never compelling enough to return to. More experiment than effective, then. *—Stephen Thomas Erlewine*

2 1/2 Years / Oct. 12, 1993 / Rykodisc ♦♦♦♦♦
Rykodisc launched its Elvis Costello reissue series with *2 1/2 Years*, a box set featuring his first three albums together with the previously promotional-only *Live at the El Mocambo*, which is only available in the box. Costello fans know the studio albums by heart and will be pleased by the remastering and bonus tracks, while the highly sought-after *Live at the El Mocambo* proves that in addition to being an extremely talented songwriter, Costello was a hell of a rocker. *—Stephen Thomas Erlewine*

Brutal Youth / Mar. 8, 1994 / Warner Brothers ♦♦♦
Perhaps realizing that *The Juliet Letters* was one step too far, especially after the willfully eclectic pair of *Spike* and *Mighty Like a Rose*, Elvis Costello set out to make a straight-ahead rock & roll record with *Brutal Youth*, reuniting with the Attractions (though Bruce Thomas appears on only five tracks) and Nick Lowe (who plays bass on most of the rest). Unfortunately, all this nostalgia and good intentions are cancelled by the retention of producer Mitchell Froom, whose junkyard, hazily cerebral productions stand in direct contrast to the Attractions' best work. Likely, Froom's self-conscious production appealed to Costello, since it makes *Brutal Youth* look less like a retreat, but it severely undercuts the effectiveness of the music, since it lacks guts, no matter how smugly secure it is in its tempered "experimentation." Costello certainly had the raw elements for a dynamic little record here—the band, when they can be heard, sound good, and many songs (highlighted by "Pony St.," "Kinder Murder," "13 Steps Lead Down," "You Tripped at Every Step," and "20% Amnesia") are fresh, effective evocations of his classic work—but it needed to be punchier to succeed. He needed to be produced by Lowe, instead of just having him sit in on bass. *—Stephen Thomas Erlewine*

● **The Very Best of Elvis Costello & the Attractions** / Oct. 25, 1994 / Rykodisc ♦♦♦♦♦
A solid complement to Ryko's Costello reissue series if you don't want to pick up each individual album. Of course, the 22 tracks (drawn from his first 11 albums and, according to the liner notes, "hand-picked by Elvis himself") also sport the crisply remastered sound featured on the rest of the series. *The Very Best Of* halts abruptly at 1986's *Blood & Chocolate*, his last release for Columbia. *—Roch Parisien*

Kojak Variety / May 9, 1995 / Warner Brothers ♦♦
With *Almost Blue*, Elvis Costello wanted to be a honkytonker. With *Kojak Variety*, he's a crooner, picking forgotten tunes by both minor and major artists (anyone from Screamin' Jay Hawkins to Bob Dylan). From his song selections to the pseudo-avant-rock/R&B band, Costello doesn't make any obvious moves. Yet that doesn't mean that the record is difficult—it just shows the depths of Costello's affection for music and record collecting (which is also clear from his loving, detailed liner notes). Costello and his band (featuring guitarists James Burton and Marc Ribot, drummer Jim Keltner and Attraction Pete Thomas play with gusto, tearing through the songs with the vigor of a bar band on a Friday night. Some of the rockers sound slightly forced, although there's no denying the power of Costello's passionate vocals, even if he stretches his range a little too much (Little Richard's "Bama Lama Bama Loo"). What matters here are the performances, and the majority of *Kojak Variety* is filled with fine interpretations. *Kojak Variety* does what any good covers album should do—it makes you want to seek out the originals. *—Stephen Thomas Erlewine*

Deep Dead Blue, Live at Meltdown / Nov. 1995 / Nonesuch ♦♦♦
A lovely, understated exercise in minimalism, *Deep Dead Blue* documents a set of otherwise unaccompanied guitar/vocal duets between Bill Frisell and Elvis Costello, recorded live at the Meltdown Festival in London's Queen Elizabeth Hall on June 25, 1995. Although the performance isn't even quite half an hour long, it's the perfect length for holding a listener's attention. Frisell co-wrote the title track, one of the five songs bearing a Costello credit; the others are underexposed items from Costello's mid- to late-'80s catalog, plus selections by Charles Mingus ("Weird Nightmare") and Lerner & Loewe ("Gigi"). Costello is once again the refined, mature vocal stylist of *Painted from Memory*, but Frisell holds the real key to the collaboration with his impeccably restrained support. He expertly controls the dynamics of each piece, often stripping his part down to single-note lines, which lends surprising emotional impact when he allows full chords to wash over Costello's voice; his articulation is crisp and clean, his chordal voicings often novel and unexpected. It's no real surprise that the two work well together, given the musical affinity demonstrated on Frisell's masterful reinterpretations of *Painted from Memory* material on his own album *The Sweetest Punch*. The pleasures of *Deep Dead Blue* are, to be sure, much subtler than either of those recordings, but they make an elegant and fascinating supplement. *—Steve Huey*

All This Useless Beauty / May 14, 1996 / Warner Brothers ♦♦♦
Following his second covers album, *Kojak Variety*, Elvis Costello set out to assemble a collection of songs he had written for other artists, but he never recorded himself—sort of a reverse covers album. As it turned out, that idea was only used as a launching pad—the resulting album, *All This Useless Beauty*, is a mixture of nine old and three new songs. Given its origins, it's surprising that the record holds together as well as it does. The main strength of *All This Useless Beauty* is the quality of the individual songs—each song can stand on its own as an individual entity, as the music is as sharp as the lyrics. Although the music is certainly eclectic, it's accessible, which wasn't the case with *Mighty Like a Rose*. Furthermore, the production is more textured and punchier than Mitchell Froom's botched job on *Brutal Youth*. *All This Useless Beauty* doesn't quite add up to a major statement, but the simple pleasures it offers makes it one of the more rewarding records of the latter part of Costello's career. *—Stephen Thomas Erlewine*

Extreme Honey: The Very Best of Warner Brothers Years / Oct. 21, 1997 / Warner Brothers ♦♦♦♦
For anyone who didn't follow the many paths Costello treaded during the '90s, *Extreme Honey: The Very Best of Warner Brothers Years* is a good way to become acquainted with the strangest portion of his career. Like the Warner years themselves, *Extreme Honey* is flawed, suffering from the same idiosyncratic compiling method as *Girls! Girls! Girls!* There are a number of hits and singles, to be sure ("Veronica," "So Like Candy," "Sulky Girl," "13 Steps Lead Down," "The Other Side of Summer"), but the bulk of the album consists of album tracks. This isn't necessarily bad, since many of Costello's best songs weren't singles, but the problem is, *Extreme Honey* doesn't necessarily contain his best songs from the era. There are a number of great moments here, whether it's the lilting "The Birds Will Still Be Singing" from the underrated *Juliet Letters* or the New Orleans-inflected "Deep Dark Truthful Mirror," but the forced cacophony of "Hurry Down Doomsday (The Bugs Are Taking Over)" merely indicates how he was prone to excess during this era. And that leaves *Extreme Honey* in a weird position—it accurately conveys the spirit of Costello's Warner recordings, but it only has a portion of his best work from those albums. Nevertheless, the fact that it captures the feeling of Costello's '90s recordings makes it a worthwhile sampler for the curious who don't want to delve into the actual albums. [In order to entice collectors and die-hard fans, *Extreme Honey* contains "My Dark Life," Costello's collaboration with Brian Eno originally on *The X-Files* soundtrack, and the new track "The Bridge I Burned," a neo-psychedelic/trip-hop number constructed from backing tapes recorded with his son and Supergrass drummer Danny Goffey once Prince denied him the permission to alter the lyrics to "Pop Life."] *—Stephen Thomas Erlewine*

Painted from Memory / Sep. 29, 1998 / Mercury ♦♦♦♦♦
Elvis Costello and Burt Bacharach first collaborated on "God Give Me Strength," a sweeping ballad that functioned as the centerpiece in Allison Anders' *Grace of My Heart*. It was a stunning song in the tradition of Bacharach's classic '60s work and it was successful enough that the composers decided to collaborate on a full album, *Painted From Memory*. Wisely, they chose to work within the stylistic parameters of Bacharach's '60s material, but *Painted From Memory* never sounds like a stylistic exercise. Instead, it's a return to form for both artists. Bacharach hasn't written such graceful, powerful melodies since his glory days, and Costello hasn't crafted such a fully realized album since *King of America*. It's a testament to both that even if the album is clearly in Bacharach's territory, it feels like a genuine collaboration. Often, the music not only evokes the spirit of Dionne Warwick, it's reminiscent of Elvis' torching ballads for *Trust*. Costello keeps Bacharach from his schmaltzier tendencies, and Bacharach keeps Costello from overwriting. With its lush arrangements, sighing brass and strings, gentle pianos, and backing vocals, it's clearly a classicist album, yet it sounds utterly timeless. Its melodies are immediate, its emotions subtle, its impact lasting—and, with that timeless sound *Painted From Memory* illustrates that craft can not only be its own reward, it can be genuinely moving. *—Stephen Thomas Erlewine*

The Very Best of Elvis Costello / Apr. 17, 2001 / Rhino ♦♦♦♦
Elvis Costello seems to have an aversion to presenting his work in a logical, comprehensive fashion, if the double-disc *The Very Best of Elvis Costello* is any indication. Like its predecessor, *Girls Girls Girls*, it sprawls over two discs, with very little regard to chronology or style, baffling and enticing listeners in equal measure. Although there are certainly some terrific songs missing, it's hard to argue with much of what's here (with the notable exception of the cuts here to lure in collectors—the Charles Aznavour cover of "She," first heard in *Notting Hill*, and a version of "That Day Is Done," recorded with the Fairfield Four, featured on their 1997 album). So, as a reasonably thorough, albeit scattershot, overview, this works pretty well, since the music itself is good, even if it doesn't make sense when presented in this fashion (if it was intended to illustrate Costello's stylistic sweep, it winds up as counterproductive, since it's confusing in this fashion, not enticing). Still, the curious will prefer the single-disc sampler, *The Best of Elvis Costello and the Attractions*, since it's not only more concise, it illustrates Costello's depth and range equally well. And if you want to dig deeper after hearing that, the original albums are worth any fan's time. *—Stephen Thomas Erlewine*

The Count Bishops

f. 1974, England, **db.** 1979

Garage Rock Revival, Garage Rock, Punk

Although amounting to little more than a footnote in the early days of English punk rock, the Count Bishops were a fine, energetic, R&B-based band capable of kicking out a fierce racket of noise that sounded like a grimier version of seminal British R&B revivalists Dr. Feelgood. Originally fronted by journeyman American singer Mike Spencer, the Count Bishops' 1975 debut EP, *Speedball*, released on Ted Carroll's wonderful Chiswick Records, was a straightahead slice of R&B that featured the spooky, exhilarating "Train, Train." Surprisingly, the band unceremoniously dumped Spencer and recorded their self-titled debut with fellow Englishman Dave Tice, who had a voice so gruff it sounded as though he gargled with ground glass. A ripsnorting live record followed (by this time they had dropped "Count" from their name), but it was clear that the band was simply treading water. By 1979, the thoroughly mediocre *Cross Cuts* was released to public apathy, guitarist Zenon de Fleur was killed in a car wreck, and lead guitarist Johnny Guitar hooked up with Dr. Feelgood. The Bishops called it a career. *—John Dougan*

● **Count Bishops** / 1977 / Dynamite ♦♦♦♦♦

Kicking off with a great cover of The Kinks' "I Need You," this solid, unpretentious debut album should belong in the home of every fan of English R&B from The Yardbirds to The Pretty Things to Dr. Feelgood. Guitarists Johnny Guitar and Zenon de Fleur keep it tight and simple, never wasting a note, and vocalist Dave Tice is so macho, it's enough to make you laugh. The originals are OK, if somewhat predictable blues-based rave-ups, but the energy and good cheer more than make up for the album's derivative nature. Not a deep album by any stretch of the imagination, just good dirty fun. *—John Dougan*

Live [12 Inch] / 1978 / Chiswick ♦♦♦

A hunk of greasy rock and R&B that's not the most original record you're likely to hear; it is fun, loud, sloppy and endearing. Vocalist Dave Tice's growl is a hoot, as are the Chuck Berry pyrotechnics of Johnny Guitar. Two great covers: Fleetwood Mac's barroom anthem "Somebody's Gonna Get Their Head Kicked in Tonight" and The Standells' "Good Guys Don't Wear White." As the old saying goes: made loud to be played loud! *—John Dougan*

The Best of the Count Bishops / Oct. 1995 / Chiswick ♦♦♦♦

The Best of the Count Bishops is exactly what it promises, the very best of a band whose four-year career swung from the snarling denouement of "Route 66," through to the less than livid (but damned good regardless) *Cross Cut* album, and barely put a foot wrong. Across its course, stinging singles, burning LPs, and some positively lethal live cuts re-establish what a lot of people knew in 1976, but which history has conveniently overlooked ever since. Without bands like the Bishops (and the Bishops in particular), punk would never have known its parents. The opening (and, in live form, closing) "Train Train" lets you know what kind of journey this will be from the outset. Featuring a feline Elvis vocal from guitarist Zenon De Fleur, the sound of the Bishops in sensitive rockabilly mode has a swirling darkness and a restless rhythm, and it rattles by as hellbound as any classic blues locomotive. Other band originals are similarly evocative, and zealously antagonistic. But the true measure of the Bishops' importance comes with the cover versions. The Bishops may have been furiously retro in their musical tastes, but their delivery was primal, young, loud, and snotty belligerence. Arguably, it was their exhumations of "I Want Candy" and Fleetwood Mac's "Someone's Gonna Get Their Head Kicked in Tonight" which inspired subsequent versions by Bow Wow Wow and the Rezillos, although it goes without saying that the Bishops' versions are by far the fiercer. Similarly, the Jam might have been the first to chart with a revved-up cover of an old forgotten Kinks song, but they weren't the first to do it—fiery recreations of "I Need You" and "Til the End of the Day" were already established Bishops staples. *—Dave Thompson*

● **Speedball Plus 11** / Feb. 1996 / Chiswick ♦♦♦♦♦

In the year or so before punk finally emerged on the London scene, the Count Bishops were the kind of band you wished everyone could sound like—without ever guessing that very soon, they would. The original *Speedball* EP featured just four tracks, including the superlative "Teenage Letter," a performance which sounds like the Flamin' Groovies if they really were on fire. The 11 extras round up a mass of material that never saw release during the band's own lifetime, but packs a similarly psychotic visceral kick. Most of the songs are covers; many, additionally, are covers of the covers which the Bishops' British beat boom heroes were wont to play. The early Stones and Pretty Things positively leer over the track listing, although in terms of gritty nastiness, the Bishops make their bad boy barrage sound like misbehaving choir boys. "Honey I Need" is positively lethal, and "I Want Candy" leaves a nasty taste before it's even been unwrapped. Overall, *Speedball Plus 11* is little more than a glimpse inside the most formative days of the Count Bishops and, in terms of sonics and content, it may leave something to be desired. But like those archive exhumations which scour the Sex Pistols' pre-*Bollocks* strivings, it has that vibrant, vitriolic vitality which inexperience alone can render realistic—and which history wishes had been recognized at the time. The Bishops have, by and large, been forgotten. This set proves how unjust that is. *—Dave Thompson*

Count Five

f. 1965, San Jose, CA, **db.** 1967

Acid Rock, Garage Rock, Psychedelic

The definitive one-hit wonders, the Count Five failed to make much of a lasting impression—but just play that one hit, "Psychotic Reaction," and almost any audience will want to hear more. Their one fault was that they could never generate more—they tried but never issued another record half as good. The Count Five started life in San Jose, California in the early '60s, still in their mid-teens and specializing in surf instrumental music before trying to pick up on the British Invasion sound. At about the time the group changed its name to the Count Five, guitarist Sean Byrne put the finishing touches on a song he'd been outlining in his head, ultimately called "Psychotic Reaction." It became a showcase for the band's abilities, and the crescendo of their stage act. A local deejay eventually got the song and the group placed with L.A.-based Double Shot Records. A chugging, fuzz-tone laden piece of punk defiance with more than a few signature licks and phrasings borrowed from Bo Diddley and the Yardbirds, plus a punk attitude worthy of the Standells, the record eventually made No. 5 nationally. An album was rushed out, containing some ill-conceived originals, but nothing that the group did after "Psychotic Reaction" seemed to work. The strain of maintaining music careers while attending college—which was essential to the members keeping their draft deferments—took its toll, as did the dwindling bookings; by the end of 1967, the Count Five ceased to exist. Their story might have ended there, but for the 1972 release of *Nuggets*, Lenny Kaye's original '60s garage/psychedelic punk compilation. Suddenly a new generation discovered the Count Five, and demand for their album resulted in several rounds of reissues on vinyl and CD. In the decades since, the group has rated at least a mention in most histories of garage rock and psychedelic punk, and "Psychotic Reaction" is a standard of the genre, still potent and enjoyable on its own terms. *—Bruce Eder*

Psychotic Reaction / 1987 / Edsel ♦♦♦♦

Includes seven cuts from their only album, and a few of their ultra-rare flop follow-ups to "Psychotic Reaction." *—Richie Unterberger*

● **Psychotic Reaction: The Very Best of Count Five** / Mar. 23, 1999 / Collectables ♦♦♦♦♦

Re-release of the earlier Count Five compilation from Performance, with new packaging and notes. There's a considerable range of material here, all of it pretty punk oriented, though very little as rewarding as the title track, a number five hit nationally that managed to incorporate the best elements of the Yardbirds' and Bo Diddley's music. The other highlights include "Pretty Big Mouth" and a very animated cover of the Who's "My Generation." The sound is ridiculously good as well, and the biographical notes are highly informative. *—Bruce Eder*

Counting Crows

f. Aug. 1991

American Trad Rock, Adult Alternative Pop/Rock, Alternative Pop/Rock

With their angst-filled hybrid of Van Morrison, the Band, and R.E.M., Counting Crows became an overnight sensation in 1994. Only a year earlier, the band was a group of unknown musicians, filling in for the absent Van Morrison at the Rock & Roll Hall of Fame ceremony; they were introduced by an enthusiastic Robbie Robertson. Early in 1993, the band recorded their debut album, *August & Everything After*, with T-Bone Burnett; it was released in the fall. It was a dark, somber record, driven by the morose lyrics and expressive vocals of Adam Duritz; the only up-tempo song, "Mr. Jones," became their ticket to stardom. What made Counting Crows was how they were able to balance Duritz's tortured lyrics with the sound of the late '60s and early '70s; it made them one of the few alternative bands to appeal to listeners who thought that rock & roll died in 1972. *Recovering the Satellites* followed in 1996, and in 1998 they issued the two-disc *Across a Wire—Live in New York*. Counting Crows' third studio album, *This Desert Life*, appeared in 1999. *—Stephen Thomas Erlewine*

● **August and Everything After** / Sep. 14, 1993 / Geffen ♦♦♦♦

When the prevailing guitar jingle of "Mr. Jones" cascaded over radio in the early '90s, it was a sure sign that the Counting Crows were a musical force to be reckoned with. Their debut album, *August and Everything After*, burst at the seams with both dominant pop harmonies and rich, hearty ballads, all thanks to lead singer Adam Duritz. The lone guitar work of "Mr. Jones" coupled with the sweet, in-front pull of Duritz's voice kicked off the album in full force. The starkly beautiful and lonely sounding "Round Here" captured the band's honest yet subtle talent for singing ballads, while "Omaha" is lyrically reminiscent of a Springsteen tune. The fusion of hauntingly smooth vocals with such instruments as the Hammond B-3 organ and the accordion pumped new life into the music scene, and their brisk sound catapulted them into stardom. On "Rain Kings," the piano takes over as its aloof flair dances behind Duritz with elegant crispness. The slower-paced "Raining in Baltimore" paints a perfectly grey picture and illustrates the band's ease at conveying mood by eliminating the tempo. Most of the songs here engage in overly contagious hooks that won't go away, making for a solid bunch of tunes. Containing the perfect portions of instrumental and vocal conglomeration, the Counting Crows showed off their appealing sound to its full extent with their very first album. *—Mike DeGagne*

Recovering the Satellites / Oct. 15, 1996 / Geffen ♦♦♦♦

For their second album, *Recovering the Satellites*, Counting Crows crafted a self-consciously challenging response to their unexpected success. Throughout the record, Adam Duritz contemplates his loss of privacy and sudden change of fortunes, among other angst-ridden subjects. In one sense, it's no difference from the subjects that dominated *August & Everything After*, yet his outlook is lacking the muted joy that made "Mr. Jones" into a hit. Similarly, the music is slightly more somber, yet the approach is harder and more direct, which gives even the ballads a more affecting, visceral feel. *Recovering the Satellites* occasionally bogs down in its own pretention—for a roots-rock band, the group certainly has a lot of artsy goals—yet when they scale back their ambitions to simple folk-rock, such as on the single "A Long December," they are at their most articulate. *—Stephen Thomas Erlewine*

Across a Wire: Live in New York / Jul. 14, 1998 / Geffen ♦♦♦

This Desert Life / Nov. 2, 1999 / Interscope ♦♦♦♦

It's likely that critics and listeners will consider Counting Crows' long-delayed third album, *This Desert Life*, another retro effort by a traditionalist band, but it's actually their most individual and finest album yet. All the familiar elements are in place, from Adam

Duritz's impassioned vocals and cryptic lyrics to the jangling instrumentation, but the laments gel better than ever before. Part of it undoubtedly has to do with David Lowery and Dennis Herring's organic production, which keeps the rough edges in place, helping the music to breathe, but the real success of the record is due to the band themselves, who have matured gracefully. They may have spent a long time recording this album, but the music feels natural and immediate. Upon closer inspection, the craft really shines through. The songs are tight, with strong hooks on the choruses, and nice, memorable melody lines; the arrangements may be earthy, but they're never cluttered. Most importantly, Duritz has reigned in his tendency to overwrite and over-emote, turning in his best sets of songs to date. But the best thing about *This Desert Life* is that it holds together as a cohesive album while providing the best individual songs in the band's catalog. And that just doesn't mean the best singles, although "Hanginaround" is their finest uptempo number to date; the album tracks are consistently compelling, ranging from the winding narrative of "Mrs. Potter's Lullaby" to the measured ballad "Speedway." These subtle differences—the confident performances, cohesion, and assured songwriting—add up Counting Crows' strongest album to date. They may still recall rock giants, but only in the best possible way—by crafting an album that ebbs and flows like the best classic rock records. —*Stephen Thomas Erlewine*

Country Joe & The Fish

f. 1966, El Monte, CA
Folk-Rock, Psychedelic

One of the original and most popular San Francisco Bay Area psychedelic bands, Country Joe & the Fish, was formed by lead singer Country Joe McDonald (b. Jan. 1, 1942). The Berkeley group still had one foot in the jugband sound on their first EP, released in 1965 (featuring a folk version of their anthem "I-Feel-like-I'm-Fixin'-to-Die Rag"). By the time of their second EP in 1966, though, they had plunged full-tilt into the burgeoning psychedelic sound, with raga-ish, heavily distorted guitars and farfisa organ, displayed to its full glory on the instrumental "Section 43." Versions of songs from those limited edition EPs were combined with other material for their first and best album, *Electric Music for the Mind and Body.* McDonald and his group combined protest politics, free love, and psychedelic drugs with a good-time humor on this 1967 release. After a similar, less impressive follow-up, the band began to disintegrate, and never recaptured the highs of their early days. McDonald went on to an intermittently successful, more folk-rock oriented solo career, achieving his greatest moment of notoriety with his version of "Fixin'-to-Die" (complete with the obscene "Fish Cheer") at the Woodstock festival. —*Richie Unterberger*

● **Electric Music for the Mind and Body** / 1967 / Vanguard ◆◆◆◆◆
Their full-length debut is their most joyous and cohesive statement, and finds the band's psychedelic swirl of distorted guitar and organ at its most inventive. Ranging in mood from good-timey to downright apocalyptic, it includes most of their best tunes. —*Richie Unterberger*

I Feel Like I'm Fixing to Die / 1967 / Vanguard ◆◆◆◆◆
The Fish's second album is quite similar to their first in its organ-heavy psychedelia with Eastern-influenced melodic lines, but markedly inferior to the debut, and much more of a period piece. There's more spaciness and less comic energy here, and while the band were undoubtedly serious in their explorations, some of these songs are simply silly in their cosmic naivete. To be crueler, there is no other album that exemplifies so strongly the kind of San Francisco psychedelia that Frank Zappa skewered on his classic *We're Only in It for the Money.* The weeping, minor-key melodies, liquid guitar lines, and earnestly self-absorbed quests to explore the inner psyche—it's almost as if they put themselves up as a dartboard for The Mothers to savage. For all that, the best songs are good; "Who Am I" and "Thursday" are touching psychedelic ballads. But more notably, the title cut—whose brash energy is atypical of the album—was a classic anti-war satire that became one of the decade's most famous protest songs, and the group's most famous track. —*Richie Unterberger*

Together / 1968 / Vanguard ◆◆◆◆◆
Together, Country Joe & the Fish's third album, was the group's most consistent, most democratic, and best-selling record. Unlike their first two albums, which were dominated by Country Joe McDonald's voice and compositions, *Together* featured the rest of the band—guitarists Barry Melton and David Cohen, bassist Bruce Barthol and drummer Chicken Hirsh—almost as prominently as McDonald. That's usually a formula for disaster, but in this case it gave the album more variety and depth: McDonald tended to favor droning mantras like the album-closing "An Untitled Protest," which worked better when contrasted with the likes of Melton's catchy anti-New York diatribe, "The Streets of Your Town," and the group-written "Rock and Soul Music." Songs like the latter cast the group as a soul revue, true, and they couldn't quite pull that off, but *Together* had the charming quality of unpredictability; you never knew what was coming next. Unfortunately, what came next in the band's career was a split. Barthol was out by September 1968, Cohen and Hirsh following in January 1969. Thereafter, McDonald and Melton fronted various Fish aggregations, but it was never the same, even when this lineup regrouped for *Reunion* in 1977. —*William Ruhlmann*

Here We Are Again / 1969 / Vanguard ◆◆

The Collected Country Joe & the Fish / 1987 / Vanguard ◆◆◆◆◆
Country Joe & the Fish are well represented on this 19-track compilation that traces their development from a politically oriented folk/jug band ensemble to a politically oriented rock and soul band. Most of the material comes from 1967, the band's high-water mark, and the centerpiece is the still-cutting "I-Feel-like-I'm-Fixin'-to-Die Rag." —*William Ruhlmann*

The First Three EPs / 1987 / Decal ◆◆◆
The first recordings by Country Joe & the Fish (1965-1966) and his early solo material (1971). It includes "I-Feel-like-I'm-Fixin'-to-Die Rag," "Superbird," and "Tricky Dicky." —*William Ruhlmann*

Live! Fillmore West 1969 / Mar. 12, 1996 / Vanguard ◆◆

Don Covay (Donald Randolph)

b. Mar. 24, 1938, Orangeburg, SC
Vocals / Deep Soul, Southern Soul, Soul

An R&B and soul songwriting great, Don Covay compositions have been recorded by everyone from the Rolling Stones to Jimi Hendrix, Gladys Knight to Wilson Pickett, and many others. Covay joined the Rainbows alongside Marvin Gaye, John Berry, and Billy Stewart in the '50s. He also performed as a solo singer with Little Richard, who recorded Covay as "Pretty Boy" on the Atlantic release "Bip Bop Bip." Covay had moderate success with the single "Pony Time," which he co-wrote with Berry, for the Arnold label in 1960. He began to hit his stride in 1964 with "Mercy Mercy," "Sookie Sookie," and "See Saw," and had tunes recorded by Gene Chandler and Aretha Franklin. Covay did both blues and soul numbers for the Janus and Mercury labels in the '70s. His most electrifying number was 1973's "I Was Checkin' Out While She Was Checkin' In," which made it to number six. Covay made one LP for Gamble and Huff's Philadelphia International label in 1976, but *Travelin' in Heavy Traffic* proved a disappointment. Covay recorded for Newman in 1980, and got his last chart single with "Badd Boy." —*Ron Wynn*

● **Mercy Mercy: The Definitive Don Covay** / Oct. 19, 1994 / Razor & Tie ◆◆◆◆◆
Mercy Mercy: The Definitive Don Covay compiles 23 tracks from throughout the soul singer's career. Encompassing everything from the R&B stomp of "Bip Bop Bip" and "Pony Time" to the seductive soul of "I Was Checkin' Out While She Was Checkin' In" and "No Tell Motel," the disc makes a convincing argument that Covay was one of the great overlooked R&B/soul artists of the '60s. —*Stephen Thomas Erlewine*

Cowboy Junkies

f. 1985, Toronto, Ontario, Canada
College Rock, Adult Alternative Pop/Rock, Alternative Country-Rock, Alternative Pop/Rock

Although it was solely a way to gain attention, the Cowboy Junkies' name goes a long way in describing the Canadian band's sound. At its core, the group's music is based in country and folk traditions, except their tempos are slow and lethargic, their guitars are languid, and Margo Timmins' vocals are lovely, yet hauntingly detached. The group recorded their first album, *Whites off Earth Now!!,* in 1986, releasing it on a Canadian independent label. Two years later, they recorded *The Trinity Sessions* in an abandoned church, using only one microphone. The album may have only cost $250 to record, but it sparked a small sensation, with the band's reworkings of "Blue Moon," "I'm So Lonesome I Could Cry," "Walking After Midnight," and "Sweet Jane" earning them a diverse and dedicated cult following. *The Caution Horses* didn't earn as much press as their previous album, yet they maintained a sizable cult, which stuck by the band through their next two records, *Black-Eyed Man* (1992) and *Pale Sun, Crescent Moon* (1993). —*Stephen Thomas Erlewine*

Whites off Earth Now!! / 1986 / RCA ◆◆◆
Featuring only one original song, the Cowboy Junkies' debut *Whites Off Earth Now!!* captures the band forming their own sound through covers, including songs by Robert Johnson and Bruce Springsteen. It's not as captivating as their later releases, but it's fascinating to hear their signature country-on-valium sound develop. Margo Timmins sings beautifully. —*Stephen Thomas Erlewine*

● **The Trinity Sessions** / 1988 / RCA ◆◆◆◆◆
Recorded in a one-night session at a Toronto church using only a DAT recorder, *Trinity Sessions* turned into the Junkies' American breakthrough thanks to the fluke success of "Sweet Jane," a cover of the Velvet Underground classic. Lou Reed himself praised it due to its inclusion of the lost verse about "heavenly wine and roses," and the four-piece do it all proud, with Margo Timmins' lovely, haunted vocal and the band's quietly narcotic performance in perfect sync. As a whole, *Trinity Sessions* captures that entire mood throughout, building on the sound established on *Whites Off Earth Now!* to create a perfect balance between older inspirations and a newer, hushed dramatic edge. The album is split evenly between covers and new cuts, with the former showing the group's many gifts at creating its own interpretations and the latter its abilities to come up with equally fine cuts. Among the originals, "Misguided Angel" is perhaps the best, a lengthy, sweetly beautiful piece that showcases the abilities of guest performers Jaro Czerwinec on accordion and Jeff Bird on mandolin and harmonica. The core quartet just nails the main performance to a T, and the end result is wondrous. As for the covers, while some of the choices are well known—Hank Williams' "I'm So Lonesome I Could Cry," Patsy Cline's "Walking After Midnight"—the Junkies effectively turn each take into their own. —*Ned Raggett*

The Caution Horses / Feb. 1990 / RCA ◆◆

Black-Eyed Man / Feb. 11, 1992 / RCA ◆◆◆
The Cowboy Junkies' *Black-Eyed Man* is an excellent return to form following their disappointing third LP, *The Caution Horses.* Where Michael Timmins' songwriting was stilted and overly self-conscious on the previous record, here his character studies are literate and finely-etched; like Robbie Robertson before him, Timmins' Canadian roots allow him to view the rural American experience with unique objectivity, and narratives like the opening "Southern Rain" and "Murder, Tonight, in the Trailer Park" are told with compassion and cinematic detail. *Black-Eyed Man* also broadens the Junkies' musical

horizons: "If You Were the Woman and I Was the Man," a duet with John Prine, is like a Fifties-era love song intercepted from an alternate reality, while tracks like the lilting "A Horse in the Country" push the group closer to the folk-pop territory of 10,000 Maniacs. At the same time, their country roots are further reinforced by a pair of outstanding Townes Van Zandt covers, "Cowboy Junkies Lament" and "To Live Is to Fly"; sandwiched between them is Timmins' own tribute, "Townes' Blues." —*Jason Ankeny*

Pale Sun, Crescent Moon / Nov. 23, 1993 / RCA ✦✦✦✦
A refreshed, revitalized sound that doesn't sacrifice the delicate touches that first made them unique; rugged, but still pristine. Much of the new spark emanates from the strings of honorary Junkie Ken Myhr, who peals out intense, biting lead guitar throughout. Especially prominent is his incendiary slide work on "Seven Years" and a spectacular cover of Dinosaur Jr.'s "The Post." Still, it's hard to imagine a ballad instrument more haunting and ethereal than Margo Timmins' voice. —*Roch Parisien*

200 More Miles, Live Performances 1985-1994 / Oct. 10, 1995 / RCA ✦✦✦
Subtitled, "Live Performances 1985-1994" (though the earliest track comes from Halloween 1986), *200 More Miles*, which concluded the Cowboy Junkies' contract with RCA, was a 17-track compilation of concert recordings. Its five and a half cover songs spanned the group's influences: "Blue Moon Revisited (A Song for Elvis)" drew upon the Rodgers & Hart song (that's the half) as interpreted by the King of Rock & Roll; "Me and the Devil Blues" came from the King of the Delta Blues Singers, Robert Johnson; "I'm So Lonesome I Could Cry" was by the King of Country Music, Hank Williams, "Walking After Midnight" by the Queen, Patsy Cline, and "State Trooper" and "Sweet Jane" came from a couple of Rock's Crown Princes, Bruce Springsteen and Lou Reed. Of course, this was for the most part downbeat material, and the Cowboy Junkies rendered it in their usual transfixing, if soporific style. They did the same on a set of Michael Timmins originals such as "Sun Comes Up, It's Tuesday Morning" and "Murder, Tonight, in the Trailer Park." (John Prine guests on "If You Were the Woman and I Was the Man.") "Before I do some rock & roll I always like to sit down," Margo Timmins noted at the outset, and she wasn't kidding. —*William Ruhlmann*

Lay It Down / Feb. 27, 1996 / Geffen ✦✦✦
Released in 1996, this CD definitively answers a question that has occasionally plagued the Cowboy Junkies—"yes, they sound good, but can they rock?" Though still laden with the melancholia that has marked previous efforts, this CD is sonically dense, guitar-drenched, and good at high volume levels. Margo Timmins' voice has never been more expressive, and the lyrics shimmer with intensity. Although the band has occasionally touched on quiet moments reminiscent of fellow Canadian Neil Young, little they have done before this album approached the emotive wail of his louder efforts. The Cowboy Junkies have proven their versatility while retaining their unique sound. —*Jeff Crooke*

Studio: Selected Studio Recordings 1986-1995 / Nov. 12, 1996 / RCA ✦✦✦✦
Studio: Selected Studio Recordings is a fine compilation of highlights from the Cowboy Junkies' albums, including such songs as "Sweet Jane" and "Misguided Angel," as well as the previously unreleased "Lost My Driving Wheel." While this is a thoughtfully compiled retrospective, *The Trinity Sessions* remains the definitive Cowboy Junkies album, although this isn't a bad way to collect much of the best material from their frequently uneven records. —*Stephen Thomas Erlewine*

Miles from Our Home / Jun. 30, 1998 / Geffen ✦✦✦
Working with producer John Leckie on *Miles from Our Home* has enlivened the Cowboy Junkies' trademark lackadaisical style somewhat. Replacing the group's calm, minimalist sound with a polished production, Leckie manages to make the record sound unlike anything else in the band's catalog. That's not to say that there's no trace of the old style—he has simply updated their sound, bringing it in line with adult alternative pop that they played a part in establishing in the late '80s. If the results aren't as magical as *The Trinity Sessions*, they're far from disappointing. Margo Timmins' voice remains as enchanting as ever and her brother Michael Timmins' songs are sturdy. There might not be any masterpieces on *Miles from Our Home*, but there aren't any misfires, either—it's simply a solid album from a reliable band. —*Stephen Thomas Erlewine*

Rarities, B-Sides and Slow, Sad Waltzes / Oct. 12, 1999 / Valley ✦✦✦

Waltz Across America / 2000 / Latent ✦✦✦

Open / May 15, 2001 / Zoe ✦✦✦
Cowboy Junkies have a sound, a vibe. There's no denying it. You can tell it's them within a few notes and each successive record seems to pick up right where the last one left off. Some, like *The Trinity Sessions*, are dark, moody, and mellow, like being coated in honey and draped in velvet. Others, take *Pale Sun, Crescent Moon* for example, seem downright energetic in comparison. *Open* is more in line with the first batch, though it has moments of near-enthusiastic revelry. With Alan Anton's plump (rather than phat) bass lines, Peter Timmins' laid-back drumming, and Michael Timmins' dirty guitars to ride on, Margo Timmins contributes her trademark sensual, yet understated vocal performances. The whole gang sounds as good as ever. And, although he may be called a songwriter, Michael Timmins is more a true poet with musical inclinations. Full of wonder and romance, fear and passion, *Open* is simply the next chapter in his sublime book of heartfelt verse. The compassionate tenderness of "Thousand Year Prayer" contrasts nicely with the harmonica and feedback duel of "Dragging Hooks." And darn if "I'm So Open" doesn't bounce right along on a little groove. They've got it all here. If nothing else, this band is one of the most consistent around. Though album sales may not always reflect it, they continually deliver strong records that refuse to be faulted for anything other than being non-mainstream. —*Kelly McCartney*

Best of Cowboy Junkies / Aug. 21, 2001 / RCA ✦✦✦✦
Like so many of their '80s contemporaries, Cowboy Junkies have never quite broken into the mainstream, yet their music has seeped into movies, television, and alternative radio. Despite their lack of fame, they still made great music that persevered through trends and imitators, and the best of that music is found on this compilation. Their early covers of "Sweet Jane" and "I'm So Lonesome I Could Cry" highlight the first third of the album, featuring Margo Timmons' whispered vocals over the lazy shuffle pumped out by the rest of the band. The up-tempo country lament "Sun Comes Up, It's Tuesday Morning" and the cheery "To Live Is to Fly" show Timmons' vocals shaping into a strong croon reminiscent of Natalie Merchant. Even their '90s work, which critics were never very kind to, still has strong representation with "Anniversary Song" and "Hard to Explain." Fans may wonder why no songs from any album past *Pale Sun, Crescent Moon* are included, as so many great songs—from "Common Disaster" to "Dragging Hooks"—could have rounded out the album. Although these albums may have been financial disappointments, they still could have included some of the stronger tracks. As it is, this is still a good retrospective of the strongest years of a band who made good albums long after the compilation's cutoff date. —*Bradley Torreano*

The Cows
f. 1985

Noise-Rock, Indie Rock, Alternative Pop/Rock, American Underground
Longtime denizens of the Minneapolis rock scene, the Cows are one of America's great degenerate punk-rock bands. Starting off as near-total incompetents, they have become more technically polished musicians over the past decade, but their white-hot noise-rock has not been tamed one bit. In many ways, the Cows remain as gloriously messy, primitive and exciting as they were the day they started. Formed in the mid-'80s by idiosyncratic lead singer Shannon Selberg, the Cows appropriated the hardcore guitar blur that characterized fellow-Twin Citians Hüsker Dü, but stripped away any and all concessions to melodies, hooks, riffs—essentially anything that remotely resembled pop. What they offered was a blazing wall of distortion that was punk rock at its crudest; a feral racket that sounded as if the guitars were being played with metal files. Above the din was Selberg, free-associating surreal vignettes about, well, God knows what, but his squealing, shrieking and general lunacy provided the bizarre, often engaging focus. He plays trumpet, too—well, not so much plays as blasts a note or two when he's tired of ranting. After the release of their first album in 1987, the Cows were roundly derided as a talentless, tasteless joke (a charge that would be levelled a few years later against Babes in Toyland). However, they've stayed true to their anti-commercial stance and punk roots, releasing a handful of weird, loud, gleefully unhinged records that seem to get better (i.e., more focused and less obtuse) and retain the band's devotion to mania. —*John Dougan*

Taint Pluribus Taint Unum / 1987 / Treehouse ✦✦✦✦
Recommended to those who want to experience The Cows at their most impenetrable and noisy. This is not to say that this record is worthless, but it is relentless. And, if you tire of guitar feedback, screeched vocals and a rhythm section that only infrequently knows what it's doing, this may be more than you can handle. However, fans of Japanese noise acts like The Boredoms and some of John Zorn's more extreme jazzcore outfits might think this is pretty cool. —*John Dougan*

Daddy Has a Tail / 1989 / Amphetamine Reptile ✦✦✦
On their Amphetamine Reptile Records debut, the Cows sound like a Midwest punk rock band who had listened to every Swans and Butthole Surfers album thousands of times, consecutively. Borrowing the former's noisiness and sonic girth, and the latter's Beefheartian weirdness, the Cows were forerunners of the noise rock scene essentially birthed by Amrep, a scene that included Helmet, Surgery, God Bullies, Unsane, and Halo of Flies. In many ways, *Daddy Has a Tail* showcases a band experimenting sonically, finding their voice—at least trying to—much in the way Butthole Surfers did with the messy *Rembrandt Pussyhorse*. *Daddy Has a Tail*'s guitars are an overdose of distortion; the bass trembles and wails far too much, and the songs just aren't quite there yet. Beyond that, Shannon Selberg hasn't fully manned his screwball vocal chariot. That would all slide into place on subsequent releases. However, songs like "Chow" stand out as Cows classics. —*Patrick Kennedy*

Effete & Impudent Snobs / 1990 / Amphetamine Reptile ✦✦

Peacetika / 1991 / Amphetamine Reptile ✦✦✦
Peacetika opens with the rollicking "Hitting the Wall," with vocalist Shannon Selberg alternately screeching and sneer-singing his way through lyrics that would certainly be catchy if you could understand them. With this album, the Cows continue to trim away at the massively noisy foundations of *Taint Pluribus, Taint Unum*, and *Daddy Has a Tail*, trimming the overload of distortion and harmonic dissonance away to slowly reveal a more potent, melodic—but still peculiar—noise rock vehicle. Eisentrager's guitar still shrieks and wails like a three a.m. cat fight, Rutmanis' bass still drips and oozes, and Selberg holds court vocally like a deranged court jester, but this time around, those elements have been tempered, and the band is beginning to fully congeal. Like most of the Cows' output, the album title is a clever linguistic finger pointing at the oddities held within, akin to the Butthole Surfers' *Locust Abortion Technician*, or *Hairway to Steven*. Though this is not the band's high-water mark, it's close, and by the time the next two albums emerged—*Cunning Stunts* and *Sexy Pee Story*—the Cows had hit their stride. —*Patrick Kennedy*

● **Cunning Stunts** / 1991 / Amphetamine Reptile ✦✦✦✦✦
The release of *Cunning Stunts* signaled a "maturity" to the Cows, but it really meant that riffs and hooks were starting to emerge from their usual tarpit of sound. Although Selberg's ranting and raving dominate the proceedings, it's guitarist Thor Eisenstrager who steals the show with his frenetic playing and bold experimentation. Not the pure noise of their earlier work, but certainly not an attempt at mainstream respectability either. The

Cows are simply too frenzied and defiantly idiosyncratic for that to happen. *—John Dougan*

Sexy Pee Story / 1993 / Amphetamine Reptile ♦♦♦♦♦
With an album title that sounds as though it was made up by a four-year-old, this follow-up to *Cunning Stunts* showed the Cows hitting their stride, producing another terrific, noisy, clamorous record stuffed to the gills with pure punk rock excitement. Never ones to miss an opportunity for humor, included on this disc is a great cover of "39 Lashes" from *Jesus Christ Superstar,* lyrics ("1, 2, 3, 4…") included. *—John Dougan*

Orphan's Tragedy / 1995 / Amphetamine Reptile ♦♦♦
It's been nearly a decade since their debut release, and the Cows show absolutely no sign of slowing down. *Orphan's Tragedy* squeals in a way that is reminiscent of early Cows, but Eisenstrager's guitar still dominates the mix with its overwhelming power. *—John Dougan*

Old Gold: 1989-1991 / 1996 / Amphetamine Reptile ♦♦♦
Serving as both an excellent introduction to the Cows' freaked-out, discordant universe and as a reissue of older, out-of-print album tracks and singles, *Old Gold* captures this quartet's arc of development from a sloppy, discordant Butthole Surfer-esque punk band to legendary noise rock merchants. Culling tracks from 1989's massively off-kilter *Daddy Has a Tail,* 1990s more developed *Effete and Impudent Snobs,* and the band's first classic album, 1991's *Peacetika, Old Gold* also contains "One O'Clock High" from the "Slapback" single. With a tone that most clearly resembles the damaging, atonal scraping Ted Falconi employed in Flipper, guitarist Thor Eisentrager's shrill feedback and distortion is perfectly foiled by Kevin Rutmanis' amorphous, melting bass tone; truly it sounds as though Rutmanis' bass is melting through the amps. As the tracks on *Old Gold* progress, so do the Cows musically, and by the time the cuts from *Peacetika* have been reached, the band is capable of harnessing and developing melody while retaining their signature noise attack. *—Patrick Kennedy*

Whorn / Apr. 1996 / Amphetamine Reptile ♦♦♦
With new drummer Freddy Votel installed behind the kit, the Cows decided to record live in the studio for this release—completely live—and the result is a loose and energetic album, rich with the obvious microphone bleeds endemic to such a recording style. The bass mic picks up drum sound, the snare mic picks up some guitar reverb, the room mics pick up everything, and so on. This is a fairly traditional, old fashioned recording method—setting up the microphones and rolling tape. This is not to say that *Whorn* isn't without problems; after all, the band peaked during *Cunning Stunts* and *Sexy Pee Story,* then opted to explore the more avant territory visited here and on the band's final, massively tweaked Beefheart-meets-Flipper-meets-Chrome opus, *Sorry in Pig Minor.* But overall, *Whorn,* with its inventive title, is pure Cows—loud, noisy, brash, cryptically odd, dense, and wonderfully strange. At times the recording style soars; at others, it sags. *—Patrick Kennedy*

Sorry in Pig Minor / Mar. 10, 1998 / Amphetamine Reptile ♦♦♦
King Buzzo, from the Melvins royalty, produces this ninth album from the very unherd-like Cows. *Sorry in Pig Minor* is a big album—huge in sound, sleek and fat. Not an easy or even listen, *Sorry in Pig Minor* rocks back and forth like a strait-jacketed lunatic ("No, I'm Not Coming Out") or bursts forth like an unleashed psychopath ("Cabin Man"). There is a wonderful disparity between the percussion (which sounds far away and primitive) and the rest of the music (which confronts and instigates). This album is the Cows at their cathartic best. The recording is psycho-grunge with punk rock horn that reaches to psychological depths. *—Thomas Schulte*

The Cowsills

f. 1966, Newport, RI, **db.** 1971
Bubblegum, Power Pop, Pop
The real-life inspiration behind the hit television series *The Partridge Family,* the Cowsills—the teen siblings Bill, Bob, Barry, John, Susan and Paul in tandem with mom Barbara—were one of the biggest pop acts of the late '60s, scoring a series of hits including "The Rain, the Park and Other Things" and "Hair" distinguished by their angelic harmonies and sun-kissed melodies. The family group began performing live as Beatlemania dawned, and recorded four singles during 1967 to negligible interest. Producer Artie Kornfeld then set up another recording date with their mother Barbara contributing vocals to the session, which yielded the stunning number two hit "The Rain, the Park and Other Things." The Cowsills' self-titled debut LP soon followed, and with the title track from 1968's *We Can Fly,* the family scored their second hit. "Indian Lake" reached the Top Ten later that year, and in 1969 the group scored their biggest chart entry with the title song from the rock musical *Hair.* By 1970, however, the Cowsills' career was on the decline, and in the wake of the 1971 LP *On My Side,* the group disbanded. In the late '70s, four siblings recorded a batch of original material, but the sessions remain unreleased. During the 1990s, Barry mounted a solo career, Bill founded the country group the Blue Shadows, and Susan joined the Continental Drifters. In 1998, the "core four"—Bob, John, Susan and Paul—recorded a new studio album, *Global.* *—Jason Ankeny*

● **20th Century Masters—The Millennium Collection: The Best of the Cowsills** / Jun. 26, 2001 / Polydor ♦♦♦♦
The Cowsills' volume of *20th Century Masters—The Millennium Collection: The Best of the Cowsills* contains nearly all of the group's biggest hits and best songs, including "The Rain, The Park, & Other Things," "Hair," and "Love American Style." Over the course of 12 songs, almost all of their hits are presented, along with Bill Cowsill's "When Everybody's Here," which means this will satisfy nearly all of their casual fans. Some diehards could use a longer collection, but the rest will find this to be a fine, entertaining collection. *—Stephen Thomas Erlewine*

Kevin Coyne

b. Jan. 27, 1944, Derby, England
Vocals, Guitar / Singer/Songwriter
There are plenty more heralded singer/songwriters, but few have produced more good work or have done so for longer than Kevin Coyne. Virtually unknown in America, Coyne has over 30 records, most of them very good, that deal primarily with outsiders: men, women, and children arbitrarily shunted to the fringes of society, or worse, locked away and left alone. He can be extraordinarily compassionate and, in the blink of an eye, angry, anguished, and accusatory. Perhaps the most durable and telling image of Kevin Coyne is the cover photo of his album *In Living Black and White.* On the front, Coyne is smiling and politely bowing to an unseen audience; the back of the album jacket is the same photo taken from the rear, with Coyne clutching an open straight razor. In 1973, Coyne began a relationship with the then-fledgling Virgin Records, who seemed willing to embrace the decidedly non-commercial, difficult performer. For the next eight years, he recorded some of his best music and, somewhat surprisingly, attained a modicum of commercial success, albeit in Europe only. These were mostly edgy, folk-rock records tinged with an avant-garde feel for performance art (Coyne is a published poet too), clearly not easy listening by any stretch of the imagination; neither were these records overly pretentious or unapproachable. By the early '80s, Coyne was recording for independent labels, making frustrating, semi-successful records that were erratically released and difficult to find. In late 1994, there was a major CD reissue series (only in England, of course) of Coyne's work. *—John Dougan*

Case History / 1971 / Dandelion ♦♦♦♦♦
Coyne's first solo recording is a triumphant, if occasionally bleak, look at life's outsiders. Using his time as social worker in a government-run mental hospital as a basis for his narratives, Coyne deals with issues of intense alienation, indifference, substance abuse (to which he was no stranger), and mental instability in a world that would rather forget these people existed, and a labyrinthine governmental bureaucracy that often denied their humanity. This is not a happy record, and is only infrequently hopeful, but it's never cynical, and neither does Coyne indulge in glib condescension. He acts as a subjective documentarian, an advocate for a group of people who desperately need one. Reissued on CD with extra tracks by the import label Dandelion/See For Miles in 1994. *—John Dougan*

● **Marjory Razorblade** / 1973 / Virgin ♦♦♦♦♦
Marjory Razorblade was Coyne's return to rock & roll after a two-year "retirement" to go back to social work. A two-LP set in England, edited to a single disc in America, it contains some of his most stunning material and, arguably, his single greatest song, "House on the Hill." A harrowing tale of institutional life, as told by an overmedicated patient, it's as emotionally complex and well-written a song as one is likely to hear. Still, tracks like "Eastbourne Ladies," which pokes fun at stylish women at English seaside resorts, proves that Coyne the satirist is capable of making people laugh as well as cry. With so many albums available, it's difficult (close to impossible) to find one Coyne recording that's vastly superior to the others. However, if you bought this or *Case History,* you'd be listening to Coyne in his prime. *—John Dougan*

Blame It on the Night / 1974 / Virgin ♦♦♦
At times it sounds like Coyne, or other forces, are attempting to make his music more commercial here, with the full, generic mid-'70s arrangements and occasional horns. That's a proposition as fruitless as selling snow to the Eskimos. Coyne is never going to be a mainstream artist; it seems more sensible to let him rip and be eccentric, playing in acoustic, stripped-down, bluesy contexts. Fortunately, that's what he does on about half the album, sounding his borderline lunatic self on "Don't Delude Me," and opting for an eerie, cryptic mood on "Blame It on the Night," and "Witch," with its flamenco guitars and undercurrent of suspicious paranoia. How not to gain commercial airplay, lesson 14: write lyrics such as "I cannot stand her friends anymore, I will wipe them across the floor" (from "Witch"). *—Richie Unterberger*

Matching Head & Feet / 1975 / Virgin ♦♦♦
By the mid-'70s, Coyne was becoming very much a "cult" artist: one that would be appreciated by a small but significant segment of fans, who would buy new releases not so much because they wanted the particular record, but because they liked the particular artist. This is the kind of collection that is going to be sought mostly by that cult, as it's not one of his stronger efforts, and not likely to be adapted by anyone who hasn't previously been exposed to Coyne. The arrangements are more conventional than most of his previous work (a pre-Police Andy Summers handles guitar), and much of the results are routine. Not lifeless, though; anything sung by Coyne will have roughness around the edges (and his voice here sometimes sounds not just raw, but downright worn). And songs about folks who carry guns, knives, and smash the faces of their wives (in "Turpentine") are not your usual rock fare. The words *are* unconventional, but the settings are average in a mid-'70s way, which dilutes the lyrics' impact, and makes this an unmemorable effort on the whole. *—Richie Unterberger*

In Living Black & White / 1976 / Virgin ♦♦♦
As with *Marjory Razor Blade,* this live recording was edited down to one disc for American consumption. My advice is to find the 2-LP import and get the whole Kevin Coyne experience. Backed by a great band (perhaps his best), with dazzling guitar playing from soon-to-be Police guitarist Andy Summers, Coyne is in great form here, bellowing and braying the songs with inexhaustible energy. Excellent versions of "House on the Hill," and the searing "Turpentine," and "Fat Girl" (about a depressed, overweight woman's suicide). A great record from start to finish. *—John Dougan*

Dynamite Daze / 1978 / Virgin ♦♦♦

Babble / 1979 / Virgin ✦✦✦
A match made in heaven: Coyne singing a series of songs about the successes and failures of communication between lovers with the female perspective provided by German chanteuse (ex-Henry Cow/Slapp Happy/Art Bears) Dagmar Krause. Rather than sing duets, Coyne and Krause trade songs in a series of statements and responses. Occasionally the songwriting is thin, but the powerful singing and intense emotions more than make up for any lapses. This is a richly rewarding and frequently compelling record about love, communication and commitment that is never sanctimonious, obvious or cloying. Difficult to find (damn near impossible), but well worth the effort. *—John Dougan*

Boxed Set: Dandelion Years / 1980 / Butt ✦✦✦✦✦
This three-disc box set includes both *Siren* and *Case History*, making it an essential release. The *Siren* material holds up extremely well, thankfully eschewing art-rock (which was becoming all the rage in late-'60s London) for a grubby, blues-based pub-rock sound. Coyne is in particularly good form (and good spirits), making this a wonderful glimpse into his early years. Unfortunately, in America, this box set seemed to disappear almost immediately after its release. Good luck finding a copy. *—John Dougan*

Peel Sessions / 1990 / Dutch East India ✦✦

Wild Tiger Love / 1991 / Golden Hind/Rockport ✦✦✦
Since his 1970s peak, Coyne's voice has deepened and lost some of its rough edge. As a poet, his powers are pretty much undimmed; even a nominally romantic song like "The Bungalow Song" has a bit of paranoid madness creeping in at the edges. When Coyne sticks primarily to acoustic guitar, the results are pretty good. Problems arise when the arrangements are filled out with a more generic rock band sound. Coyne, like so many artists, is a case of "less is more"; the more "produced" cuts, with their lazily mainstream tonal qualities, sit uneasily beside stark oddities like "Fish Brain" and "Open up the Gates." The better, more passionate cuts may make this worth tracking down for serious Coyne fans, but it's a patchy recording overall. *—Richie Unterberger*

Tough and Sweet / 1993 / Rockport ✦✦

Elvira: Songs from the Archive / 1994 / Golden Hind/Rockport ✦✦✦
A combination of two separate sessions, one from 1979, one from 1983. The 1979 tracks were originally conceived as a one-woman show about Elvira Barney, an English debutante who shot her boyfriend, although it never went into production. Almost all of the tracks feature no instrumentation save Coyne's acoustic guitar. It's suitably harrowing stuff, typical of Coyne's fine walk between sanity and instability, though here he is taking on the persona of another character (the fact that it's a female character adds another level of strangeness). The 1983 sessions, by contrast, have abrasive, sometimes chaotic backing that sometimes skirts free jazz, though Coyne's lyrics remain chillingly sardonic and neurotic. It's worth searching for if you liked Coyne's early, sparse recordings. *—Richie Unterberger*

● **Sign Of The Times** / 1994 / Virgin Records (UK) ✦✦✦✦✦
Uneasy listening for the psychotic set—if the often splintered music doesn't put you off, the tortured, lonely lyrics may, and if that doesn't do it, Coyne's hurt, angry, forceful vocals ought to do the trick. Coyne's songs come out of his experience working with psychiatric patients, people living on the edge—one of the songs in this compilation, "Witch," provides quite a graphic view of his history, with the accompanying wordless vocal turning into helpless shrieking as the main vocal sneers and snaps through a narrative that becomes gradually more psychotic as it goes on. Coyne, alas, is both brilliant and *painful*, an artist who is difficult to take in anything but small doses. This compilation touches on the highlights of the records Coyne made for Virgin and should serve as an excellent introduction to his work. *—Steven McDonald*

Case History . . . Plus / 1995 / See For Miles ✦✦✦✦✦

The Adventures of Crazy Frank / 1995 / Rockport ✦✦✦
A bit of an upturn for Coyne, this is a song cycle of sorts about a troubled, alcoholic comedian whose life bears some similarity to Coyne's own experiences. It's a more low-key, unforced affair than some of his previous '90s albums. Sometimes the rough, weathered quality of his voice makes him sound like a male counterpoint to post-*Broken English* Marianne Faithfull; at his mellowest moments, he sounds a bit like a very debauched Van Morrison. On the whole it's one of his gentlest, most compassionate works, though not one of his more impressive. *—Richie Unterberger*

Sugar Candy Taxi / Apr. 20, 1999 / Ruf ✦✦✦
"I see this record as a return to roots, as a heartfelt blast from the soul," writes Coyne in the liner notes. That's an overdone sentiment when it comes to artists promoting their latest album, but in this case it is correct. With the exception, oddly, of the title cut, which has a mainstream flavor to the arrangement that seems to have been designed with picking up some airplay or something, the production is usually spare. And that is the context in which Coyne best shines, when his scratchy voice (made scratchier by age) and jagged guitar are at the forefront. (Auteurish artists such as Coyne are *never* made better by more production.) By the time he repeats "maybe I'm paranoid" throughout the second track, "Porcupine People," you know the eccentric, quasi-disturbed Coyne is back in town. Coyne's extemporized-sounding lyrics are usually witty and occasionally gripping, sometimes getting into territory—fooling around with "My Wife's Best Friend," the deranged despair of "Normal Man"—that will unsettle those who want music to soothe rather than provoke. Although much of this is of the minimal folky art rock that typified his early '70s work, some care is taken for stylistic variety, as in the wheezy flutes that dance in the background of "Porcupine People, the free jazzy piano and sax of "Rusting Away," or the almost avant-garde gospel of the a cappella voices on "Little White Arms." *—Richie Unterberger*

Room Full of Fools / Oct. 24, 2000 / Ruf ✦✦✦
The result of his first recording sessions in the U.S., *Room Full of Fools* offers more of what we've come to expect from Coyne: anguished, sometimes verging-on-deranged narratives of life's underside. This is territory that's been mined far more in the 1980s and 1990s than it was when Coyne came to prominence in the 1970s, so you could view this as a statement from an elder statesman of the style, or something that's bound to sound less fresh than it did earlier in his career. Coyne does retain his ability to convey angst with more sincerity and humor, albeit very dark humor, than most such practitioners. It's harder-rocking than usual, which works to its disadvantage more often than not; the full blues-rock arrangements just sound too conventional in juxtaposition with Coyne's far from ordinary voice and lyrics. When he slows it down for something more acoustic and even bluesier, or the swirling organ comes more to the fore, his restrained rantings find a more suitable context. Subject-wise, Coyne casts his net over material that's run-of-the-mill for him, but not to be found in the work of many popular music singers: uncertain mental stability, incorrigible boys, and the mundane irritations of not-so-happy lives. That's balanced by some warped optimism and romantic longing, like a man who's down for a count but keeps managing to rise for more battering. It's idiosyncratic and heartfelt stuff, but apt to make any listener caught in the wrong mood feel as irritated and agitated as the mental landscape of his compositions. *—Richie Unterberger*

Cracker

f. 1991
American Trad Rock, Adult Alternative Pop/Rock, Alternative Pop/Rock
While he was the frontman for Camper Van Beethoven, it seemed that it would take nothing short of a miracle to make guitarist/singer David Lowery a favorite of mainstream rockers, but that's what he and his second band, Cracker, have become. Led by Lowery and guitarist Johnny Hickman, Cracker is much more straightforward than Camper; Cracker concentrates on rock and country, creating a twisted, rootsy rock & roll that sounds like a post-punk Rolling Stones or Little Feat. While their self-titled 1992 debut had moments of raw brilliance, Cracker's second album, 1993's *Kerosene Hat*, fulfilled their promise. Powered by the hit single "Low," the album was a hard-rocking meeting of traditional rock and post-punk sensibilities. Like Camper Van Beethoven's albums, it deserved to be heard by a wide audience; this time Lowery found a larger audience—*Kerosene Hat* eventually went gold.

Cracker released their third album, *The Golden Age*, in the spring of 1996. The album didn't repeat the success of its predecessor, falling off the charts within three months of its release. *Gentleman's Blues* followed in 1998. *—Stephen Thomas Erlewine*

Cracker / Mar. 10, 1992 / Virgin ✦✦✦✦
Apart from David Lowery's tendency to slip in some smug, self-serving lyrics, Cracker's debut is a terrific rock & roll record, full of energetic three-chord bashers and surprisingly moving ballads. *—Stephen Thomas Erlewine*

Kerosene Hat / Aug. 24, 1993 / Virgin ✦✦✦✦
With their second album, Cracker have lost the smarmy self-righteousness that plagued their otherwise fine debut, replacing it with a surprisingly solid, rocking core. *Kerosene Hat* is David Lowery's least affected album yet—its humor is no stranger than "Dead Flowers" by the Stones or "Fat Man in a Bathtub" by Little Feat, two groups that Cracker strongly recall throughout the album. *Kerosene Hat* is more blues- and country-based than their debut, but it sounds natural, since their songwriting has improved and they've grown tighter as a unit. *—Stephen Thomas Erlewine*

The Golden Age / Apr. 2, 1996 / Virgin ✦✦✦
Kerosene Hat, Cracker's second album, was an unexpected hit because of its off-kilter charm. Though Cracker rocked hard throughout the record, they also threw in fractured pop and country tunes that gave the album a broader appeal. The band's follow-up album, *The Golden Age*, tries to expand on that appeal by burying the weirdness inherent in David Lowery's songwriting with loud, grungy guitars and a more streamlined production. The change is evident from the record's leadoff track, "I Hate My Generation." With its pounding rhythms and grunge-drenched guitars, it may have been intended as a parody of '90s Generation-X angst, but the riffs and melodies are so slight that it fails embarassingly. In fact, most of the louder numbers on *The Golden Age* are forced and underdeveloped. What saves the record is when Cracker turn the volume down, whether it's the country-rock of the title track, the goofy pop of "How Can I Live Without You," or the dusty psychedelia of "Bicycle Spaniard." Once you dig past the surface of the loud guitars, it becomes apparent that there's an abundance of quiet gems scattered throughout *The Golden Age*, and that is what makes the album worthwhile listening. *—Stephen Thomas Erlewine*

Gentleman's Blues / Aug. 25, 1998 / Virgin ✦✦✦
Cracker's third album, *The Golden Age*, was uneven, but it also suffered from bad timing: When it was released in the spring of 1996, the bottom had just fallen out of alternative guitar rock, and Cracker was left without the large audience that made their first two albums hits. Realizing this conundrum, and approaching middle age, frontman David Lowery decided to stop trying to score modern rock hits and simply play for Cracker's fourth album, *Gentleman's Blues*. Picking up musical cues from *Kerosene Hat* and the quieter moments of *The Golden Age*, Lowery and his partner, Johnny Hickman, fall back to their beloved '70s album rock, mixing up blues-rock, hard rock, Southern rock, and Dead-like jams. Apart from Lowery's characteristically quirky, absurdist lyrics, *Gentleman's Blues* sounds as if it could have been recorded in the early '70s. It does sound as if they no longer care about being contemporary, but their easy charm and shambling delivery are so appealing, it doesn't matter if the album is indeed a retreat. Beneath the surface, however, there's a certain weariness unheard of in earlier Cracker albums. Many of Lowery's songs,

such as "Seven Days," have a bitterness that's barely masked by his irony and songcraft. It may be a shock to discover those sentiments lurking behind these appealing songs, but that's what makes *Gentleman's Blues* worth repeated listens. —*Stephen Thomas Erlewine*

● **Garage d'Or** / Mar. 14, 2000 / Virgin ✦✦✦✦
Garage d'Or chronicles Cracker's rise and fall, choosing to cut corners where it better suits the band's legacy. For instance, "I Hate My Generation" is nowhere to be found on the 16-track disc, but a cover of the Flamin' Groovies' "Shake Some Action" (from the *Clueless* soundtrack) is. Why, you ask? Because *Garage D'Or* is designed for Cracker's core audience—not the people who requested "Low" every hour on the hour, but those who understood all the musical references, jokes, and lyrical allusions, and cherished each little detail. Consequently, it may not be "comprehensive," in the traditional sense of the word, but there's little question that it is definitive, capturing the wry essence of the band. Based on these 16 tracks, including all their modern rock radio hits (except "Happy Birthday to Me"), Cracker might not have been the great overlooked band of the '90s, but they were still quite good. They still may not be for every listener. Fans of Camper Van Beethoven will find this a little too obvious, though they'll certainly treasure such bizarre little gems as the priceless travelogue "Euro-Trash Girl" (originally a "hidden" bonus track at the end of *Kerosene Hat*, and arguably their finest moment). Trad rock fans who might be receptive to the the general sound of the band may find the lyrical irony a little quirky for their tastes. That was their problem in a nutshell: Despite being musically accessible, they didn't appeal to everyone. Naturally, that's what makes them more lovable in the eyes of hardcore fans, and *Garage D'Or* goes a long way to proving that those fans just may be right. —*Stephen Thomas Erlewine*

Sarah Cracknell

Indie Pop, Alternative Pop/Rock
The frontwoman for beloved British club-pop trio Saint Etienne, diva Sarah Cracknell was born April 12, 1967 in Chelmsford, Essex; raised primarily in the Windsor area, as a youth she attended convent school, and later briefly studied drama. After a stint with the little-known Prime Time, in the spring of 1991 Cracknell was recruited to sing on the third Saint Etienne single "Nothing Can Stop Us"; her cool allure fit perfectly with the group's sophisticated indie-dance approach, and after contributing heavily to their 1991 debut LP *Fox Base Alpha* she was made an official member of the lineup. After completing two more Saint Etienne albums, 1993's *So Tough* and 1994's *Tiger Bay*, in the summer of 1996 Cracknell issued her debut solo single "Anymore"; an LP, *Lipslide*, followed in the spring. And in the midst of recording and releasing Saint Etienne's fifth album *Sound of Water* in summer 2000, Cracknell balanced out another solo effort entitled *Kelly's Locker*, which appeared in September. —*Jason Ankeny*

● **Lipslide** / May 1997 / Instinct ✦✦✦✦
Recorded as St. Etienne was on an extended hiatus, Sarah Cracknell's solo debut *Lipslide* is a breezy, endearing record that wears its lightweight aspirations proudly. Divided equally between Euro-dance and British Invasion pop, *Lipslide* is a triumph of style over substance, but its surfaces are so appealing that the uneven songwriting doesn't matter. And when Cracknell's writing does succeed, as on "Anymore," "Ready or Not," and "Taxi," *Lipslide* shines with both infectious, well-crafted melodies and sparkling, sunny charm. —*Stephen Thomas Erlewine*

Kelly's Locker / Sep. 12, 2000 / Instinct ✦✦✦
Saint Etienne's glossy chanteuse Sarah Cracknell picks up where her debut album *Lipslide* left off with the exclusive release of *Kelly's Locker*, an eight track look at Cracknell's sheer Europop harmonies and dreamy female grace.

She is often compared to '60s pop diva Dusty Springfield, but Cracknell is humbly her own popstar. This release is a bit more synth-driven, and songs like "Taking off for France" and "Taxi" exude a sophisticated disco flair that's naturally linked to Cracknell's sweet but smooth persona. She follows the funk, playing into quick blues tinges and frolicking drum 'n' bass. What's most alluring is Cracknell's cover version of the Charmels' 1969 Stax track "Sea Shells." It's absolutely fantastic; modern day breakbeats loosely carrying back to nostalgia. *Kelly's Locker* is a refreshing and decent solo effort for Ms. Cracknell; a fundamental addition to any Saint Etienne collection or pop music enthusiast. —*MacKenzie Wilson*

The Cramps

f. 1976, New York, NY
Psychobilly, Rockabilly Revival, Post-Punk, Alternative Pop/Rock, American Underground
The Cramps' unique sound synthesizes classic rockabilly, touches of psychedelia, and lyrical fare devoted mostly to monster movies and sleazy sex into an infectious, gloriously tasteless conglomeration of American trash culture. While their subject matter may verge on offensive to some, their obvious sense of humor and the fun, disposable feel of their best work prevent the listener from ever taking things more seriously than they should. The group was formed by vocalist Erick "Lux Interior" Purkhiser and guitarist Kirsty "Poison Ivy Rorschach" Wallace, who met in Sacramento and found they shared an affinity for obscure '50s rockabilly and surf records and junk culture. The Cramps eventually went to the legendary Sun studio with cult icon Alex Chilton producing to record several singles, later released on the *Gravest Hits* EP. Chilton also produced their minimalistic 1980 debut album, *Songs the Lord Taught Us.* Following the 1983 live EP *Smell of Female*, the Cramps sued I.R.S. for lack of support; the case was settled out of court and resulted in the band being released from the label. Nothing more was heard from them in the way of new material for years; their only new album prior to 1990, 1986's *A Date with Elvis*, was not released in the U.S. until four years later. —*Steve Huey*

Gravest Hits / Jul. 1979 / Illegal ✦✦✦
This first release by the Cramps shows the group laying out many of the aspects of their curious style in rudimentary fashion. Raw, slashing guitar playing derived mostly from rockabilly and somewhat from psychedelic and 1960s garage pop (the group would have no bass player until the mid-'80s) and primitive drumming provide the platform for Lux Interior's eccentric singing, which is best described as a hyper-crazed, reverb-drenched, exhibitionist rockabilly style complete with groaning, shouting, growling, and hiccuping effects. The only song written by the band here is "Human Fly," a skulking mid-tempo fuzz-guitar number with monster movie lyrics; the line "I got 96 tears/And 96 eyes" is a sly reference to the ? and the Mysterians garage band hit. The other selections are covers of classic 1950s and 1960s songs; these include a bizarre version of the Ricky Nelson crooning hit "Lonesome Town" that peppers the musical texture with stray guitar interjections, and a rip-snorting version of the Trashmen song "Surfin' Bird" that ends with a long, noisy improvisation section of doubtful tonal focus. The cavernous sound quality lends a certain bleak feel to the music here, but distortions on the vocal in "Human Fly" and drums on "Lonesome Town" merely sound poor. This unpolished but effective release is worth hearing. —*David Cleary*

Songs the Lord Taught Us / May 1980 / IRS ✦✦✦✦
Continuing the spooked-out and raging snarls of *Gravest Hits*, the Cramps once again worked with Alex Chilton on the group's full-album debut, *Songs the Lord Taught Us.* The jacket reads "file under: sacred music," but only if one's definition includes the holy love of rockabilly sex-stomp, something which the Cramps fulfill in spades. Having spent *Gravest Hits* mostly doing revamps of older material, the foursome tackled a slew of originals like "The Mad Daddy" and "TV Set" this time around, creating one of the few neo-rockabilly records worthy of the name. Years later *Songs* still drips with threat and desire both, testament to both the band's worth and Chilton's just-right production. "Garbageman" surfaced as a single in some areas, a wise choice given the at-once catchy roll of the song and downright frightening guitar snarls, especially on the solo. The covers of the Sonics' "Strychnine" and Billy Burnette's "Tear It Up"—not to mention the concluding riff on "Fever"—all challenge the originals. Interior has the wailing, hiccuping, and more down pat, but transformed into his own breathless howl, while Ivy and Gregory keep up the electric fuzz through more layers of echo than legality should allow. Knox helms the drums relentlessly; instead of punching through arena rock style, Chilton keeps the rushed rhythm running along in the back, increasing the sheer psychosis of it all. —*Ned Raggett*

Psychedelic Jungle / May 1981 / IRS ✦✦✦✦
Here, Kid Congo Powers and Ivy form just as fine a team as she and Gregory did on earlier releases, and if things aren't always as flat-out fried as on *Gravest Hits* and *Songs*, the same atmosphere of swampy, trashy, rockabilly-into-voodoo ramalama reigns supreme. The song titles alone show the band hasn't really changed its sights any: the opening two cuts are covers, "Green Fuz" and "Goo Goo Muck," while originals include "Caveman," "Can't Find My Mind," and the brilliant "The Natives Are Restless." Then there's "Don't Eat Stuff Off the Sidewalk," which almost sounds worthy of a Frank Zappa freakout (at least lyrically). Other legendary tracks like "Primitive" and "Green Door" get the Cramps makeover this time out, with the proper mix of respect and hot-wired energy, while "The Crusher" sounds like Interior's on the verge of going completely insane. The Cramps themselves take over the production this time out, resulting in a cleaner, crisper sound (especially when it comes to Knox's drums) that isn't quite as wired, for better or for worse. As commanding showmen, though, the quartet's style comes through big time, with Interior throwing in appropriate yells, yipes, and other sounds where appropriate; his antics at the end of "Goo Goo Muck" are especially gone. If anything, the moodier strutting throughout increases the creepiness of what's afoot; if things aren't psychedelic in the commonly accepted sense, it's certainly not easy listening. Interior sometimes sounds almost normal, but with the sense that something strange is lurking just around the corner, and Ivy is still one of the best guitarists around, her snarling reverb worth a thousand fret-shredders. —*Ned Raggett*

Smell of Female / 1983 / Capitol/Enigma ✦✦✦
One gets the feeling from the title and cover art alone that if the Cramps could have released this live document in Glorious Smell-o-rama they would have jumped at the chance. Even without it one can almost sense the whiffs of perspiration and energy the group was cooking up; recorded at New York's Peppermint Lounge with Powers on guitar, the quartet slams out a then mostly entirely new set of songs with, as expected, appropriate covers as needed. The wonderfully profane take on Hasil Adkins' "She Said" surfaces here, with Interior sounding like he's about to die more than once. The Count Five's "Psychotic Reaction" and the perfectly appropriate "Faster Pussycat," taken from the legendary Russ Meyer film of the same name, also give the band more than a little something to chew on. As for the originals, the usual mess of swampy rockabilly and industrial strength noise comes together in just the right way from the start. "Thee Most Exalted Potentate of Love" gives Interior the chance to do his undead but still wired loveman thang right from the start, while Ivy and Powers hit the twang hard and Knox keeps everything going just right. "Call of the Wighat" is another highpoint, with Knox showing that he's up to more involved pounding and percussion when the need arises. A studio cut, "Surfin' Dead," surfaces as a ringer at the end; if not quite the Cramps go Beach Boys, it arguably forecasts the Jesus and Mary Chain's "Kill Surf City" just enough. —*Ned Raggett*

● **Bad Music for Bad People** / 1984 / IRS ✦✦✦✦
An extremely skimpy compilation, *Bad Music* is only 31 minutes long. Still, this dog's breakfast of material, assembled upon the Cramps' departure from IRS, was the only place for a variety of B-sides and rarities, at least for a long while. The most well-known

is "New Kind of Kick," covered later by the the Jesus and Mary Chain. It isn't as out there sonically as that band, but it has plenty of attitude to burn, with Interior getting lyrically rude more than once and Ivy turning in some fierce, screeching guitar. Another winner is the sassy "Drug Train," originally the B-side to "Garbageman," which celebrates debauchery with the expected gusto. Knox gets to show his command for steady but right drumming on this one, while Interior and Ivy go crazy with the usual vim. The usual selection of covers of rockabilly and garage rarities surfaces, most memorably with a ripping redo of rock & roll wildman Hasil Adkins' "She Said." The rave-up qualities are brought out in a full-bodied performance, while Interior sounds like he's been either dug up from a grave or a swamp. More semi-hits like "Human Fly" and "Goo Goo Muck" surface as well, making the whole release a fine if overly short overview of the Cramps' vision of the universe. Production at points ventures into the totally primitive—all the more appropriate for the band in question, admittedly—giving everything the necessarily rough-and-ready atmosphere for the group's own brand of scummy sleaze. The artwork is notable in its own right, with the fleshless big-haired ghoul on the cover having turned into an icon for the Cramps and goth/rockabilly music worldwide. —*Ned Raggett*

Date with Elvis / 1986 / Restless ♦♦♦
After *Psychedelic Jungle*, the Cramps experienced personnel and record label difficulties; they would not release another studio album until this one, four years later. Gone here are the tinny sound quality and horror-flick-based lyrics of prior releases, replaced by clearer sonics and an often hilarious obsession with sex (examples of the latter can be found on "What's Inside a Girl?," "The Hot Pearl Snatch," "Cornfed Dames," "(Hot Pool of) Womanneed," "How Far Can Too Far Go?," and the uproarious single "Can Your Pussy Do the Dog?"). There are numerous sly references in the verses to high and low culture icons, including "Shake it one time for me" (a line from Jerry Lee Lewis' "Whole Lotta Shakin' Goin' On"), "I'll be dancing through the flames/Like a devil in disguise" (a nod to the Elvis Presley hit), and "Now there's more things in Tennessee/Than is dreamed of in your philosophy" (a paraphrase of a line from Shakespeare's *Hamlet*). Most of the songs here are in various rockabilly-derived styles featuring either garage-band fuzz or Duane Eddy twanging guitar from Poison Ivy. Vocalist Lux Interior is in excellent form here, exhibiting a fair bit of variety within his usual 1950s-derived approach. "Kizmiaz" is unique in the band's oeuvre, being a smarmy parody of 1960s hippie feel-good music; Ivy joins Interior on vocals here. Intonation is off in a few numbers (notably on "Kizmiaz," "The Hot Pearl Snatch," and "Can Your Pussy Do the Dog?"), but this is not enough to detract from the overall excellence here. This rollicking and energetic platter in particular is the equal of any in their canon and an essential listen. —*David Cleary*

Rockin' 'N Reelin' in Auckland, New Zealand / 1987 / Vengeance ♦♦♦
From 1986 to 1990, the Cramps eschewed studio work in favor of extensive touring; this album documents a live show from August 1986. The sound quality is crude at best, but the Cramps' music and attitude are just as crude, so the already wild performances are actually somewhat enhanced. The repertoire relies heavily on *A Date With Elvis* and also features covers of "Heartbreak Hotel" and "Do the Clam." —*Steve Huey*

Psychedelic Jungle/Gravest Hits / Aug. 4, 1989 / IRS ♦♦♦♦
Combining what is arguably the band's finest full-length album with their debut collection of covers, *Psychedelic Jungle/Gravest Hits* offers up a substantial dose of the Cramps' punk-strained mix of rockabilly music and '50s horror flick aesthetics. Lux Interior's ghoulishly manic vocals, Poison Ivy's treble-heavy guitar distortion, and Knick Knox's tribal beat are all ideally showcased on such Cramps classics as "Goo Goo Muck," "Primitive," "Green Door," and "The Crusher." While these are all fine covers, originals such as "Caveman," "Can't Find My Mind," and "Beautiful Garden" demonstrate the Cramps could take their rockabilly roots to fetchingly gothic extremes. Adding to the riches from *Psychedelic Jungle*, the 5-song EP *Gravest Hits* features inimitable versions of the Trashmen's "Surfin' Bird," Roy Orbison's early rockabilly side "Domino," and the Ricky Nelson hit "Lonesome Town." With quality roundups hard to come by, Cramps fans would do well to pick this two-fer of the band's prime early material. —*Stephen Cook*

Creature from the Black Leather Lagoon / 1990 / Enigma ♦♦♦
This five-song EP contains the demented sleaze of the title track and tunes like "Jackyard Backoff" and "Beat Out My Love," plus covers of "Jailhouse Rock" and a live version of Carl Perkins' "Her Love Rubbed Off." —*Steve Huey*

Stay Sick! / Jan. 1990 / Capitol/Enigma ♦♦

Look Mom No Head! / Nov. 1991 / Restless/Enigma ♦♦
The Cramps' humor has always relied on trashy tastelessness, but even at its most offensive, it is usually delivered with a wink, preventing it from degenerating into mindless vulgarity. Unfortunately, *Look Mom No Head* doesn't do a good job of retaining this balance, as the flat performances and lack of intensity and energy fail to supply the irony necessary for the Cramps' music to work well. Sleaze without fun is simply embarrassing. —*Steve Huey*

Collection / Oct. 19, 1993 / Castle ♦♦♦

Flamejob / Oct. 11, 1994 / Medicine Label/Warner Brothers ♦♦♦
Something of a return to form, *FlameJob* features the band's most committed, energetic performances in quite some time, with wild, crazed vocals from Lux Interior and sizzling guitar work from Poison Ivy enlivening some of the band's most entertainingly stupid and crude offerings in recent memory, including "Let's Get Fucked Up" and "Inside Out and Upside Down (With You)." The failed stylistic experiments of some recent work are gone, replaced by simple, straight-ahead vintage Cramps psychobilly. Also featured is a cover of "Route 66." —*Steve Huey*

Big Beat from Badsville / Sep. 23, 1997 / Epitaph ♦♦♦
As the Cramps approached their 20th anniversary, they showed no signs of changing their signature kitschy psychobilly style. In so many ways, *Big Beat From Badsville* is no different from its immediate predecessor, *Flamejob*, or any of the group's other records—it's a collection of campy songs about sex, horror, violence, leather and perversion. Sonically, it's slightly rawer than *Flamejob*, and the group's performances are as inspired here as they are on any of their other '90s albums. And the songs are uniformly good, even if there aren't any standouts. So, *Big Beat From Badsville* is the kind of record that fans will be pleased with, but newcomers will just wonder what the big deal is. —*Stephen Thomas Erlewine*

The Cranberries

f. 1990
Celtic Rock, Adult Alternative Pop/Rock, Alternative Pop/Rock
Combining the melodic jangle of post-Smiths indie-guitar-pop with the lilting, trance-inducing sonic textures of late '80s dream-pop and adding a slight Celtic tint, the Cranberries became one of the more successful groups to emerge from the pre-Britpop UK indie scene of the early '90s. Led by vocalist Dolores O'Riordan, whose keening, powerful voice is the most distinctive element of the group's sound, the group initially made little impact in the United Kingdom. It wasn't until the lush ballad "Linger" became an American hit in 1993 that the band also achieved mass success in the UK. Following the success of "Linger," the Cranberries quickly became international stars, as both their 1993 debut album, *Everybody Else Is Doing It, So Why Can't We* and its 1994 follow-up, *No Need to Argue*, sold millions of copies and produced a string of hit singles. By the time of their third album, 1996's *To the Faithful Departed*, the group had added distorted guitars to its sonic pallete and attempted to make more socially significant music, which resulted in a downturn in the band's commercial fortunes. —*Stephen Thomas Erlewine*

● **Everybody Else Is Doing It, So Why Can't We?** / Apr. 20, 1993 / Island ♦♦♦♦♦
Title aside, what the Cranberries *were* doing wasn't that common at the time, at least in mainstream pop terms; grunge and G-funk had done their respective big splashes via Nirvana and Dr. Dre when *Everybody* came out first in the U.K. and then in America some months later. Lead guitarist Noel Hogan is in many ways the true center of the band at this point, co-writing all but three songs with O'Riordan and showing an amazing economy in his playing, and having longtime Smiths/Morrissey producer Stephen Street behind the boards meant that the right blend of projection and delicacy still held sway. One can tell he likes Johnny Marr and his ability to do the job just right: check out the quick strums and blasts on "Pretty" or the concluding part of the lovely "Waltzing Back." O'Riordan herself offers up a number of romantic ponderings and considerations lyrically (as well as playing perfectly fine acoustic guitar), and her undisputed vocal ability suits the material perfectly. The two best cuts were the deserved smashes: "Dreams," a brisk, charging number combining low-key tension and full-on rock, and the melancholic, string-swept break-up song "Linger." If *Everybody* is in the end a derivative pleasure—and O'Riordan's vocal acrobatics would never again be so relatively calm in comparison—a pleasure it remains nonetheless, the work of a young band creating a fine little synthesis. —*Ned Raggett*

No Need to Argue / 1994 / Island ♦♦♦♦♦
With their surprise success behind them, the Cranberries went ahead and essentially created a sequel to *Everybody Else is Doing It, So Why Can't We* with only tiny variations, with mixed results. The fact that the album is essentially a redo of previously established stylistic ground isn't apparent in just the production, handled again by Stephen Street, or the overall sound, or even that one particularly fine song is called "Dreaming My Dreams." *Everybody* wasn't a laugh riot, to be sure, but *No Need To Argue* starts to see O'Riordan take a more commanding and unfortunately much more self-conscious role that ended up not standing the band in good stead later. Lead single "Zombie" is the worst offender in this regard—the heavy rock trudge isn't immediately suited for the band's strengths (notably, O'Riordan wrote this without Noel Hogan)—while the subject matter—the continuing Northern Ireland tensions—ends up sounding trivialized. Opening cut "Ode to My Family" is actually one of the band's best, with a lovely string arrangement created by O'Riordan, but her overdubbed vocals start showing her distinct vocal tics becoming a bit more gimmicky at the expense of the performance. Where *No Need* succeeds best is when the Cranberries stick at what they know, resulting in a number of charmers like "Twenty One," the uilleann pipes-touched "Daffodil's Lament," which has an epic sweep that doesn't overbear like "Zombie," and the evocative "Disappointment." —*Ned Raggett*

To the Faithful Departed / Apr. 30, 1996 / Island ♦♦

Bury the Hatchet / Apr. 27, 1999 / Island ♦♦♦
The Cranberries stumbled with their move toward heavier, politically fueled modern rock on *To the Faithful Departed*, losing fans enamored with their earlier sound. Like many groups that see their stardom fading, the band decided to return after a short hiatus with a mildly updated, immaculately constructed distillation of everything that earned them an audience in the first place. It's immediately apparent that *Bury the Hatchet* has retreated from the ludicrous posturing that marred *To the Faithful*. There are no blasts of distorted guitar—as a matter of fact, there are no songs that even qualify as "rockers"—and there is little preaching, even on Dolores O'Riordan's most earnest songs. Every note and gesture is pitched at the adult alternative mainstream, which is a good thing. Though they ran away from the dreamy jangle of their first hits, the Cranberries never sounded more convincing than on mid-tempo, folky pop tunes with polished productions. Sonically, that's precisely what *Bury the Hatchet* delivers, complete with little flourishes—a Bacharachian horn chart there, cinematic strings there—to illustrate that the band did indeed know what was hip in the late '90s. All this planning—some might call it calculation—shouldn't come as a surprise, since *Bury the Hatchet* is essentially a make-or-break

album, but what *is* a surprise is that the end result is the most consistent record of their career. It's not necessarily their best—it lacks the immediate singles of their first two records—but all the songs work together to form a whole; not even embarrassments like the skittering "Copycat" interrupt the flow of the record. True, the album never challenges listeners, but it delivers on their expectations—and after *To the Faithful Departed*, that comes as a relief. *—Stephen Thomas Erlewine*

Crazy Elephant

f. 1968, **db.** 1970

Bubblegum, AM Pop

Crazy Elephant was one of the seemingly endless aliases employed by the Kasenetz-Katz production duo to market their bubblegum hits of the late 1960s. Primarily a vehicle for session vocalist Robert Spencer—previously known for his lead performance on the Cadillacs' 1956 hit "Speedo"—Crazy Elephant was the name appended to the Kasenetz-Katz production of the song "Gimme Gimme Good Lovin'"; after the master was rejected by Buddah Records, the Super K Productions duo's primary outlet, they instead shopped the track to the Bell label, for whom it fell just shy of the U.S. Top Ten in 1969. Despite the single's success, however, Crazy Elephant failed to reach the charts again, instead becoming yet another interchangeable cog in the Kasenetz-Katz hit machine. *—Jason Ankeny*

Crazy Elephant / 1969 / Bell ✦✦✦

After failing to secure a recording contract with Buddah Records, the Kasenetz-Katz production team-sponsored band Crazy Elephant found a home with Bell Records and released a self-titled album. This Rock in Beat release is a straight reissue of that lone album from the band originally released in 1969 and includes one bonus track. The album contains mainly original compositions by band members and Kasenetz and Katz together with an odd psychedelic R&B cover of Otis Redding's "Respect" and the very strange heavy version of the Leonard Bernstein song "Somewhere." While the music on this album does have a bubblegum feel to it, the entire album is more overtly psychedelic with swirling organ, fuzz guitars, and even horns, in the style of a less heavy Vanilla Fudge or Rare Earth. Crazy Elephant did manage to produce a hit single in 1969 with the song "Gimme, Gimme Good Lovin'" that featured vocals by Robert Spencer, former lead vocalist from the '50s band the Cadillacs. *—Keith Pettipas*

Crazy Horse

Hard Rock, Album Rock

Out of all the backing bands that Neil Young has recorded and performed with during his long and illustrious career, the best known of the bunch remains Crazy Horse. The band's roots lay in the obscure early-'60s doo wop band Danny and the Memories, which contained future Crazy Horse members Danny Whitten, Billy Talbot, and Ralph Molina, among others. Shortly after their 1968 self-titled debut release as the Rockets, Whitten and Talbot met Neil Young, who had just left Buffalo Springfield and was about to launch a solo career. Young's sophomore effort, 1969's classic *Everybody Knows This Is Nowhere*, established Young and Crazy Horse as one of the most promising new rock bands of the time. Crazy Horse inked their own recording contract, resulting in their 1971 self-titled debut. But just as their own recording career began, Whitten became addicted to heroin, resulting in his leaving by 1972. Crazy Horse continued on with a revolving door of replacement members for a pair of lackluster albums in 1972. When Young heard about Whitten's deteriorating condition, he wanted to help out his old friend, and asked Whitten to be part of his touring band. But when Whitten proved to be too far gone during rehearsals, he was fired. On the same night he left Young and the band (November 18, 1972), Whitten overdosed and died. Devastated, Young reconvened with the surviving members of Crazy Horse by the summer of 1973, working on a set of dark songs that he'd written about the seedier side of life, which wouldn't see the light of day until 1975 as *Tonight's the Night*. The same year, the group named their official replacement for Whitten, newcomer Frank "Poncho" Sampedro. *—Greg Prato*

● **Crazy Horse** / 1971 / Reprise ✦✦✦✦✦

This was the finest album by the band that made Neil Young's music sound the way it did. There are places where you'd swear you hear Neil Young singing. Great material, including the first recordings of "Gone Dead Train" and "Beggars Day," plus Jack Nitzsche on a couple of lead vocals. Crazy Horse is a great band—dark, melancholy and bright all at once. This is worth finding and hearing often. *—William Ashford*

Loose / 1971 / Reprise ✦✦

At Crooked Lake / 1973 / Epic ✦✦

Crazy Moon / 1978 / One Way ✦✦✦

The trio of Molina, Talbot, and Sampedro is frequently joined by compatriot Neil Young on an album of hard rock with a sound not unlike that produced by them on Young's records. *—William Ruhlmann*

Cream

f. 1966, England, **db.** 1969, London, England

British Psychedelia, British Blues, Psychedelic, Hard Rock, Blues-Rock

Although Cream were only together for a little more than two years, their influence was immense, both during their late-'60s peak and in the years following their breakup. Cream were the first top group to truly exploit the power-trio format, in the process laying the foundation for much blues-rock and hard rock of the 1960s and '70s. It was with Cream, too, that guitarist Eric Clapton truly became an international superstar. Critical revisionists have tagged the band as overrated, citing the musicians' emphasis upon flash, virtuosity, and showmanship at the expense of taste and focus. This was sometimes true of their live shows in particular, but in reality the best of their studio recordings were excellent fusions of blues, pop, and psychedelia, with concise original material outnumbering the bloated blues jams and overlong solos.

Clapton had established himself as a guitar hero with the Yardbirds, and later with John Mayall's Bluesbreakers, while bassist/singer Jack Bruce and drummer Ginger Baker had both been in the British R&B combo the Graham Bond Organisation. At first Cream's focus was electrified and amped-up traditional blues, which dominated their first album, 1966's *Fresh Cream*. Originals like "N.S.U." and "I Feel Free" gave notice that the band were capable of moving beyond the blues, and they truly found their voice on *Disraeli Gears* in late 1967. The album broke the band bigtime in the States, generating their first big U.S. hit single, "Sunshine of Your Love." With the double album *Wheels of Fire*, Cream topped the American charts in 1968, though the record itself was an erratic affair dogged by the decision to present separate discs of studio and live material. Their decision to disband later that year—at a time when they were seemingly on top of the world—came as a shock to most of the rock audience. In 1969, a posthumous album featuring both studio and live material, *Goodbye*, made number two. Clapton and Baker would quickly resurface in 1969 as half of another short-lived supergroup, Blind Faith, and Clapton of course went on to one of the longest and most successful careers of anyone in the rock business. *—Richie Unterberger*

Fresh Cream / Dec. 1966 / Polydor ✦✦✦✦

All of the raw material that would make Cream one of the finest bands of their era is present here on this, their debut release. *Fresh Cream* contains the band's signature mixture of psychedelic pop songs and blues-rock improvisations. The best of one extreme is the opener "I Feel Free" (absent on the original British release of the record). It is a '60s pop gem, with a catchy opening and a haunting verse. This excellent track was made present on the American release of *Fresh Cream* in January of 1967 at the expense of the omission of "Spoonful." An excellent example of Eric Clapton's blues mastery, this reading of the Willie Dixon classic is ultimately the high point of the record. Not to downplay the contributions of Jack Bruce and Ginger Baker, but it is Clapton's incendiary playing that really makes this blues come alive. This is where his (and, by extension, Cream's) muse really lies: in the extended, high-energy, improvised explorations of traditional blues tunes. However, Clapton seems a bit lost on some of the more pop-oriented fare; his rhythm guitar playing especially is often atrocious. Bruce not only handles most of the vocal chores with panache, but also plays very innovative bass, using it both more aggressively and more melodically than most players of his generation were accustomed to doing. Baker's heavy drumming is notable throughout. His distinct, idiosyncratic style is best demonstrated by the drum solo on his own "Toad." All in all, *Fresh Cream* is a fine first album, but Baker, Bruce, and Clapton would all go on to bigger and better, both together with Cream and separately with other projects. *—Daniel Gioffre*

Disraeli Gears / Nov. 1967 / Polydor ✦✦✦✦

The threesome of Jack Bruce, Ginger Baker, and legendary guitarist Eric Clapton forming the band Cream was a monumental effort of jazz, blues, and psychedelic rock during the British rock period of the late 1960s. Cream, with their raw fury of intense sound, was renowned for their rare talent of taking songs of complex arrangements and making them an act of spontaneous beauty during live shows. *Disraeli Gears*, their second release, was an essential landmark recording that brought listeners to the direction they were soon to take with *Wheels of Fire*. Taking on a circus-spinning arsenal of sounds and effects, Cream's fashionable art is a blend of highly sustained drenched distortion, rampant percussion, and a kaleidoscope of various musical textures and colors, both in melody and rhythm. Each of *Disraeli Gears*' list of 11 tunes is original in format, containing it own unique brands of dashing blues-laden guitar riffs by Clapton, as well as thick bass lines and smashing drum leads. Highlights of the record feature Clapton's awe-inspiring and soul-gripping guitar leads, including hits such as "Sunshine of Your Love" and "Tales of Brave Ulysses." The latter is a magical poem laced into a line of mesmerizing chordal changes. *Disraeli Gears* is a definitive staple of early British rock and a sensational addition to the avid classic rock listener. *—Shawn Haney*

Wheels of Fire / Jun. 1968 / Polydor ✦✦✦✦

Wheels of Fire was a two-album set, one disc recorded in the studio, the second disc recorded on stage in San Francisco. Side three contains the definitive live version of what became Clapton's signature piece, Robert Johnson's "Crossroads," plus a version of "Spoonful" that clocks in just short of 17 minutes. On such pieces, Cream approached blues-based rock with a jazz aesthetic, using the song as a framework to begin and end a performance. The strength of the performance is in the improvisation. When it worked, as it does on "Spoonful," they were brilliant. When it didn't, as on "Traintime" and "Toad," the band became excess incarnate. The studio disc contained their second Top Ten single, Jack Bruce's "White Room," as well as a stunning cover of Albert King's "Born Under a Bad Sign." Other tracks, particularly those written by Ginger Baker, do not hold up. *—Rob Bowman*

Goodbye / Jan. 1969 / Polydor ✦✦✦

As the title implies, this is Cream's farewell. By the time it was issued, the band had broken up. Three studio recordings that were left were coupled with extended live versions of "I'm So Glad," "Politician," and "I'm Sitting on Top of the World." The live tracks burn. Clapton, Bruce, and Baker each take credit for one of the studio tracks. Clapton's cut, "Badge," was co-written by George Harrison and remains what was surely the prettiest melody to ever grace a Cream recording. *—Rob Bowman*

Live Cream, Vol. 1 / Apr. 1970 / Polydor ✦✦✦

Cream was a band born to the stage. This is their most consistently brilliant album. Four of the five cuts appeared on *Fresh Cream*. The fifth, "Lawdy Mama," is a traditional blues piece that makes its first appearance here. All but "Lawdy Mama" are given extended jazz-based treatment. The dialog among the three musicians as the jams develop is fascinating. Foreground and background seem to dissolve as all three musicians take charge, using the full range of their instruments. Performances like this single-handedly raised the stakes of musicianship in rock. —*Rob Bowman*

Live Cream, Vol. 2 / Mar. 1972 / Polydor ♦♦♦
More live Cream concentrating on material from their *Disraeli Gears* and *Wheels of Fire* albums plus an extended workout on Freddie King's "Hideaway." —*Rob Bowman*

★ **The Very Best of Cream** / May 9, 1995 / Polydor/Chronicles ♦♦♦♦♦
There have been many compilations drawn from the four albums Cream originally released between 1966 and 1969. But the one most commonly available since the early 1980s was the ten-track *Strange Brew: The Very Best of Cream* (1983) (Polydor 811 639), a bare-bones collection focusing on the group's hit singles. Note, then, that this album, despite the similar title, is a newly compiled 1995 CD/cassette containing all of the recordings on *Strange Brew*, plus ten more. It is thus the most comprehensive Cream anthology on the market, including all the group's essential tracks on a single disc with superior sound in a package containing good annotations. —*William Ruhlmann*

Those Were the Days / Sep. 23, 1997 / Polydor ♦♦♦♦
Those Were the Days is an ambitious four-disc, 63-track box set that divides Cream's career into two halves. The first two discs feature every studio track the group ever released, plus a handful of unreleased cuts, alternate takes and rarities. The other two discs are devoted to live material, which is segued together in an attempt to recreate the "ideal" Cream concert. It's a remarkably comprehensive collection, complete with an extensive booklet and remastered sound, yet it doesn't reveal any new insights about Cream, nor does it offer any invaluable rarities. Therefore, it's only for diehard collectors or listeners wanting to acquire the entire Cream catalog at once; casual fans will be satisfied with individual albums or greatest-hits collections. —*Stephen Thomas Erlewine*

20th Century Masters—The Millennium Collection: The Best of Cream / Feb. 29, 2000 / Polydor ♦♦♦
Let's be clear from the outset—*20th Century Masters* does not contain all of Cream's essential moments. It's missing such mind-warps as "SWALBR," trippy folk-psychedelia as "Anyone for Tennis," flights of fancy as "Wrapping Paper," crushingly inevitable blues as "I'm So Glad," and the brilliant throwaway "Doing That Scrap Yard Thing," all of which added to Cream's character. Still, if you're just looking for the hits, this has most of them, from "I Feel Free" and "Spoonful" to "Strange Brew," "Sunshine of Your Love," "Crossroads," "White Room," and "Badge." For those who like to skim the surface, sampling what they know, this will certainly satisfy, but if you're curious, you're advised to dig deeper than this. —*Stephen Thomas Erlewine*

The Creation

f. 1966, Middlesex, England, db. 1968
Freakbeat, British Psychedelia, Mod, Psychedelic, British Invasion, Rock & Roll
No other band came closer to emulating the feedback-ridden autodestruction of the early Who than the Creation, who had a couple minor British hit singles in 1966 with "Making Time" and "Painter Man." The sonic resemblance is hardly surprising; the Creation were produced by Shel Talmy, who also produced the Who's earliest records, and lead guitarist Eddie Phillips was even asked by Pete Townshend to join the Who as second guitarist. Phillips' feedback freakouts were grounded by solid mod power chords and British Invasion harmonies. The Creation produced several interesting singles between 1966 and 1968, and although they achieved brief stardom in Germany, they never made it big in the U.K. Ronnie Wood was briefly a member before the group disbanded in 1968. —*Richie Unterberger*

● **How Does It Feel to Feel?** / 1982 / Edsel ♦♦♦♦♦
Unquestionably the best of the several Creation repackages floating around. Includes virtually all of their 1966-68 singles and a few other stray tracks of interest from the same period. —*Richie Unterberger*

● **Our Music Is Red—With Purple Flashes** / May 5, 1998 / Diablo ♦♦♦♦
Our Music Is Red—With Purple Flashes doesn't improve on the definitive Creation collection *How Does It Feel to Feel*, nor is it any worse. Instead, it's a comprehensive, well-produced 24-track compilation that contains every one of the group's major songs, plus a couple of interesting covers, lesser-known singers and album tracks. Like *How Does It Feel to Feel* it offers a generous retrospective of the underappreciated Mod quartet and if you don't have that compilation, it's a worthwhile acquisition. If you already have that other excellent collection, *Our Music Is Red—With Purple Flashes* isn't necessary. —*Stephen Thomas Erlewine*

Complete Collection, Vol. 1: Making Time / Oct. 13, 1998 / Retroactive ♦♦♦♦
Along with its companion volume (*Biff Bang Pow*), this collects everything available by the Creation: all of their officially released tracks, rare mono and stereo mixes, and a smattering of live German TV show appearances. General fans should continue to stick with Edsel's *How Does It Feel to Feel*, a well-chosen anthology of their best 20 tracks. However, a cult band such as the Creation tends to attract fans who *do* want everything, and this two-volume series is exemplary in that regard, although much of the rare material is slightly different stereo mixes, rather than entirely new versions. The most interesting rarities on this disc are the live TV broadcasts from 1966 (including covers of "I'm a Man" and "That's How Strong My Love Is," which they never recorded in the studio), and an entirely unreleased instrumental. It also has several of their most renowned official tracks ("Making Time," "Try and Stop Me," "How Does It Feel to Feel," "Nightmares"), and the package is made more enticing with extensive liner notes by Mike Stax. —*Richie Unterberger*

Complete Collection, Vol. 2: Biff Bang Pow / Oct. 13, 1998 / Retroactive ♦♦♦
Together with its companion volume *Making Time*, this 20-track disc collects everything by the Creation. It's just as worthy as the first installment, featuring several of their most well-known tunes ("Painter Man," "Biff Bang Pow," "Life Is Just Beginning," "Through My Eyes") and a bunch more alternate stereo mixes. Tracks such as "Sweet Helen," "Like a Rolling Stone," and the instrumental "Sylvette" have been hard to find over the years, although they don't rate among their better efforts. There are also a couple of German TV show performances circa 1967 of "Painter Man" and "Try and Stop Me." By the way, the two *Complete Collection* discs don't have the rare mid-'60s singles by the Mark Four (who evolved into the Creation), some of which were quite good; for those you'll need to look for Eva's *The Mark Four/The Creation*. —*Richie Unterberger*

Creedence Clearwater Revival

f. 1967, El Cerrito, CA, db. Oct. 1972
Rock & Roll
At a time when rock was evolving further and further away from the forces that had made the music possible in the first place, Creedence Clearwater Revival brought things back to their roots with their concise synthesis of rockabilly, swamp pop, R&B, and country. Though CCR were very much a group in their tight, punchy arrangements, their vision was very much singer, songwriter, guitarist, and leader John Fogerty's. Fogerty's classic compositions for Creedence both evoked enduring images of Americana and reflected burning social issues of the day. The band's genius was their ability to accomplish this with the economic, primal power of a classic rockabilly ensemble. On their first album in 1968, the group played it both ways, offering extended, quasi-psychedelic workouts of the '50s classics "I Put a Spell on You" and "Susie Q." The latter song became their first big hit, but the band didn't really bloom until "Proud Mary," a number-two single in early 1969 that demonstrated John's talent at tapping into Southern roots music and imagery with a natural ease. It was the start of a torrent of classic hits from the gritty, Little Richard-inspired singer over the next two years, including "Bad Moon Rising," "Green River," "Down on the Corner," "Travelin' Band," "Who'll Stop the Rain," "Up Around the Bend," and "Lookin' out My Back Door." —*Richie Unterberger*

Creedence Clearwater Revival / Jul. 1968 / Fantasy ♦♦♦♦
Released in the summer of 1968—a year after the summer of love, but still in the thick of the Age of Aquarius—Creedence Clearwater Revival's self-titled debut album was gloriously out-of-step with the times, teeming with John Fogerty's Americana fascinations. While many of Fogerty's obsessions and CCR's signatures are in place—weird blues ("I Put a Spell on You"), Stax R&B (Wilson Pickett's "Ninety-Nine and a Half"), rockabilly ("Susie Q"), winding instrumental interplay, the swamp sound, and songs for "The Working Man"—the band was still finding their way. Out of all their records (discounting *Mardi Gras*), this is the one that sounds the most like its era, thanks to the wordless vocal harmonies toward the end of "Susie Q," the backward guitars on "Gloomy," and the directionless, awkward jamming that concludes "Walking on the Water." Still, the band's sound is vibrant, with gutsy arrangements that borrow equally from Sun, Stax, and the swamp. Fogerty's songwriting is a little tentative. Not for nothing were two of the three singles pulled from the album covers (Dale Hawkins' "Susie Q," Screamin' Jay Hawkins' "I Put a Spell on You")—he wasn't an accomplished tunesmith yet. Though "The Working Man" isn't bad, the true exception is that third single, "Porterville," an exceptional song with great hooks, an underlying sense of menace, and the first inkling of the working-class rage that fueled such landmarks as "Fortunate Son." It's the song that points the way to the breakthrough of *Bayou Country*, but the rest of the album shouldn't be dismissed, because judged simply against the rock & roll of its time, it rises above its peers. —*Stephen Thomas Erlewine*

Bayou Country / Jan. 1969 / Fantasy ♦♦♦♦♦
Opening slowly with the dark, swampy "Born on the Bayou," *Bayou Country* reveals an assured Creedence Clearwater Revival, a band that has found its voice between their first and second album. It's not just that "Born on the Bayou" announces that CCR has discovered its sound—it reveals the extent of John Fogerty's myth-making. With this song, he sketches out his persona; it makes him sound as if he crawled out of the backwoods of Louisiana instead of being a native San Franciscan. He carries this illusion throughout the record, through the ominous meanderings of "Graveyard Train" through the stoked cover of "Good Golly Miss Molly" to "Keep on Chooglin'," which rides out a southern-fried groove for nearly eight minutes. At the heart of *Bayou Country*, as well as Fogerty's myth and Creedence's entire career, is "Proud Mary." A riverboat tale where the narrator leaves a good job in the city for a life rolling down the river, the song is filled with details that ring so true that it feels autobiographical. The lyric is married to music that is utterly unique yet curiously timeless, blending rockabilly, country, and Stax R&B into something utterly distinctive and addictive. "Proud Mary" is the emotional fulcrum at the center of Fogerty's seductive imaginary Americana, and while it's the best song here, his other songs are no slouch, either. "Born on the Bayou" is a magnificent piece of swamp-rock, "Penthouse Pauper" is a first-rate rocker with the angry undertow apparent on "Porterville" and "Bootleg" is a minor masterpiece, thanks to its tough acoustic foundation, sterling guitar work, and clever story. All the songs add up to a superb statement of purpose, a record that captures Creedence Clearwater Revival's muscular, spare, deceptively simple sound as an evocative portrait of America. —*Stephen Thomas Erlewine*

☆ **Green River** / Aug. 1969 / Fantasy ♦♦♦♦♦
If anything, CCR's third album *Green River* represents the full flower of their classic sound initially essayed on its predecessor, *Bayou Country*. One of the differences between the two albums is that *Green River* is tighter, with none of the five-minute-plus jams that filled out both their debut and *Bayou Country*, but the true key to its success is a peak in

John Fogerty's creativity. Although CCR had at least one cover on each album, they relied on Fogerty to crank out new material every month. He was writing so frequently that the craft became second-nature and he laid his emotions and fears bare, perhaps unintentionally. Perhaps that's why *Green River* has fear, anger, dread, and weariness creeping on the edges of gleeful music. This was a band that played rock & roll so joyously that they masked the, well, "sinister" undercurrents in Fogerty's songs. "Bad Moon Rising" has the famous line "Hope you've got your things together/Hope you're quite prepared to die," but that was only the most obvious indication of Fogerty's gloom. Consider all the other dark touches: the "Sinister purpose knocking at your door"; the chaos of "Commotion"; the threat of death in "Tombstone Shadow"; you only return to the idyllic "Green River" once you get lost and realize the "world is smolderin'." Even the ballads have a strong melancholy undercurrent, highlighted by "Lodi," where Fogerty imagines himself stuck playing in dead-end towns for the rest of his life. Not the typical thoughts of a newly famous rock & roller, but certainly an indication of Fogerty's inner tumult. For all its darkness, *Green River* is ultimately welcoming music, since the band rocks hard and bright and the melancholy feels comforting, not alienating. —*Stephen Thomas Erlewine*

☆ **Willy & the Poor Boys** / Nov. 1969 / Fantasy ♦♦♦♦♦
Make no mistake, *Willie & the Poor Boys* is a *fun* record, perhaps the breeziest album CCR ever made. Apart from the eerie minor-key closer "Effigy" (one of John Fogerty's most haunting numbers), there is little of the doom that colored *Green River*. Fogerty's rage remains, blazing to the forefront on "Fortunate Son," a working-class protest song that cuts harder than any of the explicit Vietnam protest songs of the era, which is one of the reasons that it hasn't aged where its peers have. Also, there's that unbridled vocal from Fogerty and the ferocious playing on *CCR*, which both sound fresh as they did upon release. "Fortunate Son" is one of the greatest, hardest rock & rollers ever cut, so it might seem to be out of step with an album that is pretty laid-back and friendly, but there's that elemental joy that by late '69 was one of CCR's main trademarks. That joy runs throughout the album, from the gleeful single "Down on the Corner" and the lazy jugband blues of "Poorboy Shuffle" through the great slow blues jam "Feelin' Blue" to the great rockabilly spiritual "Don't Look Now," one of Fogerty's overlooked gems. The covers don't feel like throwaways, either, since both "Cotton Fields" and "The Midnight Special" have been overhauled to feel like genuine CCR songs. It all adds up to one of the greatest pure rock & roll records ever cut. —*Stephen Thomas Erlewine*

☆ **Cosmo's Factory** / Jul. 1970 / Fantasy ♦♦♦♦♦
Throughout 1969 and into 1970, CCR toured incessantly and recorded nearly as much. Appropriately, *Cosmo's Factory*'s first single was the working band's anthem "Travelin' Band," a funny, piledriving rocker with a blaring horn section—the first indication their sonic palette was broadening. Two more singles appeared prior to the album's release, backed by John Fogerty originals that rivaled the A-side or paled just slightly. When it came time to assemble a full album, Fogerty had only one original left, the claustrophobic, paranoid rocker "Ramble Tamble." Unlike some extended instrumentals, this was dramatic and had a direction—a distinction made clear by the meandering jam that brings CCR's version of "I Heard It Through the Grapevine" to 11 minutes. Even if it wanders, their take on the Marvin Gaye classic isn't unpleasant, and their faithful, exuberant takes on the Sun classics "Ooby Dooby" and "My Baby Left Me" are joyous tributes. Still, the heart of the album lays in those six fantastic songs released on singles. "Up Around the Bend" is a searing rocker, one of their best, balanced by the menacing murkiness of "Run Through the Jungle." "Who'll Stop the Rain"'s poignant melody and melancholy undertow has a counterpart in Fogerty's dope song, "Lookin' out My Back Door," a charming, bright shuffle, filled with dancing animals and domestic bliss—he had never been as sweet and silly as he is here. On "Long as I Can See the Light," the record's final song, he again finds solace in home, anchored by a soulful, laid-back groove. It hits a comforting, elegiac note, the perfect way to draw *Cosmo's Factory*—an album made during stress and chaos, filled with raging rockers, covers, and intense jams—to a close. —*Stephen Thomas Erlewine*

Pendulum / Dec. 1970 / Fantasy ♦♦♦♦
During 1969 and 1970, CCR was dismissed by hipsters as a bubblegum pop band and the sniping had grown intolerable, at least to John Fogerty, who designed *Pendulum* as a rebuke to critics. He spent time polishing the production, bringing in keyboards, horns, even a vocal choir. His songs became self-consciously serious and tighter, working with the aesthetic of the rock underground—*Pendulum* was constructed as a proper album, contrasting dramatically with CCR's previous records, all throwbacks to joyous early rock records where covers sat nicely next to hits and overlooked gems tucked away at the end of the second side. To some fans of classic CCR, this approach may feel a little odd since only "Have You Ever Seen the Rain" and maybe its B-side "Hey Tonight" sound undeniably like prime Creedence. But, given time, the album is a real grower, revealing many overlooked Fogerty gems. Yes, it isn't transcendent like the albums they made from *Bayou Country* through *Cosmo's Factory*, but most bands never even come close to that kind of hot streak. Instead, *Pendulum* finds a first-class songwriter and craftsman pushing himself and his band to try new sounds, styles, and textures. His ambition results in a stumble—"Rude Awakening 2" portentously teeters on the verge of prog-rock, something CCR just can't pull off—but the rest of the record is excellent, with such great numbers as the bluesy groove "Pagan Baby," the soulful vamp "Chameleon," the moody "It's Just a Thought," and the raver "Molina." Most bands would kill for this to be their best stuff, and the fact that it's tucked away on an album that even some fans forget illustrates what a tremendous band Creedence Clearwater Revival was. —*Stephen Thomas Erlewine*

Creedence Gold / 1972 / Fantasy ♦♦♦
Creedence Gold is a collection of Creedence Clearwater Revival's hit singles. Unfortunately, the album is a little too small to meet anybody's needs. A mere eight tracks are

featured on *Creedence Gold*. Admittedly, these are eight tracks of amazing quality, but those looking for a more thorough collection will be pleased with the much more in-depth *Chronicle, Vol. 1*. *Creedence Gold* shows off the musical talent involved in the band. The 11-plus-minute "I Heard It Through the Grapevine" is a fine showcase for Creedence's lead guitar styling, while "Born on the Bayou" is a fine sampler of how the band worked as a unit. By no means is *Creedence Gold* a bad album. Indeed, the eight tracks featured are eight of the best moments in their respective genres. As a compilation of Creedence's career, however, *Creedence Gold* fails miserably. —*Ben Davies*

Mardi Gras / Apr. 1972 / Fantasy ♦♦

★ **Chronicle, Vol. 1** / 1976 / Fantasy ♦♦♦♦♦
Chronicle, Vol. 1 contains every one of Creedence Clearwater Revival's original 19 hit singles—including "Proud Mary," "Bad Moon Rising," "Green River," "Down on the Corner," "Travelin' Band," "Up Around the Band," and "Have You Ever Seen the Rain"—plus "I Heard It Through the Grapevine," which became a hit at the same time this double-record compilation was released. It's a lean, concise collection that tells you everything you need to know about Creedence. Several of the band's individual albums are essential, but *Chronicle* is not only an excellent introduction to the group, it offers definitive proof that group was one of the definitive singles bands of the late '60s. Rarely has a greatest hits collection been so well-assembled. [The compact disc edition is hampered by the inclusion of the full-length, eleven-minute album version of "I Heard It Through the Grapevine;" its presence slows down the momentum of the collection considerably.] —*Stephen Thomas Erlewine*

The Concert / 1980 / Fantasy ♦♦♦♦
Originally released in 1980 as *The Royal Albert Hall Concert* but quickly retitled when the label discovered the show it captures was recorded in California at the Oakland Coliseum on January 31, 1970, *The Concert* is as simple as its name. The album simply captures Creedence Clearwater Revival at the height of their powers, when they were the most popular American rock & roll band. They released three albums in 1969, all of which went into the Top 10. They had three number two singles that year ("Proud Mary," "Bad Moon Rising," "Green River") and one number three single ("Down on the Corner"). They were simply a phenomenon and this record shows why. It's not as good as a compilation of hit singles; CCR were the rare excellent live band whose studio recordings were as ferocious as their stage work, and those were better detailed, too. Still, it's a pretty terrific little record, since the band is in fine form, tearing through the hits and such album favorites as "Tombstone Shadow," "Don't Look Now," "Born on the Bayou," "The Midnight Special," and "Keep on Chooglin'." Only hardcore fans really need to pick up this record and they might not even spin it all that often. But when they do, they'll wind up satisfied. —*Stephen Thomas Erlewine*

Chronicle, Vol. 2 / 1986 / Fantasy ♦♦♦♦♦
Chronicle, Vol. 2 effectively compiles all of the highlights from Creedence Clearwater Revival's career that weren't on the first volume. All of the singles were included on *Chronicle*, so *Chronicle, Vol. 2* is comprised solely of album tracks. That doesn't mean these are lesser items. On the contrary, the majority of these songs—"Born on the Bayou," "Tombstone Shadow," "Wrote a Song for Everyone," "It Came out of the Sky," "Midnight Special"—rank among their best performances. Of course, a couple of great tracks remain on CCR's individual albums, notably "Bootleg," but *Chronicle, Vol. 2* is an ideal choice for listeners that want a little more than the hits but are unwilling to delve into the proper albums. —*Stephen Thomas Erlewine*

Marshall Crenshaw

b. Nov. 11, 1953, Detroit, MI
Vocals, Guitar / College Rock, Pop/Rock, Power Pop, New Wave
Singer/songwriter Marshall Crenshaw has built up an impressive body of work over the course of his career, showing a fine craft for everything he approaches while stubbornly following his own creative muse to reach that end. To say that Crenshaw has had an interesting career so far would be putting it mildly. He's been in the movies and he's been in the road show version of *Beatlemania*. His songs have been plastered all over the soundtracks to several hit movies and covered by artists as diverse as Robert Gordon, Bette Midler, Kelly Willis, Marti Jones and the Gin Blossoms. He got a bunch of his likeminded show business acquaintances together and put out a book on all the great and lousy rock & roll movies in existence called *Hollywood Rock & Roll*. He's put together comps of his own for record companies (most notably *Hillbilly Music, Thank God!* for the short lived Bug Music label) and has contributed chapters to books on vintage guitar collecting. Crenshaw is a true rock & roll renaissance man while still remaining the everyman. —*Cub Koda*

★ **Marshall Crenshaw** / Apr. 28, 1982 / Warner Brothers ♦♦♦♦♦
On the cover of his self-titled LP, Marshall Crenshaw—complete with crew-cut, thick glasses and unfashionable suit—looks like nothing so much as the second coming of Buddy Holly, or possibly an Americanized Elvis Costello; listening to the record itself does little to alter those first impressions, and even if his subsequent LPs failed to live up to such immense promise there's no doubting this debut release's enduring greatness. Working without any kind of smoke or mirrors, Crenshaw delivers simple, straightforward pop music invested with remarkable melodic ingenuity; his material is timeless and fresh—gems like "Someday, Someway," "She Can't Dance" and "Not for Me" are the kinds of songs which would fit like a glove on both oldies radio and contemporary Top 40 playlists in any era. Witty, assured and utterly infectious, *Marshall Crenshaw* remains among the finest debuts of its day. [Rhino reissued *Marshall Crenshaw* in 2000 with nine bonus tracks, including demos, live cuts, and non-LP B-sides.] —*Jason Ankeny*

Field Day / 1983 / Warner Brothers ♦♦♦♦
Following his critically acclaimed 1982 debut and successful single "Someday, Someway," Marshall Crenshaw returned with the following year's greatly anticipated *Field Day*. Crenshaw doesn't fall prey to the sophomore jinx, delivering nine more brilliantly crafted pop/rock originals and a terrific cover of the Jive Five's "What Time Is It?" Though the record meets the high standard that Crenshaw, his brother Robert Crenshaw (drums) and bassist Chris Donato, set with the first album, many had trouble warming up to producer Steve Lillywhite's dense, more muscular production, especially Robert's explosive snare and bass drum. But while it may lack its predecessor's immediate sparkle and charm, *Field Day* is equally infectious. It also shows a newfound depth and maturity in Crenshaw's writing, which Lillywhite's sound reinforces. Like *Marshall Crenshaw*, the majority of *Field Day* deals with time-honored themes of loves lost and found, albeit from a slightly less innocent viewpoint, much like the lyrical growth of the Beatles in late 1964, early 1965, or Buddy Holly's "True Love Ways" and "Learning the Game." Previously, he would move on and "find someone better" or "feel the need to go "Rockin' Around in N.Y.C." Now, he's willing to "try with all [his] heart every day," seeing a night on the town as a "duty" that must be done before slipping back into comfortable domesticity and responsibility. Crenshaw realizes now that even true love "makes demands" amidst the fun and summer evening walks. This album brims with deceptively simple, pure pop pleasures that continue to unfold with repeated listens. Though *Field Day* didn't match the commercial promise of the first album, it was the perfect second step in Marshall Crenshaw's artistic evolution. *—Brett Hartenbach*

Downtown / 1985 / Warner Brothers ♦♦♦♦
Marshall Crenshaw entered the studio to begin work on his third album, *Downtown*, but for the first time, he was without the familiar backing of Chris Donato on bass and brother Robert Crenshaw on drums (though he does appear on two tracks). Following the dense, sonic thunder of the commercially disappointing *Field Day*, this album employed the services of various studio pros, and returned him to the roomier, more traditional tone of his first effort. Along with co-producers T-Bone Burnett and Larry Hirsch (and Mitch Easter on one track), Crenshaw creates an old-fashioned rock & roll record with the inviting warmth of '60s pop and the swing and recklessness of the '50s. And though he doesn't do anything radically new or different here, the results are once again never less than fresh or stirring. Tracks like the irresistible "Little Wild One (No. 5)," the primal beat of "Yvonne," and "(We're Gonna) Shake Their Minds," with it's syncopated guitar and drum interplay, are first-rate rockers, while Ben Vaughn's "I'm Sorry (But So Is Brenda Lee)" and Crenshaw's own "Like a Vague Memory" have the feel of classic '50s pop tunes. Though *Downtown* did little to reverse the downward slide of Marshall Crenshaw's market value, it does complete a brilliant triad of releases going back to his 1982 debut. *—Brett Hartenbach*

Mary Jean & 9 Others / 1987 / Warner Brothers ♦♦♦
Marshall Crenshaw's first three records, though each with their own distinct personality, were an irresistible combination of masterful pop and vibrant, timeless rock & roll. His fourth effort, *Mary Jean & 9 Others*, has many of these same ingredients, while at the same time lacking the impact of its predecessors. And though there isn't really a bad cut here, there isn't much that would make you think of Crenshaw as much more than a craftsman. Even the best of the originals, including the title track and "Somebody Crying," seem to lumber along, never really delivering on their promise. This may be partially due to Don Dixon's production that, though not out of place with Crenshaw's material, lacks the freshness of the first album, the allure and depth of *Field Day*, and the spirit of *Downtown*. Overall, it's the beautiful closer, "They Never Will Know," and Peter Case's "Steel Strings" that are most successful in this setting. Like the rest of Crenshaw's mid-'80s, early-'90s catalog, *Mary Jean* is difficult to find, but of this period, *Downtown*, which is also on Warner Bros., and *Life's Too Short*, his only release for MCA, are preferred. *—Brett Hartenbach*

Good Evening / Jun. 1989 / Warner Brothers ♦♦♦
While Marshall Crenshaw's first two releases were self-contained efforts, built around his voice, guitar, and songwriting, and the rhythm section/backing vocals of Chris Donato and brother Robert Crenshaw, his third, *Downtown*, brought an assortment of studio hands on board without really sacrificing what makes him special. Following a return to a scaled-down configuration for the slightly disappointing *Mary Jean & 9 Others*, *Good Evening*, like *Downtown*, employs the services of various sidemen and backup vocalists—including Kenny Aronoff, Graham Maby, Syd Straw, Robert Crenshaw, and the BoDeans—and seems to be geared towards a more contemporary, marketable sound. Producers David Kershenbaum and Paul McKenna bring a veneer to his pop/rock, adding the occasional keyboard, steel guitar, fiddle, mandolin, and accordion, while Crenshaw, for the first time, brings in a handful of ringers (Sonny Landreth, David Lindley, and James Burton) to share lead guitar chores for the majority of the record. Furthermore, for the first time, he looks elsewhere for the bulk of the record's material, with half of the songs coming from other sources (two seemingly written to order), and three of the remaining five being collaborations. Still, he slips naturally into the words and music of artists such as Richard Thompson, John Hiatt, the Isley Brothers, and Bobby Fuller, bringing as much of himself to these tunes as he does to his own. Whatever the reason for the delegation of work on *Good Evening*, the choices are good ones, and it works to varying degrees. *Good Evening*, which was his final recording for Warner Bros., may not reach the heights of the first three, but there's a spark here that was missing last time out. *—Brett Hartenbach*

Life's Too Short / May 14, 1991 / MCA ♦♦♦♦
Marshall Crenshaw entered the '90s, following his departure from Warner Bros., with a new label, his hardest rocking album to date, and hope of a rejuvenated career. Backed for the most part by the rhythm section of Kenny Aronoff (drums) and Fernando Saunders (bass), *Life's Too Short* adds to the muscle that Crenshaw had been building in recent years, while at the same time stripping away the slight sheen of his previous two releases. It's also arguably his best collection of tunes since 1983's *Field Day*. With the expectations and pressure to recapture the success of his debut seemingly behind him, Crenshaw appears to have found a renewed sense of freedom and vitality here, and not since *Downtown* has he sounded so natural and at home. The opener, "Better Back Off," kick starts the record with a quote from the Rolling Stones and then proceeds to offer words of love and encouragement, with music that's both as tough and as sweet as its sentiment. Furthermore, with cuts such as "Delilah," "Stop Doing That," "Walkin' Around," and "Fantastic Planet of Love," he strikes a nice balance between self-assured rocker and pop craftsman, while steering clear of tired, power pop clichés. He also brings an adult sensibility to the material, which effortlessly walks the line between innocent and mature, and simple and complex. Difficult to find, as well as being Crenshaw's last major label release, *Life's Too Short* is another terrific yet commercially underappreciated work by an artist that, though responsible for some of the most irresistible songs of the '80s and '90s, seems inevitably destined for cult status. *—Brett Hartenbach*

Live: My Truck Is My Home / Sep. 20, 1994 / Razor & Tie ♦♦♦
Fourteen tracks taken from various sources (soundboard tapes, etc.) from performances plucked from 1982, 1987, 1990, 1991, 1992 and 1994. Loads of great Crenshaw material ("You're My Favorite Waste of Time," "Cynical Girl"), explosive guitar that seldom surfaces on his studio efforts the way it does here, and plenty of deadpan humor (the picture of Bo "Billy, Don't Be a Hero" Donaldson on the disc itself says it all) make this a great live album with quirks that keep it ahead of the pack. *—Cub Koda*

Miracle of Science / Jul. 23, 1996 / Razor & Tie ♦♦♦
Crenshaw's first studio effort for the indie Razor & Tie imprint also marks a return to his earlier, stripped-down approach of his debut album. Playing most of the instruments himself (including drums), there's a far more organic feel to the tunes presented here than his last major-label efforts. In addition to solid Crenshaw pop originals like "What Do You Dream Of?," "Laughter," and "Starless Summer Sky," his takes on Dobie Gray's "The 'In' Crowd" and the countryish "Who Stole That Train" also show him as always to be a prime interpreter of other folks' great songs as well. *—Cub Koda*

The 9 Volt Years: Battery Powered Home Demos & Curios / 1998 / Razor & Tie ♦♦♦♦♦
Far from the collection of scraps and throw-aways its humble title would suggest, *The 9 Volt Years: Battery Powered Home Demos & Curios (1979-198?)* is instead a showcase for Marshall Crenshaw at his most engaging and refreshing. Whereas some of his studio LPs have suffered from overproduction, the bare-bones ambience of these 15 cuts—home recordings, live performances and the stray studio date—allows his songs' melodic smarts and impeccable craftsmanship to truly shine. Familiar tracks like "Someday, Someway," "Rockin' Around in NYC" and "Vague Memory" are dramatically revitalized in these spartan settings, while lost gems like "Run Back to You," "Everyone's in Love with You" and the classic B-side "You're My Favorite Waste of Time" assume their rightful place alongside Crenshaw's best work. The end result is not only a must-have for fans, but also an ideal introduction to one of the best singer/songwriters around, captured here at his purest, loosest and most honest. *—Jason Ankeny*

#447 / Sep. 28, 1999 / Razor & Tie ♦♦♦♦
Crenshaw's first album since 1998's wonderful home demo collection, *The 9 Volt Years* (and his first studio album since 1996's *Miracle of Science*), *#447* finds the singer/songwriter constructing the kind of clever pop gems that have become his trademark. "Dime a Dozen Guy," for example, is as witty a song about being cheated on as you'll ever find, with Crenshaw sarcastically repeating "I've been passed over for a dime a dozen guy" to form the hook. The singer also employs a string section to masterful use to create the melodic hook of "Television Light" and experiments with Dobro for the country & western-sounding "Glad Goodbye." Though the latter half of the album strays a bit from Crenshaw's three-minute pop gem style, favoring jazzier bass lines and chord progressions, *#447* is still a strong addition to this underrated artist's recorded work. *—Steve Kurutz*

The Best of Marshall Crenshaw: This Is Easy / Aug. 15, 2000 / Rhino ♦♦♦♦♦
Co-compiler Gary Stewart and project assistant David Gorman waste no time at all before addressing the question that has plagued rock critics and fans since 1981: "how can we rationalize the continued underappreciation of Marshall Crenshaw?" It's not just that Crenshaw is a cult favorite and critics' pet; he's also steeped in rock & roll traditions that date back to Buddy Holly and Gene Vincent, and his records are such ear candy that you'd figure they would attract a big audience. Instead, only three of Crenshaw's previous ten albums have even reached the charts, along with just one single; Stewart and Gorman hope this compilation will "set things right." If only it could. Running from 1981 to 1996, the 22-track collection gathers four tracks each from Crenshaw's first three albums, as well as his first indie single "Something's Gonna Happen," the exceptional B-side "You're My Favorite Waste of Time," and assorted tracks from four subsequent albums. Crenshaw doesn't so much write songs as he makes records, at least as interested in guitar textures and what echo is placed on his vocal as what he's singing about. For all the surface pleasure his work provides, the only depth it reveals is one of craft; one is more impressed than really involved. And yet, it would be hard for a rock & roll fan not to enjoy this record, which cherry-picks Crenshaw's albums, diminishing, for example, the inappropriately bombastic production Steve Lillywhite brought to *Field Day*. The tracks are all pop gems, and they do, as Stewart and Gorman claim, induce the fantasy of a world in which classic, 1965-vintage pop/rock was still on top 20 years later. It's a nice dream for rock & roll fans; with this album they can close their eyes and, for 75 minutes, pretend it's true. *—William Ruhlmann*

I've Suffered for My Art, Now It's Your Turn / Jul. 14, 2001 / King Biscuit ♦♦♦

The Crests

f. 1956, **db.** 1960
Doo Wop
One of the most successful integrated doo wop groups, the Crests waxed the classic ballad "16 Candles" in 1959. Formed in 1956, they began recording the next year for Joyce, where they inched onto the pop lists with "Sweetest One." Moving to the brand-new Coed logo, Johnny Maestro's (b. May 7, 1930) warm tenor made "16 Candles" a national smash, and pop/R&B hybrids like "The Angels Listened In" and "Step by Step" also did well. Maestro went solo in 1960, scoring the next year with "Model Girl" on Coed, while the Crests attempted to survive on their own. Maestro eventually reclaimed stardom as leader of Brooklyn Bridge, an 11-piece aggregation that hit with "Worst That Could Happen" in 1968. *—Bill Dahl*

• **The Best of the Crests Featuring Johnny Maestro** / 1990 / Rhino ♦♦♦♦♦
Rhino's *The Best of the Crests Featuring Johnny Maestro* is a generous 18-track collection that contains all of the doo wop group's greatest hits, along with a selection of singles, B-sides and album tracks that prove that the Crests were one of the finest outfits of their time. There may not be any earth-shaking revelations among the songs that didn't make the charts, but there is certainly a bunch of fine music, and this is worth the time of any serious doo wop fan. *—Stephen Thomas Erlewine*

The Crew Cuts

f. 1952, Toronto, Ontario, Canada, **db.** 1964
Vocal Pop
On most informed lists of rock & roll villains, the Crew Cuts would have to rank near the top. Their clean-cut Canadian harmony quartet concentrated on covers of songs originally recorded by R&B/doo wop vocal groups, with their cover of the Chords' "Sh-Boom" setting the pattern. Though the original hit the Top Ten, the Crew Cuts' cover found a far easier entrance into established radio formats and mainstream White audiences, hitting number one in 1954. The group were regular visitors to the Top 20 over the next couple of years, repeating the "Sh-Boom" syndrome with songs like "Earth Angel," their second-biggest hit at number three (though nobody remembers the Crew Cuts' version today, the Penguins' original having long established supremacy with audiences and on oldies stations). Their strategy of foraging for sources among Black R&B vocal singles was widely imitated throughout the industry, by Pat Boone, the McGuire Sisters, Georgia Gibbs, and numerous others. After Elvis, Chuck Berry, and others had staked their own claim on superstardom though, it became increasingly obvious that teenagers preferred the real article, and that the entrenchment of authentic rock & roll was inevitable. By 1958, the Crew Cuts had left their original label Mercury for stints with RCA and other labels; they broke up in 1964. *—Richie Unterberger*

• **The Best of the Crew Cuts: The Mercury Years** / Jul. 16, 1996 / Mercury ♦♦♦♦♦
Twenty-two tracks from their 1954-57 prime, with over a dozen hits, including "Sh-Boom," "Earth Angel," "Crazy 'Bout Ya Baby," and "Ko Ko Mo." Now that the original R&B/doo wop versions of most of the material is available for easy comparison, you'd have to be nuts to prefer these whitewashed covers, which sound incredibly quaint and lightweight. The Crew Cuts were never a bona fide rock & roll group, however. Judged solely within the context of other young White male harmony pop quartets of the time, such as the Four Freshmen and the Four Aces, they acquit themselves well with their accomplished vocal arrangements. *—Richie Unterberger*

Crime & The City Solution

f. 1984, **db.** 1990
Post-Punk, Goth Rock, Alternative Pop/Rock
Despite roots dating back as far as 1978, Crime & the City Solution did not truly emerge until 1984, coming to life in the wake of the dissolution of the seminal Birthday Party. The group was led by the evocative singer/songwriter Simon Bonney, a Melbourne, Australia native who led a series of bands under the verbose Crime name throughout the late '70s and early '80s; a longtime friend of the Birthday Party, he contacted former members Mick Harvey and Rowland S. Howard after the group's breakup, and following the addition of Howard's bassist brother Harry, the most successful and famed lineup of Crime & the City Solution was born.

In 1985, the quartet debuted with *The Dangling Man*, a self-produced EP quickly establishing the band's moody, atmospheric blues-based aesthetic. Former Swell Maps drummer Epic Soundtracks joined Crime after the EP's release, freeing Harvey to alternate among a variety of instruments for the haunting follow-up, *Just South of Heaven.* Their full-length bow *Room of Lights* appeared in 1986 and featured the remarkable "Six Bells Chime," which so impressed the acclaimed filmmaker Wim Wenders that he invited the band to perform the song live in his 1988 masterpiece *Wings of Desire.*

By the time the film appeared, however, the incarnation of Crime & the City Solution presented onscreen was no more; after *Room of Lights,* the Howard brothers and Soundtracks exited to form These Immortal Souls, leaving Bonney, Harvey and violinist Bronwyn Adams (also Bonney's wife and songwriting partner) to relocate to Berlin, where they recruited a number of local musicians, including Einsturzende Neubauten guitarist Alexander Hacke, to cut 1988's ornate, intoxicating *Shine.* Even more baroque was the follow-up, 1989's *The Bride Ship.*

In 1990, Crime returned to the studio one final time to record *Paradise Discotheque,* a record built around Bonney's ambitious four-part suite "The Last Dictator," a song cycle inspired by the downfall of Romanian warlord Nicolae Ceaucescu. After contributing "The Adversary" to the soundtrack of Wenders' *Until the End of the World,* Crime & the City Solution disbanded; while Harvey rejoined former Birthday Party mate Nick Cave in the Bad Seeds, Bonney began work on his 1992 solo debut, *Forever. —Jason Ankeny*

• **Just South of Heaven** / 1985 / Mute ♦♦♦♦♦
Aussies with a gothic vision of the American South. *—Robert Gordon*

Room of Lights / 1986 / Mute ♦♦

Shine / 1988 / Mute ♦♦♦
With the reconstituted line-up now including Hacke and his appropriately post-punk-into-blues guitar work—which had to have attracted inevitable comparisons to his bandmate Blixa Bargeld's role with Nick Cave—Crime & the City Solution came up with another doomy winner with *Shine.* Cave connections aside, the group is even more its own outfit than before, a touch less classically smooth and arranged, more rough around the edges and jagged, especially with Bonney's delivery. Occasional Cave-like groans aside, his lyrics come across as distinctly unfriendly to a usual verse/chorus structure, sounding like a spoken-word recitation sung a line at a time. "All Must Be Love," which also appears on the CD version at the end in a danker, slower "early version," sets the atmospheric tone to begin with, Harvey's sudden, massive drum hits and Bonney's vocal turn the highlights of an effective band performance. Adams makes her presence as strong lyrically as musically, writing the words to about half the record while also contributing her violin throughout. The three combine especially well on another track that appears twice on the CD, the anthemic "On Every Train (Grain Will Bear Grain)." The straight-up album version benefits from Harvey's roiling drum work, building up the intensity slowly but surely, as Bonney and Adams interweave carefully in combination with the brisk guitar and bass work from the rest of the band. The alternate take is shorter and brighter in feel, making for an interesting alternate take. A similar sense of steady increase towards explosion colors "Steal to the Sea," which almost feels like a slow-motion apocalypse of rural country blues gone electric and headed towards damnation. There's even a bit of chugging heavy rave-up a la the MC5 with "Hunter," though the production makes vocals much more predominant than the music. *—Ned Raggett*

Bride Ship / 1989 / Mute ♦♦♦
Starting with "The Shadow of No Man," the band's zoned atmospherics accentuated by both a nicely grimy keyboard drone and brisk pace, Crime & the City Solution continue carving its own strange path. The same line-up from *Shine* reappears here—keyboardist Haas appears only as an auxiliary member, but still adds to the music here and there, while Harvey doubtless contributes most of the organ work. Bonney continues to evolve into more of his own man—if anything, he's embracing country and western more explicitly in his singing style where Cave would prefer blues and Vegas-style show tunes. He takes over the lion's share of the lyrics this time as well, again working with the mix of sometimes cryptic, sometimes concrete imagery of empty landscapes, forlorn towns, ill-lit city streets and the people who live there. In terms of performance, the line-up carries out its shadowy brief well once again—Hacke sounds a little more integrated into the mix than before, as well as a touch more prominent, while Harvey's peerless drumming remains a delight. Adams, meanwhile, still performs her violin with skill and haunting style. A number of interesting approaches surface—consider the deeply funky guitar/keyboard intro to "Stone," which gives the track a major boost of power as well as nicely sitting apart from the band's usual approach. The second half of the album consists of a suite of songs called "The Bride Ship," starting with the track of that name and continuing through "Free World" and "New World." Bonney sometimes sounds far more like Cave than ever, but otherwise it's a dramatic conflation of everything from *Moby Dick* to modern apocalypse, with appropriately doom-laden backing. The CD version includes B-sides—"Three/Four," an okay enough track, and an alternate take on "The Bridge Ship." *—Ned Raggett*

Paradise Discotheque / 1990 / Mute/Elektra ♦♦♦♦♦
What turned out to be Crime & the City Solution's final album was in the end its most unique, striking record, with all the promise and fine fire of its past at last giving a wholly individual expression, foreshadowing Bonney's equally impressive solo career. Lead single and opening track "I Have the Gun" shows the band's new power in particular, shifting between a countryesque blend of jump blues and sorrowful twang and a snarling, forceful electric guitar build. Hacke's work on the latter part is especially impressive, while Harvey shifts between the two gears with aplomb. Bonney, meanwhile, has shaped his now slightly dryer but no less passionate vocals into a unique instrument, easily able to move from the smoky late-night jazz moods of "The Sly Persuaders" to the stunning reworking of the old traditional "Motherless Child." The band's collective grasp of mood and style make *Paradise* both the most varied and most attractive Crime album of the lot—everything's a little more on edge, tensions are higher in performance and delivery, and the mood is not simply building doom but plenty of threat along the way. "The Dolphins and the Sharks" is especially notable, with a quick but subtle bass pulse from Stern relentlessly driving the increasingly edgy performance, as Hacke's guitar and Adams' violin contribute ever more layers of shade. The combination of looped African percussion and what sounds like muffled orchestration on "The Sun Before the Darkness" is just as striking, especially in concert with Bonney's delivery. The last half of the album is a fitting farewell bow for the band—like the concluding part of *The Bride Ship,* it's an extended multi-song piece, called "The Last Dictator." With Bonney's portrayal of the titular character—a bizarre but fascinating musical/political figure—at the center, it's a tour de force for both band and singer. *—Ned Raggett*

Crispy Ambulance

f. 1977, Manchester, England, **db.** 1982
Post-Punk
Inspired after witnessing gigs by the Sex Pistols and Magazine, vocalist Alan Hempsall

formed Crispy Ambulance with guitarist Robert Davenport, bassist Keith Darbyshire, and drummer Gary Madeley. After several shows, including a support slot for Joy Division, they recorded their first single and contacted labels such as Rough Trade and Factory, only to be turned down. Upset but resourceful, the band released it on their own Aural Assault imprint. Rob Gretton (Joy Division's manager) was soon hired by Factory, and his first priority was signing Crispy Ambulance—ironic since the label had earlier rejected the band. After a couple singles were derided in the press for their resemblance to Joy Division, the band was shifted to Factory's Belgian subsidiary. Their lone proper studio LP, *The Plateau Phase*, was released in 1982 and received more comparisons to their brethren, as well as '70s prog rock. The Crispies broke up later that year, but a number of posthumous releases containing studio extras, live material, and radio sessions saw issue. Most significant were the 1999 reissues of *The Plateau Phase* and live compilation *Fin*; the band re-formed in November of that year for a reunion show in Manchester to celebrate the fact. A live documention of the show was issued the following year. *—Andy Kellman*

The Plateau Phase / 1982 / Factory Benelux ✦✦✦✦
The one studio album Crispy Ambulance put out over its career, *The Plateau Phase* boldly aimed to stand out as an experimental rock album and achieved its goal with style and power. With tips of the hat to everyone from early-'70s Pink Floyd and aggro Krautrock to the later song-smashings of Throbbing Gristle, *The Plateau Phase* isn't an out-and-out masterpiece, but comes awfully close. If anything, the comparisons at the time of release to Joy Division resulted from the label association—as a singer, Alan Hempsall had a lighter tone than Ian Curtis, while Keith Darbyshire's bass is hardly trying to clone Peter Hook's inimitable surge. *The Plateau Phase* is certainly a dark, moody experience though, and Chris Nagle turned out to be as crucial for setting a sonic mood for the Crispies as Martin Hannett did for Joy Division. Given the similar influences, the best contemporary band to draw comparisons to might be early Public Image Ltd., but with much less dub and more general melancholy. The mix is often thick, echoing, and understated, only coming up for air with some instruments at times, if at all. Consider "Travel Time," where the brisk drum hits lead the way as the guitar, bass, and especially Hempsall quietly lurk beneath, forcing attention more closely onto them as a result. Hempsall in general has some lyrics perhaps too readily calling to mind "lost in the wilderness" post-punk scenarios already becoming clichéd, but his restrained, dreamlike delivery makes them work better than a flat, declamatory style. Even the occasional wails are set back, strange and curious to hear. Song titles—"Death From Above," "We Move Through the Plateau," "Simon's Ghost"—further heighten the dark, almost psychedelic mood. Call it goth if one wants, but there's more going on here than Batcave-inspired shenanigans. Later CD reissues included the "Live on a Hot August Night" and "Sexus" singles as bonus tracks. *—Ned Raggett*

● **Frozen Blood (1980-1982)** / 2000 / LTM ✦✦✦✦
While various CD reissues had resurrected much of the Crispies' back catalog, there was still a variety of singles and random tracks kicking around by the time Les Temps Moderne embarked on a proper re-release program. As a result, the label topped everything off with *Frozen Blood*, meant to put the final seal on the group in the digital age. Starting with the long out-of-print second single *Unsightly & Serene*, the core of the release consists of two radio sessions, one for legendary U.K. DJ John Peel and another for Piccadilly Radio. Both are notable as together they contain six songs never officially recorded or released elsewhere by the group. Hempsall's vocals on the Peel session cuts are a touch hoarser than usual—explained in the exhaustive liner notes as resulting from an unfortunate cold—but collectively the band is on fire, exuding energy and confidence. "Drug User-Drug Pusher" is the winner from the Peel cuts, a six-minute rip with a fantastic mid-song break and swirling lead melody from Davenport. Derbyshire and Madeley lay down an intricate rhythm line that stops and stutters even as it grooves, and there's the strong sense that a little more time spent on the song would have made a killer single. That sense is borne out by two of the Piccadilly session cuts, "The Presence" and "Concorde Square," both sounding fine here but later turned into something epic on the *Live on a Hot August Night* release. The final seven songs are often intriguing outtakes from the various live tapes that would end up forming *Open Gates of Fire* and its CD cousin *Fin*, taken from a number of dates around Europe in 1982, plus one studio rehearsal, "Cult." Three come from the band's last ever show, at which the band played wholly new material—a fine way to go down fighting. *—Ned Raggett*

Jim Croce

b. Jan. 10, 1943, Philadelphia, PA, **d.** Sep. 20, 1973, Natchitoches, LA
Vocals, Guitar / Soft Rock, Singer/Songwriter
Arguably the worst tragedy that can befall a recording artist is to die when he or she is just beginning to break through on a national level. One such artist was Jim Croce, a songwriter with a knack for both upbeat, catchy singles and empathetic, melancholy ballads. Croce appealed to fans as a common man, and it was not a gimmick—he was a father and husband who went through a series of blue-collar jobs. And whether he used dry wit, gentle emotions or sorrow, Croce sang with a rare form of honesty and power. Few artists have ever been able to pull off such down-to-earth storytelling as convincingly as Croce. After a failed first album recorded with wife Ingrid in 1969, Jim juggled several jobs, including singing for radio commercials. Eventually he was noticed and signed by the ABC/Dunhill label, and released his second album, *Life and Times*, in 1973. The record spawned three hits: "You Don't Mess Around With Jim," "Operator (That's Not the Way It Feels)" and "Bad, Bad Leroy Brown." The latter would become Croce's breakthrough hit, shooting all the way to number one on the Billboard charts. Unfortunately, just two months after it did so, Croce's plane crashed in Natchitoches, Lousiana; he and the four other passengers were killed instantly. Ironically, Croce's career peaked after his death. In 1974, the album *I Got A Name* surfaced, containing the hit "Time in a Bottle," which would become his second #1 single. Shortly afterwards, "I'll Have to Say I Love You in a Song" reached the Top Ten. Several albums were released posthumously, most notably the greatest-hits collection *Photographs and Memories*, which became a best-seller. One cannot help but wonder how far Croce's extraordinary talents could have taken him; unfortunately, such a question may only be looked at rhetorically, but Jim Croce lives on in the impressive catalog of songs he left behind. *—Barry Weber*

● **Photographs & Memories: His Greatest Hits** / 1974 / Atlantic ✦✦✦✦✦
Though Jim Croce produced a handful of hit singles before his death, one can nonetheless argue that Croce was and is a rather underrated songwriter. This is especially evident in listening to his album tracks, many of which are remarkably potent and arguably could have been hits themselves. The numerous double-disc collections that have been released echo this factor, but for casual fans who merely want the radio favorites, the single-disc *Photographs and Memories* will suffice. All of Croce's biggest singles are here, including "Bad Bad Leroy Brown," "Time in a Bottle," and "Operator," as well as overlooked album tracks such as "New York's Not My Home" and "Lovers Cross." This is far from a perfect compilation; the album barely clocks in over 40 minutes, leaving time for numerous tracks that could have easily been added onto the same disc during the record's move from vinyl to CD. Still, it's hard to argue with what's here. While Croce's more devoted followers would prefer the double-disc *50th Anniversary Collection*, casual listeners merely in search of Croce's well-known songs would be best suited with *Photographs and Memories*. *—Barry Weber*

Time in a Bottle/Greatest Love Songs / 1977 / Atlantic ✦✦✦✦✦
Since it contains only his love ballads, fans who prefer his sweetly sentimental songs like "Operator" and "Time in a Bottle" to story-songs like "Bad, Bad Leroy Brown" and "You Don't Mess Around With Jim," will find *Time in a Bottle* the essential compilation; despite the amount of good material here, *Photographs and Memories* remains a better collection, because it presents both sides of the popular singer/songwriter. *—Stephen Thomas Erlewine*

The 50th Anniversary Collection / Sep. 22, 1992 / Saja ✦✦✦✦
For those who want to dig a little deeper into Croce's music than just his well-known songs, the double-CD set *The 50th Anniversary Collection* is a fine buy. The 49-track collection, released in 1992 to commemorate what would have been Croce's 50th birthday, includes all of his radio singles as well as many of the noteworthy album tracks that the single-disc *Photographs and Memories* overlooks. It's not quite a flawless compilation; both discs have a substantial amount of filler, but that doesn't stop the *50th Anniversary Collection* from being a great retrospective on a career that was silenced far too soon. *—Barry Weber*

David Crosby

b. Aug. 14, 1941, Los Angeles, CA
Vocals, Guitar / Pop/Rock, Folk-Rock, Singer/Songwriter
The singular odyssey of David Crosby remains one of the more remarkable tales in the annals of music history. As a founding member of the pioneering American groups the Byrds and Crosby, Stills & Nash, he helped create and popularize the highly influential folk-rock sound, forging the richly harmonic, radiantly acoustic approach which defined the West Coast music scene for years to follow. Yet despite his often overwhelming success, Crosby is recognized far less for his artistic achievements than for his larger-than-life offstage exploits, specifically a long and fantastically excessive battle with drug abuse which seemingly kept him teetering on the brink of death for over a decade.

Born in Los Angeles on August 14, 1941; he made his first recordings as a member of the Les Baxter Balladeers. Crosby cut his first solo session in late 1963; early the following year he formed the Jet Set, later rechristened the Byrds. Creative differences plagued the group throughout their career, and just three years later Crosby left the Byrds in the wake of their appearance at the Monterey Pop Festival.

In 1968 Crosby hooked up with Stephen Stills and Graham Nash. The addition of Neil Young expanded the group to a four-piece, creating a band that would reunite again and again in various configurations over the next thirty years and continue to make a major impact on folk-rock music.

Crosby's solo albums included 1971's *If I Could Only Remember My Name*; a planned second solo album, *Might as Well Have a Good Time*, was rejected by Capitol in 1980. In 1989 he managed to release a second solo effort, *Oh Yes I Can*. The '90s were marked by personal difficulties, including a motorcycle accident and an earthquake which destroyed his home. In 1994, he returned to the headlines when it was announced he was diagnosed with Hepatitis C and dying of liver failure, undergoing a successful organ transplant in 1995. In 1999, CSNY reunited for the first time in 25 years, introducing a new generation to their unforgettable sound. *—Jason Ankeny*

● **If I Could Only Remember My Name** / Feb. 22, 1971 / Atlantic ✦✦✦✦✦
David Crosby's, debut solo album *If I Could Only Remember My Name* is a one-shot wonder of dreamy but ominous California ambience. The songs range from brief snapshots of inspiration (the angelic chorale-vocal showcase on "Orleans" and the a cappella closer, "I'd Swear There Was Somebody Here") to the full-blown, rambling Western epic "Cowboy Movie," and there are absolutely no false notes struck or missteps taken. No one before or since has gotten as much mileage out of a wordless vocal as Crosby does on "Tamalpais High (At About 3)" and "Song With No Words (Tree With No Leaves)," and because the music is so relaxed, each song turns into its own panoramic vista. Those who don't go for trippy Aquarian sentiment, however, may be slightly put off by the obscure, cosmic storytelling of the gorgeous "Laughing" or the ambiguous (but pointed) social questioning of "What Are Their Names," but in actuality it is an incredibly focused

album. Even when a song as pretty as "Traction in the Rain" shimmers with its picked guitars and autoharp, the album is coated in a distinct, persistent menace that is impossible to shake. It is a shame that Crosby would continue to descend throughout the remainder of the decade and the beginning of the next into aimless drug addiction, and that he would not issue another solo album until 18 years later. As it is, *If I Could Only Remember My Name* is a shambolic masterpiece, meandering but transcendently so, full of frayed threads. Not only is it among the finest splinter albums out of the CSNY diaspora, it is one of the defining moments of hung-over spirituality from the era. *—Stanton Swihart*

Oh Yes I Can / Jan. 23, 1989 / A&M ♦♦♦

David Crosby's re-entrance into the music world after drugs and guns landed him in prison and rehab. It's a surprisingly good recording, showing his strengths as a composer of melodic acoustic music. "Melody" recalls early Crosby, Stills & Nash, and "Tracks in the Dust," featuring Graham Nash and Michael Hedges, brings back the "hippie hopefulness" that has always characterized the best of Crosby's songwriting. "Distances" is gorgeous, sounding like an outtake from 1977's *CSN*, and "Flying Man" reminds us of what a sweet sound Crosby can get out of a wordless vocal. The attempts at electric rock are less interesting, with "Drop Down Mama" and "Monkey and the Underdog" being the weakest tracks on the disc (though considering Crosby's personal history, the latter's lyrics are quite understandable). *Oh Yes I Can* represents an artistic triumph for David Crosby, one that held out hope for a continued resurrection by this rock & roll survivor. *—Jim Newsom*

Thousand Roads / May 4, 1993 / Atlantic ♦♦♦

For his third solo album, *Thousand Roads*, Crosby increased the participation of his guests and attempted to redefine himself as an artist. Where previously, regardless of who was playing or singing on the track, the song was a Crosby composition, on *Thousand Roads* Crosby acted primarily as an interpretive singer, penning only one of the ten songs and contributing to two others. The result certainly was a craftsmanlike set of songs written by pop professionals—Phil Collins, Jimmy Webb, Marc Cohn, John Hiatt, Paul Brady, Stephen Bishop—and produced by the cream of pop producers—Don Was, Glyn Johns, Phil Ramone. The failings were, first, that Crosby's individuality was lost and, second, that, as the list suggests, his choices were more calculated than inspired. The problem with David Crosby as a solo artist was not how to make him sound more conventional, it was how to make his unconventionality work. *Thousand Roads* solved the wrong problem; the album was Crosby's least successful in the record stores. *—William Ruhlmann*

It's All Coming Back Now / Jan. 24, 1995 / Atlantic ♦♦

Crosby, Stills & Nash (and Young)

f. 1968, Laurel Canyon, CA

Pop/Rock, Folk-Rock, Singer/Songwriter

The musical partnership of David Crosby, Stephen Stills and Graham Nash—with and without Neil Young—not only was one of the most successful touring and recording acts of the late '60s,'70s, and early '80s; with the colorful, contrasting nature of the members' characters and their connection to the political and cultural upheavals of the time, it was the only American-based band to approach the overall societal impact of the Beatles. The group was a second marriage for all the participants when it came together in 1968: Crosby had been a member of the Byrds, Nash was in the Hollies, and Stills had been part of Buffalo Springfield. The resulting trio, however, sounded like none of its predecessors and was characterized by a unique vocal blend and a musical approach that ranged from acoustic folk to melodic pop to hard rock. By the time of their first tour (which included the Woodstock festival), they had added Young, also a veteran of Buffalo Springfield, who maintained a solo career. The first CSN&Y album, *Déjà Vu*, was a chart-topping hit in 1970, but the group split acrimoniously after a summer tour. In 1974, CSN&Y reformed for a summer stadium tour without releasing a new record. Nevertheless, the compilation *So Far* became their third straight #1. Crosby, Stills & Nash re-formed without Young in 1977 for the album *CSN*, another giant hit. The trio remains a popular live act. *—William Ruhlmann*

☆ **Crosby, Stills & Nash** / May 29, 1969 / Atlantic ♦♦♦♦♦

The Crosby, Stills & Nash triumvirate shot to immediate superstardom with the release of their self-titled debut LP, a sparkling set immortalizing the group's amazing close high harmonies. While elements of the record haven't dated well—Nash's Eastern-influenced musings on the hit "Marrakesh Express" now seem more than a little silly, while the anti-war sentiments of "Wooden Ships," though well-intentioned, are rather hokey—the harmonies are absolutely timeless, and the best material remains rock-solid. Stills' gorgeous opener "Suite: Judy Blue Eyes," in particular, is an epic love song remarkable in its musical and emotional intricacy, Nash's "Pre-Road Downs" is buoyant folk-pop underpinned by light psychedelic textures, and Crosby's "Long Time Gone" remains a potent indictment of the assassination of Robert Kennedy. A definitive document of its era. *—Jason Ankeny*

☆ **Déjà Vu** / Mar. 11, 1970 / Atlantic ♦♦♦♦♦

The first of the group's albums to include Neil Young, *Déjà Vu* is the CSNY aggregrate's most consistent and lovely LP. Not only does Young's recruitment bring an idiosyncratic new dimension to the group's shimmering harmonies, but the addition of his guitar skills greatly broadens their musical scope; at the same time, his prodigious songwriting gifts seem to have spurred the original CSN line-up to new creative heights—the material on *Déjà Vu* is uniformly excellent, ranging from the gorgeous "Helpless" to the ambitious title cut. The star of the record is Graham Nash, who delivers a pair of classics, the country-inflected "Teach Your Children" and "Our House," written for Joni Mitchell; speaking of Mitchell, she also penned the record's centerpiece, the perennial "Woodstock," a sweeping celebration of counterculture values. *—Jason Ankeny*

Four Way Street / Apr. 7, 1971 / Atlantic ♦♦♦♦♦

This 1992 expanded version of the original double live album (originally released on April 7, 1971) by CSN&Y is now an indispensible part of any collection, with additional Neil Young and Graham Nash material (and even a version of "King Midas in Reverse," the old Hollies tune) that any serious listener will want. Some of the extended guitar jams between Stills and Young ("Southern Man") go on longer than strict musical sense would dictate, but it seemed right at the time, and they capture a form that was far more abused in other hands after this group broke up. *—Bruce Eder*

● **So Far** / Aug. 1974 / Atlantic ♦♦♦♦♦

Released to coincide with CSN&Y's 1974 reunion tour, this compilation remains the best representation of the group's early work, featuring such hits as "Teach Your Children" and "Suite: Judy Blue Eyes." It also put the one-off single "Ohio/Find the Cost of Freedom" (CSN&Y's response to the shooting of four anti-war student protestors at Kent State University) on an album for the first time. *—William Ruhlmann*

CSN / Jun. 17, 1977 / Atlantic ♦♦♦♦

The times had certainly changed since *Déjà vu*'s release in 1970. Nevertheless, there was a hunger in the musical audience for a return to the harmony-soaked idealism with which this trio had catapulted to popularity, and *CSN* consequently reached number two on the charts, behind Fleetwood Mac's mega-success *Rumours*. The music here is very good, though probably not up to the hard-to-match level of *Crosby, Stills & Nash* or *Déjà vu*. Still, the songs showed a great deal of lyrical maturity and compositional complexity compared to those earlier albums from a far more innocent time. "Just a Song Before I Go" was the latest of Graham Nash's radio-friendly acoustic numbers, and was a Top Ten single. "See the Changes" and "Dark Star" rank with the best of Stephen Stills' work, while David Crosby contributes three classics from his distinctive oeuvre: "Shadow Captain," "Anything at All," and the beautiful "In My Dreams." Nash's multi-part "Cathedral," a recollection of an acid trip taken in Winchester Cathedral on his 32nd birthday, became a staple of the group's live repertoire. *CSN* was this trio's last fully realized album. It was also the last recording on which the three principals handled all the vocal parts without the sweetening of additional voices. It has held up remarkably well, both as a memento of its time, and as a thoroughly enjoyable musical work. *—Jim Newsom*

Daylight Again / Jun. 21, 1982 / Atlantic ♦♦♦

Originally a Stills and Nash project, but with the drug-addled Crosby added virtually in name only for commercial reasons (Timothy Schmit and Art Garfunkel provide many of the harmonies), this turned out better than expected, featuring Nash's reflective "Wasted on the Way" and Stills' "Southern Cross," both hits and respectable additions to the CSN repertoire. *—William Ruhlmann*

Allies / Jun. 6, 1983 / Atlantic ♦♦

American Dream / Nov. 3, 1988 / Atlantic ♦♦

Live It Up / Jun. 11, 1990 / Atlantic ♦♦

Crosby, Stills & Nash [Box Set] / Oct. 1991 / Atlantic ♦♦♦♦♦

Seventy-seven tracks make up this four-CD boxed set retrospective of the various permutations of Crosby, Stills and Nash (and Young) from 1968 to 1990. The set is dotted with unreleased tracks from abortive album sessions (CSN&Y may have recorded only two studio albums, but they sure tried a lot of other times), and there are also good choices from both solo work and the well-known material. For a neophyte, it may be on the long side, but seasoned fans can welcome this lavish tribute. *—William Ruhlmann*

After the Storm / Aug. 16, 1994 / Atlantic ♦♦

Looking Forward / Oct. 26, 1999 / Reprise ♦♦♦

Christopher Cross

b. May 3, 1951, San Antonio, TX

Vocals / Soft Rock, Adult Contemporary

Christopher Cross was far and away the biggest new star of 1980, virtually defining adult contemporary radio with a series of smoothly sophisticated ballads including the chart-topping "Sailing"; seemingly as quickly as he shot to fame, however, his star descended, although he continued recording and touring for years to come. Born Christopher Geppert in San Antonio, TX on May 3, 1951, Cross first surfaced in the Austin-based cover band Flash before signing a solo contract with Warner Bros. in the autumn of 1978. His self-titled debut LP appeared two years later, with the lead single "Ride Like the Wind" rocketing to the number two spot; the massive success of the second single "Sailing" made Cross a superstar, and in the wake of two more Top 20 hits, "Never Be the Same" and "Say You'll Be Mine," he walked off with a record-setting five Grammys in 1981, including Best New Artist and Song of the Year for "Sailing." He soon scored a second number one as well as an Academy Award with "Arthur's Theme (Best That You Can Do)," which he co-wrote with Burt Bacharach, Carole Bayer Sager, and Peter Allen for the smash Dudley Moore film comedy *Arthur*. Cross' much-anticipated sophomore effort *Another Page* arrived in 1983, but except for the Top Ten entry "Think of Laura" (popularized through its constant presence on the daytime soap phenomenon *General Hospital*), the album failed to repeat the success of its predecessor, and somewhat amazingly, he never returned to the Top 40 again. *Every Turn of the World* appeared to little notice in 1985, and when 1988's *Back of My Mind* failed to chart altogether, Cross was dropped by Warner. His next album, *Rendezvous*, did not appear until five years later on BMG. *Window* followed in 1995, and in 1998 he signed to CMC International for *Walking in Avalon*, a two-disc effort split between new studio material and live recordings of his past hits. Cross returned in the spring of 2000 with *The Red Room*. *—Jason Ankeny*

• **Christopher Cross** / Jan. 1980 / Warner Brothers ✦✦✦✦✦
Christopher Cross' debut was a huge hit and widely acclaimed, at least among industry professionals (critics didn't give it a second listen), leading to multi-platinum success and Grammys. In retrospect, it might seem like the kind of success that's disproportional to the record itself, especially to hipper-than-thou younger generations, but in truth, *Christopher Cross* was a hell of a record—it just was a hell of a soft rock record, something that doesn't carry a lot of weight among most audiences. That doesn't erase Cross' considerable gifts as a craftsman. Yes, he does favor sentimentality and can be very sweet on the ballads, but his melodicism is rich and construction tight, so there's a sturdy foundation for the classy professional gloss provided by his studio pros and friends, including indelible backing vocals by Michael McDonald. And while the hits like the dreamy "Sailing" and the surging "Ride Like the Wind" deserved all the attention, they're hardly the only highlights here—to borrow a sports metaphor, this has a deep bench, and there's not a weak moment here. In fact, soft rock albums hardly ever came better than this, and it remains one of the best mainstream albums of its time. *—Stephen Thomas Erlewine*

Another Page / Jan. 1983 / Warner Brothers ✦✦✦
Christopher Cross had a lot to live up to in following his self-titled debut album, which had sold a million copies (now up to four million), spawned four Top 40 hits, including the #1 "Sailing," and won him five Grammy Awards, including Album of the Year, Song of the Year, Record of the Year (the last two for "Sailing"), and Best New Artist. So, he took three years to make *Another Page*, which, unsurprisingly, sounded a lot like its predecessor. Cross concentrated on smooth pop arrangements, over which be sang greeting-card romantic sentiments in an innocent, Brian Wilson-like tenor. No one would confuse the result with anything truly heartfelt or with real rock & roll, but Cross's soothing approach was still good enough to put two of his songs, "All Right" and "No Time For Talk," into the Top 40 and earn a gold record certification. Then, nearly a year after the album's release, TV soap opera *General Hospital* began featuring the maudlin ballad "Think of Laura," and *Another Page* suddenly had a third single, this one a Top Ten hit. *—William Ruhlmann*

Every Turn of the World / Nov. 1985 / Warner Brothers ✦✦

Back of My Mind / 1988 / Warner Brothers ✦✦

Rendezvous / Apr. 2, 1993 / BMG ✦✦✦

Window / Mar. 21, 1995 / Priority ✦✦

Sheryl Crow

b. Feb. 11, 1962
Singer, Vocals, Songwriter, Guitar / American Trad Rock, Adult Alternative Pop/Rock, Pop/Rock, Singer/Songwriter
Of all the singer-songwriters that emerged during the much-publicized "women in rock" explosion of the mid-'90s, Sheryl Crow was the traditionalist of the bunch, revitalizing classic rock. Her first album, 1993's *Tuesday Night Music Club*, slowly became a hit, thanks to the bouncy "All I Wanna Do," yet she found her voice over her next two albums, consolidating her fan base, earning strong reviews and winning Grammys.

Crow began her professional music career as a backing vocalist for both Don Henley and Michael Jackson. After landing a couple of original songs on other artist's records, she scored a record deal with A&M. Her first attempt at a solo album was recorded with producer Hugh Padgham. The resulting record was glossy, streamlined and calculated—enough so that she and the label shelved it. Crow headed back into the studio with producers Kevin Gilbert and Bill Botrell. They used music played during a local LA jam session called "Tuesday Night Music Club" as the inspiration for the record, eventually taking the title for her 1993 album. Initially, the record didn't make much of an impact, but the next year "All I Wanna Do" became a smash hit, sending the album into blockbuster territory. Her success was not without controversy, as members of the Music Club, led by David Baerwald, claimed that Crow took too much credit for what was essentially a collaborative effort. Determined to shed these criticisms, Crow largely abandoned the Club for her eponymous 1996 album, relying on Tchad Blake as her primary collaborator. Though it was still classicist in many ways, it was considerably more ambitious lyrically and musically, a determinedly modern record. It was another smash success, thanks to singles like "Every Day Is a Winding Road." She returned to fairly straightforward territory for 1998's *The Globe Sessions*. While it wasn't quite as popular as its two predecessors, it nevertheless went platinum. She bought time in 1999 with her fourth album, *Sheryl Crow and Friends: Live in Central Park*. *—Stephen Thomas Erlewine*

Tuesday Night Music Club / Aug. 3, 1993 / A&M ✦✦✦
Sheryl Crow earned her recording contract through hard work, gigging as a backing vocalist for everyone from Don Henley to Michael Jackson before entering the studio with Hugh Padgham to record her debut album. As it turned out, things didn't go entirely as planned. Instead of adhering to her rock & roll roots, the record was a slick set of contemporary pop, relying heavily on ballads. Upon hearing the completed album, Crow convinced A&M not to release the album, choosing to cut a new record with producer Bill Bottrell. Along with several Los Angeles-based songwriters and producers, including David Baerwald, David Ricketts, and Brian McLeod, Bottrell was part of a collective dubbed "the Tuesday Night Music Club." Every Tuesday, the group would get together, drink beer, jam, and write songs. Crow became part of the Club and, within a few months, she decided to craft her debut album around the songs and spirit of the collective. It was, for the most part, an inspired idea, since *Tuesday Night Music Club* has a loose, ramshackle charm that her unreleased debut lacked. At its best—the opening quartet of "Run, Baby, Run," "Leaving Las Vegas," "Strong Enough," and "Can't Cry Anymore," plus the deceptively infectious "All I Wanna Do"—are remarkable testaments to their collaboration, proving that roots rock can sound contemporary and have humor. That same spirit, however, also resulted in some half-finished songs, and the preponderance of those tracks make *Tuesday Night Music Club* better in memory than it is in practice. Still, even with the weaker moments, Crow manages to create an identity for herself—a classic rocker at heart but with enough smarts to stay contemporary. And that's the lasting impression *Tuesday Night Music Club* leaves. *—Stephen Thomas Erlewine*

• **Sheryl Crow** / Sep. 24, 1996 / A&M ✦✦✦✦✦
Hiring noted roots experimentalists Tchad Blake and Mitchell Froom as engineer and consultant, respectively, Sheryl Crow took a cue from their Latin Playboys project for her second album—she kept her roots rock foundation and added all sorts of noises, weird instruments, percussion loops, and off-balance production to give *Sheryl Crow* a distinctly modern flavor. And, even with the Stones-y grind of "Sweet Rosalyn" or hippie spirits of "Love Is a Good Thing," it is an album that couldn't have been made any other time than the '90s. As strange as it may sound, *Sheryl Crow* is a post-modern masterpiece of sorts—albeit a *mainstream*, post-alternative, post-modern masterpiece. It may not be as hip or innovative as, say, the Beastie Boys' *Paul's Boutique*, but it is as self-referential, pop-culture obsessed, and musically eclectic. Throughout the record, Crow spins out wild, nearly incomprehensible stream-of-consciousness lyrics, dropping celebrity names and products every chance she gets ("drinking Falstaff beer/Mercedes Ruehl and a rented Leer"). Often, these litanies don't necessarily add up to anything specific, but they're a perfect match for the mess of rock, blues, alt-rock, country, folk, and lite hip-hop loops that dominate the record. At her core, she remains a traditionalist—the songcraft behind the infectious "Change Would Do You Good," the bubbly "Everyday Is a Winding Road," and the weary "If It Makes You Happy" helped get the singles on the radio—but the production and lyrics are often at odds with those instincts, creating for a fascinating and compelling (and occasionally humorous) listen and one of the most individual albums of its era. *—Stephen Thomas Erlewine*

The Globe Sessions / Sep. 29, 1998 / A&M ✦✦✦✦
Since her dense, varied, post-modernist eponymous second album illustrated that Sheryl Crow was no one-album wonder, she wasn't left with as much to prove the third time around. Having created an original variation on roots rock with *Sheryl Crow*, she was left with the dilemma of how to remain loyal to that sound without repeating herself on her third album, *The Globe Sessions*. To her credit, she never plays lazy, not when she's turning out Stones-y rockers ("There Goes the Neighborhood") or when she's covering Dylan (the remarkable "Mississippi," an outtake from *Time Out of Mind*). However, she has decided to abandon the layered, yard-sale production and pop-culture fixations that made *Sheryl Crow* a defining album of the mid-'90s. *The Globe Sessions*, instead, is the work of a craftsman, one who knows how to balance introspective songs with pop/rockers, one who knows how to exploit their signature sound while becoming slightly more eclectic. In that sense, the album is a lot like a latter-day album from her idols, the Stones—it finds pleasures within the craft and the signature sound themselves. That means that there are no surprises (apart from the synthesized handclaps, of course)—the Celtic homage "Riverwide" may be new, but it's not unexpected, much like how the whiplash transition in "Am I Getting Through" isn't entirely out of the blue—but that's not necessarily a bad thing, since *The Globe Sessions* has a strong set of songs. Since it lacks the varied sonics, humor, and flat-out weirdness of *Sheryl Crow*, it's never quite as compelling a listen as its predecessor, yet it is a strong record, again confirming Crow's position as one of the best roots-rockers of the '90s. *—Stephen Thomas Erlewine*

Sheryl Crow and Friends: Live in Central Park / Dec. 7, 1999 / A&M ✦✦

Crowded House

f. Jul. 1985, **db.** Jun. 1996
College Rock, New Zealand Rock, Adult Alternative Pop/Rock, Pop/Rock
An institution in their homeland, a two-hit wonder in the U.S. and, during the last half of their ten-year career, bonafide stars in the U.K. and most of Europe, Crowded House recorded some of the best pop music of the late '80s and early '90s. Leader Neil Finn's carefully crafted songs, meticulous eye for lyrical detail and gift for melody are matched by few other songwriters.

Crowded House formed in the ashes of Split Enz in 1985 when Neil Finn shifted to a stripped down, back-to-basics combo featuring ex-Enz drummer Paul Hester and bassist Nick Seymour. The group headed to Los Angeles, eventually signing with Capitol Records and after several name changes, settled on Crowded House, a reflection of their living conditions in L.A. Their self-titled debut didn't gain much attention upon its release in the summer of 1986, but the band created a buzz in North America by taking an unorthodox, low-profile tour of odd venues like ethnic restaurants. On the talk-show circuit, they won over audiences with their charm and wit. By early 1987, the album eventually peaked at number 12, spawning the number two hit single "Don't Dream It's Over" and number seven "Something So Strong." In their homeland, multi-platinum success followed. 1988's *Temple of Low Men* showcased a notable progression in Finn's songcraft but the album's slightly darker tone failed to spark the interest of pop audiences. *Woodface*, released in 1991, featured several collaborations from Neil's brother (and temporary member of the band) Tim. The album certainly represents their finest recorded moments, and the smash hit "Weather with You" eventually made the band stars in the U.K. and Europe. In early 1993, they recorded their fourth album, adding American guitarist Mark Hart. *Together Alone* was released in 1993 to unanimously positive reviews. Paul Hester left the band in 1994.

Following a Finn Brothers album, Neil officially broke up Crowded House in June 1996. That same month, *Recurring Dream: The Very Best of Crowded House* was released, entering the U.K. and Australian charts at number one. After a handful of "final shows" in various locations, on Sunday November 24, 1996, Crowded House played their official farewell show at the Sydney Opera House to 100,000 fans.

By 1997, Paul Hester formed a new band, Largest Living Things, releasing two EPs and playing regular gigs in Australia. Neil Finn made his debut as a solo artist in 1998 with *Try Whistling This*. In December 1999, *Afterglow*, an album's worth of Crowded House leftovers and rarities, was issued. *—Chris Woodstra*

Crowded House / Jun. 1986 / Capitol ♦♦♦
Split Enz needed to end, particularly since founding member Tim Finn found his little brother Neil's growth spurt uncomfortable, but also because Neil was no longer writing tunes that made sense within the context of a band that ran the gamut from art rock to eccentric new wave. Neil Finn was now writing songs that were undeniably totems of popcraft, but infused with the spirit and introspection of a singer/songwriter. This formula would later become quite popular with artists from Matthew Sweet to the legions of basement auteurs in the pop underground, but this sensibility was relatively unheard of in the mid-'80s—hence the birth of Crowded House. Neil Finn retained Paul Hester from Enz, added Nick Seymour for the trio, and recorded one abandoned attempt at an album before joining with Mitchell Froom for the band's eponymous debut. At the time, Froom's clean production seemed refreshing, almost rootsy, compared to the synth-pop dominating the mainstream and college scenes at the time, but in retrospect it seems a little overreaching and fussy, particularly in its addition of echo and layers of keyboards during particularly inappropriate moments. But Finn at his best overshadowed this fairly stilted production with his expert songcraft. As it happened, the record was blessed by good timing, and the majestic ballad "Don't Dream It's Over" became an international hit, while its follow-up, the breezy "Something So Strong," also turned into a hit. Both revealed different sides of Finn's talents, with the first being lyrical and the second being effervescent, but perhaps the truest testaments to his talents are "Mean to Me," "World Where You Live," and "Now We're Getting Somewhere," songs where the lyrics meld with the melody in a way that is distinctive, affecting, and personal. If the rest of the record doesn't reach those heights, it's still good, well-constructed pop, and these aforementioned highlights point the way to *Temple of Low Men*, where Crowded House (and particularly Neil Finn) came into its own. *—Stephen Thomas Erlewine*

Temple of Low Men / Jul. 1988 / Capitol ♦♦♦♦♦
Following the success of Crowded House's debut and the band's gruelling promotion schedule, Neil Finn was clearly showing signs that he was no longer happy being New Zealand's zany ambassador to the U.S. While the material on *Temple of Low Men* demonstrates great leaps in quality over its predecessor, it is a darkly difficult album, especially for those expecting *Crowded House, Pt. 2*—in short, there are no immediately accessible singles. Instead, Finn digs into the depths of his emotional psyche with obsessive detail, crafting a set of intense, personal songs that range from the all-too-intimate look at infidelity of "Into Temptation" to the raucous exorcism of "Kill Eye." Through all of this introspective soul searching, Finn reveals most of all his true mastery of melody. *—Chris Woodstra*

Woodface / Jul. 2, 1991 / Capitol ♦♦♦♦♦
Where Crowded House's previous album, *Temple of Low Men*, showcased the often dark side of a man alone with his thoughts, *Woodface* represents the joy of reunion and the freedom of a collaborative effort—more than half of the album was originally conceived as a Finn Brothers project, which was Tim and Neil's first crack at writing together. The songs are easily their finest to date, combining flawless melodies and the outstanding harmonies of the brothers' perfectly matched voices. *—Chris Woodstra*

Together Alone / Oct. 18, 1993 / EMI-Capitol Special Markets ♦♦♦
More experimental and musically varied than any of their previous releases, *Together Alone* finds Crowded House branching out into traditional Maori music and heavy guitars, as well as the shining pop songcraft that is Neil Finn's trademark. Picking up a new guitarist and adding the production skills of ex-Killing Joke member Youth, Crowded House energizes their sound without losing sight of Neil Finn's classic pop songwriting, as "Locked Out" and "Distant Sun" prove. *—Stephen Thomas Erlewine*

● **Recurring Dream: The Very Best of Crowded House** / Jun. 24, 1996 / Capitol ♦♦♦♦♦
Recurring Dream is a 19-track collection which assembles most of the band's singles and adds three new studio tracks to entice fans—"Not the Girl You Think You Are," "Instinct" and "Everything Is Good for You." As a career summary, the collection works fairly well, though the nonchronological sequencing makes for a slightly confusing listen. Nevertheless, for a band with no shortage of great material (there's not a bad album in the bunch), *Recurring Dream* is a good place to get aquainted with them. Initial pressings also came with a second disc which compiles highlights from the band's always entertaining live shows. Maybe a disc of non-album rarities and B-sides would have been a better choice, but for fans this is an essential addition. *—Chris Woodstra*

Afterglow / Dec. 7, 1999 / Capitol ♦♦♦
Like any band, Crowded House had some unfinished business after their split. Namely, they had a number of very good songs that never appeared on an official album. These weren't rejects, per se—they were tunes that didn't have a home, so they popped up on B-sides, soundtracks and live shows, where Crowded House regularly aired unreleased and rare songs. These often became fan favorites yet they weren't readily available until the appearance of the rarities, B-sides, and "orphans" collection, *Afterglow*. Not every non-LP song made the cut, but everything here is quite strong and the album gels very well, sounding a bit like a lost album, even if the tracks were recorded between 1985 and 1994. Is it an essential collection? Well, for hardcore fans—the kind that know that with the existence of *Afterglow* they can now piece together the running order of the original *Woodface*—it certainly is. But it's not just for them, since casual fans will find several gems here. Perhaps Paul Hester's endearingly silly "My Telly's Gone Bung" will rub them the wrong way, but such gems as the pre-Crowded House tune "Recurring Dream" and the gorgeous "I Love You Dawn" rank among the group's finest, proving that Neil Finn became an exceptional songsmith during the time he led Crowded House. They, along with several other tunes, mean *Afterglow* isn't just appealing for Crowded House diehards, but for anyone with a taste for fine, well-crafted pop. *—Stephen Thomas Erlewine*

The Crust Brothers

Indie Rock, Rock & Roll
The Crust Brothers started out on December 5, 1997, when Pavement's frontman Steve Malkmus got together with the members of the Seattle/Montana trio of Silkworm. They played a benefit show together in Seattle, and the recording of this show was later turned into their first album, titled *Marquee Mark* (Telemomo). Malkmus is known for his brilliant, arcane songwriting and his powerful, precision guitar playing. Although the name of Steve Malkmus might steal some of the thunder from the lesser-known Silkworm trio, don't be fooled; the threesome posses a continuous energy that drives their instruments with confidence and delivers their songs with surprisingly introspective lyrics. The members of Silkworm include bassist/vocalist Tim Midgett, guitarist/vocalist Andy Cohen, and drummer Michael Dahlquist. These fellows met Malkmus at the 1996 Lollapalooza concert and the friendship developed from there. Malkmus later moved to Portland, and due to proximity or chemistry, he started spending more time with his friends in Seattle. Oddly enough, the four musicians began working on some "fight" songs for a National Football League commercial but things never panned out. Cohen has received credit for creating the name of The Crust Brothers. At first glance, the name would appear to have been developed for the primary purpose of tainting a date on a club's calendar, but it apparently evolved from the classic rock band The Dust Brothers. All of this makes perfect sense once you hear their first album's set of classic rock treasures. Malkmus has made big waves in the past with another one of his so-called "side-projects," The Silver Jews. The founder of this band, David Berman, points out that the Jews were formed at the University of Virginia before Pavement ever had the chance to grace us with their futuristic wisdom. *—Gregg Rounds*

Marquee Mark / Oct. 15, 1998 / Telemomo ♦♦♦
It's hard to put a finger on what makes this album a worthy purchase. It could be that it's refreshing to hear two heavyweights of the alternative rock, lo-fi movement playing—for the most part—mainstream classic rock songs. Or, maybe—to fans of earlier Silkworm and Pavement work—it's that their behavior on this album is abnormally conformist for these notoriously anti-establishment artists; however, it's probably just the fact that they play the songs so well. As far as sound quality goes, the recording of the show is commendable, but the band is rough around the edges due to their lack of practice. In reality, they are just having a good time, and the listener shouldn't look any further than this. The set list is, for the most part, a testament of respect to Bob Dylan. The first six songs of the album are Dylan's work, five of them from his legendary *Basement Tapes*. They mix one Silkworm song in the middle of the set, and the rest of the album draws tricks from Lynyrd Skynyrd, Creedence Clearwater Revival, the Rolling Stones, the Byrds, and Cheap Trick. Hidden on the B-side of the album are two fine gems. When Malkmus takes on Silkworm's "Never Met a Man I Didn't Like," he finds harmony and produces a convincing sincerity that almost seems out of place on the album. "Heard It Through the Grapevine" is also particularly powerful. Malkmus delivers some great guitar licks, and the band seems to find a common ground. The album is fun, and a treat for serious fans, but to the uninitiated, it's a bit unbearable. *—Gregg Rounds*

The Cryan' Shames

f. 1964, Chicago, IL, **db.** 1970
The Cryan' Shames were a big deal in Chicago in the mid- and late '60s when a bunch of their singles hit the local Top Ten; some of them were small national hits as well. The biggest of these was "Sugar and Spice," a cover of a Searchers song (itself a cover of a Drifters hit) that made the Top 50 in 1966 and was later featured in the *Nuggets* anthology of '60s garage bands. In their original incarnation, the Shames leaned toward the pop end of garage. Borrowing heavily from the Beatles, the Byrds, and the Yardbirds, guitarist Jim Fair wrote a clutch of energetic guitar pop/rockers with sparkling harmonies. After 1966, the group pursued an increasingly mainstream pop direction featuring saccharine arrangements and material. In this respect they uncannily mirrored the devolution of local rivals the New Colony Six, who also shifted from tough pop/rock to MOR in their bid for national success. *—Richie Unterberger*

● **Sugar & Spice (A Collection)** / Jul. 14, 1992 / Columbia/Legacy ♦♦♦♦
This 18-song compilation spans 1966 to 1969, and features their singles and key album cuts. Despite its good intentions, this well-packaged retrospective runs out of octane after the first half dozen songs. *—Richie Unterberger*

The Crystals

f. 1961, Brooklyn, NY, **db.** 1966
Girl Group
This Brooklyn female vocal group had R&B roots, but the Crystals were really a pop ensemble whose best songs perfectly expressed the romantic innocence of the early '60s. Barbara Alston, Lala Brooks, Dee Dee Kennibrew, Mary Thomas, and Patricia Wright were the original lineup; the remarkable producer Phil Spector heard them rehearsing and eventually signed them to his Philles label, where they had several classic songs. "There's No Other like My Baby" got things started in 1961; "Uptown" cracked the R&B and pop Top 20, and then came "He's a Rebel," arguably their finest song and one of the era's landmarks. Darlene Love was lead vocalist, and both "He's A Rebel," and the successful follow-up "He's Sure the Boy I Love" featured Love and the Blossoms but were

credited to the Crystals. The actual Crystals returned in 1963 and had two more huge hits, "Da Doo Ron Ron (When He Walked Me Home)" and "Then He Kissed Me" in 1963, each one making the Top Ten on both the R&B and pop lists. But the party ended in 1964, as their final two singles for Philles both flopped and relations between them and Spector degenerated. Various editions of the Crystals have been plentiful on the oldies circuit, but at last account, only Kennibrew was still involved out of the originals. *—Ron Wynn*

● **The Best of the Crystals** / Sep. 22, 1992 / ABKCO ✦✦✦✦✦
All of the Crystals' biggest hits are included on this comprehensive collection, which also features many forgotten singles and album tracks; while some of the lesser-known material might not match the standards of the classic singles, many songs do come close. *—Stephen Thomas Erlewine*

Phil Spector Wall of Sound, Vol. 3: The Crystals Sing Their Greatest Hits! / 1995 / Phil Spector International ✦✦✦
For a long time, the British Phil Spector International series was the only way you could pick up his classic early '60s productions. The Crystals volume covers all of the essential bases: the monster hits, worthy obscurities like "Please Hurt Me" and "No One Ever Tells You," and the controversial, withdrawn Goffin-King single, "He Hit Me." It's been superseded as the collection of choice by the 1992 ABKCO CD, *The Best Of The Crystals*. As this import collection is out-of-print and difficult to find, all those looking for a definitive Crystals anthology should go for the ABKCO one instead. But if you already have this vinyl LP, it essentially duplicates the contents of the CD; audiophiles may differ on the matter, but I wouldn't say it's worth the $15 or so to "upgrade." *—Richie Unterberger*

Cub

f. 1992, **db.** Jun. 1997
Twee Pop, Indie Rock
Crush-pop trio Cub formed in 1992 after vocalist/bassist Lisa Marr, guitarist Robynn Iwata and drummer Valeria Fellini met while working at the college radio station of their alma mater, the University of British Columbia. Despite no prior musical experience—throughout the band's first year, Iwata played live seated on the stage while looking at cheat sheets for chord progressions—Cub's live shows (during which the group often tossed candy to the audience) won their unique brand of simple, infectious punk-pop a cult following on the Vancouver club circuit, and in October 1992 the trio issued their debut EP, *Pep*, on Mint Records, the Vancouver-based label co-owned by Iwata's brother Randy.

Following the release of *Betti-Cola*—a superb collection of EP tracks and new recordings complete with a *Josie and the Pussycats*-styled cover by famed Archie Comics artist Dan DeCarlo—Fellini left the band; she was replaced by drummer Lisa G., whom Marr met through the pages of the fanzine *Self-Esteem Queen*. After the release of 1994's *Come Out, Come Out*, Mint signed a distribution deal with the U.S. punk label Lookout!, which brought increased visibility to the release of 1996's edgier *Box of Hair*, *Mauler*, another collection of singles, followed in early 1997. On June 10 of that year, a series of three handwritten messages posted on the Mint Records website—one from each member—announced Cub's breakup. *—Jason Ankeny*

● **Betti-Cola** / 1993 / Mint ✦✦✦✦✦
Cub's insanely catchy debut *Betti-Cola* collects the group's two early EPs *Pep* and *Hot Dog Day*, along with another 15 unreleased tracks recorded over the course of three separate 1993 sessions. While the band's primitive, sweet formula changes little over the duration of the set, the performances grow more assured with each passing track; whether tackling Lisa Marr's own infectious compositions (highlighted by the idyllic "Motel 6," the buoyant "My Chinchilla" and the wistful "Someday") or well-chosen covers (Beat Happening's "Cast a Shadow," the Beach Boys' "Surfer Girl"), Cub's naive charm is irresistible. *—Jason Ankeny*

Come Out, Come Out / 1994 / Mint ✦✦✦✦✦
Come Out, Come Out is Cub's masterpiece, transcending the cutesy limitations of cuddlecore to create music of genuine originality and meaning. Each of the 11 original tracks here is an absolute gem, buoyed by Ramones-like abandon but anchored by an ever-expanding melodic sophistication and lyrical depth; apart from almost absurdly infectious highlights like "Ticket to Spain" and "Everything's Geometry," there's also an emotional complexity to tracks like the giddy "Your Bed" and the bitter "Tomorrow Go Away," which rejects the seeming naivete of the band's music once and for all. Cuddlecore's finest hour. *—Jason Ankeny*

Box of Hair / Jul. 26, 1996 / Lookout ✦✦✦✦
This set of short, poppy and punky songs has instant appeal. The three women of Cub have found a formula that suits them: sweetly harmonized vocals, guitars that jangle and roar, and hummable melodies all set to a fast beat. Although they occasionally veer into the realm of snarled vocals and noise for its own sake, they sound more comfortable singing about boyfriends (past and future) and family. They may not be deep, but they get under your skin. An aside: beware the creaking chair sound that closes out the album, it keeps on going. *—Peter Stepek*

Mauler / Feb. 25, 1997 / Au-Go-Go ✦✦✦
An after-the-fact collection (Cub broke up in 1996, after the release of the fine *Box of Hair*) of singles, compilation appearances, and oddities, 1997's *Mauler* wraps up all of Cub's loose ends. Like most indie pop groups of the mid-'90s, Cub considered the 7" single to be sacrosanct (their second album, *Come Out Come Out*, was originally released in a limited edition of three 7" EPs), and most of their best moments took place at 45 rpm. The career-defining "New York City" and "My Chinchilla" are both here, as is the terrific "The Day I Said Goodbye," from a split single Cub shared with the pop-punk trio the Potatomen. Three covers show influences both expected (Joan Jett's "Runaway") and surprising (the Hollies' "You Know He Did," turned into a garage rock stomp halfway between "Louie Louie" and "Wild Thing," complete with a dead-on recreation of the ocarina solo from the latter; "She's Like a Rainbow," a slightly mistitled cover of the Rolling Stones' trippiest moment, "She's a Rainbow"). As is usually the case with this sort of compilation, the other tracks are pretty hit or miss. This is more for established Cub fans than newcomers, who should probably check out any of the trio's three proper albums first. *—Stewart Mason*

The Cult

f. 1984, Bradford, W. Yorks, England, **db.** 1995
Heavy Metal, Alternative Pop/Rock, Hard Rock
Following a succession of name and stylistic changes, the Cult emerged in 1984 as one of England's leading heavy metal revivalists. Picking up the pseudo-mysticism and native American obsessions of the Doors, the guitar-orchestrations of Led Zeppelin and the three-chord crunch of AC/DC, while adding touches of post-punk goth-rock, the Cult gained a dedicated following in their native Britain with mid-'80s singles like "She Sells Sanctuary" before breaking into the American metal market in the late '80s with "Love Removal Machine."

The origins of the Cult lie in the Southern Death Cult, a goth-rock outfit formed by vocalist Ian Astbury in 1981. Though it was popular, Astbury soon pulled the plug on the band, recruited guitarist Billy Duffy and bassist Jamie Stewart, and renamed it Death Cult. After recording just one EP, the group became the Cult and moved into heavy hard rock with slight psychedelic flourishes. Their debut album, 1984's *Dreamtime*, performed well and the follow-up *Love* amplified the hard rock direction with a break-out single, "She Sells Sanctuary." For their third album, the Cult hired Rick Rubin as producer and recorded *Electric*, their hardest record to date. In 1989, *Sonic Temple* became the Cult's most successful album, propelled into the American Top Ten by the hit single "Fire Woman." By the time they recorded their follow-up to *Sonic Temple* though, infighting and substance abuse had begun tearing up the band. With Astbury and Duffy the only continuing members of the band, *Ceremony*, was released in the fall of 1991 to weak reviews and disappointing sales. *The Cult* appeared in 1994, though by the following year the Cult had disbanded, with Ian Astbury forming the Holy Barbarians later in 1995. *—Stephen Thomas Erlewine*

Dreamtime / 1984 / Beggars Banquet ✦✦✦✦
Image-wise, the Cult still weren't entirely there yet, as the band photos show. Astbury's bandanna is more dated than anything else, but it's Duffy's look—a Duran Duran/Spandau Ballet wannabe, down to the haircut and suit—which is terribly amusing in context. Musically, though, on its full album debut the Cult was pretty much on its way. Duffy's dramatic, spaghetti-western tinged dark psychedelic guitar and Astbury's passionate semi-wailing set the tone from the start and throughout, while the Jamie Stewart/Nigel Preston rhythm section keep the tribal/goth feeling running equally high. Indeed, goth is still stalking the band's efforts whether the members liked it or not—consider "83rd Dream" and its distinctly creeped-out introduction, Astbury's vocals fed through extra effects. If there's not as much in the way of blunt power-chording as later, *Dreamtime* is still loaded with a variety of moody, energetic joys. "Spiritwalker" is especially fantastic, Preston's rolling drums and Duffy's epic, crystalline guitar not that far off from what U2 was after, but with arguably even more appeal. Add in Astbury's explosive singing and it's a definite treat through and through. The other strong tracks include the title effort, which may reference the native Australian concept of time but is more about wearing long hair and tripping on the shamanic vibes, and the who-else-but-the-Cult invocations of mythic America "Go West," "Horse Nation," and "A Flower in the Desert." If everything is sometimes too shrilly dramatic for easy digestion, one can't fault the band for energy, and given where they would shortly improve all around it's still an attractive enough listen. Later CD versions of the album included two reasonable enough tracks, the vaguely bluesy (and slightly silly) "Bonebag" and the dreamy "Sea and Sky," plus one total smash. "Resurrection Joe," a queasy, nervous and frenetic combination of aggro epic and swampy funk, remains an undeservedly forgotten highlight from the early eighties, only topped by the dramatic sweep of the later "She Sells Sanctuary." *—Ned Raggett*

Love / 1985 / Beggars Banquet ✦✦✦
1985's *Love* displayed a marked improvement over the Cult's early material, and though it remains underappreciated in America (worldwide it was a smash), this exceptional record has actually aged better than the band's more notorious (and equally important) releases: *Electric* and *Sonic Temple*. Equal parts psychedelic hard rock and new wave-goth, the songs on *Love* emanate a bright guitar sheen, tight arrangements, crisp drumming, and a command performance from vocalist Ian Astbury, who, as usual says a lot more with less than most singers. Overall, the album benefits from a wonderful sense of space, thanks in large part to guitarist Billy Duffy (who is much more subdued here than on future releases), whose restraint is especially notable on "Revolution" and the remarkably uncluttered title track. Duffy also provides compelling melodies ("Hollow Man," "Revolution"), driving riffs ("Nirvana," "The Phoenix"), and even a U2-like intro to "Big Neon Glitter." Also on offer is the near-perfect "She Sells Sanctuary" and the smash hit "Rain," quite possibly the band's most appealing single ever. Considering the musical schizophrenia that would plague each subsequent Cult release, *Love* just may be the band's purest moment. *—Ed Rivadavia*

Electric / 1987 / Beggars Banquet ✦✦✦✦✦
The roots of *Electric* lay in another album entirely, *Peace*, which was recorded with *Love* producer Steve Brown in a series of sessions that the band found increasingly pressure-filled and fraught with tension. A chance meeting with Def Jam supremo Rick Rubin at an American awards ceremony turned out to be the charm, resulting in the saucy

chest-baring stomp of *Electric*. Rubin chucked all the old recordings for a series of new sessions, stripping everything down and essentially transforming Duffy into the logical successor to AC/DC's Angus Young. Thankfully Astbury decided not to become Brian Johnson, and while his macho yells can't help being cartoonish, he's clearly having fun throughout. Though both band and album caught a lot of flack for its perceived wallowing in dinosaur sounds and styles, the end result is still a fist-punching yelp of energy that demands to be heard at maximum volume in arenas, with a brusque punch in Les Warner's drums to match Duffy's power-chord action. "Love Removal Machine" is still the album's calling card, another in the series of instantly catchy Cult singles. "Li'l Devil" is almost as worthy, while other cuts like "Wild Flower" and "King Contrary Man" would have sounded good in 1973 and sound just as good in a new century. There are a couple of missteps—"Peace Dog" starts good but ends up being what happens when the Doors are used as a model in the wrong way, while the version of the Steppenwolf classic "Born to Be Wild" should be taken out and shot. Otherwise, an enjoyable pleasure from start to finish—even if Astbury sings "Plastic fantastic lobster telephone" at one point. *—Ned Raggett*

Sonic Temple / 1989 / Beggars Banquet ✦✦✦

More varied than its predecessor, *Electric*, *Sonic Temple* finds the Cult trying several different metal styles, from crunchy *Electric*-era '70s grooves and the fuzzy, noisy psychedelia of *Love* to mellow ballads and commercial '80s hard rock. Not all of the experiments work, as some of the songs lean toward ponderousness, but enough of them did to send *Sonic Temple* into the Billboard Top Ten, due to the exposure provided by the hit single "Fire Woman." *—Steve Huey*

Ceremony / Sep. 24, 1991 / Beggars Banquet ✦✦

Pure Cult: The Best of the Cult (For Rockers, Ravers, Lovers & Sinners) / Feb. 16, 1993 / Beggars Banquet ✦✦✦✦✦

Say what you want about the Cult—a band which will certainly go down as one of the most schizophrenic in rock history—but singer Ian Astbury and guitarist Billy Duffy could sure write a great tune. Just glance at a few titles included on their hard-to-find, but definitely best greatest-hits collection *Pure Cult*: "Edie (Ciao Baby)," "Love Removal Machine," "She Sells Sanctuary," "Wild Flower," "Fire Woman," "Rain," "Lil' Devil," and "Sun King." Spread haphazardly across the disc (rather than in chronological order), each track's uniqueness is even more evident, further showcasing the Cult's fearless creativity. Early songs such as "Spiritwalker" and "Resurrection Joe" will surprise most fans with their class and maturity, while later cuts like "Wild Hearted Son" and "Heart of Soul" (from the disappointing *Ceremony* album) show new life when viewed on their own merits. And for those seeking some added collector's value, the band offers a fine new track in the industrial-tinged "The Witch." [After languishing for several years in an import release, Beggars Banquet released a virtually similar version of *Pure Cult* for American audiences in 2000.] *—Ed Rivadavia*

The Cult / 1994 / Beggars Banquet ✦✦✦

The self-titled follow-up to 1991's anemic *Ceremony* clearly shows a once great band trying to recapture the excitement of their earlier efforts. Sadly, for the Cult, their problems were bigger than the sum of their parts. When it boils down to it, the constant musical tug of war between Ian Astbury and Billy Duffy would result in the band losing its focus and ultimately its audience. From *Love* onwards, each Cult release would be greeted with a mix of awe, *Electric*, commercial triumph, *Sonic Temple*, and eventually, apathy as the band's fan base continued to be bedazzled and eroded due to the band's ever-changing styles. *The Cult* is a perfect case in point. If the arena rock of *Sonic Temple* proved to be Duffy's brainchild, the subsequent faux pas of *Ceremony* (Astbury's idea) only makes *The Cult* that much more confusing and frustrating. With a newfound sense of sobriety and spirituality, Astbury set out to make a record that would combine the guitar riffing of its two predecessors along with the singer's newfound love for electronica. Re-hiring producer/songwriter Bob Rock proved to be a definite step in the right direction. Whereas, songs like "Real Grrrl," the scorching "Be Free," and "Star" evoke the Cult of yore (with a more modern-day treated sound, others like the Doors pastiche of "Joy" and the oh-where-have-our-heroes-gone cheese of "Sacred Life are a mess. If anything positive came out of these sessions, it's nice to hear Astbury's voice sounding lean and mean at the forefront of Bob Rock's mix. The Cult get an A for effort/enthusiasm and a B- for execution on this one. For Cult diehards and curiosity seekers only. *—John Franck*

Best of Rare Cult / Oct. 17, 2000 / Beggars Banquet ✦✦✦

Best of Rare Cult, the companion piece to the Cult's expansive box set *Rare Cult*, features an interesting collection of rarities, unreleased material, B-sides, studio experiments, and just plain throwaways. If you're just an average fan or a curiosity seeker, the *Best of Rare Cult* single CD will do just fine. Featuring 15 cuts by, admittedly, one of England's best rock band's of the '80s and '90s, *Best of Rare Cult* gets underway with the original version of "Love Removal Machine." Yet more rarities permeate this release as "No. 13" (the B-side to "Sanctuary") and "Sea and Sky" (which dates all the way back to the band's Southern Death Cult days) are available for mass consumption here for the first time as well. Both are essential historical documents. 1984's "Go West" simply reaffirms this concept. "Join Hands" ends *Best of Rare Cult* on an anthemic note replete with na-naa-naa-naa choruses, thereby putting a lid on a hit and miss, yet fascinating collection of Cult oddities. In conclusion, it's interesting to note that through all their trials and tribulations, re-listening to these Cult tracks later, one can garner a finer appreciation for just how far this band has traveled over the years. The Cult have managed to transform themselves from innocent, cloak and dagger goth boys into a world-class, pants and flares, arena rock & roll band replete with drug and booze problems. *—John Franck*

Beyond Good and Evil / Jun. 5, 2001 / Atlantic ✦✦✦

During their late-'80s heyday, the Cult were known for their Doors-meets-Zeppelin-meets-Love and Rockets style, combining mysticism, solid three-chord guitar progressions, and goth rock stylings. In their 2001 incarnation, the Cult may be more accurately described as the Doors meets Zeppelin meets Tool. Guitarist Billy Duffy seems to have discovered distortion in the seven years since their last album. Not warm fuzz tones, but bone-crunching, mind-numbing distortion. While the music has changed, it still sounds like the Cult thanks to singer Ian Astbury's consistent wails and moans. In the opener, "War (The Process)," Astbury hollers "whoa" just like the old days, except now he does it over Duffy's Metallica-like rifts and frenetic drumming by Matt Sorum. The band also shows they've been listening to Trent Reznor with the industrial overtones of "Speed of Light," but even with heavy vocal effects, they remain the Cult, thanks to a catchy chorus. For classic Cult fans, the band throws in a couple tunes reminiscent of their *Sonic Temple* days—"Breathe," a rocker in the tradition of "Fire Woman," and "Nico," the equivalent of the power ballad "Edie." Old fans may have trouble adjusting to the Cult's updated sound, but the band manages to maintain the energy of their music, creating heavy metal for the new millennium without lapsing into the pure cliché that waylays so many angry young (and old) men. *—Michael Gowan*

Culture Club

f. 1981, London, England, **db.** 1986

Blue-Eyed Soul, Pop/Rock, New Wave

Few New Wave groups were as popular as Culture Club. During the early '80s, the group racked up seven straight Top 10 hits in the UK and six Top 10 singles in the US with their light, infectious pop-soul. Though their music was radio-ready, what brought the band stardom was Boy George, the group's charismatic, cross-dressing lead singer. George dressed in flamboyant dresses and wore heavy makeup, creating a disarmingly androgynous appearence that created a sensation on early MTV. George also had a biting wit and frequently came up with cutting quips that won Culture Club heavy media exposure in both America and Britain. Although closely aligned with the New Romantics—they were both inspired by Northern Soul and fashion—Culture Club had sharper pop sense than their peers and they consequently had a broader appeal. However, their time in the spotlight was brief. Not only could they not withstand the changing fashions of MTV, but the group was fraught with personal tensions, including Boy George's drug addiction. By 1986, the group had broken up, leaving behind several singles that rank as classics of the New Wave era. *—Stephen Thomas Erlewine*

Kissing to Be Clever / 1982 / Virgin ✦✦✦✦

Kissing To Be Clever was the album that put Culture Club on the musical map. Incorporating pop, rock, dance, new wave, soul and Caribbean rhythms (an amalgamation of "cultures"), the result was a soulful, progressive pop outing which scored several landmark international hits and made a star out of the band's outrageous front man Boy George. A couple of tracks were European dance hits, but the first "official" single, "Do You Really Want To Hurt Me," was a simple masterpiece, resonating with an ache that harked back to the classic torch songs of yesteryear. Most of the other songs were quite different, with energetic beats and sometimes silly, campy themes ("Boy Boy I'm The Boy," "White Boys Can't Control It" and "White Boy"). The album scored two other major hits, the zippy and bouncy "I'll Tumble 4 Ya" and the gorgeous "Time (Clock Of The Heart)." However, beware that "Time" is only on certain pressings of the album. When the album was issued on CD, and once the Epic label dissolved, the formerly color album cover had turned to black and white, and "Time" had been omitted, which is pretty ridiculous, considering the song was a huge number two hit, and the album was then left with only nine tracks. Still, this set is a highlight of 1980s music, and set the stage for one of the decade's most loved and oft-remembered bands. *—Jose F. Promis*

Colour by Numbers / 1983 / Virgin ✦✦✦✦✦

Colour By Numbers was Culture Club's most successful album, and, undoubtedly, one of the most popular albums from the 1980s. Scoring no less than four U.S. hit singles (and five overseas), this set dominated the charts for a full year, both in the United States and in Europe. The songs were infectious, the videos were all over MTV, and the band was a media magnet. Boy George sounded as warm and soulful as ever, but one of the real stars on this set was backing vocalist Helen Terry, who really brought the house down on the album's unforgettable first single, "Church of the Poison Mind." This album also featured the band's biggest (and only number one) hit, the irresistibly catchy "Karma Chameleon," its more rock & roll Top Five follow-up "Miss Me Blind," and the fourth single (and big club hit), "It's a Miracle" (which also featured Helen Terry's unmistakable belting). Also here are "Victims," a big, dark, deep, and bombastic power ballad which was a huge hit overseas but never released in the U.S., and other soulful favorites such as "Black Money" and "That's the Way (I'm Only Trying to Help You)," where Boy George truly flexed his vocal muscles. The 1980s music was, in many cases, flamboyant, fun, sexy, soulful, colorful, androgynous, and carefree, and this album captured that spirit perfectly. A must for any collector of 1980s music, and the artistic and commercial pinnacle of a band which still attracts new fans years later. *—Jose Promis*

Waking Up with the House on Fire / 1984 / Virgin ✦✦

The career of Boy George and Culture Club had been on a steady upward climb for two years by the fall of 1984, so the group had every reason to expect that their third album, *Waking Up With the House on Fire*, would enjoy similar success, but it was not to be. The leadoff single, "The War Song," put off many fans, but the problem may have been less the music on *Waking Up*, which was typically frothy and propulsive, than the passing of a fad. By late 1984, Boy George had been sideswiped in the image department by Michael Jackson, Prince, and Madonna. So, while it's true that *Waking Up* didn't contain any song as catchy as "Karma Chameleon," the album's real failure was one of timing. *—William Ruhlmann*

From Luxury to Heartache / 1986 / Virgin ♦♦

● **At Worst ... The Best of Boy George and Culture Club** / Nov. 2, 1993 / Virgin ♦♦♦♦♦
The success of "The Crying Game" marked a comeback for Boy George, especially in the U.S., where his solo career had never taken hold beyond the dance clubs, and SBK (distributor of his label, Virgin) took advantage of his resurgence by compiling this 75-minute, 19-track album, which combines his former group Culture Club's biggest hits with selections from his solo work. The ten Culture Club tracks are of a piece, from 1982's "Do You Really Want to Hurt Me" (which here leads off with an ominous voice intoning, "Popularity breeds contempt") to "Love Is Love," which wasn't a hit, but is a better choice than the missing "The War Song," which was. The solo tracks are a more mixed batch, and not only because Top 40 U.K. hits like "Keep Me in Mind," "Sold," and "To Be Reborn" are missing. They often rely on loud percussion tracks that strand Boy George's tender tenor somewhere in the distance. He remains most effective on rhythmic ballads, whether "Do You Really Want to Hurt Me," "Everything I Own" (his chart-topping first U.K. solo hit), or "The Crying Game." —*William Ruhlmann*

VH-1 Storytellers/Greatest Moments / Aug. 11, 1998 / Virgin ♦♦♦♦
This two-CD set is a double dose of Culture Club greatest hits: one includes a reunion show the band did for the cable music network in 1998; the other gathers 13 of the quartet's best studio tracks from 1982 to 1998 (the newly recorded "I Just Wanna Be Loved" is the first song Culture Club recorded together since their split in 1987). The *Storytellers* disc is a pretty lazy run-through of all the obvious tunes, with little spark generated on stage among the long-separated combo (and there's not much storytelling either). *Greatest Moments*, however, is a pretty thorough retrospective and glorious proof of what made Culture Club leaders of the British faux-soul invasion of the '80s. Most of the group's hits are here—"Do You Really Want to Hurt Me," "Time (Clock of the Heart)," "Church of the Poison Mind," "Karma Chameleon," "I'll Tumble 4 Ya," "Miss Me Blind," etc.—as are a couple of Boy George solo cuts ("The Crying Game" is the only one of interest). Skip the first half, soak in the second. —*Michael Gallucci*

The Cure
f. 1976, Crawley, England
College Rock, Post-Punk, Goth Rock, New Wave, Alternative Pop/Rock
Out of all the bands that emerged in the immediate aftermath of punk rock in the late '70s, the Cure was one of the most enduring and popular. Led through numerous incarnations by guitarist/vocalist Robert Smith, the band became notorious for their slow, gloomy dirges and Smith's ghoulish appearance. But the public image often hid the diversity of the Cure's music. At the outset, they played jagged, edgy pop songs and they slowly evolved into a more textured outfit. As one of the bands that laid the seeds for goth-rock, the group created towering layers of guitars and synthesizers, but by the time goth caught on in the mid-'80s, the Cure had moved away from the genre. By the end of the '80s, the Cure had crossed over into the mainstream not only in their native England, but also in the United States and in various parts of Europe. —*Stephen Thomas Erlewine*

Three Imaginary Boys / Jun. 1979 / Fiction ♦♦♦♦♦
Bursting with high-energy playing and bare-bones production, the band's first album showcases Robert Smith's most concise songwriting. Smith's now common themes of isolation, alienation and despair are present, this time presented in perfect three-minute form with a more aggressive stance. *Three Imaginary Boys* ends up sounding like a slightly more tuneful version of Wire's *Pink Flag* and quite unlike anything else they would record later on. —*Chris Woodstra*

Boys Don't Cry / Jan. 1980 / Elektra ♦♦♦♦♦
Boys Don't Cry combines the finer moments of *Three Imaginary Boys* with the singles released around the same time—the title track, "Jumping Someone Else's Train," and the often misinterpreted "Killing an Arab," as well as "Plastic Passion." The adding of the singles makes this the perfect encapsulation of the Cure's early days. —*Chris Woodstra*

Seventeen Seconds / May 1980 / Elektra ♦♦♦
Still capturing the more accessible pop elements and angular post-punk leanings of *Three Imaginary Boys*, *Seventeen Seconds* marks a move toward the despair for which the band would become best known. The tempos are slowed down considerably, and the addition of subtle synthesizers to minimalist arrangements builds a darkly evocative atmosphere of depression. —*Chris Woodstra*

Faith / Sep. 1981 / Elektra ♦♦♦
Continuing the trend set by *Seventeen Seconds*, *Faith* is an even darker affair. Smith sings with suicidal resignation through eight somber epics of gloom typified by the title track and "The Funeral Party," raising the funeral march tempo only for the single "Primary." The atmosphere created is chilling, though very few of the songs stand out. That's probably not the point anyway—as a mood-setting piece, *Faith* is quite effective. —*Chris Woodstra*

Pornography / 1982 / Elektra ♦♦♦
Pornography is the culmination of the band's gloom-and-doom period. It's not that they've changed their mood much since *Faith*—this is still pretty bleak stuff—but this album marks a more aggressive stance, incorporating faster, near-tribal rhythms and layers of heavy, distorted guitars that serve to bring out Smith's echoed vocals and doom-laden lyrics like "It doesn't matter if we all die." *Pornography* isn't their most interesting album—much of it suffers from same-sounding monotony—but it did manage to crack the U.K. Top Ten and was undoubtedly influential in the emerging goth-rock movement. —*Chris Woodstra*

Japanese Whispers / 1984 / Sire ♦♦♦
After reaching the depths of gloom, Smith recast himself as something of a British pop eccentric, releasing three singles—"The Walk," "Let's Go to Bed," and "The Lovecats"—that revealed an accessible and upbeat, nearly bubbly, side. *Japanese Whispers* collects those singles, along with their slightly less interesting b-sides. The singles were compiled on the more comprehensive *Staring at the Sea: The Singles* collection, but as a collection of Smith's brief period of whimsy, there is no better collection than *Japanese Whispers*. —*Chris Woodstra*

The Top / 1984 / Sire ♦♦
Where their previous albums were gloomy and depressing, *The Top* is downright scary in places. The opener, "Shake Dog Shake," doesn't sound too dissimilar to the songs found on *Pornography*, but the album quickly shifts gears from that point on, with rapid style and mood changes that go from manic to nightmarish near-psychedelia with disturbing themes and a swirl of odd sounds. Ultimately, *The Top* is the band's least consistent album and their most difficult listen, but it is an interesting study in paranoid chaos, and it provides a fascinating look at a band (and more specifically, leader Robert Smith) spinning out of control. —*Chris Woodstra*

Concert: The Cure Live / 1984 / Fiction ♦♦

The Head on the Door / 1985 / Elektra ♦♦♦♦♦
The Cure refocused and ultimately hit their stride with *Head On the Door*, producing an album which not only more effectively depicted gloom, but also showed enough pop smarts to make it memorable (and even danceable). The band scored a hit with the infectious, New Order-ish "In Between Days" (which managed to beat New Order at their own game) and the highly memorable "Close to Me," but the album's outstanding trait is its diversity—they managed to combine a wide variety of influences, not only that of contemporary dance-floor peers, but also incorporating rhythms from the Far East and South America to fine effect. The Cure made more accomplished albums later on and had bigger hits, but none combined artistic ambition with really catchy songs as well as *Head On the Door*. —*Chris Woodstra*

★ **Staring at the Sea: The Singles** / 1986 / Elektra ♦♦♦♦♦
Staring at the Sea: The Singles collects all of the Cure's biggest UK hits and best-known songs from the late '70s and early '80s. Spanning from "Killing an Arab" and "Boys Don't Cry" to "The Lovecats," "Inbetween Days," and "Close to Me," *Staring at the Sea* captures some of the finest—and most influential—post-punk music. At their best, the Cure were nervy, intellectual, catchy and foreboding all at once. No matter how carefully crafted the Cure's individual albums were, their finest moments occured on singles like these, when they distilled their essence into surprisingly catchy, but decidedly left-of-center, pop singles. *Standing on a Beach* not only selects highlights from their uneven early albums, it collects many of the group's terrific non-LP singles. It's a definitive retrospective of the Cure and is one of the finest albums of the '80s. [The cassette version of *Staring at the Sea* was titled *Standing on a Beach* and included several B-sides.] —*Stephen Thomas Erlewine*

Kiss Me, Kiss Me, Kiss Me / 1987 / Elektra ♦♦♦
Simultaneously more accessible and ambitious than any of the Cure's previous albums, the double-album *Kiss Me, Kiss Me, Kiss Me* finds Robert Smith expanding his pop vocabulary by tentatively adding bigger guitars, the occasional horn section, lite-funk rhythms and string sections. It's eclectic, to be sure, but it's also a mess, bouncing from idea to idea and refusing to develop some of the most intriguing detours. Even if *Kiss Me* doesn't quite gel, its best moments—including the deceptively bouncy "Why Can't I Be You?" and the stately "Just Like Heaven"—are remarkable and help make the album one of the group's very best. —*Stephen Thomas Erlewine*

Disintegration / May 1989 / Elektra ♦♦♦♦♦
Expanding the latent arena-rock sensibilities that peppered *Kiss Me, Kiss Me, Kiss Me* by slowing them down and stretching them to the breaking point, the Cure reached the peak of their popularity with the crawling, darkly seductive *Disintegration*. It's a hypnotic, mesmerizing record, comprised nearly entirely of epics like the soaring, icy "Pictures of You." The handful of pop songs, like the concise and utterly charming "Love Song," don't alleviate the doomy atmosphere. The Cure's gloomy soundscapes have rarely sounded so alluring, however, and the songs—from the pulsating, ominous "Fascination Street" to the eerie, string-laced "Lullaby"—have rarely been so well-constructed and memorable. It's fitting that *Disintegration* was their commercial breakthrough, since, in many ways, the album is the culmination of all the musical directions the Cure were pursuing over the course of the '80s. —*Stephen Thomas Erlewine*

Mixed Up / Oct. 19, 1990 / Elektra ♦♦

Wish / Apr. 21, 1992 / Elektra ♦♦♦
On the surface, *Wish* sounds happier than *Disintegration*, and the sunny British Invasion hooks of the hit single "Friday I'm in Love" certainly seem to indicate that the record is a brighter affair than its predecessor. Dig a little deeper, and the album reveals itself to be just as tortured, and perhaps more despairing. Granted, the sound of the record, with its jangling guitars and simple arrangements, is more immediately accessible than the epic gloom of *Disintegration*, but nearly every song finds Robert Smith wracked with depression. Unfortunately, the even-handed production makes the record sound very similar, so it is less compelling than it might have been, but there are a handful of gems ("High," "A Letter to Elise," "Wendy Time," "Friday I'm in Love") that make the record worthwhile. —*Stephen Thomas Erlewine*

Paris / Oct. 26, 1993 / Elektra ♦♦

Show / Nov. 23, 1993 / Elektra ♦♦

Wild Mood Swings / May 21, 1996 / Fiction/Elektra ♦♦♦
After the relatively straightforward pop of *Wish*, the Cure moved back toward stranger,

edgier territory with *Wild Mood Swings*. Actually, that's only part of the truth. As the title suggests, there's a vast array of textures and emotions on *Wild Mood Swings*, from the woozy mariachi lounge horns of "The 13th" to the perfect pop of "Mint Car" and the monolithic dirge of "Want." In between the extremes, Robert Smith and the Cure—which now features a radically reworked lineup, with several key players from *Wish* now missing—explore some simpler territory, from contemplative acoustic numbers tinged with strings to swooning neo-psychedelia. But what ties it all together is conviction—Smith sounds more content than he ever has, but he sings with more passion than he has for a number of years. Of course, the Cure haven't significantly changed their sound—tinny synthesizers and guitar effects that haven't appeared on an album since 1988 are in abundance throughout the record—but the variety of sounds and strength of performance offers enough surprises to make *Wild Mood Swings* more than just another Cure record. *—Stephen Thomas Erlewine*

Galore / Oct. 28, 1997 / Fiction/Elektra ✦✦✦✦✦
It's ironic that the Cure, a band whose albums have always seemed like definitive artistic statements, were at their best as a singles band. On the group's singles, Robert Smith's ideas reached their full potential, since they captured not only the group's off-kilter pop sense, but also the haunting melancholy and wacky humor that interlaced Smith's songs. *Galore* rounds up the singles from the second part of the Cure's career, beginning with "Why Can't I Be You?" from 1987's *Kiss Me Kiss Me Kiss Me* and ending with "Gone!" from 1996's *Wild Mood Swings*. Between those two are 15 more songs, nearly every one of which is a gem. The Cure were never a repetitive singles band, and there's a dizzying array of styles here, from infectious jangle-pop ("Friday I'm In Love," "Mint Car") and monolithic, chilly goth-rock ("Fascination Street," "Pictures of You," "Just Like Heaven") to jaunty, clever dance-club pop (the remix of "Close to Me"), eerie crawls ("Lullaby"), neo-mariachi madness ("The 13th") and even love songs ("Catch," "Lovesong"). There are a couple of missteps along the way—the pounding dance and pseudo-rap of "Hot Hot Hot!!!" sounds dated, as does the ill-conceived Madchester diversion "Never Enough"—but *Galore* emphatically confirms the Cure's status as one of the best and most adventurous alternative bands of the '80s. And the new song, "Wrong Number," is pretty good, too. *—Stephen Thomas Erlewine*

Bloodflowers / Feb. 15, 2000 / Fiction/EastWest ✦✦✦
The Cure edged into new territory with *Wild Mood Swings*, but nevertheless drew scorn from certain quarters because it eschewed goth rock for pop, both pure and twisted. For 2000's *Bloodflowers*, Robert Smith decided to give the people what they wanted: a classic Cure album, billed as the third part of a trilogy begun with *Pornography* and continued with *Disintegration*. That turns out to be more or less true, since *Bloodflowers* boasts all of the Cure's signatures: stately tempos, languid melodies, spacious arrangements, cavernous echoes, morose lyrics, keening vocals, long running times. If that's all you're looking for, *Bloodflowers* delivers in spades. If you want something transcendent, you're out of luck, since the album falls short of the mark, largely because it sounds too self-conscious. As one song segues into the next, it feels like Smith is striving to make a classic Cure record, putting all the sounds in place before he constructs the actual songs. That makes for a good listening experience, especially for fans of *Disintegration*, but it never catches hold the way that record did, for two simple reasons: there isn't enough variation between the songs for them to distinguish themselves, nor are there are enough sonic details to give individual tracks character. While *Disintegration* had goth monoliths, it also had pristine pop gems and elegant neo-psychedelia; with a couple of exceptions, the songs on *Bloodflowers* all feel like cousins of "Pictures of You." The album is certainly well made, and even enjoyable; however, its achievement is a bit hollow, since it never seems like Smith is pushing himself or the band. Nobody else can come close to capturing the Cure's graceful gloom, but it's hard to shake the suspicion that *Bloodflowers* could have been something grand if he had shaken up the formula slightly. *—Stephen Thomas Erlewine*

Curve

f. 1991, London, England
Electronica, Alternative Dance, Shoegazing, Alternative Pop/Rock
Considering Curve's towering monolith of guitar noise, dance tracks, dark goth, and airy melodies, it's strange that their two core members—guitarist Dean Garcia and vocalist Toni Halliday—met through David Stewart of Eurythmics. Halliday met Stewart while she was a teenager and they remained friends for years; Garcia played on Eurythmics' *Touch* and *Be Yourself Tonight*. The two played together in State of Play, who released one album and two singles in the late '80s to little notice. After the failure of that band, Garcia and Halliday parted ways only to reunite in the beginning of the '90s. Renaming themselves Curve, Halliday and Garcia released three EPs that became independent hits in 1991. Although they were critically acclaimed as well, some members of the U.K. press attacked Halliday for not being a genuine member of the indie scene. Despite the negative press, their next EP and first album, 1992's *Doppelganger*, hit number one on the U.K. indie charts. By the time of the following year's *Cuckoo*, Curve had added two guitarists and a drummer, with Garcia moving to bass. *Cuckoo* was noisier and more experimental than their previous releases, although it did have a couple of pop songs that were tighter than their usual singles. However, the album didn't make as big of a splash in the U.K. as previous releases; Curve split several months after its release, only to reform in 1997 with the *Chinese Burn* EP. The full-length *Come Clean* followed a year later. *—Stephen Thomas Erlewine*

● **Doppelganger** / Mar. 10, 1992 / Anxious/Charisma ✦✦✦✦✦
Following a series of single and EP releases that had found chart success in the U.K. and indie credibility in the States, the British band Curve released their full-length debut *Doppelganger* on Dave Stewart's Anxious label. Led by lead singer Toni Halliday and guitarist Dean Garcia, both of whom had toured with Robert Plant, Curve enlisted production help from Flood for this record. Roaming the same sonic landscape as My Bloody Valentine, *Doppelganger* features the breathy, dreamy vocals of Halliday over top layers of throbbing guitar, dense keyboards, and sledgehammer drumming to create formidable aural textures. At times meandering and unrelenting, tracks like "Already Yours" and "Wish You Dead" are stellar workouts full of rhythm and attitude. The few slower numbers are a nice change of pace with the best results on "Fait Accompli" and the quiet, almost dirge-like "Sandpit," where the less dense instrumentation allows Halliday's vocals to become the focal point. At times menacing and dark and other times more playful, *Doppelganger* is a bracing listening experience that earned Curve well-deserved attention on both sides of the Atlantic. *—Tom Demalon*

Pubic Fruit / 1992 / Anxious/Charisma ✦✦✦✦
Pubic Fruit is not a proper follow-up to Curve's debut full-length, but, instead, it gathers together three of the band's earlier E.P. releases which had only been released in the U.K. and adds the previously unavailable 12" version of "Fait Accompli." Despite the album being a compilation of sorts, it holds together quite nicely and provides a good look at the band's work up until their debut release. Much of the material is produced by the band and Steve Osborne and isn't nearly as dense as their debut which benefited from their work with Flood. The non-focus tracks of the E.P.s are every bit the equal of the songs that eventually found their way onto *Doppelganger* with many of them being true gems. "No Escape From Heaven" features a sultry vocal performance by Toni Halliday over a galloping percussive beat and drive-by bursts of guitar. And "Cherry" is the high-point of this collection. The song starts out quietly with hushed vocals and subtle keyboards before the drums signal a blast of fuzz guitars and everything crashes into a riveting sound collage. *—Tom Demalon*

Cuckoo / Sep. 21, 1993 / Anxious/Charisma ✦✦✦✦
Curve's second record finds more midtempo songs and a more electronic feel, although producer Flood still manages to bring out the band's dense sonic tendencies. While the music on *Cuckoo* is less aggressive than *Doppelganger*, singer Toni Halliday's lyrics are well defined and still pack a punch. Often playing the woman spurned, but not broken, Halliday takes no quarter. On "Super Blaster" she warns a companion not to start anything that they can't finish and she reads an ex-lover the riot act on "Left of Mother." The music shows more diversity, with a bit of funk injected into the guitars on "Crystal," while "Men Are From Mars, Women Are From Venus" is a hypnotic midtempo march. The album closes with the achingly confessional title cut, with Halliday showing a rare sense of vulnerability that is quite effective. Not as immediate as their earlier material and not quite as fulfilling, *Cuckoo* nonetheless will please longtime fans and is a solid introduction for potential converts. *—Tom Demalon*

Come Clean / Mar. 10, 1998 / Universal ✦✦✦✦✦
Just as fans were beginning to wonder if the duo Curve would ever return from their self-imposed exile, they've returned with their best album to date, *Come Clean*. Still combining largely electronic music with alternative hooks and lines, members Toni Halliday and Dean Garcia have returned to a now-popular form of music they helped create years ago. Although the album's two best tracks have previously appeared on their late-1997 EP *Chinese Burn* (the title tracks from both the EP and the full length), there are plenty of other strong tracks in attendance. "Something Familiar" may be the band's most melodically accessible track yet, while the extremely overdriven distortion and abrasive tones of "Dogbone" are just the opposite. Unlike many electronic bands nowadays, the duo makes it clear that they don't just go for musical overkill, as evidenced by the slow electronic groove contained in "Killer Baby," and the mid-paced dance rock of "Cotton Candy." *Come Clean* is the welcome return of a band that deserved attention when they first appeared years ago, and may get it in the electro-friendly late '90s. *—Greg Prato*

Open Day at the Hate Fest / 2001 / Curve ✦✦✦✦
Open Day at the Hate Fest isn't so much about yet another comeback from Curve as it is a reminder that they're still around, alive and kicking as ever. While locked in legal battles with the major label they began referring to as Estupendo (similar to the way a number of bands refer to another label as Neglektra, to further get the drift), it didn't stop Toni Halliday and Dean Garcia from providing B-sides and new recordings as MP3s on their website. Just as the duo had wriggled their way from their business partners—which had been holding the follow-up LP to *Come Clean* hostage for over a year—they released this web-only disc, which compiles a number of those MP3s and a couple extras to sweeten the deal. The limited availability and patchwork formation sound like the very definition of a completists-only package, but that's really not the case here. Back when Curve were releasing singles with regularity, it was apparent that Halliday and Garcia often weren't the best judges at what constituted B-material, since some of their finest moments could be found on the back side of their 12"s. At its best, this disc reminds fans of that fact; at its worst, this disc reminds fans that they very rarely released any mediocre tracks. *Hate Fest* might not surpass their previous highs, but nearly everything holds up to them quite handily. It finds Curve doing what they do best, with only slight variations on their familiar attack. In fact, this could pass as a successor to 1993's *Cuckoo*, in that it's grittier and darker than 1998's slicker *Come Clean*. And it wouldn't be a stretch to say that several will find this to be better than that record for Estupendo. [www.curve.co.uk] *—Andy Kellman*

Gift / Sep. 18, 2001 / Hip-O ✦✦✦✦
Curve has had more than their share of ups and downs. Yet even when their career looked its bleakest, the band continued to make great music. When Estupendo/Universal told the band that their album *Gift* would be shelved, they continued to write and record. As the band enjoyed brisk sales of their self-released *Open Day at the Hate Fest*, they re-

ceived word from Universal that *Gift* was put back on schedule and would be released on their Hip-O imprint. It's interesting to consider that *Gift* almost never saw the light of day. While it does fit in well with the band's efforts, it sounds different enough to reveal that the duo has fresh ideas and an ability to write great melodies without recycling old ones. As *Come Clean* kicked things off with "Chinese Burn," a gritty track featuring slick production, skittering beats, and a dirty, guitar-driven sound, "Hell Above Water" impressively introduces *Gift* with an edgy riff reminiscent of late-'90s Nine Inch Nails. While mixing elements of rock and electronica together is old news for Curve, their songwriting seems more natural on this outing. Perhaps due to their more personal nature, *Gift's* ten tracks are among Curve's best. While bringing together an all-star mix of producers and performers, including Alan Moulder, Flood, Alan Wilder (Depeche Mode, Recoil), and Ben Grosse (Filter), group members Toni Halliday and Dean Garcia showcase their unique knack for recording songs that feature an underlying darkness, even in their lighter moments. As Garbage and Sneaker Pimps have each scored commercial success with similar blends of female lead vocals, big beats, samples, and electric guitars, Curve shows that they are among the innovators of the form and prove themselves with one of their finest efforts. —*Don Kline*

Cypress Hill

f. 1988, Los Angeles, CA, **db.** 1993
Rap-Rock, Latin Rap, West Coast Rap, Hardcore Rap, Alternative Rap
Cypress Hill were notable for being the first Latino hip-hop superstars, but they became notorious for their endorsement of marijuana, which actually isn't a trivial thing. Not only did the group campaign for its legalization, but its slow, rolling bass-and-drum loops pioneered a new, stoned funk that became extraordinary influential in '90s hip-hop—it could be heard in everything from Dr. Dre's G-Funk to the chilly layers of English triphop. DJ Muggs crafted the sound, and B-Real, with his pinched nasal voice, was responsible for the rhetoric that made them famous. The pro-pot position became a little ridiculous over time, but there was no denying that the actual music had a strange, eerie power. Cypress Hill's first hit was their second album, 1993's *Black Sunday*, which entered the album charts at number one and spawned the crossover hit "Insane in the Brain." With *Black Sunday* and their subsequent tour with the fifth Lollapalooza festival, Cypress Hill's audience became predominantly white, collegiate suburbanites, which caused them to lose some support in the hip-hop community. A darker, gloomier affair than their first two records, 1995's *Temples of Boom* was greeted with mixed reviews and generally disappointing sales. Though the group appeared to be falling apart (second rapper Sen Dog departed soon afterward), another album, *IV*, appeared in 1998. —*Stephen Thomas Erlewine*

★ **Cypress Hill** / Aug. 13, 1991 / Ruffhouse/Columbia ✦✦✦✦✦
It's hard enough to transform an entire musical genre—Cypress Hill's eponymous debut album revolutionized hip-hop in several respects. Although they weren't the first Latino rappers, nor the first to mix Spanish and English, they were the first to achieve a substantial following, thanks to their highly distinctive sound. Along with the Beastie Boys and Public Enemy, Cypress Hill was also one of the first rap groups to bridge the gap with fans of both hard rock *and* alternative rock. And, most importantly, they created a sonic blueprint that would become one of the most widely copied in hip-hop. In keeping with their pro-marijuana stance, Cypress Hill intentionally crafted its music to sound stoned—lots of slow, lazy beats, fat bass, weird noises, and creepily distant-sounding samples. The surreal lyrical narratives were almost exclusively spun by B-Real in a nasal, sing-song, instantly recognizable delivery that only added to the music's hazy, evocative atmosphere; as a frontman, he could be funny, frightening, or just plain bizarre (again, kind of like the experience of being stoned). Whether he's taunting cops or singing nursery rhyme-like choruses about blasting holes in people with shotguns, B-Real's blunted-gangsta posture is nearly always underpinned by a cartoonish sense of humor. It's never clear how serious the threats are, but that actually makes them all the more menacing. The sound and style of *Cypress Hill* was hugely influential, particularly on Dr. Dre's boundary-shattering 1992 blockbuster *The Chronic*; yet despite its legions of imitators, *Cypress Hill* still sounds fresh and original today, simply because few hip-hop artists can put its sound across with such force of personality or imagination. —*Steve Huey*

Black Sunday / Jul. 27, 1993 / Ruffhouse/Columbia ✦✦✦✦✦
Black Sunday made Cypress Hill's connection to rock & roll more explicit, with its heavy metal-like artwork and noisier, more dissonant samples (including, naturally, stoner icons Black Sabbath). It's a slightly darker affair than its groundbreaking predecessor, with the threats of violence more urgent and the pot obsession played to the hilt (after all, it was a crucial part of their widespread appeal). Apart from those subtle distinctions, the sound

of *Black Sunday* is pretty much the same as *Cypress Hill*, refining the group's innovations into an accessible bid for crossover success. In fact, it's a little startling how often *Black Sunday* recycles musical ideas and even lyrical catchphrases from the endlessly inventive debut. And the rock-derived, verse-chorus song structures start to sound a little formulaic by the end of the record (how many choruses feature Sen Dog repeating part of whatever B-Real just said?). But in spite of that, *Black Sunday* still sounds vital and lively, since the group has a surer sense of craft. Most of the tracks are fleshed out into structured songs, in contrast to the brief sketches that punctuated *Cypress Hill*. The album benefits immensely from the resulting clutch of excellent singles (and songs that could have been), and while a couple of tracks feel redundant and underdeveloped, *Black Sunday* is overall a consistent, engaging listen, especially the flawless first half or so. Unfortunately, it's also the group's last great album, thanks to the musical recycling operation that began here and would handicap much of their subsequent work. —*Steve Huey*

Cypress Hill III: Temples of Boom / Oct. 31, 1995 / Ruffhouse/Columbia ✦✦

IV / Oct. 6, 1998 / Ruffhouse/Columbia ✦✦

Skull & Bones / Apr. 25, 2000 / Columbia ✦✦✦✦
Despite the best efforts of DJ Muggs, Cypress Hill ran out of gas fairly quickly, entering a tailspin as soon as their third album. Back at full strength with the return of Sen Dog, Cypress Hill devised a full-scale comeback with their fifth album, *Skull & Bones*. The idea behind the album was to divide it into two—a hip-hop disc (*Skull*) and a rock disc (*Bones*). This would guarantee some publicity, at the very least, and, hopefully, it would win over the new generation of adolescents who flipped for rap-metal acts like Kid Rock and Limp Bizkit. On paper, it's a sound theory, but there was a slight flaw—the group is kind of lame when they rock. Their band is competent enough, and B-Real's voice does sound good with overdriven guitars, but their rock songs utterly fall apart, since they have no hooks, no catchy riffs, and no character. If rap-rock was all there was to *Skull & Bones*, it would be a bit of an embarrassment. Fortunately, the *Skulls* disc is their finest effort since *Black Sunday*. Muggs is in prime form, creating funky, ominous, evocative soundscapes, which B-Real makes the most of with fluid rhymes. At times, B-Real does descend into tastelessness ("Stank Ass Hoe"), and neither he nor Sen Dog really find any new lyrical ground, but sonically, *Skulls* is a blast; B-Real's whine and Sen Dog's gruff, blunt style are the perfect match for Muggs' darkly cinematic soundscapes, and, on a purely sonic level, it's quite intoxicating. At their best, Cypress Hill is a hip-hop experience unlike any other, and, ignoring the *Bones*, this is the best they've been in a long, long time. —*Stephen Thomas Erlewine*

The Cyrkle

f. 1966, Easton, PA, **db.** 1967
Sunshine Pop, Pop
The Cyrkle didn't seem like much more than a two-hit wonder in 1966, when they charted with "Red Rubber Ball" and "Turn Down Day." Their pleasant, upbeat folk/pop/rock sound, however, coupled with the fact that they got to record two complete LPs, speaks volumes about how good music was in the years 1965-1967—even second-tier groups like this were a delight to hear. Ironically, for a group remembered for just a pair of singles, the Cyrkle were considered a promising and choice signing, and were, to different degrees, wired into the management and creative circles surrounding the Beatles and Simon & Garfunkel. Issued in April of 1966, the Paul Simon-written "Red Rubber Ball" rode the charts all that spring and got as high as number two, and earned the group a spot on the Beatles' 1966 summer tour, their final scheduled concert tour. The bandmembers themselves, who had started doing this as a lark in college and as recently as six months earlier had been playing Greenwich Village folk clubs to audiences of a couple of hundred people, were astonished to find themselves suddenly thrust into the role of an arena act. An LP titled *Red Rubber Ball* was recorded that spring under producer John Simon, utilizing the same lyrical folk-rock sound found on the 45 disc, and rose to number 47 on the charts. A second single, "Turn Down Day," was issued in the early summer of 1966, and rose to number 16, thus completing the group's stay in the pop chart annals. The group continued despite several personnel changes. Although it had some enjoyable cuts, their second album, *Neon*, wasn't nearly as strong or accessible as its predecessor, and with no hit single to follow "Turn Down Day," the group's fortunes gradually ebbed. —*Bruce Eder*

● **Red Rubber Ball (A Collection)** / 1966 / Columbia ✦✦✦✦✦
Basically a two-hit wonder of the mid-'60s ("Red Rubber Ball," "Turn-Down Day"), the Cyrkle had Beatles and Paul Simon connections and were themselves fine examples of lightweight folkie pop. Everything of note they ever did is on this album. —*Jeff Tamarkin*

D'Angelo

b. Feb. 11, 1974, Richmond, VA

Vocals / Contemporary R&B, Urban

A self-taught pianist who began playing at the age of three, D'Angelo took his soul influences (Marvin Gaye, Al Green, Stevie Wonder, Prince) and parlayed them into an EMI contract when he was 18 years old. He wrote and co-produced "U Will Know," from the soundtrack for *Jason's Lyric*. The single featured D'Angelo with Tony Toni Tone, Boyz II Men, Tevin Campbell, Gerald Levert, R. Kelly, After 7 and others. His debut, *Brown Sugar*, appeared on EMI in 1995. *Live at the Jazz Cafe* followed in 1998, and two years later D'Angelo returned with *Voodoo*. —*John Bush*

● **Brown Sugar** / 1995 / Capitol ◆◆◆◆◆

By the mid-'90s, most urban R&B had become rather predictable, working on similar combinations of soul and hip-hop, or relying on vocal theatrics on slow seductive numbers. With his debut album, *Brown Sugar*, the 21-year-old D'Angelo crashed down some of those barriers. D'Angelo concentrates on classic versions of soul and R&B, but unlike most of his contemporaries, he doesn't cut and paste older songs with hip-hop beats; instead, he attacks the forms with a hip-hop attitude, breathing new life into traditional forms. Not all of his music works—there are several songs that sound incomplete, relying more on sound than structure. But when he does have a good song—like the hit "Brown Sugar," Smokey Robinson's "Cruisin,'" or the bluesy "Shit, Damn, Motherfucker," among several others—D'Angelo's wild talents are evident. *Brown Sugar* might not be consistently brilliant, but it is one of the most exciting debuts of 1995, giving a good sense of how deep D'Angelo's talents run. —*Stephen Thomas Erlewine*

Voodoo / Jan. 11, 2000 / Virgin ◆◆◆◆

Five years after his *Brown Sugar* album helped launch contemporary R&B, D'Angelo finally returned with his sophomore effort, *Voodoo*. His soulful voice is just as sweet as it was on *Brown Sugar*, though D'Angelo stretches out with a varied cast of collaborators, including trumpeter Roy Hargrove and guitarist Charlie Hunter, fellow neo-soul stars Lauryn Hill and Raphael Saadiq, and hip-hop heads like DJ Premier, Method Man & Redman, and Q-Tip. It must have been difficult to match his debut (and the frequent delays prove it was on his mind), but *Voodoo* is just as rewarding a soul album as D'Angelo's first. —*John Bush*

Daft Punk

f. 1992, Paris, France

Electronica, Club/Dance, House

In similar company with new-school French progressive dance artists such as Motorbass, Air, Cassius and Dimitri from Paris, Parisian duo Daft Punk have quickly risen to acclaim by adapting a love for first-wave acid house and techno to their younger roots in pop, indie rock, and hip-hop. The combined talents of DJs Guy-Manuel De Homem-Christo and Thomas Bangalter, Daft Punk released their debut single, "The New Wave," in 1993 on the celebrated Soma label. Instantly hailed by the dance music press as the work of a new breed of house innovators, the single was followed by "Da Funk," the band's first true hit (the record has sold 30,000 copies worldwide and seen thorough rinsings by everyone from Kris Needs to the Chemical Brothers. The group eventually signed with Virgin, with their first long-player, *Home Work*, appearing early the following year. As with the earlier singles, the group's sound is a brazen, dancefloor-oriented blend of progressive house, funk, electro, and techno, with sprinklings of hip-hop-styled breakbeats and excessive, crowd-firing samples, similar to other anthemic dance-fusion acts such as the Chemical Brothers and Monkey Mafia. —*Sean Cooper*

● **Homework** / Jan. 20, 1997 / Virgin ◆◆◆◆◆

Daft Punk's full-length debut is a funk-house hailstorm, giving real form to a style of straightahead dance music not attempted since the early fusion days of on-the-one funk and dance-party disco. Thick, rumbling bass, vocoders, choppy breaks and beats, and a certain brash naivete permeate the record from start to finish, giving it the edge of an almost certain classic. While a few fall flat, the best tracks make this one essential. —*Sean Cooper*

Discovery / Mar. 13, 2001 / Virgin ◆◆◆◆◆

Four long years after their debut, Daft Punk returned with a second full-length, also packed with excellent productions and many of the obligatory nods to the duo's favorite stylistic speed bumps of the 1970s and '80s. *Discovery* is by no means the same record, though. Deserting the shrieking acid house hysteria of their early work, the album moves in the same smooth filtered disco circles as the European dance smashes ("Music Sounds Better With You" and "Gym Tonic") co-produced by DP's Thomas Bangalter during the group's long interim. If *Homework* was Daft Punk's Chicago house record, this is defi-

nitely the New York garage edition, with co-productions and vocals from Romanthony and Todd Edwards, two of the brightest figures based in New Jersey's fertile garage scene. Also in common with classic East Coast dance and '80s R&B, *Discovery* surprisingly focuses on songwriting and concise productions. "One More Time," the irresistible album opener and first single, takes Bangalter's "Music Sounds Better With You" as a blueprint, blending sampled horns with some retro bass thump and the gorgeous, extroverted vocals of Romanthony going round and round with apparently endless tweakings. Though "Aerodynamic" and "Superheroes" have a bit of the driving acid minimalism associated with *Homework*, here Daft Punk are more taken with the glammier, poppier sound of Euro-disco and late R&B. Abusing their pitch-bend and vocoder effects as though they were going out of style, the duo loop nearly everything they can get their sequencers on: divas, vocoders, synth-guitars, electric piano. Daft Punk are such stellar, meticulous producers that they make *any* sound work, even superficially dated. —*John Bush*

Dick Dale

b. May 4, 1937

Guitar / Surf Revival, Surf, Instrumental Rock

The father of surf music, guitarist Dick Dale to a large degree invented and defined the form in the early '60s with his pioneering use of Fender reverb, dazzling staccato playing, and thundering instrumentals that incorporated Middle Eastern and Latin melodic influences. Playing guitars strung for right-handers with his left hand (as Hendrix would years later), he had an agreement with Fender instruments to "road test" new amplification equipment before it was manufactured for the general public, and found that its hollow, sustained tones evoked the mood of surfing, then catching on in a big way in his Southern California stomping grounds. Dale's impact was largely limited to Southern California, but his influence was vast, helping ignite surf music and contributing several of the genre's most enduring classics, especially "Let's Go Trippin'" and "Miserlou" (both of which were covered by the Beach Boys on their early albums). In the 1990s, Dale made an unexpectedly successful comeback with newly recorded material that closely echoed his vintage sides. —*Richie Unterberger*

★ **King of the Surf Guitar: The Best of Dick Dale** / Aug. 4, 1989 / Rhino ◆◆◆◆

King of the Surf Guitar: Best of Dick Dale is the definitive compilation of the father of surf-rock, containing 18 of his best-known songs, including all of his biggest hits ("Miserlou," "Let's Go Trippin'"), all presented in their original versions and in excellent audio. In addition to showcasing the roots of surf, *King of the Surf Guitar* demonstrates what a skilled and eclectic guitarist Dale was. Dale was one of the first guitarists in rock & roll to rely on studio and guitar effects and fuse elements of world musics to his sound, and every one of his experiments is captured on this disc. It's a definitive retrospective. —*Stephen Thomas Erlewine*

Better Shred Than Dead: The Dick Dale Anthology / Jun. 10, 1997 / Rhino ◆◆◆◆

The big picture on Dick Dale—the inventor of surf music, the Godfather of Loud, precursor of heavy metal, the first high-energy power guitarist (all titles being proffered from the man himself to describe his contributions)—gets told in a real fine way on this two-disc, 39-track anthology. Although single-disc best-ofs exist, this is the first one to cross-license from various labels. Dale started as a vocalist who just happened to be able to furnish his own guitar solos, and it's here that the compilation starts. But by track four on the first disc, "Let's Go Trippin,'" the Dick Dale story begins in earnest. The sopping-wet surf sound hadn't been invented yet, but the staccato picking, heavy twang, and hard attack were already in place. The outboard Fender reverb tank that became part of Dale's signature found its first workout on "Miserlou" (although Dale claims otherwise), and what followed was the beginning of surf music, pure and simple. Most of the groundbreaking recordings were featured on Dale's debut disc, *Surfer's Choice*, hands down *the* surf album that started it all. From this classic comes "Shake-N-Stomp," "Take It Off," and the one that made him a California legend, "Surf Beat." The rest of the first disc carries you through his later Capitol recordings while the second disc starts with the second half of Dale's career in 1983 with live tracks from his *The Tigers Loose* album and steers you through duets with Stevie Ray Vaughan, tributes to Hendrix, and best of all, documenting his own resurrection in the '90s, totally viable and still his own man. Transfers sound a bit buzzier in an over-EQ'd way on some of the early tracks, but overall, this is one really great tribute to an original pioneer. —*Cub Koda*

The Damned

f. 1976, England, **db.** 1989

British Punk, Goth Rock, Punk

The Damned usurped the Sex Pistols, working behind their backs to become the first British punk band to release a record, the first to have a hit single (the epochal "New

Rose") and the first to tour America. That, in a nutshell, is the appeal of the Damned—they weren't revolutionaries, they were drunken louts who would do anything for a prank. Like many of their first-generation punk peers, the band were rooted in pub-rock, playing simple three-chord pounders, but the group played fast, loose and sloppy, often sounding like everything was about to fall apart. Their 1977 debut *Damned Damned Damned* epitomized this sound, and they never quite captured it again, partially because of their limited talent and partially because of their defiant, boundless stupidity. Following the debut, the Damned released a pair of similar records that weren't quite as successful before delving into a bizarre affair with goth-rock for several years in the early '80s. By the time that was worked out of their system, several key members had left the band and the group had nothing more than a cult following, yet they still managed the odd hit single in the U.K. until the late '80s, when the Damned decided to call it a day. But that wasn't the end of the story. During the '90s, the band continually reunited in various incarnations, playing concerts across England and functioning as a sort of bizarre punk nostalgia act. *—Stephen Thomas Erlewine*

★ **Damned Damned Damned** / Apr. 16, 1977 / Frontier ✦✦✦✦✦

While the Sex Pistols will always have a prominent place in the story of U.K. punk, the Damned did nearly everything first, including the first single, the smoking "New Rose," and the first album, namely, this stone classic of rock & roll fire. At just half an hour long, *Damned Damned Damned* is a permanent testimony to original guitarist Brian James' songwriting (ten of the 12 tracks are his) and the band's take no prisoners aesthetic. Starting with Captain Sensible's sharp bass line for "Neat Neat Neat," which rapidly explodes into a full band thrash, the Damned left rhetoric for the theoreticians and political posing for the Clash. All the foursome wanted to do was rock, and that they do here. Vanian already has his spooky-voiced theatrics down cold; "Feel the Pain" indulges his Alice Cooper fascination while the band creates some creepy fun behind him. Most of the time, he's yelping with the best of them, but with considerably more control than most of the era's shouters. Scabies' considerable reputation as a drummer starts here; comparisons flew thick and fast to Keith Moon, and not just for onstage antics (of which there were plenty). His sense of stop-start rhythm and fills is simply astounding, whether on "So Messed Up" or in his own one-minute goof, "Stab Yer Back." Though the Captain doesn't get his full chance to shine on bass, he's more than adequate, while James just cranks the amps and lets fly. Concluding with a version of the Stooges' "1970" which sounds hollower than the original but no less energetic, *Damned Damned Damned* is and remains rock at its messy, wonderful best. *—Ned Raggett*

Music for Pleasure / Nov. 1977 / Demon ✦✦

Quickly dismissed by critics at the time as a shocking misstep, *Music for Pleasure* is not quite as bad as the Nick Mason (Pink Floyd) production would indicate—though close. Its failure led to Stiff Records dropping them and the first of many temporary breakups. *—Chris Woodstra*

Machine Gun Etiquette / Dec. 1979 / Roadrunner ✦✦✦✦✦

Rejoining forces without James, who pursued his own interests from then on (only hooking up with the band again for a late-'80s "farewell" show), the remaining three brought in young Saints veteran Ward on bass, recorded an album, and hoped for the best. That best proved much better than expected; while singles ended up on the charts, *Etiquette* itself was deservedly hailed as another classic from the band. Over time, its reputation has grown to equal the original *Damned Damned Damned*; while no less strong than that record, the Damned here bring in a wide variety of touches and influences to create a record that most of their contemporaries could never have approached. The group's wicked way around witty punk hadn't ebbed a bit; the opening cut, "Love Song," is a hilarious trashing of romantic clichés (sample lyric: "I'll be the rubbish, you'll be the bin!") that barely lasts two minutes, while "Noise, Noise, Noise" and "Liar" work in the same general vein. These, however, only scratch the surface. "Melody Lee," written by the Captain for a favorite comic character, starts with a lovely piano intro, whereas the celebratory angst of "I Just Can't Be Happy Today" chugs along with garagey élan and keyboards á la the Electric Prunes. Other prime standouts include "Plan 9 Channel 7," a Grand Guignol of an epic about James Dean and Vampira with a fantastic Vanian vocal; the merry mayhem of "These Hands" (belonging to a killer circus clown, with appropriate carnival music, of course); and a great rip through the MC5's "Looking at You." The best moment was saved for last, though: "Smash It Up," a two-part number divided between an affecting instrumental tribute to longtime supporter and Captain hero Marc Bolan, and a perfect trash-the-rules-and-party pop/punk/R&B scorcher. *—Ned Raggett*

The Black Album / Dec. 1980 / Chiswick ✦✦✦

The fact that one of its songs is called "Hit or Miss" is quite appropriate for the double-vinyl *Black Album*; while not perfect, it's definitely got some high points on it. Given the intentionally parodic reference to the Beatles' own two-disc sprawler, perhaps the semi-schizophrenia is perfectly intentional. Some of the numbers show the band following their original punk vein, but by this point the four (joined here by a new bassist, Paul Gray) were leaving straight, three-chord thrash to the cul-de-sac revivalists. The album begins with a Damned classic, "Wait for the Blackout," a dramatic psych/punk surge infected with Vanian's glorious croon, celebrating the joys of the night while steering clear of overtly-serious goth affectations. After that, things start to vary, but tracks of note are still thick on the ground, including the Sensible-sung "Lively Arts," a nicely barbed take on culture with some harpsichord to match, and the goofy but still enjoyable "Drinking About My Baby." Regardless, things get a bit restful at points, and while Vanian often steps forward to continue carrying it along, sometimes even the band isn't happy with the results. "History of the World (Part One)" has always carried the credit "overproduced by Hans Zimmer" because they felt the guest synth player did just that! However, the final two studio tracks are doozies: "Therapy," a Sensible/Vanian-sung romp with a great chorus, and the sidelong "Curtain Call," perhaps the most unlikely thing the Damned ever did. That said, it's still a surprisingly good blast, a tour de force for Vanian particularly and a chance for the band to try everything from straightforward rock to gentler atmospherics. *—Ned Raggett*

Strawberries / 1982 / Castle ✦✦✦

Recuperating a bit from *The Black Album*'s uneven impact while still aiming to try whatever they want in studio, here the same four members, along with soon-to-be regular Roman Jugg on various keyboard parts, come up with their strongest album since *Machine Gun Etiquette*. By turns sprightly and cheerful, dark and dramatic, energetic and snarling, or all that and more at once, *Strawberries* defies usual expectations to be yet another good rock album from the band, resisting easy attempts to categorize it. Older punk fans would likely appreciate the album's initial blast of "Ignite," a driving thrasher with a fine chorus and some hilarious vamping in the end from Vanian. Immediately following is the superior "Generals," which beautifully combines piano and a crisp arrangement with Vanian's powerfully smooth mode. From there, it's almost a case of strength-to-strength as the album continues: the brass-driven "Stranger on the Town," sassy and sharp; the giddy keyboards and crunch of "Dozen Girls"; the gentler psych-pop experiments of "Gun Fury" and "The Pleasure and the Pain"; the Reagan-baiting "Bad Time for Bonzo"; and the bright beauty of "Under the Floor Again," at once mysterious and gorgeous with a particularly winning instrumental break merging some of Vanian's most positive lyrics. Captain Sensible gets two fun moments for himself in the ruminative "Life Goes On" and the album-closing fun goof, "Don't Bother Me." Meanwhile, at the album's center is the darkest, most haunting thing the band ever recorded, "The Dog." It's an astonishingly effective chiller based on the character of Claudia from Anne Rice's *Interview with the Vampire*. Cleopatra's welcome 1993 re-release added five bonus tracks, including the Captain's brief piano piece "Torture Me," which tackles the same subject as the Smiths' "Meat Is Murder" but with arguably less hectoring and more affecting results. *—Ned Raggett*

Phantasmagoria / 1985 / Off Beat ✦✦✦✦

By the time the Damned found themselves on a major label after nine years of ups, downs, and all arounds, a big change had taken place: Captain Sensible, with both his own solo successes and other pressures coming to bear, decided to depart. Keyboardist Roman Jugg took over the guitar, while Bryn Merrick remained on bass and Vanian and Scabies continued doing their thing. The first fruit of this new Damned, *Phantasmagoria*, doesn't match up to the excellent variety and performance level on *Strawberries*, but still has a lot to show while at the same time exploring new territory for the group. The cover and artwork seem to ally the Damned even more closely with goth rock than before, but Vanian thankfully has never seen fit to simply ape those clichés, steering his own powerful path. Similarly the music can be moody but never without its own distinct energy and fire—more a Cramps sense (if not sound) of loving the dark than anything, but with a clean, modern sheen and just enough Hammer horror. "Street of Dreams" makes for a powerful, anthemic opener, with some fine Scabies drumming. "Is It a Dream," the one song with a Sensible co-writing credit, is yet another fantastic Vanian vocal showcase in a career of many. The really killer tracks include "Shadow of Love," a semi-Morricone style mood-out quick shuffle with haunting guitar from Jugg, and "Grimly Fiendish," a funny bit of spooky psychedelia not all that far off from where the Dukes of Stratosphear would end up a couple of years later. *Phantasmagoria* concludes with the surging instrumental "Trojans," a strong number that showed the Damned had lots of life in them yet. *—Ned Raggett*

Anything / 1986 / MCA ✦

The Light at the End of the Tunnel / 1987 / MCA ✦✦✦✦✦

Anyone expecting a fully organized compilation from this double-disc effort will be sorely disappointed; while the years for release dates are mentioned, the sources for many of the releases aren't, leaving neophytes to the Damned a bit high and dry. Happily, an appreciative and detailed essay from one Herb Fenstein (more likely Chiswick label boss Roger Armstrong writing under a pseudonym, as he did in the liner notes to the CD version of *Machine Gun Etiquette*) helps. Even without the chronological organization, *Light* is still a great overview of the first ten years of the band's career, especially given the sheer amount of labels that they'd been on over the years (at least five, if not more!). The selection is, for the most part, quite on the money; while those who feel the group fell off dramatically with the *Phantasmagoria* and *Anything* albums will think them over-represented, it's still definitely the Damned at their best from track to track. Early punk breakouts like "Neat Neat Neat" and "New Rose" as well as turn-of-the-'80s standards such as "Plan 9 Channel 7," "Smash It Up," and "I Just Can't Be Happy Today" make a case for the band's early days. *The Black Album* is mostly ignored, but the sidelong "Curtain Call" thankfully is included, giving Vanian his well-deserved showcase. Later numbers like "Ignite," "Lovely Money," "Grimly Fiendish," and the smash single "Eloise" demonstrate that far from fading away, the Damned just found other ways to make their mark. Add to this a slew of rarities—the studio cover of the Beatles' "Help!," "Rabid (Over You)," "Disco Man," and some alternate mixes of other numbers—and *Light* remains the best place for those new to the Damned to start. Comprehensive and perfectly entertaining all at once. *—Ned Raggett*

Neat Neat Neat / Nov. 19, 1996 / Demon Duplicate ✦✦✦

That a band as irreverent and messy as the Damned has been given "proper box set treatment" just goes to show that anything can become respectable if it sticks around long enough. Or it shows that the CD reissue boom has gotten out of hand. Either way, *Neat Neat Neat* isn't really a necessary box set for anyone outside of the dedicated Damned collector. The Damned's recordings have been notoriously uneven, making them the perfect subject for a compilation, but three discs is a little too extensive, especially since it's packed with extraneous live tracks. For anyone but hardcore fans, their output could conceivably be whittled down to two discs, much like the fine but flawed *The Light at the End of the Tunnel*, but three discs tends to emphasize their early peak and quick decline more than anyone would like. —*Stephen Thomas Erlewine*

Marvellous: The Best of the Damned / 1999 / Big Beat ♦♦

It's safe to declare that no reasonable person could agree that this is "the best of the damned," subtitle be damned. What it really is, perhaps, is the best of the tracks the band did for Chiswick in the late 1970s and early 1980s. A release which has nothing from *Damned Damned Damned*, nor any of the mid-1980s singles that were small and large hits in Britain, cannot fairly be labeled a best-of retrospective of the group. The ten tracks here do cover a few of their better-known early songs, including the British hits "Love Song," "Smash It Up," and "I Just Can't Be Happy Today," the last of which is presented in its "rare radio edit," if that makes you happy. The music doesn't make a great argument for the Damned being a major punk/new wave act; it often thrashes about without first-class wit or imagination, and sometimes treads close to metal. Then again, it's probably not what the band would present as exhibit A to history anyway. With just ten tracks, no liner notes, and the misleading title, this is an uncommonly disappointing package from the Big Beat/Ace label, which usually does much to set the standard for such items on reissues. —*Richie Unterberger*

The Dandy Warhols

f. 1992, Portland, OR

Power Pop, Alternative Pop/Rock

Vocalist/guitarist Courtney Taylor played drums in a glam band called Beauty Stab before forming the Dandy Warhols in Portland, Oregon in the early '90s. He joined up with keyboard player Zia McCabe, guitarist Peter Holmstrom and drummer Eric Hedford, and recorded the album *Dandy's Rule, OK?* for Tim/Kerr Records. Tours with Electrafixion and Love and Rockets spread the word about the Dandys' grunge-inspired Brit Invasion pop; a major-label bidding war ensued, and Capitol emerged with a contract in 1996. The Dandy Warhols' first Capitol album, *The Dandy Warhols Come Down*, was released in the summer of 1997 and *Thirteen Tales from Urban Bohemia* followed three years later. —*John Bush*

Dandy's Rule OK? / Oct. 1995 / TK ♦♦♦

The Dandy Warhols seem like they *should* be a great band—they bring together shoegazing British pop, lazy grunge, and Velvet Underground-style grittiness, all with a wicked sense of humor. Despite all this—and despite the fact that *Dandys Rule OK* is fairly well written—their songs tend to slip by unnoticed, never really leaving an impression. The band seems to be at its best when it parodies *other* bands: "Lou Weed," "Ride," and "The Coffee and Tea Wrecks" are all affectionate pastiches of their namesakes, and "The Dandy Warhol's T.V. Theme Song" is a fine bit of bouncy pop. Unfortunately, none of the album's more clever segments stand out, buried as they are in a murky mess of forgettable material. —*Nitsuh Abebe*

Dandy Warhols Come Down / Jul. 15, 1997 / Capitol ♦♦♦

Power-pop bands are often caught in a quandary. Their core audience praises them for their classicist approach, but if they ever want to break out into a larger audience, they have to modernize their sound, which makes their cult angry. The problem is especially difficult for bands that came of age in the early '90s, since they were weaned on not just the Beatles and Beach Boys, but also the Pixies and Sonic Youth. As a result, bands like the Dandy Warhols are restless, anxious to make catchy pop songs while keeping indie cred, and that's why their major-label debut *The Dandy Warhols Come Down* is so uneven. The band has talent for not just punchy hooks, but for layered sonics as well, but they don't know how to meld the two together. As a result, the most immediate moments on the record are awash in a sea of feedback, which can't be trance-inducing, since its spell is punctured by pop hooks. And while those pop songs are good, they aren't enough to prevent *Come Down* from being a frustrating listen. —*Stephen Thomas Erlewine*

● **Thirteen Tales from Urban Bohemia** / 2000 / Capitol ♦♦♦♦

Though they still tend towards pastiche, the Dandy Warhols' third full-length, *Thirteen Tales From Urban Bohemia*, presents a bakers' dozen of their most focused and cohesive songs. Where their earlier albums were eclectic to the point of being scattershot, this release manages to limit the band's style-switching to dreamy, sweeping epics like "Godless" and "Nietzsche," sussed, sleazy power pop like "Horse Pills" and "Cool Scene," and country and gospel ventures like "Country Leaver" and "The Gospel." The group's increasingly strong songwriting makes most of these experiments successful and distinctive, though the Dandys fall into their old habit of appropriating sounds they like wholesale with "Shakin'," a "tribute" to Elastica's uptight yet sexy riffs and rhythms. Not surprisingly, the most successful songs on *Thirteen Tales From Urban Bohemia* are the least derivative ones, such as anxious pop songs like "Solid," "Get Off," and the delicate, lovelorn ballad "Sleep." On those tracks, as well as the satirical single "Bohemian Like You"—this year's model of their hit "Not If You Were the Last Junkie on Earth"—the Dandys reveal themselves as a savvy pop band with a voice of their own. Though they're not all the way there yet, *Tales From Urban Bohemia* is a worthwhile step in their developing creativity. —*Heather Phares*

Danielson Famile

Alternative Pop/Rock

For his senior thesis project at Rutgers University Daniel Smith handed in what became the Danielson Famile's album *A Prayer for Every Hour*, he got an A. The album was released on Tooth & Nail records in 1995. It features Smith backed by his siblings who range in age from 12 to their early 20s. *Tell Another Joke at the Ol' Choppin' Block*, pro-

duced by Kramer (Galaxy 500, Low, Palace Brothers), followed in 1997. In 1998 Smith launched Tri-Danielson to convey his three distinct musical directions: solo, with his family, and a more rock based incarnation called Danielsonship. Tri-Danielson released *Alpha* in 1998 and followed in 1999 with *Omega*. The Danielson Famile is unmistakably a Christian band, but in the same way that Flannery O'Connor was a Christian writer. They reject the conventional set of Christian symbols and subject matter while at the heart of every song, underneath the weirdness, is a perfectly orthodox Christian message; and Smith's falsetto vocals are downright shocking, an effective tool in cutting through the barriers to convey these messages. No contemporary Christian radio station in their right mind would ever play Danielson, they're just too out there. They sound like Captain Beefheart's Magic Band joined by the Partridge Family at some roadside revival along the Jersey Turnpike—definitely an acquired taste. —*Jason Nickey*

Prayer for Every Hour / Jun. 7, 1996 / Tooth & Nail ♦♦♦

A relatively stripped-down record in comparison to their later works, this is the finished product that served as lead Danielson Famile member Daniel Smith's senior thesis at Rutgers University. With guitars, bells, drums, and Smith's trademark yelp, the album takes listeners through 24 tracks (the prayers for every hour). The songs themselves are a disheveled group ranging in length from 17 seconds to over five minutes. The musical approach sees simple swipes of choppy, repeated acoustic guitar rhythms being used more as percussion, while the listener is regaled with extremely personal revelations that try to define the conflicts that arise within when dealing with religion and youth (e.g., "My loins say just one thing to me/But my brain says another thing to me"). The album has a tinny, home-recorded quality that suits these homespun flights of inspiration and tales of the faith. The call-and-response calls of "Amen, brother!" during the song "Feeling Tank" are inspired, and the joyful ranting of the opening track, "Nice of Me," is remarkable. Smith fills the record with his high-pitched asides and relays his organic, loving message amidst off-time, rattling musical backdrops and dramatic, sometimes endearingly sloppy execution. Choruses are unveiled in between bits of laughter. Voices echo and marching band dirges work alongside acoustic odes to higher powers. This first release also features some surprisingly recognizable indie rock elements with the inclusion of some louder, scratchy guitars and straightforward, propulsive arrangements. But nothing is straightforward for very long in the Danielson Famile world. If there is a fault, it is that the vocal melodies are not as well developed as the musical ideas, but the seeds for one of the more interesting independent bands recording in both the secular and nonsecular world are sewn here. —*Jon Pruett*

● **Tell Another Joke at the Ol' Choppin' Block** / Feb. 18, 1997 / Tooth & Nail ♦♦♦♦

Daniel Smith and family jump out of the gate with fervent heavens-praising energy and never let up on *Tell Another Joke at the Ol' Choppin' Block*. Sounding like a Pixies tribute band performing at a carnival sideshow, Smith and company spout strange lyrics that give props to the Lord, examine mother-child bonds, and explore the "deep kind of love" of a "Jersey Loverboy." Highlights include the banjo workout opening track where Smith proclaims, "Bring it down now...I love my Lord, I love my Lord, I love my Lord" until he's out of breath, and "Ye Olde Battleaxe" with its repeated refrain of "mothers and their daughters" and a comic highpoint of Smith nonchalantly telling one to "give it up for your momma." "Flesh Thang" is particularly thrilling, with a racing piano attempting to keep pace with Smith's Black Francis-style yelps about "looking like a baby" and "shedding withered skin." At this early stage in the band's career, their trademark sound was already fully developed with cowbells, xylophones, ragged guitars, and all sorts of whimsical gizmos making for quite a lush cacophony. Sing-song harmonies, call-and-response-style song elements, wild tempo changes, and lyrics that are about as subtle as sledgehammers rule the day. Kramer's excellent, clean production makes sure the wild arrangements never fly off the handle. *Tell Another Joke at the Ol' Choppin' Block* is an accessible, bubbly joy from start to finish. —*Tim DiGravina*

Tri-Danielson, Vol. 1 (Alpha) / May 19, 1998 / Tooth & Nail ♦♦♦♦

Beginning with the family's repeated chant of "Tri-Danielson," followed by a round of hooting and applause, the Danielson Famile's third LP is the one that sees them at their strongest. This is their brightest collection of songs so far, and it's definitely the album to start with. Beginning with "Southern Paws"—a simple acoustic melody with Daniel Smith and harmonies courtesy of sisters Megan and Rachel—it's apparent that the group has finally become comfortable enough to make the music they were on the verge of with 1997's *Tell Another Joke at the Ol' Choppin' Block*. "Rubbernecker" takes a sort of quirky, straight rhythm and punches it up with Wurlitzer effects and horns, while Daniel Smith sings about people with "hungry eyes," "homemade thighs," and "greasy talk." In the end, it sounds like nothing else and is certainly one of the tracks that will either endear you to or steer you away from the band. The carnival comparisons begin with this track, as do their ties to soul music. Other songs add banjo amidst all the pianos, and acoustic guitars amid all the tinkling keyboards. "Between the Lines of the Scout Signs" is the sound of a man possessed. "Release the social burden," he says, and "shake hands with that middle finger." However you might feel about the lyrical content, there's no doubting his zeal and there's certainly no doubting the effective, stripped-down punch of the music. Not content to take down the middle finger, the Danielson Famile speak out on "Pottymouth" about, yes, swearing. Imagine an after-school special with music done by indie rock gypsies. If that's not enough, the band throws in a (somewhat) straightforward cover of Ken Nordine's "Flesh." —*Jon Pruett*

Tri-Danielson, Vol. 2 (Omega) / Jan. 26, 1999 / Tooth & Nail ♦♦♦

Beginning with some synth-based rhythms that are by no means synthetic, *Tri-Danielson, Vol. 2* runs and skips through a collection of songs that sees the Danielson Famile coming further into their own, creating their own brand of pop-based worship and singling the band out as crazed innovators. Daniel Smith sounds especially inspired on the record, from the opening track, "Cutest Lil' Dragon," to the ending, "Deeper Than the Gov't." "Idiot Boxsen" is surely one of the strongest songs they have created, with the sisters providing some wonderfully eerie background vocals alongside the horns and flutes. Lyrically, Smith is in fine form, decrying the evils of television. Musically, they have really discovered a distinct sound in their girl group harmonies and general carnival-like atmosphere. There is the sound of soul music in here as well, although it may be a kind of carnival soul music. This is most apparent on "Failing a Test," which is about the fear of just that. During the sonorous violin drone of "Fruitful Weekend," you might notice a meshing together of genres that is not too far removed from the earliest cross-pollinations of Camper Van Beethoven. "Sold! To The Rich Man!" begins with a slight lyrical variation on "He's Got the Whole World in His Hands" (recorded live with crowd and group singalong) before turning into a completely different song. These are the hoots and hollers of a revival or an especially slapdash campfire singalong. When Smith breaks into the repeated phrase "'Tis we, not me" during the closing "Deeper Than the Gov't," it pretty much sums up the feeling of the record: This is not just one man—this is community. *—Jon Pruett*

Fetch the Compass Kids / Apr. 24, 2001 / Secretly Canadian ✦✦✦✦
Most of the attention showered on the Danielson Famile up to this release focused on the band's eccentricities—the odd rhythm shifts, the girl group harmonies, the otherworldly lyrics, and, above all, Daniel Smith's voice, which at times sounds like a pre-pubescent Frank Black—overlooking the quality of Smith's songcraft. With *Fetch the Compass Kids*, the family also broke away from longtime producer/collaborator Kramer (who worked on their previous three outings) and enlisted the ubiquitous Steve Albini to work behind the boards. And the result is an album far more accessible than anything put out previously by the band. The unpredictability and general weirdness is still fully intact—with banjos, falsetto harmonies, toy piano, and marching singsong-y tempos strewn about—but it doesn't overshadow the songs themselves. Lyrically, *Fetch the Compass Kids* is a loose concept album about finding tranquility in a fast-paced world, and the Christian concept of forgiveness, as on previous Danielson albums, plays a prominent role here. But whereas Smith came off as a mystical seer of visions on previous efforts, here that element is toned down, and much of the album is spent free of allegory and symbol in favor of the direct and literal (although there are plenty of times when this is not true, particularly on songs like "Fathom the Nine Fruits Pie" and "Good News for the Puss Pickers"). This approach comes as a refreshing change after the challenging *Tri-Danielson* albums, and although it's far from easily accessible, *Fetch the Compass Kids* provides a good introduction to the music of Danielson Famile. But, as a word of warning, all preconceived notions of what "Christian bands" sound like should be checked at the door. *—Jason Nickey*

Dantalian's Chariot

f. 1967, **db.** 1968
British Psychedelia, Psychedelic
One of the most brilliant obscure psychedelic singles of the late '60s—indeed, one of the most brilliant obscure rock singles of any kind from the era—was Dantalian's Chariot's "Madman Running Through the Fields." This 1967 effort was British pop-psych at its zenith, strongly reminiscent of (and as good as) the classic early sides by Syd Barrett's Pink Floyd. What made it all the stranger was that it was the debut single by a group of veteran musicians who, just a few months earlier, had been playing jazz/R&B fusion as Zoot Money's Big Roll Band. Such was the impact of psychedelic music in 1967, however, that by the middle of the year, Money had decided to totally revamp his sound. Zoot Money's Big Roll Band became Dantalian's Chariot. The music, written primarily by Money and a young Andy Summers (over a decade before the guitarist would reach stardom with the Police), changed as radically as the name, with airy melodies, spacy lyrics, and guitar/organ-driven arrangements. The band hit the London underground circuit and made their debut recording as Dantalian's Chariot ("Madman") in the summer of 1967. The single, innovative as it was, didn't make any commercial waves. Their new direction wasn't supported by EMI, which dropped the band. A psychedelic-minded LP was worked on, but not released. Some of the material appeared on an early 1968 record credited to Zoot Money and the Big Roll Band, which the Direction label assembled from various tunes cut over the past year. Dantalian's Chariot came to an end in the spring of 1968, with Summers joining the Soft Machine; Money would also join Eric Burdon's Animals around the same time. A collection of psychedelic-oriented Dantalian's Chariot tracks (several previously unreleased) did emerge in 1996. *—Richie Unterberger*

Chariot Rising / 1996 / Wooden Hill ✦✦✦
A close facsimile of what Dantalian's Chariot's unreleased album would have sounded like, taken from ten tracks recorded in 1967, several of which were previously unissued. "Madman Running Through the Fields" is essential listening for anyone who likes Pink Floyd, with its happy-go-mad lyrics, astral organ, Syd Barrett-esque guitar, and sudden quiet breaks into pastoral flute passages. Nothing else here is nearly as striking, but it's decent, somewhat prototypical early underground British psychedelia, though the songwriting can be kind of forced. The wistfully ebullient "Sun Came Bursting Through My Clouds" (the B side of "Madman") is probably their best secondary effort; instrumentally oriented explorations like "Soma" and "This Island" get freakier. *—Richie Unterberger*

Danzig

f. 1987
Alternative Metal, Heavy Metal
After the demise of Samhain, ex-Misfits vocalist Glenn Danzig formed his own eponymous heavy metal band in 1987, which would prove a more effective vehicle for his obsession with the dark side. But there's more than meets the eye—Danzig obviously relishes casting himself as the archetypal evil, menacing heavy metal frontman, and his theatricality often seems to indicate that his posturing is tongue-in-cheek. The darkness of Danzig's vision increasingly expressed itself over the band's career in a romanticized, gothic sensibility, more quietly sinister and darkly seductive than aggressively threatening, and the group's music has progressed from simple, blues-based metal riffs to more atmospheric, coldly haunting textures that attempt to sonically replicate the feel of the lyrics. Their self-titled debut for Rick Rubin's Def American label found Glenn Danzig playing the Satanic metal singer role to the hilt, even if the band's songs sounded much the same. *Danzig II: Lucifuge* followed in 1990, and it expanded on the simple blues riffs of the debut with more extensive forays into that style. *Danzig III: How the Gods Kill* marked a full-fledged entry into the realm of gothic romanticism, working to create moods rather than pounding heavy metal aggression. Glenn Danzig next released a solo project, *Black Aria*, a quasi-operatic attempt at classical instrumentals. The band broke through into the mainstream in 1993, when a live video for "Mother," a song originally released on *Danzig*, became an inescapable smash on MTV and even charted as a single, nearly cracking the *Billboard* Top 40. The more experimental *Danzig 4* was released in 1994 and entered the charts at number 29, but its moody, atmospheric subtlety didn't find as much favor with the band's new audience as the anthemic "Mother." Following the supporting tour, Danzig broke up the band and assembled another version more in line with his new direction. Though increasingly ignored by the press and the public, Danzig continued to release records into the new millennium. *—Steve Huey*

Danzig / 1988 / American ✦✦✦
Danzig debuts with a record of simple, pounding, bluesy metal featuring lead singer Glenn Danzig's trademark Elvis-meets-Jim Morrison bellow and outlandishly dark, evil lyrics. There isn't a great deal of musical variety or complexity here, but the band powers its way through such signature tunes as "Twist of Cain," "Am I Demon," and the (future) hit "Mother" with a primal energy. Plus, Danzig's tongue-in-cheek posturing as the ultimate unholier-than-thou heavy metal frontman gives the record a definite appeal, even if one is not inclined to view his theatrics as dangerous or threatening. *—Steve Huey*

Danzig II: Lucifuge / Jun. 1990 / American ✦✦✦✦
Danzig's second release is also their most diversified. They explore their blues roots with a couple of boogies, a slow shuffle, and a slide number, throwing in a '50s-reminiscent ballad in waltz time for good measure. Glenn Danzig's theatrical vocals don't prevent these numbers from working surprisingly well (except when he attempts a Mississippi-delta accent on "Killer Wolf"), demonstrating his talents and range of expression as a vocalist. The simple, somewhat standard blues-metal riffs of their debut are here ("Snakes of Christ" is a flat-out rewrite of *Danzig*'s "Twist of Cain"), but not as plentiful, making the record more interesting and listenable. "Her Black Wings" ranks with the band's best songs. *—Steve Huey*

● **Danzig III: How the Gods Kill** / Jul. 14, 1992 / American ✦✦✦✦
Featuring disturbing cover art from H.R. Giger, Danzig's third album continues to expand the band's musical range; rather than pounding away at simple blues riffs, the atmospheric title track (yet another rewrite of "Twist of Cain," this time at a slower tempo) and the haunting ballad "Sistinas" attempt to match their music with the darkness of Glenn Danzig's lyrics, resulting in two of the album's high points. Danzig's vocals are more subtle in places, and John Christ's guitar work continues to improve. Arguably the definitive Danzig album. *—Steve Huey*

Black Aria / 1993 / Phonographie ✦

Thrall: Demonsweatlive / May 25, 1993 / American ✦✦✦
Danzig's breakthrough EP features three new studio tracks (*Thrall*) and live performances of four of the band's most popular songs (*Demonsweatlive*). The live version of "Mother" was the hit, of course, but there are other worthwhile moments—the new tracks include "It's Coming Down," a threatening rocker, and a cover of Elvis Presley's "Trouble," and the live material is also highlighted by "Sistinas," one of the band's best songs. *—Steve Huey*

Danzig 4 / Dec. 1994 / American ✦✦✦
Danzig's experiments with using texture and atmosphere to evoke their trademark mood of darkness and evil come to the forefront on their fourth full-length album, with John Christ contributing more effects and fuller chord voicings. The band has also started to craft their songs, using different instruments and a few industrial sounds in the background of some tracks. Not all of the experiments are successful or interesting, partially due to inconsistent songwriting, but out of all their releases, the music here comes the closest to reflecting the darkness of Glenn Danzig's lyrics. Some, however, may miss their more energetic earlier albums. *—Steve Huey*

Blackacidevil / Oct. 29, 1996 / Phonographie ✦✦✦
Even though it was more metal-oriented than *4*, *Blackacidevil* fell through the cracks upon its late 1996 release. Producer Bill Kennedy gives Danzig a harder, edgier sound than before, but the group has trouble coming up with hooks, which makes Glenn Danzig's standard demonic lyrics a little tedious to anyone but hardcore fans. *—Stephen Thomas Erlewine*

6:66 Satan's Child / Nov. 2, 1999 / Phonographie ✦✦✦
Danzig's last release of the 20th century, *6:66 Satan's Child*, follows the same formula as his last album (1996's *Blackacidevil*)—gone are the straightforward Jim Morrison meets Black Sabbath-sounding songs of the band's first few albums, replaced by metallic industrial sounds (comparable to Godflesh, White Zombie, etc.). Singer Glenn Danzig is the only remaining member of his original solo lineup, and as on his previous album, handles guitar duties (filling out the lineup are Lazie on bass and Joey C. on drums). Although Danzig's musical style may have shifted over the years, the outfit's trademark sex n' Satan

imagery remains the same, as evidenced by the album title, lyrics, comic book-style cover, and the CD booklet photos. While such tracks as "Belly of the Beast" and "Lilin" move at a dirge-like pace, they also pack quite a sonic punch, courtesy of the album's production team of Glenn and Peter Lorimer (Orgy members Amir Derakh and Jay Gordon mixed several tracks as well). Longtime Danzig fans will know what to expect from such titles as "Cult w/out A Name," "Firemass," "Satans Child," and "Apokalips." *—Greg Prato*

Live on the Black Hand Side / May 8, 2001 / Restless ♦♦♦

Live on the Black Hand Side is a double-disc compilation of Danzig concert performances stretching from 1992 (just as the band was beginning to break through on MTV with the *How the Gods Kill* album) through 2000. However, the song selections date back to the group's beginnings, balancing the simple, pounding rockers of their early days with the more atmospheric recent material. Some fans might think a full second disc of the new, post-John Christ/Eerie Von/Chuck Biscuits lineup is too much, given that the album seems to be designed as an in-concert history (not to mention the sometimes dicey sound quality of that 2000-vintage material). But there are enough high points along the way to make *Live on the Black Hand Side* a treat for rabid fans. *—Steve Huey*

Terence Trent D'Arby

b. Mar. 15, 1962, New York, NY

Vocals, Saxophone, Keyboards, Drums, Guitar / Contemporary R&B, Adult Alternative Pop/Rock, Pop/Rock, Urban

Terence Trent D'Arby emerged in 1987 amid a storm of publicity. Claiming his debut record was the best since *Sgt. Pepper*, his brash arrogance captured headlines throughout the U.K., eventually winding their way back to America. D'Arby's first single, "If You Let Me Stay," rocketed into the U.K. Top Ten upon its release. Its accompanying album, *Introducing the Hardline According to Terence Trent D'Arby*, was also a massive success, hitting number one and spending over a year in the top half of the chart. D'Arby didn't have a major hit in the U.S. until 1988, when the sparse funk of "Wishing Well" hit number one. All of the success—both commercial and critical—had D'Arby poised as a major act, artistically and popularly. His mix of soul, rock, pop and R&B recalled Prince in its scope and sound, yet his sensibility was grittier and earthier. At least they were at first. By the time of his second album, 1989's *Neither Fish nor Flesh*, his ambitions were more nakedly pretentious, and the album dropped off the charts quickly, without so much as one hit single. *Terence Trent D'Arby's Symphony or Damn*—an album containing many of the same ideas as *Neither Fish Nor Flesh*, only better executed—was released in 1993 to favorable reviews, as well as some airplay on modern rock radio stations and MTV. It was enough for D'Arby to regain some credibility, yet it wasn't enough to make the album a hit. Two years later, he released *TTD's Vibrator*, which received the same fate as *Symphony or Damn*. *—Stephen Thomas Erlewine*

Introducing the Hardline According to Terence Trent D'Arby / 1987 / Columbia ♦♦♦♦

Introducing the Hardline According to Terence Trent D'Arby is a strong debut by this young, cocky Black British singer, who wrote virtually every note, played a multitude of instruments, and claimed that his was the most important album since the Beatles' *Sgt. Pepper*. Hits included "If You Let Me Stay," "Dance Little Sister," "Sign Your Name," and the #1 "Wishing Well." His first album is a curious mixture of old and new styles. Although the production is quite modern, D'Arby shows his roots in the work of older artists, borrowing a page or two from Michael Jackson and Stevie Wonder, while James Brown appears to have had the strongest influence on D'Arby's stage presence. *—Rob Bowman*

Neither Fish Nor Flesh / Oct. 1989 / Columbia ♦♦♦

Following the major success of his debut, Terence Trent D'Arby made the always-difficult sophomore effort more difficult. In addition to the brash declarations that preceded his first record, D'Arby made ultimately self-sabotaging demands upon his label, concerning *Neither Fish Nor Flesh*'s promotion and release (to coincide with the competitive Christmas market). The challenging nature of the album didn't help matters. *Neither Fish Nor Flesh* is a sprawling, overly ambitious work that incorporates Middle Eastern flavorings and even more of a gospel influence into his gritty mix of rock, R&B, and funk. Lyrically, D'Arby's pretensions run a bit wild, but the man does possess a voice that is a force to be reckoned with. Songs like the rousing, soulful "I'll Be Alright" and the sexy "To Know Someone Deeply Is to Know Someone Softly" are masterful. Other highlights include the breezy, Motown vibe of "Billy Don't Fall" (a song actually about AIDS) and the skeletal, fiery "This Side of Love." *Neither Fish Nor Flesh* crashed upon release, but the album remains a compelling, if flawed, effort from a musician that has been one of the more baffling unfulfilled talents in recent memory. *—Tom Demalon*

● **Terence Trent D'Arby's Symphony or Damn** / May 11, 1993 / Columbia ♦♦♦♦♦

Falling halfway between the modern R&B of *Introducing the Hardline* and the extravagant *Neither Fish nor Flesh*, *Symphony or Damn* is Terence Trent D'Arby's most ambitious album yet. It's also his best, because it takes the fine songwriting of his debut and melds it to the sonic excesses of *Fish*. Sure, some of it is embarassing (it's hard not to cringe during the "Welcome to My Monasteryo" declaration at the beginning of the album), but more often than not, D'Arby's experimentations succeed, and succeed grandly, at that. *—Stephen Thomas Erlewine*

TTD's Vibrator / Jun. 1, 1995 / Work ♦♦♦

Symphony or Damn was an impressive comeback for Terence Trent D'arby, pulling together the melodic songcraft of his debut and the conceptual ambitions of *Neither Fish nor Flesh*. *TTD's Vibrator* follows the same pattern of *Symphony or Damn*, only without the songs to support the ambitions. *—Stephen Thomas Erlewine*

Bobby Darin (Walden Robert Cassotto)

b. May 14, 1936, New York, NY [The Bronx], **d.** Dec. 20, 1973, Los Angeles, CA

Vocals / Traditional Pop, Brill Building Pop, Folk-Rock, Pop

There's been considerable discussion about whether Darin should be classified as a rock & roll singer, a Vegas hipster cat, an interpreter of popular standards, or even a folk-rocker. He was all of these and none of these. Throughout his career he made a point out of not becoming committed to any one style at the exclusion of others; at the height of his nightclub fame he incorporated a folk set into his act. When it appeared he could have gone on indefinitely as a sort of junior version of Frank Sinatra, he would periodically record pop-rock and folk-rock singles whose principal appeal lay outside of the adult pop market. At one point he started calling himself Bob Darin and recorded songs with vague anti-establishment overtones that could be said to be biting the largely bourgeois hands that fed his highest-paying gigs. It may be most accurate to say that Darin was, above all, a *singer* who wanted to do a lot of things, rather than make his mark as a particular stylist. That may have cost him some points as far as making it to the very top of certain genres, but also makes his work more versatile than almost any other vocalist of his era. *—Richie Unterberger*

● **The Ultimate Bobby Darin** / Jun. 1988 / Warner Brothers ♦♦♦♦♦

The Ultimate Bobby Darin remains the most thorough single-disc retrospective of the legendary singer to date, effectively capturing the stunning range of his unique musical vision. Each of its 17 songs is a gem, although the cream of the crop includes "Splish Splash," "Dream Lover," "Mack the Knife" and "Beyond the Sea." *—Chuck Donkers*

Capitol Collectors Series / 1989 / Capitol ♦♦♦♦

A compilation of Darin's mid-'60s singles, which showcase Darin's diversity even if the majority of the set leans heavily on his pop material. Comprehensive liner notes, intelligent track selection, and great fidelity make this worth picking up. *—Stephen Thomas Erlewine*

Splish Splash / Nov. 12, 1991 / Atco ♦♦♦♦♦

The first installment of a definitive two-volume Bobby Darin retrospective, *Splish Splash* concentrates on his earlier hits, including "Dream Lover," "Baby Face," "You Must Have Been a Beautiful Baby," "Multiplication," and the title track. *—Stephen Thomas Erlewine*

Mack the Knife / 1991 / Atco ♦♦♦♦♦

Darin's later hits, including "Mack the Knife," "Beyond the Sea," "Guys and Dolls," "Black Coffee," and "Artificial Flowers," are collected on this second volume of Atco's fine two-part retrospective. *—Stephen Thomas Erlewin*

Spotlight on Bobby Darin / 1995 / Capitol ♦♦♦

If you've a yen for the most pop-oriented area of Darin's repertoire, head for this disc, which presents 20 of his most mainstream Capitol outings from 1962 to 1965. Devoted to pop standards, over half of the tracks feature orchestras working under the conduction of Billy May. It also has a bit more collector appeal than the typical volume of Capitol's *Spotlight* series in that it contains six previously unreleased tracks, including versions of "Alabamy Bound," "I Got Rhythm," "I'm Sitting on Top of the World," and "All of You." *—Richie Unterberger*

As Long As I'm Singing: The Bobby Darin Collection / Nov. 21, 1995 / Rhino ♦♦♦♦♦

A four-CD box set spanning several styles, labels, and eras, this will stand as the most thorough retrospective of Darin's eclectic career, though not necessarily the best. There's a lot of material here—96 songs, including not only the hits, but obscure flops, B-sides, album cuts, and 11 previously unreleased tracks. Because Darin covered a lot of different genres, it's not programmed chronologically, but by style—one disc for "The Rock & Roll Years" (which, truth be told, were often closer to pop than rock), two to his pop sides, and one to his folk and country outings. In hindsight (and in the enclosed 64-page book), much has been made of Darin's versatility. But while it's true he could handle a range of genres competently, versatility does not automatically equate with quality. Just as a baseball player who can play all the positions is not necessarily a great player, Darin's unusual eclecticism did not mean that he was as great a singer as some legends who concentrated only on rock, or only on pop, or only on folk. There are some neat surprises here—the mid-'60s protest folk-rock of "We Didn't Ask to Be Brought Here," the full-bodied pop of "When I Get Home," the fine rendition of "Nature Boy," and the reasonably cogent and sincere late-'60s folk-rock. But a lot of it is not more than competent, and some of it (especially the slighter rock efforts) are less than that. And the almost diametrically opposed range of sounds (it's a long way from "Splish Splash" to "Mame" and "If I Were a Carpenter," after all) means that not many listeners except Darin fanatics will be able to get through the whole set without skipping over a lot of the tracks. *—Richie Unterberger*

Swingin' the Standards / May 11, 1999 / Varese ♦♦♦

All but two of these songs—all standards, natch—were released in 1966, when Darin released the LPs *Sings the Shadow of Your Smile* and *In a Broadway Bag* within months of each other. Songs from those albums form the bulk of this compilation, which also includes a couple of selections from 1967's *Sings Doctor Dolittle* and the 1966 single "Breaking Point"/"Silver Dollar." It's very credible swing-influenced pop and show tunes that aren't far from a Frank Sinatra bag, despite the attempts of some writers to establish distance between the two singers. Naturally, it isn't a complete picture of the versatile vocalist's talents. But it should also be pointed out that it's much easier to take Darin's swing-jazz-Broadway-easy listening side in one dose than it is to hear it interspersed among other styles on Darin anthologies. *—Richie Unterberger*

If I Were a Carpenter: The Very Best of Bobby Darin: 1966-1969 / Sep. 14, 1999 / Varese ♦♦♦♦

It's easy to criticize Bobby Darin as a shameless follower of trends who shifted from rock & roll to mainstream pop patterned after Frank Sinatra, when rock appeared to be on the wane at the end of the '50s. In this sense, his mid-'60s embrace of folk-rock protest music looks like just another example of opportunism. When Darin returned to Atlantic Records in 1966, he released nearly unknown folk-rock singer/songwriter Tim Hardin's "If I Were a Carpenter" as a single. Though it soared into the Top Ten, Darin didn't just become Tim Hardin's popularizer; as this collection demonstrates, he also tried the music of the Lovin' Spoonful and obtained a contribution from Alan Gordon and Gary Bonner, writers of the Turtles' hit "Happy Together." But a greater indication of the sincerity of Darin's conversion was his own songwriting. Always an excellent writer, he turned his attention to more personal and political topics. In 1968, he left Atlantic to form his own Direction Records label; by 1969, he had grown a mustache, taken to wearing blue jeans, and started calling himself Bob Darin. It didn't last. Darin's new approach was not taken to by the hippies, and it was soundly rejected by his old audience. Since Darin's death, his period as a folk-rocker has been nearly forgotten, but this album demonstrates that it contained some of his best writing and performances. Few pop vocalists were inclined or able to make music in the serious style that became popular in the mid-'60s; Bobby Darin was one of them, and it is a tribute to his talent and courage as an artist that he did. — *William Ruhlmann*

Unreleased Capitol Sides / Sep. 21, 1999 / Collectors' Choice Music ✦✦✦
While signed with Capitol records, Bobby Darin recorded a number of studio masters that went unreleased for 30 years. With three exceptions, these long-lost recordings are available for the first time on Collector's Choice Music's new CD, *The Unreleased Capitol Sides*. The exceptions are "I Got Rhythm," "Alabamy Bound," and "Standing on the Corner" which were released by Capitol on its 1995 CD *Spotlight on Bobby Darin*. This treasure trove of music is a must own for fans of Bobby Darin's swinging Capitol years. Thirteen songs from this collection were completed during Bobby Darin's most productive recording period ever. In January 1963 he entered the studio seven separate times to work on his follow-up album for Capitol, the country-themed *You're the Reason I'm Living*. But he also left these songs unreleased until now. Jumping ahead to the end of the disc, four songs from the *Venice Blue* sessions are also included. *The Unreleased Capitol Sides* is a great addition to any Bobby Darin collection, especially the one who has his biggest hits. It completes at least three major Darin releases: the out of print *Oh! Look at Me Now* (but largely available as *Spotlight on Bobby Darin*), *Venice Blue*, and Rhino's *As Long as I'm Singin'* box set. As such, it is an indispensable group of 25 archival tracks. — *JT Griffith*

The Curtain Falls: Live at the Flamingo / Oct. 17, 2000 / Collector's Choice Music ✦✦✦✦
This stellar nightclub performance, from early November 1963, somehow remained under wraps for nearly four decades. Thankfully it was discovered and issued by independent mail order specialists Collectors' Choice Music. In addition to the unique qualities of an unheard vintage recording, Bobby Darin had also cited this run—at the Flamingo Hotel and Casino in Las Vegas—to be his last lengthy tour or nightclub engagement due to increasing health concerns. So, it is indeed a special affair. It was rare for a performer to be so accepted as both a sophisticated balladeer as well as a rebellious rocker. *The Curtain Falls: Live at the Flamingo* reveals both sides of Darin's underappreciated talent of interpretation. Handling ballads such as "My Funny Valentine" and "You're Nobody 'Til Somebody Loves You" with sensitivity and control, Darin conversely rips open up-tempo numbers such as the "Hits Medley: Splish Splash/Beyond the Sea/Artificial Flowers/Clementine." Darin also swings through a spellbinding version of his trademark, "Mack the Knife." This in no way sounds like a man suffering from a rheumatic heart condition. In addition to the music, Darin offers up several spoken-word interludes. The aptly titled "Comedy Routine" features several impersonations by Darin as set to "One for My Baby (And One More for the Road)." However, when introducing the title cut, Darin is somber, leading to an emotional climax—not only for this performance, but for a brilliant live career as well. There is little information given in the liner-note text regarding the brilliant orchestra heard accompanying Darin during this run. However, their efforts are noted by the star and rightfully so, as they swing right along with him—never overpowering, but infinitely enhancing, underscoring, and punctuating the proceedings. — *Lindsay Planer*

Das EFX

f. 1991, Petersburg, VA
East Coast Rap, Hip-Hop, Golden Age
With their first album, Das EFX caused a minor revolution based on their speedy, quick-tongued stuttering; it helped that they backed their rhymes with thick, funky tracks. The album was a major success, scoring a Top 40 pop single and going gold. On their second LP, *Straight up Sewaside*, the duo of Drayz and Skoob Effect slightly altered their approach. They downplayed the high-speed stuttering, though they continued with the intense rhyming and confrontational themes that made their debut so memorable. — *AMG*

● **The Very Best of Das EFX** / Jul. 3, 2001 / Rhino ✦✦✦✦✦
Rhino/Elektra Traditions' 2001 release *The Very Best of Das EFX* is an excellent summary of the duo's seminal recordings for Elektra. When they came crashing out in 1992 with *Dead Serious*, the group was a bold change, thanks to their revolutionary quick-fire, stuttering delivery. The record was hailed as a mini-masterpiece, but like a lot of rap crews, what was praised upon the debut became ignored by the third, often because the once-fresh style now seemed stale, even if it was their signature sound. And, while the quality of their recordings did dip somewhat after the first album, they still turned out fine recordings, as this collection proves. True, it does tilt toward the debut, with no less than seven selections from *Dead Serious*, but it also contains three cuts from *Straight Up Sewaside* and four from 1995's *Hold It Down*, ending with two tracks from their final Elektra album, 1998's *Generation EFX*. This winds up as an excellent summary, providing a huge portion of their greatest album, with cuts from the other albums that prove

they hadn't lost their talents after the debut. And while *Dead Serious* remains a landmark, this may be the best choice for anybody indeed wanting to hear *The Very Best of Das EFX*. — *Stephen Thomas Erlewine*

David & David

f. 1985, **db.** 1987
Pop/Rock, Singer/Songwriter
Although they only recorded one album, the California duo of David Baerwald and David Ricketts made some of the finest mainstream pop of the '80s. With its slick surfaces and memorable melodies, 1986's *Boomtown* was deceptively smooth; beneath the production, the songs were tales of despair and broken dreams in the Reagan era. David & David scored a surprise hit in 1986 with "Welcome to the Boomtown"; it was their only single that charted. Baerwald began a critically acclaimed solo career in 1990; Ricketts has not released anything since *Boomtown*. — *Stephen Thomas Erlewine*

● **Boomtown** / 1986 / A&M ✦✦✦✦✦
David & David's *Boomtown* is a hard look at urban life in the 1980s, a time when many were fulfilling the American Dream of financial success and upward mobility. It is not an easy album to listen to, as the characters depicted in the songs are often dealing with major problems such as drugs and domestic violence. But it is an artful record, full of poetry and convincing stories of the hard times that many silently endured. At times the record is full of pop hooks, and at other stages a more bleak sound dominates. The vocals of David & David are also effective in telling the tales, as often there is a shrill, despondent quality that complements what is being related to the listener. In particular, the drums have kind of a hushed sound to them, and the guitars often purvey sounds of doom through distortion or other means. "Welcome to the Boomtown" is the hit off the album, and is one of various cuts that convincingly detail the many trials of the characters such as Kevin, who "deals dope out of Denny's keeps a table in the back." Although there are often hints of hope and seemingly a sense of compassion toward the subjects in the songs, it is not apparent that most will eventually pull themselves out of their predicaments. One may not want to listen to this record to lift the spirit, but it is a strong reminder of difficult situations faced during what can be perceived by many as the best of times. — *Michael Ofjord*

Dave Davies

b. Feb. 3, 1947, Muswell Hill, London, England
Vocals, Keyboards, Harmonica, Guitar / Album Rock, Arena Rock, Hard Rock
Although he took a largely subordinate role to his brother Ray in the Kinks, Dave's fierce guitar work and hoarse but effective background (and occasional lead) vocals were key elements of the band's appeal. Dave also occasionally wrote songs for the Kinks that showed him to be a writer of considerable skill and wit, if not up to the same level as Ray. In the late '60s, Dave made some solo singles that met with critical success in Britain, although they were unknown in the U.S. "Death of a Clown" (also included on the Kinks' *Something Else* LP) made number three on the British charts in 1967, and the follow-up "Susannah's Still Alive" also did fairly well. Dave began to consider making a solo album, but after a couple other solo singles flopped, he seemed to lose heart and abandoned his plans (some unreleased solo tracks from this period turned up on the obscure Kinks bootleg *Good Luck Charm*). In the 1980s, Dave finally began a solo career in earnest, releasing a series of mainstream rock albums that found little critical or commercial acclaim, his work neatly summarized on *Unfinished Business: Dave Davies Kronikles 1963-1998*. — *Richie Unterberger*

AFL1-3603 / 1980 / RCA ✦✦✦

Glamour / 1981 / RCA ✦✦

Chosen People / 1983 / Warner Brothers ✦✦✦
Chosen People is Dave Davies third solo album and by this release he seemed to have gotten it right. Gone is the big stadium rock sound and present is Davies' wonderful voice and melodic songs. Although this is not the album fans of "Death of a Clown" were hoping for, it is a much stronger album than 1981's *Glamour* and 1980's *AFL1-3603*. Davies still rocks out, but there are more ballads present. Also, the lyrics seem to have much more thought into them and present interesting stories and thoughts. Perhaps it is due to the use of a band and a co-producer on this album (the other two releases were primarily just Davies, although drummer Robert Henrit did drum on *Glamour*). The songs here are much more melodic and Davies finally displays that wonderful voice that was buried on the other two releases. Yes, his trademark guitar is found throughout, but so are beautiful, heartbreaking songs such as "Is It Any Wonder." Dave Davies has spent much of his career in the shadow of his brother and the band The Kinks. As good as this album is, it does not remove that shadow. This proved to be Davies only release on the Warner Brothers label. Fans of The Kinks and '80s hard rock should have this album in their collection. — *Aaron Badgley*

The Album That Never Was / 1987 / PRT ✦✦✦✦✦
When Dave Davies racked up a couple British hits in 1967, rumors were rife that The Kinks' lead guitarist would cut a solo album of his own. He never did—not in the '60s, anyway—and this album is a facsimile of what might have been, packaging some ultra-rare solo singles of the time with tracks that Dave wrote and sang on some of The Kinks' late-'60s records. They show him to be a fine, underappreciated singer and songwriter in a Dylanesque folk-rock mode. — *Richie Unterberger*

● **Unfinished Business: Dave Davies Kronikles 1963-1998 (US)** / Jan. 12, 1999 / Velvel ✦✦✦✦✦
This two-CD set compiles the other Davies brother's contributions to the Kinks as well as his own solo works. From the earliest Kinks recording, "I Believed You," penned by Dave,

to his groundbreaking guitar work on "You Really Got Me"; memorable vocal takes on "Long Tall Shorty," "C'mon Now" and "Milkcow Blues"; some less spectacular vocal turns and on through to the many songs Davies wrote and made famous for the band ("Wait Till the Summer Comes Along," "Trust Your Heart"), it's clear that melodically, Dave was his brother's equal. The title song Davies penned with the intention of recording as a Kink tune sounds absolutely contemporary—Dave's no dinosaur. And there are plenty of rarities—demos, new versions and unheard music. This is the definition of a class reissue, bittersweet in its sheer existence, but no less a huge victory. *—Denise Sullivan*

Richard Davies

b. Sydney, Australia

Vocals, Guitar / Indie Pop, Chamber Pop, Singer/Songwriter

Australian-born singer-songwriter Richard Davies formed the chamber-pop unit the Moles in Sydney in the late 1980s after growing disenchanted with studying law; concluding that he preferred composing poetry to writing essays for his class assignments, he soon began crafting his first songs. After finding some underground success in their native land as well as the U.S. and Britain, the Moles broke up around the beginning of 1993; Davies soon settled in New York City to begin a solo career, although in 1994 he released his solo debut, *Instinct*, under the Moles name. Through a mutual friendship with Sebadoh drummer Bob Fay, Davies joined forces with multi-instrumentalist and arranger Eric Matthews to form the duo Cardinal, which released their lush, symphonic self-titled debut to great acclaim in 1994. However, internal strife prompted the group to split soon after, and Davies began his solo career in earnest with 1996's baroque *There's Never Been a Crowd Like This*; on tour, he was backed by avowed fans the Flaming Lips. The superb *Telegraph* followed in 1998, and in 2000 Davies signed to the Kindercore label to issue his third solo LP, *Barbarians*. *—Jason Ankeny*

● **There's Never Been a Crowd Like This** / Mar. 26, 1996 / Flydaddy ✦✦✦✦✦

One of the best albums of the whole mid-'90s chamber pop movement, Richard Davies' *There's Never Been a Crowd Like This* isn't as completely strange as the final Moles album, 1994's *Instinct* (which was a Davies solo album in all but name). It's quite mad, though. Davies' lyrics are unfailingly peculiar, whether serving as an impressionistic diary of his early days as a transplanted New Yorker ("Sign Up Maybe for Being"), making up stories about his Australian childhood ("Transcontinental"), or concerning topics that are probably obscure even to Davies himself ("Why Not Bomb the Movies?," "Chips Rafferty"). The melodies are similarly peculiar, but they're extremely inviting. Somehow, although the album was recorded with a simple guitar-bass-drums-piano quartet, plus trumpet and a pair of backing singers, the album sounds almost orchestral. Davies' appealingly plain voice, with its thick Aussie accent and tendency toward oddly rhythmic vocal melodies (as on "Topple Into My Fantasy"), puts the focus on the melodies and arrangements instead of the often nonsensical lyrics, which has the dual effect of making the songs more immediately inviting and enhancing the oddity of the lyrics once the listener recognizes their unique qualities. Worlds better than either album by his former Cardinal partner Eric Matthews, *There's Never Been a Crowd Like This* is sort of like a mid-'90s indie version of *Smiley Smile*, right down to its abbreviated length of under 30 minutes. *—Stewart Mason*

● **Telegraph** / Mar. 24, 1998 / Flydaddy ✦✦✦✦

Telegraph offers proof positive that Richard Davies reaches new creative heights when sparked by the collaborative spirit. While by no means a dismissal of his other work, this second official solo album is far and away his most impressive record outside of the one-off *Cardinal* project, clear evidence that his fortunes rise and fall in relation to the company he's keeping. Davies' partner in crime here is former Flaming Lips guitarist Ronald Jones, who serves as co-producer, multi-instrumentalist and occasional co-songwriter; bringing to the table the same acid-pop grandeur which typified his Lips tenure, Jones colors *Telegraph* with a dreamy, vaguely psychedelic patina ideally suited to Davies' poetic lyrics and clever melodies. Tracks like the opening "Cantina," "Confederate Cheerio Call" and "Main Street Electrical Parade" are simply sublime, each a portrait of contemporary pop at its most perfect. *—Jason Ankeny*

Barbarians / Jun. 27, 2000 / Kindercore ✦✦✦

Richard Davies' third solo effort is the most straightforward guitar-pop record he's produced to date—stripped of the orchestral flourishes of his early work, as well as the psych-folk textures of the previous *Telegraph*, *Barbarians* instead favors a simple yet nuanced approach which nevertheless cuts a wide stylistic path spanning from dark, ominous garage-rock ("Great Republic") to feather-light acoustic balladry (the gorgeous "Stars"). From the Uncle Sam stars-and-stripes stovepipe hat which adorns the cover to name-checks of everything from the Rio Grande to Lewis & Clark to NASA, *Barbarians* is a pointed, if often abstract, meditation on Davies' adopted home of America—many of the songs touch on themes of exploration and migration, yet despite his obvious gifts for rich, poetic wordplay, the lyrics don't really add up to much when taken as a whole. Still, given time, Davies' lazily ingratiating melodies take hold, and the record's relaxed, spontaneous atmosphere evokes a nonchalance ideally suited to its understated ambitions. *—Jason Ankeny*

Paul Davis

b. Apr. 21, 1948, Meridian, MS

Vocals, Guitar / Soft Rock, Adult Contemporary

Spotted playing with his country-rock band by Bert Berns of Bang Records in 1970, Paul Davis was signed to the label as a solo artist. Born on April 21, 1948, in Meridian, Mississippi, his soft, country-inflected style helped win him several minor hits, including his first single, a cover of the Jarmels' 1961 doo-wop hit "A Little Bit of Soap." He released his first LP with Bang in 1972, *A Little Bit of Paul Davis*. His next album, *Ride 'Em Cowboy*, produced a signature song of the same name. He followed up that album with *Southern Tracks and Fantasies* in 1976. 1977's album, *Singer of Songs—Teller of Tales* featured the ballad "I Go Crazy," which would become his biggest hit, peaking at number 7 a full eight months after its release. Its continuing appeal helped keep it in the top 100 for 40 more weeks.

In 1981 he moved to Arista Records and recorded the LP *Cool Night* which spawned two top 20 hits, including "65 Love Affair." The album was more slickly produced and was more pop-influenced than his previous releases. The formula was not a comfortable one for Davis, however, and he reverted to country recordings, eventually issuing two country-pop duets with Marie Osmond in the late '80s. *—Stacia Proefrock*

Greatest Hits / Apr. 11, 1995 / Epic/Bang ✦✦✦✦

Based upon his songwriting and pop recordings, Paul Davis should be a superstar. But, unfortunately, he shuns the spotlight. In fact, he has not released an album of original material in over 20 years. However, there have been several collections released in the last two decades, including this *Greatest Hits* package. Notably missing from *Greatest Hits* are recordings from Davis' last and most successful album (*Cool Night*, released on Arista), including " '65 Love Affair," his highest-charting song. *Greatest Hits* focuses on Davis' Bang recordings; however, it omits "Superstar," his excellent Top 40 tribute to Elton John, Stevie Wonder, Linda Ronstadt, and Joni Mitchell. The collection does feature the gorgeous "Medicine Woman," the gospel-tinged "Do Right," and the huge hit "I Go Crazy," along with nine other excellent pop recordings. *—Tim Griggs*

● **Sweet Life: His Greatest Hit Singles** / Sep. 28, 1999 / Razor & Tie ✦✦✦✦

Razor & Tie's *Sweet Life: His Greatest Hits Singles* is the first CD compilation to draw from Paul Davis' recordings for Bang and Arista. In other words, it's the first and only definitive career retrospective, containing such '70s hits as "I Go Crazy," "Thinking of You," "Superstar," "Darlin'" and "Sweet Life," as well as the early '80s singles "Do Right," "Cool Night" and "65 Love Affair." It could be argued that the compilation should have been sequenced in chronological order, but the 14 songs flow smoothly in this incarnation, proving that Paul Davis was one of the finest soft-rock crooners of his generation. Yes, the lesser-known singles and album tracks don't really match the quality of the aforementioned hits, but they're all well-crafted and pleasant, and anyone who is a fan of one of his soft-rock classics should be pleased with this entire collection. *—Stephen Thomas Erlewine*

The Spencer Davis Group

f. 1963, Birmingham, England, **db.** 1986

Blue-Eyed Soul, British Invasion

His ferocious soul-drenched vocals belying his tender teenage years, Stevie Winwood powered the Spencer Davis Group's three biggest US hits during their brief life span as one of the British Invasion's most convincing R&B-based combos.

Guitarist Davis formed the band with Winwood on organ, his brother Muff Winwood on bass, and drummer Peter York. Signing on with producer Chris Blackwell, the quartet got their first hit (the blistering "Keep on Running") from another of Blackwell's acts, West Indian performer Jackie Edwards. After topping the British charts in 1965, the song struggled on the lower reaches of the US Hot 100.

The group's two hottest sellers were self-penned projects. "Gimme Some Lovin'" and "I'm a Man" were searing showcases for the adolescent Winwood's gritty vocals and blazing keyboards and the band's pounding rhythms. Although they burned up the charts even on this side of the ocean in 1967, the quartet never capitalized on their fame with an American tour. At the height of their power, Winwood left to form Traffic, leaving Davis without his dynamic front man. The bandleader focused on producing other acts, including a Canadian ensemble called the Downchild Blues Band during the early 80s. *—Bill Dahl*

Their First LP / 1965 / Fontana ✦✦✦

The group's first album is basically a reflection of their early repertoire and very heavy on the R&B/soul standards. Dominated by covers of Ike & Tina Turner, the Coasters, John Lee Hooker, Little Walter, Brenda Holloway, and others, only three of the tunes are original. Two of these are written by Stevie Winwood, the other by Spencer Davis; Winwood's mid-tempo soul number "It Hurts Me So" is easily the best of them. Winwood is in fine voice and the group is energetic, but this is neither as good as their best work nor nearly as good as the best British R&B albums of the era by competitors like Them and the Rolling Stones. Includes their first two British singles, "Dimples" and "I Can't Stand It." *—Richie Unterberger*

Autumn 66 / 1966 / Fontana ✦✦✦

At the peak of their popularity, the Spencer Davis Group's albums were considerably less impressive than their hits and a bit thin on imagination, although they were never less than competent. This, their third LP, relies heavily on soul covers, as well as a few oft-covered blues standards ("Midnight Special," "Mean Woman Blues," "Dust My Blues"). Highlights are their second British number one hit "Somebody Help Me," the decent group original "High Time Baby," Winwood's organ-based instrumental "On the Green Light," and "When I Get Home," which (like "Somebody Help Me") was a hit in Britain, but not the U.S. *—Richie Unterberger*

Best of the Spencer Davis Group (Island Masters) / 1967 / Island ✦✦✦✦✦

Anyone who has suffered through Capitol Records' domestic *Best of the Spencer Davis Group*, and also doesn't want to spring for the double-CD import, should look to this 14-song collection from British Island Records. All of the best-known songs are here—"I'm a Man," "Gimme Some Lovin'," "Every Little Bit Hurts," "Keep on Running," "When I Come Home," "This Hammer," etc.—in loud, robust, and richly textured sound. The organ, piano, drums, and guitars fairly leap out at you, and Winwood's vocals never sounded better or closer than they do on this CD. The double CD is a better deal and sounds superior to this collection, but it also has a lot more dross on it. The real crime is that there isn't a decent-sounding domestic best-of, but this one will do. *—Bruce Eder*

Heavies / 1969 / United Artists ♦♦♦

A hodgepodge of some of the group's lesser-known tracks, this actually contains some of their better performances. The instrumental jam "Waltz For Lumumba" sounds like a prototype for some of the ideas Winwood would employ in Traffic; the group original "Hey Darling" is a smoldering, moody blues, "Mean Woman Blues" and "Watch Your Step" are a couple of their best uptempo, and most guitar-oriented, R&B covers, "Please Do Something" is a good cover of a Don Covay tune, and "Back Into My Life Again" was co-written by Jackie Edwards, who was responsible for their first few British hits. Put together by United Artists after the group had broken up to capitalize on Winwood's ascent to superstardom in Traffic, it's nonetheless a decent compilation of some of their more interesting odds and ends. *—Richie Unterberger*

● **Best of the Spencer Davis Group** / 1985 / EMI America ♦♦♦♦♦

Somehow the same label issued two albums with the same name in the same year. This one, with 15 tracks, is vastly preferable to its 10-song counterpart. Both releases hit the high points with the irresistible "Gimme Some Lovin'," "I'm a Man," and others. With half again as many tunes, though, this album includes the minor hit "Strong Love" and "Goodbye Stevie," written by the group to commemorate the departure of sensational singer and multi-instrumentalist prodigy Steve Winwood. "Waltz for Lumumba" presages the jazzier turns he would take with Traffic. *—Mark Allan*

● **Golden Archive Series** / 1987 / Rhino ♦♦♦♦♦

The best compilation of their best moments. 14 songs, including both of their U.S. hits, "I'm a Man" and "Gimme Some Lovin'," the U.K. chart-toppers "Keep on Running" and "Somebody Help Me," the smaller U.K. hit "When I Come Home," and several fine R&B covers, all from 1964–66. *—Richie Unterberger*

Taking Out Time 1967–1969 / 1994 / RPM ♦♦

With the loss of Stevie Winwood, the Spencer Davis Group were just another rock band. But that didn't keep them from marching onwards until the end of the decade, with a few more personnel changes. This compilation of 20 previously unreleased tracks is taken from radio/TV broadcasts and studio outtakes, as well as their near-complete unreleased 1969 album, *Letters From Edith*. The 1967-1968 cuts are middling pop-flavored psychedelia that's heavy on the organ-guitar combination, with the odd slice of above-average material ("With Their New Face On") and strange stylistic detour (a couple of Jimmy Webb songs). Guitarist Ray Fenwick comes to the fore as songwriter on the *Letters From Edith* sessions. This finds them groping for a style—some country-rock here, a bit of jazzy funk there, and some lowest-common-denominator psych-prog as well—without much success, though the jazz-soul instrumental organ showcase "Firefly" isn't bad. *—Richie Unterberger*

Eight Gigs a Week: The Steve Winwood Years / Apr. 22, 1996 / Island/Chronicles ♦♦♦♦♦

This two-CD, 51-song set covers virtually everything the group recorded with Steve Winwood in the lineup from 1964-1967. The gap between the band's best and worst material was considerable; quite a few of their R&B covers are surprisingly routine, and the occasional cuts that don't have Winwood on lead vocals are downright pedestrian. Because of this inconsistency, the general fan's better off with the Rhino best-of, if it can be found. If you want to get more, though, this is the first and last place to go, with all the hit singles, everything from their three albums, an early EP, some B-sides, and a couple of previously unissued tracks. And some of the obscure material is really good, whether in a straight R&B/blues or more soulful vein. Be aware that the version of "Gimme Some Lovin'" here is the less dynamic, original British mix, minus some backup vocals and percussion. *—Richie Unterberger*

Mulberry Bush / Jan. 11, 2000 / RPM ♦♦♦

With this 17-track disc, RPM has assembled the album that the Spencer Davis Group *might* have put out in late 1967. As it was, just two singles appeared from the April-December 1967 lineup (Davis, drummer Pete York, Eddie Hardin on keyboards, and Phil Sawyer on vocals), although some material would come out on the soundtrack to *Here We Go Round the Mulberry Bush* and the 1968 *With Their New Face On* album. To make matters more confusing, some of the songs released by the group in 1967 and 1968 were re-recorded or remixed for subsequent releases, sometimes replacing or overdubbing the vocals on the first versions. The important thing, though, is: does the music merit this kind of vault combing? It's kind of ho-hum, to be honest. All of these tracks were from the lineup Davis assembled just after the departure of Stevie Winwood and Muff Winwood. They were acceptable, but just a face in the crowd, really, with the absence of Winwood. From a strictly collector-oriented viewpoint, though, this CD is valuable for the inclusion of the original single versions of "Time Seller" and "Don't Want You No More"; the fey psych-pop B-side of their second single, "Sanity Inspector"; the original versions of "Morning Sun" and "Feel Your Way"; and previously unissued alternate versions of four songs from the *Here We Go 'Round the Mulberry Bush* soundtrack. This also has all of the official versions of the songs the band got onto the *Here We Go 'Round the Mulberry Bush* soundtrack (except "Waltz for Caroline," as that was recorded with Stevie Winwood still in the lineup). Got all that? The one thing you might want to know, when all the discographical complications are pushed aside, is that this is likely the best post-Winwood Spencer Davis Group disc available. *—Richie Unterberger*

Tyrone Davis

b. May 4, 1938, Greenville, MS
Vocals / Smooth Soul, Chicago Soul, Pop-Soul, Soul

Perennially a ladies' choice, Tyrone Davis just seems to naturally appeal to women. That's not to say that gents haven't bought his churning Chicago soul records too—his impressive hit-making career harks back to 1968, and there's no end in sight.

His mentor, noted singer Harold Burrage, coached his charge well, and Davis debuted on wax in 1965 as "Tyrone the Wonder Boy" on the local Four Brothers logo. Far more wondrous were Davis' classy efforts for Chicago's Dakar label, commencing with the remorseful R&B chart-topper "Can I Change My Mind" in 1968, continuing with "Is It Something You've Got" in 1969, and the million-selling classic "Turn Back the Hands of Time" in 1970. With Willie Henderson producing, the cats at Dakar were forging a fresh, vital new Chicago soul sound, and Tyrone Davis was right there at its forefront.

Davis remained with Dakar into 1976, his warm, assured vocals powering the likes of "I Had It All the Time" and "Turning Point," before moving over to Columbia without missing a beat. After years of hopping from one label to the next, he finally landed at Malaco for a series of releases including 1996's *Simply Tyrone Davis*, 1997's *Pleasing You* and 1999's *Call Tyrone*. *Relaxin' With Tyrone* followed a year later. Davis is still no stranger to the urban contemporary charts, and the women still love him. What more could he possibly ask for? *—Bill Dahl*

The Best of Tyrone Davis: In the Mood / Jun. 4, 1996 / Columbia ♦♦♦♦

The Best Of Tyrone Davis: In The Mood offers 15 gems that center mostly on romance. The title track was Davis' biggest hit with the label. With it's boudoir-minded lyrics Davis' come-ons were forward and as he sang, "Just like ice cream and honey my love is gonna make you melt," it's almost cringe time. "Ain't Nothing I Can Do" follows the same logic and has Davis singing about a "dark, cozy room" where he's no doubt doing more than talking. During this time Davis, longtime producer Leo Graham and arranger James Mack fashioned an up-to-the-minute subtle Chicago sound. The streamlined yet hooky approach gave the proper emphasis on Davis' voice on the tracks "Be With Me" and the delicate "Let's Be Closer." Davis also did uptempo offerings as well. "Give It Up (Turn It Loose)" has the title being his pragmatic solution to put an end to going-nowhere relationships. This compilation's most overt dance track, the bass heavy, "Get On Up (Disco)" is skilled, kinetic and certainly shows Davis having a good time. As his Columbia output is often underrated *The Best Of Tyrone Davis: In The Mood* thankfully puts these tracks back in circulation and is a must for his fans. *—Jason Elias*

Greatest Hits / Aug. 11, 1998 / Brunswick ♦♦♦♦

The many R&B hits Tyrone Davis cut for the Dakar label between 1968 and 1976 are featured on this fine Brunswick collection. Along with smashes like "Turn Back the Hands of Time" and "Turning Point," other chart-toppers include "Can I Change My Mind" and "Homewreckers," one of his last hits for Dakar. Davis' pleading and sensually charged voice is in top form throughout, while Willie Henderson's production and Tom (Tom Tom 84) Washington's charts are consistently impressive, featuring a wealth of slick grooves and tasteful instrumentation. And even though the sophisticated Chicago soul sound is what dominates here, one also hears some welcome rough edges in both Davis' tone and the driving rhythm tracks. The case could be made, in fact, that the deft mix of rough and smooth in Davis' delivery is what made him a perennial ladies favorite; it's a sympathy-grabbing display of raw emotions and vulnerability heard to particularly fine effect on cuts like "I Keep Coming Back" and "Let Me Back In." Even though Davis would go on to produce fine work after leaving Dakar, this collection of hits represents the singer's high point. A definite first disc for those new to Davis' work and certainly an essential, if somewhat overlooked, soul collection. *—Stephen Cook*

● **Turning Back the Hands of Time: The Soul of Tyrone Davis** / Oct. 13, 1998 / Diablo ♦♦♦♦♦

A great anthology of Tyrone Davis' hits on the Dakar Label, covering a period from 1968 to 1976. People mistakenly labeled Davis a blues singer; he's not. Tyrone is urban R&B seasoned with southern soul. All the tunes that put him over the top are here: the shuffling, bluesy "Can I Change My Mind," the questioning, horn accented "Is It Something You've Got" and there's "Turn Back the Hands of Time," highlighted by some sweet punchy horns. And on, and on. Lesser known releases included the excellent "Could I Forget You," "I'll Be Right Here" and "Homewreckers." Davis' bluesy, baritone/tenor is soothing, assured, and remarkably believable on the 23 tracks. An excellent import CD by one of Americas most underappreciated soul singers. *—Andrew Hamilton*

Bobby Day

b. Jul. 1, 1932, Fort Worth, TX, **d.** Jul. 15, 1990
Vocals / Doo Wop, Rock & Roll

An important cog in Los Angeles's doo-wop community during the '50s, Day wrote three often-covered early rock classics in 1957-1958. Day was part of the Hollywood Flames, one of the area's top R&B vocal groups, and briefly part of Bob & Earl, later to hit without Day on "Harlem Shuffle." Day formed his own group, the Satellites, in 1957, cutting the original "Little Bitty Pretty One" for Class Records. A nearly identical cover by Thurston Harris beat the original out, so Day countered with the driving "Rockin' Robin" in 1958, an R&B chart-topper. Its flip, "Over and Over," was a hit in its own right, although the Dave Clark Five's 1965 revival is better remembered today. Day waxed a few more hits for Class in 1959, including "That's All I Want" and a derivative "The Bluebird, the Buzzard & the Oriole," flitting from label to label during the '60s. *—Bill Dahl*

● **The Original Rockin' Robin** / 1991 / Ace ♦♦♦♦

Bobby Day's "Rockin' Robin" remains a classic. That and 25 other original recordings show up on this solid British import. *—Jeff Tamarkin*

The Best of Bobby Day / Jul. 24, 2001 / Varese ◆◆◆◆

Dazz Band

f. 1977, Cleveland, OH
Funk

The Cleveland-based Dazz Band was one of the more popular funk groups of the early '80s. Bobby Harris formed the group in the late '70s, taking members from two Cleveland funk bands, Bell Telefunk and the Kinsman Grills house band. The end result was an eight-piece band featuring Harris, Skip Martin III, Pierre DeMudd on horns and vocals, guitarist Eric Fearman, bassist Michael Wiley, drummer Isaac Wiley, keyboardist Kevin Frederick, and percussionist Kenny Pettus. Harris and lead songwriter/guitarist Mike Calhoun's concept for the group was "danceable jazz;" he shortened the description to "dazz" and called the group Kinsman Dazz. Under that name, the group had two small hits in the USA during 1978 and 1979. After Calhoun left the group they changed their name to the Dazz Band in 1980 and signed to Motown.

Let the Music Play, the band's first release for the record label, was released in 1981. Once the group veered away from the more melodic, pop-oriented dance music that dominated their debut and started playing a tougher, more groove-oriented funk, the Dazz Band began racking up the hits. "Let It Whip," taken from their second album *Keep It Live* (1982), reached number five and won a Grammy Award for Best Performance by an R&B Vocal Duo or Group. While they never reached those heights again, the Dazz Band had a string of six consecutive Top 100 albums that ran until 1986; during that time, they scored two other Top 100 singles, "Joystick" and "Let It All Blow." In 1985, Fearman and Frederick left the band; they were replaced by Marlon McClain and Keith Harrison respectively. The Dazz Band switched labels to Geffen in 1986. That year they had their final charting album, *Wild and Free*. Soon after its release, the band switched to RCA. The group failed to have another hit and quietly faded away. —*Stephen Thomas Erlewine*

Greatest Hits / 1987 / Motown ◆◆◆◆

What's not to like about the Dazz Band's highly combustible "Let It Whip"? Its funky drum machine rhythms and diabolical mini-Moog bass lines are wicked. Reggie Andrews produced and co-wrote the sizzling groove that was #1 R&B chart for five consecutive weeks, and scaled to #5 Pop. "Joy Stick" is as potent as Viagra with its maniac, thumping beat. But, "Party Right Here," and "Keep It Live (On the K.I.L.)" are formulaic stiffs, all flash and no substance. "Swoop (I'm Yours)" has appeal, and some of the dance floor drawing power of "Whip." Fans of Dazz Band ballads will not have much use for this CD, only two made the disk: the ultra romantic "Invitation to Love," and the melodramatic "Knock, Knock," where lead singer Skip Martin begs like a baby. Dazz Band's honcho Bobby Harris experiments with their sound on "On the One for Fun," and "Let It All Blow," and both sound better on CD than vinyl. Each features creative fusion/funk licks, sweetened by razor-sharp horns, chant vocals and frivolous lyrics. —*Andrew Hamilton*

● **Funkology: The Definitive Dazz Band** / Nov. 15, 1994 / Motown ◆◆◆◆

Funkology: The Definitive Dazz Band is a comprehensive overview of the early-'80s funk band, featuring all of their major hits, including "Let It Whip," "One for the Fun," "Joystick" and "Let It All Blow." —*Stephen Thomas Erlewine*

20th Century Masters—The Millennium Collection: The Best of the Dazz Band / Jun. 19, 2001 / Motown ◆◆◆◆

An 11-song snapshot of the Dazz Band's Motown stint that includes the not-often-featured "To the Roof," whose origins date back to "Take It to the Woof" by Cleveland, OH-based funk band Morning Maniac led by ex-Dazz Band member Kenny Pettus who's the lead voice on the Earth, Wind and Fire-ish "I Might As Well Forget About Loving You." But other than that, there are no surprises, just straight-ahead digitally remastered Dazz Band blasts that blow you away in CD format ("Let It Whip"'s bass line is hypnotizing). For lovers, "Invitation to Love" and "Knock, Knock" are bonafide heart stirrers and the only two slow jams in the bunch. Not as complete as the 1994 *Funkology: The Definitive Dazz Band* but dazzling enough. —*Andrew Hamilton*

The dB's

f. 1978
College Rock, Jangle Pop, Power Pop, Alternative Pop/Rock

Along with Let's Active, the dB's defined the Southern power-pop/jangle-pop movement of the early-to-mid-'80s. The band's music was a quirky blend of smart pop and psychedelia crossed with the more experimental side of new wave. Though they never received widespread recognition outside of critical acclaim, they provided a key link between Big Star and '80s alternative guitar acts such as R.E.M. Formed in 1978 in Winston-Salem, NC, the original lineup of the band featured Chris Stamey (guitar, vocals, keyboards), Gene Holder (bass), and Will Rigby (drums). After relocating to New York, the dBs released their debut single, "(I Thought) You Wanted to Know," for Stamey's Car label. Guitarist/vocalist/keyboardist Peter Holsapple joined the band by the end of 1978. Holsapple and Stamey shared the songwriting chores during the band's early years. The dB's were unable to secure a U.S. recording contract, so they signed to the British Albion label. They released two albums on Albion: *Stands for Decibels* (1981) and *Repercussion* (1982). Both records received rave reviews but little sales. Stamey left in 1983 to resume a solo career. With Holsapple fronting the group, they signed to Bearsville in 1984 and released *Like This*, a more conventional jangle-pop album with strong country leanings. Bearsville's internal problems doomed the album despite its obvious hit potential. They eventually left to sign with I.R.S. Records in 1987, where they released *The Sound of Music*. By the end of 1988, the band decided to break up. —*Chris Woodstra*

● **Stands for Decibels** / 1981 / IRS ◆◆◆◆◆

On their debut, the dB's combined a reverence for British pop and arty, post-punk leanings that alternate between minimalism and a love of quirky embellishment, odd sounds, and unexpected twists; *Stands for Decibels* is clearly a collegiate pop experiment, but rarely is experimentation so enjoyable and irresistibly catchy. Singing and songwriting duties are shared equally by Chris Stamey and Peter Holsapple—Stamey, more quirky and psychedelic-leaning with a winsome, pure-pop whine, is nicely balanced by Holsapple's more earthy drawl and straightforward approach. The album stands not only as a landmark power-pop album but also as a prototype for much of the Southern jangle that would follow. [*Stands for Decibels* remained criminally unavailable in the U.S. for years. When IRS reissued it on CD in 1989, Holsapple's "Judy" was added as a bonus track.] —*Chris Woodstra*

Repercussion / 1982 / IRS ◆◆◆◆◆

Repercussion is very much of a piece with the debut, repeating much of the same formula that made *Stands for Decibels* great—terrific harmonies, winning melodies and catchy hooks with subtle quirks thrown into the mix. This time, they feature a fuller, more polished sound, but the impact of the songs isn't diminished. Stamey left shortly after *Repercussion* to pursue a solo career. ["pH Factor" was added as a bonus track to the IRS CD reissue in 1989.] —*Chris Woodstra*

Like This / 1984 / Rhino ◆◆◆

From the opening notes of "Love Is for Lovers," this is obviously no ordinary dB's record. The group, now pared down to a trio fronted by Peter Holsapple, have stripped away the arty quirks of the first two albums, opting instead for straight-ahead, rootsy rockers and country-rock romps. Amid the more muscular, guitar-based sound, Holsapple turns in his same instantly endearing melodies, especially on the album highlight, "Lonely Is as Lonely Does," their most beautiful song to date. [Rhino's CD reissue adds an unnecessary extended remix of "A Spy in the House of Love."] —*Chris Woodstra*

The Sound of Music / 1987 / IRS ◆◆◆

The years between 1984 and 1987 were not a lot of fun for The dB's; Chris Stamey left the group shortly before they began work on *Like This*, forcing them to reinvent themselves as a trio with Peter Holsapple as leader, and shortly after the album was released, their record company, Bearsville Records, went out of business, killing the record's commercial possibilities and leaving the group in legal limbo as they tried to sort out the details of their still-valid contract with a non-existent label. Consequently, 1987's *The Sound Of Music* was, in many ways, a "make or break" album for the band (and their first opportunity to release an album through a fully-functioning American label), and the band seemed determined to make the most of it. *The Sound Of Music* is easily the group's most polished and least eccentric album; Greg Edward's production is far slicker than anything The dB's had come in contact with in the past, and Peter Holsapple's songs shrewdly leaned to the most accessible side of his musical personality. In other words, if you loved the quirks and angles of *Repercussion* or *Stands For Decibels*, this is not the album you're looking for. But no one has ever denied that Peter Holsapple writes great pop tunes, and he came up with a dozen winners on *The Sound Of Music*, from the moody "I Lie" and the mournful "Never Before and Never Again" to the rollicking "Change With The Changing Times" and "Any Old Thing," these songs are smart and superbly crafted, and the band performs them with a winning enthusiasm. And the oddball racing anthem "Bonneville," the catty breakup tune "Molly Says," and the idiosyncratically anthemic closer "Today Could Be The Day" made it clear Holsapple hadn't entirely subsumed the group's personality in a bid for mainstream success. *The Sound Of Music* was the biggest reach The dB's ever made towards a larger audience, and if the masses didn't take the bait, one listen proves it was certainly their loss. —*Mark Deming*

Ride the Wild Tom Tom / Aug. 17, 1993 / Rhino ◆◆◆

In his liner essay for *Ride the Wild Tom-Tom*, former dB's member Peter Holsapple jokingly describes this collection as "the equivalent of our *Basement Tapes*," and that statement actually describes the contents fairly well, especially when one remembers that Bob Dylan's *Basement Tapes* were mostly recorded as a goof. A collection of rehearsal tapes, demos, early single sides, and inside jokes, *Ride the Wild Tom-Tom* is hardly a definitive portrait of The dB's, but anyone looking for a ragged-but-right look at the band's formative days during Chris Stamey's tenure with the band will eat it up. Along with early versions of "Soul Kiss," "Modern Boys and Girls," and "A Spy in the House of Love," *Ride the Wild Tom-Tom* features a highly individual cover of The Grassroots' "Let's Live for Today," a commercial jingle for the East Coast music magazine *New York Rocker* (the band was using their offices as a rehearsal space), and the mock-punk onslaught "Hardcore Judy." Committed dB's fans will find this to be hoot, and while it's hardly the best introduction to the band's music, the quality of Chris Stamey and Peter Holsapple's songwriting shines through on even the jokiest numbers. —*Mark Deming*

Paris Avenue / Oct. 4, 1994 / Monkey Hill ◆◆

De La Soul

f. 1987, Amityville, Long Island, NY
Alternative Rap, Hip-Hop

Long Island's De La Soul—Posdnuos (b. Kelvin Mercer), Trugoy the Dove (b. David Jolicoeur), and Pasemaster Mase (b. Vincent Mason)—formed while attending high school in the late '80s. Their demo tape came to the attention of Stetsasonic leader/producer Prince Paul, who helped the trio land a contract with Tommy Boy Records and produced their 1989 debut album, *3 Feet High and Rising*. With its colorful, neo-psychedelic collage of samples and musical styles, plus the trio's low-key, clever rhymes and goofy humor, the album sounded like nothing else in hip-hop. De La Soul was gentler and more eclectic than most of their contemporaries, and were quickly perceived as the leaders of a contingent of New York-based alternative rappers dubbed the Native Tongues Posse. In the wake of *3 Feet High and Rising*'s critical and commercial success, the '60s pop group the

Turtles won a lawsuit against De La Soul over an unauthorized sample of their song "You Showed Me." The decision had substantial impact on rap in general—all samples now had to be legally cleared, which delayed the release of De La Soul's second album, *De La Soul Is Dead*. When the record was finally released in the spring of 1991, it received decidedly mixed reviews, and its darker, more introspective tone didn't attract as big an audience. De La Soul's third album, *Buhloone Mindstate*, was harder and funkier than its predecessors, but although it received strong reviews upon its late-1993 release, the album quickly fell off the charts; the same fate greeted 1996's *Stakes Is High*. Four years later, De La Soul initiated what promised to be a three-album series with *Art Official Intelligence: Mosaic Thump*; though reviews were mixed, it was greeted warmly by record buyers, debuting in the Top Ten. *—Stephen Thomas Erlewine*

★ **3 Feet High and Rising** / 1989 / Tommy Boy ♦♦♦♦♦

The most inventive, assured, and playful debut in hip-hop history, *3 Feet High and Rising* not only proved that rappers didn't have to talk about the streets to succeed, but also expanded the palette of sampling material with a kaleidoscope of sounds and references culled from pop, soul, disco, and even country music. Weaving clever wordplay and deft rhymes across two dozen tracks loosely organized around a game-show theme, De La Soul broke down boundaries all over the LP, moving easily from the groovy my-philosophy intro "The Magic Number" to an intelligent, caring inner-city vignette named "Ghetto Thang" to the freewheeling end-of-innocence tale "Jenifa Taught Me (Derwin's Revenge)." Rappers Posdnuos and Trugoy the Dove talked about anything they wanted (up to and including body odor), playing fast and loose on the mic like Biz Markie. Thinly disguised under a layer of humor, their lyrical themes ranged from true love ("Eye Know") to the destructive power of drugs ("Say No Go") to Daisy Age philosophy ("Tread Water") to sex ("Buddy"). Prince Paul (from Stetsasonic) and DJ Pasemaster Mase led the way on the production end, with dozens of samples from all sorts of left-field artists—including Johnny Cash, the Mad Lads, Steely Dan, Public Enemy, Hall & Oates, and the Turtles. The pair didn't just use those samples as hooks or drumbreaks—like most hip-hop producers had in the past—but as split-second fills and in-jokes that made some tracks sound more like DJ records. Even "Potholes on My Lawn," which samples a mouth harp and yodeling (for the chorus, no less), became a big R&B hit. If it was easy to believe the revolution was here from listening to the rapping and production on Public Enemy's *It Takes a Nation of Millions to Hold Us Back*, with De La Soul the Daisy Age seemed to promise a new era of positivity in hip-hop. *—John Bush*

De La Soul Is Dead / May 13, 1991 / Tommy Boy ♦♦♦♦

De La Soul throws a curveball at listeners with its second album, *De La Soul Is Dead*, taking a slightly harder and tougher approach, but remaining highly musical, distinctive, and recognizable. Though not quite as consistently appealing as the debut, De La Soul is still one of rap's most inviting acts, and remain quite experimental and unpredictable. *De La Soul Is Dead* is less lighthearted than *Three Feet High and Rising*, but offerings like "Oodles of O's" and "Pease Porridge" make it clear that the group can still be enjoyably quirky and eccentric. One song that definitely isn't amusing is "Millie Pulled a Pistol on Santa," an unsettling commentary on child molestation that cuts like a knife without preaching. Like the first album, *De La Soul Is Dead* is a very abstract and cerebral effort that requires several listenings to be fully appreciated. *—Alex Henderson*

Buhloone Mindstate / Sep. 21, 1993 / Tommy Boy ♦♦♦♦

Continually trying to live up to the revolution that was their debut, *Buhloone Mindstate* is a return to Daisy Age positive vibes. The beats are big, the samples are fresh, and the melodies are enticing. While the first two albums featured intros and sidelights along the way, *Buhloone Mindstate* has only fifteen tracks (eleven songs). With help from friends Guru, Maceo Parker, and Biz Markie, De La Soul approaches the perfection of *3 Feet High and Rising*, if not the initial effect. *—John Bush*

Stakes Is High / Jul. 2, 1996 / Tommy Boy ♦♦♦

Seven years after its debut album, De La Soul was still one of the most unpredictable and risk-taking groups in rap. On the excellent *Stakes Is High*, the Long Island natives continue to thrive on the abstract and the cerebral. Instead of the lightheartedness that characterized *Three Feet High and Rising*, they favor a harder, tougher approach that's closer to their second album, *De La Soul Is Dead*. Jazz remains a strong influence for the group, who sample the improvised works of Milt Jackson, Lou Donaldson, and Chico Hamilton, as well as classic soul by the likes of the Commodores and Sly & the Family Stone. This eclectic approach certainly didn't hurt the group's popularity in alternative rock and acid jazz circles, but in 1996, rap's hardcore seemed much more interested in gangster rap. *—Alex Henderson*

Art Official Intelligence: Mosaic Thump / Aug. 8, 2000 / Tommy Boy ♦♦

Dead Boys

f. 1976, Cleveland, OH, **db.** 1978

New York Punk, Punk

Forming from the ashes of Cleveland's semi-legendary Rocket From the Tombs, the Dead Boys were one of the first punk bands to escalate the level of violence, nihilism, and pure ugliness of punk rock to extreme new levels. After they relocated to New York, ex-Rocket members Cheetah Chrome (guitar) and Johnny Blitz (drums) hooked up with guitarist Jimmy Zero, bassist Jeff Magnum, and vocalist Stiv Bators to form the Dead Boys. Their music wasn't very special; even by the relaxed standards of punk it was loose and incompetent, bordering on the stupidity of heavy metal. "Sonic Reducer" and "Ain't It Fun," the band's two best songs, were holdovers from former Rocket From the Tombs members David Thomas and Peter Laughner, who went on to form Pere Ubu. What distinguished the Dead Boys, and what makes them notorious to this day, is their pure nastiness, much of it coming from Bators. Their two albums—*Young, Loud, and Snotty* and *We Have Come for Your Children*—are brutal; wallowing in their own self-serving nihilism, they embodied the punk stereotypes held by the mainstream. After two albums, the band split. Bators formed Lords of the New Church and the rest of the members slid into obscurity. In 1990, Bators died of injuries sustained from being hit by a bus in Paris. *—Stephen Thomas Erlewine*

● **Young Loud & Snotty** / Oct. 1977 / Sire ♦♦♦♦♦

Fellow Cleveland types Pere Ubu may have won the artistic kudos for their adventurous, surprising work, but if the goal was just to rock and rock again, the Dead Boys had them totally trumped. As both title phrase and capsule description, *Young, Loud & Snotty* accurately defines the predominating aesthetic so well that one could just leave it at that, but there's a lot more going on here than on the face of it. With perhaps surprising great production from demi-famous '70s rocket Genya Ravan, the five-some found something sonically smack in-between the US garage/punk heritage of the past and the more modern thrashings from overseas. Bators sneers, gobs, gasps, and whines with the best of them, but he knows his rock history, as does his bandmates. Zero and Chrome aren't guitar virtuosos, but they do know what makes a song great and aren't afraid to concentrate on that, while the Magnum/Blitz rhythm section keeps things moving as it does. In some ways songs like "All This and More" and "I Need Lunch" simply emerge from an alternate '50s, with admittedly much more feedback and stereo sound. Stone cold rock classic "Sonic Reducer" starts things off—amusingly—with all sorts of phased drums and other fripperies that later generations wouldn't consider punk at all. That said, it's still blunt, brilliantly sung by Bators and kicks out the jams with messy energy. Other all-time greats include the perfect bored-and-needing-kicks anthem "Ain't Nothin' to Do" and the thoroughly wrong "Caught With the Meat In Your Mouth." There's even a rock oldie—a cover of "Hey Little Girl" live onstage at spiritual home CBGB's. And why not? With great punk rock and great rock, *Young, Loud and Snotty* still packs a punch. *—Ned Raggett*

We Have Come for Your Children / Jun. 1978 / Sire ♦♦♦

Highlighted by the snarling "Ain't It Fun," The Dead Boys' second album was as nasty and raw as their first. *—Stephen Thomas Erlewine*

Dead Can Dance

f. 1981, Australia

Dream Pop, Shoegazing, Alternative Pop/Rock, Ethnic Fusion

Dead Can Dance combines elements of European folk music—particularly music from the Middle Ages and the Renaissance—with ambient pop and worldbeat flourishes. Their songs are of lost beauty, regret and sorrow, inspiration and nobility, and of the everlasting human goal of attaining a meaningful existence. Over the course of their career, Dead Can Dance has featured a multitude of members, but two musicians have remained at the core of the band—guitarist Brendan Perry and vocalist Lisa Gerrard. Originally based in Australia, the duo moved to London in 1982 and signed to 4AD. Their eponymous 1984 debut was followed by *Spleen and Ideal*, an album that helped build their European cult following (it peaked at number two on the U.K. indie charts). Two more albums followed during the '80s, and after 1990's *Aion*, the group toured America for the first time. As a result, the 1991 compilation *A Passage in Time* became their first American release. Two years later, *Into the Labyrinth* was a cult success throughout the US and Europe. In the summer of 1996, Dead Can Dance released *Spiritchaser* and embarked on an international tour. *—Stephen Thomas Erlewine & Vladimir Bogdanov*

Dead Can Dance / 1984 / 4AD ♦♦♦

Early punk backgrounds and the like behind them, Perry and Gerrard created a striking, dour landmark in early-'80s atmospherics on their first, self-titled effort. Bearing much more resemblance to the similarly gripping, dark early work of bands like the Cocteau Twins and the Cure than to the later fusions of music that would come to characterize the duo's sound, *Dead Can Dance* is as goth as it gets in many places. Perry and Gerrard's wonderful vocal work—his rich, warm tones and her unearthly, multi-octave exaltations—are already fairly well established, but serve different purposes here. Thick, shimmering guitar and rumbling bass/drum/drum machine patterns practically scream their sonic connections to the likes of Robin Guthrie and Robert Smith, but they still sound pretty darn good for all that. When they stretch that sound to try for a more distinct, unique result, the results are astonishing. Gerrard is the major beneficiary here—"Frontier" explicitly experiments with tribal percussion, resulting in an excellent combination of her singing and the rushed music. Then there's the astonishing "Ocean," where guitar and chiming bells and other rhythmic sounds provide the bed for one of her trademark—and quite, quite lovely—vocal excursions into the realm of glossolalia. Perry in contrast tends to be matched with the more straightforward numbers of digital processing and thick, moody guitar surge. The album ends on a fantastic high note—"Musica Eternal," featuring a slowly increasing-in-volume combination of hammered dulcimer, low bass tones, and Gerrard's soaring vocals. As an indicator of where the band was going, it's perfect. *—Ned Raggett*

Spleen and Ideal / 1985 / 4AD ♦♦♦♦♦

With this amazing album, Dead Can Dance fully took the plunge into the heady mix of musical traditions that would come to define its sound and style for the remainder of its career. The straightforward goth affectations are exchanged for a sonic palette and range of imagination. Calling it "haunting" and "atmospheric" barely scratches even the initial surface of the album's power. The common identification of the duo with a consciously medieval European sound starts here—quite understandable, when one considers the mystic titles of songs, references to Latin, choirs, and other touches that make the album sound like it was recorded in an immense cathedral. Opening number "De Profundis" sets this mood so thoroughly, with bells and drones and more supporting another bravura performance from Gerrard, while the immediately following "Ascension" builds on this initial effort with further style and grace. It's limiting to think of either album or band strictly in terms of simple revivalism of old music. While the elements being drawn on are certainly of an older range, the results owe as much to the technologies of arrangement and production and a consciously cinematic feeling as much as they do antique pasts. Similarly, the feeling is not simply European but worldwide, with Gerrard's glossolalia intentionally reaching beyond easy understanding. Perry's vocal efforts are no less compelling, his own high point occurring with the vast-sounding "Enigma of the Absolute," as a steady, massive drum pound echoes behind a similarly treated guitar/harpsichord combination, tinged with a striking string arrangement. The overall feeling is of an ancient religious service suddenly brought to life in a truly modern way, with stunning results. *—Ned Raggett*

Within the Realm of a Dying Sun / 1987 / 4AD ✦✦✦✦
With its two sides split between Perry and Gerrard's vocal efforts, *Within the Realm of a Dying Sun* serves as both a display for the ever more ambitious band and a chance for the two to individually demonstrate their awesome talents. Beginning with the portentous "Anywhere Out of the World," a piece that takes the deep atmospherics of "Enigma of the Absolute" to a higher level with mysterious, chiming bells, simple but effective keyboard bass and a sense of vast space, the album finds Dead Can Dance on a steady roll. Once again a range of assistant musicians provide even more elegance and power to the band's work, with a chamber string quartet plus various performers on horns, woodwind, and percussion. Impressive though the remainder of the first side is, Gerrard's showcase on the second half is even more enveloping and arguably more successful. The martial combination of drums and horns that start "Dawn of the Iconoclast" call to mind everything from Wagner to Laibach, but Gerrard's unearthly alto, at its most compelling here, elevates it even higher. "Cantara" is no less impressive, a swirling, drum-heavy song that sounds equally inspired by gypsy dancing, classical orchestras and any number of Arab musical traditions. "Summoning of the Muse" is perhaps too formal in comparison, though still quite impressive, but "Persephone" is the finer effort and a good way to close. *—Ned Raggett*

Serpent's Egg / 1988 / 4AD ✦✦✦✦✦
Perry and Gerrard continued to experiment and improve with *The Serpent's Egg*, as much a leap forward as *Spleen and Ideal* was some years previously. As with that album, *The Serpent's Egg* was heralded by an astounding first track, "The Host of Seraphim." Its use in films some years later was no surprise in the slightest—one can imagine the potential range of epic images the song could call up—but on its own it's so jaw-droppingly good that almost the only reaction is sheer awe. Beginning with a soft organ drone and buried, echoed percussion, Gerrard then takes flight with a seemingly wordless invocation of power and worship—her vocal control and multi-octave range, especially towards the end, has to be heard to be believed. Nothing else achieves such heights, but everything gets pretty darn close, a deserved testament to the band's conceptual reach and abilities. Slow plainsong chants such as "Orbis De Ignis" mix with the harpischord and overlaid vocals of "The Writing on My Father's Hand" and the slow build and sweep of "In the Kingdom of the Blind the One-Eyed Are Kings." Two of Perry's finest vocal moments occur here. The first, "Severance," is a slow, organ/keyboard led number that showcases his rich, warm vocals exquisitely—it's no wonder that Bauhaus chose to cover it some years later on its reunion tour. "Ullyses," the album's closing track, makes for a fine ending as much as "The Host of Seraphim" did an opening, Perry's delivery almost like a reading from a holy book, the arrangement of strings and percussion rhythmic, addictive and lovely. *—Ned Raggett*

Aion / Sep. 1990 / 4AD ✦✦✦✦✦
Their reputation growing by leaps and bounds, including a huge underground following in the U.S.—they were able to tour there even without one domestic release available, while at one point Dead Can Dance was the biggest selling band in 4AD's history—Perry and Gerrard once again did the business with *Aion*. Its cover taken from Bosch, *Aion*'s medievalism was worn more openly than ever before, with songs adapted from centuries-old material. The beautiful, entrancing "Saltarello," with lead performance by what sounds like an old wind instrument, comes from an Italian dance of the 14th century, while the mysterious moods of "The Song of the Sibyl" derive from 16th-century Catalonia. The group's command of not merely recording possibilities—witness the exquisite layering of vocals on the opening "The Arrival and the Reunion"—but of musical traditions, instruments, and more from around the world was arguably never stronger. Gerrard's vocals in particular have an even stronger, richer feeling than before, not merely able to command with its power but softly calm and seduce. Perry, meanwhile, is no less compelling, his ever-strong, wonderful voice perfectly suited to his choice of material. The standout track is "Fortune Presents Gifts Not According to the Book" with lyrics from a Spanish poet. The musical combination of softly plucked guitar and buried organ drone is striking enough, swathed in reverb, but when Perry steps in with his vocals, matched by more sparkling keyboards, the result is yet another high point for a band laden with them. Guest performers once again assist throughout, including Perry's brother Robert on haunting, quite non-clichéd bagpipes for "As the Bell Rings the Maypole Spins" and singer David Navarro Sust, returning again to contribute some fine backing work. *—Ned Raggett*

● **A Passage in Time** / Oct. 1991 / Rykodisc ✦✦✦✦✦
It was only a matter of time before some sort of introduction to American audiences came about, especially following the band's successful tour of the States, so Rykodisc did the honors with this excellent compilation—if there's one thing anyone needs to get from the duo, it's unquestionably this. While there's no chronological order to the collection, and the sequencing and arrangement from the original albums are unfortunately if inevitably lost, the choice of songs to feature is completely spot on. The biggest gap is the lack of anything from the self-titled debut and the *Garden of the Arcane Delights* EP, including the track the collection takes its title from. As such songs would jarringly stand out sonically from the rest, though, it's an understandable omission. Nearly every undisputed highlight from the band is included, covering both Perry's and Gerrard's contributions in equal measure. "The Host of Seraphim" here forms the centerpiece of an album rather than the start, and two new tracks help to round things out—while they aren't among the most deathless numbers the band has created, they're still worth listening to. "Bird" piles on the ambient jungle noises and animal calls and cries, but is saved from neo-New Age bathos by both its arrangement and the central combination of drumming and Gerrard's singing, here a touch lighter than normal. "Spirit," in contrast, predominantly features electric guitar and strong bass pulse, feeling a bit like a number from the very first album heavily stripped down with a new tension and beauty. Perry's singing suits the performance well, another excellent effort. *—Ned Raggett*

Into the Labyrinth / Sep. 14, 1993 / 4AD/Warner Brothers ✦✦✦✦✦
With a regular American deal in place for the first time ever, thanks to 4AD's linkup with the WEA conglomerate, Dead Can Dance made a splash on commercial alternative radio with "The Ubiquitous Mr. Lovegrove," the first single from *Into the Labyrinth*. Raga drones, a strange clattering beat, a haunting wind instrument, orchestral shading, and Perry's ever-grand voice make it one of the more unlikely things to be heard on the airwaves in a while. It all begins with yet another jaw-dropper from Gerrard, "Yulunga (Spirit Dance)," with keyboards and her octave-defying voice at such a deep, rich level that it sweeps all before it. Wordless as always but never without emotional heft, the song slowly slides into a slow but heavy percussion piece that sounds a bit like "Bird" from *A Passage in Time*, but with greater impact and memorability. As the album slowly unwinds over an hour's length, the two again create a series of often astounding numbers that sound like they should be millennia old, mixing and matching styles to create new fusions. Perhaps even more impressive is that everything was performed solely by Perry and Gerrard—no outside guests here, and yet everything is as detailed, lush, and multifaceted as many of their past albums. New classics from the band appear almost track for track: Gerrard's a cappella work on "The Wind That Shakes the Barley," the gentle beauty of "Ariadne," the rhythmic drive and chants of the title song. The conclusion is a slightly surprising but quite successful cover—"How Fortunate the Man With None," an adaptation of a classic Bertolt Brecht tune about the turn of fortune's wheel. Given a restrained arrangement and Perry's singing, it brings *Labyrinth* to a satisfying end. *—Ned Raggett*

Toward the Within / Oct. 25, 1994 / 4AD ✦✦✦
A large reason that Dead Can Dance tours and performances were so praised by hardcore fans lay in the band's welcome preference for unknown and otherwise unheard material, rather than simply rehashing expected numbers. Bootlegging of these tracks and performances was understandable and widespread, so involved and passionate was the band's following. Recorded at a Los Angeles performance from the *Into the Labyrinth* tour, the astounding *Toward the Within* shows that the band's magic was clearly not simply something created in studio. Both lead performers are simply in excelsis, their vocal abilities hardly diminished by the rigors of the road—if anything, they sound even more inspired as a result. The range of instruments tackled is testimony to the group's breadth, from the yang ch'in, a Chinese equivalent to hammered dulcimer, to a wide range of drums. As for the songs, only four of the fifteen had been officially released before, including fine takes on "Cantara," "Song of the Sibyl" and "Yulunga (Spirit Dance)." As for the numerous new delights, Perry has a number of solo or near-solo tracks he performs with acoustic guitar. These include the lovely "American Dreaming" and the mystical set-closing "Don't Fade Away," calling to mind Tim Buckley's sense of scope and vision. Gerrard's unquestioned highlight is the combination of "Tristan" and "Sanvean," the latter of which is an awesome, widescreen number that became an undisputed highlight on her solo debut *The Mirror Pool*. Perhaps the most astonishing numbers are "Rakim," featuring a striking intertwining of Perry and Gerrard's singing, and a version of Sinead O'Connor's "I Am Stretched on Your Grave" that redefines passionate drama. *—Ned Raggett*

Spiritchaser / Jun. 25, 1996 / 4AD ✦✦✦✦
Dead Can Dance's final album *Spiritchaser* was something of an unusual release—it's not as much of an anomaly as the first album, but one can hear the duo wanting to stretch a bit more, however subtly. Perry and Gerrard's personal and creative tensions didn't stop them from creating another fine album, though there's a strong sense the group had finally reached a logical end. Essentially, *Spiritchaser* is a summing up rather than a push forward; it features all the usual elements of a Dead Can Dance album instead of further explorations to see what else could be done. *Toward the Within* contributors Ronan O'Snodaigh and Lance Hogan, as well as previous collaborator Peter Ulrich, appear on some tracks here, most specifically on the opening "Nierika" and "Dedicace Outro." Both are laden with lots of percussion—unsurprising when one realizes that five performers are creating the drumming! Outside of Turkish clarinet by Renaud Pion on the Beatles-sampling "Indus," it's nothing but Perry and Gerrard throughout the album, with another combination and arrangement of multiple influences coming to bear. Both Perry and Gerrard are in fine voice throughout, their strong singing still the centerpiece of their work, but there's almost an air of predictability to their approaches at this point (perhaps explaining Perry's greater experimentation on his solo debut years later). Interestingly, overtly rock elements like Morricone-styled electric guitar appear at points amid the usual melange of various percussion instruments and arrangements. It works surprisingly well, indicating where the duo might have gone had they continued on. *Spiritchaser* ends on a strong note, the gentle, mysterious "Devorzhum," a Gerrard-sung number that makes for a grand conclusion. *—Ned Raggett*

Dead Kennedys

f. 1978, **db.** 1987

Anarchist Punk, American Punk, L.A. Punk, Hardcore Punk, American Underground

The Dead Kennedys merged revolutionary politics with hardcore punk music and, in the process, became one of the defining hardcore bands. Often, they were more notable for their politics than their music, but that was part of their impact. The Kennedys were more inspired by British punk and the fiery, revolutionary-implied politics of the Sex Pistols than the artier tendencies of New York punk rockers. Under the direction of lead vocalist Jello Biafra, the Dead Kennedys became the most political and—to the eyes of many observers, including Christians and right-wing politicians—the most dangerous band in hardcore. Within a year of their formation, the band had released two of their most well-known singles, "California Über Alles" and "Holiday in Cambodia." After releasing their debut album *Fresh Fruit for Rotting Vegetables*, Dead Kennedys formed their own label, Alternative Tentacles. Two years later, the group released their second full-length album, *Plastic Surgery Disasters*. Following a three-year hiatus, 1985's *Frankenchrist* precipitated a bitter legal battle (regarding an allegedly pornographic poster included with copies of the album) that revealed Biafra as one of the most articulate advocates for free speech and vocal opponents of the PMRC (the case ended with a hung jury and was dismissed). Just before the prosecution began in 1986, the band released *Bedtime for Democracy*, which turned out to be their last official album. Biafra embarked on a solo career, releasing musical and spoken word recordings sporadically over the next decade and a half. *—Stephen Thomas Erlewine*

★ **Fresh Fruit for Rotting Vegetables** / 1980 / Alternative Tentacles ♦♦♦♦♦

A hyper-speed blast of ultra-polemical, left-wing hardcore punk and bitingly funny sarcasm, *Fresh Fruit for Rotting Vegetables* stands as the Dead Kennedys' signature statement. As one of the first hardcore albums, it was a galvanizing influence on the musical and attitudinal development of the genre, also helping to kickstart the fertile California scene. The record's tactics are not subtle in the least; Jello Biafra's odd warble and spat-out lyrics leave no doubt as to what he thinks, baiting his targets of conservatism, violence, overbearing authority, and capitalist greed with a viciously satirical sarcasm that keeps his unflinchingly political outlook from becoming too didactic. The thin production dilutes some of the music's power, but the ragged speed-blur still packs a wallop, and the hooks cribbed from surf and rockabilly give it a gonzo edge. The songwriting isn't consistent all the way through the album, but classics like "Kill the Poor," "Let's Lynch the Landlord," "Chemical Warfare," "California Über Alles," and "Holiday In Cambodia" helped define the hardcore genre and, thus, must be heard. *—Steve Huey*

In God We Trust, Inc. / Feb. 1981 / Alternative Tentacles ♦♦♦

The band didn't hold back at all when it came to the follow-up for *Fresh Fruit*—if anything, they exploded to a degree never matched by them in later years. Arguably the sheer speed and lack of any subtlety throughout most of this eight-song EP release means there's less to talk about in terms of deathless songs and more in the way of sheer breathless anger and rage. The titles say it all: "Nazi Punks Fuck Off," "Religious Vomit," "Hyperactive Child." The sheer hilarity of the band isn't lost, thankfully; "Moral Majority" may rip along as per always, but Biafra's parody of a typical TV preacher at the start is a scream. The real winners come at the end, starting with "We've Got a Bigger Problem Now." A reworking of "California Über Alles," specifically targeted at California governor turned president Ronald Reagan, benefits from an amusing jazz/lounge start and even more righteous, slow-burn bile than before. The group tops it off with a romp through Frankie Laine's "Rawhide," ending everything on a fun, kicking note. *—Ned Raggett*

Plastic Surgery Disasters / 1982 / Alternative Tentacles ♦♦♦♦♦

Having proved themselves masters of the quick, vicious smash and bash, on their second full-length album the Kennedys continued in that vein while finding other effective ways to express their all-encompassing message of resistance and satire. Absolutely nobody is safe, whether it's the more expected targets of conservative society, or those who claim to follow what the Kennedys and punk promised but only ended up acting like idiots. For the most part, though, it's a well-deserved smackdown of all the jerks the early '80s produced, set to some fantastic music. Bookended by random noise jams—the first one with a wonderfully dismissive spoken-word analysis on societal programming for The Good Life—*Plastic Surgery Disasters* shows East Bay Ray, Klaus Fluoride and D.H. Peligro turning into an even more awesome unit than before. Ray's sheet-metal intense guitar may once or twice get slammed into too much treble for its own good, but his spaghetti-western-cranked-to-ten playing is fantastic stuff at its best. The others have their moments, like Peligro's rolling drum breaks on "Government Mechanic." When the band aims for subtlety, the results are grand—the sudden silences on "Trust Your Mechanic," the goofy hipswing start to "Forest Fire." Unsurprisingly, Biafra is still at the center of it all; once again, the song titles make it clear what's at play. "Terminal Preppie," rips into an example of the type with gusto, and the wonderfully sneering "Winnebago Warrior" is just the tip of the iceberg. The real highlight can be found at the end—"Moon Over Marin," with a soaring, anthemic surf-rock line from Ray offsetting Biafra's semi-apocalyptic vision of the Bay Area's snooty region. *—Ned Raggett*

Frankenchrist / 1985 / Alternative Tentacles ♦♦♦

Released after a three-year studio hiatus, this album picks up right where *Plastic Surgery Disasters* left off. As always, the lyrics are among the most literate and angry in all of rock & roll. "Goons of Hazard" scores the culture of guns and the rednecks who love them, utilizing full-textured hard rock to set the verses. "Soup Is Good Food" lacerates the concept of disposable people in disposable jobs, pairing this idea with repeated guitar riff-based music that suggests a nightmare version of 1960s songs. "Jock-O-Rama" excoriates organized sports and macho attitudes; musically, the outer sections wed rockabilly and hardcore influences, sandwiching a slow middle section that spoofs martial numbers like Barry Sadler's "Ballad of the Green Berets." "This Could Be Anywhere" has critical lyrics about racism and classicism set to music highly reminiscent of the Sex Pistols. "Hellnation" has garbled, wide-range, muckracking verses set to stun-speed punk that recalls numbers from *In God We Trust Inc.* The excellent "MTV—Get Off the Air" lambastes the corporate influences on rock & roll; musically, the song exhibits a tripartite structure, using a vacuously poppy opening, a speed hardcore central section, and a mid-tempo rocking finale that prominently features trumpet (a very brief coda reprise of hardcore ends the number). The finest selection on this album (and perhaps in the whole Dead Kennedys' canon) is the anthemic "Stars and Stripes of Corruption." This number also utilizes a three-part construct, consisting here of a hard-rocking midsection flanked by faster, punk-oriented material. The verses here are stunningly detailed, describing what the band believes is wrong with the United States and what the solutions should be. This wonderful and challenging album is very highly recommended. *—David Cleary*

Bedtime for Democracy / 1986 / Alternative Tentacles ♦♦

The Dead Kennedys go out in a blaze of snarling, defiant glory in their final studio release. They drub a bushel basket's worth of entrenched interests, including scientists, the military, the power hungry, macho attitudes, classicism, lie detectors, Reagan and his economic policies, the press, the entertainment industry, and the commercialization of rock and revolutionary attitudes. The album's manic speed punk style recalls *In God We Trust Inc.*, particularly on the frenetic cover of Johnny Paycheck's hit "Take This Job and Shove It." When the tempo slows, a few songs resemble frantic rockabilly; of these, "Hop With the Jetset" lampoons the privileged classes, "I Spy" savages government agents, and "Where Do Ya Draw the Line" is a plea in favor of anarchy. The quiet, furtive "D.M.S.O." is a highly atypical number strongly resembling the theme to *The Pink Panther*. The lengthy, anthemic "Cesspools in Eden" is a hard rock number with unusual chord changes and lyrics railing against toxic waste; similarly, "Chickenshit Conformist" alternates slow and hyperfast sections and sports wide-ranging verses that constitute a scathing indictment of the rock music industry. As usual, the rushed hardcore numbers often garble or swallow up the well-written lyrics (if you want people to follow you into revolution, your ideas need to be intelligible). The album cover sports witheringly disparaging artwork; also included in this release are two muckraking newspapers, one containing clip art, and the other written articles about the obscenity trial embroiling the band at that point. While it's not totally successful, at least the Dead Kennedys had the satisfaction of going out on their own terms. It's all well worth hearing. *—David Cleary*

Give Me Convenience or Give Me Death / 1987 / Alternative Tentacles ♦♦♦♦♦

Hounded by political enemies and reaching their personal breaking point, the Kennedys bowed with a retrospective of some of their fiercest, finest moments. If one needs a starting point for the band's fierce, funny assault on any level of complacency imaginable, *Give Me Convenience* is indeed as convenient as it gets. Focusing for the most part on non-album cuts or various rarities, it appeals to hardcore Dead Kennedys fans as well as neophytes. The collection includes some of the band's earliest greats, like the legendary rant "Too Drunk to Fuck," as withering a depiction of getting trashed and stupid as any. While the definitive "California Über Alles" and "Holiday in Cambodia" make the cut from the first album, there are also plenty of more obscure and unknown goodies. The second half features live tracks like the hilarious "Pull My Strings," which vivisects typical rock star pomposity (knowingly quoting the Knack's "My Sharona") before shifting into an even nuttier chorus. Another screamingly funny number is the improv "Night of the Living Rednecks," done "while Ray was changing strings" at an Oregon date in 1979. After threatening to play the theme from the *Dinah Shore* show, the remaining three members light into something resembling a beat/'50s hep groove, only with Biafra recalling a tale of idiots encountered during a previous visit to Portland. Meanwhile, there's a version of "I Fought the Law," which easily trumps the Clash's version, helped by a lyric change or two along the way. Messy, nutty, and fun, *Convenience* is a treat and a half. *—Ned Raggett*

The Dead Milkmen

f. 1983, Philadelphia, PA

College Rock, Comedy Rock, Alternative Pop/Rock

Philadelphia pop-punk quartet featuring vocalist Rodney Anonymous (who sometimes adds "Amadeus" or "Mellencamp" to his name), guitarist Joe Jack Talcum, bassist Dave Blood, and drummer Dean Clean. The Milkmen are renowned for their dumb, obnoxious sense of humor, which they frequently focus on pop culture. Some critics love them, some critics hate them, but all agree that The Milkmen are sophomoric and snotty. "Bitchin' Camaro," from their debut, *Big Lizard In My Backyard*, was a minor alternative-radio hit. The band got a small measure of publicity when Detroit Tiger infielder Jim Walewander praised them in interviews, and had a minor MTV hit with *Beelzebubba*'s "Punk Rock Girl." Unfortunately, they were never as consistently funny as they tried to be, and wound up dropped from Enigma after *Metaphysical Graffiti*. Their subsequent releases found them trying to learn how to be serious, and their popularity had almost disappeared by the time they broke up in the mid-'90s. *—Steve Huey*

Big Lizard in My Backyard / 1985 / Enigma/Restless ♦♦♦♦♦

It may not be deathless, but 1984's *Big Lizard in My Backyard* is that rarest of beasts (as a random listen to any Barenaked Ladies disc will show): a collection of rock & roll silliness that outlives one playing. That mid-'80s favorite "Bitchin' Camaro" already demonstrated that ability plenty of times over. Portraying two guys yammering about Doors cover bands and "going down to the shore" before finally getting to the main point—the way-cool car of the title—it somehow finds the lost gap between pseudo-jazz grooves and punky snottiness. As left field a fluke hit single as it gets, its mix of bad taste, rock-star mockery and stoner humor still works well. As a whole, the album shows that the

Milkmen know their rock & roll history, whether tackling serious issues with sarcasm or just aiming for straight-up silliness. The opening track "Tiny Town," is a quick thrash-and-scream about small minds in small towns and the blatant idiocy of "Takin' Retards to the Zoo," which is about just what it says it is, find the Milkmen's tongues planted firmly in their cheeks. The reggae-tinged "Gorilla Girl" is about a choice in sweethearts that meets with parental disapproval, while the tense, nervous bite of "Right Wing Pigeons," trashes the Reagan administration with style and smirks. Semi-seriousness crops up on the wistfully poppy "Dean's Dream" about "a girl with long blonde hair" or the instrumental finale "Tugena," which shows that when they want to, the Milkmen can rock out with the best of them. Never too heavy but deeper than expected, *Big Lizard* captures these disaffected class clowns getting it out of their system with energy. *—Ned Raggett*

Eat Your Paisley! / 1986 / Enigma/Restless ✦✦✦
Having created a near-perfect blend of whiny humor and punk catchiness on *Big Lizard in My Backyard*, on their follow-up the Milkmen ended up falling a bit short. It's not a drastic, disastrous fall-off by any means, but part of the problem is the album's lack of a perfect single; where the past had "Bitchin' Camaro" and the future would have "Punk Rock Girl," *Eat Your Paisley* doesn't have a specific "must listen" number to recommend it. The closest might be "The Thing That Only Eats Hippies," a nutty rant about a Japanese-style movie monster out to nosh on '60s relics ("now it's got a sweet tooth for long hair") that fits the odd album title. Then there's "Beach Party Vietnam," which admittedly says it all in the title but still has a catchy chorus and appropriately off-kilter vim, and the dark cheer of "Happy Is," sunnily reflecting on corpses and death a bit like the Soft Boys' "I Wanna Destroy You." Beyond that, though, things are more hit and miss. The same overall combination of questionable taste, sometimes oddly sweet energy, and wiggy smirkiness runs rampant, but very little connects the way it should, raising a smile but not demanding repeated listens. The band is most successful when showing its continually improving musical chops, as with the ghost-of-New Order bass from Dave Blood that starts off "Fifty Things" or the appropriately winsome chime of "I Hear Your Name." There is one nicely off number at the end, "The Fez," a slow, heavy crunch that features Rodney Anonymous going off about how "ripping off the Butthole Surfers is how we make our living!" *—Ned Raggett*

Bucky Fellini / 1987 / Enigma/Restless ✦✦✦✦✦
A step up from the good but not great *Eat Your Paisley*, *Bucky Fellini* begins with a parody of the bandmember introductions from Sweet's "Ballroom Blitz" and raises another fun and funny stink. The most entertaining and ridiculous thing the band ever did takes deserved center stage—"Instant Club Hit (You'll Dance to Anything)." Consisting of drum machine fills, intentionally basic bass lines and Rodney Anonymous' instantly recognizable sneer, it's a hilarious, all-too-knowing rip on '80s new wave/dance culture. With lines like "Oh, baby, look at you, don't you look like Siouxsie Sioux" and "I met Andy Warhol at a really chic party/Blow it out your hair, dude, cuz you work at Hardee's!" it's hilarity personified (and bizarrely enough won them an appearance on an MTV dance show, where they encouraged a bout of stage diving). Nothing equals that song's sublime satire, but the Milkmen still stir things up with a touch more fire and sass than before. Naming a song "I Am the Walrus" that has absolutely nothing to do with the Beatles song proves that the jokers are in full effect. The goofy, country-tinged "Watching Scotty Die," features Joe Jack Talcum's surprisingly good Dobro playing. In honor of the album's Texas recording locale, some native sons are honored via covers. Daniel Johnston's "Rocketship" keeps its charm in a full-band arrangement, while the LeRoi Brothers' "Big Time Operator" gets an appropriate rave-up that also trashes Lone Star blowhards like Stevie Ray Vaughn and Charlie Sexton. Add in songs trashing Graceland and titles like "(Theme From) Blood Orgy of the Atomic Fern," and the result is another successful batch of silliness. *—Ned Raggett*

Beelzebubba / 1988 / Enigma/Restless ✦✦✦✦
Having built up a sizeable cult with surprising mainstream exposure here and there, the Milkmen got as close as they ever would to high-profile success with *Beelzebubba*. The basic formula and approach of the band hadn't changed a lot, but they did get it all together to create another near-perfect single, "Punk Rock Girl." Sprightly and catchy, it mixes the unexpectedly tender, sweet side of the band with the usual drawling humor from Anonymous—everything from accordion to utterly random Beach Boys (or is that the Mamas and the Papas?) references crop up. Beyond that splash, it was Milkmen time as usual: over the top, sarcastic, and more. Production was the clearest and most radio-friendly it ever was. The band's eternal hatred for trendoids, poseurs, and morons unsurprisingly continued to flourish from the first song in: "Brat in the Frat" targets the title character in question but spends some time demolishing the radical wannabe as well. Similarly amusing slams and smackdowns crop up throughout: "Bad Party," the snarky "Everybody's Got Nice Stuff But Me," and so forth. As an album through and through, *Beelzebubba* suffers from the same problem as *Eat Your Paisley* in many ways—a load of potentially inspiring ideas that often don't add up in the end. "RC's Mom" is a good example; if the music is meant to parody funk, it doesn't do it as well as, say, Led Zeppelin's "The Crunge," and if it's a celebration, it's pretty obvious and boring. As for the vocals, well, never mind. But so long as songs like "My Many Smells" and "Born to Love Volcanoes" are around, there's still hope yet. *—Ned Raggett*

Metaphysical Grafitti / Apr. 1990 / Enigma/Restless ✦✦

Soul Rotation / Apr. 14, 1992 / Hollywood ✦✦

Not Richard But Dick / Oct. 12, 1993 / Hollywood ✦✦

Chaos Rules—Live at the Trocadero / Nov. 8, 1994 / Restless ✦✦

Stoney's Extra Stout (Pig) / Nov. 7, 1995 / Restless ✦

● **Death Rides a Pale Cow: The Ultimate Collection** / Nov. 11, 1997 / Restless ✦✦✦✦✦
Death Rides a Pale Cow is an excellent, 22-track overview of the Dead Milkmen's career, containing all of their cult classics—"Bitchin' Camaro," "Instant Club Hit (You'll Dance to Anything)," "Punk Rock Girl," "Smokin' Banana Peels"—plus the previously unreleased "Labor Day" and "Milkmen Stomp," which was previously only available on a self-released cassette. For the curious or the casual fan, this contains everything you'd need, and it provides a fine, thorough introduction to the group's warped humor and amateurish punk rock. *—Stephen Thomas Erlewine*

Cream of the Crop: Best of the Dead Milkmen / Nov. 3, 1998 / BMG Special Products ✦✦✦
The title of BMG Special Products' *Cream of the Crop: Best of the Dead Milkmen* may be a little knowing, it may be a little ironic, but the fact of the matter is, this ten-track budget-line collection contains most of the group's underground favorites, including "Bitchin' Camaro, " "Instant Club Hit (You'll Dance to Anything)," "Smokin' Banana Peels" and the MTV hit "Punk Rock Girl." Sure, it may be missing some fan favorites, but it captures the feel and sound of the band, which will be enough for most casual fans. *—Stephen Thomas Erlewine*

Chris de Burgh

b. Oct. 15, 1948, Buenos Aires, Argentina
Keyboards, Guitar / Euro-Rock, Soft Rock, Prog-Rock/Art Rock, Adult Contemporary
An art-rocker that occasionally writes pop-oriented material, Chris de Burgh has never been as popular in his native Britain or the United States as he was in other areas of the world. In America, he's only managed two Top 40 hits—1983's "Don't Pay the Ferryman" and 1986's "The Lady in Red." Nevertheless, he has gained an astounding worldwide popularity, particularly Norway and Brazil. de Burgh's debut album, 1975's *Far Beyond These Castle Walls*, was a folk-tinged stab at fantasy in the tradition of the Moody Blues. Though it failed to chart in Britain, a single from the album named "Flying" stayed on top of the Brazilian charts for 17 weeks. This became a familiar pattern for the singer/songwriter, as every one of his '70s and early '80s albums failed to chart in the U.K. or U.S. while they racked up big sales in European and South American countries. Finally, de Burgh had an across-the-board success in 1986 with the languid ballad "The Lady in Red." The single became a number one hit in England (number three in America) and its accompanying album, *Into the Light*, reached number two in the U.K. de Burgh never hit the U.S. charts after 1988 and his commercial fortunes began to slide slightly in Britain in the early '90s, yet he retained a devoted following around the world. *—Stephen Thomas Erlewine*

Far Beyond These Castle Walls / 1975 / A&M ✦✦✦
On Chris de Burgh's debut album, his gentle, beguiling vocal style is introduced, which instantly trademarks him as a genuine master of the soft ballad. de Burgh's engaging dominance of words and lyrics carries both his love songs and his simple light rock tunes to a higher level, thanks to the attention and care given to each of his pieces. As an inaugural album, the songs hold well as they are delicately cushioned by his voice, but are substantially thin where melody or appealing choruses are concerned. Both "Windy Night" and "Watching the World" draw the most attention, bringing de Burgh's silkiness to the focal point. "Satin Green Shutters" beautifully illustrates his knack for sounding sincere and charismatic within the boundaries of a love song. What is most important about this album is the manner in which it reveals de Burgh as one of the finest mood-invoking artists ever. Even the last song, entitled "Goodnight," ends the album with his lush voice still hovering in the air once the music has finished. While the lyrics and recipe of the songs themselves come across as rather nimble compared to future releases, it is here that he lets his song styling make a name for himself. *—Mike DeGagne*

Spanish Train & Other Stories / 1976 / A&M ✦✦✦✦
Chris de Burgh's storytelling prowess comes into fruition on *Spanish Train and Other Stories* as he carefully grasps the listener's attention with his soft-spoken candor. With songs that are reminiscent of tales told to a young child by his bedside, de Burgh captivates his audience with his serene anecdotes that are enhanced by the music that envelops him. The opening "Spanish Train" is a mysterious yarn about a chess match between God and the Devil, where the victor inherits the soul of a dying train engineer. de Burgh's vocal escalation from serene to flamboyant makes this one of his best songs, as does the marvelous twist at the end of the story. "A Spaceman Came Travelling" has de Burgh blanketing his wispy voice in a tale about the birth of Jesus, only his version substitutes the Star of Bethlehem for an alien visitor who has arrived to reveal a startling message. With "Patricia the Stripper," de Burgh proves that his sense of humor has not escaped him, as the baroque melody and playful banter make this tune one of his most spirited. Both musically appealing and lyrically thought-provoking, it is this style of narrative that causes *Spanish Train* to be one of his best albums. Even the forlorn tone of the piano in "Lonely Sky" invokes sadness and melancholy with perfection, coupled with de Burgh's vacant air. All the songs on *Spanish Train* capture de Burgh's flair for singing elegant pieces that are sincerely attractive, all the while illustrating his pliable vocal stylishness. *—Mike DeGagne*

At the End of a Perfect Day / 1977 / A&M ✦✦✦

Crusader / 1979 / A&M ✦✦✦✦
The title track to 1979's *Crusader* is not only this album's crowning glory, but also serves as one of de Burgh's finest songs. Its narrative is based on the courageous efforts of Richard the Lion-Hearted and his spirited battle against Saladin, the king of the Saracens during the crusades that took part between the 11th and 13th centuries. Broken into four separate parts, its detailed story line and moving musical passages exemplify de Burgh's talent as an intriguing anecdotist. His seriousness and passion build the song until the very end of the "Finale," in which the moral of "Crusader" is revealed through his soft-spoken final words. Even though this track bears most of this album's weight, the rest of

the songs aren't without their merit. de Burgh still musters up enough romance to make "It's Such a Long Way Home" a likeable tune. The serenity and overall quaintness of "The Girl With April in Her Eyes" aptly display his gift of singing cobblestone courtyard love songs. These songs, along with "Quiet Moments," insure that his talent for singing gallant, gentle pieces has not escaped him. Although these songs house their own distinct beauty, this album's true value lies in "Crusader," his most moving and compelling work. —*Mike DeGagne*

Eastern Wind / 1980 / A&M ✦✦✦

● **The Getaway** / 1982 / A&M ✦✦✦✦

The Getaway gave Chris de Burgh his first charted single with "Don't Pay the Ferryman," which peaked at number 34 in 1983. A feverishly fast-paced tune, it contained vibrant keyboards and had de Burgh powerfully barking out the chorus in one of his most intense offerings. As his most spirited single up to that point, it proved that he could easily dish out a charging rock song that still harbored his enchanting brand of lyrics and mystery. Other songs carry this surging flow as well, like the flighty tempo of "The Getaway," kept together by its pop/rock stride, or the determination aching from de Burgh's voice throughout "Ship to Shore," which proves he can muster up some energy with barely any effort. de Burgh creates a tropical ambience with the calming flow of "Living in the Island" and returns to his charming form with "Crying and Laughing." *The Getaway* is made up of mostly edgier tunes from de Burgh this time around, which is a delightful transition from his usually mellow offerings. Although the odd love song creeps up here and there, they don't seem to tarnish the admirable course of the album. —*Mike DeGagne*

● **Man on the Line** / May 1984 / A&M ✦✦✦✦

The pop/rock power pent up in "High on Emotion" established the fact that Chris de Burgh could be just as energetic as he could be romantic. Its explosive chorus followed by some dynamic electric guitar riffs highlighted 1984's *Man on the Line*, making a rocker out of the usually complacent balladeer. Following suit, only with a little less vigor, is the title track that sparks a little bit of dramatic anger in de Burgh's voice. He hasn't left his mellifluous candor behind completely, though, but his slower pieces do seem to be a tad more hearty. "Sound of a Gun" deals with a civilian's outlook of living in a war-torn country, which has de Burgh singing in whispers at one point. His trademarked romantic style is brought back to life on "Head and the Heart," a gorgeous love song presented in true de Burgh fashion. The majority of the songs on *Man on the Line* are made up of catchy pop tunes, rounded out by his debonair vocal approach. Each track brandishes an early-'80s keyboard feel, resilient and bright, and quite fitting for the album's period. Its appeal still remains, and even though it isn't one of his best efforts, it does provide evidence that de Burgh could escape his stereotypical trademark as a one-dimensional artist. —*Mike DeGagne*

Into the Light / 1986 / A&M ✦✦✦

Into the Light contains Chris de Burgh's highest-charting single with the ballroom elegance of "Lady in Red," peaking at number three in 1987 and remaining on the Billboard charts for 14 weeks. This song, with it's sweeping romantic tempo and classy feel, is reminiscent of Eric Clapton's "Wonderful Tonight" as de Burgh's sincere flattery for his dame is exquisitely sung. Even his voice seems more pronounced, as it resonates and then lowers into a softer tone. Besides the hit single, much of the album remains lush and mellow in the style of de Burgh's usual ballads. On songs like "Last Night" and "Spirit of Man," his seriousness and honesty break through to showcase his passion for his work. Although the music on the album is slow paced, this doesn't take away from de Burgh's appealing blend of dignified lyrics and late-night sound. The flyaway chorus in "Saying Goodbye to It All" makes this song the second best on the album. Here, de Burgh sparks some energy with a slightly quicker stride than most of the album's material. Even "Fire in the Water" contains an attractive hitch of its own kind. While *Into the Light* may not be his best work, its lavish, posh feel sets it apart from much of his other slower recordings. —*Mike DeGagne*

Flying Colours / 1988 / A&M ✦✦✦

There really isn't any grandeur or magnificence tacked on to 1988's *Flying Colours* album, but that doesn't mean the songs themselves aren't without some worthiness. The album's atmosphere blends mild rock tunes with slower songs that rely on their demure appeal, helped by de Burgh's conservative musical style. Much like *Into the Light* but without the massiveness of "Lady in Red," the songs come off as more developed and mature sounding, especially in their combination of tempos and lyrics. The adventurous "Sailing Away," complete with gusty chorus and careless melody, makes for the album's greatest asset. Its airborne feel is much like that of "Say Goodbye to It All" or "High on Emotion," only with a lighter touch. "Missing You" and "Carry Me" fall within the boundaries of familiarity since they reflect de Burgh's knack for producing soft-centered love songs. Even "Night on the River" conjures up the romantic quiet of a moonlit evening through its faint charm and ease. Without the lure of a dominant single, *Flying Colours* remains as one of de Burgh's more typical sounding efforts, but is tainted somewhat by a lack of novel appeal. —*Mike DeGagne*

● **Spark to a Flame: The Very Best of Chris de Burgh** / Oct. 24, 1989 / A&M ✦✦✦✦✦

Covering all of his crucial eighties material, *Spark to a Flame: The Very Best of Chris de Burgh* offers up most of this songwriter's best work, while also including a few of his better pieces from early in his career. The decade took apt notice of de Burgh, giving him two Top 40 hits on Billboard with "Don't Pay the Ferryman" in 1983 and the hugely successful "Lady in Red" in 1987, which are both included on this set. Three of his most delightful narratives from the '70s show up here as well, with "Spanish Train," "A Spaceman Came Travelling," and "Patricia the Stripper," all from the highly regarded *Spanish Train and Other Stories* album. The asset of *Spark to a Flame* comes from the fact that de Burgh's best singles can be heard here without the other ho-hum material from their

respective albums getting in the way. For example, songs like "Sailing Away" and "Say Goodbye to It All" add value to this compilation, as they were easily their parent album's best material. His most explosive tune, "High on Emotion" from 1984's *Man on the Line* album, is another welcomed addition, as is the refined fervor of "Ship to Shore" from *The Getaway*. Even though "Crusader" is nearly nine minutes in length, its addition to this compilation would have raised its stakes, as it's one of his best story songs. Although many of his amiable ballads and love songs from his early albums didn't make their way to this set, *Spark to a Flame* still stands as a suitable best-of. If owned, so should 1981's *Best Moves* for a greater cross-section of de Burgh's illustrious career. —*Mike DeGagne*

● **Lady in Red: Very Best of Chris de Burgh** / 1991 / A&M ✦✦✦✦✦

Chris de Burgh is rightly described as a "songwriter's songwriter," and this new collection shows why. The 16 selections on *Lady in Red* showcase de Burgh's immaculate pop instincts. Ranging from epic Elton John-esque ballad statements such as the title track and "Here Is Your Paradise" to sprightly pop/rockers like "Don't Pay the Ferryman," de Burgh's elegant touch is truly a wondrous thing to discover. The collection is also buttressed by an unreleased composition, "There's a New Star in Heaven Tonight," which is a fitting and loving tribute to Lady Diana. —*Matthew Greenwald*

Joey Dee

b. Jun. 11, 1940, Passaic, NJ

Vocals / Rock & Roll

Joey Dee led the house band at New York's Peppermint Lounge, immortalizing the joint in his 1961 chart-topper "Peppermint Twist." Born Joseph DiNicola in Passaic, NJ, Dee teamed with veteran producer Henry Glover to cut "Peppermint Twist" for Roulette, and the huge hit led to a starring role in the film *Hey, Let's Twist*. Most of Dee's hits, including a supercharged revival of the Isley Brothers hit "Shout" in 1962, were firmly in the Twist mode, although he took a successful stab at a softer sound that year with a Johnny Nash tune, "What Kind of Love Is This." Dee gave several future stars early breaks with the Starliters, notably the Ronettes, three-quarters of the Young Rascals, and Jimi Hendrix. Dee is still active on the oldies circuit. —*Bill Dahl*

● **Best of Joey Dee and the Starliters: Hey Let's Twist** / Jun. 1990 / Rhino ✦✦✦✦✦

While Dee is generally looked upon as the quaint bearer of the twist to a mass audience (clean covers of R&B tunes palatable to White audiences), the truth is that Dee had a racially integrated band (in 1961, no less) that not only delivered the goods, but put some high voltage energy into the tunes as well. Although this 18-track compilation brings together all the chart hits ("Peppermint Twist," "Shout," "Everytime," "What Kind Of Love Is This," "I Lost My Baby," "Dance, Dance, Dance") from Dee and the Starliters' brief run for the gold, it omits several barn-burning covers from the second live album and opts for the edited 'part one' version of "Shout" as opposed to the six-minute-plus workout that's on the *Doin' the Twist* album. That said, it's still a wonderful introduction to the music of this seldom-lauded rock & roll pioneer. —*Cub Koda*

Starbright / Sep. 28, 1999 / West Side ✦✦✦✦

A two disc collection of all the group's Roulette singles, A and B sides, all the subsequent Jubilee singles and the rare 1966 album, *Hitsville*. Rounding out the rarities are both sides of a single sung in German and a premium record available from Vaseline Hair Tonic, the spoken word "Joey Dee Teaches You How To Dance The Authentic Peppermint Twist," one of the more surreal exercises in rock & roll history. —*Cub Koda*

Deee-Lite

f. 1986, New York, NY, db. 1996

Club/Dance, House, Dance-Pop

With the massive popularity of their hit single "Groove Is in the Heart," Deee-Lite brought the colorful sights and sounds of New York's club culture into the mainstream. Formed in 1986, the group comprised vocalist Lady Miss Kier, Super DJ Dmitry and Jungle DJ Towa Towa; fusing house, techno, rap, ambient and funk music with an outrageous visual flair largely influenced by the drag-queen community, Deee-Lite became hugely popular among New York club denizens, and the trio's own unique cultural make-up earned them a following which ignored racial and sexual boundaries. In 1990, they debuted with the album *World Clique*, a crossover smash thanks to hits like the loping classic "Groove Is in the Heart" and "Power of Love." With their 1992 follow-up *Infinity Within*, Deee-Lite's music turned overtly political; Towa Towa left the group soon after, and rechristened Towa Tei, he released his solo debut *Future Listening* in 1995. Kier and Dmitry, meanwhile, enlisted DJ Ani for 1994's *Dewdrops in the Garden*, a sensual outing influenced by the growing rave culture. After the release of 1996's remix album *Sampladelic Relics and Dancefloor Oddities*, Deee-Lite disbanded. —*Jason Ankeny*

● **World Clique** / Aug. 1990 / Elektra ✦✦✦✦✦

Its reputation may rest on only one hit single—but what a hit. "Groove Is in the Heart" defined the summer of 1990 on radio and MTV with its delicious combination of funk, modern dance sheen, and Lady Miss Kier's smart, sharp diva ways. Add in guest vocals and bass from Bootsy Collins (a pity his hilarious video cameo wasn't represented here), brass from the original Horny Horns duo of Fred Wesley and Maceo Parker, and a smooth mid-song rap from A Tribe Called Quest's Q-Tip, and the results sounded good then and now. The rest of *World Clique* offers variations on the song's theme, with Kier's sweet, light vocals and DJs Dimitri and Towa Tei making it work in various ways. It's still a bit surprising that Kier didn't go on to greater fame on her own, because she definitely has not merely the pipes but the personality to carry something on her own—compared to the dog-whistle vocal calisthenics of someone like Mariah Carey, there's no contest. Check out her work on songs like "Good Beat" and the amusing sass of such numbers as "Try Me on, I'm Very You." The two musicians come up with a seamless, adept flow throughout, merrily raiding whatever they so choose in the past for their own purposes. Disco is the heart of it all, with everything from hip-hop breaks to bubble-salsa piano—even early Depeche Mode!—taking a bow; hints of the future genre-mashing Towa Tei would make his own trademark are already plentiful. Bootsy and the Horny Horns crop up at other points as well, adding just enough classic funk to blend with the crisper electronic pulses and arrangements. *—Ned Raggett*

Infinity Within / Jun. 23, 1992 / Elektra ✦✦✦
Infinity Within is Deee-Lite's difficult second album. The group's social activism overtakes their instinctive infectiousness, producing well-intentioned but not especially memorable tracks like "I Had a Dream I Was Falling Through a Hole in the Ozone Layer" and "Rubber Lover." *—Heather Phares*

Dewdrops in the Garden / Aug. 2, 1994 / Elektra ✦✦✦✦
Dewdrops in the Garden sees DJ Towa Tei take a vacation from the band, replaced with DJ On-E—just one of the album's not-so-subtle rave references. The tracks on *Dewdrops in the Garden* are either pseudo-rave instrumentals or witty, funky showcases for Lady Kier's rich vocals. While it's somewhat inconsistent, songs like "Apple Juice Kissin'," "Picnic in the Summertime" and "Call Me" radiate with the group's innate charisma. *—Heather Phares*

Sampladelic Relics & Dancefloor Oddities / Oct. 29, 1996 / Elektra ✦✦✦
Something of a B-sides, remixes, and greatest-hits collection all in one, *Sampladelic* feels unfortunately less like a real career celebration and more like a hastily assembled package done at label behest. DJ Dmitry assembled the album, but the fact that most of the remixes collected were done in the year of its appearance makes it seem like one of the endless collection of mix collections on Cleopatra done solely for money. The end result is patchy at best, more of a sampler for other mixers and DJs than for the band (and the occasional inclusion of drum'n'bass loops smacks more of attempts to make the band more "relevant" for the mid-'90s). The musical fusions that helped to make the band stand out in the first place are de-emphasized in favor of a variety of various house and techno approaches straight up, rather than intermingling in true Deee-Lite style. Lady Miss Kier, meanwhile, gets some spotlight moments here and there but otherwise is in usual remix style reduced to a few lines here and there per song. She does get some a cappella between some tracks, which is quite cool but not quite enough. Taken on its own terms, though, there's some fine stuff floating around. When Dmitry tackles things himself, whether via the old "Sampladelic" mixes with the full group or in his new partnership with DJ Silver, the results are often spirited, as the just-experimental-enough tweaking of "D.M.T." and an original remix of "Groove Is in the Heart" shows. As for the outsiders, Hani's deep, moody crawl on "Say Ahh..." is a winner, high-pitched tones and a low, murky synth crunch snaking through the mix, while Carl Cox's crisp take on "Heart Be Still" and Todd Terry's in-your-face house bounce for "Bittersweet Loving" are also worth a listen. *—Ned Raggett*

Deep Purple

f. 1968, Hertford, England
British Metal, Arena Rock, Heavy Metal, British Invasion, Hard Rock
Deep Purple survived a seemingly endless series of lineup changes and a dramatic mid-career shift from grandiose progressive rock to ear-shattering heavy metal to emerge as a true institution of the British hard rock community. The group, first assembled as a session band, fused rock and classical elements on their early LPs, though guitarist Ritchie Blackmore soon took creative control of the band, steering it towards a heavier, guitar-dominated approach. Deep Purple's most enduring hit, the AOR staple "Smoke on the Water," featured on the 1972 multi-platinum classic *Machine Head*, positioned the group among rock's elite.

Long-simmering creative differences soon pushed vocalist Ian Gillan and bassist Roger Glover out of the band, the former replaced by David Coverdale. After completing 1974's *Stormbringer*, Blackmore himself left (to form Rainbow) and was replaced by Tommy Bolin. Following a 1976 tour, the group completely dissolved, with Coverdale going on to form Whitesnake and Bolin dying from a drug overdose later in the year. Most of the classic line-up reunited in 1984 for the platinum smash *Perfect Strangers*, and though Gillan again exited the group, he returned for 1992's *The Battle Rages On...* Blackmore quit the group next, replaced temporarily by Joe Satriani and later by Steve Morse. The revitalized group returned to the studio for 1996's *Purpendicular*, which proved a success among the Purple faithful. *—Jason Ankeny*

Shades of Deep Purple / 1968 / Spitfire ✦✦✦✦
This is worthwhile mainly for their psychezilla cover of Joe South's "Hush," which pits Ritchie Blackmore's flame-throwing guitar bursts against Jon Lord's chugging organ. *—Tom Graves*

Concerto for Group and Orchestra / 1969 / Warner Brothers ✦✦✦
Back in 1970, it seemed as though any British group that could was starting to utilize classical elements in their work—for some, like ELP, that meant quoting from the classics as often and loudly as possible, while for others, like Yes, it meant incorporating classical structures into their albums and songs. Deep Purple, at the behest of keyboardman Jon Lord, fell briefly into the camp of this offshoot of early progressive rock with the *Concerto for Group and Orchestra*. For most fans, the album represented the nadir of the classic (i.e., post-Rod Evans) group: minutes of orchestral meandering lead into some perfectly good hard rock jamming by the band, but the trip is almost not worth the effort. Ritchie Blackmore sounds great and plays his heart out, and you can tell this band is going to go somewhere, just by virtue of the energy that they put into these extended pieces. The classical influences mostly seem drawn from movie music composers Dimitri Tiomkin and Franz Waxman (and Elmer Bernstein), with some nods to Rachmaninoff, Sibelius, and Mahler, and they rather just lay there. Buried in the middle of the second movement is a perfectly good song, but you've got to get to it through eight minutes of orchestral noodling on either side. The third movement is almost bracing enough to make up for the flaws of the other two, though by itself, it wouldn't make the CD worthwhile—Pink Floyd proved far more adept at mixing group and orchestra, and making long, slow, lugubrious pieces interesting. As a bonus, however, the producers have added a pair of hard rock numbers by the group alone, "Wring That Neck" and "Child in Time," that were played at the same concert. They and the third movement of the established piece make this worth a listen. *—Bruce Eder*

The Book of Taliesyn / 1969 / Spitfire ✦✦✦
A year after the innovative remake of "You Keep Me Hanging On," England's answer to the Vanilla Fudge was this early version of Deep Purple, which featured vocalist Rod Evans, and bassist Nicky Simper, along with mainstays Ritchie Blackmore, Jon Lord, and Ian Paice. Also like Vanilla Fudge, the group's own originals were creative, thought provoking, but not nearly as interesting as their take on cover tunes. The Fudge did "Eleanor Rigby," and Deep Purple respond by going inside "We Can Work It Out"—it falls out of nowhere after the progressive rock jam "Exposition," Ritchie Blackmore's leads zipping in between Rod Evans smooth and precise vocals. As Vanilla Fudge was progressive leaning more towards psychedelic, here Deep Purple are the reverse. Originals "The Shield" and "Anthem" make early Syd Barrett Pink Floyd appear punk in comparison. Novel sounds are aided by Lord's dominating keyboards, a signature of this group. Though "The Anthem" is more intriguing than the heavy metal thunder of *Machine Head*, it is overwhelmed by the majesty of their "River Deep, Mountain High" cover, definitely not the inspiration for the Supremes and Four Tops 1971 hit version. By the time 1972 came around, Deep Purple immersed themselves in dumb lyrics, unforgettable riffs, and a huge presence, much like Black Sabbath. The evolution from progressive to hard rock was complete, but a combination of what they did here—words that mattered matched by innovative musical passages, would have been a more pleasing combination. *—Joe Viglione*

Deep Purple in Rock / 1970 / Warner Brothers ✦✦✦✦✦
After satisfying all of their classical music kinks with keyboard player Jon Lord's overblown *Concerto for Group and Orchestra*, Deep Purple's soon-to-be classic Mark II lineup made their proper debut on 1970's awesome *In Rock*. The cacophony of sound (led by Ritchie Blackmore's blistering guitar solo), which introduces the opener "Speed King," makes it immediately obvious that the band is no longer fooling around. The slightly less intense "Bloodsucker" allows for some breathing room before the band embarks on the album's epic, ten-minute tour de force "Child in Time." In what is arguably his greatest performance, singer Ian Gillan leads the band on a series of crescendos, from the song's gentle beginning through to its ear-shattering climax, and back again to an even more intense encore. With searing power chords, "Flight of the Rat" is another example of the band's new hard-rock stance; though at nearly eight minutes, it too finds room for some extended soloing from Blackmore and Lord. "Into the Fire" and "Living Wreck" are more concise but equally appealing, and despite the closer "Hard Lovin' Man," which waffles on a bit before descending into feedback, this is still an essential album. *—Ed Rivadavia*

Fireball / 1971 / Warner Brothers ✦✦✦✦✦
One of Deep Purple's three essential albums, 1971's *Fireball* finds the band taking the no-holds-barred, hard-rock direction of the previous year's *In Rock* to new creative heights. Metal machine noises introduce the sizzling title track, which is an explosively tight group effort with Jon Lord's organ truly shining. The somewhat repetitive "No No No" threatens to drop the ball, but the fantastic "Strange Kind of Woman" picks things up again. The innuendo-encrusted hilarity of "Anyone's Daughter" features one of singer Ian Gillan's best lyrics, and guitarist Ritchie Blackmore shows his range with one of his most uncharacteristic, bluesier performances. "The Mule" is perhaps the band's finest instrumental and they flirt with progressive rock on "Fools," which probably could have been done without the rather boring, drawn-out middle section. Closing the album is the exceptional "No One Came," which sounds so fresh that its plausible that the band improvised it on the spot. Their intertwining instrumental lines lock together beautifully, and Gillan weaves a comic, semi-autobiographical story that is equal parts rooted in fact and *Monty Python*. *—Ed Rivadavia*

★ **Machine Head** / 1972 / Warner Brothers ✦✦✦✦✦
Led Zeppelin's fourth album, Black Sabbath's *Paranoid*, and Deep Purple's *Machine Head* stand as the Holy Trinity of English hard rock. These recordings provide the blueprint followed by virtually every heavy rock & roll band since the mid-'70s. Though probably the least celebrated of the three, *Machine Head* contains the mother of all guitar riffs in "Smoke on the Water," a song that needs no further explanation. The album also features the classic "Highway Star," which epitomizes all of Deep Purple's intensity and versatility, while featuring perhaps the greatest soloing duel ever between guitarist Ritchie Blackmore and organist Jon Lord. Also in top form is singer Ian Gillan (simply one of the finest singers of his generation, bar none), who explodes with amazing power and range throughout. Gillan lets the band take over on the largely instrumental "Lazy," which would evolve into an incredible live jam. The plodding shuffle of "Maybe I'm a Leo" shows some signs of age, but "Pictures of Home" and "Never Before" remain vital, displaying Purple at their melodic best. Another tremendous Blackmore riff drives the marvelous "Space Truckin'," a fitting end to one of the essential hard-rock albums of all time. *—Ed Rivadavia*

Purple Passages / 1972 / Warner Brothers ✦✦

☆ **Made in Japan** / Dec. 1972 / Warner Brothers ✦✦✦✦✦
Recorded over three nights in August 1972, Deep Purple's *Made in Japan* was the record that brought the band to headliner status in the U.S. and elsewhere, and it remains a landmark in the history of heavy metal music. Since reorganizing with singer Ian Gillan and

bassist Roger Glover in 1969, Deep Purple had recorded three important albums—*Deep Purple in Rock*, *Fireball*, and *Machine Head*—and used the material to build a fierce live show. *Made in Japan*, its selections drawn from those albums, documented that show, in which songs were drawn out to ten and even nearly 20 minutes with no less intensity, as guitarist Ritchie Blackmore and organist Jon Lord soloed extensively and Gillan sang in a screech that became the envy of all metal bands to follow. The signature song, of course, was "Smoke on the Water," with its memorable riff, which went on to become an American hit single. But those extended workouts, particularly the moody "Child in Time," with Gillan's haunting falsetto wail and Blackmore's amazingly fast playing, and "Space Truckin'," with Lord's organ effects, maintained the onslaught, making this a definitive treatment of the band's catalog and its most impressive album. By stretching out and going to extremes, Deep Purple pushed its music into the kind of deliberate excess that made heavy metal what it became, and their audience recognized the breakthrough, propelling the original double LP into the U.S. Top Ten and sales over a million copies. On November 17, 1998, Warner Archives/Rhino issued "the remastered edition" of the album, a two-CD set that added more than 20 minutes of encores on a second disc that contained "Black Night," previously released only as a European B-side, and versions of "Speed King" and Little Richard's "Lucille" that were previously unreleased. *—William Ruhlmann*

Who Do We Think We Are / Jan. 1973 / Warner Brothers ✦✦

Burn / 1974 / Warner Brothers ✦✦✦
The departure of vocalist Ian Gillan and bassist Roger Glover seemed to rejuvenate Deep Purple, and 1974's *Burn* was a huge improvement over their previous effort, the lackluster *Who Do We Think We Are*. In an interesting twist, new recruits David Coverdale and ex-Trapeze bassist Glenn Hughes share lead vocals on virtually every track—an enviable tag team, as both possessed exceptional pipes. The title track starts things off at full speed thanks to the phenomenal drumming of Ian Paice, and the intro to "Might Just Take Your Life" is one of organist Jon Lord's finest moments. Full of starts and stops, "Lay Down, Stay Down" features a fantastic solo from guitarist Ritchie Blackmore, who, as usual, serves as the band's primal force. "What's Going On Here" is about as good a single as Purple ever wrote; "You Fool No One" is compelling in its intensity; and the funky "Sail Away" is a sign of the band's future direction. "Mistreated," a fantastic slow blues, closes the album proper (let's ignore the boring instrumental "A 200," the record's only throwaway) and showcases Coverdale on his own for the first time. So impassioned is the singer's performance that the song would remain his concert trademark long into his post-Purple career with Whitesnake. *—Ed Rivadavia*

Stormbringer / 1974 / Warner Brothers ✦✦
Stormbringer falls short of the excellence of *Machine Head* and *Who Do We Think We Are*, but nonetheless boasts some definite classics—including the fiery "Lady Double Dealer," the ominous title song (a Gothic-metal treasure), the sweaty "High Ball Shooter" and the melancholy ballad "Soldier of Fortune." Most of the other songs on the decent, if uneven, *Stormbringer* (which Metal Blade reissued on CD in the early '90s) are not essential. Like *Come Taste the Band*, *Stormbringer* will be of interest to Purple's more enthusiastic fans rather than casual listeners, who would be much better off starting out with either of the above-mentioned studio projects or the live *Made in Japan*. *—Alex Henderson*

Come Taste the Band / 1975 / Warner Brothers ✦✦✦
When Ritchie Blackmore departed Deep Purple in the mid-'70s and formed Elf (which evolved into Blackmore's Rainbow and featured Ronnie James Dio), his replacement was Tommy Bolin. To be sure, Blackmore was a darn tough act to follow, but Bolin proved himself to be a fine guitarist in his own right on *Come Taste The Band*, his first album with Purple. But unfortunately, Bolin didn't have exceptional material to work with—decent and likable, but hardly exceptional. While sweaty yet melodic cuts like "Dealer," "Lady Luck" and "You Keep On Moving" are far from bad, nothing here is in a class with "Smoke On The Water" or "Highway Star." Purple's more hardcore devotees will want this album (reissued on CD in the early 1990s), though it's far from the best representation of their '70s work. *—Alex Henderson*

Made in Europe / 1976 / Warner Brothers ✦✦✦
This live recording, made in 1975, comes from Ritchie Blackmore's last three concerts with the band before leaving to form Rainbow. It features Purple's Mark III, with David Coverdale on vocals and Glenn Hughes on bass and vocals. Coverdale is a convincing hard rock singer, though he lacks the winning quirkiness of Ian Gillan, while Hughes is a busier and more up-front player than Roger Glover. While "Burn" and "Mistreated" are worthy successors to the previous Purple, the remaining material is weaker, and overall, this stuff is definitely a couple of notches below the glory days of *Made in Japan*. But Blackmore, for his swan song, still manages to inject a good deal of excitement, and his invention and fire raise the proceedings up somewhat. *—Stephen Raiteri*

When We Rock, We Rock & When We Roll, We Roll / 1978 / Warner Brothers ✦✦✦✦✦
When We Rock, We Rock & When We Roll, We Roll is a solid, if incomplete collection from their 1968-1974 peak years. *—Dan Heilman*

Perfect Strangers / 1984 / Mercury ✦✦

The House of Blue Light / 1987 / Mercury ✦✦✦
Though it was considered a disappointment upon its release (indeed, its production was much too sleek at times and it lacked the creative daring of *Perfect Strangers*), 1987's *House of Blue Light* has actually stood the test of time just as well, if not better than its predecessor. The second effort from the re-formed Mark II lineup, this album showed Deep Purple searching for an '80s-flavored hit single, and by doing so, sounding uncomfortably similar to guitarist Ritchie Blackmore's other band, Rainbow. Virtually all of the record's first half suffers from this (especially "Unwritten Law" and "Bad Attitude"), but things improve with the eastern-flavored melodies of "The Spanish Archer" and "Strange Ways." The eerie sound textures explored on the latter evoke memories of classic Purple and finally allow some space for soloing from Blackmore and keyboardist Jon Lord. And the telltale lyrics to the equally interesting "Mitzi Dupree" (based on a true story) are vintage Ian Gillan, as the singer combines James Bond-style international intrigue with high comedy. *—Ed Rivadavia*

Nobody's Perfect / 1988 / Mercury ✦✦

Knocking at Your Back Door: The Best Of Deep Purple in the 80's / 1992 / Mercury ✦✦
Knocking at Your Back Door may be inconsistent and unsatisfying, but that's an accurate reflection of the group's career during the decade. Even though it's fitfully entertaining, *Best Of* features all of the highlights the group recorded during the '80s and it's preferable to the albums they released during the era. *—Stephen Thomas Erlewine*

Archive Alive / May 20, 1997 / Archive/Navarre ✦✦✦
Archive Alive is a double-disc set of previously unreleased live material from Deep Purple, including a complete concert from the group's peak period in the mid-'70s. In addition to the full concert, there's a selection of bonus tracks, and taken together, the set offers a good portrait of Deep Purple live on stage, making it a nice addition to the serious collector's library. *—Stephen Thomas Erlewine*

Machine Head 25th Anniversary Edition / 1998 / Warner Archives/Rhino ✦✦✦✦✦
Disc one of this two-disc 25th anniversary edition of *Machine Head* contains an excellent remaster of this classic album: heavy, hard-hitting, and historic Purple with some of their best-known songs, including the rousing "Highway Star," the mega-famous "Smoke on the Water" and overlooked gems like "Pictures of Home." Also included is the non-LP B-side "When a Blind Man Cries" (a sad song featuring an exquisite Ritchie Blackmore solo) and two alternate mixes from the quadraphonic version of the album. As if that weren't enough, disc two cranks things up yet another notch (to 12?) with a stunning new remix of the entire album (and "When a Blind Man Cries") by bassist Roger Glover, restoring lost intros and outros—including alternate guitar solos—and giving a whole new life to every song. Excellent liner notes, courtesy of Glover and Purple archivist extraordinaire Simon Robinson, only add to the appeal of a package already almost irresistible to fans of '70s hard rock. *—Stephen Raiteri*

Shades 1968-1998 / Mar. 16, 1999 / Rhino ✦✦✦✦✦
A lot of care went into the track selection and mastering on this four-CD set, devoted to 30 years in the history of Deep Purple—though for most listeners, discs one through three, devoted to the band's first eight years, are what will really count. Deep Purple recorded significant bodies of work in several styles, but the years 1968 through 1974, when they evolved out of psychedelia and into heavy metal, are the vitally important ones. The first disc is a treat not only for Deep Purple fans but '60s British rock completists, highlighted by two previously unissued tracks dating from a time when the band was apparently still known officially as Roundabout.

The band's chart singles and a beautifully lyrical and reflective version of the Beatles' "Help" open the first disk, and it's hard not to love those early singles. And then comes "Hallelujah (I Am the Preacher)," which opens the group's classic heavy metal era and heralds the arrival of Ian Gillan on lead vocals and Roger Glover on bass. From there on, and for most of the next two-and-a-half CDs, this set threatens to fry any speakers or ears in its presence. Disc two is from the core of the group's prime years, from the spring of 1971 through the end of that year. The *Fireball* and *Machine Head* albums are well represented, and some of this music is surprisingly durable. Disc three covers the peak years, closing out in 1975 at the end of the Tommy Bolin/Glenn Hughes lineup, and disc four picks up with the 1984 reunion. The packaging is slightly awkward, but it comes with a 55-page booklet giving just about the fullest easily available account of the band's impact and importance. *—Bruce Eder*

• **The Very Best of Deep Purple** / May 9, 2000 / Rhino ✦✦✦✦✦
The Very Best of Deep Purple collects 15 live performances, singles, and album tracks from the group's inception in 1968 to 1984, when the Mark II lineup (featuring vocalist Ian Gillan) reunited. Hits like "Hush," "Smoke on the Water," "Woman From Tokyo," "Kentucky Woman," and "Knocking at Your Backdoor" anchor the set, while "Black Night," "Demon's Eye," "Burn," and other staples of Deep Purple's body of work add depth to the collection. Designed to complement, not compete with, the four-disc box set *Shades (1968-1998)* that Rhino released in 1999, *The Very Best of Deep Purple* gathers the definitive tracks from one of hard rock and heavy metal's most popular and influential bands. *—Heather Phares*

Def Leppard

f. 1977, Sheffield, Yorkshire, England

New Wave of British Heavy Metal, Pop-Metal, Hair Metal, Heavy Metal, Pop/Rock, Hard Rock, British Metal

Def Leppard, in many ways, was the definitive hard rock band of the '80s. There were many bands that rocked harder, and were more dangerous, than the Sheffield quintet, but few others captured the spirit of the times quite as well. Emerging in the late '70s as part of the New Wave of British Heavy Metal, the group actually owed more to the glam-rock and metal of the early '70s—their sound was equal parts T. Rex, Mott the Hoople, Queen and Led Zeppelin. By toning down their heavy riffs and emphasizing melody, Def Leppard were poised for crossover success by 1983's *Pyromania*, but skillfully used the fledgling MTV network to their advantage. The group was already blessed with photogenic good looks, but they also crafted a series of innovative, exciting videos, which made them into stars. They intended to follow *Pyromania* quickly, but were derailed when their drummer lost an arm in a car accident, the first of many problems that plagued the group's career. Def Leppard managed to pull through such tragedies and they even expanded their large audience with 1987's blockbuster *Hysteria*. As the '90s began, mainstream hard rock shifted away from Leppard's signature pop-metal and towards edgier, louder bands, yet the group maintained a sizable audience into the late '90s and were one of only a handful of '80s metal groups to survive the decade more or less intact. —*Stephen Thomas Erlewine*

On Through the Night / 1980 / Mercury ✦✦✦
On Through the Night, Def Leppard's debut album, established the band as one of the leading lights of the New Wave of British Heavy Metal. While possessing the tight, controlled attack of comrades Judas Priest and Iron Maiden, Def Leppard was uninterested in the fantastic, menacing, and sometimes gothic themes of those bands; instead, *On Through the Night* is a collection of working-class hard rock anthems informed by the big, glittering hooks of glam-rock. It may lack the detailed production and more pop-oriented songwriting of later efforts, but it's also arguably their heaviest album, and some Leppard fans prefer this sound. —*Steve Huey*

High 'n' Dry / 1981 / Mercury ✦✦✦
Def Leppard's second album, *High 'N' Dry*, continues in the vein of the anthemic, working-class hard rock of their debut. While still opting for a controlled musical attack and melodies as big-sounding and stadium-ready as possible, the band opens up its arrangements a bit more on *High 'N' Dry*, letting the songs breathe and groove, and the rhythm section and guitar riffs play off one another. MTV helped break the album in the U.S. with its heavy rotation of the video for the unabashedly dramatic rock ballad "Bringin' On the Heartbreak." —*Steve Huey*

☆ **Pyromania** / 1983 / Mercury ✦✦✦✦✦
While Def Leppard had obviously wanted to write big-sounding anthems on their previous records, *Pyromania* was where the band's vision coalesced and jelled into something more. More than ever before, the band's songs on *Pyromania* are driven by catchy, shiny melodic hooks instead of heavy guitar riffs, although the latter do pop up once in a while. But it wasn't just this newly intensified focus on melody and consistent songwriting (and heavy MTV exposure) that made *Pyromania* a massive success and the catalyst for the '80s pop-metal movement; Robert John "Mutt" Lange's buffed-to-a-sheen production—polished drum and guitar sounds, multi-tracked layers of vocal harmonies, a general sanding of any and all musical rough edges, and a perfectionistic attention to detail—set the style for much of the melodic hard rock that followed. It wasn't a raw or spontaneous sound, but the performances were still energetic and committed. Leppard's quest for huge, transcendent hard rock perfection on *Pyromania* was surprisingly successful; their reach never exceeded their grasp, which makes the album an enduring (and massively influential) classic. —*Steve Huey*

☆ **Hysteria** / 1987 / Mercury ✦✦✦✦✦
Where *Pyromania* had set the standard for polished, catchy pop-metal, *Hysteria* only upped the ante. *Pyromania*'s slick, layered Mutt Lange production turned into a painstaking obsession with dense sonic detail on *Hysteria*, with the result that some critics dismissed the record as a stiff, mechanized pop sell-out (perhaps due in part to Rick Allen's new, partially electronic drum kit). But Leppard's music had always employed big, anthemic hooks, and few of the pop-metal bands who had hit the charts in the wake of *Pyromania* could compete with Leppard's sense of craft; certainly none had the pop songwriting savvy to produce seven chart singles from the same album, as the stunningly consistent *Hysteria* did. Joe Elliott's lyrics owe an obvious debt to his obsession with T. Rex, particularly on the playfully silly anthem "Pour Some Sugar On Me" and the British glam-rock tribute "Rocket," while power ballads like "Love Bites" and the title track lack the histrionics or gooey sentimentality of many similar offerings. The strong pop hooks and "perfect"-sounding production of *Hysteria* may not appeal to diehard heavy metal fans, but it isn't heavy metal—it's pop-metal, and arguably the best pop-metal ever recorded. Its blockbuster success helped pave the way for a whole new second wave of hair-metal bands, while proving that the late-'80s musical climate could also be very friendly to veteran hard rock acts, a lead many would follow in the next few years. —*Steve Huey*

Adrenalize / Dec. 24, 1992 / Mercury ✦✦✦
After two straight blockbusters that delivered the goods both musically and commercially, anticipation ran high for Def Leppard's follow-up to *Hysteria*, in spite of the tragic death of guitarist Steve Clark. Unfortunately, *Adrenalize* sounds somewhat tired, formulaic, and bland, qualities absent from the band's best pop-metal work. Perhaps somewhat understandably, Leppard doesn't sound like its heart is really in the party anthems, and their ballads sound more calculated and generic. But most of all, the songs don't really have the effortlessly anthemic feel Leppard achieved so well on its past two albums, even though they try mightily. *Adrenalize* is competent, workmanlike, and impeccably produced, but not much more. —*Steve Huey*

Retro Active / Oct. 5, 1993 / Mercury ✦✦✦
Retro Active is a collection of outtakes and leftovers spanning Def Leppard's entire career. Kicking off the disc, "Desert Song" and "Fractured Love" are two of its most distinctive tracks, harkening back to the band's early (pre-success) days with their rough power chords. After paying homage to some of their heroes with a set of covers (Sweet's "Action" and Mick Ronson's "Only After Dark"), the band tackles a couple of solid, but hardly groundbreaking ballads—"Two Steps Behind" and "Miss You in a Heartbeat"—before stretching out (with mixed results) on the folky "From the Inside." Taken from the *Hysteria* sessions, the classy "I Wanna be Your Hero" is another pleasant surprise, and the band reaches all the way back to the beginning by re-recording their first demo "Ride into the Sun." Overall, this is an interesting release which marks the end of a long chapter in the band's history, following the death of guitarist and guiding force Steve Clarke. While

casual fans might find it confusing, Leppard fanatics will revel in its diversity and informative liner notes. —*Ed Rivadavia*

● **Vault: Def Leppard's Greatest Hits** / Oct. 31, 1995 / Mercury ✦✦✦✦✦
Def Leppard was untouchable in the '80s. Over the course of four albums, the band established themselves as one of the best and most popular hard-rock/heavy-metal groups of the decade, scoring a long list of hit singles. *Vault: Def Leppard's Greatest Hits—1980-1995* compiles the biggest of those hits, as well as selections from their first album of the '90s, *Adrenalize*, and the outtakes collection *Retro Active*. Essentially, Def Leppard's legacy rests on two albums, 1983's *Pyromania* and 1987's *Hysteria*. On both records, the group created a sleek, shiny brand of hard rock powered by huge, catchy melodies and guitar hooks that owed more to Mott the Hoople and T. Rex than Deep Purple and Black Sabbath. It was a polished but potent sound, whether the band turned out rockers ("Photograph," "Rocket") or ballads ("Bringin' on the Heartbreak," "Love Bites"). *Vault* has all of the necessary items, from "Pour Some Sugar On Me" to "Rock of Ages." It's not a perfect collection—it's not sequenced chronologically, it includes too much material from *Adrenalize*, and the new "When Love & Hate Collide" is simply average—but that doesn't stop *Vault* from being a great greatest hits collection. —*Stephen Thomas Erlewine*

Slang / May 14, 1996 / Mercury ✦✦✦
After the lackluster performance of *Adrenalize*, Def Leppard realized it was time to abandon their trademark wall-of-guitars sound. Jettisoning producer Mutt Lange—who, admittedly, was busy producing his wife, country singer Shania Twain—the group stripped their sound to the basics for *Slang*. There are very few layers-of-guitar effects on the album, just straight, crunching chords. Most notably, Rick Allen has returned to playing acoustic drums after playing an electronic kit for nearly a decade. The change in approach is apparent and welcome—Def Leppard hasn't sounded so immediate since *Pyromania*. Furthermore, they decided to expand their musical vocabulary slightly, working in elements of R&B and funk into the rhythms. Not all of the experiments work, but Def Leppard sounds revitalized, particularly when they attack a straightforward rocker. *Slang* would have been even better if they had come up with a set of hooks that sounded as alive as their performance, but the album is a much-needed return to form for the group. —*Stephen Thomas Erlewine*

Euphoria / Jun. 8, 1999 / Mercury ✦✦✦✦
Even though *Slang* successfully revitalized Def Leppard, it didn't become a huge hit, which was a disappointment, considering that the band adjusted their sound to fit the times. Taking that into account, Def Leppard set out to make a classic Def Leppard album with *Slang*'s successor, *Euphoria*. And, surprisingly, that's exactly what they've delivered. From the outset, it's clear that *Euphoria* finds the band returning to the glam-inflected, unabashedly catchy, arena-ready pop-metal that made them stars—and it's also clear that they're not concerned with having a hit, they just want to make a good record. For them, that means returning to the pop-metal formula that made *Pyromania* and *Hysteria* blockbusters, even if they must know that this signature sound no longer guarantees a hit at the close of the '90s. It is true that this approach means *Euphoria* sounds out of time in 1999, but it's a tight, attractive album with more than its share of big hooks, strong riffs, and memorable melodies. There are a couple of slow moments here and there, but no more than those on *Hysteria*, and the best songs (particularly the opening triptych of "Demoltion Man," "Promises," "Back in Your Face," plus the jangly Beatles-esque "21st Century Sha-La-La Girl") are worthy additions to an already strong catalog. But what's best about *Euphoria* is that it's utterly not self-conscious. Def Leppard feels free to try straight pop, appropriate Gary Glitter riffs, or play straight metal, without caring whether it's hip or commercial. That doesn't mean *Euphoria* is a classic, but it does mean that it's their most appealing effort in over a decade. —*Stephen Thomas Erlewine*

The DeFranco Family

f. 1972, Port Colborne, Ontario, Canada
Bubblegum, Teen Idol
Consisting of Anthony, Benjamin, Marisa, Merlina and Nino DeFranco, the Canadian version of the Osmonds produced a number three hit in the U.S. in 1973. "Heartbeat—It's a Lovebeat" sold over two million copies, though later singles never approached the same success. An album of the same name also appeared in 1973, followed by *Save the Last Dance for Me* the next year. —*John Bush*

● **DeFranco Family: Featuring Tony DeFranco** / Apr. 18, 2000 / K-Tel ✦✦✦✦
The DeFranco Family really had only one big hit which, of course, was "Heartbeat—It's a Lovebeat," but they also reached the charts two additional times with the Top 20 "Save the Last Dance for Me" and the Top 40 "Abra-Ca-Dabra." That's still a meager base for an extensive collection like K-Tel's 22-track *DeFranco Family: Featuring Tony DeFranco*, which is certainly more than what most listeners will want to hear. And there aren't any hidden gems here—just novelties like "Love Is Bigger Than Baseball" and oldie covers like "Save the Last Dance for Me." That means that most listeners will be satisfied with "Heartbeat—It's a Love Beat" on a various-artists collection, but for the fanatics who love that sound, or have a weakness for early '70s AM pop, this has a bright, sugary sound that is sonically appealing; even if the songs don't deliver, the pop freaks might find it pleasing on the surface. —*Stephen Thomas Erlewine*

Deftones

f. 1989, Sacramento, CA
Rap-Metal, Post-Grunge, Alternative Metal, Heavy Metal, Alternative Pop/Rock
The Deftones have established themselves as one of the premier alternative-metal bands of the future. Combining elements of punk, pop, hip-hop, and traditional metal, the Deftones have succeeded in creating a unique sound while remaining accessible to a wide

variety of listeners. The Sacramento quartet, consisting of Chino Moreno on vocals, Stephen Carpenter on guitar, Chi Cheng on bass and Abe Cunningham on drums, debuted in 1995 with the release of *Adrenaline* on the Maverick label. Appearances on the soundtracks of *The Crow: City of Angels* and *Escape from L.A.* garnered the band favorable publicity, setting the stage for the release of their 1997 follow-up, *Around the Fur*. The first single from the album, "My Own Summer (Shove It)," enjoyed heavy radio airplay as well as significant exposure on MTV and M2. *White Pony* followed in mid-2000, debuting at number three on the Billboard albums chart. —*Kirk Dombek*

Adrenaline / Oct. 1995 / Maverick ✦✦✦
Another absolutely incredible aggressive-melodic band. These guys pound out rough, yet beautiful music topped off immaculately with the unique and emotional singing and lyrics of Chino. The band switches from softly sung melodies to grunting screams in a way that no other band can seem to pull off quite as well. The driving force of songs like "Root" and "Minus Blindfold," the sheer anger of "Birthmark" and "7 Words," and the overall refreshing blend of hardcore/emo/punk/rock/hip-hop prove that this is one band truly worth paying close attention to. —*Blake Butler*

● **Around the Fur** / Oct. 28, 1997 / Maverick/Warner Brothers ✦✦✦✦
While the Deftones still rely more on form than content, they have noticeably improved on their second album, *Around the Fur*. Their sound has hardened into a blunt, aggressive slab of metallic guitars and hammering drums, giving the album a visceral force. The Deftones tap into the same alternative-metal vibe as Korn and L7, and while they don't have catchy riffs or a fully developed sound, *Around the Fur* suggests they're about to come into their own. —*Stephen Thomas Erlewine*

White Pony / Jun. 20, 2000 / Maverick ✦✦✦✦
Hard rockers Deftones take their heavy post-grunge ways to another level on their third album *White Pony*. Sensing painful frustrations and personal rediscovery with its allusive microcosm of an album title, the Californian alt-rock five piece were periodically stifled while making *White Pony*. Their 1997 sophomore effort *Around the Fur* was hailed to blast out commercially, but such pressure crippled the band musically and personally. The band struggled with leading its direction, trudging through weighed emotion, but *White Pony* was the tantalizing outcome. The Deftones went soft, but in an impressive way, to twist around its signature punk thrash sound. Frontman Chino Moreno is still intense, and his sour vocals throughout the entire record growl and stomp all over mainstream movements. He is bored with it all. "Feiticeira" calls out against authority with textured guitars and gnarling percussive throws. "Elite" is sonically industrial and embryonic, as Moreno's beer-soaked vocals scream like Ministry's Al Jourgensen and Skinny Puppy's Nivek Ogre. Lyrically, Moreno is exquisitely mind-blowing, but his fear is also evident. Check out the fierce ballad-esque "Teenager"—the innocent days when life seemed easy can only be dreams now. Moreno's duet with Tool's Maynard James Keenan on "Passenger" is as equally tender. The first single, "Change (In the House of Flies)," is hardening in the way that punk can be sultry and not just pogo-skanking nonsense. It is honest, stripped, and exposed with it's flowing guitar riffs and haunting orchestral back drops. There aren't any lackluster similarities to Limp Bizkit and Korn. The Deftones have forged ahead, unafraid to delve into the influences of The Smiths and The Cure. —*MacKenzie Wilson*

Del Amitri

f. 1982, Glasgow, Scotland
College Rock, Adult Alternative Pop/Rock, Pop/Rock
Glasgow's Del Amitri gained a strong cult following for their country and folk-inflected rock & roll and the quality songwriting of bassist/vocalist Justin Currie and guitarist Iain Harvie, plus the frequently ironic lyrics of the former. Del Amitri's self-titled debut album was released in 1985 and featured a country and new wave-influenced brand of pop/rock, but unfortunately the group had appeared on the cover of *Melody Maker* two months before its release; critics slammed the album in the wake of excessive hype, while potential fans perceived the lack of product in record stores as a sign of the album's quality. However, a network of fans helped organize a low-budget Del Amitri tour of the U.S. Encouraged, the band returned to England and hammered out new material, which helped get them signed to A&M in 1987. 1990's *Waking Hours* accentuated Del Amitri's roots-rock feel and produced the British singles "Kiss This Thing Goodbye," "Nothing Ever Happens," and "Spit in the Rain"; the former scraped the lower reaches of the U.S. Top 40. The 1992 follow-up, *Change Everything*, solidified their popularity in the U.K. and produced another minor American chart single, "Always the Last to Know." —*Steve Huey*

Del Amitri / 1985 / Chrysalis ✦✦✦
Sounding like a gang of snotty pop antagonists, Del Amitri came out swinging on this quirky and often brilliant debut. Vocalist Justin Currie's lyrics were intelligent and witty, laced with sarcasm and venom. With jaunty rhythms and quirky melodies, calling them the bastard sons of XTC and Elvis Costello would not have been too far off the mark. Highlights include "Sticks and Stones Girl" and "Hammering Heart." —*Steven "Spaz" Schnee*

Waking Hours / 1989 / A&M ✦✦✦✦✦
After four years in hibernation, Del Amitri emerged as a gang of mature pop stars. Dropping their edgy quirkiness, Justin and the boys explored their Scottish folk roots, refashioned their sound, and quickly established themselves as a rock band with heart. Still retaining a bit of the Elvis Costello musical heritage, the Dels added a dose of Elvis Presley (check out Currie's sideburns!) and a healthy chunk of Van Morrison. This time, the critics flocked in droves and the public started to take notice. Highlights include "Nothing Ever Happens," "Stone Cold Sober" and "Kiss This Thing Goodbye." —*Steven "Spaz" Schnee*

Change Everything / Jun. 9, 1992 / A&M ✦✦✦✦✦
Contrary to the album's title, the Dels kept on doing what they were doing and released an even better album than *Waking Hours*. Although the songs here were not as good as any individual song from their past, the album as a whole was their best yet. —*Steven "Spaz" Schnee*

Twisted / Feb. 28, 1995 / A&M ✦✦✦✦
Taking a tiny step backwards, Del Amitri did not top their previous outing this time, but they remained true to their musical cause. The fact that they sound a bit tired may mean that it is time to re-evaluate their journey. —*Steven "Spaz" Schnee*

Some Other Sucker's Parade / Jun. 24, 1997 / A&M ✦✦✦
Twisted unexpectedly generated an American Top Ten hit for Del Amitri with "Roll to Me." Not surprisingly, that song provides the touchstone for *Some Other Sucker's Parade*, the follow-up to *Twisted*. Like that record, *Some Other Sucker's Parade* isn't that different from Del Amitri's other records—it's a collection of pleasant, jangly guitar-pop, with nice melodies and gentle hooks. It doesn't offer anything new, but that's not bad, because the group's music is appealing as it is. *Some Other Sucker's Parade* won't win Del Amitri any new fans, but to longtime followers, it's a welcome addition to their library. —*Stephen Thomas Erlewine*

● **Hatful of Rain: The Best of Del Amitri** / Sep. 29, 1998 / A&M ✦✦✦✦✦
It's likely that a large portion of the audience Del Amitri won with the lightly infectious, incessantly catchy "Roll to Me" thought of the Scottish group as a new band, not an outfit that had been recording for over a decade. That may be one of the reasons why *Hatful of Rain: The Best of Del Amitri* was released in 1998, a mere three years after "Roll to Me" climbed into the Top Ten. (It could also be that the follow-up, *Some Other Sucker's Parade*, stiffed on the charts.) In any case, *Hatful of Rain* is an excellent overview of Del Amitri's career, containing no less than 17 tracks, including all of their American and British hits. It may overlook their early independent singles, yet the consistency of their major-label work in the '80s and '90s gives the collection a sense of cohesion, even if it is sequenced out of chronological order. What matters is that *Hatful of Rain* contains everything that a casual fan could want while reconfirming their stature as a solid singles band to their core constituents—and that's everything a good greatest-hits album should do. —*Stephen Thomas Erlewine*

Del Fuegos

f. 1983, db. 1990
College Rock, Heartland Rock, Roots Rock
Part of the roots rock movement of the 1980s, the Del Fuegos hailed from Boston and released several acclaimed albums during the mid-'80s before falling into critical disfavor. The band was formed and led by brothers Dan (vocals) and Warren Zanes (guitar) and also featured a rhythm section of bassist Tom Lloyd and former Embarrassment drummer B. Woody Giessmann. Their energetic debut, *The Longest Day*, was released on the Slash label in 1984 to wide acclaim for its simple '60s-influenced rock & roll energy, high-quality songwriting, and wide emotional range. Released in 1985, *Boston, Mass.* was an homage to the group's working-class roots à la Bob Seger, but 1987's *Stand Up* was a major misstep, panned by critics as bland, boring, and indulgent. Giessmann left the band, which recorded one more album, 1989's *Smoking in the Fields*, which reflected a new-found maturity and love of R&B. In spite of their return to critical favor, the band quietly disappeared shortly after the release of *Smoking in the Fields*. —*Steve Huey*

The Longest Day / 1984 / Slash ✦✦✦✦✦
The Del Fuegos were proud sons of Boston, Massachusetts, but you might not have guessed that to listen to their debut album, *The Longest Day*, which mixed the swaggering thunder of heartland garage rock with the rootsy twang of Dixie-fried rockabilly and roots-conscious rock & roll. While the band would later claim that producer Mitchell Froom slicked back their sound considerably from the raucous club shows that earned their hometown reputation, the results actually capture the band's swing and stomp without an excess of sonic affectation (something that would later become Froom's hallmark), reveling in the crack of Brent "Woody" Giessmann's drums and the bark of Dan and Warren Zanes' guitars. And if the Zanes Brothers' songs didn't exactly stretch the boundaries of early rock archetypes, they honored the traditions in the best ways—by playing roots rock with sweat, fire, good humor, and a lot of heart and soul. And you just can't argue the genius of this line from "When The News Is On": "And sometimes love is a lot like a shoe/ You run around too much and it'll fall apart." *The Longest Day* isn't the sort of album likely to change the way you look at rock & roll, but it will probably remind you why you love the stuff, and that's more than enough reason to slap it into your stereo and turn it up. —*Mark Deming*

● **Boston, Mass.** / 1985 / Slash ✦✦✦✦✦
Building from the blue-collar foundation of *The Longest Day*, the Del Fuegos crafted another winning record of straight-ahead rock & roll with their second album, *Boston, Mass.* While the record isn't as bracing as the debut, it features a better, more consistent selection of songs, and the group's sound is clean, professional and hard-rocking, making the album an infectious and entertaining, if unassuming, collection of roots-rock. —*Stephen Thomas Erlewine*

Stand Up / 1987 / Slash ✦✦✦

Smoking in the Fields / 1989 / RCA ✦✦✦

The Del Lords

f. 1984
Roots Rock

Six years after the demise of the Dictators, guitarist Scott Kempner, no longer billed as "Top Ten," returned with a simple, no-frills rock & roll band, Bronx's Del Lords. Aided by lead guitarist Eric "Roscoe" Ambel, Kempner sang his mix of love songs, party anthems, and social examinations in an energetic, raucous fashion matched by the band behind him. The Del Lords' debut, 1984's *Frontier Days*, was basic urban rock & roll, but there was no mistaking its country and R&B roots. Their next two albums, *Johnny Comes Marching Home* and *Based On a True Story*, contained some shining moments as well. After a lackluster live EP, the Del Lords bounced back with *Lovers Who Wander*, their most critically acclaimed work. Ambel, who had recorded the solo album *Roscoe's Gang* in 1988, left the group following the release of *Lovers*. 1999 saw the release of *Get Tough: The Best of the Del Lords*. *—Steve Huey*

Frontier Days / 1984 / EMI America ♦♦♦

It's hard to say what anyone should have expected from a band fronted by the former rhythm guitarist for The Dictators and featuring Joan Jett's ex-lead guitar player, but it probably wasn't the tough, populist roots-rock of The Del Lords. The group's debut album, *Frontier Days*, proved that Scott Kempner knew enough to hold on to several of The Dictators' key virtues (quick wit and hard-rock passion) while adding a few touches of his own (left-leaning politics with a strong blue-collar stripe, a sound that blended the best of blues, country, and no-frills barroom rock), while Eric "Roscoe" Ambel hadn't lost touch with the streamlined kick-ass rock & roll that was the hallmark of his former boss Ms. Jett. The Del Lords were smart without losing touch of their streetwise instincts, and rocked hard without sacrificing melodies that would stick in your ear long after the songs were over; however, while *Frontier Days* is a reasonably accurate document of The Del Lords blazing live show, the overly tidy and oddly hollow-sounding production by Lou Whitney robs this band of a goodly share of their full power, especially in Kempner and Ambel's guitars and Frank Funaro's drums. *Frontier Days* has some great songs and spirited performances, but one senses this band wanted to rock a lot harder than the circumstances permitted—a presumption that was confirmed on their next album. *—Mark Deming*

Johnny Comes Marching Home / 1986 / EMI America ♦♦♦

The Del Lords' first album, *Frontier Days*, was flawed by a flat, hollow production that never quite captured the band's power and vibrancy; their second, *Johnny Comes Marching Home*, often manages the feat of going too far in the opposite direction. Produced by Neil Geraldo, best known for his work as Pat Benatar's guitarist (Pat sings backup on one track), *Johnny Comes Marching Home* sounds a lot brighter and more engaging than the group's debut, and the band, seasoned by plenty of roadwork, sounds tighter and firmer without sacrificing any of their swing in the process. But while the band rocks harder under Geraldo's guidance, the production also boasts many of the unfortunate hallmarks of mid-'80's record production; everything is dripping with digital reverb, and the mixes often sound like they've been processed and filtered within an inch of their life. It's a testament to the band's strength that despite the Lucite sheen of the mix, *Johnny Comes Marching Home* still sounds like a tougher and more muscular album than the debut, with the guitars of Scott Kempner and Eric "Roscoe" Ambel cutting deeper, their vocals registering with greater emotional impact, and Frank Funaro's drums sounding a hell of a lot livelier. And Kempner's songwriting continued to shine, especially on the anthemic "Heaven," the rock & roll radio tribute "St. Jake," and the rockabilly on steroids wrap-up "No Waitress No More." The Del Lords never made an album without its share of flaws (generally attributable to people outside the band), but while *Johnny Comes Marching Home* has nearly as many problems as their debut, at least it rocks harder, and that makes up for a lot. *—Mark Deming*

• **Based on a True Story** / 1988 / Enigma ♦♦♦♦♦

Kempner expands his songwriter range, but it's the celebratory party-man anthems like "The Cool and the Crazy" that make this the group's best work. *—John Floyd*

Lovers Who Wander / 1990 / Enigma ♦♦♦

The band's most ambitious work, it has complex songs and a sound that expands on their previous attack. *—John Floyd*

The Del-Tino's

Surf Revival, Garage Rock, Rock & Roll

If Cub Koda hadn't been their lead singer and guitarist, the Del-Tino's might have disappeared into the mists of undocumented garage-rock history. As it stands, the Southeastern Michigan rock & roll trio is ground zero for a man who kept the rock & roll flame burning throughout his career. In the fall of 1963, the Del-Tino's entered United Sound Studios in Detroit to cut their first single, a cover of Roy Orbison's "Go! Go! Go!," which featured "Ramrod" on the flip side. They released it independently and it made a small impact. In 1965, they released their second single, "Nightlife"/"Pa Pa Ooh Mau Mau," which was issued by Sonic Records. That spring, drummer Doug Hankes graduated from high school and went to Michigan State University in East Lansing, which meant he only occasionally came back for Del-Tino rehearsals. Knowing that the end of the group was in sight, Koda and Creech continued playing, with Hankes returning for the gigs. They stuck it out throughout the summer following Cub and Rusty's 1966 graduation, playing as the house band at the Coca Club and recording a final session in a basement in Adrian. Two songs from that session, "Ramblin' on My Mind" and "I Got My Mojo Workin'," were released as a single later that year, not long after the group went their separate ways. Cub Koda was the only member to continue working in the music biz, eventually finding fame and fortune through Brownsville Station and their hit, "Smokin' in the Boy's Room." Koda continued as a solo artist following Brownsville's breakup; he also played blues with Hound Dog Taylor's backing band, the Houserockers. He also established himself as a music journalist through his work in *Goldmine* magazine. *—Stephen Thomas Erlewine*

Go Go Go to Surfin' School / Apr. 28, 1998 / Norton ♦♦♦

There was a portion of America that hadn't been touched by the British Invasion in the mid-'60s. While many bands hunkered down in their garages attempting to transform themselves into the Beatles or Stones, there were groups that kept the music of Chuck Berry, Bo Diddley, the Beach Boys, and the Trashmen alive. Two of those bands happened to be in southeastern Michigan, and one of them happened to have Cub Koda as its leader. And if it wasn't for Koda and his passionate efforts to keep real rock & roll and blues alive, the music of the Del-Tino's and the Hesitations might never have made it to compact disc, let alone in a package as appealing as *Go! Go! Go! to Surfin' School!*. All known recordings of both the Del-Tino's and the Hesitations are featured on this generous 24-track collection. The Hesitations pound out wild surf and garage rock, while the Del-Tino's are a little more adventurous, dipping into blues as well as surf and rock & roll. Both bands are a little raw, but their energy is infectious, especially on the Del-Tino's covers. Some of the originals are a little undistinguished, but they're fun artifacts, and each group gets off at least one gem, whether it's the Del-Tino's "Cheatin'" or the Hesitations' "Wild Little Willie." You have to be an archivist or fetishist to dig this stuff, but if greasy rock & roll is your passion, you owe it to yourself to check this out. *—Stephen Thomas Erlewine*

The Del-Vikings

f. 1955, Pittsburgh, PA, **db.** 1965

Doo Wop

The story of the Dell-Vikings (or Del Vikings, or Del-Vikings) is one of the most glorious, complicated and frustrating of any successful doo wop group in music history. With two major national hits ("Come Go With Me," "Whispering Bells") to their credit—one more hit than most other successful doo wop groups ever had—they had a jump on virtually all of their competition. Just as they were ascending those heights of fame and success, however, internal fractures and some greed and misdirected ambition helped destroy any chance they had of making a lasting place for themselves at the top of their profession. They left behind two hits and a large body of very good records that weren't nearly as well known, as well as a reputation as one of the few successful integrated vocal groups of their era. *—Bruce Eder*

Dell Vikings / 1988 / Collectables ♦♦♦♦♦

Solid hits by one of doo wop's first integrated groups. *—Bill Dahl*

For Collectors Only / 1992 / Collectables ♦♦♦♦♦

This really isn't for collectors only—it is the only single collection of the group's stuff that shows the full range of this sadly underrated vocal group. As it is, its mere existence as a mid-priced double CD, alongside the presence of the two best-of compilations from MCA and Mercury, makes collecting the best Dell Vikings material extremely complicated. Collectables Records got access to the complete recordings that the original group made for Fee Bee Records, which covers their history from 1956 through 1957, overlapping with the history of the Mercury version of the group. This includes the hit version of "Come Go With Me," as well as "Whispering Bells" (both of which appear on MCA's best-of in those very same versions) and their other early tracks. Collectables also got access to an extraordinary body of outtakes—a magnificent fast version of "I'm Spinning" that's completely different from the version that appears on both the MCA and Mercury best-of discs. There are distinctive outtakes of "Willette" and oddities such as the Joey Biscoe single "What Made Maggie Run," on which the group sang backup in a hurried attempt to get them out before the public again after that first hit. More important are tracks like "Uh Uh Baby," a fast jump number that shows the group at about its rockingest and nimblest, with a killer guitar solo courtesy of the late Joe Lopes. Other highlights include radiant outtakes of "Girl, Girl" and "Cold Feet" (done a cappella), little snippets of session chatter (amazing the stuff survived 40 years), and rehearsal and audition versions of the group's songs and generally the fullest account possible of the history of the Fee Bee Records version of the group that you'll ever see. *—Bruce Eder*

The Best of the Del-Vikings: The Mercury Years / Jul. 16, 1996 / Mercury ♦♦♦

Read the title carefully, because the Del-Vikings' two great doo wop hits—"Come Go with Me" and "Whispering Bells"—were *not* recorded for Mercury, and so are not contained on this compilation. This disc has 22 sides they recorded for Mercury in 1957-58, with a lineup that had some but not all of the members that recorded "Come Go with Me" and "Whispering Bells." (To make matters more confusing, a different Del-Vikings, led by Kripp Johnson, who had sung lead on "Whispering Bells," kept recording for a different label.) The Mercury Del-Vikings did have a Top 20 hit right out of the box, "Cool Shake" (included here), but never had a big single again. Most of this is routine doo wop that's below the standards of their Dot sides, sometimes clouded by inadvisable attempts at pop-oriented material and production. It's only of value to hard-core doo wop bugs, who will appreciate the inclusion of many tracks only available on rare EPs, singles, and compilations, as well as one previously unissued in the U.S. The intro to "The Bells," by the way, bears a close similarity to the famous wordless scats that kicked off the Marcels' classic "Blue Moon" several years later. *—Richie Unterberger*

★ **Come Go With Me: The Best of the Del-Vikings–The Dot/ABC Recordings** / Jun. 17, 1997 / Hip-O ♦♦♦♦♦

As one of the first interracial vocal groups of the rock & roll era—and the first to score a Top Ten million-selling record on their very first try—the Del-Vikings seemed poised for very big things indeed. But when "Come Go With Me" became a national hit, the greed caused the Del-Vikings to split into two separate groups. Recording at various times with almost the same name, sometimes utilizing interchangeable group members as the two groups released follow-up singles on both Dot and Mercury simultaneously (with errant tracks showing up a couple of years later on a third label, Luniverse), this put the brakes on the group's success in a most confusing manner, raising the ire of disc jockeys and radio station programmers alike. This 16-track compilation from the Hip-O subsidiary is subtitled *The Dot-ABC Recordings* and does a better than average job of cherry picking through their sides for that label. Their big hit, "Come Go With Me," kicks things off, followed by the A- and B-sides of five early Fee-Bee, Dot, and ABC-Paramount singles. Filling out the compilation are the top sides of four more ABC singles. Oddly enough, the follow-up to "Come Go With Me," a two-sided rocker ("What Made Maggie Run" and "Little Billy Boy"), isn't here, making this collection somewhat incomplete. But as a basic hits primer, this tells the story of the "original Del-Vikings" in a thoroughly digestible way. —*Cub Koda*

Delaney & Bonnie

f. 1966, **db.** 1972
Album Rock, Pop/Rock, Blues-Rock
Delaney Bramlett (b. Jul. 1, 1939) and his wife Bonnie (b. Nov. 8, 1944) recorded a series of blues and country influenced albums in the late '60s and early '70s. A variety of musicians played in Delaney & Bonnie's band, including Eric Clapton, Dave Mason, Duane Allman, Leon Russell, Rita Coolidge, Jim Gordon, Bobby Whitlock, and Carl Radle; Clapton, Gordon, Whitlock, and Radle formed Derek & The Dominoes after performing together on Delaney & Bonnie's 1969-70 tour. Delaney & Bonnie's records were a strong influence on Eric Clapton's style in the '70s. The group broke up after the Bramletts' marriage collapsed in 1972. —*Kenneth M. Cassidy*

● **Delaney & Bonnie & Friends on Tour with Eric Clapton** / Jun. 1970 / Atco ✦✦✦✦
This 42-minute, eight-song live album, cut at Croydon late in 1969, is not only the peak of Delaney & Bonnie's output, but also the nexus in the recording and performing careers of Eric Clapton and George Harrison. *On Tour With Eric Clapton* features the guitarist performing the same blend of country, blues, and gospel that would characterize his own early solo ventures in 1970. He rises to the occasion with dazzling displays of virtuosity throughout, highlighted by a dizzying solo on "I Don't Want to Discuss," a long, languid part on "Only You Know and I Know," and searing, soulful lead on the beautifully harmonized "Coming Home." Vocally, Delaney & Bonnie were never better than they come off on this live set, and the 11-piece band sounds tighter musically than a lot of quartets that were working at the time, whether they're playing extended blues or ripping through a medley of Little Richard songs. It's no accident that the band featured here would become Clapton's own studio outfit for his debut solo LP, or that the core of this group—Bobby Whitlock, Carl Radle, and Jim Gordon—would transform itself into Derek & the Dominoes as well; or that most of the full band here would also comprise the group that played with George Harrison on *All Things Must Pass* and at the Concert for Bangladesh, except that the playing here (not to mention the recording) is better. Half the musicians on this record achieved near-superstar status less than a year later, and although the reasons behind their fame didn't last, listening to their work decades later, it all seems justified. One only wishes that Atlantic Records might check their vaults for any unreleased numbers from these shows that could fit on an extended CD. —*Bruce Eder*

The Best of Delaney & Bonnie / Nov. 1990 / Rhino ✦✦✦✦✦
Bonnie Bramlett released "Groupie," the song she co-wrote with Leon Russell, as an Atlantic single in December of 1969. Almost two years later in September of 1971, Karen Carpenter took it to the top of the pop and adult contemporary charts under the name "Superstar." It may not have been Bramlett's favorite rendition of one of her songs, but it was phenomenal and deserved success for the talented singer/songwriter beyond her appearances on the TV show *Roseanne.* "Groupie (Superstar)" is the highlight of a simply great collection of musical expression by the underrated and abundantly talented duo known simply as Delaney & Bonnie. *Goldmine/Discoveries* magazine contributor Joe Tortelli is very detailed in his six-page liner notes/track listing to this 18-song compilation. It includes the duo's two Top 20 hits from 1971, "Never Ending Song of Love" and "Only You Know and I Know"; the excellent double-sided minor hits "Free the People" and "Soul Shake"; three tracks from their Jimmy Miller-produced legendary live album *Delaney & Bonnie & Friends on Tour With Eric Clapton* (and George Harrison); a thrilling rendition of "Piece of My Heart" tracked two years after Janis Joplin but tipping the hat, no doubt, to Aretha's sister, Emma Franklin, who did it before both these gals—this best-of basically concentrates on the Elektra, Stax, and Atlantic recordings. The downside is that it really should be twice as long, and they have enough legitimate music to fill a double CD. For now this is a unique time capsule which lives up to the title "Best Of." —*Joe Viglione*

The Delfonics

f. 1965, Philadelphia, PA, **db.** 1974
Smooth Soul, Pop-Soul, Quiet Storm, Philly Soul, Soul
The Delfonics were one of the first groups to sing in the sleek, soulful style that became popularized (thanks to producer Thom Bell) as the "Philadelphia sound." Their roots go back to doo-wop singing at school dances in the early '60s. They were well-known in the Philly area for their supple, airtight harmonies talent that brought them to the attention of record producers, eventually landing them a contract with Cameo-Parkway. While their early records brought them little if any notice, it did bring them to the attention of producer/arranger Thom Bell who signed the band to his soon-to-be influential soul label Philly Groove. Right from the start this was a perfect match as the band released the classic "La La Means I Love You" in 1968, a song that began a string of hits lasting into the mid-'70s. The sound that Bell created for the Delfonics was the antithesis of the soul sound that came from Stax in Memphis and Muscle Shoals in Alabama. He sandpapered away the grit, lightened up on the backbeat, brought in string sections, and created a smooth, airy sound—Bell and the Delfonics were setting the stage for a different kind of groove where subtlety and nuance reigned. —*John Dougan*

● **La, La Means I Love You: The Definitive Collection** / Aug. 26, 1997 / Arista ✦✦✦✦✦
A lush collection of classy Delfonics tracks. The trio had a more soulful sound than the Stylistics whom Thom Bell (who produced the lion's share of these tracks) later produced. Initially flooring the world with "La, La Means I Love You," the Harts, William & Wilbert, Randy Cain, and later Major Harris churned out delightful ear candies for years. "I'm Sorry," "Break Your Promise," "Ready or Not Here I Come," and "You Got Yours I'll Get Mine," included here, were as potent as "La, La." But, it took the eloquent, French-horn embellished "Didn't I Blow Your Mind This Time," however, to put them on top again. "Somebody Loves You" is a luscious B-side featuring William's sweet falsetto and harmonies that run over. Later, less successful recordings provide the most thrills: "Over & Over," "Lying to Myself," "Think It Over," and "I Told You So" are as smooth and as creamy as whipped cream. "Hey Love," an exquisite slow jam, featuring Wilbert Hart's heavier tenor, has shown an amazing longevity for a flip side. Not quite definitive, they could have omitted the awkward "Funny Feeling," and "Loving Him"—a B-side—for "I Gave to You" and "Can You Remember." But this is still fantastic, and more than enough Delfonics for most; you'll want two copies—one for the car and one for the crib. —*Andrew Hamilton*

Forever New / Nov. 16, 1999 / Volt ✦✦✦
When Fantasy reactivated the Volt label in 1999, it recorded urban contemporary newcomer Angel Sessions, as well as older soul veterans like the Delfonics, the Dramatics, and Brenda Holloway. Although not in a class with the Delfonics' seminal recordings of the late '60s and early '70s, 1999's *Forever New* is an enjoyable outing that finds the group in good form 31 years after "La La Means I Love You" burned up the R&B charts. William Hart's distinctive voice has held up well over the years, and his performances on "I Will Remember You," "When You're Gone," and other selections, demonstrate that time has not robbed the Philadelphian of his charisma. Produced by Fred Pittman and Preston Glass, *Forever New* tends to favor a high-tech urban contemporary production style that is a departure from the lush orchestral approach Thom Bell was known for (although Bell arranged "She's The Kinda Girl"). The horns and strings are missed, and the Delfonics (whose lineup on *Forever New* consists of Hart, Major Harris, and Futures graduate Frank Washington) would have been better served by an honest-to-God band—even so, the material generally sounds organic rather than forced and unnatural. Also noteworthy is a remake of "Break Your Promise," which falls short of the excellence of the original version but is pleasing nonetheless. *Forever New* isn't essential—casual listeners would be better off with a collection of the Delfonics' late '60s/early '70s hits—but it's still a CD that seasoned Delfonics fans will appreciate. —*Alex Henderson*

The Dells

f. 1952, Chicago, IL, **db.** 1986
Smooth Soul, Chicago Soul, Pop-Soul, Northern Soul, Doo Wop, R&B, Soul
After nearly four decades of recording an incredible legacy of hits, the Dells have made only one personnel change in their entire professional career. Perhaps that's why the venerable R&B vocal group can boast such a remarkably consistent track record.
The quintet from Chicago's south suburbs has weathered stylistic shifts from doo wop and soul to disco and urban contemporary, and every permutation in between. Their harmony remains as striking as ever, with Marvin Junior's earthshaking lead enduring as the group's focal point.
Signing with Vee-Jay in 1955, their creamy vocal blend on "Oh, What a Night" gave the Dells their first major R&B hit the next year, but it would be nearly a decade before they returned to the winner's circle with another dreamy classic, "Stay in My Corner." By then Chicago's R&B sound had changed drastically—doo wop was dead and soul was king—but the Dells adapted effortlessly, regularly scaling the charts for the Chess subsidiary Cadet with "There Is," "Always Together," "Give Your Baby a Standing Ovation," and a marathon remake of "Stay in My Corner" that afforded Junior's booming baritone room to roam.
Seemingly an indestructible force (turning up on the R&B charts as recently as 1984), the succinct harmonies of the Dells span entire generations of R&B history. —*Bill Dahl*

Dreams of Contentment / Nov. 17, 1993 / Vee-Jay ✦✦✦✦
The Dells never made it over the hump while at Vee-Jay, despite making many impressive singles. They were a top-flight doo wop group, but they couldn't find a way to advance beyond the R&B margins. Only when they moved to Chess, changed their style, and made Marvin Junior the lead singer did they enjoy the success they deserved. Still, as this 24-track reissue shows, there wasn't anything wrong with their Vee-Jay output. They experimented on such numbers as "Lil Darlin," "It's Not for Me to Say," and "It's Not Unusual" with jazz/pop harmonies and covers. In addition, songs like "Now I Pray" and "Pain in My Heart" are wonderfully sung and harmonized, even if they weren't huge sellers. —*Ron Wynn*

Passionate Breezes: The Best of the Dells 1975-1991 / Oct. 1995 / Mercury ✦✦✦
By the last half of the '70s, the Dells had already gone through two phases in their career, transforming themselves from an R&B vocal group into a smooth soul outfit and scoring hits in both incarnations. During the late '70s and '80s, the group continued to perform, usually in the same vein as their early-'70s hits. Even if the strength of their voices hadn't diminished, their audience had. Nevertheless, much of the material they recorded during this era was fine, as *Passionate Breezes: Best of 1975-1991* proves. It's not as compulsively listenable as the group's doo wop hits or their early-'70s material, but there is still enough first-rate music here to satisfy fans. —*Stephen Thomas Erlewine*

Bring Back the Love: Classic Dells Soul / Feb. 27, 1996 / Chess ✦✦✦✦✦
Chess' *Bring Back the Love: Classic Dells Soul* doesn't contain any of the group's big hits, but that's fine, since it offers a nice, 14-song roundup of the Dells' early recordings for Chess in the '50s. These may not be well-known, but they're uniformly strong singles,

highlighted by a nice version of "The Glory of Love," "If You Really Love Your Girl (Show Her)" and "I Can't Do Enough." —*Stephen Thomas Erlewine*

★ **Anthology** / Sep. 28, 1999 / Hip-O ◆◆◆◆◆

The Dells were one of the few groups that rode the transition from doo wop to smooth soul without missing a beat and without falling off the charts. Just as remarkably, the group did so without declining much in quality, as Hip-O's definitive double-disc *Anthology* proves. Throughout these 36 tracks, the music changes, from street-corner R&B to string-drenched disco-soul, but in all their incarnations, the Dells always sound wonderful. There are a handful of minor hits missing, but all the big singles—including both the Vee-Jay and Cadet versions of "Oh, What a Nite" and "Stay in My Corner"—are here, assembled chronologically. As such, it tells an epic story of a group whose history mirrored the story of R&B vocal groups from the '50s through the '70s. The latter-day material may pale somewhat in comparison to the band's early classics, but it holds up well against other '70s soul. The final cut, the group's surprise 1991 hit "A Heart Is a House for Love"—their contribution to Robert Townsend's *The Five Heartbeats*, which was a loose tribute to the Dells themselves—illustrates that the group sounded terrific well into their third decade of performing, which is a true sign of greatness. *Anthology* is a testament to their greatness, offering solid proof that they were one of the greatest vocal R&B groups of their time. —*Stephen Thomas Erlewine*

20th Century Masters—The Millennium Collection: The Best of the Dells / Aug. 29, 2000 / MCA ◆◆◆

The Best of the Dells: The Millennium Collection gathers 11 remastered highlights from the late-'60s/mid-'70s phase of their career, including the 1969 remake of their '50s hit "Oh, What a Night," "Stay in My Corner," "Give Your Baby a Standing Ovation," and "Always Together." Though it's not quite as complete as their *Anthology* or *On Their Corner*, *The Millennium Collection* does provide a compact overview of some of the Dells' most soulful singles. —*Heather Phares*

The Very Best of the Dells / Oct. 17, 2000 / Collectables ◆◆◆◆

A fine chronological CD of the Dells' Vee-Jay recordings, from their 1955 debut "Tell the World" to 1964's immortal "Stay in My Corner"—with liner notes by Robert Prueter, the godfather of Chicago's soul scene. The original Dells recorded the bulk of these tracks with Johnny Funches; exaggerated falsetto Johnny Carter replaced Funches in 1959. Their recording debut (as the El Rays) was 1954's "Darling I Know," which didn't make the 25 tracks—nor did a few early-'60s releases on Argo Records when they broke from Vee-Jay for a spell. Singularly, and occasionally together, tenor Verne Allison and baritone Michael McGill wrote most of the material, with blustery baritone lead Marvin Junior chipping in a few tunes as well. All the Dells wrote songs but rarely together. These are the Chicago area recordings from whence the Dells' legend spread. —*Andrew Hamilton*

Sandy Denny

b. Jan. 6, 1947, Wimbledon, England, d. Apr. 21, 1978
Vocals, Piano, Guitar / British Folk-Rock, British Folk, Folk-Rock

Maddy Prior, Jacqui McShee, and June Tabor all give her a run for her money, but the late Sandy Denny remains the pre-eminent British folk-rock singer. In addition to recording several albums of her own, Denny was an integral force behind the best work of the most respected British folk-rock band of all, Fairport Convention, and also contributed mightily to recordings by the Strawbs and Fotheringay. It's impossible for words to fully evoke the haunting, spectral presence of her powerful and penetrating alto voice, which seemed to bring the mythology of English moors and folktales to life in contemporary, 20th-century settings. Her composition "Who Knows Where the Time Goes" gave Sandy her first international recognition when Judy Collins recorded it in 1968; that same year Denny was tapped to replace Judy Dyble in Fairport Convention, and is prominently featured on their late-'60s albums *What We Did on Our Holidays*, *Unhalfbricking*, and *Liege and Lief*. These are not only recognized as Fairport's best work, but as some of the finest British folk-rock records of all time. Denny left Fairport Convention in 1970, and while both she and Fairport would produce some worthwhile work in the future, it's fair to say that neither band nor singer would reach the same peaks again. Much of the best of Denny's later solo work, oddly, is found on live and BBC recordings, some of which surfaced on the box set *Who Knows Where the Time Goes?* Her final LP, *Rendezvous*, came out in 1977; the following year, she died from injuries sustained in a fall down a flight of stairs. —*Richie Unterberger*

All Our Own Work / 1968 / Pickwick ◆◆◆

Sandy Denny / 1970 / Saga ◆◆◆

North Star Grassman and the Ravens / 1971 / Hannibal ◆◆◆

Following the breakup of the short-lived Fotheringay, Sandy Denny returned with her first post-Fairport solo album, *The North Star Grassman and the Ravens*. Produced with ex-bandmate Richard Thompson and longtime engineer John Wood, who would go on to produce the bulk of Thompson's work with Linda Thompson, the record consists of eight evocative Denny originals, along with the traditional "Blackwaterside" and a pair of borrowed rockers. There's a looseness and roominess to the sound, with acoustic guitar, piano, and Thompson's electric guitar leading the sparse backing from former members of Fotheringay, along with the occasional accordion, violin, pedal steel, and strings. Songs such as "Late November," "John the Gun," and "Next Time Around" are among her best, while "Blackwaterside," featuring Thompson's guitar and accordion, continues to show her mastery of traditional music. Because her songs tend to lean towards the melancholy, and are primarily on the slow to mid-tempo side, Denny had to look elsewhere for upbeat material. Choices such as Brenda Lee's "Let's Jump the Broomstick" and a ragged, yet somewhat effective, duet with Thompson on Bob Dylan's "Down in the Flood," are

good ones, though both sound as if they were afterthoughts. Her best record was still a year away, but *The North Star Grassman* is a solid effort from Sandy Denny's sadly shortened solo career. —*Brett Hartenbach*

Sandy / 1972 / A&M ◆◆◆◆◆

Sandy Denny's second post-Fairport solo offering, produced by (then-future) husband Trevor Lucas, is a beautiful blend of the traditional style with which she is most often associated and a slightly more lavish sound that would become more prevalent in her later work. Lucas does an excellent job of balancing the two and creating an exquisite backdrop for Denny's gorgeous songs and majestic voice. Nearly every track has the radiance and timelessness of her best Fairport work, along with an accessibility she had merely hinted at prior to this. "Listen, Listen," with its soaring chorus and bed of strings and mandolin, the lovely "The Lady," and the layered a cappella vocal arrangement of Richard Farina's "Quiet Joys of Brotherhood" (featuring Dave Swarbrick's haunting solo violin coda) are perfect examples of Denny's enormous talents, and only a few of the many pleasures found here. Touches such as lush strings, Allen Toussaint's horn arrangement on "For Nobody to Hear," Sneaky Pete Kleinow's steel guitar and former Fairport partner Richard Thompson's guitars and mandolin, bring out the many dimensions in Denny's music without obscuring it. *Sandy* also boasts her best collection of original material, as well as terrific covers of Dylan's "Tomorrow Is a Long Time," featuring Linda (Thompson) Peters on backing vocals, and the aforementioned "Quiet Joys of Brotherhood." If you're simply looking for a quick introduction to a wonderful songwriter and one of the finest voices in popular music, go for the single disc best-of collection, but if you would like to hear Sandy Denny's definitive (solo) musical statement, search out *Sandy*. —*Brett Hartenbach*

The Bunch / 1972 / A&M ◆◆

Like an Old Fashioned Waltz / 1973 / Hannibal ◆◆

With *Like an Old Fashioned Waltz*, Sandy Denny expands on the more polished moments that her previous work, *Sandy* (1972), had suggested. The tone throughout most of the record is melancholy and personal, with gentle piano, rich strings, and barely a trace of her British folk roots. "Solo," one of her best songs, opens the album with a sense of apprehension and yearning, while cuts such as the beautifully vivid title track, the longing "At the End of the Day," and the evocative closer "No End" nicely follow suit. The Ink Spots covers "Whispering Grass" and "Until the Real Thing Comes Along" break the mood a bit, but it's a testament to the breadth of Denny's talent that she's able to make this sort of jazz-inflected pop work for her. These two songs seem to hint at a new direction that never really materialized in her final years, though an entire album of Ink Spots tunes was actually rumored at one point. As Sandy Denny's last solo work for four years, *Like an Old Fashioned Waltz* remains an intimate and moving record. —*Brett Hartenbach*

Rendezvous / 1977 / Hannibal ◆◆◆

With a sublime voice and a catalog full of beautiful songs, Sandy Denny left an indelible mark on British folk and popular music in her 31 years. Released in 1977, less than one year before her untimely death, the overwrought *Rendezvous* unfortunately stands as her final musical statement. Producer Trevor Lucas' use of cumbersome strings, backup singers and bloated lead guitars weigh things down and bury some otherwise fine writing. One of her best, "I'm a Dreamer," is nearly ruined by the chorus of singers and anthemic guitar at the end, while the heartfelt "One Way Donkey Ride" and the poignant "Full Moon," though more successful, never seem to quite reach their potential. Even some choice covers—including Richard Thompson's "I Wish I Was a Fool for You" (aka "For Shame of Doing Wrong"), Elton John's "Candle in the Wind," and a somber working of "Silver Threads and Golden Needles"—lack the impact she brought in the past to works by the likes of Thompson, Bob Dylan, Joni Mitchell, Richard Farina and Buddy Holly, as well as the many traditional tunes that she made her own. Few, if any of the exquisite touches that Lucas brought to Denny's superb 1972 release *Sandy* are evident here. Originally released by Island Records in the U.K., and not available in the U.S. until the mid-'80s, *Rendezvous* seems to be a flawed attempt at gaining a wider audience, by an artist who deserved better and was capable of the best. —*Brett Hartenbach*

Original Sandy Denny / 1978 / Trojan ◆◆◆

Denny's first sessions, originally recorded in 1967, are her most traditional effort. Backed only by her own acoustic guitar, Denny's voice is assured, pure, and powerful on her debut. The album features traditional folk staples like "This Train," "Make Me a Pallet On Your Floor," and "Pretty Polly," as well as covers of Tom Paxton's "Ramblin' Boy" and "Milk And Honey." There are also a couple of songs by the obscure American songwriter Jackson Frank, one of which she would soon perform with Fairport Convention ("You Never Wanted Me"). Although this has little of the folk-rock cross-pollination that Denny would soon master with Fairport and others, it is still an impressive collection that shows her voice in as haunting and commanding form as her more renowned recordings. —*Richie Unterberger*

Sandy Denny & The Strawbs / 1985 / Hannibal ◆◆◆◆

Sandy Denny was only with the Strawbs for a short period of time, but she was around long enough to make some very memorable contributions to the band. An expressive jewel of a folk singer with a rich, angelic voice, the pre-Fairport Convention Denny is clearly the main attraction on this CD. In contrast to the progressive-rock and art-rock elements the band would later embrace, these sides are acoustic-oriented and unmistakably British-sounding folk-pop. Gems like "Tell Me What You See In Me," "Nothing Else Will Do" and "Who Knows Where the Time Goes" not only illustrate how superb and moving a singer Denny was, they also demonstrate how prolific a composer Dave Cousins was. One can only speculate as to what direction the Strawbs would have taken had Denny stayed, but what we know with certainty is that her short-lived association with Cousins was lucrative and valuable. *—Alex Henderson*

Who Knows Where the Time Goes [Box Set] / 1986 / Hannibal ✦✦✦✦✦
This magnificently produced multi-disc boxed set presents a complete portrait of Sandy Denny, the haunting singer, the melodic, mournful songwriter, and the mesmerizing bandleader of Fairport Convention and Fotheringay. Much of the material is previously unheard, but it's all of a piece with Denny's accomplished work on her solo albums and in her groups. The album makes the case for Denny as a major folk artist. *—William Ruhlmann*

The Best of Sandy Denny [Best of Box] / 1989 / Hannibal ✦✦✦✦✦
The Best of Sandy Denny is a fine 16-track collection that has an excellent cross-section of her best solo recordings, including "Listen, Listen," "One Way Donkey Ride," "It'll Take a Long Time," "Farewell, Farewell," "Late November," "Solo," "Sea," "For Shame of Doing Wrong," "Stranger to Himself," "I'm a Dreamer" and "Who Knows Where the Time Goes." *—Stephen Thomas Erlewine*

Attic Tracks 1972-1984 / 1995 / Raven ✦✦✦✦✦
The perfect—and we do mean perfect—complement to Hannibal Records' *Who Knows Where the Time Goes* box. *Attic Tracks* (so named to distinguish it from Dylan's *Basement Tapes*) is an 18-song collection from Australia's Raven Records consisting of unreleased songs, outtakes, and extreme rarities, recorded by Sandy Denny and her former husband, the late Trevor Lucas. Included are tracks from Fairport's 1974 tour ("The Ballad of Ned Kelly"); Denny's beautiful, passionate French version of "Listen, Listen," entitled "Ecoute, Ecoute"; a pair of Denny demos ("One More Chance," "Rising for the Moon") given to Fairport Convention for their recording of the *Rising for the Moon* album; the lost 1975 Lucas/Fairport track "Tears"; "Losing Game," a Flying Burrito Bros. track recorded by Denny and Lucas, in a broad, brassy, hard-rocking version in 1972 and finished in 1976, but never released; the forgotten 1977 Denny B-side "Still Waters Run Deep"; Lucas' version of Bob Dylan's "Forever Young"; three songs from the last concert that Denny ever gave, including one of her longest, liveliest versions of "Who Knows Where the Time Goes" on record; and Denny's fiery reading of the Little Feat song "Easy to Slip," recorded during the making of her *Rendezvous* album. The big surprise, however, is Lucas' gently soulful cover of the Australian hit "Girls on the Avenue," on which his voice has an extraordinary "haunt count" and the accompaniment is nothing less than ravishing, in a mid-'70s pop vein—Paul McCartney should only make such records! A unique collection, and a necessary addition to the possessions of any fan of Fairport Convention or Sandy Denny. *—Bruce Eder*

The BBC Sessions 1971-1973 / 1997 / Strange Fruit ✦✦✦✦✦
This 20-track CD was available only super-briefly in the spring of 1997 before Island Records prevented further copies from being distributed. The several thousand copies that had already been released, however, were allowed to remain in circulation, meaning that this disc is difficult but not impossible to find. And if you like Sandy Denny, you need to find it, because it's some of her best material. Most of the tracks are BBC versions of songs that appeared on her first three solo albums, and most are her own compositions; all but four are performed solo on piano or guitar. In a sense, it's Sandy unplugged, although that term didn't exist in those days. Denny arguably sounds much better on these spare versions than she does on the official takes, when she had to contend with often humdrum, over-arranged session accompaniment. In this context, she comes off much more like a kindred spirit to early-'70s singer/songwriters, especially Joni Mitchell and Judy Collins, than she does a British folk troubadour. You could, indeed, make a strong argument for this as her best solo recording, with fidelity that ranges from good to excellent. While eight of these tracks previously appeared on the fine bootleg *Dark the Night*, the remaining 12 did not, making it an essential addition for Denny fans. *—Richie Unterberger*

Gold Dust: Live at the Royalty / Jun. 9, 1998 / Island ✦✦✦
Gold Dust: Live at the Royalty captures Sandy Denny's final concert. The show (performed on Sunday, November 27, 1977) was intended to be the first date of an 11-city tour, but it turned out to be her last show ever. It certainly wasn't the way anyone wanted Denny to leave the stage, but it remains an affecting, surprising farewell. There are familiar items, to be sure, but the concert also finds her breaking new ground and moving away from traditional folk-rock to an edgier sound. These are subtle distinctions that only hardcore fans will notice, but those fans will find *Gold Dust* a minor treasure. *—Stephen Thomas Erlewine*

● **No More Sad Refrains: The Anthology** / Jul. 25, 2000 / A&M ✦✦✦✦✦
Like fellow Briton Nick Drake, Sandy Denny is one of the rare lesser-known artists whose extraordinary talents have been duly represented on disc over the years. Though it may not be as expansive as the multiple disc set *Who Knows Where the Time Goes*, *No More Sad Refrains* may be the best introduction to Sandy Denny's career to hit the market: more affordable, while still covering 34 songs over two discs (as opposed to 43 over three), including a few rarities. And though the collections overlap on nearly two-thirds of the songs selected, less than a third are the same recordings, and these have been digitally remastered. The tracks are arranged chronologically from her first record with Fairport Convention in 1969 to 1977's *Rendezvous*, concentrating on her exquisite songwriting, along with a handful of well-chosen covers. And while it may emphasize her solo years, her work with Fotheringay and the one-off rock & roll tribute *The Bunch* is given a good overview as well. Fans who will have a majority of the material included here will be enticed by the previously unreleased demo version of "Stranger to Himself" and rarities such as "Here in Silence" and "Man of Iron." Still, *No More Sad Refrains* is seemingly aimed more at the uninitiated than devotees, though it does a admirable job of covering a lot of territory and trying to please both. Either way, this is a fine retrospective of a terrific songwriter and what may well have been the most stunningly beautiful voice in British folk and pop. Included is a 22-page booklet featuring musician credits, photos, and informative liner notes by Denny biographer Clinton Heylin. *—Brett Hartenbach*

John Denver

b. Dec. 31, 1943, Roswell, NM, **d.** Oct. 12, 1997
Vocals, Guitar / Folk-Rock, Soft Rock, Singer/Songwriter
One of the most popular recording artists of the 1970s, country-folk singer/songwriter John Denver's gentle, environmentally conscious music established him among the most beloved entertainers of his era; wholesome and clean-cut, his appeal extended to fans of all ages and backgrounds, and led to parallel careers as both an actor and a humanitarian. After moving to Los Angeles in 1964, he joined the Chad Mitchell Trio and helped resuscitate the group on the strength of his songwriting skills. Denver finally began a solo career in 1969 that gained him a degree of fame as the songwriter of "Leaving on a Jet Plane," an international chart-topper for Peter, Paul & Mary. Finally, with 1971's *Poems, Prayers and Promises*, he achieved superstardom as an artist, thanks to the million-selling hits "Take Me Home, Country Roads" and "Sunshine on My Shoulders." By 1974, he was firmly established as America's best-selling performer; his greatest-hits collection that year sold over ten million copies worldwide. In 1977, he moved into film but dramatically curtailed his recording output as a result. In the '80s, Denver's popularity waned as he turned his focus more towards humanitarian work. He made more news for a 1993 drunk-driving arrest than he did for records like 1991's *Different Directions*. Tragedy struck in 1997 when his experimental aircraft suddenly crashed, killing him instantly. *—Jason Ankeny*

● **Greatest Hits** / 1973 / RCA ✦✦✦✦✦
Released in 1973, *Greatest Hits* only sums up a handful of years of hitmaking for John Denver, but what years those were. Between 1971 and 1973, Denver actually didn't have that many hits, but they were songs that defined him—"Take Me Home, Country Roads," "Rocky Mountain High," and "Sunshine on My Shoulders." Those three songs, along with "Leaving on a Jet Plane"—which he wrote but Peter Paul & Mary made into a standard—are all here, along with seven other early songs recorded between 1969 and 1973 that may not be familiar to the average casual fan, and all capture Denver's warm folk-pop at its best. There may be more hits on *Greatest Hits, Vol. 2*, but this collection is every bit as engaging as that record. *—Stephen Thomas Erlewine*

Greatest Hits, Vol. 2 / 1977 / RCA ✦✦✦✦✦
Greatest Hits, Vol. 2 captures the hitmaking years, containing many of John Denver's most beloved songs: "Annie's Song," "Back Home Again," "Thank God I'm a Country Boy," "I'm Sorry," "Calypso," "Fly Away," "Grandma's Feather Bed" and "This Old Guitar." These are also the songs that found Denver enhancing his pop leanings, crafting endearingly catchy, sweet folk-pop songs that sounded more suited for airplay than singalongs around the campfire. And while the songs on the first *Greatest Hits* volume are perhaps more organic, these are impeccably crafted songs that justifiably turned Denver into a superstar. *—Stephen Thomas Erlewine*

Greatest Hits, Vol. 3 / 1985 / RCA ✦✦✦✦
By the end of the '70s, John Denver was still a star, but he didn't have many hits. That situation didn't improve in the early '80s, as his records started sliding slowly down the charts. This is the era that *Greatest Hits, Vol. 3* covers—one that found Denver's popularity fading, but not necessarily his skills. Sure, his songs don't sound as effortless or charming as they used to, but the best moments from these years (most of which are captured on this compilation) illustrate that he was still capable of crafting ingratiating folk-pop songs. It's not for every listener, but fans of Denver's classic years that want to dig a little deeper may find some gems here. *—Stephen Thomas Erlewine*

The Rocky Mountain Collection / Apr. 1996 / RCA ✦✦✦✦✦
The Rocky Mountain Collection is a double-disc, 39-track collection that features all of John Denver's greatest hits—"Leaving on a Jet Plane," "Sunshine on My Shoulders," "Take Me Home Country Roads," "Rocky Mountain High," "Annie's Song," "Thank God I'm a Country Boy," "Back Home Again," "Sweet Surrender," "Fly Away," "I'm Sorry"—plus several lesser-known but equally fine songs from throughout his career. For those who want to dig deeper than the *Greatest Hits* collections, or want to pass by those individual volumes in favor of one set, *The Rocky Mountain Collection* is an ideal purchase. *—Stephen Thomas Erlewine*

Reflections: Songs of Love & Life / Oct. 29, 1996 / RCA ✦✦✦✦
Reflections: Songs of Love & Life is a collection of John Denver's most sentimental soft-rock hits from the '70s, including "Annie's Song," "Sunshine on My Shoulders," "I'm Sorry" and "How Can I Leave You Again." Though it isn't a thorough retrospective, it is useful for casual fans who just want Denver's famous ballads. *—Stephen Thomas Erlewine*

Greatest Country Hits / Mar. 24, 1998 / RCA ✦✦✦✦✦
To the hardcore, John Denver was never really country, as evidenced by Charlie Rich's infamous protest at the Country Music Awards. Nevertheless, he was a country-pop star, scoring a number of hits on the country charts during the '70s and early '80s. *Greatest Country Hits* is a superb 18-track collection of those hits, and it's nearly as good as any of his greatest-hits collections. A few big songs, such as "Rocky Mountain High" and "Calypso," are missing, but all the familiar songs—"Take Me Home, Country Roads," "Sunshine On My Shoulders," "Annie's Song," "Back Home Again," "Sweet Surrender," "Thank God I'm a Country Boy," "I'm Sorry"—are here, along with such latter-day country hits as "Some Days Are Diamonds (Some Days Are Stone)" and "Dreamland Express." Furthermore, it's a generous, attractively packaged collection that is one of the best compilations RCA has yet assembled on John Denver, and it hopefully bodes well for upcoming reissues from the label. *—Stephen Thomas Erlewine*

Depeche Mode

f. 1980, Basildon, England

Alternative Dance, Club/Dance, Post-Punk, Alternative Pop/Rock, Synth Pop

Originally a product of Britain's New Romantic movement, Depeche Mode went on to become the quintessential electro-pop band of the 1980s; one of the first acts to establish a musical identity based completely around the use of synthesizers, the group began their existence as a bouncy dance-pop outfit but gradually developed a darker, more dramatic sound which ultimately positioned them as one of the most successful alternative bands of their era. After building a following on the London club scene, Depeche Mode scored their first major hit with "Just Can't Get Enough," and their 1981 debut LP *Speak and Spell* was also a success. Just as the group appeared poised for a major commercial breakthrough, however, principal songwriter Vince Clarke abruptly exited to form Yazoo; keyboardist Martin Gore grabbed the reins, and his ominous compositions grew more assured and sophisticated by the time of 1983's *Construction Time Again. Some Great Reward* was Depeche Mode's artistic and commercial breakthrough, as Gore's dark, kinky preoccupations with spiritual doubt ("Blasphemous Rumours") and psychosexual manipulation ("Master and Servant") came to the fore; the egalitarian single "People Are People" was a major hit on both sides of the Atlantic, and typified the music's turn towards more industrial textures. Still, despite an enormous fan base, the group was considered very much an underground cult phenomenon prior to the release of 1990's *Violator*, a Top Ten smash which spawned the hits "Enjoy the Silence," "Policy of Truth" and "Personal Jesus." *—Jason Ankeny*

Speak and Spell / 1981 / Sire ✦✦✦✦

Though probably nobody fully appreciated it at the time—perhaps least of all the band!—Depeche Mode's debut is at once both a conservative, functional pop record and a groundbreaking release. While various synth pioneers had come before—Gary Numan, early Human League, late-'70s Euro-disco, and above all Kraftwerk all had clear influence on *Speak and Spell*—Depeche became the undisputed founder of straight-up synth-pop with the album's 11 songs, light, hooky, and danceable numbers about love, life, and clubs. For all the claims about "dated" '80s sounds from rock purists, it should be noted that the basic guitar/bass/drums lineup of rock is almost 25 years older than the catchy keyboard lines and electronic drums making the music here. That such a sound would eventually become ubiquitous during the Reagan years, spawning lots of crud along the way, means the band should no more be held to blame for that than Motown and the Beatles for inspiring lots of bad stuff in the '60s. Credit for the album's success has to go to main songwriter Vince Clarke, who would extend and arguably perfect the synth-pop formula with Yazoo and Erasure; the classic early singles "New Life," "Dreaming of Me," and "Just Can't Get Enough," along with numbers ranging from the slyly homoerotic "Pretty Boy" to the moody thumper "Photographic," keep everything moving throughout. Gahan undersings about half the album, and Gore's two numbers lack the distinctiveness of his later work, but *Speak and Spell* remains an undiluted joy. *—Ned Raggett*

A Broken Frame / 1982 / Sire ✦✦✦

Martin Gore has famously noted that Depeche Mode stopped worrying about its future when the first post-Clarke-departure single, "See You," placed even higher on the English charts than anything else Vince Clarke had done with them. Such confidence carries through all of *Frame*, a notably more ambitious effort than the pure pop/disco of the band's debut. With arranging genius Alan Wilder still one album away from fully joining the band, *Frame* became very much Gore's record, writing all the songs and exploring various styles never again touched upon in later years. "Satellite" and "Monument" take distinct dub/reggae turns, while "Shouldn't Have Done That" delivers its slightly precious message about the dangers of adulthood with a spare arrangement and hollow, weirdly sweet vocals. Much of the album follows in a dark vein, forsaking earlier sprightliness, aside from tracks like "A Photograph of You" and "The Meaning of Love," for more melancholy reflections about love gone wrong as "Leave in Silence" and "My Secret Garden." More complex arrangements and juxtaposed sounds, such as the sparkle of breaking glass in "Leave in Silence," help give this underrated album even more of an intriguing, unexpected edge. Gore's lyrics sometimes veer on the facile, but Gahan's singing comes more clearly to the fore throughout—things aren't all there yet, but they were definitely starting to get close. *—Ned Raggett*

Construction Time Again / 1983 / Sire ✦✦✦

The full addition of Alan Wilder to Depeche Mode's line-up created a perfect troika that would last another 11 years, as the combination of Martin Gore's songwriting, Wilder's arranging, and David Gahan's singing and live star power resulted in an ever more compelling series of albums and singles. *Construction Time Again*, the new line-up's first full effort, is a bit hit and miss nonetheless, but when it does hit, it does so perfectly. Right from the album's first song, "Love in Itself," something is clearly up; Depeche never sounded quite so thick with its sound before, with synths arranged into a mini-orchestra/horn section and real piano and acoustic guitar spliced in at strategic points. Two tracks later, "Pipeline" offers the first clear hint of an increasing industrial influence (the band members were early fans of Einstürzende Neubauten), with clattering metal samples and oddly chain gang-like lyrics and vocals. The album's clear highlight has to be "Everything Counts," a live staple for years, combining a deceptively simple, ironic lyric about the music business with a perfectly catchy but unusually arranged blending of more metallic scraping samples and melodica amid even more forceful funk/hip-hop beats. Elsewhere, on "Shame" and "Told You So," Gore's lyrics start taking on more of the obsessive personal relationship studies that would soon dominate his writing. Wilder's own songwriting contributions are fine musically, but lyrically, "preachy" puts it mildly, especially the environment-friendly "The Landscape Is Changing." *—Ned Raggett*

People Are People / 1984 / Sire ✦✦✦

The unexpected American success of "People Are People," which remained the band's biggest U.S. hit until the start of the '90s, prompted this stateside-only compilation, very much a dog's breakfast of new and old songs alike. Earlier album cuts such as "Pipeline" and "Told You So" appear here, but the four new tracks understandably received the biggest attention. The title track itself, though the bandmembers have long since expressed embarrassment over it, still sounds like what it became, an engaging, instantly memorable pop hit—if the lyrical sentiments are among Gore's most naively sociopolitical before or since, Gahan delivers them strongly, with Gore providing a fine counterpoint vocal. Musically, the explicit use of sampled metallic crashes and detailed production throughout makes the song one of the strongest incorporations of industrial music techniques in a more listener-friendly manner. Of the three other new tracks, "Get the Balance Right" is the strongest, a wickedly barbed but beautifully sung lyric on political/lifestyle posturing with a killer synth line melody. "Work Hard" veers towards the monotonous, while "Now This Is Fun" has a nice moody intro to recommend it. Given that both "People Are People" and "Get the Balance Right" ended up on the band's first proper singles compilation, this collection is now rendered one solely for the hardcore fans. *—Ned Raggett*

Some Great Reward / 1984 / Sire ✦✦✦✦✦

The peak of the band's industrial-gone-mainstream fusion, and still one of the best electronic music albums yet recorded, *Reward* still sounds great, with the band's ever-evolving musical and production skills matching even more ambitious songwriting from Gore. "People Are People" appears here, but finds itself outclassed by some of Depeche's undisputed classics, most especially the moody, beautiful "Somebody," a Gore-sung piano ballad that mixes its wit and emotion skillfully; "Master and Servant," an amped-up, slamming dance track that conflates sexual and economic politics to sharp effect; and the closing "Blasphemous Rumors," a slow-building anthemic number supporting one of Gore's most cynical lyrics, addressing a suicidal teen who finds God only to die soon afterward. Even lesser-known tracks like the low-key pulse of "Lie to Me" and the weirdly dreamy "It Doesn't Matter" showcase an increasingly confident band. Wilder's arrangements veer from the big to the stripped down, but always with just the right touch, such as the crowd samples bubbling beneath "Somebody" or the call/response a cappella start to "Master and Servant." With *Reward*, Gahan's singing style found the metier it was going to stick with for the next ten years, and while it's never gone down well with some ears, it still has a compelling edge to it that suits the material well. *—Ned Raggett*

Catching Up with Depeche Mode / 1985 / Sire ✦✦✦✦✦

Like its predecessor, *People Are People, Catching Up With Depeche Mode* attempts to fill in gaps in the group's extensive discography by compiling singles and album tracks taken from their four previous studio LPs. Dating back to the band's Vince Clarke-penned hits ("Just Can't Get Enough," "Dreaming of Me"), the set culminates with tracks like "Master and Servant" and "Blasphemous Rumours," which bear the full fruit of Martin Gore's dark obsessions; a preview of *Black Celebration* is even offered via "Fly on the Windshield." *—Jason Ankeny*

Black Celebration / 1986 / Sire ✦✦✦✦

Whether the band felt it was simply the time to move on from its most explicit industrial pop fusion days, or whether increased success and concurrently larger venues pushed the music into different avenues, Depeche Mode's fifth studio album saw the group embarked on a path that in many ways defined their sound to the present: emotionally extreme lyrics matched with amped-up tunes, as much anthemic rock as they are compelling dance, along with stark, low-key ballads. The slow, sneaky build of the opening title track, with a strange distorted vocal sample providing a curious opening hook, sets the tone as Gahan sings of making it through "another black day" while powerful drums and echoing metallic pings carry the song. *Black Celebration* is actually heavier on the ballads throughout, many sung by Gore—the most per album he has yet taken lead on—with notable dramatic beauties including "Sometimes," with its surprise gospel choir start and rough piano sonics, and the hyper-nihilistic "World Full of Nothing." The various singles from the album remain definite highlights, such as "A Question of Time," a brawling, aggressive number with a solid Gahan vocal, and the romantic/physical politics of "Stripped," featuring particularly sharp arrangements from Alan Wilder. However, with such comparatively lesser-known but equally impressive numbers as the quietly intense romance of "Here Is the House" to boast, *Black Celebration* is solid through and through. *—Ned Raggett*

Music for the Masses / 1987 / Sire ✦✦✦✦✦

Initially the title must have sounded like an incredibly pretentious boast, except that Depeche Mode then went on to do a monstrous world tour, score even more hits in America and elsewhere than ever before, and pick up a large number of name checks from emerging house and techno artists on top of all that. As for the music the masses got this time around, the opening cut "Never Let Me Down Again" started things off wonderfully: a compressed guitar riff suddenly slamming into a huge-sounding percussion/keyboard/piano combination, anchored to a constantly repeated melodic hook, ever-building synth/orchestral parts at the song's end, and one of Gahan's best vocals (though admittedly singing one of Gore's more pedestrian lyrics). It feels huge throughout, like they taped Depeche recording at the world's largest arena show instead of in a studio. Other key singles "Strangelove" and the (literally) driving "Behind the Wheel" maintained the same blend of power and song skill, while some of the quieter numbers such as "The Things You Said" and "I Want You Now" showed musical and lyrical intimacy could easily co-exist with the big chart-busters. Add to that other winners like "To Have and to Hold," with its Russian radio broadcast start and dramatic, downward spiral of music accompanied by Gahan's subtly powerful take on a desperate Gore love lyric, and the weird, wonderful choral closer "Pimpf," and Depeche's massive success becomes perfectly clear. *—Ned Raggett*

101 / 1989 / Sire ✦✦✦✦
As an event, Depeche Mode's huge (attendance around 80,000) L.A. Rose Bowl concert in 1988 remains legendary; no single artist show had totally sold out the venue since eight years beforehand, while the film documentary done by Dylan-filmer D.A. Pennebaker based around the show clearly demonstrated fans' intense commitment to a near-decade-old band most mainstream critics continued to stupidly portray as a flash-in-the-pan synth-pop effort. This start-to-final-encore record of the concert showcases a band perfectly able to carry its music from studio to stage as well as any other combo worth its salt should be able to do. Understandably focused on *Music for the Masses* material, the album shows Depeche experimenting with alternate arrangements at various points for live performance; big numbers like "Never Let Me Down Again," "Stripped," and "Blasphemous Rumors" pack even more of a wallop here. Slower numbers and more than a couple of ballads help to vary the hit-packed set, including a fine "Somebody" and "The Things You Said" combination sung by Gore. "Pleasure Little Treasure," on record an okay B-side, becomes a monster rocker live, the type of unexpected surprise one could expect from a solid band no matter what the music. With a triumphant set of closing numbers, including magnificent takes on "Never Let Me Down Again," "Master and Servant," and the set-ending "Everything Counts," with what sounds like the entire audience singing the chorus well after the song has finally ended, *101* does far better at its task than most might have guessed. *—Ned Raggett*

Violator / Feb. 1990 / Sire ✦✦✦✦✦
In a word, stunning. Perhaps an odd word to use given that *Violator* continued in the general vein of the previous two studio efforts by Depeche Mode: Gore's upfront lyrical emotional extremism and knack for a catchy hook filtered through Wilder's ear for perfect arrangements, ably assisted by top English producer Flood. Yet the idea that this record would both dominate worldwide charts, while song for song being simply the best, most consistent effort yet from the band could only have been the wildest fantasy before its release. The opening two singles from the album, however, signaled something was up. First was "Personal Jesus," at once perversely simplistic, with a stiff, arcane funk/hip-hop beat and basic blues guitar chords, and tremendous, thanks to sharp production touches and Gahan's echoed, snaky vocals. Then "Enjoy the Silence," a nothing-else-remains-but-us ballad pumped up into a huge, dramatic romance/dance number, commanding in its mock orchestral/choir scope. Follow-up single "Policy of Truth" did just fine as well, a low-key Motown funk number for the modern day with a sharp love/hate lyric to boot. To top it all off, the album itself scored on song after song, from the shuffling beat of "Sweetest Perfection" (well sung by Gore) and the ethereal "Waiting for the Night" to the guilt-ridden and loving it "Halo," building into a string-swept pounder. "Clean" wraps up *Violator* on an eerie note, all ominous bass notes and odd atmospherics carrying the song. Goth without ever being stupidly hammy, synth without sounding like the clinical stereotype of synth music, rock without ever sounding like a "rock" band, Depeche here reached astounding heights indeed. *—Ned Raggett*

Songs of Faith & Devotion / Mar. 23, 1993 / Sire ✦✦✦✦
In between *Violator* and *Songs of Faith & Devotion*, a lot happened: Nirvana rewrote the ideas of what "alternative" was supposed to be, while Nine Inch Nails, hit the airwaves as the most clearly Depeche-influenced new hit band around. In the meantime, the band went through some high-profile arguing as Gahan turned into a long-haired, leather-clad rocker and pushed for a more guitar-oriented sound. Yet the odd thing about *Songs of Faith & Devotion* is that it sounds pretty much like a Depeche Mode album, only with some new sonic tricks courtesy of Alan Wilder and co-producer Flood. Perhaps even odder is the fact that it works incredibly well all the same. "I Feel You," opening with a screech of feedback, works its live drums well, but when the heavy synth bass kicks in with the wailing backing vocals, even most rockers might find it hard to compete. Gore's lyrical bent, as per the title, ponders relationships through distinctly religious imagery; while the gambit is hardly new, on songs like the centerpiece "In Your Room," the combination of personal and spiritual love blends perfectly. Outside musicians appear for the first time, including female backing singers on a couple of tracks, most notably the gospel-flavored "Condemnation" and the uilleann pipes on "Judas," providing a lovely intro to the underrated song (later covered by Tricky). "Rush" is the biggest misstep, a too obvious sign that Nine Inch Nails was a recording-session favorite to unwind to. But with other numbers such as "Walking in My Shoes" and "The Mercy in You" to recommend it, *Songs of Faith & Devotion* continues the Depeche Mode winning streak. *—Ned Raggett*

Songs of Faith & Devotion Live / May 1993 / Sire ✦✦

Ultra / Apr. 15, 1997 / Reprise ✦✦✦
When news surfaced in 1995 that Alan Wilder had departed Depeche to concentrate on his solo project Recoil, the immediate concern among fans was whether the band would be able to hit past heights again. Though Wilder's profile was always much lesser than that of Martin Gore and David Gahan—and almost even that of Alan Fletcher, whose non-performance live has always been a running joke in the fan community and who freely admits to generally being around merely to maintain a vibe with his childhood friend Gore—his capability at arranging the songs over the years gave the band its increasingly distinct, unique edge. Combined with Gahan's near suicide and lengthy recovery from drugs, things looked bleak. Happily, *Ultra* turned out a winner; hooking up with Tim Simenon, longtime U.K. dance maven and producer of arty fare such as Gavin Friday's *Adam and Eve*, Depeche delivered a strong album as a rejuvenated band. The most immediate change was Gahan's singing; for the first time ever, he took singing lessons beforehand, and his new control and projection simply shines, especially on the marvelous "It's No Good," a pulsing, tense yet beautiful song with another deeply romantic Gore lyric. Opener "Barrel of a Gun" continues in the vein of arena-level stompers like "Never Let Me Down Again" and "I Feel You," with huge drum slams and scratching to boot, but *Ultra* mostly covers subtler territory, such as the slightly creepy "Sister of Night" and the gentle "The Love Thieves." Gore sings two winners: the orchestral, slow dance groove "Home" and "The Bottom Line," featuring steel guitar and Can's Jaki Liebezeit on drums, distinctly different territory for Depeche. Closing with "Insight," a quite lovely, building ballad, *Ultra* showed Depeche wasn't ready to quit by any means. *—Ned Raggett*

● **The Singles 81 > 85** / 1998 / Sire ✦✦✦✦✦
Replacing the original *Catching Up with Depeche Mode* compilation, *81 > 85* subtracts two tracks—the lightweight curiosity "Flexible" and "Fly on the Windscreen," which surfaced to better effect on *Black Celebration*—and adds two, the full six-minute remix of "Just Can't Get Enough" and the original version of "Photographic," Depeche's recording debut on a 1980 compilation album. The overall collection remains the same, though, namely, a run through the peerless singles that kept the band on the charts in the U.K. and elsewhere, as well as building up their increasing cult following in America. It's an embarrassment of riches, from such bouncy early hits as "New Life," "Just Can't Get Enough," and "The Meaning of Love" to the increasingly heavier sound of "Everything Counts," "People Are People," and "Blasphemous Rumors." Nearly all the tracks appear in the original single mixes, some quite different from their album versions, others essentially the same (the one subtle difference in "Somebody" is an echoey percussion pattern buried in the mix, for instance). Two otherwise unavailable singles also appear here: "It's Called a Heart" is pleasant enough, but "Shake the Disease" is great, an obsessive love lyric matched to a wonderful, slow dance melody and an excellent pairing of Gahan's more aggressive and Gore's gentler vocals. As an introduction to Depeche's brilliant knack for catchy tunes evolving over time into a more challenging but no less popular collection of songs, at once defining and expanding the boundaries of synth-pop, look no further. *—Ned Raggett*

● **The Singles 86 > 98** / Oct. 6, 1998 / Reprise ✦✦✦✦✦
It took Depeche Mode only four years to assemble their first singles compilation, but 12 to assemble *The Singles 86 > 98*. Appropriately, the second set was much more ambitious than *The Singles 81 > 85*, spanning two discs and 20 songs, plus a live version of "Everything Counts." *The Singles 86 > 98* was an album that many fans, both casual and hardcore, waited patiently for, and for good reason—Depeche Mode was always more effective as a singles band than as album artists. That's not to say that the double-disc compilation is perfect. DM's output fluctuated wildly during those 12 years, as the group hit both career highs and lows. It's possible to hear it all on this set, from "Strangelove" and "Never Let Me Down Again," through "Personal Jesus" and "Enjoy the Silence," to "I Feel You" and "Barrel of a Gun." It's possible that some casual listeners will find that the collection meanders a bit too much for their tastes, but the end result is definitive and, along with *The Singles 81 > 85*, ranks as Depeche Mode's best, most listenable album. *—Stephen Thomas Erlewine*

Exciter / May 15, 2001 / Mute/Reprise ✦✦✦✦
It's rare to find bands capable of keeping their own best qualities to the fore while trying something new each time out, but Depeche Mode demonstrate that balance in full on the marvelous *Exciter*. Arguably the first album made by the group as a cohesive unit since *Violator* (and bearing some resemblance to that record in overall title and song names—compare "The Sweetest Condition" with "The Sweetest Perfection"), *Exciter* finds the trio again balancing pop catchiness with experimental depths. As with *Ultra*, an outside producer helps focus the end results in new, intriguing directions—in this case, said producer is Mark Bell, known for his work with Björk but also as part of Warp Records flagship act LFO, which always acknowledged their own debt to Depeche. Bell's ear for minimal, crisp beats and quick, subtle arrangements and changes suit Martin Gore's songs beautifully. If there are few storming arena-shaking numbers this time out, the exquisite delicacy throughout is addicting, with Gore's guitar providing slippery and stinging leads to the smoky, romantic flow of *Exciter*. "When the Body Speaks" is a particular winner, his gentle work and a backing string section combining just right. David Gahan's voice, already audibly benefiting from lessons on *Ultra*, is even more supple and passionate than before, ranging from the fuller delivery on the snaky charm of "Shine" to the haunting album closer "Goodnight Lovers," a romantic lullaby with perfect counterpoint backing vocals. Gore's own singing remains equally fine, as does his lyrical obsessions on, well, obsession—"Breathe," which quotes more Bible names per verse than most preachers, makes for a good example on both fronts. When the band fully crank it up, the results work there too—"The Dead of Night" makes for a far superior nod to Gore's glam roots and Depeche's own industrial-dance descendents than *Songs of Faith and Devotion*'s "Rush" did. *—Ned Raggett*

Derek & The Dominos

f. 1970, New York, NY, **db.** 1971
Album Rock, British Blues, Hard Rock, Blues-Rock
Derek & the Dominos was a group formed by guitarist/singer Eric Clapton with other former members of Delaney & Bonnie & Friends, in the spring of 1970. From late August to early October, they recorded the celebrated double album *Layla and Other Assorted Love Songs* with guitarist Duane Allman sitting in. They then returned to touring in England and the U.S., playing their final date on December 6. The *Layla* album was successful in the U.S., where "Bell Bottom Blues" and the title song charted as singles in abbreviated versions, but it did not chart in the U.K. The Dominos reconvened to record a second album in May 1971, but split up without completing it. Clapton then retired from the music business, nursing a heroin addiction. In his absence, and in the wake of Allman's death in a motorcycle accident on October 29, 1971, the Dominos and *Layla*

gained in stature. Rereleased as a single at its full, seven-minute length in connection with the compilation album *History of Eric Clapton*, "Layla" hit the Top Ten in the U.S. and the U.K. in the summer of 1972. Time has only added to the renown for the group, which is now rated among Eric Clapton's most outstanding achievements. *—William Ruhlmann*

★ **Layla & Other Assorted Love Songs** / Nov. 1970 / Polydor ✦✦✦✦✦
Wishing to escape the superstar expectations that sank Blind Faith before it was launched, Eric Clapton retreated with several sidemen from Delaney & Bonnie to record the material that would form *Layla & Other Assorted Love Songs*. From these meager beginnings grew his greatest album. Duane Allman joined the band shortly after recording began, and his spectacular slide guitar pushed Clapton to new heights. Then again, Clapton may have gotten there without him, considering the emotional turmoil he was in during the recording. He was in hopeless, unrequited love with Patti Boyd, the wife of his best friend, George Harrison, and that pain surges throughout *Layla*, especially on its epic title track. But what really makes *Layla* such a powerful record is that Clapton, ignoring the traditions that occasionally painted him into a corner, simply tears through these songs with burning, intense emotion. He makes standards like "Have You Ever Loved a Woman" and "Nobody Knows You (When You're Down and Out)" into his own, while his collaborations with Bobby Whitlock—including "Any Day" and "Why Does Love Got to Be So Sad?"—teem with passion. And, considering what a personal album *Layla* is, it's somewhat ironic that the lovely coda "Thorn Tree in the Garden" is a solo performance by Whitlock, and that the song sums up the entire album as well as "Layla" itself. *—Stephen Thomas Erlewine*

In Concert / Jan. 1973 / Polydor ✦✦✦
While it isn't nearly as intense as *Layla*, *Derek & the Dominos In Concert* offers some fine playing by Clapton and his band and easily ranks among his best live albums. *—Stephen Thomas Erlewine*

The Layla Sessions: 20th Anniversary Edition / Sep. 1990 / Polydor ✦✦✦
Featuring two discs of outtakes and jams, the three-CD box *The Layla Sessions* manages to detract from the original by surrounding it with endless, dull instrumentals. Then again, all the unreleased material proves what a well-constructed album *Layla* is. *—Stephen Thomas Erlewine*

Live at the Fillmore / Feb. 22, 1994 / Polydor ✦✦✦
In his liner notes, Anthony DeCurtis calls *Live at the Fillmore* "a digitally remixed and remastered version of the 1973 Derek and the Dominos double album *In Concert*, with five previously unreleased performances and two tracks that have only appeared on the four-CD Clapton retrospective, *Crossroads*." But this does not adequately describe the album. *Live at the Fillmore* is not exactly an expanded version of *In Concert*; it is a different album culled from the same concerts that were used to compile the earlier album. *Live at the Fillmore* contains six of the nine recordings originally released on *In Concert*, and three of its five previously unreleased performances are different recordings of songs also featured on *In Concert*—"Why Does Love Got to Be So Sad?," "Tell the Truth," and "Let It Rain." The other two, "Nobody Knows You When You're Down and Out" and "Little Wing," have not been heard before in any concert version. Even when the same recordings are used on *Live at the Fillmore* as on *In Concert*, they have, as noted, been remixed and, as not noted, re-edited. In either form, Derek and the Dominos' October 1970 stand at the Fillmore East, a part of the group's only U.S. tour, finds them a looser aggregation than they seemed to be in the studio making their only album, *Layla and Other Assorted Love Songs*. A trio backing Eric Clapton, the Dominos leave the guitarist considerable room to solo on extended numbers, five of which run over ten minutes each. Clapton doesn't show consistent invention, but his playing is always directed, and he plays more blues than you can hear on any other Clapton live recording. *—William Ruhlmann*

Rick Derringer

b. Aug. 5, 1947, Celina, OH
Vocals, Guitar, Bass / Pop/Rock, Hard Rock, Blues-Rock, Rock & Roll
It seems like Rick Derringer has been on the rock & roll scene forever—actually, it's only been since 1965, which makes him one of the more enduring veterans of his generation. Derringer's work with his band the McCoys in his mid-teens, highlighted by the bubblegum anthem "Hang on Sloopy," gave him a claim to low-level rock & roll immortality, and his subsequent playing with Johnny (and later Edgar) Winter provided him with a degree of credibility that a lot of guitar players can only envy, especially after the release of the Edgar Winter live double album *Roadwork*. Derringer began getting production experience with the McCoys, but they were never able to overcome their bubblegum rock image, and by the end of the 1960s, Derringer and his brother Randy were recruited by Johnny Winter into his band, with Derringer playing guitar and also producing. He emerged as a solo artist in the wake of his playing with Edgar Winter's White Trash. Derringer first became popular in his own right during the early '70s/mid-'70s, beginning with a new version of his own "Rock & Roll Hoochie Koo" (which Johnny Winter had covered for him a few years earlier) off Derringer's heavy metal-influenced debut album, *All American Boy*. Derringer soon had his own band, called Derringer, on the road and within a couple of years had established himself as a popular favorite. Derringer's recorded history was somewhat spotty, however, as his record sales never matched his favor with concert audiences. He spent most of the late '70s and 1980s, however, as a producer, working with artists as diverse as Bette Midler, Kiss, Meat Loaf, Cyndi Lauper, Barbra Streisand, and Weird Al Yankovic. *—Bruce Eder*

All American Boy / 1974 / Blue Sky ✦✦✦✦✦
Fresh from stints in the McCoys and Johnny Winter Band, *All American Boy* was supposed to be Rick Derringer's breakthrough solo album. For years, it was argued that the frightfully touched-up cover photo of Derringer sank the album before anyone heard it. If that's true, it's a shame, because this is simply Rick Derringer's most focused and cohesive album, a marvelous blend of rockers, ballads, and atmospheric instrumentals. Joe Walsh helps out on a couple of tracks, but mostly it's Derringer's show—multi-instrumental virtuosity in a number of styles. Consider this one of the great albums of the '70s that fell between the cracks. *—Cub Koda*

● **Rock & Roll Hoochie Coo: The Best of Rick Derringer** / Sep. 3, 1996 / Epic Associated/Legacy ✦✦✦✦✦
Rock & Roll Hoochie Coo: Best of Rick Derringer collects all of Derringer's biggest hits and his album-rock staples, making it an excellent retrospective of his heyday as a popular arena rocker in the mid-'70s. *—Stephen Thomas Erlewine*

Des'ree

Adult Contemporary, Urban
With her second album, 1994's *I Ain't Movin'*, soul singer Des'ree became a star. Des'ree's contemporary soul is smooth enough to fit into most urban contemporary playlists, yet it has enough grit and emotional style to attract fans of early-'70s R&B. Her first album—*Mind Adventures* (1992)—didn't attract an audience, yet her second record, 1994's *I Ain't Movin'*, was a pop and R&B smash; thanks to the Top Ten hit "You Gotta Be," the record sold over a million copies. *Supernatural* followed in 1998. *—Stephen Thomas Erlewine*

Mind Adventures / 1992 / Epic ✦✦✦

● **I Ain't Movin'** / 1994 / Epic/550 Music ✦✦✦
Des'ree's second album features one gem of a single, "You Gotta Be." It's as good as '90s spirit-lifting anthems go, even if it does seem more adaptable/limited to women's issues rather than to the bigger picture. Still, a major achievement on a minor album that's mostly filled out with listenable but listless people-power tunes of glory. *—Michael Gallucci*

Supernatural / Aug. 11, 1998 / 550 Music ✦✦✦
On her third album of adult R&B, new age princess Des'ree offers up more musical self-help tips and self-esteem makeovers for the chronically lovesick and spiritually downhearted. And while there's nothing as peacefully sublime as "You Gotta Be" (from 1994's *I Ain't Movin'*) on *Supernatural*, the listen is a soothing one. Credit Brit Des'ree herself for this; her voice—a reassuring tool that envelops everything around it—has never been better. Working her softened tones around the mostly forgettable material (many of the songs try to rewrite "You Gotta Be" by essentially sticking with the same formula of making sophisticated urban soul), she creates a melodic new-age tone (complete with a cover of Bruce Springsteen's "Fire") that may not stick with you a lifetime, but it sure feels like the most tranquil place on earth for its 50 minutes. *—Michael Gallucci*

Endangered Species / May 23, 2000 / Sony International ✦✦✦

Descendents

f. 1979
College Rock, L.A. Punk, Punk-Pop, Hardcore Punk, American Underground
Fueled by "rejection, food, coffee, girls, fishing and food," the Descendents sprang up during the halcyon days of the Los Angeles punk scene; fusing the blind rage of hardcore with an unexpectedly wry, self-deprecating wit and a strong melodic sensibility which set them distinctly apart from their West Coast brethren, they gradually emerged as one of the most enduring and adored bands of their time. Formed in 1979, the Descendents' first lineup consisted of vocalist/guitarist Frank Navetta, vocalist/bassist Tony Lombardo and drummer Bill Stevenson; initially sporting an edgy power-pop sound inspired by the Buzzcocks, the group issued a debut single, "Ride the Wild," and then promptly vanished from sight.

When the Descendents resurfaced in 1981, they were a four-piece fronted by vocalist Milo Auckerman, a beloved figure within the hardcore community who infused the group's identity with both unmitigated teen angst and a healthy dose of goofball humor. Amid a relentless, caffeine-powered touring schedule, the Descendents found time to record the 1981 EP *Fat*, a collection spotlighting both Auckerman's affection for fast food ("Weinerschnitzel," "I Like Food") and distaste for parental guidance ("My Dad Sucks"). A year later, the group issued their debut LP, *Milo Goes to College*; despite the considerable levity of tracks like "Bikeage" and "Suburban Home," the title was no joke—Auckerman was indeed headed off to study biochemistry, and when Stevenson joined the ranks of Black Flag, the Descendents went on sabbatical.

In 1985, the group re-formed, with SWA alum Ray Cooper replacing Navetta on guitar; after the release of the more pop-flavored album *I Don't Want to Grow Up*, ex-Anti bassist Doug Carrion assumed Lombardo's duties. A sunnier perspective informed 1986's *Enjoy!*, as evidenced by the inclusion of a cover of the Beach Boys' "Wendy," but after 1987's lackluster *All*, the group split again; after Stevenson formed a new group, also dubbed All, the only Descendents products to appear for a number of years were a pair of live releases, 1987's *Liveage!* and 1989's *Hallraker*. Somewhat surprisingly, Auckerman and Stevenson re-formed the Descendents in 1996 with All bassist Karl Alvarez and guitarist Stephen Egerton; in addition to mounting a tour, the group recorded a new album, *Everything Sucks*. *—Jason Ankeny*

Fat / 1981 / SST ✦✦✦
Quick, immediate, goofy, fun—*Fat* and the Descendents in general in a nutshell. Aukerman turned out to be the genius addition to the original trio, with the ultimate in bratty sneering whines and yelps and a perfectly gone sense of humor. He actually became even more high-pitched with time—here sometimes he sounds at points more like an early Black Flag vocalist—but he's still got it down just right. The band merrily bashes and crashes behind, combining Wire's sense of "get done and go home" with poppy L.A./O.C. hardcore hooks. The result was a hyperspeed trashing of modern youth

Kultur circa 1981, where the song titles in some cases took longer to read than to listen to the tunes as a whole. "My Dad Sucks" starts the whole thing and stops just as abruptly, only to dive into the story of "Mr. Bass," namely the adventure of said fish and his eventual appearance "on my wall." And so forth—those demanding really deep thoughts from the band's music should look elsewhere. The most appropriate track of them all is the 15-second "I Like Food"—"turkey legs and raw fish eyes/teenage girls, with ketchup too!"—while "Weinerschnitzel" is even shorter and even crazier, detailing an order at said hot dog joint with barely room to breathe. *—Ned Raggett*

Milo Goes to College / 1982 / SST ♦♦♦♦♦
And indeed, since he was heading off to do just that, the Descendents bowed out the earliest phase of its existence with another collection of blink-and-you'll-miss-it songs about life, love, girls, losers, and, of course, food. Starting with the classic rip-and-riff of "Myage," which started a long-standing trend of Descendents songs ending with "-age," the four-piece pureed everything it loved—pop hooks, punk and hardcore thrash, and whatever else it enjoyed—and came up with an unpretentious, catchy winner. The playing of the core band is even better than before, never mistaking increased skill with needing to show off; the Lombardo/Stevenson rhythm section is in perfect sync while Navetta provides the corrosive power. Add in Aukerman's in-your-face hilarity and fuck-off stance, and it's punk rock that wears both its adolescence and brains on its sleeve. Aukerman lets his heart slip through more than once amid all the hilarious descriptions and putdowns, like the slow-burn introduction to "Catalina," with Navetta's guitar the perfect snarling counterpoint. There are a couple of moments where the band's young age is all too obvious—the trendoids slammed in "Loser" deserve the total trashing given, but the casual homophobia is unfortunate no matter where you stand. As for "Kabuki Girl," you've got to wonder. Generally, though, this is smart, sly music and words coming from people interested in creating their own lives and style as opposed to following trends. There's "Tonyage," another rant against punk/new wave wannabes who "were all surfers last year"; the wise-in-advance-of-its-years "I'm Not a Punk" and perhaps the band's greatest song; and the power-singalong "Suburban Home," with its spoken word start and ending, "I want to be stereotyped, I want to be classified!" The music never stops, neither does the energy—an instant party album of its own kind. *—Ned Raggett*

Bonus Fat / 1985 / SST ♦♦♦
So-called because of the two bonus tracks that surfaced on this reissue of *Fat*, specifically the two sides from the group's original single, "Ride the Wild"/"It's a Hectic World." Aukerman hadn't joined the group yet, while the music is actually gentle, surf-inspired power pop more than anything else. "Ride the Wild" is a classic enough lament over a lyin' girl with Navetta's semi-tremolo twang doing what it can, vocals left down in the mix. "It's a Hectic World," meanwhile, is even more explicitly surfy in ways, but with a nervous, flat new wave edge to it as well—not quite Devo if they grew up on the coast, but there's something to that comparison. *—Ned Raggett*

I Don't Want to Grow Up / 1985 / SST ♦♦♦♦
What's to be expected given the title track, with a hilarious 'nyah nyah!' line on top of the chorus! Give a closer ear to the song, though—where the reason not to grow up is that it might "mean being like you"—and the band's core message of having fun and dealing with things as best one can in a stupid society is still there. When the four want to be straight up and perfectly poppy, they can and do with smashing success, with surprisingly mature, emotional lyrics and playing that doesn't rely on all-speed all the time. "Can't Go Back" is a great lost power-pop classic, with some of Aukerman's best singing, a wonderful chorus and a tuneful reflection on not reliving past mistakes. "Christmas Vacation" is another winner, a heartfelt and sharp depiction of a relationship on the skids with some great, melancholy harmonies, while "My World" draws on Aukerman's college years with a tale of personal frustration in an unfamiliar locale, all while rocking hard and strong. For all this there's ridiculous humor everywhere—thus "Pervert," which is at once frank and funny, saying "I'd hate to think that romance is just a pose/But all I want to do is rip off your clothes." "Rockstar," which immediately follows, is a hyperspeed trashing that's the understandable sequel to "Loser," demolishing the title character with a series of brief putdowns before concluding with a drawled "Let's exploit rock & roll to its fullest potential." But of course. *—Ned Raggett*

Enjoy / 1986 / SST ♦♦

All / 1987 / SST ♦♦♦♦
Just when the Descendents were thought to have gone to the world of bands who've passed their prime, they return with *All*. With this record, not only are they forgiven for the bad spots to be found on here—it's not like they can't be skipped over—but their last release (*Enjoy*) will be forgotten. With some of their best material all dealing with the traumas of a broken relationship—"Collidge" and "Clean Sheets," for example—these guys prove that the most creative comes out of personal tragedy. And as for the tearjerker "Pep Talk," it's a felony that this song wasn't included on their "best of" album, *Somery*. *—Mike DaRonco*

Liveage / 1987 / SST ♦♦♦
Recorded sometime during their *All* tour back in 1986, *Liveage* showcases the Descendents while they were at the height of their popularity. One could classify this as a best-of live album, considering that it features all the hits—"Coolidge," "Clean Sheets," "Wendy" and "Suburban Home," among others; not a "Sour Grape" to be found in the bunch. Bratty, aggravated pop-punk at its finest, the Descendents were not only way ahead of their time, but they were also one of the most influential punk bands of the '80s. *Liveage* is for all the fans who were too young to see them at their peak or too slow to get tickets before their reunion tour sold out. *—Mike DaRonco*

Two Things at Once (Milo Goes to College/Bonus Fat) / 1988 / SST ♦♦♦♦
Just like the title says, this album complies *Milo Goes to College* and the *Bonus Fat* EP, both of which are great releases, conveniently packaged on one record. All the mischievous teenage skaters could appreciate classics like "Myage," "I'm Not a Loser," "Bikeage" and "Hope." But for all those who already own their "best of" (*Somery*, which features the previously mentioned songs), other less-known hits such as "Marriage," "I'm Not a Punk" and "Catalina" are exclusive to this release. *—Mike DaRonco*

Hallraker: Live! / 1989 / SST ♦♦♦
When the Descendents finally ended their first run as an on-again/off-again pop-punk band in 1987, a pair of live albums (*Liveage* and *Hallraker*) was compiled by their only constant member, founding drummer Bill Stevenson. As Stevenson writes in the liner notes for *Hallraker*, *Liveage* was meant to "serve as a sort of 'greatest-hits' album," but too many tracks were left out, so a second LP was released, "at the request of fans." The albums do provide a fine end cap to the first part of the band's legacy, even though several early songs ("Bikeage," "Marriage," "Jean Is Dead," etc.) are unforgivably absent.

The album was assembled from live tracks recorded at two shows: one in July 1987 at First Avenue in Minneapolis, and the other in April 1987 at Berkeley Square in Berkeley. This was during the "All" and "Final" tours, as described by Stevenson, before the band switched singers to Dave Smalley to become All, and Milo Aukerman wandered off to Ph.D.-land.

The recordings here do well to capture the vitality and frenzy of the band in action, even as they were in the final throes of existence. Among the songs that are included, "Pep Talk," "Cheer," and "My World" are the highlights. Other tracks like "Iceman" and "Jealous of the World" demonstrate the metal edge that developed in the band's sound in their last couple of studio albums.

The Descendents reunited in 1996 with *Everything Sucks*, featuring the same lineup (for once!) and proving that they hadn't lost a step. For their first incarnation (as it was), *Hallraker* provides a good document after the fact. *—Jeremy Salmon*

● **Somery** / Jul. 16, 1991 / SST ♦♦♦♦♦
Somery is an overview of the Descendents' SST records, drawing equally from each record. Although this means a handful of great songs from their best albums are missing, *Somery* nevertheless selects the highlights from their occasionally uneven records, making it a useful and comprehensive retrospective. *—Stephen Thomas Erlewine*

Everything Sucks / Sep. 24, 1996 / Epitaph ♦♦♦
To hear it told, the reason why yet another Descendents reunion happened might have been because Epitaph wasn't going to sign All on their own. Then again, it all depends on who one talks to. Regardless of rationale or the nagging suspicion that the mid-'90s breakthrough of Green Day and the Offspring was the only reason this album got recorded, one fact remains: take this out of its surrounding context and this was and is a prime Descendents album. All the humor and heart-on-sleeve showcasing one could hope for are here, and if the band is essentially just All with Aukerman back on vocals, said band had been playing the old Descendents classics for long enough to know their way around great pop-punk, straight up. Aukerman's not the snot-nosed brat from *Milo Goes to College* anymore, of course, but as the logical continuation of his half-goofy/half-emotional persona from the mid-'80s he's more than fine. All it takes to demonstrate that is to hear the great, affecting "I'm the One," a perfect tug-the-heartstrings hooky roar, immediately followed by the half-minute long jokey romp "Coffee Mug." All the band members write one thing or another throughout, an admirable democracy that follows the everyone-does-something approach found on earlier albums, and the hits outweigh the misses—anyone dismissing this as just like any other pop-punk around misses the point that these characters helped found it as much as anyone! That the Descendents aren't interested in simply rehashing the past comes up more than once. Consider "Caught," which uses certain allegations about President Clinton (at least the earlier ones) as a starting point on responsibility and truth, and the just wistful and wondering enough "When I Get Old" ("will I still hate the cops/and have no class?"). A welcome, wonderful return to action. *—Ned Raggett*

Jackie DeShannon

b. Aug. 21, 1944, Hazel, KY
Vocals, Guitar / Brill Building Pop, Folk-Rock, Pop, Singer/Songwriter
Few performers have enjoyed as versatile a career as Jackie DeShannon, and although she made a couple of well-remembered Top Ten pop hits in the '60s, she's never achieved the level of success or artistic recognition she deserves. One of the first established rock figures to see the potential for crossbreeding rock and folk, she was a crucial midwife to the birth of folk-rock, with the wonderful singles "Needles and Pins" and "When You Walk in the Room." DeShannon's famous affiliations and success as a songwriter have sometimes obscured her own enormous talents. She's a superb singer, capable of both sweet ballads and (more satisfyingly) a gutsy, soulfully husky delivery. She performed her own material with an honest, vulnerable, intelligent intensity that pre-figured the singer/songwriter movement by several years, and demonstrated command of pop, soul, hard rock, girl group, and country styles. Her greatest success, however, came not with her own material, but with Bacharach-David's "What the World Needs Now Is Love," which made the Top Ten in 1965. The soft-rock "Put a Little Love in Your Heart" gave her another Top Ten hit in 1969, and she made some well-received singer/songwriter albums in the 1970s. One of the songs from her '70s LPs, "Bette Davis Eyes," became a number one hit for Kim Carnes in 1981. *—Richie Unterberger*

This Is Jackie DeShannon / Aug. 1965 / Imperial ♦♦♦
Issued in the wake of her mammoth hit "What the World Needs Now Is Love" (included here), this album saw DeShannon moving in an orchestrated ballad direction. If her work in that field doesn't hold up as well as her more rock-oriented material, she still did quite a good job of it, handling big production numbers like "Summertime," "Don't Let the Sun

Catch You Crying," "I'm Gonna Be Strong," and "Take Me Tonight" with soulful, full-throated gusto. Her best effort in this style, actually, was Bacharach-David's "A Lifetime of Loneliness," which was a small hit (and is featured on this LP). As was their wont with DeShannon, Imperial/Liberty didn't help matters by pasting on a few old tracks from her early-'60s girl group days; they're good, but out of place in the context of this album. A fairly strong but spotty recording by a great artist who was never afforded the opportunities to fulfill her potential. *—Richie Unterberger*

In the Wind / Sep. 1965 / Imperial ✦✦✦
This is a slightly altered reissue of an album, *Jackie DeShannon,* that came out on Liberty in mid-1963, more than two years before *In the Wind* was released. *In the Wind* contained ten of the twelve songs that had appeared on *Jackie DeShannon,* dropping "Betsy from Pike" and "Sing Hallelujah," and substituting the singles "Needles and Pins" and "Don't Turn Your Back on Me." Other than those singles, the album was devoted to pop-folk arrangements of contemporary and traditional folk songs, including three Bob Dylan tunes as well as "If I Had a Hammer," "Baby, Let Me Follow You Down," and "Puff (The Magic Dragon)." DeShannon was a folk-rock precursor/innovator, but these tracks were *not* folk-rock; they were pop-folk, given a bit more rhythm and added instrumentation than the standard folk albums of the early 1960s had. DeShannon does the tunes fairly well, and her gutsy delivery is enough to raise it considerably above most of the LPs of this era by other artists devoted to covers of such material. Yet this approach really wasn't DeShannon's forte; versatile pop-folk-rock-soul, often written by herself, was, as you can hear on "Needles and Pins" and "Don't Turn Your Back on Me," which are simultaneously the best songs on the album and the most ill-fitting. She invested some emotion in her covers, but didn't quite let it all hang out, although the version of Bob Dylan's "Walkin' Down the Line" is a standout, both for the earthy vocal and its obscurity (which Dylan himself did not release a version of in the 1960s). It's an interesting album in that it vaguely foreshadows the folk-rock combination of DeShannon and others, and it doesn't do DeShannon any discredit, but it's no more than an average recording, by her standards anyway. *—Richie Unterberger*

You Won't Forget Me / Sep. 1965 / Imperial ✦✦✦
This was also issued, with very minor track alterations, in 1964 on Liberty as *Breakin' It Up on the Beatles Tour!*; this version, issued after her Top Ten Ten hit "What the World Needs Now Is Love," is much easier to find. It was probably the strongest album by this mercurial artist, who never seemed to corral enough top-rank material to produce a first-rate LP, despite recording dozens of fine songs throughout the '60s. Arranged by Jack Nitzsche, it's also her most girl group and rock-oriented, featuring mostly original material, written alone or in collaboration with Nitzsche, Sharon Sheeley, and a young, unknown Randy Newman. DeShannon also acquits herself well on a couple of Buddy Holly covers, "Oh, Boy" and "Maybe Baby." *—Richie Unterberger*

Are You Ready for This? / Sep. 1966 / Imperial ✦✦✦
At this stage in her career, DeShannon had decided to pursue a sort of pop/rock-soul that found her heavily influenced by Diana Ross and Dionne Warwick, both in her singing and arrangements. The Ross influence is more dominant on this LP, a pleasant effort that nonetheless doesn't showcase her at the top of either her singing or songwriting capabilities. DeShannon running at 75% of her game is still decent, so this is nonetheless a fair if undistinguished listen. Highlighted by "Love Is Leading Me," one of the best Supremes knockoffs ever waxed. *—Richie Unterberger*

New Image / Mar. 17, 1967 / Imperial ✦✦

Put a Little Love in Your Heart / Sep. 1969 / Imperial ✦✦✦
DeShannon co-wrote her second Top Ten hit, the title track, with Jimmy Holiday and Randy Myers, and this album contains more of the fruit of their collaboration, including the follow-up, a Top 40 hit called "Love Will Find a Way." *—William Ruhlmann*

New Arrangement / Sep. 1975 / Columbia ✦✦✦
This 1975 album by Jackie DeShannon launches with a version of "Let the Sailor's Dance," a rendering that works better than the one performed by her co-songwriter/husband Randy Edelman. Edelman plays piano on "Sailor," as well as on "Boat to Sail," the second track and only tune DeShannon composes without the help of a collaborator. Truly, a *New Arrangement,* a very pleasant set of surprises from the woman who gave listeners "Put a Little Love in Your Heart" and "What the World Needs Now Is Love." The exquisite country tune that opens side two, "Bette Davis Eyes," became a huge worldwide hit for Kim Carnes six years after the release of this influential disc, proving DeShannon as powerful a songwriter as a vocalist. The title track is reflected in the cover of an impeccably dressed DeShannon with newspapers on the furniture, a bouquet of flowers on the back. "He says you're eccentric/and you swing either way/When you talked about being married/You mentioned my name," a not-so-disguised song about a husband having an affair with another man, thus, the title "New Arrangement." "Over My Head Again" might be a nod to Fleetwood Mac's breakthrough hit—DeShannon would release a very Fleetwood Mac-sounding "Don't Let the Flame Burn Out" on her 1977 album *You're the Only Dancer.* "I Wanted It All," co-written with John Bettis, has that Jackie DeShannon sound listeners love from her Burt Bacharach days, but this is her new arrangement: perfectly crafted '70s adult contemporary with nice Mark Creamer guitar lines. "Murphy," co-written with Glenn Ballentyne, is a quirky, almost country tune about an incognito detective from Scotland Yard. "Dreamin' As One" is a beautiful, almost gospel love song concluding this album with a touch of class. *—Joe Viglione*

● **Pop Princess** / 1981 / EMI Australia ✦✦✦✦✦
Rhino and EMI have come out with fairly extensive CD compilations of DeShannon's work, but this 23-song Australian album—if it can be found—is probably the best. It concentrates almost solely on her '60s recordings (one 1959 track is included), which remains her most fertile era. It also has a few excellent singles that didn't make it onto either compilation. These include the early-'60s girl group-type efforts "It's Love Baby," "Baby (When Ya Kiss Me)," "I Won't Turn You Down," and "Should I Cry?"—most written by DeShannon, all flops, and all worth hearing. Later, more mainstream efforts like "A Proper Girl" and Jim Webb's "The Girls' Song" are also not included on other reissues, and also worth a listen. The gatefold package contains informative liner notes, photos, and an exhaustive discography which also lists dozens of songs she wrote for other performers. *—Richie Unterberger*

Trouble with Jackie Dee / 1991 / Teenager ✦✦

The Best of Jackie DeShannon / Feb. 1, 1991 / Rhino ✦✦✦✦✦
This album is a fine roundup of her best moments as a singer and a writer. *—Dan Heilman*

● **What the World Needs Now . . . : The Definitive Collection** / Jul. 26, 1994 / EMI ✦✦✦✦✦
DeShannon's work is actually too diverse to be satisfactorily captured on an anthology, even one that includes 28 tracks, as this one does. Still, considering how hard the one DeShannon anthology that might be better than this one is to find (the Australian import *Pop Princess*), this has to be cited as the recommended first purchase. Focusing on her output for Liberty between 1959 and 1970, it has all the essentials: her two Top Ten hits, the minor hits like "A Lifetime of Loneliness," and the original versions of "Needles and Pins" and "When You Walk in the Room," and a host of fine girl group, ballad, folk-rock, and singer/songwriter flop singles. From the collector's viewpoint, the most interesting songs are the rarities. The six previously unreleased tracks include the exuberant "Breakaway," a hit for Irma Thomas; the rocker "Dream Boy," cut in 1964 in Britain with Jimmy Page on guitar; and a cover of Tim Hardin's "Reason to Believe." A couple of interesting rarities are "For Granted" (from the little-seen movie *C'mon, Let's Live a Little*) and the 45 version of "Splendor in the Grass," a somewhat sloppy folk-rock performance on which DeShannon was backed by the Byrds. *—Richie Unterberger*

The Very Best of Jackie DeShannon / Jun. 11, 1996 / Collectables ✦✦✦✦

You Know Me / Sep. 26, 2000 / Varese ✦✦✦✦✦
It takes a few spins to understand, and it is one of this prolific singer's many, many recordings, but when you spend some quality time with *You Know Me,* it starts unraveling its secrets in ways that only a truly great recording can. "Any Heart" is pure power, with the band weaving textures around Jackie DeShannon's distinctive vocal, the guitar relentless as it sustains the wall of sound. A true labor of love, few artists can produce a song this strong, and the fact that it follows three equally powerful compositions is evidence of the majesty that sweeps across all 14 tracks. "Steal the Thunder" opens the album with authority—the resonating grandeur Eric Carmen's "Hungry Eyes" contained, with a better hook. DeShannon places everything in perfect order, the vocal gliding over a groove that is rock-solid. "Wing Ryder" changes the pace, and you get the idea that this major songwriter is building an album more complex than Carole King's *Tapestry*—sheer art for art's sake. It ebbs and flows with an elegance younger musicians are too impetuous to seek out. And that's the secret here: DeShannon hasn't made another singer/songwriter album, she has shouldered a project akin to filming a major motion picture. Each song is an episode, with the title track a defiant affirmation of someone who has been with listeners through the years, from "Put a Little Love in Your Heart" to "Bette Davis Eyes." While Lou Adler's sparse production on *Tapestry* allowed Carole King to bare her soul, DeShannon gives us a dense production, thick and rich, a wide range of sounds that could reinvent AAA radio if given the chance to be heard with the same presence as her best-known tunes. *—Joe Viglione*

Destiny's Child

f. 1990, Houston, TX
Teen Pop, Urban

Destiny's Child is an R&B girl group from Houston, signed to Columbia and first premiered on *Men in Black: The Album* with their song "Killing Time." Early in 1998, the group released their self-titled debut album, featuring the single "No, No, No (Part II)" featuring Wyclef Jean. The quartet, including Beyoncé Knowles, Kelly Rowland (Beyoncé's cousin), LaTavia Roberson and LeToya Luckett, also toured with Jean. The group's sophomore album *The Writing's on the Wall* followed in 1999 and immediately spawned the number one smash "Bills, Bills, Bills," which topped both the pop and R&B charts. By the end of the year, "Say My Name" had duplicated the feat, and ended up becoming one of the biggest hits of 2000. But just as the group had broken through to superstardom, Roberson and Luckett abruptly left in March of 2000, filing a lawsuit against the group and manager Matthew Knowles (Beyoncé's father and Kelly's guardian). The two were replaced by similar-looking 18-year-old Farrah Franklin and 19-year-old Michelle Williams, who debuted in the video for "Say My Name" (much to some fans' surprise). Five months after her addition, Franklin announced that she too was leaving. Undaunted, the remaining trio recorded the theme song for the film revival of *Charlie's Angels*; "Independent Women" became another across-the-board smash that fall, topping the charts by the end of the year. Roberson and Luckett dropped the portion of their lawsuit directed at the group itself in early 2001; they soon formed a new group called Angel, while Farrah Franklin began work on a solo album. Meanwhile, Destiny's Child released their third album, *Survivor,* in May. *—John Bush & Steve Huey*

Destiny's Child / Feb. 17, 1998 / Columbia ✦✦✦✦
Destiny's Child isn't quite just another debut album from an R&B girl-group. The quartet worked with Wyclef Jean and Jermaine Dupri among others, and their voices sound beautiful together, but much of the album sounds indistinguishable from all the other female

groups out there. When Destiny's Child does sound different, as on the single "No, No, No (Part II)," they're more than competent. —*John Bush*

● **The Writing's on the Wall** / Jul. 27, 1999 / Columbia ◆◆◆◆

With their second album, *Writing's on the Wall*, Destiny's Child still suffers from slightly uneven songwriting, but it's nevertheless an assured step forward from the girl group. Not only are they maturing as vocalists, they are fortunate to work with such skilled, talented producers as Kevin "She'kspere" Biggs, Rodney Jerkins, Dwayne Wiggins, Chad Elliot, Daryl Simmons and Missy Elliott, who all give the quartet rich, varied music upon which to work their charm. So, even when the album fails to deliver memorable songs, it always sounds alluring, thanks to the perfect combination of vocalists and producers. —*Stephen Thomas Erlewine*

Survivor / May 1, 2001 / Columbia ◆◆◆

Nobody would have predicted that Destiny's Child would rule over the contemporary R&B scene in the beginning of the new millennium—not after "Bills, Bills, Bills" hit the top of the charts, not even after "Say My Name" became an anthem in 2000. But nobody challenged their position, so they reigned supreme in the early 2000s, eventually inheriting the title of the great girl group of their era. Since they had a couple of pretty good singles, namely the aforementioned pair, most conceded them that position, particularly since they *seemed* more talented than their peers, but *Survivor*, their first album as full-fledged superstars—also their first album since most of the group disappeared due to managerial conflicts—is as contrived and calculated as a Mariah Carey record, only without the joy. This is a determined, bullheaded record, intent on proving Destiny's Child has artistic merit largely because the group survived internal strife. This doggedness may fit on occasion, as on "Independent Women, Pt. 1," the theme to *Charlie's Angels*, but it usually takes precedence over the music. There are moments where the group makes it work, but this is a truly uneven record, bouncing between appealing mid-tempo soul numbers and hard-sell feminist anthems, where the ambition of Beyoncé and her cohorts is too naked. It's a record that tries to be a bold statement of purpose, but winds up feeling forced and artificial. —*Stephen Thomas Erlewine*

Destroy All Monsters

f. 1973, Detroit, MI, **db.** 1985

Obscuro, Detroit Rock, Proto-Punk, Hard Rock

An anti-rock band founded in direct reaction to the pretensions and complacency of 1970s pop music, the Detroit-based noise deconstructionists Destroy All Monsters earned their greatest notoriety at the peak of the punk era, thanks to a line-up which included alumni of the MC5 and the Stooges. Named after a cult-favorite Japanese monster movie, Destroy All Monsters was formed in 1973 by art students Niagara (a former model), Jim Shaw, Mike Kelley and Cary Loren; influenced by everything from underground comix to film noir to psychedelia, the highly visual group was experimental and abrasive, with Niagara's Betty Boop-vocals and squealing violin cresting atop waves of trance-like sonic dementia.

The original incarnation of Destroy All Monsters never widely released any official recordings, and by 1976 both Shaw and Kelley had exited to continue their graphic art careers, both later gaining considerable notoriety as underground talents. Niagara and Loren continued on, recruiting brothers Larry and Ben Miller (space guitar and saxophone, respectively); within six months, former Stooges guitarist Ron Asheton and one-time MC5 bassist Michael Davis had also signed on, pointing the group's sound in a more dynamic and energetic direction. Upon releasing their first-ever single, 1978's "Bored," Destroy All Monsters became darlings of the British music press, based largely upon the connection to the Stooges' legacy; "Bored" was soon set for U.K. release on the Cherry Red label, which licensed the record before ever even hearing it.

Even as a second single, "Meet the Creeper," was being readied for release, Destroy All Monsters was coming apart; tensions within the group had come to a head when Niagara left longtime boyfriend Loren to hook up with Asheton, and soon Loren, as well as the Miller brothers, were dismissed from the band. In response, Loren issued a 1979 live EP, *The Days of Diamonds*; a year later, he, the Millers and drummer Rob King formed Xanadu, recording an EP, *Black-Out in the City*, co-produced by Kelley and Shaw. Meanwhile, the remaining members of Destroy All Monsters carried on until 1985 before finally disbanding. In the wake of a 1994 box set, the original line-up occasionally reformed to play live and record new material. —*Jason Ankeny*

1974–76 / Apr. 16, 1995 / Ecstatic Peace ◆◆◆◆◆

Who knows what exactly prompted it, but one of the most unlikely box sets/multi-disc collections ever put out surfaced in 1994 courtesy of a co-release between Thurston Moore's Ecstatic Peace! and Byron Coley's Father Yod label—and even got distribution via Warner Bros. at that! Covering the years in question, *1974–76* is an exhaustive three-disc overview of Destroy All Monsters' little-known early days, when the original core quartet were doing music for themselves and nobody else, and punk was an incipient scene no matter where one looked. Given that the Ron Asheton years are the ones most people would know, it's thrilling to hear what was going on before he came along—while the Stooges were an admitted influence on the band, it was merely one of many. Mike Kelley assembled the package, providing the collage of band-created artwork and an informative history of the group, its ties to Ann Arbor, and the desire of the four to do something well beyond the surrounding milieu of post-hippie/frat row life in the town. Given that everything was recorded on cheap tape using often broken or run-down equipment, the sound is still quite good. The three discs clearly show that the band definitely had the same "try anything, screw the rules, and what is supposed to be quality" approach that fellow acts like Pere Ubu, Suicide, and Chrome were coming up with, only steering even further away from what rock was supposed to be. Some of the Asheton tracks surface

towards the end, and okay enough rock they are too, but it's the real band material that needs to be heard, and now finally can be, in spades. —*Ned Raggett*

The Deviants

f. 1967, England

British Psychedelia, Psychedelic

In the late '60s, the Deviants were something like the British equivalent to the Fugs, with touches of the Mothers of Invention and the British R&B-based rock of the Yardbirds and the Pretty Things. Their roots were not so much in the British Invasion as the psychedelic underground that began to take shape in London in 1966-1967. Not much more than amateurs when they began playing, they squeezed every last ounce of skill and imagination out of their limited instrumental and compositional resources on their debut, *Ptooff!*, which combined savage social commentary, overheated sexual lust, psychedelic jamming, blues riffs, and pretty acoustic ballads—all in the space of seven songs. Their subsequent '60s albums had plenty of outrage, but not nearly as strong material as the debut. Lead singer Mick Farren recorded a solo album near the end of the decade, and went on to become a respected rock critic. He intermittently performed and recorded as a solo artist and with re-formed versions of the Deviants. —*Richie Unterberger*

● **Ptooff!** / 1967 / Decca ◆◆◆◆

Talk today about Britain's psychedelic psyxties, and it's the light whimsy of Syd Barrett's Pink Floyd, the gentle introspection of the village green Kinks, *Sgt. Pepper*, and "My White Bicycle" which hog the headlines. People have forgotten there was an underbelly as well, a seething mass of discontent and rancor which would eventually produce the likes of Hawkwind, the Pink Fairies, and the Edgar Broughton Band. It was a damned sight more heartfelt, too, but the more some fete the lite-psych practitioners of the modern age, the further their reality will recede. Fronted by journalist/author/wild child Mick Farren, the Deviants spawned that reality. Over the years, three ex-members would become Pink Fairies; for subsequent reunions, sundry ex-Fairies would become honorary Deviants. And though only Russell Hunter is present on *Ptooff!*, still you can hear the groundwork being laid. The Pink Fairies might well have been the most perfect British band of the early '70s. The Deviants were their dysfunctional parents. The deranged psilocybic rewrite of "Gloria" which opens the album, "I'm Coming Home," still sets a frightening scene, a world in which Top 40 pop itself is horribly skewed. Move on to "Garbage," and though the Deviants' debt to both period Zappa and Fugs is unmistakable, still there's a purity to the paranoia. *Ptooff!* was conceived at a time when there genuinely was a generation gap, and hippies were a legitimate target for any right-wing bully boy with a policeman's hat and a truncheon. *IT* and *Oz*, the two underground magazines which did most to support the Deviants (Farren wrote for both), were both publicly busted during the band's lifespan, and that fear permeates this disc; fear, and vicious defiance. —*Dave Thompson*

No. 3 / 1969 / Sire ◆◆◆◆

Legendary British counter-culture figurehead Mick Farren lead this group through three astonishing albums before mutating the project into the Pink Fairies. For this 1969 recording the group consisted of Paul Rudolph on guitar, Duncan Sanderson on bass, and Russell Hunter on drums with Farren's vocals out front. While the group had previously flirted with a Frank Zappa Mothers of Invention sound and Fugs style rock-as-propaganda approach this album is a straightforward heavy psychedelic rock album almost reaching the explosive magnitude of the Stooges' *Funhouse*, the MC5 and such heavyweights. An absolute classic of proto-punk U.K. psychedelic rock, this is the essential Deviants document that set the direction for the harder sound Mick Farren and co. explored as the Pink Fairies in the '70s. —*Skip Jansenn*

Garbage / 1996 / Alive/Total Energy ◆◆

Eating Jello With A Heated Fork / 1996 / Alive ◆◆◆

Fragments of Broken Probes / 1996 / Captain Trip ◆◆◆

A companion to the compilation *This CD Is Condemned*, *Fragments of Broken Probes* is an all-encompassing roundup of the myriad nooks and crannies that have punctuated Mick Farren's career since he launched the Deviants in 1966. It is also one of the most essential releases in his entire catalog. The sleeve notation merely describes the contents as "alternative recordings, outtakes, remixes and live recordings." Closer examination, however, reveals a treasure trove of hard-to-find singles and compilation cuts: disheveled versions of "Play With Fire" and "To Know Him Is to Love Him" cut for the New York-based Ork label in 1976, "Screwed Up" and "Outrageous Contagious" from an EP recorded for Stiff in 1978, live versions of "Half Price Drinks" and "I Want to Be Called Loretta," and so on. There's also, at long last, a chance to rediscover what remains perhaps the archetypal Farren performance, his own hyper-speed rendition of "Lost Johnny," a psilocybic sci-fi nightmare co-written with Lemmy and already recorded by both Hawkwind and Motorhead, but never…ever…sounding like this. Vocals scream, guitars keen, and rhythms race by with speed metal density; though the performance pre-dated punk with barely minutes to spare, Farren's claim to godfatherhood could have no better witness. The earliest tracks date from the dog days of the Deviants in 1968-1969; sound collages, interludes, and a clutch of recent recordings take the story up to 1996 and the group's reinvention as aural terrorists for a new generation. But time neither dulls nor detracts from the consistent excellence of the material, and the often scarifying relevance of Farren's worldview. As both a performer and a writer, he was often described as being ahead of his time. With a fiery breath that still smells fresh, *Fragments* shows listeners just how far ahead he really was. —*Dave Thompson*

The Deviants Have Left the Planet / 1999 / Captain Trip ◆◆◆

Black Tracks Of Mick Farren & The Deviants 1967-96: This CD Is Condemned / Sep. 19, 2000 / Total Energy ◆◆◆◆

This 19-track, career-spanning compilation of the erratic career of Mick Farren and the Deviants might span 1967-1996, but it basically plucks from three eras. Most heavily represented is the original incarnation's punk/blues/psychedelic era, with nine tracks from the late '60s, including selections from all three of the Deviants' LPs from that era, and Farren's cover of "Mona" from his 1969 solo album. Then there are half a dozen cuts by the revived Deviants that recorded in the early punk/new wave era in 1976-1977, and as a capper there are four items from 1996 (including three from the *Eating Jello With a Heated Fork* album). This is often entertaining, and at times even inspiring, but it's kind of hit-and-miss, due both to the sometimes questionable selection of what constitutes the Deviants' "best," and because the group's basic, aggressive satire so often treads the line between stupid and clever. Where, one wonders, are first-album highlights like "I'm Coming Home" and "Child of the Sky"? Well, the latter's most likely missing because Farren has since expressed his dislike of that acoustic, pretty track, but the exclusion of the Yardbirds-like "First Line, probably the best cut off 1969's *#3*, also hurts this anthology. So do the absence of liner notes, although personnel, dates, and original release info are provided in the track listings. As a point in its favor, it's good to have the fairly humorous almost-punk 1976 cuts "Screwed Up" and "Let's Loot the Supermarket Again," with Deviants/Pink Fairies associates Paul Rudolph, Larry Wallis, and Andy Colquhoun, in the lineup. —*Richie Unterberger*

Devo

f. 1972, Akron, OH, **db.** 1991
College Rock, American Punk, Post-Punk, New Wave, Synth Pop, American Underground
One of new wave's most innovative and (for a time) successful bands, Devo was also perhaps one of its most misunderstood. Formed in Akron, Ohio in 1972 by Kent State art students Jerry Casale (bass) and Mark Mothersbaugh (vocals), along with Bob Casale (guitar), Bob Mothersbaugh (lead guitar), and Alan Myers (drums), Devo took its name from their concept of "de-evolution"—the idea that instead of evolving, mankind has actually regressed, as evidenced by the dysfunction and herd mentality of American society. Their music echoed this view of society as rigid, repressive, and mechanical, with appropriate touches—jerky, robotic rhythms; an obsession with technology and electronics (the group was among the first non-art-rock bands to make the synthesizer a core element); and often atonal melodies and chord progressions—all filtered through the perspectives of geeky misfits. After attracting the attention of luminaries like David Bowie and Iggy Pop through their soundtrack work for the short film *The Truth About De-Evolution*, Devo recorded its 1978 debut, *Q: Are We Not Men? A: We Are Devo!* under the auspices of pioneering producer Brian Eno. The record was a cult sensation, helped in part by the band's concurrent emphasis on its highly stylized visuals—videos, costumes which made the band members look alike, etc. Their third album, *Freedom of Choice*, featured a smash single in "Whip It," and the fledgling MTV network made the accompanying video into a staple. However, following those first three albums, the group began to run out of ideas, both musical and conceptual; their simple, basic electronic sound had proven very influential, and other bands were already expanding on some of Devo's ideas. After a series of largely uninteresting albums, the band called it quits early in the '90s. Casale and Mothersbaugh concentrated on other projects until a brief reunion for several dates at 1996's Lollapalooza tour. —*Steve Huey*

Q: Are We Not Men? A: We Are Devo! / Jul. 1978 / Warner Brothers ✦✦✦✦✦
Produced by Brian Eno, *Q: Are We Not Men? A: We Are Devo!* was a seminal touchstone in the development of American new wave. It was one of the first pop albums to use synthesizers as an important textural element, and although they mostly play a supporting role in this guitar-driven set, the innovation began to lay the groundwork for the synthpop explosion that would follow very shortly. *Q: Are We Not Men* also revived the absurdist social satire of the Mothers of Invention, claiming punk rock's outsider alienation as a home for freaks and geeks. While Devo's appeal was certainly broader, their sound was tailored well enough to that sensibility that it still resonates with a rabid cult following. It isn't just the dadaist pseudo-intellectual theories, or the critique of the American mindset as unthinkingly, submissively conformist. It was the way their music reflected that view, crafted to be as mechanical and robotic as their targets. Yet Devo hardly sounded like a machine that ran smoothly. There was an almost unbearable tension in the speed of their jerky, jumpy rhythms, outstripping Talking Heads, XTC, and other similarly nervy new wavers. And thanks to all the dissonant, angular melodies, odd-numbered time signatures, and yelping, sing-song vocals, the tension never finds release, which is key to the album's impact. It also doesn't hurt that this is arguably Devo's strongest set of material, though several brilliant peaks can overshadow the remainder. Of those peaks, the most definitive are the de-evolution manifesto "Jocko Homo" (one of the extremely few rock anthems written in 7/8 time) and a wicked deconstruction of "(I Can't Get No) Satisfaction," which reworks the original's alienation into a spastic freak-out that's nearly unrecognizable. But *Q: Are We Not Men?* also had a conceptual unity that bolstered the consistent songwriting, making it an essential document of one of new wave's most influential bands. —*Steve Huey*

Duty Now for the Future / Jul. 1979 / Warner Brothers ✦✦✦✦
While the most obvious flaw of Devo's *Duty Now For The Future* is that the material simply isn't as good as on their debut, their second album also captures the group in the midst of a significant stylistic shift. On their first album, for all their herky-jerky rhythms and electronic accents, Devo were pretty much a standard guitars/bass/drums rock band, albeit one with more than their share of eccentricities. *Duty Now For The Future* found them bringing the keyboards that were used as punctuation on their earlier material into the forefront, adding a new level of irony to their "little minds through big technology" philosophy. While Devo would later learn to use electronics with confidence and wit, they were still learning how to integrate them into their sound on *Duty Now*, and the results

lacked the strength and coherence of their debut. Of course, it also helped that the first album had better songs; the two instrumentals on side one are merely filler, "Pink Pussycat" and "Clockout" are jokes that just aren't funny, and "Triumph Of The Will" embraces fascism as a satirical target without bothering to make it sound as if they disapprove. But "Secret Agent Man" is a wittier devolved cover than "Satisfaction," the band rarely sounded as cheerfully creepy as on "The Day My Baby Gave Me A Surprize," and the side two rave up, "Smart Patrol/Mr. DNA" is superbly potent (for all their progressive trappings, Devo were formalists enough to know you make a big rock move near the end of side two.) *Duty Now For The Future* is hardly a bad album, but it isn't as strong as what Devo had already brought to the table—or would offer later on. —*Mark Deming*

Freedom of Choice / Jul. 1980 / Warner Brothers ✦✦✦✦✦
With *Freedom of Choice*, Devo completed their transition into a full-fledged synth-pop group, producing arguably their most musically cohesive effort in the process. Synthesizers are now fully integrated into the band's sound, frequently dominating the arrangements and at least sharing equal time with the guitars. Everything is played with a cool, polished precision that mirrors the stylized uniformity of the band's visuals; the dissonance is more subdued than in the past, and the uptight rhythms are no longer jarring, instead locking the band into a rigidly even keel. Oddly, even though the music is the least human-sounding Devo had yet produced, their social observations were growing less insular and more sympathetic. Several tunes—like the oft-covered "Girl U Want"—have a geeky (but pragmatic) romantic angst that was new to Devo albums, although the band's view of relationships is occasionally colored by their cultural themes of competition and domination. Those preoccupations also inform their breakthrough hit single, "Whip It," but elsewhere, they're finding enough connection with the rest of the world to moderate their cynicism, at least a little bit. Songs like "Gates of Steel," "Planet Earth," and the title track reveal a frustrated idealism under their irony, one that can't quite understand why Americans don't use more of their freedom to search for happiness. Altogether, there's a little less of the debut's energy, and a little less variety as well. But the songwriting is a match for consistent quality, and moreover, the music on *Freedom of Choice* is the sound that defines Devo in the minds of many. In the end, that makes it the band's only other truly necessary album. —*Steve Huey*

New Traditionalists / 1981 / Warner Brothers ✦✦✦
Devo followed up their platinum-selling pop breakthrough in typically perverse fashion: *New Traditionalists* presents a band seemingly aghast at being pegged as a novelty act by some of their own satirical targets. Apparently deciding—admittedly, not without reason—that America's comprehension of irony was sorely lacking, Devo largely abandons its sense of absurdity on *New Traditionalists*, explicitly stating their cultural views and at times calling attention (as with the otherwise terrific single "Beautiful World") to their already obvious sarcasm, in case anyone missed the point. The problem was, Devo's cult wasn't missing the point, and with all their quirky trappings, the band was hardly likely to reach most of their newfound pop audience by making their message more straightforward. Still, despite some heavy-handedness, *New Traditionalists* is hardly a total failure. The opener "Through Being Cool" actually benefits from the new outlook, making for a clear and effective statement of purpose. It sets the stage for some of Devo's angriest, most embittered songs, which often function as connections between new wave and the punk attitudes that were so crucial in its creation. Devo might have pulled it off if their songwriting hadn't also begun to slip—too many tracks end up flat-out unmemorable. They try a couple new things arrangement-wise (adding more electronic percussion), but nothing that drastically overhauls their minimalist synth-pop, and that lack of variety is more glaring when paired with the melodic deficiencies. *New Traditionalists'* repetition of musical and lyrical ideas foreshadows the band's decline, but really, at least half of the album is worthwhile. It just doesn't quite recapture the inventiveness or pointed humor of its predecessors. —*Steve Huey*

Oh, No! It's Devo / 1982 / Warner Brothers ✦✦✦
New Traditionalists seemed to indicate that Devo saw their audience as having shifted to the mainstream, and *Oh, No! It's Devo* slides further in that direction. For their first non-self-produced album since the debut, the band brings in Cars producer Roy Thomas Baker, who smooths out any remaining edges in the band's sound, and employs colder-sounding digital synths more often. As a result, it's hard to differentiate Devo from all the other new wave synth-pop acts following the trail they'd originally blazed. Topping off their increasingly generic sound is a reliance on thudding electronic percussion, which contributes heavily to the album's overall feeling of bloodlessness. Still, *Oh, No! It's Devo* is only about as uneven as *New Traditionalists*, which means that there are several quality singles, and some barely memorable album tracks. There's also a bit more novelty material, perhaps in hopes of scoring another hit on the level of "Whip It." It isn't terrible, but compared to Devo's earlier conceptual satire, it often feels distressingly pointless. Unfortunately, the comparative lack of ideas on *Oh, No! It's Devo* would only get worse on subsequent albums. —*Steve Huey*

Shout / 1984 / Warner Brothers ✦
The creative decline begun on *New Traditionalists* which continued through *Oh, No! It's Devo* becomes complete. The original music on *Shout* lacks the pointed, absurd satire of classic Devo, while the music itself is generally dull; the record's only highlight is a typically Devo-ized version of Jimi Hendrix's "Are You Experienced?" Not surprisingly, the band went on hiatus to concentrate on other projects shortly afterwards. —*Steve Huey*

E-Z Listening Disc / 1987 / Rykodisc ✦

Total Devo / 1988 / Enigma ✦

Now It Can Be Told (Devo at the Palace 12/9/88) / 1989 / Enigma ✦✦
Released as a three-sided album, Devo continued to flounder with *Now It Can Be Told*, a

live performance as undistinguished as their recent studio efforts. Again, diehards may find items such as a slowed-down, mostly acoustic rearrangement of "Jocko Homo" necessary, but few others will. *—Steve Huey*

Smooth Noodle Maps / Jun. 1990 / Enigma ✦✦

Hardcore Devo, Vol. 1: 74-77 / Aug. 1990 / Rykodisc ✦✦✦
While it is inconsistent, the first of Rykodisc's compilations of early four-track recordings made in Devo's basement is a necessary item for devoted fans. In addition to the original Booji Boy releases of "Satisfaction," "Jocko Homo," and "Mongoloid," *Hardcore Vol. 1* contains the full-length version of "Mechanical Man," the sarcastic satire of "Social Fools," and the flat-out weirdness of songs like "Golden Energy," "I'm a Potato," and "Uglatto." Most of these songs had never been previously available in an authorized format; many are reminiscent of the minimalist weirdness of the Residents. While some tracks are a bit short on melody, and the sound quality is mostly (and understandably) crude, they amply illustrate Devo's D.I.Y. garage-band origins and their seemingly inexhaustible (at that point) supply of satirically humorous ideas, as well as the fact that the band's patented sound was present right from the start of their long gestational period. *—Steve Huey*

The Greatest Misses / Dec. 1990 / Warner Brothers ✦✦✦
This compilation, released concurrently with *Greatest Hits*, collects some of the band's stranger experiments, early album tracks, and a few rarities, such as the Booji Boy releases of "Be Stiff" and "Mechanical Man" (both available on the *Hardcore* compilations) and a U.K. B-side, "Penetration in the Centerfold." It does serve as a good supplement to the *Greatest Hits* collection, even if it is a bit haphazard, but listeners who want more than one Devo disc are advised to go ahead and purchase the first three albums rather than these two compilations—it's a better way to appreciate their achievements, and it's more entertaining. *—Steve Huey*

The Greatest Hits / Dec. 1990 / Warner Brothers ✦✦✦✦
While *Greatest Hits* contains all of the truly necessary items, it also tends to overlook some of the better album tracks from Devo's early period (easily their best work) in favor of a more balanced overview, which means that later albums receive more exposure than they really deserve. The import collection *Hot Potatoes: The Best of Devo* has stronger selections and is the preferred single-disc overview of Devo's career, but if you can't find it and only want one Devo disc, this will do. *—Steve Huey*

Hardcore Devo, Vol. 2: 1974-1977 / Aug. 23, 1991 / Rykodisc ✦✦✦
Like its predecessor and true to its title, *Hardcore Vol. 2* is an indispensable item for any hardcore Devo fan. Featuring over an hour's worth of raw, four-track basement recordings from the years 1974-1977, the disc contains such necessities as the atmospheric instrumental "Booji Boy's Funeral," the mechanized blues shuffle of "37," the mock sports anthem "Let's Go," the gleeful bubblegum-pop parody "Goo Goo Itch" (revealing a surprisingly strong sense of melody), and the sheer aural dementia of "U Got Me Bugged," as well as "Be Stiff," which later became the theme song for the pioneering British indie label Stiff Records. Also featured are early versions of "Clockout" and their cover of Lee Dorsey's "Working In a Coalmine." While there are a number of misses as well—some tracks are all robotic rhythms with no melody, and others come off as the mildly misogynistic rantings of sexually frustrated misfits—the compilation again proves the depth of development and detail in Devo's satirical vision far prior to their 1978 debut album. *—Steve Huey*

Devo Live: The Mongoloid Years / Oct. 1992 / Rykodisc ✦✦

Hot Potatoes: The Best of Devo / 1993 / Virgin ✦✦✦✦✦
The import-only *Hot Potatoes* is the best available single-disc overview of Devo's career, hitting nearly all of the most significant moments from their first five albums, as well as including the non-LP singles "Be Stiff" and "Working in a Coalmine." "Whip It" and "Freedom of Choice" are here, of course, as are cult favorites "Jocko Homo," "Mongoloid," "Satisfaction (I Can't Get Me No)," plus many more. However, even if it's the best available, it isn't that *widely* available in the U.S.; plus, Devo's first three albums in particular all have at least a few fine songs that aren't included here. But if you only want one disc and don't mind hunting a bit, *Hot Potatoes: The Best of Devo* is superior to the American *Greatest Hits*, which for some reason does not feature "Mongoloid," one of the most obvious choices for a Devo hits collection. *—Steve Huey*

Adventures of the Smart Patrol / Aug. 27, 1996 / Discovery ✦✦

● **Pioneers Who Got Scalped: The Anthology** / May 9, 2000 / Rhino ✦✦✦✦
Heading into the new millennium, there was no truly definitive Devo compilation on the market, so Rhino attempted to remedy the situation with the double-disc *Pioneers Who Got Scalped: The Anthology*—and did a pretty good job, without quite pulling it off. When faced with a choice, the compilation takes the collector-oriented route by including the rarer version; as a result, buyers get a couple of early Booji Boy-label recordings, and several single and dance remixes. More problematic, though, is the anthology's attempt to present a balanced overview of Devo's career. While admirable in intent, the fact is that the group's oeuvre grew steadily weaker as time passed, and since disc one runs all the way through their first (and best) four albums, disc two is a pretty bumpy ride. Not that it's worthless—devotees will be thrilled with the inclusion of quite a few songs that had only previously appeared on movie soundtracks, and it also rescues a few worthwhile singles from obscurity. But it pales next to the first disc in terms of songwriting, musical invention, and edgy humor; plus, where the band's early covers reinvented rock standards as comments on alienation, latter-day items like "Bread and Butter" and "Itsy Bitsy Teenie Weenie Yellow Polka Dot Bikini" are nothing more than novelties. So the bottom line is, you've got to be a hardcore Devo enthusiast to fully appreciate *Pioneers Who Got Scalped*. If you are, it's a fantastic package; if you want a more basic overview, you're better off with the somewhat disorganized *Greatest Hits* or the import collection *Hot Potatoes*. It's kind of a shame, though, that in spite of the generally fine job done compiling *Pioneers*, there still isn't a Devo anthology that distills *all* the best moments from their crucial early years, and throws in just the right (small) number of later singles. *—Steve Huey*

Dexy's Midnight Runners

f. Jul. 1978, Birmingham, England, **db.** 1986
Blue-Eyed Soul, Post-Punk, New Wave

When Dexy's Midnight Runners was at their peak in the early '80s, U.K. critics hailed their lead singer/songwriter Kevin Rowland as a genius, capable of fusing soul, pop, Irish folk, new wave, and rock into one seamless, unique mix. Although the band wasn't able to fulfill their promise, the best of their music was remarkable. On their first album, *Searching for the Young Soul Rebels*, the group featured scores of horns along with accomplished songwriting from Rowland. It became a sensation in England, although it didn't dent the charts in America. After the album's release, three members of the band split and formed the Bureau, leaving Rowland to refashion Dexy's Midnight Runners. What he came up with was a departure from the debut, although they shared the same spirit. Instead of soul, the band was rooted in folk and Celtic music on their second album, *Too-Rye-Ay*, which produced the enormous international hit, "Come on Eileen." Rowland seemed lost in the wake of his success, lacking a new idea for his music; the last Dexy's album was bland and directionless, as was his solo album, 1988's *The Wanderer*. Following the album's release, Rowland entered a period of seclusion. In early 1997, he signed with Creation Records and was scheduled to deliver an album by the end of the year. *—Stephen Thomas Erlewine*

● **Searching for the Young Soul Rebels** / Jul. 1980 / EMI ✦✦✦✦✦
The crackling stations being switched on the radio and the gang shout followed by the spoken injunction to "burn it down" sound like they should be starting off a Sham 69 record. Then "Burn It Down" actually starts, with its horn section, Hammond organ and Kevin Rowland's utterly unconventional soul vocals. The cult of Dexy's, and this album in particular, were worshipped as the return of "soul" to English rock music at the dawn of Thatcherism. Exploring the myth that this album holds, especially in Brit music terms, can be a strange prospect: 20 years on it doesn't sound revolutionary, it just sounds good. And good it is, quite good, compared to where Paul Weller ended up, i.e., too reverential by half. This is vibrant, alive, and unconcerned with perfection. Rowland takes a role that Morrissey would have in 1985 and Jarvis Cocker in 1995—the unexpected but perfect voice to capture a time and moment in the U.K. His slightly strangled wail and sly, wry lyrics and song titles ("Tell Me When My Light Turns Green," "Thankfully Not Living in Yorkshire It Doesn't Apply") make this album in many ways. Musically, the group lays down R&B grooves and brassy hooks with aplomb, as on the brilliant "Seven Days Too Long" and the number one single "Geno," but throw in film noir touches, John Barry-writing-for-James Bond fare and more just as ably. The liner notes have a fun description of the group's origins and brief notes for most of the tunes—the best for the finale, "There, There, My Dear": "P.S. Old clothes do not make a tortured artist." The 2000 reissue contains a slew of extra tracks and B-sides, making it the version to find. *—Ned Raggett*

Too-Rye-Ay / Aug. 1982 / Mercury ✦✦✦✦✦
For one brief moment, Dexy's exploded into America's consciousness—and what a song to do it with! "Come on Eileen" combines ramalama rock & roll, soul delivery, and Celtic/country flavor into a perfect musical fusion and an irresistible U.K. and U.S. number one hit. Both the song and its video were such hits that years later, ska/punk band Save Ferris made a minor splash with its own version of the tune, while Garth Brooks appeared in a *Saturday Night Live* skit dressed as the capering, bedraggled Rowland. The rest of the album is nearly as successful, with quite a few numbers that should have matched "Come on Eileen"'s fame. Given that song's obvious debt to Van Morrison's similar fusions, it's no surprise that Dexy's tipped their hat with a great cover of Morrison's "Jackie Wilson Said," another big British single. Throughout the album, Rowland's distinct, unique voice takes the fore, but the revamped Dexy's lineup proves it was the original version's equal, if not better. Given that only trombonist Big Jimmy Patterson remained, and even then only for two tracks, recruiting a new band able to create the "Celtic soul" Rowland dreamed about turned out to be exactly the right move. Excellently produced by Rowland and the legendary Clive Langer/Alan Winstanley production team, *Too-Rye-Ay* sounds like an old soul revue recorded on stage, no doubt an intentional goal. Other highlights include the opening jaunt "The Celtic Soul Brothers," which just about says it all both in title and delivery; the slow swirl of "All in All"; and the vicious ballad "Liars A to E." 1996's reissue is recommended, with eight extra tracks, including some fantastic live cuts like a seven-minute "Come on Eileen," and an appreciative and thorough essay. *—Ned Raggett*

Don't Stand Me Down / Sep. 1985 / Mercury ✦✦
In the three years between the release of *Too-Rye-Aye* and *Don't Stand Me Down*, bandleader Kevin Rowland once again revamped Dexy's Midnight Runners. Musically, Rowland had evolved a combination of the soul sound of the first album and the folky approach of the second, retaining both the horns of the former and the strings of the latter. But long passages of *Don't Stand Me Down* were spoken, not sung, by Rowland in conversation with Adams. "Listen to This" proved that Rowland was still capable of turning out a catchy, Motown-derived pop song when he chose, but the bulk of *Don't Stand Me Down*, which sold disappointingly, must have sounded idiosyncratic to British listeners and nearly incomprehensible to Americans. *—William Ruhlmann*

The Very Best of Dexy's Midnight Runners / 1991 / Mercury ✦✦✦✦
Very Best of Dexy's Midnight Runners, a 19-track collection, gives a comprehensive look at the band. Though the import price tag may be prohibitive, it is notable for the inclusion

of the rare "Because of You"—the charming theme to the British television show *Brush Strokes*—unavailable elsewhere. —*Chris Woodstra*

It Was Like This / 1996 / EMI ✦✦✦✦✦

It Was like This collects the entirety of *Searching for the Young Soul Rebels* and adds all the B-sides from the album, plus alternate mixes of "Geno" and "Dance Stance," plus a version of "Respect" recorded for the BBC. The reissue is packaged with care and attention to detail, highlighted by Kevin Rowland's liner notes, making the compact disc the definitive version of Dexy's debut album. —*Stephen Thomas Erlewine*

Neil Diamond

b. Jan. 24, 1941, Brooklyn, NY

Vocals, Songwriter, Guitar / Pop/Rock, Soft Rock, Pop, Adult Contemporary

Neil Diamond built a career, first as a pop songwriter, and then as a pop singer, that has withstood the changing fashions of music, especially rock, over more than 25 years. Diamond was writing and recording in New York in his teens, and in 1965, he signed to Bang Records as an artist while also working as a songwriter. In 1966, he reached the Top Ten with his "Cherry, Cherry," while the Monkees took his "I'm a Believer" to #1. "Cherry, Cherry" was the first of five straight Top 20 hits, among them "Girl, You'll Be a Woman Soon." Diamond began to develop into more of an individual writer in the mold of Bob Dylan and Paul Simon in the late '60s, and this led to his move to Uni Records in 1968, where he continued to score hits like "Sweet Caroline," "Holly Holy," and "Cracklin' Rosie," in a pop/rock style laced with gospel and country influences. His 1976 album, *Beautiful Noise*, was produced by Robbie Robertson of the Band; it was his first album to go platinum. In 1980, Diamond starred in a remake of the film *The Jazz Singer*. Its soundtrack was another million-seller for him. Diamond had developed into a dynamic live performer over the years, and his concert recordings were among his most successful. In the late '80s and early '90s, while updating his sound, he faded from the singles charts though his albums continued to sell consistently and his shows continued to sell out. —*William Ruhlmann*

Velvet Gloves & Spit / 1968 / MCA ✦✦✦

Most of Neil Diamond's albums are cluttered with filler, but few of his records were as flat-out strange as *Velvet Gloves & Spit*. Apart from "Two Bit Manchild," the album is comprised of lesser-known material, some of it quite good ("Modern Day Version of Love," "Honey-Drippin' Times"), and some of it just weird. The unintelligible "Knackelflerg" is one thing, but "The Pot Smoker's Song" is something else entirely. With its trippy, spoken-word testimonials about the dangers of drugs (including one addict that claims to shoot heroin into his spine) punctuated by Neil's ridiculous, sing-song chorus ("Pot, pot / Gimme some pot/ Forget who you are / You can be who you're not"), it's anti-drug pontificating at its worst, but it's a strangely fascinating artifact and helps distinguish *Velvet Gloves & Spit* from Diamond's catalog of uneven albums. —*Stephen Thomas Erlewine*

Touching You, Touching Me / 1969 / MCA ✦✦✦✦✦

Diamond's first regular album release to sell in substantial numbers, *Touching You, Touching Me* contains the gold Top Ten single "Holly Holy," and a Diamond composition, but is mostly notable for its covers of standards by other songwriters: "Everybody's Talkin'," "Mr. Bojangles," "Both Sides Now," and the chart entry "Until It's Time for You to Go." These helped signal that Diamond was thinking of himself less as a Brill Building hack than as a peer of Fred Neil, Jerry Jeff Walker, Joni Mitchell, and Buffy Sainte-Marie. —*William Ruhlmann*

Tap Root Manuscript / 1970 / MCA ✦✦✦✦✦

The follow-up to *Touching You, Touching Me* was an ambitious set of songs, all originals except for a Top 20 cover of "He Ain't Heavy…He's My Brother," including the side-long suite "The African Trilogy" (which featured the hit "Soolaimon"), the #1 hit "Cracklin' Rosie" and "Done Too Soon." Going gold within two months, this album confirmed Diamond's breakthrough as a recording artist. —*William Ruhlmann*

Stones / 1971 / MCA ✦✦

Driven by the hit singles "I Am…I Said" and "Crunchy Granola Suite," *Stones* is a stronger album than most of Neil Diamond's late-'60s records. Instead of padding the album with mediocre originals, Neil picked several fine covers to fill out the remainder of the album, including Roger Miller's "Husbands and Wives," Joni Mitchell's "Chelsea Morning," Leonard Cohen's "Suzanne," Randy Newman's "I Think It's Gonna Rain," Jacques Brel's "If You Go Away" and Tom Paxton's "The Last Thing on My Mind." There are still a few weak patches on *Stones*, but the record remains an engaging collection of mainstream pop. —*Stephen Thomas Erlewine*

Moods / 1972 / MCA ✦✦✦

Moods finds Neil Diamond attempting to craft a more ambitious and substantial album than his usual pop record through heavy orchestration, but the results only work when he sticks to catchy pop-rock, as on "Song Sung Blue," "High Rolling Man" and "Play Me." —*Stephen Thomas Erlewine*

Hot August Night / 1972 / MCA ✦✦✦✦✦

This is the ultimate Neil Diamond record. Not necessarily the best—he's at his most appealing crafting in the studio—but certainly the ultimate, capturing all the kitsch and glitz of Neil Diamond, the showman. And that also means that it's not just loaded with flair, but with filler, songs like "Porcupine Pie," "Soggy Pretzels," and "And the Grass Won't Pay No Mind"—attempts to write grand, sweeping epics that collapse under their own weight. Still, that's part of the charm of Diamond and while it can sound unbearable on studio albums, it makes some sense here, surrounded by his pomp and circumstance. That spectacle is the great thing about the record, since it inflates not just his great songs, it gives

the weaker moments character. And while this does wind up being a little much—21 songs, 24 on the 2000 reissue—it nevertheless is the one record for casual Neil fans, after the hits collections, since this shows Diamond the icon in full glory. —*Stephen Thomas Erlewine*

Rainbow / 1973 / MCA ✦✦✦

Rainbow is a compilation that relies solely on compositions by folk-rock singer/songwriters and modern-day pop craftsmen, which means that the record is more consistent than the average Neil Diamond album, even if it lacks the distinctive spark that one of his originals would have lent the album. Still, there are fine performances here, and Diamond does justice to "Everybody's Talkin'," "Both Sides Now," "Chelsea Morning," and "He Ain't Heavy, He's My Brother." —*Stephen Thomas Erlewine*

Jonathan Livingston Seagull / Oct. 1973 / Columbia ✦✦✦

Columbia Records' multi-million-dollar signing of Diamond was questioned by industryites who felt president Clive Davis had paid too high a price. Davis had left the company by the time this, Diamond's first Columbia album, was released in October 1973, but it was posthumous vindication. The soundtrack to a forgettable film based on a trivial bestseller, *Jonathan Livingston Seagull*, sold two million copies, spinning off the singles "Be" and "Skybird," even if, in retrospect, it is not one of Diamond's more consistent efforts. —*William Ruhlmann*

His 12 Greatest Hits / 1974 / MCA ✦✦✦✦✦

Actually, this is 12 songs that were hits for Diamond on Uni between 1969 and 1972. "Cracklin' Rosie" is here, along with Diamond's other chart-topper of the period, "Song Sung Blue," and the Top Ten hits "Sweet Caroline" and "Holly Holy." —*William Ruhlmann*

Serenade / Oct. 1974 / Columbia ✦✦

Beautiful Noise / 1976 / Columbia ✦✦✦

A beautifully recorded concept album about Diamond's own emergence from the Brooklyn streets and from the Brill Building's Tin Pan Alley. Produced by Robbie Robertson. —*William Ruhlmann*

Love at the Greek / Jan. 1977 / Columbia ✦✦

Love at the Greek captures Neil Diamond at the height of his late-'70s excess. Considerably less kinetic and exciting than the previous double-live album *Hot August Night*, *Love at the Greek* finds Diamond at the peak of his powers as a schmaltzy showman, hamming up each of his songs for the audience. It's the kind of performance that will please both dedicated fans, who will love Neil's no-holds-barred showmanship, as well as listeners with an ear for kitsch, who will no doubt treasure Diamond's immortal introduction "Ladies and gentlemen…the Fonz! Henry Winkler!" on "Song Sung Blue." —*Stephen Thomas Erlewine*

I'm Glad You're Here with Me Tonight / Feb. 1977 / Columbia ✦✦

You Don't Bring Me Flowers / 1978 / Columbia ✦✦✦

Reprising "You Don't Bring Me Flowers" from *I'm Glad You're Here With Me Tonight*, Neil Diamond constructed his finest late-'70s record with *You Don't Bring Me Flowers*. Although the glossy production may be a little too sterile for some listeners, the shiny, radio-ready sound is appealing, and the songs—including the title track and "Forever in Blue Jeans"—are consistently entertaining, even if they are a little similar. —*Stephen Thomas Erlewine*

September Morn / 1979 / Columbia ✦✦

The Jazz Singer / 1980 / Columbia ✦✦✦✦✦

Diamond's only notable screen appearance was his starring role in this remake of the 1927 movie that was Hollywood's first real talkie and originally featured Al Jolson. Diamond wrote a new score, featuring his biggest latter-day hits, "Love on the Rocks," "Hello Again," and "America," and as a result this soundtrack album became his biggest seller ever—five million copies and counting. —*William Ruhlmann*

Heartlight / 1982 / Columbia ✦✦

12 Greatest Hits, Vol. 2 / May 1982 / Columbia ✦✦✦✦✦

Keying off the title of an earlier hits collection on another label, Columbia's *12 Greatest Hits Volume II* summed up Neil Diamond's first eight years with the label, 1973-1981, as well as his successful 1980 soundtrack for *The Jazz Singer* on Capitol Records. Five of the 12, "Longfellow Serenade," "You Don't Bring Me Flowers" (with Barbra Streisand), "Love on the Rocks," "Hello Again," and "America," were Top Ten hits. Another six, "Be," "If You Know What I Mean," "Desiree," "Forever in Blue Jeans," "September Morn," and "Yesterday's Songs," made the Top 40, and the last, "Beautiful Noise," was the title track of Diamond's best album of the period. The songs shared a catchiness that belied Diamond's shallow philosophizing and thinly veiled lust, and they made for a consistent collection out of what had been a series of uneven albums. And, since Diamond only made the Top Ten one more time, the album capped his hit-making days. This is the record to buy instead of investing in the Columbia catalog. —*William Ruhlmann*

★ **Classics: The Early Years** / 1983 / Columbia ✦✦✦✦✦

Classics: The Early Years rounds up 12 highlights from Neil Diamond's recordings for Bang Records. These, of course, were Diamond's earliest recordings and for many fans they remain among his very best work, and it's easy to see why—not only are these terrific songs, but the productions don't oversell the songs. Even when strings grace the productions, there's a dark, brooding vibe to the ballads and a crisp feeling to the pop songs. And while some of the songs won't be instantly recognizable, most of them will, because these are the tunes that made Diamond's reputation as a songwriter and performer: "Kentucky Woman," "Cherry, Cherry," "Solitary Man," "Thank the Lord for the Night Time," "I'm a Believer," "Girl, You'll Be a Woman Soon," "Shilo" and "Red, Red Wine." Diamond occasionally matched these peaks later in his career, but never again did he deliver so many great songs at such a frequency—and *Classics* conveniently collects them all in one place. *—Stephen Thomas Erlewine*

Primitive / 1984 / Columbia ✦✦

Headed for the Future / 1986 / Columbia ✦✦

Hot August Night 2 / 1987 / Columbia ✦✦

The Best Years of Our Lives / 1988 / Columbia ✦✦✦
This album came when Neil Diamond was firmly entrenched in his adult contemporary niche. A/C can be so pandering it's insulting sometimes, but when it's done with heart and smarts it can be sublime. Diamond apparently gets that and for the most part makes adult contemporary that is actually for adults. It takes a master to croon "Cause I do believe in forever/it's a place that lovers find" without making the sentiment cringe-inducing. And Diamond pulls it off. Despite that, even he can't keep from sounding creepy when he sings, "Ooh, babe, you're a hot little number" on "Everything's Gonna be Fine." Both he and this album are classier than that, and once you're into the song it's undeniable—it becomes a feel-good anthem, and it works. Diamond was wise enough to co-write a number of these songs with master producer/songwriter David Foster. Foster writes his share of pabulum, but when he's good he's great, and on this album he's in fine form. Diamond was also wise enough to tone down the production so that his rugged voice and the melancholy melodies are able to shine through. *The Best Years of Our Lives* is an album that is romantic and sentimental without being manipulative, and despite a couple of overproduced ballads that are outweighed by the other tracks, particularly the high-spirited and hopeful title cut and the subtle remorse of "This Time," it is a strong entry in Diamond's oeuvre. *—Bryan Buss*

Lovescape / Aug. 27, 1991 / Columbia ✦✦

The Greatest Hits (1966-1992) / May 19, 1992 / Columbia ✦✦✦✦
Columbia has been Diamond's label since 1973, and it acquired the rights to his Bang material of 1966-1968. But MCA still controls the recordings from 1968-1973. That's why (although you won't find out by reading the album cover) this two-disc, 37-track retrospective consists of the original versions of such hits as "Cherry, Cherry" (1966) and "You Don't Bring Me Flowers" (1978) but covers the middle period with re-recordings and live renditions of 13 of Diamond's biggest hits. As such, this collection gets only a qualified recommendation. *—William Ruhlmann*

Glory Road: 1968 to 1972 / Jun. 30, 1992 / MCA ✦✦✦✦✦
A fine two-disc retrospective of Diamond's late-'60s and early-'70s tracks, it includes some of his biggest hits—"Cracklin' Rosie," "Sweet Caroline," and "Song Sung Blue," among others. If *His 12 Greatest Hits* doesn't offer enough material, *Glory Road* is the definitive retrospective of his years with Uni/MCA. *—AMG*

Up on the Roof: Songs from the Brill Building / Sep. 28, 1993 / Columbia ✦✦✦
This is Diamond's equivalent of, say, one of Barbra Streisand's *Broadway* albums. It's Broadway that Diamond is returning to as well; specifically, the corner of 49th Street, where he and many others turned out songs for music publishers. Some of these songs were written there; most were only in the spirit of that modern Tin Pan Alley. Handling the work of his then-rivals, such as "Spanish Harlem," "A Groovy Kind of Love," and "River Deep, Mountain High," Diamond adopts his usual hammy style. Peter Asher patented a neo-'60s production style in crafting oldies for Linda Ronstadt in the '70s, and he does the same thing here. Actually, this record sounds exactly like you would expect: just call to mind a familiar song like "Will You Love Me Tomorrow" and imagine what it would sound like if Neil Diamond sang it. Fans can decide for themselves whether it's valid and, perhaps more problematic, necessary. *—William Ruhlmann*

Live in America / 1995 / Columbia ✦✦✦
Much like its predecessor *Hot August Night 2*, *Live in America* captures Neil Diamond at the height of his powers as a showman. By the time *Live in America* was recorded, it had been several years since he had a hit; in fact, the closest he had come to the top of the charts was when UB40 took a reggae remake of "Red Red Wine" to number one. That doesn't mean the album is a wash-out. Diamond hauls out his old hits—including an approximation of UB40's interpretation of "Red Red Wine"—and gives one hell of a show. It might not offer anything that the previous *Hot August Nights* do, but *Live in America* remains an entertaining listen. *—Stephen Thomas Erlewine*

Tennessee Moon / Feb. 1996 / Columbia ✦✦✦
Neil Diamond mounted a major comeback with *Tennessee Moon*, his first collection of new material in nearly five years. Instead of capitalizing on the psuedo-hipster status he had acquired with the early '90s alternative rockers, particularly Urge Overkill, Diamond headed to Nashville to write and record *Tennessee Moon*. Appropriately, the album is rooted in contemporary country, spiked with hints of the pop craftsmanship that made him popular in the '60s. Not all of the songs were written by Diamond or his collaborators, which included Raul Malo of the Mavericks; the combination of originals and professionally-written made-to-order songs works well, leaving the overall quality of the material rather high. *Tennessee Moon* suffers from an overabundance of songs, as well as a slightly sterile production, but it remains one of Neil Diamond's most successful records of the '80s and '90s. *—Stephen Thomas Erlewine*

In My Lifetime / Oct. 29, 1996 / Columbia ✦✦✦✦✦
In My Lifetime is a triple-disc, 71-track box set spanning Neil Diamond's entire career, from his early Bang hits, through his heyday at MCA to his latter-day adult contemporary hits for Columbia. Demos, alternate takes, and live cuts are interspersed throughout the box. Not all of Diamond's greatest songs are here—obscurities like "Two-Bit Manchild" would have been welcome—but all of the classics are present. Aside from the flimsy book-style packaging, the only real problem with the set are the rarities. While the songwriting demos from the beginning of his career are of interest to both dedicated and casual fans, latter-day demos and alternate takes are only of interest to hardcore collectors and break the rhythm of the set. Nevertheless, if anyone wants just one Neil Diamond album, *In My Lifetime* is the one to get—it has all the songs you know plus several great lesser-known gems, presented in crisp, clear sound and with an excellent biography and discography. *—Stephen Thomas Erlewine*

The Movie Album: As Time Goes By / Oct. 27, 1998 / Columbia ✦✦

20th Century Masters—The Millennium Collection: The Best of Neil Diamond / Mar. 9, 1999 / MCA ✦✦✦
Like any record company worth their salt, MCA knows a good gimmick when they see it, and when the millennium came around… well, the *20th Century Masters—The Millennium Collection* wasn't too far behind. Supposedly, the millennium is a momentous occasion, but it's hard to feel that way when it's used as another excuse to turn out a budget-line series. But apart from the presumptuous title, *20th Century Masters—The Millennium Collection* turns out to be a very good budget-line series. True, it's impossible for any of these brief collections to be definitive, but they're nevertheless solid samplers that don't feature a bad song in the bunch. For example, take Neil Diamond's *20th Century* volume—it's an irresistible summary of his MCA years, rivaling the previous *His Twelve Greatest Hits*. There may be a couple of noteworthy songs missing, but all the big hits of that era are here, including "Sweet Caroline," "Holly Holy," "Song Sung Blue," "Brother Love's Traveling Salvation Show," "Play Me," "Brooklyn Roads," "Crunchy Granola Suite," "Stone," "Soolaimon," "I Am… I Said" and "Cracklin' Rosie." Serious fans will want something more extensive, but this is an excellent introduction for neophytes and a great sampler for casual fans, considering its length and price. That doesn't erase the ridiculousness of the series title, but the silliness is excusable when the music and the collections are good. *—Stephen Thomas Erlewine*

★ **Collection** / Nov. 23, 1999 / MCA ✦✦✦✦✦
Not as comprehensive an anthology of Neil Diamond's eight-album, four-year affiliation with MCA as 1992's 38-track double *Glory Road*, *Collection* is a definitive single disc recap of one of his extensive career's most influential periods. At 17 songs, it's less than half as long as the two-disc set; oddly, the two live albums Diamond recorded during these years are ignored. Only a hot version of "Cherry, Cherry" from *Hot August Night*, at the time his most successful album and even one these liner notes tout as "one of the strongest live albums ever recorded," is included. *Neil Diamond Gold* is completely absent, but since it primarily consisted of inferior versions of his Bang material, that's not unusual. Instead, it's a beautifully remastered, non-chronologically arranged 67 minutes of studio highlights from Diamond's most ambitious, if not his most commercially successful years. Only his version of "He Ain't Heavy, He's My Brother," the disc's lone cover, is a questionable choice, but since it charted at number 20 in 1970, its inclusion is justified. Otherwise, this non-stop, hit-filled collection shifts from one radio standard to another, easily replacing the existing and rather anemic *12 Greatest Hits* with its sound quality, depth and breadth. Dramatic, classic mini pop-operas like "Brother Love's Traveling Salvation Show," "Cracklin' Rosie," and "Holly Holy" are as much a part of the late '60s singer/songwriter rubric as work from the era's more feted artists. The thoughtfully compiled 16-page booklet includes detailed track documentation, an extensive essay, and some rare pictures of the young artist, making this the essential single-disc representation of Neil Diamond's short, yet significant, MCA tenure. *—Hal Horowitz*

Ultimate Collection / Dec. 21, 1999 / Columbia/MCA ✦✦✦✦✦

The Dickies

f. 1977, **db.** 1989
American Punk, L.A. Punk, Comedy Rock, Punk
For the Dickies, punk rock wasn't a way to vent anger, it was a way to make fun of things. More than anything, the Los Angeles quartet was distinguished by their simplistic, nearly moronic, sense of humor. Basing their musical attack as well as their lyrical obsessions on early Ramones records, the Dickies played a speedy, hooky variation on standard three-chord rock, singing ludicrous, campy songs about the "Attack of the Mole Men." In addition to their wacky originals, the group recorded zany, jokey covers of rock & roll classics like "Paranoid," "Eve of Destruction," and "Communication Breakdown," as well as oddities like "Eep Opp Ork (Uh, Uh)," a pseudo-rockabilly number from a *Jetsons* episode.

The Dickies formed after the initial punk explosion of 1977. The band comprised vocalist Leonard Graves Phillips, guitarist Stan Lee, bassist Billy Club, keyboardist Chuck Wagon, and drummer Karlos Kaballero—all of the names were assumed, of course. Two years later, the group released their debut album, *The Incredible Shrinking Dickies*, on A&M Records. Throughout their career, the Dickies only deviated slightly from the fast and catchy punk of their debut—their earlier records leaned toward the Californian hardcore punk that was popular at the time, while the later records slow down a little, approaching heavy metal territory. Over the course of six albums between 1979 and 1989, the group's audience never grew beyond a cult following. With echoes of their music heard in Green Day's multi-platinum 1994 hit album *Dookie*, the Dickies returned to action in 1998 with *Dogs from the Hare That Bit Us*; *Still Live Even If You Don't Want Us* came out the following year and they kept the ball rolling with their release of *Stukas Over Disneyland* in 2000. *—Stephen Thomas Erlewine*

The Incredible Shrinking Dickies / 1979 / Captain Oi! ✦✦✦✦
This first release by the California-based Dickies contains songs best described as percolating, hyperactive cartoon hardcore, colored with a noticeable bit of Ramones influence. All the songs on this album are frantically fast and very short; over half the selections

here have durations under two minutes, and only the instrumental number "Rondo" is longer than three minutes. Most of the tunes here have agreeably goofball lyrics that are often only semi-intelligible. Chucklesome touches such as dog-barking vocals in "Poodle Party," a quote from the Champs' instrumental "Tequila" in "Shadow Man," cuckoo clock noises in "Mental Ward," and a rubber ducky solo in "Curb Job" help keep the songs firmly tongue in cheek. Black Sabbath's "Paranoid," the Monkees' "She," and Barry McGuire's "Eve of Destruction" are given the same dizzy treatment as everything else here. This album is good, crazy fun and worth a listen. *—David Cleary*

Dawn of the Dickies / 1979 / Captain Oi! ✦✦✦✦

The Dickies march boldly past the three-minute song duration mark on their second release. Tempos for the most part here are a little less frantic, allowing the inherent tunefulness of these songs to come through more clearly. A few selections, particularly those with monster movie lyrics, are set to noticeably slower music; one of these numbers, "Attack of the Mole Men," sports highly unusual chord progressions and comes as close to being a big production number as the group ever gets. Comparisons to the Ramones are more obvious here as well, particularly on the enjoyable could-have-been-an-avant-garde-Pep-Boys-commercial "Manny, Moe & Jack" and the frenetic "I'm a Chollo"; the latter song eventually turns into something approximating a funhouse version of a Yardbirds rave-up. The maudlin Moody Blues tune "Nights in White Satin" gets an uproariously funny trampling here; not only is the song given at breakneck speed, but in addition, the original version's expressive flute solo is played nearly note for note on grinding guitar and is further adorned with faux heavy metal embellishments. This surprisingly strong platter is well worth hearing. *—David Cleary*

Stukas Over Disneyland / 1983 / Restless ✦✦✦

This album, released after a four-year silence, shows the band training their popcorn wiseguy sights somewhat away from the hardcore and Ramones influences of earlier platters to that of power-pop and 1960s songs. The former of the two new influences is showcased in the tunefully memorable "Pretty Please Me" and "If Stuart Could Talk"; the latter is evident in "Rosemary" (with its Beatles-on-caffeine bridge), "Wagon Train" (which sports a broad tune that evokes comparisons to old television Western show theme songs), "Out of Sight, Out of Mind" (featuring a chorus that echoes the one in Ricky Nelson's "Garden Party"), and especially the title track (which exhibits noticeable surf music and Chuck Berry influences and sets ironic, humorous lyrics detailing a Disney-based world takeover). Bows to their earlier punk influences can be seen in the uproariously funny "She's a Hunchback" (complete with smart-aleck references to the Victor Hugo novel) and a giddy cover of the Led Zeppelin classic "Communication Breakdown." The 1988 re-release appends three songs ("Gigantor," "I'm Okay, You're Okay," and "Bedrock Barney") cast in their old cartoon hardcore manner; while all are likable and welcome, the addition of these numbers makes this release seem more stylistically schizophrenic than it originally was. Regardless of the version obtained, this excellent album is an enjoyable and recommended listen. *—David Cleary*

We Aren't the World! / 1986 / Combat ✦✦✦✦✦

Idiocy of a ridiculous, catchy, and hilarious kind—the best sort one can ask for. Playing up their punk inspirations as much as they did their *Mad Magazine* upbringings and varying musical touchstones of youth, it's the Dickies in the rawest form around, an hour-long laugh riot that rocks. Aside from an initial four song demo session from late 1977, with extremely rough rips through such beloved first album hits as "Hideous" and "You Drive Me Ape (You Big Gorilla)," *We Aren't the World* captures the band onstage here, there, and everywhere. Huge gigs in the U.K. during their late-'70s pop heyday and club romps and riffs in CBGB's and elsewhere are culled, with the only track duplication being a 1982 take on "You Drive Me Ape." Anyone even slightly in love with the Dickies' studio work will kill for this, but the real joy is that total neophytes to the group will probably find this as equally a perfect introduction as *Great Dictations*. While the recording quality varies, to put it mildly, hearing Phillips' often-hilarious between-song comments and introductions and Lee's full-on, balls-out rock heroics in an unrestrained live setting, not to mention rapturous audience cheers and eggings on is more than enough to make up for it. At no point do the band sound like they couldn't eat anyone else for breakfast, however wide the smiles. Highlights are legion: introducing their hyperspeed cover of "The Sounds of Silence"—"Paul Simon taught us this next tune... over a highly homosexually erotic game... of Mousetrap!" During a 1985 show, at the height of Live Aid mania—"Absolutely none of tonight's profits are going to Ethiopia!" Top it off with an abusive (and tongue-in-cheek) essay from Frontier Records boss and former Dickies fan club president Lisa Fancher, and all is well in Dickiedom. *—Ned Raggett*

Killer Klowns from Outer Space / 1988 / Enigma ✦✦✦

After paying tribute to a number of trashy B-movies and writing a number of original songs that sounded as though they were based on similar junk culture, the Dickies got to indulge their obsession in reality by contributing the theme song to the low-grade comedy/horror film *Killer Klowns From Outer Space*. The remainder of the EP is not quite as inspired, but fans will want the album for that track, as well as a cover of Jet Screamer's "Eep Opp Ork (Uh, Uh)," a rockabilly tune featured in an episode of *The Jetsons*. *—Steve Huey*

Second Coming / 1989 / Enigma ✦✦✦✦

With the *Killer Klowns* EP restoring the band to more of an active duty, the Dickies fully got their act back together with *Second Coming*, amusing angel/sainthood cover and all. The core Lee/Phillips partnership remains the same, while the core band, including bassist Lorenzo Buhne, guitarist Enoch Hain, and drummer Clifford Martinez, backs up everything with the expected elan. Things aren't quite at the same all-out just-insane-enough level of the original band in terms of performance—volumes are sometimes lower, arrangement a touch less hyperactive—but in terms of good spirit and good fun, *Second Coming* is an entertaining romp. Two covers continue the tradition of out-of-nowhere "you're covering that?" reactions—while "Hair" and "Town Without Pity" aren't given the sheer high speed/slam dance treatment of times bast, it's nice to see the group still tweaking the nose of what's hip and acceptable. The latter in particular is an amusing effort—straightforward enough, but hearing Phillips instead of Gene Pitney's wailing makes for an interesting change! As for the originals, mostly from the pen of Phillips, things are off-kilter enough, as always, to make for a good time. "Magoomba" reappears from *Killer Klowns*, guest vocals from Phillips' mom and all, while "Monster Island" celebrates the legendary locale from the *Godzilla* series with surfy vibes. "Cross-Eyed Tammy" slots into the vein of sweet and silly power pop á la "Pretty Please Me" and "Out of Sight"; "Caligula" reads like the world's weirdest Iron Maiden parody ever (and why not?); and "Booby Trap" makes for a new way to look at goth girls. Even "Goin' Homo," which on the face of it would seem insulting, is good-natured silliness at quick speed—"Why did god make men with nipples?," indeed. *—Ned Raggett*

● **Great Dictations (The Definitive Dickies Collection)** / 1989 / A&M ✦✦✦✦✦

If there's one place to plunge into the joy, madness and mayhem of the Dickies' late-'70s/early-'80s period glory days, this is it. Featuring the classic line-up, including the utterly underrated keyboardist Chuck Wagon, *Great Dictations* draws on both A&M studio albums and the slew of EPs and singles that made them demi-stars in the U.K. and cult heroes in the US. Given rock's tendency to valorize "serious" music—or fun music taken "seriously"—the Dickies are the perfect response, serious musicians unafraid to goof out and let loose. A stone-cold bunch of great performers, they knew how to rock the house, but didn't worry about looking silly. Lee's guitar work is as badass as those of his heroes in the Stooges, the arrangements are powerful and fun—the Ramones parallel is obvious, but Phillips' nutty yelp and the group's embrace of even more trash culture than the New York legends sets them apart. Where to start? The giddy "I'm OK, You're OK," rips through one of mellow '70s sillier manifestos; "Give It Back," is a tale of outwitting local bullies that turns out all wrong in the end; the brilliantly barbed "Fan Mail," a hilarious vision of said material at its most banal and obvious. Then there are the covers: "Paranoid," "Sounds of Silence," "Nights In White Satin," "Eve of Destruction," all done in ways likely unimagined by the songs' creators. Top that off with their two legendary kid show theme remakes, "Banana Splits" and "Gigantor," and a very rare romp through "Silent Night," and it doesn't get any more entertaining. *—Ned Raggett*

Idjit Savant / Jan. 17, 1995 / Relativity ✦✦✦

Six years after their first comeback, the Dickies return with another effort showing little deviation from their past work, but the band's songwriting is surprisingly consistent and melodic, and the production is more streamlined than *Second Coming*. Few would have predicted that the Dickies' tenure as active recording artists would last this long, and *Idjit Savant* is a testament to their endurance and continued ability to rock out with a healthy sense of humor. *—Steve Huey*

All This and Puppet Stew / May 22, 2001 / Fat Wreck Chords ✦✦

The Dictators

f. 1974, **db.** 1978

American Punk, New York Punk, Proto-Punk, Hard Rock

Formed in 1974, NYC's Dictators were one of the finest and most influential proto-punk bands to walk the earth. Alternately reveling in and satirizing the wanton excesses of a rock & roll lifestyle and lowbrow culture (e.g., wrestling, TV, fast food), the Dictators played loud, fast rock & roll fueled by a love of '60s American garage rock, British Invasion pop, and the sonic onslaught of the Who. Driven by the guitar barrage of Scott "Top Ten" Kempner and Ross "the Boss" Funichello and fronted by indefatigable ex-roadie and wrestler Handsome Dick Manitoba (aka Richard Blum), it seemed that nothing stood in the way of the Dictators and mega-popularity. But that's not what happened. There were complications with record companies, personnel changes, radio hated them, critical response was lukewarm, and lots of audiences didn't get the jokes; supporters remained loyal and vociferous, but it didn't turn into anything tangible. Ironically, what didn't help at all was the rise of the New York punk scene, which only diverted attention away from them and onto bands they influenced (e.g., the Ramones). They did manage to release three fine albums, but by 1978, it was over, and the Dictators broke up in the face of the public apathy and overstated accusations of sellout that greeted what was to be their final album, *Bloodbrothers*. *—John Dougan*

● **The Dictators Go Girl Crazy** / Mar. 1975 / Epic ✦✦✦✦✦

In 1975, when punk rock and heavy metal were two opposing camps who barely who acknowledged each other's existence, The Dictators' first album, *The Dictators Go Girl Crazy!*, found New York's finest trying to bring both sides together in a brave, prescient, and (at least at the time) futile gesture. The band's "smart guys who like dumb stuff" humor, junk-culture reference points, and '60s cheeze rock covers ("California Sun" *and* "I Got You Babe" on one album) would seem tailor made for the crowd at CBGB digging The Ramones and The Dead Boys, but their sludgy and stripped down hard rock (and Ross "The Boss" Funichello's neo-metal guitar solos) were something else altogether. And at a time when the arena rock audience had not yet embraced the less-than-subtle humor and theatrics of Sparks or Cheap Trick, The Dictators ahead-of-their-time enthusiasm for wrestling, White Castle hamburgers, and television confused more kids than it converted. Heard today, the album is a hoot and a half; if the tempos could often stand to be a bit livelier, Adny Shernoff's songs are still great (especially the absurdly anthemic "Two Tub Man," "I Live For Cars and Girls," and "Weekend"), the jokes still register (while the contemporary Political Correctness brigade might blanch at "Back To Africa" or "Master Race Rock," they're merely absurd in the *Mad Magazine* tradition), and "secret weapon" Handsome Dick Manitoba was truly a find. Dozens of groups borrowed wholesale from *The*

Dictators Go Girl Crazy! later on down the line, but the original is still the greatest . . . and the funniest. *—Mark Deming*

Manifest Destiny / 1977 / Asylum ♦♦♦
By this time, Manitoba was considered the full-time lead singer (although Shernoff and Kempner sing plenty) and the band was hitting its stride. Despite a longish dud track that closes side one ("Disease"), *Manifest Destiny* shows off the Dictators' strong (and often tender) pop smarts, especially on Shernoff's "Sleepin' With the Television On" and Kempner's "Hey Boys." Also, there's a fast and furious cover of the Stooges' "Search & Destroy." *—John Dougan*

Bloodbrothers / 1978 / Dictators Multimedia ♦♦♦
This was the Dictators' third album and their second for Elektra/Asylum. The band was energized after returning from a tour of England and being embraced by the emerging punk rock audience over there. As a result, this album was recorded almost 90% live and, as such, stands as a good example of what the band sounded like on a good night live. "Faster & Louder," and the kickoff track, features an unannounced guest appearance from Bruce Springsteen on backing vocals, while "Baby, Let's Twist" features guitar work far more sophisticated than the title would lead you to believe. The band may have still been trying to cast themselves as the next logical extension of the MC5 and the Stooges, but Andy Shernoff's songwriting (especially on tunes like "No Tomorrow," "Stay With Me," and "Borneo Jimmy") shows infinitely more craft than mere Motor City knockoffs. The playing is self assured and solid, the production is simple, raw and direct. In many ways, this is the Dictators' rockinest and most musical album. *—Cub Koda*

Live, Fuck 'Em If They Can't Take a Joke / 1981 / ROIR ♦♦♦

New York, New York / Oct. 27, 1998 / ROIR ♦♦♦
New York, New York is a CD reissue of the 1981 Dictators live album *Live: Fuck 'Em If They Can't Take a Joke* with three bonus tracks, among them the favorite "Master Race Rock." In his new liner notes, bassist/vocalist/songwriter Adny (or Andy) Shernoff takes issue with Richard Meltzer's original liner notes, denying that the recording, made on February 11, 1981 (the bonus tracks are from "the early '80s"), represented a reunion show since the Dictators, despite appearances, had not broken up even though "there were occasional gaps of a few years between some shows." In this case, it had been three years since the Dictators had been active, but it only took the opening chords of "Next Big Thing" to establish the band's claim to being a major influence on the Ramones and thus on the entire punk/new wave movement of the second half of the '70s. By 1981, punk had been just about absorbed into mainstream pop/rock, but the Dictators returned to their unique blend of hard rock and humor (the latter an element missing from most punk), at least for one night, adding Velvet Underground and Stooges songs to their repertoire. ROIR issued the result on cassette for a fitting coda to the band's career, and years later the album sounds as raucous as ever and at least a little bit improved sonically, though the sound quality is still nothing to write home about. *—William Ruhlmann*

Bo Diddley

b. Dec. 30, 1928, McComb, MS
Vocals, Guitar (Electric), Violin, Guitar / Rock & Roll, R&B
He only had a few hits in the 1950s and early '60s, but as Bo Diddley sang, "You Can't Judge a Book by Its Cover." You can't judge an artist by his chart success, either, and Diddley produced greater and more influential music than all but a handful of the best early rockers. The Bo Diddley beat—bomp, ba-bomp-bomp, bomp-bomp—is one of rock & roll's bedrock rhythms, showing up in the work of Buddy Holly, the Rolling Stones, and even pop-garage knockoffs like the Strangeloves' 1965 hit "I Want Candy." Diddley's hypnotic rhythmic attack and declamatory, boasting vocals stretched back as far as Africa for their roots, and looked as far into the future as rap. His trademark otherwordly vibrating, fuzzy guitar style did much to expand the instrument's power and range. But even more important, Bo's bounce was fun and irresistibly rocking, with a wisecracking, jiving tone that epitomized rock & roll at its most humorously outlandish and freewheeling. *—Richie Unterberger*

Have Guitar, Will Travel / 1960 / Chess ♦♦♦♦
Amazingly, Bo Diddley's third album—containing classics such as "Cops and Robbers," "Run Diddley Daddy," and "Mona (I Need You Baby)"—has only been reissued on vinyl, and even that's out of print. More than one British Invasion band learned what they needed to know about American rock & roll from the songs on this record (the Stones cut "Cops and Robbers" at their earliest recording session, and later released a killer version of "Mona," though the most interesting British version of the latter was done by an all-girl band with an attitude called the Liverbirds). This record is every bit as raunchy as Diddley's first two albums (the guitars may even be crunchier, and the singing shows more range), and has more than enough to recommend it to collectors and fans. This is the album that began the funny cover photos on Diddley's records. *—Bruce Eder*

Bo Diddley in the Spotlight / 1960 / Chess ♦♦♦♦
As with Bo Diddley's first five albums (except *Have Guitar Will Travel*), the most important cuts (but not all the good ones) off of this album have been included on *The Chess Box* from MCA, which doesn't mean that this record isn't a good separate issue, just somewhat redundant if you have the box. There are surprises from these 1960-vintage recordings, including the languid, Caribbean-sounding "Limber"; the soft, romantic "Love Me"; the doo wop-style "Deed and Deed I Do"; the loping "Walkin' and Talkin'"; upbeat, gospel-tinged rockers such as "Let Me In" interspersed with the hot and raunchy "Road Runner," "The Story of Bo Diddley," "Craw-Dad" (a genuine diamond in the rough), and "Signifying Blues"; and solid instrumentals like "Scuttle Bug" (really "Live My Life" with the vocals removed and Otis Spann overdubbed on piano) that make this record more than worthwhile. *—Bruce Eder*

Bo Diddley Is a Lover / 1961 / Checker ♦♦♦♦
There's not a bad song on this long-forgotten album; in fact, it's all good, and so little of it has been reissued that it's a crime. There are a lot of familiar moments here: Diddley slips most effectively into his "Say Man" groove on "Bo's Vacation"; plays some serious Chicago blues on "Call Me (Bo's Blues)" and makes it count; invades Chuck Berry territory by way of Howlin' Wolf on the window-rattling "Hong Kong Mississippi" (a track so riveting and funny, and so rippling in superb guitar work, it makes this album worthwhile on its own); bounces back to his signature beat on the title song, the hysterically funny autobiographical "Bo Diddley Is Loose," "Quick Draw," "Back Home," and "Not Guilty" (a song that deserves enshrinement as one of Diddley's best); and slips into a romantic groove on "You're Looking Good." Find it, buy it, and savor it. *—Bruce Eder*

Hey Bo Diddley! / 1962 / Chess ♦♦♦
Bo's music was beginning to slip in sales—though he remained a popular concert act—when Chess released this album in the summer of 1962. "I Can Tell," written by Samuel Smith, showed Bo trying out a slower, more seductively soulful sound, a whole four-and-a-half-minutes long—it is different, though not very distinguished. "Bo's Twist" isn't much more impressive, a fairly standard instrumental with an unusually grungy (like you were expecting Julian Bream) guitar sound, with the first prominent appearance of an organ in the backing of a Bo Diddley record; "Sad Sack" is a somewhat more successful instrumental. "Mr. Kruschev" is one of the funniest, most delightfully nonsensical pieces of topical songwriting Bo ever engaged in, writing about wanting to go into the army and go over to see the Soviet leader and get him to stop nuclear testing, to a background of "Hut, two—three four!" "You All Green" is first-rate Bo, and deserved to be anthologized somewhere. "You Can't Judge A Book By The Cover" was the one standard from the album, but other tracks deserving of better exposure include "Bo's Bounce" and "Who May Your Lover Be," which takes off from Howlin' Wolf's "Moaning At Midnight," recasting it in a Bo Diddley beat, with Bo sounding a lot like Wolf here, and "Give Me A Break (Man)," which is a very animated impromptu guitar jam. The album filler tracks include "Mama Don't Allow No Twistin'," Bo's take on "Mama Don't Like Music," a song that was old when country-and-western/novelty singer Smiley Burnette covered it successfully in the 1930s, "Babes in the Woods" (featuring a backing chorus mimicking the doo-wop parody "Get a Job") and "Diddling," a routine Bo instrumental. *—Bruce Eder*

Bo Diddley Is a Gunslinger / 1963 / Chess ♦♦♦♦
Not only does it sport one of the most striking album covers of its era (Diddley decked out in cowboy finery, about to get the drop on some unfortunate varmint with one of his fieriest guitars lying at his feet), this 1963 album contains some fine music. The title track continues the legend of you-know-who, while "Ride on Josephine" and "Cadillac" rock like hell (and Ed Sullivan must have been glad to see that Diddley finally learned "Sixteen Tons"). Two bonus cuts, "Working Man" and "Do What I Say," make this one a must. *—Bill Dahl*

Bo Diddley's Beach Party / 1963 / Checker ♦♦♦♦♦
A blistering live album, especially in genuine mono (the re-channeled stereo is barely passable)—and quite simply the finest live rock & roll album of its era, cut live by Diddley and band at Myrtle Beach, SC, on July 5 and 6, 1963. From the opening track (erroneously listed as "Memphis" and credited to Chuck Berry as composer) to the final note, this is some of the loudest, raunchiest guitar-based rock & roll ever preserved. It also bears an uncanny resemblance to the sound that the Rolling Stones achieved on their own *Got Live If You Want It*, which only shows how much the Stones learned from Diddley. Highlights include "Gunslinger," "Hey Bo Diddley," "Road Runner," and "I'm All Right." The sound doesn't necessarily translate ideally to compact disc, but that shouldn't dissuade anyone. Currently out of print but well worth the search. *—Bruce Eder & Cub Koda*

Two Great Guitars / 1964 / Chess ♦♦

Hey, Good Lookin' / Apr. 1965 / Checker ♦♦♦
One of Bo's least known albums, mostly recorded in April of 1964 and released a year later, at the point when none of his records were selling in America. With an edgy, raunchy sound and modern record techniques (it's in stereo), Bo and band come up with a solid '60s version of his original sound. The title track is a real jewel, featuring Jerome Green on the maracas and Lafayette Leake on the piano. "Mama Keep Your Big Mouth Shut" isn't a bad soul-styled number, with Bo abandoning his standard beat in favor of a smoother, more Motown-like sound. He tries for a similar sound on "I Wonder Why (People Don't Like Me)" and "Brother Bear." In addition to the title track (which is *not* the Hank Williams tune), the Bo Diddley beat gets a workout on "La La La," "Rain Man," and "Bo Diddley's Hoot'nanny." Bo gets to have some real fun on "London Stomp," his commentary on the sudden fashionability of British rock & roll, parodying the accents and attitudes of most of the bands that he encountered on his visit to England in October of 1963. Other tracks sound like they'd have worked well as part of extended jams of the kind that Bo did on stage—"Yeah Yeah Yeah," in particular, could've come from the middle of one of Bo's 15-minute shuffle-and-chant workouts, and would've been great in such a setting, although here, as a free-standing 2:25 track it's a little weak. There is some filler here, most notably "Let's Walk A While" and "Rooster Stew," but that can be forgiven in view of the strength of the rest of the material. *—Bruce Eder*

☆ **Bo Diddley/Go Bo Diddley** / 1986 / Chess ♦♦♦♦♦
There are precious few weak tracks on this combination of Bo Diddley's first two late-'50s albums for Chess/Checker, which boasts a plethora of classics ("Bo Diddley," "I'm a Man," "Before You Accuse Me," "Crackin' Up," "Little Girl," even his electric violin workout "The Clock Struck Twelve"). The only drawback: someone failed to notice that "Dearest Darling" was on both LPs, so . . . it's on here twice! *—Bill Dahl*

☆ **The Chess Box** / Jul. 26, 1990 / Chess ♦♦♦♦♦

Not every single track you'll ever want or need by the legendary shave-and-a-haircut rhythm R&B/rock pioneer, but a great place to begin. Two discs (45 songs) in a great big box with a nice accompanying booklet contain the groundbreaking introduction "Bo Diddley" (never again would he be referred to as Ellas McDaniel), its swaggering flipside "I'm a Man," the killer follow-ups "Diddley Daddy," "I'm Looking for a Woman," "Who Do You Love?," and "Hey Bo Diddley;" signifying street-corner humor ("Say Man"), piledriving rockers ("Road Runner," "She's Alright," "You Can't Judge a Book by Its Cover"), and numerous stunning examples of his daringly innovative guitar style. *—Bill Dahl*

Rare & Well Done / Sep. 10, 1991 / Chess ♦♦♦♦
Sixteen extreme rarities from the deepest recesses of the Chess vaults that date from 1955-1968. The grinding "She's Fine, She's Mine" and snarling "I'm Bad" are comparatively well known, at least to collectors; far more obscure are the previously unissued "Heart-O-Matic Love," "Cookie-Headed Diddley," and "Moon Baby." *—Bill Dahl*

Bo's Blues / 1993 / Ace ♦♦♦♦♦
Twenty-two of Bo Diddley's best blues-oriented sides from the Chess catalog, including some rare stuff—the rip-roaring 1959 outing "Run Diddley Daddy," a jive-loaded "Cops and Robbers" from 1956 that features maraca shaker Jerome Green more than Diddley, and a surging "Down Home Special." If you think that everything Bo Diddley ever made has that same shave-and-a-haircut beat, this collection will set you straight! *—Bill Dahl*

The Chess Years / 1993 / Charly ♦♦♦♦♦
Charly Records' *The Chess Years* has assembled most—though not quite all—of the music that the Originator recorded for Chess Records, which, unfortunately, means a lot of his lesser work as well—282 recordings, made between 1955 and 1974, on 12 CDs; looking at it is like staring across the Grand Canyon, except you *want* to jump into this if you have any sense. If the collection seems like overkill, that's because it is, and there's some poor material here from the late '60s/early '70s, when Bo was searching for a new commercial sound, although some of that later isn't really bad—his covers of Al Kooper's "I Love You More Than You'll Ever Know" or the Band's "The Shape I'm In" from *Another Dimension* are soulful and moving, but just aren't what one buys a Bo Diddley album to hear. Additionally, the collection gives the listener a chance to see how Bo explored different variations on his sound, adapting it to doo wop, folk, and even calypso, all of which worked better than one would have expected, plus soul and funk, which didn't. The sessionography is very detailed and pretty cool, and the notes are among the better biographical accounts of Bo's life and career—oh, and there are lots of pictures of Bo and the Duchess recreated throughout the set. There are problems with the mastering, however—momentary gaps exist in one or two songs, and the sound quality in certain places, such as the live *Beach Party* material, leaves something to be desired. But at its best, and that is often (at least through the mid-'60s), this set presents one of the primal forces in rock & roll. *—Bruce Eder*

Let Me Pass . . . Plus / 1994 / See For Miles ♦♦♦
Another British import version of a vintage Checker album, with a few highly desirable bonus cuts at the end to further recommend it. Most of the CD mirrors Diddley's 1965 *500% More Man* LP (the title track obviously being a sequel to his "I'm a Man"), but the extra items include the amusing "Mama, Keep Your Big Mouth Shut" and a danceable "We're Gonna Get Married." *—Bill Dahl*

A Man Amongst Men / May 21, 1996 / Code Blue ♦♦♦
Bo Diddley's major-label '90s comeback effort *A Man Amongst Men* is overflowing with guest stars, but it rarely gels into something distinctive. The presence of such heavyweights as Keith Richards, Ron Wood, and Jimmie Vaughan actually weighs down the set, preventing Diddley from digging deep into the grooves. The band never quite rocks hard enough and no one tears off an inspired solo—*A Man Amongst Men* is pleasant, but it never approaches compelling listening. *—Stephen Thomas Erlewine*

★ **His Best (Chess 50th Anniversary Collection)** / Apr. 8, 1997 / Chess ♦♦♦♦♦
With his various hits and anthology packages all out of print and the multi-disc deluxe box set out of pocketbook reach for most casual consumers, MCA finally comes up with a 20-track compilation that hits the bullseye and makes this rock pioneer's best and most influential work available to everyone. The song list reads like a primer for '60s British rhythm & blues and '90s blues bands: "Bo Diddley," "I'm a Man," "Diddley Daddy," "Pretty Thing," "Before You Accuse Me," "Hey! Bo Diddley," "Who Do You Love," "Mona" and "Roadrunner" are the tracks that made the legend and put his sound on the map worldwide. The transfers used on this set are exemplary, the majority of them utilizing masters that have a few extra seconds (or more) appended to the fades, which will cause even hardliners to hear these old standards with fresh ears; especially revelatory are the "long versions" of "I Can Tell" and "You Can't Judge a Book By Its Cover." If the box set is too big a trigger to pull and you want all of Bo's influential sides in one package, this one should be first-stop shopping of the highest priority. *—Cub Koda*

20th Century Masters—The Millennium Collection: The Best of Bo Diddley / Jan. 25, 2000 / MCA ♦♦♦
This fine but brief summation of Diddley's career includes all the relevant hits ("Bo Diddley," "I'm a Man") as well as a few not-so-relevant ones ("Dearest Darling," "Say Man"). Its brevity doesn't give much opportunity to cover all of Diddley's achievements —none of the *Millennium* collections really do—but for beginners it's a good place to start. *—Michael Gallucci*

Dido

Vocals / Adult Alternative Pop/Rock, Singer/Songwriter

Electronic pop chanteuse Dido entered London's Guildhall School of Music at age six, and by the time she reached her teens had already mastered piano, violin and recorder. After touring with a British classical ensemble, she accepted a publishing job, in the meanwhile singing in a series of local groups before joining the trip-hop outfit Faithless—helmed by her older brother, the noted DJ and producer Rollo—in 1995. As the group's 1996 debut *Reverence* went on to sell some five million copies worldwide, Dido began working on solo material, developing a lushly ethereal sound combining elements of acoustic pop and electronica; signing with Arista, she released her debut LP *No Angel* in mid-1999, and toured with the Lilith Fair that summer. Her biggest break, however, came the following year, when rap superstar Eminem sampled the *No Angel* track "Thank You" for the chorus of his hit single "Stan," to surprisingly touching effect. Demand for the Dido original escalated quickly, and "Thank You" became a Top Five smash in early 2001, as did the album, which topped sales of three million copies. *—Jason Ankeny*

● **No Angel** / Jun. 1, 1999 / Arista ♦♦♦♦
The title notwithstanding, this debut from the former Faithless singer is pretty angelic-sounding stuff. You're bound to think of Sinéad O'Connor, but the comparison is as misleading as it is inevitable. Granted, Dido's ethereal vocals here frequently recall O'Connor; but Dido's music—while inventively augmented with electronics—is generally less adventurous. Ditto *No Angel*'s lyrics, which focus almost exclusively on love, lust, and relationships. That said, the fact remains that this is an auspicious and highly listenable album; atmospheric, seductive, and beautifully produced and sequenced. *—Jeff Burger*

Ani DiFranco

b. Sep. 23, 1970

Vocals, Guitar / Alternative Folk, Indie Rock, Alternative Pop/Rock, Singer/Songwriter, Urban Folk, Anti-Folk

A folkie in punk's clothing, Ani DiFranco battled successfully against the Goliath of corporate rock to emerge as one of the most influential and inspirational cult heroines of the 1990s. A resolute follower of D.I.Y. ethos, DiFranco released her records through her own indie label, slowly but steadily building a devout grass-roots following on the strength of a relentless tour schedule; an ardent feminist and an open bisexual, her songs tackled issues like rape, abortion and sexism with insight and compassion, the music's empowering attitude and anger tempered by the poignant candor of singer-songwriter confessionalism. By the age of 19 DiFranco had written over 100 original songs, later relocating to New York City to further her musical aspirations. After recording a demo tape for sale at her shows, she founded Righteous Babe in 1990 to better distribute her recordings. As albums like 1992's *Imperfectly* and 1993's *Puddle Dive* expanded her musical ambitions as well as her following, DiFranco became the subject of considerable major-label interest, yet she steadfastly rejected all offers. She exploded with 1995's *Not a Pretty Girl*, which garnered notice from outlets ranging from CNN to the *New York Times*. *Dilate* even debuted in the Top 100 album charts upon release in 1996, and 1998's *Little Plastic Castle* became her highest-charting album to date, setting the stage for the release of *Up Up Up Up Up Up* the following year. *—Jason Ankeny*

Ani DiFranco / 1989 / Righteous Babe ♦♦♦♦
"I am a work in progress," appropriately announces Ani DiFranco on her debut album. Though her lyrics have the rambling style of free-form poetry and she sounds like she learned her spare, percussive style of guitar playing by listening to Suzanne Vega albums, she defines a distinct persona, that of a self-possessed, assertive woman in a tough, urban landscape who feels the need to lash out first (usually in reference to heterosexual romantic relationships) and then turn vulnerable. She justifies her chip-on-the-shoulder attitude with some telling observations and turns of phrase, even if individual lines are sometimes better than whole songs, and puts the songs across with her elastic phrasing and sheer conviction even when they're not really about much of anything. When she has a real subject, however, notably on the album's best composition, "Lost Woman Song," which concerns abortion, it all comes together and she displays a writing and performing talent that is as thrilling as it is affecting. *—William Ruhlmann*

Not So Soft / 1991 / Righteous Babe ♦♦♦
Ani DiFranco showed musical growth on her second album, playing her guitar more fluidly and adding occasional harmony vocals on the choruses and even the occasional bit of percussion. Her songs had more structured melodies with shorter, more direct lyrics that sounded more like song lyrics and less like free-form poetry than those on her first album. And her subject matter also saw changes, as she for the most part moved beyond the edgy breakup songs of her debut to less personal, more political concerns, including an attack on the music business ("The Next Big Thing"). But there still was personal material, notably two songs, "She Says" and "The Whole Night," that contemplated lesbianism. These tended to undercut the point of the album's most striking track, "Gratitude," whose general point—that women's bodies are their own and they shouldn't have to put out if they don't want to—was of course well taken, even if its specific circumstances were suspect: If you don't want a guy to put the moves on you, maybe you shouldn't get into bed with him. *—William Ruhlmann*

Imperfectly / 1992 / Righteous Babe ♦♦♦♦
Ani DiFranco continued to expand her musical palette gradually on her third album, using outside musicians on some tracks to support her acoustic guitar with bass and drums, and adding individual instruments—trumpet, viola—for color on certain tunes. But the focus was still on the evolving persona depicted in her lyrics, one who continued to flirt with lesbianism consciously on "In or Out" and "If It Isn't Her," and, perhaps unconsciously, in the what-does-she-see-in-him sentiment of "Fixing Her Hair." The larger theme of the album, also suggested in "In or Out," was the artist's inability to "fit in," either because of her sexuality, her politics, or, most tellingly, her occupation as an itinerant musician. In "Every State Line," she reflected on the difficulties of shoestring travel, and in "Good, Bad, Ugly" and "The Waiting Song," the difficulties of long-distance rela-

tionships shaped both the songwriter's anger and her self-doubt. She had not tended to question herself before this, but from its title, *Imperfectly*, on, DiFranco deconstructed her persona, asking, "What If No One's Watching" in one song and declaring, "I'm No Heroine" in another. At the same time, she upped the ante of her sexual politics, expanding from criticizing individual men to berating a culture she saw as dominated by male views in everything from the music business to architecture ("Who says I like right angles?"). But if *Imperfectly* presented the singer at her most doctrinaire, it also displayed surprising warmth for individuals, notably the uncharacteristically forgiving "Served Faithfully." *Imperfectly* was the work of a still-growing, still passionate, sometimes confused artist whose personal story in song was proving to be fascinating. *—William Ruhlmann*

Puddle Dive / 1993 / Righteous Babe ♦♦♦
Like most singer/songwriters, Ani DiFranco writes songs out of her own experience and perspective, and as of her fourth album she seems to be spending a lot of time on the road, since the life of a traveling musician is repeatedly described in the album's songs. The first two tracks, "Names and Dates and Times" and "Anyday," are about the singer's attraction to someone, but she never forgets that she won't be in town long. "4th of July" finds her passing through Iowa, and "Back Around" justifies the career of an itinerant musician as better than working in construction or retail. At times, DiFranco's bitterness gets the better of her. In "Blood in the Boardroom" she expresses her disapproval of the corporate record business (you assume—what else was she doing in a boardroom?) by staining her chair with menstrual blood. That isn't the only time that menstruation comes up on this album, either, and it is part of DiFranco's method to seize upon topics that make some people uncomfortable (and that few other songwriters bring up). Who else would use nosepicking as a metaphor for liberation? "What is it about me that offends?" she asks in "Pick Yer Nose" after having declared "I'm not hurting anyone/I'm just telling my own truth" in "Born a Lion." But of course that's disingenuous; she knows perfectly well that telling your own truth can offend people, and she sets up targets to shoot down. ("Every tool is a weapon if you hold it right," she sings in "My IQ.") Nevertheless, though *Puddle Dive* is characteristically scattershot, DiFranco as usual hits a few of those targets, even when, as not infrequently, she's aiming at herself. *—William Ruhlmann*

Out of Range / Jul. 26, 1994 / Righteous Babe ♦♦♦♦
DiFranco spruces up her sparse folk arrangements with the odd brass band, accordion, and even an electric guitar or two, but the meat of these songs is still her distinctively funky acoustic guitar style (she borrowed her rhythmic plucking technique from R&B, but unplugged it bears no resemblance to its genre of origin). Meanwhile, DiFranco's spunky activist lyrics are tempered here by a bigger dose of vulnerability than in previous albums, which allows for a unique mix of anger, humor and poignancy. The best songs this time around are not bitter but quietly reflective ("You Had Time," "Buildings and Bridges," "If He Tries Anything"). *—Darryl Cater*

Like I Said: Songs 1990-91 / Jul. 26, 1994 / Righteous Babe ♦♦♦
Like I Said: Songs 1990-91 contains reworked and re-recorded versions of 15 songs from Ani DiFranco's first two albums. These new arrangements are fleshed out with a variety of folk instruments, ranging from violin to dulcimer. By and large, these arrangements are more impressive than the originals, adding depth to songs that sounded spare in their original incarnations. Certainly, these distinctions will only be of note to hardcore fans who own the original albums, but for latter-day fans curious about her earlier work, this is a good way to sample the songs, if not the actual recordings. *—Stephen Thomas Erlewine*

● **Not a Pretty Girl** / Jul. 18, 1995 / Righteous Babe ♦♦♦♦♦
On her relatively spare sixth album (which features only one other musician, percussionist/vocalist Andy Stochansky, and, on one song, singer Kate Fenner), Ani DiFranco takes on a few expected topics, such as abortion ("Tiptoe"), capital punishment ("Crime for Crime"), and why she isn't on a major label ("The Million You Never Made"). But much of the disc is given over to introspective ruminations on personal life and love. As usual, the singer is not shy (despite a song of that title) about offering criticism of the person or persons she's addressing, but she is also self-critical and even, on "Sorry I Am," apologetic. The songs do not add up to the complete story of a relationship, but there are some deeply felt portraits here, especially "Light of Some Kind" in which the singer seems to be confessing to a man that she has been unfaithful to him with a woman. As usual, the imagery is urban and gritty; DiFranco is the kind of writer who likes to tell us that she's got last night's underwear in her back pocket as she rides home on the subway on the afternoon following an assignation. But the sometimes messy details are in the service of her view of reality, an unflinching one in which everything can be faced, even the songwriter's emotional torment. *—William Ruhlmann*

More Joy, Less Shame / 1996 / Righteous Babe ♦♦

Dilate / May 21, 1996 / Righteous Babe ♦♦♦♦
Ani Di Franco doesn't really expand her sonic palette on *Dilate*, but she doesn't need to. Di Franco racked up a dedicated cult audience on the basis of her conviction. There's not much melody on any of her songs, but there are messages and, thankfully, a fair share of humor. *Dilate* suffers from a bit too much repetition, but when Di Franco lands on a good hook—such as "Superhero" or "Done Wrong"—the results suggest that she could reach a wider audience. *—Thom Owens*

Living in Clip / Apr. 22, 1997 / Righteous Babe ♦♦♦♦♦
For all of their cult popularity, Ani DiFranco's studio albums were frequently hampered by mannered performances, which is precisely what her live shows were not. In concert, DiFranco plays her songs with infectious energy, frequently twisting the melody lines and digressing into rambling, entertaining stories and jokes. That side of Ani DiFranco is finally captured in the double-disc live album, *Living in Clip*. Supported by bassist Sara Lee and drummer Andy Stochansky, she runs through 32 songs, including the previously unreleased "Gravel," plus all of her best-known songs, occasionally spinning off stories and humorous anecdotes and illustrating exactly why a rabid cult following developed around her appealingly edgy persona and songs. *—Thom Owens*

Little Plastic Castle / Feb. 17, 1998 / Righteous Babe ♦♦♦♦
Little Plastic Castle posed an unusual challenge for Ani DiFranco. She released this record after spending a year promoting her first live CD (*Living In Clip*) by repeatedly admitting to reporters that her studio albums lack the vitality of her concert performances. Rock critics agreed en masse, and their praise for the live album helped to propel DiFranco to a new level of mainstream stardom—but it also heightened the scrutiny on her next studio recording. Fortunately, she managed to dodge several of the pitfalls of her previous albums. Her excellent band had plenty of time to jell on the road, and their performances here are as tight, driven and intense as they've ever been. Vocally, DiFranco is somewhat less affected than on previous albums, where the unnatural isolation of the studio sometimes led her to unnatural mannerisms. Her songwriting, however, is not quite up to par. While her melodies have almost never been exactly catchy, they have usually been perfect vessels for her terrifically smart lyrics. This time, the lyrical tail seems to be wagging the melodic dog willy-nilly. That's especially damaging when her songs are wallowing too comfortably in angst ("Independence Day," "Glass House"). Nonetheless, this is the most creatively produced Ani DiFranco album to date, combining her distinctively frenetic acoustic fingerstyle with computer samples, dance rhythms, mariachi brass and full-band rock jams. The result is colorful—almost cartoony—but almost never overshadows the emotional content. When Jon Hassell contributes a gorgeous jazz trumpet solo on the album's final track (the fourteen-minute "Pulse"), it blends in so perfectly that one has to remind oneself that DiFranco is one of the biggest talents in *folk* music. *—Darryl Cater*

Up Up Up Up Up Up / Jan. 19, 1999 / Righteous Babe ♦♦♦
The self-appointed CEO of intrepid indie grrrl-rock sparks one more with *Up Up Up Up Up Up*, an ebullient addition to an already prolific and deeply admirable career. The playful synthetics and occasional stabs at atypical DiFranco stylings bely the general humorlessness of her lyrics: "'Tis of Thee" is as annoyed with American TV-news culture as one can get (as might be expected of street-cynical Ani). "Come Away" is just plain corny, wistfully scrapbooking a lover away with tinkly punches on an electric piano. "Virtue" is wackier, with shades of old songs by young Edie Brickell, and "Jukebox" sounds relentlessly synthesized, funky with baffling lyrics and weird abrupt high notes like the ones we either adore or abhor from contempo sister Alanis Morissette. Some fans may continue to dream of an album wherein Ani shows off some real chops, as she'll do for lucky people in concert: she's actually a wonderful 12-string guitarist, but you can't really get a feel for that here. *—Becky Byrkit*

To the Teeth / Nov. 16, 1999 / Righteous Babe ♦♦♦
With the release of *To the Teeth*, it has been ten studio albums of original material in ten years for Ani DiFranco, and she sounds tired. The singer/songwriter has always had ample reserves of anger and criticism, some of which she has directed at herself, but here her self-questioning is unusually intense. As usual, a couple of songs deal with political topics, but much of the album is given over to songs in which the singer looks at her life and career unhappily. "Going Once" and "Swing" are in the third person, though the characters seem self-identified, with the "she" in the former wondering "how did I get here/Without even knowing where I was going?," while in the latter "she" speaks of weariness, dread, and nagging voices inside her head that say "You suck." "Freakshow," a metaphor for the performer's life, is almost unrelentingly critical, its only relief coming from the comfort that the life of a traveling entertainer is better than being stuck in a hometown. The culmination of all this comes with "Wish I May," which she closes by singing, "I don't think I am strong enough/To do this much longer." She also says she wishes the song were longer, and that wish may have been expressed in the album's musical arrangements. Employing horns (including Maceo Parker's saxophone) and other embellishments, DiFranco has written a series of downbeat riff tunes and stretched them out, in some cases to six or seven minutes, often with extended instrumental codas after the lyrics have been sung. As usual, she gives her audience a warts-and-all portrait of her current view of herself and the world. Longtime fans will find the result compelling (while perhaps fearing for their favorite's future), but this is probably not the place to start your Ani DiFranco collection. *—William Ruhlmann*

Revelling: Reckoning / Apr. 10, 2001 / Righteous Babe ♦♦

Digable Planets

f. 1991
Jazz-Rap, Alternative Rap, Urban
Though they were not the first to synthesize jazz and hip-hop, Digable Planets epitomized the laidback charm of jazz hipsters better than any group before or since. The trio's 1993 debut album *Reachin' (A New Refutation of Time and Space)* was a mellow ride packed with samples from Art Blakey, Sonny Rollins and Curtis Mayfield, and the single "Rebirth of Slick (Cool like Dat)" became a Top 20 pop hit. After embarking on an ambitious tour which included several live musicians, the Planets returned in late 1994 with their best album yet. *Blowout Comb* continued the group's jazz-rap fusion, but also saw them branching out to embrace the old-school sound of the street as well. Much stronger than its predecessor, it used fewer samples and even included several solos; with no strong single to carry it, however, *Blowout Comb* sold less well than *Reachin'*. *—John Bush*

● **Reachin' (A New Refutation of Time and Space)** / Sep. 27, 1993 / Pendulum ♦♦♦♦♦
Landing in 1993, Digable Planets' *Reachin' (A New Refutation of Time and Space)*, settled in on the consciousness of a large cross section of listeners ranging from alt rockers,

metal freaks, and headz worldwide. A surprise hit with the press and the general populace alike, *Reachin'* was released at the most opportune time of the nineties. The so-called alternative scene had just blown up in '91/'92 so commercial radio was actually playing something close to variety and major labels were signing acts and developing them at an unprecedented level. Played on rock and urban stations, Digable Planets' debut represented an actual alternative to the masses that had grown up on Van Halen and Whitney Houston and as a result, Digable Planets found themselves with a top 20 single in "Rebirth of Slick (Cool Like Dat)." In a lot ways the song paints the picture for the rest of the album with samples that are drenched in cool jazz and interlaced with smart catchy rhymes that move across the hip hop spectrum of self aggrandization and political awareness. The widespread appeal of *Reachin'* lies in Doodle, Ladybug and (head-honcho) Butterfly's smooth delivery. Never too excited but always passionate, they keep it going with seemingly light-hearted pieces like "Where I'm From." Here Butterfly almost falls into hip hop stereotype by tripping on the theme of geographical location (see: *Paul's Boutique*); but instead of really letting the listener know where they're from, they go into a chorus of "everywhere, everywhere" and thus really pointing out this record's underlying theme: Under the hood of inventive beats, and well-placed layered samples are the ideas and attitudes of universal and cosmic spirituality combined with personal consciousness expansion that crosses geographical and ethnic boundaries. Easily one of the most successful hip hop records ever made and a must have selection in most *any* collection. —*Jack LV Isles*

Blowout Comb / Oct. 18, 1994 / Pendulum ✦✦✦✦✦
After heavily favoring samples on its debut, *Reachin'*, Digable Planets shifts to more of a live band sound on this impressive sophomore release. Even in the absence of a rich store of secondary material, though, the band still creates a layered if more groove-centric album, deftly weaving its MC ruminations with some of the tightest syncopated beats in hip-hop. Core members Butterfly, Ladybug, and Doodlebug all shine atop the jazz-inflected cuts, offering wry and insightful commentary on black life, hip-hop culture, and New York living. As with fellow Day-Glo hip-hoppers De La Soul and A Tribe Called Quest, the band's lyrical honesty stands in nice contrast to the playfully funky music. The mix takes in beats both hard ("The Art of Easing") and fat ("Blowing Down"), and even includes some retro, summer-breeze soul à la War and Tower of Power ("For Corners"). Helping out in the studio are Guru from Gang Starr and jazz heavies like saxophonist Donald Harrison. Along with the equally enjoyable *Reachin'*, *Blowout Comb* is essential listening for hip-hop fans. —*Stephen Cook*

Digital Underground
f. 1987, **db.** 1996
West Coast Rap, Alternative Rap, Hip-Hop
Formed in 1987 by Shock-G (b. Gregory Jacobs), Oakland's Digital Underground built most of their music from sampled Parliament-Funkadelic records, crafting a bizarre, funky homage. They also developed a similarly weird sense of style and humor, highlighted by Shock-G's outrageous costumes, and the whole band's parade of alter egos. Of all these alter egos, Shock-G's Humpty Hump—a ridiculous figure with a Groucho Marx nose and glasses, and a goofy, stuttering voice—was the most famous, since he was immortalized on their loopy breakthrough single, "The Humpty Dance." Their 1990 debut *Sex Packets* was a platinum-selling hit, and while they never scaled such commercial heights ever again, their role in popularizing George Clinton's elastic funk made them one of the most important hip-hop groups of their era. Over the course of their career, Digital Underground featured numerous members, but throughout it all, Shock-G remained at its core. Early 1991's *This Is an EP Release* was their first recording to feature Tupac Shakur; it went gold set and the stage for their second album, *Sons of the P*, which was released that fall. On the strength of the gold single "Kiss You Back," *Sons of the P* also went gold, but it received criticism for its similarity to *Sex Packets*. By the time Digital Underground delivered its third album *The Body Hat Syndrome* in late 1993, hip-hop had become dominated by gangsta rap, particularly the drawling G-funk of Dr. Dre, which ironically was heavily indebted to George Clinton. Consequently, their fan base diminished significantly, and *The Body Hat Syndrome* disappeared shortly after its release. Nearly three years later, Digital Underground returned with *Future Rhythm*, which spent a mere three weeks on the charts; *Who Got the Gravy?* followed in 1998. —*Stephen Thomas Erlewine*

★ **Sex Packets** / Jan. 1990 / Tommy Boy ✦✦✦✦✦
With their debut album *Sex Packets*, Digital Underground kickstarted the Parliament/Funkadelic obsessions that dominated the hip-hop world of the early '90s. Digital Underground essentially create a full-length tribute to George Clinton's warped fantasy world, taking both the elastic bass lines and the goofy, surreal sense of humor and adopting it to their own purposes. With their ridiculous sense of humor and endless, loping synth-laced grooves, the two hit singles, "The Humpty Dance" and "Doowutchyalike," seem to tell the whole story, but that's not the case. Within the album tracks of *Sex Packets* are jazzy experiments, hardcore funk and loads of innovative rhymes and grooves that set the pace mucfor of the music that followed. Furthermore, the Underground has a good-natured, welcoming sense of humor that infuses everything on *Sex Packets*, particularly the tongue-in-cheek sci-fi mini-opera that comprises the title track. Although they made some musical innovations on their two subsequent albums, Digital Underground never made an album as consistently engaging as their debut. —*Stephen Thomas Erlewine*

This Is an EP Release / 1991 / Tommy Boy ✦✦✦✦
Released in the same era of expansive and humorous hip-hop debuts by De La Soul, Digable Planets, Gang Starr, and A Tribe Called Quest, Digital Underground's similarly dis-

posed first album and follow-up EP offered a party-friendly alternative to gangsta rap with a heavy dose of P-funk, jazz, and Prince's electro-funk aesthetic. The Oakland-based crew, featuring Shock-G as alter-ego and frontman Humpty Hump, would continue to ride high with *Sons of the P*, but never really captured the inspired mix of their first forays into the hip-hop arena. That said, curious fans should first check out the group's maiden *Sex Packets* release before diving into this six-song collection; while solid in its own right, the EP does contain two non-essential remixes of tracks off of *Sex Packets*. And even though new cuts like the extended funk jam "Same Song" (featuring a nasty Bernie Worrell-meets-Jimmy Smith synth-organ solo), "Nuttin Nis Funky," "Arguin' on the Funk," and "Tie the Knot" are all impressive, *This Is an EP Release* does not expand on the sound of *Sex Packets*. Still, a very enjoyable selection of cuts full of top-notch rapping, samples, scratches, and elastically funky bass and beats. —*Stephen Cook*

Sons of the P / Oct. 15, 1991 / Tommy Boy ✦✦✦✦✦
Digital Underground's love of George Clinton and Parliament/Funkadelic was still more than obvious on its second full-length album. *Sons of the P*, which falls short of the overall excellence of *Sex Packets*, but nonetheless has much to admire. This time, the Oakland group isn't as consistently lighthearted as before, and doesn't shy away from insightful social commentary on "Heartbeat Props" (which pays tribute to accomplished Black Americans in both politics and the arts), "The Higher Heights of Spirituality" and "No Nose Job." But even so, the album is a danceable, fun and delightfully quirky effort reminding us how influential Clinton's P-Funk remained 11 years after the 1970s ended. Indeed, the fact that artists as different-sounding as Digital Underground and the Red Hot Chili Peppers owe so great an artistic debt to Clinton makes it obvious just how far-reaching his influence is. —*Alex Henderson*

The Body Hat Syndrome / Oct. 5, 1993 / Tommy Boy ✦✦✦

Future Rhythm / Jun. 1996 / Radikal ✦✦

Who Got the Gravy? / Sep. 8, 1998 / Interscope ✦✦✦✦

Lost Files / Oct. 26, 1999 / Lil Butta ✦✦✦

No Nose Job: The Legend of Digital Underground / Jun. 19, 2001 / Tommy Boy ✦✦✦✦
A major part of hip-hop's explosion of creativity during the late '80s and early '90s, Digital Underground was the first major rap group to draw their inspiration from Parliament-Funkadelic. They followed that blueprint even more closely than the legions of West Coasters who walked the trail they blazed; the Underground didn't just draw from George Clinton's loose, funky beats and crazed party atmosphere, but also replicated P-Funk's extended jams (albeit without the instrumental solos). Shock-G's numerous alter egos and goofy sense of humor fit perfectly into the playful vibe of post-De La Soul, pre-Chronic hip-hop, and the group recorded more than a few terrific singles. All of those singles are present in some form on *No Nose Job: The Best of Digital Underground*, which mixes full-length album versions (including the full 6:30 of the group's signature smash "The Humpty Dance") with briefer radio edits. Those shorter versions don't quite capture the way Digital Underground sounded on album (and, for a group able to craft such excellent singles, they were surprisingly consistent and engaging on their best albums). But that actually works as a better introduction for newcomers, who get most of the group's best songs in pure concentrated form. *Sex Packets* is still an essential classic, but *No Nose Job* will likely end up a necessary purchase for many. —*Steve Huey*

Dils
f. 1977, **db.** 1980
American Punk, L.A. Punk, Hardcore Punk, Punk
The Dils were one of the biggest draws on the late '70s L.A. punk circuit. Led by harmonizing brothers Chip and Tony Kinman, the group played short, aggressive songs with political lyrics, often from a socialist viewpoint. During the group's four years of existence, it only released three 7-inch singles; all of their albums were posthumous, culled from the singles and various live performances. The group later evolved into Rank and File. —*Steve Huey*

Live! / 1987 / Iloki ✦✦✦✦
A legendary early L.A. punk band, The Dils never got to record much during their lifetime (three seven-inches), so this posthumous release actually comprises a fair chunk of their recorded legacy. Ten of the fourteen tracks were taken from a cassette recording of a gig circa 1980. The fidelity, as you might expect, is not top-notch, but gets the job done as far as capturing their adrenaline rush. Dominated by singers Chip and Tony Kinman, this actually has a fair amount of harmonies and pop power chords considering the near hardcore tempos. A chunky cover of Buddy Holly's "Modern Don Juan" is an unexpected nod to roots on this crude but effective set, which includes some considerably different versions of songs they recorded in the studio. The album closes with four songs from a show circa 1977 of distinctly raunchier fidelity and thrashier tempos. —*Richie Unterberger*

● **The Dils** / 1990 / Lost ✦✦✦✦✦
With all eight of their studio tracks (from their three singles and a 1977 demo), and 21 songs taken from four live shows in 1978 and 1979, this is the essential document of the Dils' limited legacy. As a listening experience, however, it's somewhat frustrating. The studio tracks, especially the "I Hate the Rich" and "Class War" singles, are important early California punk, comparable in energy to the early British efforts by the likes of the Clash. The live material, however, is poorly recorded; the vocals in particular are faint and usually indecipherable. Certainly it has its historical significance, but it's more a tantalizing glimpse of what the band might have achieved than a significant body of work. The many

songs from the live sets that were never recorded in the studio would have surely benefited immensely from even rudimentary clarity and production. *—Richie Unterberger*

Dino, Desi & Billy

f. 1964, **db.** 1970

Pop

A Hollywood trio that were barely into their teens when they hit the charts in 1965, Dino, Desi & Billy anticipated the bubblegum fad with records that usually featured none of their own contributions, except their characterless vocals. That may be phrasing matters too kindly. The best bubblegum is far more distinctive and catchy than the lowest-common-denominator L.A. session pop/rock that they recorded. But they knew the right people, as they say in the business, which made them stars for a brief time, although they never had an ounce of credibility. This mid-'60s trio were kind of a cross between the Monkees and Gary Lewis in a few key respects. Like Gary Lewis, their very opportunities to record came about primarily because of their distinguished Hollywood fathers. In the case of these guys, however, the nepotism was rather extreme: Dino was Dino Martin, son of singer/comedian Dean Martin, and Desi was the son of Lucille Ball and Desi Arnaz. Along with classmate Billy Hinsche, they began playing for fun. They'd barely gotten their equipment together when they auditioned for Dean Martin's buddy, Frank Sinatra—who just happened to record for and run Martin's label, Reprise. By the end of 1964, they'd released their first single for the label, although it was made clear to them that session musicians would handle the instruments. Top producers and arrangers Lee Hazlewood, Billy Strange, and Jimmy Bowen would oversee the trio's recording dates over the next couple of years. "I'm a Fool" made the Top Twenty in 1965; "Not the Lovin' Kind" got into the Top Thirty a few months later. Dino, Desi & Billy never got into the Top Forty after 1965, but they recorded singles and albums for years to come. *—Richie Unterberger*

● **Rebel Kind: The Best of Dino, Desi & Billy** / Feb. 27, 1996 / Sundazed ♦♦♦♦♦

20 songs from their 1964-70 Reprise recordings, wisely concentrating on their singles (as their albums were overpopulated with covers of familiar hits). Includes "The Rebel Kind," "I'm a Fool," and several smaller hits and non-hits, some of which were never released on album. Extensive liner notes by the Smithereens' Dennis Diken. Beach Boys fans may want to note the presence of the 1970 non-LP single "Lady Love," written by Brian Wilson and Billy Hinsche. *—Richie Unterberger*

Dinosaur Jr.

f. 1983, Amherst, MA

Indie Rock, Alternative Pop/Rock, American Underground

Dinosaur Jr. was largely responsible for returning lead guitar to indie-rock and, along with their peers the Pixies, they injected late-'80s alternative rock with monumental levels of pure guitar noise. As the group's career progressed, it turned into a vehicle for J. Mascis' songwriting and playing, which had the ultimate result of turning Dinosaur's albums into largely similar affairs. Over time, Mascis shed his hardcore punk roots and revealed himself to be a disciple of Neil Young, crafting simple songs that were delivered at a crushing volume and spiked with shards of feedback. Consequently, Dinosaur Jr.'s '90s albums—when the group was essentially a front for Mascis—don't sound particularly revolutionary, even with their subtle sonic innovations, yet their original '80s records for SST were a different matter. On their early records, Dinosaur lurched forward, taking weird detours into free-form noise and melodic soloing before the songs are brought back into relief by Mascis' laconic whine. Dinosaur's SST Records laid the foundation for alternative rock's commercial breakthrough in the early '90s, and while the band's profile was raised substantially in the wake of Nirvana's success, they never really became much bigger than highly respected cult figures. *—Stephen Thomas Erlewine*

Dinosaur / 1985 / Homestead ♦♦♦

Released before the group was forced to change their name to Dinosaur Jr. by an obscure psychedelic group, the band's debut *Dinosaur* is a noisy, impressive, but uneven array of pseudo-hardcore numbers, sonic experiments, and sprawling hard rock. Although the band doesn't land on any distinctive style, their ambition of marrying Neil Young and Sonic Youth sounds intriguing, and it has enough outstanding moments to indicate that the group was capable of the stylistic breakthrough they achieved on *You're Living All Over Me. —Stephen Thomas Erlewine*

★ **You're Living All Over Me** / 1987 / SST ♦♦♦♦♦

A blitzkrieg fusion of hardcore punk, Sonic Youth-style noise freak-outs, heavy metal and melodic hard rock in the vein of Neil Young, *You're Living All Over Me* was a turning point in American underground rock & roll. With its thin, unbalanced mix, the album sounds positively menacing and edgy—Lou Barlow's bass barrels forward over Murph's clanking drums, with J. Mascis' guitar twisting pummeling riffs and careening, occasionally atonal solos. It established guitar heroics as a part of indie-rock, bringing the noise of Sonic Youth into more conventional song structures. Also, Mascis' laconic, self-absorbed whine was a distinct departure from the furious post-hardcore rants or the mumbling Michael Stipe imitations that dominated indie-rock. While the songwriting is occasionally uneven, the best moments of *You're Living All Over Me*—"Little Fury Things," "Raisans," "In a Jar" and Barlow's proto-Sebadoh "Poledo"—retain their power, and it's possible to hear the record's influence throughout alternative rock. *—Stephen Thomas Erlewine*

Bug / 1988 / SST ♦♦♦♦♦

Relatively cleaner-produced and more accessible than *You're Living All Over Me*, *Bug* expanded on the strengths of its predecessor and established Dinosaur Jr. as a major band in the American underground. Although the majority of the album is firmly situated in the sprawling, noisy metallic fusion of hard rock and avant-noise, *Bug* also demonstrates that J. Mascis has a talent for winding folk-rock, particularly on "The Post" and "Pond Song." Like its predecessor, the songs on *Bug* are quite uneven, but it does represent a major step forward for Mascis, particularly on the masterpiece of the record, "Freak Scene," a surprisingly catchy song encapsulating the appeal and pitfalls of indie-rock within three minutes. *—Stephen Thomas Erlewine*

Green Mind / Feb. 1991 / Blanco y Negro/Sire ♦♦♦♦♦

Many consider *Green Mind* to be a weak, uninspired effort, but Dinosaur Jr.'s major-label debut is a strong, varied album, featuring some of J. Mascis' best songwriting, as well as some of his best, most fluid guitar work. Essentially a solo effort by Mascis (Murph only appears on three tracks), *Green Mind* finds him stretching and expanding his traditional sonic assault with more acoustic guitars and tighter melodies. With its gentle Mellotron and lovely, sighing melody, "Thumb" stands as one of Mascis' finest songs; "Muck" is a surprisingly enjoyable stab at funk, "How'd You Pin That One on Me" is a great guitar workout, "Puke & Cry" and "I Live for That Look" are impressive folk-punk, and "The Wagon" rivals "Freak Scene" in its depiction of the underground scene. *—Stephen Thomas Erlewine*

Fossils / Aug. 1991 / SST ♦♦♦♦

A brief, eight-song compilation of the group's SST singles, *Fossils* effectively sums up the power and vision of Dinosaur Jr.'s early work. Not only does it contain the two masterpieces from *You're Living All Over Me* and *Bug*—"Little Fury Things" and "Freak Scene," respectively—but it also gathers several excellent B-sides, including sardonic covers of Peter Frampton's "Show Me the Way" and the Cure's "Just Like Heaven," making it an excellent retrospective of Dinosaur's influential and erratic indie recordings. *—Stephen Thomas Erlewine*

Whatever's Cool With Me / Oct. 22, 1991 / Blanco y Negro/Sire ♦♦♦♦

"This is not an album," the liner notes state—and that's true enough, but some albums are almost as long. *Whatever's Cool With Me* compiles the complete "Whatever's Cool With Me" single and the the European single of "The Wagon," making it an amiable, eight-song stopgap to keep hardcore fans happy in-between albums. "Whatever's Cool With Me" itself is a loud rifer, not as memorable as "Freak Scene" or "The Wagon," but good enough. It's perhaps most memorable for being the studio debut of bassist Mike Johnson, who provided the stability needed after Barlow's departure to reestablish the trio for its most commercially successful period. Johnson also turns up on the two live tracks: a fine version of *Green Mind*'s "Thumb" and a rough rip through "Keep the Glove." One new studio track, "Sideways," starts with one of Mascis' best acoustic lines, turning into a slow, relaxed full arrangement with everything from drums to vibes played by Mascis himself. Like this song, the remaining "The Wagon" B-sides also feature Mascis as one-man-band. In context, the acoustic "Quicksand" is the most amusing number: originally from David Bowie's *Hunky Dory*, Mascis changes nothing about the arrangement, but substitutes "the wagon" for "the power" in the lyrics, and begins the song with the melody from another *Hunky Dory* number, "Andy Warhol." The other songs have more of Dinosaur Jr.'s fuzzy appeal, like the friendly roar and strum of "Not You Again" and the screaming yelps and feedback cropping up throughout "The Little Baby." *—Ned Raggett*

Where You Been / Feb. 9, 1993 / Blanco y Negro/Sire ♦♦♦♦

By the time *Where You Been* surfaced, Seattle had completely exploded, and given that Dinosaur Jr.'s sound, attitude and more were as proto-slacker as could be, the temptation must have been great to cash in. But Mascis stuck to his guns, and there's little about *Where You Been* that would have seemed out of place on *Green Mind* or even some earlier records. Recorded with a full band throughout, Johnson and Murph lay down does-the-job rhythm tracks while Mascis tackles almost everything else, *Where You Been* is occasionally moody and dark but otherwise is more rough fun. Opening track "Out There" is one of the most mournful things Mascis has recorded, with an especially yearning chorus, but his fiery solo still makes it classic Dinosaur Jr. "Start Choppin" immediately follows, its quick, catchy lead riff helping to make it as close to a radio hit as the band ever had—and, of course, a big ol' solo or two adding to the fun of it all. From there on in it's a pureed blast of punk, classic rock and more. It may be business as usual, but it's good business just the same, whether it's the gentle "Not the Same," on which Mascis does his best Neil Young impersonation, or the stuttering feedback snorts and rips on "Hide," on which he borrows a bit back from disciple Kevin Shields. Other highlights include "Get Me," a melancholic, steady cruncher with another trademark solo of the gods, and the unjustly ignored "What Else is New," which sounds like a mid-seventies rock ballad with louder volume and none of the crud, right down to the concluding string section. *—Ned Raggett*

Without a Sound / Aug. 23, 1994 / Blanco y Negro/Sire ♦♦

J. Mascis fired long-time drummer Murph before the recording of *Without a Sound*, which came as a surprise to Murph. Naturally, the change in personnel hasn't changed Dinosaur Jr.'s sound much; the only difference between *Without a Sound* and *Where You Been* is a more pronounced country leaning (particularly on the album's high point, the rollicking "I Don't Think So") and shorter, more concise performances. What hasn't changed are the overpowering fuzz tones of Mascis' guitar, which tend to hide his more expressive vocals; it also makes digging out the gems on this album a little more difficult than necessary. *—Stephen Thomas Erlewine*

Hand It Over / Mar. 25, 1997 / Blanco y Negro/Sire ♦♦♦♦

Bouncing back from the staid *Without a Sound*, J. Mascis turns in his most eclectic album since *Green Mind* with Dinosaur Jr.'s *Hand It Over*. Dinosaur's bedrock sound hasn't changed—it's still a sprawling, electric mess of hard rock filtered through folk-rock song structures—but Mascis plays with the arrangements, adding strings, trumpets and, on a handful of tracks, My Bloody Valentine's slippery guitar orchestrations and vocals (Kevin Shields and Blinda Butcher both sing on the album). These additions make the music sound fresh, but they would only be window-dressing if Mascis' songs weren't as strong as they are. Again, his progressions are subtle, but songs like "I Don't Think," "Nothin's Goin' On," "Can't We Move This" and "Sure Not Over You" are fine additions to his catalog, and help make *Hand It Over* one of Dinosaur Jr.'s most consistent and best records. —*Stephen Thomas Erlewine*

Dio

f. 1983
Heavy Metal, Hard Rock

Before he assembled Dio, Ronnie James Dio was a well-known figure in the heavy metal world. With Elf, Rainbow, and Black Sabbath, Dio was a top hard rock singer with a solid commercial appeal; he was responsible for reviving Sabbath's sagging fortunes in the early '80s. After three years with Sabbath, he left to form his own band in 1983; it featured guitarist Vivian Campbell (who would later play with Whitesnake and Def Leppard), drummer Vinny Appice, ex-Rainbow bassist Jimmy Bain, and keyboardist Claude Schnell. For the rest of the '80s, Dio was one of the top metal bands, with a crunchier, more streamlined version of Sabbath's mystical vision. In 1990, Dio disbanded the group and returned to Black Sabbath for a brief time in 1991 and 1992; he soon left the band again, assembling a revamped version of Dio and began touring again in support of LPs like 1994's *Strange Highways* and 1996's *Angry Machines*. Following 1998's two-disc *Inferno: Last in Live*, the group resurfaced in the spring of 2000 with *Magica*. —*Stephen Thomas Erlewine*

● **Holy Diver** / 1983 / Reprise ✦✦✦✦✦
After participating in five classic studio albums (three with Ritchie Blackmore's Rainbow and two with Black Sabbath) in the late '70s and early '80s, it seemed that singer Ronnie James Dio could do no wrong. And with the release of his self-monickered band's debut album, *Holy Diver*, in 1983, Dio struck gold once again by injecting catchy melodies into the classic metal riffery of his previous groups. Besides Dio's inspired songwriting, the album's consistency owes a lot to his carefully chosen bandmates, including veteran bassist Jimmy Bain and drummer Vinny Appice, and a phenomenal find in young guitarist Vivian Campbell, whose creativity and technique are quite astounding. The album opens in full-tilt metal mode with the frenetic "Stand Up and Shout," which segues into the epic title track, an album highlight thanks to it's hypnotic, mid-paced riff. Dio himself plays keyboards (badly) on the hit single "Rainbow in the Dark," and the remaining cuts range from further stabs at pop-metal ("Gypsy," "Caught in the Middle") to blatant metal anthems ("Straight Through the Heart," "Invisible"). These two facets find a perfect balance on the excellent "Don't Talk to Strangers," arguably the album's high point. —*Ed Rivadavia*

The Last in Line / 1984 / Warner Brothers ✦✦✦
After the warm reception accorded their debut, Dio decided to play it safe with their 1984 sophomore effort, *The Last in Line*—with mixed results. The in-your-face energy of the band's debut is dulled by a sleeker production job, with generous keyboards from new member Claude Schnell. And Ronnie James Dio's once-amusing Dungeons and Dragons lyrics begin sounding disturbingly repetitive, with the words "rainbow," "fire," and "stone" seemingly present in every song. Cuts like "We Rock," "Breathless," and "I Speed at Night" go from good to grating surprisingly fast, and the seven-minute epic "Egypt (The Chains Are On)" inexplicably loses it's awesome main riff halfway through. The band score some points with the driving "Evil Eyes," the theatrical "One Night in the City," and the solid title track, but the intended hit single "Mystery" is simply horrible. Still, despite the obvious signs of decline, anyone who enjoyed Dio's debut will certainly find much to like here. —*Ed Rivadavia*

Sacred Heart / 1985 / Warner Brothers ✦✦✦
Death by stagnation is the best way to describe Dio's disappointing third release, *Sacred Heart*. If only writer's block had been the problem, but the cheesy live sounds that introduce the obviously self-referential "King of Rock & Roll" clearly point to a clueless, egotistical leader instead. Throughout most of the album, singer Ronnie James Dio seems intent on strangling every last creative spark out of his backing musicians in an attempt to score an MTV pop-metal hit. The faceless but effective "Rock & Roll Children" may have done the job, but Dio's lack of sex appeal (not to mention the fact that he was over 40 at the time) killed any possibility of crossover success in image-conscious America. In the end, selling out cost him his hardcore metal following to boot. Oh yeah, and the album's title track is a cliché-ridden mess, while the dire filler material on side two is simply embarrassing. —*Ed Rivadavia*

Intermission / 1986 / Reprise ✦✦

Dream Evil / 1987 / Reprise ✦✦✦✦
On *Dream Evil*, Dio manages to record an album where the songwriting doesn't amount to an endless series of riffs. Instead, the record features real songs with actual melodies, making it their most accomplished album. —*Stephen Thomas Erlewine*

Lock up the Wolves / 1990 / Reprise ✦✦✦
Ronnie James Dio assembled a new version of Dio for *Lock up the Wolves*, to no apparant change in the band's sound. Nevertheless, the group's status in the metal community was beginning to slip, and the album was the lowest-charting Dio record apart from the live *Intermission*. —*Stephen Thomas Erlewine*

Strange Highways / 1994 / Reprise ✦✦

Diamonds: The Best of Dio / 1994 / Reprise ✦✦✦✦

Angry Machines / Oct. 15, 1996 / Mayhem ✦✦✦
Originally released on Mayhem in 1996, then reissued by Spitfire in 2000, *Angry Machines* was Dio's first effort away from Warner/Reprise, and it does find Ronnie James

Dio looking for subtle ways to push into new territory. The lyrics mostly avoid Dio's familiar medieval-fantasy D&D obsessions, instead directing their attention to more real-world concerns (albeit with the same sense of drama). Similarly, there aren't many of the gothic neo-classicisms present on the band's best-known output; and while there are a few progressive sections, *Angry Machines* is more of a straightforward metal record, full of pounding rhythms and guitars along with plenty of wailing by Ronnie James Dio. The main problem is that the band often seems to concentrate on sound more than songwriting—the album sounds good while it's playing, but not enough of the riffs or melodies stick with the listener afterwards to judge it a complete return to form. Yet there are enough moments here to make it worth the time of Dio diehards. —*Steve Huey*

Magica / Mar. 21, 2000 / Spitfire ✦✦✦✦
Dio's rock-solid 2000 concept album *Magica* would have better fit the musical climate 15-25 years beforehand, but a good album is a good album. Ronnie James Dio's band's previous studio effort, 1996's *Angry Machines*, admirably addressed modern, non-traditional heavy metal topics. But the musically superior *Magica* is rooted in the dark, mystical themes he perfected on Rainbow, Black Sabbath, and early Dio albums. One important factor is the solid lineup, particularly the return of Craig Goldy, the best guitarist Dio's had in his band besides Vivian Campbell. Bassist Jimmy Bain and drummer Simon Wright also return. Dio seems inspired, and his vocals are more textured than usual. *Magica* is a detailed fantasy epic about the struggle between good and evil. Several elements are similar to J.R.R. Tolkien's beloved *Lord of the Rings* novels, which themselves rely on traditional literary archetypes such as heroes, villains, and mythic quests. "Lord of the Last Day" builds slowly with Goldy's dirge-like guitar and Dio's menacing vocals augmented by strings. "Fever Dreams" is tightly arranged and geared for rock radio airplay with Goldy's crisp, snapping guitar and Dio's smooth, slightly edgy vocals. "Turn to Stone" is effective, traditional heavy metal based on slow, heavy rhythm guitar and drums. The most musically complex song is "Feed My Head" due to the hypnotic chorus, multi-tracked harmony vocals, clean guitar and cymbal interplay, slashing strings, and Dio's smooth vocal interlude. Although "As Long As It's Not About Love" has some of the characteristics of a basic power ballad, the arrangement is more detailed and flexible. The album ends with "Magica Story," Dio's 18 1/2-minute spoken narrative; the liner notes include a separate sheet with the complete short story. His warm, rich voice is enhanced with a little bit of echo and faint synthesizer touches occasionally add drama. —*Bret Adams*

● **The Very Beast of Dio** / Oct. 3, 2000 / Rhino ✦✦✦✦✦
The first domestically available Dio anthology (following the 1994 German import *Diamonds*), Rhino's *The Very Beast of Dio* is jam-packed with 16 tracks taken from the band's seven Warner and Reprise albums (spanning the years 1983-1994). Which is to say, it's an excellent overview of the band's career, especially given the unevenness of some of their albums. Ronnie James Dio honed his metal chops singing lead in both Rainbow and Black Sabbath, and his own band is sort of a reflection of both: the sinister, medievally gothic elegance of the former, and the crushingly heavy, doom-laden riffs of the latter. That combination, plus solid songwriting, made Dio's best work some of the most invigorating British metal of the '80s, and those qualities are best concentrated here. —*Steve Huey*

Dion (Dion DiMucci)

b. Jul. 18, 1937, New York, NY [The Bronx]
Vocals / Teen Idol, Folk-Rock, Doo Wop, Rock & Roll

Bridging the era between late-'50s rock and the British Invasion, Dion DiMucci was one of the top White rock singers of his time, blending the best elements of doo wop, teen idol, and R&B styles. Some revisionists have tried to cast him as a sort of early blue-eyed soul figure, although he was probably more aligned with pop-rock, at first as the lead singer of the Belmonts, and then as a solo star. Formed by a group of friends that sang on Bronx street corners, Dion and the Belmonts recorded a few hits including "I Wonder Why" and "A Teenager in Love," the latter pointing the way for the slightly self-pitying, pained odes to adolescence and early adulthood that would characterize much of his solo work. Dion finally made the move in 1960, handling himself with a suave, cocky ease on hits like "The Wanderer" and "Runaround Sue." After battling heroin for several years, he re-emerged in 1968 as a gentle folk-rocker with a #4 hit single, "Abraham, Martin and John." He continued recording for the LP market during the '70s, reunited with the Belmonts in 1972, and cut a disappointing record with Phil Spector as producer. He's been recording and performing fairly often over the last two decades, sometimes singing Christian music. —*Richie Unterberger*

Lovers Who Wander / 1962 / The Right Stuff ✦✦✦✦
A better-than-average early-'60s effort. Besides the oft-anthologized singles "Lovers Who Wander," "Little Diane," "Sandy," and "(I Was) Born to Cry," it has some hot covers ("The Twist," "Stagger Lee," and "Shout") that Dion makes his own. The haunting "Lost for Sure," which Dion co-wrote, is one of his best obscure Laurie-era tracks. —*Richie Unterberger*

Dion / 1968 / The Right Stuff ✦✦✦✦✦
Featuring his Top Five comeback single "Abraham, Martin and John," this folk-rock and blues-flavored effort remains his most fully realized album. In addition to the impressive anti-war original "He Looks a Lot Like Me," it contains mature interpretations, arranged both acoustically and with strings, of songs by Fred Neil, Joni Mitchell, Leonard Cohen, Bob Dylan, and Lightnin' Hopkins (though the florid version of Jimi Hendrix's "Purple Haze" is embarrassing). The CD reissue adds the highly sought-after non-LP B-side "Daddy Rollin'," a Dion original that ranks as his most country-blues-influenced performance. —*Richie Unterberger*

★ **24 Golden Greats** / 1983 / Arista ♦♦♦♦♦
24 Golden Greats contains all of Dion & the Belmonts' biggest hits, plus all of Dion's solo hits from the late '60s and early '70s, making it the definitive compilation of the vocalist's long, successful career. *—Stephen Thomas Erlewine*

Runaround Sue / 1986 / The Right Stuff ♦♦♦
Includes the title track, "The Wanderer," and the minor hit "The Majestic," covers of "Little Star," "In the Still of the Night," "Kansas City," "Dream Lover," and "Take Care of My Baby," and a few other songs that follow the blueprint of his early-'60s hits. The singing is good, but the best tracks are the hits, and they're on all the Dion compilations of note. *—Richie Unterberger*

Bronx Blues: The Columbia Recordings / Feb. 2, 1991 / Columbia ♦♦♦♦♦
After many hit singles with the Belmonts, Dion went solo and became one of the first rock & roll stars signed to the Columbia label. Although he was only with the label for four years, Dion recorded some of his most adventurous music during this period. *Bronx Blues* chronicles this phase in his career, and is the best single-disc compilation of his mid-'60s work. The first singles released were similar in style to the Belmont's recordings ("Donna the Prima Donna") and demonstrated his continued love for doo wop as he covers older songs such as the Drifters' "Ruby Baby," which peaked at number two. While the first half of this album is strong, the second half is truly revelatory; it shows Dion, who had just been exposed to the music of Robert Johnson, infusing the bravado of his streetwise persona into the blues. The results don't always work (he doesn't have the deep, powerful voice required to sing Willie Dixon's "Spoonful"), but the results are magic when he hits the mark. The best example is his own "Two Ton Feather," a song that's not pure blues, but blues interpreted by a newly converted fan of the genre. In that respect, it's not surprising that his style is similar to Bob Dylan's. In fact, the highlight of the album, and perhaps Dion's best recording ever, is his previously unreleased version of Dylan's "Baby, I'm in the Mood for You" in which he brings out all the snarl and attitude of the tune. While these years are often considered a transition period for Dion, this compilation is essential in showcasing his songwriting talents and restless spirit. *—Vik Iyengar*

The Road I'm On: A Retrospective / Feb. 18, 1997 / Columbia/Legacy ♦♦♦♦♦
Dion's mid-'60s Columbia period was a strange and rather mysterious one. After notching up some solid hits that were more or less in his early '60s rock style ("Ruby Baby," "Donna the Prima Donna"), he dove into blues, folk, and folk-rock with varying degrees of success. Although the results were usually pretty interesting, commercially he seemed to have disappeared (a situation not helped by either his heroin problems or the failure of some of the material to get released). This is a good, if imperfect, two-CD overview of the Columbia years, moving from the expected early hits to quite a few tasty surprises, including covers of Woody Guthrie, Chuck Berry, Willie Dixon, "Work Song" (penned by Nat Adderley and Oscar Brown), Tom Paxton, and Bob Dylan's "It's All Over Now, Baby Blue." There are also a number of pretty fair self-penned originals in a folk-rock, slightly Dylanish style, unsurprising considering that Dion was recording with one-time Dylan producer Tom Wilson in late '65. It doesn't make a 100% convincing argument that Dion would have matured into a top-rank blues-folk-rocker if not for his drug problems, but it has integrity, and the material is usually well-sung, whether pop or not. About half a dozen of the tracks were previously unreleased; there are also a couple of new recordings from 1996. This does not, by the way, make the 1991 *Bronx Blues* CD (much of it drawn from the same era) redundant. Almost half of the tracks from that disc don't appear, the most serious omission being the cover of Dylan's "Baby, I'm in the Mood for You," which was probably Dion's best mid-'60s recording of all. *—Richie Unterberger*

Deja Nu / Jul. 25, 2000 / Ace ♦♦♦♦♦
A major influence on artists as varied as roots rocker Dave Edmunds, Lou Reed, and Bruce Springsteen (two of whose *Lucky Town* songs he covers here), Dion effectively mixes his tough yet delicate city-styled street corner harmonies with basic Chuck Berry chords to produce evocative tunes that, although embedded in the echoes of his youth, bubble with a soothing, low-key effervescence. Dion's perennially youthful voice delightfully swoops and swirls on the autobiographical "In New York City" and the Everly Brothers-styled "Hey Suzy," but it's on the Springsteen tracks, especially the beautiful a cappella ballad "If I Should Fall Behind," which seems like it was written with this arrangement in mind, that the concept fully clicks. The band chugs behind him with shabby charm, the backing vocalists are warm and subtle, the sound sparsely clean, and the album cruises along like a shiny '50s convertible primed on hi-test. Some of these songs, like the magnificent opener "Shu Bop (The Lost Track)," although retro in concept, sound lean and fresh with little of the stylized production of the doo wop era. Dion sings with the joyous vitality of his youth throughout, making the appropriately named *Deja Nu* one of the best, and most fully realized, albums of his extensive yet uneven career. *—Hal Horowitz*

• **King of the New York Streets** / Dec. 5, 2000 / Capitol ♦♦♦♦♦
Although Dion's career wasn't over when *King of the New York Streets* appeared, this three-CD package is likely to be the most thorough overview of his output to be heard in one place. "Most thorough" is not synonymous with "best music of his career," however, and while this box contains much of major significance, it really does slide downhill after the early '70s. That point is reached around the middle of the second disc, so that leaves about half of this material as average, or duller than average, stuff. In its favor, the box set has all the familiar hits from the salad days, from the Belmonts' "I Wonder Why" through "Abraham, Martin and John," as well as a number of fine cuts that are largely known only to collectors. Those include his hard-rocking 1965 cover of the obscure Bob Dylan song "Baby, I'm in the Mood for You"; the folk-rock version of Tom Paxton's "I Can't Help but Wonder Where I'm Bound" from the same era; the little-heard 1966 ABC single "My Girl the Month of May" (with the Belmonts); the bluesy B-side "Daddy Rollin'"; and the anti-drug "Your Own Backyard." The post-early-'70s tracks do have their high points, like "(I Used to Be a) Brooklyn Dodger," but they're just not remotely on the same level as what precedes them. Anyone wanting to focus on Dion's best music can get more of it, in more concentrated doses and for about the same amount of money, by purchasing several other less extensive compilations that target a specific period of his work. *—Richie Unterberger*

Sit Down Old Friend/You're Not Alone / Jun. 12, 2001 / Ace ♦♦♦
Dion's early-'70s albums have been quite overlooked, even in comparison to his similar late-'60s folk-rock records, and even by many Dion fans. This single-disc CD pairs 1970's *Sit Down Old Friend* with 1971's *You're Not Alone*, both records showing Dion continuing to mature as a singer/songwriter and blender of folk, rock, and blues stylings. *Sit Down Old Friend* was a change of pace even by the standards of his mellower, folk-rockish late-'60s comeback records. This was Dion unplugged: just him on acoustic guitar (both classical and steel string), and no other accompaniment, with all but three of the songs written or co-written by the singer. It's a wistful and reflective set, as unplugged acoustic guitar albums tend to be. But the inherent mellowness of the format is given a harder and more emotional edge by Dion's blues leanings, and the sense of a man emerging from hard times into something better. *You're Not Alone* was a low-key record in which Dion continued his explorations into introspective music that bridged the folk-rock and singer/songwriter styles. Whereas *Sit Down Old Friend* was solo acoustic, though, Dion did revert to full-band arrangements for the follow-up. Fortunately, the backing was tastefully understated, which would not often be the case the further Dion moved into the 1970s. It's respectable, yet not as good as *Sit Down Old Friend* and his best late-'60s folk-rock records, with a slight slide in the quality of the material, and less of the near-naked atmosphere that made *Sit Down Old Friend* stand out. Most of the set is self-composed, and it's fair but not exceptional singer/songwriting, with covers varying from effective (Melanie's "Close to It All") to unimaginative (the Beatles' "Let It Be"). *—Richie Unterberger*

Celine Dion

b. Mar. 30, 1968, Charlemagne, Quebec, Canada
Vocals / Adult Contemporary
Rising from humble beginnings in the small town of Charlemagne, Quebec, Celine Dion became one of the biggest international stars in pop music history, selling more than 100 million albums worldwide. The youngest in a family of 14 children, her parents and siblings were important figures in the early development of her singing career. By the age of 12 she had written one of her first songs, "Ce N'etait Qu'un Rêve" ("It Was Only a Dream"), which she recorded with the help of her mother and brother and shipped off to a manager named Rene Angelil, who mortgaged his house to pay for her first two albums and became a driving force in the career that would make her an international star.

1990's *Unison* was her breakthrough album, but it was her duet with Peabo Bryson on the theme song of Disney's *Beauty and the Beast* that was her true breakthrough. The song reached number one on the pop charts and won both a Grammy and an Academy award. It was also featured on her second English album, 1992's *Celine Dion.*

During this time there were also important developments in Dion's personal life. In 1988 Angelil crossed the line from manager to romantic partner when he kissed Dion one night after a show in Dublin. Fearful that fans would find the 26-year difference in their ages unsettling, the couple kept their relationship a secret for several years, eventually marrying in 1994.

Dion recorded six albums between 1992 and 1996, when *Falling Into You* took her to a new level of stardom. Dion's longest tenure on the pop charts would come the following year, however, when she recorded "My Heart Will Go On," the theme song for James Cameron's blockbuster movie *Titanic.*

The continuing popularity of her recordings and live performances made her 1999 sabbatical seem like a tragedy to her fans, but Dion needed a break after more than a decade and a half of breakneck pace. After undergoing fertility treatments, she announced her pregnancy in June, 2000, declaring "There is no hiding happiness… the dream dearest to our hearts has come true." *—Stacia Proefrock*

Unison / Aug. 21, 1990 / Epic ♦♦♦
A fine, sophisticated American debut from this popular Canadian singer, featuring the hit singles "(If There Was) Any Other Way" and "Where Does My Heart Beat Now." *—Stephen Thomas Erlewine*

Celine Dion / Mar. 31, 1992 / Epic ♦♦♦♦
Featuring the hit singles "Beauty and the Beast," "Love Can Move Mountains," and "If You Asked Me To," Celine Dion's follow-up to her successful American debut is an even stronger and more accomplished record than her previous album. *—Stephen Thomas Erlewine*

The Colour of My Love / Nov. 9, 1993 / 550 Music/Epic ♦♦♦
The Colour of My Love follows the same pattern as Celine Dion's eponymous breakthrough, and while the songs aren't quite as consistent this time around, the record is nevertheless quite successful, thanks to the careful production, professional songwriting (highlighted by "When I Fall in Love," "The Power of Love" and "Think Twice") and Dion's powerhouse performances. *—Stephen Thomas Erlewine*

Dion Chante Plamondon / 1994 / Epic ♦♦♦
In 1990, Celine Dion had enjoyed her first taste of success in the United States with her English-language debut album *Unison.* The album's first single, "Where Does My Heart Beat Now," was a number four hit, and the follow-up, "(If There Was) Any Other Way," made the Top 40. Her 1994 album, *Dion Chante Plamondon,* was her first U.S. French-language release, and found the singer interpreting the songs of renowned French-

Canadian lyricist Luc Plamondon. On this relatively early album, Dion sounds as self-assured and mature as on her latter-day recordings as a world-class superstar. Her voice exudes a passion beyond her young years, especially on the album's rocking opener, "Des Mots Qui Sonnent." As is often the case with Dion records, this album spans a wide musical spectrum, including the dramatic "Le Fils de Superman," the funk-tinged "Je Danse Dans Ma Tete," the bluesy "Les uns Contres les Autres," and the mega-power ballad "Le Blues du Businessman." Also on this album is one of her biggest French-language hits, "Un Garçon Pas Comme les Autres (Ziggy)," as well as a song that was an English-language European hit for Cyndi Lauper, "Le Monde Est Stone" ("The World Is Stone"). This album was a labor of love for the composer and the singer. Despite some middle-of-the-road fare, this is a strong collection of songs and a must for the singer's legions of fans. — *Jose Promis*

Falling into You / Mar. 12, 1996 / 550 Music/Epic ✦✦✦✦
Celine Dion's *Falling into You* returned the Canadian vocalist to the top of the American charts, and for good reason. Although the album is formulaic, it is a well-executed, stylish, and catchy formula, accentuating her natural vocal charm. Dion shines on ballads like "Because You Love Me" and mock-epics like Jim Steinman's "It's All Coming Back to Me Now." Between those two peaks, she tackles dance-pop and love songs with grace; that effortless elegance saves the mediocre material on the album from being tedious. Though there are a couple of weak tracks, *Falling Into You* is a remarkably well-crafted set of adult contemporary pop and Dion's best album. — *Stephen Thomas Erlewine*

Let's Talk About Love / Nov. 18, 1997 / 550 Music ✦✦✦✦
Falling Into You finally established Celine Dion as a superstar in America, so its sequel, *Let's Talk About Love*, was designed to consolidate her position as a newly-minted star. The album was constructed as a blockbuster, featuring Dion's trademark melodramatic ballads, some carefully-tailored dance-pop, a bevy of duets with the likes of Barbra Streisand and the Bee Gees and production and songs from adult contemporary gurus David Foster, Jim Steinman and Walter Afanasieff. Given that so many talented craftsmen worked on *Let's Talk About Love*, it makes sense that a number of the cuts succeed according to adult contemporary terms—they are predictably sweeping showcases for Dion's soaring, technically skilled voice. As usual, the singles (including the Streisand duet "Tell Him" and the *Titanic* love theme "My Heart Will Go On") shine the most brilliantly, but even the filler is immaculately produced. If the end result doesn't quite gel as an album, that shouldn't be surprising—this is music by committee, a product that was made to appeal to the widest possible audience. Such a calculated execution guarantees that anyone that liked one of the singles shouldn't be disappointed by *Let's Talk About Love*, but it doesn't necessarily mean they'll remember all of the record after it's finished playing. — *Stephen Thomas Erlewine*

These Are Special Times / Nov. 3, 1998 / 550 Music/Epic ✦✦✦
In the wake of her *Titanic* success, Celine Dion produced two new albums for the holiday season of 1998. One was a new French album, and the other was *These Are Special Times*, her first Christmas album. *These Are Special Times* is an especially successful holiday album, since Dion wisely balances popular carols ("The Christmas Song," "Blue Christmas," "Feliz Navidad") with new songs ("Don't Save it All for Christmas," the R. Kelly duet "I'm Your Angel"), hymns ("Ave Maria," "Adeste Fidelis") and Christmas songs with a distinct religious theme ("O Holy Night," the Andrea Bocelli duet "The Prayer"). At times, the production is too slick, at other times Dion's vocals are a little mannered, but overall, *These Are Special Times* is very effective, because the songs are good and she's committed to the material. Any fan of Dion, or of '90s adult contemporary pop in general, should find this very enjoyable. — *Stephen Thomas Erlewine*

• **All the Way: A Decade of Song** / Nov. 16, 1999 / 550 Music ✦✦✦✦
There aren't a lot of greatest-hits albums with seven new songs, which is exactly what *All the Way: A Decade of Song* is. There are just nine hits on this hits collection, and of those, only a handful—"If You Asked Me To," "Beauty and the Beast," "The Power of Love," "Because You Loved Me," "It's All Coming Back to Me Now," and "My Heart Will Go On"—were huge hits in the U.S. Her first American hit, "Where Does My Heart Beat Now," isn't here, nor is her duet with Barbra Streisand, "Tell Him." Naturally, this means it's not a definitive collection, but rather an unsatisfying album that feels suspiciously like a piece of product. The best of the hits, like the Meat Loaf-ian epic "It's All Coming Back to Me Now" and "My Heart Will Go On," are certainly among the best adult contemporary songs of the decade, and the new stuff would pale in comparison, even if it was very good—which, by and large, it is not. Two numbers, the danceable "That's the Way it Is" and the pretty ballad "If Walls Could Talk," work, but the cover of "The First Time Ever I Saw Your Face" falls flat and "All the Way," complete with old vocals from Sinatra, is a disaster. The remaining three aren't bad, but they're not particularly memorable, especially compared to the hits. And that's the problem with *All the Way*—if it had been a straight hits collection, with "That's the Way it Is" and "If Walls Could Talk" added to the end, it would have been fine, but padding it with nearly a full album worth of new material hurts it. — *Stephen Thomas Erlewine*

The Collector's Series, Vol. 1 / Oct. 24, 2000 / 550 Music ✦✦

Dire Straits

f. 1977, London, England, db. 1995
Album Rock, Pop/Rock

Dire Straits emerged during the post-punk era of the late '70s, and while their sound was minimalistic and stripped-down, they owed little to punk. If anything, the band was a direct outgrowth of the roots-revivalism of pub rock, but where pub rock celebrated good times, Dire Straits were melancholy. Led by guitarist/vocalist Mark Knopfler, the group built their sound upon the laid-back blues-rock of J.J. Cale, but they also had jazz and

country inflections, occasionally dipping into the epic song structures of progressive rock. The band's music was offset by Knopfler's lyrics, which approximated the winding, stream-of-conscious narratives of Bob Dylan. As their career progressed, Dire Straits became more refined and their new maturity happened to coincide with the rise of MTV and the compact disc. These two musical revolutions from the mid-'80s helped make Dire Straits' sixth album, *Brothers in Arms*, an international blockbuster. The band—along with Eric Clapton, Phil Collins, and Steve Winwood—become one of the leaders of a group of self-consciously mature veteran rock & rollers in the late '80s that designed their music to appeal to aging baby boomers. Despite the band's international success, they couldn't sustain their stardom, waiting a full six years to deliver a followup to *Brothers in Arms*, by which time their audience had shrunk significantly. — *Stephen Thomas Erlewine*

Dire Straits / Oct. 1978 / Warner Brothers ✦✦✦✦
Dire Straits' minimalistic interpretation of pub-rock had already crystallized by the time they released their eponymous debut. Driven by Mark Knopfler's spare, tasteful guitar lines and his husky warbling, the album is a set of bluesy rockers. And while the bar-band mentality of pub-rock is at the core of Dire Straits—even the group's breakthrough single, "Sultans of Swing," offered a lament for a neglected pub-rock band—their music is already beyond the simple boogies and shuffles of their forefathers, occasionally dipping into jazz and country. Knopfler also shows an inclination toward Dylanesque imagery, which enhances the smoky, low-key atmosphere of the album. While a few of the songs fall flat, the album is remarkably accomplished for a debut, and Dire Straits had difficulty surpassing it throughout their career. — *Stephen Thomas Erlewine*

Communiqué / Jun. 1979 / Warner Brothers ✦✦✦
Rushed out less than nine months after the surprise success of Dire Straits' self-titled debut album, the group's sophomore effort, *Communiqué* seemed little more than a carbon copy of its predecessor with less compelling material. Mark Knopfler and Co. had established a sound (derived largely from J.J. Cale) of laidback shuffles and intricate, bluesy guitar-playing, and *Communiqué* provided more examples of it. But there was no track as focused as "Sultans of Swing," even if "Lady Writer" (a lesser singles chart entry on both sides of the Atlantic) nearly duplicated its sound. As a result, *Communiqué* sold immediately to Dire Straits' established audience, but no more, and it did not fare as well critically as its predecessor or its follow-up. — *William Ruhlmann*

Making Movies / Oct. 17, 1980 / Warner Brothers ✦✦✦✦✦
Without second guitarist David Knopfler, Dire Straits began to move away from its roots-rock origins into a jazzier variation of country-rock and singer-songwriter folk-rock. Naturally, this means that Mark Knopfler's ambitions as a songwriter are growing, as the storytelling pretensions of *Making Movies* indicate. Fortunately, his skills are increasing, as the lovely "Romeo and Juliet," "Tunnel of Love" and "Skateaway" indicate. And *Making Movies* is helped by a new wave-tinged pop production, which actually helps Knopfler's jazzy inclinations take hold. The record runs out of steam toward the end, closing with the borderline offensive "Les Boys," but the remainder of *Making Movies* ranks among the band's finest work. — *Stephen Thomas Erlewine*

Love over Gold / Sep. 1982 / Warner Brothers ✦✦✦✦
Adding a new rhythm guitarist, Dire Straits expands its sounds and ambitions on the sprawling *Love Over Gold*. In a sense, the album is their prog-rock effort, containing only five songs, including the 14-minute opener "Telegraph Road." Since Mark Knopfler is a skilled, tasteful guitarist, he can sustain interest even throughout the languid stretches, but the long atmospheric instrumental passages aren't as effective as the group's tight blues-rock, leaving *Love Over Gold* only a fitfully engaging listen. — *Stephen Thomas Erlewine*

Twisting by the Pool / Feb. 1983 / Warner Brothers ✦✦✦
Dire Straits followed the ponderous *Love Over Gold* five months later with a three-song EP paced by its title track, which lived up to its name by adopting a twist beat, making it the closest thing to exuberant rock & roll this seemingly humorless band had ever attempted. "Two Young Lovers" had the same early rock feel, and even "If I Had You" was taken at a quicker tempo than had become common on Dire Straits albums. *Twisting by the Pool* didn't quite turn Dire Straits into a dance band, but it went a long way toward lightening up the group's image and repertoire. — *William Ruhlmann*

Alchemy: Dire Straits Live / Mar. 1984 / Warner Brothers ✦✦✦
There is an interesting contrast on this 94-minute double-disc live album (recorded at London's Hammersmith Odeon in July 1983) between the music, much of which is slow and moody, with Mark Knopfler's muttered vocals and large helpings of his fingerpicking on what sounds like an amplified Spanish guitar, and the audience response. The arena-size crowd cheers wildly and claps and sings along, when given half a chance, as though each song were an uptempo rocker. When they do have a song of even medium speed, such as "Sultans of Swing" or "Solid Rock," they are in ecstasy. That Dire Straits' introspective music loses much of its detail in a live setting matters less than that it gains presence and a sense of anticipation. Alan Clark's keyboards help to fill out the sound and give Knopfler's spare melodies a certain majesty, but Dire Straits remains an overgrown pub band with a Bob Dylan fixation, and that's exactly how the crowd likes it. [The CD version of the album contains one extra track, "Expresso Love," which adds a needed change of pace to the otherwise slow-moving first disc.] — *William Ruhlmann*

• **Brothers in Arms** / May 1985 / Warner Brothers ✦✦✦✦
Brothers in Arms brought the atmospheric, jazz-rock inclinations of *Love Over Gold* into a pop setting, resulting in a surprise international best-seller. Of course, the success of *Brothers in Arms* was helped considerably by the clever computer-animated video for "Money for Nothing," a sardonic attack on MTV. But what kept the record selling was

Knopfler's increased sense of pop songcraft—"Money for Nothing" had an indelible guitar riff, "Walk of Life" is a catchy uptempo boogie variation on "Sultans of Swing," and the melodies of the bluesy "So Far Away" and downtempo Everly Brothers-style "Why Worry" were wistful and lovely. Dire Straits had never been so concise or pop-oriented, and it wore well on them. Though they couldn't maintain that consistency through the rest of the album—only the jazzy "Your Latest Trick" and the flinty "Ride Across the River" make an impact—*Brothers in Arms* remains one of their most focused and accomplished albums and, in its succinct pop sense, it is distinctive within their catalog. *—Stephen Thomas Erlewine*

Money for Nothing / Oct. 1988 / Warner Brothers ♦♦♦♦
Released in late 1988, as everyone was waiting for the follow-up for *Brothers in Arms*, the 12-track *Money for Nothing* does an adequate job of summarizing hits and highlights from Dire Straits. Since the group only released one studio album after this compilation, and that really didn't produce any blockbusters, *Money for Nothing* winds up being a pretty good career summary. Far from perfect, though: too many album rock hits, such as "Expresso Love" and "Skateaway," are missing, plus there are two live cuts and the new cut "Where Do You Think You're Going?" doesn't go anywhere. Discounting these, the remainder of the compilation does hit many of the big songs, relying heavily on *Brothers in Arms*. *Sultans of Swing*, the post-*On Every Street* collection, is a better overview, yet this still has enough of the best-known tracks to satisfy the majority of casual fans. *—Stephen Thomas Erlewine*

On Every Street / Sep. 1991 / Warner Brothers ♦♦

On the Night / May 11, 1993 / Warner Brothers ♦♦

Live at the BBC / Jun. 26, 1995 / Warner Brothers ♦♦♦
Always a quiet act, Dire Straits dissolved quietly in 1995 as Mark Knopfler prepared his first full-fledged solo album. Meanwhile, this documentary effort, the group's third live recording, appeared to chronicle their early days. Most of it was recorded in July 1978, so it is in effect a concert version of the self-titled debut album. Tacked on at the end is a 12-minute version of "Tunnel of Love" from 1981, bringing the total time to 46 minutes. It's a modest effort from a modest band and, in that sense, a better representation of them than *Alchemy* or *On the Night*, both of which reflected their worldwide popularity. *—William Ruhlmann*

● **Sultans of Swing: The Very Best of Dire Straits** / Nov. 10, 1998 / Warner Brothers ♦♦♦♦
Exactly ten years after Dire Straits' first compilation, *Money for Nothing*, appeared in the stores, their second, *Sultans of Swing: The Very Best of Dire Straits*, was released. Though a decade is a significant span of time, Dire Straits had released just two subsequent albums—1991's *On Every Street* and 1993's *On the Night*, a live album culled from tapes of the record's supporting tour. Not quite enough material for a new greatest-hits album, but it had been years since Dire Straits had released an album of any sort (a compilation of BBC sessions snuck into the stores in 1995)—hence the birth of *Sultans of Swing*. Unsurprisingly, it covers much of the same ground as *Money for Nothing*, containing all the essentials ("Sultans of Swing," "Romeo and Juliet," "Tunnel of Love," "Private Investigations," "Twisting by the Pool," "Money for Nothing," "Brothers in Arms," "Walk of Life"), with the exception of "Telegraph Road," which was left on the earlier compilation. A live "Love Over Gold," "Lady Writer" and "So Far Away" replace "Down to the Waterline," "Where Do You Think You're Going" and a live "Portobello Belle," which is really just a trade-off, since they're all equal in quality. Then there are the three hits from *On Every Street* ("Calling Elvis," "Heavy Fuel," "On Every Street"), all of which are pleasant recreations of the *Brothers in Arms* sound; a live version of "Your Latest Trick" from *On the Night*, and, inexplicably, Mark Knopfler's "Wild Theme (Theme from Local Hero)." Fine tunes all, but none of them are reason enough to replace *Money for Nothing* with *Sultans of Swing*. For casual fans or curious listeners looking for an introduction/sampler, it's the better choice, simply because it covers more ground and contains more music while remaining quite listenable and entertaining. *—Stephen Thomas Erlewine*

Dirty Looks

f. 1979, **db.** 1981
Power Pop, New Wave, Rock & Roll
Dirty Looks (not to be confused with the late-'80s metal band of the same name) were formed in the late '70s in Staten Island, New York. Composed of Patrick Barnes (guitar/vocals), Peter Parker (drums/vocals) and Marco Sin (bass/vocals), the trio began playing their hard-rocking power-pop at Max's Kansas City and CBGB's where they were discovered by Stiff Records' Dave Robinson. Robinson signed them, anticipating they were "the next big thing." After releasing one brilliant single ("Let Go"), a good but unfortunately overlooked debut LP for Stiff, and a mediocre follow-up, the band faded into obscurity. *—Chris Woodstra*

● **Dirty Looks** / 1980 / Stiff ♦♦♦♦♦
The band's self-titled debut showed a lot of promise with its lean, hard-driving power-pop and near-perfect single, "Let Go." Just barely out of touch with the times, they drifted a little too close to bar-band territory to fit in with the new wave of the time. *—Chris Woodstra*

Turn It Up / 1981 / Stiff ♦♦♦♦
After failing with the edgy approach, the band enlisted Nick Garvey, ex-Ducks Deluxe/Motors, for production and moved toward a slicker, more mainstream sound—a poor choice, considering that Garvey was probably better suited to bring out the rock & roll side of the band. None of the songs really approach the last batch and the arrangements rarely rise above run-of-the-mill new wave. A sad end to a band that could have been . . . *—Chris Woodstra*

Dirty Three

f. 1992, Melbourne, Australia
Experimental Rock, Indie Rock, Post-Rock/Experimental, Instrumental Rock
Melancholy instrumental trio Dirty Three formed in Melbourne, Australia in 1992, led by classically-trained violinist Warren Ellis, who began writing and performing music for art openings and plays and also tenured in the groups Blackeyed Susans, Paranoid and the Nursing Mothers. After enlisting Blackeyed Susans' guitarist Mick Turner and drummer Jim White—veterans of Melbourne bands including the Sick Things, the Moodists, Fungus Brain and Venom P. Stinger—Ellis formed the Dirty Three; at the group's debut performance, he used a rubber band to attach a guitar pickup to his violin, giving the instrument a distorted, feedback-drenched feel far removed from its original sound. Recorded as a demo, the trio's debut *Sad & Dangerous* appeared in 1994; subsequent tours in support of Pavement, Sonic Youth and John Cale helped win the Dirty Three a deal with the Touch & Go label, which issued a 1995 eponymous effort and 1996's acclaimed *Horse Stories*. In 1998, the Dirty Three resurfaced with *Ocean Songs*; *Whatever You Love, You Are* followed two years later. *—Jason Ankeny*

Sad & Dangerous / 1994 / Poon Village ♦♦♦
On their debut, Dirty Three seems to be working out future ideas. Most of the songs are quite lengthy, and some of the more repetitive numbers are often hurt by this ("Kim's Dirt," "Turk Reprise"). As a result of the band's experimentation, however, we see a different side of the group not witnessed on later efforts. For instance, Warren Ellis sets down his violin to play bass on "Jim's Dog," a song that seems like it would fit perfectly on a film-noir detective movie soundtrack. One of the greatest moments on the record arrives in the form of "Turk," appropriately the last song and the biggest epic. Here, Dirty Three emits dark Eastern melodies that build until they finally climax into a shrieking, stuttered middle section. In the end, there are two sides to the material on the album: pure emotional feeling and meandering filler. *—Stephen Howell*

Dirty Three / 1995 / Touch & Go ♦♦♦♦
There have been many attempts to integrate instrumentation, other than the guitar, bass, and drums format, into so-called rock music. Many bands have gone through an Eastern or psychedelic phase, adding strings, tabla, or some other seemingly eccentric instrument to their sound. For the most part, bands like the Rolling Stones, the Beatles, and others make these new instruments sound out of place in a rock setting. But the Dirty Three—an aptly-named Australian drum, guitar, and violin trio—create an hour of music on this self-titled album that takes the experiments of their predecessors and coalesces them into a beautiful whole. Violinist Warren Ellis is a magician—the sounds he coaxes out of the instrument range from conventional melody to washed-out feedback noise. On "Indian Love Song" Ellis starts off with a gentle plucking of the strings, but midway though this ten minute drone he's on another planet, wailing away in a Pete Townshend meets Thurston Moore vein. This album does not follow a strict melody-cacophony structure though. Mick Turner plays along perfectly with Ellis, crafting subtle guitar lines that complement his counterpart. All the while drummer Jim White uses a keen selection of shells, tambourines, and God knows what else to keep a beat. The band seems equally assured in playing quiet pastoral passages ("Kim's Dirt") and ferocious rock ("Everything's Fucked"). Their music is cinematic—moving at varying paces through different emotions. Where most bands have come up short in both creativity and execution, the Dirty Three have it right. *—Marc Gilman*

Horse Stories / Sep. 10, 1996 / Touch & Go ♦♦♦♦♦
Dirty Three have a gift for creating unforgettably emotive instrumental soundscapes, and *Horse Stories* demonstrates this to great effect. The versatility of Warren Ellis' violin playing is what drives *Horse Stories*, but although the violin is the focal point, Mick Turner's guitar and Jim White's drumming are vital elements in making Dirty Three's sound so compelling. The tracks here are widely varied, from slow, languid pieces like "1000 Miles" and "At the Bar" and wild dances like "Red" and "I Remember a Time When Once You Used to Love Me" to stunningly beautiful tracks like the aptly titled "Hope." It is fitting that *Horse Stories* helped Dirty Three reach a wider audience than they had with their earlier efforts, as it was an album that saw them reach new heights in creativity. *—Jonathan Lewis*

● **Ocean Songs** / Mar. 31, 1998 / Touch & Go ♦♦♦♦♦
The Dirty Three's fourth venture into long-play territory is easily their most controversial, and a decided change in direction. While the band's previous recordings—*Sad & Dangerous*, *Dirty Three*, and *Horse Stories*—have all, in some way, attempted to capture the trio's live show, where slow, winding patterns and riffs become a swirling churning blast of emotional cacophony for both musicians and listeners, *Ocean Songs* takes a very different tack to achieve an end that is similar, but more focused. There is an aesthetic at work on *Ocean Songs*, from the cover through to the last note of the original recordings (early issues of the CD came with a second CD with three bonus tracks, all of which have surfaced elsewhere), the purpose of which is held in the somewhat mysterious title. The music is what makes it so. Are D3 playing songs inspired by or seemingly "created" from the ocean? Or are they paying homage to the ocean? The music here keeps all tempos reigned in and all instrumental flurries to a minimum, creating the feeling of waves lapping and pouring into and out of one another. On *Ocean Songs*, the Dirty Three have expanded themselves immeasurably as a band by holding themselves in to listen, and have made some of the most haunting, poetically profound, and emotionally honest music ever to come out of the "rock" world. *—Thom Jurek*

Whatever You Love, You Are / Mar. 7, 2000 / Touch & Go ♦♦♦♦
The Dirty Three have created their own brand of violin-infused rock and carry this torch of innovation even further with *Whatever You Love, You Are*. There are some characteristic Dirty Three moments on this album; the final song "Lullaby for Christie" would have fit in perfectly on their first self-titled album. The song swoons and breaks with a delicate

yet powerful melody. There are some key explorations on this album that, even if they don't always succeed, depict a band that is far from comfortable with the status quo. "I Offered It up to the Stars and the Night Sky" experiments with overlapping violin tracks and ends up sounding more like a chamber work by Steve Reich than the Dirty Three. Although it's not the album's most listenable song, it sounds incredibly different than anything else the band has done. Another new direction for the band is in terms of production; much of the album contains overdubs and has a much smoother, but not always better, sound. Perhaps the only aspect of *Whatever You Love* that is lacking is the rough "live" sound that the other albums have had. The production takes away from some of the band's spontaneity but also allows it to refine the subtleties of their sound. Hopefully, with time, the Dirty Three will be able to fuse their rough-edged sound with technological advancements to achieve a perfect synthesis. *—Marc Gilman*

Praise! / Apr. 4, 2000 / Festival ♦♦♦

If ever a band were suited to soundtrack work, it's Australia's violin, guitar, and drums trio the Dirty Three. From the outset an instrumental band, D3 have created a music in which dynamic and drama are equal partners with melody and dissonance. *Praise* is an Aussie independent film directed by John Curran and based upon the down and dirty novel by Andrew McGahan. The film stands on its own as a work of creative and artistic Aussie cinema and should be sought out on video. But the music, which adds so much to its effect, is another thing entirely. Perhaps everything that the Dirty Three lend to a soundtrack is summed up in the opening sequence, "I Remember When You Used to Love Me," taken from the band's *Horse Stories* album. Of eight D3 tunes on the soundtrack, three are from previously released albums; the other two are "Toaster" from *Ocean Songs* and "Devil in the Hole" from *Sad & Dangerous*. Fans of D3 know the reputation of these selections, especially "Devil in the Hole." But the other five, which are featured prominently on the soundtrack—that also includes Tex Williams, John Ellis, and the band Crow—are the backbone of the score, beginning with the mournful "Lights Are Yellow & the Night Is Slow." This is music that sets up dramatic situations, languid, sad, empty, and lonesome. *—Thom Jurek*

Dismemberment Plan

f. Jan. 1, 1993, Washington, D.C.

Indie Rock, Post-Punk, Alternative Pop/Rock

Washington, D.C.-based emo quartet the Dismemberment Plan—frontman Travis Morrison, guitarist Jason Caddell, bassist Eric Axelson and drummer Joe Easley—debuted in 1994 with the single "Can We Be Mature?," signing to DeSoto to release the full-length *!* in the fall of 1995. *The Dismemberment Plan is Terrified* followed a year and a half later, and after releasing 1998's *The Ice of Boston* EP on major label Interscope, the group returned to DeSoto for 1999's *Emergency & I*. In early 2001, the Dismemberment Plan and Juno issued the *Split Release* EP, which featured new songs and covers from each of the bands. *—Jason Ankeny*

! / Oct. 2, 1995 / DeSoto ♦♦♦

It's one of the punchier titles around, and happily the Dismemberment Plan live up to it on their full debut album. Carrying over a new version of "Wouldn't You Like to Know" (a track from "Can We Be Mature?," their first single), the Plan—here with original drummer Steve Cummings—are a fairly thrash-crazed example of what the term "emo" used to mean. There aren't any apologetic weepouts, just calmer moments amidst pretty explosive performances. The group's debt to the Cure, whom they had covered on the *Give Me the Cure* benefit/tribute CD, actually surfaces in the more openly tuneful passages—it's more pop Cure than the angst-y version though, since the young band's own screaming frustration derives from other sources. There are hometown faves like the Rites of Spring, naturally, but one can also catch the intensity of Drive Like Jehu, if slightly smoothed out and made more accessible. Compared to the group's later, more open embrace of different rhythmic approaches and influences, here it's a touch more straightforward—Cummings by now means a bad drummer, just not as totally impressive and fluid as Joe Easley. Travis Morrison casts around for a variety of vocal guises rather than settling on one, sometimes chatty and relaxed, other times amping up the screams, and at still other times trying for a bit of soul/lounge shtick. It's an odd combination, but still has a certain something, while the overall combination on such winners as "OK Jokes Over," an analysis of a shredded relationship with a great high-speed rush in the music, is pure delight. For all that the quartet is still a straight-up rock band, there's plenty of hints of their future subtlety and sonic joy—the chimes and handclaps in "Soon to Be Ex Quaker," the stuttering stop-start rumble of "13th and Euclid." *—Ned Raggett*

Dismemberment Plan is Terrified / Mar. 17, 1997 / DeSoto ♦♦♦

A four-piece outfit brandishing erratic musical directions, punk-rock energy and experimental songwriting may not sound like major-label material, but sure enough, based upon the strength of *... Is Terrified*, the Dismemberment Plan were scooped up by biggie Interscope Records. The group's sophomore outing is not as neatly reigned in as its predecessor *!*, but pleasures abound: "That's When the Party Started," with a cool synth-pop sheen, sounds like an aggro Talking Heads, while the monologue that drives "The Ice of Boston" demonstrates singer Travis Morrison's lyrical chops. *—Brian Raftery*

● **Emergency & I** / Oct. 26, 1999 / DeSoto ♦♦♦♦♦

The band's third full album is a firecracker, showing their at once passionate and sly approach to music—take in everything, put it back out, and give it its own particular sheen and spin—is in no danger of letting up. Knowing fans of the quartet have spoken on how it's clear that the bandmembers listen to everything from old soul to hip-hop and techno and back again, and there's no argument here based on the evidence of this disc. Travis Morrison's unusual vocals make a brilliant calling card for the band, high, a touch quavery, but never out of control, slipping into the mix like another instrument. Though the comparisons to fellow D.C. musical figure Craig Wedren are understandable, Morrison's voice isn't as piercing, with a warm, light undertow that's quite affecting. When he hits his best moments, like the downright anthemic but never breast-beating "What Do You Want Me to Say?," it's a wonder more people aren't talking about the guy. The rest of the band turn the indie rock stereotype on its head, avoiding aimless shambling jangle or emo's straightjacketing stereotype in favor of an unsettled mix that embraces sampling's jump-cut techniques and shifting rhythms where prominence is equally given to guitar, keyboards, and beat. It can be late-night jazzy mood-out or sudden thrash, but the quartet handles all approaches with aplomb and creative arrangements to boot. Drummer Joe Easley may be the band's secret weapon, able to keep the pace and swing just enough, though bassist Eric Axelson is by no means a slouch himself—the dub-touched "Spider in the Snow" is a great showcase for both. The fact that "You Are Invited" is conceivably the world's greatest synth-pop/electro/guitar chime/post-punk song about trying to get to the right party—and is emotional without being overwrought—gives a sense as to this album's considerable strengths. *—Ned Raggett*

The Divine Comedy

f. 1989, Londonderry

Chamber Pop, Alternative Pop/Rock

The Divine Comedy is the alias for Neil Hannon, a British pop singer/songwriter with aspirations of becoming a new wave fusion of Scott Walker, Morrissey, and Electric Light Orchestra. During the early '90s, he built up a strong cult following with a pair of idiosyncratic, critically acclaimed records before his third album, *Casanova*, became a mainstream success in the wake of Brit-pop and Pulp's popularity. "Becoming More Like Alfie" and "Something for the Weekend," both pulled from *Casanova*, became hits after receiving significant airplay from Radio One DJ Chris Evans, and the Divine Comedy moved from British indie rock favorites to a minor mainstream cult in their own right. Hannon was appearing not only on the cover of Melody Maker, but there were articles about him throughout mainstream press, from The Guardian to Just Seventeen. The Divine Comedy supported the single "The Frog Princess" with a tour with a 30-piece orchestra, culminating with a concert at Lond Shepherds Bush Empire, which provided the basis for the band's next album, *A Short Album About Love*. Released to coincide with Valentine's Day 1997, *A Short Album About Love* was greeted with positive reviews and the strongest initial sales of any Divine Comedy record to date. *—Stephen Thomas Erlewine*

Liberation / Aug. 1993 / Setanta ♦♦♦

Jettisoning the rest of the band but keeping the name, Hannon as the Divine Comedy becomes as art-pop as it gets with his first full album, but with an extreme Englishness that even Ray Davies might be hard-pressed to keep up with. *Liberation* is mostly a self-composed and performed release, aside from a couple of string players, a French horn performer, and a drummer, plus a song lyric borrowed from Wordsworth, giving "Lucy" a crisp, gentle rock recasting here. Otherwise it's Hannon's hyper-elegant show all the way, practically begging to be equally played in a Victorian drawing room, at a swank '20s club, at a swinging beautiful people party in London, or at an end-of-the-century Britpop disco. Slightly more rock/poppy tunes like "Bernice Bobs Her Hair" groove along with MOR backing vocals and understated energy, while others pile on the artsy touches: the harpsichord underlying the entirety of "Death of a Supernaturalist" and the mournful string arrangement which provides all of the music on "Timewatching." A few songs rock in a more straightforward manner, but often only just so: "I Was Born Yesterday" interrupts its persistent pounding with a spoken-word break referring to ballerinas and standing en pointe while a cello plays; the acoustic guitar-based "Victoria Falls" has a fragile, frosty feeling to it. Hannon, meanwhile, belies his Northern Ireland upbringing to an astounding degree with his clipped, toff singing style. As for subject matter, Hannon tackles everything from borrowing "Your Daddy's Car" to the jaunty, XTC-inspired "The Pop Star's Fear of the Pollen Count," slipping in as much wry humor as he does gentle pathos and reflection—plenty of all three. "Europop" is particularly sharp—a self-descriptive new-wave synth plus guitar dance tune with rather lugubrious vocals from Hannon, reflecting on everything from science and finance to the strange nature of love. *—Ned Raggett*

Promenade / Mar. 1994 / Setanta ♦♦♦♦

While In appearance, it seems like a sequel to *Liberation*—a similar cover shot down to the typeface is on the front, in this case showing Hannon in front of the I. M Pei-designed entrance to the Louvre, while the back shows a similarly rococo piece of decoration—*Promenade* is in fact even more extremely and defiantly non-rock than its predecessor. With a larger number of string performers to accompany him, not to mention someone on oboe, sax, and cor anglais (English horn), Hannon retains only drummer/co-producer Darren Allison from the previous record to make what remains his most self-conscious art release to date. The opening "Bath" sets the course, with seacoast sounds and a brief spoken word bit which turns into a minimalist Michael Nyman homage before slamming into the song proper, where the guitars and bass take a back seat to the choir, strings, and woodwinds, all the while driven along by Allison's solid percussion. From there all kinds of twists and turns emerge in an alternate universe where classical instrumentation offers as much pop as a guitar strum. The extreme archness of "Going Downhill Fast" is also a pub sing-along, while "Don't Look Down" builds to a dramatic, striking ending. Hannon's wickedly sharp wit informs almost everything; "The Booklovers" is the clear winner on that count, as Hannon tremulously recites a number of authors' names (with an appropriate accompanying sample or aside, often quite hilarious) over a stately arrangement. "A Seafood Song" and "A Drinking Song" celebrate exactly what they say they do, the latter offering up the great line "All my lovers will be pink and elephantine!" At the same time the tender side of Hannon, which has sometimes been ignored, surfaces more than once, with "The Summerhouse," a nostalgic, wonderfully gentle piece on a lost season of love. This turns out to be one of Hannon's best songs ever. —*Ned Raggett*

● **Casanova** / 1996 / Tristar ◆◆◆◆◆

Turning back to a slightly more straightforward rock/pop format turned out to be advantageous for Hannon; *Casanova* turned into a smash hit in the U.K., while the singles "Something for the Weekend" (at once soaring, cheeky, leering, and truly weird, with lyrics detailing a guy led astray by his lover and attacked by her secret thug companions) and "Becoming More Like Alfie" (a sly '60s acoustic pop number with solid percussion, sampling the Michael Caine movie in question and reflecting on how all the wrong people in life seem to get the girls) became Top Ten charters. Recruiting the equivalent of a full orchestra didn't hurt either, fleshing out the classical/art/pop Divine Comedy fusion to even more expansive ranges than before, while drummer Allison and Hannon continued overseeing and co-producing everything, again demonstrating their careful collective ear for the proceedings. Hannon's lyrical music fires on all cylinders as well, from the cock-eyed vision of romance in "The Frog Princess" (with more than one low-key French reference in both lyrics and sweeping music) to the wickedly funny and elegant "Songs of Love," detailing how boys and girls seem to be in heat everywhere while all the songwriters are stuck alone writing the title objects in question. In the meantime, there are great one-off moments scattered throughout *Casanova*. For instance, Hannon's impersonation of a modern dandy as fortune teller at the start of "Middle-Class Heroes" is to die for. He also does one of the best Barry White takeoffs yet recorded in the mid-song break of "Charge," packed with Tennyson references and army commands amidst swirling strings and an increasingly loud beat. After topping that off with "Theme From Casanova," a slightly tongue-in-cheek number detailing all the basic credits and inspiration for the album, the result is a massive project that hits the jackpot with smiles all around. —*Ned Raggett*

A Short Album About Love / Feb. 1997 / Setanta ◆◆◆◆◆

Following the success of *Casanova*, Neil Hannon decided to indulge his Scott Walker fetish by recording a lush, symphonic mini-album with a 30-piece orchestra. Released to coincide with Valentine's Day, *A Short Album About Love* is, if anything, an even better record than *Casanova*, simply because Hannon holds nothing back. These are grandiose, extravagant songs that work because of their very pretensions. His deep, baritone croon has never sounded more affecting, and his songs are easily among his best, making *A Short Album About Love* much more than a record for hardcore fans. Several months later, a re-release of the album added four bonus tracks. —*Stephen Thomas Erlewine*

Fanfare for the Comic Muse / Sep. 22, 1998 / Setanta ◆◆◆

Fin de Siecle / Dec. 8, 1998 / Setanta ◆◆◆◆

Fin de Siecle contains many of the touching, excellent, and suave sort of songs for which Neil Hannon and the Divine Comedy are known. There are quite a few stellar tracks to be found on this, their final full-length album of new material for Setanta Records. Humorous, stylish songs are present in the form of "Generation Sex" and "Sweden." "Generation Sex" contains some simply joyous wordplay, alluding to the death of Princess Diana, the struggle between the classes worldwide, and genetic engineering in the cosmetic industry. "Sweden" is a tongue-in-cheek exploration of the beauty of Swedish citizens, which culminates in the loud proclamation of an obsession about Nina Persson of the Cardigans. The other high points of the album are in the emotional extremes of "Commuter Love" and the monumentally touching "Sunrise." "Commuter Love" is a touching ode to subway love. "Sunrise" is perhaps the most pristine, chilling, and heart-wrenching song ever written or recorded dealing with the swirling chaos of unrest in Northern Ireland. Any music critics who have dismissed Hannon as an empty mimic of Scott Walker would eat their words after hearing "Sunrise." The remainder of the album is quite strong, though "Thrillseeker" and "Here Comes the Flood" are a bit too bombastic to be completely enjoyable. The band is simply too talented, though, for a few missteps to darken the charms of its albums. With "Sunrise" and much of *Fin de Siecle*, the Divine Comedy continue in the mode of beautiful ballads and pop divinity found on *A Short Album About Love*. The band has raised the bar sky high for any future releases. —*Tim DiGravina*

Secret History: Best of the Divine Comedy / Sep. 21, 1999 / Tristar ◆◆◆◆

For those who want lyrical bones to chew on, there's no denying Neil Hannon's sly appeal. To dismiss him as "baroque" would be as misleading as pegging him as the missing link between Noel Coward, Anthony Newley, and Scott Walker. But Hannon's highly evolved song constructions, grandiose orchestral pretensions, and baritone crooning seem as much quaint classicism as a bicycle built for two—even as his deft, complex, ambitious arrangements are contemporary. (He's no Leon Redbone.) In the end, his consummate skills as a writer come across most. You hang on the surprise of every wily word, wrapped around venerable melody. Distilled here to a best-of, Hannon makes one of his strongest cases for his dashing, romantic charm. It's this sweeping romanticism, the thick violins and pianos like spectacular sunsets spurring his yearning singing, that transcends his occasional lapses into naughty schoolboy leering. One listen to *Fin de Siècle*'s triumphant "The Certainty of Chance" or *A Short Album*'s cascading "In Pursuit of Happiness" is to open the blinds in a dark room that emit bursts of blinding light; the sweep of the orchestra playing madly, as if running to catch a train, and Hannon's voice bawling along, carried away, shedding its sporadic smugness. Today's Divine Comedy is a lot sweeter and emotional than Dante's. As a word of caution, the uninitiated might find the opening "National Express" and the so-so "Generation Sex" tough going. But with the early help of Hannon's first English hits "Something for the Weekend" and "Becoming More Like Alfie," one can get hooked into Hannon's passion play without realizing it. Pop can mean something more than momentary, torpid trifle again, if only those stifling blinds can be lifted. —*Jack Rabid, The Big Takeover*

Gin Soaked Boy / Jan. 4, 2000 / Setanta ◆◆◆

Regeneration / Mar. 12, 2001 / Parlophone ◆◆◆

Choosing a new direction is a hard and serious business for any band, but perhaps more so for listeners, who, for better or worse, have grown to expect a certain mood and style from their favorite artists. *Regeneration*, the Divine Comedy's first album for Parlophone Records, finds Neil Hannon and company parting ways with the playful, coquettish songs of *Casanova* and *Fin De Siecle* and taking a serious look at the duality of "town" and "country." Many bands have tackled the subject of the "haves and have-nots," and that may be a bit of a problem here, as both Pulp and the Divine Comedy themselves have done a much better job of illustrating the point than songs like "Lost Property" or "Bad Ambassador." By shedding the smirking artifice that served *Casanova* so well, and hiring producer Nigel Godrich, the Divine Comedy may be treading dangerously close to the sounds of countrymen Radiohead, but the Divine Comedy are smart enough to give listeners just enough lyrical bit to throw them off the scent. Perhaps the true art of the Divine Comedy was the artifice that is missing on *Regeneration*, but it is more likely that Hannon has found different things to say, and wanted to find a different language in which to say them. Although not as musically striking or original as *Casanova*, there is still a great commentary on celebrity in "Timestretched," and Hannon's unmistakable croon saves the record's obvious single, "Love What You Do," by adding just enough sincerity to make its listeners believers. —*Terry Miles*

The Divinyls

f. 1981, Sydney, Australia, db. 1996
Arena Rock, Pop/Rock, New Wave, Hard Rock

The Divinyls' Christina Amphlett is the most dynamic live female performer Australia has ever produced, let alone sent out into the world. With the help of an ever changing Divinyls lineup, Amphlett and guitarist Mark McEntee have created a legacy of powerful pop records. In December of 1980 they started performing in the sleazy bars of Sydney. They had only just started performing live when the group was spotted by film director Ken Cameron who was looking for a group to appear in his film *Monkey Grip*. Cameron was so impressed by Amphlett he invented a small speaking part for her. What he also hadn't imagined was finding a group capable of providing the movie with a soundtrack. The single from the soundtrack mini-album, "Boys in a Town," came with an eye-catching video of Amphlett at her provocative best, dressed in a school uniform and fishnet stockings, filmed from below as she performed on top of a metal grill. The single made the Australian Top Ten. With just one hit to their credit the Divinyls were able to sign a worldwide deal with Chrysalis. While the group toured the world extensively in the years that followed, the lineup kept changing around the Amphlett-McEntee team. The group's output on record has been hindered by the struggle to get all the pieces together long enough to release albums. In 1991, the Divinyls stirred up a storm again with the song "I Touch Myself" and a video with a tied-up Amphlett back in fishnets. The ensuring controversy helped make the song a huge hit around the world: number one in Australia, Top Ten in America. —*Ed Nimmervoll*

Desperate / 1983 / Chrysalis ◆◆◆

What a Life! / 1985 / Chrysalis ◆◆

● **Essential** / 1987 / Chrysalis ◆◆◆◆◆

Essential Divinyls is a terrific 12-track compilation of the Australian duo's early- and mid-'80s singles, including such songs as "Pleasure and Pain," "Temperamental," "Back to the Wall" and "Boys in Town," offering a good overview of their pre-"I Touch Myself" records. —*Stephen Thomas Erlewine*

Temperamental / 1988 / Chrysalis ◆◆◆

The Divinyls' third album, *Temperamental*, is a marked improvement over *What A Life!* in that the songs are stronger, have more of an edge and contain less of the failed experiments found on the previous album. Highlighted by the single "Back to the Wall," which was featured in *Nightmare on Elm Street 4: The Dream Master, Temperamental* is the Divinyls' most hard-rocking, straight-ahead rock album. The entire set is arena-ready and uptempo, and includes such highlights as the rollicking "Better Days," the '50s-ish rock & roll of "Hey Little Boy," "Fighting" and the speedy title track, which features some of guitarist Mark McEntee's finest work. Apart from the fact that there is no single as strong as "Pleasure and Pain" or "Boys In Town," *Temperamental* is the Divinyls at their best. —*Jason Damas*

Divinyls / Jan. 29, 1991 / Virgin ◆◆◆

In 1991, Australia's Divinyls generated some controversy in the U.S. when lead singer Chrissie Amphlett sang about female masturbation on "I Touch Myself." Far from explicit, the PG-rated hit shouldn't have come as such a shock to American ears. At any rate, this self-titled CD offers exactly what one generally expects from the Divinyls: rockin' intensity combined with new wave-ish quirks and a strong melodic sense. Though not mind-blowing, it's respectable and generally appealing. Hardcore Divinyls enthusiasts will find the eerie "Love School" and infectious offerings like "Make Out Alright," "Bless My Soul (It's Rock-N-Roll)" and "I Touch Myself" to be well worth acquiring. *Desperate* would be a better introduction to the Divinyls, but this is a release with many more strengths than weaknesses. —*Alex Henderson*

Underworld / Nov. 11, 1996 / RCA ◆◆◆

After the success of "I Touch Myself," the Divinyls became the victims of a severe backlash. Because of this, they waited six years before releasing their follow-up album, but the wait proved to be worth it. Darker and with more of an emphasis on ballads than any of their previous albums, *Underworld* is the Divinyls' most accomplished release to date. Mark McEntee's guitar work is as dark and grungy as ever, and Christina Amphlett's vocals continue to be ragged and charismatic. The album survives on the strength of the singles, which include "Heart of Steel" (a slick, AOR-ready ballad), "I'm Jealous" (a vengeful ballad also featured on *Melrose Place*, "Sex Will Keep Us Together" (a Stonesy rocker) and "Human on the Inside" (a tender, hurtful ballad about spousal abuse). This Australia-only release is a must-have for any fans of the band. After the release of this album, the band went on hiatus again as Amphlett decided to temporarily pursue her acting career. —*Jason Damas*

The Dixie Dregs

f. 1975, db. 1982
Southern Rock, Fusion
One of the top jazz-rock fusion ensembles ever, the Dixie Dregs combined virtuoso technique with eclecticism and a sense of humor and spirit too frequently lacking in similar projects. Guitarist Steve Morse and bassist Andy West played together as high school students in Augusta, Georgia in a conventional rock band called Dixie Grit. When Morse was expelled from school for refusing to cut his hair, he enrolled at the University of Miami School of Music, where he met violinist Allen Sloan, who had played with the Miami Philharmonic, and drummer Rod Morgenstein. The three decided to form a band, and Morse convinced West to come to Miami and join. The Dixie Dregs completed their lineup with keyboardist Steve Davidowski. Their first album, *The Great Spectacular*, was recorded for a class project in 1975 and later released by the band (it is long out of print). Following graduation, the quintet began playing live around the South and got their break after opening for Sea Level on 1976, when a representative from Capricorn Records was impressed enough to sign them. Mark Parrish, a former member of Dixie Grit, replaced Davidowski for their official debut, 1977's *Free Fall*. Their follow-up, *What If*, proved to be one of their most artistically successful albums, and the Dregs played at the 1978 Montreux Jazz Festival with T Lavitz replacing Parrish. Half of *Night of the Living Dregs* contains excerpts from that concert. The group shortened their name to the Dregs for 1981's *Unsung Heroes*, and added both vocalists and three-time national fiddling champ Mark O'Connor, whose old-timey playing style added another dimension to the group's sound, for *Industry Standard*. The Dregs then disbanded; the highly respected Morse formed his own band and recorded several albums, later joining Kansas from 1986 to 1988, while Morgenstein hooked up with pop-metallists Winger.

The Dregs reunited briefly in 1988 for a series of live dates, but a full-fledged reunion didn't take place until 1992, with Morse, Lavitz, Morgenstein, and Dave LaRue of the Steve Morse Band in West's place. Allen Sloan rejoined only briefly, with his position then filled by ex-Mahavishnu Orchestra member Jerry Goodman. *Bring 'Em Back Alive* was culled from the group's tour, and 1994's *Full Circle* was also well-received. *California Screamin'* followed in early 2000. —*Steve Huey*

● **The Best of the Dixie Dregs: Divided We Stand** / Jul. 1989 / Arista ✦✦✦✦
Although brief, *Divided We Stand: The Best of the Dixie Dregs* is a good overview of highlights of the jazzy Southern rock group's stint at Capricorn Records. A live version of "Refried Funky Chicken" is added as bait for hardcore fans, but its true strength is how it offers an even-handed retrospective of what is arguably the group's prime period. —*Stephen Thomas Erlewine*

Don Dixon

Vocals, Keyboards, Guitar, Bass / College Rock, Jangle Pop, Singer/Songwriter
Best known among the key producers to emerge from the American underground's jangle-pop movement of the early 1980s, Don Dixon also enjoyed a cult following as a solo performer. A native of North Carolina, he dwelled in relative obscurity for well over a decade as a member of the little-known Arrogance before attracting his first significant notice around 1983 after co-producing with Mitch Easter R.E.M.'s landmark debut LP *Murmur*. Subsequent work on Chris Stamey's *It's a Wonderful Life*, the Windbreakers' *Terminal* and Tommy Keene's *Run Now* solidified his reputation among jangle-pop aficionados, and in 1985 Dixon recorded his solo debut *Most of the Girls Like to Dance But Only Some of the Boys Do*, a further affirmation of his love of classic pop melodies and spiky, Nick Lowe-inspired wordplay. After producing wife Marti Jones' *Unsophisticated Time*, he released his second solo effort *Romeo at Juilliard* in 1987, and the live *Chi-Town Budget Show* a year later. After 1989's *EEE*, Dixon's recording career went into mothballs for several years and he returned to producing, helming efforts for the Smithereens, Richard Barone and James McMurtry before finally releasing *Romantic Depressive* in 1995. Another lengthy hiatus preceded the early 2000 release of *The Invisible Man*. —*Jason Ankeny*

Most of the Girls Like to Dance but Only Some of the Boys Do / 1985 / Dixon Archival ✦✦✦✦✦
Dixon put together *Most of the Girls Like to Dance but Only Some of the Boys Do* out of demos cut from 1981-1984. It's a kind of best-of from a man with a pure pop sensibility and a wicked sense of humor when it comes to matters romantic. [The 1986 CD version adds two songs to make a total of 16.] —*William Ruhlmann*

Romeo at Juilliard / Sep. 1987 / Enigma ✦✦✦✦✦
Dixon's domestic debut featured more of his skewed songs, and here he was aided and abetted by such compatriots as Mitch Easter and Marti Jones (who is his wife). —*William Ruhlmann*

Chi-Town Budget Show / 1988 / Enigma ✦✦✦
An intimate live album featuring many of the best songs from the two previous albums. —*William Ruhlmann*

EEE / Sep. 20, 1989 / Enigma ✦✦✦

● **If I'm a Ham, Well You're a Sausage** / Mar. 3, 1992 / Restless ✦✦✦✦✦

While he is known mainly through his production work, this extensive best-of collection shows Dixon to be an equally sharp songwriter and performer, collecting the highlights of his albums as well as a handful of rare tracks. —*Chris Woodstra*

Romantic Depressive / Mar. 28, 1995 / Sugar Hill ✦✦✦✦✦
Don Dixon is known primarily as a producer, but this rock-solid collection of original songs will make you wish he'd step out from behind the board more often. Nothing on this album is especially groundbreaking—not his gravelly baritone, not his Memphis soul beats or his late-'50s chord progressions—but everything here sheds new light on old traditions. A multi-instrumentalist as well as a fine songwriter, Dixon plays almost everything on the album, and the sound is dense without being muddy, snappy without being shallow. You'll recognize both the rhythms and the sentiments on "Angel, Angel," but Dixon's delivery and his way with a melody make it all sound brand new even while it takes you back 20 or 30 years; the album's best track, "Giving Up the Ghost," is timeless in its gutbucket romantic desperation. Dixon does sometimes succumb to cleverness (remember his earlier album called *Romeo at Juilliard*?), and you can't help but suspect that the lackluster instrumental toward the end of the album was just an excuse to use the title "Good Golly Svengali." It's also true that "Lottery of Lives," an anti-Vietnam song, is not only dated, but also comes off as a by-the-numbers diatribe. However, by "Never Slow Down," it's hard to tell whether he's tweaking the left or the right, and at that point he wisely puts down his pen and slips quietly away. Highly recommended. —*Rick Anderson*

The Invisible Man / Mar. 7, 2000 / Gadfly ✦✦✦
A superstar who took five years to follow up an album that, in turn, had been his first in six years would be matching the marketplace these days, but for a guy like Don Dixon, such a schedule indicates either a casual attitude toward his solo career or trouble interesting a record company in releasing his discs. Vermont indie Gadfly has taken on *The Invisible Man*, which may be the quirkiest release yet from a notably quirky artist. "This record is about mortality & redemption," Dixon notes in the CD booklet. "Many different characters appear as singers ... I am none of them & all of them." He then helpfully lists the ages of the characters by song. The problem of appreciating Dixon's concept is immediately apparent. While one can expect, and find, a distinction in the authorial voice by very different ages, most of the characters fall into middle age, a period that certainly has its stages, but not ones as clearly defined. This is some hint to the general obscurity of the album's lyrics. While titles like "Tax the Churches" and "Digging a Grave" seem to announce their subjects right off, they don't turn out to be that clear. And not all the songs are all that musically accessible. *The Invisible Man* is an often puzzling album created almost single-handedly by a highly individual singer-songwriter who has made some attempts to create commercial music in the past, but this time seems to have followed his muse without much concern about whether anyone would be able to follow him. —*William Ruhlmann*

DJ Jazzy Jeff & The Fresh Prince

Pop-Rap, Urban, Hip-Hop
If you're looking for bubble-gum rap, these guys are your best bet. The Prince spins his teen-suburban tales in a pleasant, if facile fashion, and Jeff isn't bad on the turntable. Don't look for anything gritty or street-smart: when Jeff boasts that he can beat Mike Tyson, that's about as menacing as it gets. The Fresh Prince starred in the early-'90s TV sitcom, *The Fresh Prince of Bel Air*. Will Smith, the "Fresh Prince" part of the team, has greatly expanded his horizons in the '90s. He appeared in the films *Six Degrees of Separation* and *Bad Boys*, and also tried to expand his hip-hop horizons enough to offset the talk that his raps had become hopelessly whitebread and irrelevant. *Homebase* in 1991 included "Dog Is a Dog" and the Top Ten pop hit "Summertime," with Smith's rap done in a leaner, harder fashion even if the lyrics were pretty much family hour. But by *Code Red* in 1993 it seemed Smith had made peace with his image and was back to laid back, pop-oriented material such as "Boom! Shake the Room," "I Wanna Rock," and "Can't Wait to Be with You" which had a guest stint from Christopher Williams. A *Greatest Hits* collection followed in 1998. —*John Floyd*

Rock the House / 1987 / Jive/Novus ✦✦✦

He's the D.J., I'm the Rapper / 1988 / Jive/Novus ✦✦✦✦✦

And in This Corner ... / Oct. 1989 / Jive/Novus ✦✦✦

Homebase / Jul. 23, 1991 / Jive/Novus ✦✦✦✦✦

Code Red / Oct. 12, 1993 / Jive ✦✦✦

● **Greatest Hits** / Apr. 28, 1998 / Jive ✦✦✦✦✦
DJ Jazzy Jeff & the Fresh Prince actually turned out better albums than many of their pop-rap contemporaries, but like their peers, they excelled at singles, not albums. That's what makes the appearance of *Greatest Hits* welcome. Although it has its flaws—the sublime "Summertime" is here twice, but only as an "Extended Club Mix" and a "'98 remix"—it remains an excellent summation of their career, boasting such hits as "Girls Ain't Nothing But Trouble," "I Think I Can Beat Mike Tyson," "Parents Just Don't Understand," "Boom! Shake the Room," "Ring My Bell," "A Nightmare On My Street" and, as a bonus, Will Smith's 1997 solo hit "Men in Black." —*Stephen Thomas Erlewine*

DJ Shadow (Josh Davis)

b. 1973, Hayward, CA
DJ, Producer / Turntablism, Electronica, Ambient Breakbeat, Trip-Hop, Hip-Hop, DJ
DJ Shadow's Josh Davis is widely credited as a key figure in developing the experimental instrumental hip-hop style associated with the London-based Mo'Wax label. His early singles for the label, including "In/Flux" and "Lost and Found (S.F.L.)," were all-over-the-map mini-masterpieces combining elements of funk, rock, hip-hop, ambient, jazz, soul, and used-bin incidentalia. Although he'd already done a scattering of original and pro-

duction work (during 1991-92 for Hollywood Records) by the time Mo'Wax's James Lavelle contacted him about releasing "In/Flux" on the fledgling imprint, it wasn't until his association with Mo'Wax that his sound began to mature and cohere. Mo'Wax released his longest work to date in 1995—the 40-minute single in four movements, "What Does Your Soul Look Like," which topped the British indie charts—and Davis has gone on to co-write, remix, and produce tracks for labelmates DJ Krush and Doctor Octagon. Shadow's first full-length, *Endtroducing*, was released in late 1996. —*Sean Cooper*

★ **Endtroducing . . .** / Nov. 19, 1996 / Mo' Wax/ffrr ♦♦♦♦♦
As a suburban Californian kid, DJ Shadow tended to treat hip-hop as a musical innovation, not as an explicit social protest, which goes a long way toward explaining why his debut album *Endtroducing . . .* sounded like nothing else at the time of its release. Using hip-hop, not only its rhythms but its cut-and-paste techniques, as a foundation, Shadow created a deep, endlessly intriguing world on *Endtroducing*, one where there are no musical genres, only shifting sonic textures and styles. Shadow created the entire album from samples, almost all pulled from obscure, forgotten vinyl, and the effect is that of a hazy, half-familiar dream—parts of the record sound familiar, yet it's clear that it only suggests music you've heard before, and that the multi-layered samples and genres create something new. And that's one of the keys to the success of *Endtroducing*—it's innovative, but it builds on a solid historical foundation, giving it a rich, multi-faceted sound. It's not only a major breakthrough for hip-hop and electronica, but for pop music. —*Stephen Thomas Erlewine*

Preemptive Strike / Jan. 13, 1998 / Mo' Wax/ffrr/London ♦♦♦♦
DJ Shadow assembled the singles collection *Preemptive Strike* as a way for American audiences to catch up on his career prior to his debut album, *Endtroducing*. The 11-track album contains three new interludes and three complete singles that he released on Mo'Wax—"In/Flux," "What Does Your Soul Look Like," and "High Noon"—and a bonus disc, "Camel Bobsled Race," which is a megamix of DJ Shadow material by DJ Q-Bert. Given that *Endtroducing* was a masterpiece of subtly shifting texture, *Preemptive Strike* almost seems purposely incoherent, even though the tracks are sequenced chronologically. The jerky flow can make the album a little difficult to assimilate on first listen, but it soon begins to make sense, even if it never achieves the graceful flow of the album. Several of the selections on *Preemptive Strike* were available in different forms on *Endtroducing*—parts four and one of "What Does Your Soul Look Like" are in their original forms here, presented along with one and three, and there's the "extended overhaul" of "Organ Donor." All of these are significantly different than the LP versions, and "What Does Your Soul Look Like" is necessary in its original, half-hour, four-part incarnation. But the key moments are the seminal "In/Flux," which arguably created trip-hop, and "High Noon," the dynamic, fuzz-drenched single that was his first single release since *Endtroducing*. Those three A-sides are reason enough for any serious fan of the debut to pick up *Preemptive Strike*, but the B-sides and "Camel Bobsled Race" are equally intriguing, making the package a nice summation of DJ Shadow's most important singles through the end of 1997. —*Stephen Thomas Erlewine*

DMX (Earl Simmons)

b. Dec. 18, 1970
Vocals / Hardcore Rap, East Coast Rap
It's obvious that hip-hop has finally come into its own when one of its most respected rappers (among all kinds of fans) is also one of its best-selling artists, and a successful crossover act to rock fans as well. DMX built himself an excellent reputation in the rap game, working the fragile territory between intense, metaphysical lyrical concerns and his image as a canine-obsessed personality who often uses a backing track to bark assent to his own raps. All this from a tremendously successful chart act, whose first three albums debuted at number one and sold well over ten million records in just a year and a half. With Nas and Jay-Z (both of whom also made it on an artistic and commercial level), DMX is the kingpin of hip-hop in the years after the twin giants, Biggie and 2Pac, were gunned down.

A rough-toned Yonkers MC who debuted with hometown friends the Lox on a DJ Clue mix-tape, DMX hit the big time in early 1998 when his single "Get at Me Dog" became a club and radio smash. The rapper had first appeared seven years earlier however, in an "Unsigned Hype" column by *The Source* back in 1991. He was signed to Columbia a few years later, but the deal fell through before recording had even begun. DMX guested on tracks by LL Cool J, Mase and Mic Geronimo (among others), then signed to Def Jam in 1997. His debut album *It's Dark and Hell Is Hot* debuted at number one in May 1998, and eventually sold platinum four times over. *Flesh of My Flesh, Blood of My Blood* followed just six months later (also debuting at the top), and in late 1999 DMX returned with *. . . And Then There Was X*. Once again, he entered the charts at number one. —*John Bush*

● **It's Dark and Hell Is Hot** / May 12, 1998 / Def Jam ♦♦♦♦
A startling debut, *It's Dark and Hell Is Hot* catapulted DMX to instantaneous icon status. Before even listening to the album, DMX's persona pervades via the album title and the cover art. And as one song succeeds another, it quickly becomes evident that DMX's most impressive talent isn't so much his lyrics, or his flow, or his songwriting, or his producers; these are all impressive, no doubt, but it is his dramatic stance as the ideological zenith of urban manhood that makes his music so potent. It's no coincidence that DMX stands tattooed and shirtless on his album cover with a grim expression and high-held face—it's all part of his well-crafted persona. And he spends the entirety of this album theatrically illustrating this dramatic persona. On "Intro," he introduces himself via an extended monologue that seems more of an imposing threat than an introduction. Next comes "Ruff Ryders' Anthem," a simple yet powerful summation of his ethic, followed by one song after another that similarly explores DMX's diametric world of dogs and bitches, heaven and hell, respect and pity, power and weakness, and so on. Not only is this persona crafted with perfection, but it's also accompanied by a myriad of talents: DMX's rousing lyrics, aggressive flow, sincere delivery, and producers Swizz Beatz and Dame Grease's inventive beats are all dazzling. Though he would quickly dilute himself with succeeding albums, DMX is at his peak here, succinctly showcasing one of rap's most well-crafted personas ever. —*Jason Birchmeier*

Flesh of My Flesh, Blood of My Blood / Dec. 15, 1998 / Def Jam ♦♦♦♦
On the heels of his multi-platinum debut *It's Dark and Hell Is Hot*, DMX unleashed his dogs again on an album overflowing with raw energy and spiritual catharsis. The irascible Yonkers MC, 27 at the time of this recording, continues the Ruff Ryder legacy on this follow-up release. DMX's canine split-personality flow is like none other, not only rhyming over tracks, but barking expression over explosive beats. Production here—by Swizz Beats, PK, DJ Shok, Dame Grease—is mostly stripped-down, pure high-tech drum machine and synthesizer combinations that are sure to inspire emotional and adrenal responses in listeners. Although DMX is no new jack, he is a part of a no-frills new breed of MCs that hold nothing back on the microphone; emphasis is on emotion rather than on wordbending. Standout cuts include "Blackout," with guest appearances from fellow hip-hop heavyweights the Lox and Jay-Z; "Coming From," a duet with the queen of hip-hop/R&B, Mary J. Blige, which stuns the ears with a haunting piano loop; "The Omen," a bout with the devil featuring the demonic Marilyn Manson on the hook; and the opening cut on Side B, "Slippin'," an introspective look inside DMX's struggle to stay on top of his art while dealing with the perils of his reality. This is a very spiritual album, a testimony to one artist's struggle with the manifestations of good and evil. The final cut, "Ready to Meet Him," a conversation between DMX and his god, punctuates this realness. —*Michael Di Bella*

. . . And Then There Was X / Dec. 21, 1999 / Def Jam ♦♦♦♦
Though it's DMX's third album in two years, *. . . And Then There Was X* doesn't show much sign of burnout. True, it's similar to his last, which balanced new-school gangsta tracks ("The Professional," "Make a Move") with a couple that question the inevitable trappings that come with success ("Fame," "One More Road to Cross"). And the productions by Swizz Beats, P. Killer Trackz, and Shok—all part of Ruff Ryder Productions, Inc.—are heavily synthesized and occasionally melodramatic, just like both of his previous albums. Even when Swizz Beats' usually reliable productions fall through, DMX brings it all back with his tough rhymes and inventive wordplay. He's still torn between the thug life and spiritual concerns (even including a long prayer in the liner notes), but the most exciting tracks on *. . . And Then There Was X* are good-time joints like "Party Up" and "What's My Name?" —*John Bush*

The D.O.C.

Vocals / West Coast Rap, Gangsta Rap
After the release of his debut album, the career of Texas-born rapper the D.O.C. was shattered by a car crash that almost took his life. Although he could no longer rap like he used to, his former producer Dr. Dre featured the rapper on his groundbreaking album *The Chronic*, which built on the foundation laid by the D.O.C.'s *No One Can Do It Better*. He was also featured on Snoop Doggy Dogg's *Doggystyle*. The D.O.C. returned in early 1996 with *Helter Skelter*, his first album in nearly seven years. The album received mixed reviews and failed to earn a large audience, leaving the charts a few months after its release. —*Stephen Thomas Erlewine*

★ **No One Can Do It Better** / 1989 / Ruthless ♦♦♦♦♦
Despite the D.O.C.'s connection to the members of N.W.A.—including its producer, Dr. Dre and Ruthless Records' founder, the late Eazy-E—not a trace of gangsta rap is to be found on the Dallas rapper's debut album, *No One Can Do It Better*. N.W.A.'s influence on this enjoyable, though not remarkable, disc is musical rather than lyrical. Avoiding social or political commentary, the D.O.C. devotes himself almost entirely to rap's time-honored tradition of boasting. What makes this album come alive is his strong technique and Dre's imaginative production. At a time when so many East Coast rappers were content to sample James Brown over and over—often sounding tired and clichéd in the process—Dre took a much more musical, though equally aggressive approach, emphasizing melody and harmony as well as beats. On *No One*, everything from reggae to heavy metal is fair game for Dre and the D.O.C. This album was still burning up the charts when a car crash almost killed the D.O.C., greatly hindering his rapping abilities. —*Alex Henderson*

Helter Skelter / Jan. 23, 1996 / Giant ♦♦♦
After releasing his debut album *No One Can Do It Better*, the D.O.C. suffered a severe car accident which did irreparable damage to his vocal chords. It left him with a thin, raspy voice that was simply unusable for several years. In 1996, he made his comeback with *Helter Skelter*, an album that illustrated how ragged his voice was. While the backing tracks to *Helter Skelter* are solid, if generic, gangsta rap recorded by a live band, the D.O.C. simply doesn't have enough power to make the songs interesting. Sometimes, the harsh growl of his voice sounds threatening, giving the tracks a menacing power. Too often, the D.O.C. simply sounds tired and worn. It's admirable that he attempted the comeback, but the musical results don't justify the effort. —*Stephen Thomas Erlewine*

Dr. Buzzard's Original Savannah Band

f. 1974, New York, NY, **db.** 1979
Disco
Dr. Buzzard's Original Savannah Band was one of the most original musical ensembles of the disco era. They were formed in the Bronx in 1974 by Stony Browder, Jr. (b. 1949), his brother August Darnell (born Thomas Browder, 1951), singer Cory Daye (b. 1952),

Andy Hernandez (b. 1950), and Mickey Sevilla (b. 1953). The concept of the group was the re-creation of a '30s dance band... a la Cab Calloway, with witty lyrics and a disco beat. All of this was in evidence on their debut album, *Dr. Buzzard's Original Savannah Band*, released in 1976. It produced the dance-floor hit "Cherchez La Femme" and went gold. A follow-up album, *Dr. Buzzard's Original Savannah Band Meets King Pennett*, was less successful. After the release of a third album, *James Monroe HS Presents Dr. Buzzard's Original Savannah Band Goes to Washington*, the group fragmented, with Darnell and Hernandez going off to form Kid Creole & the Coconuts. Browder reorganized and issued a Dr. Buzzard's Savannah Band (dropping the "original") album titled *Calling All Beatniks!* in 1984. *—William Ruhlmann*

● **The Very Best of Dr. Buzzard's Original Savannah Band** / Jul. 2, 1996 / RCA ✦✦✦✦✦
Cherchez La Femme: The Very Best of Dr. Buzzard's Original Savannah Band compiles the highlights from the group's first two albums, which featured the kitschy, big band-influenced disco group at the height of their powers. All of the group's hits—"I'll Play the Fool," "Whispering/Cherchez La Femme/Se Si Bon," "Sour and Sweet/Lemon in the Honey"—are included on the collection, as well as a number of first-rate album tracks, making it not only the perfect place to start, but also the only Dr. Buzzard album any fan needs to own. *—Stephen Thomas Erlewine*

Dr. Dre (Andre Young)

b. Feb. 18, 1965
Producer, Vocals, Keyboards / West Coast Rap, G-Funk, Gangsta Rap
More than any other rapper, Dr. Dre was responsible for moving away from the avant-noise and political stance of Public Enemy and Boogie Down Productions, as well as the party vibes of old school rap. Instead, Dre pioneered gangsta rap and his own variation of the sound, G-Funk. BDP's early albums were hardcore but cautionary tales of the criminal mind, but Dre's records with N.W.A. celebrated the hedonistic, amoralistic side of gang life. Dre was never much of a rapper—his rhymes were simple and his delivery was slow and clumsy—but as a producer, he was extraordinary. With N.W.A. he melded the noise collages of the Bomb Squad with funky rhythms. On his own, he reworked George Clinton's elastic funk into the self-styled G-Funk, a slow-rolling variation that relied more on sound than content. When he left N.W.A. in 1992, he founded Death Row Records with Suge Knight, and the label quickly became the dominant force in mid-'90s hip-hop thanks to his debut, *The Chronic*. Soon, most rap records imitated its sound, and his productions for Snoop Doggy Dogg, Warren G and Blackstreet were massive hits. For nearly four years, G-funk dominated hip-hop, and Dre had enough sense to abandon it and Death Row just before the whole empire collapsed in late 1996. Dre retaliated by forming a new company, Aftermath, and while it was initially slow getting started, his bold moves forward earned critical respect. *—Stephen Thomas Erlewine*

★ **The Chronic** / Dec. 15, 1992 / Death Row ✦✦✦✦✦
With its stylish, sonically detailed production, Dr. Dre's 1992 solo debut *The Chronic* transformed the entire sound of West Coast rap. Here Dre established his patented G-funk sound: fat, blunted Parliament-Funkadelic beats, soulful backing vocals, and live instruments in the rolling bass lines and whiny synths. What's impressive is that Dre crafts tighter singles than his inspiration George Clinton—he's just as effortlessly funky, and he has a better feel for a hook, a knack that improbably landed gangsta rap on the pop charts. But none of *The Chronic*'s legions of imitators were as rich in personality, and that's due in large part to Dre's monumental discovery, Snoop Doggy Dogg. Snoop livens up every track he touches, sometimes just by joining in the chorus—and if *The Chronic* has a flaw, it's that his relative absence from the second half slows the momentum. There was nothing in rap quite like Snoop's singsong, lazy drawl (as it's invariably described), and since Dre's true forte is the producer's chair, Snoop is the signature voice. He sounds utterly unaffected by anything, no matter how extreme, which sets the tone for the album's misogyny, homophobia, and violence. The Rodney King riots are unequivocally celebrated, but the war wasn't just on the streets; Dre enlists his numerous guests in feuds with rivals and ex-bandmates. Yet *The Chronic* is first and foremost a party album, rooted not only in '70s funk and soul, but also that era's blue party comedy, particularly Dolemite. Its comic song intros and skits became prerequisites for rap albums seeking to duplicate its cinematic flow; plus, Snoop and Dre's terrific chemistry ensures that even their foulest insults are cleverly turned. That framework makes *The Chronic* both unreal and all too real, a cartoon and a snapshot. No matter how controversial, it remains one of the greatest and most influential hip-hop albums of all time. *—Steve Huey*

First Round Knock Out / May 21, 1996 / Triple X ✦

Back N Tha Day / Sep. 24, 1996 / Blue Dolphin ✦

Dr. Dre Presents the Aftermath / Nov. 26, 1996 / Aftermath/Interscope ✦✦✦
Dr. Dre shifted directions drastically half-way through 1996, leaving Death Row Records and abandoning gangsta rap, claiming that he had "Been There, Done That." So, Dre founded a new record label, Aftermath, and built an artist roster consisting entirely of new, unproven talent. He also decided not to concentrate on rap, signing urban R&B acts as well as hip-hop. Aftermath's initial release was the various-artists compilation *Dr. Dre Presents... The Aftermath* and one listen proves that Dre wasn't kidding when he said he wasn't interested in gangsta anymore. There are a number of rappers on *The Aftermath*, even a handful of hardcore rappers, but nothing fits into the standard G-funk template. The true revelation of the album is Dre's skill for urban R&B and soul, all of which sounds fresh and exciting compared to several of the fairly pedestrian hip-hop tracks. Despite the success of these urban productions, none of the actual performers make much of an impact—the tracks are impressive only because it demonstrates Dre's musical versatilty and skill. In fact, the two tracks that really stand out—Dre's stately, sexy "Been There, Done That" and the powerful "East Coast / West Coast Killas," which features cameos by B-Real, KRS-1, Nas and RBX—are a combination of terrific production and personality, which is usually what results in great singles. But that doesn't mean that *The Aftermath* is a wash-out. Instead, it's a promising fresh start for Dr. Dre that is full of potential and enough great music to make it a vital listen. *—Stephen Thomas Erlewine*

2001 / Nov. 16, 1999 / Aftermath/Interscope ✦✦✦✦
The *Slim Shady* LP announced not only Eminem's arrival, but it established that his producer Dr. Dre was anything but passé, thereby raising expectations for *2001*, the long-anticipated sequel to *The Chronic*. It suggested that *2001* wouldn't simply be recycled *Chronic*, and, musically speaking, that's more or less true. He's pushed himself hard, finding new variations in the formula by adding ominous strings, soulful vocals, and reggae, resulting in fairly interesting recontextualizations. Padded out to 22 tracks, *2001* isn't as consistent or striking as *Slim Shady*, but the music is always brimming with character. If only the same could be said about the rappers! Why does a producer as original as Dre work with such pedestrian rappers? Perhaps it's to ensure his control over the project, or to mask his own shortcomings as an MC, but the album suffers considerably as a result. Out of all the other rappers on *2001*, only Snoop and Eminem—Dre's two great protégés—have character and while Eminem's jokiness still is unpredictable, Snoop sounds nearly as tired as the second-rate rappers. The only difference is, there's pleasure in hearing Snoop's style, while the rest sound staid. That's the major problem with *2001*: lyrically and thematically, it's nothing but gangsta clichés. Scratch that, it's über-gangsta, blown up so large that it feels like a parody. Song after song, there's a never-ending litany of violence, drugs, pussy, bitches, dope, guns, and gangsters. After a full decade of this, it takes real effort to get outraged at this stuff, so chances are, you'll shut out the words and groove along since, sonically, this is first-rate, straight-up gangsta. Still, no matter how much fun you may have, it's hard not to shake the feeling that this is cheap, not lasting, fun. *—Stephen Thomas Erlewine*

Dr. Feelgood

f. 1971
Pub Rock, Rock & Roll
Dr. Feelgood was the ultimate working band. From their formation in 1971 to lead vocalist Lee Brilleaux's untimely death in 1994, the band never left the road, playing hundreds of gigs every year. Throughout their entire career, Dr. Feelgood never left simple, hard-driving rock & roll behind, and their devotion to the blues and R&B earned them a devoted fan base. That following first emerged in the mid-'70s, when Dr. Feelgood became the leader of the second wave of pub-rockers. Unlike Brinsley Schwarz, the laidback leaders of the pub-rock scene, Dr. Feelgood was devoted to edgy, Stonesy rock & roll, and their sweaty live shows—powered by Brilleaux's intense singing and guitarist Wilko Johnson's muscular leads—became legendary. While the group's stripped-down, energetic sound paved the way for English punk rock in the late '70s, their back-to-basics style was overshadowed by the dominance of punk and new wave, and the group had retreated to cult status by the early '80s. *—Stephen Thomas Erlewine*

Down by the Jetty / Jan. 1975 / Grand ✦✦✦✦✦
The CD reissue of this album is a must-own release, even for those who already have one of the Dr. Feelgood anthologies currently available, neither of which has more than three of the 13 tracks here. The 1975 album, a magnificent first album, recorded in pure mono, has been transferred to CD in exemplary form, a clean, sharp, crunchy, close sound that recalls the sonic textures of the Rolling Stones' first album, even as they cross swords with the Stones' arch-rivals of the era, the Animals, with a superb version of "Boom Boom." Released amid the burgeoning radio presence of acts like Thin Lizzy, Blue Öyster Cult, and Kansas, and the growing self-conscious profundity of Bruce Springsteen, *Down by the Jetty* was as refreshingly lean as anything the headline-grabbing '70s punks would later loose on the world, and as stripped down as the most basic roots rock. Lee Brilleaux's singing could go up against Eric Burdon's or Cyril Davies, and even take on elements of a thick rasp vaguely reminiscent of Howlin' Wolf (listen closely to "Roxette"), certainly better than Mick Jagger ever did; and guitarist Wilko Johnson could play Jimmy Reed, Chuck Berry, or Bo Diddley licks with equally imposing (and seemingly effortless) virtuosity. This record was one of the great '70s rock & roll albums, right up there with the Groovies' *Shake Some Action* and anything CCR left listeners, and ran circles around the Rolling Stones' post-*Exile on Main Street* output. The final cut, a killer live medley of "Bonie Maronie"/"Tequila" with guests Brinsley Schwarz and Bob Andrews blowing saxes, was a taste of what they did on stage with astonishing regularity, and could have sent the Ramones back to the drawing board if the Queens-based quartet had heard it. *—Bruce Eder*

● **Malpractice** / Feb. 1975 / Columbia ✦✦✦✦✦
Guitarist Wilko Johnson's songs shine against such inspired covers as "Riot in Cell Block #9." And his Stonesy playing takes no prisoners. *—Bruce Eder*

Stupidity / 1976 / Grand ✦✦✦✦✦
Comprised of recordings taken from 1975 tours, the live *Stupidity* finally captures the relentless, hard-driving energy of Dr. Feelgood at their peak. All the music on *Stupidity* is presented raw and without overdubs, making it clear that the dynamic friction between guitarist Wilko Johnson and vocalist Lee Brilleaux could propel the band toward greatness. While many of the versions here don't differ in form from the original studio versions, these unvarnished performances are considerably more exciting, revealing the Johnson originals "She Does It Right" and "All Through the City" as minor rock & roll classics. *—Stephen Thomas Erlewine*

Sneakin' Suspicion / 1977 / Grand ✦✦✦✦
Wilko Johnson's last album with Dr. Feelgood continues to be dominated by his tough guitar playing, although fewer of his songs are heard. *—Bruce Eder*

Be Seeing You / 1977 / Grand ✦✦✦✦
The Nick Lowe-produced *Be Seeing You*, Dr. Feelgood's first album with guitarist John Mayo, was only slightly weaker than the group's previous records. Although Mayo was still working his way into the band's sound, Dr. Feelgood retained their tough, hard-rocking appeal. *—Stephen Thomas Erlewine*

Private Practice / 1978 / United Artists ✦✦
Although producer Richard Gottehrer gives *Private Practice* a sound that's just a little too clean and restrained, the album nevertheless is a fine set of professional R&B and rock & roll. The material on the album is a little uneven, but with the assistance of Nick Lowe, the Feelgoods wrote a pair of tight, catchy rockers in "Milk and Alcohol" and "It Wasn't Me," which stood out among the entertaining, yet generally generic, songs. *—Stephen Thomas Erlewine*

As It Happens / 1979 / United Artists ✦✦

Let It Roll / 1979 / United Artists ✦✦

A Case of the Shakes / 1980 / United Artists ✦✦✦
A Case of the Shakes, the group's second album recorded with Nick Lowe, proved that Dr. Feelgood's last three records simply captured the band in a transitional phase. On *Shakes*, the band returns to form, ripping through a set of catchy three-chord rockers that are invigorated by Lowe's new wave-tinged production. *—Stephen Thomas Erlewine*

On the Job / 1981 / Liberty ✦✦

Casebook / 1981 / Liberty ✦✦✦✦✦
Although it's far from perfect—"I Can Tell" and "Keep It Out of Sight" are both missing, for instance—*Casebook* is an adequate overview of the group's early records, featuring enough classic material ("Roxette," "She Does It Right," "She's a Wind Up," "Milk and Alcohol") to make it an effective, if flawed, retrospective and introduction. *—Stephen Thomas Erlewine*

Fast Women & Slow Horses / 1982 / Chiswick ✦✦

Doctor's Orders / 1984 / Demon ✦✦✦
Lee Brilleaux returned with a completely new lineup of Dr. Feelgood for *Doctor's Orders*, a record that returned the band to its piledriving R&B and rock & roll roots. At this stage, the band sounds more accomplished and professional than ever before—there's little of the wild energy that distinguished their first records—but that's actually not a bad thing, because they have enough sensibility to be skilled, not slick. Supported by the new band, Brilleaux manages to turn in the grittiest Dr. Feelgood record in years, making *Doctor's Orders* a fine comeback from a band that seemed to have lost the plot. *—Stephen Thomas Erlewine*

Mad Man Blues / 1986 / ID ✦✦✦✦✦
Lee Brilleaux and Dr. Feelgood sound positively revitalized on *Mad Man Blues*, a collection of raw versions of blues standards that is their best album since 1977's *Be Seeing You*. *—Stephen Thomas Erlewine*

Brilleaux / 1986 / Grand ✦✦✦
Lee Brilleaux invested in the groundbreaking British independent label Stiff when it was being launched in the mid-'70s, so it is sort of appropriate that Dr. Feelgood eventually recorded for the label. The only trouble is, it wasn't in 1976, when Stiff and Feelgood were at their peak; it was in 1986, as Stiff was sliding toward bankruptcy and the Doctors were far from their popular heyday. Dave Robinson, in his infinite wisdom, decided that the way to restore both his label and the Feelgoods to their proper glories was by refashioning the band as radio-ready, R&B-tinged popsters. Of course, that ran contrary to the group's entire career, but they decided to follow his advice, and with producer Will Birch, the group assembled their most eclectic batch of songs ever. Although the smoother sound strips much of Feelgood's gritty essence, *Brilleaux* remains a varied, entertaining record—it's a welcome change of pace from the driving rockers, even if it wasn't welcomed by radio as originally planned. *—Stephen Thomas Erlewine*

Classic / 1987 / Stiff ✦
By 1987, Dr. Feelgood had been churning out their raw variety of Canvey R&B for so long that even the newest songs sounded ferociously familiar. But *Classic* probably wasn't the most aptly named album in their canon, simply because it is anything but. No complaints about the music, even allowing for a less-than-enthused take on "See You Later, Alligator." A gritty cover of Dylan's "Highway 61" is utterly inspired, while Will Birch and Kevin Morris had moved firmly ahead as the band's most dynamic source of new material. Even astride the broadest stage on the planet, the Feelgoods were a bar band, grinding out their gravel-edged blues with a bottle in one hand and a switchblade in the other, and *Classic*'s contents spell that out from the start. But somewhere between stage and studio, it all went horribly wrong, and *Classic* emerges so absurdly over-produced that you need to physically hack your way through the horns and backing singers in the hope of finding the band... yes, that's them, that bad-tempered grumble at the back of the room, somewhere behind producer Pip Williams' apparent conviction that a song the caliber of "I Just Wanna Make Love to You" has spent its entire life crying out for a keyboard wash. The Feelgoods made a lot of great albums and a lot of so-so ones. *Classic*, however, is the first that can be called truly awful. And it seems to know it as well—the best song is called "Quit While You're Behind." *—Dave Thompson*

Case History / 1987 / EMI ✦✦✦✦✦
Case History—The Best of Dr. Feelgood is a fine, basic primer of the group's best moments, featuring such Feelgood staples as "She Does It Right," "Roxette," "As Long as the Price Is Right," "She's a Wind Up," "Down at the Doctors" and "Milk and Alcohol." It does shortchange the group's early records somewhat, but it remains a fine single-disc introduction. *—Stephen Thomas Erlewine*

Singles—The UA Years / 1989 / Liberty ✦✦✦✦✦
Singles—The UA Years is a terrific double-album set that chronicles all of Dr. Feelgood's major singles, from 1976's "Roxette" to 1986's "See You Later Alligator." Although the hits-only approach leaves out some major Feelgood songs, *Singles* remains a first-rate retrospective, and for many years, it was the best Dr. Feelgood collection available. The 1997 double-disc *Twenty Five Years of Dr. Feelgood* later replaced *Singles* as the definitive retrospective, yet there are enough songs on this collection to make it worthwhile for serious fans who don't want to spring for either the box set *Lookin' Back* or the entire catalog. *—Stephen Thomas Erlewine*

Live in London / 1990 / Grand ✦✦✦✦

Down at the Doctors / 1995 / Grand ✦✦✦
Down at the Doctors captures Lee Brilleaux's last concert before his death in the spring of 1994. Culled from concerts performed on January 24 and 25, 1994, the set features many of Feelgood's classic songs, including "Milk and Alcohol" and "Down at the Doctors," plus unexpected, delightful covers of Nick Lowe's "Heart of the City" and "Road Runner." It's a surprisingly energetic and thoroughly enjoyable record that serves as an excellent epitaph for Brilleaux, who remained one of the hardest-working performers in rock & roll until the very end. *—Stephen Thomas Erlewine*

Looking Back / Nov. 1995 / EMI ✦✦✦
Theoretically, Dr. Feelgood could have produced a fine multi-disc box set, yet the four-disc *Looking Back* isn't it. Although it contains the group's very best songs, including large portions of *Down by the Jetty* and *Malpractice*, it is cluttered with mediocre latter-day material, and the entire final disc is devoted to Lee Brilleaux discussing his cancer. Although his testimonial is moving, it would have been better heard on a separate disc, not as part of a comprehensive retrospective. Then again, *Looking Back* is filled with so many songs that only serious fans, the kind that would want an interview disc, will find it necessary. For most fans, even those with a fairly deep interest in the band, the comprehensive double-disc *Twenty Five Years of Dr. Feelgood* is a more logical choice. *—Stephen Thomas Erlewine*

25 Years of Dr. Feelgood / Feb. 9, 1999 / Grand ✦✦✦✦
Distilled from the five-CD *Looking Back* box set, *25 Years* is basically everything you want to know about Dr. Feelgood before you take the major step which we all know is inevitable—discovering everything you *need* to know about them. 40 tracks pursue the band from start to finish and beyond—the final rush of cuts includes material from vocalist Lee Brilleaux's last ever live show (the full concert appears on the *Down at the Doctors* album), together with four more from *On the Road Again*, the reborn Doctor's first album with new vocalist Pete Gage. It's stirring, sterling stuff throughout. With only the occasional lapse, the Feelgoods quality control never lapsed for more than a song or two, none of which are included. Rather, this is the Feelgoods for perfectionists, the story of what could have been the most righteous firestorm ever to explode out of mid-'70s Britain. It begins with a clutch of songs drawn from the Wilco Johnson heyday, which put the band on the map and made punk rock a reality. No surprises, no shocks, no disappointments—"Roxette," "She Does It Right," "Back in the Night," "I Can Tell," you can guess the rest. From there, album by album is raised up for inspection, milked of its might and then placed gently down again—only the self-confessedly dire *Classic* is given anything resembling short shrift. Only occasionally do you listen to one song and wish another had taken its place. In fact, the only regret in the whole blessed package is that we will never hear their like again. But at least we heard it once. *—Dave Thompson*

Chess Masters / May 16, 2000 / Grand ✦✦✦
It's easy to be suspicious of the 2000 incarnation of Dr. Feelgood since it not only doesn't contain Lee Brilleaux, the Feelgoods' leader throughout their history, but it doesn't contain any original members at all. Still, the group's comeback effort *Chess Masters* (they should be docked points for titling the record so it seems as if it was part of a reissue series of classic Chess recordings) is a damn good album, one that will surprise neophytes and longtime fans alike. According to Kevin Morris' brief liner notes, he was inspired to give the Feelgoods another chance after Will Birch encouraged him and the band while he was preparing the excellent pub rock history, *No Sleep Til Canvay Island*. Morris agreed with Birch and put together a new version of the band, with the idea of essaying a tribute to Chess Records with their new album (hence the name *Chess Masters*). It is a real testament to Dr. Feelgood that *Chess Masters* doesn't sound rote, even though it contains a number of familiar tunes from the Chess catalog ("Who D You Love," "Killing Floor," "Suzie Q," "Talkin' Bout You," "Don't Start Me Talking," "Hoochie Coochie Man"). They did sprinkle the album with some lesser-known tunes, but the selection of songs matters less than the feeling of the performance. Thankfully, the Feelgoods have captured the sound of a first-rate bar band on a hot night, which means that *Chess Masters* is just a fine listen, from start to finish. Will it make you forget the glory days of *Down by the Jetty*? No, it won't. The band isn't volatile or hot, but it is a lot looser and fun, which is something that many modern-day blues-rock outfits can't claim as characteristics. That's why *Chess Masters* winds up being a better record than even the diehards could have expected, and even if it doesn't find its way onto your turntable all that often, it'll always sound good when it's spun. *—Stephen Thomas Erlewine*

Complete BBC Sessions: 1973-1978 / Sep. 25, 2001 / Grand UK ✦✦✦✦✦

Dr. Hook

f. 1968, New Jersey, **db.** 1972
Pop/Rock, Soft Rock, Country-Rock, AM Pop
This American country-rock band was originally named Dr. Hook and the Medicine Show. Formed in New Jersey in 1968, the original members included Ray Sawyer (b. 1937), Dennis Locorriere (b. 1948), Bill Francis, John David, and George Cummings. First

coming to prominence with material written by Shel Silverstein, the looniness of their stage show transferred to records well, reaching its peak with the mega-hit "The Cover of the Rolling Stone" in 1972. They mellowed their style on record, hitting the charts with ballads as the decade wore on, but they were still crazy in live performances. Sawyer continues to front versions of the band to this day on various oldies package shows, while once lead singer Dennis Locorriere went on to pursue a solo career. —*Cub Koda*

● **Greatest Hits (And More)** / May 1987 / Capitol ✦✦✦✦
It includes "Sexy Eyes," "Sylvia's Mother," "Only Sixteen," "When You're in Love with a Beautiful Woman," and "Cover of the Rolling Stone." —*AMG*

Dr. John (Mac Rebennack)
b. Nov. 21, 1940, New Orleans, LA
Vocals, Keyboards, Piano, Guitar / New Orleans R&B, Piano Blues, Rock & Roll
Although he didn't become widely known until the 1970s, Dr. John had been active in the music industry since the late '50s, when the teenager was still known as Mac Rebennack. A formidable boogie and blues pianist with a lovable growl of a voice, his most enduring achievements have fused New Orleans R&B, rock, and Mardi Gras craziness to come up with his own brand of "voodoo" music. He's also quite accomplished and enjoyable when sticking to purely traditional forms of blues and R&B. On record, he veers between the two approaches, making for an inconsistent and frequently frustrating legacy that often makes the listener feel as if the Night Tripper (as he's nicknamed himself) has been underachieving. Rebennack renamed himself Dr. John the Night Tripper when he recorded his first album, *Gris-Gris*. According to legend, this was hurriedly cut with leftover studio time from a Sonny & Cher session, but it never sounded hastily conceived. In fact, its mix of New Orleans R&B with voodoo sounds and a tinge of psychedelia was downright enthralling, and may have resulted in his greatest album. He began building an underground following with both his music and his eccentric stage presence, which found him conducting ceremonial-type events in full Mardi Gras costume. Dr. John was nothing if not eclectic, and his later albums were granted mixed critical receptions because of their unevenness and occasional excess. —*Richie Unterberger*

Gris-Gris / 1968 / Collectors' Choice Music ✦✦✦✦✦
The most exploratory and psychedelic outing of Dr. John's career, a one-of-a-kind fusion of New Orleans Mardi Gras R&B and voodoo mysticism. Great rasping, bluesy vocals, soulful backup singers, and eerie melodies on flute, sax, and clarinet, as well as odd Middle Eastern-like chanting and mandolin runs. It's got the setting of a strange religious ritual, but the mood is far more joyous than solemn. —*Richie Unterberger*

Babylon / 1969 / Atco ✦✦✦
Dr. John's ambition remained undiminished on his second solo album, *Babylon*, released shortly after the groundbreaking voodoo-psychedelia-New Orleans R&B fusion of his debut, *Gris-Gris*. The results, however, were not nearly as consistent or impressive. Coolly received by critics, the album nonetheless is deserving of attention, though it pales a bit in comparison with *Gris-Gris*. The production is sparser and more reliant on female backup vocals than his debut. Dr. John remains intent on fusing voodoo and R&B, but the mood is oddly bleak and despairing, in comparison with the wild Mardi Gras-gone-amok tone of his first LP. The hushed, damned atmosphere and after-hours R&B sound a bit like Van Morrison on a bummer trip at times, as peculiar as that might seem. "The Patriotic Flag-Waiver" (sic), in keeping with the mood of the late '60s, damns social ills and hypocrisy of all sorts. An FM underground radio favorite at the time, its ambitious structure remains admirable, though its musical imperfections haven't worn well. To a degree, you could say the same about the album as a whole. But it has enough of an eerie fascination to merit investigation. —*Richie Unterberger*

Remedies / 1970 / Atco ✦✦

The Sun, Moon & Herbs / Sep. 1971 / Atco ✦✦✦
Originally intended as a triple album, *The Sun, Moon & Herbs* was chopped up, whittled down and re-assembled into this single-disc release, and while Dr. John never liked this version much, perhaps this single disc is testament to the "less is more" theory. The seven cuts are all quite lengthy and the spells Dr. John and his consorts weave are dark and swampy. "Black John the Conqueror" comes from old Cajun folklore which the good Dr. has modernized and given a beat. The swampy "Craney Crow" is the younger sibling of his earlier "Walk on Guilded Splinters" and has a similar effect on the listener. "Pots on Fiyo (Fils Gumbo)" combines Latin American rhythms with lots of Cajun chants and spells. The vocals are nearly incomprehensible and actually serve as another instrument in the mix. "Zu Zu Mamou" is so thick that you can almost cut the music with a knife. Here, the atmosphere takes on a whole other meaning altogether. *The Sun, Moon & Herbs* is best listened to on a hot, muggy night with the sound of thunder rumbling off in the distance like jungle drums. Dr. John was definitely on to something here, but just what is left up to the listener. —*James Chrispell*

Dr. John's Gumbo / Apr. 1972 / Atco ✦✦✦✦✦
Dr. John's Gumbo bridged the gap between post-hippie rock and early rock & roll, blues and R&B, offering a selection of classic New Orleans R&B, including "Tipitina" and "Junko Partner," updated with a gritty, funky beat. There aren't as many psychedelic flourishes as there were on his first two albums, but the ones that are present enhance his sweeping vision of American roots music. And that sly fusion of styles makes *Dr. John's Gumbo* one of Dr. John's finest albums. —*Stephen Thomas Erlewine*

In the Right Place / Mar. 1973 / Atco ✦✦✦
Dr. John finally struck paydirt here and was certainly *In the Right Place*. With the hit single "Right Place Wrong Time" bounding up the charts, this fine collection saw many unaware listeners being initiated into New Orleans style rock. Also including Allen Tou-

ssaint's "Life" and a funky little number entitled "Traveling Mood," which shows off the good doctor's fine piano styling, and with able help from the Meters as backup group, *In the Right Place* is still a fine collection to own. —*James Chrispell*

Desitively Bonaroo / Apr. 1974 / Atco ✦✦✦
When you latch on to a hit formula, don't mess with it, and that is just what the doctor ordered with *Desitively Bonaroo*. With installment #3 of Dr. John's funky New Orleans styled rock & roll, trying to strike gold again proved elusive. There wasn't the big hit single this time around to help boost sales, and the tunes were starting to sound a little too familiar. While not a carbon copy of his previous releases, *Desitively Bonaroo* was a disappointment to his fans. Good as it was, it was the end of an era for Dr. John and his type of music. —*James Chrispell*

Mos' Scocious: Anthology / Oct. 19, 1993 / Rhino ✦✦✦✦✦
Over his 35 years of recording, Mac "Dr. John" Rebennack has worn many hats, from '50s greasy rock & roller to psychedelic '70s weirdo to keeper of the New Orleans music flame. All of these modes, plus more, are excellently served up on this two-disc anthology. From the early New Orleans sides featuring Rebennack's blistering guitar work ("Storm Warning" and "Morgus the Magnificent") to the fabled '70s sides as the Night Tripper to his present-day status as repository of the Crescent City's noble musical tradition, this is the one you want to have for the collection. —*Cub Koda*

Cut Me While I'm Hot: The Sixties Sessions / 1995 / Magnum ✦✦✦
The liner notes for this 19-song compilation are brief, but at least have the honesty to admit that "the precise details of the circumstances surrounding these recordings may be lost forever." It speculates that the first half of the outtake-sounding program was cut in New Orleans during the first half of the 1960s, while the latter part dates from L.A. sessions from 1965-1967. It actually sounds like much of this postdates the mid-'60s, with a feeling not unlike his early-'70s work. Most of the titles are self-penned, and there are also a few Professor Longhair covers. The material isn't really up to the level of his better early records, and the earlier tracks boast muffled audio (though fidelity is listenable throughout). At the same time, if you like vintage Dr. John, this is not much worse than the official stuff, the jiving throaty vocals, humorous songwriting, and distinctive keyboard playing all in place. It's low on outstanding compositions, but isn't bad at all, meaning there's no need to rush out and buy it, but also that committed fans won't mind having it around. —*Richie Unterberger*

● **The Very Best of Dr. John** / Apr. 25, 1995 / Rhino ✦✦✦✦✦
The Very Best of Dr. John compiles the best moments from the comprehensive double-disc *Anthology*, making it a more effective, and cheaper, introduction for casual fans. —*Stephen Thomas Erlewine*

Medical School: The Early Sessions of Mac "Dr. John" Rebennack / Jun. 22, 1999 / Music Club ✦✦✦✦
Dr. John's early work as a producer, sessionman, and songwriter for Ace Records is legendary, not only among fans of Mac Rebennack but among devotees of New Orleans R&B. Unfortunately, there was no easy way to hear this material until Music Club's 1999 release, *Medical School: The Early Sessions of Mac "Dr. John" Rebennack*. Clocking in at 18 tracks, the disc isn't complete, but it is definitive—all the best-known cuts are here, along with a generous selection of little-known gems. To anyone but scholars and aficionados, most of the names on the compilation will not be familiar (The Ends, Al Reed, Ronnie & the Delinquents, Sugar Boy Crawford, Bobby Hebb, among others), and many of these cuts have never been well-circulated, or even released, but that's what makes the compilation so special. Not only are these lost classics from Dr. John, but these are lost gems from the prime period of New Orleans R&B. And this is not hyperbole—listening to *Medical School*, it's hard not to escape the feeling that almost every song is a hit you've never heard or have forgotten about. The instrumentals are not weak, the novelties (such as "Morgus the Magnificent") are fun, and cuts like "It Ain't No Use," "Bad Neighborhood," "You Don't Leave Me No Choice," and "Keeps Dragging Me On" are simply fantastic, sounding for all the world like classics, not throwaways. And that's the reason why *Medical School* isn't simply a necessary addition to Dr. John's catalog—it's an essential addition to any New Orleans R&B library. —*Stephen Thomas Erlewine*

Hoodoo: The Collection / Jul. 25, 2000 / Music Club ✦✦✦✦

Dr. Octagon (Keith Thornton)
Vocals / Underground Rap, Electronica, Trip-Hop, Hip-Hop
After single-handedly redefining "warped" as the mind and mouth behind the Bronx-based Ultramagnetic MCs, "Kool" Keith Thornton headed for the outer reaches of the stratosphere with this solo project. A one-time psychiatric patient at Bellevue, Keith's lyrical thematics are as free-flowing here as they ever were with the NY trio, connecting up complex meters with fierce, layers-deep metaphors and veiled criticisms of those who "water down the sound that comes from the ghetto." The debut Octagon single, "Earth People," was quietly released in late 1995 on the San Francisco-based Bulk Recordings, and the track spread like wildfire through the hip-hop underground, as did the subsequent self-titled full-length released the following year. *Dr. Octagon's* left-field fusion of sound collage, fierce turntable work, and bizarre, impressionistic rapping found audiences in the most unlikely of places, from hardcore hip-hop heads to jaded rock critics. Although a somewhat sophomoric preoccupation with body parts and scatology tends to dominate the album, Keith's complex weave of associations and shifting references is quite often amazing in its intricacy. By 1999 however, Keith had "killed off" Dr. Octagon and released one album as Kool Keith (*Black Elvis/Lost in Space*) and one as Dr. Dooom (*First Come, First Served*). —*Sean Cooper*

● **Dr. Octagonecologyst [Dr. Octagon]** / May 6, 1996 / DreamWorks ✦✦✦✦✦

Ultramagnetic MC Kool Keith's best-known solo pseudonym is a psychotic gynecologist with a soft spot for porn samples and lazy, textured production by DJs Automator and Shadow. If the slightly misogynistic lyrics get occasionally tedious, most of the rest of this album is next-style, James-Joyce-on-acid-in-the-medical-textbook-section hip-hop, with expert scratches by DJ Q-Bert and consistently inventive (if somewhat lo-fi) production. Originally released on underground hip-hop imprint Bulk Recordings, *Dr. Octagon* was picked up for U.K. release by trip-hop label Mo'Wax (an instrumental version of the album, *Instrumentalyst* was also issued by the label toward the end of the year). Confusingly, the album was then issued again by Geffen sublabel Dreamworks (with whom Keith signed in 1997), adding a few new tracks. *—Sean Cooper*

The Instrumentalyst: Octagon Beats / Dec. 9, 1996 / DreamWorks ♦♦♦
This is essentially the entire *Dr. Octagon* album sans vocals and slightly remixed. If any other artist released an album such as this it would be considered throwaway trash… something for the hardcore fans. But Dr. Octagon's backing tracks are so fresh and original, it's actually nice to just hear the beats minus the rhymes. *—Kembrew McLeod*

Dokken

f. Germany
Pop-Metal, Hair Metal, Heavy Metal, Hard Rock
At a time when the charts were ruled by pop-metal acts, Dokken was a major attraction throughout the 1980s. With vocalist Don Dokken's captivating stage presence and guitarist George Lynch's high-energy style, the band combined rockers and power ballads in order to create a number of best-selling albums. Dokken's roots date back to the late '70s, when Lynch, along with drummer Mick Brown, teamed up with Don Dokken to form the Boyz. In 1981, Don moved to Germany and was signed to Carerre Records. The band, now simply known as Dokken, recorded and released *Breaking the Chains*, their first studio album, in 1983. While the record failed to retain a decent chart position in the U.S., the group was immensely popular in Europe. After a tour in Germany, Dokken was signed to Elektra Records. In 1984, the band released *Tooth and Nail* and found themselves topping the charts worldwide, selling over one million copies in the U.S. alone. Following a tour with the Scorpions, the group recorded *Under Lock and Key* in 1985, which had a similar success due. In 1987, the band released *Back for the Attack*, which featured a track they had written as the subtitle for the third *Nightmare on Elm Street* film, "Dream Warriors." The coinciding music video was their most popular ever, and *Back for the Attack* became Dokken's third record to reach platinum status. The album's subsequent tour resulted in a live compilation, *Beast From the East*, which was released shortly before the band broke up in 1988 due to creative differences. After the disbanding of Dokken, Don pursued a solo career with *Up From the Ashes*, and Lynch formed the Lynch Mob, releasing an album in 1990; both releases failed to chart. In 1992, the band reunited. *—Barry Weber*

The Very Best of Dokken / Jul. 6, 1999 / Rhino ♦♦♦♦♦
Dokken was one of the finest bands to come out of the Los Angeles hair metal scene of the '80s, and *The Very Best of Dokken* proves it. Don Dokken was a terrific singer, and guitarist George Lynch's splashy fretwork was a superb fit. (Bass guitarist Jeff Pilson and drummer Mick Brown were important factors in the group's songwriting as well.) Perhaps it's no surprise that tensions were high between Don Dokken and Lynch, continuing a long tradition pioneered by the Rolling Stones' Mick Jagger and Keith Richards and Deep Purple's Ian Gillan and Ritchie Blackmore. By 1999, Lynch had left the band and been replaced by Winger alumnus Reb Beach. *The Very Best of Dokken* is a great 16-song compilation arranged in chronological order; it's essential listening for anyone interested in Reagan-era hard rock and heavy metal. Dokken's '80s studio albums were occasionally uneven, so this collection, which also includes decent liner notes, is the best place for the uninitiated to start. Highlights include "Breaking the Chains," "Into the Fire," "Just Got Lucky," "Alone Again" (one of the finest power ballads ever), "In My Dreams," "Dream Warriors," and "Burning like a Flame." Other notable tracks include the fiery instrumental "Mr. Scary"; "Walk Away," the sole studio cut on Dokken's 1988 live album, *Beast from the East*; "Mirror Mirror," from Don Dokken's 1990 solo album, *Up from the Ashes*; and the anti-drug "Too High to Fly," from the somewhat underrated yet aptly titled 1995 reunion album, *Dysfunctional*. *—Bret Adams*

Thomas Dolby

b. Oct. 14, 1958, Cairo, Egypt
Vocals, Keyboards, Guitar, Synthesizer / New Wave, Synth Pop
Though he never had many hits, Thomas Dolby became one of the most recognizable figures of the synth-pop movement of early-'80s new wave. Largely, this was due to his skillful marketing. Dolby promoted himself as a kind of mad scientist, an egghead that had successfully harnassed the power of synthesizers and samplers, using them to make catchy pop and light electro-funk. Before he launched a solo career, Dolby had worked as a studio musician, technician, and songwriter; his most notable work as a songwriter was "New Toy," which he wrote for Lene Lovich, and Whodini's "Magic's Wand." In 1981, he launched a solo career, which resulted in a number of minor hits and two big hits—"She Blinded Me with Science" (1982) and "Hyperactive" (1984). Following "Hyperactive," his career faded away, as he began producing more frequently, as well as exploring new synthesizer and computer technology. Dolby continued to record into the '90s, but by that time, he was strictly a cult act. *—Stephen Thomas Erlewine*

The Golden Age of Wireless / Mar. 1982 / Capitol ♦♦♦♦♦
Talk to anyone who was the right age in the early '80s for both pop radio and the dawn of MTV and "She Blinded Me With Science" will inevitably come up. The most famous song from the reissued version of the album, it's a defiantly quirky, strange number that mixes its pop hooks with unusual keyboard melodies pitched very low and a recurrent spoken-word interjection ("Science!") from guest vocalist/video star Magnus Pike. To Dolby's credit, the rest of the album isn't simply that song over and over again, making *Golden Age of Wireless* an intriguing and often very entertaining curio from the glory days of synth-pop. Part of the album's overall appeal is the range of participating musicians, no doubt thanks in part to Dolby's own considerable range of musical work elsewhere. "She Blinded Me With Science" itself features Kevin Armstrong on guitar, Matthew Seligman on bass, megaproducer Robert "Mutt" Lange on backing vocals, and co-production with Tim Friese-Greene. Elsewhere, Andy Partridge contributes harmonica, Mute Records founding genius Daniel Miller adds keyboards, and Lene Lovich adds some vocals of her own. The overall result is still first and foremost Dolby's, with echoes of David Bowie's and Bryan Ferry's elegantly wasted late-'70s personae setting the stage. If anything, *Golden Age of Wireless* is the friendlier, peppier flip side of fellow Bowie obsessive Gary Numan's work, where the melancholy is gentle instead of harrowing. Dolby's melodies are sprightly without being annoyingly perky, his singing warm, and his overall performance a pleasant gem. Especially fine numbers include the amusing romp "Europa and the Pirate Twins" and the nostalgia-touched, just-mysterious-enough "One of Our Submarines." *—Ned Raggett*

The Flat Earth / Feb. 1984 / Capitol ♦♦♦♦♦
A departure from the style of his debut, this moody and atmospheric album adds jazz and Joni Mitchell-esque elements to warm his synth textures. Only "White City" and the single, "Hyperactive!," feature the hard dance beats of his early hits. *—Scott Bultman*

Aliens Ate My Buick / Apr. 1988 / EMI-Manhattan ♦♦
Thomas Dolby didn't do his career much good by waiting four years between album releases. Pop music trends shifted away from the quirky synth-pop Dolby had pioneered in 1983-1984, and though he employed a heavy funk beat aimed at the discos and even covered a George Clinton song, Dolby seemed less a true dancefloor king than a commentator on the same, especially in such songs as the (non-charting) single "Airhead," "Pop Culture," and "The Ability to Swing." Dolby's flirtation with film had also added an eclecticism to his style that embraced '40s jazz vocalese ("The Key to Her Ferrari") and European balladeering ("Budapest By Blimp"). As ever, Dolby was a man of many ideas, but on *Aliens Ate My Buick* they failed to add up to a coherent statement. *—William Ruhlmann*

Astronauts & Heretics / Jul. 1992 / Giant ♦♦♦

Gate to the Mind's Eye / Oct. 18, 1994 / Giant ♦♦♦♦
Soundtrack work suits Thomas Dolby, who here turns in a variety of musical settings for a computer animation video that include everything from moody electronic instrumentals and dance tracks to a '30s pop pastiche complete with horn section ("Nuvague"). Five of the nine tracks have vocals, two of which are contributed by Dr. Fiorella Terenzi. Dolby himself sings, raps, and even murmurs Napoleon's words of love to Josephine. As a non-visual listening experience, it all seems scattered, but *The Gate to the Mind's Eye* demonstrates Dolby's continuing inventiveness. *—William Ruhlmann*

● **The Best of Thomas Dolby: Retrospectacle** / Apr. 4, 1995 / Capitol ♦♦♦♦♦
After what had seemed like a promising start with "She Blinded Me With Science" in 1983, Thomas Dolby only charted with two other singles in the U.S. (though he had nine chart singles in his native U.K., 1981-1992). This 16-track compilation, embracing both his Capitol/EMI and Warner Bros. recordings, demonstrates that Dolby deserved better. His synthesizer-based songs are consistently catchy and clever, and especially notable are early songs like "Urges" and "Leipzig" that have not previously appeared on a U.S. album. "One of Our Submarines," Dolby's cover of Dan Hicks' "I Scare Myself," and "Hyperactive!" all hold up well. Some of the later (non-hit) material from the albums *Aliens Ate My Buick* and *Astronauts & Heretics* is less impressive; a better choice could have been made from those records. But for the most part, this is an efficient collection that justifies its name. *—William Ruhlmann*

Fats Domino (Antoine Domino)

b. Feb. 26, 1928, New Orleans, LA
Vocals, Leader, Songwriter, Piano / New Orleans R&B, Piano Blues, Rock & Roll, R&B
The most popular exponent of the classic New Orleans R&B sound, Fats Domino sold more records than any other Black rock & roll star of the 1950s. His relaxed, lolling boogie-woogie piano style and easygoing, warm vocals anchored a long series of national hits from the mid-'50s to the early '60s. Through it all, his basic approach rarely changed. He may not have been one of early rock's most charismatic, innovative, or threatening figures, but he was certainly one of its most consistent. Domino's first single, 1949's "The Fat Man," is one of the dozens of tracks that have been consistently singled out as a candidate for the first rock & roll record. The record made number two on the R&B charts, sold a million copies, and established a vital production partnership between Fats and Imperial A&R man Dave Bartholomew. Domino didn't really cross over into the pop charts in a big way until 1955, when "Ain't That a Shame" made the Top Ten. Between 1955 and 1963, he racked up an astonishing 35 Top 40 singles, the best (and best-remembered) of which was probably 1956's "Blueberry Hill." Although an active performer in the ensuing decades, his career as an important artist was essentially over in the mid-'60s. He did stir up a bit of attention in 1968 when he covered the Beatles' "Lady Madonna" single, which had been an obvious homage to Fats' style. *—Richie Unterberger*

★ **My Blue Heaven: The Best of Fats Domino** / Jul. 30, 1990 / EMI America ♦♦♦♦♦
For the budget-minded fan, this 20-track single-disc compilation of Fats Domino's Imperial smashes will serve nicely. Not much of his early pre-rock stuff—"The Fat Man" and "Please Don't Leave Me" are all that are here—but there's plenty of his hit-laden output from 1955 on—"Ain't It a Shame," "Blue Monday," "I'm in Love Again," "Blueberry Hill,"

"I'm Ready," among others. One small but substantial difference between this set and the larger packages: It uses non-sped-up masters of his mid-'50s material (some of his hits from this era were mastered slightly faster than true pitch). Even if they're not historically correct, these versions actually sound better. —*Bill Dahl*

☆ **They Call Me the Fat Man: The Legendary Imperial Recordings** / Oct. 22, 1991 / EMI America ✦✦✦✦✦

If you can't quite finance the Bear Family box, this four-disc compilation is the next best thing; an even 100 of the best Imperial sides, including a great many from 1958 on that turn up in crystal-clear stereo (as they also do on the Bear Family package). All the hits are aboard, along with a nice cross section of the important non-hits. The saxes (usually including Herb Hardesty and sometimes Lee Allen) roar with typical Crescent City power, Fats rolls the ivories, and magic happens—over and over again! Another nice booklet with plenty of photos (but a less detailed discography without sideman credits). —*Bill Dahl*

Out of New Orleans / 1993 / Bear Family ✦✦✦✦✦

An amazing piece of work—a massive eight-disc boxed set that contains every one of Fats Domino's 1949-1962 Imperial waxings. That's a tremendous load of one artist, but the legacy of Domino and his partner Dave Bartholomew is so consistently innovative and infectious that it never grows tiresome for a second. From the clarion call of "The Fat Man," Domino's 1949 debut, to the storming "Dance with Mr. Domino" in 1962, he typified everything charming about Crescent City R&B, his Creole patois and boogie-based piano a non-threatening vehicle for the rise of rock & roll. A thick, photo-filled book accompanies the disc, and there's an exhaustive discography that makes sense of Domino's many visits to Cosimo Matassa's studios. If you care about Fats Domino, this is the package to purchase! —*Bill Dahl*

Fat Man: 25 Classic Performances / Aug. 20, 1996 / Capitol ✦✦✦✦

Ostensibly replacing the compact disc *My Blue Heaven* as the definitive single-disc collection of Fats Domino's biggest hits singles, *Fat Man: 25 Classic Performances* features most of Fats Domino's biggest hits, but it inexplicably neglects such hits as "Walking to New Orleans," "Be My Guest" and "I'm Gonna Be a Wheel Someday." The only justification for the omission of so many hits is that the intent of the collection is to portray Fats Domino as the R&B master that he undoubtedly is, but seldom receives credit for being. Nevertheless, *Fat Man* masquerades as a greatest hits collection, billing itself as "25 Classic Performances," which leads you to believe that it is simply another hits collection. As an R&B compilation, *Fat Man* is strong—and, like any proper R&B collection, it presents the singles at the speed they were recorded at, not the sped-up versions that became hits—but because it lacks these hits, *My Blue Heaven* remains a preferable collection and introduction to Fats. —*Stephen Thomas Erlewine*

☆ **Legends of the 20th Century** / Nov. 2, 1999 / Capitol ✦✦✦✦✦

Released as part of Capitol/EMI's *Legends of the 20th Century* series, this single-disc collection is an excellent summary of Fats Domino's legendary singles. Technically, it doesn't have all the hits—it's missing such gold singles as "Bo Weevil," "It's You I Love," and "Wait and See"—but it has every classic: "The Fat Man," "Ain't It a Shame," "I'm In Love Again," "My Blue Heaven," "Blueberry Hill," "Blue Monday," "I'm Walkin'," "Whole Lotta Loving," "I'm Ready," "I Want to Walk You Home," "I'm Gonna Be a Wheel Some Day," "Be My Guest," "Walking to New Orleans," "My Girl Josephine," and "Let the Four Winds Blow," among others. Yes, it's essentially the same as many of the other greatest hits collection, but it's done well, sounds good, and, at 25 tracks, is quite generous, making it an ideal choice for most listeners. —*Stephen Thomas Erlewine*

Don & Dewey

f. 1957, Pasadena, CA
R&B

Wailing in tandem like twin Little Richards, Don & Dewey cut numerous blistering rockers for Specialty from 1957 to 1959 without registering a single hit, only to see other acts revive their songs to much greater acclaim. Don Harris (b. 1938) and Dewey Terry (b. 1938) were born and raised in Pasadena, CA, joining a group called the Squires and recording for Vita before branching off on their own. Their Specialty output included the savage rockers "Jungle Hop," "Koko Joe" (written by Sonny Bono), and "Justine," the latter pair later covered by the Righteous Brothers. Don & Dewey's Specialty discography also includes the original "I'm Leavin' It up to You," a hit for Dale & Grace; "Big Boy Pete," ditto for the Olympics; and "Farmer John," the Premiers' only smash. Don laid down his guitar for a violin during the '60s and, billed as "Sugarcane" Harris, sawed his rocked-out fiddle beside John Mayall and Frank Zappa. —*Bill Dahl*

● **Jungle Hop** / 1991 / Specialty ✦✦✦✦✦

Wild '50s rock & roll duets from Don "Sugarcane" Harris and Dewey Terry, backed by the same Specialty house band that recorded with Little Richard and others. A lot of these songs were covered by other people, but *Nobody* cut these guy's versions. —*George Bedard*

Don & Juan

f. 1962
Doo Wop

Don & Juan, born Claude Johnson and Roland Trone, scored one big hit in 1962 entitled "What's Your Name." The single has become a doo-wop classic, but also its smooth ballad style also hints at the beginning of the emergence of soul.

Johnson and Trone got their start in a Brooklyn band called the Genies. In 1959 they released an uptempo single entitled "Who's That Knocking" on Shad records. The song reached number 71 on the U.S. charts. They were unable to reproduce that success and were dropped from the label. Johnson and Trone continued to perform sporadically while working as painters on Long Island, and were rediscovered by an agent named Peter Paul who

arranged for them to sign with Big Top Records. They changed the name of their duo to Don & Juan and recorded "What's Your Name," which eventually peaked at number 7 on the charts. Only one other single, "Magic Wand," charted, though the band continued to record until 1967. Trone died in 1983 and Johnson later revived the act with another former member of the Genies, Alexander Faison, who stepped in as the new Juan. —*Stacia Proefrock*

What's Your Name: Golden Classics / 1995 / Collectables ✦✦✦✦✦

A nice 14-track collection of this obscure one-hit wonder duo from the early '60s. Apartment painters Claude Johnson and Roland Trone—Don and Juan respectively—contributed one hit to the history of rock & roll, "What's Your Name," a track that skirts the fine line between old '50s doo wop and the emerging proto-soul style waiting in the wings. The duo never found another hit, but tracks like "Chicken Necks," "Two Fools Are We," and "Magic Wand" are equally fine examples of their sound. A minor collection by these one-hit wonders, but great fun anyway. —*Cub Koda*

Bo Donaldson

b. Jun. 13, 1954, Cincinnati, OH
Vocals / Bubblegum

Bo Donaldson & the Heywoods shot to prominence in 1974 with "Billy, Don't Be a Hero." Sales that topped three million copies brought the group a gold record. The single spent two weeks in the top spot on the charts. The number one single was the band's greatest success, but it didn't mark the first time that the group charted. Bo Donaldson & the Heywoods made a showing on the charts with "Someone Special" in 1972 and "Deeper and Deeper" the following year. The band was ten years old when "Billy, Don't Be a Hero" made such a splash, and it had already performed as the opening act for such artists as Herman's Hermits, the Box Tops, the Osmond Brothers, the Rascals, the Grass Roots, and Paul Revere & the Raiders. The group also performed on *American Bandstand.* After "Billy, Don't Be a Hero," the band took "Who Do You Think You Are" into the Top 20. "The Heartbreak Kid" followed, reaching the Top 40. The group charted again with "House on Telegraph Hill" and "Our Last Song Together."

Donaldson, whose real name is Robert Walter Donaldson, sang and played keyboard and the trumpet. The group also included lead vocalist James Michael Gibbons on bass and trumpet; lead vocalist Richard Leon Joswick on percussion; Gary James Coveyou on vocals, woodwinds, and reeds; David Alan Krock on vocals, trumpet, and bass; Richard Brunetti on vocals, percussion, and drums; and Earl Baker Scott on vocals and guitar. Danny Loveland, a co-vocalist on the Heywoods' number one single, dropped out in 1975 to pursue a solo career and record "Black Is Black." Originally a drummer, Loveland began singing because the group kept losing its lead singers. When he gave up singing, the Kansas native launched a disco that he named Backstage. He went on to establish a restaurant in Bangkok, Thailand. —*Linda Seida*

● **The Best of Bo Donaldson and the Heywoods** / Jun. 18, 1996 / Varese Sarabande ✦✦✦✦✦

Bo Donaldson & the Haywoods are remembered for one hit—the silly number one hit "Billy, Don't Be A Hero." They happened to have four other hits—"Special Someone," "Who Do You Think You Are?," "The Heartbreak Kid," and "Our Last Song Together"—but "Billy, Don't Be A Hero" was one of the cornerstone songs of early '70s AM radio and overshadowed the rest of their material. That's not the case on Varese Sarabande's *Best of Bo Donaldson & the Haywoods*, a single-disc collection which is easily the most comprehensive compilation that could ever be assembled on the pop group. Most of the songs sound like variations on "Billy, Don't Be A Hero" or are sweet, polished love ballads. Certainly, the quality of the songwriting isn't very high, but fans of the *sound* of early '70s pop should find much of this collection enjoyable. Nevertheless, the compilation doesn't do much to erase the image of Bo Donaldson & the Haywoods as a one-hit wonder. —*Stephen Thomas Erlewine*

Lonnie Donegan

b. Apr. 29, 1931, Glasgow, Scotland
Vocals, Guitar, Banjo / British Folk, Rockabilly, Skiffle

To look at Lonnie Donegan today, in pictures taken 40 years ago when he was topping the British charts and hitting the top Ten in America, dressed in a suit, his hair cut short and strumming an acoustic guitar, he looks like a musical non-entity. But in 1954, before anyone (especially anybody in England) knew what rock & roll was, Donegan was cool, and his music was hot. He's relatively little remembered outside of England, but Donegan shares an important professional attribute with Elvis Presley, Bill Haley, the Beatles, the Rolling Stones, and the Sex Pistols—he invented a style of music, skiffle, that completely altered the pop culture landscape and the youth around him, and for a time completely ruled popular music through that new form. What's more, his music, like that of Presley and Haley, was vital to the early musical careers and future histories of the Beatles, the Stones, and hundreds of other groups. And he did it in 1954, before Elvis was known anywhere outside of Memphis and before Bill Haley was perceived as anything but a western swing novelty act. —*Bruce Eder*

● **The EP Collection** / 1992 / See For Miles ✦✦✦✦✦

In England, before the Beatles and the Rolling Stones came along, EPs (four-song extended play singles) outsold albums. This compilation of the best of Donegan's EPs is the definitive Lonnie Donegan collection, eclipsing any album or CD that existed previously on his work. It is certainly the best hits compilation there ever has been on him, containing the 1956 hit "Rock Island Line" and its B-side, "Digging My Potatoes," plus 23 more fairly hard-rocking tracks dating up through 1962, all very crisply remastered, with original artwork represented and a very detailed biography. —*Bruce Eder*

More Than "Pie in the Sky" / 1993 / Bear Family ✦✦✦✦✦

Eight CDs, and nearly 10 hours of music may seem like overkill to most onlookers, but this is a boxed set that truly justifies itself, once you've listened to it. What is here is amazing—this set presents Lonnie Donegan as the prodigious musical talent he actually was, a white bluesman extraordinaire and a country, rockabilly, and gospel singer of no small merit as well. No, he didn't have Elvis Presley's voice, or his way with the girls, but Donegan had musical talent by the ton—his blues stylings on songs like the previously unreleased alternate take of Lonnie Johnson's "I've Got Rocks In My Bed" or Leroy Carr's "Hoe Long How Long Blues" will astonish anyone who thinks that British blues began with the Rolling Stones or even with Alexis Korner (who had never been anywhere near a recording studio when Donegan cut some of this stuff); his covers of numbers by Cole Porter (in a blues style, no less) and Bob Dylan (from Donegan's final Pye album) will amaze anyone who never got past "Rock Island Line." And the unedited live set from Conway Hall in 1957 will delight anyone who likes great, exciting concert recordings. And most of the rest is of as high quality as these rarities. The only drawback is the $180 price-tag, but that's the cost of quality. The profusely annotated and illustrated booklet is an added bonus. —*Bruce Eder*

The EP Collection, Vol. 2 / 1994 / See For Miles ✦✦✦✦
Surprisingly strong (and nearly as important as Volume One) collection of the rest of Donegan's classic skiffle material, including the complete contents of his live EP *Donegan on Stage*. The novelty tunes share space with some surprisingly solid early rock & roll, and all of it is fast-paced and entertaining. —*Bruce Eder*

Showcase . . . Plus / Mar. 2000 / Sequel ✦✦✦✦✦
Sequel Records has decided to honor Lonnie Donegan with its *Lonnie 2000* series, reissuing all of his classic Pye/Nixa sides from 1955 through 1962, and *Showcase . . . Plus* is the place to begin. The first 13 tracks on this 26-song CD are from various EPs and singles cut by Donegan in late 1955 and early 1956, doing a wide range of country blues and folk material, with repertory by Leroy Carr, Leadbelly, and Woody Guthrie interspersed among country and cowboy numbers, work songs, and field hollers that go back too far for authorship to be identified. There's also one fine Chris Barber/Lonnie Donegan original, "Harmonica Blues," dating from 1955 and never before issued. Apart from the excellent sound, the surprising element of this body of songs is just how bracing it remains almost 50 years after it was recorded—the tendency is to dismiss the skiffle boom as an embarrassing fluke, but in fact the level of musicianship achieved by Donegan and company (especially guitarist/singer Dick Bishop) was exceptional, and their feel for the material was a match for that of any white Americans this side of Bob Dylan. Additionally, Donegan was extremely charismatic as a performer, and not just within the context of his time—he would have found some kind of audience at almost any point in the 1950s in England. —*Bruce Eder*

Lonnie . . . Plus / Apr. 2000 / Sequel ✦✦✦✦✦
This expanded version of Lonnie Donegan's second album (a 10" LP) from September 1958 reaches all the way to late 1957 and forward to the spring of 1959 for singles and B-sides to add on, and it is also augmented by several outtakes—Leadbelly's "Shorty George" and two alternate versions of the Woody Guthrie-associated number "Hard Travellin'," plus the rebel song "My Only Son Was Killed in Dublin (The Dying Rebel)." The original album contained what was probably the best single blues number of Donegan's career, the five and a half minute long "I've Got Rocks In My Bed." It is still the major track on this CD, but the mix of sounds—particularly folk and gospel—makes this a very diverse album, and the additional singles only enhance its value. The husband-and-wife folk duo Miki and Griff are present on five songs, singing and playing behind Donegan on blues-influenced folk numbers like "Sally Don't You Grieve" and cheerful ballads like "Nobody Loves Like an Irishman." We're also treated to the B-side "Grand Coulee Dam," which was featured in a live performance clip in the 1957 movie *The Six-Five Special*; bluesy outings like "Ham 'n' Eggs" and "Hard Travellin'" (which appears in three completely difference versions, each better than the last) on which Donegan is near his best, bracing and exciting; and he gives us a sample of his skills as a jazz interpreter on "Baby Don't You Know That's Love." His singing range is more than a little impressive, and the only flaw in this album, as opposed to its predecessor, is that Jimmy Currie simply isn't as aggressive or inventive a guitarist as his two predecessors, Dickie Bishop and Denny Wright. —*Bruce Eder*

The Donnas
Punk-Pop, Punk Revival, Alternative Pop/Rock, Hard Rock
Still having to deal with the ordeals of final exams, dumb jocks and other typical high school melodramas was when the Donnas first got together. While everybody else in their grade was more concerned about whom they should take to the prom, vocalist Donna A., guitarist Donna R. bassist Donna F. and drummer Donna C. were all about rock & roll and flipping the bird to everyone they couldn't stand in their class. After releasing a handful of singles and a self-titled LP on the small Superteem label, Lookout! Records released *American Teenage Rock & Roll Machine* in 1998. Upon graduating from high school, the Donnas released the *Speedin' Back to My Baby* EP along with the re-issue of their first full-length, followed by a tour of the United States and Japan, all while under the label support of Lookout! Records. After a split EP with New York's the Toilet Boys, the group released the full-length *Get Skintight* in 1999. *The Donnas Turn 21* followed in 2001. —*Mike DaRonco*

American Teenage Rock & Roll Machine / Jan. 27, 1998 / Lookout ✦✦✦
The Donnas' *American Teenage Rock & Roll Machine* recalls the trashy spirit of the Runaways or the Ramones, delivering infectious punk-pop workouts like "You Make Me Hot," "Leather on Leather" and "Speed Demon." —*Jason Ankeny*

Donnas / Jul. 28, 1998 / Lookout ✦✦✦✦✦

The Donnas' self-titled debut album presents the girls as the most convincing Ramones ripoff band ever. Song titles like "Get Rid of That Girl," "I Don't Want to Go to School" and "Teenage Runaway" should make this painfully obvious. Their three-chord punk songs have an innocent sound which is upended, as most of their lyrics consist of tales of teenage rebellion ("I Don't Wanna Go" and "Get Rid of That Girl") and drug use ("Huff All Night," "Everybody's Smoking Cheeba" and "Friday Fun"). What makes this slight record so much fun is the tempo of the music, the lo-fidelity recording, and high-school cheerleader backing vocals that give the songs a "rah-rah" excitement. Like most complaints about the Ramones, all of the songs on *The Donnas* sound the same—but at least it's a good song. —*Brian Flota*

● **Get Skintight** / Jun. 8, 1999 / Lookout/Mordam ✦✦✦✦
It took almost no time for the Donnas to become an underground rock sensation, favorites of punk scensters and journalists. Almost overnight, the teen quartet released their debut, graduated from high school and then started popping up in the most unlikely places, including the Rose McGowan teen flick, *Jawbreaker*. It wasn't exactly like they were omnipresent, but the Donnas certainly were primed to break into the major leagues with their second set of Ramones-styled punk-pop, *Get Skintight*. Stylistically, there is no change from the debut, but *Get Skintight* does boast a better, catchier set of songs and a ferocious group of performances. The Donnas are undeniably good—they have the songs and the hooks, a great attitude and a great look—but there's something a little strange about a group of teens hero-worshipping music that was made before their birth. It could be argued that the Ramones did the same thing, but not only did they build on music from their youth, they bent the rules. The Ramones were ironic post-modernists, twisting around bubblegum, surf and teen-pop with campy glee. It made their music vibrant and unpredictable and deep, while still being pure fun. The Donnas, in turn, play by the rules the Ramones wrote with their debut album, without any irony or camp—it's straight-ahead party music, with no apologies. It's the primary difference between the two groups, what separates a good party band from a transcendent one. Ultimately, such criticisms seem like quibbling, because *Get Skintight* isn't meant as anything other than a great punk party record, which is exactly what it is. But that difference is why listeners raised on old-school punk may find the album a little off. —*Stephen Thomas Erlewine*

The Donnas Turn 21 / Jan. 23, 2001 / Lookout ✦✦✦
There's a double-edged sword in the title of *The Donnas Turn 21*—they're now old enough to drink, but a little too old for Barely Legal, thereby whittling their core audience of frustrated middle-aged rockers by a third, maybe. Then, there's the sound itself, which is less Ramones than retooled Runaways, a band that was never as wild, popular, or good as their revisionist reputation claims. The girls do their best to seem like crazy sluts, "spending every night in a different state/spending every night with a different date—I'd do them all if I could," which just winds up just sounding a little desperate. Screwing police officers, wearing hot pants, dissing critics that gave them bad reviews, huffing and binge-drinking, giving midnight blowjobs, covering Judas Priest, and giving props to Cheech, Chong, and Schlitz—if this is the music of young rock & rollers, then Neil Sedaka is still hip. At least this time they wrote their own tunes, so I guess they mean it, man, but it can't help but feel a little pre-packaged and processed for an audience that was into this music before the Donnas were born. Occasionally, the band winds up with a hook and some momentum, as on "Drivin' Thru My Heart," but musically they're never as gaudy and raunchy as they should be; it says something if the Judas Priest cover is the only thing that really hits hard. Face it, if *The Donnas Turn 21* sounded as shamelessly sexy as the lyrics and tarted-up images, it'd be a hell of a little rock & roll record. Instead, this inspires feelings of guilt instead of guilty pleasure. —*Stephen Thomas Erlewine*

Donovan
b. May 10, 1946, Glasgow, Scotland
Vocals, Harmonica, Guitar / British Psychedelia, Psychedelic Pop, British Folk, Folk-Rock, Psychedelic, British Invasion, Singer/Songwriter
Upon his emergence during the mid-'60s, Donovan was anointed "Britain's answer to Bob Dylan," a facile but largely unfounded comparison which compromised the Scottish folk-pop troubadour's own unique vision. Where the thrust of Dylan's music remains its bleak introspection and bitter realism, Donovan fully embraced the wide-eyed optimism of the flower-power movement, his ethereal, ornate songs radiating a mystical beauty and child-like wonder. For better or worse, his recordings remain quintessential artifacts of the psychedelic era, capturing the peace-and-love idealism of their time to perfection. Born in Glasgow in 1946, Donovan Leitch was tapped as a regular on the television pop showcase *Ready, Steady, Go!* He soon issued his debut single "Catch the Wind," earning the first round of Dylan comparisons with his ramshackle folk sound and ragamuffin look. Signing with Epic in 1966, he released his breakthrough album, *Sunshine Superman*, which in its exotic arrangements and pointedly psychedelic lyrical outlook heralded a major shift from his previous work; the title track topped the charts on both sides of the Atlantic, with the enigmatic "Mellow Yellow" reaching the number two spot a few months later. Donovan remained a chart fixture throughout 1967, generating a series of hits including "Epistle to Dippy," "There Is a Mountain," and "Wear Your Love Like Heaven." In 1968 Donovan scored a Top Five smash with the hallucinatory title cut of *The Hurdy Gurdy Man*. He retreated to Ireland in 1970, and California in 1974, living quietly and emerging only occasionally. In 1996, Donovan released his comeback LP, *Sutras*, helmed by producer-du-jour Rick Rubin. —*Jason Ankeny*

Catch the Wind / Jun. 1965 / Castle ✦✦

Fairytale / Nov. 1965 / Castle ✦✦

Sunshine Superman / Sep. 1966 / Epic ✦✦✦✦
Paced by the title track, one of Donovan's best singles, 1966's *Sunshine Superman* heralded the coming psychedelic age with a new world/old world bent: several ambitious psychedelic productions and a raft of wistful folk songs. Producer Mickie Most fashioned a new sound for the Scottish folksinger, a sparse, swinging, bass-heavy style perfectly complementing Donovan's enigmatic lyrics and delightfully skewed, beatnik delivery. The two side-openers, "Sunshine Superman" and "Season of the Witch," are easily the highlights of the album; the first is the quintessential bright summer sing-along, the second a chugging eve-of-destruction tale. The rest of *Sunshine Superman* is filled with lengthy, abstract, repetitive folk jams, perfect for lazy summer afternoons, but more problematic when close attention is paid. Accompanied by acoustic guitar and a chamber quartet, the second track, "Legend of a Girl Child Linda," plods on for nearly seven minutes, Donovan's hippie-dippie delivery rendering "lace" into "layyyzzz." After that notable low point, he performs much better, tingling a few spines with his enunciation on the ancient-sounding folksongs "Guinevere," "Three King Fishers," and "Ferris Wheel." Elsewhere, he salutes the Jefferson Airplane on "The Fat Angel" and fellow British folkie Bert Jansch on "Bert's Blues." Donovan's songs are quite solid, but Mickie Most's insistence on extroverted productions (it would grow even more pronounced with time) resulted in a collection of songs that sound good on their own but aren't very comfortable in context. *—John Bush*

Mellow Yellow / Jan. 1967 / Epic ✦✦✦✦
Mellow Yellow is actually more diverse in its sounds than *Sunshine Superman*, drawing on some of the same era's better follow-up material but also reaching back somewhat further for repertory. It was, as one could rightly guess, a by-product of the late-1966 hit title track, but the songs dated back in some instances as much as a year, to a point prior to Donovan's having made the leap from folk to pop artist. "Mellow Yellow" itself was cut after "Sunshine Superman" and boasted one of the earliest arrangements by John Paul Jones to achieve international recognition (although not without some resistance from Donovan himself), with its broad, biting brass sound. The next two tracks, however, reached back to the singer-songwriter's earlier acoustic/folk songbag, and a very different point in his career—the reflective, somber "Writer in the Sun" was written in Greece during the spring of 1966, when it looked as though Donovan's career was in danger of ending due to legal problems. By contrast, the hauntingly beautiful "Sand and Foam" dated from a somewhat happier visit to Mexico. "The Observation" manages to quote the album's title tune obliquely in its bass-line, even as the singer veers close to a beat-style poetry recital. "Museum," which sounds at times almost like an artier sequel to "Sunshine Superman" and a precursor to "There Is a Mountain" in its word pattern, breaks up the succession of blues settings on the album's second side, as does the jazz-flavored "Hampstead Incident." The album ends with "Sunny South Kensington," an upbeat number driven by radiant (albeit name-dropping) lyrics, Eric Ford's crunchy guitar (emulating his contribution to "Sunshine Superman"), Shawn Phillips' sitar, and an economical arrangement by John Cameron (who also plays the harpsichord). *—Bruce Eder*

For Little Ones / Dec. 1967 / Epic ✦✦

Wear Your Love Like Heaven / Dec. 1967 / Epic ✦✦✦✦✦
Separately released in the US as the "pop" record from 1967's double-LP *A Gift from a Flower to a Garden*, *Wear Your Love Like Heaven* stands on its own as one of the brightest, most pleasant works Donovan ever recorded. The title track and "Oh Gosh" were the only nods to the charts (and tellingly, the only songs produced by Mickie Most). For once in Donovan's career, the remainders far outshone the singles, with brisk, breezy productions and the thoughtful playing of an actual band behind Donovan—usually just bass, keyboards, and soft, whisking drums or bongos. Donovan's voice is better than ever, playful and unassuming on romps like "Mad John's Escape," "Skip-A-Long Sam," and "Oh Gosh," while expressive and controlled for the slower material. He also makes evocative folkie nostalgia work much better than it should on "Sun" and "Little Boy in Corduroy," helped by the breathy flute playing of Harold McNair. *—John Bush*

A Gift from a Flower to a Garden / Dec. 1967 / Collectors' Choice Music ✦✦✦✦✦
Rock music's first two-LP box set has been reissued on one CD. Even better, enough time has passed that the music has overcome its original shortcomings and now stands out as a prime artifact of the flower-power era that produced it. The music still seems a bit fey, and overall more spacy than the average Moody Blues album of this era, but the sheer range of subjects and influences make this a surprisingly rewarding work. Essentially two albums recorded simultaneously in the summer of 1967, the electric tracks include Jack Bruce among the session players. The acoustic tracks represent an attempt by Donovan to get back to his old sound and depart from the heavily electric singles ("Sunshine Superman," etc.) and albums he'd been doing—it is folkier and bluesier (in an English folk sense) than much of his recent work. *—Bruce Eder*

Donovan in Concert / Jul. 1968 / Epic ✦✦

Hurdy Gurdy Man / Oct. 1968 / Epic ✦✦✦
Having Mickie Most as producer could be a double-edged sword. On *The Hurdy Gurdy Man*, his over-ambitious nature and scattershot production sense occasionally sabotaged Donovan's songs rather than emphasizing their strengths. (The credits shamelessly list "Produced by Mickie Most" *and* "A Mickie Most Production," right next to each other.) As with the last few LPs, the program began with the hit title track (one of Donovan's best singles), a dim, dark song balancing psychedelia with the heavier, earthier rock championed during 1968 by Dylan and the Beatles. Though the next two tracks—an eerie, trance-like "Peregrine" and the endearing acoustic number "The Entertaining of a Shy Girl"—are excellent performances, any sense of mood is soon shattered by a hopelessly overblown music-hall showtune, "As I Recall It." This terrible problem of pacing and song placement continually afflicts *The Hurdy Gurdy Man*, rendering ineffective many solid songs. As for the writing, Donovan certainly wasn't expanding his songbase; as usual, the album overflowed with playful songs on girls ("West Indian Lady," "Jennifer Juniper") and pastoral themes ("The River Song," "A Sunny Day," "The Sun Is a Very Magic Fellow"). Most of these featured more inventive, sympathetic accompaniment, combined with Donovan's usual spot-on delivery. Despite the great songs and (usually) solid performances though, *The Hurdy Gurdy Man* is a very difficult listen. *—John Bush*

Barabajagal / Aug. 11, 1969 / Epic ✦✦✦✦
Barabajagal found Donovan making a tentative move from folkie psychedelia into acid-rock, drafting the Jeff Beck Group for instant credibility. Though Beck appeared on only two tracks, Donovan actually worked very well fronting a rock band, getting into a vicious groove on the title track. Elsewhere, things were much the same, paced by a yearning end-of-summer tale ("Where Is She"), an innocent, child-like round ("Happiness Runs"), and the downright dippy "I Love My Shirt." Also included was "To Susan on the West Coast Waiting," Donovan's first direct protest song in several years ("From Andy in Vietnam fighting/To Susan on the West Coast waiting"). The song was recorded in Los Angeles, along with the extended jam "Atlantis," a sub-aquatic fairy tale reminiscent of "Hey Jude." *Barabajagal* hangs together better than most Donovan LPs; it has more of a consistent sound than earlier LPs, and the songs are among his best. *—John Bush*

Open Road / 1970 / Epic ✦✦✦
Although it was a disappointing seller and signaled the start of Donovan's commercial decline, *Open Road* could have been a new beginning for the singer. Stripping down to a "Celtic rock" format that managed to be hard and direct, yet still folkish, Donovan turned out a series of excellent songs, notably the minor hit "Riki Tiki Tavi," that seemed to show him moving toward a roots-oriented sound of considerable appeal. Unfortunately, he was derailed by record company hassles and perhaps his own burnout, and *Open Road* turned out to be a sidestep rather than a step forward. *—William Ruhlmann*

Cosmic Wheels / Mar. 1973 / Epic ✦✦

Essence to Essence / Dec. 1973 / Epic ✦✦

7-Tease / Nov. 1974 / Epic ✦✦

Slow Down World / May 1976 / Epic ✦✦

Donovan / 1977 / Castle ✦✦

Spotlight / 1981 / PRT ✦✦✦✦✦
Donovan's acoustic, pre-psychedelic work was shoddily packaged in the United States, spread out over several albums in a haphazard fashion. This 24-track double LP reissue covers most of his work from this period (basically, 1965), including the hits "Catch the Wind" and "Colours," as well as his cover of Buffy St. Marie's "Universal Soldier" and the memorable originals "Josie" and "Hey Gyp." This early phase is often unfairly dismissed as sub-Dylan musings by critics; Donovan was indeed the closest counterpart to Bob in the mid-'60s, but was distinctly more pop-oriented, and had a gentle, wistful songwriting voice all his own, even if it wasn't as complex as Dylan's. While this material lacks the punch of his best psychedelic work, it is of a consistently high standard, and lacks the occasional overly cosmic vision that has dated some of his later '60s recordings. While this reissue captures all the essential highlights of Donovan's pre-electric career, it's missing a few cuts and is packaged rather tackily; a comprehensive double-CD compilation of the thirty or so tracks he recorded for the British Pye label during this time would be welcome. *—Richie Unterberger*

Lady of the Stars / 1983 / Allegiance ✦✦

The Classics Live / 1991 / Great Northern Arts ✦✦✦
Fresh stage recordings of Donovan's '60s hits, well-produced and arranged, and laced with a certain amount of humor from the passage of time and the druggy sensibilities behind them. "Sunshine Superman" is an intrinsically good song, although the infectious beat of the original Mickie Most-production is missed in spite of the good playing. *—Bruce Eder*

Live in Concert / 1992 / QED ✦✦✦
Like a lot of 1960s folk-rock veterans, Donovan has found his biggest modern audience in new recordings of his classic hits. This British release is one of them, a 1990s all-acoustic show running an hour and covering such material as "Sunshine Superman," "Jennifer Juniper," "Catch the Wind," "The Hurdy Gurdy Man," "Universal Soldier," "Atlantis," "Colours," "Cosmic Wheels," "Young Girl Blues," and "Wear Your Love Like Heaven," among others. His voice is better here than it was for many a '60s performance, and the recording quality is excellent. The old Columbia *Live In Concert* still has a certain dopey (in more ways than one) charm, having been recorded in the midst of flower power, but these performances are more engaging and include a bigger cross-section of his repertory. "Hurdy Gurdy Man," for example, works amazingly well without the psychedelic guitar of the studio original, complete with Donovan's wry recollections of his time with the Maharishi, the Beatles, Mia Farrow et al., and an extra verse associated with George Harrison; and "Sunshine Superman" (which includes Donovan's harmonica playing), "Cosmic Wheels," and "Atlantis" are better songs here than their originals. A couple of numbers that should be here aren't ("Hey Gyp" would be welcomed, and one is surprised that Donovan doesn't do more with "There Is a Mountain," given how famous the song is courtesy of the Allman Brothers), but this is still a pleasure. *—Bruce Eder*

Troubadour: The Definitive Collection 1964-1976 / Aug. 4, 1992 / Epic/Legacy ✦✦✦✦✦
This two-disc, 44-track retrospective album (initially released as a boxed set) chronicles Donovan's decade-long career at Epic Records, with the few folk hits he recorded before joining the label and a couple of early demos added. All the hippie hits of the '60s are in-

cluded, plus a judicious selection of the less successful '70s recordings. Good liner notes by Brian Hogg and Derek Taylor. —*William Ruhlmann*

Sutras / Oct. 15, 1996 / American ♦♦♦
Like Johnny Cash before him, Donovan was selected by producer Rick Rubin as a childhood hero he would like to restore to glory. With Rubin's encouragement and production, Donovan does make an impressive comeback with *Sutras*, which is reminiscent of his earliest records. *Sutras* abandons the colorful psychedelic pop of his best-known songs for the spare acoustic folk of his first records, and while Donovan's songwriting is a little uneven, the warmth of the performances is charming and welcoming, especially for longtime fans. —*Stephen Thomas Erlewine*

★ **Greatest Hits [Expanded Edition]** / Mar. 30, 1999 / Epic/Legacy ♦♦♦♦♦
Epic/Legacy's 1999 reissue of *Greatest Hits* improves on the original 1969 collection in a number of ways. First of all, the original Hickory versions of "Catch the Wind" and "Colours" are included instead of re-recordings, which is enough to make this new version preferable, but the compilers have also chosen to include the original mono version of these hits instead of the stereo cuts that were on the first edition. Plus, they've added four excellent bonus tracks: "Atlantis," "To Susan on the West Coast Waiting," "Barabajagal" and "Riki Tiki Tavi." All of that means that this expanded and updated *Greatest Hits* is a near-perfect single-disc summary of Donovan's most popular material and hit singles. As these songs prove, Donovan and producer Mickie Most could craft irresistible folkrock and psychedelic-pop singles. Some of the sounds and sentiments may sound a little dated, but the productions and the songs—"Sunshine Superman," "Jennifer Juniper," "Wear Your Love Like Heaven," "Season of the Witch," "Mellow Yellow," "Hurdy Gurdy Man," "Epistle to Dippy," "There Is a Mountain," "Lalena," plus the aforementioned bonus tracks—have proven to be classics of the era, and this is the best place to get them all on one collection. —*Stephen Thomas Erlewine*

Summer Day Reflection Songs / Apr. 25, 2000 / Castle ♦♦♦♦
In 1965, before Donovan's U.S. contract was transferred to Epic, he made 30-plus recordings for Pye in the U.K., all in an acoustic folk mold (with occasional additional instruments and percussion). It would not seem to be such a heroic feat to gather all of that material in one place, but prior to this double-CD compilation, that had never occurred. This is the anthology to rectify that gap permanently. The two CDs contain all 34 known songs from this era, including a few rarities: the original single versions of "Catch the Wind" and "Colours," an alternate take of "The Ballad of a Crystal Man," and "Every Man Has His Chain," which during the '60s only showed up on a French EP. These rarities aren't so amazing that you necessarily need to shell out if you already have most of the cuts, but for historical completism's sake their presence is most satisfying. The historical liner notes, covering the pre-"Sunshine Superman" period almost exclusively, are thorough and excellent. And the music is fine, quite consistent folk or pre-folk-rock that should permanently put an end to all the unwarranted dismissals of his early work as twee Dylan imitation. Donovan was his own man, even at this young age, and hard to beat as far as tuneful yet meaningful mid-'60s folk went. —*Richie Unterberger*

Mellow Yellow/Wear Your Love Like Heaven / Jan. 16, 2001 / Collectables ♦♦♦
Collectables' two-fer of *Mellow Yellow/Wear Your Love Like Heaven* offers both of Donovan's 1967 albums on one CD. Of the two, *Mellow Yellow* is the more diverse and developed work; the title track, "Bleak City Woman," "Writer in the Sun," and "Sand and Foam" blend folk, pop, and blues elements in their creative arrangements (courtesy of John Paul Jones and John Cameron). Originally one half of Donovan's *A Gift from a Flower to a Garden*, *Wear Your Love Like Heaven* captures some of the larger work's poppiest moments, such as the beautiful title track, "There Was a Time," "Someone Singing," and "Little Boy in Corduroy." On their own, neither of these albums are Donovan's strongest, but together they provide an entertaining look at the peak of his psych-pop years. —*Heather Phares*

The Doobie Brothers

f. Mar. 1970, San Jose, CA, db. 1982
Album Rock, Blue-Eyed Soul, Boogie Rock, Pop/Rock, Soft Rock
As one of the most popular Californian pop/rock bands of the '70s, the Doobie Brothers evolved from a mellow, post-hippie boogie band to a slick, soul-inflected pop band by the end of the decade. Along the way, the group racked up a string of gold and platinum albums in the US. Driven by the singles "Listen to the Music" and "Jesus Is Just Alright," 1972's *Toulouse Street* became the group's breakthrough. *The Captain and Me* (1973) was even more successful, spawning the Top 10 hit "Long Train Runnin'" and "China Grove," while 1974's *What Once Were Vices Are Now Habits* launched their first number one single, "Black Water."

Jeff "Skunk" Baxter officially joined the Doobie Brothers for 1975's *Stampede*. Prior to the release of *Stampede*, singer/guitarist Tom Johnston was hospitilized with a stomach ailment, and was replaced for the supporting tour by keyboardist/vocalist Michael McDonald. Although it peaked at number four, *Stampede* wasn't as commercially successful as its three predecessors, and the group decided to let McDonald and ex-Steely Dan member Baxter, who were now official Doobies, revamp the band's light country-rock and boogie. The new sound was showcased on 1976's *Takin' It to the Streets*, a collection of light funk and jazzy pop that resulted in a platinum album. In 1977, the group released *Livin' on the Fault Line*, which was successful without producing any big hits. Johnston left the band after the album's release to pursue an unsuccessful solo career. Following his departure, the Doobies released their most successful album, *Minute By Minute* (1978) which spent five weeks at number one on the strength of the number one single "What a Fool Believes." —*Stephen Thomas Erlewine*

The Doobie Brothers / Apr. 1971 / Warner Brothers ♦♦♦
One of the most inauspicious debuts by a major rock group, this subdued slice of coun-

try boogie might be called the missing link between Moby Grape and the later, revved-up Doobies of "Listen to the Music." Only a handful of West Coast hippies bought this record originally, but it lays the blueprint for the Doobies' future radio-friendly sound: chugging rhythm guitar, stretched-out harmonies, Tom Johnston's joyful R&B vocals, and Patrick Simmons' acoustic picking. A muffled mixing job helped keep this album in the morgue, which is sad, because "Nobody" and "Greenwood Creek" rate with some of Johnston's best tunes, and they deserve issuance on a definitive Doobie Brothers compilation. —*Peter Kurtz*

Toulouse Street / Jul. 1972 / Warner Brothers ♦♦♦♦
After a promising but ill-formed debut, The Doobie Brothers returned with *Toulouse Street*, a better-written and more energetically performed effort that became a platinum record on the strength of its catchy single, "Listen to the Music." —*Stephen Thomas Erlewine*

The Captain & Me / Mar. 1973 / Warner Brothers ♦♦♦♦♦
Their best early album features "China Grove." —*Dan Heilman*

What Were Once Vices Are Now Habits / Feb. 1974 / Warner Brothers ♦♦♦
Apart from the tight "Black Water," The Doobie Brothers' follow-up to their breakthrough *The Captain and Me* was a tepid affair, lacking the strong material of the previous album. —*Stephen Thomas Erlewine*

Stampede / May 1975 / Warner Brothers ♦♦
With the addition of ex-Steely Dan guitarist Jeff "Skunk" Baxter, the Doobie Brothers became a more musically ambitious and accomplished band, without sacrificing their capability to rock & roll. However, *Stampede* suffers from the same flaw as *What Were Once Vices*—a lack of consistent material. —*Stephen Thomas Erlewine*

Takin' It to the Streets / Mar. 1976 / Warner Brothers ♦♦♦♦♦
Under keyboardist/vocalist Michael McDonald's direction, the group departed from their trademark bluesy country-rock on *Takin' It to the Streets*, taking a laidback pop-soul approach that touched on jazz and White funk. The result was a commercial and artistic success, providing a blueprint for the band's next two records. —*Stephen Thomas Erlewine*

Best of the Doobies / Nov. 1976 / Warner Brothers ♦♦♦♦♦
Featuring 11 of the group's best-known songs from their first five albums (from 1971's *The Doobie Brothers* to 1976's *Takin' it to the Streets*), *The Best of the Doobie Brothers* contains the boogie-rock band's very best songs, including the big hits "Listen to the Music," "Jesus Is Just Alright," "Long Train Runnin'," "China Grove," "Black Water," and "Takin' It to the Streets." For most casual fans, *The Best of the Doobie Brothers* is the perfect summation of the group's early career, before they turned into a slick, jazzy blue-eyed soul band in the late '70s. —*Stephen Thomas Erlewine*

Livin' on the Fault Line / Aug. 1977 / Warner Brothers ♦♦♦♦
Livin' on the Fault Line follows the same pattern as *Takin' It to the Streets*, yet it lacks the fine songwriting of its predecessor. —*Stephen Thomas Erlewine*

Minute by Minute / Dec. 1978 / Warner Brothers ♦♦♦♦♦
Due to health problems, founding member Tom Johnston departed after *Livin' on the Fault Line*, leaving Michael McDonald as the leader of The Doobie Brothers. McDonald, in turn, wrote his finest set of songs for *Minute by Minute*, highlighted by the number one single "What a Fool Believes." —*Stephen Thomas Erlewine*

One Step Closer / Oct. 1980 / Warner Brothers ♦♦♦♦
One Step Closer was less impressive than *Minute by Minute* not only because it lacked the strong songwriting of the previous album, but because the band sounded tired and uninspired. Unsurprisingly, it was the final studio album The Doobie Brothers made before breaking up. —*Stephen Thomas Erlewine*

Best of the Doobies, Vol. 2 / Nov. 1981 / Warner Brothers ♦♦♦♦♦
This is the best of the Michael McDonald era. —*Dan Heilman*

Cycles / May 17, 1989 / Capitol ♦

Very Best of the Doobie Brothers / May 24, 1993 / Elektra ♦♦♦♦
Until the release of Rhino's 2001 collection, the import collection *The Very Best of the Doobie Brothers* was the most comprehensive Doobie Brothers overview on the market. Containing 19 songs, this features all of the big hits, minus any of the reunion cuts, but featuring a single edit of "Long Train Runnin'" and an alternate "Listen to the Music," in addition to the album versions of both songs. It's a good collection, containing everything most listeners could want, but compared to the Rhino collection, it's not markedly better, and the Rhino disc is cheaper and easier to find. —*Stephen Thomas Erlewine*

Long Train Runnin' 1970-2000 / Sep. 14, 1999 / Rhino ♦♦♦♦
There's little question that the four-disc box set *Long Train Runnin' 1971-2000* is only for hardcore Doobie Brothers fans, since it not only spans 79 tracks, but it also contains a full disc of rarities. The sheer abundance of material makes it unnecessary for anyone that isn't already a dedicated fan, either of the Doobies or of album rock, and even those listeners may find *Long Train Runnin'* a little long. After all, the Doobies' hit-making years end around the end of disc two, even though a few hits spill over to the beginning of disc three. That means the first half of the box is essentially an expanded greatest hits, featuring all the '70s singles—from "Listen to the Music" to "Dependin' on You"—balanced by a handful of album tracks. There is some elaboration of these years on disc four, but it takes a while to get there, since disc three chronicles the '80s and beyond. In the early '80s, the Doobies had only one Top Ten hit with "Real Love" before going on hiatus. They reunited in 1989 and continued to tour and record throughout the '90s. Those two decades comprise disc three and while it has its moments, it pales considerably next to the Doobies' prime material. The rarities disc is similarly uneven, but more interesting because much of the music dates from the '70s. Also, the mix of solo songs, alternate

mixes, and demos illuminates those classic years somewhat, throwing out a handful of gems along the way. It's a nice bonus for the dedicated, but they really are the only audience for this set. —*Stephen Thomas Erlewine*

● **Greatest Hits** / Sep. 4, 2001 / Rhino ✦✦✦✦✦
Apart from the four-disc Rhino box and an import collection, there was no comprehensive Doobie Brothers collection, spanning the Tom Johnston and Michael McDonald eras alike, until Rhino's 2001 collection, *Greatest Hits*. This, needless to say, is a welcome development, since it does have all the big songs, from "Listen to the Music" and "China Grove" through "Takin' it to the Streets" and "What a Fool Believes" to their reunion single, "The Doctor," providing an excellent introduction-cum-summary of one of the singles-oriented pop/rock bands of the '70s. —*Stephen Thomas Erlewine*

The Doors

f. Jul. 1965, Los Angeles, CA, **db**. 1973
Album Rock, Proto-Punk, Psychedelic, Rock & Roll
The Doors, one of the most influential and controversial rock bands of the 1960s, were formed by UCLA film students Ray Manzarek and Jim Morrison with drummer John Densmore, and guitarist Robby Krieger. The group never added a bass player, and their sound was dominated by Manzarek's electric organ work and Morrison's deep, sonorous voice, with which he sang and intoned his highly poetic lyrics. The group signed to Elektra Records in 1966 and released its first album, *The Doors*, featuring the hit "Light My Fire," in 1967. Blending blues, classical, Eastern music, and pop into sinister but beguiling melodies, the band sounded like no other. From the start, the Doors' focus was the charismatic Morrison, who proved increasingly unstable over the group's brief career. In 1969, Morrison was arrested for indecent exposure during a concert in Miami, an incident that nearly derailed the band. Nevertheless, the Doors managed to turn out a series of successful albums and singles through 1971, when, upon the completion of their final album, *L.A. Woman*, Morrison decamped for Paris. He died there, apparently of a drug overdose. The three surviving Doors tried to carry on without him, but ultimately disbanded. In 1991, director Oliver Stone made *The Doors*, a feature film about the group starring Val Kilmer as Morrison. —*William Ruhlmann & Richie Unterberger*

☆ **The Doors** / Jan. 1967 / Elektra ✦✦✦✦✦
A tremendous debut album, and indeed one of the best first-time outings in rock history, introducing the band's fusion of rock, blues, classical, jazz, and poetry with a knockout punch. The lean, spidery guitar and organ riffs interwove with a hypnotic menace, providing a seductive backdrop for Jim Morrison's captivating vocals and probing prose. "Light My Fire" was the cut that would top the charts and establish the group as stars, but most of the rest of the album is just as impressive, including some of their best songs: the propulsive "Break On Through" (their first single), the beguiling Oriental mystery of "The Crystal Ship," the mysterious "End of the Night," "Take It As It Comes" (one of several tunes besides "Light My Fire" that also had hit potential), and the stomping rock of "Soul Kitchen" and "Twentieth Century Fox." The eleven-minute Oedipal drama "The End" was the group at their most daring and, some would contend, overambitious. It was nonetheless a haunting cap to an album whose nonstop melodicism and dynamic tension would never be equaled by the group again, let alone bettered. —*Richie Unterberger*

Strange Days / Oct. 1967 / Elektra ✦✦✦
Many of the songs on *Strange Days* had been written around the same time as the ones that appeared on *The Doors*, and with hindsight one has the sense that the best of the batch had already been cherry-picked for the debut album. For that reason, the band's second effort isn't as consistently stunning as their debut, though overall it's a very successful continuation of the themes of their classic album. Besides the hit "Strange Days," highlights included the funky "Moonlight Drive," the eerie "You're Lost Little Girl," and the jerkily rhythmic "Love Me Two Times," which gave the band a small chart single. "My Eyes Have Seen You" and "I Can't See Your Face In My Mind" are minor but pleasing entries in the group's repertoire that share a subdued Eastern psychedelic air. The eleven-minute "When the Music's Over" would often be featured as a live showstopper, yet it also illustrated their tendency to occasionally slip into drawn-out bombast. —*Richie Unterberger*

Waiting for the Sun / Jul. 1968 / Elektra ✦✦✦
The Doors' 1967 albums had raised expectations so high that their third effort was greeted as a major disappointment. With a few exceptions, the material was much mellower, and while this yielded some fine melodic ballad-rock in "Love Street," "Wintertime Love," "Summer's Almost Gone," and "Yes the River Knows," there was no denying that the songwriting was not as impressive as it had been on the first two records. On the other hand, there were first-rate tunes such as the spooky "The Unknown Soldier," with antiwar lyrics as uncompromisingly forceful as anything the band did, and the compulsively riff-driven "Hello, I Love You," which nonetheless bore an uncomfortably close resemblance to the Kinks' "All Day and All of the Night." The flamenco guitar of "Spanish Caravan," the all-out weirdness of "Not to Touch the Earth" (which was a snippet of a legendary abandoned opus, "The Celebration of the Lizard"), and the menacing closer "Five to One" were also interesting. In fact, time's been fairly kind to the record, which is quite enjoyable and diverse, just not as powerful a full-length statement as the group's best albums. —*Richie Unterberger*

The Soft Parade / Jul. 1969 / Elektra ✦✦✦
The weakest studio album recorded with Morrison in the group, partially because their experiments with brass and strings on about half the tracks weren't entirely successful. More to the point, though, this was their weakest set of material, lowlights including filler like "Do It" and "Runnin' Blue," a strange bluegrass-soul blend that was a small hit. On the other hand, about half the record is quite good, especially the huge hit "Touch Me"

(their most successful integration of orchestration), the vicious hard-rock riffs of "Wild Child," the overlooked "Shaman's Blues," and the lengthy title track, a multi-part suite that was one of the band's best attempts to mix rock with poetry. "Tell All the People" and "Wishful Sinful," both penned by Robby Krieger, were uncharacteristically wistful tunes that became small hits, but were not all that good, and not sung very convincingly by Morrison. —*Richie Unterberger*

Morrison Hotel / 1970 / Elektra ✦✦✦✦✦
The Doors returned to crunching, straightforward hard rock on an album that, despite yielding no major hit singles, returned them to critical favor with hip listeners. An increasingly bluesy flavor began to color the songwriting and arrangements, especially on the party and booze anthem "Roadhouse Blues." Airy mysticism was still present on "Waiting for the Sun," "Queen of the Highway," and "Indian Summer"; "Ship of Fools" and "Land Ho!" struck effective balances between the hard rock arrangements and the narrative reach of the lyrics. "Peace Frog" was the most political and controversial track, documenting the domestic unrest of late-'60s America before unexpectedly segueing into the restful ballad "Blue Sunday." "The Spy," by contrast, was a slow blues that pointed to the direction that would fully blossom on *L.A. Woman*. —*Richie Unterberger*

Absolutely Live / Sep. 1970 / Elektra ✦✦

L.A. Woman / Apr. 1971 / Elektra ✦✦✦✦✦
The final album with Morrison in the lineup is by far their most blues-oriented, and the singer's poetic ardor is undiminished, though his voice sounds increasingly worn and craggy on some numbers. Actually, some of the straight blues items sound kind of turgid, but that's more than made up for by several cuts that rate among their finest and most disturbing work. The seven-minute title track was a car-cruising classic that celebrated both the glamour and seediness of Los Angeles; the other long cut, the brooding, jazzy "Riders on the Storm," was the group at their most melodic and ominous. It and the far bouncier "Love Her Madly" were hit singles, and "The Changeling" and "L'America" count as some of their better little-heeded album tracks. An uneven but worthy finale from the original quartet. —*Richie Unterberger*

Other Voices / Oct. 1971 / Elektra ✦✦

Full Circle / Jul. 1972 / Elektra ✦✦

Alive, She Cried / Oct. 1983 / Elektra ✦✦

★ **The Best of the Doors [1985]** / 1985 / Elektra ✦✦✦✦✦
Ideally, one would avoid compilations of the Doors' work, except perhaps for the hit singles and moments when one wanted very light listening. This was a band that took itself very seriously, almost to the point of self-parody at times, and their music ought to be discovered in the setting and context in which it was intended, but assuming that one needs a Doors anthology, this 18-track collection (19 on CD) is the place to start. It started life during the quadrophonic era as a single LP of the same title, with programming intended to combine the concepts behind two earlier compilations, *13* and *Weird Scenes Inside the Goldmine*, under one cover. In 1985, the two-LP version, the fourth compilation of the group's work, and the most comprehensive, was released, providing a good overview to the most obvious different sides of the group's output, and in 1991 this was remastered for CD with improved sound and an extra track. Good as it is, the compilation misleads somewhat by removing the material from its original context and also shuffling the order, so that songs off of *The Soft Parade* bump up against tracks from *L.A. Woman*. The hits can stand on their own, but overall the music lacks the broader impact that it was intended to have when heard juxtaposed with the other tracks on their respective original albums. The 1996 *Greatest Hits* CD, with its remastered sound, and the remastering of their individual albums that began in the year 2000, also renders this collection somewhat less attractive than it was on its initial release. —*Bruce Eder*

In Concert / May 21, 1991 / Elektra ✦✦✦
The Doors could be erratic live, as this double CD shows. Still, it's a fair example of their in-concert charms. —*Jeff Tamarkin*

Greatest Hits / Oct. 15, 1996 / Elektra ✦✦✦✦✦
Although the version of "The End" included on *Greatest Hits* is taken from the *Apocalypse Now* soundtrack and filled with sound effects, this single-disc collection remains a terrific overview of the Doors' career, featuring all of their biggest hits and best-known songs, and thereby functioning as a fine introduction for neophytes. —*Stephen Thomas Erlewine*

The Doors Box Set / Oct. 28, 1997 / Elektra ✦✦✦
Fans of the Doors waited many years for *The Doors Box Set* to be released, and when it finally arrived in the fall of 1997, it was a bit of a mixed blessing. The classic conundrum for box sets is how much rare and unreleased material to showcase, and in this case, the producers opted for three discs of rarities, devoting the last disc to "band favorites," instead of hits. This means, of course, that the casual fan is not going to be well-served by the box, since it not only doesn't contain studio versions of such staples as "Five to One," but it doesn't even have versions of "People Are Strange" and "Touch Me." Furthermore, diehards might very well be frustrated by the quality of the rarities. The first disc and third disc are peppered with live cuts, outtakes and the legendary 1965 demos for Columbia Records. The quality of the music is uneven—the demos are interesting but mainly from a historical standpoint, the live cuts vascillate in sonic and performance quality, and outtakes like the plodding, 17-minute "Rock Is Dead" encapsulate much of what was wrong with the band—but much of it is worth hearing once, unlike the second disc, "Live in New York," which is startlingly similar to *Alive She Cried*. In the end, the sheer abundance of rare material makes the set of interest to diehard fans, but they might find that the collection falls short of their expectations. Listeners that have a passing interest in the Doors are advised to stick to the double disc set, *The Best of the Doors*. —*Stephen Thomas Erlewine*

Complete Studio Recordings / Nov. 9, 1999 / Elektra ♦♦♦♦
As the title says, *The Complete Studio Recordings* contains all of the Doors' studio recordings in one convenient box set. All six of the band's studio albums have been given 24-bit remasters, and the lyrics for all the albums are included for the first time. Also, a couple of minor edits on *The Doors* have been fixed— Jim Morrison's vocals at the end of "The End" are brought up in the mix, and his exclamation of "she gets high!" on "Break on Through" has been restored. The box set includes a seventh disc comprised of nothing but rarities, including some live cuts. Most of these rarities were debuted on *The Doors Box Set*, but there is one previously unreleased outtake, "Woman is a Devil," which isn't great but isn't bad, and it will certainly be worth the time of collectors. Then again, this whole set is basically for collectors only, since it's lavish and expensive. But, it may be worth it, since the booklet is nice and the sound is very, very good. However, hardcore fans who want the rarities and the remastered sound but don't want to spend the money—or want the discs available in jewel boxes instead of the sturdy cardboard sleeves designed to look like little records (complete with replicas of the inner paper sleeves)—are advised to wait, since the individual albums, plus the *Essential Rarities* disc, will be released separately sometime in 2000. —*Stephen Thomas Erlewine*

Essential Rarities / Jun. 20, 2000 / Elektra ♦♦♦
Originally released as part of the box set *The Complete Studio Recordings*, *The Essential Rarities* essentially gathers a bunch of odds and ends, not just previously unreleased studio cuts, but also live cuts, composites, stage chatter, alternate takes, and demos. In other words, it's a bunch of stuff that only hardcore fans need, and they've likely already purchased it as part of the box set or as bootlegs. If not, this is a good way to get a bunch of pretty good cuts, highlighted by the 1969 outtakes "Woman Is a Devil" and "Who Scared You" and the 1965 demo "Moonlight Drive." It must be said, however, that this is really just for the hardcore fans since there just isn't anything (apart from possibly those three previously mentioned tracks, yet those still are specialized items) that is noteworthy for the casual listener. As a way of tying up loose ends, *The Essential Rarities* is necessary for collectors, but for everybody else, it's hardly essential. [By the way, there are almost no liner notes to speak of, only four photos (not counting the cover shot) and two track listings, only one with the sources. The rest of the information details the reissue producers, but there are no liner notes to explain the origins of these cuts.] —*Stephen Thomas Erlewine*

★ **The Very Best of the Doors** / Sep. 18, 2001 / Rhino ♦♦♦♦♦
This is very, very close to being *The Very Best of the Doors*, and it does indeed contain most of the group's biggest hits and best-known songs, but this 2001 compilation does not supplant 1985's double-disc set *The Best of the Doors* as being the best Doors compilation on the market. It's not because the disc is sequenced non-chronologically, since it does have a momentum of its own (plus it does contain full-length album versions), but because it simply misses too many big songs. "The WASP (Texas Radio and the Big Beat)," "Peace Frog," and even the group's version of "Back Door Man" may be fan favorites, but they do not replace "Five to One," "Alabama Song," "Waiting for the Sun," or "When the Music's Over," all missing here. That's not to say what's here isn't good, since it is, and it is given the same exceptional remastering heard on the 1999 set, *The Complete Studio Recordings*. So, it is indeed a good sampler—but just don't think that it is a proper introduction, or exhaustive retrospective. —*Stephen Thomas Erlewine*

Lee Dorsey

b. Dec. 24, 1924, New Orleans, LA, **d.** Dec. 1, 1986, New Orleans, LA
Vocals / New Orleans R&B, R&B, Soul
The effervescent approach of Lee Dorsey perfectly summarizes the infectious charm of early-'60s New Orleans R&B. Dorsey specialized in good-humored music with a touch of second-line funk thrown in to make it all the more irresistible. Although he had already waxed a couple of singles, Dorsey caught the country by total surprise in 1961 with his deceptively simply nursery-rhyme-style "Ya Ya" on Bobby Robinson's Fury label. Arranged by prolific New Orleans pianist Allen Toussaint, the track proved an R&B chart-topper and a major pop hit to boot.

Dorsey's laconic vocal charms served him well on "Ya Ya" and the Earl King-penned follow-up "Do Re Mi," and the mid-'60s found him working with Toussaint on the funky smashes "Ride Your Pony" and "Working in a Coal Mine," this time for Amy Records. It's little remembered that Dorsey was responsible for the original 1970 version of Toussaint's "Yes We Can," revived to much greater acclaim by the Pointer Sisters (who tacked on an extra "Can"). From all accounts, Dorsey remained an exceedingly humble R&B star who preferred tinkering with cars to extensively touring the country. He died of emphysema in 1986. —*Bill Dahl*

Ya Ya / 1962 / Relic ♦♦♦♦♦
This terrific overview of the good-humored New Orleans singer's early-'60s classics (for Bobby Robinson's Fury label) features direct-from-masters sound quality. —*Bill Dahl*

The New Lee Dorsey / 1966 / Sundazed ♦♦♦
Less than a year had passed between this and Dorsey's previous LP *Ride Your Pony*, and Allen Toussaint was again the prime creative force, writing material and co-producing. The sound, however, had definitely taken a step in a funkier direction. It's still lighthearted, though not lightweight, soul music with a New Orleans bounce, paced by the Top Ten hit "Working in a Coal Mine" and also including the Top 30 follow-up "Holy Cow." Other than those hit singles, the songs, though not exactly throwaways, aren't up to the same level. The original LP duplicated four songs from *Ride Your Pony*, and the 2000 Sundazed CD reissue has taken intelligent liberties with the track sequence. It removes the four duplicated songs and replaces them with rare singles from the era, most notably the uncommonly moody 1967 45 "Rain Rain Go Away." Furthermore, an additional dozen tunes are added as bonus tracks, most taken from rare 1968-1970 singles, with a couple of previously unissued cuts and a 1968 recording ("Lottie Mo '68") that didn't show up until 1997. These bonus items are on the whole more worthy of investigation than the slightly earlier rarities that fill out Sundazed's *Ride Your Pony* CD, as Dorsey and Toussaint (who was, still, writing virtually everything) venturing into deeper funk, sometimes with backup by the Meters. Maybe you don't need the five-minute reading of "What Now My Love," but "Little Ba-By," the self-fulfilling prophecy "Everything I Do Gonh Be Funky (From Now On)," and "What You Want (Is What You Get)" are decent soul-funk. Of the previously unavailable songs, "A Mellow Good Time Pt. 2" is an instrumental continuation of one of the songs on *The New Lee Dorsey*, while "I'm the One" is a serviceable 1970 Toussaint number. —*Richie Unterberger*

Ride Your Pony / 1966 / Sundazed ♦♦♦
Aside from the title track and the oft-covered, ultra-funky "Get Out of My Life, Woman," none of the 12 songs on this early 1966 album are familiar to most listeners. As it turns out it's a quality full-length bridging early-'60s New Orleans R&B with soul, even if the songs tend to be on the light partying side. That's part of the main draw of much New Orleans music, of course, and few were better at projecting a relaxed sense of fun than Dorsey. It helped that all but two of the songs were written by co-producer Allen Toussaint; the Crescent City giant doesn't get nearly as much attention as Smokey Robinson, but as with Smokey, one wonders if Toussaint ever slept in the 1960s, so prolific and generally fine was his output. The Sundazed CD reissue is recommended even if you have the (by now hard to find) original LP, since it nearly doubles the length with almost a dozen tracks from rare 1966-1968 singles. These are more rare than exciting, to be honest, but Toussaint wrote all of these (sharing songwriting credit on one tune, "My Old Car"), and they're more good-time New Orleans soul with gradually modernizing production, even if the tunes weren't memorable enough to reach classic status. Certainly the most interesting is the two-part 1968 45 "Four Corners," an unabashed "Tighten Up" takeoff with bits of James Brown and the Meters rattling around the corners; there's also a 1967 duet single with Betty Harris. —*Richie Unterberger*

★ **Wheelin' and Dealin': The Definitive Collection** / Aug. 26, 1997 / Arista ♦♦♦♦♦
Wheelin' and Dealin': The Definitive Collection pretty much lives up to its title, presenting 20 choice selections from one of the greatest figures of New Orleans R&B. All of his big singles are here—"Ya Ya," "Do-Re-Mi," "Ride Your Pony," "Get Out of My Life Woman," "Working in the Coal Mine," "Holy Cow," "Everything I Do Gonh Be Funky (From Now On)"—along with lots of great lesser-known singles like "Confusion," "Can You Hear Me" and "My Old Car." There are some really good songs missing, both from his prime Bell Recordings and such latter-day singles as "Sneaking Sally Through the Alley," but that's primarily because everything Dorsey cut was consistently enjoyable; even when the quality of the material dipped, the band and Dorsey remained appealing. So, even if there's a handful of songs that could have been here, it's impossible to argue with what is, since it does result in a wonderful, endlessly listenable collection. —*Stephen Thomas Erlewine*

The EP Collection / Mar. 21, 2000 / See For Miles ♦♦♦♦♦
See for Miles' series *The EP Collection* is always fascinating, since it not only provides collectors with a nifty compilation of pop artifacts, but it also provides a chance-taking, unpredictable singles collection. Such is the case with Lee Dorsey's *The EP Collection*. There's not a bad track to be found on this dynamite 26-track collection that boasts three original British EPs, two French EPs, and six A-sides from "Ya Ya" to "Sneakin' Sally Through the Alley." The very fact that there aren't any weak moments is a testament to just how damn good Lee Dorsey was. It wasn't just that he was backed by stellar musicians under the direction of Allen Toussaint—it was that he was a supremely gifted vocalist with a sly turn of phrase. He could make throwaway songs sound substantial, and he brought unexpected twists to stronger numbers. These talents are readily apparent on any Dorsey collection, but this is one of the very finest, ranking just beneath the slightly tighter Arista compilation, *Wheelin' and Dealin'*. The truth of the matter is this—Lee Dorsey sounds terrific in any context and the singles sound great in any sequence, so even if you buy this for the handful of tracks that you don't have, you'll be satisfied. And if you get this as your first Lee Dorsey album, you're bound to be converted. —*Stephen Thomas Erlewine*

Working in a Coalmine: The Very Best of Lee Dorsey / Apr. 24, 2001 / Music Club ♦♦♦♦
Music Club's *Working in a Coalmine: The Very Best of Lee Dorsey* contains a few songs that don't normally make it on Dorsey collections, from both his Bell recordings and late-'60s/early-'70s funky Allen Toussaint-produced recordings. "Hoodlum Joe," "Messed Around (And Fell in Love)," "People Sure Act Funny," "Can I Be the One?," and "If She Won't" all don't regularly make it on Dorsey collections, which means this is something more for collectors than the neophyte who the title suggests this is aimed at. On that level, it's a neat item to pick up, even if does contain the usual suspects that any Dorsey fan has many times over. If it's viewed as an introduction, however, it falls short—for that, get *Wheelin' and Dealin'* first, then move to this to fill in some holes later. —*Stephen Thomas Erlewine*

Doves

f. 1998, Manchester, England
Dream Pop, Space Rock, Britpop, Alternative Pop/Rock
The Manchester, England epic pop trio the Doves reunited Jimi Goodwin (vocals/bass) with twin brothers Jez (guitar) and Andy Williams (drums) for a stunning musical collaboration mimicking the likes of Radiohead, The Verve, and Ocean Colour Scene. Doves, all of whom previously joined forces in the dance combo Sub Sub, are best known for

their club smash "Ain't No Love (Ain't No Use)." Debuting in October of 1998 with the *Cedar* EP, Doves quickly sold out the record's limited pressing, earning "next big thing" status in the British press; "Sea Song" followed in the spring of 1999, and upon issuing *Hear It Comes* that autumn, the group signed to the Heavenly label. They inked an American deal with Astralwerks in summer 2000 and the band's first full-length effort *Lost Souls* was released in the U.S. that October. *—Jason Ankeny*

● **Lost Souls** / Apr. 4, 2000 / Heavenly ✦✦✦✦
Hailing from the scene that brought the defining sounds of the Smiths, the Stone Roses, Oasis, James, and the Charlatans U.K., Doves is another Brit-pop band playing around with depressing lyrical imagery and embryonic soundscapes that made the Mancunian circuit so popular throughout the '80s and '90s. Gloriously basking in the ethereal ones before them, their debut *Lost Souls* is a shoegazing twist of emotional bliss. Music hasn't sounded so heavenly since Radiohead and The Verve.

The dozen-track look into streaming psychedelia taps into melodic waves of love lorn and sadness, especially on songs like "Rise" and "Lost Souls." The mood rouses and the positive clamor of "The Cedar Room" becomes the album's brassy anthem, very Oasis-like. Frontman/bassist Jimi Goodwin drools like a swooning Damon Albarn during "Here It Comes" and whooshing guitar licks from Jez Williams recall the sounds of Noel Gallagher. NME boldly claims it as the best debut album since *Definitely Maybe.* They're onto something good. If only Liam and Noel could calm down a bit and find that mesmerizing nature once again. [In October 2000, *Lost Souls* was issued in America on Astralwerks with three added bonus tracks not included on the import version.] *—MacKenzie Wilson*

The Downliners Sect

f. 1963, **db.** 1967
British Invasion
Of all the British R&B bands to follow the Rolling Stones' footsteps, the Downliners Sect were arguably the rawest. The Sect didn't as much interpret the sound of Chess Records as attack it, with a finesse that made the Pretty Things seem positively suave in comparison. Long on crude energy and hoarse vocals, but short on originality and songwriting talent, the band never had a British hit, although they had some sizable singles in other European countries. Despite their lack of commercial success or appeal, the band managed to record three albums and various EPs and singles between 1963 and 1966, with detours into country-rock and an EP of death-rock tunes. Although they recorded afterwards, it is the Sect's early work that continues to attract connoisseurs of '60s garage and punk. *—Richie Unterberger*

● **The Sect** / 1964 / Columbia ✦✦✦✦✦
Their rawest and most R&B-oriented, firmly rooted in the same influences as The Stones and Pretty Things. Includes punk covers of Chuck Berry, Bo Diddley, Muddy Waters, Jimmy Reed, et al., and a few originals in the same vein. *—Richie Unterberger*

Nite at Gt. Newport Street / 1964 / RBC ✦✦

The Country Sect / 1965 / Columbia ✦✦

Sect Sing Sick Songs / 1965 / Columbia ✦✦

The Rock Sect's In / 1966 / Columbia ✦✦✦
Their wildly erratic third album includes some tepid material, but also has some of their best tracks, especially their vicious run-through of the early British rock & roll standard "Brand New Cadillac." It's most notable for the appearance—through God-knows-what channels—of "Why Don't You Smile Now," which was written by Lou Reed, John Cale, and two unknowns before the Velvet Underground formed. *—Richie Unterberger*

I Want My Baby Back / 1978 / Charly ✦✦✦
A collection of 1960s tracks that is now supplanted in value, content, and sound by the See For Miles Records *Definitive Downliners Sect.* *—Bruce Eder*

Be a Sect Maniac / 1983 / Out Line ✦✦

Definitive Downliners Sect: Singles A's & B's / Dec. 1994 / See For Miles ✦✦✦
Definitive, yes—both sides of all eight of their Columbia singles, both sides of their one Pye single, their 1965 *The Sect Sing Sick Songs* EP, their ultra-rare self-released *Nite at Gt. Newport Street* EP from early 1964, and demos of "Cadillac" and "Roll over Beethoven" from '63 and '64, respectively. Twenty-nine songs in all, spanning 1963-67, many of which didn't make it onto the three albums they released during this period. Good? No, not really. As performers the Sect didn't only verge on inept, they were at times downright careless, as if they couldn't be bothered to polish things a bit in the studio. As (infrequent) songwriters, their talent was nearly nonexistent. It's hard to believe anyone thought most of these sides had any commercial potential, either in the band or at the record label; the material is largely lackluster, and not even especially well chosen (a few of the songs on their first and third LPs would have been much better bets). Highlights are the *Newport* EP, which at least finds them playing things a bit straight and passionate, with a ramshackle version of "Green Onions" and a good cut of Bo Diddley's "Nursery Rhymes"; the 1965 single "Bad Storm Coming" is a fairly moody number. That's a pretty low return on a band that enjoys a vociferous following among some collectors, although they were really a pedestrian British R&B band with a propensity toward parched humor and odd novelty tunes that hasn't aged well. *—Richie Unterberger*

Nick Drake

b. Jun. 19, 1948, Rangoon, Burma, **d.** Nov. 25, 1974, Tanworth-in-Arden, England
Vocals, Piano, Guitar / British Folk-Rock, Baroque Pop, Progressive Folk, British Folk, Folk-Rock, Singer/Songwriter
A singular talent who passed almost unnoticed during his brief lifetime, Nick Drake produced several albums of chilling, somber beauty. With hindsight, these have come to be recognized as peak achievements of both the British folk-rock scene and the entire rock singer/songwriter genre. Sometimes compared to Van Morrison, Drake in fact resembled Donovan much more in his breathy vocals, strong melodies, and the acoustic-based orchestral sweep of his arrangements. His was a much darker vision than Donovan's, however, with disturbing themes of melancholy, failed romance, mortality, and depression lurking just beneath, or even well above, the surface. Ironically, Drake has achieved a far greater stature in the decades following his death, with an avid cult following that grows by the year. In the manner of the young romantic poets of the 19th century who died before their time, Drake is revered by many listeners today, with a following that spans generations. Baby boomers who missed him the first time around found much to revisit once they discovered him, and his pensive loneliness speaks directly to contemporary alternative rockers who share his sense of morose alienation. *—Richie Unterberger*

★ **Five Leaves Left** / 1969 / Hannibal ✦✦✦✦✦
It's little wonder why Drake felt frustrated at the lack of commercial success his music initially gathered, considering the help he had on his debut record. Besides fine production from Joe Boyd and assistance from folks like Fairport Convention's Richard Thompson and his unrelated bass counterpart from Pentangle, Danny Thompson, Drake also recruited school friend Robert Kirby to create most of the just-right string and wind arrangements. His own performance itself steered a careful balance between too-easy accessibility and maudlin self-reflection, combining the best of both worlds while avoiding the pitfalls on either side. The result was a fantastic debut appearance, and if the cult of Drake consistently reads more into his work than is perhaps deserved, *Five Leaves Left* is still a most successful effort. Having grown out of the amiable but derivative styles captured on the long-circulating series of bootleg home recordings, Drake assays his tunes with just enough drama—world-weariness in the vocals, carefully paced playing, and more—to make it all work. His lyrics capture a subtle poetry of emotion, as on the pastoral semi-fantasia of "The Thoughts of Mary Jane," which his soft, articulate singing brings even more to the full. Sometimes he projects a little more clearly, as on the astonishing voice-and-strings combination "Way to Blue," while elsewhere he's not so clear, suggesting rather than outlining the mood. Understatement is the key to his songs and performances' general success, which makes the combination of his vocals and Rocky Dzidzornu's congas on "Three Hours" and the lovely "'Cello Song," to name two instances, so effective. Danny Thompson is the most regular side performer on the album, his bass work providing subtle heft while never standing in the way of the song—kudos well deserved for Boyd's production as well. *—Ned Raggett*

☆ **Bryter Layter** / 1970 / Hannibal ✦✦✦✦✦
With even more of the Fairport Convention crew helping him out—including bassist Dave Pegg and drummer Dave Mattacks along with, again, a bit of help from Richard Thompson—as well as John Cale and a variety of others, Drake tackled another excellent selection of songs on his second album. Demonstrating the abilities shown on *Five Leaves Left* didn't consist of a fluke, *Bryter Layter* featured another set of exquisitely arranged and performed tunes, with producer Joe Boyd and orchestrator Robert Kirby reprising their roles from the earlier release. Starting with the elegant instrumental "Introduction," as lovely a mood-setting piece as one would want, *Bryter Layter* indulges in a more playful sound at many points, showing that Drake was far from being a constant king of depression. While his performances remain generally low-key and his voice quietly passionate, the arrangements and surrounding musicians add a considerable amount of pep, as on the jazzy groove of the lengthy "Poor Boy." The argument could be made that this contravenes the spirit of Drake's work, but it feels more like a calmer equivalent to the genre-sliding experiments of Van Morrison at around the same time. Numbers that retain a softer approach, like "At the Chime of a City Clock," still possess a gentle drive to them. Cale's additions unsurprisingly favor the classically trained side of his personality, with particularly brilliant results on "Northern Sky." As his performances on keyboards and celeste help set the atmosphere, Drake reaches for a perfectly artful reflection on loss and loneliness and succeeds wonderfully. *—Ned Raggett*

☆ **Pink Moon** / 1972 / Hannibal ✦✦✦✦✦
After two albums of tastefully orchestrated folk-pop, albeit some of the least demonstrative and most affecting around, Drake chose a radical change for what turned out to be his final album. Not even half-an-hour long, with 11 short songs and no more—he famously remarked at the time that he simply had no more to record—*Pink Moon* more than anything else is the record that made Drake the cult figure he remains. Specifically, *Pink Moon* is the bleakest of them all; that the likes of Belle and Sebastian are fans of Drake may be clear enough, but it's doubtful they could ever achieve the calm, focused anguish of this album, as harrowing as it is attractive. No side musicians or outside performers help this time around—it's simply Drake and Drake alone on vocals, acoustic guitar, and a bit of piano, recorded by regular producer Joe Boyd but otherwise untouched by anyone else. The lead-off title track was eventually used in a Volkswagen commercial nearly 30 years later, giving him another renewed burst of appreciation—one of life's many ironies, in that such an affecting song, Drake's softly keened singing and gentle strumming, could turn up in such a strange context. The remainder of the album follows the same general path, with Drake's elegant melancholia avoiding sounding pretentious in the least thanks to his continued embrace of simple, tender vocalizing. Meanwhile, the sheer majesty of his guitar playing—consider the opening notes of "Radio" or "Parasite"—makes for a breathless wonder to behold. If anyone needs confirmation as to why artists like Mark Eitzel, Elliot Smith, Lou Barlow, or Robert Smith hold Drake close to their hearts, it's all here, still as beautiful as the day it was released. *—Ned Raggett*

☆ **Fruit Tree** / 1986 / Hannibal ✦✦✦✦✦
Fruit Tree is a four-disc box set featuring all three of Nick Drake's studio albums (*Five*

Leaves Left, Bryter Layter, Pink Moon) and the rarities collection *Time of No Reply*. In other words, it contains every known recording Drake made during his brief lifetime, and listening to the set, the depth of his talent becomes abundantly clear. And the four discs are *not* overkill. The quality of Drake's songs was startlingly high, and anyone who purchases one disc will eventually need the other three albums, making *Fruit Tree* a logical way to acquire all of the records at once. *—Stephen Thomas Erlewine*

Time of No Reply / 1986 / Hannibal ♦♦♦

Released in the mid-'80 during one of the many Drake revivals over the years, combining tracks from the original *Fruit Tree* box set and other outtakes unreleased until then, *Time of No Reply* is a fine coda to Drake's all too brief recording career. A collection of outtakes and alternate versions of more familiar songs, it parallels *Pink Moon* in that all songs but two are simply Drake on his own, his guitar and his voice doing all that needs to be done. The majority of the recordings come from the late '60s, from the slew of sessions and home recordings predating the release of *Five Leaves Left*. They still show Drake working in a touch more traditional mode, but his unmistakable vocal approach is well in place throughout. The title track itself is a gem, raising the question as to why Drake thought it unworthy for initial release, with a softly catchy chorus and sweet, reflective lyrical cast. The takes on "Man in a Shed" and "The Thoughts of Mary Jane," with Richard Thompson adding electric guitar on the latter, make for an intersting contrast to their more familiar studio incarnations. The release concludes with the "final session," four last songs recorded two years after *Pink Moon*, shortly before his death. The songs included on *Time of No Reply* should be considered demos and experiments, but there's no questioning Drake's power for understated exploration of darker moments and emotions remained. *—Ned Raggett*

● **Way to Blue: An Introduction to Nick Drake** / Oct. 4, 1994 / Hannibal ♦♦♦♦

A selection of 16 tracks from all three of his studio albums and the *Time of No Reply* collection, compiled by Drake's producer, Joe Boyd. Of course the music is excellent, but Drake's albums stand so well on their own that this collection of piecemeal offerings hardly works as the best way to experience his distinctively haunting brand of folk-rock. *—Richie Unterberger*

Dramarama

f. 1983, Wayne, NJ, **db.** 1994

Alternative Pop/Rock, Rock & Roll

Blending hard rock wallop, alternative rock smarts, power pop songcraft, and punk rock urgency, Dramarama was a band who seemed on the verge of a major commercial breakthrough several times during their 11-year career. Puzzlingly, it never arrived, though the band developed a potent following in their native New Jersey as well as the West Coast; their almost-hit, "Anything Anything (I'll Give You)," was cited by L.A.'s KROQ-FM, arguably America's most influential alternative rock outlet, as the most requested song in the station's history. Formed in Wayne, NJ, by vocalist and songwriter John Easdale in 1983, Dramarama self-released a single and a five-song EP before a French label commissioned a full-length album from the band, which recycled material from both previous releases. The result, 1985's *Cinema Verite*, featured "Anything Anything," which began scoring airplay after the album was picked up by Chameleon Records in the United States. The group relocated to California in time for their second LP, *Box Office Bomb*, which earned enthusiastic reviews but not significantly greater sales. As the band was completing their fourth studio album, *Vinyl*, in 1991, Chameleon Records went bankrupt, and as the band scrambled to come up with the cash to finish the project, the elusive major-label deal finally materialized when Elektra picked up the project. However, while the success of Nirvana in 1991 would seemingly have broken open radio for bands as adventurous as Dramarama, their sound was too far from grunge to capitalize on the new openness, and the band's 1993 album, *Hi-Fi Sci-Fi*, failed to make an impact outside the band's devoted cult following. Dramarama called it a day after a farewell show at Asbury Park's the Stone Pony in 1994; four years later, John Easdale returned to the music business with a solo album. *—Mark Deming*

Cinéma Vérité / Nov. 1985 / Chameleon ♦♦♦♦♦

Probably the greatest rock release from 1985 that almost no one has ever heard, *Cinema Verite* is a simply fantastic album. Blending everything from British Invasion panache and glam influences to punk energy and back again, its cult legend was established by L.A. DJ legend Rodney Bingenheimer. He played "Anything, Anything (I'll Give You)" to death on his show and created a sizeable following for the New Jersey band in Southern California. It's no surprise why: "Anything, Anything" simply smokes, a rave-up for the modern day that starts with a blasting riff before hitting a high-speed punch that doesn't stop, while singer John Easdale details the highs and lows of a relationship with a breathless yowl. There's much more to *Cinema Verite* than that song, though, as even a casual listen demonstrates. Guitarists Mr. E Boy and Peter Wood distill the kick of performers like Keith Richards, Mick Ronson, and Mott the Hoople-era Mick Ralphs into a hot-wired combination, while rhythm section Chris Carter (bass) and Jesse (drums) hit the beat with heart and talent. Add in keyboardist Theothorous Athanasious Ellenis for final flair and the results are jaw dropping. "Scenario," for instance, is the greatest song the Psychedelic Furs never wrote, with a chugging beat, cut-to-the-chase solos, and Easdale's delicious Dylan-into-Ian Hunter-via-Bowie vocals creating the definition of energetic melancholia. Speaking of Bowie, there's a fantastic cover of his "Candidate," the freaked-out psychosis fully intact, not to mention a nicely dissipated take on the Velvet Underground's "Femme Fatale." Add in everything from the anguished kick of "Questions?" and the building explosion of "Some Crazy Dame" to the concluding elegance of "Emerald City," and this isn't a cult classic, but classic, period. Rhino's welcome reissue in 1995 tacked on eight bonus tracks, including demo takes and sparer, nervous early singles, and two extensive essays celebrating both the band and this wonderful record. *—Ned Raggett*

Box Office Bomb / 1989 / Chameleon ♦♦♦♦

Blessed and cursed with the cult classic "Anything, Anything (I'll Give You)"—it became the group's calling card, though many music fans never took the time to look beyond that one song—the band moved to Southern California and created its inspired follow-up to *Cinema Verite*. Tongue firmly in cheek regarding the title, *Box Office Bomb* still lived up to its name as it didn't create as much of a buzz as Dramarama's debut, keeping the group's West Coast following more than happy while unfortunately never doing much elsewhere in the world. Regrettably so, for *Box Office Bomb* is another strong blast of energetic classic rock-via-punk treats that shows the band still in outrageously good form. Lyrically reflecting the group's transplantation to Hollywood's environs in more ways than one, including the album's slamming lead single "It's Still Warm," an unsure, uneasy reflection on their new locale and the cost it incurred, musically *Box Office Bomb* otherwise stayed true to its roots. Once or twice the band sounded like it wanted to aim for huge venues—the brilliant opener "Steve and Edie" sounds like what would happen if U2's guitar pyrotechnics were transferred to a less full-of-itself outfit—and a few songs sound like semi-retreads of *Cinema Verite* tracks. For the most part, though, this is intelligent but never pretentious red-blooded rock that avoids gravelly rootsiness in favor of flash and style, worth every note. Standouts include the clearly Stooges-inspired "Spare Change" and the smart ghost-of-Blondie rush of "Out in the Rain." Rhino's reissue of the album is the equal to its similar revival of *Cinema Verite*; besides more entertaining liner notes, six bonus tracks appear, including a great demo take on the later *Stuck in Wonderamaland* standout "Last Cigarette" and a solid cover of the New York Dolls' "Private World." *—Ned Raggett*

Stuck in Wonderamaland / 1989 / Chameleon ♦♦♦♦

Continuing its regret-tinged look at the life of the almost-famous in L.A., Dramarama on its third album continued polishing its abilities at both straight-ahead rock and gentler affairs on *Stuck in Wonderamaland*. Beginning and, in a brief acoustic reprise, concluding with the title track, a wistful strum with some prime feedback burn added in the mid-section, the band happily turned firmly away from the bad-glam-addled idiocies of late-'80s Sunset Strip sleaze to keep pursuing its own muse. The sly choice of a cover song, Mott the Hoople's bitter, knowing demolition of the rock dream "I Wish I Was Your Mother," betrays the emotional sucker punch prevalent throughout. With no changes outside of the departure of keyboardist Ellenis, adequately replaced here and there by Tommy T, also tackling guitar as needed, the group still kicks with a sharp energy even at its calmest moments. Easdale's signature semi-rasp if anything became even more emotive with time, while the guitar team of Wood and Mr. E Boy remained able to tackle full-on riffing to softer shades with aplomb. Carter's bass work here is some of his best, warm and flowing, while drummer Jesse similarly does the business. The great "Last Cigarette" continues the Dramarama tradition of strong lead singles, hitting and ripping with the prime energy of early New York glam/punk and even earlier rave-ups without sounding dated in the least. Then there's "70s TV," which makes the addiction to such a seeming pit of hell downright cool. When the group tries for calmer material, it does so in ways that make the then-prevalent "power ballad" trend look like the weak cheese it was. "Fireplace, Pool and Air Conditioning" hits a lovely slow burn that sounds like an updated Love if Tom Waits was the lyricist, while "Try" simply shimmers with a gorgeous acoustic/electric combination, a lovely eternal sunset. *—Ned Raggett*

Live at the China Club / 1990 / Chameleon ♦♦♦♦

Recorded as something of a stopgap between albums, *Live* is just that, a great six-song document of the band in its 1990 incarnation, touching briefly on all its previous albums with fire and panache. Perhaps inevitably, "Anything, Anything (I'll Give You)" leads off the disc, and while it's a brilliant performance of a brilliant song, it's not the sole reason to pay attention (indeed, the even quicker rush of the live take may signal a desire on the band to get it over with). Another highlight of the first album, "Some Crazy Dame," barrels out nonstop from the speakers, sly cool and high-speed power intact, while the sly, Stooges quoting *Box Office Bomb* cut "Spare Change" gets a well-deserved rampage. Meanwhile, more recent history is touched on with a commanding rave-up and burn-down-the-house rip on "Last Cigarette," as well as another *Stuck in Wonderamaland* number, "Would You Like," its slow, reflective pace the one moment of breath in the otherwise nonstop rush of the EP. The one rarity is a fun, kicking version of "Private World," the New York Dolls classic, whose studio version didn't surface on a Dramarama release until the reissue of *Box Office Bomb* some years later. Easdale's vocal abilities really shine here, his just raspy enough but never burnt out singing taking deserved charge. Meanwhile, the Mr. E Boy/Wood guitar team blasts along loud and proud, one of the most underrated combinations since Rick Nielsen and Robin Zander of Cheap Trick first plugged in and fired up. Original drummer Jesse takes what turned out to be his final bow with the band here, style and power intact and still working hand in glove with bassist Carter. A full album would have been fantastic, but in its absence this is a more than fine substitute. *—Ned Raggett*

Vinyl / 1991 / Chameleon ♦♦♦♦♦

Finding itself on a major label for the first time in its career, Dramarama maintained the overall course of its career with *Vinyl*, combining smart pop/rock kicks and a sense of hip cool for grand overall results. With Brian Macleod taking over the drum duties from departed sticksman Jesse and keyboard/guitar player Tommy T stepping in on a track or two, the otherwise still-in-one-piece group creates and performs up to the best of its considerable abilities. Guest help doesn't hurt either, most often coming from Tom Petty keyboardist Benmont Tench, but *Vinyl* is still clearly Dramarama's vision rather than anything else. "Haven't Got a Clue" keeps up the winning streak of brilliant first singles from the band's releases, starting with a sample from the legendary Tube Bar crank call series and hitting a great mid-paced groove with a gently descending glam melody. "I've Got Spies" is equally brilliant, a nugget of romantic paranoia that rivals the Who's "I Can See for Miles," with delicious singing from Easdale and a great main melody. Another great moment comes with "Classic Rot"—a knowing trashing of groups that have lasted way too long, it draws the line clearly between simply re-creating and re-listening to the same old hash and, as the band itself does, taking inspiration from the past and creating their own sound. Even tastier is the identity of the guest guitar player—as the liner notes proudly say, "THE Mick Taylor, of Rolling Stones fame." The Stones themselves—or more accurately Mick Jagger—are the beneficiaries of the cool cover version this time out, in this case a fine take on "Memo From Turner." All in all, *Vinyl* shows Dramarama still in rude creative health, right down to the neat artwork and the bold Marc Bolan song lyric on the back of the CD booklet: "John Lennon knows your name/and I've seen his." *—Ned Raggett*

Hi-Fi Sci-Fi / 1993 / Chameleon ♦♦♦♦
Hi-Fi Sci-Fi proved to be the swan song for New Jersey's Dramarama, but the band goes down blazing with an excellent effort. Produced by bassist Chris Carter and lead vocalist John Easdale, the band brings the well-traveled Clem Burke into the fold on drums, and he provides this album with more muscle than their prior release, *Vinyl*. The raucous, pile-driving intro title "Introduction/Hey Betty" leads into the almost radio hit "Work for Food." With Dwight Twilley lending a hand on backup vocals, "Work for Food" is a driving and delightfully hooky tale of resilience from the point of view of a homeless person—the twist being that the protagonist is revealed to be a failed musician. Other standouts on this consistently engaging album are numerous. Benmont Tench appears again playing piano on the lovely ballad "Senseless Fun," which also benefits from Martin Tillman's cello, and "Right on Baby, Baby," is another ballad with intelligent, poignant lyrics, Pete Wood's slide guitar, and Nicky Hopkins' added piano. On the rocking side, "Don't Feel Like Doing Drugs" is an amusing take on the aftermath of such endeavors. *Hi-Fi Sci-Fi* is, perhaps, the finest moment for an underappreciated band. *—Tom Demalon*

• **The Best of Dramarama: 18 Big Ones** / Oct. 29, 1996 / Rhino ♦♦♦♦♦
Despite all of their good reviews, Dramarama was never able to break into the mainstream. Nevertheless, they left behind a number of terrific rock & roll albums, which found a dedicated cult following. For anyone interested in joining that cult, *Best of Dramarama: 18 Big Ones* provides an excellent primer, featuring 16 of the group's best songs—including "Last Cigarette," "Anything, Anything (I'll Give You)," "Scenario," "Work for Food," "Haven't Got a Clue," "Wonderamaland" and "What Are We Gonna Do?"—plus two previously unreleased cuts, "Going Blind" and "You're So Rude." *—Stephen Thomas Erlewine*

The Dramatics

f. 1962, Detroit, MI, **db.** 1983
Smooth Soul, Quiet Storm, Soul
Before assuming the name the Dramatics, the vocal sextet that was comprised of Rob Davis, Ron Banks, Larry Reed, Robert Ellington, Larry "Squirrel" Demps and Elbert Wilkens initially released two singles as the Dynamics on the Wingate imprint that saw no chart action. The group became a quintet upon Ellington's exit, and also changed their name to the Dramatics. They migrated to the Sport label and in 1967 released their first single to hit the charts, "All Because of You," which peaked at #42 on the Billboard R&B charts. However, in spite of the exposure and limited record sales, some group members became discouraged, which facilitated a major personnel change. William "Wee Gee" Howard replaced lead singer Reed, and Willie Ford of the Capitols replaced bass Rob Davis. Also during this time, the Dramatics had signed with producer Don Davis' productions company.

The group wouldn't see a major hit for four years until "Watcha See Is Watcha Get" was released, peaking at number three on the Billboard R&B charts, and sustaining chart action for 15 weeks. That single was followed by the R&B Top Ten single "Get Up and Get Down." Several other hits followed, including "In the Rain."

In 1973 Larry "L.J." Reynolds replaced Howard and Lenny Mayes replaced Wilkens. Wilkens formed his own band under the same name, which led the original Dramatics to be briefly known as Ron Banks and the Dramatics while the legal battles ensued.

The Dramatics' success continued with mainly R&B Top 20 hits during the heyday of disco, cracking the R&B Top Ten just once more with "Welcome Back Home" in 1980. In 1981, Reynolds went solo and the group disbanded after Banks' exit in 1983. *—Craig Lytle*

• **The Best of the Dramatics** / 1976 / Stax ♦♦♦♦♦
In the 1960s, Stax Records was best known for raw southern soul that rejected the type of sleekness and pop sensibilities favored by the northern soulsters at Motown. But by the early '70s, Memphis soul was losing its popularity, and Stax's A&R department started to emphasize northern and so-called "uptown" soul in order to stay competitive. One of Stax/Volt's biggest sellers was the Dramatics, a Detroit group that, like the Temptations at Motown and the O'Jays in the Gamble & Huff camp, effectively combined gritty soul belting with a sleek production style. Thanks to major hits ranging from the delightfully funky "Whacha See Is Whacha Get" to slow jams and ballads like "Hey You! Get Off My Mountain," "Toast to the Fool" and the melancholy "In the Rain," the Dramatics were on quite a roll in the early-to-mid-'70s. All of those gems are included on the hour-long CD, *The Best of the Dramatics*, which offers a fine overview of the quintet's Stax/Volt years. Many Dramatics albums are worth owning, but if a listener were allowed to own only one Dramatics CD, this would be it. *—Alex Henderson*

Be My Girl: Their Greatest Love Songs / Jan. 27, 1998 / Hip-O ♦♦♦♦
During the 1970s, the Dramatics were one of the smoothest purveyors of romantic ballads, and this 16-track collection brings together some of their best moments in that genre. Highlights include "In the Rain," "Fall In Love, Lady Love," "The Stars In Your Eyes," "Door to Your Heart," "Do What You Want to Do," "Ocean of Thoughts and Dreams" and "You're the Best Thing In My Life." The Dramatics are hard to beat for romantic ambience, and this collection brings together some of their very best work. *—Cub Koda*

Shake It Well: The Best of the Dramatics 1974-1980 / Oct. 20, 1998 / MCA ♦♦♦
A nice collection of this Detroit-based group's best records for the Cadet and ABC-MCA labels between 1974-1980. Besides the title track (a #5 R&B hit that crossed over to the pop charts), highlights include "I Can't Get Over You," "Be My Girl," "You're Foolin' You," "Love Is Missing From Our Lives," "Don't Make Me No Promises" and the pop crossover smash "Do What You Want, Be What You Are." Although their earlier sides for Wingate, Sport and Volt aren't on here (thus leaving off their biggest hit, "Whatcha See Is What You Get"), this is still a nice collection of tunes by one of the '70s' most prolific and dependable R&B acts. *—Cub Koda*

Ultimate Collection / Sep. 19, 2000 / Hip-O ♦♦♦♦
Spanning their biggest singles from the '70s and '80s, the Dramatics' *Ultimate Collection* includes staples like "In the Rain," "Whatcha See Is Whatcha Get," and "Be My Girl." "You're Fooling You," "Welcome Back Home," "I'm Going By the Stars in Your Eyes," and "Me and Mrs. Jones" are some of the other notable tracks from this retrospective, which covers the group's years with Stax, ABC, and Volt. Though it doesn't go into as much depth as some previous Dramatics collections, *Ultimate Collection* does a good job of presenting highlights from the majority of the group's career. *—Heather Phares*

The Dream Academy

College Rock, Dream Pop, New Wave, Alternative Pop/Rock
The airy, baroque British pop trio dubbed the Dream Academy emerged in the mid-'80s as one of the leading lights of the psychedelic revival movement. The group was led by vocalist/guitarist Nick Laird-Clowes, a former member of the short-lived Act; also comprised of multi-instumentalist Kate St. John (an alumna of the Ravishing Beauties) and keyboardist Gilbert Gabriel, the Dream Academy issued their eponymously titled debut LP in 1985. Co-produced by David Gilmour, the atmospheric lead single "Life in a Northern Town," an elegy for Nick Drake, quickly reached the Top 20 of the U.K. charts; issued in the U.S. the following year, it became a Top Ten hit.

The trio's follow-up single, "The Love Parade," failed to repeat the success of its predecessor, however, and the Dream Academy's commercial momentum stalled. After 1987's *Remembrance Days* quickly dropped from sight, the group went into seclusion; when their 1991 comeback *A Different Kind of Weather* failed to restore their chart luster, the Dream Academy promptly disbanded. In subsequent years, St. John was the trio's most visible graduate; in addition to touring with Van Morrison, she teamed with Roger Eno, Bill Nelson and others in the group Channel Light Vessel, and in 1996 issued her solo debut *Indescribable Night*. *—Jason Ankeny*

The Dream Academy / 1985 / Reprise ♦♦♦♦
Dream Academy was the self-titled debut release for the art-school trio led by lead singer/guitarist Nick Laird-Clowes. Produced by David Gilmour and Laird-Clowes, the group was rounded out by vocalist/multi-instrumentalist Kate St. John and keyboard player Gilbert Gabriel, and they struck the first time out with the album's standout track "Life in a Northern Town," which became a Top Ten smash in the spring of 1986. *Dream Academy* used lush string arrangements and choir-like background vocals to create a sumptuous backdrop for their paisley-tinged pop. It works to best effect on "Life in a Northern Town," a slice of watercolored nostalgia with its memorable chant-like hook. Other highlights include the sax-driven "The Edge of Forever," the gentle dream recollection of "In Places on the Run," and "This World," with its somber, stark portrayal of the downtrodden. Laird-Clowes' vocals are thin, a shortcoming masked by the soft-focus of the material, and the album falters a bit during the second half; however, the best material on this record leaves you longing for more. *—Tom Demalon*

Remembrance Days / 1987 / Reprise ♦♦♦
Attempting to follow up the enormous success of their debut proved to be a difficult task for the British trio Dream Academy. Hugh Padgham (Genesis, the Police) came on board to produce the band with frontman Nick Laird-Clowes, resulting in a more glossy sheen to much of the material. "Indian Summer" kicks things off, and while echoing the wistfulness and even incorporating a chant-like chorus similar to their massive hit "Life in a Northern Town," it fails to impress in a similar manner. "Here" is a lovely, understated ballad that concludes with a flourish and Kate St. John playing oboe, and "Ballad in 4/4" is a Beatlesque tale of infidelity featuring Laird-Clowes adding harmonica. *Remembrance Days*, however, failed to make a splash commercially and received more exposure through the use of "Power to Believe" during a key scene of the hit movie *Planes, Trains, and Automobiles* than through airplay. Not a bad record, just a pale imitation of the first. *—Tom Demalon*

A Different Kind of Weather / 1990 / Reprise ♦♦♦♦
Nick Laird-Clowes and company return for what would prove to be their swan song. If *A Different Kind of Weather* failed to reach the heights of the band's debut, it outshone *Remembrance Days* and proved to be a fitting close on one of the 1980s' overlooked delights. It also marked the return of David Gilmour's involvement with the band in a production capacity with Laird-Clowes and adding guitar. The band stretches a bit on their version of John Lennon's "Love," which opens the album. Building the song around a drum loop and Indian instrumentation, they don't fully succeed. However, the rest of the album contains several moments of pure pop pleasure like "Gaby Says," a dramatic expression of longing to get away; "Twelve-Eight Angel," a punchy song about regret with a sax solo by

Kate St. John; and "It'll Never Happen Again," a lovely laid-back gem with an undercurrent of Gilmour's guitar work and breezy background vocals. Overall, a graceful bow by Dream Academy that is a worthwhile addition to their catalog. —*Tom Demalon*

● **Somewhere in the Sun: Best of the Dream Academy** / Mar. 28, 2000 / WEA International ✦✦✦✦

This 18-song import is probably the place to start and finish with the Dream Academy, encompassing as it does the best songs off of all three of their albums, spiced with the extended mix of "Life in a Northern Town," an acoustic version of "The Party," and the "Hare Krishna Mix" of "Love." The only track not here that definitely ought to be is "Gaby Says" from *A Different Kind of Weather*. All of the lyrics are reprinted along with full instrumental credits. —*Bruce Eder*

Dream Syndicate

f. 1981, Los Angeles, CA, db. 1989
College Rock, Jangle Pop, Paisley Underground, Alternative Pop/Rock, American Underground

Dream Syndicate are at the foundation (alongside the Velvet Underground, the Stooges and R.E.M.) of contemporary alternative music sheerly because at the time when most bands were experimenting with new technology, the Syndicate deigned to bring back the guitar. Fronted by Steve Wynn, the band debuted with a self-titled, unbelievably Velvet Underground-like EP on Wynn's own Down There label. It was shortly off to Ruby/Slash for *Days of Wine and Roses*, the most lauded record on the college charts that year. The record has been cited as influential from artists as diverse as Kurt Cobain to the Black Crowes' Chris Robinson. Live, they had developed into an assaultive guitar band prone to jamming which helped earn them the tag as leaders of L.A.'s Paisley Underground movement. 1984's *Medicine Show* was met with mixed response by the college crowd. Wynn took his cues from Neil Young and Crazy Horse on the record rather than Lou Reed (who was considered a preferable source at the time), and the rootsier sound caused a backlash with the fan base. In 1986, a new lineup and a flailing morale, as the band label-hopped, spawned *Out of the Grey* and the Elliot Mazer-produced *Ghost Stories* in 1988. —*Denise Sullivan*

The Days of Wine & Roses / 1982 / Slash ✦✦✦✦✦

On the one hand, where the Dream Syndicate came from was so obvious that it almost hurt. The Velvet Underground was a clear touchstone (if not quite the original LaMonte Young ensemble the band name referred to), as were the Doors, the Byrds, and any number of blues and country traditions and more. Had they been around in the late '60s, one might have wondered whether they would have garnered much attention in comparison. But the early '80s was the band's time and place, and their fusions of all the above and more via punk-inspired energy achieved its own level of deserved attention. Capturing the original killer Wynn/Precoda/Smith/Duck lineup performing with inspiration throughout, *The Days of Wine and Roses* trumps the "paisley underground" tag the band was saddled with by being a great rock record, full on. While Wynn received the lion's share of attention thanks to his ghost-of-Lou Reed vocals and frontman status, arguably it's Precoda who is the real reason to listen in. Both his rave-ups and gentler shadings are phenomenal, as a random listen of songs like "Definitely Clean" and the sweet, Smith-sung "Too Little, Too Late" show. The Smith/Duck rhythm section grooves along fairly enough, at its best on the Krautrock-inspired chug of Precoda's composition "Halloween." Highlights include the romping "Then She Remembers," with a much more direct Wynn vocal that makes for good in-your-face fun, and the mid-tempo moodout of "When You Smile," Precoda's screeching feedback playing around the mix's edges. Concluding with the epochal title track, which builds to a frenetic climax not once but twice, *The Days of Wine and Roses* is a grand treat. —*Ned Raggett*

Medicine Show / 1984 / A&M ✦✦✦✦✦

More Neil Young and Crazy Horse than the previous Lou Reed and the Velvet Underground-inspired album, the Syndicate rip through eight fairly traditional (save for the feedback) rock songs. The CD reissue includes *This Is Not the Dream Syndicate Album ...Live!*, five songs performed from the album. "The Medicine Show" and the similar "John Coltrane Stereo Blues" are the keepers, and check the guitar on "Bullet With My Name on It." The record wrestles with American roots music in a way college rockers probably weren't familiar with, and thus it was almost universally hated at the time. Wynn admits in the liner notes to the CD reissue that this is his favorite release with the band. —*Denise Sullivan*

This Is Not the New Dream Syndicate / 1984 / A&M ✦✦

Dream Syndicate / 1985 / Demon ✦✦✦

Out of the Grey / 1986 / Atavistic ✦✦✦

Like nearly everything released that year, *Out of the Grey* suffered from a touch of the post-new wave flu. But "50 in a 25 Zone" has that old, bluesy Syndicate spirit, as does "Now I Ride Alone," and Steve Wynn is still an exceptional vocal stylist, bringing heart and meaning to every word he writes. —*Denise Sullivan*

50 in a 25 Zone / 1987 / Big Time ✦✦

Ghost Stories / 1988 / Restless ✦✦✦

Opening with the self-referential "The Side I'll Never Show," and produced by Neil Young and Crazy Horse vet Elliot Mazer, Wynn and Co. mine the dark and rusty terrain of folk and blues-rock that they ultimately made work to their advantage on this very straight-ahead rock album. Wynn's vocal style and forthright lyrics never really connected with the masses at the time, but years later, it's clear he was making music for the ages. —*Denise Sullivan*

Live at Raji's / 1989 / Enigma ✦✦✦✦

A fond farewell from the preeminent '80s distorto-rock band. All the classics are here: "Days of Wine and Roses," "The Medicine Show," "That's What You Always Say." Even the previously uninspired "Forest for the Trees" sounds good on this night. Lucky for them, they were particularly on fire, because tape was rolling. —*Denise Sullivan*

● **Tell Me When It's Over: The Best of Dream Syndicate** / Jun. 23, 1992 / Rhino ✦✦✦✦✦

While the Dream Syndicate's 1982 debut album, *The Days of Wine and Roses*, made them an immediate sensation on the post-punk underground scene, their subsequent body of work rarely received the same degree of attention, partly because of the band's deliberate swing away from noisy neo-Velvet Underground jamming after the departure of guitarist Karl Precoda and partly because most of their subsequent albums lacked the sonic and thematic consistency of their debut. The shame of this was that leader Steve Wynn grew steadily as a songwriter through the band's career, and even their patchiest albums had at least two or three cuts worth hearing. Thankfully, *Tell Me When It's Over: The Best of the Dream Syndicate* sets the record straight about this misunderstood band's career, offering about half of *The Days of Wine and Roses* (and a cut from the band's first self-released EP) alongside nine neglected gems like "Merrittville," "Now I Ride Alone," and "Loving the Sinner, Hating the Sin"; there's also a hard rocking cover of Eric Clapton's "Let It Rain" thrown in for good measure. Anyone wanting a crash course in the Dream Syndicate's challenging body of work could hardly do better than to give *Tell Me When It's Over* a listen. —*Mark Deming*

3 1/2: The Lost Tapes: 1985-1988 / 1995 / Normal ✦✦✦

So-called because it mostly consists of sessions and takes recorded in between *Out of the Grey* and *Ghost Stories*, *3 1/2* makes for an entertaining coda for the dedicated Dream Syndicate fan and has some points of interest for the general listener. While Precoda is understandably missed, Cutler was no slouch as a replacement guitarist, and the recordings here generally have a good, rootsy feeling to them. Most were recorded during mid-1987 with Vitus Matare manning the boards and Green on Red mainstay Chris Cacavas guesting on keyboards and vocals. Cutler throws in some okay feedback squeals and blasts, while Cacavas adds a further barrelhouse/bar band jam touch to the material, especially on the cover of Rodney Crowell's "I Ain't Living Long Like This." Wynn's in OK voice and everything sounds pleasant, though frankly less of the hot-wired inspiration of the band's early years appears—it's reverential without being revelatory, where a band like the Walkabouts took many similar influences to wider conclusions. Most of the remaining tracks come from earlier recordings in 1985 shortly after the band was reactivated with Cutler as the new guitarist. Hearing him play distinctly non-chaotic/goth music so soon after 45 Grave's dissolution is perversely amusing, but the real point is that he brings a fine sense of performance to Wynn's material, especially to the disc-concluding "Blood Money," a solid rocker. One final ringer is an outtake from the *Live at Raji's* album, a nice version of "When You Smile," introduced with an amusing admonition for the crowd to scream so "we can run a loop of that whole thing" throughout said record's length. In general, *3 1/2*, while nowhere near the real heights of the Precoda years, is listenable and intriguing if not deathless. —*Ned Raggett*

Dream Warriors

f. 1988, Toronto, Ontario, Canada
Jazz-Rap, Political Rap

The Juno Award winning hip-hop and jazz-rap group Dream Warriors was made up of three members at first, King Lou, Capital Q, and Spek. The friends from Toronto, Ontario, Canada came together about 1988 and soon began doing a number of performances and later some independent recordings. Those first efforts impressed the right people in the right places.

In 1991 the Dream Warriors completed a debut album, *And Now the Legacy Begins*. It was released under the Island Records label. A short year later the group came home with a Juno Award, thanks to the tunes on that first album. In 1994 the threesome became a foursome with the addition of member Luv. Dream Warriors also switched to a new label, EMI, and released a sophomore album that year, *Subliminal Simulation*. It was followed two years later by *The Master Plan*. After the third album hit the market, Spek decided to move on to a new project. The other members tried to hold on, but failed to recapture the early success the group had gained so easily and quickly.

Some of the songs done by Dream Warriors are "Wash Your Face in My Sink," "Voyage Through the Multiverse," "Do Not Feed the Alligators," "Maximum 60 Lost in a Dream," and "Answer for the Owl." —*Charlotte Dillon*

● **Anthology: A Decade of Hits 1988–1998** / Jun. 22, 1999 / Priority ✦✦✦✦✦

Though often neglected within the jazz-rap community during their brief, three-album run, Dream Warriors recorded a legion of interesting tracks, and *Anthology* does a better job than either of those albums in summarizing what made them so great. Featuring two versions of their nearest thing to a hit, "My Definition of a Boombastic Jazz Style," the album also scores with a few collaboration tracks including others in the jazz-rap royalty—"It's a Project Thing" with DJ Premier, "I've Lost My Ignorance" with Premier and Guru (i.e., Gang Starr), and "Tricycles and Kittens" with Digable Planets. Elsewhere, Dream Warriors salute their Caribbean influences with tracks like "Sound Clash" with Beenie Man and "Dem No Ready" with General Degree. It's a great look at one of the better hip-hop groups of the '90s. —*Keith Farley*

The Drifters

f. May 1953, New York, NY
Doo Wop, R&B, Soul

Originally a backup group formed around the soaring vocal talents of Clyde McPhatter, the Drifters—like their '50s counterparts, the Platters and the Coasters—have turned out to be one of the most enduring "franchises" in rock & roll. Though it's been years since any of the original members have been involved (almost all of them being long deceased), chances are if there's an oldies but goodies stage show happening somewhere tonight, there's a 50-50 shot that some form of the Drifters will be up on that stage, singing the hits that made the original group a legend. Unlike other groups who lost key members along the way and never regained their artistic or commercial footing, the various incarnations of the Drifters produced distinctly memorable material every step of the way. Depending on what time frame you come in on during their 40-plus years as a group, you'll discover that they turned from a hard rhythm and gospel doo wop aggregation to one of the smoothest and most romantic ever to grace an AM radio. One of the first Black R&B groups to utilize a string section on their records ("There Goes My Baby," 1959), their middle period sound defined universal love and the good life as seen through the eyes of the ghetto, an arresting combination that won them crossover appeal. That they not only moved, but prospered, with the times is testimony enough to their rightly deserved longevity. *—Cub Koda*

☆ **Let the Boogie-Woogie Roll: Greatest Hits 1953-1958** / 1988 / Rhino/Atlantic ✦✦✦✦✦
This is a repackaged and re-sequenced version of the similarly titled 1988 Atlantic double CD, containing the 40 songs recorded by the early Drifters in their Clyde McPhatter, David Baughan, and Johnny Moore eras—and it's as fine a body of rhythm & blues-cum-rock & roll as you'll ever find. The work runs from the ethereal, soulful balladry ("Gone") to bluesy laments ("Don't Dog Me") and distinctive reinterpretations of classic songs ("White Christmas," "The Bells of St. Mary's") to out and out rock & roll ("Money Honey," "Let the Boogie Woogie Roll," "Bip Bam"), with lots of classic moments and songs. Certainly Clyde McPhatter never cut better music than the 20 tracks he did with the Drifters, all laid out on disc one. Their string of hits was unbroken by the arrival of Johnny Moore, so the second disc in this set is as enjoyable as the first. The improvement to this set over the original includes a bigger typeface for the notes, and the altered sequencing, which puts everything in order of recording, not release, thus, presenting the way the group evolved, step by step and song by song. The sound, in addition to showing off the group's extraordinary vocal prowess, also highlights the playing of guitarist Mickey Baker and saxman Sam "The Man" Taylor. *—Bruce Eder*

☆ **All-Time Greatest Hits & More: 1959-1965** / 1988 / Rhino/Atlantic ✦✦✦✦✦
If Rhino's *Very Best of the Drifters* is a fine R&B snack, then *All-Time Greatest Hits & More: 1959-1965* is a three-course gourmet meal with dessert built on the same ingredients. Forget about the higher price and the fact that 40 songs might seem to be more Drifters than most casual listeners would want—*All-Time Greatest Hits & More: 1959-1965* is a towering and magnificent collection of some of the best popular R&B ever done this side of Sam Cooke. And, as with Sam Cooke, the beautiful part of the Drifters' work during this period is that any look beyond and behind their hits reveals a lot more songs that were every bit as good as those hits. There's not even a slightly weak track anywhere on *All-Time Greatest Hits & More*, which contains the biggest hits Ben E. King, Rudy Lewis, and Johnny Moore sang for the group. "There Goes My Baby," "This Magic Moment," "Save the Last Dance for Me," "Sweets for My Sweet," "I Count the Tears," "Some Kind of Wonderful," "Up on the Roof," "On Broadway," and "Under the Boardwalk" are all here, mastered in surprisingly good sound for the late '80s. There's a lot more than that, however—the producers have also included killer B-sides (such as "Let the Music Play") that hadn't been in print since the mid-'60s, and they've dug even deeper to throw in finished tracks that were left in the vaults until the '70s. The notes by Colin Escott are an added bonus, displaying his usual command for historical detail. *—Bruce Eder*

★ **The Very Best of the Drifters** / Apr. 20, 1993 / Rhino ✦✦✦✦✦
This mid-priced 16-song collection is the successor to the old Atlantic Records *Drifters Golden Hits*, covering the group's very best songs from "There Goes My Baby" in 1959 on up through 1964 in a more comprehensive way. Very pleasingly remastered and handy on its own terms, *The Very Best of the Drifters* also provides just a taste of what the post-1958 group had to offer, even in terms of singles. No one will dislike anything about it, but those who have heard even part of the two-CD package *All-Time Greatest Hits & More* will recognize *The Very Best of the Drifters* as nothing but a superficial sampler of what the Ben E. King/Rudy Lewis/Johnny Moore version of the group left behind. *The Very Best of the Drifters* is a great place to start, but the leap from this material to the rest of the Drifters' best is such a short one that, unless time or budgetary limitations dictate otherwise, it can be bypassed in favor of Atlantic's double-disc *All-Time Greatest Hits & More*. *—Bruce Eder*

Rockin' & Driftin': The Drifters Box / 1996 / Rhino ✦✦✦✦✦
This triple-disc 79-song compilation looks pretty impressive, and in some ways it is, representing most of the best work of each incarnation of the Drifters from 1953 through 1976. There's a lot of classic music here, including all of the big hits and many interesting (even musically glorious) flops and B-sides, but the limitations of three CDs make this less than ideal. Atlantic had already released a pair of two-CD sets, *Let the Boogie Woogie Roll: Greatest Hits 1953-58* and *All-Time Greatest Hits & More: 1959-1965*, eight years earlier, each of which covers those major periods in question far more generously than does this box—although it must be conceded that the sound on the cuts included on *Rockin' & Driftin'* is improved over those late-'80s digital transfers, good as they seemed at the time. Additionally, almost concurrent with this release from Rhino Records in America, Sequel Records in England issued its Drifters *Anthology* series, assembling the group's complete Atlantic Records output on seven separate CDs, organized somewhat awkwardly at times but also including a number of outtakes, so serious fans may want to opt for that group of discs. This set, had it gone to four CDs, could have been truly comprehensive, covering all of those bases by grabbing some of the best of those genuinely beautiful outtakes, such as "In the Park"—as it is, the only unreleased cut here is the group's version of "Only in America"—and oddities like the achingly soulful "She Never Talked to Me That Way," plus all of the official live recordings that they left behind from the mid-'60s. At three CDs, it's a little squeezed, especially as the producers devote some space and attention on concurrent solo hits by Clyde McPhatter and Ben E. King. *—Bruce Eder*

Ducks Deluxe

f. 1972, **db.** 1975
Pub Rock, Rock & Roll
If the old scientific adage is true—that for every action there is an equal and opposite reaction—then British pub-rockers Ducks Deluxe were purely and simply a reaction. With the mid-'70s English pop scene dominated by glitter/glam-rockers like Gary Glitter, Sweet, or blustery, chops-heavy art-rockers like Yes, Tull, Genesis, etc., then Ducks Deluxe represented none of the above. One of the first pub-rock bands, the Ducks played basic American-style blues and boogie with remarkable panache and thorough disregard for the whims of the zeitgeist. They never were hugely popular, but the unpretentious, do-it-yourself, working-class attitude they and their contemporaries (most notably seminal pub-rockers Dr. Feelgood) exuded influenced the English punk scene that was right around the corner. With friends like Dave Edmunds producing their records, the Ducks (guitarist/vocalist Sean Tyla, guitarist Martin Belmont, bassist Nick Garvey, and keyboardist Andy McMasters) came up with engaging, though not life-changing, records that celebrated the simple joys of rock & roll. Sure, much of it sounds like recycled Chuck Berry, but there's an infectious enthusiasm that the fan in you, who simply wants to hoist a pint of lager and hear some Little Richard, will love. Ironically, to get the biggest promotional boost in America, the *Ducks Deluxe* LP was released three years after they'd split up. This little bit of shift marketing came as a result of ex-Ducks going on to more prominent bands like the Motors, the Rumour and the Tyla Gang. *—John Dougan*

● **Ducks Deluxe/Taxi to the Terminal Zone** / 1974 / Edsel ✦✦✦✦✦
Both of the group's albums, *Ducks Deluxe* and *Taxi to the Terminal Zone*, compiled on one CD with one song from each removed to fit the format's time restriction—really a best-of, and worth any three Led Zeppelin albums. *—Bruce Eder*

All Too Much / 1975 / Skydog ✦✦✦✦✦
The final studio work by the band—Sean Tyla (vocals, guitar), Martin Belmont (guitar), Mick Groom (bass), and Tim Roper (drums)—is as good as anything the group ever did on RCA. This album, an expanded version of their *Jumpin'* EP from Skydog, opens up with a high-energy version of "I Fought the Law" that makes Bobby Fuller's original sound like the work of a high-school band. Two very different versions of "Something's Going On," a killer version of "Here Comes the Night," the romantic rocker "Amsterdam Dog" (highlighted by some great electric slide), the funky "Cannons of the Boogie Night," and the anthem-like "Rock & Roll for Every Boy and Girl" (which opens almost like a burlesque of the finale of the Who's "Won't Get Fooled Again") are some of the remaining highlights. The nine Ducks Deluxe tracks are rounded out with two lesser Sean Tyla-produced songs from Left Hand Drive, and all of it is played with a drive, passion, and precision that makes *All Too Much* all-too-difficult to resist, especially as a standard price release. (Japanese import) *—Bruce Eder*

Don't Mind Rockin' Tonite / 1978 / RCA ✦✦✦
After RCA failed to do much for the band when the label released their self-titled debut record in 1974, the powers that be decided that this collection of material from their two previous LPs, along with some outtakes and B-sides, would engender more interest in the band now that they had some punk/new wave credibility. Well, it was a good thought, but it didn't work. Marketing avarice notwithstanding, this is a fine, loose-limbed, fast, and funky record chock full of guitar bombs from Martin Belmont and some macho growling from Sean Tyla. The pure pop of "Love's Melody" (written by McMaster) is jarring in juxtaposition to all the blues-based grunting, but nothing detracts from the good vibe this record and the Ducks produced in their short existence. *—John Dougan*

Living on the Front Line / 1994 / Magnum ✦✦✦✦
This compilation (credited to "The Heroes of Pub Rock") opens with five tracks by Ducks Deluxe, two studio recordings (one the original version of "Somethin's Goin' On") and three decent sounding, intense live tracks (including renditions of "Little Queenie" and "Route 66") recorded at the band's farewell gig at the 100 Club in London, where they're joined by Nick Lowe, Lee Brilleaux, and Martin Stone. Also contains tracks by Nick Lowe, Mick Green, the Pirates, Wilko Johnson and the Lew Lewis Band, and Das Luftwaffegeschaft, all of whom are worthwhile in their own right. (British import) *—Bruce Eder*

The Dukes of Stratosphear

f. 1985
College Rock, British Psychedelia, Neo-Psychedelia, Psychedelic, Alternative Pop/Rock
In 1985, the British pop band XTC recorded an EP of affectionate parodies of '60s psychedelia and guitar-pop called *25 O'Clock*. Instead of releasing the EP under their own name, they released the record under the name the Dukes of Stratosphear. Working with producer John Leckie, all three members of the group adopted pseudonyms—Andy Partridge was Sir John Johns, Colin Moulding was the Red Curtain and David Gregory was Lord Cornelius Plum. For this one project Gregory's brother Ian joined the band under the name Ian E.I.E.I. Owen. The EP was released without mention of XTC's name anywhere on the record, and the group claimed they had nothing to do with the project.

Two years after the appearance of *25 O'Clock*, the Dukes of Stratosphear released a full album, *Psonic Psunspot*. By the time *Psonic Psunspot* appeared in 1987, XTC were beginning to admit in interviews that they were indeed the Dukes of Stratosphear. Later in 1987, both the EP and album were released on a single compact disc, *Chips from the Chocolate Fireball*. *—Stephen Thomas Erlewine*

● **Chips from the Chocolate Fireball** / 1987 / Geffen ✦✦✦✦✦
During the mid-'80s, XTC developed a deep fascination with '60s psychedelia that manifested itself on their late-1986 masterpiece *Skylarking*. While *Skylarking* was filled with lush pop reminiscent of the Beatles and Beach Boys, it was generally a sober affair, since they decided to leave many of the lighter songs off the album for B-sides and future albums. During this time, they decided to develop their alter egos of the Dukes of Stratosphear, a way to let all of their infatuation with psychedelia flourish. Both the EP *25 O'Clock* and the full-length *Psonic Psunspot*, collected on the single-disc *Chips From the Chocolate Fireball*, capture the sound of '60s psychedelia remarkably well. All of the sonic details, from the fuzz guitars to the cavernous echoes and sound effects, are in place, as are the self-consciously trippy lyrics. But what makes the Dukes of Stratosphear far more than a comedy band are the songs, which happen to be some of the best pure pop tunes XTC ever wrote: "My Love Explodes" has a tense, spiraling guitar line and melody; "Little Lighthouse" and "You're My Drug" are wonderful pastiches; "The Mole From the Ministry" is a devilish homage to "I Am the Walrus" and Bowie; and the group rarely wrote a song as infectious as the bright, jangling "Vanishing Girl." Despite the clever craftsmanship, XTC has never sounded so carefree or effortless, been quite as immediately catchy or consistent—*Chips From the Chocolate Fireball* is too good to be overlooked as a side-project folly, because it truly is some of the best music XTC ever made. And, coincidentally, it's some of the best psychedelic pop ever recorded as well. *—Stephen Thomas Erlewine*

Duran Duran

f. 1978, Birmingham, England
New Romantic, Pop/Rock, New Wave, Synth Pop, Dance-Pop
Duran Duran personified New Wave for much of the mainstream audience. And for good reason, too. Duran Duran's reputation was built through music videos, which accentuated their fashion-model looks and glamourous sense of style. Without music videos, it is likely that the band's pop-funk—described by the group as the Sex Pistols meets Chic—would never have made the group international pop stars. While Duran Duran did have sharper pop sensibilities than their New Romantic contemporaries like Spandau Ballet and Ultravox, none of their peers exploited MTV and music video like the Birmingham-based quintet. Each video the group made was distinctive, incorporating a number of cinematic styles to showcase the band as either part of the jet-setting elite ("Rio") or as worldly adventurers ("Hungry Like the Wolf"). While early videos like "Girls on Film" and "The Chaffeur" sparked controversy in England over their sexual content, their best-known clips were often based on hit contemporary movies. "Hungry Like the Wolf" uncannily recalled *Raiders of the Lost Ark*, while "Union of the Snake" and "The Wild Boys" brought to mind *The Road Warrior*. The clever videos helped make Duran Duran's rise to popularity remarkably swift. Between 1982 and 1984, they rocketed from underground British post-punk sensations to teen idols. But their fall from grace was equally fast. By the late '80s, the group's lineup had fragmented, and the remaining members had trouble landing hit singles. Nevertheless, the group pulled off a surprising, if short-lived, comeback in the early '90s as a sophisticated soft-rock trio. *—Stephen Thomas Erlewine*

Duran Duran [First] / 1981 / Capitol ✦✦✦✦✦
Duran Duran's self-titled debut effectively established their slick, catchy synth-pop sound. Featuring the decadent "Girls on Film" and "Planet Earth," the album set the pace for scores of new wave bands in the early '80s, which were subsequently dubbed the new romantics. *—Stephen Thomas Erlewine*

Rio / 1982 / Capitol ✦✦✦✦✦
From its Nagel cover to the haircuts and overall design—and first and foremost the music—*Rio* is as representative of the eighties as it gets, at its best. The original Duran Duran's high point, and just as likely the band's as a whole, its fusion of style and substance ensures that even two decades after its release it remains as listenable and danceable as ever. The quintet integrates its sound near-perfectly throughout, the John and Roger Taylor rhythm section providing both driving propulsion and subtle pacing. For the latter, consider the lush semi-tropical sway of "Save a Prayer" or the closing paranoid creep of "The Chauffeur," a descendant of Roxy Music's equally affecting dark groover "The Bogus Man." Andy Taylor's muscular riffs provide fine rock crunch throughout, Rhodes' synth wash adds perfect sheen, and Le Bon tops it off with sometimes overly cryptic lyrics that still always sound just fine in context courtesy of his strong delivery. *Rio*'s two biggest smashes burst open the door in America for the New Romantic/synth rock crossover. "Hungry Like the Wolf" blended a tight, guitar-heavy groove with electronic production and a series of instant hooks, while the title track was even more anthemic, with a great sax break from guest Andy Hamilton adding to the soaring atmosphere. Lesser known cuts like "Lonely In Your Nightmare" and "Last Chance on the Stairway" still have pop thrills a-plenty, while "Hold Back the Rain" is the sleeper hit on *Rio*, an invigorating blast of feedback, keyboards and beat that doesn't let up. From start to finish, a great album that has outlasted its era. *—Ned Raggett*

Seven and the Ragged Tiger / 1983 / Capitol ✦✦✦
Seven and the Ragged Tiger was released at the height of Duran Duran-mania and it shows. Throughout the album, the group replicates the sound of *Rio*, yet they have failed to write strong material. Although they are catchy, the singles "Union of the Snake" and "The Reflex" aren't on par with "Hungry like the Wolf" and "Rio." Only the brooding "New Moon on Monday" matches the inspired pop-craft of *Rio*. *—Stephen Thomas Erlewine*

Arena / 1984 / Capitol ✦✦
Seeing Duran Duran in concert in 1984 was like seeing a video come to life. The group put on a spectacular show, filled with impressive light shows and videos. Since the concerts featured so many visuals, the band could not vary the tempos greatly, resulting in music that nearly replicated the studio versions of the songs. *Arena* accurately reproduces the sound and feeling of these concerts. Duran Duran sounds tight and professional (probably due to studio overdubbing), yet Simon Le Bon sounds a little winded, possibly because of all the dancing he had to do during the course of the show. The new Nile Rodgers-produced single "The Wild Boys" was added to the album as bait and the strategy worked—peaking at number four, *Arena* was Duran Duran's highest-charting album and it sold over two million copies. Nevertheless, it's the most inconsequential album in their entire catalog, even if it's fun. *—Stephen Thomas Erlewine*

Notorious / 1986 / Capitol ✦✦✦
After a brief hiatus, Duran Duran returned as a trio in 1986 with *Notorious*. The spare groove of the title track made it clear that the band was trying to shed its teeny-bopper image and refashion themselves as a pop band for yuppies. Thanks to Nile Rodgers' polished, radio-friendly production, *Notorious* was a success, as the band found a middle ground between synth-pop and White funk. *—Stephen Thomas Erlewine*

Big Thing / 1988 / Capitol ✦✦
Big Thing replicated the clean, mechanized funk of *Notorious*, yet the band failed to come up with a batch of strong songs. The naggingly catchy "I Don't Want Your Love" made it into the Top Ten, but the remainder of the album was bland and undistinguished. *—Stephen Thomas Erlewine*

Decade: Greatest Hits / Nov. 15, 1989 / Capitol ✦✦✦✦✦
Decade is an excellent singles compilation, featuring all of the highlights from Duran Duran's heyday—"Planet Earth," "Girls on Film," "Rio," "Is There Something I Should Know," "Union of the Snake," "The Reflex," "The Wild Boys," "Save a Prayer," "A View to a Kill"—plus late-'80s hits like "Notorious," "Skin Trade," "I Don't Want Your Love" and "All She Wants Is." By juxtaposing their stylish new wave pop against their latter-day lite-funk experiments, the group's decline becomes shockingly evident, but no other Duran Duran album sums up their appeal like *Decade*, and it's hard to imagine another compilation working the same ground as effectively. *—Stephen Thomas Erlewine*

Liberty / Aug. 13, 1990 / Capitol ✦

Duran Duran [The Wedding Album] / 1993 / Capitol ✦✦✦✦
Duran Duran came back out of nowhere in early 1993 with a new album and a huge hit, "Ordinary World." The group sounds more relaxed and mature than it did during their glory days, but not all that much has changed; instead of personifying the days of early-'80s synthesized dance-pop, the music is smooth dance-pop for the '90s. Taken on its own terms, *Duran Duran* works every bit as well as *Duran Duran*, *Rio* or *Seven and the Ragged Tiger*. "Ordinary World" and "Come Undone" are wonderful pop singles that sit between some passable album tracks and the occasional embarrassment, namely the wretched cover of The Velvet Underground's "Femme Fatale." In other words, Duran Duran are back and as good as they ever were. *—Stephen Thomas Erlewine*

Thank You / Apr. 1995 / Capitol ✦

Medazzaland / Oct. 14, 1997 / Capitol ✦✦✦

● **Greatest** / Nov. 3, 1998 / Capitol ✦✦✦✦✦
Twenty years since their pop music debut, Duran Duran issued another greatest-hits collection. As if 1989's *Decade* wasn't stellar enough, this select package was much more solid. *Greatest* showcased the band's early days of glam rock décor and new romanticism to the alluring sophistication Duran Duran exuded throughout the '90s. The typical synth-powered pop hits are included—"Girls on Film," "Rio," "A View to a Kill"—as well as the signature ballads—"Save a Prayer"—but it might also receive criticism due to its chronological disarray. Still, that gives no reason to fret, for other goodies can be found throughout. The much-neglected "New Moon on Monday" is featured, as well as the band's mature eclecticism of such songs from the self-titled *Wedding Album*—"Ordinary World" and "Come Undone." The band's experimentation with new millennium electronica found on "Electric Barbarella" again refocuses on Simon LeBon as the center of the band. A continuity blatantly obvious on *Greatest* and the strong commercialism that progressed throughout the band's healthy evolvement is not denied. Those chart-smashing singles from the 1980s made them a force to be reckoned with and an arena favorite. The songs are nearly ageless and they get their due here. It's a cheeky production and a definitive depiction of one of rock's biggest pop bands. *—MacKenzie Wilson*

Pop Trash / Jun. 13, 2000 / Hollywood ✦✦

Ian Dury

b. May 12, 1942, Upminster, Essex, England, **d.** Mar. 27, 2000
Vocals, Songwriter / British Punk, Pub Rock, New Wave, Punk, Disco
Rock & roll has always been populated by fringe figures, cult artists that managed to develop a fanatical following because of their outsized quirks, but few cult rockers have ever been quite as weird, or beloved, as Ian Dury. As the leader of the underappreciated and ill-fated pub-rockers Kilburn & the High Roads, Dury cut a striking figure—he remained handicapped from a childhood bout with polio, yet stalked the stage with dynamic charisma, spitting out music-hall numbers and rockers in his thick Cockney accent. Dury was 28 at the time he formed Kilburn, and once they disbanded, conventional wisdom would have suggested that he was far too old to become a pop star, but conventional wisdom never played much of a role in Dury's career. Signing with the fledgling indie label Stiff in 1978, Dury developed a strange fusion of music-hall, punk rock and disco that brought him to stardom in his native England. Driven by a warped sense of humor and a pulsating beat, singles like "Hit Me With Your Rhythm Stick," "Sex & Drugs & Rock & Roll" and "Reasons to Be Cheerful (Part 3)" became Top Ten hits in the U.K., yet Dury's

most distinctive qualities—his dry wit and wordplay, thick Cockney brogue, and fascination with music-hall—kept him from gaining popularity outside of England. After his second album, Dury's style became formulaic, and he faded away in the early '80s, turning to an acting career instead. *—Stephen Thomas Erlewine*

New Boots & Panties!! / 1977 / Demon ✦✦✦✦✦

Ian Dury's primary appeal lies in his lyrics, which are remarkably clever sketches of British life delivered with a wry wit. Since Dury's accent is thick and his language dense with local slang, much of these pleasures aren't discernable to casual listeners, leaving the music to stand on its own merits. On his debut album, *New Boots and Panties!*, Dury's music is at its best, and even that is a bizarrely uneven fusion of pub rock, punk rock, and disco. Still, Dury's off-kilter charm and irrepressible energy make the album gel, with the disco pulse of "Wake Up and Make Love With Me" making perfect sense next to the gentle tribute "Sweet Gene Vincent," the roaring punk of "Blockheads," and the revamped music hall of "Billericay Dickie" and "My Old Man." [Repertoire's 1996 CD reissue adds five essential singles—"Sex and Drugs and Rock & Roll," "Razzle in My Pocket," "You're More Than Fair," "England's Glory," "What a Waste"—that nearly make the disc a Dury best-of.] *—Stephen Thomas Erlewine*

Do It Yourself / 1979 / Demon ✦✦✦✦

Ian Dury's music always bordered on the functional, since it was used as a backdrop for his wry vignettes and stories, but on his second album *Do It Yourself*, that aspect came to the fore. Largely abandoning the punk inflections that were scattered throughout *New Boots and Panties!*, *Do It Yourself* is a record of mid-tempo pub rock disco—competently played, but rarely engaging. Dury's stories are all wonderful, filled with humor and penetrating detail, but only a handful of tracks, such as the terrific "Inbetweenies," are married to actual hooks, and by the end of the record, the steady disco throb has become a little numbing. Even with these faults, *Do It Yourself* remains one of Dury's very best records, since his lyrical facility throughout the album is simply amazing. [Repertoire's 1996 CD reissue of *Do It Yourself* improves the album considerably by adding several singles—"Hit Me With Your Rhythm Stick," "There Ain't Half Been Some Clever Bastards," "Reasons to Be Cheerful, Part 3," "Common As Muck," "I Want to Be Straight"—that are far more successful disco/pub rock fusions than anything on the album.] *—Stephen Thomas Erlewine*

Laughter / 1980 / Stiff ✦✦✦

Working with lead guitarist Wilko Johnson (Dr. Feelgood), Ian Dury gradually moves away from disco with his third album, *Laughter*. The steady dance pulse is still apparent, but it's balanced by rockers and pub singalongs that give the album more depth. That doesn't necessarily make it a better album, however. Dury's humor is at its most basic, as the titles of "Uncoolohol," "Take Your Elbow out of the Soup You're Sitting on the Chicken," "Oh Mr. Peanut," and "Fucking Ada" indicate, and his lyrics aren't quite as stunningly fluid as before. Still, the record is fun, and "Superman's Big Sister," "Yes & No (Paula)," and "Over the Points" are pretty infectious, but the record can't help but illustrate that Dury's peak period is over. *—Stephen Thomas Erlewine*

● **Jukebox Dury** / 1981 / Stiff ✦✦✦✦✦

Although Ian Dury's albums all had their share of high points, he functioned best as a singles artist, and *Jukebox Dury* is the definitive singles collection. Not only are his four Top 40 hits all featured ("What a Waste," "Hit Me With Your Rhythm Stick," "Reasons to Be Cheerful (Pt. 3)," "I Want to Be Straight"), but so are Stiff singles and album tracks like "Wake Up and Make Love to Me," "Razzle in My Pocket," "Common as Muck," "Inbetweenies," "Sweet Gene Vincent" and "Sex and Drugs and Rock & Roll"—in other words, it has every essential song Dury ever recorded. Rhino's *Sex & Drugs & Rock & Roll* compilation used this as its foundation, but eliminated two of its best songs, "Wake Up" and "Sweet Gene Vincent," and added several other tracks to give it a more comprehensive overview. So, *Juke Box Dury*, with its concise 12 tracks, remains the one definitive compilation. *—Stephen Thomas Erlewine*

Lord Upminster / Nov. 1981 / Polydor ✦✦✦

When Ian Dury left Stiff Records, he also left the Blockheads behind, recording *Lord Upminster* with reggae superstars Robbie Shakespeare and Sly Dunbar as producers. *Lord Upminster* turned out to be a set of uninspired funk that lacks the joyful energy of his three previous records. *—Stephen Thomas Erlewine*

4000 Weeks Holiday / 1984 / Polydor ✦✦

4000 Weeks Holiday suffers from a polished, radio-ready production that is entirely devoted to Ian Dury's fascination with disco and lite-funk. Over these slick backing tracks, Dury runs through a familiar litany of working-class anthems, love songs, social commentaries and bad jokes, all delivered with noticeably less inspiration than before. Despite a couple of bright moments, *4000 Weeks Holiday* represents Dury at a creative nadir. *—Stephen Thomas Erlewine*

Apples / 1989 / WEA ✦✦✦

Rebounding from the tepid *4000 Weeks Holiday*, Ian Dury delivers the low-key and thoroughly charming *Apples*. Although the music is considerably more relaxed than any other Dury album, it's the perfect backdrop for Dury's clever, literate stories, which resonate with great humor and detail. *Apples* does lack a standout song or melody, but the whole of the record is quite engaging, and it represents a respectable and modest comeback from Dury. *—Stephen Thomas Erlewine*

The Bus Driver's Prayer and Other Stories / 1992 / Demon ✦✦✦

Picking up where *Apples* left off—it even includes that record's "The Bus Driver's Prayer," a clever Cockney rewrite of the Lord's Prayer, as the title track—*The Bus Driver's Prayer and Other Stories* is an engaging collection of character sketches and stories from Ian Dury. The album may lack strong hooks and melodies, yet Dury diehards will find that his wry observations are just as subtle and humorous as ever. *—Stephen Thomas Erlewine*

● **Sex & Drugs & Rock & Roll: Best of Ian Dury and the Blockheads** / Apr. 28, 1992 / Rhino ✦✦✦✦✦

Ian Dury could make wonderful albums (and sometimes did, most notably the inarguable classic *New Boots and Panties!!*), but he saved many of his finest moments for his singles, which justifiably made him a legend in his native England between 1977 and 1980. With the most notable exception of Ray Davies and Paul Weller, few U.K. rockers embraced their Britishness with greater fervor than Dury, and he mined his for a wit, gleeful eccentricity, and street-smart intelligence no one could touch. And his band, the Blockheads, were as musos stronger than anyone to emerge during the British new wave explosion (their years of slogging it out on the pub circuit certainly paid off), but their curiously refreshing light funk also boasted an oddball good humor and cleverness that was the equal of their leader (no small feat). *Sex & Drugs & Rock & Roll: The Best of Ian Dury and the Blockheads* collects 18 superb sides from the band's glory days, and while the bigger hits like "Hit Me With Your Rhythm Stick," "Reasons to Be Cheerful, Part 3," and the title cut are just as good as you remember, there are plenty of pearly lesser-knowns on board, such as the childhood tale of daring "Razzle in My Pocket," the charming "Common As Muck," the hilariously anthemic "I Want to Be Straight," and the odd but captivating prognostication of "You'll See Glimpses." While Dury made plenty of other records worth investigating, if you're only going to own one Ian Dury album, this is certainly the one to get, and it truly does capture the man's singular magic at its best. *—Mark Deming*

Mr. Love Pants / 1998 / Ronnie Harris ✦✦✦✦✦

The most remarkable thing about Ian Dury's 1998 reunion with his legendary Blockheads is that it sounds like the 15 years separating *Mr. Love Pants* from their last album haven't happened at all. Sure, the production might be a little cleaner and modern, but, musically, they still kick out disco-ized funk grooves, mild new wave pop, and relaxed pub rock that provides the perfect setting for Dury's clever tales and character sketches. No, they don't rock nearly as hard as they did during the *New Boots & Panties* era, but it's not missed, because there's a genuine warmth to the performances that gives real resonance to this familiar sound. Better still, the songs are considerably better than those that made up the last proper Blockheads record, and they're better than those on Dury's solo records. There aren't any classics along the lines of "Sex & Drugs & Rock & Roll," "I'm Partial to Your Abracadabra," "Common as Muck," or "Hit Me with Your Rhythm Stick," but they're all charming examples of Dury's strengths as narrator and the band's supple musicianship. Sadly, *Mr. Love Pants* turned out to be Dury's last recording, but his body of work is much stronger with this as his final album. *—Stephen Thomas Erlewine*

Live! All the Best, Mate / Aug. 22, 2000 / Music Club ✦✦✦✦

The title *All the Best, Mate* is a valedictory drawn from Ian Dury's song "My Old Man" about his late father. In this case, it refers to Dury himself, who died five months before the release of this album. The phrase also signals the disc's contents, as it is a live set containing performances of most of Dury's best-known songs. He staged a reunion with his band the Blockheads in September 1990 to play a series of benefits for Blockheads drummer Charlie Charles, who was suffering from cancer. After Charles' death, they stayed together, and the show contained here was recorded December 22, 1990, at Brixton Academy in London. Nine of the 15 songs are drawn from Dury's 1977 debut album, *New Boots and Panties!!!*, among them the Top Ten British hit "What a Waste!" Also included are the Top Five British hits "Hit Me With Your Rhythm Stick" and "Reasons to Be Cheerful Pt. 3." The band, led by Chaz Jankel and featuring Wilko Johnson (who replaced Jankel in the Blockheads in 1980), sounds as good as ever, and so does the always roughly engaging frontman. Fans may note the omission of an occasional favorite ("Sex & Drugs & Rock & Roll," a song that bequeathed a slogan to popular culture, is particularly missed), but this is a solid set of Dury's best material. That it is being sold at what is called a "lite price" despite a CD-busting running time of over 78 minutes only adds to the value. The studio versions are preferred, but this is a strong performance before an enthusiastic audience, bringing out the best in the material. *—William Ruhlmann*

Dyke & The Blazers

f. 1964, **db.** 1971

Pop-Soul, Funk, Soul

Dyke & the Blazers were one of the first acts—possibly *the* first notable act—to play funk other than James Brown. Indeed, they often sounded like a sort of junior version of the JB's, playing songs in which the rhythms and riffs mattered more than the tune. Similarly, vocalist Dyke Christian sang-grunted words that mattered more for the feeling and rhythm than the content. Their best-known track, "Funky Broadway," was covered for a bigger hit by Wilson Pickett, though Dyke & the Blazers got a few more R&B hits before Dyke was shot to death in 1971. Arlester "Dyke" Christian was born in Buffalo, NY, in 1943, and by the mid-'60s was singing and playing bass with the O'Jays' backing band, the Blazers. Dyke and some of the other Blazers were stranded in Phoenix when the O'Jays couldn't afford to bring them back to Buffalo, and the Blazers based themselves in Phoenix, having no means to travel elsewhere. Their "Funky Broadway" was released on the Phoenix indie Artco in late 1966, and picked up for distribution by the L.A.-based Original Sound label. It became a sizable R&B hit (and a small pop one), and may have been the first record to use the word "funky" in the title. In the late '60s and early '70s, Dyke and the band issued a series of gutbucket funk singles with scratchy guitar riffs, greasy organ, hoarse vocals, and jazzy horns—all traits that Brown and his band had developed, admittedly. But Dyke did the style well (right down to issuing several two-part singles), although not with a great deal of variety. Dyke, sadly, was fatally shot on the street in Phoenix on March 13, 1971. *—Richie Unterberger*

● **So Sharp** / 1983 / Kent ♦♦♦♦♦
The best Dyke & the Blazers collection has 24 tracks, including all the key singles: "Funky Broadway," "Uhh," "Runaway People," "We Got More Soul," "Let a Woman Be a Woman—Let a Man Be a Man," "Funky Walk," "Funky Bull" (like James Brown, Dyke was not a man averse to milking an idea with a series of similar song titles). What's more, the disc includes parts one and two of the multi-sided singles "Funky Broadway," "Funky Walk," "Funky Bull," and "Uhh." Not much development of style or ideas over the four years or so encompassed by this anthology, but that's not the main point of funk dance music. "Runaway People" does look forward to the more sophisticated urban funk of the early 1970s with its addition of strings—reminiscent, ironically, of the production eventually adapted by Dyke's old buddies the O'Jays. Note that *So Sharp!* was originally issued by Kent on LP in 1983, but the CD version has extra tracks. *—Richie Unterberger*

Funky Broadway: The Very Best of Dyke & the Blazers / Mar. 23, 1999 / Collectables ♦♦♦♦
Give Collectables Records credit for compiling the most comprehensive Dyke & the Blazers collection to date. The Buffalo band launched their recording career in Phoenix, AZ, with the chart-busting "Funky Broadway," a gritty introduction to Dyke's sandpaper-rough vocal style. Many of the 18 tracks like "Broadway Combination" are "Funky Broadway" clones, but "We Got More Soul," "Let a Woman Be a Woman, Let a Man Be a Man," "Funky Walk," and other funky charmers keep boredom at bay; just when you think Dyke, who "wrote" 17 of the 18 tracks, has depleted his creative juices, up cues a "Shotgun Slim" or "Funky Bull," and you're bouncing again. You also get a glimpse of Dyke, the balladeer, on "I'm So All Alone"; thankfully, he didn't do them very often. *—Andrew Hamilton*

Bob Dylan (Robert Allen Zimmerman)

b. May 24, 1941, Duluth, MN
Vocals, Keyboards, Songwriter, Piano, Harmonica, Guitar / Album Rock, Folk-Rock, Singer/Songwriter, Country-Rock, Rock & Roll, Political Folk
Bob Dylan's influence on popular music is incalculable. As a songwriter, he pioneered several different schools of pop songwriting, from confessional singer/songwriter to winding, hallucinatory, stream-of-conscious narratives. As a vocalist, he broke down the notions that in order to perform, a singer had to have a conventionally good voice, thereby redefining the role of vocalist in popular music. As a musician, he sparked several genres of pop music, including electrified folk-rock & country-rock. And that just touches on the tip of his achievements. Dylan's force was evident during his height of popularity in the '60s—the Beatles' shift toward introspective songwriting in the mid-'60s never would have happened without him—but his influence echoed throughout several subsequent generations. Many of his songs became popular standards, and his best albums were undisputed classics of the rock & roll canon. Dylan's influence throughout folk music was equally powerful, and he marks a pivotal turning point in its 20th-century evolution, signifying when the genre moved away from traditional songs and toward personal songwriting. Even when his sales declined in the '80s and '90s, Dylan's presence was calculable. *—Stephen Thomas Erlewine*

Bob Dylan / Mar. 19, 1962 / Columbia ♦♦♦♦
Bob Dylan's first album is a lot like the debut albums by the Beatles and the Rolling Stones—a sterling effort, outclassing most, if not all, of what came before it in the genre, but similarly eclipsed by the artist's own subsequent efforts. The difference was that not very many people heard *Bob Dylan* on its original release because it was recorded with a much smaller audience and musical arena in mind. At the time of *Bob Dylan*'s release, the folk revival was rolling, and interpretation was considered more important than original composition by most of that audience. A significant portion of the record is possessed by the style and spirit of Woody Guthrie, whose influence as a singer and guitarist hovers over "Man of Constant Sorrow" and "Pretty Peggy-O," as well as the two originals here, the savagely witty "Talkin' New York" and the poignant "Song to Woody." There's a punk-like aggressiveness to the singing and playing here. His raspy-voiced delivery and guitar style were modeled largely on Guthrie's classic 1940s and early-'50s recordings, but the assertiveness of the bluesmen he admires also comes out, making this one of the most powerful records to come out of the folk revival of which it was a part. Within a year of its release, Dylan, initially in tandem with young folk/protest singers like Peter, Paul & Mary and Phil Ochs, would alter the boundaries of that revival beyond recognition, but this album marked the pinnacle of that earlier phase, before it was overshadowed by this artist's more ambitious subsequent work. In that regard, the two original songs here serve as the bridge between Dylan's stylistic roots, as delineated on this album, and the more powerful and daringly original work that followed. *—Bruce Eder*

★ **The Freewheelin' Bob Dylan** / May 27, 1963 / Columbia ♦♦♦♦♦
It's hard not to overestimate the importance of *Freewheelin' Bob Dylan*, the record that firmly established Bob Dylan as an unparalleled songwriter, one of considerable skill, imagination, and vision. At the time, folk had been quite popular on college campus and bohemian circles, making headway onto the pop charts in diluted form, and while there certainly were a number of gifted songwriters, nobody had transcended the scene as Dylan did with this record. There are a couple (very good) covers, with "Corrina Corrina" and "Honey Just Allow Me One More Chance," but they pale with the originals here. At the time, the social protests received the most attention, and deservedly so, since "Blowin' in the Wind," "Masters of War," and "A Hard Rain's A-Gonna Fall" weren't just specific in their targets, they were gracefully executed and even melodic. Although they've proven resilient throughout the years, if that's all *Freewheelin'* had to offer, it wouldn't have had its seismic impact, but this also revealed a songwriter who could turn out whimsy ("Don't Think Twice, It's All Right"), gorgeous love songs ("Girl From the North Country"), and cheerfully absurdist humor ("Bob Dylan's Blues," "Bob Dylan's Dream") with equal skill. This is rich, imaginative music, capturing the sound and spirit of America as much as that of Louis Armstrong, Hank Williams, or Elvis Presley. Dylan, in many ways, recorded music that equaled it, but he never topped it. *—Stephen Thomas Erlewine*

The Times They Are A-Changin' / Jan. 13, 1964 / Columbia ♦♦♦♦♦
If *The Times They Are A-Changin'* isn't a marked step forward from *The Freewheelin' Bob Dylan*, even if it is his first collection of all originals, it's nevertheless a fine collection all the same. It isn't as rich as *Freewheelin'*, and Dylan has tempered his sense of humor considerably, choosing to concentrate on social protests in the style of "Blowin' in the Wind." With the title track, he wrote an anthem that nearly equaled that song, and "With God on Our Side" and "Only a Pawn in Their Game" are nearly as good, while "Ballad of Hollis Brown" and "The Lonesome Death of Hattie Carroll" are remarkably skilled re-castings of contemporary tales of injustice. His absurdity is missed, but he makes up for it with the wonderful "One Too Many Mornings" and "Boots of Spanish Leather," two lovely classics. If there are a couple of songs that don't achieve the level of the aforementioned songs, that speaks more to the quality of those songs than the weakness of the remainder of the record. And that's also true of the album itself—yes, it pales next to its predecessor, but it's terrific by any other standard. *—Stephen Thomas Erlewine*

☆ **Another Side of Bob Dylan** / Aug. 8, 1964 / Columbia ♦♦♦♦♦
The other side of Bob Dylan referred to in the title is presumably his romantic, absurdist and whimsical sides—anything that wasn't featured on the staunchly folky, protest-heavy *Times They Are A-Changing*, really. Because of this, *Another Side of Bob Dylan* is a more varied record and it's more successful, too, since it captures Dylan expanding his music, turning in imaginative, poetic performance on love songs and protest tunes alike. This has an equal number of classics to its predecessor, actually, with "All I Really Want to Do," "Chimes of Freedom," "My Back Pages," "I Don't' Believe You," and "It Ain't Me Babe" standing among his standards, but the key to the record's success are the album tracks, which are graceful, poetic, and layered. Both the lyrics and music have gotten deeper and Dylan's trying more things—this, in its construction and attitude, is hardly strictly folk, it encompasses far more than that. The result is one of his very best records, a lovely intimate affair. *—Stephen Thomas Erlewine*

☆ **Bringing It All Back Home** / Mar. 22, 1965 / Columbia ♦♦♦♦♦
With *Another Side of Bob Dylan*, Dylan began pushing past folk, and with *Bringing It All Back Home*, he exploded the boundaries, producing an album of boundless imagination and skill. And it's not just that he went electric, either, rocking hard on "Subterranean Homesick Blues," "Maggie's Farm," and "Outlaw Blues," it's that he's exploding with imagination throughout the record. After all, the music on its second side—the nominal folk songs—derive from the same vantage point as the rockers, leaving traditional folk concerns behind and delving deep into the personal. And this isn't just introspection, either, since the surreal paranoia on "It's Alright, Ma (I'm Only Bleeding)" and the whimsical poetry of "Mr. Tambourine Man" are individual, yet not personal. And that's just the tip of the iceberg, really, as he writes uncommonly beautiful love songs ("She Belongs to Me," "Love Minus Zero/No Limit") which sit alongside uncommonly funny fantasias ("On the Road Again," "Bob Dylan's 115th Dream"). This is the point where Dylan eclipses any conventional sense of folk and rewrites the rules of rock, making it safe for personal expression and poetry, not only making words mean as much as the music, but making the music an extension of the words. A truly remarkable album. *—Stephen Thomas Erlewine*

★ **Highway 61 Revisited** / Aug. 30, 1965 / Columbia ♦♦♦♦♦
Taking the first, electric side of *Bringing It All Back Home* to its logical conclusion, Bob Dylan hired a full rock & roll band, featuring guitarist Michael Bloomfield, for *Highway 61 Revisited*. Opening with the epic "Like a Rolling Stone," *Highway 61 Revisited* careens through nine songs that range from reflective folk-rock ("Desolation Row") and blues ("It Takes a Lot to Laugh, It Takes a Train to Cry") to flat-out garage rock ("Tombstone Blues," "From a Buick 6," "Highway 61 Revisted"). Dylan had not only changed his sound, but his persona, trading the folk troubadour for a streetwise, cynical hipster. Throughout the album, he alternates between druggy, surreal imagery, which can either have a sense of menace or beauty, and the music reflects that, jumping between soothing melodies to hard, bluesy rock. And that is the most revolutionary thing about *Highway 61 Revisited*—it proved that rock & roll needn't be collegiate and tame in order to be literate, poetic and complex. *—Stephen Thomas Erlewine*

☆ **Blonde on Blonde** / May 16, 1966 / Columbia ♦♦♦♦♦
If *Highway 61 Revisited* played as a garage rock record, the double album *Blonde on Blonde* inverted that sound, blending blues, country, rock and folk into a wild, careening and dense sound. Replacing the fiery Michael Bloomfield with the intense, weaving guitar of Robbie Robertson, Dylan led a group comprised of his touring band the Hawks and session musicians through his richest set of songs. *Blonde on Blonde* is an album of enormous depth, providing endless lyrical and musical revelations on each play. Leavening the edginess of *Highway 61* with a sense of the absurd, *Blonde on Blonde* is comprised entirely of songs driven by inventive, surreal and witty wordplay, not only on the rockers but also on winding, moving ballads like "Visions of Johanna," "Just Like a Woman," and "Sad Eyed Lady of the Lowlands." Throughout the record, the music matches the inventiveness of the songs, filled with cutting guitar riffs, liquid organ riffs, crisp pianos and even woozy brass bands ("Rainy Day Women #12 & 35"). It's the culmination of Dylan's electric rock & roll period—he would never release a studio record that rocked this hard, or had such bizarre imagery, ever again. *—Stephen Thomas Erlewine*

★ **Bob Dylan's Greatest Hits** / Mar. 27, 1967 / Columbia ♦♦♦♦♦
Arriving in 1967, *Greatest Hits* does an excellent job of summarizing Dylan's best-known

songs from his first seven albums. At just ten songs, it's a little brief, and the song selection may be a little predictable, but that's actually not a bad thing, since this provides a nice sampler for the curious and casual listener, as it boasts standards from "Blowin' in the Wind" to "Like a Rolling Stone." And, for collectors, the brilliant non-LP single "Positively Fourth Street" was added, which provided reason enough for anybody that already owned the original records to pick this up. This has since been supplanted by more exhaustive collections, but as a sampler of Dylan at his absolute peak, this is first-rate. —*Stephen Thomas Erlewine*

☆ **John Wesley Harding** / Dec. 27, 1967 / Columbia ♦♦♦♦♦
Bob Dylan returned from exile with *John Wesley Harding*, a quiet, country-tinged album that split dramatically from his previous three albums. A calm, reflective album, *John Wesley Harding* strips away all of the wilder tendencies of Dylan's rock albums—even the then-unreleased *Basement Tapes* he made the previous year—but it isn't a return to his folk roots. If anything, the album is his first serious foray into country, but only a handful of songs, such as "I'll Be Your Baby Tonight," are straight country songs. Instead, *John Wesley Harding* is informed by the rustic sound of country, as well as many rural myths, with seemingly simple songs like "All Along the Watchtower," "I Dreamed I Saw St. Augustine" and "The Wicked Messenger" revealing several layers of meanings with repeated plays. Although the lyrics are somewhat enigmatic, the music is simple, direct and melodic, providing a touchstone for the country-rock revolution that swept through rock in the late '60s. —*Stephen Thomas Erlewine*

☆ **Nashville Skyline** / Apr. 9, 1969 / Columbia ♦♦♦♦♦
John Wesley Harding suggested country with its textures and structures, but *Nashville Skyline* was a full-fledged country album, complete with steel guitars and brief, direct songs. It's a warm, friendly album, particularly since Dylan is singing in a previously unheard gentle croon—the sound of his voice is so different it may be disarming upon first listen, but it suits the songs. While there are a handful of lightweight numbers on the record, at its core are several excellent songs—"Lay Lady Lay," "To Be Alone With You," "I Threw It All Away," "Tonight I'll Be Staying Here With You," as well as a duet with Johnny Cash on "Girl from the North Country"—that have become country-rock standards. And there's no discounting that *Nashville Skyline*, arriving in the spring of 1969, established country-rock as a vital force in pop music, as well as a commercially viable genre. —*Stephen Thomas Erlewine*

Self Portrait / Jun. 8, 1970 / Columbia ♦♦
There has never been a clearer attempt to shed an audience than *Self-Portrait*. At least, that's one way of looking at this baffling double album, a deliberately sprawling affair that runs the gamut from self-portrait to self-parody, touching on operatic pop, rowdy *Basement Tapes* leftovers, slight whimsy, and covers of wannabe Dylans from Paul Simon to Gordon Lightfoot. To say the least, it's confusing, especially arriving at the end of a decade of unmitigated brilliance, and while the years have made it easier to listen to, it still remains inscrutable, an impossible record to unlock. It may not be worth the effort, either, since this isn't a matter of deciphering cryptic lyrics or interpreting lyrics, it's all about discerning intent, figuring out what the hell Dylan was thinking when he was recording—not trying to decode a song. There are times where it's quite clearly played for a laugh—if his shambling version of "The Boxer" isn't a pointed parody of Paul Simon, there was no reason to cut it—but he's poker-faced elsewhere, and the songs (apart from such earthed gems as "Mighty Quinn," which aren't presented in their best versions) are simply not worth much consideration. But, in a strange way, *Self Portrait* is, because decades have passed and it still doesn't make much sense, even for Dylanphiles. That doesn't necessarily mean that it's worth the time to figure it out—you're not going to find an answer, anyway—but it's sort of fascinating all the same. —*Stephen Thomas Erlewine*

New Morning / Oct. 21, 1970 / Columbia ♦♦♦♦♦
Dylan rushed out *New Morning* in the wake of the commercial and critical disaster *Self Portrait*, and the difference between the two albums suggests that its legendary failed predecessor was intentionally flawed. *New Morning* expands on the laidback country-rock of *John Wesley Harding* and *Nashville Skyline* by adding a more pronounced rock & roll edge. While there are only a couple of genuine classics on the record ("If Not for You," "One More Weekend"), the overall quality is quite high, and many of the songs explore idiosyncratic routes Dylan had previously left untouched, whether it's the jazzy experiments of "Sign on the Window" and "Winterlude," the rambling spoken-word piece "If Dogs Run Free" or the Elvis parable "Went to See the Gypsy." Such offbeat songs make *New Morning* a charming, endearing record. —*Stephen Thomas Erlewine*

☆ **Bob Dylan's Greatest Hits, Vol. 2** / Nov. 17, 1971 / Columbia ♦♦♦♦♦
Where Dylan's first *Greatest Hits* took its title literally, *Greatest Hits, Vol. 2* is a greatest hits album only in the loosest sense of the term. While the double album does contain several genuine hits—"Lay Lady Lay," "Tonight I'll Be Staying Here With You," the non-LP "Watching the River Flow"—it is largely comprised of album tracks which became classics, either through Dylan's own version or through covers. These include "Don't Think Twice, It's All Right," "All I Really Want to Do," "My Back Pages," "Maggie's Farm," "She Belongs to Me," "If Not for You," and "Just Like Tom Thumb's Blues," among many others. There are also a number of rarities scattered throughout the 21 songs, including a live version of "Tomorrow Is a Long Time" from 1963, a live take of "The Mighty Quinn (Quinn, the Eskimo)" and the *Basement Tapes* songs "I Shall Be Released," "Down in the Flood" and "You Ain't Goin' Nowhere." While some of the cuts may not be immediately familiar to some listeners, *Greatest Hits, Vol. 2* in many ways is a more accurate picture of the depth and breadth of Dylan's talents, making it an excellent introduction. And it's not just for casual fans, because the rarities and sequencing are revealing for even devoted Dylan fans. [*Greatest Hits, Vol. 2* was reissued with 24-bit remastering in the summer of 1999.] —*Stephen Thomas Erlewine*

Pat Garrett & Billy the Kid [Soundtrack] / Jul. 13, 1973 / Columbia ♦♦
Dylan / Nov. 16, 1973 / Columbia ♦
Commonly regarded as the worst album in Bob Dylan's catalog, *Dylan* is a collection of nine outtakes from the *Self Portrait* album Columbia assembled after the singer briefly jumped ship for David Geffen's fledgling Asylum Records. Dylan didn't want the record to be released, and it's easy to see why—the album is a collection of covers which are poorly performed on purpose. Tackling both contemporary writers (Joni Mitchell's "Big Yellow Taxi," Jerry Jeff Walker's "Mr. Bojangles"), pop songs ("Can't Help Falling in Love," "A Fool Such as I"), and traditional numbers ("The Ballad of Ira Hayes," "Spanish Is the Loving Tongue"), Dylan attempts to sabotage each number, but none of the results is quite so shocking, or funny, as the deconstructions on *Self Portrait*. While *Dylan* is indeed a negligible album, it isn't unlistenable—it has a pleasant pop-rock sheen and Dylan sings in his *Nashville Skyline* croon. Nevertheless, it adds nothing to his canon, and only diehard fans with a perverse sense of humor will find the record worth a listen. —*Stephen Thomas Erlewine*

Planet Waves / Jan. 17, 1974 / Columbia ♦♦♦
Re-teaming with the Band, Bob Dylan winds up with an album that recalls *New Morning* more than *The Basement Tapes*, since *Planet Waves* is given to a relaxed intimate tone—all the more appropriate for a collection of modest songs about domestic life. As such, it may seem a little anticlimactic, since it has none of the wildness of the best Dylan and the Band music of the '60s—just an approximation of the homespun rusticness. Considering that the record was knocked out in the course of three days, its unassuming nature shouldn't be a surprise, and sometimes it's as much a flaw as a virtue, since there are several cuts that float into the ether. Still, it is a virtue in places, as there are moments—"On a Night Like This," "Something There Is About You," the lovely "Forever Young"—where it just gels, almost making the diffuse nature of the rest of the record acceptable. —*Stephen Thomas Erlewine*

Before the Flood / Jun. 20, 1974 / Columbia ♦♦♦♦♦
Bob Dylan and the Band both needed the celebrated reunion tour of 1974, since Dylan's fortunes had been floundering since *Self Portrait* and the Band stumbled with 1971's *Cahoots*. The tour, with its attendant publicity, definitely returned both artists to center stage, and it definitely succeeded, breaking box office records and earning great reviews. *Before the Flood*, a double-album souvenir of the tour, suggests that these were generally dynamic shows, but not because they were reveling in the past, but because Dylan was fighting the nostalgia of his audience—nostalgia, it must be noted, that was promoted as the very reason behind these shows. Yet that's what gives this music such kick—Dylan reworks, rearranges, reinterprets these songs in ways that are still disarming, years after its initial release. He could only have performed interpretations this radical with a group as sympathetic, knowing of his traits as the band, whose own recordings here are respites from the storm. And this is a storm—the sound of a great rocker, surprising his band and audience by tearing through his greatest songs in a manner that might not be comforting, but it guarantees it to be one of the best live albums of its time. Ever, maybe. —*Stephen Thomas Erlewine*

☆ **Blood on the Tracks** / Jan. 17, 1975 / Columbia ♦♦♦♦♦
Following on the heels of an album where he repudiated his past with his greatest backing band, *Blood on the Tracks* finds Bob Dylan, in a way, retreating to the past, recording a largely quiet, acoustic-based album. But this is hardly nostalgia—this is the sound of an artist returning to his strengths, what feels most familiar, as he accepts a traumatic situation, namely the breakdown of his marriage. This is an album alternately bitter, sorrowful, regretful, and peaceful, easily the closest he ever came to wearing his emotions on his sleeve. That's not to say that it's an explicitly confessional record, since many songs are riddles or allegories, yet the warmth of the music makes it feel that way. The original version of the album was even quieter—first takes of "Idiot Wind" and "Tangled Up in Blue," available on *The Bootleg Series, Vols. 1-3*, are hushed and quiet (excised verses are quoted in the liner notes, but not heard on the record)—but *Blood on the Tracks* remains an intimate, revealing affair, since these harsher takes let his anger surface the way his sadness does elsewhere. As such, it's an affecting, unbearably poignant record, not because it's a glimpse into his soul, but because the songs are remarkably clear-eyed *and* sentimental, lovely and melancholy at once. And, in a way, it's best that he was backed with studio musicians here, since the professional, understated backing lets the songs and emotion stand at the forefront. Dylan made albums more influential than this, but he never made one better. —*Stephen Thomas Erlewine*

☆ **The Basement Tapes** / Jun. 26, 1975 / Columbia ♦♦♦♦♦
The official release of *The Basement Tapes*—which were first heard on a 1968 bootleg called *The Great White Wonder*—plays with history somewhat, as Robbie Robertson overemphasizes the Band's status in the sessions, making them out to be equally active to Dylan, adding in demos not cut at the sessions and overdubbing their recordings to flesh them out. As many bootlegs (most notably the complete five-disc series) reveal, this isn't entirely true and that the Band were nowhere near as active as Dylan, but that ultimately is a bit like nitpicking, since the music here (including the Band's) is astonishingly good. The party line on *The Basement Tapes* is that it is Americana, as Dylan and the Band pick up the weirdness inherent in old folk, country, and blues tunes, but it transcends mere historical arcana by being lively, humorous, full-bodied performances. Dylan never sounded as loose, nor was he ever as funny as he is here, and this positively revels in its weird, wild character. For all the apparent antecedents—and the allusions are sly and obvious in equal measures—this is truly Dylan's show, as he majestically evokes old myths and creates new ones, resulting in a crazy quilt of blues, humor, folk, tall tales, inside jokes, and rock. The Band pretty much pick up where Dylan left off, even singing a couple of his tunes, but they play it a little straight, on both their rockers and ballads.

Not a bad thing at all, since this actually winds up providing context for the wild, mercurial brilliance of Dylan's work—and, taken together, the results (especially in this judiciously compiled form; expert song selection, even if there's a bit too much Band) rank among the greatest American music ever made. *—Stephen Thomas Erlewine*

Desire / Jan. 16, 1976 / Columbia ✦✦✦✦✦
If *Blood on the Tracks* was an unapologetically intimate affair, *Desire* is unwieldy and messy, the deliberate work of a collective. And while Dylan directly addresses his crumbling relationship with his wife, Sara, on the final track, *Desire* is hardly as personal as its predecessor, finding Dylan returning to topical songwriting and folk tales for the core of the record. It's all over the map, as far as songwriting goes, and so it is musically, capturing Dylan at the beginning of the Rolling Thunder Revue era, which was more notable for its chaos than its music. And, so it's only fitting that *Desire* fits that description, as well, as it careens between surging folk-rock, mideastern dirges, skipping pop, and epic narratives. It's little surprise that *Desire* doesn't quite gel, yet it retains its own character—really, there's no other place where Dylan tried as many different style, as many weird detours, as he does here. And, there's something to be said for its rambling, sprawling character, which has a charm of its own. Even so, the record would have been assisted by a more consistent set of songs; there are some masterpieces here, though—"Hurricane" is the best-known, but the effervescent "Mozambique" is Dylan at his breeziest, "Sara" at his most nakedly emotional, and "Isis" is one of his very best songs of the '70s, a hypnotic, contemporized spin on a classic fable. This may not add up to a masterpiece, but it does result in one of his most fascinating records of the '70s and '80s—more intriguing, lyrically and musically, than most of his latter-day affairs. *—Stephen Thomas Erlewine*

Hard Rain / Sep. 10, 1976 / Columbia ✦✦
Hard Rain is a snapshot of Bob Dylan's fabled Rolling Thunder Revue, a traveling circus that was more notable for its excess and character than the music. *Hard Rain* bears this out, being neither as sacrilegious or as exciting as *Blood on the Tracks*, and never seeming necessary—after all, it arrives just two years after the last live album. There are some new interpretations along the lines of what appeared on *Before the Flood*, but this lacks kinetic energy, rolling along on its own sense of inevitably. That's not to say there isn't good material tucked away here, as a few of the new versions hit home and Dylan is generally spirited throughout, but ultimately, this remains the province of the dedicated. *—Stephen Thomas Erlewine*

Street Legal / Jun. 15, 1978 / Columbia ✦✦✦
Arriving after the twin peaks of *Blood on the Tracks* and *Desire*, *Street Legal* seemed like a disappointment upon its 1978 release, and it still seems a little subpar, years after its release. Perhaps that's because Dylan was uncertain himself, not just writing a set of songs with no connecting themes, but replacing the sprawl of the Rolling Thunder Revue with a slick, professional big band, featuring a horn section and several backing vocalists. The interesting thing about this is that the music and slick production don't jibe with the songs, which are as dense as anything Dylan has written since before his motorcycle accident. So, *Street Legal* becomes an interesting dichotomy, filled with songs that deserve close attention but recorded in arrangements that discourage such listening. As such, *Street Legal* is fascinating just for that reason—in another setting, these are songs that would have been hailed as near-masterpieces, but covered in gloss, they seem strange. Consequentially, it's not surprising that there are factions of Dylanphiles that find this worth the time, while just as many consider it a missed opportunity. *—Stephen Thomas Erlewine*

At Budokan / 1979 / Columbia ✦✦
On his third live album in a mere five years, Bob Dylan brings the big, professional showmanship of *Street Legal* to the stage, recasting recent and classic favorites into that album's image—and, he does that over the course of two albums, no less. It's a bit much, even for the diehards, even if moments work pretty well. Nevertheless, those moments work because of pizzazz, although those are the very moments that will make most long-term Dylan fans bristle. Which, of course, raises the question—who is this for? The dedicated aren't going to be dazzled by the slickness and the casual fans certainly aren't going to pay much attention to a live album from 1978. Interesting historically, perhaps, but only marginally. *—Stephen Thomas Erlewine*

Slow Train Coming / Aug. 20, 1979 / Columbia ✦✦✦
Perhaps it was inevitable that Dylan would change direction at the end of the '70s, since he had dabbled in everything from full-on repudiation of his legacy to a quiet embrace of it, to dipping his toe into pure showmanship. Nobody really could have expected that he would turn to Christianity, embracing a born-again philosophy with enthusiasm. He has no problem in believing in a vengeful god—you gotta serve somebody, after all—and this is pure brimstone and fire throughout the record, even on such lovely testimonials as "I Believe in You." The unexpected side-effect of his conversion is that it gave Dylan a focus he hadn't had since *Blood on the Tracks*, and his concentration carries over to the music, which is lean and direct in a way that he hadn't been since, well, *Blood on the Tracks*. Focus isn't necessarily the same thing as consistency, and this does suffer from being a bit too dogmatic, not just in its religion, but in its musical approach. Still, it's hard to deny that Dylan doesn't sound revitalized here and the result is a modest success that at least works on its own terms. *—Stephen Thomas Erlewine*

Saved / Jun. 20, 1980 / Columbia ✦✦
If *Saved* did anything, it proved that the born-again Christianity of *Slow Train Coming* wasn't merely a passing fad, and that it did, in fact, mean something significant to Dylan. Whether it meant something significant to his audience was another matter entirely, since this is where his religion overshadows his music, turning the album into a sermon to an audience that is nearly certainly unconverted—and never will be, either. Dylan himself may be part of that audience, since he did back away from such a staunchly dogged viewpoint not long afterward, but that doesn't change *Saved*'s status as being a fairly flat—and, for Dylan, fairly pedestrian—testament to his faith. And, if *Slow Train Coming* found him at a fairly creative peak of songwriting and supported by a supple backing band, he's turning out routine songs here, and the backing follows suit, resulting in his flattest record yet. *—Stephen Thomas Erlewine*

Shot of Love / Aug. 12, 1981 / Columbia ✦✦
Shot of Love finds Dylan still in born-again mode, but he's starting to come alive again—which isn't as much a value judgment as it is an observation that he no longer seems beholden to repeating dogma, loosening up and crafting songs again. And it's not just that his writing is looser, the music is, too, as he lets himself—and his backing band—rock a little harder, a little more convincingly. *Shot of Love* still isn't a great album, but it once again has flashes of brilliance, such as "Every Grain of Sand," which point the way to the rebirth of *Infidels*. *—Stephen Thomas Erlewine*

Infidels / Nov. 1, 1983 / Columbia ✦✦✦✦
Infidels is the first secular record Bob Dylan recorded since *Street Legal*, and it's far more like a classicist Dylan album than that, filled with songs that are evocative in their imagery and direct in their approach. This is lean, much like *Slow Train Coming*, but its writing is closer to the peak of the mid-'70s, and some of the songs here—particularly on the first side—are minor classics, capturing him reviving his sense of social consciousness and his gift for poetic, elegant love songs. For a while, *Infidels* seems like a latter-day masterpiece, but toward the end of the record it runs out of steam, preventing it from being a triumph. Still, in comparison to everything that arrived in the near-decade before it, *Infidels* is a triumph, finding Dylan coming tantalizing close to regaining all his powers. *—Stephen Thomas Erlewine*

Real Live / Dec. 3, 1984 / Columbia ✦✦✦
It may be his first live album in six years, but *Real Live* still is his fourth live album in ten years, and, as such, it still feels a little redundant. Nevertheless, it doesn't feel anywhere nearly as unnecessary as *At Budokan* and if it doesn't capture a historically significant tour, as *Hard Rain* did with the Rolling Thunder Revue, this is a better record all the same, capturing a working band—a working band featuring ex-Stones guitarist Mick Taylor, no less—on a pretty good night. That means there are few revelations—though diehards will certainly revel in "Tangled Up in Blue," which has several brand-new (not necessarily better) verses—but it's still pretty good all the same, providing lean, relatively muscular renditions of Dylan's great songs. This isn't an important, necessary Dylan record, but it's a good, solid live album, his best live album since *Before the Flood*, even if it's hardly as monumental as that. *—Stephen Thomas Erlewine*

Empire Burlesque / Jun. 8, 1985 / Columbia ✦✦✦✦✦
Say what you want about *Empire Burlesque*—at the very least, it's the most consistent record Bob Dylan has made since *Blood on the Tracks*, even if it isn't quite as interesting as *Desire*. However, it is a better set of songs, all deriving from the same place and filled with subtle gems—the most obvious being "Tight Connection to My Heart (Has Anybody Seen My Love?)," but also "Emotionally Yours" and "Dark Eyes"—proving that his powers are still there. The rest of the album may not be as graceful, but it's still well-crafted songwriting that never fails to be interesting. The record's biggest flaw is its state-of-the-art production; this is every bit as slick as *Street Legal*, but now sounds more focused and more of its time—thanks to a reliance on synthesizers and mildly sequenced beats—than it did upon its original release. All this makes *Empire Burlesque* seem more transient than it actually is, since—discounting the production—this is as good as Dylan gets in his latter days. *—Stephen Thomas Erlewine*

☆ **Biograph** / Oct. 28, 1985 / Columbia ✦✦✦✦✦
Historically, *Biograph* is significant not for what it did for Dylan's career, but for establishing the box set, complete with hits and rarities, as a viable part of rock history. Following *Biograph*, multi-disc box sets for veteran rockers became accepted and almost the norm, but that doesn't discount this set's strengths as a summary of Dylan's career, using the familiar and the rare to draw a fully rounded portrait of his strengths as a songwriter, musician, and record-maker in a way that conventional choices alone couldn't achieve. Certainly, the chief attraction of this set, even years after its initial release, is its smattering of rarities that aren't just rare, but revealing—ranging from forgotten rock B-sides and singles to demos, alternate takes, and unreleased songs that rival official releases. But *Biograph* is really remarkable for weaving these songs into a fabric that reveals the true trajectory of Dylan's career, offering as much to the curious as it does to the dedicated. That sets a standard for box sets that has rarely been matched, making *Biograph* all the more impressive in retrospect. *—Stephen Thomas Erlewine*

Knocked Out Loaded / Aug. 8, 1986 / Columbia ✦✦
It's easy to dismiss *Knocked Out Loaded* out of hand, considering it an extension of the slick professionalism of *Empire Burlesque*, only not written completely by Dylan. He collaborates with everyone from Tom Petty to Sam Shepard, relying on recordings cut at various times in the mid-'80s, which makes its scattershot effect perhaps not so surprising. Still, that scattershot approach has its charms, especially when it results in winding epics like the Shepard collaboration "Brownsville Girl." But even with songs as good and interesting as that, the record follows too many detours to be consistently compelling, and some of those detours wind down roads that are indisputably dead ends. By 1986, such uneven records weren't entirely unexpected by Dylan, but that didn't make them any less frustrating. *—Stephen Thomas Erlewine*

Down in the Groove / May 31, 1988 / Columbia ✦✦
If the diffuseness of *Knocked Out Loaded* was excusable due to its collaborators and various recording sessions, *Down in the Groove* has less of an excuse, since it's relatively from the same time period, even if it's culled from several different sessions with several

different backing band. Nevertheless, the main difference is that, while *Down in the Groove* was ambitious, this is positively unassuming, at best hoping to capture the mellow roots rock of the Grateful Dead (which it does, on Dylan's irresistible collaborations with Robert Hunter, "Ugliest Girl in the World" and "Silvio"). The rest of the record strolls through covers with amiable ease, whether he's backed by ex-punks or lifetime pros. That may not make for a great record by any stretch, but it's a rather ingratiating one, a little more focused than *Knocked Out Loaded* and a little looser and funkier than *Empire Burlesque*. Actually, not as heavy on great moments as either (especially *Burlesque*), but it's still rather nice in its low-key way —*Stephen Thomas Erlewine*

Dylan & the Dead / Feb. 6, 1989 / Columbia ✦

Oh Mercy / Sep. 22, 1989 / Columbia ✦✦✦
Oh Mercy was hailed as a comeback, not just because it had songs noticeably more meaningful than anything Dylan had recently released, but because Daniel Lanois' production gave it cohesion. There was cohesion on *Empire Burlesque*, of course, but that cohesion was a little too slick, a little too commercial, whereas this record was filled with atmospheric, hazy production—a sound as arty as most assumed the songs to be. And Dylan followed suit, giving Lanois significant songs—palpably social works, love songs, and poems—that seemed to connect with his past. And, at the time, this production made it seem like the equivalent of his '60s records, meaning that its artiness was cutting edge, not portentious. Over the years, *Oh Mercy* hasn't aged particularly well, seeming as self-conscious as such other gauzy Lanois productions as *So* and *The Joshua Tree*, even though it makes more sense than the ersatz pizzazz of *Burlesque*. Still, the songs make *Oh Mercy* noteworthy; they find Dylan quietly raging against the materialism of Reagan and accepting maturity, albeit with a slight reluctance. So, *Oh Mercy* is finally more interesting for what it tries to achieve than for what it actually does achieve. At its best, this is a collection of small, shining moments, with the best songs shining brighter than their production or the album's overall effect. —*Stephen Thomas Erlewine*

Under the Red Sky / Sep. 11, 1990 / Columbia ✦✦
Dylan followed *Oh Mercy*, his most critically acclaimed album in years, with *Under the Red Sky*, a record that seemed like a conscious recoil from that album's depth and atmosphere. By signing Don Was, the king of mature retro-rock, as producer, he guaranteed that the record would be lean and direct, which is perhaps exactly what this collection of simplistic songs deserves. Still, this record feels a little ephemeral, a collection of songs that Dylan didn't really care that much about. In a way, that makes it a little easier to warm to than its predecessor, since it has a looseness that suits him well, especially with songs this deliberately lightweight. As such, *Under the Red Sky* is certainly lightweight, but rather appealing in its own lack of substance, since Dylan has never made a record so breezy, apart from (maybe) *Down in the Groove*. That doesn't make it a great, or even good, record, but it does have its own charms that will be worth searching out for Dylanphiles. —*Stephen Thomas Erlewine*

Bootleg Series, Vols. 1-3: Rare & Unreleased, 1961-1991 / Mar. 26, 1991 / Columbia ✦✦✦✦✦
This three-disc box set is what Dylanphiles have been waiting for, sitting patiently for years, even decades. And, even after its 1991 release, it retains the feeling of being a special, shared secret among the hardcore, since—no matter the acclaim—it's the kind of record that only the hardcore will seek out. Of course, the great irony is that even casual Dylan fans will find much to treasure in this three-disc set of unreleased material. They'll find songs as good as anything that made the records (sometimes surpassing the official releases, especially on the last disc), plus alternate versions (including original versions of songs on *Blood on the Tracks*) and long-fabled songs, from the incomplete "She's Your Lover Now" to songs cut from *The Freewheelin' Bob Dylan*. This doesn't just function as an alternate history of Dylan, but as an expansion of Dylan's history, enriching what is already known about the greatest songwriter of his era—after all, every song here would qualify as the best song on anybody else's album. And that's no exaggeration. —*Stephen Thomas Erlewine*

Good as I Been to You / Oct. 27, 1992 / Columbia ✦✦✦
Given the acclaim of *The Bootleg Series* and the perceived disappointment of *Under the Red Sky*, it seemed like it was time for Dylan to bounce back with a convincing album of original material. Instead, he delivered a record of folk songs, his first straight covers album ever, not to mention his first guitar, harmonica, and voice record since the early '60s. That alone would make it an anomaly, but *Good as I Been to You* is more than that, because it's a really good traditional folk album, having just enough familiar tunes— "Frankie & Albert," "Blackjack Davey," "Sittin' on Top of the World," "Froggie Went a Courtin'"—to provide an entryway to the less familiar numbers, which are delivered equally well. Yes, this could be seen as a rather unassuming record, but that's what's special about it. In 1992, not even folksingers were working with this material, but Dylan did, reviving folk's (and rock's) ties to the past at an unexpected time and with unexpectedly strong results. A minor high point in his catalog. —*Stephen Thomas Erlewine*

World Gone Wrong / Oct. 28, 1993 / Columbia ✦✦✦
If *Good as I Been to You* was a strong traditionalist folk record, *World Gone Wrong* was an exceptional one, boasting an exceptional set of songs given performances so fully realized that they seemed like modern protest songs. Much of this record is fairly obscure to anyone outside of dedicated folk fans; "Delia" (covered by Johnny Cash the following year) and "Stack-A-Lee" are the most familiar items, yet they're given traditional readings, meaning that the latter doesn't quite seem like "Stagger Lee." But even if these are traditionalist, they're spirited and lively renditions, and Dylan seems more connected to the music than he has in years. That sense of connection, plus the terrific choice of songs, makes this one of his best, strongest albums of the second half of his career. —*Stephen Thomas Erlewine*

Greatest Hits, Vol. 3 / Nov. 15, 1994 / Columbia ✦✦✦✦
Dylan's first greatest hits album was released in 1967, and his second in 1971. Twenty-three years later comes his third, and it's a reasonable compilation of the better-known songs he has produced over the period, notably standards like "Knockin' on Heaven's Door" and "Forever Young," Dylan chart hits like "Tangled Up in Blue" and "Hurricane," songs that have been covered extensively by other singers, such as "Ring Them Bells," and some of the better album tracks, such as "Changing of the Guard" and "Brownsville Girl." In an effort to span the period, a few lesser, later songs, such as "Silvio" and "Under the Red Sky" are included, while some stronger, earlier songs are not ("Simple Twist of Fate," "Senor," "Emotionally Yours," and "Everything Is Broken"). But on the whole, the selection is excellent, and this is the album to get for that Dylan fan who stopped listening to him at the end of the '60s. [Includes the previously unreleased 1989 track "Dignity."[—*William Ruhlmann*

MTV Unplugged / Apr. 25, 1995 / Columbia ✦✦
This show, taped for MTV, finds Dylan turning in an 11-song set, with eight of the songs dating from his 1963-67 heyday, including such standards as "The Times They Are A-Changin'" and "Like A Rolling Stone." ("John Brown," a powerful anti-war song from 1963, had not been released on a Dylan album previously.) The '70s are represented by "Knockin' On Heaven's Door," and the '80s by "Shooting Star" and "Dignity" (a trunk song, the studio version of which had emerged only the previous November on *Bob Dylan's Greatest Hits, Volume 3*). Dylan, accompanied by a competent five-piece band, approaches his material in a gentler fashion than on some of the originals—"The Times They Are A-Changin'" and "With God On Our Side," for example, seem sadder and less defiant than they did back in 1964. Otherwise, unlike some other *Unplugged* performances, this one doesn't offer a noticeably different view of the artist's work. But then, Dylan has been unplugged for much of his career, anyway. —*William Ruhlmann*

Time Out of Mind / Sep. 30, 1997 / Columbia ✦✦✦✦
After spending much of the '90s touring and simply not writing songs, Bob Dylan returned in 1997 with *Time Out of Mind*, his first collection of new material in seven years. Where *Under the Red Sky*, his last collection of original compositions, had a casual, tossed-off feel, *Time Out of Mind* is carefully considered, from the densely detailed songs to the dark, atmospheric production. Sonically, the album is reminiscent of *Oh Mercy*, the last album Dylan recorded with producer Daniel Lanois, but *Time Out of Mind* has a grittier foundation—by and large, the songs are bitter and resigned, and Dylan gives them appropriately anguished performances. Lanois bathes them in hazy, ominous sounds, which may suit the spirit of the lyrics, but are often in opposition to Dylan's performances. Consequently, the album loses a little of its emotional impact, yet the songs themselves are uniformly powerful, adding up to Dylan's best overall collection in years. It's a better, more affecting record than *Oh Mercy*, not only because the songs have a stronger emotional pull, but because Lanois hasn't sanded away all the grit. As a result, the songs retain their power, leaving *Time Out of Mind* as one of the rare latter-day Dylan albums that meets his high standards. —*Stephen Thomas Erlewine*

☆ Bootleg Series, Vol. 4: Live 1966—Royal Albert Concert / Oct. 13, 1998 / Columbia/Legacy ✦✦✦✦✦
The most famous bootleg in rock history, with the possible exception of Dylan's own *Basement Tapes*, finally makes its official appearance 32 years after the event, and nearly 30 years after it started circulating in the underground. Although often identified as a Royal Albert Hall show, this May 17, 1966, concert, in which Dylan played electric material in front of a British audience, was actually recorded in Manchester (hence the unwieldy title with quotes around "Royal Albert Hall"). Even those who've owned this recording for many a year might be tempted by this official package, as it has been expanded into a two-CD set that not only includes the eight electric rock songs from the original bootleg, but also the seven solo acoustic performances that comprised the first half of the show. It's all in very good fidelity, about as good as any copies you could find through unofficial sources. More importantly, the electric half in particular is an important document of rock history. It captures the point at which Dylan was at his most controversial and hard rocking as he blazes through mid-'60s classics such as "Like a Rolling Stone" and "Ballad of a Thin Man," radical electric arrangements of songs that had originally been recorded acoustically ("One Too Many Mornings," "I Don't Believe You"), and the hard rocker "Tell Me, Momma," which Dylan never recorded in the studio. The acoustic disc is not as epochal, but on par with the electric half in the quality of material and performance. On top of everything else there's a 56-page booklet with a fine essay by Dylan's friend Tony Glover (a notable folk musician in his own right). It's not just an interesting adjunct to Dylan's '60s discography; it's as worthy of attention as anything else he recorded during that decade. —*Richie Unterberger*

● Essential Bob Dylan / Oct. 31, 2000 / Columbia ✦✦✦✦
A double-disc set released for the holiday season of 2000, *The Essential Bob Dylan* is a fine choice for the casual listener that just wants all the songs they know on one collection—it's Dylan's equivalent of *Beatles One*. Outside of the remastering and the previously non-LP (and very good) "Things Have Changed," there's nothing here for collectors, but, then again, that's not who this was designed for. This collection is for the listener that wants "Blowin' in the Wind," "Like a Rolling Stone," "All Along the Watchtower," "Quinn the Eskimo," "Lay Lady Lay," and "Tangled Up in Blue" in one tidy place. Yes, it's easy to find great songs missing, but for those casual fans, and for those looking for a fairly comprehensive yet concise entry point, *The Essential Bob Dylan* comes close to living up to its title. —*Stephen Thomas Erlewine*

Love and Theft / Sep. 11, 2001 / Columbia ✦✦✦✦✦
Time Out of Mind was a legitimate comeback, Bob Dylan's first collection of original songs in nearly ten years and a risky rumination on mortality, but its sequel, *Love and*

Theft, is his true return to form, not just his best album since *Blood on the Tracks*, but the loosest, funniest, warmest record he's made since *The Basement Tapes*. There are none of the foreboding, apocalyptic warnings that permeated *Time Out of Mind* and even underpinned "Things Have Changed," his Oscar-winning theme to Curtis Hanson's 2000 film *Wonder Boys*. Just as important, Daniel Lanois' deliberately arty, diffuse production has retreated into the mist, replaced by an uncluttered, resonant production that gives Dylan and his ace backing band room to breathe. And they run wild with that liberty, rocking the house with the grinding "Lonesome Day Blues" and burning it down with the fabulously swinging "Summer Days." They're equally captivating on the slower songs, whether it's the breezily romantic "Bye and Bye," the torch song "Moonlight," or the epic reflective closer, "Sugar Baby." Musically, Dylan hasn't been this natural or vital since he was with the Band, and even then, those records were never as relaxed and easy or even as hard-rocking as these. That alone would make *Love and Theft* a remarkable achievement, but they're supported by a tremendous set of songs that fully synthesizes all the strands in his music, from the folksinger of the early '60s, through the absurdist story-teller of the mid-'60s, through the traditionalist of the early '70s, to the grizzled professional of the '90s. None of this is conscious, it's all natural. There's an ease to his writing and a swagger to his performance unheard in years—he's cracking jokes and murmuring wry asides, telling stories, crooning, and swinging. It's reminiscent of his classic records, but he's never made a record that's been such sheer, giddy fun as this, and it stands proudly among his very best albums. —*Stephen Thomas Erlewine*

The E-Types

f. 1966, **db.** 1967
Garage Rock

In the mid-'60s, this group from Salinas, California, (near San Jose) played a pleasant blend of British Invasion-inspired pop/rock and a touch of garage. With prominent keyboards, three-part harmonies, and original material with minor-keyed shifts, they sounded something like a mix between the Zombies and the Turtles. Very popular within their (pretty limited) stomping grounds, they made no impact whatsoever on a national level, issuing four singles on small labels (most of them with producer Ed Cobb, who also handled the Standells and the Chocolate Watch Band). Certainly they were a promising outfit, capable of offering strong original material (most of which, oddly, was penned by a friend who wasn't in the band, Larry Hosford). They didn't have enough time to convert that promise into truly significant work, however. They disbanded in 1967, when their carefully executed pop/rock was falling out of fashion in California, in favor of psychedelia. —*Richie Unterberger*

● **Introducing . . . The E-Types** / 1995 / Sundazed ♦♦♦♦♦
Twenty-two tracks, including both sides of their four singles and previously unissued demos, outtakes, and live performances. The four singles are legitimately fine finds if you collect obscure '60s pop-garage. "Long Before," "I Can't Do It," and "Put the Clock Back on the Wall" are outstanding, and the cover of Lennon-McCartney's "Love of the Loved" (which the Beatles never officially released themselves) rates as one of the best unknown Beatle covers of the '60s. Most of the rest of this archival compilation is padding, though, consisting largely of faithful British Invasion covers and some outtakes that are markedly inferior to their singles. It's an enjoyable listen for collectors of mid-'60s rock, boasting considerably more pop-oriented material and accomplished production than the garage norm. But it couldn't be considered in the top drawer of this sort of thing. —*Richie Unterberger*

The Eagles

f. 1971, Los Angeles, CA, **db.** 1982
Album Rock, Pop/Rock, Folk-Rock, Soft Rock, Country-Rock

The Eagles were among the most successful rock groups of the '70s, and their blend of country, folk, and rock continues to sell well in catalog. The group's four original members—Glenn Frey, Bernie Leadon, Randy Meisner, and Don Henley—were Los Angeles session veterans assembled as backup musicians for Linda Ronstadt. Signed to Ronstadt's Asylum label, they found a couple of Top 40 hits with their eponymous 1972 debut. The third Eagles LP, 1974's *On the Border*, was their breakthrough record; it went gold in three months and produced the number one hit "Best of My Love." The follow-up, *One of These Nights*, was the first of four straight albums to top the charts. The Eagles' 1976 greatest-hits album became the best-selling record of all time, now standing at 22 million sales. Soon after, they suffered the loss of Leadon, who was replaced by Joe Walsh. At the end of the year, the Eagles released *Hotel California*, including hits with the ominous title track, "New Kid in Town," and "Life in the Fast Lane." After Meisner left, he was replaced by Timothy B. Schmit. It took the group until the fall of 1979 to complete *The Long Run*, another million-seller featuring the chart-topper "Heartache Tonight." By 1981, the Eagles had split up. A dozen years later, the group reunited for a summer stadium tour and recorded an album for *MTV Unplugged*. Released in 1994, *Hell Freezes Over* debuted at number one and sold over six million copies. —*William Ruhlmann*

The Eagles / Jun. 1, 1972 / Asylum ♦♦♦
Balance is the key element of the Eagles' self-titled debut album, a collection that contains elements of rock & roll, folk, and country, overlaid by vocal harmonies alternately suggestive of doo wop, the Beach Boys, and the Everly Brothers. If the group kicks up its heels on rockers like "Chug All Night," "Nightingale," and "Tryin'," it is equally convincing on ballads like "Most of Us Are Sad" and "Train Leaves Here This Morning." The album is also balanced among its members, who trade off on lead vocal chores and divide the songwriting such that Glenn Frey, Bernie Leadon, and Randy Meisner all get three writing or co-writing credits. (Fourth member Don Henley, with only one co-writing credit and two lead vocals, falls a little behind, while Jackson Browne, Gene Clark, and Jack Tempchin also figure in the writing credits.) The album's overall balance is worth keeping in mind because it produced three Top 40 hit singles (all of which turned up on the massively popular *Eagles: Their Greatest Hits 1971-1975*) that do not reflect that balance. "Take It Easy" and "Peaceful Easy Feeling" are similar-sounding mid-tempo folk-rock tunes sung by Frey that express the same sort of laid-back philosophy, as indicated by the word "easy" in both titles, while "Witchy Woman," a Henley vocal and co-composition, initiates the band's career-long examination of supernaturally evil females. These are the songs one remembers from *Eagles*, and they look forward to the eventual dominance of the band by Frey and Henley. But the complete album from which they come

belongs as much to Leadon's country-steeped playing and singing and to Meisner's melodic rock & roll feel, which, on the release date, made it seem a more varied and consistent effort than it did later, when the singles had become overly familiar. —*William Ruhlmann*

Desperado / Apr. 17, 1973 / Asylum ♦♦♦
If Don Henley was the sole member of the Eagles underrepresented on their debut album, *Eagles*, with only two lead vocals and one co-songwriting credit, he made up for it on their follow-up, the "concept" album *Desperado*. The concept had to do with Old West outlaws, but it had no specific narrative. On *Eagles*, the group had already begun to marry itself to a Southwest sound and lyrical references, from the Indian-style introduction of "Witchy Woman" to the Winslow, AZ, address in "Take It Easy." All of this became more overt on *Desperado*, and it may be that Henley, who hailed from Northeast Texas, had the greatest affinity for the subject matter. In any case, he had co-writing credits on eight of the 11 selections and sang such key tracks as "Doolin-Dalton" and the title song. What would become recognizable as Henley's lyrical touch was apparent on those songs, which bore a serious, world-weary tone. Henley had begun co-writing with Glenn Frey, and they contributed the album's strongest material, which included the first single, "Tequila Sunrise," and "Desperado" (strangely never released as a single). But where *Eagles* seemed deliberately to balance the band's many musical styles and the talents of the band's members, *Desperado*, despite its overarching theme, often seemed a collection of disparate tracks—"Out of Control" was a raucous rocker, while "Desperado" was a painfully slow ballad backed by strings—with other band members' contributions tacked on rather than integrated. Randy Meisner was down to two co-writing credits and one lead vocal ("Certain Kind of Fool"), while Bernie Leadon's two songs, "Twenty-One" and "Bitter Creek," seemed to come from a different record entirely. The result was an album that was simultaneously more ambitious and serious-minded than its predecessor and also slighter and less consistent. —*William Ruhlmann*

On the Border / Mar. 22, 1974 / Asylum ♦♦♦
The Eagles began recording their third album in England with producer Glyn Johns, as they had their first two albums, but abandoned the sessions after completing two acceptable tracks. Johns, it is said, tended to emphasize the group's country elements and its harmonies, while the band, in particular Glenn Frey and Don Henley, wanted to take more of a hard rock direction. They reconvened with a new producer, Bill Szymczyk, who had produced artists like B.B. King and, more significantly, Joe Walsh. But the resulting album is not an outright rock effort by any means. Certainly, Frey and Henley got what they wanted with "Already Gone," the lead-off track, which introduces new band member Don Felder as one part of the twin guitar solo that recalls the Allman Brothers Band; "James Dean," a rock & roll song on the order of "Your Mama Don't Dance"; and "Good Day in Hell," which is strongly reminiscent of Joe Walsh songs like "Rocky Mountain Way." But the album also features the usual mixture of styles typical of an Eagles album. For example, "Midnight Flyer," sung by Randy Meisner, is modern bluegrass; "My Man" is Bernie Leadon's country-rock tribute to the recently deceased Gram Parsons; and "Ol' 55" is one of the group's well-done covers of a tune by a singer-songwriter labelmate, in this case Tom Waits. The title track, meanwhile, points the band in a new R&B direction that was later pursued more fully. Like most successful groups, the Eagles combined many different elements, and their third album, which looked back to their earlier work and anticipated their later work, was a transitional effort that combined even more styles than most of their records did. —*William Ruhlmann*

One of These Nights / Jun. 10, 1975 / Asylum ♦♦♦♦
The Eagles recorded their albums relatively quickly in their first years of existence, their albums succeeding each other by less than a year. *One of These Nights*, their fourth album, was released in June 1975, more than 14 months after its predecessor. Anticipation had been heightened by the belated chart-topping success of the third album's "The Best of My Love"; taking a little more time, the band generated more original material, and that material was more polished. More than ever, the Eagles seemed to be a vehicle for Don Henley (six co-writing credits) and Glenn Frey (five), but at the same time Randy Meisner was more audible than ever, his two lead vocals including one of the album's three hit singles, "Take It to the Limit," and Bernie Leadon had two showcases, among them the cosmic-cowboy instrumental "Journey of the Sorcerer" (later used as the theme music for the British television series *The Hitchhiker's Guide to the Galaxy*). Nevertheless, it was the team of Henley and Frey that stood out, starting with the title track, a number one single, which had more of an R&B—even disco—sound than anything the band had attempted previously, and continuing through the ersatz Western swing of "Hollywood Waltz" to "Lyin' Eyes," one of Frey's patented folk-rock shuffles, which became another major hit. *One of These Nights* was the culmination of the blend of rock, country, and folk styles the Eagles had been making since their start; there wasn't much

that was new, just the same sorts of things done better than they had been before. In particular, a lyrical stance—knowing and disillusioned, but desperately hopeful—had evolved, and the musical arrangements were tighter and more purposeful. The result was the Eagles' best-realized and most popular album so far. *—William Ruhlmann*

★ **Their Greatest Hits (1971-1975)** / Feb. 17, 1976 / Asylum ♦♦♦♦♦

On their first four albums, the Eagles were at pains to demonstrate that they were a group of at least near-equals, each getting a share of the songwriting credits and lead vocals. But this compilation drawn from those albums, comprising the group's nine Top 40 hits plus "Desperado," demonstrates that this evenhandedness did not extend to singles—as far as those go, the Eagles belong to Glenn Frey and Don Henley. The tunes are melodic, and the arrangements—full of strummed acoustic guitars over a rock rhythm section often playing a shuffle beat, topped by tenor-dominated harmonies—are immediately engaging. There is also a lyrical consistency to the songs, which often concern romantic uncertainties in an atmosphere soaked in intoxicants. The narrators of the songs usually seem exhausted, if not satiated, and the loping rhythms are appropriate to these impressions. All of which means that, unlike the albums from which they come, these songs make up a collection consistent in mood and identity, which may help explain why *Eagles: Their Greatest Hits 1971-1975* works so much better than the band's previous discs and practically makes them redundant. No wonder it was such a big hit out of the box, topping the charts and becoming the first album ever certified platinum. Still, there must be more to it, since the album wasn't just a big hit, but one of the biggest ever, becoming one of the very few discs to cross the threshold of 20 million copies and competing for the title of best-selling album of all time. There may be no explaining that, really, except to note that this was the pervasive music of the first half of the 1970s, and somehow it never went away. *—William Ruhlmann*

☆ **Hotel California** / Dec. 8, 1976 / Asylum ♦♦♦♦♦

The Eagles took 18 months between their fourth and fifth albums, reportedly spending eight months in the studio recording *Hotel California*. The album was also their first to be made without Bernie Leadon, who had given the band much of its country flavor, and with rock guitarist Joe Walsh. As a result, the album marks a major leap for the Eagles from their earlier work, as well as a stylistic shift toward mainstream rock. An even more important aspect, however, is the emergence of Don Henley as the band's dominant voice, both as a singer and a lyricist. On the six songs to which he contributes, Henley sketches a thematic statement that begins by using California as a metaphor for a dark, surreal world of dissipation; comments on the ephemeral nature of success and the attraction of excess; branches out into romantic disappointment; and finally sketches a broad, pessimistic history of America that borders on nihilism. Of course, the lyrics kick in some time after one has appreciated the album's music, which marks a peak in the Eagles' playing. Early on, the group couldn't rock convincingly, but the rhythm section of Henley and Meisner has finally solidified, and the electric guitar work of Don Felder and Joe Walsh has arena-rock heft. In the early part of their career, the Eagles never seemed to get a sound big enough for their ambitions; after changes in producer and personnel, as well as a noticeable growth in creativity, *Hotel California* unveiled what seemed almost like a whole new band. It was a band that could be bombastic, but also one that made music worthy of the later tag of "classic rock," music appropriate for the arenas and stadiums the band was playing. The result was the Eagles' biggest-selling regular album release, and one of the most successful rock albums ever. *—William Ruhlmann*

The Long Run / Sep. 24, 1979 / Asylum ♦♦♦

Three years in the making (which was considered an eternity in the '70s), the Eagles' follow-up to the massively successful, critically acclaimed *Hotel California* was a major disappointment, even though it sold several million copies and threw off three hit singles. Those singles, in fact, provide some insight into the record. "Heartache Tonight" was an old-fashioned rock & roll song sung by Glenn Frey, while "I Can't Tell You Why" was a delicate ballad by Timothy B. Schmit, the band's newest member. Only "The Long Run," a conventional pop/rock tune with a Stax Records R&B flavor, bore the stamp and vocal signature of Don Henley, who had largely taken the reins of the band on *Hotel California*. Henley also dominated *The Long Run*, getting co-writing credits on nine of the ten songs, singing five lead vocals, and sharing another two with Frey. This time around, however, Henley's contributions were for the most part painfully slight. Only "The Long Run" and the regret-filled closing song, "The Sad Café," showed any of his usual craftsmanship. The album was dominated by second-rank songs like "The Disco Strangler," "King of Hollywood," and "Teenage Jail" that sounded like they couldn't have taken three hours much less three years to come up with. (Joe Walsh's "In the City" was up to his usual standard, but it may not even have been an Eagles recording, having appeared months earlier on the soundtrack to *The Warriors* where it was credited as a Walsh solo track.) Amazingly, *The Long Run* reportedly was planned as a double album before being truncated to a single disc. If these were the keepers, what can the rejects have sounded like? *—William Ruhlmann*

Eagles Live / Nov. 7, 1980 / Asylum ♦♦♦

Although *Eagles Live* includes four tracks recorded in the fall of 1976 (thus allowing for the inclusion of departed singer Randy Meisner on "Take It to the Limit"), the bulk of the album comes from the end of the Eagles' 1980 tour, just before they broke up, and it reflects their late concert repertoire, largely drawn from *Hotel California* and *The Long Run*. The occasional early song such as "Desperado" and "Take It Easy" turn up, but many of the major hits from the middle of the band's career—"The Best of My Love," "One of These Nights," "Lyin' Eyes"—are missing, replaced by such curiosities as two extended selections from Joe Walsh's solo career, "Life's Been Good" and "All Night Long." At least Walsh introduces some live variations to his material; the rest of the Eagles seem determined to recreate the studio versions of their songs in concert, which may work for them live but almost makes a live recording superfluous. The previously unrecorded rendition of Steve Young's "Seven Bridges Road" is welcome, and the album would have benefited from more surprises as well as a livelier approach to a live recording. *—William Ruhlmann*

The Eagles Greatest Hits, Vol. 2 / Oct. 1982 / Asylum ♦♦♦♦

With the Eagles having officially disbanded in May 1982, leaving behind eight Top 40 hits that followed the release of the spectacularly successful *Eagles: Their Greatest Hits 1971-1975*, Asylum Records naturally compiled a second hits collection for fall 1982 release. Seven of those hits were included (the exception being the seasonal "Please Come Home for Christmas"), along with three LP tracks, one each from *One of These Nights*, *Hotel California*, and *The Long Run*. Disdained by longtime fans and by the Eagles themselves, the collection was perfect for listeners who knew the band through number one radio hits like "New Kid in Town," "Hotel California," and "Heartache Tonight." It also spared them having to buy mediocre albums like *The Long Run* and *Eagles Live* just to have copies of the best-known songs from those releases. No wonder, then, that over the years *Eagles Greatest Hits, Vol. 2* achieved multi-platinum status. *—William Ruhlmann*

Hell Freezes Over / Nov. 8, 1994 / Geffen ♦♦♦

The Eagles' first newly recorded album in 14 years gets off to a good start with the rocker "Get Over It," a timely piece of advice about accepting responsibility, followed by the tender ballad "Love Will Keep Us Alive," the country-styled "The Girl From Yesterday," and "Learn to Be Still," one of Don Henley's more thoughtful statements. Unfortunately, that's it. *Hell Freezes Over* contains an EP's worth of new material followed by a live album. The Eagles, known for meticulously recreating their studio recordings in concert, nevertheless released *Eagles Live* in 1980. Six songs from that set reappear here, and only one is in a noticeably different arrangement, "Hotel California," which gets an acoustic treatment. As was true on *Eagles Live*, the group remains most interested in their later material, redoing five songs from the *Hotel California* LP and two from its follow-up, *The Long Run*, but finding space for only three songs from their early days, "Tequila Sunrise," "Take It Easy," and "Desperado," the last two of which were also on *Eagles Live*. As such, *Hell Freezes Over* is hard to justify as anything other than a souvenir for the Eagles' reunion tour. That, however, did not keep it from topping the charts and selling in the millions. *—William Ruhlmann*

Selected Works: 1972-1999 / Nov. 14, 2000 / Elektra ♦♦♦♦

The relative sonic neglect suffered by the Eagles' catalog was the fault of the band's consistent success—with the original albums and hits collections still selling year after year, why bother to upgrade? Finally, however, longtime Eagles producer Bill Szymczyk remastered their albums in 1999, and the band put together a box set. Including most of their hits (the exception is "Seven Bridges Road") and lots of album tracks, the four-CD set regroups the Eagles' material into three categories: "The Early Days," which consists of 13 tracks from their first four albums; "The Ballads"; and "The Fast Lane," i.e., rhythm songs. The fourth disc is drawn from their millennium concert at the Staples Center in Los Angeles. While their early albums balanced the contributions of their members, "The Early Days" is dominated by Glenn Frey and Don Henley; that means a few worthy efforts are missing, but the selection is generally good. "The Ballads" is a straightforward collection of popular slow songs. Along with their more uptempo hits, "The Fast Lane" contains what little unreleased material there is, but anyone hoping for greatness is going to be disappointed. The Eagles have gone out of their way in "The Millennium Concert" to perform songs out of their usual repertoire, including several solo hits and both sides of their 1978 seasonal single, "Please Come Home for Christmas" and "Funky New Year." Much of this is minor or atypical material, but at least the unusually animated band members were trying (though it sounds like there was plenty of studio overdubbing). The overall result is a nearly four-hour collection that is something of a hodgepodge. There are enough rarities to bait the hook for hardcore Eagles fans, but not really satisfy them, and casual fans will probably be better off with the two single-disc hits collections. *—William Ruhlmann*

Earth, Wind & Fire

f. 1969, Chicago, IL

Blaxploitation, Smooth Soul, Quiet Storm, Urban, Disco, Funk, Soul

Earth, Wind & Fire was the most successful R&B group of the second half of the '70s. Founded by Maurice White and his brother Verdine in Chicago in 1969, they released their self-titled debut album on Warner Bros. in 1970. EWF encapsulated many strains of black pop from before their time—their high-pitched harmony vocals called to mind groups such as the Temptations, while their funkiness was reminiscent of Sly and the Family Stone, and their horn section sometimes evoked the work of James Brown and others. Over this, Maurice White laid his own brand of African-inspired kalimba music for a thorough synthesis that nonetheless bore a particular musical stamp unique to Earth, Wind & Fire. The band began to break through with its fourth album, *Head to the Sky*, in 1973. Their first R&B Top Ten hit was "Mighty Mighty," from their first gold album, *Open Your Eyes*, which also contained the R&B hit "Kalimba Story." EWF's breakthrough to a mass audience, however, came in 1975 with the release of *That's the Way of the World*, the soundtrack to a film in which the group appeared. Led by its gold-selling number one single, "Shining Star," the album topped the pop charts. After the relative failure of *Electric Universe* in 1983, EW&F disbanded. It re-formed for the 1987 release *Touch the World*. *—William Ruhlmann and Ron Wynn*

Earth, Wind & Fire / 1971 / Warner Brothers ♦♦♦

Earth, Wind & Fire is the debut album from the band of the same name. Originally released in 1971, it contains all of the trademarks of the best soul music from the early part of that decade, as well as some of the distinguishing characteristics that have made Earth, Wind & Fire such a consistently successful soul/R&B aggregate ever since.

Earth, Wind & Fire approximates the sound of the Isley Brothers from this same period, both in style—the rhythms beat with the strong pulse of soul, R&B, funk, *and* rock & roll, with a freewheeling sense of improvisation that feels like jazz, in hard-rocking tempos, with plenty of singalong chanted vocals and screaming (if not psychedelic) electric guitar—and in substance, with most songs addressing social issues under titles such as "Help Somebody," "Love Is Life," "C'Mon Children," and "This World Today." "Bad Tune" features the kalimbas of Maurice White, along with the soaring vocal harmonies and spiritual air of the lyrics that were among the primary trademarks of this band. White & Co. went on to further distill and then elaborate on their sound, most notably with the later assimilation of Philip Bailey as lead vocalist, but *Earth, Wind & Fire* presents them at the point from which it all began. —*Chris Slawecki*

The Need of Love / 1971 / Warner Brothers ✦✦✦
The Need of Love is R&B "head music," with Earth, Wind & Fire mixing all the psychedelia and experimentation going on in rock and jazz in 1971 into their R&B/soul repertoire. So *The Need of Love* begins with a free-form, ten-minute opus titled "Energy," with wind and brass solos squirming around and above and rumbling, percussion rhythm beds of varying time signatures (sort of like a Pharoah Sanders take on R&B). Other titles include "Beauty" and "Everything Is Everything" (which suggests jazz-R&B fusioneers from this same period such as Roy Ayers). The ballad "I Think About Lovin' You" provides some much-needed grounding, with composer Sherry Scott's soft and tender lead vocal couched in vocal harmonies straight from a starlit, warm doo wop summer's night. —*Chris Slawecki*

Last Days & Time / 1972 / Columbia ✦✦✦
Earth, Wind & Fire were nothing if not ambitious, and by the time of their third album they had forged an individual sound by absorbing nearly everything that had gone before them in the previous ten years. It was as if they were trying to encapsulate every eclectic foray pursued by Motown, from catchy, rhythmic pop to churning funk, and even from Stevie Wonder singing borrowed folk songs like "Blowin' In The Wind" (here, Bailey did "Where Have All the Flowers Gone") to the schmaltzy, string-filled pop that spelled legitimacy to Motown. Not only that, they wanted to incorporate Sly and the Family Stone's horn-filled, gutbucket R&B and some of the fusion style of Weather Report. On *Last Days and Time*, they succeeded in pulling all that into their orbit, but they hadn't yet managed one crucial thing: they hadn't learned to write hits. That would come next. —*William Ruhlmann*

Head to the Sky / May 1973 / Columbia ✦✦✦
As phenomenally popular as Earth, Wind & Fire was from the mid-1970s to the early 1980s, it's easy to forget that the band was hardly an overnight success. With *Head to the Sky*—EWF's fourth album overall, second with Philip Bailey and second for Columbia—Maurice White's very spiritual and ambitious brand of soul and funk was starting to pay off commercially. The Latin-influenced "Evil" became the soulsters' biggest hit up to that point, and material ranging from the hauntingly pretty title song (which boasts one of Bailey's finest performances ever) to the jazz-fusion gem "Zanzibar" is just as rewarding. The lineup White unveiled with *Last Days and Time* was working out beautifully; Bailey was clearly proving to be a major asset. Also worth noting is the presence of singer Jessica Cleaves, who left after this album and, several years later, resurfaced in George Clinton's eccentric female group the Brides of Funkenstein. EWF still had what was basically a cult following, but that was beginning to change with *Head to the Sky*. And when EWF took off commercially in 1974 and 1975, many new converts went back and saw for themselves just how excellent an album *Head to the Sky* was. —*Alex Henderson*

Another Time / 1974 / Warner Brothers ✦✦✦
Once Earth, Wind & Fire became the top black music band in the world, Warner Bros. realized the mistake they had made in not giving Maurice White complete creative freedom. They rushed out this anthology featuring the group's early music, hoping to piggyback off their huge Columbia hits. These songs are certainly worth hearing again, but few people who hadn't originally purchased the Warner Bros. tracks were enticed to get them. —*Ron Wynn*

Open Our Eyes / Mar. 1974 / Columbia/Legacy ✦✦✦
Finally, after almost half a decade of serious dues-paying, Earth, Wind & Fire took off commercially with its fifth album, *Open Our Eyes*. EWF had been delivering great albums since 1971, but it wasn't until 1974 that the public proved genuinely receptive to Maurice White's mystical and unorthodox take on soul and funk. No longer would EWF enjoy only a small cult following. Thanks to treasures like "Kalimba Song," the gritty funk smoker "Mighty Mighty," and the unforgettable "Devotion," *Open Our Eyes* became EWF's first gold album and went to the top of the R&B charts. It's also interesting to note that with this album, singer Jessica Cleaves was gone, resulting in the first time EWF had an all-male lineup. The 2001 CD reissue adds four previously unreleased bonus tracks, one of them a "Walkin' in N'awlins" mix of "Fair But So Uncool," though the other three songs did not appear on the original album in an alternate form. —*Alex Henderson*

That's the Way of the World / Mar. 1975 / Columbia/Legacy ✦✦✦✦✦
Earth, Wind & Fire has delivered more than its share of excellent albums, but if a person could own only one EWF release, the logical choice would be *That's the Way of the World*, which was the band's best album as well as its best-selling. *Open Our Eyes* had been a major hit and sold over half a million units, but it was *World* that established EWF as major-league, multi-platinum superstars. Fueled by gems ranging from the sweaty funk of "Shining Star" and "Yearnin', Learnin'" to the gorgeous ballad "Reasons" and the unforgettable title song, EWF's sixth album sold at least five million units. And some of the tracks that weren't major hits, such as the exuberant "Happy Feelings" and the gospel-

influenced "See the Light," are equally powerful. There are no dull moments on *World*, one of the strongest albums of the 1970s and EWF's crowning achievement. The 1999 CD reissue has five previously unreleased "sketches" from late 1974, including much briefer instrumental run-throughs of "Shining Star" and "That's the Way of the World," the first take alternate vocal of "All About Love," an alternate of "Happy Feelin'," and the jazz-oriented jam "Caribou Chaser" (the only one of the five not to be represented in a different version on the proper album). —*Alex Henderson*

Gratitude / Dec. 1975 / Columbia/Legacy ✦✦✦✦✦
With *That's the Way of the World* having made Earth, Wind & Fire one of the best-selling soul bands of the 1970s, Maurice White & Co. had no problem filling large arenas. As dynamic as EWF was on stage, it's a shame that there isn't more documentation of the band's live show. Only one live EWF album was released by a major label in America, the superb *Gratitude*. First a two-LP set and later reissued on CD, *Gratitude* brilliantly captures the excitement EWF generated on stage at its creative peak. Neither hardcore EWF devotees nor more casual listeners should deprive themselves of the joys of the live versions of "Shining Star" and "Yearnin', Learnin'." Maurice White is magnificent throughout, and Philip Bailey truly soars on extended versions of "Reasons" (which boasts a memorable alto sax solo by guest Don Myrick) and "Devotion." The album also introduced some excellent new studio songs, including the haunting "Can't Hide Love" and the uplifting "Sing a Song." One could nitpick and wish for live versions of "Evil," "Keep Your Head to the Sky," and "Kalimba Song," but the bottom line is that *Gratitude* is one of EWF's finest accomplishments. —*Alex Henderson*

Spirit / Sep. 1976 / Columbia/Legacy ✦✦✦✦✦
With *That's the Way of the World* having enjoyed multi-platinum success, Earth, Wind & Fire had a lot to live up to when the time came for another studio project. And the soul powerhouse didn't let anyone down (either commercially or creatively) on the outstanding *Spirit*, which boasted hits ranging from the optimistic "On Your Face" and the passionate funk classic "Getaway" to the poetic ballad "Imagination." Philip Bailey is as charismatic as ever on "Imagination" and the gorgeous title song. Maurice White's message and vision (an interesting blend of Afro-American Christianity and Eastern philosophy) was as positive and uplifting as ever, and as always, EWF expressed this positivity without being Pollyanna-ish or corny. And even if one didn't take EWF's calls for unity, hard work, self-respect, and faith in God to heart, they had no problem with their solid grooves. The 2001 CD reissue adds five previously unreleased bonus tracks, including an alternate mix of "Saturday Nite," an "Angels Mix" of "Imagination," "Departure (The Traveler)," and two songs that did not appear on the original album in an alternate form. —*Alex Henderson*

All'n All / Nov. 1977 / Columbia/Legacy ✦✦✦✦
Earth, Wind & Fire's artistic and commercial winning streak continued with its ninth album, *All 'N All*, the diverse jewel that gave us major hits like "Serpentine Fire" and the dreamy "Fantasy." Whether the visionary soul men are tearing into the hardest of funk on "Jupiter" or the most sentimental of ballads on "I'll Write a Song for You" (which boasts one of Philip Bailey's many soaring, five-star performances), *All 'N All* was a highly rewarding addition to EWF's catalogue. Because EWF had such a clean-cut image and fared so well among pop audiences, some may have forgotten just how sweaty its funk could be. But "Jupiter"—like "Mighty, Mighty," "Shining Star," and "Getaway"—underscores the fact that EWF delivered some of the most intense and gutsy funk of the 1970s. The 1999 CD reissue adds three bonus tracks: "Would You Mind" (a demo version of "Love's Holiday"), the "original Hollywood mix" of "Runnin'," and a live version of "Brazilian Rhyme," recorded live in 1980. —*Alex Henderson*

☆ **The Best of Earth, Wind & Fire, Vol. 1** / Nov. 1978 / Columbia ✦✦✦✦✦
Best of Earth, Wind & Fire, Vol. 1 contains the bulk of their hits from the mid-'70s, including "Shining Star," "September," "Got to Get You into My Life," "Sing a Song," "Getaway," and several other hits. The 1999 CD reissue has a bonus track, the late 1990s dance-mixed EWF hit medley "Mega Mix 2000," along with a radio edit of the same. —*Stephen Thomas Erlewine*

I Am / Jun. 1979 / Columbia ✦✦✦
Disco was at the height of its popularity in 1979, when Earth, Wind & Fire responded with its most disco-influenced single ever, the glossy and infectious "Boogie Wonderland." Up to that point, EWF had pretty much ignored disco, and when the band finally acknowledged the style, the soulsters weren't about to inundate listeners with it. "Boogie Wonderland" (which features the Emotions, a female group for whom Maurice White had been producing major hits) isn't representative of *I Am* on the whole. From the hit ballad "After the Love Has Gone" to the exuberant "Let My Feelings Flow," *I Am* isn't a radical departure from its predecessor, *All N' All*. Though not in a class with *That's the Way of the World*, *Spirit*, or *All N' All*, *I Am* is a rewarding album that has a lot going for it. —*Alex Henderson*

Faces / Oct. 1980 / Columbia ✦✦✦
Although they were catching more flak from critics for an alleged obsession with sociopolitical commentary and quasi-mystical references, R&B audiences hadn't yet tired of Earth, Wind & Fire. While this album admittedly had less memorable material and was more dependent on what had become production cliches and stock devices, it still landed plenty of hits on the charts. But it was becoming clear to even the most devoted fans that songs like "In The Stone" and "Let Me Talk" weren't their finest hour. —*Ron Wynn*

Raise! / Oct. 1981 / Columbia ✦✦

Powerlight / Feb. 1983 / Columbia ✦✦✦✦

Electric Universe / Nov. 1983 / Columbia ✦✦

Touch the World / Oct. 1987 / Columbia ✦✦✦

The Best of Earth, Wind & Fire, Vol. 2 / 1988 / Columbia/Legacy ✦✦✦✦✦
The second collection covering hit singles from the '70s top funk and soul band, Earth, Wind & Fire. This anthology has recently been supplanted by a box set covering virtually all of their big Columbia singles and some early Warners material. If you enjoyed their disco and late '70s cuts more than the early tracks, this anthology is worth getting. The 2000 CD reissue has two bonus tracks: the moderate 1973 hit "Keep Your Head to the Sky" and "I'll Write a Song for You," from the 1977 album *All 'n All.* —*Ron Wynn & Richie Unterberger*

Heritage / Jan. 1990 / Columbia ✦✦

The Eternal Dance / Sep. 8, 1992 / Columbia/Legacy ✦✦✦✦✦
Covering three discs and including all the hits, as well as a healthy selection of rarities, *The Eternal Dance* is not designed for the casual listener; only hardcore fans will remain enthralled through the numerous rarities. Most listeners will be content with the two greatest hits collections, but this comprehensive box set remains essential for hardcore Earth, Wind & Fire fans. —*Stephen Thomas Erlewine*

Millennium / Sep. 14, 1993 / Reprise ✦✦

★ **Greatest Hits** / Nov. 17, 1998 / Columbia/Legacy ✦✦✦✦✦
Columbia's 1998 collection of Earth, Wind & Fire's *Greatest Hits* in many ways stands as the group's definitive compilation. Even though there have been more extensive overviews of the group's work, such as the triple-disc set *The Eternal Dance,* this is the first collection to contain all of the group's biggest hits on one disc. All but one ("Love Music") of the ten songs from 1978's *The Best of Earth, Wind & Fire* are included, while six of the ten songs from *The Best Of, Vol. 2* are featured; the remaining two cuts on the 17-track collection are the minor early single "Kalimba Story" and the album cut "Gratitude." These are fine additions to the album, but the true meat of the collection lies in the hits—"Shining Star," "That's the Way of the World," "Sing a Song," "Getaway," "Got to Get You Into My Life," "September," "Boogie Wonderland," "After the Love Has Gone," "Let's Groove," and so many others. They might not be presented in chronological order (the only flaw in this otherwise flawless collection), but it's a sheer delight to have all of the hits on one terrifically entertaining and valuable disc. —*Stephen Thomas Erlewine*

Sheena Easton

b. Apr. 27, 1959, Belshill, Scotland
Vocals / Pop/Rock, Soft Rock, Adult Contemporary, Dance-Pop
1980s pop diva Sheena Easton was born Sheena Shirley Orr in Belshill, Scotland on April 27, 1959. Inspired to pursue a singing career after seeing Barbra Streisand in *The Way We Were,* she later attended the Royal Scottish Academy of Music and Drama while moonlighting with the group Something Else. Exposure on the BBC television production *The Big Time: Pop Singer* not only resulted in a record deal with EMI but also pushed Easton's 1980 debut singles, "Modern Girl" and "9 to 5," into the U.K. Top Ten, and she became the first female artist to score two simultaneous Top Ten hits. Her self-titled debut LP followed in 1981, while "9 to 5" was reissued in America under the title "Morning Train" to avoid confusion with Dolly Parton's recent hit of the same name; regardless, the single topped the U.S. pop charts, with "Modern Girl" cracking the Top 20 a few months later. After earning a Grammy as Best New Artist, Easton was tapped to sing the title theme of the latest James Bond film, *For Your Eyes Only;* in 1983, she duetted with Kenny Rogers on the smash "We've Got Tonight," returning to the Top Ten later that year with "Telefone (Long Distance Love Affair." However, with 1984's *A Private Affair,* Easton retooled her squeaky clean image, following the sassy "Strut" with the salacious "Sugar Walls," written and produced by one Alexander Nevermind (a.k.a. Prince, to whose "U Got the Look" she contributed vocals in 1987). She followed a stint as Don Johnson's ill-fated TV wife on *Miami Vice* by scoring the number two smash "The Lover in Me" in 1989; however, 1991's "What Comes Naturally" proved to be Easton's last chart entry, and after starring in a musical revival of *Man of La Mancha* she spent much of the decade on stage, also appearing in a revival of *Grease* as well as on the seasonal tour *The Colors of Christmas.* —*Jason Ankeny*

● **The World of Sheena Easton: The Singles Collection** / 1993 / EMI America ✦✦✦✦✦
Sheena Easton never achieved red-hot status, but she remained consistent for nearly a decade—a much more difficult feat—and this generous collection showcases a long (in terms of pop stardom) career of adult contemporary ballads, R&B-flavored dance tunes, and straight-up pop. What's nice about this collection is that it includes monster hits like the fluff of "Telefone (Long Distance Love Affair)" and "Morning Train (Nine to Five)," as well as smaller hits like the beautifully written but sadly over-synthesized "When He Shines" and the plucky "Modern Girl," while also including cuts like the proud but humbled "I Wouldn't Beg for Water" and the Motown throwback "Jimmy Mack" that didn't get much action on the U.S. charts. Easton wraps her pipes around each song, turning vamp ("Strut") then drama queen ("Almost Over You") then country chanteuse ("We've Got Tonight") without ever missing a beat. Her strong point is good material, though it oftentimes gets overshadowed by less than worthy production. As extensive as this collection is, however, it's unfortunate her singles with Prince and "The Lover in Me" are missing. Otherwise, this is an almost-perfect greatest-hits compilation. —*Bryan Buss*

The Easybeats

f. 1963, Sydney, Australia, **db.** 1970
British Invasion, Pop, Rock & Roll
The most successful Australian rock group of the 1960s, the Easybeats were nearly as popular as the Beatles in their homeland in the mid-'60s. In 1965 and 1966, they ran off a rapid string of seven Top Ten singles in Australia with peppy variations on the early Beatle and Merseybeat sound. With a nervous energy that featured staccato guitar lines, unexpected tempo changes, and strong original material, they also betrayed strong debts to the Kinks, Who, and Small Faces, although their songs were generally cheerier and more lightweight. Like all of the aforementioned bands, the Easybeats stand as one of the earliest and foremost exponents of pure power-pop. In late 1966, the Easybeats moved to London and hooked up with legendary producer Shel Talmy (Who, Kinks) in an attempt to crack the international pop market. Against all the odds, they did so the first time out with the classic "Friday on My Mind," which hit the British Top Ten and the American Top 20. Some ill-chosen follow-ups, however, deflated their momentum, although the group—led by the increasingly adventurous combination songwriting/production team of guitarists George Young and Harry Vanda—were keeping up with the tenor of their times by expanding the scope of their lyrics and arrangements. —*Richie Unterberger*

Easy / 1965 / Repertoire ✦✦✦✦
Their first album, not available outside Australia until the 1990s. The Vanda/Young songwriting partnership had yet to dominate the band in their early days, and most of the (entirely original) material here comes from the pens of George Young and singer Stevie Wright. It's more Merseybeatish and less oriented toward power-pop and staccato guitar attacks than their subsequent releases, which isn't really detrimental; it doesn't scale the peaks the band would shortly climb, but neither does it have the overdone good-time mania that made some of their efforts hard to take in more than limited doses. A fairly consistent, if not incredibly remarkable, relic from the Beat era, with some very Beatlesque tracks, including "It's So Easy," "I Wonder" (on which Harry Vanda sounds a lot like a young George Harrison circa "Do You Want to Know a Secret"), and cuts that could pass for the Searchers ("I'm Gonna Tell Everybody"), Gerry & the Pacemakers ("Hey Girl," "A Letter"), the Merseybeats ("Cry Cry Cry"), the Kinks ("You'll Come Back Again"), and Peter & Gordon ("Girl on My Mind"). Stuck in the middle of all of those delightfully derivative treasures is the most defiantly original track off the album, and (not coincidentally) their first big Australian hit, "She's So Fine," which doesn't sound like anything else here, pulsing with energy, a hot pumping bass part, and a ferocious guitar break. The Repertoire Records CD reissue enhances the original album significantly with the addition of eight bonus tracks, including five jewels from the Vanda/Young songwriting team. —*Richie Unterberger & Bruce Eder*

It's 2 Easy / 1966 / Repertoire ✦✦✦✦
The Easybeats' second album was an Australia-only release that only got out elsewhere 27 years later. It was vaguely similar in spots to the band's first—many of the songs, particularly the hits "Women" and "Sad and Lonely and Blue," were heavily influenced by 1964-vintage Merseybeat groups. Those songs are somewhat deceptive, however, for the group was stretching out stylistically on much of *It's 2 Easy.* Sharing space with bright, heavily harmonized numbers like "Let Me Be" and "You Are the Light" is a string of songs integrating elements of blues, folk, and even a certain novelty feel, similar to the work of the Kinks. "Come and See Her" and "I'll Find Somebody to Take Your Place" abandon those Beatlesque melodies in favor of dissonances and a punk attitude. Featuring some gloriously crisp and slashing lead guitar over pleasantly crunchy rhythm playing, "Easy as Can Be" is a catchy, loud, fiercely posturing declaration of lust that could almost pass for a piece of American garage rock.

Most of this album is a respectable piece of mainstream rock & roll, inspired and full of surprises. With the addition of 11 more songs, the original LP has been expanded to 25 tracks and 62 minutes' running time. The added tunes are an uneven lot, derived from various singles, B-sides, and other sources. Some of it is rather lugubrious, but none of it detracts from the value of the original album, which remains one of the best bodies of music in the late British invasion style ever produced. —*Bruce Eder*

Volume 3 / 1966 / Albert ✦✦✦
The hardest Easybeats album to find (now available on CD) contains some of their rarest material, never issued outside of Australia. It's actually not worth making a special effort for unless you're a big fan of the group. Like their first two Australia-only LPs, it's accomplished guitar pop/rock with a heavy British Invasion influence, but not outstanding. The best songs ("Sorry," "Funny Feelin'") have been reissued on Easybeats anthologies. —*Richie Unterberger*

Friends / 1969 / Repertoire ✦✦

The Shame Just Drained / 1977 / Albert ✦✦✦
For a group that really only scored one major international hit, the Easybeats' songwriting team—Harry Vanda and George Young—were very busy bees indeed in the studio in the late '60s. All but one of the songs on this 15-track compilation are taken from sessions between late 1966 and late 1968 that were unreleased at the time; five come from an album that was canned at the last minute. Apparently there were about 20 more outtakes where that came from. Don't pay any mind to the ridiculous claim in the sleeve note that "had all the material been released in the sequence (and quantity) it was created, then the Easybeats' impact might have been far more notable and we might today be comparing their albums alongside *Rubber Soul, Aftermath,* and other rock milestones." This is cheery late-'60s pop with mild psychedelic influences, echoing the Small Faces, the Turtles, and especially the Kinks. The cheeriness, in fact, verges on childish and sickly sweet in places. It's not bad. In fact, it's occasionally pretty good; it's just not incredibly significant. By far the best track is "Mr. Riley of Higginbottom & Clive," a bit of dry class satire that compares well with Ray Davies' vignettes from the same era. —*Richie Unterberger*

Absolute Anthology / 1980 / EMI ✦✦✦✦✦
A two-CD package from Australia, with ear-stunning sound and two hours of golden classics. The collection of choice. —*Bruce Eder*

Raven Ep Lp, Vol. 2 / 1982 / Raven ♦♦♦

A compilation of three EPs originally released on the Australian reissue label Raven, hence the strange title. The Easybeats recorded extremely prolifically during their five-year career, and this gathers about a dozen unreleased tracks, a few stray cuts that ended up on fairly rare LPs or EPs, and three (yes, three) Coke jingles. The best of these offerings are six demos from early 1965; all originals, they show the band at their most British Invasion-influenced and have a mawkish, innocent charm, though they're hardly classic. The rest of the material is typical mid- to late-period Easybeats: extremely clever insofar as quirky songwriting and guitar playing, cheerful almost to the point of being grating, and not nearly as lasting or important as their obvious reference points (the Beatles, Kinks, Who, and Small Faces). Also includes a couple unimpressive covers (of "Hound Dog" and the Nashville Teens' "Find My Way Back Home"). *—Richie Unterberger*

The Best of the Easybeats [Rhino] / 1985 / Rhino ♦♦♦♦♦

A well-devised collection that pales in sound and content next to its Australian competitor. *—Bruce Eder*

The Best of the Easybeats [Repertoire] / 1995 / Repertoire ♦♦♦

A better title for this 58-minute, 20-song CD might have been "The Best of the Easybeats 1967-1969." Like virtually all of the compilations of this band's work (with the notable exception of *Absolute Anthology*), Repertoire Records' best-of ignores the group's 1965 and early-1966 Australian sides and their early hits in that country in favor of distilling down the group's work beginning with "Friday on My Mind." That might be the work that is best known to most listeners outside of Australia, but it also gives a skewed perspective of the group's work—similar to if someone started a Beatles best-of with "Penny Lane." Neophytes might think from this that the Easybeats started out as a psychedelic rock outfit, when they actually made some punchy British Invasion-style music for a couple of years. In fairness, the sound here is excellent, and the choice of songs is good within the confines of the disc—one just wishes that some of the more forced "good time" music was supplemented with a few of those early rockers, perhaps in place of a couple of the later, serious songs. The annotation, surprisingly, is minimal, without even the inclusion of release dates or histories on the individual songs. *—Bruce Eder*

● **Aussie Beat That Shook the World: The Definitive Anthology** / 1996 / Repertoire ♦♦♦♦♦

This two-CD, 56-song anthology is an excellent value even at an import price. It contains all their Australian hits, lots of album tracks, and some rarities that don't show up very often, like the 1965 B-side "The Old Oak Tree." It may be too lengthy an introduction or overview for some, though; some of their LP tracks weren't memorable, and one gets the feeling that some of the rarities and cover versions were put on here because they were rare, not because of their musical quality. In addition, all of the Easybeat rarities you could want have been placed on Repertoire's reissues of individual Easybeats albums as bonus tracks. The 48-page booklet does have interview material with Harry Vanda, including comments on each song in the set. *—Richie Unterberger*

Eazy-E (Eric Wright)

b. Sep. 7, 1964, Compton, CA, **d.** Mar. 26, 1995

Vocals / Dirty Rap, West Coast Rap, Hardcore Rap, Gangsta Rap

After leaving N.W.A., rapper Eazy-E led a career that was filled with controversy and was considerably successful commercially, even if it never matched the creativity of his previous band. Eazy-E began his solo career in 1988 with *Eazy-Duz-It*; it was his only full-length album.

Eazy-E left N.W.A. after 1991's *Niggaz4Life* hit the top of the charts. The breakup of N.W.A. was extremely bitter and Eazy in particular earned the wrath of Dr. Dre. Dre and Eazy carried out their feud on record throughout the early '90s.

Even though he released several hit EPs, Eazy's career was in decline when he announced he was suffering from AIDS in early March of 1995; he only learned that he had the disease in the previous month. Three weeks later, the rapper died on March 26, 1995—he was 31 years old. *—Stephen Thomas Erlewine*

Eazy-Duz-It / 1988 / Ruthless ♦♦♦

A second-rate companion to *Straight Outta Compton*, Eazy-E's Dr. Dre-produced *Eazy-Duz-It* stands primarily as an artifact of the time when gangsta rap was still developing and has little other value. Sure, Eazy-E was an undeniable superstar at the time, but due mostly to his charisma more than to his admittedly poor rapping skills. Furthermore, Dre doesn't deliver that rousing of production here, as if he was saving his more striking beats for the N.W.A. album. There are a few moments when this album enters notable territory, particularly on the Ice Cube-penned "Boyz-N-the Hood" and also on "Eazy-Er Said Than Dunn" and "Eazy-Duz-It"; "We Want Eazy," a highly derivative interpolation of a Bootsy Collins track, also stands out. But, ultimately, even these highlights aren't that notable in retrospect, and the other tracks are undeniably throwaways. At this point in his career, Eazy wasn't a strong MC and relied on Dre's beats and his own charisma to carry him. At the time of its release, the album did seem significant, but time quickly corrected that—this album has not aged well at all. Eazy's later contributions to N.W.A.'s *100 Miles and Runnin'* and *Niggaz4life* releases found him vastly improved as a rapper with more wit and better flow; furthermore, his *It's On (Dr. Dre) 187um Killa* release showed that he was indeed improving with every passing year. *—Jason Birchmeier*

5150 Home 4 Tha Sick / Dec. 28, 1992 / Priority ♦

It's On (Dr. Dre) 187um Killa / Nov. 5, 1993 / Ruthless ♦♦♦♦♦

Though not necessarily one of rap's most shining moments by any means, *It's On (Dr. Dre) 187um Killa* does stand as Eazy-E's best moment outside of N.W.A., showcasing his amazingly sarcastic and downright ruthless sense of wit. More than anything else, this EP was thrown together as a quick answer to Dr. Dre's *The Chronic*, an album ridden with lyrical shots at Eazy. Songs here such as "Real Muthaphuckkin G's" and "It's On" are pointed directly at Dre and Snoop Dogg, with Eazy showing no remorse whatsoever. The irony of this is the fact that Eazy co-opts Dre's style for this EP, rapping over production that is obviously modeled after Dre's signature flute- and synth-laden G-funk melodies of the time (produced, in part, by Dre's old partner, Yella). Sure, this release is definitely lacking in quantity (being forced to yet again resurrect "Boyz-N-the Hood"), and Eazy doesn't have much to say outside of his relentless Dre-aimed disses and his odes to sex and drugs. But despite these complaints, "Real Muthaphuckkin G's" and "It's On" remain some of Eazy's best solo songs ever, and "Gimmie That Nutt" remains a timeless nasty club anthem. Though it's a bit odd to consider a quickly thrown-together EP such as this to be the highlight of Eazy-E's brief solo career, it's hard to say that it isn't. It seems Dre's disses were the best motivation for Eazy's often half-hearted rap career. *—Jason Birchmeier*

Str8 off Tha Streetz / 1995 / Relativity ♦♦♦

At the time of his death, Eazy-E was completing a comeback album that was intended to restore his street credibility, which had taken a savage beating in the early '90s. *Str8 Off the Streetz of Muthaphukkin Compton*, the album he left unfinished, does show more ambition than his previous *It's On*, but it's unlikely that it would have made him a star again. Collaborating with his former N.W.A. partners Ren and Yella, Eazy-E sounds revitalized, but the music simply isn't imaginative. Instead of pushing forward and creating a distinctive style, it treads over familiar gangsta territory, complete with bottomless bass, whining synthesizers, and meaningless boasts. The occasional track, like the surrealistic "The Muthaphukkin Real" and the menacing "Ole School Shit," illustrate what Eazy-E could have done if hadn't been tied to his pedestrian production, but the majority of *Str8 Off the Streez* is depressingly by-the-books. Sadly, the album is the farthest thing from a graceful departure. *—Stephen Thomas Erlewine*

● **Eternal E** / Dec. 1995 / Ruthless/Priority ♦♦♦♦

During his short career, Eazy-E only released one full-length album but managed to release a number of tracks on EPs and with N.W.A.; most of the notorious rapper's best moments from these releases are included here on *Eternal E*, which is essentially a greatest-hits collection. Unfortunately, as great as it is to hear some of Eazy-E's best moments—"Boyz-N-the Hood," "8 Ball," "Eazy-Duz-It," "Only If You Want It"—there are several unacceptable exceptions. Most notably, the material from his most realized moment, *It's On (Dr. Dre) 187um Killa*, is nowhere to be found. Furthermore, the majority of his solo material pales in comparison to his work with N.W.A. on tracks such as "Fuck the Police" and "100 Miles and Runnin'," and this collection sadly only features four N.W.A. songs. So it's almost ironic that this greatest-hits collection ignores his greatest hits (most likely for the licensing costs required to secure the absent material). It would also be nice to have some of Eazy-E's posthumously released material from the *Str8 off tha Streetz of Muthaphukkin Compton* sessions included here. So even though this album is still the best introduction to his canon of work for novices, it functions poorly as a comprehensive representation of Eazy-E's short career, as it ignores much of his best work. *—Jason Birchmeier*

Echo & The Bunnymen

f. Sep. 1978, Liverpool, England

College Rock, Dream Pop, Neo-Psychedelia, Post-Punk, Alternative Pop/Rock

Echo & the Bunnymen's dark, swirling fusion of gloomy post-punk and Doors-inspired psychedelia brought the group a handful of British hits in the early '80s, while attracting a cult following in the United States. Formed around vocalist Ian McCulloch and guitarist Will Seargent, the group's debut album, 1980's *Crocodiles*, reached number 17 on the U.K. charts. The more ambitious and atmospheric *Heaven Up Here* (1981) became their first U.K. Top Ten album, and two years later, *Porcupine* appeared, becoming the band's biggest hit (peaking at No. 2 on the U.K. charts) and launching the Top Ten single, "The Cutter." "The Killing Moon" became the group's second Top Ten hit at the beginning of 1984, and the album *Ocean Rain* was the Bunnymen's first album to chart in the US Top 100. Just after their eponymous 1987 album became their biggest American hit, peaking at number 51, McCulloch left for a solo career while the band continued on for one more album before quitting. McCulloch and Sergeant reunited for a 1995 album as Electrafixion, then re-formed Echo and the Bunnymen two years later, issuing two LPs in the late '90s. *—Stephen Thomas Erlewine*

Crocodiles / Jul. 18, 1980 / Sire ♦♦♦♦♦

Inspired by psychedelia, sure. Bit of Jim Morrison in the vocals? Okay, it's there. But for all the references and connections that can be drawn (and they can), one listen to Echo's brilliant, often harrowing debut album and it's clear what a unique, special band presents itself. Beginning with the dramatic, building climb of "Going Up," *Crocodiles* at once showcases four individual players sure of their own gifts and their ability to bring it all together to make things more than the sum of their parts. Will Sergeant in particular is a revelation—arguably only Johnny Marr and Vini Reilly were better English guitarists from the '80s, eschewing typical guitar-wank overload showboating in favor of delicacy, shades, and inventive, unexpected melodies. More than many before or since, he plays the electric guitar as just that, electric not acoustic, dedicated to finding out what can be done with it while never using it as an excuse to bend frets. His highlights are legion, whether it's the hooky opening chime of "Rescue" or the exchanges of sound and silence in "Happy Death Men." Meanwhile, the Pattinson/De Freitas rhythm section stakes its own claim for greatness, the former's bass driving yet almost seductive, the latter's percussion constantly shifting rhythms and styles while never leaving the central beat the song to die. "Pride" is one standout moment of many, Pattinson's high notes and De Freitas' interjections on what sound like chimesor blocks inspired touches. Then there's McCulloch himself, and while the imagery can be cryptic, the delivery soars, even while his semi-wail conjures up, as on the nervy, edgy picture of addiction "Villiers Terrace," "People rolling round on the carpet/Mixing up the medicine." Brisk, wasting not a note and burning with barely controlled energy, *Crocodiles* remains a deserved classic. *—Ned Raggett*

Heaven Up Here / May 30, 1981 / Sire ♦♦♦
While darker and more intense than *Crocodiles*, Echo and the Bunnymen's sophomore effort lacks the immediacy of their debut; the songs are subpar, relying too much on atmosphere and texture instead of substance. Although a few of the tracks, including "A Promise" and "All I Want," are keepers, the vast majoirity of *Heaven Up Here* is too self-indulgent and ridiculously gloomy to warrant serious consideration among the group's most enduring work. *—Jason Ankeny*

Porcupine / Feb. 4, 1983 / Sire ♦♦♦
The group's third album is a solid outing, a noticeably better listen than its predecessor, *Heaven Up Here*. Songs are intriguing and elaborate, often featuring swooping, howling melodic lines. Arrangements here owe a lot to 1960s psychedelia and feature lots of reverb, washed textures, intricate production touches, and altered guitar sounds. Ian McCulloch's vocals are yearning, soaring, and hyper-expressive here, almost to the point of being histrionic, most notably on "Clay," "Ripeness," and the title track. Driving bass and drums lend the songs urgency and keep the music from collapsing into self-indulgence. Parallels between the group's U.S. contemporaries such as Translator, Wire Train, and R.E.M. can be drawn, though all seem to have developed aspects of this style at about the same time—and none utilize it as flamboyantly as the Bunnymen do. Highlights here include "Back of Love" (with its galloping drumbeat and fragmented, yet ardent vocal line) and "Gods Will Be Gods" (which gradually speeds up from beginning to end, working itself into a swirling frenzy). This album is well worth hearing. *—David Cleary*

Ocean Rain / May 4, 1984 / Sire ♦♦♦♦♦
Channeling the lessons of the experimental *Porcupine* into more conventional and simple structural parameters, *Ocean Rain* emerges as Echo and the Bunnymen's most beautiful and memorable effort. Ornamenting Ian McCulloch's most consistently strong collection of songs to date with subdued guitar textures, sweeping string arrangements and hauntingly evocative production, the album is dramatic and majestic; "The Killing Moon," *Ocean Rain*'s emotional centerpiece, remains the group's unrivalled pinnacle. *—Jason Ankeny*

● **Songs to Learn & Sing** / Nov. 15, 1985 / Sire ♦♦♦♦♦
Liverpool's favorite lads Echo & the Bunnymen battled the cathartic reign of the Smiths and the enigmatic synth-pop of Depeche Mode and New Order throughout the '80s movement of redesigned post-punk, and they became a staple image as well. *Songs to Learn & Sing* marked the Bunnymen's cemented place in new wave and relished the crooning ambience of frontman Ian McCulloch. This collection recalls the rise and steadfast career of the band, highlighting the Bunnymen's work between 1980 and 1985 and collecting the most prominent tracks that made the band the waxed poetics the British press hailed them to be (specifically on older cuts like "Do It Clean" and "Rescue"). Frequent use of the band's classic drum machine or "echo" was also a major feature in Bunnymen tracks, especially on the vibrant dance cuts "Never Stop" and "Back of Love." With various production work from Lightning Seeds' Ian Broudie and Chameleons and Zoo labelmates David Balfe and Bill Drummond (the KLF), Echo & the Bunnymen achieved great cult status throughout the '80s stream of U.K. pop music. *Songs to Learn & Sing* is a solid and comprehensive collection of the band's material, also introducing the previously unissued album track "Bring on the Dancing Horses," which was featured on the soundtrack to the Molly Ringwald film *Pretty in Pink* (1986). *—MacKenzie Wilson*

Echo & the Bunnymen / Jul. 6, 1987 / Sire ♦♦♦
This fine release (not to be confused with the self-titled 1983 EP) is the Bunnymen's best since their debut, *Crocodiles*. The album catches the group at a fortuitous career juncture; the clutch of songs here is among the hookiest and most memorable the band would ever write, while the arrangements are noticeably clean and punchy, mostly eliminating strings and similar clutter to focus almost exclusively on guitars, keyboards, drums, and occasional percussion touches. The warmly expressive "All My Life," and which might perhaps have received an overheated arrangement on prior albums, benefits especially from this approach. The band rocks out convincingly on other selections, such as "Satellite" and "All in Your Mind." Pete DeFreitas' solid drumming at times veers toward the danceable on tracks like "Lost and Found," "Lips Like Sugar," and the overtly Doors-influenced "Bedbugs and Ballyhoo." Surprisingly, vocalist Ian MuCulloch appears to have rediscovered the maxim "less is more"; his singing is comparatively restrained and tasteful here, resulting in a more natural, unforced emotiveness that is extremely effective. Production values are excellent, with many subtle touches that do not detract from the album's overall directness. In short, doing it clean really pays off here; this energetic, top-notch album is highly recomended. *—David Cleary*

Reverberation / Dec. 1990 / Sire ♦♦

Ballyhoo / 1997 / Korova/WEA International ♦♦♦♦♦
Released to coincide with Echo & the Bunnymen's 1997 comeback, the 18-track *Ballyhoo* is an attempt to assemble a definitive overview of the group's seminal '80s material, yet it falls short of the mark. *Ballyhoo* essentially replicates the bulk of 1985's *Songs to Learn & Sing*, adding three tracks from their eponymous 1987 album and their non-LP cover of "People Are Strange." Meanwhile, four songs ("Angels and Devils," "Simple Stuff," "Pride and the Puppet," "Read It In Books") are elminated in favor of "All That Jazz," "Villiers Terrace," "Over the Wall" and "The Disease." Those four songs are good, and the remaining singles—"The Cutter," "The Killing Moon," "Bring on the Dancing Horses"—are post-punk classics, but *Ballyhoo* still overlooks too much fine material to be a definitive retrospective. Instead, it's simply a respectable, solid introduction. *—Stephen Thomas Erlewine*

Evergreen / Jul. 1, 1997 / London ♦♦♦
The cover alone is a dead giveaway, echoing as it does the cover of *Crocodiles*, with what looks like a set of trees and a car in place of De Freitas. But that telling and unavoidable absence alone puts the promise and problem of Echo's comeback album in perspective—McCulloch and Sergeant had been working together again and Pattinson returned to the fold, but without De Freitas something remained unavoidably absent. Replacement drummer Michael Lee fills in adequately but not completely, rendering what was a special group something less so. The remaining core three discharge their duties well enough, but the focus is unavoidably on McCulloch this time around, rendering Sergeant and Pattinson to the status of talented backing players and making *Evergreen* seem like an extension of McCulloch's solo career more than anything. While Sergeant in particular shows many flashes of the brilliance of Echo's first phase, his work is more conventional here, perhaps the result of his experimental tendencies with his solo project, Glide. As an album *Evergreen* is closest to *Ocean Rain* due to the liberal appearance of the London Symphony Orchestra throughout, sometimes with impressive results, though without achieving the total heights of artistry of that earlier collection. There's nothing quite like "The Killing Moon" or "Ocean Rain" itself this time around. For all that, when *Evergreen* shines at its best, it's still an attractive piece of work. The album's most successful number, the gently epic "Nothing Lasts Forever," gets an extra boost from an uncredited backing singer, Oasis' Liam Gallagher, while "I Want to Be There (When You Come)," the title track, and the moody "Just a Touch Away" kick up some smoke. *—Ned Raggett*

What Are You Going to Do with Your Life? / Jun. 1, 1999 / London ♦♦♦♦
Echo & the Bunnymen made a dignified return in 1997 with *Evergreen*, but that record displayed some hints of rustiness and a desire to stay hip—two things notably absent from its superb sequel, *What Are You Going to Do With Your Life?* Trimmed to just the duo of Ian McCulloch and Will Sergeant, Echo has succeeded where many of their peers have failed—they have matured without getting stodgy, they have deepened their signature sound without appearing self-conscious. Indeed, *What Are You Going to Do With Your Life?* feels of a piece with their earlier albums, not only sonically, but in terms of quality. Clocking in at just 38 minutes, the record is concise and dense with detail, finding the precise tone between the floating grandeur of early Echo and the timeless romanticism of classic torch songs. It's melancholy without ever being self-pitying and it never once sounds gloomy or depressing. The key is that McCulloch and Sergeant never push too hard. They never force themselves to play up-tempo, nor do they try to recapture their "edge"—they settle into a sad groove and find all the possible variations in the sound, both sonically and emotionally. The perfect thing is, this is exactly the kind of record a post-punk band should be making as they reach their 20th anniversary—it speaks to where they are now, and it speaks to their aging fans. *—Stephen Thomas Erlewine*

Flowers / May 22, 2001 / Cooking Vinyl ♦♦♦
Still clinging to the post-punk snarl that made them cult favorites during the '80s, Echo and the Bunnymen's Ian McCulloch and Will Sergeant maintain a stunning inventiveness as they enter into the third decade of the band. They're older, but an ignited passion remains central. *What Are You Going to Do With Your Life?* was more or less a lackluster Ian McCulloch effort, but the mediocrity of that album was twisted into a clear beauty for Echo's ninth album, *Flowers*. After contractual battles with London Records, a deal with SpinArt contributed to the redefined structure of the band, and *Flowers* solidified McCulloch's and Sergeant's brotherly musical jaunt, reaching a respectable status. McCulloch isn't an angst-ridden punk—he's aged with class—and Sergeant's typically moody guitar work has mellowed. The alluring rawness of the band is intact, and songs such as "King of Kings" and "Hide & Seek" are playful cuts with reminiscent production work of 1983's musical prize, *Ocean Rain*. "It's Alright" rolls with layered guitars, and McCulloch experiments vocally for a rough-edged spiral of psychedelics and '60s pop flair. "Everybody Knows" and "An Eternity Turns" get back to basics, circa *Crocodiles*, and they are the most consistent set of songs on the new album. Ian McCulloch is at his finest with a lyrical clarity that is typically dark, intelligent and swaggering. Sergeant's rippling accompaniment is rightfully complimentary to define that Echo and the Bunnymen have stayed in tune to what makes them an effective unit. *Flowers* doesn't possess the initial fiery power of the band's first four albums, but the underlying concept that brought McCulloch and Sergeant together in 1978 is what matters, and this album holds true to such a bond. *—MacKenzie Wilson*

Crystal Days: 1979-1999 / Jul. 17, 2001 / Rhino ♦♦♦♦♦
The answer is a resounding yes—Echo & the Bunnymen's *Crystal Days: 1979-1999*, a four-disc set boasting a great built-in book with a biography and track-by-track commentary, is worth every penny. Through 71 tracks, it does an excellent job by catering to the longtime fan and merely curious, running through all the hits and selecting standout album tracks, rarities, and unreleased curiosities, all worthwhile. The very fact that compilation producer Andy Zax was driven to put this project into motion after realizing he just *had* to find a way to get stellar B-sides like the Velvets-meets-Byrds heaven of "Angels and Devils" and the Peel Session version of the experimental "No Hands" into circulation tells you right off that you're in good hands. If this great-sounding box proves anything, it's that the Bunnymen don't deserve to be merely regarded as an excellent '80s band; sure, they've had some bumps along the road, but despite having thrived in a decade known for plasticity and fad crazes, this collection establishes that their legacy exists apart from the negative connotations the " '80s band" tag carries. And by carefully selecting songs from their '90s incarnation, they throw a pie in the face of those who

believe all reunions are artistic no-nos. The first three discs run chronologically through the band's first 20 years, occasionally throwing surprises into the mix with alternative versions and outtakes. The only gripe one might have is the favoring of the "All Night Version" of "The Killing Moon" over the original, which would be nitpicky. The final disc is chiefly occupied by live covers, including a great set-closing combo of the Velvets' "Heroin" and their own "Do It Clean." This is no mere nostalgia kick—it's just solid, ageless rock & roll with attitude and brains. *—Andy Kellman*

Echobelly

f. 1992, London, England

Indie Pop, Brit-pop, Alternative Pop/Rock

Led by vocalist Sonya Aurora Madan, Echobelly fused the ironic, self-absorbed viewpoint of the Smiths with stylish Blondie posturing and a solid guitar crunch. Defiantly politically correct, the group cultivated a fair amount of praise within the British press at the beginning of their career, but as the Brit-pop craze of the mid-'90s wore on, the group was slowly eclipsed by such contemporaries as Elastica and Sleeper. Nevertheless, Echobelly earned a dedicated cult following in the U.S. and U.K., as well as a devoted fan base within Japan.

Madan formed Echobelly circa 1992 with Glenn Johansson (guitar), Debbie Smith (guitar), Alex Keyser (bass), and Andy Henderson (drums). The group's first single, "Bellyache," was released in late 1993 to positive reviews from the U.K. weekly music press and managed to debut at number 15 on the indie charts. By early 1994, they broke the Top 40 with "I Can't Imagine the World Without Me." *Everybody's Got One*, the band's debut album, was released in the fall of 1994 to positive reviews and strong sales within the U.K.; it was released in the U.S. in the spring of 1995 to little attention.

By the summer of 1995, British indie-guitar music had overtaken the pop consciousness, and Echobelly were poised to break into the mainstream. Though the band was plagued by some behind-the-scenes problems—bassist Alex Keyser was replaced by James Harris after the recording of their second album, *On*—they didn't quite manage to make the leap. "Great Things," the first single from *On*, entered the charts at number 13, but each subsequent single, and the album itself, didn't fare as well. Nevertheless, the group retained a strong following within Japan over the course of 1995, where they were considered superstars. In 1997 Echobelly issued *Lustra*. *—Stephen Thomas Erlewine*

Everybody's Got One / Oct. 25, 1994 / Epic ♦♦♦♦

The album is *Everybody's Got One* or EGO for short, thus the pun and point of the title. Given that Echobelly's work clearly echoes one of the great English self-obsessives, Morrissey, it's an appropriate enough tag for the quintet's full debut. Madan perhaps gained a little too much U.K. press attention based over the surprising fact that she was non-Caucasian and non-male as opposed to her own qualities straight up—a pity, because they're considerable. While her singing voice comes across a touch weak here and there compared to the crunch of her band, lessening the overall impact as a result, she hits the spot more than once to make an impact. That she does indeed have something of Morrissey's vocal swoops and tics, and that guitarist Glenn Johansson knows his Johnny Marr and more, means Echobelly aren't a truly distinct and great group, but certainly have the foundations for a good one, as shown throughout. Madan's own life experiences provide some sharp grist for the mill. "Father Ruler King Computer" obliquely tackles the expectations from her Anglo-Indian family background of being a housewife and solely that, while "Give Her a Gun" heats up the feminist rhetoric further with smart, sharp lines like "Half the population/one percent of the wealth/blame the mother/sell the sister." At the band's best, though, Madan grapples with personal politics and dreams full on—"Insomniac" and "Close... But," with its pictures of relationships fracturing on all fronts and resolution to look beyond them for something better, make for entertaining blasts of inspiration. Perhaps most outrageous and outrageously successful is the group's best single, "I Can't Imagine the World Without Me." With trumpet and strings adding to the anthemic rip and soar of the mid-song break, it's a sparkling mini-masterpiece of Brit-pop; sassy, tuneful and memorable all at once. *—Ned Raggett*

On / Oct. 17, 1995 / Work ♦♦♦♦

Gaining a different bassist and having longtime studio hound B.J. Cole in on some guest slide guitar didn't appreciably alter the Echobelly approach much—the post-glam/punk feeling of the poppy music still predominates and Madan still claims the sharp and sly frontwoman role with fire. If nothing on *On* reaches the total heights of "I Can't Imagine the World Without Me," it still possesses a few fine moments of note, otherwise generally killing time in its own fashion well enough. Johansson's guitar playing and Madan's singing and lyrics still inevitably call the Smiths shades to the forefront, no matter what. It's something they seem comfortable with at this point, though, and the rest of the band jointly adds a touch more fuzz and sludge in contrast, which makes a nice combination. Touches like the singsong sass on "Go Away," which suits the sentiment of the lyrics to a T, while Johansson usually comes up with one killer riff or part per song that elevates what would be okay tunes just that little bit higher. Cole's own contributions, like the great electric slide wail on "Something Hot in a Cold Country," don't hurt either. Sean Slade and Paul Kolderie's production remains up to the general level of that noted duo's other work: loud, cutting, and sounding great. "King of the Kerb," an album standout and a fine single from the band, benefits not merely from the strange, nagging lead guitar melody from Johansson but said production, with a rich sound in the instrumental lead-in and a well-mixed chorus. Madan's wittiest moment probably comes with "Pantyhose and Roses," a cutting portrayal of sexual objectification and fantasy, while her most heartfelt is the passionate "Nobody Like You," a fun and desire-filled celebration of a loved one. *—Ned Raggett*

Lustra / 1997 / Epic ♦♦♦

It's funny how a band can lose momentum in two years, especially in British pop. Either because of changes in the musical climate or changes in the band, a group that was at the top of charts one year can return 24 months later and find that everything has shifted 180 degrees. Such was the case with Echobelly and their third album, *Lustra*. There were a few upheavals in the band, and they decided to hire Gil Norton, a producer renowned for his work with the Pixies, to give them a change in sound. Norton does lend his signature clean-but-loud style to *Lustra*, giving it a bit more volume than Echobelly's first two records, but that ultimately doesn't amount to much of a change in sound. Similarly, no matter how they try to mature, Echobelly simply can't successfully develop their fusion of the Smiths and Blondie into something new. Unfortunately, they can't come up with many memorable hooks, either. There are a handful of solid songs on *Lustra*, but they lack the spark of "Insomniac" or "Car Fiction"—they simply sound tired. What makes this really disappointing is that Echobelly sounded fresh and inspired on both *Everybody's Got One* and *On*, but with their attempt to sound mature, they've snuffed out their spark. Hopefully, *Lustra* is simply a misstep, not the end of the line. *—Stephen Thomas Erlewine*

People Are Expensive / May 21, 2001 / Fry Up ♦♦♦

After the weary *Lustra*, Echobelly found themselves on the receiving end of negative press, corrupt accountants, and the frustrations of starting out on their own independent record label. But all is well in the unwell for the band's fourth album, with Sonya Aurora Madan sounding as progressively paranoid as ever—in "Ondine," she sings "But this is the plastic age/The quiet rage is damned and civilised"; in "Digit," "There's no disease, the human race is digital/Pacified by fluoride, genetically modified"—and the undercooked production catching and redirecting her stark rhymes without undermining their meaning. In fact, the open-aired, twilight hum that co-producer Ben Hillier creates goes some way to expand what was once Echobelly's unobstructed angst. "Kali Yuga" is exclamatory yet by no means overbearing. There's a relaxed hope in normally melancholic lines like "I'm dying, give me symphonies," with sketched out sonics recalling those summertime nights of pensive stargazing when a cold soda and the right tune could make you believe that no matter how tempting or attractive a sense of futility may be, it's lazy and destructive, and probably a religion for poets lacking imagination. In a sense, Echobelly are more bleak than ever before but with considerable more confidence. They've managed to ignore their ill fortune and suffer through the hecklers, and have—in the best possible way—given listeners a 54-minute soundtrack for the paper bag scene in *American Beauty*. *—Dean Carlson*

● **Best of Echobelly: I Can't Imagine World Without Me** / Sep. 11, 2001 / Sony International ♦♦♦♦

Eddie & The Hot Rods

f. 1975

British Punk, Pub Rock, Power Pop, New Wave, Punk

Arriving during the waning days of pub rock, Eddie & the Hot Rods helped usher in punk rock in the United Kingdom. Working from the same bluesy, Stonesy three-chord foundation as contemporaries like Dr. Feelgood, the Hot Rods were faster, tougher, wilder and louder than any other pub-rock band. They also celebrated adolescent abandon, unlike their peers, who usually concentrated on working-class subjects. Developing a substantial cult following by touring the pub circuit relentlessly, Eddie & the Hot Rods, with their fast, tough rock & roll, made the pub-rock taverns more willing to book wilder acts like the Damned and the Sex Pistols, thereby firing the first shot in the U.K. punk revolution. They also made some inroads on the pop charts with their 1976 debut EP *Live at the Marquee* and the singles "Teenage Depression" and "Do Anything You Wanna Do," but by the time the latter reached the Top Ten in the summer of 1977, Eddie & the Hot Rods and their bar-band demeanor had already begun to appear outdated. The group's following declined sharply over the next two years, and they disbanded in 1980. Although they never wound up as stars, the band undeniably made an impact in the birth of punk rock. *—Stephen Thomas Erlewine*

Live at the Marquee / Aug. 1976 / Island ♦♦♦♦♦

Eddie & the Hot Rods were first and foremost a great live band so it makes perfect sense for their debut EP to show the band in their natural setting. *Live at the Marquee*, though only four songs (all covers), clearly shows how the band's wild and raw energy helped to inspire the punk explosion. *—Chris Woodstra*

Teenage Depression / Dec. 1976 / Captain Oi! ♦♦♦

The band's first studio album is a fine effort in the spirit of Dr. Feelgood, bridging the gap between pub rock and punk rock. Wild, raw and rebellious—everything a rock & roll album should be. *—Chris Woodstra*

Life on the Line / 1977 / Captain Oi! ♦♦♦♦♦

Life on the Line adds guitarist Graeme Douglas (ex-Kursaal Flyers), helping to bring out the band's pure pop sensibility. This is their finest moment and also their last really great album. Includes the brilliant "Do Anything You Want to Do," a British hit. *—Chris Woodstra*

Thriller / 1977 / Island ♦♦

Fish & Chips / 1980 / EMI ♦♦

● **End of the Beginning: The Best of Eddie & the Hot Rods** / 1994 / Island ♦♦♦♦♦

A nearly flawless collection, *End of the Beginning* documents the band's golden period of 1976-1979 with the infectious singles, inspired live workouts, album tracks and a rarity or two for the collectors. This is an important, though unfortunately overlooked, part of British punk rock's roots that shouldn't be missed. *—Chris Woodstra*

Duane Eddy

b. Apr. 26, 1938, Corning, NY
Guitar / Instrumental Rock, Rock & Roll

If Duane Eddy's instrumental hits from the late '50s can sound unduly basic and repetitive (especially when taken all at once), he was vastly influential. Perhaps the most successful instrumental rocker of his time, he may have also been the man most responsible (along with Chuck Berry) for popularizing the electric rock guitar. His distinctively low, twangy riffs could be heard on no less than 15 Top 40 hits between 1958 and 1963. He was also one of the first rock stars to successfully crack the LP market. It was his second single, "Rebel Rouser," that really broke him as a national star, reaching the Top Ten in 1958. Opening with a down-and-dirty, heavily echoed guitar riff, it remains the tune with which he's most often identified. Eddy's phenomenally successful run of hits over the next few years was to some extent a variation on the "Rebel Rouser" theme. Duane would have his biggest hit, however, in 1960, when he sweetened the twang with strings for the movie theme "Because They're Young." After Eddy signed with RCA in 1962, his albums—often based on loose themes, like *A Million Dollars Worth of Twang, Twisting with Duane Eddy*, and *Surfing with Duane Eddy*—kept him afloat to some degree, though his style doggedly refused evolution. Paul McCartney, George Harrison, Ry Cooder, and Jeff Lynne all helped produce a 1987 album. —*Richie Unterberger*

Have 'Twangy' Guitar-Will Travel / 1958 / Jamie/Guyden ✦✦✦✦
Eddy's debut album was a good value by the standards of the era, with several of his early hits and favorites ("Rebel Rouser," "Cannonball," "Ramrod," "Movin' and Groovin'," and "3:30 Blues") included. Many of the songs, though, appear on whatever greatest-hits anthology you're likely to pick up; Rhino's *Twang Thang*, for instance, has no less than nine of the 12 tracks. The 1999 CD reissue (which is in stereo) adds three 1958 B-sides that *aren't* always likely to show up on anthologies—"Up and Down," "The Walker," and "Mason-Dixon Line"—as well as historical liner notes. The album was also issued on a two-fer CD by Motown, teamed with the 1960 album *$1,000,000 Worth of Twang*. —*Richie Unterberger*

Especially for You / 1959 / Jamie/Guyden ✦✦✦
Eddy's second LP contained just one hit, "Yep," although "Peter Gunn" would enter the Top 40 when it was issued later in 1960. Unlike his debut *Have "Twangy" Guitar Will Travel*, it was not built around singles and a few songs to stretch it to album length, with all of the songs (except "Yep") being recorded in a week. Give Eddy this much credit: at a time when virtually all rock & roll LPs were hasty knocked-together jobs, he did at least try to vary the program. There was slow blues ("Only Child"), pop standards (Rodgers & Hart's "Lover"), a rather long jazzy workout ("Quiniela"), original material in the mold of his hits, sax-driven R&B (a cover of Noble Watts' "Hard Times"), and poppy stuff with strings and wordless female backup vocals that sounded like themes for B-movie westerns ("Along the Navajo Trail"). It still added up to a pretty inconsequential instrumental album in which the hits ("Peter Gunn" and "Yep") boasted much more arresting hooks than the surrounding tunes. Eddy sounds like he's tearing a page from Les Paul's book on "Lover," with its very atypical (for Eddy) arrangement of hyper-fast guitar licks. The 2000 CD reissue has five previously unreleased bonus tracks, but all of these are in fact alternates: "Some Kinda Earthquake" (a hit single recorded at the sessions but held off the album) and "Only Child" with alternate overdubs, take one of "Yep," "St. James" (actually a retitled version of "Quiniela"), and an undubbed version of "First Love, First Tears," a ballad that was also held off the LP. —*Richie Unterberger*

★ **Twang Thang: Anthology** / May 18, 1993 / Rhino ✦✦✦✦✦
Duane Eddy was America's first bona-fide rock & roll guitar hero, playing minimalistic riffs that any kid with a pawnshop guitar could aspire to with a little determination and elbow grease. This two-CD anthology offers the finest retrospective of his career available, with all facets of his career being well documented, from the early hits to later collaborations with the famous rockers he initially inspired. Featuring just enough rarities to keep it from being merely a greatest-hits package, this truly showcases Duane at his best. —*Cub Koda*

Twangin' from Phoenix to L.A. / Nov. 29, 1994 / Bear Family ✦✦✦✦✦
Bear Family's *Twangin' from Phoenix to L.A.* is a 133-track, eight-disc box set that contains all of Duane Eddy's early recordings, from his early singles for Ford, through his recordings for Jamie. Since it's complete, that's an awful lot of material and while Eddy had a distinctive, pioneering sound, it wasn't particularly varied, and it can become a little tiring over the course of this set. Furthermore, outside of the big hits and a handful of other sides, there aren't that many hidden gems, which means this is a set only for the strong of heart, even among the dedicated. —*Stephen Thomas Erlewine*

That Classic Twang / Apr. 4, 1995 / Bear Family ✦✦✦✦✦

Edison Lighthouse

Bubblegum, AM Pop

The British pop group Edison Lighthouse was primarily the vehicle of session vocalist Tony Burrows; the group's lone hit, 1970's "Love Grows (Where My Rosemary Grows)," was one of four simultaneous U.K. Top Ten records scored by Burrows under different names (the others were White Plains' "My Baby Loves Lovin'," the Pipkins' "Gimme Dat Ding," and the Brotherhood of Man's "United We Stand"). In truth, Edison Lighthouse was merely the alias of songwriters and producers Tony McCauley and Barry Mason, although members of the group Greenfield Hammer were eventually brought in to perpetuate the image of a real working band; after the success of "Love Grows," Burrows exited to pursue other projects, and McCauley, who owned the copyright to the Edison name, simply assembled another group to record under the alias. The second Edison Lighthouse barely

cracked the U.K. Top 50 with the single "It's Up to You, Petula" before vanishing. —*Jason Ankeny*

● **Best of Edison Lighthouse** / May 8, 2001 / Repertoire ✦✦✦✦✦
Repertoire's *Best of Edison Lighthouse* proves that while the studio-created group was a one-hit wonder, they nevertheless recorded several other bubblegum AM pop songs that were equally engaging and frothy. These may not be substantial songs, but they're well-crafted, appealingly silly, and certain to engage anybody who loved "Love Grows Where My Rosemary Grows." This is pretty much as good as bubblegum got. —*Stephen Thomas Erlewine*

Dave Edmunds

b. Apr. 15, 1944, Cardiff, Wales
Vocals, Keyboards, Guitar, Bass / Pub Rock, New Wave, Roots Rock, Rock & Roll

Roots-rockers are seldom as purist as Dave Edmunds. Throughout his career, he stayed true to '50s and '60s rock & roll—for Edmunds, rock & roll history stopped somewhere in 1963, after the Beach Boys' first singles but before the Beatles' hits. After establishing himself as a hotshot lead guitarist in the blues-rockers Love Sculpture, he launched his solo career by painstakingly re-creating oldies in his own studio, usually recording every track by himself. Through all of his efforts, he learned how to uncannily replicate the sound of Sun, Chess, and Phil Spector records, which not only helped him garner several U.K. hits in the early '70s, but also led to successful production work with artists like the Flamin' Groovies and Brinsley Schwarz. In the late '70s, he hit the peak of his career when he teamed up with former Schwarz bassist Nick Lowe to form Rockpile. For several years, Edmunds recorded albums with Rockpile and toured relentlessly with the band, which resulted in a string of hit U.K. singles. After the group imploded in the early '80s, he slowly disappeared from the mainstream, even as he made his most commercial music with producer Jeff Lynne; Edmunds eventually retreated to cult status in the '90s. —*Stephen Thomas Erlewine*

Rockpile / 1972 / Mamou ✦✦✦✦
Dave Edmunds' debut album *Rockpile* established his sound—not only his revivalist tendencies, but also his method of meticulously recreating the sound and style of classic early rock & roll, R&B, and country records. Edmunds plays nearly every instrument on the album, with bassist John Williams being the only full-time collaborator. As a result, the record doesn't sound "live," it has a pinched, precise quality that may contradict the spontaneity that was at the core of the original singles, but it does offer an otherworldly quality that makes the record distinctive. Take the hit "I Hear You Knocking," which has a mechanical rhythm and a weird, out-of-phase vocal that qualifies as an original interpretation, unlike his by-the-book take on Chuck Berry's "The Promised Land," which suffers from the stiff rhythms. Still, the best moments on *Rockpile* come from songs like "Down, Down, Down," an obscure gem that manages to recreate not only the sound, but the feeling of classic rock & roll, perhaps because Edmunds wasn't concerned with recreating one of his beloved singles. —*Stephen Thomas Erlewine*

Subtle As a Flying Mallet / 1975 / One Way ✦✦✦
Taking the one-man band aesthetic to an extreme, Dave Edmunds recorded nearly all of his second album *Subtle As a Flying Mallet* on his own, hiring a bassist and a drummer for only a pair of tracks. Edmunds took several years to complete the record, probably because it took a considerable amount of effort to recreate these songs so throughly—he spends so much attention on detail that he refuses to change the sex on "Da Doo Ron Ron." Alternating between Spector classics, the Everly Brothers, Chuck Berry, and a variety of R&B, country, and pop numbers, Edmunds hits on all the styles of the late '50s and early '60s, but he spends so much time on duplicating the sound that he sucks the joy out of the music; it is positively eerie to hear these songs performed by one man, who spent weeks overdubbing himself to sound like his own wall of sound. And the main problem with *Subtle As a Flying Mallet* is that these are not reinterpretations, they are recreations, and there's little point in hearing a one-man version of rock classics if he offers new ideas. When Edmunds works with obscure material, like the Chordettes' "Born to Be With You," or with newer items like Nick Lowe's "She's My Baby," the results are better, because the songs are less familiar, which makes his painstaking production exciting, but his isolation makes *Subtle As a Flying Mallet* sound less like a revival and more like a creepy science experiment. —*Stephen Thomas Erlewine*

Get It / 1977 / Swan Song ✦✦✦✦✦
Get It marks a significant departure from Dave Edmunds' early records, as it is the first time he's backed by a full band. Most of *Get It* was recorded with a fledgling version of Rockpile, with other session men filling in when necessary, and the live band gives the album a lively feel which he had previously ignored. Just as importantly, the song selection is more carefully considered than before, containing only a handful of classics and obscure rock & roll, and concentrating on pub rock staples ("Get Out of Denver," "Back to School Days," "JuJu Man") and songs written or co-written by Nick Lowe, which gives the album a freshness lacking on his early records. Lowe's homages to the Everly Brothers ("Here Comes the Weekend"), Chuck Berry ("I Knew the Bride"), and Phil Spector ("Little Darlin'") are more appealing than Edmunds' recreations of the originals, because Nick's songs are lyrically and musically clever. But Dave knows how to make them sound like forgotten classics, and that's why *Get It* is one of his very best albums. —*Stephen Thomas Erlewine*

Dave Edmunds, Rocker: Early Works 1968/1972 / 1977 / Parlophone/EMI ✦✦✦✦
Dave Edmunds, Rocker: Early Works 1968/1972 is a good double-LP set that features highlights from Edmunds' recordings with Love Sculpture, a handful of solo singles, and the 1972 *Rockpile* album, which was rarely reissued after its initial release, despite the

fact that it spawned the hit single "I Hear You Knocking." If you can find it, it's an excellent summary of Edmunds' first recordings. *—Stephen Thomas Erlewine*

Tracks on Wax 4 / 1978 / Swan Song ✦✦✦✦✦
Tracks on Wax 4 is the first official Rockpile collaboration and its hard-driving, unified sound makes it one of Dave Edmunds' very best records. Like *Get It*, *Tracks on Wax 4* relies primarily on originals and contemporary pub rock songs, leaving behind the classic oldies; the older songs on the record are obscurities like Chuck Berry's "It's My Own Business" and Jan & Dean's "Thread Your Needle." Built on such fine songs as the rockabilly tinged "Trouble Boys," the Everly-esque "Never Been in Love," "Television," "Readers Wives," and "Deborah," *Tracks on Wax 4* is a tight, snappy rock & roll record that is only derailed by a version of Nick Lowe's classic "Heart of the City," where Lowe's original vocal is stripped away and replaced by a new take by Edmunds. Only then does the record recall Edmunds' perfectionist nature. *—Stephen Thomas Erlewine*

Repeat When Necessary / 1979 / Swan Song ✦✦✦✦✦
Recorded simultaneously with Nick Lowe's *Labour of Lust*, *Repeat when Necessary* continues the winning streak of *Get It* and *Tracks on Wax 4* simply by sticking to the formula. Though Rockpile's sound is a little cleaner here than before, nothing's changed but the songs, which are uniformly excellent. Culled primarily from pub-rock contemporaries (and containing no Lowe songs whatsoever), the record contains four classics: Elvis Costello's galloping "Girls Talk," and Graham Parker's relentless "Crawling From the Wreckage," the funny (a rarity of Edmunds) "Creature From the Black Lagoon," and the country-rocker "Queen of Hearts," which would later become a hit for Juice Newton in exactly the same arrangement. A few songs come close to meeting this high standard, but they are occasionally hampered by a tightness similar to the pinched rhythms of *Subtle As a Flying Mallet*;—in particular, the early Huey Lewis song "Bad Is Bad" and the old Brinsley Schwarz number "Home in My Hand" are hurt by this. But these are minor flaws—*Repeat When Necessary* is an energetic, old-fashioned rock & roll record that ranks as Edmunds' last great album. *—Stephen Thomas Erlewine*

Twangin' / 1981 / Swan Song ✦✦✦
Twangin' was recorded as Rockpile was in the process of breaking up, and the record suffered as a result. Where the previous Rockpile collaborations were loose and rocking, *Twangin'* is tight and precise, as if Edmunds recorded it on his own. Only on "The Race Is On" does the record truly cut loose, and he's backed by the Stray Cats on that one. Still, there are a number of fine moments on the record, particularly in the pseudo-new wave pulse of John Hiatt's "Something Happens," the pub rock of Mickey Jupp's "You'll Never Get Me Up (In One of Those)," and the gorgeous Everly-esque "(I'm Gonna Start) Living Again if It Kills Me." The rest of the record is pleasant filler which could have used some of the old Rockpile spark. *—Stephen Thomas Erlewine*

The Best of Dave Edmunds / 1981 / Swan Song ✦✦✦✦✦
The Best of Dave Edmunds is a terrific single-disc retrospective picking highlights from Edmunds' best albums, which were all recorded with Rockpile. While Edmunds' tight-assed covers of "Singin' the Blues" and John Fogerty's "Almost Saturday Night" should never have been included, the rest of the album captures the rock revivalist at his best, containing nearly all of his finest moments ("Deborah," "Girls Talk," "I Knew the Bride," "Here Comes the Weekend," "Trouble Boys," "Crawling From the Wreckage," "JuJu Man," "Queen of Hearts"). *—Stephen Thomas Erlewine*

D.E. 7th / 1982 / Columbia ✦✦✦
Dave Edmunds assembled a self-consciously eclectic root-rock album for *D.E. 7th*, his first post-Rockpile effort. Instead of returning to a one-man band status, Edmunds hired a new band, which prevented him from returning to the studied perfectionism of his early work. Nevertheless, *D.E. 7th* lacks the pop sensibilities that made early Edmunds a guilty pleasure, concentrating instead on roots musics. While that occasionally means there's missteps like "Deep in the Heart of Texas," but it also means the wonderful bluegrass-stomp "Warmed Over Kisses (Left Over Love)," the country-rocker "Bail You Out," the cajun-tinged "Louisiana Man" and the excellent Springsteen cover "From Small Things (Big Things One Day Come)." The rest of *D.E. 7th* is uneven, but there a few enjoyable cuts, and compared to what came later, it's certainly more fun. *—Stephen Thomas Erlewine*

Information / 1983 / Columbia ✦✦
For some inexplicable reason, Dave Edmunds decided to shoot for mass success with *Information*, enlisting Jeff Lynne of the Electric Light Orchestra to give him a contemporary, synthesized sheen. Since Edmunds always sounded reluctant when Rockpile strayed too close to new wave, the sudden change of heart is puzzling, especially considering the weakness of the material. Lynne steers the guitarist toward generally undistinguished material, with the exception of his own "Slipping Away," which pulsates with a surprisingly infectious synthetic beat and an undeniably catchy hook that manages to be both contemporary and rootsy. If the rest of *Information* had the same vibe, it would have been a success, but the synthesizers dominate the record, making it a lifeless album. *—Stephen Thomas Erlewine*

Riff Raff / 1984 / Columbia ✦✦
Since "Slipping Away" was a minor hit, Edmunds brought Jeff Lynne back to produce *Riff Raff*, a record that essentially replicates the sound and style of *Information*. Lynne has a tighter hold on the album than before, and Edmunds rarely sounds as energetic as he does on his best records, mainly because the processed rhythms are at odds with his roots-rock sensibilities. Like *Information*, there are a few good moments on the record, particularly in the giddy "Rules of the Game," but overall, *Riff Raff* is Edmunds' weakest record. *—Stephen Thomas Erlewine*

Dave Edmunds Band Live: I Hear You Rockin' / 1987 / Columbia ✦✦✦
Dave Edmunds was always notorious for his perfectionist approach to studio recordings, so his skills as a live performer were often overlooked. Although it has been doctored slightly in the studio, *Dave Edmunds Band Live: I Hear You Rockin'* is an energetic, enjoyable record that demonstrates that the roots-rocker can be a fun, charismatic performer when he chooses. The album's set list draws heavily from his classic late-'70s records ("Girls Talk," "Here Comes the Weekend," "Queen of Hearts," "Crawling From the Wreckage," "I Knew the Bride," "Ju Ju Man"), adding the hits "I Hear You Knockin'" and "Slipping Away," plus "Information" for good measure. It's a basic primer, delivered with passion, making it a fine record for diehard fans. *—Stephen Thomas Erlewine*

Closer to the Flame / 1990 / Capitol ✦✦
The wait between *Riff Raff* and its follow-up was a full six years, so it isn't surprising that *Closer to the Flame* finds Dave Edmunds abandoning the new wave flourishes of his Jeff Lynne productions for a straightforward roots-rock sensibility. The record still suffers from a stiff production—the rhythms are extremely mannered, and the sound of the record is slightly sterile—but Edmunds manages to tear into a handful of driving rockers, including Mickey Jupp's "Don't Talk to Me" and "Stockholm," and his version of Al Anderson's "Never Take the Place of You" is his most affecting performance in years. *—Stephen Thomas Erlewine*

The Early Edmunds / 1991 / EMI ✦✦✦✦
In print for a brief time in the early '90s, EMI's double-disc set *Early Edmunds* is a valuable entry in Dave Edmunds' catalog, not just because it collects all of Love Sculpture's albums, but because it is the only time his first solo album, *Rockpile*, has appeared in complete form on compact disc. Combining those two worlds might result in a collection that's a little skewed—a disc-plus of Love Sculpture's gonzo blues-psych is actually miles away from the solo stuff—but it's a godsend for collectors, particularly because that solo debut is really fine stuff. It's not as consistent as he was just a record later, but his homespun take on classic rock & roll not only set the blueprint for his solo career, it was a little weirder (check the phoned-in vocals on the hit "I Hear You Knocking," or the general razor-thin quality of the production), and it proves that he was hip even before Nick Lowe, Elvis Costello, and Graham Parker were giving him songs (cherry picking "Outlaw Blues" from Dylan, taking Neil Young's "Dance Dance Dance," and reviving Roy Davies' "It Ain't Easy" before Bowie's classic performance on *Ziggy Stardust* does qualify as hip). That, along with getting all the Love Sculpture stuff at once, makes this worth tracking down at any price for the dedicated Edmunds fan. *—Stephen Thomas Erlewine*

● **The Anthology (1968-1990)** / Apr. 20, 1993 / Rhino ✦✦✦✦✦
A double-disc set covering Dave Edmunds' entire career, the 41-song *Anthology (1968-1990)* does a fine job of capturing his musical evolution, even if it is not without its faults. To a certain extent, *Anthology* is a definitive compilation, since it begins with Love Sculpture's infamous "Sabre Dance" and runs through his early solo recordings ("I Hear You Knocking"), before hitting Rockpile ("Trouble Boys," "Deborah," "Girls Talk," "Crawling From the Wreckage," "Queen of Hearts") and Edmunds' overly synthesized recordings with Jeff Lynne, adding a couple of rarities like the excellent Carlene Carter duet "Baby Ride Easy" along the way. However, the track selection is uneven, including far too many Love Sculpture songs and Lynne collaborations, which tends to dilute the spirit of Edmunds' best music. Still, *Anthology* is the best overview of Edmunds' entire career, even if the single-disc *The Best of Dave Edmunds* may be better, more consistent introduction for many listeners. *—Stephen Thomas Erlewine*

Plugged In / Jul. 19, 1994 / Forward/Rhino ✦✦

The Edsels

f. 1959, Youngstown, OH, **db.** 1961
Doo Wop
A brief encounter with fame came for the Edsels when they recorded the doo wop masterpiece "Rama Lama Ding Dong." Originally released in 1959, the single became a hit some three years after its intial release, thanks to the efforts of diligent record collectors and disc jockeys.

Taking their name from Ford's legendary failed automobile, the Edsels formed in in the tiny mill town of Campbell, OH in the late '50s. The group consisted of lead vocalist George Jones Jr., James Reynolds, Marshall Sewell, Harry Greene, and Larry Greene. The group audtioned for a local Ohio music publisher in 1958. Through the publisher, the group landed a record deal with the small Dub Records. The Edsels' first single was a song Jones had written, "Rama Lama Ding Dong." The first pressings on Dub Records were mislabelled "Lama Rama Ding Dong."

"Rama Lama Ding Dong" became a local hit, but made no impact nationally. In 1961, disc jockeys began playing the song again because it sounded similar to the Marcels' current hit, "Blue Moon." Within a few months, the single was re-released on Twin Records—this time with the correct song title—and it quickly scaled the pop charts, peaking at number 21. Ironically, the group had broken up by the time "Rama Lama Ding Dong" became a hit in 1961. *—Stephen Thomas Erlewine & Cub Koda*

● **Rama Lama Ding Dong** / 1992 / Relic ✦✦✦✦✦
A complete 16-track collection of the group's best sides, including the title track, one of the great nonsense doo wop sides of all time. *—Cub Koda*

Jonathan Edwards

b. Jul. 28, 1946, Aitkin, MN
Vocals, Harmonica, Guitar / Folk-Rock, Singer/Songwriter, Progressive Bluegrass
Best remembered for his crossover hit "Sunshine," country and folk singer/songwriter Jonathan Edwards got his start in the blues band Sugar Creek, debuting with the 1969 LP *Please Tell a Friend*. Wanting to pursue acoustic performing, he left the group to record a solo album. Near the end of the 1970 sessions, one of the finished tracks, "Please Find

Me," was accidentally erased, forcing Edwards to instead record a brand new composition. The song was "Sunshine," and when it was released as a single the following year, it quickly became a Top Five pop hit. With the release of 1972's *Honky-Tonk Stardust Cowboy*, Edwards' music began gravitating toward straight-ahead country; his label was at a loss as to how to market the record, however, and over the course of two more albums, 1973's *Have a Good Time for Me* and the following year's live *Lucky Day*, his sales sharply declined. A cameo on Emmylou Harris' *Elite Hotel* resulted in a new record deal and the LP *Rockin' Chair*, recorded with Harris' Hot Band. Edwards eventually moved to Nashville; his 1989 album *The Natural Thing* generated his biggest country hit, "We Need to Be Locked Away." —*Jason Ankeny*

● **Jonathan Edwards** / 1971 / Atco ✦✦✦✦
This album is best known for Edwards' hit, "Sunshine" and the song "Shanty," which radio stations around the country call "The Friday Song." If either of these songs is as far as you've gotten with this album, you are missing a great deal. Edwards has a great sense of melody, which means there is not a weak track on this record. Aside from the previously mentioned numbers, one or two of the songs on the record have taken on a life of their own. "Don't Cry Blue," for instance, has been knocking around bluegrass circles for some years. One listen and you'll know why this album has never gone out of print. —*Jim Worbois*

Honky-Tonk Stardust Cowboy / 1972 / Atco ✦✦✦✦
Edwards continues where the first record left off and continues to grow as an artist. In addition to his own fine songs, Edwards chose to include a few covers like Jesse Colin Young's "Sugar Babe," The Mills Brothers' "Paper Doll" (complete with faux "trombone" solo), and the title track. The title track did receive some airplay on country radio in 1972 but was never the hit it should have been. If you find a copy of this one, grab it. —*Jim Worbois*

Have a Good Time for Me / 1973 / Atco ✦✦✦

Lucky Day / 1974 / Atco ✦✦✦

Rockin' Chair / 1976 / Reprise ✦✦

Sailboat / 1977 / Reprise ✦✦

Eels

f. 1995
Adult Alternative Pop/Rock, Post-Grunge, Alternative Pop/Rock
Several years before he formed the Eels in 1995, vocalist/guitarist (E) released two underrated solo albums for Polydor. Taking the same idiocratic pop sensibility but with an increased use of trip-hop technology, the Eels—(E) plus Tommy Walter and Butch Norton—signed to the Dreamworks label and released *Beautiful Freak* in mid-1996. The single "Novocaine for the Soul" became a number one hit on alternative radio. *Electro-Shock Blues* followed in 1998, and two years later the group returned with *Daisies of the Galaxy*. —*John Bush*

● **Beautiful Freak** / Aug. 13, 1996 / DreamWorks ✦✦✦✦
Eccentric and quirky are the best ways to describe the Eels' debut effort, *Beautiful Freak*. Concise pop tunes form the backbone of the album, yet tinges of despair and downright meanness surface just when you've been lulled into thinking this is another pop group, as titles like "My Beloved Monster," "Your Lucky Day in Hell" and "Novocaine for the Soul" indicate. All in all, *Beautiful Freak* is a satisfying first record. —*James Chrispell*

Electro-Shock Blues / Oct. 20, 1998 / DreamWorks ✦✦✦✦✦
The Eels' second release, *Electro-Shock Blues*, is a much darker album than their underrated debut, 1996's *Beautiful Freak*, but just as rewarding. Singer/guitarist/songwriter (E) experienced many upheavals in his personal life between albums (the passing of several family members and close friends), and decided to work his way through life's tribulations via his music. The result is a spectacular epic work, easily on par with such classic albums cut from the same cloth—Neil Young's *Tonight's The Night*, Lou Reed's *Magic And Loss*, etc. For some of the most introspective and haunting tunes of recent times, look no further than the title track, "Last Stop: This Town," and "Elizabeth on the Bathroom Floor." And although the lyrics deal almost entirely with mortality, the music for "Hospital Food," "Cancer for the Cure," and "Going to Your Funeral Part I" is comparable to Beck's funky noise, while "Efils' God," "The Medication Is Wearing Off," and "My Descent Into Madness" are all ethereal, soothing compositions. One of the finest and fully realized records of 1998, a must-hear. —*Greg Prato*

Daisies of the Galaxy / Mar. 14, 2000 / DreamWorks ✦✦✦
The Eels were always a vehicle for a songwriter called (E), but by the point of their third album, 2000's *Daisies of the Galaxy*, they were his and his alone. When it came time to deliver a follow-up to the intimate, tortured *Electro-Shock Blues*, (E) couldn't help but deliver a lighter album, but he'd already turned so far into himself that his music was entirely insular. Of course, his music had always been fairly insular, but if *Daisies of the Galaxy* is any indication, he's gone so far in, he can't really come out. He's certainly not as extreme as Brian Wilson or Syd Barrett, but he's at the level of XTC or Roy Wood, making pop music for an already-established audience. Nothing on *Daisies of the Galaxy* will draw in casual listeners the way "Novocaine for the Soul" did, since everything is in miniature, from the yardsale production to the poetic scrawlings. Unlike its predecessor, the album doesn't play like (E)'s private diary; instead, it feels as if one is rummaging through his sketchbook. And, like many sketchbooks, some moments have blossomed, and others remain just intriguing, unformed ideas. For the dedicated, it's worth sifting through the album to find the keepers, since there are enough moments of quirky genius. But not all longtime fans will find this rewarding, since (E) has spent more time in creating mood than crafting songs. There are very few melodies that resonate like his best

work, and the stripped-down, yet eccentric production—sounding much like a cross between Jon Brion and Beck—never feels realized. That's the problem with an offbeat, gifted musician becoming too insular; there are still clear clues of why he has his reputation, but there's not enough to justify exactly why he does. —*Stephen Thomas Erlewine*

Eggs over Easy

Pub Rock
Historically renowned as the band which launched the entire British pub rock scene, the all-American Eggs over Easy originally arrived in the U.K. to cut a record with producer Chas Chandler in 1970. Sessions at Olympic Studios went well, but escalating problems with the group's American backers, Cannon Films, saw the project run aground in the new year and the group moved onto the live circuit while they sought a new deal. They played a number of college gigs around the country, but it was at the Tally Ho pub in London's Kentish Town neighborhood, just around the corner from the band's communal home, that they made their reputation—and forged an entire new musical movement.

Originally booked to play the traditionally slack Monday night at a venue which had hitherto favored jazz performers, Eggs over Easy's reputation quickly spread, not only to the public but also among other bands. The members of Brinsley Schwarz were early admirers, frequently attending the band's Tally Ho dates and often joining them onstage—before long, Brinsley Schwarz, too, was concentrating their attention on the pub circuit. With other bands hastening to join them, by early fall 1971, interest and enthusiasm was so high that Eggs over Easy was able to organize a city-wide tour of Inde Coope brewery pubs. They followed through with a 12-date U.K. tour supporting John Mayall, Eggs over Easy's country rock-flavored repertoire offering a fascinating counterpoint to Mayall's then rampant jazz-blues fixation.

The group's U.K. sojourn was coming to an end, however. Despite having recorded an album, a record deal remained elusive, while the band's work permits were also expiring. On November 7, 1971, Eggs over Easy played their final Tally Ho show, then returned to the U.S. They would disband shortly after, but before they did, they signed with A&M and finally consigned a fraction of their repertoire to vinyl—according to Brinsley Schwarz's Nick Lowe, the band had over 100 songs at their fingertips. Just one-tenth of that catalog appeared on *Good'N'Cheap*, the band has also been enshrined on EMI's *Naughty Rhythms: The Best of Pub Rock* CD anthology. —*Dave Thompson*

Good 'n' Cheap / 1972 / A&M ✦✦✦✦

808 State

f. 1988, Manchester, England
IDM, Club/Dance, Acid House, House
A pioneer of the acid house sound, 808 State formed in Manchester, England in 1988 when Martin Price, the owner of the city's legendary record store Eastern Bloc and the founder of the independent label Creed, first joined forces with local musician and producer Graham Massey. After teaming with collaborator Gerald Simpson, 808 State recorded its debut EP *Newbuild* in 1988, and also began remixing tracks for groups like the Inspiral Carpets. After Simpson exited to form his solo project A Guy Called Gerald, Price and Massey enlisted DJs Andrew Barker and Darren Partington (known together as the Spinmasters) for the recording of 1989's *Quadrastate* EP, which earned a huge club hit with the track "Pacific." After signing with ZTT, they released the album *808:90*, which was embraced by the burgeoning rave culture. 808 State's next single, "The Only Rhyme That Bites," recorded with hip-hopper MC Tunes, marked a dramatic shift into hardcore rap, but was another huge hit. In 1992, Price left to work as a solo producer, later forming his own label, Sun Text. The remaining trio continued on in 1993 with *Gorgeous*, and handled remix work for the likes of David Bowie, Soundgarden, and Bomb the Bass before returning with the experimental *Don Solaris* in 1996. —*Jason Ankeny*

● **808:88:98** / Jun. 2, 1998 / ZTT/Universal ✦✦✦✦✦
Celebrating, as the title hints at, ten years of work together, *808:88:98* makes the brilliant case for 808 State's place as a modern techno pioneer. Time has shown that while a rougher breakbeat approach ended up defining much of dance in the broad public eye during the '90s, 808 State's own slightly cleaner approach was no less energetic and instantly compelling. Starting with the hyperactive shimmer and smooth flow of "Pacific," an instant trip back to the acid house days of the late '80s, *808:88:98* merrily makes its way through the years, touching on both the smash hits and some side diversions. The guitar mania and prototypical synth riff blare of "Cubik" provides the second blast, while both tunes reappear at the end in 1998 remixes. 808 State practically invented the "famous guest vocalist" cameo in techno and a slew of its various collaborations are sprinkled throughout. Bernard Sumner and Ian McCulloch aren't included, while regretfully the resolutely unspectacular MC Tunes is ("The Only Rhyme That Bites" isn't even much musically), but otherwise it's a feast of choices. Björk's playfully dark spin on "Ooops" (the clear harbinger of her eventual solo career), the Manic Street Preachers' James Dean Bradfield's winsome turn on "Lopez," and even UB40's work on "One in Ten" all make for reasonable crossover winners, though Lamb's Louise Rhodes steals the show with "Azura." For all that, the group's own work stands out most of all, from the threatening vocal snippets and drum slams of "In Yer Face" to the multi-percussive clatter and charge of "Bombadin." An appreciative essay makes the case for the band's landmark work and broad appeal, among other things noting that 808 State played for American crowds numbering in the thousands well before the major labels thought techno even existed. —*Ned Raggett*

Einstürzende Neubauten

f. Apr. 1, 1980, Berlin, Germany
Experimental Rock, Dark Ambient, Post-Punk, Alternative Pop/Rock, Industrial
Along with Cabaret Voltaire and Throbbing Gristle, Germany's Einsturzende Neubauten

("collapsing new buildings") helped pioneer industrial music with an avant-garde mix of white-noise guitar drones, vocals verging on unlistenable at times, and a clanging, rhythmic din produced by a percussion section consisting of construction materials, hand and power tools, and various metal objects. Neubauten was founded by vocalist/guitarist Blixa Bargeld and percussionist and American expatriate N.U. Unruh in Berlin as a performance art collective; their early activities included a seemingly inexplicable half-naked appearance on the Berlin Autobahn, where the duo spent some time beating on the sides of a hole in an overpass. Their earliest recordings are mostly unstructured, free-form noise issued on various cassettes and singles, including their first single, "Fuer den Untergang," 1981 EP *Schwarz*, and 1982 album *Kollaps*. A tour of England opening for the Birthday Party resulted in a contract with Some Bizarre Records, which released the slightly more structured *Portrait of Patient O.T.*, as well as consternation from club owners and journalists over Neubauten's stage demolitions and frequent ensuing violence. *—Steve Huey*

Zeichnungen des Patienten O.T. / 1983 / Some Bizarre ♦♦♦

• **Strategies Against Architecture '80-'83** / 1984 / Mute ♦♦♦♦♦
Einsturzende's first compilation album summed up all that was brilliant and thrilling about the young band, who perhaps more than anyone else encapsulated exactly what "industrial" consisted of—honest-to-goodness mechanistic pummeling and *musique concrete* remade for a newer generation. Selections from *Schwarz* and *Kollaps* feature, along with single-only cuts and various live performances as well, giving a striking picture of the group's varying approaches. Bargeld's rasped, whispered vocals and sudden screams crawl with threat and dread in a consciously dramatic but never overtly hammy fashion, while the rough rhythms and harsh clattering which serves as a bed for his delivery touches on everything from free jazz to minimal Krautrock rhythms. That the volume often gets amped to its absolute highest is only to be expected, but silence and space between sound matters just as much, especially on a slew of songs toward the end. Guitars and bass appear more often than might be expected, but the way they're played is something else entirely, muddied deep in the mix or roaring as undifferentiated noise stabbing in here and there. It's also interesting to hear the earlier version of the band in contrast with the later, when a slightly more formal rock presentation took the fore. Given that on the recordings here the group consisted mostly of percussionists beating on metal and whatever else was to hand, it's little wonder things sound even more aggressive. Maybe for some this will only sound like the backing music on a *Sprockets* sketch, but the impact on any number of sound terrorists then and since from this album can't be measured. *—Ned Raggett*

2X4 / 1984 / ROIR ♦♦♦

Fuenf Auf Der Nach Oben Offenen Richterskala / 1987 / Thirsty Ear ♦♦♦♦♦
Imagine a child that's been given a toy with detailed directions. Frustrated with its complexities, the child throws out the directions and chucks the toy against a wall, proceeding to step on it, bite it, smash it, and ultimately break it into as many pieces as he can. Bored with merely making as much noise as possible with the toy, the child begins to examine its parts and how it works. Though the child puts it together in a way that was not intended, the child becomes enamored with the new toy. *Funf Auf Der Nach* is where Neubauten truly grab hold of their broken elements and fashion them into something completely unique and (relatively) contemporary at the same time. Take their sleazy, spaghetti-westernized cover of Tim Rose's "Morning Dew" for instance, and the *structured* manner in which the record glides by. Very subdued and darkly ambient throughout, it's nowhere near the aural riots of yesteryear. For its lack of cacophony, and as restrained and formed as it is, Neubauten are just as unsettling, gripping, and tension-ridden as ever—they're just finding a new way to be all of that. You expect the big release during the closer, "Kein Bestandteil Sein," but you don't get it. *Funf auf der Nach* is like watching a stalker cleverly follow its prey for miles, only to watch it shy away just short of lodging a knife into the back of the followed. *—Andy Kellman*

Haus der Luege / 1989 / Thirsty Ear ♦♦♦♦♦
The final Einsturzende album of the 1980s found the group wrapping up that decade on a high note; while *Haus der Luege* barely lasts over half an hour, it's designed for maximum impact, and that it creates. The seasoned five-person lineup clatters and bangs away with fire, though the focus is more on straightforward industrial-tinged rock, as opposed to full-on industrial banging and relentless sonic experimentation. Things fully fire after an alternating voice/noise "Prolog" with "Feurio!," one of the band's strongest singles. With an ominous death-disco rhythm stop-starting under it all, swirling wails and cries in the mix, and sudden guitar lines filling out the sound, Bargeld's declamatory vocal approach in full effect. It's perhaps one of the most "industrial dance" songs the group's ever done, but it feels like a logical conclusion of their sound rather than a sudden embrace of Wax Trax! esthetics. Equally impressive is the title track, starting with a soft chime before turning into a dangerously funky aggro-crawl. Much of the album's second half is taken up by the lengthy "Fiat Lux," broken into three separate sections. Low in volume and astonishingly subtle until its final, overtly rhythmic conclusion, it's a testament to Einsturzende's abilities at the opposite end of where they are most often stereotyped as working, ambient instead of full-on noise. Bargeld's singing and a soft, central keyboard loop provides the main hooks for the piece, even when an array of random samples and noises starts surfacing about halfway through the track. Add in some blunt, interesting cover art and an appreciative essay from writer Biba Kopf, and *Haus der Luege* is another Einsturzende success. *—Ned Raggett*

Strategies Against Architecture II / May 21, 1991 / Mute ♦♦♦♦
Complementing the original *Strategies* collection, this double-disc affair covers the years 1984 to 1990, featuring the noted Bargeld/Unruh/Einheit/Chung/Hacke lineup of the group. With an informative, witty booklet providing a slew of pictures and complete liner notes for each track, *Architecture II* focuses on the band's continued rude creative health through the rest of the decade, inventing and perfecting a wide variety of approaches that would help define industrial music. Power tools and heavy machinery still get used and abused throughout, Bargeld's vocals remain in extremis screeching or nervy, unsettlingly calm semi-crooning, both loud and soft tracks appear with regularity. It's abrasive and strangely beautiful at its best, art music via studio manipulation turned into gripping aural entertainment. As with the first *Strategies*, studio recordings get mixed with various live efforts as well—in one instance, a fiery rip through "Haus der Luege" is grafted with the audience reaction from a completely separate concert once the quintet lit the stage on fire! Many highlights appear—besides the aforementioned "Haus der Luege," there are a number of versions of the fierce "Abfackeln!," a blistering concert take on "Yu-Gung," the centuries-old death shuffle of "Ein Stuhl in der Hoelle." Two interesting diversions capture the sly humor of the group—first, there's the 1985 studio take on the Lee Hazlewood/Nancy Sinatra song "Sand," partial evidence of Bargeld's dual alliance with Nick Cave via the Bad Seeds, perhaps. The liner notes claim that the group "detected a Neubaten feel" in the original—but if the idea means use of studio sonics, why not? Meanwhile, one of the variants of "Abfackeln!" is a 1988 Jordache jeans ad, of all things—brief, but amusing, with the store's name bleeped out at the end because they refused to pay up! *—Ned Raggett*

Tabula Rasa / Feb. 16, 1993 / Elektra ♦♦♦♦
A surprisingly restrained Neubauten outing, *Tabula Rasa* favors mood and atmosphere over noise and fury. *—Jason Ankeny*

Ende Neu / Jul. 23, 1996 / Mute ♦♦♦
On their 1996 release *Ende Neu* (ending-new), the quintessential scientists of the post-avant-garde abstain from focusing on listener disintegration tactics as they did on prior albums, but opt instead to hone their craftsmanship in new compositional areas. Some followers of their earlier material might object to the obvious and comparatively conventional song structure and style that is displayed on *Ende Neu*—picking up a power tool to highlight a piece rather than centering the entire work around it, or leaving a stage before setting it ablaze—but the destruction has already been performed, and now they are erecting the brave new anti-building of musical art. Exploring intricate processions of time and toying with melodious harmonies, Blixa Bargeld and Co. seem to have matured gracefully. The opening cut, "Was ist ist," is a furious, fast-paced slander on the constant wanting of mankind while simultaneously serving as a tongue-in-cheek remark on how absolute, scientific power overrules impossibility. From there, *Ende Neu* continues to musically rewrite the band's style, using familiar topics such as ethereal chaos ("Die Explosion Im Festspielhaus"), cosmic complacency ("The Garden"), revolt ("Installation No.1"), and even a Kafka-esque piece, "Der Schacht Von Babel." This is the first release since the departure of founding band member Mark Chung, and it is obvious that the remaining members have taken the time to contribute to the void left by his departure. *Ende Neu* delivers a precision-fed matrix of audio-encrypted knowledge in a manner not like the chaotic Neubauten of the early '80s, but more strategic, and more mature. *—Greg Matherly*

Ende Neu Remixes / Sep. 8, 1997 / Mute ♦♦

Silence Is Sexy / May 23, 2000 / Mute ♦♦♦♦
Odds are *no one* banked on Einstürzende Neubauten lasting 20 years. What were the odds of such a destructive band surviving two decades? Did the Stooges ever stand a chance of writing a song called "1989"? More importantly, who would have thought that the milestone year would see the release of one of Neubauten's finest records? Though *Silence Is Sexy* might retain some of the band's recent song-based developments that have left some fans puzzled, its closest touchstone is 1987's *Richterskala*. They might not be as unsettling or destructive as they were in their early days, but they still know how to capture the imagination and warp the senses. As with *Richterskala*, restraint is a key element. The schlock of recent outings is done away with to focus more on stark restraint. Bargeld doesn't *really* let his vocal chords rip often, and their trademark clangorous overload isn't resorted to much. "Sabrina" is one of the tracks that brings to mind their excellent album from 1987. Swaying strings and plaintive percussive taps frame Blixa Bargeld's whispers as he waxes like a bawdier Bryan Ferry. Those who reveled in Neubauten's familiar undead bass sound will find the record goes down a treat. At nearly 70 minutes, it's a bit sprawling, but it allows the gang to represent every element that has made them vital and influential to experimental music throughout the last twenty years. Irregardless of your pickiness with Neubauten's material—what you like/hate about them—anyone could piece together 40 minutes of the record for an ace *Cliff's Notes* version. [Early editions came with a second disc, consisting solely of the 19-minute long "Pelikanol." A scraping, hypnotic track, Bargeld uses his voice as a drone instrument to great effect.] *—Andy Kellman*

Mark Eitzel

b. Jan. 30, 1959, Walnut Creek, California
Vocals, Guitar / Sadcore, Adult Alternative Pop/Rock, Indie Rock, Alternative Pop/Rock, Singer/Songwriter
As both a solo artist and the frontman for enduring cult favorites American Music Club, Mark Eitzel established himself among the truly powerful forces in contemporary music; a hauntingly evocative singer, he earned even greater notoriety for his brilliance as a composer, combining the energy of punk, the pastoral beauty of folk, and the melodrama of lounge music to build one of the most impressive and darkly poetic bodies of songs in the modern pop canon. Born January 30, 1959 in Walnut Creek, CA, Eitzel's military upbringing led him everywhere from Great Britain to Columbus, OH; as a teen, he became a born-again Christian, but at the age of 16, he rejected religion in favor of alcohol, his

love/hate relationship with the bottle going on to fuel much of his subsquent work as a performer. Inspired by punk, he eventually formed his own group, the Naked Skinnies, and with them relocated to San Francisco in 1980; there the band quickly dissolved, and three years later he formed American Music Club.

AMC's 12-year existence was tumultuous, to say the least; Eitzel, prone to facing his demons while onstage, earned a notorious reputation as a loose cannon, and despite the lavish critical praise heaped on albums like 1991's *Everclear* and 1993's *Mercury*, the group never rose beyond a fierce cult following. Eitzel quit the band on numerous occasions, once joining another Bay Area group, the Toiling Midgets; in 1991, while still fronting American Music Club, he issued his solo debut, *Songs of Love*, a live acoustic set recorded in London (British audiences being much more receptive to his music than their American counterparts). A subsequent solo single on Matador, the lovely "Take Courage," increased rumors of the band's impending breakup, but they did not truly implode until after the release of 1994's *San Francisco*. At that point, Eitzel began pursuing his solo career in earnest, debuting in 1996 with the jazzy *60 Watt Silver Lining*; for 1997's *West*, he co-wrote all of the songs with R.E.M. guitarist Peter Buck. Early the following year, he resurfaced with *Caught in a Trap and I Can't Back Out 'Cause I Love You Too Much, Baby.* —*Jason Ankeny*

Songs of Love: Live at the Borderline—1/19/91 / 1991 / Demon ✦✦✦

In between American Music Club albums, and also in between labels, Mark Eitzel was offered a deal to fly to London and play a solo show with the intention of releasing the results. To the dismay of many within the AMC camp, Eitzel accepted the deal, as he would have complete control over whatever came of it. *Songs of Love Live* is the result, a documentation of his show at London's Borderline. Though he played nearly half of what would become AMC's best work (*Everclear*), most of the CD is made up of gripping versions of earlier favorites, such as "Outside This Bar" and "Gary's Song" (from *Engine*), as well as "Firefly" and "Blue and Grey Shirt" (from *California*). The only missing element is the trademark banter between Eitzel and his audience. To paraphrase *Saturday Night Live's* Dieter from "Sprockets," Eitzel masks his self-depracation with the subtlety of a flying mallet, and when combined with his razor-sharp wit, it can lead to some hilarious and sometimes uncomfortable exchanges with the crowd. The closing songs "Take Courage" (a one-off Matador solo single) and "Nothing Can Bring Me Down" were actually recorded by Eitzel in a small room at Demon's offices. Fitting perfectly with the AMC mystique, *Songs of Love Live* was the best selling Eitzel record to date, despite it's U.K.-only release. A key possession for any AMC fan, it provides an unfiltered, uncompromised, raw vision of Mark Eitzel's songs. —*Andy Kellman*

60 Watt Silver Lining / Mar. 19, 1996 / Warner Brothers ✦✦✦

Mark Eitzel's *60 Watt Silver Lining* is the first step in a new direction for the former leader of American Music Club. With its trimmed-down percussion and bass, the clear, calm lines of Bruce Kaphan's piano, and the unhurried rhythms and atmospheric moods of the songs, you could almost call *60 Watt Silver Lining* a jazz album. But on the whole, the record is not a radical departure from his previous work; Eitzel is and always has been a sincere and deeply introspective songwriter, and many of the album's best songs share a grounding in real-life people and places. He takes his newfound freedom as a solo artist to the furthest extreme with "Wild Sea"—a free-form, stream-of-consciousness ramble through visions of "old ghosts," "drowned words," and "frozen prayers"—but never completely abandons rock & roll or his sense of humor: "Cleopatra Jones," as much of a rocker as anything here, follows directly behind "Saved," a love song Eitzel says he wrote for Barbra Streisand. It's clear that this is a songwriter who will continue to surprise us for a long, long time. —*Kurt Wolff*

Lover's Leap USA / 1997 / [self released] ✦✦✦

In 1997 Eitzel put together an album of unreleased songs which would be sold only at his live shows. The resultant *Lover's Leap USA* consisted of demos and session outtakes of 13 songs that hadn't made the grade on his previous solo albums; only 500 copies were made, each featuring a doodle on the sleeve drawn personally by Eitzel himself, and while there were four variations on his one-paragraph liner notes (some featuring jokes about patriotism or the poor quality of the album), each featured the polite request to potential bootleggers, "Don't make any f—king copies of this. DON'T." As a result, *Lover's Leap USA* has become a highly sought after collector's item among Eitzel's small but passionately loyal circle of fans, though after a listen it's not difficult to see why this material didn't make the cut on one of Eitzel's "real" albums. Eitzel goes a bit far when he says, "The first two songs are truly bad," but "Have No Words" and "The Big House" certainly aren't up to his usual high standards, and while there were more than a few examples of Eitzel's brilliance as a songwriter—the quietly bitter "How Will You Face Yourself in Sleep," the witty but pained "Steve I Always Knew," and the cynical groove of "Nice Nice Nice"—there's more filler and less top-shelf genius than one usually expects from him. As a souvenir for hardcore fans (which is what it was intended to be), *Lover's Leap USA* features a few pearly moments, and it deserves to be heard by a wider audience than 500 people, but it's hardly an essential release, and the unconverted needn't search it out. —*Mark Deming*

● **West** / May 5, 1997 / Warner Brothers ✦✦✦✦✦

For his sophomore solo effort *West*, Mark Eitzel teamed with R.E.M. guitarist Peter Buck; given that several of the songs recorded during the sessions were originally intended as material for Buck's day job, it's no great surprise that the album sounds much like R.E.M. circa *Out of Time* or *Automatic for the People*, favoring gorgeously spare acoustic arrangements. Eitzel has never sounded looser or more carefree than he does here—tracks like "Free From Harm" and the exhilarating "In Your Life" are positively sunny by his usual standards, upbeat declarations of love and commitment lifted by Buck's trade-

mark guitar jangle; even the drinking songs, like "Fresh Screwdriver," offer an uncharacteristic ray of hope.

Still, while *West* is an improvement over Eitzel's solo debut *40 Watt Silver Lining*, it nevertheless suffers in comparison to his work with American Music Club; without the galvanizing eclecticism of his old band, his songs occasionally lack distinction, but at his best—the opening "If You Have to Ask," "Then It Really Happens"—Eitzel remains one of the most transcendent figures on the musical landscape. —*Jason Ankeny*

Caught in a Trap and I Can't Back Out 'Cause I Love You Too Much, Baby / Jan. 20, 1998 / Matador ✦✦✦✦✦

Neither as polished and loose as *West* nor as studiously serene as *60 Watt Silver Lining*, *Caught in a Trap and I Can't Back Out 'Cause I Love You Too Much, Baby* is the liveliest record Mark Eitzel has recorded since the demise of American Music Club. Eitzel's songs always flourish when stripped down and delivered directly, and the stark production of *Caught* emphasizes his wry lyricism and wrenching emotions. Much of the music on the album was written before *West*, his collaboration with Peter Buck, and the songs do sound like a bridge between that record and *60 Watt*. In many ways, it's his finest solo record yet, because the largely acoustic setting is quite affecting, and the handful of electric tracks—recorded with Sonic Youth drummer Steve Shelley and Yo La Tengo bassist James McNew—have a nervy power reminiscent of the best AMC tracks. —*Stephen Thomas Erlewine*

The Invisible Man / May 22, 2001 / Matador ✦✦✦✦✦

Mark Eitzel seems to have had no problems writing songs since the breakup of American Music Club, but finding a musical setting for them that suits him as well AMC's brooding folk-punk has proven to be a daunting task. After the neo-jazz of *60 Watt Silver Lining*, the warm R.E.M.-ish pop of *West*, and the stark postmodern folk of *Caught in a Trap* …, Eitzel takes yet another left turn with *The Invisible Man*, his first album after a three-year layoff. This time out, Eitzel has built his arrangements around spare keyboard lines, atmospheric electronic samples, and percussion loops that blend with his voice and acoustic guitar to create an effect that suggest a more spare, organic version of Portishead, or a Jon Brion production that's stuck in a blue funk. But the new surroundings suit the songs quite well, and surprisingly enough, by Eitzel's standards *The Invisible Man* doesn't sound especially doomstruck. Anyone looking for his usual failed-romantic gloom will find plenty of it on songs like "Sleep," "Bitterness," and "Steve I Always Knew," the latter in a take markedly superior to that on the limited-edition *Lover's Leap USA*. But there's also a haunting wistfulness to the lovelorn "Anything" and "Without You,"; "Can You See" and "Seeing Eye Dog" are love songs that at least acknowledge the possibility of a functional relationship with wit and compassion; and the surreal humor of "Christian Science Reading Room" is a welcome reminder of how funny Eitzel can be when he feels like it. And the final track, "Proclaim Your Joy," is shocking in its good cheer—it's a goofy Lou Reed-esque talking blues that winds into a rollicking singalong chorus that's the most life-affirming message Eitzel has offered to date. As a writer, Eitzel hasn't sounded this warm and approachable since American Music Club's *California*, and musically, this his most satisfying work since going solo; on all levels, *The Invisible Man* is an experiment that succeeds. —*Mark Deming*

The El Dorados

f. 1954, Chicago, IL, **db.** 1958

Doo Wop, R&B

One of the leading R&B vocal groups on Vee Jay, the El Dorados had a relatively short career with their first lineup, during which they scored a massive crossover hit, 1955's "At My Front Door." The El Dorados' first single, a bluesy ballad called "My Loving Baby," was issued in September 1954, and was a popular regional seller. Their next effort had the group backing up Hazel McCollum on "Annie's Answer," which was Vee Jay's contribution to the ongoing "Annie" saga begun by Hank Ballard and the Midnighters. During the third week of September 1955, Vee Jay released the group's "At My Front Door," which stormed the Billboard R&B charts on September 24th and the Top 100 on October 15th. The song featured Al Duricati's pounding drum rhythm and a rousing sax solo. The so-called "baby talk" pre-finale by Moses Jr. made the record soar even further, and the lyrics about that "crazy little mama" became as legendary as the Annie saga. By the end of the year it had climbed to number 17 on the pop charts and number one R&B, where it remained for 18 weeks. (Pat Boone later did a cover version that charted at number seven pop). They managed only one other charting record, 1956's "I'll Be Forever Loving You." It was a rocker that exuded jazz, pop, and R&B overtones, but although it made it to number eight R&B in February 1956, it never charted on the pop lists. A few additional singles performed well in certain U.S. cities, but didn't measure up to their prior hit status. Subsequent lineups and name changes (and alterations) brought no further success, but they continued performing well into the '80s. —*Bryan Thomas*

● **Bim Bam Boom** / Nov. 17, 1993 / Vee-Jay ✦✦✦✦✦

The El Dorados didn't enjoy sustained success or notoriety and really weren't a top-echelon doo wop group. They did make one superb song in 1955: "At My Front Door" is a landmark of the genre; it had every ingredient, from a simple, catchy theme to first-rate harmonizing and Pirkle Moses' finest lead. The El Dorados made many other good tunes, and an occasionally inspired one like "I'll Be Forever Loving You" or "A Fallen Tear," before quitting Vee-Jay in a money dispute and subsequently disbanding. Almost their entire output is available on this 25-song reissue. It's a chance for fans to revisit triumphs and newcomers to hear why they did have a brief time in the spotlight. —*Ron Wynn*

Elastica

f. Oct. 1992, **db.** Oct. 2001

Post-Grunge, Punk Revival, Brit-pop, Alternative Pop/Rock

Elastica's brief, angular, and catchy punk rock became a hit on both sides of the Atlantic in 1995. While the group reworks both the sound and the image of new wave and punk rockers like Adam & the Ants, Wire, the Buzzcocks, and Blondie, the band's songs are more pop-oriented and hook-driven than most of their influences and Justine Frischmann's cool sexuality is earthier, yet more detached, than Debbie Harry's. Frischmann, the original guitarist of Suede, left the group soon after her relationship with frontman Brett Anderson ended. She then formed Elastica in 1991, and gained rave reviews for the group's first single, the roaring three-chord, two-minute punk rocker "Stutter." Two subsequent singles, "Line Up" and "Connection," sold well but suffered from claims the band swiped riffs from Wire (the band's publishers later built a case that was settled out of court). Entering the charts at number one, Elastica's self-titled first album became the fastest-selling debut in the U.K., beating the record Oasis' *Definitely Maybe* set only seven months earlier. Like Oasis, Elastica managed to have a hit single in America with "Connection"; the single was a major modern rock radio hit, as well as reaching the Top 60 on the singles chart. A follow-up LP ended up being years in the making however, and Elastica's future became the subject of considerable media speculation. —*Stephen Thomas Erlewine*

● **Elastica** / Mar. 14, 1995 / DGC ✦✦✦✦✦

Elastica's debut album may cop a riff here and there from Wire or the Stranglers, yet no more than Led Zeppelin did with Willie Dixon or the Beach Boys with Chuck Berry. The key is context. Elastica can make the rigid artiness of Wire into a rocking, sexy single with more hooks than anything on *Pink Flag* ("Connection") or rework the Stranglers' "No More Heroes" into a more universal anthem that loses none of its punkiness ("Waking Up"). But what makes *Elastica* such an intoxicating record is not only the way the 16 songs speed by in 40 minutes, but that they're nearly all classics. The riffs are angular like early Adam & the Ants, the melodies tease like Blondie, and the entire band is as tough as the Clash, yet they never seem anything less than contemporary. Justine Frischmann's detached sexuality adds an extra edge to her brief, spiky songs—"Stutter" roars about a boyfriend's impotence, "Car Song" makes sex in a car actually sound sexy, "Line Up" slags off groupies, and "Vaseline" speaks for itself. Even if the occasional riff sounds like an old wave group, the simple fact is that hardly any new wave band made records this consistently rocking and melodic. —*Stephen Thomas Erlewine*

The Menace / Apr. 2000 / Atlantic ✦✦✦✦

The wait. That's all anybody listening for the first time to Elastica's second album, *The Menace*, will have in mind. Inevitably, with a five-year buildup, the first listen to *The Menace* will be a letdown, especially for diehards who bought the *6-Track EP*—the full-length album contains four of those songs, albeit in (mostly) re-recorded versions. That initial disappointment fades fairly quickly, however, since this is an ideal second Elastica record. Where *Elastica* was smart, sexy, and hooky, *The Menace* is cerebral, dense, harsh, and dissonant, a culmination of their obsession with such detached avatars of post-punk cool as Wire and the Fall. It's a subtle shift, since much of their signature sound remains in place—angular riffs, spiky hooks, Justine Frischmann's cool vocals—but it's noticeable nevertheless, especially since there is no obvious single. A handful of cuts are still just as catchy in their own way as the hits on *Elastica*; what separates them is that here, the band is as enamored with chaos as they are with hooks. Other than that, the main difference is the preponderance of eerie, slower numbers, something totally absent from the debut. It may not be the huge progression that some groups make after five years, but it is certainly a consolidation of their strengths and a restatement of purpose as Elastica the art-punk band. So it's a pretty damn terrific second album, a tight yet layered record that delivers—albeit incrementally—on the promise of the debut. —*Stephen Thomas Erlewine*

Electric Flag

f. Apr. 1967, Chicago, IL, **db.** 1974

Jazz-Rock, Psychedelic, Blues-Rock

When guitarist Mike Bloomfield left the Paul Butterfield Blues Band in 1967, he wanted to form a band that combined blues, rock, soul, psychedelia, and jazz into something new. The ambitious concept didn't come off, despite some interesting moments; maybe the Electric Flag was *too* ambitious to hold all that weight. Oddly, before even playing any live concerts, the group recorded the soundtrack for the 1967 psychedelic exploitation movie, *The Trip*, which afforded them the opportunity to experiment with some of their ideas without much pressure. *A Long Time Comin'* was an erratic affair, predating Blood, Sweat & Tears and Chicago as a sort of attempt at a big band rock sound. Calling it an early jazz-rock outing is not exactly accurate; it was more like late '60s soul-rock-psychedelia that sometimes (but not always) employed prominent horns. Indeed, it sometimes didn't always sound like the work of the same band—or, at least, you could say that it seemed torn between blues-rock, soul-rock, and California psychedelic influences. —*Richie Unterberger*

● **Old Glory: The Best of Electric Flag** / Oct. 1995 / Columbia/Legacy ✦✦✦✦✦

The Electric Flag was Michael Bloomfield's doomed-from-the-start musical vision of an American Music band that played it all and sometimes mixed it all up together. This 17-track set brings together all the highlights from their two albums (with and without Bloomfield), some unissued demos, and a pair of live tracks from the group's debut at the Monterey Pop Festival in 1967. A nice collection that serves their musical legacy well, with great notes from Jeff Tamarkin to recommend it. —*Cub Koda*

Electric Light Orchestra

f. Oct. 1970, Birmingham, England, **db.** 1988

Album Rock, Pop/Rock, Prog Rock/Art Rock

The Electric Light Orchestra's ambitious yet irresistible fusion of Beatlesque pop, classical arrangements, and futuristic iconography rocketed the group to massive commercial success throughout the 1970s. ELO was formed in Birmingham, England in the autumn of 1970 from the ashes of the eccentric art-pop combo the Move, reuniting frontman Roy Wood with guitarist/composer Jeff Lynne, bassist Rick Price, and drummer Bev Bevan. Announcing their intentions to "pick up where 'I Am the Walrus' left off," the quartet embellished their engagingly melodic rock with classical flourishes for their self-titled debut LP (issued as *No Answer* in the U.S.). *Electric Light Orchestra* sold strongly, buoyed by the success of the U.K. Top Ten hit "10538 Overture." Wood soon left ELO to form Wizzard, taking two members with him. Bevan and Lynne restructured the group; Lynne assumed vocal duties, with his Lennonesque tenor proving the ideal complement to his increasingly sophisticated melodies. With 1973's *ELO II*, the group returned to the Top Ten with their grandiose cover of the Chuck Berry chestnut "Roll Over Beethoven"; the record was also their first American hit, with 1974's *Eldorado* yielding their first U.S. Top Ten, the lovely "Can't Get It Out of My Head." Despite Electric Light Orchestra's commercial success, the band remained relatively faceless; the lineup changed constantly, with sole mainstays Lynne and Bevan preferring to let their elaborate stage shows and omnipresent spaceship imagery instead serve as the group's public persona. 1975's *Face the Music* went gold, while the follow-up, *A New World Record*, sold five million copies internationally thanks to standouts like "Livin' Thing."

The platinum-selling double-LP, *Out of the Blue*, appeared in 1977. Beginning with 1979's *Discovery*, the group launched their own Jet imprint. In the wake of ELO's best-selling *Greatest Hits* compilation, Lynne wrote several songs for the soundtrack of the Olivia Newton-John film *Xanadu*, including the hit title track. *Time* (1981) generated their final Top Ten hit, "Hold on Tight." Following 1983's *Secret Messages*, Bevan left the group to join Black Sabbath, although he returned to the fold for 1986's *Balance of Power*, which received little interest from fans and media alike. —*Jason Ankeny*

No Answer / 1972 / Jet ✦✦✦✦

Electric Light Orchestra's debut album is an astonishing creation in its own right, but neophyte listeners should be aware that it bears very little resemblance to the sound for which ELO would become known on its subsequent records. *No Answer*, as it ended up being called in America through a miscommunication with ELO's U.S. label, is a minimalist work by comparison with anything on the band's later albums. The core trio of Roy Wood, Jeff Lynne, and Bev Bevan, augmented by one horn player and a violinist, approaches the music alternately like a hard rock band attacking a song and a string ensemble playing a chamber piece. Filled with surprisingly loose playing and sounds throughout, and with a psychedelic aura hovering over most of the music, *No Answer* is unique in ELO's output. Written and sung by Lynne, "10538 Overture" is the opener and the best song on the album. Wood's "Look at Me Now," by comparison, plays like a sweet, melodic follow-up to "Beautiful Daughter" from the Move's *Shazam*, with some digressions on the oboe and a cello and violin subbing for the guitars.

The rest moves from period-style popular songs to strangely cinematic conceptual pieces, on which the rock elements almost disappear in favor of quasi-classical playing by all concerned. A beautiful acoustic guitar workout by Wood, "1st Movement" also features the song's composer on the oboe, while "Mr. Radio," an exercise in 1920s nostalgia written and sung by Lynne, digresses for a moment into 1940s-style classical piano pyrotechnics. His "Whisper in the Night" ends the album with a lean and textured acoustic sound that, ironically, disappeared from ELO's repertory when he exited the lineup following these sessions. —*Bruce Eder*

Electric Light Orchestra II / Feb. 1973 / Jet ✦✦

Cut during the fall of 1972, *Electric Light Orchestra II* was where Jeff Lynne started building (or, more correctly, rebuilding) the sound of Electric Light Orchestra following the departure of Roy Wood from the original lineup. It was as personal an effort as Lynne had ever made in music, showcasing his work as singer, songwriter, guitarist, sometime synthesizer player, and producer, and it is somewhat more focused than its predecessor but also retains some of the earlier album's lean textures. Lynne, drummer Bev Bevan, bassist Mike D'Albberquerque, and keyboardist Richard Tandy comprise the basic core of the band, with two cellists and a violinist sawing away around them. There were holes in their sound that made the group seem somewhat ragged, as on the pounding "In Old England Town (Boogie #2)"; Lynne's singing would also have to develop, and some of the material also showed the need of an editor. On the other hand, "From the Sun to the World (Boogie #1)" was a succinct progressive rock workout, and "Kuiama" was a decent showcase for the different sides of the group that worked about as well as any 11-minute progressive rock track of the period. But the very fact that the group's cover of "Roll Over Beethoven" was the hit off of this album also showed how far Lynne had to go as a songwriter—there's nothing else here one-quarter as good as that as a song, and the fact that the band attacked it like a buzzsaw made it one of the most bracing pieces of progressive rock to make the charts. As a patchwork job, the album holds up well, and it and the single did go a long way toward getting them the beginnings of an audience in America. —*Bruce Eder*

On the Third Day / Dec. 1973 / Jet ✦✦✦

The group's third album showed a marked advancement, with a fuller, more cohesive sound from the band as a whole and major improvements in Jeff Lynne's singing and songwriting. This is where Electric Light Orchestra took on its familiar sound, Lynne's voice suddenly showing an attractive expressiveness reminiscent of John Lennon in his early solo years, and also sporting a convincing white British soulful quality that was utterly lacking earlier. The group also plugged the holes that made its work seem so close to being ragged on those earlier records. "Showdown" and "Ma-Ma-Ma Belle" (the latter featuring Marc Bolan on double lead guitar with Lynne) became AM radio fixtures while "Daybreaker" became a concert opener for the group and, along with "In the Hall of the Mountain King," kept the group's FM/art rock credentials in order. *—Bruce Eder*

☆ **Eldorado** / Oct. 1974 / Jet ✦✦✦✦✦
This is the album where Jeff Lynne finally found the sound he'd wanted since co-founding ELO three years earlier. Up to this point, most of the group's music had been self-contained—Lynne, Richard Tandy, et al. providing whatever was needed, vocally or instrumentally, even if it meant overdubbing their work layer upon layer. Lynne saw the limitations of this process, however, and opted for the presence of an orchestra—it was only 30 pieces, but the result was a much richer musical palette than the group had ever had to work with, and their most ambitious and successful record up to that time. Indeed, *Eldorado* was strongly reminiscent in some ways of *Sgt. Pepper's Lonely Hearts Club Band*. Not that it could ever have the same impact or be as distinctive, but it had its feet planted in so many richly melodic and varied musical traditions, yet made it all work in a rock context, that it did recall the Beatles classic. It was a very romantic work, especially on the opening "Eldorado Overture," which was steeped in a wistful 1920s/1930s notion of popular fantasy (embodied in movies and novels like James Hilton's *Lost Horizon* and Somerset Maugham's *The Razor's Edge*) about disillusioned seekers. It boasted Lynne's best single up to that time, "Can't Get It out of My Head," which most radio listeners could never get out of their respective heads, either. The integration of the orchestra would become even more thorough on future albums, but *Eldorado* was notable for mixing the band and orchestra (and a choir) in ways that did no violence to the best elements of both. The album has appeared on CD twice as of early 2001, from Sony Music, and from DCC in a gold-plated audiophile CD, with significantly better sound. [The 2001 CD reissue on Epic/Legacy adds two previously unreleased bonus tracks: an eight-minute "Eldorado Instrumental Medley," and the 46-second home demo "Dark City," described by Jeff Lynne as an "early idea for 'Laredo Tornado'."] *—Bruce Eder*

Face the Music / Oct. 1975 / Jet ✦✦✦✦
The group's more modest follow-up to *Eldorado* is a very solid album, if not as bold or unified. It was also their first recorded at Musicland in Munich, which became Jeff Lynne's preferred venue for cutting records. At the time, he was also generating songs at a breakneck pace and had perfected the majestic, quasi-Beatles-type style (sort of high-wattage *Magical Mystery Tour*) introduced two albums earlier. The sound is stripped down a bit on *Face the Music*, Louis Clark's orchestral contributions generally more subdued than on *Eldorado*, even when they compete with the band, as on "Strange Magic." The soulful "Evil Woman" was one of the most respectable chart hits of its era, and one of the best songs that Lynne ever wrote (reportedly in 30 minutes), while "Strange Magic" showed off his writing in a more ethereal vein. "One Summer Dream," which is written in a similar mode, also has a touchingly wistful mood about it but is a somewhat lackluster finale compared to the albums that preceded and followed this one. The requisite rock & roll number, "Poker," is a quicker tempo than anything previously heard from the band, the guitar is pumped up louder than ever. And "Down Home Town," an experiment in achieving a country & western sound, is fresh at this point and more interesting than the equivalent material of *Out of the Blue*. *—Bruce Eder*

Ole' ELO / 1976 / Jet ✦✦✦✦✦
The early hits, marred only by the unnecessary cutting of "Roll over Beethoven." *—Bruce Eder*

A New World Record / Nov. 1976 / Jet ✦✦✦✦✦
Jeff Lynne reportedly regards this album and its follow-up, *Out of the Blue*, as the high points in the band's history. One might be better off opting for *A New World Record* over its successor, however, as a more modest-sized creation chock full of superb songs that are produced even better. Opening with the opulently orchestrated "Tightrope," which heralds the perfect production found throughout this album, *A New World Record* contains seven of the best songs ever to come out of the group. The Beatles influence is present, to be sure, but developed to a very high degree of sophistication and on Lynne's own terms, rather than being imitative of specific songs. "Telephone Line" might be the best Lennon-McCartney collaboration that never was, lyrical and soaring in a way that manages to echo elements of *Revolver* and the Beatles without ever mimicking them. The original LP's second side opened with "So Fine," which seems like the perfect pop synthesis of guitar, percussion, and orchestral sounds, embodying precisely what Lynne had first set out to do with Roy Wood at the moment the ELO was conceived. From there, the album soars through stomping rock numbers like "Livin' Thing" and "Do Ya," interspersed with lyrical pieces like "Above the Clouds" (which makes striking use of pizzicato bass strings). The album was a jewel on vinyl, especially coming out at a time when disco was starting to undermine the airwaves. "Do Ya," in particular, was a breath of fresh air. The album has held up well on CD and, along with the rest of ELO's catalog, is slated for upgrading on CD in the year 2001, with the addition of extra songs. Any version of this album is worth hearing, however, if only to savor the production, which recalls the glory days of psychedelic pop/rock. *—Bruce Eder*

Out of the Blue / Nov. 1977 / Jet ✦✦✦
The last ELO album to make a major impact on popular music, *Out of the Blue* was of a piece with its lavishly produced predecessor, *A New World Record*, but it's a much more mixed bag as an album. For starters, it was a double LP, a format that has proved daunting to all but a handful of rock artists, and was no less so here. The songs were flowing fast and freely from Jeff Lynne at the time, however, and well more than half of what is here is very solid, at least as songs if not necessarily as recordings. "Sweet Talkin' Woman" and "Turn to Stone" are among the best songs in the group's output, and much of the rest is very entertaining. The heavy sound of the orchestra, however, as well as the layer upon layer of vocal overdubs, often seem out of place. All in all, the group was trying too hard to generate a substantial sounding double LP, complete with a suite, "Concerto for a Rainy Day." The latter is the nadir of the album, an effort at conceptual rock that seemed archaic even in 1977. Another chunk is filled up with what might best be called art-rock mood music ("The Whale"), before you finally get to the relief of a basic rocker like "Birmingham Blues." Even here, the group couldn't leave well enough alone—rather than ending it on that note, they had to finish the album with "Wild West Hero," a piece of ersatz movie music that adds nothing to what you've heard over the previous 65 minutes. In its defense, *Out of the Blue* was massively popular and did become the centerpiece of a huge worldwide tour that earned the group status as a major live attraction for a time. *—Bruce Eder*

ELO's Greatest Hits / 1979 / Jet ✦✦✦✦
By ignoring the band's first two albums, the Roy Wood-dominated *Electric Light Orchestra* and the transitional *ELO II*, the 1979 singles compilation *ELO's Greatest Hits* presents a somewhat skewed vision of the band. Ironically, this revision has become the normative view of the band: slick, almost mechanical purveyors of undeniably catchy but somewhat soulless hit singles. "Evil Woman," "Showdown," "Turn to Stone," "Telephone Line," "Strange Magic"—anyone who was anywhere near a radio in the latter half of the '70s knows them all by heart, whether they like them or not. But *ELO's Greatest Hits* does a far graver disservice to the Electric Light Orchestra's oeuvre. For some reason, the original vinyl LP sounded somewhat muffled and distant, as if the EQ was perceptibly off. The CD was apparently mastered from the same poor-quality tapes. The result is while this is otherwise a fine survey of Jeff Lynne's most successful—if not necessarily his best—songs, it just doesn't sound very good. The ELO catalog has since been carefully remastered, and sounds worlds better. The two-disc *Strange Magic* and three-disc *Flashback* compilations trump *ELO's Greatest Hits* in both sound quality and historical accuracy. *—Stewart Mason*

Discovery / Jun. 1979 / Jet/Epic/Legacy ✦✦
ELO continued on their winning Top 40 ways with the release of *Discovery*. Now pared down to the basic four-piece unit, Jeff Lynne continued to dominate the band and they still got their hits (this time around it was the smash "Don't Bring Me Down." Elsewhere on the disc there was, of note, "Last Train to London" and "Confusion." Though *Discovery* charted well, it was becoming obvious that ELO were starting to run themselves out of useful Beatles hooks with which to fuel their hit-making machine. [The 2001 CD reissue on Epic/Legacy adds three previously unreleased bonus tracks: a home demo of "On the Run," a home demo of "Second Time Around" (a song Lynne never finished for the album), and a cover of Del Shannon's "Little Town Flirt."] *—James Chrispell*

Time / Aug. 1981 / Jet ✦✦
Time takes its cues more from such bands as the Alan Parsons Project and Wings than from Jeff Lynne's fascination with *Pepper*-era Beatles. Sure, all the electronic whirrs and bleeps are present and accounted for, and *Time* did spawn hit singles in "Hold on Tight" and "Twilight," but on the average, ELO had begun to get too stuck on the same structure and content of their releases. "The Way Life's Meant To Be" echoes very early ELO hits like "Can't Get It Out Of My Head," and the "Prologue" and "Epilogue" segments try to bring about a unifying concept which doesn't quite hold up upon listening all the way through. *Time* proves to be competent ELO but not great ELO. (The 2001 CD reissue on Epic/Legacy adds three bonus tracks, all B-sides of singles: "The Bouncer," "When Time Stood Still," and "Julie Don't Live Here.") *—James Chrispell*

Secret Messages / Jun. 1983 / Jet ✦✦

Balance of Power / Mar. 1986 / Epic ✦✦

Afterglow / Jun. 1990 / Epic ✦✦✦✦
Although it contains all the hits and the remastering sounds superb, the three-disc box set *Afterglow* is likely to be more ELO than anyone but the most devoted fans would want from an anthology. *—Stephen Thomas Erlewine*

★ **Strange Magic: The Best of Electric Light Orchestra** / Apr. 11, 1995 / Epic Associated/Legacy ✦✦✦✦✦
ELO's smart blend of pop and rock with modernly orchestrated classical music flourished throughout the '70s and '80s, since their sound was one of a kind. Plush arrangements that drowned themselves in bright synthesizers and vibrant guitar gave way to a brand new type of music, giving the Electric Light Orchestra a distinguished setting atop the vast rock & roll mantle. *Strange Magic* is a two-CD set of their most illustrious songs from their lengthy career. Every one of their charted hits, except three, appear here, leaving out "I'm Alive," "All Over The World," and the famed "Xanadu" with Olivia Newton John. These deletions aside, this generous 29-song compilation is a splendid cross-section of the group. The first disc is highlighted by the eight-plus minutes of "Roll Over Beethoven," which combines their trademarked classical and rock sound, and the guitar driven allure of "Ma-Ma-Ma Belle" showcases their edginess. ELO's most gracious offering, the beautiful "Can't Get It Out of My Head," appears here as well, with its grandeur stemming from its exquisite string work. The synth-saturated "Strange Magic" is one of their most colorful songs, and "Evil Woman" has Jeff Lynne showing off his concealed yet masterful voice. The second disc begins to show their drift into disco, with the keyboards front and center on "Shine a Little Love" along with the computerized texture of both "Turn to Stone" and "Sweet Talkin' Woman." The wispy synthesized tinkle of "Confusion" is a nice addition, bringing their domination of electric music to its full capacity. ELO's glide into the '80s found them playing more rock-infused music, relying on the keyboards a little less. Songs like "Hold on Tight," with its slippery rhythm, and the '60s-tinged sound of "Rock & Roll Is King" proved that Lynne could pump out amiable rock tunes that

befriended radio in a new decade. *Strange Magic* sums up this innovative group's musical career with an abundant amount of hits, bettered only by the box set. *—Mike DeGagne*

Flashback / Nov. 21, 2000 / Epic/Legacy ✦✦✦✦✦
The very fact that Electric Light Orchestra released a second three-disc box set is a tacit admission that, yes, 1987's *Afterglow* wasn't everything it should be. Happily, 2000's *Flashback* is. Assembled with the cooperation of Jeff Lynne, *Flashback* covers all the bases, featuring all the hits, a good selection of album tracks, and seven previously unreleased tracks, two alternate mixes and "After All," previously unavailable on CD. The sequencing is roughly chronological, with each of the three discs spotlighting a different era, then sequenced for maximum listenability within that—so "10538 Overture" segues to "Showdown" and "Ma-Ma-Ma Belle" then doubles back to the first album. It's a gambit that works, since *Flashback* winds up flowing as gracefully as ELO's best albums. And, make no mistake, this is one of their best albums, a rare box set that satisfies the needs of both casual and mildly dedicated fans, while offering the hardcore not just a bunch of rarities but an enjoyable album with its own character. So, it trumps *Afterglow* in every possible way, then, and thereby eliminates the need for yet another three-disc ELO box. *—Stephen Thomas Erlewine*

Zoom / Jun. 12, 2001 / Epic ✦✦✦✦
Fifteen years after Jeff Lynne masterminded the last official Electric Light Orchestra album and ten after his solo debut, Lynne recorded *Zoom*—an ELO album that he recorded nearly entirely by himself. So why isn't this a solo album? Well, not only does Lynne own the ELO name, so he can do whatever he wants, but he designed this to be a return to the classic ELO sound. Which it is, more so than any album since the early '80s. There are lush, heartbreaking ballads and '50s-styled rockers with an endearingly robotic pulse and Beatlesque harmonies. Better than that, the songwriting is melodic and memorable, the strongest Lynne has done in decades, resulting in the most consistent record released under the ELO banner since *Discovery*. On top of that, the production, while clearly not a product of the '70s, avoids all the pitfalls of modern record production, sounding warm, welcoming and right. So, why was *Zoom* largely ignored upon its release in the summer of 2001? Probably because no matter how good it is, there weren't a lot of listeners clamoring for a new ELO album and even some dedicated fans may have wondered if they needed a new ELO record, since for all its strengths, *Zoom* doesn't deliver any knockout punches, even on the level of "Calling American" or "Four Little Diamonds." Without a great lead single (and, even if there had been, there wouldn't have been any place for it to receive airplay), there was nothing to bring the doubters into the fold, so they couldn't discover that *Zoom* was a very good ELO album, certainly more than just an album for the true believers—which is what it wound up being. *—Stephen Thomas Erlewine*

The Electric Prunes

f. 1965, Los Angeles, CA, **db.** 1970
Acid Rock, Garage Rock, Psychedelic
The Electric Prunes were not so much a self-contained group as a front for some talented L.A. songwriters and producers; they by and large played the music on their records, but the vision and inspiration came from elsewhere. Nonetheless, they produced a few great psychedelic garage songs, especially the scintillating "I Had Too Much to Dream Last Night," which mixed distorted guitars and pop hooks with inventive oscillating reverb. Songwriters Annette Tucker and Nancie Mantz wrote much of the Prunes' material, much of which in turn was crafted in the studio by Dave Hassinger, who had engineered some classic Rolling Stones sessions in the mid-'60s. "Too Much to Dream" was a big hit in 1967, and the psychedelized Bo Diddley follow-up "Get Me to the World on Time" was just as good, and also a hit. Nothing else by the group made it big, and their initial pair of albums were quite erratic, although a few scattered tracks were nearly as good as those singles. Their third LP, *Mass in F Minor*, was a quasi-religious concept album of psychedelic versions of prayers; a definitively excessive period piece, its best song ("Kyrie Eleison") was lifted for the *Easy Rider* soundtrack. None of the original Prunes were still in the lineup when the band dissolved, unnoticed, at the end of the '60s. *—Richie Unterberger*

The Electric Prunes (I Had Too Much to Dream) / Apr. 1967 / Collector's Choice Music ✦✦✦✦
The Electric Prunes' self-titled debut was an interesting but wildly erratic psychedelic album. The hits "I Had Too Much to Dream (Last Night)" and "Get Me to the World on Time" led off sides one and two, respectively, and were easily the highlights of a set that boasted continuously imaginative production but inconsistent songwriting. There were some tracks that proved the group were more than two-hit wonders. The group original "Train for Tomorrow," for instance, had the edgy melody and atmosphere typical of several Tucker/Mantz compositions of the time, unexpectedly ending with a jazz guitar coda; the nutty "Sold to the Highest Bidder" boasted a futuristic sped-up guitar that sounded like a berserk balalaika; and "Try Me on for Size" recalled a punked-out Paul Revere & the Raiders. On the downside, there were some positively frightful quasi-psychedelic vaudevillian fairy-tale tunes; it's hard to believe that the same songwriting team who wrote the brilliant "Get Me to the World on Time" was also responsible for "Tunerville Trolley" and "About a Quarter to Nine." Part of the problem was that the group's identity was so beholden to the material and production given them by outside songwriters and producers (the band themselves wrote only two of the album's tracks). There's about two-thirds of a good album here, though, chock-full of intriguing and sometimes wacky reverberation and guitar effects. The Collector's Choice reissue also included both sides of the "Ain't It Hard"/"Little Olive" single as bonus tracks. *—Richie Unterberger*

Underground / Aug. 1967 / Collector's Choice Music ✦✦✦
The Electric Prunes' second album was just as uneven as their debut and lacked the obvious hit material its predecessor had boasted in "I Had Too Much to Dream (Last Night)" and "Get Me to the World on Time." However, at least a more consistent tone and recognizable group identity had asserted itself, as the band wrote half the material. In addition, the airy-fairy vaudevillian misfires that had dotted the first LP were thankfully abolished. Many of the tunes—whether from the band or from their frequent outside contributors Annette Tucker and Nancie Mantz—had floridly inscrutable lyrics ("The Great Banana Hoax," "Children of Rain," "Dr. Do-Good," "Antique Doll") of the kind that some hip critics like to scorn as dated and naïve flower-power relics. At the best points of this album, though, the Prunes conjured a menacing psychedelic pop atmosphere that, in conjunction with their flair for unusual guitar reverb and sundry special effects, sounded fetchingly spooky and seductive. "Hideaway," with its killer bass riff, and the demented "Dr. Do-Good," a crazed children's hour theme gone amok, were standouts in this regard, while "Long Day's Flight" is one of their best psych-garage tracks. On a more straightforward level, "I Happen to Love You" is one of the best obscure Goffin/King covers you're likely to hear, and one of the bluesiest too. The Collector's Choice reissue also includes the bonus tracks "Everybody Knows You're Not in Love" and "You Never Had It Better." *—Richie Unterberger*

Mass in F Minor / Jan. 1968 / Collector's Choice Music ✦✦

● **Long Day's Flight** / 1986 / Demon ✦✦✦✦✦
This 18-track compilation includes the best cuts from their first two albums, as well as a couple of non-LP singles. Pruned down to the best six or seven cuts, it would have made a ferocious EP; some of the material is simply unmemorable, as the band pounds away in a sub-Stones bluesy fuzz style in the mode of the Standells or Chocolate Watch Band. Besides the two hits, there are a few first-rate cuts that meld garage pop to inspired psychedelic production, like "Train for Tomorrow," "Hideaway," "Long Day's Flight," "You Never Had It Better," "Sold to the Highest Bidder" (featuring an organ made to sound like a balalaika), and their cover of Goffin/King's "I Happen to Love You." *—Richie Unterberger*

Lost Dreams / Feb. 13, 2001 / Birdman ✦✦✦✦
Aside from the British anthology *Long Day's Flight*, this is (as of its 2001 release) the only legit Electric Prunes best-of ever issued. For the most part it succeeds in encapsulating the band's finest moments, adding a few rarities that will make it a desirable acquisition for completists. Their best singles are here, including the hits "I Had Too Much to Dream (Last Night)" and "Get Me to the World on Time," of course, as well as "Dr. Do-Good," "Long Day's Flight ('Til Tomorrow)," and their non-LP debut, "Ain't It Hard"/"Little Olive." Outstanding album tracks like "I Happen to Love You," "Sold to the Highest Bidder," and "Train to Tomorrow" are on board as well. The truly awful cuts from their first LP are omitted, although the exclusion of decent items from *Underground*, particularly "Antique Doll" and "Children of Rain," could be questioned. As for the rarities, there's "Shadows," a creepy item from an excruciatingly rare non-LP 1968 promo single; an inconsequential cover of the Hollies' "I've Got a Way of My Own"; the previously unreleased "World of Darkness," an amiably bouncy but inessential number; and their infamous 1967 commercial for Vox wah-wah pedals (unlisted on the sleeve). For those who care about such things, "Dr. Do-Good" and "Long Day's Flight ('Til Tomorrow)" have elongated fadeouts not present on the more commonly circulated versions. The slightly shorter Edsel compilation *Long Day's Flight* is probably a better listen overall (and *does* include "Children of Rain" and "Antique Doll"), but either one makes for a satisfactory overview. Like *Long Day's Flight*, however, this has nothing from their *Mass in F Minor* album, which might be viewed as either a loss or a gain by Electric Prunes fans according to their tastes. As a minor drawback, *Lost Dreams* does not document the original release dates of any of the tracks. *—Richie Unterberger*

Electronic

f. 1989, Manchester, England
Alternative Dance, Alternative Pop/Rock
One of the first supergroups from post-punk Great Britain, Electronic is the on-off project formed by New Order's Bernard Sumner and Johnny Marr, former guitarist of the Smiths. The duo released "Getting Away with It" in December 1989, with both Sumner and Neil Tennant of the Pet Shop Boys on vocals. The single just missed the Top Ten in England, but was the end of Electronic for over two years; Sumner and Tennant returned to their respective groups while Marr played on albums by The The and Billy Bragg.

Electronic's sophomore single "Get the Message" finally appeared in April 1991, and an eponymous debut album followed in June. The non-album single "Disappointed" was released just over a year later. Sumner then returned to New Order to record their sixth album *Republic*, while Marr returned to his sideman role with The The and the Pretenders. The duo reunited to record again—this time with help from former Kraftwerk member Karl Bartos—and released *Raise the Pressure* in July 1996. Newly signed to the Koch label, Electronic issued their third full-length *Twisted Tenderness* four years later. *—John Bush*

● **Electronic** / May 28, 1991 / Warner Brothers ✦✦✦
Electronic's debut album fuses Marr's impeccable riff-oriented songwriting, Sumner's yearning vocals, and mid-tempo post-acid-house beats not quite as hard-hitting as New Order's recent *Technique* LP. The singles "Getting Away With It" (with the Pet Shop Boys' Chris Lowe and Neil Tennant) and "Get the Message" are solid pop songs just as sublimely infectious as the best of New Order. The only misstep is "Feel Every Beat," a lightweight rap featuring none other than Sumner on vocals. *—John Bush*

Raise the Pressure / Jul. 9, 1996 / Warner Brothers ✦✦✦
By the time Electronic's long-delayed second album appeared in 1996, the zeitgeist in Britain had completely shifted from its members' parent bands to a new generation of groups, with Oasis, who shared management with Sumner and Marr's project, standing

forth out of a horde of newer Brit-pop acts. Electronic itself chose not to try and compete, following its own low-key path while working with a variety of guest musicians, including returning singer Denise Johnson. The intriguing surprise came courtesy of an additional keyboardist—none other than Kraftwerk veteran Karl Bartos, who also co-wrote nearly half the release with Sumner and Marr. In the same way that the group's debut promised more than it delivered, though, *Raise the Pressure*—theoretically a dream collaboration between key members of three groundbreaking bands—ends up being more pleasant than necessary. About the only concession to changing times from the band is a more open embrace of gentle pop/rock as opposed to specifically dance-based compositions—if the debut was a little more New Order, many times on *Raise the Pressure* things are a touch more Smiths. But it's more accurate to say it's a bit more Lightning Seeds, frankly—polite, chiming, keyboard-touched but not much more. There's little of the superior takes on rough, modern rock styles both New Order and the Smiths are known for (and certainly no Kraftwerk per se outside of some brisk synth work here and there). What more, specifically dance/synth efforts appear to follow in the lead of the first album's quietly epic romance, such as the charging, acid-meets-strings "Dark Angel" and the slightly gospel-touched "Second Nature," which all sound much better than the more rock-focused songs. A pity there's not more of that on *Raise the Pressure*, but such is life. *—Ned Raggett*

Twisted Tenderness / Apr. 26, 1999 / Parlophone ♦♦♦♦

Twisted Tenderness, Electronic's third album, is certainly a vast improvement from their sophomore effort, 1996's *Raise the Pressure*. It steps back into Marr's talented guitar work: carefree, a bit rollicking at times, but classic Electronic fashion. The obvious rock-laden riffs carry the typical synth-generated backdrops, and Sumner's cheeky lyrics are stylish and breezy. Sumner, who experienced writer's block during the mid-'90s and resorted to Prozac to break his creative blindness, isn't exquisitely sharp or wholly impressive when it comes to being a songwriter. He's simple, and that's what makes Electronic and his work with his original band so alluring. But it's Marr's maddening style that carries things along. Songs like "Late at Night" and "Breakdown" fiercely showcase his spiraling guitar loops, not overshadowing Sumner's storybook visions of love, deceit, passion, and desire. And what makes *Twisted Tenderness* so vibrant is how Electronic placated their lushness for more of a moody demeanor, mysteriously similar to the likes of U2's electric distortion found on 1997's *Pop*. "Make It Happen" is nearly an eight-minute sonic bombast of churning bass lines and swirling techno beats, and Marr's layering is raucous. He is so underrated as a mastered player, but outlets like Electronic and his new band the Healers make it easy for him to fully deliver his great skills. "Haze" showcases Sumner's snarling sauciness, which comes out occasionally, and is darkly wistful. But that's what New Order/Smiths fans are looking for. Electronic doesn't have to prove that they can write decent pop songs. Their musical brashness is expected, and *Twisted Tenderness* is their best yet. Marr and Sumner have already laid down the gravel in their previous musical lives—Electronic is just an extra treat. *—MacKenzie Wilson*

Eleventh Dream Day

f. 1981

Indie Rock, Alternative Pop/Rock

One of the most resilient and criminally underappreciated bands to rise from the Midwestern underground community, the career of the noisy guitar unit Eleventh Dream Day was a textbook study in alt-rock endurance; despite a nightmarish major-label tenure, ill-timed roster changes and commercial indifference, the group persevered, ultimately emerging as elder statesmen of the fluorishing Chicago independent scene of the mid-'90s.

Eleventh Dream Day's origins dated to 1981, when singer/guitarist Rick Rizzo met vocalist/drummer Janet Beveridge Bean at the University of Kentucky. Inspired by punk, Rizzo taught himself to play guitar with the aid of Neil Young's *Zuma* songbook; Young remained the group's major inspiration throughout their career, his incendiary aesthetic informing much of Rizzo's own raw, rootsy style. The couple soon relocated to Chicago, where they teamed with bassist Douglas McCombs and guitarist Baird Figi; after several years of honing their explosive live set, Eleventh Dream Day finally recorded their eponymous debut EP for the Amoeba label in 1987.

The full-length *Prairie School Freakout*, recorded in one six-hour span with a buzzing, dilapidated amplifier, followed in 1988, and brought Eleventh Dream Day to the attention of Atlantic Records, which signed the group for 1989's assured *Beet*. Despite critical acclaim, the record failed to find an audience; *Lived to Tell* followed in 1991 and suffered the same fate as its predecessor. In the middle of a tour to promote the album, Figi abruptly quit, and was replaced by Bodeco's Matthew "Wink" O'Bannon prior to 1993's superb *El Moodio*.

After three commercial strikes, Atlantic unceremoniously dropped the group; following a hiatus which allowed Rizzo and Bean to concentrate on raising their newborn child, Eleventh Dream Day enlisted co-producers Brad Wood and John McEntire (McCombs' partner in the post-rock supergroup Tortoise) for 1994's *Ursa Major*, released on City Slang. After another break—during which time Rizzo returned to college, Bean focused on her country side project Freakwater and O'Bannon exited to return to Bodeco—Eleventh Dream Day signed to the Chicago-based indie Thrill Jockey to record 1997's *Eighth*. *—Jason Ankeny*

Prairie School Freakout / 1988 / Amoeba ♦♦♦

Beet / Nov. 1989 / Collector's Choice Music ♦♦♦

Beet only hints at what was to come, but in retrospect it holds up pretty well. The songs are strong, the playing is energetic, but this is not the place where the epiphanies are. *—John Dougan*

● **Lived to Tell** / Jan. 16, 1991 / Collector's Choice Music ♦♦♦♦♦

Recorded, as the credits state and a photo in the album artwork confirms, "in a tobacco barn on the Niland's farm in Cub Run, Kentucky." Whether that provided the air of ripping, fiery country-goes-to-hell guitar work that permeates *Lived to Tell* may not be known, but clearly the setting didn't hurt the band any. Whatever pressure from Atlantic came down to record something user friendly, Eleventh Dream Day stuck to its guns with fine results on its second major-label effort. Rizzo and Beveridge Bean make a fantastic pair of front singers, strong without being overbearing, on joint harmonies hitting something not far off from the brilliant combination of X's John Doe and Exene Cervenka. "I Could Be Lost" isn't merely a great example of that but one of the album's best songs, leading into a blasting instrumental break and brilliant guitar solo while the band raves it up behind. When Beveridge-Bean takes over lead, as on "You Know What It Is," nothing about the intensity or ability differs—Freakwater's frontwoman had already proved herself times over before that band had issued a note. Figi's electrified lapsteel, as noted, adds fierce explosive power to songs like "Dream of a Sleeping Sheep." Together, he and Rizzo kick out the jams so righteously it almost hurts—the rise of grunge in public eyes may have made people think then of Neil Young, but it's clear he already had two solid disciples. Even slower numbers like "Frozen Mile" crackle with a sharp energy. A few guest performances don't hurt at all—some tenor sax on "There's This Thing" and both calliope and cello on the waltz-time "Daedalus"—but mostly this is Eleventh Dream Day ripping through a set of smart songs with all the wired passion one could ever want. *—Ned Raggett*

El Moodio / Apr. 6, 1993 / Atlantic ♦♦♦♦♦

Beveridge-Bean gets to lead off the album with the wonderful "Makin' Like a Rug," delivering her vocal with side-of-the-mouth twang and sass—it's not quite like a rural Pixies, but the combination of restrained verses and Rizzo-accompanied explosive choruses gives it the same good feeling. Sometimes the lyrics get a bit lost in the din, but close attention proves rewarding—the cryptic, tense scenario of "Murder" details what might be a romantic breakdown, or what might be something more, with sharp detail. Rizzo and O'Bannon both continue the tradition of kick-butt riffs and solos; producer Jim Rondinelli lets them explode forth just the way they should, with enveloping blasts and razor-sharp whines. The McCombs/Beveridge-Bean rhythm section keep up the rear with equally inspired vim and skilled playing, both able to convey restraint (consider the gentle mood-out into lovely zone of "Figure It Out") with just as much passion as raging rush. More calmer moments surface here than on *Lived to Tell*, but far from seeming like a toning down songs like the power poppy "After This Time Has Gone" and the lengthy, beautifully melancholy rumination "Honeyslide" just seem to be a new way for the band's abilities to shine. As for the concluding "Rubberband," the group's love of Neil Young reaches new and impressive heights, which the fantastic solo confirms. Otherwise, as before, all Eleventh Dream Day needs to create their fantastic work are their own considerable talents. *—Ned Raggett*

Ursa Major / 1994 / Atavistic ♦♦♦

Now recording for an indie label, guitarist Wink O'Bannon quit before the recording of *Ursa Major*, and Janet Bean was also consumed with her excellent side band Freakwater, but this record was winner number three. A tad more experimental (and some would argue less accessible, though not me) than earlier records, *Ursa Major* is still loaded with supple, pretty melodies and intense, rampaging guitars. *—John Dougan*

Eighth / Feb. 11, 1997 / Thrill Jockey ♦♦♦♦♦

In their first outing minus guitarist Matthew O'Bannon, Eleventh Dream Day continue to focus their post-punk avant-rock leanings. Although songs like "Two Smart Cookies" and "View From the Rim" rock out, most cuts are the kind of slow to mid-tempo dirgelike-tunes-with-guitar-atmospherics that Sonic Youth does so well. Rick Rizzo steps to the front being the sole guitar player, as well as handling all lead vocal duties, while drummer/wife Janet Beveridge Bean contributes only backing vocals this time out. Rizzo has a feedback laden, howling guitar tone much like Karl Precoda from Dream Syndicate, and he puts it to good use on nearly every track. The instrumental "Motion Sickness" really showcases Rizzo's controlled mayhem guitar style, sounding at times like Sonny Sharrock, but even the slowest cuts have moments where he's letting loose. Good pacing and nice production touches help keep *Eighth* from becoming a bit monotonous. *—Sean Westergaard*

Stalled Parade / Sep. 5, 2000 / Thrill Jockey ♦♦♦♦

After a three-year hiatus, Eleventh Dream Day is back with another solid album, *Stalled Parade*, with a slightly broader sonic palette than its predecessor, *Eighth*. Don't worry, Rick Rizzo's overdriven guitars are still generally set for stun, but you can hear a little more in the way of acoustic guitars throughout the record, and Janet Beveridge Bean steps up to sing lead vocals on a few tracks. One of these, "Valrico74," strongly evokes "Cloak of Frogs" from Freakwater's *End time*, but Rizzo's atmospheric guitar plonking and John McEntire's understated keyboards give it a flavor all its own. The way this slow, haunting track gives way to the out and out Crazy Horse-isms of "In the Style Of...." is indicative of the effective pacing of *Stalled Parade* overall, eliciting a wide range of moods and tempos from track to track. The ethereal backing vocals and dream pop leanings of "Stalled Parade" quickly give way to the insistent post-punk of "Ice Storm," then to the brief abstract experimentalism of "On Ramp," and so on.

A well-sequenced album is one thing, but Eleventh Dream Day really shines when they just rock out. "Interstate" is a case in point, with its catchy boy/girl chorus, and "In the Style Of..." and "Way Too Early" give Rizzo a chance to flex his Neil Young guitar muscles. Bean and bass player Douglas McCombs are a tight rhythm section, and McCombs's bandmate from Tortoise, John McEntire, adds just the right touch on keyboards on several tracks, "Bite the Hand" in particular. With the success of the band members' other projects (Freakwater, Tortoise, Brokeback), and the fact that Eleventh Dream

Day is no longer a touring band, it's a shame logistics conspire to keep them from making albums more often. —*Sean Westergaard*

Elf Power

f. Athens, GA
Indie Pop, Indie Rock, Lo-Fi

The Athens, Georgia-based Elf Power emerged as part of the second wave of bands linked to the Elephant 6 Recording Company collective, a coterie of like-minded, lo-fi indie groups—including the Apples (in stereo), Neutral Milk Hotel, and the Olivia Tremor Control—who shared musicians, ideas and sensibilities. Formed by singers/multi-instrumentalists Andrew Rieger and Laura Carter, Elf Power debuted in 1995 with the self-released *Vainly Clutching at Phantom Limbs*, followed a year later by *The Winter Hawk EP*, which heralded the additions of bassist Bryan Helium and drummer Aaron Wegelin. The excellent *When the Red King Comes* appeared in late 1997, and two years later the group returned with *A Dream in Sound*; also in the spring of 1999, a series of live dates with the Olivia Tremor Control yielded the tour-exclusive EP *Come On. Winter Is Coming* followed a year later. —*Jason Ankeny*

Vainly Clutching at Phantom Limbs / 1995 / Arena Rock Recording ♦♦
Lo-fi production can produce a captivatingly personal album experience for the listener like no other, but when it goes awry, without the gossamer sheen of that same polish to smoothen the sting of rockier terrains, that same listener can be in for one hopelessly excruciating ride. Elf Power's 1995 debut, *Vainly Clutching at Phantom Limbs*, roughly falls somewhere in between these two destinations. On one hand, Andrew Rieger has a definite melodic talent that gives most of the material here an inherent listenability despite its slovenly intent, and regardless of the reigning juvenile weirdness of the lyrics, several of the better songs manage to make lasting first impressions ("Finally Free," "Circular Malevolence," and the title track being the best of these). Furthermore, there is strange, experimental affection surrounding the songs that borders on the mystically surreal, and if nothing else, is intriguing enough in itself to make the album worthwhile; this is especially true on later versions of the disc that include the five songs consisting of the group's *Winterhawk* EP. The problem here is that the songs are so poorly recorded (even more so than most lo-fi projects), they aren't really done any justice by an approach of such defiant trashiness, and Rieger's songwriting talents only serve to make the frequent obstructions of sonic disarray and derangement that much more frustrating. Fortunately, all this slapdash procedure is easily excusable when one takes into consideration the fact that this is merely the debut release of a band who would go on to see their vision bear much greater fruition with their next album, *When the Red King Comes*, so in the end, while everything here does sound like a really cheap home recording, it paints a very interesting early portrait. —*Mathias Sheaks*

When the Red King Comes / Oct. 1997 / Arena Rock/Elephant 6 ♦♦♦♦
As the Elephant 6 catalog continues to expand, it becomes increasingly obvious that many of the label's bands are concerned not merely with creating fresh and exciting music but rather entire mythologies, crafting obscure concept records exploring the intricacies of strange pocket universes. Existing in the musical gray area between Olivia Tremor Control and Neutral Milk Hotel—both of whose members make cameos here—Elf Power's superb *When the Red King Comes* is a heady journey to a psychedelic utopia, a travelogue with such destinations as "The Secret Ocean," "The Separating Fault," and "The Silver Lake." As imagined primarily by singer/songwriter Andrew Rieger, the album is a odyssey "Into the Everlasting Time," and true to its word, it seems to exist outside of any obvious era—the fuzzy, lo-fi production is an Elephant 6 hallmark, but the unique instrumentation (electric horns, pump organs, even Nepalese percussion) and cryptic, stream-of-consciousness wordplay suggest something altogether different; perhaps most telling is *When the Red King Comes* cover, a crazed map suggesting something out of a J.R.R. Tolkien fever dream. —*Jason Ankeny*

● **A Dream in Sound** / May 11, 1999 / Arena Rock Recording ♦♦♦♦
The aptly titled *A Dream in Sound* is Elf Power's creative breakthrough—inventively produced by the great Dave Fridmann, the record is a great leap forward from the previous *When the Red King Comes*, boasting a bright, majestic sheen (the richest to grace an Elephant 6 release to date) that illuminates the striking pop melodies once buried below the group's fuzz-drenched surface. Although song titles like "High Atop the Silver Branches" and "Simon (The Bird With the Candy Bar Head)" serve notice that the Elves' psychedelic tendencies are still in full bloom, there's a new emotional complexity behind the songs as well—Andrew Rieger's high, plaintive vocals lend a strange poignancy to his surreal narratives, and tracks like the lovely "Jane" possess genuine sweetness and warmth. A major addition to the E6 canon, *A Dream in Sound* pushes Elf Power to the label's front lines alongside Olivia Tremor Control and Neutral Milk Hotel—lofty company indeed. —*Jason Ankeny*

The Winter Is Coming / Oct. 17, 2000 / Sugar Free ♦♦♦
The Winter Is Coming continues the darker, more complex sound Elf Power forged on its landmark album *A Dream in Sound*, enriching its brand of tripped-out pop with more emotional depth. Recorded over the course of nine months at the band's home studio, *The Winter Is Coming* seems mellow; however, melancholy and tense undercurrents lay just beneath its surface. Dense, droning songs like "Embrace the Crimson Tide" and "Wings of Light" are some of the best examples of the band's increasingly intricate sound, but "The Sun Is Forever," "Birds in the Backyard," and the title track prove that Elf Power hasn't sacrificed its catchiness for experimentalism's sake. Though the slightly silly bubblegum march "The Great Society"—which almost sounds like an Elephant 6 parody—seems out of place with the rest of the album's tone, the fuzzy-yet-brooding "Skeleton" more than makes up for it. Though it may not be quite as immediate or coherent as *A*

Dream in Sound, The Winter Is Coming marks another step forward for this consistent—and consistently evolving—band. —*Heather Phares*

Missy Misdemeanor Elliott (Melissa Elliott)

b. Portsmouth, VA
Vocals / Alternative Rap, Urban, Hip-Hop

A female jack-of-all-trades in the hip-hop world, Missy Misdemeanor Elliot rode into the rap mainstream by the usual route for female MCs (guesting on every track in sight) but proved to be so much more than a rapper: a prolific songwriter, a great R&B singer, director of her own videos and an astute businesswoman who wrangled an entire sub-label out of her initial Elektra Records deal. She first hooked up with a female R&B group called Sista; though Elliott wrote most of the material for their debut album, it went nowhere and they broke up soon after. Elliott continued to write songs, though, and placed one with former *Cosby Show* sprite Raven-Symone. She also began appearing on several popular singles, like SWV's "Can We," Aaliyah's "If Your Girl Only Knew," and a remix of Gina Thompson's "The Things You Do." Granted her own record deal by 1996, Elliott responded with *Supa Dupa Fly*, which featured much of her own songwriting and production by her friend Timbaland. The album peaked at number three on the album charts, and went platinum soon after its release. The duo teamed up again for 1999's *Da Real World*. —*John Bush*

● **Supa Dupa Fly** / Jul. 15, 1997 / The Gold Mind/EastWest/EEG ♦♦♦♦♦
On her debut album, *Supa Dupa Fly*, Missy "Misdemeanor" Elliott skillfully blends classic soul with modern R&B and street hip-hop rhythms. It's funky and melodic, with strong song sense and startlingly fresh production courtesy of Elliott and her partner, Timbaland. It's a refreshingly ambitious and successful urban R&B debut that reveals the weaknesses of her contemporaries as much as it emphasizes her strengths. —*Leo Stanley*

Da Real World / Jun. 22, 1999 / The Gold Mind, Inc./EastWest ♦♦♦♦
It's really not that difficult to hurdle the sophomore blues provided that you're an excellent songwriter and performer, that you have the same, equally excellent producer behind the scenes who contributed to the first album, and most importantly, that you haven't tampered with the hit-making formula from the first. Thankfully, *Da Real World* is clearly a Missy Elliott album in most respects, with Timbaland's previously trademarked, futuristic-breakbeat production smarts laced throughout. The churchgoing Elliott has often remarked that she wishes she didn't need profanity to get attention, and the album accordingly includes satirical nods to other clichéd notions of hip-hop—the single "She's a Bitch" is the best example, wherein Elliott reappropriates the insult to refer to strong females. She also takes on the cartoonish Eminem for "Bus a Rhyme," a track that turns out to be one of the best on the album. Da Brat and Aaliyah make repeat appearances, and Redman and Outkast's Big Boi also contribute to this excellent follow-up. —*Keith Farley*

Miss E . . . So Addictive / May 15, 2001 / The Gold Mind, Inc./Elektra ♦♦♦♦♦
Sounding more assured of her various strengths than at any time since her startling debut, Missy "Misdemeanor" Elliott broke in several directions for 2001's *Miss E . . . So Addictive*. At the same time, she's a sexed-up rapper demanding respect from men, a loved-up club diva leading the charge of rappers into the brave new world of dance culture, and a sensitive female spreading syrup over a few great ballads. It's a tribute to her incredible songwriting skills and Timbaland's continuing production excellence that she can have it any way she wants it and still come away with a full-length that hangs together brilliantly. She definitely starts out hardcore, with a pair of self-explanatory titles ("Dog in Heat," "One Minute Man") featuring Elliott cooling down on a trio of rappers (Redman, Method Man, Ludacris) and definitely getting the best of them. By "Get Ur Freak On," the lead single, she's changed angles and become a new-millennium diva straddling the worlds of hip-hop and commercial dance with bumping club tracks like "Scream a.k.a. Itch" and "4 My People." But before listeners can reconcile Elliott the club kid, special guest Ginuwine takes the album into love-ballad territory with "Take Away," a half-step ballad with an irresistible plucked-string production from Timbaland. Though *Miss E . . . So Addictive* is undeniably Elliott's affair, Timbaland's production really stretches out and pulls the album together. He's less reliant on his oft-copied trademarks, and more willing to experiment with left-field samples and seemingly odd bridges that always work despite the audio high-wire act. Though it fails to come up with anything to top her big singles hit, "The Rain (Supa Dupa Fly)," *Miss E . . . So Addictive* is her best album so far. —*John Bush*

Joe Ely

b. Feb. 9, 1947, Amarillo, TX
Vocals, Guitar / Americana, Outlaw Country, Country-Rock, Progressive Country

In the '70s, country & western was full of artists referred to as outlaws, mavericks who bucked the stodgy Nashville music establishment by writing their own songs, recording with their road bands, and producing their own records. The genre produced a slew of acts, but Amarillo, TX native Joe Ely epitomized the form. Unlike most of that era's big names, Ely remained a viable artist. He got his start back in the early '70s, working with Butch Hancock and Jimmie Dale Gilmore in a group called the Flatlanders. Their only album didn't go far, and the group broke up. (Rounder reissued the album in 1990.) Around the mid-'70s, Ely formed an eclectic group who was able to swing from Cajun and western to honky tonk stomps and rockabilly; they were signed to MCA in 1977. Ely released an eponymous debut that year, using songs written by ex-Flatlanders Gilmore and Butch Hancock and throwing in some of his own road-worn, oddly poetic originals. The next year brought *Honky Tonk Masquerade*, the cornerstone of Ely's legacy and one of modern country's most ambitious albums. Further albums (especially *Live Shots*, recorded during his European tour with the Clash) brought Ely to the attention of rock fans and netted ecstatic reviews in country and pop magazines (but, mysteriously, produced no hits). MCA dropped Ely in 1983, and he woodshedded until 1987, when the independent Hightone label signed him and released *Lord of the Highway*. Another Hightone album followed before Ely (whose influence was being felt by the new breed of country neo-traditionalists) re-signed with MCA, releasing another live set and *Love and Danger*. *Twistin' in the Wind* followed in 1998, and *Live at Antone's* arrived two years later along with MCA-Nashville's *Best Of* collection. Ely remained an energetic and passionate live performer and an occasionally inspired songwriter. —*John Floyd*

Joe Ely / 1977 / MCA ✦✦✦✦✦
Ely's first album came out while country's outlaw movement was in full swing, but *Joe Ely* took it one better. This is a roots-rocking country album with tunes by Jimmie Dale Gilmore ("Treat Me Like a Saturday Night") and Butch Hancock ("She Never Spoke Spanish to Me," "If You Were a Bluebird") that deserve the near-classic status their cult of fans has bestowed on them. —*Brian Mansfield*

☆ **Honky Tonk Masquerade** / 1978 / MCA ✦✦✦✦✦
Ely's best album, *Honky Tonk Masquerade* contains everything from Texas weepers ("Because of the Wind") to roadhouse rockers ("Fingernails"). Among the best tunes are Jimmie Dale Gilmore's "Tonight I Think I'm Gonna Go Downtown" and Butch Hancock's "West Texas Waltz." Nobody made country records like this in 1978. Come to think of it, they still don't. —*Brian Mansfield*

Down on the Drag / 1979 / MCA ✦✦✦
Simply another set of decent country songs. Ely's momentum was gone: his band, for the first time, sounded like tired and bored pros. —*John Floyd*

Live Shots / 1980 / MCA ✦✦✦✦✦
Ely partakes of the musical diversity of his hometown, Lubbock, TX, freely mixing country, rock, Tex-Mex, and hard honky-tonk music in excellent songs he writes himself or borrows from his friend Butch Hancock. This is a live best-of covering his first three albums, recorded on tour in England. —*William Ruhlmann*

Musta Notta Gotta Lotta / 1981 / MCA ✦✦✦
If you're making a tape of Ely's greatest hits, *Musta Notta Gotta Lotta* is a must—"Dallas" and "Wishin' for You" ensure its necessity. But anyone who has shed tears (and danced them away) to *Honky Tonk Masquerade* will feel cheated by such obvious covers as Roy Brown's "Good Rockin' Tonight" and Buddy Holly's "Rock Me My Baby." —*John Floyd*

Hi-Res / 1984 / MCA ✦✦
Lord of the Highway / 1987 / Hightone ✦✦✦
After a long recording layoff, Ely picked up where he'd left off in 1984 with this typical collection, whose best songs—"Me and Billy the Kid" and "Are You Listenin' Lucky?"—were Ely originals. —*William Ruhlmann*

Dig All Night / 1988 / Hightone ✦✦✦
Dig All Night follows in the direction of *Lord of the Highway*, finding Joe Ely concentrating on hard-kicking roots-rock and rockabilly. The country influences are now just flavoring, not the focal point, and that's not a bad thing, since *Dig All Night* is a lean, mean record that rocks harder than nearly any roots record of its era. —*Thom Owens*

Milkshakes & Malts / 1988 / Sunstorm ✦✦✦
Live at Liberty Lunch / Sep. 1990 / MCA ✦✦✦
This live album was recorded over two days at Liberty Lunch in Austin, TX. Ely's band has evolved from a country band with Tejano roots to a hard-rocking Texas ensemble highlighted by guitarist David Grissom, who later defected to John Cougar Mellencamp. —*Brian Mansfield*

Love & Danger / Sep. 29, 1992 / MCA ✦✦✦✦✦
Ely is stark and restless...His muse still roams the highways in search of whatever, his romance doomed by a twist of fate. He's a more objective observer; a storyteller who captures the tragic side to the well-defined characters of "The Road Goes on Forever" and "Every Night About This Time." Ely conveys much—if not most—of a song's emotion through his inspired electric guitar playing. The string-bending is at high-pressure intensity for "Love Is the Beating of Hearts," then drops deep, sonorous and echoed for "Slow You Down." —*Roch Parisien*

No Bad Talk or Loud Talk 1977-'81 / Apr. 25, 1995 / Edsel ✦✦✦✦✦
Edsel's *No Bad Talk or Loud Talk 1977-'81* is an exhaustive, 18-track collection that culls many highlights from his first five albums, including "Honky Tonk Masquerade," "Fingernails," "Tonight I Think I'm Gonna Go Downtown," "Treat Me Like a Saturday Night," "Maria," "Musta Notta Gotta Lotta," "Suckin' a Big Bottle of Gin," and "She Never Spoke Spanish to Me." While *Honky Tonk Masquerade* and *Live Shots* remain excellent albums in their own right, this is a superb collection, capturing the excitement of Ely's music and offering a definitive introduction to his peak years. —*Stephen Thomas Erlewine*

Letter to Laredo / Aug. 29, 1995 / MCA ✦✦✦✦✦
Flamenco guitarist Teye is the dominant instrumentalist on a Joe Ely album that fits the "unplugged" tag—drums, electric bass, and various, mostly acoustic guitars and occasional accordion and harmonica—and that could be played without complaint in any cantina along the Rio Grande. Ely is joined in his story songs about Southwest life and romantic devotion by Raul Malo, Jimmie Dale Gilmore, and Bruce Springsteen, while Butch Hancock and Tom Russell contribute the strongest material; Hancock's is a sequel, "She Finally Spoke Spanish To Me," and Russell's is the tragic story of a man who bets his future on a cock fight. *Letter To Laredo* is a mood piece with less of the raw energy of many of Ely's albums, but the singer is in his element and his mastery of the form is obvious. —*William Ruhlmann*

Time for Travellin': The Best of Joe Ely, Vol. 2 / Aug. 6, 1996 / Edsel ✦✦✦✦
Time for Travellin': The Best of Joe Ely, Vol. 2 fills the gaps left by Edsel's previous Ely compilation, *No Bad Talk or Loud Talk*, offering 19 tracks from Ely's first four albums that weren't featured on that collection. It's a testament to Ely's talent and the quality of the records that these aren't lesser songs—they're just a little less celebrated. Just a cursory listen to "Tennessee's Not the State I'm In," "Jericho (Your Walls Must Come Tumbling Down)," "I'll Be Your Fool," "She Leaves You Where You Are," "Wishin' For You," and "I Keep Gettin' Paid the Same" reveals that these songs are every bit as good as those on the first volume. In many ways, it makes more sense to acquire the original albums, since the songs that didn't make these collections are also quite good, but if you want to take the compilation route, neither *Time for Travellin'* or *No Bad Talk or Loud Talk* will disappoint. —*Stephen Thomas Erlewine*

Twistin' in the Wind / May 12, 1998 / MCA ✦✦✦✦
Joe Ely, like fellow Texans Billy Joe Shaver, Guy Clark, and Townes Van Zandt, is pure originality. An artist whom other artist seek to emulate, he never disappoints. With this release, Ely continues his wild ride into the heart and soul of a man and the landscape he inhabits. Effective as a songwriter and performer, Joe Ely becomes more potent with each passing year. His diversity buoys him up as he works his way through both the dark and the light. The title cut, "Up on the Ridge," and "You're Workin' for the Man" display his ability to cast a deep shadow upon life's more rugged passages. "Sister Soak the Beans" and "If I Could Teach My Chihuahua to Sing" are light and humourous, reflective of Ely's geography, Texas, and create a balance that too few artists ever find. With "Gulf Coast Blues" and a wonderful honky tonk concerto, "I Will Lose My Life," Ely proves to be a master painter who creates his songs from a vast palette of colors, textures and experiences. —*Jana Pendragon*

Live at Antone's / Jun. 6, 2000 / Rounder ✦✦✦✦
Live at Antone's is Joe Ely's third release mixing his rock, country, folk, and Tex-Mex-fueled live show for an appreciative Texas audience. This retrospective was recorded by the Rounder label January 22 and 23, 1999, and showcases the heartfelt romanticism and storytelling on compositions by Jimmie Dale Gilmore, Tom Russell, Butch Hancock, Robert Earl Keen, Utah Phillips, and Ely. Pedal steel guitarist Lloyd Maines and the accordion of Joel Guzman add extra spice to this already high-energy performance. Favorites like "The Road Goes on Forever," "Me and Billy the Kid," "Dallas," "Road Hawg," and the obligatory Buddy Holly cover "Oh! Boy" are featured on another recommended Joe Ely live set. —*Al Campbell*

★ **The Best of Joe Ely** / Nov. 21, 2000 / MCA ✦✦✦✦✦
For all his critical hosannas, Joe Ely is something of an acquired taste, since his rebellious neo-traditionalist country fluctuates between heartfelt honky tonk evocations, self-conscious modern-day mocking, and material that falls somewhere in between. He did cut a series of albums that were acclaimed and influential, including the rollicking *Live Shots*, one the great country live albums of its time, but MCA Nashville's 2000 *The Best of Joe Ely* is the best introduction to his sound and aesthetic. Spanning his career from his 1977 debut to 1995's *Letter to Laredo*, this touches on every defining moment Ely had, including songs that he initially cut with the Flatlanders. In this setting, his blend of honky tonk, folk, and rock & roll is remarkably effective and consistent, with "She Never Spoke Spanish to Me," "Tonight I Think I'm Gonna Go Downtown," "Musta Notta Gotta Lotta," and "Letter to Laredo" all standing out as progressive/alternative country classics. Given his cult status—the kind of cult where all his recordings are acclaimed equally—this is the best way for outsiders to fall in love with Ely. —*Stephen Thomas Erlewine*

Emerson, Lake & Palmer

f. 1970, Bournemouth, Dorset, England. **db.** Dec. 1978
Album Rock, Prog Rock/Art Rock

Emerson, Lake & Palmer were progressive rock's first supergroup. They succeeded in broadening the audience for progressive rock from hundreds of thousands into tens of millions of listeners, creating a major radio phenomenon as well. Their flamboyance on record and in the studio proved that classical rockers could compete for that arena-scale audience, paving the way for bands like Yes. Upon officially teaming in 1970, keyboardist Keith Emerson (formerly of the Nice) and singer/bassist Greg Lake (ex-King Crimson) auditioned several drummers before they approached Carl Palmer, a former member of the Crazy World of Arthur Brown. The group's self-titled debut album was released in November 1970 and was an instant success. The title track of their second album, 1971's *Tarkus*, was an extended suite that ultimately defined the ELP sound as most people understood it—loud, dense, and bombastic, somewhat gloomy in its lyrical tone, and exultant in its instrumental power. After *Tarkus* hit number one on the English charts and reached the Top Ten in America, a concert featuring the group's adaptation of Mussorgsky's *Pictures at an Exhibition* was recorded for release, and became another major hit. 1972's *Trilogy* found each member taking an equal share of musical responsibility. *Brain Salad Surgery* was released in 1973 on their own record label, Manticore. Their string of successes came to a halt with 1977's *Works*; at the time, each member was feeling constrained by the presence of the others, and the resulting album consisted of three solo sides and a collaborative fourth side. *Works* fared poorly and destroyed ELP's unity, and their main motivation for recording seemed only to be their contractual obligations. Plus, the public's taste was changing—extended suites, conceptual rock albums, and classical-rock fusion seemed hopelessly ponderous and pretentious with the rise of punk rock and disco. ELP split up in 1979, but reunited in 1991 for an album called *Black Moon*, followed by a fairly successful tour. However, Emerson developed of a repetitive stress disorder in one hand which required surgery and restricted the group's ability to record or perform. —*Bruce Eder*

Emerson, Lake & Palmer / 1970 / Rhino ✦✦✦✦✦
Lively, ambitious, almost entirely successful debut album, made up of keyboard-dominated instrumentals ("The Barbarian," "Three Fates") and romantic ballads ("Lucky Man") showcasing all three members' very daunting talents. This album, which reached the Top 20 in America and got to number four in England, showcased the group at its least pretentious and most musicianly—with the exception of a few moments on "Three Fates" and perhaps "Take a Pebble," there isn't much excess, and there is a lot of impressive musicianship here. "Take a Pebble" might have passed for a Moody Blues track of the era, but for the fact that none of the Moodies' keyboardmen could solo like Keith Emerson. Even here, in a relatively balanced collection of material, the album shows the beginnings of a dark, savage, imposingly Gothic edge that had scarcely been seen before in so-called "art-rock," mostly courtesy of Emerson's larger-than-life organ and synthesizer attacks. Greg Lake's beautifully sung, deliberately archaic "Lucky Man" had a brush with success on FM radio, and Carl Palmer became the idol of many thousands of would-be drummers based on this one album (especially for "Three Fates" and "Tank"), but Emerson emerged as the overpowering talent here for much of the public. The reissues of this album on either the Victory or Rhino labels are much superior in sound and graphics to the older Atlantic compact disc. *—Bruce Eder*

Tarkus / Jun. 14, 1971 / Rhino ✦✦✦
This album nearly broke the trio up, but instead its title track delivered the first definitive ELP composition, an apocalyptic piece that gave most listeners their first experience of the full range of the Moog synthesizer. The rest is pretty forgettable, and since the title track also appears on the group's box set, owners of the latter may skip this release. The Mobile Fidelity, Victory, or Rhino versions are all worth owning, however, over the Atlantic version. *—Bruce Eder*

Pictures at an Exhibition / Jan. 1972 / Rhino ✦✦✦
One of the seminal documents of the progressive rock era, a record that made its way into the collections of millions of high school kids who never heard of Mussorgsky and knew nothing of Russia's Nationalist "Five." It does some violence to Mussorgsky, but it is also the most energetic and well-realized live release in the trio's catalog, and it makes a fairly compelling case for adapting classical pieces in this way. At the time, it introduced "classical rock" to millions of listeners, including the classical community, most of whose members regarded this record as something akin to an armed assault. The early-'70s live sound is a little crude by today's standards, but the tightness of the playing (Palmer is especially good) makes up for any sonic inadequacies. Emerson is the dominant musical personality here, but Lake and Palmer get the spotlight enough to prevent it from being a pure keyboard showcase. *—Bruce Eder*

Trilogy / Jul. 6, 1972 / Rhino ✦✦✦✦
The first real group effort once ELP was established, a very romantic-sounding album, with a very restrained use of the synthesizer, which stands in for an orchestra here, rather than setting new boundaries in electronic sound. Mobile Fidelity, Victory, and Rhino each has an excellent version of this disc out. *—Bruce Eder*

Brain Salad Surgery / Nov. 19, 1973 / Rhino ✦✦✦✦✦
The trio's most successful and well-realized album (after their first), and their most ambitious as a group, as well as their loudest, is also their most electronic sounding one. The main focus, thanks to the three-part "Karn Evil 9," is sci-fi rock, approached with a volume and vengeance that stretched the art rock audience's tolerance to its outer limit, but also managed to appeal to the metal audience in ways that little of *Trilogy* did. Indeed, "Karn Evil 9" is the piece and the place where Emerson and his keyboards finally matched in both music and flamboyance the larger-than-life guitar sound of Jimi Hendrix. Pete Sinfield's lyrics, while not up to his best King Crimson-era standard, were better than anything the group had to work with previously, and Lake pulled out all the stops on his heaviest singing voice in handling them, coming off a bit like Peter Gabriel in the process. The songs (except for the throwaway "Benny the Bouncer") are also among their best work—the group's arrangement of Sir Charles Hubert Parry's setting of William Blake's "Jerusalem" manages to be reverent yet rocking, while Emerson's adaptation of Alberto Ginastera's music in "Tocatta" outstrips even "The Barbarian" and "Knife Edge" from the first album as a distinctive and rewarding reinterpretation of a piece of serious music. Lake's "Still... You Turn Me On" is his last great ballad with the group, possessing a melody and arrangement sufficiently pretty to forgive the presence of the rhyming triplet "everyday a little sadder/a little madder/someone get me a ladder." The Rhino CD is to be preferred over all other domestic reissues, as it features an improved remastering, an interview, and packaging with a very cool 3-D cover design. *—Bruce Eder*

Welcome Back, My Friends, to the Show That Never Ends—Ladies and Gentleman / Aug. 19, 1974 / Victory Music ✦✦

Works, Vol. 1 / Mar. 17, 1977 / Rhino ✦✦✦✦
Though no one talked about it at the time of its release, this album reflected a growing split within the group. Originally, the trio's members, tired of sublimating their musical identities within the context of ELP, each intended to do a solo album of his own. Reason prevailed, however, probably aided by the group's awareness that the combined sales of the solo albums issued by the five members of Yes the previous year were a fraction of the sales of Yes' most recent records. The result was this double LP; essentially three solo sides and one group side, it is the most complex and demanding of the group's albums. Keith Emerson's "Piano Concerto" is on the level of a good music-student piece, without much original language. Where Emerson, in conjunction with his conductor and co-orchestrator, John Mayer, succeeds admirably is in writing beautiful virtuoso passages for the piano. Greg Lake's romantic songs mark the final flowering of his work in this vein—and perhaps its going to seed, since "C'Est la Vie," the featured single, says little that "Still... You Turn Me On," from their previous album, didn't say better and shorter. Carl Palmer's side is the most accessible of the three solo sides for casual rock listeners, rocking hard on the classical adaptations and featuring Joe Walsh on lead guitar for one song. The group's two tracks, "Fanfare for the Common Man" and "Pirates," cover a lot of old ground, albeit in ornate and stylish fashion. Having used Copland's "Hoedown" as a concert showstopper for four years, the trio takes "Fanfare" to new heights of indulgence, and it actually works, up to a point—like CCR's extended version of "Heard It Through the Grapevine," this is just a little too much of a good thing. *—Bruce Eder*

Works, Vol. 2 / Nov. 10, 1977 / Rhino ✦✦✦
After the relentlessly dull *Works, Vol. 1*, the highly underrated *Works, Vol. 2* is a godsend. *Works, Vol. 1* took their pompous, bombastic, keyboard-driven prog-rock epics to the limit; had it been stripped of its excesses and coupled with the strongest cuts from *Works, Vol. 2*, the band may have had an enormous success with critics and fans alike. *Volume 2*'s brief, eclectic compositions cover an array of musical styles, combining stimulating originals and handsomely orchestrated renditions of "Maple Leaf Rag," "Honky Tonk Train Blues," and "Show Me the Way to Go Home." Lake peppers the tunes with guitar and bass flourishes, resulting in some of his most challenging instrumental work, and both he and Palmer deliver incredibly strong performances. Meanwhile, Peter Sinfield contributes some of his most mature and accomplished lyrics. Emerson's work is solid and creative, but sounds a bit dated, which is part of why the band couldn't endure. Unlike some ELP albums, *Volume 2*'s brief pieces sustain interest; there really isn't a weak tune in the set. The five instrumentals are highlighted by two short prog-rock tunes, including the jazzy "Bullfrog," which features Lake's brief jazz bass solo and Palmer's fluid, versatile drumming. "Barrelhouse Shake-down" and "Maple Leaf Rag" showcase Emerson's superb ragtime and barrelhouse piano playing, and Palmer's jazz fusion/marching band piece, "Close but Not Touching," features horns and Lake's psychedelic electric guitar lines.

The vocal pieces are equally interesting. "Brain Salad Surgery" is progressive jazz-rock that bears some resemblance to King Crimson's "Cat Food," unsurprising since each features Lake singing Sinfield's lyrics. And, of course, there is the hit "I Believe in Father Christmas," a beautiful Lake/Sinfield composition that highlights Lake's strong voice and vibrant acoustic guitar. *—David Ross Smith*

Love Beach / Nov. 18, 1978 / Rhino ✦

In Concert / Oct. 1979 / Atlantic ✦

The Best of Emerson, Lake & Palmer [Atlantic] / Nov. 1980 / Atlantic ✦✦

Black Moon / Jun. 27, 1992 / Rhino ✦✦

Live at the Royal Albert Hall / Oct. 1992 / Victory ✦✦✦✦
Known for their on-stage energy and full force musical prowess, *Live at the Royal Albert Hall* is the farthest from disappointment a live album can get. Each member of ELP exhibits his individual talents on this astonishing audio spectacle that doesn't let up at any point. Spearheading the 11 songs on the album that runs almost 70 minutes is keyboardist Keith Emerson, whose earsplitting synthesizer rumbles and squeals with devastating vigor. His playing is loose and freewheeling, characterizing his devil-may-care style, and bursting with emotion. Equally forceful is Carl Palmer behind the drums, especially on "Lucky Man" and "Karn Evil No. 9" where he showcases both his subtle mechanics and his frantic arm swirling. On guitar, Greg Lake fills in with some stellar bass work, whose impact can be felt even above the grandiose of the other two. The songs that work best live from ELP are all included, amassing all the ardor and extravagance surrounding this threesome. In front of their home audience in England, they really steal the show with a nine-minute outpouring of "Tarkus," as the combination of all their talents are fused together in instrumental wonderment. Even better is the grand finale, a 14-minute medley of "Fanfare for the Common Man," "America," and "Rondo." A truly volcanic display of keyboard driving from Keith Emerson sends this intense montage into a frenzy, ending the album on a fierce high. *Live at the Royal Albert Hall* has the grandfathers of progressive rock sounding like sonically intoxicated teenagers. *—Mike DeGagne*

Works Live / Nov. 2, 1993 / Victory Music ✦✦

The Return of the Manticore / Nov. 16, 1993 / Rhino ✦✦✦✦✦
It's hard not to mention progressive rock without bringing up Emerson, Lake & Palmer. Ever since their first major live gig at The Isle of Wight Festival in 1970, they've been a staple in symphonic rock history. *The Return of the Manticore* is a beautifully packaged four-disc set that gathers essential tracks, covering ELP's best albums and offering up some re-recorded favorites as well. The first disc begins with an alternate version of 1986's "Touch and Go" that emphasizes Carl Palmer's presence. The disc also includes a cover of "Hang on to a Dream," originally by Keith Emerson's former band The Nice, and King Crimson's *pièce de résistance* "21st Century Schizoid Man." A new recording of the Crazy World of Arthur Brown's "Fire" rounds out Disc 1's novelties. The remaining discs overflow with ELP's greatest creations, pleasing the most avid fan and saturating the curious beginner. A new, extended recording of "Pictures at an Exhibition" is a must-hear, accompanied by a choir and recorded in full surround sound. A stunning unreleased version of "Rondo" and a bizarrely entertaining adaptation of "Bo Diddley" are also highlights. The improved, remastered sound stands out on "Karn Evil 9," "Fanfare for the Common Man," and "Knife Edge." "Prelude And Fugue," previously unreleased, finds Emerson molesting the piano, releasing all its unbridled energy. An excellent collection, *Return of the Manticore* bridges ELP's symphonic work with their classical work, and unites their dazzling electronic pieces with their ragtime and blues efforts. The band's essence, as well as each member's individual talents, stands out on every song, defining the sole purpose of a box set. *—Mike DeGagne*

● **The Best of Emerson, Lake & Palmer [Rhino]** / 1994 / Rhino ✦✦✦✦
Serves up a more digestible portion than the box set, focusing mostly on key early

material. Fourteen tracks isn't skimpy in the ELP context; "Tarkus" is represented, for instance, in all of its 20-minute glory. The set also includes the original single version of "I Believe in Father Christmas." *—Roch Parisien*

The Very Best of Emerson, Lake & Palmer / Oct. 17, 2000 / Rhino ♦♦♦
It may seem that it's impossible to summarize an album act like ELP on a single-disc, 13-track collection like Rhino's *The Very Best of Emerson, Lake & Palmer*, but this disc does summarize the prog-rock trio's strengths very well. Yes, it might not have the sweep of one of their proper studio albums, or the consistency of tone, but for the casual fan, this is all that they need since it contains "Lucky Man," "Fanfare for the Common Man," and "Still... You Turn Me On," along with several key album tracks, plus three live selections at the end of the record. This contains no rarities, so diehards will probably not need it (even if the liner notes are quite good), but since it condenses much of the band's noteworthy moments to one disc, casual fans will likely find this a collection to embrace. *—Stephen Thomas Erlewine*

EMF

f. Oct. 1989, Forest of Dean, England
Alternative Dance, Club/Dance, Euro-Dance, Dance-Pop
Best remembered for the international smash "Unbelievable," the British dance-rock quintet EMF formed in Cinderford, England in October 1989. All five members—vocalist James Atkin, guitarist Ian Dench, keyboardist Derry Brownson, bassist Zachary Foley, and drummer Mark Decloedt—were veterans of the local music scene before founding EMF, whose name supposedly stood for "Epsom Mad Funkers" (although it was widely speculated that the initials instead represented "Ecstasy Mind Fuckers"). Within two months of formation, the group played its first gig; after unearthing a Casio sampler and sequencer in a local thrift shop, a light techno element was added to their rock-oriented sound.

By the end of 1990, EMF's infectious debut single "Unbelievable" had conquered the U.K. charts; it hit number one in the U.S. the following year. The 1991 album *Schubert Dip* was also successful, spawning another hit single in "Lies." (The LP also garnered considerable press when Yoko Ono objected to the group's use of a voice sample of Mark David Chapman, the murderer of John Lennon; the offending sound bite was later removed from future pressings.) In 1992, EMF returned with the EP *Unexplained* and the full-length effort *Stigma*; both releases performed badly on the charts, however, and the band effectively vanished from sight until 1995's *Cha Cha Cha*. *—Jason Ankeny*

Schubert Dip / 1991 / EMI America ♦♦♦
"Unbelievable" was so insanely infectious that many who were introduced to EMF by that single went out and purchased *Schubert Dip* in the hope that the rest of the album would be equally strong. But unfortunately, most of the CD fell short of "Unbelievable"'s excellence. This isn't to say that *Schubert Dip* is a bad album—far from it, in fact. But weighed against "Unbelievable"'s dizzying infectiousness, distinctly British dance/rock/pop offerings like "Girl of an Age," "Children," and the follow-up single "Lies" are fairly catchy, but nonetheless mildly disappointing. The only song that comes close to packing the punch of "Unbelievable" is the intoxicating "Long Summer Days." For the most part, *Schubert Dip* is a prime example of an album that is simply decent when it should have been excellent. *—Alex Henderson*

Stigma / 1992 / Capitol ♦♦♦
To everyone's surprise, EMF proved that they had the musical capability to be more than a one-hit wonder with their second album, *Stigma*. To no one's surprise, the record-buying public treated them as a one-hit wonder and the record bombed. Anyone who liked "Unbelievable" that cares to take a listen to *Stigma* will find much more than rewrites of their hit single; the band shows some skill and variety. *—Stephen Thomas Erlewine*

Back 2 Back Hits / 1998 / EMI-Capitol Special Markets ♦♦♦♦
This is one of the rare instances where the *Back 2 Back Hits* concept fulfills its potential. Not only did EMF and Jesus Jones explore a watered-down Madchester and dance-pop hybrid, but they both only had one true hit single, followed by a couple of near-hits that made a slight impression on the charts and in the pre-Nirvana alt-rock consciousness. They're all here—EMF's "Unbelievable," "I Believe," "Children," and "Lies," Jesus Jones' "Right Here, Right Now," "Real Real, Real," "International Bright Young Thing," and "The Devil You Know." Since neither group had a real deep catalog, this is as close to as definitive collection for either EMF or Jesus Jones as most listeners will need. And the pairing actually results in a more consistently entertaining collection than a full-fledged hits compilation from either artist. *—Stephen Thomas Erlewine*

● **The Best of EMF: Epsom Mad Funkers** / Jul. 3, 2001 / EMI ♦♦♦♦
Regrettably, England's EMF had been seared with the curse of premature victory, sometimes belting out "Unbelievable" two or three times per show, and many assumed they'd be forever damned to run from their own success until the day they took off their long shorts and cut their hair. But *Epsom Mad Funkers*, an emphatic and touching tribute with new songs and a second disc of remixes, proves that what saved them from disaster was an anarchic instinct for just how to nail together the flotsam and jetsam of late-20th century chart music without sounding totally contrived. One moment you could get "Girl of an Age," the great, cherubic baggy anthem that never was, the next you'd be swimming about in megalomaniac, brain-rammed funk ("Perfect Day," "They're Here") or even a sort of facetious revelry, such as the live classic "EMF," which would rather stack up stylistic Lego blocks and smash them to pieces than try to mimic the picture on the box. For better or worse, nobody else sounded like this. They weren't the Happy Mondays, they weren't Take That—in the end perhaps the only band in history to sound like both. *—Dean Carlson*

Eminem (Marshall Mathers)

b. Kansas City, MO
Vocals / Hardcore Rap, Hip-Hop
A protege of Dr. Dre, rapper Eminem was born Marshall Mathers in St. Joseph, MO (near Kansas City), spending the better part of his impoverished childhood shuttling back and forth between his hometown and the city of Detroit. Initially attracted to rap as a teen, Eminem began performing at age 14, later earning notoriety as a member of the Motor City duo Soul Intent. He made his solo debut in 1996 with the independent release *Infinite*, soon followed by the *Slim Shady* EP; both records made a huge splash in the hip-hop underground, earning notice not only for Eminem's exaggerated, nasal-voiced rapping style but also for his skin color, with many quarters dubbing him the music's next "great white hope." According to legend, Dr. Dre discovered his demo tape on the floor of Interscope label chief Jimmy Iovine's garage, although it was not until Eminem took second place in the freestyle category at 1997's Rap Olympics MC battle in Los Angeles that Dre agreed to sign him. The best-selling *Slim Shady LP* followed in early 1999, scoring a massive hit with the single and video "My Name Is," plus a popular follow-up in "Guilty Conscience"; over the next year, the album went triple platinum. With such wide exposure, controversy ensued over the album's content, with some harshly criticizing its cartoonish, graphic violence; others praised its edginess and surreal humor, as well as Eminem's own undeniable lyrical skills and Dre's inventive production. In between albums, Eminem appeared on Dre's *Dr. Dre 2001*, with his contributions providing some of the record's liveliest moments. *The Marshall Mathers LP* appeared in the summer of 2000, moving close to two million copies in its first week of release on its way to becoming the fastest-selling rap album of all time. *—Jason Ankeny*

The Slim Shady LP / Feb. 23, 1999 / Interscope ♦♦♦♦♦
In all the press surrounding the release of Eminem's debut *The Slim Shady LP*, journalists, critics, and Em himself went out of the way to clarify that the songs on the record were not autobiographical—he was merely playing a corrupt character called Slim Shady. Such a practice is common in hip-hop, but it seems disingenuous coming from the mouth of Marshall Mathers, a white-trash kid from the streets of Detroit whose fictional creation is a white-trash kid from the streets of Detroit. The line between fact and fiction seems a little blurry, and it would be more so if Eminem's lyrics weren't ridiculous, violent fantasies. That doesn't quite excuse the endless dreams of rape, murder, and dope that provide the core of *The Slim Shady LP*, but the cartoonish exaggerations do explain why certain journalists were eager to embrace the record as an inspired, surrealistic parody of Jerry Springer-fueled pop culture and gangsta rap. It also helps that Eminem was endorsed by Dr. Dre, not only because he provides a strong, Beasties-meets-Wu-meets-Dr. Octagon musical backdrop, but because his presence is almost code, proving that Mathers is not a racist. Eminem is clearly a gifted rapper, twisting and turning his words with ease, knowing how to accentuate the strengths of the music with the rhythm of his rhymes. Still, that doesn't erase the uneasiness that his grotesque caricatures and stories leave behind. For many discerning listeners—especially the countless teens who have been raised on a diet of *WWF*, *Faces of Death*, slasher films, porn, and No Limit records—it's clear that this is all intended as a joke. That may be, but it's hard to escape the impression that if a black artist had released *The Slim Shady LP*, it wouldn't have been embraced as satire. *—Stephen Thomas Erlewine*

● **The Marshall Mathers LP** / May 23, 2000 / Interscope ♦♦♦♦♦
It's hard to know what to make of Eminem, even if you know that half of what he says is sincere and half is a put-on; the trick is realizing that there's truth in the joke, and vice versa. Many dismissed his considerable skills as a rapper and social satirist because the vulgarity and gross-out humor on *The Slim Shady LP* were too detailed for some to believe that it was anything *but* real. To Eminem's credit, he decided to exploit that confusion on his masterful second record, *The Marshall Mathers LP*. Eminem is all about blurring the distinction between reality and fiction, humor and horror, satire and documentary, so it makes perfect sense that *The Marshall Mathers LP* is no more or no less "real" than *The Slim Shady LP*. It is, however, a fairly brilliant expansion of his debut, turning his spare, menacing hip-hop into a hyper-surreal, wittily disturbing thrill ride. It's both funnier and darker than his debut, and Eminem's writing is so sharp and clever that the jokes cut as deeply as the explorations of his ruptured psyche. The production is nearly as evocative as the raps, with liquid bass lines, stuttering rhythms, slight sound effects, and spacious soundscapes. There may not be overpowering hooks on every track, but the album works as a whole, always drawing the listener in. But, once you're in, Eminem doesn't care if you understand exactly where he's at, and he doesn't offer any apologies if you can't sort the fact from the fiction. As an artist, he's supposed to create his own world, and with this terrific second effort, he certainly has. It may be a world that is as infuriating as it is intriguing, but it is without question his own, which is far more than most of his peers are able to accomplish at the dawn of a new millennium. *—Stephen Thomas Erlewine*

The Emotions

f. 1968, Chicago, IL, **db.** 1986
Smooth Soul, Quiet Storm, Disco, Soul
A trio of sisters with a strong gospel base, the Emotions were one of the leading female R&B acts of the '70s. Lead singer Sheila Hutchinson and her sisters Wanda and Jeanette were only teenagers when they crashed the soul charts in 1969 with the engaging "So I Can Love You," but they sang gospel as children and enjoyed secular fame locally before signing with Memphis-based Volt and working with producers Isaac Hayes and David Porter. When Stax folded in 1975, the group hooked up with Maurice White of Earth, Wind & Fire, an association that led to the number one pop/R&B hit "Best of My Love"

in 1977. Two years after, White and the Emotions collaborated on "Boogie Wonderland," which was both a number two R&B and number six pop hit. They issued three more albums on White's ARC label from 1979 to 1981, but were unable to duplicate their earlier success. *—Bill Dahl and Ron Wynn*

• **Best of My Love: The Best of the Emotions** / Mar. 12, 1996 / Columbia/Legacy ♦♦♦♦♦
This 16-track, 69-minute disc surveys the Emotions' five-year, five-album stay on Columbia Records (and the custom label ARC), which was the group's most successful period, featuring the gold number one hit "Best of My Love" and the gold Top Ten hit "Boogie Wonderland" (on which the Emotions backed their mentors, Earth, Wind & Fire), both of which are heard here, along with four other songs that saw action on the pop charts. Surprisingly, the Emotions' five singles that only made the R&B charts are excluded in favor of album tracks. Unlike their earlier period at Stax, at Columbia the Emotions essentially were an adjunct to EWF and its leader, Maurice White, and since EWF featured tenor and falsetto vocals, the similarity was often heightened, especially on "Boogie Wonderland." Nevertheless, the sisters sang well over the horns and disco rhythms that characterized the pop/R&B music of the period. *—William Ruhlmann*

So I Can Love You/Untouched / Mar. 19, 1996 / Stax ♦♦♦♦♦
Combining their first two albums onto one CD, this is the best compilation of the group's Stax material, offering polished sweet soul with a gospel tinge. *—Richie Unterberger*

Love Songs / Apr. 6, 1999 / Columbia/Legacy ♦♦♦♦
A fine companion piece to the earlier *The Best of My Love: The Best of the Emotions*, this 13-track compilation focuses on the trio's most affecting songs of love, not only of the romantic variety but the spiritual as well. The majority of the songs are drawn from the group's mid-1970s efforts *Flowers* and *Rejoice*; the former, produced by Maurice White and the great Charles Stepney, remains the Emotions' most personal and accomplished work, a gorgeously arranged set that showcases both their solo and harmony vocals to beautifully ethereal effect. *—Jason Ankeny*

En Vogue

f. Jul. 18, 1988
New Jack Swing, Club/Dance, Urban
The female vocal quartet En Vogue was conceived and put together by the production team of Denzil Foster and Thomas McElroy, both former members of Club Nouveau. Foster and McElroy wanted a vocal group who could exude sultriness and intelligence in addition to vocal proficiency, and as producers, they wanted material that would fuse R&B and girl-group traditions with hip-hop and new jack swing rhythms. The two held auditions and settled on a membership of former Miss Black California Cindy Herron, Maxine Jones, Dawn Robinson, and Terry Ellis. The producers crafted an image of them as stylish, sophisticated, and sexy. En Vogue's debut album, *Born to Sing*, appeared in 1990 and launched the pop crossover smash "Hold On," which peaked at number two and helped the album go platinum. When En Vogue returned in 1992 with *Funky Divas*, critical and commercial response was overwhelming. The album's wide array of styles, from pop, rock, and R&B to rap, rock, and reggae, were lauded in print; the first three singles—"My Lovin' (You're Never Gonna Get It)," "Giving Him Something He Can Feel" (both covers of songs written by Curtis Mayfield), and "Free Your Mind"—reached the Top Ten, and the album went multiplatinum. As En Vogue was recording its third album, Dawn Robinson left the group. *—Steve Huey*

Born to Sing / 1990 / Atlantic ♦♦♦♦
A youthful unit with classic girl-group chops. *—Ron Wynn*

Funky Divas / Sep. 1, 1992 / East West ♦♦♦♦♦
En Vogue are incredible singers, which is what makes *Funky Divas* a delight. Naturally, the singles are the high points on the album, but the rest of the album is hardly filler—it proves that En Vogue possess great talent. *—Stephen Thomas Erlewine*

Runaway Love / Sep. 21, 1993 / East West ♦♦

EV3 / Jun. 17, 1997 / Elektra/Asylum ♦♦♦

• **Best of En Vogue** / Jun. 1, 1999 / Elektra ♦♦♦♦♦
En Vogue did make some fine albums, but they always shone on singles. As a matter of fact, the best of their hits—"My Lovin' (You're Never Gonna Get It)," "Whatta Man," "Runaway Love," "Free Your Mind," "Hold On," "Don't Let Go (Love)"—were among the very best singles of the '90s, regardless of genre. That's why *The Best of En Vogue* is such a welcome addition to their catalog. Serious and casual fans alike will find this 14-track collection a captivating listen, since there's a certain intoxicating thrill in hearing each great single flow into the next. It can be argued that the high quality of the material makes this En Vogue's best record, but at the very least, *The Best of En Vogue* is a dynamite, definitive compilation. *—Stephen Thomas Erlewine*

Masterpiece Theatre / May 23, 2000 / Elektra/Asylum ♦♦♦♦
Whether it was caused by Dawn Robinson's absence or the questionable manipulations of their production team, En Vogue's first release as a trio, *EV3*, was a disappointment. *Masterpiece Theatre*, their second album since Robinson's departure, shows the group in much finer form. The silky-smooth harmonies are still there, combined with forceful solos and sassy and intelligent lyrics. "Love U Crazay" and "Those Dogs" both explore the liabilities of love in an aggressively funny way, set to famous classical music melodies, while still keeping funky R&B flavors. More traditional love songs pepper the rest of the album, but throughout, *Masterpiece Theatre* manages to accomplish what few albums do—being clever and classy at the same time. *—Stacia Proefrock*

• **Very Best of En Vogue** / Aug. 21, 2001 / Rhino ♦♦♦♦
En Vogue may not have been as visionary as TLC, but they were still one of the best female urban groups of the '90s, which is why their *Very Best* collection works so well. Album by album, they delivered terrific singles, from the swaggering "My Lovin' (You're Never Gonna Get It)" and "Free Your Mind" to the yearning "Don't Let Go (Love)" and "Hold On," plus such wonderful duets as "Whatta Man," where they team with Salt-N-Pepa to deliver a songs so sexy it hurts (but, as John Mellencamp says, it hurts so good). All these are here on this 16-track collection, along with several other singles that didn't climb as high on the charts, plus album tracks, and, well, filler, like a remix of "Hold On." This collection gets the nod over 1999's *Best Of* because it has a sharper selection of songs that really make a good case for their gifts. It may have benefited from fewer songs, since it would be a better listen if it was nothing but their ten best songs, but it still offers the best encapsulation of their talents imaginable. *—Stephen Thomas Erlewine*

England Dan & John Ford Coley

f. 1970, Austin, TX, **db.** 1981
Pop/Rock, Soft Rock, Singer/Songwriter, Country-Rock
The 1970s produced relatively little popular music displaying elegance and unassuming charm—often identified by pop historians as the "me" decade, it was an era of tremendous self-indulgence, in music and everywhere else, marked most strikingly by open, almost frenzied sexual exploration. Running almost counter to these currents were a handful of pop/rock acts of the period that managed to make some headway against the twin assaults of disco and punk on the musical consciousness, and got listeners to slow down and appreciate life. England Dan & John Ford Coley were one of the better such acts. Although considered a mid-'70s phenomenon, and often misidentified in peoples' memories as a one-hit act—they actually charted six Top 40 pop singles, four of them Top Ten, in just four years—their history actually goes back a decade prior to their first and biggest hit, "I'd Really Love to See You Tonight." Even if their biggest hits were authored by other composers, England Dan & John Ford Coley had a knack for capturing an elusive yet reassuring component of life in the 1970s. If one was in college or just out of it in the mid-'70s, their music seemed to say that life (and love) were these wonderful components of existence worth exploring and experiencing, slowly and not frantically—it sang of an innocence in the air, before the Iran hostages, AIDS, the schisms of the Reagan era, and the open cultural warfare of the 1980s. *—Bruce Eder*

• **The Very Best of England Dan & John Ford Coley** / Nov. 19, 1996 / Rhino ♦♦♦♦♦
Sixteen songs by the soft rock duo, cut between March of 1976 and early 1980, that sum up most of their best work. It's unfortunate that the producers couldn't have salvaged one or two cuts from their A&M years, just to delineate the development of their sound, but limited to 16 songs that might not have been possible. This is a handy volume, with excellent sound and ample annotation and session information, which tells the listener a lot about the duo that is often overlooked. For starters, they took care of their own—their one-time '60s-era partner Shane Keister played keyboards on the *Nights Are Forever* album. And Jim Seals accompanied them on acoustic guitar, with Janie Fricke appearing on backing vocals, on the same album. The team were never too far from country music, even when they were topping the pop and adult contemporary charts, but their genius (and that of producer Kyle Lehning) lay in applying the most compatible country players to the most melodic attributes of pop/rock. The music is as smooth and virtuosic as the best country-rock, comparable to the work of Firefall but also more personal. *—Bruce Eder*

England's Glory

f. 1973, **db.** 1974
Proto-Punk, Hard Rock, Rock & Roll
Several years before Peter Perrett came to prominence in the new wave band the Only Ones, he was doing his best to imitate Lou Reed in an outfit called England's Glory. The group—dominated by Perrett's vocals and songs and including future Squeeze bassist Harry Kakoulli—cut a bunch of demos in early 1973, but never got anywhere on record or as a performing act. In the late '80s, long after the Only Ones had disbanded, many of these demos finally saw the light of day on an archival reissue. *—Richie Unterberger*

• **The Legendary Lost Album** / 1994 / Anagram ♦♦♦♦
This CD includes all ten of the demos on the *Legendary Lost Recordings* album, and adds three songs from somewhat later that feature ex-Pretty Things guitarist Gordon Edwards and some session players. It retains Pete Makowski's *Legendary Lost Recordings* liner notes, but adds additional notes by England's Glory drummer Jon Newey. This material marks Perrett as the most obsessed, and accurate, Lou Reed imitator ever captured on tape. No doubt the result of endless hours spent kneeling at Reed's 1972 *Transformer* album as it was spinning round the turntable, Perrett didn't miss a trick in emulating his hero of the moment. Tuneful power chords, sluggish keyboards, vulnerable-to-the-point-of-shaking love songs, and tossed-off, sing-speak vocals—it's all here, such an uncanny imitation that it could easily fool unwary listeners into believing they've stumbled on a stash of early-'70s Reed outtakes. No, it's not original, but it is pretty good—not as good as *Berlin*, but certainly better than some of *Transformer*, if not up to that album's best songs. Imagine Reed's 1972-1973 work without the orchestration or anonymous session musicians, and you get the picture. Perrett isn't as good a singer or as direct a lyricist as Reed. But looking past the obvious imitation, Reed fans could do worse than check this out, and Only Ones fans will find this a fascinating glimpse into Perrett's beginnings. The three new cuts are consistent with the quality of the ten previously circulated demos, and are perhaps a tad more polished in production; none of the songs were included in different versions on *Legendary Lost Recordings*. *—Richie Unterberger*

The English Beat

f. 1978, Birmingham, England, **db.** 1983
College Rock, Ska Revival, New Wave
One of the earliest and most important ska-revivalist groups, Birmingham's the Beat

formed in 1978 (the band had to change their name to the English Beat in the U.S. to avoid confusion with Paul Collins' band of the same name). The multiracial band carved a distinct sound through the use of alternating lead vocals by guitarist Dave Wakeling and punk-toaster/rapper Ranking Roger, while the addition of 50-year-old saxophonist Saxa, who originally played with Prince Buster and Desmond Dekker, gave the band credibility and fleshed out its sound. Signing to 2-Tone, they released the hit single "Tears of a Clown," a wonderful version of the Smokey Robinson classic. In 1980, the band decided to form their own 2-Tone inspired label, Go-Feet. A string of hit singles followed in the U.K., including "Mirror in the Bathroom." Their debut LP, *I Just Can't Stop It*, combined the early hits with other pop/ska-oriented material. "Stand Down Margaret," with its anti-Thatcher stance, found the band moving in a more political direction. Musically, the Beat slowed down the tempo for a more traditional reggae sound showcased on 1981's *Wha'p-pen*. Featuring a more pop-oriented approach, 1982's *Special Beat Service* helped the band increase its U.S. fan base through MTV exposure of "Save It for Later" and "I Confess," but the band members decided to call it quits later that same year. Wakeling and Ranking Roger went on to form General Public, and guitarist Andy Cox and bassist Dave Steel formed Fine Young Cannibals. —*Chris Woodstra*

☆ **I Just Can't Stop It** / Oct. 1980 / Sire ✦✦✦✦✦
The Beat's debut is a true landmark of the period, perfectly blending intense politics with a playful, yet driving dance beat. While the sound could be mimicked by other revivalists, the top-notch songwriting represented on this album is what set them apart. *I Just Can't Stop It* plays like a Greatest Hits album (most of their hits are found here) and still holds up today. —*Chris Woodstra*

Wha'ppen? / Jun. 1981 / Sire ✦✦✦
After the nearly perfect debut, the Beat seem somewhat directionless on *Wha'ppen?* No longer instantly danceable, the tunes have slowed to sub-Reggae tempo with more political content (though less focused this time around). The two unmemorable singles, "Drowning" and "Doors of Your Heart," failed to make an impact in the charts and only "Dreamhome in N.Z." leaves any lasting impression. —*Chris Woodstra*

Special Beat Service / 1982 / Sire ✦✦✦✦✦
The final Beat album focuses less on politics and more on the subject of personal relationships. Their most polished effort, the band leaves behind their early ska influences in favor of jangly pop that, at times, delves into African and Latin rhythms. Includes the flawless singles "Save It for Later" and "I Confess." —*Chris Woodstra*

● **What Is Beat?** / 1983 / IRS ✦✦✦✦
Little surprise that the Beat (or English Beat, depending on what country the band found itself in) quickly achieved a cult status that has yet to die. A perfect blend of Madness' warm, winning spin on ska and the early Specials' tenser, darker sound, the septet created pop/rock/ska fusions that were instantly memorable and rewarded repeated listens. This compilation showcases many of the band's strongest points, including its two biggest American hits in the incipient alternative scene. "Mirror in the Bathroom" is a crisp, to-the-point picture of self-doubt with great, unnerving sax on the breaks, while "Save It for Later" remains one of the few pop songs about holding off on sex instead of taking the plunge. The latter appears in its fine 12" remix version, one of several rarities making *What is Beat?* of interest to hardcore fans. Most are U.K.-only singles that never appeared on any of the group's three albums, including the almost sprightly "What's Your Best Thing" and "Too Nice to Talk To"'s just-dark-enough nervous dance. Two other remixes turn up: the cover of "Can't Get Used to Losing You" moves with moody, string-touched atmosphere, while noted early-'80s dance producer John "Jellybean" Benitez does a salsa-tinged revamp of "I Confess." More familiar cuts include the captivating remake of Smokey Robinson and the Miracles' "Tears of a Clown," the shuddering "Twist and Crawl," and "Doors of Your Heart," which features Ranking Roger's toasting skills quite nicely. The album wraps up with a fiery live medley of "Get a Job" and "Stand Down Margaret," recorded in Boston in late 1982, a bonus that captures the band at a definite highpoint. —*Ned Raggett*

B.P.M.: The Very Best of the English Beat / Nov. 1995 / Arista ✦✦✦✦✦
B.P.M.... the Very Best of the Beat nearly duplicates the original *What is Beat?* collection—covering all of the band's hit singles. Initial runs of the album came with an additional disc of remixes and dub versions making it a nice, though not necessary, addition for fans and completists. —*Chris Woodstra*

Enigma

f. 1990, Ibiza, Spain
Club/Dance, Ethnic Fusion
With their 1991 hit "Sadeness," Enigma brought the new age fascination with Gregorian chants and old-world culture to the clubs; the resulting single was both unique and irresistible. The rest of the album followed that pattern successfully, although without quite matching the stunning success of the hit single. On their second album, 1994's *Cross of Changes*, some of the old-world elements remained, but the new age angle came to the forefront in a set of slick, radio-friendly dance-pop. *Enigma 3: Le Roi Est Mort, Vive le Roi* followed in 1996. A side project, Trance Atlantic Airwaves, issued *The Energy of Sound* in 1998. The fourth Enigma record, *The Screen Behind the Mirror*, followed in early 2000. —*Stephen Thomas Erlewine*

● **MCMXC A.D.** / 1990 / Charisma ✦✦✦
It's a scam, sure. But like the best of scams, it also succeeds. Cretu's attempt at fusing everything from easy listening sex music and hip-hop rhythms to centuries-old Gregorian chants couldn't have been more designed to tweak the nose of high art, a joyously crass stab straight at a mainstream, do not pass go, do not collect 200 dollars. The result is something that shouldn't exist, but in its own way results in as much of a cultural

scramble and explosion as anything Public Enemy were doing around the same time, crossing over the Eurodisco and new age spheres with style. Credit Cretu for an open ear for whatever works, which is precisely why "Sadeness," the first part of a longer track called "Principles of Lust," turned into a fluke worldwide hit. Snippets of monks invoking the Almighty effortlessly glide in and out of a polite but still strong breakbeat, shimmering, atmospheric synth and flute lines and a Frenchwoman whispering in a way that sounds distinctly more carnal than spiritual (as her gasps for breath elsewhere make clear). Guitar and male vocals add to the album version's try-anything-that-works approach, as do attempts at shuffling jazz beats and horns. If nothing quite equals that prime moment elsewhere on the album, *MCMXC* still trips out on the possibilities as it can, right from the opening "Voice of Enigma," inviting all listeners to sit back, relax, and take a gentle trip. Cretu certainly isn't trying to hide anything—"Callas Went Away" goes right ahead and adds a sample of Maria Callas herself to the chirping birds and soft beats, while elsewhere the flutes, beats, monks, and French voices merrily go about their glossy business. About the only thing missing is the kitchen sink, making the entire album the "Macarthur Park" of its day. —*Ned Raggett*

The Cross of Changes / Feb. 8, 1994 / Charisma ✦✦✦✦
Cretu being no fool, he figured if it worked the first time, no need to change things much for the second. But he also knew not to simply go ahead and just rehash his debut for *Cross of Changes*, resulting in a just different enough effort along the same overall lines. The usual air of tasteful middle-of-the-road spirituality takes precedence, right down to the cover art and appropriately pantheistic quote from Persian mystic poet Rumi in the CD booklet. Needless to say, the music attempts to match the same throughout, and often succeeds. Things kick off with more of the synth-whale song noises and atmospherics from *MCMXC*, however there aren't any monks to be found this time around, but what sounds like the same whispering woman talking about "clearing the debts of many hundred years" and the like. From there, Cretu merrily takes the same plunge—some of his sample choices this time around show he's got a decent record collection, including parts from *Songs From the Victorious City*, the striking fusion of Egyptian and Western musics from Anne Dudley and Jaz Coleman. His work with beats and loops noticeably shows a more developed edge—while hardly an innovator, there's a bit more grime and loud in his rhythms, which in combination with extra electric guitar make a reasonable contrast to the smoother elements. Consider the rampaging conclusion to "I Love You ... I'll Kill You," which while sharing some cheese with the title itself still works surprisingly well, right down to a clever Robert Plant vocal sample at the end. "Return to Innocence" was the big single from this one, not quite up there with "Sadeness" in the popular culture in the U.S. but almost inescapable elsewhere. There's another Led Zeppelin sample (this time John Bonham) and a haunting male vocal providing oomph under the fuzzy-headed greeting card philosophy of the main lyrics. It's an impressive effort, showing Cretu had a definite something in his own way. —*Ned Raggett*

Le Roi Est Mort, Vive Le Roi / Nov. 26, 1996 / Virgin ✦✦✦
Enigma burst on the scene in the early '90s with a pretty nifty schtick: dance beats and lush chord washes underpinning such exotica as muttered French sex talk and Gregorian chant, all unified by a bizarre theme somehow related to the Marquis de Sade. The concept was never as original as some people thought (Mark Stewart's "Maffia" had set plainchant to electro-funk as far back as 1984), but it worked nicely, and "Sadeness" (har har) was an international dance club hit. Two albums later, Michael Cretu (the individual who records under the Enigma moniker) doesn't seem to have done much to expand upon his original ideas. The monks are still there, floating in a murky club mix, though this time they're joined by a cool Mongolian ensemble as well. Cretu is singing more, which is unfortunate since his voice is mediocre and his lyrics silly, but the occasional high point does emerge, such as the darkly lovely "The Child in Us." Most of the album, however, is twaddle. Song titles like "Morphing Thru Time," "Beyond the Invisible" and (seriously) "Odyssey of the Mind" will give you a good idea of what to expect—lots of atmosphere, lots of reverb, lots of sternly intoned lyrics about, er ... something or other. What's missing is musical interest. Overall, the cool packaging is the only thing noteworthy about this disappointing effort. —*Rick Anderson*

The Screen Behind the Mirror / Jan. 18, 2000 / Virgin ✦✦
Enigma's fourth album *The Screen Behind the Mirror* continues Michael Cretu's explorations into ambient new age, Gregorian chant, world music, and dance rhythms. Cretu's vocals play a more prominent role than on earlier Enigma albums, which, unfortunately, often detracts from the songs' other diverse elements—which include church bells, Middle Eastern and European choirs, sensuous female vocals, and a wide array of ethnic percussion and instruments. The album's pieces are mixed together continuously and are united thematically by samples and reinterpretations of Orff's "O Fortuna" and other material from *Carmina Burana*, giving songs like "Endless Quest," "The Gate," and "Smell of Desire" a flowing, cohesive feel. Though it doesn't reveal significant growth or change in Enigma's work, *The Screen Behind the Mirror* will please fans of the group's other atmospheric works. —*Heather Phares*

Brian Eno (Brian Peter George St. Baptiste de la Salle Eno)

b. May 15, 1948, Woodbridge, Suffolk, England
Producer, Vocals, Keyboards, Arranger, Synthesizer / Experimental Rock, Proto-Punk, Experimental, Glam Rock, Prog Rock/Art Rock, Ambient, Electronic
Ambient pioneer, glam-rocker, hit producer, multimedia artist, technological innovator, worldbeat proponent and self-described non-musician—over the course of his long, prolific and immensely influential career, Brian Eno was all of these things and much, much more. Eno championed theory over practice, serendipity over forethought, and texture over craft; in the process, he forever altered the ways in which music is approached,

composed, performed and perceived, and everything from punk to techno to new age bears his unmistakable influence. In 1971 he rose to prominence as a member of the seminal glam band Roxy Music, playing the synthesizer and electronically treating the band's sound. A flamboyantly decked-out enigma, his presence threatened the focal dominance of frontman Bryan Ferry, and he exited after just two LPs. Eno's first solo project, the frenzied and wildly experimental *Here Come the Warm Jets*, reached the U.K. Top 30 in 1974. A 1975 car accident left Eno bedridden for several months and resulted in perhaps his most significant innovation, the creation of ambient music. Unable to move to turn up his stereo to hear above the din of a rainstorm, he realized that music could blend thoroughly into its given atmosphere without upsetting the environmental balance. Heralded by 1975's minimalist *Another Green World*, Eno plunged completely into ambient with the instrumental *Discreet Music*. After returning to pop structures for 1977's *Before and After Science*, Eno continued his ambient experimentation with albums like 1978's *Music for Airports*; concurrently, he became a much-sought-after collaborator and producer, including a landmark teaming with David Bowie. In 1978, he began a long, fruitful union with Talking Heads; friction with David Byrne's bandmates hastened Eno's departure, but in 1981 he and Byrne reunited for *My Life in the Bush of Ghosts*, which fused electronic music with a pioneering use of Third World percussion. His collaboration with Acadian producer Daniel Lanois would emerge as one of the most commercially successful production teams of the 1980s, most notably helming records for U2. Eno remained dedicated to his solo work, and frequently ventured into other realms of media as well. *—Jason Ankeny*

☆ **Here Come the Warm Jets** / Jan. 1974 / EG ✦✦✦✦✦

Eno's solo debut, *Here Come the Warm Jets*, is a spirited, experimental collection of unabashed pop songs on which Eno mostly reprises his Roxy Music role as "sound manipulator," taking the lead vocals but leaving much of the instrumental work to various studio cohorts (including ex-Roxy mates Phil Manzanera and Andy Mackay, plus Robert Fripp and others). Eno's compositions are quirky, whimsical, and catchy, his lyrics bizarre and often free-associative, with a decidedly dark bent in their humor ("Baby's on Fire," "Dead Finks Don't Talk"). Yet the album wouldn't sound nearly as manic as it does without Eno's wildly unpredictable sound processing; he coaxes otherworldly noises and textures from the treated guitars and keyboards, layering them in complex arrangements or bouncing them off one another in a weird cacophony. Avant-garde yet very accessible, *Here Come the Warm Jets* still sounds exciting, forward-looking, and densely detailed, revealing more intricacies with every play. *—Steve Huey*

☆ **Taking Tiger Mountain (By Strategy)** / Nov. 1974 / EG ✦✦✦✦✦

Continuing the twisted pop explorations of *Here Come the Warm Jets*, Eno's sophomore album, *Taking Tiger Mountain (By Strategy)*, is more subdued and cerebral, and a bit darker when he does cut loose, but it's no less thrilling once the music reveals itself. It's a loose concept album—often inscrutable, but still playful—about espionage, the Chinese Communist revolution, and dream associations, with the more stream-of-consciousness lyrics beginning to resemble the sorts of random connections made in dream states. Eno's richly layered arrangements juxtapose very different treated sounds, yet they blend and flow together perfectly, hinting at the directions his work would soon take with the seamless sound paintings of *Another Green World*. Although not quite as enthusiastic as *Here Come the Warm Jets*, *Taking Tiger Mountain* is made accessible through Eno's mastery of pop song structure, a form he would soon transcend and largely discard. *—Steve Huey*

★ **Another Green World** / Nov. 1975 / EG ✦✦✦✦✦

A universally acknowledged masterpiece, *Another Green World* represents a departure from song structure and toward a more ethereal, minimalistic approach to sound. Despite the stripped-down arrangements, the album's sumptuous tone quality reflects Eno's growing virtuosity at handling the recording studio as an instrument in itself (à la Brian Wilson). There are a few pop songs scattered here and there ("St. Elmo's Fire," "I'll Come Running," "Golden Hours"), but most of the album consists of deliberately paced instrumentals which, while often closer to ambient music than pop, are both melodic and rhythmic; many, like "Sky Saw," "In Dark Trees," and "Little Fishes," are highly imagistic, like paintings done in sound which actually resemble their titles. Lyrics are infrequent, but when they do pop up, they follow the free-associative style of albums past; this time, though, the humor seems less bizarre than gently whimsical and addled, fitting perfectly into the dreamlike mood of the rest of the album. Most of *Another Green World* is like experiencing a soothing, dream-filled slumber while awake, and even if some of the pieces have dark or threatening qualities, the moments of unease are temporary, like a passing nightmare whose feeling lingers briefly upon waking but whose content is forgotten. Unlike some of his later, full-fledged ambient work, Eno's gift for melodicism and tight focus here keep the entirety of the album in the forefront of the listener's consciousness, making it the perfect introduction to his achievements even for those who find ambient music difficult to enjoy. *—Steve Huey*

Discreet Music / Dec. 1975 / EG ✦✦✦✦✦

Taking a cue from Satie's idea of "musique d'ameublement" (furniture music), music that just exists like furnishings in an apartment, played so as not to draw attention to itself (not really Muzak, a company which seeks to produce a more intentional work-product effect), Eno created several albums of what he termed "ambient music" which combined a softer style of pattern music (influenced by Bryars, Nyman, Harold Budd) with environmental noises. *Discreet Music* is probably the best of these, using an Oliveros-style tape delay arrangement to slowly change patterns of repeating sounds. *—"Blue" Gene Tyranny*

☆ **Before and After Science** / 1977 / EG ✦✦✦✦✦

Before and After Science is really a study of "studio composition" whereby recordings are created by deconstruction and elimination: tracks are recorded and assembled in layers, then selectively subtracted one after another, resulting in a composition and sound quite unlike that at the beginning of the process. Despite the album's pop format, the sound is unique and strays far from the mainstream. Eno also experiments with his lyrics, choosing a sound-over-sense approach. When mixed with the music, these lyrics create a new sense or meaning, or the feeling of meaning, a concept inspired by abstract sound poet Kurt Schwitters (epitomized on the track "Kurt's Rejoinder," on which you actually hear samples from Schwitters' "Ursonate"). *Before and After Science* opens with two bouncy, upbeat cuts: "No One Receiving," featuring the offbeat rhythm machine of Percy Jones and Phil Collins (Eno regulars during this period), and "Backwater." Jones' analog delay bass dominates on the following "Kurt's Rejoinder," and he and Collins return on the mysterious instrumental "Energy Fools the Magician." The last five tracks (the entire second side of the album format) display a serenity unlike anything in the pop music field. These compositions take on an occasional pastoral quality, pensive and atmospheric. Cluster joins Eno on the mood-evoking "By This River," but the album's apex is the final cut, "Spider and I." With its misty emotional intensity, the song seems at once sad yet hopeful. The music on *Before and After Science* at times resembles *Another Green World* ("No One Receiving") and *Here Come the Warm Jets* ("King's Lead Hat") and ranks alongside both as the most essential Eno material. *—David Ross Smith*

☆ **Ambient 1: Music for Airports** / 1978 / EG ✦✦✦✦✦

Four subtle, slowly evolving pieces grace Eno's first conscious effort at creating ambient music. The composer was in part striving to create music that approximated the effect of visual art. Like a fine painting, these evolving soundscapes don't require constant involvement on the part of the listener. They can hang in the background and add to the atmosphere of the room, yet the music also rewards close attention with a sonic richness absent in standard types of background or easy-listening music. *—Linda Kohanov*

Music for Films / Oct. 1978 / EG ✦✦✦

Recorded intermittently between 1975 and 1978, *Music for Films* compiles moody, instrumental electronic pieces intended as soundtrack material for imaginary motion pictures; the songs are brief and fragmentary, ranging from the haunting "Sparrowfall" to the luminous, densely layered "Quartz." *—Jason Ankeny*

After the Heat / 1978 / Sky ✦✦✦

The second album collaboration with Dieter Moebius and Hans-Joachim Roedelius of Cluster consists of slow-moving instrumentals full of repeated synthesizer sound patterns and sustained guitar notes in the ambient style familiar from Eno's collaborations with Robert Fripp and albums of his own, such as *Discreet Music*. (One song, "Broken Head," features recited vocals by Eno, and on another, "The Belldog," he sings. On "Tzima N'arki," he sings backwards.) *—William Ruhlmann*

Fourth World, Vol. 1: Possible Musics / 1980 / EG ✦✦✦

Fourth World Vol. 1: Possible Musics is a collaboration between the trumpeter Jon Hassell (who gets top billing) and synthesizer player Brian Eno. The "fourth world" seems to be located somewhere in the Sudan, if the album's cover picture is any indication. (That's in the middle of Africa, just south of Egypt, for you geography neophytes.) And the music consists of Hassell's haunting trumpet sounds, coupled with Eno's atmospheric synthsizer sounds and "treatments," playing over a variety of percussion instruments. Typical of both musicians, the music is slow and trance-like, and typical of Middle Eastern music, it has an odd, often wailing tonality that is, however, more otherworldly than, um, fourth-worldly. *—William Ruhlmann*

Ambient 3: Day of Radiance / 1981 / EG ✦✦✦

My Life in the Bush of Ghosts / Feb. 1981 / Sire ✦✦✦✦✦

A pioneering work for countless styles connected to electronics, ambience, and third-world music, *My Life in the Bush of Ghosts* expands on the fourth-world concepts of Hassell/Eno work with a whirlwind 45 minutes of worldbeat/funk-rock (with the combined talents of several percussionists and bassists including Bill Laswell, Tim Wright, David van Tieghem, and Talking Heads' Chris Frantz) that's also heavy on the samples—from radio talk-show hosts, Lebanese mountain singers, preachers, exorcism ceremonies, Muslim chanting, and Egyptian pop, among others. It's also light years away from the respectful, preservationist angles of previous generations' field recorders and folk song gatherers. The songs on *My Life in the Bush of Ghosts* present myriad elements from around the world in the same jumbled stew, without regard for race, creed, or color. As such, it's a tremendously prescient record for the future development of music during the 1980s and '90s. *—John Bush*

Ambient 4: On Land / Apr. 1982 / EG ✦✦✦✦

On Land represented a significant move away from the strategies Brian Eno had employed in earlier ambient releases such as *Discreet Music* and *Music for Airports*. Instead of using a specific process to generate music with minimal interference from the composer, he here opts for a more gestural and intuitive approach, creating dreamy pictures of some specific geographical points or evocative memories of them. It's quite easy to imagine these works as soundtracks to mysterious footage of imprecisely glimpsed landscapes. *On Land* is an album that would become highly influential with the rising tide of new age composers, though few if any would capture the chilly beauty or latent romanticism that is part and parcel of Eno. The first piece, "Lizard Point," includes an early recorded performance of Bill Laswell on bass, and one imagines that his association with Eno was a crucial factor in the ambient directions his later work would sometimes take. *On Land* remains a landmark event in the genre, as well as one of its high-water marks, and sounds entirely up to date 20 years after its initial release. A superb effort. *—Brian Olewnick*

Working Backwards 1983-1973 / 1983 / EG ✦✦

Working Backwards was a box set from EG Records containing all of Eno's solo albums up to 1983. Pointless? Yes, if you had them already, but as a catch it contained two total rarities: *Music for Films, Vol. 2* and the *Rarities* EP. (Both have readily separated themselves from the pack and are in record-collector stores and eBay.) The tracks from *Music for Films, Vol. 2* made up a lot of *Apollo: Atmospheres & Soundtracks*, though there are a few unreleased songs. All of *Rarities* is now available on the Eno *Vocals* box set, the price of which may be the same as a used copy of the vinyl EP. Tracks include his cover of "The Lion Sleeps Tonight," the *Warm Jets*-era "Seven Deadly Finns," and three early-'80s instrumentals, "More Volts," "Strong Flashes of Light," and "Mist/Rhythm." *—Ted Mills*

Apollo: Atmospheres & Soundtracks / 1983 / EG ✦✦✦✦✦
An exquisite experiment, *Apollo* takes Eno's spacescapes from albums like *Another Green World* and arranges them with some heavenly pedal steel guitar by Daniel Lanois. The recording engulfs the listener and captures the feel of space travel, weightlessness, and other sensations vividly. It's also perhaps Eno's warmest record ever. In the end, it comes off sounding not unlike a Grateful Dead experiment, with Lanois' lazy pedal steel sounding quite similar to Jerry Garcia's playing on David Crosby's "Laughing." An excellent nighttime vehicle. *—Matthew Greenwald*

Music for Films, Vol. 2 / 1983 / EG ✦✦✦
Like its predecessor, *Music for Films, Vol. 2* collects more of Eno's scores for nonexistent motion pictures. *—Jason Ankeny*

Begegnungen / 1984 / Gyroscope ✦✦✦✦
A prime compilation from the Eno/Cluster family, *Begegnungen* features previously released solo, duo, and trio recordings circa 1976-1984. These include pieces from various configurations of Eno, Moebius, Roedelius, Plank, and percussionist Mani Neumeier. The compositions are strong and inventive, and the music, an eclectic mix of progressive Krautrock and artistic, ambient electronica, is the best of its genre. All the material is synth-based and mostly upbeat, even bubbly at times, as in the jumpy "Nervos" (from Moebius' *Tonspuren*) and the quirky, rhythmic "Pitch Control" (from the exquisite *Zero Set*), which features electronic horse whinnies.

"Johanneslust" and "The Belldog" are highlights. From Roedelius' *Durch die Wuste*, the vibrant, reflective "Johanneslust" stands out with its acoustic guitar-like synthesizers and ambient landscape; and "The Belldog" (*After the Heat*), the only vocal track on the album, benefits from industrial overtones, musically and lyrically. Based in a warm, synthetic rhythm, "The Belldog" features beautifully mood evoking Eno vocals. And the song takes on an air of importance and sophistication with its epic quality. Honorable mention goes to Moebius and Plank's "Two Oldtimers," a bright, almost playful composition from *Rastakraut Pasta*.

The album's cover photograph by Michael Weisser is one of several photos he created for Sky Records, including *Begegnungen II* and *Old Land*. *Begegnungen II* is an excellent follow-up, released the same year as the first. It contains different songs from *Begegnungen* but draws from most of the same album sources. And *Old Land*, strictly an Eno/Cluster compilation, contains all of the Eno/Cluster tracks found on the *Begegnungen* pair, plus more. *—David Ross Smith*

Begegnungen II / 1985 / Gyroscope ✦✦✦✦
More offerings from Eno, Moebius, Roedelius, Plank, and Neumeier, *Begegnungen II* is the equivalent of its predecessor. The tracks on the compilation (recorded in 1976-1983) are an appealing mix of artsy electronic ambiance and progressive Krautrock. Eno's mechanical "Broken Head" stands out as the only vocal track—a dark, almost oppressive industrial tune not unlike early Gary Numan, but warmer. "Speed Display," originally recorded for Moebius, Plank, and Neumeier's *Zero Set*, is a fantastic showcase for Mani Neumeier's speed and endurance as a percussionist. He generates an incredible rhythmic groove, supplemented by sparkling synthesizer flourishes. Roedelius shines with two contributions to the set. His atmospheric "Mr. Livingstone," an Asian-influenced synth piece with complementary percussion, is pleasantly reminiscent of the opening to "The Colony of Slippermen" from Genesis' *Lamb Lies Down on Broadway*. Along similar lines, the warm colors of "Langer Atem" may have been inspired by Eno's more melodic ambient work, perhaps *Music for Films*. Elsewhere on the record, Moebius and Plank's "Conditionierer" scores as upbeat, quirky synth rock. The well-crafted recordings on the *Begegnungen* albums are easily some of the most interesting compositions by all involved; the albums therefore serve as excellent introductions to the musicians' work. *—David Ross Smith*

More Blank Than Frank / 1986 / EG ✦✦

Desert Island Selection / 1986 / EG ✦✦✦✦✦
A CD-only survey of Eno's first four albums, with songs hand-picked and annotations written by Eno himself. *—John Floyd*

Music for Films, Vol. 3 / 1988 / Opal ✦✦✦

Wrong Way Up / Oct. 1990 / Opal ✦✦✦✦✦
Both Eno and Cale have always flirted with conventional pop music throughout their careers, while reserving the right to go off on less accessible experiments, which means they've always held out the promise that they would make something as attractive as this synthesizer-dominated collection, on which Eno comes as close to the mainstream as he has since *Another Green World* and Cale is as catchy as he's been since *Honi Soit*. The result is one of the best albums either one has ever made. *— William Ruhlmann*

Nerve Net / Sep. 1992 / Opal ✦✦✦
For the record, this was not Brian Eno's first attempt at rock & roll. Not counting his time with Roxy Music (hardly rock & roll, let's face it), he also made several solo albums in the 1970s that were clearly intended as approaches to pop music—they were sideways approaches, of course, shaped by the intellectual distance he has always kept between himself and the music that arises from the forces that he puts into motion, and they were far from unqualified successes. But this is his most rocking solo album in years, and also his funkiest. That's not say it's either funky or rock & roll, but it does manage to be lots of fun in a slightly inhuman, claustrophobically funky sort of way. The list of participants includes several of the usual suspects (Robert Fripp, Robert Quine, Roger Eno), as well as a few surprises (Benmont Tench, John Paul Jones) and a raft of unknowns. The sound, which doesn't vary much from track to track, is compressed and dense, with lots of heavily treated and synthesized percussion. On "What Actually Happened," for example, drummer Richard Bailey plays a distinctly organic funk part through what sounds like a battery of effects, while a bassist and guitarist do indistinguishable things and Eno messes around with everything and throws in samples. "Juju Space Jazz" features both Quine and Fripp (the latter credited with "early '50s club guitar") as well as Eno playing such instruments as "African organ" and "tenor fax" (har har). Overall, this album is quite fun but nothing to get too awfully excited about. *—Rick Anderson*

The Shutov Assembly / Oct. 1992 / Opal ✦✦✦
If *The Shutov Assembly* is reminiscent of Brian Eno's earlier "ambient" music projects dating back to *Discreet Music* (1975), it shouldn't be surprising. Recorded between 1985 and 1990, the atmospheric, slow-moving sound patterns are more, the artist contends, like paintings than music. *The Shutov Assembly*, dedicated to Russian painter Sergei Shutov, is, like the similar works in his catalog (he cites *Music for Films, On Land, Music for Airports, Thursday Afternoon*, and *Nerve Net*, as well as *Discreet Music*), as much a concept as a record. *— William Ruhlmann*

Neroli / Aug. 3, 1993 / Gyroscope ✦✦✦✦
As beautiful and sparse as anything produced to date, ambient pioneer Brian Eno sets a mood of quiet contemplation that, as he himself states in the liner notes, is a piece to "reward attention, but not (be) so strict as to demand it." Single notes resonate like heavy drops in deep water in a seemingly random but harmonic pattern that shifts quietly for close to an hour. "Neroli" brings a sense of weightlessness; it feels as much like an installation piece as it does an actual song. To that end, *Neroli* has been implemented into some maternity wards, both to instill a sense of calm as well as enhance the organic nature of childbirth (it was said that Eno even planned to release a longer version of this piece for such purposes). A secondary title for *Neroli* is "Thinking Music, Part IV." Indeed, a strong meditative quality can come over the listener without any particular emotion attached to it, making it ideal for all sorts of calming applications in the home, office, spa, or space station. It's like having a painting on the wall with an on/off switch; the piece simply exists, rather than evolves. This is the sound of a constellation of stars quietly minding its own business. A simple, unique masterpiece. *—Keir Langley*

Eno Box II: Vocals / Nov. 16, 1993 / Virgin ✦✦✦✦✦
The first of two retrospective box sets devoted to the groundbreaking work of Brian Eno, *Eno Box II* concentrates on his pop and vocal material, including some selections from the unreleased *My Squelchy Life*. Although his music still makes the most sense in the context of his albums, *Eno Box II* is solid crash-course introduction to his work, which remains as revolutionary today as it was when it was released. *—Stephen Thomas Erlewine*

Eno Box I: Instrumentals / Mar. 22, 1994 / Virgin ✦✦✦✦✦
This is one of the nicest box sets released in a while, from the outer box to the design of the accompanying booklet. The selection of tracks covers everything from Eno's earliest instrumental explorations through to an assortment of collaborations with artists such as David Bowie and Jon Hassell. This is a great set for owners of CD changers—the structure of these three discs allows a continuous performance in which the music develops over a period of almost four hours. Despite the ambient nature of some of the material, it's never boring. An excellent job. *—Steven McDonald*

The Drop / Jul. 7, 1997 / Thirsty Ear ✦✦✦
The Drop finds Brian Eno replicating the floating, trancy sound of *Neroli*, creating a shimmering collection of ambient music. Although *The Drop* illustrates that ambient doesn't all sound the same—it can be soothing and scary, sometimes both at once—the album doesn't particularly hold the listener's interest, as the shifting electronic soundscapes never reveal any substantial compositions. It's intriguing for a while, but by the time the 74 minutes of *The Drop* have finished, the album has made little lasting impression. *—Stephen Thomas Erlewine*

Sonora Portraits / Aug. 10, 1999 / Materiali ✦✦

Drawn from Life / May 15, 2001 / Astralwerks ✦✦✦
Following four years after *The Drop, Drawn from Life* sees Brian Eno collaborating with German DJ J. Peter Schwalm. (2000's *Music for Onmyo-Ji*, a previous Eno/Schwalm work, was released in Japan only.) Those who soured at the distant crispness of *The Drop* will find this to be a more inviting listen, even more so than Eno's 1996 collaboration with bassist Jah Wobble on *Spinner*. Jazzy, shuffling rhythms and strings that sway from cutting to sighing lay the foundation of most of the tracks, with some repetitive nonmusical effects often falling somewhere in the mix. If there is a fault of the record, it's that the vocals often get in the way of some fine background listening. If you don't have an affinity for Laurie Anderson's voice, you might be troubled that "Like Pictures Part #2," which otherwise happens to be one of the record's most melodic and tranquil tracks, is interrupted by her intonations. One might find that the babbling contributions from Eno's young daughters on "Bloom" to be far less obstructive, but that's because they're more part of the fabric of the song, rather than an interruption or distraction. There's plenty to enjoy for devoted Eno fans, though nothing truly sticks in the mind after the most attentive listen-through. *—Andy Kellman*

Enuff Z'nuff

f. 1984

Power Pop, Hard Rock, Hair Metal

If there is such a thing as false advertising in rock & roll, then Enuff Z'Nuff are one of its textbook examples. Packaged in garish peace-glam attire by their record company, the group was quickly lumped in with the disposable pop-metal stars of the era (Poison, Warrant, etc.), rather than appreciated for the truly gifted power pop act that they were. By the time they finally managed to shed their deceptive camouflage, it was much too late to turn public opinion or their fortunes around. Released in August 1989, Enuff Z'Nuff's self-titled debut scored a couple of hit singles with "New Thing" and "Fly High Michelle," but the frustrated band discovered themselves receiving more attention for their over-the-top, brightly colored peace sign-infested wardrobe than their superlative hard rock songs. By the time they unleashed 1991's *Strength* album, the band had noticeably toned down their image and turned up their creative ambitions to deliver a masterful '90s take on the crunchy power pop sound of Cheap Trick and Badfinger. America's new alternative rock regime was not impressed, however, and they were dismissed from Atco due to disappointing sales. Group founders Donnie Vie and Chip Z'Nuff hit rock bottom in 1994. With no record deal in sight and amidst deepening drug addiction, they decided to re-release their original 1985 demos as the next Enuff Z'Nuff album, simply calling it *1985*. The album proved a godsend, doing enough business domestically and in Japan (remember the production costs were negligible) to pad the band's coffers, and get the boys back on their feet. It also allowed them to record two new albums in 1995: *Tweaked* and the Japan-only *Chip & Donnie: Brothers*—later re-released in 1997 as *Seven*. —*Ed Rivadavia*

Enuff Z'nuff / 1989 / Atco ♦♦♦

Often overlooked because of their role in the ill-fated hair-metal craze of the late '80s, Enuff Z'nuff actually shares more common ground with power-pop luminaries Cheap Trick and Badfinger than with the lipstick-and-leather crowd. Their self-titled major label debut boasts one of the best power-pop singles of the late '80s with "New Thing," which features Donnie Vie's raspy vocals set against a backdrop of whimsical guitar-powered melody. "For Now" captures more of the same magic that makes "New Thing" so refreshing, while "Fly High Michelle" reveals the band's fondness for psychedelic ballads. The contemplative "I Could Never Be Without You" shows a serious streak that offsets the obviously lighthearted approach of boisterous tracks like "Hot Little Summer Girl" and "Kiss the Clown." Where Enuff Z'nuff falters is their tendency to let songs get bogged down by excessive guitar ramblings. The nearly seven-minute long "In the Groove" falls victim to this unfortunate fate, sputtering and failing to ever really get off the ground. Overall, the good far exceeds the bad on this impressive debut, proving that Enuff Z'nuff deserves more respect than they'll probably ever receive. —*Michael Frey*

● **Strength** / 1991 / Atco ♦♦♦♦♦

At the start of their career, Chicago's Enuff Z'Nuff were touted as the rightful heirs to Cheap Trick thanks to their uncanny talent for combining alluring pop melodies with controlled hard rock crunch. Like their late-'70s heroes, Enuff Z'Nuff took most of their inspiration from a single influence: the Beatles. And where the Trick imbued their initially innocent-seeming pop gems with a dark, sinister edge, Enuff Z'Nuff, in accordance with their environment (late-'80s pop-metal), spun their music with a liberal dose of decadence and debauchery. Indeed, raunchy rockers such as "Heaven or Hell" and "Missing You" (like the bulk of their self-titled debut) stick close to this formula. But *Strength* soon introduces an entirely deeper side of the band, with lush string arrangements and chorused vocals contrasting perfectly with the ascending and descending chords of the title track. From here on out, anything goes, as the foursome rip through racy hard rock gems like "In Crowd" and "The World Is a Gutter," then relax into stunning power ballads like "Goodbye" and "Blue Island." The material which lies between is even better, and the two tracks which kick off the album's second half, "Mother's Eyes" and "Baby Loves You," are simply unbelievable pop songs. Take away three or four of its 14 tracks, and *Strength* would be a perfect album, but a little extra fat never hurt anyone. Arguably the greatest *Abbey Road* tribute and/or rip-off of the early '90s (depending on who you ask), *Strength* was sadly lost in the shuffle of the alternative rock revolution and through sheer record company incompetence, and Enuff Z'Nuff would sadly never recover. —*Ed Rivadavia*

Animals with Human Intelligence / 1992 / Arista ♦♦♦

Enuff Z'Nuff's fortunes were quickly spiraling out of control by the time they released their third album, *Animals with Human Intelligence*, in 1993. The previous year had seen them dropped by record company Atco (which had somehow managed to completely bury their incredible sophomore album, *Strength*), only to be snapped right back up by Arista Records—not exactly a force in hard rock circles either. Still, the band rose to the challenge with a strong, if erratic, effort, featuring such awesome examples of post-Cheap Trick melodic rock like "Right by Your Side" and "One Step Closer to You," as well as noticeably forced metallic numbers like "Black Rain" and "Master of Pain." Also on offer is one of the band's most psychedelic moments ("The Love Train"), a ballad to die for ("Innocence"), and an unquestionable career highlight in "Mary Anne Lost Her Baby," whose at once beautiful and terrifying melodies perfectly complement its painful portrayal of abortion-related guilt. Sadly, the band's new label proved as incompetent as their last and this album too would sink without a trace. Spectacularly named drummer Vikki Foxx added insult to injury by quitting to join Vince Neil's band as soon as the sessions for *Animals* wrapped; and with lead guitarist Derek Frigo also with one foot out the door, Enuff Z'Nuff's tragic, comic career began to slide into obscurity. —*Ed Rivadavia*

1985 / Apr. 29, 1994 / Big Deal ♦♦

Tweaked / Nov. 1995 / Mayhem ♦♦

Peach Fuzz / Feb. 27, 1996 / BD ♦♦♦

A collection of demos with a variety of guests rather than an official album per se, *Peach Fuzz* is still a delightful treat—one can understand the band's stated claim that every song they write is supposed to sound like a hit after giving this a listen. Ricky Parent provides most of the drums, but otherwise it's Donnie Vie and Chip Z'Nuff continuing their productive partnership. No specific date for recording is provided, but it seems to be around the *Tweaked* era or just after it, given that Gino Martino has once again taken a powder from the band. With muscular power pop gems aplenty, *Peach Fuzz* has plenty to recommend it (even just a random listen to perfectly catchy numbers like "Let It Go" makes one wonder why the Enuff Z'Nuff cult isn't as big as, say, that of Shoes). The duo's eternal worship of the Beatles again makes itself known throughout, as the opening lines and notes of "Vacant Love" make totally clear. One feels John Lennon would approve of the spirit of 1965 being so enjoyably summoned from the past. An even more delightful tip of the hat comes with the sincerely dippy-but-right sentiments of "Message of Love," as great a call to stop fighting and start loving as any. It's immediately followed with the huge, crunching build of "Happy Holiday," with one of the band's best ever all-around performances and an absolutely killer chorus, easily *Peach Fuzz*'s nuclear strength highlight. Compared to the fraught *Tweaked*, *Peach Fuzz*'s sentiments are generally sunnier, though the odd downer or two slips through, notably the tale of a drawn-out breakup, "So Long." As is the Enuff Z'Nuff way, the song itself is a hummable and personable treat that could almost be mistaken for a cheery rocker unless one actually pays attention to the lyrics. —*Ned Raggett*

Seven / Feb. 18, 1997 / Mayhem ♦♦♦

Following on from *Peachfuzz* and very appropriately titled—it was, indeed, the band's seventh record—*Seven* finds the latter day Enuff Z'Nuff line-up finally in place with guitarist Monaco joining the band and various folks, including sax player Mars Williams and violinist Johnny Frigo, filling in the corners. There's no big surprises on *Seven*, but those who appreciate the band's ever-enjoyable aim at feeding the Beatles and Cheap Trick through power pop, glam, and metal of all stripes will enjoy this once again. "Wheels" starts off the album on an utterly predictable but still flat-out great note—"Strawberry Fields Forever" keyboards, "Penny Lane" trumpet, harmonies, solos, a lyrical picture of being just on the edge and more, and there's not one thing wrong with any of it. From there the foursome, with Vie and Z'Nuff handling production and doing a great job of it, make their fine, hummable way through a dozen tracks. Both singers sound wonderful, with plenty of chances to showcase their sweetly fragile vocals on any number of dramatic yet never melodramatic songs. "On My Way Back Home," a nicely anthemic number with a killer end section, the descending chord structure of "Down Hill" and the unplugged, folky vibe of "It's No Good" and (partially) "We Don't Have to Be Friends," one of the band's best anti-love songs, are all great numbers. There are a couple of odd misfires—"LA Burning" has the weird, out-of-it feeling down, like an even more screwy version of *Tweaked*'s "Stoned," though the group was about five years late to make a topical statement about the Rodney King reaction. The later reissue of *Seven* included three bonus tracks, most notable of which is another open tip of the hat to eternal band inspiration John Lennon, a cover of "Jealous Guy." —*Ned Raggett*

Paraphernalia / May 4, 1999 / Spitfire ♦♦♦

Accepting the fact that they're unlikely to become anything bigger than a cult band has actually done wonders for Enuff Z'Nuff. Instead of shooting for the stars, they're simply working on their craft, sharpening their melodic skills and trying different things. They've returned to hard rock, but haven't left their popcraft or studio mastery behind. In turn, *Paraphernalia* is their best album since *Tweaked*. Where that album found the band exploring their dark side, this is a lighter album that has a winning mixture of rockers, pop tunes and ballads, with nothing more in mind than having a good time. And it is a good time—the band has found a great blend of metal and power-pop which would make their idols Cheap Trick proud (and it probably does, since Rick Nielsen cameos on the record.) [*Paraphernalia* was originally released on the Japanese label Pony Canyon in 1998. The following spring, it was issued in America on Spitfire. The American version features Billy Corgan's guest guitar on "Everything Works if You Let It," plus two new tracks: "No Place to Go" and "Save Me."] —*Stephen Thomas Erlewine*

10 / Apr. 25, 2000 / Pony Canyon ♦♦♦

Enuff Z'Nuff really knows how to make killer hard-edged pop music with great retro leanings. On this, their tenth CD, they continue that tradition in fine form. The band has put together a collection of pieces that should really please both the longtime listener and the new fan. The material on the CD ranges from bouncy pop in the vein of early Beatles to harder edged power pop to heavy metal and even ELO-oriented sounds. Smashing Pumpkin's Billy Corgan joins the group on a dark, hard edged take on the Cheap Trick number "Everything Works if You Let It." —*Gary Hill*

Enya (Eithne Ní Bhraonáin)

b. May 17, 1961, Gweedore, Donegal, Ireland

Vocals, Keyboards / Celtic New Age, Contemporary Celtic, Adult Alternative Pop/Rock, Contemporary Instrumental, Ethnic Fusion, Adult Alternative

With her blend of folk melodies, synthesized backdrops, and classical motifs, Enya created a distinctive style that more closely resembled new age than the folk and Celtic music that provided her initial influences. Her first professional experience came with the Irish band Clannad, a group that already featured her older brothers and sisters. She stayed with Clannad from 1980 to 1982, then recorded one album (a BBC television score named *The Celts*) before making her proper solo debut with 1988's *Watermark*. "Orinoco Flow," the first single pulled from the album, became a number one hit in Britain, helping the album eventually sell four million albums worldwide. She finally released *Shep-*

herd Moons, her follow-up to *Watermark*, in 1991. *Shepherd Moons* was more successful than its predecessor, entering the U.S. charts at number 17 and eventually selling over ten million copies worldwide. Enya was slow to follow up on the success of *Shepherd Moons*, spending nearly four years working on her fourth album. The record, entitled *Memory of Trees*, entered the U.S. charts at number nine in 1995 and sold over two million copies within its first year of release. *—Stephen Thomas Erlewine & William Ruhlmann*

Celts / 1987 / Reprise ✦✦✦

Initially released simply as *Enya*, *The Celts* shows that the style she became famous for on *Watermark* was already well under way. With production and lyrical help fully in place thanks to her husband-and-wife gurus Nicky and Roma Ryan, Enya's combination of Celtic traditionalism and distinctly modern approach finds lush flower here. All the elements that characterize her music—open, clear nods to her Irish heritage, any number of vocal overdubs to create an echoing, haunting feeling, and layers of synth and electronic percussion—can be found almost track for track. The flip side is that those who find such a combination to be gloopy mush won't be at all convinced further by her work here. It's understandable why folk music traditionalists and anti-mainstream types would get the hives, but those not coming from that angle will find much that's rewarding. Given that *The Celts* is a commissioned piece of work, it actually stands on its own quite well. The charging surge of the title track functions both as a fine introduction and its own stirring, quietly powerful anthem, a good sign for the rest of the album. There are a couple of slight missteps—an electric guitar solo disrupts the string-and-vocal flow of the truly lovely "I Want Tomorrow," for instance. Generally, though, her musical instincts serve her very well, with many striking highlights. The appropriately three-part "Triad" showcases her ear for vocal work excellently, while both versions of "To Go Beyond," especially the second, which closes the disc with an exquisite extra string part, also are worthy of note. *—Ned Raggett*

● **Watermark** / 1988 / Reprise ✦✦✦✦✦

Thanks to its distinct, downright catchy single "Orinoco Flow," which amusingly referenced both her record company boss Rob Dickins and co-producer Ross Cullum in the lyrics, Enya's second album *Watermark* established her as the unexpected queen of gentle, Celtic-tinged new age music. To be sure, her success was as much due to marketing a niche audience in later years equally in love with Yanni and Michael Flatley's Irish dancing, but Enya's rarely given a sense of pandering in her work. She does what she does, just as she did before her fame. Admittedly, avoiding overblown concerts run constantly on PBS hasn't hurt. Indeed, the subtlety that characterizes her work at her best dominates *Watermark*, with the lovely title track, her multi-tracked voice gently swooping among the lead piano, and strings like a softly haunting ghost, as fine an example as any. "Orinoco Flow" itself, for all its implicit dramatics, gently charges instead of piling things on, while the organ-led "On Your Shore" feels like a hushed church piece. Elsewhere, meanwhile, Enya lets in a darkness not overly present on *The Celts*, resulting in work even more appropriate for a moody soundtrack than that album. "Cursum Perficio," with her steady chanting-via-overdub of the title phrase, gets more sweeping and passionate as the song progresses, matched in slightly calmer results with the equally compelling "The Longships." "Storms in Africa," meanwhile, uses drums from Chris Hughes to add to the understated, evocative fire of the song, which certainly lives up to its name. *Watermark* ends with a fascinating piece, "Na Laetha Geal M'Oige," where fellow Irish modern/traditional fusion artist Davy Spillane adds a gripping, heartbreaking uilleann pipe solo to the otherwise calm synth-based performance. It's a perfect combination of timelessness and technology, an appropriate end to this fine album. *—Ned Raggett*

Shepherd Moons / Nov. 1991 / Reprise ✦✦✦✦✦

Calling *Shepherd Moons* a near carbon copy of *Watermark* puts it quite mildly. Like *Watermark*, *Shepherd Moons* opens with the title track, a calm instrumental, has another brief instrumental titled after a *Dora Saint* book smack in the middle ("No Holly for Miss Quinn"), and concludes with a number incorporating a striking uilleann pipes solo, "Smaointe...." In general, Enya's own musical style and work remains the same, again assisted on production by Nicky Ryan and with lyrics by Roma Ryan. *Shepherd Moons* does have one key factor that's also carried over from *Watermark*—it's quite good listening. Though the total continuity means that those who enjoy her work will again be pleased and those who dislike it won't change their minds, in terms of finding her own vision and sticking with it, Enya has increasingly polished and refined her work to a strong, elegant degree. "Caribbean Blue," the lead single, avoids repeating the successful formula of "Orinoco Flow" by means of its waltz time—a subtle enough change, but one that colors and drives the overall composition and performance, the closest Enya might ever get to a dance number. Some songs call to mind traditional Irish music even more strongly than much of her earlier work, while two other tracks are haunting rearrangements of old, traditional numbers. With her trademark understated drama in full flow many other places, especially on the wonderful "Book of Days" (replaced on later pressings with an English language version done for the film *Far and Away*), Enya shows herself to still have it, to grand effect. *—Ned Raggett*

The Memory of Trees / Dec. 5, 1995 / Reprise ✦✦✦

No surprises here, of course—Enya didn't achieve new-age superstardom by challenging anyone's expectations. This album is every bit as hushed, lovely, and soulless as everything else she's ever done; like a perfect angel food cake, it's sweet, soft, and utterly lacking in nutritive substance. There's nothing the matter with angel food cake, of course, and there's also nothing really the matter with *The Memory of Trees*, though its Druidic theme does smell awfully trendy (nothing was quite so hip as neopaganism in 1995), and it steers so strictly the same melodic and textural course she's been following throughout her solo career that you're tempted to wonder why anyone would want to spend the money on what amounts to a complete rehash of her earlier work. While other cultural influences play a greater part in this album, the beautiful and brooding Celtic melodies she brought with her from her earlier work with Clannad are still the primary raw materials, and her skillful use of them is still the main thing that sets her apart from the new age pack. She also has a truly lovely voice, and there's no point trying to resist the gentle charm of "China Roses" and the incantatory power of "Anywhere Is." But so little of the album lives up to the promise of these and one or two other tracks that it's hard to recommend it very enthusiastically. *—Rick Anderson*

● **Paint the Sky With Stars: The Best of Enya** / Nov. 11, 1997 / Reprise ✦✦✦✦✦

Paint the Sky With Stars: The Best of Enya is an excellent 16-song overview of Enya's career, containing 14 selections from *The Celts*, *Watermark*, *Shepherd Moon*, and *The Memory of Trees*—including "Caribbean Blue," "Anywhere Is," "Marble Halls," "Book of Days," and, of course, "Orinoco Flow (Sail Away)"—as well as two previously unreleased songs ("Only If...," "Paint the Sky With Stars") that fit comfortably with her past work. Although Enya is, in many ways, an album artist that creates a mood and sustains it through the course of one disc, this is a fine sampler for listeners that only want the hits and highlights. *—Stephen Thomas Erlewine*

A Day Without Rain / Nov. 21, 2000 / Reprise ✦✦✦

Enya's first full-length album of new material in five years (and her fourth in 12 years) will have a familiar sound to the millions who have followed her career so far. As usual, the slow songs sound like "Silent Night" being performed in a cathedral, and the less slow songs are paced by rhythm patterns that would be called pizzicato passages if they were being played on real strings instead of string-like synthesizers. Over the music, Enya sings in her multi-tracked, ethereal voice, making Roma Ryan's lyrics, which are full of pastoral imagery and abstract romantic sentiments, seem even more insubstantial than they already are. In the press materials accompanying the release, Enya explains why it took her five years to come up with less than 34 and a half minutes of music that sounds like most of her earlier music by noting that she plays all the instruments and does all the singing herself without using samples. It might be more accurate to say that there is no need for her to release albums any more frequently than she does, since each one sells over a long period of time. And since her listeners are more concerned with the mood she sets than with musical content, the similarity to her other albums is a good thing. This is music that works almost entirely as a surface pleasure; strip it of its pretensions, and it's just contemporary easy listening music. *—William Ruhlmann*

Episode Six

f. 1965, **db.** 1969

British Invasion

Most famous for including bassist Roger Glover and singer Ian Gillan before they joined Deep Purple, Episode Six managed to release no less than nine British singles between 1966 and 1969 without coming close to a hit record or establishing a solid identity. Also prominently featuring organist/singer Sheila Carter-Dimmock, the group's 1966-1967 singles were rather light pop/rock harmony numbers, with an occasional ballad and a bit of a soul influence. Light years removed from Deep Purple, Episode Six was nothing if not eclectic in their choice of material, trying their hands at numbers by the Hollies, the Beatles, the Tokens, and Charles Aznavour, as well as a British hot-rod tune (written by Glover). While their repertoire lacked focus, their singles were actually pleasant and their fine cover of Tim Rose's "Morning Dew" would have been a deserving hit.

In 1967, they began to fuse pop and psychedelia with reasonably impressive results, especially the single "I Can See Through You" (written by Glover), one of the finest British psychedelic obscurities. Their final two singles showed the band going in a much more progressive direction and anticipating some of the most indulgent art rock of the '70s with "Mozart Versus the Rest," which assaulted one of the composer's most famous riffs with manic electric guitars. Episode Six folded in 1969, after Gillan and Glover had joined Deep Purple. *—Richie Unterberger*

Put Yourself in My Place / 1987 / PRT ✦✦✦

Although it's more a reflection of the pop trends of the day than an original vision, this compilation of their first seven singles (from 1966-67) is enjoyable listening, with some fine harmonies and reasonably strong material. Unfortunately, it's missing their final three singles from 1968 and 1969. *—Richie Unterberger*

● **The Roots of Deep Purple: The Complete Episode Six** / 1994 / Collectables ✦✦✦✦

This is not a Deep Purple album: it's a compilation of the singles released in the mid-to-late-'60s by Episode Six (Ian Gillan and Roger Glover's pre-Purple band). Six previously unreleased songs, and solo singles by two members, are also included. For Purple fans, it's interesting for Glover's early compositions (including a hot-rod parody song called "Mighty Morris Ten") and to hear Gillan, in a style very different from his well-known one, sing the Beatles' "Here There and Everywhere." "Mr. Universe," a late single, is the only track that really sounds close to Purple, with its air of menace, distorted guitar fills, and screams of "Ow!" from Gillan (and a title that Gillan later used for a solo album). For '60s fans, there's some above average period material here, from a beaty version of Willie Dixon's "My Babe" to the later psychedelic-influenced "I Can See Through You." Sheila Carter's orchestrated solo single ("I Will Warm Your Heart"/"Incense") is surprisingly good, but some of the poppier material is less interesting. A wide variety of covers are included, from the Tokens ("I Hear Trumpets Blow") to the West Coast Pop Art Experimental Band ("I Won't Hurt You") to Mozart ("Mozart vs. the Rest," which copies Love Sculpture's "Sabre Dance" idea of supercharging a classical theme). *—Stephen Raiteri*

EPMD

f. 1987

Hardcore Rap, East Coast Rap, Golden Age

On the surface, Erick Sermon and Parrish Smith had little to recommend themselves—sample-reliant production and a monotone rapping style—but their recordings as EPMD were among the best in hip-hop's underground during the late '80s and early '90s. Over the course of four albums (from the 1988 classic *Strictly Business* to 1992's *Business Never Personal*), they rarely varied from two themes, dissing sucker MCs and recounting sexual exploits. But a closer look reveals that the duo's rhymes were nothing less than incredible, simply undervalued because of their lack of intonation during delivery. EPMD also had a feel for a good groove, and created numerous hip-hop classics, including "It's My Thing," "You Gots to Chill," and "Rampage." *—John Bush*

★ **Strictly Business** / 1988 / Priority ♦♦♦♦♦

Erick Sermon is a classic example of using a disadvantage to one's advantage. Having a lisp and a slight speech impediment didn't prevent Sermon from pursuing a career as a rapper—and in fact, his lisp caught on in a big way and was a key element of EPMD's distinctive sound. In contrast to the hyper, forceful tendencies of many rappers, Erick and partner Parrish Smith's style of rapping is relaxed and deadpan. On *Strictly Business*, their gold debut album, the Long Islanders aren't very substantial lyrically—all they talk about is how strong their rapping skills are and how pathetic sucker MCs are. But their sound was so unique, fresh, and distinctive that such classics as "You Gots to Chill," "Strictly Business," and "The Steve Martin" proved impossible to resist. *—Alex Henderson*

Unfinished Business / 1989 / Priority ♦♦♦♦♦

EPMD avoided the dreaded sophomore curse and kept its artistic momentum going on its second album, *Unfinished Business*. Once again, the duo triumphed by going against the flow—when MCs ranging from Public Enemy to Sir Mix-A-Lot to N.W.A. weren't hesitating to be abrasive and hyper, EPMD still had a sound that was decidedly relaxed by rap standards. For the most part, EPMD's lyrics aren't exactly profound—boasting and attacking sucker MCs is still their favorite activity. However, Erick and Parrish do challenge themselves a bit lyrically on "You Had Too Much to Drink" (a warning against drunk driving) and "Please Listen to My Demo," which recalls the days when they were struggling. But regardless of subject matter, they keep things exciting by having such an appealing, captivating sound. *—Alex Henderson*

Business as Usual / 1990 / Def Jam ♦♦♦

Business as Usual is an ironic title for EPMD's third album—for in terms of production, it was anything but business as usual for the Strong Island rappers. While *Strictly Business* and *Unfinished Business* favored a very simple and basic approach to production consisting primarily of samples (many of them clever) and drum machines, the production is busier and more involved this time—and even suggests Marley Marl. Unfortunately, the sampling isn't as clever as before. What didn't change was EPMD's relatively laid-back approach to rapping and a preoccupation with sucker MCs. Though not as inspired as its two predecessors, the album does have its moments—including "Rampage" (which unites EPMD with LL Cool J), "Give the People," and "Gold Digger," a candid denunciation of "material girls" who exploit and victimize men financially after a divorce. *—Alex Henderson*

Business Never Personal / Jul. 28, 1992 / Def Jam ♦♦♦♦♦

EPMD's terse, thick-tongued rapping style was back on point with their fourth album. Although behind-the-scenes turmoil finally split Erick Sermon and Parrish Smith up, they were together and cooking on this 1992 record. They scored their final signature single with "Crossover," a dead-on commentary directed at rappers putting pop hopes ahead of hip-hop values. "Headbanger" and "Can't Hear Nothing but the Music" were other sterling tracks from their last great album. *—Ron Wynn*

Back in Business / Sep. 16, 1997 / Def Jam ♦♦♦

Out of Business / Jun. 29, 1999 / Def Jam ♦♦♦♦

After the popular, praised 1997 comeback album *Back in Business*, Erick Sermon and Parrish Smith returned with another solid effort that proved they remained one of the best combos in hip-hop, as relevant and tight in 1999 as they were ten years earlier. Most of the tracks are in-house productions (either Sermon or Smith), a true rarity in the '90s hip-hop world, and they lend the album a continuity sorely lacking considering the legion of rap albums that feature a different producer for each track. And as the duo has done for ages, EPMD does more than just trade in familiar riffs to drive the tracks on *Out of Business*. The only familiar sample is on the "Intro," and even there, Sermon and Smith turn "Fanfare for Rocky" into something over and above the original. The pair's raps have definitely progressed in the past ten years, as "Pioneers," "U Got Shot," "Right Now," and "Hold Me Down" more than prove. One of the album highlights is the anti-crossover diatribe "Rap Is Still Outta Control," featuring Busta Rhymes (another rapper who's been around long enough to know) and including great lines like, "They took our music and our beat and tried to make it street/And then got in the magazine to try to sound all sweet." Still, EPMD occasionally falls prey to current trends, with obligatory string-sample productions on "Symphony" and "Symphony 2000" (the latter with Redman, Method Man, and Lady Luck) that serve only to obscure the great guest raps. Despite the title, in the liner notes EPMD dispels any rumors that this could be the duo's last album. *—John Bush*

Greatest Hits / Nov. 23, 1999 / Def Jam ♦♦♦♦♦

Greatest Hits is a 13-track overview of EPMD's first five albums, culling many of the group's best moments into a fantastic set of loose, flowing grooves. There's a major problem with the compilation, though, and it isn't the fact that a few classics are missing (where are "Let the Funk Flow" and "The Steve Martin"?), though that could be a problem for some. No, the problem is that *Greatest Hits* was released only as a bonus disc that was packaged in a limited-edition issue of the 1999 album *Out of Business*. Which was one of the better albums in the EPMD catalog, but it's doubtful that anyone looking for an overview of the group's career will want to spring for it. As an introduction to the group and an indicator of their accomplishments, *Strictly Business* still can't be beat. *—Steve Huey*

The Equals

f. 1965, North London, England

Psychedelic Pop, Bubblegum, Funk

An energetic East London combo, the Equals balanced maximum R&B with plenty of pop, plus a few nods to vocalist Eddy Grant's West Indian background. Grant, born in British Guyana, moved to England with his family at the age of 12, and formed the Equals several years later with four schoolmates. The band began gigging around London, amazing audiences with their apparently limitless energy and a distinct style fusing pop, blues, and R&B plus elements of ska and bluebeat.

The single that made the Equals' reputation, "Baby, Come Back," was the flipside of the band's first single. It hit the top of the charts in Germany and the Netherlands during 1967, made number one in Britain one year later, and brushed the charts in America. Subsequent singles lacked the immediate punch of "Baby, Come Back," however, and the Equals landed only two more Top Ten hits: "Viva Bobby Joe" and "Black Skin Blue Eyed Boys," the latter an apt message track from one of the few racially mixed bands of the era. Grant left the Equals for a solo career in 1971, and though the band never charted again, they remained a popular live act, especially on the continent. *—John Bush*

● **First Among Equals: The Greatest Hits** / 1995 / ICE ♦♦♦♦♦

This two-CD, 40-song compilation is not so much a greatest hits as a lengthy retrospective. In any case, the designation "greatest hits" is pushing it in the U.S., where only "Baby Come Back" (included here, of course) made the Top 40. Forty songs might seem like too much, but actually it should be your first choice, because of both its consistent quality and the consideration that it's more available, and no more expensive, than whatever other Equals compilations you might find (which will invariably be imports). Much of this is good-time romantic rock-soul-ska, occasionally lifting or varying some well-known soul and rock riffs, sometimes with a touch of British mod rock (as on "I Can See, But You Don't Know" and "Fire"). Political and racial concerns occasionally make themselves known (as on "Police on My Back," covered by the Clash, and the British hit "Black Skin Blue Eyed Boys"); even more occasionally, there is a spacy lyricism ("Give Love a Try," "Reincarnation," "Let's Go to the Moon"). Interesting, accomplished (if sometimes too similar-sounding) stuff from Eddy Grant's formative years, though it's marred by the almost total absence of details about the Equals' career in the liner notes. *—Richie Unterberger*

Erasure

f. 1985, London, England

College Rock, Alternative Dance, Club/Dance, Alternative Pop/Rock, House, Dance-Pop

Following the disbandment of the short-lived synth-pop group Yazoo, former Depeche Mode member Vince Clarke formed Erasure in 1985 with singer Andy Bell. Like Yaz and Depeche Mode (both formed by Clarke), Erasure was a synth-based group, but they had stronger dance inclinations, as well as a sharper, more accessible sense of pop songcraft, than either of Clarke's previous bands. Furthermore, Erasure had the flamboyantly eccentric Andy Bell as its focal point. One of the first openly gay performers in pop music, his keening, high voice and exaggerated sense of theatrically became the band's defining image. After a failed debut album, Erasure followed with the single "Sometimes," a number two hit in Britain. *The Innocents*, Erasure's third album, became their first number one album in Britain upon its release in 1988. The album also featured the group's first American hits, the Top 20 entries "Chains of Love" and "A Little Respect." Subsequent albums *Wild!* and *Chorus* both topped British charts, and their tribute EP *Abba-Esque* became their first number one single. The duo's its fifth album, *I Say, I Say, I Say*, featured "Always," their first American hit since 1988. Erasure's eponymous sixth album was released in the fall of 1995. It was followed in the spring of 1997 by *Cowboy*. *—Stephen Thomas Erlewine*

Wonderland / May 1986 / Sire ♦♦♦♦♦

The duo's full debut was a sparkling collection of synth-pop tunes that made up in enthusiasm and immediate catchiness what it lacked in overall variety or any sense of artistic progression from Clarke's past. Though the production, one of Flood's earliest high-profile efforts, is detailed and often lush, anyone who had followed Clarke's career wouldn't be surprised by anything on *Wonderland*. Bell's vocals merely tie the connections to the past further, his at-times too-shrill-for-comfort falsetto inevitably echoing Yaz's Alison Moyet as well as one-time Assembly vocalist Feargal Sharkey. Allowing for all these inevitable reminders, though, still means *Wonderland* is well worth a listen. The key reason is the smash U.K. single "Oh l'Amour," which rapidly became a staple for American modern rock stations as well. A lovely a cappella opening and instantly catchy hook, not to mention sprightly performances from Clarke and Bell both (the latter wisely undersings rather than pushing the flamboyance, letting loose more on the chorus), ensured its classic status. The two other singles, "Who Needs Love Like That" and "Heavenly Action," aren't quite as strong but work in the general formula quite well regardless. Other album cuts are a touch more scattered in quality; nothing is awful, but there are some definite highlights. The slightly slower "Cry So Easy" has a great chorus, giving Bell a chance to show his chops, while "March on Down the Line" moves with a fine positive energy, an anthem without calling attention to itself as such. "Say What" is an interesting mostly instrumental, aside from a gang shout or two of the title, letting Clarke's compositional abilities come to the fore on their own. *—Ned Raggett*

The Circus / Mar. 1987 / Sire ✦✦✦
Having gotten familiar with each other and the public on *Wonderland*, Clarke and Bell aim their sights higher with its follow-up, a more distinct all-around album. Flood once again mans the production boards, helping bring out Clarke's greater number of individual touches and approaches to great effect. It can be the queasy synth whoosh on "Don't Dance," the chunky pseudo-guitar blasts on lead track and single "It Doesn't Have to Be," or the funhouse keyboards on the title song, a cautionary environmental tale, all testaments to Clarke's ever-strengthening pushback of synth-pop's presumed sound and cliches. Bell in turn is finding more to do with his voice, his breathy crooning more seductive and affecting, while his high-volume calls to musical arms generally avoid hyper-ear-piercing levels in favor of general appeal. Exceptions do crop up, admittedly "Sexuality," which has a slightly clumsy chorus to begin with, and Bell's histrionics don't help it. But when the two members are on, they're on in a big way, and the two major hit singles from *The Circus* are prime examples of Erasure in excelsis. "Victim of Love" has Bell showing off some great soul chops right from the start over an inspiring, charging melody, while "Sometimes" contains a strong dance beat and Clarke's synth/acoustic guitar mix underscoring Bell's call for love. Elsewhere, the band's social conscience makes itself known without sounding obvious, especially on "Hideaway." Detailing the coming-out of a young man to his family and his resultant need to leave home, it makes its point with drama but not histrionics, Bell's multi-tracked chorus at once uplifting and empathetic. *—Ned Raggett*

The Two Ring Circus / Dec. 1987 / Sire ✦✦

The Innocents / Apr. 1988 / Sire ✦✦✦✦✦
Having built up a strong fan base and back catalogue in just a couple of years, Erasure turned into a full-blown pop phenomenon thanks to *The Innocents*, winning the British equivalent of the Grammy for album of the year and spawning a big American hit single, "Chains of Love." Stephen Hague took over as producer from Flood, perhaps smoothing out some points for a more general mainstream appeal but otherwise letting the strengths of the songs speak for themselves. It begins with another single and stone-cold classic, "A Little Respect," with a charging beat/acoustic guitar/synth arrangement and a flat-out fantastic performance from Bell, especially on the ascending chorus. Guest performances help flesh out a number of songs quite well. Wheeler and others reappear on "Yahoo!," a gospel-touched (musically and lyrically) number, while noted session performers the Kick Horns add just that to the "please come back" punch of "Heart of Stone." On their own, though, the duo continues in the same general vein of earlier releases while the Erasure formula of dance/synth/soul was now clearly established through and through, thankfully the combination of slight variety and overall performance prevents the album from dragging. *The Innocents'* ballads are perhaps a touch prettier than the lyrics would make them out to be, but if the sheen of songs like "Hallowed Ground" cuts away from the sometimes blunt images of poverty and hopelessness Bell calls up, the music still has a solid power. The CD version adds a fine original, "When I Needed You," and a fun cover of the Phil Spector/Ike and Tina Turner classic "River Deep, Mountain High." *—Ned Raggett*

Crackers International / Sep. 1988 / Sire ✦✦✦
This six-track EP helped bridge the gap between the April 1988 release of *The Innocents* and the October 1989 release of *Wild!* "Stop!" and "Knocking on Your Door" (both heard in original and 12" remix versions) were typical hi-NRG Erasure tracks, with driving dance beats and forceful tenor vocals by Andy Bell, but they did not embrace the broader pop audience the group had reached with the 1988 singles "Chains of Love" and "A Little Respect." "She Won't Be Home" was a Christmas song, reflecting the seasonal release of the EP in November 1988 in the U.K. *—William Ruhlmann*

Wild! / Oct. 1989 / Sire ✦✦

Chorus / Oct. 1991 / Sire ✦✦

Abba-esque [EP] / Jun. 30, 1992 / Mute ✦✦✦✦
Erasure had never hidden its love for ABBA, with one of its earliest B-sides being an enthusiastic remake of "Gimme Gimme Gimme," a version of which later popped up on *The Two-Ring Circus*. Come 1992 and Clarke and Bell decided to take the full plunge on a tribute EP with great results, including getting to the top of the charts in England. All four songs are indeed ABBA covers, including some of that supergroup's best: "Lay All Your Love on Me," "S.O.S.," "Take a Chance on Me," and "Voulez-Vous." Overall arrangements and pace differ little if at all from the original, so those expecting or desiring more variety or creative intrigue in remakes will find this underwhelming. As an energetic salute to a past influence, though, *Abba-esque* is a freewheeling blast. Bell's in wonderful voice throughout, and if nobody could truly match Agnetha and Frida in full effect, Bell's usual way with vocal overdubs makes for an adequate substitute. Clarke's revamping of the Ulvaeus/Andersson team's killer melodies, meanwhile, keeps all of the sprightly, addictive punch while more modern dancefloor rhythms step up here and there. About the only out-of-nowhere touch is the ragga break from MC Kinky halfway through "Take a Chance on Me," but it's not too intrusive or strange. *—Ned Raggett*

• **Erasure Pop!: The First 20 Hits** / Nov. 24, 1992 / Sire ✦✦✦✦✦
On a roll from its U.K. chart-topping success with the *Abba-esque* EP, Erasure celebrated with the baldly titled *Pop!* While scant in terms of general info, as a no-frills hit-for-hit collection *Pop!* lives up to its considerable brief. Taken out of context from the various albums, hearing one straight-up smash after enough becomes a pure delight. It's intriguing to hear how the pure synth-pop/soul fusions of the earliest years give way to a more fluid style, almost as if the notoriously hard-to-stay-satisfied Clarke, having finally found a perfect partner in Bell, found the time and inclination to explore other options. As for Bell, hearing his evolution from an all-too-obvious clone of Clarke's Yaz partner Alison Moyet into his own English soul style makes for a treat. Picking out highlights from already powerful material almost begs the question, but hearing the stretch of brilliant songs from the soothing jump of "Oh L'Amour" to the explosive, infectious energy of "Stop!" makes for great listening, Clarke's arrangements and Bell's passionate vocals hitting everything song for song. Calling a straightforward, chronologically organized singles collection one of "hits" would be arrogant if it weren't for the fact that it was also true, almost every number a Top 40 placer at home, more than half hitting the Top Ten—and it's never hard to hear why. There is one wryly funny and informative bonus in the liner notes—without explanation, though unquestionably written by self-confessed gearhead Clarke, a list of classic keyboards he's used on Erasure's hits appears with this note: "This is a general list of synthesizers you may or may not be interested in. It is not a product endorsement." *—Ned Raggett*

I Say I Say I Say / May 17, 1994 / Mute/Elektra ✦✦✦
Released three years after *Chorus*, *I Say I Say I Say* found Erasure for the first time fully interested in essentially staying in place. The album as a whole is at base an attractively redressed version of what the duo had already done, the occasional slight surprise notwithstanding. While Clarke in particular shows some virtuosity with his performances, helped by Human League/Heaven 17 veteran Martyn Ware's production, *I Say* lacks any real novelty (certainly Bell's singing isn't going to change any earlier perceptions, positive or negative). It's not as experimentally indulgent as the self-titled album or unfortunately unmemorable as *Cowboy*, but it's still not quite the group at its sharp pop finest track for track. When it does succeed, though, it has plenty of the flash and verve of old. "Always," the wonderful ballad that was the album's lead single, with a slightly quirky opening, strong verses both musically and lyrically, and a flat-out brilliant chorus, Bell's impassioned delivery one of his finest moments. *I Say*'s lead-off one/two combination is also a winner; "Take Me Back" also plays the sweeping, slow card effectively, Bell in particular getting in some fine singing. "I Love Saturday," meanwhile, neatly balances pepped up energy on Clarke's part with a lower-key delivery from Bell, a striking combination that makes for a better result than the strident, full-on pep of "Run to the Sun." Other winners include "Man in the Moon," which has a delightful chorus with a sweetly silly pipe/synth melody, "So the Story Goes," and "Miracle," the last two of which feature the singing of a cathedral choir. It's a nice look ahead to the reach of the self-titled record, though, with more pop-friendly song lengths and two of Bell's best, strongest performances on the album. *—Ned Raggett*

Erasure / Oct. 24, 1995 / Elektra ✦✦✦
Having continued course on *I Say I Say I Say* without adding much to its overall reputation, Erasure took a surprising turn on its self-titled album. With statements at the time indicating Clarke claimed inspiration from the complexity and reach of prog-rock keyboard experiments, the duo entered a less pop-friendly turn for this extensive record. Clarke definitely aims for a more spacy atmosphere throughout Erasure, assisted by sometime Orb compatriot Thomas Fehlmann. While the catchy hooks with which Clarke made his name remain, the arrangements show more grandiose reflections and less full-on dancefloor fun, more Jarre than Moroder. Songs are often much longer than the quick, punchy numbers the duo became known for, sometimes getting a bit lost along the way as a result. Bell, to his credit, matches Clarke's ambitions well, trying different vocal deliveries, especially with his trademark backing vocal overdubs—"Rescue Me" being a great example of that. While the overall results don't lead to a fully spectacular record, it's certainly Erasure's most experimental, an indulgence that pays off in surprising ways. One of the more interesting features of the album is who helps out on it—the London Community Gospel Choir takes a wonderful bow on two tracks, the quietly intoxicating lead single "Stay With Me" and the gentle shimmer of "Rock Me Gently." In one of the more unlikely guest appearances of the time, meanwhile, Mute labelmate Diamanda Galas delivers haunting solo turns on "Rock Me Gently" and "Angel." If not as harrowing as much of her own work, it does provide an interesting addition to a duo not known for its particularly dark vision of life. *—Ned Raggett*

Cowboy / Apr. 22, 1997 / Elektra ✦✦✦
The calmer inner meditations of *Erasure* behind them, the duo found themselves on Madonna's label in America and released the notably more upbeat *Cowboy* in 1997. The zeitgeist which the duo perfectly encapsulated in the late '80s had long been left behind, resulting in an album that sounds like it wants to keep the party going when all the guests had long gone home. While *Erasure* itself could drag here and there, it was still an honestly intriguing combination of new and old for the band, something the pleasant (but little more than that) *Cowboy* can't claim. At base, the problem is that while the basic Erasure knack of hummable hooks and fine singing remains unchanged, something seems missing—what made songs like "A Little Respect," "Stop!," and "Chorus" more than enjoyably catchy pop isn't there. *Cowboy* is amiable but not memorable. Clarke to his credit doggedly resists flat out following current pop trends in the hopes of greater relevance, so there's something to be said for sticking to one's guns. His usual preferred combination of gentler lead synths and rougher bass tones sounds enjoyably supple as well, with perhaps the only concession to late-'90s pop being a greater use of hip-hop beats. Bell's voice as always hits its fine sweet-sounding heights. But beyond a cut or two, very little honestly connects beyond that, sad to say. "In My Arms," released as a single, has an attractive air to it, with a nicely sweeping chorus, but feels a little too relaxed, not as flat out energetic as it could be. *—Ned Raggett*

Loveboat / Oct. 31, 2000 / Mute ✦✦✦✦
Erasure perfected their synth-pop/dance sound in the mid-'80s, and over the course of the next decade and a half they continued within that structure. By 1997's *Cowboy*, the band lost some of their melodic sense in exchange for the techno dance trip. It is nice to say that on this release Erasure went back to doing what they do best: strong melodic pop

music full of angst and pain. There's no real experimentation, just the old form of song-writing. This will not win new fans, but it might win back those few who were turned off by the group's dive into techno. Since 1997, Vince Clarke has collaborated on two experimental projects: 1999's Clarke & Ware Experiment with Martin Ware of Heaven 17 fame and the Family Fantastic album. Neither were too successful, but they did provide platforms for Clarke to expand his writing and playing beyond the pop song format. His return is very much welcomed. Andy Bell's voice has never sounded better, and as usual it fits the music perfectly. A strong album, with some of the best songs they have ever produced (including the wonderful "Freedom" and "Surreal"), this is a classic sounding Erasure album, and it could not be better. —*Aaron Badgley*

Eric B. & Rakim

f. 1985, db. 1992
East Coast Rap, Hip-Hop, Golden Age

One of rap's most influential acts during the 1980s, Eric B. & Rakim made the sampling of James Brown records the main source for hip-hop's sound during the late '80s and early '90s, beginning with their stellar debut, *Paid in Full*. While Eric B. dazzled listeners with his turntable techniques, Rakim pointed the way toward the easy-rollin' style of the '90s with his laid-back raps, though forceful in content. Each of the duo's first three albums achieved gold status, and they even managed the Top Five R&B hit "Friends" in 1989.

While working as a mobile DJ for New York's WBLS during 1985, Eric Barrier met William Griffin, a top MC who had grown up on Long Island. The two began recording together and emerged with "Eric B. Is President." The single appeared in 1986 on Harlem's Zakia label, and became a street sensation. Signed to 4th & Broadway the following year, Eric B. & Rakim released their debut album, *Paid in Full*. The LP's success led to a contract with Uni/MCA in 1988, and their second album, *Follow the Leader*, was released that year. Two more albums followed, *Let the Rhythm Hit 'Em* (1990) and *Don't Sweat the Technique* (1992), after which the duo broke up. By the mid-'90s, Eric B. had emerged as a solo act on his own 95th Street label. —*John Bush*

★ **Paid in Full** / 1987 / 4th & Broadway ✦✦✦✦✦
The 1987 release of *Paid In Full* marked the arrival of a hip-hop legend, Long Island's own Rakim Allah. With one of the rawest and fiercest deliveries on the microphone, Rakim's voice hit listeners' eardrums from somewhere beyond the clouds. Here was an otherworldly MC whose penetrating lyrics flowed seemingly without effort. This album would be a classic purely on the strength of three of hip-hop's all-time top 50 songs (maybe even top 20): opener "I Ain't No Joke," title cut "Paid in Full," and "Eric B. Is President." Volumes could be written on the legacy and import of these three songs alone. "I Ain't No Joke," Rakim grabs the listener by the throat and illustrates his mastery of the rhyming craft over a simple James Brown loop produced by Eric B. The other half of the dynamic duo, Eric B. was a master of the minimal beat and one of the first producers to truly scratch the surface of James Brown's work. Eric B. just stripped his beats down and let his partner do his thing, and Rakim shows his appreciation on "Eric B. Is President," a track originally recorded in 1986 along with another entry in the hip-hop canon, "My Melody." "Paid in Full" is the theme the album rests on, outlining one of hip-hop's primary objectives: to get paid and stay paid. However, Eric B. & Rakim sought this goal with originality and superior skills, rather than succumbing to trends or sacrificing their creativity. *Paid in Full* demonstrates the importance of getting paid without diluting one's art; in Eric B. & Rakim's era, anything else was unthinkable. —*Michael Di Bella*

☆ **Follow the Leader** / 1988 / UNI ✦✦✦✦✦
On their second album, Eric B. & Rakim deliver an album that expands on the power of their debut. Taking a cue from the Coldcut remix of "Paid in Full" that became a hit after the release of *Paid In Full*, *Follow the Leader* has a looser, wilder beat than its predecessor. Eric B. uses the spare, James Brown-influenced grooves that dominated *Paid in Full* as a starting point, adding all kinds of production flourishes that flesh out the funk without watering it down. Not only are Eric B.'s musical accomplishments impressive, but so are Rakim's rhymes, which are more detailed and complex than before, even if his subject matter didn't change much. In short, *Follow the Leader* is the second hip-hop classic Eric B. & Rakim delivered in a row—it captures the duo at the top of their game. —*Leo Stanley*

Let the Rhythm Hit 'Em / May 1990 / MCA ✦✦✦
One thing the rap audience will never be accused of is having the world's longest attention span. Even some of the most celebrated hip-hoppers can fade in popularity after only a few albums. Eric B. & Rakim were extremely popular in the mid- to late 1980s, but by 1990, rap buyers were starting to lose interest in them. Not much different from *Paid in Full* or *Follow the Leader*, *Let the Rhythm Hit 'Em* makes rapping technique its number one priority. At time when West Coast MCs like Ice-T and Ice Cube were mainly interested in getting a political message across, Rakim's goal was showing us how much technique he had. Rakim may rap in a deadpan tone, but "Step Back," "No Omega," and other tunes leave no doubt that he had sizable chops. There are a few message raps (including "In the Ghetto"), although Rakim spends most of his time finding tongue-twisting ways to boast and brag about his microphone skills. The overall result is a CD that is enjoyable, yet limited. —*Alex Henderson*

Don't Sweat the Technique / 1992 / MCA ✦✦✦✦
Starting with their 1986 debut, *Paid in Full*, Eric B. and Rakim earned raves for Eric B.'s often flawless, judicious productions and Rakim's serious yet relentlessly rhythmic rhyming style. This 1992 album finds the duo picking up from where they left off of 1990's *Let the Rhythm Hit 'Em*. "What's on Your Mind" has Rakim with intents to woo under a bubbling track with an adroit interpolation of D Train's 1983 hit of the same name. That track aside, *Don't Sweat the Technique* has Rakim in bleak spirits as thoughts of combat,

revenge, and unfortunate "accidents" are not far from his mind. "Casualties of War" has Rakim as an all-purpose psycho with the unsettling hook, "I get a rush when I see blood and dead bodies on the floor." Although it's supposed to be gripping, the thought of a war-ravaged Rakim with his pistols blazing after hearing a truck backfiring is hilarious. All of *Don't Sweat the Technique* would be more disturbing if it wasn't for the brilliant ear of Eric B. who can cut the tension and exact magic out of a going-nowhere track. Although the lyrics and premise of "What's Going On" aren't extremely sharp, the cracking snare drums and low bass riffs are a perfect compliment to Rakim's delivery. The title track is also jazz influenced, but not as potent as the Simon Law and Mr. Lee's Funky Ginger remixes that don't appear here. Like many albums of this type, *Don't Sweat the Technique* ends on tracks of little distinction but it is another strong effort from one of rap's most respected acts. —*Jason Elias*

20th Century Masters—The Millennium Collection: The Best of Eric B. & Rakim / Jun. 19, 2001 / Hip-O ✦✦✦✦✦
Eric B. & Rakim really didn't have crossover hits, but anybody that paid any attention to hip-hop in the late '80s didn't just know of them, they considered them one of the greatest outfits working. Even in the '90s, Rakim was considered one of the greatest MCs ever to hit the mic, and it's easy to see why—great voice, unbelievable flow, cutting lyrics. Both *Paid in Full* and *Follow the Leader* are widely considered to be pinnacles of hip-hop's golden age, but they never had a full-fledged hits collection until 2001's *20th Century Masters—The Millennium Collection*. Actually, that's not entirely true, since Rakim's solo debut, *The 18th Letter*, was initially released with a bonus disc containing the group's greatest hits. That collection is more comprehensive than this 11-track overview, but this still gets the job done effectively. Some might complain that "Paid in Full" is included in the British hit Coldcut remix instead of the original, but the basic lay of the land remains the same—all the major songs (minus "My Melody") are here, and the results are pretty stunning. Both Eric B. and Rakim were visionaries, and while some of the productions may now sound a little dated, years after their initial release the urgency of the performances and freshness of the ideas have not been diluted. This record, as much as any other they released, vividly captures their brilliance. —*Stephen Thomas Erlewine*

Eric's Trip

f. 1990, db. 1996
Indie Rock, Alternative Pop/Rock

A product of the same Eastern Canada indie-rock community which also gave rise to the superb Jale and Sloan, the noise-pop quartet Eric's Trip formed in Moncton, New Brunswick in 1990. The group, which took their name from a Sonic Youth song, dated back to 1989, when singer/guitarist Rick White and guitarist Chris Thompson teamed in the Forest; they recruited vocalist/bassist Julie Doiron-Claytor the following year, and when drummer Mark Gaudet joined some months later, Eric's Trip was born. The band debuted with a self-titled 1990 cassette; with the floodgates duly opened, a massive amount of material followed, stretching across the 1991 tapes *Caterpillars* and *Drowning*, the 1992 EPs *Warm Girl* and *Belong*, and 1993's *Peter*. After becoming the first Canadian artist signed to Sub Pop, Eric's Trip issued the EP *Songs About Chris*, followed by *Julie and the Porthole to Dimentia* (recorded for the tiny Sappy label), before finally closing out 1993 with their full-length Sub Pop debut *Love Tara*. After 1994's *Gordon Street Haunting* EP and the *Forever Again* LP, Doiron-Claytor's pregnancy forced the group into a hiatus; following 1996's *Purple Blue*, Eric's Trip announced their breakup. —*Jason Ankeny*

Love Tara / Jun. 1993 / Sub Pop ✦✦✦
Their full-length debut, *Love Tara*, introduced this lo-fi pop band to the world with beautiful and noisy tracks like "Smother." This record was also one of the first to mark Sub Pop's journey from the Seattle grunge scene to a lighter, more melodic form of music. —*Heather Phares*

● **Forever Again** / 1995 / Sub Pop ✦✦✦✦✦
At 17 tracks, the group's expansive follow-up *Forever Again* could be considered too long to hold attention, but Eric's Trip's power to soothe and seethe at the same time remains captivating. Tracks like "New Love" confirm that the band's sound is a study in contradictions: It's instantly catchy, but it sounds like it was recorded on an answering machine; it's punk rock, but it's dreamy, too. The sound effects on the album—a rainy day and a busy street—heighten the album's entrancing mood. —*Heather Phares*

Purple Blue / Jan. 16, 1996 / Sub Pop ✦✦

Long Day's Ride / Oct. 7, 1997 / Sonic Unyon ✦✦✦

Roky Erickson

b. Jul. 15, 1947, Dallas, TX
Vocals, Guitar / Garage Rock, Psychedelic, Rock & Roll

Like Syd Barrett, a common point of reference, Roky Erickson rose to cult-hero status as much for his music as for his tragic personal life; in light of his legendary bouts with madness and mythic drug abuse, the influence exerted by his garage-bred psychedelia was often lost in the shuffle. After dropping out of high school to become a professional musician, he penned his most famous composition, "You're Gonna Miss Me," in 1965 and joined the psychedelia-influenced 13th Floor Elevators. The band soon took "You're Gonna Miss Me" onto the pop charts in 1966. As the band's fame grew, so did their notoriety with local law enforcement officials, who took exception to the group's heavy experimentation with (and public support of) marijuana and LSD. After Erickson was arrested for the possession of one lone joint in 1969, he pleaded insanity to avoid a prison term and spent over three years in a state mental hospital. Erickson was never the same person after his reemergence; he returned to performing, but his songs found little success. By the 1990s, he was struggling to survive and was briefly re-institutionalized. In 1990, however, artists including R.E.M., ZZ Top, John Wesley Harding, and the Jesus & Mary Chain recorded his songs for the tribute album *Where the Pyramid Meets the Eye*, which brought his work to a wider audience than ever before. In 1995, a new Erickson album titled *All That May Do My Rhyme* was released on Trance Syndicate. —*Jason Ankeny*

Roky Erickson & The Aliens / 1980 / CBS ✦✦✦✦

Like Syd Barrett and Robyn Hitchcock, Roky Erickson is one of rock & roll's genuine crazies, and this album does nothing to dispel that image. As the song titles accurately suggest, the lyrics here all draw their subject matter from satanic and horror-movie subjects. Musically, the album is quite appealing. If the ghouls in the 1960s song "Monster Mash" were really hip, they'd be partying down to "Don't Shake Me Lucifer," a rollicking 1950s-inspired number with clear nods to Little Richard, and they'd be slow-dancing to "I Walked With a Zombie," a demented early-'60s ballad update. A number of other songs here suggest a drier, mid-tempo version of the garage psychedelia of Erickson's legendary 1960s band 13th Floor Elevators, especially "I Think of Demons," "Cold Night for Alligators," and the feedback-laden anthem "Two-Headed Dog." "Night of the Vampire" and "Stand for the Fire Demon" are ominously effective slow-tempo production numbers. The sound quality on this album is a bit trebly, but not bad. In general, this is an excellently listenable album. Note that this release's title as it appears on the disc label and jacket spine is five runic symbols unreproducible with a standard typewriter keyboard; other review sources give the eponymous title which has been listed above. —*David Cleary*

Holiday Inn Tapes / 1987 / Fan Club ✦✦✦

Listeners primarily familiar with Erickson via his deranged vocals and compositions with the 13th Floor Elevators and as a solo act may be shocked by the low-key, acoustic intimacy of this album. Recorded on December 1, 1986 at the Holiday Inn Red River in Austin, TX, Erickson's acoustic guitar and vocals are the whole show on this ten-song performance. Going easy on the horror/monster/mystical imagery, Erickson reprises a couple of Buddy Holly classics, traditional folk tunes, and the Elevators' "May the Circle Remain Unbroken." Just to remind you that this is Roky Erickson, "The Singing Grandfather" (different versions of which open and close this album) begins with the line "The singing grandfather will saw off your head." Sound (played into a portable recorder) is fair but quite listenable, and Erickson's plaintive, yearning vocals are quite touching. His acoustic picking isn't bad either, although he stumbles or loses the beat once in a while (and for Erickson, once in a while is quite an acceptable margin of error). This doesn't deliver the outrage that many have come to expect from Erickson, but shows a glimpse of the man behind the madness. —*Richie Unterberger*

• You're Gonna Miss Me: The Best of Roky Erickson / Sep. 27, 1991 / Restless/Enigma ✦✦✦✦✦

The title is not entirely truthful, as this compilation covers only Roky Erickson's '80s work for the Enigma/Pink Dust/Restless family of labels, and much of the Texas singer/songwriter's best work, including the title track (showcased here in a 1981 live performance in his hometown of Austin), was recorded in the '60s. Still, this is the best overview of a confusing period in Erickson's career, when the same basic set of songs were recorded several times and released on a variety of labels around the world. (Versions of these songs, most of them recorded in the early '80s, were still showing up in the late '90s.) The versions collected here tend to be the definitive ones, most of them produced by ex-Creedence Clearwater Revival bassist Stu Cook in the late '70s and early '80s.

There's an unfortunate element of "Hey! Lookit the weird crazy guy!" in some circles of Erickson's admirers, a disturbingly voyeuristic quality that largely ignores the fact that although Erickson's legendary mental problems are part of his mystique, he's also an incredibly gifted songwriter. There are songs on here, particularly the remarkably catchy Buddy Holly tribute "Starry Eyes," the manic rocker "Don't Slander Me" and the dreamy "I Have Always Been Here Before," that would cement Erickson's place in the underappreciated pop genius category even without the legacy of his early '70s stay in a Texas state mental hospital. However, he will unfortunately always be better known for inferior but more lyrically provocative tunes like "Creature With the Atom Brain" and "I Walked With a Zombie." Despite its flaws, *You're Gonna Miss Me* does a fair job of summarizing this sad state of affairs. —*Stewart Mason*

All That May Do My Rhyme / Feb. 13, 1995 / Trance Syndicate ✦✦✦

His mind may be fried, but Roky's vocal talents are relatively intact on this mid-1990s effort, which turns out be one of his more subdued, folkier outings. (About half of the tracks, however, are actually remixes of sessions from the mid-'80s.) Roky's most excessive traits are mostly absent; he sounds sort of like an eccentric, updated Buddy Holly. It's the kind of roots rock that may well please the more open-minded fans of, for instance, John Fogerty or Van Morrison, although the compositions are more pleasant than inspired. Charlie Sexton and Butthole Surfer Paul Leary make low-key session appearances; Texas singer Lou Ann Barton duets with Roky on "Starry Eyes" (reprised at the end with a version on which Roky handles all the vocals). A significant bonus, not listed on the sleeve, is "We Got Soul," the rare and fine mid-'60s single cut by Roky's first group, the Spades, before Erickson joined the 13th Floor Elevators. —*Richie Unterberger*

Never Say Goodbye / Feb. 9, 1999 / Emperor Jones ✦✦✦✦✦

Never Say Goodbye features previously unreleased Roky Erickson material from 1971 to 1985. Much of the music is of a stripped-down or solo acoustic nature; the five solo 1971 cuts were recorded, for instance, at Rusk State Mental Hospital (where Erickson was an inmate). Although a sticker on the cover notes that these are "lo-fidelity field recordings," in fact the sound quality is listenable and not a hindrance, save for a brittle (and brief) version of "I Pledge Allegiance." Erickson's solo recordings are noted for their preoccu-

pations with ghouls and comic book imagery, but these songs (which are not available in any other form)—particularly those from 1971-1974—omit those traits almost entirely. Instead, they are tender, sincere, and melodic performances, with a naked vulnerability shining through both in Erickson's yearning vocals and the folk-rockish turns of phrases. There is little else in the Erickson catalog to compare it to, other than maybe the *Holiday Inn* tapes, except that the performances here are far more committed and together. Erickson's colorful bouts with mental instability, both inside and outside his recordings, have tended to overshadow his more straightforward musical gifts. This is the recording, above all others, that demonstrates the strengths of his uniquely gentle and mystical writing and singing, when these qualities are not subsumed by his inner demons. —*Richie Unterberger*

The Escorts

British Invasion

A distinctly lower-echelon Merseybeat band, the Escorts' commercial impact was slight indeed. Only one of their six singles made the British Top 50, and at number 49 at that. They covered "Dizzy Miss Lizzie" before the Beatles, and the single made some noise in Texas, but besides that they were unheard beyond their Liverpool hometown. Their 45s were pleasant, moderately catchy, and featured close harmonies, but were basically unmemorable. The Escorts lacked a distinctive sound and wrote virtually none of their own material (many of their A-sides were tame covers of U.S. rock and R&B hits; many of their B-sides were shallow Merseybeat numbers written by their manager). After a lineup change in 1966, the group recorded their sixth single with Paul McCartney on tambourine, showing a much more pronounced soul feel. Guitarist Terry Sylvester left the Escorts near the end of their recording career to join the Swinging Blue Jeans, and eventually replaced Graham Nash in the Hollies in the late '60s. —*Richie Unterberger*

From the Blue Angel / 1982 / Edsel ✦✦✦

The only Escorts LP, this compiles both sides of their six 1964-66 singles. It's lovingly packaged, complete with a four-page history of the group, but one has to wonder whether the effort was really necessary for such a slight band. —*Richie Unterberger*

Alejandro Escovedo

Vocals, Guitar / Americana, Alternative Country-Rock, Roots Rock, Progressive Country, Singer/Songwriter

Alejandro Escovedo's family tree includes former Santana percussionist Pete Escovedo and Pete's daughter, Sheila E (also Prince's former drummer and later a pop star). He began his music career with the Nuns, a mid-'70s punk band based in San Francisco. He co-founded the cowpunk band Rank and File in 1979, which moved to Austin, TX, in 1981 after a stint in New York City. The band released *Sundown* on Slash Records; shortly after, Escovedo left to form the True Believers with brother Javier. The band recorded two albums for EMI (the second was never released, a fact that eventually caused the band to break up in 1988) and toured the country, often as an opening act for Los Lobos. Escovedo released a solo album in 1992 on Watermelon Records, *Gravity*, uniting his wide variety of styles; the album was produced by Stephen Bruton of Bonnie Raitt's band. After 1996's *With These Hands*, he also began recording with the group Buick MacKane. The solo *Bourbonitis Blues* followed in 1999. —*John Bush*

• Gravity / 1992 / Watermelon ✦✦✦✦✦

While Alejandro Escovedo had shown plenty of versatility over the first 15 years of his career in music—playing with early punk ravers the Nuns, prescient alt-country upstarts Rank and File, and roots rock firebrands the True Believers, among many others—it wasn't until the Believers took shape that he began to display his formidable gifts as a songwriter, and with his first solo album, *Gravity*, Escovedo belatedly made it clear that he possessed one of the strongest and most distinctive lyrical voices of his generation. Opening with "Paradise," a haunting first-person narrative of a man about to be hanged, *Gravity* is a strikingly accomplished set of songs that deal with love ("Broken Bottle," "Five Hearts Breaking"), death ("She Doesn't Live Here Anymore"), and loss ("The Last to Know," the title song) in deeply personal terms, and Escovedo tells his stories with a talent for finely woven detail that would be the envy of a first-rate novelist. And the diversity of Escovedo's years of musical experience shows in the album's arrangements, which range from quiet, contemplative pieces structured around cello and piano ("Broken Bottle," "She Doesn't Live Here Anymore") to full-on, amped-up barrelhouse rock & roll ("Oxford," "One More Time"); Turner Stephen Bruton's clean, unobtrusive production gets all the details on tape with admirable clarity. Not every songwriter has the luxury of spending a decade and a half on the sidelines honing his craft before making a solo bow, but even with that advantage, there are few people who have the talent and vision to create an album as strong and moving as *Gravity*; to call it an "auspicious debut" is to risk understatement. —*Mark Deming*

Thirteen Years / 1994 / Watermelon ✦✦✦✦

The Austin singer-songwriter reaches deep once again, adding triple violins, harp, and cello to his palette of movingly introspective material. Overall, the expanded lineup provides for plenty of tonal space. Before the mood ever gets maudlin, Escovedo cranks up the volume with guest guitarist Charlie Sexton for "Losing Your Touch," and a playful rocker that could have come from The Replacements/Paul Westerberg camp. With the exception of this track, "Mountain of Mud," and the John Cougar-ish "The End," *Thirteen Years* keeps to fragile, graceful interiors. —*Roch Parisien*

The End/Losing Your Touch / 1994 / Watermelon ✦✦✦

With These Hands / Jun. 18, 1996 / Rykodisc ✦✦✦✦

After recording two superb albums for the tiny independent label Watermelon Records, Alejandro Escovedo moved up, if not to the big leagues, then at least to AAA ball, when he signed with Rykodisc for his third solo set, *With These Hands*. While Escovedo's arrangements (he calls his band an orchestra without exaggeration) and Turner Stephen Bruton's production on *Gravity* and *Thirteen Years* were strikingly ambitious given their tiny budgets, *With These Hands* found them with a bit more money at their disposal, and if their approach wasn't remarkably different, the results display more polish and audibly greater depth than before, and Escovedo was able to bring along a few celebrity guests—among them Willie Nelson, Jennifer Warnes, and his cousin Sheila Escovedo (aka Sheila E)—who add to the music without calling undue attention to themselves. Lyrically, after the deeply (and sometimes painfully) personal material of *Gravity* and *Thirteen Years*, *With These Hands* found Escovedo stepping a bit outside himself to tell stories less obviously based on his own life, though the results are as compelling (and ring as true) as his more autobiographical material, especially the failed rock star's lament of "Pissed Off 2 A.M.," the dead of night heartache of "Sometimes," and "Nickel and a Spoon"'s story of a devastated family. If *With These Hands* seems less immediately striking than the two albums that preceded it, that's only because it's less surprising—with his first two solo albums, Alejandro Escovedo announced himself as a world class talent with a singular style, and if *With These Hands* doesn't break much new ground for him, it shows he's still in full command of his considerable gifts as a musician, and it's an impressive achievement. *—Mark Deming*

More Miles Than Money: Live 1994-1996 / Feb. 24, 1998 / Bloodshot ✦✦✦✦✦

Bourbonitis Blues / May 14, 1999 / Bloodshot ✦✦✦

After Alejandro Escovedo's relationship with Rykodisc came to a sudden halt following the release of an album by his glam punk side project Buick MacKane, he released two stopgap albums while writing the material for 2001's masterful *A Man Under the Influence*. *More Miles Than Money: Live 1994-96* was a superb document of Escovedo's startlingly intimate live shows, but *Bourbonitis Blues* sounds like an odds-and-ends EP of covers, live tracks, and a few token new cuts that was somehow stretched to a 38-minute LP. The disc only features four original songs (one of which, "Guilty," is a remake of a tune from *With These Hands*), and while "I Was Drunk" is excellent, "Sacramento and Polk" and "Everybody Loves Me" suggest he was saving most of his A-list material for his next proper album. The rest of *Bourbonitis Blues* is filled up with covers, most of which are well worth hearing, especially his heart-rendering reading of Ian Hunter's "Irene Wilde," and a slow, ominous take on the Gun Club's "Sex Beat." But since Jon Langford happens to be singing lead on the take of "California Blues" featured here, it's not certain just what it's doing on an Alejandro Escovedo record. There isn't anything bad on *Bourbonitis Blues*, but there isn't a lot that's truly distinguished, either, and it's something of disappointment coming from one of the best singer/songwriters to emerge in the 1990s. *—Mark Deming*

A Man Under the Influence / Apr. 24, 2001 / Bloodshot ✦✦✦✦

"It's all about this love/It's all about this pain/It's all about the loss/We take to live again." Those lines hardly tell you everything there is to know about Alejandro Escovedo's songwriting, but he's rarely expressed his key themes with such strength and concision as he does in the first verse of "About This Love," and while Escovedo's fifth studio album, *A Man Under the Influence*, doesn't stray far from the musical and lyrical themes that have dominated his previous work, he's rarely (if ever) put the pieces together quite as well as he does here. Escovedo's latest lineup of his orchestra—anchored by Brian Standefer on cello, Eric Heywood on pedal steel, Mike Daly on keyboards and guitar, Hector Munoz on drums, and Cornbread on bass—sounds like his strongest and best controlled to date, as comfortable with the subtleties of "Wave" as the full-on rock of "Castanets." Quite simply, Escovedo has never sung better than he does on this set, running the emotional spectrum from plaintive longing to swaggering contempt and never sounding less than convincing at any stop along the way. And while Turner Stephen Bruton's production on Escovedo's first three studio albums was intelligent and intuitive, Chris Stamey's work on *A Man Under the Influence* suits him just as well while sounding clearer, sharper, and better focused; the sound catches the full range of Escovedo's personality while adding the sonic details that sometimes got lost on his previous records. And if love and loss still remain Escovedo's favorite themes, like Hank Williams or Leonard Cohen he seems to have something new and telling to say about them each time out; each of this album's 11 songs is worth hearing, and the cumulative effect is nothing less than stunning. No one who's heard Escovedo's work doubts his status as one of the finest singer/songwriters of his day, and he's never been heard to better advantage on disc than on *A Man Under the Influence*. *—Mark Deming*

ESG

f. 1978, South Bronx, New York City, NY

Old School Rap, Electro, Club/Dance

An art-funk ensemble from the South Bronx, ESG was formed by sisters Renee, Valerie, and Marie Scroggins, all of whom handle vocals and percussion, and friend Leroy Glover (bass). ESG's music is centered around the sisters' complex polyrhythms, with atmosphere supplied by bass and pop-flavored guitar. During their first incarnation, the group signed with 99 Records and issued a debut self-titled EP in 1981 that featured three live and three studio songs, the latter produced by the legendary Martin Hannett (Joy Division, etc.). 1982's *ESG Says Dance to the Beat of the Moody* EP continued in a similar vein, as did their first full-length album, 1983's *Come Away With ESG*. ESG disbanded shortly thereafter, but unexpectedly re-formed in the early '90s, heralding their comeback with a self-titled 1991 compilation of previously released material. The group's work had become popular among hip-hop artists searching for samples, with such acts as TLC, the Wu-Tang Clan, the Beastie Boys, Big Daddy Kane, and indie rockers Unrest all making use of ESG beats; the group addressed this issue on the 1992 12" EP *Sample Credits Don't Pay Our Bills*. *ESG Live!* appeared in 1995, featuring both old and new material. The group continued to record during the late '90s, and even added Scroggins' daughters Chistelle and Nicole. The major retrospective *A South Bronx Story* appeared on Universal Sound in 2000. *—Steve Huey*

● **A South Bronx Story** / 2000 / Universal Sound ✦✦✦✦✦

With their limited resources, the Scroggins sisters put the boogie down in the Boogie Down Bronx. Major kudos to Universal Sound for compiling ESG's best works for *A South Bronx Story*, a crucial document of sparse, old school funk. Until 2000, the group's scant material had been nearly impossible to find. The most legendary inclusion is the Martin Hannett-produced 7" EP that was originally released on Factory (later released as a 12" in the U.S. by 99 with live tracks backing it). This release featured their trademark "Moody," which ended up being listed as a Top 50 classic by nearly all of New York's dance clubs; it was also immortalized on a volume of Tommy Boy's excellent *Perfect Beats* series, lodged between Liquid Liquid and Strafe. Like the remainder of their recorded output, it featured the three "R"s: rhythm, rhythm, and more rhythm. Also on the debut EP was their most sampled "UFO"; the nauseous siren trills at the beginning found sped-up use in at least half a dozen rap tracks in the late '80s and early '90s. Big Daddy Kane and LL Cool J used it, and the Bomb Squad slyly swiped it for Public Enemy's "Night of the Living Baseheads." But arguably their best moment was "Dance" with its jumpy Motown rhythm, post-punk bass, and narrative/old school vocals. It sounds like a wild mix of the Supremes and *Metal Box*-era Public Image Limited. Deborah's bass, though not as musicianly, captures the spirit of PiL's Jah Wobble copping Motown session bassist James Jamerson. It's that sort of sprited, unconscious hybrid that made ESG so unique. After all, they played the opening night of Manchester's Factory club and the closing night of Larry Levan's Paradise Garage. *—Andy Kellman*

Esquerita

b. New Orleans, LA, **d.** Oct. 23, 1986, Harlem, NY

Vocals, Piano / Rock & Roll

With a six-inch pompadour, brocaded shirts, rhinestone shades, and a rhythmic, belligerent style of piano playing, Esquerita was the original Little Richard, years before Mr. Penniman tutti-frutti'd his way to stardom. Working around the Dallas-New Orleans circuit in the early '50s, Esquerita's shot at the big time came when Capitol Records decided they needed their own version of Little Richard, after signing their answer to Elvis, Gene Vincent. The resulting recordings, though smartly produced, stand as some of the most untamed and unabashed sides ever issued by a major label. Long revered by rock & roll fans the world over, they make Little Richard's Specialty sides look highly disciplined by comparison. Though Esquerita continued to record in a tamer style through the '60s, his Capitol sides stand as a monument to the potential of rock & roll's lunatic power and the off-kilter genius of Esquerita. *—Cub Koda*

● **Rockin' the Joint** / 1998 / Collectables ✦✦✦✦

Rockin' the Joint is a reissue of the 1990 *Capitol Collectors Series* anthology with a new name and different cover, but otherwise the two are the same. Since many of the discs in the *Capitol Collectors Series* have been deleted, Collectables has given a few of them facelifts and another crack at the marketplace. Esquerita, the R&B pianist who profoundly influenced Little Richard, is at the top of his game on these recordings from the late '50s. He somehow managed to convince the Jordanaires to drop by the studio and lay down some vocal tracks on their way to the funeral of Elvis Presley's mother, and they appear on "I Live the Life I Love" and "This Thing Called Love." The 28 tracks on this collection constitute Esquerita's complete Capitol recordings, and they are a vital addition to the collection of any enthusiast of '50s rock & roll or R&B. *—Greg Adams*

The Essex Green

Indie Pop, Neo-Psychedelia, Indie Rock

Neo-psychedelic pop outfit the Essex Green was formed in mid-1997 after four members of the Burlington, VT-based Guppyboy—singer/guitarist Chris Ziter, singer/keyboardist Sasha Bell, guitarist Jeff Baron, and bassist Mike Barrett—relocated to Brooklyn, NY. Completing the lineup with drummer Tim Barnes, the group appeared at various New York City clubs before touring the East Coast with Aden and Saturnine, releasing a split single with the Sixth Great Lake in the spring of 1999. The Essex Green's full-length debut *Everything Is Green* appeared on Kindercore later that year, and a self-titled EP on Elephant 6 followed in early 2000; concurrently, both Bell and Baron also played in the like-minded Ladybug Transistor. *—Jason Ankeny*

● **Everything Is Green** / Nov. 16, 1999 / Kindercore ✦✦✦✦✦

The Essex Green's debut album captures the sound and spirit of the psychedelic era with an uncanny accuracy which makes the rest of the Elephant 6 collective seem positively postmodern by comparison. It's hardly paint-by-numbers, however—for all of its colorful guitar effects, orchestral spangles, and studio trickery, what's impressive about *Everything Is Green* is the subtle mastery with which the band deploys these cues, soaring so far beyond their music's superficial similarities to psychedelia that the album seems less like a latter-day homage to the late '60s than an actual artifact of the times; songs like "Primrose" and the majestic "Mrs. Bean" are both wonderfully unique and instantly familiar, evoking not merely the sonic grandeur of pop's past but its limitless possibilities as well. *—Jason Ankeny*

The Essex Green / Apr. 25, 2000 / Elephant 6 ✦✦✦✦

Bands of the Elephant 6 collective usually fall into two categories: those who function simply as rock historians recreating the sounds of the '60s (Of Montreal anyone?) and those who are able to extrapolate those influences into originality (the brilliant Olivia Tremor Control, Elf Power). From the first song on the EP, the effervescent "Fabulous

Day," the Essex Green firmly place themselves into the second group. So while their pop is heavily indebted to the likes of the Kinks and the Strawberry Alarm Clock, they manage to measure in just enough originality to eclipse mimicry, making the Essex Green's music at once familiar and innovative, classic and fresh. As with their full-length, *The Essex Green* is a consistent listen, with each of the five tracks possessing a definite hook and embodying a different variation on summer of love era pop. *—Ari Wiznitzer*

Gloria Estefan

b. Sep. 1, 1957, Havana, Cuba

Vocals / Tropical, Club/Dance, Adult Contemporary, Latin Pop, Dance-Pop

As one of the biggest new stars to emerge during the mid-1980s, singer Gloria Estefan predated the coming Latin pop explosion by a decade, scoring a series of propulsive dance hits rooted in the rhythms of her native Cuba before shifting her focus to softer, more ballad-oriented fare. Born Gloria Fajardo in Havana on September 1, 1957, she was raised primarily in Miami, FL . In the fall of 1975, Fajardo and her cousin Merci Murciano auditioned for the Miami Latin Boys, a local wedding band headed by keyboardist Emilio Estefan; with their addition, the group was rechristened Miami Sound Machine, and four years later, Fajardo and Estefan were wed. As Miami Sound Machine began composing their own original material, their fusion of pop, disco, and salsa earned a devoted local following, eventually bursting onto the national stage.

The band recorded several albums, each progressively giving more credit to Gloria until 1989's *Cuts Both Ways* was credited to Estefan alone. Unfortunately, while touring in support of the album, on March 20, 1990 her bus was struck by a tractor-trailer, resulting in a broken vertebrae which required extensive surgery and kept her off the road for over a year. She resurfaced in 1991 with *Into the Light*, again topping the charts.

With 1993's *Mi Tierra*, Estefan returned to her roots, recording her first Spanish-language record in close to a decade and earning a Grammy Award for Best Tropical Latin Album. Another all-Spanish effort, *Abriendo Puertas*, earned the Grammy as well. In 1999, she also made her feature film debut alongside Meryl Streep in *Music of the Heart*, recording the film's title song as a duet with 'N Sync and scoring both a massive pop hit and an Oscar nomination in the process. A new Spanish-language album, *Alma Caribeña*, followed in the spring of 2000. Several months later, Estefan was awarded a Grammy for Best Music Video for "No Me Dehes De Querer at the first annual Latin Grammy Awards. *—Jason Ankeny*

● **Greatest Hits** / Oct. 6, 1992 / Epic ✦✦✦✦

In 1985, she started off as the lead singer of Miami Sound Machine. By 1987, after scoring four big hits from their first major U.S. album, they became Gloria Estefan and Miami Sound Machine, and by 1989, after even bigger success, it was simply Gloria Estefan. This greatest-hits collection covers the years 1985 to 1992, featuring most of the pop confections that propelled her to the top of the charts and to international stardom. Among the hits included are her three number ones: "Anything for You," "Coming Out of the Dark," and "Don't Wanna Lose You," as well as other Top Ten hits including "Conga," "Words Get in the Way," "Rhythm Is Gonna Get You," "Can't Stay Away From You," "Here We Are," and the single mix of "1-2-3." There are a few glaring omissions, however. "Bad Boy," her second Top Ten hit, was left off, and that is unfortunate because the hit version was a remix of the original album version and is extremely difficult to find on CD. Other omissions include "Dr. Beat," "Falling in Love (Uh-Oh)," "Oye Mi Canto," "Live for Loving You," and "Can't Forget You." To round off the set are four new recordings, including the album's first single "Always Tomorrow," the Jon Secada-penned "I See Your Smile," the irresistible Latin-flavored dance track "Go Away," and the semi-tepid holiday tune "Christmas Through Your Eyes." This is a good collection from a great artist that could have been a great collection had they included all the hits. *—Jose Promis*

Greatest Hits, Vol. 2 / Feb. 6, 2001 / Epic ✦✦✦✦

Gloria Estefan's second volume of greatest hits seems more progressive than her first, considering the techno-leaning sounds of her 1990s hits which dominate this set as compared to the more straight-ahead pop from her 1980s hits. This collection assembles nearly all of her Hot 100 hits since her last *Greatest Hits* album (only "Don't Let This Moment End" is missing). Most of the songs are included in their original album versions, save for a couple which may be of interest to the collector. "If We Were Lovers," one of her loveliest and classiest ballads, was originally on the *Mi Tierra* album in its Spanish-language form, titled "Con Los Anos Que Me Quedan." The English version of the song had never been available on any of her albums until now. Also making its first appearance on a Gloria Estefan album is her duet with 'N Sync, "Music of My Heart." "You'll Be Mine (Party Time)" and "I'm Not Giving You Up" are featured in remixed forms which had previously only been available as singles. The real treat, however, are the three new songs, which rank among the singer's best, especially "You Can't Walk Away From Love," a dramatic, sweeping, Middle Eastern-tinged ballad. Also included is an updated remix of her first U.S. hit, "Conga." All in all, this is a fine greatest-hits album, almost superior to her first, with classy ballads, great pop songs, and high-energy dance numbers. *—Jose Promis*

Melissa Etheridge

b. May 29, 1961, Leavenworth, KS

Vocals, Guitar / Heartland Rock, Adult Alternative Pop/Rock, Singer/Songwriter

Melissa Etheridge's gutsy electric blues-rock has earned her favorable comparisons to Rod Stewart and Janis Joplin, as well as a considerable fan base across America. Not only is she a solid live performer, but she has written several songs that have became AOR favorites since the late '80s, including "Bring Me Some Water" and "Similar Features." Although she earned some fans with her debut in 1988, her audience has increased with each new album. When she revealed that she is a lesbian in 1992, her commercial fortunes were not hurt at all; in fact, her audience continued to grow. Because it is rooted in the heartbreak and turmoils of everyday life, Etheridge's music has a widespread appeal that makes her one of the top concert draws and AOR acts of the '90s. *—Stephen Thomas Erlewine*

● **Melissa Etheridge** / 1988 / Island ✦✦✦✦✦

This was one of the most stunning debut albums of the 1980s. Given the domination of synthesizer pop on the radio, Melissa Etheridge was a breath of fresh air when she burst out of the gate with this roots-rock album sung with a sensitive bravado often compared to Janis Joplin. Although the passionate vocal deliveries are similar, the comparisons end there: Etheridge is a Midwesterner who was clearly influenced by classic rock artists such as Bruce Springsteen and John Cougar Mellencamp. The main theme explored is the emotional complexity of relationships, and throughout the album she sings about the hunger for affection, the pain of unrequited love, and the fire of obsessive romance. While the limited scope of the songwriting requires the listener to enter her world and exorcise the demons of relationships past, the album is full of infectious, up-tempo songs that propel the album forward. Etheridge's true talent, however, is reconciling uncontrollable emotions such as jealousy with a strong and fiercely independent spirit ("Similar Features," "Like the Way I Do"). Perhaps that's why Etheridge became a role model for a generation of young women who found her to be an uncompromising artist unafraid to expose (and celebrate) her strengths and weaknesses. This is a fine introduction to Melissa Etheridge, and it is one of her most enjoyable albums. *—Vik Iyengar*

Brave and Crazy / Sep. 1989 / Island ✦✦✦

Not a trace of the dreaded sophomore curse was to be found on Melissa Etheridge's second album. On *Brave and Crazy*, the throaty singer/guitarist/composer is slightly more reflective than on her first release, but no less confident. Nor is she is any less rootsy. Etheridge's earthiness is a large part of her appeal, and she uses it most advantageously on the gutsy rockers "Skin Deep" and "Let Me Go," as well as more reflective pieces such as "Testify," "You Used to Love to Dance" and "You Can Sleep While I Drive" (which, like a lot of Bruce Springsteen's songs, equates long drives with freedom and liberation). As introspective as things get on this CD, Etheridge never becomes wimpy or self-pitying. For all its vulnerability, *Brave and Crazy* is the work of someone who comes across as a survivor. *—Alex Henderson*

Never Enough / Mar. 17, 1992 / Island ✦✦✦

Never Enough displays a newfound maturity for Etheridge. While the songs feature the same sandpaper on barbed wire voice, there's more range and diversity to the material. Fans of Etheridge's full-throttle material may protest, but there are no less than five thoughtful ballads on *Never Enough*, the most successful moodscape being "Dance Without Sleeping," featuring chiming, U2-ish guitar. The album's highlight is also the most unusual addition to the Etheridge catalog. "2001" is a smoldering number set to a hypnotic funk rhythm and a swampy, grungy guitar line. The overall effect is truly memorable. Some will miss the relentless urgency of Etheridge's previous releases; others will be happy to curl up comfortably in the spaciousness of this latest effort. *—Roch Parisien*

Yes I Am / Sep. 21, 1993 / Island ✦✦✦✦

Melissa Etheridge wasn't out of the closet when she released *Yes I Am* in 1993, yet it's hard not to notice the defiant acclamation in the album's title. This barely concealed sense of sexual identity seeps out from the lyrics, and it informs the music as well, which is perhaps the most confident she has ever been. It's also the most professional she's ever been (perhaps not a coincidence), as she belts out these unapologetically anthemic numbers with a sense of finesse that's suited to lifestyle newspaper pages, not rock & roll, thereby setting herself up for her bout with celebrity during the second half of the '90s. *Yes I Am* wouldn't have been as convincing if it wasn't so slick, though; her Springsteen-isms and Janis tributes are tempered by songs that work as album rock favorites, even if they aren't as epic or passionate as their inspirations. She may not have songs as great as she did the first time out—"Somebody Bring Me Some Water" remains her finest moment—but she has a sense of purpose and identity that suits her well. And that identity wound up being the touchstone for the rest of her career. *—Stephen Thomas Erlewine*

Your Little Secret / Nov. 14, 1995 / Island ✦✦

Breakdown / Oct. 5, 1999 / Island ✦✦✦

Shortly after becoming a household name, Melissa Etheridge released *Your Little Secret* in 1995, an album that performed well but didn't quite receive the acclaim or sales of her 1993 breakthrough, *Yes I Am*. Following its release, she took some time off and became a parent. During her self-imposed hiatus, pop music underwent a quiet revolution, as female artists accounted for the majority of record sales and radio play. There were rootsy singer/songwriters in the same vein as Etheridge, but by and large they were overshadowed by the bouncy pop of the Spice Girls and their ilk, Alanis Morissette and her offspring, and Sarah McLachlan and the Lilith Fair crowd. If this affected Etheridge at all, it's not apparent from her comeback, *Breakdown*. There are a couple of concessions to the late '90s, primarily in the presence of subdued, vaguely hip-hop-influenced rhythms that underpin some mid-tempo cuts, but *Breakdown* is the work of an artist who is assured and comfortable, meaning that she's not afraid to play straight-ahead music or to delve deep into her soul. Consequently, it's the most intimate album she's ever made. A by-product of this development is that the record isn't as visceral or immediate as her earlier work, and some of the songs need a few plays before they sink in completely. That may mean that some listeners will not have the patience to truly hear *Breakdown* for what it is—a low-key but revealing record that is intimate even when it rocks the hardest. But those who do will discover that its best moments—whether it's "Scarecrow," her moving tribute to hate-crime victim Matthew Shepard, or the nakedly autobiographical "Mama I'm Strange"—find Etheridge exploring new, refreshingly honest territory that suits this subdued musical style quite well. *—Stephen Thomas Erlewine*

Skin / Jul. 10, 2001 / Island ✦✦✦

If ever there was a perfect breakup album, this is it. *Skin* is Melissa Etheridge's first album since she split with her long-term partner and it takes you on a tour of the hurt, healing, and the journey of making sense of it all. Travel through the pain, longing, and lamenting along with Etheridge herself as she goes "looking for a little salvation." In her own raw, strength-of-heart style and that husky voice of hers, Etheridge sings about the long, trying process that one usually undergoes in order to find the answers, forgiveness, and clues about losing and staying in the game of love. The opening track, "Lover Please," is an aggressive tune where your heroine, wounded heart in hand, sings with true emotion, asking, "Didn't I love you right?" Yet as the songs progress, so does Etheridge's strength. Known for her sensibility for raw emotion, Etheridge delivers nothing less. And on the nostalgic track "Walking on Water," you can sense that she is gaining some footing on her pain and beginning to pick herself up again. But the ballad-like "Down to One" knocks your heart out with one whack as she croons, "My heart is a traitor." Back to square one. The album climaxes and Etheridge sorts through her demons with simple, heartfelt lyrics that hit the spot right through to the truth. But it is her unbridled honesty that drives this album right into your gut. She reveals the depth of her pain on the dark track "Heal Me." Like love, this album simply leaves that infamously ambiguous mystery lingering in the air: Why do people pay so much for love? And Etheridge does it with such conviction, you cannot help but listen closely. —*Kerry L. Smith*

E.U.

f. 1970, Washington, D.C.
Go-Go, Funk

E.U. is one of D.C.'s original go-go bands, but they never scored a pop hit until 1988, when "Da Butt" became a dance sensation, thanks to Spike Lee's *School Daze* movie. While they didn't record many great albums—1989's *Livin' Large*, which was riding on the success of "Da Butt," came the closest—each of their records has something that would appeal to hardcore funk fans. But E.U.'s strength was never captured on vinyl—it was their energetic, groove-oriented live shows that earned them a large following in the '80s, not their records. —*Stephen Thomas Erlewine*

E.U. Live: Two Places at the Same Time / 1986 / Island ✦✦

Go Ju Ju Go / 1987 / E. Unlimited ✦✦✦

● **Livin' Large** / 1989 / Virgin ✦✦✦✦✦

Rare go-go tracks to get national exposure in 1989. —*Ron Wynn*

Cold Kickin' It / 1990 / Virgin ✦✦

Europe

f. 1981, db. 1991
Arena Rock, Hair Metal, Heavy Metal, Hard Rock

Originally a progressive rock group, Europe didn't achieve any success until they reworked their sound into a bombastic yet melodic pop-metal. In their first incarnation, the Swedish band was called Force. The band—featuring the core members Joey Tempest (vocals), John Norum (guitar), and John Leven (bass)—won a national talent contest in the early '80s, which led to a record contract. After changing their name to Europe and releasing two albums in Sweden (*Europe* and *Wings of Tomorrow*), the band landed an international deal with Epic Records. By this time, Norum had left the group and was replaced by Kee Marcello; drummer Ian Haughland and keyboardist Michael Michaeli also joined the lineup.

In 1986, Europe released *The Final Countdown*. On the album, Michaeli's keyboards took a prominent role (they provide the main riff in the hit title track), which nicely complimented the band's smoother pop melodies. The change in style proved successful, as the record became a Top Ten hit in the U.S. and U.K.; both "The Final Countdown" and "Carrie" became Top Ten singles as well. Delivered two years later, *Out of This World* continued the formula of the previous record. It also was a success, although its numbers didn't match those of *The Final Countdown*. Two years later, Europe released their final album, *Prisoners of Paradise*, to little attention. —*Stephen Thomas Erlewine*

● **1982-1992** / 1993 / Epic ✦✦✦✦✦

1982-1992 is a 17-track compilation that contains all of Europe's greatest hits ("The Final Countdown," "Carrie," "Rock the Night," "Cherokee," "Superstitious"), plus several album tracks and a pair of rarities, the single version of "Prisoners in Paradise," and the acoustic version of "I'll Cry for You." While this is certainly the way to go for most fans—only diehards need the original studio albums, which are rather spotty—it may be a bit too much for some casual fans, since much of the material not released as singles simply wasn't as strong or catchy as the hits. —*Stephen Thomas Erlewine*

Eurythmics

f. 1980, London, England, db. 1990
Pop/Rock, New Wave, Synth Pop

Eurythmics were one of the most successful duos to emerge in the early '80s. Where most of their British synth-pop contemporaries disappeared from the charts as soon as new wave faded away in 1984, Eurythmics continued to have hits until the end of the decade, making vocalist Annie Lennox a star in her own right, as well as establishing intstrumentalist Dave Stewart as a successful, savvy producer and songwriter. Originally, the duo channelled the eerily detached sound of electronic synthesizer music into pop songs driven by robotic beats. By the mid-'80s, singles like "Sweet Dreams (Are Made of This)" and "Here Comes the Rain Again" had made the group into international stars and the group had begun to experiment with their sound, delving into soul and R&B. As the decade wore on, the duo's popularity eroded somewhat—by the late '80s, they were hav-

ing trouble cracking the Top 40 in America, although they stayed successful in the U.K. During the early '90s, Eurythmics took an extended hiatus as both Lennox and Stewart pursued solo careers. —*Stephen Thomas Erlewine*

In the Garden / 1981 / RCA ✦✦✦

Eurythmics' debut album, *In the Garden*, is the missing link between the work of the Tourists, who included both Dave Stewart and Annie Lennox, and 1983's commercial breakthrough, *Sweet Dreams (Are Made of This)*. Co-produced by Kraftwerk producer Conny Plank at his studio in Cologne, Germany, it has some of the distant, mechanistic feel of the European electronic music movement, but less of the pop sensibility of later Eurythmics. The chief difference is in Lennox's singing; even when the musical bed is appealing, Lennox floats ethereally over it, and the listener doesn't focus on her. As a result, *In the Garden* wasn't much of a success, though when Eurythmics streamlined their sound and emphasized Lennox's dominating voice on subsequent releases, they found mass popularity. —*William Ruhlmann*

Sweet Dreams (Are Made of This) / Jan. 1983 / RCA ✦✦✦✦✦

The Eurythmics' breakthrough album is a deft mix of electronic thrills, new wave chills, and sultry R&B, the latter supplied by Annie Lennox's warm tenor. Pretty much relying on themselves, Lennox and Dave Stewart slip past the music's usual coldness and into a territory all their own. It can be smug (the new wave here is served with a side of irony) and a tad dull (the long, operatic pieces serve little purpose), but the payoffs—"Love Is a Stranger" and, especially, the magnificent title tune—are among the finest the genre has to offer. —*Michael Gallucci*

Touch / Nov. 1983 / RCA ✦✦✦✦✦

The follow-up to the success of *Sweet Dreams* showed a more confident Lennox and Stewart, ready to expand their stylistic range. It contains the Top 40 hits "Here Comes the Rain Again," "Who's That Girl," and "Right by Your Side." —*Scott Bultman*

1984 (For the Love of Big Brother) / Nov. 1984 / RCA ✦✦

While it is not billed as an Original Motion Picture Soundtrack, this album does contain, as a jacket note indicates, "music derived from Eurythmics." The original score of the motion picture *1984*, it was treated as a side project for marketing purposes, not as Eurythmics' full-fledged fourth new studio album. Fair enough. Much of the album is instrumental, and the closest thing to a pop song, "Sexcrime (Nineteen Eighty-Four)" (which was a Top Ten hit in the U.K.), like the other vocal numbers, relates to the movie's future fiction theme. As such, the album is substandard if judged as an independent Eurythmics album, adequate if judged as a soundtrack. —*William Ruhlmann*

Be Yourself Tonight / May 1985 / RCA ✦✦✦✦

On *Be Yourself Tonight*, Eurythmics' most commercially successful and hit-laden album, the duo meticulously blended the new wave electronic elements that dominated their previous sets with the harder straight-edged rock and soul that would dominate later sets to come up with a near-perfect pop album. This disc scored no less than four hit singles and kept them a mainstay on MTV's play lists during the channel's heyday. Fusing pop, soul, rock, electronic beats, and even gospel, this is arguably the duo's finest moment. The first hit, "Would I Lie to You," is a straight-forward rocker, complete with great guitar licks, a soulful horn section, and Annie Lennox sounding as vicious and vivacious as ever. The second single, which was a huge chart topper in Europe, "There Must Be an Angel," is nothing short of shimmering beauty, with Lennox providing truly angelic vocals and Stevie Wonder lending an enchanting harmonica solo. Aretha Franklin lends her powerhouse pipes for the duet "Sisters Are Doin' It for Themselves," which has gone on to become an immortal feminist anthem. From the soulful electronic beats (a rarity) in "It's Alright (Baby's Coming Back)" to the beauty of the Elvis Costello duet "Adrian" to the pain and longing of the sorrowful rocker "Better to Have Lost in Love (Than Never to Have Loved at All)," this album runs a wide array of musical styles, each song standing tall on its own two feet. This disc is, without a doubt, one of the best rock/pop albums from the 1980s and one of the grandest, most creative albums delivered by the ever-appealing and innovative duo of Annie Lennox and Dave Stewart. A true classic. —*Jose Promis*

Revenge / Jul. 1986 / RCA ✦✦✦

On their fifth album, Eurythmics moved away from the austere synth-pop of their previous work and toward more of a neo-'60s pop/rock stance. "Missionary Man" (which went Top 40 as a single in the U.S. and charted in the U.K.) featured a prominent harmonica solo, while "Thorn in My Side" had a chiming guitar riff reminiscent of the Searchers and a fat sax solo. Of course, the primary element in the group's sound remained Annie Lennox's distinctive alto voice, which was still impressive even if the material was slightly less so. *Revenge* was a successful album, reaching the Top Ten in the U.K. and going gold in the U.S., but it was a disappointment compared to their last three albums. And creatively, it was a step down as well—there was nothing here that they hadn't done a little better before. —*William Ruhlmann*

Savage / Nov. 1987 / RCA ✦✦

We Too Are One / Sep. 1989 / Arista ✦✦✦

Switching to Arista Records in the U.S., Eurythmics made their last album together with *We Too Are One*, and they went out in style. Calling upon a broad pop range, their seventh album was their best since *Be Yourself Tonight* in 1985. The sound was varied, the melodies were strong, and the lyrics were unusually well-crafted. In retrospect, the album can be seen as a dry run for Annie Lennox's debut solo album, *Diva* (1992); songs like "Don't Ask Me Why" (which grazed the U.S. Top 40) serve as precursors to the dramatic ballads to come. There is, however, an air of romantic resignation throughout *We Too Are One*, appropriate to its valedictory nature. The disc spawned four chart singles in the U.K. and returned Eurythmics to number one in the album charts, but it did not substantially improve Eurythmics' reduced commercial standing in the U.S., confirming that it was time for Lennox and Dave Stewart to pursue other opportunities. *—William Ruhlmann*

- **Greatest Hits** / May 1991 / Arista ✦✦✦✦✦

It may have taken them a little while to get going, but when the Eurythmics hit their stride with their second album *Sweet Dreams (Are Made of This)*, they began a hit streak that defined them as one of the most commercially successful and musically satisfying new wave bands of the '80s. For six years, the group was reliable, turning out at least one great single on each album, none of which sounded identical, yet all were recognizable as the work of Dave Stewart and Annie Lennox. *Greatest Hits* summarizes those glorious years and while it misses a couple of hits—a bad thing when the sublime "Right by Your Side" is concerned, but not when "Sexcrime (Nineteen Eighty-Four)" is—it remains an excellent collection. It might not follow a strict chronological order, but it flows nicely, revealing that the band that produced such chilly synth-pop classics as "Sweet Dreams," "Here Comes the Rain Again," "Love Is a Stranger," and "Who's That Girl?" were capable of delivering equally captivating light pop and ballads ("There Must Be an Angel (Playing With My Heart)," "Don't Ask Me Why," "Thorn in My Side"), ersatz soul ("Sisters Are Doin' It for Themselves"), and hard-driving rock & roll ("Missionary Man," "I Need a Man"). Few of their contemporaries were capable of such range and *Greatest Hits* proves that the best of the Eurythmics' work were undeniable pop classics. *—Stephen Thomas Erlewine*

Live 1983-1989 / Nov. 15, 1993 / Arista ✦✦

Peace / Oct. 19, 1999 / Arista ✦✦✦

Nearly a decade after Eurythmics went on an unannounced, virtually unnoticed hiatus in 1990, Annie Lennox and Dave Stewart returned with the heavily publicized *Peace*. Both Lennox and Stewart had been silent since 1995, which means that reuniting really wasn't a sacrifice, since their solo careers had stalled. In fact, it was a wise idea to re-team, both commercially and artistically, since their best and most popular music was made together. What's odd is that *Peace* strongly resembles Lennox's *Diva*. True, Eurythmics were moving toward the melodramatic grandeur of *Diva* on their final '80s album, *We Too Are One*, yet they still had an innate sense of quirkiness and a desire to take risks. In 1999, they're more about craft, which only emphasizes the maturity of the music. That's not entirely a bad thing, even if it means that *Peace* needs a couple of spins before the songs begin to register. Lennox and Stewart know how to write gently insinuating melodies and how to layer their tracks with small sonic details, weaving lush tapestries of sound. *Peace* keeps its alluring mood throughout; even when they attempt to revisit their Stones-y tendencies, the songs play as sleekly and smoothly as the ballads that dominate the record. In one sense, that's good, because it means that *Peace* keeps a consistent tone from front to back, but it also means that most of the songs blend together. There are no standout singles here, and that's the hardest thing to accept about the record since Eurythmics were one of the best singles bands of the '80s. Even so, *Peace* is a successful debut for Eurythmics, Mark II—it's classy adult pop, delivered with style and grace. *—Stephen Thomas Erlewine*

Faith Evans

Vocals / Urban, Hip-Hop

Perhaps not as well known as her late husband, the Notorious B.I.G., Faith Evans has actually been in the music business for a longer period of time as a singer and songwriter. Evans began singing at age two in her Newark, NJ, church, going on to perform in high school musicals, study both jazz and classical music, and even win the title of New Jersey Miss Fashion Teen. She attended Fordham University for a year, but left to pursue a career in the music industry. She wrote songs and sang background vocals for artists such as Pebbles, Color Me Badd, and Mary J. Blige before meeting rap sensation Biggie Smalls at a photo shoot. The two were married nine days later, and Evans guested on B.I.G.'s "One More Chance." Her self-titled debut album was released in 1995 and featured the hit single "You Used to Love Me." Separated from Smalls prior to his 1997 murder, Evans was nevertheless prominently featured on Puff Daddy's tribute to the late rapper, the monster hit "I'll Be Missing You"; her own *Keep the Faith* album followed in 1998, scoring with the single "Never Gonna Let You Go." *—Steve Huey*

Faith / 1995 / Bad Boy ✦✦✦

Faith Evans had written songs for a variety of new jack and hip-hop artists (including Mary J. Blige, Al Be Sure!, Pebbles, and Christopher Williams) before releasing her first album, *Faith*. The record proves that she is as powerful in the spotlight as she is behind the scenes. Evans builds on a basic, hip-hop-influenced funk, alternating between simmering grooves and sultry ballads. *Faith* does have a couple of dull spots, but the album is a first-class debut. *—Stephen Thomas Erlewine*

- **Keep the Faith** / Oct. 27, 1998 / Bad Boy ✦✦✦✦

Faith Evans' second album, *Keep the Faith*, was met with quite a bit of anticipation. The album was released three years after her acclaimed, soulful, and raw debut, *Faith*, and in that time she had witnessed the murder of her husband, the Notorious B.I.G., which led to the biggest hit of her career, the tribute "I'll Be Missing You" (in collaboration with Puff Daddy). *Keep the Faith* proved to be a success, and she happily avoided the curse of the sophomore slump. The album scored two Top Ten singles with the irresistible dance/R&B cut "Love Like This" and its follow-up, the equally intoxicating "All Night Long." Aside from those two dance numbers, the rest of the album falls somewhere between heavy ballads and mid-tempo grooves. Ms. Evans shines when she sings fast or mid-tempo songs, such as the slick "Life Will Pass You By," but the ballads weigh too heavily on this otherwise fine album. Some of the ballads stand tall, such as the gorgeous "My First Love" and the inspiration-tinged "Keep the Faith," while others are about as entertaining and inspired as tree sap ("Anything You Need" and the yawn-inducing interludes). Unfortunately, these ballads are all lumped together on this album, to the point where they almost blend into one long drip of molasses. However, the classy Ms. Evans possesses a beautiful voice, is a gifted songwriter, and happily steers clear of the tacky clichés that burden so much contemporary R&B. So despite the heavy reliance on ballads, this is actually a fine album, and is without a doubt a highlight of 1990s soul-pop music. *—Jose Promis*

Everclear

f. 1992, Portland, OR

Grunge, Alternative Pop/Rock, Hard Rock

Though Everclear's Northwestern grunge-punk style was hardly revolutionary when the band became popular in 1995, the band's superb songs and Art Alexakis' us-against-them lyrics were taken to heart by bored Gen-X teens. Also elemental to Everclear's success is their obsessive touring schedule and agressive self-promotion. The death of both his brother and girlfriend by drug overdoses convinced Alexakis to kick his own cocaine habit in the mid-'80s, and he later formed a country-punk band named Colorfinger. In 1992, he met Craig Montoya and Everclear's first drummer, Scott Cuthbert; the trio recorded a demo EP that was released on Portland, OR's Tim/Kerr label. Alexakis grew frustrated with the company's lack of promotion, so he hired an independent promoter to push the EP and personally mailed copies to media outlets and distributors. Everclear then added several songs to the EP and released it as *World of Noise* in 1993. During 1994, the group toured relentlessly, replaced Cuthbert with Greg Eklund, and signed to Capitol in June. Their second album *Sparkle and Fade* appeared in 1995, and alternative radio quickly picked up on the singles "Santa Monica" and "Heroin Girl." *So Much for the Afterglow* followed in 1997. *—John Bush*

World of Noise / 1995 / Capitol ✦✦✦

World of Noise is an album of alternately crisp and noisy indie-punk. Great melodies (especially on "Fire Maple Song") and A.P. Alexakis' witty, gravelly vocals make this album a left-hook of a debut. *—John Bush*

Sparkle and Fade / May 23, 1995 / Capitol ✦✦✦✦

Everclear's major label debut is a tough, melodic set of gnarled, post-punk hard rock. An easy comparison is Nirvana, but Everclear's music is closer to the country-rock leanings of Screaming Trees—underneath their loud, grungy guitars there is a distinct rootsiness lacking in most Seattle bands and that give *Sparkle and Fade* its edge. *—Stephen Thomas Erlewine*

- **So Much for the Afterglow** / Oct. 7, 1997 / Capitol ✦✦✦✦

Sparkle and Fade became a surprise hit thanks to "Santa Monica," a gritty, infectious grunge hit that captured Everclear at their best. Like many grunge and post-grunge rockers, however, Everclear's leader Art Alexakis felt constrained by his modest success and its implications, deciding to take his band in new experimental directions for their follow-up album, *So Much for the Afterglow*. As the title suggests—as well as song titles like "One Hit Wonder," "White Men in Black Suits" and "Everything to Everyone"—Alexakis is feeling a bit ambivalent about his success, believing that it's only a transient thing. He may be right—*So Much for the Afterglow* lacks anything as catchy as "Santa Monica." He attempts to compensate by adding a more elaborate production, complete with Beach Boys harmonies and guest musicians. The result sounds cluttered, not symphonic, and distracts from Everclear's strength as a straight-ahead grunge trio. There are several songs on the album that do showcase the group at their best, but they aren't enough to excuse the confused attempts at progression that make *So Much for the Afterglow* a muddled affair. *—Stephen Thomas Erlewine*

Songs from an American Movie, Vol. 1: Learning How to Smile / Jul. 11, 2000 / Capitol ✦✦✦✦

If the two-part title wasn't a tip-off, let's make this clear: *Songs From an American Movie, Vol. 1: Learning How to Smile* is a concept album, based on Everclear leader Art Alexakis' divorce. Many pop musicians have mined this territory before, but Alexakis pulls off an ingenious move by dividing his divorce album in two parts and two records, separating falling in love from the fallout. *Learning How to Smile* is the courtship album, painting a picture of when everything was wonderful. He goes back further than that, returning to his childhood, specifically the sparkling, catchy late-'60s and '70s pop that provided the soundtrack to his coming of age. It's all innocent, from the sounds and melodies to the aesthetic; at first, it's hard to tell that this music was made in the wake of a divorce. As the album unfolds, certain themes of regret, sadness, and longing run to the surface, but they're all coated in glittering pop melodies and big rock riffs that mask the emotions of the songs. And, make no mistake, Alexakis is digging deep into his psyche, especially at the end of the record as the romance begins to fall apart. What makes *Learning to Smile* work—and an album this ambitious could easily have collapsed under its own weight—is that the songs are strong and smart and are given savvy productions that make them sound even smarter. Very few of Everclear's peers could have pulled off an album that skillfully balances such an arty concept with such strong, strikingly revealing songs. *Songs From an American Movie, Vol. 1* is their best, most consistent effort to date—and certainly whets the appetite for the sequel. *—Stephen Thomas Erlewine*

Songs From an American Movie, Vol. 2: Good Time for a Bad Attitude / Nov. 21, 2000 / Capitol ✦✦✦

Everclear separated their double album into two different albums, isolating the poppier songs (thematically, the courtship songs) onto the first album, leaving *Songs From an American Movie, Vol. 2: Good Time for a Bad Attitude* as the hard rock record (thematically, the divorce songs, or, as Art Alexakis puts it, "When It All Goes Wrong Again"). This may have concentrated their talents a little bit too much, but it does result in two pretty dynamic, effective records—albums whose connections only become apparent through close listening, which is a compliment. If *Good Time* pales slightly to its predecessor, it's because it isn't as sonically varied as *Vol. 1*, even if it's still quite catchy. And this is the great thing about Everclear's advanced age, compared to their peers—they not only have a greater musical reach, they are stronger craftsmen, not afraid to give their big riffs big melodies and pacing the record well, even if it winds up being heavy on hard-rockers. Yes, sometimes they seem a little out of step—the Spike character on "Babytalk" seemed just as out of date when Tom Petty wrote about him on 1986's *Southern Accents*—but this is still a stronger post-grunge record than most, heavy on heavy rock, fine songcraft, and lyrics. If Alexakis occasionally delves into inadvertent misogyny, he balances it with sharp wit and warm humanity, plus fine riffs and melodies. —*Stephen Thomas Erlewine*

Betty Everett

b. Nov. 23, 1939, Greenwood, MS, **d.** Aug. 17, 2001, Beloit, WI
Vocals, Piano / Pop-Soul, Soul
Betty Everett sang gospel growing up in Greenwood, MS, before relocating to Chicago and moving into secular music. She began recording for Cobra in 1958, then joined Vee-Jay in the early '60s and started to land hit records. Her original version of "You're No Good," though sung with fire and verve, didn't make much impact until it was turned into a number one pop hit by Linda Ronstadt in 1975. Her next single, "The Shoop Shoop Song (It's in His Kiss)," was her first major release, peaking at number six pop in 1964. Her next success was the duet "Let It Be Me" with Jerry Butler, a soul version of the Everly Brothers tune that reached number five R&B that same year. Everett's finest song as a solo act was 1969's "There'll Come a Time," which reached number two on the R&B charts and also cracked the pop Top 30 at number 26. Everett was now on Uni, where she remained until 1970. She continued recording for Fantasy until 1974 and made one other record for United Artists in 1978. A comeback performance for the 2000 PBS special *Doo Wop 51* was her last public appearance; she died at her Wisconsin home in August 2001. —*Ron Wynn*

There'll Come a Time / 1969 / Varese Sarabande ✦✦✦✦✦
Everett made her best records for Vee-Jay in the mid-'60s, but this album, originally released on Uni in 1969, isn't far behind in merit. Featuring her number two R&B single (and Top 40 pop hit) "There'll Come a Time," this has much more of a sweet soul flavor than her Vee-Jay sides, at times blending the trademarks of her brassy native Chicago scene with a Philadelphia influence. It's far from too sweet, though, with strong material, punchy arrangements, and Everett's always dependably energetic and warm vocals. It also contains the R&B hit "I Can't Say No to You." The CD reissue adds three valuable 1969-1970 singles that were previously unavailable on album, including the Top 20 R&B hit "It's Been a Long Time," arranged by Donny Hathaway and written by Kenny Gamble, Leon Huff, and Jerry Butler. —*Richie Unterberger*

● **The Shoop Shoop Song** / Nov. 22, 1993 / Vee-Jay ✦✦✦✦
Though sometimes classified as a girl group singer because of the Top Ten success of "The Shoop Shoop Song," Betty Everett's main thrust was much more in the R&B/soul vein. This excellent 25-track anthology of her 1963-1965 material shows her facility with various soul, R&B, and pop styles. She had three other minor hits—the original hit version of "You're No Good," the energetic Goffin/King pop/rocker "I Can't Hear You," and Van McCoy's soulful "Gettin' Mighty Crowded"—all of which are featured here. But most of the other material is equally enjoyable, including other early efforts by McCoy, Valerie Simpson, and Nick Ashford, and even P.F. Sloan (whose "Can I Get to Know You" is presented in a much earthier, slower version here than the Turtles' rendition several years later). This CD doesn't include her hit duets with fellow Chicago soulster Jerry Butler, but is a consistently enjoyable retrospective of an underrated singer who straddled the soul and pop worlds. —*Richie Unterberger*

The Fantasy Years / Oct. 3, 1995 / Fantasy ✦✦✦
For the first half of the 1970s, Everett recorded updated soul-pop for the Fantasy label with mixed but generally positive results. This 18-track compilation features cuts from two mid-'70s LPs, as well as various singles from the early '70s, including the R&B hits "I Got to Tell You," "Ain't Nothing Gonna Change Me," and "Sweet Dan." Not nearly as pop-oriented as her more famous mid-'60s recordings, this finds Everett in fine, expressive voice, but somewhat at the mercy of the quality of the material, which is variable. The selections from the 1975 *Happy Endings* album are kind of anonymous, but much of the rest is good, gutsy '70s soul. Johnny "Guitar" Watson helps out on a few numbers, as co-producer, guitarist, and occasional songwriter, and a couple were cut in Memphis with the Hi Rhythm Section. —*Richie Unterberger*

● **The Shoop Shoop Song (It's in His Kiss)** / Jun. 20, 2000 / Collectables ✦✦✦✦✦
These are Betty Everett recordings, minus the duets with Jerry Butler, from 1963 to 1966—the Vee Jay years. A thorough overview for the period covered, but not a definitive collection of Everett's career because it doesn't include earlier tracks (she began recording in 1961), or later recordings on ABC, Uni ("There Come a Time"), Fantasy, Soundstage, United Artists, or 20th Century Fox Records. But if you want her solo Vee Jay Records' story, this is it, includes the substantial hits "The Shoop, Shoop Song" and "You're No Good," Van McCoy's unsung "Getting Mighty Crowded," as well as three early Valerie Simpson/Nicholas Ashford/Joshie Armstead compositions, "Too Hot to Hold," "The Real Thing," and "The Shoe Won't Fit." —*Andrew Hamilton*

Everlast (Eric Schrody)

Vocals / Rap-Rock, Hardcore Rap, Alternative Rap
Once best known for his tenure in the rap unit House of Pain, Everlast successfully reinvented himself in 1998 with the best-selling *Whitey Ford Sings the Blues*, a largely

acoustic, hip-hop-flavored effort in the genre-crossing mold of Beck. Born Erik Schrody, Everlast first surfaced in Los Angeles as a member of Ice-T's Rhyme Syndicate Cartel, issuing his debut album *Forever Everlasting* in 1990. When the album failed to find an audience, he formed House of Pain with MC Danny Boy and DJ Lethal; carving out an image which drew heavily on Everlast and Danny Boy's shared Irish heritage, the trio managed to overcome the stereotypes facing white rappers and scored a massive hit with their 1992 single "Jump Around." Their self-titled debut LP also went platinum, but when follow-ups including 1994's *Same as It Ever Was* and 1996's *Truth Crushed to Earth Shall Rise Again* failed to repeat House of Pain's early success, the group disbanded. Everlast then returned to his solo career, but while recording *Whitey Ford Sings the Blues* he suffered a massive cardiac arrest stemming from a congenital defect, resulting in heart bypass surgery and an artificial valve implant. Following his recovery, he completed the album, which appeared in the fall of 1998 to strong commercial notices: hitting the Top Ten, going platinum, and launching the Top 40 single "What It's Like." After appearing on Santana's vaunted comeback album *Supernatural*, Everlast began work on a follow-up with an eclectic group of guest artists. Titled *Eat at Whitey's*, the album was released in late 2000. —*Jason Ankeny*

Forever Everlasting / Mar. 27, 1990 / Warner Brothers ✦✦✦
Here's a little known fact of rap history: before Everlast enjoyed recognition as a member of House of Pain, he pursued a career as a solo artist. *Forever Everlasting*, his first and only pre-Pain solo album, is a decent, though not outstanding release proving that he had strong rapping skills long before becoming well known. Ice-T, who serves as this CD's executive producer, once said of Everlast, "Hearing him rap, you'd never know he was white"—and to be sure, the L.A.-based MC is far from a pop rapper. Though most of his lyrics aren't remarkable, this CD definitely has its moments—most notably, "Speak No Evil" (a reflection on injustice in America) and the angry "Fuck Everyone." —*Alex Henderson*

● **Whitey Ford Sings the Blues** / Sep. 8, 1998 / Tommy Boy ✦✦✦✦✦
Saying that Everlast showed a great deal of artistic growth between his first and second solo albums would be a understatement. While 1989/1990's *Forever Everlasting* was a decent, if uneven, debut, Everlast's second solo album, *Whitey Ford Sings the Blues* is an amazingly eclectic gem that finds him really pushing himself creatively. Between those two albums, Everlast joined and left House of Pain, which evolved into one of the most distinctive rap groups of the 1990s. While Pain's albums thrived on wildness for its own sake, *Whitey Ford* has a much more introspective and serious tone. Everlast, who was born with a heart defect, was in the process of recording the album when he needed life-saving open-heart surgery; in fact, he was lucky that he was around to see *Whitey Ford* completed and released. Though not without its share of hardcore B-boy rap, *Whitey Ford* also finds Everlast playing acoustic guitar, doing some singing and exploring folk-rock, Memphis soul and heavy metal. As a singer, Everlast has a relaxed style that sounds a bit like Gil Scott-Heron. "Today (Watch Me Shine)," "Ends" and "What It's Like" venture into Neil Young/Bob Dylan territory, while "Hot to Death" is blistering metal with industrial touches. And the plot thickens—on "The Letter," he raps over a jazz-influenced piano. Given how rap's hardcore tends to frown on rappers crossing over to rock, it took guts for Everlast to be so diverse. But it's a good thing that he did, for his risk-taking pays off handsomely on this outstanding release. —*Alex Henderson*

Eat at Whitey's / Oct. 17, 2000 / Tommy Boy ✦✦✦✦
Nobody ever would have guessed that the leader of House of Pain would come back after a bout of obscurity and a serious heart attack to reinvent himself as a hip-hop troubadour, rasping out bluesy folk-rock to a steady-rolling beat. The fact that Everlast had the vision to change his tune was surprising enough, but the fact that it worked *and* found a wide audience was stunning. When it came time to deliver *Eat at Whitey's*, the follow-up to *Whitey Ford Sings the Blues*, in 2000, Everlast was smart enough to expand on a good thing, turning out a sequel that built on the folk-rap-rock that rejuvenated his career, while adding slight new twists. The problem is, the new twists, particularly in the guise of cameos from rockers like Carlos Santana and Warren Haynes, don't work particularly well. Also, whenever he veers toward straight rap, such as on the B-Real duet "Deadly Assassins," the music falls a little flat—just like it did on the predecessor. Still, these not-quite successful moments don't detract from an album that delivers on the promise of *Whitey Ford*. Whenever Everlast lays back and spins stories and tall tales on his own, his blend of folk, rock, blues, rap, and pop culture clicks. It can be a little silly—his rhymes are occasionally goofy, his growl a little too raspy—but at its best, it's evocative, catchy, and ingratiating. If he can't sustain the quality of the first three songs throughout the record, at least it connects several more times, enough to make *Eat at Whitey's* satisfying for listeners that want a little more of "What It's Like." —*Stephen Thomas Erlewine*

The Everly Brothers

f. 1954, **db.** 1973
Close Harmony, Folk-Rock, Pop, Rockabilly, Country-Rock, Rock & Roll
The Everly Brothers were not only among the most important and best early rock & roll stars, but also among the most influential rockers of any era. They set unmatched standards for close, two-part harmonies and infused early rock & roll with some of the best elements of country and pop music. Their legacy was and is felt enormously in all rock acts that employ harmonies as prime features, from the Beatles, Simon & Garfunkel, and legions of country-rockers to modern-day roots rockers like Dave Edmunds and Nick Lowe (who once recorded an EP of Everlys songs together). 1957's "Bye Bye Love" began a phenomenal three-year string of classic hit singles for Cadence, including "Wake Up Little Susie," "All I Have to Do Is Dream," "Bird Dog," "('Til) I Kissed You," and

"When Will I Be Loved." The Everlys sang of young love with a heart-rending yearning and compelling melodies. The harmonies owed audible debts to Appalachian country music, but were imbued with a keen modern pop sensibility that made them more accessible without sacrificing any power or beauty. They were not as raw as the wild rockabilly men from Sun Records, but they could rock hard when they wanted. In 1960, the Everlys left Cadence for a lucrative contract with the then-young Warner Bros. label (though it's not often noted, the Everlys would do a lot to establish Warners as a major force in the record business). It's sometimes been written that the duo never recaptured the magic of their Cadence recordings, but actually Phil and Don peaked both commercially and artistically with their first Warners releases. "Cathy's Clown," their first Warners single, was one of their greatest songs and a number one hit. The hits kept coming for a couple of years, some great ("Walk Right Back," "Temptation"), some displaying a distressing, increasing tendency toward soft pop and maudlin sentiments ("Ebony Eyes," "That's Old Fashioned"). In the late '60s, they also helped pioneer country-rock with the 1968 album *Roots*, their most sophisticated and unified full-length statement. *—Richie Unterberger*

The Everly Brothers / 1958 / Rhino ✦✦✦✦✦
Although the Everlys hadn't quite fully matured as artists, their debut is a fine, consistent effort divided between original material and respectably energetic covers of early rockers by Little Richard, Gene Vincent, and Ray Charles. Besides their first few hits, it includes some superb, underappreciated tracks that are nearly as good, like "Should We Tell Him" and "I Wonder if I Cared as Much." *—Richie Unterberger*

Songs Our Daddy Taught Us / 1959 / Rhino ✦✦✦
The Everlys had reached their commercial peak when they made this album of sparsely arranged traditional songs, a concept that was quite a surprise from a top rock & roll act, and considerably ahead of its time. It's actually not as enduring as their early rockers and pop ballads, but the singing is superb on their interpretations of standards like "Barbara Allen" and "Kentucky." *—Richie Unterberger*

The Fabulous Style of the Everly Brothers / 1960 / Rhino ✦✦✦✦✦
The best of their original Cadence albums, packed with hits ("Bird Dog," "All I Have To Do Is Dream," "When Will I Be Loved," "'Til I Kissed You") and other classic tracks ("Devoted to You," "Let It Be Me," "Since You Broke My Heart," "Like Strangers"). Almost all of the songs show up on their greatest hits collections, so it might be a superfluous purchase for all but serious fans, despite its top-drawer quality. *—Richie Unterberger*

It's Everly Time / 1960 / Warner Brothers ✦✦✦✦✦
While the Everlys' sound was diluted by more elaborate production in the '60s, that's not at all true on this LP, which is one of their very best. Not a stiff among the 12-tracks, most of which are barely known outside of serious Everly fans. Includes six stellar contributions by Boudleaux and Felice Bryant, one of Don Everly's best compositions ("So Sad"), and incredible harmony singing throughout. *—Richie Unterberger*

A Date with the Everly Brothers / 1961 / Warner Brothers ✦✦✦✦✦
Although the material is not on the killer level of *It's Everly Time*, there are some very fine songs on their second Warner LP. Includes "Cathy's Clown," their raucous cover of Little Richard's "Lucille," "Love Hurts" (which preceded Roy Orbison's hit version), and "So How Come" (covered by the Beatles in 1963 on the BBC). *—Richie Unterberger*

The Very Best of the Everly Brothers / Aug. 1964 / Warner Brothers ✦
The operative word here is: beware. This does indeed have 12 of their biggest hits, but half of them are re-recorded versions of Cadence-era material. It's not that they're bad or radically different (after all, they were recorded only a few years later). But why settle for these when only the originals will do? *—Richie Unterberger*

Gone, Gone, Gone / 1965 / Warner Brothers ✦✦

Two Yanks in England / 1966 / Demon ✦✦✦✦
At first glance, this seems like a cash-in on the British Invasion. Recorded in London in 1966, no less than eight of the 12 songs were written by the Hollies (who released their own versions of many of the tunes). There are also covers of hits by the Spencer Davis Group and Manfred Mann. With a harder rock guitar sound (though not overdone or inappropriate) than previous Everlys discs, the duo's interpretations are actually worth hearing in their own right. The harmonies are fabulous, and indeed, the Everlys improve a few of the Hollies' songs substantially. "So Lonely" and "Hard Hard Year," in particular, have a lot more force, transforming the tunes from decent Hollies album tracks to excellence. Because so much of the material is non-original, this couldn't be placed in the top rank of Everly Brothers recordings. But it is a good effort that shows them, almost ten years after "Bye Bye Love," still at the top of their game and still heavily committed to a rock & roll sound. This was a bold contrast to other '50s white rock & rollers with roots in country, most of who had retreated to tamer country-oriented sounds by the mid-'60s. *—Richie Unterberger*

Roots / 1968 / Warner Brothers ✦✦✦✦✦
Considered one of the finest early country-rock albums, this showed the Everlys, unlike virtually every other top rock & roll act of the '50s, keeping abreast of contemporary rock and pop trends. In the manner of their 1958 LP *Songs Our Daddy Taught Us*, the concept was to cover songs by performers and composers that had been influential on the duo, including Jimmie Rodgers, Merle Haggard, traditional standards, and a couple of numbers by Ron Elliott of the Beau Brummels. Although this laid-back, tasteful, acoustic-oriented recording isn't as outstanding as their classic early hits, the vocals are superb, conveying qualities of innocence tempered by experience. *—Richie Unterberger*

Nashville Tennessee Nov 1955 / 1981 / Bear Family ✦✦

The Reunion Concert / 1984 / Mercury ✦✦✦
Lively, if ultimately too slick, this concert recording ties up a few loose ends. *—Bruce Eder*

EB 84 / 1984 / Razor & Tie ✦✦✦
After their televised reunion concert, the Everlys made a commercial and artistic comeback with *EB 84*. With Dave Edmunds producing, Phil and Don brought their sound into the '80s while maintaining their trademark harmonies. Lifted by Paul McCartney's "Wings of a Nightingale" and Jeff Lynne's ethereal "The Story of Me," this record has more to offer than simply nostalgia. *—J.P. Ollio*

All They Had to Do Was Dream / 1985 / Rhino ✦✦✦
Alternate takes of much of their strongest material from the Cadence era, cut between 1957 and 1960. A bit more tentative than the familiar renditions, these aren't as good as the versions that ended up on official releases, but are enjoyable and fascinating glimpses of works in progress, and the singing is excellent throughout. Includes different versions of hits like "Wake Up Little Susie," "All I Have to Do Is Dream," "'Til I Kissed You," and "When Will I Be Loved." *—Richie Unterberger*

★ **Cadence Classics: Their 20 Greatest Hits** / 1986 / Rhino ✦✦✦✦✦
The single-disc collection *Cadence Classics: Their 20 Greatest Hits* compiles all of the Everly Brothers' hits, plus many terrific album tracks, from the duo's recordings for Cadence Records in the late '50s. Every one of the Everlys' biggest hits, including "Bye Bye Love," "I Wonder If I Care As Much," "Wake Up, Little Susie," "This Little Girl of Mine," "All I Have to Do Is Dream," "Claudette," "Bird Dog," "Devoted to You," "Problems," "Message to Mary," "(Til) I Kissed You," "Let It Be Me," and "When Will I Be Loved." *Cadence Classics* misses no essential track, making it a definitive collection and the perfect introduction to the duo's sound. *—Stephen Thomas Erlewine*

Hidden Gems from the Warner Years / 1989 / Ace ✦✦✦✦✦
This collects 14 songs that originally appeared on non-hit singles between 1962 and 1965; many of them had never been on LP. This material strongly counters the view that the Everlys faded artistically after "Cathy's Clown." The writing credits for these strong compositions read a bit like a who's who of early-'60s pop/rock, with contributions from Gerry Goffin, Mann/Weill, Doc Pomus and Mort Shuman, Sonny Curtis, Boudleaux and Felice Bryant, and the Everlys themselves. The singing is fabulous, and the arrangements still strong, rock-oriented, and tastefully produced. Tracks like "Nancy's Minuet" (1963), a great Don Everly original and one of their best paeans to lovelorn melancholia, and "You're the One I Love" (1964), a fine, brooding mid-tempo rocker, stand with their very best work. Only three of these appear on the '60s Everlys anthology *Walk Right Back*, making this a necessary purchase for Everlys fans. *—Richie Unterberger*

Best of the Everly Brothers: Rare Solo Classics / 1991 / Curb ✦✦✦
Between their breakup in 1973 and their reunion in 1983, Don and Phil Everly did a lot of recording on their own without achieving much in the way of commercial success, though Phil did reach the U.K. Top Ten in a duet with Cliff Richard on the excellent "She Means Nothing to Me" in 1983. You won't find that song here, but you will find 18 performances in 50 minutes of songs mostly released on singles—by Don on Hickory Records in 1976-77, by Phil on Curb Records in 1980-81. There's more of Don (who made the 1977 *Brother Juke-Box* album for Hickory) than there is of Phil, but the tracks are all mixed up, the singers are not identified on the jacket, and we bet you'll have trouble telling them apart. One hint: Don, freed of the brotherly harmonies, usually likes to sing solo lead against backup choruses, while Phil often recreates brother-like duo vocals. In either case, the brothers separately pursued a country-rock-pop style similar to what they did together. There are some good performances here, but as you might expect, this is a record more for Everly fans than first-time listeners. *—William Ruhlmann*

Classic Everly Brothers / 1992 / Bear Family ✦✦✦✦✦
The three-disc box set *Classic Everly Brothers* collects all of their Cadence recordings, including alternate takes, as well as several early radio shows and the four tracks the duo recorded for Columbia in 1955. While this music is the most essential the brothers ever made, the disc of rarities is only of interest to devoted fans. Nevertheless, the sound on the box is stellar, the liner notes are excellent, and the whole package is wonderful; for hardcore fans, the set is worth the money. *—Stephen Thomas Erlewine*

The Mercury Years / Jul. 20, 1993 / Mercury ✦✦✦✦
Mercury Years collects all of the finest moments from their two 1980s albums; its best moments, like "On the Wings of a Nightingale," are surprisingly strong. *—Stephen Thomas Erlewine*

☆ **Walk Right Back: The Everly Brothers on Warner Bros.** / Sep. 14, 1993 / Warner Archive ✦✦✦✦✦
This two-CD, 50-track compilation assembles the Everly Brothers' most memorable recordings of the 1960s. Although their work from this period has sometimes been criticized as inferior to their classic '50s recordings for Cadence, the best of these songs are a match for anything the duo recorded. As it happens, the strongest of these tunes are drawn from their first two albums for Warners in the 1960s, including the hits "Cathy's Clown" and "So Sad." In the following years, their material suffered from increasing inconsistency and ill-suited production. Yet the Brothers continued to intermittently hit the mark squarely—not only with early-'60s hits like "Crying in the Rain" and "Temptation," but neglected flop singles like "Nancy's Minuet" and "You're the One I Love," as well as the hard-rocking minor 1964 hit "Gone Gone Gone" (their last Top 40 single). They also showed a willingness to incorporate the hard-rocking beat of the British Invasion into their work that was not shared by any of the other major stars of the '50s. This compilation misses a number of fine B-sides and non-hit singles from the early and mid-'60s (check the Ace import collection *Hidden Gems* for those) and perhaps leans too heavily on their tepid late-'60s country-rock. But it's a good overview of a body of work that is often unfairly overlooked. *—Richie Unterberger*

☆ **Heartaches & Harmonies [Box Set]** / Oct. 18, 1994 / Rhino ♦♦♦♦♦
This four-CD, 102-song set includes all of their key performances, as well as many overlooked ones, dating from a previously unreleased 1951 radio performance of "Don't Let Our Love Die" to a 1990 live rendition of the very same tune. Opening with a disc's worth of classic Cadence performances, most of the next three CDs are given over to their largely overlooked Warner Bros. '60s output, including many interesting flop singles and album tracks, as well as top-notch rarities like an alternate version of the supremely moody "Nancy's Minuet" and the mid-'60s outtake "And I'll Go." Fine liner notes with detailed comments from the Everlys themselves, but it still manages to miss some great tunes (like the 1964 single "You're the One I Love" and various tracks from their late-'50s and early-'60s LPs), and shouldn't be considered a definitive collection of all their great performances. And the hard fact is, a lot of their post-1966 material (which comprises some of disc three and all of disc four) is kind of boring. *—Richie Unterberger*

● **All-Time Original Hits** / Nov. 2, 1999 / Rhino ♦♦♦♦♦
Rhino's 16-track collection *All-Time Original Hits* provides a useful service by compiling the Everly Brothers' greatest hits from both Cadence and Warner onto one disc. This, of course, means that many great songs are missing, particularly from the Cadence era, since only the A-sides of Top Ten singles were chosen for inclusion (which means such classics as "I Wonder if I Care As Much," "This Little Girl of Mine," "Claudette," "Poor Jenny," and "Like Strangers" are absent). Still, it's nice to have "Bye Bye Love," "Wake Up Little Susie," "Bird Dog," "('Til) I Kissed You," "When Will I be Loved," "Cathy's Clown," "Ebony Eyes," "Walk Right Back," and "Crying in the Rain" on one disc, which may make it preferable to *Cadence Classics* and *Walk Right Back: The Everly Brothers on Warner Bros.* for some casual fans. One caveat: the mixes on *All-Time Original Hits* sound wrong, with the voices pushed too far up in the mix and the instruments a little bit muted. At times, these mixes are disarming enough to distract from the actual music, at least to listeners well-acquainted with other mixes that are closer to the originals. *—Stephen Thomas Erlewine*

The Complete Cadence Recordings: 1957-1960 / Apr. 3, 2001 / Varese ♦♦♦♦♦
Strictly speaking, the title of this two-CD, 47-song collection is not accurate. This does have every recording the Everly Brothers released while they were on the Cadence label in 1957-1960, and does also include at least one version (always the more familiar one, in case only one is used) of every *song* the pair recorded for the label. However, it does not include most of the alternate versions that were released on the Rhino collection *All They Had to Do Was Dream.* That technicality out of the way, this is a very good collection for those who want more early Everly Brothers than a Cadence best-of disc, but may not want to have every last thing (and you can always pick up *All They Had to Do Was Dream* as a supplement), though it does have everything from their Cadence singles and LPs. Serious fans and collectors, however, are going to be tempted to fork out for this even if they have all that stuff already, since this has four previously unreleased demos, all Phil Everly songs, none dated, but almost certainly recorded in the late '50s. These are just okay, not great, and sound like Phil Everly solo acoustic numbers rather than full duo performances, but they're certainly worth having if you love your Everlys. Also of value are a couple of demos of Don Everly originals, "Give Me a Future" and "Life Ain't Worth Living," that aren't that easy to come by either, although they've been previously released on Bear Family's *Classic Everly Brothers* box set; "Give Me a Future" uses, according to Varese Sarabande, an improved source from the one used on the Bear Family collection. *—Richie Unterberger*

Everything But the Girl

f. 1982, Hull, England
College Rock, Alternative Dance, Club/Dance, Alternative Pop/Rock, Sophisti-Pop
Originating at the turn of the 1980s as a leader of the lite-jazz movement, Everything But the Girl became an unlikely success story more than a decade later, emerging at the vanguard of the fusion between pop and electronica. The duo of Tracey Thorn and Ben Watt debuted in 1982 and hit the British Top 40 two years later with the single "Each and Every One." The jazz-pop confections of the group's early work gave way to shimmering jangle-rock and occasional subtle country influences. The 1988 single "I Don't Want to Talk About It" became the pair's biggest hit to date, landing at the number three spot on the British charts. After the slick, L.A.-recorded *The Language of Life* and a return to pop textures for 1991's *Worldwide*, Everything But the Girl released *Acoustic*, the results of a series of club performances which presaged the coming ascendancy of the "Unplugged" concept. In 1994, EBTG collaborated with dub-trance innovators Massive Attack on their LP *Protection*; Thorn's vocal turn highlighted the hit title track, and the cinematic Massive Attack sound clearly informed Everything But the Girl's own 1994 effort *Amplified Heart.* In 1995 the soulful single "Missing" was innovatively remixed by Todd Terry, and soon became a club sensation and major international hit, reaching the number two position on the U.S. pop charts. With 1996's brilliant *Walking Wounded*, Everything But the Girl dove headfirst into electronica, crafting sophisticated, assured excursions into trip-hop, drum 'n' bass and jungle. *—Jason Ankeny*

Everything But the Girl / 1984 / Blanco y Negro/Sire ♦♦♦
The music fad of the moment in 1984 in England was a revival of the early-'60s Brazilian pop sound of Antonio Carlos Jobim, Astrud Gilberto, and Stan Getz, updated to current sensibilities, and the two main practitioners were Sade and Everything But the Girl. On this revised version of their U.K. debut album, *Eden*, altered for U.S. consumption, the duo of Tracey Thorn and Ben Watt performed their three U.K. chart singles, "Each and Every One," "Mine," and "Native Land," in a calm, unruffled style keyed to Thorn's warm, if slightly unfocused, vocal style. If the music had a flaw, it was that the sound, with its light sambas and steady ballads, spare instrumentation, and careful sax solos, impressed more than individual songs did, perhaps because Thorn's way of phrasing meant you could listen to "Mine," for example, several times before catching on to its feminist theme. Still, Everything But the Girl was more direct and had less of the exotic affectation of Sade (which, however, may help explain why it was she, and not they, who succeeded in America). *—William Ruhlmann*

Love Not Money / Apr. 1985 / Blanco y Negro/Sire ♦♦♦
On their second album, Everything But the Girl took a more contemporary pop approach while retaining the spareness of their debut. They also upped the ante in their songwriting, tackling a range of issues from the Irish troubles to the troubles of movie star Frances Farmer, with lots of criticism of the stratification and sexism of the current social and economic system thrown in. Tracey Thorn's careworn voice proved an excellent vehicle for such essentially pessimistic sentiments, and even if *Love Not Money* made for a dour listening experience, it was nevertheless compelling. (The "special U.S. edition" of the album, released by Sire Records, differed from the Blanco Y Negro version from the U.K. in that it featured the pop-sounding "Heaven Help Me" and a cover of the Pretenders' "Kid." Neither enhanced the album's commercial appeal; it made the Top Ten back home, but did not chart stateside.) *—William Ruhlmann*

Baby, the Stars Shine Bright / Aug. 1986 / Blanco y Negro/Sire ♦♦♦
On their third album, Everything But the Girl tries another departure on their craftsmanlike ballad style, hiring a full orchestra to give a lush backing to songs usually concerned more with sexual than national politics. Their last album, *Love Not Money*, may have boasted a considerable social agenda, but here Tracey Thorn sings of romantic disappointment and illicit liaisons, only occasionally bowing to such favorite themes as the lure of fame ("Country Mile"), fantasies about American movie stars ("Sugar Finney," which is "for Marilyn Monroe," and has the chorus, "America is free, cheap and easy"), and fears of fascism ("Little Hitler"). Thorn's throbbing voice is well-suited to the emotional concerns of the lyrics, and Ben Watt creates attractive, string- and horn-filled backings for them. So, Everything But the Girl has found yet another way effectively to vary what would have seemed to be a limited musical style. *—William Ruhlmann*

Idlewild / Feb. 1988 / Blanco y Negro/Sire ♦♦♦♦♦
Thorn and Watt made a couple of albums with a cocktail-jazz backup and one with strings before trying a small unit for the intimate songs of their most accessible recording. The setting is perfect for such moving compositions as "Love Is Here Where I Live" and "Apron Strings." Start here, then go on to the rest of this remarkable group's catalog. *—William Ruhlmann*

The Language of Life / Jan. 1990 / Atlantic ♦♦
It may have been the logical extension of Everything But the Girl's ersatz cool-jazz approach to finally go all the way by hiring veteran producer Tommy LiPuma and a studio full of fusion stars like Joe Sample (the Crusaders), Russell Ferrante (the Yellowjackets), Michael Brecker, and, finally, Stan Getz, whose early-'60s albums of Brazilian jazz are a main touchstone for the group. With such firepower, *The Language of Life*, at least musically, may be the album that Ben Watt and Tracey Thorn have been trying to make from the beginning. But it falls down in its songwriting, largely because of the near-disappearance of Thorn and her edgy lyrics; Watt takes over for a series of so-so love songs. And the bottom of the barrel is hit with a cover of Womack and Womack's "Take Me," intended as an erotic come-on and sounding more like a lullaby. *—William Ruhlmann*

Worldwide / Sep. 1991 / Atlantic ♦♦♦
Ben Watt and Tracey Thorn returned to the direct record-making style of their first two albums on *Worldwide.* Here, the music was carried largely by Watt's bank of keyboards. But the duo's lyrical concerns reflected their recent frenetic lifestyle. Sooner or later, every group that lasts makes a road album, and this was the one for Everything But the Girl, its songs nostalgically reminiscing about childhood back in England, along with reflections on the big-time touring life in America. Happily, there was still room for a few of Everything But the Girl's complicated adult love songs, notably Thorn's "Understanding," though even that one talked about how love "depends on geography." The breezy subject matter contrasted with the more contemplative music. *—William Ruhlmann*

Acoustic / Jun. 1992 / Atlantic ♦♦♦
Acoustic presents two side projects in one. The first half of it consists of Everything But the Girl's covers of six songs by other contemporary performers. The second half contains two live recordings and four re-recordings of songs from Everything But the Girl's repertoire. All of the songs are performed with spare, acoustic instrumentation. The group's favorites are predictable—Bruce Springsteen, Elvis Costello, and Tom Waits at their quietest—and while the choices are indisputably good ones—"Alison," "Downtown Train," Cyndi Lauper's "Time After Time"—they are also familiar, and Ben Watt and Tracey Thorn don't bring anything new to them. Their own material is calm and contemplative anyway, so stripping away the synthesizers doesn't affect the arrangements much. *Acoustic* is a pleasant-sounding, inessential Everything But the Girl album. *—William Ruhlmann*

Amplified Heart / Jul. 19, 1994 / Atlantic ♦♦♦♦♦
Despite its title, *Amplified Heart* is one of Everything But the Girl's more acoustic works. A simple instrumentation of guitars and keyboards, augmented here and there by British folk-rock veterans like Richard Thompson, Danny Thompson, and Dave Mattacks, serves to set up a series of songs of romantic disillusionment. Declaring "My life is just an image of a roller coaster, anyway" and "I don't understand anything," among other things, over and over the songs speak of confusion and disappointment deriving from failed love affairs. The approach is much more introspective than that taken on the group's last new original album, *Worldwide*, but Tracey Thorn and Ben Watt's musical restraint supports it well. This is an album to listen to when you've just broken up with your lover, or even

when you're just in the mood to think about lost lovers from long ago—self-pity set to music. —*William Ruhlmann*

The Best of Everything But the Girl / 1996 / Blanco Y Negro ✦✦✦✦
The Best of Everything But the Girl is divided between selections from their early records and remixes of '90s hits, such as "Missing." Consequently, the album draws a slightly misleading portrait of their career, yet it still functions as an excellent introduction to the band, since it features many of their best songs, including "Apron Strings." —*Stephen Thomas Erlewine*

● **Walking Wounded** / May 21, 1996 / Atlantic ✦✦✦✦✦
With *Walking Wounded*, Everything But the Girl puts an acceptable face on trip-hop, jungle, and techno, opening up the world of experimental dance music to a new audience. At its core, Everything But the Girl is a pop group, which means they automatically abandon the free-form song structures that characterize most of trip-hop and techno. In a sense, that dilutes the impact of the music, but the duo found a way around that by seamlessly incorporating the rhythms into carefully crafted songs. They work the same ground as Massive Attack, but their songwriting is more accessible and less adventurous than the groundbreaking Bristol group. Furthermore, Everything But the Girl never approaches the tarnished glamour of Portishead, the kineticism of Björk, or the brilliantly evocative soundscapes of Tricky. Essentially, the beats are used as window dressing—the group's music hasn't changed that much. —*Stephen Thomas Erlewine*

Everything But the Girl Vs. Drum & Bass / Oct. 22, 1996 / Atlantic ✦✦✦✦
The *Everything But the Girl Vs. Drum & Bass* EP is comprised of remixes of several tracks from Everything But the Girl's first full-fledged dance album, *Walking Wounded*. Most of the EP consists of fine remixes of the album's title track, but the best cut is a version of "Single" remixed by Photek. —*Stephen Thomas Erlewine*

Temperamental / Sep. 28, 1999 / Atlantic ✦✦✦✦✦
Everything But the Girl's resurrection as a sophisticated electronica outfit may have been unpredictable, but it certainly revitalized the duo's music. Prior to 1996's *Walking Wounded*, the duo had taken their charming, jazzy acoustic pop as far as it could go. Adding electronica, primarily drum'n'bass and trip-hop, to the equation broke their potential wide open, as the captivating, seductive *Walking Wounded* proved. It was such a drastic, fulfilling departure that it did raise the question of where they go from here; its 1999 sequel, *Temperamental*, answers that by offering more of the same, except just a little different. *Temperamental* tempers the lightly skittering drum'n'bass and eliminates trip-hop, yet retains the same feel as *Walking Wounded*. House music—everything from classic '80s house to contemporary house—serves as the musical foundation, which actually opens the doors for slight jazzy inflections, along with long, hypnotizing instrumental passages (most notably on "Compression"). Weirdly, it also serves as a good setting for a batch of songs that are essentially in the singer/songwriter vein. In fact, there aren't as many clear pop hooks here as there were on *Walking*. "Five Fathoms," "Tempermental," and a couple of other tracks work as singles, but the album is a more of a meditative, reflective piece, like a singer/songwriter album—except it's dressed in sultry, evocative electronic dance music. That means, of course, that *Temperamental* isn't all that different than its predecessor, but its blend of house, electronica, pop, jazz, and folk is equally satisfying as that landmark album. —*Stephen Thomas Erlewine*

Back to Mine / May 29, 2001 / Ultra ✦✦✦✦
Long-time music connoisseurs and taste-makers Everything But the Girl (aka Ben Watt and Tracey Thorn) were naturals to take over the stereo for a volume in the chill-out mix series *Back to Mine* and, as could be expected, the mix is tasteful, wide-ranging, and above all, astonishingly well-paced. Beginning with a down-tempo hip-hop cut by French DJ Cam and moving into Slick Rick's excellent message track "All Alone (No One to Be With)," *Back to Mine* moves from jazzy rap and trip-hop into moody techno and deep house, with vocal tracks—everyone from Beth Orton to Mary Margaret O'Hara to Donny Hathaway—mixing very well with the instrumentals. Also appearing are two tracks by Detroit techno legends: a mix of "The Flow" by Juan Atkins' Model 500 and "A Wonderful Life from Carl Craig's *Landcruising* LP of 1995. *Back to Mine* is an excellent addition to the scads of mix albums on the shelves, as conscious of perfect transitions and solid mixing as any out there. —*John Bush*

The Exciters

f. 1961, Jamaica, NY
Brill Building Pop, Girl Group
Despite the presence of lone male Herb Rooney, the Exciters made some of the best girl-group records of the early '60s. Led by vibrant-voiced Brenda Reid, the originally all-female quartet came from Jamaica, NY, as the Masterettes. After signing on with saxist Al Sears as their manager, they switched their name to the Exciters and cut "Tell Him" in 1962 for United Artists. Produced by Jerry Leiber and Mike Stoller, the brilliant uptown soul effort proved a major smash. Reid's roaring pipes were expertly spotlighted on the follow-ups "He's Got the Power," "Get Him," and their original reading of "Do-Wah-Diddy," immortalized later that year by Manfred Mann. The group later appeared on Roulette, Bang, Shout, and RCA. Reid and Rooney were married for a time, and Reid now performs with her children backing her. —*Bill Dahl*

● **Tell Him** / 1995 / Collectables ✦✦✦✦✦
A reissue of a reissue, this 1995 Collectables package is the same as EMI's 1991 *Legendary Masters* entry on this New York vocal group from the early 1960s. Hits like the title track, "He's Got the Power" and the original version of "Do-Wah-Diddy" are class-A New York rock & roll all the way, and lead singer Brenda Reid's chops are as exciting, always making the material more interesting than it sometimes is. Very interesting are the inclusion of the longer unedited versions of "Tell Him" and "He's Got the Power," both remixed here in true stereo. Though not *technically* a girl group (they featured a male bass singer in the lineup), the Exciters were one of the best working in the genre. —*Cub Koda*

Extreme

f. 1985, **db.** 1996

Hair Metal, Heavy Metal, Pop/Rock, Hard Rock, Pop-Metal

Although guitarist and band mastermind Nuno Bettencourt's style was derived from Eddie Van Halen, his heart is with the progressive hard rock of Queen, as well as Beatlesque pop and touches of lounge jazz. Consequently, Extreme's music is never easy to classify; it's not just heavy metal, hard rock, or pop—their albums cover all of that territory, with a sweeping ambition and a social conscious to match. By the time of their second album, *Pornograffiti*, Bettencourt was already well-respected in the heavy metal world but it was the Everly Brothers-style acoustic ballad, "More Than Words," that crossed them over into the mainstream—it hit number one and the follow-up single, the acoustic-based pop rocker "Hole Hearted," hit number four. Extreme's third album, *Extreme III: Three Sides to Every Story*, was an over-ambitious follow-up that sold well at first, but didn't have the staying power of their previous album. Extreme's fourth album, 1995's *Waiting for the Punchline*, suffered from a similar lack of sales. —*Stephen Thomas Erlewine*

Extreme / 1989 / A&M ✦✦✦
Extreme's first album shows the band struggling to shed their influences, particularly Van Halen, and develop a style of their own; consequently, it's wildly uneven, but guitarist Nuno Bettencourt is always worth hearing. —*Stephen Thomas Erlewine*

Extreme II: Pornograffiti / 1990 / A&M ✦✦✦✦
Extreme came into its own on the concept album *Pornograffiti*, with the band's strongest set of songs and an intellectual theme revolving around the struggle for genuine love and romance in a sleazy, decadent society full of greed and corruption. The band shows a strong desire to experiment and push the boundaries of the pop-metal format, adding a funky horn section on "Get the Funk Out" and displaying progressive compositional leanings throughout, and virtuoso Nuno Bettencourt put down his guitar for the enjoyable pseudo-lounge piano ballad of "When I First Kissed You." But of course, the album is best known for its two acoustic-guitar-only hits, the number one ballad "More Than Words" and the equally fine full-band rocker "Hole Hearted." Other highlights include "Decadence Dance" and "Song for Love." —*Steve Huey*

III Sides to Every Story / 1992 / A&M ✦✦✦
Extreme's brand of hard rock balanced ambitious, progressive tendencies with catchy melodies owing more to the Beatles than anthemic arena rock; on *III Sides to Every Story*, the former tends to dominate. The album is divided into three "sides of the story"—roughly speaking, "Yours" concentrates on politically oriented rockers showing off Nuno Bettencourt's virtuosity; "Mine" leans toward pop songs with warmly romantic sensibilities, plus an occasional philosophical lament; and "The Truth" tries to wrap things up into a coherent whole but dissolves into indigestible prog-rock excess. Thus, the thematic material can be likened to a less focused version of *Pornograffiti*. The album is wildly uneven, but amidst the indulgences there are some fine songs to be found: "Rest in Peace" displays both Bettencourt's technique and melodicism as a soloist, while "Seven Sundays" continues in their occasional lounge ballad vein, and "Tragic Comic" and "Stop the World" are two more intelligent, wounded-romantic pop gems. —*Steve Huey*

● **The Best Of Extreme: An Accidental Collision of Atoms** / Feb. 15, 2000 / Interscope ✦✦✦✦
To some listeners, *Best Of: An Accidental Collision of Atoms* may not seem necessary, since Extreme's two hits were already on one album, yet for casual fans who don't have *Pornograffiti*, or want highlights from the other records, this is a strong, representative collection. Sure, dedicated fans will find some favorites missing—after all, these are pulled from records that were designed as albums—but all the singles are here, including such European releases as "Get the Funk Out" and "Tragic Comic," along with such strong album tracks as "Decadence Dance." There's only one semi-rarity to snag the faithful—the "Horn Mix" of "Cupid's Dead"—but these fans are likely to stick with the original albums, no matter what. And, truth be told, there's some relevance in that, since the albums were cohesive works, but *An Accidental Collision of Atoms* remains a first-rate sampler that proves Extreme were better than the vast majority of their Bush-era hard-rock and pop-metal peers. —*Stephen Thomas Erlewine*

F

Fabian

b. Feb. 6, 1943, Philadelphia, PA

Vocals / Tropical, Brill Building Pop, Teen Idol

Thanks to a series of performances on Dick Clark's *American Bandstand*, Fabian rocketed to stardom in the late '50s. With his stylish good looks and mild rock & roll, he became one of the top teen idols of the era; luckily, he had the support of the legendary songwriting team of Doc Pomus and Mort Shuman, who provided him with "Turn Me Loose," "Hound Dog Man," and "I'm a Man," among other songs. Fabian's fame peaked in 1959 with the million-selling "Tiger" single; after that, he valiantly tried to become a movie star. When Congress fingered him as one of the performers who benefited from payola, his already-ailing career was given a nearly fatal blow; under questioning, Fabian explained that his records featured a substantial amount of electronic doctoring in order to improve his voice. After the hearings, he starred in some more movies in the '60s, without regaining the audience of his peak years. —*Stephen Thomas Erlewine*

● **This Is Fabian! (1959-61)** / 1991 / Ace ◆◆◆◆
It's true that Fabian couldn't sing, but that's really beside the point. He worked with talented instrumentalists and songwriters (Mort Shuman and Doc Pomus to name a couple), rocked harder than the average teen idol, and stuck with material that didn't challenge his already challenged vocal talents. *This Is Fabian* collects 26 original recordings for the Chancellor label, including all ten of his Billboard hits. "Tiger," "Turn Me Loose," and "Hound Dog Man" are the ones people remember, but some of the non-hits are fine as well (check out the amazing guitar solo on "Mighty Cold" for one example). Collectables has issued an equally generous Fabian anthology domestically, but *This is Fabian!* remains a fine and comprehensive collection of his hit recordings. —*Greg Adams*

● **The Best of Fabian** / Jun. 6, 1995 / Varese Vintage ◆◆◆◆
Compared to some import collections that are available, this ten-song CD is on the skimpy side. But it does include all of his late-'50s and early-'60s chart hits, which should satisfy all but obsessively rabid collectors, and as a domestic release, it's considerably cheaper and more readily available than the other comps. —*Richie Unterberger*

The Fabulous Thunderbirds

f. 1974, Austin, TX

Modern Electric Texas Blues, Electric Texas Blues, Blues-Rock, Rock & Roll

With their fusion of blues, rock & roll, and R&B, the Fabulous Thunderbirds helped popularize roadhouse Texas blues with a mass audience in the '80s and, in the process, helped kick-start a blues revival during the mid-'80s. During their heyday in the early '80s, they were the most popular attraction on the blues bar circuit, which eventually led to a breakthrough to the pop audience in 1986 with their fifth album, *Tuff Enuff*. The mass success didn't last too long, and founding member Jimmie Vaughan left in 1990, but the Fabulous Thunderbirds remained one of the most popular blues concert acts in America during the '90s.

Vaughan formed the group with vocalist/harpist Kim Wilson in 1974. Within a few years, the Thunderbirds became the house band for the Austin club Antone's, and by the end of the decade, they had built a strong fan base and recorded their eponymous debut. It attracted the attention of Chrysalis, which released three largely unsuccessful albums during the early '80s. Although the Fabulous Thunderbirds had become favorites of fellow musicians (they opened shows for the Rolling Stones and Eric Clapton), they were without a record contract for several years, until signing to Epic/Associated in 1985. After entering a London studio and recording *Tuff Enuff* with producer Dave Edmunds, the title track hit the American Top Ten and the album went platinum. The follow-up, 1987's *Hot Number*, quickly fell off the charts. Furthermore, its slick, radio-ready sound alienated their hardcore following of blues fans. After another poorly received album, Jimmie Vaughan left the band to play with his brother, Stevie Ray Vaughan. The Fabulous Thunderbirds replaced Vaughan with two guitarists, Duke Robillard and Kid Bangham. The first album from the new lineup, *Walk That Walk, Talk That Talk*, appeared in 1991. After three years in limbo, the band re-assembled in 1994 and recorded their ninth album, *Roll of the Dice*. Following its release, the band returned to actively touring the United States. —*Stephen Thomas Erlewine*

The Fabulous Thunderbirds / 1979 / Chrysalis ◆◆◆◆◆
Their debut album, with the original lineup of Wilson, Vaughn, Buck, and Ferguson stompin' through a roadhouse set of covers and genre-worthy originals. One of the few white blues albums that works. —*Cub Koda*

What's the Word / 1980 / Benchmark ◆◆◆◆◆
Second album, equally powerful. Some of their best, including the off-kilter "Los Fabulosos Thunderbirds" and "Running Shoes." The 2000 CD reissue on Benchmark adds

three bonus tracks, one of them the aforementioned "Los Fabulosos Thunderbirds," the other two recorded live in an Austin, TX, bar. —*Cub Koda*

Butt Rockin' / 1981 / Benchmark ◆◆◆◆
As with most bands who reach back into styles more than a couple of decades old for their chief inspirations, the limitations of the Fabulous Thunderbirds' approach was becoming apparent by this, their third album. Granted they were still more competent and enthusiastic at their specialty than most of their competition, and they did expand their recorded sound a bit by using some members of Roomful of Blues on sax and piano. Ultimately, though, it's an average if well-done set of roots rock with strong echoes of the blues, New Orleans R&B, and swamp-pop. The program's split between Kim Wilson originals (one of which, "One's Too Many," was co-written with Nick Lowe) and covers, including an unpredictable version of "Cherry Pink and Apple Blossom White." Actually the highlight is the instrumental "In Orbit," which features excellent Little Walter-styled harmonica by Wilson. The 2000 CD reissue on Benchmark adds liner notes by producer Denny Bruce and three bonus tracks, although no details about the extra cuts are provided. —*Richie Unterberger*

T-Bird Rhythm / 1982 / Benchmark ◆◆◆◆
After using manager Denny Bruce as producer for their first three albums, the Fabulous Thunderbirds tapped Nick Lowe for their fourth outing, *T-Bird Rhythm*. It was more of the same stew of rock, blues, R&B, and lowdown swamp music for which the early Thunderbirds were known. That was a good thing for anyone just in love with the sound and who wanted more. Those for whom one Thunderbirds album is good but enough, however, might not have seen much point to investing in another similar recording. Whatever the case, *T-Bird Rhythm* is solid, though not innovative, with the usual roots sounds that alternate between Kim Wilson originals and well-chosen covers of obscure non-hit oldies. The 2000 CD reissue on Benchmark adds historical liner notes. —*Richie Unterberger*

Tuff Enuff / 1986 / Epic Associated ◆◆◆
Their breakthrough success. The title track and soul covers point the band in a new, more mainstream direction. —*Cub Koda*

Hot Number / 1987 / Epic Associated ◆◆

Powerful Stuff / 1989 / Epic Associated ◆◆

The Essential / Jun. 18, 1991 / Chrysalis ◆◆◆◆
Nice compilation of the early Chrysalis albums on one CD. —*Cub Koda*

Walk That Walk, Talk That Talk / Dec. 1991 / Epic Associated ◆◆◆
Walk That Walk, Talk That Talk is the first album the Fabulous Thunderbirds recorded without Jimmie Vaughan. It takes two guitarists—two good guitarists, by the way—to fill his place and even with Duke Robillard and Kid Bangham on board, there is something missing. Though the T-birds have returned to straightahead blues-rock, abandoning the overly commercial production of their previous three albums, they don't sound as distinctive as the did with Vaughan. Kim Wilson blows some good harp, Robillard throws out a few stellar solos and Bangham can almost keep up with him, but on the whole, the album is a disappointment. —*Thom Owens*

● **Hot Stuff: The Greatest Hits** / Aug. 25, 1992 / Epic Associated ◆◆◆◆◆
The best tracks from the Fabulous Thunderbirds' more rock-oriented years at CBS Associated Records are collected on this single-disc compilation. —*Stephen Thomas Erlewine*

Roll of the Dice / Aug. 1, 1995 / Private Music ◆◆◆
The Fabulous T-Birds' second album without Jimmie Vaughan is an improvement over *Walk That Walk, Talk That Talk*, featuring a tighter, more focused band and hotter playing. Nevertheless, the band takes a couple of missteps, particularly with a limp version of "Zip-a-Dee-Doo-Dah." —*Stephen Thomas Erlewine*

Different Tacos / 1996 / Country Town Music ◆◆◆
For Fabulous Thunderbirds fanatics, or anyone longing for the raw gutbucket blues-rock of their early recordings, *Different Tacos* is something of a godsend. Essentially, the disc is a rarities collection, boasting nine outtakes from their first four studio albums, a couple of live cuts from various U.K. tours, and a nearly complete set from an Austin club gig in the late '70s. Each track is straightforward, take-no-prisoners Texas blues, played with astonishing fervor and grit. There are alternate takes and live versions of familiar T-Birds items, plus covers and songs that were reworked or abandoned for the original albums. Certainly, the nature of this live and rarities set makes *Different Tacos* primarily of interest to hardcore fans, but those fans will find it a most welcome addition to their Thunderbirds collection. —*Stephen Thomas Erlewine*

Best of the Fabulous Thunderbirds / 1997 / EMI ◆◆◆◆
The Best of the Fabulous Thunderbirds is a terrific 22-track U.K. collection hitting all the

highlights of the group's first four albums and offering a nearly flawless overview of the band's bluesiest period. *—Stephen Thomas Erlewine*

High Water / Aug. 12, 1997 / High Street ✦✦

Girls Go Wild / 2000 / Benchmark ✦✦✦✦✦

Although there was no Fabulous Thunderbirds album by the name of *Girls Go Wild* prior to this 2000 release, this is actually a repackaged version of their self-titled 1979 debut. It has all of the songs from *The Fabulous Thunderbirds*, in the same sequence, but adds three bonus tracks, as well as liner notes by producer Denny Bruce. Why the title change? Well, because the lettering "Girls Go Wild" was so prominent on the cover, it became unofficially known as their "*Girls Go Wild*" album, and for this reissue, the title change is official. At any rate, it's still the group at their early bluesy best. No hard info about the bonus cuts though, except that all three, oddly, were recorded *after* drummer Fran Christina (who did not play on the debut album) joined. One of those bonus songs, "Things I Forgot to Do," is an outtake from the band's third album, *Butt Rockin'*, and features members of Roomful of Blues. *—Richie Unterberger*

Faces

f. Mar. 1969, London, England, **db.** Sep. 1975

Album Rock, Proto-Punk, Hard Rock, Rock & Roll

When Steve Marriott left the Small Faces in 1969, the three remaining members brought in guitarist Ron Wood and lead singer Rod Stewart to complete the lineup and changed their name to the Faces, which was only appropriate since the group now only slightly resembled the mod-pop group of the past. Instead, the Faces were a rough, sloppy rock & roll band, able to pound out a rocker like "Had Me a Real Good Time," a blues ballad like "Tell Everyone," or a folk number like "Richmond" all in one album. Stewart, already becoming a star in his own right, let himself go wild with the Faces, tearing through covers and originals with abandon. Notorious for their hard-partying, boozy tours and ragged concerts, the Faces lived the rock & roll life-style to the extreme. They never sold that many records and were never considered as important as the Stones, yet their music has proven extremely influential over the years. Many punk rockers in the late '70s learned how to play their instruments by listening to Faces records; in the '80s and '90s, guitar-rock bands from the Replacements to the Black Crowes took their cue from the Faces as much as the Stones. Their reckless, loose and joyous spirit has stayed alive in much of the best rock & roll of the past two decades. *—Stephen Thomas Erlewine*

First Step / 1970 / Warner Brothers ✦✦✦✦✦

On their first album, the Faces established the pattern they would follow throughout their four albums—a ragged mix of breakneck rockers ("Shake, Shudder"), sensitive yet gritty ballads ("Devotion"), folk songs ("Stone"), revelatory covers (Bob Dylan's "Wicked Messenger"), and relaxed, friendly rockers ("Three Button Hand Me Down"). Although two instrumentals on the second side is one too many (Ron Wood's "Pineapple and the Monkey" is pretty great), the Faces seldom got better than the first half of *First Step*. *—Stephen Thomas Erlewine*

☆ **Long Player** / 1971 / Warner Brothers ✦✦✦✦✦

With their second effort, the Faces grew more muscular and loose, rocking with loose abandon on "Bad N' Ruin" and "Had Me a Real Good Time," two of their best songs. At the same time, their ballads also improved, with Stewart's "Tell Everyone" and Lane's "Richmond" rivaling each other for the most touching number on the album. Out of the two live tracks, "I Feel So Good" goes on a little too long, but "Maybe I'm Amazed" is tremendous—the Faces tear into the song, transforming it from a McCartney ballad to a heartfelt cry of devotion. *Long Player* is a sloppy, terrific record; although it may have a couple of weak moments, it has the heart and soul of the band. *—Stephen Thomas Erlewine*

☆ **A Nod Is as Good as a Wink . . . To a Blind Horse** / 1971 / Warner Brothers ✦✦✦✦✦

Boasting "Stay With Me," the only hit the Faces ever had, *A Nod is As Good As a Wink* is their most consistent record, and arguably their best. "Stay With Me" and "Miss Judy's Farm" showcase the band at their best—they're all over the place, threatening to fall apart altogether before they snap it all back into place. Nobody rocked better than this, and the album is full of such terrific moments, including a rollicking cover of Chuck Berry's "Memphis." As with all of the Faces' albums, it's a little messy, but it is a classic rock & roll band at the top of their form. *—Stephen Thomas Erlewine*

Ooh La La / 1973 / Warner Brothers ✦✦✦

Although it's routinely lambasted as an uninspired effort or a sell-out, *Ooh La La* is a tight rock & roll album, with its best moments—"Cindy Incidentally" and "Borstal Boy"—ranking among the Faces' best songs. *—Stephen Thomas Erlewine*

Snakes & Ladders / 1976 / Warner Brothers ✦✦✦

Snakes & Ladders is a fine 12-song overview of the Faces, containing some of the group's best songs ("Had Me a Real Good Time," "Stay With Me," "Miss Judy's Farm," "Sweet Lady Mary," "Ooh La La," "Cindy Incidentally"), along with a couple of mediocre cuts ("Pineapple and the Monkey," "Flying") and the unremarkable, single-only "Pool Hall Richard." Though it gives a sense of what made the Faces a great rock & roll band, it falls far short of being a definitive retrospective or introduction. *—Stephen Thomas Erlewine*

★ **The Best of Faces: Good Boys When They're Asleep** / Aug. 17, 1999 / Rhino ✦✦✦✦✦

Twenty years after their breakup, the Faces remained one of the most beloved bands in rock history, but it wasn't until 1999 that they were rewarded with a genuine collection, one that worked as an introduction while satisfying the dedicated with a truly listenable, terrific album. Not that the 19-track *Good Boys When They're Asleep: Best of Faces* contains everything worthwhile from the band—the absence of the extraordinary live version of Paul McCartney's "Maybe I'm Amazed" is the most egregious omission, and there are a number of remarkable songs missing as well—but it's hard to quibble with anything that is here. As a matter of fact, listening to *Good Boys When They're Asleep* is quite a thrilling ride, since it emphasizes their two sides—the rowdy, party-addled rockers and the melancholy ballads. Collectors will be happy to have the previously unreleased "Open to Ideas," along with the non-LP selections "Pool Hall Richard" and "You Can Make Me Dance, Sing or Anything," but the real news about the disc is that it offers a genuine retrospective that's every bit as good as the band itself, while arguably being a better, more cohesive record than any of the original albums. For longtime fans, as well as neophytes who have read about the Faces but never dived into the records, it's an album that's worth the wait. *—Stephen Thomas Erlewine*

Donald Fagen

b. Jan. 10, 1948, Passaic, NJ

Vocals, Keyboards, Synthesizer / Jazz-Rock, Pop/Rock, Soft Rock

Donald Fagen was one of the two masterminds behind Steely Dan, the seminal jazz-pop band of the '70s. Fagen's solo work has been a continuation of the band's work of the early '80s—carefully constructed and arranged, intricately detailed pop songs that are more substantial than their stylish surface may indicate. His 1982 solo debut, *The Nightfly*, was the best album he had made in years; it covered the same ground as the last two Steely Dan albums, yet surpassed it in terms of ambition and achievement.

After the success of *The Nightfly*, Fagen suffered a case of writer's block; for the rest of the decade he contributed music to the occasional film and briefly wrote a column for Premiere magazine in the mid-'80s. In the early '90s, he toured with the New York Rock & Soul Revue as he finished the material for his second album. With his former Steely Dan partner Walter Becker producing, 1993's *Kamakiriad* sounded like *Aja* recorded with '90s technology. It had some success on the adult contemporary charts, but it was overshadowed by the duo's decision to re-form Steely Dan and tour for the first time in nearly 20 years; the tour was a massive success. *—Stephen Thomas Erlewine*

● **The Nightfly** / Oct. 1982 / Warner Brothers ✦✦✦✦✦

A portrait of the artist as a young man, *The Nightfly* is a wonderfully evocative reminiscence of Kennedy-era American life; in the liner notes, Donald Fagen describes the songs as representative of the kinds of fantasies he entertained as an adolescent during the late '50s and early '60s, and he conveys the tenor of the times with some of his most personal and least obtuse material to date. Continuing in the smooth pop-jazz mode favored on the final Steely Dan records, *The Nightfly* is lush and shimmering, produced with cinematic flair by Gary Katz; romanticized but never sentimental, the songs are slices of suburbanite soap opera, tales of space-age hopes (the hit "I.G.Y.") and Cold War fears (the wonderful "The New Frontier," a memoir of fallout-shelter love) crafted with impeccable style and sophistication. *—Jason Ankeny*

Live at the Beacon / Sep. 1991 / Giant ✦✦✦

Not much was heard from Donald Fagen following the release of his debut solo album *The Nightfly* in 1982 for the rest of the decade. But in the early '90s, Fagen began turning up in clubs in New York City as part of a loose affiliation of performers that came to be called the New York Rock & Soul Revue. This album captures a two-day stand by the Revue, March 1-2, 1991, at the Beacon Theater. The principal performers, in addition to Fagen, who performs originals, oldies, and Steely Dan tunes, are Michael McDonald, Phoebe Snow, Boz Scaggs, Charles Brown, and Eddie and David Brigati. So, you get to hear favorites from the repertoires of those stars and their old groups, such as the Doobie Brothers and the Rascals. Of course, it would have been better to have been there, but this makes an entertaining souvenir. *—William Ruhlmann*

Kamakiriad / May 25, 1993 / Reprise ✦✦✦

Donald Fagen's second solo album is a song cycle of sorts, following the adventures of an imaginary protagonist as he travels the world in his car, a brand-new Kamakiri. It is an odd concept, and one that is not obvious to the listener, but reflection upon Fagen's liner notes while listening to the album does tend to evoke a vision of a non-apocalyptic near future, where swingers sip cocktails and fresh vegetable juices as they groove to synthesized jazz-rock. Evocative or not, this is not Fagen's best effort. The songs on *Kamakiriad* are mainly static one-chord vamps, with little of the interesting off-beat hits or chord changes that characterized most of Steely Dan's corpus (although, it must be said, *Two Against Nature* isn't too far conceptually from what Fagen is doing here). There is a slightly antiseptic feeling to *Kamakiriad*. Although the drum tracks are not synthesized, they sure sound that way, and even the horns sound electronic at times, a far cry from the lush arrangements of *Aja*. Another shortcoming of this record is the fact that the verse melodies don't sound very developed. The choruses are as catchy and cryptic as you would expect from Donald Fagen, but the verses are less than memorable. Walter Becker, who produced the record, as well as contributing bass and guitar, also co-wrote "Snowbound." Perhaps not surprisingly, it does the best job at evoking classic Steely Dan. *Kamakiriad* is pleasant as background music, but in the end it doesn't provide enough interesting moments to rank as a must-have. The static grooves, coupled with the long song lengths, and general lack of dynamic movement makes this record one of the least essential of Fagen's recorded output. However, Steely Dan completists will certainly find enough here to keep them happy. *—Daniel Gioffre*

Jad Fair

b. Ann Arbor, MI

Vocals, Guitar / Experimental Rock, Indie Rock, Post-Punk, Alternative Pop/Rock, American Underground

There are plenty of performers rock critics compliment by using the label "primitive," but few, if any, can hold a candle to the greatest American rock primitive, Jad Fair. With his fantastic and increasingly influential band Half Japanese or as a solo performer, Fair has constructed a prolific and extremely interesting career, writing and recording songs that display an uncomplicated emotional directness, unselfconscious (almost hokey) charm and warmth, and a genial simplicity that is simply beyond words. Although Fair's recent recordings are certainly more accessible—in some ways resembling those of another great American primitive, Jonathan Richman—his stock-in-trade is still the ability to compose and play music without any discernable (i.e., traditional) musical talent. Although he has "played" guitar since the mid-'70s, Fair, according to past and present members of Half Japanese, still can't name a chord, and plays riffs almost by accident, and wouldn't have it any other way. Fair's career as a solo artist began in 1980. It wasn't that he was particularly upset or unhappy with the direction he and brother David were leading Half Japanese, but rather that he needed another outlet with which to satiate his obsessive desire to make music. The first efforts were tentative, and in terms of the noise versus music factor (more noise than music), akin to early Half Japanese records. But by the mid- to late '80s, Fair's solo records were becoming more accessible due to the contributions of celebrities and huge Half Japanese fans such as Dinosaur Jr.'s J. Mascis, NRBQ's Terry Adams, and Gumball mastermind Don Fleming. And while the records got a little more polished, they certainly never lost a bit of Fair's childlike view of the world, nor his explosive, giddy belief in rock's liberating potential and endless possibilities. *—John Dougan*

Everybody Knew . . . But Me / 1982 / Press ♦♦♦
Early, more extreme Jad. His singing is surrounded by metallic clattering and only the barest concessions to traditional pop song forms. The songs tend to be about love and, uh, love, but the rather limited narratives in no way detract from what is a mostly wonderful listening experience. Although this is an accurate portrait of what Jad was up to at the time, it's recommended for adventure seekers, noise-pop fans, and those who unequivocally loved the first two Half Japanese records. *—John Dougan*

● **Jad Fair and Daniel Johnston** / 1989 / Homestead ♦♦♦♦♦
Those not familiar with Daniel Johnston's work should know that his approach to pop songwriting is similar to Fair's, with the exception that he suffers from serious bouts with manic depression and severe delusional behavior. That said, this pairing of these two musical savants is a successful foray into pop music as therapy. Neither one is blessed with a great voice (or technically, a good voice), the songs tend to be about simple pleasure, and the instrumentation is sparse. Despite both of them having flashes of happiness, this is by and large not a happy record; it's more of a soul-baring exercise. *—John Dougan*

The Sound of Music / 1990 / Shimmy-Disc ♦♦♦
Jad Fair and Kramer's first collaboration in over a decade resulted in 1999's *The Sound of Music*, released on Kramer's Shimmy Disc label. As on their first effort, 1988's *Roll the Barrel*, a sense of inventiveness and whimsy threads through each song. On *The Sound of Music*, Kramer focused on just that, composing and recording all of the music before Fair stepped in the studio, imagining Fair's voice and its possibilities. Fair then listened to the songs and wrote some of his signature abstract-yet-accurate lyrics; this time, the subject matter was the women he had met in the last year. The offbeat creativity of this dynamic duo makes *The Sound of Music* an engaging and decidedly different album. *—Heather Phares*

I Like It When You Smile / 1992 / Psycho ♦♦♦
This is the Fair release with the largest number of heavy hitters providing musical support (Terry Adams, J Mascis, Don Fleming) and some of it rocks in a radio-friendly (for Jad anyway) fashion that's downright jarring. But there is enough of the trademark Fair mania and out-of-tune playing (a downright messy, atonal cover of "On the Sunny Side of the Street") to keep diehards happy, while expanding the minds of newcomers to Jad Fair's warm and wonderful world. *—John Dougan*

26 Monster Songs for Children / May 12, 1998 / Kill Rock Stars ♦♦♦
Twenty-six monsters, one for each letter of the alphabet, are appraised in this offbeat and humorous album. A young child introduces each track with an epigrammatic description of the creature. The beasties range from legendary personalities like Dracula to more modern myths like E.T. and such ghost story stars as Headless Horseman to crypto-zoological question marks as Sasquatch. The music is largely simple, with quirky guitar duets or similarly simple instrumentation. The effect is one of exaggerated and mock creepiness that mates with the verses well. David Fair gave us the lyrics and lends his sonorous tone to much of the material, sometimes with Jad. The CD insert is decorated with children's illustrations. The album is delightful, unique and deserves to be a classic with children and adults that still like Halloween and Godzilla movies. *—Thomas Schulte*

Strange But True / Oct. 20, 1998 / Matador ♦♦

Fairport Convention

f. 1967

British Folk-Rock, Progressive Folk, British Folk, Folk-Rock

The best British folk-rock band of the late '60s, Fairport Convention did more than any other act to develop a truly British variation on the folk-rock prototype by drawing upon traditional material and styles indigenous to the British Isles. While the revved-up renditions of traditional British folk tunes drew the most critical attention, the group were also (at least at the outset) talented songwriters as well as interpreters. They were comfortable with conventional harmony-based folk-rock as well as tunes that drew upon more explicitly traditional sources, and boasted some of the best singers and instrumentalists of the day. A revolving door of personnel changes, however, saw the exit of their most distinguished talents, and basically changed the band into a living museum piece after the early '70s, albeit an enjoyable one with integrity. Fairport didn't reach their peak until 1968 and the addition of singer Sandy Denny, whose penetrating, resonant style qualified her as the best British folk-rock singer of all time and provided the band with the best vocalist they would ever have. *What We Did on Our Holidays* (1969) and *Unhalfbricking* (1969) are their best albums, mixing strong originals, excellent covers of contemporary folk-rock songs by the likes of Joni Mitchell and Bob Dylan, and imaginative revivals of traditional folk songs that mixed electric and acoustic instruments with a beguiling ease. With *Liege and Lief* (1969), critical thought diverges; some insist that this is unequivocally their peak, marking a final escape from their '60s folk-rock influences into a much more original style. This school of thought severely underestimates their songwriting talents, and others feel that they were at their best when mixing original and outside material, and contemporary and traditional styles, in fact becoming more predictable and derivative when they opted to concentrate on British folk chestnuts. *—Richie Unterberger*

Fairport Convention / Jun. 1968 / Polydor ♦♦♦♦♦
By far the most rock-oriented of Fairport's early albums, this was recorded before Denny joined the band (Judy Dyble handles the female vocals). Unjustly overlooked by listeners who consider the band's pre-Denny output insignificant, this is a fine folk-rock effort that takes far more inspiration from West Coast '60s sounds than traditional British folk. Good originals and excellent covers of a variety of obscure tunes by Joni Mitchell, Dylan, Emmitt Rhodes, and Jim & Jean. *—Richie Unterberger*

What We Did on Our Holidays / Jan. 1969 / Hannibal ♦♦♦♦♦
Sandy Denny's haunting, ethereal vocals give Fairport a big boost on her debut with the group. A more folk-based album than their initial effort, divided between original material and a few well-chosen covers. This contains several of their greatest moments: Sandy Denny's "Fotheringay," and Richard Thompson's "Meet on the Ledge," the obscure Joni Mitchell composition "Eastern Rain," the traditional "She Moves Through the Fair," and their version of Dylan's "I'll Keep It With Mine." *—Richie Unterberger*

★ **Unhalfbricking** / Jul. 1969 / Hannibal ♦♦♦♦♦
Richard Thompson and Sandy Denny shine throughout this record, which is considered by some to be their Fairport peak together. The second album by a tragically short-lived Fairport Convention lineup. It seems top-heavy with Dylan tunes, three of them included, but they're done with such verve and freshness that they seem perfectly appropriate. As for the rest, Denny's performance on "Autopsy" is outshone only by her work on the apocalyptic nine-minute "A Sailor's Life," which is one of the great English folk-rock showcases ever recorded, a rival to such works as Phil Ochs' "Crucifixion" and Bob Dylan's "Desolation Row," as a song that just makes the listener "white out" inside, mouth open, when its over. Also highlighted by the definitive Denny recording of "Who Knows Where the Time Goes." And take in the powerhouse drumming, and realize what the band lost when Martin Lamble died. *—William Ruhlmann & Bruce Eder*

☆ **Liege and Lief** / Dec. 1969 / A&M ♦♦♦♦♦
For their fourth album, Fairport Convention released what is regarded by many as not only the best record in their history but also one of the seminal English folk-rock albums of all time. This was also the album that marked the transformation of the group from, essentially, a rock band that utilized folk music (in tandem with modern singer/songwriter material) as a source for part of their sound, and an inspiration for their own songwriting, into a group specializing in reinterpreting traditional English songs. There's only one original number here, the soaring "Come All Ye," the rest being adaptations of old English folk songs; at the time, however, very few groups were doing this with any success, or mixing acoustic and electric sounds quite as adeptly, with the result that *Liege and Lief* was practically a consciousness-raising album for a lot of listeners. "Farewell Farewell," "Matty Groves," "Reynardine," and "Tam-Lin" were highlights of an LP filled with gems in this style, ornamented with gorgeous harmonies and striking instrumental virtuosity. Sadly, this lineup was in the process of splitting up virtually as the record was being made—after Sandy Denny's and Ashley Hutchings' exits, it would be remembered with a tone of nostalgia that was somewhat unfair to the equally impressive lineup that followed. The CD edition of *Liege and Lief* is decent, although, as with almost any A&M CD release dating before the end of the 1990s, the album could use a 24-bit remastering one of these days. *—Bruce Eder*

Full House / Jul. 1970 / Hannibal ♦♦♦♦♦
Fairport Convention is a group that has always beaten the odds—that's why a version of the band is working in the 21st century. By the time of this, the group's fifth album, key members Ashley Hutchings and Sandy Denny had exited the lineup, yet the group continued here without skipping a beat, for the first time without a female singer—and it turned out not to make a major difference. Richard Thompson and Dave Swarbrick took over as singers, and Dave Pegg (more recently of Jethro Tull) joined on bass, and the resulting album was actually more viscerally exciting than its predecessor, *Liege and Lief*, if not quite as important as that record, since it came first. Even vocally, this version of the group needed offer no apologies. Thompson, Swarbrick, Pegg, and Simon Nicol harmonize beautifully around strong lead vocals. Not only does the singing here retain the high standard of the earlier incarnation of the group (check out the harmony singing on "Sir Patrick Spens" and "Flowers of the Forest"), but the playing throughout has greater urgency and punch, from the rousing Thompson-Swarbrick opener "Walk Awhile" to the haunting, moody, dazzling nine-minute "Sloth," which remained part of the group's live set for years. An indispensable recording, and one that anybody who wants to truly know this band, or to take in some of the best work of Richard Thompson's career, must own (his playing on "Sloth" and "Doctor of Physick" makes it worthwhile). Swarbrick's fiddle and viola playing is also among the best of his career. Ironically, Thompson would make this his last full-time studio venture with Fairport, but what a way to go! *—Stephen Winnick & Bruce Eder*

Angel Delight / Jun. 1971 / Island ✦✦✦
Richard Thompson exits the Fairport lineup, leaving the band reduced to a quartet of Simon Nicol, Dave Swarbrick, Dave Pegg, and Dave Mattacks. The loss of big guns Thompson and Denny was felt, but amazingly, although it isn't nearly as well known as *Liege and Lief* or *Full House*, this record reached the highest chart position of any Fairport LP, making number eight in England. Swarbrick led the group in even more of a traditional British folk vein. By now everybody involved was singing (with Nicol and Swarbrick usually alternating on lead), and they managed to pull it off, mostly by virtue of the honesty of their voices and instrumental work almost as vital and animated as any in their history. From the beautifully sung and exciting opener "Lord Marlborough," the album should strike a responsive chord with any folk or folk-rock enthusiast—especially enjoyable are the singing on the buoyantly humorous title track and the viola/violin duet between Swarbrick and Nicol on "Bridge Over The River Ash." *—Bruce Eder & William Ruhlmann*

Babbacombe Lee / Nov. 1971 / Island ✦✦✦
The group's only concept album (similar in some ways to the Pretty Things' *S.F. Sorrow*), built around the life story of John "Babbacombe" Lee, a Victorian-era condemned murderer. Lee's story, from his boyhood poverty to his time in the Royal Navy, his being invalided out and forced to work in the service of Miss Keyes, to her murder and his sentence of death, and the failure of the gallows three times, is told in song, and all but one of those songs are originals. The all-male Fairport seldom sang better, nor did the post-Thompson band ever play with more panache, and some of the songs are beautiful—but a few are lugubrious, and as with most other concept albums, the fit between the songs and the larger subject ultimately isn't entirely comfortable for the listener. All of the material was confusing because the group, for some reason, never put titles on the individual songs, instead stringing them together in longer sections. The critics loved it, but the listeners stayed away in droves for the first time since the band's debut album. *—Bruce Eder*

History of Fairport Convention / Nov. 1972 / Island ✦✦✦✦✦
Originally a double album, this 18-song CD is a good selection of the better songs recorded by the group from *What We Did on Our Holidays* thru *Babbacombe Lee*, including "Sailor's Life," "Who Knows Where The Time Goes," "Meet On the Ledge," "Si Tu Dois Partir," "Matty Groves," "Sloth," and "Angel Delight." It's no substitute for any of the albums up to and including *Full House*, but it's adequate for someone on a limited budget. As with most Fairport albums, the notes are virtually nonexistent, but in place of a historical essay, the CD reproduces the original album's group family tree by Pete Frame, covering the seven lineups of the group (and the prior and subsequent activities of all members) as of the fall of 1972—it was already pretty complex at that point, though someday that account has to be extended to the end of the century. (British import) *—Bruce Eder*

Rosie / Mar. 1973 / Island ✦✦✦
Following the departure of Simon Nicol, the group was reconstituted with the addition of Sandy Denny's husband Trevor Lucas and Jerry Donahue, both formerly of Fotheringay. Their first album was also a miscalculation, a failed attempt to crack the pop music market. There are lots of original songs done in a modern folk-rock sound, many written by Lucas, although the best was the title track by Swarbrick (which featured Denny and Thompson as well as Thompson's future wife Linda Peters, as guest artists). The Lucas compositions were all pleasant (especially "Knights of the Road" and the haunting "The Plainsman"), but tend to make one think more of Gordon Lightfoot sounding archaic than of previous incarnations of Fairport. The only exceptions are "Peggy's Pub" and "The Hens March Through the Midden," instrumentals that recall the group's old sound. *—Bruce Eder & William Ruhlmann*

Nine / Oct. 1973 / A&M ✦✦
Fairport Convention's ninth album is their most uneven. The group shows extraordinary virtuosity and musical instincts on folk-based tracks such as "The Hexamshire Lass" and "The Brilliancy Medley & Cherokee Shuffle" (which features some of the best mandolin playing you're ever likely to hear from an English band), but on numbers like "Polly on the Shore" and "To Althea From Prison," where the band supplies the music to traditional lyrics, they simply fall flat—it isn't even that the playing is bad, so much as that the failed numbers are uniformly lugubrious in the way they're treated. Part of the problem lies with the fact that while Lucas and Donahue were good guitarists, they weren't terribly interesting—where Richard Thompson always came up with something surprising and unexpected on Fairport's songs, Lucas and Donahue stick with fairly routine pop music sounds, more in keeping with the Eagles than the group that recorded *Liege and Lief*, *Full House*, and *House Full*. Lucas's "Bring 'Em Down" is a decent song, with some strong singing and playing by the composer and a lovely and powerful fiddle solo by Swarbrick, but it overstays its welcome and loses its cohesion—"Sloth" it is not. Too much of the album is taken up by easily forgotten contemporary-style rockers like "Big William" and throwaways such as the countrified "Pleasure and Pain"; not even the upbeat, riff heavy "Possibly Parsons Green" makes up for this problem. And the rather plain cover art didn't help matters any when it came to selling this record. *—Bruce Eder*

A Fairport Live Convention / Jul. 1974 / Island ✦✦✦
The presence of Sandy Denny raises expectations for the group's first released live album. Recorded on the band's 1973 world tour, it features songs such as "Matty Groves" and "Sloth," as well as the Swarbrick instrumental "Fiddlestix," their then current single "Rosie," and a nod to the group's origins as interpreters of American rock & roll and folk-rock, in the form of Dylan's "Down in the Flood" and Chris Kenner's "Something You Got." Denny's solo abilities are showcased on "John the Gun." The problem is the uneven quality of the recording, from three different venues, each seemingly lacking intimacy and warmth. This may explain why it was never released in America, and why Island released the superior *Live At the L.A. Troubadour/House Full* just two years later. As the only live document of Denny with the band, however, this record is vital to Fairport completists. *—Bruce Eder & William Ruhlmann*

Rising for the Moon / Jun. 1975 / Island ✦✦✦
Although there's nothing here as overpowering as "Sailor's Life" or "Sloth," this record is still a choice release, as Sandy Denny's official return to Fairport. She wrote or co-wrote seven of its 11 songs, and dominates most of the others with her voice. This lineup (Denny, Dave Swarbrick, Dave Pegg, Jerry Donahue, Trevor Lucas, and Bruce Rowland, with Dave Mattacks—who quit partway through—drumming on some of the tracks) went for the gold with rock veteran Glyn Johns in the producer's spot. The result was the only Fairport album done after the departure of Richard Thompson that doesn't sound anemic in the electric guitar department. Some of the songs, especially the title track and "Restless," have the feel of compact, breezy pop/country-rock, reminiscent of the Eagles or Firefall, although it's hard to imagine either of those groups turning in anything with with ethereal beauty of Denny's performance on "White Dress" or "Dawn." Those songs and "Stranger To Himself" could easily have been on one of her solo albums. Others, like Trevor Lucas's "Iron Lion," sound almost like Fairport's version of the Rolling Stones' "Dead Flowers." Only the Swarbrick/Pegg "Night-time Girl" resembles Fairport's established work from their earlier history. This was the last album and the last incarnation of Fairport Convention to present itself to the public as a contemporary rock group, and their last (apart from 1987's *In Real Time*) release on a major label. Beyond this point, they became part of the folk revival circuit, albeit with a huge audience. (British import) *—Bruce Eder*

Gottle O'Geer / May 1976 / Island ✦✦

Live at the L.A. Troubadour / 1977 / Island ✦✦✦
With Fairport off the label, Island Records reached back and released this live recording from 1970, featuring the last Richard Thompson lineup of the band. It was a forceful album, but it has since been superseded by *House Full*, a revised version of the same material. *—William Ruhlmann*

Bonny Bunch of Roses / Feb. 1977 / Vertigo ✦✦

Tipplers Tales / May 1978 / Vertigo ✦✦✦
Some of Fairport's finest traditional song performances are here, from yet another lineup. Singer/guitarist Simon Nicol, the only original Fairporter left, begins to take a more active role. *—Steve Winick*

Farewell, Farewell / 1979 / Simon's ✦✦✦
Originally recorded as a memento of the group's "final" tour from May to August of 1979, *Farewell, Farewell* was intended as Fairport's last release. It hasn't worked out that way, luckily, as the re-formed version of the group has done some good work, but this was still a rarity, about 23,000 copies (distributed by the bandmembers) ever pressed on vinyl. It's not in league with *House Full*, but it is a worthwhile album, featuring the final version of Fairport Convention in its unbroken line from the original group—here including Simon Nicol, Dave Swarbrick, and Dave Pegg—in good form, covering a cross section of their history. Songs include a crunchy version of "Mr. Lacey"; faithful, emphatic renditions of "John Lee" and "Sir Patrick Spens"; a lustily sung "Walk Awhile"; and a warmly nostalgic "Meet on the Ledge"; with a finale of Mike Waterson's "Rubber Band." Reissued in 1997 with bonus tracks. *—Bruce Eder*

Moat on the Ledge / 1982 / Stony Plain ✦✦✦
Fairport Convention officially disbanded in 1979, only to become the hosts of a yearly folk festival/reunion concert every August in England. This album is taken from the 1981 show. It features original Fairport members Simon Nicol, Judy Dyble, and Richard Thompson, plus later members Dave Swarbrick, Dave Pegg, Dave Mattacks, and Bruce Rowland, and it's a good recapitulation of the band's style, with such numbers new to the repertoire as Bob Dylan's "Country Pie" and Thompson's "Woman or a Man." *—William Ruhlmann*

Gladys' Leap / 1985 / Varrick ✦✦✦
After six years, Fairport re-formed and released this fine record featuring mostly newly composed material. *—Steve Winick*

Expletive Delighted! / 1986 / Varrick ✦✦✦
The group's only all-instrumental album is alternately enjoyable and maddening. On the down side, there was no earthly reason why Dave Mattacks' drums had to be recorded as loud as they are on certain tracks. But "Portmeirion" and "Expletive Delighted" are as delicate and beautiful as any work that this version of the band has done. Richard Thompson and Jerry Donahue turn up on electric guitar for the rippling finale "Hanks For the Memories," a reconsideration of instrumentals ranging from "Apache" and "Pipeline" to "Peter Gunn." *—Bruce Eder*

House Full / 1986 / Hannibal ✦✦✦✦✦
Although its release date is 16 years later, this 1970 live recording is of a piece with *Full House* and should be discovered in tandem with the studio album. A revised version of *Live at the L.A. Troubadour* (originally released on vinyl in 1976), with different takes and/or songs, taken from a group of September 1970 concert performance by the Richard Thompson-led 1970 lineup of Fairport, one of its strongest incarnations. A 12-minute-long version of "Sloth" dominates the proceedings, but even better is the fact that, at 48 minutes, this is one of Fairport's longer albums, so there is lots of room for other material, including a shattering Thompson-sung rendition of "Matty Groves," and a pair of numbers, "Staines Morris" and "Banks of the Sweet Primroses," scheduled for this group's never-realized second studio album (though the latter made it into the studio history of the four-man Fairport that followed). *—Bruce Eder & William Ruhlmann*

Heyday: BBC Radio Sessions, 1968-1969 / 1987 / Hannibal ✦✦✦✦✦

Fairport Convention has long been British folk-rock with the emphasis on British and folk, but listeners most familiar with their revved-up interpretation of traditional English ballads (and like-minded originals) often forget that the band started out as the U.K.'s response to Jefferson Airplane. *Heyday* collects 12 performances (ten of them covers) recorded for the BBC during the early period when Sandy Denny and Ian Matthews were both singing for the group (and a bus accident had not yet taken the life of original drummer Martin Lamble). While most of the songs were written by noted American folk-rockers of the day, the Fairports put a very individual stamp on every selection here; if you don't think you ever need to hear another version of Leonard Cohen's "Suzanne" or Bob Dylan's "Percy's Song," you might well change your mind after hearing Fairport work their magic with them, and their takes on Joni Mitchell's "I Don't Know Where I Stand" and Gene Clark's "Tried So Hard" actually improve on the very worthy originals. Fairport Convention approaches these songs with taste, skill, and subtle but potent fire, and Richard Thompson was already growing into one of the most remarkable guitarists in British rock (and if you're of the opinion that he doesn't know how to be funny, check out his goofy double entendre duet with Sandy, "If It Feels Good, You Know It Can't Be Wrong"). While Fairport Convention would create their most lasting work with *Liege and Leif* and *Full House, Heyday* offers delightful proof that this band's talents (and influences) took many different directions, and it captures one of the band's better lineups in superb form. —*Mark Deming*

In Real Time: Live '87 / 1987 / Island ✦✦

Red & Gold / 1989 / Rough Trade ✦✦

Five Seasons / Dec. 1990 / Rough Trade ✦✦✦

Fairport Convention's 17th studio album in 22 years finds them a competent, craftsman-like unit led by Simon Nicol, who has developed into a strong singer. If they never aspire to the heights achieved with more impressive lineups, they nevertheless continue to find traditional and new material that suits them, sometimes by turning to newest members Ric Saunders and Martin Allcock, who are accomplished instrumentalists. —*William Ruhlmann*

25th Anniversary / Oct. 10, 1994 / Woodword ✦✦✦

Recorded live to DAT at a performance that had fiddler Chris Leslie filling in for Ric Sanders, who had injured himself in an accident involving a plate glass window (Sanders was able to provide keyboards, however). A festive outing, with numerous guests (including Fairport founders Richard Thompson and Ashley Hutchings), the two-disc set ranges from the sublime (a ferocious, Boiled In Lead-style take of "Matty Groves") to the slightly surreal ("John Barleycorn" with the lyrics screwed up). The sound is unfortunately too bright and metallic, and the mix, taken from the soundboard, is sometimes atrocious, but trimming the highs helps with the former, while the latter, in the spirit of live shows, can simply be ignored. Not the best example of Fairport, but *highly* entertaining. —*Steven McDonald*

Jewel in the Crown / Jun. 6, 1995 / Green Linnet ✦✦✦

On their first album in five years, Fairport Convention, which now boasts a steady lineup (nearly a decade together!) for the first time in its history, carries on two traditions. The shorter-term one is the tradition of Fairport itself, a band intended to blend contemporary rock with folk, often in the form of work by current singer/songwriters, here including Clive Gregson and Leonard Cohen. The longer term one is the tradition of Scots-Irish music, with its jigs and reels and story songs that date back to the Middle Ages. Sometimes, the band combines the two traditions, recording songs like Steve Tilston's "The Naked Highwayman" and Ralph McTell and band member Maartin Allcock's "The Islands," which update traditional themes in interesting ways. (Allcock, by the way, has added an extra "A" to his first name since we last heard from him.) Simon Nicol, the only original member of Fairport Convention dating back to 1967, has developed into a sturdy baritone singer, and multi-instrumentalist Allcock carries the bulk of the musical burden. *Jewel in the Crown* is a well-balanced collection of songs that is true to the spirit of Fairport Convention and its antecedents. —*William Ruhlmann*

Old-New-Borrowed-Blue / Jul. 16, 1996 / Green Linnet ✦✦✦✦

This is Fairport Convention's first all-acoustic album in their 29 year history. The material, recorded variously in the studio and at December 30, 1995 concert, displays the eclectic nature of the 1990's version of the band, folk-styled originals such as "There Once Was Love/Innstruck" juxtaposed with covers of James Taylor and Loudon Wainwright III songs, reprises of vintage Fairport numbers like Richard Thompson's "Genesis Hall," "Crazy Man Michael," and the epic "Matty Groves," and even some vintage swing elements. The playing is exquisite and the vocalizing by Simon Nicol and Dave Pegg is extraordinary, particularly on "There Once Was Love," "Frozen Man," "The Hiring Fair," and "Lalla Rookh." —*Bruce Eder*

● **Meet on the Ledge: The Classic Years (1967-1975)** / Jul. 27, 1999 / A&M ✦✦✦✦✦

Fairport Convention have had their fair share of anthologies, but the double-disc set *Meet on the Ledge: The Classic Years (1967-75)* is arguably the best yet, rivaling the classic *Fairport Chronicles*, which was released just as the classic lineup was splitting apart. *Meet on the Ledge* is more exhaustive than that collection, and it also boasts a number of rarities, including the previously unreleased "Bonny Bunch of Roses" and "Poor Will and the Jolly Hangman." Undoubtedly, those will be of interest to collectors, but the 32-track set is still primarily targeted at neophytes and casual fans. Happily, it fulfills its goal of offering a flawless introduction—not only does it provide a concise history of the band, but it's also tremendously entertaining. Which means that even if it satiates some appetites, it will whet others. But the best thing is that the compilation works well enough to remain entertaining, even if you know the albums inside out. —*Stephen Thomas Erlewine*

The Wood and the Wire / Jul. 25, 2000 / Compass ✦✦✦✦

There's no doubt that Fairport Convention chose the right man for the job upon Martin Allcock's departure after *Old-New-Borrowed-Blue* (1996). His replacement, Chris Leslie (Whippersnapper and Albion Band), has assumed an obvious leadership position within this legendary band. He either wrote or co-wrote (with writing partner Nigel Stonier) nine of the selections on *The Wood and the Wire* and sang lead on seven cuts. With a voice that resembles onetime Fairport member Ian Matthews, a fiddle and mandolin style that recalls one of the most beloved Fairport alumni Dave Swarbrick, and a songwriting style that conveys folk imagery in the inimitable Fairport manner, Leslie seems to have been part of this "moveable feast" for much longer than three years. While a fiddler by trade, Leslie relinquishes that instrument for most of this album in favor of the mandolin and bouzouki; the role of longtime violin player Ric Sanders has been unaffected as a result of Leslie joining the band. Fairport Convention has long possessed the knack of selecting songs from outside sources (Bob Dylan, Ralph McTell, Huw Williams, et al.) and transforming them into classics of their own. On this album they appear to continue the trend with three choice songs—"The Heart of the Song" by Peter Scrowther, "Western Wind," a traditional piece brought to their attention by Susan McKeown, and Steve Tilston's "Rocky Road," all sung venerably by guitarist Simon Nicol with Leslie and bassist Dave Pegg sharing the lead on the final selection. Drummer Gerry Conway appears with the band for the first time since 1973's *Rosie*. —*Dave Sleger*

Faith No More

f. 1982, San Francisco, CA, **db.** Apr. 20, 1998

Alternative Metal, Funk Metal, Heavy Metal, Alternative Pop/Rock

With their fusion of heavy metal, funk, hip-hop, and progressive rock, Faith No More earned a substantial cult following. By the time they recorded their first album in 1985, the band had already had a string of lead vocalists, including Courtney Love; their debut, *We Care a Lot*, featured Chuck Mosley's abrasive vocals but it was driven by Jim Martin's metallic guitar. Faith No More's next album, 1987's *Introduce Yourself*, was a more cohesive and impressive effort; for the first time, the rap and metal elements didn't sound like they were fighting each other. In 1988, the rest of the band fired Mosley; he was replaced by Bay Area vocalist Mike Patton during the recording of their next album, *The Real Thing.* Patton was a more accomplished vocalist, able to change effortlessly between rapping and singing, as well as adding a considerably more bizarre slant to the lyrics. Besides adding a new vocalist, the band had tightened their attack and the result was the genre-bending hit single, "Epic," which established them as a major hard-rock act. Following up the hit wasn't as easy, however. Faith No More followed their breakthrough success with 1992's *Angel Dust*, one of the more complex and simply confounding records ever released by a major label. Upon the conclusion of a tour in support of *Album of the Year*, Faith No More announced it was disbanding in April 1998. —*Stephen Thomas Erlewine*

We Care a Lot / 1985 / Mordam ✦✦✦

After listening to Faith No More's debut, *We Care a Lot*, it's hard to believe that this is the same band that we know today. They sound more like early Public Image Limited than the FNM that would eventually assault your senses with *Angel Dust* and *Album of the Year*. Obviously, one of the major reasons is because current singer Mike Patton is not on the album. Original frontman Chuck Mosley handles the vocal duties, and his singing style is the complete opposite of Patton's. While Patton is extremely talented and versatile (he can sing every style of music imaginable, including foreign music), Mosley's voice is often off-key, fairly monotonous, and colorless (but with lots of attitude). Musically, the group shows glimpses of the killer genre-bending band they would become in the near future. The original version of the title track is an anthem in typical twisted FNM style: it contains irresistible melodies and riffs, but challenges you lyrically (the words deal with the hypocritical situation surrounding the millionaire musicians who participated in 1985's Live Aid concert). The song is still featured at their concerts, as is the keyboard-laced "As the Worm Turns." Other highlights include the furious instrumental "Pills for Breakfast" and the near dance-track "Arabian Disco." Although most of FNM's important components are present—airy keyboards, tribal drumming, heavy metal guitar, and sturdy bass—the big picture is not as focused as it would eventually be. And it becomes more and more evident that the missing piece of the puzzle is Mike Patton. —*Greg Prato*

Introduce Yourself / 1987 / Slash/Rhino ✦✦✦✦

On Faith No More's major-label debut, *Introduce Yourself*, the Faith No More that you've grown to know and love finally rears it's ugly head (much more so than on their 1985 independent release *We Care a Lot*). All the ingredients are there, but like its predecessor there's one crucial item missing, super-vocalist Mike Patton. This would be original singer Chuck Mosley's last outing with the band, before he was ejected due to erratic and unpredictable behavior. Still, the album is consistent and interesting, with Mosley's out-of-tune vocals being an acquired taste to most. "The Crab Song" is one of their most underrated tracks, which packs quite a wallop when guitarist Jim Martin's heavily saturated guitar kicks in. The title track is an enjoyable and brief rant, and the loopy bass and irresistible melodicism of "Anne's Song" should have been a hit. There's also a slightly updated version of "We Care a Lot" included, and the resulting video gave the band their first taste of MTV success (but nothing compared to what they'd experience with their heavily rotated breakthrough "Epic"). A step in the right direction toward the deliciously twisted sound they'd achieve on later releases. —*Greg Prato*

● **The Real Thing** / Jun. 1989 / Slash ✦✦✦✦

Starting with the careening "From Out of Nowhere," driven by Bottum's doomy, energetic keyboards, Faith No More rebounded excellently on *The Real Thing* after Mosley's firing.

Given that the band had nearly finished recording the music and Patton was a last minute recruit, he adjusts to the proceedings well. His insane, wide-ranging musical interests would have to wait for the next album for their proper integration, but the band already showed enough of that to make it an inspired combination. Bottum, in particular, remains the wild card, coloring Martin's nuclear-strength riffs and the Gould/Bordin rhythm slams with everything from quirky hooks to pristine synth sheen. It's not quite early Brian Eno joins Led Zeppelin and Funkadelic, but it's closer than might be thought, based on the nutty lounge vibes of "Edge of the World" and the Arabic melodies and feedback of "Woodpeckers From Mars." "Falling to Pieces," a fractured anthem with a delicious delivery from Patton, should have been a bigger single that it was, while "Surprise! You're Dead!" and the title track stuff riffs down the listener's throat. The best-known song remains the appropriately titled "Epic," which lives up to its name from the bombastic opening to the concluding piano and the crunching, stomping funk metal in between. The inclusion of a cover of Black Sabbath's "War Pigs" amusingly backfired on the band—at the time, Sabbath's hipness level was nonexistent, making it a great screw-you to the supposed cutting edge types. However, all the metalheads took the band to their hearts so much that, as a result, the quintet dropped it from their sets to play "Easy" by the Commodores instead! *—Ned Raggett*

Angel Dust / 1992 / Slash ✦✦✦✦✦

Warner Bros. figured that lightning could strike twice at a time when oodles of (most horribly bad) funk-metal acts were following in Faith No More and Red Hot Chili Peppers's footsteps. In response, the former recorded and released the bizarro masterpiece *Angel Dust*. Patton's work in Mr. Bungle proved just how strange and inspired he could get given the opportunity; now, in his more famous act, nothing was ignored. "Land of Sunshine" starts things off in a vein similar to *The Real Thing*, but Patton's vocal role-playing is smarter and more accomplished, with the lyrics trashing a smug bastard with pure inspired mockery. From there, *Angel Dust* mixes the meta-metal of earlier days with the expected puree of other influences, including a cinematic sense of atmosphere. The album ends with a cover of John Barry's "Midnight Cowboy," which suits the mood perfectly, but the stretched-out, tense moments on "Caffeine" and the soaring charge of "Everything's Ruined" make for other good examples. Even a Kronos Quartet sample crops up on the frazzled sprawl of "Malpractice." Other sampling and studio treatments come to the fore throughout, adding quirks like the distorted voices on "Smaller and Smaller." The band's sense of humor crops up frequently—there's the hilarious portrayal of prepubescent angst on "Kindergarten," made all the more entertaining by the music's straightforward approach, or the beyond-stereotypical white trash cornpone narration of "RV," all while the music breezily swings along. Patton's voice is stronger and downright smooth at many points throughout, the musicians collectively still know their stuff, and the result is twisted entertainment at its finest. *—Ned Raggett*

King for a Day, Fool for a Lifetime / Mar. 28, 1995 / Slash/Reprise ✦✦

Album of the Year / Jun. 3, 1997 / Slash/Reprise ✦✦✦✦

Faith No More's 1997 release *Album of the Year* featured the talents of another new guitarist, Jon Hudson, who replaced Dean Menta (Menta only toured with the group in support of *King for a Day* before being dismissed). Like *King for a Day, Album* is more straightforward musically than past releases and remains one of FNM's most focused and concise works. Recorded in bassist Billy Gould's home studio, *Album of the Year* would turn out to be their last studio recording before splitting up in 1997. A trio of outstanding tracks—"Stripsearch," "Last Cup of Sorrow," and "Ashes to Ashes"—blend hard rock and pop melodicism the way only FNM can, while "Helpless" is an unpredictable composition that alternates between heavy guitar riffing and Mike Patton's tempered vocals. The explosive album opener, "Collision," and "Naked in Front of the Computer" show that the band can still compose prime heavy rockers, while other musical forms were included as well (the romantic ballad "She Loves Me Not," the evil boogie of "Home Sick Home," and the Middle Eastern sounds of "Mouth to Mouth"). For the gripping album closer "Pristina," the 1990s' turmoil in Yugoslavia is used as a backdrop for a tale of lovers being separated due to war. *Album of the Year* was a fitting way for one of alt-rock's most influential and important bands to end their career. *—Greg Prato*

Who Cares a Lot: Greatest Hits / Nov. 24, 1998 / Slash/Reprise ✦✦✦

For a band that only scored one true hit single (1989's "Epic"), the "Greatest Hits" tag appended to *Who Cares a Lot* is deceptive—most of Faith No More's airplay occurred on MTV, as well as some more open-minded rock radio stations. That's what the 15 tracks collected here represent: singles and songs that were promoted for radio airplay, not necessarily the "best of" Faith No More. The compilation wisely selects only two key tracks from the Chuck Mosley era, and while it's missing the band's collaboration with the Boo-Y.A.A. Tribe for the *Judgment Night* soundtrack, it does include the non-LP covers of the Commodores' "Easy" and the Bee Gees' "I Started a Joke." However, because the emphasis is on commercially promoted material, there are only five total entries from the group's two defining albums (*The Real Thing* and *Angel Dust*); there are three apiece from the somewhat less interesting *King for a Day, Fool for a Lifetime* and *Album of the Year*. The adrenaline rush of a good Faith No More album lies in the way the band walks the fine line between eclecticism and disjointedness; concentrating only on their most commercially accessible selections simply can't capture that feeling. Granted, *Who Cares a Lot* is not without its uses; it will satisfy fans who just want the band's recognizable songs on one disc, or who don't have the patience to sort through the more uneven albums. But if its aim is to be a definitive Faith No More retrospective, *Who Cares a Lot* falls well short of the mark. [Some pressings featured an eight-song bonus rarities CD.] *—Steve Huey*

Marianne Faithfull

b. Dec. 29, 1946, Hampstead, London, England
Vocals / Girl Group, British Invasion

Few stars of the 1960s have reinvented themselves as successfully as Marianne Faithfull. Coaxed into a singing career by Rolling Stones manager Andrew Loog Oldham in 1964, she had a big hit in both Britain and the U.S. with her debut single, the Jagger/Richards composition "As Tears Go By" (which prefaced the Stones' own version by a full year). Considerably more successful in her native land than the States, she had a series of hits in the mid-'60s that set her high, fragile voice against delicate orchestral pop arrangements—"Summer Night," "This Little Bird," Jackie De Shannon's "Come and Stay With Me." She offered a taste of things to come with her compelling 1969 single "Sister Morphine," which she co-wrote (and which the Stones released themselves on *Sticky Fingers* later). In the 1970s, Faithfull split up with Mick Jagger, developed a serious drug habit, and recorded rarely, with generally dismal results—until late 1979, when she pulled off an astonishing comeback with *Broken English*. Displaying a croaking, cutting voice that had lowered a good octave since the mid-'60s, Faithfull had also begun to write much of her own material, and addressed sex and despair with wrenching realism. After allowing herself to be framed as a demure chanteuse by songwriters and arrangers throughout most of her career, Marianne had found her own voice, and suddenly sounded more relevant and contemporary than most of the stars she had rubbed shoulders with in the '60s. *—Richie Unterberger*

Marianne Faithfull / May 1965 / Deram ✦✦✦

Her erratic, self-titled debut features lovely baroque arrangements by Mike Leander and decent tunes like "As Tears Go By," and Jackie DeShannon's "Come and Stay With Me" and "In My Time of Sorrow," and Bacharach/David's "If I Never Get to Love You," as well as fairly crummy covers of hits by the Beatles, Herman's Hermits, and Petula Clark. Look for the Japanese CD reissue: It adds six non-LP bonus tracks from mid-'60s singles, including a couple (the girl-groupish "The Sha La La Song," the melancholy "The Morning Sun") that rank among her best '60s recordings. *—Richie Unterberger*

Dreaming My Dreams / Jan. 1977 / Nems ✦✦✦

Marianne Faithfull's first new album in a decade revealed the weathered voice she later would put to good, if harrowing, use in a series of albums for Island Records starting with *Broken English* in 1979. Here, that voice was smoothed out and used for pop and country material including such songs as "I'll Be Your Baby Tonight," "I'm Not Lisa," and "It Wasn't God Who Made Honky Tonk Angels." Faithfull had loosened up considerably since the chaste schoolgirl days of "As Tears Go By," and *Dreaming My Dreams* suggested that her hard life could be analogous to that of a country music star. Faithfull didn't have the accent to match that assertion, but she did have the attitude. (Rereleased in slightly altered form as *Faithless* in March 1978.) *—William Ruhlmann*

Faithless / Mar. 1978 / Columbia ✦✦✦

Marianne Faithfull's first new album in a decade revealed the weathered voice she later would put to good, if harrowing, use in a series of albums for Island Records starting with *Broken English* in 1979. Here, that voice was smoothed out and used for pop and country material including such songs as "I'll Be Your Baby Tonight," "I'm Not Lisa," and "It Wasn't God Who Made Honky Tonk Angels." Faithfull had loosened up considerably since the chaste schoolgirl days of "As Tears Go By," and *Faithless* suggested that her hard life could be analogous to that of a country music star. Faithfull didn't have the accent to match that assertion, but she did have the attitude. (*Faithless* was a slightly altered version of the January 1977 album *Dreaming My Dreams*. It was reissued on CD in 1991 with four bonus tracks.) *—William Ruhlmann*

● **Broken English** / Nov. 1979 / Island ✦✦✦✦✦

After a lengthy absence, Faithfull resurfaced on this 1979 album, which took the edgy and brittle sound of punk rock and gave it a shot of studio-smooth dance rock. Faithfull's whiskey-worn vocals perfectly match the bitter and biting "Why'd Ya Do It" and revitalize John Lennon's "Working Class Hero." *—John Floyd*

Dangerous Acquaintances / Sep. 1981 / Island ✦✦✦

A rather lukewarm, disappointing follow-up to *Broken English*, on which Faithfull seemed to be retreating from that album's sonic and lyrical risks. Although *Broken English* had found most of its audience with the new wave/alternative crowd (songs like "Why'd Ya Do It," after all, were too shocking to get much commercial airplay), *Dangerous Acquaintances* seemed to be moving back to more mainstream rock territory, particularly in the arrangements. It's always a possible sign of trouble when there are over a dozen session musicians in the credits, and much of the record's music has a sort of anonymous feel. The songs, too, are less striking (and less angrily risque) than those of *Broken English*, although Faithfull was still carving her own identity with lyrics about romantic duplicity. The most commercially accessible track, "For Beauties Sake," was co-written by Faithfull and Steve Winwood. *—Richie Unterberger*

A Childs Adventure / Mar. 1983 / Island ✦✦

Marianne Faithfull's Greatest Hits / 1987 / ABKCO ✦✦✦✦✦

While missing a few fine album tracks, this is an excellent 16-song distillation of her '60s recordings. Includes all of her British and American hits—"As Tears Go By," "This Little Bird," "Summer Nights," and "Come and Stay With Me." Bonuses include "In My Time of Sorrow," an obscure mid-'60s folk-rocker co-written by Jackie DeShannon and Jimmy Page, and her 1969 single "Sister Morphine" (co-written with the Rolling Stones), predating the *Sticky Fingers* version; it's easily her most powerful performance of the decade. *—Richie Unterberger*

Strange Weather / Jul. 1987 / Island ✦✦✦✦✦

Faithfull's 1987 release recast her as a nicotine-stained chanteuse, approaching such standards as "Boulevard of Broken Dreams" and "Penthouse Serenade" with a ravaged, world-weary demeanor that recalls the latter-day recordings of Billie Holiday. She also tackles some blues and jazz material and turns "As Tears Go By" into the gut-wrenching torch ballad neither the Stones nor Faithfull could ever have done in the '60s. A dark, challenging masterpiece. *—John Floyd*

Blazing Away / Mar. 1990 / Island ♦♦♦♦
Fully established as a dramatic, innovative singer with astonishing appeal and energy thanks to her string of excellent '80s releases, Faithfull concluded her renaissance decade with *Blazing Away*, an excellent live album recorded in New York's St. Anne's Cathedral. The crackerjack backing band deserves note in and of itself, including members ranging from the Band's Garth Hudson to Dr. John, plus regular collaborators Marc Ribot, Fernando Saunders, and her key partner Barry Reynolds. Faithfull and the players fit hand in glove track for track, with the emphasis on subtler arrangements and performances suiting the hushed, striking atmosphere of the performance. When the band shows its muscle, as with the snarling strut of "Guilt," there's no question of this being anything like easy listening. In general, though, the sense of cabaret meets modern nightclub dominates, with Faithfull's singing capturing the cracking tug of her vocals just so. The selection of songs ranges from the intriguingly obscure to the familiar enough—"As Tears Go By" and "Broken English" take unsurprising bows, as does a lengthy brood on "Sister Morphine," "She Moved Through the Fair," and a commanding rip through the harrowing "Why'd Ya Do It?" There are two new numbers as well. The title track is the one song recorded in studio, with Reynolds and Saunders, plus a number of other musicians; it's got a nice steel guitar twang to it, and Faithfull tries for the high lonesome sound in her own wonderful way. Other flat-out highlights include a grand take on "Times Square" and a slow crawl through "Working Class Hero" that seethes with fire, both from the musicians and Faithfull. *—Ned Raggett*

Faithfull: A Collection of Her Best Recordings / Aug. 23, 1994 / Island ♦♦♦
This best-of basically covers the years 1979 to 1994, though it reaches back to 1964 for Marianne Faithfull's first recording and first hit, "As Tears Go By," and includes "She," slated for the upcoming 1995 album *A Secret Life*. Five of the 11 songs are drawn from Faithfull's strongest album, 1979's *Broken English*, including the bitter title track and "Why'd Ya Do It." Otherwise, compiler Chris Blackwell makes little attempt to present a balance among Faithfull's recordings—there is nothing at all from *Dangerous Acquaintances* or *A Child's Adventure*, and only one track each from *Strange Weather* and *Blazing Away*. But there is a good newly recorded cover of Patti Smith's "Ghost Dance" co-produced by Keith Richards and featuring other members of the Rolling Stones, and Blackwell rescues Faithfull's rendition of the title theme for the movie *Trouble in Mind* from the soundtrack album. It adds up to an excellent compilation that highlights Faithfull's strengths as a singer. *—William Ruhlmann*

A Secret Life / Mar. 21, 1995 / Island ♦♦♦
For her first studio album comprised of mostly original material in over a decade, Faithfull enlisted noted composer Angelo Badalamenti (who collaborated with David Lynch for the *Twin Peaks* TV soundtrack) to write music for her lyrics and produce. Faithfull is still in rippingly fine voice, and her words still penetrate. But while Badalamenti's densely orchestral arrangements can be effectively noirish, they can also create an inappropriately cold and detached ambience, despite standout tracks like "Flaming September" and "She." *—Richie Unterberger*

20th Century Blues / Jan. 14, 1997 / RCA ♦♦♦♦
As the liner notes to this intriguing release tell, Faithfull had a long-simmering interest in German cabaret, particularly the work of Kurt Weill. It came fully to life via her role as Pirate Jenny in a staging of *The Threepenny Opera* in Dublin as translated by Frank McGuinness and her attendance at a workshop organized by Allen Ginsburg. After a series of initial performances with pianist Paul Trueblood, Faithfull took her revue of many classic songs from the mid-century, titled "An Evening in the Weimar Republic," to the road. This particular recording is from a performance in Paris in 1996, showcasing both a smart selection of songs to work with and Faithfull's own dramatic, interpretive skills with them. Kicking off with the aggressive-then-smooth bite of the Brecht/Weill standard "Alabama Song," Faithfull and Trueblood show they make a great team—her distinct vocals seem almost born for the material, while Trueblood is a sure hand on the keys, both playful and polished. Weill remains the centerpiece of the show, in both his various collaborations with Brecht—standout tracks include withering versions of "Pirate Jenny," "Salomon Song," and "Surabaya Johnny"—and with other partners, including "Complainte de la Seine" and "Mon Ami, My Friend." Friedrich Hollaender gets the nod twice, with a take on the eternal classic "Falling in Love Again" almost rivaling Marlene Dietrich's original interpretation. The title track, a noted Noel Coward number, gets a fine performance, as does the one nod to more contemporary times, a rendition of Harry Nilsson's "Don't Forget Me." One nod to Faithfull's previous recording past appears via a new version of "Boulevard of Broken Dreams," originally covered by her on *Strange Weather*. Faithfull throughout introduces songs with humor and reflection, a perfect MC for her own performance. *—Ned Raggett*

The Seven Deadly Sins / Sep. 15, 1998 / RCA ♦♦♦♦
If you're looking for the angelic Marianne Faithfull of *As Tears Go By*, or the angry diva of *Broken English*, or the lush but piercingly acute imagery of her work with Angelo Badalamenti, you will not find it here. What you will find is a fully orchestrated work that she has been selling out houses with in Europe—a parable of commerce called *The Seven Deadly Sins*, with the Vienna Radio Orchestra and Dennis Russell Davies conducting. These are the songs of Kurt Weill, composer, and Bertolt Brecht, lyricist. This work is a perfect match of voice timbre and sound wished for by the composer. The husky and weary-voiced Faithfull does these songs as they were intended to be done. Weill's music tends toward a formality and somberness that shadows the concerns of the songs. Here, Brecht's lyrics tell the moribund story of a girl placed on a tour by her family to earn money for their luxury; her voice reflects the weariness that becomes the ideal vehicle for her travails and lacerations. According to the tabloids, if they are to be believed, Faithfull has spent her life researching this work. She displays that rare intelligence that allows all "misfortunes" to be converted to her benefit. There is a detachment that allows one to be intimately involved with, but not consumed by this type of work. This is her best work in quite some time. She deserves all the accolades that come her way as a serious singer who can pull off the piece. A wonderful disc from one whose live presence must be counted as miraculous considering what she has lived through. *—Bob Gottlieb*

Perfect Stranger: The Island Anthology / Oct. 27, 1998 / Island ♦♦♦♦♦
Because more than half of the 35 songs on this two-disc retrospective of Marianne Faithfull's 1979-95 output come from her three great albums—*Broken English, Dangerous Acquaintances*, and *Strange Weather*—or are previously unreleased outtakes or B-sides from them, *A Perfect Stranger: The Island Anthology* makes a fine primer to Faithfull's often challenging, always mesmerizing (or would that be always challenging, often mesmerizing?) music. "Ballad of the Soldier's Wife," her solid contribution to 1985's *Lost in the Stars: The Music of Kurt Weill*, is also included, giving Faithfull's hauntingly tragic voice the resonance and attention it demands. Weill and Faithfull seem made for each other, as the bulk of the second disc (comprised of songs from her 1990 live album and the underachieving *A Secret Life*, as well as the career-capping *Strange Weather*) makes clear. But there's also a strain to some of these tracks, as if Faithfull's aesthetic wandering eventually will bring her to that elusive cabaret of her dreams. On her best recordings, it indeed sounds like she's home. *—Michael Gallucci*

It's All Over Now Baby Blue / Mar. 28, 2000 / Repertoire ♦♦♦
Marianne Faithfull, who gained her notoriety in the '60s as much for her relationships with famous musicians like Mick Jagger as she did for her own music, descended into a heavy drug habit in the '70s that sapped her underappreciated creative talent. This compilation documents a time when she was beginning to crawl out again—the late '70s and early '80s—and draws from three of her albums for Nems Records, *Dreaming My Dreams, All I Wanna Do in Life*, and *The Way You Want Me to Be*. The music here is not among her most polished, indeed it is the rawness of the songs that make them intriguing. No other female vocalist can make a guttural growl sound musical the way that Faithfull can and here it is showcased at its unadorned best. The title track aches with sadness, a cover of Bob Dylan's "Visions of Johanna" shines, and "Dreamin' My Dreams" expresses an almost existential longing. Overall this is a fine collection that highlights the best from an undervalued era in Faithfull's musical career. *—Stacia Proefrock*

True / Sep. 26, 2000 / Music Club ♦♦♦
In early 1971, Marianne Faithfull—whose personal life was not in the best shape and whose commercial prospects were idle as she had released just one single since early 1967—recorded an album's worth of material with producer Mike Leander, who had worked with Faithfull in the 1960s. Leander hoped to place the album with Bell Records, but despite some initial positive feedback, Bell rejected the record after it was completed. The 12 songs on this CD were cut at these 1971 sessions and eventually released in the mid-'80s on the Castle compilation *Rich Kid Blues*, which added most of the material from her 1978 album *Faithless*. Now isolated on a disc of their own, these early-'70s performances turn out to be surprisingly worthwhile, even if they're not among her very best work. Faithfull's voice had now lowered about a full octave (actually it had already done so by her 1969 single "Sister Morphine"), and she gave dignified, knowing interpretations to songs with a folk-rock and country-rock bent, with suitably understated, low-key arrangements. Bob Dylan, Phil Ochs, James Taylor, Tim Hardin, and Cat Stevens were among the composers covered, and pure country ("Long Black Veil") and folk ("Corinne, Corinna") tunes were also part of the program. This is best when the arrangements are stripped down to little more than guitar and Faithfull's sensually low voice, as on "Sad Lisa," "Southern Butterfly," and "Visions of Johanna." When a fuller electric band backing's employed, there's a more dated early-'70s mellow-rock sluggishness. Still, at its best this is actually very good stuff, and even at less than its best, it has its good points. A worthy transition from her '60s pop days into more serious material, it's worth finding (and has often been overlooked) by Faithfull fans. *—Richie Unterberger*

Jason Falkner

b. 1968, Los Angeles, CA

Vocals, Guitar, Bass / Pop Underground, Indie Pop, Chamber Pop, Adult Alternative Pop/Rock, Alternative Pop/Rock

A one-time member of the West Coast neo-psychedelic bands the Three O'Clock and Jellyfish, Jason Falkner went out on his own by 1996, playing jagged power-pop with impeccable arrangements, a clue to both his classically trained childhood and additional time spent working on the first LP by another classical popster, Eric Matthews. Leaving Jellyfish after their 1990 debut *Bellybutton*, Falkner vowed to never play in another band again, bending the promise not long after by joining the loose collective known as the Grays, four musicians who hated the confines of most groups and thus decided to do everything in their power to avoid the pitfalls. Being such a laid-back band, however, resulted in the release of just one album, 1994's *Ro Sham Bo*. Again on the dole, Falkner worked with Eric Matthews on the 1996 LP *It's Heavy in Here*, and finally got what he had been looking for all the time: a solo deal. Through Elektra Records, he released *Presents Author Unknown*, also in 1996. The following year, he played on Matthews' second album, *The Lateness of the Hour*, and in early 1999 issued his own sophomore effort, *Can You Still Feel?* *—John Bush*

● **Presents Author Unknown** / Aug. 13, 1996 / Elektra ♦♦♦♦♦
You may remember Jason Falkner from helping out buddy Eric Matthews craft a tasty bit

of pop music in 1995. Well, he's done it again, only all by himself this time. Writing, producing, singing, and playing nearly everything except the occasional guitar overdub (and strings), Jason has released a one-man pop tour de force. Hooks abound and won't let you down. The more you listen, the more you'll find yourself humming along. Standout tracks include "I Go Astray" and "Don't Show Me Heaven," but all are worthy of a listen. It's good ol' pop music. Better still, it's good music. —*James Chrispell*

Can You Still Feel? / Feb. 23, 1999 / Elektra ✦✦✦✦
Jason Falkner's second album is another set of pop gems given his own wildly inventive production support—besides playing each of the instruments heard (except for a few strings and reeds), Falkner also co-produced the record with Nigel Godrich. Sweeping pop epics like "Author Unknown" and "Holiday" are quite solid—even while sounding quite similar to songs from the debut album—but the highlight proves to be the bitter-toned downtempo number "I Already Know," which reveals a bridge complete with a heart-wrenching jagged guitar line. There's a (barely) perceptible drop in the songwriting quality from his practically flawless debut, but *Can You Still Feel?* is overall a worthy follow-up. —*John Bush*

Necessity: The 4-Track Years / Apr. 24, 2001 / spinART ✦✦✦
Jason Falkner's excellent third solo release may be subtitled *The 4-Track Years*, but that doesn't mean the album is a mishmash of throwaways and unfinished filler. On the contrary, even when his songs are "all crackly and intimately recorded in various apartment-bed-living rooms"—as the liner notes describe the album's demos and rarities—Falkner plays pristine power pop that's radio-ready from the get-go. From the opening Matthew Sweet-styled "She's Not the Enemy" to the closing "I Go Astray," the ex-Jellyfish member doesn't let a single dud creep onto *Necessity*. His are songs that jingle-jangle like Sloan and resonate with the emotional weight of Michael Penn. And while nearly half of these songs are original versions of previously released songs, consider their inclusion less a lazy way to fill the album's 45-minute running time than a closer look into Falkner's superb songwriting. After all, when someone's odds 'n' ends are better than many musicians' final polished products, listeners should be so lucky as to acquire them. —*Jimmy Draper*

The Fall

f. 1977, Manchester, England
College Rock, British Punk, Post-Punk, Alternative Pop/Rock, Punk, Indie Rock
Out of all the late-'70s punk and post-punk bands, none were longer-lived or were more prolific than the Fall. Throughout their career, the band underwent a myriad of lineup changes, but at the center of it all was vocalist Mark E. Smith. With his snarling, nearly incomprehensible vocals and consuming bitter cynicism, Smith became a cult legend in indie and alternative rock. Over the course of their career, the Fall went through a number of shifts in musical style, yet the foundation of their sound was a near-cacophonic, amelodic jagged jumble of guitars, sing-speak vocals, and keyboards. During the late '70s and early '80s, the band was at their most abrasive and atonal. In 1984, Smith's American wife Brix joined the band as a guitarist, bringing a stronger sense of pop melody to the group. By the mid-'80s, the band's British following was large enough to result in two U.K. Top 40 hits, but in essence, the group has always been a cult band—their music was always too abrasive and dense for the mainstream. Only hardcore fans can differentiate between the Fall's many albums, yet the Fall, like many cult bands, inspired a new generation of underground bands, ranging from waves of sound-alike indie-rockers in the U.K. to acts in America and New Zealand, which is only one indication of the size and dedication of their small, devoted fan base. —*Stephen Thomas Erlewine*

Live at the Witch Trials / Jan. 1979 / Resurgent ✦✦✦✦
That the first Fall album in a near endless stream would not only not sound very punk at all but would be a downright pleasant listen at the start (thanks to Yvonne Pawlett's electric piano on "Frightened") seems perfectly in keeping with Smith's endlessly contrary mind. His inimitable drawl/moan and general vision of the universe (idiots are everywhere and idiotic things are rampant) similarly sprawls all over the music—there's no question who this is or whose band it is as well. That said, most of *Live at the Witch Trials* is co-written with Martin Bramah, whose guitar work here is noticeably much more inclined to chime and ring instead of brutally scratching away like Craig Scanlon's awesome work would soon do. Bramah's not just there to sound tuneful, though, and the killer Marc Riley/Karl Burns rhythm section both keeps up the energy and provides surprising grooves. On chugging tracks like "Two Steps Back," it's not hard to tell Smith's Krautrock fandom is coming into play. With Pawlett's keyboards providing a pretty garage kick on top of it all, the result is an all-around treat. Brilliantly scabrous tracks are everywhere, one of the most memorable being "Rebellious Jukebox," simultaneously one of the most tuneful and aggressive songs from the early lineup, Smith pouring it on along with the band as a whole. The driving funk of "Music Scene," meanwhile, redefines misanthropy (and more) with a particularly central Smith target in mind. "No Xmas for John Quays," meanwhile, almost establishes the Fall formula on its own—Smith chanting and yelling over a quick, semi-rockabilly shamble and attack punctuated with unexpected stops and starts. Note—the Cog Sinister CD re-release of the album, in keeping with similar perverse reissues in the Fall's back catalog, is mastered directly from vinyl, and more than once sounds it. —*Ned Raggett*

Dragnet / Oct. 1979 / Step Forward ✦✦✦
The Fall's second album was also one of the hardest to find in later years, getting only sporadic represses and reissues. Though some opinions would have it that there was a good reason for this—namely, that it was something of a dead end sonically—it's not as bad as all that. It's true that more than a few tracks come across as Fall-by-numbers (even then, already better than plenty of other bands), but there are some thorough standouts

regardless. There's also another key reason to rate *Dragnet*—it's the debut album appearance of Craig Scanlon, who picked up on the off-kilter rockabilly-meets-art rock sensibilities of the initial lineup and translated it into amazing guitar work. No less important is the appearance of Steve Hanley, who would soon take over fully on bass from Marc Riley, who in turn moved to guitar, forming one heck of a partnership with Scanlon that would last until Riley jumped ship to form the Creepers. Generally the songs which work the best on *Dragnet* throw in some amusingly odd curves while still hanging together musically. The full winner is unquestionably "Spectre vs. Rector," an amazing combination of clear lead vocals and buried, heavily echoed music and further rants, before fully exploding halfway through while the rhythm obsessively grinds away. Another odd and wonderful cut is "Muzorewi's Daughter," which starts out sounding like stereotypical Hollywood music for Native American tribes before shifting between that and quicker choruses. "Dice Man," with its rave-up melody and slower vocal- and guitar-only chorus, not to mention the weird muttering elsewhere in the mix, says it all in under two minutes and has fun while doing it. Through it all, Smith rants and raves supreme, spinning out putdowns, cracked vocals, and total bile with all the thrill and energy one could want from a good performer. —*Ned Raggett*

Totale's Turns (It's Now or Never) / May 1980 / Rough Trade ✦✦✦
The first of what would be a veritable flock of live albums, some legit and some hovering on the edge of it, *Totale's Turns*, with the same lineup as *Dragnet*, found the Fall in a hilariously aggressive mood, as the statement of purpose "Intro" demonstrates. "The difference between you and us is that we have brains!" proclaims Smith, and from there it's off into their version of rock & roll hell. Song choices range over the first two albums and various singles, delivered with the at-once on form and shambling elan that characterized the band's rough and ready early days. The Riley/Scanlon guitar team performs their own brand of anti-guitar hero guitar heroics, scratchy, twanging, cutting, kicking into rave-up energy more often than not. The Leigh/Hanley rhythm section matches it all quite well, leaving Smith to be the howling, sneering, gurgling, and perfectly charismatic center of attention. There aren't as many one-off side comments as might be thought, but at one point he does note to the audience that "last orders are at half past ten." Some brilliant performances are to be had—"Rowche Rumble" kicks into gear with just Leigh and Smith setting the rhythm and the pace before everyone else pours it on, a straightforward, endlessly cycling riff driving everything before it. "Muzorewi's Daughter" immediately follows, its tense exchange between slow, rolling beats and explosive chorus fully intact and even more ragged. Two of the band's most famous early numbers get some great runthroughs—"Spector vs. Rector" has a brief intro about "those flowers, take them away" before shifting into a stuttering, lurching groove somehow perfectly suited to Smith's delivery. Meanwhile, "No Xmas for John Quays" concludes the album with all the murky and righteous kick one could want, the keyboards at the end adding even more craziness. —*Ned Raggett*

Grotesque (After the Gramme) / Nov. 1980 / Essential ✦✦✦✦
Kicking off with the thrilling bite of "Pay Your Rates," on *Grotesque*, the Fall really started hitting its stride, with Marc Riley and Craig Scanlon now a devastatingly effective combination, somehow managing to sound exactly placed between random sloppiness and perfect precision. The sharp rockabilly leads and random art rock racket thrived on both counts, with Smith as always the mad jester ripping into anything and everything while having a great time doing so. The final song of the album was especially fierce—"The N.W.R.A.," short for "the north will rise again," Smith's own take on the long-standing "soft south/grim north" dichotomy in English society given extremely bitter life. Throughout the record, a slew of really good producers keep an eye on things—besides the band themselves, there are Grant Showbiz, Geoff Travis, and Mayo Thompson all contributing. The end result is crisp without being polished, rough while packing its own smart punch (though "W.M.C.-Blob 59" intentionally sounds like it was recorded eight rooms over). Some nice variety starts appearing more and more in the Fall approach as well—"C'n'C-s Mithering," a brilliant vivisection of California and its record business, and the attendant perception of the Fall themselves, relies on acoustic guitars instead of electric, creating an understated but still great groove. "Impression of J. Temperance" fits more immediately with what had come before, but the martial drums from Paul Hanley and Riley's freaky keyboards create some crazy atmospheres. Of course, Smith sends everything over the top, whether it's his rant about governments, dead neighbors, and scandals on the hilarious romp "New Face in Hell" or "In the Park." As a side note, the hilarious music scene caricatures on the front cover and wind-up liner notes add just the right level of acidic wit to the proceedings. —*Ned Raggett*

Early Years, 1977-1979 / 1981 / Resurgent ✦✦✦✦
Though *Live at the Witch Trials* was the first Fall album, the band already had some singles and recordings under its belt, conveniently collected on the self-descriptive *Early Years*, along with a few post-*Witch Trials* efforts. Various initial lineups appear—some tracks have Martin Bramah on guitar, others with Marc Riley after he switched from bass, while Craig Scanlon first steps out with the commanding rave-up "Rowche Rumble." Then there's the keyboard work of Una Baines, later Bramah's partner in the Blue Orchids, who brings her own semi-psych feel to the proceedings. No matter who's around, though, it's still very much the Fall, Smith's immediately identifiable vocals leading the way. It's terribly amusing to hear the semi-conventional punk edge in his voice on some of the earliest songs, but that said, his approach did more or less appear fully formed, down to the drawling "-uh" at the end of nearly every word. Bramah's guitar work contains a delicacy that wouldn't last, at least quite the same way, while first and future drummer Karl Burns throws in his own flair more often than not (including the near-disco moves on "Psykick Dancehall"). There are even some gently pretty moments when least expected—consider the flow of "In My Area," a portrait of urban breakdown that's almost

winsome, or would be if Smith was a conventionally calm singer. The leadoff track—actually a B-side for the first single, "Bingo Master's Breakout"—is pretty much the Fall manifesto in a nutshell: "Repetition," drawing together punk's obsession with the basics with avant-garage art rock focus courtesy of Krautrock. The long-overdue CD version included the two cuts from the *Short Circuit* live album: "Stepping Out" and "Last Orders," neither of which are deathless but still have that certain Fall something. *—Ned Raggett*

Hex Enduction Hour / Mar. 1982 / Resurgent ♦♦♦♦
The Fall already had a slew of brilliant records under its belt by the time *Hex Enduction Hour* emerged, but when it did, the result was a bona fide classic on all fronts. Honing the vicious edge of his lyrics to a new level of ability, Smith led his by-now seasoned band—at this time sporting the double-drumming lineup of Paul Hanley and Karl Burns—to create a literal hour's worth of entertaining bile. The Marc Riley/Craig Scanlon team had even more of a clattering, industrial edge than before, now inventing its own style of riff and melody that any number of later groups would borrow, with varying degrees of success. "Iceland" itself tips its hat toward where part of the album was recorded, and it's little surprise that the Sugarcubes and any number of contemporaneous bands from that country ended up with a deep Fall fetish. Of the many song highlights, perhaps the most notorious was the opening "The Classical," an art-rock groove like no other, racketing around with heavy-duty beats and stabbing bass from Steve Hanley. Apparently, the band was on the verge of signing with Motown, at least until they heard Smith delivering the poisonous line "Where are the obligatory niggers? Hey there, fuckface!" Politically correct or not, it set the tone for the misanthropic assault of the entire album, including the hilarious dressing down of "misunderstood" rock critics, "Hip Priest" ("He ... is ... not ... apPRE-ciated!") and the targeting-everyone attack "Who Makes the Nazis?" Musically, all kinds of approaches are assayed and the results are a triumph throughout, from "Hip Priest" and its tense exchange between slow, dark mood and sudden guitar bursts to the motorik drone touch of "Fortress/Deer Park." As a concluding anti-anthem, "And This Day" ranks up with "The N.W.R.A.," ten minutes of ramalama genius. *—Ned Raggett*

Perverted by Language / Dec. 1983 / Essential ♦♦♦♦
Punk may have been the initial spark for the Fall, but by 1983 they had made it clear that whatever trend was next was not for them. Brix Smith made her debut with the band on *Perverted by Language*, helping to introduce the slightly more pop-friendly era of the group with another fine album. She takes lead vocals at various points throughout, notably "Hotel Bloedel," while her husband plays violin and adds extra spoken word thoughts along the way. The hints of strange beauty that the Fall can sometimes let into its world appear here more than once—whether it's Brix's influence or not isn't clear, and why not? "Garden" still hits hard while using a softer chime at its heart, while "Hexen Definitive" is almost a country (and western) stroll. Even for all the slightly more accessible touches for a wider audience, the Fall remain the Fall. "Smile" shows the band's abilities at tense audio drama excellently, a relentless, steady build with the Steve and Paul Hanley and Karl Burns rhythm section leading the way, winding up to a total explosion that never comes. Smith's increasingly frenetic vocals match the looming dread of the track to a T. "Neighbourhood of Infinity," notable for its appearance on *Palace of Swords Reversed*, crops up here in a studio take, again a sequel of sorts to "The Man Whose Head Expanded." Musically it hits its own stride, another of the many motorik-tinged tunes that helped give the Fall its own particular edge ("I Feel Voxish" also fills that bill, and quite well at that). "Eat Y'Self Fitter," touching on everything from meeting heroes (maybe) to returning late rental videos, makes for a great start to things, an endlessly cycling rockabilly chug with extra keyboard oddities and sudden music-less exchanges for the chorus. *—Ned Raggett*

Wonderful and Frightening World of the Fall / Sep. 1984 / Beggars Banquet ♦♦♦♦♦
The high point of the "Brix Period" may well have been the release of *Wonderful and Frightening World of the Fall*. Where before the music was tense, jumpy, and anarchic, here it was focused, harder-hitting, and rocked more. To some, it signaled the end of the Fall, but that was an unfair assessment. Granted, the music changed slightly, but it didn't diminish the band's potency. And, for all the time that Mark Smith had dominated the band, it was becoming clear that Brix's talents as a writer and musician were formidable and deservedly taking some of the spotlight. *—John Dougan*

Hip Priests and Kamerads / Mar. 1985 / Atlantic ♦♦♦♦
So named due to this being a collection of stuff released on the Kamera label, for a long time *Hip Priests* was the only way to listen to material from the mighty *Hex Enduction Hour* album, as well as *Room to Live* and related singles like "Lie Dream of a Casino Soul" and "Look, Know." For that reason alone it was a useful collection, though it was also flawed in that nearly everything was mastered for CD from vinyl, a harbinger of what would eventually happen in the late '90s with any number of early Fall reissues. It's especially noticeable on "Hip Priest" itself. Whether or not one wants to debate the aesthetics of such an approach, it's still more than a little frustrating. Thankfully, the song selection is nearly impeccable—omissions are unavoidable, but there's no overlap with *Palace of Swords Reversed*, and the highlights are legion: "Hip Priest," "The Classical," "Mere Psued Mag. Ed.," "I'm Into C.B.!," and the absolutely wonderful B-side "Fantastic Life." The CD and cassette versions both include a useful bonus of interest to hardcore fans—four live cuts of varying fidelity of other material from that time. "Who Makes the Nazis?" is OK enough, but the take on "Just Step Sideways" gets delivered with rough, fiery authority. At the end of the collection, meanwhile, there's an extremely muddy take on "Jawbone and the Air-Rifle" that will likely cause immediate departures on the part of neighbors and friends. A full quarter-hour ramble and stumble through "And This Day" concludes the release as a whole; it's a great performance that at nearly every point sounds like it'll collapse into formless chaos. Mark E. Smith is his typically contrarian self, while the lineup has its usual off-center way with the proceedings. *—Ned Raggett*

This Nation's Saving Grace / Sep. 1985 / Beggars Banquet ♦♦♦♦♦
"Feel the wrath of my Bombast!" exhorts Smith on this follow-up to their groundbreaking *Wonderful and Frightening World of... the Fall*, and this collection is ample proof of the pure confidence the group had at this time. Stompers like "Barmy," "What You Need," and the mighty "Gut of the Quantifier" are all led by Brix Smith's twanging lead hooks, filled by distorted guitars and bludgeoning drums, on top of which Smith rants with conviction. But it's the departures from this sound that mark the real interest here: The synth-driven "L.A." looks ahead to the Fall's experiments with electronica; "Paint Work" is an impressionist piece interrupted by Smith accidentally erasing over some of the track at home; and "I Am Damo Suzuki," a tribute to Can's lead singer, which borrows its arrangement from several of that group's songs. The Fall sound mysterious, down-to-earth, and hilarious all at the same time. The CD reissue adds the singles "Cruiser's Creek" and "Couldn't Get Ahead" as well as their B-sides making this an essential purchase. *—Ted Mills*

Bend Sinister / Oct. 1986 / Beggars Banquet ♦♦♦
Again working with John Leckie on production, the Fall's third Beggars album, *Bend Sinister*, was a distinctly down affair—not that the Fall were ever a shiny happy band, of course, but both music and lyrics seemed like a darker corner to dwell in. Happily there was no worry that the Fall would ever go goth; one suspects Smith would rather have his tongue removed. Still, opening track "R.O.D." makes for a distinctly lower-key start in comparison to recent lead-offs like "Lay of the Land" and "Bombast," almost sounding a bit like fellow Mancunian legends Joy Division, Smith's lyric his own depressing vision of a beast slouching toward Bethlehem. Leckie's production emphasizes space in the recording, while the band as a whole sounds generally more deliberate and understated, even Scanlon's guitar not leaping quite as much to trebly life as is normally the case. Songs like "Gross Chapel—British Grenadiers" favor Hanley's bass work as much as anything, while the almost industrial/hip-hop beat of "US 80s-90s" sets the tone for a glowering vision of the States from, as Smith puts it, "the big-shot original rapper." Elsewhere, there's Smith's vision of the eternal outsider comes to life once again—"Shoulder Pads #1," a hardly disguised sneer against being surrounded by people who "can't tell Lou Reed from Doug Yule," for all that there's a slightly quirky arrangement thanks to Simon Rogers' keyboards. Still, there are certainly moments of sheer fun—in keeping with the band's regular ear for good cover versions, this time around psych-era obscurities the Other Half get the nod with a brisk rip through the obvious drug references of "Mr. Pharmacist." Brix again shares vocal leads with Smith at various points, notably "Dktr. Faustus," a distinctly reworked version of that particular legend that turns into a frantic, audibly unhappy dance groove. *—Ned Raggett*

Domesday Pay-Off (Triad Plus) / 1987 / Big Time ♦♦♦
This is effectively the American version of the British release *Bend Sinister*. As well as an amended running order, the album also includes the singles "Hey! Luciani" and a workmanlike cover of R. Dean Taylor's "There's a Ghost in My House." As neither constitutes a classic moment in the Fall's distinguished history, you're better off with *Bend Sinister*, the album the Fall intended you to hear. *—Alex Ogg*

The Peel Sessions [EP] / May 1987 / Strange Fruit ♦♦♦
Disc jockey John Peel talked at great length over several years about the eventual release of "the Fall sessions"—his favourite band having recorded at least 20 times for the BBC. However, the old man river of U.K. indie pop simply could not decide what to choose. He insisted he wanted to include every song the band ever recorded (60+ for the Peel programme alone, at least 20 more for other BBC DJs). When this proved impracticable, this EP emerged, featuring a December 1978 session (with Marc Riley on bass)—the Fall's second for the programme. These versions of "Put Away," "No Xmas For John Quay," "Like to Blow," and "Mess of My" arguably outshine their studio counterparts—as was the case with many early punk bands, the BBC offered a comparatively professional studio environment and facilities. As for the box set of Fall sessions—we wait expectantly. *—Alex Ogg*

The Fall In: Palace of Swords Reversed / Nov. 1987 / Cog Sinister-Rough Trade ♦♦♦♦♦
Calling this collection absolutely essential damns it with faint praise. A near-perfect compilation of the Fall's early-'80s singles minus a track or two ("Lie Dream of a Casino Soul" and "Look, Know," in particular), plus most of the *Slates* EP, *Palace of Swords Reversed* serves up 14 tracks of audio and lyrical brilliance. Nearly split evenly between the Marc Riley/Craig Scanlon days and when Scanlon was sole guitarist, *Palace* covers three years during which the band couldn't seem to make a wrong step. Smith's focus dwells on everything from the anxiety of influence to soccer hooliganism and video games, all grist for his dismissive mill. The trashing of neo-imperialist pretensions thanks to the Thatcher government and the Falkland Islands, "Marquis Cha-Cha" may not have the emotional tug of Elvis Costello's "Shipbuilding," but its black humor and vicious cut-downs on all fronts packs its own punch. Meanwhile, the anti-London demolition of "Leave the Capitol" is pure destruction, band and singer matched in equal power. Musically, meanwhile, there's everything from nervous minimalism to brawling noise, everything turned toward the band's own goal. "Totally Wired" features a great opening drum break from Paul Hanley before everyone piles into a building crash of sound, Smith, riding it all like a wave while trading off call and response vocals with his band about having "a jar of coffee/and then I took some of these!" There's the barbed synth-pop nod on "The Man Whose Head Expanded," sudden tempo shifts on "Pay Your Rates" and "Putta Block"—two of the band's best charge-ahead-then-think-about-it numbers—and the slow upward crawl of "An Older Lover," stripped down and the more unsettling for it. Special bonus points for the occasional bits of live performances, including the hilarious introduction to "Putta Block," where after an audible screw-up Smith dryly notes, "Another dynamic entrance!" *—Ned Raggett*

The Frenz Experiment / Mar. 1988 / Beggars Banquet ♦♦♦♦
After the dark morass of *Bend Sinister*, the sound of 1988's *Frenz Experiment* comes as

a bit of a shock. The arrangements are spare and broken down to the essentials, with the distorted guitars brought down low and Wolstencroft's drums high in the mix. Marcia Schofield had also joined the band to add keyboards. With most of the songs credited only to Smith himself, this could be seen as a solo album of sorts, or an indication of some rift within the group—it certainly doesn't translate into the music. For the first time too, his vocals are loud and clear, though certainly not comprehensible; "Bremen Nacht" hints at some sort of run in with a ghost in Germany, "Athlete Cured," with its Spinal Tap-borrowed riff, tells of a "German athletic star" made ill from unusual circumstances—the narrative turns strange, then funny until wandering off, a classic Smith tactic. Their cover of the Kinks' "Victoria" marked the Fall's first entry into the British charts, but also fit in with Smith's continuing explorations of Britain's history and how it translates into issues of class identity. The CD contains their other two singles from this time—"Hit the North" and a cover of R. Dean Taylor's "There's a Ghost in My House," which the group makes their own—plus several B-sides. *—Ted Mills*

I Am Kurious Oranj / Oct. 1988 / Beggars Banquet ♦♦♦
The last thing most Fall fans expected the group to do in 1988 was provide music for a ballet, but in fact this is what they did. Of course, it helped that the Michael Clark company of dancers were some of the most avant-garde at the time in Britain and were inspired originally by the Fall's "Hey! Luciani" single. The concept, very loosely, centers around William and Mary of Orange, and finds Smith arranging William Blake's "Jerusalem" for the band, adding his own lyrics ("It was the fault of the government," providing ironic contrast to the self-sufficiency espoused in Blake). As a cohesive Fall album it fails: The strongest tracks are those that have little to do with the ballet (and are available elsewhere). "New Big Prinz" updates their own "Hip Priest" into one of their heaviest tracks full of threat and wonder. "Cab It Up!" features all forward momentum and jingling keyboards. For the first time tracks felt like filler, and indeed they were. The CD booklet contains photographs from the performance full of giant pop art hamburgers and cans of baked beans suggesting *I Am Kurios Oranj* would have been more interesting to see than hear. *—Ted Mills*

Seminal Live / Jun. 1989 / Beggars Banquet ♦♦

Extricate / Feb. 1990 / Resurgent ♦♦♦♦
The Smiths had divorced around the time of *Extricate*, but Brix's presence could still be felt on Fall records. Some thought the mid-'80s signaled an end to the ragged, jagged Fall of old; the '90s must have made them apoplectic. Working with producers Rex Sergeant, Craig Leon, and Adrian Sherwood, the post-apocalyptic sound of the '70s had been smoothed to a sheen. There were still moments of anarchy and dissonance, but generally they were swaddled in synth-driven beats and high-tech production that smoothed out any remaining rough edges. Again, this was not a bad thing; after all, Mark E. Smith was still upfront and still ranting, but even he was singing more, and shocking as that was, it made for even better music. For this period, the place to start is *Extricate*, which proved beyond a doubt that the Fall were not too old to still be a part of this punk rock thang. Since this record follows on the heels of the Smiths' divorce, it's tempting to assume that Mark E. Smith's ranting has a more conspicuous target, but enigmatic as he tends to be, this is mere speculation. Still, "Sing! Harpy" and the title track will give you pause as to the source of Smith's considerable consternation. The band sounds great, especially long-time members Stephen Hanley and Craig Scanlon. Extra kudos to the solid backbeat provided by Simon Wolstencroft. *—John Dougan*

★ **458489 A-Sides** / Sep. 1990 / Beggars Banquet ♦♦♦♦♦
Bypassing their edgy, early singles and concentrating on their artier, more eclectic work of the mid- and late '80s, *458489 A-Sides* encapsulates nearly all of the Fall's many attributes. All of the singles on *A-Sides* are culled from the era when Brix Smith was in the band, arguably the band's most cohesive and rewarding years. Drawing from their strongest albums—*The Wonderful and Frightening World of the Fall, This Nation's Saving Grace, Bend Sinister, The Frenz Experiment*—*A Sides* offers an excellent introduction to the Fall. It is both a useful retrospective and a kind of road map, pointing out the differences between albums. For neophytes and the uninitiated, there is no better sampler, and for long-time fans, the collection reiterates what a fine singles band the Fall were in their heyday. *—Stephen Thomas Erlewine*

458489 B-Sides / Dec. 1990 / Beggars Banquet ♦♦♦♦♦
The title cleverly encapsulates the contents—the Fall's B-sides (45s) from 1984 to 1989. The Fall were a first-rate singles band, and the flip sides were often their equals. There is the odd dud here—there are a thousand Fall songs to hear and "Clear Off" and "Mark'll Sink Us" wouldn't be high on ones list of priorities. But there are also many genuinely great tracks: "Petty Thief Lout," "Australians in Europe," "No Bulbs." It should be noted that in the Fall's turbulent history, their six-year spell at Beggars Banquet was their most productive and artistically rewarding. There are actually 31 tracks on view here, including a handful of remixes—rich pickings (the album was never originally issued outside of Europe). *—Alex Ogg*

Shift-Work / Apr. 1991 / Fontana ♦♦♦
Shift-Work marked the sophomore effort from a new Brix-less Fall and is a slightly more subdued effort than the raging *Extricate*. It also marked a new direction for Mark E. Smith and the band as what once was repetitious grooves became interspersed with pop song structures. Don't worry, the classic riffage is still here in "The War Against Intelligence," "Idiot Joy Showland," and "So What About It." But there does seem to be a softening of Smith, albeit slightly. He still rails against foolish pop stars, mass media, and the spawn of the Manchester scene (side two is headed "Notebooks Out Plagiarists") but also here are paeons to Edinburgh ("Edinburgh Man," surprisingly malice-free), social observation ("Shift Work" looks at a modern marriage and is more wistful than angry), and an electronics and violin led portrait of a DJ ("The Mixer"). Probably what's most surprising is that in retrospect most of this works, although begins to run out of steam near the end. There are hooks and melodies here, and the group ineffably remain the Fall. The following year's *Code: Selfish* would return to a much harder sound, leaving this a melancholic, introspective album. *—Ted Mills*

Code: Selfish / Mar. 1992 / Fontana ♦♦♦
An underrated and hard-to-find Fall album, this 1992 release returned to a harder, more caustic band than found on the previous year's *Shift Work*. Slimmed down to a four-piece (with added keyboards by David Bush) and produced by Craig Leon and Simon Rogers, the Fall yet again returned with an experimental and menacing collection of songs. The centerpiece and only single off the album was "Free Range," a bit of Mark E. Smith's "prepsicognition" about the coming Balkan wars. "Pressure guilt! Grudge match!" Smith yelps, stringing together images and streams of consciousness. "It pays to talk to no-one!" Years later, it has the same chilling foresight of Yeats's "The Second Coming." Smith's writing was beginning to pare itself down to the essence, relying on repetition and imagery, while the backing of Scanlon, Wolstencroft, and Hanley were translating the feel of sequenced techno into their guitars and drum attack (especially on "Immortality" and "So Called Dangerous"). An album that improves with age. *—Ted Mills*

The Infotainment Scan / May 18, 1993 / Matador ♦♦♦♦
Returning to the indie label world with a bang, the Fall unleashed a winner and a half with *Infotainment Scan*, one of the band's most playful yet sharp-edged releases. The choice of covers alone gives a sense of where Smith's head was at—tackling Lee Perry's "Why Are People Grudgeful?" is one tall order to start with, while a cover of the novelty tripe "I'm Going to Spain" is just silly fun (even if the guitar does sound like early Cure!). Even more astounding, though, is what the band does to the Sister Sledge disco classic "Lost in Music"—nobody will ever mistake Smith's singing for that of the threesome, but the band's overall performance is an honest-to-god tribute to the tight but full Chic Organization sound. Craig Scanlon throws in some scratchy work around the edges, but otherwise the group takes it as it is and does a great job. As for the originals, Smith and crew are in fine form once again, Scanlon, Steve Hanley, Dave Bush, and Simon Wolstencroft once again a dynamic, inventive unit. After the explicitly techno nods of the recent past, *Infotainment* balances that off with more straight-ahead rock, though with Wolstencroft's strong, sharp drumming still setting a brisk, danceable pace while Scanlon whips up his usual brand of tight, memorable riffing and Bush adds subtle textures and catchy melodies. One of the best numbers is the explicitly Gary Glitter-styled romp "Glam-Racket," a great shout-along, while the beat-crazy "A Past Gone Mad" wins for this line alone: "And if I ever end up like U2/slit my throat with a garden vegetable." "The League of Bald Headed Men" also deserves note, as does another strong motorik-inspired number, "It's a Curse." Best song title of the bunch? "Paranoia Man in Cheap Shit Room," with a high-strung and aggressive arrangement to boot. *—Ned Raggett*

The Collection / Oct. 19, 1993 / Castle ♦♦♦
The surplus of unnecessary, often downright insulting Fall compilation CDs can be confusing. Though they provide employment for underused sleevenote writers, all they otherwise serve to do is misdirect attention away from a perfectly adequate selection of official releases. This is a prime suspect, with its "seen it, done it" running order, though it deserves some sort of mention for being among the most widely distributed of Fall compilations. *—Alex Ogg*

Middle Class Revolt / May 1994 / Matador ♦♦♦♦♦
A mixture of lackluster performances and songs filled with vigor and fury, *Middle Class Revolt* is a puzzling proposition from the Fall. After two opening tracks that seem ready to convince worried fans that Smith couldn't care less ("15 Ways" and "Reckoning") there follows the poppish "Behind the Counter" and their devilish cover of Henry Cow's "War," with Smith making up half the lyrics. Other highlights include the furious "Hey! Student" (a rewrite of a 1977 tune, "Hey! Fascist"), and yet another Monks cover: "Shut Up!" All find Smith in fine form, impassioned and deeply sarcastic. The band experiments with some techno, some tape manipulation, and sparse rock arrangements, though the vocals on this disc are the most layered of any Fall release. There's also some local (Manchester, that is) social criticism going on in tracks, such as "M5#1" and "City Dweller," which takes on the aborted attempt to hold the Olympic games in Smith's city (the nerve!). *—Ted Mills*

Cerebral Caustic / May 18, 1995 / Permanent ♦♦♦
Smith once again landed on his feet after departing a label, ditching Matador in favor of Permanent, but *Cerebral Caustic* is notable for many other reasons. First, of all people, Brix Smith (still going by the name) rejoined the lineup, while future events made this the last studio album featuring Craig Scanlon. Though not an original member, his guitar playing for many made the Fall as much as Smith's vision and vocals, and knowing in retrospect that this was his unintentional final bow makes *Cerebral* that much more of interest. On top of that, Dave Bush would also leave after this album and its tour to join Elastica. Musically, *Cerebral* followed in the vein of recent albums like *Infotainment Scan*, blending techno-derived touches and glam-era sonic tributes to the usual stew of approaches. Generally the band sounds like they're having a great time, pulling out some odd arrangements and fun little touches, like the rising and falling melody of "Life Just Bounces." Smith himself sounds a touch disconnected around the edges, but makes up for it with some interesting vocal treatments and sudden interjections to leaven things up. Perhaps the strangest of the bunch is "Bonkers in Phoenix," with Brix's voice turned into overdubbed Chipmunks while the music combines a soft, low volume lope with sudden bursts of noise and Smith rants. One of the sharpest songs in context is "Don't Call Me Darling"—while the truth can't be known, hearing Brix deliver the chorus with a roaring edge in response to Smith's verses makes a listener wonder. As is often the case, a cover version helps to spice things up—having paid tribute to Frank Zappa elsewhere,

here the band cover his "I'm Not Satisfied" in low-key but well-paced fashion. Smith has good fun blurring and double-tracking his vocal, and the result is another winner in the Fall's series of remakes. —*Ned Raggett*

Twenty Seven Points / Sep. 5, 1995 / Permanent ◆◆◆

The follow-up to *Cerebral Caustic* turned out as one of the strangest things the Fall had yet released, though it was also fairly prescient in terms of what would follow. A slew of incredibly random live cuts, outtakes, and other otherwise unreleased material from throughout the first half of the 1990s, *Twenty Seven Points* (actually 28 tracks long) is first and foremost a catchall. There's no sense of any particular order or overriding theme—the liner notes are fragmentary at best—but for all that there's some good stuff to be had on a generally up-and-down release. Compared to the slew of similar live/demo/whatever collections that would appear with numbing regularity and much less quality over the next few years, meanwhile, *Twenty Seven Points* is practically essential. Smith himself presumably compiled the contents with an eye towards perversity, which explains the truncated version of "Idiot Joy Showland" that ends after 40 seconds, Smith promising a quick return to the stage. Even crazier is "Glam Racket/Star," which ends up splicing together two different versions of the song (one with Brix, one without) from separate shows. As for straightforward performances, happily, there are plenty to choose from. From the first disc, "Ladybird (Green Grass)" could use a touch clearer sound but runs its motorik-inspired chug quite well, while "The Joke," when it gets started, turns into a sharp, crisp rocker. On the second disc, studio cut "Cloud of Black" creates some murky dance atmosphere; a rough cover of "Strychnine" is another treat. There are spoken word pieces of collected insults and dressing downs, conversations about Frank Zappa books, sudden cuts between tracks, and all sorts of other demolitions of typical live album experiences. It's not necessarily a deathless record, but it's still more of a treat than might be guessed. —*Ned Raggett*

The Light User Syndrome / 1996 / Jet ◆◆◆

The Fall's first post-Craig Scanlon album also introduced Julia Nagle, who took over keyboards from the departing Dave Bush and also contributed some guitar. Brix Smith and Karl Burns covered the rest of the guitar, and while Scanlon is missed, the end results work well enough. The crisp live edge to the recording is attractive, but oddly enough leaves a lot of space in the mix—Mark E. Smith and Nagle's keyboards have pride of place along with Steven Hanley's bass guitar (give an ear to "Das Vulture Ans Ein Nutter-Wain" for an example). Smith himself seems to be searching for lyrics more than once, and while he comes up with a usual collection of acid-tongued zingers, other times he seems to be making vocal noise for the sake of it—nothing wrong with that, but still, one expects more. Though the album takes a little while to get started, when it does, the winners start coming in droves, such as the attractive Smith/Brix duet "Spinetrap" and the nervy, brisk bite of "Oleano," which sounds like an endless alarm bringing out the paranoia. There's some fiery aggression flaring up more than once as well, as "He Pep!" and especially the lengthy, roaring clatter and blast of "Interlude/Chilinism" in particular show. The addition of another pretty/sharp exchange between Brix and Smith makes the latter all the more entertaining. In terms of unexpected covers, the Fall do have another winner—Johnny Paycheck's "Stay Away (Old White Train)," sung by Smith with an appropriate if terribly amusing drawl. Speaking of singing—more than once co-producer Mike Bennett shares the vocals with Smith, a surprising change to say the least! The odd geographical confusion track "Cheethan Hill" shows how well that can actually work, with Bennett taking a clearer lead while Smith, unsurprisingly, does the "sing from one room over" approach. —*Ned Raggett*

Levitate / Sep. 1997 / Artful ◆◆◆◆

Mark E. Smith was always in step with progressing musical styles, even if his vocal delivery and abstract material placed him square against the mainstream, so it's not a huge surprise to find breakbeat jungle on *Levitate*'s first track, "Ten Houses of Eve." And the Fall frontman doesn't just add moderate elements of drum'n'bass, he bends electronics to his own will; the synth lines on "Masquerade" and "Jungle Rock" function in the same fashion as ragged guitar lines did on previous albums—repetitive music for Smith to vamp over, which places him right in the center of the mix. Most of the rest of the album is signature Fall, with raunchy garage-rock covers (the completely obscure "I'm a Mummy") and noisy percussive post-punk ("41/2 Inch," "Spencer Must Die") alternating with abstract pieces, instrumental or otherwise. Longtime guitarist Craig Scanlon is missing (and definitely missed), but songwriter/programmer/keyboard player Julia Nagle helps contribute to Mark E. Smith's twisted vision. (A special two-disc issue adds five extra tracks.) —*John Bush*

The Marshall Suite / Oct. 12, 1999 / Artful ◆◆◆◆

With the release of *The Marshall Suite*, there are probably an even dozen comeback albums in the Fall discography. Featuring virtually a new lineup comprised of untested musicians, *The Marshall Suite* returns Mark E. Smith to the music industry after a debacle of sorts. Given his unswerving control of any new Fall material that appears on the shelves, it's unsurprising that this edition of the band sounds similar to its recent forebears—this is still a shambling, energetic garage band whose members record right next to their mics for maximum speaker-thrashing. If anything, this group is even more propulsive and noise-oriented than other editions of the Fall, which suits Smith perfectly. He sounds much more focused than he's been in a while, working in that marvelous state of genius artistry that resists any attempt to explain how it's happened. The album is a three-part suite that cycles through a variety of roughshod originals and a few excellent covers (Tommy Blake's "F-'Oldin' Money," the Saints' "This Perfect Day"). In many ways, *The Marshall Suite* is similar to previous Fall albums—a couple of British psychobilly stomps balanced with several experimental pieces featuring Smith ranting over a skeletal musical framework. Though it appears to usher in a new era of the Fall's incredible

history, *The Marshall Suite* also thankfully displays that Mark E. Smith is still in complete control of his unique artistic vision. —*John Bush*

A Past Gone Mad: The Best of 1990-2000 / Sep. 5, 2000 / Artful ◆◆◆◆

Family

f. 1967, Leicester, England, **db.** 1973
British Psychedelia, Prog Rock/Art Rock, Blues-Rock

A blues-based band with art-rock inclinations, Family was one of the more interesting groups of hippie-era Britain. Fronted by the deft and frequently excellent guitar playing of John "Charlie" Whitney and the raspy, whisky-and-cigarette voice of Roger Chapman, Family was much loved in England and Europe but barely achieved cult status in America. While bands like Jethro Tull, Ten Years After, and the Keith Emerson-led Nice (and later Emerson, Lake, and Palmer) sold lots of records, Family, which frequently toured with these bands, was left in the shadows, an odd band loved by a small but rabid group of fans. With Whitney and Chapman leading the way, Family delivered their debut record in 1968, *Music in a Doll's House*. *Doll's House* is pop music redolent of the zeitgeist: Chapman's voice is rooted in the blues and R&B, but the record is loaded with strings, mellotrons, acoustic guitars, horns, essentially all the trappings of post-psychedelia and early art-rock. Almost completely ignored in the states, *Doll's House* was a hit in Britain and Family began a string of less art-rock, more hard rock albums that ended, as did the band, with the release of *It's Only a Movie* in 1973. After Family's demise, Whitney and Chapman formed the blues-rock Streetwalkers. A fine, occasionally great band, Family deserved more recognition (at least in America) than they received. —*John Dougan*

● **Music in a Doll's House** / 1968 / See For Miles ◆◆◆◆◆

Not the greatest psychedelic record ever made, but a damn fine one. *Doll's House* is dripping with pretension, but that doesn't make it a bad record, rather a record that reflects its time. Chapman's voice, booming and bellowing one moment, quiet and understated the next, is a revelation, as is Charlie Whitney's deft guitar playing and songwriting. As early British hippie rock goes, this is a record well worth having. —*John Dougan*

Family Entertainment / 1969 / See For Miles ◆◆◆◆

With cover art that Roger Chapman admits was an idea stolen from the Doors LP *Strange Days*, *Entertainment* leaves some of the excess of *Doll's House* behind for a more aggressive, blues-drenched assault. Chapman really lets loose on this record, especially on "Hung Up Down," and it is easy to see why rock critics were comparing him to Rod Stewart and Joe Cocker—yes, he sings that well. In England, *Entertainment* did very well as a follow-up to *Doll's House*, but in America it was greeted with almost total apathy, something that even a Family tour did little to fix. —*John Dougan*

A Song for Me / 1970 / Castle Music America ◆◆◆

Twenty-seven years after the fact, this might well be the best of the early Family recordings. A combination of hard rock (bordering on metal) and wistful folk-rock (it sounds as if Chapman and Whitney were listening to a lot of Incredible String Band), *A Song for Me* veers toward early progressive rock, but isn't as nakedly indulgent as some early prog-rock recordings (e.g., they didn't try to sound like a jazz band, they wanted to sound like a rock band screwing around with jazz). Perhaps their most experimental record, it seems as though the credo in making this disc was that anything went. And on tracks like "Drowned in Wine," it works quite well. Again, Chapman offers more proof of his vocal greatness, and again the record sells large quantities in England and nearly nothing in America. —*John Dougan*

Anyway / 1970 / Castle Music America ◆◆

Fearless / 1971 / Castle Music America ◆◆◆

An improvement over *Anyway*, but at this juncture Family was floundering. Grech was gone, and the other personnel changes began limiting the band's cohesiveness. Although *Fearless* is (again) saved by Chapman and Whitney, the record's eccentricities work against them, and the hard rock moves (i.e., blues/boogie nonsense) sound forced. Chapman's drunken machismo makes "Sat'd'y Barfly" a winner. —*John Dougan*

Bandstand / 1972 / Castle Music America ◆◆◆◆◆

Now this was more like it. Kicking off with the wickedly salacious "Burlesque," *Bandstand* was the best of the late Family recordings. For a band that for the most part eschewed riffs and hooks, both are in plentiful supply here. More important, by the time of *Bandstand*'s release, Family had reconciled the war between their art-rock and hard rock tendencies; that is to say, there is more of the latter and less of the former. So, the record doesn't have the internal stress of their earlier releases, but what it does have is Chapman shouting like he could take on the world and Whitney playing like he must have when he formed the Farinas in 1962. A corker from the word go. —*John Dougan*

It's Only a Movie / 1973 / Castle Music America ◆◆◆

For a swan song, this is pretty a good one. Generally, at this point in a band's career, when personnel changes become more frequent, live shows become more unpredictable, and substance use seems to become more central to the band than singing and songwriting, you would think that Family (a band that partied as hard as any) would simply cough up a final piece of dreck and say so long. But *Movie* is a relaxed, funny and funky record, almost sunny in disposition. The songs take a while to worm their way in, but once they do, tracks like "No Money Down" and "Boom Bang," with their swagger and sway, end up sounding as good as any of the band's previous work. Totally ignored upon release, *Movie* was one of those records that seemed to go directly into the cutout bins (I paid $1 for my copy more than 20 years ago), a fitting end to Family's career in America. —*John Dougan*

Merrell Fankhauser

b. Dec. 23, 1943

Vocals, Guitar / Folk-Rock, Psychedelic, Prog Rock/Art Rock, Singer/Songwriter

One of the most interesting cult figures in rock history, Fankhauser's best work came as the leader of several interesting groups during the '60s and early '70s: the Impacts (instrumental surf), Merrell & the Exiles (solid British Invasion-style rock), Fapardokly (great Byrds-ish folk-rock), the H.M.S. Bounty (fine late-'60s folk-rock), and Mu (spaced-out progressive blues/psychedelia). When Mu broke up in the mid-'70s, Fankhauser began working as a solo artist, issuing a series of independent albums. These usually show him in a considerably mellower and more mainstream folk-rock mood than his earlier work, sometimes recalling Crosby, Stills, & Nash and often featuring violinist Mary Lee. —*Richie Unterberger*

● **Things** / 1968 / Sundazed ✦✦✦✦

Fine, tuneful '60s psychedelia with a pop edge, featuring Fankhauser's first-rate songwriting and warm vocals. About half of the tunes are excellent, especially the country-rocker "Your Painted Lives," and the folk-rock ballad "Ice Cube Island," and "A Visit With Ashiya," one of the best raga-rock songs ever cut. The reissue adds a bluesy non-LP B-side, "Flying Home," that looks forward to the innovations of Mu; it also includes fine, lengthy liner notes detailing Fankhauser's fascinating and winding career. —*Richie Unterberger*

The Maui Album / 1988 / Reckless ✦✦✦✦✦

Fankhauser's first solo outing, originally titled *Merrell Fankhauser* and released in 1976, remains his best post-Mu work. Very light and serene folk-rock that owes little to trends of its era, predominantly acoustic in feel, often featuring Mary Lee on violin and harmony vocals. The 1988 reissue is enhanced by four previously unreleased Mu tracks, dating from 1974. —*Richie Unterberger*

Early Years 1964-1967 / 1994 / Legend Music ✦✦

Credited to Merrell & the Exiles, this is a selection of rarities and unreleased material by Fankhauser's mid-'60s band, essentially the one that cut the great rare psych-folk-rock album that was credited to Fapardokly. It's pretty much a collection of outtakes with a few rare non-LP singles thrown in, and as such doesn't measure up to the best of Fankhauser's '60s material. Often derivative of the British Invasion, folk-rock, and early '60s teen pop, it's not bad, just not terribly memorable. The fake British Invasion of cuts like "Send Me Your Love" rank as the highlights. It also has his late-'60s non-LP single cover of Fred Neil's "Everybody's Talkin'," although for some reason it's missing one of his mid-'60s non-LP 45s, "Can't We Get Along"/"That's All I Want From You"—it was reissued on a rarities tape that Merrell himself released, if you can find it. Future Mu and Captain Beefheart guitarist Jeff Cotton appears on most of the tracks; future Beefheart drummer John French also appears on a few. —*Richie Unterberger*

Fapardokly

f. 1965, db. 1966

Folk-Rock, Psychedelic

Though they were considered an enigma in the world of '60s rock collectibles, there was never a group called Fapardokly; the 12 songs on their self-titled album were recorded by Merrell & the Exiles, a Southern California group headed by legendary cult folk-rocker Merrell Fankhauser. That group cut several singles for the tiny Glenn label before heading off in a psychedelic direction and mutating into H.M.S. Bounty. The equally tiny UIP label decided to gather a few of the Glenn singles, add a few more psychedelically oriented tracks that Merrill and his group had recorded, and release the package as the work of a group called Fapardokly. Although it was not recorded or intended as a unified work, it stands as one of the great lost folk-rock classics of the '60s. Fankhauser went on to make more excellent obscure recordings with H.M.S. Bounty in the late '60s and Mu in the early '70s. —*Richie Unterberger*

● **Fapardokly** / 1966 / Sundazed ✦✦✦✦✦

One of the most sought-after rock rarities of the '60s, this album was stylistically uneven, as can be expected from an LP cobbled together from recordings spanning a few years. About half, however, is sparkling psychedelic folk-rock, recalling *Fifth Dimension* Byrds with its shimmering twelve-string guitars, multipart harmonies, and occasional trippy lyrics. Although the early material is more pop-oriented and doesn't fit in as well, it's pretty solid, recalling the Zombies and (in the very earliest tracks) Ricky Nelson. "Lila," "Tomorrow's Girl," and "Super Market" are genuine lost '60s treasures, and much of the rest of the album isn't far behind. —*Richie Unterberger*

Richard & Mimi Fariña

f. 1964, db. 1966

Folk Revival, Folk-Rock, Singer/Songwriter, Traditional Folk

Richard Fariña was a noted countercultural author and folksinger in the early '60s. Married for a time to folksinger Carolyn Hester, he was an early intimate of Bob Dylan, and in fact recorded a collectable album with Dylan (playing under the pseudonym Blind Boy Grunt) and Ric Von Schmidt in 1963. After marrying Joan Baez's sister, Mimi, he formed a folk-rock duo who released two acclaimed albums in the mid-'60s. Unlike folk-rock figureheads like the Byrds, the Fariñas were far more firmly rooted in folk than rock.

Their recordings effectively flavored their material (mostly written by Fariña) with jangling electric guitars and a rhythm section, ably assisted by such session players as guitarist Bruce Langhorne (who also played on Dylan's first electric recordings), bassist Felix Pappalardi, and harmonica player John Hammond. The Fariñas themselves also played guitar, autoharp, and dulcimer. Least successful with blues, they recorded some effective Appalachian-flavored material, and several excellent bona fide mid-tempo folk-rockers

and ballads. Their best songs effectively balanced world-wise, sardonic observations with good-natured, melodic optimism.

The Fariñas' promising career ended prematurely with the death of Richard Fariña in a motorcycle accident on his birthday in 1966. His novel of the same year, *Been Down So Long It Looks Like up to Me*, became a cult favorite. Since Richard Fariña's death, Mimi Fariña has sporadically recorded and performed as a solo act. —*Richie Unterberger*

Celebrations for a Grey Day / 1965 / Vanguard ✦✦✦

The duo's debut effectively laid out their approach: Appalachian-like instrumentals that put the dulcimer to the fore alternate with strong contemporary folk compositions, which are by turns mournful and high-spirited. The world-weary "Reno Nevada" (a part of Fairport Convention's repertoire in their early days) is the duo's best song. —*Richie Unterberger*

Reflections in a Crystal Wind / 1965 / Vanguard ✦✦✦

Basically a continuation of the first album with a slightly more electric feel, finding Richard developing deeper insight and a subtler touch. —*Richie Unterberger*

Memories / 1968 / Vanguard ✦✦✦

A posthumous collection of odds and ends, this actually holds considerable appeal for anyone who likes their pair of fully realized albums. The 12 songs include a few studio outtakes, a few solo turns by Mimi on compositions written by Richard but incompletely recorded at the time of his death, a couple performances from the 1965 Newport Folk Festival, and a couple of Joan Baez tracks from sessions for an aborted album Richard was producing with her. These leftovers are generally up to the standard of the two "real" albums, especially "The Quiet Joys of Brotherhood" (covered by Fairport Convention) and "Morgan The Pirate" (a farewell to Bob Dylan, according to the sketchy liner notes). The two cuts by Baez (which Richard wrote or co-wrote), especially the compellingly melancholy "All The World Has Gone By," are excellent, leading one to wonder if the projected album they came from would have been one of Baez's best if it had been completed. These may be leftovers, but it's a worthwhile collection nonetheless. —*Richie Unterberger*

The Best of Mimi and Richard Fariña / 1971 / Vanguard ✦✦✦✦✦

While a 20-song double album is not ordinarily recommended as the best introduction to such a short-lived act, the Fariñas' work was so consistent that it makes sense to pick up this compilation, which combines *Celebrations for a Grey Day* and *Reflections in a Crystal Wind* into one package. —*Richie Unterberger*

★ **Pack up Your Sorrows: Best of Vanguard Years** / Sep. 28, 1999 / Vanguard ✦✦✦✦

When Vanguard Records issued their double album *The Best of Mimi & Richard Fariña* in 1971, five years after the motorcycle crash that claimed Richard Fariña's life, the label simply repackaged the duo's two regular album releases, *Celebrations for a Grey Day* (1965) and *Reflections in a Crystal Wind* (1966). In 1988, when it reissued the package on CD, Vanguard cut six songs to fit *The Best Of* on a single disc, leaving 20. Eighteen of those tracks are repeated on *Pack Up Your Sorrows: Best of the Vanguard Years*, which restores one of the cut songs and adds two tracks from the 1968 outtakes album *Memories*, plus one previously unreleased instrumental, "Tuileries." All of that makes the new compilation a slight improvement in terms of selection, while the CD remastering improves the sound. (Ed Ward's enthusiastic but ill-informed liner notes—he confuses the Big Sur Folk Festival with the Newport Folk Festival and makes other errors—are not a plus.) As a lyricist, Fariña matched the elliptical style of mid-'60s Bob Dylan image for image, and tracks such as "Hard Loving Loser" are stylistically identical to the folk-rock of Dylan's *Bringing It All Back Home*, partly because they employ some of the same sidemen. But Fariña and his wife Mimi gave his words a sweet-and-sour harmony style, and their most distinctive music was made when they duetted on autoharp and dulcimer, as on the instrumentals that make up a good part of the song list. Richard Fariña's early death robbed the music world of an important singer/songwriter (not to mention robbing literature of a promising novelist), but the work he left behind ranks with the best folk-rock of the 1960s. —*William Ruhlmann*

The Farm

f. 1983, Liverpool, England, db. 1994

Madchester, Club/Dance, Alternative Pop/Rock

One of the stranger overnight success stories in pop history, the chameleon-like Farm was formed in Liverpool, England, in 1983 by singer Peter Hooton, a onetime youth worker searching for a musical outlet to voice his political concerns. Rounded out by guitarist Stevie Grimes, bassist Phil Strongman, and drummer Andy McVann, the first incarnation of the Farm recalled both the leftist identity and horn-powered sound of the Redskins. Despite a handful of independent singles and the addition of a full-time brass section, the Farm found little interest in their pop-flavored Northern soul. Still, they soldiered on, even weathering the 1986 death of McVann. The Farm dropped their horn section and added keyboardist Benjamin Leach and second guitarist Keith Mullen, resulting in a move toward synth pop. Still, the Farm struggled; finally, in 1990 they approached dance producer Terry Farley, who agreed to produce a sample-heavy cover of the Monkees' "Stepping Stone." The single fell just shy of the Top 40, and suddenly the group found themselves aligned with the baggy-pants club culture movement. The Farm's next single, "Groovy Train," hit the U.K. Top Ten, while the anthemic follow-up "All Together Now" landed in the Top Five. Eight years after their inception, the Farm finally issued their debut LP, *Spartacus*, in 1991; the album entered the British charts at number one. The band's moment in the limelight was a brief one, however; their next two singles, "Don't Let Me Down" and "Mind," both failed to penetrate the Top 30, and 1991's quickly produced follow-up LP, *Love See No Colour*, sank without a trace. Aside from a Top 20 cover of the Human League's "Don't You Want Me?" in 1992, the Farm essentially vanished from sight, releasing 1994's *Hullabaloo* to minimal notice. *—Jason Ankeny*

- **Spartacus** / Apr. 17, 1991 / Sire ✦✦✦✦
The Farm's debut album *Spartacus* is one of the more ridiculous by-products of baggy, containing all of its rolling, neo-psychedelic grooves and blissfully colorful pop hooks, yet very little of its charm, character, or substance. Since baggy was never about substance, this is particularly damning. Still, the Farm manages to turn out a couple of goofily endearing singles with "Groovy Train" and "All Together Now," but the group shows no real feeling for dance-club rhythms, or even pop hooks. As an artifact, *Spartacus* is fascinating, since it demonstrates how far the over the top the entire Madchester phenomenon went, even if the record itself isn't necessarily good listening. *—Stephen Thomas Erlewine*

Love See No Colour / Nov. 3, 1992 / Sire ✦✦✦
Love See No Colour is essentially a retread of *Spartacus* without the benefit of a single as catchy as "Groovy Train" or "All Together Now," which means that it's characterless baggy without hooks or distinctive rhythms. It demonstrates that the Farm have run out of what few ideas they had, recycling them with diminishing returns. Again, it's interesting as a period piece, but little else. *—Stephen Thomas Erlewine*

Hullabaloo / May 10, 1994 / Sire ✦✦
The Farm had hit the end of the road with 1992's *Love See No Colour*, which means 1994's *Hullabaloo* was unnecessary. Indeed, the album is comprised entirely of bland, colorless material that recycles baggy for no apparent reason. It sounds purposeless on the originals, but when the group covers the Flamin' Groovies' "Shake Some Action," the results are simply ridiculous. *Hullabaloo* wasn't a particularly graceful way to end the band's career, but then again, the Farm were never a band that handled their career gracefully. *—Stephen Thomas Erlewine*

- **The Best of the Farm** / May 1998 / Essential ✦✦✦✦
The Farm were never one of the great Madchester bands, writing only one truly memorable single ("All Together Now") and turning out a bunch of pleasant, nondescript baggy. *The Best of the Farm* collects all of the singles and highlights from the group's three albums. There aren't any hidden treasures here, but anyone nostalgic for the pleasures of loping beats, baggy clothes, neo-psychedelia and buckets of Ecstasy should be pleased with this collection. [The first pressings of *The Best of the Farm* included a bonus remix disc.] *—Stephen Thomas Erlewine*

Fastbacks

f. 1981, Seattle, WA
Punk-Pop, Indie Rock, Alternative Pop/Rock
Seattle's Fastbacks were one of the few first-wave punk bands to make it to the end of the century with their original sound and focus intact. In classic punk rock fashion, Fastbacks were born when Lulu Gargiulo saw a terrible band at a local punk club and was convinced even she could do better. She and her high school friends, Kurt Bloch and Kim Warnick began playing—along with vocalist Shannon Wood—in 1979, and played their first gig the following February. Though Bloch and Warnick began playing guitar in high school, Gargiulo took lessons in classical guitar but never played rock & roll until joining the band. When Wood left, Warnick took over vocal duties, Bloch became lead guitarist and the band hired 15-year-old Duff McKagen, the first of a very long line of drummers; McKagen left a year later for Los Angeles, where he later joined Guns & Roses. Their 1981 debut single, "It's Your Birthday"/"You Can't Be Happy" defined their sound: loose, scrappy punk with strong pop hooks, punctuated by Bloch's Rick Nielsen-meets-Johnny Ramone guitar solos ad Warnick and Gargiulo's singalong harmonies. During the '80s, the band remained a local phenomenon; their debut album *... And His Orchestra* didn't arrive until 1987. Bloch played guitar with the Young Fresh Fellows and worked as a producer, Warnick worked at the offices of Sub Pop records and Gargiulo pursued her career as a cinematographer. But when Nirvana and Seattle reshaped rock in 1992, the Fastbacks finally received national attention. Sub Pop released the odds-n-sods collection *The Question Is No*, which became their first widely distributed album. They stayed with Sub Pop for three more albums and opened for famous local fans like Mudhoney and Pearl Jam. SpinArt released *The Day That Didn't Exist* in 1999. Though the Fastbacks never achieved rock stardom, they've managed to mature while remaining true to their original sound and vision, and their work is still as fresh, enthusiastic, and powerful as when they began. *—Mark Deming*

... And His Orchestra / 1987 / Pop Llama ✦✦✦✦
Fastbacks' first album was slapped together from three sessions tracked out over 11 months (one in an actual recording studio, two on TEAC four-tracks in rehearsal studios), and as a result it lacks some of the punch and cohesion of their best work. But Kurt Bloch's songs were well worth hearing from the start, and *... And His Orchestra* features several winners, including "K Street," "Seven Days," and the horn-enhanced "Wrong, Wrong, Wrong." And the band sounds tight and enthusiastic throughout, even if the audio sometimes lets them down; Fastbacks also come clean on their fondness for '70s hard rock with a ragged-but-right take on Sweet's "Set Me Free." A more than promising start for a band destined for better (if not always bigger) things. The CD reissue tacks on nine songs from the group's first two self-released EPs as a bonus. *—Mark Deming*

Very, Very Powerful Motor / 1990 / Pop Llama ✦✦✦✦✦
1990 was a difficult time for Fastbacks; after nearly a decade together, the band had failed to gain a significant audience outside the Pacific Northwest, and Lulu Gargiulo opted to take a sabbatical from the group. *Very, Very Powerful Motor*, the band's second album, seems to reflect the problems facing the group; while it's tighter, snappier, and rocks a good bit harder than their debut, *... And His Orchestra*, it's also one of the group's edgiest, most angst-filled recordings. Alongside such pop-punk gems as "In the Summer" and "Says Who?" are a number of longer tunes where Kurt Bloch leaves himself plenty of space to work out on guitar (like "What to Expect/Dirk's Car Jam" and "Last Night I Had a Dream That I Could Fly"), and lyrically the overall tone of the album is one of anxiety and doubt. But while Fastbacks sounded gifted but tentative on their debut, here the band sounds like they were finally living up to their potential; *Very, Very Powerful Motor* is the first Fastbacks album to capture the group's qualities at full power. *—Mark Deming*

- **The Question Is No** / Jun. 19, 1992 / Sub Pop ✦✦✦✦✦
Featuring 14 songs spanning 12 years (and five drummers), *The Question Is No* is not only a terrific introduction to Fastbacks, but an excellent summary of the early years when they were one of the dozens of Seattle punk bands who couldn't get a hearing outside of Washington. While from the start Fastbacks were a band that loved first-wave pop-punk (think Ramones, Buzzcocks, and Rezillos), theirs was pop-punk with a difference; Kurt Block was willing to betray his fondness for '70s rock in his guitar solos, and his lyrics suggested the confused and angst-ridden internal monologue of an adolescent while dealing with the hopes, fears, and everyday realities of an adult. Bloch managed all this in a manner that was at once personal and unpretentious, thanks in part to the vocals of Kim Warnick and Lulu Gargiulo, who blend the offhand blather of punk with a sweetness that gives this band a very human warmth. Compiling singles, compilation tracks, and a few unreleased tunes (including one with a teenage Duff McKagan behind the traps), *The Question Is No* is as good as collection as you could ask for of the band's formative period and features some of their most energetic, rollicking performances. *—Mark Deming*

Zucker / Jan. 29, 1993 / Sub Pop ✦✦✦✦✦
After the compilation *The Question Is No* catapulted them from their lowly status as a local cult item to their new role as a national cult item, Fastbacks sounded a good bit more cheerful and a lot more confident on their third proper album, *Zucker*. Roaring right out of the box with three hooky classics in a row ("Believe Me Never," "Gone to the Moon," and "Hung on a Bad Peg," *Zucker* manages to be one of Fastbacks' most rocking *and* most pop-influenced albums at once; "When I'm Old" is a lovely bit of mid-tempo contemplation replete with acoustic guitars, and Fastbacks even cover a Bee Gees tune (don't fret, "Please Read Me" dates from the Gibbs' Brit-pop period rather than the disco era). And if Kurt Bloch still sounds a bit uncertain about the world around him, he and his partners Kim Warnick, Lulu Gargiulo, and drummer of the moment Rusty Willoughby sound energetic enough to roar right over the bad times. Witty, muscular, and packed with great songs, *Zucker* ranks with Fastbacks' very best work. *—Mark Deming*

Bike-Toy-Clock-Gift / 1994 / Lucky ✦✦✦

Answer the Phone Dummy / Oct. 25, 1994 / Sub Pop ✦✦✦
After 14 years of dealing with the "drummer problem," *Answer the Phone Dummy* was the album where Fastbacks cheerfully decided to give up the fight, at least for a while; the disc's 15 songs are divided between six different percussionists borrowed from other bands, including Jason Finn (from the Presidents of the United States of America), Dan Peters (from Mudhoney), Mike Musburger (of the Posies), and Rusty Willoughby (from Flop, who also played on Fastbacks' previous long-player, *Zucker*). Perhaps due to the lack of a consistent rhythm section, *Answer the Phone Dummy* doesn't sound as solid and consistent as *Zucker*, the band's high-water mark at that time; while Kurt Bloch wrote a batch of great tunes (as usual), this set lacks a certain aural cohesion the pacing is inconsistent, with the album sometimes struggling to maintain a steady momentum. *Answer the Phone Dummy* is a good album from a great band, but beginners are advised to check out *Zucker* or *The Question Is No* instead. *—Mark Deming*

New Mansions in Sound / Jun. 18, 1996 / Sub Pop ✦✦✦✦
Fastbacks managed to pare themselves down to a mere three drummers while recording *New Mansions in Sound* (Mike Musburger played on 13 of the album's 15 cuts, while Jason Finn and Nate Johnson each sat in for one song), and the resulting album is a good bit stronger than their previous set, *Answer the Phone Dummy*. Fastbacks' punk quotient isn't especially high on this set (though "555 (Part One)" and "The Bitter Drink" will satisfy those looking for a fast-loud fix), but their pop side is in unusually solid form; Kim Warnick and Lulu Gargiulo have rarely sang so harmoniously, and songs like "Fortune's Misery" and "No Information" are so catchy it's hard to imagine anyone being able to resist them. The band's choice of covers on this set also makes for a lovely balance of sublime vs. ridiculous, facing "Space Station #5" by Montrose against "Girl's Eyes" by the Who. Solid, joyous, occasionally poignant, and lots of fun—in short, another slice of brilliance from Fastbacks. (By the way, the "e.v." credited with singing backup on "Girl's Eyes" is noted Fastbacks fan Eddie Vedder, who can be heard offering the engineer 100 dollars if he'll please erase his vocal and let him try it again.) *—Mark Deming*

The Day That Didn't Exist / Oct. 5, 1999 / spinART ✦✦✦✦✦
The Fastbacks return with more snappy, happy, bright and buzzy punk pop on 1999's *The Day That Didn't Exist*. With "if it ain't broke, don't fix it" as their motto, the trio cranks out more sugar-fueled, rapid-riff pop moments like "Maybe" and "One More Hour," and their charming, quirky songwriting comes to the front on "New Book Of Old," "Dreams I Have Seen," and the title track. *The Day That Didn't Exist* continues to prove that the Fastbacks' speedy sound is also surprisingly durable. *—Heather Phares*

The Fat Boys

f. 1982, Brooklyn, NY
Comedy Rap, Old School Rap, Hip-Hop
One of early rap's most successful acts, the Fat Boys parlayed a combined weight of over 750 pounds into a comic novelty act that sustained them through several albums and hit singles. Originally known as the Disco 3, Brooklynites Mark "Prince Markie Dee" Morales, Damon "Kool Rockski" Wimbley, and Darren "Buff the Human Beat Box"

Robinson recorded a series of good-time party anthems and songs humorously exploiting their weight; their first few records were produced by Kurtis Blow and feature fusions of hip-hop with reggae and rock. The Fat Boys hit their commercial peak with 1987's platinum LP *Crushin'*, a collection of entertaining party tunes that included a hit collaboration with the Beach Boys, "Wipeout." The group took the opportunity to star in the comedy film *Disorderlies* that year. *Coming Back Hard Again* essentially repeated the formula of *Crushin'*; the cover this time was "The Twist (Yo' Twist)," which featured backing from Chubby Checker. However, audience tastes were changing, and the Fat Boys' gimmicky novelty act was quickly becoming passe. Robinson died of a heart attack in December 1995. *—Steve Huey*

- **All Meat No Filler: The Best of Fat Boys** / Mar. 18, 1997 / Rhino ✦✦✦✦✦

All Meat No Filler: The Best of the Fat Boys is an excellent 18-track compilation of all of the Fat Boys' biggest hits, including "Fat Boys," "Human Beat Box," "Jail House Rap," "Can You Feel It," "The Fat Boys Are Back," "Hard Core Reggae," "Failling In Love," "Wipeout" (with the Beach Boys), and "The Twist (Yo, Twist!)" (with Chubby Checker). Although some of the latter-day cuts have aged poorly, the Fat Boys' earliest singles are groundbreaking and timeless records, proving that they weren't merely a novelty act. *—Stephen Thomas Erlewine*

Fatboy Slim (Norman Cook)

b. Jul. 13, 1963, Bromley, England

DJ, Producer / Big Beat, Funky Breaks, Electronica, Trip-Hop, Club/Dance

Norman "Jacker-Of-All-Genres" Cook, in addition to his former occupations as bassist for the Housemartins and one third of acid-house hitmakers Pizzaman, is also the man behind one of the most popular of the new flock of English "brit hop" producers, Fatboy Slim. Releasing his Fatboy material through club staple Skint, Cook's raucous blend of house, acid, funk, hip-hop, electro, and techno has added to his already formidable reputation as one of the foremost all-around producers on the U.K. club scene. In addition to his FBS work, Cook also recorded the *Skip to My Loops* sample CD, a popular studio tool sporting a melange of sample-ready drum loops, analog squelches, and assorted noises. In early 1998, his remix of Cornershop's "Brimful of Asha" spent several weeks at number one in the British charts. His eagerly anticipated second LP *You've Come a Long Way Baby* followed later that year, launching the breakthrough hits "Rockafeller Skank" and "Praise You." *—Sean Cooper*

Better Living Through Chemistry / 1996 / Astralwerks ✦✦✦✦

Fatboy Slim is one of DJ Norman Cook's many aliases, and has proven to be his most popular and successful yet. Although he consistently racks up dance hits in his native England (each under a different surname), he didn't achieve global success until the release of *Better Living Through Chemistry* in '97. On the insistence of his friends the Chemical Brothers, Cook released the track "Going Out of My Head" as the album's first single. Due to its popular video and instantly catchy sample from the Who classic "I Can't Explain," Cook earned his first U.S. hit. Another unlikely sample used to great effect was featured in the track "Michael Jackson," which used a snippet of Negativland's "Negativland." "The Weekend Starts Here" is similar to the Beastie Boys' funk instrumentals, featuring distant organ and lazy harmonica-blowing (which sounds an awful lot like the harmonica phrase at the beginning of Black Sabbath's "The Wizard"). Recommended to those who can't get enough of today's popular technoid-sampled-alternative-dance style. *—Greg Prato*

- **You've Come a Long Way, Baby** / Oct. 12, 1998 / Skint ✦✦✦✦✦

Fatboy Slim's debut album, *Better Living Through Chemistry*, was one of the surprises of the big beat revolution of 1996—an eclectic blowout, all tracked to thunderous loops and masterminded by Norman Cook, a former member of the British pop band the Housemartins. It might not have been as startlingly fresh as the Chemical Brothers, but the hard-hitting beats and catchiness, not to mention consistency, of *Better Living* was a shock, and it raised expectations for Fatboy Slim's second album, *You've Come a Long Way, Baby*. And that record itself was something of a surprise, since it not only exceeded the expectations set by the debut, but came damn close to being the definitive big beat album, rivaling the Chemicals' second record, *Dig Your Own Hole*. The difference is, Cook is a record geek with extensive knowledge and eclectic tastes. His juxtapositions—the album swings from hip-hop to reggae to jangle pop, and then all combines into one sound—are wildly original, even if the music itself doesn't break through the confines of big beat. Then again, when a record is this forceful and catchy, it doesn't need to break new stylistic ground—the pleasure is in hearing a master work. And there's no question that Cook is a master of sorts—*You've Come a Long Way, Baby* is a seamless record, filled with great imagination, unexpected twists and turns, huge hooks, and great beats. It's the kind of record that gives big beat a good name. *—Stephen Thomas Erlewine*

Halfway Between the Gutter and the Stars / Nov. 7, 2000 / Astralwerks ✦✦✦✦

The cover of Norman Cook's breakout Fatboy Slim album, *You've Come a Long Way, Baby*, was a good clue to the contents, picturing as it did thousands of LPs straining the racks in Cook's record room—undoubtedly just a small portion of his massive collection of sampling material. Inside, Cook unfolded a party record for the ages, long on fun (though understandably short on staying power), chock full of samples pillaged from all manner of obscure soul shouters and old-school rap crews, triggered and tweaked *ad nauseam*. With his third LP, *Halfway Between the Gutter and the Stars*, Cook pulls away slightly from the notoriously fickle pop charts and crossover kids courted on his last record. Instead, he makes a conscious attempt to inject some real hedonism back into the world of dance—he *is* a DJ, after all. On advice from friends the Chemical Brothers, Cook recruited collaborators for the first time—nu-soul diva Macy Gray, funk legend Bootsy Collins, fellow superstar DJ/producer Roger Sanchez—and the two tracks with Gray, "Love Life" and "Demons," are arguably the highlights of the entire album. In all, *Halfway Between the Gutter and the Stars* is possibly Norman Cook's best possible statement after being—nearly simultaneously—picked up by a multitude of notoriously fickle pop consumers and thrown away by his previously rock-solid dance fan base. The hooks are unmissable and there's plenty of big-beat techno from a master of the form, but there's also a good amount of mature material that would undeniably appeal to many listeners in the dance world if they ever condescended to give it an objective listen. *—John Bush*

Faust

f. 1971, Wumme, Germany

Experimental Rock, Kraut Rock, Experimental, Prog Rock/Art Rock

"There is no group more mythical than Faust," wrote Julian Cope in his book *Krautrocksampler*, which detailed the pivotal influence the German band exerted over the development of ambient and industrial textures. Issued on clear vinyl in a transparent sleeve, Faust's eponymously-titled debut LP surfaced in 1971; although sales were notoriously bad, the album—a noisy sound collage of cut-and-paste musical fragments—did earn the group a solid cult following. Another lavishly-packaged work, *Faust So Far*, followed in 1972, and earned the group a contract with Virgin, who issued 1973's *The Faust Tapes*—a fan-assembled collection of home recordings—for about the price of a single, a marketing ploy which earned considerable media interest. After *Outside the Dream Syndicate*, a collaboration with Tony Conrad, the band released 1973's *Faust IV*, a commercial failure which resulted in the loss of their contract with Virgin, who refused to release the planned *Faust 5*. They disbanded in 1975, and the members scattered throughout Germany; however, after more than a decade of playing together in various incarnations, Faust officially reunited during the early 1990s. *—Jason Ankeny*

Faust / 1971 / Recommended ✦✦✦✦✦

The impact of Faust cannot be overstated; their debut album was truly a revolutionary step forward in the progress of "rock music." It was pressed on clear vinyl, packaged in a clear sleeve, with a clear plastic lyric insert. The black X-ray of a fist on the cover graphically illustrates the hard core music contained in the grooves, an amalgamation of electronics, rock, tape edits, acoustic guitars, musique concrete, and industrial angst. The level of imagination is staggering, the concept is totally unique and it's fun to listen to as well. *—Archie Patterson*

Faust So Far / 1972 / Recommended ✦✦✦✦✦

Faust's second album moves closer to actual song structure than their debut, but it still remains experimental. Songs progress and evolve instead of abruptly stopping or cutting into other tracks. The opening song "It's a Rainy Day, Sunshine Girl" begins as a repetitive 4/4 beat played on toms and piano with the title sung over the top. But for seven minutes the song adds instruments, including a lush analog synth line, and ends in a memorable sax riff. Faust's lyrical side appears on the acoustic "Picnic on a Frozen River" and "On the Way to Adamäe," whereas its abrasive side pops up on "Me Lack Space." "So Far," a jam shared by guitar, horns, and tweedy keyboard, rolls along with a funky hypnotic beat and wailing processed synths. And on "No Harm," the crazed delivery of such lines as "Daddy, take the banana, tomorrow Sunday" makes one want to believe something profound is going down. In terms of scope and the wealth of ideas, this is probably the most balanced of their first four albums. *—Ted Mills*

The Faust Tapes / 1973 / Cuneiform ✦✦✦✦

This was the release that "broke" Faust to a British audience, mostly because of a marketing gimmick whereby the then-infant Virgin label sold it in shops for half a pound. Still, it's no mean feat to sell 50,000 copies of rock this avant-garde, no matter what the cost. A continuous 43-minute piece with about 26 discrete passages (which makes it hell to zero in on a specific bit on CD), it roams from crash'n'mash drums and fierce art rock jamming to rather pretty, if inscrutable, bits of folk-rock and spoken word, with odd shards of melody sticking out like glass in a tire. There are rough reference points to Zappa in the torrid editing and British Canterbury bands in the goofier, more rock-driven parts, but this is even less immediately accessible, taking a few plays to get a grip on, though most pop-oriented listeners won't get that far. *—Richie Unterberger*

Faust IV / 1973 / Virgin ✦✦✦✦✦

Coming on the heels of the cut-and-paste sound-collage schizophrenia of *The Faust Tapes*, *Faust IV* seems relatively subdued and conventional, though it's still a far cry from what anyone outside the German avant-garde rock scene was doing. The album's disparate threads don't quite jell into something larger (as in the past), but there's still much to recommend it. The nearly 12-minute electro-acoustic opener "Krautrock" is sometimes viewed as a comment on Faust's droning, long-winded contemporaries, albeit one that would lose its point by following the same conventions. There are a couple of oddball pop numbers that capture the group's surreal sense of whimsy: one, "The Sad Skinhead," through its reggae-ish beat, and another, "It's a Bit of a Pain," by interrupting a pastoral acoustic guitar number with the most obnoxious synth noises the band can conjure. Aside from "Krautrock," there is a trend toward shorter track lengths and more vocals, but there are still some unpredictably sudden shifts in the instrumental pieces, even though it only occasionally feels like an idea is being interrupted at random (quite unlike *The Faust Tapes*). There are several beat-less, mostly electronic soundscapes full of fluttering, blooping synth effects, as well as plenty of the group's trademark Velvet Underground-inspired guitar primitivism, and even a Frank Zappa-esque jazz-rock passage. Overall, *Faust IV* comes off as more a series of not-always-related experiments, but there are more than enough intriguing moments to make it worthwhile. Unfortunately, it would be the last album the group recorded (at least in its first go-round). *—Steve Huey*

Munich and Elsewhere / 1986 / Recommended ✦✦✦

Leftovers from the early part of the '70s that are consistent enough with the Faust anything-goes vibe to be considered worthy of investigation by anyone who values their proper albums as well. There's no consistent focus, which in turn is entirely consistent with the nature of a band so enigmatic. It's been reissued in its entirety on the *Seventy One Minutes Of* CD, which adds a substantial amount of additional rare material, and is thus the recommended alternative to hunting down the original release. *—Richie Unterberger*

Rien / Oct. 24, 1995 / Table of the Elements ✦✦✦

It took 20 years to get the mysterious Faust back in the studio, and *Rien* was the baffling result. With only two members of the original group left, the sounds on *Rien* owe more to their impromptu, anarchic, industrial noise concerts in 1992 than any of their original work and should be taken on a different level as almost a different group. With the weight of nostalgic expectations against them, Faust did what they could to separate themselves from their past. The first track, for instance, is pure silence; the second is mostly feedback, with segues into environmental sounds of a cold (presumably) windy day, children playing in the background. Gone are the lyricism and melody, and even the prog-rock aesthetics of the original group. Only track five, a drum and drone with the lyric "listen to the fish," retains some of the early style. Producer Jim O'Rourke wisely refrains from copying Uwe Nettlebeck's work with the group but gives shape to Faust's sound. Older fans will be puzzled, newer ones will be interested. *—Ted Mills*

71 Minutes of Faust / 1996 / Cuneiform ✦✦✦✦

Basically an expanded version of *Munich and Elsewhere* (which was itself a compilation of unreleased material), with the addition of the unreleased LP *Faust Party Three* (parts of which had previously appeared only as limited-edition EPs and singles), as well as two previously unreleased tracks. Parts wed brutal drum patterns to insistently repetitive guitar riffing; there are prog rock keyboard passages that slightly recall Soft Machine; and "Don't Take Roots" sounds like an unintentional satire of the cheap California psychedelia that you might hear on a late-'60s youth culture exploitation flick. Sometimes it even sounds like a parody of early King Crimson-type pomp rock. It would be nice to have some liner notes explaining exactly what comes from where, but basically what you need to know is that it was all recorded in Germany from 1971 to 1975 and is on par with the quality of the albums they actually released during that time. *—Richie Unterberger*

You Know FaUSt / Feb. 25, 1997 / Recommended ✦✦✦

Faust's comeback album *You Know FaUSt* is a surprisingly vital return, finding the group at the wild, recklessly experimental peak of *The Faust Tapes* and *Faust IV*. Largely shedding the blistering *musique concrete* of their reunion concerts, the band concentrates on creating mainly instrumental soundscapes of synthesizers, organs, horns, droning guitars and pulsating rhythms. While the sound isn't as revolutionary as it once was, it is undeniably more accomplished—and frequently just as exciting—as their earlier recordings. *—Stephen Thomas Erlewine*

● **Faust/Faust So Far** / Oct. 3, 2000 / Collectors' Choice Music ✦✦✦✦✦

Faust/Faust So Far is an excellent, timely reissue of the first two LPs from the monolithic Krautrock band. Included are the complete contents of two full albums of wildly experimental head music, a portrait of a group rarely happy with what's going on unless they're moving to something else. Though the material ranges far and wide—from the distorted rock freakout of "Why Don't You Eat Carrots?" to the experimental, heavily processed "Miss Fortune" to the tribal, trance-inducing pop on much of *Faust So Far*—the results are radical and astonishing, some of the most breathtaking experimental music recorded during the '70s. *—John Bush*

The Wumme Years: 1970-73 / Nov. 7, 2000 / Recommended Records ✦✦✦✦✦

The Wumme Years: 1970-73, titled for the studio where the band created much of its magic, documents an output that simply defies belief. Throughout the period under consideration, Faust recorded two albums, but created sufficient material for three more—with the first of them funded by a major record label that not only didn't know what would be delivered at the end, but wasn't even sure that the players were really musicians. The entire thing was set up by a German journalist, who wondered what would happen if a bunch of untried avant-garde instrumentalists were given free rein in the studio for as long as they wanted. Polydor, to its everlasting credit, shared his curiosity. That the *Faust* and *So Far* albums (completely unadorned, the first two discs in this package) emerged as both critical and cult successes during 1971 and 1972 was, then, as much a triumph for performance art as it was for the art of performance. A handful of these songs have been released in the past, chiefly during the 1980s, when they were spread across the *Munich and Elsewhere*, *Last LP*, and *Faust Party Three* albums and EPs; this, however, marks their first appearance in anything approaching a cohesive whole, reconstructed not only in the fashion that the band originally envisioned them, but also completely remastered. Not all of these latter two discs can be called essential listening. More than a few things fall horribly flat; one or two are even embarrassingly inept. But there's enough to make this box worthwhile, even if you already own all the Faust you think you need. *—Dave Thompson*

Charlie Feathers

b. Jun. 12, 1932, Holly Springs, MS, **d.** Aug. 29, 1998

Vocals, Songwriter, Guitar / Rockabilly, Traditional Country

Charlie Feathers was many things to many fans of rock and country music. To some, he was a superb country stylist who could take almost any piece of material and stamp it with the full force of his personality. To others, he was one of rockabilly's great pioneers, there at the dawn of Sun Records. And Feathers' stubborn insistence on combining elements of country, raw blues, and bluegrass to make his own version of the rockabilly experience showed him to be one of the genre's most original and enduring artists. By 1954, Feathers was working his way into the confines of Sam Phillips' Memphis Recording Service, with an eye toward getting something released on Sun Records. When Phillips decided to start a local non-union label called Flip, he released the first Feathers single on that label, the classic "Peepin' Eyes" coupled with "I've Been Deceived." The record kicked enough noise locally to get Charlie transferred to Sun for a second single, but the artist had bigger visions. Although Phillips saw him as "a superb country stylist," Feathers wanted to rock and cut many Sun demo sessions in that style. When Phillips turned a deaf ear to it all, Charlie's impatience led him to Memphis rival Meteor Records, where he waxed the two-sided rockabilly classic "Tongue-Tied Jill" and "Get With It." This single garnered enough Memphis airplay to cement him a deal with King Records, and it is here that the Charlie Feathers as rockabilly legend story begins in earnest. The dozen or so sides he cut as singles for King are the greatest '50s rockabilly tracks to escape the hegemony of the Sun studios with "One Hand Loose," "Bottle to the Baby," "Everybody's Lovin' My Baby," and "I Can't Hardly Stand It" all becoming classics of the genre. *—Cub Koda*

Live in Memphis / 1979 / Barrelhouse ✦✦✦

Loose early-'70s recordings. Great, but unfortunately out of print. *—Cub Koda*

Rockabilly Rhythm! / 1981 / Cowboy Carl ✦✦✦✦

The career of this top-notch rockabilly artist certainly had its downs and downs, as one can ascertain from the fact that it is a rare Charlie Feathers session that was released anytime near the date it was recorded. These sides languished for nearly a decade, although the playing is great and Feathers is in fine vocal form. He assembled a minimalist group—no drums, although it is a rare listener that even notices this because the rhythm sound is so happening thanks to popping bass playing from both Charlie and Bubba Feathers. The program is mostly cover versions, which was an area where this artist really shone. Very few recording artists could take something such as "Roll Over Beethoven" and make something personal out of it, but this is just what Feathers does in his jaunty, medium-tempo version complete with goofy background singers. Some of these tunes are ones Feather recorded over and over, such as "I'm Movin' On" by Hank Snow, perversely done at a tempo slow enough to suggest a broken down truck rather than a smoothly running eight-wheeler. Other song transformations are done with such simplicity of technique that it is remarkable, such as the laid-back but still threatening cover of Johnny Cash's "Folsom Prison Blues." *—Eugene Chadbourne*

Jungle Fever / 1987 / Kay ✦✦✦✦✦

Boasting a generous twenty tracks, *Jungle Fever* is the best available compilation of Charlie Feathers' original rockabilly recordings; all of his best-known songs are collected here, including "Get With It" and "Tongue-Tied Jill." *—Stephen Thomas Erlewine*

Rock-a-Billy / May 1991 / Zu-Zazz ✦✦✦✦✦

This 1998 Bear family reissue of a CD originally issued in 1990 on Colin Escott's ZuZazz imprint gathers together the absolute cream of Charlie Feathers' unreleased and alternate recordings. Usually an album of outtakes would infer a compilation of less than releasable material. But Charlie Feathers' unreleased demos and outtakes are every bit as illuminating and wonderful as his better-known singles, making this just as good as any Feathers collections out there, save for the two-disc Revenant anthology, which contains all of his '50s recordings intact. Here are 1954 living-room rehearsals for his first Sun session ("Defrost Your Heart," "Runnin' Around," "I've Been Deceived"), outtakes from his second ("Wedding Gown of White," "Defrost Your Heart"), the 1956 Sun demo session ("Corrine Corrina," "Frankie & Johnny," "So Ashamed," "Honky Tonk Kind" and an early stab at "Bottle to the Baby" with different lyrics), rowdier and looser King outtakes ("Bottle to the Baby," "One Hand Loose," "Everybody's Lovin' My Baby" and "I Can't Hardly Stand It"), rare singles for local labels like Wal-May, Memphis and Kay ("Dinky John," "Today and Tomorrow" and "Wild, Wild Party"), rounded out by some great '60s and early-'70s sides cut at the Sun and Select-O-Hits studios (a recut of "Tongue Tied Jill," "Gone! Gone! Gone!," "Where's She at Tonight," and "Wild Side of Life"). Some—but not all—of this also appears on Revenant's *The Definitive Recordings* two-disc set. This particular edition, however, sports superior sound and mastering. *—Cub Koda*

Uh Huh Honey / Nov. 16, 1993 / Norton ✦✦✦

An important part of any Charlie Feathers or rockabilly collection, this brings together all of his late-'60s recordings for the Memphis-based Philwood label, along with some fascinating live TV recordings from 1978. Charlie is in rare form on these explosive sides, turning in the best version of "Tear It Up" ever recorded, with its legendary B-side, "Stutterin' Cindy." The television broadcast from Houston finds Charlie in a drummer-less trio format—as real as rockabilly gets—running through an inspired set that covers everything from the ballad "We're Getting Closer to Being Apart" to his classic "Get With It." Even if you already have the double set of Feathers classics on Revenant, here's the companion volume. *—Cub Koda*

Tip Top Daddy / 1995 / Norton ✦✦✦

Call this one "Charlie Feathers Unplugged" if you want to, but what we have here is a bushelbasket of unissued acoustic demos from 1958 to 1973 from the King of Rockabilly. It doesn't much matter when Feathers cut something as long as he was into it when the tape was rollin' and here's 23 tracks that bear that simple fact out. It also doesn't seem to matter much if Feathers wrote the tune or not, because everything he puts his pipes to—along with his consummate arranging talents—stamps it with the crazed redneck mark of hizzown personality. Electric guitar fleshes out a couple of tracks here and there, but in the main it's pure, unvarnished Charlie Feathers and that's worth more than the next dozen hat hunk albums that come down the pike. *—Cub Koda*

● **Get With It: The Essential Recordings (1954-1969)** / Jul. 21, 1998 / Revenant ✦✦✦✦✦

After decades of Feathers' best recordings being scattered piecemeal across various compilations (sometimes as little as just a few tracks on a various-artists collection), this two-disc, 42-track deluxe edition finally gathers up the most essential of them, making this the most complete overview of his career yet to be assembled. All of his original Sun, Meteor, King, Kay, Walmay, and Holiday Inn masters are here; only the 1961 Memphis single of "Wild Wild Party" and the 1968 Philwood single of "Tear It Up" and "Stutterin' Cindy" keeps this super deluxe package from being complete (both sides of the latter single available on Norton's *Uh Huh Honey*), curious omissions to say the least, especially in light of what follows. The second disc brings together a great deal of the known extant unissued material from the same time period (1954 to 1969), featuring Sun demos, King alternates, even duets with blues singer Junior Kimbrough, although still missing a lot of stuff to be considered a complete overview. With excellent liner notes from Peter Guralnick, Jim Dickinson, and Colin Escott, this becomes the most in-depth look at Feathers' music yet assembled by anyone. Consider this compilation the new standard bearer and definitely the place to start your Charlie Feathers collection. *—Cub Koda*

Rock-A-Billy: Rare & Unissued Recordings / Nov. 25, 1998 / Bear Family ♦♦♦♦♦
Spanning 26 tracks, Bear Family's *Rock-A-Billy: Rare & Unissued Recordings* has a wealth of little-heard Charlie Feathers songs from his prime. This may not contain anything that qualifies as a flat-out classic, but for rockabilly fanatics—who are the people that will be buying this set—this is an engaging, even exciting, collection of tunes that lives up to Feather's reputation as the rockabilly cat's rockabilly cat. *—Stephen Thomas Erlewine*

The Feelies

f. 1977, Hoboken, NJ, **db.** 1992
College Rock, Jangle Pop, Alternative Pop/Rock, American Underground
Of the countless bands to emerge from the New York City underground during the post-punk era, few if any were as unique and influential as the Feelies; nerdy, nervous and noisy, even decades later their droning, skittering avant-pop remains a key touchstone of the American indie music scene. Formed in suburban New Jersey in 1976, the group made its NYC debut and quickly created a buzz throughout the city's new wave circuit. In 1979, the Feelies cut their debut single "Fa Ce-La" for the British indie Rough Trade, though their refusal to work with outside producers jeopardized their immediate hopes for a major-label deal. Their brilliant 1980 LP *Crazy Rhythms* instead appeared on another U.K. indie, Stiff; although it made little impact outside of underground circles, many latter-day acts—R.E.M. chief among them—cited the album as a major influence. After Stiff pressured the Feelies for a hit single, the group was forced into a kind of suspended animation which saw them out of action for the better part of the early '80s. Frontmen Bill Million and Glenn Mercer reactivated the Feelies banner in 1983, and finally released their second album, *The Good Earth*, three years later. A&M released the follow-up *Only Life* in 1988, and *Time for a Witness* followed in 1991, but later that year the Feelies played their final show at the Hoboken club Maxwell's. Mercer and drummer Dave Weckerman later re-teamed in two bands, Wake Ooloo and Sunburst. *—Jason Ankeny*

★ **Crazy Rhythms** / Apr. 1980 / A&M ♦♦♦♦♦
Even the cover is a winner, with a washed-out look that screams new wave via horn-rimmed glasses, even more so than contemporaneous pictures of either Elvis Costello or the Embarrassment. But if it was all look and no brain, *Crazy Rhythms* would long ago have been dismissed as an early-'80s relic. That's exactly what this album is not, right from the soft, haunting hints of percussion that preface the suddenly energetic jump of the appropriately titled "The Boy With the Perpetual Nervousness." From there the band delivers seven more originals plus a striking cover of the Beatles' "Everybody's Got Something to Hide" that rips along even more quickly than the original. The guitar team of Mercer and Million smokes throughout, whether it's soft, rhythmic chiming with a mysterious, distanced air or blasting, angular solos. But Fier is the band's secret weapon, able to play straight-up beats but aiming at a rumbling, strange punch that updates Velvet Underground/Krautrock trance into giddier realms. Mercer's obvious Lou Reed vocal inflections make the VU roots even clearer, but even at this stage of the game there's something fresh about the work the quartet does, even 20 years on—a good blend of past and present, rave-up and reflection. When the group's later label, A&M, finally got around to reissuing the album for the first time stateside, a curious bonus was included: a version of the Rolling Stones' "Paint It, Black," recorded by the later lineup of the band in 1990. Mercer's voice is noticeably different from his decade-old self, but it's an enthusiastic rendition not too far out of place. *—Ned Raggett*

No One Knows / 1986 / Coyote ♦♦♦
This brief EP takes two excellent songs from the album *The Good Earth* and pairs them with two covers. "The High Road" and "Slipping (Into Something)" both utilize strummed acoustic guitar textures, submerged Lou Reed-style vocals, and a vibrant New South sound. The former is a midtempo loping number, while the latter is faster and more jittery; the final section of "Slipping (Into Something)" also layers on nervous electric guitar lines and speeds up the tempo. The Beatles' "She Said, She Said" gets a faithful, if understated reading, while Neil Young's "Sedan Delivery" alternates between sections that are by turns punky fast and grandiosely slow. This is an attractive release worth hearing. *—David Cleary*

The Good Earth / 1986 / Twin/Tone ♦♦♦
After the various side projects and explorations the band got up to for most of the early '80s, not to mention switching some members around (with bassist Sauter and drummer Demeski now forming the rhythm section), the Feelies made a fine return with *The Good Earth*. With co-production from noted fan Peter Buck, the group exchanged some of the understated tense frazzle of *Crazy Rhythms* for a gentler propulsion without losing its trancy edge. Compared to the wispy jangle rock that passed for much of college radio at the time, the Feelies proposed a different path with the songs' steady pace and murkier feeling. Demeski's a more than fine replacement for Fier (his martial playing on "Tomorrow Today" is one of his many entertaining touches), Sauter's playing emphasizes controlled understatement, and the Million/Mercer guitar duo still nails it. The brisker jauntiness of songs like "The Last Roundup," which wears just enough of a country & western edge without seeming like a parody or half-assed, varies the calmer moods elsewhere very well. At the album's considerable best, such as the brief but really lovely acoustic/electric blend of "When Company Comes" or the title track, with an almost epic ending, Million and Mercer sound like they inhabit the same body playing two guitars, everything's that much in lovely sync. Their vocals ride low in the mix this time out, but thankfully the sometimes all-too-obvious hints of Lou Reed in Mercer's style have been replaced with a more unique, stronger edge—not that the connection still isn't there on a track like the building groove of "Slipping (Into Something)." Reed would also love its concluding guitar solo! Perhaps the only criticism is a slight sameness between a few songs, but there's more sly variety on display to offset this gentle treasure. *—Ned Raggett*

Only Life / 1988 / A&M ♦♦♦♦
With an unchanged lineup but more attention due to their A&M deal, the Feelies hit the jackpot with their third album, a warm, inviting collection that finally addresses the endless Lou Reed comparisons with a cover of his "What Goes On." With its clearer feeling and peppier overall delivery, it avoids simply cloning the original arrangement and performance. The rest of the album shows off the band's distinctive yet flexible sound, as much jangle as it is quietly moody. Mercer and Million's previously tense guitar power becomes attractive shadings, implying a louder approach without always delivering it, while the Demeski/Sauter rhythm team takes the lead throughout; his steady drums and her low, rolling performances giving the guitarists something to play around instead of dominate. The Feelies always make this tranced-out rock their own, but this time around it's as quietly thrilling, if not more so, than ever. "Higher Ground" is a great example, with Mercer and Million trading off not merely notes and passages but differing approaches, whether laden with distortion or chiming clearly. Though Weckerman's work, as earlier, isn't easily distinguished from Demeski's, from the sound of it everything fit in right when recording. Where appears more audibly, as on the start of "The Undertow," his percussion adds an intriguing wild card to the proceedings, aiming at the same goal with slightly different sonics. Mercer's ghost-of-you-know-who vocals still pop up at times, but here his own ability to actually sing and hold notes comes forward, giving him a technical edge that he uses to great effect on the brisk "Away." *—Ned Raggett*

Time for a Witness / Mar. 5, 1991 / A&M ♦♦♦
The final Feelies album didn't change much in the way the band operated, but as a conclusion to the band's active days, it makes for a fine coda. Million and Mercer peel out some amazing frazzled solos, the rhythm section knows the virtues of raving it up and keeping the beat steady and flowing, and the ghost of various earlier inspirations plays around without dominating things. If anything, the concluding cover this time around makes for an intriguing difference away from the Velvets—namely, the Stooges, in a gentle rip through "Real Cool Time." But even though there's nothing "new" to report about the Feelies and the members' way of doing things, as a well-played and written collection of low-key rock with non-mainstream aims and goals, *Time for a Witness* makes for a fine listen. One of the band's best songs surfaces here, the lengthy "Find a Way," which showcases both the noted Million/Mercer guitar interplay, solo filigrees, and soft chimes passed back and forth, and the complex layering of Weckerman's percussion with the core rhythm section. It's a virtuoso performance from a band that doesn't need to create pointless flash with its abilities, a fine balance all told. Other smart performances crop up song for song, including some really fine, energetic performances such as "Sooner or Later" or "Doin' It Again." "Invitation" deserves more attention—in its own way it indicates where the Feelies could have gone next, with a lovely vocal arrangement on the chorus and a slightly varied mix that steps away from the usual clear flow for a hazier yet still strong end result. The lead guitar melody in particular is a charmer, and the whole thing kicks up its heels with delight, a bit like a happier "Boys Don't Cry." *—Ned Raggett*

Felt

f. 1979, **db.** 1989
Indie Pop, Post-Punk
Felt was the project of Britain's enigmatic Lawrence Hayward, a singer/songwriter who transformed his long-standing obsession with the music of Tom Verlaine and Television into an impressive catalog of minimalist pop gems and, ultimately, cult stardom. The first Felt single, "Index," was produced by Lawrence alone in his bedroom on a portable cassette player; released in 1979, its primitive, impressionistic sound stood in stark contrast to the sleek solemnity of the new wave, and as a result the record became the subject of lavish critical praise. Hayward then set about assembling a band, although Felt was clearly his project and his alone. After a series of roster shuffles, a steady group including guitarist Maurice Deebank and drummer Gary Ainge began to take shape in time to record 1981's *Crumbling the Antiseptic Beauty* EP. After one more EP, 1984's *The Splendour of Fear*, Felt issued its long-awaited full-length *The Strange Idols Pattern and Other Short Stories* in 1984. The group's ranks swelled to include keyboardist Martin Duffy prior to recording 1985's *Ignite the Seven Cannons* with producer Robin Guthrie. Despite their success, internal friction plagued the group, and finally Deebank left for good prior to the release of 1986's *Ballad of the Band* EP, Felt's first effort for the Creation label. In the wake of the guitarist's exit, the group's next album, 1986's *Let the Snakes Crinkle Their Heads*, became a brief instrumental outing, but its follow-up, *Forever Breathes the Lonely Word*, was acclaimed as Felt's masterpiece. Two dramatically different LPs, *The Pictorial Jackson Review* and *Train Above the City*—the latter of which did not even include Hayward—followed in 1988, and upon issuing 1989's *Me and a Monkey on the Moon*, Felt announced its breakup. *—Jason Ankeny*

Crumbling the Antiseptic Beauty / 1981 / Cherry Red ♦♦♦

On *Crumbling the Antiseptic Beauty*, there are hints of Felt's later English pop grandeur—on the instrumental opener "Evergreen Dazed," for example, which (sans rhythm section) pits guitarist Maurice Deebank's cascading, euphoric noodlings against Lawrence Hayward's clear acoustic strums—but overall this is a fairly primitive affair. There is a stripped-down psychedelic feel to certain tracks, with drums pounding out a tribalistic, rolling beat beneath Deebank's complex guitar runs and Hayward's obtuse vocals. Later in their career, particularly on 1985's *The Strange Idols Pattern and Other Short Stories*, Felt would finally curb all that minimalist atmosphere into three-minute pop gems (while maintaining their skewed, unconventional palette); here, however, the pieces are in place but the overall vision is still rudimentary. *—Erik Hage*

The Splendour of Fear / 1984 / Cherry Red ♦♦♦

The Strange Idols Pattern and Other Short Stories / 1984 / Cherry Red ♦♦♦♦

On *The Strange Idols Pattern and Other Short Stories*, Felt finally transforms its oft-mentioned Television influence into the band's own, distinctly English brand of elegant guitar pop. Guitarists Lawrence Hayward and the classically trained Maurice Deebank work against each other in breathtakingly cascading figures while Hayward drapes his deadpan vocal delivery across the shimmering bliss of tracks like "Sunlight Bathed the Golden Glow," "Crystal Ball," and "Whirlpool Vision of Shame." This is the pinnacle of Felt's Cherry Red catalog, evolving from the starker stance of the group's first two releases—*Crumbling the Antiseptic Beauty* and *The Splendour of Fear*—to a skewed yet gorgeous pop vision that eludes comparison. Producer John Leckie (XTC, the Stone Roses, the Fall) understands the source of the group's power and highlights the crisp, effects-free guitars chattering incessantly beneath Hayward's poetically charged lyrics. *—Erik Hage*

Ignite the Seven Cannons/The Strange Idols Pattern and Other Short Stories / 1985 / Cherry Red ♦♦♦♦

On *Ignite the Seven Cannons*, Felt brings in Cocteau Twin Robin Guthrie to produce. While Guthrie brings along bandmate Elizabeth Fraser to add her typically ethereal vocals to "Primitive Painters"—earning Felt a minor U.K. hit—the collaboration doesn't work as well as one would hope. John Leckie's clear, simple production on the group's previous album, *The Strange Idols Pattern and Other Short Stories*, highlighted the shimmering guitar work and infused the album with odd yet breathtaking beauty. However, the guitars are deeper in the mix here, at times buried beneath Guthrie's atmospheric production and the addition of keyboardist Martin Duffy (later of Primal Scream). Lawrence Hayward has noted that this album sounds different than other Felt albums because Guthrie simply did what he did with the Cocteau Twins. And, while there is a new urgency to Hayward's singing—bringing him even closer to the anti-vocals of his hero Tom Verlaine—and some gorgeous guitar moments from the classically trained Maurice Deebank, this album falls short of the high-water mark set by the group's previous effort. *—Erik Hage*

Ignite the Seven Cannons / 1985 / Cherry Red ♦♦♦♦

Crumbling the Antiseptic Beauty/Splendour of Fear / 1986 / Cherry Red ♦♦♦

On *Crumbling the Antiseptic Beauty*, there are hints of Felt's later English pop grandeur—on the instrumental opener "Evergreen Dazed," for example, which (sans rhythm section) pits guitarist Maurice Deebank's cascading, euphoric noodlings against Lawrence Hayward's clear acoustic strums—but overall, this is a fairly primitive affair. There is a stripped-down psychedelic feel to certain tracks, with drums pounding out a tribalistic, rolling beat beneath Deebank's complex guitar runs and Hayward's obtuse vocals. Later in their career, particularly on 1985's *The Strange Idols Pattern and Other Short Stories*, Felt would finally curb all that minimalist atmosphere into three-minute pop gems (while maintaining their skewed, unconventional palette); here, however, the pieces are in place but the overall vision is still rudimentary. On *The Splendour of Fear*, Felt still hasn't figured out how to tame all that glorious atmosphere into a distinct vision. The classically trained Deebank can unravel glistening guitar scales like nobody's business—and Lawrence's obtuse vocal delivery certainly possesses an uncanny charm—but this release can be monotonous at times, lapsing too often into meandering guitarscapes. The tone of the album is set on the first track, which opens with an extended dirge-like instrumental that finally gives way to Lawrence's vocals. The eight-minute-plus track "The Stagnant Pool" is a highlight here, simply because it seems purposeful—with Lawrence's ominous vocals giving way to an emotional, melodic guitar jam that anticipates the later work of the Smiths' Johnny Marr. *—Erik Hage*

Forever Breathes the Lonely Word / 1986 / Creation ♦♦♦♦♦

Let the Snakes Crinkle Their Heads to Death / 1986 / Creation ♦♦♦

Felt's other instrumental album, *Train Above the City*, was created without the involvement of frontman Lawrence (beyond the naming of the songs), but with *Let the Snakes Crinkle Their Heads to Death* Lawrence got in on the act, authoring or co-authoring nine of the ten brief instrumental tracks and playing guitar. Without a doubt the most minor, disposable record in Felt's catalog, *Let the Snakes*... sounds like backing tracks awaiting vocal overdubs. No memorable melodies or interesting textures fill the void created by the absence of vocals, and as a result most of the compositions seem unfinished or simply unremarkable. At the very least, *Felt*'s albums usually have inventive song titles, but game efforts such as "Voyage to Illumination" and "Sapphire Mansions" suggest the silliest of New Age pap. Leave this one for the completists. *—Greg Adams*

Poem of the River / 1987 / Creation ♦♦♦♦

Pictorial Jackson Review / 1988 / Creation ♦♦♦♦

More evidence of Felt's odd approach to a career in rock music. Side one is eight songs in the classic indie-pop vein. The guitars ring loudly, Hammond organs swoop in and out, Lawrence's flat and reedy vocals sing songs of bitterness and irony. Indie pop unequaled by any other band of their era. Each song as catchy and memorable as the last. "Don't Die on My Doorstep" deserving extra credit for having one of the best song titles of the '80s. Then you flip the record over and are met by a 12-minute ambient piano piece. Martin Duffy presses softly on the keys and the melody that results is not unaffecting, in fact, it is kind of pretty in a new-agey way. Still, you have to wonder what they were thinking. Careers are made by delivering what the peole expect and only that, over and over, until they get bored and find the next big thing. Following your own path usually leads to nothing but heartbreak, poverty, and the occasional great pop record. Like this one. *—Tim Sendra*

Poem of the River/Forever Breathes the Lonely Word / 1988 / Creation ♦♦♦♦♦

Train Above the City / 1988 / Creation ♦♦♦

Lawrence has said that this is his favorite Felt record. Which is funny because all he does on the album is title the songs. He does a fine job however; "Run Chico Run" and "Press Softly on the Brakes, Holly" are two titles most songwriters would give at least five bucks for. The music itself is for the most part cocktail jazz, vibes, and piano with a splash of percussion. The melodies are nice, if sometimes a little new-agey. Still, when the album is finished one is hard pressed to see what Lawrence is on about. Perhaps his fondness stems from the concept behind the record. No pop band in their right mind would release an album of inconsequential tinklings when all around them bands are changing the face of music or scaling the charts or desperately trying to get ahead. Nobody but Felt. Well, that's Lawrence for you. A man with his own peculiar and quite amusing ways. Give the record's concept five stars but don't bother listening to it. *—Tim Sendra*

Me and a Monkey on the Moon / 1989 / Cherry Red ♦♦♦♦♦

Felt's head man, Lawrence, had a plan. Ten years, ten records, then break up the band. This is that tenth record and Felt goes out on a high note. *Me and a Monkey on the Moon* is the most musically accomplished and personal record of the band's career. It is emotional, funny, and loaded with memorable melodies, some of Lawrence's best. Felt always came across as incredibly remote and icy. The sound was sparse and jagged, the lyrics—when not vague—were hostile and acerbic, and Lawrence's vocals were pitched somewhere between Lou Reed and talking in his sleep. *Me and a Monkey on the Moon* is so intimate and personal that it almost sounds like a different band. The record sounds like Lawrence's autobiography, with songs about childhood, family, lost love, and the end of Felt; eight of the ten songs have "I" in the first line and they are all sung in a voice aching with loss and regret. The emotional nature of the lyrics and singing is bolstered by the lush and autumnal musical backing provided by the band. Martin Duffy is amazing here; he plays a wide range of keyboards from piano to mellotron to ARP string ensemble with just the right notes and feeling. The record is filled with instrumentation that was totally new to Felt, like long rock & roll guitar solos, pedal steel guitars, and female backup vocals. It all works to create a rich and heartfelt farewell to Felt, full of sentiment but not sentimental—the sound of a band reaching its potential and kissing it goodbye. As great as Lawrence's next band, the glam and novelty rock-inspired Denim, was, it is too bad he didn't further explore the adult and emotional sounds of *Me and a Monkey on the Moon*. *—Tim Sendra*

Bubblegum Perfume / 1990 / Creation ♦♦♦♦♦

● **Absolute Classic Masterpieces** / 1992 / Futurist ♦♦♦♦♦

Absolute Classic Masterpieces documents the dark jangle pop of Felt between the years of 1979 and 1985; it's a best-of collection for a band that always deserved more attention. The tracks run in reverse chronological order, starting with "Primitive Painters," a song that charts the territory where the Cocteau Twins, the Fall, and the Smiths overlap, and ending with the very first demo single "Index." The order of the tracks means that you are listening to the band devolve into its influences, and the effect is enjoyable. "Primitive Painters" is a lost treat if ever one existed; along with the next three tracks, it was produced by Robin Guthrie of the Cocteau Twins. "Primitive Painters" also features Elizabeth Frazer of the Cocteau Twins on vocals. Guthrie is not the only famed producer whose work appears here; three John Leckie tracks are also included, from the *Strange Idols Pattern & Other Short Stories* album. While most of the slower songs appear toward the end of the album, making it a somewhat sleepy affair as it winds down, there are charms like "The World Is as Soft as Lace" to liven things up. "Penelope Tree" sounds a bit like Lou Reed fronting the Cure. There's great material to be found throughout the work of Felt, so this collection would work regardless of its running order. Newcomers looking for their first Felt album should start here, with the knowledge that there is quite a bit of dark atmosphere layered over the pop charms within. While these songs might not be masterpieces, as the album title would have you believe, there are many near-masterpieces of moody jangle pop just waiting to be rediscovered. *—Tim DiGravina*

Bryan Ferry

b. Sep. 26, 1945, Washington, England

Vocals, Keyboards, Piano, Harmonica / Album Rock, Pop/Rock, Glam Rock, Prog Rock/Art Rock

While his tenure as the frontman for the legendary Roxy Music remained his towering achievement, singer Bryan Ferry also carved out a successful solo career which continued in the lush, sophisticated manner perfected on the group's final records. He began his musical career as a singer with the rock outfit the Banshees before joining the Gas Board, a soul group featuring bassist Graham Simpson; in 1970, Ferry and Simpson formed Roxy Music. Within a few years, the group had become phenomenally successful, affording Ferry the opportunity to cut his first solo LP in 1973. Far removed from the group's arty glam-rock, *These Foolish Things* established the path which all of his solo work would take, focusing on elegant synth-pop interpretations of '60s hits rendered in the singer's distinct, coolly dramatic manner. His third solo venture, 1976's *Let's Stick Together*, featured remixed, remade, and remodeled versions of Roxy Music hits as well as the usual assortment of covers. 1977's *In Your Mind* was Ferry's first collection of completely original material. 1985's *Boys and Girls* was Ferry's first "official" solo release following the Roxy breakup. For 1987's *Bete Noire*, he was joined by former Smiths guitarist Johnny Marr on the shimmering "The Right Stuff," and notched his only U.S. Top 40 hit with "Kiss and Tell." *—Jason Ankeny*

These Foolish Things / Oct. 1973 / Virgin ♦♦♦♦
Much like his contemporary David Bowie, Ferry consolidated his glam-era success with a covers album, his first full solo effort even while Roxy Music was still going full steam. Whereas Bowie on *Pin-Ups* focused on British beat and psych treasures, Ferry for the most part looked to America, touching on everything from Motown to the early jazz standard that gave the collection its name. Just about everyone in Roxy Music at the time helped out on the album—notable exceptions being Andy Mackay and Brian Eno. The outrageous take on Bob Dylan's "A Hard Rain's A-Gonna Fall," with Ferry vamping over brassy female vocals, sets the tone for things from the start. All this said, many of the covers aim for an elegant late-night feeling not far off from the well-sculpted Ferry persona of the '80s and beyond, though perhaps a touch less bloodless and moody in comparison. In terms of sheer selection alone, meanwhile, Ferry's taste is downright impeccable. There's Leiber & Stoller via Elvis' "Baby I Don't Care," Lesley Gore's "It's My Party" (with narrative gender unchanged!), Smokey Robinson and the Miracles' "The Tracks of My Tears," and more, all treated with affection without undue reverence, a great combination. Ferry's U.K. background isn't entirely ignored, though, thanks to two of the album's best efforts—the Beatles' "You Won't See Me" and the Stones' "Sympathy for the Devil." Throughout Ferry's instantly recognizable croon carries everything to a tee, and the overall mood is playful and celebratory. Wrapping up with a grand take on "These Foolish Things" itself, this album is one of the best of its kind by any artist. *—Ned Raggett*

Another Time, Another Place / Jul. 1974 / Virgin ♦♦♦♦
Another Time, Another Place isn't as immediately thrilling as Ferry's solo debut, but still is a great listen. The same core band that backed Ferry up on the earlier record stays more or less in place here. If, like Roxy over the years, this collection is a touch less frenetic at points in comparison to Ferry's earlier solo stab, the opening blast through "The 'In' Crowd" doesn't show it. Porter's guitar rips along as intensely as Phil Manzanera's can, and the whole thing makes Elvis' original take seem pretty tame. Beyond that, things will be familiar to anyone who's heard *These Foolish Things*—same general atmosphere, same overall approach of Ferry taking classic originals and putting his own proto-lounge-lizard stamp on them, mixing energetic versions with far calmer ones. A very intriguing development is his inclusion of efforts from up-and-coming country writers and singers—thus, a loud and groovy cover of "Funny How Time Slips Away" by Willie Nelson and another of Kris Kristofferson's "Help Me Make It Through the Night." Other country atmospheres slip in here and there via another nod to Elvis ("Walk a Mile in My Shoes," originally by Joe South), while other classics get tapped with versions of "Smoke Gets in Your Eyes" and Sam Cooke's "(What A) Wonderful World." The album as a whole feels a touch more formal than its predecessor, but Ferry and company, plus various brass and string sections, turn on the showiness enough to make it all fun. A harbringer of solo albums to come appears at end—the title track, a Ferry original. *—Ned Raggett*

Let's Stick Together / Sep. 1976 / Virgin ♦♦♦♦
As Roxy approached its mid- to late-'70s hibernation, Ferry came up with another fine solo album, though one of his most curious. With Thompson and Wetton joined by U.K. journeyman guitarist Chris Spedding, Ferry recorded an effort that seemed as much of a bit of creative therapy as it was music for its own sake. On the one hand, he followed the initial formula established for his solo work, looking back to earlier rock, pop, and soul classics with gentle gusto. The title track itself, a cover of the fluke Wilbert Harrison '60s hit, scored Ferry a deserved British hit single, with great sax work from Chris Mercer and Mel Collins and a driving, full band performance. Ferry's delivery is one of his best, right down to the yelps, and the whole thing chugs with post-glam power. Other winners include the Everly Brothers' "The Price of Love" and the Beatles' "It's Only Love," delivered with lead keyboards from Ferry and a nice, full arrangement. On the other hand, half of the album consisted of Ferry originals—but, bizarrely, instead of creating wholly new songs, he re-recorded a slew of earlier Roxy classics. Fanciful fun or exorcising of past demons? It's worth noting that most of the songs come from the Eno period of the band, and consequently the new versions steer clear of the sheer chaos he brought to the original Roxy lineup. As it is, the end results are still interesting treats—"Casanova" exchanges the blasting stomp of the original for a slow, snaky delivery that suggests threat without sounding too worried about it. "Re-Make/Re-Model," meanwhile, turns downright funky without losing any of its weird lyrical edge. Others have subtler differences, as when the stark, stiff midsection of "Sea Breezes" becomes a looser, slow jam. *—Ned Raggett*

In Your Mind / Feb. 1977 / Virgin ♦♦♦
With Roxy Music set aside for the time being, Ferry took the solo plunge with an album of totally original material. As such, the underrated *In Your Mind* makes a logical follow-on from Roxy's *Siren*, especially since usual suspects—Thompson, Manzanera, Wetton, and many more—assist him in the brief eight-song effort. While lacking early Roxy's long-gone freakouts *In Your Mind* still burns more fiercely than both the later solo and group albums, at least on certain tracks—like *Siren*, it balances between rockier and smoother paths, most often favoring the former. Ferry's lyrics remain in his own realm of intelligent, romantic dissipation, and are some of his best efforts. The strong opener "This Is Tomorrow" starts with Ferry and keyboards before moving into a big, chugging full band arrangement and a wistful chorus: "This is tomorrow callin'/Wish you were here." When Ferry aims for a calmer mood, rather than stripped-down melancholia, he lets everyone play along. Sometimes the arrangements almost swamp the songs, but "One Kiss'" combination of female backing vocals, sax, and straight-up rock for instance, make it a great woozy, end-of-the-night singalong before the bars close. There are a few blatant misfires—"Tokyo Joe" has the chugging, dark funk/rock beat down cold, but the lyrics play around too much with Asian stereotypes (and let's not mention the opening gong and all too obvious attempts at "atmosphere" via the strings). On balance, though, *In Your Mind* remains the secret highlight of Ferry's musical career, an energetic album that would have received far more attention as a full Roxy release. *—Ned Raggett*

The Bride Stripped Bare / Sep. 1978 / Virgin ♦♦♦
When Jerry Hall, front-cover model on Roxy's *Siren*, left Ferry for Mick Jagger, his response was this interesting album, not a full success but by no means a washout. In part Ferry returned to the model of his solo work before *In Your Mind*, with half the tracks being covers of rock and soul classics. Thus, Sam and Dave's "Hold On (I'm Coming)," Al Green's "Take Me to the River" (which arguably sounds like a strong influence on Talking Heads' near contemporaneous version) and even the Velvet Underground's "What Goes On," among others, take a bow. Unfortunately Ferry's backing performers, mostly drawing on studio pros like Waddy Wachtel, don't seem to have the real affinity for the material like his earlier solo-effort cohorts did. If anything, though, there's also the sense of Ferry channeling his romantic gloom through a number of the songs, giving them a strong personal bite. The guitar and bass-only version of the traditional folk tune "Carrickfergus" works best of all, its lovelorn sentiments and slow pace connecting just right. As for Ferry's originals, his sentiments are all the more clear, right from the abbreviated charge of the opening "Sign of the Times," its fractured sentiments of disturbed, vicious romance matched by the clipped punch of the music and Ferry's own brisk delivery. The other originals don't cut quite so bloodily, but the sense of loss and confusion is all there, from the opening line "Well I rush out blazin'/My pulse is racin'" on "Can't Let Go" to the lonely sense of mystery on "This Island Earth," the album's conclusion. *—Ned Raggett*

● **Boys and Girls** / May 1985 / Virgin ♦♦♦♦
Having at last laid Roxy to bed with its final, intoxicatingly elegant albums, Ferry continued its end-days spirit with his own return to solo work. Dedicated to Ferry's father, *Boys and Girls* is deservedly most famous for its smash single "Slave to Love." With a gentle samba-derived rhythm leading into the steadier rock pace of the song, it's '80s Ferry at his finest, easy listening without being hopelessly soporific. As a whole, *Boys and Girls* fully established the clean, cool vision of Ferry on his own to the general public. Instead of ragged rock explosions, emotional extremes, and all that made his '70s work so compelling in and out of Roxy, Ferry here is the suave, debonair if secretly moody and melancholic lover, with music to match. Co-producer Rhett Davies, continuing his role from the latter Roxy albums, picks up where *Avalon* left off right from the slinky opening grooves of "Sensation." The range of people on the album is an intriguing mix, from latterday Roxy members like Andy Newmark and Alan Spenner to avid Roxy disciples like Chic's Nile Rodgers. Everyone is subordinated to Ferry's overall vision, and as a result there's not as much full variety on *Boys and Girls* as might be thought or hoped. The album's biggest flaw is indeed that it's almost too smooth, with not even the hint of threat or edge that Ferry once readily made his own. As something that's a high cut above the usual mid-'80s yuppie smarm music, though, *Boys and Girls* remains an enjoyable keeper that has aged well. *—Ned Raggett*

Street Life: 20 Greatest Hits / Apr. 1986 / EG ♦♦♦♦♦
Covering both Ferry and Roxy Music's best-known songs, *Street Life* is the best introduction to the stylish art-rocker's career. *—Stephen Thomas Erlewine*

Bête Noire / Oct. 1987 / Reprise ♦♦♦♦
Hooking up with regular Madonna collaborator Patrick Leonard as the co-producer of this album proved to be just the trick for Ferry. *Bete Noire* sparkles as the highlight of Ferry's post-Roxy solo career, adding enough energy to make it more than *Boys and Girls* part two. Here, his trademark well-polished heartache strikes a fine balance between mysterious moodiness and dancefloor energy, and Leonard adds more than a few tricks that keep the pep up. Five out of the nine songs are Ferry/Leonard collaborations; all succeed, from "Limbo"'s opening punch and flow to the cinematic (and unsurprisingly French-tinged) feeling of the title track. The atmospheric, almost chilling "Zamba"'s minimal, buried drums, soft synths and doomy piano, make it the best of that bunch. Ferry's best moment here is all his own, though—the great single "Kiss and Tell," with a steady, bold bass line leading the way for his slightly dissolute portrayal of mating rituals and all they entail. Like *Boys and Girls*, the album's supporting cast mixes a lengthy list of session pros with a few guest stars. David Gilmour returns, but even more interesting is the appearance of a more recent guitar hero—none other than Johnny Marr, hot on the heels of the Smiths' dissolution. He took the music of a Smiths instrumental, "The Draize Train," and made it the basis of a full collaboration, "The Right Stuff." Marr shows a little more fluidity than usual, likely thanks to the rhythm section's smooth, effortless groove, while Ferry steps to the fore with gusto. In sum, a great listen from start to finish. *—Ned Raggett*

Taxi / Mar. 1993 / Reprise ♦♦♦
Taxi shows a mature Bryan Ferry, suave and controlled, very much in line with his general career from 1979 on. The choices of songs to cover doesn't make for any surprises—the same selections of classic rock, pop, and soul numbers dominate, with an interesting ringer here and there like "Amazing Grace." As with his other recent solo records, a cast of thousands supports him, ranging from the Grid's Richard Norris on synth programming to Brit guitar legends Robin Trower and Michael Brook, plus vocalist Carleen Anderson. All four feature on the opening "I Put a Spell on You," which manages the neat trick of sounding almost exactly like a Ferry original—what Screamin' Jay Hawkins would have made of it is anyone's guess. The rest of the album takes a similar tone, either crackling with low-key energy or aiming for a more gentle approach. The former style turns up in

some welcome guises—thus the take on Fontella Bass' "Rescue Me," here benefiting from a quick beat, mysterious samples and noises buried in the mix and near-subliminal guitar. An overall highlight is the take on the Velvet Underground's "All Tomorrow's Parties," which balances a certain winsomeness with a subtle air of threat, the music just beautiful enough on the one hand and just creepy enough on the other. Ferry's treated vocals, made to sound weirdly flat and compressed, heightens the curious mood. *—Ned Raggett*

Mamouna / Sep. 20, 1994 / Virgin ♦♦♦

Sufficiently recharged via *Taxi*, Ferry got down to business and the following year released *Mamouna*, notable among other things for being his first recordings with the help of Brian Eno since the latter split from Roxy Music back in 1973. Rather than playing the wild card as he so often did, though, Eno concentrates on (to use his own descriptions in the credits) "swoop treatment" and "sonic awareness." Slightly more to the fore are Ferry's usual range of excellent musicians and pros. Steve Ferrone once again handles drums as he did on *Taxi*, while Richard Norris also reappears on loops and programming; other familiar faces include Nile Rodgers, Robin Trower (the album's co-producer), and Carleen Anderson. One of the most intriguing guest appearances comes at the very start—"Don't Want To Know" has no less than five guitarists, including none other than Roxy's own Phil Manzanera. Whereas his '80s work seemed to fit the times just so, with his own general spin on things providing true individuality as a result, on *Mamouna* Ferry seems slightly stuck in place. Compared to the variety of *Bete Noire*, *Mamouna* almost seems a revamp of *Boys and Girls*. Combine that with some of Ferry's least compelling songs in a while, and *Mamouna* is something of a middling affair, almost too tasteful for its own good (and considering who this is, that's saying something). There are some songs of note—"The 39 Steps" has a slightly menacing vibe to it, appropriate given the cinematic reference of the title, while the Ferry/Eno collaboration "Wildcat Days" displays some of Eno's old synth-melting flash. Overall, though, *Mamouna* is pleasant without being involving. *—Ned Raggett*

● **More Than This: The Best of Bryan Ferry and Roxy Music** / Oct. 5, 1999 / Virgin ♦♦♦♦

It may seem that the same *Best of Roxy Music & Bryan Ferry* keeps being reissued under different names, first *Street Life* in 1986 and then *More Than This* in 1999, because in a way it is. *More Than This* shares no less than 15 tracks with the 20-track *Street Life*. Instead of giving time to the great, arty side of Roxy Music, it concentrates on Bryan Ferry the crooner, which means "Pyjamarama" and "Do the Strand" are no longer here, but such latter-day solo cuts as "Don't Stop the Dance," "Kiss and Tell," and "I Put a Spell On You" (all not on *Street Life*) are, along with "I'm in the Mood For Love," a "preview" of his standards album *As Time Goes By*, which was released just a week after *More Than This*. All this track shuffling doesn't result in a radically different collection, though it is one that is slightly worse than its predecessor, since it doesn't really do Roxy justice. If it had been assembled as a collection of Ferry's solo material, it might have been a little more useful (then again, the casual fan who would buy a collection of Ferry hits would probably want the latter-day Roxy singles, since Ferry just didn't have that many hits on his own), but as it stands, *More Than This* is just an acceptable, entertaining sampler. *—Stephen Thomas Erlewine*

As Time Goes By / Oct. 19, 1999 / Virgin ♦♦♦

Bryan Ferry invests considerable time and energy in cover albums (he should, considering that they compose a good portion of his solo catalog), treating them with as much care as a record of original material. He's always found ways to radically reinvent the songs he sings, so it's easy to expect that his collection of pop standards, *As Time Goes By*, would re-imagine the familiar. Instead, *As Time Goes By* is his first classicist album, containing non-ironic, neo-traditionalist arrangements of songs associated with the '30s. That doesn't mean it's a lavish affair, dripping with lush orchestras—it's considerably more intimate than that. Even when strings surface, they're understated, part of a small live combo that supports Ferry throughout the record. He's made the music as faithful to its era as possible, yet instead of rigidly replicating the sounds of the '30s, he's blended Billie Holiday, cabaret pop, and movie musicals into an evocative pastiche. Ferry is at his best when he's exploring the possibilities within a specific theory or concept; with *As Time Goes By*, he eases into these standards and old-fashioned settings like an actor adopting a new persona. Since Ferry has always been a crooner, the transition is smooth and suave. He makes no attempt to alter his tremulous style, yet it rarely sounds incongruous—he may sound a little vampirish on "You Do Something to Me," but that's the rare case where he doesn't seamlessly mesh with his romantic, sepia-toned surroundings. On the surface, it may seem like a departure for Ferry, but in the end, it's entirely of a piece with his body of work. True, it may not be a major album in the scheme of things, but it's easy to be seduced by its casual elegance. *—Stephen Thomas Erlewine*

Slave to Love: Best of the Ballads / Aug. 8, 2000 / Virgin ♦♦♦♦

When *Slave to Love: The Best of the Ballads* was released in 2000, there hadn't been a true Roxy Music compilation in print for years. *Street Life* and *More Than This* were both grab bags of Roxy Music singles and material from Bryan Ferry's solo career. While it's logical to assume that fans of one artist would certainly be interested in the other, the approach never made for a unified compilation—Roxy Music's sound shifted quite a bit over the years, and their earlier, edgier singles never sat well next to the smooth balladeering of Ferry's companion career. However, *Slave to Love* is the first Ferry/Roxy grab bag to make internal sense, because it's thematically limited to the Roxy material that most resembles Ferry's crooning solo style. By the time of 1982's *Avalon*, the gap between the two had narrowed so much as to be virtually indistinguishable, and this compilation captures the elegantly romantic sound that came to be inextricably linked to Ferry. *Slave to Love* shouldn't be taken as comprehensive, even in this narrower vein (there are several excellent late-period Roxy Music singles missing), but as an encapsulation of one specific part of their appeal, it makes for a strong listen. *—Steve Huey*

The Field Mice

f. 1988, **db.** 1991

Indie Pop, Twee Pop

The flagship band of the legendary Sarah Records, the Field Mice neatly encapsulated the label's trademark wispy, lovelorn pop sound and remain among the most beloved British cult bands of their time. Debuting in 1988 with the single "Emma's House," the Field Mice were originally comprised of singer/guitarist Robert Wratten and bassist Michael Hiscock; initially dismissed in the U.K. press as little more than twee-pop fluff, over the course of subsequent releases like 1989's "Sensitive" and the *So Said Kay* EP, the group earned not only a devout following but also grudging critical respect, in the process becoming Sarah's best-selling band. Later growing to a quintet with the additions of guitarist Harvey Williams, keyboardist Annemari Davies, and drummer Mark Dobson, the group held fast to their label's singles-only policy until a much-requested compilation LP, *Coastal*, was finally released in mid-1991; a studio album, *For Keeps*, appeared just a few months later. However, in the wake of a November, 1991 Glasgow live date which ended in onstage fisticuffs, the Field Mice essentially disbanded, playing one final London farewell gig before splitting for good; Wratten, Davies, and Dobson later reunited in Northern Picture Library and Trembling Blue Stars. *—Jason Ankeny*

For Keeps / 1991 / Sarah ♦♦♦♦

What turned out to be the only full studio album the Field Mice released was also nothing less than a quietly triumphant masterpiece. Building on the strength of its string of great singles while keeping its own particular character and mood, *For Keeps*—a sly and sharp title, given how many of the band's songs reflected both love's creation and dissolution—found the five piece full of gently impassioned creativity. It could be the subtle funk wah-wah guitars on the opening "Five Moments" or the blissout psych droning of "Tilting at Windmills," but writing the Field Mice off as simple twee-pop types would be a hard task for anyone after a listen to this album. In the end, the group stood apart from all the early '90s scenes swirling around it to make its own mark. Davies' softly cool vocals, winsome without being cloying, brought both greater variety and range of emotion to the songs. Wratten's still in fine voice, and together their duets work perfectly, almost defining the form that many other bands clearly inspired by them would take. On his own Wratten experiments with his voice, adding flanging to the just-epic-enough guitar build of "This Is Not Here" and elsewhere piling on the echo and other tricks for fine variety. The subtle musical nods all over the map fit the band's impressive range of influences, while avoiding drowning in them. There's the hint of late-'50s/early-'60s tearjerker drama in "Star of David," for instance, heightened by the sharp growl of the guitars against the slow, building punch of the drums. In the end it's the Field Mice, but it's a much more accomplished and intriguing Field Mice than the band's detractors (and possibly many of its followers) would ever give it real credit for. *—Ned Raggett*

● **Where'd You Learn to Kiss That Way?** / 1998 / Shinkansen ♦♦♦♦♦

Although revered in certain indie circles, for far too long the Field Mice appeared in danger of languishing as the great lost pop band of the early '90s, their records out of print and fetching obscene prices on the collector market; a lavish two-disc retrospective worthy of their growing legacy, the extraordinary *Where'd You Learn to Kiss That Way?* finally restores the group to their rightful prominence, assembling all of the key tracks they released on the legendary Sarah label between 1988 and 1991. With their shimmering guitars, indelible melodies, lush arrangements, and Bobby Wratten's heartbreaking songs, in retrospect the Field Mice now seem like the missing link between the Smiths and Belle & Sebastian—at their best ("Emma's House," "This Love Is Not Wrong," "Coach Station Reunion," and countless others), they achieve the same kind of pop transcendence, spinning tales of love and loss with an elegance and grandeur that are often breathtaking. And while it's a shame Shinkansen didn't opt to include a third disc and release the band's complete recorded output, each of the 36 tracks which did make the cut sparkles; no longer lost, the Field Mice were simply a great pop band, and with *Where'd You Learn to Kiss That Way?*, their music might finally reach the wide audience it so richly deserves. *—Jason Ankeny*

Fields of the Nephilim

f. 1984, **db.** 1991

Goth Rock, Alternative Pop/Rock

Of all the bands involved in Britain's goth-rock movement of the 1980s, Fields of the Nephilim were the most believable. The group's cryptic, occult-inspired songs were sung in a guttural roar by vocalist Carl McCoy. Live appearances were shrouded with dim light and smoke machines, while bandmembers stalked the stage in black desperado gear inspired by western dress. The group was also one of the longest lived of the original goth-rock groups, finally breaking up in 1991 when McCoy left for another project.

Fields of the Nephilim formed in 1984, in Stevenage, Hertfordshire, with an original lineup of McCoy, guitarist Paul Wright, his brother Nod on drums, saxophonist Gary Whisker, and bassist Tony Pettit. The quintet played many live shows and released the EP *Burning the Fields* in late 1984. Whisker then left the band, just as Peter Yates was added as a second guitarist. Beggar's Banquet, also the home of goth-rockers Southern Death Cult and Bauhaus, signed the Nephilim and released the singles "Power" and "Preacher Man" in 1986. Both did well on the independent charts; "Preacher Man" made it to number two, increasing the expectation for debut album *Dawnrazor*, which appeared in 1987. The album also did well on the indie charts, but later that year Fields of the Nephilim finally cracked the pop singles chart with "Blue Water." In June 1988, second album *The Nephilim* reached number 12 in the pop charts, while the single "Moonchild" made number 28. A live video titled *Forever Remain* was also released in 1988.

The May 1989 single "Psychonaut" also cracked the Top 40, but the resulting *Elyzium* (1990) proved to be the group's last studio effort. The live double album *Earth Inferno* was also released in 1990, and the singles "For Her Light" and "Sumerland (Dreamed)" both charted, but Carl McCoy left the band—and took the name with him—in October 1991. Remaining members Yates, Pettit, and the Wright brothers added vocalist Alan Delaney and released *What Starts, Ends* (1992) as Rubicon; McCoy formed Nefilim, and began releasing material, including the 1996 album *Zoon*. Beggar's Banquet issued a two-disc retrospective in 1994 titled *Revelations*. —*John Bush*

Returning to Gehenna / 1986 / Supporti ✦✦✦

Dawnrazor / 1987 / Beggars Banquet ✦✦✦

The Nephilim / 1988 / Beggars Banquet ✦✦✦✦✦
Having built a considerable and passionate fanbase, the Nephilim approached their second album with confidence and a clutch of stunning new songs. The resulting, semi-self-titled release blows away the first by a mile (the art design alone, depicting an ancient, worn book with strange symbols, is a winner), being an elegantly produced and played monster of dark, powerful rock. Even if McCoy's cries and husked whispers don't appeal to all, once the listener gets past that to the music, the band simply goes off, incorporating their various influences—especially a good dollop of pre-*Dark Side of the Moon* Pink Floyd (think songs like "One of These Days")—to create a massive blast of a record. Buchanan again produces with a careful ear for maximum impact, whether it be the roaring rage of "Chord of Souls" or the minimal guitar and slight keyboard wash of "Celebrate"; McCoy's vocal on the latter is especially fine as a careful, calm brood that matches the music. Perhaps most surprising about the album is that it yielded an honest-to-goodness U.K. Top 40 hit with "Moonchild," which is very much in the vein of earlier songs like "Preacher Man" but with just enough of a catchier chorus and softer guitar part in the verse to make a wider mark. Though the first part of the album is quite fine, including such longtime fan favorites as "The Watchman" and "Phobia," after "Moonchild" the record simply doesn't let up, building to a fantastic three-song conclusion. "Celebrate" is followed by "Love Under Will," a windswept, gloomily romantic number with a lovely combination of the band's regular push and extra keyboards for effect. "Last Exit for the Lost" wraps everything up on an astonishing high; starting off softly with just bass, synths, one guitar, and McCoy, it then gently speeds up more and more, pumping up the volume and finally turning into a momentous, unstoppable tidal wave of electric energy. —*Ned Raggett*

Elizium / 1990 / Beggars Banquet ✦✦✦✦✦
For the first time since *Dawnrazor*, the Nephilim worked with someone other than Bill Buchanan as producer; whatever Andy Jackson's particular qualifications, happily he knew not to ruin a good thing. The end result was the band's best all-around album, consisting of four lengthy pieces that showcase their now near-peerless abilities to create involved, textured, driving, and loud pieces of rock. It was still goth as all heck, but like the best bands in any genre, the Nephilim transcended such artificial limitations to create their own sound. McCoy still comes up with an occasionally curious lyric, to put it mildly, but such is the power of his performance as well as the band's that, at least for the time it's playing, *Elizium* really does sound like it's about to call up darkling spirits from the nether planes. The opening song is divided into four parts but mainly known by its second, "For Her Light," which was edited into a single. It moves from initial crashes of noise, feedback, and keyboards to catchier brooding and riff action, a calmer midsection with appropriate samples of Alistair Crowley, and a last slamming run to the song's conclusion. "Submission" stands on its own, switching between minimal bass with guitar stabs and massive crescendos. "Sumerland (What Dreams May Come)" takes the apocalyptic element of the Nephilim to its furthest extent; its relentless pulse supports some of the most powerful guitar out there while McCoy achieves a similar high point with his commanding voice. "Wail of Sumer" concludes *Elizium* on a striking two-part note, gently floating rather than exploding over its length, while McCoy's lost, regretful voice drifts along with it as a soft, yet still unnerving conclusion. Combine that with another fantastic job on art design, and *Elizium*, once you accept the Nephilim's basic conceits, simply stuns. —*Ned Raggett*

Earth Inferno / 1991 / Beggars Banquet ✦✦✦

● **Revelations** / 1994 / Beggars Banquet ✦✦✦✦✦
Intelligently selected and sequenced, this near-complete overview of the Nephilim's career, excepting the earliest EPs, is both the best starting point for newcomers to the band as well as convincing evidence for the band's compelling blend of styles and sources into a commanding combination. Nearly all of the hits are here—"Moonchild," "Preacher Man," "Psychonaut" (in its "Lib III" incarnation), "For Her Light," and "Power"—plus a judicious choice of album cuts. "Chord of Souls" and "Watchman" make the grade, though surprisingly neither the album version nor the single take of "Sumerland" appears. Some of the single edits do bear remarkable differences from the album takes. "For Her Light," as an example, gets a calmer mid-song break, while its conclusion consists of McCoy's vocals run backward over a fade of the main melody, instead of the sudden end on *Elizium*. Generally, though, these are the album cuts as recorded, filling out the CD's length to the max. A wise nod to *Earth Inferno* appears at the end when the insanely powerful live cut of "Dawnrazor" appears instead of the studio take. Horror novelist Storm Constantine provides appreciative liner notes, detailing the history of the band quite thoroughly and making especial note of the Nephilim's awesome live shows and artistic promotional videos. As a further enticement, initial copies included a second bonus disc with a grab bag of B-sides, alternate takes, and other rarities. —*Ned Raggett*

From Gehenna to Here / Jul. 17, 2001 / Santeria ✦✦✦

The 5th Dimension

f. 1966, Los Angeles, CA
Sunshine Pop, Pop-Soul, Pop
They didn't sound anything like an R&B group, and their soaring, lighter-than-air harmonic blend frequently proved more palatable to pop audiences than to black record buyers but did not suggest, even for a second, that the 5th Dimension was in any way lacking in soul.

Formed as the Versatiles in 1965, the slick quintet changed its name at the request of Johnny Rivers, who had just signed them to his brand new label, Soul City. Up-and-coming songwriter Jimmy Webb supplied the group with their first pop smash "Up, Up and Away," in 1967, and the group's monumental rise mirrored the song's high-flying imagery. Another prolific composer, Laura Nyro, handed the 5th Dimension several megahits, notably "Stoned Soul Picnic" and "Wedding Bell Blues," but their biggest seller hailed from the groundbreaking musical *Hair*. The Grammy-winning "Aquarius/Let the Sunshine In" held down the number one slot on the pop lists for six weeks in 1969.

After several more hits, Marilyn McCoo and Billy Davis Jr., who had married while part of the group, successfully branched off as a duo, while Lamonte McLemore, Ron Townson, and Florence LaRue kept the 5th Dimension on the soul charts, losing a head-to-head battle with Diana Ross for hit status on "Love Hangover" in 1976. —*Bill Dahl*

Up, Up and Away / May 1967 / Buddha ✦✦✦

The Magic Garden / Dec. 1967 / Buddha ✦✦✦
This record did contain the small hits "Paper Cup" and "Carpet Man," but the group, or more likely arranger/conductor Jim Webb, was probably shooting for something a bit higher than the Top 40. Aside from a misfired cover of the Beatles' "Ticket to Ride," Webb wrote everything on this album, which—with between-track segues, lyrics expounding dreams and possibility, and dense orchestral settings—seemed to be aiming for a song cycle of sorts. It's not *Pet Sounds*, however, or even Van Dyke Parks' *Song Cycle*. It's over-ambitious MOR pop-soul with mild psychedelic colors, and a bit ludicrous, though not unattractive due to the typically conscientious harmonies. "Orange Air" is probably the group's best shot at pseudo-psychedelia; "The Girls' Song," on much firmer MOR territory, was done much better by Jackie DeShannon; and "The Worst That Could Happen," Webb at his most disagreeably sentimental, was covered for a huge hit by the Brooklyn Bridge about a year later. A recent biography of cult singer/songwriter Nick Drake, by the way, revealed that this album, along with such estimable underground classics as Love's *Forever Changes* and Van Morrison's *Astral Weeks*, was a special favorite of his because of its combination of rock and orchestration. That means it might suddenly become a lot harder to find in the dollar bins, although many of those copies will probably find their way right back there after Drake fans play it once or twice. [The album was also reissued by Soul City under the title *The Worst That Could Happen*.] —*Richie Unterberger*

Stoned Soul Picnic / Aug. 1968 / Buddha ✦✦✦
One of the 5th Dimension's finest all-around albums, *Stoned Soul Picnic* is not only home to the title tracks, but also to the hits "Sweet Blindness" and "California Soul." All three of these songs provide excellent examples of the band's sunny and buoyant appeal. Although the singers' awesome vocal gifts deserve all the credit they get, it's also important to realize the immense contributions from producer Bones Howe and vocal arranger Bob Alcivar. The group was far more than a black version of the Mamas & the Papas. There are also some excellent album cuts here, such as Jeff Companor's "It'll Never Be the Same Again," where Ron Townson's exquisite soul pipes get off an amazing solo around an excellent Motown-driven arrangement. If you're going to pick up one 5th Dimension album (aside from a greatest hits package), you'd be hard-pressed to find a better one than this. —*Matthew Greenwald*

The Age of Aquarius / May 1969 / Buddha ✦✦✦✦
The Age of Aquarius, the 5th Dimension's fourth album, was the group's commercial peak. They had already topped the charts with their medley of two songs from the Broadway musical *Hair*, "The Age of Aquarius" and "Let the Sunshine In (The Flesh Failures)," a platinum single that would earn them Grammy Awards for Record of the Year and Best Contemporary Vocal Performance, Group, when they released this album. It turned out that was only the tip of the iceberg: They returned to number one with another platinum single, "Wedding Bell Blues," penned by Laura Nyro, who had given them "Stoned Soul Picnic" the year before. And the album also spawned Top 40 hits in Nyro's "Blowing Away" and Neil Sedaka's "Workin' on a Groovy Thing." The 5th Dimension were the successors to the L.A. vocal group mantle passed on by The Mamas and the Papas (they even inherited the studio band of Hal Blaine, Joe Osborne, and Larry Knechtel). They smoothed out and commercialized everything they sang, and their work had a sheen and a zest that sometimes contrasted with the original tone of the material. On Broadway, the *Hair* songs seemed full of hippie rebellion; here, they seemed enthusiastic and optimistic. In a conflicted time, the 5th Dimension thrived on their ability to equivocate, and this album was their triumph—just listen to them harmonize on "Sunshine of Your Love"! —*William Ruhlmann*

Portrait / Apr. 1970 / Buddha ✦✦✦✦
Along with *Stoned Soul Picnic*, this may very well be the 5th Dimension's finest album. Home to one of their finest singles ever—the Bacharach/David "One Less Bell to Answer," on which Marilyn McCoo gives the vocal performance of her career—the record also contains the surprisingly funky and rocking "Puppet Man." Some great covers also include Dave Mason's "Feelin' Alright," Jimmy Webb's gorgeous "This Is Your Life," and Laura Nyro's anthemic "Save the Country." This vibe is echoed by the album's centerpiece, a medley of "A Change Is Gonna Come" and "People Gotta Be Free" preceded by "The Declaration." It's an ambitious suite, yet one that works well; it provides a great marriage between the group's pop leanings and the counterculture of the late '60s. Progressive, yet

still encapsulating, which is the 5th Dimension's sunny appeal, *Portrait* is a minor masterpiece. Famed expressionist artist Leroy Neiman's appropriate cover and liner paintings are literally icing on the cake. *—Matthew Greenwald*

• **Greatest Hits on Earth** / Sep. 1972 / Arista ♦♦♦♦♦
Until Rhino issued its anthology, this was the best hits package for the 5th Dimension, a group that in its peak was among the best at doing lighthearted pop with a soulful foundation. Certainly, they weren't a hardcore R&B or earthy singing group, but they did put some punch into songs that were really kind of silly otherwise, like "Wedding Bell Blues." *—Ron Wynn*

Up Up & Away: The Definitive Collection / May 20, 1997 / Arista ♦♦♦♦♦
The subtitle on this anthology is correct: This is truly the definitive collection of the 5th Dimension's music, including all the hits and most of the album cuts that anyone could want. The 20-bit digital mastering provides a crisp, bright audio experience, and the joyous harmonies bring back the positive side of the late '60s/early '70s era in which the songs were recorded. The megahits are all here: Jimmy Webb's "Up Up and Away," Laura Nyro's "Stoned Soul Picnic" and "Wedding Bell Blues," the Bacharach/David opus "One Less Bell to Answer," the beautiful "(Last Night) I Didn't Get to Sleep at All" and the Grammy-winning number one smash from the spring of 1969, "Aquarius/Let the Sunshine In" from *Hair.* There are not-quite-Top-Ten hits like "Sweet Blindness," "Go Where You Wanna Go," "California Soul," "Workin' on a Groovy Thing," "Blowing Away," "Save the Country," and "Love's Lines, Angles and Rhymes." What a run this quintet had on the pop charts from 1967 to 1972. This two-disc set successfully makes the case for the 5th Dimension to be remembered among the finest purveyors of pop song vocal harmony in the rock era. Baby Boomers will delight at the memories this collection conjures up and will find surprises they may have forgotten or never known: "Paper Cup," "Carpet Man," "Puppet Man," "Light Sings," and the group's medley of "The Declaration/A Change Is Gonna Come/People Gotta Be Free." Listening to *Up Up and Away: The Definitive Collection* is a great antidote for the blues, lifting the listener up with a smile and reminding those who may have forgotten that there once was a time when it seemed that music really could bring us all together. *—Jim Newsom*

The Master Hits: The 5th Dimension / Jul. 27, 1999 / Arista ♦♦♦♦
Arista celebrated its 30th anniversary by releasing *The Heritage Series*, spotlighting the most popular artists on the label. The Fifth Dimension installment in *The Heritage Series* is pretty much a straight hits collection—the first such assembled on the pop-soul group. While they were at Arista, the Fifth Dimension had such hits as "Up Up and Away," "Go Where You Wanna Go," "Stoned Soul Picnic," "Aquarius/Let the Sunshine In," and "Wedding Bell Blues." All those songs are here, along with some highlights from their albums, providing a nice retrospective of their time with Arista. *—Stephen Thomas Erlewine*

Fine Young Cannibals

f. 1984, Birmingham, England
College Rock, Blue-Eyed Soul, Pop/Rock
When the Beat (known as the English Beat in the U.S. only) split in 1983, it came as a surprise to guitarist Dave Cox and bassist David Steele. The first time they realized that the group's vocalists, Ranking Roger and Dave Wakelin, had gone off to form a group without them was when their accountant phoned to finalize the divorce. While the defectors had formed General Public, Cox and Steele set about creating something new of their own. Apart from not wanting to repeat the mistakes the Beat made, and a vague notion of adding both jazz and soul to the Beat's ska roots (they also decided to feature a strong vocalist), there was no real master plan. They found Roland Gift singing with a barroom R&B band named the Bones, looking like Sidney Poitier but sounding like Otis Redding. He was their man. Gift had spent his teenage years in youth theatre, until the advent of punk made music his main passion. As punk gave way to the two-tone ska, which gave rise to groups like Madness and, ultimately, the Beat, Gift took up saxophone and singing in a local band. Keeping live work down to just the occasional one-off date, the Fine Young Cannibals signed to London Records in early 1985. Resisting the record company's attempts to team them up with a producer, the Fine Young Cannibals released a demo version of "Johnny Come Home" as their first single. Its instant success allowed them to team up with a compatible producer, Robin Miller, for the first Fine Young Cannibals album. Five years later, a second album emerged, *The Raw and the Cooked.* The single "She Drives Me Crazy" was a worldwide number one hit. Since then, the Fine Young Cannibals have remained elusive. *—Ed Nimmervoll*

Fine Young Cannibals / Dec. 1985 / IRS ♦♦♦♦
When Dave Wakeling and Ranking Roger split from the rest of the English Beat to form General Public, Andy Cox and Dave Steele originally advertised on MTV for a new lead singer for the Beat. When that didn't pan out (although it did work for Wall of Voodoo), Cox and Steele hooked up with the unique and soulful singer Roland Gift and formed the Fine Young Cannibals. Though the trio first hit the mass U.S. consciousness with 1989's electronic dance-pop *The Raw and the Cooked,* their 1985 debut was a soul-jazz pop charmer that's more low key but every bit as entertaining. Along the lines of early Everything But the Girl (the two groups share a producer, Robin Millar) with a heavier Motown influence, the songs on *Fine Young Cannibals* are uniformly strong. The singles "Johnny Come Home" (a plea to a runaway that sounds like the Beat's ska stripped down to its tense and obsessive essentials) and "Blue" (one of the more oblique and successful anti-Margaret Thatcher tracks of its era) are terrific, but album tracks like the casually devastating "Funny How Love Is" and the manic "Like a Stranger" (which incongruously ends with a female chorus shrieking "You've been too long in an institution!" repeatedly while Gift tries out his Otis Redding impression) are even better. The album's highlight, though, is a reworking of "Suspicious Minds" (with scarifying backing vocals by Jimmy Somerville) that, while it doesn't replace Elvis' version, certainly takes the song into an interesting new direction. Although often overlooked, especially in the U.S., in the wake of their massively successful follow-up, *Fine Young Cannibals* is a powerful and satisfying debut. The U.S. CD adds two extended remixes of "Johnny Come Home" and "Suspicious Minds." *—Stewart Mason*

• **The Raw & the Cooked** / Feb. 20, 1989 / IRS ♦♦♦♦♦
One of the most exciting albums released during a decade of artifice and extravagance, in a mere ten songs and 35 minutes the Fine Young Cannibals created a masterpiece. Admittedly the trio had some help—backing singers, guest musicians (including former Squeeze pianoman Jools Holland and Talking Heads' Jerry Harrison)—but that doesn't take away the band's own accomplishment. Remaining true to the FYC's vision of tying past and present musical styles together into artful new pop packages, *The Raw & the Cooked* features a shopping list of genres. Mod, funk, Motown, British beat, R&B, punk, rock, and even disco are embedded within the songs, while the rhythms, many synthetically created, are equally diverse. Two-thirds of the record were released as U.K. singles, all were hits, and each one proudly boasted a distinctly different blend of styles. "Good Thing," for example, was the trio's tribute to the legendary all-night Northern soul parties of the '60s, but is much more than a mere meld of mod and Motown. It's actually built round a slinky R&B riff, fueled by a boogie-woogie piano, and slammed home with a cracking beat. "I'm Not the Man I Used to Be" is a torrid torch song, but fired by a futuristic jungle beat and an almost housey production. Then, of course, there's "She Drives Me Crazy," which features the most unique, and instantly identifiable, beat/riff combination of the decade. Even the four tracks that didn't make the singles cut could have, if MCA had the audacity to keep releasing them. Every one of *Raw's* tracks simmers with creativity, as the hooks, sharp melodies, and irrepressible beats are caressed by nuanced arrangements and sparkling production. Never has music's past, present, and future been more exceptionally combined. *—Jo-Ann Greene*

Finest / Nov. 26, 1996 / MCA ♦♦♦♦♦
Fine Young Cannibals only released two albums, so it's slightly unusual that they even have a greatest hits collection like *Fine Young Cannibals Finest.* After all, a dedicated fan will have both records, and casual fans will only want the singles on *The Raw and the Cooked,* thereby eliminating the audience for the collection. Despite these misgivings, *Finest* does its job well, featuring 12 of their biggest hits and best-known songs ("She Drives Me Crazy," "Johnny Come Home," "Good Thing," "Suspicious Minds," "Don't Look Back"), plus two unreleased cuts ("The Flame" and "Since You've Been Gone") to entice collectors. If you want the highlights, *Finest* is fine, but most fans will want to stick with the two original albums. *—Stephen Thomas Erlewine*

Finn Brothers

f. 1994
Adult Alternative Pop/Rock, Pop/Rock
Brothers Tim and Neil Finn have been making music together since their childhood in Te Awamutu, New Zealand, continuing through to international success in Split Enz and Crowded House. However, it wasn't until late 1989 that they actually started writing together—a reunion that yielded more than a dozen songs for a proposed Finn Brothers side project. That album was scrapped and most of the material was absorbed by Crowded House's *Woodface* (1991) and *Together Alone* (1993), as well as Tim's 1993 solo album, *Before & After.* The brothers' project resumed in late 1994, and in four weeks, they completed an album called simply *Finn.* The album, released in the fall of 1995 (the summer of 1996 in the U.S.), showed a much more casual side of the Finns and was less pop-oriented than their previous musical collaborations—the brothers play nearly all of the instruments themselves, ranging from the primitive to the exotic. After initial pressings of *Finn,* the duo changed their name to the Finn Brothers to avoid confusion with a band going under a similar name. *—Chris Woodstra*

• **Finn** / Oct. 1995 / Discovery ♦♦♦♦♦
Finn is the long rumored and awaited collaboration between brothers Tim and Neil Finn. The first reports of the project in 1990 promised an album of "just acoustic guitars and lots of harmonies," and when that material was absorbed by Crowded House for *Woodface,* it was proven that the team was capable of making near-perfect pop. Those expecting Woodface Part 2, however, are in for a surprise—*Finn* is a moody, atmospheric album that shows a more spontaneous and experimental side with the brothers playing all of the instruments, including ukuleles, Chamberlain keyboards, mellotron, and tea chest bass. Though most projects of this nature get hung up on the "concept," this one succeeds because the Finns' pop songwriting sense allows the songs to come first. Despite the lack of polish and the odd setting, the material on this album is among the pair's finest, together or apart. *—Chris Woodstra*

Neil Finn (Neil Mullane Finn)

b. May 27, 1958, Te Awamutu, New Zealand
Vocals, Guitar / New Zealand Rock, Adult Alternative Pop/Rock, Singer/Songwriter
Neil Finn has consistently proven his knack for crafting high quality songs that combine irresistible melodies with meticulous lyrical detail, from his beginnings as the precocious junior member of Split Enz, through his leadership of Crowded House, earning commercial success, respect from his peers, praise from critics, and a devoted fan base.

Born Neil Mullane Finn, May 27, 1958, in Te Awamutu New Zealand, Finn cut his musical teeth as a child by performing for family friends, harmonizing with elder brother Tim. Finn took up piano, studying the songcraft of the Beatles, Elton John, and David Bowie, while watching his brother Tim's band, Split Enz, become a musical force in Australia. Following a few opening slots for Split Enz in 1976, he formed the After Hours.

The group showed a great deal of promise, but came to a relatively quick end when Phil Judd left Split Enz and brother Tim offered the slot to Neil. Just before his 19th birthday, even though he'd never played electric guitar, Neil joined Split Enz as lead guitarist.

Neil stayed in the background for the first two albums of his membership—1977's *Dizrhythmia* and 1978's *Frenzy*—but emerged with the infectious "I Got You" for *True Colours*. The single was an immediate hit, saving the band from obscurity and, most likely, from imminent breakup. Split Enz enjoyed moderate international success for the next several years until disbanding in 1985. Neil followed with Crowded House, a combo that found both critical acclaim and massive commercial success internationally. In 1996, Neil decided to dissolve the band in favor of a solo career.

In 1998, he released his first solo album, the critically acclaimed *Try Whistling This*. That same year, he contributed a cover of "I Can See Clearly Now" to the animated feature *Antz* and, in mid-1999, he released the charity single, "Can You Hear Us?" In 2001 Finn prepared to release his second solo album, *One Nil*. *—Chris Woodstra*

● **Try Whistling This** / Jun. 16, 1998 / Work ✦✦✦✦✦
When Neil Finn closed the doors on Crowded House, all signs seemed to point to a more experimental direction for future solo releases; even the title of his first solo album, *Try Whistling This*, implies a reaction against his reputation for well-crafted, highly melodic songs. However, from the opening track, the light and breezy "Last One Standing," Finn puts all fears to rest. *Try Whistling This* does dabble in experimentation—most notably in the feedback and distorted vocals of the parnoid "Twisty Bass" and the mild trip-hop groove of "Sinner"—but thoughout, he shows restraint, tastefully incorporating more exotic effects while staying true to his high melodic standard and meticulous songcraft. Finn seems clearly freed from the restraints of being in a band, allowing him to try a lot of different ideas, from the sweeping "Souvenir" to the instant pop classic of "She Will Have Her Way" to more delicate atmospheric pieces like the title track, ultimately creating his most complex and diverse set to date. And though many of the songs take time to reveal their treasures, it's worth the effort. *Try Whistling This* features some of Finn's best work yet, and in a nearly flawless catalog like his, that's quite impressive. *—Chris Woodstra*

One Nil / Mar. 19, 2001 / EMI ✦✦✦✦✦
In retrospect, *Try Whistling This*, Neil Finn's solo debut, seems like a conscious effort to distance himself from Crowded House. Filled with studio trickery, distorted microphones, and trendy vague trip-hop beats, the album was a deliberate move to establish himself as a separate, more adventurous entity from Crowded House—yet one that remained a gifted, melodic songwriter. This is all put into sharp relief by his second solo album, *One Nil*, a record that finds him returning to solid ground, delivering his most straightforward album since Crowded House's *Woodface*. Curiously, for an album that plays to his strengths, a good portion is the result of a fruitful collaboration with Wendy & Lisa, plus a production pairing with Tchad Blake and numerous cameo spots, including Sheryl Crow, Lisa Germano, and Mitchell Froom. For all the guests and star power, the record is surprisingly subtle, lacking the knockout punches of *Try Whistling This*, where the singles leapt out of the grooves. This time around, the songs are gently insinuating, slowly working their way into the subconscious. Even the songs with the biggest hooks, such as the first single "Rest of the Day Off," aren't as immediate as "She Will Have Her Way." Yet, on repeated plays, the record begins to gel, revealing itself as a reliably solid effort from Finn. There may not be any new revelations, yet the little details—the turns of phrase, the gently persuasive melodies, the slyly detailed productions—all confirm his status as a gifted craftsman. *—Stephen Thomas Erlewine*

Tim Finn (Brian Timothy Finn)

b. Jun. 25, 1952, Te Awamutu, New Zealand
Vocals, Keyboards, Guitar, Drums, Piano / College Rock, Adult Alternative Pop/Rock, New Wave, Singer/Songwriter
Singer/songwriter keyboardist/guitarist Tim Finn was born in Te Awamutu, New Zealand. Influenced by not only British Invasion acts like the Beatles, the Move and the Kinks, but also his Catholic upbringing and the communal sing-alongs of the native Maori people, Finn founded the '70s art-rock turned new wave band Split Enz, leading the band through several albums to moderate international success. The success of the between-albums solo project, *Escapade*, led to his leaving the band in 1983. He followed with the more ambitious second album, *Big Canoe* (1985) which went virtually ignored (it was unreleased in the U.S. until the success of his brother's band, Crowded House, stirred up enough interest by 1988). Finn returned in 1989 with a self-titled album for Capitol Records. Despite good reviews, this too failed to make much impact. He joined his brother Neil Finn's band, Crowded House, for their *Woodface* album but left mid-tour and released his fourth solo album, *Before and After* in 1993. In 1995, he joined with Hothouse Flowers' Liam O Maonlai and Andy White, releasing an album under the group name ALT. A long-rumored collaboration between the Finn brothers was finally released in late 1995 under the name Finn Brothers (it was released in the spring of 1996 in the U.S.). Finn returned to his solo career by the fall of 1996. In 1999, Finn completed work on his fifth solo album, *Say It Is So*, which was released early the following year. *—Scott Bultman and Chris Woodstra*

Escapade / 1983 / A&M ✦✦✦
Following Split Enz's *Time & Tide*, Tim Finn took his first break from the band with *Escapade*, a collection of light pop songs, some of which dated back to the late '70s but never seemed to quite fit in the Enz format. A flawed though fun album, *Escapade* managed several hits in Australasia and Europe and revealed a considerably brighter, more mainstream aspect to Finn's writing. And while the album was successful and a satisfying diversion, it unquestionably served to derail the forward momentum of Split Enz and led to Finn's leaving the band the following year. *—Chris Woodstra*

Big Canoe / 1985 / Virgin ✦✦✦
Tim Finn teamed up with playwright Jeremy Brock for his second solo outing, *Big Canoe*. Although the collaboration is predictably ambitious—probably Finn's most ambitious since the early days of Split Enz—beneath all the overblown arrangements and slightly dated production lie some terrific songs. Material like "No Thunder No Fire No Rain," "Hyacinth," and "Carve You in Marble" deserves a better setting, but the album is still able to shine, and some minor flaws are forgivable, especially to diehard fans. *Big Canoe* also marks a welcome reunion between Finn and ex-Enz collaborator Phil Judd, who contributes sitar and rhythm guitar to a couple of tracks. *—Chris Woodstra*

● **Tim Finn** / 1989 / Capitol ✦✦✦✦✦
Perhaps in response to the failed big production of *Big Canoe* and the success of brother Neil's back-to-basics outfit, Crowded House, Finn simplified his approach for his self-titled album, joining forces with Crowded House producer Mitchell Froom. A touching and intensely personal album, Finn bares all, revealing self-doubts, regrets, and a failed relationship with intricate detail. And despite the subject matter, the album has an optimistic, uplifting overall tone, with tasteful adult-pop arrangements perfectly complementing his strongest melodies and finest songwriting to date. Though the sound and sentiments could have (and should have) easily found an audience in the emerging "adult alternative pop" format, the album went virtually ignored. *—Chris Woodstra*

Before & After / Aug. 10, 1993 / Capitol ✦✦✦✦✦
On his fourth solo album, Finn dabbles in dance-pop, pseudo-reggae, and folky ballads, with a different set of producers on nearly every track. While this leads to a certain lack of consistency, Finn's songwriting has never been stronger. He has the most success on the self-produced, stripped-down tracks where his strong sense of melody and knack for catchy pop hooks are allowed to be in the forefront. "Persuasion," co-written by Richard Thompson and "In Love With It All," written with his brother Neil Finn (Crowded House) are highlights. *—Chris Woodstra*

Say It Is So / Feb. 29, 2000 / W.A.R.? ✦✦✦✦
Seven years separated Tim Finn's fourth album, 1993's *Before & After*, and his fifth, *Say It Is So*, by which time he was left without a label. With a backlog of songs and inspiration from American alt-country acts, Finn went to Nashville in late 1998 to record with producer and multi-instrumentalist Jay Joyce, lacking any clear idea where or when the record would be released. He eventually put it out himself, through Sonny's Pop Records, and it certainly sounds like his first full-fledged independent release. For the first time, Finn sounds entirely unconscious of the charts, which, coupled with his voice's new deep, gravelly texture, may be disarming at first. Although he hasn't concentrated on writing shiny pop songs, he also hasn't abandoned melody—it's just that this time, he writes melodies like singer/songwriters do, resulting in songs that take a little longer to take hold. They're coupled to production that is fairly stripped down, yet also atmospheric, with its blend of dry guitars, old keyboards, muted drums, and the occasional distorted meaning—an apt match for Finn's most shaded lyrics to date. All of these sonic textures and elliptical, yet vaguely rootsy songs are quite different from any of Finn's previous solo works. Consequently, *Say It Is So* may take some time before it reveals its rewards, but it eventually emerges as one of Finn's finest efforts. There may not be any initial standouts, but overall, there are no weak moments, and it's some of the sturdiest, most consistent songwriting he's ever done on one record. Some listeners may miss the pop sheen or Finn's good humor—this is a relatively sober affair, unlike much of his catalog—but *Say It Is So* feels like one of his strongest and most personal records. *—Stephen Thomas Erlewine*

Together in Concert: Live / Feb. 13, 2001 / Era/Epic ✦✦
Three of New Zealand's most talented and treasured singer-songwriters, Tim Finn, Dave Dobbyn, and Bic Runga, embarked on a 26-date theater tour of their homeland in August 2000; *Together in Concert: Live* offers a sampling of these highly successful performances. The three musicians share the stage while performing some of the best-known songs from each man's catalog, including Tim Finn's "Six Months in a Leaky Boat" and "Persuasion," Bic Runga's "Sway" and "Drive," and Dave Dobbyn's "Whaling" and "Just Add Water," among others. While this show has the warmth one would expect, it's far from being just an "evening with" nicety; playing with a tight band, minus the expected acoustic guitars, they rock really hard at times, especially on the Split Enz classic "I See Red." *—Chris Woodstra*

Feeding the Gods / Sep. 25, 2001 / What Are? ✦✦✦

Firefall

f. 1975, Boulder, CO, **db.** 1983
Pop/Rock, Soft Rock, Country-Rock
The mellow, easy country-rock sounds of Firefall, coupled with the group's penchant for pop melodies and high-pitched harmonies, produced a series of successful LPs in the late '70s and a series of chart singles, including the Top Ten hit "You Are the Woman." The group was formed by former Flying Burrito Brother Rick Roberts, who handled vocals, guitar, and most of the songwriting duties; he was joined by fellow ex-Burrito and Byrd Michael Clarke on drums, ex-Spirit and Jo Jo Gunne bassist Mark Andes, guitarist/vocalist Jock Bartley, guitarist/vocalist/songwriter Larry Burnett, and keyboardist/woodwind player David Muse, who joined in 1977. The group recorded its self-titled debut in 1976; it and its follow-up, *Luna Sea*, both went gold, and their third album, *Elan*, went platinum. However, the group's commercial fortunes began to decline, and even though Muse experimented with adding different instruments to the overall sound, Firefall's relaxed, toned-down approach simply wore out its welcome as pop trends moved elsewhere. Jock Bartley reformed the group in 1994 for the album *Messenger*. *—Steve Huey*

Firefall / 1976 / Rhino ✦✦✦✦

Given Firefall's pedigree of former Spirit and Flying Burrito Brothers members, it may seem that the group would have been a little more adventurous than the band that gave us the soft-rock classic, "You Are the Woman." Thing is, they were—the song was just so successful, it's overshadowed the fact that their 1976's eponymous debut was a varied, satisfying record. Yes, most of it was within the province of mellow Californian soft-rock, but they do display their country-rock roots, along with some searching musicality throughout the record. And while a couple of the songs coast by on sound, they could also craft a good tune, with the singles "Livin' Ain't Livin'" and "Cinderella" standing proudly alongside "You Are the Woman." It's a fine, understated country-rock debut that remains one of the more underrated items of its kind—it holds its own next to Poco, Pure Prairie League, and the Eagles. —*Stephen Thomas Erlewine*

● **Greatest Hits** / Sep. 1, 1992 / Rhino ✦✦✦✦

Sharing a light, lush airiness with bands like Poco, America, and Air Supply, Firefall sang fluffy love songs that were weak in lyrical nutrients but abundant with softened chords and harmonies. When radio was saturated with light rock in the mid- to late-'70s, they were right in the heart of it, reaching number nine on Billboard's Top 40 with the gentle "You Are the Woman," which remained on the charts for a startling 15 weeks. Firefall's greatest hits collects all of their mellow rock favorites in one place, presenting some thin but not unlistenable soft rock tunes. Lead singer Rick Roberts pours his heart out but still manages to stir up a decent tempo with "Just Remember I Love You," their second biggest single. The blue of the Colorado skyline, the band's home state, is visioned on the soothing flow of "Break of Dawn," and a slight attractiveness is felt throughout "Strange Way," another chart single in 1978. Roberts, who replaced Gram Parsons in the Flying Burrito Brothers, and drummer Michael Clarke, a onetime Byrds member, did give Firefall a talented history within its lineup, but the music being produced contained ample amounts of schlock that soon faded as radio became tired of this shallow drivel. Sometimes harboring a country feel a la Michael Martin Murphy best heard in songs like "Someday Soon" and "It Doesn't Matter," it was evident that the band had only one direction, which was that of a folk-rock sound. Since their material never strayed from this subtle easiness, Firefall's greatest hits is their most worthwhile offering. —*Mike DeGagne*

fIREHOSE

f. 1985, db. 1994

College Rock, Post-Punk, Alternative Pop/Rock, American Underground

In 1985, after D. Boon's tragic death at age 28 signalled the end of the Minutemen, bassist Mike Watt and drummer George Hurley threw in their lot with then-22-year-old former Ohio State University student, guitar player, and Minutemen fanatic Ed Crawford to form fIREHOSE. Taking their group name from a line in Bob Dylan's "Subterranean Homesick Blues," fIREHOSE continued in the Minutemen tradition of breathtaking musicianship combined with caustic lyrical fusillades inspired by the writing of the Beat Generation and the erect-middle-finger indignation of the Blank Generation. However, with Crawford's decidedly folkie bent insinuating itself into the mix, fIREHOSE's songs began to expand into more traditional verse-chorus-verse songwriting symmetry. And although fIREHOSE never equaled the Minutemen's output in terms of sheer audacity and emotional depth, Crawford, Watt, and Hurley recorded rock that was muscular, dense, and daring, along with being tremendously heartfelt. They never patronized audiences or comported themselves as "rock stars"; they were instead the quintessential post-punk "peoples' band." Although they achieved wider notoriety than did the Minutemen (eventually recording for a major label), fIREHOSE called it quits in early 1994 after a desultory, dispirited final LP (*Mr. Machinery Operator*). Still, nearly all of their recorded work stands as some of the best late-'80s/early-'90s indie rock. —*John Dougan*

Ragin', Full-On / 1986 / SST ✦✦✦

When the Minutemen were forced to split up in December of 1985 due to the untimely death of singer/guitarist D. Boon, the remaining members (bassist Mike Watt and drummer George Hurley) were so devastated that they considered giving up music all together. Shortly afterwards though, a college student and major Minutemen fan, Ed Crawford, convinced the remaining members to soldier on. And soldier on they did, taking Crawford (known as "Ed fROMOHIO," due to his signature on a letter) as their new singer/guitarist, and dubbing the new outfit fIREHOSE, after the famous Bob Dylan song "Subterranean Homesick Blues." Their first album was issued less than a year after Boon's death, 1986's *Ragin', Full On* for SST, and surprisingly, the new band sounded completely different than it's predecessor (for example, Crawford had more of a real singing voice than Boon, the music was less unpredictable and more focused, etc.). Ex-Black Flag bassist Kira (and eventual wife of Watt) helped co-write several tracks: the hyper instrumental "Under the Influence of Meat Puppets," plus "It Matters," "Locked In," "Perfect Pairs," "Relatin' Dudes to Jazz," and "Things Could Turn Around." Other highlights included "Brave Captain," "Candle and the Flame," "Choose Any Memory," and "Caroms." While fIREHOSE would perfect their highly original sound on future albums (*Flyin' the Flannel, Mr. Machinery Operator*, etc.), *Ragin', Full On* still proved to be a worthwhile, interesting debut. —*Greg Prato*

● **If'n** / 1987 / SST ✦✦✦✦✦

Whereas fIREHOSE's debut, 1986's *Ragin', Full On*, was issued quickly to get the new outfit off the ground (two of the three members were still reeling from the death of their previous band's frontman, the Minutemen's D. Boon), their sophomore effort, 1987's *If'n*, included more cohesive and focused songwriting. Touring together had obviously made Watt-Hurley-Crawford tighter as a unit, and several of their best all-time compositions reside here. Although the debut incorporated other musical forms besides punk and hard rock (funk, jazz, etc.), *If'n* was the first fIREHOSE release to feature folk-style originals—

such as Crawford's "In Memory of Elizabeth Cotton." Standouts include the album opening highway anthem "Sometimes," the groovy '50s feel of "Honey, Please," the laid-back "Backroads," and the irate rockers "Anger" and "For the Singer of R.E.M." Also featured are several Mike Watt lead vocal spots—the perennial concert favorite "Making the Freeway" (included on the 1993 mini-album *Live Totem Pole* EP), the humorous "Me & You Remembering," "Operation Solitaire," and the closing epic "Thunder Child." —*Greg Prato*

Sometimes / 1988 / SST ✦✦✦

Bridging their *If'n* (1987) and *fROMOHIO* (1989) albums, this three-track EP incorporates two songs recorded at the sessions for the former album and an additional track. It's better to stick with the albums, though this does include their ode to Michael Stipe—"For the Singer of REM." —*Alex Ogg*

Fromohio / 1989 / SST ✦✦✦✦✦

fIREHOSE's second release, 1987's *If'n*, was a major improvement over their 1986 debut, *Ragin', Full On*. And while their third album, 1988's *fROMOHIO*, was another solid set and contained its share of highlights, it seemed to be cut from the same musical cloth as its predecessor rather than a true progression. Again, the playing is inspired, and the new band had already established an original, identifiable sound. The best tracks prove to be Ed Crawford originals—"In My Mind" and "Time With You" (the latter was an MTV video), while "Whisperin' While Hollerin'" and "What Gets Heard" soon became concert staples. The band's appreciation of folk shines through with a reading of the traditional Black folk song "Vastopol" and the original "Liberty For Our Friend," and drummer George Hurley takes center stage on a pair of short, unaccompanied drum solos—"Let the Drummer Have Some" and "'Nuf That Shit, George." Other highlights include the album opener "Riddle of the Eighties," the funky "Mas Cojones," the laid-back rock of "If'n" and "Understanding," plus the lethargic album closer, "The Softest Hammer." —*Greg Prato*

Flyin' the Flannel / Apr. 23, 1991 / Columbia ✦✦✦

It was a pretty big deal in the underground rock community when fIREHOSE made the jump from an independent record label to a major one (Columbia) with their fourth full-length record, 1991's *Flyin' the Flannel*. But fans shouldn't have worried; the trio didn't change their sound to fit their new label, although the songwriting did become more succinct, which only improved the album's outstanding 16-tracks (resulting in fIREHOSE's finest album). The album-opening anthem, "Down With the Bass," is a Mike Watt tribute to his beloved four-string, while the band rocks out throughout the album: "Up Finnegan's Ladder," "Can't Believe," the title track, "O'er the Town of Pedro," "The First Cuss," "Anti-Misogyny Maneuver," and "Town' the Line" are all standouts. Like all fIREHOSE albums, *Flyin' the Flannel* includes it's share of soothing moments, such as "Toolin'," "Walking the Cow," the downtrodden album closer "Losers, Boozers, and Heroes," and perhaps the best song on the album, the swirling jazz of "Epoxy, for Example." *Flyin' the Flannel* is one of the great lost rock gems of the '90s. Super highly recommended. —*Greg Prato*

Live Totem Pole / 1992 / Columbia ✦✦✦

fIREHOSE's seven-track mini album from 1992, *Live Totem Pole EP*, proved to be a strong testament to the trio's high-energy live show. Recorded live at the Palomino in North Hollywood, CA on August 16, 1991, Mike Watt & Co. sound possessed as they thrash their way through five covers and two overlooked originals from yesteryear. Although the fIREHOSE precursor band, the Minutemen, had covered Blue Oyster Cult's "The Red and the Black" previously, the album-opening version included here simply shreds all previous versions (including BOC's original). Other covers include Public Enemy's "Sophisticated Bitch," The Butthole Surfers' "Revolution (Part Two)," Superchunk's "Slack Motherfucker," and Wire's "Mannequin." A pair of short Watt-penned compositions, "What Gets Heard" and "Makin' the Freeway" (the latter contains a humorous stage warning from Watt to a fan who's "throwing shit"), fit in well with the other selections. Shortly after it's release, *Live Totem Pole EP* was discontinued, and has become a collector's item amongst fIREHOSE/Watt fans. —*Greg Prato*

Mr. Machinery Operator / Feb. 16, 1993 / Columbia ✦✦

Fishbone

f. 1979

Ska-Punk, Funk Metal, Alternative Pop/Rock

Combining equal parts of deep funk, high energy punk, and frantic ska, the Los Angeles-based Fishbone were one of the most distinctive and eclectic alternative rock bands of the late '80s. With their hyperactive, self-conscious diversity, goofy sense of humor, and sharp social commentary, the group gained a sizable cult following during the late '80s, yet they were never able to earn a mainstream audience. Led by vocalist/saxophonist Angelo Moore, the group formed in 1979 while the band was still in junior high. After performing in local clubs during the early '80s, the group signed with Columbia Records in the mid-'80s, releasing a self-titled EP in 1985. The following year, Fishbone released their first full-length album, *In Your Face*. While it was marred by a somewhat slick production, the sheer energy of their performances burned through the slightly polished surface. *Truth and Soul* (1988), Fishbone's second album, captured the band at their most ambitious. The album expanded their audience and charted at number 153. However, the band didn't record a new album for another three years. *The Reality of My Surroundings* (1991) didn't depart from the band's reckless eclecticism, it refined it. The album was a hit, peaking at number 49 and receiving positive reviews. However, the record didn't establish the band as a mainstream success, nor did 1993's *Give a Monkey a Brain*, despite their appearance at the third Lollapalooza. Even when the third wave of ska revival began to rise to popularity in 1996, Fishbone were left behind, as their 1996 record, *Chim Chim's Bad Ass Revenge*—their first album for Arista—was ignored, as was the double-disc compilation *Fishbone 101: Nuttasaurusmeg Fossil Fuelin.* Despite their poor sales, the group remained a popular concert attraction. *—Stephen Thomas Erlewine*

Fishbone / 1985 / Columbia ✦✦✦

While it wasn't as jaw-droppingly brilliant as such future releases like 1988's *Truth and Soul* and 1991's *The Reality of My Surroundings* would be, Fishbone's self-titled debut from 1985 sounded, at the time, totally unlike anything on the music scene. Although it only contains six songs total and their more hard-rocking direction of the future isn't yet present, it remains Fishbone's most ska-based work. By incorporating the energy and unpredictability of punk rock, however, the EP was an obviously important influence on the 1990s popular alterna-ska scene (No Doubt, Sublime, etc.). One of the band's perennial concert favorites, "Party at Ground Zero," is included and remains an invigorating listen years later. Other lesser-known highlights include the cutting edge sounds of "? (Modern Industry)," in which the bandmembers shout out radio station call letters as opposed to conventional lyrics, as well as "Another Generation." While the album opener "Ugly" was an early fan favorite, the lyrics are quite silly, and the closing track, "Lyin' Ass Bitch," hasn't aged well either, especially when heard in the politically correct '90s. Still, *Fishbone* remains an important album for the now commonplace, genre-jumping alternative music scene. *—Greg Prato*

In Your Face / 1986 / Columbia ✦✦✦

Fishbone's first full-length release, 1986's *In Your Face* was a far more focused affair than their self-titled debut EP from 1985, but the band was still honing their original and genre-spanning sound. While it would not be perfected until their 1988 release *Truth and Soul, In Your Face* remains an important musical stepping-stone for Fishbone. Few other bands at the time (perhaps only the Red Hot Chili Peppers) were attempting to merge different musical styles together as they were. Ska, funk, and punk rock are again put into the musical blender this time around, along with often thought-provoking lyrics, resulting in several strong compositions. The opening track "When Problems Arise" is an enjoyable, stomping little ditty for which a rarely aired video clip was filmed, while other highlights include the up-tempo numbers "A Selection" and "Give It Up," the Caribbean-tinged "Cholly," the desperate plea of "I Wish I Had a Date," and the gorgeous ballad "Movement in the Light." Also featured are the funk-workouts "In the Air" and "Knock It," the furious punk-rocker "Simon Says the Kingpin," and the goofy, album-closing instrumental "Post Cold War Politics." *—Greg Prato*

Truth and Soul / 1988 / Columbia ✦✦✦✦✦

By 1988, alternative/college rock was becoming a recognizable force in the mainstream. Several bands were big enough to play arenas, and many even earned gold and platinum albums. The tide was clearly changing for such previously misunderstood bands such as Fishbone. Their second full-length release *Truth and Soul* was issued that year, and remains one of the band's (and the '80s) very best. On past albums, Fishbone's sound was a melting pot of ska, punk, and funk. This time, hard rock has been added to the mix—especially evident in guitarist Kendall Jones' six-string work, with often-spectacular results. Also, the songwriting has improved tremendously and has become much more focused here. The party anthem "Bonin' in the Boneyard" is one of the band's finest (with superhuman bass work by Norwood Fisher), as is the ska-based "Ma and Pa," and a cover of Curtis Mayfield's early-'70s hit "Freddie's Dead." Also featured are several musically varied tracks that deal with the same topic: racism, past and present ("Deep Inside," "One Day," "Subliminal Fascism," "Slow Bus Movin'," "Ghetto Soundwave"). *Truth and Soul* remains Fishbone's most consistent album. *—Greg Prato*

● **The Reality of My Surroundings** / Apr. 23, 1991 / Columbia ✦✦✦✦✦

When Fishbone's *The Reality of My Surroundings* was released in 1991, several critics went as far as comparing its all-encompassing brilliance to that of *Sgt. Pepper's*. While it may have been too high of a praise, Fishbone's third full-length album was indeed exceptional. While their preceding album, *Truth & Soul*, was straightforward in its approach, *Reality* was more unpredictable and off-the-wall, but just as gripping. While not all of the selections exactly hit the spot (the pointless four-part "If I Were a... I'd," "Naz-Tee May'en," and "Babyhead"), its many bright spots outshine the misfires. Fishbone continues to explore their hard rock side on such standouts as "Fight the Youth," "Behavior Control Technician," "Those Days Are Gone," and the crushing album closer, "Sunless Saturday." But as on their older releases, other music styles are digested and spit out—the wonderful tribute to Sly & the Family Stone, "Everyday Sunshine," the reggae-tinged "Pray to the Junkiemaker," the explosive punk rocker "Pressure," and the humorous funk of "Housework." *The Reality of My Surroundings* would prove to be Fishbone's last great album, unfortunately. *—Greg Prato*

Give a Monkey a Brain and He'll Swear He's the Center of the Universe / May 25, 1993 / Columbia ✦✦

Chim Chim's Badass Revenge / Apr. 1996 / Arista/Rowdy ✦✦

Fishbone 101: Nuttasaurusmeg Fossil Fuelin / Sep. 24, 1996 / Columbia/Legacy ✦✦✦✦

Comprised of one disc of hits and one disc of rarities, the double-disc retropective *Fishbone 101: Nuttasaurusmeg Fossil Fuelin* attempts to fulfill the needs of both the collector and the casual fan and winds up satisfying neither. The first disc, featuring hits and cult classics "Freddie's Dead" and "Everyday Sunshine," is a fine overview of their career, hitting nearly all of the band's best moments. On its own, it would be the album to own for casual fans. However, the second disc, while of utmost interest to dedicated followers, is filled with B-sides, demos, alternate takes, and rarities that will simply bore neophytes. Of course, all of this material is all necessary for collectors, but they will probably be frustrated by the extraneous hits collection on the set. If *Fishbone 101* had been separated into two individual collections, both albums would have fulfilled their goals perfectly. As it stands, it's a set that is bound to frustrate both casual and hardcore fans, and thereby can only be recommended with reservations. *—Stephen Thomas Erlewine*

The Five Americans

f. 1965, Dallas, TX, **db.** 1969

Bubblegum, Garage Rock

In 1966-67, this Dallas group enjoyed some modest national success with the number five hit "Western Union," as well as a few other Top 40 entries, "I See the Light," "Zip Code," and "Sound of Love." Dominated by high, bubbling organ lines and clean harmony vocals, the group favored high-energy pop/rock far more than British Invasion or R&B-inspired sounds, although a bit of garage/frat rock raunch could be detected in their stomping rhythms. Recording prolifically throughout the last half of the '60s (often with ex-rockabilly star Dale Hawkins as producer), and writing much of their own material, they were ultimately too lightweight and bubblegumish to measure up to either the era's better pop/rock or garage bands. Their 1966 hit "I See the Light" is their toughest and best performance. *—Richie Unterberger*

I See the Light / 1966 / Sundazed ✦✦✦✦

If you're curious enough about the five Americans to want more than a greatest hits collection, this 1966 album is a worthwhile supplement. Ten of the 12 cuts are group originals, and they lean toward the gutsier side of what this sometimes pop-oriented act could offer, with occasional influences of Beau Brummels-like folk-rock. Most of the songs are not on their CD best-of (*Western Union*), and this disc adds previously unreleased alternate takes of "The Train" and "Good Times." *—Richie Unterberger*

● **Western Union** / 1989 / Sundazed ✦✦✦✦

Twenty-song best-of includes all their big and small hits, as well as quite a few rarities and an extensive group history. *—Richie Unterberger*

The "5" Royales

f. 1952, Winston-Salem, NC, **db.** 1965

R&B

The "5" Royales were a relatively unheralded, but significant, link between early R&B and early soul in their combination of doo wop, jump blues, and gospel styles. Their commercial success was relatively modest—they had seven Top Ten R&B hits in the 1950s. A few of their singles would prove extremely popular in cover versions by other artists, though—James Brown and Aretha Franklin tore it up with "Think," Ray Charles covered "Tell the Truth," and the Shirelles (and later the Mamas & the Papas) had pop success with "Dedicated to the One I Love." Almost all of their material was written by guitarist Lowman Pauling, who influenced Steve Cropper with his biting and bluesy guitar lines, which at their most ferocious almost sound like a precursor to blues rock. After forming as the Royal Sons Quintet, the group made their debut on the R&B charts in 1953 with a pair of number one singles for Apollo, "Baby Don't Do It" and "Help Me Somebody." After being lured away to King in 1954, they entered the R&B Top Ten only two more times, though they recorded for the label throughout the 1950s. After leaving King and recording some more sides in the early '60s, they finally broke up by 1965. *—Richie Unterberger*

★ **Monkey Hips and Rice: The "5" Royales Anthology** / Mar. 8, 1994 / Rhino ✦✦✦✦✦

The "5" Royales certainly did their share of forgettable period-piece tunes, but they also had transcendent songs like "Think," "Just as I Am," and "Dedicated to the One I Love." They enjoyed a lengthy run, creating many hits plus a few gems, which are all available on this sparkling two-disc set. The opening disc sets the stage, showing their gospel origins and also the rather routine cuts the band did in its formative period. They began to evolve into a more substantial unit in the mid-'50s, and by the late '50s were a sterling unit cutting emphatic, appealing numbers. Most of these appear on the second disc. By the early '60s, they had run their course, but their legacy and impact was secure. This offers the most complete picture of the "5" Royales and their superb music. *—Ron Wynn*

● **Apollo Sessions** / Sep. 1, 1995 / Collectables ✦✦✦✦✦

Although not the career-long survey of the Rhino anthology, this 23-song, 62-minute collection covers the Five Royales' very best years, spent with Apollo Records from 1951 until 1955, first as the Royals ("Give Me One More Chance") and then as a quintet under their more familiar name. Their sound here is vocally very smooth yet passionate, but the instrumental backings are exuberant and raunchy, the kind of combination that made acts like this such a threat to the established popular music of the era. The mix of jump blues with accomplished gospel-influenced harmony singing (best represented on the delightful "What's That" or "All Righty," or, most startling of all, "Baby Take All of Me," with its abandoned wailing in the background) helped make their music some of the most expressive and satisfying of the period. Their way with a chorus and a phrase made the Royals one of the top R&B acts of their era, although it wasn't until much later that they made the jump to pop stardom. Unfortunately, during the period represented here, they were one of those R&B acts whose radio play exceeded their record sales (at least, as reported by Apollo, one reason they jumped to King Records). From 1951 until 1955, they helped provide the soundtrack against which mainstream rock & roll was born and took root with the public. On that basis alone, this material is worth hearing and owning; it was the soil in which rock & roll sprouted, the stream in which other acts' commercial hits were spawned and nurtured. They later had their share of successes, but this is their real sound, raw, sweet and elegant all at the same time. *—Bruce Eder*

All Righty!: Apollo Recordings / Mar. 3, 1999 / West Side ✦✦✦✦

All Righty! is the first complete collection of the "5" Royales' recordings for Apollo Records from 1951 to 1955, including even their gospel sides (recorded as the Royal Sons Quintet). *—John Bush*

Take Me With You Baby / Mar. 14, 2000 / Cleopatra ♦♦♦♦
A nice collection of the group's latter-day material originally waxed for the Memphis House of Blues imprint. Some of these sides were later issued on Vee-Jay and ABC/Paramount, but the Memphis stamp of Willie Mitchell's early work is all over these tracks. Highlights include the previously unissued "Show Me," "I Got to Know," "She Did Me Wrong," and a nice stab at James Brown's "Please Please Please." Usually, latter-day sides are a load of diminished returns, but these tracks are every bit as enjoyable as their more famous counterparts. Well worth adding to the shopping cart. *—Cub Koda*

The Five Satins

f. 1956, New Haven, CT, **db.** 1961
Doo Wop
The Five Satins are best-known for the doo wop classic "In the Still of the Night," a song that was popular enough to make the group one of the most famous doo wop outfits, although they never had another hit of the same magnitude. Led by Fred Parris, the group recorded for their first single "In the Still of the Night," a song Parris had recently written, in the basement of a local church. Released in early 1956, it became a huge hit by the end of the year, peaking at number three on the R&B charts and number 25 on the pop charts. Though Parris spent more than a year in the Army just after the Five Satins' big success, Bill Baker temporarily took over lead vocals for another big hit, "To the Aisle." When Parris returned, he reorganized the group and had a minor hit in 1959 with "Shadows." During the remainder of the '60s and early '70s, Parris led various incarnations of the Five Satins through oldies revues in America and Europe; they also recorded occasionally during this time. After moderate success during the mid-'70s under the name Black Satin, the group reverted to the Five Satins and performed regularly at oldies shows in America and Europe. *—Stephen Thomas Erlewine*

The Five Satins Sing Their Greatest Hits / 1982 / Collectables ♦♦♦♦♦
Collectables' *Five Satins Sing Their Greatest Hits* may not have the fanciest packaging, and the sound is merely adequate, but it remains a hell of a good Five Satins collection, containing a robust 24 tracks. That means it doesn't just have "In the Still of the Night," it has a wealth of other singles that prove that the group were one of the finest doo wop outfits. Perhaps it could have been presented with a little more care, but it's still a terrific overview. *—Stephen Thomas Erlewine*

● **In the Still of the Night** / 1990 / Relic ♦♦♦♦♦
Everything you need from this sumptuous and smoochy late-night doo wop quintet is here. The title cut is a work of art worth listening to over and over. *—John Floyd*

The Five Stairsteps

f. 1965, Chicago, IL, **db.** 1976
Chicago Soul, Soul
The Five Stairsteps were "The First Family of Soul," a title bestowed upon the Chicago-based teenaged group in part because of their astounding five-year run of hits, which included the 1970 million-selling single "O-o-h Child." The Five Stairsteps were formed in 1958 as a five-member brother-and-sister teenaged vocal group. The group got its name, "the Five Stairsteps," when "Momma Stairsteps," as Betty Burke was affectionately called, noticed that her kids looked like stair steps when stood next to each other according to age. After winning first prize in a talent contest at the legendary Regal Theater, the Five Stairsteps were deluged with recording contract offers. Neighbor and family friend Fred Cash of the Impressions introduced the group to Curtis Mayfield. Signing with Mayfield's Windy City label, distributed by Philadelphia-based Cameo Parkway Records, their first single was the Burke-written ballad "You Waited Too Long" b/w the upbeat "Don't Waste Your Time," a Mayfield song. A double-sided hit in Chicago, the A-side charted number 16 R&B on Billboard's charts in the spring of 1966. More hits followed, most of collected on the LP *The Five Stairsteps*. The group's second album, *Family Portrait*, whose cover was a collection of Burke family photos, was recorded and produced in Chicago by Clarence Jr. With the addition of their three-year-old brother, the group became the Five Stairsteps & Cubie. Signing with Buddah Records, the group was once again known as the Five Stairsteps. In the spring of 1970, the group released their sole certified million-seller and biggest pop hit, "O-o-h Child" (written by Stan Vincent), which hit number 14 R&B and number eight pop. *—Ed Hogan*

● **Greatest Hits** / Apr. 18, 1990 / Collectables ♦♦♦♦
This hits package examines the adolescent Chicago soul group from their mid-'60s beginning with their 1970 bubblegum soul hit "O-o-h Child." *—Bill Dahl*

Comeback: The Best of the Five Stairsteps / Aug. 19, 1996 / Sequel ♦♦♦♦
Comeback: The Best of the Five Stairsteps contains all of the group's major R&B hits, from "You Waited Too Long" and "World of Fantasy" to "O-o-h Child." For some listeners, there may be a little bit too much material here, especially since their lesser-known singles weren't quite as good as the hits, but this remains the definitive overview of the group's career. *—Stephen Thomas Erlewine*

The Fixx

f. 1980
Pop/Rock, New Wave
A London-based new wave group that managed to sustain a successful career in America for several years in the mid-'80s, the Fixx always flirted with mainstream pop with their catchy, keyboard-driven pop. They released their debut album, the Rupert Hine-produced *Shuttered Room*, in 1982. The record spawned two minor U.K. hits, "Stand or Fall" and "Red Skies," and spent a short time in the charts. In America, none of the singles were hits, yet the album stayed on the charts for nearly a year. *Reach the Beach*, released in 1983, established them as a hit-making force in the U.S. The terse, pulsating "One Thing Leads to Another" became a number four hit, sending the album into the Top Ten. *Reach the Beach* would go platinum by the end of the year, launching two more Top 40 singles—"Saved by Zero" and "Sign of Fire." Despite all of their American success, the Fixx failed to break back into the British charts with *Reach the Beach*; in fact, they never had another British hit in their career. The Fixx returned in 1984 with *Phantoms*. While it performed well—it peaked at number 19 and went gold—it didn't match the success of *Reach the Beach*; after it launched the number 15 single "Are We Ourselves?" the record fell off the charts. Although their audience was shrinking, the band kept their basic, synth-driven sound intact for 1986's *Walkabout*, which featured the hit "Secret Separation." *—Stephen Thomas Erlewine*

Shuttered Room / 1982 / Fuel 2000/Varese ♦♦♦
The Fixx' debut album *Shuttered Room* suffers from inconsistent and unmelodic songwriting, but producer Rupert Hine helps turn the group's generic new wave into engaging synth-pop. Even with Hine's support, only a couple of tracks ("Red Skies," "Stand or Fall," "Shuttered Room") stand out, yet the band's clean, mechanical attack makes the record enjoyable *—Stephen Thomas Erlewine*

Reach the Beach / 1983 / MCA ♦♦♦♦♦
Reach the Beach is a significant step forward from the Fixx' debut album *Shuttered Room* simply because the band can now craft immediately accessible, incessantly catchy pop/rock melodies. "One Thing Leads to Another" has a big, ringing guitar hook hammered home by the dance beat, while "Saved by Zero" and "The Sign of Fire" are cool, robotic slices of synth-pop. Although the rest of the album isn't quite as catchy as those three hits, *Reach the Beach* remains a pleasant collection of immaculately produced and stylishly danceable new wave. *—Stephen Thomas Erlewine*

Phantoms / 1984 / MCA ♦♦♦
The Fixx had a banner year in 1983, as their second album, *Reach the Beach*, broke down doors and gave the band a huge hit with "One Thing Leads to Another." *Phantoms* wasn't as good as *Reach the Beach*, not just because it had that hit, but also because it was simply a really good mainstream new wave record. *Phantoms* was a little more serious, a little more lugubrious, a little directionless, but it still was a pretty good record, all the same. The reason why? The Fixx were a good band. They had an original sound, thanks to the echoing synths, clean processed guitars, cavernous drums, and Cy Curnin's soaring voice, which soared over the precise arrangements to make it sound human. The wondrous thing about this combination is that it sounded appealing even when the material wasn't the equal of the sound, which is often the case on *Phantoms*. That's not to say it's a disaster, because it hardly is—the band sounds good, and the record is a shining example of post-new wave production. But, it does play a bit as singles and filler, with the Top 20 hit "Are We Ourselves" shining brightly among the record's 12 songs, but "Lose Face," the reggae-tinged "Sunshine in the Shade," and "Woman on a Train" all were fine Fixx songs, standing proudly among the perfectly acceptable, but rather undistinguished, cuts that formed the rest of the album, including a preponderance of long, moody synth ballads. Even if it was an uneven record, its ratio of hits to filler was no greater than most pop albums. However, *Phantoms* had the misfortune of arriving in one of the greatest years for pop music, a year where every kind of style was in full bloom. So, *Phantoms* fell by the wayside, but, in retrospect, it was an admirable successor to an album that defined a band's career. *—Stephen Thomas Erlewine*

Walkabout / 1986 / MCA ♦♦♦
With its layered, synthesized textures and ponderous songs, *Walkabout* displays a bit more ambition than the average Fixx album, yet its best moments arrive when the group concentrates on pop songs, such as the trancy "Secret Separation." Unfortunately, only a handful of songs on *Walkabout* come close to matching the hooks of "Secret Separation," suggesting that the Fixx have begun to run out of ideas. *—Stephen Thomas Erlewine*

React / 1987 / MCA ♦♦

Calm Animals / 1988 / RCA ♦♦♦
The Fixx attempted to redefine themselves as a guitar-driven mainstream rock band for 1988's *Calm Animals*, their first album for RCA Records. Although their stylistic revamping isn't embarrassing, it isn't executed well, particularly because the group has failed to write any memorable songs. Consequently, *Calm Animals* produced no hits, and the group left RCA after releasing this lone album. *—Stephen Thomas Erlewine*

One Thing Leads to Another: Greatest Hits / Oct. 1989 / MCA ♦♦♦
The Fixx's music stood out from '80s radio, even though they shared the airwaves with numerous techno bands and new wave groups. They had an intangible quality to their lyrical flow and musical rhythm that kept them from sounding like everyone else. On *One Thing Leads to Another*, the indistinguishable characteristics become evident as all of their best songs are played out, making for quite an amusing compilation. Four tracks do hover above the rest on this 12-song offering, opening with the clang and push of the title track, their highest charting single (number four on Billboard in 1983). The mechanical dream-like pulse of "Secret Separation" contains an unavoidable attractiveness in it's chorus, and the wispy but haunting "Saved by Zero" reflects a certain science fiction motif. The paranoid "Are We Ourselves" has lead singer Cy Cumin coming off like Peter Schilling, with the chorus one step behind him in the background. The other eight songs are far from dry, complete with a hustle-and-bustle flux incorporated by clean synthesizers and ridged pop tempos, tied up with a rock styled flavor. This hits package is an enjoyable wallow through some music that surprisingly has a difference. *—Mike DeGagne*

Ink / Feb. 19, 1991 / Impact ♦♦

● **Ultimate Collection** / Nov. 9, 1999 / MCA ♦♦♦♦♦
At their very best, the Fixx were one of the great singles bands of the new wave era. They

often don't get credit for it because they were a little out of step with the times. They certainly weren't as dark as the legions of critically acclaimed post-punk bands like the Cure and Gang of Four, nor were they as lightly quirky as many of the early-MTV one-hit wonders or as fashionable as the new romantics. Instead, the Fixx picked up the album-rock side of David Bowie, which meant that they were briefly in step with the times in the early '80s but then could carry on in the years immediately following new wave, since they were just slightly more traditional than their peers. In both their new wave and post-new wave incarnations, the Fixx turned out a handful of terrific singles—"Saved by Zero," "The Sign of Fire," "Are We Ourselves," "Secret Separation," and "One Thing Leads to Another," which sounds as startlingly fresh years after its recording as it did at the time. All of these songs are on the aptly-titled *Ultimate Collection.* In addition to the hits, the 17-track compilation contains a number of lesser-known singles and album tracks, and while they're not quite as good as the classic singles, they're still solid songs in the same vein, and anyone that believes that the Fixx's five best singles are indeed classics should find plenty to enjoy here. *—Stephen Thomas Erlewine*

20th Century Masters—The Millennium Collection: The Best of the Fixx / Oct. 17, 2000 / MCA ♦♦♦♦
20th Century Masters: The Millennium Collection comes very close to being a flawless singles collection of one of the most underrated mainstream new wave singles bands of the early '80s. Yes, the latter-day moderate hit "Driven Out" is entirely absent, but the true complaint is that "Stand or Fall" and "Red Skies" are included in live incarnations. This, of course, isn't the first Fixx collection to suffer from that problem—the live "Stand or Fall" was also on the first Fixx compilation—but it's still irksome. Still, it's easy to forgive that flaw when you look at the bulk of the disc, which includes the sublime "One Thing Leads to Another," "Saved by Zero," "The Sign of Fire," "Are We Ourselves," and the great "Secret Separation." Those five songs hold their own with many mainstream, new wave-tinged songs from their era, while "One Thing Leads to Another" virtually defines it. All this makes this edition of *20th Century Masters: The Millennium Collection* recommended, even if that original version of "Stand or Fall" is missing. *—Stephen Thomas Erlewine*

Roberta Flack

b. Feb. 10, 1939, Ashville, NC
Vocals, Piano / Smooth Soul, Quiet Storm, Soft Rock, Urban, Soul
Classy, urbane, reserved, smooth, and sophisticated—all of these terms have been used to describe the music of Roberta Flack, particularly her string of romantic, light-jazz ballad hits in the 1970s, which continue to enjoy popularity on MOR-oriented adult contemporary stations. Her first two albums were well received but produced no hit singles; however, that all changed when a version of Ewan MacColl's "The First Time Ever I Saw Your Face," from her first LP, was included in the soundtrack of *Play Misty For Me.* The single zoomed to number one in 1972 and remained there for six weeks, becoming that year's biggest hit. Flack followed it with the first of several duets with Howard University classmate Donny Hathaway, "Where Is the Love." "Killing Me Softly With His Song" became Flack's second number one hit (five weeks) in 1973. She charted several more times over the next few years, but a major blow struck in 1979 when Hathaway committed suicide. Devastated, Flack was forced to find another partner and eventually did in Peabo Bryson, with whom she toured in 1980. The two recorded together in 1983, scoring a hit duet with "Tonight, I Celebrate My Love." *—Steve Huey*

First Take / 1969 / Atlantic ♦♦♦♦
The album that launched Roberta Flack's career. She had been doing background vocals and also recording with Les McCann, who helped her land at Atlantic. The single "The First Time Ever I Saw Your Face" zoomed into the pop stratosphere after it was included in Clint Eastwood's film *Play Misty For Me. —Ron Wynn*

Chapter Two / Aug. 1970 / Atlantic ♦♦♦♦♦
A great album and the release that made Roberta Flack a major soul and R&B artist in the early '70s. She had a soft, compelling, alluring voice, and was able to convincingly switch gears and also convey anger, regret, hurt, or despair. Those who thought Flack was a one-hit wonder, or didn't think she could make the transition from doing mostly jazz to other styles, were convinced otherwise. *—Ron Wynn*

Quiet Fire / Nov. 1971 / Atlantic ♦♦♦♦♦
Quiet Fire proves to be an apt title, as Flack's MOR-informed jazz and gospel vocals simmer just below the surface on the eight sides here. Forgoing the full-throttled delivery of, say, Aretha Franklin, Flack translates the pathos of gospel expression into measured intensity and sighing, elongated phrases. There's even a bit of Carole King's ashen tone in Flack's voice, as manifested on songs like "Let Them Talk," Van McCoy's "Sweet Bitter Love," and a meditative reworking of King's "Will You Still Love Me Tomorrow." The album's other high-profile cover, "Bridge Over Troubled Waters," features the ideal setting for Flack's airy pipes with a tasteful backdrop of strings and a chorus featuring soul songstress Cissy Houston (Whitney's mom). Switching from this hushed sanctity, Flack digs into some groove-heavy southern soul on "Go Up Moses," "Sunday and Sister Jones," and an amazing version of the Bee Gees hit "To Love Somebody" (this perennial number has been done by everyone from Rita Marley to Hank Williams Jr.). Flack finally completes the modern triumvirate of southern music, adding the country tones of Jimmy Webb's "See You Then" to the *Quiet Fire*'s stock of gospel and soul. And thanks to top players like guitarist Hugh McCracken, organist Richard Tee, bassist Chuck Rainey, and drummer Bernard Purdie, the varied mix all comes off sounding seamless. One of Flack's best. *—Stephen Cook*

Roberta Flack & Donny Hathaway / Apr. 1972 / Atlantic ♦♦♦♦♦
A duet classic, and perhaps the most popular album Roberta Flack made. Their single "Where Is the Love" dominated urban contemporary radio for almost the entire year, while "You've Got a Friend" was just as influential and was later covered by numerous artists (of course they didn't write it, but a lot of folks thought they did). It did so well that Flack eventually did other duet material and also became very close to Hathaway. *—Ron Wynn*

Killing Me Softly / Aug. 1973 / Atlantic ♦♦♦♦♦
The title track was another smash for Roberta Flack, and the album continued in the same tradition as *Chapter Two* and *A Quiet Fire.* She made simmering ballads, declarative message songs, and better-than-average up-tempo numbers, and at the time was among the top-selling female vocalists in any style. *—Ron Wynn*

Feel Like Makin' Love / Mar. 1975 / Atlantic ♦♦♦

Blue Lights in the Basement / Dec. 1977 / Atlantic ♦♦♦

Born to Love / Jul. 1983 / Capitol ♦♦♦

● **Softly With These Songs: The Best of Roberta Flack** / Jun. 22, 1993 / Atlantic ♦♦♦♦♦
Roberta Flack was blessed with one of the loveliest, most soothing voices in the music industry. In the 1970s, she not only appealed to pop and R&B audiences, but also fit in with the era's more serious, sensitive singer/songwriters. She scored some of the decade's biggest hits with classics such as "The First Time Ever I Saw Your Face," "Killing Me Softly With His Song," and "Feel Like Making Love," as well as her legendary duets with Donny Hathaway, all which have gone on to become standards in the pop pantheon. This single-disc set attempts at collecting her best and most successful recordings from the 1970s to the 1990s, when she enjoyed the success of another Top Ten hit with Diane Warren's "Set the Night to Music" (with Maxi Priest). However, this ambitious collection, even with such stellar material, proves a little frustrating due to the omission of several key tracks from Flack's catalog, among those "Jesse," "If I Ever See You Again," "You've Got a Friend," and several others. It does, however, manage to incorporate other Flack collectibles, including her soundtrack hit "Making Love," her hit with Peabo Bryson, "Tonight I Celebrate My Love," her lovely, breezy, chart-topping 1988 R&B hit "Oasis," and a sleek 1990s house track, "Uh-Uh Ooh-Ooh Look Out (Here It Comes)." This ambitious yet frustrating collection not only highlights Flack's long, illustrious career, but also brings to attention the fact that a multi-disc retrospective on this legendary singer would be a most welcome addition to her catalog. *—Jose F. Promis*

The Flamin' Groovies

f. 1965, San Francisco, CA, **db.** 1979
Proto-Punk, Power Pop, Rock & Roll
One of America's greatest, most influential, and legendary cult bands, the Flamin' Groovies came out of the San Francisco area in 1965 playing greasy, bluesy, rock & roll dashed with a liberal sprinkling of British Invasion panache in an era soon to be dominated by hippie culture and hyperextended raga-rock freakouts. Caught in a double bind of playing the wrong kind of music at the wrong time (as well as not looking the part), the Groovies were almost completely forgotten as the Fillmore/Avalon Ballroom scenes, dominated by the Dead, the Jefferson Airplane, et al., rendered them anachronistic. The plain truth, however, was that despite not being in tune with the zeitgeist, the Groovies made great music, and managed to sustain a career that lasted for over two decades. *—John Dougan*

Sneakers [10 Inch] / 1968 / Snazz ♦♦♦
The group's earliest release, recorded in early 1968, was originally issued as a seven-song 10". Featuring mostly Roy Loney originals, the band mashed together garage rock, San Francisco psychedelia, the Lovin' Spoonful, and blues for this derivative set. Nonetheless, there was a good deal of charm in the over-amped, hyper-speedy execution—less finesse than their more renowned Bay Area peers, but less pretension than most of them. The easygoing blues-rock of "The Slide," and the tunefully moody "Lovetime," and the insanely fast fusion of '20s pop and '60s rock on "My Yada" were standouts. The entire record has been reissued on CD as part of Sundazed's *Supersneakers,* which also includes ten live tracks recorded in 1968. *—Richie Unterberger*

Supersnazz / 1968 / Sundazed ♦♦♦♦♦
For an unknown band, Epic sank a lot of money into this record, and wasn't happy when it didn't sell. But that's hardly the fault of the band, who sound great despite the intrusive overproduction of novice knob-twiddler Steve Goldman. Loney's yelping lead vocals are in fine form, and the rest of the band rocks with a reckless abandon and stunning succinctness that was totally out of step with the times. *—John Dougan*

Flamingo / 1970 / Kama Sutra ♦♦♦♦♦
While the Flamin' Groovies' first album, *Supersnazz,* loaded their high-octane retro-rock down with a loving but overly intrusive production, their next long-player, *Flamingo,* went in exactly the opposite direction; for their second time at bat (and their second major label), the Groovies cranked up their amps and kicked up the tempos, while producer Richard Robinson stripped the band's sound to the bone. If *Flamingo* has a flaw, it's that the album is just a bit *too* basic; the recording sounds a bit flat and muddy, and it isn't very flattering to either Tim Lynch's guitar or Danny Mihm's drums (and who fell in love with the panning control while they were mixing?). But if *Flamingo* sometimes sounds more like a demo than a finished album, it's a demo of a great band firing on all cylinders; with "Gonna Rock Tonite," the album starts out in fifth gear and never stops, with even the less manic tunes (such as the bluesy "Childhood's End") sounding sharp and full of fire, and the many rave-ups raving mighty fine indeed (notable exception: the trippy "She's Falling Apart," which proves these guys didn't understand psychedelia and had no business playing it, which was a considerable virtue in the Bay Area during the late '60s and early '70s). If the engineering sometimes lets them down, *Flamingo* does a far, far

better job of capturing what made the Groovies a great band than their debut and ranks alongside their very finest work. (Buddha Records' 1999 CD reissue tacks on six potent bonus tracks from a live-in-the-studio session which appeared in part on the 1976 compilation *Still Shakin'*.) *—Mark Deming*

Teenage Head / 1971 / Buddha ✦✦✦✦✦
Miriam Linna once opined that the Roy Loney-era line-up of the Flamin' Groovies suggested what the Rolling Stones would have sounded like if they'd sworn their allegiance to the sound and style of Sun Records instead of Chess Records. If one wants to buy this theory (and it sounds reasonable to me), then *Teenage Head* was the Groovies' alternate-universe version of *Sticky Fingers*, an album that delivered their toughest rock & roll beside their most introspective blues workouts. (In his liner notes to Buddha's 1999 CD reissue of *Teenage Head*, Andy Kotowicz writes that Mick Jagger noticed the similarities between the two albums and thought the Groovies did the better job.) While the Flamin' Groovies didn't dip into the blues often, they always did right by 'em, and "City Lights" and "Yesterday's Numbers" find them embracing the mournful soul of the blues to superb effect, while their covers of "Doctor Boogie" and "32-20" honor the originals while adding a energy and attitude that was all their own. And the rockers are among the best stuff this band ever put to tape, especially "High Flying Baby," "Have You Seen My Baby?," and the brilliant title track. And unlike *Flamingo*, *Teenage Head* sounds just as good as it deserves to; Richard Robinson's production is clean, sharp, and gets the details onto tape with a clarity that never gets in the way of the band's sweaty raunch. While *Flamingo* rocks a bit harder, *Teenage Head* is ultimately the best album the Flamin' Groovies would ever make, and after Roy Loney left the band within a few months of its release, they'd never sound like this again. *—Mark Deming*

☆ **Shake Some Action** / 1976 / Aim ✦✦✦✦✦
The Groovies disappeared into the wilds of Europe after *Teenage Head*, which barely earned them a cult following over here. They went through a few personnel changes, honed their sound to an even finer point, and developed a few more musical smarts. Then came *Shake Some Action*, the debut of the Flamin' Groovies' Mark II, where they rocked out British-style for most of it (while still acknowledging their American roots), only louder and more passionately than any British Invasion band had played since 1964. The sound was a complete anachronism in the mid-'70s, but it got them noticed and earned them a cult following. The guitar sound is straight 1964 Beatles (a la "Not a Second Time") alternating with Kinks material of the same era, the vocals are the plaintive wailing of lovesick young rock gods, and the effect is stunning even 20 years on. Maybe the greatest British Invasion album since 1964. Reissued by Australia's AIM Records on CD, and well worth tracking down as an import. *—Bruce Eder*

Still Shakin' / 1976 / Buddah ✦✦✦✦✦
Buddah Records, the successor to Kama Sutra, seeing that the boys were finally getting their due in the rock press, put together this cool little cash-in effort, which combined the best tracks from *Flamingo* and *Teenage Head* with a bunch of outtakes into a sort of "best-of" the Mark I Groovies. The leftover tracks are even rawer and better than the released material, and this record only added to the passion that fans old and new felt for the band. *—Bruce Eder*

The Flamin' Groovies Now! / 1978 / Sire ✦✦✦✦✦
It looks like listeners are destined to rely on imports for most of the Groovies' Sire catalog. In 1978, the group was getting all kinds of great press, and even some radio play from their comeback *Shake Some Action* album on Sire, and embarked on a national tour playing clubs like the Bottom Line in New York in front of every rock V.I.P. who could wangle a ticket. And to accompany the tour, they put out *Flamin' Groovies Now!*, an album of more British Invasion tracks. The sound on this record, produced and engineered by Dave Edmunds, was a notable improvement over *Shake Some Action*, and the group had lost none of its flair for the period or the style, though there was also precious little new ground covered. The range of styles embraced on this record was astonishing—"Between the Lines" and "Take Me Back," and especially "Good Laugh Mun" were examples of Edmunds emulating Phil Spector, and had the Groovies sounding like the Beach Boys of "Don't Worry Baby" and recalled the way the early Kinks covered American music; "House of Blue Lights" gave nods to both Merrill Moore and Chuck Berry, as well as the Stones. The songs off of side two were harder, giving them more the kind of edge one associated with the Stones or the Rockin' Vickers. But their version of Gene Clark's "Feel a Whole Lot Better" was the crowning achievement on this record, the best contemporary cover of a Byrds track ever done, and one so good that some fans thought a re-formed Byrds should have done a cover of the Groovies' "Shake Some Action" in return. *—Bruce Eder*

Jumpin' in the Night / 1979 / Sire ✦✦✦
The Groovies' third British Invasion-revival style album was actually even better than the second, but Sire by this time was hedging its bets, replacing a cover of the Rolling Stones' "19th Nervous Breakdown" with Warren Zevon's "Werewolves of London" on the U.S. version. It didn't gain the band any added sales, and alienated hardcore fans, who had to buy the import to get the Stones cover. The record company was losing interest and the band was going through major personnel changes as well, and it would be a while before the Groovies turned up on another full-length album again. *—Bruce Eder*

Flamin' Groovies Studio '68 / 1984 / Eva ✦✦✦
The very earliest Flamin' Groovies material ever to be issued, taken from live studio tapes cut on January 10, 1968. Lead singer Roy Loney's songs dominate this session, which also includes a couple of Lovin' Spoonful numbers and a version of the blues "Sportin' Life"; a couple tunes would later show up on their *Sneakers* EP. Most of this material is good-timey, blues/R&B-influenced rock, in the spirit of the earliest recordings of the Charlatans, Dead, and Big Brother. The jugband influence of the Lovin' Spoonful also pervades a few tracks, in an unimpressive fashion. This hardly stacks up with the best San Francisco rock of the time; its appeal will largely lie with Groovies fanatics (a not inconsiderable audience) looking for a glimpse of the group's roots. By far the most impressive track is "Good Morning, Mr. Stone," a seven-minute psychedelic workout with guitar work inspired by Jeff Beck, Pete Townshend, and Jorma Kaukonen, as well as a brief lift of a snatch of the Who's "A Quick One." *—Richie Unterberger*

The Gold Star Tapes / 1984 / Skydog ✦✦✦

● **Groovies' Greatest Grooves** / Jul. 1989 / Sire ✦✦✦✦✦
During their early period with Roy Loney as lead singer, the Flamin' Groovies made one great album (*Teenage Head*), one very good one (*Flamingo*), and one that was flawed but enjoyable (*Supersnazz*). When Cyril Jordan took over as the band's unquestioned leader following Loney' s departure, the Groovies shifted gears from supercharged roots rock to neo-British Invasion pop, and while every record they released had more than a few brilliant moments, they seemed incapable of making an album that was solid from front to back. Thankfully, some bright penny at Sire Records got the idea of putting together a Flamin' Groovies compilation CD, and the result, *Groovies' Greatest Grooves*, makes a superb case for the inconsistent but undeniable brilliance of their post-Loney repertoire. *Groovies' Greatest Grooves* harvests pretty much every great track from the group's three albums for Sire (*Shake Some Action*, *Flamin' Groovies Now!*, and *Jumpin' in the Night*) and tosses in one superb cut with Loney (the masterful "Teenage Head"), two hard-to-find ravers with short-time vocalist Chris Wilson (including the much-covered "Slow Death"), and a rough but exciting demo of "River Deep, Mountain High" cut for a proposed collaboration with Phil Spector. While Jordan's edition of the Flamin' Groovies may not have rocked as hard as Loney's, that doesn't say that they couldn't rock hard when they wanted to, as "Jumpin' in the Night," "Tallahassee Lassie," and "Please Please Girl" easily prove, and "Shake Some Action," "You Tore Me Down," and "All I Wanted" are as transcendent as pop music gets. A satisfying 75 minutes of pure bliss, *Groovies' Greatest Grooves* is a one-stop shopping place for anyone wanting the cream of the Flamin' Groovies' faux-Brit era, and a fine introduction to one of the best American bands of the period. *—Mark Deming*

Sixteen Tunes / 1995 / Munster ✦✦✦✦
Or "the great lost Groovies album," filling some holes in the group's discography. *Sixteen Tunes* combines the contents of the EPs *Grease*, *Supergrease*, and *The Gold Star Sessions* on one disc. The sound isn't ideal, due to the fact that much of the material was outtakes and demos, and because Skydog never had ideal sources. Still, these are the Groovies in their prime years, and their energy and enthusiasm compensate for a multitude of technical flaws. The best songs include "River Deep Mountain High," "And Your Bird Can Sing," "She Don't Care About Time," "Feel a Whole Lot Better," "Do I Love You" (maybe the best song here, as well as the most improbable number for the group), "Sweet Little Rock & Roller," "Jumpin' Jack Flash" (based on the seldom-seen 1968 video of the song, not the single), "Paint It Black," the Groovies' own "Slow Death," and their original version of "Shake Some Action," which sounds a lot darker than the familiar Sire version. A few of these tracks are available elsewhere, but most of them aren't—all of it is either live in the studio with un-retouched vocals or genuine concert recordings. "Sweet Little Rock & Roller" may come the closest to emulating Chuck Berry's sound by any white band; the originals hold their own and then some in this company. The notes are in French and Japanese. *—Bruce Eder*

Supersneakers / Nov. 19, 1996 / Sundazed ✦✦✦✦
A combination of the *Sneakers* indie 10" from 1968 and ten tracks from a 1968 gig at a San Francisco club. (The live material had previously been issued on the French import *Flamin' Groovies '68* in the mid-'80s.) The studio tracks from *Sneakers* decidedly outshine the looser, more indulgent live takes, several of which duplicate *Sneakers* material. It's the definitive document of their pre-major label days, though, when they fused garage rock with blues, psychedelia, and the Lovin' Spoonful, complete with historical liner notes. *—Richie Unterberger*

In Person! / May 6, 1997 / Norton ✦✦✦
There are loads of Flamin' Groovies live recordings out there, some more legitimate than others, but until now all of them have required some allowances in the mind of the listener to their sonic and musical shortcomings. Not *In Person!*, which actually works as an album. The first ten tracks on this disc were taped for radio broadcast during the final week of the Fillmore West's existence, on June 30, 1971, and capture the Roy Loney lineup of the group at the peak of its form, grinding their way in high style through "Slow Death," "Shakin' All Over," "Teenage Head," "Walkin' the Dog," "Sweet Little Rock & Roller," and "Have You Seen My Baby," among others. There's one bit of little dropout and hints of some slight sound leakage—overall, the audio quality is maybe two steps above that of, say, *The Live Kinks* album (by Muswell Hill's own precursors to the Groovies, natch)—but the balance between the voices and the instruments is about as good as any Groovies concert recording, and for a change, the "room" ambience, as it were, works in the group's favor—the guitars are all nicely represented. Moreover, the performance by Loney, Jordan, and company does work as an audio release—there's nothing here that you had to be here to see. The set is rounded out by "I'm a Man" and "Headin' for the Texas Border" from a Matrix show from a year earlier. Leave it to a label run by members of the A-Bones to get out the best live classic Flamin' Groovies album ever. *—Bruce Eder*

Absolutely the Best / May 11, 1999 / Varese ✦✦✦✦
Since it contains ten classics and five latter-day live tracks, it's hard to agree with the assessment of the title of Varese's *Absolutely the Best*. This 15-track collection certainly contains a selection of the Flamin' Groovies' best material—after all, "Slow Death," "Teenage Head," and "I Can't Hide" are among their best rockers, and "Shake Some Action" and "You Tore Me Down" are two definitive power-pop songs—but the five live tracks keep

this one back, even if hearing the group tear through "A Million Miles Away" may please some hardcore fans. Those fans won't need this collection and the less dedicated should seek out Sire's *Groovies Greatest Grooves*, whose 24 songs paint the definitive portrait of the Flamin' Groovies. *—Stephen Thomas Erlewine*

Flaming Ember

f. 1967, Detroit, MI, **db.** 1972
Blue-Eyed Soul, Soul

A blue-eyed Detroit soul group that enjoyed a short time in the spotlight during 1970-1971, they were initally known as the Flaming Embers. The band included guitarist Joe Sladich, pianist Bill Ellis, bassist Jim Bugnel, and drummer Jerry Plunk. They first recorded for Ric-Tic in 1968, then moved to Hot Wax and dropped the "s." The songs "Mind, Body and Soul," "Westbound #9," and "I'm Not My Brother's Keeper" each made the pop Top 40 and R&B Top 20. But "Stop the World and Let Me Off" flopped, despite being released on both Hot Wax and Radio Active Gold. The group later changed its name to Mind, Body and Soul and became a fixture on the Detroit bar scene through the late '70s. *—Ron Wynn*

● **The Best of Flaming Ember** / 1992 / Fantasy ✦✦✦✦✦

The Flaming Lips

f. 1983, Oklahoma City, OK
Experimental Rock, Dream Pop, Neo-Psychedelia, Alternative Pop/Rock, Noise Pop, American Underground

Of the innumerable one-hit wonders littering the cultural landscape, few, if any, were so brave, so frequently brilliant, and so deliciously weird as the Flaming Lips. To even classify the Lips as merely a one-hit wonder is to do the group a grave injustice: although their standing as a commercial entity proved little more than a blip on the radar screen, their moment of Top 40 success was simply another pit-stop on one of the more surreal and haphazard career trajectories in pop music—an acid-bubblegum band with as much affinity for sweet melodies as blistering noise assaults, their off-kilter sound, uncommon emotional depth, and bizarre history (packed with tales of self-immolating fans and the like) firmly established them as one of the true originals of the post-punk era. Conventional wisdom dictates that artists lose their edge when they sign to a major label, but the Lips' tenure at Warner Bros. is irrefutable proof that some bands in fact reach new creative heights when allowed to romp around in the corporate sandbox. 1992's *Hit to the Death in the Future Head*, their Warner debut, bridged the gap between the monolithic noise of past efforts with a melodic beauty still in its embryonic stages—their first truly accessible effort to date, at the same time it somehow retains all of the idiosyncratic force of their prior white-noise freakouts. The hit "She Don't Use Jelly" aside, 1993's *Transmissions from the Satellite Heart* is even more strangely compelling—sonically dense, lyrically addled, and melodically haywire, it's an idiot-savant classic. 1995's *Clouds Taste Metallic* is quite possibly a masterpiece, the *Lips'* very own *Pet Sounds* (complete with animal noises); it was followed by one of the most unique major label releases ever—1997's *Zaireeka*, a logistically nightmarish set of four CDs designed to be played simultaneously. 1999's *The Soft Bulletin* might just be the best album of the decade, period. And somehow, in the midst of it all the band even guest starred on *Beverly Hills 90210*—go figure. *—Jason Ankeny*

The Flaming Lips / 1985 / Restless ✦✦

Hear It Is / 1986 / Restless/Enigma ✦✦✦

Hearing *Hear It Is* years later, after all the band had done up to the new century, makes for an almost surreal experience. No swirling orchestral parts, no Beach Boys-on-Mars homages, even Wayne Coyne's immediately recognizable cracked fracture of a voice isn't present. Instead, it's raunchy bar-band-gone-insane fun or calmer but not too wracked ruminations from Coyne, with music to match. It isn't as completely discontinuous as might be thought, though—Coyne's vision was already distinctly gone, in ways that most bands would kill for. The gentle acoustic strumming that starts the album on "With You" or the steady pace and mournful singing on "Godzilla Flick" shows that subtlety was as much a part of the game as stomping, fried electric guitar insanity. Throughout *Hear It Is*, there's a gleeful "try what works" approach that would only become stronger later—the band may have been punk-inspired and birthed, but Coyne and company drew on everything from country & western to classic rock crunch and more; there are even some clear early goth-rock touches. If anybody was kin at the time, it would be the Meat Puppets, with perhaps a little less interest in high lonesome sounds. Texas psych types like the 13th Floor Elevators and the Red Krayola were clear forebears—one can easily imagine Roky Erickson coming up with shaggy dog stories and music for the likes of "Trains, Brains and Rain." The group's own uniqueness comes through, though. Consider the blunt imagery of "Jesus Shootin' Heroin" or the clearly humorous yells and climax of "Charlie Manson Blues" as two examples of many. Initial CD versions of the album included the self-titled EP, while later pressings only added an enthusiastic fuzz-take of Eddie Cochran-via-Blue Cheer's "Summertime Blues." *—Ned Raggett*

Oh My Gawd!!! . . . The Flaming Lips / 1987 / Restless/Enigma ✦✦✦

Starting with either a sample or a cool replication of a legendary one-off line in the Beatles' "Revolution No. 9"—"Take this, brother, may it serve you well!"—the Lips dive head-on into rock dreams on *Oh My Gawd!!!* Coyne's sudden resemblance vocally to Paul Westerberg is its own curiosity, but the Replacements never quite got so fried—drunk, yes, but not fried. The cover, one weird-ass collage of skullmonsters, random photographs of landscapes, dogs and things, and, on the back, somebody literally burning up serves to set the mood just as much as the rampaging fun of "Everything's Exploding." The same combination of this and that which made *Hear It Is* a fun listen takes precedence here—Coyne and company can strum along softly or crank everything up to ten and back as they please, and they do. Coyne's knack for utterly brilliant song titles also takes full life here—how else to explain such hilarities as "Maximum Dream for Evil Knievel" or the flatly phrased "Prescription: Love," a groovy mindbender and arty rave-up all at once. While the Lips here are still a rock band par excellence, evidence of the band's increasing ambition kicks in with the simultaneously mocking and celebratory Pink Floyd vibes of "One Million Billionth of a Millisecond on a Sunday Morning." All ten minutes of it should really be on *Ummagumma*—Richard English's drums are pure Nick Mason from the get-go—but darn if it doesn't sound equally great here, as Coyne idly wonders what to do with himself in the time allotted. Other songs throw in everything from Led Zeppelin drum stomps to Mountain/Deep Purple raspy rock bellowing and more besides—theoretically everything mid-'80s American indie rock wasn't, making the Lips that much more of a fun, unique trip. *—Ned Raggett*

Telepathic Surgery / 1989 / Restless/Enigma ✦✦✦

With a few more studio tweaks and tricks at play, part of the band's continual efforts to find out just what could be done with a studio, *Telepathic Surgery* is pretty much the companion piece to *Oh My Gawd!!!*, blending the same great crazy combination of influences into the mix. That the opening track has everything from a rushed Sonic Youth rhythm roil to heavily flanged guitar solos that are all treble and back again isn't surprising at all, really. Coyne later described the album as more open-ended experimentation with overdubs than a collection of songs per se—some of the random orchestral samples and other drop-ins indicate as much—but *Telepathic Surgery* has its joys, as much garage rock nuttiness as fried, off-kilter post-punk. Coyne himself is still in rough voice plenty of places, but finding his own bit by bit; he still doesn't really sound like he would in the '90s, but the gentler side creeps in here and there. "Chrome Plated Suicide," another in the string of Lips songs with brilliant titles, has him sounding a lot more wistful than on numerous other full-on crunch monsters. Call it the bells on "Chrome Plated Suicide" itself that also help the slightly dreamier feeling, even as Coyne peels off a nicely zonked guitar solo halfway through. Other fun titles (and fine songs) include "Redneck School of Technology" and "The Spontaneous Combustion of John," the latter a short but fun little track. Then there's the cryptic subtitle of "Hari-Krishna Stomp Wagon"—"fuck Led Zeppelin"—which may yet forever remain a mystery given the Lips' own clear influence by said group. The most notorious track actually only surfaced on the CD version—"Hell's Angel's Cracker Factory," a nearly 25-minute long zone through backwards-run vocals, endless solos, trance drums, and more. *—Ned Raggett*

In a Priest Driven Ambulance / Sep. 1990 / Restless/Enigma ✦✦✦✦

In a Priest Driven Ambulance ranks as the first truly brilliant Flaming Lips album; the first effort to feature guitarist Jonathan "Dingus" Donahue, it's a loose concept record which brings Wayne Coyne's long-standing obsessions with religion bubbling to the surface. The thematic glue creates a structural framework unlike anything found on previous albums, resulting in a newfound sense of cohesion and depth: songs like "Rainin' Babies" and "Five-Stop Mother Superior Rain" offer unforeseen levels of poignancy, while guitar freak-outs such as "Unconsciously Screamin'" and "Mountain Side" slash and burn with remarkable potency. For the Lips, the future begins here. *—Jason Ankeny*

Hit to Death in the Future Head / Aug. 11, 1992 / Warner Brothers ✦✦✦

With *Hit to Death in the Future Head*, the Lips make the leap to major-label status as though it were the moment they've been waiting for all their lives. Though not as conceptually tight as *In a Priest Driven Ambulance*, the album is no less cohesive or imaginative, and in its way serves as the bridge between the band's noisier, more hallucinatory indie work and the acid-bubblegum aesthetic perfected on their later Warner Bros. albums. Nowhere are the band's pop smarts more evident than on "The Sun," which freely quotes Carole King's "So Far Away," or on the undeniably catchy "Gingerale Afternoon (The Astrology of a Saturday)" and "Frogs"; tracks like "Felt Good to Burn" and "Halloween on the Barbary Coast," meanwhile, indulge fully in the trademark weirdness that got the group this far. (And speaking of indulgence, check out the unlisted bonus track, which offers some 29 minutes of speaker-hopping static assault.) *—Jason Ankeny*

● **Transmissions from the Satellite Heart** / Jan. 1993 / Warner Brothers ✦✦✦✦✦

The addition of guitarist Ronald Jones and drummer Steven Drozd recharges the Lips' batteries for the superb *Transmissions from the Satellite Heart*, another prismatic delicacy which continues the group's drift toward pop nirvana. In typical fashion, the record's left-field hit, the freakshow sing-along "She Don't Use Jelly," bears little resemblance to the album as a whole; the remainder of *Transmissions* is much more sonically and structurally ambitious—the towering "Moth in the Incubator" keeps generating new layers of noise before erupting into an amphetamine waltz, "Pilot Can at the Queer of God" dive-bombs with kamikaze recklessness, and the slow-burning "Oh My Pregnant Head" is as mind-expanding as its title. *—Jason Ankeny*

Clouds Taste Metallic / Sep. 19, 1995 / Warner Brothers ✦✦✦✦✦

The same extraordinary madness which infected the best work of Brian Wilson rears its head on the shimmering and melodic *Clouds Taste Metallic*, a masterful collection which completes the Flaming Lips' odyssey into the pop stratosphere. The *Pet Sounds* comparisons are obvious—two of the highlights are titled "This Here Giraffe" and "Christmas at the Zoo"—yet not unfair; like Brian Wilson, Wayne Coyne has refined his unique vision into something both highly personal and powerfully universal. Similarly, while Coyne's lyrics remain as acid-damaged and inscrutable as ever, his densely-constructed songs convey emotional complexities far beyond the scope of their head-case titles ("Psychiatric Explorations of the Fetus with Needles," "Guy Who Got a Headache and Accidentally Saves the World"); galvanized by equal parts newfound maturity and childlike wonderment, *Clouds Taste Metallic* is both the Flaming Lips' most intricate and most irresistible work. *—Jason Ankeny*

Zaireeka / Oct. 28, 1997 / Warner Brothers ✦✦✦✦

A combination of the words "Zaire" and "Eureka," *Zaireeka* is a term coined by Flaming Lips frontman Wayne Coyne symbolizing the fusion of anarchy and genius. It's a perfect title; *Zaireeka* is the culmination of the Lips' helter-skelter brilliance. Pushing the concept of interactive listening into new realms of possibility, the work extends Coyne's infamous "parking lot experiments" into not merely one album, but four separate discs that can be played separately or in groups of two, three, and four with multiple stereos. (Properly synchronized multi-disc playback requires more than one person—it's literally a party album.) Between combining the discs and toying with volume, balance, fidelity, etc., the options are truly limitless. No two multi-disc performances can be repeated, thanks to the space-time continuum and discrepancies from one CD player to another. Musically as well as conceptually, the Lips are defiantly experimental throughout *Zaireeka*; individually, each disc sounds more like free jazz than pop, although Coyne's diamond-sharp melodic sensibilities prevail even during the most chaotic moments. With each additional disc, the music's force and ingenuity reveals itself: "Riding to Work in the Year 2025 (Your Invisible Now)" is an epic orchestral noise suite, "Thirty-Five Thousand Feet of Despair" is a multi-narrative plane-crash drama remarkably evocative in its depiction of fear and chaos, and "How Will We Know? (Futuristic Crashendos)" features such extreme high and low frequencies that it can lead to disorientation, confusion, or nausea (the track is not recommended to be played while operating a motor vehicle or in the presence of infants). Logistical nightmares aside, *Zaireeka* is a dense, difficult work, recommended only for the hardiest Flaming Lips fetishists; however, they're in for the musical experience of a lifetime. —*Jason Ankeny*

A Collection of Songs Representing an Enthusiasm for Recording . . . By Amateurs / Sep. 29, 1998 / Restless ✦✦✦✦✦

With the exception of the superb *In a Priest Driven Ambulance*, the Flaming Lips' early albums for the Restless label are at best hit-or-miss affairs; *A Collection of Songs Representing an Enthusiasm for Recording . . . By Amateurs* sifts through the debris to rescue the most enduring material from those LPs, revealing a band still struggling to discover their voice but on occasion capable of flickers of startling brilliance. The best tracks here—"Unconsciously Screamin'," "Jesus Shootin' Heroin," and "One Million, Billionth of a Millisecond on a Sunday Morning"—rival anything in the group's catalog, while even the weaker selections still suggest a truly original musical vision in embryo. Complete with a batch of unreleased covers making the set as valuable to longtime fans as more recent converts, *A Collection of Songs* proves once and for all that the Lips didn't simply become a great band overnight—they always had it in them, with the best still yet to come. —*Jason Ankeny*

The Soft Bulletin / Jun. 22, 1999 / Warner Brothers ✦✦✦✦✦

So where does a band go after releasing the most defiantly experimental record of its career? If you're the Flaming Lips, you keep rushing headlong into the unknown—*The Soft Bulletin*, their follow-up to the four-disc gambit *Zaireeka*, is in many ways their most daring work yet, a plaintively emotional, lushly symphonic pop masterpiece eons removed from their past efforts' mind-warping noise of their past efforts. Though more conventional in concept and scope than *Zaireeka*, *The Soft Bulletin* clearly reflects its predecessor's expansive sonic palette. Its multidimensional sound is positively celestial, a shape-shifting pastiche of blissful melodies, heavenly harmonies, and orchestral flourishes; but for all its headphone-friendly innovations, the music is still amazingly accessible, never sacrificing popcraft in the name of radical experimentation. (Its aims are so perversely commercial, in fact, that hit R&B remixer Peter Mokran tinkered with the cuts "Race for the Prize" and "Waitin' for a Superman" in the hopes of earning mainstream radio attention.) But what's most remarkable about *The Soft Bulletin* is its humanity—these are Wayne Coyne's most personal and deeply felt songs, as well as the warmest and most giving. No longer hiding behind surreal vignettes about Jesus, zoo animals, and outer space, Coyne pours his heart and soul into each one of these tracks, poignantly exploring love, loss, and the fate of all mankind; highlights like "The Spiderbite Song" and "Feeling Yourself Disintegrate" are so nakedly emotional and transcendently spiritual that it's impossible not to be moved by their beauty. There's no telling where the Lips will go from here, but it's almost beside the point—not just the best album of 1999, *The Soft Bulletin* might be the best record of the entire decade. —*Jason Ankeny*

The Flamingos

f. 1952, Chicago, IL
Doo Wop

Both prolific and seminal in their influence and impact, the Flamingos may have been the greatest harmonizing vocal ensemble ever, and were certainly among the premier units of the doo wop/R&B era. Cousins Jake and Zeke Carey formed the group in Chicago, and added lead vocalist Sollie McElroy just before their recording debut for the Chance label, 1953's "If I Can't Have You." After McElroy left and was replaced by Nate Nelson, the Flamingos enjoyed their first chart success with Checker, scoring a Top Ten R&B hit with "I'll Be Home" in 1956. Signed to End in 1958, the following year's "I Only Have Eyes for You" became their biggest hit, peaking at number three R&B and number 11 pop. It was the start of a productive period that saw the Flamingos issue four albums for End and get two more R&B Top 30 singles, one the Sam Cooke composition "Nobody Loves Me Like You" in 1960. The group returned briefly to Checker in 1964 and later recorded for Phillips, Julman and Polydor, but couldn't regain their former standing. They remained among the genre's most beloved groups, and anthologies of their material on Chance and Checker have been reissued. In 1993, *The Flamingos Meet the Moonglows* was reissued by Vee-Jay. —*Ron Wynn*

★ **The Doo Bop She Bop: The Best of the Flamingos** / May 1990 / Rhino ✦✦✦✦
The Doo Bop She Bop: Best of the Flamingos is an 18-track collection that compiles all of the Flamingos' biggest hits and best songs. *The Doo Bop She Bop* ignores the group's latter-day soul hits and concentrates solely on their doo wop material, which makes for a stronger, more cohesive collection. "I Only Have Eyes for You" is the acknowledged classic, while "I'll Be Home" and "A Kiss from Your Lips" were hits in their own right, but the compilation proves that the Flamingos were one of the greatest doo-wop groups with its lesser-known numbers like "The Vow" and "The Ladder of Love." —*Stephen Thomas Erlewine*

For Collectors Only / Feb. 21, 1992 / Collectables ✦✦✦✦✦

The title on this two-CD set is more than a little unfair—in fact, it's downright inaccurate. *For Collectors Only* is one of the more impressive collections of material by this celebrated R&B vocal group, consisting entirely of songs cut for George Goldner's Gone Records, which was their most successful commercial period and arguably represents the group's best years. The 42 songs here include three tracks ("I'll Be Home," "A Kiss From Your Lips," "Lovers Never Say Goodbye") which are either previously unissued outtakes or previously unreleased altogether, and they're icing on the cake. This collection's real virtue is its assembly of the previously issued numbers; the highlights are, of course, the group's treatment of ballad standards such as "I Only Have Eyes for You," "My Foolish Heart," and "Love Walked In," but this set also includes unusual parts of their repertory, like the riveting, fast-paced Gone Records version of "Jump Children" (to which they were seen miming brilliantly, in a stunning performance clip, in the 1959 movie *Go Johnny Go*). Its presence, along with the outtakes, makes this double disc preferable to Rhino Records' *Best of*, and essential listening for anyone who owns MCA's compilation of the group's Chess recordings. The annotation is especially frustrating, however—it consists of a reprinted interview with two of the group's original members discussing their days with Chance Records, which considerably predates any of the songs here. The sound is acceptable if unexceptional, and has been outstripped by the audio quality on West Side's recent two-LP-on-one-CD reissues of the Flamingos' albums. —*Bruce Eder*

Complete Chess Masters Plus / May 20, 1997 / Chess ✦✦✦✦✦

The Flamingos didn't have many hits while they were at Checker, but those two singles—"I'll Be Home" and "A Kiss from Your Lips"—were terrific, sketching out the lush sound they would later blossom on "I Only Have Eyes for You." *Complete Chess Masters Plus* contains all 18 songs, including two previously unreleased tracks, the group recorded for Checker and Chess. Although it's not a definitive career overview, it's an essential item for collectors of doo wop and vocal R&B, since it's lovingly packaged and contains numerous gems, including "The Vow" and "Dream of a Lifetime." —*Stephen Thomas Erlewine*

Fleetwood Mac

f. 1967, London, England
Album Rock, British Blues, Pop/Rock, Soft Rock, Adult Contemporary, Blues-Rock

While most bands undergo a number of changes over the course of their career, few groups experienced such radical stylistic changes as Fleetwood Mac. Initially conceived as a hard-edged British blues combo in the late '60s, the band gradually evolved into a polished pop-rock act over the course of a decade. Throughout all of their incarnations, the only consistent members of Fleetwood Mac were drummer Mick Fleetwood and bassist John McVie—the rhythm section who provided the band with its name. Ironically, they had the least influence over the musical direction of the band. Originally, guitarists Peter Green and Jeremy Spencer provided the band with its gutsy, neo-psychedelic blues-rock sound, but as both guitarists descended into mental illness, the group began moving toward pop-rock with the songwriting of pianist Christine McVie. By the mid-'70s, Fleetwood Mac had relocated to California, where they added the soft-rock duo of Lindsey Buckingham and Stevie Nicks to their lineup. Obsessed with the meticulously arranged pop of the Beach Boys and the Beatles, Buckingham helped the band become one of the most popular groups of the late '70s. Combining soft-rock with the confessional introspection of singer-songwriters, Fleetwood Mac created a slick but emotional sound that helped 1977's *Rumours* become one of the biggest-selling albums of all time. The band's retained their popularity through the early '80s, when Buckingham, Nicks, and Christine McVie all began pursuing solo careers. The band reunited for one album, 1987's *Tango in the Night*, before splintering in the late '80s. Buckingham left the group initially, but the band decided to soldier on, releasing one other album before Nicks and McVie left the band in the early '90s, hastening the group's commercial decline. —*Stephen Thomas Erlewine*

Peter Green's Fleetwood Mac / Feb. 1968 / Blue Horizon ✦✦✦✦✦

Fleetwood Mac's debut LP was a highlight of the late-'60s British blues boom. Green's always inspired playing, the capable (if erratic) songwriting, and the general panache of the band as a whole placed them leagues above the overcrowded field. Elmore James is a big influence on this set, particularly on the tunes fronted by Jeremy Spencer ("Shake Your Moneymaker," "Got to Move"). Spencer's bluster, however, was outshone by the budding singing and songwriting skills of Green. The guitarist balanced humor and vulnerability on cuts like "Looking for Somebody" and "Long Grey Mare," and with "If I Loved Another Woman," he offered a glimpse of the Latin-blues fusion that he would perfect with "Black Magic Woman." The album was an unexpected smash in the U.K., reaching number four on the British charts. —*Richie Unterberger*

Mr. Wonderful / Aug. 1968 / Castle ✦✦

Although it made number ten in the U.K., Fleetwood Mac's second album was a disappointment following their promising debut. So much of the record was routine blues that it could even be said that it represented something of a regression from the first LP, despite the enlistment of a horn section and pianist Christine Perfect (the future Christine

McVie) to help on the sessions. In particular, the limits of Jeremy Spencer's potential for creative contribution were badly exposed, as the tracks that featured his songwriting and/or vocals were basic Elmore James covers or derivations. Peter Green, the band's major talent at this point, did not deliver original material on the level of the classic singles he would pen for the band in 1969, or even on the level of first-album standouts like "I Loved Another Woman." The best of the lot, perhaps, is "Love That Burns," with its mournful minor-key melody and sluggish, responsive horn lines. *Mr. Wonderful*, strangely, was not issued in the U.S., although about half the songs turned up on its state-side counterpart, *English Rose*, which was fleshed out with some standout late-'60s British singles and a few new tracks penned by Danny Kirwan (who joined the band after *Mr. Wonderful* was recorded). *—Richie Unterberger*

English Rose / Jan. 1969 / Epic ✦✦✦✦✦
Under the direction of Peter Green, Fleetwood Mac is heard as a British blues group, although its most notable performances are on Green's original tunes "Black Magic Woman" and "Albatross," both British hits. *—William Ruhlmann*

● **Pious Bird of Good Omen** / Aug. 1969 / Columbia ✦✦✦✦✦
This is a compilation of Fleetwood Mac's early period, 1967-1968, featuring both sides of its debut single, "I Believe My Time Ain't Long"/"Rambling Pony" and many blues covers, as well as the hits "Albatross" and "Black Magic Woman." *—William Ruhlmann*

Then Play On / Oct. 1969 / Reprise ✦✦✦✦
This Peter Green-led edition of the Mac isn't just an important transition between their initial blues-based incarnation and the mega-pop band they became, it's also their most vital, exciting version. The addition of Danny Kirwan as second guitarist and songwriter foreshadows not only the soft-rock terrain of "Bare Trees" and "Kiln House" with Christine Perfect-McVie, but also predicts *Rumours*. That only pertains to roughly half of the also excellent material here, though; the rest is quintessential Green. The immortal "Oh Well," with its hard-edged, thickly layered guitars and chamber-like sections, is perhaps the band's most enduring progressive composition. "Rattlesnake Shake" is another familiar number, a down-and-dirty, even-paced funk, with clean, wall-of-sound guitars. Choogling drums and Green's fiery improvisations power "Searching for Madge," perhaps Mac's most inspired work save "Green Manalishi," and leads into an unlikely symphonic interlude and the similar, lighter boogie "Fighting for Madge." A hot Afro-Cuban rhythm with beautiful guitars from Kirwan and Green on "Coming Your Way" not only defines the Mac's sound, but the rock aesthetic of the day. Of the songs with Kirwan's stamp on them, "Closing My Eyes" is a mysterious waltz love song; haunting guitars approach surf music on the instrumental "My Dream"; while "Although the Sun Is Shining" is the ultimate pre-*Rumours* number someone should revisit. Blues roots still crop up on the spatial, loose, Hendrix-tinged "Underway," the folky blues tale of a lesbian affair on "Like Crying," and the final outcry of the ever-poignant "Show Biz Blues," with Green moaning "do you really give a damn for me?" *Then Play On* is a reminder of how pervasive and powerful Green's influence was on Mac's originality and individual stance beyond his involvement. Still highly recommended and a must-buy after all these years, it remains their magnum opus. *—Michael G. Nastos*

Kiln House / Sep. 1970 / Reprise ✦✦✦
Fleetwood Mac's first album after the departure of their nominal leader, Peter Green, finds the remaining members, Mick Fleetwood, John McVie, Jeremy Spencer, and Danny Kirwan (plus McVie's wife, Christine) trying to maintain the band's guitar-heavy, blues-rock approach, with the burden falling on Spencer and Kirwan. They don't embarrass themselves, but none of this is of the caliber of Green's work. *—William Ruhlmann*

Future Games / Nov. 1971 / Reprise ✦✦✦
By the time of this album's release, Jeremy Spencer had been replaced by Bob Welch and Christine McVie had begun to assert herself more as a singer and songwriter. The result is a distinct move toward folk-rock and pop; this album sounds almost nothing like Peter Green's Fleetwood Mac. Welch's eight-minute title track has one of his characteristic haunting melodies, and with pruning and better editing could have been a hit. Christine McVie's "Show Me a Smile" is one of her loveliest ballads. Initial popular reaction was mixed: the album didn't sell as well as *Kiln House*, but it sold better than any of the band's first three albums in the U.S. In the U.K., where the original lineup had been more successful, *Future Games* didn't chart at all, the same fate that would befall the rest of its albums until the Lindsey Buckingham-Stevie Nicks era. *—William Ruhlmann*

Bare Trees / Mar. 1972 / Reprise ✦✦✦✦
Arguably the first consistently strong album Fleetwood Mac ever recorded, 1972's *Bare Trees* is also the album where the band finally defines its post-blues musical personality. Low-key but less narcoleptically mellow than 1971's sleepy *Future Games*, *Bare Trees* is a singer/songwriter album in the traditional early-'70s style, backed up with just enough musical muscle to keep from sounding like weedy soft rock in the manner of Bread or Cat Stevens. This is the one Fleetwood Mac album on which singer/guitarist Danny Kirwan is the dominant figure, writing five songs to Christine McVie and Bob Welch's two apiece. Impressively, all three writers get off a small masterpiece on side two; McVie's "Spare Me a Little of Your Love" sounds like a dry run for the string of hits she would start writing with 1975's *Fleetwood Mac*, and it's her first really good pop song. By comparison, Kirwan and Welch's best songs are all-time career highlights. Kirwan's "Dust" combines a gentle, gliding melody with resigned, melancholy lyrics and his most memorable chorus. Welch's "Sentimental Lady" was, of course, his first solo hit in its 1977 re-recorded version, but this original take is far superior, and one of the great lost pop songs of the early '70s. The rest of the album is less magical, but the instrumental "Sunny Side of Heaven" and the downright funky "Danny's Chant" are impressive in their use of atmospheric arrangements and so point toward the subtle but effective production choices that would make *Fleetwood Mac* and *Rumours* among the most listenable albums of their time. *Bare Trees* isn't in that league, but it shows that after five years of false starts and failed experiments, Fleetwood Mac were finally on their way. *—Stewart Mason*

Penguin / Mar. 1973 / Reprise ✦✦

Mystery to Me / Oct. 1973 / Reprise ✦✦✦
At this point the band was best known as a British blues unit. Slowly but surely the band was becoming more acclimated with a production style that was reminiscent of the California pop sound. With the majority of the blues and psychedelic behind them, *Mystery to Me* finds Fleetwood Mac in a more ruminative vein. American guitarist Bob Welch established that path. Despite the all-encompassing ethos, Welch's songwriting skills made him walk a fine line between the mystical and the silly. But luckily most everything works here. The leadoff song, the laid-back "Emerald Eyes" matches Welch's spacey lyrics and vocals as Christine McVie provides great backing help. The album's best track, the gorgeous and lyrically strong "Hypnotized" has Welch matching an effortless, soothing croon with jazzy guitar riffs. Throughout *Mystery to Me* the amazing and almost telepathic drums and bass of Mick Fleetwood and John McVie give this effort more panache and muscle than was represented on this effort's predecessor, *Bare Trees*. The best Christine McVie offering, "Keep on Going," has a strong, soulful string arrangement and her customary sensual and poised vocals. The only weak spot is the ill-advised cover of "For Your Love" that's steeped in hackneyed, post-psychedelic style. *Mystery to Me*'s interesting sound is directly attributed to the fact that it was recorded on the Rolling Stones Mobile Unit. This effort is custom-made for those who like thoughtful offerings and is a valuable set in the scheme of the band. *—Jason Elias*

Heroes Are Hard to Find / Sep. 1974 / Reprise ✦✦✦
Welch's peak as a songwriter (with new highs by Christine McVie) is also his swan song with the group. *—William Ruhlmann*

Fleetwood Mac in Chicago / 1975 / Sire/Warner Bros./Blue Horizon ✦✦

☆ **Fleetwood Mac** / Jul. 1975 / Reprise ✦✦✦✦✦
"Monday Morning," a sunny slice of folk-rock with Beach Boys harmonies, opens *Fleetwood Mac* and makes it clear that the band is no longer a blues-rock outfit. Lindsey Buckingham and Stevie Nicks were the catalyst for Fleetwood Mac's successful re-emergence as a mainstream pop/rock band. While Buckingham only contributed three songs, he helped the band develop a coherent vision, providing crystal-clear backings for Nicks' hippie anthems and Christine McVie's remarkably improved pop-soul. McVie dominates the album, contributing some of her finest songs, including the sighing "Over My Head" and the bouncy "Say You Love Me." Nicks' songs function as folky counterpoints to McVie's sweet pop, and she rarely ever wrote songs as memorably affecting as "Rhiannon" or "Landslide." Remarkably, *Fleetwood Mac* is a blockbuster album that isn't dominated by its hit singles, and its album tracks ("World Turning," "Sugar Daddy," "Crystal") demonstrate a depth of both songwriting and musicality that would blossom fully on *Rumours*. *—Stephen Thomas Erlewine*

Original Fleetwood Mac / 1977 / Sire ✦✦
This collection of outtakes from the group's early days probably dates from 1967-68, and finds the band at their most reverently bluesy. Peter Green wrote most of the material on this set, which is quite similar to the band's first couple of albums in its purist British take on traditional electric blues forms. The material, however, isn't nearly as strong as the best early Fleetwood Mac; not that the band should be faulted for that, as this is an outtake collection, after all. A couple of the tunes featuring Jeremy Spencer are actually taken from an audition that Spencer's pre-Fleetwood Mac outfit, the Levi Set, recorded for the Blue Horizon label in England. The best track is the driving instrumental "Fleetwood Mac," and has been rumored to be an outtake from Green's days with John Mayall's Bluesbreakers. *—Richie Unterberger*

★ **Rumours** / Feb. 4, 1977 / Reprise ✦✦✦✦✦
The new lineup that Fleetwood Mac successfully unveiled with their eponymous 1975 album became even more successful with the multi-platinum *Rumours*, which became the band's most celebrated album and one of the best-selling albums of all time. To be sure, this was a very different sounding Fleetwood Mac than the blues-rock outfit of the late '60s. This edition of the band generally wasn't well received by rock critics (who tend to be critical of all things commercial). But as commercial and slick as *Rumours* is, the music has a lot of heart and never comes across as insincere. From Christine McVie's optimistic "Don't Stop" (which President Bill Clinton used as his campaign theme song in 1992) to Lindsey Buckingham's remorseful "Go Your Own Way," *Rumours* is consistently memorable. And the folkish "Gold Dust Woman" (covered by Courtney Love and Hole in 1996) and the melancholy hit "Dreams" made it quite clear just how much depth and substance Stevie Nicks was capable of. *—Alex Henderson*

Tusk / Oct. 1979 / Reprise ✦✦✦✦✦
Where *Rumours* achieved greatness through turmoil, its double-album follow-up, *Tusk*, is the sound of a band imploding. Lindsey Buckingham began to assume control of Fleetwood Mac during the *Rumours* sessions, but he dominates *Tusk*, turning the album into a paranoid roller coaster ride where sweet soft rock is offset by feverish cocaine fantasies. Christine McVie and Stevie Nicks don't deviate from their established soft-rock and folk-rock templates, and all their songs are first-rate, whether it's McVie's "Over and Over" or Nicks' "Sara." Buckingham gives these mainstream-oriented songs off-kilter arrangements, so they can fit neatly with his nervy, insular, yet catchy songs. Alternating bracing pop-rockers like "The Ledge" and "What Makes You Think You're the One" with melancholic, Beach Boys-style ballads like "Save Me a Place" and "That's All For Everyone," Buckingham subverts pop/rock with weird arrangements and unpredictable melodies, which are nevertheless given accessible productions. Even the hit title track is a strange, menacing threat punctuated by a marching band. This is as strange as mainstream pop

gets, even pushing on the borders of the avant-garde. Because of its ambitions, *Tusk* failed to replicate the success of its two predecessors (it still went double platinum, though), yet it earned a dedicated cult audience of fans of twisted, melodic pop. *—Stephen Thomas Erlewine*

Fleetwood Mac Live / Dec. 1980 / Reprise ♦♦♦
Fleetwood Mac's first live album finds it at its popular height, pumping out hit after hit. To its credit, the group nevertheless puts out: Fleetwood drums like a demon and Buckingham plays fiercely. All the hits you'd expect are here, spread across two discs, and there's also a charming backstage rendition of the Beach Boys' "Farmer's Daughter." *—William Ruhlmann*

Mirage / Jun. 1982 / Reprise ♦♦♦
Fleetwood Mac retreated from the insular strangeness of *Tusk* and returned to straightforward pop songcraft for *Mirage*. Boasting a glossy, friendly production that makes even the lesser numbers pleasant and ingratiating, *Mirage* nonetheless suffers from a lack of substance. *Rumours* had raw emotion to give it a core, and *Tusk* had Lindsey Buckingham's runaway ambition. For its part, *Mirage* sounds as if its sole goal is to sustain Fleetwood Mac's popularity, and while there may be a handful of terrific songs—notably the hit singles "Gypsy," "Love in Store," and "Hold Me"—it simply isn't as compelling as the group's previous three albums. *—Stephen Thomas Erlewine*

Tango in the Night / 1987 / Reprise ♦♦♦
Artistically and commercially, the Stevie Nicks/Lindsey Buckingham/Mick Fleetwood/ Christine and John McVie edition of Fleetwood Mac had been on a roll for over a decade when *Tango in the Night* was released in early 1987. This would, unfortunately, be Buckingham's last album with the pop/rock supergroup—and he definitely ended his association with the band on a creative high note. Serving as the album's main producer, Buckingham gives an edgy quality to everything from the haunting "Isn't It Midnight" to the poetic "Seven Wonders" to the dreamy "Everywhere." Though Buckingham doesn't overproduce, his thoughtful use of synthesizers is a major asset. Without question, "Family Man" and "Caroline" are among the best songs ever written by Buckingham, who consistently brings out the best in his colleagues on this superb album. *—Alex Henderson*

Greatest Hits / Nov. 1988 / Reprise ♦♦♦♦♦
Greatest Hits is a fine overview of Fleetwood Mac's hit-making years, containing the bulk of the group's Top 40 hits of the late '70s and '80s, including "Over My Head," "Rhiannon," "Say You Love Me," "Go Your Own Way," "Dreams," "Don't Stop," "Tusk," "Sara," "Hold Me," "Gypsy," and "Little Lies." Minor hits like "Think About Me," "Love in Store," and "Seven Wonders" are missing, making room for the new songs "As Long As You Follow" (which actually became a hit) and "No Questions Asked.," but overall, *Greatest Hits* is an excellent choice for casual listeners. *—Stephen Thomas Erlewine*

Behind the Mask / Apr. 10, 1990 / Reprise ♦♦
Lindsey Buckingham's departure proved to be a severe blow when Fleetwood Mac unveiled a new lineup with the disappointing *Behind the Mask*, Stevie Nicks' last album with the band. Nicks, Christine and John McVie, and Mick Fleetwood are joined by new members Rick Vito (vocals, lead guitar) and Billy Burnette (vocals, guitar) on this generally weak effort. The production (courtesy of Greg Ladanyi and Fleetwood Mac) is often bland and faceless, and most as the songs are among the least inspired the band ever recorded. The album has a few strong points, including "Save Me" and "Freedom," a haunting number featuring Nicks. But most of the material is quite forgettable. And there would be even less reason for optistim by 1993, when Nicks left as well. *—Alex Henderson*

25 Years: The Chain / Nov. 24, 1992 / Reprise ♦♦♦
Overall, Fleetwood Mac's four-CD box set, *25 Years: The Chain*, contains a lot of great music, with plenty of the 1970s hits that made them one of the biggest bands in the world. It fails as a complete chronicle; not enough weight is given to the early, blues-based Mac with Peter Green, and there are too many songs (nearly a whole disc's worth) from the lightweight 1980s albums. Also, the haphazard song sequencing doesn't help matters—it doesn't make the case for Fleetwood Mac's music as a body of work, and it doesn't trace the evolution, which should be apparent from the diversity of the music. If nothing else, *25 Years—The Chain* offers evidence that Lindsey Buckingham was a brilliant pop composer and that the band's '70s success was well deserved. *—Stephen Thomas Erlewine*

Peter Green's Fleetwood Mac Live at the BBC / Oct. 1995 / Castle ♦♦

Time / Oct. 10, 1995 / Warner Brothers ♦♦
Fleetwood Mac suffered more personnel changes following the release of *Behind the Mask* in 1990, with Stevie Nicks and Rick Vito leaving, to be replaced by newcomer Bekka Bramlett (daughter of Delaney and Bonnie) and veteran Dave Mason. As a result, the group slipped down another notch in terms of quality and attention. Christine McVie could always be relied on to turn in her quotient of four or five perky songs of romantic devotion; Mason checked in with "Blow by Blow," a statement of renewed purpose that was braver than it was accurate; and Bramlett was an appealing, emotive singer. But despite the familiar rhythm section, this simply was not the group that made the great blues-rock of the 1960s or the group that made the great pop-rock of the '70s. And nobody was fooled: *Time* didn't even make the charts. *—William Ruhlmann*

The Dance / Aug. 19, 1997 / Reprise ♦♦♦
Two years after the Buckingham/Nicks/Christine McVie-less incarnation of Fleetwood Mac crashed and burned, their classic '70s lineup reunited for an *MTV Unplugged* session and an accompanying tour. Although it's likely that the reunion was for monetary purposes, it made creative sense as well—no members were as compelling solo as they were with the group. Despite this, the *Unplugged* setting wasn't ideal for a reunion, since the group decided to devote nearly a quarter of *The Dance* to new material, inevitably resulting in unfair comparisons to their warhorses. Since there's so much new material, *The Dance* can't be a truly nostalgic experience either, because the new songs interrupt the flow. Not that they're bad—Buckingham's gentle "Bleed to Love Her" and nervy "My Little Demon" are first-rate, and Nicks' "Silver Springs" finds her at her hippie best—but they aren't given the full-fledged production they deserve. Similarly, the older songs suffer from the slightly hollow unplugged production. All the hits are performed in nearly identical arrangements to the originals, with the exception of Buckingham's solo "Big Love" (an improvement on the original) and the addition of *Tusk*'s marching band to "Don't Stop," which makes the differences all too apparent. Much is the same—McVie and Nicks sound terrific, and the band is tight and professional—but Buckingham has lost some of his range, which undercuts some of his songs. Still, that isn't enough to prevent *The Dance* from being an entertaining listen; it just isn't a substantial one. *—Stephen Thomas Erlewine*

The Vaudeville Years 1968-1970 / Oct. 13, 1998 / Receiver ♦♦♦
Two long CDs' worth of outtakes, alternate versions, and full-length versions from the Peter Green era, most in exemplary sound quality. Although much of this is interesting, and it's occasionally very good, it resembles *Peter Green's Fleetwood Mac Live at the BBC* in its unevenness, both in aesthetic quality and in stylistic tone. One is struck by how much the numbers featuring Green's singing and songwriting surpass those in which the other guitarists come to the fore. When Jeremy Spencer's in charge, it means you get 1950s rock pastiches and blues satires (though he does an okay Elmore James schtick with "Talk to Me Baby" and "My Baby Is Sweeter"). These aren't without their amusing points—there's the entire session of songs that would have made a bonus EP with *Then Play On*, on which Spencer does fairly humorous impressions of Alexis Korner and John Mayall—but deathless art it's not. Green shines on a live version of "Oh Well" (everything else here, incidentally, is from the studio) and alternates of "Showbiz Blues" and "Love that Burns." There are also alternates of "Man of the World" and "The Green Manalishi," though frankly these aren't so different from the familiar renditions that they'll jar you into taking notice. Some of the cuts are nothing more than shapeless jams or instrumental tracks with ideas that sometimes got pumped up into full tunes on official albums. So it's kind of like having a high-quality, easily available bootleg of the Green-era Mac, accent on the *Then Play On* era. But those who like that period of Fleetwood Mac a lot will want to hear this, its luster enhanced by a 48-page booklet with an essay by Green biographer Martin Celmins. *—Richie Unterberger*

The Complete Blue Horizon Sessions: 1967-1969 / Oct. 19, 1999 / Sire ♦♦♦
A six-CD set of everything Fleetwood Mac recorded for the British Blue Horizon label. Wait, you're saying, didn't they only do two albums for Blue Horizon before leaving the company in early 1969? True, but there were also the non-LP singles that comprised the bulk of the U.K. compilation *The Pious Bird of Good Omen*, the two albums of blues jams in Chicago that came out later in 1969, and the 1971 LP *The Original Fleetwood Mac*, comprised of early outtakes. Make each of those half-dozen LPs a CD, add some outtakes and alternate takes to each, and you've got a pretty full box. Unintentionally, this box makes the Mac a candidate for Most Erratic Major Rock Group of the Late 1960s, ranging from the sheer brilliance of Peter Green's songs to rote blues covers that are downright mundane, particularly some of the Jeremy Spencer showcases and Chicago blues jams. If you're a committed enough fan to consider buying this box, you already know that; you're probably more concerned with whether the previously unreleased material merits the cost. Those extras are marginal, to be honest, comprised largely of false starts, incidental studio chatter, and alternate versions that are pretty close to the official takes. Certainly the highlight of those newly unearthed tracks is the 37 minutes of alternate takes of "Need Your Love So Bad." It's also nice that the Danny Kirwan tracks that appeared only on the U.S. album *English Rose* are here as well. Unfortunately, this is not a complete retrospective of the Peter Green era, whose best material was recorded for Reprise; there's also a lot of noteworthy live stuff that appeared on different labels. Looking for more reasons to get the box anyway? There are extensive notes by producer Mike Vernon, which incorporate a few comments from Green. *—Richie Unterberger*

Vaudeville Years 1968-1970, Vol. 2: Show-Biz Blues / Jun. 26, 2001 / Receiver ♦♦♦
The title of this double CD might be a bit confusing to neophytes. It's basically a second helping of rarities, all previously unreleased, from the Peter Green era from Receiver. That label also put out what might be classified as "volume one" of this series. Since much of this is alternate studio or live versions of songs that are available in more polished form, it's something that should primarily be investigated by early Fleetwood Mac/Peter Green buffs. If you're among that crowd, though, there's a good deal of interest and even pleasure to be had. For instance, there are the three previously unissued 1966 instrumentals in the Booker T. & the MG's mode by the Peter B's, a pre-Mac band that Green and Fleetwood played in even before their stints in John Mayall's Bluesbreakers. Other high spots take in a cover of Otis Rush's characteristically spooky minor-key blues "I Have to Laugh" (with Jeremy Spencer on piano and vocals), and working versions of "Show-Biz Blues," one of Green's most scorching, soul-baring originals. Then there's the nice alternate take of "World in Harmony," and "Leaving Town Blues," an oddity in that it has violin by Nick Pickett. Disc two is comprised entirely of live 1970 material, the first two songs from Boston February 1970, the rest from a gig simply identified as London 1970. The sound quality on the live stuff is okay and the performances good, though so much live Mac from this time has already appeared that it's not a revelation. The 52-page booklet, by Green biographer Martin Celmins, is certainly a vital bonus, though, with commentary on both the Peter Green era as a whole and the tracks on *Show-Biz Blues* in particular. *—Richie Unterberger*

The Fleetwoods

f. 1958, Olympia, WA, **db.** 1963

Doo Wop, Pop

Although the Fleetwoods' sound was smooth, without many of the rougher edges of doo wop groups, they were one of the few white vocal groups of the late '50s and early '60s to enjoy success not only on the pop charts, but also the R&B charts. The Fleetwoods' forte was ballads, beginning with their 1959 debut single "Come Softly to Me" and continuing through the next three years. The group broke up in 1963, but their songs became pop-rock classics of the pre-British Invasion era. A trio of Gretchen Christopher, Barbara Ellis, and Gary Troxell, the group wrote "Come Softly to Me" quite early and released the single on Seattle's Dolphin (later Dolton) label. The song became an instant hit, climbing to number one on the American charts and the Top Ten in the UK. Later that year, "Mr. Blue" became their second chart-topper. After vocalist Troxell was drafted just at the height of their popularity though, the Fleetwoods hit the Top Ten just once more, with 1961's "Tragedy." Disbanded in 1963, the group reunited occasionally throughout the ensuing decades, including a 1973 recording session and a 1990 oldies tour following Rhino's release of *The Best of the Fleetwoods*. *—Stephen Thomas Erlewine*

● **The Best of the Fleetwoods** / May 1990 / Rhino ✦✦✦✦

Rhino's *Best of the Fleetwoods* contains all of their hits ("Come Softly to Me," "Mr. Blue," and 16 other songs) on a smartly assembled collection. *—Stephen Thomas Erlewine*

Come Softly to Me: The Very Best of the Fleetwoods / Aug. 10, 1993 / EMI ✦✦✦✦

While the single-disc collection *Come Softly to Me—The Very Best of the Fleetwoods* is a treasure for devoted fans, featuring alternate takes, radio commercials, a comprehensive discography, fine liner notes, and unreleased tracks. Casual listeners will find all of this material extraneous; they will find everything they need on Rhino's collection. *—Stephen Thomas Erlewine*

Flesh for Lulu

f. 1982, England, **db.** 1991

Goth Rock, Alternative Pop/Rock

Fusing the strut and swagger of the Rolling Stones and New York Dolls with the dank coldness of goth-rock, Flesh for Lulu arose from Brixton to build their initial reputation in London's so-called "Batcave" scene. Vocalist/guitarist Nick Marsh, drummer James Mitchell, guitarist Rocco Barker (formerly of Wasted Youth), and bassist Glen Bishop made enough of an impression with their leather, mascara, and lipstick to cut a single for Polydor, "Restless," after which Bishop departed in favor of Kevin Mills. The singles "Roman Candle" and "Subterraneans" followed, with new member Derek Greening joining to play keyboards and guitar, and a self-titled album appeared in 1984. It proved quite unsuccessful, and Flesh for Lulu found themselves back in the world of indie labels for the 1985 EP *Blue Sisters Swing*, which attracted attention for its possibly blasphemous cover art (two nuns kissing) more than the band's greatly improved music. The improvement continued on that year's full-length *Big Fun City*, an eclectic outing that aroused the interest of the Beggars Banquet label. With a new rhythm section of Mike Steed (bass) and Hans Perrson (drums), 1987's *Long Live the Flesh* was a stab at success on mainstream and/or college radio, and "I Go Crazy" proved a minor hit on the latter. Commercial aspirations got the better of the band on the somewhat generic *Plastic Fantastic*, a 1989 record that spelled the end of Flesh for Lulu's career. *—Steve Huey*

Flesh for Lulu / 1984 / Polydor ✦✦✦

● **Big Fun City** / 1985 / Statik ✦✦✦✦✦

Underneath the black clothes and eyeliner, Flesh for Lulu were no more nor less than a pop/rock band, forever cursed by their post-punk past. Born a dozen years too late, the group were condemned to the corners of the indie scene and the edges of the U.S. charts, virtually neglected by the American rock masses that were their natural audience. At least the U.K. indie kids took them to heart, but *Big Fun City* deserved so much more than that. Having shaken off their cobwebs on *Blue Sisters Swing*, Flesh came to NYC (thus the new album's title) to record with producer Craig Leon. A less sympathetic producer would have destroyed this record, either by foisting a thoroughly '80s slickness into the mix, or lazily permitting the group's retro sound to run rampant. Instead, Leon respected the group's vision, creating a modern album that remains a tribute to rock's rich past. A motherlode of riffs are the song's sturdy foundation blocks, mostly mined from a rich R&B vein. The Stones are an obvious influence, although Flesh never plunder directly, instead creating the best riffs Keith Richards never played. Lou Reed and the Velvet Underground also played a major role in the members' youths, while country & western and the blues continued to make welcome appearances. Thus the band touch all the major rock roots before tossing them into their own indie blender. Perhaps Flesh were just too adventurous for the rock community, too willing to take chances, too energetic, too pop, too different. Too bad for the rockers for missing out on such a classic record. The CD also included the *Blue Sisters Swing* EP as an added incentive. *—Jo-Ann Greene*

Long Live the New Flesh / 1987 / Capitol ✦✦✦✦✦

Determined that an American breakthrough was now within their grasp, Flesh for Lulu gambled the farm on *Long Live the New Flesh*. In the short term it was a smart move and placed the band right on the verge of stardom, but in the long term it was, in retrospect, suicide. In an altered reality kind of way, *New* and its predecessor, *Big Fun City*, correspond virtually track for track, with the rockers frontloaded and the softer numbers mainly in the second half. But the title tells the whole story, and indeed launched a very new Flesh upon the world. Gone were the masses of R&B riffs and punky rhythms that fired their last album; in came a new arena sound. The pop/rock melodies still remained, but were now fleshed out (so to speak) with synths, female backing vocalists, big rock guitar, and a Gary Glitter stomping beat. Of course, the British found this new Flesh bloated to obesity, but this was what America wanted, and the band were happy to dish it up. But even while toning done their punkier sound and R&B riffs, at least the band remained diverse. Going down *Fun*'s genre checklist, *Live* also includes country & western hybrids, a bit of blues, a nod to U2 ("Sleeping Dogs"), and a closing experimental track. So what *Fun* was for the Brits—a classic pop/rock album in an indie mold—*Live* was for Americans—a classic pop/rock album in an arena mold. Pick your poison, both records are excellent, but few but the most die-hard fans will find them both equally appealing. *—Jo-Ann Greene*

Plastic Fantastic / Sep. 20, 1989 / Capitol ✦✦✦

The Fleshtones

f. 1976, Queens, New York, NY

Garage Rock Revival, Jangle Pop, Indie Rock, New Wave, Alternative Pop/Rock, American Underground

Tagged as garage-rock revivalists, the Fleshtones mix the fuzz-guitar and Farfisa organ sounds of that genre with rockabilly, '50s R&B, and surf into a potent retro-rock stew. The group formed in 1976 in Queens with vocalist/keyboardist Peter Zaremba, guitarist Keith Strong, bassist Jan Marek Pukulski, and drummer Bill Milhizer and aimed to return to the simplicity and unself-consciousness of '50s and early-'60s rock & roll. The group fit nicely into New York's punk and new wave scene, and an early single, "American Beat," attracted the attention of independent label Red Star and, in time, I.R.S. The group's debut EP, *Up-Front*, was released in 1980 and was followed by their first full-length album, *Roman Gods*, and *Blast Off!*, an unreleased studio album recorded in 1978. 1983 produced *Hexbreaker*, regarded as the Fleshtones' finest album. The band continued to record through the '80s and released *Powerstance* in 1992 and *Beautiful Light* in 1994. Fleshtones side projects include Keith Streng's band Full Time Men, who worked with R.E.M. guitarist Peter Buck, and Peter Zaremba's Love Delegation. *—Steve Huey*

Blast Off! / 1982 / ROIR ✦✦

Roman Gods / Mar. 1982 / A&M ✦✦✦✦✦

In the 1980s, of the dozens of bands who were mining the sounds of '60s garage rock for inspiration, few were smarter or wittier about it than the Fleshtones; lots of folks might have sounded more like the Knaves or the Remains or whatever band they chose to embrace as a sonic template, but Peter Zaremba, Keith Streng, and their partners in Super Rock were able to communicate heart, soul, and actual thought instead of a mere awestruck nostalgia. The Fleshtones could also rock pretty hard, and were willing to mix up their influences a bit (not many *nuevo garage* bands would pick Lee Dorsey as the source of their album's sole cover tune). There's never been a real substitute for seeing the Fleshtones live (not even their live album quite fills the quota), but *Roman Gods* does a fine job of getting their ideas down on plastic with muscle, enthusiasm, and creative thinking, and it boasts several of their best songs, including the hard-charging "R-I-G-H-T-S," the moody "Shadow Line," the rollicking "I've Gotta Change My Life" (good advice!), and the title cut, easily the finest Kingsmen tune ever written by some guys from New York 20 years after "Louie Louie" was a hit. It's cool, it's not dumb, and it sounds great at a party—*Roman Gods* is everything you've ever wanted in a garage revival album, and more! *—Mark Deming*

Hexbreaker / 1983 / A&M ✦✦✦✦✦

Speed Connection II: The Final Chapter / 1985 / IRS ✦✦✦

There's a difference between being a great band and making great records, and that's the rub that's long dogged the Fleshtones; they're smart, funny, and a great live act, but they haven't always had the best of luck in the studio, where their best qualities often evaporate in overly sterile conditions. *Speed Connection II*, recorded live in front of a well-oiled crowd in Paris, doesn't perfectly capture the charm and wild energy of their stage show, but it comes close enough to be one of their most purely enjoyable albums—when the band starts shouting out "5! 10! 15! 20!" like it's the Rosetta Stone as Bill Milhizer's drums stomp out the beat and Jan Pakulski's bass makes with the fuzz in the opening seconds of "Hide and Seek," you know you're hearing the Fleshtones the way they were meant to be heard. You get a "Kingsmen-Like Medley" alongside one of the greatest fake Kingsmen tunes of all time ("Return to the Haunted House," which true to '60's form appears to be a stray studio cut overdubbed with crowd noise), an "Extended Super Rock Medley" that lives up to the billing, a frat-rock classic waiting to happen in "B.Y.O.B.," and Peter Buck from R.E.M. adding extra guitar power on two songs (including the Athens boys' own "Windout." (And no matter what the songwriting credits might say, that isn't T-Bone Burnett's "When the Night Falls" they're covering, but the Mod classic by the Eyes.) At one point, an especially drunken fan bellows "We haven't had enough! We want intoxication of the Fleshtones!" Peter Zaremba, cool as a cuke, responds "We're workin' on it, baby." And you know what? By the end of the album, they just about make it. (By the way, *Speed Connection II* is a decidedly different album than it's European counterpart, *Speed Connection*, and in this case you're better off with the domestic edition.) *—Mark Deming*

Speed Connection / 1985 / IRS ✦✦✦

Fleshtones Vs. Reality / 1987 / Emergo ✦✦✦

The Fleshtones opted to produce themselves (with the help of James A. Ball) for their fourth studio album, *Fleshtones Vs. Reality*, and it turned out to be an inspired choice; it's one of the best-sounding Fleshtones records ever, bright and lively, with the wild-party undertow they so dearly love flowing through nearly every track and the mid-60's ambience unencumbered by unnecessary studio murk. Peter Zaremba is in inspired voice (and his keyboards fit like a glove), Keith Streng's guitar work is near the top of his game, and the rest of the band sounds locked, loaded, and ready to wail. If the songs were as good as the performances and the production, *Fleshtones Vs. Reality* would rank with the band's finest work, but sadly that's not quite the case; while there are a few winners here, there are just as many obvious miscalculations, and it's hard to say if "Way up Here" rips off the Kinks quite as obviously as "Mirror, Mirror" rips off the Rolling Stones. Significantly, the most memorable tune here is a wild cover of "Treat Her Like a Lady," and the lack of top-shelf material is what prevents this from being one of the band's finest albums—*Fleshtones Vs. Reality* will sound great at your next party, but chances are you won't remember much of it the next morning. *—Mark Deming*

- **Living Legend Series** / 1989 / IRS ♦♦♦♦♦

An essential collection for those wanting to find out more (the more so because the IRS material is thoroughly out of print, including this disc itself), *Living Legend Series* draws on the debut *Upfront* EP, *Roman Gods, Hexbreaker*, and various other goodies. It makes a great overview of the early band in one place, accompanying by celebratory liner notes from critic Chris Morris. Compared to some of the wilder and meaner examples of garage/psych revivalism that future years produced, the early Fleshtones sound almost sweetly tame in comparison—something that Zaremba and his compatriots would likely consider a horrifying prospect. In context, though, the band kicked against prevailing trends with inspired fire, while years later their stuff holds up just fine. Spaeth's sax work in particular often makes them sound like logical forebears to the likes of Rocket From the Crypt (check out the opening "Theme From 'The Vindicators'," originally from the *Upfront* EP). Nearly everything sounds like it should be on the *Nuggets* box set—or at least one of many *Pebbles* collections—but that's not so much a criticism as a basic description of what it is. Zaremba's sometimes hiccuping, sometimes engagingly smooth white soul moves entertain just as they should, while the band pulls out all the needed riffs and grooves (the Milhizer/Pakulski rhythm section deserves particular credit). The rarities interspersed throughout the disc make for an interestingly mixed bunch, drawn on foreign and domestic singles and B-sides, not to mention a smart redo of "American Beat" originally recorded for, of all things, Tom Hanks' pre-serious persona film *Bachelor Party*. A couple of unreleased covers surface as well, including a fine romp through the Dantee's "Can't Get Enough of Your Love." Good sound and great cover art make for the icing on the cake. *—Ned Raggett*

Soul Madrid / 1989 / Impossible ♦♦♦

Powerstance / 1992 / Naked Language ♦♦♦

Beautiful Light / 1994 / Naked Language ♦♦

Laboratory of Sound / Oct. 1995 / Ichiban ♦♦

Fleshtones / Oct. 22, 1996 / Restless ♦♦♦

Hitsburg, USA / Jun. 17, 1997 / Telstar ♦♦♦

More Than Skin Deep / Jan. 13, 1998 / Ichiban ♦♦♦

The Fleshtones haven't changed at all in their 20 years together, which is both for better and for worse. On one hand, there's nobody—*nobody*—that delivers retro-garage raunch as consistently enjoyable as these guys. On the other hand, there isn't much stylistic variation between their albums, which means almost all of their records—especially the latter-day efforts, after the group's raw energy settled down a little bit—are interchangeable. *More Than Skin Deep*, recorded nearly 20 years into the group's career, is essentially the same as all their other records, filled with primal riffs and garagey raunch. A few of the songs are great, a few are terrible, many simply make the grade. If you've been following the group for any length of time, you won't be surprised and you won't be disappointed. If you haven't heard any of their other records, you may wonder what the fuss is about. *—Stephen Thomas Erlewine*

Angry Years / Mar. 10, 1999 / Amsterdamned ♦♦♦♦

Return to Hitsburg / Jul. 22, 2000 / Telstar ♦♦♦

Les Fleur de Lys

f. 1965, **db.** 1969

Freakbeat, British Psychedelia, Mod, Psychedelic, British Invasion

Although several of their singles are coveted by collectors of British '60s rock, Les Fleur de Lys remain obscure even by cultist standards. That's partly because they never came close to getting a hit, but also because their furious pace of lineup changes makes their history very difficult to trace and also precluded any sense of consistent style or identity. The group did release a number of fine singles in the mod-psychedelic style that has latterly become known as "freakbeat," with more of a soul music influence than most such British acts.

Les Fleur de Lys changed lineups about half a dozen times during their recording career, which roughly spanned 1965-69. Drummer Keith Guster was the only constant member; some of the musicians passing through went on to commercial success with Journey and Jefferson Starship (keyboardist Pete Sears) and King Crimson (bassist Gordon Haskell). At the outset they recorded a couple of singles for the Immediate label that were produced by Jimmy Page (there remains some controversy about whether he played guitar on these as well). A cover of the Who's "Circles" featured the fluid, slightly distorted guitar lines that would become Fleur de Lys' most distinguishing characteristic. The 45s made no commercial impact, however, and Fleur de Lys helped sustain themselves in the late '60s by backing relocated South African singer Sharon Tandy.

Continuing to record intermittently on the side, the band managed a few decent slabs of freakbeat with "Hold On," "Mud in Your Eye," and their most psychedelic outing, the memorably titled "Gong With the Luminous Nose. As if the musical chairs of personnel weren't enough, they further confused record buyers with tracks issued under different names like Shyster and Chocolate Frog, as well as playing on singles by Tandy, Waygood Ellis, and John Bromley. One single issued under the moniker Rupert's People, the Procol Harum-like "Reflections of Charlie Brown," became a European hit of sorts; subsequent singles by Rupert's People, however, are *not* Fleur de Lys playing under an assumed name. The confusing saga came to an end in the late '60s. Several of the group's better tracks repeatedly showed up on collector-oriented reissues of rare British '60s rock, and an entire CD of their work was issued in 1996. *—Richie Unterberger*

- **Reflections 1965-1969** / 1996 / FDL ♦♦♦♦♦

Sprawling 24-track comp of the rare recordings of this enigmatic band. Includes 14 songs issued under the Les Fleur de Lys name, singles that they issued under the Rupert's People, Chocolate Frog, and Shyster pseudonyms, and releases on which they backed Sharon Tandy, John Bromley, and Waygood Ellis. It goes without saying that such a manic hodgepodge is geared toward the hardcore collector market. But if you like mid-to-late '60s mod-psych, it's a decent item to have around, with some sparkling (occasionally crazed) guitar work, unusually constructed tunes that sometimes meld soul and psychedelia, and nice harmonies. "Circles" and "Mud in Your Eye" are first-rate pounding mod guitar tunes; "Gong With the Luminous Nose" is pop-psych at its silliest; "Reflections of Charlie Brown" is pop-psych at its most introspective; and Sharon Tandy's "Daughter of the Sun" is a lost near-classic with witchy vocals and sinister psychedelic guitar. *—Richie Unterberger*

Flipper

f. 1978, San Francisco, CA, **db.** 1993

L.A. Punk, Hardcore Punk, Alternative Pop/Rock, American Underground

They came, they saw, and they conquered—sort of. Never topping the charts, nor possessing a huge following, San Francisco's Flipper have always been considered a fringe act. But, in 1982, they were the toast of rock critics across the country with their post-hardcore punk masterpiece "Sex Bomb." Clocking in at over seven minutes, possessing one riff played over and over (and sloppier and sloppier), with vocalist Will Shatter screaming rather than singing (total lyrics: "She's a sex bomb/My baby/yeah"), it was a remarkable record: loud, proud, defiantly obnoxious, and relentlessly dumb. But in its own gleeful and intentionally moronic way it was (and remains) a perfect record. With "Sex Bomb" providing the impetus, Shatter and his fellow Flippers—vocalist/bassist Bruce Loose, drummer Steve DePace, and guitarist Ted Falconi—emerged from the fractious muck of the California hardcore punk scene with a crushingly loud, slowed-down sound that resembled the Stooges at their most drug addled. Their debut album, *Album—Generic Flipper*, included "Sex Bomb" along with a handful of good-to-great songs about anonymity and desperation that were not all bleak, nor without moments of humor. With much of the rock press singing their praises (and deservedly so), Flipper went on to demi-celebrity status as the reigning kings of American underground rock, for a few years. They never released anything as mind-blowingly good as *Album*, but until they split up in 1987, the music was usually very good. Precipitating their breakup was Shatter's death from a heroin overdose, with the remaining members spending the next half-dozen years stepping in and out of music. In 1992, Rick Rubin encouraged the remaining members to record a new album. The subsequent effort, *American Grafishy*, only hinted at their greatness. *—John Dougan*

- **Album—Generic Flipper** / 1982 / Def American ♦♦♦♦♦

If great rock & roll is supposed to be about breaking the rules, then Flipper's still-astonishing debut, *Album—Generic Flipper*, confirms their status as one of the great rock bands of their day. *Album* captures a band who not only refused to obey the accepted guidelines of rock & roll, they didn't even bother to pay much attention to their *own* rules. On the opening cut, "Ever," the band displays a willful contempt for rhythm, playing in a sludgy mid-tempo that wavers back and forth—and then they add a snappy (if casually executed) clap track over the top, making the sloppy mess seem almost catchy. Flipper slogs along through a slow, noisy swamp through most of the album, only to snap-to with a dose of up-tempo hardcore near the end on "Living for the Depression," and then close out with the brilliant "Sex Bomb," the closest thing '80s punk ever created to the beer-fueled genius of the Kingsmen's "Louie Louie," and a song with a great beat that you just can't dance to. About the only accepted rule of rock that seems to mean anything to Flipper is that music isn't worth playing if it doesn't have passion; every noisy moment of *Album—Generic Flipper* sounds like Flipper was willing to live and die for this music (and in a sense, that's just what Will Shatter did). On *Album—Generic Flipper*, Flipper play noise rock with none of the pretension that later bands brought to the form, proving that music doesn't have to be fast to be punk, and creating a funny, harrowing, and surprisingly engaging masterwork that profoundly influenced dozens of later bands without sounding any less individual two decades later. *—Mark Deming*

Gone Fishin' / 1984 / Subterranean ♦♦♦

After the glow of *Album*, *Gone Fishin'* may sound like a bit of a disappointment primarily due to the cleaned up (for Flipper anyway) sound, but that shouldn't stop you from enjoying this record. Not as confrontational nor as gloriously unhinged, *Gone Fishin'* still has moments that will poleaxe you with their power. *—John Dougan*

Blow'n Chunks / 1984 / Combat ♦♦♦♦

If not quite as rarity-collecting as the brilliant *Sex Bomb Baby* overview, *Blow'n Chunks* is still actually a great place for a Flipper newcomer to begin. Taking from a show at CBGB's in late 1983, *Blow'n* finds the band smashing and crashing through a combination of older and newer numbers both, including some that had yet to be officially recorded. The sound quality is good without being too pristine—something about Flipper, at least back then, seems to resist a clean recording as being disruptive of the thick flow of sludge created. What's especially interesting in the light of history is that no matter how many bands from Seattle in particular claim Flipper as an influence, the quartet themselves never sounds like slow, dire grunge. Tracks like "Way of the World," "In Life My Friend," and "Shed No Tears" keep all the strong, lumbering energy familiar from the studio versions, sounding practically quick and speedy, even while the feedback walls and bass trudges set the way. Those numbers that are actually slow, like "The Lights, the Sound, the Rhythm, the Noise" and "Life Is Cheap" definitely betray the Black Sabbath influence long credited to the band, but with an economy that group seemed to lose somewhere along the way (if it ever had it). Both Lose and Shatter bark and scream out their vocals, and for all the implicit drama they never sound like they're putting on an act—it's all natural, fitting right in with the powerful music. Fun examples of humor: quick snippets that appeared at the ends of the separate sides on the original tape release, with dogs barking and the band urging the listener to either "turn the tape over!" or to realize "it's finished!" Bio notes from the band and critic Michael Goldberg make for good liner info as well. *—Ned Raggett*

Public Flipper Limited / 1986 / Subterranean ✦✦✦
A two-record set of live material recorded between 1980-82, this is as good as *Blow'n Chunks* and essential for born-again Flipperphiles. The sound is messy and grimy, but that enhances the experience, but it's also easy to see that *Album* was without a doubt their benchmark record and that even the good material released after it (like this LP) couldn't equal its high (low?) standards. *—John Dougan*

Sex Bomb Baby / 1988 / Subterranean ✦✦✦✦
Originally released by Subterranean in 1987 and buffed up for a fine Infinite Zero/American reappearance in the mid-'90s, with hilarious and heartfelt liner notes from hardcore fan Mark Arm, *Sex Bomb Baby* is a blast and a half, drawing together singles, compilation appearances, and other oddities. The emphasis is on earlier days—nothing on the album comes from later than 1982—and the sheer amount of cool, obscure material in one place is a dream. "Sex Bomb" itself starts everything off in its scuzzy, frenetic glory, from the whistling bomb sounds to the thunder and rain opening, not to mention the explosive, oppressive crunch of the band and Shatter's almost crazed yelps. From there it's a dip into both more familiar numbers like "Love Canal" and a sometimes nutty range of covers and originals both. "Ha Ha Ha" is humor of the blackest kind—it almost shouldn't work, but Lose's extreme cackling in the chorus over the idiocies of modern life succeeds and then some. Despite the familiar name, "Lowrider" is an amusing, semi-jazzy original about supposedly being cool, but the real trip when it comes to interpreting others' material is the nursery rhyme "The Old Lady Who Swallowed a Fly." A slew of live and live in studio recordings also surface, including a great rant through "Ever" that has the band trashing idiotic audience members for crushing younger people among their number. Throughout, though the band works with a variety of producers, its bloody-minded aesthetic comes through clearly—take it at the speed necessary, be deliberate but don't worry about being sloppy around the edges. Balanced off just enough with their own kind of musical hooks, it made for a great fusion that blows out speakers the right way 20 years later. *—Ned Raggett*

American Grafishy / Jan. 12, 1993 / Warner Brothers ✦✦✦

Flo & Eddie

Pop/Rock
Self described as the Partridge Family and Redd Foxx on one album, Mark Volman and Howard Kaylan, otherwise known as Flo & Eddie, presented one of the more eclectic duos in the history of rock & roll. Their friendship and musical partnership, which began in their high school choir in Westchester, CA, led at first to a surf band called the Crossfires, which changed its name to the Turtles after its members graduated high school. The Turtles had some of the sweetest, most feel-good sounds in pop music, but underneath the melodic pop there was always an undercurrent of mischief. When the band broke up in 1970, Volman and Kaylan became members of Frank Zappa's Mothers of Invention, which provided them a perfect breeding ground for their quirky ways. Performing under the name The Phlorescent Leech & Eddie, they eventually shortened their monicker to Flo & Eddie. They recorded seven solo albums, eventually producing inexplicably weird reggae albums, but their real name was made by their radio show, which started out in the mid '70s in Detroit, but eventually ended up on KROQ in California and was syndicated by nearly 50 stations at its peak. Flo & Eddie scored two low budget films, Dirty Duck and Texas Detour, and, surreally enough, also worked on music for several kids' television shows, including the animated series Strawberry Shortcake and the Care Bears. *—Stacia Proefrock*

● **The Best of Flo & Eddie** / 1987 / Rhino ✦✦✦✦
Mark Volman (Flo) once described the music created under the Flo & Eddie guise as embracing the Partridge Family and Redd Foxx on the same record. Rhino's 1987 *Best of Flo & Eddie* compilation captures that juxtaposition vividly. Mark Volman and Howard Kaylan (Eddie) were the voices and the main creative drive behind the Turtles. When that band disintegrated amidst financial and personnel problems in 1970, they were asked by Frank Zappa to join the Mothers of Invention, where they metamorphosed into the musical equivalent of Dr. Jeckyll and Mr. Hyde. Zappa encouraged them to interject and utilize the venom and anger they had harnessed during their troublesome Turtle years. What would eventually came out captured the power-pop drive of the Small Faces, the Raspberries, and Badfinger with lyrics ranging from downright hostility toward the music business and it's stars, manic melancholia drenched with impeccable harmonies, delivered with a smile that implied "the joke's on you." *The Best of Flo and Eddie* is taken from four albums released in the early to mid-'70s and includes a few songs they scored for two low budget films, *Dirty Duck* and *Texas Detour.* This material is matched only by a few other like-minded songs of the time; Nilsson's "You're Breaking My Heart" would be a fair comparison. These arrangements were tailor made as AM radio hits, but ended up being so lyrically outlandish they instead were embraced only by a handful of "hip" underground FM stations. WABX in Detroit was even brave enough to play host to the short-lived "Flo & Eddie Radio Show" in the '70s before they moved on to wreak havoc at KROQ in California. Volman and Kaylan made recordings that gleefully welcomed failure—but only on their terms. They took an uncompromising stand and did their best to bully the very music business that had provided them with so much earlier success in the Turtles. The ultimate payback and essential listening. *—Al Campbell*

A Flock of Seagulls

f. 1980, Liverpool, England
New Romantic, New Wave, Synth Pop
As well known for their bizarrely teased haircuts as their hit single "I Ran (So Far Away)," A Flock of Seagulls were one of the infamous one-hit wonders of the new wave era. Growing out of the synth-heavy and ruthlessly stylish New Romantic movement, the band was a little too robotic and arrived a little too late to be true New Romantics, but their sleek dance-pop was forever indebted to the short-lived movement. From their eponymous 1982 debut album, "I Ran (So Far Away)" was quickly picked up by MTV for its icily attractive video and made the American Top Ten. "Wishing (If I Had a Photograph of You)" hit the British Top Ten later that year, and reached the Top 40 in America. From the group's second album, 1983's *Listen,* the single "Wishing" was moderately successful though the band's fortunes crashed shortly after its release. After one more album, a splintered lineup bowed out with 1986's *Dream Come True.* In 1989, frontman Mike Score assembled a new lineup of A Flock of Seagulls, though the band failed to make an impact. They continued to tour worldwide, and in 1996 released a new album: *The Light at the End of the World.* *—Stephen Thomas Erlewine*

A Flock of Seagulls / 1982 / Jive ✦✦✦✦✦
The Liverpool quintet A Flock of Seagulls first gained attention in the dance clubs with "Telecommunication," included on this debut release. The band benefited from heavy play on MTV and quickly became known for their outrageous fashion and lead singer Mike Score's waterfall-like haircut. However, their self-titled debut is an enjoyable romp that was set apart from other synth-heavy acts of the time by Paul Reynolds' unique guitar style. The kinetic "I Ran (So Far Away)" became a video staple and a Top Ten radio hit. "A Space Age Love Song," with its synthesizer washes and echo-laden guitar, also managed to score at radio. The rest of the album consists of hyperactive melodies, synthesizer noodlings, and electronic drumming. The lyrics are forgettable. In fact, they rarely expand on the song titles, but its all great fun and a wonderful collection of new wave ear candy. *—Tom Demalon*

Listen / 1983 / Jive ✦✦✦
Following their gold-selling Top Ten debut, A Flock of Seagulls returned in 1983 with *Listen.* Mike Howlett again handled the production chores, but the band errantly chose to pursue even more reliance on electronics, which gives *Listen* a bit of a sterile feel. Nonetheless, there are still several tracks here that are as strong as their debut, even if, as a whole, the album isn't as consistent.

Listen spawned only one hit, but it's a gem; the multi-layered, hypnotic "Wishing (If I Had a Photograph of You)." Other standouts include the eerie, moody "Nightmares," with its sparse guitar and synthesizer squawks and a surprisingly effective ballad "Transfer Affection." Ultimately, the band loses the plot on the second half, when they seem to forget melodies and focus on hardware. Although, the Bill Nelson-produced "(It's Not Me) Talking" is a bracing, breakneck tempo return to their interest in aliens. *Listen* is most likely to be enjoyed most by fans of the band only. *—Tom Demalon*

The Story of a Young Heart / Aug. 1984 / Jive/Arista ✦✦✦
Faced with declining sales and a sound that was already becoming considered passé, A Flock of Seagulls retooled a bit for their third album *The Story of a Young Heart.* Steve Lovell stepped into the producer's role and the band eased up on their heavily synthesized approach for more of a Europop feel to no avail. The less-cluttered, more-polished sound of album is undermined by the limited vocal ability of singer Mike Score. His monotone delivery fails to imbue the songs with any warmth. "The More You Live, the More You Love" is as good as anything they've done and gave the band one final chart hit, stalling at number 54. Otherwise, the best stuff is near the end and sounds most reminiscent of their debut. "Over My Head" and "Heart of Steel" bound along but sound thin. However, they almost recapture their hyperkinetic glory with "Remember David." *The Story of a Young Heart* is the sound of a band slowly losing momentum. *—Tom Demalon*

The Best of A Flock of Seagulls [Jive] / 1987 / Jive ✦✦✦✦✦
Liverpool's A Flock of Seagulls are best remembered for lead singer Mike Score's hair [and their number ten hit "I Ran (So Far Away)"]. The quartet actually scored three lesser hits aside from that archetypal '80s smash. The kinetic "A Space Age Love Song"; the cascading, multi-layered "Wishing (If I Had a Photograph of You)"; and the sweeping "The More You Live, the More You Love" are also included here. The set is fleshed out with non-hits and album cuts that most listeners will find pleasant but unessential (although the neurotic "Nightmares" is quite fun). It's an interesting curio from synth-rock's heyday and all the Flock of Seagulls that anyone aside from ardent fans or '80s junkies needs. *—Tom Demalon*

Telecommunications / 1995 / Elite ✦✦✦✦
At 16 tracks, *Telecommunications* contains nearly twice the number of songs as *The Best of a Flock of Seagulls* (excluding that set's two remixes). While that is probably much more than most listeners will want of A Flock of Seagulls, more interested fans will be delighted. *Telecommunications* includes all four of the Liverpool quartet's American chart singles and the other songs are primarily from the band's early period. Some of their stronger album tracks such as the hyperkinetic delights "Modern Love Is Automatic" and "(It's Not Me) Talking" flesh things out with enjoyable, unreleased material like "Committed" and "Living in Heaven." Fairly extensive liner notes add to the quirky, mindless

fun. For fans who recall more than "I Ran," *Telecommunications* is a fine snapshot of one of the better-remembered icons of early-'80s synth-rock. *—Tom Demalon*

Light at the End of the World / Jun. 25, 1996 / SAVA ♦♦

• **The Best of A Flock of Seagulls [Music Club]** / Jun. 30, 1998 / Music Club ♦♦♦♦
Music Club's *The Best of a Flock of Seagulls* is an excellent 16-track roundup of A Flock of Seagulls' best material. Their catalog wasn't particularly deep outside of the hits "Wishing (If I Had a Photograph of You)" and "I Ran (So Far Away)," but they did do some good New Romantic synth-pop, particularly on cuts like "Nightmares," "A Space Age Love Song," and "Telecommunications," all of which are here. As a matter of fact, this really does contain all of the group's best material, and while new wave fetishists will likely go for the actual albums anyway, most listeners will be more than satisfied with this. *—Stephen Thomas Erlewine*

Eddie Floyd

b. Jun. 25, 1935, Montgomery, AL
Vocals / Soul

Eddie Floyd came aboard the good ship Stax at the behest of his friend Al Bell and immediately made himself useful as a composer for labelmates Carla Thomas, William Bell, Otis Redding (originally intended to be the recipient of "Knock on Wood"), and Atlantic's Wilson Pickett.

Floyd's own mid-'60s output included "Raise Your Hand," which utilized the same Booker T. & the MGs-powered thrust as "Knock on Wood," and "Big Bird," written partially in shocked response to the tragic death of Redding. Floyd remained loyal to Stax right up to its bitter demise, his engaging vocals resulting in major hits with the gentle "I've Never Found a Girl" and a lively remake of Sam Cooke's "Bring It on Home to Me."

Whenever Floyd re-teams with his old Stax pals—guitarist Steve Cropper, bassist Duck Dunn, and sometimes Booker T. Jones on organ—the long-ago Memphis magic instantly returns. With Floyd happily leading the throngs through "Raise Your Hand" and "Knock on Wood," it's 1966 all over again. *—Bill Dahl*

Knock on Wood / 1967 / Stax ♦♦♦♦
In contrast to the 1970s—when artists ranging from Curtis Mayfield to Parliament/Funkadelic were praised for their albums—singles defined soul music in the 1960s. It has often been pointed out that many Stax and Motown albums of the '60s had their share of filler—nonetheless, others were full of gems that should have been released as singles. Reissued on CD in 1991, *Knock On Wood* is one of Eddie Floyd's best albums. The soul shouter successfully embraced sleeker northern soul on other projects, but here he sticks to the type of raw, hard-edged Memphis soul that Stax was first known for. From the unforgettable title song (a number one R&B hit) to covers of J.J. Jackson's "But It's Alright," Jerry Butler's "I Stand Accused," and Wilson Pickett's "634-5789," this CD beautifully illustrates the splendor of down-home Southern R&B. *—Alex Henderson*

• **Chronicle** / 1979 / Stax ♦♦♦♦♦
Singer/songwriter/producer Eddie Floyd, a former member of the Falcons, shines on originals such as "Soul Street" and "I've Got to Have Your Love" as well as covers such as Sam Cooke's "Bring It on Home to Me" and Smokey Robinson's "My Girl." This 1979 collection includes all of Floyd's singles between 1968 and 1974.

Rare Stamps / Mar. 21, 1993 / Stax ♦♦♦♦♦
A pair of remarkable soul hits, "Knock on Wood" and "I've Never Found a Girl," enabled Eddie Floyd to attain national success in 1968. But the longtime singer and composer, whose roots dated back to the Detroit group the Falcons in the late '50s, was a steady, if not spectacular, performer for many years before and after those two songs. Several of Floyd's finest pieces are compiled on the 25-track CD *Rare Stamps*, including a wonderful testimonial to Otis Redding, "Big Bird." There are also two super duets with Mavis Staples, "Never Let You Go" and "Ain't That Good," which rank with anything that the label issued. *—Ron Wynn*

The Flying Burrito Brothers

f. 1969, Nashville, TN
Country-Rock

The Flying Burrito Brothers helped forge the connection between rock and country, and with their 1969 debut album, *The Gilded Palace of Sin*, they virtually invented the blueprint for country-rock. Though the band's glory days were brief, they left behind a small body of work that proved vastly influential both in rock and country.

Gram Parsons and Chris Hillman formed the Burrito Brothers after leaving the Byrds in 1968, adding pedal steel guitarist "Sneaky" Pete Kleinow and bassist Chris Ethridge to the lineup. *The Gilded Palace of Sin* was released in the spring of 1969. Although the album only sold 40,000 copies, the band developed a devoted following, including many prominent Los Angeles musicians, Bob Dylan, and the Rolling Stones. Around this time, Parsons and Stones guitarist Keith Richards became good friends, which led to Parsons losing interest in the Burritos. Ethridge left the band before their second album; he was replaced by Bernie Leadon, and ex-Byrd Michael Clarkewas hired as their drummer.

Burrito Deluxe, the group's second album, was released in the spring of 1970. After its release, Parsons left the group and was replaced by Rick Roberts, a local Californian songwriter, who was featured on 1971's *The Flying Burrito Brothers*. After its release, Kleinow left the band and Leadon departed to join the Eagles. They were replaced by Al Perkins and Roger Bush, respectively, and guitarist Kenny Wertz and fiddler Byron Berline were added to the lineup. This new version of the group recorded the 1972 live album *The Last of the Red Hot Burritos*. Before its release, the band splintered apart. Berline, Bush, and Wertz all left to form Country Gazette, while Hillman and Perkins joined Manassas. After a European tour led by Roberts, the group disbanded. Throughout the remainder of the '70s, '80s and '90s, different incarnations of the Burrito Brothers, usually led by Kleinow, would form for recordings and tours, yet the band remains famous for their first two records. *—Stephen Thomas Erlewine*

☆ **The Gilded Palace of Sin** / Feb. 1969 / Edsel ♦♦♦♦♦
By 1969, Gram Parsons had already built the foundation of the country-rock movement through his work with the International Submarine Band and the Byrds, but his first album with the Flying Burrito Brothers, *The Gilded Palace of Sin*, was where he revealed the full extent of his talents, and it ranks among the finest and most influential albums the genre would ever produce. As a songwriter, Parsons delivered some of his finest work on this set; "Hot Burrito #1" and "Hot Burrito #2" both blend the hurt of classic country weepers with a contemporary sense of anger, jealousy, and confusion, and "Sin City" can either be seen as a parody or a sincere meditation on a city gone mad, and it hits home in both contexts. Parsons was rarely as strong as a vocalist as he was here, and his covers of "Dark End of the Street" and "Do Right Woman" prove just how much he had been learning from R&B as well as C&W. And Parsons was fortunate enough to be working with a band who truly added to his vision, rather than simply backing him up; the distorted swoops of Sneaky Pete Kleinow's fuzztone steel guitar provides a perfect bridge between country and psychedelic rock, and Chris Hillman's strong and supportive harmony vocals blend flawlessly with Parsons' (and he also proved to be a valuable songwriting partner, collaborating on a number of great tunes with Gram. While *The Gilded Palace of Sin* barely registered on the pop-culture radar in 1969, literally dozens of bands (the Eagles most notable among them) would find inspiration in this music and enjoy far greater success. But no one ever brought rock and country together quite like the Flying Burrito Brothers, and this album remains their greatest accomplishment. *—Mark Deming*

Burrito Deluxe / Apr. 1970 / Edsel ♦♦♦♦♦
Gram Parsons had a habit of taking over whatever band he happened to be working with, and on the first three albums on which he appeared—the International Submarine Band's *Safe at Home*, the Byrds' *Sweetheart of the Rodeo*, and the Flying Burrito Brothers' *The Gilded Palace of Sin*—he became the focal point, regardless of the talent of his compatriots. *Burrito Deluxe*, the Burritos' second album, is unique in Parsons' repertoire in that it's the only album where he seems to have deliberately stepped back to make more room for others; whether this was due to Gram's disinterest in a band he was soon to leave, or if he was simply in an unusually democratic frame of mind is a matter of debate. But while it is hardly a bad album, it's not nearly as striking as *The Gilded Palace of Sin*. Parsons didn't deliver many noteworthy originals for this set, with "Cody Cody" and "Older Guys" faring best but paling next to the highlights from the previous album (though he was able to wrangle the song "Wild Horses" away from his buddy Keith Richards and record it a year before the Rolling Stones' version would surface). And while the band sounds tight and they play with genuine enthusiasm, there's a certain lack of focus in these performances; the band's frontman sounds as if his thoughts are often elsewhere, and the other players can't quite compensate for him, though on tunes like "God's Own Singer" and a cover of Bob Dylan's "If You Gotta Go (Go Now)," they gamely give it the old college try. *Burrito Deluxe* is certainly a better than average country-rock album, but coming from the band who made the genre's most strongly defining music, it's something of a disappointment. *—Mark Deming*

The Flying Burrito Brothers / May 1971 / A&M ♦♦♦
On their first post-Parsons album, the Burritos (now led by Hillman and Rick Roberts, and with future Eagle Bernie Leadon replacing Ethridge) make an honest step forward in country-rock. Includes the Roberts song "Colorado." *—William Ruhlmann*

Dim Lights, Thick Smoke and Loud, Loud Music / Mar. 1987 / Edsel ♦♦♦
The British Edsel label's *Dim Lights, Thick Smoke and Loud, Loud Music*, the first try at a Flying Burrito Brothers compilation in a decade, is not a best-of. Because the label had recently reissued the Burritos' first two albums, *The Gilded Palace of Sin* and *Burrito Deluxe*, this 13-song collection is drawn from the rarities and outtakes first released on the A&M albums *Close Up the Honky-Tonks* and *Sleepless Nights* after the original group's (and Gram Parsons') demise. Specifically, as the album notes report, "... [I]t brings together for the first time on one record all the Burritos' material that features Gram Parsons and that wasn't on those first two LPs." The songs are for the most part covers of country music standards presented as demos or working versions that probably never would have been released if it were not for Parsons' death. Parsons, of course, is the reason the Burritos continue to interest fans, and he sings well here, but this half-finished material does not compare to the first two albums. *—William Ruhlmann*

★ **Farther Along: The Best Of** / 1988 / A&M ♦♦♦♦♦
Farther Along: The Best of the Flying Burrito Brothers is a nearly flawless compilation, containing a full 21 tracks of the pioneering group's best material. All but two of the songs from *The Gilded Palace of Sin* are included on the collection, as are all of the highlights from *Burrito Deluxe* and a handful of rarities and outtakes. In short, it's a definitive collection containing all of the Burrito Brothers' finest moments. It's indespensible to any rock or country collection. *—Stephen Thomas Erlewine*

☆ **Hot Burritos! The Flying Burrito Brothers Anthology: 1969-1972** / Apr. 18, 2000 / A&M ♦♦♦♦♦
There's little question that the double-disc collection *Hot Burritos! The Flying Burrito Brothers Anthology: 1969-1972* is comprehensive, since it contains the entirety of the band's first three albums plus a bevy of rarities, including six songs from *Close Up the Honky-Tonks*, two cuts from *Sleepless Nights*, two tracks from *The Last of the Red Hot Burritos*, the non-LP single "The Train Song," and "Six Days on the Road," originally released on the 1988 collection, *Farther Along: The Best of the Flying Burrito Brothers*. That pretty much covers *everything* they cut during those four years. Since the Burritos were

truly great while Gram Parsons was in the band—once he left, they were still solid, thanks to Chris Hillman—this may border on overkill for some listeners, especially since the Parsons years are covered expertly by *Farther Along*, which contained all but one song from *The Gilded Palace of Sin*, plus the best songs from *Deluxe* and rarities and highlights from posthumous releases. For neophytes, that's a better bet, yet the converted will find this quite nice. Apart from "The Train Song," which rarely shows up on collections, there aren't any revelations or even new songs, but there are nice liner notes, great outtakes from the photo shoot for *Gilded Palace*, and exquisite remastered sound. And, for Parsons fanatics, the Hillman-led *Flying Burrito Brothers* may seem like a new record, too, since they may have previously overlooked it. So, diehards get all the Parsons material in one place, while neophytes with a serious attention span will be introduced to one of the great bands of the last 25 years of the 20th century—and, yes, that means it qualifies as definitive. —*Stephen Thomas Erlewine*

Flying Saucer Attack

f. 1993, Bristol, England

Ambient Pop, Experimental Rock, Dream Pop, Space Rock, Indie Rock, Post-Rock/Experimental

Formed in Bristol, England in 1993, the elusive avant-noise project Flying Saucer Attack primarily comprised the duo of singers/guitarists David Pearce and Rachel Brook, refugees from the group Lynda's Strange Vacation who formed FSA as an outlet for their interest in home-recording experimentation. Drawing influence from Krautrock, folk, and dream-pop, they bowed with the single "Soaring High," followed by an eponymously-titled 1993 debut LP which buried the group's narcoleptic vocals and amorphous songs under dense, organic sheets of feedback.

After 1994's *Distance*, a collection of atmospheric singles and unreleased material, FSA emerged in 1995 with *Further*, a remarkably evocative work which transported the group's hypnotic guitar wash into a uniquely pastoral setting. *Chorus*, another singles compilation, followed later in the year, and with it came a declaration of the end of the group's initial phase, setting the stage for Flying Saucer Attack's continued evolution as one of the decade's most innovative and ambitious groups. 1997's *New Lands* was the first fruit of this new FSA, now a Pearce solo project exploring the possibilities of sampling; Brook, meanwhile, focused on her side group Movietone, a similarly blissed-out excursion into sound. FSA followed up *New Lands* three years later with *Mirror*. —*Jason Ankeny*

Flying Saucer Attack / 1994 / VHF ✦✦✦✦

Seemingly emerging out of nowhere following an initial single or two, Flying Saucer Attack's debut album crystallized an incipient 1990s underground as in thrall to folk music as to feedback blasts and Krautrock influences. The description the band members themselves used, also considered by some as an alternate title to this album, was "rural psychedelia," and rarely has form so readily followed function. The original duo of Pearce and Brook, with some help from friend/Third Eye Foundation mainman Matt Elliott on percussion and clarinet (thus creating an even more alien atmosphere on "Moonset"), created a thick, evocatively haunting collection of modern mind-blowers. If any one thing could be singled out about the album, it's the continual contrast between Pearce's soft, reflective singing, often sunk deep into the overall mix and treated with heavy-duty echo, and his often tremendous guitar work, electric squalls, and drones piled atop one another. Songs like the exultant "Wish" and "A Silent Tide" are the breathtaking results. Initial comparisons were made to My Bloody Valentine and the shoegazing crowd, but they're misplaced—it's a consciously different style employing some similar elements, but with notably varying results. Two astonishing drone/tribal instrumentals are named "Popol Vuh 2" and "Popol Vuh 1," both open tips of the hat to the long-lived German experimental group. The completely out-of-left-field number, though, is the cover of Suede's "The Drowners"—changing nothing about the pace but overdriving the feedback and relentlessly toning down the vocals, FSA turn the neo-glam piece into a noisefest beyond description. Compared to later albums, *Flying Saucer Attack* sets more of an immediately consistent mood—some numbers aside, the dreamy singing, the seemingly straightforward guitar parts that get more involved the more one listens, and more continue from track to track, generally speaking. The end results, though, are more than worth it. —*Ned Raggett*

Distance / 1994 / VHF ✦✦✦

Not waiting long to do so, Flying Saucer Attack followed up its full-length debut with a singles collection—understandable, given how fond the band was from the start for releasing 7" vinyl as part of its *modus operandi* (nearly every FSA release has a pro-vinyl statement somewhere in the artwork). Described by Pearce in the liner notes as "the second FSA album but not album number two," *Distance* hangs together quite as well as the debut album, exploring various sides of the band's noted "rural psychedelia" approach. Two tracks, "Oceans 2" and "November Mist," were previously unreleased; otherwise, the remaining selections come from FSA's first three singles. "Oceans" itself makes for a lovely start, with Matt Elliott of the Third Eye Foundation adding rolling tribal percussion gently beneath an ever-evolving web of open-ended electric guitar and Brook's subtle bass. It calls to mind a dreamier take of Ash Ra Tempel's early days and stands up well in comparison. Another guest appearance is the semi-mysterious Rocker, a longtime collaborator of Pearce and company, who adds his computer—with no indication as to what it does—on the heavy electronic screams and mechanistic rhythms of the title track. One song from the self-titled debut also released as a single, "Wish," appears here as "Instrumental Wish" and lives up to the name, a truly beautiful combination of low drones, rolling feedback rhythms, and more echoing off into the beyond. Most of the tracks continue the established FSA approach, with Pearce's sometimes barely audible vocals coming across almost as wordless sighs through the thick but somehow never overbearing

guitar crunches and riffs. On "November Mist" and "Soaring High," the folk influence in FSA comes through the clearest, the latter living up to the title on a beautiful post-Byrds guitar chime then treated with FSA's own brand of avant-garde lo-fi production. —*Ned Raggett*

● **Further** / Apr. 17, 1995 / Drag City ✦✦✦✦✦

Thanks to its release on Drag City and an increasingly higher profile (and rabid fan base), *Further* turned out to be FSA's breakthrough, at least in cult terms. Even Rolling Stone reviewed the album (amusingly pairing it with a modern Pink Floyd live release), but *Further* was anything but a corporate sellout. Rather, the twosome achieved a new balance of delicacy and power, heightened in noticeable part by Pearce's increasingly assertive singing. His vocal approach of extended sigh as singing hadn't changed, but his words had a new clarity and crisper delivery, with fine results. Otherwise, FSA stayed the same general course musically, but again the arrangements provide the difference, with the unplugged folk side of Pearce's music now firmly taking the fore on songs like the extended, multipart "For Silence," often with gentle reverb or extra studio effects that make the songs all that much more intriguing. It's not quite Bert Jantsch or John Fahey redux, but there's a definite sonic connection there that's well worth the hearing. Other highlights are the clear acoustic notes cutting through the hum and drone of the majestic "In the Light of Time" or the buried waves of electric guitar in counterpoint to the gentle picking on "Come and Close My Eyes"—the latter accompanied at the end with what sounds like a typewriter, without sounding jarring or out of place. No compromises were aimed at radio-friendly unit shifters—opening track "Rainstorm Blues," a roaring feedback squall ascending and descending in volume, got further accompaniment from hard-to-place crumbles and squeals, Brook's growling bass work setting the mood even stranger. Brook herself gets a lovely moment of vocal glory on "Still Point," her voice even more soft and restrained than Pearce's, rising through a striking squall of sound and, once again, upfront acoustic guitar. —*Ned Raggett*

In Search of Spaces / 1996 / Corpus Hermeticum ✦✦✦

An unusual and striking document of the FSA live experience, *In Search of Spaces* consists of instrumental snippets from a series of shows in the early '90s with a rotating lineup, including Matt Elliott of Third Eye Foundation. The number of shows FSA has ever done is nearly nil to begin with, and no live lineup was ever quite the same. Corpus Hermeticum/A Handful of Dust mainman Bruce Russell then edited and wove everything together, creating a single-track CD that runs for 50 minutes. *In Search of Spaces* definitely rewards the patient as a result, but those willing to take the plunge will be well-rewarded. Given the general FSA recording approach of home-taping and anti-gloss, the crumbling and murky results aren't too far off from the band's studio releases (indeed, the liner notes claim the recordings come from audience tapes rather than soundboard streams). If there's little or none of the sudden crispness that makes songs like "In the Light of Time" so striking, the moody, post-psychedelic reach of the performances more than makes up for it. As there's no way to tell when or how anything was done, making judgments on the basis of improved abilities over the time or the like is impossible—*In Search of Spaces* needs to be taken at face value. Elliott's contributions likely result in the occasional drums, but Pearce's unearthly guitar howls and shattering, abrasive yet lovely feedback arcs take understandable pride of place. Singling out particular moments to concentrate on can take some patience, but there's a lengthy jam starting around ten minutes in with a low, rumbling rhythm providing the background for some wonderful guitar craziness from Pearce and others. —*Ned Raggett*

Chorus / Jan. 1996 / Domino ✦✦✦✦

As the liner notes put it, "This album marks the end of FSA phase one." Pearce later described the whole "phase one/phase two" business as something of a joke, but for a while it seemed FSA was going to call it quits in the mid-'90s, partially due to Brook's departure to concentrate on Movietone. Thankfully, the projected end of FSA turned out to be false, but it's easy to see *Chorus* as an intentional wrapping up (though in fact the four songs that appeared on the *Outdoor Miner/Land Beyond the Sun* EP did not surface here). Bringing together a scattered variety of tracks in the same way that *Distance* did, *Chorus* includes songs from singles, compilation cuts, and the entirety of a John Peel session for good measure. Two cuts appear twice in alternate versions—the appropriately titled "Feedback Song," which also crops up in a demo take, and "There but Not There," appearing as well in a dub take and both featuring the talents of regular FSA collaborator Rocker. Even more so than *Distance*, *Chorus* captures FSA trying out a wide variety of approaches, from minimal, acoustic arrangements, as on the Brook-sung "Beach Red Lullaby," to more of the fierce and somehow elegant guitar sound swells (the mind-melting "Second Hour" providing an astonishing instance of the latter). Some fairly conventional numbers, for FSA at least, turn up—"Always" has a lovely, pop-friendly melody that places the song much closer to out-and-out shoegazing than most of the band's other work. Pearce's singing generally favors the more shadowy, buried approach of earlier efforts than the somewhat clearer approach on *Further*, but still haunting and mysterious in contrast to the web of music surrounding it. Here and there various references to earlier work crop up—continuing the series started on the self-titled debut, the stripped-down "Popul Vuh III" takes a bow. —*Ned Raggett*

Distant Station / Dec. 12, 1996 / Drag City ✦✦✦

Recorded and released when Flying Saucer Attack was on its semi-hiatus around 1996, *Distant Stations* isn't actually an FSA album per se, but a collaborative remix project done by fellow U.K. experimental artist Tele:funken (real name Tom Fenn), named after a German company. Consisting of two sidelong (or on CD, simply long) dark ambient-themed songs, it seems to be something of a tribute to older FSA inspirations like Ash Ra Tempel, also fond of similarly lengthy and moody numbers. As a result, or maybe just as a sly nod to the rampant Krautrock and space rock worship of the mid-'90s in hipster indie circles, the liner notes warn, "Achtung! Diese Platte ist Moog-frei!"—which may or may not be grammatically accurate, but still makes for a good in-joke. Tele:funken himself took a variety of samples and elements of FSA's work; no specific origin for any of the sounds is indicated but one collaborator is mentioned, Rosie Cuckston of Pram, who adds "toy sampler" on the first track. Tele:funken's remix work doesn't so much turn FSA into blissful relaxation as it increases the edgy, uneasy qualities, all while still being engagingly atmospheric. The first track, with its opening of stretched-out guitar feedback in rhythmic cycles, up and down, back and forth in the mix, is a particular gem, turning into a haunting haze of floating high-pitched tones before a relentless, low rhythmic burble combines with it to conclude the song. The second piece starts in the most low-volume and minimal way possible, with barely on-the-edge-of-hearing percussion and squiggly loops only just gaining in general intensity in the opening minutes. This then turns into an intriguingly open-ended combination of oscillating, constantly varying tones and feedback wails, distorted and pushed to the edge. Sonically, *Distant Stations* feels like a kissing cousin to Main's similarly extreme work—not a bad situation to be in. —*Ned Raggett*

Goodbye/And Goodbye/Whole Day / Jan. 21, 1997 / VHF ✦✦✦
Allegedly at one point the farewell release by Flying Saucer Attack, at least if the title indicated as much, *Goodbye* brings together "by chance," to quote the liner notes, three separate recordings. More or less the last release featuring Brook, who can just barely be seen with Pearce on the back cover, *Goodbye* finds FSA pushing into even more abstract realms than before. Even the most outré FSA songs beforehand had central melodies or vocal hooks, but the series of edits that make up the title track lead from one slice of randomness to another, feedback loops to out-of-nowhere squalls and guitar grind to a soft piano figure. A useful comparison point would be Main, but with less obvious structure. "And Goodbye" is a separate instrumental recorded live, featuring one of Pearce's heroes, cult New Zealand guitarist Roy Montgomery, jamming with the band. Montgomery is credited with the lead, his own considerable talents perfectly suited for the exploratory work of FSA, though he intriguingly doesn't play a "typical" Montgomery guitar part, instead matching the band's own general aesthetic direction. Recorded on Dictaphone, the sound quality is anything but clean, but it actually adds to the song's weird charm, adding even more murkiness than usual. The last track, "The Whole Day," is actually an instrumental preview of the song of similar name from *New Lands*. The ambient feedback introduction to the song was not repeated on the later release, giving this version its own unique appeal—otherwise, the steadily paced guitar shimmer here is the same as on *New Lands*, drizzling down like electric rain. —*Ned Raggett*

New Lands / Oct. 14, 1997 / Drag City ✦✦✦✦
Likely titled *New Lands* due to Flying Saucer Attack being lauched upon "phase two" (as the liner notes put it), this release finds FSA down to Pearce and Pearce only, as before with a bit of help here and there from Rocker and, on "Present," the co-writing skills of two members of Amp. That the first two tracks are called "Past" and "Present" and that the first has more of a "classic" FSA sound with a steady rhythm and huge solo while the second revolves around a buried, near inaudible series of loops, seems to be part of the album's plan, such as it is. *New Lands* in general showcases Pearce in testing mode, seeming to see what works and what doesn't, looking backward as much as forward. Indeed, the lengthy, majestic steady build of "Whole Day Song" reappears from the *Goodbye/and Goodbye* EP, this time with vocals and a low-key, softly intoxicating piano line. While the more experimental parts of *New Lands* aren't really Pearce completely trashing his general aesthetic and trying something new, they do show him attempting and often succeeding at introducing further variety to his murky, intriguing field. Thus, "Up in Her Eyes" has a very familiar vocal and guitar style, but the obsessive, upfront yet still shadowy percussion—sounding more like a chugging train engine than anything else—dominates the track, at least up until its slightly more ambient, free-flowing end. Other curious rhythms, reminiscent of past comparisons to the work of Main, crop up more than once—the near arrhythmic, squealing loop that introduces "Respect" or the blunt, brusque punch of "The Sea." Through it all, the combination of Pearce's tender, dark folk vocals and skybursting guitar provides the central point of the experience, making for some fascinating, entrancing results. —*Ned Raggett*

Mirror / Jan. 18, 2000 / Drag City ✦✦✦
The sweeping billows of sound that begin "Space (1999)," the opening track of *Mirror*, Flying Saucer Attack's first album of the 21st century, set the tone for this ride on the clouds. The blurring of lines between noises and notes, of sounds and music, give this album a soothing and ambient feel. Atmospheric guitars layer the background, simple bass lines provide the anchor, and sound effects take the sound further into space. Dave Pearce's gentle vocals keep the album a mellow affair throughout, except for the out of place "Chemicals," which unfortunately breaks the mood with its quasi-industrial feel. Some of the songs do seem to wander aimlessly, however, and *Mirror* occasionally gets tangled in its own loose web. Overall, these surges of sound are best enjoyed in the late evening or early morning hours, depending on your intention. Both results are great. Either you will enter one of your most relaxed states of sleep or will awaken as if by a wave of feathers. —*Jason Kane*

Focus

f. 1969, Amsterdam, The Netherlands
Prog Rock/Art Rock

Best remembered for their bizarre chart smash "Hocus Pocus," Dutch progressive rock band Focus was formed in Amsterdam in 1969 by vocalist/keyboardist/flutist Thijs van Leer, bassist Martin Dresden, and drummer Hans Cleuver. With the subsequent addition of guitarist Jan Akkerman, the group issued its debut LP, *In and Out of Focus*, in 1970, earning a European cult following thanks to the single "House of the King." Dresden and

Cleuver were replaced by bassist Cyril Havermanns and drummer Pierre Van der Linden for the English-language follow-up, *Moving Waves*; the record generated the hit "Hocus Pocus," a hallucinatory epic distinguished by Akkerman's guitar pyrotechnics and van Leer's demented yodeling. Easily one of the flat-out strangest songs ever to crack the American pop charts, the single peaked at number nine in the spring of 1973, by which time Focus had already exchanged Havermanns for bassist Bert Ruiter and issued their third album, *Focus III*, which yielded the minor hit "Sylvia." In the wake of 1974's *Hamburger Concert*, the band streamlined the classical aspirations of earlier efforts to pursue a more pop-oriented approach on records like *Ship of Memories* and *Mother Focus*; though roster changes regularly plagued Focus throughout the period, none was more pivotal than the 1976 exit of Akkerman, who was replaced by guitarist Philip Catherine for 1978's *Focus con Proby*, cut with British pop singer P.J. Proby. Focus then disbanded, with the original lineup reuniting in 1990 for a Dutch television special. —*Jason Ankeny*

In and Out of Focus / 1970 / IRS ✦✦✦
This debut album is gentler and more low-key and vocal-oriented than their subsequent efforts; fans of Jan Akkerman's pyrotechnics may be disappointed by his relatively restrained presence, but others may be pleasantly surprised to find a more economic group than they remember. A fair collection of progressive rock tunes without a clear focus, the material is dominated by Thijs Van Leer, often introducing classical sensibilities. But at least as often, it sticks with fairly conventional period folk-rock and blues influences, with occasional jazzy shadings. Akkerman's "House of the King" is the most accurate Jethro Tull imitation ever recorded. —*Richie Unterberger*

Moving Waves / 1971 / IRS ✦✦✦✦
The album that boosted Focus into at least semi-fame outside of continental Europe, *Moving Waves* blasts off with their hit single "Hocus Pocus." Built around a killer guitar hook by Akkerman and a series of solo turns by the band, this instrumental replaced "Wipeout" as a staple of FM radio. The bizarrely hilarious vocal and accordion solos by Thijs van Leer—one of which absurdly concludes with rousing stadium cheers—have to be heard to be believed. After this over-the-top performance, the other tracks seem comparatively constrained: the gentle "Le Clochard" features some gorgeous classical guitar over Mellotron strings. The album concludes with "Eruption," which while mimicking the multi-suite nomenclature of Yes and King Crimson, is essentially a side-long jam session. Stop-time Emersonian organ solos alternate with languid sections of jazzy guitar redolent of Santana, while still other sections are flat-out electric blues-rock stomps. It's impressive playing, though it comes off as a bit meandering after the tightly structured solos that began the album. —*Paul Collins*

● **Focus III** / 1972 / IRS ✦✦✦✦✦
Riding on the success of their hit single "Hocus Pocus" from the revolutionary *Moving Waves* album, Focus got to work on this, their third LP in four years. While the debut album features a style not too dissimilar to the Bonzo Dog Doodah Band, Focus' second LP *Moving Waves* is purely instrumental and wholly serious-minded. *Focus III* keeps this same sound, but approaches it with a jollier, more accessible tone. As with its predecessor, *Focus III* features only one tune that would be in with a chance of being a hit single. The enjoyable rhythm of "Sylvia," partnered with Jan Akkerman's victorious guitar solo, some of Van Leer's finest organ-work, Bert Ruiter's tight bass lines, and Pierre Van Der Linden's mellow drumming assured the track classic status. "Sylvia" found worldwide success and gained the band valuable radio and press exposure. The song remains one of the most loved and best remembered songs from Focus' catalog. The consistence in musical quality throughout *Focus III* is enough to merit any listeners' respect. To be frank, this LP has it all: diverse songs, astounding musicianship, one of the finest singles ever released—*Focus III* should unquestionably be ranked alongside the likes of *Revolver* and *Dark Side of the Moon* and any others of rock's greatest. —*Ben Davies*

Live at the Rainbow / Dec. 1973 / Sire ✦✦✦

Hocus Pocus: Best of Focus / 1994 / EMI ✦✦✦✦
Since the band has a seven-album strong catalog, each with many highlights, compiling a Focus "best of" could never be an easy task. Fortunately, the people behind this release have done a super job. Although it includes none of the band's lengthy jams which made up the bulk parts of *Focus III*, *Moving Waves*, and *Hamburger Concerto*, *Hocus Pocus* is one of the best releases to highlight what Focus were all about. Featuring all of the hits and semi-hits the band were ever known for ("Sylvia," "Hocus Pocus," "House of the King"), as well as the fans favorites ("Focus [Instrumental]," "Harem Scarem," "Anonymous") this release highlights the musical ability and amazing songwriting talent that were part and parcel of Focus. There is, unfortunately, a little too much of the track listing hailing from the band's rather weak funk/rock album *Mother Focus*. There are also a few exclusions that could have added to the album's diversity, namely "Moving Waves," "Love Remembered," and "Round Goes the Gossip." Although the band's seminal album, *Focus III*, perhaps provides a more accurate picture of their overall makeup, *Hocus Pocus* will unquestionably gratify the purchaser. —*Ben Davies*

Dan Fogelberg

b. Aug. 13, 1951, Peoria, IL
Vocals, Keyboards, Guitar / Soft Rock, Singer/Songwriter

Peoria, IL native Dan Fogelberg has built a devoted following over the years with his laidback, folky singer/songwriter style. A pianist since 14, Fogelberg switched to guitar and played local coffeehouses while majoring in art at the University of Illinois, where he met ex-student and REO Speedwagon manager Irving Azoff. Fogelberg relocated to Los Angeles and played the folk circuit while doing session work, landing a tour spot with Van Morrison at one point. Fogelberg's 1972 debut, *Home Free*, didn't make much of an impact, and he was dropped from Columbia. However, Fogelberg's connection with Azoff led to a deal with Epic. Fogelberg's Epic debut, *Souvenirs*, became his first in a string of seven consecutive platinum albums. He increased his visibility by touring with the Eagles in 1975. Fogelberg's popularity peaked in 1980 with the release of *Phoenix*, which contained the number two hit single "Longer." His follow-up, *The Innocent Age*, was a double concept album, and four Top 20 singles were pulled from it. Following the release of a greatest hits package, Fogelberg's commercial appeal began to evaporate; none of his subsequent albums have gone platinum, but continue to sell well to a core of fans. 1993's *River of Souls* saw Fogelberg experimenting with worldbeat sounds as a backdrop for his lyrical musings. *No Resemblance Whatsoever*, a collaboration with Tim Weisberg, followed in 1995, and four years later Fogelberg returned with *First Christmas Morning*. *Live: Something Old New Borrowed and Some Blues* appeared in mid-2000. *—Steve Huey*

Greatest Hits / 1982 / Full Moon/Epic ✦✦✦✦
Greatest Hits may ignore some of his better album tracks, but it does contain what the title says—Dan Fogelberg's biggest hits, prior to its release date of 1982. Really, that means only one big hit—"The Language of Love"—is missing, since his peak of popularity arrived in the early '80s, when "Longer," "Same Old Lang Syne," "Hard to Say," and "Leader of the Band" all made the Top Ten, and "Heart Hotels," "Run for the Roses," "Missing You," and "Make Love Stay" cracked the Top 40. All of those songs, along with his first hit "Part of the Plan," are here, on a collection that remains the best, most concise chronicle of his hitmaking years yet assembled. *—Stephen Thomas Erlewine*

Portrait: The Music of Dan Fogelberg From 1972-1997 / Jun. 3, 1997 / Full Moon/Epic ✦✦✦✦
Portrait: The Music of Dan Fogelberg 1972-1997 is an extensive, four-disc box set that covers the singer-songwriter's entire career in detail. In addition to all of the hits and favorite album tracks, the box also features the B-side "Hearts and Crafts" and four previously unreleased tracks, including the newly recorded "Don't Lose Heart." Those five songs aren't quite enough to entice hardcore Fogelberg collectors, who are the only listeners that will be interested in such a substantial box set, since casual fans will find the sheer length of this set intimidating and maybe even tedious. But for any devoted Fogelberg fan who doesn't already own his entire catalog, *Portrait* is a worthwhile purchase. *—Stephen Thomas Erlewine*

• **The Very Best of Dan Fogelberg** / Jul. 3, 2001 / Epic/Legacy ✦✦✦✦
Although nine of the ten songs on Fogelberg's 1982 release *Greatest Hits* also show up here, this is a definite improvement on that prior disc. It has more songs (17), and extends its chronological reach all the way up to 1993. A few post-1982 chart singles are on here that weren't on *Greatest Hits*, though only one of them, "The Language of Love," was a big hit, and it could be argued that Fogelberg's most popular and familiar material is adequately summarized by *Greatest Hits* anyway. *—Richie Unterberger*

John Fogerty

b. May 28, 1945, Berkeley, CA
Vocals, Guitar / Heartland Rock, Roots Rock, Rock & Roll
John Cameron Fogerty achieved fame as the lead singer/songwriter and guitarist in Creedence Clearwater Revival and has since gone on to a chart-topping solo career. Born in Berkeley, CA, Fogerty and his brother Tom organized the group that would become Creedence as the Golliwogs in the late '50s. As Creedence, they released nine Top Ten singles, all written by Fogerty, between 1969 and 1971, starting with the standard "Proud Mary." They also scored eight gold albums between 1968 and 1972, all fueled by Fogerty's simple, driving rock songs and his burly baritone, intoning deceptively poetic ("Bad Moon Rising") and even political ("Fortunate Son") lyrics.

Creedence split up in 1972. Fogerty at first confused his considerable following by releasing an album of covers, on which he played all the instruments, under the name the Blue Ridge Rangers in 1973. This was followed by a formal solo album, *John Fogerty*, in 1975, and then silence for more than nine years while the artist worked out business problems with Creedence's old label. But Fogerty returned at the end of 1984 with a Top Ten single, "The Old Man Down the Road," and a number one album, *Centerfield*. *Eye of the Zombie* was a less successful follow-up in 1986. Following the failure of *Eye of the Zombie*, Fogerty went into seclusion. For the next 11 years he remained quiet, finally resurfacing in 1997 with *Blue Moon Swamp*; the live *Premonition* appeared just a year later. *—William Ruhlmann*

Blue Ridge Rangers / 1973 / Fantasy ✦✦✦
Fogerty as a one-man country band paying tribute to his honky-tonk roots. *—Jeff Tamarkin*

John Fogerty / 1975 / Asylum ✦✦✦✦
This one-man extravaganza finds John Fogerty plowing the same ground he worked with Creedence Clearwater Revival. This mix of originals and rock & roll classics finds him in fine voice, with the familiar vocal scream and hot guitars augmented in places by saxophones reminiscent of CCR's "Travelin' Band." Several of these songs rank with the top tier of Fogerty's Creedence material, particularly "The Wall," "Almost Saturday Night," and the anthemic "Rockin' All Over the World." He also delivers satisfying versions of Jackie Wilson's "Lonely Teardrops" and Frankie Ford's "Sea Cruise" (written by Huey "Piano" Smith. The closer, "Flying Away," could have come off the Doobie Brothers' *Toulouse Street*. This underappreciated album is worth checking out. *—Jim Newsom*

• **Centerfield** / Jan. 1985 / Warner Brothers ✦✦✦✦✦
"Put me in coach, I'm ready to play." These are lines familiar to any baseball fan, for John Fogerty's "Centerfield" has become the unofficial song of our national pastime. Those lines also signaled Fogerty's return to the music business after a ten-year absence. The music is mighty familiar, as Fogerty works the same terrain he mined for gold with Creedence Clearwater Revival from 1968-1972. The riff of the opening track, "The Old Man Down the Road," sounds so much like the Creedence hit "Run Through the Jungle" that Fogerty was sued by his former record company for plagiarizing himself. (He won the suit, the court upholding a composer's right to sound like himself.) "Old Man" was a Top Ten single, and this album reached number one itself. "Big Train (From Memphis)" is a rockabilly salute to Elvis, while "I Saw It on TV" takes us on a trip through the '50s and '60s "from Hooter to Doodyville," via the boob tube. "Searchlight" recalls "Keep On Chooglin" and the other extended one-chord jams of the Creedence days. Fogerty also lashes out at his old nemesis Saul Zaentz, head of that former label, Fantasy Records, with whom he had battled (and lost) over rights to his own catalog of Creedence songs. On "Mr. Greed" and "Zanz Kant Danz" (renamed "Vanz Kant Danz" on later pressings due again to the threat of lawsuit), he vents his anger over these past legal battles and foretells the one to come over "Old Man."

Fans hoped *Centerfield* would indeed mark the return of John Fogerty to the playing field, but after releasing the bitter *Eye of the Zombie* the following year, he disappeared again, not to return until 1997's *Blue Moon Swamp*. *—Jim Newsom*

Eye of the Zombie / 1986 / Warner Brothers ✦✦

Blue Moon Swamp / May 20, 1997 / Warner Brothers ✦✦✦✦✦
Listening to the easy roots-rock shuffle of *Blue Moon Swamp*, it's hard to believe that it took John Fogerty a full decade to write and record the album. It's not just because the album isn't a great stylistic departure from his past work, it's because *Blue Moon Swamp* sounds so natural and unforced. Nothing on the album sounds fussy, nor does it sound like a meticulous reconstruction of the past. Instead, Fogerty's songs and performances are richly evocative of tradition, but they're vibrant and living for the present, which makes the rockabilly, blues, country, and swampy rock & roll sound fresh. It's not as raw or as hooky as Creedence Clearwater Revival, nor as pop-oriented as *Centerfield*, but it's a warm, laid-back and mature record of roots rock at its very best. *—Stephen Thomas Erlewine*

Premonition / Jun. 9, 1998 / Warner Brothers ✦✦✦✦
Upon its release in the spring of 1997, John Fogerty's long-awaited comeback album *Blue Moon Swamp* was lavished with praise—it didn't become the crossover hit that *Centerfield* was, but it earned great reviews and a solid cult audience. Furthermore, his tour—his first ever to feature classic Creedence material—was, if anything, even better received than *Blue Moon Swamp*, so it made some sense that he quickly released *Premonition*, his first solo live album, in 1998. *Premonition* is frighteningly good—Fogerty doesn't sound like a veteran rocker, he sounds nearly as powerful as he did on old Creedence live shows. He also sounds more mature, bringing increased depth to his older songs as he energizes recent material from "The Old Man Down the Road" to "Walking in a Hurricane." *Premonition* is essentially the province of dedicated Fogerty fans—there's only one new song, and the differences in the live performances are things only the hardcore will spot—but they'll be delighted with the quality of the music. *—Stephen Thomas Erlewine*

Foghat

f. 1971, London, England, **db.** 1984
Album Rock, Boogie Rock, Arena Rock, Heavy Metal, Hard Rock, Blues-Rock
Foghat specialized in a simple, hard-rocking blues-rock, releasing a series of best-selling albums in the mid-'70s. While the group never deviated from their basic boogie, they retained a large audience until 1978, selling out concerts across America and earning five gold albums, as well as two platinum. Once punk and disco came along, the band's audience dipped dramatically, yet the group continued performing until 1980. With its straight-ahead, three-chord romps, the band's sound was American in origin, yet the members were all natives of England. Guitarist/vocalist "Lonesome" Dave Peverett, bassist Tony Stevens, and drummer Roger Earl were members of the British blues band Savoy Brown who left the group in the early '70s. Upon their departure, they formed Foghat with guitarist Rod Price. Foghat moved to the United States, signing a record contract with Bearsville Records, a new label run by Albert Grossman. Their first album, *Foghat*, was released in the summer of 1972 and became a hit on album rock radio. For their next album, the group didn't change their formula at all—in fact, they didn't even change the title of the album. Like the first record, the second was called *Foghat*; it was their first gold record, and it established them as a popular arena rock act. Their next five albums all were best-sellers and all went at least gold. "Slow Ride," taken from *Fool for the City*, was their biggest single, peaking at number 20. *Foghat Live* was their biggest album, selling over two million copies. In the early '80s, Foghat's commercial fortunes declined rapidly, with their last album, 1983's *Zig-Zag Walk*, barely making the album charts. The group broke up shortly afterward, although they have reunited for various tours in the late '80s and early '90s. *—Stephen Thomas Erlewine*

• **The Best of Foghat** / Oct. 1990 / Rhino ✦✦✦✦
Rhino's *Best of Foghat* is an excellent 16-track collection featuring every one of the hard-rocking boogie band's best-known songs, from "Slow Ride" and "I Just Want to Make Love to You" to "Fool for the City," "Drivin' Wheel," and "Ride, Ride, Ride." In short, it's all the Foghat most fans will ever need. *—Stephen Thomas Erlewine*

The Best of Foghat, Vol. 2 / Jan. 24, 1992 / Rhino ✦✦✦
If *Best of Foghat* made you hungry for more, *Best of Foghat, Vol. 2*, with no hit singles, only album tracks, and including two live cuts and an outtake, should satiate your desire. *—Stephen Thomas Erlewine*

Ben Folds

Vocals, Piano / Pop Underground, Adult Alternative Pop/Rock, Alternative Pop/Rock, Singer/Songwriter
Singer/pianist Ben Folds (born Sept. 12, 1966 in Winston-Salem, NC) is best known as

the leader of the power-pop trio Ben Folds Five, but he has also struck out on his own as a solo artist. Despite playing in bands in high school, his musical career didn't really get off the ground until the late-80's, as a bassist for Majsha. Proving his multi-instrumental talents, Folds also played drums in as a session musician in Nashville. Moving back to North Carolina, Folds formed Ben Folds Five in 1994. Whereas most alternative bands of the '90s specialized in distorted teen angst rock, the guitarless trio was a refreshing break from the norm. The band was signed to the independent Caroline Records shortly afterward, resulting in their self-titled debut one year later. Due to airings of their humorous anthem, "Underground" (which poked fun at the politics of the punk/alternative scene) on MTV's *120 Minutes* and constant touring, quite a buzz was stirring for the band by the time of their second album. Released in 1997, *Whatever and Ever Amen* was pure pop perfection and easily one of the year's best releases (and perhaps the best power-pop release of the '90s). While 1998 didn't see a new studio album by the band, BF5's former label issued a 16-track rarities collection (*Naked Baby Photos*), as Folds released his first solo album, *Volume 1*, under the pseudonym Fear of Pop. Although the album went largely unnoticed, it included the song "In Love," which included overly dramatic vocals from none other than Captain Kirk himself, Mr. William Shatner. Ben Folds Five regrouped with 1999's *The Unauthorized Biography of Reinhold Messner*, which was a more mature work than its predecessors, although the energetic lead-off single, "Army," showed that Folds' humorous approach hadn't dulled at all. *—Greg Prato*

● **Ben Folds Five** / Aug. 8, 1995 / Passenger ✦✦✦✦

The debut album from piano-playing Ben Folds' smart-ass trio is a potent, and extremely fun, collection of post-modern rock ditties that comes off as a pleasantly workable combination of Tin Pan Alley showmanship, Todd Rundgren-style power pop, and a myriad of alt-rock sensibilities. The gimmick here is that not a single guitar was used on the 12 songs; but the way that Folds and his bandmates unravel their instruments (piano, bass, and drums make up this combo), even the most hardened noise enthusiasts will hardly miss it (it's the melodies that carry this album, and Folds has plenty of them up his sleeve). Some of it is a bit coy—Folds plays the joker as much as he does the musician—but with the dead-on "Underground," they manage to skewer, and pay loving tribute, to the oh-so-hip indie scene from which they came. *—Michael Gallucci*

Whatever and Ever Amen / Mar. 18, 1997 / 550 ✦✦✦✦

Expanding on the hook-laden songcraft of their eponymous debut, the Ben Folds Five turn in another glitzy array of Todd Rundgren-esque, piano-driven pop on their second album, *Whatever and Ever Amen*. Though it isn't as consistently tuneful and clever as their first record, *Whatever and Ever Amen* has a snazzy sense of popcraft—the hooks of "The Battle of Who Could Care Less," "Brick," and "Fair" sink in nearly as effortlessly as Billy Joel, Elton John, or Joe Jackson—which makes the record enjoyable ear candy. Occasionally, Folds' smug humor—whether it's the alternative-rock skewering of "The Battle" or the borderline misogynist humor of "Song for the Dumped"—can undercut his melodic gifts, but *Whatever and Ever Amen* is confirmation that the showy pop pleasures of his first record were no fluke. *—Thom Owens*

Naked Baby Photos / Jan. 13, 1998 / Caroline ✦✦✦

As the title suggests, *Naked Baby Photos* opens the vaults to capture Ben Folds Five in their developmental stages, splitting its 16 tracks evenly between studio rarities and live performances; about half have never been available before in any recorded form. In addition to those previously unavailable tracks, Folds collectors will be enticed by the band's rare debut 7", "Jackson Cannery," and the original demo of "Bad Idea," which the band considers superior to the version released on the *Truth About Cats and Dogs* soundtrack. *—Steve Huey*

Fear of Pop, Vol. 1 / Nov. 17, 1998 / 550 ✦✦✦

Ben Folds' first solo project away from the ultra-pop of Ben Folds Five is not the upbeat, piano banging you would expect after listening to his previous work. As his project's name spells out in bold letters, *Fear of Pop* collects all of the nasty little demons running through Folds' mind when he's singing his sweet ditties. The biggest distinction is the addition of guitar, a BF5 no-no. Screeching chords christen the album's title track as Folds howls at his most unharmonic. From there, every track continues on in a different experimental vein which paints Folds as some manic child who has just gotten a recording studio for Christmas. 1970s sleaze funk mixes with avant-garde flute and muffled crime-scene samples on "Kops"; "Blink" sounds like background music at a planetarium laser light show; the synth-pop throwback "Avery M. Powers Memorial Speedway" sounds like a lost Heaven 17/Sigue Sigue Sputnik collaboration. Most interesting of Folds' experiment is "In Love" which gives William Shatner, Mr. Golden Throat himself, a chance to mutter suave, obscure poetry over a sea of smooth backing vocals and tinny drum machines. Shatner's appearance is enough to clue us in that Folds is anything but serious with this eclectic surge of energy. If anything, the bizarre humor mixed with the swift sounds and firm beats makes *Volume 1* a danceable novelty record with a justified sense of end-of-the millennium attention deficit disorder. *—Jason Kaufman*

The Unauthorized Biography of Reinhold Messner / Apr. 27, 1999 / 550 ✦✦✦✦

The follow-up to the popular *Whatever and Ever Amen*, Ben Folds Five's third LP, *The Unauthorized Biography of Reinhold Mesner*, continues the eclectic and clever songwriting that has become the group's trademark. Like other piano-based rock composers such as Randy Newman and Todd Rundgren, principal songwriter and *de facto* leader Ben Folds combines an offbeat worldview with equally off-kilter musical arrangements to create a thoroughly original sound. The pseudo-lounge break in "Regrets," for example, or the downright sillyness of "Your Redneck Past" set the Ben Folds Five apart from the hundreds of the sound-alike bands that the group competes with for radio space. What makes Ben Folds Five, and *The Unauthorized Biography of Reinhold Mesner*, relevant is their willingness to take musical risks, an anomaly in today's scene. On an album where there is a lack of instantly catchy hooks, Folds has the audacity to add a bizarre Burt Bacharach-ish horn section to "Don't Change Your Plans," one of the few radio friendly tracks on the album. And in "Most Valuable Possession," the band uses studio trickery and an answering machine message left by Folds' father to create a bizarre spoken word pastiche. It is this willingness to forge a unique sound that makes *The Unauthorized Biography of Reinhold Mesner* such an interesting album to listen to. There is care to these songs and, what's even more significant and fresh, there is also intelligence. *—Steve Kurutz*

Rockin' the Suburbs / Sep. 11, 2001 / Epic ✦✦✦✦✦

Superficially, there's not much separating Ben Folds' first official solo album, *Rockin' the Suburbs*, from his records with Ben Folds Five. It's hard to note any difference, really, since he still works from the same vantage point, borrowing equally from new wave, '90s irony, and a love of classic pop. Still, there is a difference, even if it's hard to pinpoint—perhaps it's an increased focus, perhaps it was a hot streak from Folds, or perhaps the Five really were more of a group than they seemed and he's benefited by working according to his own patterns. Regardless, *Rockin' the Suburbs* is as good a record as any he's made, possibly his best. It's still possible to hear his influences—Joe Jackson still stands out, as do elements of Billy Joel and Todd Rundgren—but there's no shame there, and he's accepted it as part of his musical personality so much that it sounds like him, even when it sounds familiar. Better still, he's tempered his tendency to be a collegiate wiseass—it pokes through on the title track, but that's the rare time that it's brought to the forefront—which helps his songs shine brighter. And while there are no surprises here to anybody familiar with his work, it's a remarkably consistent record, filled with great mid-tempo pop tunes and nicely sentimental ballads. It's simply a good, solid record that captures Ben Folds at his most engaging, and that's more than enough. *—Stephen Thomas Erlewine*

Folk Implosion

f. 1993

Indie Rock, Lo-Fi, Alternative Pop/Rock

Lo-fi duo the Folk Implosion was one of the many side projects of the ubiquitous Lou Barlow, this time out in tandem with fellow singer/songwriter John Davis. The two began playing together in 1993 after Davis sent Barlow a tape of home recordings inspired by the latter's work with his primary musical outlet, Sebadoh; dubbing themselves the Folk Implosion, the duo soon issued a self-titled cassette on the Chocolate Monk label, followed in 1994 by the 7" *Walk Through This World With the Folk Implosion* and an EP, *Take a Look Inside the Folk Implosion*. The following year the duo recorded a series of songs for the soundtrack of the controversial Larry Clark film *Kids*, scoring an unlikely pop radio hit with "Natural One." The full-length *Dare to Be Surprised* followed in 1997, and two years later the Folk Implosion released their Interscope debut *One Part Lullaby*. *—Jason Ankeny*

Take a Look Inside / Aug. 15, 1994 / Communion ✦✦✦

With 14 songs whizzing by in 22 jam-packed minutes *Take a Look Inside* is just a lo-fi blur on the first few listens. But eventually the great songs stand out, and it becomes clear that this short-form approach to songwriting suits Lou Barlow well. So instead of the rip-off one would expect from a 22-minute full-length, *Take a Look Inside* stands as one the Folk Implosion's best releases. By limiting each song to three minutes, Barlow and bandmate John Davis reign in their stranger "freak-out" tendencies, exposing a cache of pop gems. So it's worth wading through the murk of "Spiderweb-Butterfly" to get to the serene "Had to Find Out," or the drone of "Boyfriend, Girlfriend" to reach the superb trio "Shake a Little Heaven," "Waltzin' With Your Ego," and the funky "Take a Look Inside." *—Ari Wiznitzer*

● **Dare to Be Surprised** / Apr. 29, 1997 / Communion ✦✦✦✦

The surprise success of "Natural One" affected the Folk Implosion in a surprising way. Instead of running from success and shunning melody, Lou Barlow and John Davis decided to embrace pop on their own terms. That means the Folk Implosion remains an indie-rock band, recording on cheap equipment and layering brittle guitars for the basic tracks, but they write impossibly catchy hooks, such as the amazing single "Pole Position." At its best, *Dare to Be Surprised* is spare, tuneful and infectious, and at its worst, it's merely underwritten. Nevertheless, Barlow has rarely been as succinct and consistent as he is here, and Davis' songs are uniformly strong as well, making *Dare to Be Surprised* one of the finest items in their respective catalogs. *—Stephen Thomas Erlewine*

One Part Lullaby / Sep. 7, 1999 / Interscope ✦✦✦

Folk Implosion disappeared from view not long after *Dare to Be Surprised*, which failed to capitalize on "Natural One"'s surprise success. Perhaps the group effort of 1998's *The Sebadoh* made Lou Barlow want to claim control of Folk Implosion on *One Part Lullaby*. Though John Davis is credited with co-writing the songs, "Lou sang lead vocal and wrote most of the words," making this feel like a Barlow solo project blessed with greater popcraft. It's more cohesive than *Dare to Be Surprised*, built around the trip-hop/new wave blend that made "Natural One" a hit, but that turns out to be a mixed blessing. Part of the charm of Folk Implosion was that it felt like two friends just kicking back, making weird noises, and writing quirky songs. Some of that remains, especially in the cheap synths and other electronic instrumentation, but *One Part Lullaby* is far more measured, filled with songs performed at the same basic tempo, with similar hooks and arrangements. It's not mellow, necessarily, but has a meditative mood, which fits Barlow's disarmingly introspective lyrics—something familiar to Sebadoh and solo albums, but previously unheard of on Implosion albums. Parts of *One Part Lullaby* work very well, but it's also curiously flat. The modern rock production feels two years out of date—shiny and commercial for 1996-1997, but an anomaly in 1999. Barlow's writing is too emotionally insular and musically similar for it to be truly engaging throughout and mutes the carefree spirit of previous Implosion albums; worst of all, it feels like he's repeating himself. That's not to say *One Part Lullaby* is a failure—when Barlow and Davis pull it all together, the results are as strong as anything else the duo has recorded. As a whole, however, it winds up being strangely unengaging. *—Stephen Thomas Erlewine*

Wayne Fontana & The Mindbenders

f. 1963, Manchester, England, **db.** 1968

Merseybeat, British Invasion

Lester Bangs said it best in his essay on the British Invasion in *The Rolling Stone Illustrated History of Rock & Roll*: "Wayne Fontana & the Mindbenders may have been a one-shot group, but what a shot. "The Game of Love," with its heavy bass, "Louie Louie" chording, Bo Diddley break, and Fontana's rich, wailing vocals, was an instant classic, a perfect example of the rock & roll band of no apparent distinction but with a masterpiece in them anyway." Make that two masterpieces, although Fontana had split for a solo career before the group topped the charts again with "A Groovy Kind of Love." The Manchester, England, group was composed of competent and energetic performers, but suffered the bane of many early British Invasion acts in the ultra-competitive days of 1966—they didn't write strong material for themselves. After some low-charting follow-ups to "Game of Love," Fontana left for a solo career which saw him only gaining a couple British hits: "Come on Home" and Graham Gouldman's "Pamela, Pamela." After "A Groovy Kind of Love," the Mindbenders had another British Top 20 hit with "Ashes to Ashes," then cut a string of flop singles and made a memorable appearance in the film *To Sir With Love*. Graham Gouldman was briefly a member before the group called it a day in 1968, though he and Mindbenders singer/guitarist Eric Stewart would work together again in 10cc. *—Richie Unterberger*

Hit Single Anthology / 1991 / Fontana ✦✦

In 1965, Wayne Fontana & the Mindbenders struck with one of the British Invasion's greatest one-shots, the number one hit "Game of Love." After Fontana split for a solo career shortly afterwards, the Mindbenders scored another mammoth hit that was nearly as memorable, "A Groovy Kind of Love." This 23-song anthology—featuring the most successful singles by Fontana & the Mindbenders, both together and as separate entities—does not, unfortunately, offer anything in the same league as those two smashes. They did manage a couple other U.K. hits, "Um Um Um Um Um Um" and "Just a Little Bit Too Late" (both included here), in their original incarnation, but neither are especially memorable. Dependent upon outside writers for virtually all of their material, Fontana & Co. had little to distinguish them from literally hundreds of other middling British Invasion-era groups except their extraordinary luck in latching on to a couple of pieces of great material. Upon splitting from the Mindbenders, Fontana pursued a Tom Jones-like balladeering direction that has worn badly; the Mindbenders, while remaining rock-oriented, offered nearly as little. Stick with the two hit singles, on which they miraculously secured masterful pieces of tuneful and dynamic British Invasion pop. *—Richie Unterberger*

● **The Best of Wayne Fontana & the Mindbenders** / 1994 / Fontana ✦✦✦✦✦

Well-chosen 20-track anthology, covering the hits and the best of their rare 1964-68 singles, as well as a couple rare cuts from U.K. LPs and EPs. It's actually a distinct improvement upon its U.K. counterpart *Hit Single Anthology*, as it includes the fine "It's Getting Harder All of the Time"/"Off and Running" single from the *To Sir With Love* soundtrack, and eliminates some of the weak covers and Wayne Fontana solo singles. *—Richie Unterberger*

The World of Wayne Fontana & the Mindbenders / 1996 / Spectrum ✦✦✦

Following reasonably warm on the heels of Polygram's domestic *Best Of*, this set opens with the understandable duplication of the band's greatest hits. But while the last release just marched straightforwardly chronological, this one really goes walkabout. And if it's true that the Mindbenders are better remembered for featuring one half of 10cc (guitarist Eric Stewart and last days bassist Graham Gouldman), you wouldn't know it from this remarkably egalitarian collection. Stewart cops just one co-writing credit, Gouldman scores two. The emphasis, then, is on the less well-walked passages. Early singles and B-sides which don't figure on the domestic compilation include the band's storming debut "Hello Josephine," alongside "It's Just a Little Bit Too Late," a surprisingly strong cover of the Boxtops' "The Letter," "Long Time Coming," and "Like I Did," while original frontman Wayne Fontana's solo career is healthily represented by "It Was Easier to Hurt Her," "Storybook Children," "Something Keeps Calling Me Back," "Come on Home," "Words of Bartholomew," and "Goodbye Bluebird"—some of the greatest and most underrated pop of the mid- to late '60s. It would, of course, have been preferable to see the story split into individual collections—having shared a common destiny for three years, Fontana and the Mindbenders not only went their separate ways in 1966, they also launched increasingly divergent careers. Fontana went for classy pop, the band slammed from a groovy kind of bubblegum to a rough approximation of proto-hard rock. Still, any chance to pick up songs which, in their original form make hen's teeth seem plentiful, is gratifying and, if history is ever to rehabilitate the Mindbenders beyond the dubious charms of "Um Um Um Um Um Um," *The World Of* is a good place to start. *—Dave Thompson*

Foo Fighters

f. 1995, Seattle, WA

Grunge, Alternative Pop/Rock, Post-Grunge

While he was drumming with Nirvana, Dave Grohl was recording original songs at home that never received public release. Those tapes would become the foundation of the Foo Fighters, the band he formed in 1995. Like Nirvana, the Foo Fighters melded loud, heavy guitars with pretty melodies and mixed punk sensibilities with a sharp sense of pop songwriting. Following Kurt Cobain's suicide in 1994, the drummer kept quiet for several months, but then recorded the album that became the Foo Fighters' debut in a week. In no time, Dave Grohl's solo project became the object of a fierce record-company bidding war. Less than a year after its release, the album was certified platinum in the US. Throughout 1996, the Foo Fighters supported the album with an extensive tour, enjoying a crossover hit with "Big Me" that spring. *The Colour and the Shape*, the Foo Fighters' second album, was released in 1997. *—Stephen Thomas Erlewine*

● **Foo Fighters** / Jul. 4, 1995 / Roswell/Capitol ✦✦✦✦

Essentially a collection of solo home recordings by Dave Grohl, the Foo Fighters' eponymous debut is a modest triumph. Driven by big pop melodies and distorted guitars, Foo Fighters does strongly recall Nirvana, only with a decidedly lighter approach. If Kurt Cobain's writing occasionally recalled John Lennon, Dave Grohl's songs are reminiscent of Paul McCartney—they're driven by large, instantly memorable melodies, whether it's the joyous outburt of "This Is a Call" or the gentle pop of "Big Me." That doesn't mean Grohl shys away from noise; toward the end of the record, he piles on several thrashers that make more sense as pure aggressive sound than songs. Since he recorded the album by himself, they aren't as powerful as most band's primal sonic workouts, but the results are damn impressive for a solo musician. Nevertheless, they aren't as strong as his fully formed pop songs, and that's where the true heart of the album lies. *Foo Fighters* has a handful of punk-pop gems that show, given the right musicians and songwriters, the genre had not entirely become a cliche by the middle of the '90s. *—Stephen Thomas Erlewine*

The Colour and the Shape / May 20, 1997 / Capitol ✦✦✦✦

Since the first Foo Fighters album was a collection of Dave Grohl solo recordings, their second album *The Colour and the Shape* is in many ways their official debut, and it certainly does sound different than its predecessor. Producer Gil Norton has tightened up the sound considerably—his control was so tight that drummer William Goldsmith left the band during the recording, leaving Grohl to record the rhythm tracks for the bulk of the album. Certainly, Norton's big, shiny sound makes *The Colour and the Shape* sound more professional than the debut, but the presence of a full band makes a difference, too. The full Foo Fighters make Grohl's songs heavier, not punkier, which may be a little unsettling to fans of the debut's ragged, amateurish edge. It's also strange that the album has such a glossy, arena-ready sound, since Grohl's songs are introspective, quite different than the endearing punk-pop of its predecessor. They're also not quite as catchy as before, but the band compensates by delivering them with a brutal energy. Still, the lack of immediate hooks prevents *The Colour and the Shape* from truly catching fire. *—Stephen Thomas Erlewine*

There Is Nothing Left to Lose / Nov. 2, 1999 / RCA ✦✦✦✦

Foo Fighters were the most unexpectedly mercurial band in '90s rock, boasting a different lineup for each of their three albums. The ever-shifting lineup didn't help erase the image that the group was merely a vehicle for Dave Grohl, and made it seem like Grohl was something of a dictator, at least to some biased outside observers. That's why their third record *There is Nothing Left to Lose* comes as somewhat of a surprise. It is the first Foo Fighters album that sounds like the work of a unified, muscular band, and the first one that rocks *really* hard. A lot of credit should go to Adam Kasper, who produced the record with the band. *There is Nothing Left to Lose* has a stripped-down sound and an immediate attack that makes even the poppier numbers rock hard. The organic, natural sound is welcome, but the album also benefits from the strongest set of songs Grohl and the Foo Fighters have yet written. There are the typical strong singles, but there's no fat or filler; each track has a memorable hook or melody, and they seem all the more catchy because they're delivered with conviction and confidence. And that's why the album sounds like the first true band album Foo Fighters have made—the group sounds assured and confident, where they previously seemed like they had something to prove. It's as if they know they have few peers in straight-ahead, post-grunge hard rock, so they're willing just to lay back and turn out a solid set of 11 songs. They make it sound easy and fun, and that's what really sets them apart from their contemporaries. That, and the fact that they're getting better as they're losing members and growing older, which is certainly a rarity in rock & roll. *—Stephen Thomas Erlewine*

Steve Forbert

b. 1955, Meridian, MS

Vocals, Harmonica, Guitar / Contemporary Folk, Singer/Songwriter

Annointed "the new Dylan" upon his recording debut, folk-rock singer/songwriter Steve Forbert was born in Meridian, MS in 1955. After learning guitar at age 11, he spent his high school years playing in a variety of local bands before quitting his job as a truck driver and moving to New York City at the age of 21. There, he performed for spare change in Grand Central Station before working his way up to the Manhattan club circuit.

After signing to Nemperor, Forbert debuted in 1978 with *Alive on Arrival*, which earned critical acclaim for its taut, poetic lyrics. The follow-up, 1979's *Jackrabbit Slim*, was his most successful outing, reaching the Top 20 on the strength of the hit single "Romeo's Tune" (allegedly inspired by the late Supreme Florence Ballard). However, both 1980's *Little Stevie Orbit* and a self-titled 1982 effort fared poorly, and Forbert was dropped by his label. He spent much of the decade in Nashville, where he continued honing his songwriting skills and performed regularly throughout the South. In 1988, he signed to Geffen, where the E Street Band's Garry Tallent produced his comeback album, *Streets of This Town*. Pete Anderson took over the production reins for 1992's *The American in Me*, but Forbert's continued lack of chart success prompted the label to cut him loose. After 1994's live effort *Be Here Now*, he recorded *Mission of the Crossroad Palms* for

Giant the next year. *Rocking Horse Head* followed in 1996, and in early 2000 Forbert returned with *Evergreen Boy*. The fierce driving *Young Guitar Days* appeared in spring 2001. *—Jason Ankeny*

Alive on Arrival / 1978 / Nemperor ♦♦♦
Steve Forbert's youthful features and boyish voice certainly become misleading once his lyrics are heard. His folk-rock styled songs are usually centered around life's ups and downs and the problems of adulthood, portraying him as an artist who's just trying to get by. *Alive on Arrival* is an album full of earnest tunes about loneliness, self-worth, aspirations, and disappointments. Forbert's wispy, innocent sounding voice floats gently (and cuts roughly) over his acoustic guitar to homespun ditties with a down-to-earth feel. This album represents Forbert's music perfectly, and even though his latter albums sound less subtle, it is *Alive on Arrival* that so aptly personifies him. "Going Down to Laurel" has his voice aching about the dirtiness of the city and the beauty of his true love, and "Steve Forbert's Midsummer Night's Toast" is an interesting musical jaunt through the bittersweet world of growing up. Forbert really comes to life on "What Kinda Guy?," humorously explaining what a simplified, easygoing chap he is. The kick-back aura of *Alive on Arrival* puts the emphasis on the down and out Forbert while feelings of sentiment and adolescence slowly emerge with each passing song. This album makes for a great late-night listen. *—Mike DeGagne*

Jackrabbit Slim / Oct. 1979 / Columbia ♦♦♦♦♦
Although *Jackrabbit Slim* was Steve Forbert's best-selling album, containing his only Top 40 hit, "Romeo's Tune," and his only other chart single, "Say Goodbye To Little Jo," it took Nemperor (formerly part of CBS, now part of Sony) 17 years to put it out on CD (on Sept. 3, 1996). It sounds as good as it did before, thanks both to Forbert's excellent songwriting (also included: "January 23-30, 1978," one of his best diary songs) and to John Simon's production. In a newly added note, Forbert says Simon was a late addition, after his producer was stolen by Barbra Streisand. If he means Gary Klein, who handled Streisand's 1979 *Wet* album, one can only concluded that he traded up. Simon, whose previous credits included the Band, understood Forbert's folk-rock-pop style perfectly, making this the best marriage of artist and producer on what is also the artist's best material. *—William Ruhlmann*

Little Stevie Orbit / Sep. 1980 / Nemperor ♦♦♦
Little Stevie Orbit was seen as a disappointment at the time of its release because it did not generate a hit single on the order of "Romeo's Tune," and thus failed to consolidate the commercial success Steve Forbert had achieved with his second album, *Jackrabbit Slim*. In retrospect, however, it is a spirited, rollicking collection on which Forbert sounds increasingly comfortable fronting a rock band on a series of lighthearted songs such as "I'm an Automobile" and "If You've Gotta Ask You'll Never Know." It may not have made him a superstar, but *Little Stevie Orbit* provided some strong additions to Steve Forbert's concert repertoire for years to come. *—William Ruhlmann*

Steve Forbert / Jul. 1982 / Nemperor ♦♦
Steve Forbert hit quite a few stylistic bases on his fourth, self-titled album, maybe too many. From the horn-filled, Motown-tinged "Ya Ya (Next to Me)" to a faithful cover of Jackie DeShannon's mid-'60s classic "When You Walk in the Room" to the lush, string-heavy "Oh So Close (And Yet So Far Away)" to the up-tempo country two-step "You're Darn Right," Forbert couldn't be pinned down to a genre (certainly not folk-rock). But there was too little of the spunky tone of songs like "It Takes a Whole Lotta Help (To Make It on Your Own)" that had sparked Forbert's previous albums. (Unfortunately, Forbert's proposed fifth album was rejected by his record company in 1984, and it took him six years to follow this album.) *—William Ruhlmann*

Streets of This Town / Apr. 1988 / Geffen ♦♦♦
Coming back after a six-year layoff, Forbert displays a previously unheard edge of bitterness that only deepens his thoughtful lyrics. And he rocks harder than ever. *—William Ruhlmann*

The American in Me / Jan. 1992 / Geffen ♦♦♦
Steve Forbert never had a chance of living up to the "new Dylan" kiss of death that critics smeared on his collar with his first releases in the late '70s. Four albums of wit and optimism gave way to a six-year drought without a record contract. With *The American In Me*, Forbert has found a healthier, more balanced perspective. The pressures and uncertainties of growing up, taking on responsibilities, and looking back on missed opportunity makes up the central theme linking the disc's ten songs. This isn't a disc for the kids. It's for the parents out there who can still touch the rebel spirit within themselves and who have no desire to age gracefully. *—Roch Parisien*

● **The Best of Steve Forbert: What Kinda Guy?** / Apr. 13, 1993 / Columbia/Legacy ♦♦♦♦
The storytelling precision of Steve Forbert shines brightly on this generous collection of his finest songs, answering the interrogative title *What Kinda Guy?* with 19 tracks. From the addictive piano melody of "Romeo's Tune" off of *Jackrabbit Slim* to the philosophical "Thinkin" from *Alive on Arrival*, the exuberance and grit of Forbert is well represented through each and every song. The five unreleased songs, four of them live, are wonderful add-ons, especially the juvenile flair of "Schoolgirl" and the compelling honesty of "Complications." Forbert's humble character and boyish simplicity sparks a yearning deep down inside anyone who pays close attention to his unpretentiousness. Bits and pieces of life's hardships and tribulations weave themselves through his yarns in ballads and in the energetic jangle of his guitar. Ending with the realistic "It Isn't Gonna Be That Way," listeners are left with a loneliness and a coziness, intermingled by way of Forbert's folk-roots approach. This set is a superb gathering of tunes from this underestimated singer. *—Mike DeGagne*

Mission of the Crossroad Palms / Mar. 28, 1995 / Giant ♦♦♦
Steve Forbert turns in an album of craftsmanlike tunes on his seventh album, including story songs such as "It Sure Was Better Back Then" (a working man's reminiscence) and "The Trouble With Angels" (in which an ex-beauty queen robs the till to pay for her infertility treatments). There is also one of Forbert's philosophical treatises ("It Is What It Is [And That's All]") and the humorously multi-referential "Lay Down Your Weary Tune Again" (risky territory for a former "new Dylan"). But the best song may be Forbert's ode to infidelity, "Don't Talk to Me." The point, though, is that Forbert has flowered into a distinctive, broad-based songwriter and that, in E Street Band bassist Garry Tallent, he has found a sympathetic producer able to showcase his voice and lyrics properly. Now, if he could just reconnect with his audience. *—William Ruhlmann*

Rocking Horse Head / Sep. 24, 1996 / Giant ♦♦♦

Here's Your Pizza / Nov. 4, 1997 / Paladin ♦♦♦♦
Steve Forbert may have been *Alive on Arrival* (the title of his 1978 debut), but it took him another 19 years to get around to releasing a live album. He dug into the vaults to do it, waxing a concert he recorded with his band, the Rough Squirrels, in a small Florida club back in 1987. "Yes there's some tape hiss here, some distortion," and Forbert admits in the liner notes, but there are also performances that "more than make up for any technical imperfections." For the most part, that's true, although you do have to wade through a few throwaways to get to the goodies. Don't look here for "Goin' Down to Laurel," or many of Forbert's other best-known tunes; with a couple of exceptions—most notably a great version of the midtempo "Song for Katrina," one of his best love songs—this is an album of covers and obscurities, not greatest hits. There's a taste of the '50s (a cover of Bobby Day's "Rockin' Robin" and a tribute to Ritchie Valens that includes a snippet of his "La Bamba"), a nod to the Beatles ("One After 909"), and a surprisingly successful version of Tommy Roe's "Sweet Pea," the 1966 bubblegum hit. There's also ample evidence of Forbert's wacky sense of humor on "Everybody Does It in Hawaii," the yodel-spiced "Years Ago," and his own "What Kinda Guy?" [Note: Keep listening after the last listed track, and you'll hear an unadvertised bonus: affecting versions of "If You're Waiting on Me" and "You Cannot Win 'Em All," both of which first surfaced on Forbert's *The American in Me* album.] *—Jeff Burger*

Evergreen Boy / Jan. 25, 2000 / Koch ♦♦♦
Steve Forbert couldn't have picked a more appropriate title than *Evergreen Boy* for his latest effort. It contains the same sturdy roots rock that Forbert's been sending our way for years. Forbert's yarns about relationships and daily life, like "Breaking Through" and "Trusting Old Soul," are spawned from the same spool of Americana that's served Bruce Springsteen and John Mellencamp so well. Although Forbert will probably never be as popular or acclaimed as those two, he's carved his own niche, with mature, mellow music that can still rock when necessary. *—Mark Morgenstein*

Young, Guitar Days / Mar. 20, 2001 / Madacy ♦♦♦♦
Far from being a collection of second-rate unfinished songs, B-sides, and live tracks that didn't make the cut because they were subpar, *Young, Guitar Days* is a treasure trove of 20 terrific gems from Steve Forbert's early-'80s years that sounds as fresh and inspired as anything he's released. Not only a treat for established fans, there is also enough great music here to convince even newcomers of his remarkable talents. The singer/songwriter's voice and approach have changed little over the course of his career, so these songs—all of which originate from the early '80s—sound like recent recordings. From the good-time pedal steel-driven country & western of "The Weekend" to the appropriately bluesy slide guitar of "No Use Running From the Blues" to the impassioned cover of Terry Stafford's "Suspicion" (complete with '60s-styled backing vocals and an early indication of Forbert's love of AM radio fare that later resulted in his take on "When You Walk in the Room"), the styles are varied but still completely identifiable as emanating from Forbert's uniquely Americana-based approach. The sound is beautifully clear, exuding an airy unforced quality, as the performances brim with the youthful enthusiasm of an artist who has already found his voice and is excited about his future. The music is contagious in its rootsy joy and the songs stand as some of the best in his catalog. Since he wrote the liner notes and chose the tracks, it's clear that Forbert agrees, making this an essential addition to his discography and a wonderful collection of songs—regardless of why they were left to languish in obscurity for almost 20 years between their recording and 2001 release. *—Hal Horowitz*

Force M.D.'s

f. 1983, Staten Island, NY
Quiet Storm, New Jack Swing, Urban
Although not as well known as other New York hip-hop acts of the early '80s, Staten Island's Force M.D.'s were a vital crew in the early history of street hip-hop and one of the first vocal groups to fuse doo wop-influenced harmonies with hip-hop beats. Originally a street troupe known as the LD's, the group sang and danced on Greenwich Village street corners and the Staten Island ferry. By the time they signed to Tommy Boy in 1984 as the Force M.D.'s (M.D. standing for "musical diversity"), they had evolved into a more straightforward R&B vocal group, distinguished mostly by their street attitude. The M.D.'s had a string of R&B hits through the '80s, but their only pop hit was the Top Ten Jimmy Jam/Terry Lewis-penned ballad "Tender Love," which was featured in the movie *Krush Groove*. 1987 produced the group's first R&B number one, "Love Is a House," but their popular appeal began to ebb the following year. *—Steve Huey*

Love Letters / 1984 / Tommy Boy ♦♦♦

Chillin' / 1986 / Tommy Boy ♦♦♦♦♦

Touch & Go / 1987 / Tommy Boy ♦♦♦

Step to Me / Sep. 4, 1990 / Tommy Boy ♦♦♦

● **For Lovers & Others: Greatest Hits** / Feb. 18, 1992 / Tommy Boy ♦♦♦♦
This is a solid collection of captivating love songs, featuring singles taken from the quartet's previous albums. However, of the 12 selections presented, four never charted, the most notable being "Sweet Dreams." Groomed around the smooth-sailing falsetto of the late Antoine "T.C.D." Lundy, the single is augmented by the group's faintly audible background vocals. With this album's debut, the label seized the opportunity to release "Your Love Drives Me Crazy"; previously appearing on the quartet's gold-selling album *Touch and Go*, Antoine Lundy humbly steps into the intro with a juvenile vocal expression, which does not discredit his delivery. As the melody develops, Lundy's voice graciously amplifies with maturity and emotion. The featured single on this compilation release, "Your Love Drives Me Crazy" peaked at 78 after only six weeks on the Billboard R&B charts. This is a classic R&B cut among many. —*Craig Lytle*

● **Let Me Love You: The Force M.D.'s Greatest Hits** / Mar. 20, 2001 / Tommy Boy ♦♦♦♦
The Force M.D.'s predated the explosion of new jack swing in the late '80s, but they definitely helped lay the groundwork, fusing R&B vocal harmonies with street-level hip-hop beats. Their most popular material, however, tended to concentrate more on the urban R&B end of that spectrum, as displayed on *Let Me Love You: The Force M.D.'s Greatest Hits*. The collection gathers a generous 17 cuts, making it the definitive overview of the group's achievements. —*Steve Huey*

Frankie Ford

b. Aug. 4, 1939, Gretna, LA
Vocals / New Orleans R&B, Rock & Roll
It's ironic that some of the greatest New Orleans R&B of the 1950s was sung by a white man. Although he could have passed for a teen idol, Frankie Ford sang with as much grit as anyone of any color in the Crescent City. He recorded some fine singles for the Ace label in the late '50s, particularly the pounding "Sea Cruise," which made the Top 20 in 1959 and remains one of the hits most identified with the classic New Orleans R&B sound. "Sea Cruise" actually began life as a Huey "Piano" Smith song with Bobby Marchan on vocals, but producer Johnny Vincent had the inspired idea of dubbing Ford's singing on top of Smith's backing track. "Sea Cruise," with its bleating foghorn and irresistible piano groove, was an impossible act to follow, and Ford never approached the Top 20 again. But he cut several more gutsy sides for Ace that featured top New Orleans players like Huey Smith and saxophonist Red Tyler; one of the best, "Roberta," was covered by the Animals in the mid-'60s. A few of his singles found him following ill-advised swing jazz and teen idol directions, and he faded from view in the 1960s, although he made a cameo appearance in the film version of Alan Freed's life. —*Richie Unterberger*

Sea Cruise: The Very Best of Frankie Ford / Jun. 16, 1998 / Music Club ♦♦♦♦
Frankie Ford's one big hit, "Sea Cruise," is one of the truly great one-shot marvels of rock & roll history, all noise and groove and a big invitation to the party. But Ford also knew how to sell a song and the efforts of his recorded legacy at Ace Records is slimmed down to essentials on this 18-track very-best-of collection. Both sides of his debut single ("Cheatin' Woman" and "Last One to Cry") are aboard, along with Ford's later recordings, where the move into nightclub respectability all but quenches the rock & roll fire out of his music. This budget package features nine less tunes than the more deluxe Westside package and duplicates everything there. But the transfers are crisp and clear and if you still want the bare bones essentials, this also makes a recommended purchase. —*Cub Koda*

Cruisin' with Frankie Ford / Nov. 24, 1998 / Ace ♦♦♦
This has both sides of all six singles Ford did for Imperial from 1960-62 and a couple of unissued tracks from the same era, as well as his 1984 Ace recording *New Orleans Dynamo*. The main attraction is the Imperial material, which was very hard to find before this reissue. Ford's association with Imperial wasn't very fruitful commercially, producing just a couple of small hits in covers of Joe Jones' "You Talk Too Much" and Boyd Bennett's "Seventeen." This batch lacks anything on the order of "Sea Cruise," but it's still pretty solid vintage New Orleans R&B, produced by Dave Bartholomew. Some of the cuts are sweetened up with strings and backup female singers, but it's mostly on the earthy side; when he slows the pace down on "Dedicated to Fats" and "One Hour," he can sound uncannily like Fats Domino. *New Orleans Dynamo* is well above average for a 1980s effort by a 1950s rocker; nothing new here (in fact, many of its songs are covers of old New Orleans classics), but Ford and the London musicians execute the Crescent City R&B sound convincingly. —*Richie Unterberger*

● **Let's Take a Sea Cruise** / Aug. 24, 1999 / Ace ♦♦♦♦♦
Fine collection of 18 vintage sides, including "Sea Cruise" and "Roberta," establishes Ford's claim as one of the first of the great white R&B singers. Most of this is first-rate New Orleans R&B with a swinging bounce, enhanced by Ford's cool and cocky vocals, although a few tracks are lame excursions into trad jazz or teen idol fare. For now it's the definitive Ford anthology, but there's room for improvement: documentation for when the tracks were originally released is nonexistent, and much of the music was obviously dubbed from vinyl records, not from master tapes. —*Richie Unterberger*

Foreigner

f. 1976, New York, NY
Album Rock, Arena Rock, Pop/Rock, Hard Rock
Foreigner was formed in 1976 by Mick Jones (ex-Spooky Tooth) and Ian McDonald (ex-King Crimson). The band was an instant success with the release of their debut album in 1977, which showcased the talents of guitarist Jones and lead singer Lou Gramm. Jones and Gramm also wrote most of the band's material. The songs, mainly hard rock, boasted strong melodies and memorable guitar riffs. The band never strayed far from this formula

but, to keep things fresh, added some interesting touches. For example, Junior Walker's sax on "Urgent" and the gospel vocals of Jennifer Holliday and the New Jersey Mass Choir on "I Want to Know What Love Is" helped elevate these songs above the ordinary. Gramm left the band in the late '80s for a solo career. Foreigner recruited a new lead singer but Gramm's writing and distinctive vocals are sorely missed. —*Kenneth M. Cassidy*

Foreigner / 1977 / Atlantic ♦♦♦♦
Although punk rock's furious revolution threatened to overthrow rock's old guard in 1977, bands like Foreigner came along and proved that there was plenty of room in the marketplace for both the violent, upstart minimalism of punk and the airbrushed slickness of what would be called "arena rock." Along with Boston, Journey, Heart, and others, Foreigner celebrated professionalism over raw emotion. And, looking back, it's easy to see why they sold millions; not everyone in the world was pissed off, dissatisfied with the economy, or even necessarily looking for a change. In fact, for most suburban American teens, *Foreigner*'s immaculate rock sound was the perfect soundtrack for cruising through well-manicured neighborhoods in their Chevy Novas. The album spawned some of the biggest FM hits of '77, including the anthemic "Feels Like the First Time" and "Cold as Ice," both of which were anchored—like most of Foreigner's songs—by the muscular but traditional riffing of guitarist Mick Jones, the soaring vocals of Lou Gramm, and the state-of-the-art rock production values of the day, which allowed the band to sound hard, but polished. As pure rock craftsmanship goes, Foreigner was as good as it got in the late seventies. —*Andy Hinds*

Double Vision / 1978 / Atlantic ♦♦♦♦
Foreigner promptly followed up its blockbuster debut with the equally successful *Double Vision* LP in 1978, which featured the FM mega-hits "Hot Blooded" and the driving title track. Opting not to mess with a good formula, the band wisely stick to the polished hard rock sound that made its first record such a hit. Aside from the big singles, other highlights include the swaggering "Love Has Taken Its Toll" and the more restrained "Blue Morning, Blue Day." As always, Lou Gramm's impeccable rock vocals lead the way, supported by Mick Jones' tasteful, arena-sized guitar riffs. —*Andy Hinds*

Head Games / 1979 / Atlantic ♦♦♦
Foreigner continues its platinum winning streak on *Head Games*, the band's third album. By the time *Head Games* was released, FM radio had fully embraced bands like Foreigner, Journey, and Boston, whose slick hard rock was tough enough to appeal to suburban teens, but smooth enough to be non-threatening to their parents. Tailor-made for the airwaves, "Dirty White Boy" and "Head Games" kept Foreigner at the top of the arena rock heap as the decade came to a close; and the supergroup's successes would continue well into the '80s. —*Andy Hinds*

4 / 1981 / Atlantic ♦♦♦♦♦
Over the course of their first three late-'70s albums, Foreigner had firmly established themselves (along with Journey and Styx) as one of the top AOR bands of the era. But the band was still looking for that grand slam of a record which would push them to the very top of the heap. 1981's *4* would be that album. In producer Robert John "Mutt" Lang—fresh off his massive success with AC/DC's *Back in Black*—guitarist and all-around mastermind Mick Jones found both the catalyst to achieve this and his perfect musical soul mate. Lang's legendary obsessive attention to detail and Jones' highly disciplined guitar heroics (which he never allowed to get in the way of a great song) resulted in a collaboration of unprecedented, sparkling efficiency where not a single note is wasted. "Nightlife" is only the first in a series ("Woman in Black," "Don't Let Go," the '50s-tinged "Luanne") of energetic, nearly flawless melodic rockers; and with "Juke Box Hero," the band somehow managed to create both a mainstream hit single and a highly unique sounding track, alternating heavy metal guitar riffing, chorused vocals, and one of the ultimate "wanna be a rock star" lyrics. As for the mandatory power ballad, the band also reached unparalleled heights with "Waiting for a Girl Like You." One of the decade's most successful cross-genre tearjerkers, it has since become a staple of soft rock radio and completely eclipsed the album's other very lovely ballad, "Girl on the Moon," in the process. And last but not least, the surprisingly funky "Urgent" proved to be one of the band's most memorable and uncharacteristic smash hits thanks to Junior Parker's signature saxophone solo. All things considered, *4* remains Foreigner's career peak. —*Ed Rivadavia*

Records / 1982 / Atlantic ♦♦♦♦♦

Agent Provocateur / 1984 / Atlantic ♦♦♦
It took Foreigner three years to release a follow-up to its 1981 blockbuster, *4*. Perhaps that wait wasn't long enough, because *Agent Provocateur* is a prime example of the best and worst traits of AOR—a handful of remarkable songs padded by toothless filler. Despite contributing a few killer riffs to Foreigner's '70s canon, guitarist/keyboardist Mick Jones isn't known for his six-string abilities. His biggest strength is his knack for melody as a songwriter, keyboardist, and producer, and all these qualities are evident on *Agent Provocateur*. Of course, vocalist/songwriter Lou Gramm is indispensable as the band's golden-throated frontman. Jones largely guided things behind the studio console, but a co-producer usually helped, such as Alex Sadkin on this album. "I Want to Know What Love Is" became Foreigner's first and only number one single, and it's not hard to see why. Its dreamy, hypnotic feel is due in part to Gramm's soulful lead vocals and the New Jersey Mass Choir's background vocals. Jennifer Holliday and the Thompson Twins' Tom Bailey help out as well. "That Was Yesterday," a terrific hit single, features a catchy chorus and a nifty synthesizer lick. "Reaction to Action" and "Down on Love" were both minor hits, but there's a huge difference in quality between the two; the former is the epitome of bland, formulaic AOR, while the latter includes a pleasant chorus and a warm keyboard melody. "A Love in Vain" and "Growing Up the Hard Way" have a few good moments too. —*Bret Adams*

Inside Information / 1987 / Atlantic ♦♦♦
Foreigner was arguably the finest band of AOR's late-'70s and early-'80s heyday. Unfortunately, after a decade of monstrous success and raking in truckloads of cash for themselves and Atlantic Records, 1987's *Inside Information* showed that the songwriting gas tank of guitarist/keyboardist Mick Jones and vocalist Lou Gramm was running low. Impeccable studio craftsmanship can't compensate for the lack of quality songs. There are a few solid tracks, but the album only sold a million copies—paltry when compared to previous releases—and it currently ranks as Foreigner's last major commercial success. The proceedings start promisingly enough with "Heart Turns to Stone," an energetic rock number that became a minor hit. "Say You Will" was Foreigner's last great Top Ten single. It's loaded with killer vocal and keyboard hooks. The bloodless, pleasantly tepid ballad "I Don't Want to Live Without You" actually made the Top Five; it has neither the passion of "Waiting for a Girl Like You" nor the soul of "I Want to Know What Love Is." "Inside Information" experiments a little with odd rhythms. "The Beat of My Heart" is notable only for the Spanish guitar intro by guest Hugh McCracken. The gritty "Face to Face" is an excellent album track. "Out of the Blue" is the only song written by the entire band—Jones, Gramm, bassist Rick Wills, and drummer Dennis Elliott—and that does give it a slightly more organic feel. *—Bret Adams*

Unusual Heat / Jun. 17, 1991 / Atlantic ♦♦♦

● **The Very Best . . . and Beyond** / Sep. 22, 1992 / Atlantic ♦♦♦♦
Very Best . . . and Beyond not only collects all the major hits from Foreigner's early years ("Feels Like the First Time," "Head Games," "Hot Blooded"), but also features their hits from the late '80s ("I Want to Know What Love Is," "Say You Will"), making the set preferable to *Records*. *—Stephen Thomas Erlewine*

Mr. Moonlight / 1995 / Valley ♦♦

● **Jukebox Heroes: The Foreigner Anthology** / Aug. 15, 2000 / Rhino ♦♦♦♦♦
It's easy to say that Rhino's *Jukebox Heroes: The Foreigner Anthology* is the definitive Foreigner retrospective, simply because there's so much music here: 39 tracks over the course of two discs, including all the hits, the bulk of notable album tracks, solo cuts from Lou Gramm and Mick Jones, plus two tracks from Jones-era Spooky Tooth. Clearly, that does amount to a clearly comprehensive collection, but the question is, is this a clear-cut choice for most fans? Well, it all depends on a listener's needs. This will be too much Foreigner if you're just looking for nothing but hits, especially since the classic era (roughly defined as pre-*Agent Provocateur*) stops at the end of the first disc. But, anyone that truly enjoys Foreigner's big, glossy arena rock will find that this doesn't test their patience, even if it runs out of steam toward the end of the collection. *Anthology* keeps interest because of canny selection and sequencing. The addition of Gramm and Jones songs on the second disc works wonders, since it not only strengthens its value for consumers—it's terrific to be able to have all Foreigner and Foreigner-related songs in one place, especially since Gramm's peerless "Midnight Blue" is not just the best thing here, it's the last great single of the album-rock era—it accelerates the pace and keeps things interesting just as the band's output gets a little patchy. So, *Anthology* winds up more consistently entertaining than skeptics could have imagined. It still may not convert those skeptics, but it will prove to the listener with the curiosity to delve deeper than the hits that it's worth doing so. *—Stephen Thomas Erlewine*

Fotheringay

f. 1970
British Folk-Rock, British Folk
A short-lived offshoot of Fairport Convention, featuring key member and leader Sandy Denny. A second album was planned but never completed; tracks from it turn up on the triple-CD Denny anthology *Who Knows Where the Time Goes*. This is far more interesting and beguiling than their work with Fairport Convention, especially the Bob Dylan songs, but it lacks Fairport's precision and focus. *—Bruce Eder & William Ruhlmann*

● **Fotheringay** / 1970 / Hannibal ♦♦♦♦♦
Also featured are Trevor Lucas and Jerry Donahue, both of whom eventually joined Fairport when Denny rejoined. The album is a close relative of Denny's other solo and group work and features several of her flowing ballads, showcasing her lovely voice. A footnote, but a pleasing one. *—Bruce Eder & William Ruhlmann*

The Foundations

f. 1967, England, **db.** 1970
Pop-Soul, Soul
The Foundations are a surprisingly obscure late-'60s outfit, considering that they managed to reach the tops of the both the British and American charts more than once in the space of a year and had a solid three years of recordings. At the time of their debut in mid-1967, they were hailed for being the first British band to come up with an authentic soul sound, and the fact that they were first multiracial band to top the British charts only made their success that much more impressive (at a time when England was beginning to come to grips with its own racial attitudes). What's more, the group had the goods to back up the press' accolades. Their performances revealed a seasoned, well-rehearsed, exciting stage presence and a bold, hard soul sound that most British bands managed to imitate only in the palest manner, if at all. "Baby Now That I've Found You," "Build Me Up Buttercup," and "In the Bad, Bad Old Days" were the biggest hits for this multiracial octet, made up of Londoners and West Indians. The band's success finally faltered when producer/songwriter Tony Macaulay exited Pye Records. As he later revealed, he was still being paid solely as a producer and he received no royalties for his songs, despite millions of copies sold. With his departure, the group were cut off from the only composer who'd written all of their hits. Additionally, the sounds of soul were changing faster than the group could assimilate it all—they tried for a funkier, James Brown-type sound on their last recordings together in 1970 but failed to attract any attention. *—Bruce Eder*

● **Baby Now That You've Found Me** / May 11, 1999 / Sequel ♦♦♦♦♦
The proof of a reputation is in the listening, and this double CD just oozes proof in its 41 songs, 23 of them off of *From the Foundations* and *Digging the Foundations*. At their worst, the Foundations sound like early Rare Earth (or maybe Three Dog Night) on a really good day, and most of this collection is a lot better than that: smooth, slightly poppy but eminently danceable soul, stuff that Berry Gordy and company and their fans lived for—*and* it's beautifully remastered and very carefully put together to make the most of the CD format. Ironically, the hits are among the least interesting of the songs here, although they'll sell the set. Two of the bonus tracks, "I Need Your Love" and "Something for My Baby" by the New Foundations (Colin Young with new backup), are lost treasures that ought to have filled the international airwaves in 1976, when they were cut. And the utterly infectious "Where the Fire Burns," recorded by the original band in 1970, is a lost funk-instrumental jewel, with soaring horns and thick, twangy rhythm guitars. An astonishing, glorious collection, only missing cuts off the live second album, *Rocking the Foundations*, which is due for a separate reissue. *—Bruce Eder*

Fountains of Wayne

f. 1996
Pop Underground, Indie Pop, Alternative Pop/Rock
The New York City-based power-pop band Fountains of Wayne was anchored by the singer/songwriter duo of Adam Schlesinger and Chris Collingwood, who first teamed in 1986 while studying at Massachusetts' Williams College. Sharing a mutual affection for melodic British pop, they formed a series of short-lived bands before recording an LP under the name Pinnwheel; legal hassles blocked the album's release, however, and the duo went their separate ways, with Schlesinger resurfacing in the NYC indie-pop band Ivy and Collingwood joining the Boston country group Mercy Buckets. They reunited in 1996 as Fountains of Wayne (so named in honor of a New Jersey gift shop), issuing their acclaimed self-titled LP on Atlantic; that same year, Schlesinger also enjoyed success as the author of the title theme to Tom Hanks' rock & roll movie *That Thing You Do!* Their sophomore effort, *Utopia Parkway*, followed in 1999. *—Jason Ankeny*

● **Fountains of Wayne** / Oct. 1, 1996 / Tag/Atlantic ♦♦♦♦
Every so often, a band comes along that digs back into what pop music is all about—good, fun tunes. Fountains of Wayne is one such band. The wonderful thing about the duo (singer Chris Collingwood and bassist Adam Schlesinger of Ivy) is that they manage not to be overtly retro—the album is a wholly modern production. The only non-modern aspect of it is the fact that the songwriting is so straightforward and wonderful; nearly every song is a pop gem. The result is an album that's almost innovative, when you really think about it—very few albums released in the '90s have been this pleasant, charming, and all-around likeable. The obvious reference points would be Teenage Fanclub, Big Star, and the Posies, but even these don't quite capture the duo's sound. Think of some of They Might Be Giants' best pop tunes and scrape away every trace of silliness, and you'll be a little closer. *—Nitsuh Abebe*

Utopia Parkway / Apr. 6, 1999 / Atlantic ♦♦♦♦
There's no denying that Fountains of Wayne know how to craft a great pop record. They know how to write a hook, they can pull of mild rockers and sweet ballads with equal aplomb and they write melodies that feel like half-forgotten favorites. They have all the elements of a classic power-pop band but they suffer from that peculiar '90s ailment—detachment. For all their flair, talent, and craftsmanship, the band doesn't really dig deeper than the surface. Of course, that doesn't mean they make bad records and their second album, *Utopia Parkway*, if anything, is every bit as good as their fine debut. All the songs immediately make a connection and all of their melodic attributes simply strengthen with repeated listens. However, those repeated listens reveal that Fountains of Wayne don't have a lot to say. That's not a cardinal sin in guitar-pop, since most bands simply recycle the same lovelorn themes, but the Fountains choose to have fun with cliches, throwing in goofy asides even in their ballads. Throughout the record, they seem like the well-read, pop culture-saturated kids that sat in the back of the classroom, cracking jokes that only they can understand. Depending on your view, this either enhances the fun or keeps the record at a distance, because if you don't share their disdain for hippies, laser shows, proms, malls, and bikers, it will be a little hard to sing along with those glorious melodies. For some, this may be a minor point, but consider this: emotional depth is what lifted Matthew Sweet's *Girlfriend* to classic status and what keeps *Utopia Parkway* from truly soaring, despite its many virtues. *—Stephen Thomas Erlewine*

The Four Seasons

f. 1961, Newark, NJ
Pop
Although they were one of the very biggest rock & roll groups of the 1960s, the Four Seasons—unlike, say, the Beatles, Rolling Stones, or the Byrds—don't excite virtually automatic respect from listeners and critics. A big factor is their most distinguishing trademark, the shrill falsetto vocals of their lead singer, Frankie Valli. Many also find their material—gently moralistic, romantic tunes with tightly arranged group harmonies that updated doo wop ethos into the 1960s—too cornball and clean-cut. Whatever your feelings about the group, though, there's no denying their considerable importance. No other white American group of the time save the Beach Boys boasted such intricate harmonies, though the Four Seasons were much more firmly in the Italian-American doo wop tradition. Their uptown production values were contemporary and, in certain respects, innovative. The R&B influence in their music was large, and some of their early singles

enjoyed success with the R&B audience; in fact, some listeners thought that the Four Seasons were black when the group landed their first hits. And they were immensely successful, making the Top 10 thirteen times between 1962 and 1967 with hits like "Sherry," "Big Girls Don't Cry," "Dawn," "Rag Doll," and "Let's Hang On." *—Richie Unterberger*

25th Anniversary Collection / 1987 / Rhino ✦✦✦✦✦
This three-CD set is a reminder of just how rich and diverse the work of Frankie Valli and the Four Seasons was, beyond their ubiquitous chart hits. Those songs have been available from various labels over the years, but this collection is the best available look at the true range of their work, covering their history (and Valli's solo career) from 1962 through 1978 beyond the hits, including good B-sides and oft-overlooked album tracks. The group had a lot to offer on repertory beyond the Bob Gaudio-Bob Crewe originals through which they became famous. The 36 songs on disc one and two, covering the years 1962-1967, illustrate precisely how the quartet's sound evolved, and the complexity that it achieved. Moreover, the presence of these sides makes this collection far more interesting and exciting than just another compilation of hits by the group. The presence of cuts such as their parody of Bob Dylan's "Don't Think Twice, It's Alright" (credited to "The Wonder Who") and tracks off of the controversial *Genuine Imitation Life Gazette* album makes this a truly ambitious effort. Valli's solo sides, including "The Sun Ain't Gonna Shine Anymore," are certain to add to the appeal of this disc. One comes away with far greater admiration for the group and, if anything, a desire to hear more of their work. Although this set was produced in the middle to late '80s, the production and engineering holds up surprisingly well, even in the wake of the huge advances in digital audio technology in the years since. This still may be more appropriate as a holiday gift than a casual purchase, but this set holds up remarkably well, and it will offer even the casual listener a range of delightful surprises. *—Bruce Eder*

★ **Anthology** / 1988 / Rhino ✦✦✦✦✦
Over the course of 20 tracks, *Anthology* covers all of the Four Seasons' essential hits, as well as Valli's solo "Can't Take My Eyes off You"; it's the definitive collection. *—Stephen Thomas Erlewine*

Off Seasons: Criminally Ignored Sides From Frankie / May 15, 2001 / Rhino ✦✦✦✦✦
This extra volume in the Four Seasons' anthology series seems unnecessary—why didn't they just assemble a box set? It focuses on what producer Gary Stewart calls "criminally ignored sides." Whatever. What this set reveals are two things: one is that there were a lot of Four Seasons B-sides that could have been issued as front-side singles. The reason they weren't is simply because the group recorded constantly. They issued 23 singles in only four years and some of these tracks backed them. The other reason a lot of these tracks didn't warrant any attention is because they were so out to lunch. Take "Cry Myself to Sleep," from the Four Seasons' "folk" album, *Born to Wander.* The songwriting and production pair of Bob Gaudio and Bob Crewe spent an awful lot of time listening to the Beach Boys' "In My Room," but with the glockenspiel and off-kilter melody it came off as an almost psychedelic depression ballad than anything else. The same goes for "Hugging My Pillow" from 1965, where the glockenspiel is as prominent as the vocals and the track ends with a tympani roll. The next few cuts seem to ape the Beatles in total. *—Thom Jurek*

In Season: The Frankie Valli and the 4 Seasons Anthology / May 15, 2001 / Rhino ✦✦✦✦
To the people of New Jersey and other parts of America, the Four Seasons were every bit as much a part of the early pop scene as the Beatles and the Beach Boys. Rhino Records it seems is in agreement with this premise and has undertaken a crusade to convince critics and the general public that somehow a group that sold literally millions of records has not been given enough attention. To this end they've issued this two-disc anthology and a separate disc of B-sides and other underappreciated "golden nuggets" by the classic Four Seasons lineup of Valli, Bob Gaudio, Tommy DeVito, and Nick Massi. Evidenced by this anthology alone, there is no disputing that the Four Seasons were very special, a singular East Coast supergroup who managed to keep rock & roll exciting and surprisingly whitebread at the same time. The music here contains all the hits: "Sherry," "Big Girls, Don't Cry," "Stay," "Walk Like a Man," "Dawn (Go Away)," "Candy Girl," "Let's Hang on to What We've Got," and so on. Disc one alone contains 23 essential Four Seasons sides from 1962 to 1966—all of which charted. That's a hell of a run. *—Thom Jurek*

The Four Tops

f. 1956, Detroit, MI
Pop-Soul, Motown, Soul
The Four Tops are the most stable, consistent, and dependable of the successful R&B/pop vocal acts to emerge from Motown Records in the 1960s. Unlike the Temptations, they have had no personnel changes; unlike the Supremes and the Miracles, their lead singer never felt the need to step out on his own. At the same time, the Four Tops personified the musical hybrid Motown sought—they had the grittiness of gospel and R&B, but they were smooth enough to appeal to pop audiences. Their first substantial hit came in 1964, one year after signing to Motown. "Baby, I Need Your Loving" set the pattern for a series of songs showcasing lead vocalist Levi Stubbs' emotive wail set against a solid harmony line. Need and longing would be the group's hallmarks on their biggest hits, the charttoppers "I Can't Help Myself" and "Reach Out, I'll Be There." In 1967, the Four Tops' main songwriting and production team (Holland-Dozier-Holland) left Motown, though the group continued to pace the R&B charts with hits like "(It's the Way) Nature Planned It," before moving to Dunhill and later Casablanca for a steady series of moderate chart entries. The group recorded again for Motown during the mid-'80s, and remained a solid concert draw into the '90s. *—William Ruhlmann*

☆ **Anthology** / Jul. 1974 / Motown ✦✦✦✦✦
Until they get the deluxe box set CD treatment, this three-record/two-CD set qualifies as the ultimate Four Tops Motown statement. It includes all the landmark hits, plus good numbers from their final days at Motown in the 1970s (they did return in the mid-'80s), such as "Still Water" and "Just Seven Numbers." *—Ron Wynn*

Until You Love Someone: More of the Best (1965-1970) / Feb. 16, 1993 / Rhino ✦✦✦✦
This compilation gathers 18 non-hit album tracks from eight LPs that the Four Tops cut for Motown between 1965 and 1970 (some of which appeared on B-sides). A major soul group they might have been, but the Tops' pinnacle was actually quite brief, and that's reflected in this collection. No less than two-thirds of the songs date from 1965 and 1966, six from 1965's *Second Album* alone. Not so coincidentally, all but one of those cuts were written by the legendary Holland/Dozier/Holland songwriting team. The production is faultless, the songs very characteristically HDH, and Levi Stubbs' lead vocals are unfailingly gritty and pleasurable. Yet none of these have the unforgettable hooks of their hit singles of the period like "Reach Out, I'll Be There" and "I Can't Help Myself." As enjoyable as the formula is, the uniformity of the sound limits this disc's appeal to serious Motown and soul collectors. Curiosities among the non-HDH cuts include little-known tunes by Smokey Robinson and Stevie Wonder, and a non-hit single from 1969, "What Is a Man." *—Richie Unterberger*

Keepers of the Castle: Their Best 1972-1978 / Jul. 29, 1997 / MCA ✦✦✦✦
When the Four Tops moved from Motown to Dunhill in the early '70s, they encountered the dilemma faced by most '60s soul giants, from Motown or elsewhere: how to update their sound while maintaining some degree of personality. Commercially at least, things got off to a smashing start with "Keeper of the Castle," "Ain't No Woman (Like the One I Got)," and "Are You Man Enough?" (all included here). Yet it was evident that the Four Tops, removed from the magic of '60s Motown, would be trend followers rather than pacesetters. Most of this 14-song compilation shows them as a competent but rather generic '70s soul vocal group, adding Philly soul and funk elements to their sound without asserting much of an identity. Even "Are You Man Enough?," as good as it is, is something of a son-of-"Back Stabbers"; "Ain't No Woman," similarly, could be easily mistaken for a Spinners cut by the unschooled. Save the occasional standout like "Love Music," not much else here measures up to the early Dunhill hits, though if you want one post-early-'70s Four Tops compilation, this is probably the best. *—Richie Unterberger*

★ **The Ultimate Collection** / Oct. 7, 1997 / Motown ✦✦✦✦✦
Featuring 25 tracks on a single disc, *The Ultimate Collection* nearly lives up to its billing, featuring all of the group's pop Top Ten hits for Motown, plus all but three of their Top Ten R&B hits. For most casual fans, this well-assembled compilation will be the definitive overview. *—Stephen Thomas Erlewine*

Lost and Found: Breaking Through / Sep. 28, 1999 / Motown ✦✦✦
The Four Tops' early years as a jazz-vocal group are generally glossed over in capsule histories. Long before they signed to Motown—nearly a full decade as a matter of fact—they had been one of the popular Detroit jazz-vocal groups, earning the admiration of such luminaries as Smokey Robinson and Billy Eckstine, whom the group supported. After some persuasion, the group signed with Motown on the condition that they could record jazz. Over the course of a year, they cut nearly two albums' worth of material, which boiled down to one album, *Breaking Through.* Berry Gordy pulled the record at the last minute, believing that it would have been a commercial failure. Gordy's fears were not unfounded—indeed, had the album that comprises *Breaking Through (1963-1964)* been put out in 1964, it likely wouldn't have found much of an audience. Still, *Breaking Through* is a strong record, firmly within its tradition and working well on those terms. The Four Tops may not sound as distinctive singing jazz as they did with pop-soul, but they are convincing, as are the Motown house band. Neither of them take many chances, however. The songs are primarily standards, plus four new songs that feel like standards, all given good generic arrangements. This may sound like a dismissal, but it isn't; it's hard to do this kind of music right, but the group most certainly does. And it's not just one member that shines; everyone gets to take a lead, and the results are uniformly strong. Even so, *Breaking Through* appeals primarily to hardcore fans of the group, plus a handful of straight-ahead vocal-jazz aficionados. Reminiscent of a cross between Eckstine and the Four Freshmen, it's good stuff, but it's essentially a curiosity. *—Stephen Thomas Erlewine*

20th Century Masters—The Millennium Collection: The Best of The Four Tops / Nov. 30, 1999 / Motown ✦✦✦
Though they have been around for nearly 40 years, the Four Tops were never stronger than during the '60s and early '70s. With a dozen Top 20 and five Top Ten hits, the Tops were just as their name implies. As part of their *Millennium Collection,* Motown has selected 11 of these hits for consideration as one of the pre-eminent groups of the era. From the trademark stylings of Holland-Dozier-Holland to a tune by Smokey Robinson (who himself once considered the Tops to be "the baddest group around"), this best-of set is pretty much what it says to be. Though a cover of "If I Were a Carpenter" and a hyper-produced version of Robinson's "Still Water (Love)" may not reach the reminiscent heights of "Reach Out I'll Be There" and "I Can't Help Myself (Sugar Pie, Honey Bunch)," the Tops' devotions to originally named girls like "(Walk Away) Renee" and "Bernadette" and their tales of love wanted, won, and lost easily make them one of the best-loved groups of the last century, if not the last millennium. *—Matthew Robinson*

Peter Frampton

b. Apr. 22, 1950, Beckenham, Kent, England
Vocals, Guitar / Album Rock, Arena Rock, Pop/Rock
Before he shot to solo superstardom in the mid-'70s, guitarist Peter Frampton was a British teen idol in the late '60s thanks to his work with the Herd and looks worthy of being named "Face of 1968" in several British magazines. The following year, Frampton

joined ex-Small Faces front man Steve Marriott in Humble Pie, remaining for two years before departing for a solo career. He recorded his solo debut *Wind of Change* in 1972; recorded at San Francisco's Winterland, 1976's double album *Frampton Comes Alive* was a staggering success, selling over six million copies and becoming the biggest-selling live rock album ever at that time. It showcased Frampton's mastery of the talk-box guitar effect and his penchant for in-concert theatrics, and produced three hit singles ("Show Me the Way," "Baby, I Love Your Way," and "Do You Feel Like We Do"). The follow-up LP, *I'm in You*, produced Frampton's biggest hit in the title track, but his career was temporarily put on hold by a near-fatal car crash in the Bahamas in 1978. Personal problems halted a full-scale comeback following Frampton's recovery; he recorded sporadically throughout the '80s, but none of these efforts caught fire with the public. *—Steve Huey*

Wind of Change / 1972 / A&M ♦♦♦♦
Peter Frampton's solo debut after leaving Humble Pie (as they stood on the brink of stardom) spotlights Frampton's well-crafted, though lyrically lightweight, songwriting and his fine guitar playing. The songs on *Wind of Change* are built primarily around acoustic guitar foundations, but "It's a Plain Shame" and "All I Want to Be (Is by Your Side)" sound like they could have been lifted off Humble Pie's *Rock On*. The sound is crisp, the melodies catchy, and Frampton's distinctive, elliptical Gibson Les Paul guitar leads soar throughout. A comparison between this album and Humble Pie's post-Frampton turn to generic boogie-rock shows why Frampton left that group. Although Humble Pie's *Smokin'* was much more successful, hitting the Top Ten in the spring of 1972, *Wind of Change* was far superior musically. With its mix of ballads and upbeat numbers with just enough of a rock edge, *Wind of Change* showed Frampton at his creative peak. The band here includes Ringo Starr, Billy Preston, and Klaus Voorman. *—Jim Newsom*

Frampton's Camel / 1973 / A&M ♦♦♦♦♦
Named after Frampton's touring band at the time, *Frampton's Camel* has a harder-rocking feel than its predecessor *Wind of Change*, with Mick Gallagher's percussive electric piano and organ taking a prominent position in the mix and Frampton getting a harder sound from his electric guitars (though his acoustic playing is so lush and lyrical that it dominates the album here and there in its quiet way). The sound on this recording lays out the formula that Frampton would take to mega-success three years later with the release of *Frampton Comes Alive*. The songs are all first-rate or close to it—included here is the original studio version of the group composition "Do You Feel Like We Do," a quicker-tempo, extended (albeit less majestic) version of which appeared on the latter album and became a staple of classic-rock radio, but the Frampton-composed "I Got My Eyes on You" and "Don't Fade Away" and the Frampton-Gallagher "All Night Long" are also compelling examples of '70s hard rock at its commercial best. This album also includes a nice cover of Stevie Wonder's "I Believe (When I Fall in Love With You It Will Be Forever)," the power ballad "Lines on My Face," the rollicking "White Sugar," and Frampton's gorgeously lyrical, all acoustic "Just the Time of the Year." As on *Wind of Change*, Frampton's use of dynamics and mix of acoustic and electric guitars keeps the music from becoming one-dimensional. The October 2000 CD reissue, remastered in state-of-the-art sound, adds an even more expansive feel to this album and enhances its melodic richness. *—Jim Newsom & Bruce Eder*

Something's Happening / 1974 / A&M ♦♦♦
Peter Frampton's third album in as many years is much weaker than its predecessors, beginning with the lyrics, which sound forced on most of the songs. The production also lacks the crispness of his earlier releases, or their clarity; where *Wind of Change* had an airy feel because of the prominence of acoustic guitars, and *Frampton's Camel* had a percussive electric piano drive, *Somethin's Happening* originally sounded more like mud, with a clutter of electric guitars attempting to make up for lack of originality. The October 2000 remastered CD edition does alleviate a multitude of the original's sonic sins, however: Neither "I Wanna Go to the Sun" nor "Magic Moon" are among Frampton's most inspired songs, but the soaring guitars that highlight both now sound like they're practically in your lap, and one can also appreciate the quieter, subtler, more lyrical sounds of "Waterfall" and "Sail Away" and the elegant piano contribution of Nicky Hopkins behind Frampton's acoustic and electric playing, respectively. At this point, Frampton was touring constantly, following manager Dee Anthony's belief that a reputation for exciting live performances would lead to increased record sales. This strategy ultimately proved successful two years later when *Frampton Comes Alive* was released, but it also undoubtedly contributed to the decreasing quality of Frampton's original material. *—Jim Newsom & Bruce Eder*

Frampton / 1974 / A&M ♦♦♦♦
Frampton exited Humble Pie because that group fell into a loud, hard-rock groove that overwhelmed the technical skills he'd spent years working on as a guitarist; he poured a lot of that into this highly melodic mid-tempo rock album. In the days before it saturated the airwaves in the version from *Frampton Comes Alive*, "Show Me the Way" was just a nice, very pleasant love song that benefited from a mix of acoustic and electric guitar textures spun out over a great beat and some excruciatingly memorable hooks, vocal and instrumental. It was surrounded by a lot more like it, including "Baby, I Love Your Way" in its original studio form, "The Crying Clown," "Nowhere's Too Far (For My Baby)," and most of the rest, although apart from the two hits, the playing and singing is often better than the songs themselves. This prevents the Frampton album from being a true classic, but it is one of the better albums from its all-too-mellow era. *—Bruce Eder*

Frampton Comes Alive / 1976 / A&M ♦♦♦♦♦
In the 1980s and '90s, many artists (especially in R&B and urban contemporary) have been so reliant on technology that they their live shows pale in comparison to their studio recordings. But in the '70s, the opposite was sometimes true. Compared to *Frampton Comes Alive*—the best-selling live album ever—Peter Frampton's studio efforts sound downright tame. The Humble Pie graduate packed one hell of a punch onstage—where he was obviously the most comfortable—and in fact, the live versions of "Show Me the Way," "Do You Feel Like I Do," "Something's Happening," "Shine On," and other album-rock staples are much more inspired, confident, and hard-hitting than the studio versions. Commercially as well as artistically, this package (a two-LP set that later became a two-CD set) was undeniably Frampton's crowning achievement. Period. *—Alex Henderson*

I'm in You / 1977 / A&M ♦♦♦♦
It was almost inevitable that *I'm in You* would be thought of as a letdown no matter now good it was. Following up to one of the biggest selling albums of the decade, Peter Frampton faced a virtually impossible task, made even more difficult by the fact that in the two years since he'd cut any new material, he had evolved musically away from some of the sounds on *Frampton Comes Alive*. The result was mostly a surprisingly laid-back album steeped in lyricism and craftsmanship, particularly in its use of multiple overdubs even on the harder rocking numbers. From the opening bars of "I'm in You," dominated by the sound of the piano (played by Frampton) and an ARP synthesizer-generated string section, rather than a guitar, it was clear that Frampton was exploring new sides of his music. Cuts like "Won't You Be My Friend," a piece of white funk that might've been better at six minutes running time, seemed to be dangerously close to self-indulgence at eight minutes long. The high points also include the title track, "Don't Have to Worry," and a killer cover of Stevie Wonder's "Signed, Sealed Delivered (I'm Yours)"; a couple of solid rock numbers, "Tried to Love" and the crunching "(I'm A) Roadrunner" also work their way in here to pump up the tension and excitement. *I'm in You* was successful on its own terms, and had Frampton recorded it before the live album, it would probably be very fondly looked back on. As it was, many listeners were not impressed. The spring 2000 reissue in 20-bit audio recreates the original album artwork and notes and is the best way to appreciate the multi-layered sound (and the crunchier rock moments) on this album. *—Bruce Eder*

Shine On: A Collection / Oct. 20, 1992 / A&M ♦♦♦♦♦
Shine On: A Collection is a double-disc, 30-song set featuring all of Peter Frampton's best-known songs and biggest hits, plus a couple of rarities and unreleased cuts for hardcore fans. While the collection is far too thorough for casual listeners, any fan who wants to dig deeper than *Frampton Comes Alive!* should start with *Shine On*, particularly since most of Frampton's individual older albums have been out of print for years. *—Stephen Thomas Erlewine*

Peter Frampton / Jan. 25, 1994 / Sony Legacy ♦♦

● **Greatest Hits** / Jun. 18, 1996 / A&M ♦♦♦♦♦
By compiling all of Peter Frampton's biggest hits—in their hit versions, so "Show Me the Way" and "Baby, I Love Your Way" are from *Frampton Comes Alive*, not the studio albums—onto one disc, *Greatest Hits* functions as the definitive retrospective on the guitarist. It has a better selection than the single disc *Classics, Vol. 12*, and it is more concise and listenable than the double-disc box *Shine On: A Collection*, which means it's the only collection that provides an effective, manageable overview of Frampton. *—Stephen Thomas Erlewine*

The Very Best of Peter Frampton / Aug. 4, 1998 / A&M ♦♦♦♦
Yet another Frampton compilation, this one a mid-priced ten-song (45-minute) assembly of his most well-known songs from the middle/late-1970s. Drawn primarily from *Frampton Comes Alive*, *Frampton*, *Wind of Change*, *Frampton's Camel*, and *I'm In You*, the material ranges from passionate, midtempo romantic rock to harder numbers. This CD has the virtue of using fresh, glittering 1998 remasterings, making for some pretty impressive listening. "Show Me the Way" is the live cut, but everything else, including "Baby I Love Your Way" and "Do You Feel Like We Do," is represented by its studio version. There are no notes, but as a mid-priced item, there didn't have to be—the sound is superb, and the price, if caught in the right sale mode, is about a third of the double-disc sets out on Frampton. *—Bruce Eder*

● **Anthology: The History of Peter Frampton** / Jul. 24, 2001 / A&M ♦♦♦♦
Most Peter Frampton collections concentrate simply on his solo career. A&M's 2001 retrospective *Anthology: The History of Peter Frampton* takes a broader view, containing a cut from his first band the Herd and five songs from Humble Pie, plus all the solo heavy-hitters from the '70s—and all in the space of a 16-track single-disc collection. This is a nice tactic, especially since it downplays his famous *Frampton Comes Alive* (only one song, "Show Me the Way"; "Baby I Love Your Way" is present in the studio version), thereby offering an introduction not just for the utter neophyte, but for those that only know that blockbuster. Some may argue that all the Humble Pie material takes up space that could have been dedicated to solo cuts, especially since this ignores anything recorded past 1979, but the end result winds up being the lone, concise summation of Frampton's strengths as both a solo artist and guitarist. *—Stephen Thomas Erlewine*

Connie Francis

b. Dec. 12, 1938, Newark, NJ
Vocals / Brill Building Pop
Considered the leading pop female singer of her era, Connie Francis usually sang of her latest broken heart with a teardrop in her voice. The Newark, NJ native started performing as a child, signing with MGM Records in 1955, but she suffered two years of bombs before the torch ballad "Who's Sorry Now" shot up the charts in 1958. Although she specialized in sobbing tales of woe, Francis proved she could rock with Neil Sedaka's "Stupid Cupid" in 1958 and "Lipstick on Your Collar" the next year. Francis scored two number one hits in 1960—the twangy "Everybody's Somebody's Fool" and "My Heart Has a Mind of Its Own," and she branched into acting with a starring role in *Where the Boys Are*, the archetypal spring-break movie. "Don't Break the Heart That Loves You" was

Francis' last pop chart-topper in 1962, but she continued to rank high in the pop pantheon throughout the decade, with forays into ethnic and country idioms. *—Bill Dahl*

- **The Very Best of Connie Francis** / Oct. 1963 / Polydor ♦♦♦♦♦

Though many best-of's exist on the market, this one leans more heavily toward her earlier rock & roll hits. (Originally released in October 1963 as a 15-track LP by MGM Records, *The Very Best of Connie Francis* was reissued in 1986 on CD with six bonus tracks by Polydor Records.) *—Cub Koda*

White Sox, Pink Lipstick . . . & Stupid Cupid / Jul. 1993 / Bear Family ♦♦♦♦♦

Anyone who thinks they appreciate Connie Francis probably doesn't know half of what she could do as a singer—this five-CD box will set them straight. The revelation of Disc one lies in the fact that the three included demos and the other "failures" from her early career are all worthwhile, even inspired recordings. Francis had a superb voice, richly emotive and evocative, with an alluringly delicate enunciation when she wanted it. Listening to these sides today, one hears an extraordinary talent that was ignored until "Who's Sorry Now." After that, things really get going, because Francis was working under a contract that nobody—not even Frank Sinatra—had: the right to choose her own material. Disc two picks up her career after the explosive success of "Who's Sorry Now"; these are more confident performances, and reveal Francis as not only a dazzlingly talented singer but an excellent judge of songs and arrangements. Disc three showcases Francis' efforts in the long-player market, where she was really aiming her best work. The outstanding material here is the product of her Feb. 1959 New York sessions and the sessions a month later at Abbey Road in London; here she's starting to sound like a female analog to Sinatra, just when Sinatra was at his coolest and swinging-est. But at this point, it was the rock & roll singles that were moving, and she cut a whole album of standards in that genre, represented on Disc four; also featured are her country sides. Disc five is mostly made up of unissued tracks and various alternate takes. They're all first-rate, and a few should have been hits and could have redefined her career. The lavish booklet and the detailed notes and sessionography cap this reissue, which puts Polygram's efforts with Francis to shame. *—Bruce Eder*

Kissin', Twistin', Goin' Where the Boys Are / Apr. 16, 1996 / Bear Family ♦♦♦♦♦

Five more CDs of Connie Francis, picking up right where Bear Family's earlier *White Sox, Pink Lipstick* set left off, in 1960—although its 300-plus minutes of music only cover the period of 1960 to 1962. By this time, Connie Francis was established as one of the top female vocal talents of her generation, and she was ready to experiment—you hear her successful move into country music, wonderful outtakes, and never-issued songs from her early-'60s sessions. Disc one has more highlights than most greatest-hits albums, notable among them a pair of unissued "Swinging Medley" tracks, and tracks from the most daring of all of her albums, *Songs to a Swinging Band.* Disc two includes the rest of the *Swinging Band* album and also highlights her first Nashville folk-style sessions with the Jordanaires. Disc three is devoted to the rest of Francis' Nashville sessions, including her outstanding covers of movie theme songs (one of her top-selling albums) and the folk-type songs with the Jordanaires. Disc four is given over to her recordings of Irish songs and, more significantly, Francis' 1962 *Twist* album, including the first release of the risqué-sounding "Lovey Dovey Twist." Disc five features more of her Irish songs, as well as a number of hit singles, but the highlight is the previously "lost" original recordings from Francis' April 1962 sessions in Rome, which were believed lost when the accompaniments from those sessions were wiped and replaced by new orchestrations. This set is a major investment of time and attention, but it is rewarding—Francis is one of those performers who seems hardly ever to have recorded anything second-rate. The booklet is lively, entertaining, and lavishly illustrated. *—Bruce Eder*

Souvenirs / Oct. 22, 1996 / Polydor ♦♦♦♦

Seen by many as one of rock & roll's greatest enemies during the Elvis-Beatles gap, Francis is really no more offensive than any of the other bland, adult, faceless pop princes and princesses reaching the airwaves in the early '60s. This four-CD box gathers just about everything anyone could ever want from the pleasantly white Francis, laying out a thoughtful chronological assessment of her accomplishments. She is pretty lifeless, though. Even the big hits "Everybody's Somebody Fool," "My Heart Has a Mind of Its Own," "Together," and "Don't Break the Heart That Loves You" sound anonymous in the setting. *—Michael Gallucci*

- **20th Century Masters—The Millennium Collection: The Best of Connie Francis** / Oct. 5, 1999 / Polydor ♦♦♦♦

MCA's *20th Century Masters: The Millennium Collection* is a good, basic collection of Connie Francis' biggest hits—including "Who's Sorry Now," "Stupid Cupid," "Lipstick on Your Collar," "My Heart Has a Mind of Its Own, " "Where the Boys Are," and "Vacation"—available at a budget price. Although there are a couple of hits and good songs missing, this has enough of the best-known tunes to make it worthwhile for casual listeners on a budget. *—Stephen Thomas Erlewine*

Frankie Goes to Hollywood

f. 1980, Liverpool, England, **db.** 1987

Club/Dance, New Wave, Dance-Pop

Mixing slick dance-pop and a savvy publicity campaign, Liverpool's Frankie Goes To Hollywood dominated British music in 1984. Their music was a glossy version of hi-NRG, but the group's marketing—which included slogans, T-shirts, and homoerotic videos—created controversy in England and some buzz in the U.S. But their popularity was fleeting: the group's audience disappeared by the release of their second album.

Ex-Big in Japan vocalist Holly Johnson, vocalist Paul Rutherford, guitarist Nasher Nash, bassist Mark O'Toole, and drummer Peter Gill formed the band in 1980. Originally called Hollycaust, they switched to Frankie Goes to Hollywood—an old headline about Frank Sinatra's acting career—by the year's end. In 1982 they appeared on the British television program "The Tube" with a rough version of the video for "Relax"—a driving dance number with suggestive lyrics—which won them a deal with producer Trevor Horn's ZTT label. He also produced most of their material, including their 1983 debut single "Relax"/"Ferry Cross the Mersey."

Frankie's publicity director Paul Morley promoted the single with T-shirts that read "Relax" and "Frankie Says . . . ," and emphasized the band's stylish, homosexual imagery in their video for "Relax." British TV banned it and a new version was shot, but Radio 1 and the rest of BBC's radio and television networks banned the single; it shot to number one in early 1984, selling over a million copies. Frankie's double-album debut *Welcome to the Pleasuredome* and the singles "Two Tribes," and "The Power of Love" also topped the charts that year. Gradually, Frankie-mania reached the States: "Relax" hit number 67 and "Two Tribes" grazed the Top 40 in 1984; *Pleasuredome* reached number 33 in 1985 and "Relax" was re-released, making the American Top Ten.

1986's single "Rage Hard" peaked at number four in the U.K. and the second album *Liverpool* reached number five. The band began their final tour in early 1987 and broke up that spring. After legal battles with ZTT, Johnson pursued a solo career, as did Rutherford. Johnson retired from music after he was diagnosed with AIDS in the early '90s. *—Stephen Thomas Erlewine*

Welcome to the Pleasuredome / 1984 / ZTT/Island ♦♦♦♦

Strip away all the hype, controversy, and attendant craziness surrounding Frankie—most of which never reached American shores, though the equally bombastic "Relax" and "Two Tribes" both charted well—and *Welcome to the Pleasuredome* holds up as an outrageously over-the-top, bizarre but fun release. Less well-known but worthwhile cuts include by-definition-camp "Krisco Kisses" and "The Only Star in Heaven," while U.K. smash "The Power of Love" is a gloriously insincere but still great hyperballad with strings from Anne Dudley. In truth, the album's more a testament to Trevor Horn's production skills than anything else. To help out, he roped in a slew of Ian Dury's backing musicians to provide the music, along with a guest appearance from his fellow Yes veteran Steve Howe on acoustic guitar that probably had prog rock fanatics collapsing in apoplexy. The end result was catchy, consciously modern—almost to a fault—arena-level synth rock of the early '80s that holds up just fine today, as much an endlessly listenable product of its times as the Chinn/Chapman string of glam rock hits from the early '70s. Certainly the endless series of pronouncements from a Ronald Reagan impersonator throughout automatically date the album while lending it a giddy extra layer of appeal. Even the series of covers on the album at once make no sense and plenty of it all at once. While Edwin Starr's "War" didn't need redoing, Bruce Springsteen's "Born to Run" becomes a ridiculously over the top explosion that even out rocks the Boss. As the only member of the band actually doing anything the whole time (Rutherford pipes up on backing vocals here and there), Johnson needs to make a mark and does so with appropriately leering passion. He didn't quite turn out to be the new Freddie Mercury, but he makes a much better claim than most, combining a punk sneer with an ear for hyperdramatic yelps. *—Ned Raggett*

Liverpool / 1986 / ZTT/Island ♦♦♦

Frankie Goes to Hollywood's first double-album was a huge hit. Their second offering also met with some success, although it is not as well remembered. And yet, on many accounts, *Liverpool* can be considered as an improvement over its predecessor. For one thing, the album is shorter, more conventional. While *Welcome to the Pleasuredome* had some strong material, the length weakened the whole in many places. Here, the band focused on eight tracks and the result is somewhat more convincing. "Warriors of the Wasteland," "Rage Hard," and "Watching the Wildlife" were all minor hits back in 1986, and the other tracks are, for the most part, of the same quality, with, perhaps, "For Heaven's Sake" standing out as a favorite. Again, Trevor Horn was involved in the production (the band was signed to his famous Zang Tuum Tumb label, so it's no big surprise)—thus the production is impeccable, as one would expect from a Horn-produced album. Worth a listen if you like the band or have an interest for '80s music—of which this is not such a bad sample. *—Alex S. Garcia*

- **Bang! . . . The Greatest Hits of Frankie Goes to Hollywood** / Mar. 22, 1994 / ZTT/Island ♦♦♦♦♦

Frankie Goes to Hollywood hyped their debut album *Welcome to the Pleasuredome* so much that when their second record, *Liverpool,* failed to live up to expectations, their career was effectively over. That didn't stop them from releasing greatest-hits albums, however, nor did it stop the inevitable wave of '80s nostalgia that surged forth in the '90s. To cash in on whatever meager Frankie nostalgia that may have existed, *Bang! . . . Greatest Hits of Frankie Goes to Hollywood* appeared in 1994 and was reissued in 1998, when the rights shifted to Universal Records. *Bang!* is as good a compilation of Frankie's material as could be assembled, featuring no less than eight songs from *Pleasuredome* (including, of course, "Relax," "Two Tribes," "The World is My Oyster," and "Bang") and five songs from *Liverpool.* There were a couple of good songs stranded on the second album ("Ferry Cross the Mersey," "Rage Hard") and certain casual fans may enjoy having those singles on the same disc with the hits, but the fact remains that Frankie can only truly be understood (and, to a certain extent, truly enjoyed) on *Pleasuredome.* That debut stood on its own, sounding unlike any other record of its time, and it contained all of the big hits in the first place. Consequently, many casual listeners will be satisfied with simply acquiring that record, even if the album versions were slightly different than the singles. If they feel otherwise, *Bang!* will serve as the definitive singles collection, satisfying both the hardcore and casual fan. *—Stephen Thomas Erlewine*

Aretha Franklin

b. Mar. 25, 1942, Memphis, TN

Vocals, Piano / Deep Soul, Southern Soul, Quiet Storm, Black Gospel, Urban, R&B, Soul
Aretha Franklin is one of the giants of soul music, and indeed of American pop as a whole. More than any other performer, she epitomized soul at its most gospel-charged. Her astonishing run of late-'60s hits with Atlantic Records—"Respect," "I Never Loved a Man," "Chain of Fools," "Baby I Love You," "I Say a Little Prayer," "Think," "The House That Jack Built," and several others—earned her the title "Lady Soul," which she has worn uncontested ever since. Yet as much of an international institution as she's become, much of her work—outside of her recordings for Atlantic in the late '60s and early '70s—is erratic and only fitfully inspired, making discretion a necessity when collecting her records. When Franklin left Columbia for Atlantic, producer Jerry Wexler was determined to bring out her most soulful, fiery traits. As part of that plan, he had her record her first single, "I Never Loved a Man (The Way I Love You)," at Muscle Shoals in Alabama with esteemed Southern R&B musicians. The combination was one of those magic instances of musical alchemy in pop: the backup musicians provided a much grittier, soulful, and R&B-based accompaniment for Aretha's voice, which soared with a passion and intensity suggesting a spirit that had been allowed to fly loose for the first time.

In the late '60s, Franklin became one of the biggest international recording stars in all of pop. Many also saw Franklin as a symbol of Black America itself, reflecting the increased confidence and pride of African-Americans in the decade of the civil rights movements and other triumphs for the black community. Franklin was able to maintain creative momentum, in part, because of her eclectic choice of material. Franklin's commercial and artistic success was unabated in the early '70s, during which she landed more huge hits with "Spanish Harlem," "Bridge Over Troubled Water," and "Day Dreaming." Critically, as is the case with many '60s rock legends, there have been mixed responses to her later work. In the meantime, despite her lukewarm recent sales record, she's an institution, assured of the ability to draw live audiences and immense respect for the rest of her lifetime, regardless of whether there are any more triumphs on record in store. —*Richie Unterberger*

☆ **I Never Loved a Man (The Way I Love You)** / 1967 / Rhino ✦✦✦✦✦
While the inclusion of "Respect"—one of the truly seminal singles in pop history—is in and of itself sufficient to earn *I Never Loved a Man (The Way I Love You)* classic status, Aretha's Atlantic label debut is an indisputable masterpiece from start to finish. Much of the credit is due producer Jerry Wexler, who finally unleashed the soulful intensity so long kept under wraps during her Columbia tenure; assembling a crack Muscle Shoals backing band along with an abundance of impeccable material, Wexler creates the ideal setting to allow Aretha to ascend to the throne of Queen of Soul, and she responds with the strongest performances of her career. While the brilliant title track remains the album's other best-known song, each cut on *I Never Loved a Man* is touched by greatness; covers of Ray Charles' "Drown in My Own Tears" and Sam Cooke's "Good Times" and "A Change Is Gonna Come" are on par with the original recordings, while Aretha's own contributions—"Don't Let Me Lose This Dream," "Baby Baby Baby," "Save Me" and "Dr. Feelgood (Love Is a Serious Business)"—are perfectly at home in such lofty company. A soul landmark. —*Jason Ankeny*

Aretha Arrives / 1967 / Rhino ✦✦✦
Recorded in 1967 after the first flush of back-to-back successes with "Respect" and "I Never Loved a Man," this captures Aretha Franklin in peak form. Lady Soul provides her own piano accompaniment on the majority of tracks here, and the core band is the same one that provided the fire on her previous album. The tunes are an eclectic batch, and while "Baby, I Love You" was the hit of the album, Franklin turns in strong versions of "Satisfaction," "You Are My Sunshine," "Night Life," "Ain't Nobody (Gonna Turn Me Around)," and a quirky cover of "96 Tears" for good measure. An essential addition to her discography. —*Cub Koda*

☆ **Lady Soul** / 1968 / Rhino ✦✦✦✦✦
Great personnel again—King Curtis, Bobby Womack, Frank Wess, and others, including a guest spot by Eric Clapton. Several classic songs, including the lesser-known "Ain't No Way" by Carolyn Franklin and the hits "Chain of Fools" and "Natural Woman." —*George Bedard*

Aretha in Paris / 1968 / Rhino ✦✦✦
Atlantic's Jerry Wexler once said that this concert album was an embarrassment to him, criticizing the inferior band (actually, the musicians that usually accompanied her live in the late '60s). Composed of her first few big singles and cuts from her first three albums, it doesn't match the classic studio versions and could be considered her least essential '60s Atlantic LP. That's not to say, though, that it doesn't sound pretty good, with fine if basic readings of a lot of her most popular late-'60s material, although the horns fall distressingly out of tune at a key point in the instrumental break of "Chain of Fools." —*Richie Unterberger*

Aretha Now / 1968 / Rhino ✦✦✦✦✦
Though a bit short on running time at ten songs, this still caught Franklin at the peak of her early form. "Think," "I Say a Little Prayer," "See Saw," and "I Can't See Myself Leaving You" were all big hits. Her choice of cover material included some of her most R&B-drenched early Atlantic cuts, like "Night Time Is the Right Time," "You Send Me," and "I Take What I Want." —*Richie Unterberger*

Soul '69 / 1969 / Rhino ✦✦✦✦✦
One of her most overlooked '60s albums, on which she presented some of her jazziest material, despite the title. None of these cuts were significant hits, and none were Aretha originals; she displayed her characteristically eclectic taste in the choice of cover material,

handling compositions by Percy Mayfield, Sam Cooke, Smokey Robinson, and, at the most pop-oriented end of her spectrum, John Hartford's "Gentle on My Mind" and Bob Lind's "Elusive Butterfly." Her vocals are consistently passionate and first-rate, though, as is the musicianship; besides contributions from the Muscle Shoals rhythm section, session players include respected jazzmen Kenny Burrell, Ron Carter, Grady Tate, David Newman, and Joe Zawinul. —*Richie Unterberger*

This Girl's in Love With You / 1970 / Rhino ✦✦✦
The title song (a cover of Herb Alpert's "This Guy's in Love With You") might lead you to believe this is one of Aretha's more pop-oriented albums, but in fact, this is the only song of the sort on this solid and fairly earthy effort. Besides the hit singles "Call Me" and "Share Your Love With Me," it also includes her most well-known Beatle covers ("Eleanor Rigby" and "Let It Be"), and her interesting version of "The Weight," a Top 20 single featuring slide guitar by Duane Allman. —*Richie Unterberger*

Sweet Bitter Love / 1970 / Columbia ✦✦

Spirit in the Dark / 1970 / Rhino ✦✦✦✦✦
Spirit in the Dark was one of Aretha Franklin's more overlooked albums from her Atlantic prime, despite the inclusion of a couple hit singles (the title track and "Don't Play That Song"). The disc includes five of her own compositions (the most she ever recorded for a single album) and her usual eclectic choice of cover material. On this record, the covers ranged from B.B. King and Dr. John to Jimmy Reed and Goffin/King's "Oh Not My Baby." The album also benefits from great backup players: Both the Muscle Shoals rhythm section and the Dixie Flyers contributed to the sessions, and Duane Allman lends his guitar to a couple of tracks. Though it doesn't rank with her very best Atlantic LPs, it's an exuberant and remarkably consistent effort. The 1993 CD reissue has detailed liner notes on the songs and sessions by David Nathan. —*Richie Unterberger*

Aretha Live at Fillmore West / 1971 / Rhino ✦✦✦
Aretha Franklin's 1971 album *Live At Fillmore West* was as seminal a soul breakthrough as Albert King's visit had been for blues. It finally cemented her status beyond soul audiences as both a recording and live attraction, and it matched her with a phenomenal rhythm section in King Curtis and the Kingpens. Franklin adroitly mixed pop, rock, and soul material throughout the three nights, including Stephen Stills' "Love the One You're With," and Bread's "Make It With You," and the Beatles' "Eleanor Rigby," as well as tried and true favorites "Respect," "Don't Play That Song," and "Spirit in the Dark," which brought Ray Charles out of the audience for a spirited duet. There's more than enough here to make this absolutely essential. —*Ron Wynn*

Young, Gifted & Black / 1971 / Rhino ✦✦✦✦✦
It's near impossible to single out any of Aretha Franklin's early '70s albums for Atlantic as being her best, particularly given the breadth of her output during this era. In terms of albums rather than singles, it's probably her strongest era, and if you count live albums like *Amazing Grace*, choosing a standout or a favorite record isn't any easier. Yet of this stunning era, *Young, Gifted & Black* certainly ranks highly among her studio efforts, with many arguing that it may be her greatest. And with songs like "Rock Steady," that may be a valid argument. But there's much more here than just a few highlights. If you really want to go song by song, you'd be hard-pressed to find any throwaways here—this is quite honestly an album that merits play from beginning to end. You have upbeat songs like the aforementioned "Rock Steady" that will get you up out of your seat moving and grooving, yet then you also have a number of more introspective songs that slow down the tempo and are more likely to relax than rouse. And if that wide spectrum of mood isn't enough reason to celebrate this album, you get some unlikely songs like a take on "The Long and Winding Road." Plus, you also have to keep in mind that Franklin was in her prime here, not only in terms of voice but also in terms of confidence—you can just feel her exuding her status as the best of the best. Furthermore, her ensemble of musicians competes with any that she had worked with on previous albums. So even if this isn't *the* greatest Aretha album of the early '70s, it's certainly a contender at the least, the sort of album that you can't go wrong with. —*Jason Birchmeier*

Amazing Grace / 1972 / Atlantic ✦✦✦✦✦
Aretha Franklin disproved the notion that once you leave the church, you can't go back. She returned in triumph on this 1972 double album, making what might be her greatest release ever in any style. Her voice was chilling, making it seem as if God and the angels were conducting a service alongside Franklin, Rev. James Cleveland, the Southern California Community Choir, and everyone else in attendance. Her versions of "How I Got Over" and "You've Got a Friend" are legendary. —*Ron Wynn*

Hey Now Hey (The Other Side of the Sky) / 1973 / Rhino ✦✦✦
Hey Now Hey (The Other Side of the Sky) was just about Franklin's last gasp before succumbing to disco. This odd album, with its cheesy, junky artwork, contains some gems—notable are a poignant cover of Bernstein's "Somewhere," and a sparkling "Moody's Mood," and the beautiful Carolyn Franklin composition "Angel." —*George Bedard*

With Everything I Feel in Me / 1974 / Atlantic ✦✦✦
This respectable but not earth-shattering release was part of the gradual decline of Franklin's artistic and commercial achievements at Atlantic. The leadoff track, "Without Love," was a Top Ten R&B hit, and the title track, written by Franklin, was Top 20 R&B. There were a couple of familiar but completely rearranged Burt Bacharach tunes and a contribution from Stevie Wonder. Franklin was in good voice, and the studio band was accomplished, but this was all a far cry from the standard Franklin had set in the late '60s. It was also a far cry from the sales she enjoyed then: This was her first new album since her 1967 breakthrough to peak below the Top 30. —*William Ruhlmann*

Let Me in Your Life / 1974 / Rhino ✦✦✦
A nice, if at times overbearing, mid-'70s Franklin set. She was still singing with the

stunning delivery, amazing timing, and majestic soul that highlighted her late-'60s releases. Her version of "Until You Come Back to Me (That's What I'm Gonna Do)" is the only one that might be superior to Stevie Wonder's great original, while "I'm In Love" and the title cut are prime Franklin. *—Ron Wynn*

You / 1975 / Atlantic ✦✦

Sparkle / 1976 / Rhino ✦✦✦✦
Aretha Franklin's career was in a down period in the mid-'70s when she collaborated with Curtis Mayfield to sing his compositions for the film *Sparkle*. The film proved a non-event, but for Franklin it marked a return to glory. Once again she was the Queen of Soul, doing the chilling, spectacular leaps, cries, whoops, and shouts that defined secularized gospel in the late '60s. The title cut was a sizable hit, while "Giving Him Something He Can Feel" became an anthem. Mayfield's lyrics and production shouldn't be overlooked; he added just the right amount of background trappings, and the Kitty Haywood Singers provided Franklin's best continuing backgrounds since the Sweet Inspirations. *—Ron Wynn*

Love All the Hurt Away / 1981 / Arista ✦✦

Jump to It / 1982 / Arista ✦✦✦
Aretha Franklin scored some hits with this early '80s album and managed to make concessions to urban contemporary tastes without totally distorting her classic soul sound. While it's certainly not in the class of past recordings, the title cut gave Franklin her first number one of the '80s, and "Love Me Right" was a decent follow-up. *—Ron Wynn*

Get It Right / 1983 / Arista ✦✦✦
Luther Vandross scored a popular success with *Jump to It*, but this follow-up is less impressive and proved less successful. Vandross wrote most of the material, including the number one R&B title track and the R&B Top Ten hit "Every Girl (Wants My Guy)," although he also has Franklin tackle the Temptations hit "I Wish It Would Rain," in a painfully overwrought production. With this record, what had seemed to be an artist/producer marriage made in heaven hit the rocks. *—William Ruhlmann*

Never Grow Old / 1984 / Chess ✦✦✦
Actually credited to "Reverend C.L. Franklin and Aretha Franklin," this album was recorded live—very live—in church. The Reverend Franklin takes most of the leads on traditional gospel songs, with keyboard accompaniment, shouting and singing, although his daughter also has a couple of spotlights. The music is moving, and the audience is moved: one or two of them scream uncontrollably. *—William Ruhlmann*

Who's Zoomin' Who? / 1985 / Arista ✦✦✦
After nearly a two-year hiatus from the charts, the Queen of Soul returns in style with three Billboard R&B Top Ten singles, including the number one smash hit "Freeway of Love." With its festive rhythm arrangement and electric sax solo by Clarence Clemons, Aretha Franklin injects her lively vocals. It held the number one spot for five straight weeks. The title track, "Who's Zoomin' Who," has a more soulful bounce, including Franklin's delivery. Its sputtering bass line and chiming keyboards are augmented by Franklin's soulful delivery; her improvising ad libs are laudable to say the least. The single peaked at number two for four consecutive weeks. She had another Top Ten hit with "Another Night," a mid-tempo number with a light rock feel. It was a number nine hit. Her duet with Eurythmics, "Sisters Are Doin' It for Themselves," faltered at number 66. This album has a slight pop texture. Narada Michael Walden is credited with the majority of the production on this sound outing. *—Craig Lytle*

Aretha / 1986 / Arista ✦✦

★ **30 Greatest Hits** / 1986 / Atlantic ✦✦✦✦✦
The double-disc set *30 Greatest Hits* contains all of Aretha Franklin's greatest hits from the '60s and early '70s, from 1967's "I've Never Loved a Man (The Way I Love You)" and "Respect" to 1973's "Until You Come Back to Me (That's What I'm Gonna Do)." It's an essential, comprehensive collection—the ideal purchase for fans that want more than just the biggest hits, but don't want to invest in the box set. *—Stephen Thomas Erlewine*

One Lord, One Faith, One Baptism / 1987 / Arista ✦✦✦

Through the Storm / 1989 / Arista ✦✦✦

Jazz to Soul / Jul. 14, 1992 / Columbia/Legacy ✦✦✦

☆ **Queen of Soul: The Atlantic Recordings** / 1993 / Rhino ✦✦✦✦✦
The Queen of Soul: The Atlantic Recordings is an 86-track, four-disc box set that covers Aretha Franklin's Atlantic career, spanning from 1967's "I Never Loved a Man (The Way I Love You)" to 1976's "Something He Can Feel." Over the course of the set, all of Aretha's best-known songs, including all of her Top Ten pop and R&B singles, are included. For fans that only know the singles, the set is primarily notable for the wealth of album tracks and forgotten singles that are included, which nearly equal the hits in terms of quality. Stopping just short of her move to disco, *The Queen of Soul* just misses being a totally comprehensive collection, but it remains definitive—it may miss some of her later hits, but every one of her greatest tracks is on the box. *The Queen of Soul* is one the cornerstones of any soul collection. *—Stephen Thomas Erlewine*

Greatest Hits (1980-1994) / Feb. 22, 1994 / Arista ✦✦✦
Greatest Hits (1980-1994) rounds up the biggest hits from the latter part of Aretha Franklin's career, including "Jump to It," "Freeway of Love," "Who's Zoomin' Who," and "I Knew You Were Waiting (For Me)," a duet with George Michael. The album does a good job of selecting the highlights from a slightly uneven era for Aretha. *—Stephen Thomas Erlewine*

The Very Best of Aretha Franklin, Vol. 1 / Mar. 22, 1994 / Rhino ✦✦✦✦✦
30 Greatest Hits is still the preferred essential document for the Atlantic years, but this is certainly an excellent 16-track primer of her most popular late-'60s tracks. Most of them are also on *30 Greatest Hits*. But if you've got a particular yen for Aretha's early Atlantic period (which was also her very best), you'll find all the biggest smashes from that era here, including "Respect," "Chain of Fools," "Think," "The House That Jack Built," "Baby I Love You," "I Never Loved a Man," and so forth. *—Richie Unterberger*

The Very Best of Aretha Franklin, Vol. 2 / Mar. 22, 1994 / Rhino ✦✦✦✦✦
Covering 1970-76, this isn't quite as top-notch as *The Very Best of, Vol. 1*. And, like *Very Best of, Vol. 1*, much of this is also found on the more comprehensive *30 Greatest Hits* (although some of it is not). Still, it contains the prime stuff from the first half of the '70s, including "Spanish Harlem," "Don't Play That Song," "Bridge Over Troubled Water," and "Until You Come Back to Me," along with less-traveled items like "Oh Me Oh My" and "Brand New Me." *—Richie Unterberger*

Early Years / Feb. 11, 1997 / Columbia/Legacy ✦✦✦
When Aretha was recording for Columbia in the 1960s, the label didn't seem to know what to do with her. Now that they're reissuing material from that time on CD, they *still* don't know what to do with her. It's hard to determine why someone would pick this over the far more extensive double-disc, *Jazz to Soul*, that covers the some era. Nevertheless, about half of this doesn't show up on that collection, which means short value overall, but some value at least. It's generally considered that Aretha's Columbia output has been somewhat undervalued, and this is a good cross-section of ballads and grittier R&B-influenced items. It's usually overproduced, but not in as unlistenable fashion as some old-school critics might have you believe. But it's hard to determine what focus (if any) this collection has, especially as it's missing her most soulful (and therefore best) Columbia cuts, "Lee Cross" and "Soulville." *—Richie Unterberger*

The Delta Meets Detroit: Aretha's Blues / Jan. 13, 1998 / Rhino ✦✦✦
The Delta Meets Detroit: Aretha's Blues is one of the few non-hits compilations that makes sense. Selecting 16 tracks from her Atlantic recordings, the disc spotlights Aretha at her bluesiest—there are no hits here, but there's also no shortage of remarkable songs here, as "Today I Sing the Blues," "Night Life," "Night Time is the Right Time," "Good to Me As I Am to You," "Going Down Slow," "Drown in My Own Tears," and "Dr. Feelgood (Love Is a Serious Business)" rank among her grittiest performances. If you're only familiar with the hits, this is an excellent way to dig deeper into her catalog, and if you already have this material on their original albums, *The Delta Meets Detroit* actually offers some revelations you may not have expected. *—Stephen Thomas Erlewine*

A Rose Is Still a Rose / Mar. 10, 1998 / Arista ✦✦✦✦
For much of the '90s, Aretha Franklin acted as if she couldn't even care about appealing to a younger audience. She rarely recorded, and when she did, it was usually slick adult contemporary material. That's what makes the fresh *A Rose Is Still a Rose* such a surprise. Although it certainly has its share of predictably glossy ballads fit for adult radio (usually produced by Narada Michael Walden or Michael Powell), the most notable element of the album is that Franklin collaborates with a fresh talent, all of whom are either prominent rap figures or at least fluent in hip-hop. That's not to say that *A Rose Is Still a Rose* is a rap album—it simply illustrates that the album sounds contemporary, which is the last thing most observers would have expected from Aretha in 1997. That in itself is heartening, but that doesn't necessarily mean everything works. Lauryn Hill's "A Rose Is Still a Rose" is a perfect match, lyrically and musically, but it only shows how shallow Puff Daddy's writing really is on "Never Leave You Again." Still, Dallas Austin's "I'll Dip," Jermaine Dupri's "Here We Go Again" and "Every Lil' Bit Hurts," and Daryl Simmons' "In the Morning" and "In Case You Forgot" all work, and Franklin's original "The Woman" is arguably her most soulful performance in years. These make the awkward moments forgivable because they find Aretha sounding vital, which is something that has not happened throughout the '90s. *—Stephen Thomas Erlewine*

Amazing Grace: The Complete Recordings / May 4, 1999 / Rhino ✦✦✦✦✦
Among Aretha aficionados, *Amazing Grace* has long been considered one of her high-water marks, since it captured her glorious return to her gospel roots in front of a live audience. The original 1972 album contained just 14 tracks, culled from two live performances with the Southern California Community Choir, Ken Lupper, and the Rev. James Cleveland at the New Temple Missionary Baptist Church in Los Angeles. Fans have long wished for the release of the two complete concerts—which is exactly what Rhino's *Amazing Grace: The Complete Recordings* gives them. Over the course of two discs and 29 tracks, every performance Franklin gave that January, along with comments from Cleveland and solo tracks from Lupper and the Choir, is unfurled, and if anything, the music is even more impressive when heard complete and unedited. Of course, the nature of this set makes it of interest primarily to dedicated fans, but they'll likely be delighted by the entire package. *—Stephen Thomas Erlewine*

Aretha's Best / May 15, 2001 / Rhino ✦✦✦✦✦
Rhino's *Aretha's Best* is notable for attempting to squeeze highlights of every era of Aretha's career onto one disc. Unfortunately, the compilers threw logic and chronology out the window, preferring to vacillate between classic Atlantic recordings and very good latter-day Arista recordings. There are certainly some great performances missing, but this pretty much hits the majority of the big numbers, from "Respect" to "Freeway of Love." Unfortunately though, it does this within the course of three songs, which gives the compilation no grounding whatsoever. But if you're looking for just the basics—just the basic hits without any rhyme or reason to the presentation—this will suit your needs. The compilation would have been close to essential, however, if it had just made some sense. *—Stephen Thomas Erlewine*

Freakwater

f. 1987, Louisville, KY

Alternative Country, Alternative Country-Rock, Traditional Country, Neo-Traditional Folk

An acoustic side project of the Eleventh Dream Day family tree featuring Dream Day drummer/singer Janet Bean (who plays guitar in Freakwater) and her friend, Catherine Ann Irwin, with contributions from various other musicians. This is only alternative rock in the marketing sense; the Kentucky-bred singers largely stick to acoustic folk/country with close harmonies and strong Appalachian overtones, sometimes employing fiddle, pedal steel, mandolin, and Dobro. Mixing strong original material (mostly written by Irwin) with traditional numbers and songs by the likes of Bill Monroe, Freakwater's albums stand as some of the finest maverick, progressive acoustic records of recent years. —*Richie Unterberger*

Freakwater / 1989 / Amoeba ✦✦✦

Their debut, a short LP or a long EP, depending on how you look at it, presents plaintive, raw country-folk in a modern context without sounding forced. —*Richie Unterberger*

● **Dancing Under Water** / 1991 / Thrill Jockey ✦✦✦✦✦

Feels Like the Third Time / May 23, 1995 / Thrill Jockey ✦✦✦

Freakwater's third album finds them treading similar ground to their first two albums, but since no one else really does what they do, more of the same is welcome. The beautiful harmonies of Catherine Irwin and Janet Bean remain the focus, and Dave Gay, as always, provides solid support on the upright bass; this time out augmented by Brian Dunn on guitar and Lisa Marsicek on fiddle and mandolin. Cathy Irwin's songwriting continues to progress, as this time she accounts for half of the album's tunes. Janet Bean contributes one song with choice covers by the likes of Woody Guthrie, Conway Twitty, and Nick Lowe. Similar in sound to the Carter Family and Gillian Welch, Freakwater stands apart because their lyrics are so firmly rooted in the modern world; no dustbowl ballads here. Sounding more traditional than most neo-traditional country acts with lyrics that have a more modern bite than most contemporary country, it's Freakwater's ability to effortlessly straddle these two worlds that makes them such a special band. —*Sean Westergaard*

Old Paint / Oct. 10, 1995 / Thrill Jockey ✦✦✦✦✦

After a four-year gap since their second album, Freakwater returned with another solid effort that's not as bare-bones as their debut, but a little earthier than *Dancing under Water*. Not a lot of new ground is broken, yet it somehow doesn't sound at all tiresome. All of their strengths remain in place: fine, mournful harmonies, good original songs, some well-chosen covers (Loudon Wainwright's "Out of This World" is a particular highlight), and nice unobtrusive touches of pedal steel and fiddle embellishing the acoustic guitars. This is modern country-folk at its best, and in fact would really be more suitable for the roots-country audience, except that the execution is too direct, the production too basic, and the songwriting too heartfelt for the contemporary country marketplace. Thus it is that the group's primary listenership is the alternative rock community, which is country's loss: Few performers today are performing roots music so convincingly, without sounding forced or dated. —*Richie Unterberger*

Springtime / Jan. 20, 1998 / Thrill Jockey ✦✦✦✦✦

A consolidation of Freakwater's status as one of the best—perhaps *the* best—1990s exponents of the folk-country tradition. The Appalachian flavor is, if anything, a little more pronounced than usual, but the songwriting is utterly contemporary, and the Irwin-Bean harmonies among their best. "Binding Twine," with its delectably sad melody and vocals, has the makings of a modern classic; "Jesus Year" has some great trembling harmonies; and "Slowride," more unexpectedly, has the country-rock punch of the late-'60s Byrds in that group's better moments. Most unusual lyrical twist: "Louisville Lip," inspired by Muhammad Ali's toss of his gold medal into the Ohio River after getting denied service at a restaurant. Max Konrad Johnston, formerly of Wilco, helps out on guitar, fiddle, banjo, Dobro, mandolin, and vocals, helping devise a sound that is both spare and textured. —*Richie Unterberger*

End Time / Sep. 7, 1999 / Thrill Jockey ✦✦✦✦✦

With Freakwater records, continuity is a far greater trait than change or innovation. Yet this album does represent a significant advancement for the group, without altering the sound in any way that would alienate fans of their previous discs. The arrangements are fuller than ever before, without sounding overproduced—it's the first Freakwater record to have a full drum kit, and a three-piece string section appears on some tracks. This is also the first Freakwater album consisting entirely of compositions by the core duo of Catherine Irwin and Janet Bean. More noteworthy than any of these details, however, is the sheer level of vocal, musical, and lyrical accomplishment throughout, as well as the attention to diversity and nuance within their country/folk/alt-rock niche. At times this sounds like a pure country record (with lots of pedal steel) that's too country for Nashville; on "Good for Nothing" there's a Band-like organ that puts this in an early-'70s mood; "Sick, Sick, Sick" is just voice and what sounds like Dobro, getting close to country blues territory; "Dog Gone Wrong" has a honky tonk feel; and "All Life Long" is nearly Appalachian folk. It makes a reasonable contender for the best Freakwater release to date, as Bean and Irwin also maintain their high standard of moving vocal harmonies and clever, emotionally complex lyrics. —*Richie Unterberger*

John Fred

b. May 8, 1941, Baton Rouge, LA

Vocals / Blue-Eyed Soul

Remembered only for his fluke 1968 number one hit "Judy in Disguise," John Fred actually made quite a few records in the '60s. Though he was from Louisiana, Fred's vocals strongly recall Eric Burdon at times and Georgie Fame at others. A capable songwriter ("Judy in Disguise" was an original), he also cut several fine, deep Southern soul ballads that distinguish him as one of the best American white R&B singers. —*Richie Unterberger*

History of John Fred & the Playboys / 1991 / Paula ✦✦✦✦

Eclectic 26-song assortment of pop/rock/soul/R&B. Highlights are his 1964 cover of John Lee Hooker's "Boogie Chillen," which stands up to the best early British R&B; the odd, moody "Agnes English" and "Sun City," which shows a strong Animals influence, and of course "Judy In Disguise." A 1958 track that he cut as a teenager recalls a frat-rock Frankie Ford with its low-wattage emulation of the New Orleans sound. Unfortunately there are little in the way of liner notes here, but the grooves prove Fred to be a versatile stylist with much greater depth than the usual one-shot. —*Richie Unterberger*

● **With Glasses: The Best of John Fred & His Playboys** / Apr. 3, 2001 / Varese ✦✦✦✦

Freddie & The Dreamers

f. 1961, Manchester, England, **db.** 1968

Merseybeat, British Invasion

Freddie & the Dreamers were the clowns of the British Invasion, playing their pop music for laughs while the other groups of the time were dead serious. Lead singer Freddie Garrity (b.Nov 14, 1940) began playing in skiffle groups in the late '50s, switching to rock & roll in the early '60s. After the Beatles broke the American market wide open, Freddie & the Dreamers followed in the flood of acts that tried to duplicate the overwhelming success of the Beatles. The group's hits were more numerous in the U.K. than in America, where they had only one Top Ten hit, the number one "I'm Telling You Now." As 1965 turned into 1966, the group stopped charting in the U.S. and the hits began to dwindle in the U.K.; by 1968 the original group disbanded. Garrity continues to tour with a new version of the Dreamers. —*Stephen Thomas Erlewine*

The Best of Freddie & The Dreamers / Jun. 2, 1992 / EMI America ✦✦✦✦✦

Yes, "I'm Telling You Now" is here, and so is "Do the Freddie," an absurd attempt at fashioning a dance craze, but so are "How About Trying Your Luck With Me," "When I'm Home With You," and "Brown and Porters (Meat Exporters) Lorry." In other words, it's more than a definitive collection, with 25 tracks (many previously unreleased in the U.S.) and a comprehensive discography. —*Stephen Thomas Erlewine*

Free

f. 1968, London, England, **db.** 1973

Album Rock, Hard Rock, Blues-Rock

Famed for their perennial "All Right Now," Free helped lay the foundations for the rise of hard rock, stripping the earthy sound of British blues down to its raw, minimalist core to pioneer a brand of proto-metal later popularized by 1970s superstars like Foreigner, Foghat, and Bad Company. Although both of their first two albums fared poorly on the charts, 1970's *Fire and Water* became a tremendous hit on the strength of the primal "All Right Now," a Top Five smash powered by frontman Paul Rodgers' gritty, visceral vocals. After headlining 1970's Isle of Wight festival, the group appeared destined for superstardom, but the LP *Highway* did not fare nearly as well as anticipated, and after a grueling tour which yielded 1971's *Free Live*, the band dissolved amidst ego clashes and recriminations. The original lineup of Free re-formed to record 1972's *Free at Last*, which launched the hit "Little Bit of Love." However, drug problems nagged the group, and soon they disbanded again, this time for good; Rodgers and drummer Simon Kirke went on to found Bad Company. —*Jason Ankeny*

Tons of Sobs / 1968 / A&M ✦✦

Free / 1969 / A&M ✦✦✦

Fire and Water / 1970 / A&M ✦✦✦✦✦

If Fleetwood Mac, Humble Pie, and Foghat were never formed, Free would be considered one of the greatest post-Beatles blues-rock bands to date, and this record shows why. Conceptually fresh, with a great, roots-oriented, Band-like feel, Free distinguished itself with the public like bands like Black Sabbath and Deep Purple did (in terms of impact, only) in 1970. A lot of people thought that they were in the same league, but buttressed by the FM hit "All Right Now," the entire album and group presented itself to the world as a complete band, in every sense of the word. From Paul Kosoff's exquisite and tasteful guitar work, to Paul Rodgers' soulful vocals, this was a group that was easily worthy of the Cream, Blind Faith, or Derek and the Dominos mantle. —*Matthew Greenwald*

Highway / Feb. 1971 / A&M ✦✦✦

Free Live / Sep. 1971 / A&M ✦✦✦✦✦

Although Free made excellent studio records, this live album is perhaps the best way to experience the band in all its glory. Led by singer-guitarist Paul Rodgers and lead guitarist Paul Kosoff, the band swings through nine songs with power, clarity, and a dose of funk. Of course, the hit single "All Right Now" is gleefully extended, much to the audience and listener's delight. Superbly recorded by Andy Johns, this is one of the greatest live albums of the 1970s. —*Matthew Greenwald*

Free at Last / 1972 / A&M ✦✦✦

The Best of Free / 1973 / A&M ✦✦✦

One of Britain's most underrated rock acts, Free produced a number of quality albums until the band's breakup in 1973. From the bluesy debut album, through the rocky *Fire and Water*, and on to the haunting *Heartbreaker*, Free's albums were consistently loaded with impressive music and catchy melodies. *The Best of Free* attempts to capture the highlights of the bands seven albums on one disc. The major and semi hits that the band ever enjoyed are featured, including "All Right Now," "Fire and Water," and "I'm a Mover." *The Best of Free* fails, however, through its stupidly small track list. So many more tracks should have been added to this compilation that *The Best of Free* is embarrassing in the light of Island's near-perfect best of, *The Free Story*. —*Ben Davies*

Heartbreaker / 1973 / Island ♦♦♦

● **Molten Gold: The Anthology** / Oct. 5, 1993 / A&M ♦♦♦♦♦
With their big riffs and bluesy melodies, Free virtually defined hard rock in the early '70s, and *Molten Gold: The Anthology* shows that this wasn't such a meager achievement. Throughout the two discs, it becomes clear that the key to Free's rock & roll was their rhythm section, which powered their riffs to perfection. This is the definitive Free, two discs of pure hard rock. —*Stephen Thomas Erlewine*

Songs of Yesterday / Oct. 10, 2000 / Island ♦♦♦♦♦
It's strange that a band with a song as immediate as "All Right Now" is a bit of an acquired taste, but it's the truth. Free was a powerful, majestic hard rock band at their peak, but they were also a little obtuse; a lot of their power came from their playing, and their songwriting was epic, but often elliptical. As such, they're for hard rock connoisseurs—a band who gained a spirited, dedicated following largely because they took devotion to unlock their treasures, especially in the years following their breakup. For those fans, the five-disc *Songs of Yesterday* is a godsend. This is not a box for listeners with less than a consuming interest in the band (even if you think you want total immersion in Free, this will not be as effective as purchasing each of their albums) since this contains a wealth of unreleased material. Very few of the tracks are actual album tracks, most are alternate mixes or alternate versions, plus there are a lot of live tracks in the mix, as well. As long as you know what you're getting into, this isn't bad, especially since it refurbishes the band's canon for the dedicated, giving them fresh insights to familiar songs (even if the new mixes aren't necessarily better than the originals—they just sound a bit brighter and more modern). For anyone else, it's a bit much, and it doesn't quite tell the story in the right fashion, since it really offers a mirror image, alternate version rather than the real thing. —*Stephen Thomas Erlewine*

The Free Design

Sunshine Pop, Baroque Pop
The commercial failure of the Free Design remains one of the most baffling mysteries in the annals of pop music—with their exquisitely celestial harmonies, lighter-than-air melodies, and blissful arrangements, the group's records were on par with the work of superstar contemporaries like the Beach Boys, the Association, and the Cowsills, yet none of their singles even cracked the Hot 100. The Free Design originally comprised siblings Chris, Bruce, and Sandy Dedrick, natives of Delevan, NY, whose father, Art, served as a trombonist and arranger with Vaughn Monroe; when Chris moved to New York City in 1966 to attend the Manhattan School of Music, he recruited Bruce and Sandy to form a folk group, and soon the trio emerged as a popular attraction on the Greenwich Village coffeehouse circuit. In time Chris began composing original material for the Free Design to perform, and with the assistance of their father, the siblings cut a demo, ultimately signing with producer Enoch Light's audiophile label Project 3. The title track from their 1967 debut LP, *Kites Are Fun*, was also their first single, cracking the Top 40 on the Billboard adult contemporary chart but reaching only number 114 on the pop chart—somewhat amazingly, it was the Free Design's biggest hit. Another Dedrick sister, Ellen, joined the group after graduating high school, making her debut on 1968's *You Could Be Born Again*. By the 1990s, hipster favorites including Cornelius, Pizzicato 5, and Louis Philippe were regularly citing the Free Design as a key influence, resulting in the 1998 release of *Kites Are Fun: The Best of the Free Design*. The new millennium saw the Free Design convene for another album—2001's *Cosmic Peekaboo*—which gathered Sandy, Chris, and Bruce Dedrick back together again. —*Jason Ankeny*

● **Kites Are Fun: The Best of the Free Design** / Jul. 28, 1998 / Varese ♦♦♦♦
The Free Design was the product of the Dedricks, a group of former folk singing siblings who left folk behind in the suburbs of Delevan, NY and headed for the Big Apple in 1966. By 1967, they hooked up with lightweight big-band maestro Enoch Light, who promptly signed them to his Project 3 record label. The best of their recorded output is available on this fine collection from Varese Sarabande. The Free Design were excellent vocalists, able to handle a variety of pop styles. The vocals are reminiscent of the Swingle Singers and Lambert, Hendricks & Ross (although that may be a stretched analogy). The material is decidedly lightweight, and obviously aimed at the preteen market. Fans of groups like Harpers Bizarre and the Association will probably find the music enjoyable, although the material does not have the edge of those fine groups. This is a bit more in the Brady Bunch/Partridge Family arena, but its fine production and engineering make it quite enjoyable. An invaluable gift for the younger brother or sister, provided they are under 12. —*Matthew Greenwald*

Cosmic Peekaboo / Mar. 6, 2001 / Marina ♦♦♦♦
For the 2000 release of the superb Beach Boys tribute album *Caroline Now!*, the legendary Free Design reunited for the first time in three decades, stealing the spotlight from the band's indie-pop descendants with a beautifully poetic rendition of "Endless Harmony." The full-length follow-up *Cosmic Peekaboo* restores the group's brilliance to its original luster, reassembling the founding lineup of siblings Chris, Sandy, and Bruce Dedrick for a remarkable comeback effort that more than lives up to the standard of their past classics. Resisting the temptation to incorporate even a dash of the electronic pop approaches of avowed acolytes like Stereolab, the High Llamas, and Cornelius, on *Cosmic Peekaboo* the group picks up right where it left off—although the harmonies are deeper and even richer than before. The infinite warmth and affection at the heart of all the Dedricks' work remains intact, with every note utterly free of the irony and detachment prevalent throughout so much of the music produced in their absence. Although *Cosmic Peekaboo*'s incandescent performances and majestic arrangements barely acknowledge the 30-year gap, the lyrics cast a knowing eye on the Free Design legacy—the elegiac "Younger Son" evokes vintage classics like "Kites Are Fun" and "My Brother Woody," while "The Hook" updates the group's still-relevant chart lament "2002—A Hit Song," gently chiding a new generation of navel-pierced pop icons while taking to task the music industry's reliance on style over substance. The record's emotional centerpiece is the haunting "Day Breaks," a sweepingly angelic tribute to sister Stefanie, to whose memory *Cosmic Peekaboo* is lovingly dedicated. —*Jason Ankeny*

Bobby Freeman

b. Jun. 13, 1940, San Francisco, CA
Vocals, Songwriter / Pop-Soul, Northern Soul, R&B
Bobby Freeman's energetic vocals punctuated two R&B dance hits in the late '50s and mid-'60s. The San Francisco performer started the Romancers as a 14-year-old and later formed the West Coast Vocaleers, whose sound was much more pop-oriented than the Harlem group of the same name. Freeman's single "Do You Want to Dance" just missed topping the R&B charts in 1958, staying at number two for two weeks (number five pop). It was one of three hits he enjoyed that year on Josie, although "Betty Lou Got a New Pair of Shoes" and "Need Your Love" only reached numbers 20 and 29, respectively. "C'Mon and Swim" parlayed the 1964 dance craze into his second Top Ten R&B hit, reaching number five. But the follow-up went to the water once too often, as "S-W-I-M" fizzled at number 56. Both were for Autumn. It was also Freeman's final visit to the R&B charts. —*Ron Wynn*

● **Best of Bobby Freeman** / 1992 / Sequel ♦♦♦♦♦
It's a shame that most listeners only know Bobby Freeman's "Do You Wanna Dance" in the Beach Boys' or Cliff Richard's cover versions, which is lively enough but still a white-bread workout compared to the 1958 original. This 20-song collection, covering "Do You Wanna Dance" on Josie-Jubilee, up through his last hit, the Sylvester (Sly) Stewart co-authored "C'Mon and Swim," does a lot to restore Freeman's name to the consciousness, and not just through shouters like "Do You Wanna Dance" and "Betty Lou Got a New Pair of Shoes." He acquits himself well on ballads like "Need Your Love" and standards like "Ebb Tide." The collection, mostly made up of the dance numbers that Freeman made his specialty, also includes one previously unissued cut, the doo wop style "Follow the Rainbow," and the notes provide a detailed account of the confusing state of Freeman's recording history (at one point, he seems to have been working for two labels simultaneously). The sound is somewhat uneven, a bit tinny on certain cuts, while others, especially on the later tracks, are above average, giving a good account of his solid backing band on those cuts. —*Bruce Eder*

C'Mon and S-W-I-M / Jun. 26, 2000 / Ace ♦♦♦♦
Although this has the same title as Freeman's only Autumn album, 1965's *C'mon and S-W-I-M*, this is in fact a retrospective of Freeman's entire stint with the label. In addition to all 12 songs from the original *C'mon and S-W-I-M* LP, it has five non-LP cuts from 1963-65 singles, and seven previously unissued outtakes and alternates. At the very least, it's enjoyable up-tempo party soul. At its most ambitious, there are fusions of rock and soul elements—hard slicing guitars, unusual and crafty melodic lines—that point to the directions explored, in much deeper and more effective fashion, by Sly Stone a few years later. That should not come as a great surprise, given that Sly Stone, then known as Sylvester Stewart, produced this material, in which he was also involved as arranger and frequent songwriter. In fact, "I'll Never Fall in Love Again" (heard here in both its LP version and faster single version) would be done on Sly & the Family Stone's *Dance to the Music* album, although Larry Graham and not Sly Stone would do lead vocals. More impressive than the energetic dance outings with live-in-the-studio-sounding party noise are Stone/Stewart's pop-soul-rock compositions, including "I'll Never Fall in Love Again"; "That Little Old Heartbreaker Me"; "Friends," with its James Brown-like horns and Latin rhythms; and the idiosyncratically, melodically twisting "Cross My Heart." (The last of these only appeared on 45 originally.) The outtakes and alternates, incidentally, are pretty worthwhile, and not just footnotes, particularly as they include a few Sly Stone-penned tunes. Of those, "Swing Me" is a pretty good Motown approximation, while "Honest" gets into some more personal, melancholy writing that certainly anticipates some of Stone's work a few years down the line. Not a brilliant disc, but a good one that has more historical importance in the rock and soul lineage than has been recognized. —*Richie Unterberger*

The Friends of Distinction

f. 1968, Los Angeles, CA, **db.** 1973
Sunshine Pop, Pop-Soul, Quiet Storm, Soul
Founded by Harry Elston and Floyd Butler, the Friends of the Distinction also comprised of Jessica Cleaves, Barbara Jean Love, and Charlene Gibson, who was Love's replacement during her pregnancy. After polishing up their act for roughly six months in the year of 1968, the group hit the local tour circuit in Los Angeles. The day following a performance at a Beverly Hills club one night, Elston began receiving phone calls from record companies that were interested in signing the group. With their well-developed talent and the support of their well-known manager, former football great Jim Brown, the group signed with RCA Records. In 1969, the Southern California-based act released their first single, "Grazing in the Grass." Originally recorded by famed trumpeter Hugh Masakela, Elston wrote the lyrics to Masakela's trumpet lead, and the song became a smash hit. Four months later, the second release, "Going in Circles," surpassed its predecessor. It climbed its way to number three after a prosperous 19 weeks. Three more singles charted for the group: "Love or Let Me Be Lonely," "Time Waits for No One," and "I Need You." None were as rewarding as the group's first two hits. "Love or Let Me Be Lonely" came the closest.

It peaked at 13 on the Billboard R&B charts and six on the pop charts. The group encountered some personnel changes following the two smash hits. Jessica Cleaves and Barbara Love both departed the group. Cleaves joined up with other R&B acts (Earth, Wind & Fire, Parliament, etc.). After the release of their fifth and final single, the decline of Friends of Distinction was on the horizon. By the mid-'70s, the group's well had run dry. —*Craig Lytle*

● **The Best of the Friends of Distinction** / Nov. 26, 1996 / RCA ✦✦✦✦✦
It's the summer of 1969, and the whole world is joyfully singing, "Grazing in the grass is a gas, baby, can you dig it!" The Friends of Distinction's debut single was a made-for-radio pop masterpiece that captured the ebullience of that last summer of the '60s in its three minutes of harmonic exuberance. While the group never quite reached those heights again, the Friends did produce a small body of work in their brief lifetime that has held up well. The foursome's two other major hit singles, "Love or Let Me Be Lonely" and "Going in Circles" have joined "Grazing in the Grass" in the permanent rotations of most "fun and oldies" formats. Other highlights of this 20-song compilation include "Grazing's" flipside, "I Really Hope You Do," the group's reading of the Four Tops' hit "Ain't No Woman (Like the One I've Got)," David Gates's "It Don't Matter to Me," and the beautifully baritoned "Love Can Make It Easier." —*Jim Newsom*

The Frogs

f. 1980
Indie Rock, Alternative Pop/Rock, Novelty
Thanks to their 1989 pseudo-gay album *It's Only Right and Natural*, the Frogs became a hip name to drop as fans like Nirvana, Pearl Jam, and Smashing Pumpkins ascended to superstardom in the 1990s. Milwaukee brothers Dennis (drums) and Jimmy Flemion (guitar) have an edgy sense of humor, skewering stereotypes—sometimes racial, but mostly homosexual—by pretending to be the minorities they sing about. Some critics have blasted the Frogs as juvenile and insensitive, especially when the duo wallows in graphic sexual imagery, but with such politically correct bands affirming themselves devotees, it's clear whose side of the fence the Frogs are ultimately on. The Flemion brothers began performing in local coffeehouses in 1980, when both were in their early twenties. Bassist Jay Tiller (also of Couch Flambeau) was added in 1983, the same year Jimmy debuted his trademark stage gimmick—a pair of six-foot bat wings. In between live shows, the Frogs developed a voluminous home-taping habit, which eventually resulted in a collection of self-released material. Further home tapes found their way to Homestead Records head Gerard Cosloy, who issued a collection of 12 tracks under the title *It's Only Right and Natural*. And then, the Frogs fell silent. Not by choice, but due more to a series of record company difficulties and bankruptcies. In particular, an album called *Racially Yours*, which featured one Flemion brother in blackface and one in white, went unreleased due to squeamishness over songs like "Purification of the Race," although the record contained pro-black anthems like "Freedom" as well. A slew of releases shut out the '90s. —*Steve Huey*

The Frogs / 1988 / Frogs ✦✦✦
Released in 1988, the Frogs' self-titled debut is basically pure power pop, largely without the bizarre humor that made them an indie favorite. It's still quirky, though, and fans who go in without expecting to find another "Hot Cock Annie" will likely be pleased with what they find. The 1999 reissue on Jim O'Rourke's Moikai label features liner notes by Steve Albini. —*Steve Huey*

● **It's Only Right and Natural** / 1989 / Positive ✦✦✦✦
If *Right and Natural* isn't quite yet the *White Light/White Heat* of a new generation, it's getting close—unknown upon release, venerated by multitudes of listeners and bands since all out of proportion to its public profile. The insane secret of the record is its perfect—if not note-perfect—combination of hooks, folky influences (especially from the U.K.—"Baby Greaser George" is practically an acoustic T. Rex homage), and utterly outrageous, hilarious lyrics and stories. Nothing is sacred, but the methods used would probably frighten even *Monty Python* or *South Park*'s creators at their prime. The centerpiece to everything is gay love, lust, and more at its most crazed—song titles like "These Are the Finest Queen Boys I've Ever Seen" and the sweetly catchy celebration "Homos" help say it all. Right from the start, when Dennis Flemion slurs "I've got drugs...that'll blow your mind tonight...out of your mind tonight" on "Out of the Mist," things can't help but be more than gone. By the time the song gets to the priest with drug-filled lips, listeners will have decided whether to stay the course or get out while the getting's good. One definite fun point about *Right and Natural* is seeing how it influenced future artists. Beck sampled the double-tracked claim, "That was a good drum break"—even though the break is audibly terrible—from "I Don't Care if You Disrespect Me (Just So Long as You Love Me)" for "Where It's At." The Blake Babies, meanwhile, took the song title "Rosy Jack World" for an album, and so forth. What makes the album all the more grand is its ear for tenderness in unexpected areas—"Been a Month Since I Had a Man" is gently melancholy, and more straightforward (if not straight) than anything else around it. —*Ned Raggett*

My Daughter the Broad / Jun. 11, 1996 / Matador ✦✦✦✦
After *Racially Yours* couldn't be released in 1992, the Frogs spent several years recording away happily by themselves, creating a series of 'Made-Up Songs' tapes that they sold and circulated to fans in between finding themselves feted by the alternative rock empire of the early nineties. A slew of selections from these tapes ended up forming *My Daughter the Broad*, a nicely rough counterpoint to the slicker, near-contemporaneous *Starjob* EP. To say that *My Daughter the Broad* is clearly a Frogs album and nobody else's is like saying the Pope is Catholic—there's no question about it, it simply is. Some of the more insane song titles will confirm that much: "Which One of You Gave My Daughter

the Dope?," "April Fools (He Had the Change Done at the Shop)," "Children Run Away (The Man With the Candy)," and the immortal wrongness of "Who's Sucking on Grandpa's Balls Since Grandma Ain't Home Tonight?" As before, the split between the two singers—Dennis Flemion's rasping multiple characters and Jimmy Flemion's sweetly vile troubadour—makes for even more entertainment. When they both try out on an occasional duet, the results are even more disturbing—"Where's Jerry Lewis?" tears down that particular icon and more in a mere one and a half minutes. Musically the duo still know how to make astoundingly epic rock & roll, fractured folk, and heaven knows what else out of their particular stew, and as seems to be their preferred style, they're at their most outrageous when creating the most accessible music. "The Boys With the Boys" rides its gently strummed melody along to rather disturbing ends, while "God is Gay" is calmly sung and softly performed, yet will never fit into any Christian church's hymnal. And who could knock the weepy piano ballad "I'm Sad the Goat Just Died Today"? —*Ned Raggett*

Bananimals / Oct. 12, 1999 / Four Alarm ✦✦✦✦
Once again unexpectedly emerging with an official album after a long silence, the Frogs stepped back from the smooth sounds of *Starjob* with a new collection of often rough, perversely charming, and always entertainingly offensive tracks. A fair number of songs could easily constitute a part two of *It's Only Right and Natural*, mixing the same elements of sweet folkiness and gay-themed lyrics. "La Da Da Da, La Da Da Dee, La Da Da Dum Dum"—indeed the title as well as the chorus—talks about French kissing some guy and not minding his dentures. Meanwhile, "Love in the Sand" lazily describes a scenario with another fellow where he "blew me...a kiss." Not everything is quite so focused—thus, of course, "Love Me or Die, Bitch" ("...make up your mind which!"), with alternately beautiful and stomped piano. An even more perversely pretty example is "Golden Showers," where the music and tender singing is quite lovely, even if the water sports being celebrated aren't swimming and water polo. The hints of melancholia and distress which underpin a lot of the band's best work crop up more than once, sometimes in the simplest of ways, as they do in the lead piano on "One of Them Wore Wings, the Other Did the Painting." Dennis Flemion is still in fine, scraggly voice—alternately breathy, aggressively camp, or just plain screwed up (refer to "Evil Arnold (With the Ugly Name)" for a good example of the latter). When he gets to slamming down some of the morons of the world—thus, "U Bastards" ("you should be sent to hellll...you rotten motherfuckers")—his singing is at its sweetest. "Fur z Musik Biz (10 Years to Waste)" is perhaps the perfect epitome of such an approach—a sickly sweet, tenderly arranged "up yours" to the industry that is simply mind-blowing. —*Ned Raggett*

Racially Yours / 2000 / Four Alarm ✦✦✦
A sticker on the front of *Racially Yours* proclaims it "The Most Controversial Album of All Time," but, like most of what the Frogs do, that statement is quite over the top. Sure, the album's topic is inherently controversial and the cover art features drummer Dennis Flemion costumed in blackface. But upon listening to the record—and, more importantly, reading its lyrics, which are included—it becomes obvious that the Frogs aren't crazed racists filled with hate. No, they're just a pair of white guys interested, as always, in examining the limits of what is socially acceptable. Rather than making fun of blacks, on many of the songs, they simply pretend to be black, much like they pretended to be gay on their landmark album, *It's Only Right and Natural*. And, on close inspection, it's clear that the majority of the songs are intended to be quite anti-racist, although in a bizarre fashion. "Now You Know You're Black" asserts that God is black; "Massa" is a first-person account of a slave murdering his keeper. In fact, "Prejudiced" is the only outright offensive song, but it's so obviously over the top and not serious that it becomes simply another joke—albeit a joke, like most Frogs' jokes—in poor taste. Which leaves very little to recommend this album, except to Frogs completists. It's certainly not their funniest work (that'd be the fantastic *My Daughter the Broad*) or their most politically engaging. Recorded in 1993, *Racially Yours* sat unreleased for almost seven years, supposedly because no one wanted to be associated with such controversial material. Now that it's been exposed to the light of day, it becomes clear that the album isn't only not terribly controversial, but not terribly interesting either. —*Josh Modell*

Hopscotch Lollipop Sunday Surprise / Feb. 6, 2001 / Scratchie ✦✦✦✦
The idea that the Frogs would release an album with such a gooey, sticky title seems completely ridiculous on first blush—but then again, nothing is forbidden in the realm of the Frogs, which perhaps explains the bunny costumes on the front cover. At once an extension of the usual realm of obsessions and taboos that make the duo so distinctive and a dive into crisper, focused musical realms, *Hopscotch* could almost be called a stab for mainstream attention if it weren't so enjoyably wrong. Compared to the rougher joys of *Bananimals*, *Hopscotch* generally but not entirely relies on drum machines, clean arrangements, and straightforward hooks for most of its length, with smart, subtle production touches filling out things. It's not quite *Starjob* all over again, but there's a similar dissonance between the radio-friendly music and the subject matter. There's doomy metal drama, Nine Inch Nails industrial beats, sweet, dinky synth-pop, and more—even a soaring arrangement of Bob Dylan's "Billy." Longtime fan Billy Corgan again anonymously helps out as Johnny Goat on the completely straight-faced end-of-a-romance number "The Longing Goes Away." Jimmy Flemion takes the vocal duties for the most part, his warm voice effortlessly delivering lines that still leave one wondering just how serious the proceedings are. For all the trappings, though, this is still the Frogs, and that means, well, consider some song titles for a start: "Nipple Clamps," "Better Than God," "Fuck Off," "Bad Daddy" (and, but of course, "Bad Mommy"). "Bad Daddy" itself is a complete scream, with soft orchestration and bells—even harmonica—gently supporting lines like "Bad daddy's children on crutches/At 4:30 takes one out of the oven." The album wraps up on its strongest number, "Enter I," another spin on the rock messiah pose the

band works with so well, with suitably over the top music heightening its sheer pleasure. May the Frogs continue to thrive. *—Ned Raggett*

Front 242

f. Oct. 1981, Brussels, Belgium

Electro-Industrial, Industrial Dance, Industrial Metal, Alternative Metal, Industrial

One of the most consistent industrial bands of the 1980s, even though they regularly pursued a more electronic variant of the sound that swept into vogue during the '90s, Front 242 was the premier exponent of European electronic body music. Not dissimilar to Depeche Mode and other synthesizer bands (at least in the early '80s), the band began to grow more aggressive with 1984's *No Comment* EP and in 1987 gained an American contract through Chicago's Wax Trax!. The first Front 242 LP to coalesce as a consistent recording, 1988's *Front by Front* was undoubtedly their best yet, with more emphasis on song structure than loose mechanistic grooves on the club hits "Headhunter" and "Never Stop." By the end of the decade, Front 242 had become the first Wax Trax! artist to make the jump to a mainstream label (Epic), and the single "Tragedy (For You)" became yet another club hit. Though the group was, with Ministry and Skinny Puppy, one of the most well-known industrial acts in music around that time, two simulataneously released 1993 LPs—*06:21:03:11 Up Evil* and *05:22:09:12 Off*—were not well received in an industrial climate that had begun pushing unrestrained angst and raging guitars in the vein of Nine Inch Nails. Quiet for the most part while flocks of industrial crossovers invaded the charts during the mid- to late '90s, Front 242 returned in 1997 for a tour and the live album *Re: Boot*. *—John Bush*

Geography / 1982 / Epic ✦✦✦

Official Version / 1987 / Epic ✦✦✦✦

On this amazing album, Front 242 came into its own, its brutal electrobeat now helping to fully define industrial in the broadest sense of the term. Daniel B and Codenys together whip out a series of chilling but always just danceable enough full body slams, showing an increased depth and sophistication in the overall arrangements, while 23 and de Meyer deliver their shouted and emotionless vocals with the force of full command. When the two share their vocals via traded-off lines or, often, simultaneous singing, the contrast between 23's slightly more breathless and de Meyer's sterner approach increases the overall appeal. The band's ear for vivisection by sampling reaches new heights: endless series of cries, random words, and more are looped and tweaked throughout nearly every song, a good example being the title word on "Aggressiva Due." The two peaks of the album are its singles, both of which showcase equally gripping approaches. "Masterhit," appearing in its full seven-minute version, is a full-on dancefloor monster, with a weirdly pretty chorus that makes it even more striking and memorable. "Quite Unusual," meanwhile, combines an almost quizzical lyrical portrait of a cryptic (romantic?) situation with a cinematic synth arrangement and the ever important pounding beat, varied at numerous points for even greater effect. At points on *Official Version* one can still hear the hints of the band's calmer start, but otherwise all is brusque yet chilly energy. The random metal guitar samples in said tune aren't quite up to the level of the Young Gods, but they're cool regardless. The 1992 reissue makes a great album even better with four fine bonus cuts, including an alternate take of "Quite Unusual." The two remixes of "Masterhit," "Masterblaster" and "Hypnomix," are both fine examples of the art, especially the former. *—Ned Raggett*

Back Catalogue / 1987 / Wax Trax! ✦✦✦

A collection of early 12" singles, *Back Catalogue* is the best way to get acquainted with Front 242's early days. *—Stephen Thomas Erlewine*

● **Front by Front** / 1988 / Epic ✦✦✦✦✦

Official Version was fantastic, but this album was something else again. Easily one of the greatest industrial albums ever made, bar none, *Front by Front* hit like a bombshell on its listeners and influenced more bands and songs than can be counted. Even the album art design, with everything from a rough pixel computer font cover to harsh video stills and blunt slogans, is a work of art, perfectly in sync with the electric mania inside. From the rampaging start of the album, "Until Death (Us Do Part)," not a single note, sample, guttural syllable, or headache-inducing drum hit is out of place. The album's most deservedly famous track can make an equally good case for being the definite EBM song—"Headhunter." A portrait of capitalism as mercenary terrorism with a wickedly compelling mock orchestral bass providing lead melody, "Headhunter" deserves notice not merely for the pounding music but the astonishing vocal arrangements. 23 and de Meyer serve up the memorable step-by-step chorus in perfect balance, the latter delivering each step like an order from on high while 23's singing adds on even more frenetic energy. The overall feeling of militaristic, blunt efficiency encompasses music, artwork, and lyrics both—thus utterly appropriate songtitles like "Circling Overland" and "First In/First Out." "In Rhythmus Bleiben" stands out as a particularly fine song in a series of them, the melange of computer squeals and glitches, building percussion, chaotic vocal samples, and a downright anthemic chorus resulting in one killer tune. The flipside from the original "Headhunter" single only appeared on the CD version of *Front by Front*, but it's almost as incredible as the song itself; the wickedly funny "Welcome to Paradise," sampling TV preachers like mad and subverting their messages all to another great rhythm. The 1992 reissue does the original CD one better by also including another mix of "Headhunter," as well as the entire *Never Stop* EP. *—Ned Raggett*

Tyranny (For You) / Jan. 24, 1991 / Epic ✦✦✦

What should have been an amped-up consolidation of the group's considerable strengths, coming off the blazingly brilliant *Front by Front* album, instead was a sometimes successful but sometimes repetitive effort. As a major label debut, *Tyranny (For You)* shows no sign of compromise for greater airplay—it's Front 242 straight up, powerful, pounding, and following its own muse. It's just not quite as spot-for-spot successful as *Front by Front*, though technically the group sound even more comfortable with sampling and the art of atmospherics. Where it falls apart is the relentless one-note nature of the experience, with only the occasional variety in the beats per minute on tracks. Front 242 shouldn't be sounding like uninspired imitators who have only the one idea, but more than once songs like "Trigger 2" seem to be just that. The high points of *Tyranny*, though, are stunners. With the cinematic, slow groove of "Sacrifice" leading things off—a wonderful, threatening start, heightened by compressed orchestral samples and the heavy echo and low whispers of de Meyer and 23—the group collectively pour it on for "Rhythm of Time," a great, charging single. Even more compelling is the sheer mania of "Tragedy (For You)," the lead-off single from the album as a whole, starting with a quick collage of random sounds before settling into the aggressive, nervous bass line. De Meyer's straightforward delivery of the cryptic lyrics, notably about the only time on *Tyranny* that he's quite so noticeable and upfront, immeasurably adds to the track's power, with 23 topping things off on the choruses. Another winner is "Neurobashing," one of the band's best instrumentals, with yells and crowd chants turned into a mesmerizing call-and-response exchange over an absolutely nonstop beat. *—Ned Raggett*

Angels Versus Animals / 1993 / RRE ✦✦✦

06:21:03:11 Up Evil / May 25, 1993 / Epic ✦✦✦

The first of two releases for Front 242 in 1993, *06:21:03:11 Up Evil* (aka Fuck Up Evil) found the foursome rebounding from the somewhat sterile *Tyranny (For You)* with a varied, vicious assault. Incorporating guitar noise more readily than ever before, but most often chopped up and heavily treated for the band's own particular purposes, *06:21:03:11 Up Evil* contains some of the band's most virulent, explosive songs. All titles are one word long, simple and straightforward, with names like "Flag," "Mutilate," and "Crapage." There's almost a straight-up rock feel to a number of tracks as well, as the drumming on "Waste" and the quite anthemic "Melt" shows. It's hardly Front 242's grunge move, though—Jean-Luc de Meyer and the generally little-heard Richard 23 may have a more openly emotional rasp and rage in their voices, especially de Meyer, but the relentless beat of industrial/electronic body music lives on. Leadoff single "Religion" continues the group's winning vein on that front, feedback roars and a huge beat setting an edgy pace before a body slam of a chorus kicks in, de Meyer raging over the top, "Let me burn you down!" The winning secret of the album is that a fair number of songs also demonstrate a careful subtlety, as with the sly mood-setting of "Skin," with its chopped-up electro/hip-hop beats providing the propulsion behind desperate whispers and ominous synth buzzes. The immediately following "Motion" provides an even more upfront blend of styles, with a quiet start and gentle singing suddenly shifting into a pounding call-to-arms percussion attack, all while de Meyer chants "progress, progress!" again and again. Other successes in this vein include the strange prettiness of "Stratoscape," featuring a low, purring bass line and crisp beats offset against soft keyboard sparkles and chimes, and "Fuel," which includes minimal ambient buzz, more upfront dance/beat chaos, and varying combinations of the two. *—Ned Raggett*

05:22:09:12 Off / Nov. 2, 1993 / Epic ✦✦✦✦

A combination remix collection and wholly separate album, *05:22:09:12 Off* (aka Evil Off) is a semi-sequel to *06:21:03:11 Up Evil*, appearing about six months after the release of the first disc. Not only is it a fine companion piece to the earlier disc, it easily stands on its own, finding the band thoroughly engaged in some of its most extreme, experimental music ever. A fair amount of the record is given over to darker plunges, with grinding industrial noise and moody, rumbling sonics used as the basis for many a composition, while other songs explicitly flirt with hardcore techno via hyperactive rhythms. More than a few compositions—the rhythms on "GenEcide" being a great example—sound like they're forecasting a lot of subsequent avant techno work on Warp Records and elsewhere. Another radical departure involves the use of female vocals throughout; no direct credits are given for the singer or singers, unfortunately, but contemporary interviews referred to a New York-based trio that would be appearing on the album. Combined with Daniel Bressanutti and Patrick Codenys' thrilling reinvention of their sound throughout—little here sounds like the "typical" Front 242 familiar from *Front by Front* or the like—the vocals make *05:22:09:12 Off* a fascinating listen. The key tracks are "Animal" and "Angel," both of which crop up in a variety of different forms throughout *05:22:09:12 Off*. "Animal" itself appears in three radically different versions at the start of the disc, ranging from understated minimalism to crisp but oddly distanced rhythms, as well at least one other take later on. "Angel," meanwhile, surfaces as both "Modern Angel," with the female singer delivering her lines with sheer threat and command over the acid-touched forward crunch of the music, and the appropriately titled "Speed Angel." Three songs reappear from *06:21:03:11 Up Evil* in remix form, including a fair take on "Melt" and a wonderful mix of "Crapage" called "Junkdrome." *—Ned Raggett*

Mut@ge.Mix@ge / Dec. 17, 1996 / RRE ✦✦

Headhunter 2000 / Dec. 1, 1998 / Metropolis ✦✦✦

Edith Frost

Singer, Vocals, Songwriter / Alternative Country-Rock, Indie Rock, Lo-Fi, Alternative Pop/Rock, Singer/Songwriter

Alternative country-rock singer/songwriter Edith Frost was born in San Antonio, TX on August 18, 1964. As a child, her family moved sporadically between San Antonio, Austin, and Guadalajara, Mexico; after college she relocated to Brooklyn, where by day she worked as an Internet programmer and by night fronted three different groups: the Holler Sisters (an old-time country covers band), the Marfa Lights (a western swing outfit), and Edith & Her Roadhouse Romeos (a rockabilly unit). By 1992, Frost was performing her own songs, and inspired by her love for Will Oldham's Palace projects, she sent her demo tape to his label, a receptive Drag City; in the wake of a divorce from her husband, she also relocated to Chicago. After a self-titled EP collection of demo material appeared in the summer of 1996, Frost began recording her debut LP with members of Gastr del Sol, Eleventh Dream Day, and the High Llamas; the result, the superb *Calling Over Time*, was issued in 1997. *Telescopic* followed a year later. *Love Is Real* (1999) featured artwork by Sea and Cake's Sam Prekop. *Wonder Wonder*, which followed in summer 2001, included production works by Steve Albini. *—Jason Ankeny*

● **Calling over Time** / Apr. 22, 1997 / Drag City ♦♦♦♦♦
Like Drag City stablemates Palace (a major influence), Edith Frost haunts the more oddball fringes of country music; recorded with members of Gastr del Sol, *Calling Over Time* is a contemplative and atmospheric collection, its gentle, downcast songs accented by slightly off-kilter organ drones and muted piano fills. Frost is a tremendous songwriter and a poignant lyricist, as well as a wonderfully expressive singer; her music is both fresh and strangely familiar, and her best efforts—"Temporary Loan," "Pony Song" and the stunning "Give Up Your Love"—are powerful expressions of soul-baring beauty. A stellar debut. *—Jason Ankeny*

Telescopic / Oct. 20, 1998 / Drag City ♦♦♦♦

Wonder Wonder / Jul. 17, 2001 / Drag City ♦♦♦

Fruupp

f. 1971, **db.** 1976
One of the hardest-working progressive bands to end up languishing in relative obscurity, Fruupp was begun in 1971 by guitarist Vincent McCusker. After a brief musical apprenticeship in London, McCusker returned to Belfast and quickly pulled together a group of largely clasically trained musicians; the lineup was unusual in that keyboardist Stephen Houston doubled on the oboe. (The unusual band name was taken from a Lectreset sheet.) The band's resulting sound is not unlike Spring or early Genesis, with primary composers McCusker and Houston acting as foils for each other—Houston's cello, oboe, and violin typically lend dark folk textures beneath McCusker's aggressive guitar parts and Farrelly's Celtic-influenced vocals. After two years of gigging, they shopped their demo tape around and were picked up by Pye Records for their Dawn label. Between 1973 and 1975 they released four albums, the last of which was produced by King Crimson alum Ian McDonald; the band also toured in support of Crimson. Despite playing hundreds of gigs per year throughout the U.K. and Europe during this period, their record sales never quite took off, and the band closed up shop after a London final gig at the Roundhouse in 1976. *—Paul Collins*

Future Legends / 1973 / Dawn ♦♦♦♦
A strong debut effort that, despite some searing guitar work by McCusker and a well-placed howl by Peter Farrelly in "Decision," remains a strangely low-key work. This may be due to the contemplative nature of Stephen Houston's keyboard and string parts. The erstwhile title tracks that bookend the album are instrumental throwaways, but several of the intervening numbers are impressive in their range and instrumental prowess. "Olde Tyme Future" is an ultimately hopeful elegy for an Irish homeland that seems unable to escape its own bitter past, alternating stark vocals and organ-driven instrumentals. "Song for Thought" uses the old progressive structure of spiraling fugues easing into slow blues on the verses, and it works wonderfully here. *—Paul Collins*

Prince of Heaven's Eyes / 1974 / Dawn ♦♦♦

Seven Secrets / 1974 / Dawn ♦♦♦
Seven Secrets is a pensive follow-up that shows the band stretching out into lengthy and varied suites like "Garden Lady." The album's dynamics can be a bit irritating at times—the production too often toys with very soft passages that may cut it in the symphony hall, but get tiresome anywhere else. Still, "Elizabeth" is one of the band's best compositions, an ambitious fulfillment of their talents at both string arrangements and progressive rock instrumentation, and "Three Spires" is a fine showcase for Farrelly's wistful vocals. As on their debut, the title track is a rather fey little bit of filler, but it hardly detracts from the overall high level of the album. *—Paul Collins*

Modern Masquerades / 1975 / Dawn ♦♦♦

The Prince of Heaven's Eyes/Modern Masquerades / 1996 / See For Miles ♦♦♦♦
Fruupp is primarily memorable for their wonderful name, but they nevertheless delivered some nice, warped British pysch-prog in the '60s. See for Miles' two-fer features their first two albums, *Prince of Heaven's Eyes* and *Modern Masquerades*, and while they're fairly generic, it's in a good way, especially for the psych collectors that will seek this kind of music out. No, it's not a great find, the kind you'll play for fellow record geeks, but it's enjoyable enough to pick up. *—Stephen Thomas Erlewine*

● **Future Legends/Seven Secrets** / 1997 / See For Miles ♦♦♦♦
See For Miles reissued Fruup's first two albums, *Future Legends* and *Seven Secrets*, on a single disc in 1997. *—Stephen Thomas Erlewine*

Fugazi

f. 1988, Washington, DC
Emo, Indie Rock, Post-Punk, Hardcore Punk, American Underground
If history is kind to Fugazi, their records won't be overshadowed by their reputation and methods of operation. Instead of being known for their community activism, five-dollar shows, ten-dollar CDs, resistance to mainstream outlets, and the laughably fictitious folklore surrounding their lifestyle, they will instead be identified as setting a high bar for artistic excellence that is frequently aimed for but seldom achieved with great frequency. During their existence, the four piece created some of the most intelligent, invigorating, and undeniably *musical* post-hardcore rock & roll. Along with their stridently underground ethics—which were more out of pragmatism and modesty than anything else—they gained an extremely loyal and numerous global following. More than anything, Fugazi inspired; they showed that art can prevail over commerce.

Drummer Brendan Canty, bassist Joe Lally, and guitarists/vocalists Ian MacKaye and Guy Picciotto formed the band in 1987, debuting on vinyl with two EPs recorded during 1988-89 (later coupled on CD as *13 Songs*). Their full-length debut, 1990's *Repeater*, was generally regarded as a classic, though it suffered slightly from lyrical shortcomings. Released in 1991, *Steady Diet of Nothing* branched out lyrically and limited the finger pointing, with more imaginative arrangements and less visceral qualities. Two years passed until *In on the Killtaker*, the band's most abrasively black-and-white record. As Fugazi's recordings and tours became more sporadic, *Red Medicine* was released another two years after *In on the Killtaker*, chipping away some of the latter's abrasion in favor of more jam-oriented experiments. The even wilder *End Hits* came in 1998, amidst rumors of the band being put to rest. One year later, the *Instrument* video and soundtrack hit the shelves. *—Andy Kellman*

Repeater / 1990 / Dischord ♦♦♦♦♦
With its righteous disdain for capitalism and the almighty dollar, *Repeater* sounds like an angrier American update of Gang of Four's *Solid Gold*. Lines/slogans like "When I need something/I reach out and grab it," "You are not what you own," "I was caught with my hand in the till," and "Everything is greed" bear this out. Though not lacking any sense of conviction, *Repeater* honestly gets a little stifling. It's not too difficult to see why the band was allegedly lacking a sense of humor at this stage. But—and that's a *big* but—*Repeater* nearly matches the *Fugazi* and *Margin Walker* EPs with its musical invention and skill, spewing out another group of completely invigorating songs, which makes the subject matter and finger-pointing a little easier to swallow. Few rhythm sections of the time had the great interplay of Joe Lally and Brendan Canty. Likewise, the guitar playing and interaction of Ian MacKaye and Guy Picciotto almost always get overlooked, thanks to all the other subjects brought up when the band is talked about. Anemic revs spiked by pig squeals (or is it a screeching train?) highlight the title track, one of the band's finest moments. As always, MacKaye and Picciotto's noise-terrorism-as-guitar-joust avoids flashiness, used as much as rhythm as punctuation device. Sharp, angular, jagged, and precise. Other gnarling highlights include the preachy "Styrofoam," the late-breaking "Sieve-Fisted Find," and the somewhat ironic "Merchandise," which skewers Mr. Business Owner by asking, "What could a businessman ever want more/than to have us sucking in his store?" Plenty of fans had to suck in someone's store to get this record, after all. [The CD version of *Repeater* added the *3 Songs* 7" as a bonus, titled as *Repeater + 3 Songs*.] *—Andy Kellman*

★ **13 Songs** / Apr. 1990 / Dischord ♦♦♦♦♦
Disregarding all the wordiness and adjectives that can be heaped like a pile of horse dung at Disneyland upon great, timeless albums, the importance of this record can perhaps be more suitably measured by the number of people who remember the first time they heard it. *13 Songs* (a combination of the *Fugazi* and *Margin Walker* EPs) is usually amongst the first records that spring to mind when defining alternative rock. Furious, intelligent, artful, and entirely musical, it's a baker's dozen of cannon shots to the gut—not just a batch of emotionally visceral and defiant songs recorded by angry young men, but something greater. Nearly every song here reaches an anthemic level without falling prey to pomposity.

Most of these songs are anthems of the self rather than a rallying cry of accusation or unification, with "Waiting Room" and "Suggestion," serving as two examples. The attention-getting drop into silence that occurs at the 22-second mark of the former is instantly memorable. The relentless ska/reggae-inflected drive of the song is equally effective, as Ian MacKaye tells everyone listening to get off their behinds and do what they want. During the Meters-meets-Ruts thrust of "Suggestion," MacKaye switches genders for an entirely convincing rant on the objectification of women. Guy Picciotto takes on the persona of an addict on "Glue Man," whose blurred sense of reality is also conveyed in the warped, psychedelic guitars. Picciotto threatens to set himself on fire during "Margin Walker"; given the spirited play of the remaining members, it sounds like the same could be said for the rest of them. Foreshadowing the band's knack for introspective and mid-tempo concluding tracks, the disc ends with MacKaye's "Promises," examining the pitfalls of trust in relationships of any nature. A landmark record. *—Andy Kellman*

Steady Diet of Nothing / Jul. 1, 1991 / Dischord ♦♦♦♦
From the opening swarms of "Exit Only," you can tell *Steady Diet of Nothing* will differ from Fugazi's earlier records. *Repeater*'s excellence can't be denied, but the band stood in danger of stagnating its sound. To its benefit, Fugazi made some changes, employing more herk-a-jerk rhythms and dub influences, and changing up the lyrical focus. Actually, the lyrics get a bit vague—bordering on equivocal at times—which has its advantages and disadvantages.

With *Steady Diet*, Fugazi gets more economical and less forceful. Though not nearly as neck-gnawing as *Repeater*, *Steady Diet* still packs a sizable wallop, but with slower tempos and less deliberate instrumentation. As always, a poison-tipped dart is pointed at the government, media, and major entertainment outlets. Ian MacKaye's "destroy your television" rant on "Polish" is one of the more direct and simple songs. His "KYEO" comes straight from the rice paddy or homefront, depending on interpretation. It urges the listener to always remain aware, whether awaiting the enemy's next battle move or remaining blissfully unaware of how people can be taken advantage of by others.

As with the rest of the band's catalog, lyrics are provided in the booklet. This makes things much easier on the intent listener, as both Picciotto and MacKaye have weird voices that become unintelligible when howled over their instrumental din. The lyric sheet is most useful on Picciotto's "Latin Roots." He's not warning you that "it's time to meet Jamaicans," as it sounds, but rather "it's time to meet your makers." Not quite lending itself to "Purple Haze"-like levels of butchery, but important to point out nonetheless. *—Andy Kellman*

In on the Kill Taker / Jun. 30, 1993 / Dischord ♦♦♦♦

In on the Kill Taker is like scrubbing your face with steel wool. It finds the band relying on rusty guitar shards that scrape, seethe, and hiss, further removing itself from the sound of *13 Songs* and *Repeater.* Harsh and grating, Fugazi surprisingly produces sheer noise at times, best witnessed in the lengthy closing of "23 Beats Off" and the unintentional *Gremlins* homage that opens "Walken's Syndrome." Joe Lally's bass and Brendan Canty's drums are relegated to acting as a guide; they're pushed—but not squashed—down in the mix, allowing for Ian MacKaye and Guy Picciotto's guitars to take control, corrosively so. It's probably Fugazi's least digestible record from front to back, but each track has its own attractive qualities, even if not immediately perceptible. "Facet Squared" and "Public Witness Program" open the record furiously, but the majority of the following "Return the Screw" is hardly audible, aside from occasional vocal tantrums. A good amount of time is spent alternating between low-key guitar noodling and intrusive bursts of aggression. They're smart with their sequencing, placing the gentle instrumental "Sweet and Low" (the only track where Lally plays a prominent role) after the exhaustive cacophony of "23 Beats Off," and generally piecing together a set of rather diverse tracks that flows well. Picciotto's anti-Hollywood rant on the properly titled "Cassavetes" is a classic Fugazi moment, as is his similarly name-dropping "Walken's Syndrome." Buried at the end of the record are two excellent lurchers, MacKaye's "Instrument" and Picciotto's "Last Chance for a Slow Dance." Not Fugazi's finest hour, but one of its most daring and rewarding. *—Andy Kellman*

Red Medicine / Jun. 1995 / Dischord ♦♦♦♦♦

Retreating from the skinned-knee production values of *In on the Kill Taker, Red Medicine* packs more rhythmic punch and shows more range. With more drive and playful goings-on, the arrangements sound much looser than on *Kill Taker,* while remaining just as gut-kicking and brainy. The experimentation, which adds liveliness, doesn't sound measured. Even Joe Lally is allowed to sing, and it just happens to be one of the best songs on the record. Running against the theory that Fugazi is a pack of killjoys, numerous instances pop up where the band's twisted sense of humor is apparent. The sinister ha-has that open "Birthday Pony," the android sample in the pleasant (!) instrumental "Combination Lock," and random piano plinks all manage to find a welcome place. But the most uncharacteristic track is the "Blade Runner in Kingston" slo-mo instrumental "Version," featuring clarinet skronks, dubwise rhythm, incidental zaps, and—get this—no guitars. Picciotto declares in the immediately following "Target" that he hates the sound of guitars. What gives? It's clearly a rumination against corporate America's capitalization/bastardization of "punk" aesthetics. If anyone had the right to comment, it was Fugazi. "Back to Base" and "Downed City" (another dubby intro here) return to more standard issue, hardcore roots Fugazi, full of the soaring guitars that the band is most known for. Closing out the nearly flawless second side is yet another contemplative exit track, "Long Distance Runner." Acting as a daily affirmation of sorts to combat lethargy, MacKaye opines, "If I stop to catch my breath/I might catch a piece of death." *—Andy Kellman*

End Hits / Apr. 28, 1998 / Dischord ♦♦♦

Scary—"Closed Captioned" through "Foreman's Dog" provides the worst stretch of material the Fugazi has recorded, full of disjointed patches and awkward moments. There's a virtually complete disregard for linearity that makes things seem stitched together, rather than the seamlessness you've grown accustomed to. Within that chunk and various points in the remainder, the arrangements sound like they're on the verge of collapse, and not in a violently riveting manner. One thing comes to mind, and that's boredom—perhaps not for the artists involved, but likely for the listener.

There are some great moments, however, so *End Hits* only dips its toes in failure. The epileptic "Lust for Life"-style "Five Corporations" has the riffs and rage, with Ian MacKaye taking the music industry to task for being the slow, incestuously festering beast that it is. Though the band seems to lack the stamina for instrumental wowing they once had, the songwriting is still there. On point as always, MacKaye remains lyrically immolated: "Check the math here/Check in ten years/Clusterfuck theory/Buy them up and shut them down/Then repeat in every town/Every town will be the same." Nigh on two decades of punk army service, MacKaye is still far away from running out of relevant things to say. Other highlights include "Break" and "Place Position." MacKaye and Picciotto's mantra-like barking of "yawn yawn yawn" during the latter could stop you to think "Wait, that was kind of funny" amidst all the fist pumping. Altogether, the least of the band's LPs so far; yes kids, even Fugazi makes mistakes. A minor blebby, it's nothing to disown the band for. *—Andy Kellman*

Instrument / Mar. 23, 1999 / Dischord ♦♦♦

Fugazi finally released a career retrospective after more than a decade together, though in true indie fashion, *Instrument* is far from your average band's greatest-hits collection. In truth, it's the soundtrack to a documentary produced by the band with filmmaker Jem Cohen. While the film contains footage from live dates, studio work, and intimate home-movie tapes, the soundtrack itself focuses on unreleased studio tracks and outtakes with never-before-heard songs, including "I'm So Tired," "Swingset," "Slo Crostick," and "Turkish Disco." *—John Bush*

The Argument / Oct. 15, 2001 / Dischord ♦♦♦♦♦

It's unfortunate that a band so forward looking as Fugazi has been criticized over and over for not remaking "Waiting Room," or "Repeater." Some have called them sellouts, regardless of the band's integrity and class, while others consider them elitists, "guiding" the Washington, D.C. scene. This could not be further from the truth. As the film and soundtrack to *Instrument* proved, this is a band that is only concerned with musical growth, with each album improving on its predecessor.

But no album they have put together has the jump ahead that *The Argument* has. Being both ear shattering and spine tingling at once, this is Fugazi at their "musical" best. Incorporating melody with texture and their signature angular approach, the band has raised the bar for themselves and others once again. The first "full" track, "Cashout," (an anti-gentrification anthem) is classic stuff, with a subtle guitar line exploding into a screaming chorus, but this time there is less of an emphasis on the screaming and more on the gentle melody of the verse. Slower tracks like "The Kill," and "Life and Limb," touch on strange new territory. Gentle with sense of swagger, these songs lack none of the power that the band is known for. While the two drum assault of "Ex-Spectator" (courtesy of Brendan Canty and second drummer Jerry Busher) has just as much potency on disc as it does live. And the final song, "Argument," with its rolling guitar lines, dreamy breakdown, and vocals that build from gentle to screaming, may be the best closer on a Fugazi record since "Promises." Listeners may be surprised to hear strings open up the record, or piano guiding the brilliant "Strangelight," but this is the album that proves once and for all that Fugazi has become a purely musical force.

Fifteen years in and Fugazi is still progressing. It makes one wonder what they're capable of in the future. *—Chris True*

The Fugees

f. 1987

East Coast Rap, Alternative Rap, Hip-Hop

The Fugees translated an intriguing blend of jazz-rap, R&B, and reggae into huge success in the mid-'90s, when their sophomore album *The Score* hit number one on the pop charts and sold over five million copies. The trio formed in the late '80s in the New Jersey area, where Lauryn Hill and Prakazrel Michel ("Pras") attended a local high school and began working together. Michel's cousin Wyclef Jean ("Clef") completed the group, whose debut album, *Blunted on Reality* was quite solid, although it reflected a prevailing gangsta stance that may have been forced by the record label. No matter how pigeonholed the Fugees may have sounded on their debut, the group had obviously asserted their control by the time of their second album, *The Score*—with just as much intelligence as their jazz-rap forebears, the trio also worked with surprisingly straightahead R&B on the soulful hit "Killing Me Softly with His Song." Elsewhere, Clef and Pras sampled doo wop and covered Bob Marley's "No Woman No Cry," giving the record familiarity for the commercial mainstream, but keeping it real with insightful commentary on their urban surroundings. *The Score* became one of the surprise hits of 1996, making the Fugees one of the most visible rap groups around the world. *—John Bush*

Blunted on Reality / Feb. 1, 1994 / Ruffhouse/Columbia ♦♦♦

Given the brilliance of *The Score* and the shortage of Fugees albums in the '90s, many fans probably sought out *Blunted on Reality.* Those fans no doubt were a little shocked, though, by what they found. Yes, *Blunted* features Wyclef, Lauryn Hill, and Pras, but it's not quite the same trio that fans of *The Score* have come to know. Here they offer their take on rap circa 1993. However, rather than use rap as a starting point and depart from there into a myriad of other directions as they did on *The Score,* they used rap as a starting point and never depart, instead emulating the popular style of the era. In that sense, it comes across as a bit derived and undoubtedly confined by its stifled creative ambitions. If you think back, you'll probably remember 1993 as being the pinnacle of gangsta rap—Dr. Dre's *The Chronic* was ubiquitous with not only its reach but also its influence, and Death Row was literally changing the game. If you keep this context in mind, it's a little easier to understand why *Blunted on Reality* sounds nothing like *The Score.* It's essentially the Fugees trying to earn respect in an era of gangstas, chronic, bitches, and guns by trying to come across as being hardcore. And, unfortunately, as hard as the Fugees portray themselves here, it can't help but seem a little silly in retrospect. It's an album that is best seen as novelty. Devoted fans may wish to seek it out for curiosity's sake, and that's understandable, but no one should approach this album expecting the prequel to *The Score.* *—Jason Birchmeier*

★ **The Score** / Feb. 1996 / Ruffhouse/Columbia ♦♦♦♦♦

An open, yet funky, collage of hip-hop, soul, blues, jazz, and reggae, the Fugees' second album, *The Score,* is a great step forward for the New York trio. On their debut, the group had sketched out a pattern similar to the multi-ethnic, edgy music on *The Score,* but they didn't deliver it with the authority that they do here. The Fugees cover Bob Marley's "No Woman, No Cry" and Roberta Flack's "Killing Me Softly," which gives an idea of their range, as well as their intent to carry on the soul/R&B tradition. They pull it off with a surprisingly amount of style and innovation—with its intelligent, gritty lyrics and brave eclecticism, *The Score* simply sounds like few rap records of the mid-'90s. *—Stephen Thomas Erlewine*

The Fugs

f. 1964, **db.** 1970

Comedy Rock, Proto-Punk, Folk-Rock, Psychedelic

Arguably the first "underground" rock group of all time, the Fugs formed at the Peace Eye bookstore in New York's East Village in late 1964. The nucleus of the band throughout its many personnel changes was Peace Eye owner Ed Sanders and fellow poet Tuli Kupferberg. Sanders and Kupferberg had strong ties to the beat literary scene, but charged, in the manner of their friend Allen Ginsberg, full steam ahead into the maelstrom of '60s political involvement and psychedelia. Surrounded by an assortment of motley refugees from the New York folk and jugband scene, some of whom could barely play their instruments, the group nonetheless was determined to play rock & roll their way—which meant rife with political and social satire, as well as explicit profanity and sexual references, that were downright unheard of in 1965. Starting on the legendary avant-garde ESP label, the Fugs' debut was full of equal amounts of chaos and charm, but their songwriting and instrumental chops improved surprisingly quickly, resulting in a great second album that was undoubtedly the most shocking and satirical recording ever to grace the Top 100 when it was released. Moving on to Frank Sinatra's Reprise label, unleashing a few more albums of equally satirical material that was more instrumentally polished, but equally scathing lyrically. *—Richie Unterberger*

The Fugs First Album / 1965 / Fantasy ✦✦✦
A loping, ridiculous, and scabrous release, the Fugs' debut mashed everything from folk and beat poetry to rock and rhythm & blues—all with a casual disregard for sounding note perfect, though not without definite goals in mind. Actually compiled from two separate sessions originally done for Folkways Records, and with slightly different lineups as a result, it's a short but utterly worthy release that pushed any number of 1964-era buttons at once (and could still tick off plenty of people). Sanders produced the sessions in collaboration with the legendary Harry Smith, who was able to sneak the collective onto Folkways' accounts by describing them as a "jug band," and it's not a far-off description. A number of songs sound like calm-enough folk-boom fare, at least on casual listening, though often with odd extra touches like weirdly muffled drums or out of nowhere whistles and chimes. Others, meanwhile, are just out there—thus, the details of the perfect "Supergirl," who, among other things, can "poop like a devil." Then there's "Boobs a Lot," the post-toke/acid lament "I Couldn't Get High," and the pie-in-the-face to acceptable standards of the time, "Slum Goddess." Throughout it all, the Fugs sound like they're having a perfectly fun time; the feeling is loose, ragged, but right, and while things may be sloppy around the edges, often that's totally intentional. Certainly little else could explain the random jamming and rhythmic chanting/shouting on "Swinburne Stomp." Good as the original album is, the CD version is what any serious fan needs to find, thanks to the inclusion of 11 bonus tracks. Some come from the original sessions, including the signature tune "We're the Fugs" and "The Ten Commandments," while others appear from various live jams. Then there's the self-explanatory "In the Middle of Their First Recording Session the Fugs Sign the Worst Contract Since Leadbelly's." *—Ned Raggett*

Virgin Fugs / 1966 / ESP ✦✦✦✦✦
These are outtakes from the April 1965 and July 1965 sessions that yielded the Fugs' first album. Since *The Fugs First Album* was itself a pretty wild and loose affair, you'd better believe that these leftovers are even more ramshackle. While that might serve as a hearty recommendation to some, the racket teeters on the edge of cacophony more often than it should. Sure, this is the product of bohemian poets having fun, and sure it's witty at times. But even in comparison to the first official album, it's untutored, musically speaking, and so tuneless and arrhythmic that's it's sometimes hard to bear in sustained doses. It does, however, contain some barrier-breaking (in terms of subject matter) compositions of note, such as "Coca Cola Douche," "CIA Man," "The Ten Commandments" (credited to GOD and Tuli Kupferberg), and "I Saw the Best Minds of My Generation Rot," which is Allen Ginsberg prose set to music by Ed Sanders. Several of the songs were given far more professional, full rock arrangements on the live album *Golden Filth* (recorded in 1968), if you want to hear them in less grating contexts. *—Richie Unterberger*

● **The Fugs** / 1966 / Fantasy ✦✦✦✦✦
At the time of its release, the Fugs' second (self-titled) album contained the most outrageous lyrics ever heard on a Top 100 rock & roll LP. The group, with roots in New York's underground folk and poetry scenes, flung themselves wholeheartedly into all-out rock & roll on this 1966 record, which addresses concerns like free love, the madness of war, and government repression. The CD reissue of this classic includes two previously unreleased live performances and three tracks from the unreleased album they recorded for Atlantic in 1967. *—Richie Unterberger*

Tenderness Junction / 1967 / Reprise ✦✦✦
The band opted for a considerably more conventional rock sound more in keeping with the era's psychedelic tenor on their first major-label release. The material isn't as strong and the satirical humor not as biting as their earlier efforts, though it's characteristically witty stuff. Highlights include "Turn On/Tune In/Drop Out" and "War Song"; "Aphrodite Mass" is an ambitious if not terribly memorable five-part suite. *—Richie Unterberger*

It Crawled into My Hand, Honest / 1968 / Reprise ✦✦✦
Having attained a professional rock band sound on *Tenderness Junction*, the Fugs seemed determined to further expand their arrangements (aided, perhaps, by a major label budget) on *It Crawled Into My Hand, Honest*. Indeed, the album is ridiculously eclectic. There's stoned psychedelic folk-rock ("Crystal Liaison"); cry-in-your-beer country music with vehemently satirical or surrealistic lyrics ("Ramses II Is Dead My Love," "Johnny Pissoff Meets the Red Angel"); grand, sweeping classical orchestration ("Burial Waltz"); a Gregorian chant about "Marijuana"; down-home gospel with lyrics that no preacher would dare enunciate ("Wide Wide River," with the line "I've been swimming in this river of shit/more than twenty years and I'm getting tired of it"); and, almost buried along the way, the kind of tuneful, countercultural folk-rock Tuli Kupferberg contributed to earlier albums ("Life Is Strange"). Choral backup vocals abound, and the mere presence of a half dozen outside arrangers testifies to how much the group's attitude toward exploiting the studio had developed since the bare-bones ESP albums. Generally the songs (most written by the core trio of Sanders, Kupferberg, and Weaver) are more concerned with deft poetry and humor than political statements, although the customary social satire and calls for sexual freedom and drug use are present in diminishing degrees. Although side one is five discrete tracks, side two is a side-long cut-and-paste of tracks varying in length from three seconds to four minutes, the stylistic jump-cuts similar to those employed by *the Mothers of Invention* in the same era. It's an impressive and, usually, fun record, but it's also less lyrically cogent and powerful than their early albums. One senses that the Fugs' personality and individuality was ultimately somewhat muted by the more ambitious production values and frequent use of external musicians and arrangers. *—Richie Unterberger*

Golden Filth / 1969 / Reprise ✦✦✦
By the time of this recording on June 1, 1968 at the Fillmore East, the Fugs had evolved from their primitive beginnings into a pretty full and tight rock band. They'd also grown into a pretty large group, in fact, with ten musicians, including two drummers. However, most of the material was initially recorded between 1965 and 1966, ESP era. While some listeners might be disappointed by the absence of live versions of highlights from their Reprise records, this release actually has more value than the typical live album because it has notably different arrangements of well-known songs. On the Fugs' first recordings in particular, the sound and execution was pretty primitive, and it's good to have full, together rock versions of notable songs like "Slum Goddess," "Supergirl," "Nothing," "I Couldn't Get High," "Coca-Cola Douche," and "How Sweet I Roamed." The spoken intros haven't dated as well, with Sanders' monologues about lesbian dwarfs and zebra puke, and Kupferberg moaning at one point, "I want a titty"; what was once a shocking and taboo-breaking is now superfluous to the music. The reissue of this on Edsel in Britain may be easier to find now than the original LP. *—Richie Unterberger*

The Belle of Avenue A / 1969 / Reprise ✦✦
The Fugs sounded a little weary and burnt out on their final studio album of the 1960s. The psychedelic experimentation and orchestral arrangements of 1968's *It Crawled into My Hand, Honest* were ditched in favor of basic rock or even, at times, acoustic performances. The title track and "Queen of the Nile" are essentially Ed Sanders solo cuts, with acoustic guitar accompaniment by Dan Hamburg; "Bum's Song" is likewise pretty much a Tuli Kupferberg recording, with just his voice and Hamburg's guitar. The sexually and politically charged heart of the band continued to beat on songs like "Chicago" (originally written for the soundtrack of a Yippie movie about Chicago police riots at the 1968 Democratic Convention) and "The Belle of Avenue A," about a quickie between a hippie and a truck driver. But the production and adrenaline levels are kind of flat. The country influence that was always present in Ed Sanders' singing and songwriting started to really flower on this LP, where his yodeling vocal style—which was less than an acquired taste—prefigured the country satire of his 1969 debut solo album, *Sanders' Truckstop*. It was up to Tuli Kupferberg to provide the record's highlight, the sincere ballad "Flower Children." *—Richie Unterberger*

The Fugs Second Album [With Additional Live & Studio Tracks From the Early Fugs] / 1993 / Fantasy ✦✦✦✦✦
The Fugs Second Album finds them sounding more professional than on their debut, and still sounding very ahead of their time lyrically, expressing sentiments in ways that just hadn't been done before. Lyrically, many of the tracks on this album wouldn't be out of place on any Dead Kennedys record, but like the Dead Kennedys, the Fugs' weakness for crude humor puts a damper on the whole affair. Sometimes the jokes work ("Dirty Old Man"), sometimes they don't ("Mutant Stomp"), but they're always entertaining. At times, Ed Sanders' nasal whine and clichéd hippie posturing can grow tiresome ("Frenzy," "Group Grope"), but a few true gems do manage to shine through. "Morning Morning" and "I Want to Know," which wouldn't have been out of place on *The Velvet Underground & Nico*, are true highlights. Like Reed, the revolutionary tag is placed on the Fugs for the sheer frankness they used to deal with the taboo. But whereas Reed dealt with the dark sides of promiscuity and drug use, the Fugs celebrate it, and most times in a very exhibitionist way. Biting social commentary, as on "Doin' All Right," is articulately done, and while being listenable, is not outstanding in musical terms. Bonus tracks, such as "Carpe Diem," are nice additions, and "Wide Wide River," which has a faux gospel feel, is appropriate for the sermonizing the Fugs do on the song, as throughout the album. Overall, *The Fugs Second Album* is an interesting historical footnote. *—Matt Fink*

Live from the '60s / 1994 / Big Beat ✦✦✦✦✦
For anyone who thinks the the Velvet Underground was as outré as successful cult 1960s bands got, this is the *real* stuff: taken from the personal tape collection of Ed Sanders, it's 50 minutes of unadulterated live Fugs, from their first concert in Greenwich Village through to a bunch of dates from Sweden, Wisconsin, and Texas played between 1967 and 1969. All of it is pretty raw, but that's good, because it's real. The material represents the different sides of the group's sound very well—"The Swedish Nada" has them sounding like the punk equivalents of the Doors, while "The Garden Is Open" ventures into VU territory, with Dan Kooch's violin creating a positively demonic sound, and "The Exorcism of the Grave of Senator Joseph McCarthy" (conducted at the senator's grave with Allen Ginsberg present) is like little else ever recorded by an alleged rock group. There's a lot of history here, and some fascinating music captured in generally fair fidelity. The perfect gift for anyone who already has all of the Velvets' material, or thinks the Doors were poet poseurs. *—Bruce Eder*

Electromagnetic Steamboat: The Reprise Recordings / Sep. 2001 / Rhino Handmade ✦✦✦✦

Bobby Fuller

b. Oct. 22, 1942, Baytown, TX, **d.** Jul. 18, 1966, Los Angeles, CA
Vocals, Guitar / Rock & Roll
With his blatant reverence for Buddy Holly, fellow Texan Bobby Fuller was a bit of an anomaly in the mid-'60s. With his Stratocaster guitar and brash, full sound, at his best Fuller sounded like Holly might have had he survived into the '60s. Cracking the Top 30 in 1966 with a cover of Holly's "Love's Made a Fool of You" and the Top Ten with "I Fought the Law" (written by one-time Cricket Sonny Curtis), Fuller had just become a star when he died in mysterious circumstances in a parked car in Hollywood (the police thought it

was a suicide, just about everyone who knew him disagreed). Fuller's relatively short period of national stardom actually crowned a good half-dozen years of recording, during which he released many outstanding tracks. After a few local singles in his hometown of El Paso in the early '60s, he moved to California with his combo in 1964 and briefly had aspirations of playing surf music before hooking up with producer Bob Keene. In the short time he recorded for Mustang in 1965 and 1966, he waxed quite a few tracks (most self-penned) in addition to his hits, including "Let Her Dance," "Another Sad and Lonely Night," "My True Love," "Never to Be Forgotten," "Fool of Love," and "The Magic Touch." Rocking, tuneful, and infectiously joyous, they showed Fuller to be a worthy inheritor of early rock & roll and rockabilly traditions without sounding self-consciously revivalist. While it's hard to imagine Fuller maintaining his success in the era of psychedelia, he no doubt would have gone on to produce interesting work. A talented and prolific songwriter and a studio whiz who drew from Eddie Cochran and (though only slightly) the full guitar sound of the British Invasion as well as Buddy Holly, he recorded a great deal of unreleased studio and live material that was issued in the '80s, when the depth of his loss began to be appreciated. —*Richie Unterberger*

● **The Best of Bobby Fuller Four** / 1981 / Rhino ✦✦✦✦✦
A great 18-track compilation of his best work that is truly all killer, no filler. While there's some other good Fuller to be found, this is definitely the prime stuff from his mid-'60s recordings for Mustang: "I Fought the Law," "Let Her Dance," "The Magic Touch," "Love's Made a Fool of You," "Fool of Love," "My True Love," and other equally fine if lesser-known sides. —*Richie Unterberger*

Bobby Fuller Tapes, Vol. 1 / 1983 / Rhino ✦✦✦
Not released until nearly 20 years after his death, this rare material—recorded in El Paso between 1960 and 1964—is less polished and even more overtly Buddy Holly-influenced than his mid-'60s tracks. But they're nearly as affecting and tuneful, and feature many strong Fuller originals. —*Richie Unterberger*

Live Again / 1984 / EVA ✦✦✦
According to legend, the Bobby Fuller Four were one hell of a live band. These previously unreleased live recordings from 1964 are indeed accomplished, but keep in mind that in those days, unestablished acts stuck mostly to well-known cover versions, and Fuller was no exception. Most of this set was composed of R&B/rock chestnuts along the lines of "Whole Lotta Shakin' Goin' On," "Night Train," "Peggy Sue," and "Little Bitty Pretty One"; there's a slight nod to the raging British Invasion with "From Me to You" and "House of the Rising Sun." Good though not imperfect fidelity on these cleanly executed but hardly revelatory interpretations. Fuller showed the true scope of his talents on his studio recordings of 1965 and 1966, and though this album demonstrates the bandmembers were first-class live players, it shows nothing of their originality. As such, it is only recommended to serious fans. —*Richie Unterberger*

Bobby Fuller Tapes, Vol. 2 / 1984 / Voxx ✦✦✦
The second major excursion into the vaults for previously unreleased Fuller material isn't nearly as interesting as *Vol. 1*, primarily because this collection of rare singles, alternate versions, live recordings, and outtakes from 1960-1964 is composed mostly of cover versions. Still, Fuller's brash vocals and guitars are worth hearing, though they don't redefine Little Richard, Jerry Lee Lewis, and Buddy Holly's originals. The best of the lot are the versions of "Pretty Girls Everywhere," "Baby I Don't Care," and the sizzling five-minute instrumental version of "Miserlou." Also includes the original 1964 version of "I Fought the Law," the first-class Fuller rockabilly original "Bodine," and a haunting instrumental version of "My True Love." "Shakedown" is as raw and dirty as he ever got, but unfortunately, the version on this LP was mastered from a scratchy rare single (though the fidelity on the rest of the album is excellent). —*Richie Unterberger*

Shakedown! The Texas Tapes Revisited / Oct. 1996 / Del-Fi ✦✦✦✦✦
Although a lot of this has previously appeared on various out-of-the-way reissues, this is the best compilation to date of the material Fuller recorded between 1961 and 1964 prior to signing with the Mustang label. The two-disc, 52-track package has both sides of the seven singles he made for the Yucca, Eastwood, Exeter, and Todd labels, as well as a wealth of unreleased cuts and alternate versions. It's not as polished as his more renowned mid-'60s records, and it's more derivative of his '50s heroes, particularly Buddy Holly. But it's almost as good as Bobby's most celebrated work, marked by a combination of incessant brash energy and infectious Hollyesque melodies. Fuller's confident vocals and guitar playing, even at this early stage, were equally capable of delivering raucous rockabilly and sensitive, emotional performances. Completists should note that although some of this hasn't seen the light of day before, this reissue doesn't gather *everything* he did during these years; other cuts are scattered on other compilations. Much of the previously released tracks, though, appear here in much better fidelity, and the discs are carefully sequenced to spread the alternate takes far apart from each other, icing the cake of an excellent reissue. —*Richie Unterberger*

Never to Be Forgotten: The Mustang Years / 1998 / Del-Fi ✦✦✦✦✦
A three-CD box set that includes everything Fuller recorded for Mustang between 1964 and 1966: all the LP and 45 tracks, the previously import-only album recorded at PJ's on Sunset Strip, over a dozen cuts that were unreleased during Fuller's lifetime, and rarities. Although much of the music is excellent, it should be stressed that this is for the Bobby Fuller fanatic; most fans will be quite content with the all-killer no-filler distillation of his best mid-'60s cuts on Rhino's *Best Of* compilation. Fuller's albums were filled out with some unmemorable hot rod tunes and generic rockers that seemed to have been cranked out under pressure for product. The rare selections (some of which, despite being designated as unreleased, have shown up elsewhere) are largely alternates of songs that were already available, and although these are occasionally interesting, the variations are mostly on the slight side. A couple of cuts by the Randy Fuller Four (led by Bobby's

brother and bassist) don't measure up to his sibling's output in the least, sounding jarring and clumsy by contrast. The *Live at PJ's* disc is disappointing: it consists mostly of covers of familiar rock standards, for one thing, and neither the sound quality nor performance match the excitement that Fuller routinely generated in the studio during this time. But make no mistake, this is a good thing for fans to have, and is superbly packaged, with a 64-page booklet of critical essays, speculation on his mysterious death, and an interview with Randy Fuller. —*Richie Unterberger*

I Fought the Law: The Best of the Bobby Fuller Four / Mar. 20, 2001 / Del-Fi ✦✦✦✦

Fun Boy Three

f. 1981, db. 1983
New Wave
The Specials were one of the most popular and influential bands in the U.K., scoring a streak of seven straight Top Ten singles. The 1981 chart-topper "Ghost Town" was the last to feature Terry Hall and the original lineup—after its release Hall split with the group's other two vocalists, Lynval Golding and Neville Staples, to form the Fun Boy Three. Where the Specials were a ska-revival band, the Fun Boy Three was a new wave pop group with distinctly weird, skeletal, and experimental overtones. They released their eponymous debut in the spring of 1982. That summer, they had a hit with a cover of George Gershwin's "Summertime." The group recorded a second album with Talking Heads leader David Byrne late in 1982. The resulting album, *Waiting,* appeared in the spring of 1983, concurrently with the Top Ten singles "The Tunnel of Love" and "Our Lips Are Sealed," a song Hall wrote with Jane Wiedlin, who already made it into a hit the previous year with her group, the Go-Go's. By the summer of 1983, the Fun Boy Three were peaking in popularity and Hall disbanded the group. —*Stephen Thomas Erlewine*

The Fun Boy Three / Mar. 1982 / Chrysalis ✦✦✦✦✦
"Where do we go from here, what kind of sound do we follow?" muses Terry Hall on "Way on Down," a track from the Fun Boy Three's eponymous debut album. It was a question on numerous lips, ever since Hall and his fellow ex-Specials Neville Staples and Lynval Golding announced the formation of their new group. It's doubtful that anyone came even close to the correct answer. The album was built firmly around tribal drumming, whose percussive possibilities were inspiring a number of groups at the time. Most notably, Adam Ant had merged the beats with a Gary Glitter stomp and a military tattoo, and was now riding the rhythms toward world domination. The Boys, however, were taking the same African influence in an entirely different, and even more innovative, direction. Most surprisingly, or perhaps not, considering the size of their former band, was how minimalistic the music was. Many of the songs were stripped down to bare vocals and percussion, while even those tracks which did sport other instruments mostly utilized them as mere embellishments around the showcased rhythms. Long before modern rap and techno placed all its focus on the beats, the Boys were diligently working around this same concept. Three of the album's tracks—"The Lunatics," "It Ain't What You Do It's the Way That You Do It," and "The Telephone Always Rings"—snaked their way into the U.K. Top 20. The album pulsated all the way number seven. It also introduced the world to Bananarama, who provided backing vocals on many of the record's tracks. "One of the most wonderful recordings of our time," the album sleeve boldly stated, and it was absolutely true. —*Jo-Ann Greene*

Waiting / Feb. 1983 / Chrysalis ✦✦
David Byrne-produced second album contains the Boys' own version of their song "Our Lips Are Sealed," a hit for the Go-Go's. —*William Ruhlmann*

● **The Best of Fun Boy Three** / 1984 / Chrysalis ✦✦✦✦✦
This collects all of the essential moments of the short-lived band. Two non-LP tracks are an added bonus: a cover of Gershwin's "Summertime" and their collaboration with Bananarama, "Really Saying Something." —*Chris Woodstra*

The Best of Fun Boy Three: Really Saying Something / 1997 / Chrysalis ✦✦✦
Instead of concentrating on the single versions of hits like "Our Lips Are Sealed," *The Best of Fun Boy Three—Really Saying Something* includes remixed versions of nearly all of the group's best-known songs. While this is a selling point for some collectors—after all, many of these 12" mixes have not been on CD before—for most fans, it makes the compilation an ultimately frustrating listen, since the extended mixes and alternate versions aren't nearly as infectious as the originals. —*Stephen Thomas Erlewine*

Fun Lovin' Criminals

f. 1993
Alternative Rap, Alternative Pop/Rock
Much like G. Love and Special Sauce, the New York trio known as Fun Lovin' Criminals hit the alternative airwaves with a blend of hip-hop beats, alternative style, and bluesy rhythms. The group was formed in 1993 by bassist Fast and drummer Steve, who had met in Syracuse while going to school; the pair formed a techno group, but later moved back to New York City, where they hooked up with vocalist/guitarist Huey. FLC played around the area, and released their self-titled debut album in 1995 on the Silver Spotlight label. Signed to Capitol the following year, the group gained an alternative radio hit with their single "Scooby Snacks," from *Come Find Yourself. 100% Colombian* followed in 1998. —*John Bush*

Fun Lovin' Criminals / Nov. 1995 / Silver Spotlight ✦✦✦

● **Come Find Yourself** / Feb. 20, 1996 / Capital ✦✦✦✦
In some circles, the Fun Lovin' Criminals were touted as the heir apparent to the Beastie Boys. There were two problems, however, with this contention: the Beastie Boys weren't going away, and the Fun Lovin' Criminals certainly were not pushing anybody with this

major-label debut. Aside from the radio hit "Scooby Snacks," nothing on the album had anywhere near enough staying power to distinguish the Criminals as anything more than a run-of-the-mill one-hit wonder. While the music of the Beastie Boys is eclectic, dynamic and laden with amusing pop-culture references, the music of the Fun Lovin' Criminals is predictable, unimaginative, and downright boring for the most part. While the band attempted to mix in some elements of the Beastie Boys and also tried to cash in on the same fusion of rock, rap, and punk, the results were decidedly inferior. *—David M. Childers*

100% Colombian / Nov. 17, 1998 / Virgin ✦✦✦✦

Fun Lovin' Criminals got a lot of mileage out of their Scorsese-meets-Beasties-meets-*Reservoir Dogs* schtick on their first-full length album, *Come Find Yourself.* Their stoned, funky grooves brought them an MTV hit in America and, inexplicably, critical acclaim in the U.K., where their New York attitude came across as... well, not genuine, but at least an authentic parody from a knowing source. Eventually, the British acclaim eclipsed the moderate U.S. success, so it shouldn't be surprising that they tailored their follow-up, *100% Colombian,* to the very things the British press loved—the tongue-in-cheek humor, the cartoonish gangsterism, the dope, the funk- and rap-inflected grooves, the cheeky pop culture references. It's a little jazzier, a little slower, a little more cinematic than its predecessor, which means it's more cohesive, as well as more sonically appealing. Of course, it's possible that the average listener—one who wasn't charmed or amused by *Come Find Yourself* and "Scooby Snacks"—will never discover this, since Huey's self-satisfied rapping and smug lyrics can be exceptionally grating if you're not smirking along with him. But if his '70s mob movie fetishism and ironic celebration of da streets uv Noo Yawk seem humorous, chances are *100% Colombian* will feel even better than *Come Find Yourself.* Everything's cool, everything's shmoove, put the money in the bag... *—Stephen Thomas Erlewine*

Mimosa / Dec. 7, 1999 / EMI ✦✦✦✦✦

Smooth New York jazz rappers Fun Lovin' Criminals have quietly built their popularity stateside and particularly in Europe over the last six years by wrapping their tales of the Big Apple's underbelly with sweet grooves and live instrumentation akin to Cake, the Roots, and Luscious Jackson. The smoothness of their grooves and underground culture has always been just a stone's throw away from lounge-lizard heaven. With *Mimosa,* the band gives in to their Velveeta-smooth cheese urges and delivers a quirky collection of far-out covers and retoolings of their own songs.

It's an interesting collection, and works best when they stick to their own material. Reworked originals like "Scooby Snacks" and the excellent "I Can't Get With That" have a great, easy, witty feel not terribly far from the original recordings. Some tracks, like "The Summer Wind," with the surprising guest Ian McCullough, showcase the band's strong live performances. Others are just plain whacked out, like the ultra-wimpy '70s weepers "I'm Not In Love" and "Shining Star" (not the Earth, Wind & Fire song, another one). It seems like they might have taken a miscue from Cake, whose 1996 cover of "I Will Survive" is both hilarious but true to the spunk of the original. These covers lack the irony or campiness needed to make it interesting. *—Theresa E. LaVeck*

Funkadelic

f. 1968, **db.** 1981

Psychedelic, Hard Rock, Funk, Soul

Though it often took a back chair to its sister group Parliament, Funkadelic furthered the notions of black rock begun by Jimi Hendrix and Sly Stone, blending elements of '60s psychedelia and blues plus the deep groove of soul and funk. Led by sound architect George Clinton, the band pursued album statements of social/political commentary while Parliament stayed in the funk singles format, but Funkadelic nevertheless paralleled the more commercial artist's success, especially in the late '70s when the interplay between bands moved the Funkadelic sound closer to a unified P-Funk style. After debuting with an eponymous 1970 LP, the group hit its stride with acid-rock extravaganzas like the following year's *Maggot Brain.* By their mid-'70s major-label debut, 1976's *Hardcore Jollies,* the Funkadelic sound had gelled with cornerstones like bassist Bootsy Collins and keyboardist Bernie Worrell. The band's next studio LP, 1978's *One Nation Under a Groove,* became their biggest hit—the title track hit number one on the R&B charts (and the Top 40) while the album went platinum. In 1979, Funkadelic's "(Not Just) Knee Deep" hit number one as well, and its album (*Uncle Jam Wants You*) reached gold status. At just the point that Funkadelic appeared to be at the top of its powers, the band began to unravel. A splinter group also known as Funkadelic even hit the charts in 1981, and after George Clinton began a solo career the following year, Funkadelic effectively disbanded. *—John Bush*

Funkadelic / 1970 / Westbound ✦✦✦✦

Funkadelic's self-titled 1970 debut is one of the group's best early- to mid-'70s albums. Not only is it laden with great songs—"I'll Bet You" and "I Got a Thing..." are obvious highlights—but it retains perhaps a greater sense of classic '60s soul and R&B than any successive George Clinton-affiliated album. Recorded for the Detroit-based Westbound label, at the time Funkadelic were in the same boat as psychedelic soul groups such as the Temptations, who had just recorded their landmark *Cloud Nine* album across town at Motown, and other similar groups. Yet no group had managed to effectively balance big, gnarly rock guitars with crooning, heartfelt soul at this point in time. His songs are essentially conventional soul songs in the spirit of Motown or Stax—steady rhythms, dense arrangements, choruses of vocals—but also with a loud, overdriven, fuzzy guitar lurking high in the mix. And when Clinton's songs went into their chaotic moments of jamming, there was no mistaking the Hendrix influence. Furthermore, Clinton's half quirky, half trippy ad libs during "Mommy, What's a Funkadelic?" and "What Is Soul" can be mistaken for no one else—they're pure-cut P-funk. Successive albums found the group drifting further toward rock, funk, and eventually disco, especially once Bernie Worrell began playing a larger role in the group. Never again would they be this attuned to their '60s roots, making this a revealing and unique record that's certainly not short on quality songs. *—Jason Birchmeier*

Free Your Mind . . . And Your Ass Will Follow / 1970 / Westbound ✦✦✦✦

It's one of the best titles in modern musical history, for song and for album, and as a call to arms mentally and physically the promise of funk was never so perfectly stated. If it was just a title then there'd be little more to say, but happily, *Free Your Mind* lives up to it throughout as another example of Funkadelic getting busy and taking everyone with it. The title track itself kicks things off with rumbling industrial noises and space alien sound effects, before a call and response chant between deep and chirpy voices brings the concept to full life. As the response voices say, "The kingdom of heaven is within!" The low and dirty groove rumbles along for ten minutes of dark fun, with Worrell turning in a great keyboard solo toward the end—listening to it, one gets the feeling that if Can were this naturally funky, they'd end up sounding like this. From there the band makes its way through a total of six songs, ranging from the good to astoundingly great. "Funky Dollar Bill" is the other standout track from the proceedings, with a great, throw-it-down chorus and rhythm and a sharp, cutting lyric that's as good to think about as it is to sing out loud. The closing "Eulogy and Light," meanwhile, predates Prince with its backwards masking and somewhat altered version of the Lord's Prayer and Psalm 23. At other points, even if the song is a little more straightforward, there's something worthwhile about it, like the random stereo panning and Hazel's insane guitar soloing on "I Wanna Know If It's Good for You," with more zoned and stoned keyboard work from Worrell to top things off. The amount of drugs going down for these sessions in particular must have been notable, but the end results make it worthy. *—Ned Raggett*

★ **Maggot Brain** / 1971 / Westbound ✦✦✦✦✦

It starts with a crackle of feedback shooting from speaker to speaker and a voice intoning "Mother Earth is pregnant for the third time, for y'all have knocked her up" and talking about rising "above it all or drown in my own shit." This could only have been utterly bizarre back in 1971 and it's no less so 30 years on; though the Mothership was well on its way already, *Maggot Brain* really helped it take off. The instrumental title track is the key reason to listen, specifically for Eddie Hazel's lengthy, mind-melting solo. Clinton famously told Hazel to play "like your momma had just died," and the resulting evocation of melancholy and sorrow doesn't merely rival Jimi Hendrix's work but arguably bests a lot of it. Accompanied by another softer guitar figure providing gentle rhythm for the piece, the end result is simply fantastic, an emotional apocalypse of sound. *Maggot Brain* is bookended by another long number, "Wars of Armageddon," a full-on jam from the band looping in freedom chants and airport departure announcements to the freak-out. In between are a number of short pieces, finding the collective merrily cooking up some funky stew of the slow and smoky variety. There are folky blues and gospel testifying on "Can You Get to That" (one listen and a lot of Primal Scream's mid-'90s career is instantly explained) and wry but warm reflections on interracial love on "You and Your Folks, Me and My Folks," its drum hits distorted to give a weird electronic edge to the results. "Super Stupid" is a particular killer, pounding drums and snarling guitar laying down the boogie hard and hot, while "Hit It and Quit It" has a great chorus and Bernie Worrell getting in a fun keyboard solo to boot. *—Ned Raggett*

America Eats Its Young / 1972 / Westbound ✦✦✦

A double album and worth every minute of it, *America Eats Its Young* makes for a freaky, funky, and aware good time. Compared to the endless slabs of double-album dreck that came out around the same time from all sources, here Funkadelic brought life, soul, and much more to the party. With Clinton credited only for arranging and producing, here the mad cast he brought together went all out. Worrell in particular now had a new importance, credited as co-arranger with Clinton as well as handling string and horn charts on a number of songs. His surging, never-stop keyboards, meanwhile, took control from the start, with his magnificent lead break on the opening "You Hit the Nail on the Head" making for one of the best performances ever on Hammond organ. Bootsy Collins (credited as William) is also somewhere in the crowd on bass and vocals, while old favorites like Hazel and Fulwood, among many others, can be found. Perhaps to fill in the time, a few numbers from the first Parliament album *Osmium* two years before cropped up, namely "Loose Booty" and the hilariously sleazy "I Call My Baby Pussycat," here performed with a noticeably slower, dirty groove. The straightforward social call to arms appears throughout, with one song title saying it all—"If You Don't Like the Effects, Don't Produce the Cause." Other winners include the vicious title track, combining everything from mysterious, doom-laden voices and weeping wails to slow, sad music, and the concluding "Wake Up," while "Everybody Is Going to Make It This Time" is a lovely, gospel-informed ballad that heads for the skies and hearts. There are more mundane concerns as well, such as "There Was My Girl," a quirky weeper, and the weird if smoothly delivered "Miss Lucifer's Love," with more than one target in mind. *—Ned Raggett*

Cosmic Slop / 1973 / Westbound ✦✦✦✦

With a much more stripped-down version of the band, if the credits are to be believed (five regular members total, not counting any vocalists), Funkadelic continued its way through life with *Cosmic Slop.* A slightly more scattershot album than the group's other early efforts, with generally short tracks (only two break the five-minute barrier) and some go-nowhere ballads, *Cosmic Slop* still has plenty to like about it, not least because of the monstrous title track. A bitter, heartbreaking portrait of a family on the edge, made all the more haunting and sad by the sweet vocal work—imagine an even more mournful "Papa Was a Rollin' Stone"—the chorus is a killer, with the devil invited to the dance while the band collectively fires up the funk. Elsewhere, the band sounds like it's more interested in simply hitting a good groove and enjoying it, and why not? If introductory track "Nappy Dugout" relies more on duck calls and whistles than anything else to give it identity, it's still a clap-your-hands/stomp-your-feet experience, speeding up just a little toward the end. As for the band members themselves, Worrell still takes the general lead thanks to his peerless keyboard work, but the guitar team of Gary Shider and Ron Bykowski and the rhythm duo of Lampkin and Mosson aren't any slouches, either. Clinton again seems to rely on the role of ringleader more than anything else, but likely that's him behind touches like distorted vocals. Certainly it's a trip to hear the deep, spaced-out spoken word tale on "March to the Witch's Castle," a harrowing picture of vets returning from Vietnam—and then realizing that Rush ripped off that approach for a song on its *Caress of Steel* album a year or two later! *—Ned Raggett*

Standing on the Verge of Getting It On / 1974 / Westbound ✦✦✦

Expanding back out to a more all-over-the-place lineup—about 15 or so people this time out—Funkadelic got a bit more back on track with *Standing on the Verge*. Admittedly, George Clinton repeats a trick from *America Eats Its Young* via another re-recording of an *Osmium* track, namely leadoff cut "Red Hot Mama." However, starting as it does with a hilarious double soliloquy (with the first voice sounding like the happier brother of Sir Nose D'Voidoffunk) and coming across with a fierce new take, it's a good omen for *Standing on the Verge* as a whole. Eddie Hazel's guitar work in particular is just plain bad-ass; after his absence from *Cosmic Slop*, it's good to hear him fully back in action with Bernie Worrell, Cordell Mosson, Gary Shider, and the rest. In general, compared to the sometimes too polite *Cosmic Slop*, *Standing on the Verge* is a full-bodied, crazy mess in the best possible way, with heavy funk jams that still smoke today while making a lot of supposedly loud and dangerous rock sound anemic. Check out "Alice in My Fantasies" if a good example is needed—the whole thing is psychotic from the get-go, with vocals as much on the edge as the music—or the wacky, wonderful title track. There are quieter moments as well, but this time around with a little more bite to them, like the woozy slow jam of "I'll Stay," which trips out along the edges just enough while the song makes its steady way along. In an unlikely but effective turn, meanwhile, "Jimmy's Got a Little Bit of Bitch in Him" is a friendly, humorous song about a gay friend; given the rote homophobia of so much later hip-hop, it's good to hear some founding fathers have a more open-minded view. *—Ned Raggett*

Let's Take It to the Stage / Apr. 1975 / Westbound ✦✦✦✦

One of Funkadelic's goofiest releases, *Let's Take It to the Stage* also contains more P-Funk all-time greats as well, making for a grand balance of the serious and silly. Perhaps the silliest is at the end—there's not much else one can call the extended oompah/icing rink start of "Atmosphere." The title track is as much a call to arms as "Free Your Mind and Your Ass Will Follow" is, but with a more direct musical performance and a more open nod to party atmospheres (not to mention the source of one of Andrew Dice Clay's longest-running bits). The targets of the band's good-natured wrath are, in fact, other groups—"Hey, Fool and the Gang! Let's take it to the stage!" There's no mistaking the track that immediately follows makes it even more intense—"Get Off Your Ass and Jam" kicks in with one bad-ass drum roll and then scorches the damn place down, from guitar solo to the insanely funky bass from Bootsy Collins. It may only be two and a half minutes long, but it alone makes the album a classic. Hearing Collins' unmistakable tones is usually enough to get anything on the crazy tip, but "Be My Beach" just makes it all the more fun, as does the overall air of silly romance getting nuttier as it goes. "Good to Your Earhole" sets the outrageous mood just right—it's one of the band's tightest monsters of funk, guitars sprawling all over the place even as the heavy-hitting rhythm doesn't let one second of groove get lost. Of course, there's also one totally notorious number to go with it, but "No Head No Backstage Pass" has one of the craziest rhythms on the whole album, not to mention lip-smackingly nutty lines delivered with the appropriate leer. *—Ned Raggett*

Hardcore Jollies / 1976 / Priority ✦✦✦✦

Funkadelic's major-label jump brought its version of life more into line with Parliament, though the crucial difference between the two—Funkadelic's guitars vs. Parliament's horns—remained intact. Eddie Hazel, as ever, is missed, but Gary Shider and Mike Hampton do fine work. Whoever peels off the concluding solo at the end of "Comin' Round the Mountain" deserves credit, even if it's sometimes flash for flash's sake. Similar exercises in feedback can be found on the title track and elsewhere, sometimes great, sometimes timekeeping. Still, after all, the album itself is dedicated "to the guitar players of the world," so it can't be said that Clinton and company aren't keeping the proper focus on things. Generally things are fairly light on *Hardcore Jollies*, though a remake of earlier highlight "Cosmic Slop" retains the sharp sentiments, if not quite as strongly delivered as before (musically it's much more centered around the bass and drums, though things get duly crazed all around toward the end). Otherwise, the emphasis is on fairly clean jams and rhythms, with lower-key goofiness than before but still merrily out there. If it's not truly gone and great like *Maggot Brain* or *Let's Take It to the Stage*, it's still good listening at its best moments. "If You Got Fun, You Got Style" makes for a better chat-up dancefloor appreciation than most, while "Soul Mate" balances out obvious "want you bad" sentiments with squirrelly lead vocals that don't quite fit the subject at hand. And who could knock the use of the "there's a place in France/where the ladies wear no pants" melody in "You Scared the Lovin' Outta Me"? Pedro Bell does some of his best work ever for the cover and inside art, while the accompanying short story is hilarious. *—Ned Raggett*

Tales of Kidd Funkadelic / 1976 / Westbound ✦✦✦

Some leftover jams, songs, and funk pieces from the Funkadelic era. George Clinton was in the midst of moving Funkadelic to another label, and the Westbound folk released a bunch of vault material to get another Funkadelic album on the market. There were still some fine cuts, but the random element prevented it from being a great album because it lacked the thematic organization and vision Clinton provided for the concept LPs. *—Ron Wynn*

★ **One Nation Under a Groove** / 1978 / Priority ✦✦✦✦✦

Funkadelic continued its late-'70s ways with *One Nation Under a Groove*, betraying more than once the then-commercial dominance of disco but still getting away with things, if not as consistently successful as before. Shider and Hampton remain the lead guitarists while any number of bassists and drummers keep things going—usual folks like Collins and Lampkin, among others—while Worrell is still the keyboardist extraordinaire. The title track itself is the one most addicted to the mirrorball atmosphere of the time, though there are more than a few nutty voices and surprising choruses to leaven things nicely. Still, it's a surprising thing to hear from any branch of the P-Funk empire, even if Parliament had its own similar slip with "Party People"—it's not that it's bad disco, it's just not what Funkadelic is capable of. There are a number of highlights which put that track in the shade, notably the nutty "Promentalshitbackwashpsychosis Enema Squad," where a ten-minute loverman funk groove gets ranted and chanted over by the assembled with all sorts of hilariously foul sentiments and bizarre proclamations. Perhaps the oddest song in context is "Who Says a Funk Band Can't Play Rock?!" Lyrically it's a brilliant slam regarding said idiotic stance and the larger question of race and music, but compared to past feedback-drenched highlights, it's simply too crisp and clean, the solos too dedicated to showing off for showing off's sake. Far more to the point—and far more of a great song—is the vicious snarl and yelp of "Lunchmeataphobia (Think! It Ain't Illegal Yet!)," with Worrell's crunching keyboard work adding to the heavy-riffing punch. A surprising kicker comes at the end, with a live version of the early classic "Maggot Brain" taking a bow. *—Ned Raggett*

Uncle Jam Wants You / 1979 / Priority ✦✦✦✦✦

Almost as if Clinton and company wanted to atone for parts of *One Nation Under a Groove*, *Uncle Jam Wants You* takes not merely a more daring musical approach but a more forthright political stance. The cover art alone is brilliant, front and back showing Clinton in Huey P. Newton's famous Black Panther pose. The main goal is the cover subtitle's stated claim to "rescue dance music 'from the blahs,'" and "Uncle Jam" itself does a pretty funny job at doing that, starting out like a parody of patriotic recruitment ads before hitting its full, funky stride. It's still very much a disco effort, but one overtly spiking the brew even more than before with P-Funk's own particular recipe, mock drill instructors calling out dance commands and so forth. The absolute winner and most famous track, without question, is the 15-minute deep groove of "(Not Just) Knee Deep." It'd be legend alone for being the musical basis for De La Soul's astonishing breakthrough a decade later with "Me, Myself and I," but on its own it predates the mutation of disco into electro thanks to the stiff beat and Worrell's crazy keyboards. Elsewhere there are pleasant enough jams like "Field Maneuvers," kicking around some good guitar work amidst the hop-and-skip beat, and the weepy ballad "Holly Wants to Go to California," intentionally undercut by all the cheering and noise deep in the mix. It's not to say that Funkadelic hasn't left the entire world of coke spoons and pointing to the sky behind them, as "Freak of the Week" shows, which isn't entirely far off from the early Sugar Hill party/zodiac aesthetic. Then again, lines like "disco-sadistic, that one beat up and down, it just won't do" amidst the whistles and screams have their own impact. *—Ned Raggett*

The Electric Spanking of War Babies / 1981 / Priority ✦✦✦✦✦

With George Clinton, a humorous phrase could be nothing more than playful tomfoolery, or it could be a double entendre with a deep political meaning. The phrase "electric spanking of war babies" falls into the latter category—it referred to what the funk innovator saw as the U.S. government using the media to promote imperialistic wars. To Clinton, the American media functioned as a propaganda machine during wartime. But whether or not one cares to examine its hidden political messages, *Electric Spanking* is an above-average party album. *Spanking* falls short of the excellence of *One Nation Under a Groove* and *Uncle Jam Wants You* and didn't boast a major hit single, but amusing funk smokers like "Electro-Cuties" and "Funk Gets Stronger" aren't anything to sneeze at, nor is the reggae-influenced "Shockwaves." *Spanking* turned out to be the last album Clinton would produce under the name Funkadelic—when he hit the charts again in 1983, Mr. P-Funk was billing himself as a "solo artist." *—Alex Henderson*

Who's a Funkadelic / 1981 / Rhino ✦

Connections & Disconnections / 1981 / LAX ✦

★ **Music for Your Mother** / Mar. 31, 1993 / Westbound ✦✦✦✦✦

Though *Tales of Kidd Funkadelic* brought together some oddballs and rarities from Funkadelic's early- to mid-'70s existence, it wasn't until *Music for Your Mother* came out that there was a full compilation of all the band's singles from birth to the mid-decade switch to Warner Bros. And what a compilation it is: Bringing together some of the band's best material as well as some of its craziest, *Music for Your Mother* does the business for any self-respecting P-Funk clone. Given that the focus is on A- and B-sides rather than album cuts, it isn't a truly exhaustive overview—that would require the inclusion of songs like "Maggot Brain" and "Free Your Mind and Your Ass Will Follow," for a start. It's a small quibble in context, though, especially given the inclusion of a number of songs that never made it onto the original eight albums. Most notable is a curious rarity, the semi-smooth soul "I Miss My Baby" single, which was credited to U.S., with music by Funkadelic (U.S. being a group led by eventual P-Funk guitarist Gary Shider). As for the other B-sides and uncollected numbers, they're an understandably mixed but often interesting bunch, including alternate instrumental takes of "Music for Your Mother" and "I Wanna Know if It's Good to You," the unreleased "Can't Shake It Loose" single, the gospel/feedback freak-out "Open Our Eyes," and the hilariously titled "Fish, Chips and Sweat." The amazing bonus to the whole collection is the exhaustive 24-page booklet, reviewing the entire early history of Funkadelic via archival photos and a slew of interviews with the surviving participants. Plenty of fun tales are told, but George Clinton didn't participate—not surprising, given the unflattering picture eventually painted of him—while the depressing fates of Eddie Hazel and Tawl Ross get deserved attention. *—Ned Raggett*

Live: Meadowbrook, Rochester, Michigan 12th September 1971 / 1996 / Westbound ✦✦✦

Not released until 1996, this was an unusual gig for the band, who were breaking in a new rhythm section (this may have been their first show) without much or any rehearsal. You can't tell from this 77-minute disc, which offers a typically amorphous, freefloating set of black rock—which is to say, judged by most standards, it's not typical music at all. Seguing from spaced-out jams to occasional numbers with vocals by George Clinton, and throwing in imaginative improvisations by guitarist Eddie Hazel and keyboardist Bernie Worrell, it sounds something like a combination of Jimi Hendrix, James Brown, and Sun Ra. The 14-minute "Maggot Brain" verges on prog rock/psychedelia (in the good sense), with its almost mystical guitar lines; earthier pleasures are offered with cuts like "I Call My Baby Pussycat" (two versions). The fidelity is pretty good, though the vocals lack the presence of the instruments. Funkadelic is still shown to their best advantage on their studio recordings of the era, but this is certainly a fascinating find for fans, augmented by detailed liner notes about the gig by Rob Bowman. *—Richie Unterberger*

Finest / 1997 / Westbound ✦✦✦✦

Contains their Westbound singles from 1969 to 1976, including Funkadelic's first significant single "I Bet You," co-written by George Clinton while under contract to Motown for five fruitless years. Motown never released it or any other Parliament song. Billy Butler's rendition of "I Bet You" preceded Funkadelic's stoner version. Guitars dominate every track, either as lead instruments or as electric wallpaper; Bernie Worrell's keyboard and synthesizer skills glue everything together. The erotic "I Wanna Know if It's Good for You" messes with your head for ten funky minutes. Worrell plays a multitude of keyboards on the musically happy "A Joyous Process." They emulate the Temptations on "You Can't Miss What You Can't Measure" by bouncing the lead around like a hot potato. "Red Hot Mama" scorches, "Hit It and Quit It" has an orgasmic, jerky beat. In-your-face openers "Let's Take It to the Stage" and "Get Off Your Ass & Jam" have been P-Funk concert staples for more than 25 years. "Cosmic Slop" and "Undisco Kidd" display a trend toward commercialism that crystallized and paid dividends on *One Nation Under a Groove*. A live version of "Maggot Brain" featuring guitarist Michael Hampton is a bonus. *—Andrew Hamilton*

Nelly Furtado

Alternative Pop/Rock, Singer/Songwriter, Adult Alternative Pop/Rock

Singer/songwriter Nelly Furtado heavily credits her ethnic background and childhood for culturally and crucially spawning her creativity as a female and as an inspiring musician. Born and raised in Victoria, British Columbia, Canada, Furtado's working-class parents, whom are of Portuguese decent, instilled a hardcore work ethic during her upbringing. She spent eight summers working as a chambermaid with her housekeeping mother, quickly realizing what it meant to honestly make a living. She turned to music for enjoyment, learning to play the guitar and the ukulele, and listened to mainstream R&B like Mariah Carey, TLC, Jodeci, Salt-N-Pepa, and Bell Biv DeVoe. Later, she delved into her older brother's collection of Radiohead, Pulp, Oasis, Portishead, the Verve, and U2, pushing Furtado to fully embrace different musical genres, specifically Brazilian music and material by Nusrat Fateh Ali Khan and Amalia Rodrigues. Hip-hop was also a big catalyst in shaping Furtado's musical appreciation. After high school, she headed to Toronto where she worked at an alarm company by day and experienced the music scene by night. She joined a hip-hop duo tagged Nelstar, and this opportunity led Furtado back to her hip-hop influences of De La Soul and Digable Planets. This also allowed her to get comfortable with writing her own melodies and freestyle rhymes. It was when Furtado cut loose at a local Toronto club where her musical aspirations began to swirl. Brian West and Gerald Eaton, who were of the Canadian funk-pop group the Philosopher Kings, were instantly impressed by her strong sense of performing and asked to produce her demo. During those sessions, Furtado created some of the moving work which landed on her debut for Dreamworks; these solid collaborations led to the pertinent introduction of Nelly Furtado and the critical acclaim of her debut *Whoa Nelly!*, released in fall 2000. *—MacKenzie Wilson*

• **Whoa, Nelly!** / Oct. 24, 2000 / DreamWorks ✦✦✦✦

Nelly Furtado's *Whoa, Nelly!* is one of those albums that's designed to be a surprising, precocious debut—the kind of record that's meant to make a listener exclaim, well, "whoa nelly" upon the first spin. From that first play, it's evident that Furtado is indeed an audacious songwriter, not at all hesitant to bare her emotions, tackle winding melodies, and bend boundaries to the point that much of the record sounds like folk-pop tinged with bossa nova and backed by a production designed for TLC. Clearly, this is a musician with big, serious ambitions, a notion that is supported not only by her naked lyrics but especially by her singing. Furtado is a restless vocalist, skitting and scatting with abandon, spitting out rapid repetitions, bending notes, and frequently indulging in miasmas. This, more than anything, makes her a bit of an acquired taste, since her relentless vocalizing can obscure hooks that are nevertheless there. Once you appreciate (or grow to understand) her quirks, *Whoa, Nelly!* unfolds as a rewarding, promising debut, albeit one with its flaws. True, most of those flaws arise from its naïveté. You either choose to be annoyed by these quirks or become charmed by them, realizing it's a first album, and savoring the talent that's apparent on much of the album. Many of her blends of pop, folk, dance, and Latin are beguiling; she has a knack for strong pop hooks; her lyrical imagery can be evocative; she has a sly sense of humor; and, when she doesn't get carried away, she's an inventive, endearingly eccentric vocalist. These are the things that endure after that first slightly bewildering spin of *Whoa, Nelly!* and those are the things that make you wonder where she goes from here. *—Stephen Thomas Erlewine*

Billy Fury

b. Apr. 17, 1941, Liverpool, England, **d.** Jan. 28, 1983

Vocals / Early British Pop/Rock, Rock & Roll

Billy Fury was the most prodigiously talented and fondly remembered of his generation of British rock & roll singers, a songwriter of considerable ability and a decent actor as well. He was born Ronald Wycherley in Liverpool, and was discovered singing backstage at a concert. Fury's recording career began early in 1959; he revealed himself capable of dark, brooding, intensely sexual performances, but also of gentle, vulnerable ballads. Coupled with his good looks, he became a major star in short order. After a string of hit singles, Fury cut his debut album, *The Sound of Fury*, in early 1960; it was the best rock & roll platter to come out of England up to that time. Fury's early-'60s recordings moved toward a more sophisticated pop-rock sound. 1961's orchestrated "Halfway to Paradise" began his brief assault on the top of the charts, followed by two more Top Five hits, "Jealousy" and "I'd Never Find Another You." By 1962, Fury was the top rock & roll attraction in England; only the Beatles ended his dominance. He got a television show in late 1964, but by then his records seldom charted better than the mid-20s; additionally, Fury's health began to deteriorate. In 1966, he signed a five-year contract with Parlophone Records, during which he would see some very modest success. Fury underwent heart surgery in 1970 and another in 1971, and resumed performing the following year. A 1976 heart operation brought an end to Fury's musical career, except for occasional recording and television appearances. In 1982, Fury collapsed and nearly died while working on his farm. He went back on tour that summer and managed to place two singles on the English charts, but on January 27, 1983, he was found unconscious in his home, and died that same day in hospital. *—Bruce Eder*

We Want Billy!/Billy / 1963 / BGO ✦✦

The Billy Fury Story / 1977 / Decca ✦✦✦

Fury has been repackaged ad infinitum in the U.K. This double LP is one of the better sets to pick up if you still prefer vinyl, including the entirety of his 1960 album *The Sound of Fury* and various singles from 1958 to 1965. *The Sound of Fury* is respectable rockabilly-inspired material; the singles are largely faithful, forgettable covers of American rock and pop hits, the moody 1960 ballad "Wondrous Place" and the brassy pop of 1965's "In Thoughts of You" (his final British Top Ten hit) being standouts. *—Richie Unterberger*

Sound of Fury Plus 10 / 1988 / PolyGram ✦✦✦✦✦

The best rock album recorded in England before the rise of the Beatles (Andy White, the guest drummer on "Love Me Do," plays the skins on this, too). A hard-rocking gem driven by Fury's powerful voice and Joe Brown's superb guitar. This reissue has ten bonus tracks. *—Bruce Eder*

40th Anniversary Anthology / 1998 / Deram ✦✦✦✦✦

The idea behind this ultimately very persuasive two-CD, 63-song anthology is a good one, and short of a Billy Fury box set, it was probably the way to go, albeit with a few flaws—the producers admit that they were unable to include any tracks off of what they describe as his most representative album, the live *We Want Billy*. All of the singles, however—even the very attractive flop records—are here, along with the better B-sides, which are augmented by album, EP, and movie tracks and four previously unissued songs from 1963 to 1966. All have been transferred from the original session tapes, which is the first stereo appearance of some songs, and the first CD appearance of the original mono versions of others. Even the softer pop-type numbers stay within a certain range of softer rock acceptability, and some of it is first-rate hard rock & roll, on which Fury and the backing group the Four Jays sound like nothing less than Buddy Holly. His subsequent material, from the early 1960s, does veer into teen-pop, though he's a good enough singer to keep most of it interesting amid the swirling strings and soaring female choruses. By the end of 1963, Fury was again toughening up his sound, getting bluesy and trying to come to terms with the Liverpool sound embodied by the Beatles. Still, the record label found it easier to sell Fury as a pop-rock crooner, and the public found him easier to hear in that vein. The second disc in this collection shows Fury trying to balance his repertory between that brand of pop/rock and blues. His last chart records of the 1960s show him stepping away completely from rock & roll, although he still cut decent (and better than decent) tracks in a rock vein around them. The set closes with two very good ballads which were buried so deeply in the vaults that they didn't even have songwriting credits attached to them. (British import) *—Bruce Eder*

• **The Sound of Fury: 40th Anniversary** / Jun. 2000 / Decca ✦✦✦✦✦

The Sound of Fury was the best rock & roll album to come out of England's original beat boom of the late '50s, and it was a singular achievement for its artist, Billy Fury, who wrote every song on the 10" LP. A singer of extraordinary power and sensitivity, the Liverpool-born Fury was the closest thing to Elvis Presley that England produced. The record was a miraculous piece of rock & roll, ten hard rocking songs that could've passed for Memphis originals. "My Advice," "Turn My Back on You," "Don't Say It's Over," "Since You've Been Gone," and "It's You I Need" could stand next to the best work that Elvis Presley cut between 1955 and 1957, running that gamut from hot rockabilly blow-outs to hard white blues. The 40th Anniversary reissue is on two CDs, the first of which contains the mono mix of the original 22-minute 10" LP, and the second of which has stereo masters of nine of the ten original tracks, along with the inexplicably failed single "My Christmas Prayer" and four B-sides. The sound throughout is impeccable, but so was the quality of the old *Sound of Fury + 10* CD from 1988; what sets this apart are those bonus cuts and the booklet, which contains the best account ever given of the recording sessions that led to this extraordinary album. *—Bruce Eder*

Future Bible Heroes

Indie Rock, Lo-Fi

The Future Bible Heroes are one of several lo-fi projects headed by vocalist/keyboardist/songwriter Stephen Merritt (others include Magnetic Fields and the 6ths). 1997's *Memories of Love* featured songwriting and production contributions from Chris Ewen and vocals by longtime Merritt collaborator Claudia Gonson. —*Steve Huey*

Memories of Love / May 20, 1997 / Slow River ♦♦♦♦♦

The lyric sheet for *Memories of Love* is composed of a variety of wacky puzzles—anagrams, cryptograms, jumbles and the like—that you need to solve to get to the words. This sets the tone for the entire album—a playful collection of puzzlers that's more fun than the Sunday crossword. Stephin Merritt has a facility for twisting clichés and hackneyed images into delightful new shapes. This—along with his inherent tunefulness—puts him in the same league as songwriters like Robyn Hitchcock and Elvis Costello. "Death Opens a Boutique" is a case in point. It recounts the tale of a specialty shop that sells dangerous commodities such as poison, Black Plague, and socialism to universal acclaim: "There was no reason to exist if you weren't on the mailing list." Merritt and Claudia Gonson share vocal duties, Gonson with her breathy and delicate chords giving perfect counterpoint to Merritt's dour delivery. And Merritt works with Christopher Ewen, formerly of Figures on a Beach, to create musical soundscapes that seamlessly blend electronics with acoustic instruments that have been treated almost to the point of being non-recognizable. The resulting tunes are surprisingly organic and, above all, catchy. —*Michael Jourdan*

G. Love & Special Sauce

f. 1992, Philadelphia, PA

Alternative Rap, Post-Grunge, Indie Rock, Alternative Pop/Rock

G. Love & Special Sauce is a trio from Philadelphia, PA. Their laid-back, sloppy blues sound is quite unique, as it encompasses the sound/production of classic R&B and recent rap artists (the Beastie Boys, in particular). The group—G. Love (real name: Garrett Dutton) on guitar/vocals/harmonica, Jeff Clemens on drums, and Jim Prescott on upright bass—released their self-titled debut in 1994 on Okeh/Epic. It received enthusiastic reviews and nearly went gold on the strength of the MTV-spun video for "Cold Beverage." The group toured heavily, also landing a subsequent spot on the H.O.R.D.E. tour, and found a receptive young audience. They followed up this success with the more mature *Coast to Coast Motel* in 1995. Although it didn't sell as well as the debut, it was definitely a stronger album. On tour, the group nearly broke up due to bickering over finances. They decided to take a break from each other, while G. Love worked on a new album with three different bands (All Fellas Band, Philly Cartel, and King's Court) and special guest Dr. John. Soon, though, G. Love & Special Sauce made amends, and the next album featured Special Sauce plus combinations of the three other groups. *Yeah, It's That Easy* was released in October of 1997, and it turned out to be a soul-inflected effort, more similar to the debut than their second album. G. Love & Special Sauce soon embarked on another world tour, returning in 1999 with *Philadelphonic. Electric Mile*, issued in spring 2001, depicted another sultry and provocative mix from G. Love. —*Greg Prato*

G. Love & Special Sauce / 1994 / Epic/OKeh ♦♦♦

Although this is G. Love & Special Sauce's most popular album (approaching gold status), it is not their best. Although there are quite a few musical surprises, the overall sound and quality of the compositions are neither as focused nor as rewarding as future releases would be. "Cold Beverage" became the band's signature tune and a fan favorite, featuring lighthearted jive lyrics and funky musical accompaniment, and its popular MTV video putting them on the map. "This Ain't Living" is a precursor to the comforting Philly soul style that would be explored more thoroughly on 1997's *Yeah, It's That Easy*. "Town to Town" adds variety to the album with its slow-as-molasses blues style. Most of the other tracks tend to blend into each other after awhile, because of their similar sound and feel ("Rhyme for the Summertime," "Shooting Hoops," etc.). Even with its mishaps, G. Love & Special Sauce's debut serves as the musical foundation on which the group would build their future sound. —*Greg Prato*

● Coast to Coast Motel / Sep. 19, 1995 / Epic/OKeh ♦♦♦♦

Although not as commercially successful as their self-titled debut, *Coast to Coast Motel* is a definite improvement. The band keeps their hip-hop influence (much more prevalent on the debut) in check here, concentrating more on creating a mighty instrumental groove. It's also more of a traditional rock & roll approach for the band, with the results quite often being successful. The opening "Sweet Sugar Mama" is bass-driven and funky; other highlights include the smooth "Nancy," the uplifting "Chains #3," and the startling Led Zeppelin attack (musically, anyway) of "Small Fish." "Kiss and Tell" is an obvious attempt at a hit single, while some may consider the lyrics to "Soda Pop" a bit too foolish. As mentioned earlier, however, the group achieves some great, groovy interplay which can easily suck the listener in. Jimmy Prescott's upright bass playing and Jeff Clemens' drumming are tight and locked together, as G. Love adds his scratchy blues guitar on top. These guys have found the groove. —*Greg Prato*

Yeah, It's That Easy / Oct. 28, 1997 / Epic/OKeh ♦♦♦♦

On G. Love's third release, he's joined by his trusty band, Special Sauce, as well as combinations of three others: The All Fellas Band, Philly Cartel, and King's Court. The reason for the joint effort was that prior to the writing/recording of *Yeah, It's That Easy*, the group split up. G. Love soldiered on with the three other bands, but there was a reconciliation with Special Sauce during the album's recording. Hence, others (including the legendary Dr. John on piano and organ) join in with Special Sauce. The group sheds its raw rock & roll vibe, gloriously present on 1995's *Coast to Coast Motel*, and replaces it with the soothing sounds of early-'70s Philly soul. The album's approach resembles their 1994 self-titled debut more than their last release, which seems like a step back for the group. Still, the band presents plenty of compositions worthy of the G. Love & Special Sauce name, and there is more consistency and maturity with the lyrics, which deal with such heavy topics as drug abuse and senseless violence, among other things. One of the best songs, "You Shall See," sports a tribal feel, with the drums and guitar playing together percussively. And "Stepping Stones," "Lay Down the Law," and "Take You There" do a good job of introducing the listener to the band's new soul-oriented approach. The words to "I-76" are about G. Love's hometown of Philadelphia, and the title track preaches harmony between races. A solid album, but not quite as satisfying as their last. Now if the band

could just mix the groove-laden music of their second album with the thoughtful lyrics of this record… —*Greg Prato*

Philadelphonic / Aug. 3, 1999 / OKeh/550 Music ♦♦♦

The title of G. Love & Special Sauce's fourth album illustrates their desire to play up their Philadelphia roots, emphasizing classic Philly soul along with their blues-rap melange. *Philadelphonic* isn't entirely unsuccessful on that front, either. The group's laid-back, groove-oriented sound benefits from the sophisticated, sultry sound of Philly soul, as the single "Rodeo Clowns" illustrates. The problem is, G. Love & Special Sauce still winds up sacrificing songs for groove and feel. That wouldn't be so bad if *Philadelphonic* was simply a series of jams, but they continue to write material that feels like songs but never gels. They turn out to be vehicles for jams and half-hearted, muttered raps, neither of which provide hooks or memorable turns of phrase. That doesn't mean *Philadelphonic* doesn't sound good, since the group does have a way with a groove—it just never really rises above the level of a groove-jam album. —*Stephen Thomas Erlewine*

The Electric Mile / Apr. 24, 2001 / OKeh/550 Music ♦♦♦

Like G. Love & Special Sauce's previous albums, *The Electric Mile* isn't easy to categorize. Is it alternative rock, psychedelic rock, retro-soul, funk, or hip-hop? Actually, this diverse, unpredictable CD is a combination of those things—and the group also shows its appreciation of reggae, blues, and folk. True to form, vocalist G. Love and his colleagues keep things unpredictable; you never know from one song to the next if they will tend to favor retro-soul ("Night of the Living Dead"), hip-hop ("Parasite," "Electric Mile"), folk-rock ("Sara's Song"), psychedelic blues-rock ("Poison"), or reggae ("Unified"). And the impressive thing is that G. Love can go in so many different directions and never fail to sound distinctive, which is something he has in common with Prince and David Bowie. But while *The Electric Mile* (which is G. Love's fifth album) has more plusses than minuses, it isn't perfect. A few of the tunes sound unfocused, and not everything that G. Love & Special Sauce try is successful—occasionally, a song will miss its mark. But more often than not, the trio's risk-taking pays off on this generally rewarding, if imperfect, CD. —*Alex Henderson*

Peter Gabriel

b. Feb. 13, 1950, London, England

Producer, Vocals, Keyboards, Percussion, Flute, Synthesizer / College Rock, Album Rock, Pop/Rock, Prog Rock/Art Rock

As the leader of Genesis in the early '70s, Peter Gabriel helped move progressive rock to new levels of theatricality. In his solo career, Gabriel was no less ambitious, but he was more subtle in his methods. With his first eponymous solo album in 1977, he began exploring darker, more cerebral territory, incorporating avant-garde, electronic, and world-beat influences into his music. The record, as well as its two similarly titled successors, established Gabriel as a critically acclaimed cult artist, and with 1982's *Security*, he began to move into the mainstream; "Shock the Monkey" became his first Top 40 hit, paving the way for his multi-platinum breakthrough *So* in 1986. Accompanied by a series of groundbreaking videos and the number one single "Sledgehammer," *So* became a multi-platinum hit, and Gabriel became an international star. Instead of capitalizing on his sudden success, he began to explore other interests, including recording soundtracks and running his company Real World. By the time he returned to pop with 1992's *Us*, his mass audience had faded away, and he spent the remainder of the '90s working on multimedia projects for Real World. —*Stephen Thomas Erlewine*

Peter Gabriel [1] / 1977 / Atco ♦♦♦♦♦

Peter Gabriel tells why he left Genesis in "Solsbury Hill," the key track on his 1977 solo debut. Majestically opening with an acoustic guitar, the song finds Gabriel's talents gelling, as the words and music feed off each other, turning into true poetry. It stands out dramatically on this record, not because the music doesn't work, but because it brilliantly illustrates why Gabriel had to fly on his own. Though this is undeniably the work of the same man behind *The Lamb Lies Down on Broadway*, he's turned his artiness inward, making his music coiled, dense, vibrant. There is still some excess, naturally, yet it's the sound of a musician unleashed, finally able to bend the rules as he wishes. That means there are less atmospheric instrumental sections, as there were on his last few records with Genesis, but unhinged bizarreness in the arrangements, compositions, and productions, as the opener "Morbund the Burgermeister" vividly illustrates. He also has turned sleeker, sexier, capable of turning out a surging rocker of "Modern Love." If there is any problem with *Peter Gabriel*, it's that Gabriel is trying too hard to show the range of his talents, thereby stumbling occasionally with the doo wop-to-cabaret "Excuse Me" or the cocktail jazz of "Waiting for the Big One" (or, the lyric "you've got me cookin'/I'm a hard-boiled egg" on "Humdrum"). Still, much of the record teems with invigorating energy (as on "Slowburn," or the orchestral-disco pulse of "Down the Dolce Vita"), and the closer

"Here Comes the Flood" burns with an anthemic intensity that would later become his signature in the '80s. Yes, it's an imperfect album, but that's a byproduct of Gabriel's welcome risk-taking—the very thing that makes the album work, overall. *—Stephen Thomas Erlewine*

Peter Gabriel [2] / 1978 / Atco ✦✦✦

The pairing sounds ideal—the former front man of Genesis, as produced by the leading light of King Crimson. Unfortunately, Peter Gabriel's second album (like his first, eponymous) fails to meet those grandiose expectations, even though it seems to at first. "On the Air" and "D.I.Y." are stunning slices of modern rock circa 1978, bubbling with synths, insistent rhythms, and polished processed guitars, all enclosed in a streamlined production that nevertheless sounds as large as a stadium. Then, things begin to drift, at first in a pleasant way ("A Wonderful Day in a One-Way World" is surprisingly nimble), but by the end, it all seems a little formless. It's not that the music is overly challenging—it's that the record is unfocused. There are great moments scattered throughout the record, yet it never captivates, either through intoxicating, messy creativity (as he did on his debut) or through cohesion (the way the third *Peter Gabriel* album, two years later, would). Certain songs work well on their own—not just the opening numbers, but the mini-epic "White Shadow," the tight "Animal Magic," the tense yet catchy "Perspective," the reflective closer "Home Sweet Home"—yet for all the tracks that work, they never work well together. Ironically, it holds together a bit better than its predecessor, yet it never reaches the brilliant heights of that record. In short, it's a transitional effort that's well worth the time of serious listeners, even it's still somewhat unsatisfying. *—Stephen Thomas Erlewine*

★ Peter Gabriel [3] / 1980 / Geffen ✦✦✦✦✦

Generally regarded as Peter Gabriel's finest record, his third eponymous album finds him coming into his own, crafting an album that's artier, stronger, more song oriented than before. Consider its ominous opener, the controlled menace of "Intruder." He's never found such a scary sound, yet it's a sexy scare, one that is undeniably alluring, and he keeps this going throughout the record. For an album so popular, it's remarkably bleak, chilly, and dark—even radio favorites like "I Don't Remember" and "Games Without Frontiers" are hardly cheerful, spiked with paranoia and suspicion, insulated in introspection. For the first time, Gabriel has found the sound to match his themes, plus the songs to articulate his themes. Each aspect of the album works, feeding off each other, creating a romantically gloomy, appealingly arty masterpiece. It's the kind of record where you remember the details in the production as much as the hooks or the songs, which isn't to say that it's all surface—it's just that the surface means as much as the songs, since it articulates the emotions as well as Gabriel's cubist lyrics and impassioned voice. He wound up having albums that sold more, or generated bigger hits, but this third *Peter Gabriel* album remains his masterpiece. *—Stephen Thomas Erlewine*

Security / 1982 / Geffen ✦✦✦

Security—which was titled *Peter Gabriel* everywhere outside of the U.S.—continues where the third Gabriel album left off, sharing some of the same dense production and sense of cohesion, yet lightening the atmosphere and expanding the sonic palette somewhat. The gloom that permeates the third album has been alleviated and while this is still decidedly somber and serious music, it has a brighter feel, partially derived from Gabriel's dabbling in African and Latin rhythms. These are generally used as tonal coloring, enhancing the synthesizers that form the basic musical bed of the record, since much of this is mood music (for want of a better word). *Security* flows easily and enticingly, with certain songs—the eerie "San Jacinto," "I Have the Touch," "Shock the Monkey"—arising from the wash of sound. That's not to say that the rest of the album is bland easy listening—it's designed this way, to have certain songs deliver greater impact than the rest. As such, it demands close attention to appreciate tone poems like "The Family and the Fishing Net," "Lay Your Hands on Me," and "Wallflower"—and not all of them reward such intensive listening. Even with its faults, *Security* remains a powerful listen, one of the better records in Gabriel's catalog, proving that he is becoming a master of tone, style, and substance, and how each part of the record enhances the other. *—Stephen Thomas Erlewine*

Plays Live / 1983 / Geffen ✦✦✦

Released after *Security* brought Peter Gabriel a gold record and Top 40 hit, the double-album *Plays Live* summarizes his first four solo albums quite well. Though these performances aren't as fearless as the ones that accompanied his first solo tours, they are surging and tight. Gabriel is a consummate performer and even if the tapes were slightly cleaned up in the studio, his passion is apparent throughout the record. It's a very good live album, but it really is only necessary for die-hard fans. *—Stephen Thomas Erlewine*

Birdy / 1985 / Geffen ✦✦✦✦

An intriguing film score created by Gabriel for a film by Alan Parker. Gabriel utilized both existing material (remixing, editing, and adding to as needed, after stripping away the vocal material) and newly recorded pieces. The result was both familiar and different as a result, an album with some haunting passages that demand repeat play. *—Steven McDonald*

So / 1986 / Geffen ✦✦✦✦

Peter Gabriel introduced his fifth studio album *So* with "Sledgehammer," an Otis Redding-inspired soul-pop raver that was easily his catchiest, happiest single to date. Needless to say, it was also his most accessible, and, in that sense it was a good introduction to *So*, the catchiest, happiest record he ever cut. "Sledgehammer" propelled the record toward blockbuster status, and Gabriel had enough songs with single potential to keep it there. There was "Big Time," another colorful dance number; "Don't Give Up," a moving duet with Kate Bush; "Red Rain," a stately anthem popular on album rock radio; and "In Your Eyes," Gabriel's greatest love song which achieved genuine classic status after being featured in Cameron Crowe's classic, *Say Anything*. These all illustrated the strengths of

the album: Gabriel's increased melodicism and ability to blend African music, jangly pop, and soul into his moody art rock. Apart from these singles, plus the urgent "That Voice Again," the rest of the record is as quiet as the album tracks of *Security*. The difference is, the singles on that record were part of the overall fabric; here, the singles *are* the fabric, which can make the album seem top-heavy (a fault of many blockbuster albums, particularly those of the mid-'80s). Even so, those songs are so strong, finding Gabriel in a new-found confidence and accessibility, that it's hard not to be won over by them, even if *So* doesn't develop the unity of its two predecessors. *—Stephen Thomas Erlewine*

Passion / Jun. 1989 / Geffen ✦✦✦✦

Passion is in actuality Peter Gabriel's soundtrack to the Martin Scorsese film *The Last Temptation of Christ*, retitled as a result of legal barriers; regardless of its name, however, there's no mistaking the record's stirring power. Like much of Gabriel's solo work, the album is a product of his continuing fascination with world music, which he employs here to create an exceptionally beautiful and atmospheric tapestry of sound perfectly evocative of the film's resonant spiritual drama; inspired by field recordings collected in areas as diverse as Turkey, Senegal, and Egypt, *Passion* achieves a cumulative effect clearly Middle Eastern in origin, yet its brilliant fusion of ancient and modern musics ultimately transcends both geography and time. Remarkably dramatic, even visual, it is not only Gabriel's best film work but deserving of serious consideration as his finest music of any kind; equally worthwhile is *Passion: Sources*, which assembles the original native recordings which served as his creative launching pad. *—Jason Ankeny*

Shaking the Tree: Sixteen Golden Greats / Dec. 1990 / Geffen ✦✦✦✦

Greatest-hits albums are a traditional way of buying time for artists between albums. Peter Gabriel's, entitled *Shaking the Tree: Sixteen Golden Greats*, arrived in December of 1990, as he was toiling away at the follow-up to his smash *So*, which was four years old at that point. As greatest-hits albums go, it's pretty good, containing all the hits, plus an effective re-recording of "Here Comes the Flood" and a good new song in the form of the title track. While the sequencing may leave something to be desired—it is neither chronological, nor as supple as a good mix tape—it does contain nearly everything a casual fan could want (nothing from the second album, though; both "On the Air" or "D.I.Y." would have been nice additions), making it an effective sampler. *—Stephen Thomas Erlewine*

Us / Sep. 29, 1992 / Geffen ✦✦✦

Six years after earning his first blockbuster, Peter Gabriel finally delivered *Us*, his sequel to *So*. Clearly, that great span of time indicates that Gabriel was obsessive in crafting the album, and *Us* bears the sound of endless hours in the studio. It's not just that the production is pristine, clean, and immaculate, it's that the music is, with only a handful of exceptions (namely, the "Sledgehammer" rewrite "Steam" and the fellatio ode "Kiss That Frog"), remarkably subtle and shaded. It's also not a coincidence that *Us* is, as Gabriel says in his liner notes, "about relationships," since the exquisitely textured music lets him expose his soul, albeit in a typically obtuse way. Since the music is so muted, it's no surprise that the album failed to capture a mass audience the way *So* did, but it's foolish to expect anyone but serious fans to unravel an album this deliberate. Gabriel is as adventurous as ever, yet he is relentlessly sober about his experiments, burying exotic sounds and percussion underneath crawling tempos measured atmospherics—this is tastefully two-toned music, assembled by a consummate craftsman who became too immersed in detail to make anything but an insular, introspective work. Some gems are easier to unearth than others—"Digging in the Dirt" has an insistent pulse, "Blood of Eden" and "Come Talk to Me" are quite beautiful, "Secret World" is quietly anthemic—yet, given enough time, the record's understated approach and reflection becomes its most attractive element. But it takes a lot of spins and patience to get to that point, since this is an album he made for himself, and only those dedicated to the artist will have the patience to decode it. *—Stephen Thomas Erlewine*

Revisited / Nov. 10, 1992 / Atlantic ✦✦✦

A good but useless compilation of Peter Gabriel's first two solo albums. *Revisited* contains some wonderful music, but fans would be better served by the individual albums, and casual fans will prefer *Shaking the Tree*, which has all of his big hits, including material featured here. *—Stephen Thomas Erlewine*

Secret World Live / Sep. 13, 1994 / Geffen ✦✦

Serge Gainsbourg (Lucien Ginzburg)

b. Apr. 2, 1928, Paris, France, d. Mar. 2, 1991, Paris, France
Vocals, Piano, Guitar / French Rock, Baroque Pop, Foreign Language Rock, French Pop, Cabaret, Jazz-Pop

Serge Gainsbourg was the dirty old man of popular music; a French singer/songwriter and provocateur notorious for his voracious appetite for alcohol, cigarettes, and women, his scandalous, taboo-shattering output made him a legend in Europe but only a cult figure in America. Gainsbourg initially wanted only to carve out a niche as a composer and producer, though he began recording in 1958 and followed with strong, jazz-inflected efforts like 1961's *L'Etonnant Serge Gainsbourg* and 1964's *Gainsbourg Confidentiel*. Still, his songwriting proved more successful than his performing until the late '60s, when he befriended the actress Brigitte Bardot. With Bardot as his muse, Gainsbourg's lushly-arranged music suddenly became erotic and delirious. His affair with Bardot was brief, but its effects were irrevocable: after he became involved with constant companion Jane Birkin, they recorded the 1969 duet "Je T'Aime...Moi Non Plus." Banned in many corners of the globe, it reached the top of the charts throughout Europe and grew in stature to become an underground classic. Gainsbourg returned in 1971 with *Histoire de Melody Nelson*, a dark, complex song cycle which signalled his increasing alienation from modern culture; his his work gradually grew more esoteric, inflammatory, and outrageous with each passing release. He remained an imposing and controversial figure throughout

Europe, where he was both vilified and celebrated for his shocking behavior. Along with his pop music oeuvre, Gainsbourg scored a number of films, and also directed and appeared in a handful of features. He died on March 2, 1991. *—Jason Ankeny*

Histoire de Melody Nelson / 1971 / Polydor ♦♦♦♦♦

You don't need to speak a word of French to understand *Histoire de Melody Nelson*—one need only to look at the front cover (with its nearly pornographic portrait of a half-naked nymphet clutching a rag doll) or hear the lechery virtually dripping from Serge Gainsbourg's sleazily seductive voice to realize that this is the record your mother always warned you about, a masterpiece of perversion and corruption. A concept record exploring the story of—and Gainsbourg's lust for—the titular teen heroine, *Histoire de Melody Nelson* is arguably his most coherent and perfectly realized studio album, with the lush arrangements which characterize the majority of his work often mixed here with funky rhythm lines which underscore the musky allure of the music; perhaps best described as a dirty old bastard's attempt to make his own R&B love-man's record along the lines of a *Let's Get It On* (itself still two years away from release), it's by turns fascinating and repellent, hilarious and grim, but never dull—which, in Gainsbourg's world, would be the ultimate (and quite possibly the only) sin. *—Jason Ankeny*

● **Comic Strip** / Feb. 11, 1997 / Polydor ♦♦♦♦♦

Serge Gainsbourg's remarkable pop hits are best represented on *Comic Strip*, an indispensable set collecting 20 tracks recorded between 1966 and 1969. In addition to the lushly erotic "Je T'Aime...Moi Non Plus"—Gainsbourg's best-known record—*Comic Strip* includes the title track and "Bonnie and Clyde," his collaborations with Brigitte Bardot, as well as "Initials B.B.," a sweeping paean to his duet partner, "the most beautiful woman on earth." Other highlights include "Chatterton" (a bouncy celebration of suicide), "Torrey Canyon" (a prescient warning against threats to the environment), and the self-explanatory "Soixante Neuf Annee Erotique" ("69 Erotic Year"). *—Jason Ankeny*

Couleur Café / Feb. 11, 1997 / Polydor ♦♦♦♦

A French craze for exotic rhythms and dances like the cha-cha and the mambo inspired Serge Gainsbourg to explore Latin and Caribbean rhythms at the outset of his career; *Couleur Cafe* collects 20 of these beat-driven recordings, which span from 1959 to work from as late as 1974. More than his jazz performances of the same period, the earliest songs on the set presage the direction taken on his pop records; in addition to the distinctly snotty attitude which pervades cuts like "Laissez-Moi Tranquille" and "L'Anthracite," the nine tracks taken from the 1964 recording *Gainsbourg Percussions* innovatively embrace African rhythms while focusing on the thematic concerns (specifically cigarettes, American culture and young girls) of his seminal later work. *—Jason Ankeny*

Du Jazz Dans Le Ravin / Feb. 11, 1997 / Polydor ♦♦♦♦

While Serge Gainsbourg rose to infamy as a pop star, he actually got his start playing jazz; the 20-track collection *Du Jazz Dans le Ravin* samples his early work from between 1958 and 1964, at which point he chose to "go commercial." While neither as imaginative nor as distinctive as his pop material, Gainsbourg's jazz sides clearly presage his future work; bright and colorful, cuts like "Requiem Pour un Twisteur" and "Ce Mortel Ennui" offer much of the same attitude and outlook which defined his later, more provocative music. *—Jason Ankeny*

Galaxie 500

f. 1986, Boston, MA, **db.** 1991

College Rock, Indie Pop, Slowcore, Dream Pop, Indie Rock, Shoegazing, Alternative Pop/Rock

Though criminally overlooked in their own lifetime, Galaxie 500 later emerged as one of the pivotal underground groups of the post-punk era; dreamy and enigmatic, their minimalist dirges presaged the rise of both the shoegazer and slowcore movements of the 1990s. The group formed in Boston, MA in 1986 and comprised vocalist/guitarist Dean Wareham, bassist Naomi Yang, and drummer Damon Krukowski. Named after a friend's car, Galaxie 500 began performing live throughout Boston and New York before recording a three-song demo tape which they sent to Shimmy Disc honcho Kramer, who agreed to become the trio's producer. After bowing in early 1988 with the singles "Tugboat" and "Oblivious," they issued their full-length debut, *Today*, which highlighted the group's distinct, evolving sound pitting Wareham's eerie, plaintive tenor, elliptical songs and slow-motion guitar textures against Yang's warm, fluid bass lines and Krukowski's lean drumming. After signing to the U.S. branch of Rough Trade, Galaxie 500 issued its defining moment, 1989's evocative *On Fire*, a remarkably assured and rich record including the superb singles "Blue Thunder" and "When Will You Come Home." The group returned in 1990 with *This Is Our Music*; following a subsequent tour, Galaxie 500 disbanded after Wareham phoned Yang and Krukowski to say he was quitting the group. A few months later, Wareham formed his new band, Luna, while Krukowski and Yang later recorded as Damon and Naomi. *—Jason Ankeny*

Today / 1988 / Rykodisc ♦♦♦♦

Galaxie 500's debut doesn't merely live up to the sweet promise of the band's debut single "Tugboat," *Today*'s final song, but almost without trying becomes its own gently powerful touchstone. While the influences are clear—third album Velvet Underground, early non-dance New Order, psychedelic haze and fuzz thanks to the reverb Kramer piled on as producer—the resulting brew easily stands on its own. By never feeling the need to conventionally rock out, the Krukowski/Yang rhythm section comes up with its own brand of intensity. Sometimes the two are persistently skipping along without Krukowski having to bash the hell out of the drums (the downright delightful "Oblivious" is a good example), other times they simply play it soft and slow. Meanwhile, Wareham's low-key chiming and slightly lost, forlorn singing, at places wry and whimsical, often achingly sad, forms the perfect counterpoint to the songs' paces, feeling like a gauzy dream. When he comes up with his own brand of electric guitar heroics, it's very much in the Lou Reed and such descendants vein of less being more, setting the moods via strumming and understated but strong soloing. One particular descendant gets honored with a cover version—Jonathan Richman, whose "Don't Let Our Youth Go to Waste" is turned into a deceptively calm epic, with marvelous playing by all three members. It's easier to lose oneself in the flow of the sound rather than worry about any deep meaning, making the stronger images that come to the fore all that more entertaining, like "watching all the people fall to pieces" in "Parking Lot." "Tugboat" itself, meanwhile, remains as wonderful as ever, a cascading confession of love at the expense of everything else, somehow mournful and triumphant all at once. Later CD versions included the "Tugboat" B-side, "King of Spain." *—Ned Raggett*

● **On Fire** / 1989 / Rykodisc ♦♦♦♦♦

Having already made a fine account of themselves on *Today*, the three members of Galaxie 500 got even better with *On Fire*, recording another lovely classic of late '80s rock. As with all the band's work, Kramer once again handles the production, the perfect person to bring out Galaxie 500's particular approach. The combination of his continued use of reverb and the sudden, dramatic shifts in the music—never exploding, just delivering enough of a change—makes for fine results. Consider "Snowstorm," with Krukowski's soft-then-strong drums and Wareham's liquid solo and how they're placed in the mix, leading without dominating. Yang's vocals became more prominent and her bass work more quietly narcotic than before, while Krukowski adds more heft to his playing without running roughshod over everything, even at the band's loudest. Wareham in contrast more or less continues along, his glazed, haunting voice simply a joy to hear, while adding subtle touches in the arrangements—acoustic guitar is often prominent—to contrast his beautifully frazzled soloing. Leadoff track "Blue Thunder" is the most well-known song and deservedly so, another instance of the trio's ability to combine subtle uplift with blissed-out melancholia, building to an inspiring ending. There's more overt variety throughout *On Fire*, from the more direct loner-in-the-crowd sentiments and musical punch of "Strange" to the Yang-sung "Another Day," a chance for her to shine individually before Wareham joins in at the end. Again, a cover makes a nod to past inspirations, with George Harrison being the songwriter of choice; his "Isn't It a Pity" closes out the album wonderfully, Kramer adding vocals and "cheap organ." Inspired guest appearance—Ralph Carney, Tom Waits' horn player of choice, adding some great tenor sax to the increasing volume and drive of "Decomposing Trees." Later CD pressings included the bonus tracks from the *Blue Thunder* EP. *—Ned Raggett*

This Is Our Music / 1990 / Rykodisc ♦♦♦♦♦

What turned out to be the final Galaxie 500 album was also arguably the band's most accomplished. Not that the earlier records lacked either charm or ability, but right from the charging, chugging start of "Fourth of July," the amazing single and leadoff song from *This Is Our Music* (even including a cheeky Velvet Underground reference from "Candy Says"), the trio here sounds like they could take on anyone. Kramer's production and the use of reverb from past releases all once again contribute to Galaxie 500's magic, while the individual members continue to sound fantastic. Somehow, though, everyone aims higher, Wareham's singing among his finest and his guitar going for the truly epic more than once, Krukowski and Yang even more perfectly in sync than before, often being very bold without losing their intrinsic warmth. From a generally different approach, Galaxie 500 here easily equaled the heights of their U.K. shoegaze contemporaries and often trumped them—"Summertime" in particular is a stunner—while making a lot of contemporary American indie rock seem fairly dull and workaday. The choice of cover version this time out is astonishing—Yoko Ono's "Listen, The Snow Is Falling," with Yang singing beautifully over, initially, Wareham's echoed guitar strums, and Krukowski's barely-there percussion cascade. The switch to a full-band arrangement, far from destroying the song's spell, makes it even more intense and gripping a listen. The subtle touches throughout the album add immeasurably to its magic—the soft ringing bells shimmering through "Hearing Voices," quiet synth on "Spook," and Kramer's self-described "cheap flute" on "Way up High." It all concludes with "King of Spain, Part Two," a reworking of the flip side to "Tugboat"—while it wasn't a planned finale, as an unexpectedly right bookend to a career, it ends both Galaxie 500 and *This Is Our Music* on a perfect note. Later CD versions include a cover of the Velvet Underground's "Here She Comes Now," originally the B-side from "Fourth of July." *—Ned Raggett*

Galaxie 500 / Sep. 24, 1996 / Rykodisc ♦♦♦♦♦

Happily putting the entirety of Galaxie 500's work in one place, this truly appealing box set—Naomi Yang did the overall design, which really looks wonderful—is well worth the price for any hardcore fan. Besides having all three of the original albums—*Today*, *On Fire*, and *This Is Our Music*—each disc includes at least one bonus track and a video, each directed by Sergio Huidor. Rykodisc's usual quality of remastering comes through, not least because the group's regular producer Kramer oversaw it, keeping the sound right where it should be. A further bonus disc—*The Uncollected Galaxie 500*—compiles every last one of the band's other cuts from demos and compilation appearances, along with a slew of unreleased tracks. While an uneven listen, it's still a fine treat, containing many notable numbers. The nuttiest is first—a cover of the Rutles' "Cheese and Onions," tweaking Neil Innes' accomplished Beatles parody track into the trio's own unique style. The Beatles themselves get a similar treatment with a frenetic, speaker-shredding live medley of "Rain" and Jonathan Richman's "Don't Let Our Youth Go to Waste," while the Young Marble Giants' "Final Day" takes a studio bow. Among the band originals are alternate takes of studio cuts, including a great version of "Blue Thunder" with Ralph Carney on sax. As for unheard numbers, "Them," one of the last songs the group recorded, gives a taste where the three might have gone next, with some artful guitar/feedback arrangements suggesting more complex approaches in future. In an interesting contrast, the three songs from the band's original demo tape appear, helping show how Kramer transformed the trio's strong enough work into something much more unique. A booklet with rare photos, recording details, and reminiscences from all three band members completes this truly worthy model of what a box set should be like. *—Ned Raggett*

Copenhagen / Apr. 29, 1997 / Rykodisc ♦♦♦♦
A presumably final punctuation mark on Galaxie 500's work, *Copenhagen*, released in 1997, is actually a recording from the last date of the band's late 1990 European tour, captured for radio broadcast in the Danish capital in front of a vocally appreciative crowd. One main reason to listen in is hearing how the band's studio approach clearly differed from the concert arena—while Kramer handles the live sound, the cocooning web of reverb familiar from the records isn't present here. As a result, the performances have a more direct approach, Wareham's voice a little more naked, his thoughts on emotional connection, and the oddities of life easier to capture. Yang's bass gains in prominence as well, almost more so than Wareham's guitar at points, while Krukowski as always keeps the beat well, adding subtle flourishes and touches as he goes. All this would be mere technical notation if the performance itself wasn't worthy, though, and that it is. Touring for *This Is Our Music* as the trio was, the set list is mostly focused on that, though a fine version of "Decomposing Trees" starts things off. Three of the band's favored covers close the set—Yoko Ono's "Listen, the Snow Is Falling," the Velvet Underground's "Here She Comes Now," and a version of Jonathan Richman's "Don't Let Our Youth Go to Waste" that provides a great final kick. For all the excellence of the show, one can hear a little more than once in Wareham's soloing what Yang and Krukowski later described as his tendency to play the big rock star toward the end of the band's life. It's not bad work, but the cracks were starting to show. Longtime Galaxie 500 fanatic Byron Coley provides the detailed essay in the booklet, a useful history of the group and its influence. *—Ned Raggett*

● **Portable Galaxie 500** / Sep. 29, 1998 / Rykodisc ♦♦♦♦♦

Game Theory

f. 1982, Sacramento, CA, **db.** 1990
College Rock, Jangle Pop, Paisley Underground, Power Pop, Alternative Pop/Rock, American Underground
Game Theory formed on the fringe of the Paisley Underground movement of the early-'80s and though they certainly had a retro-'60 sound with psychedelic leanings, the band owed its greatest debt to the proto-power pop of Big Star. Leader Scott Miller's song craft, distinctive voice (self-described as a "miserable whine"), and intelligent lyrics (often obscure but rarely pretentious) carved a sound that, while firmly rooted in traditional pop, was truly original and defined an era of college rock. The band's first album, *Blaze of Glory*, was a pleasant amalgam of '60s pure pop and the quirkier elements of new wave, but only hinted at the band's potential. In 1985, with the help of producer Mitch Easter, they recorded their first proper album—*Real Nighttime*—for Enigma. With a radically different lineup spearheaded by Miller and Easter, 1986's *Big Shot Chronicles* showed great leaps in quality. Miller seemed to accept the destiny of the band (obscurity) when he created his most excessive, and ultimately most enjoyable album, 1987's *Lolita Nation*, a sprawling double album riddled with experimental sounds and song fragments. They took one more stab at the mainstream with the more accessible *Two Steps From the Middle Ages* in 1988, but its commercial failure led to several more personnel changes including the temporary exit of Miller himself. Miller finally dissolved the band in 1990 to form the similar-sounding, though more ecclectic, Loud Family. *—Chris Woodstra*

Blaze of Glory / 1982 / Alias ♦♦♦
Game Theory's 1982 debut is about as DIY as it gets. *Blaze of Glory* was recorded in leader Scott Miller's old bedroom at his parents' house in Sacramento, CA, and you can just barely hear his mom running the vacuum cleaner downstairs at one point. Not able to afford printing costs for jackets once the records were pressed, the group simply slipped the discs into white plastic garbage bags with a Xeroxed sheet of paper.

Despite the funky homemade feel of the album, *Blaze of Glory* is a clear signpost towards the hyperactively literate art pop of Game Theory's later albums. The songwriting is extremely inconsistent, with a couple of songs, "Stupid Heart" and "Tin Scarecrow," that are just plain terrible, and the overall feel is along the lines of the manic synth-pop of early Devo, or perhaps more overtly, Sacramento new wave legends the Twinkeyz. Yet although *Blaze of Glory* sounds far more dated than any of Game Theory's other records, it has a handful of early gems. The giddy and galloping "Date With an Angel" is one of Miller's sunniest-sounding songs, and the jangly guitar-led arrangement predates the Paisley Underground-influenced sound of 1985's *Real Nighttime*. Even better, the wry collegiate angst of "Bad Year at UCLA" and the stark "It Gives Me Chills" are two of Miller's best early songs, and the jubilant "Sleeping Through Heaven" has remained a fan favorite.

All 12 songs from *Blaze of Glory* ended up on the 1994 compilation *Distortion of Glory*. Re-recorded versions of "Bad Year at UCLA" (with the grammatical mistake in the first verse corrected) and "Sleeping Through Heaven" were released on 1990's *Tinker To Evers To Chance*. *—Stewart Mason*

Real Nighttime / 1985 / Alias ♦♦♦
While Game Theory had released three EPs between 1982 and 1984, their first full-length album, *Real Nighttime*, was where the band truly found their voice on vinyl. With Mitch Easter on board as producer, the band was finally working with a sympathetic craftsman who knew how to make the most of the band's sound, and Scott Miller was maturing into one of the finest and most distinctive pop songwriters in America. While Game Theory's most obvious influence was certainly Big Star (the album even features a cover of "You Can't Have Me" that sounds slightly more deranged than the original), *Real Nighttime*'s loose narrative suggested a mid-'80s smart-pop update of *Pet Sounds*, as it followed a young man from blissful innocence on "24" to crushing romantic defeat on "I Turned Her Away." Always tuneful, and by turns rollicking and heartbreaking, *Real Nighttime* was the album that announced Game Theory as one of the major talents to emerge from California's "Paisley Underground" scene. *—Mark Deming*

Big Shot Chronicles / 1986 / Alias ♦♦♦♦♦
Scott Miller broke in a new Game Theory lineup on *The Big Shot Chronicles* (a revolving-door cast of musicians was something he would get used to over the next decade or so), and if the album lacks the narrative cohesion of the group's first full-length effort, *Real Nighttime*, it's obvious from the album's first cut that the addition of Shelley LaFrenier on keyboards, Suzi Ziegler on bass, and Gil Ray on drums made Game Theory a stronger band in every respect. While Game Theory's attempts to rock out on *Real Nighttime* sometimes sounded a bit tentative, *The Big Shot Chronicles* reveals a band that's equally adept at flexing their muscles ("I've Tried Subtlety" and "Make Any Vows") or easing into a song's subtleties ("Regenisraen" and "Like a Girl Jesus"). As a songwriter, Scott Miller continued to grow ("Erica's Word" and "Don't Look Too Closely" are both smart pop heaven on Earth), and while he's fond of referring to his voice as a "miserable whine," he sure knows how to make it communicate. Finally, Mitch Easter's production guides the record through moody neo-psychedelia and up-tempo hard pop with an equally sure hand; the record sounds just as good as the band plays. A superb set from one of the best (and most underappreciated) bands of the 1980s. *—Mark Deming*

Lolita Nation / 1987 / Enigma ♦♦♦♦♦
Game Theory leader Scott Miller has never made much of a secret of his fondness for Big Star, but while *Real Nighttime* favored the sound of *#1 Record* and *The Big Shot Chronicles* suggested the harder-edged tone of *Radio City*, *Lolita Nation* sounded like Game Theory's variation on the themes of Big Star's masterfully damaged swan song, *Third/Sister Lovers*. Certainly Game Theory's most ambitious album, *Lolita Nation* was a two-LP set that combined some of Miller's most user-friendly power pop with dark, moody ruminations on betrayal, failed love, and mortality, bursts of avant-garde noise, and fragments of unclassifiable studio doodling, all thrown into a sonic Cuisinart through Miller's aggressive use of aural montage. *Lolita Nation* is more than a bit disorienting on first listen, though it finds the band playing at the top of their form on challenging material (new guitarist Donnete Thayer makes an impressive debut), and there are more than a few flat-out brilliant tracks (such as "Chardonnay," "The Waist and the Knees," and "The Real Shelia") alongside such head-scratchers as "Turn Me on Dead Man," "Watch Who You're Calling Space Garbage Meteor Mouth," and the 22nd track (which stubbornly defies titling). Taken as a whole and given time to fully absorb, *Lolita Nation* is probably Game Theory's finest and most impressive album, though it's also the worst place for a beginner to start examining their work. *—Mark Deming*

Two Steps from the Middle Ages / 1988 / Enigma ♦♦♦♦
Many fans of 1987's sprawling and often bizarre masterwork *Lolita Nation* felt that 1988's comparatively concise and straightforward *Two Steps from the Middle Ages* was a step backwards for Scott Miller and company. Listened to on its own merits, however, *Two Steps* is clearly one of Game Theory's finest efforts and an entirely worthy follow-up to *Lolita Nation*. Squeezing that album's love for odd sounds and unexpected musical detours into a 13-song stretch of relatively "normal" pop song structures, this is a musically and lyrically satisfying album with none of the filler that marks earlier records like *The Big Shot Chronicles*. Guitarist Donnette Thayer's helium-pitched harmony vocals are better integrated into the songs than they had been on *Lolita Nation*, and her lead on "Wyoming" is her best vocal performance ever. (It helps that, unlike her wretched contributions to *Lolita Nation*, that album's only flaws, she didn't write the song.) The songs are uniformly terrific, with at least half a dozen all-time Game Theory classics including the opening "Room For One More, Honey"; led by Gil Ray's walloping drums and featuring two intertwining vocal lines on the chorus by Thayer and keyboardist Shelley LaFreniere, this song pulls off the difficult trick of being simultaneously mid-tempo and hyperactive. Other gems include the delightful "Rolling with the Moody Girls," with its "Baker Street"-like sax interjections, and the brilliant "Throwing the Election," chosen as Scott Miller's best song ever in an online fan poll. This turned out to be Game Theory's final album, as Thayer left the group and Ray was seriously injured in a mugging shortly after the album's release, leading to a period of personnel instability that eventually led to the group's dissolution in 1990. It's a shame, as a similarly strong follow-up to *Two Steps From the Middle Ages* could have put Game Theory one step closer to escaping the near-total oblivion they operated in for most of their career. *—Stewart Mason*

● **Tinker to Evers to Chance (Selected Highlights 1982-1989)** / Mar. 1990 / Enigma ♦♦♦♦♦
Scott Miller compiled and annotated this career-spanning retrospective of his band Game Theory, and anyone looking for a convenient introduction to the band's arch and intelligent power pop could hardly do better than to pick this up. *Tinker to Evers to Chance* boasts 22 songs that offer representative selections from the band's four studio albums and three EPs, including their relative "hits" (well, "Erica's Word" and "The Real Shelia" got some college radio airplay and made brief appearances on MTV in the middle of the night), as well as hard-to-find material from their early 12"s. For the completists, Miller also re-recorded two very early Game Theory tracks with the band's final lineup and even reworked "Beach State Rocking" by his pre-Game Theory combo Alternate Learning. A nice mix of obscurities and favorites for the fans, and a revelation for the uninitiated, *Tinker to Evers to Chance* is hardly the only Game Theory album worth owning, but it may well be the best way to go if you're only going to buy one. *—Mark Deming*

Distortion of Glory / 1994 / Alias ♦♦♦
Distortion of Glory is a 1994 CD compilation of all of 1982's *Blaze of Glory* and most of

the two following EPs, 1983's *Pointed Accounts of People You Know* and 1984's Michael Quercio-produced *Distortion*, plus a rare flexidisc track, "Dead Center." *Blaze of Glory* is a clear signpost toward the hyperactively literate art pop of Game Theory's later albums. Scott Miller's songwriting is inconsistent, and the overall feel is along the lines of the herky-jerky synth-pop of early new wave. However, it has a handful of early gems, particularly the wry collegiate angst of "Bad Year at UCLA" and the jubilant "Sleeping Through Heaven." *Pointed Accounts* and *Distortion* are much improved, and each features some stellar material. The heartbreaking "The Red Baron," an anguished acoustic lost-love song leavened by keyboardist Nancy Becker's mocking "Fifty or more" backing vocal on the last chorus (think of the Royal Guardsmen's "Snoopy Versus the Red Baron"), the glorious sci-fi singalong "Nine Lives to Rigel Five" and the thumping "Shark Pretty" (featuring guest lead guitar by former Bowie sideman Earl Slick) are *Distortion*'s highlights, with the sneering rocker "Metal and Glass Exact" and the winsome "Penny Things Won't" supporting *Pointed Accounts*. The freaky opening of the otherwise undistinguished "Dead Center," featuring layered voices, odd sounds and snatches of bandmember interviews, foreshadows the sonic experiments of 1987's classic *Lolita Nation*.

Unfortunately, *Distortion of Glory* stumbles a bit in terms of what it chose to leave out, especially concerning bassist Fred Juhos' material. The sarcastic fake rap of "Kid Convenience" made the cut, but neither of Juhos' other, much better, Game Theory offerings did. Either the haunting "37th Day" or the bitter "I Wanna Get Hit by A Car" (which was actually one of Game Theory's most popular early songs on college radio) would have better commemorated Juhos' tenure in the band. Also, for no apparent reason, Miller's then-wife, Shalini Chatterjee, overdubs vocals and bass on the ghostly "It Gives Me Chills," making it sound oddly out of place amidst its unretouched fellows. Other than those minor flaws, though, *Distortion of Glory* is an essential release for Game Theory fans, making these otherwise impossible to find songs available again. *—Stewart Mason*

Gang of Four

f. 1977, Leeds, England, **db.** 1984

College Rock, Post-Punk, New Wave, Alternative Pop/Rock

Gang of Four produced some of the most exhilarating and lasting music of the early English post-punk era of 1978-1983. Fueled by the fury of punk rock and radical political theory, the group successfully welded the two in an inspired display of polemics and music that addressed the vagaries of life in the modern world (including love and romance) as matters of political inquiry. What made Gang of Four's polemical clang 'n' roll so compelling was that it worked as harsh, bracing, and ultimately liberating rock & roll. Andy Gill didn't play guitar as much as emit thick wads of semi-tuneful distortion, while vocalist Jon King "sang" in a dry, declamatory fashion similar to that of the Fall's Mark E. Smith. The group openly challenged the audience's preconceived notions about rock music, performance, the cult of celebrity, and the nature of politics; in doing so, GOF conveyed rage, confusion, and loss of identity as well as any band of its time. After three consecutive sensational albums, bassist Dave Allen left in 1982 to form the more danceable and less overtly political Shriekback, while the remaining trio recorded the misguided "radical soul/R&B" record *Hard*. After calling it quits in 1984, King and Gill put together a new Gang of Four in the early '90s for two albums, 1991's *Mall* and 1995's *Shrinkwrapped*. *—John Dougan*

★ **Entertainment!** / 1979 / Infinite Zero ♦♦♦♦♦

Entertainment! is one of those records where germs of influence can be traced through many genres and countless bands, both favorably and unfavorably. From groups whose awareness of genealogy spreads wide enough to openly acknowledge Gang of Four's influence (Fugazi, Rage Against the Machine), to those not in touch with their ancestry enough to realize it (rap/metal, some indie rock)—all have appropriated elements of their forefathers' trailblazing contribution. It's vaguely funky rhythmic twitch, its pungent, pointillistic guitar stoccados, and its spoken/shouted vocals have all been picked up by many.

Lyrically, the album was apart from many of the day, and it still is. The band rants at revisionist history in "Not Great Men" ("No weak men in the books at home"), self-serving media and politicians in "I Found That Essence Rare" ("The last thing they'll ever do?/Act in your interest"), and sexual politics in "Damaged Goods" ("You said you're cheap but you're too much"). Though the brilliance of the record thrives on the faster material—especially the febrile first side—a true highlight amongst highlights is the closing "Anthrax," full of barely controlled feedback squalls and moans. It's nearly psychedelic, something post-punk and new wave were never known for. With a slight death rattle and plodding bass rumble, Jon King equates love with disease and admits to feeling "like a beetle on its back." In the background, Gill speaks in monotone of why Gang of Four doesn't do love songs. Subversive records of any ilk don't get any stronger, influential, or exciting than this. [In 1995, *Entertainment!* was reissued on Warner subsidiary Infinite Zero/American, with the *Yellow* EP appended.] *—Andy Kellman*

Solid Gold / May 1981 / Warner Brothers ♦♦♦♦♦

Gang of Four's existence had as much to do with Slave and Chic as it did the Sex Pistols and the Stooges, which is something *Solid Gold* demonstrates more than *Entertainment*. Any smartypants can point out the irony of a band on Warner Bros. railing against systematic tools of control disguised as entertainment media, but Gang of Four were more observational than condescending. True, Jon King and Andy Gill might have been hooting and hollering in a semiviolent and discordant fashion, but they were saying "think about it" more than "you lot are a bunch of mindless puppets." Abrasiveness was a means to grab the listener, and it worked. Reciting *Solid Gold*'s lyrics on a local neighborhood corner might get a couple interested souls to pay attention. It isn't poetry, and it's no fun; most within earshot would just continue power-walking or tune out while buffing the SUV.

Solid Gold has that unholy racket going on beneath the lyrics, an unlikely mutation of catchiness and atonality that made ears perk and (oddly) posteriors shake. With its slightly ironic title, *Solid Gold* is more rhythmically grounded than the fractured nature of *Entertainment!*, a politically charged, more teutonic take on funk. It's a form of release for paranoid accountants. Financial concerns form the basis of the subject matter; the hilarious but realistic "Cheeseburger" is a highlight with its thinly veiled snipe at America: "No classes in the U.S.A./Improve yourself, the choice is yours/Work at your job and make good pay/Make friends, great/Buy them a beer!" This is a nickel less spectacular than the debut, but owning one and not the other would be criminal. [*Solid Gold* was reissued in 1995 on Warner subsidiary Infinite Zero/American, with *Another Day, Another Dollar* appended.] *—Andy Kellman*

Songs of the Free / 1982 / Warner Brothers ♦♦♦

Only within the context of *Entertainment!* and *Solid Gold* does *Songs of the Free* seem truly weak; otherwise, it has its merits and lasting value but doesn't hold up in invention and influence like its predecessors. Clunky rhythms, lumpen tempos, and morbid existentialism dampen some the songs, making the record seem less assertive and defiant. Funk plays more of a definitive role here, defenestrating the frenetics that characterized the earlier records. With bassist Dave Allen out of the fold in Shriekback, the rhythmic chemistry isn't what it used to be. Replacement Sara Lee is excellently skilled, but she doesn't have the rapport with drummer Hugo Burnham that Allen had.

There's a certain dour moodiness apparent in the production, most obvious in Andy Gill's guitar on "Call Me Up"; he's less incisive, used more as an atmospheric and rhythmic device than for the dagger shots he provided before. "I Love a Man in a Uniform" wound up being the band's most well-known song, which is something of a shame. Not weak in any manner, it's just unfortunate that more exciting singles like "At Home He's a Tourist" and "Damaged Goods" didn't catch fire. Nonetheless, "Uniform" found its spot down on the disco floor; ironically, odds are pretty good that most didn't realize the lyrical content of the song. With its chorus led by female singers, "Uniform could be mistaken for something similar in subject to "It's Raining Men." Not the case, as the song is laden with just as much irony as Go4's early album titles. Soldiers sexy! Rifles erotic! Amputations—well, the picture is clear. [*Songs of the Free* was reissued in 1995 on Warner subsidiary Infinite Zero/American, with a dub mix of "I Love a Man in Uniform."] *—Andy Kellman*

Hard / 1983 / Warner Brothers ♦♦♦

The final studio LP released prior to the group's 1984 dissolution, *Hard* continues Gang of Four's long-standing tradition of ironic LP titles; this time, however, the joke's on them—produced by Ron and Howard Albert, best known for their work with Crosby, Stills & Nash and Firefall, *Hard* is anything but. The taut, bracing energy of past glories has fallen by the wayside, replaced by morose, uninspired dirges; a strangely apolitical album, even Jon King's lyrics lack bite, and his vocals lack any sense of urgency. *—Jason Ankeny*

At the Palace / 1984 / Mercury ♦♦

Peel Sessions / 1990 / Dutch East India ♦♦♦♦

In later years, some bandmembers claimed that the best Gang of Four album of all was, in fact, this collection of three separate sessions from 1979 and 1981. It's little surprise why—recorded with brisk, blunt immediacy, *Peel Sessions* is both a showcase for the band's sheer power and amazing transformation of funk and punk for its own virulent ends, with all three sessions featuring the full original lineup. Good production from Bob Sargeant, who produced all tracks except the last three, helps immensely, while there's no track repetition at all. A gripping version of "I Found That Essence Rare" begins the collection, Andy Gill's guitar slashing like a vicious weapon and Jon King's vocals getting even more wired and intense as the song continues. As for the Dave Allen/Hugo Burnham rhythm section, it sounds like it could beat down walls. From there, *Peel Sessions* serves up one highlight after another. Also from the first session, "Return the Gift" builds to a powerful climax, King's plaintive call "Please send me evenings and weekends" echoing into the distance, while "At Home's He's a Tourist" is stripped-down aggression at its finest. On the second session, "Natural's Not in It" is the standout, featuring some of Burnham's best drumming ever, while Gill's clipped riff gets a deservedly strong performance. King's singing sends everything over the top, while his work on "Ether" is equally strong, balanced between collapsing quaver, simmering outrage, and smooth passion (consider his delivery of the final "white noise in a white room" in the midsong break). His occasional melodica, as heard on "Not Great Men," adds to the performances nicely. As for the last session, the murky, dislocated performance of "History's Bunk" makes for a fascinating, weird listen, while "To Hell With Poverty" tops things off with some brutal disco. *—Ned Raggett*

● **A Brief History of the Twentieth Century** / Dec. 1990 / Warner Brothers ♦♦♦♦♦

Gang of Four emerged from the wreckage of punk rock in the early 1980s with a sound all their own. Characterized by blatantly political lyrics that were chanted, sung, and yelled over spare, funky drumbeats and Andy Gill's scratch-and-kill guitar, the Gang's particular brand of angular dance punk was as refreshing as ice water in the face, and, as this collection shows, still holds up well almost 20 years later. Back when the members of Rage Against the Machine were still in grade school, Gang of Four's explicit politics were something of a curiosity; the desultory feminism of "It's Her Factory" and the pessimistic Marxist economic forecasting of "Capital (It Fails Us Now)" were not exactly common lyrical conceits in the immediate post-disco era. Those who know their Chinese history will recognize the band's name, though whether it was meant ironically or as a genuine tribute to the counterrevolutionist faction led by Lady Mao is unclear. This generous best-of recaps some of the Gang's finest moments, and will serve as a perfectly sufficient precis for all but completist fans. Half of the Gang's first full-length album (cheerfully titled *Entertainment!* as in "guerrilla war struggle is the new entertainment") is here, and so are some of the better tracks from their EPs. It also brings together some of the brighter moments from the band's protracted decline into synthesized dribble, such as the immortal "I Love a Man in a Uniform." There are occasional disappointments (the studio version of "To Hell With Poverty" was much better than the so-so live version included here), but overall this is an excellent collection. *—Rick Anderson*

Mall / May 7, 1991 / Polydor ✦✦

Shrinkwrapped / Sep. 19, 1995 / Castle ✦✦✦

Bleak and unforgiving, *Shrinkwrapped* picks up where the preceding *Mall* (and, for that matter, *Entertainment!*) left off, exploring life in a consumer culture under the specter of capitalism on tracks like "The Dark Ride," "Unburden," and its companion piece "Unburden Unbound." Less glossy and overproduced than other recent efforts, cuts including "Better Him Than Me" and "I Parade Myself" restore the group to their noisy roots. *—Jason Ankeny*

A 100 Flowers Bloom / Nov. 3, 1998 / Rhino ✦✦✦✦

Two-CD, 40-song compilation that draws from all of their albums (including the ones from the 1990s) and a couple of early EPs, throwing in eight previously unreleased live performances, demos, and remixes (as well as the 7" single version of "To Hell With Poverty"). Although this is only two discs, it opens itself up to the usual box set criticisms. It's likely that anyone who has followed Gang of Four has already picked up the albums they want, and will thus need to shell out more money than they want for a bunch of not-too-essential rarities. For those who just want a compilation, the single-disc *Brief History of the Twentieth Century* is better and more economical, even though it has no '90s material. Most puzzling is the decision to present the tracks out of chronological sequence, meandering from 1979 to the 1990s and back again while visiting all points in between. All this taken into consideration, there's a lot of music here that Gang of Four fans will consider among the band's most essential, and the package is made more appealing with a 52-page booklet that has a lengthy band history by noted British punk historian Jon Savage. *—Richie Unterberger*

Gang Starr

f. 1988

Jazz-Rap, East Coast Rap, Hip-Hop, Political Rap, Golden Age

Never overly prolific and never overly popular, Gang Starr nonetheless became and remain one of hip-hop's most admired acts ever, its legacy nothing short of legendary in terms of influence. DJ Premier and Guru, the duo's respective producer/DJ and lyricist/MC, began humbly enough, releasing *No More Mr. Nice Guy* in 1989, an ambitious debut album that sought to heavily incorporate a jazz aesthetic into hip-hop. Ambitious or not, the formative album didn't impress many, and Gang Starr took two years to reconsider their approach. They returned in 1991 with a new record label and a fresh approach. It worked marvelously. That album, *Step in the Arena*, set new standards with not only its beats but also its lyrics. Premier had blossomed into one of New York's most savvy producer/DJs, capable of using samples in ways never before imagined and garnered much acclaim for his subtle use of jazz. Similarly, Guru's literate, thoughtful, and most of all earnest lyrics stood out among the brash materialism increasingly plaguing the genre, and his trademark monotone delivery didn't hurt either. A year later came *Daily Operation*. If *Step in the Arena* had been and remains a masterpiece, this album is nothing short of that mark—a longtime topic of debate among East Coast fanatics.

While both *Step in the Arena* and *Daily Operation* astounded critics, they never inspired any breakthrough hits, and Gang Starr remained somewhat of a cult favorite. When the duo returned in 1994 with *Hard to Earn* and later in 1998 with *Moment of Truth*, they remained so, even though the 1999 best-of *Full Clip* made evident just how many brilliant songs Gang Starr had performed. Though the duo quietly put the Gang Starr moniker to rest, they remained active over the years: Guru released a series of acclaimed jazz-rap albums, and DJ Premier produced countless tracks for countless East Coast rappers, many of which became more successful than anything he had produced for his own group. While that's somewhat ironic, the fact of the matter is that Gang Starr never attained commercial success because of their uncompromising, somewhat high-brow style—something which they refused to dilute with accessibility and essentially the reason why their influence has proven timeless. *—Jason Birchmeier*

● **Full Clip: A Decade of Gang Starr** / Mar. 23, 1999 / Cooltempo ✦✦✦✦✦

Considering that the only previous hip-hop hits collection to stretch two full CDs came from 2Pac (and only after his death), Gang Starr's *Full Clip* is a surprising release, though it's incredibly welcome. The duo of DJ Premier and Guru has been one of the longest continuous acts on the rap scene, beginning with 1989's *No More Mr. Nice Guy* and a spot on the soundtrack to Spike Lee's 1990 film *Mo' Better Blues*. And as demonstrated by Premier's stunning productions on classic early tracks like "Who's Gonna Take the Weight," "Words I Manifest," and "Just to Get a Rep," Gang Starr hit its stride early, and just kept on hitting peak after peak during the '90s with "Speak Ya Clout," "Code of the Streets," "Tonz 'O' Gunz," and "You Know My Steez." And new tracks, usually the bane of any best-of collection, provide quite a few highlights here—including "Full Clip," "Discipline" (featuring Total), and "All 4 Tha Ca$h." Also, the set compiles several notable B-sides—"The ? Remainz," "Credit Is Due," and "You Know My Steez (Remix)"—as well as soundtrack works like "1/2 & 1/2" (from *Blade*), "Gotta Get Over" (from *Trespass*), and "The Militia II (Remix)" (from *Belly*). Though Guru's monotone raps can grate over the course of two hours, *Full Clip* documents one of the best, most underrated hip-hop groups ever, from their jazzy beginnings into Premier's harder productions from the mid-'90s and beyond. *—John Bush*

The Gap Band

f. 1967, Tulsa, OK

Quiet Storm, Funk, Soul

A funk septet led by brothers Ronnie (vocals, trumpet, keyboards), Charles (lead vocals, keyboards), and Robert Wilson (vocals, bass), all cousins of Bootsy Collins, the Gap Band enjoyed a successful run on the R&B charts during the '80s with its Sly Stone-influenced boogie. The brothers met Leon Russell in 1974, who signed them to his Shelter label; this led to a recording session with A&M, a self-titled debut on Tattoo/RCA, and a deal with Mercury. A string of R&B Top Ten hits followed, including "I Don't Believe You Want to Get Up and Dance (Oops, Up Side Your Head)"; by the time of *Gap Band III*, the group was established as hitmakers, and the album and its follow-up went platinum on the strength of hits like "Burn Rubber (Why You Wanna Hurt Me)," "Early in the Morning," and "Outstanding." The Gap Band resumed recording after a six-year hiatus in 1995 with *Ain't Nothin' But a Party*, which was followed in 1996 by *V Jammin. Funkin' 'Til 2000 Comz* followed in May of 1999. *—Steve Huey*

● **Ultimate Collection** / Feb. 6, 2001 / Hip-O ✦✦✦✦✦

This 19-track collection does come very close to fulfilling its promise of delivering the *Ultimate Collection*, delivering all the group's big hits—"Shake," "Burn Rubber (Why You Wanna Hurt Me)," "I Don't Believe You Want to Get up and Dance (Oops up Side Your Head)," "Early in the Morning," "You Dropped a Bomb on Me"—as it stretches through all of the Gap Band's recordings for Mercury/Total. In some ways, it might stretch a little bit too far, as it extends all the way into two 1990 tracks, but as a relatively comprehensive, far-reaching retrospective of the band at its peak, this fills the bill (plus, it's topped off by nice packaging and good notes by Sean Ross). *—Stephen Thomas Erlewine*

Garbage

f. 1993, Madison, WI

Alternative Dance, Alternative Pop/Rock

Garbage built on the sonic landscapes of My Bloody Valentine, Curve, and Sonic Youth, adding a distinct sense of accessible pop songcraft. The brainchild of producers Butch Vig, Duke Erikson, and Steve Marker, the group began as an informal jam session between the three producers, of whom Vig was by far the most successful, having helmed breakout records by numerous American alternative superstars (Nirvana, Smashing Pumpkins, Sonic Youth). After recruiting vocalist Shirley Manson, Garbage released their eponymous first album in 1995 on Almo Sounds. After receiving support from radio and MTV, the album began to climb the charts toward the end of 1995, when the second single, "Queer," received heavy airplay. By the summer of 1996, *Garbage* had gone gold in the United States, and shortly afterward it achieved platinum status, as "Only Happy When It Rains" and "Stupid Girl" became radio hits. After a brief break, Garbage began work on their second album in the summer of 1997. The record, entitled *Version 2.0*, was released in May the following year, preceded by the single "Push It." *—Stephen Thomas Erlewine*

● **Garbage** / Aug. 15, 1995 / Almo Sounds ✦✦✦✦✦

Garbage's self-titled debut has all the trappings of alternative rock—off-kilter arrangements, occasional bursts of noise, a female singer with a thin, airy voice—but it comes off as pop, thanks to the glossy production courtesy of drummer Butch Vig. Not only is the sound of the record slick and professional, but all the songs are well-crafted pop songs. Unfortunately, only a handful of the songs are memorable, but those that are—"Vow" and "Queer," in particular—are small, trashy alternative pop gems. *—Stephen Thomas Erlewine*

Version 2.0 / May 12, 1998 / Almo Sounds ✦✦✦

Neither a flat-out retread nor a full-fledged progression, *Version 2.0* is almost too accurate a title for Garbage's second album. Everything that made *Garbage* a success is here—Shirley Manson's seductive strength, strong pop sensibility, a production that falls halfway between alternative rock and techno—presented in a slightly newer form. *Version 2.0* may be gilded with fresh drum loops and shiny, computerized production, but it lacks the thrilling immediacy of the debut. It isn't that Garbage's sound is no longer appealing—it's that high-tech production has a tendency to make the songs sound the same. That was a problem with the debut as well, but it's discouraging to find that those flaws are repeated, not solved. Still, when Garbage pulls it all together, the results are irresistible, and there are just enough moments on the album—including "Special," "Push It," "Temptation Waits," and "I Think I'm Paranoid"—to make it a successful follow-up, even if it isn't a brave step forward. *—Stephen Thomas Erlewine*

Jerry Garcia

b. Aug. 1, 1942, San Francisco, CA, **d.** Aug. 9, 1995, San Francisco, CA

Vocals, Guitar (Electric), Guitar / Folk-Rock, Country-Rock, Rock & Roll

Jerry Garcia was the lead guitarist, vocalist, and spokesman for the seminal '60s rock & roll band the Grateful Dead. Throughout his career, he led the Dead through numerous changes, becoming one of the most famous figures in the history of rock & roll. Simultaneously, Garcia pursued an eclectic array of side projects, ranging from the bluegrass group Old & In the Way to his folky solo recordings. He entered music in the '60s, playing in numerous bluegrass and folk bands before forming the Grateful Dead in 1966. Garcia began a solo career five years later with *Hooteroll?* and recorded solo albums frequently during the next few years, often with keyboardist Merl Saunders. Though his solo efforts slowed in the early '80s, he returned later in the decade with several acoustic duet records with David Grisman and a handful of live tours and albums with the Jerry Garcia Acoustic Band. While attempting to recover from heroin addiction in 1995, Garcia died in his sleep of a heart attack. *—Stephen Thomas Erlewine*

• **Garcia** / Jan. 1972 / Grateful Dead ♦♦♦♦♦
In essence, this is a Grateful Dead record, featuring as it does the band's leader/singer/guitarist, its drummer, and its lyricist. Except for the few instrumental/experimental cuts, the material has been incorporated into the Dead's concert repertoire. In fact, this is a perfect follow-up to the folk-rock song albums the Dead produced in 1970, *Workingman's Dead* and *American Beauty*—albums the band itself has never really followed up. *—William Ruhlmann*

Reflections / Jan. 1976 / Grateful Dead ♦♦♦
Again, a Dead album in everything but name, with several tracks featuring the entire band, perhaps most memorably on "It Must Have Been the Roses." *—William Ruhlmann*

Cats Under the Stars / 1978 / Arista ♦♦♦
The first real "Garcia Band" album is paced by songs that would not sound out of place at a Dead concert. As a matter of fact, the album has garnered increased interest in the '90s as the Dead added the leadoff track "Rubin and Cherise" to its repertoire. *—William Ruhlmann*

Run for the Roses / 1982 / Arista ♦♦♦
Jerry Garcia has been stuck in the same groove for too long to concede anything to a new decade, so it's no surprise that his first solo album in the '80s, *Run for the Roses*, sounds just like his music from the '70s. And for anyone who enjoyed Garcia's laid-back melodies on albums like *Terrapin Station* and *Go to Heaven*, *Run for the Roses* is recommended. Garcia assembles the usual band of suspects—Robert Hunter, John Kahn, Michael Omartian, and Merl Saunders—for a mix of originals and covers that go down like a cool drink on a hot summer's day. Both "Run for the Roses" and "Leave That Little Girl Alone" are breezy pop songs rendered in Garcia's trademark style, and a hiccupy version of the Beatles' "I Saw Her Standing There" is a real treat. The record adds a few slow songs to keep its balance, featuring some fine vocals from Garcia for a cover of Clyde McPhatter's "Without Love" (the only track on here to use horns). Two originals—the still "Midnight Getaway" and the good love gone bad of "Valerie"—benefit from Garcia's twangy whine. Perhaps the most intriguing track for Dead fans is a reggae-fied cover of Bob Dylan's "Knockin' on Heaven's Door," suggesting what Dylan and the Dead's version might have sounded like minus the composer's own caterwauling. Of interest: Melvin Seals, whose distinctive organ plays a prominent role on this album, reappeared with the Jerry Garcia Band in the '90s. *—David Connolly*

Almost Acoustic / Dec. 1988 / Grateful Dead ♦♦♦
Garcia got his start in bluegrass, and here he assembles the Jerry Garcia Acoustic Band (some of whom he started playing with) to handle a live set full of Jimmie Rodgers, Mississippi John Hurt, and traditional mountain music. *—William Ruhlmann*

Compliments of Garcia / 1989 / Grateful Dead ♦♦

Jerry Garcia & David Grisman / 1991 / Acoustic Disc ♦♦♦

Jerry Garcia Band / Aug. 27, 1991 / Arista ♦♦♦
A double live album recorded in 1990 and featuring extended versions of songs by Bruce Cockburn, Bob Dylan, Smokey Robinson, the Beatles, the Band, Los Lobos, and others. The Garcia Band serves a kind of songbook function for its listeners (as, indeed, does the Dead), which may mean that its chief virtue is as instruction: if you're familiar with the originals, you don't really need to hear Garcia's covers, but if, like many Deadheads, you don't hear much music outside the band's orbit, this may help lead you to other good music. *—William Ruhlmann*

Not for Kids Only / Oct. 1993 / Acoustic Disc ♦♦♦
On their second duo album, Jerry Garcia and David Grisman play songs either written for or applicable to children, among them Elizabeth Cotten's "Freight Train" and "Teddy Bears' Picnic." It's a delightful record that lives up to its title, and also marks the development of Garcia/Grisman as a full partnership, with Grisman contributing as many vocals as Garcia and the two trading off on guitar and mandolin. *—William Ruhlmann*

Shady Grove / 1996 / Acoustic Disc ♦♦♦
In the last five years of his life, Jerry Garcia frequently dropped in on his old friend, mandolin player David Grisman, to play and record the kind of folk, bluegrass, and old-time music they had both begun their careers with in the early 1960s. Grisman released two Garcia/Grisman albums on his Acoustic Disc label during Garcia's lifetime, and this is the first to be compiled since his death. In a note, Grisman writes, "I decided to organize this material by genre; this first volume is comprised of traditional folk songs and ballads." Indeed, among the 13 tracks here are versions of child ballads and other ancient songs that formed the repertoire of some of the folk groups that both players belonged to. Grisman has included a lavish CD booklet containing thorough annotations by New Lost City Ramblers member John Cohen that trace the origins of each of the songs and detail Garcia and Grisman's backgrounds. One gets the sense that Cohen and Grisman are trying to provide a tutorial to Deadheads who may be puzzled. The effect of all the scholarship is to imply that the sessions are more deliberate than a hearing suggests, however. The playing is loose and spontaneous, and Garcia is not always in the best voice. Nevertheless, Grisman is right to begin his documentation of Garcia's last sessions with an album that ties directly into the guitarist's initial musical passions. *—William Ruhlmann*

How Sweet It Is / Apr. 15, 1997 / Arista ♦♦♦

So What / Aug. 18, 1998 / Acoustic Disc ♦♦♦♦
Jerry Garcia of the Grateful Dead and David Grisman were friends for over 30 years. On an occasional basis they would get together and jam, and Grisman would tape the results. Sometimes they would play rock, folk music, country, or free improvisation, but the music on this CD put out by Grisman's Acoustic Disc label is strictly straight-ahead jazz. Joined by two (or sometimes three) sidemen from the mandolist's regular band (bassist Jim Kerwin, Joe Craven on percussion, and, on two numbers, flutist Matt Eakle), the co-leaders perform three versions of "So What," and two apiece of "Bag's Groove" and "Milestones," and one of Grisman's "16/16." Garcia is quite credible as a jazz improviser without attempting to be a virtuoso; he apparently loved the music and does not sound at all like a rock player. The versatile Grisman effectively updates his swing style, and the rhythm section is driving and supportive despite being quite light in volume. Even with the repetition of titles (only the last version of "So What" sounds like a rehearsal rather than a regular recording session), the music holds one's interest throughout. A nice surprise that is well worth checking out. *—Scott Yanow*

The Pizza Tapes / Apr. 25, 2000 / Acoustic Disc ♦♦♦
Jerry Garcia and David Grisman released two albums on the latter's Acoustic Disc label during the last years of Garcia's life, and since his death in 1995, Grisman has culled a series of albums from other sessions the two recorded together. *Shady Grove* (1996) presented traditional folk and country material, while *So What* (1998) contained jazz compositions. *The Pizza Tapes* (so named because Garcia's cassette of the sessions supposedly was stolen by a pizza delivery boy and circulated clandestinely) chronicles two nights worth of sessions that Garcia and Grisman shared with guitarist Tony Rice. The Grisman albums with Garcia have become increasingly informal as he has delved into picking dates that may have been intended as rehearsals or just get-togethers, and *The Pizza Tapes* carries that trend further. There's lots of conversation (delineated by the five "Appetizer" titles), along with false starts, mistakes, and fragments of songs, and there is some repetition of tunes (though not performances) from previous albums. "Shady Grove" and "Louis Collins" from *Shady Grove* are here, as is "So What" from *So What*. But the two guitarists show a genuine rapport as they range from pop/jazz standards like "Summertime" to folk songs like "Man of Constant Sorrow" and folk-rock fare like "Knockin' on Heaven's Door." "I'm having a great time," declares Garcia enthusiastically, and his pleasure comes across. Dead Heads long ago found that Garcia was at his best away from the formal restrictions and pressures of recording, and the same thing seems to hold for the Garcia/Grisman albums. Rice, meanwhile, more than holds his own. *—William Ruhlmann*

Don't Let Go / Jan. 23, 2001 / Arista ♦♦♦♦
During the 20-month hiatus that the Grateful Dead took from the road, lead guitarist Jerry Garcia began fronting and touring with one of the premier cover bands of the time. *Don't Let Go* captures this powerhouse rhythm section in the intimate confines of San Francisco's Orpheum Theatre only a few weeks prior to the Dead's resuscitation. This all-star incarnation of the Jerry Garcia Band includes Dead members Keith Godchaux on piano and Donna Jean Godchaux on vocals. Since the late '50s, Bay area bassist John Kahn had been performing with the likes of blues legends John Lee Hooker, Michael Bloomfield, and Nick Gravenites. Kahn remained with the band until they disbanded following Garcia's death in August of 1995. Ron Tutt, while perhaps best remembered as Elvis Presley's favorite drummer, has also performed on more Top 40 singles and albums than almost any other drummer—the notable exception being Hal Blaine. This band is about infectious rhythms and soul. Garcia plays with an energy and freedom of spirit which he rarely achieved during his final two decades with the Grateful Dead. This was likely due, at least in part, to the encyclopedic catalog of material—drawing from such disparate sources as Allen Toussaint's "I'll Take a Melody," J.J. Cale's "After Midnight," and Bob Dylan's "Knocking on Heaven's Door." The band uses the structure of each song as a platform for their unique brand of instinctual aural acrobatics. The interplay amongst the instrumental quartet is best described as inspired telepathy. For instance, between the verses of Hank Ballard's "Tore Up Over You" the rhythmic pockets left by Garcia's incendiary guitar leads are filled in with a swing time precision and grace that harkens back to Benny Goodman or Duke Ellington's orchestra. *Don't Let Go* is highly recommended for the curious enthusiast as well as the insatiable Deadhead. *—Lindsay Planer*

Shining Star / Mar. 20, 2001 / Arista ♦♦♦♦
While the Grateful Dead will always be considered Jerry Garcia's primary outlet, the Jerry Garcia Band often proved the most musically satisfying of the two. *Shining Star* is a double-disc anthology featuring Garcia's *other* band, and is comprised entirely of cover tunes derived from concert recordings made between 1989 and 1993. The late '80s and early '90s were sporadic in terms of performance consistency for the Grateful Dead; however, "the Jerry band"—as Deadheads refer to this aggregate—proved to be vibrant, funky, and alarmingly agile. "Ain't No Bread in the Breadbox" is a textbook example. This inspiring four-way musical conversation allows Garcia the room to wield, as well as yield, his fluid fretwork in order to assemble an ideal congregational sound from the band. Especially tasty are the licks he trades with organist Melvin Seals. Also worthy of note is the sweet gospel blend provided by backing vocalists Jackie LaBranch and Gloria Jones. While all of the material Garcia chose to cover with "the Jerry band" was at the very least unique, tracks such as Irving Berlin's "Russian Lullaby" and the Smokey Robinson-penned "When the Hunter Gets Captured By the Game" rate as diverse in any comparison of 20th century popular music. What is more, Garcia and company are able to transform these pieces in a way that is unparalleled—yoking them stylistically with respectful abandon. Garcia's longtime friend and occasional bandmate Peter Rowan contributes two compositions to this set, "Mississippi Moon" and "Midnight Moonlight," the former being among the finest works on this collection. Its drop-dead cadence blended with some truly psychedelic guitar playing more than compensates for the price of admission—and continues to upon every subsequent visitation. Other highlights include a uniquely structured reading of Solomon Burke's "Everybody Needs Somebody to Love" and Bob Dylan's "Positively 4th Street." *—Lindsay Planer*

Art Garfunkel

b. Nov. 5, 1941, Queens, NY
Vocals / Soft Rock, Adult Contemporary
After Simon & Garfunkel, one of the most successful duos in pop history, split up in 1970, Art Garfunkel became a solo artist, as well as pursuing an acting career. Garfunkel's pure, high tenor had been one of the most distinctive elements of the duo's music, yet he wasn't responsible for the songwriting—Simon wrote all of the group's hits. Not surprisingly, Garfunkel relied on other songwriters, from Jimmy Webb and Randy Newman to rock & roll standards like "I Only Have Eyes for You," throughout his solo career. As a solo performer, he was never quite as successful as he was with Simon & Garfunkel, yet he did have a number of Top 40 hits in the mid-'70s. *Angel Clare*, his first solo record, was co-produced with Simon & Garfunkel producer Roy Halee and released in the fall of 1973. It established the style—a light, carefully arranged and constructed melodic soft rock—he would follow throughout his solo career. Two years later, he returned with the Richard Perry-produced *Breakaway*, the most successful album of his solo career. In the fall of 1977, Garfunkel released his third album, *Watermark*, which primarily consisted of Jimmy Webb covers. The following year, *Fate for Breakfast* appeared. Although it performed well in Britain, reaching number two, the album signaled that his American audience was beginning to shrink: none of the singles made the Top 40 and the album only reached number 67. *Scissors Cut*, a reunion with producer Roy Halee released in 1981, did nothing to reverse his sliding commercial potential. After a lengthy quiet period, Garfunkel re-emerged in 1988 with *Lefty*, which spent a mere eight weeks in the American charts and failed to make the British charts. *—Stephen Thomas Erlewine*

Angel Clare / Sep. 1973 / Columbia ✦✦✦✦✦
Garfunkel (he was billed without his first name here) had a lot riding on his debut solo album, and *Angel Clare*, named after a character in Thomas Hardy's novel *Tess of the D'Urbervilles*, lived up to the heightened expectations for the man who had sung "Bridge over Troubled Water" and other Simon And Garfunkel favorites. Garfunkel took no chances, issuing as the first single Jimmy Webb's "All I Know," which was arranged in a similar style to "Bridge" and made the Top Ten. Elsewhere on the record, Garfunkel took a more spirited approach, notably on a version of Van Morrison's "I Shall Sing" that was reminiscent of Simon And Garfunkel's "Cecilia" and made the Top 40. Certainly, there was enough firepower on the record, which featured guitarists Jerry Garcia and J.J. Cale. But much of it was filled with stately, orchestra-laden ballads, sung by Garfunkel in his naive, breathy tenor. If Simon & Garfunkel had been the thinking man's Everly Brothers, Garfunkel alone turned out to be the thinking man's Johnny Mathis. *—William Ruhlmann*

Breakaway / Oct. 1975 / Columbia ✦✦✦
The second time around, Art Garfunkel turned to pop producer Richard Perry, who liked to record in studios rather than cathedrals and who replaced the angelic style of the first album with a lush pop approach. The result was Garfunkel's best-selling album. The title track and a cover of "I Only Have Eyes for You" reached the Top 40 (the latter topped the U.K. charts), though the most prominent song was the Simon & Garfunkel reunion single "My Little Town." But the album was full of wise pop choices, among them Bruce Johnston's "Disney Girls," Stevie Wonder's "I Believe (When I Fall in Love It Will Be Forever)," and Hal David and Albert Hammond's "1199 Miles from L.A." Perry proved that, given the right material and production, the problem of the relative sameness of Garfunkel's vocal approach could be overcome. *—William Ruhlmann*

Watermark / Oct. 1977 / Columbia ✦✦✦
The original idea was for Art Garfunkel to record an album of songs written by Jimmy Webb. But when the leadoff single, "Crying in My Sleep," failed to make the charts, Columbia Records withdrew the album and induced Garfunkel to put together a cover of Sam Cooke's "(What A) Wonderful World" with Paul Simon and James Taylor harmonizing. The single and a revised version of the album then made the Top 40. But it's still a Garfunkel-Sings-Webb album, except for one song. And the initial idea was a good one: Garfunkel handles Webb's wistful pop songs well, and he has made good choices from Webb's songbook, dating back to the 1960s, though avoiding his big bits. The result is Garfunkel's most cohesive solo album. (The original version of *Watermark*, on test pressings and only a very few commercial copies, was available briefly in October 1977. The revised version, containing "[What A] Wonderful World," was released in January 1978.) *—William Ruhlmann*

Fate for Breakfast / Mar. 1979 / Columbia ✦✦

Scissors Cut / Aug. 1981 / Columbia ✦✦

Lefty / Mar. 1988 / Columbia ✦✦

● **Garfunkel: Best Of** / Oct. 1990 / Columbia ✦✦✦✦✦
Released in 1990, *Garfunkel: Best Of* is a good summary of Art Garfunkel's solo career, even if it doesn't feature all of his charting hits. For instance, "I Shall Sing" and "Second Avenue," two Top 40 songs from his first album, are missing, which may irritate some casual fans (as well as completists). Still, this winds up being a very good overview of his solo years, since it touches on the rest of his hits—such as "I Only Have Eyes for You," "Break Away," "(What A) Wonderful World," and "A Heart in New York"—are all here, along with a couple of Jimmy Webb songs. Since this hits collection winds up showing the weaknesses of Garfunkel's solo material, it's a representative cross-section of his career, but it derives its greatest strength by just being a solid singles sampler. *—Stephen Thomas Erlewine*

Up 'til Now / Oct. 28, 1993 / Columbia ✦✦

Across America / May 27, 1997 / Virgin ✦✦

Leif Garrett

b. Nov. 8, 1961, Hollywood, CA
Vocals / Teen Idol, Pop/Rock
Leif Garrett, with his tousled blonde hair, big trusting eyes, and sexy yet boyish good looks, set many a teen girl's heart to racing in the '70s. He started working at the tender age of five, appearing in movies like *Skateboard*. In 1977, at the ripe old age of 16, Garrett was still acting, making two new films that year, and two new television movies. He was also singing by this point in his career. That same year he signed a recording contract with Atlantic Records and released a self-titled debut album. He quickly hit the charts with remakes of the songs "Surfin' USA" and "The Wanderer." His biggest musical hit was a song titled "I Was Made for Dancing." The smash disco single topped the charts in both the United States and the United Kingdom. Teen magazines like Teen Beat and Tiger Beat couldn't feature enough about the hot pop star. He seemed at the height of his career in 1978, yet no one knew that his fall was drawing ever nearer, even as he stood in the spotlights smiling. Garrett was 17 by this point, and enjoying the lifestyle of a rock star when the fall came in the form of a car crash. He was the driver, and a close friend, Roland Winkler, was in the passage seat. The needless wreck left Winkler in a wheelchair for the rest of his life and a devastated Garrett on a path of self-destruction. Garrett held on long enough to make two more albums: *Same Goes for You* in 1979, and then *My Movie of You* in 1981. He worked on a few more films and television shows, but no one seemed to notice much. *—Charlotte Dillon*

● **The Leif Garrett Collection** / Jan. 13, 1998 / Scotti Bros. ✦✦✦✦✦
Scotti Bros.' *Leif Garrett Collection* may not seem particularly extensive, weighing in at only 12 tracks, but it does contain every single one of his ten charting singles, with two other cuts thrown in for good measure. In other words, it's as thorough as a compilation as anyone could hope for, and while his music hasn't dated particularly well, it will give a nostalgic ride to anyone that thrilled to his episode of *Behind the Music*. *—Stephen Thomas Erlewine*

Gastr del Sol

f. 1991, Louisville, KY
Math Rock, Experimental Rock, Indie Rock, Post-Rock/Experimental
Gastr del Sol was the most prominent vehicle of indie-rock stalwart David Grubbs, a former member of Squirrel Bait, Slint and Bastro. With Gastr del Sol, the Louisville, Ky-born vocalist/guitarist/pianist's evolution from conventional rock music into more intricate and sophisticated tone patterns became complete; debuting with the 1993 EP *The Serpentine Similar*, the group—a shifting aggregate of talents which initially inclued bassist Bundy K. Brown and drummer John McEntire—began exploring their new approach, taking off from often improvisational performances to embark on highly idiosyncratic sonic adventures. With the single "20 Songs Less," guitarist, composer, and tape manipulator Jim O'Rourke signed on, and following the departure of Brown, and with the decreased involvement of McEntire, Gastr del Sol became a kind of catchall tag for Grubbs and O'Rourke's many eclectic projects; the acoustic *Crookt, Crackt, or Fly* followed in 1994, as did the EP *Mirror Repair*. With 1995's *The Harp Factory on Lake Street*, Grubbs and O'Rourke composed a single 17-minute orchestral piece, while with 1996's *Upgrade and Afterlife* they returned to more more traditional dynamics to create their most beautiful and intriguing work to date. O'Rourke left Gastr del Sol in 1997, shortly after completing work on *Camoufleur*, which was released in Janurary 1998. *—Jason Ankeny*

The Serpentine Similar / 1993 / Dexter's Cigar/Drag City ✦✦✦✦

Crookt, Crackt, or Fly / 1994 / Drag City ✦✦✦✦
At this point, Gastr del Sol was pretty much just David Grubbs and Jim O'Rourke, though John McEntire was still around here and there on a couple of songs. There are a few other guests at points—percussion from Steve Butters and clarinet from Gene Coleman, both on the lengthy, mysterious "Work From Smoke"—but otherwise this was just the partnership going at it. Acoustic guitars were all the rage for the duo and that's what a listener will hear a lot of over *Crookt*'s eight-song length. Other instruments and approaches do surface—"Every Five Miles" adds electric guitar to the predominantly unplugged approach, while "Is That a Rifle When It Rains?" is actually a full-on rocker, with McEntire hitting the skins—but generally electricity was only used for the microphones. Some numbers are near fragments, like the opening "Wedding in the Park," while others extend to over ten minutes. Anyone expecting, say, the fluid genre hopping of John Fahey or the more abrupt but still uncategorizable leaps of the Sun City Girls will find *Crookt* a different experience. Generally, there are abrupt, quick chord runs or soft, repetitive figures, often with plenty of pauses, over which Grubbs and O'Rourke do or don't quietly sing, as the mood takes them. One of the shorter numbers is among the most intriguing—"Paranthetically," with only Grubbs and his piano over a minute and 20 seconds. Conversational in tone, it's an interesting if too brief approach. "The Wrong Soundings" ends the album on a nicely ragged note, starting with one of the calmer guitar leads on the album before moving into a seemingly random cutup of everything from full electric riffing to low-volume percussion hits and back. Indie obsessives who favor the Thrill Jockey stable will be pleased to hear "The C in Cake," the name of which indeed was the inspiration for McEntire's The Sea and Cake. *—Ned Raggett*

The Harp Factory on Lake Street / Aug. 1, 1995 / Table of the Elements ✦✦✦
The Harp Factory on Lake Street is an intentional departure from Gastr del Sol's main line of work—aside from the formality of a name change, it could almost be considered a one-off side project. The record consists of one 17-minute orchestral composition, recruiting various Chicago musicians (Jeb Bishop, John McEntire, Bob Weston) to create a decidedly abstract and ambient work from largely traditional instruments. The result is

sparse and unstructured and times, and adopts a wall-of-sound approach at others; some of David Grubbs' melodic piano work emerges at points as well. *The Harp Factory on Lake Street* may not be of much interest to those who enjoy the pop aspects of Gastr del Sol's other work, but it fits well with the more experimental work of Chicago's post-rock and avant-jazz musicians. —*Nitsuh Abebe*

Upgrade & Afterlife / Jun. 17, 1996 / Drag City ✦✦✦✦
Somewhere along the line, *Upgrade & Afterlife's* original concept—a set of conventional song made up of "normal" chords and accessible melodies—must have been abandoned. Instead, David Grubbs and Jim O'Rourke's fifth album as Gastr del Sol abounds with elliptical melodies, broken by silence and noise, that avoid resolution. The antithesis of a pop lyricist, Grubbs' elusive wordplay and vague, surreal imagery matches his music, particularly on "Rebecca Sylvester." Random noise interrupts throughout the album, bursting and seeping through song surfaces, wreaking havoc on the compositions. A fanfare of destructive screeches announces "Hello Spiral." On "The Sea Incertain," they emerge from the stops and starts of the piano's careful explorations, pushing the instrument out of focus and out of the picture. A paranoid hum underpins "The Relay" and "Crappie Tactics." There is beauty throughout *Upgrade & Afterlife,* but it's almost entirely on Gastr's terms. Grubbs' gorgeous vocal melody on "The Relay" carries some of his most cryptic imagery. "Cooked corn in formaldehyde/Popcorn in an airtight jar," he sings, backed by a dissonant piano. The album's biggest surprises are its bookends: "Our Exquisite Replica of 'Eternity'" (an absurd opening statement) may someday be recognized as the perfect piece of film music, capable of communicating as much paranoia, suspense, and terror as a director could with his/her camera. It's an ominous drift fractured by shards of electronic feedback, breaking through and breaking down like static between alien stations before closing with mournful trumpets. Meanwhile, Jim O'Rourke's performance of John Fahey's "Dry Bones in the Valley" ends the album with pure fresh air, resolving every awkward moment offered up in the preceding 37 minutes. Joined by Tony Conrad, the pair embark on an exploration of the violinist's micro-tonal drones that follow the album into the sunset. —*Nathan Bush*

● **Camoufleur** / Jan. 20, 1998 / Drag City ✦✦✦✦✦
Jim O'Rourke's last album with Gastr del Sol is a subdued, meditative affair, bringing together elements of folk, jazz, film music, and the avant-garde. "The Seasons Reverse" opens the album with a deceptive, gentle melody and strummed, hushed guitars. Its sound and leisurely pace set the tone, but not the style, for the rest of the album. Each track is intricate and layered, but the music isn't overly complex. Instead, *Camoufleur* is quiet and minimal, requiring attentive listening. Only "The Seasons Reverse" and the closer "Bauchredner," with its unexpected, catchy horn-driven coda, are straightforward. The remainder of the album demands concentration. Given some time, the album opens up, revealing layers of modest beauty. It's a nice way for O'Rourke to leave the fold, and it certainly suggests that David Grubbs is far from finished musically, whether he chooses to continue with Gastr del Sol or not. —*Stephen Thomas Erlewine*

Marvin Gaye (Marvin Pentz Gay, Jr.)

b. Apr. 2, 1939, Washington, D.C., **d.** Apr. 1, 1984, Los Angeles, CA
Vocals, Keyboards, Drums / Blaxploitation, Smooth Soul, Quiet Storm, Motown, Urban, R&B, Soul
One of the most gifted, visionary, and enduring talents ever launched into orbit by the Motown hit machine, the career of Marvin Gaye blazed the trail for the continued evolution of popular black music: moving from lean, powerful R&B to stylish, sophisticated soul to finally arrive at an intensely political and personal form of artistic self-expression, his work not only redefined soul music as a creative force but also expanded its impact as an agent for social change. With 1963's "Pride and Joy," Gaye scored his first Top Ten smash, but often found his role as a hitmaker stifling—his desire to become a crooner of lush romantic ballads ran in direct opposition to Motown's all-important emphasis on chart success, and the ongoing battle between his artistic ambitions and the label's demands for commercial product continued throughout Gaye's long tenure with the company. After the chart-topping 1968 success of "I Heard It Through the Grapevine," his biggest hit and arguably the pinnacle of the Motown Sound, he increasingly found the material he recorded for the label to be increasingly irrelevant in the face of the tremendous social changes sweeping the nation; spending the majority of 1970 in seclusion, Gaye resurfaced early the next year with the self-produced *What's Going On,* a landmark effort heralding a dramatic shift in both content and style which forever altered the face of black music. A highly percussive album which incorporated jazz and classical elements to forge a remarkably sophisticated and fluid soul sound, *What's Going On* was a conceptual masterpiece which brought Gaye's deeply held spiritual beliefs to the fore to explore issues ranging from poverty and discrimination to the environment, drug abuse and political corruption; chief among the record's concerns was the conflict in Vietnam, as Gaye structured the songs around the point of view of his brother Frankie, himself a soldier recently returned from combat. The album's success guaranteed Gaye continued artistic control over his work and helped loosen the reins for other Motown artists, most notably Stevie Wonder, to also take command of their own destinies. —*Jason Ankeny*

That Stubborn Kinda Fellow / Jan. 31, 1963 / Motown ✦✦✦

When I'm Alone I Cry / Apr. 1, 1964 / Motown ✦✦

Marvin Gaye and Kim Weston / 1966 / Motown ✦✦✦

☆ **Marvin Gaye's Greatest Hits, Vol. 2** / 1967 / Motown ✦✦✦✦✦
Other than the *Anthology* line, this was for quite a while the best single album set featuring Gaye's early and mid-'60s hits. There isn't a dud in the bunch, but both the *Super Hits* and Anthology line give you more cuts, while the boxed set has more variety. But this isn't by any stretch a bad release. —*Ron Wynn*

M.P.G. / Apr. 30, 1969 / Motown ✦✦✦
An underrated late '60s album, this one has sometimes been overlooked because it seemed like a generic throwaway. But it included some outstanding songs. Motown wisely has included it on their list of Gaye albums that got reissued on CD. —*Ron Wynn*

That's the Way Love Is / Jan. 8, 1970 / Motown ✦✦✦
The title cut was another Gaye classic, while much of the other material was equally impressive. Gaye was beginning to become disillusioned with Motown, but that hadn't affected his album output or his singing. Anyone hearing this wouldn't have suspected that Gaye was about to unleash *What's Going On. —Ron Wynn*

☆ **What's Going On** / May 20, 1971 / Motown ✦✦✦✦✦
Shortly after Marvin Gaye turned 30, he became the first Motown artist with a measure of creative control. *What's Going On* was the result, surely Marvin's finest moment and, along with a number of Stevie Wonder's early-'70s releases, one of a handful of great Motown albums. A concept album, *What's Going On* chronicled a multitude of societal ills. Ironically, Motown owner Berry Gordy did not want to release it. He was convinced it held no commercial potential. Gordy couldn't have been more wrong: *What's Going On* catapulted Marvin Gaye into superstardom. Three number one singles were pulled from the album: the title song, "Mercy Mercy Me (The Ecology)," and "Inner City Blues (Make Me Wanna Holler)." This was the first album where Marvin overdubbed his voice multiple times, creating a one-man vocal group. The result was a level of timbral integration in the harmonies that became a Gaye trademark. —*Rob Bowman*

Trouble Man / Dec. 8, 1972 / Motown ✦✦✦
Marvin Gaye turned to soundtracks in the early '70s, and came out with one that ranked right alongside the epic scores done by Curtis Mayfield and Isaac Hayes. The film itself was a typical '70s "blaxploitation" effort, but Gaye's vocals, seamless production, and a nice mix of up-tempo funk, light ballads, and pseudo-macho camp were brilliant. —*Ron Wynn*

☆ **Let's Get It On** / Aug. 28, 1973 / Motown ✦✦✦✦✦
After brilliantly surveying the social, political, and spiritual landscape with *What's Going On,* Marvin Gaye turned to more intimate matters with *Let's Get It On,* a record unparalleled in its sheer sensuality and carnal energy. Always a sexually charged performer, Gaye's passions reach their boiling point on tracks like the magnificent title hit (a number one smash) and "You Sure Love to Ball"; silky and shimmering, the music is seductive in the most literal sense, its fluid grooves so perfectly designed for romance as to border on parody. With each performance laced with innuendo, each lyric a come-on, and each rhythm throbbing with lust, perhaps no other record has ever achieved the kind of sheer erotic force of *Let's Get It On,* and it remains the blueprint for all of the slow jams to follow decades later—much copied, but never imitated. —*Jason Ankeny*

Live / Jun. 19, 1974 / Motown ✦✦✦
Appearing during Marvin Gaye's extended sabbatical following *Let's Get It On, Live* features the erratic soul superstar moving briskly through some of his biggest hits. This brisk tempo acts as a double-edged sword, though, on the one hand establishing an up-tempo, kinetic sense of euphoria never dulled by any lulls. However, on the other hand, the dizzying sense of energy overwhelms you, never letting you relax and fully soak up the music's exuded beauty. Either way, Gaye's in top form here, delivering nothing but perennial anthems to a rabid crowd. The album-opening "Trouble Man" wields considerable weight, instantly establishing an engaging tone. From there Gaye moves toward an 11-minute medley of his '60s classics that comes across as almost a montage of nostalgia, evoking wistful memories of a more innocent and untainted Marvin. Following this medley, the album hits its fiery peak with versions of "Let's Get It On" and "What's Going On," his two biggest hits of the era. *Live* isn't quite as accomplished as 1977's *Live at the London Palladium,* being a bit too rushed and not instrumental or funky enough. It's still a great snapshot of the artist at a landmark point in his career, the sabbatical from which he would never return the same. Furthermore, *Live* serves as an artifact that revealingly alludes to Gaye's disposition: elated, crowd-pleasing, and quite uncomfortable. —*Jason Birchmeier*

I Want You / Mar. 16, 1976 / Motown ✦✦✦✦
Together with Leon Ware, Gaye created 1976's *I Want You.* Some of these tracks were to go on Leon Ware's Motown debut, *Musical Massage* until Berry Gordy got a listen and decided that they'd be even better for Gaye, as the artist had not released a studio album since 1973's *Let's Get It On.* The title track to *I Want You* was the album's most successful effort, but certainly not the best. Like many of his albums, *I Want You* has Gaye's peaks not so much coming from the singles but rather the album cuts and the totality of the effort itself. Not that all of the lyrics and intentions here are crystal clear, though. In fact, Gaye does sound somnolent in spots, and it gives credence to the rumors that he did some of the tracks lying on a couch. "Come Live With Me," produced by Ware and Hal Davis, is the most focused track here. The refined and atmospheric "Feel My Love Inside" has Gaye giving a commanding upper-register vocal and has some doo wop backing vocals thrown in for good measure. To most fans, *I Want You* probably sounds unlike anything Gaye recorded. They're not wrong. In fact, this has the feel of a Leon Ware album with a more persuasive voice on top. "Since I Had You" typifies that idea as Gaye skillfully maneuvers through Ware's compelling and complicated arrangement, and he puts an accent on notes that other singers wouldn't even think to. *I Want You* is one of Gaye's best albums, and the production set a standard that few have been able to match. —*Jason Elias*

Here, My Dear / Dec. 15, 1978 / Motown ✦✦✦✦✦
On one of the stranger releases in popular music, *Here, My Dear,* Gaye stands emotionally naked. Over the course of this two-album set, Marvin chronicles the dissolution of

his marriage (to company president Berry Gordy's sister Anna). The level of detail is nearly painful as Marvin accuses Anna of keeping him from seeing his son, having a restraining order issued against him, and holding their separation up for ransom. Marvin also tells us of his cocaine habit and his obsession with prostitutes. In a trace of irony not lost on the singer, Anna received all royalties from the album as per their divorce agreement. Upon hearing it, she reportedly contemplated suing for invasion of privacy. *—Rob Bowman*

In Our Lifetime / Jan. 15, 1981 / Motown ♦♦♦♦
This album came after the confessional and meadering double album 1978's *Here My Dear*. Although this better set does seem effortlessly conceived, it wasn't that simple. Gaye originally envisioned a "party" album and almost released one called *Love Man*. After some consideration, Gaye nixed the idea and aimed for an effort that would spotlight his religious concerns. Thankfully *In Our Lifetime* splits the difference between the two mindsets. The first single from the aborted *Love Man* shows up here. "Ego Tripping Out" works as both a parody of the "love man" with a few autobiographical flourishes as he sings, "Got a sweet tooth / For the chick on the floor." Slowly but surely the religious matters do surface here. The buoyant "Praise," has a blithe riff inspired and or lifted from Stevie Wonder and has Gaye getting his message across without being preachy. Although no song is especially brilliant here, the level of Gaye's musical sense and his vocal prowess carries him throughout. The unfinished and non-Gaye approved, "Far Cry" has lyrics that are steam of conscious and are barely decipherable. The mesmerizing "Love Me Now or Love Me Later" that has Gaye examining both good and evil with equal skill. The last track, the title song, has Gaye back in the party frame of mind and has great horn charts and a propulsive beat. *In Our Lifetime* is one of his finest later albums and captures him as his craft was maturing and becoming more multi-faceted. *—Jason Elias*

Midnight Love / Oct. 1982 / Columbia/Legacy ♦♦♦♦
Larkin Arnold, former CBS Records (Sony Music) senior executive VP, convinced Marvin Gaye to leave his flat in Belgium and sign with Columbia Records; the result would become the soul singer's last album before his untimely death. Of all his number one songs, this album's first release, "Sexual Healing," became his longest running number one single on the Billboard R&B charts (ten straight weeks). With the exception of the guitar, the Washington, D.C. native performed every instrument on this classic hit. Gaye concocted a pioneering percussive sound that was balladic in taste but stimulating in feel. As this project may not be an absolute erotic expression or a socially challenging plea from Gaye like on some of his previous albums, nonetheless, *Midnight Love* is a classic Marvin Gaye effort. In addition to this project thriving with Gaye's enthusiastic spirit, it has his harmonious background vocals, his stunning vocal arrangements and his creative penmanship, as he wrote all the selections. The 2000 CD reissue on Sony/Legacy adds historical liner notes by Gaye biographer David Ritz and a bonus track, an instrumental version of "Rockin' After Midnight" (which actually does feature a bit of vocalizing by Gaye). *—Craig Lytle*

The Marvin Gaye Collection / Sep. 1990 / Motown ♦♦♦
Marvin Gaye has more than enough great music to make a superb box set, but the haphazard *Marvin Gaye Collection* isn't it. The four discs within the set are arranged thematically: one terrific disc of hits, one good disc of duets, one largely uninteresting disc of rarities, and one wildly uneven disc of ballads. By spreading out the material this way, Motown shortchanges Gaye's musical accomplishments; there is no sense of growth or innovation. Although many of the songs are wonderful, some of the selections are puzzling—they seem to be chosen because they're arcane, not because they're significant. This very quality makes *The Marvin Gaye Collection* essential for his most devoted fans; however, most fans will find this box set disappointing. *—Stephen Thomas Erlewine*

Seek & You Shall Find: More of the Best (1963-1981) / 1993 / Rhino ♦♦♦♦♦
Full of album tracks and B-sides, *Seek & You Shall Find: More of the Best* is a great compliment to Gaye's greatest-hits collections. *—AMG*

Norman Whitfield Sessions / Aug. 23, 1994 / Motown ♦♦♦
All of Gaye's recordings with producer Norman Whitfield are collected on the appropriately titled *The Norman Whitfield Sessions*. The sessions proved beneficial to both Gaye and Whitfield, as they produced the classic "I Heard It Through the Grapevine." While nothing on the set matches that seminal single, most of the music is captivating. Nevertheless, the disc will appeal mainly to the devoted Marvin Gaye collector, since most of the material is either alternate takes or outtakes. *—Stephen Thomas Erlewine*

The Master 1961-1984 / Apr. 25, 1995 / Motown ♦♦♦♦♦
The average fan is better off with *Anthology*, which covers almost all of Gaye's true classics. But for those who want the hits and then some, and have the budget and interest to go further, this four-CD box set is an excellent retrospective of his career. The 89 tracks include all the chart hits (both on his own and with Mary Wells, Kim Weston, Tammi Terrell, and Diana Ross) and many interesting B-sides, album tracks, and misses. There are also over a dozen previously unreleased cuts, most dating from the early part of his career; they don't rank among his best work, but they're almost all good and interesting. With a long essay by his biographer, David Ritz, this is the best overview of Gaye's evolution and versatility, and a much-recommended alternative to the previous Gaye box, *The Marvin Gaye Collection*. *—Richie Unterberger*

★ **Anthology** / Aug. 22, 1995 / Motown ♦♦♦♦♦
The Marvin Gaye Anthology released in 1995 is an entirely different compilation from the three-LP *Anthology* originally released in 1974 and reissued as a double CD in 1986. The earlier version contained 40 tracks, starting with "Stubborn Kind of Fellow" and running through "Trouble Man." The new one, on two CDs or cassettes, contains 47 tracks, also starting with "Stubborn Kind of Fellow," but running through "Heavy Love Affair." As such, it is more comprehensive, containing such later hits as "Let's Get It On," "I Want You," and "Got to Give It Up, Pt. 1" that were not featured on the earlier edition (but not "Sexual Healing," which Gaye recorded after leaving Motown). Only a couple of Gaye's Top Ten R&B/Top 40 pop hits are missing, and there is a smattering of rarities. The 1995 *Anthology* falls neatly between the single-disc *Every Great Motown Hit* and the four-disc boxed set *The Master 1961-1984* as a thorough hits collection at a reasonable price. *—William Ruhlmann*

Vulnerable / Mar. 25, 1997 / Motown ♦♦♦
Vulnerable is the end result of a project entitled The Ballads that Marvin Gaye began in 1966. Gaye intended the project as a showcase for his crooning, as well as a way to pay tribute to the pop and jazz standards he loved. It was a labor of love that took him 12 years to complete, and even after it was finished, the record wasn't released until 1997. Was it worth the wait? For dedicated fans, it certainly was, since Gaye's voice is as beautiful and soulful as ever. However, anyone who is not a dedicated fan will find *Vulnerable* intriguing but significantly flawed, especially since several of the songs seem ill-suited for Gaye's seductive vocals. Which means that even though *Vulnerable* is a nice addendum to his catalog, it's little more than a curiosity. *—Stephen Thomas Erlewine*

Midnight Love & the Sexual Healing Sessions / Nov. 10, 1998 / Columbia/Legacy ♦♦♦♦♦
After a series of business and personal upheavals as well as a couple of artistically satisfying but commercially disappointing albums, Marvin Gaye scored a final triumph with *Midnight Love* on which he embraced dancefloor rhythms derived from Rick James, horn charts that echoed Earth, Wind & Fire, and the kind of lover-man lyrics he himself had pioneered on earlier hits such as "Let's Get It On." The breakthrough track was his last major hit, "Sexual Healing," a relaxed groove tune with burbling percussion, doo wop backup vocals, and a new twist on the old romantic come-on. But the album as a whole made Gaye's case as a contemporary R&B artist. Then he was gone.

This reissue compilation contains the entire *Midnight Love* album on the first disc, followed by a full, 74-minute disc of previously unreleased work tapes and alternate takes of most of the album's songs, among them four versions of "Sexual Healing." Since Gaye developed the tracks himself, playing keyboards and percussion, the alternates illuminate his creative process, but they contain no real revelations and will be of interest primarily to Gaye fans and hip-hop musicians searching for samples. Everybody else can stick with the original album. *—William Ruhlmann*

Lost and Found: Love Starved Heart [Expanded Edition] / Sep. 28, 1999 / Motown ♦♦♦♦
Originally issued as part of a 1994 box set and newly expanded here with nine additional performances, *Love Starved Heart* assembles 25 unreleased tracks recorded by Marvin Gaye between 1963 and 1971, Motown's golden era. That it took three decades for these songs to see the light of day speaks far more to the intensity of the label's assembly line production ethic than to the quality of the material itself—at their most pedestrian, these are fine performances simply lost in the shuffle, but at moments like "It's a Desperate Situation," "When I Feel the Need," and "This Love Starved Heart of Mine (It's Killing Me)," Gaye achieves the same peaks of his hits of the era, crafting performances of such sublime beauty and haunting poignance that their failure to reach the masses until now is nothing short of remarkable. Still, where classics like "I Heard It Through the Grapevine" and "Ain't That Peculiar" tend to suffer from years of oldies radio wear and tear, *Love Starved Heart* sounds positively refreshing—in their own way, these long-lost songs reaffirm the timelessness of Marvin Gaye's brilliance even more than the familiar hits on which his reputation rests. *—Jason Ankeny*

Gloria Gaynor

b. Sep. 7, 1949, Newark, NJ
Vocals / Disco
Gaynor sang with the Soul Satisfiers band before being discovered at the Wagon Wheel in New York in the early '70s. Probably the first "disco queen," Gaynor helped popularize, through her music, the "segue" or "extended mix" that came to represent disco music. Her 1979 cut, "I Will Survive," became a woman's anthem in the vein of Helen Reddy's "I Am Woman." She continued to thrive in Europe during the '80s and continued recording throughout the following decade. *—Bil Carpenter*

I Will Survive: The Anthology / Apr. 21, 1998 / Polydor/Chronicles ♦♦♦♦
Gloria Gaynor was one of the main disco divas, scoring a number of crossover hits, including "I Will Survive" and "Never Can Say Goodbye," in addition to pioneering extended mixes on her 12" singles. Instead of relying on her hit singles, all of which are compiled on *Greatest Hits*, the double-disc *I Will Survive: The Anthology* concentrates on her dancefloor classics. In other words, if you're looking for brief, catchy disco-pop, look elsewhere; this has nothing but full-length album tracks and three extended disco medleys, each running around 18 minutes—the length of one side of a 12" single. For some, this will be tedious listening, but any disco fanatic will find plenty of interesting material here, and for those with hardcore dance tastes, *I Will Survive* may even be preferable to *Greatest Hits*. *—Stephen Thomas Erlewine*

● **20th Century Masters—The Millennium Collection: The Best of Gloria Gaynor** / Sep. 26, 2000 / Polydor ♦♦♦♦
The Millennium Collection: The Best of Gloria Gaynor gathers highlights from her soul and disco years, including "How High the Moon," "Casanova Brown," "Let Me Know (I Have the Right)," and "I Will Survive." "This Love Affair," "(If You Want It) Do It Yourself," and "Walk on By" are some of the other highlights of this compact but entertaining compilation. Though it's not as extensive as some of the other available Gaynor collections,

The Millennium Collection gives casual fans a taste of her powerful sound. —*Heather Phares*

J. Geils Band

f. 1967, Boston, MA, **db.** 1985

Album Rock, Boogie Rock, Arena Rock, Pop/Rock, Hard Rock, Blues-Rock, Rock & Roll

The J. Geils Band were one of the most popular touring rock & roll bands in America during the '70s. Where their contemporaries were influenced by the heavy boogie of British blues-rock and the ear-splitting sonic adventures of psychedelia, the J. Geils Band were a bar band pure and simple, churning out greasy covers of obscure R&B, doo wop, and soul tunes, cutting them with healthy dose of Stonesy swagger. While their muscular sound and the hyper jive of frontman Peter Wolf packed arenas across America, it only rarely earned them hit singles. Seth Justman, the group's main songwriter, could turn out catchy R&B-based rockers like "Give It to Me" or "Must of Got Lost," but these hits never led to stardom, primarily because the group had trouble capturing the energy of their live sound in the studio. In the early '80s, the group tempered their driving rock with some pop, and the makeover paid off with the massive hit single "Centerfold," which stayed at number one for six weeks. By the time the band prepared to record a followup, tensions between Justman and Wolf had grown considerably, resulting in Wolf's departure, which quickly led to the band's demise. After working for years to reach to top of the charts, the J. Geils couldn't stay there once they finally achieved their goal. —*Stephen Thomas Erlewine*

The J. Geils Band / 1970 / Atlantic ✦✦✦✦✦

Their debut paid homage to the likes of Otis Rush, John Lee Hooker, and Motown through blistering covers, but originals such as "Wait" and "What's Your Hurry" more than hold their own. Magic Dick steals the show on this one. —*John Floyd*

The Morning After / 1971 / Atlantic ✦✦✦

It's rare when a group's sophomore effort is as good as their debut. *The Morning After* by the J. Geils Band is that, and in some ways, even better. Tighter and more focused than their debut, the band found success on the singles charts with "Looking for a Love." Again, they laid original material alongside blues covers, but the sound was always their own—exciting, enjoyable rocking blues. —*James Chrispell*

Full House Live / 1972 / Atlantic ✦✦✦✦✦

Live is the way the J. Geils Band should be experienced; they put on a show like few others, and *Full House* is the proof. From start to finish, there is not one bad cut. From the opener, "First I Look at the Purse" right on through "Looking for a Love," these guys don't give up an inch. —*James Chrispell*

Bloodshot / 1973 / Atlantic ✦✦

More hot, rockin' rhythm & blues from these guys out of Boston. *Bloodshot* includes their Top 40 hit "Give It To Me," as well as the great opener, "(Ain't Nothin' But A) House Party," plus soulful struts and bluesy shuffles in between. It's a wonder these guys could tour almost constantly and still turn out great albums one after another. On *Bloodshot*, the J. Geils Band make it appear easy. —*James Chrispell*

Ladies Invited / 1973 / Atlantic ✦✦✦

On this, their first album of all original material, something appeared to be amiss. Perhaps it was road fatigue—only the band knows for sure, but *Ladies Invited* didn't burn up the charts like their previous efforts, nor did it have that all-important hit single. It's well done and worthwhile, but lacks spark. —*James Chrispell*

Nightmares . . . and Other Tales from the Vinyl Jungle / 1974 / Atlantic ✦✦✦

After a brief sidestep, the J. Geils Band came roaring back with a very urban-jungle sort of album which percolates with beat and rocks with enthusiastic excitement. Here lies the reggae-ish "Give It to Me," as well as the concert staple "Detroit Breakdown." A fertile release from some of the hardest rockers of the '70s. —*James Chrispell*

Hotline / 1975 / Atlantic ✦✦

Blow Your Face Out / 1976 / Rhino ✦✦✦✦✦

If you're looking to put on a party record from the mid-'70s, grab a hold of *Blow Your Face Out* and crank up the volume. Always known as a great live band, J. Geils and Co. stomp through one of the most exciting live sets put on vinyl (and tape and CD). The title says it all. —*James Chrispell*

Monkey Island / 1977 / Atlantic ✦✦✦✦✦

One of the great lost albums, *Monkey Island* is where the Geils Band make the blues their own. It's an elaborately produced, adventurous set that analyzes their commerical failure and looks for answers to hard-to-ask questions. Unlike their 1972 live album *Full House*, *Monkey Island* refuses to pander to blues conservists or boogie-rock hammerheads; the album is steeped in the kind of pathos and bitterness that infuse the Stones' *Sticky Fingers*. The album flopped, but it remains the group's most personal statement. —*John Floyd*

Sanctuary / 1978 / Razor & Tie ✦✦✦

Hot on the heels of the band's excellent but completely overlooked *Monkey Island*, the J. Geils Band severed ties with Atlantic and signed a fresh deal with EMI Records. The band's tenure with Atlantic only yielded a few successes, and on paper, teaming up with producer Joe Wissert, the man responsible for many of Earth, Wind & Fire's and Boz Scaggs' biggest hits, seemed like an odd choice. However, *Sanctuary* was a rebirth of sorts for the sextet: Wissert crystallized the band's attack, working off their leaner songwriting and simplifying their arrangements. Keeping their boogie-woogie bar band attack intact, Peter Wolf and Seth Justman delivered first-rate material, including the down and dirty opener "I Could Hurt You," the sublime title track and the lovely "One Last Kiss," which cracked the Top 40 in early 1978. The Stevie Wonder-ish "Take It Back," also a mild hit, predicted the commercial direction the band took on *Freeze Frame* three years later. The beautiful "Teresa," a heartbreaking ballad executed with help of a simple vocal/piano arrangement courtesy of the Wolf/Justman team, and "Wild Man," which sounds like a leftover from the Atlantic years, are also highlights. *Sanctuary*'s final song, the rollicking, Magic Dick-driven "Just Can't Stop Me," encapsulates everything magical (pun intended) and soulful about this band. With its effortless playing and a breakdown that'll have you on the edge of your seat, it served as the band's call into battle for the Freeze Frame tour. The Razor & Tie reissue features covers of "I Do" and "Land of a Thousand Dances" from the band's live record *Showtime*, recorded at the height of their *Freeze Frame* period. "Land of a Thousand Dances" in particular reminds you just how incredible these guys were live. —*John Franck*

● **The Best of the J. Geils Band** / 1979 / Atlantic ✦✦✦✦

Contractual obligations aside, *The Best of the J. Geils Band* is a worthy and yet somewhat disjointed collection of the band's more popular radio songs taken from their eight Atlantic records. Released just a year after J. Geils' EMI debut *Sanctuary*, one listen to these two works back to back can make an extraordinary argument for the band's growth. Or lack of it, depending on whom you ask. On their eight years with Atlantic, Peter Wolf and company released some of THE "best white R&B" records of all time. Some sold well, some sold moderately, and some just plain tanked. The one thing that remained a constant was the band's monolithically inspired live performances. Unfortunately for Atlantic, as soon as the band left the label, almost overnight, with a newly retooled, more compact sound, success would find the six-piece on 1980's *Love Stinks* and, of course, on the gigantic blockbuster *Freeze Frame*. If you want to find out just how powerful these guys were, this "best collection" is a decent starting point. Songs like joyous "Give It to Me" or the colossal "Detroit Breakdown" are just some of the highlights. For a brief overview, pick up this set, but if it's a college education that you're after, pick up the band's Rhino anthology, *Houseparty* (a much more worthy compilation replete with killer liner notes). —*John Franck*

Love Stinks / 1980 / EMI America ✦✦✦

Released some two years after the band's EMI debut, *Sanctuary*, the *Love Stinks* project would see the J. Geils Band going in an even more commercial-leaning direction than its predecessor. Taking over the main production duties, keyboard player/main songwriter Seth Justman set out to better the band's gold-plus-selling *Sanctuary*. And to some degree, he wildly succeeded. Although not as consistent or diverse as *Sanctuary*, *Love Stinks* would feature one of the band's most recognizable FM songs ever—the album's infectious title track "Love Stinks." In a live setting, the track would often turn into a veritable *tour de force* only to be outdone by Peter Wolf's hilarious rap about "Adam and Eve in the Garden of Eden smoking weed together," which would introduce the song (often on a nightly basis). "Night Time" is another great, although somewhat typical "rave-on" type of J. Geils song; "No Anchovies Please" is a little strange; and closer "Till the Walls Come Tumblin' Down" is, as the song title hints, just that. Bolstered by "Just Can't Wait," another good album opener, *Love Stinks* turns out to be solid effort, but one that sounds a little outdated at times due to its acerbic, synth textures. Not one of the band's best overall records but one that would allow the band to outdo itself with the classic *Freeze Frame* a year later. —*John Franck*

● **Freeze Frame** / 1981 / EMI America ✦✦✦✦✦

Tempering their bar band R&B with a touch of new wave pop production, the J. Geils Band finally broke through into the big leagues with *Freeze Frame*. Fans of the hard-driving rock of the group's '70s albums will find the sleek sound of *Freeze Frame* slightly disorienting, but the production gives the album cohesion. Good-time rock & roll remains at the core of the group's music, but the sound of the record is glossier, shining with synthesizers and big pop hooks. With its singalong chorus, "Centerfold" exemplifies this trend, but it's merely the tip of the iceberg. "Freeze Frame" has a great stop-start chorus, "Flamethrower" and "Piss on the Wall" rush along on hard-boogie riffs, and "Angel in Blue" is terrific neo-doo wop. There are still a handful of throwaways, but even the filler has a stylized, synthesized flair that makes it enjoyable, and the keepers are among the band's best. —*Stephen Thomas Erlewine*

Showtime! / 1982 / BGO ✦✦

You're Gettin' Even While I'm Gettin' Odd / 1984 / EMI ✦✦

This doesn't sound like the J. Geils Band folks know and love, since Peter Wolf has left the band; *You're Gettin' Even While I'm Gettin' Odd* is mainly keyboardist Seth Justman's baby, and he uses banks and banks of synths along with more traditional keyboards to come up with the palette of sounds used here. The cut "Californicating" glides along courtesy of J. Geils' guitar and there's a slow blues titled "The Bite from Inside," but other than that, much of what's here is simply ordinary. Justman and drummer Stephen Bladd cover the vocals this time out, but they are no match for Wolf's old growl. Lots of production dazzle with none of the bite of old. —*James Chrispell*

Flashback / 1988 / EMI America ✦✦✦

Featuring a hodgepodge of material taken from the band's three biggest career selling records (all on EMI), *Flashback* is an all too brief ten-track affair which includes a handful of classics like "Love Stinks," "Centerfold," "Freeze Frame," and a couple of other essential J. Geils Band "deep" cuts like "Flamethrower" and the terrific "Just Can't Wait." Incomprehensibly, other essentials like "Sanctuary," "Teresa," "Just Can't Stop Me," "Nightime," and even the hilarious "Piss on the Wall" (not so essential) are nowhere to be found. Glancing over the track listing, it's obvious that EMI spent next to no time putting together this compilation and decided to issue it as some sort of contractual obligation (even though Peter Wolf would continue to release solo records for the label in years to come) or perhaps as a forgone catalog piece. And that's too bad. It sure would have been nice to hear the live version of "Love Stinks" from *Showtime* (which is introduced by Wolf's now legendary, "Adam and Eve were smoking weed in the Garden of Eden" rap) or perhaps some other un-released live gems from the band's Freeze Frame tour—their biggest outing ever. Wisely, the label chose to completely shun the band's god-awful post-Peter Wolf release *You're Getting Even While I'm Getting I'm Getting Odd*. As far as compilation records go, this one's the weakest of all the J. Geils Band anthologies. For a more thorough appreciation, invest in the much superior Rhino collection *Houseparty: Anthology*. Better yet, pick up one of the band's old live records like *Blow Your Face Out* or even *Full House* (both feature material from the band's superior Atlantic releases). —*John Franck*

● **Houseparty: Anthology** / 1992 / Rhino ✦✦✦✦

The superb two-disc anthology *Houseparty* concentrates on the rousing, full-throttle blues-boogie of their heyday, including a full album's worth of live material (ten songs from their three live albums). The pop success of *Love Stinks* and *Freeze Frame* makes sense in the context of the set, but the songs that cut the deepest are the blues-rock numbers on the first disc and the live songs. Thankfully, the compilers (Trouser Press editor Ira Robbins and band members Peter Wolf and Seth Justman) end *Houseparty* with three songs from *Sanctuary*, helping secure the image of the J. Geils Band as one of America's top rock & roll groups. —*Stephen Thomas Erlewine*

Gene

f. 1993, England
Britpop, Alternative Pop/Rock

Gene will forever be haunted by comparisons to the Smiths, especially since lead singer Martin Rossiter favors the same strangled croon and tortured loneliness of Morrissey. Nevertheless, under the direction of guitarist Steve Mason, Gene developed a tougher sound than the Smiths, drawing not only from the fey tradition of British indie-pop, but also from the three-chord raunch of the Faces, the working-class punk of the Jam, and the soulful stomp of Motown. Most critics didn't hear such subtle differences, and the group earned as many detractors as supporters upon the release of their first single in 1994. Nevertheless, Gene developed a devoted following with their debut *Olympian*, emerging as one of the leading artists of the Brit-pop second tier in 1995, even if the band had trouble breaking into the States. Gene's success in its homeland was short-lived as well. *Olympian* may have debuted in the Top 10, but 1996's *To See the Lights*, a collection of B-sides and BBC sessions, played only to the fans, and 1997's *Drawn to the Deep End* was greeted with mixed reviews and quickly fell down the charts. Nevertheless, the group's core audience remained loyal, supporting them through a third album and a live record in 2000 with a passion similar to … well, Morrissey's devotees. —*Stephen Thomas Erlewine*

● **Olympian** / Jun. 6, 1995 / Polydor ✦✦✦✦

Kicking off with the sprightly "Haunted by You," *Olympian* immediately conjures images of the Smiths, particularly "This Charming Man." Martin Rossiter's voice also sways like Morrissey, yet his band plays their songs as if they were hard rockers, bringing a desperate edge to their best material. Most of *Olympian*'s finest moments were singles—aside from "Haunted by You," the epic sweep of "Sleep Well Tonight" and the gentle urgency of the title track form the heart of the album; two other singles were added to the American version, including the stellar "Be My Light, Be My Guide." While Gene manages to carve out an identity indebted to the Smiths but not dominated by them, they also fail to produce an album of consistently compelling material—considering that it's a debut album, that's not a fatal flaw. And Gene's best material shows they are capable of transcending their influences. —*Stephen Thomas Erlewine*

To See the Lights / Jan. 1996 / Costermonger ✦✦✦✦

The easy joke is, *To See the Lights* is Gene's *Hatful of Hollow*. True, the album is a collection of B-sides, non-album singles, radio sessions, and live tracks but, like the Smiths' *Hatful of Hollow* before it, the album illustrates the band's strengths more effectively than their debut album, *Olympian*. Several of Gene's greatest songs, including the roaring title track, the anthemic "Be My Light, Be My Guide," and the gorgeous "I Can't Decide If She Really Loves Me," are all rounded up on the album and they are frequently stronger than some of the material that appeared on the *Olympian* singles are better, illustrating that the band can rock with a vengeance. It might appear to be an album designed solely for fans, but *To See the Lights* is a better, more compulsively listenable album than *Olympian*. —*Stephen Thomas Erlewine*

Drawn to the Deep End / Mar. 1997 / Polydor ✦✦✦

Gene thrashes all over the place on their second album *Drawn to the Deep End*, as if they were anxious to shake off any comparison to the Smiths. Opening with the textured, near-art-rock of "New Amusements" and moving into the revamped pop-soul stomp of "Fighting Fit," the record initially doesn't sound like the tragically doomed bed-sit pop of *Olympian*, and it seems like *Drawn to the Deep End* might be a great leap forward. Unfortunately, Gene doesn't quite have the vision to carry through with their promise. Quite a few cuts kick with either a self-determined drive ("Speak to Me Someone") or a sense of tragic grace ("Where Are They Now?") or, at best, both, like on "We Could Be Kings." But the band quickly becomes victims of their own ambition and botched execution. The record becomes bogged down with turgid ballads or failed experiments that come off as weak art-rock. Still, the Queen-styled chorus of "I Love You, What Are You?" are charming, and it is endearing to hear the band try so hard to move forward, but the lack of focus makes the album less affecting than the hero-worship of *Olympian*. —*Stephen Thomas Erlewine*

Revelations / 1999 / Polydor ✦✦✦

Gene more or less disposes of the Mancunian monkeys on their backs (the Smiths) with *Revelations*. Not as thick, emotionally draining, or cinematic as 1997's *Drawn to the Deep End*, Gene enlists another excellent producer in the form of Hugh Jones. Surprisingly,

Jones doesn't add the graceful, rich luster to *Revelations* that he did to other great records like the Kitchens of Distinction's *Strange Free World* or the Teardrop Explodes' *Kilimanjaro*. Instead, the sound is sharp and heavy on the high end. With Martin Rossiter getting hitched and becoming a father, his writing material is now focused more on politics than heartbreak. And yes, there's an ode to his "Little Child."

Their dramatics haven't been sacrificed by any stroke, but *Revelations* feels more like a batch of songs in the manner of their debut than their cinematic studio offering from 1997. The band might be running low on ideas, but they still sound full of fire. More than anything, they deserve credit for fearlessly maintaining an emotional edge that so few of their peers in the British scene lack or avoid. And Steve Mason is surely one excellent guitarist who's gone overlooked far too long. —*Andy Kellman*

Rising for Sunset / Aug. 16, 2000 / Contra ✦✦✦

It's a strange move. After the critical and public antipathy towards Gene's third proper studio album *Revelations*, the band packed their bags, flew to Los Angeles to play some small shows, and recorded their performances for a live album. Strangest of all, this is one of Gene's best releases. More bands should be this peculiar. Though they're playing in a venue more the size of a swimming pool than an airport hangar, they sound absolutely wonderful: "Where Are They Now?" is more subtly elegant than ever; "Speak to Me Someone" reaches an unstoppable, euphoric crescendo. Hearing a bunch of Californians singing along to "London, Can You Wait?" or "The British Disease" is also amusing. The album only sags during the repetitive "Mayday" (and sadly lacks the new song "Who Said This Was the End?"). While guitarist Steve Mason is inevitably compared to The Smiths' Johnny Marr, these performances prove that Mason's playing is more fluid and wistful than Marr's hard-lined melodic style. At times, as on "As Good As It Gets'" rolling bridge, it's actually far more effective than anything the Smiths recorded. It helps that the new songs sound promising for a band relegated to "always the bridesmaid" status: the string-driven title-track and the delicate finale "Somewhere in My World" are fitting teases for things to come. A year after the world considered the band down and out, Gene are still alive and kicking with grace. Martin Rossiter jokingly tells the crowd a few times during the concert, "Oh shut up," but fans listening to *Rising For Sunset* can know how much the band deserves to hear the opposite. —*Dean Carlson*

● **As Good As It Gets** / May 28, 2001 / Costermonger ✦✦✦✦✦

General Public

f. 1983, **db.** 1987
Club/Dance, Ska Revival, New Wave

This U.K. duo of vocalist Dave Wakeling (b. Feb 19, 1956) and "toaster" Ranking Roger (b. Feb 21, 1961) was formed from the split of the English Beat in 1983. General Public released two albums before they split. In 1994, General Public reunited and had a surprise hit single with their UB40-style interpretation of the Staple Singers' "I'll Take You There," taken from the *Threesome* soundtrack. This led to the release of a new album, *Rub It Better*, in 1995. —*William Ruhlmann*

● **All the Rage** / 1984 / IRS ✦✦✦✦

The vocal duo from the English Beat turn in an album of passionate pop-rock, little of which bears the ska style of the parent group. Most effective are the uptempo, Motown-style songs, especially the Top 30 hit "Tenderness." —*William Ruhlmann*

Hand to Mouth / 1986 / IRS ✦✦✦

Although it still has some of the pop smarts that informed *All the Rage*, General Public has toned down their ska and reggae roots, making *Hand to Mouth* a more professional, but less exciting, album. —*Stephen Thomas Erlewine*

Rub It Better / Apr. 4, 1995 / Epic ✦✦✦

General Public earned a second shot with its Top 40 cover of "I'll Take You There" in 1994. But the group took a year to complete this reunion album, which did not include the hit. Instead, Dave Wakeling and Ranking Roger alternated tracks, with Wakeling's employing the dense, multi-rhythmic sound found on producer Jerry Harrison's solo albums and Roger's in a more conventional reggae-with-toasting style. Only occasionally (for example, on "Handgun") did Wakeling display the talent for catchy pop he had previously displayed on songs like "Save It for Later" and "Tenderness." *Rub It Better* suggested that General Public had reformed without a clear idea of what kind of music it wanted to make or who its audience was. Wakeling and Roger remained a talented twosome, but one in need of direction. —*William Ruhlmann*

Generation X

f. 1976, **db.** 1981
British Punk, Punk

An early London punk band (1978-1981), Generation X featured Billy Idol and Tony James (later to form Sigue Sigue Sputnik). Often criticized as being too commercially minded, Gen X was definitely the smoothest and most pop-oriented of their rebellious crowd. Their first album is considered the best, with the U.S. version offering a slightly improved song set. Their third and last, *Kiss Me Deadly*, was more an Idol/James project than a band effort and was produced by Keith Forsey, who shaped Idol's solo sound. This album contained an early version of "Dancing With Myself," which was eventually Idol's first big solo pop success. As to whether they were a band of crass opportunists or true champions of the punk spirit, Billy Idol's career and Sigue Sigue Sputnik's dubious distinction of having the first advertisement on a pop record speak volumes. —*Scott Bultman*

Generation X [UK Version] / 1979 / Chrysalis/EMI ✦✦✦✦✦

Generation X had punk attitude and subject matter on their debut album, which includes their answer song to the Who, "Your Generation," and the generic "One Hundred Punks."

But the group's music already had more of a melodic mainstream rock sound than punk's raw assault, and frontman Billy Idol's snarl was straight out of Elvis Presley. *—William Ruhlmann*

Valley of the Dolls / 1979 / Chrysalis ✦✦
Billy Idol's solo posturing and Tony James' excruciating work with Sigue Sigue Sputnik have long provided cheap targets for rock critics (and cheap-seat entertainment for undiscriminating fans). But ridicule should not be so readily heaped on former employers, Generation X. Never in the same league as the Clash or the Pistols, the group nevertheless kicked up a fair amount of dust and recorded some memorable singles and a classy debut album. They were, after all, the first of the punk bands to truly embrace the rock industry and all its trappings. But on this, their second album, the band's limitations are self-evident. Produced by glitter rock veteran Ian Hunter, "King Rocker" and "Running With the Boss Sound" prove the only diverting moments in this bleak parade of glam punk by numbers. *—Alex Ogg*

Kiss Me Deadly / 1981 / Chrysalis ✦✦✦
Idol and bassist Brian James rehearse for their post-Gen X careers, respectively as a solo artist and as the leader of Sigue Sigue Sputnik. This album contains the dance hit "Dancing With Myself." *—William Ruhlmann*

● **Perfect Hits 1975-1981** / 1985 / Chrysalis ✦✦✦✦
Besides attempting to be the definitive Generation X compilation, *Perfect Hits 1975—1981* seeks to give the band punk credibility with its erroneous title (the band formed in late 1976). The collection wisely focuses on their vastly superior debut LP by incorporating two more songs than on *The Best of Generation X*, though "Wild Dub" should have been omitted. What's missing are subsequent album tracks like "Running With the Boss Sound," "Night of the Cadillacs," and "Revenge," all included on *The Best of Generation X*. The compilers try to please collectors, but miss the mark with a poorly mixed BBC version of "Day by Day," an unspecified take of John Lennon's "Gimme Some Truth" (marred by an out-of-tune guitar), and the obscurity "New Order," which is only a mediocre tune, at best. *—Bart Bealmear*

Genesis

f. 1966, Godalming, England
Album Rock, Pop/Rock, Soft Rock, Prog Rock/Art Rock, Adult Contemporary
One of the most successful rock acts of the 1970's, 1980's, and 1990's, Genesis enjoyed a longevity exceeded only by the likes of the Rolling Stones and the Kinks, in the process providing a launching pad for the superstardom of members Peter Gabriel and Phil Collins. The theatrical attributes of Gabriel's singing fit in well with the group's live performances, and he began to make ever more extensive use of masks, make-up, and props in concert, telling framing stories in order to set up their increasingly complicated songs. When presented amid the group's very strong playing, this aspect of Gabriel's work turned Genesis's performances into multi-media events. *Foxtrot*, issued in the fall of 1972, was the flashpoint in Genesis' history, and not just on commercial terms. The writing was as sophisticated as anything in progressive rock, and the lyrics were complex, serious and clever, a far cry from the usual overblown words attached to most prog rock. The release of the ambitious double LP *The Lamb Lies Down on Broadway* in late 1974 marked the culmination of the group's early history; in 1975, Gabriel announced that he was leaving Genesis. Drummer Collins took over the role of lead singer, and the resulting *Trick of the Tail* made number three in England and number 31 in America, the best chart showing up to that time for a Genesis album. In 1978, Genesis released *And Then There Were Three*, which abandoned any efforts at progressive rock in favor of a softer, much more accessible and less ambitious pop sound. After a flurry of solo projects, the group reconvened for 1980's *Duke*, which became their first chart-topper in England while rising to number 11 in America. *Abacab*, released in late 1981, was another smash, and 1983's self-titled *Genesis* furthered the group's record of British chart-toppers and American top 10 hits, becoming their second million-selling U.S. album while also yielding their first American Top Ten single, "That's All." Two years later, the group outdid themselves with the release of their most commercially successful album to date, *Invisible Touch*. Their 1991 album *We Can't Dance* debuted at number one in England and got to number four in America; it was Collins' last album with the group. *—Bruce Eder*

From Genesis to Revelation / Mar. 1969 / Decca ✦✦
This collection of music, which has appeared under license to various labels in addition to Decca and London in different configurations, is largely of historical interest. The group was still in its formative stages, the members barely past their 18th birthdays and still working out what they wanted to sound like. Mostly they sound like the Bee Gees trying to be the Moody Blues (picture something similar to the sound of the former group's *Odessa* album). "The Silent Sun" and "Where the Sour Turns to Sweet" are pleasant enough, but scarcely indicate the true potential of the group or its members. A pleasant enough piece of pop-psychedelia/art-rock, but not a critically important release, except to the truly dedicated. *—Bruce Eder*

Trespass / Oct. 1970 / MCA ✦✦
The group's first truly progressive album, and their first record for the Charisma label (although *Trespass* was released in America by ABC, which is how MCA comes to have it today), is important mostly as a formative effort. Peter Gabriel, Tony Banks, and Michael Rutherford are here, but the guitarist is Anthony Phillips, and the drummer is John Mayhew. Gabriel, Banks, Phillips, and Rutherford are responsible for the compositions, which are far more ambitious than the group's earlier efforts ("Silent Sun," etc.). Unfortunately, much of what is here is more interesting for what it points toward than what it actually *does*—the group reflects a peculiarly dramatic brand of progressive rock, very theatrical as music, but not very successful. The lyrics are complex enough, but lack the unity and clarity that would make Genesis' subsequent albums among the most interesting of prog-rock efforts to analyze. Gabriel's voice is very expressive but generally lacks power and confidence, while the conventional backup vocalizing by the others is wimpy, and Phillips' playing is muted. Tony Banks' keyboards are the dominant instruments, which isn't that bad, but it isn't the Genesis that everyone came to know. The soft, lyrical "Visions of Angels" and "Stagnation" are typical, gentle works by a band that later learned how to rock much harder. Only one of the songs here, "The Knife"—which rocks harder than anything else on *Trespass* and is easily the best track on the album—lasted in the group's concert repertory past the next album. The MCA CD sounds good enough, though it was not remastered at the time the Charisma/Atlantic output by the band was redone. *—Bruce Eder*

Nursery Cryme / Nov. 1971 / Atco ✦✦✦
The group's first fully realized, mature album is still somewhat uneven, but the stuff that does work well works so well that it carries the record. This includes "The Musical Box," which became a highlight of the group's live shows, presenting Gabriel's extraordinary abilities as a singer/actor as well as hinting at a level of lyrical sophistication that dazzled many fans and onlookers. "Return of the Giant Hogweed" was an even better showcase for the group's playing. The "Definitive Edition Remaster" version runs circles around the sound on all previous versions, although a certain weakness in the engineering (obviously in the original recording, and beyond repair) remains, especially where the presence of Collins' drums in relation to the rest of the band (particularly on the acoustic passages) is concerned. *—Bruce Eder*

☆ **Foxtrot** / Oct. 1972 / Atco ✦✦✦✦✦
This was the point where all of the talent simmering and occasionally boiling up out of Genesis blew the lid off the pot. There isn't a weak song here, and the two showpieces, "Watcher of the Skies" and "Supper's Ready," presented the group at its strongest in medium-length and extended-length songs. The lyrical complexities of the latter were not easily sorted out, but they were clever enough and inviting enough not to put off any potential fans, and as handled by Gabriel, they demanded attention. And not only is the band playing loud on a lot of this album, but the engineer captured them perfectly. The Definitive Remastered Edition released in 1995 supplants all prior versions of the compact disc. *—Bruce Eder*

Genesis: Live / Jun. 1973 / Atco ✦✦✦
Essentially a live best-of with one glaring omission, *Live* was issued in America nearly a year after it reached the Top Ten in England. A well-recorded showcase of the early group's concert sound, much of what is here actually works better than the studio versions of the same songs—"The Musical Box," "The Knife," "Return of the Giant Hogweed," and "Watcher of the Skies" are heard in livelier, tighter versions than their excellent originals. The only drawback is that in preparing to CD, nobody thought to try and retrieve the performance of "Supper's Ready" from the same set of tapes that yielded the original LP—it would've been a nice CD bonus. The Definitive Remastered Edition is not only superior to earlier versions of this disc, but is easier to find as well. *—Bruce Eder*

★ **Selling England by the Pound** / Nov. 1973 / Atco ✦✦✦✦✦
By the Ezra Pound, no doubt—seriously, the influence of T.S. Eliot and other early 20th-century literary figures crops up throughout the opening and closing portions of this album, with the rest of the songs given over to more conventional subject matter. The original group's strongest single album and, for those not predisposed to enjoy the double-disc *Lamb Lies Down on Broadway*, the peak of their output. The production is note-perfect, and not an instrument is out of place. The Definitive Remastered Edition from 1996 is a significant improvement, in sound and packaging, over the earlier version from Atlantic. *—Bruce Eder*

★ **The Lamb Lies Down on Broadway** / Nov. 18, 1974 / Atco ✦✦✦✦✦
The group's only double studio album was the culmination of their early period, featuring Peter Gabriel in a bravura performance in the role of Rael, a New York street hustler, in this musical drama. The singing and playing are all strong, and the remastered edition from 1995 is the first CD edition that sounds as good as (or better than) the superb original Atco pressing from 1975. The piece's length makes it something of an acquired taste, but most serious fans regard this as the best record the group ever cut. *—Bruce Eder*

Trick of the Tail / Feb. 2, 1976 / Atco ✦✦✦✦✦
The quality of the group's first post-Peter Gabriel album astonished everyone, especially coming out after an 18-month gap following *The Lamb Lies Down on Broadway*. The opening number, "Dance on a Volcano," almost deliberately recalls "Cinema Show" from *Selling England by the Pound* in melody and structure, and Phil Collins sounds more like Peter Gabriel than Gabriel himself did. Tony Banks' and Steve Hackett's "Entangled" was the prettiest song the group had recorded up to that time, a gossamer-textured piece about sleep and dreaming in which a strummed acoustic guitar makes its most prominent appearance ever on a Genesis song, supported by the sweetest singing of Collins' career. Not all of the material is in league with these two songs, but all of it has some moments of tremendous beauty, and Tony Banks' "Robbery, Assault and Battery," with its bold, hard-rocking choruses and extended song structure, would have been worthy of inclusion on any of the group's earlier records. Even "Los Endos," an instrumental finale that ought to be considered a cop-out in the absence of a good song, provides the quartet with an opportunity to showcase its still considerable collective skills to which few fans could object. The 1995 "Definitive Edition Remaster" is a vast improvement in sound and packaging over the earlier CD version and is the one worth picking up. *—Bruce Eder*

Wind & Wuthering / Dec. 27, 1976 / Atco ✦✦✦✦
For many veteran fans, *Wind & Wuthering* was the last near-great Genesis album, as well as their last album to feature a progressive rock sound. The group's second (and last)

album as a quartet, it features the requisite long-form songs, complete with slashing guitars, rippling synthesizers, sweeping Mellotron passages, and elegant piano parts, along with some beautifully complex and poetic lyrics. Songs like "Eleventh Earl of Mar," "One for the Vine," and "All in a Mouse's Night" are the equals of the better (but not the best) work from the band's Peter Gabriel era, but the most important song on this album was Michael Rutherford's "Your Own Special Way," an edited version of which became their first single to make the American charts (and only their second British chart hit). Although most of the songs are more complex and challenging, they also present a sense of marking time, while "Your Own Special Way" pointed the way toward the simpler, more accessible sound that the group was moving toward. The 1995 reissue, part of Atco's "Definitive Edition Remaster" series, from the original master tapes is considerably more impressive than the original late-'80s CD, and includes full lyrics and production credits as well. *—Bruce Eder*

Seconds Out / Nov. 1977 / Atlantic ♦♦
On its second live album (a double), recorded in 1976 and 1977, Genesis tried to make the case that its two manifestations, Genesis-with-Peter Gabriel and Genesis-without-Peter Gabriel, were actually one entity. They didn't really succeed, sounding instead like, on the one hand, the new post-Gabriel Genesis on side one and most of side four, and on the other hand, a Gabriel/Genesis soundalike band on sides two and three, on which Phil Collins handled Gabriel's vocals on such favorites as "Supper's Ready." *—William Ruhlmann*

And Then There Were Three / Mar. 23, 1978 / Atlantic ♦♦♦
Having lost frontman Peter Gabriel and guitarist Steve Hackett during the preceding three years, Genesis soldiered on as a trio with this 1978 release. They had previously scaled the prog-rock heights in their own very English, literate, and dramatic way, producing a relatively tuneful and provocative mix out of Tony Banks, Mike Rutherford, and Hackett's architectronic charts; Collins' fluidly sophisticated drumming; and Gabriel's theatrics. Foreshadowing the band's later incarnation as a very pop-friendly, chart-topping outfit, *And Then There Were Three* straddles the divide between the band's earlier, often times verbose explorations and later radio-issue tracks, like 1986's "Invisible Touch." With Collins' ascendancy not too far off, Banks and Rutherford hold court with impressive ballads like "Many Too Many" and "Snowbound." While a tad overarching in spots, the sentiment is generally well-framed. Rutherford furthers his credibility on the jazz-tinged, barroom ballad "Say It's Alright Joe." When the trio teams up on multi-tempo/mood sides like "Ballad of Big," though, the going gets confusing, with nicely turned bursts of melody often giving way to leaden passages. But somehow they find an unadulterated groove on their first major hit, "Follow You Follow Me," setting the stage for the many smashes that would follow. Sure, there are cringe-inducing guitar breaks and questionable synthesizer textures along the way, but both the Genesis purist and latter-day fan should still find much to enjoy here. *—Stephen Cook*

Duke / Mar. 31, 1980 / Atlantic ♦♦♦
Released in April 1980, *Duke* found Genesis completely geared up as a maker of concise, appealing pop singles, and it was an immediate, across-the-board hit, topping the U.K. chart and almost making the U.S. Top 10, while the singles "Misunderstanding" and "Turn It On Again" became radio favorites on both sides of the Atlantic. *—William Ruhlmann*

● **Abacab** / Sep. 14, 1981 / Atlantic ♦♦♦♦♦
After gaining some limited commercial success with *Duke*, Genesis went for the jugular of American radio with the well-crafted pop of *Abacab*. While there are still some traces of their art rock past, the album is primarily filled with a new wave sound and concise songs. Phil Collins, who replaced Peter Gabriel years earlier as the lead vocalist, was finally comfortable with his role as the leader of the band, and his influence is more prominent. Although he's not a strong vocalist, Collins more than makes up for it with passionate performances. "Man on the Corner," a modest hit, managed to make social commentary about the homeless without feeling preachy. *Abacab* rose to number seven on the charts, which is a tribute the band's ability to bring intellectual pop to the masses with catchy melodies. Genesis is no ordinary pop band—they use driving beats and unusual syncopation (by pop standards) on the title track and "No Reply at All," a song that employs the horn section from Earth, Wind & Fire. This album is one of their most enjoyable, and it gave Genesis the success and recognition they deserved. *—Vik Iyengar*

Three Sides Live / Jun. 1982 / Atlantic ♦♦♦
On its third live album (another double), Genesis brought listeners up to date on the trio version of the group and its recent hit singles from *Abacab* and *Duke*. The U.K. version of the album (Charisma GE 2002), despite the title, was an all-live album, while the American version (Atlantic SD 2-2000), had three live sides and a fourth side of studio material, including the Top 40 hit "Paperlate" (which appeared in the U.K. as part of an EP called *3 By 3*). *—William Ruhlmann*

Genesis / Oct. 1983 / Atlantic ♦♦♦♦
If Genesis still had one foot in the art rock world with *Abacab*, they jumped into pop with both feet on their eponymous release. Genesis used crisp, glossy production and mid-tempo arrangements designed for pop radio in the 1980s. After years of relative obscurity on this side of the Atlantic, one cannot blame the band, especially one so talented. There were many hits, the biggest of which were the slower easy listening songs such as "That's All" or "Taking It All Too Hard." While all the songs are unbelievable catchy, they often mask inane lyrics ("Illegal Alien") and the lack of musical innovation that fans had come to expect was a little disappointing. Although they had lost their edge, Genesis still had the ability to craft catchy songs. *Genesis* still represents the best pop radio of that era, and the album is still recommended for fans looking for 1980s nostalgia or fans of Phil Collins' solo work. *—Vik Iyengar*

Invisible Touch / Jun. 1986 / Atlantic ♦♦♦
The biggest Genesis hit to date, this multi-million-selling release features five Top Five hits, including the number one title track, "Throwing It All Away," "Land of Confusion," "Tonight, Tonight, Tonight," and "In Too Deep." *—William Ruhlmann*

We Can't Dance / Oct. 28, 1991 / Atlantic ♦♦♦
After spending the 1980s moving in an increasingly pop-friendly direction, 1991's *We Can't Dance* marked a return to earlier aesthetics for Genesis. Edgier with more prominent guitars and live drums than on *Invisible Touch*, the record was the band's strongest musical statement in over a decade. With "Driving the Last Spike" and the dark "Dreaming While You Sleep" the group revisited one of their forgotten strengths; telling extended stories. That's not to say the album is a return to *The Lamb Lies Down on Broadway* or *Trick of the Tail*. Indeed, while there are several extended pieces on the record, there is none of the eccentricities, odd meters, or extended virtuoso solos of the band's progressive heyday. The album's closer, "Fading Lights," comes the closest, featuring an outstanding instrumental mid-section. Unfortunately, the record also contains some gutless ballads and peons for world understanding that sound miles away from any immediacy. However, the surprisingly gritty singles "No Son of Mine," "Jesus He Knows Me," and "I Can't Dance" help make up for the album's weaker moments. *—Geoff Orens*

Genesis Live: The Way We Walk, Vol. 1 (The Shorts) / Nov. 17, 1992 / Atlantic ♦♦

Genesis Live: The Way We Walk, Vol. 2 (The Longs) / Feb. 9, 1993 / Atlantic ♦♦♦
The second CD culled from the We Can't Dance tour, *The Way We Walk Volume Two: The Longs* was designed to draw interest from Genesis' older fans, featuring the more progressive material from their shows. However, no music here outside of the "Old Medley" predates 1983, and while the band continued to write decent longer material through 1991's *We Can't Dance*, those songs were nowhere near as eclectic and experimental as the group's earlier work. That said, both "Domino" and "Home by the Sea" sound tighter and more powerful than on their already solid studio versions. And while the unfortunate "Old Medley" leaves the heart out of the band's earlier material, "Driving the Last Spike" and "Fading Lights" sound great live and are less polished than the studio versions on *We Can't Dance*. In the end, the album is fine way to catch up on the group's post-progressive days for those who do not want to deal with the pop songs that dominate their later records. *—Geoff Orens*

Calling All Stations / Sep. 2, 1997 / Atlantic ♦♦
Phil Collins left Genesis following the *We Can't Dance* tour and many obersvers expected Tony Banks and Michael Rutherford to finally call it a day. They decided to persevere instead, hiring former Stiltskin vocalist Ray Wilson to replace Collins. Given that Stiltskin was a European neo-prog band, it isn't a total surprise that Genesis returned to their art-rock roots on *Calling All Stations*, their first album with Wilson. The music on *Calling All Stations* is long, dense, and lugubrious, but it's given the same immaculate, pristine production that was the hallmark of their adult contemporary work with Collins. It wants to be an art-rock album, but not at the expense of losing the pop audience—which makes it all the stranger that the group doesn't really *write* pop songs on *Calling All Stations*. That may be because Wilson's voice isn't suited for pop, but works well with languid, synthesized prog settings. But even ponderous prog rock has to have musical themes worth exploring, and on that level, Genesis comes up dry on *Calling All Stations*. *—Stephen Thomas Erlewine*

Genesis Archives, Vol. 1: 1967-1975—The Gabriel Years / Jun. 16, 1998 / Atlantic ♦♦♦♦
Prog-rock audiences have always been receptive to box sets, especially sets that include an abundance of rare material—witness the success of the numerous King Crimson sets. When it came time to assembling their own box sets, Genesis chose to follow the path of rarities instead of merely rehashing their old hits. That means, of course, that *Genesis Archives, Vol. 1: 1967-75—The Gabriel Years* is the province of hardcore fans and collectors, not casual listeners, since there is nothing but unreleased material on the four-disc set. The first two discs are devoted to a live performance of *The Lamb Lies Down on Broadway* at the Shrine Auditorium in Los Angeles on January 24, 1975; the third has a selection of live material from the London Rainbow Theatre on October 20, 1973, plus a handful of rare singles and a BBC session; the fourth has alternate mixes, BBC sessions and demos from 1967-1969. It's a virtual cornucopia of rare material, much of which will be necessary to dedicated fans. However, for some listeners, the set may be frustrating, and not because it contains rarities—it's because those rarities have been tampered with. Peter Gabriel recut some of his vocals for *The Lamb* in 1998, claiming that he didn't give his best possible performance because his elaborate costumes were constricting. Steve Hackett followed suit and "brushed up" some guitar lines. This may frustrate some fans who would prefer to have the original tapes preserved, but it may be a minor thing to collectors, who will likely delight in having all these rare recordings—many of which are quite terrific—in one place. *—Stephen Thomas Erlewine*

● **Turn It On Again: The Hits** / Oct. 26, 1999 / Atlantic ♦♦♦♦
Originally, there were plans for two Genesis box sets—one covering the classic Peter Gabriel era, the other chronicling the band's development into hit-makers under the direction of Phil Collins. The Gabriel set was released in 1998, but instead of a second box following it in 1999, the single-disc *Turn It On Again: The Hits* appeared. Truth be told, it was a wise move, because even if the Collins set appears, there will be a market for a concise collection of hits, which *Turn It On Again* more or less is. Since Genesis had such a prolific career and had so many hits, it should come as no surprise that the compilation isn't complete, but it's a little disappointing to discover that such latter-day nonentities as "Hold on My Heart" (from the last Collins album, *We Can't Dance*) and "Congo" (from the post-Collins album, *Calling All Stations*) are included in favor of such fine singles as "Paperlate" or "Man on the Corner." But that's nitpicking, since all the big hits are here:

"Turn It On Again," "Invisible Touch," "Follow You, Follow Me," "Tonight, Tonight, Tonight," "In Too Deep," "That's All," "Misunderstanding," "Throwing It All Away"...the list goes on and on. True, the sublime Gabriel number "I Know What I Like (In Your Wardrobe)" sounds completely out of place sandwiched between "Abacab" and "No Son of Mine," but it's nice to have it here. Similarly, "The Carpet Crawlers 1999," reworked as a duet between Collins and Gabriel, is a surprisingly effective re-recording, and a nice inclusion. It may not be enough to convince hardcore fans that they need *Turn It On Again*, but this album is really for listeners who've thought of Genesis as a singles act, and they're not going to be disappointed by this. *—Stephen Thomas Erlewine*

Genesis Archives, Vol. 2: 1976-1992 / Nov. 7, 2000 / Atlantic ✦✦✦

The first *Genesis Archive* made sense. It covered the Peter Gabriel years, an era that was not only supremely creative for the band, but filled with rarities, forgotten tracks, outtakes, B-sides, BBC sessions, and live performances begging for a collection. It was a box set for fans and it filled its purpose splendidly. Its sequel, *Genesis Archive 2: 1976-1992*, attempts to fill the role for the Genesis Mach II, otherwise known as the Phil Collins years, but the problem is, the Collins era was completely different from Gabriel's. It wasn't just that the band became progressively more pop oriented during these 16 years—besides, they never totally abandoned their prog roots—but the late '70s and '80s simply were not conducive to the kind of rarities that made the first *Archive* valuable. They didn't need to do BBC sessions, they didn't do non-LP rarities live, and their B-sides were often devoted to extended mixes for the dance club or live cuts. If there were outtakes, they were often left in the can because they simply didn't meet quality-control standards. All of this is borne out by the three-disc *Archive 2*. Although there are some nice moments scattered throughout the record, it all winds up feeling rather unnecessary. None of the remixes are particularly interesting and the live tracks, while listenable, are never revelatory—and those wind up forming the bulk of the set. There's some value in the outtakes, but most of them are historical curiosities; only a handful, such as the *Abacab* leftover "You Might Recall" and an early version of "Paperlate," are truly worthwhile. For anyone other than hardcore fans, this can easily be overlooked. *—Stephen Thomas Erlewine*

Genius (Gary Grice)

b. New York, NY

Vocals / Hardcore Rap, East Coast Rap, Hip-Hop

Inside and outside of the Wu-Tang Clan, the inventive hip-hop supergroup he co-founded, Staten Island, NY native GZA/Genius likes to make his own rules when it comes to his music. GZA/Genius grew up in a large, musically inclined family that included cousins Ol' Dirty Bastard and RZA; as the eldest of the three, he was the first to absorb hip-hop culture and the first to make a record. 1989's *Words From the Genius* was released on Cold Chillin' Records; when problems with the label stifled record sales, GZA/Genius saw the other side of the record industry. This inspired him to join forces with Ol' Dirty Bastard and RZA among others as the Wu-Tang Clan; the group's clever wordplay, twisted humor, and innovative production techniques provided them with platinum-level success on their own terms. It also provided Genius the opportunity to have an equally lucrative solo career, which started with the 1995 album *Liquid Swords* and continued with 1999's *Beneath the Surface*. As with other Wu-Tang side-projects, Genius/GZA's albums featured guest appearances from most of the other Wu-Tang Clan members. *—Heather Phares*

★ **Liquid Swords** / Nov. 1995 / Geffen ✦✦✦✦✦

Contending with Raekwon's *Only Built for Cuban Linx* for the status of being the overall best Wu-Tang solo album of the 1990s, the Genius' *Liquid Swords* ultimately proves so effective due to the synergy of the rapper's ultra-literate rhymes and RZA's consistently foreboding production. What proves to be even more amazing is how both the Genius and RZA maintain their stellar efforts from the album's kung-fu flick intro to the album's prophetic conclusion—this album features no filler. In a way, the album is the perfect medium between the cinematic decadence of *Only Built for Cuban Linx* and the lyrical heights of Method Man's *Tical*; it has both the evocative production and the dizzying rhymes that made these two albums so wonderful, with few interruptions by outside producers or outside rappers. It is this very attribute that makes *Liquid Swords* such a consistent album from beginning to end. Yet this consistency ultimately ends up being the album's only debatable flaw; if anything, the Genius' well-conceived rhymes come across almost too clinically, as if he's reciting from a book rather than flowing lucidly. As talented as he is, he could use a partner, similar to how Ghostface Killah accompanies Raekwon on *Only Built for Cuban Linx*. Granted, this is a minor complaint; for the most part, this is a nearly flawless album—surely one of the decade's best—and it stands as a benchmark for all Wu-Tang albums to be judged against. And judging by successive RZA-produced albums and the Genius' long-awaited follow-up, *Below the Surface*, this is an album that even its creators struggled to match. *—Jason Birchmeier*

Beneath the Surface / Jun. 29, 1999 / MCA ✦✦✦✦✦

There were so many Wu-Tang-related projects released during 1998 and 1999 that listeners—and even fans—could be forgiven for a bit of apathy regarding the second solo effort by Wu-Tang's Genius/GZA. The collective's trademark detuned strings had gone from *de rigueur* to downright dated by mid-1999, and except for a well-received RZA solo album earlier in the year, the lead in hip-hop's hype game appeared to have been taken over by Timbaland's brand of future funk. It may not have proved the commercial smash of a proper Wu-Tang LP, but Genius/GZA's *Beneath the Surface* is a worthy continuation and development of the Wu-Tang Clan conglomeration. The best tracks here, "Amplified Sample" and "Crash Your Crew," are quintessentially Wu-Tang, but with important tweaks to the trademark sound. The crisp, clean production—by Wu associates Inspectah Deck, Mathematics, and Arabian Priest—sounds much better than any project that had been recently issued (even RZA's *Bobby Digital*), and GZA's raps prove he's the most innovative and talented vocalist Wu-Tang had to offer. The only failure (at least in terms of sound) is "Victim," a cloying track with a bit of scratched acoustic guitar and some *X Files*-styled strings. Other than a few "skits" that disturb the flow, *Beneath the Surface* is arguably the best thing to come out of the Wu camp since their second proper album, *Forever*. *—John Bush*

Gentle Giant

f. 1969, **db.** 1980

Prog Rock/Art Rock

Formed at the dawn of the progressive rock era in 1969, Gentle Giant seemed poised for a time in the mid-'70s to break out of its cult band status, but somehow never made the jump. Somewhat closer in spirit to Yes and King Crimson than to Emerson, Lake & Palmer or the Nice, their unique sound melded hard rock and classical music with an almost medieval approach to singing. Born out of the ruins of the R&B group Simon Dupree & the Big Sound, brothers Derek, Ray, and Phil Shulman formed Gentle Giant and released their self-titled first album in 1970. After the group's third LP, *Three Friends*, earned release in America on Columbia, fourth album *Octopus* looked poised for a breakthrough. The group began falling apart in 1974, however, with Phil Shulman exiting the band and Columbia rejecting their subsequent album. In 1976, Gentle Giant released *Free Hand*, their most commercial album, but then followed it up with the jarringly experimental *Interview*. The group later went through another change of heart and issued a series of albums aimed at mainstream audiences, even approaching disco, but by the end of the 1970s their popularity was in free-fall. Ray Shulman later became a producer and had considerable success in England working with bands like the Sundays and the Sugarcubes, while Derek Shulman became a New York-based record company executive. *—Bruce Eder*

Gentle Giant / 1970 / Polydor ✦✦✦✦

Astonishingly daring debut album, not as focused or overpowering as King Crimson's first but still crashing down barriers and steamrolling expectations. The mix of medieval harmonies and electric rock got stronger on subsequent albums, but the music here is still pretty jarring. Kerry Minear was probably the only prog-rock keyboard player of the era who allowed his synthesizers to sound like themselves and not mimic orchestras; Gary Green's guitars are alternately loud and brittle or soft and lyrical, and always surprising; and the presence of saxes and trumpets (coutesy of Phil Shulman) was unusual in any rock band of the era—all of which explains how Gentle Giant managed to attract a cult following but hadn't a prayer of moving up from that level of recognition. "Funny Ways" was the softest prog-rock song this side of Crimson's "I Talk to the Wind," but a lot of the rest is pretty intense in volume and tempo changes. "Nothing At All" by itself is worth the price of the CD, the release of which marked the first appearance of this album in the U.S. catalog, 20 years after it was recorded. *—Bruce Eder*

Acquiring the Taste / 1971 / Polydor ✦✦✦✦✦

The band's second album is a major advance on its first, featuring superior singing, playing, and songwriting, as well as a more unified sound, without sacrificing the element of surprise in the first record. Many of the melodies and even the riffs here (check out Gary Green's first guitar flourish on "Pantagruel's Nativity") have a pretty high haunt count, and all of the musicianship displays an elegance seldom heard even in progressive circles—but the record also, amazingly enough, rocks really hard as well. Elements of hard rock and Gregorian chants mix freely and, amazingly enough, *well* throughout this album. *—Bruce Eder*

Gentle Giant/Three Friends / 1972 / Vertigo ✦✦✦

Vertigo released two of Gentle Giant's early albums—*Gentle Giant* and *Acquiring the Taste*—as a double-LP set. While this is a nice way to acquire the music on the albums, most fans will be satisfied with the original releases or the CD reissues and won't need to seek this out. *—Stephen Thomas Erlewine*

Three Friends / 1972 / Columbia ✦✦✦✦✦

The band's third album (and their first self-produced effort, Tony Visconti having run the sessions on the two previous records) was another advance, this time in the direction of a harder rock sound—everything sounds turned up here, especially the guitars, the bass, and the electronic keyboards. *Three Friends* hardly sacrificed any of the group's progressive intentions, however, and there are some softer moments here, such as the playful, sprightly first half of "Schooldays"; the harmonies and arrangements still had a distinctly medieval feel, and the melodies, though a little harder to discern here (which made them even more appealing when they did become obvious) were quite engaging. This is supposed to be a concept album, about the relationship between three friends across a lifetime, and the original notes and lyrics have been reprinted, but none of that is necessary in order to enjoy the songs here. *—Bruce Eder*

● **Octopus** / 1972 / Columbia ✦✦✦✦✦

Octopus is Gentle Giant's *magnum opus*, where all the disparate elements of *Acquiring the Taste* come together with bizarre, intertwining vocals. Though it is slightly less extreme than its predecessor, it is actually more accomplished, demonstrating new levels of near-mathematical complexity—it's an album that reaches nearly as far as an octopus itself. It's a singular achievement few other prog-rock groups could equal. *—Daevid Jehnzen*

In a Glass House / 1973 / Dressed to Kill ✦✦✦✦✦

Precisely why this album, recorded in 1973, has never been released in the United States is one of those minor mysteries of the pop music business. The group was reduced to a quintet here with the departure of elder brother Phil Shulman, but its sound is unchanged, and the group may actually be tighter without the presence of his saxophones. The time signatures are still really strange, and the tempo changes are sometimes jarring, as is the wide range of dynamics, but this is also one of the group's most pleasing records—they rock out in various places, and elsewhere perform all kinds of little experiments with percussion instruments ("An Inmate's Lullaby"), or create a strange, otherworldly sort of modern medieval-style music ("Way of Life"). None of it except possibly "A Reunion" is light listening, but the challenge does yield some rewarding sounds. —*Bruce Eder*

The Power and the Glory / 1974 / One Way ✦✦

Free Hand / 1975 / One Way ✦✦✦✦✦

This is perhaps Gentle Giant's most realized effort. After the excellent *In a Glass House*, the group further developed their Renaissance-medieval approach, producing one of the most creative and complex recordings in progressive rock history. Their vocal approach to the four-part fugue "On Reflection" was revolutionary for its time and is looked upon as one of the genre's defining moments. Despite the complexity of the arrangements, the music never sounds academic and in fact is very accessible thanks to several melodic hooks. The combination of superb musicianship, dry wit, and creative compositions make this an essential and historical recording. —*Robert Taylor*

The Missing Piece / 1977 / One Way ✦✦

Giant for a Day! / 1978 / One Way ✦✦

Civilian / 1980 / One Way ✦✦

Collection / Oct. 19, 1993 / Castle ✦✦✦

Playing the Fool: The Official Live / Mar. 19, 1996 / One Way ✦✦✦

This live album (originally a double LP but put onto one CD) was released in the wake of a single-disc bootleg of the same name taken off of an FM radio concert. The repertory includes lots of stuff off of their early albums, including the never-released-in-the-U.S. *In a Glass House*. The sound is very vivid and close, whether the band is rocking to "Just the Same" or recreating the medieval-style a cappella vocals to "On Reflection." One Way has done an unusually good job with the sound on this album, and the original art has also been nicely recreated. This disc will obviously appeal to serious fans most of all, but even neophytes might consider this as an early acquisition. —*Bruce Eder*

Edge of Twilight / 1997 / Vertigo ✦✦✦✦✦

Edge of Twilight is a thorough overview of Gentle Giant's years at Vertigo Records, containing nearly every highlight from each of their early records. As a result, it's not only a perfect introduction to the strange, provocative world of Gentle Giant, it could be all the Gentle Giant most prog-rock fans need. —*Daevid Jehnzen*

Out of the Fire: Live on the BBC 1973 & 1978 / Nov. 17, 1998 / Hux ✦✦✦

Gentle Waves

Indie Pop, Twee Pop

The orchestral folk-pop of the Gentle Waves was primarily the brainchild of singer/songwriter Isobel Campbell, best known as the cellist and occasional vocalist for Scottish twee phenoms Belle and Sebastian. Recorded with the aid of fellow B&S members Stuart Murdoch, Richard Colburn, Chris Geddes, Mick Cooke, and Stevie Jackson following the group's 1998 U.S. tour, the Gentle Waves' debut LP *Green Fields of Foreverland* was released on Jeepster Records the following spring. *Swansong for You* was issued in fall 2000. —*Jason Ankeny*

● **Green Fields of Foreverland ...** / May 4, 1999 / Jeepster ✦✦✦✦

Green Fields of Foreverland delivers upon the promise of Isobel Campbell's sparkling contributions to the albums and singles of Belle and Sebastian—highlights like "Dirty Snow for the Broken Ground" and "Rose I Love You" are exquisite folk-pop gems in the vein of *The Boy with the Arab Strap*'s "Is It Wicked Not to Care?," and with bandmates like Stuart David and Stevie Jackson on board, it's the next best thing to a new B&S album. —*Jason Ankeny*

Swansong for You / Nov. 7, 2000 / Jeepster ✦✦✦✦

Swansong for You picks up right where the debut *The Green Fields of Foreverland* left off, which is to say with more gentle waves of pure orchestral pop loveliness. All the same characterizations hold true. Isobel Campbell's compositions are hauntingly wistful and dreamy, with many of the same echoes from her work in Belle & Sebastian and a plethora of nods to the softer strains of '60s pop, while retaining a diffuse and ethereal haze, like the dew-dappled light of morning, or perhaps like Scottish winters. The music often sounds like a delicate web being torn apart, but even in its most hushed moments it teems with intensity. The album's centerpiece is the completely groovy, left-field departure, "Sisterwoman," which can only (though nervously) be classified as garage pop. Opening with a ridiculously simple beat and piano groove reminiscent of the Violent Femmes classic "Raisin in the Sun," Campbell proceeds to layer on and incorporate fabulously unforeseen musical elements: rock & roll rhythm guitar, Booker T. & the MG's organ fills, incredible Stax-style horn charts. On top of it all, she gives a subtly campy vocal performance, at once recalling the Go-Go's and literal go-go singers of the '60s, specifically Nancy Sinatra, as well as British waifs like Lulu. It is unlike anything else of the Belle & Sebastian catalog or, for that matter, anything recorded previously by the Gentle Waves. It doesn't entirely fit with the rest of the album in sound or spirit, but nevertheless displays a different side of Campbell and, hopefully, points to an avenue ripe for future exploration by this most delightful of side projects. —*Stanton Swihart*

Barbara George

b. Aug. 16, 1942, New Orleans, LA

Vocals / New Orleans R&B, Soul

George's "I Know (You Don't Love Me No More)" topped the R&B charts in 1961 and has

proven a popular cover item ever since. The New Orleans native had never been in the studio before she brought her extremely catchy melody to Harold Battiste's fledgling A.F.O. label. Benefiting from her pleasing, unpolished vocal and a melodic cornet solo by Melvin Lastie, the tune caught fire, vaulting high on pop playlists. Amazingly, nothing else George did ever dented the charts, although she waxed some listenable follow-ups for A.F.O. and Sue. —*Bill Dahl*

● **I Know (You Don't Love Me Anymore): Golden Classics** / 1962 / Collectables ✦✦✦✦✦

Part of the label's *Golden Classics* series, this is a straight-up reissue of Barbara's A.F.O. album from 1962. With her lone smash hit as the centerpiece, the album is surprisingly free of filler, almost a prerequisite in those singles-dominated times. Her follow-up hit, "Talk About Love," is also aboard, and other highlights include nice takes of "Since I Fell for You," the bouncy "Don't Ask Me No Questions," and the soulful ballad "Honest I Do." With top-notch playing from Harold Battiste and others, this is classic early-'60s New Orleans music all the way. —*Cub Koda*

Lowell George

b. Apr. 13, 1945, Hollywood, CA, **d.** Jun. 29, 1979, Arlington, VA

Slide Guitar, Vocals, Guitar / Album Rock, Boogie Rock, Southern Rock, Hard Rock, Singer/Songwriter, Blues-Rock, Rock & Roll

As Little Feat was disbanding in late 1978, their lead guitarist/songwriter Lowell George recorded a solo album, *Thanks I'll Eat It Here*, that sounded as loose and funky as the band in their prime. After its release the following year, he set out on tour to support the album. Sadly, George died of a heart attack while on the road; he left behind a body of gritty, eclectic, and funky rock & roll. On the first five Little Feat albums, his songwriting and instrumental talents are more apparent than on his solo effort, yet that doesn't detract from the record's pleasures. —*Stephen Thomas Erlewine*

● **Thanks I'll Eat It Here** / 1979 / Warner Brothers ✦✦✦✦✦

Thanks I'll Eat it Here is strikingly different from the fusion-leanings of Little Feat's last studio album, *Time Loves a Hero*. Lowell George never cared for jazz-fusion, so it should be little surprise that there's none to be heard on *Thanks*. Instead, he picks up where *Dixie Chicken* left off (he even reworks that album's standout "Two Trains"), turning in a laidback, organic collection of tunes equal parts New Orleans R&B, country, sophisticated blues, and pop. George wasn't in good health during the sessions for *Thanks*, which you wouldn't tell by his engaging performances, but from the lack of new tunes. Out of the nine songs on the album, only three are originals, and they're all collaborations. That's a drawback only in retrospect—it's hard not to wish that the last album George completed had more of his own songs—but Lowell was a first-rate interpreter, so even covers of Allen Toussaint ("What Do You Want the Girl to Do"), Ann Peebles ("I Can't Stand the Rain") and Rickie Lee Jones ("Easy Money") wind up sounding of piece with the original songs. George's music rolls so easy, the album can seem a little slight at first, but it winds up being a real charmer. Yes, a few songs drift by and, yes, Jimmy Webb's vaudevellian "Himmler's Ring" feels terribly out of place, but Lowell's style is so distinctive and his performances so soulful, it's hard not to like this record if you've ever had a fondness for Little Feat. After all, it's earthier and more satisfying than any Feat album since *Feats Don't Fail Me Now* and it has the absolutely gorgeous "20 Million Things," the last great song George ever wrote. —*Stephen Thomas Erlewine*

Lightning-Rod Man / Nov. 2, 1993 / Bizarre/Straight ✦✦✦

Before emerging as a cult star in the 1970s, Lowell George was a presence on the L.A. folk-rock/psychedelic scene in the 1960s. With his group the Factory, he only managed to release one single during this time. *Lightning-Rod Man* rescues 15 tunes cut by this unit, including the single and over a dozen outtakes and demos. Almost exclusively original material, most of these tracks were recorded in 1966 and 1967. They show the group pursuing a slightly eccentric folk-rock vision that neither bears much similarity to George's more famous work nor matches the best work done in this genre by their L.A. peers. At times they echo Kaleidoscope in their vaguely spacy, good-natured folkish rock; just as often, they take cues from Captain Beefheart and Frank Zappa in their skewed blues-rock and obtuse songwriting. In fact, Zappa himself produced and played on a couple of the demos, and one-time Mothers of Invention members Elliot Ingber and Roy Estrada show up on a few others. A few songs edging toward the end of the decade feature a heavier, bluesier sound that show George edging in a different direction. An enjoyable vault find, but not a major revelation. —*Richie Unterberger*

The Georgia Satellites

f. 1980, Atlanta, GA

American Trad Rock, Roots Rock, Hard Rock, Rock & Roll

At a time when rock & roll didn't care about its roots, the Georgia Satellites came crashing into the charts in 1986 with "Keep Your Hands to Yourself," a surprise hit single to remind everybody where the music had come from, rocking as hard as an old Chuck Berry song as well as being almost as clever. The Satellites weren't a back-to-basic roots band, either—their straightforward sound borrowed equally from Berry, the Rolling Stones, the Faces, Little Feat, and AC/DC, with a Southern backwoods bent. At their best, the Satellites were just a damn good rock & roll band, driven by the classic, yet fresh, songwriting of lead singer/guitarist Dan Baird. On the strength of "Keep Your Hands to Yourself," their first major-label album sold well, but the follow-up, *Open All Night*, did not; radio and MTV had treated the band as a kind of novelty—a bunch of hicks kicking out rock & roll offered a break between the slick pop-metal of Bon Jovi and Peter Gabriel's introspective pop. After one more album, 1989's *In the Land of Salvation and Sin*, the band called it quits. Baird pursued a solo career and had a small hit in late 1992 with "I Love

You Period." The Georgia Satellites reunited without Baird to release *Shaken Not Stirred* in 1997. *—Stephen Thomas Erlewine*

Georgia Satellites / 1986 / Elektra ✦✦✦✦✦
Dirty Rolling Stones-like guitar grunge played by Rick Richards and topped by the adenoidal singing of Dan Baird. Especially enjoyable on the hits "Keep Your Hands to Yourself" and "Battleship Chains." *—William Ruhlmann*

Open All Night / 1988 / Elektra ✦✦✦
The Georgia Satellites' follow-up to their surprise hit is as loose and rocking as their previous album, but wasn't as successful. The few who did buy the album were treated to some of the rawest and funniest pure rock & roll of the 1980s, highlighted by the sleazy humor of "Mon Cheri" and the title track, as well as the stomping cover of the Beatles' "Don't Pass Me By." *—Stephen Thomas Erlewine*

In the Land of Salvation and Sin / Oct. 1989 / Elektra ✦✦✦
On the Georgia Satellites' final album, Dan Baird decides that he's a songwriter like Lowell George—a traditionalist who adds a healthy dose of ironic humor without losing respect for the music's roots. While his ambitions are ripe with pretensions, his band keeps him in check, and *In the Land of Salvation and Sin* is a terrific record, full of intelligent songs that are never pompous and never fail to rock like hell. *—Stephen Thomas Erlewine*

• **Let It Rock: The Best of the Georgia Satellites** / Jan. 19, 1993 / Elektra ✦✦✦✦✦
Most of the band's best tracks are on this generous compilation, which not only features their hits ("Keep Your Hands to Yourself" and "Battleship Chains"), but also includes rarities like their sublime John Fogerty medley "Almost Saturday Night/Rockin' All Over the World" from the *Rubaiyat* collection. *—Stephen Thomas Erlewine*

Shaken Not Stirred / 1997 / 3NM ✦✦

The Geraldine Fibbers

f. 1993, Los Angeles, CA
Alternative Country-Rock, Indie Rock, Grunge, Alternative Pop/Rock, Neo-Traditional Folk
The Geraldine Fibbers was the bluesy, country-tinged vehicle of singer/songwriter Carla Bozulich, a longtime veteran of the Southern California post-punk scene who previously tenured in Ethyl Meatplow and Neon Vein. After the former's 1993 breakup, Bozulich formed the Fibbers with guitarist Daniel Keenan, bassist William Tutton, violinist Jessy Greene, and drummer Kevin Fitzgerald, debuting the following year on the Sympathy for the Record Industry label with the EP *Get Thee Gone*. After signing to Virgin, the group issued 1995's acclaimed *Lost Somewhere Between the Earth and My Home*; *Butch*, a more rock-oriented effort recorded with new guitarist Nels Cline, followed in 1997. *—Jason Ankeny*

• **Lost Somewhere Between the Earth and My Home** / 1995 / Virgin ✦✦✦
Carla Bozulich's distorted folk tales for the desolate got their start on this debut album from her punky alterna-country performance outfit the Geraldine Fibbers, and what an introduction it is. Defying labels across the board, and turning old-style ancestral narratives into brutal and harrowing portraits of life on the edge of nowhere, the Fibbers wrap each of *Lost Somewhere Between the Earth and My Home*'s 12 songs into a ball of fury and toss it against the wall of tradition, just to see what happens. The results, wickedly conveyed through Bozulich's often androgynous and twangy tones, are among the most original, if not always successful, conceived in the cookie-cutter '90s. Chaotic noise breakdowns give way to melodic singalongs, songs twist and turn through several side paths before reaching their destination, and everything sounds as if total annihilation is imminent. Scary, thoughtful and highly inventive (plus a bit one-noted), *Lost* is the sound of country gone to hell. *—Michael Gallucci*

What Part of "Get Thee Gone" Don't You Understand? / Feb. 11, 1997 / Sympathy for the Record Industry ✦✦✦
While most of the material on this compilation was recorded prior to the release of the Geraldine Fibbers' first album, *Lost Somewhere Between the Earth and My Home*, *What Part of "Get Thee Gone" Don't You Understand?* stylistically straddles a middle ground between the group's first long-player and their second (and apparently final) album, *Butch*. The set's first seven songs originally appeared on the band's first EP, *Get Thee Gone* (two of the tracks were re-recorded for *Lost*), and the performances are leaner and more direct than those on *Lost*; while they jibe with the more country-accented approach of that disc, the pared-down arrangements also recall the philosophy (if not the sound) of the rawer, more aggressive *Butch*. The rest of the set is comprised of single tracks, demos, and a variety of live cuts, many of which anticipate *Butch*'s blunter approach, particularly "They Suck," "She's a Dog," and a striking cover of Bobbie Gentry's "Fancy," a tale of a young girl forced into prostitution by her mother that Carla Bozulich wrings for every bit of its drama (and how is it some other bunch of cowpunks didn't run across this lost classic first?). A number of other covers dot the rest of the collection, which show how *Bozulich* and her bandmates could honor the emotional power of classic country while bending its structures to their own will; her version of George Jones' "The Grand Tour" is turned into a same-sex breakup song that's just as devastating as Ol' Possum's recording, and while Daniel Keenan's guitar solo on "Hands on the Wheel" takes it someplace very different than Willie Nelson's original, it doesn't lose a bit of its heart-tugging undertow. *Lost Somewhere Between the Earth and My Home* remains the Geraldine Fibbers' greatest moment on plastic, but this collection proves they were already had a strong and distinctive sound well before that and were already looking to other places; it's invaluable for fans and not bad for beginners. *—Mark Deming*

Butch / Jul. 1, 1997 / Virgin ✦✦✦
Despite again working with Steve Fisk, *Butch* doesn't quite put it all together like the marvelous debut *Lost Somewhere Between the Earth and My Home*, if only because it's not as much of a total reach of styles as that record. By no means is Carla Bozulich's ear for, or abilities at, various country and traditional approaches gone—the opening track "California Tuffy" shows her vocals, in-your-face as always, have that great, deep twang. Generally, though, *Butch* isn't so much the work of a band crossing readily between musical realms as coming down firmly on the rock side with definite country touches. On that level, however, it's a great effort, with Bozulich more than once returning to her more strident Ethyl Meatplow roots, at least in terms of overall volume if not industrial beats. "Toybox" is a massive, brawling monster of a track, where Nels Cline's guitar and Kevin Fitzgerald's blasting drums set the pace even as Jessy Greene's violin slices through the mix like a demented banshee. Throughout the album all the band members pull off some amazing performances—it's little surprise Cline continued to work with Bozulich in Scarnella based on his sometimes aggressive, sometimes calm contributions. Perhaps the most surprising touch is the inclusion of a cover of Can's Krautrock classic "Yoo Doo Right," but much like fellow Californians Thin White Rope, the Fibbers work their own magic on the song, with Bozulich commandingly leading everyone through a fierce take. Little on the album is quiet, but there are songs where taking a softer touch at points comes up trumps, like the sweet, seaside push of "Trashman in Furs," which is able to sound epic without having to hammer it home. When the band lets go and gets completely down-home, like on the enjoyable romp "Folks Like Home" and the slow singalong "Pet Angel," it's among *Butch*'s best moments. *—Ned Raggett*

Lisa Germano

b. 1958, Mishawaka, IN
Vocals, Violin, Fiddle / Dream Pop, Alternative Pop/Rock
Violinist Lisa Germano became known for her fluid, gutsy style through her work with John Mellencamp, which is captured on the *Big Daddy* and *Lonesome Jubilee* albums. Germano's solo work is much more dark and atmospheric than Mellencamp's albums; her 1991 solo debut, *On the Way Down From Moon Palace*, displayed some promising songwriting along with her acclaimed instrumental prowess. Germano's second album, 1993's *Happiness*, was even better, but the record didn't sell very well when it was first released on Capitol, prompting her to change record labels in 1994. She signed with 4AD, who released a re-sequenced and remixed *Happiness* in the spring of 1994; the new version of the album emphasized her music's underlying dark melancholy, which the original version only hinted at. Later in 1994, she released *Geek the Girl*, her first album for 4AD, to very positive reviews. Two years later, Germano released *Excerpts From a Love Circus*. *Slide* followed in 1998. *—Stephen Thomas Erlewine*

On the Way Down From the Moon Palace / 1991 / Koch ✦✦✦
Lisa Germano's debut album *On the Way Down From the Moon Palace* is considerably rootsier and poppier than her later efforts, but the album showcases her skills as an arranger and her wonderfully expressive, versatile violin playing, particularly on the title track, "Dark Irie," and "Screaming Angels Dancing in Your Garden." The album's somewhat glossy production makes pop-oriented songs like "Guessing Game (or The Music Business)," "Cry Baby," and "Dig My Own Grave" sound more mainstream than they actually are. However, pretty, meditative instrumentals like "Calling" and "Simply Tony"—which feature guitar, mandolin, accordion, and piano as well as Germano's violin—hint at the ethereal folk she'd perfect on albums like *Geek the Girl* and *Excerpts From a Love Circus*. On "Blue Monday," Germano's whispery voice provides a clever contrast with the song's tough, earthy melody and lyrics, making it a bit of an anomaly in her career, but the lush strings and plaintive melody of "The Other One," the delicate, wistful pop of "Hangin' With a Deadman," and the spooky folk of "Riding My Bike"—about the stalker who inspired several of Germano's other songs—point the way toward her more developed work. An accomplished debut, *On the Way Down From the Moon Palace* introduced her unique, uncompromising talent, and suggested she had much more to offer. *—Heather Phares*

• **Happiness** / Jul. 27, 1993 / 4AD ✦✦✦✦✦
On 1993's *Happiness*, Lisa Germano delivered on the promise that her debut *On the Way Down From the Moon Palace* suggested she had. Both more ambitious and more accessible than her first album, *Happiness* swaths her ethereal-yet-earthy melodies in a rich, shimmering production courtesy of Malcom Burn. Originally released by Capitol, 4AD re-released the album once Germano switched labels; the label's head, Ivo Watts-Russell, remixed certain tracks like the folky dream pop of "Destroy the Flower" and the scathing "Sycophant," bringing out the songs' melancholy, wistful tendencies. However, even the Capitol version of *Happiness* has plenty of both of those qualities. Just as Germano mixes the delicate with the down-to-earth in her music, she uses her fragile voice to express uncomfortable, sad, and occasionally funny sentiments, as on the bitchy, jaded "Bad Attitude," where she sings "You wish you were pretty/But you're not/Ha ha ha" with equal amounts of cynicism and idealism. With "The Dresses Song," she turns what would be a flirty pop song in anyone else's hands into an ambivalent compliment: "You look at me so fragile/You make me think about nothing/It feels so good like that." *Happiness* also expands Germano's musical palette, ranging from jangly pop like "Puppet" and "Energy," to the brooding, droning rock of the title track and "Everyone's Victim," to the haunting, proto-trip-hop instrumental "Miamo-Tutti" (named for one of Germano's cats). The spooky, vulnerable final song "The Darkest Night of All" is a forerunner of the dark, riveting territory she'd cover on *Geek the Girl*; as a whole, *Happiness* finds Germano moving toward a remarkable emotional honesty, which makes the album all the more captivating. *—Heather Phares*

Geek the Girl / Oct. 25, 1994 / 4AD ✦✦✦✦✦
With 1994's *Geek the Girl*, Lisa Germano found the perfect balance of her work's inherent

contrasts. On songs like "My Secret Reason," soft, intricate arrangements surround her raw, whispery vocals and unflinching lyrics, making it even easier for them to get unsettlingly close to you. A largely autobiographical album about a girl's emotional and sexual coming of age, each of *Geek the Girl*'s songs—particularly the title track—fairly tremble with awkward sadness and self-discovery. Shimmering, hesitant songs like "Trouble" sound like they might float off the album, but Germano's delivery of lyrics like "Little by little you touched my heart / Where they had touched it too" gives them a delicate determination. *Geek the Girl* also braves the uglier possibilities of adolescent girlhood, whether it's rape ("Cry Wolf") or growing up too fast ("Sexy Little Girl Princess"). The album's centerpiece, "... A Psychopath," inspired by Germano's own experiences with a stalker, mixes excerpts of a 911 caller confronting an intruder, Germano's deadpan delivery of lyrics like "A baseball bat beside my bed / You win again / I am alone / And paralyzed" and brooding, scraping violins. *Geek the Girl* never feels whiny, thanks to Germano's abstract lyrics and the album's clever structure: snippets of whimsical Italian folk tunes bookend *Geek the Girl*'s darkest, most intense moments, offering a tiny bit of comic relief. Similarly, "Cancer of Everything," a harshly funny cry for attention, borrows *Happiness*'s ironic humor. Hypnotic instrumentals like "Phantom Love" and "Just Geek" also provide respites from the album's wrenching emotions, but songs like "... Of Love And Colors" and "Stars" end the album with something more important: hope. *Geek the Girl*'s brave whispers hit on more emotional truths than the self-important screams of Germano's mid-'90s, women-in-rock contemporaries. *—Heather Phares*

Excerpts From a Love Circus / Sep. 9, 1996 / 4AD ♦♦♦♦
After the wrenching but rewarding *Geek the Girl*, Lisa Germano widens her focus and brightens her outlook on *Excerpts from a Love Circus*. Of course, *Love Circus* is a Lisa Germano album, but it's a slightly lighter take on her vulnerable, folky dream-pop: only she could make the refrain "Bruises, bruises, bruises" equally catchy and disturbing. As the title suggests, *Excerpts From a Love Circus* collects vignettes about hating the one you love and loving the one you hate; once again, Germano captures awkward, abstract feelings with her dreamy arrangements, hooky songwriting, and unflinching lyrics. Passive-aggressive love songs like "I Love a Snot" sport flourishes like toy pianos and tablas, and incisive comments like "A Beautiful Schizophrenic"'s "I know you like my bad side / I love you like my good side." Germano's dark, self-effacing sense of humor surfaces on "Victoria's Secret," which answers the question "What is Victoria's Secret?" for once and all: "She says 'You are ugly / I am pretty / Your man wishes / You looked like me.'" Musically, *Excerpts from a Love Circus* is her most grounded and eclectic work since *Happiness*, spanning the intricate, spooky pop of "Baby on the Plane," the folky "Forget It, It's A Mystery," the menacing, Eastern-influenced "Lovesick," and the jangly "Small Heads." Germano closes the album on a gentle, hopeful note, suggesting with a trio of ballads—"Singing to the Birds," "Messages from Sophia," and "Big Big World"—that finding and losing love isn't the worst thing in the world, as long as you don't lose yourself in the process. It's not quite as gripping as some of her other albums, but *Excerpts From a Love Circus* is still a genuine, thoughtful album and a welcome addition to Germano's body of work. *—Heather Phares*

Slide / Jul. 21, 1998 / 4AD ♦♦♦♦
Name almost any under-recognized artist and someone will say that if he or she were only marketed correctly or heard by the right people, a star would be born. It's hard to imagine anyone making that claim about the under-recognized Lisa Germano, whose songs are so personal, ambiguous, and unsettling that even sympathetic listeners can find it hard to gain entry. Still, *Slide* is one of the more accessible albums in Germano's catalog, lacking both the harrowing sexual dramas of *Geek the Girl* and the overt self-loathing of *Happiness*. The songs here feature Germano's trademark carnival-music textures, but are both subtler and prettier than usual, which sometimes makes them even more disturbing: "No Color Here" and "Crash," both about depression, are so tender and closely observed they're nearly fetishistic. Elsewhere, Germano lets some air into her universe: the lilting "Electrified" remembers a time when "playing was everything," "Wood Floors" is a beautiful piano ballad, and "Turning Into Betty" is a darkly humorous song about the fear of turning into one's mother. Even Germano's lighter moments are disorienting, though; when she sings "I'm giving in to beauty," it sounds less like an epiphany than a potentially fatal error. *—Kristi Coulter*

The Germs

f. 1977, **db.** 1980
American Punk, L.A. Punk, Hardcore Punk, Punk, American Underground
Living fast and dying young is one of rock's great cliches, but no phrase better describes the reasons for the demise of L.A. punkers the Germs. Capable of creating a firestorm of noisy, confrontational music, they were ultimately undone by their perversely charismatic lead singer, madman Darby Crash, who died Sid Vicious-style out on the mainline at age 22. The Germs kicked up a hellacious racket that strayed from fast/loud punk into art-damage and garage grunge. On stage, their gigs bordered on performance art, with Crash in full Iggy frenzy, diving into the crowd, adorning himself with whatever foodstuffs the audience provided, wearing less and less clothing, all done with the band cranking out noisy spasms of simple, but effective, rock noise. Never capturing this mania on record (how could you?) the Germs' recording career is based on the sole record made during Crash's short life. *(GI)* was a fine hunk of early L.A. punk rock that was more literate and compelling that what was being offered by lesser local luminaries such as the Zeroes and the Weirdos. It may not be life-changing music, but the white-hot, adrenal rush is a little bit of heaven. *—John Dougan*

(GI) / 1979 / Slash ♦♦♦♦♦
A blast of self-lacerating L.A. punk in its original glory, *(GI)* is simply classic; a commanding, rampaging sneer at everyone and everything infused with a particular, disturbed vision. Said vision belongs to Darby Crash, whose proclivities for charismatic manipulation were already well established before he fully spelled them out in lyrics like "Lexicon Devil," here featuring in a re-recording, and "Richie Dagger's Crime." His David Bowie worship was also paramount—"Land of Treason," "Communist Eyes," and "Strange Notes" are just three numbers featuring his transformation of the apocalyptic aesthetics of albums like *Diamond Dogs* and *Station to Station* towards bruter ends. Practically speaking, his snarling star quality comes through more than his words, but it's more than enough on that front. Pat Smear has an equal claim to being the album's star, though, and for good reason—not only did he co-write everything, his clipped, catchy monster riffing was as pure punk in the late '70s sense as anything, wasting no time on anything extraneous. Lorna Doom and Don Bolles keep up the side as a kickass rhythm section, Bolles in particular making a good mark in the first of his many drumming stints over the moons. Joan Jett's production got knocked at the time for perceived thinness, but she and engineer Pat Burnette actually did a great job at recording the band with crisp, strong results. The notorious closing number "Shut Down (Annihilation Man)" makes for a nicely balanced contrast to the 42-second opener "What We Do Is Secret." While the latter song is pure hyperspeed, Crash sounding like he's about to run out of breath on the shout-along chorus, "Shut Down (Annihilation Man)," recorded at a club gig, shows how the Germs could (quite intentionally) tick off an audience via long, meandering numbers if they so chose. *—Ned Raggett*

What We Do is Secret / 1981 / Slash ♦♦♦
Originally released as a 12" mini-album, *What We Do Is Secret* did much to propagate the myth of Darby Crash and the Germs on release in 1981 (especially in Europe). It's a companion volume to the (superior) *(GI)*, featuring a version of Chuck Berry's "Round and Round" recorded in 1977, live tracks recorded through 1980 and a *(GI)* out-take. Everything the Germs did was messy, and this collection is no different. But that's half the appeal of the band, and fans will makes allowances for it. *—Alex Ogg*

• **Germs (M.I.A.)—The Complete Anthology** / Aug. 3, 1993 / Slash/Rhino ♦♦♦♦♦
There are other collections with rarer material out there, notably the live *Germicide* and *Media Blitz*, but unless one is a rabid must-have-everything-Crash-breathed-on fanatic, *(M.I.A.)* is everything one could ever want from the Germs in one perfect collection. Not simply a reissue of *(GI)*—thus the joke of the title—*(M.I.A.)* pulls together everything from the very first recordings to the last efforts of the classic lineup, namely six songs done for the film *Cruising*. Only one was ever actually released on the soundtrack, "Lions Share," so hearing the others in studio form is welcome and long overdue, including the only Crash/Lorna Doom co-write, the brusque strutter "Now I Hear the Laughter." The debut single, the primitive blast "Forming," and its hilarious, chaotic live B-side, "Sexboy," bottles breaking while Crash practically attacks the audibly scared audience, understandably start the collection. Meanwhile, the alternate "Forming 2" (featuring DJ Bonebrake and recorded by Chris Ashford, as compared to the un-produced and proud of it original) wraps it up just as well. All three tracks from the *Lexicon Devil* EP appear, including the slightly slower original recording of the title song and the sly, self-referential "Circle One," as well as two selections from the *What We Do Is Secret* EP, with Bonebrake again turning up on a live rip through Chuck Berry's "Round and Round." To be fair, on that number Crash reaches new depths of sheer incoherence. In terms of presentation, one couldn't ask for more—even the CD case itself has a classic Germs blue tint. There's two separate articles from Pleasant Gehman; the first a piece from 1982 giving a useful history of the group and the second from a decade later reflecting on the band's impact and place in history. Complete lyrics also appear, along with a slew of pictures of the band and Crash in his various incarnations, including one hilarious photo with him sticking his tongue out while a cigarette is propped in his ear. *—Ned Raggett*

Lisa Gerrard

Vocals / Adult Alternative Pop/Rock, Alternative Pop/Rock, World Fusion
In collaboration with Brendan Perry, Lisa Gerrard is half of the duo Dead Can Dance, which has been releasing arty goth-rock on the 4AD label since the mid-'80s. Gerrard began her solo career with the 1995 release *The Mirror Pool*, which contained a lot of work that wouldn't fit comfortably into the DCD oeuvre. Combining these fragments with music that she composed and arranged digitally before reconfiguring them into scores that could be performed, it also draws on a composition by Handel and traditional Iranian music. Recorded and produced largely at her home in rural Australia, it extends the world music inclinations of recent Dead Can Dance albums by featuring bouzouki, tablas, and camel drums, though the somber, orchestrated pomp of Dead Can Dance is also present in her operatic, often wordless vocals, and string/woodwind passages (some of which were performed by Australia's Victorian Philharmonic Orchestra). Gerrard released her second album, *Duality*, in the spring of 1998. *Duality* was written and performed with Pieter Bourke. *—Richie Unterberger*

• **The Mirror Pool** / Aug. 22, 1995 / 4AD ♦♦♦
Lisa Gerrard was so indelibly and obviously a part of what made Dead Can Dance what it is that it's little wonder that *The Mirror Pool* feels essentially like a continuation of that band's haunting, vast atmospheres. Without Brendan Perry's deep, rolling voice as a contrast, Gerrard's sky-sweeping abilities transform the entire recording into a truly mystical experience. The use of Australia's Victorian Philharmonic Orchestra on many tracks continues the tradition of strong arrangements in Gerrard's work, thanks to the abilities of John Bonnar, who conducts as well as performs at other points. Future collaborator Pieter Bourke contributes everything from vocals to tabla and claps, while other guests add similar touches. Gerrard handles everything else, as always demonstrating her

excellent abilities on the yang t'chin, while when it comes to singing she again is practically peerless, her multi-octave range demonstrating both power and astonishing control. If there is a slight criticism of *The Mirror Pool*, it's that as a collection it's almost too overwhelming—the contrast between more direct and loftier performances on Dead Can Dance releases add immeasurably to their impact. It's hard to argue with the end results, though—Gerrard's singing is just so rich and dramatic that even the smallest complaint seems puny. Her overdubbed choir effects are particularly striking, especially when she's exploring different styles within the same song. Several cuts make their studio debut after having been part of the Dead Can Dance live repertoire, as partially captured on *Toward the Within*; two standouts in particular are "Sanvean" and "Persian Love Song." Others, such as "Ahjon" and the immediately following "Glorafin" seem to derive from Gerrard's Dead Can Dance piece "Bird." There's even an attractive adaptation of Handel's composition "Largo," which suits the mood perfectly, and on which Gerrard's vocals are absolutely perfect. —*Ned Raggett*

Duality / Apr. 14, 1998 / Warner Brothers ◆◆◆
Having already worked with Pieter Bourke on *The Mirror Pool*, Lisa Gerrard created her second album, *Duality*, with him as a full partner. It's literally just the two of them, recorded at a home studio in Australia. Bourke's work in Eden—which had often been tagged with a Dead Can Dance wannabe brush—actually meant that he knew more than most where Gerrard was coming from with her all-encompassing vision of music from different locales and times. Compared to the often overwhelming feeling of *The Mirror Pool*, *Duality* is no less mysterious and captivating, but still maintains a more intimate, close atmosphere. The echoing depths that characterize Gerrard's work again appear, as much a tribute to excellent production as it is an artistic choice, and there are wondrous parts with haunting string arrangements, but there are no huge, heavenly orchestras or the like dominating this time out. Meanwhile, the mysterious folk/dance side of Gerrard's work remains intact, percussive instruments of all sorts to the fore, blending Arabic, Mediterranean, South Asian, and other styles into a mystic whole, as on tracks like "Shadow Magnet" and "Nadir (Synchronicity)." Where there are rhythmless tracks, such as "The Unfolding" and the minimal beauty of "The Circulation of Shadows," the scale is less dominating, more directly connecting. As always, Gerrard's voice is simply breathtaking, the vaunted and well-earned reputation for her singing range completely intact. Perhaps most surprising is when she sings in clear, straightforward English on "The Human Game," compared to her usual glossolalia when singing her own lyrics; in context, it's a fascinating switch. Bourke's own contributions—it's not immediately clear if those include vocals, given Gerrard's own abilities in both high and low registers—mesh excellently with her instrumental work and, since no specific credit appears instrument for instrument, everything works as a true partnership. —*Ned Raggett*

Gerry & The Pacemakers

f. 1959, Liverpool, England, **db.** 1990
Merseybeat, British Invasion
As unfathomable as it seems from the distance of over 30 years, for a few months, Gerry & the Pacemakers were the Beatles' nearest competitors in Britain. Managed (like the Beatles) by Brian Epstein, Gerry Marsden and his band burst out of the gate with three consecutive number one U.K. hits in 1963, "How Do You Do It," "I Like It," and "You'll Never Walk Alone." If the Beatles defined Merseybeat at its best in early 1963, Gerry & the Pacemakers defined the form at its most innocuous, performing bouncy, catchy, and utterly lightweight tunes driven by rhythm guitar and Marsden's chipper vocals. Compared to the Beatles and other British Invasion heavies, they sound quaint indeed. That's not to say the group were trivial; their hits were certainly likable and energetic and are fondly remembered today, even if the musicians lacked the acumen (or earthy image) to develop their style from its relentlessly upbeat and poppy base. —*Richie Unterberger*

The EP Collection / 1987 / See For Miles ◆◆◆◆◆
A truly definitive collection, with all the hits and the most interesting non-hits. Includes the ultra-rare live *Gerry in California* concert recording from 1966. —*Bruce Eder*

● **The Best of Gerry & the Pacemakers: The Definitive Collection** / Oct. 15, 1991 / EMI America ◆◆◆◆◆
The title promises more than it really delivers in content, if not sound. It'll do for the casual listener. —*Bruce Eder*

● **Gerry Cross the Mersey: All the Hits of Gerry and the Pacemakers** / Oct. 1995 / Razor & Tie ◆◆◆◆◆
Sixteen-track best-of includes all of their British and American hits, as well as some of their best B-sides. The more extensive EMI America best-of has all of these songs and more, and so is still recommended as the first purchase. But for just about everybody, this has all the Gerry & the Pacemakers you need, and all but two of the songs are in stereo, if that's an important consideration. —*Richie Unterberger*

Magic Moments / Jul. 2, 1996 / Varese Sarabande ◆

Get Up Kids

f. 1994, Kansas City, MO
Emo, Indie Rock
Kansas City's Get Up Kids play melodic, pop-inflected emo similar to the Promise Ring and Braid, with whom the band released a split single in 1998. The group debuted in 1996 with a slew of 7"s, including "Shorty" on the Huey Proudhon label and "All Stars" on Doghouse Records, which became their main record label. 1997 saw the release of their debut full-length *Four Minute Mile*, which they recorded with Bob Weston. In 1998 the group toured extensively and released more singles, including "I'm a Loner, Dottie, a Rebel," which also appeared on their 1999 album *Something to Write Home About*. The

band resurfaced two years later, re-releasing some of their early works and hitting the road with Green Day and Weezer. —*Heather Phares*

Four Minute Mile / Sep. 30, 1997 / Doghouse ◆◆◆◆
The album that put this Kansas City, MO band on the map as everyone's favorite emo-pop rockers of late, with catchy lyrics, fairly unique and powerful pop/rock composition, and an overall sense of energy. Their lyrical content is centered around remembering painful relationships, regret of past mistakes, and longing for that special someone. Favorite tracks on this one would be "Coming Clean," "Stay Gold, Ponyboy," and "Fall Semester." If you don't have this and you enjoy poppy, catchy emo, you'd love it. —*Blake Butler*

● **Something to Write Home About** / Sep. 21, 1999 / Vagrant ◆◆◆◆
Imagine if the kids that got made fun of on the back of the bus ended up being the coolest ones in the school. Not through any kind of terrorist revenge fantasy or post-apocalyptic last-people-alive-on-Earth scenario, but what if they were actually the most interesting, most sincere, most talented kids around? That is exactly the impression given by the Get up Kids on their 1999 album *Something to Write Home About*. That although they are struggling with stumbling relationships and the pervasive frustrations of being young men in their generation, they still are able to process the complexities of their daily lives through music. This is a heavy statement concerning a power pop band, but these guys are doing it right.

Rocketing out of the gates with a blast of punk bravado and true emo energy, guitarists Matthew Pryor and Jim Suptic sing as if the more forcefully they belt it out, the sooner their dilemmas will be solved. Incorporating Fender Rhoades electric piano and Moog synthesizers (played sparingly by James Dewees) adds an element that Weezer introduced to smart post-punk bands, allowing the sound to be cool and geeky at the same time. The cross-town traffic ballad "Ten Minutes" is a stuttering ode where the singer's girlfriend lives, hoping for understanding but expecting an argument. The sincere combination of excitement and concern in Suptic's voice gives the listener a genuine feeling for the situation. Shifts in tempo and punchy guitar riffs separate the Get up Kids from their emo contemporaries who often seem too comfortable with their guitar-bass-drums formula. The pleading acoustic "Out of Reach" showcases the bright harmonies and raw emotion of the band as it builds into a piano-driven, swaying lost love torch song, quite unusual for the genre. "I'm down for whatever," Pryor sings on "Action & Action," and it is that kind of apathetic optimism that makes *Something to Write Home About* worthy of the critical praise and dedicated fanbase it has earned. —*Zac Johnson*

Red Letter Day/Woodson / Jan. 9, 2001 / Doghouse ◆◆◆
This CD combining two hard to find EPs (1997's *Woodson* 7" and 1999's *Red Letter Day* 10") provides an entertaining glimpse into two of the more raw and punk-edged stages in the evolution of the Get Up Kids. A brash but melodic nine songs, the thing that really jumps out is the transition that this group made in the two years between recordings. The four songs from *Woodson* (positioned last on this collection) are very rough-edged and full of furious energy, while the songs that originally appeared on *Red Letter Day* foreshadow the band's now trademark harmonies and dynamic songwriting. The urgent "Forgive and Forget" is contrasted by the poetic and yearning "Mass Pike," and both are jarred off balance by the indie punk of "Second Place." This pair of recordings serves not only as a fine introduction to one of emo's premier acts, but also as an interesting window into the growth of the band. [The second track appears in an even more refined form on 1999's sublime *Something to Write Home About*.] —*Zac Johnson*

Geto Boys

f. 1986
Southern Rap, Hardcore Rap, Gangsta Rap
Though the controversial subject matter of gangsta rap wasn't much of a barrier to popular success during the '90s, the Geto Boys' recordings proved almost too extreme for widespread exposure. Based in Houston's 5th Ward, the trio of Scarface, Willie D., and Bushwick Bill signed to Rap-A-Lot Records and recorded their first album in 1990. The group was blocked from releasing it by distributor Geffen, who insisted that "Mind of a Lunatic," a track dealing with necrophilia as well as murder, was a step too far. By late 1990, another distributor was found and the album was released—as *Grip It! On That Other Level*—in 1990. The controversy, which occurred two years earlier than similar censorship incidents involving Ice-T and 2 Live Crew, gave the Geto Boys a large amount of publicity and their second album *We Can't Be Stopped* eventually hit platinum. The trio of Scarface, Willie D., and Bushwick Bill began to fracture by 1993, and they went their separate ways after that year's *'Til Death Do Us Part*. Each mounted several solo projects before reuniting in 1996 for their most praised album yet, *The Resurrection. Da Good, Da Bad & Da Ugly* followed in 1998. —*John Bush*

Grip It! On That Other Level / 1990 / Rap-A-Lot ◆◆◆

Geto Boys / 1990 / Rap-A-Lot/Def American ◆◆◆◆
This disturbing CD inspired quite a bit of controversy when Geffen Records refused to distribute it unless the Geto Boys agreed to tone down their violent and profane lyrics. American Records founder Rick Rubin (who had produced everyone from L.L. Cool J to Slayer to the Beastie Boys) countered that the Houston gangsta rappers shouldn't have to compromise their artistic vision, and sought distribution elsewhere. When the Geto Boys was finally released, it hadn't been toned down a bit. Adding a horror-movie element to their accounts of inner-city crime and violence, the Geto Boys paint a brutally honest and sobering picture of urban life. The members of this group grew up in the tough Houston ghetto known as the 5th Ward and don't hesitate to inform listeners just how ugly things can get in so oppressive an environment. From "Assassins" (originally released in 1988) to "Mind of a Lunatic" (a shocking depiction of a mental patient's psychopathic terror

spree), this album proves that Rubin did the right thing by holding his ground. *—Alex Henderson*

We Can't Be Stopped / Jul. 1, 1991 / Rap-A-Lot/Priority ♦♦♦♦♦

The cover of the Geto Boys' *We Can't Be Stopped* shows a member with his eye poked out. It's grotesque, but realistic—a realistic cover for an album whose violent, profane lyrics paint a vivid and accurate picture of life as the Geto Boys knew it growing up in Houston's tough ghetto known as the Fifth Ward. This CD isn't as thought-provoking as Ice-T, N.W.A., or Ice Cube can be—nor is it the Geto Boys' best offering. But it's an engaging, disturbing effort that comes across as much more heartfelt than the numerous gangster rap albums by the N.W.A. and Cube clones and wannabes who jumped on the gangster bandwagon in the early '90s. *We Can't Be Stopped* serves as an unsettling reminder of the type of ugly social conditions that were allowed to fester in poor inner-city neighborhoods. *—Alex Henderson*

● **Uncut Dope: Geto Boys' Best** / 1992 / Rap-a-Lot/Priority ♦♦♦♦♦

With various members opting for solo projects and the group disintegrating, Rap-A-Lot Records primed the pump one last time with what was essentially a greatest hits CD. It wasn't totally a retrospective because it included "Damn It Feels Good to Be a Gangsta," the ultimate genre definition piece and the last significant Geto Boys composition. "And My Word," "Actions Speak Louder Than Words," and "The Unseen" were other fresh jams that joined the Geto Boys anthems "Mind Playing Tricks on Me," "Assassins," "Scarface," and "Mind of a Lunatic," among others. The old/new menu made this the one to grab if one Geto Boys CD is all you need. *—Ron Wynn*

Till Death Do Us Part / Mar. 19, 1993 / Rap-A-Lot ♦♦♦

Makin' Trouble / 1994 / Rap-A-Lot ♦♦

The Resurrection / Apr. 2, 1996 / Rap-A-Lot/Noo Trybe ♦♦♦♦

After spending nearly five years apart, the Geto Boys reunited in 1996 and released *The Resurrection.* Since they were more notorious for their lyrical violence than their music—only 1991's "We Can't Be Stopped," with its stunning single "Mind Playing Tricks on Me," showed the band experimenting musically—it comes as a suprise that *The Resurrection* is such a strong album. Although the band never deviates from their standard blood-guts-sex lyrical routine, they have a greater sense of humor throughout the album. More importantly, they perform with energy and their backing tracks are vigorous and funky. As a result, *The Resurrection* outstrips every other Geto Boys record in every sense—it is the leanest, meanest, and funkiest thing they've ever recorded. *—Stephen Thomas Erlewine*

Da Good Da Bad & Da Ugly / Nov. 17, 1998 / Virgin ♦♦♦

Ghost

f. 1988, Tokyo, Japan

Neo-Psychedelia, Indie Rock, Alternative Pop/Rock

A collective of psychedelic-minded Japanese musicians headed by guitarist Masaki Batoh, Ghost records commune-minded free-range psychedelia with equal debts to the Can/Amon Düül axis of Krautrock, as well as West Coast psych units like Blue Cheer and Jefferson Airplane. Batoh grew up in Kyoto, where he attended a private school well-geared to spark his interest in rock music, from Dylan and Pink Floyd to the Velvet Underground. Later, he formed Ghost with a large and varying lineup, centered around contributors such as Michio Kurihara, Kazuo Ogino, and Taishi Takizawa. According to reports, the group lived a nomadic existence, drifting from ruins of ancient temples to disused subway stations around the Tokyo area.

The band began releasing their work with the albums *Ghost* and *Second Time Around,* each appearing during 1991-92. The American independent Drag City licensed each of the albums for distribution, and L.A.'s The Now Sound picked up two of Batoh's solo albums, *A Ghost From the Darkened Sea* and *Kikaokubeshi* (released together as well under the title *Collected Works*). Two more Ghost titles, *Tune In, Turn On, Free Tibet* and *Snuffbox Immanence,* were released simultaneously in 1999. A year later, the group teamed with kindred spirits Damon and Naomi for *Damon and Naomi With Ghost.* *—John Bush*

Ghost / Jul. 8, 1991 / Drag City ♦♦♦♦

Give points to Ghost for defying expectations right from the start of its first album, at least if one is coming in merely expecting a drifty, new age type of experience. "Sun is Tangging" may start off fairly quietly, but then it explodes in a noise fest and then returns to a calmer acoustic serenity throughout. With that as a fine surprise starting point, Batoh and company enter fully into their fascinating acid-folk-jam world with a strong number of songs. The group and its many guests—no less than 11—explore everything from droning mysticism that sounds like it was recorded in mist-shrouded jungle temples to heavy duty percussion-led songs that will make any Amon Düül fan smile in happiness. Given this wide range, Batoh's particular vision feels not merely like a tribute to his musical forebears but a striking new synthesis, while his main collaborators at this point match his dreams well. Mu Krishna, the chief percussion player, does a particularly fine job on his own or with various guests throughout, also contributing 'whisper,' as the credits name it. One moment where Batoh gets to step fully to the fore is the lovely "I've Been Flying," where his soft acoustic playing and understated but still strong singing floats above a lovely electric guitar solo from then guest performer Kurihara. The immediately following "Ballad of Summer Rounder" is just as grand, Batoh's tender, evocative singing and playing accompanied about four minutes in by Takizawa's flute and guest drummer Shigeru Konno's steady, restrained percussion. It eventually ends in a classic jam, Takizawa switching to sax and going off over the head-nodding beat as Batoh seems almost to be speaking in tongues or mantras. "Rakshu" wraps up this quite fine debut with an intoxicating, hushed blend of percussion—gongs, bells, blocks—and Batoh's prayerful singing. *—Ned Raggett*

● **Second Time Around** / 1992 / Drag City ♦♦♦♦♦

Ghost's second album, following one year on from the self-titled debut, saw a slight shift in the lineup, with Krishna out on percussion, replaced by Iwao Yamazaki. Guest performer Kazuo Ogino also became permanent, introduced from the start with his Celtic harp on the opening "People Get Freedom," while multi-instrumentalist Takizawa and bassist/singer Kohji Nishino continued from before. Batoh as always remained the center around which all revolved, with even more eerily beautiful and powerful music than before. All members were credited with a large number of percussion instruments, from bell tree and Tibetan bells to "some nameless bells and stones," further intensifying the aura of ancient and mysterious rites that hangs through Ghost's music. The blend of influences both Western and Eastern results in a series of fine syntheses, perhaps even stronger than on *Ghost.* "Higher Power," with oboe and finger cymbals among much more, and "First Drop of the Sea," which could almost be a calmer Scott Walker number from the late '60s at points, both capture this sense of broad listening to grand effect. Batoh can be straightforward as he chooses, thus the title track, for one example. He almost sounds a bit like Bowie in lighter cabaret mode (an approach he generally maintains throughout the record) even while the acid folk atmosphere gently kicks along, sometimes with quiet drama in the arrangements. When the band fully kicks in, as on the rolling "Forthcoming From the Inside," everything achieves powerful heights as a result. His lyrics throughout are often quite striking—his images of ceremonies, seeking the spiritual amid the mundane and more often make a lot more sense than the fuzzier hoo-hah coming from his West Coast psych/Krautrock forebears. This is especially saying something the case of the former, given that English isn't his first language. *—Ned Raggett*

Lama Rabi Rabi / Nov. 19, 1996 / Drag City ♦♦♦

Temple Stone / Jul. 8, 1997 / Drag City ♦♦♦♦

A live album, but a live album unlike any other, *Temple Stone* is, as the liner notes indicate, a record of "some experimental performances at sacred places in recent years," in many but not all cases favoring acoustic over electric instruments (a notable exception is a great version of "Rakshu"). Playing at various temples and churches in Japan, Ghost mostly drew on songs from the self-titled debut and *Second Time Around,* with most of the recordings coming from sessions in 1993. The various selections aren't arranged in any particular order, while there's no hint if songs listed as taken from a performance at a particular site are all from the same or different evenings, so anyone expecting a straight record of the Ghost live experience at the time won't find it here. Those expecting more of the mysterious, fascinating acid folk-rock drama of early Ghost, though, will find plenty of that here. Not merely recreating the album recordings, the four piece lineup, supplemented at many different points by other guests, add further explorations to the arrangements, while the quality of the delivery alone makes the cuts rival the studio versions. "Guru in the Echo" is one standout; Taishi Takizawa's performance on flute is absolutely wonderful, while Batoh's impassioned singing makes it one of his finest recorded moments as well. "Sun Is Tangging," meanwhile, is pure a Amon Düül-style mega-jam at the end, an absolutely stunning all-around effort. Of the unfamiliar cuts, the most interesting is a reworking of the traditional "Blood Red River." Batoh plays it fairly straight himself in terms of singing and guitar, but the band as a whole turn it into a noisy freak-out not far distant from the Birthday Party's similarly insane exorcisms of the blues. The sheer chaos at the end is a wonder to behold. *—Ned Raggett*

Snuffbox Immanence / Apr. 20, 1999 / Drag City ♦♦♦♦♦

With a slightly reshuffled lineup—Ogino now clearly became Batoh's chief collaborator, while new percussionist Setsuko Furuya accompanied the returning Kurihara, cellist Hiromichi Sakamoto and two brass players—Ghost on *Snuffbox* created another striking, beautiful album. With its senses of fusions now firmly grasped, able to slide from trumpet and flute-accompanied folk on the opening "Regenesis" to the initially acoustic then ragingly electric "Sad Shakers," Ghost achieved levels of inspiration that easily equaled many of Batoh's original role models. One of those early sources gets saluted in a sharp way—the Rolling Stones' "Live With Me" gets a piano/vibe-heavy remake here, with Furuya getting to showcase his abilities in particular. Another neo-psych masterpiece is the title track—Batoh's truly cool, spaced-out lyric gets backed perfectly by Ogino's harpischord, his own acoustic and crunching electric guitar work, and plenty of production effects and tweaking for effect. The at-times-underrated sense of playfulness which crops up in Ghost's work gets some airing here. "Soma" ends by shifting from a gentler flow to a quicker ending led by Batoh's banjo, while "Fukeiga" has similar fun with the vibes and Batoh's electric soloing offset against his clear acoustic work. Still, though, it's the sense of spiritual power and mantra-based music and performance that comes through the strongest on *Snuffbox,* a mostly calm and understated affair for its length. The fine instrumental "Daggma," with Ogino and Furuya's combination of keyboard and percussion instruments backed by Sakamoto's cello, is at once melancholic and uplifting. Batoh also clearly feels thoroughly comfortable with switching between his native tongue and English, splitting the amount sung in each language down the middle. "Hanmiyau" closes *Snuffbox* with a flourish, piano, guitar reverb, and more, Batoh's serene lyrics echoing up from the depths. *—Ned Raggett*

Tune In, Turn On, Free Tibet / Apr. 20, 1999 / Drag City ♦♦♦♦

Conceived as a companion release to *Snuffbox*—the two albums were released within a few weeks of each other and share some art—*Free Tibet* is definitely much more the socially forceful flipside to that lovely album. The same core five-person lineup records here, but as photos and an impassioned essay from the liaison office of the Dalai Lama demonstrate, the goal is what's stated right in the title. Given Batoh's open inspiration, spiritually and musically, from that region, recording what amounts to both a celebration and call to action makes perfect sense. Certainly Ghost aren't interested in simply recording a tribute to Tibetan music—while the opening track "We Insist" starts with various Tibetan wind instruments, the focus is on Batoh, who speaks rather than sings, his words distorted heavily, the effect almost that of a government official dictating one's fate. The same sense of beautiful serenity that so often pervades Ghost's work is more than clear here—all it takes is a listen to the grand "Way of Shelkar" to show that, its blend of Batoh, guitars, keyboards, and other instruments achieving a wondrous calm. Other songs like "Lhasa Lhasa" and "Change the World" deliver the key message with the same sweet grace. The album climaxes with the mind-blowing title track, the longest thing the group has ever done at over half an hour long. Whether it was carefully planned or a jam session, it's a stunner, ranging from acoustic gentility to percussion craziness to nuclear-strength electric roars, sometimes switching from one section to another on a dime. There's one interesting link to *Snuffbox* in terms of music—as on that album, Ghost here salute a musical forebear, in this case Tom Rapp. His Pearls Before Swine track "Images of April" gets a stripped-down, softly whispered cover here, both a worthy tribute to the original and a showcase for Batoh's own considerable work. *—Ned Raggett*

Ghostface Killah (Dennis Coles)

Vocals / Hardcore Rap, East Coast Rap, Hip-Hop

As one of the original members of the seminal '90s rap crew the Wu-Tang Clan, Ghostface Killa (a.k.a. Tony Starks) made an impact before he released his debut album, *Iron Man*, late in 1996. Like all members of the Wu-Tang Clan, the rapper used the group as a launching pad for a solo career, which was assisted greatly by other members of the Clan, particularly producer the RZA/Prince Rakeem. Ghostface Killah had rapped on Wu-Tang's 1993 debut *Enter the Wu-Tang*, but he didn't distinguish himself until 1995, when he was showcased on fellow Wu member Raekwon's *Only Built 4 Cuban Linx*. Ghostface received good reviews for his appearance on the record, and his contribution to the soundtracks for *Sunset Park* and *Don't Be a Menace to South Central While You're Drinking Your Juice in the Hood* also were well received. All of these guest appearances and soundtrack contributions set the stage for Ghostface Killah's solo debut, *Iron Man*, in late 1996. Like all Wu-Tang projects, it was produced by the RZA and it was quite successful in the large hip-hop/rap underground, debuting at number two on the pop charts upon its release. *Iron Man* was also the first album to be released on Razor Sharp Records, the RZA's record label on Epic Records. *Supreme Clientele* followed in early 2000. *—Stephen Thomas Erlewine*

● **Ironman** / Oct. 29, 1996 / Columbia ✦✦✦✦✦

Every Wu-Tang Clan solo project has a different flavor, and Ghostface Killah's *Iron Man* is no exception. Though it boasts cameos from nearly every other Wu-Tang member—notably Raekwon and Cappadonna—*Iron Man* is unlike any other record in RZA's catalog of productions, particularly because it is significantly lighter in tone. There are still touches of the Wu's signature urban claustrophobia throughout the record, but the music is largely built on samples of early '70s soul, from Al Green to the Delfonics, who make a guest appearance on "After the Smoke Is Clear." Consequently, the mood of the album can switch tones at the drop of the hat, moving from hard funk like "Daytona 500" to seductive soul with the Mary J. Blige duet "All That I Got Is You." *Iron Man* bogs down slightly in the middle, yet the record is filled with inventive production and rhymes, and ranks as another solid entry in the Wu-Tang legacy. *—Stephen Thomas Erlewine*

Supreme Clientele / Jan. 25, 2000 / Razor Sharp/Epic Street ✦✦✦✦

Most of the members of rap's Roman Empire, the Wu-Tang Clan, experienced sophomore slumps with their second solo releases, whether artistically or commercially (usually both). The second offerings from Method Man, Ol' Dirty Bastard, GZA, and Raekwon featured some of the old Wu magic, but not enough to warrant a claim to their once total mastery of the rap game. Just as the Wu empire appeared to be crumbling, along came the second installment from the Clan's spitfire element, Ghostface Killah (aka Tony Starks, aka Ironman). Every bit as good as his first release, *Supreme Clientele* proves Ghost's worthiness of the Ironman moniker by deftly overcoming trendiness to produce an authentic sound in hip-hop's age of bland parity. Some of the Wu's slump could be contributed to Wu-Abbott's (aka RZA) relative sabbatical. This album has RZA's stamp all over it, but the guru himself only provides three tracks. On this effort, the Wu-pupil producers at times seem to outdo their teacher. RZA's best composition is the piano-driven, double-entendre-laced childhood retrospective "Child's Play." But of the many standout cuts, it's the slew of disciple producers paying homage to the Wu legacy that truly makes this album fresh-sounding: "Apollo Kids" (Hassan), "Malcolm" (Choo the Specialist), "Saturday Nite" (Carlos "Six July" Broady), "One" (JuJu of the Beatnuts), "Cherchez la Ghost" (Carlos Bess), "Wu Banga 101" (Allah Mathematics). While the album is complete and characteristically Wu-sounding, each track is distinctive lyrically, thematically, and sonically. Ghostface's *Supreme Clientele* is a step toward the Wu-Tang Clan's ascent from the ashes of their fallen kingdom. The once slumbering Wu-Tang strikes again. *—Michael Di Bella*

Debbie Gibson

b. Aug. 31, 1970, Long Island, NY

Vocals, Piano / Teen Idol, Pop/Rock, Dance-Pop

Debbie Gibson became a pop phenomenon in the late '80s, scoring a string of hit singles when she was only 17. Although she was still a teenager, Gibson showed signs of being a talented pop craftsman, capable of making catchy dance-pop in the style of Madonna, as well as lush, orchestrated ballads. Gibson's time at the top of the charts was brief, but it was quite successful, producing five Top Five singles, including two number ones, and two multi-platinum albums. While she was still in high school, Debbie Gibson signed with Atlantic Records and began recording her debut album with producer Fred Zarr. "Only in My Dreams," her debut single, climbed to number four when it was released in the summer of 1987. It was followed in the fall by the dance-oriented "Shake Your Love," which also peaked at number four. *Out of the Blue*, her debut album, was released in the fall of 1987, and by the spring of 1988, it had reached the American Top Ten. The title track became a number three hit that spring and it was followed by her first number one single, "Foolish Beat," making her the youngest artist ever to write, perform, and produce a number one single. Following the success of "Foolish Beat," Gibson graduated from Calhoun High School in Merrick, NY, with honors. "Lost in Your Eyes," the first single from her second album, *Electric Youth*, became Gibson's biggest hit early in 1989, staying at number one for three weeks. *Electric Youth*, released in the spring of 1989, also hit number one, spending five weeks at the top of the charts. However, her popularity began to slip by the end of the year. *—Stephen Thomas Erlewine*

Out of the Blue / 1987 / Atlantic ✦✦✦✦✦

Mention the name Debbie Gibson and you're likely to elicit either a derisive snort or embarrassment from your conversant about ever having owned a Gibson album. Chances are that anyone who falls into the latter category—and there are several million of them—bought her debut, *Out of the Blue*. While *Out of the Blue* does possess the slick, processed dance-pop production and squeaky-clean innocence of most '80s teen-pop, it stands out from the competition due to Gibson's talent as a singer, musician, pop songwriter, arranger, and even producer. Five of this album's ten tracks hit the Top 40, with four of those going Top Five, and Gibson's youthful exuberance and energy shine through infectiously. Despite her reputation, it's some of the best teen-pop you're likely to hear. *—Steve Huey*

Electric Youth / 1989 / Atlantic ✦✦✦

Following up her enormously popular debut, *Out of the Blue*, Debbie Gibson sought to grow from the teen fan base she had established, while not alienating those who made her a household name. The result is slickly produced teen pop, like her debut, but it's not as squeaky clean or as compulsively likable. That is not to say it's a bad album. "Lost in Your Eyes" is a pretty ballad that showcases her songwriting skills, her clear voice, and her talent on the piano. "Electric Youth" is a bouncy, frenetic song that is ridiculously singalongable, but at the same it is time hard to really identify with it unless you're 12 (or at least young at heart). "We Could Be Together," in which she basically tells her friends and family to go fly a kite, is practically anthemic in its joy at taking a risk on love: "I'll take this chance/I'll make this choice/I'll give up my security/for just the possibility/that we could be together/for a while." It's teen pop at its best: it makes you feel young, it makes you want to sing, it makes you want to fall in love. "Silence Speaks (A Thousand Words)" is a beautiful ballad about lack of communication that is vastly different from any of her other work, with a flute solo and lyrics that many adult songwriters can't nail. The same can be said for "No More Rhyme," a minor hit about a relationship's first hurdle. Gibson really exercised her writing chops on those songs, but much of the rest the album is only passable filler; "Who Loves Ya Baby?," "Helplessly in Love," and "Over the Wall" do little more than give her voice a reason to shine, while "Shades of the Past" is excruciatingly grating. *—Bryan Buss*

Anything Is Possible / 1990 / Atlantic ✦✦

Body Mind Soul / 1993 / Atlantic ✦✦✦

Think With Your Heart / 1995 / EMI ✦✦

● **Greatest Hits** / Jan. 1996 / Atlantic ✦✦✦✦✦

Say what you will about the slickly produced teen pop of the late '80s and its revival in the late '90s: Debbie Gibson made some of the best of either era. Her best material (nearly all of which she wrote herself) displayed superior pop craftsmanship at a surprisingly young age, and she was no slouch as a producer or arranger, either. Perhaps that's why *Greatest Hits* still sounds so much less calculated and contrived than a lot of the artists working similar territory. Rant and rave all you want about corporate pandering; Gibson's love of pure pop is obvious (so it shouldn't be a surprise that she later moved into musicals). Yes, this music is almost painfully clean-cut and sugary-sweet, but Gibson imbues it with a refreshing sincerity which comes directly from the fact that this is *her* music (unlike teen queens who rely on middle-aged men for material). *Greatest Hits* features all of her hit singles, and while both the upbeat dance-pop and the adult contemporary ballads sound very much of their time, that's not a bad thing at all—they're very good, very well-crafted pop songs, and they hold up surprisingly well because of that. *—Steve Huey*

Deborah / May 27, 1997 / Espiritu ✦✦✦

What You Want / Oct. 24, 2000 / Espiritu ✦✦✦

M.Y.O.B / Mar. 6, 2001 / Golden Egg ✦✦✦

Nick Gilder

b. Nov. 7, 1951, London, England

Vocals, Songwriter / Pop/Rock, Soft Rock

Nick Gilder began playing with Vancouver-based Sweeney Todd. The band split in 1977 after two albums (*Sweeney Todd* and *If Wishes Were Horses*) when he and bandmate Jimmy McCullouch moved to Los Angeles. That same year, Gilder began a solo career, signing to Chrysalis and releasing *You Know Who You Are*. His second album, *City Nights*, produced the platinum number one single "Hot Child in the City" in 1978. Though Gilder released several other albums (including 1979's *Frequency* and 1981's *Body Talk Muzak*), he never approached his earlier success. *—John Bush*

● **The Best of Nick Gilder: Hot Child in the City** / Mar. 20, 2001 / Razor & Tie ✦✦✦✦

"Hot Child in the City" is a great single: a song about Hollywood hookers that encapsulates everything cool about late-'70s summer nights. But even better is "Roxy Roller," a groupie ode Gilder recorded with his former band, Sweeney Todd, named after the infamous Fleet Street barber. In fact, "Got to Get Out," "Runaways in the Night," and "Tantalize" (also a Sweeney Todd number) are stone-cold classics. Featuring killer Gilder tracks that have never been reissued, *The Best of Nick Gilder* is a composite of Gilder's three '70s solo releases: *You Know Who You Are, City Nights*, and *Frequency*. Each is an excellent platter and Nights features production from glam-master Mike Chapman in the midst of conquering America (he also had number ones with Blondie and Exile during 1978). Chapman then worked on Pat Benatar's debut, *In the Heat of the Night*, which featured Gilder's "Rated X," a consummate carnal confection that Gilder serves up even better on this disc. Gilder compresses a bubblegum blast comparable to T. Rex or Cheap Trick. At least now there's a CD to prove it. *—Doug Stone*

Gin Blossoms

f. 1987, **db.** Dec. 1997

Adult Alternative Pop/Rock, Pop/Rock, Alternative Pop/Rock, Power Pop

Alternative power popsters the Gin Blossoms were formed in 1987 in Tempe, AZ, by longtime friends Bill Leen (bass) and Doug Hopkins (guitar), with an initial lineup also featuring vocalist Jesse Valenzuela, guitarist Richard Taylor, and drummer Chris McCann. The following year saw several personnel shifts as the band struggled to solidify—McCann was replaced by Dan Henzerling and, shortly thereafter, Phillip Rhodes, while Taylor was fired and replaced by guitarist Robin Wilson. Wilson and Valenzuela subsequently switched roles, and the band recorded a self-released album, *Dusted*, in 1989. A&M signed them the following year. After an impressive 1991 debut EP, *Up and Crumbling*, the Gin Blossoms rocketed out of the college pop charts and into the mainstream with their 1993 hit single "Hey Jealousy." Combining the ringing guitar hooks of the Byrds and R.E.M. with a solid, rootsy drive, the band's breakthrough full-length album, *New Miserable Experience* (which had actually been released the previous year), was filled with songs equally as strong as "Hey Jealousy," including the second hit single, "Found Out About You." *New Miserable Experience* and its singles dominated radio and MTV for the following year—"Hey Jealousy" and "Found Out About You," both penned by Hopkins, were in heavy radio rotation nearly a year after their initial release—pushing the sales of their debut album to over one million copies. However, all was not well. Doug Hopkins' battle with alcoholism and depression had taken its toll on the band during the sessions for *New Miserable Experience*, and he was fired shortly after the record's release, with guitarist Scott Johnson taking his place. Speculation abounded as to whether the band would be able to maintain their success without Hopkins' melancholy songwriting voice. Tragically, on December 5, 1993, Hopkins shot and killed himself, even as the songs he had written were blanketing the airwaves.

In the summer of 1995, the Gin Blossoms contributed "'Till I Hear It From You," a song they co-wrote with Marshall Crenshaw, to the soundtrack of the film *Empire Records*. "'Till I Hear It From You" became a major radio hit, but was never released as an official single until it was the B-side of "Follow You Down," the first single from the group's second album, *Congratulations... I'm Sorry*. Upon its release in February of 1996, *Congratulations... I'm Sorry* charted well, but within six months, it had disappeared from the charts. Following the supporting tour, the Gin Blossoms disbanded in 1997. *—Stephen Thomas Erlewine*

Up & Crumbling / 1991 / A&M ✦✦✦

The Gin Blossoms' debut EP *Up & Crumbling* is an appealing five-song slice of jangly power-pop, filled with ringing hooks and sweet melodies. Since two of the songs (including "Alison Road") wound up on their full-length debut *New Miserable Experience* and a couple others became B-sides, its value has decreased somewhat, but it remains an engaging listen. *—Stephen Thomas Erlewine*

● **New Miserable Experience** / Aug. 4, 1992 / A&M ✦✦✦✦

The Gin Blossoms were one of the more truly damned rock & roll bands to grace the pop charts in the early 1990s. The group was founded and spiritually led by singer-guitarist Doug Hopkins, who also wrote the band's best songs; by the time *New Miserable Experience*, the band's major-label debut, was released, Hopkins had been kicked out (his bandmates had apparently tired of dealing with his alcoholism). Shortly after the album's release Hopkins killed himself, and the band subsequently enjoyed the biggest hit of its career with "'Til I Hear It From You" (which, perversely, never appeared on a Gin Blossoms album, but only on the *Empire Records* soundtrack). The band dropped from sight not long after. *New Miserable Experience* remains the best and most representative document of the group's existence, a tight and lean collection of brilliant, edgy pop music. "Hey Jealousy" and "Until I Fall Away" are the two songs that leave the deepest impression, but the crunchy melodicism and lyrical desperation of "Hold Me Down" sticks with you as well. Two dilettantish genre pieces—"Cajun Song" and a country weeper called "Cheatin'" (as in "you can't call it cheatin' 'cause she reminds me of you")—provide the program's two low points, but even those aren't completely without charm. *—Rick Anderson*

Congratulations... I'm Sorry / Feb. 13, 1996 / A&M ✦✦✦

Most observers wondered if the Gin Blossoms would be able to deliver a consistent second album after the departure (and subsequent suicide) of Doug Hopkins, their former guitarist who wrote "Hey Jealousy" and "Found Out About You," the two big hits from the band's debut. *Congratulations... I'm Sorry* proves that they can. The Gin Blossoms haven't backed away from the sound that made *New Miserable Experience* a hit. It's filled with chiming guitars, sweet melodies, and simple, catchy hooks, as well as a sturdy grasp of traditional pop/rock songwriting that results in a number of gems. The only fault of *Congratulations... I'm Sorry* is that it sounds a bit *too* close to the debut—there's virtually no difference in terms of style and production. As such, it builds a case for their craftsmanship. The Gin Blossoms may not have much new to say, but they say it well throughout *Congratulations... I'm Sorry*. *—Stephen Thomas Erlewine*

● **Outside Looking In: The Best of the Gin Blossoms** / Oct. 19, 1999 / Interscope ✦✦✦✦

In December 1997, the Gin Blossoms announced their breakup, and the lines of communication were severed so severely that the band didn't realize their former label was assembling a hits collection, *Outside Looking In: The Best Of*. The album may not have been compiled with the complete authorization of the band, but that doesn't mean it isn't good or useful. Aside from the live version of "Whitewash," a sap to collectors, this is a tight distillation of the band's two A&M albums, noteworthy for the first album appearance of "Til I Hear It From You." Some might think that a compilation of two albums is stretching the definition of compilation a little bit too much, but that's really just a reflection of the industry in the '90s—two albums and one non-LP single *was* the end result of a decade's worth of work. Ultimately, *Outside Looking In* is a good listen, from the hits to the album tracks, and it confirms that the Gin Blossoms were one of the first bands to really carve out the sound later known as adult alternative pop/rock. *—Stephen Thomas Erlewine*

Ginger

f. 1992, **db.** 1997

College Rock, Adult Alternative Pop/Rock

When vocalist/guitarist and founding member Kevin Kane left Canada's acclaimed Grapes of Wrath due to the cliched musical and personal differences, the remaining members—Chris Hooper (drums), Tom Hooper (vocals, bass, guitars), and Vincent Jones (keyboards)—carried on with the like-sounding and equally enjoyable Ginger. The band returned to Nettwerk Records (Grapes of Wrath's original label), releasing a self-titled, Canadian-only EP in 1993 and the full-length *Far Out* in 1994. *Far Out* was eventually released in the U.S. in 1995. The band followed with *Suddenly I Came to My Senses* in late 1996 for EMI Canada. *—Chris Woodstra*

Ginger / 1993 / Nettwerk ✦✦✦

The combo's first release picks up effectively where Grapes of Wrath left off with five songs of pleasantly jangly folk-pop that occasionally flirt with pseudo-psychedelia. Only "The Earth Revolves Around You" appears on *Far Out*, so fans are advised to seek this out. *—Chris Woodstra*

● **Far Out** / 1994 / Nettwerk ✦✦✦✦

Far Out is a well-paced album that clearly stands alongside the finer moments of Grapes of Wrath, alternating quieter, introspective moments with upbeat rockers and pure Beatlesque pop. *—Chris Woodstra*

Ginuwine

Contemporary R&B, Club/Dance, Urban, Hip-Hop

Ginuwine (born Elgin Lumpkin) is a Washington, DC-based contemporary soul artist who released his debut album, *Ginuwine: The Bachelor*, to great acclaim in the fall of 1996. *100% Ginuwine* followed three years later, generating the hit "So Anxious." Another monumental effort *Life* was issued in early 2001. *—Stephen Thomas Erlewine*

● **Ginuwine... The Bachelor** / Oct. 8, 1996 / 550 Music/Epic ✦✦✦✦

Ginuwine's debut album *The Bachelor* is an audacious fusion of Prince-style funk, hip-hop, and swingbeat soul, led by the updated electro-funk of the hit single, "Pony." Throughout the rest of *The Bachelor*, Ginuwine proves that "Pony" is no fluke, as he demonstrates his songwriting skills with songs like "Do Anything/I'm Sorry" and his vocal talents with a cover of Prince's "When Doves Cry." *—Leo Stanley*

100% Ginuwine / Mar. 16, 1999 / 550 Music/Epic ✦✦✦✦

Ginuwine's debut album certainly sounded like little else in the modern soul front. Thanks to Timbaland's inventive production, it blended classic soul songwriting with inventive sonic textures, borrowed equally from hip-hop, trip-hop, and electro-funk. For the follow-up, Ginuwine and Timbaland decided that if it ain't broke, just spiffy it up a little bit—which means *100% Ginuwine* uses *The Bachelor* as a blueprint but goes further, boasting more inventive productions and a stronger set of songs. If nothing grabs the ear like "Pony," most of the songs slowly work their way underneath the skin, revealing themselves as either seductive ballads or ingratiating dance-floor numbers. Timbaland continues to prove that he's one of the savviest producers in modern hip-hop and soul, but Ginuwine remains the star of the show, thanks to his rich, inviting voice. *—Stephen Thomas Erlewine*

The Life / Apr. 3, 2001 / Epic ✦✦✦

On his third album, Ginuwine is even more of a practiced R&B loverman than he was on his first two releases. Big Dog Productions, Inc. and the team of Troy Oliver and Cory Rooney produce the bulk of the beats here, which, as usual, mostly range from slow to very slow tempos with such trendy touches as acoustic guitar passages. But all that just serves as a bed for Ginuwine's elastic tenor and his message to the women in his audience. The singer sounds like he's been reading women's magazines and tried to construct a persona that's as appealing as possible. "Baby," he croons in "Why Did You Go," "I'm sorry for whatever I've done and I want you to be my wife." In "Differences," he talks about how much he has improved since meeting the woman he's addressing, concluding, "I'm so responsible." Even when he's criticizing a woman, as he does in the album's first single, "There It Is," it's because she's not contributing to the relationship, while he's holding down a steady job and paying the bills. It's only in the album's eighth cut, "How Deep Is Your Love" (an original, not the Bee Gees song), that he begins to apply pressure for sex, ungallantly suggesting that if the woman doesn't come across he'll start cheating on her. "Show After the Show" is a come-on to a post-concert groupie, which seems to negate what's gone before, and "Role Play" moves on to kinky sex, but in the album-closing "Just

Because," Ginuwine acknowledges the temptations of his occupation and pleads, "I'm trying to learn to be committed." It's hard to believe that anyone who's swallowed his line before is going to become skeptical now, so *The Life* looks like another winner for him. *—William Ruhlmann*

Glitter Band

f. 1972

Glitter, Glam Rock

Named for their associations with glam idol Gary Glitter, the Glitter Band originally came together in 1972, following Glitter's own breakthrough with the hit "Rock & Roll." With his first major concert tour looming, Glitter and producer/co-conspirator Mike Leander required a full-time backing band, one which would—though they could never have dreamed it at the time—ultimately become almost as successful, and certainly as well known, as Gary Glitter himself. Although the band was not physically present on any of Glitter's own hits (according to the singer, Mike Leander alone played every instrument himself), the Glitter Band not only accompanied Glitter on each of his tours and television appearances, they also racked up seven hits of their own, six of them also making the Top Ten. Even more impressively, while the band's original sound was indeed firmly cut in the style of their namesake, by the end of their career, the group had developed into a wholly original and utterly captivating act in their own right. The Glittermen, as the group was originally known, was built around an idea which Glitter and Leander had first experimented with during the mid-'60s, a sprawling combo whose sound and visuals were based upon a unique (for British acts) core of two drummers and two saxophonists. Evidence that the Glitter Band were capable of meeting greater challenges than the Glitter sound normally offered was delivered in early 1975 by their fourth single, the soft rock ballad "Goodbye My Love." An absolute departure, "Goodbye My Love" climbed to number two. *—Dave Thompson*

● **The Bell Singles Collection** / Sep. 26, 2000 / 7T's ♦♦♦♦

Between 1974-76, the Glitter Band released a total of nine singles on the U.K. Bell label, running up seven Top 20 hits, one American club smash, and emerging, at the end of the day, with two bona fide classics—their debut, "Angel Face," and, precisely midway through the sequence, "Goodbye My Love." All have now been recycled so many times that there can barely be an interested soul in the world who does not own the entire catalog in one permutation or another. Far from screaming its own redundancy from the rooftops, however, this collection distinguishes itself by returning to the original source—all nine singles, all nine B-sides, presented in strict chronological order. We can get the hits out of the way with barely a second glance; from the sublime (the aforementioned giants) to the ridiculous (the glitter-by-numbers "Let's Get Together Again," "Just for You"), the sequence encompasses a surprising array of directions and some remarkably consistent visions as well. Flip over the Beach Boys-esque "Love in the Sun" and find the band returning to the well of their inspiration, with the delicious "I Can Hear Music." Dig beneath the yearning "The Tears I Cried" and find the superb "Until Tomorrow." And upend the gratuitously irritating "People Like You, People Like Me," a last-ditch attempt to return to the glitter sound after some more adventurous efforts had failed to chart, and marvel at the instrumental "Makes You Blind," a squelching, pulsing slab of electro-disco-hard rock which came within a hair's breadth of breaking the American chart. As you'd expect from any compilation which takes half its weight from B-sides, it's an inconsistent collection. By and large, the Glitter Band's A-sides represent the peak of their powers; with only a handful of exceptions, the B-sides don't. But glam rock was a singles-driven phenomenon, and bands didn't come much glammier than the Glitters. No matter what the songs are like, this is history as it happened. *—Dave Thompson*

Gary Glitter

b. May 8, 1940, Banbury, Oxfordshire, England

Vocals / Glitter, Pop/Rock, Glam Rock, Hard Rock

Although the late '90s apparently saw the end of Gary Glitter's career, following his conviction for sexual offenses, there is no doubting that for a full 25 years before that tragic denouement, Glitter ranked among Britain's best-loved performers of all time. The hits which catapulted him to fame in the early '70s, the anthemic "Rock & Roll" of course, but also the likes of "I'm the Leader of the Gang," "Do You Wanna Touch Me," and "I Love You Love Me Love," still have the capacity to stir an audience. Glitter lived up to his image with a vengeance as well. He poured a fortune into his wardrobe—at one point he owned 30 glitter suits and 50 pairs of monstrous silver platform boots. But it was worth it. Glittermania was breaking out everywhere during his early-'70s reign before the singer suddenly announced his retirement in early 1976. For the next year, Glitter existed in a twilight world of rumor alone, as financial and psychological pressures pushed him to the brink. A half-hearted return to action saw him take the lead role in a New Zealand production of *The Rocky Horror Show* and score a pair of minor U.K. Top 30 hits during 1977. But it was 1980 before he truly began to come out his shell again, launching a series of low-key concerts for a post-punk audience which had, somewhat curiously, embraced him as a figurehead of sorts. By 1984, he was playing upwards of 80 gigs a year, mainly around the college and club circuit, and returned to the charts. *—Dave Thompson*

● **Rock & Roll: The Best of Gary Glitter** / 1990 / Rhino ♦♦♦♦♦

Anyone actually interested in collecting Gary Glitter albums for their non-hit tracks is barking up the wrong tree, to put it mildly. More than most, Glitter was all about the hit single, an exponent of an approach already outdated thanks to the sales focus on albums but of prime importance to earlier glam avatars like Marc Bolan and the Sweet. His own background as a failed '60s' rocker aiming for just one breakthrough hit certainly didn't hurt this approach, and that's what makes *Rock & Roll: The Best of Gary Glitter* such a definitive collection. Honestly, the collection could be trimmed by a few tracks and few would cry—his lesser hits were such obvious clones of his bigger ones that it wasn't until the Ramones came along that recycling a definitive rock formula would be so obvious. As for the big ones, though, look out. "Rock & Roll Part Two" and its eventual adaptation as the ultimate sports anthem in America during the late '80s and '90s is its own phenomenon, and certainly reducing everything to just gleeful yells and that brilliant compressed guitar is its own stroke of genius. "Do You Wanna Touch Me? (Oh Yeah)" and "I'm the Leader of the Gang (I Am!)" are both equally brilliant, the former's relentless, meaty beat contrasted by the equally fun gang-shout and regular tempo changes of the latter, shifting up and down like the motorcycle kicking it off. Beyond the main trio, there are more than a few goodies to be found that had later influence—"Hello! Hello! I'm Back Again," covered or adapted in later years by such distinctly different outfits as the Young Gods and Oasis, and "I Love You Love Me Love," a slower number sometimes played live by Depeche Mode's Martin Gore. The usual good Rhino remastering job, hilariously over-the-top photos and fine liner notes—written years before his eventual troubles with the law—complete the package. *—Ned Raggett*

Rock & Roll: Gary Glitter's Greatest Hits / Jan. 13, 1998 / Rhino ♦♦♦♦♦

In 1998, Rhino Records reissued *Rock & Roll: Gary Glitter's Greatest Hits* with artwork that wasn't quite as silly as its original incarnation, with the intention of snagging sports fans who hold "Rock & Roll, Pt. 2" dear to their hearts. In either incarnation, *Rock & Roll* is the definitive Gary Glitter collection, containing all of his singles, including "Do You Wanna Touch Me (Oh Yeah!)," "I'm the Leader of the Gang," and "Hello! Hello! I'm Back Again." *—Stephen Thomas Erlewine*

32 Glam Hits: The Ultimate Gary Glitter / May 25, 1999 / Cleopatra ♦♦♦

The two-disc, 32-track anthology *The Ultimate (Best Of)* is perhaps the largest Gary Glitter package it would be reasonable to assemble; for the casual fan, two discs of Glitter may be slightly wearing, but for the hardcore fan who has to have all of Glitter's best moments and doesn't mind a little inconsistency, *Ultimate* is a purchase that's hard to argue with. *—Steve Huey*

The Go

Garage Punk, Alternative Metal, Indie Rock, Rock & Roll

Part of the emerging Detroit garage-rock scene of the late '90s along with their more famous brethren, the White Stripes, the Go formed in 1998. Vocalist Bobby Harlow, guitarist John Krautner, and drummer Mark Fellis grew up together as kids—the addition of guitarist Steve Nawara and bassist Dave Buick made the band complete and they began playing gigs in the Detroit area. An opening slot for fellow Detroiters ? and the Mysterians helped get them the attention of Sub Pop, who signed the band and issued their debut album, *Whatcha Doin'* in 1999. Featuring a little help from Jack White on guitar and vocals, the album has an aggressive, noisy sound that still manages to still work in lots of references to R&B and soul, providing a fun, stylish, messy romp. *—Stacia Proefrock*

Whatcha Doin' / Sep. 7, 1999 / Sub Pop ♦♦♦♦

The Go's debut album *Whatcha Doin'* introduces the Detroit group's aggressive, authentic update of late '60s garage rock. Songs like the snarling "Meet Me at the Movies" and blissed-out "Summer Sun Blues" display the group's fuzzy, driving guitars, half-shouted, half-sung vocals and swaggering beats, while the poppier "It Might Be Good" and the "Get Off of My Cloud"-esque "You Can Get High" add another dimension to the Go's straight-up rock sound. *Whatcha Doin*'s final song "Time for Moon" is one of the album's best, combining a primal beat with dashes of backwards guitar and raw vocals. Though the occasionally muddy sound of the album takes the Go's quest for '60s-style authenticity a bit too far and fails to capture the group's live energy, *Whatcha Doin'* is a good introduction to one of the Motor City's most explosive bands. *—Heather Phares*

The Go-Go's

f. 1978, Los Angeles, CA, **db.** May 1985

Pop/Rock, New Wave

The Go-Go's were the most popular all-female band to emerge from the punk/new wave explosion of the late '70s and early '80s, becoming one of the first commercially successful female groups that wasn't controlled by male producers or managers. While their hit singles—"We Got the Beat," "Our Lips Are Sealed," "Vacation," "Head Over Heels"—were bright, energetic new wave pop, the group was integral part of the Californian punk scene. And they did play punk rock, even if many of their rougher edges were ironed out by the time they recorded their first album, 1981's *Beauty and the Beat.* Even as they became America's darlings, the Go-Go's lived the wild life of rockers, swallowing as many pills and taking as much cocaine as possible, trashing hotel rooms and just generally being bad. More importantly, their earliest music—now collected on *Return to the Valley of the Go-Go's*—was raw and rocking; it may not have directly inspired the female alternative rockers and riot grrrls of the '90s, but it certainly foreshadowed it. *—Stephen Thomas Erlewine*

Beauty & the Beat / Jul. 1981 / IRS ♦♦♦♦♦

Although the relatively polished production belies the Go-Go's' punk roots, *Beauty & the Beat* remains one of the cornerstone albums of new wave, bristling with energy, revamped surf-rock and girl-group hooks, and an intoxicating sense of fun. The infectious, bouncy "We Got the Beat" and the pulsating "Our Lips Are Sealed," which Jane Wiedlin co-wrote with Terry Hall, sent *Beauty & the Beat* to unexepected hit status, but they only scratch the surface of the wonderful pop songs that comprise the record. Nearly every song on the record is a delight, propelled by big, catchy hooks and an exuberant sense of fun. "Lust to Love," "Skidmarks on My Heart," "Tonite," and "Fading Fast" could have been hits in their own right, but as it stands, they help make *Beauty & the Beat* into a terrifically exciting pop album. *—Stephen Thomas Erlewine*

Vacation / Aug. 1982 / IRS ✦✦✦

The surprise success of *Beauty & the Beat* meant that the Go-Go's were expected to remain hitmakers, so perhaps it shouldn't have come as a surprise that their second album, *Vacation*, was a considerably slicker affair than their debut. Sporting a glossy yet alluring finish, the album had an appealing, radio-ready sound, but it was at the expense of the giddy sense of fun that made *Beauty & the Beat* such a vibrant record. However, *Vacation* is far from a washout. Although half the album is padded with filler, the very best moments are terrific pop songs, highlighted by the bouncy "This Old Feeling" and the classic title track. —*Stephen Thomas Erlewine*

Talk Show / 1984 / IRS ✦✦✦

For their third album, the Go-Go's abandoned all pretense of being punk, or even new wave, and went for an unabashed mainstream pop masterpiece. They nearly achieved their goal with *Talk Show*, an album filled with great pop songs but undermined by its own ambition. *Talk Show* has a sharper sound than its predecessors, with bigger guitars and drums, which helps drive home the accomplished pop hooks of "Turn to You," "I'm the Only One," and "Yes or No." However, the record is cluttered with half-realized songs and an overly detailed production which occasionally prevents the songs from reaching their full potential. But when the production and song are teamed well, the results are incredible, such as the surging "Head Over Heels," another classic single. Unfortunately, those moments don't arrive frequently enough to make *Talk Show* the new wave classic that it wants to be. —*Stephen Thomas Erlewine*

Greatest / Oct. 1990 / IRS ✦✦✦✦

The hits collection *Greatest* tries to reduce the Go-Go's' career to that of a mainstream pop/rock band, downplaying their punk and new wave roots. Of course, those can't be entirely erased, especially since the hits "Our Lips Are Sealed" and "We Got the Beat" form the core of the collection, but the song selection on the 14-track compilation leans a little too heavily on latter-day material and lesser songs, including an extraneous, previously unreleased cover of "Cool Jerk" that was added as bait for collectors. As a brief overview, *Greatest* is adequate, since it does contain all the hit singles, but it's also misleading, since it doesn't capture the group's punky spirit. Nevertheless, it's a cheaper, more manageable introduction than the double-disc set *Return to the Valley of the Go-Go's*, even though serious fans should choose that collection instead. —*Stephen Thomas Erlewine*

Return to the Valley of the Go-Go's / Oct. 18, 1994 / IRS ✦✦✦✦✦

Of all the various best-ofs and compilations that have come out over time that cover the Go-Go's career, this one is the clearest winner, by a long shot. Though by default it doesn't tell the full story, appearing as it did in 1994, in terms of containing both the famous hits and a slew of rarities and unreleased tracks, *Return to the Valley of the Go-Go's* is equally valuable for both neophytes and hardcore fans. The first 11 tracks alone make for an entertaining peek into the band's earliest days, with a slew of live cuts from both early rehearsals and gigs, including a number of songs taped at the legendary SF punk venue the Mabuhay Gardens. Everything's rough, energetic, and merry fun—while it's no surprise why some compositions remained unheard in later years, it's still worth hearing how the group pureed everything from straight-up punk to spaghetti Western guitar and girl group right from the start. A real treat is a romp through "Johnny, Are You Queer?" which would later get a more famous (and much more sedate!) take by Josie Cotton. Plenty of rare B-sides from the group's commercially dominant days surface here and there, and as for the big hits, they're available a-plenty: "We Got the Beat," "Vacation," "Our Lips Are Sealed," "Head Over Heels," "Turn to You," and more. Choice album cuts include "Skidmarks on My Heart" and "This Town." Closing things out is an acoustic live take on "Mercenary" from the band's 1990 reunion and three wholly new songs from 1994, including the enjoyable "The Whole World Lost Its Head." Topping things off is a great booklet featuring a hilarious collection of photos and ephemera from early days on, with plenty of amusing comments from the bandmembers, along with an enjoyable history of the group and reflections from all five on their favorite songs. —*Ned Raggett*

● **VH-1 Behind the Music: Go-Go's Collection** / May 23, 2000 / Interscope ✦✦✦✦

Just in time for the debut of their episode of VH1's *Behind the Music* comes *VH1 Behind the Music: Go-Go's Collection*, which features 17 of the group's definitive tracks, including "We Got the Beat," "My Lips Are Sealed," "Head Over Heels," "Vacation," and "Turn to You." Not as exhaustive as the *Return to the Valley of the Go-Go's* but not as slight as the *Greatest* album, *Go-Go's Collection* strikes a nice balance between the group's early, punky days and their later work as new wave divas. —*Heather Phares*

God Bless the Go-Go's / May 15, 2001 / Beyond ✦✦✦

The Go-Betweens

f. 1978, Brisbane, Australia, **db.** Dec. 31, 1989
College Rock, Indie Pop, New Wave, Alternative Pop/Rock

The Go-Betweens were perhaps the quintessential cult band of the '80s: they came from an exotic locale (Brisbane, Australia), moved to a major recording center (in their case, London) in a sustained bid to make a career out of music, released album after album of music seemingly tailor-made for the radio in spite of their having little use for contemporary Top 40 musical/lyrical formulas and earned considerable critical praise and a small but fervent international fan base. Though they split up at the end of the decade, both songwriters have moved onto respectable solo careers, that, while rarely reaching the heights the Go-Betweens scaled, continue to uphold their legacy. Robert Forster and Grant McLennan began as a pair of teenagers obsessed with the earthy rock of Dylan, CCR, and the Velvet Underground and encouraged by the Australian punk of the Saints. As collected on *The Able Label Singles*, their first two singles show a fondness for scruffy, British Invasion/new wave-influenced pop rock. Picking up permanent drummer Lindy

Morrisson, they recorded their debut LP, moved to England, and signed a short-lived deal with Rough Trade. Going for a lush, tuneful sound crammed with nonstandard rock instrumentation, they went on to record five more excellent LPs. Though their pre-Beggars Banquet albums were traditionally hard to find in the States, that label finally reissued all six albums on CD in 1996. 2000 saw a reunion of the band with the production of a new album, *The Friends of Rachel Worth* which also featured all three members of Sleater-Kinney. —*Michael Ribas*

Send Me a Lullaby / 1981 / Beggars Banquet ✦✦✦

The first official album from the Go-Betweens, after a slew of earlier recordings and initial singles, was described by Forster and McLennan in later years as sounding like a practice room session, "metallic folk in a way." It's a fair assessment, and certainly while it's the work of a young band, *Send Me a Lullaby* is still a promising start, showing that the original trio had an aesthetic and the talent to carry its work over an album's length. Another McLennan comment, that it's the 1981 version of the Pixies, is partially accurate—there's no walls of feedback or screaming, but the songs are short, brisk, angular. The not-so-secret weapon, as one can imagine, is the singing of Forster and McLennan, investing even the sharpest songs and most cutting rhythms (check out the relentless rhythms of the art-funk "The Girls Have Moved") with a sometimes desperate and sometimes withdrawn emotion. At points the vocals are forced, as can also be heard on *Very Quick on the Eye*, but both are starting to audibly try out other approaches. As musicians, the three definitely had something of that 'metallic folk' thing about them, with Morrison's drumming adding a sometimes brusque but (except for part of "Eight Pictures") never brutal touch to the proceedings that holds up quite well. Forster's guitar work and McLennan's bass are both interesting to hear in context given how much of an influence they would exert in later years. Rather than sounding like they're trying to recodify rock & roll or the like, it's a series of often gentle explorations in restraint, saying more with less. There are definitely more thrashy numbers that live might well have completely rocked out—"People Know," with its squirrelly guest saxophone from James Freud, is the most likely candidate of all. —*Ned Raggett*

Very Quick on the Eye / 1982 / Man Made ✦✦✦

Before Hollywood / 1983 / Beggars Banquet ✦✦✦✦✦

The Go-Betweens were already a good band well before they made *Before Hollywood*, but this second album is what proved for many listeners that they were great. For good reason—both Forster and McLennan's singing sounds much more honestly theirs, finding their own voices, while collectively the trio create a series of intricate, surprising melodies and songs which balance past and present beautifully. Strange as it may sound, the band's peers at this point could and did range from the Cure (for both melancholic intensity and guitar—check some of the electric work on "Ask") to more obvious cohorts as Orange Juice, but the Go-Betweens already had its own identity firmly established. For many the album's reputation rests on the presence of one song alone, and understandably so: "Cattle and Cane." Arguably the band's absolute highlight of its earliest years and one of the early '80s' utter classics, the combination of McLennan's nostalgia-laden but not soppy lyric, his flat-out lovely singing and overdubbed backing vocals, and the catchy, beautifully elegant acoustic/electric arrangement is simply to die for. There are plenty of other songs that demonstrate the threesome's collective strength. "Two Steps Step Out" is a prime example, with sudden tempo shifts, from a more straightforward beat on the chorus to the sudden breakdown on the brisk chorus, and McLennan's lovelorn lyric and quietly impassioned singing making an instant winner. Another McLennan winner is "Dusty in Here," soft piano from Bernard Clarke adding just enough to the spare but warm arrangement. Forster gets his own share of memorable moments, not least of which is the title track, not to mention the edgy, desperate "By Chance" and slightly calmer "On My Block." Morrison's abilities as a drummer are similarly improved, the at-times strident work of *Send Me a Lullaby* here replaced with a good balance between impact and steady swing. —*Ned Raggett*

Spring Hill Fair / 1984 / Beggars Banquet ✦✦✦

With Robert Vickers and his more straightforward style of bass introduced to the band, McLennan switched fully over to guitar and the quartet entered the studio with producer John Brand for *Spring Hill Fair*. A slightly more conventional but no less entrancing collection of songs in comparison to *Before Hollywood*, *Spring Hill Fair* contains its fair share of Go-Betweens classics, with the rough, barbed emotional edge of many lyrics getting almost gentle arrangements. There's more appearances from guest musicians than ever before, with contributions running from string arrangements to trumpet and saxophone. It's all still the Go-Betweens' own style of chiming guitar rock, able to switch between restraint and a hard-swinging (definite credit again to Morrison—check out her glammy stomp on "The Old Way Out") but not hard-riffing punch. Leadoff track "Bachelor Kisses," with its subtly intense mid-song break, McLennan's suddenly nervous singing matched by a quiet intensity in the music, is easily matched at the end with Forster's "Man O' Sand to Girl O' Sea," its pounding chorus one of the band's best captured moments of desperation. If McLennan had ultimate pride of place on *Before Hollywood* with "Cattle and Cane," Forster comes to the fore here with the just tense enough "Draining the Pool for You." It's a blackly humorous portrait of a maintenance worker and the faded superstar who hired him that also succeeds as a perfect kiss-off, with a memorable chorus to boot. Other Forster-sung standouts include "Part Company," an almost-Smiths-like all-around performance on the verses spiked with an at once inspirational and regret-laden chorus. Throughout the album one can not only hear the expanded lineup testing things out, but individual players adding their own particular flair—the brush-and-shuffle percussion from Morrison on "Five Words," McLennan's great lead guitar solo on "You've Never Lived," Vickers' ability with crisp funk on "Slow Slow Music." —*Ned Raggett*

Metal and Shells / 1985 / PVC ♦♦♦
This vinyl-only compilation was useful in acquainting at least a few Americans with the Go-Betweens' early (and in the U.S., otherwise unissued) recordings. Though fans are best served by the complete albums, it's worth picking up used for the curious non-fan since it contains among its treasures one of the best tracks from *Spring Hill Fair* not included on *1978-1990*, "Unkind & Unwise." *—Michael Ribas*

Liberty Belle and the Black Diamond Express / 1986 / Beggars Banquet ♦♦♦♦♦
Robert Forster's endearingly fey persona, equal parts Bryan Ferry and gangly bookstore clerk, reaches full flower on the Go-Betweens' fourth album, which tempers the angularity and occasional claustrophobia of the band's previous work with a new airiness and nervous romanticism. The lighter sound can be partly attributed to the growing influence of co-leader Grant McLennan, whose wistful "Cattle and Cane" and "Bachelor Kisses" lent grace to the Go-Betweens' sometimes stilted early records. McLennan's touch is all over *Liberty Belle and the Black Diamond Express*—his "In the Core of a Flame," a love song that manages to be at once tenderhearted and impatient, is a highlight—but this is still mostly Forster's show, and as such is a revelation. The merry, pastoral opener "Spring Rain" serves as notice that this will be a less dour affair than usual, yet, rather than negating Forster's pained, self-doubting lyrics, the comparatively gentle songs set them off beautifully. "You opened my mail apart at the seams/and now you know I live beyond my means," he sings at the outset of the swaying "Bow Down," and the prettiness of the melody makes him sound all the more uneasy. Other highlights include the sublime "Head Full of Steam," a tale of infatuation so strong that Forster breathlessly reports what his beloved's parents do for a living before realizing that such trivia is probably "of no importance at all" to anyone but him (which doesn't stop him from blurting out just a few lines later the earth-shattering news that neither he nor his object of desire have ever had a nickname). Protestations aside, the urgency in his voice makes it clear that the minutiae of love matter very much indeed, and anyone who's been there will sympathize. *Liberty Belle* is by no means free of the old Go-Betweens edge (the brooding "Twin Layers of Lightning" is proof of that), but it is the pervading warmth and rueful humor of this release that make it so accessible and such a delight. *—Kristi Coulter*

The Able Label Singles / 1986 / Situation Two ♦♦♦
Snatch up this U.K./Australian-only EP if you see it; it reissues Forster and McLennan's fascinating earliest recordings, revealing an endearingly goofy bubblegum streak that's most effective when they subvert it on the Modern Lovers-ish "Karen." *—Michael Ribas*

Tallulah / 1987 / Beggars Banquet ♦♦♦
The band lineup changed again with the inclusion of violinist/oboeist Amanda Brown before *Tallulah*'s recording sessions began, and in keeping with the group's near-perfect streak of releases *Tallulah* itself is a delight. This said, there are one or two slips over its course—"The House That Jack Kerouac Built" is burdened down by its title from the start, while some tracks are gently relaxed without being very involving. There's also the slightly curious decision by Morrison to create drum machine lines for some songs instead of playing them herself, which ends up unfortunately dating the record to the late-'80s' period of its creation. It's the about the only flaw on the ravishing opening song, though. "Right Here," with one of McLennan's most affecting vocals and a shimmering, memorable chorus, also has a completely wonderful full band performance, Brown's violin adding an inspired extra element to the familiar Go-Betweens approach. It's also only one of two songs produced by Craig Leon on the album, apparently both being done as potential singles (the other, "Cut It Out," sounds like an attempt at a Top-40 yuppie dance groove but is saved by a great chorus). The remainder do have a less immediately radio-friendly feel, though one can hear a lot of extra touches in the arrangements, especially on keyboards. Both Forster and McLennan are again in fine voice, their individual singing styles long since their own particular trademarks working in tandem, while Brown's own backing vocals slot in very nicely on many songs. Full on winners this time around—"I Just Get Caught Out," another in the line of Go-Betweens "upbeat but nervous" classics, the reflective personal study "The Clarke Sisters," and "Bye Bye Pride," another Forster success with a killer chorus. *—Ned Raggett*

16 Lovers Lane / 1988 / Capitol ♦♦♦♦♦
Finally, after years of critical acclaim, a Go-Betweens album was released in the U.S. by a major label and given a reasonable promotional push. Though it's unusual for final albums by long-standing bands to be much good, *16 Lovers Lane* was an improvement over *Tallulah*. The sound was more radio-friendly than ever (and the "big" single, "Streets of Your Town," even got a little airplay) but it was all for naught. *—Michael Ribas*

● **1978-1990** / Aug. 27, 1990 / Capitol ♦♦♦♦♦
A summation of the Go-Betweens' rewarding body of work. Frustratingly, several of their best numbers were left off in favor of some so-so ones. Even so, this collection is invaluable because besides a complete discography, personnel history, and liner notes courtesy of Forster and McLennan, it contains a few interesting unreleased tracks, two good early singles ("People Say" and "I Need Two Heads"), as well as some of the best of the Go-Betweens' frequently amazing B-sides, including the shimmering "Rock & Roll Friend." From that perspective, it's a worthy epitaph for a special band. [Collectors/world travelers: Look out for the double-CD/record Japanese/U.K. versions that include all the tracks mentioned above—the U.S. release is a single CD that eliminates six of the rarities.] *—Michael Ribas*

'78 Till '79: The Lost Album / Apr. 6, 1999 / Jetset ♦♦♦♦
The 1960s always provided major stimulus for Robert Forster and Grant McLennan, permeating a large portion of their catalog. The lineage of that influence is tracked to its source on this collection of their earliest, chiefly unreleased songs. Unearthed after 20 years, *78 'til 79* is an actual lost album that precedes any of the band's official albums, and it is saturated by the duo's reverence for the era. The band's first two singles bookend the album, and the music that occurs in between is, in a sense, a matter of hero worship. Dylan's hand is particularly felt. In addition, "Summer's Melting My Mind" dives full-body into psychedelia, "Day for Night" has mod written all over it, and "The Sound of Rain" was almost certainly an effort, even if it only a subconscious one, to rewrite the Rolling Stones' "As Tears Go By." But they also surprisingly show an affinity for the Ramones ("Just Hang On") and for the then en vogue London punk scene, while simultaneously reaching back to their precedents in garage rock, which the album frequently echoes. The recording levels rise and fall (most the songs were recorded live to McLennan's two-track in Forster's bedroom), feedback escapes from speakers, mistakes remain intact, McLennan and Tim Mustapha's rhythmic underpinning is rudimentary in the most terrifically thudding way, and the hooks and melodies are relatively simplistic. Forster and McLennan could never bypass hooks, however, and they don't do so on these songs, no matter how raw and youthfully reckless they are. The duo's songcraft was already in place, and while boldly insolent and unsophisticated, the album nevertheless displays a unique talent that was soon to flower fully. *—Stanton Swihart*

● **Bellavista Terrace: Best of the Go-Betweens** / May 18, 1999 / Beggars Banquet ♦♦♦♦
Not quite as comprehensive or well chosen as the earlier (and now out-of-print) *1978-1990* retrospective, *Bellavista Terrace* is nevertheless a fine introduction to the Go-Betweens' enduring brilliance. As Robert Forster's liner notes point out with painful accuracy, this 14-track compilation could scarcely be called a greatest-hits collection as none of the band's singles actually charted, a mystery which has only deepened with the passing years—that perfect pop confections like "Head Full of Steam," "Bye Bye Pride," and the sublime "Streets of Your Town" could fail to reach an audience is a crime. ("...Anyway, we were too good for the bloody charts," Forster continues—damn right.) There is consolation to be had in that these songs all sound as good today as when they first appeared—if the Go-Betweens' refusal to bow to current trends was a liability during their own era, that same timelessness is their music's greatest strength in the here-and-now. *—Jason Ankeny*

The Friends of Rachel Worth / Sep. 19, 2000 / Jetset ♦♦♦♦♦
Twelve years after disbanding the Go-Betweens, Melbourne-based singer/songwriters Robert Forster and Grant McLennan reformed the band they began in 1978 for their seventh album. While they haven't quite picked up where they left off (none of the other original members hopped on board), and the violin/viola that was such an integral aspect of their last few albums appears sporadically, this isn't a huge departure from the trademarked Go-Betweens sound. Poetic, languid, spoken/sung vocals similar to Lou Reed weave between lovely melodies whose appeal unfolds with repeated listens. Strummed guitars and sympathetic drums (sadly, the marvelous percussionist Lindy Morrisson, a mainstay of the band, is missing) spar with Forster and McLennan's breathy, often stream-of-consciousness vocals. But since the singer/songwriters evenly split the ten tracks, this sounds more like a combination of two solo albums rather than one from a cohesive unit. The backing musicians, which include Olympia's similarly hyphenated Sleater-Kinney, are generally faceless except on the riff-rocking "German Farmhouse" where the band sounds even more like the Velvet Underground than usual. Forster's ode to Patti Smith, the album closing "When She Sang About Angels," is occasionally gorgeous, with half-recited lyrics that sometimes flow yet often sound uncomfortably meshed with the beautiful melody. But on the effervescent "Going Blind," the duo returns to the uncluttered, wistful, folk-pop sound of their best work. While it won't garner new fans, or even make newcomers search out their earlier work, *The Friends of Rachel Worth* is a convincing if inconsistent return to form. Its highlights recall the past glories of this commercially overlooked band and add a handful of keepers to their best work. *—Hal Horowitz*

Godspeed You Black Emperor!

f. 1994, Montreal, Quebec, Canada
Experimental Rock, Space Rock, Indie Rock, Post-Rock/Experimental
The instrumental, multi-media Montreal group Godspeed You Black Emperor! creates extended, repetition-oriented chamber rock. The minimal and patient builds-to-crescendo of the group's compositions result in a meditative and hypnotic listen that becomes almost narrative when combined with found sound splices and the films of their visual collaborators. GYBE! formed in 1994, and that year self-released a limited-run (33 copies) cassette entitled, *All Lights Fucked on the Hairy Amp Drooling*. The band's next recording, *F#A#(Infinity)*, was initially a limited run release of 550 LPs on the Canadian label Constellation, but was picked up by Kranky and released onto CD as well. Early 1999 brought the EP *Slow Riot for New Zero Kanada* (released by both labels) and increased recognition for a band intent on retaining anonymity. Nevertheless, interest in GYBE! only continued to grow among new music fans with much positive attention from The Wire magazine, the band's participation in the John Peel-produced Peel Session for the London BBC, and the group's consistently impressive live shows, including their performance at Quebec's 1999 new music festival, FIMAV, and the tour with Labradford later that year. GYBE! performances generally include at least nine or more musicians and a projectionist. The instrumentation consists of three guitars, two basses, French horn, violin, viola, cello, and percussion. 2000 brought about the release of *Lift Your Skinny Fists Like Antennas to Heaven*, pushing their diverse orchestral rock sound even further into the universe. *—Joslyn Layne*

F# A# (Infinity) / 1996 / Kranky ♦♦♦
F# A# (Infinity) contains three compositions that run the gamut from grotesque to sublime. The term "composition" seems an appropriate one to use as this band does not write songs. Each piece is at least 14 minutes in length, consisting of three to four sections. The band, a nine-member unit consisting of guitar, drums, bass, strings, keyboard, marimbas, and woodwinds, intersperses voice-over narrative with sprawling instrumental melodies.

The arrangements move slowly, building from hushed silence to cathartic crescendo and back again. The narratives that accompany the music meditate on the corruption of the American government and the seeming emptiness of the postmodern era. At times, it seems that the music might offer hope, but alternatively, the haunting melodies can serve to emphasize the confusion encountered in these stories. As "Dead Flag Blues," the album's first track, unfolds, the speaker's voice is undercut by a poignant string melody and the piece builds to a beautiful peak. "Dead Flag Blues" is a four-part arrangement in an apparently symphonic pattern. A theme is stated, followed by a quiet interlude out of which the tension builds to disaster/epiphany and finally a quiet reprise of the initial melody is given. The album's second piece, "East Hastings," follows a similar pattern producing brilliant results. "Providence" is the album's final piece, a bit longer than the others, but lacking the consistency and unity of its counterparts. The music on this album is unique and powerful. Its origins are as much avant-classical as they are rock & roll, and the band has achieved a true synthesis of the two forms, expanding them to new boundaries. This music is inherently inexplicable, and this is its beauty. —*Marc G. Gilman*

● **Lift Your Skinny Fists Like Antennas to Heaven** / Sep. 12, 2000 / Kranky ✦✦✦✦✦
Lift Your Skinny Fists Like Antennas to Heaven, the much-anticipated follow-up to Godspeed You Black Emperor's *Slow Riot*, is a double-disc achievement of four works (each with multiple parts): "Storm," "Static," "Sleep," and "Antennas to Heaven." It is a windfall for any fan of ambient pop, orchestral rock, space rock, or simply lush string arrangements who understands how powerful love, melancholy, and frustration can be. The main complaint voiced by critics of Godspeed's music is that their works just repeat the same pattern: start out sparse and slow, build-build-build, crescendo. While there are certainly crescendos, there is no such predictable pattern repeated among the works on *Lift Your Skinny Fists Like Antennas to Heaven*—it's loaded with dynamics, unexpected sections, strong emotions, and beauty. The album opener, "Storm," is a leap that, alone, makes this release worth getting. It's a rapturous work that rises with a potent melancholy, driven by heartrending emotions. "Storm" vents a powerful frustration (each listener can insert their own reasons why) with majestic screams of strings, guitars, and layers, resulting in a climactic and passionate soaring. It eventually winds down into an exhausted aftermath of piano, underlying drones, and frustrated rants. The second piece, "Static," is a wandering, isolationist piece of bleak expanses shaded with darker emotions, but the remaining two works raise the album back up to the impressive standard set by the opening cut, though with less furor and even more loveliness. During most of *Lift Your Skinny Fists Like Antennas to Heaven*, musical and emotional opposites alternate as regularly, and naturally, as breathing: delicate string work and rock-out guitar and drums, spoken word and walls of sound, gracious and possessed, tip-toes and cliff-diving, dark hallways and blinding sunshine. —*Joslyn Layne*

The Godz

Arena Rock, Heavy Metal, Hard Rock
Not to be confused with the 1960s/early-'70s psychedelic band that was also called the Godz, this foursome was an obscure hard rock/arena rock outfit of the late '70s and '80s. This band was formed in the Midwest in 1976, when bassist/producer Eric Moore got together with lead guitarist Mark Chatfield, rhythm guitarist/keyboardist Bob Hill, and drummer Glen Cataline. All four of them contributed lead vocals. The Godz signed with Casablanca in 1977, which was also the year in which they had an opening spot on Kiss' Love Gun Tour. (Cheap Trick was the other opening act on that tour.) The Midwesterners recorded two little-known albums for Casablanca: 1978's *The Godz* and 1979's *Nothing Is Sacred*, both of which received very little attention. Some more albums followed in the 1980s, including 1985's *I'll Get You Rockin'* on Heavy Metal America and 1987's *Mongolians* on Grudge. —*Alex Henderson*

● **The Godz** / 1978 / PolyGram ✦✦✦✦
Essentially a biker band, the Godz put out a hard rock type of music that was fun-loving and rough around the edges. They made no apologies and put on no airs. The result was a good fun-time, hard-rocking album in the vein of such groups as Grand Funk Railroad and Starz. The extended cut "Gotta Keep A Runnin'" is the highlight of the disc. It got a decent amount of airplay on AOR stations and includes a great extended spoken word section. If you like your rock hard-edged and with no pretenses, this is a good, fun album to pick up. —*Gary Hill*

Nothing Is Sacred / 1979 / RCA ✦✦
It's merely a coincidence that two bands called themselves the Godz: The psychedelic Godz of the late '60s and early '70s had no connection to the Midwestern hard rock/arena rock foursome of the late '70s. And the two bands didn't sound anything alike—the first, quite honestly, were a lot more creative and experimental. Released in 1979, *Nothing Is Sacred* is the second of two albums that the second Godz recorded for Casablanca. The tunes on this LP are routine, generic hard rock and arena rock. None of the material is very distinguished, and the band isn't the least bit distinctive. But the Godz, who sound like a neighborhood bar band that somehow managed to land a deal with a well-known label, do come up with some catchy grooves here and there. "Rock Yer Sox Auf," "Gotta Muv," and the Kiss-like "Luv Kage" won't win any awards for originality, but they are likable and fairly catchy. However, *Nothing Is Sacred* wasn't any more successful commercially than the Godz' first album, and Casablanca ended up dropping the band. —*Alex Henderson*

The Godz

f. 1966, db. 1973
Proto-Punk, Experimental, Psychedelic
Few bands in the annals of rock & roll were stranger than the New York City-based Godz.

Recording for the wonderfully idiosyncratic ESP-DISK label from the mid-'60s until the early '70s (although nothing they recorded after 1968 is worth hearing), the Godz coughed up some of the strangest, most dissonant, purposely incompetent rock noise ever produced. Part of the Lower East Side scene that produced post-beat avant-hippie rockers/performance artists the Fugs and the Holy Modal Rounders, as well as honest-to-God beat performers like Allen Ginsberg, the Godz recorded the most extreme music while being secretive about themselves. In fact, there are few, if any, detailed histories about this enigmatic band. What is known is that the Godz consisted of guitarist Jim McCarthy, bassist Larry Kessler, autoharpist Jay Dillon, and drummer Paul Thornton. McCarthy, the ostensible leader of the group, went solo in 1973, but the Godz were pretty much over by that point. As to what happened after they split, none of that is as interesting as the three squalling bits of avant-garde noise/junk they recorded from 1966-1968. Sounding like a prototype for Half Japanese or the Shaggs, the Godz play as if they discovered their instruments ten minutes before the tape started rolling. The singing is intentionally off-key, almost parodic, and the songs—well, they sound more like improvised snippets than actual compositions. And while that may not be your idea of pop music, this works, in large part due to the absolute glee and unself-consciousness with which the these clowns approached their peculiar brand of aural nonsense. You may not want to play this every day, but if your tastes run to the fringes of popular music, missing out on the Godz would be unforgivable. —*John Dougan*

Contact High with the Godz / 1966 / ESP ✦✦✦✦✦
Clocking in at a hair over 25 minutes, *Contact High* is an unholy mess of a record. Opening with the track "White Cat Heat," which consists of clumsily strummed acoustic guitars, arhythmic percussion, and Jim McCarthy and Larry Kessler screeching like a couple of, uh, cats in heat, it gets weirder. Best tracks are "1+1 Equals?" and the hilarious "Lay in the Sun" (total lyrics: "All I want to do is lay in the sun"). For those who like their pop on the cutting edge, begin here and don't turn back. —*John Dougan*

● **Godz Two** / 1967 / ESP ✦✦✦✦✦
Only a label as adventurous as ESP would allow a band like The Godz to make second record, and *Godz Two* is as extreme as *Contact High*, and as good. A little more psychedelic sound here, but nothing that detracts from The Godz' relentless amateurish spirit and abilities. If you were sold on *Contact High*, having this is important. —*John Dougan*

Third Testament / 1968 / ESP ✦✦✦
Although they went on to record into the 1970s, this is the last decent Godz record, primarily because it's the last one that incorporates their distinctive meandering and lack of technical merit with their growing interest in psychedelic rock. True Godz fanatics will tell you that *Third Testament* is a significant dropoff from *2*, but not to these ears. And while it doesn't pack the visceral wallop of *Contact High*, there's enough dementia here for a lifetime of fun. —*John Dougan*

Godzhunheit / 1973 / ESP ✦✦✦

Alien / 1973 / ESP ✦✦

Godz Bless California / 1974 / ESP Disk ✦✦

Andrew Gold

b. Aug. 2, 1951, Burbank, CA
Multi Instruments, Vocals, Keyboards, Guitar / Pop/Rock, Soft Rock
Best remembered for his mid-1970s smashes "Lonely Boy" and "Thank You for Being a Friend," pop singer/songwriter Andrew Gold is the son of composer Ernest Gold and vocalist Marni Nixon. He began his musical career in the Los Angeles band Bryndle. In 1973, Gold joined Linda Ronstadt, appearing on 1974's *Heart Like a Wheel* and 1975's *Prisoner in Disguise*. A noted arranger as well as a skilled multi-instrumentalist, Gold swiftly emerged as one of the most sought-after session musicians on the West Coast scene, and his resume—including dates with James Taylor, Carly Simon, Loudon Wainwright III, and J.D. Souther—reads like a Who's Who of the singer/songwriter movement.

In 1975 Gold released his self-titled solo debut; its follow-up, *What's Wrong with This Picture?*, was his commercial breakthrough, notching an international hit with "Lonely Boy." "Never Let Her Slip Away," from 1978's *All This and Heaven Too*, reached the British Top Five, but its most enduring moment remains "Thank You for Being a Friend," which would later become the theme song for the hit sitcom *The Golden Girls*. Once 1980's *Whirlwind* stiffed, Gold was cut loose from his contract with Asylum. After touring with Ronstadt, he teamed with 10cc alumnus Graham Gouldman to form Common Knowledge, recording a self-titled LP in 1984. Gold and Goldman then rechristened their duo project Wax UK, notching a minor hit in 1986 with "Right Between the Eyes." After 1989's *A Hundred Thousand in Fresh Notes* Wax UK disbanded. Returning to his solo career, Gold issued *Home Is Where the Heart Is* in 1991, before immersing himself in production work. In 1995, he joined a reunited Bryndle for an eponymous LP. The next year, he released ... *Since 1951*, as well as the children's album *Halloween Howls*. *Leftovers*, a collection of unreleased material, followed in 1998. —*Jason Ankeny*

● **Thank You for Being a Friend: The Best of Andrew Gold** / Jun. 24, 1997 / Rhino ✦✦✦✦✦
Thank You for Being a Friend: The Andrew Gold Collection is a comprehensive 20-track overview of Gold's career, featuring not only hits like "Lonely Boy," "Thank You for Being a Friend," and "Final Frontier (Theme From *Mad About You*)," but also an abundance of fine album tracks and two brand new songs, "Can You Feel It" and "King of Showbiz." It may be a bit too much for the casual fan, but it's hard to imagine a more thorough Andrew Gold retrospective than this. —*Stephen Thomas Erlewine*

Golden Earring

f. 1964

Arena Rock, Hard Rock

Best known in the U.S. for its hard rock material, Golden Earring has been the most popular homegrown band in the Netherlands since the mid-'60s, when they were primarily a pop group. The group was founded by guitarist/vocalist George Kooymans and bassist/vocalist Rinus Gerritsen, then schoolboys, in 1961; several years and personnel shifts later, they had their first Dutch hit, "Please Go," and in 1968 hit the top of the Dutch charts for the first of many times with "Dong-Dong-Di-Ki-Di-Gi-Dong," a song that broadened their European appeal. By 1969, the rest of the lineup had stabilized, with lead vocalist and multi-instrumentalist Barry Hay and drummer Cesar Zuiderwijk. They experimented with their style for several years before settling on straightforward hard rock initially much like that of the Who, who invited them to open their 1972 European tour. Golden Earring signed to the Who's Track label, which released a compilation of Dutch singles, *Hearing Earring*, helping the group break through in England. 1974's *Moontan* LP spawned the single "Radar Love," a Dutch number one, U.K. Top Ten, and U.S. number thirteen hit. The group toured America opening for the Doobie Brothers and Santana, but the lack of a follow-up ensured that their popularity remained short-lived in America, even though they remained a top draw in Europe over the rest of the 1970s. 1982 saw a brief American comeback with the album *Cut* and the Top Ten single "Twilight Zone," but as before, Golden Earring could not sustain its momentum and faded away in the U.S. marketplace. All of Golden Earring's basic lineup has recorded as solo artists in Europe. "Radar Love" enjoyed a second round of popularity when pop-metal band White Lion covered the song in 1989. *—Steve Huey*

Just Earring / 1965 / Polydor ✦✦✦

Long before Golden Earring were an international act, they were a typical Continental beat group, billing themselves initially as "the Golden Earrings." Their 1965 debut was a lightweight but enjoyable effort, highly derivative of British beat circa 1964-65, especially the Beatles, Kinks, and Zombies; all but one of the tunes were original compositions. *—Richie Unterberger*

● **The Continuing Story of Radar Love** / Oct. 1989 / MCA ✦✦✦✦

The Continuing Story of Radar Love is a 12-song hits collection from Dutch rock band Golden Earring, containing both the chug-a-long rock staple "Radar Love" and the full eight-minute version of "Twilight Zone." These two songs are the most renowned on this compilation and both cracked the Top 20, with "Radar Love" hitting number 13 in 1974 and "Twilight Zone" peaking at number ten nine years later. The other ten songs on the album consist of long, heavy guitar-filled runs that surround obscure lyrics, sometimes sounding like modern psychedelia. Some of the songs, like "The Vanilla Queen" and "Mad Love's Comin'" harbor a distinguishable progressive edge, thanks to woven keyboard and guitar interplay. A mild blues and rock feel creep into such tunes as "Candy's Going Bad" and "Lost and Found" but fail to ignite any type of serious musical flare compared to their two singles. Much of Golden Earring's music consists of average rock riffs that are either sped up or slowed down by accompanying synthesizer, helped along by the mysteriousness of Barry Hay's voice. Even though this compilation is a dozen songs deep, it still holds as a worthy best-of. *—Mike DeGagne*

The Golden Palominos

f. 1981, Cleveland, OH

Ambient Pop, Experimental Rock, Alternative Pop/Rock, College Rock

The Golden Palominos were not a group per se, but rather the revolving-door project of drummer, programmer, and bandleader Anton Fier who formed the band after stints in the Feelies and Pere Ubu. Fier founded the first Golden Palominos lineup in 1981. In its primary live incarnation, the band was an avant-funk supergroup comprised of Fier, David Moss, John Zorn, Arto Lindsay, Bill Laswell, and Jamaaladeen Tacuma; on their self-titled 1983 debut, the Palominos were augmented by Fred Frith, Nicky Skopelitis, and Mark Miller.

Over the next few years, Fier moved away from the first record's experimental noise into far more traditional pop territory; simultaneously, he largely jettisoned the first album's lineup in favor of an ever-changing collection of punk legends, post-punk superstars, up-and-comers, and NYC-scene vets, including Michael Stipe, John Lydon, Richard Thompson, and Syd Straw. The revamped Golden Palominos reached an early peak with 1985's *Visons of Excess*.

With 1986's *Blast of Silence*, the group flirted with elements of country and folk; while Stipe and Lydon were noticeably absent, many of the other players featured on *Visions of Excess* remained. On 1989's moody *A Dead Horse*, Fier again shifted gears, settling on a constant lineup of Laswell, Skopelitis, Kidney, and ex-Information Society vocalist Amanda Kramer along with a handful of guests, including former Rolling Stone Mick Taylor.

1991's *Drunk With Passion* returned to the all-star format; Stipe and Thompson again rejoined the fold, welcoming newcomers like Sugar's Bob Mould. *This Is How It Feels*, a sophisticated concept album inspired by the Graham Greene novel *The End of the Road* followed in 1993; along with core, the record spotlighted vocalists Lori Carson and Lydia Kavanaugh as well as bass great Bootsy Collins. 1994's *Pure* featured many of the same principal players, while 1996's *Dead Inside*, essentially from a trio comprised of Fier, ex-Psychedelic Furs guitarist Knox Chandler, and vocalist/lyricist Nicole Blackman, explored electronic and ambient soundscapes. *—Jason Ankeny*

The Golden Palominos / 1983 / Celluloid ✦✦✦

The first effort from Anton Fier's revolving-door band is the record which most reflects the group's downtown New York origins. Recalling the avant-funk of Material, *The Golden Palominos* spotlights a core roster of Fier, guitarists Arto Lindsay and Fred Frith, bassist Bill Laswell, and multi-instrumentalist John Zorn; the music is wildly experimental, incorporating turntables and other hip-hop staples (a rather adventurous notion back in 1983) as well as other oddball ideas (clarinets played underwater and the like) which miss the mark as often as they hit, but make for fascinating listening nevertheless. *—Jason Ankeny*

Visions of Excess / 1985 / Celluloid ✦✦✦✦✦

The first in a long series of about-faces and left turns, *Visions of Excess* forgoes the noise-funk of the Golden Palominos' debut in favor of more pop-oriented material and staggering lineup of underground luminaries. Built around a nucleus of Anton Fier, bassist Bill Laswell, guitarist Jody Harris, and keyboardist Bernie Worrell, the album recruits vocalists from Jack Bruce to John Lydon to, most impressively, Michael Stipe, who turns in striking performances on the opening "Boy (Go)" (featuring guitarist Richard Thompson), the Jefferson Airplane-like "Clustering Train," and a cover of Moby Grape's "Omaha." The real find of the record is singer Syd Straw, who makes her debut on the lovely "(Kind of) True" and "Buenos Aires" and more than holds her own with the big guns. *—Jason Ankeny*

Blast of Silence / 1986 / Celluloid ✦✦✦

With *Blast of Silence* the group that began as an outlet for drummer Anton Fier and his friends in the New York avant-garde scene (Arto Lindsay, Fred Frith, etc.) unexpectedly veers off into country-rock and folk, of all places. But with Fier's reputation, listeners should realize from the start this is not country-rock in the New Riders of the Purple Sage fashion. Rather, Fier and company, which includes singers Syd Straw and Mathew Sweet, organist Bernie Worrell, and guitarists T-Bone Burnett and Don Dixon, experiment with confidence on songs like Lowell George's "I've Been the One," adding raga percussion to the C&W ballad. The rest of the album is filled with such musical daring and is a worthy addition for fans of both Palominos and the avant garde scene alike. *—Steve Kurutz*

A Dead Horse / 1989 / Celluloid ✦✦✦

By and large, *A Dead Horse* tosses out the supersession approach of previous Golden Palominos efforts to concentrate on a steady core roster of Anton Fier, Bill Laswell, and Nicky Skopelitis; vocal chores are evenly divided among the Numbers Band's Robert Kidney and Amanda Kramer, formerly of Information Society. A subdued, moody effort, *A Dead Horse* lacks the energy and spark of the group's earlier work; only Kramer's lovely "Darklands" makes much of a lasting impression. *—Jason Ankeny*

Drunk With Passion / Sep. 17, 1991 / Nation/Charisma ✦✦✦✦

The 1991 album *Drunk With Passion* is the fifth installment of drummer Anton Fier's ongoing, ever-changing project known as Golden Palominos. As always, there's no shortage of musical heavyweights plying their trade on this edition. Guitarist Richard Thompson and bassist Bill Laswell are Palomino veterans. The vocal chores are handled by ex-Information Society singer Andrea Kramer, and Bob Mould sings lead on "Dying From the Inside Out." The emphasis here is on mood, which is decidedly ethereal, starting with the album's lead track "Alive and Living Now," featuring Michael Stipe on vocals and Carla Bley adding Hammond organ. The song is a buoyant, mid-tempo celebration of life. Other highlights include "The Haunting," with lovely vocals from Kramer, and "When the Kingdom Calls," which has some fluid, melodic guitar work from Thompson. The proceedings are so dreamy that the album threatens to float away at times. However, Mould opens "Dying From the Inside Out" with a blood-curdling howl and the band follows his lead with a primal stomp. A very classy album. *—Tom Demalon*

A History (1982-1985) / Jul. 21, 1992 / Metrotone/Restless ✦✦✦✦✦

This is a fine sampler of the Golden Palominos' first two records. *—AMG*

A History (1986-1989) / Jul. 21, 1992 / Metrotone/Restless ✦✦✦

The second in a two-disc retrospective of early work by the Golden Palominos, this disc contains most of *Blast of Silence* and *A Dead Horse*, leaving out only "Brides of Jesus" from the former and "Over" from the latter. The Palominos were a constantly shifting group of medium-to-big-name studio musicians that revolved around drummer and organizer Anton Fier, and these two albums do not represent the band at its best either in terms of material or membership. This was the post-Arto Lindsay and pre-Lori Carson period, which is to say the Syd Straw and Robert Kidney period. The *Blast of Silence* sessions suffered from serious stylistic confusion, with pseudo-country ("I've Been the One") thrown in next to punky rock ("The Push and the Shove") and no one really sounding sure of what's going on. Don Dixon contributes the raw and wonderful "Faithless Heart," but the quality of both his singing and his song just makes everyone else look that much worse. Serious sound problems pound the final nail in this album's coffin. The tracks from *A Dead Horse* are something of an improvement. The singing and songwriting are split between Robert Kidney, who rocks, and Amanda Kramer, who meanders. Kidney's "Wild River" is great rock & roll, but Kramer's aimless and uninvolving "Angel of Death" is a disgrace. This compilation is for fans only. *—Rick Anderson*

This Is How It Feels / Sep. 28, 1993 / Restless ✦✦✦✦

Lori Carson comes aboard for the sixth album from Anton Fier's Golden Palominos. Her writing and singing provides the emotional backbone of *This Is How It Feels*, while a usual collection of stellar musicians ranging from bassist Bill Laswell to guitarists Bootsy Collins and Nicky Skopelitis gives the record its sonic grooves. *This Is How It Feels* offers the same ethereal textures of its predecessor, *Drunk With Passion*, but the feel is rooted in chugging, hypnotic dance rhythms. "Prison of the Rhythm" is slightly funky as Carson delivers a breathy vocal on the clever word play on betrayal. "I'm Not Sorry" has a rhythmic, percussive beat and a self-confident lyric about a woman laying down the law to her lover. The strongest, most alluring cut is the midtempo shuffle "To a Stranger." Lydia Kavanagh gives a sultry vocal performance on this tale of a physical encounter with a stranger over a pulsating beat complete with moans. *This Is How It Feels* is another strong entry into the catalog of the Golden Palominos. — *Tom Demalon*

Pure / Oct. 11, 1994 / Restless ✦✦✦✦

If you live in New York, then chances are good that either you or someone you know has once been the Golden Palominos' singer. With *Pure* it was Lori Carson's turn, and she was just what this occasionally brilliant but frequently unfocused band needed. This is probably the Palominos' first great album (unless you count the group's brilliantly abrasive debut). What's the difference this time? Easy: focus, cogency, and discipline. Also funky, up-to-the-minute beats percolating under Carson's diaphanous vocals and supporting her intelligent (if sometimes overly precious) lyrics. Notice how her unbelievably sexy whisper on "Heaven" rubs up against Bill Laswell's ironclad bass; try not to notice the lyrics on "No Skin" ("This dark and secret crime/Cruelty masked as something kind"), and instead luxuriate in the dark and lovely atmospherics. Very, very nice. That's Bootsy Collins playing rhythm guitar, by the way. — *Rick Anderson*

No Thought, No Breath, No Eyes, No Heart / Mar. 14, 1995 / Restless ✦✦✦

Dead Inside / Oct. 8, 1996 / Restless ✦✦✦

Unlike previous Golden Palominos records, which boasted a bevy of guest stars, Anton Fier worked only with one other musician for *Dead Inside*—poet Nicole Blackman. With Blackman providing appropriately bleak poetry, Fier has created one of the most evocative and disturbing soundscapes to grace any Golden Palominos album. Though that means *Dead Inside* is darker than any of the group's other albums, it isn't necessarily more challenging—it's just hard to get inside these detached and death-obsessed sounds. — *Stephen Thomas Erlewine*

● **Best of the Golden Palominos** / Jul. 1, 1999 / Music Club ✦✦✦✦✦

More concise and user-friendly than *History*, *The Best of the Golden Palominos* is a solid collection that draws from all of the group's albums, providing a good sampler of Anton Fier's many moods, styles and shifts in direction. It's not a definitive overview, since it lacks some essential songs, but it acts as a nice introduction for the curious. — *Stephen Thomas Erlewine*

Surrealistic Surfer / Jan. 30, 2001 / Dressed To Kill ✦✦✦

Surrealistic Surfer is neither a greatest-hits collection nor a new release. It's an oddball compilation of the Golden Palominos' early days, up until 1989's *Dead Horse* LP. It showcases a healthy sampling of Anton Fier's revolving door of musical accomplices, including Amanda Kramer and Robert Kidney. Two versions of "The Animal Speaks" also appear, the most notable of which features John Lydon on his trademark long-winded, soap box-like vocals. It's basically an early years mix tape that's being sold to the public. Which is curious, not because the album isn't good, but because it's a mystery why they felt compelled to release it. — *Kieran McCarthy*

Goldfrapp

Electronica, Alternative Pop/Rock

Bath, England's singer/composer/keyboardist Allison Goldfrapp began exploring music as a part of her studies as a Fine Art Painting major at Middlesex University, mixing sound, visuals, and performances in her installation pieces. While she was still in college, she appeared on her friend Tricky's 1995 debut *Maxinquaye*, which led to appearances on albums from other cutting-edge electronic artists, including Orbital's *Snivilisation* and Add N to X's *Avant Hard*. By the late '90s, Goldfrapp began honing her own compositions; one of her friends passed some of her demos on to composer Will Gregory. Finding much in common in their musical tastes and approaches, the duo took Allison's surname as the name for their collaboration. After signing to Mute in 1999, Goldfrapp delivered their debut album, *Felt Mountain*, in fall 2000. — *Heather Phares*

● **Felt Mountain** / Sep. 19, 2000 / Mute ✦✦✦✦

Though her collaborations with Tricky, Orbital, and Add N To X focused on the sheer beauty and power of her singing, on her debut album *Felt Mountain* Allison Goldfrapp also explores more straightforward styles. Together with composer/multi-instrumentalist Will Gregory, Goldfrapp wraps her unearthly voice around songs that borrow from '60s pop, cabaret, folk, and electronica without sounding derivative or unfocused. From the sci-fi/spy film hybrids "Human" and "Lovely Head" to the title track's icy purity, the duo strikes a wide variety of poses, giving *Felt Mountain* a stylized, theatrical feel that never veers into campiness. Though longtime fans of Goldfrapp's voice may wish for more the exuberant, intoxicating side of her sound, lovelorn ballads like "Pilots," "Deer Stop," and "Horse's Tears" prove that she is equally able at carrying—and writing—more traditional tunes. A strange and beautiful mix of the romantic, eerie, and world-weary, *Felt Mountain* is one of 2000's most impressive debuts. — *Heather Phares*

Goldie (Clifford Price)

b. 1966, Walsall, England

DJ, Producer / Electronica, Jungle/Drum 'N Bass, Club/Dance

The first superstar produced by the breakbeat jungle movement, Goldie popularized drum'n'bass as a form of musical expression just as relevant for living-room contemplation as techno had become by the early '90s. Though he hardly developed the style, and his reliance on engineers like Rob Playford and Optical to capture his sound puts into question his true musical importance, Goldie became one of the first personalities in British dance music, his gold teeth and b-boy attitude placing him leagues away from the faceless bedroom boffins which had become the norm in intelligent dance music. For the first time, England had a beat-maestro and tough-guy head that could match the scores of larger-than-life hip-hop stars America had produced, and the high profile of drum'n'bass as the first indigenously British dance music made Goldie a figure of prime importance. After spending several years working on his production skills at Reinforced

Records (the home of 4 Hero), he founded Metalheadz Records, which released seminal dark-yet-intelligent singles by Source Direct, Photek, J. Majik, Optical, Lemon D, Wax Doctor and Peshay, among others. In 1995, Goldie released *Timeless*, one of jungle's first and best full-length works of art. The album put him squarely at the top of the drum'n'bass heap—at least in the minds of critics and mainstream listeners—though his follow-up *SaturnzReturn* displayed an ambitious, personal side of Goldie hardly in keeping with jungle's producer mentality. — *John Bush*

★ **Timeless** / Aug. 1995 / ffrr ✦✦✦✦✦

Respected by the underground for his production skills and lauded by the press for his star potential, Goldie's album debut proved he was no fluke on either count. But from the first few minutes of *Timeless*, new listeners might wonder what's so different about jungle and its first superstar. The sweeping synths and lilting female vocals that form the intro to the title-track opener could be taken from any above-average house anthem. All questions are answered, however, once the beat kicks in. Manic, echoey percussion rolls around and through the song while a muscular dub bass line pounds additional sonic territory. The beat fades in and out, appearing and re-appearing with all the stealth of a charging rhino. The seven other tracks are just as uncompromising, even adopting a hip-hop beat for the R&B flavor of "State of Mind." Though jungle might be jarring for first-time listeners unused to mid-tempo melodies functioning as a bed for hyperspeed beats, *Timeless* makes it a much smoother ride. — *John Bush*

SaturnzReturn / Jan. 27, 1998 / ffrr ✦✦

Ring of Saturn / Dec. 8, 1998 / London ✦✦✦✦

After the negative response to his two-disc sophomore album *SaturnzReturn*, Goldie's next major release was (thankfully) an EP, albeit a ten-track, 60-minute EP. Fortunately, *Ring of Saturn* returns the producer to exactly what made his reputation: the tightest breakbeats and most original effects around. *Ring of Saturn* begins with a VIP remix of "Mother"—a track whose album version was over an hour long—that drastically improves the original simply by trimming the endless wash of swirling orchestration that began and closed the track in its original incarnation. Signs of Goldie's particular affinity for excess (read: super-slick jazz-fusion) are still noticeable; the emphasis single is a cover of Bobby Caldwell's quiet-storm chestnut "What You Won't Do for Love" with longtime Goldie collaborator Diane Charlemagne on vocals. The other unreleased tracks however, are leaner and much more tied to underground jungle than anything on *SaturnzReturn*, and it's a much better release. Rounding out the EP are remixes—by Optical and Grooverider—of the Noel Gallagher collaboration "Temper Temper," and both are excellent examples of twisted industrial tech-step. — *John Bush*

INCredible Sound of Drum'n'Bass / May 3, 1999 / Ovum ✦✦✦✦

He's known more for his production expertise and musical vision than his skills behind the turntables, but Goldie has been a DJ almost as long as he's been a producer. And despite the fact that it's not his specialty, *INCredible Sound of Drum'n'Bass* is a solid album. Though his mixing isn't up there with the best (Grooverider, Fabio, Bukem), Goldie's track selection is excellent. Almost half of the tracks either originally appeared on Goldie's Metalheadz label or were produced by close compatriots. The nepotism is hardly a problem, however, since Metalheadz released a raft of crucial singles—"Pulp Fiction" by Alex Reece, "The Angels Fell" by Dillinja, "To Shape the Future" by Optical, "The Warning" by Grooverider's Codename John project, "Here Come the Drumz" by Doc Scott, "Your Sound" by J. Majik—that can only help any collection they're on. The second disc also includes two of Goldie's earliest productions, "Manslaughter" and "Terminator." Goldie usually plays out most of the songs before moving on to the next, but drops in plenty of twists to keep listeners into it. True, a better mix album by a less popular name would never sell in the numbers this one has, but Goldie proves with *INCredible Sounds of Drum'n'Bass* that his status as jungle superstar number one is untouched. — *John Bush*

Bobby Goldsboro

b. Jan. 18, 1941, Marianna, FL

Vocals, Guitar / AM Pop, Nashville Sound/Countrypolitan, Soft Rock, Pop, Country-Pop

Best remembered for his 1968 chart-topper, "Honey," singer/songwriter Bobby Goldsboro was born January 18, 1941 in Marianna, FL. After relocating to Dothan, AL while in his teens, he went on to study at Auburn University, quitting school after his sophomore year to pursue music full-time. During the early 1960s, Goldsboro played guitar in Roy Orbison's backing band, mounting a solo career in early 1964 and soon scoring a Top Ten hit with the self-penned "See the Funny Little Clown." His sophisticated yet sentimental vocal style yielded Top 40 entries throughout the middle of the decade, among them "Whenever He Holds You," "Little Things," "Voodoo Woman," "It's Too Late," and "Blue Autumn"; though Goldsboro primarily wrote and recorded his own material, he also notched a minor hit with the Burt Bacharach/Hal David novelty "Me Japanese Boy I Love You." "Honey," a maudlin tale about the tragic death of a young bride, remained at number one for five weeks in the spring of 1968, reaching the number two spot in the U.K. soon after and falling just shy of the top spot upon re-entering the British charts in 1975.

However, "Honey" was far and away the biggest of Goldsboro's career, and after returning to the Top 40 twice more in 1968 with "Autumn of My Life" and "The Straight Life," he was absent from the charts for over two years. He made an unexpected comeback in early 1971 when "Watching Scotty Grow" nearly reached the Top Ten, but outside of the follow-up, "Summer (The First Time)," his commercial heyday was over. Between 1973 and 1975 he hosted the syndicated television variety series *The Bobby Goldsboro Show*, next forming the Nashville-based House of Gold Music publishing firm. Goldsboro retired from performing during the mid-1980s to producing children's entertainment, including a number of audiobooks and television specials, the first of which, *Easter Egg Mornin'*, premiered on the Disney Channel in 1991. Concurrently, he scored the CBS sitcom *Evening Shade*, and in 1995 launched the children's series *The Swamp Critters of Lost Lagoon*. —*Jason Ankeny*

Greatest Hits / 1990 / Curb ✦✦✦

Greatest Hits is a budget-priced, ten-track selection of some of Bobby Goldsboro's hits, and while there are some essential items missing, it still functions as a good, affordable sampler featuring such hits as "Honey," "Watching Scotty Grow," "See the Funny Little Clown," "Straight Life," "Autumn of My Life," "Little Things," and "With Pen in Hand." —*Stephen Thomas Erlewine*

● **The Best of Bobby Goldsboro: Honey** / 1991 / EMI America ✦✦✦✦✦

A definitive 23-track collection of all the Bobby Goldsboro you'll ever need. —*Stephen Thomas Erlewine*

The Golliwogs
Garage Rock, Rock & Roll

Of all the vault recordings by '60s rock groups that were unearthed and repackaged, few are less indicative of future fame and greatness than the Golliwogs'. With no changes in personnel, the group became superstars as Creedence Clearwater Revival. As the Golliwogs, they issued seven singles in the mid-'60s; all flops, they were eventually repackaged as a retrospective. These 45s liberally borrowed from the British Invasion and other rock and R&B trends of the day without displaying a shred of distinction, or even an especially high energy level. It doesn't take a genius to figure out what the problem is; over half the songs were sung not by John Fogerty, but his brother, Tom. The half-dozen numbers sung by John are indeed more palatable, but even so, his songwriting had a distance to go before attaining maturity. The Golliwogs' recordings are interesting for their historical insight, but listeners shouldn't approach them expecting anything on the level of Creedence. —*Richie Unterberger*

Golliwogs (Pre Creedence) / 1975 / Fantasy ✦✦✦

Both sides of all seven of their singles, originally issued on Fantasy and Scorpio. It is odd to hear the group casting about for an identity; songs variously bring to mind The Zombies, Them, Merseybeat, even hints of The Beach Boys. "Fight Fire" was their best early number, and has a fairly high reputation among garage fans. The later cuts (all sung by John) show the group starting to develop a rootsier, funkier approach more in line with Creedence. Has early versions of "Walking on the Water" and "Porterville," which were included on the first Creedence album. —*Richie Unterberger*

Gomez
f. 1996
British Trad Rock, Brit-pop, Alternative Pop/Rock

The British band Gomez is a five-piece, consisting of Ben Ottewell (vocals, guitar), Tom Gray (vocals, guitar, keyboards), Paul Blackburn (bass, guitar), Olly Peacock (drums), and Ian Ball (vocals, guitar, harmonica). Whereas the majority of up-and-coming British bands are either retro-pop (a la Oasis), trip-hop (Portishead), or space-rock (Verve, Radiohead), Gomez is one of the few to contain bluesy elements in their rock. Their debut for Virgin Records, *Bring It On*, was praised in the rock press on both sides of the Atlantic. They also received the distinguished Mercury Music Prize for "1998 Album of the Year" in England, where they edged out such stiff competition as Massive Attack's *Mezzanine* and The Verve's *Urban Hymns*. They completed their inaugural U.S. tour opening for Eagle Eye Cherry in October 1998, while the press still offered praise—Spin magazine called *Bring It On* "a damn beautiful album," giving it an 8/10 rating. *Liquid Skin* followed in 1999 and the rarities and B-sides compilation *Abandoned Shopping Trolley Hotline* was issued a year later. —*Greg Prato*

● **Bring It On** / May 1998 / Virgin ✦✦✦✦✦

On their debut album, *Bring It On*, England's Gomez introduces their original take on bluesy roots rock. Unlike the Jon Spencer Blues Explosion, this isn't amphetamine-fueled freak-out music, but similar at times to Beck's acoustic-based work (*One Foot in the Grave*), with more going on vocally. The band has a total of three strong vocalists, who can switch from pretty harmonies to gutsy blues outpourings in the blink of an eye. The band manages to cover a lot of ground convincingly on *Bring It On*, which is unusual, since it commonly takes bands the course of a few releases to hone their sound. The three British singles released from the album are definite highlights—"Get Myself Arrested," "Whippin' Piccadilly," and "78 Stone Wobble," the latter containing a beautifully haunting acoustic guitar riff similar to the Nirvana unplugged version of the Meat Puppets' "Plateau." All the praise that Gomez' debut is receiving is definitely not hype, the album is consistently great, as proven by such tracks as "Tijuana Lady," "Love Is Better Than a Warm Trombone," and "Get Myself Arrested." —*Greg Prato*

Liquid Skin / Sep. 21, 1999 / Virgin ✦✦✦

In the wake of Brit-pop's unraveling and the legitimization of prog rock by Radiohead and Spiritualized, Gomez was seen as the future of Brit-rock upon their debut. *Bring It On* was caught between those two poles: traditionalist on one hand, yet striving for a larger goal. Gomez's secondhand appropriations of American music, crossed with ambling arrangements and a hazy atmosphere indigenous to home recordings, won them a larger audience who expected the group's second album, *Liquid Skin*, to be a great breakthrough. They may be disappointed to find that it's not. Instead, *Liquid Skin* is a cleaner, more streamlined version of the debut; it's clear that the band made the move from the garage into a professional studio. In doing so, they wound up with a dead ringer for Pearl Jam's *No Code*, in which America's best traditionalist band of the '90s strove for a glorious, pan-ethnic mess and pretty much succeeded. *Liquid Skin* doesn't rival *No Code*, not just because Gomez isn't as passionate, but also because Pearl Jam didn't sound as self-conscious or predictable when they decided to stretch out. Throughout the record, Gomez

betrays their age, playing music that they believe to be experimental or rootsy, but not quite going far enough in either direction. This was true of *Bring It On* as well, but the cleaner sound and improved focus brings these factors to the forefront. And, frankly, that's not such a bad thing, either. In this context, they might not seem as adventurous (and, therefore, important), but they do bring back varying strands in interesting ways. They still seem to be trying too hard, and treading water in doing so. Still, *Liquid Skin* will satisfy fans of the first record, just as it will undoubtedly frustrate those who didn't get with them the first time. —*Stephen Thomas Erlewine*

Abandoned Shopping Trolley Hotline / Oct. 10, 2000 / Virgin ✦✦✦✦

Abandoned Shopping Trolley Hotline is a collection of B-sides, outtakes, and live radio sessions courtesy of Gomez. Interestingly, this collection allows Gomez to better define themselves as a band by allowing them to indulge in some of their more experimental tendencies. "Emergency Surgery" is a fine example, with its treated vocals and electro-dub musical setting. The freaky loops and overall bizarre production of "Steve McCroski" belie its live-in-the studio origins. Production touches are more subtle on "Flavors" but still give an other-worldly feel.

The familiar is rendered unfamiliar with "We Haven't Turned Around" getting a radical reworking with the X-ray mix. The vocal track takes center stage, accented by a bowed bass loop and Mellotron reminiscent of the intro to "Strawberry Fields Forever." "78 Stone Wobble" from *Bring It On* becomes "78 Stone Shuffle" when played live in the studio; the lyrics are the same, but the song has been reinvented.

"Bring Your Lovin' Back Here" gets back to that "classic Gomez" sound, as does the eight-plus minute "Buena Vista," despite its Flock of Seagulls-esque guitar intro. The Beatles' "Getting Better" is also included, and sounds much better (and more like Gomez) in its entirety than excerpted on that commercial.

Despite the fact that this is a collection of odds and ends, *Abandoned Shopping Trolley Hotline* holds together remarkably well as an album, due to good track selection and intelligent segueing; in fact, some of the songs actually run together quite smoothly, with no break between songs. Rarely does a rock band forge such a strong identity so early in their career. This collection shows Gomez to be an extremely self-indulgent band, but their instincts are so good they pull it off without a hitch. (Initial pressings include the five-song *Machismo EP* as a bonus disc.) —*Sean Westergaard*

Ian Gomm
b. Mar. 17, 1947, Ealing, England
Vocals, Guitar / Pub Rock, New Wave, Rock & Roll

Former guitar player in England's greatest pub-rock band, Brinsley Schwarz, Gomm went on to an understated, yet fairly rewarding solo career in the late '70s and early '80s. Playing more power-pop than pub-rock as a solo artist, Gomm was a strong, if derivative, singer-songwriter whose clear, warm voice made up for the occasional banality of his lyrics. But even at his most obvious and cloying, Gomm was likable and winning, if only because of his sunny disposition and his way with a guitar riff. Curiously, after three good solo records, he pretty much disappeared. His best album is his first, *Summer Holiday*, which was released in England only. His American releases for Stiff/Epic (some of which included material from *Summer Holiday*) are solid, at times inspired, craftsmanship. —*John Dougan*

Gomm with the Wind / 1978 / Stiff ✦✦✦✦

Part of the ill-fated marriage of the great English independent label Stiff and the massive distribution power of the CBS subsidiary label Epic, *Gomm With the Wind* was probably the most ignored of all the records released under this agreement but, like *Summer Holiday*, it's a sturdy piece of pop with Gomm acquitting himself quite nicely on Johnny Rivers' schmaltz-pop classic "Swaying to the Music (Slow Dancin')." —*John Dougan*

● **Summer Holiday** / 1978 / Albion ✦✦✦✦

With his "hit" "Hold On" here, *Summer Holiday* is a wonderful record. Loaded with chiming guitars, snappy songs, and Gomm's earnest vocals, only the world's meanest musical Scrooge could hate a record like this. By no means a record that will change your life; few people make records like this anymore, at least not without sounding smug and calculated. —*John Dougan*

What a Blow / 1980 / Stiff ✦✦✦

Gomm's *What a Blow* continues in a similar vein as his highly enjoyable *Summer Holiday*. More power pop crossed with pleasing Chuck Berry riffs adds up to satisfying listening. Highlights include "Oh, What a Night," the Berryish "Jaguar," and the poppy title cut. —*James Chrispell*

The Village Voice / 1982 / Albion ✦✦

Images / 1986 / Decal ✦✦

Come On / 1997 / Line ✦✦✦✦

Following Brinsley Schwarz's disbandment, Ian Gomm launched a solo career that fell somewhere between power pop and the new wave roots-rock of Rockpile, which was co-led by his former Brinsley colleague, Nick Lowe. Gomm wasn't as sharp a songwriter as Lowe, nor was he as accomplished a recordmaker. Instead, he was a solid, workmanlike pub-rocker with pop aspirations. Each of his albums had several fine pop gems, but Gomm tended to undersell his songs and rely on slick production that now sounds dated. However, these are minor flaws if you're already a fan of either pub rock or power pop, and if that's the case, you'll likely excuse the somewhat uneven albums. Or you could choose *Come On*, a solid collection that culls 18 highlights from Gomm's first three albums (*Summer Holiday, What a Blow, Village Voice*). His hit, "Hold On," is fairly atypical—the song makes him sound like a soft-rock crooner, but the rest of the collection enjoyably falls into the power pop and pub-rock traditions, even if the production may be a little glossy for Brinsley fans. *—Stephen Thomas Erlewine*

Gong

f. 1968

Canterbury Scene, British Psychedelia, Space Rock, Psychedelic, Prog Rock/Art Rock, Electronic, Experimental Rock

Gong slowly came together in the late '60s when Australian guitarist Daevid Allen (ex-Soft Machine) began making music with his wife, singer Gilli Smyth, along with a shifting lineup of supporting musicians. Albums from this period include *Magick Brother, Mystic Sister* (1969) and the impromptu jam session *Bananamoon* (1971) featuring Robert Wyatt from the Soft Machine, Gary Wright from Spooky Tooth, and Maggie Bell. A steady lineup featuring Frenchman Didier Malherbe (sax & reeds), Christian Tritsch (bass), and Pip Pyle (drums) along with Allen (glissando guitar, vocals) and Gilli Smyth (space whisper vocals) was officially named Gong and released *Camembert Electrique* in late 1971, as well as providing the soundtrack to the film *Continental Circus* and music for the album *Obsolete* by French poet Dashiel Hedayat.

Camembert Electrique contained the first signs of the band's mythology of the peaceful Planet Gong populated by Radio Gnomes, Pothead Pixies, and Octave Doctors. These characters along with Zero the Hero are the focus of Gong's next three albums, the *Radio Gnome Invisible Trilogy,* consisting of *Flying Teapot* (1973), *Angel's Egg* (1974), and *You* (1975). On these albums, protagonist Zero the Hero is a space traveler from Earth who gets lost and finds the Planet Gong, is taught the ways of that world by the gnomes, pixies, and Octave Doctors and is sent back to Earth to spread the word about this mystical planet. The band themselves adopted nicknames—Allen was Bert Camembert or the Dingo Virgin, Smyth was Shakti Yoni, Malherbe was Bloomdido Bad de Grasse, Tritsch was the Submarine Captain and Pyle the Heap. Over the course of the trilogy, Tritsch and Pyle left and were replaced by Mike Howlett (bass) and Pierre Moerlen (drums). New members Steve Hillage (guitar) and Tim Blake (synthesizers) joined.

After *You,* Allen, Hillage, and Smyth left the group due to creative differences as well as fatigue. Guitarist Allen Holdsworth joined and the band drifted into virtuosic if unimaginative jazz fusion. Hillage and Allen each released several solo albums and Smyth formed Mothergong. Nevertheless the trilogy lineup has reunited for a few one-off concerts including a 1977 French concert documented on the excellent *Gong est Mort, Vive Gong* album. Allen also reunited with Malherbe and Pyle as well as other musicians he had collaborated with over the years for 1992's *Shapeshifter* album. Hillage also worked as the ambient-techno alias System 7. A number of Gong-related bands have existed over the years, including Mothergong, Gongzilla, Pierre Moerlin's Gong, NY Gong, Planet Gong, and Gngmaison. During the new millennium Gong material continued to be released, including *Live to Infinitea* issued in fall 2000. *—Jim Powers*

Magick Brother / 1970 / Affinity ✦✦✦

In 1970, the world got its first taste of the original pothead pixie, Daevid Allen's Gong, as *Magick Brother* was released in France on the BYG label. Allen's wife, Gilli Smyth, penned all the tunes on the album, and Allen's now-classic "Ph.P." drawing style graces the inside of the gatefold. Leaning a little toward the pop end of the spectrum, *Magick Brother* is a fairly light album, devoid of the blatant psychedelic/hippie qualities which shine through so brilliantly on the later *Camembert Electrique.* Smyth's "space whispering" makes its debut on the opening track, though the album is not as spacy as it is ethereal. "Gong Song" is a highlight, with lyrics describing a pothead pixie who came down from the planet Gong to sing his green song—the roots of the Gong myth. Allen's guitar sound is a bit flat and hollow throughout the project, dynamics taking a back seat in most of these recordings. He relies on distortion and various guitar augmentations, but this all works quite well in the context of the collective sound. Much of the vocal harmonizing on the album is typical of many '60s pop troupes and sounds fairly dated today. Didier Malherbe's sax and flute playing spices up this mostly pop-oriented prog-rock outing, helping to make this a cut above the radio norm. Although this is an interesting release, especially for its status as the first Gong project, it is not typical Gong and is not recommended as a starting point for sampling the band's recordings. *—David Ross Smith*

Camembert Electrique / 1971 / Charly ✦✦✦✦✦

This is a classic, the epitome of the band's early Daevid Allen phase with Ph.P.'s (pothead pixies) in full, blazing glory. In its infancy, Gong was a unique prog-rock band that branched out in all directions at once while most other prog bands chose simply one path or another. *Camembert Electrique* is a testament to that. The band's eclectic "electric cheese" rock is a mixture of psychedelic rock, spacy atmospherics and lyrics, and doses of jazz often presented with a pop sensibility, yet always intense. From the first cut on *Camembert,* you are transported to planet Gong via the voice of a "radio gnome" who drops in intermittently to remind you you're not in Kansas anymore. Daevid Allen leads the band through several compositions musically (not lyrically) reminiscent of, and possibly influenced by, early King Crimson—a hard, raw-edged sound propelled by a strong guitar-sax-percussion combo. Drummer Pip Pyle played on only a few Gong sessions; he is a major figure here, as is saxophonist Didier Malherbe. Both are up front on the wailing progressive rocker "You Can't Kill Me," which also features guitarist Allen in top form. Allen's declarative "I've Bin Stone Before," the first part of an inventive three-song medley, is of particular interest; introductory church organ and avant-garde sax make this another unique Gong experience. But the real gem on *Camembert* is "Tropical Fish: Selene." This jazzy composition is the most involving and intricate piece on the recording. The band moves tightly through several progressive movements and Gilli Smyth scores with her trademark "space whispering." *Camembert Electrique* remains undated after almost 30 years and hovers "strong and steamin'" over most of the Gong catalog. *—David Ross Smith*

The Flying Teapot (Radio Gnome Invisible, Pt. 1) / 1973 / Charly ✦✦✦✦

Produced by Giorgio Gomelsky, notable for his work with the Yardbirds, Brian Auger, and Magma, this relatively early Gong project is a great representation of the Daevid Allen-era Gong. Though not as intricate as its follow-up companion piece, *Angel's Egg, The Flying Teapot* is more of a true prog/space rock outing, where hippie-trippy lyrics and space whispering abound, as evidenced in the opening track, "Radio Gnome Invisible." The following cut, "Flying Teapot," is the sprawling highlight of the album. At times reminiscent of some early Weather Report jams, though not as jazzy, the tune features prominent bass, standout percussion/drums, and space whispering courtesy of Smyth. Improvisational groaning and percussion bring this jam to a close. "Pothead Pixies" is a fun pop (pot?) tune which probably received very little, if any, airplay due to the lyrics, followed by Blake's brief synth interlude, "The Octave Doctors and the Crystal Machine." "Zero the Hero and the Witch's Spell," another lengthy composition, features Malherbe's sax playing, which, at this early point in the Gong evolution, is credited for most of the jazz sounds heard in the music (remember, Pierre Moerlen has yet to join the band). This cut becomes quite heavy near its end before making a clever transition into the final cut, "Witch's Song/I Am Your Pussy." Here you hear Smyth's strange, sexually explicit lyrics, which she embellishes with ethereal voicings and cackling. This, combined with a jazzy sax from Malherbe and some very groovy musical lines near the closing, make for another fun tune. *—David Ross Smith*

Angel's Egg (Radio Gnome Invisible, Pt. 2) / 1973 / Blue Plate ✦✦✦✦

The companion piece to *The Flying Teapot, Angel's Egg* is not your usual progressive rock album. Very quirky, with many, mostly brief compositions, the album is a tad less spacy than *Teapot,* with just a few psychedelic-inspired lyrics, and it's very technically adept. *Angel's Egg* opens with a true space rock cut (one of the few on the album), filled with the usual Smyth space whispering and Allen voicings, then leads into the cleverly titled "Sold to the Highest Buddha," with Hillage and Malherbe prominent figures. The instrumental "Castle in the Clouds" finds Hillage coming into his own, with a sound identical to his solo work. "Givin' My Love to You" sounds like a bar song, with no music and a cluster of seemingly drunken fellas trying to sing. The instrumental "Flute Salad" gives way to "Oily Way," a showcase for Malherbe's jazzy flute. "Inner Temple," an instrumental space rock track, moves along with a jazz edge, provided by Didier's sax. The final three tracks are the real highlights on *Angel's Egg.* "I Never Glid Before" is a fantastic prog-rock tune, replete with blistering Hillage solo, primo Allen lyrics and vocal, and the precise percussion of new bandmember Pierre Moerlen. This eclectic composition travels through several movements and time changes, and comes across as a perpetually progressing piece. The imaginative and jazzy "Eat That Phone Book Coda" brings the album to a close. *—David Ross Smith*

Gazeuse! / 1976 / Virgin ✦✦✦✦✦

Gazeuse! was the first in a successful line of strictly jazz-rock sessions for percussionist Pierre Moerlen and company—compositions that stressed jazz more than rock and which generally strayed away from lyrical content. This 1976 recording, also released under the title *Expresso,* was the band's first completely instrumental album, a companion piece to the later, somewhat warmer *Expresso II,* which is quite similar in sound and structure. To say *Gazeuse!* is percussive is an understatement. Drummer Moerlen is accompanied by brother Benoit and Mirielle Bauer on vibraphones with Mino Cinelu playing other assorted percussion. "Percolations" is a showcase for this foursome: Part one, a display of beautiful vibes and xylophones; part two, a technically superb drum solo. Pierre's playing is fierce in this second part, exhibited by some truly volatile drumming near the close. Allan Holdsworth is the sole guitarist on the album and contributes two of his own compositions. His "Night Illusion" is a standout and reminiscent of Bill Bruford's *Feels Good to Me* on which Holdsworth collaborated around the same time. Longtime Gong member Didier Malherbe adds spice to the proceedings with jazzy flute on "Shadows Of" and prominent sax on the slightly funky "Esnuria." *—David Ross Smith*

Shamal / 1976 / Virgin ✦✦✦

Between Daevid Allen's departure from the band and Pierre Moerlen's official takeover of the band, there is *Shamal.* This transitional album contains none of the Allen-inspired psychedelia, but also very little of Moerlen's jazz influence. *Shamal* is, for the most part, a progressive rock album, half vocal, half instrumental. Its most accessible tune, the opening "Wingful of Eyes," had the potential for airplay if only it hadn't been so lengthy. Penned by Mike Howlett, his not-so-great-but-appealing vocal style and lyrics will grow on you, given the opportunity. "Bambooji," mostly instrumental, opens with Didier Malherbe's flute, which at times gives this tune an Asian sound. Percussion and flute dominate and yield a Scottish feeling as well. "Mandrake" is the soft, laid-back piece on the album, followed by the closing title cut, a slight foreshadowing of the sound Pierre Moerlen and company assumed on the next several albums. Moerlen, an outstanding, classically trained drummer/percussionist, along with Jorge Pinchevsky on violin color this piece with a Mahavishnu Orchestra hue, although it's still distinctly Gong. *—David Ross Smith*

Live Etc. / 1977 / Virgin ✦✦✦✦✦

The essential *Live Etc.* sports incredible live versions of material from four Gong albums (*Camembert Electrique, Flying Teapot, Angel's Egg, You*) and one studio track which had been recorded in 1974 as an attempt at a single. The live material, recorded 1973-1975, consists of performances from several different incarnations of the band, making this an excellent starting point for anyone interested in sampling Gong. Abundant and overflowing with infusions of space, prog, and jazz, this melting pot of a band stands alone in its eclectic delivery of the goods. Highlights include Moerlen's percussion solo on "Flying Teapot," Malherbe's sax solo on "Zero the Hero . . . ," and Hillage's guitar work on the spacy "Radio Gnome Invisible." "Where Have All the Flowers Gone" is Gong's attempt at a single; while somewhat mainstream, even this piece pushes the envelope for the airwaves. "6/8 Tune" is a superb jazzy instrumental, a kind of foreshadowing to the CD's final four tracks, which are for the most part instrumental and very progressive. The tracks blend together to form the climax and highlight of this great live album, and exhibit the jazziness that would become an integral sound in the band's future releases. Recorded after Allen's departure, this is the personnel that would go on to record *Shamal*, though no tracks from that album show up here. *Live Etc.* originally ended with the tune "Ooby-Scooby Doomsday" (another attempt at a pop hit), but at 79 minutes, the CD format could not hold it, and it has been tacked on to the end of the *Angel's Egg* compact disc release. *—David Ross Smith*

Expresso II / 1978 / Virgin ✦✦✦✦✦
As interesting and fun as the Daevid Allen period was, the name Gong became more meaningful in the context of the music as percussionist Pierre Moerlen assumed the role of bandleader. An emphasis on percussives of all sorts became clear on *Gazeuse*, the band's first completely instrumental album, and the music became much jazzier, though never considered jazz.

Expresso II finds Pierre Moerlen's Gong at their peak. Like their previous studio release, *Gazeuse!*, the album is instrumental, the music is very polished, the sound very clean. Vibes and xylophone dominate on this album, somewhat reminiscent of the sound Zappa achieved through Ruth Underwood on *One Size Fits All* just three years earlier. The first two tracks, "Heavy Tune" and "Golden Dilemma," are the highlights here, partially due to the fact that the rest of the cuts all blend together and sound quite similar. The listener is pleasantly assaulted with a barrage of vibes, yet what a unique sound it is when heard on a rock-oriented album. Guitar combos rarely get much better than on "Heavy Tune," as Mick Taylor rips out leads over Allan Holdsworth's grinding rhythm guitar. The collective guitar sound achieved is one of restrained power; however, the piece can comparatively be considered a rocker. Gong shifts to a different gear with the following track, "Golden Dilemma," a faster-paced, jazzy piece with incredible solos from guitarist Bon Lozaga. Formerly of Curved Air, Darryl Way's violin is a highlight on "Sleepy" and "Boring" (neither of which apply). "Sleepy," which combines Way's violin with Holdsworth's guitar leads, prefigures the sound of the first U.K. album (Holdsworth went on to form U.K. with violinist Eddie Jobson). A very short album, *Expresso II* is possibly the strongest of the post-Allen Gong, and an essential album. *—David Ross Smith*

Downwind / 1979 / Arista ✦✦✦✦✦
The impressive *Downwind* is the first release from the band under their new moniker, Pierre's Gong Moerlen, as Moerlen assumes creative control and dominance. The release marks a return to vocals/lyrics, which proves only partially successful. Moerlen's voice is a hit on the opener, the rocking "Aeroplane," and the collective vocals on the fast-paced, percussive "Jin-Go-Lo-Ba" (popularized by Santana) are right on target. His singing is weak, though, on "What You Know" and detracts from the song's quality. Mick Taylor makes his only appearance here with an exceptional guitar solo.

Downwind is also a return to compositions dominated by rock structures and styles, the jazz element minimal this time around. The instrumental cuts are sublime: "Emotions" and "Xtasea" are relaxing; "Crosscurrents" and "Downwind" are energetic and exciting. The title cut is easily the highlight of the album, featuring guest appearances by Steve Winwood (moog, synth) and guitarist Mike Oldfield.

At almost 13 minutes, this thrilling composition resembles the early work of Oldfield, particularly strains of "Tubular Bells, Part One," and specifically the section used for the film *The Exorcist*. On "Downwind" Moerlen's percussives are ablaze, recalling his "Percolations" performance from *Gazeuse*. Bassist Hanny Rowe is prominent, and saxophonist Didier Malherbe, a longtime Gong staple, makes his only appearance on the album. *—David Ross Smith*

Time Is the Key / 1979 / Arista ✦✦✦✦
The instrumental *Time Is the Key* ushers Moerlen's Gong into the new age. A lighter version of their previous release, *Downwind*, the band plays mostly progressive rock-based compositions with a drastically different personnel. Peter Lemer's keys, coupled with the sound of vibes and electravibe in particular, give the music a generic, new age sound at times. Hanny Rowe is a prominent figure on most of the cuts, his playing being one of the most memorable aspects of this album. Gong never had such a strong bassist—their music never stressed it—but Rowe is up front here, displaying leadership capabilities by occasionally carrying the music. This is most evident on the carnival-like "Supermarket" and "An American in England." As on *Downwind*, the jazz element is minimal, showing up only in "Arabesque Intro & Arabesque," the most impressive material on the disc. Here, Allan Holdsworth (who appears on only three cuts) plays lead over Bon Lozaga's rhythm, and Moerlen's heavyweight percussion and tympani take the prize. Other percussive highlights include the opener, "Ard Na Greine" (vibes and tympani), and the guitar-rocking "Bender." *—David Ross Smith*

● **Pre-Modern Wireless: The Peel Sessions 1971-1974** / Feb. 1996 / SFR ✦✦✦✦✦
Pre-Modern Wireless: The Peel Sessions 1971-1974 consists of nine tracks taken from three BBC sessions and is an essential archive release that would provide a perfect introduction to an interested newcomer to Gong, or provide the experienced Gong fan with some fine live material from throughout the peak of Gong's career. In addition, the album features the only tracks recorded during Kevin Ayers' tenure with the band; one of the three tracks with Ayers is an impromptu first take of "Clarence in Wonderland," lighter in spirit than the version on Ayers' *Shooting at the Moon*. The first session from 1971 was Britain's first glimpse of the band, as it was based in France at the time. In those days, BBC staff was probably wary of Gong members' eccentric appearance and lighthearted spirit. However, drummer Pip Pyle recollects on the session he participated in, "Playing on the BBC was always an interesting experience. The technicians (even in those days) are very proficient, rather straight, and armed with very singular ideas about how to record things. To be fair, they normally get a pretty impressive sound in no time at all. They might have been surprised by certain aspects of Gong, but I imagine once you've done sessions with people like Keith Moon you're pretty much ready for anything." An extended workout of "Crystal Machine" featuring Tim Blake is another highlight. As live BBC sessions, the band fits the concepts from its "Radio Gnome Trilogy" albums into medleys that get the point across, rendering this an ideal Gong anthology. *—Jim Powers*

Goo Goo Dolls

f. 1985
Adult Alternative Pop/Rock, Post-Grunge, Alternative Pop/Rock, Hard Rock
Early in their career, Buffalo natives the Goo Goo Dolls were frequently dismissed by critics as mere imitators of the Replacements; however, the band refined and mainstreamed their sound enough to become of the most popular adult alternative rock bands of the latter half of the '90s, selling millions of records to audiences largely unfamiliar with their inspirations. That's no knock on the band, either—their music simply improved in craft and accessibility as the years progressed, and radio happened to be receptive to what a decade earlier would have been considered collegiate power pop. Their early sound recalled the Replacements' origins as a bratty punk band (circa *Sorry, Ma, Forgot to Take Out the Trash*)—melodic and a little bit thrashy. That sound was the reason the band attracted the interest of the heavy metal label Metal Blade, which issued their debut album in 1987. A college-radio breakthrough came with their third album, 1990's *Hold Me Up*, a later-Replacements-ish power-pop record. 1993's *Superstar Car Wash* was the Goo Goo Dolls' artistic breakthrough; it was a finely crafted pop/rock record, and its lead single, "We Are the Normal," was co-written with Replacements leader Paul Westerberg himself. *Superstar Car Wash* wasn't the commercial force the band hoped it would be, but that all changed with 1995's *A Boy Named Goo*, which produced the Top Five acoustic-driven ballad "Name" and went platinum. The band next contributed the ballad "Iris" to the soundtrack of *City of Angels* in 1998; appearing that April, the song was a monster smash, spending nearly a year on Billboard's airplay charts, including an astonishing 18 weeks at number one. The band's next album, *Dizzy Up the Girl*, was released in September and sold over three million copies. Its clean, polished sound completed the Goo Goo Dolls' transformation into mainstream pop-rockers who happened to have alternative roots. *—Steve Huey*

First Release / 1987 / Metal Blade ✦✦

Jed / 1989 / Metal Blade ✦✦

Hold Me Up / 1990 / Metal Blade ✦✦✦
The Goos' third album was in part seen as their commercial step up, though in fact the real breakthrough didn't come along for a few more years. It's little surprise why there was more of a push for this album, though. If it wasn't as powerfully distinct as Nirvana's *Nevermind*, *Hold Me Up* is as much a product of '80s underground punk and indie (and dollops of bands like Cheap Trick) as its more famous counterpart. The Replacements Jr. tag that dogged the Goos in early years still has a connection here, unquestionably. But considering at that point Paul Westerberg was starting down his road toward tasteful irrelevance, *Hold Me Up* is the perfect stand-in for those who wanted a little more energy with their catchy but emotional rock. If anything, Rzeznik's agreeably ragged and certainly Westerberg-inspired vocals start to really come into their own even more than before, now a great contrast to Takac's amiable brattishness. The latter can have his own impact, though—check out the opening "Laughing" or "So Outta Line," both hyperactive numbers with heart. There's no question Rzeznik steals the show with the album's lead single—"There You Are," with a brilliant, descending lead guitar figure and a sprawling, sloppy/tight performance that's pure gold. Throughout the album, all the bandmembers sound just great, peeling off some wonderfully catchy numbers one after another—"Just the Way You Are," "Hey," the fine instrumental "Kevin's Song," and the acoustic pointer to the future, the concluding, wistful "Two Days in February." In keeping with past guest appearances, the Incredible Lance Diamond takes an amazing lead vocal turn on a wonderful cover of Prince's "I Could Never Take the Place of Your Man," while Rzeznik himself burns down the house on a triumphant rip through the Plimsouls' "A Million Miles Away." *—Ned Raggett*

● **Superstar Car Wash** / 1993 / Metal Blade ✦✦✦✦
The hard rock rawness of Buffalo's Goo Goo Dolls makes *Superstar Car Wash* an album that is high on amicable guitar riffs and attractive hooks, with an edge that never goes away. All the choruses are sandwiched perfectly between the crunching throttle of electric guitar and pleasing rock rhythms, changing pace and style just a notch in each of the 14 songs. Heavy but far from pretentious, songs like "Fallin' Down," "Cuz You're Gone," and "We Are the Normal," co-written by Paul Westerberg, combine pleasing elements of rough harmonies with infectious runs of six-string grit. John Rzeznik's vocals resonate with a reckless, punk-soaked ardor that lifts their music above and beyond the norm of power pop. The attitude that surrounds the album makes Goo Goo Dolls out to be a rough and tumble outfit, outlining all the tunes with a rebellious tone. Quite different from their platinum *A Boy Named Goo* album, which sounded smoother and refined, *Superstar Carwash* has the band sounding loose and freewheeling, making the best of any musical misdirection. Before radio adopted their polished glimmer, they let loose and channeled their playful immaturity throughout the attractive impurity of this album. *—Mike DeGagne*

A Boy Named Goo / 1995 / Metal Blade ✦✦✦✦✦
Produced by Lou Giordano with his trademark full-bodied, immediately accessible, but never washed-out sound, *A Boy Named Goo* finally got the band across to a wide audience, and deservedly so. Right from the start, the Goo Goo Dolls sound perfectly on the right track after *Superstar Car Wash*'s OK but ultimately go-nowhere feeling—"Long Way

Down" is another stone-cold classic of wounded romanticism wedded to catchy Cheap Trick-tinged punk-pop, Rzeznik's singing the not-so-secret weapon. Hearing him on the descending chorus, matching the just-sad-enough guitar crunch, makes one realize that there's always hope for full-bodied rock & roll. The eternal Replacements tag now makes less sense than ever—the Goos have their own enjoyable sound, Rzeznik's a more individual singer than ever, and all three rock out accordingly. Takac similarly has his own sonic improvements, his formerly rasped high register now just a little more controlled but no less affecting, as winners like "Burnin' Up" and "Somethin' Bad" easily demonstrate. Rzeznik-sung highlights are equally everywhere—the commercial but never stupid "Naked," with a great chorus and immediately radio-friendly music, the equally sharp "Only One," and the mighty fine "Ain't That Unusual." There's no question what the highlight is, though—however untypical of the rest of the album's mid-range feedback fun, "Name," with its sweet but sad acoustic arrangement, made perfect sense as the Goos' long-delayed radio breakthrough. Rzeznik's empathetic vocal, delivering one of his best lyrics on favored subjects of friendship, loss, and fame, matches unfolky strumming and quiet energy, creating a song that feels like both a farewell to the American Dream and to a long-lost partner. All this without sounding a Bruce Springsteen sermon—a rare thing indeed. *—Ned Raggett*

Dizzy up the Girl / Sep. 22, 1998 / Warner Brothers ✦✦✦✦

"Name" changed the game for the Goo Goo Dolls. Prior to that unexpected hit ballad, the Buffalo trio was pretty much content to turn out amiably sloppy rock & roll in the style of the Replacements. Like the latter-day 'Mats, they weren't adverse to cleaning up their sound a little bit, but once they had a hit, they were happy to jump head-first into the mainstream, cleaning up their rockers until they shone and embracing acoustic power ballads instead of shunning them. In fact, "Iris"—their contribution to the *City of Angels* soundtrack and lead single for their sixth album, *Dizzy Up the Girl*—is a virtual rewrite of "Name." The funny thing is, where most college-rock bands of the Bush era sounded awkward as mainstream rockers, the Goo Goo Dolls actually sound *better* as a mainstream band, partially because they were hardly underground in the first place. Like a less mannered and conflicted *Let Your Dim Light Shine*-era Soul Asylum, the trio balances hard rockers with ballads. The difference is, they enjoy the mainstreaming of their music, and respond with one of their catchiest sets of songs. There's nothing new on the record apart from their willingness to polish their music so it reaches the widest audience. That will alienate whatever hardcore followers they have left, but that attitude will likely please anyone brought aboard with "Name" and "Iris." *—Stephen Thomas Erlewine*

Ego, Opinion, Art & Commerce / May 29, 2001 / Warner Brothers ✦✦✦✦

It's hard to discern what exactly the purpose of *Ego, Opinion, Art & Commerce* is. It's a compilation, boasting remixes and remastered tracks, but it misses all of the Goo Goo Dolls' biggest hits. So, the best guess for its reason to be is to provide latter-day fans with a basic idea of what the Goos were about before "Iris" and "Name"—and, if that's the case, its release in 2001 is a little puzzling, since it's been years since they've broken through into the mainstream. In any case, this isn't a bad disc at all, since it does cherry-pick the Goos' albums rather gracefully, balancing almost-hits like "We Are the Normal" with a good selection of album tracks. Still, the audience for this must be pretty small—not the hardcore fans, since they already have all this, but fans of the early stuff won't need it, nor will the really casual fans, who just want the hits, since they're not here. So, it's for the listener that either wants an overview of the early years—and it's good at that—or for the listener that has "Name" and "Iris" and wants to dig deeper, without getting the actual albums. Small audiences in both respects, but for those that belong to that audience, it's a good bet. *—Stephen Thomas Erlewine*

Lesley Gore

b. May 2, 1946, New York, NY

Vocals / Brill Building Pop, Girl Group, Pop

The most commercially successful solo singer to be identified with the girl group sound, Lesley Gore hit the number one spot with her very first release, "It's My Party," in 1963. She wasn't the most soulful girl-group singer by a long shot, but she projected an archetype of female adolescent yearning. Her best songs survive as classics, particularly the irrestistibly melodic "Maybe I Know," "Look of Love," and "You Don't Own Me," an anthem of independence with a feminist theme that was considerably advanced for early 1964. The singles were also very well produced, with orchestral arrangements (by Quincy Jones and later Claus Ogermann) that hewed closer to mainstream pop than Phil Spector's Wall of Sound. Gore appeared on the legendary *T.A.M.I. Show* alongside such heavyweights as the Rolling Stones, James Brown, and Smokey Robinson, but after 1964 her star plummeted rapidly. Mercury was still investing a lot of care in her sessions throughout the rest of the '60s, and her material and arrangements showed her capable of greater stylistic range than many acknowledged. "Sunshine, Lollipops and Rainbows" (1965) and "California Nights" (1967) would be her only Top 20 entries after 1964. She played the cabarets after her days as an active recording artist, and eventually had some success as a songwriter for other performers. *—Richie Unterberger*

It's My Party: The Mercury Anthology / Jun. 18, 1996 / Mercury ✦✦✦✦✦

Fifty-two-track double CD has all the hits and then some. It may seem excessive for those who *only* want the hits, and some of the selections (particularly from the late '60s) are weak. But Gore had more worthy B-sides, album cuts, and low-charting singles than most people assume, and there are a good number of those on this collection: "Wonder Boy" (a white Martha & the Vandellas cop), "Off and Running" (covered by the Mindbenders in the *To Sir with Love* film), "Look of Love" (one of Greenwich-Barry's greatest girl-group-style songs), a cover of Laura Nyro's "Wedding Bell Blues" (which lost out on the charts to the Fifth Dimension's version), and interesting little-known compositions by Goffin-King, Paul Anka, Van McCoy, Marvin Hamlisch, and Lesley herself. Gore covered more territory than the teen self-pity anthems for which she's most remembered, and this anthology, while not enough to make you demand her election to the Rock & Roll Hall of Fame, is not nearly as relentlessly lightweight as her detractors would have you imagine. Includes some tracks that were previously unavailable on album, or previously unreleased in the U.S. *—Richie Unterberger*

● **Sunshine, Lollipops & Rainbows: The Best of Lesley Gore** / Jun. 16, 1998 / Rhino ✦✦✦✦✦

During the girl-group era of the early 1960s, no female singer broke down the barriers for women the way Lesley Gore did. She was battling it out in a totally dominated man's world, sending sentiments to the top of the charts that most women only whispered about at the time, years before it was hip, cool, politically correct, and resolvable by the ACLU. This makes her music not only important from a historical standpoint, but a quick listen to this 20-track best-of will also reveal that it's some of the classiest music from that era as well. With Quincy Jones producing your sessions and the top songwriters money can buy (Ellie Greenwich, Carole King, and Marvin Hamlisch, just for openers), it's no small wonder that records like "It's My Party," "Maybe I Know," "You Don't Own Me," "I Don't Wanna Be a Loser," "Judy's Turn to Cry" and the title track shine so brightly. The transfers on this disc shine equally as bright, with heavy prominence given to Gore's incredibly tight and impeccable double-tracked vocals. If you think of Lesley Gore as a one-hit wonder from a pre-feminist dark age of rock & roll, you *really* need to hear this collection. *—Cub Koda*

20th Century Masters—The Millennium Collection: The Best of Lesley Gore / Sep. 26, 2000 / Mercury ✦✦✦✦

The Millennium Collection: The Best of Lesley Gore gathers a dozen of Gore's hits, including the two-part soap opera of "It's My Party" and "Judy's Turn to Cry," the sweeping, melodramatic "You Don't Own Me," and lighthearted "Sunshine, Lollipops and Rainbows." Though it's nowhere near as extensive as collections like *It's My Party: The Mercury Anthology* or *Sunshine, Lollipops & Rainbows: The Best of Lesley Gore*, *The Millennium Collection* does include slightly obscure tracks such as "The Look of Love," "My Town, My Guy and Me," and "California Nights," her last Top 20 hit from 1967. A good collection for casual fans, even at just 12 songs long, *The Millennium Collection* showcases Gore's distinctive and surprisingly versatile sound. *—Heather Phares*

Gorillaz

f. 2000

Alternative Rap, Alternative Pop/Rock, Hip-Hop

Conceived as the first virtual hip-hop group, Gorillaz blends the musical talents of Dan "The Automator" Nakamura, Blur's Damon Albarn, Cibo Matto's Miho Hatori, and the Tom Tom Club's Tina Weymouth and Chris Frantz with the arresting visuals of Jamie Hewlett, best known as the creator of the cult comic *Tank Girl*. Nakamura's Deltron 3030 cohorts Kid Koala and Del tha Funkee Homosapien round out the creative team behind the Gorillaz quartet, which includes 2-D, the cute but spacy singer/keyboardist, Murdoc, the spooky, possibly Satanic bassist who is the brains behind the group, drummer Russel, who is equally inspired by "Farrakhan and Chaka Khan" and is possessed by "funkyphantoms" that occasionally rise up and provide some zombie-style rapping, and last but not least, Noodle, a ten-year-old Japanese guitar virtuosa and martial arts master. The group's website, www.gorillaz.com, showcases Hewlett's visuals and the group's music in eye- and ear-catching detail. Gorillaz debuted in late 2000 with the *Tomorrow Comes Today* EP, which they followed early the next year with the *Clint Eastwood* single; their self-titled full-length debut arrived in spring 2001 in the U.K. *—Heather Phares*

● **Gorillaz** / Apr. 24, 2001 / Virgin ✦✦✦✦

It's tempting to judge Gorillaz—Damon Albarn, Tank Girl creator Jamie Hewlett, and Dan "The Automator" Nakamura's virtual band—just by their brilliantly animated videos and write the project off as another triumph of style over substance. Admittedly, Hewlett's edgy-cute characterizations of 2-D, Gorillaz' pretty-boy singer (who looks a cross between the Charlatans' Tim Burgess and Sonic the Hedgehog), sinister bassist Murdoc, whiz-kid guitarist Noodle, and b-boy drummer Russel are so arresting that they almost detract from Gorillaz' music. The amazing "Thriller"-meets-*Planet of the Apes* clip for "Clint Eastwood" is so visually clever that it's easy to take the song's equally clever, hip-hop tinged update of the Specials' "Ghost Town" for granted. And initially, Gorillaz' self-titled debut feels incomplete when Hewlett's imagery is removed; the concept of Gorillaz as a virtual band doesn't hold up as well when you can't see the virtual band members. It's too bad that there isn't a DVD version of *Gorillaz*, with videos for every song, a la the DVD version of Super Furry Animals' *Rings Around the World*. Musically, however, *Gorillaz* is a cutely caricatured blend of Albarn's eclectic Brit-pop and Nakamura's equally wide-ranging hip-hop, and it sounds almost as good as the band looks. Albarn has fun sending up Blur's cheeky pop on songs like "5/4" and "Re-Hash," their trip-hop experiments on "New Genious" and "Sound Check" and "Song 2"-like thrash-pop on "Punk" and "M1 A1." Despite the similarities between Albarn's main gig and his contributions here, *Gorillaz* isn't a Damon Albarn solo album in disguise; Nakamura's bass-and-beat-oriented production gives the album an authentically dub and hip-hop inspired feel, particularly on "Rock the House" and "Tomorrow Comes Today." Likewise, Del tha Funkee Homosapien, Miho Hatori, and Ibrahim Ferrer's vocals ensure that it sounds like a diverse collaboration rather than an insular side-project. Instead, it feels like a musical vacation for all parties involved—a little self-indulgent, but filled with enough fun ideas and good songs to make this virtual band's debut a genuinely enjoyable album. *—Heather Phares*

Gorky's Zygotic Mynci

f. 1990

Neo-Prog, Neo-Psychedelia, Brit-pop, Alternative Pop/Rock

Sounding like a bizarrely sweet and whimsical cross between progressive rock, psychedelia, and pure pop, Gorky's Zygotic Mynci were one of the most original and distinctive bands to emerge from the vital post-Brit-pop Welsh scene of the mid-'90s. Gorky's music followed unconventional time signatures and structures, as well as instrumentation (boasting everything from droning moog synthesizers to slurring trombones and steel guitars) and melodic patterns. Furthermore, the band's lyrics were rarely about conventional pop/rock subjects, and they frequently sang in Welsh, which made their already odd music sound even more alien to most listeners. Nevertheless, Gorky's developed a strong cult following in Britian, as well as America, ranking behind Super Furry Animals as the most popular band to emerge from the mid-'90s Welsh scene.

Ironically, Gorky's Zygotic Mynci formed long before Super Furry Animals. Unlike many Welsh bands of their age, the members of Gorky's did not begin a band after Manic Street Preachers appeared in the early '90s—they began playing in the mid-'80s, when the band members were barely in their teens. Euros Childs (vocals, keyboards), Megan Childs (violin), John Lawrence (guitar), Richard James (bass), and Euros Rowlands (drums) were all attending school in Carmarthen, Wales, when they formed the group. Lawrence, James, and Euros Childs began making tapes in the bedroom, and they eventually added Euros' sister Megan and Euros Rowlands to the lineup. All of the group members came from upper-middle-class families, with Rowlands' father, Dafydd, being a poet who is the archdruid of the Welsh culture celebration Eisteddfod, while Lawrence's mother is a politician. The connections helped Gorky's Zygotic Mynci enter the Welsh culture quite rapidly. Throughout their teens, the band recorded and played festivals, as well as appearing on local television and radio. Eventually, the band signed with the Welsh independent label, Ankst.

Gorky's Zygotic Mynci released three albums on Ankst—*Tatay, Bwyd Time, Llanfwrog*—before moving to Mercury Records in 1996. Their last album for Ankst reached number one on the U.K. independent charts. In 1996, their first American album, *Introducing Gorky's Zygotic Mynci*, was released. A compilation of their early Welsh albums and EPs, the record received positive reviews, yet it failed to make significant inroads for the group in America. *Barafundle* followed in 1997, and two years later the group returned with *Spanish Dance Troupe*. Issued in early 2001, *The Blue Trees* featured acoustic material from the band's two Mynci 2000 tours. Their seventh album, the intimate *How Long to Feel That Summer In My Heart*, followed several months later. —*Stephen Thomas Erlewine*

Patio / 1994 / Ankst ✦✦✦✦

The earliest work of Welsh darlings Gorky's Zygotic Mynci can be found on the *Patio* CD, which compiles the band's 1991-1993 radio and studio sessions. For fans of the beauty of their largely subdued recent work, it is revelatory and essential, as it showcases the vocal and melodic gifts of Euros Childs and his band in their teenage years, when his voice was much higher, and the guitars were often much louder, but the reach for beautiful pop verses and choruses proved no less fruitless. Mix in a burgeoning folk and psychedelic sensibility characterized by keyboard smashing, plenty of sound, vocal and violin effects, and you have a set that shows just how much of a running start talentwise this group had prior to the numerous CDs and EPs they'd record. As the tracks progress chronologically, you can hear Childs' voice start to grow deeper and an increasing attention being paid to tighter structures and ideas. The final songs, recorded in late 1992 and early 1993, reveal vocal and studio experimentation that their next two CDs, *Tatay* and *Bwyd Tyme*, would develop even more. —*Jonathan Druy*

Bwyd Time / 1995 / Ankst ✦✦✦✦

The Welsh are a strange people at the best of times. *Bwyd Time* is one of the few albums to have put their peculiarity into a recording. The psychedelic pop/rock fusion that Gorky's Zygotic Mynci created has never been better captured than on this, the band's debut album. With obvious influences from Robert Wyatt, the Kinks, and even the Bonzo Dog Doodah Band, you know you're in for an abnormal affair with *Bwyd Time*. Even a mere peek at the front cover proves that. With Gorky's, however, abnormality can be made into greatness. Their amazingly original sound is both fun and musically interesting. *Bwyd Time* succeeds in holding listeners' attention throughout its 50 minutes, while songs such as "The Game of Eyes," "Miss Trudy," and "Bwyd Time" will stay with you long after the album has finished. This release is a rather eccentric album that, while not appealing to the masses for its mystic and at first inaccessible values, will ingratiate the keen listener. —*Ben Davies*

Introducing Gorky's Zygotic Mynci / Aug. 20, 1996 / Polygram ✦✦✦✦✦

Introducing Gorky's Zygotic Mynci compiles highlights from the Welsh band's first two U.K. albums, plus their singles and EPs for the Ankst record label. While it might not be an official album, it is an excellent introduction to Gorky's wild, sunny eclecticism, featuring everything from warped art-pop to homages to the Soft Machine's Kevin Ayers. What stops the music from becoming too precious is the group's surprising facility for pop hooks and their cheerful sense of humor—it might be bizarre music, but it is never alienating. —*Stephen Thomas Erlewine*

Barafundle / Apr. 7, 1997 / Fontana ✦✦✦✦✦

Recorded with the help of Welsh production guru Gorwel Owen and featuring past guests Simon James and Martin Smith from the Wizards of Twiddly throughout on various brass and wind instruments, *Barafundle* found Gorky's merrily coming to grips with major-label status without a worry. If anything, *Barafundle* did showcase where the band would go in future years, toning down the crazier side of the group in favor of a calmer, more quietly inventive approach, though not without some high-volume parts. John Lawrence still keeps the fractured side of things going, though it's no surprise he would leave after a couple more albums, taking the more overtly "mushroom" qualities with him—he still gets in some fun zingers here, though, including the nutty "The Wizard and the Lizard." Otherwise, though, this is an album soundtracking rural Welsh summers that may only exist in myth, but still work well for that. The two singles from the album are both great—"Diamond Dew," a folk/psych trip with a nicely rocking chorus, and "Patio Song," a winning stroll through winsome romance spiked with just the right odd bits ("isn't it a lovely day?/my patio's on fire"). The album as a whole merrily moves along, bringing in a bit of drama here and there ("The Barafundle Bumbler" and its just-edgy-enough verses, the full on electric crunch of "Meirion Wyltt") but otherwise things are sweetly sedate, as with the instrumental "Cursed, Coined and Crucified." Childs' singing is as wonderful as always—the man was just born to sing in that gentle, honeyed fashion—while Lawrence's no less fine vocals add just the right glaze to songs like the suddenly medieval "Starmoonsun" and "Sometimes the Father is the Son." U.S. versions added the later single "Young Girls and Happy Endings" as a bonus. —*Ned Raggett*

Gorky 5 / 1998 / Mercury ✦✦✦

● **Spanish Dance Troupe** / Oct. 19, 1999 / Beggars Banquet ✦✦✦✦✦

Gorky's Zygotic Mynci's sixth album, *Spanish Dance Troupe*, is also their first for their U.S. label, Beggar's Banquet. As with *Barafundle* and *Gorky 5*, this collection of songs focuses on the accessible side of the group's gently iconoclastic folk-rock. That doesn't mean that *Spanish Dance Troupe* has much in common with the rest of the late '90s music scene, however. Though psychedelic, country, and '70s pop elements spring up here and there, the Gorkys' songs are untouched by musical trends or fashions. The wistful violins, piano, and brass on "Don't You Worry," "Murder Ballad," and "She Lives on a Mountain" seem more inspired by traditional folk songs and vaudeville tunes than any hyphenated, postmodern genres. Acoustic interludes like "Drws" and "The Fool" are scattered throughout the album, drawing it even further away from modern rock's increasingly self-referential tendencies. But when the Gorkys decide to go pop, they do it wholeheartedly. Noisy guitars and smooth harmonies make "Poodle Rockin'"—a song that's as cute and weird as the title suggests—and "Desolation Blues" as distinctive as *Spanish Dance Troupe's* quieter moments. "Faraway Eyes" is a wonderful, bittersweet country song disguised as pop, uniting the group's sometimes contradictory musical ideas into a cohesive sound. Above all, the group's sincerity shines through on *Spanish Dance Troupe*, inviting listeners along for an eclectic, entertaining ride. —*Heather Phares*

The Blue Trees / Feb. 20, 2001 / Beggars Banquet ✦✦✦✦

The Blue Trees shows Gorky's Zygotic Mynci taking a giant leap toward maturity. Having started out like their Welsh peers Super Furry Animals as neo-psychedelic, rambunctious jangle-pop merchants, the band here takes a folk turn toward elegiac tunes praising the four seasons and nature. With subtle, rolling guitars, sometimes sounding as if they're being played by Leo Kottke himself, the band mines a similar territory as Badly Drawn Boy's *The Hour of Bewilderbeast*. But *The Blue Trees* doesn't strive toward pop sensibilities or languish in tired instrumentals like *Bewilderbeast*. Sure, these eight songs are appropriately memorable and melodic and there are more than a few instrumentals, but all of the songs take on a quiet, contemplative air. There's simply not a drop of pretension to be found, as if every acoustic instrument is covered in a subtle dew. Perhaps things slow down too much on "Foot and Mouth," but the track would be worthy of inclusion on the score to any film with introspective scenes. "Wrong Turnings" seems infused with the spirit of Nick Drake; it paints a serene picture of rural bliss. The band picks up the pace on "Fresher Than the Sweetness in Water," while maintaining the grace of earlier tracks with the addition of what sounds like a mandolin and a violin (or fiddle). *The Blue Trees* is quite an accomplishment; it's a continuation of the maturity and grace found on *Spanish Dance Troop*. Anyone who's written off Gorky's Zygotic Mynci might want to give this new-look band a second chance. The slow-burning songs of *The Blue Trees* are delicately serene and of a charmed beauty. —*Tim DiGravina*

Graham Gouldman

b. May 10, 1946, Manchester, England

Vocals, Songwriter, Guitar, Bass / British Invasion

Before forming 10cc with Eric Stewart, Graham Gouldman was a major presence in the British Invasion, writing hits for the Yardbirds, the Hollies, Herman's Hermits, and others; "For Your Love," "Bus Stop," "Look Through Any Window," "Heart Full of Soul," and "No Milk Today" are among his most famous compositions. Gouldman wrote some of the finest tunes of the era, using haunting, shifting minor key melodies as effectively as similar efforts by the Zombies and the Beatles. He also cut a lengthy string of flop singles, both as a solo artist and with his group the Mockingbirds, and released a solo album of his own in the late '60s. —*Richie Unterberger*

● **Graham Gouldman Thing** / 1968 / Edsel ✦✦✦✦✦

Gouldman issued this solo album in 1968, featuring his own versions of the hits "For Your Love," "Bus Stop," and "No Milk Today" with eight other original tunes. The album blends pensive, acoustic-guitar driven compositions with light orchestral arrangements. It's a pleasant record, but ultimately does not measure up to the monster hit covers of his tunes. He's only an adequate singer, and the slower, more elaborately produced versions of "Bus Stop" and "For Your Love" are not nearly as good as the hard-charging renditions by The Yardbirds and Hollies. A decent curio, though, highlighted by "Pawnbroker" and "Upstairs Downstairs," which would have fit in well on the Hollies' 1966-67 records. —*Richie Unterberger*

Davey Graham

b. Nov. 22, 1940, Leicester, England
Vocals, Guitar / British Folk-Rock, Progressive Folk, British Folk

One of the most eclectic guitarists of the 1960s, Graham's mixture of folk, blues, jazz, Middle Eastern sounds, and Indian ragas was an important catalyst of the British folk scene. Like Sandy Bull and John Fahey—two folk-based guitarists with a similar taste for genre-bending experimentation—Graham could not be said to be a rock musician. But like Bull and Fahey, he shared the eagerness of the '60s psychedelic rockers to stretch out and incorporate unpredictable influences into his music. While he wasn't much of a singer, Graham's taste in material was broad and shrewd, encompassing blues, ragas, Joni Mitchell, Charles Mingus, and the famous instrumental "Anji," which Graham recorded in 1962, way before the more famous versions by Bert Jansch and Simon & Garfunkel. Besides cutting several albums of his own work in the 1960s with sympathetic, low-key rhythm sections, he also recorded with traditional folk singer Shirley Collins and British blues father Alexis Korner. Graham recorded only sporadically after the 1960s, although he performed with the renowned acoustic guitar wizards Stefan Grossman and Duck Baker. —*Richie Unterberger*

The Guitar Player . . . Plus / 1963 / See For Miles ✦✦✦✦
Graham established himself as one of the most innovative players in acoustic music with his 1963 debut, *The Guitar Player*. With this album, he became one of the first folk guitarists to fuse traditional virtuosity with cross-currents from contemporary jazz and blues. Accompanied by drummer Bobby Graham (a top British sessionman who played on many British Invasion rock records, including several by the Kinks), Davey invigorates pop and traditional standards, as well as compositions by Sonny Rollins, the Adderleys, and Ray Charles. Neither jazz nor folk, Graham displays eclectic bounce that was quite visionary for its time and remains fresh today; in his subsequent 1960s' recordings, he would branch out into Middle Eastern and psychedelic sounds as a natural extension of his experimental bent. As a significant bonus, the 1992 CD reissue of this album includes the three tracks from his rare 1962 EP, *3/4 A.D.* One of these is the original version of "Anji," which was reworked by Simon & Garfunkel on one of their early albums; another features British blues-rock godfather Alexis Korner on second guitar. —*Richie Unterberger*

Folk Roots, New Routes / 1964 / Decca ✦✦✦✦✦
This pairing of one of British folk's finest voices (Shirley Collins) with one of the country's finest acoustic guitarists (Davey Graham) had a notable influence on the U.K. folk scene, although it eluded wide acclaim at the time. Collins' rich, melancholy vocals were most likely an influence on Sandy Denny, Maddy Prior, and Jacqui McShee. Graham helped redefine the nature of folk accompaniment with his imaginative, rhythmic backing, which drew from jazz, blues, and a bit of Middle Eastern music as well as mainline British Isles folk. Performed with tasteful restraint and selected with imaginative eclecticism, it also includes an instrumental showcase for Graham in "Rif Mountain," which acts as evidence of his clear influence on guitarists such as Bert Jansch and John Renbourn, and the acoustic style of Jimmy Page. —*Richie Unterberger*

Folk, Blues & Beyond / 1964 / Decca ✦✦✦✦✦
This was Graham's most groundbreaking and consistent album. More than his solo debut *The Guitar Player* (which was pretty jazzy) or his previous collaboration with folk singer Shirley Collins, *Folk Roots, New Routes*, this established his mixture of folk, jazz, blues, and Middle Eastern music, the use of a bassist and drummer also hinting at (though not quite reaching) folk-rock. "Leavin' Blues," "Skillet (Good'n'Greasy)," and "Moanin'" are all among his very best folk-blues-rock performances, while on "Maajun" he goes full-bore into Middle Eastern music on one of his most haunting and memorable pieces. Covers of traditional folk standards like "Black Is the Colour of My True Love's Hair" and "Seven Gypsies" combine with interpretations of compositions by Bob Dylan ("Don't Think Twice, It's Alright"), Willie Dixon ("My Babe"), Charles Mingus ("Better Git in Your Soul"), and Reverend Gary Davis ("Cocaine") for an eclecticism of repertoire that wasn't matched by many musicians of any sort in the mid-1960s. If there is one aspect of the recording to criticize, it is, as was usually the case with Graham, the thin, colorless vocals. The guitar playing is the main attraction, though; it's so stellar that it makes the less impressive singing easy to overlook. Ten of the 16 songs were included on the compilation *Folk Blues and All Points in Between*, but Graham fans should get this anyway, as the level of material and musicianship is pretty high throughout most of the disc. —*Richie Unterberger*

Midnight Man / 1966 / Decca ✦✦✦✦✦
Graham went into a somewhat harder-rocking bluesy groove on this record, though a strong jazz feel was always present in the rhythm especially. More than any other Graham LP, this offers proof that the guitarist would have established himself as a major star on the folk circuit in the '60s—if only his singing was better. As a guitarist, he's simply wonderful, combining folk, jazz, and blues styles into an invigorating, idiosyncratic style that can both swing and attain a delicate sadness. As an interpreter, he's relentlessly imaginative, breathing new vigor into overdone R&B standards, or devising fresh folk arrangements for Beatles and Paul Simon tunes. But as a vocalist, he's adequate at best; if he had even possessed the modest expressiveness of a Bert Jansch, the material would be that much more striking. Almost none of these tracks are available on Graham compilations, and this rare LP is definitely worth seeking by those who are familiar with some of his other '60s work. Especially excellent are the jazzy "Hummingbird" and the instrumental cover of Lalo Schifrin's "The Fakir," which blends the rhythmic drive of Charles Mingus with hypnotic raga-esque riffs. —*Richie Unterberger*

Large as Life & Twice as Natural / 1968 / London ✦✦✦✦
With the exception of 1964's *Folk, Blues & Beyond*, this is Graham's finest non-compila-

tion album. It's also his most fully arranged and rock-influenced effort, with backing by a meaty ensemble featuring Danny Thompson (of Pentangle) on bass and British blues stalwarts Jon Hiseman and Dick Heckstall-Smith (Graham Bond, Colosseum) on drums and sax respectively. Even Davey's singing sounds better than usual. Graham offers some decent blues, but more interesting are his frequent excursions into raga folk-rock of sorts, especially on "Blue Raga" (learned from Ravi Shankar and Ali Akbar Khan). The raga-jazz interpretation of Joni Mitchell's "Both Sides Now," which moves from meditative opening drones into a freewheeling explosion of modal folk-rock, is one of the highlights of Graham's career on record and one of the best expressions of his ability to make a standard his own. —*Richie Unterberger*

Hat / 1969 / Decca ✦✦✦
There's no such thing as a bad Graham album from the 1960s. While *Hat* isn't necessarily the first one you should dig into, it offers the standard pleasures that you expect from his records: excellent, feverishly imaginative acoustic guitar playing; vibrant jazz-blues arrangements; and covers of blues numbers, Paul Simon, and Lennon-McCartney. He's just as capable of good-time blues ("I'm Ready") and a folk cover of "Getting Better" from *Sgt. Pepper* as dark, slightly dissonant instrumentals with a modal/Eastern flavor. As is the case with most of his '60s albums, it's very hard to find, especially in the U.S., where Graham did not have a record deal. —*Richie Unterberger*

Holly Kaleidoscope / 1970 / Decca ✦✦✦
Graham's final Decca LP was co-billed to his wife at the time, Holly Gwyn (credited simply as "Holly"), although she only appears on a few tracks. While it's a characteristic Graham effort, right down to the token Beatles covers (here they're "Blackbird" and "Here, There and Everywhere"), it's somewhat more sparsely arranged than most of his previous records. Given that Graham was never that good a singer, enlisting a female vocalist seemed a sensible enough move. But although Holly is a better singer than Davey, she's nothing special, with her presence amounting to neither a plus nor a minus on the whole. It's not one of Graham's more notable albums, but it's respectable, and the guitar work, of course, is nothing less than stellar. —*Richie Unterberger*

Godington Boundary / 1970 / See for Miles ✦✦✦
This isn't Graham's most focused or impressive album, but is basically in the same league as most of his early catalog. It's more jazz-oriented than most of his work; he sings rather less than usual and occasionally goes into lengthy improvisations (as on his cover of "The Work Song"). Graham's wife, Holly, gets co-billed, as she did on his previous album, *Kaleidoscope*, but actually she contributes only to a few numbers; she's more of a guest artist than a true collaborator. Indian/raga influences come into play once in a while, and on the whole it's somewhat quirkier than his previous string of albums. It would also be the last the public would hear from Graham on record for quite some time, as he found himself without a contract for most of the 1970s. —*Richie Unterberger*

The Complete Guitarist / 1980 / Kicking Mule ✦✦✦✦
To those who are unfamiliar with Davey Graham's work, *The Complete Guitarist* might seem like a lofty title for this album. But it's a title that the Scottish musician, who has commanded a lot of respect in U.K. folk circles since emerging in the 1960s, lives up to on these unaccompanied acoustic solo-guitar recordings from the late 1970s. Diversity is the rule on this album, and Graham successfully turns his attention to an abundance of traditional Celtic songs (both Scottish and Irish) as well as everything from Bach's "Ein Feste Burg" to blues classics like Big Bill Broonzy's "When I Been Drinking" and Memphis Slim's "How Come You Do Me Like You Do." Whether it's Celtic music, classical, blues, or jazz, Graham has no problem tackling a variety of styles and demonstrating that he really is the complete guitarist. Originally released as a vinyl LP in the late 1970s, *The Complete Guitarist* was, in 1999, reissued on CD with eight bonus tracks from 1979-1980 added. —*Alex Henderson*

● **Folk Blues and All Points in Between** / 1985 / See For Miles ✦✦✦✦✦
Side one includes ten songs from his 1964 album *Folk, Blues & Beyond*; Side two features seven tracks from three of his late-'60s LPs. The 1964 record was probably his most accomplished, as Graham handled blues, jazz, and Northern African music with aplomb. His other '60s recordings were more erratic, but the highlights gathered here matched his mid-1960s work, peaking with the original "No Preacher Blues," his folk-jazz cover of Joni Mitchell's "Both Sides Now," and the Indian-influenced "Blue Raga." —*Richie Unterberger*

After Hours at Hull University / 1997 / Rollercoaster ✦✦✦

Lou Gramm

b. May 2, 1950, Rochester, NY
Vocals, Percussion / Album Rock, Pop/Rock, Adult Contemporary, Hard Rock

First rising to prominence as the frontman for platinum-selling hard rock combo Foreigner, Lou Gramm later mounted a successful solo career, cracking the Top Five in 1987 with "Midnight Blue." Born in Rochester, NY on May 2, 1950, Gramm first surfaced as the drummer with the band Black Sheep, assuming lead vocal duties prior to recording the group's self-titled 1975 Capitol debut; although neither the album nor its follow-up *Encouraging Words* earned much mainstream notice, they did capture the attention of journeyman guitarist Mick Jones, best known for his stint with a latter-day incarnation of Spooky Tooth. Jones soon tapped Gramm to front his new group Foreigner, and together they began writing songs, co-authoring the smash "Cold as Ice" from their best-selling 1977 eponymous debut LP. Gramm's powerfully distinctive vocals were inescapable in the years to follow as Foreigner reeled off an impressive series of pop radio hits including "Hot Blooded," "Double Vision," "Urgent," and "Waiting for a Girl Like You," culminating in 1984's chart-topping power ballad "I Want to Know What Love Is." With Foreigner on hiatus, Gramm made his solo debut in 1987 with *Ready or Not*, scoring a major hit with "Midnight Blue"; that same year, Foreigner issued *Inside Information*, but with the success of the 1989 solo effort *Long Hard Look* and its attendant single "Just Between You and Me," the singer left the group to form his own band, Shadow King, which released its self-titled debut on Virgin in 1991. Shadow King proved short-lived, however, and in 1994 Gramm and Jones revived Foreigner for *Mr. Moonlight*. In the spring of 1997, on the eve of the band's planned Japanese tour, Gramm was diagnosed with a benign brain tumor; surgery preceded a year of rehabilitation and radiation treatment, although the singer made a full recovery and resumed touring in 1999. —*Jason Ankeny*

● **Ready or Not** / 1987 / Atlantic ✦✦✦✦✦

Foreigner vocalist Lou Gramm's 1987 solo album *Ready or Not* is a winner. It came at a precarious time for Foreigner, despite coming off the success of 1985's *Agent Provocateur* and the band's first number one single, "I Want to Know What Love Is." *Ready or Not* is rich with melody and snap, but its sound does vary just enough from Foreigner that Gramm can't really be accused of stealing from himself. The production by Gramm and Pat Moran definitely has that bright 1980s style. Gramm's main sidemen include guitarist Nils Lofgren, keyboardist Philip Ashley, bassist/guitarist/keyboardist Bruce Turgon, and drummer Ben Gramm. Side one absolutely sizzles. "Ready or Not" is a strong, hard-rocking leadoff track and it was a minor hit single. The melodic, lyrical, and vocal hooks on "Heartache" are massive and Lofgren's guitar solo adds an edgy bite. The Top Five hit "Midnight Blue" is a terrific pop/rock song; despite its hit status, it's one of the decade's truly underappreciated singles. Lofgren's rolling, effective guitar riffing and a captivating chorus make "Time" one of the best cuts. Foreigner helped create and master the rock power ballad, and Gramm utilizes that gift on the dark, ethereal "If I Don't Have You." Side two is generally a letdown considering the high quality of the first half. Fortunately, there are two exceptions, "Arrow Thru Your Heart" and "Until I Make You Mine." The commercial and artistic success of *Ready or Not* was a turning point for Gramm. Foreigner issued the lackluster *Inside Information* late in 1987, and Gramm followed that troubled project with a second moderately successful solo album, *Long Hard Look*, in 1989 and then left the band for a few years before returning. —*Bret Adams*

Long Hard Look / 1989 / Atlantic ✦✦

The Best of the Early Years / Nov. 12, 1993 / Collectables ✦✦✦

Grand Funk Railroad

f. 1968, Flint, MI, **db.** 1976

Detroit Rock, Album Rock, Boogie Rock, Arena Rock, Hard Rock

One of the 1970s' most successful hard rock bands in spite of critical pans and somewhat reluctant radio airplay (at first), Grand Funk Railroad built a devoted fan base with constant touring, a loud, simple take on the blues-rock power trio sound, and strong working-class appeal. Formed by guitarist/songwriter Mark Farner and drummer Don Brewer with bassist Mel Schacher, the band gained a contract with Capitol. While radio shied away from Grand Funk Railroad, the group's strong work ethic and commitment to touring produced a series of big-selling albums over the next few years; five of their eight releases from 1969 to 1972 went platinum, and the others all went gold. The group finally scored a big hit single (number one, in fact) with the title track of the Todd Rundgren-produced *We're an American Band*. The follow-up, *Shinin' On*, contained another number one hit in a remake of Little Eva's "The Loco-Motion." However, following Grand Funk's next album, *All the Girls in the World Beware!!*, interest in the group began to wane. They remained together in 1976 solely to work with producer Frank Zappa on *Good Singin', Good Playin'*. Grand Funk Railroad re-formed in 1981 for two albums but disbanded once more. —*Steve Huey*

● **Capitol Collectors Series** / Feb. 26, 1991 / Capitol ✦✦✦✦

Grand Funk Railroad was at best a singles band, capable of turning a couple of crunching rockers and hooky singles out with each album. Though it may be missing a fan favorite or two—and that could mean something concise and catchy or meandering jams like "T.N.U.C."—this does have the overwhelming majority of their best songs, including not just hits like "We're an American Band" and "Some Kind of Wonderful," but also album tracks. Some longtime fans, like Homer Simpson, may find favorites missing, but this remains a nearly ideal summary. —*Stephen Thomas Erlewine*

Thirty Years of Funk: 1969-1999 / Jun. 29, 1999 / Capitol ✦✦✦✦

Thirty Years of Funk is a three-CD boxed set anthology of the music of one of America's premier heavy rock bands, Grand Funk Railroad. This set covers the music of the band from 1969, when the band first burst onto the music scene and ushered in a post-British Invasion alternative to the progressive movement, until they broke up in 1976 to subsequently reform in the mid-'90s.

Although Grand Funk Railroad was officially formed in 1969, some band members played together as Terry Knight and the Pack in the mid-'60s and this set opens with three songs from the Pack from 1968. The set concentrates on being a complete anthology of Grand Funk material with only two to three songs from each one of the band's 16 studio albums. All of the band's albums are represented in this collection except for one album that was released on the Warner Bros. label in 1983. The set also contains a number of previously unreleased alternate recordings, outtakes, and live material to add appeal to fans. In 1997, Grand Funk performed a concert for Bosnia and in 1998 got together in the studio and for a tour and recorded a number of new tracks, three of which are contained on this set. Although a number of the band's early songs and some fans' best-of tracks are not contained on this set, thus making it flawed according to fans, it is the best retrospective package of Grand Funk Railroad's music available to date on the market. The set's booklet contains detailed information on the history of the band, a discography, album jacket photos, and detailed song information. —*Keith Pettipas*

Grandaddy

f. 1992, Modesto, CA

Indie Rock, Alternative Pop/Rock

Solar-powered space-pop combo Grandaddy was formed in Modesto, CA in 1992 by singer/guitarist/keyboardist Jason Lytle, bassist Kevin Garcia, and drummer Aaron Burtch; although a noisy, lo-fi approach characterized early recordings like 1994's *Complex Party Come Along Theories*, with the 1995 additions of guitarist Jim Fairchild and keyboardist Tim Dryden the group's sound expanded exponentially over the course of subsequent efforts including the unreleased *Don't Sock the Tryer* and the 1996 EP *A Pretty Mess by This One Band*. Originally issued on indie label Will Records, 1997's acclaimed full-length *Under the Western Freeway* proved Grandaddy's creative breakthrough, and the following year the album was reissued on major-label V2, with "Summer Here Kids" earning Single of the Week honors in the pages of the NME. *The Broken Down Comforter Collection*, a compilation of singles tracks, preceded the 1999 *Signal to Snow Ratio* EP, which heralded a movement toward the vintage electronic textures further in evidence on 2000's superb *Sophtware Slump*. —*Jason Ankeny*

A Pretty Mess by This One Band / 1996 / Will ✦✦✦

Modesto, CA. Other than bringing back memories of George Lucas' *American Graffiti*, there isn't much else to think about the town. Well, except of course for the fact that it is also the hometown of indie's Grandaddy. So in *A Pretty Mess by This One Band*—a very early mini-album/EP—we are given a brief look into the lo-fi stuttering of a band constantly hoping to grow out of their own limitations. Which has mixed results. The album works at its weakest when the band seems to reproduce far too many American college-favored indie bands already out there. For instance, after a brief intro, the first full song—"Taster"—fails precisely because it never ascends out of its mound of discordant guitars and mumbling drawls. It's not bad songwriting, but it comes across as so many countless other college bands that it never turns any heads. Songs like "Kim, You Bore Me to Death," however, are on better footing: unlike most of the rest of the release, it seems less like Pavement's post-modernism and more like Pixies' squalls (lead singer Jason Lytle even lets his voice climax into effective Black Francis-like screeches). Continuing the trend, the album speeds past some more unexciting tracks to reach its closing "Egg Hit and Jack Too." This closer has such an impressive mix of Yo La Tengo's more melodious thrashes and the band's own dusty restlessness that one has to wonder if the band has in it them for a truly great release sometime down the road. Until then, *A Pretty Mess by This One Band* remains a decent litmus test for the band's own potential. Definitely not as pretty as the title might suggest, but still one of the better, flawed messes from America's indie underground. —*Dean Carlson*

Under the Western Freeway / Oct. 21, 1997 / Will ✦✦✦✦

Being from northern California, Grandaddy always gets compared to Pavement—and rightly so, in some respects—but this probably isn't the best way to start on the band. Some of the tracks on *Under the Western Freeway* are more in the Weezer vein ("Summer Here Kids," "A.M. 120"), and the few that are truly reminiscent of Pavement are more like *Crooked Rain, Crooked Rain*'s drawling "Range Life" than the angular guitar work more usual from Pavement. Comparisons aside, what's important is that *Under the Western Freeway* is a fairly brilliant album, combining a warm, earnest, and rustic feel with sometimes goofy experimentation (looped drums, bleeping keyboard hooks)—and it's all very pleasant and friendly. And what's more, these guys can write a solid, catchy melody. A couple listens to tracks like "Nonphenomenal Lineage" and "Go Progress Chrome" make this all too clear. —*Nitsuh Abebe*

Broken Down Comforter Collection / 1999 / 1/2 ✦✦✦

A collection of B-sides, EP, and rare tracks, this release proves just how consistent Grandaddy is. Their enjoyable, but highly eccentric style was just as well-performed on the early tracks as on the recent songs. Indeed, Grandaddy's noisy-yet-melodic approach has never sounded rawer than on the 1994 track "Kim You Bore Me to Death." *The Broken Down Comforter Collection* is, however, rather sparse in places. "Gentle Spike Resort," this compilation's opener, showcases the dull, passive side of the band. Fortunately, these low points come around rarely, and are far outnumbered by the quality tracks. Grandaddy, being the superbly original band that they are, will not please all listeners. Those with an open mind and a taste for something a little abnormal, however, will lap up *The Broken Down Comforter Collection* and all its eccentricities. —*Ben Davies*

● **The Sophtware Slump** / 2000 / V2 ✦✦✦✦✦

Picking up where their *Signal to Snow Ratio* EP left off, Grandaddy's wittily named second album *The Sophtware Slump* upgrades the group's wry, country-tinged rock with electronic flourishes that run through the album like fiber-optic lines. Arpeggiated keyboards sparkle on "Hewlett's Daughter" and "The Crystal Lake," and wind, birds, and transmissions hover around the songs' peripheries, suggesting a Silicone Valley landscape. Jason Lytle's frail, poignant vocals provide a bittersweet counterpoint to the chugging guitars and shiny electronics that envelop him like a cockpit or a cubicle on "Chartsengrafs" and "Broken Household Appliance National Forest" and set the tone for melancholy ballads like "He's Simple, He's Dumb, He's the Pilot," "Miner at the Dial-a-View," and "Jed the Humanoid," the story of a forgotten, alcoholic android. Lost pilots, robots, miners, and programmers try to find their way on *The Sophtware Slump*, an album that shares a spacy sadness with Sparklehorse's *Good Morning Spider* and Radiohead's *OK Computer*. Though it's a little more self-conscious and not quite as accomplished as either of those albums, it is Grandaddy's most impressive work yet and one of 2000's first worthwhile releases. —*Heather Phares*

Grandmaster Flash (Joseph Saddler)

b. Jan. 1, 1958, Barbados, West Indies

DJ, Producer, Leader / Old School Rap, Electro, Club/Dance, Hip-Hop, DJ

DJ Grandmaster Flash and his group the Furious Five were hip-hop's greatest innovators, transcending the genre's party-music origins to explore the full scope of its lyrical and sonic horizons. Flash began spinning records as a teen growing up in the Bronx, and first worked with the Furious Five (rappers Melle Mel, Cowboy, Kid Creole, Mr. Ness, and Rahiem) during 1978-79. After one single on Enjoy, they signed with the famed Sugar Hill label in 1980 and released their first truly landmark recording one year later. "The Adventures of Grandmaster Flash on the Wheels of Steel" introduced Flash's "cutting" techniques to create a stunning sound collage from snippets of songs by Chic, Blondie, and Queen. Flash and the Five's next effort, 1982's "The Message," was even more revelatory—for the first time, hip-hop became a vehicle not merely for bragging and boasting but for trenchant social commentary, with Melle Mel delivering a blistering rap detailing the grim realities of life in the ghetto. Following 1983's anti-cocaine polemic "White Lines," relations between Flash and Melle Mel turned ugly, and the rapper soon left the group. After a series of Grandmaster Flash solo albums during the 1980s, he reformed the original lineup for a charity concert and a new LP, 1988's *On the Strength*. Another reunion followed in 1994, when Flash and the Five joined a rap package tour also including Kurtis Blow and Run-DMC. —*Jason Ankeny*

The Message / 1982 / Sugar Hill ✦✦✦✦✦

Grandmaster Flash & the Furious Five merged the Afrocentric consciousness expressed by such early rappers as Gil Scott-Heron and The Last Poets with b-boy production to create "The Message," an all-time rap anthem. It was the focal point of this LP, which also included "It's Nasty" and "Scorpio," two other strong cuts that might have been winners on their own. Unfortunately, rather than a starting point, this album proved to be their ultimate peak. —*Ron Wynn*

The Source / 1986 / Elektra ✦✦✦

Grandmaster Flash's follow-up to *The Message* was his first minus the Furious Five. Things weren't the same from a compositional or performance standpoint, as his raps seemed weaker and his rhymes almost devoid of crispness, humor, or insight. Only "Ms. Thang" and "Street Scene" offered any hint of the incisiveness or vision depicted in "The Message." —*Ron Wynn*

Da Bop Boom Bang / 1987 / Elektra ✦✦

On the Strength / 1988 / Elektra ✦

★ **Message from Beat Street: The Best of Grandmaster Flash** / Apr. 19, 1994 / Rhino ✦✦✦✦✦

Grandmaster Flash was one of the most important, groundbreaking rap artists of the early '80s, and all of his most important records—with and without Melle Mel and the Furious Five—are collected on this essential 11-track disc, which includes the classic tracks "The Message" and "White Lines (Don't Don't Do It)." —*Stephen Thomas Erlewine*

Adventures of Grandmaster Flash, Melle Mel & The Furious Five: More of the Best / Jul. 1996 / Rhino ✦✦✦✦✦

Although much of Grandmaster Flash's best, biggest, and most groundbreaking work was compiled on *Message From Beat Street: The Best Of, The Adventures of Grandmaster Flash: More of the Best* is necessary for any comprehensive rap collection. The rest of Grandmaster Flash's most important singles, many of which have not appeared on compact disc before, are corralled onto this single-disc. On the whole, the album concentrates on the group's latter-day efforts for Elektra Records, but the cream of the album is the handful of singles for Sugar Hill, including the pioneering "The Adventures of Grandmaster Flash on the Wheels of Steel," which presents the group at its freshest and most innovative. Some of the Elektra recordings are a little rote and by-the-book, but the Sugarhill songs help make this an essential purchase. —*Stephen Thomas Erlewine*

Adventures on the Wheels of Steel / 1999 / Sugarhill/Sequel ✦✦✦✦✦

For old-school fanatics who need still more Sugar Hill material, even after Rhino's massive five-disc set *The Sugar Hill Records Story*, Sequel packaged a three-disc box of material recorded by Grandmaster Flash and the Furious Five (plus a few cuts headed by Grandmaster Melle Mel). *Adventures on the Wheels of Steel* spans all the way from their earliest, pre-Sugar Hill recordings (the great singles "Super Rappin' No. 1" and "Flash to the Beat") to the mid-'80s material recorded after Grandmaster Flash split from Sugar Hill (both he and Melle Mel headed collectives composed of former members of the Furious Five). Of course, anyone even vaguely interested in this set is already going to own quite a few of these tracks, from the big Furious Five hits "The Message" and "White Lines" to much-anthologized classics like "Birthday Party," "New York New York," "The Showdown," "Scorpio," and "Message II (Survival)." Where this collection really begins to excel, and attract collectors, is the large number of rarities included. Sure, most old-school fans have "The Adventures of Grandmaster Flash on the Wheels of Steel," but how many have even heard Melle Mel's 1984 update "The New Adventures of Melle Mel"? And the Furious Five were well known for their social critiques, but after Grandmaster Flash left the fold the group continued to record solid message tracks like "Jesse" (for Jesse Jackson's 1984 presidential campaign), the con-man game "Hustlers Convention," and "Vice." Truth to tell, there are only a pair of unreleased tracks on *Adventures on the Wheels of Steel*, but at least half of these 34 tracks have never been seen on compact disc. —*John Bush*

Grant Lee Buffalo

f. 1992, Los Angeles, CA, **db.** Jun. 9, 1999

Americana, Adult Alternative Pop/Rock, Alternative Pop/Rock

Under the leadership of guitarist/songwriter Grant Lee Phillips, Grant Lee Buffalo became a major buzz band in 1993 with their debut album, *Fuzzy*. The band's searching, often political, folk-rock has shades of everyone from David Bowie and John Lennon to R.E.M. and Bob Mould. Phillips' songwriting received a great deal of critical praise, as did the band's electrifying live performances. The band captured a larger following in Europe than their native America, earning near-universal critical praise upon the release of *Fuzzy*. During 1993, the band toured constantly, building a solid cult following all over the world. The following year they delivered their second record, *Mighty Joe Moon*. In 1996, they released *Copperopolis*, followed two years later by *Jubilee*. Grant Lee Buffalo disbanded in mid-1999. —*Stephen Thomas Erlewine*

Fuzzy / Feb. 23, 1993 / Slash ✦✦✦✦✦

While Grant Lee Phillips' songwriting is quite impressive, what makes Grant Lee Buffalo's debut album, *Fuzzy*, memorable is the band's muscular folk-rock. Equally adept at propulsive rock & roll and haunting ballads, the band turns Phillips' best songs into rough gems, as "Jupiter and Teardrop" and "Fuzzy" prove. —*Stephen Thomas Erlewine*

● **Mighty Joe Moon** / Sep. 20, 1994 / Slash/Reprise ✦✦✦✦

With their second album, Grant Lee Buffalo strips back their sound to its bare essentials, which accentuates Grant Lee Phillips' rural myths. Not only does the approach make songs like "Lone Star Song" rock viciously, but it also makes the bittersweet beauty of ballads like the gorgeous "Mockingbirds" all the more poignant. —*Stephen Thomas Erlewine*

Copperopolis / Jun. 1996 / Slash/Reprise ✦✦✦

With their third album, *Copperopolis*, Grant Lee Buffalo headed farther into the dense Americana fusions that permeated their first two albums. Although there are hints of Bowie-esque art rock on the fringes of *Copperopolis*, most of the album is informed by rootsy amalgams of Dylan, R.E.M., Pearl Jam, and the Pixies—it's political, anthemic rock that doesn't make any literal sense. Every once and a while, Grant Lee Phillips pulls out an evocative metaphor or a provocative melody, but too frequently the band's concepts are more admirable than their music. And that is more true of *Copperopolis* than any of their other albums, simply because their fusion is becoming more cerebral and less natural as time passes. —*Stephen Thomas Erlewine*

Jubilee / Jun. 9, 1998 / Slash/Reprise ✦✦✦✦

With the departure of bassist Paul Kimble, Grant Lee Buffalo has become the sole province of singer/songwriter Grant Lee Phillips; he may still be supported by drummer Joey Peters, but now, more than ever, he is the main focal point. With Kimble left some of the band's appealingly messy ambition has been reigned in, resulting in a brighter, sharper sound. And that means *Jubilee*, the group's fourth record, doesn't quite hit the heights of *Fuzzy* and *Mighty Joe Moon*, but it's arguably their most consistent effort yet, simply because it puts Phillips' songwriting on full display. He still has eclectism in his blood—there's everything from lumbering hard rock to sweet country tunes on the album—but his skills have grown; he now has the ability to make it all sound like it was coming from the same source, instead of different planets. Consequently, *Jubilee* does sound joyous—Grant Lee Buffalo fills the record with more genuine ambition and accomplishment than many of their peers have managed. —*Stephen Thomas Erlewine*

The Grapes of Wrath

f. 1983, **db.** 1992

College Rock, Jangle Pop, Alternative Pop/Rock

The Grapes of Wrath was a jangly alternative folk-pop quartet formed in Kelowna, British Columbia, in 1983 by brothers Chris Hooper (drums) and Tom Hooper (bass) along with vocalist/guitarist Kevin Kane (later adding keyboardist Vincent Jones). In 1984, they signed to Nettwerk Records and relocated to Vancouver where they recorded a four-song self-titled EP that earned the band some initial local exposure. 1985's full-length *September Bowl of Green*, however, gave them national recognition and critical acclaim. Ready to make a stab at the U.S., they enlisted the help of Tom Cochrane (ex-Red Rider) for production of the follow-up *Tree House*. Though it failed to break big, it did yield a hit single in Canada with "Peace of Mind." Subsequent singles and two more albums, *Now and Again* (1989) and *These Days* (1991), did well in their homeland but earned little sales elsewhere. In 1992, Kane left the band and the remaining members went on to become Ginger. Ginger released *Far Out* on Nettwerk in 1994 (released in the U.S. in 1995) and followed with *Suddenly I Came to My Senses* in late 1996. Kevin Kane released a solo album, *Neighborhood Watch* in 1996 for On/Off Record in Canada.

In early 2000, Grapes of Wrath reunited as a three piece, featuring original members Tom Hooper and Kevin Kane along with a new member, drummer Matt Brain. —*Chris Woodstra*

September Bowl of Green / 1986 / Capitol ✦✦✦

Their first LP shows a band unsure whether to follow R.E.M.'s folky lead or post-punk's dreamy abstraction. Fortunately, the jangly guitars and harmonies win out for a pleasing, though unspectacular, debut. Highlights include the single "Misunderstanding," as well as "Love Comes Around" and "A Dream (About You)." The CD version adds two previously unreleased tracks. —*Chris Woodstra*

Treehouse / 1987 / Capitol ✦✦✦✦✦

Early comparisons to R.E.M. are clearly justified on *Treehouse*, a jangly folk-pop masterpiece. On this, their second album, the band seem considerably more confident and focused. Crisp and bright production, courtesy of Tom Cochrane (ex-Red Rider), compliment the glorious harmonies and melancholy, introverted songs perfectly. A sadly overlooked classic of '80s guitar rock. —*Chris Woodstra*

● **Now & Again** / Sep. 1989 / Capitol ✦✦✦✦✦

These Days / Aug. 27, 1991 / Capitol ♦♦♦

Seems Like Fate 1984-1992 / 1994 / Nettwerk/EMI ♦♦♦

Seems Like Fate is a 20-track collection which attempts to chronicle the band's career. Unfortunately the disc's emphasis on non-LP material, unnecessary remixes over the original single versions, and nonchronological sequencing creates confusion, ultimately doing a disservice to one of Canada's best bands of the late '80s. As an introduction, it fails miserably, though as a rarities compilation, fans will probably find it an essential addition to their collection. —*Chris Woodstra*

Field Trip / Sep. 2000 / Song Corporation ♦♦♦♦♦

And then it's like nothing ever happened. The Grapes of Wrath split up very acrimoniously following the release of 1991's *These Days* album, casting serious doubt on the possibility of a follow-up release. It took nearly ten years, and the fact that both of them had recently become fathers, for Tom Hooper and Kevin Kane to dispense with the lawyers, remember their long friendship, and get back to the business of making music. When the first song hits the speakers it seems like time has changed them ("Black Eye" is far more hard rocking than anything that had come before), but everything that follows sounds like vintage Grapes. In fact, after only a couple of listens the songs seem like ones that you've known for years and years, even though it's really only Hooper and Kane left from the original lineup (both Chris Hooper and Vince Jones declined the opportunity to rejoin the band). For those that thought the Grapes were one of the best things to come out of Canada's music scene, it's a welcome return. As a bonus on the first run, a six-song EP is included, featuring reworkings of four older tracks and two cover tunes. —*Sean Carruthers*

The Grass Roots

f. 1964, Los Angeles, CA

AM Pop, Sunshine Pop, Pop, Folk-Rock

The Grass Roots are one of the more enduring Top 40 acts from the late 1960's and early 1970's, with a series of major hits—most notably "Let's Live for Today," "Midnight Confessions," "Temptation Eyes," and "Two Divided by Love"—that help define the essence of the era's best AM radio in the minds of millions of listeners. Although the group's members weren't even close to being recognizable, and their in-house songwriting was next to irrelevant, the Grass Roots managed to make a mark on popular music about as important (though not as successful) as that of their Dunhill Records labelmates Three Dog Night, with 14 Top 40 hits charted between 1966 and 1973, including seven gold singles and one platinum single during that period, and two hits collections that effortlessly went gold. Moreover, their influence can be found even in the work of such superstars of subsequent decades as Bruce Springsteen. —*Bruce Eder*

Where Were You When I Needed You? / 1966 / Varese Sarabande ♦♦♦♦

Before the Grass Roots reached the peak of their pop/rock popularity, they were a much more folk-rock-oriented outfit. Indeed, this debut album is a matter of much confusion; apparently the original Grass Roots were pretty much a front for the songwriting team of P.F. Sloan and Steve Barri, who ended up performing on much of the album themselves. In any case, this is decent, though not top-of-the-line, early folk-rock, falling about halfway between the Byrds and more pop-oriented peers like the Turtles and the Mamas and the Papas. Highlights include the hit title track and other Sloan-Barri originals like "Lollipop Train," "Look Out Girl," "This Is What I Was Made For," and "You Baby," which was a hit for the Turtles. The CD reissue adds six bonus tracks from rare singles, the best of which is the uncharacteristically tough "Tip of My Tongue" (not the obscure Lennon-McCartney composition). —*Richie Unterberger*

Let's Live for Today / 1967 / MCA ♦♦♦

Feelings / 1968 / Dunhill ♦♦♦

● **Anthology: 1965-1975** / Jul. 2, 1991 / Rhino ♦♦♦♦♦

It may be expensive, and two CDs of their work may seem like overkill, but this double-disc set is the one to get. Not only does it contain every hit and each single, and every B-side, from 1965's "Where Were You When I Needed You" through 1975's glorious "Mamacita," but the sound is extraordinary, far better than on any of the other hits compilations, and provides several revelations about the quality of their work. Highlights, in addition to the expected hits ("Let's Live for Today," "Midnight Confessions," "Two Divided by Love" etc.), include tracks like "Is It Any Wonder," with a chorus as radiant as anything the Mamas and the Papas ever recorded, and the seldom heard, vibrant "Mamacita." If you could never imagine listening to 120 minutes of Grass Roots material (this reviewer couldn't, either), this set will make you feel differently. —*Bruce Eder*

All Time Greatest Hits / Jul. 1996 / MCA ♦♦♦♦♦

This low-priced disc is far and away the best single-CD compilation ever issued of the Grass Roots' work, 16 chart singles covering every phase of their history, from 1966's "Where Were You When I Needed You" (in its actual hit version) thru "Let's Live for Today" and "Midnight Confessions" to their last hit, 1972's "The Runway." Listening to this 44-minute compilation, one not only encounters a superb array of catchy songs (and even some of the lesser hits, like the number 61-charting "Come On and Say It" and the number 34-charting "Glory Bound," are compelling pieces of soul-based pop/rock) but also virtuoso production and playing. The material has been remastered in state-of-the-art sound, giving one a chance to appreciate the production and engineering as well as the playing, which (regardless of whether it was provided by L.A.'s best session musicians or members of the actual band) is extraordinarily polished and quite powerful—the piano, drums, and bass on "Sooner or Later" sound like they're in the same room with the listener, and the singing seems even more up-close and personal. The annotation also explains the group's somewhat confusing formation, and their evolution from a folk-rock

band to one of the most successful white pop-soul outfits of their era, closer in spirit to the Fifth Dimension than to Bob Dylan, Roger McGuinn, et al. —*Bruce Eder*

20th Century Masters—The Millennium Collection: The Best of the Grass Roots / Jul. 10, 2001 / MCA ♦♦♦♦

This seems like an unnecessary collection, considering that *All Time Greatest Hits*—released on the same label, just five years previously—has all 12 songs on this grandly titled "*20th Century Masters*" edition, and adds four tracks not on this collection. If it's just the big hits you're looking for, and as a matter of convenience it's easier to acquire this title, it does have the main familiar hits, from "Where Were You When I Needed You" and "Let's Live for Today" to "Temptation Eyes" and "Sooner or Later." Those wishing for more obscure, worthy early cuts like "Mr. Jones (Ballad of a Thin Man)," "Tip of My Tongue," and "Feelings" need to go to Rhino's two-CD *Anthology*. —*Richie Unterberger*

The Grateful Dead

f. 1965, San Francisco, CA, db. 1995

Album Rock, Folk-Rock, Psychedelic, Country-Rock, Jam Bands

Rock's longest, strangest trip, the Grateful Dead were the psychedelic era's most beloved musical ambassadors as well as its most enduring survivors, spreading their message of peace, love, and mind-expansion across the globe throughout the better part of three decades. The object of adoration for popular music's most fervent and celebrated fan following—the Deadheads, their numbers and devotion legendary in their own right—they were the ultimate cult band, creating a self-styled universe all their own; for the better part of their career orbiting well outside of the mainstream. The Dead—originally singers/guitarists Jerry Garcia and Bob Weir, singer/keyboardist Ron "Pigpen" McKernan, bassist Phil Lesh, and drummers Bill Kreutzmann and Mickey Hart—became superstars solely on their own terms, tie-dyed pied pipers whose epic, free-form live shows were rites of passage for an extended family of listeners which knew no cultural boundaries. —*Jason Ankeny*

The Grateful Dead [1967] / Mar. 17, 1967 / Warner Brothers ♦♦

The Grateful Dead's debut album finds them uncomfortable in the studio, rushing tempos and otherwise failing to reproduce the feel of their live shows. Nevertheless, the group covers much of its then-current repertoire, including such long-term favorites as "Beat It on Down the Line," "Cold Rain and Snow," and "New, New Minglewood Blues." —*William Ruhlmann*

Anthem of the Sun / Jul. 18, 1968 / Warner Brothers ♦♦♦♦

The Grateful Dead spent six months recording their second album in studios and at concerts. The result came closer to an accurate portrait of them, highlighted by the four-part, 12-minute "That's It for the Other One." Still, the extensive mixing and editing made the sound dense and uninviting, especially to those not yet converted to the group's approach. —*William Ruhlmann*

Aoxomoxoa / Jun. 20, 1969 / Warner Brothers ♦♦♦

The addition of poet Robert Hunter as lyricist marked the beginning of a consistent set of imagery in the Dead's words to match their musical interplay, especially on songs like "St. Stephen" and "China Cat Sunflower." But the aural experiments were still making for trying listening as the Dead continued to search for a way to capture their concert feel on disc. —*William Ruhlmann*

Live/Dead / Nov. 10, 1969 / Warner Brothers ♦♦♦♦♦

Long, trancelike songs with allusive lyrics (such as the classic "Dark Star") and R&B workouts featuring Pigpen's bluesy voice characterize this album, which is the basic document in the early Dead catalog—it's what most fans would like them to sound like every night. —*William Ruhlmann*

☆ **Workingman's Dead** / May 1970 / Warner Brothers ♦♦♦♦♦

The Grateful Dead were already established as paragons of the free-form, improvisational San Francisco psychedelic sound when they abruptly shifted gears for the acoustic *Workingman's Dead*, a lovely exploration of American roots music illuminating the group's country, blues, and folk influences. The lilting "Uncle John's Band," their first radio hit, opens the record and perfectly summarizes its subtle, spare beauty; complete with a new focus on more concise songs and tighter arrangements, the approach works brilliantly. Despite its sharp contrast to the epic live space jams on which the group's legend primarily rests, *Workingman's Dead* nonetheless spotlights the Dead at their most engaging, stripped of all excess to reveal the true essence of their craft. —*Jason Ankeny*

★ **American Beauty** / Nov. 1970 / Warner Brothers ♦♦♦♦♦

A companion piece to the luminous *Workingman's Dead*, *American Beauty* is an even stronger document of the Grateful Dead's return to their musical roots. Sporting a more full-bodied and intricate sound than its predecessor thanks to the addition of subtle electric textures, the record is also more representative of the group as a collective unit, allowing for stunning contributions from Dave Torbert (the poignant opener "Box of Rain") and Bob Weir ("Sugar Magnolia"); at the top of his game as well is Jerry Garcia, who delivers the superb "Friend of the Devil," "Candyman," and "Ripple." Climaxing with the perennial "Truckin'," *American Beauty* remains the Dead's studio masterpiece—never again would they be so musically focused or so emotionally direct. —*Jason Ankeny*

The Grateful Dead [1971] / Oct. 1971 / Warner Brothers ♦♦♦

The Dead's second double live album (now on a single CD) introduces a couple of excellent Garcia/Hunter compositions, "Bertha" and "Wharf Rat," and allows Bob Weir to indulge his taste for what Deadheads would come to call "cowboy songs": Merle Haggard's "Mama Tried" and Kris Kristofferson's "Me & Bobby McGee." The album became the Dead's first gold record, probably on the momentum of *Workingman's Dead* and *American Beauty*. It also failed to match *Live/Dead* as a concert album, so that, coming off the band's recent peaks, it seemed less effective than it was. Now, it seems like one of the Dead's better, more coherent records. [Not to be confused with *The Grateful Dead*, the band's debut album. They resorted to *Grateful Dead* as a title when Warner wouldn't let them call the album "Skull Fuck."] *—William Ruhlmann*

Europe '72 / Nov. 1972 / Warner Brothers ✦✦✦✦✦
Released as a three-record set, *Europe '72* is now a double CD. But it's still a long album, notable for introducing more Garcia-Hunter songs, especially "Brown-Eyed Woman," and for incorporating onto one album the variety of musical styles to be heard at a Dead concert, as well as the sheer duration necessary to appreciate the experience. Which means that while this may not be the place a new fan wants to start, it's a Deadhead favorite. *—William Ruhlmann*

History of the Grateful Dead, Vol. 1 (Bear's Choice) / Jul. 13, 1973 / Warner Brothers ✦✦✦
This is a contractual obligation album, a record given to Warner Bros. to complete the Dead's commitment to the label. It was recorded in February 1970 and is something of a tribute to the late keyboardist/vocalist Ron "Pigpen" McKernan, who is heard frequently. Pigpen highlights an 18-minute version of Howlin' Wolf's "Smokestack Lightnin'." But this is a nonessential Dead album. "Bear" is the band's friend/soundman/drug manufacturer Owsley Stanley. The album is misnamed: it does not provide a "history" and there was never any Volume 2. *—William Ruhlmann*

Wake of the Flood / Nov. 15, 1973 / Grateful Dead ✦✦✦✦✦
The Grateful Dead's first studio album in three years was also their first for their own record label. It's a strong collection, featuring such Garcia-Hunter songs as "Mississippi Half-Step Uptown Toodleoo," "Row Jimmy," and "Stella Blue," songs that would become concert staples, as well as Bob Weir's "Weather Report Suite." *—William Ruhlmann*

Skeletons From the Closet: The Best of the Grateful Dead / 1974 / Warner Brothers ✦✦✦
This is an 11-song compilation, five of whose songs come from *Workingman's Dead* or *American Beauty*. It presents a sampling of the Dead's 1967-1972 period, focusing on their more accessible material. In that sense, it is recommended to the uninitiated who want to get a feel for the group; not surprisingly, it is a perennial seller, turning up week after week on Billboard magazine's Top Pop Catalog chart. The initiated, however, despise it: In a survey of Deadheads conducted by DeadBase, it was rated above only *Dylan & the Dead* as the worst Grateful Dead album. *—William Ruhlmann*

The Grateful Dead From the Mars Hotel / Jun. 27, 1974 / Grateful Dead ✦✦✦
The Grateful Dead made their reputation on the road with their live shows, and they have always struggled to capture that magic in the studio. *From the Mars Hotel*, while not a classic, represents one of their better studio albums. Jerry Garcia sounds engaged throughout and takes the vocal reigns for most of the songs on the album—although he's not the most gifted vocalist, he proves himself able and versatile. He sings the rollicking opener "U.S. Blues" with a tongue-in-cheek seriousness that gives the political song an edge, and he lends emotional sincerity to the atmospheric ballad "China Doll." Garcia shines on guitar during the funk workout "Scarlet Begonias," but the ensemble work is best displayed on the album's centerpiece, "Unbroken Chain." During this song, all the musicians are allowed to shine: Phil Lesh, the bassist and songwriter, provides tender vocals over a piano-based arrangement while the bridge allows the guitars and drums to stretch out in classic Grateful Dead style. This album is highly recommended for fans, but casual listeners should start with *American Beauty* or *Workingman's Dead*. *—Vik Iyengar*

Blues for Allah / Sep. 1, 1975 / Grateful Dead ✦✦✦✦✦
Opening with the suite that has become a concert favorite, "Help on the Way"/"Slip Knot!"/"Franklin's Tower," and also containing the anthemic "The Music Never Stopped," *Blues for Allah* is another Grateful Dead album containing a few band classics and a lot of filler. Note, however, that some fans seem to like the filler. In its survey of Deadheads, DeadBase found *Blues for Allah* to be the band's most popular studio album after *Workingman's Dead* and *American Beauty*. *—William Ruhlmann*

Steal Your Face / Jun. 26, 1976 / Grateful Dead ✦✦
A double live album recorded in October 1974 just before the start of a hiatus in performing by the Dead and not released until 20 months later, to coincide with the feature film *The Grateful Dead Movie*, shot at the same shows. It is universally hated by Deadheads, and why would anyone else want to listen to it? Primary evidence that the Dead needed to take a break from touring in 1974. *—William Ruhlmann*

● **What a Long Strange Trip It's Been** / 1977 / Warner Brothers ✦✦✦✦✦
This is a two-disc compilation of the Grateful Dead covering its tenure at Warner Bros., 1967-1972, and as such the most extensive sampler of their work in existence. Well-chosen, it contains many of their best songs from the period and is notable for giving album release to the studio-recorded single version of "Dark Star," the Dead's most requested song. Relative newcomers to the band (those who bought *Skeletons from the Closet* and liked it) can get a stronger dose here, and then perhaps go on to the individual albums. Of course, Deadheads hate this record. *—William Ruhlmann*

Terrapin Station / Jul. 27, 1977 / Arista ✦✦
It is generally agreed that the Grateful Dead's late-'70s studio releases left even the most enthusiastic Deadheads longing for something more. The theory being that the band's momentum is best experienced during the ebb and flow of a live performance rather than the somewhat clinical tedium of a recording studio. *Terrapin Station* marks several milestones for the Grateful Dead: It was the band's first studio album in two years, as well as their return to a major label—in this case Arista Records. More significant however is the use of an outside (read: non-Grateful Dead) producer. This was only the second time in which the Dead did not seize complete control. And the first time in a decade that they would relinquish their production reigns. They chose Keith Olson—a former member of the '60s garage rock band Music Machine—whose production roster also included other Bay Area notables including the Sons of Champlin and Santana. Musically, *Terrapin Station* offers a few choice glimpses of the band doing what they do best. While the most prominent example is the album's extended title suite, there are a few others such as the cover of the Rev. Gary Davis' gospel-blues "Samson and Delilah" and a resurrection of the Martha & the Vandellas hit "Dancin' in the Streets." The latter tune was originally performed by the Dead in their mid-'60s repertoire. What was once a garage rock and psychedelic reading has evolved into a 4/4-time, brass-influenced disco arrangement. Luckily, their extended versions during concert performances were infinitely more tolerable. Parties interested in examining the contrast between the studio and live performance versions of *Terrapin Station* material should seek the archival concert release *Dick's Picks, Vol. 3*. This two-disc set not only captures the band exactly two months and two days prior to the release of *Terrapin Station*, it also features stellar performances of every track from the album sans the up-tempo rocker "Passenger." *—Lindsay Planer*

Shakedown Street / Nov. 15, 1978 / Arista ✦✦
Using Little Feat leader Lowell George as producer should have been a great idea, but somehow it didn't work out. The Dead have salvaged "Fire on the Mountain" and "I Need a Miracle" for live work from this collection, but it's one of their least satisfactory studio ventures. *—William Ruhlmann*

Go to Heaven / Apr. 28, 1980 / Arista ✦

Reckoning / Apr. 1, 1981 / Arista ✦✦✦
Having given up on studio work after the disaster of *Go to Heaven*, the Dead recorded a series of concerts in New York and San Francisco in October 1980 for two live albums. This is the first, a set of acoustic material that will remind many listeners of the rustic feel of the classic *Workingman's Dead* and *American Beauty* albums, although much of it consists of traditional and bluegrass material favored by Jerry Garcia. [The original two-LP set was fit onto one CD in 1987 by eliminating the Dead's cover of Elizabeth Cotten's "Oh Babe It Ain't No Lie."] *—William Ruhlmann*

Dead Set / Aug. 1981 / Arista ✦✦✦
The second of the Dead's two live albums recorded at shows in October 1980, this presents an electric set featuring some material previously heard on Jerry Garcia solo albums and some of the group's less successful '70s material. As such, it is far from the Dead's best live album, but it is representative of their work at the time. *—William Ruhlmann*

In the Dark / Jul. 6, 1987 / Arista ✦✦✦✦✦
The comeback, with "Touch of Grey," "West L.A. Fadeaway," and "Black Muddy River." For anyone who wondered how these old hippies could have such a following 20 years after the hippies disappeared, here's the answer. *—William Ruhlmann*

Built to Last / Oct. 31, 1989 / Arista ✦✦
Supposedly, the Dead had broken their studio jinx with *In the Dark* and finally learned how to make good albums without an audience in front of them. So why was this follow-up such a letdown? Perhaps because they hadn't taken seven years to write and perfect new material as they had with the previous album. The dominant songwriter here was keyboard player Brent Mydland (who died the following year), while the crucial songwriting team of Garcia and Hunter contributed only minor efforts. Chastened, the Dead once again retreated from studio work. *—William Ruhlmann*

Without a Net / Sep. 1990 / Arista ✦✦✦
A double-CD live album notable for featuring performances by jazz saxophonist Branford Marsalis and the Dead's version of Traffic's "Dear Mr. Fantasy," a concert favorite. Unintentionally, the album serves as the epitaph to keyboard player Brent Mydland, who died shortly after its completion, bringing about another change in the band's direction. *—William Ruhlmann*

One from the Vault / Apr. 15, 1991 / Grateful Dead ✦✦✦
With this album, issued on the group's own merchandising label, the Grateful Dead began to address the needs of an audience that had long since taken to making their own tapes of every Dead performance. Such an audience, of course, would be interested in record releases containing vintage live shows, and the Dead began by issuing this 16-year-old concert, which occurred shortly after they completed their 1975 album *Blues for Allah* and while they were nominally retired from live work. It contains all the material featured on that album, plus such recent Dead songs as "U.S. Blues" and such favorites as "The Other One." It made for a modest beginning to the Dead's archival investigations, and only whetted fans' appetites for what might follow. *—William Ruhlmann*

Infrared Roses / Nov. 1, 1991 / Grateful Dead ✦✦
Each Grateful Dead concert includes a long instrumental section, part of which is devoted to a drum solo and part to group improvisation, the parts dubbed "Drums" and "Space" by Deadheads. This two-disc set consists of excerpts from such performances, as electronically treated by Dead soundman Bob Bralove. It is one of the Dead's more esoteric releases and not to be confused with a regular, song-filled album. For fans and aficionados of experimental music only. *—William Ruhlmann*

Two from the Vault / 1992 / Grateful Dead ✦✦✦
Two discs' worth of the Dead in all their psychedelic glory, this second volume of live material from the archives stems from two shows in August 1968, when their improvisational headiness balanced out with Pigpen bringing the proceedings solidly back down to Earth. For those who may have wondered what *Anthem of the Sun* might have sounded like minus the studio collage mix—here's the answer. *—Steve Aldrich*

Dick's Picks, Vol. 1 / Dec. 1993 / Grateful Dead ✦✦✦
This recording of a Grateful Dead concert performed in Tampa, FL, on December 19,

1973, inaugurates a new series of archival releases that differs from the band's already established *From the Vaults* series in that it is to feature somewhat lower-fidelity, "what you hear is what you get" tapes, as the liner notes put it, subject to editing problems, incompleteness, etc. Perhaps to make up for that, this double-CD album was not offered to retail, but distributed only through mail order, and it was sold at a discount price. For all that, this is a good, if laid-back, Dead set, led off by a 14-minute version of "Here Comes Sunshine." That song comes from *Wake of the Flood*, which was the band's current album release at the time, and much of that LP's other material turns up–notably, a complete, 16-minute "Weather Report Suite," along with favorites like "Truckin'" and "Playing in the Band," the latter at a running time of 21 minutes. As promised, the recording quality is noticeably unenhanced, but Deadheads won't mind, and casual fans won't bother. *—William Ruhlmann*

Dick's Picks, Vol. 2 / 1995 / Grateful Dead ♦♦♦
The second of the Grateful Dead's low-fidelity archival series of live concerts on CD finds the group in Columbus, OH, on Halloween 1971, This was a relatively low-key time for the band, which had been reduced to a quintet by the temporary departure of second drummer Mickey Hart and in which original keyboard player/vocalist Ron "Pigpen" McKernan had been replaced by Keith Godchaux. They open with a 23-minute version of "Dark Star," segue into "Sugar Magnolia" and "St. Stephen," and conclude with a medley of "Not Fade Away" and "Going Down the Road Feeling Bad," filling one 58-minute disc. The performance is representative of the group and the period, not perhaps as impressive as *The Grateful Dead* album, a live record released the month this concert occurred. For non-Deadheads, all this will seem redundant; for Deadheads, it's another show to add to the collection. *—William Ruhlmann*

Hundred Year Hall / Sep. 26, 1995 / Grateful Dead ♦♦♦
Hundred Year Hall was the archival release of an abridged Frankfurt, Germany show from the Grateful Dead's famed *Europe '72* tour. The set represents an interesting transitional point in the band's history: the 1972 Dead was a seven-member outfit that still contained Ron "Pigpen" McKernan, though his replacement, Keith Godchaux, had already joined, along with his wife, Donna Jean. The group had only one drummer, Bill Kreutzmann, during this stage, so the extended improvisations came mostly from the team of Jerry Garcia, Bob Weir, and Phil Lesh. But if the band was in transition, it was also still riding the performing and composing high of the early '70s, and both the recent original songs (including standards like "Truckin'") and the jams were frequently inspired—an epic medley of "Turn on Your Lovelight" and "Going Down the Road Feelin' Bad," two favorite covers, was a directed, energetic performance with a minimum of noodling. *—William Ruhlmann*

Dick's Picks, Vol. 3 / Nov. 7, 1995 / Grateful Dead ♦♦♦
The third volume of the Grateful Dead's mail-order-only series of unenhanced live recordings takes us to Pembroke Pines, FL, on May 22, 1977, for a two-CD, two-hour-and-20-minute set focusing on material from the group's most recent album, *Blues for Allah*, and its upcoming one, *Terrapin Station*. Typical of The Dead's archival releases, this one contains extended performances (average length of the 16 tracks: 8 3/4 minutes) that normally never would be released on disc, performances that constitute the essence of the Dead for their fans. A good example is the nearly 16-minute version of "Sugaree," on which Jerry Garcia turns in the kind of solo work that defines him as a guitarist—unhurried, lovely note series that seem directionless and yet, cumulatively, produce the indefinable transportive effect of the Grateful Dead at its best. The whole set finds Garcia in top form, and since this album was released only three months after his death, it made a fitting epitaph, even if there doubtless was more to come. *—William Ruhlmann*

★ **Dick's Picks, Vol. 4** / Mar. 1, 1996 / Grateful Dead ♦♦♦♦♦
Though this is the third Grateful Dead album to be released since the death of bandleader Jerry Garcia and the group's subsequent decision to disband, it is the first one that wasn't in the pipeline already. Its release offers evidence that the Dead organization, which had begun releasing selected recordings of live shows as a courtesy to fans while raking in most of its revenues through roadwork, has changed its priorities. *Dick's Picks, Volume 4* isn't just another Grateful Dead concert recording, it's *the* recording: February 13-14, 1970, the Dead's debut at the Fillmore East, and a show consistently ranked by Deadheads as among the five best live tapes ever. This stand, some of which was released in 1973 on the *History Of The Grateful Dead, Vol. 1 (Bear's Choice)* (there is no overlap with this album) finds the Dead gearing up to record *Workingman's Dead*, and already songs like "Casey Jones" and "Dire Wolf" have crept into the set. But there is so much more: half-hour versions of "That's It for the Other One," "Turn on Your Lovelight" (a showcase for Pigpen), and, in a near-definitive performance, the Dead's signature song, "Dark Star." Much of the then recently released *Live/Dead* material is heard, not to mention a rare performance of "Mason's Children." But it isn't just the set list that makes this a legendary show, it's the playing; amazing interaction among the players on every song, with Garcia noodling his way to nirvana. While it would be an exaggeration to say that if you own this three-CD, three-hour-and-ten-minute album you have all you need of the Grateful Dead on disc, the overstatement is only slight. As Bob Weir says at the outset, "This ain't a show, it's a party." *—William Ruhlmann*

The Arista Years / Oct. 15, 1996 / Arista ♦♦♦♦♦
This well-chosen compilation makes the best of the eight albums (five studio LPs and three live collections) the Grateful Dead released on Arista Records between 1977 and 1990. The first three studio albums are not well regarded, but by focusing on the stronger compositions, such as "Estimated Prophet," "Terrapin Station," "Fire on the Mountain," "I Need a Miracle," and "Saint of Circumstance," the compilers have made them seem better than they did when they were released. It doesn't hurt that these are the songs that emerged as concert favorites, and if these performances often sound like distilled, sometimes stilted versions for those familiar with the live shows, they nevertheless serve as a kind of blueprint for the music the Dead played in the late '70s and '80s. A more confident band emerges in the later tracks, in part because the material is superior—not only the hit "Touch of Grey," but also "Black Muddy River" and "Foolish Heart," among others—but also because the performances are seasoned by frequent live playing of the songs. The album concludes with the group's 1990 live recording of "Eyes of the World" with Branford Marsalis sitting in from *Without a Net*. *The Arista Years* presents the sound of a band compromising with, but not capitulating to, the demands of the conventional record industry. Even the Dead themselves were never really able to capture lightning in a bottle, but, as one of their better songs here puts it, they managed to shine "Just a Little Light." *—William Ruhlmann*

Dozin' at the Knick / Oct. 29, 1996 / Arista ♦♦♦♦
Drawing upon the same spring 1990 East Coast tour that produced *Without a Net, Dozin' at the Knick* mixes performances from three successive shows performed at Knickerbocker Arena in Albany, NY, March 24-26. It contains most of the first set from March 26, all of the second set from March 24, and the second half of the second set from March 25. Deadheads might have preferred that the March 24 show be presented in its entirety instead, but at least the best feature of that show is included, namely a nearly eight-minute version of the rarely performed (and never before released on record) jam "Your Mind Has Left Your Body," here playfully renamed "Mud Love Buddy Jam." The Dead had reinvigorated their live shows in the fall of 1989, meanwhile reintroducing many of their older songs. By the spring of 1990, they were back to a more conventional repertoire (though this album contains such fairly unusual selections as "The Wheel" and the a cappella "And We Bid You Goodnight"), but their performance standard remained high, as demonstrated on this well-performed collection. *—William Ruhlmann*

Live at Fillmore East 2-11-69 / Oct. 28, 1997 / Grateful Dead ♦♦♦♦
Performing two hour-long sets as the opening act to Janis Joplin's New York debut as a solo star, the Grateful Dead turned in a characteristic performance for this period in their career. In between the release of their second and third albums, they devoted much time to the songs that would turn up several months later on *Aoxomoxoa*, including acoustic renditions of "Dupree's Diamond Blues" and "Mountains of the Moon." Pigpen dominated the first set, singing the blues standards "Good Morning Little Schoolgirl," "I'm a King Bee," and "Turn on Your Lovelight." But a large part of both sets was given over to the group's extended medleys, in the first set "Cryptical Envelopment/The Other One," in the second "Dark Star/St. Stephen/The Eleven." These involved, largely instrumental pieces set the tone for the Dead at the end of the '60s and produced their breakthrough with *Live/Dead*, which was recorded within weeks of this show. There is also a game version of "Hey Jude," the biggest hit of the previous year, to end the first set, and an unlisted, interrupted performance of "Cosmic Charlie" as a second-set encore. *—William Ruhlmann*

So Many Roads (1965-1995) / Nov. 9, 1999 / Arista ♦♦♦♦♦
By the late '90s, box sets increasingly addressed the desires of ardent fans; since the uninitiated were satisfied with smaller compilations, a box set consisting mostly or entirely of unissued material often seemed more appropriate. Even within this paradigm, however, the Grateful Dead are an anomaly—most of their studio recordings are disdained by fans devoted to privately distributed tapes of their live performances. How, then, to approach a Dead box set? The compilers have scoured the group's extensive vault for a five-CD set which includes only a few tracks that have ever been released in any medium. Adopting a roughly chronological sequencing, they sought out rare songs and, especially, performance highlights spanning the Dead's 30-year career. The compilers are second-generation Deadheads, fans who came to the band in the '70s and '80s, responding to the marathon-length live instrumental improvisations. Time and again, the songs here begin in normal fashion and then take off into uncharted territory; as long as the soloing is interesting, it doesn't matter if lyrics are blown or the singing is off-key. In many cases, the compilers are so enamored of the group's interplay that they include excerpts without the songs that begin or conclude them. The rare songs include selections from the Dead's unreleased 1965 sessions for Autumn Records, outtakes from *Workingman's Dead* and *American Beauty*, and rehearsals and live performances of songs intended for a Dead album that was never formally recorded. In short, *So Many Roads (1965-1995)* was obviously made by Deadheads for Deadheads. The Dead have succeeded over the years by addressing the interests of a cult that welcomes neophytes but also revels in its exclusivity; it's no surprise that their version of a box-set retrospective holds true to that course. *—William Ruhlmann*

The Golden Road (1965-1973) / Oct. 16, 2001 / Rhino/Warner Archive ♦♦♦♦♦

David Gray

Vocals, Guitar / Adult Alternative Pop/Rock, Indie Rock, Alternative Pop/Rock, Singer/Songwriter, Folk-Pop

When most people think of English music, the Beatles obviously come to mind, along with the punk of the Sex Pistols, the glam rock of David Bowie, and maybe the soft pop of Elton John. Few would immediately think of David Gray and his acoustic guitar, but he's on a mission to change all that. Born in Manchester in 1970, Gray grew up in Wales before attending the University of Liverpool. Following a move to London, Gray signed to Hut Records in the U.K. and Caroline Records in the U.S., releasing the single *Birds Without Wings* in 1992. The next year saw his debut album, *A Century Ends*. Through his emotional tales of anger and passion, love, and solitude, Gray's trademark style of fiery intensity countered with tender poignancy started to find an audience. However, the wonderfully raw and powerful *Flesh* was released in 1994 to an underwhelming response. Although he was dropped from his label, EMI Records saw his potential and talent and quickly signed him to a new deal. Meanwhile, a quiet buzz was building in

Ireland. Hanging on to that thread, *Sell, Sell, Sell* came out in 1996 in limited release. Gray hitched up his touring boots and hit the road again, this time opening for such heavy hitters as Radiohead and Dave Matthews Band. That still didn't do the trick, and he again parted ways with his major label. Recapturing and embracing his independence, Gray self-financed his fourth album, *White Ladder*. Recorded in a London apartment with an easy blend of samplers and acoustic guitar, *White Ladder* was a sublime leap forward. Ireland certainly recognized its brilliance, as the record immediately went into the Irish Top 30. *The EPs 92-94* followed in July 2001, coinciding with the reissues of *A Century Ends* and *Flesh*. *—Kelly McCartney*

A Century Ends / 1993 / Caroline ✦✦✦

Every note on David Gray's debut album, *A Century Ends*, is sung with raw heartfelt emotion. Gray's lyrics depict a man broken by love and wanting to escape the boredom and monotony of his current station in life. On the title track, Gray challenges himself to make changes in his life before the next millennium. Gray's coffeehouse acoustic guitar and gritty Welsh-accented voice provide the backdrop for a majority of the tracks. The two exceptions are "A Century Ends" and "Wisdom," an upbeat ode to regret, complete with the only catchy chorus on the album. However, this album is not about hooks and feel-good melodies—Gray grabs the listener with his poetic lyrics and takes off on an introspective ten-song ride through desperation, regret, lost love, and a longing for change. If *A Century Ends* is an indicator of things to come, then Gray has the potential to become a prolific singer/songwriter. *—Erik Crawford*

Flesh / 1994 / Vernon Yard/Virgin ✦✦✦✦

On *Flesh*, David Gray's 1994 release, the Welsh singer/songwriter wraps his rough-hewn voice around ten self-penned songs that deal mainly with relationships. Delivered in his earnest voice, the highly literate observations of the lyrics and the folk-tinged feel of the music is easily compared to the work of Mike Scott of Waterboys fame. "What Are You?" kicks things off with an aggressive, bracing vocal growl from Gray over a tumbling rhythm. "Made Up My Mind" features a determined lyric of resilience and moving on. There isn't a weak cut on this record, but the highlights are the more sparse, reflective numbers which highlight the gentleness of Gray's guitar playing and the flawless phrasing of his vocal delivery. "Falling Free" and "Mystery of Love" are two of the best examples with the romantic longing of their lyrics. Neill Maccoll adds some wistful slide guitar to the latter. A must listen for any fan of Mike Scott or just anyone that appreciates well-done, acoustic-based rock. *— Tom Demalon*

Sell, Sell, Sell / Apr. 1996 / EMI ✦✦✦

On *Sell, Sell, Sell*, David Gray plugs in and cranks it up a notch higher than on his previous release, *Flesh*. Where once there were sparse arrangements of acoustic guitar and piano, now there are live jangling electrics and drums. Gray's voice, however, is just as raw and piercing as ever, in a good way. No matter the instrumentation, his vocal performances always best convey the message, whether urgent or tender. He does have a few quiet moments sprinkled throughout *Sell, Sell, Sell*, but the larger scheme is loud, driving, and powerful. "Hold on to Nothing," "Smile," and "Gutters Full of Rain" are songs that bear the torch of longing that filled so much of *Flesh*. Naked Gray, coffeehouse Gray—that's what they seem to recall, and quite well. That's not to say that the rocking stuff is no good. It's good. It's smart, melodic folk-rock done up with emotion and talent. As a writer, Gray's vision has expanded to include more social observations along with his personal tribulations. The loss of faith and innocence and the coldness of winter and greed are both reoccurring themes throughout the album. Even the titles suggest the importance of what lies within the melodic lines—"Faster, Sooner, Now," "Sell, Sell, Sell," "Everytime," "Forever Is Tomorrow Is Today." The pace and tone are set from the word go, or "hey" as the case may be. All in all, this is a fine next step in the evolution of a wonderfully talented young artist. *—Kelly McCartney*

● **White Ladder** / 1999 / IHT ✦✦✦✦✦

David Gray's fan base is strong and active. They have seen him through his years with Virgin Records, during which time he was applauded for his talent, emotive voice, and songwriting skills yet never quite broke through to a mainstream audience. *White Ladder* showcases Gray like never before; it's an album of such depth and quality that one would be hard-pressed to ignore his talent. Each song is strong and superbly crafted, both in terms of arrangement and delivery. The standouts, "Please Forgive Me" and "This Year's Love," are touching and likely to bring a tear to the eye of the listener. This album is definitely a much-needed addition to any quality music collection. With any justice, it will finally bring David Gray the success that he so rightly deserves. *—Jaime Ikeda*

Lost Songs 95-98 / Apr. 17, 2001 / RCA ✦✦

Singer/songwriter David Gray may have finally achieved mainstream respect with his fourth album *White Ladder*, but he's not one to forget the tumultuous time spent prior to such praise. He was a confused artist during the recording of that album, adding emotion to countless tracks that never made it on to *White Ladder*. *Lost Songs 95-98* recognizes that songwriting period of personal dysfunction. It's also a definitive selection of moods, atmospheric definitions, and self-awareness, for Gray composed some of his most beautiful ballads yet. Clearly it isn't a follow-up. It's merely an additive for a fan's collection. It combines classic acoustics and simplistic lyrical stories while his Welsh brogue captures the most heartfelt moments on the record. It's not massively produced, and that's what's classic about Gray as an artist. He allows the complexities of a song—"Wurlitzer," "Red Moon," and "Tidal Wave"—to shape its fundamentals in a nature all its own. *Lost Songs* showcases what was supposed to be for David Gray, without the bitterness, of course. *—MacKenzie Wilson*

The EP's 92-94 / Jul. 10, 2001 / Caroline ✦✦✦

Once David Gray finally became a household mainstay on the radio and on VH1, this incredible singer/songwriter received overdue props with a sold-out tour and the reissue of

his first four albums. Caroline Records also participated by releasing this rare collection of combined EP tracks showcasing Gray's early period of musical bleakness. *The EP's 92-94* comprises Gray's first three U.K. singles from *A Century Ends* and extra bonus tracks. Songs such as "L's Song" and "Brick Walls" are delicately woven around signature acoustics and Gray's gritty howl. "The Rice" is a bit more upbeat with glossy bass loops cradling Gray's strumming, but optimism shines with plucking mandolin riffs for an Irish tinge. "Coming Down" from Gray's second album *Flesh* is beaming with heartfelt emotion internally churning due to Gray's personal hardships with the music industry during the mid-'90s. It's a solid collection, but only for the most dedicated fans. The majority of the songs selected are found on his first two albums, but having videos for "Shine" and "Wisdom" also makes this inviting compilation more worthy. *—MacKenzie Wilson*

Dobie Gray

b. Jul. 26, 1943, Brookshire, TX

Vocals / Pop-Soul, Country-Soul, Disco, Soul

Journeyman soul singer, composer, and actor Gray has had a checkered career, scoring hit records in two different decades, acting on Broadway, and appearing in the Los Angeles production of *Hair*.

After moving to Nashville in 1978, Dobie Gray resurfaced in the late '80s as a country songwriter and performer. Previously he remade "The In Crowd" for an LP on Infinity, *Dobie Gray*, that was a hit in England. David Ruffin also recorded his song "City Stars." The LP *Back Where I Belong* in the early '80s was a competent bit of country-soul, but failed to secure Gray a niche in Nashville's tight-knit fraternity. He continues performing and making occasional appearances on The Nashville Network.*—Cub Koda and Ron Wynn*

● **Drift Away: His Very Best** / Jul. 23, 1996 / Razor & Tie ✦✦✦✦

Razor & Tie's *Drift Away: His Very Best* is the definitive Dobie Gray collection, containing all of his Top 40 pop hits and all of his charting R&B singles—"The 'In' Crowd," "Drift Away," "Loving Arms," "Find 'Em, Fool 'Em & Forget 'Em," "You Can Do It")—plus 12 other lesser-known singles and album tracks. A few of the songs may fall flat, but there are more hidden gems on the collection than you might expect; in particular, the country-soul of "There's a Honky Tonk Angel" and "Watch Out for Lucy" sounds particularly good. Either way, *Drift Away* captures the full range of Gray's talent and provides an excellent summation of his career. *—Stephen Thomas Erlewine*

● **Ultimate Collection** / Apr. 3, 2001 / Hip-O ✦✦✦✦

Listening to Dobie Gray's *Ultimate Collection* is like going through a musical time capsule. This collection includes his first charted single, "Look at Me," his first big hit "The In Crowd" and its follow-up, "See You at The Go-Go," all which have a distinctive, mid-1960s big go-go sound. Other early songs, such as "Out on the Floor," are full of contemporary colloquialisms (such as "groovy" and "the chicks are outta sight!"). By the time the album reaches his stellar version of "Rose Garden," the music shifts into more mid-1970s adult leaning material, especially evident by his signature, much-loved anthem "Drift Away." Then there's the soul-country/rock of "The Time I Loved You Most," the lamenting ballad "Loving Arms," the total country of "Watch Out for Lucy," and the disco of the "Stayin' Alive" sound-alike "You Can Do It" (his last Top 40 hit). Also included is his 1986 country hit "That's One To Grow On." This album collects all three of his U.S. Top 40 hits, as well as most of his other charted singles (unfortunately "Find 'Em, Fool 'Em, Forget 'Em" was omitted), and stands as a testament to an artist who was totally unafraid to sing what he wanted, whether it be rock & roll, soul, or country. And best of all, he always sounded as if he was having the time of his life. *—Jose Promis*

Macy Gray

Vocals / Contemporary R&B, Adult Alternative Pop/Rock, Urban

Alternative R&B singer Macy Gray was born and raised in Canton, OH, growing up on a steady diet of classic soul and early hip hop. A classically trained pianist, she only began singing while studying screenwriting at the University of Southern California, recording a demo with a group of musician friends after the scheduled vocalist failed to show up at the studio. From there Gray sang with a local jazz band, also becoming a sought-after session vocalist; signing to Epic, she issued her debut album *On How Life Is* in mid-1999. What followed was critical praise and comparison, a string of live performances and awards. *—Jason Ankeny*

● **On How Life Is** / Jul. 27, 1999 / Epic ✦✦✦✦

Macy Gray is such an assured, original vocalist that it's hard to believe *On How Life Is* is her debut album. She recalls a number of other vocalists, particularly jazz singers like Billie Holiday and Nina Simone, but she is unquestionably from the post-hip-hop generation, which is evident not just from the sound of the record, but the style of her songwriting, which is adventurous and unpredictable. Thankfully, she's worked with a producer (Andrew Slater, who pulled a similar trick with Fiona Apple's debut, *Tidal*) that lets her run wild and helps her find sounds that match her ideas. That's not to say that *On How Life Is* is a perfect album—at times, Gray attempts more than she can achieve—but it's always captivating, even during its stumbles. And when it works, it soars higher than most contemporary R&B. *—Stephen Thomas Erlewine*

The Grays

f. 1993, **db.** 1994

Alternative Pop/Rock, Pop Underground

A ramshackle collective of four musicians who all hated playing in bands, the Grays comprised ex-Jellyfish members Jason Falkner and Jon Brion, Buddy Judge, and Dan McCarroll. After coming together in 1993, the group released just one album, *Ro Sham*

Bo, before amicably packing it in. Falkner later began a solo career, while Brion worked with Aimee Mann, eels, and Jimmie Dale Gilmore. —*John Bush*

● **Ro Sham Bo** / 1994 / Epic ✦✦✦✦✦
Ro Sham Bo was an interesting experiment, and it remains one of the curious, off-the-path milestones of '90s pop. Four accomplished musicians disillusioned with being in rock bands formed the Grays based on utopian ideals: all members contributing songs, recording together and fleshing out each other's ideas, and playing each other's instruments when it fit certain songs, so no one was the true "leader." In practice, however, the members' strong personalities clashed and brought the project to an end soon after the recording of *Ro Sham Bo*. It's a very eclectic pop record, stemming from the fact that the different songwriters bring distinct styles to the table. Buddy Judge and Dan McCarroll's tunes tend to be more rhythmically focused jams, like "Everybody's World" and "Is It Now Yet," while Jon Brion and Jason Falkner stick to ultra-cool '70s-style pop/rock, Brion's harmonic melancholy on "Nothing Between Us" contrasting with Falkner's unabashedly catchy jubilation on "Both Belong." But everyone seems to have input into each track, and the result is a nice musical stew, none of the ingredients outshining the others in contribution to the overall taste. Although they weren't able to align musically for more than this one record, all members' attentions seem very focused on fully realizing the tunes on *Ro Sham Bo*. The instrumentation is thick and hearty, sometimes with four or five overlapping guitar parts and keyboards propelling a song toward its climax. Splashes of psychedelia (backwards tape loops, oddly distorted vocal harmonies) accentuate some of the later tunes, and Falkner displays some rare vitriolic screaming on "Spooky." —*Troy Carpenter*

Great Lakes
f. Athens, GA
Indie Pop, Neo-Psychedelia
Yet one more outgrowth of the ever-expanding Elephant 6 family tree, Athens, GA-based psychedelic pop combo the Great Lakes began as the high school project of longtime friends Dan Donahue and Ben Crum. Multi-instrumentalist Jamey Huggins (also the drummer for local favorites Of Montreal) later joined the core roster, with Todd Kelley and Joel Evans also serving as frequent collaborators; the live Great Lakes lineup often expanded to as many as 11 members, among them the Gerbils' Scott Spillane and Of Montreal's Kevin Barnes, Dottie Alexander, and Derek Almstead. The group's self-titled debut LP followed on Kindercore in mid-2000. —*Jason Ankeny*

Great Lakes / May 23, 2000 / Kindercore ✦✦✦✦
From a purely critical standpoint, one can't help but wish that sooner or later, a new Elephant 6 release will dramatically differ from its predecessors in either quality or chemical makeup if for no other reason than the opportunity to use a different set of adjectives and reference points in discussing the record's merits (or relative lack thereof); nevertheless, the Great Lakes' self-titled debut is another worthy addition to the label's ever-expanding output, a luminous paean to late-'60s psych-pop crafted with obvious skill and affection. Among fellow E-6'ers, Great Lakes have most closely to the pop classicism of the Apples in Stereo (whose Robert Schneider mixed the album) and the Essex Green, favoring a sunny, carnival-esque approach that lends the band's buoyant melodies a vividly psychedelic patina; nothing new there, granted, but still it never ceases to amaze how so many records can sound so similar and yet so consistently great. —*Jason Ankeny*

The Great Society
f. 1964, **db.** 1966
Psychedelic
Before joining Jefferson Airplane, Grace Slick sang lead and played various instruments for the Great Society, who were nearly as popular as Jefferson Airplane in the early days of the San Francisco psychedelic scene. Instrumentally, the Great Society were not as disciplined as Airplane. But they were at least their equals in imagination, infusing their probing songwriting with Indian influences, minor key melodic shifts, and groundbreaking, reverb-soaked psychedelic guitar by Slick's brother-in-law, Darby Slick. Darby was also responsible for penning "Somebody to Love," which Grace brought with her to Airplane, who took it into the Top Five in 1967. The Great Society broke up in late 1966 after recording only one locally released single; after Jefferson Airplane became stars, Columbia issued a couple of live albums of the Great Society performing at San Francisco's Matrix Club in 1966. —*Richie Unterberger*

● **Collector's Item** / 1971 / Columbia ✦✦✦✦✦
This CD reissue combines both of the Great Society's live albums onto one disc, and features "Somebody to Love" in its original slower, more menacing version. It also includes the Society's extended version of Grace Slick's "White Rabbit," along with several other haunting originals which strike an exhilarating balance between tight songwriting and psychedelic jamming. This is far more than a "Collector's Item"; it's a genuinely exciting glimpse into the birth of psychedelic music. —*Richie Unterberger*

Born to Be Burned / 1995 / Sundazed ✦✦✦
An interesting if marginal collection of previously unreleased material from late 1965. Recorded at a pretty early stage in the band's development, this is largely comprised of demos that the group recorded during their short-lived association with the Autumn label. Both the songwriting and execution are pretty sketchy and tentative, sounding considerably closer to garage rock than their later psychedelic recordings. Certainly there's a fair amount of promise here, particularly in the songs by Grace and Darby Slick, which far outshine the basic Rolling Stonesy derivations by the band's other songwriter, David Miner. Miner, a below-average garage growler, unfortunately shared the lead vocal duties with the immeasurably superior Grace Slick, who already sounds searing and confident.

But unlike *Collector's Item*, which contains some of the finest (and most unjustly overlooked) psychedelic music ever recorded, this is really mostly of interest to scholars and collectors. The material is far weaker here, and the ragaish Indian influences that characterized their most innovative work had yet to surface. It does include some songs that also appear on *Collector's Item* ("Born to Be Burned," "Daydream Nightmare," "That's How It Is," "Father Bruce"), but these versions are far more skeletal and less forceful. The highlight is their lone, rare single, which featured the first (pre-Jefferson Airplane) version of "Somebody to Love" and the flipside "Free Advice," one of the first examples of raga-rock. —*Richie Unterberger*

Great White
f. 1982
Pop-Metal, Hair Metal, Heavy Metal, Hard Rock
For most intents and purposes, Great White wasn't that different from the glut of mid-'80s hard rock/heavy metal bands. Their songs were derivative of Led Zeppelin, AC/DC, and Mott the Hoople, and lead singer Jack Russell had Robert Plant's wail down cold. Despite their lack of originality, the band was a tight unit that knew the value of a good song—they covered Hunter twice, including their hit single "Once Bitten, Twice Shy." However, Great White could never write as clever and mean as Hunter, nor could they crank out the riffs like Jimmy Page or Angus Young, which made their time in the spotlight very brief. The band continued to record and tour, but they did not regain the audience 1989's *Twice Shy* captured with records like 1994's *Sail Away* and 1996's *Let It Rock*. In 1999, they saluted their biggest influence with *Great Zeppelin: A Tribute to Led Zeppelin*; *Can't Get There From Here* appeared later that same year. 2000's *Latest & Greatest* featured newly recorded versions of their hits. —*Stephen Thomas Erlewine*

● **Greatest Hits** / Jun. 5, 2001 / Capitol ✦✦✦
A cursory glance at Great White's discography would suggest that they don't need another compilation. But Capitol Records' 1993 kiss-off *The Best of Great White: 1986-1992* was a skimpy set that omitted the Top 40 pop hit "The Angel Song" and other key tracks; *Back to Back Hits* was shared with April Wine and contained only five Great White tracks; the 2000 *Best of Great White* was a ten-track budget album from Capitol Special Markets; and *Latest & Greatest* consists of re-recordings. Thus, *Greatest Hits* is the first thorough compilation of the band's EMI and Capitol recordings, 1984-1992. Most of Great White's pop and album rock hits are included in their original versions, though the minor album rock chart entry "Lady Red Light" is missing, and the versions of "House of Broken Love" and "Desert Moon" are live recordings, the former previously issued only as a single B-side, the latter from the Japan-only album *Live in New York*. Other rarities include a bluesy alternate mix of "Face the Day" from a cassette EP, the novelty non-LP B-side "Wasted Rock Ranger," and a non-LP single cover of Led Zeppelin's "Babe I'm Gonna Leave You" from the band's 1990 *MTV Unplugged* appearance that emphasizes their similarity to the earlier group, especially Jack Russell's Robert Plant sound-alike vocals. Capitol has not acquired any tracks from Great White's recordings for subsequent labels, so that, for example, the Top Ten album rock track "Sail Away," originally released on Zoo, is not here. But this is a good survey of Great White's most popular recordings, and it deserves its name. —*William Ruhlmann*

Green Day
f. 1989, Berkeley, CA
Punk-Pop, Post-Grunge, Punk Revival, Alternative Pop/Rock
Out of all the post-Nirvana American alternative bands to break into the pop mainstream, Green Day was second only to Pearl Jam in terms of influence. At their core, Green Day were simply punk revivalists, recharging the energy of speedy, catchy three-chord punk-pop songs. Though their music wasn't particularly innovative, they brought the sound of late-'70s punk to a new, younger generation with *Dookie*, their 1994 major-label debut. Green Day wasn't able to sustain their sucess—*Dookie* sold over eight million, while its follow-up *Insomniac* only sold a quarter of its predecessor—yet their influence was far-reaching, since they opened the doors for a flood of American neo-punk, punk metal, and third-wave ska-revivalists. Led by childhood friends Billie Jo Armstrong and Mike Dirnt, the band had cultivated a cult following since their album debut, 1989's *39/Smooth*. The underground success of 1992's *Kerplunk* led to a wave of interest from major record labels, and Green Day's subsequent Reprise debut *Dookie* became a major hit in 1994 (thanks to MTV support for the initial single "Longview") and eventually sold eight million copies in America. Green Day quickly followed up *Dookie* in 1995 with *Insomniac*, an album that performed comparatively poorly (it sold only two million copies). The band spent much of 1996 resting and writing new material, issuing *Nimrod* in 1997. —*Stephen Thomas Erlewine*

1039/Smoothed Out Slappy Hour / 1991 / Lookout ✦✦✦

Kerplunk / Jan. 17, 1992 / Lookout ✦✦✦✦

● **Dookie** / Feb. 1, 1994 / Reprise ✦✦✦✦✦
Green Day couldn't have had a blockbuster without Nirvana, but *Dookie* wound up being nearly as revolutionary as *Nevermind*, sending a wave of imitators up the charts and setting the tone for the mainstream rock of the mid-'90s. Like *Nevermind*, this was accidental success, the sound of a promising underground group suddenly hitting its stride just as they got their first professional, big-budget, big-label production. Really, that's where the similarities end, since if Nirvana was indebted to the weirdness of indie rock, Green Day was a straight-ahead punk revivalist through and through. They were products of the underground pop scene kept alive by such protagonists as the Jam and Buzzcocks. On their first couple records, they showed promise, but with *Dookie*, they

delivered a record that found Billie Joe Armstrong bursting into full flower as a songwriter, spitting out melodic ravers that could have comfortable sat alongside *Singles Going Steady*, but infused with an ironic self-loathing popularized by Nirvana, whose clean sound on *Nevermind* is also emulated here. Where Nirvana had weight, Green Day is deliberately adolescent here, treating nearly everything as joke and having as much fun as snotty punkers should. They demonstrate a bit of depth with "When I Come Around," but that just varies the pace slightly, since the key to this is their flippant, infectious attitude—something they maintain throughout the record, making *Dookie* a stellar piece of modern punk that many tried to emulate but nobody bettered. *—Stephen Thomas Erlewine*

Insomniac / Oct. 10, 1995 / Reprise ✦✦✦✦
Dookie gave Green Day success, but it was never really clear whether they wanted it in the first place. However, given the incessantly catchy songwriting of Billie Joe, the success made sense. Green Day were traditionalists without realizing it, learning all of their tricks through secondhand records and second-generation California punk bands. They didn't change their sound in the slightest after signing to a major label, which meant that they couldn't revert back to a harsher, earlier sound as a way to shed their audience for *Dookie*'s follow-up, *Insomniac*. Instead, they kept their blueprint and made it a shade darker. Throughout *Insomniac*, there are vague references to the band's startling multi-platinum breakthrough, but the album is hardly a stark confessional on the level of Nirvana's *In Utero*. It's a collection of speedy, catchy songs in the spirit of the Buzzcocks, the Jam, the Clash, and the Undertones, but played with more minor chords and less melody and recorded with a bigger, hard rock-oriented production. While nothing on the album is as immediate as "Basket Case" or "Longview," the band has gained a powerful sonic punch, which goes straight for the gut but sacrifices the raw edge they so desperately want to keep and makes the record slightly tame. Billie Joe hasn't lost much of his talent for simple, tuneful hooks, but after a series of songs that all sound pretty much the same, it becomes clear that he needs to push himself a little bit more if Green Day ever wants to be something more than a good punk-pop band. As it is, they remain a good punk-pop band, and *Insomniac* is a good punk-pop record, but nothing more. *—Stephen Thomas Erlewine*

Nimrod / Oct. 14, 1997 / Reprise ✦✦✦
Following the cool reception to *Insomniac*, Green Day retreated from the spotlight for a year to rest and spend time with their families. During that extended break, they decided to not worry about their supposedly lost street credibility and make an album according to their instincts, which meant more experimentation and less of their trademark pop-punk. Of course, speedy, catchy punk is at the core of the group's sound, so there are plenty of familiar moments on the resultant album, *Nimrod*, but there are also new details that make the record an invigorating, if occasionally frustrating, listen. Although pop-punk is Green Day's forte, they sound the most alive on *Nimrod* when they're breaking away from their formula, whether it's the shuffling "Hitchin' a Ride," the bitchy, tongue-in-cheek humor of "The Grouch," the surging surf instrumental "Last Ride In," the punchy, horn-driven drag-queen saga "King for a Day," or acoustic, string-laced ballad "Good Riddance." It's only when the trio confines themselves to three chords that they sound tired, but Billie Joe has such a gift for hooky, instantly memorable melodies that even these moments are enjoyable, if unremarkable. Still, *Nimrod* suffers from being simply too much—although it clocks in at under 50 minutes, the 18 tracks whip by at such a breakneck speed that it leaves you somewhat dazed. With a little editing, Green Day's growth would have been put in sharper relief, and *Nimrod* would have been the triumphant leap forward it set out to be. As it stands, it's a muddled but intermittingly exciting record that is full of promise. *—Stephen Thomas Erlewine*

Warning / Oct. 3, 2000 / Adeline ✦✦✦✦✦
By 2000, Green Day had long been spurned as un-hip by the fourth-generation punks they popularized, and they didn't seem likely to replicate the MOR success of the fluke smash "Good Riddance (Time of Your Life)." Apparently, the success of that ballad freed the band from any classifications or stigmas, letting them feel like they could do anything they wanted on their fifth album, *Warning*. They responded by embracing their fondness for pop and making the best damn album they've ever made. There's a sense of fearlessness on *Warning*, as if the band didn't care if the album wasn't punk enough, or whether it produced a cross-platform hit. There are no ballads here, actually, and while there are a number of punchy, infectious rockers, the tempo is never recklessly breakneck. Instead, the focus is squarely on the songs, with the instrumentation and arrangements serving their needs. It's easy to say that Green Day has matured with this album, since they've never produced a better, more tuneful set of songs, or tried so many studio tricks and clever arrangements. However, that has the wrong connotation, since "mature" would indicate that *Warning* is a studious, carefully assembled album that's easier to admire than to love. That's not the case at all. This is gleeful, unabashed fun, even when Billie Joe Armstrong is getting a little cranky in his lyrics. It's fun to hear Green Day adopt a Beatlesque harmonica on "Hold On" or try out Kinks-ian music hall on "Misery," while still knocking out punk-pop gems and displaying melodic ingenuity and imaginative arrangements. *Warning* may not be an innovative record per se, but it's tremendously satisfying; it finds the band at a peak of songcraft and performance, doing it all without a trace of self-consciousness. It's the first great pure pop album of the new millennium. *—Stephen Thomas Erlewine*

Green on Red

f. 1981, Tucson, AZ, **db.** 1993
Americana, Paisley Underground, Roots Rock, Alternative Pop/Rock, College Rock
Always wary of their Paisley Underground tag, it was only Green on Red's debut EP that leaned on the psychedelic sounds of the '60s before they traded it in for a boozy, all-American sound. They have been credited as latter-day forbears to the No Depression sound forged by Wilco and Son Volt.

Singer and songwriter Dan Stuart, Chris Cacavas (keyboards), and Jack Waterson (bass) formed their first group in Tucson, AZ in 1979. Relocating to L.A., drummer Steve MacNicol joined up and the band released their debut EP on Steve Wynn's Down There label in 1982. By 1983, the band dumped the trippy psychedelic stuff for *Gravity Talks*, their Slash debut. By the time 1985's *Gas Food Lodging* rolled around and the band had added guitarist Chuck Prophet, they were earning critical accolades, but their greatest success came overseas with the release of 1985's *No Free Lunch* (Polygram). Between albums, Stuart paused to work with Steve Wynn and a smattering of their respective band members for their *Danny and Dusty* album, a record which allowed Stuart to play on his "drunken bum" persona. Prophet and Stuart continued to hone their darkish, down-and-out loser blues on *The Killer Inside Me* (1987, Mercury) and *Here Come the Snakes* (1989, Mercury), but by the time 1989's *This Time Around* (Mercury) came out, interest in their work stateside had ceased. Cacavas had since left the fold to begin what had become a consistent, albeit overlooked solo career. The Prophet/Stuart duo found an audience for their music in Europe for *Scapegoats* (1991, China) and *Too Much Fun* (1992, Off Beat), but ultimately traded in the madness of what had become their collaboration for quieter lives. Stuart relocated to Spain and Prophet continues the solo career he launched in 1990. His 1997 release *Homemade Blood* (Cooking Vinyl) bears little resemblence to the ramshackle outfit that was Green on Red. As it turns out, Prophet was a sleeper. *—Denise Sullivan*

EP / 1981 / Green on Red ✦✦✦
Chris Cacavas' organ drives the band's sound on this debut recording which pegged Green on Red as part of the Paisley Underground movement of L.A. bands devoted to '60s guitar rock. The swirling sound of "Death and Angels" and "Aspirin" sometimes recall the riffage of the Seeds and Love, thus the tag. But the band soon would shed its novice skin, so this EP turns out to be a neat curiousity. *—Denise Sullivan*

Green on Red / 1982 / Down There ✦✦✦

Gravity Talks / 1983 / Slash ✦✦✦✦
Green on Red's tinge of psychedelia was provided by Chris Cacavas' organ. But already, the band had traded in most psychedelic references for an Americana influence, along the lines of John Fogerty spiked with Roky Erickson. Completists might find they need it, but better work comes on the band's next record, *Gas Food Lodging*. *—Denise Sullivan*

Gas Food Lodging / 1985 / Enigma ✦✦✦✦
Much like their pals the Dream Syndicate, Green on Red used up nearly all their psychedelic influences early on, and 1985's *Gas Food Lodging* found Dan Stuart and company veering into country-inflected roots rock that dovetailed nicely with the populist themes Stuart had begun to explore in his lyrics. Opening with "That's What Dreams," a tough but moving first-person tale of a working man struggling to hold on to his dignity, *Gas Food Lodging* takes a long look at the sometimes-fractured state of the American psyche during the Reagan years, as seen through the eyes of a low-budget rock band out on the road. Of course, Dan Stuart's America is populated by drunks, losers, drifters, and psychopaths, but there's a genuine measure of compassion in his portrayal of this collection of lost souls, and this lineup of the band—with Chuck Prophet IV on guitar and Chris Cacavas on organ—created evocative music that added depth and detail to Stuart's grubby vision. *Gas Food Lodging* set a template for the music Green on Red would make in the future, but they rarely hit their targets as squarely as they did here; there's an emotional weight and a ring of truth to this material that missing from much of the band's later work, and while closing with "We Shall Overcome" might seem like an especially obvious gesture, through sheer bloodshot sincerity this band makes it work—and makes it genuinely moving. *Gas Food Lodging* is too loose and deliberately ramshackle to support the title of masterpiece, but calling it Green on Red's best album will do nicely. *—Mark Deming*

No Free Lunch / 1985 / One Way ✦✦✦
The critical hosannas lavished upon the album *Gas Food Lodging* earned Green on Red a major-label deal, though, with appropriate irony, this very American band found themselves contracted to the British branch of Polygram. The label's American imprint, Mercury, picked up their option several months after the group's big-label debut, *No Free Lunch*, was released in the U.K. An EP running a bit under 24 minutes (a later reissue padded it out to full length with a 13-minute blues workout on "Smokestack Lightning"), *No Free Lunch* covers territory not dissimilar to that on *Gas Food Lodging*; nomadic musicians on the road ("Keep on Moving" and the title cut), out-of-work sad sacks ("Honest Man"), families confronted with death and loss ("Jimmy Boy"), and the struggle to believe in something despite it all ("Time Ain't Nothing"). The band even throws in a pretty good cover of "Funny How Time Slips Away," and their performances are noticeably tighter and sharper than on their previous albums (the time on the road after *Gas Food Lodging* seems to have paid off), while the engineering by Steven Street and Simon Humphries is crisper and better detailed than the sometimes muddy tone of *Gas Food Lodging*. But while the band sounds game, the songs are good, and Dan Stuart is unusually strong voice (with the exception of "The Ballad of Guy Fawkes," where he lapses into a curious fake Brit accent, perhaps in tribute to his new corporate sponsors), at only seven songs *No Free Lunch* sounds oddly incomplete sounding less like a self-contained short work than an album that somehow didn't get finished. There's nothing wrong with what's here, but it's hard not to wish the band had made more of it at the time. *—Mark Deming*

The Killer Inside Me / 1987 / Mercury ✦✦✦
After the creative breakthrough of *Gas Food Lodging* and the surprising discovery that they responded well to a touch of production polish on *No Free Lunch*, Green on Red seemed poised to move on to new heights, both artistically and commercially, with their

first full-length for a major label, *The Killer Inside Me.* Jim Dickinson, noted R&B pianist and studio helpmate to such expressive eccentrics as Alex Chilton and Paul Westerberg, was tapped to produce, but while the pairing looked great on paper, the results sounded just a bit muddy and cluttered, lacking the tense clarity of *No Free Lunch* and the more organic sloppiness of *Gas Food Lodging.* While the musicians are a bit better focused here than on their earlier recordings, the overly boomy audio does little to flatter this band's newfound precision. As a singer, Dan Stuart long had a tendency toward sloppy histrionics when he wasn't held in check, and here Dickinson seemed content to let Stuart's performances go wherever they will, and with a chorus of far more gifted soul singers offering backup, his craggy tone and faux-wino bellowing have rarely sounded more obvious or less effective. Most importantly of all, *The Killer Inside Me* lacks material on a par with the two released that preceded it, and while Dan Stuart is too gifted a tunesmith to not come up with a few songs worth hearing (most notably "Mighty Gun," "We Ain't Free," and the title cut), many of these songs sounds like retreads of ideas Green on Red tackled more effectively in the past, and the album's darker tone often feels forced, without the faint hope of redemption that made *Gas Food Lodging* so powerful. While *The Killer Inside Me* isn't Green on Red's weakest album, it didn't live up to nearly anyone's expectations, and suggested this band's moment of glory might have been starting to fade away. *—Mark Deming*

Here Comes the Snakes / 1989 / Restless ✦✦✦✦
Produced by Jim Dickinson and Joe Hardy, Dan Stuart and Chuck Prophet finally cracked the Memphis sound by steeping themselves in the environment and surrounding themselves with the musicians who made their name there. From the get-go, Prophet's guitar is the cornerstone to the *Let It Bleed* mood that fires this record from "Keith Can't Read" throughout, though it ends up with the very Neil Young-like "D.T. Blues." *—Denise Sullivan*

Live at the Town & Country / 1989 / Polydor ✦✦

This Time Around / 1989 / Mercury ✦✦✦
The band was reduced to essentially a two-piece, Dan Stuart and Chuck Prophet, and some hired help, including Eagle Bernie Leadon. The album's best tracks are the slow ones; "Good Patient Woman" and the crawling "You Couldn't Get Arrested." Produced by Glyn Johns, it's an OK record; it's just that by this time Stuart's drunken-loser schtick has worn thin. Really thin. *—Denise Sullivan*

Scapegoats / 1991 / China ✦✦✦

● **The Best of Green on Red** / 1995 / China ✦✦✦✦✦

Gas Food Lodging/Green on Red / Jan. 15, 1996 / Mau Mau ✦✦✦✦✦

Green River

f. 1983, db. 1988
Grunge, Alternative Pop/Rock
In the mid-'80s, before the word grunge became a specific musical style, before Sub Pop was considered a training league for major labels, many post-punk fans didn't believe Seattle had a worthwhile musical scene. Green River helped change that. With their ugly, loud, sub-Stooges guitar grind, Green River was the first band to make Sub Pop a hip underground label. At their best, the band made powerful, brutal guitar rock that merged '70s heavy metal and '60s garage punk with '80s post-punk; at their worst, they were a sludgy, depressing mess.
    Green River was together for three years before the band splintered apart. Singer Mark Arm and occasional guitarist Steve Turner formed Mudhoney. Guitarist Stone Gossard and bassist Jeff Ament formed Mother Love Bone (who would eventually turn into Pearl Jam after the band's demise). The roots of Mudhoney's garage grunge and Pearl Jam's revisionist '70s hard rock can be heard on Green River's three EPs. *—Stephen Thomas Erlewine*

Come on Down / 1985 / Homestead ✦✦✦
Green River was the mid-'80s supergroup that introduced members of both Mudhoney and Pearl Jam to the alternative world. Despite their Seattle pedigree, this album is exactly what you would expect from a pairing of the two groups. Mudhoney fans will probably not like the heavy metal dynamics of the group, while Pearl Jam fans might not appreciate the raspy voice of Mark Arm and the sleazy guitar work from Steve Turner. But in reality, it is a good album from a band that never quite gelled together. "Come on Down" might be the best song here; with its descending riff and Arm's passionate wails, it sounds like a distant cousin to Mudhoney's "Here Comes Sickness." "Swallow My Pride" would go on to be their "biggest" song, featured on a few compilations and covered by the Fastbacks. Oddly enough, the version found here is not that exciting, mostly because Arm just does not sound like he cares. Although this problem arises a few more times, the rest of the album is like a heavy metal version of Mudhoney, which is not really a bad thing. Bassist Jeff Ament and guitarist Stone Gossard, both self-proclaimed Iron Maiden fans, wrote most of the riff-oriented music. Mark Arm keeps this from really going too far into metal territory with his Iggy-like screaming. But in the end, Green River is a worthwhile listen but not something that points towards the bright futures that its band members would enjoy. *—Bradley Torreano*

Dry as a Bone / 1986 / Sub Pop ✦✦✦
Arguably Green River's strongest individual release, *Dry as a Bone* finds the group perfecting their sleazy, raucous fusion of '70s hard rock and post-hardcore punk. *Dry as a Bone* was later combined with *Rehab Doll* for release as a two-fer, which remains the definitive Green River purchase. *—Steve Huey*

● **Rehab Doll/Dry As a Bone** / 1987 / Sub Pop ✦✦✦✦✦
Collecting Green River's second and third releases, plus three rare tracks, *Dry As a*

Bone/Rehab Doll is a near-definitive look at the Seattle band that, along with the Melvins and Soundgarden, virtually invented grunge. Out of all the bands that branched out from the Green River family tree, the originals sound most like Mudhoney upon first listen. That's due both to their punky aggression and the fact that Mark Arm's signature sneer is firmly in place. However, the differences reveal themselves rather quickly. Where Mudhoney was sort of the Ramones of grunge—their best material consisting of simple, catchy, highly similar garage rockers—Green River's instrumental attack was much more intricate and complex. That's because it was anchored by the inseparable team of guitarist Stone Gossard and bassist Jeff Ament, whose work here mixes the swagger of '70s hard rock (particularly Aerosmith) and the ferocity of hardcore punk. Melody and hooks aren't exactly Green River's strong point; their music gets over on straight-from-the-gutter attitude, kicking up a filthy, distorted racket punctuated by Arm's nauseous moan. Since *Dry As a Bone/Rehab Doll* is more energetic and less murky than many proto-grunge artifacts, it's arguably the most effective and enduring building block in the music's early evolution. *—Steve Huey*

Rehab Doll / 1988 / Sub Pop ✦✦✦
The final Green River release (with a fun rant through David Bowie's "Queen Bitch" on the cassette version) found the quintet switching from Jack Endino to another producer, resulting in a record that sounded caught somewhere between grunge mania and metal/corp rock folly. The weird thing is that the quality of the recording actually went down—Arm sounds like he's singing from across the room much of the time, for one thing. *Come On Down*'s utterly unsubtle "Swallow My Pride" resurfaces here in a new take, the Blue Oyster Cult-inspired "this ain't the summer of love" part actually coming across pretty well, as does most of the performance. Other moments of worth include moments of psychotic acoustic freakouts, Arm's voice providing most of said psychosis, and a slew of the song titles ("Porkfist," "One More Stitch"), but generally speaking, *Rehab Doll*, like Green River itself, is most noteworthy for what the people involved did next. *—Ned Raggett*

Al Green

b. Apr. 13, 1946, Forrest City, AR
Vocals / Smooth Soul, Memphis Soul, Pop-Soul, Contemporary Gospel, Soul
Al Green was the first great soul singer of the '70s and arguably the last great Southern soul singer. With his seductive singles for Hi Records in the early '70s, Green bridged the gap between deep soul and smooth Philadelphia soul. He incorporated elements of gospel, interjecting his performances with wild moans and wails, but his records were stylish, boasting immaculate productions that rolled along with a tight beat, sexy backing vocals, and lush strings. The distinctive Hi Records sound that the vocalist and producer Willie Mitchell developed made Al Green the most popular and influential soul singer of the early '70s, influencing not only his contemporaries, but also veterans like Marvin Gaye. Green was at the peak of his popularity when he suddenly decided to join the ministry in the mid-'70s. At first, he continued to record secular material, but by the '80s, he was concentrating solely on gospel. During the late '80s and '90s, he occasionally returned to R&B, but he remained primarily a religious performer for the rest of his career. Nevertheless, Green's classic early '70s recordings retained their power and influence throughout the decades, setting the standard for smooth soul. *—Stephen Thomas Erlewine*

Back Up Train / 1967 / Hot Line ✦✦✦
The album that launched the career of Al Green, the '70s reigning soul king and '80s gospel giant. While there were some problems with material, Al Green's smooth, soulful, exuberant voice quickly established him as a dominant, compelling artist. He also still had the buoyant, innocent quality that, unfortunately, time and personal problems ultimately wore away. *—Ron Wynn*

Green Is Blues / 1970 / The Right Stuff ✦✦✦
The first album linking the soul-singing greatness of Al Green with the production brilliance and expertise of Willie Mitchell. The results were mutually beneficial; Green got the great production, arrangements, and backing from the Hi Rhythm section that often turned good songs into classics, and he sang with the conviction and talent that provided the final component in an artistically and commercially satisfying union. *—Ron Wynn*

Gets Next to You / 1971 / The Right Stuff ✦✦✦✦✦
After the shaky start of *Green Is Blues*, Al Green and producer Willie Mitchell established their classic sound with Green's second album, *Gets Next to You.* The main difference is in the rhythm section. Abandoning the gritty syncopations of deep Southern soul, the Hi Rhythm Section plays it slow and seductive, working a sultry, steady pulse that Green exploits with his remarkable voice. Alternating between Sam Cooke's croon and Otis Redding's shout, Green develops his own distinctive style, and *Gets Next to You* only touches the surface of its depth. Although the album is filled with wonderful moments, few are as astonishing as Green and Mitchell's reinterpretation of the Temptations' "I Can't Get Next to You," which turns the original inside out. *—Stephen Thomas Erlewine*

☆ **Let's Stay Together** / Feb. 1972 / The Right Stuff ✦✦✦✦✦
Prior to this album, Al Green never had a number one song. The title track, "Let's Stay Together," achieved that status and held it for nine consecutive weeks. Green's ingenuity produced one of the all-time classics, which has the bounce of a dance cut and the passion of a ballad. The dynamic soul singer's whispers, animated cries, and riffing enhance his already stirring delivery. This album was sold on the strength of the title track as there were no other selections to grace the Billboard charts. However, this album includes the timeless gem "How Can You Mend a Broken Heart" and lesser-known beauties like the exulting "Judy," the cookin' testimonial "I Never Found a Girl," and the soothing blues effort "It Ain't No Fun to Me." The Arkansas native and his creative partner Willie Mitchell

season these selections with lucid rhythm arrangements complemented by the faint strums of a guitar and brawn, unchiding horns. —*Craig Lytle*

☆ **I'm Still in Love With You** / Dec. 1972 / The Right Stuff ✦✦✦✦✦
I'm Still in Love With You shares many surface similarities to its predecessor, *Let's Stay Together*, from Al Green and Willie Mitchell's distinctive, sexy style to the pacing and song selection. Despite those shared traits, *I'm Still in Love With You* distinguishes itself with its suave, romantic tone and its subtly ambitious choice of material. Green began exploring country music with this album, performing a startling version of Kris Kristofferson's "For the Good Times," as well as a wonderful, slow reinterpretation of Roy Orbison's "Oh Pretty Woman." And the soul numbers are more complex than they would appear—listen to how the beat falls together at the beginning of "Love and Happiness," or the sly melody of the title track. There isn't a wasted track on *I'm Still in Love with You*, and in many ways it rivals its follow-up *Call Me* as Green's masterpiece. —*Stephen Thomas Erlewine*

☆ **Call Me** / Jul. 1973 / The Right Stuff ✦✦✦✦✦
Al Green reached his creative peak with the brilliant *Call Me*, the most inventive and assured album of his career. So silky and fluid as to sound almost effortless, Green's vocals revel in the lush strings and evocative horns of Willie Mitchell's superbly intimate production, barely rising above an angelic whisper for the gossamer "Have You Been Making Out O.K."; with barely perceptible changes in mood, *Call Me* covers remarkable ground, spanning from "Stand Up"—a call to arms delivered with characteristic understatement—to renditions of Hank Williams' "I'm So Lonesome I Could Cry" and Willie Nelson's "Funny How Time Slips Away," both of them exemplary fusions of country and soul. Equally compelling are the album's three Top Ten hits—"You Ought to Be With Me," "Here I Am (Come and Take Me)," and the shimmering title cut. A classic. —*Jason Ankeny*

Livin' for You / Dec. 1973 / The Right Stuff ✦✦✦
Starting in 1971 with his release *Al Green Gets Next to You*, Green's albums became necessities. *Livin' for You* is Green's sixth album and the fourth one to be certified gold. The predecessor, the classic *Call Me*, was still on the charts when this was released. As a testament to Green and producer Willie Mitchell's innovative skills, *Livin' for You* does not attempt to make a formulaic follow-up. All of Green's albums with Mitchell are singular and have their own distinct style. *Livin' for You* is no exception and takes a more relaxed approach and offers some of his best ballads. The title track is Green at his most engaging, even when he sang potentially mood-interrupting lines like, "I'm tired of your bright ideas about leaving me." "Home Again" and "So Good to Be Here" both are romantic if not hypnotic, offering subtle drumming, economical keyboards, and gentle vocals. The biggest track here, the proficient and smooth "Let's Get Married" has Green being a little wishy-washy as he sings, "I didn't mean to say all the things I said/The way I felt in my heart it came out that way." The song's grievances are worked out as he makes a few utterances that proved he was having "fun." Although the originals here rank with his best, Green also did good cover work here, too. The often useless "Unchained Melody" shows up here and benefits from Green's methodical delivery. In many ways, *Livin' for You* is the perfect, intimate album for his fans. —*Jason Elias*

Al Green Explores Your Mind / 1974 / The Right Stuff ✦✦✦✦
By this point, this version of the Memphis sound was the production style for only a handful of artists. With producer Willie Mitchell's lighter touch for his most famous artist, this is all but crafted into the Al Green sound. Despite his skills, Green never falls into mannerism here and gives heartfelt and cogent vocals rooted in intelligence and technique. *Al Green Explores Your Mind* is Green's fifth gold album, and marks the point when he was the reigning sex symbol in music. "Sha-La-La (Make Me Happy)," although lyrically slight, has the artist's charisma and Mitchell's pop chops. As that song was the big single, *Explores Your Mind* also includes a song that has taken on a life of its own. With its perfect backing from Hi Rhythm and a horn and string arrangement, "Take Me to the River" has Green at his most persuasive. Despite the most notable tracks, this set is not so much perfect song but amazing cohesion and a testament to the artist's vocal prowess. "Hangin' On'" has an airy arrangement and derives its strength from the beautifully sung chorus. The last track, "School Days," has Green longing for a school girlfriend and despite the potentially sappy sentiment, it works like a charm. *Explores Your Mind*'s greatness comes from a collective effort, including James Mitchell's dreamlike string arrangements and the always skilled backing vocals of Rhodes, Chalmers, and Rhodes. But the biggest draw here is Green's phrasing and intimate vocals, which makes *Explores Your Mind* an extremely strong effort. —*Jason Elias*

★ **Al Green's Greatest Hits** / Apr. 1975 / The Right Stuff ✦✦✦✦✦
Upon its original release in 1975, *Al Green's Greatest Hits* pretty much summed up everything about Green, containing his ten biggest hits up to that point. A few years later, it was followed by a second volume, which contained hit singles that charted since the release of the first collection. In 1995, the Right Stuff reissued *Al Green's Greatest Hits*, adding five of the highlights from the second volume of greatest hits as bonus tracks. The result was a definitive single-disc compilation, featuring 15 of Green's absolute best songs, including "Tired of Being Alone," "Let's Stay Together," "I'm Still in Love With You," "Call Me," "Here I Am," "Sha-La-La (Make Me Happy)," "L-O-V-E (Love)." The original version of *Greatest Hits* was great, but the revision made it nearly perfect. —*Stephen Thomas Erlewine*

Al Green Is Love / Oct. 1975 / The Right Stuff ✦✦✦✦
In a short time, Al Green became a premier singer in R&B and pop. With songs like "Look What You've Done for Me" and "Here I Am (Come and Take Me)," among many others, Green and producer Willie Mitchell refined the sounds of each genre. As *Al Green Explores Your Mind* was the peak of Green's insouciance, *Al Green Is Love* finds a starker reality as the majority of the tracks here are ruminative but not always coherent. More often that not, every utterance here from Green is extremely entertaining. The first track, the propulsive "L-O-V-E (Love)," would be even more believable if Green didn't sound so ambivalent. Other up-tempo tracks, "I Gotta Be More" and "Rhymes" are edgy and dark and have great riffs from guitarist Mabon Hodges. The cutesy "Oh Me Oh My (Dreams in My Arms)" represents the only false moment. The heart of *Al Green Is Love* is the ballads. Green's not too happy here, however, and those looking for heartwarming thoughts on romance won't find it here. "The Love Sermon" and the even better "I Didn't Know" both are spare and have dirge-like paces that give Green a great opportunity to turn in raw and emotion-filled performances. "I Wish You Were Here" and "Could I Be the One" have producer Willie Mitchell offering suitably bleak arrangements to go with Green's airy vocals. The best track here, "There Is Love" strikes a balance between the customary production grace and the album's pervading sorrow. *Al Green Is Love* might be too depressing for some, but his fans will find Green's truthfulness appealing and some of the songs among his best. —*Jason Elias*

Full of Fire / Apr. 1976 / The Right Stuff ✦✦✦
Full of Fire is the second to last '70s effort that Green co-produced with Willie Mitchell. Even at this time, their work preceded them. Albums including *I'm Still in Love With You*, *Call Me*, and *Al Green Explorers Your Mind* spotlighted Green's skill at doing songs filled with romance and longing. The subtext to most of the work, however, was sex. That being said, *Full of Fire* has Green less concerned with matters of the heart and more centered on his burgeoning religious nature. Although that may seem slightly boring, this effort is better structured and, as a whole, comes off even better than *Al Green Is Love* did. The first track, "Glory, Glory," sneaks in religion so deftly that even Willie Mitchell probably didn't even get it until the track was done. One of the few romantic tracks, the sweet and old-fashioned "Always" has him in coming on soft with much charm. "I'd Fly Away" and "Soon as I Get Home" both have Green fantasizing about heaven, but they are more spacey rather than morbid. Green's changing priority rings loud and clear on one particular song. His take on of Buck Owens' "Together Again" doesn't exactly have Green over the top with emotion, and it works less effectively than his previous country & western covers. The last track, the hard-edged "Let It Shine" is enlivened by Howard Grimes' patently surprising drumming. Although Green doesn't seem to be all here on *Full of Fire*, his co-production with Mitchell and the playing of Hi Rhythm makes this an essential offering. —*Jason Elias*

Have a Good Time / Dec. 1976 / Hi ✦✦✦
Al Green was riding right along, still singing with confidence, power, and authority. Although this was kind of a transition effort, with Green beginning to head toward gospel, his vocals retained their edge and relaxed fire. Mitchell and Hi Rhythm did their usual excellent supporting job. —*Ron Wynn*

The Belle Album / Dec. 1977 / The Right Stuff ✦✦✦✦
Al Green severed his ties with longtime producer Willie Mitchell in 1977, establishing his own backup band and seizing the production reins. But he hadn't yet made the final break with soul; this was the last secular work he would make for many years, and it was brilliant, even though it didn't come close to equaling his previous commercial heights. In retrospect, many just didn't understand where he was going, while others were turned off by the blurred lyrical focus of songs like "Belle." But "I Feel Good" had as much danceable energy and soulful fire as any Green up-tempo tune, and "Lovin' You" and "Dream" were sorely underrated compositions. —*Ron Wynn*

Truth & Time / 1978 / Hi ✦✦✦
Returning to the formula of his classic Hi albums, Al Green assembled a fine collection of originals and covers for *Truth & Time*. Although Green is in good voice, and his version of "Say a Little Prayer" is impressive, the album feels a bit like a holding pattern, simply repeating ideas that were more fruitful the first time around. Given the generally listless nature of *Truth & Time* and the way Green sounds vaguely uninterested in the material, it's not a surprise that it was his last secular record for a very long time. —*Stephen Thomas Erlewine*

The Lord Will Make a Way / 1980 / Myrrh ✦✦✦

Tokyo Live / 1981 / The Right Stuff ✦✦✦✦

Higher Plane / Feb. 1981 / Hi ✦✦✦✦

He Is the Light / 1985 / A&M ✦✦✦

Love Ritual / 1989 / MCA ✦✦✦

I Get Joy / May 1989 / A&M ✦✦✦

One in a Million / 1990 / Word ✦✦✦✦✦
A compilation from Green's gospel recordings, it reveals the emotional depth of his religious work. —*Brian Mansfield*

The Supreme Al Green: The Greatest Hits / 1992 / Hi ✦✦✦✦✦
Released by the British division of Hi, *Supreme Al Green: The Greatest Hits* is a terrific 18-track collection that contains almost all of Green's hits, including "Tired of Being Alone," "Call Me," "I'm Still In Love With You," "Let's Stay Together," "I Can't Get Next to You," "Love and Happiness," "Sha-La-La (Make Me Happy)," "Take Me to the River," and "How Can You Mend a Broken Heart." Although it inexplicably overlooks "Here I Am (Come and Take Me)" and contains a bit too much latter-day material for some tastes, it's still one of the best single-disc collections yet assembled on Green, rivaling the revamped *Greatest Hits* the Right Stuff released in the mid-'90s. —*Stephen Thomas Erlewine*

Love Is Reality / 1992 / Word/Epic ✦✦✦
After years of refusing to sing anything but gospel, Green decided the time had finally come to fuse the godly and the secular elements of his soul. *Love Is Reality* made an overt play for the mainstream R&B market. Unfortunately, Christian dance-pop producer Tim

Miner works from formulas, while Green runs on inspiration. Green sounded great, but the final result paled in comparison to the rest of his catalog. *—Brian Mansfield*

Your Heart's in Good Hands / Nov. 7, 1995 / MCA ♦♦♦
Designed as Al Green's triumphant comeback to the R&B mainstream, *Your Heart's in Good Hands* is a mixed blessing. Although Green's voice is still astonishing, the album is undermined by a sterile urban R&B production that fails to capture the sensuality inherent in his music. As a result, *Your Heart's in Good Hands* is quite frustrating—you can hear Green hit new heights with his performance, but the music is constantly reined in by the lifeless production and the lackluster songs. *—Stephen Thomas Erlewine*

Anthology / Feb. 11, 1997 / Capitol ♦♦♦
Theoretically, an Al Green box set should be easy to assemble, given the overall excellence of his material, but the four-disc *Anthology* is a botch job. Instead of simply condensing the best of Green's prolific output, including all of the hits, the compilers were concerned with telling a story—literally. Three of the discs are spiked with lengthy interview segments; furthermore, most of the rarities are concert tracks, which means classics like "I Can't Get Next to You," "How Can You Mend a Broken Heart," "Love and Happiness," and "Sha-La-La (Make Me Happy)" are presented in inferior live versions. The live cuts, interviews, and rarities cut severely into the set's pacing, and they don't make *Anthology* useful for the fan that wants one, definitive collection—their appeal is solely for collectors, who already have the material elsewhere. Consequently, *Anthology* isn't useful for either the casual or dedicated fan, both of whom would be better off with the original albums and the *Greatest Hits* collection, which does contain the essence of Al Green, and most of his hits, on one disc. *—Stephen Thomas Erlewine*

More Greatest Hits / Jan. 27, 1998 / Right Stuff ♦♦♦♦
For its 1995 reissue, the Right Stuff revamped Al Green's *Greatest Hits*, adding five bonus tracks, four of which were featured on the original *Greatest Hits, Vol. 2*. As a result, when it came time to reissue *Greatest Hits, Vol. 2*, the Right Stuff decided to replace it with *More Greatest Hits*, since they would simply be replicating a good portion of their previous collection. However, *More Greatest Hits* isn't exactly the perfect supplement to *Greatest Hits*. Combining minor hits, album tracks, and rarities, the collection doesn't have the cohesiveness of its predecessor. Furthermore, tracks like "Back Up Train" (his first charting single, previously available only on the box set), the long version of "Let's Stay Together" (exclusive to this compilation), and 1968's "Guilty" are strong, but are mainly here to bait collectors, while his latter-day duets with Al B. Sure ("As Long As We're Together") and Lyle Lovett ("Funny How Time Slips Away") pale next to "Livin' for You" and "Love and Happiness," two highlights from *Vol. 2* that are curiously missing here. Even with these flaws, *More Greatest Hits* does contain more than its share of great moments—no Green collection is complete without "Take Me to the River," "For the Good Times," and "How Can You Mend a Broken Heart"—and in that sense, it acts as a nice supplement to the expanded *Greatest Hits*. Nevertheless, it doesn't act as a substitute for such classic albums as *Call Me* and *I'm Still in Love With You*, which is where anyone digging deeper into Green's catalog should start after they've exhausted *Greatest Hits*. *—Stephen Thomas Erlewine*

Hi And Mighty: The Story Of Al Green (1969-1978) / Oct. 27, 1998 / Hi ♦♦♦♦♦
This 37-track CD covers Green's work from 1969-78. This import takes tracks from all of Green's 69-78 recordings and is in chronological order. All of the big hits are here except for 1972's "Look What You've Done for Me," and although that omission is glaring, it's the only misstep. Due to the no-frills mix of this entire project, tracks like the single version of "Let's Stay Together" and "I'm Still in Love With You" closely resemble the way they originally sounded. *Hi And Mighty-The Story Of Al Green (1969-78)* also warmly brings together tracks that usually don't show up on Green compilations. Patented album tracks "What a Wonderful Thing Love Is" and the perfect "Funny How Time Slips Away" give a listener a sense of who Green is, more so than say, "Love and Happiness" or "How Can You Mend a Broken Heart." Those two tracks are included here as well. Disc two covers his 74-78 work. This set also earns raves for showing all aspects of Green's personas. The nervous ballads "The Love Sermon" and a single B-side "Strong As Death (Sweet As Love)" both have Green coming unhinged as his eccentricity began to reign supreme. Although this can't make any of the tracks from *Have a Good Time* sound any more useful than they are, this set takes four tracks from 1977's *The Belle Album*. His first set without Willie Mitchell finds Green sounding renewed on the best tracks "Belle" and the awe-inspiring "Loving You." Although there are no doubt more technologically savvy compilations available, *Hi And Mighty-The Story Of Al Green* attains the cohesion inherent in Green's best work. *—Jason Elias*

Master Hits: Al Green / Jul. 27, 1999 / Arista ♦♦♦♦
Most of the entries in Arista's *Heritage Master Hits* series are good compilations, but Al Green's volume is different—and it's a distinction Green fanatics will be eager to embrace. His *Arista Heritage Master Hits* is a remastered reissue of his debut album, *Back Up Train*, which was previously unavailable on CD. The record wasn't a masterpiece, yet it wasn't bad at all, showing that Green's talent was blindingly evident even at the inception of his career. This is a grittier sound than his classic Hi recordings, which doesn't always suit Green's sweet vocals, and the songs are a little spotty. Nevertheless, the album is highly enjoyable, especially for the hardcore fans that have been longing for this record to finally be available on CD. And to make a good package even nicer, the disc boasts two previously unreleased songs from the sessions: "What's It All About" and "A Lover's Hideaway." *—Stephen Thomas Erlewine*

Greatest Gospel Hits / Mar. 28, 2000 / Capitol ♦♦♦
If you like Al Green's gospel material but are hesitant to check this out since there was a previous best-of-Green's-gospel compilation—*One in a Million*—there are a few good reasons not to be wary. Right off the bat, it should be clear that there is little duplication between *Greatest Gospel Hits* and *One in a Million*, as only two songs from the latter ("Amazing Grace" and "Where Love Rules") are on the former. Also, *Greatest Gospel Hits* has 17 tracks, whereas *One in a Million* only has ten. Plus, it definitely seems as though *Greatest Gospel Hits* has been conceived as a more accessible introduction to Green's gospel world: *One in a Million* was heavy on spiritual standards, while *Greatest Gospel Hits* leans toward gospel with a soul bent. That's evidenced by the greater presence of more contemporary material, including songs written or co-written by Green, and covers of Bill Withers' "Lean on Me" and Curtis Mayfield's "People Get Ready." The chronological span is also wider, covering 1974-1995, although the focus is largely upon his 1980s work. As for the music, there are two ways of looking at this. One is that it's going to have far more secular appeal than most gospel, since Green is an excellent soul singer in both the pop and gospel contexts and uses much the same style in gospel as he did on his classic soul sides. On the other hand, it's the 1970s soul records that are stronger, musically speaking, and which will be preferred by most casual listeners, even if his vocals on the gospel sides are equal in ability and command to those on the soul discs. It's still a decent overview, particularly for those who want a taste of Green's gospel material without getting deep into his gospel catalog. *—Richie Unterberger*

The Hi Singles: A's and B's / Aug. 15, 2000 / Hi ♦♦♦♦♦
A marvelous idea that hopefully other companies emulate, these 43-tracks feature both sides of Al Green's Hi Records singles, in sequence. The uneven number of tracks (43), suggests that a track or two might have served double duty as the flip side of more than one single. The engaging B-sides include "Wish You Were Here," "What Am I Gonna Do With Myself," "All Because," "Ride Sally Ride," "I'm Glad You're Mine," "Old Time Lovin'," "What a Wonderful Thing Love Is," and "School Days." The A-sides are familiar to everyone: "Lets Stay Together," the Beatles' remake "I Want to Hold Your Hand," and "Tired of Being Alone." Some excellent album cuts like "Have You Been Making Out Okay" didn't fit the format so there's more Green to get to complete your library of one of the all-time greats. *—Andrew Hamilton*

Take Me to the River / Sep. 12, 2000 / Capitol ♦♦♦♦♦
As this two-CD best-of draws wholly from Green's prime as a Hi artist, and, as it contains almost everything from his *Greatest Hits* collection, one might reasonably assume that it's a good investment for those looking for a greatest hits anthology that's deeper than the single-disc *Greatest Hits*. Generally that's true, but there are some shortcomings to the packaging that might give you pause. The version of "Sha-La-La (Make Me Happy)" here is a live performance, not the original studio one, and his 1975 Top 30 hit "Full of Fire" (which *is* on *Greatest Hits*) is missing. It's also too bad that no original release dates are given for specific tracks in the sleeve notes and that the cuts are only sort of sequenced chronologically. This does have almost all of his Top 40 hits and some significant songs that are not on *Greatest Hits*, particularly "Take Me to the River" itself and his cover of "How Can You Mend a Broken Heart." Still, the material present on this collection that is not on *Greatest Hits* is definitely not as essential as his big single. If you're just concerned with whether this is a good collection of major soul music, of course it is, covering virtually all of Green's major highlights and then some. *—Richie Unterberger*

Testify: The Best of the A&M Years / Sep. 25, 2001 / A&M ♦♦♦

Norman Greenbaum

b. Nov. 20, 1942, Malden, MA

Vocals, Guitar / AM Pop, Jesus Rock, Soft Rock

Best known for his 1970 hit "Spirit in the Sky," singer/songwriter Norman Greenbaum was born November 20, 1942 in Malden, MA. He began his musical career while a student at Boston University, playing area coffeehouses before relocating to the West Coast during the mid-1960s and forming a kind of psychedelic jug band dubbed Dr. West's Medicine Show and Junk Band. After issuing the 1966 single "The Eggplant That Ate Chicago," which fell just shy of reaching the Top 50, the group disbanded, and Greenbaum subsequently formed a series of short-lived acts before finally returning to his solo career in 1968. A year later he issued his debut LP, *Spirit in the Sky*, releasing several unsuccessful singles before reaching the Top Three with the smash title track, which sold some two million copies. It proved to be Greenbaum's only hit, however, as follow-ups like 1970's "Canned Ham" and the next year's "California Earthquake" tanked; after the release of 1972's *Petaluma*, he retreated from music to focus on his California dairy farm, but returned to show business during the mid-1980s in a managerial capacity, also promoting a number of concerts. *—Jason Ankeny*

● **The Best of Norman Greenbaum: Spirit in the Sky** / Oct. 10, 1995 / Varese Sarabande ♦♦♦♦♦

"Spirit in the Sky" was a classic one-shot hit: an unforgettable fuzz guitar riff, those eerie descending glissando psychedelic guitar effects, a soulful female backup chorus, and a rare gospel-rock song that explored a religious theme without sounding dogmatic or sappy. Greenbaum had more depth than the usual one-shot artist, but the fact is that he never came up with anything else remotely on the level of "Spirit in the Sky," as this 15-song anthology demonstrates. He was a witty, droll songwriter with slightly absurd tunes that didn't quite descend into novelty, as on "Canned Ham" and "The Day the Well Went Dry." Selections from his early-'70s Reprise albums comprise most of half of this disc, and they're amiable, mildly humorous good-time rock that isn't even as penetrating as the rawer and goofier stuff he did before his solo career as the leader of Dr. West's Medicine Show and Junk Band. Four Dr. West songs are on this CD, including the minor 1966 hit "The Eggplant That Ate Chicago," as well as a previously unreleased 1977 recording, "The Day They Sold Beer in Church." *—Richie Unterberger*

Clive Gregson

b. Jan. 4, 1955
Vocals, Guitar / Contemporary Folk, Adult Alternative Pop/Rock, Folk-Rock, Singer/Songwriter

Clive Gregson and Christine Collister were the most moving and memorable U.K. folk-rock duo to emerge since Richard and Linda Thompson. Gregson's wry tales of the ins and outs of love, sung in Collister's heartbreaking voice have earned the duo (and subsequent solo work) respect and a devoted following though commercial success and mainstream recognition have eluded them. Gregson was the founder of Any Trouble, a pub rock/new wave quartet, in Manchester in 1975. The band's sound, and Gregson's songwriting and singing, reminded some of Elvis Costello, and Any Trouble was signed by Stiff, Costello's label. The band made several well-remembered but poor-selling albums, then split up in 1984. That same year Gregson discovered Collister singing in a folk club and, impressed by her talents, he offered to work with her on future projects. In 1985, Gregson made a solo album, *Strange Persuasions*, with Collister singing backup on a few tracks. The two began performing as a duo on the folk club circuit shortly thereafter. The duo's first release was a homemade tape sold at gigs, later released as *Home and Away*. It was followed by their first formal album, *Mischief*, in 1987, and by *A Change in the Weather* in 1989. *Love Is a Strange Hotel*, released later the same year, was an album of cover versions of Gregson and Collister's favorite songs. By 1992, the stress of constant touring and working together without substantial success finally took its toll on them. The two decided to go their separate ways after one parting shot, *The Last Word*, and one final tour. They both continued on as solo acts. *—Chris Woodstra and William Ruhlmann*

Strange Persuasions / 1985 / Compass ✦✦✦
Strange Persuasions came out in England in 1985, but it wasn't released in North America until 1995. After leaving his group, Any Trouble, Gregson made a name for himself in the States as a member of Richard Thompson's band and later as half of the Gregson and Collister duo. *Strange Persuasions* provides a missing link between his pub/pop days with Any Trouble and the more subtle, folkier tendencies of his later work. Some tracks sound like big L.A. pop productions with a dash of Squeeze thrown in, while others, "Jewel in Your Crown," for example, offer his sophisticated ballad writing. Perhaps this is what Ralph McTell would have sounded like had he chosen a more produced musical road; the melodies are often rooted firmly in the late-'60s and '70s folk singer/songwriter genre with enough pop sense to things interesting. While there is nothing revelatory here—Gregson would perfect the formula later—*Strange Persuasions* is a good album. *—Chris Woodstra and Richard Meyer*

Home and Away / 1986 / Flying Fish ✦✦✦✦
Home and Away is a collection of songs recorded during an early acoustic tour in 1986—originally a cassette-only release to be sold at gigs, reportedly it cost under $60 to make. Despite the low budget and seemingly disposable nature of a release like this, the album has become a favorite among fans for its faithfull representation of the duo's charming acoustic shows. The duo run through new originals, some songs from Gregson's Any Trouble days, and a few well-chosen covers in a warm, intimate setting. *—Chris Woodstra*

Mischief / 1987 / Rhino ✦✦✦✦
Clive Gregson's songs treat romance with ironic charm: "We're Not Over Yet" is a compendium of reasons why they ought to be over, and "Everybody Cheats on You" is about more than just romantic infidelity. Christine Collister gives the songs a depth that often keeps them from being a bit too glib and clever, as do the folk-pop arrangements. *—William Ruhlmann*

● **A Change in the Weather** / 1989 / Rhino ✦✦✦✦✦
The self-insight continues in Gregson's lyrics, but the concerns are expanded. Collister does a fine job covering "Tryin' to Get to You." *—William Ruhlmann*

Welcome to the Workhouse / 1990 / Special Delivery ✦✦✦✦✦
Welcome to the Workhouse is a collection of Gregson's home demos and outtakes and while most albums of this sort appeal only to the diehard fans, this one stands out as one of his finest recorded moments, working surprisingly well as an album. The recordings span 1980 to 1985 and provide a good bridge between his work with Any Trouble and his partnership with Christine Collister. *—Chris Woodstra*

Love Is a Strange Hotel / Nov. 1990 / Rhino ✦✦✦
A departure from the expansive arrangements of the previous two albums, *Love Is a Strange Hotel* is a low key acoustic collection of covers. Even unlikely choices, like Aztec Camera's "How Men Are" and 10cc's "Things We Do for Love" are pulled off in their own subtle and charming way. *—Chris Woodstra*

The Last Word / Mar. 24, 1992 / Rhino ✦✦✦✦
By 1992, the Gregson and Collister team had fallen apart, and the two had decided to record one more album before calling it quits. *Last Word* gives all the intimate details of a dissolving relationship, packed with real emotion and a dignified, stylish execution. In many ways, the duo tied things up with the high point of their career—their extraordinary harmonies and cool mix of folk, jazz, country, and blues have never sounded better. And though the subject matter doesn't stray far from Gregson's usual themes, knowing the circumstances of the recording brings a new dimension to the songs, making the statements all the more powerful and touching. *—Chris Woodstra*

Carousel of Noise / 1995 / Gregsongs ✦✦✦
This mail-order-only "official bootleg" release serves as something of a sequel to *Home and Away*, this time with Gregson alone tackling old favorites like the Any Trouble classic "Second Choice" in an intimate live setting. As with *Home and Away*, *Carousel of Noise* is a charming document, essential for his devoted following. *—Chris Woodstra*

People & Places / Apr. 25, 1995 / Compass ✦✦✦
One hears more of Elvis Costello and Richard Thompson's influence on this release. Still the songs are strong and the production crisp with enough unusual dynamics to keep you listening. His literate lyrics are short domestic stories told in a generally straightforward way ("Mary's Divorce" or "My Eyes Gave the Game Away"). The Ralph McTell comparison still stands, and it's meant as a compliment. *—Richard Meyer*

I Love This Town / Aug. 20, 1996 / Compass ✦✦✦✦
Clive Gregson's solo work and collaborations with Christine Collister were marked by craftsmanlike quality, always subtle and tasteful. Despite the remarkable consistency of his output, there was always an unspoken desire for him to return to the pop days of Any Trouble among elements of his fan base. With *I Love This Town*, Gregson makes this return, pulling out a batch of upbeat, musically irresistible tunes. Certainly the album is more AAA-oriented than the new wave/pub rock of the Any Trouble days, but the change of pace is a welcomed one. *—Chris Woodstra*

Happy Hour / Mar. 23, 1999 / Compass ✦✦✦
Recorded at his home studio in Nashville, *Happy Hour* is a do-it-yourself collection of 13 new originals produced and performed by Clive Gregson. The arrangements are kept sparse and simple, built around guitar or piano accompaniment with light touches of bass, keyboards, guitar, percussion, harmonica, and on the opener, "I Get What I Deserve," banjo. Anything but happy, *Happy Hour* is a dark, somber, yet intelligent and honest look at love, life, and longing, beautifully wrapped in Gregson's fetching melodies. It's to his credit that he's able to sustain this mood without becoming tiresome or falling into confessional self-pity. Because of the dour themes and stark, laid-back sound, some of the songs may take a few listenings to distinguish themselves, though a little time spent will reward you with a number of small gems. *—Brett Hartenbach*

Grifters

f. Memphis, TN
Indie Rock, Lo-Fi, Alternative Pop/Rock

If Guided by Voices are the Beatles of the mid-'90s lo-fi scene, then the Grifters' big, bluesy racket could certainly qualify as the Stones. Deliberately noisy, sloppy, and out-of-tune, the band masks their melodies under a heavy static fuzz of distortion. Based in Memphis and definitely influenced by their surroundings, the Grifters recall as well the proto-lo-fi musings of Royal Trux and Half Japanese—unlike GbV, who arrived at the lo-fi sound by simply recording pop songs at home on sub-standard equipment. Formed in the late '80s, initially as a band Called Bud, with vocalist/guitarist Scott Taylor, bassist Tripp Lamkins, and drummer Dave Shouse, the band released only a single and an obscure tape consisting of front-room recordings. By the turn of the decade, Shouse had begun sharing songwriting and guitar chores with Taylor, while Stan Gallimore replaced him on drums. The four-piece debuted on vinyl with the 1990 single "Disfigurehead" on Doink Records. In 1992, the band issued their debut album, *So Happy Together*, on the evidently like-minded Sonic Noise label. The LP continued the Sonic Youth approach to punk prevalent on the initial recordings, though the following year's *One Sock Missing* showed a more mature Grifters—that is, the songs were slower, but no less skewered with distortion and tape splices. The album was the first released on their own Shangri-La label, which has also issued a single from A Band Called Bud as well as recordings from Taylor's side-project, Hot Monkey.

With the ascension of Pavement and the emergence of Guided by Voices, the lo-fi scene became much more viable by 1994, especially in the world of indie rock. The Grifters' third album, *Crappin' You Negative*, emphasized the bluesy swagger that had been only understated before, and with the addition of somewhat proper melodies—actually the repetition of jagged riffs—the album became an underground hit. The band signed with Sub Pop later that year, and after the release of 1995's *Eureka* EP, issued *Ain't My Lookout* in 1996. *Full Blown Possession* followed in 1997. *—John Bush*

So Happy Together / 1992 / Sonic Noise ✦✦✦

One Sock Missing / 1993 / Shangri-La ✦✦✦✦
Certainly the most low-key (if not lo-fi) of the Grifters' early records, 1993's *One Sock Missing* is less noisy and aggressive than its immediate predecessor, *So Happy Together*, but that doesn't mean it's mellow. Not even close, in fact. The Memphis foursome play with the swaggering-and-staggering intensity of the circa-'84 Replacements channeling the circa-'68 Stones, and for once, the lo-fi pretense (abrupt fade-outs, jerky tape splices, audible coughs and background noise, more distortion than a Sonic Youth record) actually enhances the funky charms of the songs instead of serving as a distraction. Dig the way "Encrusted" is gradually swallowed up by the background noise until the song finally bursts through again for a triumphant climax. The swirling, almost psychedelic "#1," the strings-enhanced (!!) "Wonder" and the choogling opener "Bummer" are among the band's best-ever songs, and the filler that mars most of the Grifters' albums (even gems like *Ain't My Lookout*), is largely absent. The more in-your-face *Crappin' You Negative* got better press at the time, but in the long run, *One Sock Missing* is by far the best of the Grifters' pre-Sub Pop albums. *—Stewart Mason*

● **Crappin' You Negative** / May 16, 1994 / Shangri-La ✦✦✦✦✦

Ain't My Lookout / Feb. 1996 / Sub Pop ✦✦✦
Ain't My Lookout is the Grifters' tightest and cleanest record to date, but that's only a relative term—the band's previous records were so noisy and sloppy that it was occasionally difficult to discern melodies and hooks within the song. Apart from the band's sharper attack, things haven't' changed that much on *Ain't My Lookout*. The songs are still based in rootsy, Stonesy rock & roll, but run through the shredder, making the riffs jagged and the chords angular. Although it has slightly higher production values than their early singles, the sound remains endearingly lo-fi and ragged. The Grifters haven't changed their sound

enough to be labeled a sellout by their indie fans, but they may have opened it up enough to welcome in new fans. —*Stephen Thomas Erlewine*

Full Blown Possession / Sep. 9, 1997 / Sub Pop ✦✦✦✦
After all the years the Grifters have been playing together, they can't help but sound like a band. That wasn't always the case, but on *Full Blown Possession*, they sound seasoned, sure of themselves, and much more into the task of making a concise disc. "Sweetest Thing" is an acoustic country-blues, while "Re-Entry Blues" rocks you with just the right attitude to make you want to hear it again and again. If it's true that alt-rock has gone mainstream, then the Grifters have all oars in the water and are paddling ahead at full speed. —*James Chrispell*

Grin

f. 1969, db. 1973
Rock & Roll
Before he was under the wing of Neil Young and before he made a series of underappreciated solo albums, guitarist Nils Lofgren formed Grin, a trio who was devoted to simple, basic rock & roll, in 1969. None of Grin's albums were commercially successful—they only received good reviews, not sales—but each showed a promising, dynamic group. Unfortunately, the group never fulfilled their potential, but the finest of their albums featured some terse, brilliant guitar from Lofgren that ranks with the best of his later work, highlights later collected on the 1999 retrospective *The Very Best of Grin Featuring Nils Lofgren*. —*Stephen Thomas Erlewine*

Grin-1+1 / 1972 / Spindizzy ✦✦✦✦
Kicked off by the delicious pop confection "White Lies," *1 + 1* is the best of Nils Lofgren's work with his trio Grin. That single never got higher than number 75, though, and the album sold very little outside of Lofgren's home base in the northern Virginia and Maryland suburbs of Washington, D.C. Nonetheless, this is an enjoyable recording produced by Neil Young associate David Briggs. Lofgren's guitar playing is strong throughout, and the songs are often cleverly constructed and quite catchy, if lightweight. His high-pitched singing voice sounds better when he's not trying to be gravelly and works fairly well in the power-pop settings that inform most of this disc. —*Jim Newsom*

● **The Best of Grin** / 1976 / Epic ✦✦✦✦✦
While *1+1* remains Grin's most consistent record, *The Best of Grin* pieces together ten compelling cuts from their three CBS albums. As a writer and player, Nils Lofgren was adept at dreamy love songs ("Like Rain") and straightforward rock & roll ("Direction"). Despite its brevity, this compilation spotlights both tendencies. —*J.P. Ollio*

The Very Best of Grin / Jun. 8, 1999 / Spindizzy/Epic Associated/Legacy ✦✦✦✦✦
The failure of Grin to sell large numbers of records in the early 1970s is one of those mysteries of popular music. They seemed to have everything, all in the person of leader Nils Lofgren, an accomplished guitarist and songwriter with a connection to the CSNY axis who had played on Neil Young's *After the Goldrush* when he was only 18. He was still under 21 when the first, self-titled Grin album was released in 1971. Maybe his youth had something to do with the band's limited commercial success; he often let other band members take lead vocals on the songs he wrote, preferring a group context that sometimes hid his talents. Nevertheless, the band's albums garnered good reviews and the first three (of four) made the charts, with "White Lies" charting as a single. Those albums were stylistically diverse and somewhat uneven, but contained catchy pop-rock songs ("Like Rain," "Love or Else," "Sad Letter"), any one of which could have changed Grin's story with the right promotion. This well-chosen best-of (actually the second one, following a 1976 LP, despite a sticker on the CD proclaiming "1st-Ever GRIN 'Best-Of' Collection!"), containing a couple of previously unreleased tracks and a non-LP B-side, accurately portrays the band's pop-folk-rock-country sound, from "Everybody's Missin' the Sun" (which could have fit on *After the Goldrush* easily) to "You're the Weight," from the band's 1973 swan song *Gone Crazy*, licensed from A&M Records. Lofgren, of course, went on to a more successful solo career from the mid-'70s to the mid-'80s before becoming "the most overqualified second guitarist in rock" in Bruce Springsteen's E Street Band, as Springsteen himself put it. But the work of Grin is more than juvenilia: In the early '70s, it was good enough to make fans frustrated that the band didn't get more of a hearing. And it sounds just as good more than 25 years later. —*William Ruhlmann*

The Groundhogs

f. 1963, db. 1976
British Psychedelia, Album Rock, Heavy Metal, Prog Rock/Art Rock, Hard Rock, Blues-Rock
The Groundhogs were not British blues at their most creative; nor were they British blues at their most generic. They were emblematic of some of the genre's most visible strengths and weaknesses. They were prone to jam too long on basic riffs, they couldn't hold a candle to American blues singers in terms of vocal presence, and their songwriting wasn't so hot. On the other hand, they did sometimes stretch the form in unexpected ways, usually at the hands of their creative force, T.S. (Tony) McPhee. For a while they were also extremely popular in Britain, landing three albums in that country's Top Ten in the early '70s. The power-trio setup, as well as McPhee's vaguely Jack Bruce-like vocals, bore a passing resemblance to the sound pioneered by Cream. McPhee's lyrics, particularly on their commercial breakthrough, 1970's *Thank Christ for the Bomb*, were murky, sullen anti-establishment statements that were often difficult to decipher, both in meaning and actual content. They played it straighter on the less sophisticated follow-up, *Split*, which succumbed to some of the period's blues-hard-rock indulgences, putting riffs and flash over substance. *Who Will Save the World? The Mighty Groundhogs!* (1972), their last Top Ten entry, saw McPhee straying further from blues territory into somewhat progressive

realms. They've remained active as a touring and recording unit since the '70s, playing to a small following in the UK and Europe. —*Richie Unterberger*

● **Thank Christ for the Bomb** / 1970 / BGO ✦✦✦✦✦
Their most popular album, and probably their most representative, although *Who Will Save the World?* may be more imaginative. McPhee's guitar playing is impressive, and the songs, if not terribly compelling, at least take some lyrical and instrumental chances, building off of a blues-rock base instead of being a slave to it. McPhee seems to be struggling with some very ambitious concepts here, but lacks the clarity and vision to fashion a truly out-of-the-ordinary statement. —*Richie Unterberger*

Split / 1971 / BGO ✦✦✦
Closer to the British blues norm than some of their previous work, this boasts some of the lesser crowd-pleasing annoyances of the age—basic bluesy thumpers and extended, not-terribly-brilliant riffing. McPhee's songwriting suffered, and the band devoted half of the eight-song record to the four-part title track. That didn't prevent the album from being a big hit in Britain, but it hasn't dated well, unless you have an uncritical yen for middling 1970-era blues-rock/hard-rock hybrids. —*Richie Unterberger*

Who Will Save the World? / 1972 / BGO ✦✦✦✦
McPhee took the unusual step of adding progressive rock elements on this album, especially in his use of mellotron and harmonium. Blues rock and progressive rock is not exactly a fashionable combination among critics these days, but McPhee at least deserved credit for trying something a little bit different instead of endlessly recycling the blues-rock cliches he'd mastered. Lyrically, he reached back to the socially conscious (if not terribly clear) musings on war, peace, and philosophy that had preoccupied him on the *Thank Christ for the Bomb* album. It wasn't gripping enough to add up to something notable, and the band were still prone to wander off into headache-inducing extended riffs, as on the closing track, "The Grey Maze." —*Richie Unterberger*

The Groundhogs Best 1969-72 / 1974 / One Way ✦✦✦

Joe Grushecky

Heartland Rock, Rock & Roll, Bar Band
When Pittsburgh-based Joe Grushecky's band the Iron City Houserockers turned up on MCA Records in 1979, their driving bar-band rock & roll and working-class lyrics earned them critical kudos but also made them Johnny-come-latelies in a crowded field headed by Bruce Springsteen and including Bob Seger, John Cafferty, and John Mellencamp. Nevertheless, they managed to release four albums through 1983. Grushecky reorganized, keeping only the bass player for the new edition launched under his own name in 1989, but the approach and sound are the same. —*William Ruhlmann*

Love's So Tough / 1979 / MCA ✦✦✦✦
The Houserockers' first album, originally released in 1979, sounds like the work of a great, battle-hardened bar band who is still learning how to make their sound work in the studio. The arrangements suggest an imaginative cross between Bruce Springsteen's E-Street Band and the J. Geils Band's early period, and the band is tight and skillful throughout. But the production is a bit flat, and the sound lacks the presence and punch this material needs. And while Joe Grushecky would mature into a top-shelf songwriter by the time the band released their second album, most of the tunes on *Love's So Tough* are standard issue cars-and-girls stuff, though the two numbers about the sorry state of rock & roll ("Heroes Are Hard to Find" and "I'm Lucky") cut deep, and "I Can't Take It" kicks things off with a bang. Even at it's weakest moments, *Love's So Tough* burns with a passion and fire that makes clear the Iron City Houserockers were true believers in the power of rock & roll. —*Mark Deming*

● **Have a Good Time but Get Out Alive** / 1980 / MCA ✦✦✦✦✦
The Iron City Houserockers' first album sounded like the work of a better than average bar band with the potential to grow into something more; 1980's *Have a Good Time but Get out Alive* was where they proved just how good they could be. While the band sounded solid on their debut, here they landed with the impact of a Louisville slugger connecting with a fastball (especially drummer Ned E. Rankin and harmonica player Marc Reisman), and producer Mick Ronson managed to get their nuances on tape with tightly focused clarity. (Ian Hunter and Steve Van Zandt also helped with the production and arrangements, and their hard rock smarts certainly show in the final product.) But what really sets *Have a Good Time but Get Out Alive* apart from the work of dozens of "Heartland Rockers" who emerged in Bruce Springsteen's wake is Joe Grushecky; his songwriting and lead vocals seethe with a furious passion that's never less than convincing, and if the details of his songs sometime lean towards clichés, the total commitment of his performance, delivered with the conviction of a man fighting for his life, brings these stories to vivid, sweaty life. Lots of songwriters have written about desperate guys on the wrong side of the tracks, but on "We're Not Dead Yet," "Runnin' Scared," and the title cut, Grushecky makes them sound as real as the guy who mugged you last week and turns their stories into something both tragic and compelling. *Have a Good Time but Get Out Alive* is a masterpiece of hard-bitten Rust Belt rock, and the remastered CD reissue released in 1999 is a major improvement over the noisy vinyl pressings of the album's original release. —*Mark Deming*

● **Pumping Iron & Sweating Steel: The Best of the Iron City Houserockers** / 1992 / Rhino ✦✦✦✦✦
A generous compilation of the best of an underrated rock & roll band from the late '70s and early '80s. Some of Joe Grushecky's songs on *Pumping Iron & Sweating Steel* equal the best of Bruce Springsteen, Tom Petty, and Bob Seger during this period. Fans of those artists will definitely find the Iron City Houserockers worth investigating. —*Stephen Thomas Erlewine*

Guadalcanal Diary

f. 1981, **db.** 1989

Jangle Pop, Alternative Pop/Rock, College Rock

Thanks to R.E.M., there was no shortage of Southern guitar pop bands in the early '80s, but Guadalcanal Diary was different from the rest. While their songs and melodies were as melodic and approachable as R.E.M., the Byrds, or any of their imitators, singer/guitarist Murray Attaway's lyrics were bizarre treatises of his favorite obsessions—American history and mythology, religion, and the supernatural. What kept them from becoming unbearably precious was their natural pop sense and eclecticism, which added a rich musical variety to the diverse and strange subject matter. After four albums, the group disbanded in 1989. *—Stephen Thomas Erlewine*

Walking in the Shadow of the Big Man / 1984 / Elektra ✦✦✦

Like R.E.M., the B-52's, and Pylon, this fine band hailed from the unlikely independent-rock hotbed of Athens, GA. The long jangle-pop shadow of R.E.M. is extremely strong on this release, with seven of the ten tracks showing either full or partial influence of that group. Fortunately, the songs here are excellent, exhibiting much variety within this style. "Trail of Tears," a haunting antiwar number, sounds the most like their Athens counterparts. "Fire from Heaven" is more up-tempo, intense, and dynamic, while "Sleepers Awake" is an ominous, slowly unfolding song. "Ghost on the Road" is primarily a fast country-punk number that saves its R.E.M. stylings for its yearning chorus. "Gilbert Takes the Wheel" and the title track are jangly instrumentals, the former being a fast rocker with a thudding beat, the latter being a lengthy slow-tempo selection exhibiting noticeable psychedelic traits. Other territory is touched on as well. "Pillow Talk" is a winsomely energetic Everly Brothers-influenced song. The brilliant "Watusi Rodeo" is a jumpy pop number sporting over-the-top surf guitar licks and inspired hilarious-yet-uncomfortable lyrics about "Ugly American" cowboys in Africa. There's also an eccentric cover of the missionary hymn "Kum Ba Yah," complete with appreciative background audience shouting, an energetic drum solo, and extreme contrasts of loud and soft dynamics (sometimes within the same verse line). This odd yet strong album is well worth hearing. *—David Cleary*

Jamboree / 1986 / Elektra ✦✦✦

The first six selections on this release encompass some of the best R.E.M.-style songs never written by that band. "Michael Rockefeller" is a breathlessly rushed masterpiece with echoes of that other Athens band's "West of the Fields." "Pray for Rain" is a howling, intense number that snitches the opening two chords of Jefferson Airplane's "3/5 of a Mile in 10 Seconds" for its own beginning. Weighty concerns about religion are voiced in the ringing "Fear of God"; this song borrows the opening guitar riff from "I Call Your Name" by the Beatles. "Spirit Train" is a slower, intensely foreboding selection that suggests a highly charged version of R.E.M.'s "Old Man Kensey." What follows all this are a clutch of songs with bizarre or puckish lyrics in a wild array of pop styles. "T.R.O.U.B.L.E." is a hot jazz-influenced track with goofy lyrics about sibling rivalry. "I See Moe" is a jumpy country-punk number that compares the speaker's personality dysfunction to that of the Three Stooges. "Dead Eyes" is a thundering, hard-rocking cut with threatening verses about unknown terrors and things that go bump in the night, resulting likely from too much booze. And "Cattle Prod" has to go down as one of the strangest pop songs ever written, a grindingly grandiose number with arena-rock touches that has creepy lyrics about bestiality. This is an excellent, if sometimes bewildering album very much worth hearing. *—David Cleary*

• **2X4** / 1987 / Elektra ✦✦✦✦✦

This wonderful, hard-rocking release shows Guadalcanal Diary moving away from the obvious R.E.M. influences exhibited on their first two releases. Only "Where Angels Fear to Tread" and "Winds of Change" (both excellent songs) sound like the music of their Georgia cousins. Styles explored here are surprisingly diverse. "Let the Big Wheel Roll" is a souped-up rockabilly-influenced number with nutty lyrics that make fun of junk-pop culture in general and television commercials in particular; appropriately enough, the Monkees song "For Pete's Sake" is closely referenced in the song's chorus. "3 AM" is an affectingly haunting and beautiful low-key stunner about alcoholism. Touches of funk and psychedelic-era Beatles inform the driving "Lips of Steel." "Under the Yoke" weds booming arena-rock touches to a growled vocal, wailing harmonica, and oppressive lyrics. John Lennon and Greg Lake are the obvious touchstones for the uneasy slow-tempo song about paranoia and superstition entitled "Little Birds." "Things Fall Apart" comes across as a stumbling quintuple-meter burlesque of Jethro Tull's more bombastic numbers. And the soaring "Litany" is a powerfully exuberant selection with a walloping drum beat and vibrant guitar work. This fine album is well worth purchasing. *—David Cleary*

Flip-Flop / 1989 / Elektra ✦✦✦

Guadalcanal Diary's final album is simultaneously their most stylistically consistent and their least effective. Most of the songs on this release uneasily mix walloping rock, arena stylings, and ringing R.E.M. touches; most have clearer, somehow less effective lyrics, some of which (most notably in "The Likes of You") are riddled with cliches. The temptation to think that the band is going for chart success in a big way is very strong here. A few off-style excursions can be found, all but one showing strong ties to songs on earlier albums. "Ten Laws" has the slow, ominous feel of "Spirit Train." "... Vista" mixes musical elements of "Country Club Gun" and "T.R.O.U.B.L.E." in an uneasy alliance with nonsense lyrics. And "Fade Out" (probably the album's best track) is a further excursion into paisley-period Beatles that recalls "Lips of Steel." The one surprise here is the power-pop selection "Always Saturday." A number of the songs on this release have sour, angry lyrics excoriating such things as out-of-control drunks ("Whiskey Talk") and women both snooty ("The Likes of You") and vacuous ("Pretty Is as Pretty Does"). In short, the group seems to be stagnating. Fans of this band will likely find this release to be a letdown from earlier efforts. *—David Cleary*

The Guess Who

f. 1963, Winnipeg, Manitoba, Canada, **db.** 1975

Album Rock, Boogie Rock, Pop/Rock, Hard Rock

While the Guess Who did have several hits in America, they were superstars in their home country of Canada during the 1960s and early '70s. The band grew out of a Winnipeg-based group named the Expressions, formed by Chad Allan and Randy Bachman. After hitting the American Top 40 with 1965's "Shakin' All Over," the Expressions recorded an album that necessitated a name-change after the Quality label released it and listed their name as "Guess Who?" on the jacket, hoping to fool record buyers into thinking that it was a more famous group in disguise. Allan departed soon after and was replaced on lead vocals by Burton Cummings, though further American success eluded the Guess Who until the 1969 Top Ten hit "These Eyes." In 1970, the band released the cuttingly sarcastic riff-rocker "American Woman," which, given its anti-American putdowns, ironically became their only U.S. chart-topper. Trouble was brewing on the horizon, though. Bachman left the group that year, and formed Brave Belt with Chad Allan, which later evolved into Bachman-Turner Overdrive. The Guess Who returned to the Top Ten at the end of the year with "Share the Land," and hit one last time in 1974 with "Clap for the Wolfman" before disbanding in 1975. The lineup from the Guess Who's glory years reunited in 1983, and a version of the group with constantly shifting musicians (occasionally original members) continued to tour into the '90s. *—Steve Huey*

Shakin' All Over / 1965 / Scepter ✦✦

Canned Wheat / 1969 / Buddha ✦✦✦✦✦

As far as late-'60s and early-'70s rock bands go, the Guess Who has been both blessed and cursed. Blessed because their songs are still played quite frequently on oldies radio stations, cursed because they're only remembered for those songs. Truth be told, the Guess Who was a darn good rock band: Burton Cummings's great rock & roll voice—similar in power to Bad Company's Paul Rodgers—keeps even the most overdone Guess Who song fresh, and Randy Bachman's underrated guitar work always serves the song's needs. "Undun"'s wonderful, jazzy riff, which fits the song perfectly, is associated with the overall sound of the Guess Who, not Bachman. 1969's cleverly-titled *Canned Wheat* introduced several of the band's most remembered songs: "Laughing," "Undun," and "No Time." The album also has six other keepers, including the mellow "6 A.M. or Nearer," complete with jazzy guitar and flute, and the lovely ballad "Minstrel Boy." The original version of "No Time" is fun, even if it isn't radically different; little nuances, like the fade out, shake the listener out of the "I've heard this song a thousand times" syndrome. There are a couple of throwaway bonus tracks, "Species Hawk" and "Silver Bird," that are nice to have, even if they aren't up to the other material. The liner notes are helpful, and it's funny to learn that radio stations ordered copies of "Undun" for airplay, not realizing that it was the B-side of "Laughing." *Canned Wheat* still sounds incredibly fresh, a product from the heyday of classic rock. For those who want to dig beneath the band's "oldie" status to find the real thing, this album shouldn't be missed. *—Ronnie Lankford, Jr.*

Share the Land / 1970 / Buddha ✦✦✦

Recorded in the immediate aftermath of lead guitarist Randy Bachman's departure from the group, *Share the Land* was a better album than anyone could rightfully have expected, and it was the biggest selling original album in their entire output, appearing in the wake of "American Woman" and lofted into the Top 20 (with a lot of advance orders) with a pair of hits of its own. The music ranges from the catchy, anthem-like title tune to proto-metal excursions, with coherent digressions into blues and country ("Comin' Down off the Money Bag"/"Song of the Dog"). Burton Cummings is in excellent voice on the lead vocals, and the other members provide some of the finest harmonies ever heard on a Guess Who album, on "Do You Miss Me Darlin'" and "Three More Days." The new double lead guitar team of Kurt Winter and Greg Leskiw gave the band a greater range than they'd ever had, moving freely in various rock and blues idioms, and the rhythm section was as solid as ever. That having been said, however, the music hasn't necessarily aged well (or, perhaps, those who've achieved a maturity level beyond age 18 have aged past it)—listening to details such as Winter's shouts of "Freedom!" and "Paint me a picture" on "Three More Days," one can't escape the thought that at least half of this album not only wasn't aimed at the overachieving end of the high school and college populations, but was aggressively *not* aimed at them. And from here on, beyond whatever virtuosity the members brought to their sound, it seemed as though the group was working from formula rather than inspiration. The fall 2000 reissue on the Buddha label features a high-resolution remastering, and includes a pair of very good lost numbers from the early sessions for the record, "Palmyra" and "The Answer," featuring Bachman on guitar. *—Bruce Eder*

American Woman / Jan. 1970 / Buddha ✦✦✦✦

The Guess Who's most successful LP, reaching number nine in America (and charting for more than a year), has held up well and was as close to a defining album-length statement as the original group ever made. It's easy to forget that until "American Woman," the Guess Who's hits had been confined to softer, ballad-style numbers—that song (which originated as a spontaneous on-stage jam) highlighted by Randy Bachman's highly articulated fuzz-tone guitar, a relentless beat, and Burton Cummings moving into Robert Plant territory on the lead vocal, transformed their image. As an album opener, it was a natural, but the slow acoustic blues intro by Bachman heralded a brace of surprises in store for the listener. The presence of the melodic but highly electric hit version of "No Time" (which the band had cut earlier in a more ragged rendition) made the first ten minutes a hard rock one-two punch, but the group then veers into progressive rock territory with "Talisman." Side two was where the original album was weakest, though it started well enough with "969 (The Oldest Man)." "When Friends Fall Out," a remake of an early Canadian release by the group, attempted a heavy sound that just isn't sustainable, and "8:15" was a similar space filler, but "Proper Stranger" falls into good hard rock groove. In August of 2000, Buddha Records issued a remastered version of this album with a bonus track from a subsequent session, "Got to Find Another Way." Ironically, *American Woman* was the final testament of the original Guess Who—guitarist/singer Randy Bachman quit soon after the tour behind this album; the group did endure and even thrive (as did Bachman), but *American Woman* represented something of an ending as well as a triumph. —*Bruce Eder*

The Best of the Guess Who / 1971 / RCA ✦✦✦✦✦
A fine single-disc collection of most of the band's greatest hits, it's perfect for listeners who don't want to invest in the double-disc *Track Record.* —*AMG*

Live at the Paramount / 1972 / Buddha ✦✦✦✦
The August 2000 reissue of *Live at the Paramount* on the Buddha label has 13 songs, the whole 75 minutes of music from the first of two shows, and provides the best explanation of how the Guess Who endured as a major concert draw years after their biggest hits were behind them; when they were spot-on, as they were that night, they gave an exciting show. Remixed and remastered properly, this is now a killer concert album, showing off the double lead guitar attack that was a hallmark of their live sound in blazing glory, energizing even familiar songs like "New Mother Nature," and Burton Cummings near the peak of his form with the band as a singer. Surprisingly, the songs that were left off of the original LP included several hits, both vintage ("These Eyes," "No Time") and relatively recent ("Rain Dance," "Share the Land"), though the highlight is "Sour Suite," which is a dazzling showcase for Cummings as a singer and pianist. The remixing also helps the material that was on this album originally, pumping up the volume on the bluesy jam that opens "American Woman," which also sounds a lot better (and is worth hearing in the 15 minute jam version featured here). "Share the Land" comes off better here than its official version, set ablaze by Kurt Winter's and Don McDougal's guitars and a spirited vocal performance. —*Bruce Eder*

Track Record: The Guess Who Collection / 1988 / RCA ✦✦✦✦
Even with the release of 1997's three-disc *The Ultimate Collection*, which is poorly sequenced and has few rarities, *Track Record* remains the definitive collection for the Guess Who. It hits all the band's commercial highs, and has two sets of song by song liner notes written by producer Jack Richardson and Burton Cummings. Flexible yet distinctive, everything they played was unmistakably the Guess Who: the aggressively melodic "Laughing," the quasi-jazz of "Undun," the defiant "Hand Me Down World." Though they were Canadian, they ruled the American pop charts; even "American Woman"'s vaguely anti-American sentiment couldn't slow its chart ascent. The lovely pop of "These Eyes" and the communal hymn "Share the Land" are faultless Top 40 pop/rock gems that capture the rage, idealism, and romanticism of late-'60s and early-'70s youth culture. The Guess Who had their fingers on the era's pulse, and an ominous foreboding bled its way into their melodies and performances. Cummings's voice ranged from an intense croon to a scratchy banshee yodel ("...it would have been nice to be both Robert Plant and Jim Morrison at once," he writes in his liners, and he came close), and Randy Bachman, Kurt Winter, and Greg Leskiw were all nervy guitarists who created tense, memorable guitar riffs. Though their later singles didn't match the early hits' commercial heights or cultural prescience, they were strong cuts. "Albert Flasher" is a wonderful honky tonk blues; "Rain Dance" is both poignant and vehement; and "Follow Your Daughter Home" is a Calypso-tinged jewel. Disc two is not as consistently listenable as the first, but includes the smash "Clap for the Wolfman" and B-sides and LP cuts like 1972's "Guns Guns Guns." But there is plenty of good Guess Who music not present on *Track Record.* —*Stanton Swihart*

The Ultimate Collection / Jan. 28, 1997 / RCA ✦✦✦✦
A seemingly well-assembled package that fails to go quite as far as it should, sticking closely to the charted material and rarely delving into the vaults for interesting oddities—three rehearsal takes are tacked onto the end of the third disc in the set, providing little of interest to collectors or to the curious. The booklet does a workmanlike job of tracking the progress of the band, but there are few insights to be found in the difficult-to-read text.

The set is built around the A and B sides of singles, with album cuts salted in between. This is effective in charting the band's progression from melodic popsters to hard rockers and back to the pop-inflected music that closed out their career. The highlights are scattered throughout—"American Woman," of course; "Rain Dance," with its unnerving echoes of American massacres, the funky, improvised live "Truckin' off Across the Sky," even the goofy "Clap for the Wolfman," which came when the Guess Who were all but finished.

The Ultimate Collection works well as an introduction to the Guess Who, but will not gratify anyone with more than a basic need to know. On a sonic level, the set sounds good, however. —*Steven McDonald*

● **Greatest Hits** / Feb. 23, 1999 / RCA ✦✦✦✦✦
There have been plenty of Guess Who collections on the market, from the original *Best of the Guess Who* to the multi-disc *Track Record.* Of all of these, the best is the 1999 collection *Greatest Hits*, which contains a generous 18 songs, including all but two of their charting American singles—not counting 1965's "Shakin' All Over," the missing songs are "Broken" (the B-side to "Albert Flasher") and "Runnin' Back to Saskatoon" (which barely scraped the charts). Although the Guess Who's albums are distinctive (more so than their reputation would lead you to believe), there's little question that they're best heard as a singles band, and this is the best place to hear them that way. After a spin of *Greatest Hits*, it's clear that the Guess Who made some of the best mainstream rock of their era—

and while they never received much critical respect (apart from iconoclast Lester Bangs, of course), their music holds up better than much of their peer's, which means that the Guess Who deserves to have the last laugh. —*Stephen Thomas Erlewine*

Guided by Voices

f. 1985, Dayton, OH
Indie Rock, Lo-Fi, Alternative Pop/Rock
Inspired equally by jangle-pop and arty post-punk, Guided by Voices created a series of trebly, hissy indie-rock records filled with infectiously brief pop songs that fell somewhere between the British Invasion and prog rock. After recording six self-released albums between 1986 and 1992, the Dayton, OH-based band attracted a handful of fans within the American indie-rock underground. With the 1994 release of *Bee Thousand*, the group became an unexpected alternative rock sensation, winning positive reviews throughout the mainstream music press and signing a larger distribution deal with Matador Records. Despite all of the attention, the band never changed their aesthetic, continuing to record their albums on cheap four-track tape decks and thereby limiting their potential audience, yet that devotion to lo-fi indie rock helped Guided By Voices maintain a sizable cult during the late '90s. —*Stephen Thomas Erlewine*

Propeller / 1992 / Scat ✦✦✦
Propeller was an album that Guided By Voices released themselves originally in 1992 and was eventually reissued on the Scat label one year later. All of the ingredients that make the group totally original are present—rough production, strong melodies courtesy of Robert Pollard, and an overall sound straight out of the British clubs back in the mid-'60s. The opening epic, "Over the Neptune/Mesh Gear Fox," is two different songs sewn together (similar to T. Rex's "Tenement Lady" off their classic *Tanx* album). It starts off as a rock & roller and later changes into space-rock, while "Quality of Armor" starts off as a cross between the Beatles and Elvis Costello's "(What's So Funny 'Bout) Peace Love and Understanding?" But Guided By Voices have a style all their own, evidenced by the irresistible combination of chromatic guitar riffs and anthemic choruses contained in "Exit Flagger," and the experimental song splices throughout "Back to Saturn X Radio Report." "Circus World" is pure guitar-pop, as is the now-classic "Weedking." *Propeller* proved to be an important stepping stone for the group, helping to set the stage for such later triumphs as *Bee Thousand* and *Alien Lanes.* —*Greg Prato*

Vampire on Titus/Propeller / 1993 / Scat ✦✦✦✦✦
The home-crafted appeal of Guided By Voices finally reached the general public when *Vampire on Titus* was released in 1993. The band was on a roll at the time, pumping out creative gems like a band possessed. With one of their very best lineups, they explore the many aspects of their limited production skills without any pretension. Bandleader Robert Pollard found his voice around this time, going from a tuneful yelp to a dark croon effortlessly. And the marvelous Tobin Sprout was still with the band at the time, contributing several memorable songs that mixed up things nicely. Songs float in and out with a tight efficiency that is not typical of many likeminded artists. But without one extra second wasted on a melody, the album's strengths are only made more evident. Pollard's voice had never sounded as dark and anxious as it does on "#2 in the Model Home Series," yet on most tracks he shows an endless optimism that brings to mind *Warehouse*-era Bob Mould. The beautiful "Marchers in Orange" is where his voice gets its best showcase, wailing away despite the weak production. The band really does display a tremendous amount of power and creativity on this effort, and fans of indie rock should try and find this as soon as possible. Like the Replacements' *Hootenanny* or Pavement's *Slanted and Enchanted*, this kicked off a several-album streak of brilliance that went unnoticed by the mainstream but collected quite a following in the underground. —*Bradley Torreano*

● **Bee Thousand** / Jun. 20, 1994 / Matador ✦✦✦✦✦
The cult of indie rock thrives on the unexpected discovery, and in 1994 Guided By Voices was just the sort of musical phenomenon no one figured was still out there—thirtysomething rock obsessives cranking out fractured guitar-driven pop tunes in a laundry room. Robert Pollard and his stable of beer buddies/backing musicians had been churning out stuff like *Bee Thousand* for years, but the album's surprise critical success marked the first time the group found a significant audience outside their home town, and it made a clear case for Guided By Voices' virtues—as well as their flaws. From the moment "Hardcore UFOs" kicks in, it's obvious that Robert Pollard has an uncanny gift for a hook and a melody, and *Bee Thousand*'s 20 cuts are dotted with miniature masterpieces like "Echos Myron," "Smothered in Hugs," and "Queen of Cans and Jars." However, there are also more than a few duds that threaten to cancel out the goodwill the great songs generate, and Pollard is an acquired taste as a lyricist—his freakishly poetic verse has a real charm, but it's hard to figure out what he's on about. (GBV's other principal songwriter, Tobin Sprout, contributes less often, but manages a higher batting average.) The lo-tech rumble of the album's DIY production also wavers between being a help and a hindrance, depending on the songs, and as musicians Guided By Voices veer between sounding like inspired amateurs and...well, just amateurs. On *Bee Thousand*, Guided By Voices sounds like a passionate and gloriously quirky garage band fronted by a thrillingly and maddeningly idiosyncratic songwriter; its many pearly moments make it a fascinating discovery for rock enthusiasts, but a few years would pass before this band was fully earning the new accolades showered upon it. —*Mark Deming*

Box / Feb. 28, 1995 / Scat ✦✦✦
Compiling all of Guided By Voices' '80s albums—*Devil Between My Toes, Sandbox, Self-Inflicted Aerial Nostalgia,* and *Same Place the Fly Got Smashed* (the vinyl version includes *Propeller,* which was on the *Vampire on Titus* CD)—and adding a collection of rarities called *King Shit and the Golden Boys, Box* is a bit of an intimidating listen for some

devoted fans, let alone beginners. On each of their albums, Guided By Voices packs their records full of brief songs—if they reach the three-minute mark, it's an epic for the band. That can make such a massive collection of music rather daunting; it all seems to speed by without much distinction, if you're listening casually, but on closer inspection, it withstands repeated listens. The first records, *Devils* and *Sandbox*, are unpolished versions of R.E.M.'s *Murmur*. On the next two albums, the group's distinctive, British Invasion-inspired abbreviated pop begins to coalesce; their music sounds more like messages than songs, albeit messages that are driven by undeniable hooks. Retailing for under $50, *Box* is a worthwhile investment for dedicated fans. *—Stephen Thomas Erlewine*

Alien Lanes / Mar. 28, 1995 / Matador ♦♦♦
It's surprising what a difference it makes when a musician knows someone will actually be hearing his work. After 1994's charmingly sloppy *Bee Thousand* gained Guided By Voices a nationwide cult following (instead of the local cult following they were accustomed to), 1995's *Alien Lanes* found Robert Pollard and his partners in hard pop cleaning up their act a bit. For the most part, *Alien Lanes* isn't radically different from *Bee Thousand*—it was primarily recorded on a four-track cassette machine (and sounds like it), and Guided By Voices was still a garage band with more in the way of inspiration than chops. But the musicians have put a bit more care and focus into their performance on this set; the playing is tighter and sharper, and the band plays toward their strengths, pushing their occasional sloppiness into a harder, more rock-oriented direction. And if Pollard and Tobin Sprout were still obsessed with tiny fragments of pop song wonderment, they also rounded up a more consistent collection of them; there aren't quite as many obvious masterpieces as on *Bee Thousand*, but also fewer obvious mistakes, and the sequencing gives the album a more consistent flow than before. Pollard also made genuine inroads into more lyrically cognizant material (though don't fret, "Auditorium" and "Blimps Go 90" are as cryptic as ever), and "Watch Me Jumpstart," "Striped White Jets," and "Motor Away" are simply superb pop/rock songs. (Sprout also gets a few shining moments on "A Good Flying Bird" and "Straw Dogs.") Both *Bee Thousand* and *Alien Lanes* sound like they were made by a band of inspired amateurs with great ideas; the difference is that *Alien Lanes* suggests that Guided By Voices wanted to prove that they could turn pro some day. *—Mark Deming*

Under the Bushes Under the Stars / Mar. 26, 1996 / Matador ♦♦♦
After firmly establishing themselves as America's most original and interesting band of part-time, over-30 garage rockers, *Under the Bushes Under the Stars* found Guided by Voices dipping their toes into something resembling professionalism. Leaving behind the homemade studio craft of their previous work, this album was recorded in a pair of actual recording studios, and the sessions boasted an outside producer (friend and temporary fellow Ohioan Kim Deal); while no one would mistake the results for the latest Bob Rock project, the set sounded more like a "real" record than anything GBV had attempted up to that time. The new edition of the band attempted to rise to the occasion, and though the performances lack the passion of *Bee Thousand* and *Alien Lanes*' finest moments, the stronger playing and cleaner production honors the pop sensibilities of Robert Pollard's songwriting. Pollard was also reaching for a better controlled style as a songwriter; *Under the Bushes Under the Stars* boats a mere 18 songs (as opposed to the 30 on *Alien Lanes*), and most sound like full fledged pop tunes, with fewer shards of musical fancy littering the way. While Pollard's tighter reign over the band and new sense of self-control made this album a more solid and consistent album than GBV had made in the past, it's also not as exciting as *Alien Lanes*; Pollard's songs lack a certain fire here (though "Man Called Aerodynamics," "Your Name Is Wild," and "The Official Ironmen Rally Song" sound just fine), and the band sounds more stifled than enthused by their new grasp of the material. There's plenty to enjoy here, but it also appeared to have caught Guided by Voices in a transitional stage; just how much they were changing would be revealed on their next two albums. *—Mark Deming*

Mag Earwhig! / May 20, 1997 / Matador ♦♦♦♦
After *Bee Thousand* gave Guided By Voices a wider audience, it became evident that Robert Pollard saw himself as more than just the band's songwriter and frontman, and as his career ambitions grew, he became increasingly frustrated with the limitations of his band. Matters came to a head prior to the recording of *Mag Earwhig!* as Pollard broke ties with longtime guitarist and fellow songwriter Tobin Sprout and fired the rest of the group. While Pollard and Sprout soon buried the hatchet, Sprout opted not to stay on as a full-time member of the group, and Pollard was now Guided By Voices' uncontested leader. He hired Cleveland-based blues/garage rockers Cobra Verde as his backing band for the next GBV album, and *Mag Earwhig!* sounded a good bit different as a result; while there were a few stray four-track experiments with Sprout scattered about, most of the album had a solid, professional sheen, and Cobra Verde rock harder and sound tighter than any of the lineups Pollard had worked with in the past. Unfortunately, his songwriting wasn't quite up to his usual standards, which the new clarity of this album makes all the more evident. Pollard is incapable of making an album without a few fine songs, and "Bulldog Skin," "Sad If I Lost It," "Not Behind the Fighter Jet," and "Portable Men's Society" certainly fill the bill, but it may well be significant that *Mag Earwhig!*'s most exciting song, the joyous "I Am a Tree," was written by Cobra Verde's Doug Gillard. While there's plenty to enjoy here, Robert Pollard's next experiment in hi-fi record making, *Do the Collapse*, would prove to be much more successful. *—Mark Deming*

Do the Collapse / Aug. 3, 1999 / TVT ♦♦

Suitcase: Failed Experiments and Trashed Aircraft / Sep. 19, 2000 / Luna ♦♦♦
Only a fool would argue Robert Pollard's talent as a songwriter, but even the most loyal fans may find room to question his decision-making process. As the frontman, benevolent dictator, and sole constant member of Guided By Voices, the ever-prolific Pollard writes songs the way most people eat potato chips (one right after another), but while a surprising number of them are good, he doesn't always appear to know which songs are keepers and which would be best left in his basement. The majority of Guided By Voices' albums have at least two or three songs that are purposeless fragments (often more), and it's significant that GBV's most consistent (if not their best) album, *Do the Collapse*, was the first with a "real" producer (Ric Ocasek) on hand to assist in the editing process. Pollard's issues with quality vs. quantity are practically the *raison d'être* of *Suitcase: Failed Experiments and Trashed Aircraft*, a four-CD box set that collects homemade recordings of 100 songs that didn't make the grade on GBV's albums, from a tune Pollard wrote and recorded while a junior in high school to several tunes rejected for *Do the Collapse*. Like most of Guided By Voices' previous releases, just about everything here was recorded on cassette machines in basements or rec rooms, and it sounds like it. And true to form, each disc has several songs that sound unfinished, go in the wrong direction, or are simply dumb jokes that don't communicate outside the rehearsal room. In many ways, *Suitcase* plays like *Bee Thousand* or *Vampire on Titus* expanded to epic length—the work of a bunch of inspired semi-pros serving up a little noisy crap alongside a healthy portion of unpolished genius. *—Mark Deming*

Isolation Drills / Apr. 3, 2001 / TVT ♦♦♦♦
Guided by Voices fans who embraced them as the saviors of lo-fi pop after discovering such four-track-in-a-basement masterpieces as *Bee Thousand* and *Alien Lanes* had better learn to live with the fact those days are gone for good—the high-gloss production of 1999's *Do the Collapse* made it clear that GBV topkick Robert Pollard wanted his band to compete in rock's big leagues, and *Isolation Drills* only confirms that notion, sounding even more polished and precise than its precursor. However, if you loved GBV for their songs rather than their sometimes-charming sloppiness, then you'll be glad to hear that Pollard and Company have never used professionalism to better advantage than they do here. While Ric Ocasek's production on *Do the Collapse* was sympathetic, he clearly favored the pop side of the band's personality at the expense of their muscle (most clearly evidenced by the pseudo-new wave keyboard patches). But with Rob Schnapf behind the controls, *Isolation Drills* sounds like the real rock album GBV have always wanted to make; Pollard's hooky-but-rollicking melodies pay audible tribute to his great love for mid-'70s rock throughout, while Doug Gillard and Nate Farley's guitars finally crunch as much as they chime, making the band's rock moves as credible as their pop gestures. And Guided by Voices has never made an album this consistently strong from start to finish. God knows if the indie rock audience will ever forgive him for such obvious craft, but the side of Pollard's personality that thought touring with Cheap Trick was a great idea finally gets the album he's been waiting for with *Isolation Drills*. *—Mark Deming*

Gun Club

f. 1980, Los Angeles, CA, **db.** 1996
College Rock, Psychobilly, Indie Rock, Roots Rock, Alternative Pop/Rock, Hard Rock, American Underground

Tribal, psychobilly blues is the best way to describe Gun Club's energetic death rock, but the band's career seemed doomed from the get-go due to leader Jeffrey Lee Pierce's reputation as an unreliable wildman, and well-publicized bouts of drunkenness dogged him throughout his career. Formed in Los Angeles in the early '80s, the band were vaguely aligned with similarly roots-inspired groups like X and the Blasters, but later picked up and relocated to the Lower Eastside, resting more comfortably around the New York downtown set and Pierce's mentors, Debbie Harry and Chris Stein. Their 1981 debut, *Fire of Love*, was a punk/blues hybrid—intense energy fueled Pierce's exorcism-in-progress delivery and the band's frenetic style. It looked as if that was that when, save for some live recordings and posthumous releases, Pierce launched his solo career in 1985 with the EP *Flamingo* and *Wildweed* album for the Statick label. But it wasn't quite over; in 1987 Pierce came back with a realigned Club and the album *Mother Juno*, which earned them a wider following than ever. In 1996, after drying-out, but suffering from persistent health problems, Pierce passed away from a brain hemorrhage. *—Denise Sullivan*

• **Fire of Love** / 1981 / Slash/Rhino ♦♦♦♦♦
The Gun Club's debut is the watermark for *all* post-punk roots music. This features the late Jeffrey Lee Pierce's swamped-out brand of roiling rock, swaggerific hell-bound blues, and gothic country. With Pierce's wailing high lonesome slide guitar twinned with Kid Congo Powers' spine-shaking riffs and the solid yet off-the-rails rhythm section of bassist Rob Ritter and drummer Terry Graham, the Gun Club burst out of L.A. in the early '80s with a bone to pick and a mountain to move—and they accomplished both on their debut album. With awesome, stripped to the frame production by the Flesh Eaters' Chris D., *Fire of Love* blew away all expectations—and with good reason. Nobody has heard music like this before or since. Pierce's songs were rooted in his land of Texas. On "Sex Beat," a razor-sharp country one-two shuffle becomes a howling wind as Pierce's wasted, half-sung half-howled vocals relate a tale of voodoo, sex, dope, and death. As if the opener weren't enough of a jolt, the Gun Club follow this with a careening version of House's "Preachin the Blues," full of staccato phrasing and blazing slide. But it isn't until the anthemic, opiate-addled country of "She's Like Heroin to Me" and the truly frightening punk-blues of "Ghost on the Highway" that the listener comes to grip with the awesome terror that is the Gun Club. The songs become rock & roll ciphers, erasing themselves as soon as they speak, heading off into the whirlwind of a storm that is so big, so black, and so awful one cannot meditate on anything but its power. *Fire of Love* may be just what the doctor ordered, but to cure or kill is anybody's guess. *—Thom Jurek*

Miami / 1982 / IRS ♦♦♦♦
The sophomore record by the Gun Club bore the curse of having to follow a monolith of the group's own making. *Fire of Love* sold extremely well for an independent; it was a favorite of virtually every critic who heard it in 1981. *Miami* showcased a different lineup

as well. Ward Dotson replaced Congo Powers (temporarily, at least) on guitar, and there were a ton of guest performances, including Debbie Harry and Chris Stein. Stein produced the album. Off the bat the disc suffers from a thin mix. Going for a rougher sound, Stein left the instruments at one level and boosted Pierce's vocal. There is plenty of guitar here, screaming and moping like a drunken orphan from the Texas flatlands, but next to its predecessor it sounds drier and reedier. Ultimately it hardly matters. Going for a higher, more desolate sound, frontman and slide player Jeffrey Lee Pierce and his band were literally on fire. The songs here centered themselves on a mutant form of country music that met the post-punk ethos in the desert, fought and bloodied each other, and decided to stay together. Dotson proved to be a fine replacement for Congo Powers, in that his style was pure Telecaster country (à la James Burton) revved by the Rolling Stones and Johnny Thunders. *Miami* was given a rough go when it was issued for its production. But in the bird's-eye view of history its songs stack up, track for track, with *Fire of Love* and continue to echo well into this long good night. —*Thom Jurek*

Death Party / 1983 / New Rose Blues ✦✦✦
Some potent stuff, all right. Jeffrey Lee Pierce slowed down the tempo for the garage-rock dirge "Death Party," while "Come Back Jim" hearkens back to the debut album, and "The House on Highland Ave." is a modern-day murder ballad set to a straight-ahead rock melody. Always death-obsessed, Pierce may have been at his lowest ebb personally, but this set the stage for his strong solo work to come. —*Denise Sullivan*

The Birth, The Death, The Ghost / 1984 / ABC ✦✦

The Las Vegas Story / 1984 / IRS ✦✦✦
Original guitarist Kid Congo Powers returned to the Gun Club for *The Las Vegas Story*, an ambitious effort which lifts up the rock covering America's seamy underbelly to see what crawls out. A swamp-rock opus which bears a considerable debt to John Fogerty, Jeffrey Lee Pierce's reach often exceeds his grasp—while some of his cultural insights hit the mark, others offer only a hint of truth. Covers of Pharoah Sanders' "Master Plan" and George Gershwin's "My Man's Gone Now" (from *Porgy and Bess*) serve only to further blur whatever statement the album is attempting to make. —*Jason Ankeny*

Sex Beat 81 / 1984 / Lolita ✦✦

Danse Kalinda Boom / 1985 / Roadrunner ✦✦✦
Recorded in 1983, *Danse Kalinda Boom: Live in Pandora's Box* suffers from abysmal sound quality, although the performances are electric; Jeffrey Lee Pierce and Kid Congo Powers sound like men possessed on scorching readings of "Sleeping in Blood City" and a cover of Robert Johnson's "Preaching the Blues." —*Jason Ankeny*

Two Sides of the Beast / 1985 / Dojo ✦✦
Another stopgap collection released during one of the Gun Club's frequent dissolutions, *Two Sides of the Beast* is a double-LP set spanning both studio and live material. —*Jason Ankeny*

Mother Juno / 1987 / Buddha ✦✦✦✦✦
The Gun Club collapsed within a year of the release of 1984's *The Las Vegas Story*, so more than a few fans were surprised in 1987 when Jeffrey Lee Pierce and Kid Congo Powers returned with a new version of the band, featuring Romi Mori (Pierce's significant other) on bass and Nick Sanderson (ex-Clock DVA) on drums. Even more startling was that the group's comeback album, *Mother Juno*, was produced by Robin Guthrie of the Cocteau Twins, who would hardly have seemed a likely choice to channel the Gun Club's fiery blues-punk assault onto vinyl. But against the odds, *Mother Juno* turned out to be one of the band's best albums; the hard rock overtones of *The Las Vegas Story* were replaced by a more direct, streamlined sound that suggested *Miami* without the twangy undertow, and while "Bill Bailey" and "Thunderhead" proved this band could rock as hard as they ever had before, Pierce's songs were also venturing into new musical territory, as evidenced by the slow, slinky R&B of "Yellow Eyes," the atmospheric carnival-pop of "The Breaking Hands," and the contemplative "Port of Souls." And as a vocalist, Pierce's trademark just-off-pitch style had gained no small amount of nuance in the six years since *Fire of Love*, and whether he's shouting the blues or crooning sadly, Pierce shows he'd moved into a whole new class as a singer. Sadly, *Mother Juno* didn't earn a United States release until the 1990s, which is a shame; it not only made clear that the Gun Club were still alive and kicking, it showed they had lost none of their old power as they cleared out some new territory in the process. Buddha's 2000 reissue adds two solid bonus tracks, the scrappy "Crab Dance" and the moody "Nobody's City." —*Mark Deming*

Pastoral Hide and Seek / 1990 / Fire ✦✦✦✦
Recorded in Brussels, *Pastoral Hide and Seek* continues the Gun Club's sudden resurgence; "Emily's Changed" is a provocative and gripping character study, while the country-inflected "I Hear Your Heart Singing" is one of Jeffrey Lee Pierce's most moving songs to date. —*Jason Ankeny*

Divinity / 1991 / New Rose ✦✦✦
Noisy and intricate, *Divinity* ranks among the Gun Club's most ambitious efforts; however, the dissonant production often tends to muddy Jeffrey Lee Pierce's songs, which, conversely, are some of his most simple and straightforward. —*Jason Ankeny*

Live in Europe / 1992 / Triple X ✦✦✦
The first live Gun Club release in some years, *Live in Europe* concentrates on material from later efforts like *Mother Juno* and *Pastoral Hide and Seek*, although the group occasionally dips into its past to tackle songs like "Sex Beat" and "Preaching the Blues." —*Jason Ankeny*

In Exile / May 4, 1992 / Triple X ✦✦✦✦
In Exile compiles the majority of the Gun Club's *Mother Juno* and *Pastoral Hide and Seek* albums, and tracks from the mini-album *Divinity*. There is one bonus track included, the

title track for *Pastoral Hide and Seek* that was never previously released because of an argument about the mix. What these recordings offer is a view of a band that everybody—in America at least—had given up on. Given the band's wildly erratic live performances and Jeffrey Lee Pierce's struggles with both heroin and alcohol that led to his premature death in 1996, every track goes against the grain of who they had been and who they were expected to be. On the tracks from *Mother Juno*, such as "These Breaking Hands," "Lupita Screams," and "Yellow Eyes," there is the influence of the Cocteau Twins of all bands, with Robin Guthrie and Simon Raymonde lending production help. The bluesy aspect of the band's former sound remains intact, but they're no longer played with bowl-you-over intensity. Pierce had grown enough as a songwriter to know that that sound had its limits if the Gun Club were to remain a functioning entity. But he couldn't quite become the ballad singer he wanted to be in the context of the Gun Club either. The tension heard in the *Mother Juno* material, the band's most criminally underappreciated album, bears witness. For *Pastoral Hide and Seek*, the Gun Club was all over the map. And then there's the material from *Divinity* with its creepy Velvets-like tribute to serial killer Richard Speck and the warped metallic blues of "Black Hole." Every one of these tracks is done with sincerity and with a schizophrenic pathos that pulls in too many directions to properly focus the material. —*Thom Jurek*

Lucky Jim / 1994 / Triple X ✦✦✦✦
The final Gun Club album, *Lucky Jim*, was released in 1994, less than two years before frontman Jeffrey Lee Pierce's death at the age of 37 from complications due to liver disease. Pierce was a wasted, hollow-eyed ghost when he and the last incarnation of the Gun Club convened in Holland. Haunted from a trip to South Vietnam and Cambodia, Pierce wrote 11 new songs for the sessions and forged ahead despite the departure of longtime mate and fellow guitar slinger Kid Congo Powers, who left to concentrate on his own band, Congo-Norvell. There is tenderness in all the pain on *Lucky Jim*; it's as if Pierce had accepted that this was always going to be his lot, and knew that much of the struggle was his own fault. The set closes with "Anger Blues," the purest take on this genre the Gun Club ever recorded. The grain in Pierce's voice is an erasure, a ghost, a hunted soul who has nothing left to lose but the very thing that keeps him alive and simultaneously destroys him. As Pierce slashes out Texas blues riffs and single-string flurries, he longs for a kind of life that he knows isn't available to him, a present future free of rage. His solo is among the most expressive and genuinely engaging that he ever played, digging deep into the tradition for its mud, sweat, and bone in order to tie himself to his origins in perpetuity. It's a roar and a final gasp, kissed by Bart van Poppel's Hammond B-3, and drenched in sorrow and resignation. —*Thom Jurek*

Pastoral Hide and Seek/Divinity / 1997 / Buddha ✦✦✦✦
It was both ironic and appropriate that Jeffrey Lee Pierce, a man who worshiped at the altar of American blues and jazz, found himself in the late '80s with a much larger and more loyal audience in Europe and Holland than in the United States, much like the musicians who had first inspired him. As a result, several of the Gun Club's later albums were slow to find release in the United States, and this CD combines two European efforts that had previously traveled in the United States only as imports. On 1990's *Pastoral Hide and Seek*, Jeffrey Lee Pierce had promoted himself to lead guitar (Kid Congo Powers was still on hand to provide slide licks), and his concise, stripped-down guitar lines lead the band away from the blues structures of their earlier work and into a leaner, more contemporary R&B-styled direction (especially on "St. John's Divine" and "The Straits of Love and Hate"), though the passion and attack of the band is still pure rock & roll throughout. While Pierce's vocals aren't quite as strong as on the preceding album, *Mother Juno*, his songwriting chops were in fine form. 1991's *Divinity* is a bit more problematic; featuring four new songs and three live remakes of older tunes, *Divinity* sounds a bit more murky. While the opening guitar workout, "Sorrow Knows," proves that Pierce had grown into a impressive axeman, its seven-minute length is a bit excessive, and while the other three new cuts are strong, they don't hold together terribly well, sounding like fragments from an aborted album rather than an EP meant to stand on its own. An unreleased take of "Crab Dance" is added to the disc as a bonus. —*Mark Deming*

Guns & Roses

f. 1985
Album Rock, Heavy Metal, Hard Rock
At a time when pop was dominated by dance music and pop metal, Guns & Roses brought raw, ugly rock & roll crashing back into the charts. They were not nice boys; nice boys don't play rock & roll. They were ugly, misogynist, violent; they were also funny, vulnerable, and occasionally sensitive, as their breakthrough hit "Sweet Child O' Mine" showed. While Slash and Izzy Stradlin ferociously spit out dueling guitar riffs worthy of Aerosmith or the Stones, Axl Rose screeched out his tales of sex, drugs, and apathy in the big city; bassist Duff McKagan and drummer Steven Adler were a limber rhythm section that kept the music loose and powerful. Guns & Roses' music was basic and gritty, with a solid hard, bluesy base; they were dark, sleazy, dirty, and honest—everything that good hard rock and heavy metal should be. There was something refreshing about a band that could provoke everything from devotion to hatred, especially since both sides were equally right. There hadn't been a hard-rock band this raw or talented in years, and they were given added weight by Axl Rose's primal rage, the sound of confused, frustrated white trash vying for his piece of the pie. As the '80s became the '90s, there simply wasn't a more interesting band around, but owing to intraband friction and the emergence of alternative rock, Rose's supporting cast gradually disintegrated, as he himself spent several years in seclusion. —*Stephen Thomas Erlewine*

★ **Appetite for Destruction** / 1987 / Geffen ✦✦✦✦✦
Guns & Roses' debut *Appetite for Destruction* was a turning point for hard rock in the

late '80s—it was a dirty, dangerous, and mean record in a time when heavy metal meant nothing but a good time. On the surface, Guns & Roses may appear to celebrate the same things as their peers—namely, sex, liquor, drugs, and rock & roll—but there is a nasty edge to their songs, since Axl Rose doesn't see much fun in the urban sprawl of L.A. and its parade of heavy metal thugs, cheap women, booze, and crime. The music is as nasty as the lyrics, wallowing in a bluesy, metallic hard-rock borrowed from Aerosmith, AC/DC, and countless faceless hard-rock bands of the early '80s. It's a primal, sleazy sound that adds grit to already grim tales. It also makes Rose's misogyny, fear, and anger hard to dismiss as merely an artistic statment—this is music that sounds lived-in. And that's exactly why *Appetite for Destruction* is such a powerful record—not only does Axl have fears, but he also is vulnerable, particularly on the power-ballad "Sweet Child O' Mine." He also has a talent for conveying the fears and horrors of the decaying inner city, whether it's on the charging "Welcome to the Jungle," the heroin ode "Mr. Brownstone," or "Paradise City," which simply wants out. But as good as Axl's lyrics and screeching voice are, they wouldn't be nearly as effective without the twin-guitar interplay of Slash and Izzy Stradlin, who spit out riffs and solos better than any band since the Rolling Stones, and that's what makes *Appetite for Destruction* the best metal record of the late '80s. *—Stephen Thomas Erlewine*

G N' R Lies / 1989 / Geffen ✦✦✦

Once *Appetite for Destruction* finally became a hit in 1988, Guns & Roses bought some time by delivering the half-old/half-new LP *G N' R Lies* as a follow-up. Constructed as a double-EP, with the "indie" debut *Live ?!*@ Like A Suicide* coming first and four new acoustic-based songs following on the second side, *G N' R Lies* is where the band metamorphosized from genuine threat to joke. Neither recorded live nor released by an indie-label, *Live ?!*@ Like A Suicide* is competent bar-band boogie, without the energy or danger of *Appetite for Destruction.* The new songs are considerably more problematic. "Patience" is Guns & Roses at their prettiest and their sappiest, the most direct song they have recorded to date. Its emotional directness makes the misogyny of "Used to Love Her (But I Had to Kill Her)" and the pitiful slanders of "One In a Million" sound genuine. Although the cover shrugs them off as a "joke," Axl's venom is frightening—there's little doubt that he truly does believe "faggots" come to America from another country, and that "niggers" should stay out of his way. Since he wasn't playing a character on the remainder of the album, there's little doubt that this is from the heart as well. And what makes it harder to dismiss is the musical skills of the band, who make the country-fried boogie of "Used to Love Her," the bluesy revamp of "You're Crazy," and the tough, paranoid fever-dream of "One In a Million" indelible. So, you either listen to the music and are satisfied, or listen to the lyrics and become disturbed not only by Axl's intentions, but the millions of record-buyers that identified with him. *—Stephen Thomas Erlewine*

Use Your Illusion I / Sep. 1991 / Geffen ✦✦✦✦✦

The "difficult second album" is one of the perennial rock & roll cliches, but few second albums ever were as difficult as *Use Your Illusion, Pts. I & II.* Not really conceived as a double album, but impossible to separate as individual works, *Use Your Illusion* is a shining example of a suddenly successful band getting it all wrong and letting their ambitions run wild. Taking nearly three years to complete, the recording of the album was clearly difficult, and tensions between Slash, Izzy Stradlin, and Axl Rose are evident from the start. The two guitarists, particularly Stradlin, are trying to keep the group closer to their hard-rock roots, but Axl has pretentions of being Queen and Elton John, which is particularly odd for a notoriously homophobic midwestern boy. Conceivably, the two aspirations could have been divided between the two records, but instead they are just thrown into the blender—it's just a coincidence that *I* is a harder-rocking record than *II.* Stradlin has a stronger presence on *I,* contributing three of the best songs—"Dust N' Bones," "You Ain't the First," and "Double Talkin' Jive"—which help keep the album in Stonesy Aerosmith territory. On the whole, the album is stronger than *II,* even though there's a fair amount of filler, including a song that takes its title from the Osmonds' biggest hit and a dippy psychedelic collaboration with Alice Cooper. But it also has two ambitious set-pieces, "Novermber Rain" and "Coma," which find Axl fulfilling his ambitions, as well as the ferocious metallic "Perfect Crime" and the original version of the power-ballad "Don't Cry." Still, it can be a chore to find the highlights on the record amid the overblown production and endless amounts of filler. *—Stephen Thomas Erlewine*

Use Your Illusion II / Sep. 1991 / Geffen ✦✦✦✦✦

Use Your Illusion II is more serious and ambitious than *I,* but it's also considerably more pretentious. Featuring no less than four songs that run over six minutes, *II* is heavy on epics, whether it's the charging funk-metal of "Locomotive," the anti-war "Civil War," or the multi-part "Estranged." As if an attempt to balance the grandiose epics, the record is loaded with an extraordinary amount of filler. "14 Years" may have a lean, Stonesy rhythm, and Duff McKagan's Johnny Thunders homage "So Fine" may be entertaining, but there's no forgiving the ridiculous "Get in the Ring," where Axl threatens rock journalists *by name* because they gave him bad reviews; the misinterpretation of Dylan's "Knockin' On Heaven's Door"; *another* version of "Don't Cry"; and the bizarre closer "My World," which probably captures Axl's instability as effectively as the tortured poetry of his epics. That said, there are numerous strengths to *Use Your Illusion II*; a couple of songs have a nervy energy, and for all their pretensions, the overblown epics are effective, though strangely enough, they reveal notorious homophobe Axl's aspirations of being a cross between Elton John and Freddie Mercury. But the pompous production and poor pacing make the album tiring for anyone who isn't a dedicated listener. *—Stephen Thomas Erlewine*

The Spaghetti Incident? / Nov. 23, 1993 / Geffen ✦✦

As punk albums go, *The Spaghetti Incident?* lacks righteous anger and rage. As Guns & Roses albums go, it's a complete delight, returning to the ferocious, hard-rocking days of *Appetite for Destruction.* The Gunners play Stooges and New York Dolls songs exactly as they do Nazareth—as straight-ahead, driving riff-rockers. After the epic *Use Your Illusions,* the band sounds like it's having fun, not caring about making "art" like "November Rain" or "Estranged." Unfortunately, the tacked-on Charles Manson song leaves a bad aftertaste, but not because of the song itself; the inclusion of the song seems like a publicity-seeking stunt, a way to increase their sales while trying to regain their street credibility. And as *The Spaghetti Incident?* proves, they didn't need to stoop so low. *—Stephen Thomas Erlewine*

Live Era: '87-'93 / Nov. 23, 1999 / Geffen ✦✦✦

The double-disc *Live: Era '87-'93* was designed to do two things—satiate diehard fans longing for old-school G N' R, while clearing decks for a new studio album. It sounds good in theory, yet it suffers from in its execution, since it relies on tapes "recorded across the universe between 1987 and 1993." That's not what G N' R fans want—they want the band in its nervy late-'80s prime, when it seemed like they could self-destruct at any second. *Live: Era* offers the polar opposite with slick, professional tracks that sound pieced together from various performances. Axl's vocals are not only distant—as though they were sung in a booth, separate from the band—but also amazingly mannered, sounding for all the world as if they were redone in the studio. Meanwhile, the band's performances are either brushed up or heavily edited, so it's impossible to tell if any of this was recorded during *Appetite*-era shows. Certainly, much of this derives from the *Illusions* tour: there are backing vocals, horns, and just what every fan wants—lots and lots of Dizzy Reed. And if that isn't indicative of Axl's mindset, there is the priceless moment on "Knockin' on Heaven's Door," when he shrieks "Gimme some reggae!" and the band collapses in a sunsplash groove. So, this is heavy on Axl pretensions and short on pure, brutal rock & roll. At its best, it may come closer to vintage G N' R than the *Illusions* did, but the missing ingredients are all too apparent, and in this context, their absence is all the more painful. *—Stephen Thomas Erlewine*

Guru

Vocals / Jazz-Rap, Alternative Rap, Acid Jazz

The main cog behind Gang Starr, rapper/composer Guru stepped out on his own in 1993 with the album *Jazzmatazz.* Enlisting support from the hip-hop and jazz communities, he received help from Roy Ayers and Donald Byrd to N'Dea Davenport of Brand New Heavies. Guru later did selected club dates with some of the *Jazzmatazz* personnel before returning to straighter hip-hop on Gang Starr's *Hard to Earn.* In 1995, he recruited Ramsey Lewis, Branford Marsalis, and Jamiroquai to help out on *Jazzmatazz, Vol. 2: The New Reality.* After a five-year break, Guru's Jazzmatazz released *Streetsoul* in 2000, with collaborative tracks featuring Herbie Hancock, Isaac Hayes, the Roots, Erykah Badu, and Macy Gray, among others. *—Ron Wynn*

● **Jazzmatazz, Vol. 1** / 1993 / Chrysalis ✦✦✦✦

Gang Starr's Guru has put together the best hip-hop/jazz outing issued yet, at least on these shores. Instead of merely wedding rap to recycled jazz samples, Guru and a cast of jazz, fusion, and R&B stars actually converge performance-wise, with the jazz musicians playing and the rappers and vocalists singing fresh material. The results are never less than enjoyable, and occasionally inspirational. Guru's deadpan rap style works, as do N'Dea Davenport's sultry vocals, and Roy Ayers, Donald Byrd, and Lonnie Liston Smith sound more convincing doing these songs than they have on any recent release of their own. *—Ron Wynn*

Jazzmatazz, Vol. 2: The New Reality / Jul. 18, 1995 / Chrysalis ✦✦✦

The follow-up to the heavily acclaimed *Jazzmatazz, Vol. 1.* This album might not have quite as much jazz-rap power as the first volume did, but it's still quite good. Some of the big guns of jazz found their way into the album, including Branford Marsalis (who, of course, had already experimented with urban beats a bit with his Buckshot Lefonque project), Freddie Hubbard, Ramsey Lewis, and Kenny Garrett. Underground rapper Kool Keith (at this point still a member of the Ultramagnetics) also makes an appearance. Dancehall reggae princess Patra is included on a track, as are Chaka Khan and Me'Shell N'Degeocello; Jamiroquai helps out in another. In some ways, the personnel on this album may be slightly superior to the first outing, but the music also seems a tiny bit blander. Still, what makes the *Jazzmatazz* albums special is the live synthesis of jazz and rap. With Guru's vocals over the top of live jazz performers (as opposed the usual samples), interplay is facilitated between the two, and thus a whole new dimension is added to the fusion. For someone interested in jazz-rap in general, the first album is a higher priority (as would be Us3's albums, with extensive Blue Note sampling), but this album is still high on the list. *—Adam Greenberg*

Streetsoul / Sep. 26, 2000 / Virgin ✦✦✦

Give Keith Elam credit for knowing how to surround himself with great talent. It's a fact that has guided his career from the early days of Gang Starr—the group he formed with one of the greatest hip-hop producers of all time, DJ Premier—to his solo *Jazzmatazz* albums, recorded with a host of jazz legends including Roy Ayers, Donald Byrd, Freddie Hubbard, and Branford Marsalis. This third volume in Guru's *Jazzmatazz* series came not only after a five-year break, but at a time when the notion of jazz-rap was almost as antiquated as the '70s jazz-funk sound it helped resurrect back in the late '80s. Guru undoubtedly realized this, so instead of focusing strictly on jazz this time out, he made *Streetsoul* more of a roots album. With all the great contemporary R&B talent on display, though, any jazz-rap fans still left could hardly be annoyed with Guru's shift in focus from jazz to soul. A trinity of late-'90s soul divas—Macy Gray, Erykah Badu, and Kelis—each have features, and the swing-to-urban production behind Badu's contribution frames her vocal excellently. DJ Premier also shows up, contributing his usual excellent trackmaster skills to "Hustlin' Daze," with vocals by Donell Jones. Fellow rapcentrics the Roots make an appearance on the fight-for-your-right anthem "Lift Your Fist," and Guru inserts two pioneer tracks, Herbie Hancock's "Timeless" and Isaac Hayes' "Night Vision" near the end. Unfortunately, the one caveat to *Streetsoul*—Guru's rapping talent hasn't improved at *all*—is practically unavoidable considering he pops up for a verse or two smack-dab in the middle of almost every track here. —*John Bush*

Baldhead Slick and Da Click / Sep. 25, 2001 / Landspeed ✦✦✦

Arlo Guthrie

b. Jul. 10, 1947, Coney Island, NY
Vocals, Guitar / Contemporary Folk, Folk-Rock, Singer/Songwriter, Political Folk
Like his father Woody Guthrie, Arlo Guthrie has carved out a career as a folksinger and songwriter with a social conscience who leavens political messages with humor. Though Woody Guthrie was hospitalized for much of Arlo's youth, the youngster nevertheless grew up in a musical community that included Pete Seeger, Leadbelly, and Cisco Houston. He learned to play the guitar at age six and was performing in coffeehouses by his late teens.

Guthrie's early fame was based on his anti-Establishment shaggy-dog story in song, "Alice's Restaurant," actually a comic monolog about the singer's troubles with the police and the draft board that was extremely timely when it appeared on record in 1967. The *Alice's Restaurant* album became Guthrie's only gold record, but he made a series of folk-rock records through the '70s, filling them with his own songs and those of his contemporaries, notably Steve Goodman's "The City of New Orleans," which became Guthrie's sole hit single in 1972.

Guthrie's commercial fortunes, like those of most folkies, declined by the end of the '70s, and he made his last album for Warner Bros. in 1981. Since then, he has launched his own label, Rising Son, which has reissued his Warner albums and released his new recordings. He continues to tour extensively and to work for such causes as environmentalism, issuing *Mystic Journey* in 1998. —*William Ruhlmann*

★ **Alice's Restaurant** / 1967 / Reprise ✦✦✦✦✦
In 1967 when this album came out it was totally radical, directly political, and so deliciously funny that it deflated a great deal of the seriousness of the growing anti-war movement. In this one stroke Guthrie established himself as more than the son of the famous man and major star. Aside from the title cut, people often forget about the "Motorcycle Song" and "Chilling of the Evening," which were on side two. —*Richard Meyer*

The Best of Arlo Guthrie / 1977 / Reprise ✦✦✦✦✦
Son of folk legend Woody Guthrie, Arlo was always a hit with the hippie crowd. Most of his most well-known musical moments focused on the humorous side of his career but, as this collection shows, he could definitely be serious as well. The highlights of the disc include a rousing version of his tongue-in-cheek anti-war epic "Alice's Restaurant" and especially silly "Motorcycle (Significance of the Pickle) Song." The serious and evocative side is best showcased here with the classics "Coming Into Los Angeles" and "City of New Orleans." This compilation is a great introduction to the works of this artist and may well be the only CD casual listeners will ever need in their Arlo Guthrie collections. —*Gary Hill*

Guy [1]

f. 1987
New Jack Swing, Club/Dance, Urban
The seminal R&B trio Guy was the first group to sport the new jack swing sound, essentially traditional soul vocals melded to hip-hop beats, with credit for the genre's invention going to founder, multi-instrumentalist, and superproducer Teddy Riley. Their self-titled

debut album was an instant smash, producing the R&B hits "I Like," "Groove Me," "Spend the Night," and "Teddy's Jam." Meanwhile, Riley found himself in strong demand as a songwriter and producer; in 1988, Riley produced Bobby Brown's *Don't Be Cruel*, the album that helped new jack swing cross over into the pop mainstream. By 1989, however, Guy was in turmoil; Riley's brother Brandon Mitchell was killed in a shooting, and Guy became involved in an acrimonious split with manager Gene Griffin over money. 1990's *The Future* spawned R&B hits in "Let's Chill," "Do Me Right," "D-O-G Me Out," and "Long Gone." However, by the time Riley and Guy finally started to attract media attention for their innovative and influential work, the trio had broken up. Riley concentrated on his production and songwriting career for several years before forming the band Blackstreet. —*Steve Huey*

● **Guy** / 1988 / MCA ✦✦✦✦✦
One of the most seminal and influential releases of late '80s, Guy's self-titled debut album did more than its part to popularize new jack swing, a style that would soon become inescapable on urban contemporary radio. Teddy Riley didn't actually invent new jack swing with Guy—he'd already gotten the ball rolling on Keith Sweat's 1987 debut *Make It Last Forever*—but this album did more than any other to make it so incredibly popular in the R&B world. With their tough blend of hip-hop, R&B, and Gap Band-influenced funk, hits like "Groove Me" and "Teddy's Jam" defined new jack swing and served as the blueprint for countless new jack recordings in the late '80s and early to mid-'90s. One shameless Guy clone after another would pop up on urban radio, the vast majority of whom weren't even a fraction as inventive as Riley's distinctive trio. For anyone with even a casual interest in new jack, this CD is absolutely essential. —*Alex Henderson*

The Future / 1990 / Uptown/MCA ✦✦✦
New jack swing, a hard-edged, high-tech blend of funk, R&B, and rap/hip-hop, has been milked for all it's worth and run into the ground by Guy's numerous imitators in the late '80s and early- to mid-'90s. But in the hands of its highly influential orginators, Guy, it sounds fresh and inspired. Though not as strong as the debut album of 1988, *The Future* is one of the more appealing—and certainly more authentic—examples of "new jack swing." Lead by the ubiquitous producer/songwriter Teddy Riley, the trio brings a definite urgency to grinding, forceful funk like "Teddy's Jam 2" and "Her" and to such slow jams as "Do Me Right" and "Tease Me Tonight" (both of which recall the Gap Band a la "Outstanding"). Especially riveting is the all-rap number "Total Control," a brutally honest commentary on exploitation in the music business. It's important to absorb Guy's music and realize that it is proof, in the interest of understandable complaints about the glut of faceless "new jack swing" artists saturating the market, that it wasn't always cheap and formulaic. —*Alex Henderson*

Guy III / Jan. 25, 2000 / MCA ✦✦✦✦
More than ten years after their sophomore album—titled, ironically, *Future*—appeared to draw the curtain on urban forerunners Guy, Teddy Riley, Aaron Hall, and Damion Hall came back for their third album. In the interim, both Hall brothers released solo albums, and Riley continued his hit-making success by producing Bobby Brown, Michael Jackson, Stevie Wonder, and SWV (among others), and by appearing in yet another superstar group, Blackstreet. After Blackstreet's third album *Finally* failed to chart as high as its predecessor, Riley and the Halls re-formed. Guy was always more than just an above-average soul group, and though Riley's production schedule slowed slightly during the late '90s, he was still one of the biggest names in contemporary R&B. *Guy III* equals the extraordinary expectations that any new material from Guy provokes, occasionally exceeding their work in the past. —*Keith Farley*

Sammy Hagar

b. Oct. 13, 1947, Monterey, CA
Vocals, Guitar / Arena Rock, Heavy Metal, Hard Rock

After spending several years as the lead vocalist and rhythm guitarist for the mid-'70s hard-rock band Montrose, Sammy Hagar began a solo career that produced several hits and made him an album rock favorite. Hagar became a true star once he joined Van Halen in 1985, but he was a popular hard rocker ever since his first album with Montrose. Former Edgar Winter guitarist Ronnie Montrose asked Hagar to join his band in 1973. Hagar recorded two albums with Montrose before going solo in 1976. Hagar's eponymous debut was his first chart entry, and his 1981 album *Standing Hampton* went platinum. His 1984 album *VOA* contained the hit single "I Can't Drive 55," which peaked at number 26. In 1985, Hagar replaced David Lee Roth in Van Halen; his first album with the group was 1986's *5150.* Hagar stayed with Van Halen through the remainder of the '80s and half of the '90s before tensions began to surface between Hagar and the rest of the band. In the summer of 1996, Hagar either quit Van Halen or was fired. The entire incident became a media sensation, ensuring that Hagar's 1997 solo album *Marching to Mars*—his first in ten years—would be greeted with much media-generated fanfare. *Red Voodoo* followed two years later. —*Stephen Thomas Erlewine*

All Night Long / 1978 / One Way ♦♦♦

All Night Long is better than most hard rock live albums not only because Sammy Hagar is at his best when he's on stage, but because the set list includes only his best songs, eliminating the filler that tends to clutter his albums. —*Stephen Thomas Erlewine*

Standing Hampton / 1981 / Geffen ♦♦♦♦♦

After releasing several competent but more or less undistinguished albums on Capitol, Sammy Hagar switched to Geffen in 1981 and released *Standing Hampton*, a polished but tough record that showed a surprising amount of pop songcraft. The added production gloss and improved melodic sense proved commercially successful—the album was his first million-seller and it cracked the Top 30—and artistically successful as well; the record was the most consistent and memorable album he recorded to date, featuring the singles "I'll Fall in Love Again," "Baby's on Fire," and "There's Only One Way to Rock." —*Stephen Thomas Erlewine*

Rematch / 1982 / Capitol ♦♦♦♦

As Sammy Hagar's career was at its height in the early '80s, Capitol, his '70s record label, released *Rematch*, a compilation of highlights from his six albums with the label. Like *All Night Long* before it, *Rematch* cuts away all the fat from Hagar's '70s catalog, leaving only his best rockers, including the scorching "I've Done Everything for You," "Plain Jane," "Turn Up the Music," and "Trans Am (Highway Wonderland)." Even though the track listing is well chosen, his Capitol records weren't as impressive as his albums for Geffen, meaning *Rematch* is only the best of a specific era of Hagar's career, not his entire career. —*Stephen Thomas Erlewine*

Three Lock Box / 1983 / Geffen ♦♦♦♦♦

Continuing the sleek, driving pop-oriented sound of Hagar's breakthrough *Standing Hampton*, *Three Lock Box* equals its predecessor, featuring such highlights as the double entendres of the title track and the hit single "Your Love Is Driving Me Crazy." —*Stephen Thomas Erlewine*

VOA / 1984 / Geffen ♦♦♦♦

VOA was the last album Hagar recorded before he became the lead singer of Van Halen and the record shows why he was invited to join the band. With songs like "I Can't Drive 55" he adds a simple melody to the song which never distracts from the all-important hard-driving riff. On "Two Sides of Love," he shows that he has the ability to pull off a power ballad, wrenching every bit of feeling out of the song. Like Hagar himself, *VOA* is never subtle, but in hard rock, that's a positive attribute. —*Stephen Thomas Erlewine*

I Never Said Goodbye / 1987 / Geffen ♦♦

Sammy Hagar / 1987 / One Way ♦♦♦

Sammy Hagar, the singer's last solo album, was released a year after his first album with Van Halen, 1986's *5150.* Although it charted the highest of any of his records, peaking at number 14, it wasn't as successful as his three previous albums, suffering from a slick, synthesized production and a lack of consistent material. The power ballad "Give to Live" was a hit and a couple of the rockers raised above the pedestrian level, yet the overall product was rather faceless. Perhaps sensing the lackluster quality of the record, Hagar launched an MTV promotion to re-title the record; the winning entry was *I Never Said Goodbye*, and the album was titled that way in subsequent pressings. The 1994 *Unboxed* compilation also called the album *I Never Said Goodbye*, not *Sammy Hagar.* —*Stephen Thomas Erlewine*

The Best of Sammy Hagar / Nov. 16, 1992 / Capitol ♦♦♦♦

A CD-era collection of Hagar's Capitol work that supplants *Rematch*, *The Best of Sammy Hagar* has a nearly identical track listing as the previous collection and suffers from the same flaws. —*Stephen Thomas Erlewine*

● Unboxed / Mar. 15, 1994 / Geffen ♦♦♦♦♦

In between his days with hard-rocking Montrose in the early '70s and his takeover of lead singing duties from David Lee Roth in Van Halen, Sammy Hagar had a moderately successful solo career. Many of his singles didn't receive the recognition they deserved, which were either staid guitar-driven party anthems or infectious AOR tunes with punchy choruses. *Unboxed* is a hits collection that takes Hagar's best work from *Standing Hampton*, *I Never Said Goodbye*, *VOA*, and *Three Lock Box*, plus two other fiery singles, and puts them all on one disc, which is both convenient and entertaining. Hagar did crack Billboard's Top 40 with three of the songs on this hits set, including the friendly six-string pounce of "Two Sides of Love," which hit number 38 in 1984. His most popular solo effort, the speed inducing raucous of "I Can't Drive 55," highlights the album, proving that the vocal abilities of Hagar are anything but limited. His semi-slower material is equally justified, especially the surprising sincerity found within "Give to Live," which broke the Top 30 in 1987. The thunderous chorus of "Heavy Metal," which is twice as fast as the rest of the song, spotlights Hagar at his most fervent and is outlined with raw chord-crunching power. Surprisingly, Sammy Hagar's highest-charting single up to the release of *Unboxed*, the radio-friendly "Your Love Is Driving Me Crazy," is missing from this collection. Nonetheless, this greatest hits presents Hagar in a light that many have either sidestepped or completely disregarded, but with all his best material in one place, his musicianship is better appreciated. —*Mike DeGagne*

Marching to Mars / May 20, 1997 / MCA ♦♦♦♦

Evidently, being kicked out of Van Halen revitalized Sammy Hagar, since *Marching to Mars* is among his best solo albums. A lean, tough collection of by-the-books hard-rockers, *Marching to Mars* stands out because of its immediate sound and Hagar's sense of purpose. He's out to prove himself, to illustrate that he wasn't just Van Halen's mouthpiece or a blowhard. Subtlety still remains a weak point with Hagar, but he's rarely sounded quite as convincing as he does here, tearing through a set of surprisingly well-written songs with such guest artists as Huey Lewis, Slash, Mickey Hart, and Bootsy Collins. There's still a handful of weak moments, but the record is one of his strongest, and with bluesy cuts like "Little White Lie," it's also one of his more ambitious. —*Stephen Thomas Erlewine*

Red Voodoo / Mar. 23, 1999 / MCA ♦♦♦

When Sammy Hagar's 11 years with Van Halen came to an end, he delivered some of the best solo albums of his career. The rocker's post-Van Halen albums weren't much different from his pre-Van Halen albums of the late '70s and early to mid '80s—Hagar was still playing the type of commercial hard rock and arena rock that put him on the map, and he was doing so with a lot of conviction. The Californian was in his early fifties when *Red Voodoo* came out in 1999, but it hardly sounds like the work of someone who was mellowing with age. Ballsy, in-your-face rockers like "Mas Tequila" (which incorporates Gary Glitter's "Rock & Roll, Part 2"), "Don't Fight It (Feel it)," "Shag," and the AC/DC-ish "High and Dry Again" are oozing with confidence—in fact, it's almost as though Hagar is shaking his fist at the Van Halen brothers and letting them know that he can do quite well without them, thank you. To some proponents of '90s alternative rock, Hagar and other arena rock veterans were anachronistic—and, to be sure, this CD won't win any awards for being innovative or groundbreaking. Nonetheless, *Red Voodoo* is among the most passionate, focused, and inspired albums of Hagar's career. —*Alex Henderson*

Nina Hagen

b. Mar. 11, 1955, Berlin, Germany
Vocals / Post-Punk, New Wave, Alternative Pop/Rock

Born in East Germany, Nina Hagen had already gained a reputation as a flamboyant rock singer by the time she emigrated to the West in 1976, where she formed a band, signed to CBS Germany, and released their debut album, *Nina Hagen Band*, in 1978. It was followed in 1980 by *Unbehagen*. Hagen's first U.S. release, *Nina Hagen Band EP* (1980), was a four-song EP consisting of songs drawn from her two German releases. She moved to New York and made her first English-language LP, *Nunsexmonkrock*, in 1982. That and its follow-up, the Giorgio Moroder-produced *Fearless* (1983), charted briefly, and "New York New York" was a Top Ten dance club hit. But Hagen left CBS after *Nina Hagen in Ekstacy* (1985). In 1988, she celebrated her marriage with the EP *Punk Wedding*, released in Canada, and in 1989 she returned to the German market with *Nina Hagen.* —*William Ruhlmann*

● **14 Friendly Abductions: The Best of Nina Hagen** / Mar. 26, 1996 / Columbia/Legacy ✦✦✦✦✦

Nina Hagen is a unique vocalist, ranging from a coloratura soprano to a guttural alto and phrasing in surprising, dramatically changing ways, so that her performances are musical roller coasters, full of sudden shifts in mood and volume. Singing alternately in German and English, Hagen is backed by rock tracks leaning toward punk on some songs, and by producer Giorgio Moroder's signature Eurodisco synth-dance sounds on others on this 14-track, 74-minute compilation. Want to hear a German-language version of the Tubes' "White Punks on Dope"? How about a performance of "My Way" (also in German) that rivals Sid Vicious' for outrageousness? Ultimately, Nina Hagen may be a period novelty act of the early '80s, a mixture of Toni Basil, Falco, and a hyena. But she gets your attention. *—William Ruhlmann*

Haircut 100

f. 1980, Beckenham, Kent, England, **db.** 1983

New Wave

Combining light funk with frothy pop, Haircut 100 was one of the cleanest and most accessible new wave groups. Formed in 1980, the British band's core members were vocalist Nick Heyward, bassist Les Nemes, and guitarist Graham Jones; the following years drummer Memphis Blair Cunningham, saxophonist Phil Smith, and percussionist Mark Fox joined the group. Once the band was signed to Arista Records, they were put in the direction of producer Bob Sargeant, who helped them polish their stylish pop. Released in late 1981, Haircut 100's first single, "Favourite Shirts (Boy Meets Girl)," managed to reach number four in the U.K., establishing the group's widespread appeal. The band released their debut album, *Pelican West*, in early 1982. Their next single, "Love Plus One," was a bigger hit, making the band one of the hottest British pop groups of the year. However, their momentum crashed to a halt when Heyward decided to pursue a solo career. Fox became the lead vocalist in early 1983, yet Haircut 100 could not replicate their previous success; they broke up after the release of their second album, 1984's *Paint and Paint*. *—Stephen Thomas Erlewine*

Pelican West / Feb. 1982 / Arista ✦✦✦✦

Haircut 100's debut album *Pelican West* is a widely uneven concoction of lite-funk and jazzy new wave pop. Although the group's music was frequently so light it virtually disappeared, they did record a pair of classic new wave singles with the effervescent "Love Plus One" and "Favourite Shirts (Boy Meets Girl)." Although much of the record lacks the hooks of those two tracks, there's a handful of enjoyably breezy pop songs on *Pelican West*, such as "Fantastic Day" and "Snow Girl," that makes it worth investigating for new wave fetishists. Still, there's no denying that Haircut 100's material was often inadequate—a situation only emphasized on the American edition of the album, which places the singles at the front—and that the record sounded like a period piece just a few years after its release. *—Stephen Thomas Erlewine*

Paint and Paint / 1984 / Polydor ✦✦

Nick Heyward left Haircut 100 for a solo career shortly after the success of *Pelican West*, so the group decided that percussionist Mark Fox would be an adequate lead vocalist for their second album, *Paint and Paint*. In many ways they were right, since Fox has a pleasantly thin voice that blends easily into the band's lightly jazzy pop and funk. However, he lacks both the fey wit and easy melodicism of Heyward and, as a result, the group fails to produce anything as effortlessly catchy and memorable as "Love Plus One." It's no surprise that the group disappeared shortly after the release of *Paint and Paint*. *—Stephen Thomas Erlewine*

● **The Best of Haircut 100** / 1994 / Camden ✦✦✦✦

The Best of Haircut 100 is a 14-track collection featuring all of the lite new wave group's biggest hits, including "Favourite Shirts (Boy Meets Girl)" and "Love Plus One," plus several of Nick Heyward's solo singles, like "Whistle Down the Wind." Track for track, it's the most consistent album by either Haircut 100 or Heyward, even though several of the cuts are little more than pleasant artifacts from the early '80s. However, the three previously mentioned singles are all minor new wave classics, and it's nice to have them collected on one disc. *—Stephen Thomas Erlewine*

Bill Haley

b. Jul. 6, 1925, Highland Park, MI, **d.** Feb. 9, 1981, Harlingen, TX

Vocals, Guitar / Rockabilly, Western Swing, Rock & Roll

The Bill Haley and the Comets recording of "Rock Around the Clock," which topped the charts for eight weeks in 1955, is remembered as the beginning of the rock era. It also represented Haley's peak as a performer; his career had begun some time before and would continue for a long time after. Haley began leading Western swing bands under various names in the late '40s, slowly incorporating elements of R&B. Haley was among the first performers—perhaps he was even the very first—of any color to combine R&B and C&W in a way that can readily be identified by listeners of any era as bona fide rock & roll. His early-'50s sides rank among his most exciting, steering country and big-band forms into uncharted regions. Haley also wrote much of his own material, and one of his compositions, "Crazy, Man, Crazy," became one of the first Top 20 rock & roll hits in 1953. In 1954, he moved to the major Decca label, where his sides became increasingly formulaic, though for a time very successful, after "Rock Around the Clock." Haley was largely eclipsed as the king of rock & roll by Elvis Presley and others who followed him from 1956 on. Nevertheless, he continued to perform overseas and in oldies shows in the United States. *—William Ruhlmann & Richie Unterberger*

★ **From the Original Master Tapes** / 1985 / MCA ✦✦✦✦✦

This is it—the Bill Haley record to own! Compiled by producer Steve Hoffman from the original session masters (you even get studio chatter ahead of "Rock Around the Clock"), this 20-song collection is the definitive Haley hits collection, with every song of consequence that he recorded for Decca Records during the years 1954-56. The sound is extraordinary—you haven't really heard Haley's music till you've heard this disc—and the sessionography adds a great deal to our knowledge of the players. From "Rock Around the Clock" and "Thirteen Women" to "Don't Knock the Rock," this is the best representation of Haley's peak years. *—Bruce Eder*

The Decca Years & More / 1991 / Bear Family ✦✦✦✦

The Decca Years are where Bill Haley and his Comets had their greatest success, bringing rock & roll into the mainstream with the seminal "Rock Around the Clock." That track kicks off the exhaustive six-disc set *The Decca Years & More*, which covers all of the group's recordings (including unreleased cuts) over the course of 132 tracks. This, to be sure, is something that only the dedicated will have the patience to sort through, not because the music is bad, but because there's so much of it and so much of it is at the same level—good, but not great, jumping R&B, rock, and country boogie. The Comets are often hot, Haley is a pretty good frontman, but as a full set it's simply too much for anybody outside of Haley's dedicated fanbase (and that includes hardcore fans of '50s rock & roll, who will be better-served with *From the Original Master Tapes*). *—Stephen Thomas Erlewine*

Rock the Joint! / Apr. 5, 1995 / Schoolkids ✦✦✦✦✦

A 22-track collection that collects sides from 1951-1953. Those who haven't heard this material before will be astonished to discover bona fide rock & roll dating from three to four years earlier than the era (1954-1955) more commonly associated with the music's birth. Haley's sound is similar to the country-boogie of the late '40s, retaining the steel guitar prominent in much of the era's country music, but it's clearly more driving and forward-looking. The songs owe a lot to jump R&B but are transformed into the basic model of rock & roll with slapping bass, ricky-tick drums, and extended electric guitar riffing. Listen to his version of Jackie Brenston's "Rocket 88" (which has itself been pegged as one of the first rock & roll records) and you'll be astounded to note the basics of rockabilly already in place—in 1951. The low buzzing, distorted guitar on "Green Tree Boogie" (also from 1951) is also a revelation, as is the guitar solo on 1952's "Rock the Joint," which is almost identical to the much more famous one on "Rock Around the Clock." The later sides introduce a honking sax, which would become such a prominent feature in 1950s rock & roll. Includes "Crazy Man Crazy," the first rock & roll song to make the Top 20. *—Richie Unterberger*

The Warner Brothers Years & More / Jun. 23, 1999 / Bear Family ✦✦✦

The companion piece to Bear Family's *The Decca Years and More*, *The Warner Brothers Years & More* picks up where its predecessor left off, offering every recording Billy Haley & the Comets made for Warner over the course of eight discs and 158 songs. If that set was for the dedicated, this is for the fanatical, since it covers the non-hit years. Haley remained an appealing, everyman frontman and his band (now not stable, changing every so often) remained professional and entertaining, but the choice of the material became a little questionable and the productions didn't always showcase the band at its best. In other words, this is truly for serious Haley listeners that will not really mind the unevenness of the material (they may even dig it, actually). It's superbly assembled, of course, but it's for hardcore fans only. *—Stephen Thomas Erlewine*

Half Japanese

f. 1977

Experimental Rock, Indie Rock, Post-Punk, Alternative Pop/Rock, American Underground

Depending on your point of view, Half Japanese is either a celebration of the pure, amateurish, do-it-yourself rock & roll spirit or a pretentious, highly irritating example of noisy, self-conscious experimental rock at its most extreme. Formed by Jad and David Fair in 1977, the group started bashing out music in their parents' basement in Maryland, recording their debut EP by themselves. By the time Half Japanese recorded their debut album, the three-record box set *1/2 Gentlemen/Not Beasts*, they had acquired a full-time drummer plus a saxophonist, yet their music was no less noisy and primitive; if anything, it was more atonal and difficult than before.

For the rest of their career, the band has proudly displayed nothing approaching instrumental virtuosity. David Fair left the band after their third record, rejoining briefly for 1988's *Charmed Life*. Throughout the years, the lineup has changed frequently—at times it has included Velvet Underground drummer Maureen Tucker and guitarist Don Fleming, as well as occasional contributions from Fred Frith and John Zorn—but Jad Fair has remained. That doesn't necessarily mean the music hasn't changed; their later records are slightly more musically varied and accessible, yet no less challenging. Fair has released a few solo albums that are stranger (believe it or not) than the typical Half Japanese release. *—Stephen Thomas Erlewine*

1/2 Gentlemen/Not Beasts / 1980 / T.E.C. Tones ✦✦✦✦✦

As with any album that is three records long, *1/2 Gentlemen/Not Beasts* unwittingly shows Half Japanese's true roots. Over the three records, the band "covers" such minimalists as the Velvet Underground, the Stooges, and Jonathan Richman, as well as deconstructing such wordsmiths as Bruce Springsteen and Bob Dylan. Although they would have you believe that their untuned, almost unlistenable, instrumental clatter is the result of being so enthusiastic that they didn't bother to learn how to play their instruments, it's just the logical, inevitable intellectual extension of Richman's naivete and the Velvet Underground's stripped-down guitar. Half Japanese is consciously primitive and amateurish. *—Stephen Thomas Erlewine*

Loud / 1981 / Armageddon ✦✦✦

Music to Strip By / 1987 / 50 Skidillion Watts ✦✦✦

Charmed Life / 1988 / 50 Skidillion Watts ✦✦✦✦✦

While *Charmed Life* is the band's most accessible record, it doesn't even come close to the mainstream's concept of what constitutes pop music. Yet when Jad Fair sings about love and joy on *Charmed Life*, he is as straightforward and direct as he ever gets. —*Stephen Thomas Erlewine*

The Band That Would Be King / 1989 / 50 Skidillion Watts ✦✦✦✦

This 1993 new edition of *The Band That Would Be King* comes with 11 previously unreleased songs and a second and outstanding version of "Sugarcane." The album is a perfect medley of humorous lo-fi, rock & roll hit singles, and little experimentations. The band lineup for this album is Jad Fair, Don Fleming from Gumball and Mark Jickling, credited here as Mr. J. Rice. And icing on the cake: Kramer, Georges Cartwright, Fred Frith, and John Zorn are in on this. —*Romain Guillou*

We Are They Who Ache With Amorous Love / 1990 / T.E.C. Tones/Elemental Music ✦✦✦

● **Greatest Hits** / Mar. 13, 1995 / Safe House ✦✦✦✦✦

As Byron Coley says in his entertaining piece in the liner notes, "They have no hits by standards that Howard Cosell would appreciate." But by the time *Greatest Hits* came out, Half Japanese had gained an international fan base, released more records than many well-known bands have ever done, and had Kurt Cobain singing their praises. So even if the title is curious, the impulse behind the collection isn't and, given the scattered discography of the band, *Greatest Hits* is the perfect place for a neophyte to take the plunge. Two discs packed to the brim with Jad Fair and company's particular rock & roll vision means a lot of listening, but there's no pretense at any one way to give the release an ear—there's no chronological order, just a slew of songs that one can dip in and out of at leisure. Pretty much every album up to that point is represented at least once, from the original *1/2 Gentlemen/Not Beasts* set to 1992's *Boo!* and, while lineups and fidelity fluctuates wildly, not to mention the particular styles tried out, it's all clearly one particular approach at heart. Jad Fair's love-it-or-hate-it voice (and sometimes David Fair's more conventional approach) tackles everything from "My Sordid Past" to "Salt and Pepper" and back again, and his fluctuating crew keeps everything a ragged delight. For the hardcore, five otherwise unreleased tracks do surface. A cover of Jimmie Rodgers' "T for Texas" features Eugene Chadbourne as a duet partner, while the on-the-face-of-it surprising 1993 remake of Primal Scream's "Movin' on Up" becomes an enjoyable rave-up in the band's own garage-y way. "King Kong" makes for an amusing biography of said character, while "Amazing Clock" and "Identical Twins" are also enjoyable. David Fair's enjoyable and encouraging essay "How to Play Guitar" makes for a great final touch. —*Ned Raggett*

Hot / Aug. 22, 1995 / Safe House ✦✦✦

This album is aptly titled: On *Hot*, Jad Fair straightens out his overt quirkiness into pure white punk riot ("Drum Straight"), shimmying garage rock ("Well"), bouncy indie pop ("True Believers"), and ominous metal ("Part of My Plan"). The result is (gasp!) a highly listenable record. The direction on the album has a lot to do with the creative energy of this Half Japanese lineup, which consists of guitarist John Sluggett (who plays drums for Moe Tucker), Mick Hobbs, Jason Willett, and Gilles Rieder. This is a nice mix between in-your-face noise and thoughtful, not too schticky indie-pop. —*Erik Hage*

Heaven Sent / Nov. 4, 1997 / Emperor Jones ✦✦✦✦

Jad Fair's voice waxes between an unstable nasal falsetto and Lou Reed on the 64-minute title track. I hear the rhyming stream-of-consciousness lyrics as a psychological chronicle of "falling in like" with someone. Nine additional tracks of sparse lo-fi music and Fair's near conversational observations are "remixes" of "Heaven Sent" and seem to tell the crumbling tale of like waning into disinterest. Spend an hour and some minutes in Jad's dream. It's not quite Technicolor, but I think every shade of gray is represented. —*Thomas Schulte*

Hello / Feb. 20, 2001 / Alternative Tentacles ✦✦✦

Hall & Oates

f. 1972

Blue-Eyed Soul, Pop/Rock, Folk-Rock, Soft Rock

With their savvy contemporary take on blue-eyed soul—spiked equally with pop skills, new wave flourishes, and rock production—Hall & Oates had a wave of chart-topping singles in the early '80s that broke records set by the Everly Brothers. Despite their success, they weren't critically respected at the time, although their catalog of songs, in retrospect, is one of the finest mainstream pop had to offer in their era.

Hall & Oates began their recording career with *Whole Oates*, an album that was closer to folk-rock. They wove soul into 1973's *Abandoned Luncheonette*, which resulted in their first moderate hit, "She's Gone." After the Todd Rundgren-produced *War Babies* stiffed, they left Atlantic Records for RCA. Their eponymous 1975 debut for the label was where they discovered their signature mix of rock, pop, and soul, resulting in a Top 20 album and Top ten single, "Sarah Smile." *Bigger Than the Both of Us* was even bigger, thanks to "Rich Girl," their first number one single. Hall & Oates couldn't sustain that success and their next three records failed to make as large an impact. With 1980's *Voices* they had their first blockbuster, as the record launched two Top five singles ("Kiss on My List," "You Make My Dreams"), staying on the charts for 100 weeks and making the duo stars. *Private Eyes* reached the Top Ten on the back of two number ones ("Private Eyes," "I Can't Go for That No Can Do"), and *H20* continued their winning streak in grand fashion, going double platinum and producing their biggest hit, "Maneater." *Big Bam Boom* (1984) went double platinum and featured a number one hit ("Out of Touch"), but it was their last album to enjoy this kind of success. Hall & Oates went on hiatus the following year.

When they regrouped for 1988's *Ooh Yeah!*, their first record for Arista, they had another platinum album, but they'd lost their momentum. Following 1990's *Change of Season*, they quietly retreated from the spotlight. —*Stephen Thomas Erlewine*

Whole Oates / 1972 / Atlantic ✦✦✦

Hall & Oates' debut album was a tentative effort, with the two singers hesitantly working their way around slick but relatively undistinguished material that displayed their folk roots more than any other record they would later make. —*Stephen Thomas Erlewine*

Abandoned Luncheonette / 1973 / Atlantic ✦✦✦✦✦

Abandoned Luncheonette, Hall & Oates' second album, was the first indication of the duo's talent for sleek, soul-inflected pop/rock. It featured the single "She's Gone," which would become a big hit in 1975, when it was re-released following the success of "Sara Smile." —*Stephen Thomas Erlewine*

War Babies / 1974 / Atlantic ✦✦

After crafting the fitfully accomplished blue-eyed Philly soul-pop of *Abandoned Luncheonette*, Hall & Oates retreated to a more rock-oriented sound on *War Babies*, recorded with producer Todd Rundgren. Some of the tracks work, but the duo's performance sounds forced throughout much of the record. —*Stephen Thomas Erlewine*

Daryl Hall & John Oates / Sep. 1975 / Buddha ✦✦✦✦✦

Switching to RCA, Daryl Hall & John Oates recorded a self-titled album that fulfilled their early promise as pop-savvy blue-eyed soul craftsmen. A few of the tracks fall flat—including the reggae-tinged "Soldering" and the pompous "Ennui on the Mountain"—but much of the album is lush and catchy, featuring ballads and mid-tempo numbers that are nearly as engaging as their breakthrough single "Sara Smile." —*Stephen Thomas Erlewine*

Bigger Than the Both of Us / 1976 / RCA ✦✦

No Goodbyes / 1977 / Atlantic ✦✦

Beauty on a Back Street / 1977 / RCA ✦✦✦

Beauty on a Back Street isn't quite as accomplished as its two predecessors, yet it is more ambitious and diverse, as Hall & Oates begin to add some arena-rock conventions to their sound, particularly distorted guitars and anthemic choruses. On *War Babies* they had tried a similar attack, but on *Beauty on a Back Street*, the duo's songwriting was stronger, which meant that the instrumental approach didn't overwhelm the actual songs. —*Stephen Thomas Erlewine*

Along the Red Ledge / Sep. 1978 / RCA ✦✦✦

Continuing the more rock-oriented approach of *Beauty on a Back Street*, *Along the Red Ledge* is more successful than its predecessor, as the duo landed on a polished melodic pop/rock style that managed to retain their Philly soul influences without drowning their voices in distorted guitar flourishes. They would refine this sound two years later on *Voices*, the record that established them as pop/rock superstars. —*Stephen Thomas Erlewine*

X-Static / 1979 / Buddha ✦✦✦✦

After coming up with a sleek and soulful template on *Along the Red Ledge*, Hall & Oates took a temporary detour on *X-Static*, concentrating on disco rhythms. A few tracks were successful—in particular, "Wait for Me"—but the record sounds unfocused and misguided. —*Stephen Thomas Erlewine*

Voices / 1980 / RCA ✦✦✦✦✦

This is the album that took Hall & Oates from being a successful '70s pop duo to being one of the four biggest singles acts of the '80s (the others: Michael Jackson, Prince, and Madonna). The sound is a wonderful pop pastiche, from the Beatlesque "How Does It Feel to Be Back" to the neo-Philadelphia soul of the hits "Kiss on My List" and "You Make My Dreams." —*William Ruhlmann*

Private Eyes / 1981 / RCA ✦✦✦✦

Voices brought Hall & Oates into the new wave era, establishing their sleek fusion of synthesizers, Philly soul, mechanical beats, and pop hooks, but they didn't quite perfect it until *Private Eyes*. Powered by no less than three Top Ten singles, the album is filled with effortlessly catchy hooks and a handful of great songs that don't stop at the hits. Sure, "Private Eyes," "I Can't Go for That (No Can Do)," and "Did It in a Minute" all have remarkably graceful melodies, but what's unexpected is how flat-out terrific the pounding soul of "Looking for a Good Sign" is, or how deftly the arena-rock hooks of "Head Above Water" are executed. There's still a bit of filler, highlighted by John Oates' supremely silly "Mano a Mano," but Hall & Oates never made a record quite as good as *Private Eyes* ever again. —*Stephen Thomas Erlewine*

H2O / 1982 / RCA ✦✦✦✦✦

From the Motown beat of "Maneater" to the lush ballad "One on One," Hall & Oates continue to make the top pop of the early '80s. Also contains "Family Man." —*William Ruhlmann*

☆ **Rock 'n' Soul Pt. 1: Greatest Hits** / 1983 / RCA ✦✦✦✦✦

Not a perfect hits collection but nonetheless an excellent compilation, *Rock 'n' Soul, Pt. 1: Greatest Hits* contains nine of Hall & Oates' biggest hits from 1974's "She's Gone" to 1983's "One on One," adding new songs—the wonderful "Say It Isn't So," plus "Adult Education"—plus a live take of "Wait for Me" for good measure. While several terrific singles are missing—particularly "Did It in a Minute" and "Family Man"—all the essential items are here, and they illustrate the duo's expertise in crafting soulful pop songs, making a convincing argument that Hall & Oates were the last great blue-eyed soul group. —*Stephen Thomas Erlewine*

Big Bam Boom / 1984 / RCA ♦♦♦
The last of the major Hall & Oates albums of the '80s features more of their patented soul-rock sound on the hits "Out of Touch" and "Method of Modern Love." *—William Ruhlmann*

Live at the Apollo / 1985 / RCA ♦♦

Ooh Yeah! / 1988 / Arista ♦♦

Change of Season / 1990 / Arista ♦♦
Apart from the hit "So Close," *Change of Season* is largely undistinguished, relying more on sound than songcraft. Not surprisingly, it was Hall & Oates' lowest-charting album of original material since 1974's *War Babies*, even if it did go gold. *—Stephen Thomas Erlewine*

● **The Atlantic Collection** / Jan. 23, 1996 / Rhino ♦♦♦♦♦
Drawing from Hall & Oates' four Atlantic albums and adding one previously unreleased song, *The Atlantic Collection* is a definitive overview of the duo's early years. Although they only had one hit during this period—"She's Gone," which is included here in its full-length album version—their early recordings contained some of their richest, most diverse music. Much of the material is based in soul, particularly the smooth Philly soul of the early '70s, yet it also has strong folk overtones, as well as distinct pop/rock leanings. Within these 21 tracks, it is possible to hear the roots of their later hits, as well as directions they never wound up pursuing. For serious Hall & Oates fans, *The Atlantic Collection* can be a revelatory listen. *—Stephen Thomas Erlewine*

Marigold Sky / Sep. 30, 1997 / Push ♦♦♦
After spending several years on hiatus, Hall & Oates reunited in 1997 for *Marigold Sky*, their first album since 1990's *Change of Season*. Where its predecessor found the duo struggling to stay contemporary, *Marigold Sky* finds them relaxing into maturity, recording a collection of appealingly smooth, well-crafted soul-pop. There isn't anything as energetic as their early-'80s hits, nor is there anything unforgettably catchy, but it's a well-made album with a number of winning songs illustrating that even if Hall & Oates are past their peak, they nevertheless are capable of making engaging music. *—Stephen Thomas Erlewine*

Master Hits: Hall and Oates / Jul. 27, 1999 / Arista ♦♦♦♦
Arista celebrated its 30th anniversary by releasing *The Heritage Series*, spotlighting the most popular artists on the label. The Hall & Oates installment in *The Heritage Series* is pretty much a straight hits collection, featuring highlights from their stint at the label. Since they arrived on Arista after their peak years at RCA, their biggest hits aren't here, but this does function as a nice supplement to *Rock N Soul, Pt. 1*, containing such latter-day hits as "Everything Your Heart Desires," "So Close," "Starting All Over Again," and "Change of Season." The remaining 11 songs don't quite meet the standards of the singles, nor are they as good as their RCA also-rans, but this is an excellent, concise portrait of Hall & Oates' Arista years. *—Stephen Thomas Erlewine*

★ **The Very Best of Daryl Hall & John Oates** / Jan. 23, 2001 / RCA ♦♦♦♦♦
There's one thing wrong with *The Very Best of Daryl Hall & John Oates*, and it's minor—the promotional 12" mix of "Adult Education" is included in favor of the 7" version. This isn't a big deal and it doesn't mar what is the best overview of Hall & Oates' RCA years, the era when they became the biggest-selling duo in the history of rock. If the Atlantic years were more adventurous, dabbling in folk and album rock, *The Very Best of* demonstrates the virtues of consistency, since these blue-eyed soul songs rank among the very finest singles (and songs) of their time. And Hall & Oates weren't *un*adventurous, either, since they deftly blended elements of new wave, contemporary soul, and soft rock into their signature sound. Most impressively, smaller hits like "Wait for Me" and the splendid "Did It in a Minute" (easily one of the greatest songs they ever cut) more than hold their own alongside familiar items like "Sara Smile," "You Make My Dreams," "Private Eyes," and "Maneater." Hall & Oates may not have been hip, but they made addictive soul-pop that not only rocketed to the top of the charts but has stood the test of time as some of the best pop made during the early '80s. *—Stephen Thomas Erlewine*

Daryl Hall

b. Oct. 11, 1946, Philadelphia, PA
Vocals, Songwriter, Piano / Blue-Eyed Soul, Pop/Rock
Known for being part of the '70s and '80s duo Hall & Oates, Daryl Hall attended Temple University where he met future partner John Oates. They played together for a short time in the late '60s, until Oates decided to transfer schools. Hall did not let this discourage his musical career though and he began playing with the rock group Gulliver. The band produced one album on Elektra before disbanding. Hall then became a backup musician. Upon Oates' return to Philadelphia in 1972, the two got back together and formed the band Hall & Oates. The duo performed folk-rock tunes, most of which placed on the musical charts. Tommy Mottola became the group's manager and got them a contract on the Atlantic record label. The group's first album, *Whole Oates*, was released in 1972. Hall & Oates left Philadelphia for New York in 1976. They signed with RCA and produced their first Top Ten hit, "Sara Smile," in 1976. The '80s saw Hall & Oates producing many albums including *Private Eyes* and *H2O*, which became a double platinum success for the duo. Because of all their chart-topping hits, by 1984 Hall & Oates became the most chart-topping duo in history. Despite the outrageous success of the band, Hall & Oates disbanded. Both Hall and Oates pursued solo careers only to reunite in 1988 for the album *Ooh Yeah!* *—Kim Summers*

● **Sacred Songs** / 1980 / RCA ♦♦♦♦♦
In what must be the most bizarre coupling ever, Hall is accompanied by none other than King Crimson figurehead Robert Fripp on production and, of course, on guitar. This record suffered at the hands of record company mismanagement. Originally recorded in 1977, *Sacred Songs* wasn't granted a release until 1980. RCA worried about Hall's lack of commercial vision. However Hall and Fripp's creativity strangely works. Sure, there are pieces that wouldn't do as singles, but for an album regarded as being so uncommercial, there are plenty that could have been: the wacky title song, "Something in 4/4 Time," "Farther Away," and "Why Was It So Easy" (the latter being one of Hall's best ballads). Most bonkers of all is "Babs and Babs," a straight-ahead Daryl Hall track until a Fripp soundscape kicks in from nowhere! Fripp's own "Urban Landscape" shows him having withdrawal symptoms from Bowie's infamous *Heroes* sessions. The onward march of studio technology means that the sound here is slightly dated. Still, it's a must-have purchase, ending with another killer ballad "Without Tears"—Earth magic indeed. *—Kelvin Hayes*

3 Hearts in the Happy Ending Machine / 1986 / RCA ♦♦♦♦
Arriving just at the end of Hall & Oates' phenomenal streak of success in the early '80s, *3 Hearts in the Happy Ending Machine*, Daryl Hall's second solo album, was viewed as the first overture in a solo career but, in retrospect, its kinship with his first solo effort, 1980's *Sacred Songs*, is apparent. There is some indication that Hall had to make, or wanted to make, some concessions to bring it onto the charts—how could he not, he was one of the most popular musicians of his era—but that's not particularly evident on the tremendous lead single, "Dreamtime," a swirling slice of arty new wave psychedelia that stands in direct contrast to anything Hall & Oates sent into the Top Ten—it might have belonged on *Sacred Songs* or *X-Static*, but it could only have been cut in the mid-'80s when Hall had the freedom to make a record like this. That does mean *3 Hearts* is a bit tied to the time, particularly in its production with its clean synths and cavernous drum machines, but that's not necessarily a bad thing since it's primarily of interest as a portrait of where Hall was in 1986. He's not as insistently melodic as he is with Oates, nor is he as experimental as he was on *Sacred Songs*, and that does mean that *3 Hearts* falls in a middle ground that's a bit neither here nor there. And that means it's not particularly cohesive, but it does have its moments, the brightest of which is "Dreamtime," one of his greatest achievements. *—Stephen Thomas Erlewine*

Soul Alone / 1993 / Epic ♦♦♦
Released ten years after Hall & Oates' heyday and seven after Daryl Hall's last solo venture, *Three Hearts in the Happy Ending Machine*, *Soul Alone* finds Hall on unsure ground. It had been only three years since he had seen the upper reaches of the charts, yet it felt like much more time had passed since he had truly reigned over mainstream pop/rock. From the sounds of *Soul Alone*, he longed for those days, but not as much as longed for his youth in Philadelphia, and with it, the Philly soul and folk-rock that was so close to his heart. As a result, the album is lost in limbo between affectionate homages to years past and a need to regain his status as a hitmaker. Not surprisingly, it's the homages that hold up, largely because they give Hall a chance to shine as a songsmith and a vocalist. The other material largely sounds forced, although there are glimmers of brilliance every now and then. Mostly, *Soul Alone*—like his two previous solo ventures, which arrived at similar lulls in Hall & Oates' career—is interesting as a chapter in Hall's life, in the way it reflects where he was psychologically and musically at that point in time. Which means, of course, that it's primarily of interest to any listener who has followed him long enough to recognize that. *—Stephen Thomas Erlewine*

Terry Hall

b. Mar. 19, 1959, Coventry, England
Vocals / College Rock, Adult Alternative Pop/Rock, Pop/Rock, New Wave
In the strictest sense, Terry Hall isn't a musician. He doesn't play an instrument and his singing is generally flat and detached. But Terry Hall is a great pop star, with a perfect look, a cooly laconic voice, and a knack for anticipating pop trends. As the frontman for the Specials, Hall shot to stardom in Britain in the early '80s, singing such classic ska-revival singles as "Gangsters," "Nite Klub," and "Ghost Town" before leaving with the group's other vocalists to form the new wave pop group the Fun Boy Three. That trio began a long line of projects Hall pursued over the next decade. None of his groups recorded more than two albums, and each had a taste of British success. Of all these, the Fun Boy Three was the most successful, but he disbanded them within two years to form Colourfield, which led to Terry, Blair, and Anouchka and then to a duo with David Stewart, called Vegas. Each group led Hall closer to the pop mainstream, yet he remained an outsider, since he had no desire for stardom. While his polished recordings only bore a slight resemblance to his seminal work with the Specials and the Fun Boy Three, Hall's presence was stronger than ever in the mid-'90s, as a new generation of alternative artists, including Blur and Tricky, acknowledged his influence. All the praise coincided with the release of *Home*, Hall's first official solo album, which appeared in 1995, well over 15 years after he began his professional musical career.

● **The Collection** / Jul. 13, 1993 / Chrysalis ♦♦♦♦♦
The Collection compiles 22 highlights from Terry Hall's long, eclectic career, spanning from his groundbreaking work with the Specials to his '90s collaboration with Dave Stewart, Vegas. In between, all of the major hits Hall has sung are covered—from the Specials' "Gangsters," "Nite Klub," and "Ghost Town" to the Fun Boy Three's "The Lunatics (Have Taken Over the Asylum)," "It Ain't What You Do (It's the Way That You Do It)," "Summertime," and "Our Lips Are Sealed," as well as Colourfield's "Thinking of You." Several failed singles from the Colourfield, Terry, Blair, and Anouchka, and Vegas are included, as are interesting B-sides and rarities. And even with these rarities, *The Collection* remains the definitive compilation of Terry Hall's career, since it boils down an uneven, but always interesting, career to the essentials. *—Stephen Thomas Erlewine*

Home / 1995 / Anxious ♦♦♦
Home, Terry Hall's first solo album, is a surprisingly polished collection of mainstream

pop/rock produced by the Lightning Seeds' Ian Broudie. Theoretically, the setting is entirely too smooth for Hall's limited vocal skills, but the results are quite enjoyable, since he and Broudie have cleverly arranged each song to emphasize the strengths of Terry's detached vocals. While there is a bit of filler scattered throughout the album, the record is supported by pleasantly jangling pop songs that help make *Home* Hall's strongest effort since the Colourfield. —*Stephen Thomas Erlewine*

Laugh / 1997 / South Sea Bubble ✦✦✦✦
Terry Hall is most engaging when he is miserable. Hall, formerly of the Specials and Fun Boy Three, began delving into his shattered heart with the Colourfield in the mid-'80s. On his second solo album, *Laugh*, Hall is again weeping in his ale despite the cheerful appellation. On the surface, this album is distilled sunshine: The blanket of tastefully strummed acoustic guitars of "Love to See You," the crystalline jangle and sweet harmonies of "Sonny and His Sister," and the soaring chorus of "Take It Forever" seduce the listener into singing along to Hall's lyrics without realizing how tormented they are. Like Morrissey and Robert Smith of the Cure, Hall can sweep his angst underneath toe-tapping hooks. The shimmering guitar pop of "Summer Follows Spring" sounds as if it were made for a Sunday afternoon stroll, but it's a booby trap; the track is actually about his lover having an affair. "Last night you slept with someone else," Hall plaintively sings, while ex-Smiths member Craig Gannon paints fluffy white clouds with his six-string. While Hall mined the '60s with the Colourfield, his affection for '70s AM radio fodder is proudly displayed on *Laugh*. The songs are straightforward and immaculately produced, lacking any quirks or rough edges. If Hall didn't have such poetic and biting lyrics, this could be described as an easy listening record. Nevertheless, his mournful voice merges beautifully with the soft rock of his band. On "Ballad of a Landlord," Hall's whispery tone is matched by subtle strings; the music slowly builds volume and tempo with the rising emotion in Hall's vocals and lyrics. When he exclaims, "So now the place lies in ruin/the way you lied and ruined me," the guitars suddenly become louder, capturing the pain and resentment in his voice and words. Hall chooses to cover Todd Rundgren's "I Saw the Light" at the album's end; however, beneath its bouncy, infectious beat, there are no barbed confessions. Then again, Hall didn't write it. —*Michael Sutton*

Pete Ham

b. Apr. 27, 1947, Swansea, South Wales, **d.** Apr. 23, 1975, London, England
Vocals, Guitar / Pop/Rock, Power Pop, Singer/Songwriter
Although every member of Badfinger composed material for the group, Pete Ham was probably the most important songwriter in the band. He wrote all of their hits, and also co-wrote "Without You," which was covered by Nilsson for a number one single. He did not release any solo records during his lifetime, which ended with his suicide in 1975 (brought on by the band's horrific legal and financial problems). However, he merits an entry as a solo artist because of the posthumous 1997 compilation of Ham solo studio demos, *7 Park Avenue*. Recorded on two-track in the late '60s and early '70s and mostly unrecorded by Badfinger, they bear, as did much of Badfinger's material, a strong resemblance to the work of Paul McCartney in their ingenious melodicism. They do a good deal to flesh out appreciation of Ham's talents, showing on the whole a more tender side than was usually expected from Badfinger. A second volume of home-studio demos was released in 1999 under the title *Golders Green*. —*Richie Unterberger*

● **7 Park Avenue** / Mar. 18, 1997 / Rykodisc ✦✦✦
Only two of these 18 tracks ("No Matter What" and "Matted Spam") were recorded by Badfinger. But the rest of these solo studio demos are quite up to scratch with Badfinger's usual standards: it's not nearly as good as Paul McCartney's late Beatle tracks, for instance, but it's actually better than McCartney's typical early solo material. Ham is a thinking listener's rock romantic, offering emotional, wistful words and melodies without sounding sappy. Purists should be aware that, although Ham played most of the instruments here, some overdubs were added in the 1990s by other musicians, for the purpose of giving the tracks a fuller, more balanced sound. It's difficult to judge whether this decision was justified without hearing the original versions, though one wonders whether diehard Badfinger fans (the primary audience for this release) would really care that much about any sonic imperfections in the originals. In any case, the end result sounds pretty tasteful, without any obvious concessions to dressing up the essential sounds in modern technology. —*Richie Unterberger*

Golders Green / Jul. 13, 1999 / Rykodisc ✦✦✦
This second collection of previously unreleased home demos by Ham is almost as worthwhile and satisfying to the ear as its predecessor, *7 Park Avenue*. Again, some musicians (including Bob Jackson, who was in Badfinger for a while shortly before Ham's death) enhanced these recordings with overdubs. And as with *7 Park Avenue*, while it's impossible to tell if these were truly necessary without comparison to the original unadorned versions, these overdubs do not seem intrusive (as they are on most productions of this sort). Although there are 20 tracks, it's not as bountiful a platter as one might hope (adding up to only 42 minutes), as some of the songs are quite short, and three are nothing more than fragments lasting less than a minute. In the main, though, these are quality, sometimes enchantingly tuneful and tender performances, sometimes exhibiting a Beach Boys bent that's not so evident on Badfinger's official recordings. The cut to attract the most attention will be a demo of "Without You," although Ham's version is an incomplete skeleton of the track that Badfinger would record (and Nilsson would cover for a chart-topping hit), missing the chorus added by fellow Badfinger member Tom Evans. Otherwise, a highlight is "Makes Me Feel Good," two drastically different versions (one slow, one fast) which open and close the disc; it sounds like it could have made a first-rate Monkees track (which is a compliment, not a knock). On the whole, the effect of this CD, as was the case with *7 Park Avenue*, is to make one wish that Badfinger had recorded more of Ham's

material and had made less room for the songwriting efforts of the lesser composers in the band. —*Richie Unterberger*

Hampton Grease Band

f. 1968, **db.** 1973
Psychedelic, Prog Rock/Art Rock
Hampton Grease Band may have ultimately been a band easier to appreciate in concept than to listen to in practice. They are also, for most listeners, a band that's much more fun to read about than to hear. For a brief period, though, they were offering some of the wackiest rock ever to be found on a major label. Clearly influenced by both Zappa and Beefheart, but more grating and even less accessible to the rock underground, they took early-'70s avant rock aesthetics near their extremes. This guaranteed an eternal cult reputation for the group but also ensured that their commercial success in their own time was virtually nil. Hampton Grease Band began as a blues-rock-oriented outfit in the late '60s in Atlanta. The group steadily developed a more original sound, emphasizing intricate, Zappa-esque guitar lines and Bruce Hampton's off-the-cuff, non sequitur lyrics, usually shouted in a throaty, scratchy wheeze that made Beefheart sound like Pavarotti. The band often betrayed the Zappa influence in their theatrical, sometimes confrontational stage show, in which Hampton would throw chairs at the audience, or sing while standing on a pizza. They polarized audiences, to say the least. Hampton Grease Band generated enough of a reputation, though, to pique the interest of Columbia Records, whose curiosity incited Allman Brothers manager Phil Walden to sign the group. The Grease Band quickly recorded two albums worth of material that could in no way be construed as having money-making potential. Confronted with the tapes, Columbia reacted most unpredictably, deciding to make the band's debut (and, as it turned out, only) record a double album, *Music to Eat*. Legend has it that it was, at the time of its release, the second-lowest selling LP in the Columbia catalog. Shortly after its release, Hampton Grease Band began to disintegrate. —*Richie Unterberger*

● **Music to Eat** / 1971 / Columbia ✦✦✦✦✦
Hampton Grease Band's only album, now reissued as a double CD, is a one-of-a-kind item, drawing upon jazz, progressive/psychedelic guitar rock, and a generally surrealist bent to back Bruce Hampton's idiot-savant ravings. Comparisons with Zappa and Beefheart are really inevitable, though Hampton Grease Band really weren't on the level of those two fellow weirdos. They were definitely on their own wavelength, though, carving out a more guitar-oriented sound that skirted even closer to the lunatic fringe. The reissue's enhanced with a lengthy history by guitarist Glenn Phillips that's crammed with believe-it-or-not anecdotes from the group's fascinating career. —*Richie Unterberger*

Handsome Boy Modeling School

Underground Rap, Alternative Rap, Alternative Dance, Hip-Hop
A collaboration between two of the most innovative producers in hip-hop, Handsome Boy Modeling School united Prince Paul (best known for his work with De La Soul) and Dan "The Automator" Nakamura (the mastermind behind Kool Keith's *Dr. Octagon* project). The duo's debut record, *So...How's Your Girl?*, appeared on Tommy Boy Records in the fall of 1999. —*Jason Ankeny*

So . . . How's Your Girl? / Oct. 19, 1999 / Tommy Boy ✦✦✦✦
Handsome Boy Modeling School comes from the mind of Prince Paul and Dan "The Automator" Nakamura, or as they're known on this album, Nathaniel Merriweather and Chest Rockwell. Both men were fans of the Fox television comedy *Get a Life*. In one episode the main character (played by comedian Chris Elliott) goes to the handsome boy modeling school. Clips from the television show appear in the songs "Look at This Face" and "Modeling Sucks." Joining producers Prince Paul and Dan the Automator are Del the Funkee Homosapien, Miho Hatori of Cibo Matto, Grand Puba, Sadat X, J-Live, DJ Shadow, De La Soul, Sean Lennon, and Father Guido Sarducci of *Saturday Night Live* fame, among others. Usually when an attempt at such an ambitious project as this is made, the product has a few good songs while the rest miss the mark, but not in this case. From front to back this is a well-produced, creative album. The only song that doesn't work is "Megaton B-Boy"; its blown-speaker beat, produced by Alec Empire, is too distracting to hear the lyrics of El-P. As far as standouts go, this release is full of them, one being "The Truth," during which Roisin of Moloko sings to the jazzy beat; then after almost three minutes, J-Live jumps in to add his touch. The finished product is a great song. *Handsome Boy Modeling School* succeeds where so many compilations fail. It's a great album from start to finish. —*Dan Gizzi*

Handsome Family

f. Chicago, IL
Alternative Country, Indie Rock, Neo-Traditional Folk
Husband and wife duo the Handsome Family has been labeled both alt-country and traditionalist, but truthfully their often-dark music lies in a unique space somewhere in between, blending the sounds of traditional country and bluegrass (and, especially, murder ballads) into a more modern scenery. Vocalist and composer Brett Sparks hails from Texas where he studied music and briefly worked around the oil rigs. By the mid-'90s, he resided in Chicago with his wife Rennie Sparks, a fiction writer originally from Long Island. Brett persuaded Rennie to write lyrics for him, leading to the unusual and striking form of the Handsome Family's songs—evocative scenes and brief tales (of both the daydream and ghost story varieties) in lieu of the standard verse-chorus-verse structure. The Handsome Family's debut album, entitled *Odessa*, was released in January 1995 on the independent label Carrot Top. *Odessa* unfortunately made few waves. With *Milk and Scissors*, the duo had traded in their previous rock edges for more traditional country

sounds. The resulting album won praise from the critics. This was not, however, an easy period for the Handsome Family. Brett suffered an emotional breakdown during this time, which resulted in his hospitalization and diagnosis as manic-depressive. *Through the Trees*, the Handsome Family's third album, was written and recorded in the aftermath of these troubles. With this recording, the Handsome Family came into their own sound and received widespread attention as a result. This was the Handsome Family's breakthrough album, which continued to increase in popularity over the next several years, allowing Brett and Rennie Sparks to quit their day jobs and focus on music full-time. Following the album's release, the duo began touring extensively. *—Joslyn Layne*

● **Odessa** / Jan. 9, 1995 / Carrot Top ♦♦♦♦
The Handsome Family's first album certainly stands apart from their later work; at this point, the group still had a live drummer, they were playing more rock-oriented material (the noisy guitars on "Here's Hopin'" and "One Way Up" would have sounded rather out of place on *Through the Trees*), and there's a bit more upfront humor than in their later work. The key phrase, however, is "a bit"; the creepy but amusing Freudianisms of "Pony," the drunkard's hymn of "Water Into Wine," and the morning-after lament of "She Awoke With a Jerk" are witty enough, but there's a dark undertow that wavers between cynicism and hopelessness which allows these songs to sit side by side with the album's takes of murder ("Arlene"), urban alienation ("Moving Furniture Around"), and corrupted faith ("Everything That Rises Must Converge"). Brett Sparks' plain but resonant Midwestern twang gives the songs on *Odessa* the ring of common truth, and he and Rennie Sparks had already established themselves as writers to be reckoned with, conjuring a lyrical voice that sounds homey and terribly alienated at the same time. Listening to *Odessa* today, it's obvious the Handsome Family had a way to travel before they would create their strongest work, but it's obvious they already had the talent and the ideas that would make them one of the most interesting and intelligent bands to emerge from Chicago's alt-country scene. *—Mark Deming*

Milk and Scissors / 1996 / Carrot Top ♦♦♦

● **Through the Trees** / Jan. 26, 1998 / Carrot Top ♦♦♦♦
Spooky is the only way to describe the music that the Handsome Family makes. These are bitter tales of love and loss, alcohol, and death, each with a scary majesty all its own. Wilco's Jeff Tweedy lends a hand, as well as the recording equipment, but that's about the only connection to today's current trends of alt-country, or anything else modern. The cuts here are almost from another age, another dimension. Echoing the old-time tunes which came from the mountain folk of Appalachia, Brett & Rennie Sparks use dobros, banjos, pianos, autoharps, guitars, and drum machines to produce a rich, dark tapestry of sound. Highlights include "Weightless Again" and the after-hours waltz of "Last Night I Went Out Walking." There are ghosts in these tunes and they leave the listener feeling, well, spooky. *—James Chrispell*

In the Air / Feb. 15, 2000 / Carrot Top ♦♦♦♦
If their last album, *Through the Trees*, came to us from the darkness at the bottom of a well (or a liquor bottle), *In the Air* holds sounds of the Handsome Family after they made it out of the depths and up onto the grass—and are now adjusting to a less desperate life. Not to say that it's sunny, exactly. Lyricist Rennie Sparks still presents us with dark and bloody tragedies, as well as whimsical fairytales about lonely, but hopeful figures. The difference between *In the Air* and the Handsome Family's last album seems to be the presence of a calm (as opposed to disturbed restraint) and certain warmth pervading this album. Brett Sparks' vocal delivery comes across as more relaxed and natural and in lieu of the occasional, creepy vocal effects used on the last album. The colorful, sad, and disturbed scenes are usually delivered with a country flavor and a folk instrumentation, and include songs that are the rightful offspring of Appalachian murder ballads, such as "My Beautiful Bride" and "Up Falling Rock Hill," and southern hymns ("Never Grow Old"). The Handsome Family's songs are imbued with a tender romanticism and love of the fantastic—and of a world that, for all it's real twists and sadness, still holds moments of childlike wonder and fairy-tale possibilities.

In the Air was recorded, as were their three previous albums, in the Handsome Family living room, this time with live percussion (provided by Brett) instead of a drum machine. Also heard are guest musicians Darrell Sparks, who sings backup and plays guitar on two songs, and violinist Andrew Bird (formerly of the Squirrel Nut Zippers, now leader of his own roots music-based band) who contributes to "Poor, Poor Lenore," "Up Falling Rock Hill," and "When That Helicopter Comes," a hellfire and brimstone, foot-stomping number with a sparse, bluegrass delivery: "It's gonna rain champagne/and the hills are gonna dance ... The sky will swim in lightning fire and the trees will shake and scream." *—Joslyn Layne*

Hanson

f. 1992, Tulsa, OK
Teen Pop, Pop/Rock
Sounding like a revamped Jackson 5 for the '90s, Hanson came storming out of Tulsa, OK in 1997 blessed with photogenic looks and a surprisingly infectious sense of melody. Hanson had a sunny pop sense that stood in direct contrast to the gloomy grunge that dominated the '90s, yet they also arrived with hip credentials—a handful of the cuts on their debut were produced by the Dust Brothers and the rest were produced by Steve Lironi.

Isaac, aged 16 at the time of their major-label debut, played guitar; 13-year-old Taylor sang lead and played keyboards; drummer Zac was 11 years old. As children in Tulsa, they sang around the dinner table, often '50s and '60s rock and R&B standards and gospel songs. While waiting for a major label contract, the brothers recorded *Boomerang*, an indie record and began playing their own instruments. The group signed with Mercury Records on the strength of their song, "MMMBop," and they were hooked up with producer Steve Lironi, who helped the band with arrangements. Prior to the spring 1997 release of their debut album, *Middle of Nowhere*, Mercury put the publicity machine in full gear. Hanson became major teen idols, and as the holidays approached they issued a Christmas LP, *Snowed In*; in 1998, they reissued their earlier independent recordings as *Three Car Garage*, and also released a concert album, *Live From Albertane*.

Following that flurry of activity, Hanson remained largely silent while they worked on the proper follow-up to *Middle of Nowhere*. They finally emerged in the spring of 2000 with *This Time Around*, a more mature, measured record that represented a bid for credibility outside their primarily teenage audience; the album reflected the new influence of trad-rockers like Matchbox 20. *—Stephen Thomas Erlewine*

● **Middle of Nowhere** / May 5, 1997 / Mercury ♦♦♦♦
Sounding like a post-alternative version of the Jackson 5—complete with effervescent harmonies, sunny melodies, rolling hip-hop beats, and dense, layered productions—Hanson is positively bubbling energy throughout their surprisingly infectious and melodic debut, *Middle of Nowhere*. It's hard not to hear the lead single "MMMBop," and or the similiary infectious "Where's the Love," and not get caught up in the joy of making music. Although the boys co-wrote nine of the 13 songs with professional writers, and the producers do offer a distinctive stamp, the personalities that shine through are Hanson's—youthful, exuberant, and positively joyous. A few of the songs may run on a bit too long, and there are a couple of borrowed melodies and silly lyrics, but *Middle of Nowhere* is a delight. *—Stephen Thomas Erlewine*

Three Car Garage: Indie Recordings 1995-1996 / May 5, 1998 / Mercury ♦♦♦
As any dedicated Hanson fan knows, the trio recorded two self-released records before hitting the big time in 1997 with their first major-label album, *Middle of Nowhere*. Of course, once the group became international sensations, it was impossible to find these records, so Mercury did the smart thing—they repackaged the highlights as *Three Car Garage: Indie Recordings 1995-1996*. It's a little disingenuous to call these "indie" recordings, considering that their father is a multi-millionare who financed them himself, but that's beside the point—all that's important is the fact that these are the early recordings. And they're not bad for early recordings. It's true that the Dust Brothers brought the sparkle to "MMMBop" that made it a hit, but there's a certain boyish enthusiasm to these performances that is quite infectious. Don't expect great things from the songs that didn't make *Middle of Nowhere*—they're occasionally fun, but not particularly well-crafted—but that's really the rule of thumb with early recordings, anyway: if you go in with diminished expectations, you'll be pleased with what you find. *—Stephen Thomas Erlewine*

This Time Around / May 9, 2000 / Island ♦♦♦♦
Give Hanson credit for making a second album (not counting live affairs, demo collections, and holiday records) that virtually ignores the teen-pop boom they kick-started in 1997 with their debut album, *Middle of Nowhere*. *This Time Around* doesn't ditch the musical principles laid out on *Middle of Nowhere*—it expands them. Hanson winds up synthesizing its influences—still primarily classic pop tunes from the late '60s and early '70s, staples of oldies radio—into a bright, melodic sound of its own. Problem is, you can occasionally hear them working at it. Much of *This Time Around* feels like a conscious attempt at furthering their craft, defining their sound, and honing their songwriting skills. It's a stab at maturity. Not only are the performances measured and the production restrained, but the album features cameos by virtuosos like John Popper and Jonny Lang, just to prove that Hanson can hang with the big boys. They can, but so what? Jams and instrumental interludes are not the reason to listen to Hanson, records that sparkle with effervescent melodies and joyous hooks is. They haven't lost these gifts, even if the tempered production and overly earnest performances occasionally make the band's classicist instincts sound stuffy. There's something to be said for self-conscious maturity; by carefully watching over every aspect of the album's creation, Hanson and producer Stephen Lironi wind up with a record that is better paced and more consistent than the debut. It's hard not to miss the thrilling way *Middle of Nowhere* leapt out of the speakers upon its first spin with giddy fun, yet with its carefully considered craft and warmly ingratiating pop songs *This Time Around* is winning entertainment. *—Stephen Thomas Erlewine*

Happy Mondays

f. 1985, Manchester, England, **db.** 1992
Madchester, Alternative Dance, Club/Dance, Alternative Pop/Rock, House
Along with the Stone Roses, the Happy Mondays were the leaders of the late-'80s/early-'90s dance club-influenced Manchester scene, experiencing a brief moment in the spotlight before collapsing in 1992. While the Stone Roses were based in '60s pop, adding only a slight hint of dance music, the Happy Mondays immersed themselves in the club and rave culture, eventually becoming the most recognizable band of that drug-fueled scene. The Mondays' music relied heavily on the sound and rhythm of house music, spiked with '70s soul licks and swirling '60s psychedelia. It was bright, colorful music that had fractured melodies that never quite gelled into cohesive songs. Unwittingly or not, the Happy Mondays personified the ugly side of rave culture. Under the leadership of vocalist Shaun Ryder, the group sounded and acted like thugs. Ryder's lyrics were twisted and surrealistic, loaded with bizarre pop culture refrences, drug slang, and menacing sexuality. Appropriately, their music was as convoluted. The Happy Mondays were one of the first rock bands to integrate hip-hop techniques into their music. They didn't sample, but they borrowed melodies and lyrics and, in the process, committed rock blasphemy. For a band that celebrated their vulgarity and excessiveness, the Happy Mondays appropriately came undone by their addictions, but they left behind a surprisingly influential legacy,

apparent in everyone from dance bands like the Chemical Brothers to rock & rollers like Oasis. *—Stephen Thomas Erlewine*

Squirrell & G-Man Twenty-Four Hour Party People Plastic Face Carnt Smile / Apr. 1987 / Factory ✦✦✦

Bummed / Nov. 1988 / Elektra ✦✦✦✦
Happy Mondays first essayed their fusion of dance-club beats, hip-hop, funk, and rock & roll on *Bummed*. A considerable improvement from the unfocused *Squirrel and G-Man*, *Bummed* is slightly inconsistent, but the group's sound is beginning to gel. In particular, Shaun Ryder's incoherent bluster of non sequiturs, surreal imagery, and verbal threats is coming into its own, and it adds a sense of menace to dark grooves like "Lazy Itis," "Mad Cyril," and "Wrote for Luck." The latter was remixed by Vince Clarke after the album's release and the new version, which was included on later pressings, was the hardest dance the group had yet attempted, suggesting the direction they would follow on their next album. *—Stephen Thomas Erlewine*

★ **Pills 'n' Thrills & Bellyaches** / Apr. 1990 / Elektra ✦✦✦✦✦
A swirling, neo-psychedelic kaleidoscope of hallucinogenic drugs, trippy beats, borrowed hooks, and veiled threats, *Pills 'n' Thrills & Bellyaches* is Happy Mondays' masterpiece and the peak of the entire Madchester craze. Where the Stone Roses were pop classicists, Happy Mondays pushed pop into the ecstasy age. The Mondays' cut-and-paste rhythms and melodies are clearly influenced by hip-hop and electronic dance music, and their songs have the same sort of twisted internal logic, subverting conventional pop song structures while reinterpreting oldies, occasionally stealing entire songs and claiming them as their own (John Kongos' "He's Gonna Step on You Again" is transformed into "Step On," LaBelle's "Lady Marmalade" provides the basis for "Kinky Afro"). Most of the musical collage is the creation of producers Paul Oakenfold and Steve Osborne, but the vision of *Pills 'n' Thrills & Bellyaches* belongs to Shaun Ryder, who reveals himself as a surreally gifted lyricist. Lifting melodies at will, Ryder paints a bizarre vision of modern urban life, fueled by sex, drugs, violence, and dead-end jobs—and instead of lamenting the state of affairs, he celebrates them in his hoarse, arrhythmic, tuneless holler. His thuggishly surreal sense of humor and appropriation of hooks became enormously influential on British rock & roll in the '90s, particularly on Oasis' sense of style. *—Stephen Thomas Erlewine*

Live / Nov. 19, 1991 / Elektra ✦✦

Yes, Please / Sep. 22, 1992 / Elektra ✦

Double Easy: The U.S. Singles / Sep. 14, 1993 / Elektra ✦✦✦✦✦
Oddly enough, a greatest-hits set from the Mondays surfaced in America first rather than the U.K. but, whatever the reason for its existence, *Double Easy* is a nicely random treat. Arranged more or less in chronological order, with the exception of the killer one-two punch of "W.F.L. (Think About the Future)" and the club mix of "Hallelujah" at the end of the disc, *Double Easy* makes a good primer for the baggy era's notorious group. Though leaving out a variety of strong album cuts means that it's by default an incomplete collection (and probably a couple of *Yes, Please* cuts could have been dropped from the running order), enough good times are in the grooves to summon up instant party vibes. Ryder and company's genius was that, unlike any number of stereotypical indie Brit groups, they felt the funk—if the likes of early Kool & the Gang and Funkadelic were the true gods, at the very least the Mondays were good disciples. Combine that with a healthy take on everything from Mark E. Smith's ramalama style to electro beats and Beatles references and more, and what *Double Easy* demonstrates best in the end is that Beck's own formula had already been established years before. "Wrote for Luck," "Lazyitis," the MacColl mix of "Hallelujah," the "stuff it in" mix of "Step On," "Kinky Afro," and the 12" version of "Loose Fit" help make this a great starting point for new fans, but hardcore followers will appreciate some rarities beyond the remixes. "Tokoloshe Man"—like "Step On" a John Kongos cover, in this case recorded for the *Rubaiyat* tribute album—makes for an intense romp, a bit Madchester by numbers but with a fine slick speed to it. Meanwhile, the underrated groove of "Judge Fudge" makes its first debut on album after its stand-alone appearance in 1991, with what sounds like a Marlena Shaw sample adding a swooping, just-paranoid-enough atmosphere to the proceedings. *—Ned Raggett*

Loads (& Loads More) / Oct. 30, 1995 / London ✦✦✦✦✦
With the exception of *Pills 'n' Thrills and Bellyaches*, the Happy Mondays had difficulty expanding their ideas into full albums, which makes the singles compilation *Loads* all the more useful. It contains all of the band's hit singles—"Step On," "Kinky Afro," "Hallelujah," "Lazyitis," "W.F.L.," "Tokoloshe Man," "Loose Fit," "Bob's Yer Uncle," "24 Hour Party People," "Mad Cyril"—plus several important album tracks, making it an excellent distillation of the band's career; as an album, only *Pills 'n' Thrills* provides better listening, and *Loads* is arguably just as good as an introduction, especially for casual fans. The first 10,000 copies of *Loads* included an extra disc, *Loads More*, a compilation of remixes making their debut appearance on CD, including Bernard Sumner's "Freaky Dancing," Mike Pickering's "Delightful," Martin Hannett's "Lazyitis," and Vince Clarke's "W.F.L."; all of the remaining mixes are by Paul Oakenfold. Since the remixes date from the height of Happy Mondays' career, they provide useful insight on the band's talents as a dance group. *—Stephen Thomas Erlewine*

Tim Hardin

b. Dec. 23, 1941, Eugene, OR, **d.** Dec. 29, 1980
Vocals, Keyboards, Songwriter, Guitar / Folk-Rock, Singer/Songwriter
A gentle, soulful singer who owed as much to blues and jazz as folk, Tim Hardin produced an impressive body of work in the late '60s without ever approaching either mass success or the artistic heights of the best singer/songwriters. By the time of his 1966 debut, he was writing confessional folk-rock songs of considerable grace and emotion. The first album's impact was slightly diluted by incompatible string overdubs (against Hardin's wishes), but by the time of his second and best LP, he'd achieved a satisfactory balance between acoustic guitar-based arrangements and subtle string accompaniment. It was the lot of Hardin's work to achieve greater recognition through covers from other singers, such as Rod Stewart (who did "Reason to Believe"), Nico (who covered "Eulogy to Lenny Bruce" on her first album), Scott Walker (who sang "Lady Came From Baltimore"), and most especially Bobby Darin, who took "If I Were a Carpenter" into the Top Ten in 1966. His end was not a pretty one: due to accumulated drug and health problems, as well as a scarcity of new material, he didn't complete any albums after 1973, dying of a drug overdose in 1980. *—Richie Unterberger*

Tim Hardin 1 / 1966 / Verve ✦✦✦✦✦
Although Tim Hardin would go on to make many other fine records, his debut album is a true pioneering folk-rock classic. It's a virtual template for the form and also gives a fantastic overview of Hardin's awesome songwriting talents. "Don't Make Promises" and "Reason to Believe" were covered by dozens of artists following this album's release, and that should be reason enough to believe in this giant's talent. Aside from the excellent writing, the sound and feel of the record can easily be seen as a template for such groups as Buffalo Springfield and others who followed. If you own just one Hardin album, make it this one. *—Matthew Greenwald*

Tim Hardin 2 / 1967 / Verve ✦✦✦✦✦
Probably his best single album, on which he eschewed blues nearly entirely and forged a distinctive, folk-rock voice, occasionally embellished by tasteful full arrangements. "Lady Came From Baltimore," "Red Balloon," and especially "If I Were a Carpenter" rank among his best and most famous songs. *—Richie Unterberger*

This Is Tim Hardin / 1967 / Edsel ✦✦✦
Hardin's very earliest recordings from approximately 1964, not issued until the late '60s, when he had achieved some success with his albums for Verve. Accompanied by nothing besides his own guitar, Hardin's arrangements are far sparser and bluesier than his folk-rock work for Verve. Over half of the ten tracks are traditional blues numbers like "Hoochie Coochie Man" and "Hoouse of the Rising Sun," and even the four originals (one co-written by future Holy Modal Rounder Steve Weber) are in a very similar straight blues style. The material isn't nearly as distinctive as the best of Hardin's work, but the performances rank with Dave Van Ronk and Fred Neil as the best white blues/acoustic folk to emerge from the early-'60s Greenwich scene (indeed, Hardin covers Neil's "Blues on the Ceiling" here). The hollow, reverbed, one-man-sitting-alone-in-an-empty-room production gives this album a haunting, somber feel (though not to its detriment). While not as good as Fred Neil's similar material from this era, it's still well worth tracking down. *—Richie Unterberger*

Live in Concert / 1968 / Polydor/Chronicles ✦✦✦
Originally titled *Tim Hardin 3*, this set was recorded live in 1968 with a backing band comprised primarily of jazz musicians. The support crew is a bit tentative; it's evident that they hadn't played much with Hardin, and in places the tempo comes close to breaking down. It's still a good, effective performance; Hardin is in good voice (a condition which apparently couldn't be readily counted on, even in his early days), and on the songs that had already been released on his first two albums, the arrangements vary from the recorded versions in interesting fashions. *Live in Concert* includes renditions of most of his best early compositions ("If I Were a Carpenter," "Red Balloon," "Reason to Believe," "Misty Roses," "Lady Came From Baltimore," "Black Sheep Boy") and half a dozen Hardin originals that didn't make it onto his first pair of albums. The best of these is the Lenny Bruce tribute, "Lenny's Tune," which Nico covered on her first solo album (where it was retitled "Eulogy to Lenny Bruce"). The 1995 CD reissue of this album adds three previously unreleased bonus tracks from the same concert. *—Richie Unterberger*

Tim Hardin 4 / Feb. 1969 / Verve ✦✦

● **Reason to Believe** / Oct. 25, 1990 / Polydor ✦✦✦✦✦
The great early work of this top-flight '60s singer/songwriter includes the title track, "If I Were a Carpenter" and "Misty Roses." *—Kenneth M. Cassidy & William Ruhlmann*

● **Hang On to a Dream: The Verve Recordings** / Feb. 22, 1994 / Polydor ✦✦✦✦✦
Double-CD set of 47 tracks that Hardin recorded for Verve between 1964 and 1966. His expressive, blues-inflected vocals and confessional songwriting are heard on covers and famous compositions like "If I Were a Carpenter," "Lady Came From Baltimore," and "Reason to Believe." The compilation includes every studio recording that Hardin released on the Verve label, as well as two alternate takes and 15 previously unreleased tracks. *—Richie Unterberger*

Simple Songs / Sep. 3, 1996 / Columbia/Legacy ✦✦✦✦
Hardin's Columbia period, lasting from the late '60s to the early '70s, was a troubled one that saw his songwriting muse wither and his personal life start to dissolve. Although his best work was behind him, he was still capable of recording good material. This 17-song collection is a good distillation of the highlights of his three Columbia LPs, which largely still found his voice in good shape. Original tunes were more of a problem: although the best of his compositions were on a rough par with his Verve work, by the time of 1972's *Painted Head*, he was devoting himself entirely to covers of songs by others. The *Painted Head* selections are the least impressive on this anthology, the spare folk-rock of the earlier Columbia sessions giving way to slicker arrangements that don't highlight his sad, wavering voice nearly as effectively. The remainder is pretty good, with the significant bonus of his sole chart single, a 1969 cover of Bobby Darin's "Simple Song of Freedom," and five decent (if sometimes unpolished) previously unreleased outtakes from late 1968. *Simple Songs* is the one album of post-Verve Hardin music to own. *—Richie Unterberger*

John Wesley Harding

b. Oct. 22, 1965

Vocals, Guitar / College Rock, Alternative Folk, Contemporary Folk, Adult Alternative Pop/Rock, Alternative Pop/Rock, Singer/Songwriter, Urban Folk

John Wesley Harding may take his name from a Bob Dylan album and he's a modern day folk singer, but with the biting, cynical observations in his songs and sharp sense of humor combined with winning melodies, he shows his true forefathers are Elvis Costello and Nick Lowe with a hint of Billy Bragg. Far from being a follower or strict revivalist, however, Wes draws on a wide assortment of musical influences, pushing the boundaries of the all-too-often formulaic singer/songwriter tag to create something all his own. An opening slot for John Hiatt attracted the attention of Demon Records who signed him and released the live *It Happened One Night*; in 1990, he teamed up with producer Andey Paley and members of Elvis Costello's Attractions (the association would cause Costello comparisons that would continue to haunt him) to record *Here Comes the Groom* for Sire. While he received consistently good reviews, expanded on his cult following through constant touring, and finally shook (for the most part) the Elvis Costello comparisons, lack of a substantial push from Sire led to his leaving the label by the mid-'90s. *—Chris Woodstra*

It Happened One Night / 1988 / Rhino ✦✦✦✦✦

This solo acoustic outing, recorded live in England in 1988, seems like an odd choice for a debut, but it comes off very well. Capturing both John Wesley Harding's folk roots and a wonderful sense of humor, *It Happened One Night* gives a very representative picture of the singer/songwriter. Included are early versions of songs appearing on the following two albums as well as unreleased gems such as his fun account of Live Aid ("July 13th 1985") and a cover of Prince's "Kiss." *—Chris Woodstra*

● **Here Comes the Groom** / 1989 / Sire ✦✦✦✦✦

His second album has him working in the studio with a band called the Good Liars, including Pete Thomas, and Bruce Thomas of the Attractions. Not surprisingly, *Here Comes the Groom* has a feel similar to classic Elvis Costello. Harding's articulate and biting vocal delivery, also reminiscent of Costello, retains a good dark sense of humor. *—Chris Woodstra*

The Name Above the Title / Feb. 19, 1991 / Sire ✦✦✦

The follow-up to *Here Comes the Groom* continues in the same direction. This time the arrangements are filled out with horn sections and strings, but the overall folky feel remains. *—Chris Woodstra*

Why We Fight / Mar. 1992 / Sire ✦✦✦

This 1992 release is more low-key and moody than any of his previous work. The subject matter is darker, though the melodies are still catchy and instantly memorable as always, this time with smoother production. Even a discussion about Hitler in the bizarre fantasy of "Hitler's Tears" is musically irresistible, placing him in the ranks of Nick Lowe and Elvis Costello. *—Chris Woodstra*

John Wesley Harding's New Deal / Feb. 13, 1996 / Rhino ✦✦✦

Four years passed since John Wesley Harding's previous long-player and it seems he spent the time "growing up" a bit, shaking once and for all the image of Elvis Costello's smart-ass kid brother. *John Wesley Harding's New Deal* (the title presumably refering to his parting of ways with Sire and his new signing to Forward Records) finds a gentler Harding doing some soul searching on his most introspective outing to date. Continuing in the trend set by 1992's *Why We Fight*, the album's warmer production—bare-boned arrangements consisting mainly of acoustic guitar with subtle use of violin, cello, hammond organ, and pedal steel—create the appropriate intimate setting for the subject matter. Thankfully the new John Wesley Harding's songs are still as clever as ever and, in a different way, just as catchy and memorable. *—Chris Woodstra*

Dynablob / Jun. 1996 / Mod Lang ✦✦✦

Dynablob is a collection of previously unreleased studio recordings from John Wesley Harding's first recording session in 1986 to 1994 with track-by-track commentary by Wes himself. This is obviously an essential purchase for fans, but it is also surprisingly consistent enough to offer a good listen and a good look at the artist in a more traditional singer/songwriter setting. Points should also be given for the detail of the Dylan-esque cover design. *—Chris Woodstra*

Dynablob 2: It Happened Every Night / 1998 / Wow [Fanclub only] ✦✦✦

Awake / Mar. 10, 1998 / Zero Hour ✦✦✦✦

Billed as John Wesley Harding and the Gangsta Folk, *Dare* seems to be an attempt to recast the singer/songwriter in a different light, incorporating elements of electronica to earn more street cred. The Gangsta Folk are in truth not a band, but rather Harding handling multiple instruments (often of the more exotic variety like e-bow, moogs, and mellotron), along with a few guests like Scott McCaughey, Robert Lloyd, Kelly Hogan, and pop purist Chris von Schneidern. And while the experimentation is implemented quite well—especially in the lighter-and-match-strike percussion loop of "Burn"—Harding's craft remains untouched. His acid-tongued, always-clever phrasing, folky leanings, and strong sense of melody show him to be one of the finest (and unfairly overlooked) songwriters of the '90s. *—Chris Woodstra*

Dynablob 3: 26th March 1999 / 1999 / Wow [Fanclub Only] ✦✦✦

Trad Arr Jones / Feb. 9, 1999 / Zero Hour ✦✦✦

Both an acknowledgment to his roots and a tribute to British folky Nic Jones, *Trad Arr Jones* is an album of traditional folk songs based on Jones' sympathetic and unique arrangements. "The Singer's Request," with its gothic melody, sounds as if it was meant to be played in a monastery, and "William Glenn" tells the story of a mysterious sailing

trip—in other words, the album's subject matter harkens back to a much earlier time. Seeing as how the instrumentation is little more than an acoustic guitar, it's only through Harding's conviction and compelling voice that he is able to get away with such an obscure project, and even then, this album is really only for diehard fans of English folk. *—Steven Kurutz*

Confessions of St. Ace / Aug. 29, 2000 / Mammoth ✦✦✦✦

John Wesley Harding has tried to shake comparisons to Elvis Costello for years, and this album, with its smooth yet acerbic vocals, won't do much to further his cause. However, it is one of his best in years and is filled with witty, thoughtful songwriting and polished instrumentation that works together to make a seamless album, engaging the listener. Best songs include "She's a Piece of Work" and "I'm Wrong About Everything." *—Stacia Proefrock*

Françoise Hardy

b. Jan. 17, 1944, Paris, France

Vocals, Guitar / French Pop, Girl Group, Vocal Pop, Pop

Usually thought of as a middle-of-the-road popular singer, Françoise Hardy—at the beginning of her career, at least—covered more stylistic ground and owed more debts to pop/rock than she's given credit for. Immensely popular in her native France, the chanteuse first displayed her breathy, measured vocals in the early and mid-'60s. Her (mostly self-penned) recordings from that era draw from French pop traditions, lightweight '50s teen-idol rock, girl groups, and sultry jazz and blues—sometimes in the same song. The material is perhaps too unreservedly sentimental for some (in the French tradition), but the songs are invariably catchy and the production, arrangements, and near-operatic backup harmonies excellent, at times almost Spector-esque. Fans of Mariane Faithfull's mid-'60s work can find something of a French equivalent here, though Hardy's material was stronger and her delivery more confident. *—Richie Unterberger*

Ma Jeunesse Fout Le Camp / 1967 / Virgin [Vogue] ✦✦✦

Hardy moved toward a more adult, sedate form of orchestrated pop balladry on this 1967 album. Nothing wrong with that per se; what makes it less exciting than her previous work, though, was that in general the material lacked the bounce and melodic strength of her best recordings. "Il N'y a Pas D'Amour Heureux" ("There is No Happy Love") she sings in one of the tracks, and that sets the mournful tone for much of the tunes (half of which were written by herself), which often deal with sentimental themes of sad farewells. Still, it's delivered with classy grace and ornate period production, and the uplifting "Voila" (easily the best cut here) is one of her top classics. John Paul Jones (presumably the future Led Zeppelin bassist) was one of the arrangers. *—Richie Unterberger*

Comment Te Dire Adieu / 1968 / Virgin [Vogue] ✦✦✦

This may not rate as highly as her best mid-'60s recordings, which are less MOR-oriented. That stated, it's about as good as late-'60s MOR Continental pop gets, with tastefully imaginative orchestration, strong melodies, and sexy vocals. It's perhaps even sadder and more sentimental than was the norm for Francoise—she perpetually seems to be singing as though she's gazing out of a deserted chateau on a rainy afternoon. She largely forsakes original material here (although a couple cuts bear her writing credit), and offers fine, haunting French interpretations of Leonard Cohen's "Suzanne," and Phil Ochs' "There But for Fortune," and Ricky Nelson's "Lonesome Town." *—Richie Unterberger*

Françoise Hardy en Anglais / 1969 / Sonopress ✦✦

Soleil / 1970 / Virgin ✦✦✦

One of Hardy's less colorful efforts. The orchestration leans toward MOR at times, and she only had a hand in writing about half the material, which zigzags between rock, sad ballads, sentimental pop, and chirpy show-biz. It can't be written off, though, as it contains one of her best-ever songs, "Fleur de Lune," with its beautifully moody melody, descending guitar lines, and sultry vocal. Actually, most of the rest isn't bad, whether it's the acoustic balladry of "Soleil," the pensive "L'Ombre," or the unexpectedly forceful "Le Crabe." *—Richie Unterberger*

La Question / 1971 / Virgin [Sonopresse] ✦✦✦✦✦

Throughout her career, most of Hardy's arrangements have tended to the lush, though in a good way. This record is lush too, but it's one of her most sparsely produced efforts, usually finding her voice accompanied by little more than an acoustic guitar, touches of bass, and very subtle orchestration. Much of the record's lights-low ambience could be attributed to Tuca (no last name given), who played guitar, co-arranged, and co-wrote most of the tunes (though Hardy did contribute to the composition of a few tracks). It may be her best post-'60s effort, songs like "Chanson D'O" and "Le Martien" featuring some of her most whispery, seductive vocals. As fireside romantic music goes, it beats the hell out of Jose Feliciano. *—Richie Unterberger*

Et Si Je Je M'en Vais Avant Toi / 1972 / Virgin [Sonopresse] ✦✦

Message Personnel / 1973 / Warner Brothers ✦✦

All Over the World / 1988 / Vogue ✦✦

Story 1962-1964 / 1989 / Vogue ✦✦✦

The *Story* series, with three separate volumes covering the period from 1962-1967, presents this immensely popular French chanteuse at her best. This first volume, which features 20 songs, is perhaps the most innocuous of the lot, which isn't to say it isn't good. Her 1962 single "Le Temps De L'Amour" is perhaps her best recording, featuring snaky spy guitars and a minor-key melody in an unlikely but wonderful marriage of early-'60s rock and a film-noirish atmosphere. *—Richie Unterberger*

● **Story 1964-1965** / 1989 / Vogue ✦✦✦✦✦

Perhaps Hardy's finest compilation, although *Story 1962-64* is almost as good. This

20-song CD finds her at her most girl group-influenced; you don't need to understand French to catch the infectious melodies and sultry, almost hushed vocals. Highlights include the magnificently moody ballad "Tu Peux Bien"; "Non Ce N'est Pas Un Reve," with melodramatic Spectorish production that recalls the Righteous Brothers at their peak; and the tense, romantic yearning of "Il Se Fait Tard." All of these *Story* discs have apparently been remixed for CD release, although the differences are slight, giving more prominence to the percussion and Hardy's vocals. *—Richie Unterberger*

Story 1965-1967 / 1989 / Vogue ♦♦♦
The third 20-song anthology of work from Hardy's early (and best) years is perhaps the least essential of the trio. Several of the ballads and acoustic numbers are unmemorable, suffering from weak material and/or soppy, orchestrated arrangements. These sometimes recall a modified Petula Clark, which can be good or (more often) bad. But the best cuts here stand up to her best material from the decade. "Surtout Ne Vous Retournez Pas" and "Qu'ils Sont Hereux" are among her best ballads, "Je Ne Suis La Pour Personne" is a snappy folk-rocker, and "Voila" is her best grandiose, heart-on-the-sleeve orchestral production. All of the aforementioned highlights were Hardy originals. In the late '60s, Hardy moved toward more middle-of-the-road material (often sung in English), perhaps in an attempt to crack the international market; the three volumes of *Story* remain her most impressive work. *—Richie Unterberger*

L' Integrale Disques Vogue 1962/1967 (The Complete Vogue Recordings) / 1995 / Vogue ♦♦♦♦♦
Four-CD, 83-track box retrospective of her first five (and best) years on record (1962-1967), including everything except the English-language versions she recorded for foreign markets. It's expensive and hard to find in the U.S. But it's worth the investment for Hardy fans, as her early material was very consistent and has usually been reissued in piecemeal fashion; this puts it in all in one place, chronologically sequenced. *—Richie Unterberger*

Le Danger / Sep. 12, 1996 / Virgin ♦♦♦
Francoise Hardy is mostly known as a pop chanteuse with mild rock influences. It comes as something of a shock, then, to stick this into the CD player and hear her backed by assertive, guitar-oriented modern rock arrangements. Hardy's delivery hasn't changed much; it's still a mixture of fetching sensuality and composed reserve. What has changed is the music, with its emphasis upon gutsy guitar textures that sound influenced by '90s alternative rock—a bit of grungetone here, some Brit-pop energy there, some rootsy slide work (on "Ici Ou La?") in the mold of Ry Cooder. Many middle-aged pop singers move from gritty rock to lighthearted MOR. Hardy, unusually, seems determined to move in exactly the opposite direction. It's not as good as, or very similar to, the charming sentimental pop of her youth. Yet it's not at all embarrassing, with a couple of tunes ("Dix Heures En Ete" and "Contre-Jour") that would have definite hit potential, in the best sense of the word, were they sung in English. Whatever you think, one would be hard-pressed to name other rock singers in their early fifties, from France or anywhere else, that managed to sound unassumingly contemporary in the mid-'90s. *—Richie Unterberger*

Steve Harley (Steven Nice)

b. Feb. 27, 1951, London, England
Vocals, Songwriter, Synthesizer / Album Rock, Pop/Rock, Glam Rock
British rocker Steve Harley was born Steven Nice in London on February 27, 1951; the son of a jazz singer, he was stricken with polio at age two and spent the better part of his adolescence in and out of hospitals. After trying his hand at journalism, by the early '70s Harley was busking throughout London, forming the band Cockney Rebel in 1973 with guitarist Jean Paul Crocker, bassist Paul Jeffreys, keyboardist Milton Reame James, and drummer Stuart Elliott. Signing to EMI, the group debuted with *The Human Menagerie*; the single "Judy Teen" followed in early in 1974, becoming Cockney Rebel's first hit. *Psychomodo* was also a success, but as Harley's combative relationship with the press worsened he dissolved the group soon after. A Harley solo single, "Big Big Deal," preceded the formation of a new Cockney Rebel lineup, which again featured drummer Stuart Elliott in addition to new guitarist Jim Cregan, bassist George Ford, and keyboardist Duncan McKay.

1975's *The Best Years of Our Lives* generated Harley's first U.K. chart-topper, "Make Me Smile (Come Up and See Me)," on its way to selling over a million copies; the follow-up *Love's a Prima Donna* also launched a Top Ten hit with its cover of the Beatles' "Here Comes the Sun." But in the wake of 1977's *Face to Face—A Live Recording*, Harley again disbanded Cockney Rebel and relocated to the U.S., recording the better part of *Hobo With a Grin* in Los Angeles before returning to Britain. 1979's *The Candidate* failed to restore his commercial lustre, and with the exception of a minor 1983 hit "Ballerina (Prima Donna)" he spent the better part of the '80s removed from the pop scene. When his recording of "Mr. Soft" experienced a rebirth thanks to its use in a television commercial, Harley assembled a hits collection of the same name. Soon after he formed a new incarnation of Cockney Rebel and regularly toured into the following decade. 1999's *Stripped to Bare Bones* documents an acoustic set recorded the year previous. *Yes You Can* was issued in summer 2000. *—Jason Ankeny*

The Human Menagerie / 1974 / EMI ♦♦♦♦♦
A handful of *Human Menagerie*'s songs might seem slight today, maybe forced, certainly indicative of the group's inexperience. But others—the labyrinthine "Sebastian," the loquacious "Death Trip," in particular—possess a confidence, an arrogance, and a doomed, decadent madness which still astounds, all these decades later. Subject to ruthless dissection, Steve Harley's lyrics are essentially nonsense, a stream of disconnected images whose most gallant achievement is that they usually rhyme. But what could have been perceived as a weakness—or, more generously, an emotionally overwrought attempt to blend Byron with Burroughs—is actually a strength. Few of the songs are about anything in particular. But with Roy Thomas Baker's sub-orchestral production driving strings and things to unimaginable heights, and Cockney Rebel's own unique instrumentation—no lead guitar, but a killer violin—pursuing its own twisted journey, those images gel more solidly than the best constructed story. Unquestionably, he drew from many of the same literary, artistic, and celluloid sources as both David Bowie and Bryan Ferry, the only performers who could reasonably claim to have preempted his vision. But he went far beyond them, through the Berlin of Isherwood to the reality of the Weimar, past the Fritz Lang movies which everyone's seen to the unpublished screenplays which no one has read. And though Harley might not have been the first cultural genius of his age, he was the first who wasn't content to simply zap the prevailing zeitgeist. He wanted to suck out its soul. And he very nearly succeeded. *—Dave Thompson*

Psychomodo / 1975 / EMI ♦♦♦♦♦
If *The Human Menagerie*, Cockney Rebel's debut album, was a journey into the bowels of decadent cabaret, *Psychomodo*, its second, is like a trip to the circus, except the clowns are more sickly perverted than clowns normally are, the funhouse is filled with rattlesnakes and spiders, and you know how pink cotton candy always looks like a stickful of blood-soaked hair...? Steve Harley's themes remained essentially the same as last time out—fey, fractured alienation; studied, splintered melancholia; and shattered shards of imagery which mean more in the mind than they ever could on paper. Reversing the nature of *The Human Menagerie*, the crucial songs here are not those extended epics. Rather, it is the paranoid vignette of "Sweet Dreams," surely written in the numbing first light of that precipitous fame; the panicked brainstorm of the title track; and the stuttering, chopping, hysterical nightmare of "Beautiful Dream" (absent from the original LP, but restored as a CD bonus track), which stake out the album's parameters. The hopelessly romantic "Bed in the Corner" opens another door entirely—relatively straightforward, astoundingly melodic, it was (though nobody realized it at the time) the closest thing in sight to the music Harley would be making later in the decade. Here, however, it swerves in another direction entirely as the dawn of a closing triptych—completed by "Sling It" and "Tumbling Down"—which encompasses ten of the most heartstoppingly breathless and emotionally draining minutes in '70s rock history. "Oh dear!" Harley intones, "look what they've done to the blues." The fact is, he did it all himself—and people have been trying to undo it ever since. *—Dave Thompson*

Best Years of Our Lives / 1975 / EMI ♦♦♦
By his third album, Steve Harley had developed a strong grasp on how to combine his artistic ambitions with strongly crafted pop tunes that win the casual listener over to his artsy cause. The result was *The Best Years of Our Lives*, the finest album of his mid-1970's heyday. This album was a big hit in his native England, thanks to the fact that it spawned two major hit singles. The first was "Mr. Raffles (Man It Was Mean)," a surreal yet romanticized portrait of a convention-flaunting outlaw. The odd lyrics work thanks to the phenomenal tune backing them up, which contrasts gentle verses built on piano and acoustic guitar with choruses that work in a surprising but slickly integrated reggae beat. The second and even more impressive hit was "Make Me Smile (Come Up and See Me)," a romantic pop tune that pairs Harley's clever wordplay with a clever pop tune that boasts an inventive stop-start arrangement and a lovely flamenco-styled acoustic guitar solo. The rest of the songs on the album aren't always as strong as these singles ("It Wasn't Me" has an atmospheric synthesizer-dominated soundscape but lacks any memorable hooks or surprising twists in its arrangement), but there are plenty of highlights for the Harley fan. Some of the other standout tracks on the album include "Mad Mad Moonlight," a driving rocker with humorous lyrics about a romantic encounter with an unlikely female suitor, and the title track, a touching acoustic ballad that highlights some of Harley's most direct and emotional lyrics. All in all, *The Best Years of Our Lives* is a fine, slickly crafted album that will delight Steve Harley enthusiasts and will also appeal to fans of glam-oriented 1970's English rock. *—Donald A. Guarisco*

● **Greatest Hits** / 1987 / EMI ♦♦♦♦
Of all the glam-rock acts to hit it big in England during the 1970's, Steve Harley & Cockney Rebel were second only to David Bowie himself in terms of artsy ambition. Tunes like "Judy Teen" and "Love's a Prima Donna" may have been poppy enough to sail into the English singles charts, but they also boasted unconventional instrumentation (no Cockney Rebel single ever featured an electric guitar) and poetic lyrics with lots of surreal, Bob Dylan-esque wordplay. The result was a string of intelligent yet catchy singles, all of which are compiled on this collection. Songs like "Make Me Smile (Come Up and See Me)" and "Mr. Raffles (Man It Was Mean)" still sound fresh today thanks to their ability to mix insistent pop hooks into their mix of unconventional sounds and oblique lyrics. *Greatest Hits* also includes a generous array of album favorites like "Sling It," an apocalyptic rocker driven by frenetic electric-violin riffs, and "Tumbling Down," a beautifully orchestrated epic that takes Cockney Rebel's penchant for fatalistic melodrama to operatic heights. Another interesting aspect of this collection is that it highlights Harley's oft-underrated skill with ballads: a particular highlight in this area is "(Love) Compared with You," a delicate, subtly-orchestrated tune where Harley drops his yen for surrealistic lyrics to communicate in direct and elegantly romantic terms. The only real downside of *Greatest Hits* is that its surprisingly short track list omits some early gems like "Hideaway" and "Ritz": the compilers could have easily thrown in another two or three songs to fully flesh out the track selection. Despite this quibble, *Greatest Hits* is a fine collection that includes the majority of Cockney Rebel's finest moments and makes a great introduction to this group's ambitious, artsy style of pop. *—Donald A. Guarisco*

Stripped to Bare Bones / Aug. 3, 1999 / Pilot ♦♦♦
Steve Harley is generally known as the leader of the glam rock group Cockney Rebel, so it might come as a surprise to casual fans that he recorded a live acoustic album in 1998 at London's Jazz Cafe. That live album, *Stripped to Bare Bones*, happens to be proof that

Harley was a solid song-craftsman and a fine performer, more than just a glam has-been. His relaxed yet energetic performances and ease at storytelling make *Stripped to Bare Bones* a highly entertaining album, even for listeners that aren't familiar with his body of work. Since the record is effectively a document of a full concert, complete with schtick, it isn't something that would make its way to the stereo all that often, but when it's on, it will likely make you smile. —*Stephen Thomas Erlewine*

Harmony Rockets

Indie Rock, Experimental, Alternative Pop/Rock
For all intents and purposes, Harmony Rockets was really the New York-based avant-pop unit Mercury Rev in disguise; containing the same core players—primarily singer/guitarist Jonathan Donahue and lead guitarist Grasshopper—the side project allowed the group to pursue their most arcane musical ideas to their fullest. The first Harmony Rockets release, 1995's *Paralyzed Mind of the Archangel Void*, was a single 42-minute ambient noise piece, a portrait of the group at their most defiantly experimental; the follow-up, 1997's *Golden Ticket* EP, moved in the opposite direction to offer a disco cover of a song from the movie *Charlie and the Chocolate Factory*. —*Jason Ankeny*

● **Paralyzed Mind of the Archangel Void** / Oct. 10, 1995 / Big Cat ✦✦✦✦✦
The brain-searing *Paralyzed Mind of the Archangel Void* is a trip into the furthest reaches of sound, a complete immersion into space noise and melodic chaos. Comprised of a single, 42-minute live performance piece, the Harmony Rockets' guise allows Mercury Rev the opportunity to push their music to its breaking point; instead of the ear-splitting avant freak-out one might have expected, however, the disc seems to exist in slow motion, characterized by ominous waves of sound. Guitars drone, trumpets throb, and Jonathan Donahue's vocals float in and out of the mix like random messages intercepted from another galaxy; the cumulative effect is an amazing distortion of the time-space continuum, a shape-shifting aural world almost alien in its dementia. —*Jason Ankeny*

Ben Harper

b. Oct. 28, 1969, Pomona, CA
Vocals, Guitar (Steel), Guitar / Jam Bands, Adult Alternative Pop/Rock, Singer/Songwriter
Combining shuddering, groove-laden funky soul and folky, handcrafted acoustics, singer/songwriter Ben Harper cultivated a cult following during the course of the '90s that gained full fruition toward the end of the decade. Harper combined elements of classic singer/songwriters, blues revivalists, Jimi Hendrix, and '90s jam bands like Blues Traveler, Hootie & the Blowfish, and Phish, which meant that he was embraced by critics and college kids alike.

A native of California, Harper grew up listening to blues, folk, soul, R&B, and reggae. After steady gigging in the Los Angeles area, Harper scored a deal with Virgin Records in 1992. He released his debut album, *Welcome to the Cruel World*, two years later to positive reviews.

Released in 1995, the politically-heavy *Fight for Your Mind* made for a strong sophomore effort, an obvious growth in musical experimentation and individual declamation. Harper's third album, 1997's *The Will to Live*, pushed his blues-oriented alternative folk into the middle mainstream, becoming a mainstay at college radio and making inroads at adult alternative radio. Recorded over two years of touring in support of *Fight for Your Mind*, *The Will to Live* introduced the Innocent Criminals, Harper's supporting band.

His most successful album thus far, 1999's *Burn to Shine* blended Harper's fondness of '20s jazz compositions and urban beatboxing, resulting in a clever and passionate collection of songs. "Steal My Kisses" and "Suzie Blue" were radio favorites, landing him two headlining world tours and an opening spot on the Dave Matthews Band's summer 2000 tour. —*MacKenzie Wilson*

Welcome to the Cruel World / Feb. 8, 1994 / Virgin ✦✦✦
The full range of Harper's influences would not come to bear until later albums, but this debut lays a strong foundation. "Like a King" and "Take That Attitude to Your Grave" burn with a political conviction rarely heard during the 1990s. "Forever" has a tenderness which demonstrates Harper's emotional range. Lackluster hippie jams that cultivated his early following may have served a purpose, but feel fluffy by comparison when compared to the meatier tracks. Ben closes the album with a song that frequently closes his concerts, "I'll Rise." This song, built around Maya Angelou's 1979 poem *"And I Still Rise,"* reminds us of art's ability to pierce through society, self, and the soul. —*Ryan Randall Goble*

● **Fight for Your Mind** / 1995 / Virgin ✦✦✦✦
Fight for Your Mind fully embraces Harper's influences (Dylan, Marley, Havens, and Hendrix) into a complete sound while simultaneously broadening his thematic and musical palette. Oliver Charles' tactile drumming and Leon Mobley's percussion work give a sparkle to Harper's music that was absent on his debut. Songs like "Gold to Me" and "Excuse Me Mr." show Harper growing as a poet, approaching ideas via more subtle avenues. The single "Ground on Down" and epic jam "God Fearing Man" capture some of the explosive energy of his live performances. The latter makes allusions to "While My Guitar Gently Weeps," and that's exactly what Harper does—allows his trademark Weissenborn guitar to scream out to his audience. The only misstep on this album is his sophomoric weed anthem "Burn One Down," but one might argue that a little tarnish adds character. —*Ryan Randall Goble*

The Will to Live / Jun. 17, 1997 / Virgin ✦✦✦✦
On his third album *The Will to Live*, Ben Harper strengthens his populist folk with a grittier groove, which even borders on funk, that makes his music more immediate. Harper still has a tendency to preach, yet his melodies are catchier than before, and he has a better sense of rhythm, helping his bluesy songs catch hold. —*Leo Stanley*

Burn to Shine / Sep. 21, 1999 / Virgin ✦✦✦✦
Burn to Shine presents proof positive that you can always distill the essence of rock & roll down to a solitary man alone with his guitar and conscience. It sounds inventive yet firmly rooted in the blues-rock singer/songwriter/guitarist tradition of Taj Mahal and of Neil Young and Cat Stevens at their most confessional. Harper's guitar with falsetto vocal in "The Woman in You" even suggests a Curtis Mayfield tune in the hands of Prince. "Steal My Kisses" is one of those uncluttered, radio-friendly rock shuffles that simply makes you bob your head and feel better. Even Harper's detours—like the wobbling New Orleans shuffle with the Real Time Jazz Band, "Suzie Blue," and charred Black Sabbath metal in "Less"—prove worth exploring. Other cameos include guitarists David Lindley and former Bob Marley sideman Tyrone Downey. *Burn to Shine* is a minor masterpiece that may prove to be not so minor. —*Chris Slawecki*

Live From Mars / Mar. 27, 2001 / Virgin ✦✦✦
Ben Harper is a road dog. He and his band, the Innocent Criminals, travel around the world playing nearly 200 shows a year; therefore, it was only a matter of time before this guitar virtuoso made a live album. *Live From Mars*, an enigmatic two-disc set of 25 songs, celebrates the rise of Harper, his incredible live presence between 1998 and 2000, and the appreciation between him and his audience. His fragile acoustics have been thrown into a massive guitar storm on disc one, a thunderous combination of his signature folky blues-funk rock & roll. He's soulful and approachable on "Excuse Me Mr." and "Burn One Down," but he reaches for something tangible on Marvin Gaye's "Sexual Healing." The vibe is calm and cool while Harper's vocals scale between a sweet falsetto and a rugged twang. "Faded" exudes Harper's electric twitching, and its perfection swaggers into a riveting cover of Led Zeppelin's "Whole Lotta Love" for a near ten-minute car crash of pure rollicking. He switches from his electric to an acoustic for disc two, making his informality even more enticing. "Waiting on an Angel" is delicate, similar to the likes of Jeff Buckley, but it's the beauty of the Verve's "The Drugs Don't Work" that truly captures the standard of excellence that Harper depicts as a performer. Acoustically, he's honored and such praise is deserved. He's practically flawless. He's a modest artist, and such humility is found among his songs. He's achieved respectability with his fans that only so many artists are able to attain. *Live From Mars* is a proper release and certainly an inviting look into Harper and the showmanship he projects while spending time on the road. —*MacKenzie Wilson*

Roy Harper

b. Jun. 12, 1941, Manchester, England
Vocals, Keyboards, Guitar, Bass / British Folk-Rock, Album Rock, British Folk, Folk-Rock, Singer/Songwriter, Blues-Rock
Roy Harper is an idiosyncratic British singer/songwriter acclaimed for his deeply personal, poetic lyrics and unique guitar work. He toured with his brothers' skiffle band, before leaving home at the age of 15 to enter the Royal Air Force; he subsequently secured a discharge by claiming insanity, resulting in a long period marked by frequent stays in mental institutions and prison. By 1965, he was a mainstay at a folk club in London and he released his debut LP *The Sophisticated Beggar* one year later. After 1967's *Come Out Fighting Genghis Smith*, Harper signed to EMI's Harvest subsidiary for 1970's *Flat Baroque and Berserk*; that same year marked the appearance of *Led Zeppelin III* and its track "Hats Off to Harper," a tribute penned by longtime friend Jimmy Page. Upon relocating to Big Sur, California, Harper recorded 1971's *Stormcock*, regarded by many as his finest record. In 1975, Harper recorded *HQ* but also took lead vocals on "Have a Cigar," a track on Pink Floyd's *Wish You Were Here*. Two years later he resurfaced with *Bullinamingvase*; the single "One of Those Days in England," with guest vocals from Paul and Linda McCartney, nearly even became a hit. Due to financial problems, he did not issue another album until 1980's bleak *The Unknown Soldier*. Upon leaving EMI, Harper founded his own label, Public Records, releasing *Work of Heart* in 1982. Harper re-signed to EMI in 1986 and recorded the double live LP *In Between Every Line. Descendants of Smith* appeared two years later, and when the record stiffed he moved to the Awareness label, issuing *Once* in 1990. After the release of 1992's *Death or Glory?*, Awareness folded, again leaving Harper without label support. He soon founded his own company, Science Friction. —*Jason Ankeny*

Sophisticated Beggar / 1966 / Resurgent ✦✦✦
Recorded under primitive circumstances and not distributed well on initial release, Harper's debut proves that the definitive cult folk-rock singer's idiosyncratic weirdness was firmly in place from the start. Mostly but not wholly acoustic, there are lingering similarities to Donovan and Bert Jansch, as well as a light similarity to Al Stewart on occasion. But Harper's scrambled lyricism is already his own, as is his peculiar melismatic phrasing. Those two traits combine to give the impression of a singer-songwriting dyslexic, not able or willing to write words that are easily digested and apparently unsequenced in any linear fashion. That isn't the most appetizing recipe, but it's leavened by fairly attractive British folk melodies and very accomplished guitar work (the liner notes infer that John Renbourn and Ritchie Blackmore helped out). Although this is largely acoustic, electric guitar and backing are used from time to time, as well as reverb and backwards effects that give it a dated charm. Certainly the most uncharacteristic arrangement is "Committed," a crunching, ominous rock tune whose first-person account of madness recalls Syd Barrett's most distraught work (and is if anything more distraught than Barrett's loony tunes). And speaking of Pink Floyd, "October 12th" makes you wonder if Harper's influence didn't find its way into the post-Syd Floyd on tunes like "Grantchester Meadows." —*Richie Unterberger*

Come Out Fighting Ghengis Smith / 1967 / Griffin Music ✦✦✦
On Harper's second album (and first for a major label), he strode further into folk-rock as

opposed to folk, with sympathetic production from Shel Talmy; there was light electric backing and drums, as well as occasional orchestration. Harper remained, however, overly verbose, his observational lyrics tending to jam too many thoughts into too little time. Often this is stream-of-consciousness songwriting, proving that such a strain existed in alternative rock long before Jandek and Lambchop's Kurt Wagner. Harper is far more tuneful, and a much better singer and instrumentalist, than either Jandek or Wagner, which makes this much more accessible on a surface level. Still, it's music that demands a lot of concentration to apprehend, and ultimately doesn't fully reward the effort, the listener's attention tending to drift off amidst Harper's inscrutability. Far be it from a mere critic to suggest such a thing decades after the fact, but it may have been that Harper could have well done with a songwriting collaborator who could have extracted Roy's most coherent ideas and sanded off the most incoherent ones. Especially befuddling are the epic-length cuts ("Circle" and the title track), which seem to wish to be making a grand point, but are only intermittently interesting winding roads, the pseudo-humorous spoken dialogue in "Circle" falling especially flat. He is best when he is most restrained, as on "All You Need Is" and "What You Have." The CD reissue on Science Friction adds seven bonus tracks. Two are from his 1969 album *Folkjokeopus*; two are from a 1967 single that is only marginally more commercial than the album; and the remaining three are from 1969-70 BBC sessions. *—Richie Unterberger*

Folkjokeopus / 1969 / Griffin Music ✦✦
This Shel Talmy-produced album is as sprawling and unwieldy as its title. Always a determined eclectic, Harper tries to cover a lot of ground here, and while his effort is impressive, the result is unnervingly inconsistent. The influences of Bob Dylan, Bert Jansch, Donovan, and maybe even early Al Stewart hover over most of this folk-rock. Harper tries to cram too many musical and (especially) lyrical ideas together here, and several of his heart-on-the-sleeve narrative folktales ramble on for too long, with an obscurity that verges on maddening. Some pretty, melodic passages here and there, with adequate folk singing that cracks when he even approaches the upper register. The acoustic guitar work is uniformly excellent, making this confused late-'60s timepiece sound rather more impressive than it should. *—Richie Unterberger*

Flat Baroque & Berserk / 1970 / Science Friction ✦✦✦
Roy Harper's fourth album found him in an acoustic folkie mode more often than not, though as usual (for circa late-'60s Harper) there were detours into pretty rocky items on occasion. It's not much of either a progression or a slide from the lyrically convoluted, somewhat but not incredibly melodic path he had established with his prior work. "I Hate the White Man," however, is certainly one of his most notable (and notorious) compositions, a spew of lilting verbiage that's hard to peg. It could be irony, it could be ironic self-hatred, it could be muddled reflections on the chaos that is the modern world, or it could be a combination of all of them. There are gentler items, sometimes with subdued harmony vocals and orchestration, that sound rather like Harper's most acerbic side sanded off with edges of Al Stewart, Donovan, or Tim Hardin; "Another Day" is the prettiest of those. The atypical "Hell's Angels," on the other hand, has a twisted, chunky rock feel rather like the solo work of another of producer Peter Jenner's clients, Syd Barrett. *—Richie Unterberger*

● **Stormcock** / 1971 / Resurgent ✦✦✦✦✦
With only four tracks (three of which are quite long), this is Harper's most serious, focused work. Not as melancholy as Nick Drake, it has a similar moody appeal and features lots of fine acoustic guitar work. "The Same Old Rock" feature virtuosic acoustic lead from none other than Jimmy Page (playing under the pseudonym S. Flavius Mercurius), and one can detect Harper's influence in the acoustic-oriented Led Zep recordings of the early '70s. *—Richie Unterberger*

Lifemask / 1973 / Resurgent ✦✦✦
Lifemask is an album of music recorded for the film *Made*, in which Harper starred with Carole White. It was reissued on Harper's Science Friction imprint in 1997. Highlights include "Highway Blues," "South Africa," and the five-part, 23-minute epic "The Lord's Prayer," which features a guest appearance by Jimmy Page on guitar. *—Steve Huey*

Flashes from the Archives of Oblivian / 1974 / Resurgent ✦✦✦
Fourteen tracks recorded at various concerts in England. Some of his most influential work. An obscene cover photo. *—Michael G. Nastos*

Hats Off / Jun. 19, 2001 / Capitol ✦✦✦✦
"This CD is not a 'best of' record and does not attempt to be so," declares the first sentence of the liner notes. So, what do you call it, exactly, considering that its 14 songs span much of the 35-year period Harper had recorded during prior to its release? A 60th birthday commemoration, perhaps, or a reasonably listener-friendly introduction to Harper's quite variable output. The songs seem to have been selected with an eye to highlighting his collaborations with high-profile guests like Jimmy Page, Kate Bush, David Gilmour, Ian Anderson, and Paul McCartney, though it doesn't suffer for that. With a guy who's done about 30 records, a single-disc distillation is inevitably going to leave major gaps. But it does a fair job at assembling some of his more accessible tunes, all but four of them from the 1970s, though it does go as chronologically far as 1998. On the whole it's decent folk-influenced British rock that sounds less eccentric than many isolated Harper albums. The cuts on which Page plays are the most interesting, particularly "Same Old Rock" from 1971's *Stormcock*. Note, though, that several of the tracks are edited down from the original versions. These are sometimes minor and will not be noticed by neophytes, but in the case of "Me and My Woman," one of his finest songs (again from *Stormcock*), a track that originally took up most of an LP side has been whittled down to four minutes. In the liner notes, Harper contributes observations about the songs that are no less oblique than the lyrics he writes. *—Richie Unterberger*

Harpers Bizarre

f. 1963, Santa Cruz, CA, **db.** 1970
Sunshine Pop, Baroque Pop, Vocal Pop, Pop
The eclectic pop group Harper's Bizarre was formed in Santa Cruz, CA, in 1963 by Ted Templeman (b.Oct. 24, 1944, Santa Cruz, CA) (vocals, drums, trumpet), Dickie Scoppettone (b.Jul 5, 1945, Santa Cruz, CA) (guitar, vocals), Eddie James (b.Santa Cruz, CA) (guitar, vocals), and Dick Yount (b.Jan. 9, 1943) (guitar, bass, drums). John Peterson (b.Jan. 8, 1945, San Francisco) (drums) joined in 1966. After gaining attention as the surf-oriented Tikis in San Francisco, they were signed to Warner Bros. Records by producer Lenny Waronker, and they scored one of the sunniest hit singles of the 1967 Summer of Love with a version of Paul Simon's "The 59th Street Bridge Song (Feelin' Groovy)." Their brand of wistful, Roaring '20s pop enjoyed only a brief vogue, roughly from late 1966 to mid-1967, but they managed to get a few more minor chart singles, notably Van Dyke Parks' "Come to the Sunshine" and covers of "Anything Goes" and "Chattanooga Choo Choo" and released four albums before disbanding in 1970. Templeman went on to become one of Warner Bros.' primary staff producers. *As Time Goes By* (1976) marked a partial reunion of the group. *—William Ruhlmann*

● **Feelin' Groovy: The Best of Harpers Bizarre** / Feb. 25, 1997 / Warner Brothers ✦✦✦✦
The 14-track anthology *Feelin' Groovy* collects the majority of Harper's Bizarre's chart hits as well as rare material like the non-LP single "Poly High." Along with the group's intricate harmonies, the set spotlights songs from the likes of Randy Newman, Van Dyke Parks, Harry Nilsson, and Paul Simon. *—Jason Ankeny*

Wynonie Harris

b. Aug. 24, 1915, Omaha, NE, **d.** Jun. 14, 1969, Los Angeles, CA
Vocals, Leader, Drums / Jump Blues, R&B
No blues shouter embodied the rollicking good times that he sang of quite like raucous shouter Wynonie Harris. "Mr. Blues," as he was not-so-humbly known, joyously related risque tales of sex, booze, and endless parties in his trademark raspy voice over some of the jumpingest horn-powered combos of the postwar era.

Those wanton ways eventually caught up with Harris, but not before he scored a raft of R&B smashes from 1946 to 1952. The shouter debuted in 1945 at an L.A. date for Philo with backing from drummer Johnny Otis, saxist Teddy Edwards, and trumpeter Howard McGhee. A month later, he signed on with Apollo Records, an association that provided him with two huge hits in 1946: "Wynonie's Blues" (with saxist Illinois Jacquet's combo) and "Playful Baby." Harris's own waxings were squarely in the emerging jump blues style then sweeping the West Coast, and after he joined the star-studded roster of Cincinnati's King Records in 1947, his sales really soared. Few records made a stronger seismic impact than Harris's 1948 chart-topper "Good Rockin' Tonight." Ironically, Harris shooed away its composer, Roy Brown, when he first tried to hand it to the singer; only when Brown's original version took off did Wynonie cover the romping number. With Hal "Cornbread" Singer on wailing tenor sax and a rocking, socking backbeat, the record provided an easily followed blueprint for the imminent rise of rock & roll a few years later. After that, Harris was rarely absent from the R&B charts for the next four years, his offerings growing more boldly suggestive all the time. "Grandma Plays the Numbers," "All She Wants to Do Is Rock," "I Want My Fanny Brown," "Sittin' on It All the Time," "I Like My Baby's Pudding," "Good Morning Judge," "Bloodshot Eyes," and "Lovin' Machine" were only a portion of the ribald hits Harris scored into 1952 (13 in all). *—Bill Dahl*

Everybody Boogie! / Aug. 2, 1945-Dec. 1945 / Delmark ✦✦✦✦
This is one marvelous collection of 1945 recordings made for Apollo Records with Harris's powerhouse vocals backed by jump blues bands led by jazz greats Illinois Jacquet, Oscar Pettiford, and Jack McVea. No real honking and bar walking going on here; quite the opposite, as the Pettiford tunes have bop lines creeping in throughout. But Harris seems oblivious to it all as tracks like "Time to Change Your Town," "Here Come the Blues," "Stuff You Gotta Watch," and "Somebody Changed the Lock on My Door" are on an equal par for sheer bravado and intensity with the best of his later work for King. A welcome compilation. *—Cub Koda*

☆ **Good Rocking Tonight** / 1990 / King ✦✦✦✦✦
Equally splendid compilation of the raspy shouter's King label output from the British Charly logo. Contains 20 sides, including a few essentials that Rhino didn't bother with: a roaring "Rock Mr. Blues" that grants Harris vocal group backing; the lascivious rocker "I Want My Fanny Brown" and "Lollipop Mama," and a celebratory "Mr. Blues Is Coming to Town." Harris and King always used inexorably swinging bands—saxists include Red Prysock, David Van Dyke (who duel it out on the amazing "Quiet Whiskey"), Big John Greer, Hal Singer, and Tom Archia. *—Bill Dahl*

★ **Bloodshot Eyes: The Best of Wynonie Harris** / 1993 / Rhino ✦✦✦✦✦
Wynonie Harris was a hard-living, rousing R&B shouter who made some of the most sexually explicit songs in modern popular music history. Harris didn't leave much to the imagination, but he also possessed a booming voice with wonderful tone and range and the comedic skill to execute these tunes without becoming raunchy. There are many hilarious cuts on this 18-track anthology, among them "I Like My Baby's Pudding," "Grandma Plays The Numbers," and "Good Morning Judge." Harris roars, struts, and wails over equally feverish arrangements and earns a draw with Joe Turner on "Battle of the Blues." These songs give a good portrait of a delightful, often spectacular vocalist who could be both provocative and compelling. *—Ron Wynn*

Women, Whiskey & Fish Tails / 1993 / Ace ✦✦✦✦
British compiler Ray Topping focuses on Harris' 1952-1957 King output on this 21-song collection, when he was undeniably on the downslide as far as making hits. But there was still plenty of wind in the shouter's sails, judging from "Greyhound," "Christina," "Shake

That Thing" (an update of an ancient blues theme), "Git to Gittin' Baby," and "Mr. Dollar." Harris even supplied a savvy sequel to one of his immortal numbers with "Bad News Baby (There'll Be No Rockin' Tonite)." *—Bill Dahl*

1945-1947 / Nov. 3, 1998 / Classics ♦♦♦♦♦

The second Classics CD to feature blues singer Wynonie Harris' recordings as a leader finds him in the period right before he signed with the King label. The five four-song sessions on this disc (all quite jazz oriented) were cut for Hamp-Tone, Bullet, and Aladdin. First, Harris (who sounds quite enthusiastic in every setting) sings three numbers (including a two-part "Hey! Ba-Ba-Re-Bop") with a combo taken from the Lionel Hampton big band. The Bullet date was quite rare. Recorded in Nashville, it finds Harris backed by local players including Sun Ra in his first recording. Ra's piano is well featured throughout including on "Dig This Boogie." Harris is also heard with a Leonard Feather-organized band that includes trumpeter Joe Newman, altoist Tab Smith, and tenor-saxophonist Allen Eager ("Mr. Blues Jumped the Rabbit" is the best-known selection), with an obscure backup band in New York (including for "Ghost of a Chance," an odd departure with a vocal group) and sharing the spotlight with Big Joe Turner on three numbers (including a slightly disorganized two-part "Battle of the Blues"). Throughout, Wynonie Harris sounds like he was ready for stardom. Recommended. *—Scott Yanow*

George Harrison

b. Feb. 25, 1943, Liverpool, England, **d.** Nov. 29, 2001, Los Angeles, CA

Slide Guitar, Vocals, Guitar (Electric), Guitar / Album Rock, Experimental Rock, Pop/Rock, Psychedelic, Singer/Songwriter

As lead guitarist for the Beatles, George Harrison provided the band with a lyrical style of playing in which every note mattered. The Beatlemania years, from 1963 through 1966, were a mixed blessing for Harrison, as his lead guitar was buried beneath the chiming chords of John Lennon's instrument. Additionally, he was thwarted as a songwriter by the presence of Lennon and McCartney—the quality and prolificacy of their output left very little room for songs by anyone else. In 1966, Harrison finally seemed to find his voice, with two of his songs on the *Revolver* album, "Taxman" and "Love You Too." In the wake of the group's decision to stop touring, Harrison's playing and songwriting grew exponentially. The period from 1968 onward was Harrison's richest with the Beatles. He displayed a smooth, elegant slide guitar technique that showed up on their last three albums, and contributed two classic songs, "While My Guitar Gently Weeps" and "Here Comes the Sun," along with "Something," which became the first Harrison song on the A-side of a Beatles single. For his first solo record following the group's 1970 breakup, *All Things Must Pass*, Harrison collaborated with producer Phil Spector, whose so-called "wall of sound" technique adapted well to Harrison's voice. *All Things Must Pass* and the accompanying single "My Sweet Lord" had the distinction of being the first solo recordings by any of the Beatles to top the charts following their breakup. Subsequent Harrison albums from the 1970s into the '80s always had an audience, but except for *Somewhere in England* (1981), released in the wake of the murder of John Lennon with the memorial song "All Those Years Ago," none seemed terribly well crafted or executed. In 1987, Harrison made a return to the top of the charts with his album *Cloud Nine*, which featured his most inspired work in years. In 1988, Harrison, Bob Dylan, Tom Petty, Jeff Lynne, and Roy Orbison formed the Traveling Wilburys, whose eponymous debut was very successful. Following a second Wilburys album and a 1991 tour of Japan, Harrison retreated from the public spotlight in the '90s, resurfacing only for the Beatles' *Anthology* project, which was unveiled in 1995. In 1999, Harrison was assaulted in his home and seriously injured by a deranged fan, but he recovered and in 2000 he began work on remastering and expanding his classic *All Things Must Pass* album. The reissue of that album at the outset of 2001 heralded an unusually public publicity campaign by Harrison, who accompanied its re-release with an interview record that anticipated the eventual reissue of the rest of his catalog. Harrison had been treated for throat cancer in the late 1990's, but in 2001 it was revealed that he was suffering from an inoperable form of brain cancer; he succumbed to the disease on November 29, 2001. *—Bruce Eder*

Wonderwall Music / Dec. 2, 1968 / Capitol ♦♦♦

The first Beatle solo album—as well as the first Apple album—was a minor eruption of the pent-up energies of George Harrison, who was busy composing this offbeat score to the film *Wonderwall* as *Magical Mystery Tour* raced up the charts. With the subcontinental influence now firmly in the driver's seat, the score is mostly given over to the solemn, atmospheric drones of Indian music. Yet as a whole, it's a fascinating, if musically slender mishmash of sounds from East and West, everything casually juxtaposed or superimposed without a care in the world. Harrison himself does not appear as a player or singer; rather he presides over the groups of Indian and British musicians, with half of the cues recorded in London, the other half in Bombay. The Indian tracks are professionally executed selections cut into film cue-sized bites, sometimes mixed up with a rock beat, never permitted to develop much. Touches of George's whimsical side can be heard in the jaunty, honky-tonk, tack piano-dominated "Drilling a Home" and happy-trails lope of "Cowboy Museum," as well as a title like "Wonderwall to Be Here." Occasionally you can hear the overt footsteps of a Beatle: "Party Secombe" is a medium-tempo rock track that should remind the connoisseur of "Flying"; "Dream Scene" has Indian vocals moving back and forth between the loudspeakers over backwards electronic loops. As this and George's second experimental release *Electronic Sound* undoubtedly prove, pigeonholing this Beatle is a dangerous thing. *—Richard S. Ginell*

Electronic Sound / May 26, 1969 / Zapple ♦♦

Hard as it is to believe, George Harrison, guitar picker, was also an electronic music pioneer—as these two lengthy, abstract tone poems for early-vintage Moog synthesizer reveal. A naif in the electronic sphere, George had a lot of help putting this music together, particularly from ace California electronic composer Bernie Krause. Interestingly, Krause was originally given prominent credit in George's childlike artwork on the LP cover, but when the album came out, Krause's name was almost, but not quite, obscured by silver paint, and the CD erases it entirely. The main difference between the CD reissue and the original LP is that the identities of the two works apparently have been reversed; "Under the Mersey Wall" is really "No Time or Space" and vice-versa. Accordingly, Krause is given "assistance" credit for the latter piece instead of the former—which is significant because "No Time Or Space" is the masterpiece of the record. Dramatically structured, unearthly in its pitchless writhing, flamboyantly manipulating pink and white noise from the opening electronic gun battle onward, "No Time or Space" is still an entertaining listening experience—and some of its passages would turn up later in the "I Remember Jeep" jam from Harrison's *All Things Must Pass* album. The shorter "Mersey Wall," recorded in Harrison's Esher bungalow with his own Moog, is a low-key, drifting affair, not quite as virtuosic in its handling of abstract sound, nor nearly as theatrical. The sound is slightly sharper in the CD remastering, exposing more extraneous distortion and hum. Though scoffed at when they were released, these pieces can hold their own and then some with many of those of other, more seriously regarded electronic composers. And when you consider that synthesizers were only capable of playing one note at a time and sounds could not be stored or recalled with the push of a button, the achievement becomes even more remarkable. Alas, George has yet to follow up on this direction which, like the Zapple label, was abandoned after this release. *—Richard S. Ginell*

★ **All Things Must Pass** / Nov. 27, 1970 / Capitol ♦♦♦♦♦

Without a doubt, Harrison's first solo recording, originally issued as a triple album, is his best. Drawing on his backlog of unused compositions from the late Beatle era, George crafted material that managed the rare feat of conveying spiritual mysticism without sacrificing his gifts for melody and grand, sweeping arrangements. Enhanced by Phil Spector's lush orchestral production and Harrison's own superb slide guitar, nearly every song is excellent: "Awaiting on You All," "Beware of Darkness," the Dylan collaboration "I'd Have You Anytime," "Isn't It a Pity," and the hit singles "My Sweet Lord" and "What Is Life" are just a few of the highlights. A very moving work, with a very significant flaw: the jams that comprise the final third of the album are entirely dispensable, and have probably only been played once or twice by most of the listeners that own this record. *—Richie Unterberger*

The Concert for Bangladesh / Dec. 20, 1971 / Capitol ♦♦♦♦♦

Hands down, this epochal concert in New York's Madison Square Garden—first issued on three LPs in a handsome orange-colored box—was the crowning event of George Harrison's public life, a gesture of great goodwill that captured the moment in history and, not incidentally, produced some rousing music as a permanent legacy. Having been moved by his friend Ravi Shankar's appeal to help the homeless Bengali refugees of the 1971 India-Pakistan war, Harrison leaped to action, organizing on short notice what became a bellwether for the spectacular rock & roll benefits of the 1980s and beyond. The large, almost unwieldy band was loaded with rock luminaries—including Beatle alumnus Ringo Starr, Eric Clapton, Badfinger, and two who became stars as a result of their electric performances here, Leon Russell ("Jumpin' Jack Flash/Youngblood") and Billy Preston ("That's the Way God Planned It"). Yet Harrison is in confident command, running through highlights from his recent triumphant *All Things Must Pass* album in fine voice, secure enough to revisit his Beatles legacy from *Abbey Road* and the *White Album*. Though overlooked at the time by impatient rock fans eager to hear the hits, Shankar's opening raga, "Bangla Dhun," is a masterwork on its own terms; the sitar virtuoso is in dazzling form even by his standards—and in retrospect, he, Ali Akbar Khan, and Alla Rakha amount to an Indian supergroup themselves. The high point of the concert is the surprise appearance of Bob Dylan—at this reclusive time in his life, every Dylan sighting made headlines—and he read the tea leaves perfectly by performing five of his most powerful, meaningful songs from the '60s. *—Richard S. Ginell*

Living in the Material World / May 30, 1973 / Capitol ♦♦♦♦

How does an instant multimillion-selling album become underrated? George Harrison's follow-up to *All Things Must Pass* was necessarily a letdown for fans and critics, appearing after a two-and-a-half-year interval without the earlier album's backlog of excellent songs to draw from. And it does seem like Harrison narrowed his sights and his vision for this record, which has neither the bold expansiveness nor the overwhelming confidence of its predecessor. And some of the most serious songs here, such as "The Light That Has Lighted the World," seem dirge-like. What *Living in the Material World* shows off far better than the earlier record, however, is Harrison's guitar work—he's the only axeman on *Material World*, and it does represent his solo playing and songwriting at something of a peak. Most notable are his blues stylings and slide playing, glimpsed on some of the later Beatles sessions but often overlooked by fans. "Don't Let Me Wait Too Long" is driven by a delectable acoustic rhythm guitar and has a great beat. The title track isn't great, but it does benefit from a tight, hard band sound; and "The Lord Loves the One (That Loves the Lord)," despite its title, is the high point of the record, a fast, rollicking, funky, bluesy jewel, with a priceless guitar break (maybe the best of Harrison's solo career) that should have been at the heart of any of Harrison's concert set. Vocally, he isn't as self-consciously pretty or restrained here, but it is an honest performance, and his singing soars magnificently in his heartfelt performance on "The Day the World Gets Round." Perhaps a less serious title would have represented the album better, but nobody was looking for self-effacement from any ex-Beatle except Ringo (who's also here, natch) in those days. *—Bruce Eder*

Dark Horse / Dec. 9, 1974 / Capitol ♦♦♦

With his first solo tour looming ahead in November and December of 1974, George Harrison felt impelled to rush out a new album—and even a steadily worsening case of laryngitis wouldn't stop him. Would that it did, for the appallingly weak state of Harrison's voice would torpedo this album and the tour, to his great embarrassment. "Hari's on Tour (Express)"—with Tom Scott's L.A. Express churning out all-pro L.A.-studio jazz/rock—gets the doomed project off to a spirited start, but it's an instrumental, and George's vocal distress becomes obvious to all in the next track, "Simply Shady." Some of George's tunes—particularly the title track and the exquisite "Far East Man"—might have benefited from waiting for a better time to record, while others probably could not have been saved. The recording quality, like the voice, has a raw, coarse-grained sound that belies the impeccable musicianship. *Dark Horse* is perhaps most notorious for Harrison's bitter, slipshod rewrite of the Everly Brothers' hit "Bye Bye Love"—referring openly to George's wife Pattie running off with Eric Clapton and, for good measure, having both of them on the session! Dark Horse would also be the name of Harrison's soon-to-be-formed new label, as well as a metaphor for the underestimated Beatle who leaped artistically and commercially ahead of his three colleagues immediately after the Beatles' breakup. Unfortunately, this album—despite its humorous *Sgt. Pepper* parody on the cover and outright plea to critics on the margins of the inside jacket to go easy on its contents—would only undermine Harrison's hard-fought campaign for respect. *—Richard S. Ginell*

Extra Texture / Sep. 22, 1975 / Capitol ♦♦♦
Despite George Harrison's reputation for solemn, lugubriously paced albums in the early '70s—and this one is mostly no exception—the jacket is full of jokes, from the eaten-away Apple logo (the Apple label would expire at year's end) to the punning title, the list of non-participants, and the mischievous grin of the ex-Beatle above the arch caption "OHNOTHIMAGEN" ("Oh, not him again!"). The record gets off to a great start with the instantly winning single, "You"—a bit of which is then repeated to open Side two—but here, the basic idea and instrumental track come from Feb. 1971 during George's most fertile period, dressed up with vocals and string synthesizer four years later. One of George's most beautifully harmonized, majestic, strangely underrated ballads "The Answer's at the End"—whose inspiring lyric was based upon an inscription on George's home by its builder, Sir Frank Crisp—comes next, followed by "This Guitar (Can't Keep From Crying)," an attractive sequel to "While My Guitar Gently Weeps." At this point, the devoted fan's hopes go up; could this be an unsung masterpiece. But George has fired off his best stuff first—and the record slowly and inexorably tails off, closing with a baffling salute to ex-Bonzo Dog Band member "Legs" Larry Smith. Yet despite its stretches of treadmill material, *Extra Texture* has worn better as a whole than its Apple neighbors *Dark Horse* and even much of *Living in The Material World*; for even the lesser tunes reveal a few musical blossoms upon re-listening and the front-loaded songs are among the best of his solo career. *—Richard S. Ginell*

The Best of George Harrison / Nov. 8, 1976 / Capitol ♦♦♦
The Harrison material is matched with some Beatles numbers in a good but routine collection. *—Bruce Eder*

33 & 1/3 / Nov. 24, 1976 / Dark Horse ♦♦♦♦♦
Having suffered the humiliation of being sued successfully over "My Sweet Lord," Harrison turned the ordeal into music, writing "This Song," a Top 25 hit. Even better was "Crackerbox Palace," which would have fit in nicely on any Beatles album. The rest was slight, although Harrison covering Cole Porter's "True Love" is an interesting idea. This was Harrison's first album on his Dark Horse custom label, formed after the completion of his contract with EMI/Capitol in June 1976 and initially distributed by A&M. *—William Ruhlmann*

George Harrison / Feb. 14, 1979 / Dark Horse ♦♦♦
George Harrison is, except for the overdubbed London strings, a painstakingly polished L.A.-made product—and not a particularly inspired one at that, an ordinary album from an extraordinary talent. "Love Comes to Everyone" leads it off on a depressing note, a treadmill tune with greeting card verses, and there are too many other such half-hearted songs lurking here, although some are salvaged by a nice instrumental touch—a catchy recurring guitar riff on "Soft Touch," some lovely slide guitar on "Your Love Is Forever." Compared to the original tougher Beatles version that was left off the White Album, the remake of "Not Guilty" is an easy-listening trifle, though it was a revelation when it came out (the original had to wait until 1996 and Anthology 3 for an official release), and the succeeding "Here Comes the Moon" is a lazy retake on another Beatles song. "Blow Away" would be the record's most attractive new song—and a number 16 hit—but "Faster," a paean to George's passion for Formula One auto racing, probably better reflected where George's head was at this time. There are a few quirks; "Soft-Hearted Hana" being a strange, stream-of-consciousness Hawaiian hallucination, and "Dark Sweet Lady" is a Latin-flavored tune written for his new wife Olivia. Finally, the inevitable spiritual benediction "If You Believe" offers some thoughtful philosophy to ponder, if not an especially memorable tune. *—Richard S. Ginell*

Somewhere in England / Jun. 1, 1981 / Dark Horse ♦♦♦
This record had a troubled birth, for when Harrison originally submitted it for release in Nov. 1980, Warner Bros. rejected it, claiming that four songs—"Flying Hour," "Lay His Head," "Sat Singing," and "Tears of the World" (once available on the bootleg *Ohnothimagen*)—were not worthy of being issued. George was forced to go back into the studio to cut four new tunes, delivering a bitterly barbed thrust at his record label in "Blood From a Clone," (which they did release!), and a tune originally meant for Ringo but rewritten as a remembrance after John Lennon's assassination ("All Those Years Ago"), as well as "Teardrops" and "That Which I Have Lost." As a result, the most compelling issue of this album is the contest of wills betwen the artist and the suits. Now how do the four deleted tunes stack up against the ones that replaced them? The four missing tunes are of generally even quality, even similar in sound, although "Tears of the World" is a strident attack against corporate and political masters that probably unnerved the executives the most. Actually, the six tunes that Warner Bros. spared should have been more likely candidates for the hook, including the curious covers of two Hoagy Carmichael songs, "Baltimore Oriole" and "Hong Kong Blues." Yet in general, the new ones are indeed superior, more varied, with more of a punch than the ones they replaced. The bouncy "All Those Years Ago" is a definite gain, being the most heartfelt song on the record as well as a de facto Beatles reunion (Ringo plays drums and Paul and Linda McCartney overdubbed backing vocals)—and it was justly rewarded with a number two showing on the singles charts. One of these days, all 14 songs will be put out on a single CD; until then, the official release is slightly preferable over the bootlegs of the original. *—Richard S. Ginell*

Gone Troppo / Oct. 27, 1982 / Dark Horse ♦♦

Cloud Nine / Nov. 2, 1987 / Dark Horse ♦♦♦♦♦
Teaming with legendary Beatles obsessive Jeff Lynne, George Harrison crafted a remarkably consistent and polished comeback effort with *Cloud Nine*. Lynne adds a glossy production, reminiscent of ELO, but what is even more noticeable is that he's reined in Harrison's indulgences, keeping the focus on a set of 11 snappy pop-rock numbers. The consistency of the songs remains uneven, but the best moments—"Devil's Radio," "Cloud 9," "Just for Today," "Got My Mind Set on You," and the tongue-in-cheek Beatles pastiche "When We Was Fab"—make *Cloud 9* one of his very best albums. *—Stephen Thomas Erlewine*

The Best of Dark Horse (1976-1989) / Oct. 1989 / Dark Horse ♦♦♦♦♦
George Harrison's albums have been notoriously uneven, but despite the rough patches, his talent for songcraft never really left him, as the compilation *The Best of Dark Horse (1976-1989)* proves. A 15-song retrospective covering five albums, *The Best of Dark Horse* contains nearly every gem from *33 1/3, George Harrison, Somewhere in England, Gone Troppo*, and *Cloud Nine*, including "Crackerbox Palace," "All Those Years Ago," "Got My Mind Set on You," "Cloud 9," "When We Was Fab," and the lovely "Blow Away." For most casual fans, the record will be a welcome summation of a hit-and-miss era of Harrison's career. *—Stephen Thomas Erlewine*

Live in Japan / Jul. 1992 / Dark Horse ♦♦
George Harrison returned to the stage for the first time in years in 1991; that Japanese tour is documented on the fine double-disc set *Live in Japan*. Backed by a stellar supporting band led by Eric Clapton, Harrison turns in surprisingly strong versions of his best solo material; it easily surpasses Paul McCartney's double-disc *Tripping the Live Fantastic* or *Paul Is Live*. Not bad for a guy who doesn't like to give concerts. *—Stephen Thomas Erlewine*

☆ **All Things Must Pass [30th Anniversary Edition]** / Jan. 23, 2001 / Capitol ♦♦♦♦♦
All Things Must Pass has long been one of the more vexing classic albums to make it to CD. It appeared previously in two distinctly different (yet confusingly similar) packagings in the late '80s, one from England and one from America, both of which were straight reissues of the original triple LP. Neither was a wholly satisfactory release—originally recorded using lots of tracks (and no noise reduction technology) to achieve a very big sound, the album was impressive on vinyl but had a lot of noise when processed digitally for CD. This expanded and remastered edition solved most of those problems as well as offering five additional tracks. The remastering has imparted greater resolution to the music without losing the wall-of-sound effect that most of the album was intended to display. In the process, it's possible to discern the various guitars at work far better than on the original LP set and to better appreciate the virtuosity of the playing involved as well as the sheer size of the ensemble Harrison assembled. Additionally, and almost more important in terms of enjoying the album as a whole, the new edition captures the warmth and nuances of Harrison's singing. Of the five bonus tracks, one is an entirely new song from the original sessions, and three more are outtakes of existing songs in versions that have appeared on various bootlegs, while "My Sweet Lord (2000)" is a stripped-down reconsideration of the song. The so-called "Apple Jam" tracks that comprised disc three of the original LP have also been remastered, to their considerable advantage. The new edition comes in a box with each CD in a separate slipcase and a booklet containing photos from the original sessions, full lyrics, recording credits, and an essay by Harrison. *—Bruce Eder*

Wilbert Harrison

b. Jan. 5, 1929, Charlotte, NC, **d.** Oct. 26, 1994, Spencer, NC
Vocals, Drums, Piano, Guitar / East Coast Blues, Rock & Roll, R&B, Soul
Perceived by casual oldies fans as a two-hit wonder (his 1959 chart-topper "Kansas City" and a heartwarming "Let's Work Together" a full decade later), Wilbert Harrison actually left behind a varied body of work that blended an intriguing melange of musical idioms into something quite distinctive. He recorded briefly for Miami's Rockin' label and New Jersey's Savoy during the mid-'50s, but didn't find any success until he recorded "Kansas City" in 1959 for the Fury label. With a barbed-wire guitar solo by Wild Jimmy Spruill igniting Harrison's no-frills piano and clenched vocal, "Kansas City" paced both the R&B and pop charts soon after its issue. Contract wrangles with Savoy stalled the momentum for any Fury follow-ups, despite fine attempts with "Cheatin' Baby," the sequel "Goodbye Kansas City," and the original "Let's Stick Together." Harrison bounced from Neptune to Doc to Constellation to Port to Vest with little in the way of tangible rewards before unexpectedly making a comeback in 1969 with his infectious "Let's Work Together" for Sue. The two-part single proved a popular cover item—Canned Heat and Brian Ferry later revived it—though it was an isolated happenstance. After "My Heart Is Yours," a bottom-end chart entry on SSS International in 1971, no more hits were in Wilbert's future. He soldiered on, sometimes as a one-man band, for years to come. *—Bill Dahl*

● **Kansas City** / 1992 / Collectables ♦♦♦♦♦
Finally, paydirt! Harrison smashed the charts in 1959 with his massive hit "Kansas City" for Bobby Robinson's Fury logo. Here we have 22 fine sides from the Fury hookup, some in stereo and many with Wild Jimmy Spruill on lead guitar. "Cheatin' Baby," "C.C. Rider," "1960," and the inevitable sequel "Goodbye Kansas City" are prime examples of Harrison's slightly off-kilter approach to his craft, while this infectious "Let's Stick

Together" developed into the more worldly "Let's Work Together" toward the end of the decade. *—Bill Dahl*

Grant Hart

Vocals, Drums / Punk-Pop, Indie Rock, Alternative Pop/Rock, American Underground

As one of the co-leaders of the seminal post-hardcore punk group Hüsker Dü, Grant Hart was one of the most influential musicians of the '80s, blending raw sonic aggression with pop melodies and songs. Following the group's demise in 1987, he launched a solo career which was marked by an erratic work schedule. After releasing one solo album, he formed a trio called Nova Mob in 1989, which released two albums between 1991 and 1994, when Hart became a solo artist again. Playing drums and singing lead, Hart formed Hüsker Dü along with Bob Mould (lead vocals, guitar) and Greg Norton (bass) in the late '70s in St. Paul. Over the course of the early '80s, the group initially built a strong following in the U.S. hardcore punk underground, eventually breaking into wider recognition with their 1984 album *Zen Arcade*. In the spring of 1988, Hart became the first Hüsker Dü member to release a solo recording when his primarily acoustic *2541* EP (named after the address of the group's old office and studio) was released on the band's old record label, SST. The following year, he released the full-length *Intolerance*, which he recorded as a one-man band. Later in 1989, Hart formed Nova Mob, which released its first single, "All of My Senses," in 1990. A year later, the group released the EP, *Admiral of the Sea*, on Rough Trade. Nova Mob's first album, a rock opera named *The Last Days of Pompeii*, appeared in 1991. Following its release, the group was dormant for several years, eventually reemerging in 1994 with an eponymous album. Hart quietly split up the trio after *Nova Mob*, and disappeared for two more years. *—Stephen Thomas Erlewine*

● **Intolerance** / 1989 / SST ♦♦♦♦

A one-man-band album of driving (but not punk) rock, much of it sounding Dylanesque. Many of its lyrics seem to refer to the acrimonious breakup of Hart's old group, Hüsker Dü. *—William Ruhlmann*

Ecce Homo / Jan. 1996 / World Service ♦♦♦

Grant Hart released this live acoustic record at the height of the "unplugged" craze. While this move could be seen as jumping on the proverbial bandwagon, *Ecce Homo* was actually supposed to be a concert recording of his group Nova Mob, but the band broke up shortly before the performance date. Besides, Hart's undeniable sense of melody, combined with the intensity and singalong nature of his songs, fits perfectly in the "campfire" setting. (The album was taped in front of a small, appreciative audience.) The CD highlights Hart's entire career to date: from overlooked contributions to Hüsker Dü's legacy, to his work with Nova Mob, to solo gems (including the oft-covered "2541"). The sound quality is a tad on the lo-fi side, but *Ecce Homo* is still a rewarding purchase for both longtime and new fans of this largely neglected figure. *—Bart Bealmear*

Good News for Modern Man / Nov. 30, 1999 / Pachyderm ♦♦♦

As soon as the opening notes of Grant Hart's *Good News for Modern Man* hit the ears, the listener realizes that no matter how long between records, whether solo or within the confines of a band, Grant Hart never changes.

This statement has two sides; the first is that it's very comfortable and easy to slip into one of his records again. The genius pop sensibilities that Hart has exercised since his days behind the drum kit in Hüsker Dü are quite apparent on this recording. Everything that made Hart and Hüsker Dü forefathers of the alternative rock movement of the late 1980s and early 1990s are evident here.

Yet the flip side of this statement is, simply, that Grant Hart never changes. As his former bandmate Bob Mould seems to run from his past with each new recording, Hart seems to be constantly reminiscing, searching for what could have been. It has been over ten years since his first full solo release, 1989's *Intolerance*, but many of the songs on this record could have come from the same sessions.

Ultimately, as a complete package, *Good News for Modern Man* will bring a smile to the face of any fan. In true Grant Hart style, he combines interesting percussion with psychedelic organs as well as lyrical experimentation with pop harmonies. Optimism has given way to wisdom, but it is still the same old Grant Hart. *—Michael Cusanelli*

Harvey Danger

Post-Grunge, Alternative Pop/Rock

The alternative pop quartet Harvey Danger was formed in Seattle in 1994 by University of Washington students Sean Nelson (vocals), Jeff Lin (guitar), Aaron Huffman (bass), and Evan Sult (drums). Initially setting out merely to play Nirvana and Mudhoney covers at area parties, in time the group developed a rabid cult following, and in 1996 they teamed with renowned local producer John Goodmanson to record the tracks which were ultimately shaped into their 1997 debut LP *Where Have All the Merrymakers Gone?* Originally issued on the indie label Arena Rock, the album was soon picked up by Slash Records after the infectious single "Flagpole Sitta" became a local hit; released nationally, the track became a national smash during the summer of 1998. Two years later, the follow-up *King James Version* arrived. *—Jason Ankeny*

● **Where Have All the Merrymakers Gone?** / Jul. 29, 1997 / Never ♦♦♦

"I'm not sick, but I'm not well" whines vocalist Sean Nelson in "Flagpole Sitta," the first single released from Harvey Danger's 1998 debut album. Such studied bile and wry wordplay abound on this lyrically and musically very solid first effort. Rather than pigeonholing themselves into a sub-genre, Harvey Danger seem to have incorporated a variety of "alternative" influences—notably the Pixies, the Wedding Present, and Joy Division—plus bits of Gang of Four, Sonic Youth, the Smiths, Hole, Green Day, Buzzcocks, Ride, and Iggy Pop. The band's use of dynamics on this album is subtle and skillful, gliding within one song from a whisper to a wall of noise and back again seamlessly. With its melodic basslines and roomy, fuzz-box guitars chugging away at forceful riffs that straddle the line between '70s brit-punk and '80s indie, *Where Have All the Merrymakers Gone?* should be immediately accessible to fans of intelligent, sardonic, hard-edged rock. In "Private Helicopter," Nelson sneers "If you've got greatness in you, would you do us all a favor and keep it to yourself?" Fortunately, Harvey Danger have chosen not to take their own advice. *—David Kent-Abbott*

King James Version / Sep. 12, 2000 / Sire ♦♦♦

Quirky post-grungers Harvey Danger maintain their gnarling punk influences on their second effort *King James Version*. Still playful for the mainstream and indie enough for the college kids, Harvey Danger are fresh and witty, continuously satirical throughout the dozen-song set list. Frontman Sean C. Nelson sings like a 12-year-old boy, and Jeff Linn's guitar hooks are fetching enough to make Harvey Danger's sophomore release undoubtedly solid. Nelson makes hilarious calls on pop culture—Kip Winger, the Marlboro Man—and twists new wave ambience with jaunty fragments of '80s anthem punk rock. Songs such as "(Theme From) Carjack Fever" and "Meetings With Remarkable Men (Show Me the Hero)" are wry, whereas others "Why I'm Lonely" and "You Miss the Point Completely I Get the Point Exactly" reflect on bittersweet heartbreaks. Harvey Danger aren't afraid to be funny, poking fun at what's supposed to be taken seriously. And if 1998's "Flagpole Sitta" didn't indicate such sharpness, the material rollicking on *King James Version* will. *—MacKenzie Wilson*

PJ Harvey

b. Oct. 9, 1969, Yeovil, England

Vocals, Guitar / Adult Alternative Pop/Rock, Indie Rock, Alternative Pop/Rock, Singer/Songwriter

During the early-'90s alternative rock explosion, several female singer/songwriters rose to prominence, but few were as distinctive or as widely praised as Polly Jean Harvey. Over the course of three albums, Harvey established herself as one of the most individual and influential songwriters of the '90s, exploring themes of sex, love, and religion with unnerving honesty, dark humor, and a twisted theatricality. Her career began in 1991 with the formation of a trio named PJ Harvey, whose singles "Dress" and "Sheela-Na-Gig" received lavish praise in the U.K. music press. The band's debut album *Dry* earned American distribution through Island, and the group hired former Big Black frontman Steve Albini as the producer of their second album, *Rid of Me*. The album became a major critical success and expanded Harvey's cult greatly. At the end of the year, Harvey released *4-Track Demos*, a collection of her original versions of the songs on *Rid of Me*. Following the *Rid of Me* tour, Harvey became a solo act and recorded her third album *To Bring You My Love* with producer Flood; the album was hailed as a masterpiece by many critics and became a moderate commercial hit as well, entering the U.S. charts at number 40. During 1996 she was relatively quiet, only appearing twice on record: once in a duet with Nick Cave on his *Murder Ballads* album and singing on John Parish's *Dance Hall at Louse Point*. *Is This Desire* followed in 1998. *—Stephen Thomas Erlewine*

Dry / Jun. 30, 1992 / Too Pure/Indigo ♦♦♦♦♦

Polly Jean Harvey arrives fully formed as a songwriter on PJ Harvey's debut album, *Dry*. Borrowing its primitive attack from post-punk guitar-rock and its form from the blues, *Dry* is a forceful collection of brutally emotional songs, highlighted by Harvey's deft lyricism and startling voice, as well as her trio's muscular sound. Her voice makes each song sound like it was an exposed nerve, but her lyrics aren't quite that simple. Shaded with metaphors and the occasional biblical allusion, *Dry* is essentially an assault on feminine conventions and expectations, and while there are layers of dark humor, they aren't particularly evident, since Harvey's singing is shockingly raw. Her vocals are perfectly complemented by the trio's ferocious pounding, which makes even the slow ballads sound like exercises is controlled fury. And that's the key to *Dry*: the songs, which are often surprisingly catchy—"Dress" and "Sheela-Na-Gig" both have strong hooks—are as muscular and forceful as the band's delivery, making the album a vibrant and fully realized debut. *—Stephen Thomas Erlewine*

● **Rid of Me** / May 4, 1993 / Island ♦♦♦♦♦

Dry was shockingly frank in its subject and sound, as Polly Harvey delivered post-feminist manifestos with a punkish force. PJ Harvey's second album, *Rid of Me*, finds the trio, and Harvey in particular, pushing themselves to extremes. This is partially due to producer Steve Albini, who gives the album a bloodless, abrasive edge with his exacting production; each dynamic is pushed to the limit, leaving absolutely no subtleties in the music. Harvey's songs, in decided contrast to Albini's approach, are filled with gray areas and uncertainties, and are considerably more personal than those on *Dry*. Furthermore, they are lyrically and melodically superior to the songs on the debut, but their merits are obscured by Albini's black-and-white production, which is polarizing. It may be the aural embodiment of the tortured lyrics, and therefore a supremely effective piece of performance art, but it also makes *Rid of Me* a difficult record to meet halfway. But anyone willing to accept its sonic extremities will find *Rid of Me* to be a record of unusual power and purpose, one with few peers in its unsettling emotional honesty. *—Stephen Thomas Erlewine*

4-Track Demos / Oct. 19, 1993 / Island ♦♦♦♦

Since Steve Albini gave *Rid of Me* such an uncompromisingly noisy finish, it may have made sense for Polly Harvey to release her original demos, augmented by several unreleased songs, six months later as an album. After all, the initial British pressings of *Dry* came with a bonus disc of her demos. Still, the official, independent release of *4-Track Demos* suggests that Harvey wanted to give these songs another chance for listeners who found *Rid of Me* too abrasive. Even for those who enjoyed *Rid of Me*, *4-Track Demos* is a revelatory experience, since it arguably captures the raw emotion of the songs better the official record. A handful of songs from the record aren't repeated in demo form—namely

"Missed," "Man-Size," "Highway 61 Revisited," "Dry," and "Me-Jane"—but they're replaced by the previously unreleased "Reeling," "Driving," "Hardly Wait," "Easy," "M-Bike," and "Goodnight," most of which are easily the equal of the songs that were actually released, and that's what makes *4-Track Demos* necessary for every Harvey fan, not just collectors. —*Stephen Thomas Erlewine*

To Bring You My Love / Feb. 28, 1995 / Island ✦✦✦✦✦

Following the tour for *Rid of Me*, Polly Harvey parted ways with Robert Ellis and Stephen Vaughn, leaving her free to expand her music from the bluesy punk that dominated PJ Harvey's first two albums. It also left her free to experiment with her style of songwriting. Where *Dry* and *Rid of Me* seemed brutally honest, *To Bring You My Love* feels theatrical, with each song representing a grand gesture. Relying heavily on religious metaphors and imagery borrowed from the blues, Harvey has written a set of songs that are lyrically reminiscent of Nick Cave and Tom Waits' literary excursions into the gothic American heartland. Since she was a product of post-punk, she's nowhere as literally bluesy as Cave or Waits, preferring to embellish her songs with shards of avant-guitar, eerie keyboards and a dense, detailed production. It's a far cry from the primitive guitars of her first two albums, but Harvey pulls it off with style, since her songwriting is tighter and more melodic than before; the menacing "Down by the Water" has genuine hooks, as does the psychostomp of "Meet Ze Monsta," the wailing "Long Snake Moan," and the stately "C'Mon Billy." The clear production by Harvey, Flood, and John Parish makes these growths evident, which in turn makes *To Bring You My Love* her most accessible album, even if the album lacks the indelible force of its predecessors. —*Stephen Thomas Erlewine*

Is This Desire? / Sep. 29, 1998 / Island ✦✦✦

Retreating from the limelight after the tour for *To Bring You My Love*, PJ Harvey returned to her small hometown of Yeovil and isolated herself from most pop trends, eventually writing the material that would come to comprise her fourth album, *Is This Desire?* Released over three and a half years after *To Bring You My Love*, *Is This Desire?* has all the hallmarks of a record written in isolation: subtle, cerebral, insular, difficult to assimilate, it's the album where Polly Harvey enters the ranks of craftsmen, sacrificing confession for fiction. It's an inevitable transition for any artist, especially one as lyrically gifted as Harvey, and though her words are more obtuse and not as brutal, painful, or clever, she still draws some effective character sketches. Similarly, the music on *Is This Desire?* is hardly the immediate, blunt force that characterized her first albums, nor is it the grand theater of *To Bring You My Love*—it takes its time, slowly working its way into the subconsciousness. There are a few guitar explosions scattered throughout the record, but it's primarily a series of layered keyboards, electronic rhythms, and acoustic guitars; it's so quiet that at times it barely rises above a murmur, and occasionally floats away without leaving a lasting impression. It seems to challenge the listener to accept it on its own grounds, but once you dig deeper, it winds up offering diminishing rewards. It is more concerned with texture than any of her previous records, but it doesn't push forward enough—it's either standard hard rockers or mournful ballads underpinned by lite electronica beats, which would have more impact if they were more pronounced. Since Harvey is an extraordinarily gifted songwriter, the album is hardly devoid of merit, but it's her least focused or successful record to date. —*Stephen Thomas Erlewine*

Stories From the City, Stories From the Sea / Oct. 24, 2000 / Island ✦✦✦✦

During her career, Polly Jean Harvey has had as many incarnations as she has albums. She's gone from the Yeovil art student of her debut *Dry*, to *Rid of Me*'s punk poetess to *To Bring You My Love* and *Is This Desire?*'s postmodern siren; on *Stories From the City, Stories From the Sea*—inspired by her stay in New York City and life in the English countryside—she's changed again. The album cover's stylish, subtly sexy image suggests what its songs confirm: PJ Harvey has grown up. Direct, vulnerable lyrics replace the allegories and metaphors of her previous work, and the album's production polishes the songs instead of obscuring them in noise or studio tricks. On the album's best tracks, such as "Kamikaze" and "This Is Love," a sexy, shouty blues-punk number that features the memorable refrain "I can't believe life is so complex/When I just want to sit here and watch you undress," Harvey sounds sensual and revitalized. The New York influences surface on the glamorous punk rock of "Big Exit" and "Good Fortune," on which Harvey channels both Chrissie Hynde's sexy tough girl and Patti Smith's ferocious yelp. Ballads like the sweetly urgent, piano and marimba-driven "One Line" and the Thom Yorke duet "This Mess We're In" avoid the painful depths of Harvey's darkest songs; "Horses in My Dreams" also reflects Harvey's new emotional balance: "I have pulled myself clear," she sighs, and we believe her. However, "We Float"'s glossy choruses veer close to Lillith Fair territory, and longtime fans can't help but miss the visceral impact of her early work, but *Stories From the City, Stories From the Sea* doesn't compromise her essential passion. Hopefully, this album's happier, more direct PJ Harvey is a persona she'll keep around for a while. —*Heather Phares*

Hassles

f. 1964, **db.** 1969
Blue-Eyed Soul, Rock & Roll
The Hassles found their place in music history as Billy Joel's first recorded moment but musically, they deserve more. Though they only released two albums, the Hassles were a pretty proficient, highly enjoyable, though not particularly groundbreaking act that saw a fair amount of local attention in the Long Island area.

The Hassles were a blue-eyed soul band, modeled somewhat after the Rascals, formed in Long Island in 1964 by drummer Jon Small, singer John Dizek, organist Harry Webber, and guitarist Richie McKenna. Webber was fired from the band in 1966 due to erratic behavior and Billy Joel, who had earned a local reputation as a keyboardist with the Echoes, the Lost Souls, and the Commandos (as Billy Joe Joel), was enlisted to take his

place on the condition that the band also take on bassist Howie Blauvelt. Though still a teenager, Joel was also able to add prodigiously soulful lead vocals and harmony. The group's new sound quickly found a following through constant gigging throughout Long Island. United Artists signed the band in 1967, releasing their self-titled debut by November the same year. The single, a cover of Sam & Dave's "You've Got Me Hummin'" made it to Billboard's number 112 but the album failed to make an impact outside of the band's local following. In 1968, they followed with the more psychedelically-inclined *Hour of the Wolf*.

The group disbanded the following year when Small and Joel left to form the heavier organ-and-drums duo, Atilla. Atilla released one album for Epic in early 1970 that went justifiably unnoticed at the time and remains an embarrassment for Joel to this day. Joel went on to an incredibly successful solo career and Small went on to become a video producer. In 1999, *You've Got Me Humming* compiled the best of the Hassles' recordings, adding four unreleased cuts as well. —*Chris Woodstra*

● The Hassles / 1967 / United Artists ✦✦✦✦

On the Hassles' self-titled debut, the band displayed a naive enthusiasm and a slightly better-than-average blue-eyed soul, covering several hits and standards like "A Taste of Honey," "Fever," and "You've Got Me Hummin'," as well as "Coloured Rain" (before Traffic recorded it) in standard Rascals style. Most of the album is nothing spectacular, but a pair of Billy Joel's tracks—"Every Step I Take (Every Move I Make)" and "I Can Tell"—show a budding songwriting talent, with the material fitting in quite nicely alongside established songs. [In 1992, the album was reissued on CD as part of EMI's "Legends of Rock & Roll" series with a generous eight bonus tracks recorded around the same time. The disc was pulled off the market shortly after its release at the request of Joel, who still seems embarrassed by his juvenilia despite the charm of the album.] —*Chris Woodstra*

Hour of the Wolf / 1968 / United Artists ✦✦✦

Hour of the Wolf showed a great leap in ambition and moved away from blue-eyed soul in favor of hippyish near-psychedelia, this time with Joel handling the songwriting himself (with a couple of co-writes with bandmates). Some of the stuff is certainly cringe-worthy—none so much as the title track, a 12-minute epic which boasts lyrics like "…God has loosed a hellhound freed to feed upon the prey of his desire/Death is borne alive akin a creature with eyes of burning fire…" (there's even a middle bit featuring the band imitating wolf noises). Embarrassing? Yes, but probably no more so than much of the other music from the era. Musically, the album shows the group dabbling in several styles, at times hinting at the more singer/songwriter-oriented direction Joel would take in the early '70s, as well as displaying his strong melodic sense. [*Hour of the Wolf* was set for release on CD in 1992, presumably with bonus tracks like the first album, but it was cancelled at the last minute when *The Hassles* was pulled.] —*Chris Woodstra*

● The Best of the Hassles: You've Got Me Humming / Apr. 27, 1999 / Razor & Tie ✦✦✦✦

Best of the Hassles: You've Got Me Humming collects nearly the entire recorded output of the Long Island blue-eyed soul group best remembered as Billy Joel's early band. The first album is presented in its entirety, and the second album loses only one track—oddly, they chose to drop "Hotel St. George," an excellent song which really should have made the cut. Added are four non-LP session outtakes which were also included on the CD reissue of the first album. —*Chris Woodstra*

Juliana Hatfield

b. Jul. 27, 1967, Wiscarset, ME
Vocals, Guitar, Bass / Adult Alternative Pop/Rock, Jangle Pop, Alternative Pop/Rock
When the jangle-pop trio the Blake Babies disbanded in 1990, guitarist John Strohm and drummer Freda Boner formed Antenna, while singer/bassist Juliana Hatfield launched a solo career. In 1991, she played bass on the Lemonheads' *It's A Shame About Ray*, which became the band's commercial breakthrough. The album's success stirred interest in Hatfield's 1992 solo debut, *Hey Babe*, which was released on Mammoth Records. Acclaimed for its sweet, confessional songs, the album became a college radio and MTV hit, leading to a major-label contract for Hatfield with Atlantic. Hatfield formed the Juliana Hatfield Three with bassist Dean Fisher and drummer Todd Phillips, and the group recorded its debut with R.E.M. producer Scott Litt. While working on the record, Hatfield became a minor media sensation, appearing in fashion layouts in *Vogue* and *Sassy* and becoming the subject of gossipy tidbits about her speculated romance with Lemonhead Evan Dando and her assertion that she was still a virgin at age 25. In light of such exposure, her 1993 album *Become What You Are* was expected to be her mainstream breakthrough, but despite the moderate hits "My Sister" and "Spin the Bottle," the album didn't make her a star. Hatfield never gained a mainstream audience like the Lemonheads did; 1995's *Only Everything* appeared as alternative rock's declined, and the album to slipped down the charts quickly. Despite keeping a low profile for the rest of the '90s, Hatfield continued to release material, including 1997's *Please Do Not Disturb* EP and 1998's full-length *Bed*. She stayed busy in 2000, releasing the quiet, reflective solo album *Beautiful Creature* and *Total System Failure*, a collection of louder, poppier material, on the same day. *Total System Failure* featured Hatfield, former Weezer bassist Mike Welsh, and drummer Zephan Courtney as a new band, Juliana's Pony, which was a trio similar to the Juliana Hatfield Three. —*Stephen Thomas Erlewine*

● Hey Babe / Mar. 17, 1992 / Mammoth ✦✦✦✦

Hey Babe is Juliana Hatfield's terrific solo debut, filled with effortless melodies and catchy guitar riffs. Hatfield's thin, girlish voice can be slightly wearing over the course of an entire album, but her intelligent, hook-laden songs make up for that minor flaw. —*Stephen Thomas Erlewine*

Become What You Are / Aug. 3, 1993 / Mammoth ✦✦✦

Although she desperately tries to hide behind a grungier guitar sound, Hatfield is still a talented practitioner of girlish power pop. Because she tries so hard to put the innocent pleasures of her debut behind her, *Become What You Are* isn't as satisfying. Most of the loud rave-ups betray her true gifts with a melody, which most definitely has not disappeared; her hooks are so strong that she can bring over such cringe-inducing lyrics as those of "For the Birds" and "Mabel" rather effortlessly. Hatfield's strongest points are apparent on "Supermodel," "My Sister," and "Spin the Bottle"—catchy, honest, and incisive portraits of adolescence, rendered truthful by her girlish, singsong vocals. Fortunately, her talents are strong enough to carry the album over the weak spots. —*Stephen Thomas Erlewine*

Only Everything / Mar. 28, 1995 / Mammoth/Atlantic ✦✦✦
The Juliana Hatfield Three folded soon after the supporting tour for *Become What You Are*, yet Hatfield hasn't abandoned the basic approach of the band—she still rocks out, supporting her singsong melodies with massive, grungy guitars. If anything, her new backing band rocks harder than the Hatfield Three, with a better, looser sense of rhythm as well. Even with the improved musicianship, Hatfield isn't able to deliver consistently impressive songs, occasionally relying on her cuteness to cover underdeveloped lyrics and pedestrian melodies. Most of the record doesn't drag, however—it's a fun, engaging pop album, yet its best moments follow the strengths of her earlier songs, without doing much to expand her formula. —*Stephen Thomas Erlewine*

Bed / Aug. 25, 1998 / Zoe ✦✦✦
Despite a promising start, the world of major labels did not treat Juliana Hatfield well. *Become What You Are* generated a handful of alt-rock hits, but its follow-up, *Only Everything*, barely registered, and her third album for Mammoth/Atlantic, *God's Foot*, was never released. Frustrated, she severed ties with Mammoth/Atlantic and released a tension-breaking EP, *Please Do Not Disturb*, for Bar/None in 1997 before following with her fourth official solo album, *Bed*, in late summer 1998. Recorded in just three days, *Bed* has an immediacy lacking in all of her albums since *Hey Babe*, but truth be told, there's little to stylistically differentiate it from any of her records. Hatfield remains loyal to jangly guitar-pop dusted with the occasional grungy guitars, and she still balances precariously between charmingly innocent and cloying, which can often disguise the subversive themes or tortured emotions of her songs. For much of the album she's in good form, delivering strong songs with memorable melodies, but she fails to keep the momentum going throughout *Bed*, which has been a common problem on all of her records since *Hey Babe*. There are enough good songs to make it worthwhile for the committed fan, but at this point, unfortunately, those are the only ones who are still listening. —*Stephen Thomas Erlewine*

Juliana's Pony: Total System Failure / May 16, 2000 / Zoe ✦✦
Beautiful Creature / May 16, 2000 / Zoe/Island ✦✦✦✦
Considering that Juliana Hatfield hadn't been a serious contender for either the alt-rock charts or critical acclaim since 1995's *Only Everything*, her simultaneous release of two new albums in the spring of 2000 was slightly puzzling. Surely, her dedicated cult would purchase both at once, but it was too much music for anyone outside of her hardcore following. To her credit, *Beautiful Creature* and its sibling *Total System Failure* was not one album spread over two lengthy records, but two albums with their own distinctive characters. *Beautiful Creature* is a return to classic, *Hey Babe*-era Hatfield, whereas *Total System Failure* is a loud rock album. It was almost as if Hatfield couldn't decide which approach would make for a stronger comeback in 2000, so she put them both out. Of the two, *Beautiful Creature* is not only the superior record, it's the best album she's made since made since the heyday of *Hey Babe*. Melodic, wistful, whimsical, reflective, yet clever, the album showcases Hatfield at her peak, crafting fragile, endearing post-jangle pop songs that reveal themselves shyly and sweetly. Her girlish voice and almost painfully introspective vantage may still be an acquired taste, but she hasn't sounded as focused and consistently tuneful as she has here in many a year. —*Stephen Thomas Erlewine*

Donny Hathaway

b. Oct. 1, 1945, Chicago, IL, d. Jan. 13, 1979, New York, NY
Vocals, Keyboards, Piano / Chicago Soul, Soul
Donny Hathaway was a marvelous composer and vocalist. His sound, delivery, and timbre have influenced singers from Stevie Wonder to George Benson, while his compositions have been recorded by an array of artists from Cold Blood to Jerry Butler, the Staple Singers, Carla Thomas, and Aretha Franklin. Hathaway was born in Chicago, but grew up in St. Louis and began singing gospel at age three. He attended Howard University on a fine arts scholarship and was a classmate of Roberta Flack. He began recording for Curtis Mayfield's Curtom label in 1969, then signed with Atco. His single "The Ghetto" was a mild hit, but the duet "You've Got a Friend" with Flack was his first Top Ten R&B hit. The duo would later score two number one hit duets, "Where Is the Love" and "The Closer I Get to You," each of which was also a Top Ten pop hit. The duo had two final hits, "You Are My Heaven" and "Back Together Again," in 1980, after Hathaway stunned everyone by committing suicide in 1979 at age 33. —*Ron Wynn*

Extension of a Man / 1973 / Rhino ✦✦✦✦✦
This 1973 album (reissued on CD in 1993) was among Hathaway's most ambitious. It included a stunning two-part gospel tune, "I Love the Lord," a revamped version of "Valdez in the Country," a magnificent "We'll All Be Free," and a soulful remake of Blood, Sweat & Tears' "I Love You More Than You'll Ever Know." Hathaway's gorgeous voice and superb delivery, timing, pacing, and style made him unsurpassed among soul artists of his generation, and his arranging skills were equally brilliant. This album ranks as a masterpiece, along with his self-titled debut. —*Ron Wynn*

● **A Donny Hathaway Collection** / Apr. 12, 1990 / Atlantic ✦✦✦✦✦
Boasting many of his essential offerings, this CD underscores the fact that Donny Hathaway was one of the most riveting male soul singers of the 1970s. Hathaway's social concerns are illustrated by "To Be Young, Gifted and Black," a powerful live version of Marvin Gaye's "What's Goin' On" and his hit "The Ghetto," but more often that not, romance is his topic of choice. Indeed, R&B ballad singing doesn't get much more powerful than the Chicagoan's interpretations of Leon Russell's "A Song for You" and the remorseful "Giving Up" (an early Gladys Knight & the Pips hit written by Van McCoy of "The Hustle" fame). Hathaway and Roberta Flack usually made for a strong combination, and this holds true on duets ranging from the melancholy "Where Is the Love" to the ethereal "The Closer I Get to You" to the catchy "Back Together Again." Most of Hathaway's Atlantic albums are well worth hearing, but for novices, this CD is the most logical starting point. —*Alex Henderson*

Richie Havens

b. Jan. 21, 1941, Brooklyn, NY
Vocals, Sitar, Guitar / Folk-Rock, Singer/Songwriter
Born in the Bedford-Stuyvesant section of Brooklyn, Richie Havens moved to Greenwich Village in 1961 in time to get in on the folk boom then taking place. He had a distinctive style as a folksinger, appearing in such clubs as the Cafe Wha? His guitar set to an opening tuning, he would strum it while barring chords with his thumb, using it essentially as percussion while singing rhythmically in a gruff voice for a mesmerizing effect. Havens was signed to Douglas Records in 1965 and recorded two albums that gained him a local following. In 1967, the Verve division of MGM Records formed a folk section (Verve Forecast) and signed Havens and other folk-based performers. The result was Havens's third album, *Mixed Bag*. It wasn't until 1968 and the *Something Else Again* album, however, that he began to hit the charts. In 1969 came the double album *Richard P. Havens 1983*. Havens's career benefited enormously from his appearance at the Woodstock festival in 1969. His first album after that exposure, *Alarm Clock*, made the Top 30 and produced a Top 20 single in "Here Comes the Sun." These recordings were Havens's commercial high-water mark, but by this time he had become an international touring success. —*William Ruhlmann*

● **Resume: The Best of Richie Havens** / Apr. 6, 1993 / Rhino ✦✦✦✦✦
Havens's output has been so extensive that picking tunes for a single-disc anthology would be a difficult task for any label. Rhino has done a respectable job in compiling 17 selections, although there was no material from the LPs *Stonehenge* or *1984*, and while he certainly performed them his way, neither Ray Charles' "Drown in My Own Tears" nor Billie Holiday's "God Bless the Child" were among Havens' best songs. By comparison, "Handsome Johnny," "Freedom," "Here Comes the Sun," "The Klan," and "Just Like a Woman" had a strength and power that came partly from being ideally suited for Havens' style. This isn't the comprehensive or qualitative anthology Havens deserves; just a decent hits collection. —*Ron Wynn*

Dale Hawkins

b. Aug. 30, 1938, Goldmine, LA
Vocals, Guitar / Rockabilly, Rock & Roll
This Louisiana guitarist's 1957 hit "Suzy Q," with its crackling bluesy guitar and insistent cowbell, was one of the most exciting early rockabilly singles. Recording for Chess (as one of its few white artists) between 1956 and 1961, Hawkins never quite duplicated its success, either commercially or artistically, but came close enough on a number of occasions to warrant respect as one of the better rockabilly singers. His drawling delivery, sense of humor, affinity for blues, and sharp guitar work (which was actually provided by such ace players as Roy Buchanan, Scotty Moore, and James Burton) are heard to good effect on his 1958 album and a number of non-hit singles. Hawkins went on to become a producer of some note in the 1960s, working with the Five Americans and Bruce Channel. —*Richie Unterberger*

Susie Q / 1958 / Chess ✦✦✦✦✦
A way-above-average '50s rock & roll album, including both sides of Dale's first four singles. Highlights are "Suzie Q," its killer B-side ("Don't Treat Me This Way"), and the goofy "See You Soon Baboon" and "Mrs. Mergitory's Daughter." —*Richie Unterberger*

My Babe / 1987 / Argo ✦✦✦
Rare singles and other interesting material that Hawkins cut, mostly for Chess, between 1958 and 1962. Includes his sole Top 40 hit besides "Suzie-Q" ("La-Do-Dada") and some fine rockabilly interpretations of blues hits. —*Richie Unterberger*

● **Oh Suzy Q** / Oct. 24, 1995 / Chess ✦✦✦✦✦
Eighteen tracks from Hawkins' Chess prime, all but one from the late '50s. Includes "Susie Q" and some obscure rockabilly cuts that are nearly as good, such as "Don't Treat Me This Way," "Liza Jane," and "Ain't That Lovin' You Babe." James Burton, Roy Buchanan, and Scotty Moore are the most prominent of the excellent guitarists to be heard on these sides. One could quibble over the absence of "Mrs. Mergitory's Daughter," "Yea Yea (Class Cutter)," and the post-Chess single "Stay at Home Lulu," but this is definitely the best Hawkins compilation ever assembled. —*Richie Unterberger*

Daredevil / May 13, 1997 / Norton ✦✦✦✦
These 12 tracks, compiled from Hawkins' own personal stash of well-worn acetates, brings together the rarest of the rare of this Louisiana rockabilly songwriter/producer. The centerpiece of this 12-track collection is the first-time appearance of the original 1956 demo version of Dale's big hit, "Susie-Q." Recorded by country songwriter Merle Kilgore, the original demo is looser and faster than the better-known hit version, moved along with two raw guitar solos from a 16-year-old James Burton (this now becoming his debut

recording) and a surprise solo from saxman Sheldon Bazelle. The sound is raw and overamped, the feel of a band taking a bandstand jam and trying to shape it into something that would fit onto one side of a phonograph record. The flip side of this scratchy 78 acetate is perhaps an even bigger surprise, Hawkins and band playing an impromptu slow blues entitled "If You Please Me." Equally fine is a version of Tarheel Slim's "Number Nine Train" featuring explosive guitar work from Carl Adams and the rare appearance of a slappin' upright bass. This collection also features Hawkins in a supporting role, while his original band moonlights behind Maylon Humphries on "Weep No More," another cowbell rocker, this time in a minor key. Another noteworthy inclusion is "Superman," featuring Margaret Lewis on backup vocal, Roy Buchanan on guitar, and D.J. Fontana on drums. The title track, a wild instrumental with Adams driving the band on an agitated riff, later became the blueprint for "Lovin' Bug." Later cuts from the early '60s flesh things out, but these half dozen tracks—and especially the "Susie-Q" demo—are the main reasons to grab this one and add it to the MCA/Chess best-of compilation. *—Cub Koda*

Rock & Roll Tornado / Oct. 27, 1998 / Ace ♦♦♦♦♦
At first glance, this 30-track compilation of Dale Hawkins' late-'50s and early-'60s Checker sides might seem like a preferable collection to MCA's briefer (18-song) best-of. Actually, however, this only repeats 11 of those 18 tracks, with the emphasis on some cuts that haven't been on CD before, as well as no less than eight previously unreleased songs. It's hard to figure if this was meant as a best-of compilation or just a disc that mixes some of his biggest and best singles with obscure items; the omissions of "Ain't That Lovin' You Baby" (which is on the MCA collection) alone prevents this from being definitive. It does include a couple of songs that should be on any Dale Hawkins collection, "Yea-Yea (Class Cutter)" and "Mrs. Merguitory's Daughter," that do *not* appear on the MCA anthology. As for the more obscure material that's only on *Rock & Roll Tornado*, it's largely respectable, but not so essential that you would compare it to "Susie Q," "La-Do-Dada," or others considered among Hawkins' best performances. Sometimes it's heavily derivative—"Boy Meets Girl" sounds like it's trying very hard to imitate Jerry Lee Lewis, and "Someday, One Day" is quite Buddy Holly-like—and some of the unreleased cuts, like the cover of "Caldonia" and the country-soul ballad "Convicted," show him trying styles removed from rockabilly. In all, a good compilation that Hawkins fans should get even if they have the one on MCA. But if you just want one, it's a pretty tough call, each disc containing worthy selections not on the other, though each has his most essential recordings (i.e., "Susie Q," "Liza Jane," "La-Do-Dada"). *—Richie Unterberger*

Wildcat Tamer / Apr. 13, 1999 / Lightyear ♦♦♦♦
Hawkins' first record in over 30 years shows that he had plenty of gas left in the tank as the new century approached. From the opening title track (complete with chaotic false start) to the closing recut of "Susie Q" (done more in a Creedence style than Hawkins' original), it's very obvious that Hawkins is absolutely delighted to be making records again. His bluesy style is put to great use on funky remakes of Leadbelly's "Goodnight Irene" and "Going' Down the Road (Feelin' Bad)" while his country side comes up for air on the whimsical summer hit in the making, "Summertime Down South," which features Vassar Clements on fiddle. Some great rockin' that recalls his Chess salad years without Xeroxing it. *—Cub Koda*

Ronnie Hawkins

b. Jan. 10, 1935, Huntsville, AR
Vocals, Guitar / Rockabilly, Rock & Roll
Hawkins is a rockabilly singer who formed his original backing band, the Hawks, while attending the University of Arkansas. After auditioning unsuccessfully for Sun in 1957, he started working regularly in Canada the following year, eventually taking up permanent residence there. After one release on the Canadian Quality label, he signed with Roulette in New York in 1959, having hits with "Forty Days" and "Mary Lou." The live fervor of Hawkins (known as Mr. Dynamo) & the Hawks' show continued in Canada after all the original members except Levon Helm headed back to the U.S. Hawkins quickly hired Canadian players Robbie Robertson, Garth Hudson, Rick Danko, and Richard Manuel as the new Hawks. They stayed with him until 1963, but later became Bob Dylan's backing group and went on to a career of their own as the Band. Hawkins has remained a legend in Canada, recording unrepentant rockabilly sides and gigging constantly. He's still the original Mr. Dynamo, capable of shaking the walls down any old time he feels like it. *—Cub Koda*

● **The Best of Ronnie Hawkins & His Band** / Jun. 1990 / Rhino ♦♦♦♦♦
In the late 1950s and early 1960s, Ronnie Hawkins was one of the few rock & rollers committed to performing and recording unapologetic rockabilly while others were returning to their country roots or going the teen-idol route. This 18-song compilation focuses mostly on his initial burst of activity for Roulette in 1959 and 1960, with a few later odds and ends thrown in. While he deserves respect for keeping the torch of rock & roll's roots burning during some of its leaner years, he didn't match the greatness of rockabilly's kingpins. His voice and performance were energetic but not brilliant; his material was a bit pedestrian. The best of these tunes are "Mary Lou" (his sole Top 30 hit), "Forty Days" (an update of Chuck Berry's "Thirty Days"), and "One of These Days" (later covered by the Searchers). What he's really known for, of course, is giving a bunch of mostly Canadian kids their start as his backing band, the Hawks. A later edition of the Hawks eventually toured with Bob Dylan and evolved into the Band. Only two of these songs, though, feature that lineup (the 1963 single "Bo Diddley"/"Who Do You Love"). On "Who Do You Love" especially, Robbie Robertson lets rip with a roaring solo that's a good few years ahead of its time in its manic distorted intensity. It's by far the most exciting track on this compilation of a respectable but minor performer from rock's early days. *—Richie Unterberger*

The Roulette Years / 1995 / Sequel ♦♦♦♦♦
This 57-track double-CD set seems like a no-brainer—get almost all of Ronnie Hawkins' rock & roll recordings in one place. The packaging here is good, thoughtful, and legitimate, but could also be a little misleading to those who are buying this expecting to hear a lot of early work by the musicians who later became the Band—Levon Helm was aboard on drums from the Hawks' first official recordings, but the remainder didn't begin arriving on the scene until almost two years later; they're only on hand more than one or two at a time for less than half of what's here. Additionally, taken on its own terms, this is about as solid a rock & roll collection by a single white artist from this period as you're going to find—in 1959-60, as Elvis Presley, et al. were generally softening their sounds, Ronnie Hawkins was staying a true rock & roller. The alternate takes and demos featured here are about as worthwhile as any of Hawkins' hits, and the quality of everything about this set makes it practically scream to be purchased—the detailed notes, the complete sessionography, the bright, clean yet raunchy sound on the masters. A straight, enjoyable (and probably revelatory to some) rock & roll document, Sequel deserves an award for this release—only Bear Family does it better, and this is a lot cheaper than one of their double CDs. *—Bruce Eder*

Screamin' Jay Hawkins

b. Jul. 18, 1929, Cleveland, OH, **d.** Feb. 12, 2000, Paris, France
Vocals, Piano / Jump Blues, Rock & Roll, R&B
Screamin' Jay Hawkins was the most outrageous performer extant during rock's dawn. Prone to emerging out of coffins onstage, a flaming skull named Henry his constant companion, Screamin' Jay was an insanely theatrical figure long before it was even remotely acceptable. He debuted on wax for Gotham in 1952 with "Why Did You Waste My Time," backed by Grimes and his Rockin' Highlanders. Singles for Timely ("Baptize Me in Wine") and Mercury's Wing subsidiary (1955's otherworldly "[She Put the] Wamee [on Me]," a harbinger of things to come) preceded Hawkins' immortal 1956 rendering of "I Put a Spell on You" for Columbia's Okeh imprint. Hawkins originally envisioned the tune as a refined ballad. After he and his New York session aces (notably guitarist Mickey Baker and saxist Sam "The Man" Taylor) had imbibed to the point of no return, Hawkins screamed, grunted, and gurgled his way through the tune with utter drunken abandon. A resultant success despite the protests of uptight suits-in-power, "Spell" became Screamin' Jay's biggest seller. He cut several amazing 1957-58 follow-ups in the same crazed vein—"Hong Kong," a surreal "Yellow Coat," the Jerry Leiber/Mike Stoller-penned "Alligator Wine"—but none of them clicked the way "Spell" had. Hawkins' next truly inspired waxing came in 1969 when he was contracted to Philips Records (where he made two albums). His gross "Constipation Blues" wouldn't garner much airplay, but remains an integral part of his legacy to this day. *—Bill Dahl*

● **Voodoo Jive: The Best of Screamin' Jay Hawkins** / Feb. 1990 / Rhino ♦♦♦♦♦
Some maintain that Hawkins was a one-hit fluke and a one-dimensional performer with a limited singing voice and no other discernible skills. Others insist that Hawkins was a decent R&B and blues singer and an excellent entertainer and personality whose real talents were overshadowed by the success of "I Put a Spell on You." This anthology doesn't convincingly answer the argument, but it does collect 17 Hawkins singles from Okeh, Enrica, and Phillips, including all of his major hits. The high (or low) point is perhaps 1969's "Constipation Blues." *—Ron Wynn*

Cow Fingers & Mosquito Pie / 1991 / Epic ♦♦♦♦♦
Magically weird 19-song collection of the bizarre shouter's mid-'50s OKeh/Epic output, when he was at the height of his strange and terrifying vocal powers. In addition to the prerequisite "I Put a Spell on You" and the surreal rockers "Yellow Coat," "Hong Kong," "Alligator Wine," and "Little Demon," there's the amusing "There's Something Wrong With You," a previously unissued "You Ain't Foolin' Me," and a deranged takeoff on the cowboy ditty "Take Me Back to My Boots and Saddle" (and what Jay does to the formerly stately "I Love Paris" and "Orange Colored Sky" is truly indescribable!). *—Bill Dahl*

Spellbound! 1955-74 / 1991 / Bear Family ♦♦♦
Bear Family's *Spellbound! 1955-74* is a double-disc set that captures highlights from Screamin' Jay Hawkins' recordings for Wing, Decca, Phillips, and RCA. It's not quite the bargain it seems. Half of the 48 tracks were already issued on two Phillips albums, which were combined on one Edsel CD. Furthermore, most of these songs date from the '60s, with only a handful coming from Hawkins' '50s peak. Strangely, of those songs, not one of them is the original "I Put a Spell On You," which makes this hardly the definitive overview that it should be. Instead of focusing on the best of Screamin' Jay Hawkins' best material, it has the campy, silly stuff from the '60s, which will try the patience of anyone outside devoted fans—and those devoted fans will prefer more complete compilations than this strangely scattershot effort from Bear Family. There are some good moments here, but overall, it has to rank as a disappointment. *—Stephen Thomas Erlewine*

Best of the Bizarre Sessions: 1990-1994 / Jul. 11, 2000 / Manifesto ♦♦♦
This 18-song compilation is taken from three albums that Screamin' Jay Hawkins recorded in the early '90s for Bizarre/Straight Records: *Black Music for White People*, *Stone Crazy*, and *Somethin' Funny Goin On*. While these albums contain some spirited performances, including the hysterical operatic version of "Ol Man River," they do not contain the fire or spontaneity of his classic '50s recordings. Some of the material may have been too sincere for Hawkins' style, such as the two songs penned by Tom Waits: "Ice Cream Man" and "Heart Attack and Vine." While "Ignant and Shit," "Shut Your Mouth When You Sneeze," and "Swamp Gas" swing in the opposite direction, proving the song titles funnier than the actual songs. *Best of the Bizarre Sessions: 1990-1994* has its moments, but for a clearer glimpse of Hawkins original R&B theatrics which created such a

stir in the '50s check out the Rhino compilation *Voodoo Jive: The Best of Screamin' Jay Hawkins*. *—Al Campbell*

Sophie B. Hawkins

b. New York, NY [Manhattan]

Vocals / Adult Contemporary, Singer/Songwriter

A New York-based pop singer/songwriter, Sophie B. Hawkins' music ranges from dance-pop to folky introspection. She began performing professionally as a percussionist with Bryan Ferry in the early '80s. Hawkins released her first solo album, *Tongues and Tails*, in 1992; it launched the number five hit "Damn I Wish I Was Your Lover." Released two years later, *Whaler* was a flop upon its release, yet a year later the single "As I Lay Me Down" broke into the singles charts. *Timbre* followed in 1999. *—Stephen Thomas Erlewine*

● **Tongues and Tails** / 1992 / Columbia ✦✦✦✦

A New York eccentric type, Sophie B. Hawkins began her music career studying ethnic percussion. She moved to jazz, then was a drummer in a punk band while sidelining as an actor and performance artist. Hawkins' debut disc *Tongues and Tails* is as eclectic as her career choices. The songs ranges from the hook-filled mainstream pop of "Damn I Wish I Was Your Lover" to an off-center rant about mothers in "Carry Me" that dissolves into feedback mayhem. Hawkins stitches together bits of jazz, folk, tribal, rock, and atmospheric new age noodling while efficiently camouflaging the seams. Somehow, it all works with repeated listens. The common thread is her distinctive, streetwise but unjaded voice. *—Roch Parisien*

Whaler / 1994 / Columbia ✦✦✦✦

Sophie B. Hawkins' second album was a commercial disaster when it was released late in the summer of 1994. A year later, she had a Top Ten single with "As I Lay Me Down." That slow climb to the top is a fairly good indication of both the pleasures and flaws of *Whaler*. More subdued than *Tongues and Tails*, the songs on *Whaler* have subtler melodies and arrangements which take a while to sink in. Although the album isn't quite as energetic as *Tongues and Tails*, *Whaler* is a more consistent record, with a number of engaging songs. *—Stephen Thomas Erlewine*

Timbre / Jul. 20, 1999 / Columbia ✦✦✦✦

Since she works in a genre commonly tagged as adult contemporary pop, it's easy for some critics to dismiss Sophie B. Hawkins, but she's much more adventurous than most of her adult-pop peers. That wasn't immediately evident on her debut *Tongues and Tails*, even if "Damn, I Wish I Was Your Lover" playfully twisted sexual conventions, but *Whaler* showed significant progress. Her third album, *Timbre*, explores even greater territory, even if it's in subtle ways. Hawkins favors strong melodies and clean, polished productions, which makes her music enjoyable on a surface level, but it also reveals more upon each subsequent play. Certain quirks are self-evident upon an initial listen—the beatnik pretensions of "The Darkest Childe," which ultimately sinks under its own poetic weight—but the genuinely intriguing moments, such as the weirdly exotic instrumentations and evocative lyrics, only appear upon repeated spins. By that point, *Timbre* has slowly, surely worked its way into the subconscious—Hawkins' songs are melodic, yet they blossom and become memorable over time. She has crafted two rewarding albums prior to *Timbre*, yet this may be her best yet. It lacks a standout single on the lines of "Damn, I Wish I Was Your Lover" or "As I Lay Me Down," but song-for-song, it's impressively consistent, and her performances are remarkably assured, elevating *Timbre* to her finest moment yet. *—Stephen Thomas Erlewine*

Ted Hawkins

b. Oct. 28, 1936, Biloxi, MS, **d.** Jan. 1, 1995, Los Angeles, CA

Vocals, Guitar / Contemporary Blues, Singer/Songwriter, Modern Acoustic Blues, Soul-Blues, Soul

Overseas, he was a genuine hero, performing to thousands. But on his L.A. hometurf, sand-blown Venice Beach served as Ted Hawkins's makeshift stage. He'd deliver his magnificent melange of soul, blues, folk, gospel, and a touch of country all by his lonesome, with only an acoustic guitar for company. Passersby would pause to marvel at Hawkins's melismatic vocals, dropping a few coins or a greenback into his tip jar on the way by. That was the way Ted Hawkins kept body and soul together until 1994, when DGC/Geffen Records issued *The Next Hundred Years*, his breakthrough album. Suddenly, Hawkins was poised on the precipice of stardom. And then, just after Christmas that same year, in a bout of cruel irony, he died of a stroke. After growing up in Mississippi, Hawkins moved to L.A. in 1966 and cut his debut 45, the soul-steeped "Baby"/"Whole Lot of Women," for Money Records. He also recorded some material in 1971, which appeared on Rounder in 1982 (as *Watch Your Step*). The album gained a five-star review from *Rolling Stone*, and Hawkins recorded another album, *Happy Hour*, in 1986. He moved to England later that year and became a well-known presence performing around Europe and even Japan. After returning to America in the early '90s, DGC ever so briefly propelled him into the major leagues. *Love You Most of All: More Songs From Venice Beach* was issued posthumously in 1998. *—Bill Dahl*

Watch Your Step / 1982 / Rounder ✦✦✦

Guitarist/vocalist Ted Hawkins was an instant sensation when this session was originally released in 1982. At a time when slick, heavily produced urban contemporary material was establishing its domination on the R&B scene, Hawkins' hard-edged, rough, cutting voice, plus his crisp acoustic guitar accompaniment and country-blues roots, seemed both dated and extremely fresh. This 15-track CD includes four numbers with Hawkins backed by Phillip Walker and his band, and others ranging from the humorous "Who Got My Natural Comb?" to the poignant "If You Love Me" and two versions of the title track. He also teamed with his wife Elizabeth on "Don't Lose Your Cool" and "I Gave It All I Had" for moving duets. *—Ron Wynn*

Happy Hour / 1986 / Rounder ✦✦✦✦✦

Guitarist/vocalist Ted Hawkins' second Rounder record enhanced his reputation. *Happy Hour* features Hawkins' memorable compositions, plus a wonderful version of Curtis Mayfield's "Gypsy Woman." Hawkins' vocals were even more gritty and striking, as was his acoustic guitar backing and chording. He teamed with his wife Elizabeth on "Don't Make Me Explain It," "My Last Goodbye," and "California Song," and with guitarist Night Train Clemons on "Gypsy Woman" and "You Pushed My Head Away." Hawkins blended soul and urban blues stylings with country and rural blues inflections and rhythms, making another first-rate release. *—Ron Wynn*

The Next Hundred Years / Mar. 29, 1994 / DGC ✦✦✦

The former L.A. street musician's major label breakthrough was in a great many ways a far weaker outing than what came before, largely due to a plodding band unwisely inserted behind Hawkins that tends to distract rather than enhance his impassioned vocals and rich acoustic guitar strumming. Mostly originals ("There Stands the Glass" returns, as does "Ladder of Success") that would have sounded so much better in an intimate solo context. *—Bill Dahl*

The Kershaw Sessions: Live at the BBC / 1995 / Varese ✦✦✦

The material on *The Kershaw Sessions: Live at the BBC* was recorded for disc jockey Andy Kershaw's BBC radio show between 1986 and 1989. It captures Ted Hawkins in an intimate, unvarnished setting that strips his music down to its purest essentials, making it an intriguing listen for fans who want more of Hawkins' bare-bones street-troubadour sound. Only a little over half the songs are Hawkins compositions; the high percentage of covers and the minimalist production give *The Kershaw Sessions* a vibe similar to *Songs From Venice Beach*. This is the way many British listeners were introduced to Hawkins' music, and it makes an excellent listen for American devotees as well. *—Steve Huey*

Songs From Venice Beach / Oct. 1995 / Evidence ✦✦✦✦

Blending every form of roots music imaginable into his own singular soulful stew, the incomparable Ted Hawkins stuck mostly to R&B covers on this splendid 1985 solo outing—songs by Sam Cooke (his idol), Jerry Butler, Bobby Bland, the Temptations, and Garnet Mimms receive gorgeous readings by the acoustic guitarist. But even though he only contributed one original, the touching "Ladder of Success," to the set, Hawkins wasn't content to remain in one genre—his commanding revival of Webb Pierce's hillbilly weeper "There Stands the Glass" ranks with the disc's very best moments (of which there are many). *—Bill Dahl*

● **The Ted Hawkins Story: Suffer No More** / Jan. 13, 1998 / Rhino ✦✦✦✦✦

Taken individually, Hawkins' albums didn't measure up to his critical reputation, due to uneven material, occasionally inappropriate production, and overreliance upon covers. More than most best-ofs, this 20-song compilation is a revelation of sorts. By focusing on his best moments, it's much easier to make a convincing case for Hawkins as a major, if erratic, roots-music performer who sounded like a coarsened, acoustic-oriented Sam Cooke. The set goes all the way back to both sides of his rare (and good) 1966 soul single on the Money label and highlights the best originals from the '70s and '80s sessions released on Rounder, wisely selecting sparsely from his cover-dominated albums of the mid-'80s. The songs from his major-label finale *The Next Hundred Years* can veer toward production slickness, but there's a pleasing bonus in three acoustic, previously unreleased cuts from the early 1990s. It's an intelligently selected, well-rounded disc, presenting several sides of this idiosyncratic artist: composer, folky interpreter of material by Sam Cooke and Brook Benton, and country-tinged soul artist. *—Richie Unterberger*

The Final Tour / Jan. 13, 1998 / Evidence ✦✦✦✦✦

Ted Hawkins' story is one of the most interesting—and tragic—in the history of R&B. Who'd have thought that a fifty-something street singer who performed 1960s-type soul in Venice Beach, CA. would have signed with Geffen's DGC label after decades of obscurity? That's exactly what happened, but tragically, a 58-year-old Hawkins died from a diabetes-related stroke just when things were really looking up for him. Recorded live at three 1994 concerts and released in 1998, *The Final Tour* shows how great Hawkins was sounding during the last months of his life. Nothing slick or elaborate happens on this album—it's just the charismatic Hawkins and his acoustic guitar, drawing on Sam Cooke's influence but always sounding like his own man. Those familiar with Hawkins' Rounder output will be familiar with heartfelt originals like "Bad Dog," "Bring It On Home, Daddy" and "Revenge of Scorpio," all of which demonstrate that he was as superb a composer as he was a singer. Hawkins is equally captivating on interpretations of Brook Benton's "I Got What I Wanted" and "All I Have to Offer You Is Me," a hit for country great Charley Pride that easily lends itself to Hawkins' brand of acoustic R&B. Soul lovers who haven't experienced the joys of Hawkins' music should make a point of obtaining this magnificent album. *—Alex Henderson*

The Unstoppable Ted Hawkins / Feb. 27, 2001 / Catfish ✦✦✦

Ted Hawkins had been accepted more warmly in England in the late '80s than he had been in his native America. To his countrymen, he was a has-been soul singer, ex-junkie, and ex-con who'd never made it and was now a busker on the Venice Beach boardwalk. What America wouldn't get until his major label debut in 1994 was something the Brits seemed to grasp instinctively—Ted Hawkins was one of the great soul singers, a very decent writer, but an interpreter of other peoples' material blessed with a perfect insight to bring things to life. And he proves that here, on what was meant to be just a soundboard cassette recording. From Sam Cooke to Brook Benton, even the maudlin "Please Come to Boston" takes on a magic and depth in his voice, while something as innocuous of "Zip

Pe Dee Doo Dah" positively brims over with spirit. His guitar work was never more than rudimentary, strumming an open chord, his left hand gloved to protect it, but it did the perfect job of framing that magnificent voice, which, as this album shows, was best heard live, where he could open up and let his dramatic tendencies take over without ever going overboard. His own writing coexists well with the better-known work, "Bring It on Home Daddy" a good juxtaposition to "Your Cheating Heart." But genre never mattered—it was about whether the song worked, be it something as wonderful as his take on Otis Redding's "Dock of the Bay" or John Denver's "Country Roads," his set closer. Saying it's all good can cheapen things. But in the case of Ted Hawkins, it really *was* all good. —*Chris Nickson*

Hawkwind

f. 1969, England
British Psychedelia, Heavy Metal, Prog Rock/Art Rock, Hard Rock
Any sci-fi fan with long memories probably remembers those 1970's DAW paperback editions of Michael Moorcock's sword-and-sorcery novels, with their images of heavily armored, very muscular warriors, carrying large swords and standing against eerie land- and starscapes. Take that imagery, throw in some terminology and names seemingly lifted from the Marvel Comics of the era (The Watcher, etc.) and particle physics articles of the period, translate it into loud but articulate hard rock music, and that's more or less what Hawkwind is about. One of England's longest-enduring heavy metal bands, Hawkwind was formed during the late '60s, just as art-rock was coming into its own. They combined bold guitar, synthesizer, and Mellotron sounds, creating heavy metal music that seemed to cross paths with Chuck Berry and the Moody Blues without sounding like either of them. At their best, their early records sounded like the Beatles of "Yer Blues" combined with the Cream of "I Feel Free." The introduction of lyrics steeped in science fiction and drug effects on their second album helped define the group and separate them from the competition—in some ways they were like Pink Floyd with more of a rock & roll beat and a vengeance. They've never charted a record anywhere near the heights that *Dark Side of the Moon* has achieved, but it's a sign of the dedication of the fans they do have that the group has about 30 CDs out, including archival releases of decades-old live shows and multiple compilations. —*Bruce Eder*

Hawkwind / 1970 / One Way ✦✦✦
At the time of its original appearance, this album was a complete anomaly, a loud, basic, hard-rocking long-player that flew in the face of the tinkly psychedelia and blues ramblings that were all the rage in England at the time. Not exactly the material the group is remembered for, but worthwhile. —*Bruce Eder*

● **In Search of Space** / 1971 / One Way ✦✦✦✦✦
The group's first real foray into progressive-sounding space-rock, which began to solidify the group's image. Distinctive artwork (and set designs on stage), better songwriting, and richer production made it superficially more sophisticated, and the 15-minute version of "You Shouldn't Do That" shored up the musical end, the song becoming a centerpiece of their live sets. —*Bruce Eder*

Doremi Fasol Latido / 1972 / One Way ✦✦✦
The band's first enduring studio album, completely awash in science-fiction lyrics, with electronic keyboards vying with the guitars for attention. They make Yes sound like a folk outfit at times, which was both their virtue and their limitation in terms of finding a mass audience. This is also where Lemmy joins up, giving the band a big boost in energy, not only on the bass, guitar and vocals, but personality as well. —*Bruce Eder*

Space Ritual / 1973 / United Artists ✦✦✦✦✦
The group's magnum opus at the time, derived from live performances that showed the band at its very best and honed on stage. Both Lemmy and Bob Calvert are on hand in good form, representing the two sides of the band's personality. —*Bruce Eder*

Hall of the Mountain Grill / 1974 / One Way ✦✦✦✦✦
The band's best studio album, coming off of the success of *Space Ritual*. The group's rock roots are juxtaposed effectively with the swelling synthesizer flourishes and pretentious song ideas, creating the quintessential guitar-oriented space-rock record—the highlight was the live recording of "You'd Better Believe It," with its crunchy guitars, but nobody minded keyboardman Simon House's languid synthesizer-laden "Hall of the Mountain Grill" (especially as it was followed by the Lemmy-sung "Lost Johnny," a great all-out rocker). The sound, especially the mix of ballsy high-volume guitar playing and soaring electronic keyboards ("The Psychedelic Warlords," "D-Rider"), would later get co-opted by outfits such as Blue Oyster Cult ("Don't Fear the Reaper") and Kansas. Overall, this is the sound and imagery that the punkier kids and druggies who went to shows like Laserium were looking for, and if the producers of Laserium had devised something hooked around this record, it could have run 20 years or better. —*Bruce Eder*

Warrior on the Edge of Time / 1975 / Atco ✦✦✦✦
Michael Moorcock's influence shows up, at least in the title, as the band takes on all of the accoutrements of a prog-rock group with balls. Unfortunately, this was where the core lineup began to disintegrate, and their subsequent efforts were marred by a revolving-door membership. —*Bruce Eder*

Astounding Sounds, Amazing Music / 1976 / Charisma ✦✦

Masters of the Universe / 1977 / United Artists ✦✦✦✦
A collection of the group's early sides, including "Hurry on Sundown" and other material from their days as Hawkwind Zoo. —*Bruce Eder*

The Chronicle of the Black Sword / 1985 / Gopaco ✦✦✦
Hawkwind and science-fiction/fantasy author Michael Moorcock had been hovering around each other's vicinities for years before they finally got around to recording this

adaptation of Moorcock's "Elric" novels (long a favorite on the old DAW paperback line). They seemed made to order for the project, and by and large they are; the band rocks their way through the story of Elric and the sword that becomes the basis for his survival and his doom, breaking it up with a few ethereal keyboard-dominated interludes. "Needle Gun" could have been a single by the original band had it been released a few years earlier. They aren't quite as melodic here in their writing, singing, or playing as they might have been, say, a decade earlier, and some of the songs are a bit predictable, but overall this is a fairly successful contribution to rock's rarefied body of literary adaptations, well suited to its subject. The lineup here, for anyone who cares, is Brock (vocals, guitar, keyboards), Bainbridge (keyboards, vocals), Langton (lead guitar, vocals), Alan Davey (bass), Danny Thompson (drums), and Dave Charles (percussion). —*Bruce Eder*

Best & the Rest of Hawkwind / 1990 / Trojan ✦✦✦
Eight tracks from an uncredited period in the group's history (but obviously around 1979), and not bad, either. The band is found covering classic material ("Silver Machine," "Urban Guerilla") and much-requested album numbers ("Space Is Deep"), as well as more recent stuff like "British Tribal Music," in better-than-decent sound with lots of wattage and enthusiasm. Not necessarily the best versions of these numbers—they've recorded so many live albums at this point that one could do a box set of nothing but concert recordings—but an OK single-CD choice. —*Bruce Eder*

Stasis: The U.A. Years, 1971-1975 / 1990 / One Way ✦✦✦✦
This isn't a full history of Hawkwind's first five years with United Artists Records, the period in which their reputation was made. It is a killer 75-minute-plus collection of many of their most well-known and oft-requested tracks, with rare and forgotten original mixes (most notably on "Silver Machine," "You'd Better Believe It," and "Psychedelic Warlords") included, and a ton of live material is here as well. Some of the spacier, more pretentious stuff doesn't hold up too well ("Seven by Seven," Michael Moorcock's "The Black Corridor"), although they do present part of what the group was about. Most of this material, however, especially the early singles, showcases a first-rate group going where no band had ever rocked before. The sound is good, although the mixes on some of the early singles seem rough, but that was what the producers had in mind—the wash of guitars, synthesizer, and bass on "Silver Machine" or the monumental live "Space Is Deep" is one of the few psychedelic/space-rock sounds that really holds up today. And Paul Cox's notes give a reasonably understandable account of the group's history and their twisted membership dynamics. —*Bruce Eder*

Mighty Hawkwind Classics (1980-1985) / 1992 / Griffin ✦✦✦✦
Various tracks from across their history, including "Hurry on Sundown" and Lemmy's "Motorhead." —*Bruce Eder*

Friends and Relations: The Rarities / Dec. 1995 / Griffin ✦✦

Isaac Hayes

b. Aug. 20, 1942, Covington, TN
Vocals, Saxophone, Leader, Keyboards, Arranger, Songwriter, Piano / Blaxploitation, Disco, Funk, Soul
Few figures exerted greater influence over the music of the 1960s and 1970s than Isaac Hayes; after laying the groundwork for the Memphis soul sound through his work with Stax-Volt Records, Hayes began a highly successful solo career which predated not only the disco movement but also the evolution of rap. In 1964, Hayes began playing sax with the Mar-Keys, which resulted in the beginning of his long association with Stax Records. After playing on several sessions for Otis Redding, Hayes was tapped to play keyboards in the Stax house band, and eventually established a partnership with songwriter David Porter. Under the name the Soul Children, the Hayes-Porter duo composed some 200 songs, rattling off a string of hits for Stax luminaries like Sam and Dave (the brilliant "When Something Is Wrong With My Baby," "Soul Man," and "Hold On, I'm Comin'"), Carla Thomas ("B-A-B-Y"), and Johnnie Taylor ("I Got to Love Somebody's Baby," "I Had a Dream"). In 1967, he issued his debut solo LP *Presenting Isaac Hayes*, and with the release of 1969's landmark *Hot Buttered Soul*, he made his commercial breakthrough, as the record's adventuresome structure (comprising four lengthy songs), ornate arrangements, and sensual grooves—combined with the imposing figure cut by his shaven head, omnipresent sunglasses, and fondness for gold jewelry—made Hayes one of the most distinct figures in music. He reached his commercial zenith in 1971 with the release of *Shaft*, the score from the Gordon Parks film of the same name. Not only did the album win Hayes an Academy Award for Best Score (the first African-American composer to garner such an honor), but the single "Theme From 'Shaft'," a masterful blend of prime funk and pre-rap monologues, became a number one hit. —*Jason Ankeny*

Presenting Isaac Hayes / 1967 / Stax ✦✦✦
Isaac Hayes' earliest single efforts, and he hadn't yet perfected his lengthy raps and symphonic soul formula. These were rather the same type of songs he and David Porter turned into classics for many other Stax artists. They were mostly short gospel and country-tinged soul ballads, vamps, and up-tempo numbers. Hayes sang them well, his domineering baritone revealing itself as a potent weapon. While none of them did that well, the album revealed the enormous potential Hayes would begin to fulfill with his next album. —*Ron Wynn*

☆ **Hot Buttered Soul** / 1969 / Stax ✦✦✦✦✦
Released at the tail end of the '60s, *Hot Buttered Soul* set the precedent for how soul would evolve in the early '70s, simultaneously establishing Isaac Hayes and the Bar-Kays as major forces within black music. Though not quite as definitive as *Black Moses* or as well-known as *Shaft*, *Hot Buttered Soul* remains an undeniably seminal record; it stretched its songs far beyond the traditional three-to-four-minute industry norm,

featured long instrumental stretches where the Bar-Kays stole the spotlight, and it introduced a new, iconic persona for soul with Hayes' tough yet sensual image. With the release of this album, Motown suddenly seemed manufactured and James Brown a bit too theatrical. Surprising many, the album features only four songs. The first, "Walk on By," is an epic 12-minute moment of true perfection, its trademark string-laden intro just dripping with syrupy sentiment, and the thumping mid-tempo drum beat and accompanying bass line instilling a complementary sense of nasty funk to the song; if that isn't enough to make it an amazing song, Hayes' almost painful performance brings yet more feeling to the song, with the guitar's heavy vibrato and the female background singers taking the song to even further heights. The following three songs aren't quite as stunning but are still no doubt impressive: "Hyperbolicsyllabicsequedalymistic" trades in sappy sentiment for straight-ahead funk, highlighted by a stomping piano halfway through the song; "One Woman" is the least epic moment, clocking in at only five minutes, but stands as a straightforward, well-executed love ballad; and finally, there's the infamous 18-minute "By the Time I Get to Phoenix" and its lengthy monologue which slowly eases you toward the climactic, almost-orchestral finale, a beautiful way to end one of soul's timeless, landmark albums, the album that transformed Hayes into a lifelong icon. *—Jason Birchmeier*

Isaac Hayes Movement / 1970 / Stax ✦✦✦✦✦
His second huge hit album and a great follow-up to the superb *Hot Buttered Soul.* Those critics who thought there was no way Hayes could repeat that triumph got fooled. He included a brilliant remake of Jerry Butler's "I Stand Accused" and also did a 12-minute version of the Beatles' "Something," complete with a wailing violin solo from jazz-rocker John Blair. This album showed that Hayes was going to be around for a long time and perform just as consistently on his own as he did teaming with Porter. *—Ron Wynn*

To Be Continued / 1970 / Stax ✦✦✦✦
Released in late 1970 on the heals of two chart-topping albums, *Hot Buttered Soul* (1969) and *The Isaac Hayes Movement* (also 1970), Isaac Hayes and the Bar-Kays retain their successful approach on those landmark albums for *To Be Continued,* another number one album. Again, the album features four songs that span far beyond traditional radio-friendly length, featuring important mood-establishing instrumental segments just as emotive and striking as Hayes' crooning. Nothing here is quite as perfect as "Walk on By," and the album feels a bit churned out, but *To Be Continued* no doubt has its share of highlights, the most notable being "You've Lost That Lovin' Feelin'." The album's most epic moment opens with light strings and horns, vamping poetically for several minutes before Hayes even utters a breath; then, once the singer delivers the song's orchestral chorus, the album hits its sentimental peak—Hayes elevating a common standard to heavenly heights once again. Elsewhere, "Our Day Will Come" features a nice concluding instrumental segment driven by a proto-hip-hop beat that proves just how ahead of his time Hayes was during his early-'70s cycle of Enterprise albums. It's tempting to slight this album when holding it up against Hayes' best albums from this same era, but a comparison such as this is unfair. Even if Ike isn't doing anything here that he didn't do on his two preceding albums—*Hot Buttered Soul, The Isaac Hayes Movement*—and isn't quite as daring as he is on his two successive albums—*Black Moses, Shaft*—*To Be Continued* still topples any Hayes album that came after 1971. It didn't top the R&B album chart for 11 weeks on accident—this is quintessential early-'70s Isaac Hayes, and that alone makes it a classic soul album. *—Jason Birchmeier*

Black Moses / 1971 / Stax ✦✦✦
For many, this is Ike's finest overall effort, and despite the ego trippin' title—*Black Moses*—the music backs the brag. Hayes' low register is mesmerizing on 14 refurbished R&B and pop songs. Every track is carefully crafted and well spaced. "Ike Raps" enhances and bands them all together. The key is balance, while there's nothing as mournful as "By the Time I Get to Phoenix," soulful as "I Stand Accused," or bad as "Do Your Thing," every cut is a close second. "Going in Circles," "Man's Temptation," "Need to Belong to Someone," "Never Can Say Goodbye," and the rest are done with maturity and reverence by the self-acclaimed One. *—Andrew Hamilton*

Shaft / 1971 / Stax ✦✦✦✦✦
Of the many wonderful blaxpoitation soundtracks to emerge during the early '70s, *Shaft* certainly deserves mention as not only one of the most lasting but also one of the most successful. Isaac Hayes was undoubtedly one of the era's most accomplished soul artists, having helped elevate Stax to its esteemed status; therefore, his being chosen to score such a high-profile major-studio film shouldn't seem like a surprise. And with "Theme From Shaft," he delivered an anthem just as ambitious and revered as the film itself, a song that has only grown more treasured over the years, after having been an enormously popular hit at the time of its release. Besides this song, though, there aren't too many more radio-targeted moments here. "Soulsville" operates effectively as the sort of down-tempo ballad Hayes was most known for, just as the almost 20-minute "Do Your Thing" showcased just how impressive the Bar-Kays had become, stretching the song to unseen limits with their inventive, funky jamming. For the most part, though, this double-LP features nothing but cinematic moments of instrumentation, composed and produced by Hayes while being performed by the Bar-Kays—some down-tempo, others quite jazzy, nothing too funky, though. Even if it's not quite as enjoyable as Curtis Mayfield's *Superfly* due to its emphasis on instrumentals, *Shaft* still remains a powerful record; one of Hayes' pinnacle moments for sure. *—Jason Birchmeier*

Live at the Sahara Tahoe / 1973 / Stax ✦✦

Joy / Dec. 1973 / Stax ✦✦

Tough Guys / Mar. 1974 / Enterprise ✦✦
This 1974 soundtrack sounds pretty much like what you would expect—period funk, mostly instrumental. It's much more effective as background to screen action than home listening, where it sounds like backing tracks in search of vocals, or incidental grooves that need much more flesh on their bones. It's been combined with another 1974 Hayes soundtrack, *Truck Turner,* on the double CD reissue *Double Feature. —Richie Unterberger*

Truck Turner / Jul. 1974 / Enterprise ✦✦✦
This soundtrack was considerably lengthier and more varied than the one Hayes had released earlier in 1974 (*Tough Guys*), including Holiday Inn funk, a lugubrious vocal ("You're in My Arms Again"), and some jazz and blues riffs peppering the instrumental grooves. While the length ensured more variety, though, it also makes it a challenge to sit through the hour-plus program when you don't have images to fit the music. It's been combined with *Truck Turner* on the double-CD reissue *Double Feature. —Richie Unterberger*

Chocolate Chip / 1975 / Stax ✦✦✦
A fine mid-'70s album on which Isaac Hayes adapted to the disco era. His productions were already ideal for dance floors, and he now updated his charts to include some stomping segments with horns and layered beats, while maintaining his soulful vocals on both up-tempo tunes and ballads. This album got two Top 20 hits for Hayes and was his last really big hit album in the '70s. *—Ron Wynn*

The Best of Isaac Hayes, Vol. 1 / 1986 / Stax ✦✦✦✦✦
A decent attempt to present some of Isaac Hayes' past hits on an anthology. But as one of R&B and soul's first concept and album artists, it's impossible to appreciate his contributions out of sequence. His early and mid-'70s albums helped change the course of contemporary black music production approaches, and that can't be understood by listening to condensed versions of hit singles, or even just by hearing the singles themselves removed from the album context. *—Ron Wynn*

The Best of Isaac Hayes, Vol. 2 / 1986 / Stax ✦✦✦✦✦
These two compilations dutifully boil down Isaac Hayes' sometimes long-winded albums to their essential parts—in other words, they're both singles collections, highlighted by '70s landmarks such as "Theme From *Shaft*" and "By the Time I Get to Phoenix." Fanatics may want to investigate *Hot Buttered Soul* and *Black Moses. —John Floyd*

● **Greatest Hit Singles** / Jun. 11, 1991 / Stax ✦✦✦✦✦
The place to start (and probably the place to end), with nearly an hour of music and 12 of his best-known singles, including "Theme From 'Shaft,'" "By the Time I Get to Phoenix," "Walk on By," "Never Can Say Goodbye," "Do Your Thing," and "Joy (Part 1)." There's a separate two-volume series of Stax Hayes hits for those who want a little more, but this is the essential dose. *—Richie Unterberger*

Double Feature: Truck Turner/Tough Guys / 1993 / Stax ✦✦✦✦
Isaac Hayes not only was an innovative composer, songwriter, producer, and performer in the '60s and '70s, he was also an actor and appeared in several "blaxploitation" films during the early '70s. Hayes did double duty on these projects, writing and conducting the soundtracks for several, including the two featured on this twin-CD reissue. Neither *Truck Turner* nor *Tough Guys* was a particularly memorable film, but Hayes' effective use of symphony orchestras and strings against a vocal backdrop often made the music the best part of the movie. *—Ron Wynn*

Branded / May 23, 1995 / Pointblank ✦✦✦
Isaac Hayes launched a comeback in the spring of 1995 by releasing two records, *Branded* and *Raw and Refined. Branded* was a vocal album, while *Raw and Refined* was comprised of instrumental jams. Neither of them were a departure from the music Hayes made in the '70s—*Branded* was filled with laid-back, lush soul and *Raw and Refined* was a deep, dirty funk workout—but they were effective reminders of Hayes' influence on '90s soul. *—Stephen Thomas Erlewine*

Raw and Refined / May 23, 1995 / Pointblank ✦✦✦
Isaac Hayes launched a comeback in the spring of 1995 by releasing two records, *Branded* and *Raw and Refined. Branded* was a vocal album, while *Raw and Refined* was comprised of instrumental jams. Neither of them were a departure from the music Hayes made in the '70s—*Branded* was filled with laid-back, lush soul and *Raw and Refined* was a deep, dirty funk workout—but they were effective reminders of Hayes' influence on '90s soul. *—Stephen Thomas Erlewine*

The Best of Isaac Hayes: The Polydor Years / Feb. 6, 1996 / Polydor/Chronicles ✦✦✦✦✦
Isaac Hayes' stint with Polydor in the late '70s isn't always looked at as being one of his better eras. In fact, it's not looked upon highly at all by many of his fans. It's important to keep in mind, though, that Hayes had already seen enormous success and had released a sizable amount of legendary albums by the time the late '70s came around. In this respect, you really can't expect his later work to be on par with his classic early-'70s era with Stax—no one could one-up albums like *Shaft* and *Black Moses.* Plus, the late '70s wasn't a kind era for any early-'70s soul icons as disco and funk moved black music from behind closed doors and into the clubs. Hayes had learned this the hard way during his short-lived mid-'70s run with ABC Records where he struggled to even chart, not to mention score a big hit. So when you really look at things from a wider view, sure, Hayes' Polydor years—which began with *New Horizons* (1977) and ended with *Lifetime Thing* (1981)—weren't on par with his Stax years, but they were still successful nonetheless. Hayes became more of a singles artist than an album artist as he had been with Stax. Because of this, it's perhaps best to seek out a best-of such as *The Polydor Years* rather than bother with his individual albums. This album collects 12 of his best moments from the era such as the somewhat notorious "Moonlight Lovin' (Menage a Trois)" and other disco-flavored songs like "Zeke the Freak" that may have not stormed up the charts but did fill the dancefloor on occasion. This collection provides the insight for fans about a difficult

period in Hayes' career where he struggled to age gracefully and adjust to the jarring force of disco. It shows that contrary to popular belief, Hayes did find success during this era, even if it was only sporadic. —*Jason Birchmeier*

Ultimate Collection / Apr. 11, 2000 / Hip-O ✦✦✦✦

Since the majority of Hayes' most memorable work was during the 70's, this collection nabs 13 of its 16 tracks from that decade. The two later cuts that close the disc—especially the meandering "Ike's Rap" from 1986—are disposable. More problematic though is the surreptitious editing of Hayes' longer material like "Never Can Say Goodbye," "Walk on By," and "Joy" (although interestingly not the nine minute "Hyperbol"), which are all severely shortened from their original versions. Unfortunately that essential information is nowhere to be found on the outside sleeve or liner notes. That said, the meat of those extended songs is still represented in the edits, and Hayes' trademarked slow-burn soul/funk permeates the bulk of this collection. The decision to eliminate most of his soundtrack work—save for two tracks from *Shaft*—was a smart one, and except for the cliché disco of "Don't Let Go" and the upbeat rubber band groove of "Out of the Ghetto," the album sticks primarily to Hayes' unhurried funk. Not as good as it could have been even with the single disc restrictions, the *Ultimate Isaac Hayes* is a reasonable place to start exploring, but falls short of providing a well-rounded look at the legendary musician. —*Hal Horowitz*

Lee Hazlewood

b. Jul. 9, 1929, Mannford, OK

Producer, Vocals, Songwriter / Obscuro, Baroque Pop, Pop, Country-Pop, Country-Rock
Lee Hazlewood has had his hand in so many pies it's hard to know where to start in describing his long and varied music career. He's recorded an impressive number of pop and country albums himself—immediately distinguished by his deep, dark vocal style and playfully existential lyrics—but he's best known for two accomplishments: Discovering Duane Eddy (he created Eddy's trademark twangy guitar sound), and producing and writing the song "These Boots Are Made for Walking" and other hits for Nancy Sinatra, which turned her into a 1960s icon of sassy miniskirt pop. Initially, it was songwriting success that enabled Hazlewood to form his own Phoenix-based Jamie label in the '50s, which became the launching pad for Eddy's career. (Hazlewood wrote and produced most of the guitarist's major hits.) By the late '60s, Hazlewood had begun working as a producer for Reprise, where he eventually hooked up with Nancy Sinatra and turned her career into a goldmine with songs like "Boots" and "Sugar Town." The pair also recorded several singles together, eventually released on the album *Nancy and Lee*. Hazlewood's own solo singles and albums are some of the era's most unique pop and country creations, with material walking the line between dark, philosophical introspection and wry, playful humor (often on the same song). Hazlewood retreated into obscurity in the 1970s, but continued recording and performing in Europe. He briefly resurfaced in 1995 to tour with Nancy Sinatra, then four years later he released *Farmisht, Flatulence, Origami, ARF!!! and me…*, his first proper solo album in over 20 years. —*Kurt Wolff*

Trouble Is a Lonesome Town / 1963 / Smells Like ✦✦✦

Trouble Is a Lonesome Town was Lee Hazlewood's first proper solo album, following his prosperous late-'50s partnership with Duane Eddy and prior to his mentoring and making of '60s boot-walker Nancy Sinatra. Hazlewood considered it a "writer's album" from which other artists could cull songs, but *Trouble* is a perfectly legitimate effort in its own right and characteristically wonderful Hazlewood. The songs are succinct, country-drenched cowboy ballads given a certain undeniable authority by Hazlewood's warm, bottomless baritone, which booms out of the music like a voice amplified from the heavens. The album runs through jail songs ("Six Feet of Chain"), railroad songs ("The Railroad"), traveling songs ("Long Black Train"), and cold-hearted love songs ("Look at That Woman") peppered with outlaws, itinerants, dead-end women, card players, and beat-down heroes, too. Between the songs, Hazlewood shows his storyteller's gift by offering up bits of narration, and the album itself is a storyteller's record. *Trouble* is like a cross between a novel full of idiosyncratic character studies (à la Faulkner) and a John Wayne Western, with Hazlewood—looking a lot like a dharma bum on the album cover, sitting on the railroad tracks with his guitar and a dangling cigarette—spinning out intricate yarns about all manner of interesting souls with names like Orville Dobkins and Emory Zickfoose Brown, all residents of the hard-scrabbled fictitious town Trouble ("nothing with a railroad running through it"), which is loosely based on his birthplace. The music is as somber and loping as such subject matter demands, mostly consisting of strummed acoustic guitars and woeful harmonica wails that weep the blues. But it is in the purposefully humorous, sympathetic, and colorful storytelling that the distinct, dead-on Americana heart of *Trouble* lays. —*Stanton Swihart*

Love and Other Crimes / 1968 / Reprise ✦✦✦✦✦

If you're looking for evidence of Lee Hazlewood the weirdo, this album will not disappoint. As pure music it's another story. Hazlewood usually sounds like Johnny Cash gone pop, after gargling with razor blades; sometimes he sounds like a drunk taking over the cocktail piano, with soused accompaniment by such estimable session greats as guitarist James Burton and drummer Hal Blaine. Check out "She's Funny That Way," which suddenly fades into a silly excerpt of Ray Charles' "Drown in My Own Tears"; there's also "Pour Man'" (sic), a jaunty ballad sung by a convicted murderer on his last night of life. "Forget Marie" is reasonably solid country-pop in the style of the material he fashioned for Nancy Sinatra, but overall this has the ambience of a tax write-off or a vanity project, knocked off with a bit of extra studio time. —*Richie Unterberger*

Nancy & Lee / 1968 / Reprise ✦✦✦✦✦

Lee's first duet album with Nancy Sinatra is a classic of '60s pop. He plays the leering, deep-throated, trail-worn cowboy to her bright-eyed girl-child, and the match on songs

like "Summer Wine," "Sand," "Jackson," and "Some Velvet Morning" is a smart, sexy, lip-smacking bowl of mind candy. —*Kurt Wolff*

The Cowboy & the Lady / 1969 / Smells Like ✦✦

This doesn't come close to his duet work with Nancy Sinatra, and it lacks even a single Hazlewood composition, but "No Regrets" and "Greyhound Bus Depot" are standouts, and the inside cover art is well worth the price of admission. —*Kurt Wolff*

Cowboy in Sweden / 1970 / Smells Like ✦✦✦✦

At the turn of the '60s, Lee Hazlewood decided to leave America for Sweden. He had already spent time in the country, appearing as an actor in two television productions, so his decision wasn't completely out of the blue—especially since he had become close with the Swedish artist/filmmaker Torbjörn Axelman. The year that he arrived in Sweden, he starred in Axelman's television production *Cowboy in Sweden* and cut an album of the same name. Judging by the album alone, the film must have been exceedingly surreal, since the record exists in its own space and time. At its core, it's a collection of country and cowboy tunes, much like the work he did with Nancy Sinatra, but the production is cinematic and psychedelic, creating a druggy, discombobulated sound like no other. This is mind-altering music—the combination of country song structures, Hazlewood's deep baritone, the sweet voices of Nina Lizell and Suzi Jane Hokom, the rolling acoustic guitars, ominous strings, harpsichords and flutes, eerie pianos, and endless echo is stranger than outright avant-garde music, since the familiar is undone by unexpected arrangements. Though the songs are all well written, *Cowboy in Sweden* is ultimately about the sound and mood it evokes—and it's quite singular in that regard. —*Stephen Thomas Erlewine*

Requiem for an Almost Lady / 1971 / Smells Like ✦✦✦✦

Requiem for an Almost Lady is the rarest of Lee Hazlewood's albums because it was released in 1971 exclusively in Sweden (where Hazlewood also completed his cult classic *Cowboy in Sweden* album) and the United Kingdom. The album is one of the most beautifully agonizing breakup records to ever hit wax, culled from a composite of Hazlewood's relationships gone wrong. Spoken-word introductions precede each of the ten brief songs and reveal Hazlewood's poetic soul, while the songs themselves are full of longing and witty, clever cynicism coupled with a sad-eyed idealism that paints the music even more visceral and grievous. Hazlewood spares none of his past loves. *Requiem* is often cutting, even harsh, evident with a songs such as "I'd Rather Be Your Enemy" and "I'm Glad I Never…" (as in never owned a gun), but there is an underlying feeling of tenderness, as if Hazlewood is only talking tough to hide his own deep hurt. The album creates an impossibly cavernous warmth with only acoustic guitar and electric bass backing provided by Jerry Cole, Donnie Owens, and Joe Cannon. Although there are hints of Hazlewood's cowboy sound on "L.A. Lady" and "Must Have Been Something I Loved," *Requiem* actually steers much closer to folky psychedelic-pop territory, particularly the sound of California at the end of the '60s. The subject matter is sophisticated and somatic, but the tone of the music veers much more toward the mystical, existential, and hippie-ish. Hazlewood is meditative without seeming overly fragile. His perspective is world-weary, but it doesn't stop him from tossing in a campy sense of humor to leaven his obvious, passionate disappointment, and it makes the album that much more lyrical, intelligent, and emotionally poignant. —*Stanton Swihart*

13 / 1972 / Smells Like ✦✦✦

One of the rarest of Lee Hazlewood's original LPs, *13* is a surprisingly swinging album completely indicative of the year of its recording, 1972. But though it's undeniably a period piece, in many ways it's dated in all the right ways. The opener, "You Look Like a Lady," is a gem, complete with soaring horn section, a roving bassline, and scads of wah-wah guitar. Oddly, over-production never hurt Hazlewood's gravelly, off-key delivery, and though the arrangements here aren't always sympathetic to the songwriting ("Tulsa Sunday" is particularly jarring), they're usually entertaining. "She Comes Running," a song originally recorded for 1968's *Love and Other Crimes*, makes another appearance, though with a much more commercial production. The lyrics are vintage Hazlewood, and "Ten or 11 Towns Ago" is a highlight: "Met a girl in Baltimore / Nothing less and nothing more / She was rich and I was poor / So I let her take me on a small vacation" and "One week in San Francisco, existing on Nabisco / Cookies and bad dreams / Sad scenes and dodging paranoia." Not all of the songs are up to Hazlewood's level; "Toocie and the River" and "Rosacoke Street" are both, relatively speaking, duds. But Hazlewood fans will love to hear these songs, especially since none have been collected on the quasi-legal compilations available at the nation's better record stores. Out of print for decades, *13* returned in early 2000 thanks to a reissue campaign by Smells Like Records. —*John Bush*

Fairy Tales and Fantasies / 1989 / Rhino ✦✦✦✦✦

This CD compilation includes the entire *Nancy & Lee* album and four songs from their followup: "Did You Ever," "Down From Dover," "Paris Summer," and "Arkansas Coal (Suite)." —*Kurt Wolff*

● The Many Sides of Lee / 1991 / Request ✦✦✦✦✦

Twenty-five-song import compilation of rare Hazlewood tracks, most or all dating from the 1960s, including solo numbers and collaborations with Suzi Jane Hokom, the Shacklefords, and Mark Robinson. The most country-ish cuts are like a debauched Johnny Cash; the bullfighter narrative "Jose" is Hazlewood at his most compellingly cheesy and melodramatic; and there are shades of his Duane Eddy roots in the more rock-oriented cuts, like the grungy "Della" and the rockabilly tinged "Pretty Jane." There are also solo renditions of several songs that he produced for Nancy Sinatra, although Sinatra's versions are uniformly better. You could justifiably call this the work of an idiot savant, or (at its worst) just a plain idiot, but it is, like much of Hazlewood's stuff, intriguing in its blend of banal '60s pop-country and eccentric production, lyrics, and vocals. It would have been nice to have even a shred of documentation as far as dates and sources, and there's no question that his collaborations with Nancy Sinatra offer a much better context for his work as a songwriter and producer. But this is the best available distillation of the man's erratic and large solo output into one place, if you can find it. —*Richie Unterberger*

Farmisht, Flatulence, Origami, ARF!!! and me... / Apr. 27, 1999 / Smells Like ✦✦✦
Some may be disappointed that Lee Hazlewood's first album in over 25 years is a collection of standards, but given time, *Farmisht, Flatulence, Origami, ARF!!! and me...* will work its considerable charms. Essentially an outgrowth of Al Casey's Sidewinder project, which featured Hazlewood's vocals on a pair of tracks, *Farmisht* is a laid-back, jazzy affair, with Hazlewood contributing surprisingly supple and inventive readings of such standards as "Honeysuckle Rose," "It Had to Be You," "She's Funny that Way," "Don't Get Around Much Anymore" and "Am I Blue." The album is as much Casey's as it is Hazlewood's, since his small group strikes a wonderful balance of jazz, pop and country—it's loose but never sloppy, sophisticated but never pretentious. Thanks to Casey's fleet leadership and Hazlewood's rich vocals—which weathered far better than anyone could have predicted—*Farmisht* is one of the few standards albums that actually works, since it is faithful to the songs while creating an identity of its own. It's a modest achievement, but it's not a bad way to return to recording at all. —*Stephen Thomas Erlewine*

Roy Head

b. Jan. 9, 1943, Three Rivers, TX
Vocals / Pop-Soul, Blue-Eyed Soul, Traditional Country, Rock & Roll
Actually a country and rock vocalist rather than an R&B star, Roy Head nevertheless cut one of the great pieces of up-tempo soul in the mid-'60s. "Treat Her Right" on Back Beat made it to number two on the R&B charts and number two pop, and the fact that Head was white was soft-pedaled in R&B circles while the song made its way up the charts. That performance alone was enough to qualify Head as one of the finest blue-eyed soul singers of the 1960s. But in fact, Roy was one of the most versatile stylists of the era, capable of hard R&B/rock tunes, mournful, soul-tinged country, and straight R&B and blues covers. The Texan singer is remembered as a one-shot artist, but he actually cut many records (some under the auspices of noted producer Huey Meaux) throughout the 1960s on a confusing variety of labels. A few of these were tiny hits in the wake of "Treat Her Right," only a couple ("Just a Little Bit" and "Apple of My Eye") sneaking into the Top 40. Quite a few of his records were dynamic, sleek hybrids (in varying degrees) of soul, rock, and country, all featuring Head's cocky, confident vocals. In the 1970s, after several years without success in the rock or R&B fields, Head returned to country, and landed quite a few chart hits in the arena between 1974 and 1985. —*Ron Wynn & Richie Unterberger*

Treat Me Right / 1965 / Bear Family ✦✦✦✦✦
Read the title carefully; it's not "Treat Her Right," the title of Head's 1965 megasmash, but *Treat Me Right*, an entirely different song. Yes indeed, this is an exploitation release of material Head cut for a different label than the one that issued "Treat Her Right," repackaged after the hit to capitalize on its unexpected success. The final punchline is that, as exploitative as this LP is, it's quite good. The ten songs—mostly revved-up R&B, with a bit of country-soul thrown in—are solid evidence of Head's stature as one of the finest white soul singers of the '60s. The small combo R&B arrangements are spare and tight, investing even overdone standards like "Money" with excitement. Long out of print, it still shows up in the used bins from time to time and is worth picking up. —*Richie Unterberger*

Slip Away: His Best Recordings / Aug. 5, 1993 / Collectables ✦✦✦
Not only are these *not* his best recordings by a long shot—this package also matches the shoddiest standards of the Collectables label, a company often (justly) criticized for a variety of inadequacies. The documentation on these 14 tracks is totally nonexistent—not a clue as to when they were first released or recorded. A good many came out in the mid-'60s (though "Treat Her Right" and most of the other best Back Beat singles are absent); others have a heavier soul/blues feel that sounds as though they might date from a few years later, or even much later. What's more, a few tracks that appear (in better fidelity) on the Varese Sarabande compilation are presented here with different track titles, although you might mistakenly think at a glance that it doesn't duplicate anything from that anthology. There *are* a few very good cuts here that aren't on *The Best of Roy Head*, such as the talking soul rap "Slip Away," the deep soul ballad "The Feeling Is Gone," and the zany psychedelic/jazz-flavored "Easy Loving Girl" (written by Johnny Winter, who plays fuzz guitar on the song). Just be warned that this is a carelessly assembled package, much inferior to the Varese Sarabande compilation, if you only want one disc. —*Richie Unterberger*

● **Treat Her Right: The Best of Roy Head** / Aug. 29, 1995 / Varese ✦✦✦✦✦
A long overdue anthology of Head's best sides, mostly recorded for the Back Beat label in the mid-'60s. Besides "Treat Her Right," it has all five of his other singles that dented the charts at the time. These aren't necessarily the highlights of these 18 tracks; "Pain" is country-soul moan at its best (although it's a thinly veiled rewrite of Lonnie Mack's "Why"), "To Make a Big Man Cry" is his best foray into country-pop from the period, and "You're (Almost) Tuff" is one of his toughest rockers, with a sound that almost verges on Texas garage. This collection is the most solid evidence of Head's superb talents, which were never rewarded with the consistent material or national recognition he deserved. —*Richie Unterberger*

Heart

f. 1973, Seattle, WA
Album Rock, Arena Rock, Pop/Rock, Hard Rock
Sisters Ann and Nancy Wilson were the creative spark behind Heart, a hard-rock group who initially found success in the mid-'70s, only to reach greater heights after engineering a major comeback a decade later. Based in Vancouver, Heart was actually formed as

an all-male vocal group. After arriving in the group, both Ann and Nancy became romantically involved with other members of the band. One year later, the group's debut album *Dreamboat Annie* eventually sold platinum in the U.S. A legal battle after moving to the CBS affiliate Portrait delayed Heart's second album *Little Queen*, though it also went platinum.

After one more album, both of the band romances ended and precipitated a massive lineup change. The next two Heart albums failed miserably, and though the band moved to Capitol, it was largely written off by industry watchers. The band emerged in 1985 with a self-titled effort which ultimately sold more than five million copies on its way to launching four Top Ten hits (including the chart-topping "These Dreams"). The follow-ups, *Bad Animals* and *Brigade*, continued their comeback success. In the early '90s, the Wilson sisters took a brief hiatus from Heart to form the acoustic group the Lovemongers. Heart returned in 1993 with *Desire Walks On* and on 1995's *The Road Home* they enlisted onetime Led Zep bassist John Paul Jones to produce a live acoustic set reprising several of their hits. —*Jason Ankeny*

Dreamboat Annie / Mar. 1976 / Capitol ✦✦✦✦✦
In the 1980s and '90s, numerous women recorded blistering rock, but things were quite different in 1976—when female singers tended to be pigeonholed as soft-rockers and singer/songwriters and were encouraged to take after Carly Simon, Melissa Manchester, or Joni Mitchell rather than Led Zeppelin or Black Sabbath. Greatly influenced by Zep, Heart did its part to help open doors for ladies of loudness with the excellent *Dreamboat Annie* (reissued on a gold audiophile CD by DCC Compact Classics in 1995). Aggressive yet melodic rockers like "Sing Child," "White Lightning and Wine," and the rock radio staples "Magic Man" and "Crazy on You" led to the tag "the female Led Zeppelin." And in fact, Robert Plant did have a strong influence on Ann Wilson. But those numbers and caressing, folkish ballads like "How Deep It Goes" and the title song also make it clear that the Wilson sisters had their own identity and vision early on. —*Alex Henderson*

Little Queen / May 1977 / Portrait ✦✦✦✦✦
After acquiring a substantial following with *Dreamboat Annie*, Heart solidified its niche in the hard-rock and arena-rock worlds with the equally impressive *Little Queen*. Once again, loud-and-proud, Led Zeppelin-influenced hard rock was the thing that brought Heart the most attention. But while "Barracuda" and "Kick It Out" are the type of sweaty rockers one thought of first when Heart's name was mentioned, hard rock by no means dominates this album. In fact, much of *Little Queen* consists of such folk-influenced, acoustic-oriented fare as "Treat Me Well" and "Cry to Me." Anyone doubting just how much Heart's ballads have changed over the years need only play "Dream of the Archer" next to a high-volume power ballad like "Waiting for an Answer" from 1990's *Brigade*. —*Alex Henderson*

Magazine / Apr. 1978 / Cema Special Markets ✦✦
A collection of early demos and outtakes released when the group changed record labels, *Magazine* accentuates Heart's folkie roots, but that's not what makes the album such an unengaging listen. Instead, the album is mediocre because most of the material is underdeveloped and directionless. —*Stephen Thomas Erlewine*

Dog & Butterfly / Sep. 1978 / Portrait ✦✦✦
Using the age-old rock tradition of, in this case, rough and light, Heart continued to turn out top-selling albums as well as Top 40 hits. *Dog & Butterfly* includes the rough rockin' "Straight On" and the lighter title track. It appeared, at this time, that the Wilson sisters and Heart, in general, could do no wrong. —*James Chrispell*

Bebe Le Strange / Feb. 1980 / Epic ✦✦✦✦
Heart continued to pass their message over the airwaves with the release of *Bebe Le Strange* and spawned two smash hits, "Silver Wheels" and the rocking "Even It Up" in the process. Unfortunately, the rest of the disc was a bit of a letdown as Heart began to suffer from that same-old-same-old tradition, but they still sold like hotcakes. —*James Chrispell*

Heart Greatest Hits: Live / Nov. 1980 / Epic ✦✦✦✦✦
Released in 1980, just as Heart's first wave of popularity was fading, *Heart Greatest Hits: Live* contains a side of the group's most popularity songs—such as "Barracuda," "Crazy on You," and "Dreamboat Annie"—balanced by a side's worth of live tracks, including versions of "Magic Man," "Dog & Butterfly," and "Bebe Le Strange," plus a medley of the Beatles' "I'm Down/Long Tall Sally" and Zeppelin's "Rock & Roll." Though a straight greatest hits album would have been preferable, this is still a good overview, showcasing Heart's hooks and live power. Most casual fans should turn to one of their latter-day CD hits collections, but this does have most of their '70s hits, in one form or another, and it's worthwhile for that. —*Stephen Thomas Erlewine*

Private Audition / May 1982 / Epic ✦✦

Passionworks / Aug. 1983 / Epic ✦✦

Heart / Jun. 1985 / Capitol ✦✦✦✦✦
Heart was pretty much considered washed up when they released *Heart* in 1985. They learned a few important things while they had taken a short sabbatical—they knew that hooks were important and they knew they could play up their looks for MTV. So, they delivered both with *Heart*, giving their audience anthemic hooks and tightly corseted bosoms, leading to the most popular album they ever had. This doesn't mean it's the best, since its calculated mainstream bent may disarm some long-term fans, but it is true that they do this better than many of their peers, not just because they have good polished material from professional songwriters but because they can deliver this material professionally themselves. Yes, "These Dreams," "Never," and "What About Love" don't quite fit into the classic Heart mode, but they are good mid-'80s mainstream material, delivered as flawlessly as possible. There's still a lot of filler on this record, but the

best moments are among the best mainstream AOR of its era. — *Stephen Thomas Erlewine*

Bad Animals / May 1987 / Capitol ✦✦✦

Switching from Epic to Capitol with 1985's *Heart* proved to be a wise move for the Wilson sisters, who experienced a major resurgence in popularity and gained many new followers. Heart's arena rock sound had become even glossier, and the band was selling more albums than ever. But for all its production gloss (courtesy of Ron Nevison) and pop slickness, *Bad Animals* comes across as sincere rather than formulaic or cynical. From the rockers "You Ain't Too Tough" and "Easy Target" to the power ballads "Alone" and "Wait for an Answer," all of the songs are quite memorable. The folk elements and acoustic leanings that characterized many of Heart's early ballads were long gone, and the Wilson sisters keep the volume high but slow the tempo. — *Alex Henderson*

Brigade / Mar. 26, 1990 / Capitol ✦✦

Desire Walks On / Nov. 1993 / Capitol ✦✦✦

The Road Home / Nov. 1995 / Capitol ✦✦✦

On *The Road Home*, Heart re-records some of their biggest hits acoustically live in concert. It's interesting to hear these arena rock and AOR standards—including "Barracuda," "Crazy on You," "Dreamboat Annie," and "All I Wanna Do Is Make Love to You"—recast as intimate numbers; Heart manages to find new layers in all of these warhorses, partially due to the sublime production of John Paul Jones. The result is Heart's best album in years—the old material sounds more alive than anything they have written in a decade. — *Stephen Thomas Erlewine*

● **Greatest Hits** / Aug. 25, 1998 / Epic/Legacy ✦✦✦✦✦

Heart had a pair of greatest hits collections to their credit by 1997, but both did not contain all the renowned studio versions of their classic hits from the '70s (both 1980's *Greatest Hits/Live* on Epic and 1997's *Greatest Hits* on Capitol contained half studio and half live material). 1998's *Greatest Hits* on Epic/Legacy finally corrected this once and for all—collecting all of Heart's '70s studio hits on a single disc. Nearly all of the songs have become classic rock staples, the best known being the Zep-esque rockers "Crazy on You," "Barracuda," and "Magic Man," while the more subdued acoustic material ("Dreamboat Annie," "Love Alive," "Dog & Butterfly") showcases the immense talents of vocalist Ann Wilson. Other notables include "Kick It Out," "Heartless," "Bebe Le Strange," "Straight On," and "Even It Up," while an all-new studio cut recorded in 1998 ("Strong, Strong Wind") and a live cover of Led Zeppelin's "Rock & Roll" from 1980 are included as bonuses. While Heart may have enjoyed their biggest commercial success in the '80s with pop-oriented material, their more straight-ahead '70s work, showcased on *Greatest Hits*, has stood the test of time incredibly well. — *Greg Prato*

● **Greatest Hits: 1985-1995** / Jun. 27, 2000 / Capitol ✦✦✦✦

Heart had a second run on the charts in 1985 when they signed to Capitol Records and refashioned themselves as a mainstream pop/rock band, heavy on melodies and power ballads. The payoff came immediately, as they scored four Top Ten hits from *Heart*, their first record for the label: "What About Love?," "Never," "These Dreams," and "Nothin' At All." Heart kept up their hot streak for several more years, reaching the Top Ten three other times with the number one hit "Alone," "Who Will You Run To," and "All I Wanna Do Is Make Love to You." All of those songs are on *Greatest Hits: 1985-1995*, along with 11 other tracks, including the semi-rarities of the Ann Wilson and Robin Zander duet "Surrender to Me" and the "studio version" of "You're the Voice." It may run a little long for the more casual fans, but overall, this is an excellent overview of the era, perfect for fans that don't need the full-length studio albums. — *Stephen Thomas Erlewine*

The Heartbeats

f. 1955, Jamaica, NY, **db.** 1958

Doo Wop, R&B

Lead singer James "Shep" Sheppard co-wrote a series of velvety doo wop ballads for the Heartbeats during the mid-'50s; one entry, "A Thousand Miles Away," was a huge R&B seller in 1956. The Queens, NY, quintet began their string of street-corner classics with "Crazy for You" and "Darling How Long," culminating with "A Thousand Miles Away." The Heartbeats recorded for Hull, Rama, Roulette, Gee, and Guyden before packing it in. In 1961 the lead singer formed a new trio, Shep & the Limelites, and scored on the charts with a heartwarming sequel to his first hit, "Daddy's Home," for Hull. "Our Anniversary" also sold well for the trio the next year, but they broke up soon thereafter. Sheppard was found dead in his auto on the Long Island Expressway in 1970. — *Bill Dahl*

● **The Best of the Heartbeats** / Apr. 1990 / Rhino ✦✦✦✦✦

Here's a one-stop shopper that really rings the bell. This 20-track set not only brings all of the cool tracks by the Heartbeats together (their biggie was "A Thousand Miles Away"); it also ropes in the later hits by Shep & the Limelites, who followed the storyline in subsequent efforts like "Daddy's Home" and "Our Anniversary." The song selection is primo, the sound is stellar, and the notes from doo wop mavens Phil Groia and Donn Fileti are exhaustive and informative. Vocal group compilations don't get much better than this. — *Cub Koda*

Hearts & Flowers

f. 1965

Folk-Rock, Country-Rock

Of the many folk-rock groups in Southern California in the '60s, Hearts & Flowers was one of the relatively few that was closer to folk than rock. Founding guitarist Larry Murray was a member of the Scottsville Squirrel Barkers bluegrass group in the late '50s and early '60s; Chris Hillman and Bernie Leadon were also members of that group for a time.

Murray teamed up with David Dawson and Rick Cunha to form Hearts & Flowers, a self-described "Georgia country-folk meets Hawaiian ukelele folk-rock group," in the mid-'60s. They released a couple albums of country/folk-rock in the late '60s. — *Richie Unterberger*

Now Is the Time for Hearts and Flowers / 1967 / Capitol ✦✦✦✦✦

This debut album is an overlooked precursor to country-rock, echoing the late-'60s Byrds, Stone Poneys, Gene Clark, and most especially, as Brian Hogg points out in his lengthy liner notes, the Dillards. Earnest vocals and conscientious harmonies on this subdued, acoustic and countrified take on folk-rock, with mild Eastern/psychedelic dabs of autoharp. The songs mix original tunes with covers of Donovan, Tim Hardin, Hoyt Axton, Kaleidoscope, and Carole King. There's little to criticize, but it lacks the innovative spark that characterizes the best folk-rock of the time. — *Richie Unterberger*

Of Horses, Kids and Forgotten Women / 1968 / Capitol ✦✦✦✦✦

Future Flying Burrito Brother/Eagle Bernie Leadon replaced Rick Cunha for the group's second and final album, which is actually a considerably more L.A. pop-flavored production than their debut. Country-seasoned folk-rock remains at the core of the group's sound, but producer Nik Venet provides occasional tasteful, psychedelic-tinged orchestral arrangements. The material—about half original—is fairly strong, especially their covers of Arlo Guthrie's "Highway in the Wind" and Jesse Lee Kincaid's "She Sang Hymns Out of Tune" (also covered by Harry Nilsson on his first album). The unquestioned highlight is Larry Murray's "Ode to a Tin Angel"; by far the group's most psychedelic slice of folk-rock, with its swimming strings, tripped-out lyrics, and sweet harmonies, it's also their most atypical track. A slicker, but better, album than their first effort. — *Richie Unterberger*

● **Now Is the Time for Hearts and Flowers/Of Horses, Kids and Forgotten Women** / Oct. 1995 / Edsel ✦✦✦✦✦

Edsel does '60s collectors a favor by combining both of Hearts & Flowers' hard-to-find LPs onto one compact disc, which puts the group's entire repertoire in one place. — *Richie Unterberger*

Heaven 17

f. Oct. 1980, London, England, **db.** 1988

New Romantic, New Wave, Synth Pop

Taking their name from the Anthony Burgess novel *A Clockwork Orange*, the U.K. techno-pop trio Heaven 17 grew out of the experimental dance project the British Electric Foundation, itself an offshoot of the electro-pop outfit Human League. The core of Heaven 17 was comprised of Martyn Ware and Ian Craig Marsh, a pair of onetime computer operators who first teamed in 1977 as the Dead Daughters, which integrated synthesizer patterns with a heavy reliance on tape loops. Soon, Ware and Marsh were joined by Philip Oakey and Adi Newton and changed their name to the Human League, where they remained before exiting together in 1980.

As a means of establishing the synthesizer as an expressive, human instrument, Marsh and Ware formed the British Electric Foundation, a production project which employed a variety of musicians and singers including Tina Turner, Sandie Shaw, and Gary Glitter. The B.E.F.'s debut, 1980's *Music of Quality and Distinction, Vol. 1*, also included vocalist Glenn Gregory, a former photographer whom Ware and Marsh met at a Sheffield drama center; in 1981, the duo enlisted Gregory for Heaven 17, the first and most successful B.E.F. alter ego, and debuted with the single "(We Don't Need This) Fascist Groove Thang," a minor hit banned by the BBC over its title. An album, *Penthouse and Pavement*, followed the same year.

By the release of 1983's *The Luxury Gap*, the B.E.F. had fallen by the wayside, and Heaven 17 had become Ware and Marsh's primary focus; the LP proved highly successful, spawning the hit singles "Temptation," "Come Live With Me," "Crushed by the Wheels of Industry," and "Let Me Go." The follow-up, *How Men Are*, was another British hit, but the group receded from view after its release; when they returned in 1986 with the album *Pleasure One*, it was with a number of guest musicians and vocalists.

After the commerical failure of 1988's *Teddy Bear, Duke & Psycho*, Heaven 17 officially disbanded; Ware focused on production chores and worked on Terence Trent D'Arby's debut *Introducing the Hardline According to Terence Trent D'Arby*. In 1990, he and Marsh resurrected the B.E.F. aegis, releasing *Music of Quality and Distinction, Vol. 2* the following year. In 1996, a reformed Heaven 17 returned with *Bigger Than America*. — *Jason Ankeny*

● **The Best of Heaven 17: Higher & Higher** / Aug. 24, 1993 / Virgin ✦✦✦✦✦

The Best of Heaven 17: Higher & Higher is an extensive, 17-track collection that contains all of the group's best moments, including "Temptation" and "(We Don't Need This) Fascist Groove Thang," plus several album tracks, lesser-known singles, and remixes of their two greatest hits. It's too much music for casual fans, especially since the sequencing is slightly illogical, and it's not comprehensive enough for dedicated collectors, but *Higher & Higher* remains an adequate overview of the synth-pop band's career. — *Stephen Thomas Erlewine*

Heavy D & The Boyz

f. 1986, Mt. Vernon, NY

Pop-Rap, Club/Dance, Urban, Hip-Hop

Jamaican-born Heavy D (b. Dwight Myers) sports a 260-pound frame but can move and dance with agility and verve. He wisely chose sensitivity, rather than obesity or verbosity, as his framework, and many of his lyrics emphasize his search for a mate of similar qualities. He's also done good cover songs and penned cultural awareness tunes and tributes to black women. Heavy D has managed perhaps the ultimate balancing act. He's remained a positive figure with close ties to his mother and is arguably the most admired male rap figure among African-American feminists. At the same time he's been willing to take chances musically, never embracing hardcore gangsta rap, but yet able to include snatches of pop, R&B, reggae, and funk into his music without being assaulted with cries of sellout. —*Ron Wynn*

● **Heavy Hitz** / Sep. 12, 2000 / MCA ✦✦✦✦✦
Heavy Hitz is a near-definitive overview of Heavy D & the Boyz' pop-friendly dance-rap style, featuring not only the group's two big hits—"We Got Our Own Thang" and the Top Ten "Now That We Found Love"—but 13 more of their best tracks as well. And that's not as excessive as it might sound to casual observers; Heavy D had not only a good-natured persona and sense of humor, but also a deceptively nimble delivery on the mic, which helps enliven these already infectious party tunes. Heavy D also had a socially conscious side, recording the occasional ode to harmony between genders and races, but that isn't explored very much here; nonetheless, *Heavy Hitz* will likely be perfectly satisfactory for most listeners. —*Steve Huey*

Helium

f. 1992, Boston, MA
Noise Pop, Indie Rock, Alternative Pop/Rock
Helium is essentially the project of Mary Timony, formerly of the girl punk band Autoclave. Helium formed in 1992 with Brian Dunton on bass and Shawn King Devlin and started releasing 7"s like 1993's *The American Jean*. 1994 saw the band release the *Pirate Prude* EP, an interesting but somewhat inaccessible exercise in mixing radical feminism with punk rock. *The Dirt of Luck*, released in 1995, was an improvement and embellishment of the sound laid forth in *Pirate Prude*: Heavy, sluggish guitars, spooky keyboards, and Timony's breathy alto laid over an understated rhythm section. That year, Polvo's Ash Bowie also joined the lineup, replacing Dunton on bass. In 1997, the group returned with the *No Guitars* EP. Helium is a challenging listen but also a rewarding one. —*Heather Phares*

Pirate Prude / Apr. 5, 1994 / Matador ✦✦✦
The group's debut EP is an uncompromising introduction to Mary Timony's mix of radical feminism and warped pop sensibilities. Songs like "XXX," "OOO," and "Baby Vampire Made Me" are alluring and vicious, made all the more startling by their sonically droning and lyrically violent contrasts. Timony murmurs sentiments like "your love is a fad/and you're a drag" and "you're gonna pay me with your life" in a schoolgirlish alto, adding to the intriguing contradictions in her work. Though it requires some concentrated listening, *Pirate Prude* ultimately rewards its listeners. —*Heather Phares*

● **The Dirt of Luck** / Apr. 1995 / Matador ✦✦✦✦✦
Helium's first full-length album expands on Timony's feminist lyrical bent and adds more colors to the band's musical palette. Full of what Timony calls "cartoon and monster movie music" *The Dirt of Luck* is a tight, focused album that is also diverse. The sludgy "Pat's Trick" mingles with the sweet-sounding and sweetly named "Honeycomb," which shares space with the nasty-sultry sounds of "Medusa" and the shimmery drone-pop of "Baby's Going Underground." It's tied together by the album's spacious sound and Timony's singing, which is fuller and richer than on the group's debut. —*Heather Phares*

Magic City / Sep. 9, 1997 / Matador ✦✦✦✦✦
The *No Guitars* EP suggested that Helium was expanding their sound past the wonderful, angular indie-rock of *The Dirt of Luck*, and *The Magic City* confirms that suspicion. A rich, colorful array of sounds, *The Magic City* blends lo-fi indie-rock with '70s prog rock. Mary Timony is a sharp songwriter, and she balances her instrumental excesses with remarkable introspective lyrics. Surprisingly, the sitars, keyboards, and harpsichords are not indulgences—they're integral to the sound of the record, making *The Magic City* sound alternately fantastical and frightening. It's an impressive leap forward, confirming Helium's status as one of the '90s' best indie-rock bands. —*Stephen Thomas Erlewine*

Richard Hell (Richard Myers)

b. Oct. 2, 1949, Lexington, KY
Vocals, Bass / American Punk, New York Punk, Proto-Punk, Punk
Some people will tell you Richard Hell was the main catalyst behind the birth of New York punk and its sensibilities. That's hardly true, but he's been around forever and did influence a number of budding punks (the Sex Pistols among them). In 1971 Hell and former high school buddy Tom Verlaine formed a group called the Neon Boys, who later became Television; he also cofounded the Heartbreakers with ex-New York Doll Johnny Thunders. In 1976 Hell formed the Voidoids, a caustic congregation that included guitarists Ivan Julian and Robert Quine and soon-to-be Ramones drummer Marc Bell. Hell's apocalyptic lyrics were steeped in alienated poetry, and his anguished howl of a voice set the pattern for scores of Bowery rockers. —*John Floyd*

● **Blank Generation** / 1977 / Sire ✦✦✦✦✦
When punk rock first began to emerge in New York City, Richard Hell was one of the first men on the scene as an early member of both Television and the Heartbreakers (he left both groups before they could record), but his own version of punk wasn't much like anyone else's. While Hell's debut album, *Blank Generation*, remains one of the most powerful to come from punk's first wave, anyone expecting a Ramones/Dead Boys-style frontal assault from this set had better readjust their expectations. "Love Comes in Spurts" and "Liar's Beware" proved The Voidoids could play fast and loud when they wanted to, but for the most part this group's formula was much more complicated than that; guitarists Robert Quine and Ivan Julian bounced sharp, edgy patterns off each other that were more about psychological tension than brute force (though Quine's solos suggest a fragile grace beneath the surface of their neo-Beefheart chaos), and while most punk nihilism was of

the simplistic "Everything Sucks" variety, Hell was (with the exception of Patti Smith) the most literate and consciously poetic figure in the New York punk scene. While there's little on the album that's friendly or life-affirming, there's a crackling intelligence to songs like "New Pleasure," "Betrayal Takes Two," and "Another World" that confirmed Hell has a truly unique lyrical voice, at once supremely self-confident and dismissive of nearly everything around him (sometimes including himself). Brittle and troubling, but brimming with ideas and musical intelligence, *Blank Generation* was ground-breaking punk rock that followed no one's template, and today it sounds just as fresh—and nearly as abrasive—as it did when it first hit the racks. —*Mark Deming*

Destiny Street / 1982 / Razor & Tie ✦✦✦✦
No one ever accused Richard Hell of being the hardest working man in rock & roll, and not only did it take him five years to get around to making a follow-up to his first album, the remarkable *Blank Generation*, but he didn't even bother to come up with a full LP's worth of new material for 1982's *Destiny Street*; the opening song, "The Kid With the Replaceable Head," first appeared as a B-side to a single in 1979, and three of the album's ten tunes are covers, which hardly speaks well of his productivity. But if it's hard to imagine why it took five years to come up with *Destiny Street*, there's little arguing that Hell's second album is nearly as strong as his first. While the covers might seem like padding, the interpretations of the Kinks' "You Gotta Move" and Them's "I Can Only Give You Everything" are wildly passionate and overflowing with ideas and energy, and Hell's dour, jagged take on Dylan's "Going Going Gone" nearly surpasses the original. Robert Quine's guitar work on *Blank Generation* staked his claim as one of the most interesting and intelligent guitarists to emerge from the New York underground scene, and if anything he was in even stronger form on *Destiny Street*, while new members Naux (on guitar) and Fred Maher (on drums) give him all the support he needs. And though *Blank Generation* made it clear Hell was among the brainiest members of punk's first graduating class, the handful of new originals here showed he'd actually grown since his debut. *Destiny Street* sounds looser and more spontaneous than Hell's debut, but it's just as smart and every bit as powerful, and it's a more than worthy follow-up. —*Mark Deming*

R.I.P.: The ROIR Sessions / 1984 / ROIR ✦✦✦✦✦
The Richard Hell compilation *R.I.P., ROIR Sessions* was originally released in 1984 as a cassette-only release, and has finally been re-released on CD (different cover, same track listing). *R.I.P.* collects a total of 14 tracks (most studio, some live), and serves as a solid anthology/greatest hits compilation. The selections span his career from 1975-1984, from one of his first bands (the legendary Heartbreakers with Johnny Thunders) up until a later incarnation of the Voidoids. The sound quality is consistent for the most part, and the music is rough, raw, and rocking…in other words, classic Richard Hell. An early version of "Love Comes in Spurts" kicks off the album, and with a Heartbreakers' backup, is proof that Hell would have made a more-than-capable leader of the band (Thunders eventually gained control, effectively ending the original lineup). Also included is the depressed ballad "Betrayal Takes Two," the N.Y. new wave of "I'm Your Man," as well as the saxophone-laced "The Hunter Was Drowned." The only criticism of *R.I.P.* is the omission of one of Hell's best-known tunes, "Blank Generation," but otherwise it's highly recommended. —*Greg Prato*

Helmet

f. 1989, New York, NY
Alternative Metal, Heavy Metal, Alternative Pop/Rock
Like many influential bands, Helmet was born out of an unusual set of influences. Oregon-born guitarist and founder Page Hamilton had actually moved to New York City to study jazz, but found inspiration in the late '80s through post-punk acts Sonic Youth, Killing Joke, and Big Black, and envisioned a group that combined then-unusual tunings (particularly dropped-D) with uneven and jazz-like time signatures and harmonies. The result was Helmet, the East Coast's answer to Seattle's then-underground sensation Soundgarden. Hamilton recruited bassist Henry Bogdan from Oregon, along with Australian guitarist Peter Mengede and Florida drummer John Stanier for the group's first incarnation. Helmet's independent-label debut EP, *Strap It On*, showcased the group's raw power—both instrumentally and in Hamilton's growling vocals. Signed to the Interscope label soon thereafter, the same lineup released its breakthrough 1992 CD, *Meantime*. MTV aired three videos by Helmet, then the only band close to the Seattle grunge sound on the East Coast, in "Give It," "In the Meantime," and the distorted, stop-and-start showcase "Unsung." Replacing Mengede with guitarist Rob Echeverria on 1994's *Betty*, Hamilton crafted an album even more versatile—and at times even heavier—than *Meantime*. Yet *Betty* proved to be a critical success but a commercial failure, its versatility relegating it to the cut-out bins. Echeverria left Helmet in the mid-'90s to join Biohazard, and the band bought time to refocus by releasing the *Born Annoying* collection of B-sides in 1995. Hamilton played all the guitar parts for Helmet's swan song, the 1997 CD *Aftertaste*—but his vocals sounded like his heart just wasn't in a group in which he couldn't keep a rhythm guitarist, and *Aftertaste* proved a disappointment. After touring with Orange 9mm's Chris Traynor on guitar and after much deliberation, Helmet disbanded in 1999. —*Bill Meredith*

Strap It On / Nov. 1991 / Interscope ✦✦✦
Helmet's debut isn't as accomplished or powerful as *Meantime*, but it still provides enough gut-busting crunch to satisfy their fans. —*AMG*

● **Meantime** / Jun. 1992 / Interscope ✦✦✦✦✦
In 1991, Interscope won a ferocious multi-label bidding war (which according to first-hand accounts, pitted an estimated 18 to 22 different labels against each other) and signed Helmet for a reported cool one million-plus dollars. Under the watchful eye of the record biz, and on the heels of Nirvana's huge commercial breakthrough, Helmet were curiously

touted as the next big thing. Unsurprisingly, expectations would never be fully realized. Arguably one of the most influential and overlooked rock records of the '90s, *Meantime* not only threw the rulebook out the window, it rewrote it, redefined it, and shook it to its core. Led by the classically trained Page Hamilton, Helmet's bludgeoning riffs combined with their noise-like, stop-go-stop-go minimalist attack unknowingly changed the face of aggro-rock as we know it. Its importance cannot be overstated. Relistening to *Meantime* today it's easy to understand why. From the Steve Albini-produced title track through "Role Model," the band is relentless. On "Give It," Hamilton spews "killing hurts/has to be done/peace and love/who's number one," and later "the right to give/learn to bleed/it's free/pain is outside/lift it up to see." As the hypnotic riff and John Stanier's piccolo snare echo throughout, the band thrashes through the song like a ten-ton hammer. Again, every song is colored by Teutonic riffs with only "Unsung" hinting at a gasp of commercial accessibility. At the end of the day, try to think of one successful aggro-rock band around today that isn't indebted to the N.Y. quartet—you won't find one. *Meantime's* influence is alive and well and lives on today in the music of the Deftones, Static X, Korn, Sepultura, and especially Pantera. *—John Franck*

Betty / Jun. 1994 / Interscope ✦✦✦

With the corporate rock cognoscenti frothing at the mouth to sign the next Nirvana, in 1991 a seemingly "nerdy" band from New York by the name of Helmet was about to set the world on fire—at least on paper. Seemingly overnight, the Amphetamine Reptile faves had a fat check in their pockets and an astounding major-label debut by the name of *Meantime.* Eschewing Cobain's neo-punk/power pop instincts, Helmet opted instead for a more a minimalist approach, whereby rhythmic tension over 4/4 melodies reigned supreme. Now poised to step into their role as future darlings of a sound that can only be described as bludgeoning aggro-punk-atonal-rock, the band was propelled by a massive hype campaign and heralded as East Coast tastemakers du jour. But for all its accolades (mostly well deserved), *Meantime's* commercial success sadly fell short of expectations and by 1994 Helmet was giving it another try with *Betty*—its second effort for Interscope. Label pressure notwithstanding, *Betty* had a lot more riding on it than even perhaps Hamilton was willing to admit. Lacking some of the tightly focused ferocity of *Meantime, Betty* appears to be an almost too well-thought-out affair and, ultimately, its songs miss out on some of the discreet melodic accents that had served to underpin even the most bludgeoning noise-fests on *Meantime.* Songs like "Wilma's Rainbow," "Biscuits for Smut," and especially "Milquetoast" have their moments, but don't quite live up to expectations. And although Helmet's tuned down, stop-go-stop dynamic (originally pioneered by New Yorkers Prong) would go on to influence hundreds of up-and-coming acts, their complete lack of image or star quality (a key ingredient to Cobain's magnetism, as much as he himself despised it) would play a major role in eventually doing them in. *Betty* initiated a commercial spiral for the quartet that not even the return to form and progress displayed by 1997's massive sounding *Aftertaste* could reverse. *—John Franck & Ed Rivadavia*

Aftertaste / Mar. 18, 1997 / Epitaph ✦✦

Help Yourself

Pub Rock, Folk-Rock, Country-Rock

Help Yourself was formed in the London area of England in 1970 initially as a backup band for Malcolm Morley. The band consisted of Richard Treece (guitars/vocals/harmonica), Dave Charles (drums/percussion/vocals), Ken Whaley (bass), and, of course, Malcolm Morley (guitars/keyboards/vocals). Help Yourself recorded their debut album self-titled album in early 1971. The songs on that album were completely written by Morley. Whaley left the band after the debut to be replaced by Ernie Graham (guitars), who had just released his solo album on Liberty. Help Yourself was experiencing some financial difficulties at this time, as were a number of other bands in England, so they teamed up with bandmembers from Brinsley Schwarz and moved into a rented house in Headley in 1971/1972 called the Grange, where Led Zeppelin had recorded *Led Zeppelin IV* earlier that year. While at the Grange, the band recorded their second album, *Strange Affair,* released in early 1972, with the addition of Graham and Jonathan (Jojo) Glemser to the band. Graham and Glesmer left during the recording of *Strange Affair* and were replaced by Paul Burton for the completion of the album. The lineup of Burton, Morley, Treece, and Charles recorded another album almost immediately, called *Beware of the Shadow,* which was released at the end of 1972. None of the first three albums were big sellers. The Helps, as they were called by fans, appealed to a hippie audience and found moderate success in the U.S., where they appealed to Deadheads and fans of such bands as Quicksilver. In 1973, Whaley returned to the band and the Helps recorded an album that was appropriately called *The Return of Ken Whaley.* Shortly after this release, Help Yourself broke up. *—Keith Pettipas*

Return of Ken Whaley/Happy Days / 1973 / United Artists ✦✦✦✦

BGO's two-fer of *Return of Ken Whaley* and *Happy Days* reissues Help Yourself's second and fourth albums. This provides somewhat incongruous listening, but Help Yourself was an incongruous band, never quite making sense all the way through their albums, even if they were always fascinating. They skipped through folk-rock, both American and British, country, pub rock, prog rock, blues, and general oddities. Often, it gelled brilliantly, but it also could be maddening, but that was one of the pleasures of listening to the band. To really understand this two-fer, you will also need the other Help Yourself two-fer that BGO put out, but once you acquire a taste for this, you won't need too much convincing to seek either of these out. *—Stephen Thomas Erlewine*

● **Strange Affair/The Return of Ken Whaley Plus Happy Days** / Aug. 25, 1999 / BGO ✦✦✦✦✦

This reissue on the British-based BGO label contains the band's second (*Strange Affair*) and fourth (*The Return of Ken Whaley*) albums along with the bonus LP *Happy Days,* which was included free with the *Ken Whaley* album. The LPs were originally released on the United Artists/Liberty Records label in 1972 and 1973, respectively. Help Yourself remained on the second tier of British bands and was never able to break out commercially. On this set, the band blends its hippie pastoral sounds with a West Coast-styled psychedelia that will appeal to fans of such acts as the Grateful Dead, Quicksilver Messenger Service, or even Phish. While the band did achieve some degree of success in the early '70s and developed a large fan base, it broke up after *The Return of Ken Whaley.* The 15 songs on this two-CD set include some beautiful Crosby, Stills & Nash-styled harmonies together with stunning jams and melodic acoustic tunes with a rural feel. The albums have been remastered from original master tapes and the package contains an in-depth essay on the history of the band, along with photos and reproductions of the original album graphics. A companion piece to a reissue of the band's first and third albums by the same label, this is a superb package that highlights a relatively unknown British band with an American sound. *—Keith Pettipas*

Jimi Hendrix

b. Nov. 27, 1942, Seattle, WA, **d.** Sep. 18, 1970, London, England

Vocals, Leader, Guitar (Electric), Songwriter, Guitar / Album Rock, Acid Rock, Psychedelic, Hard Rock, Blues-Rock

In his brief four-year reign as a superstar, Jimi Hendrix expanded the vocabulary of the electric rock guitar more than anyone before or since. Hendrix was a master at coaxing all manner of unforeseen sonics from his instrument, often with innovative amplification experiments that produced astral-quality feedback and roaring distortion. His frequent hurricane blasts of noise and dazzling showmanship—he could and would play behind his back and with his teeth and set his guitar on fire—has sometimes obscured his considerable gifts as a songwriter, singer, and master of a gamut of blues, R&B, and rock styles. *Are You Experienced?* was an astonishing debut, particularly from a young R&B veteran who had rarely sung, and apparently never written his own material before the Experience formed. What caught most people's attention at first was his virtuosic guitar playing, which employed an arsenal of devices, including wah-wah pedals, buzzing feedback solos, crunching distorted riffs, and lightning, liquid runs up and down the scales. But Hendrix was also a first-rate songwriter, melding cosmic imagery with some surprisingly pop-savvy hooks and tender sentiments. He was also an excellent blues interpreter and passionate, engaging singer (although his gruff, throaty vocal pipes were not nearly as great assets as his instrumental skills). *Are You Experienced?* was psychedelia at its most eclectic, synthesizing mod pop, soul, R&B, Dylan, and the electric guitar innovations of British pioneers like Jeff Beck, Pete Townshend, and Eric Clapton. Amazingly, Hendrix would only record three fully conceived studio albums in his lifetime. *Axis: Bold as Love* and the double-LP *Electric Ladyland* were more diffuse and experimental than *Are You Experienced?* On *Electric Ladyland* in particular, Hendrix pioneered the use of the studio itself as a recording instrument, manipulating electronics and devising overdub techniques to plot uncharted sonic territory. *—Richie Unterberger*

★ **Are You Experienced?** / 1967 / MCA ✦✦✦✦✦

One of the most stunning debuts in rock history, and one of the definitive albums of the psychedelic era. On *Are You Experienced?* Hendrix synthesized various elements of the cutting edge of 1967 rock into music that sounded both futuristic and rooted in the best traditions of rock, blues, pop, and soul. It was his mind-boggling guitar work, of course, that got most of the ink, building upon the experiments of British innovators like Jeff Beck and Pete Townshend to chart new sonic territories in feedback, distortion, and sheer volume. It wouldn't have meant much, however, without his excellent material, whether psychedelic frenzy ("Foxy Lady," "Manic Depression," "Purple Haze"), instrumental freak-out jams ("Third Stone From the Sun"), blues ("Red House," "Hey Joe"), or tender, poetic compositions ("The Wind Cries Mary") that demonstrated the breadth of his songwriting talents. Not to be underestimated were the contributions of drummer Mitch Mitchell and bassist Noel Redding, who gave the music a rhythmic pulse that fused parts of rock and improvised jazz. Many of these songs are among Hendrix's very finest; it may be true that he would continue to develop at a rapid pace throughout the rest of his brief career, but he would never surpass his first album in terms of consistently high quality. The British and American versions of the album differed substantially when they were initially released in 1967; MCA's 17-song CD reissue does everyone a favor by gathering all of the material from the two records in one place, adding a few B-sides from early singles as well. *—Richie Unterberger*

☆ **Axis: Bold as Love** / 1967 / MCA ✦✦✦✦✦

When the Experience recorded their second album, they were in the process of solidfying their international stardom. That meant access to more studio time and more sophisicated technology, but not, alas, a great deal of time to write the material. That may be why *Axis* isn't quite as much of a tour de force as *Are You Experienced?,* but it's nevertheless another major effort, showing Hendrix continuing to grow, particularly in his increasing mastery of the studio and more sophisticated lyrics. Soul and R&B influences are more prominent here than on his debut, though psychedelic experimentalism ran rampant (to great effect) on "If 6 Was 9," "Spanish Castle Magic," "Up From the Skies," "You Got Me Floatin'," and "Castles Made of Sand" all had funky grooves that gave the spiraling guitars and crunchy rhythm section a much-needed buoyancy. The best song, though, might have been the mellowest: "Little Wing" was Hendrix at his most delicate, and perhaps his most personal. *—Richie Unterberger*

☆ **Electric Ladyland** / Oct. 1968 / MCA ✦✦✦✦✦

With *Electric Ladyland,* Hendrix took psychedelic experimentation as far as he could within the original Experience trio format. That meant pushing the barriers of late-'60s studio technology as far as they could bend, particularly with regard to multi-tracking and effects that could only be achieved through certain treatments and manipulation of the tape itself. It also meant greater freedom and looseness in the playing and the songwriting, which could be both a plus and a drawback, as the compositions became both less constricted and less concise. Not all of the material here is top-of-the-line, but certainly much of this is Hendrix at his best: the dreamy wah-wah guitars of "Rainy Day, Dream Away" were only matched by the dreaminess of the lyrics, and "Have You Ever Been (To Electric Ladyland)" and "Gypsy Eyes" were also standouts. "1983... (A Merman I Should Turn to Be)" and "Voodoo Chile" were lengthy cuts dominated by jam-like instrumental passages; "Crosstown Traffic" and a cover of Dylan's "All Along the Watchtower," by contrast, were two of his catchiest and most pop-friendly tunes. "Voodoo Chile," "Voodoo Child (Slight Return)," and a cover of Earl King's "Come On" are three of his most determined forays into the blues, albeit the blues as fed through a nearly avant-garde filter. Originally released as a double album, the CD reissue fits the entire recording onto one 75-minute disc. *—Richie Unterberger*

Smash Hits / Jul. 1969 / Reprise ✦✦✦✦✦
One of the first hits compilations assembled of Hendrix's catalog, *Smash Hits* remains one of the best, since it keeps its focus narrow and never tries to extend its reach. Basically, this album contains the songs everybody knows from Hendrix, drawing heavily from *Are You Experienced?*, plus adding the non-LP "Red House," "51st Anniversary," and "Highway Chile." Those non-LP selections may still make this worth seeking out, even if they've appeared on subsequent hits collections, but the main strength of *Smash Hits* is that it contains the best-known, big-name songs in one place. Maybe not enough to make the collection essential, but still enough to make it a representative, accurate, sampler. *—Stephen Thomas Erlewine*

Band of Gypsys / 1970 / Capitol ✦✦✦✦✦
Band of Gypsys was the only live recording authorized by Jimi Hendrix before his death. It was recorded and released in order to get Hendrix out from under a contractual obligation that had been hanging over his head for a couple years. Helping him out were longtime friends Billy Cox on bass and Buddy Miles on the drums because the Experience had broken up in June of 1969, following a show in Denver.

These new surroundings pushed Hendrix to new creative heights. Along with this new rhythm section, Hendrix took these shows as an opportunity to showcase much of the new material he had been working on. The music was a seamless melding of rock, funk, and R&B, and tunes like "Message to Love" and "Power to Love" showed a new lyrical direction as well. His absolute mastery of his guitar and effects is even more amazing considering that this was the first time he used the Fuzz Face, wah-wah pedal, Univibe, *and* Octavia pedals on stage together. The guitar tones he gets on "Who Knows" and "Power to Love" are powerful and intense, but nowhere is his absolute control more evident than on "Machine Gun," where Hendrix conjures bombs, guns, and other sounds of war from his guitar, all within the context of a coherent musical statement. Two Buddy Miles compositions are also included, but the show belongs to Jimi all the way. *Band of Gypsys* is not only an important part of the Hendrix legacy, but one of the greatest live albums ever. *—Sean Westergaard*

The Cry of Love / 1971 / Reprise ✦✦✦✦
This was the first of the posthumous releases in the Hendrix catalog and probably the best from the Alan Douglas years, as it collected most of the studio tracks that were either completed or very near completion before Hendrix died. Some of these tunes, like "Angel" and "Ezy Rider," have become well-known pieces in the Hendrix canon, but they sit alongside lesser-known gems like "Night Bird Flying" and the Dylanesque "My Friend." *Cry of Love* as an album has been rendered as a footnote, since the Hendrix estate has recompiled, to Hendrix' specifications, *First Rays of the New Rising Sun.* This (originally) double-album set contains not only the entire *Cry of Love* LP, but the best studio tracks from *Rainbow Bridge*, *War Heroes*, and *Crash Landing*, presented in drastically improved sound. *—Sean Westergaard*

Live at Winterland / 1987 / Rykodisc ✦✦✦✦✦
Jimi Hendrix's sonic assaults and attacks hypnotized, frightened, and amazed audiences in the late '60s. His studio recordings helped him attain his reputation, but his live works validated it. That's the case on the 13 songs from a 1968 Winterland concert that made their way onto CD in 1987. Whether he was doing short, biting songs like "Fire" or stretching out for sprawling blues statements like "Red House" and "Killing Floor," Jimi Hendrix turned the guitar into a battering ram, forcing everyone to notice and making every solo and note a memorable one. *—Ron Wynn*

Radio One / 1989 / Rykodisc ✦✦✦✦✦
Seventeen songs from 1967 BBC broadcasts, when the Experience had yet to burn out from the wheel of constant touring, management hassles, and internal strife. They're in good, enthusiastic form as they run through early gems like "Hey Joe," "Foxy Lady," "Fire," and "Stone Free," the lack of studio polish giving these versions a loose feel. The Experience studio albums are still considerably superior to this set, but it's certainly worth acquiring by any serious Hendrix fan, not least because it has several covers that didn't make it onto the three proper Experience LPs. Several of these ("Hoochie Koochie Man," "Killing Floor," "Catfish Blues") reveal his sometimes overlooked affinity for Chicago-style electric blues; there are also a couple of surprises ("Hound Dog" and "Day Tripper"). With good sound, it's a solid addition to the Hendrix library, demonsrating his versatility in various rock, soul, and blues styles. *—Richie Unterberger*

Blues / Apr. 26, 1994 / MCA ✦✦✦✦
While Hendrix remains most famous for his hard rock and psychedelic innovations, more than a third of his recordings were blues-oriented. This CD contains 1 blues originals and covers, eight of which were previously unreleased. Recorded between 1966 and 1970, they feature the master guitarist stretching the boundaries of electric blues in both live and studio settings. Besides several Hendrix blues-based originals, it includes covers of Albert King and Muddy Waters classics, as well as a 1967 acoustic version of his composition "Hear My Train A-Comin'." *—Richie Unterberger*

First Rays of the New Rising Sun / Apr. 22, 1997 / MCA ✦✦✦✦
Because Hendrix's death in September 1970 occurred before his work on these tunes was completed, the questions still abound as to what Hendrix's ultimate vision for this double album would have been. Minus the worthless—though well-intentioned—overdubs and remix manipulation that occurred when this material was issued piecemeal over the years on *The Cry of Love*, *War Heroes*, *Rainbow Bridge*, and the disappointing *Voodoo Soup*, this collection finally gets listeners back to the master tapes residing in the *Electric Ladyland* vaults. This gets the listener as close to what Hendrix had in mind as possible, (as subject to change as these versions obviously were), and also places the tunes in their original context as an album. Because this collection utilizes mixes that Hendrix and engineer Eddie Kramer were working on at the time, the tracks perhaps lack the sonic wallop of the first three Experience albums but have much more to offer than the stripped-away and re-dubbed versions that have been on the market. If one views *First Rays of the New Rising Sun* as an almost-completed work in progress, then it becomes obvious that Hendrix was heading into a new direction and sound, one rife with funk and rhythm & blues as a bedrock foundation. The psychedelic workouts got more jamlike and experimental, and the ballads got prettier and even more dreamlike in their background soundscapes. What he would have eventually come up with and released as his next musical statement is anyone's guess, but this gets you as close to that answer—and that vision—as you're ever likely to get. *—Cub Koda*

South Saturn Delta / Oct. 7, 1997 / MCA ✦✦✦
Shortly after the Hendrix family reacquired the rights to Jimi's catalog, they signed a long-term deal with MCA Records and pulled many of the compilations of unreleased material and rarities off the shelves, with the intent of re-releasing the material in better collections. *First Rays of the New Rising Sun*, an attempt at assembling Hendrix's uncompleted last album, was the first release from Experience Hendrix, and it was followed months later by *South Saturn Delta*, a collection of rarities—all but one of the 15 tracks were never officially released in the U.S.—that spans his entire career. Its intent is to capture the full range of Hendrix's music through an alternate history, and it works pretty well. Among the highlights are tracks from the *War Heroes* and *Rainbow Bridge* albums ("Look Over Yonder," "Tax Free," "Midnight," "Pali Gap," "Bleeding Heart"), "Sweet Angel" (an early version of "Angel"), an instrumental "Little Wing," a solo take on "Midnight Lightning," and a studio version of "Message to the Universe (Message to Love)." There are also alternate mixes of "All Along the Watchtower," "Power of Soul," "Drifter's Escape," "South Saturn Delta," and "The Stars That Play with Laughing Sam's Dice." It's an intelligently sequenced, listenable collection of some of the very best outtakes and rarities from Hendrix, and is another sign that Experience Hendrix's restoration of Jimi's catalog will be smart, stylish, and logical. *—Stephen Thomas Erlewine*

BBC Sessions / Jun. 2, 1998 / MCA ✦✦✦✦
These are the recordings that Jimi Hendrix made for BBC radio in the late 1960s. As such, they're loose, informal, and off-the-top-of-his-head improvisational fun. These versions of the hits "Foxy Lady," "Fire," two versions of "Purple Haze," and "Hey Joe" stay surprisingly close to the studio versions, but the tone of Hendrix's guitar on these is positively blistering and worth the price of admission alone. There's also a lot of blues on this two-disc collection, and Hendrix's versions of "Hoochie Coochie Man" (with Alexis Korner on slide guitar), "Catfish Blues," "Killing Floor," and "Hear My Train A-Comin'" find him in excellent form. But perhaps the best example of how loosely conceived these sessions were are the oddball covers that Hendrix tackles, including Stevie Wonder's "I Was Made to Love Her" (featuring Wonder on drums), Dylan's "Can You Please Crawl Out Your Window?," the Beatles' "Day Tripper" and, in recognition of his immediate competition, Cream's "Sunshine of Your Love." No lo-fi bootleg tapes here (everything's from the original masters and gone over by Eddie Kramer), the music and sound are class-A all the way, making a worthwhile addition to anyone's Hendrix collection. *—Cub Koda*

● **Experience Hendrix: The Best of Jimi Hendrix** / Nov. 3, 1998 / MCA ✦✦✦✦✦
Experience Hendrix: The Best of Jimi Hendrix is a terrific 20-track collection that features all of Hendrix's most essential material, from "Purple Haze" and "Hey Joe" to "All Along the Watchtower" and "Star Spangled Banner." There are a few fine moments missing, but everything a casual fan needs is here, making it a great introduction to the groundbreaking guitarist. *—Stephen Thomas Erlewine*

Live at the Fillmore East / Feb. 23, 1999 / MCA ✦✦✦✦
A series of performances from the *Band of Gypsys* concerts finally gets the deluxe treatment from MCA and Experience Hendrix, as tapes from both first and second shows are brought together, correctly identified (1986's *Band of Gypsys 2* actually featured three tracks that weren't by the band at all) in one deluxe two-disc set. This newly expanded edition contains the only live versions of "Earth Blues," "Auld Lang Syne," "Stepping Stone," and "Burning Desire"; Hendrix tunes specifically worked up for the performance that rarely surfaced again like "Izabella," "Power of Soul," and "Who Knows"; newly remastered versions of "Stop" and "Hear My Train A-Comin'" (both originally presented on *Band of Gypsys 2* in horrendous sound) and classic performances of "Stone Free," "Changes," "Voodoo Child (Slight Return)," and "Wild Thing." Equally as revelatory is one of the two alternate versions included of "Machine Gun," every bit as stunning as the better-known version. Though this new edition hardly makes all previous incarnations obsolete, it presents the man at his most challenged and brilliant. *—Cub Koda*

Live at Woodstock / Jul. 6, 1999 / MCA ✦✦✦
In August 1994, MCA Records released *Jimi Hendrix: Woodstock*, a single-disc collection

of highlights from Hendrix's legendary closing set at Woodstock. Less than a year later, Al Hendrix won the rights to his son's recordings, and his company, Experience Hendrix, began reissuing definitive masters of Jimi's catalog. In the summer of 1999, Experience Hendrix rolled out *Live at Woodstock*, which features the entire set over the course of two discs. Hearing Hendrix's complete concert isn't as revelatory as you'd think, since it just emphasizes that he overcompensated for his under-rehearsed band by jamming. And does he ever jam—almost everything clocks in at over five minutes, with a couple weighing in at over ten minutes. Naturally, this will hardly be seen as a detriment by legions of Hendrix fans, and that's who this set is for. Listening to all of *Live at Woodstock* takes dedication and an active interest in the subtleties of Jimi's playing. He had disbanded the Experience only eight weeks before and was teamed with players who wanted to follow him, no matter where he went. Unfortunately, the lack of rehearsal meant that they were often striving to keep up with him; in turn, Hendrix runs wild, spinning off dizzying solos that are as fascinating as they are frustrating. Taken individually, these performances are usually enthralling, but *Live at Woodstock* will exhaust the average listener. Which is not to say it isn't a worthwhile experience. As a historical document, it is interesting and revealing, and Hendrix historians undoubtedly will find several of these performances necessary. But this not an essential addition to the average fan's library, simply because Hendrix blew minds at Woodstock through excess, not focus. —*Stephen Thomas Erlewine*

The Jimi Hendrix Experience / Sep. 12, 2000 / MCA ✦✦✦✦
The Hendrix family continued its reissue campaign with the release of *The Jimi Hendrix Experience*, a lavish four-disc box set that should be a boon to Hendrix collectors everywhere. With a beautiful 80-page booklet, and purporting to have 46 unreleased tracks, further inspection actually reveals less than meets the eye, at least for collectors. The problem is that real collectors have already heard most of this material, and not only through bootleg sources. Many of the previously unreleased tracks are just *new mixes* of live tracks that were issued as part of *Stages*, *Live at Monterey*, and *Lifelines*. While the sound quality is somewhat better (handled by the expert Eddie Kramer), the new mixes do not differ substantially from the earlier versions. With the inclusion of virtually all of *In the West*, and a few quality tracks from *Rainbow Bridge* and *Crash Landing* (without the wretched mid-'70s overdubs), *The Jimi Hendrix Experience* almost seems like a shelf-clearing exercise, taking care of the leftover tracks that fans have been clamoring for *en masse*. The real highlights of the set are the early studio outtakes, presumably from the cache that Chas Chandler withheld from Alan Douglas for so many years. All in all, *The Jimi Hendrix Experience* is a fine addendum to the Hendrix legacy, but not the place to start; this is a set for someone who already has the studio albums and can't get enough of his genius. The disappointment a hardcore collector might feel at having heard most of this material already should be outweighed by the beautiful, warm sound achieved by Eddie Kramer and the general high quality of the package. —*Sean Westergaard*

Voodoo Child: The Jimi Hendrix Collection / May 8, 2001 / MCA ✦✦✦
Wading through the repackagings of Jimi Hendrix musical legacy is a daunting task which has not been made any easier in the digital age. This double-CD set features a disc of 'studio' and 'live' performances including several alternate and hard-to-find recordings of familiar classics. While nearly impossible to include everyone's favourites, this collection is a superior primer for those seeking a thumbnail sketch of Hendrix in both a studio and concert environment. Disc one cuts a chronological path through nearly 70 minutes of peak moments from Hendrix studio recordings as the leader of the Jimi Hendrix Experience and the Band of Gypsys. The sound is impeccable and the song selection hits most of the highlights. Conspicuously absent are vital contributions such as "If 6 Was 9," "Manic Depression," and "Can You See Me." In their stead are alternate versions of "Highway Chile," "All Along The Watchtower," "Stone Free," and "Spanish Castle Magic"—all of which are available elsewhere. The rare 45 featuring the *Band of Gypsys* on "Isabella" and "Stepping Stone" is a nice inclusion for collectors. Disc two highlights Hendrix concert performances, including several generation defining moments—such as the reinvention of the electric guitar during "Wild Thing" at the Monterey Pop Festival as well as his inimitable "Star Spangled Banner" solo from the Woodstock Music and Arts Fair. Other highlights include a couple of oft overlooked later-era pieces featuring the *Band of Gypsys*. "Red House" from the New York Pop Festival and the previously unissued—on CD at least—"Foxey Lady" from Maui, Hawaii are both stellar performances from July 1970. All in all, *Voodoo Child: The Jimi Hendrix Collection* is a great touchstone for anyone wishing to begin their Jimi Hendrix experience. —*Lindsay Planer*

Don Henley

b. Jul. 22, 1947, Gilmer, TX
Vocals, Drums, Percussion / Pop/Rock, Soft Rock, Adult Contemporary, Singer/Songwriter

Out of all of the Eagles, Don Henley had the most successful solo career. After the group broke up in 1982, Henley released his first solo album, *I Can't Stand Still*. Although it wasn't as successful as an Eagles record, the album peformed respectably, launching the number three single "Dirty Laundry" and going gold. *Building the Perfect Beast* followed two years later and established Henley as a solo star in his own right. Featuring the Top ten hits "Boys of Summer" and "All She Wants to Do Is Dance," the album sold over two million copies and stayed on the charts for over a year. Henley's third album, 1989's *The End of the Innocence*, was his most ambitious record yet, as well as his most commercially successful. The album sold over three million copies and stayed on the charts for nearly three years, launching the hit singles "The End of the Innocence," "Heart of the Matter," "New York Minute," "How Bad Do You Want It?," and "The Last Worthless Evening." Henley reunited with the Eagles in 1994, embarking on a worldwide tour. —*Stephen Thomas Erlewine*

I Can't Stand Still / 1982 / Warner Brothers ✦✦✦
Don Henley's first solo album may still have had the ghost of the Eagles lingering in the corners, but for the most part it showcases his stalwart partnership with producer and songwriter Danny Kortchmar. Lyrically, Henley's songs are a tad weak, but for an inaugural album from a man who had spent most of his career surrounded by multi-talented musicians and writers, on the whole it fairs quite well. His material deals with the hardships of love, the fickleness of the media, and the declining state of education, all induced with a friendly pop sound. The title track, a trouble-in-paradise love song, has Henley pouring his heart out with sugary angst, but is helped along with some avid keyboard work. "Dirty Laundry" is Henley's attack on the shallowness of the network newsperson that peaked at number three on Billboard's Top 40. Its bouncy chorus and contagious organ riffs proved that his role as a musician could conform to any style. His social commentary comes into fruition with "Johnny Can't Read," loosely based on the increasing amount of high-school dropouts at the time and helped bolster Henley's reputation as a musician with a concern for pressing issues. Numerous musicians help him out on this album as well, including former Eagles members Timothy B. Schmidt, Joe Walsh, and J.D. Souther; drummer Jeff Porcaro and guitarist Steve Lukather, both from Toto; and even Warren Zevon. Don Henley's adept combination of lyrical wit and thought-provoking staidness begins to materialize on *I Can't Stand Still*, paving the way for an extremely accomplished solo career. —*Mike DeGagne*

Building the Perfect Beast / 1984 / Geffen ✦✦✦✦✦
After experimenting with synthesizers and a pop sound on his solo debut, Don Henley hits the mark on his sophomore release, *Building the Perfect Beast*. This album established Henley as an artist in his own right after many successful years with the Eagles, as it spawned numerous hits. While the songs seem crafted for pop radio, it's hard to fault him for choosing arrangements that would get his messages to the masses. Unlike most pop in the 1980s, however, Henley had deep intellectual themes layered beneath the synthesizer sounds and crisp production. In the opening song "Boys of Summer," he talks about trying to recapture the past while knowing that things will never be the same. Henley has a gift for writing about the heart and soul of America and for mixing his love for the country and small-town life ("Sunset Grill") with cynicism about government ("All She Wants to Do Is Dance") and modernization ("Month of Sundays"). Although the politics and the sound of the album make the decade of release easy to place, Henley's earnest delivery and universal messages give many of the tracks a timeless feel, which is no small feat. This is Henley's most consistent album, and it is the place to start for those wanting to sample his solo work. —*Vik Iyengar*

The End of the Innocence / Jun. 1989 / Geffen ✦✦✦✦
Don Henley took some time before completing his highly anticipated third album, *The End of the Innocence*. Although he manages to duplicate much of the magic of his previous album, Henley has backed off of the synthesizers and expanded his musical palette. He uses background vocals to great effect, whether it's the tragic ballad "New York Minute" (with vocal group Take 6) or the angry rocker "I Will Not Go Quietly" (with Axl Rose of Guns & Roses). His collaboration with Bruce Hornsby on the opening title track show a mature Henley singing about disillusionment over a beautiful piano riff that gives the song a timeless air of nostalgia. While he still tackles political issues and writes about small-town life in America, Henley also mixes in romantic ballads, including the closer "Heart of the Matter." In this epic song, Henley explores the emotional complexity of relationships and coming to terms with oneself during the aftermath. Throughout the album, he manages to balance being cynical yet hopeful, and his great melodies allow his poignant lyrics to penetrate. This album is highly recommended for those who like their pop music with a message. —*Vik Iyengar*

● **Actual Miles: Henley's Greatest Hits** / Nov. 21, 1995 / Geffen ✦✦✦✦✦
Although it is drawn from only three albums (with only one track, "Dirty Laundry," from *I Can't Stand Still*), *Actual Miles* was a well-chosen best-of from an artist who had had just enough hits to justify one. Five tracks each came from *Building the Perfect Beast* and *The End of the Innocence*, and they included all of Don Henley's Top 40 hits. The album was filled out with a cover of Leonard Cohen's "Everybody Knows" and two new tracks, among them the ambitious "The Garden of Allah," which seemed to be an attempt to create a new allegorical masterpiece along the lines of "Hotel California," but managed to be only pretentious. Still, the bulk of this album was the sound of AOR radio in the mid-1980s. That, of course, was the catch—this album should have come out about four years before it did, and probably would have if Henley hadn't been suing Geffen Records. Though destined to be a successful catalog item, in 1995 it was more a historical artifact than a major release. —*William Ruhlmann*

Inside Job / May 23, 2000 / Warner Brothers ✦✦✦
Don Henley essentially sat out his '90s recording contract, waiting until he could sign to another label that would allow him greater artistic freedom and royalties. He finally signed to Warner and released his fourth solo album, *Inside Job*, in the spring of 2000. Considering his long absence from recording, it shouldn't come as a total surprise that the album sounds as if it could have been cut in 1990 or even 1986 (check out the obnoxious synth solo on the opening track). That is not entirely a bad thing, however. It would have been rather embarrassing if Henley was trying to run with the young boys, and he sounds very comfortable settling into a role that is something less than an old master and something more than a crotchety old-timer. It falls somewhere between that, since his simmering anger—always apparent but raised to the surface on his solo records—still can be heard, which makes him seem a little cranky on occasion, when he gets carried away with his temper. For the most part, though, he sounds relaxed, comfortable, and reflective on *Inside Job*, more so than he ever has. The heart of the record is in the slower numbers, where he honestly lays out his feelings about his new love and

marriage. Whenever he sticks to personal relationships, and thereby gentler music, *Inside Job* stays winning. It's brought down when he steps up to the podium to rail against the modern world, but this isn't quite enough to sink the record. *Inside Job* lacks the melodic craftsmanship that made *Building the Perfect Beast* a blockbuster, and it isn't as focused as *The End of the Innocence*, but it is a solid comeback record from an artist who spent a little too long out of the spotlight. —*Stephen Thomas Erlewine*

Clarence "Frogman" Henry

b. Mar. 19, 1937, Algiers, LA
Vocals, Trombone, Songwriter, Piano / New Orleans R&B, R&B
He could sing like a girl, and he could sing like a frog. That latter trademark croak, utilized to the max on his 1956 debut smash "Ain't Got No Home," earned good-natured Clarence Henry his nickname and jump-started a rewarding career that endures to this day around the Crescent City. Henry improvised the basic idea behind "Ain't Got No Home" on the bandstand one morning in the wee hours; when the crowd responded favorably, he honed it into something unique. Local DJ Poppa Stoppa laid the "Frogman" handle on the youngster when he spun the 45 (issued on the Chess subsidiary Argo), and it stuck. Despite some fine follow-ups—"It Won't Be Long," "I'm in Love," the inevitable sequel "I Found a Home"—Frog sank back into the marsh sales-wise until 1960, when Allen Toussaint's updated arrangement melded beautifully with a country-tinged Bobby Charles composition called "(I Don't Know Why) But I Do." Henry's rendition of the tune proved a huge pop smash in early 1961, as did a Domino-tinged "You Always Hurt the One You Love" later that year. Frogman continued to record a variety of New Orleans-styled old standards and catchy originals for Argo, but the hits dried up for good after 1961. —*Bill Dahl*

● **Ain't Got No Home: The Best of Clarence "Frogman" Henry** / 1994 / Chess/MCA ✦✦✦✦✦
The New Orleans R&B singer with the joyous frog's croak in his voice is served well by this 18-song collection of his 1956-1964 output for the Chess subsidiary Argo Records. It begins with his definitive "Ain't Got No Home," and follows with his vicious Crescent City rockers "Troubles, Troubles," "It Won't Be Long," and "I'm in Love," and visits his comeback hits "But I Do" and "You Always Hurt the One You Love." —*Bill Dahl*

Joe Henry

Vocals, Guitar / Americana, Adult Alternative Pop/Rock, Alternative Country-Rock, Singer/Songwriter
Joe Henry is best known for his two country-influenced albums, 1992's *Short Man's Room* and 1993's *Kindness of the World*, both of which feature members of the country-rock band the Jayhawks, but his musical direction has actually changed several times over the course of his recording career, reflecting his restless, adventurous spirit. After his little-heard 1986 debut, *Talk of Heaven*, Henry signed to A&M in 1989 for the rock & roll album *Murder of Crows*. From there he pared down to the quiet, entirely acoustic moods of *Shuffletown* (1990) before shifting into country- and folk-influenced territory. Henry's lyrics are a central focus of his songwriting, but even though he often writes in the first person, his songs are not "personal" in the manner of musicians who are often called singer/songwriters (a genre he doesn't like to be associated with). He's recorded some excellent country covers, but he's equally interested in soul, funk, and rock & roll. On *Trampoline*, released in 1996, Henry veered his music in an edgier, more rhythm-oriented direction. —*Kurt Wolff*

Talk of Heaven / 1986 / Profile ✦✦
Murder of Crows / 1989 / Mammoth ✦✦
Shuffletown / Aug. 1990 / Mammoth ✦✦✦
All-acoustic album with a quiet, laid-back, late-night vibe. Recorded live to two-track and produced by T-Bone Burnett. The lineup includes jazz trumpeter Don Cherry. —*Kurt Wolff*

● **Short Man's Room** / Jun. 16, 1992 / Mammoth ✦✦✦✦✦
A stunning collection of beautiful country- and folk-inflected songs that shift and sway with spare acoustic arrangements. While the songs are not autobiographical per se, the lyrics are a central focus, bringing a rich assortment of complex characters to life with abstract but vividly rendered details. The band includes Gary Louris and Marc Perlman from the Jayhawks. —*Kurt Wolff*

Kindness of the World / Sep. 28, 1993 / Mammoth ✦✦✦✦
On this album of more strong songs, some have definite country leanings. Henry covers Tom T. Hall's "I Flew over our House Last Night," and he wrote "She Always Goes" with George Strait in mind. —*Brian Mansfield*

Trampoline / Mar. 26, 1996 / Mammoth ✦✦✦
On *Trampoline*, Joe Henry moves away from the country-rock that earned his reputation in the early '90s. Though there are still some remnants of his Gram Parsons and Neil Young influences, Henry attempts a more atmospheric, rock-based sound on *Trampoline*, which explains his choice of Helmet guitarist Page Hamilton as musical collaborator. The shift in sound is effective, but it does sound as if the singer/songwriter is still trying to become comfortable with his new direction. It doesn't help that the album is slightly uneven, as Henry tries to write more literate lyrics, making his songs almost into short stories. When his ambitions do work, *Trampoline* is a stark, affecting listen, and even when they don't, the album is admirable. —*Stephen Thomas Erlewine*

Fuse / Mar. 9, 1999 / Mammoth ✦✦✦
Henry has often made stylistic departures, so *Fuse* shouldn't be all that shocking. Yet, "Fat" sounds freaky till the beats soak in; the faux soul of "Want Too Much" is cloying.

But ultimately, the new groove-a-delic Henry knows how to work the sound as he mixes and matches old and new, as on the Dylan-y bits with a "millennial" backing track (Daniel Lanois and T-Bone Burnett step in to mix); the subtle, catchy chorus in the opener "Monkey"; the laid-back and fuzzy "Angels"; and the fantastically evocative and poetic mysticism in the title song. There's upbeat melodicism in (I love you with my) "Skin and Teeth." But *why* that George Benson-like guitar solo during "Curt Flood"? —*Denise Sullivan*

Scar / May 2001 / Mammoth ✦✦✦✦
For the five years preceding this album's release, Joe Henry gradually took his songwriting into hidden areas, exploring the different textures of shadow with occasional forays into the twilight of the human heart. Longing has been painted upon the smoky backdrop of every song he's written. On *Scar*, his eighth album, Henry follows his other obsession down the rabbit hole: the myriad ways in which sound and texture can become musical instruments themselves in order to paint a song properly. *Scar*, his highly textured sonic meditation on love and its twisted redemptive power, features a list of highly visible musicians that help make this the album Henry's been trying to make his entire adult life. The final track, the album's namesake, is an opus at 14:21. Lyrically it's as direct as anything Henry's ever written, but it's an entire film score rolled into one love song. It's poetry too genuine, so metaphorical and rich in imagery, that it would be a disservice to quote from it. It is the most beautiful of the many beautiful songs Henry has written. *Scar*, with its rich poetic tapestries and complex musical and atmospheric architectures, is Henry's highest achievement thus far. He has moved into a space that only he and Tom Waits inhabit in that they are songwriters who have created deep archetypal characters that are composites—metaphorical, allegorical, and "real"—of the world around them and have created new sonic universes for them to both explore and express themselves in. —*Thom Jurek*

Herman's Hermits

f. 1964, Manchester, England, **db.** 1970
Merseybeat, British Invasion, Pop
Herman's Hermits began life in 1963 in Manchester, England; the group got its name when they were joined by 16-year-old TV actor Peter Noone, who was thought to resemble the Sherman character on the *Rocky & Bullwinkle* TV cartoon. Pop producer Mickie Most, induced to see the group by their managers, thought Noone looked like a young John Kennedy and agreed to sign them. Most chose the group's material, from revamped oldies and pub songs to tunes submitted by professional songwriters like Gerry Goffin and Carole King, and produced the recordings, generally using Noone as singer and a group of studio musicians. The result was two years of solid hits, starting with "I'm Into Something Good," which topped the U.K. charts and broke the group in America. There were 11 Top Ten hits in the U.S. through 1967, among them the number one gold singles "Mrs. Brown You've Got a Lovely Daughter" and "I'm Henry VIII, I Am." Inevitably, the group's teenage heartthrob appeal waned, and they never became the kind of self-sustaining musical unit that could outlive that initial infatuation. —*William Ruhlmann*

Their Greatest Hits / 1973 / ABKCO ✦✦✦✦✦
When it first appeared on CD around 1987, this 16-song compilation was easy to justify, as there are no other domestic compilations of the group's work and imported CDs were difficult to come by. And it isn't bad, as far as it goes—encompassing all of the significant American chart singles and their most recognizable songs. This disc is probably the most easily available Herman's Hermits CD that there is, and it could be the place to start and finish with the group as far as any awareness of their popularity goes. Over the years, however, EMI in England has issued far more generous and better-sounding collections of the group's work, with the result that *Their Greatest Hits* is no longer competitive on that level, nor is it remotely the place to get the fullest account of the group's range, which went considerably beyond AM radio hits. EMI's *The Very Best of Herman's Hermits* offers more songs (and better sound) at a lower price, and any of the Repertoire Records reissues of their albums, though the hits aren't all represented, will give the listener a fuller account of the group's full capabilities, which were highly underrated. —*Bruce Eder*

● **The Very Best of Herman's Hermits** / Apr. 3, 2001 / EMI ✦✦✦✦✦
This 65-minute, 25-song compilation—at least the third distinct time that EMI Records UK's Music For Pleasure line has anthologized the group's work and the second time they've used this title—offers nine more songs than the equivalent ABKCO Records Herman's Hermits collection; lists for about six dollars less; and was mastered almost a decade later, with resulting superior sound. All of the U.K. and U.S. hit singles are represented, from 1964's "I'm Into Something Good" to "Lady Barbara" in 1970, along with a handful of B-sides. That's more songs than most listeners probably realized the group ever charted, and the only flaw is that flops like "Museum" (admittedly, the most interesting of all of their singles) are overlooked. The annotation is surprisingly thorough for a collection like this and gives some idea of the real story behind the group's music, which has aged better than anybody could have predicted at the time. Anyone buying this or any other singles collection by the group, however, should think about getting one of their better albums, such as *There's a Kind of a Hush All Over the World*, *Both Sides of Herman's Hermits*, or *Blaze*, to get the fuller story of the group and its sound. —*Bruce Eder*

Kristin Hersh

b. Aug. 7, 1966, Atlanta, GA
Vocals, Guitar / Adult Alternative Pop/Rock, Alternative Pop/Rock, Singer/Songwriter
After the release of Throwing Muses' fifth album, *Red Heaven*, Kristin Hersh, the band's lead singer/songwriter, took a break from the group and issued her first solo album, the acoustic *Hips and Makers*, in early 1994. Thanks to the airplay the single "Your Ghost"—

a duet with R.E.M.'s Michael Stipe—received, the album sold more copies than any of the Muses' releases. Later that year, Hersh also released the *Strings* EP, which featured versions of selected songs from the album recorded with a string quartet, and did a solo tour. Despite her success as a solo artist, she kept the Muses going as well, releasing their next record, *University*, in February 1995. Throwing Muses and Hersh as a solo artist moved from Sire to Rykodisc, forming the boutique label Throwing Music in 1996; the label's first release was the final Muses album *Limbo*, which appeared that summer. Before the Muses hit the road in support of *Limbo*, Hersh began work on her second solo album, wrapping it up in early 1997. At the completion of the *Limbo* tour, Hersh disbanded Throwing Muses, claiming that it was no longer economically feasible to continue with the band. The acoustic-based *Strange Angels*, her first post-Muses album, was released by Rykodisc in February 1998. That year, she also released *Murder, Misery and Goodnight*, a collection of lullabies and Appalachian folk songs, as a Throwing Music exclusive. In 1999, Hersh and Throwing Music returned to her original label 4AD for *Sky Motel* and 2001's *Sunny Border Blue*. Hersh also established the *Works in Progress* series, a subscription service of exclusive rarities, through Throwing Music's website, www.throwingmusic.com. *—Stephen Thomas Erlewine*

• **Hips and Makers** / Feb. 1, 1994 / Sire/Reprise ✦✦✦✦✦
Hersh dug into her backlog of compositions for material of an intensely personal nature that she felt wouldn't be suitable for her band on her solo debut, *Hips and Makers*. In stark contrast to her work with Throwing Muses, *Hips and Makers* is almost entirely acoustic. Hersh embellishes her waifish voice and acoustic guitar with touches of cello and piano on this album, which offers a despairing and introspective tone that fails to submerge her considerable inner strength and fortitude. Recorded in a mere two weeks, this collection of haunting and confessional songs was produced by ex-Patti Smith Group guitarist Lenny Kaye, who has also produced Suzanne Vega. Hersh's voice and lyrical tone, however, are considerably brittler and coarser than Vega's. The opening track, "Your Ghost," features a duet with R.E.M. singer Michael Stipe. *—Richie Unterberger*

Murder, Misery, and Then Goodnight / 1998 / 4AD ✦✦✦✦
By listening to interpretations of the Appalachian folk songs that Pa Hersh played for her six year-old daughter prior to nighty night, the explanation as to how Kristin Hersh became such an exceptional songwriter becomes increasingly clear. Her dark humor—alternating between frightening and hilarious with a creepy level of dexterity—is showcased on *Murder, Misery, and then Goodnight*. "What'll We Do With the Baby-O" sounds inoffensive enough just going by the title, and the music is deceptively bouncy and playful. But wow—give a listen to the lyrics! "Every time the baby cries, stick my finger in the baby's eyes / Every time he starts to grin, give the baby a bottle of gin." Liquor is a common theme, given especially blurry focus on the first-person tale "Three Nights Drunk." But really, the subjects are more well-rounded than the title indicates. It's not as if every song here is capable of spooking youngsters. Or you, for that matter. Most could totally miss the words, given Hersh's calming voice. Each of these songs are traditional, with arrangements coming from the artist. Her acoustic work is spectacular as ever, and she's accompanied by her son Ryder on backing vocals and piano. So she's truly passing the songs to the next generation. It's doubtless that young Ryder will be able to pass these songs down to his kids, but whether or not you would want to depends on how playfully twisted you are as a parent. Few could do these songs as well as Hersh. Though not as essential as her "regular" records, it deserves official release; 4AD released it as part of their limited mail-order series in 1998. It might not exactly be *Soothing Sounds for Baby*, but *Murder* is still a sinister, lulling pre-slumber treat. *—Andy Kellman*

Strange Angels / Feb. 3, 1998 / Rykodisc ✦✦✦
Due to economic reasons, Kristin Hersh reluctantly disbanded the Throwing Muses in 1997, claiming that the trio could no longer afford to tour and record. So, she was essentially forced back to recording a solo acoustic album in the vein of *Hips and Makers*, her revelatory 1994 solo debut. *Strange Angels* isn't the equal of that minor masterpiece, partially because the songwriting, while solid, is a little samey, but also because Hersh sounds as if she'd rather be with the Muses. That's not to say her performances are bored—they're often more inspired than the last Muses album, *Limbo*—but they have a melancholy undertone and are occasionally a little listless. These, however, are minor flaws, because *Strange Angels* is overall a strong collection of songs. Hersh's obtuse, poetic lyrics remain a little impenetrable, yet her melodicism makes them intriguing, even for the curious. And for some longtime fans, that may be a problem—*Strange Angels* is the most accessible album in her catalog, because her vocal idiosyncracies are tamed and the production is a little too clean. Perhaps these are signs of maturity, or perhaps it's an attempt to gain a wider audience, but either way it's a mixed blessing, because the songs cry out for a more varied production to make the record more compelling. *—Stephen Thomas Erlewine*

Sky Motel / Jul. 6, 1999 / 4AD ✦✦✦✦
Kristin Hersh's third solo album *Sky Motel* finds her picking up the electric guitar again for a collection of mature, mercurial, parallel-dimension pop. The album fuses the restraint of her acoustic work with the lush textures of Throwing Muses' later albums, adding Latin percussion and keyboards for a further update on Hersh's signature sound.

A subtle and layered album, *Sky Motel*'s pop songs create the most immediately arresting moments. The album opener "Echo" pairs a jazzy electric piano with Hersh's sweetly abrasive harmonies, then explodes into a riot of spiky guitars as she snarls lyrics like "I'm loving everybody / I'm hating everyone I see." "Fog" and "A Cleaner Light" mine similar territory, delivering the kind of angular, bouncy yet slightly menacing guitar pop that made Muses albums like *The Real Ramona* and *University* college-rock favorites. Though the gentler songs on *Sky Motel* take more time to reveal their charms, songs like "White Trash Moon," "Costa Rica," "Caffeine," and "Husk," with their undulating guitars and quietly compelling vocals, make the album increasingly rewarding with each listen. *—Heather Phares*

Sunny Border Blue / Mar. 6, 2001 / 4AD ✦✦✦✦
In her solo career, Kristin Hersh alternates between acoustic-based work like *Hips and Makers* and spiky, Throwing Muses-esque punk-pop. *Sunny Border Blue*, her fourth officially released effort, is considerably folkier than its predecessor, *Sky Motel*, but borrows enough of its rock vitality to avoid *Strange Angel*'s sluggishness. Unfortunately, the album doesn't quite escape the slightly samey quality of Hersh's work since the Muses' 1996 album *Limbo*—a few too many songs share tempos, melodies, and moods to make this a great Kristin Hersh album, but it's still a very good one that her longtime fans will appreciate. Hersh's gift for crafting fascinating and often disturbing lyrics remains; even relatively weak songs suggest intriguing stories with lines like "Candyland"'s "It's like this boy took all my clear cold nights/Left me hot and dry/And when he falls, I can't hear it." Musically, piano and brass flourishes give the album a more fleshed-out, dynamic sound than some of Hersh's previous solo work; impressively, she played virtually all of the instruments on *Sunny Border Blue* herself. Much of the album seems more like a suite than a collection of songs; winding, hypnotic folk-pop tracks like "Flipside" and "Silica" almost feel like different movements of a larger work. However, the rolling opener "Your Dirty Answer" showcases Hersh's husky, slightly raw vocals; the understated yet gripping "37 Hours" rivals any of the songs on *Hips and Makers*; and the slightly countrified cover of Cat Stevens' "Trouble" is another of *Sunny Border Blue*'s highlights. The beautifully fractured pop song "Ruby" may be the most luminous moment, though frustratingly, it comes near the album's end. But it's "Spain," a seemingly gentle ballad that turns furious, that recalls the mercurial spark that initially ignited Hersh's music. It's not an entirely successful song, but it's a glimmer of excitement and unpredictability from an artist who used to define those words. *—Heather Phares*

Richard X. Heyman

Vocals / Power Pop

Richard X. Heyman is one of the sadly overlooked pop craftsmen of the '90s but his albums are widely regarded in power-pop circles as instant classics. Heyman began recording in the late '80s in the tradition of the studio nerd/one man band, playing all instruments himself in his upper west side Manhattan apartment living room, named Brontasaurus, presumably after the classic song by the Move. He released the independent *Actual Size* EP in 1987 and followed with the full-length *Living Room!!* in 1988. Considerable word-of-mouth exposure led to the album being reissued by Cypress Records in 1990 in slighltly modified form. He signed to Sire in 1990 and released one album for the label, the Andy Paley produced, *Hey Man!* in 1991. Poor sales led to him being dropped by the label but he has continued recording (several albums' worth by his estimations) while shopping for the elusive new deal. *Cornerstone* was completed by 1996 but it wasn't released nationally until early 1998 by Permanent Press Records. In late 2000 Heyman issued Heyman, Hoosier & Herman, an EP featuring former Herman's Hermits Peter Noone on vocals for the title track and six outtakes from the Cornerstone sessions. *—Chris Woodstra*

Living Room!! / 1988 / N.R. World ✦✦✦

• **Hey Man!** / May 28, 1991 / Sire ✦✦✦✦✦
In the early 1990s, Richard X. Heyman exemplified the type of artist who enjoys rave reviews from rock critics but doesn't break through commercially. The fact that the New York-based singer/composer's second album, *Hey Man!*, wasn't a big hit commercially certainly wasn't due to a lack of first-class writing. Drawing on influences ranging from Tom Petty and Elvis Costello to the Byrds, *Hey Man!* is a gem-laden CD that, sadly, got lost in the corporate shuffle. Melodic power pop treasures like "In the Scheme of Things," "Falling Away," and "Bad Business in Town" show just how prolific and thoughtful a songwriter this guy is, and should have made him well known. For power-pop enthusiasts, *Hey Man* is well worth searching for. *—Alex Henderson*

Cornerstone / Feb. 10, 1998 / Turn-Up ✦✦✦✦✦
After being dropped by Sire/Warner Bros. in 1991, Richard X. Heyman went six long years before recording another CD. When his third album, the superb *Cornerstone*, was released, it was clear that the New Yorker's singing and writing hadn't deteriorated a bit during his absence from the studio. Heyman's influences still ranged from Elvis Costello and Tom Petty to the Byrds, and continued to demonstrate how rewarding powerpop and jangly guitar rock can be on songs ranging from the dispirited "Out of My Hands" and the nostalgic "When It Was Our Time" to the exuberant "Ask Anyone Who's Tried," the reflective "From This Day Forever," and the poignant "All I Have." On some of the songs, Heyman plays all of the instruments himself, and he is heard on everything from guitar, piano, and bass as well as drums. An artist this talented should not be neglected. *—Alex Henderson*

Heyman, Hoosier & Herman / Dec. 26, 2000 / Turn Up ✦✦✦✦
Subtitled "The Cornerstone Outtakes," this seven-track mini-album is an enjoyable collection of leftovers from pop tunesmith Richard X. Heyman's stellar 1998 effort "Cornerstone," along with one track featuring former Herman's Hermits frontman Peter Noone. Heyman cuts loose on this informal outing, comfortably wearing his influences on his sleeve via a bare-bones rhythm section, thoughtful arrangements, and soulful vocals. "A Little Drive" is pure Beach Boys circa 1965 with harmonies that Brian Wilson and company would mistake for their own. The raucous "Why Can't She See Me" evokes the Who's "Happy Jack" halcyon days while "Monk's Hollow" ghosts the easygoing classic country rock fusion of Gram Parson's Flying Burrito Brothers almost effortlessly. "Hoosier Girl" is a paean to Noone's legendary outfit, and the fact that the head Hermit agreed to sing the lead on the opening cut adds to the overall authenticity. Heyman's clever, low-key

production and ability to inject his own indelible style on each song sidesteps the retro/nostalgia tag, making this disc a likable exercise. *—Tom Semioli*

John Hiatt

b. 1952, Indianapolis, IN

Slide Guitar, Vocals, Piano, Guitar / College Rock, Heartland Rock, Americana, New Wave, Roots Rock, Singer/Songwriter, Country-Rock

John Hiatt's sales have never quite matched his reputation. Hiatt's songs were covered successfully by everyone from Bonnie Raitt, Ronnie Milsap, and Dr. Feelgood to Iggy Pop, Three Dog Night, and the Neville Brothers, yet it took him 13 years to reach the charts himself. Of course, it nearly took him that long to find his own style. Hiatt began his solo career in 1974, and over the next decade he ran through a number of different styles from rock & roll to new wave pop before he finally settled on a rootsy fusion of rock & roll, country, blues, and folk with his 1987 album *Bring the Family.* Though the album didn't set the charts on fire, it became his first album to reach the charts, and several of the songs on the record became hits for other artists, including Raitt and Milsap. Following its success, Hiatt became a reliable hit songwriter for other artists, and he developed a strong cult following that continued to gain strength into the mid-'90s. *—Stephen Thomas Erlewine*

Hangin' Around the Observatory / 1974 / Epic ✦✦✦

John Hiatt mixed pop, folk, rock, R&B, country, and gospel on his debut album, immediately becoming an uncategorizable (and thus uncommercial) entity. Although this album was cut in Nashville, it owes more to Van Morrison than it does to Conway Twitty, and like the Belfast bluesman, Indianian Hiatt came to his influences somewhat secondhand, however sincerely he evoked them. What he really was, of course, was a singer/songwriter, albeit not in a style easily recognizable in 1974. The title indicates his position: Hiatt's songs show him an acute observer. But the performances require him to dig in, and although he does so with alacrity, the result is too diffuse. Nevertheless, Hiatt earned critical kudos for this album, and Three Dog Night (who knew good songwriting when they heard it) covered "Sure As I'm Sittin' Here," getting a Top 40 single out of it. *—William Ruhlmann*

Overcoats / 1975 / Epic ✦✦

John Hiatt is better at imitating Howlin' Wolf than he is James Taylor, and that he tries both here as well as Bob Dylan and Ben E. King is some indication of his ambition, if not his accomplishment. Conversely, be began to become more himself on his second album, at least on such songs as "I'm Tired of Your Stuff" and "I Killed an Ant With My Guitar," if not on the more lugubrious numbers, such as "Distance" or on the ones that sounded like publishing demos for a more popular singer, such as "Down Home." *—William Ruhlmann*

Slug Line / 1979 / MCA ✦✦✦

Conventional wisdom at the time was that MCA Records had signed John Hiatt (who had languished without a record contract for four years) with the idea that he would be their Elvis Costello—a singer/songwriter in the fashionable punk/new wave style. Certainly, Hiatt has stripped down and roughed up from his Epic records here, fronting a straight-ahead guitar rock band (that was capable, of course, of playing the obligatory reggae number), eschewing the stylistic diversity he reveled in before, and throwing out snappy, aphoristic lyrics in a highly processed voice. None of this quite turns him into Elvis Costello, although the mean streak he reveals would serve him well later. *—William Ruhlmann*

Two Bit Monsters / 1980 / MCA ✦✦✦

At the time of its release, *Two Bit Monsters* was perceived by critics who had caught up with John Hiatt on *Slug Line* as a less impressive follow-up to that record. In retrospect, it may be the better of the two albums, boasting an even more simplified musical approach and such notable songs (and future Rosanne Cash covers) as "Pink Bedroom" and "It Hasn't Happened Yet." Hiatt here was starting to emerge from the "new Elvis Costello" tag that had been affixed to him with *Slug Line*, but his reviewers, however well meaning, seemed determined to keep him in that category. (In any case, record buyers were paying little attention—*Slug Line* was Hiatt's fourth straight album to miss the charts, and MCA dropped him as Epic had before.) *—William Ruhlmann*

All of a Sudden / 1982 / Geffen ✦✦✦

Hiatt's fifth album and his first for Geffen, his third record label, was given a somewhat inappropriate big-gloss production (all shimmering keyboards and filtered vocals) by Tony Visconti, known for his work with David Bowie. What counts with Hiatt, though, is the songs, and this album contains "I Look for Love," as knowing a dissection of the dating scene as anyone has yet attempted. *—William Ruhlmann*

Riding With the King / 1983 / Geffen ✦✦✦✦✦

John Hiatt's talents as a singer and songwriter have never been a matter of question, but for the longest time neither Hiatt nor his various record labels seemed to know what to do with him. Epic Records thought he was some sort of a folky, while MCA figured, since his songs were often cranky and angular, he could be sold as a skinny-tie new wave guy. Neither idea made much of a dent in the marketplace, and by the time Hiatt cut his second album for Geffen, *Riding With the King*, someone had come to the reasonable conclusion that Hiatt was a roots-rocker at heart—but what *kind* of roots-rocker? Side one of *Riding With the King* was produced by Ron Nagel and Scott Matthews of the Durocs, with Hiatt singing and playing guitar and Matthews handling everything else; the results have a thick, glossy retro-pop sound with a vague '50s undercurrent, complete with twinkly keyboards and honking saxophones. Side two was cut with Nick Lowe at the controls, featuring a band assembled from Lowe's touring unit (which at one time included Hiatt); these tunes are leaner and bluesier, but also a bit more laid-back. While the two halves of the album have decidedly different sonic personalities, the consistent strength of Hiatt's witty, sweet-and-sour songwriting holds the album together, balancing punchy rockers like "Say It With Flowers" and "Falling Up" against soulful contemplations of the ups and downs of love, such as "She Loves the Jerk" and "You May Already Be a Winner." And while Hiatt's voice doesn't boast much range, he knows how to make the most of what he's got, and his vocals here sound a lot more subtle and incisive than the albums that preceded it. *Riding in the Family* may be a bit mixed-up, but it was certainly a step in the right direction for Hiatt. *—Mark Deming*

Warming Up to the Ice Age / Jan. 1985 / Geffen ✦✦✦

Hiatt turned to veteran country producer Norbert Putnam here, but the result still rocked hard, with the occasional soul touch (notably those obnoxious thumb-struck bass lines that are so prevalent in '80s music). Highlights here are "The Usual," later covered by Bob Dylan, and "She Said the Same Things to Me." There is also an odd duet with Elvis Costello on the old Spinners hit "Living a Little, Laughing a Little" (try and tell them apart). Critics' darling or not, when this album went into the tank, Geffen became the third label to drop Hiatt. *—William Ruhlmann*

● **Bring the Family** / May 1987 / A&M ✦✦✦✦✦

In 1987, John Hiatt, clean and sober and looking for an American record deal, was asked by an A&R man at a British label to name his dream band. After a little thought, Hiatt replied that if he had his druthers, he'd cut a record with Ry Cooder on guitar, Nick Lowe on bass, and Jim Keltner on drums. To Hiatt's surprise, he discovered all three were willing to work on his next album; Hiatt and his dream band went into an L.A. studio and knocked off *Bring the Family* in a mere four days, and the result was the best album of Hiatt's career. The musicians certainly make a difference here, generating a lean, smoky groove that's soulful and satisfying (Ry Cooder's guitar work is especially impressive, leaving no doubt of his singular gifts without ever overstepping its boundaries), but the real triumph here is Hiatt's songwriting. *Bring the Family* was recorded after a period of great personal turmoil for him, and for the most part the archly witty phrasemaker of his earlier albums was replaced by an wiser and more cautious writer who had a great deal to say about where life and love can take you. Hiatt had never written anything as nakedly confessional as "Tip of My Tongue" or "Learning How to Love You" before, and even straight-ahead R&B-style rockers like "Memphis in the Meantime" and "Thing Called Love" possessed a weight and resonance he never managed before. But *Bring the Family* isn't an album about tragedy, it's about responsibility and belatedly growing up, and it's appropriate that it was a band of seasoned veterans with their own stories to tell about life who helped Hiatt bring it across; it's a rich and satisfying slice of grown-up rock & roll. *—Mark Deming*

Slow Turning / 1988 / A&M ✦✦✦✦✦

After the success of *Bring the Family,* John Hiatt originally intended to reunite that album's all-star backing band (Ry Cooder, Nick Lowe, and Jim Keltner) for a follow-up. Hiatt's "dream band" proved to be unavailable, and he ended up cutting *Slow Turning* with his road band, the Goners, but the finished product proves he remembered well the lessons learned from *Bring the Family. Slow Turning* is a lighter and wittier affair than *Bring the Family*; the outlaw rocker "Tennessee Plates" and its more subdued companion piece, "Trudy and Dave," are more rambunctious than anything on the previous album, and the tempos are sharper this time out, with a bit less blues and a touch more twang in the melodies. But *Slow Turning* is also an album of hard-won lessons about life and love, placing a subtle but pronounced emphasis on the nuts and bolts of family life with the mingled joys and annoyances of parenthood dominating both "Georgia Rae" and the title cut, and the newfound maturity that made *Bring the Family* so special is still very much in evidence. And while the Goners aren't quite up to the standards of the quartet that recorded *Bring the Family* (and who, pray tell, is?), they're still a stronger and more empathetic band than Hiatt usually had in the studio, with Sonny Landreth's guitar work a standout. Following the best album of your career is no easy task for most performers, but with *Slow Turning* John Hiatt made it clear that the excellence of *Bring the Family* was no fluke. *—Mark Deming*

Y' All Caught? The Ones That Got Away 1979-1985 / Sep. 1989 / Geffen ✦✦✦

Bypassing 1974's *Hanging Around the Observatory* and 1975's *Overcoats, Y'all Caught?* is still an enjoyable collection of John Hiatt's early-'80s material, taking some of the best tracks from albums such as *Slug Line, Two Bit Monsters,* and *Warming up to the Ice Age.* Hiatt's blues-based guitar playing and down-home songwriting wonderfully rises to the surface throughout these 13 songs, spotlighting his material before he took on a more commercial rock & roll sound. The rustic simplicity of songs such as "Love Like Blood" and "Pink Bedroom," the latter covered by Roseanne Cash, is helped along by Hiatt's countrified vocal yammering and the looseness of his guitar strumming. 1979's *Slug Line* is represented by the title track, as well as "Radio Girl" and the solemn-sounding "Washable Ink," eventually covered by the Neville Brothers. Slightly more poetic and intricate than Hiatt's usual work, these tracks signify a change in his style, with catchier hooks and a slant toward a more modern rock feel. 1983's *Riding With the King* spawned both the title track and "Love Like Blood," both with the help of musician/producer Nick Lowe. "Riding With the King" was redone superbly almost 17 years later by the tandem of B.B. King and Eric Clapton on their collaborated album. Hiatt's more radio-friendly persona begins to take shape on tunes like "She Said the Same Things to Me" and "The Crush" from *Warming Up to the Ice Age,* as his guitar playing and lyrical makeup tends to grow flashier, busier, and less laid-back than the material that made up most of his career to that point. In 1987, Hiatt released *Bring the Family,* one of his best albums, which was where he united blues and rock to perfection, thus starting the second part of his career with a string of successful albums. As far as compilations go, *Y'all Caught* is a friendly romp through Hiatt's early days and is good to have in the collection. *—Mike DeGagne*

Stolen Moments / Jun. 1990 / A&M ✦✦✦
John Hiatt's highest-charting album yet is a step down from the dizzy heights of *Bring the Family* and *Slow Turning*, as he abandons his more acid commentaries and turns in a self-deprecating set full of promises of reformation and celebrations of marriage and family life. But the observations remain acute, and Hiatt's singing (so much camouflaged in his early days) is becoming his secret weapon. *—William Ruhlmann*

Perfectly Good Guitar / Sep. 7, 1993 / A&M ✦✦

Hiatt Comes Alive at Budokan? / Nov. 22, 1994 / A&M ✦✦✦

Walk On / Oct. 24, 1995 / Capitol ✦✦✦

Little Head / Jul. 1, 1997 / Capitol ✦✦

The Best of John Hiatt / Aug. 25, 1998 / Capitol ✦✦✦✦
John Hiatt finally achieved some sort of fame in 1987, when his comeback album *Bring the Family* sparked a career renaissance. For the next decade, his albums sold well and his songs were continually covered by other artists, all of which earned him acclaim as one of the finest songwriters of his era. Despite its title, *The Best of John Hiatt 1973-1998* is a chronicle of those successful ten years. Only two songs—"Riding With the King" and "Take Off Your Uniform"—date from before 1987, which means that the collection effectively sidesteps Hiatt's years of searching for a style; it chooses to ride with him once he settled on roots rock. Of course, that's where he did the bulk of his best work, and *The Best Of* does offer a good overview of his prime period. Since much of his best work was recorded for labels other than Capitol, the label releasing *The Best Of*, Hiatt entered the studio to record two new songs ("Love in Flames," "Don't Know Much About Love") and cut his first version of "Angel Eyes," the song he gave to Jeff Healey, who turned it into a hit in 1989. He also re-recorded "Have a Little Faith in Me" and "Drive South," two of his best songs from the late '80s. Although these new versions are OK, they don't compare with the originals and only hammer home the fact that this is merely an acceptable compilation, instead of the perfect one that it could have been. Nevertheless, it's a good sampler for the curious, and the hardcore fan will not be disappointed with the new material, even if they're frustrated that they have to purchase a whole new album to acquire it. *—Stephen Thomas Erlewine*

● **Greatest Hits: The A&M Years '87-'94** / Oct. 27, 1998 / A&M ✦✦✦✦✦
Two months after Capitol's *The Best of John Hiatt 1973-1998* hit the stores, A&M released *Greatest Hits: The A&M Years '87-'94*. It's hard to surmise what weird licensing agreements led to this release pattern, since the similarities will cause confusion even among dedicated fans, but there are notable differences between the two discs. Since Hiatt's albums for A&M in the late '80s were his creative peak, it's not surprising that *Greatest Hits*, which concentrates his A&M work, is a more consistent album than *The Best of John Hiatt*, which balances classic A&M cuts with two re-recorded songs, highlights from his two Capitol albums and two new songs. Aside from the inexplicable omission of "Slow Turning," and one of his best rockers, *Greatest Hits* contains all the A&M songs that are on *The Best of John Hiatt* ("Thing Called Love," "Memphis in the Meantime," "Child of the Wild Blue Yonder," "Drive South," "Buffalo River Home," "Feels Like Rain," "Perfectly Good Guitar," "Tennessee Plates"), plus the original versions of "Drive South" and "Have a Little Faith in Me" (only available in butchered remakes on the Capitol disc), a live take of "Angel Eyes," and several fine numbers, such as "Thank You Girl," "Real Fine Love," "Paper Thin," "Lipstick Sunset," and "Through Your Hands." There are some excellent songs from *Bring the Family* and *Slow Turning* missing, but *Greatest Hits* remains the compilation to get for casual fans. *—Stephen Thomas Erlewine*

Crossing Muddy Waters / Sep. 26, 2000 / Vanguard ✦✦✦
John Hiatt's 16th effort is a marked departure from his work of the previous 25 years, and a vast improvement over 1997's disappointing *Little Head*. Hiatt retrenched and recorded his first drummer-less, predominantly acoustic record for Vanguard. It's a sympathetic match and a smart move, since the company has a long, rich history working in the unplugged medium before it became trendy. The result is the most natural and relaxed John Hiatt album in years, and a welcome addition to his extensive catalog. With just a duo of acoustic multi-instrumentalists, Davey Faragher and David Immergluck (both longtime associates), Hiatt pulls out some of the most earnest, down-to-earth songs of his career. He sings like a man rejuvenated, totally at ease with his surroundings, and plays with the laid-back, homespun honesty that has infused his best work. Although some comical lyrical touches remain, the majority of the album is a sober reflection on lost love ("What Do We Do Now," the title track) and the resulting psychological scars. Hiatt's voice has never sounded better; its coarse edges sometimes straining for high notes works perfectly with this craggy, unpolished music. The mandolin is the most distinctive instrument here, and its brittle, trebly, crisp tone gives the disc an underlying tension, especially on the ballads that comprise the majority of the album. Heart-rending, sincere, stripped down yet multi-faceted, John Hiatt has taken a step forward by taking a small step back. Although not quite in a class with career highlights like *Bring the Family* or *Slow Turning*, *Crossing Muddy Waters* is a subtle treat and an album whose watercolor brush strokes paint a vibrant picture of stirring delicacy. *—Hal Horowitz*

Anthology / Aug. 7, 2001 / Hip-O ✦✦✦✦✦
As of its 2001 release, there are at least three other single-disc compilations of John Hiatt's prolific career available, but none truly does justice to his immense body of work. Until now. This intelligently collected, sequenced, and annotated double pack delivers 40 tracks covering 15 of Haitt's albums from his inauspicious yet refreshingly naive debut (1974's *Hangin' Around the Observatory*) to 2000's all-acoustic *Crossing Muddy Waters*, a return of sorts to his rural roots. Fans may quibble with the song selection, lack of previously unreleased material, and the inclusion of only one rarity ("Spyboy," his Jack Nitzsche-produced contribution to the obscure *Cruising* soundtrack), but this is as close to a perfect summation of Hiatt's career through 2001 as one could hope for without expanding to the box set he probably deserves. Hip-O thoughtfully licenses tracks from Sony, Capitol, Reprise (for Little Village's "Don't Think About Her . . ."), and Vanguard, in addition to including hefty chunks of his defining A&M years as well as the more spotty yet essential MCA and Geffen work. The overall effect is staggering in its stylistic diversity and sheer volume of ruggedly melodic singer/songwriter tunes. Whether it's his vaguely new wave rockers like "Doll Hospital," country weepers such as "The Way We Make a Broken Heart," the twangy pop of "Memphis in the Meantime," heartfelt, emotionally tugging ballads like "Lipstick Sunset" and "Feels Like Rain," or the Stones-y crunch of "Paper Thin," there are precious few clinkers here. Each disc maxes out at 78 minutes, the 16-page book is filled with an informative essay, quotes from the artist, and rare pictures (but surprisingly lacks specific-track personnel, a major omission considering Hiatt has worked with a stellar assortment of talented musicians), and the 24-bit remastered sound is crisp, lean, and clean. As of its 2001 release date, the modestly titled *Anthology* is the definitive portrait of one of America's most talented, respected, and eclectic songwriters. *—Hal Horowitz*

The Tiki Bar Is Open / Sep. 11, 2001 / Vanguard ✦✦✦✦
On a creative roll after 2000's acoustic *Crossing Muddy Waters*, John Hiatt returns rejuvenated as well as electric. Old backing band the Goners have returned for his 17th—and best—album in the 13 years that have passed since the same outfit accompanied him on 1988's classic *Slow Turning*. Unlike its intentionally cheesy tongue-in-cheek title, *Tiki Bar* is a keenly constructed collection of heartfelt, bluesy tunes that rock—and often rock hard—with tremendous soul. Subtle use of drum loops and the occasional overdub enhances, but doesn't update, Hiatt's roots approach. Like the Band, whose "The Weight" he evokes on "Hangin' Round Here," these songs seemingly spring from a bottomless well of melodies and hooks, all energized by his raw, throaty vocals. The famed Goners guitarist, Louisiana's Sonny Landreth, positively burns throughout, especially on slide, and the group consistently coalesces like Crazy Horse on a hot night. They follow their eclectic leader through waltzy ballads, folksy love songs, mid-tempo burners, and even an unusual album closing ten-minute psychedelic romp, "Farther Stars," that takes the Beatles' "Tomorrow Never Knows" to the Middle Eastern swamps. Far from winding down in his fifties, John Hiatt is releasing the most inspired work of his life. Fans will be thrilled that he has found his muse, and newcomers who start here will be elated to know there is more where this came from. Not quite as magical as his high-water mark, *Bring the Family*, this is still a superbly crafted disc whose songs quickly sink in and stay lodged in your brain. Come in and have a taste; the tiki bar is open. *—Hal Horowitz*

Bertie Higgins

b. Dec. 8, 1944, Tarpon Springs, FL
Soft Rock
Rembered for his lone Top ten single "Key Largo," a soft-rock fantasy about living in a Humphrey Bogart film, Bertie Higgins was a professional musician that made the leap to solo performing in the early '80s. His 1982 debut *Just Another Day In Paradise* was actually a comeback of sorts—it was the first musical venture he had undertaken since 1968, when he retired to his hometown of Tarpon Springs, FL after the breakup of his group, the Roemans. Between 1964 and 1968, Higgins drummed with the Roemans, who recorded a series of singles for ABC-Paramount, which were all ignored. More importantly, the group supported vocalist Tommy Roe on tour, which was how they sustained an income. Following the breakup of the Roemans, he returned to Tarpon Springs and over the course of the '70s, he slowly built up a collection of songs which formed the basis of *Just Another Day in Paradise*. Released on the independent label Kat Family in 1982, the record became a hit as the single "Key Largo" climbed its way into the Top ten. "Key Largo" was the only hit from the record, although the title track did reach the Top 50. For the next 12 years, Higgins was quiet, releasing *Then and Now* on Epic Records in 1994 to little attention. *—Stephen Thomas Erlewine*

● **Just Another Day in Paradise** / 1982 / Epic ✦✦✦✦✦
Sonically, *Just Another Day in Paradise* is standard-issue soft-rock, featuring light, catchy melodies, cooing backing vocals, and lush arrangements that can blend into the background. What makes it distinctive is Bertie Higgins' bizarre obsession with '40s movies and Humphrey Bogart in particular. No less than two songs, "Key Largo" and "Casablanca," mention Bogie films by name, while the entire album is driven by a romantic fantasy of adventure and old-fashioned love affairs. Higgins' melodic skills might not be exceptional, but they are pleasant enough to make his cinematic obsessions engaging, particularly on the hit single "Key Largo," which has an exceptionally smooth chorus—"We had it all / Just like Bogie and Bacall." It doesn't really matter that the only thing Bogart and Higgins have in common is that they've both seen *Casablanca*, because Bertie's affection makes *Just Another Day in Paradise* an enjoyable soft-rock artifact. *—Stephen Thomas Erlewine*

The High Llamas

f. 1991, London, England
Indie Pop, Chamber Pop, Post-Rock/Experimental, Alternative Pop/Rock
Although the High Llamas are nominally a group, they're pretty much the brainchild of singer and guitarist Sean O'Hagan. O'Hagan did some time in the London-by-way-of-Dublin band Microdisney, in which he was the songwriting partner of Cathal Coughlan. After Microdisney split in 1988 (Coughlan forming Fatima Mansions), O'Hagan released a couple of import-only solo albums before forming the High Llamas. The Llamas issued their debut, *Gideon Gaye*, in 1994 to high praise in the British press; it was released in the States a year later almost as an afterthought, with virtually no fanfare. Comparisons of the High Llamas/O'Hagan to Brian Wilson/the Beach Boys are unavoidable, and not just

from arcane critics. Anyone with a large Beach Boys collection will detect the uncanny resemblance to 1966-70 Beach Boys, with the sophisticated melodies, the beautiful harmonies, and the elaborate production, with the emphasis on layered keyboards and orchestration. Echoes of *Pet Sounds, Smile, Wild Honey,* and *Surf's Up* predominate, though O'Hagan also claims Burt Bacharach as a major inspiration. At this point, however, the strong resemblance to Wilson's meisterwerks place O'Hagan closer to imitation than originality. Considering that he's been making records for about a decade, he might want to start aiming his sights higher. Subsequent efforts include 1996's *Hawaii,* 1997's *Cold and Bouncy* and 1999's *Snowbug. Buzzle Bee* arrived the following year, featuring a more stripped-down sound and guest vocals from Mary Hansen from Stereolab. *—Richie Unterberger*

● **Gideon Gaye** / 1994 / V2 ✦✦✦✦✦
Despite what Don Was, Van Dyke Parks, and others might be claiming, Brian Wilson is *not* going to return to the peak of his powers. In his absence, Sean O'Hagan might be the best available substitute. He's obviously done his homework, listening not only to all the albums between *Pet Sounds* and *Surf's Up,* but the widely circulated *Smile* bootlegs as well. Cheeky references to cuts like "Let's Get Away for a While" and "Surf's Up" pop up from time to time on this lush set, which takes its cues from both Wilson's most melodic and most eccentric qualities (though the ten-minute flute solo on "Track Goes By" does this to excess). It's an impressive outing that sounds like little else in the alternative rock world of the mid '90s. But it only establishes O'Hagan and his various pals as charming emulators, rather than true innovators. *—Richie Unterberger*

Hawaii / 1996 / V2 ✦✦✦✦
Sean O'Hagan has a gift for orchestral pop, creating lush soundscapes that are awash with sonic detail. He clearly owes a lot to Brian Wilson, and *Hawaii,* the High Llamas' third album, falls somewhere between *Pet Sounds* and *Smile.* Sonically, the rich, orchestrated production is reminiscent of the former, but *Hawaii* is paced like *Smile,* with brief instrumentals and song fragments framing the full-fledged songs. Each is carefully arranged and recorded, offering an inviting tapestry of strings, guitars, keyboards, brass, and percussion. For much of *Hawaii,* the sound of the record is intoxicating, but the album drags over the course of 77 minutes. Among the 29 tracks, there are some beautiful moments and gorgeous songs, but *Hawaii* winds up being too much of a good thing, lacking the focus of *Gideon Gaye.* [The American edition of *Hawaii* contains a 40-minute, six-track bonus disc, containing material previously unreleased in the U.S., including the B-sides for the *Nomads* single.] *— Stephen Thomas Erlewine*

Cold and Bouncy / Jan. 27, 1998 / V2 ✦✦✦✦
Cold and Bouncy is an accurate description of the High Llamas' music, in many ways. On the surface, it's light and airy, with sprightly or sighing melodies, sometimes quite detailed, but that very attention to detail keeps the music at an emotional distance—it's easy to admire Sean O'Hagan's skill, but a little more difficult to be moved by it. Still, there's a lot to be said for being evocative, which the High Llamas certainly are. Like its predecessor *Hawaii, Cold and Bouncy* floats between involved instrumentals and songs, relying on texture more than actual songwriting. O'Hagan is beginning to break away from his Brian Wilson obsessions, even if echoes of *Smile* and *Pet Sounds* are evident throughout the record. However, it sounds more than ever like original work, thanks to a subtle incorporation of retro-electronic textures, straight out of his work with Stereolab. Those keyboards open the sound up just enough to make *Cold and Bouncy* the group's most inviting release since *Gideon Gaye,* but it still suffers from O'Hagan's meandering tendencies. While its not the marathon of *Hawaii,* the album still runs way too long, lasting well over an hour. Instead of adding depth, the length makes O'Hagan's ideas difficult to assimilate, and by the end of the record, it sounds like he only has variations on a handful of themes. But when the album is consumed in small doses, however, O'Hagan's flair for arrangement and sonic detail burns brightly. *— Stephen Thomas Erlewine*

Lollo Rosso / Oct. 13, 1998 / V2 ✦✦✦✦
As was the fashion in the '90s, the High Llamas handed off the master tapes of *Cold and Bouncy* to some of the hottest, most cutting-edge remixers of the day for some cutting and pasting. While many such projects smell of quick moneymakers, this record actually works. The remixers manage to retain the late-period Beach Boys sound that the Llamas so lovingly re-create while at the same time adding their own distinctive touches. Mouse on Mars turns "Showstop Hip Hop" into a hiccuping carnival ride of happy bleeps and bloops, Cornelius sprinkles hi-tech fairy dust over "Homespin Rerun," and Kid Loco revamps "Homespin Rerun" into a sleek techno track that breaks into a sunny acoustic guitar-spun melody about half way through. Best of all is Jim O'Rourke's epic remix of "Mini-Management." For over eight minutes he weaves the piano, vibes, and banjos into a beautiful and strange wall of sound that keeps shifting, reshaping, and all sorts of neat things before finally exploding into a burst of electronic noise that leaves the listener saying, boy, I wish all remixes could be this inventive and interesting. Not a waste of time or money, this record is an entertaining listen as well as proof that all High Llamas records don't sound exactly the same. *— Tim Sendra*

Snowbug / Oct. 26, 1999 / V2 ✦✦✦
Sean O'Hagan makes records the way some people make miniature models, slaving over the little details. At first, it's hard not to be impressed by the glittering surface, but after a while—either upon closer examination or repeated exposure to similar works—the initial thrill fades away, and the actual content isn't that impressive. But that's not the only reason why *Snowbug,* the fifth full-length album by O'Hagan's High Llamas, feels like their weakest effort yet. With *Snowbug,* O'Hagan is utterly complacent, perfectly content to roll out his old bag of tricks, whether it's something he used on *Hawaii* or his production work for Stereolab. If you haven't heard his other work, perhaps the little trademark flourishes will be charming, but this is the least involving record he has

yet cut, either as an artist or producer. All the melodies are self-consciously designed to be frothy and hummable, yet none of them wind up being memorable, largely because more time has been spent on the recording than the writing. To a certain extent, that's been true of his previous records, but here, it seems as if he's spending all his energy creating a painstakingly detailed replica of his past work. That may be enough for some fans, those who simply revel in the sheer construct of the sound, but it sounds increasingly like a dead end for O'Hagan. At one point, there was charm and invention to his music, even if it was merely an homage, but now that it's become the patented High Llamas sound, it's clear that he's boxed himself into a corner, and worse, he doesn't seem that concerned about it. The end result may be something to admire based on one quick glance, but upon closer inspection, it's too easy to see the seams in the construction. *— Stephen Thomas Erlewine*

Buzzle Bee / Oct. 24, 2000 / V2 International ✦✦✦
It's probably critical overkill to point out that the High Llamas are the prime inheritors of the lush soundscapes that Brian Wilson and Burt Bacharach perfected (each in his own way) during the '60s and early '70s. On the other hand, it's also abundantly obvious that the English quartet never seems to tire of mining Bachrach's hits and Wilson's masterworks—namely *Pet Sounds* and the aborted *Smile* album—for new ideas. *Buzzle Bee* might just be the group's most out-there production yet, as the Llamas churn out eight tracks full of gorgeous symphonic-pop arrangements and aloof, lazy melodies that dart in and out of all kinds of studio tinkering. If this is, in fact, something Wilson and Bacharach would have made, they would have had to have made it while under the influence of some very potent psychedelics. Still, too much of it sounds like background buzz, the sort of stuff that Wilson rightly left on the cutting room floor during the *Pet Sounds* sessions. What would be really interesting is if these guys struck some sort of sitcom-worthy bargain with their heroes: The Llamas would teach Wilson and Bacharach to be hip, if those two would lend the Llamas some hooks. *—Christian Hoard*

Dan Hill

b. Jun. 3, 1954, Toronto, Ontario, Canada
Vocals, Guitar / Adult Contemporary, Soft Rock
Born in Toronto, Hill is an unabashedly sentimental singer/songwriter. As a teenager, Hill was a major fan of vocalists like Frank Sinatra. He became popular in Canada, and his debut album was released in 1975. In 1977, he co-wrote the highly emotional "Sometimes When We Touch" with Barry Mann, and it became a Top Ten smash in the U.S. After a few lesser hits, he seemingly disappeared, but mounted a comeback in 1987, scoring another Top Ten hit with "Can't We Try," a duet with Vonda Sheppard. He has charted a few times on *Billboard*'s Adult Contemporary chart since then. *—Steve Huey*

Greatest Hits & More / 1994 / Spontaneous ✦✦✦
The "more" in *Greatest Hits & More* doesn't just stand for the album tracks that the word usually signifies, it also signals that this collection is not quite just the greatest hits—these are actually remakes, along with new songs. While that's not necessarily a bad thing, it does make this less than a compelling purchase for the casual fans it's aimed at. *—Stephen Thomas Erlewine*

Jessie Hill

b. Dec. 9, 1932, New Orleans, LA, d. Sep. 17, 1996, New Orleans, LA
Vocals / New Orleans R&B, R&B
Loose and wild, Jessie Hill cut a New Orleans party classic with his crazed "Ooh Poo Pah Doo." The two-sided single, a 1960 Allen Toussaint production on Minit, has Hill shouting the nearly unintelligible lyrics over a strong Crescent City groove, while the flip is an instrumental featuring saxist David Lastie. Hill cut several more boisterous outings with Toussaint at the helm before heading to the West Coast, where he made a disappointing album for Blue Thumb in 1970. *—Bill Dahl*

● **Golden Classics** / 1989 / Collectables ✦✦✦✦✦
Good-time New Orleans R&B from the early '60s, produced by prolific pianist Allen Toussaint. *—Bill Dahl*

Lauryn Hill

b. May 26, 1975
Vocals / Contemporary R&B, Alternative Rap, Urban, Hip-Hop
Call Lauryn Hill the Mother of Hip-Hop Invention: With her 1998 solo debut *The Miseducation of Lauryn Hill,* the Fugees' most vocal member not only established herself as creative force on her own, but also broke new ground by successfully integrating rap, soul, reggae, and R&B into her own sound. Her on-again, off-again stint in the Fugees began at the age of 13 but was often interrupted by both the acting gigs and her enrollment at Columbia University. With the multi-platinum *The Score,* the Fugees (and especially the camera-friendly Hill) achieved international success, though some pundits took shots at their penchant for cover songs. That criticism made *Miseducation* even more of a surprise. Hill wrote, arranged, or produced just about every track on the album, which is steeped in her old-school background, both musically (the Motown-esque singalong of "Doo Wop (That Thing)" and lyrically (the nostalgic "Every Ghetto, Every City"). By the end of the year, as the album topped virtually every major music critic's "best-of" list, she was being credited for helping fully assimilate hip-hop into mainstream music, culminating in the February 1999 Grammy awards, during which Hill took home five trophies—the most ever for a woman. *—Brian Raftery*

● **The Miseducation of Lauryn Hill** / Aug. 25, 1998 / Columbia ✦✦✦✦✦
This highly anticipated album from Lauryn Hill features a mix of soul, rap, and reggae. Hill, who gained national attention by singing in the movie *Sister Act II,* is also a mem-

ber of the hip-hop trio the Fugees, which consists of her partners Wyclef Jean and Prakazrel "Pras" Michel. This, her first solo album, houses some hip-hop-induced soul numbers. "Ex-Factor" has a bouncing flow, an enticing change-up, and a supplicating vamp accentuated by a soothing melody. The charged rhythm of "Doo Wop (That Thing)" presses on with Hill rapping and singing from verse to chorus augmented by some juiced-up horns and a whopping bass line. "Nothing Even Matters," a duet with soul singer D'Angelo, breezes in its dulcet rhythm. Their vocals maintain that consistent pitch throughout the song as they humbly complement each other from their cries to their lyrical sighs. There is much here to savor for aficionados of rap, reggae, and hip-hop/soul music. The Fugees alumna is eloquent throughout the set with her message of love, education, peace, perseverance, understanding, and patience. While the young talent is fluent in each respective genre she embraces, the ambience she exudes with her singing has a magnetic, mesmerizing feel. A great effort by a rising star. —*Craig Lytle*

His Name Is Alive

f. 1989, Livonia, MI

Experimental Rock, Dream Pop, Indie Rock, Alternative Pop/Rock

Named after history class notes on Abraham Lincoln, the Livonia, MI-based sonic manipulators His Name Is Alive formed when multi-instrumentalist/producer Warren Defever (also of shockabilly group Elvis Hitler) was still in high school. Defever, former schoolmate Karin Oliver (vocals), and drummer Damian Lang released self-produced cassettes of their music, one of which made its way to Ivo Watts-Russell, founder of the pioneering art label 4AD. Intrigued with His Name Is Alive's blend of spectral vocals, poetic lyrics, and textural guitars, Watts signed the band. The group recorded their first release for the label, *Livonia*, in Defever's home studio. The album features Oliver's shivery vocals along with tape loops, samples, and guitar blasts, for a noise-damaged, ethereal collection of songs about ghosts, reincarnation, and dreams. An epic 23 songs long, 1992's *Home is in Your Head* ranges from folky ballads to electrifying guitar maelstroms and tape collages. In 1993, His Name Is Alive released two albums: *King of Sweet*, a limited edition release that mixed tape effects, samples, demos, and unreleased songs, and *Mouth By Mouth*, which added more pop structure into the group's inherently experimental and dreamy sound, resulting in their most accessible and diverse album to that date. Defever's diverse interests influenced His Name Is Alive's next release, 1996's *Stars on ESP*. Very little of the group's original ethereal sound remained, augmented instead with touches of dub, folk, gospel, and early to mid-'60s pop like the Beach Boys' *Pet Sounds*. The following year's *Nice Day* EP reached to garage rock and '60s R&B for its inspiration, and featured some of the gospel singers from *Stars on ESP*, including Lovetta Pippen, whose singing also gave His Name Is Alive's 1998 LP *Fort Lake* an earthy sensuality. —*Heather Phares*

Livonia / 1990 / 4AD ✦✦✦

His Name is Alive's debut album, *Livonia*, is the group's artiest, most explicitly experimental release. It's also the most haphazard, in terms of musical success: the affecting ("If July," "Fossil") sits next to the affected ("You and I Have Seizures," "Reincarnation"). Even at its most contrived, however, *Livonia* features the elements the group used later to create their distinctive style: Karin Oliver's shimmery, ghostly voice and Warren Defever's open-minded production. Defever commented later that he saw himself as an avant-garde composer during the *Livonia* period; the album's found sounds, tape loops, and samples do give it an artsy and occasionally precious patina. At its best, *Livonia* explores death, dreams, and spirituality with transcendent music and lyrics. At its worst, it's an ambitious debut, introducing a creative, aspiring band. —*Heather Phares*

Home is in Your Head / Jul. 23, 1992 / Rykodisc ✦✦✦✦

Dark, disturbing, and beautiful, His Name Is Alive's *Home Is in Your Head* develops the deceptively simple, abstractly emotional music they introduced on *Livonia*. Held together by Warren Defever's artful production, its 23 songs range from jealous contemplation to spiritual concerns, from gentle folk to white noise guitar outbursts. Karin Oliver's supple voice lends itself to an array of musical and emotional settings: she's acidly sweet on "The Charmer"'s brittle taunt "Where is your head now?/I should nail it to her door/Where are your hands now?/I know what you'd use them for." On "Why People Disappear," she's pensive: "Maybe I know as much as I ever will/We've been forever." The numerous instrumentals and interludes add to the overall yearning, searching mood. "Her Eyes Were Huge Things" builds subtle strumming and Oliver's sighs into an evocative spell, while "Hope Called in Sick" crashes in with loud, wailing guitars. The group's sound collages also find more purpose here than on *Livonia*; the chanting children on "Put Your Finger in Your Eye" are downright unnerving, and "Spirit and Body" conjures a story of loss out of a ticking watch and just-audible snippets of conversation. With the oddly comforting finale, "Dreams Are of the Body," *Home is in Your Head* completes a seamless exploration of music and emotion. The Rykodisc reissue also includes the group's hard-to-find *The Dirt Eaters* EP. Named for Defever's rock-oriented side project, it features the spooky, subtly dissonant cover of Rainbow's "Man on the Silver Mountain," Ivo Watts-Russell's bleak remix of "Are We Still Married?," and "The Dirt Eaters'" pastoral art folk. Added to *Home Is in Your Head*, it represents the band's best early work. —*Heather Phares*

King of Sweet / 1993 / Perdition Plastics ✦✦✦✦

Released in a limited edition of 2,000 copies by the Chicago-based Perdition Plastics label, *King of Sweet* features demos and alternate takes of songs that appeared on *Home Is in Your Head* and future releases, as well as material that is unavailable elsewhere. In many ways, *King of Sweet* captures the experimental, abstract essence of His Name Is Alive better than the group's other releases; the album's open-ended song collages reflect His Name Is Alive's willingness to reuse, remix, and reform any ideas that cross its radar. "Take a Look Around You" gives *Home Is in Your Head*'s "Why People Disappear" an elec-

tric guitar makeover, while "This Weekend," "Are You Coming Down This Weekend," and "Meet Me by Moonlight, Alone" recast the same song in pensive, ethereal, and breezy pop settings. Other parts of the album toss the riff from Neil Young's "Hey Hey, My My," hip-hop scratches, and jazzy samples in with Karin Oliver's sweet vocals and Defever's layered, versatile guitars. Jangly little pop songs are surrounded by interludes of found noises and sound effects, as on "Honey Babe, My Blue-Eyed Babe," and "Soul Resides in the Horse Barn," both of which the band reworked later. Though not His Name Is Alive's most accessible album, *King of Sweet* showcases the band's ability to make divergent elements sound completely natural together, as well as its constant change and invention. —*Heather Phares*

● Mouth by Mouth / Apr. 13, 1993 / 4AD ✦✦✦✦

1993's *Mouth by Mouth* marks a high point in His Name Is Alive's career, consolidating the band's musical elements—sweet vocals, technicolor production, evocative guitar work, and arty arrangements—into 16 songs that are as diverse as they are cohesive. Memories of Michigan summertimes, Theodore Roethke's poetry, and sensuality collide, creating the fractured sugar-pop of "Baby Fish Mouth" and "Lip," which sit comfortably beside the stark, cello-driven "Cornfield." The band's sinister side pops up on "Ear," a deadpan retelling of Vincent van Gogh's self-amputation. *Mouth by Mouth* "rocks" more than any of the band's previous work, thanks to the continued involvement of the Dirt Eaters; they are credited with the album's louder songs, such as the fuzzed-out "Drink, Dress and Ink" and "The Torso." An electrified version of "The Dirt Eaters" rounds out *Mouth by Mouth*, hinting at the group's increasing pop tendencies. His Name Is Alive's spooky, ethereal side is here too, evident on songs like the spiritually inclined "Lord, Make Me a Channel of Your Peace" and the gamelan-pop of "Sort Of." "Can't Go Wrong Without You" manages to be creepy, catchy, and beautiful all at once (surreal stop-motion filmmakers The Brothers Quay made a fittingly eerie video for this song). The blissed-out cover of Big Star's "Blue Moon" and the Roethke-inspired "Where Knock Is Open Wide" add a dreamy, folky feel to *Mouth by Mouth*'s stylistic mix. A transitional work for a group whose very style is change, *Mouth by Mouth* begins His Name Is Alive's embrace of more traditional pop styles (for their own purposes, of course) and the departure from their overtly ethereal sound. It's a fresh, fascinating album that improves with repeated listening. —*Heather Phares*

Stars on ESP / Jul. 1996 / 4AD ✦✦✦✦

As usual, Michigan-based sonic envelope-pushers His Name Is Alive continue to boggle expectations with their beautiful, exciting music. On their fourth album for 4AD, *Stars on ESP*, the group mixes dub, dream pop, surf, country, and *Pet Sounds*-era Beach Boys into something altogether unique. The songs range from the deceptively simple, folky "Answer to Rainbow at Midnight" and "Famous Goodbye King" to bouncy pop like "Bad Luck Girl," "The Bees," and "Across the Street." Then there are the songs that defy easy description, like the beautiful, lilting "Dub Love Letter" and the "Good Vibrations" pastiche "Universal Frequencies." On the whole, *Stars on ESP* is their most acoustic-based since 1992's *Home is in Your Head* and their brightest-sounding since *Mouth by Mouth*. However, the trademark strange, spacy noises that peppered the band's other releases can still be found on this album, particularly on "What Else is New List" and "Wall of Speed." An eclectic, unique album—it even includes a gospel song—from an eclectic, unique band, *Stars on ESP* features His Name Is Alive at their most accessible and exciting. —*Heather Phares*

Stars on ESP/Nice Day / Jul. 7, 1998 / 4AD ✦✦✦✦

This reissue collects His Name Is Alive's fourth album and third EP, which explore the group's fascination with older pop and R&B styles. While the layered vocals, buzzing background noises, and other Defever production trademarks remain, *Stars on ESP/Nice Day* really pays tribute to '60s-era Motown and Beach Boys pop sensibilities. But what might be pastiche elsewhere is timeless and unique here. Though "Universal Frequencies" comes the closest to a remake, with its heavy debt to "Good Vibrations," the homages to surf, dub, folk, and gospel are filtered through the band's distinctive approach. So, *Stars on ESP* features three renditions of "This World Is Not My Home"—based on the Woody Guthrie tune of the same name—a blistering, blues rock version, a folky version, and last but not least, a version with a full gospel choir. Summer memories about catching fish and warm weather take the shape of girl-group pop on "Bad Luck Girl" and "What Are You Wearing Tomorrow." "Answer to Rainbow at Midnight" mixes dubby bass, surf guitar, and white noise, and "Wall of Speed" and "Across the Street" are unclassifiable, other than that they're both sweetly sad, abstract love songs. *Nice Day* tackles the gutsier, R&B side of His Name Is Alive's retro recasting. The EP gets even closer to reproducing the '60s vibe on the soulful garage rock of "Crashed Up on the Corner." It's possible to do the hitchhike to "Whale, You Ease My Mind," while Lovetta Pippen's sultry vocals fuel the group's slow-burn cover of "Sinnerman." As always, the band finds room for sweet, jangly pop like "Nice Day" and "Drive Around the Clock" in the midst of their new rootsiness. As a bridge between the more experimental *Mouth by Mouth* and the funkier *Fort Lake*, *Stars on ESP/Nice Day* captures His Name Is Alive at an evolutionary stage of their music. —*Heather Phares*

Ft. Lake / Aug. 25, 1998 / 4AD ✦✦✦✦

His Name Is Alive's fifth 4AD release, *Ft. Lake*, is their most complex and accomplished, pulling together the dreamy experimentalism of their early work with the poppy, soulful tendencies of *Stars on ESP* and *Nice Day*, and adding a few new twists. "The Waitress" adds drum machines and keyboards for a new wave sheen, while the slinky "No Hiding Place Down Her" has enough soul for a dozen Top 40 R&B singles. As on the *Nice Day* EP, Lovetta Pippen's voice sounds wonderful, whether she's dueting with Karin Oliver on "Everything Takes Forever" or taking center stage on the epic, Hendrix-inspired "Wish I Had a Wishing Ring." Steve King and Warren Defever's smooth, sonically rich production makes the most of the band's versatility, and Defever's guitar work sounds especially expressive on tracks like "Wishing Ring" and "Little Red Haired Girl," which shifts between bouncy rockabilly licks and noisy, neo-shoegazing leads. The retro-futuristic synth interludes, courtesy of Defever's Robot World side project, offer a nice contrast to the guitar-heavy aspects of the album. Despite the album's eclectic sound, *Fort Lake*'s one constant is its elliptical, yet emotional songwriting; lyrics like "Answer comes from behind/I've been here all this time" from "Spirit Needs a Spirit Tool" (another of the album's highlights) are strangely poignant and resonant. "How It's Gotta Be," co-written by Defever and bassist Chad Gilchrist, has the sweet, sad feel of classic girl-group songs, while "Rock & Roll Girl From Rock & Roll City"'s repeated refrain of "Come and play/Don't make me wait" adds a new urgency to the band's sound. Though His Name Is Alive defy simple classification at any point in their career, *Fort Lake* might be the best example of their wide-reaching abilities. *—Heather Phares*

Always Stay Sweet / Feb. 23, 1999 / 4AD ✦✦✦✦✦
A 21-song compilation spanning the group's first five albums, *Always Stay Sweet* emphasizes the darker undercurrents of the band's sound. Many tracks, like "How Ghosts Affect Relationships" and "Are We Still Married?" come from *Livonia* and *Home Is in Your Head*. A previously unreleased song, "Underwater," is a different take of "Honey Babe, My Blue Eyed Babe" from *King of Sweet*, and "Sitting Still Moving Still Staring Out," (featured on the *Jerry Maguire* soundtrack) is also included. Though it doesn't paint a complete portrait of His Name Is Alive, *Always Stay Sweet* presents many aspects of the band in a compelling, well-edited collection. *—Heather Phares*

When the Stars Refuse to Shine / 2000 / Time Stereo ✦✦✦
Since shedding their gauzy, ethereal, almost gothic sound, His Name Is Alive have picked up a number of adjunct members, left some old ones behind, and taken a path that one probably wouldn't have expected upon hearing their 4AD debut, *Livonia*. With *When the Stars Refuse to Shine*'s rather minimal execution, there appears to be no more than three instruments accompanying Lovetta Pippen's glorious and soul-inflected vocals at any time. Truly, Pippen's inclusion in the band (she joined during the recording of 1996's *Stars on ESP*) seems to be a marker for His Name Is Alive's shift towards the bluesy, Motown-influenced sound that they possess on both *When the Stars Refuse to Shine* and 1998's *Ft. Lake*. *When the Stars…* is remarkably divergent from earlier albums, and certain tracks on the record are virtually unrecognizable as the group's music. The sparse violin and piano orchestration of "Why Is This Night Different Than All Others" and "Lotus Blossom 1" recalls Rachel's *Music For Egon Schiele*, and their cover of Van Morrison's "Moondance" seems suitable for performance in a seedy jazz club. This album helps to illustrate the depth of Warn Defever's musical lexicon with a fine mix of contempo classical and soulful blues. Not the typical HNIA fare, but a welcome departure nonetheless. *—Ken Taylor*

Someday My Blues Will Cover the Earth / Aug. 21, 2001 / 4AD ✦✦✦
Over the years, His Name is Alive's sound has spanned everything from musique concrete-tinged soundscapes to ethereal pop, gospel, and Hendrix-channeling guitar pyrotechnics. In a less-talented group, these stylistic shifts would seem unfocused, but with His Name is Alive, constant change *is* their style. So it's not unusual that *Someday My Blues Will Cover the Earth* is another departure, but it is a bit surprising that the group, which features Warn Defever, Lovetta Pippen, and Flashpapr's Fred Thomas this time around, picks one style and sticks to it for the whole album. It's still more surprising that the style is smooth urban ballads—in a way, it's His Name is Alive's most startling change since they lightened and brightened their music on *Mouth by Mouth*. However, it's not necessarily a step forward for the group; with their similar beats and tempos, songs like "One Year" and "Our Last Affair" are the musical equivalent of treading water. The album's best moments come near the beginning, when the concept of His Name is Alive doing sleek urban pop like "Nothing Special" still seems fresh. The slinky, sexy "Happy Blues" and "Write My Name in the Groove"—which sounds like a dreamy, distant cousin of TLC's "Waterfalls"—also make the album momentarily convincing. But overall, it sounds too spare and restrained, especially when compared to artists like Aaliyah, Alicia Keys, and the aforementioned TLC, whose work expands the boundaries of urban music in much the same way that His Name is Alive redefines experimental pop. *Someday My Blues…* isn't a bad album: it showcases Pippen's remarkable voice and offers a bit of variety to with the smoky "Solitude" and "Karin's Blues." But compared to the rest of their work, it's His Name is Alive's least satisfying effort since *Livonia*; with any luck, their next experiment will be more successful. *—Heather Phares*

Robyn Hitchcock

b. Mar. 3, 1953, London, England

Vocals, Guitar, Bass / College Rock, Neo-Psychedelia, Jangle Pop, Folk-Rock, Alternative Pop/Rock, Singer/Songwriter

Robyn Hitchcock is one of England's most enduring contemporary singer/songwriters and live performers, although he's been branded eccentric and quirky during the course of his long career. Hitchcock started his recording career with the Soft Boys, a punk-era band specializing in melodic pop merged with comedic lyrics. His voice veers between John Lennon and Syd Barrett, helping to nurture his madman reputation, but his true influences lie more in English folk-rock; his guitar and vocal style and lyrical inanities recall Incredible String Band or Roy Harper. Hitchcock's solo debut, 1981's *Black Snake Diamond Role*, helped consolidate his reputation as an oddball, and was followed by the psychedelia of *Groovy Decay* in 1982 and the all-acoustic *I Often Dream of Trains* in 1984. By 1985, his penchant for zaniness and songsmithing coalesced with *Fegmania*. Three years later, Hitchcock landed his first major U.S. label contract with A&M Records and released *Globe of Frogs* in 1988 and *Queen Elvis* in 1989. He sustained and probably even grew his career; however, by this time, critical approval had fallen off for his work. It wasn't until the 1996 release of *Moss Elixir* that Hitchcock returned to form and fully embraced his folk roots. *Storefront Hitchcock*, the soundtrack to the Jonathan Demme-directed concert film, followed in 1998. *—Denise Sullivan*

Black Snake Diamond Role / 1981 / Rhino ✦✦✦
Robyn Hitchcock's first album after leaving the Soft Boys isn't that far removed from the edgy, warped guitar pop of his former band, which isn't surprising, considering the presence of former Soft Boys bassist Andy Metcalfe and drummer Morris Windsor. However, *Black Snake Diamond Role* removes much of the sharp, cutting guitars of *Underwater Moonlight* and replaces them with friendlier, ringing riffs. But that doesn't mean Hitchcock has gone soft—he's just refined his technique. And that doesn't mean his songwriting has improved. Cut by cut, *Black Snake Diamond Role* is weaker than *Underwater Moonlight*, but that's relative—the album contains pretty and twisted pseudo-psychedelic pop like "Brenda's Iron Sledge," "Acid Bird," "The Man Who Invented Himself," and "Do Policemen Sing?" which all rank among his finest songs. *—Stephen Thomas Erlewine*

Groovy Decay / 1982 / Combat ✦✦

I Often Dream of Trains / 1984 / Rhino ✦✦✦✦✦
Hitchcock was so shaken by the entire *Groovy Decay* disaster that he retired from recording for two years. When he returned in 1984 with *I Often Dream of Trains*, it was clear that the time off had affected his music. A collection of spare, acoustic-based pop-folk songs, *I Often Dream of Trains* is one of Hitchcock's most introspective and charming records. Instead of creating an impenetrably personal album, the stripped-down instrumentation actually opens up the songwriter's world, allowing the ballads ("Trams of Old London," "Cathedral," "Flavour of Night") to sit comfortably next to the jokes ("Uncorrected Personality Traits"). Alternating between acoustic guitars and solo piano, the music is never fragile, adding a strong support to Hitchcock's eccentric lyrics. *—Stephen Thomas Erlewine*

Fegmania! / Mar. 1985 / Rhino ✦✦✦✦✦
After the stripped-back collection *I Often Dream of Trains*, Hitchcock slowly formed a backing band called the Egyptians with ex-Soft Boys Andy Metcalfe and Morris Windsor and keyboardist Roger Jackson over the course of the next year. *Fegmania!*, the Egyptians' first album, was a distinct departure from both the Soft Boys' and Hitchcock's previous solo work, featuring layered, intertwining guitars and keyboards that created lush and thick sonic textures. Even with the more detailed arrangements, the songs remained twitchy and off-kilter, with melodies that usually went in willfully unpredictable directions, yet remained catchy all the while. *Fegmania!* was Hitchcock's most consistent work to date, featuring such highlights as the Eastern-tinged "Egyptian Cream," and the creepy "My Wife & My Dead Wife," and the relatively straightforward "The Man with the Lightbulb Head." *—Stephen Thomas Erlewine*

● **Gotta Let This Hen Out** / Oct. 1985 / Rhino ✦✦✦✦✦
Recorded at the Marquee in London shortly after the release of *Fegmania!*, the live *Gotta Let This Hen Out!* is a tense and exciting record, finding the raw energy that usually goes untapped in Hitchcock's music. Although the album makes the Egyptians sound more like a rock & roll band than they actually were—they never played with such wreckless abandon before or since—the driving performances don't wreck the melodic and lyrical eccentricities of the songs; instead, the increased vigor gives the music a searing power, obliterating the notion that his songs are delicate and precious. The set list also accentuates Hitchcock's strengths, relying on his most accessible and melodic material, whether it's recent material like "Egyptian Cream," "Sometimes I Wish I Was a Pretty Girl," and "Acid Bird" or Soft Boys' tracks like "Kingdom of Love," "Only the Stones Remain," "The Face of Death," and "Leppo and the Jooves." *—Stephen Thomas Erlewine*

Groovy Decoy / Dec. 1985 / Relativity ✦✦

Element of Light / 1986 / Rhino ✦✦✦✦✦
Element of Light, Hitchcock's second studio album with the Egyptians, remains one of his finest moments and offers a convincing argument for his talents as a pop craftsman. Using John Lennon's work for *Revolver* and *The Beatles* as a template, Hitchcock wrote an elegant set of songs for *Element of Light*, songs that contained all of his cryptic lyrical sensibilities, yet featured more refined melodies and song structures. The Egyptians play with a subtle grace, moving between the stately "Winchester" and light psychedelia of "If You Were a Priest" to the bracing attack of "Tell Me About Your Drugs" with ease. While it sacrifices some of the edgy tension of Hitchcock's earlier work, *Element of Light* is his most melodic and eerily beautiful record. *—Stephen Thomas Erlewine*

Invisible Hitchcock / 1986 / Rhino ✦✦✦
As the reference to the Soft Boys' rarities collection, *Invisible Hits*, suggests, *Invisible Hitchcock* gathers together a selection of obscurities and non-album tracks Robyn Hitchcock recorded between 1980 and 1986. Granted, the material is a bit uneven, but the album holds together well, as it emphasizes Hitchcock's gift for warped wordplay and appealingly convoluted melodies. Upon its original release, the running order for *Invisible Hitchcock* was considerably different in Britain and America; Rhino's 1995 reissue standardized the album, including all the material from both versions of the album (with the exception of "Grooving on a Inner Plane," which appeared as a bonus track on the company's reissue of *Black Snake Diamond Role*), as well as adding two songs that never appeared on either version of the record. *—Stephen Thomas Erlewine*

● **Globe of Frogs** / 1988 / A&M ✦✦✦✦✦
Hitchcock's first foray into U.S. major-label territory disappointed some critics but helped expand his audience beyond the realm of college radio, thanks to the radio-friendly "Balloon Man." Aided by his band the Egyptians, it's the production that mars this record,

along with half of the songs. "Sleeping With Your Devil Mask," "Chinese Bones," and "Flesh Number One (Beatle Dennis)," which features Peter Buck on guitar and Squeeze's Difford and Tilbrook on vocals, are the reasons to own this record. *—Denise Sullivan*

Queen Elvis / 1989 / A&M ♦♦♦
Hitchcock redeemed himself on this collection—song for song more vital than *Globe of Frogs*. "Madonna of the Wasps" is a timeless pop song, but the record is mired in modern-rock production and synthesizer sounds. "One Long Pair of Eyes" remains a Hitchcock standard, and the bizarre "Wax Doll" and "Veins of the Queen" kept Hitchcock at the fore of eccentric rock, making him the only appropriate heir to the English king-loony throne formerly occupied by Syd Barrett. *—Denise Sullivan*

Eye / 1990 / Rhino ♦♦♦♦♦
Robyn Hitchcock recorded *Eye*, his fourth proper solo album, after the disappointing *Queen Elvis*. *Eye* marked a return to the acoustic-oriented folk-pop of *I Often Dream of Trains*, featuring a collection of his most personal songs. Where *I Often Dream of Trains* was a kaleidoscopic journey through a colorfully twisted world, *Eye* sounds more confessional, although Hitchcock's exact lyrical sentiments can be difficult to sort out through his dense and willfully obscure imagery. Nevertheless, the immediacy of the music—which is delivered on acoustic guitars and piano—and the simple, delicate grace of Hitchcock's melodies make even the most cryptic lines sound direct and straightforward. *—Stephen Thomas Erlewine*

Perspex Island / Aug. 6, 1991 / A&M ♦♦
By this time, Hitchcock could be counted on for a couple of exceptional songs per album plus a preponderance of less than astonishing material. "So You Think You're In Love" was the keeper from this set, a rollicking, cautionary tale about the joys of early love. Wisely, Hitchcock and the Egyptians gave up producing themselves, but Paul Fox's attempt was still muddled and misguided and ultimately didn't showcase the band to the best of their abilities—although the lack of quality material could also explain the lapse. *—Denise Sullivan*

Respect / Feb. 23, 1993 / A&M ♦♦

Gravy Deco (The Complete Groovy Decay/Decoy Sessions) / Jan. 1995 / Rhino ♦♦

You & Oblivion / Mar. 1995 / Rhino ♦♦

Moss Elixir / Aug. 1996 / Warner Brothers ♦♦♦
Wisely, Hitchcock chucked the band sound (though longtime associates Morris Windsor and Andy Metcalfe continue to lend their services on some tracks) and returned to the spare singer-songwriter format for his best set of songs in more than ten years. Everything is here: the quirky on "Man With a Woman's Shadow," and the elegant on "Beautiful Queen," and the straight-ahead Beatlesque music in which Hitchcock excels in the perfect pop of "Alright, Yeah." Finally, Hitchcock embraced his folk-guitar roots, which hearken back to the days of the Incredible String Band and Roy Harper, while imprinting his indelible lyrical and vocal stamp, one of the true leading lights of contemporary alternative music. *—Denise Sullivan*

Greatest Hits / Sep. 9, 1996 / A&M ♦♦♦♦♦
Disappointingly, the 1980s failed to recognize the genius of Robyn Hitchcock. As a member of the Soft Boys until they broke up in 1981, Hitchcock went on to write some extremely witty, off-the-wall, and peculiarly clever music. With a sound reminiscent of Lloyd Cole and even Elvis Costello at times, Hitchcock's jangly Brit-pop is made up of sharp lyrical craftsmanship and a frolicsome weightlessness that gives his music a distinct charisma. This hits collection is a fine example of his work with the Egyptians dating back to their formation in 1987, made up of album selections, rarities, B-sides, and promotional singles, most of which failed to surface on any of their albums. Riding on the strength of college radio, tunes like "A Globe of Frogs" and "Balloon Man" eventually gained popular admiration, even if it was for a short while. The tongue-in-cheek subtlety of "Legalized Murder" is typical of Hitchcock's humor, and the bizarre effusiveness of "Madonna of the Wasps" is fittingly left of center. The band's cover of Roxy Music's "More Than This" holds up a little better than their attempt at the Byrds' "Eight Miles High," but is a valiant effort nonetheless. Intriguing pieces like "The Yip Song," "Dark Green Energy," and "She Doesn't Exist" confirm that Robyn Hitchcock & the Egyptians possess a unique imagination as well as an adept spiritedness, which should have led to wider attention. *—Mike DeGagne*

Uncorrected Personality Traits: The Robyn Hitchcock Collection / Aug. 5, 1997 / Rhino ♦♦♦♦
Hitchcock is an album-oriented artist with an extensive oeuvre, so this 20-track anthology of '80s material is best valued as a summary of selected career highlights for those who don't want to collect all of his full-length efforts. As such, it does a decent job, offering college radio hits like "Egyptian Cream," "My Wife & My Dead Wife," "The Man with the Lightbulb Head," and "Heaven," along with less-heard cuts from early-'80s albums that some listeners may have missed. This has nothing from his A&M records of the late '80s and early '90s and so couldn't properly be considered a career-spanning best-of (highlights of the A&M period are on A&M's *Greatest Hits*). It's well-packaged, though, with liner notes featuring detailed comments on the tracks by Hitchcock himself. *—Richie Unterberger*

Storefront Hitchcock: Music from Demme Picture / Oct. 27, 1998 / Warner Brothers ♦♦♦♦
On Hitchcock's last U.S. tour, he played Hendrix's "The Wind Cries Mary" as well as "Are You Experienced," sometimes within the same set. It's the kind of act that defines his performing genius as a whimsical iconoclast; but then Hitchcock once performed most of Dylan's "Royal Albert Hall" concert, so such live acts of devotion shouldn't come as entirely unexpected.

Though only "Mary" is included here, Hitchcock's wacky essence is captured on the soundtrack to the Jonathan Demme picture which chronicles a couple of evenings during the aforementioned U.S. tour; both documents demand patience, but by the third song and final guitar of "I'm Only You," if you ain't hooked, I'll buy yours. Drawing from a variety of eras (the slice of life "The Yip! Song" and the electrified riff of "Freeze" are familiar Egyptians songs; love stories "Beautiful Queen" and "Alright, Yeah" are from *Moss Elixir*, "1974" and "I Don't Remember Guildford" are newer, personal-ish songs), the tie that binds this collection is feelings, instead of those proverbial Hitchcock symbols for them: fish and birds. What a relief. And who knew he was such an accomplished folk *and* electric guitarist? *Storefront Hitchcock* reveals his humanness, with all of his flaws, foibles, and mid-life revelations: "I'm completely gray, you're completely mad, you're a middle-aged baby and the world is bad," in "Let's Go Thundering"; "I know who wrote the book of love... it was an idiot, it was a fool..." in "Freeze." To the best of his ability, the Hitchcock persona has become "sensitive male" while still maintaining his absurd sense of humor. In the process, he's made one dictionary-definition, jaw-dropping live singer/songwriter album. Listen closely for the nod to "Purple Haze." *—Denise Sullivan*

Jewels for Sophia / Jul. 20, 1999 / Warner Brothers ♦♦♦
The slight failure of Robyn Hitchcock's *Jewels for Sophia* is by no means the fault of his songs—they are as tuneful and ridiculous as ever. But after his close-to-the-bone *Moss Elixir*, Hitchcock's regressed into goofiness, hiding behind a noisy band on some tracks. Compadre Tim Keegan on guitar and producers Jon Brion and Pat Collier come up with the best work like the techno/folk "Dark Princess" and the acoustic, Dylanesque "You've Got a Sweet Mouth on You, Baby." The jangling "Sally Was a Legend" reunites Hitchcock with ex-Soft Boy Kimberly Rew on guitar. Yet the ramshackle inanity of "Viva! Sea Tac" and "Elizabeth Jade," provided by Peter Buck, three-fourths of the Young Fresh Fellows, and a recording crew in Seattle, are silly self-parody. Conversely, the gentle "I Feel Beautiful" with Grant Lee Phillips on harmony and the bonus song, "Don't Talk to Me About Gene Hackman," are the kinds of spare composition at which Hitchcock has come to master. *—Denise Sullivan*

Hoku

Teen Pop, Euro-Pop
Hawaiian singing star, Don Ho, is the father of ten children. One of them is Hoku. She decided to follow her father's musical example, but in her own way. Before her 20th birthday, Hoku had completed a self-titled debut album. One of the tracks, "Another Dumb Blonde," added to the soundtrack from the hit movie, *Snow Day*. It became a Top Ten video on MTV—and her first single hit gold. Kind of fitting if you consider the fact that her name, translated into English, means star. Hoku was born in Hawaii in 1981. She got used to singing in front of large audiences by frequently performing on-stage with her famous father. Before reaching her teens, there was already no mistaking her talent. Her lovely voice was always a crowd pleaser, soon she was doing more and more solo numbers, and then doing shows of her own.

After being raised in Hawaii, Hoku left the beautiful island and her family behind to move to California to continue her education. It was there, in the latter part of 1999, that she signed a contract with the Geffen Records label. The next year her self-titled debut album was recorded. Shortly after the release, one of her tunes, "Another Dumb Blonde," hit the Billboard charts. Some of her other songs are "You First Believed," "Just Enough," "What You Need," and "Oxygen." Most critics quickly began comparing her to young stars like Christina Aguilera and Britney Spears, but Hoku has a style all her own. Some of it probably comes from the fact that she is a practicing Pentecostal Christian and refuses to showcase her performances with some kind of sex kitty act. *—Charlotte Dillon*

● **Hoku** / Apr. 18, 2000 / Interscope ♦♦♦
What separates Hoku's self-titled debut album from the glut of shiny teen pop that flooded the market in late 1999/early 2000 is that it never tries to sound wiser than its years and it never seems to pander to commercial concerns. Sure, it's commercial—that's what teen pop is all about—but never once do the record makers decide to push Hoku as a nymphet. Her songs are never sexual the way those of Britney Spears and Christina Aguilera surely are. These are sunny, innocent songs, from the bright dance numbers to the slow ballads. That's appropriate because Hoku has a girlish voice; she sounds young, so it makes sense that her record is targeted toward middle-school daydreams and junior-high dances. Thankfully, producer Antonio Armato keeps things light and sparkling, helping to keep the record fun even through a couple of slow stretches. Make no mistake, *Hoku* isn't a masterpiece, but it *is* a really fun, lightweight pop record that is better than most teen-pop wannabes from its era. Also, it suggests that Hoku could stick around and be more than a one-hit wonder (though that one hit, the exuberant and slyly clever "Another Dumb Blonde," would be good enough for most dance-pop divas); she wrote, performed, and produced the final track, the Jewel-ish ballad "You First Believed." It may be a little sophomoric, but it's sweetly so, and that sweetness is apparent throughout the record and is what makes it a winning debut. *—Stephen Thomas Erlewine*

Hole

f. 1989, Los Angeles, CA
Grunge, Alternative Pop/Rock
Throughout Hole's career, Courtney Love's notorious public image has overshadowed her band's music. In its original incarnation, Hole was one of the noisiest, most abrasive alternative bands performing in the early '90s. By the time of their second album, 1994's *Live Through This*, the band had smoothed out many of their rougher edges, as well as adding more melody and hooks to their songwriting. Through both versions of Hole, Love's combative, assaultive persona permeated both the group's music and lyrics, giving the band a tense, unpredictable edge even at their quietest moments. Hole's debut record,

1991's *Pretty on the Inside*, received numerous positive reviews, especially in the British weekly music press. One year later, Courtney Love married Kurt Cobain, the lead singer/songwriter of Nirvana. For a couple of months, the couple were the king and queen of the new rock world. Halfway through 1993, Love reassembled Hole and recorded the group's first major-label album, the more pop-oriented *Live Through This*. Four days before the album was released, Kurt Cobain's body was discovered in the couple's Seattle home; he died of a self-inflicted shotgun wound three days before. Two months after Cobain's death, Hole bassist Kristen M. Pfaff died of a heroin overdose. After *Live Through This* went gold in the summer of 1995, Hole toured with the fifth Lollapalooza tour. The often-delayed *Celebrity Skin* followed in 1998. *—Stephen Thomas Erlewine*

Pretty on the Inside / Jul. 1, 1991 / Caroline ♦♦♦
With the assistance of producers Kim Gordon and Don Fleming, Hole records a brutally uncompromising debut with *Pretty on the Inside*. The jagged white noise and buzzing guitars articulate Courtney Love's pent-up rage as well as her lyrics, and while that might make the album difficult to absorb in one sitting, it also makes it a singular achievement. *—Stephen Thomas Erlewine*

● **Live Through This** / Apr. 12, 1994 / DGC ♦♦♦♦
Courtney Love completely revamped Hole before recording their second album, keeping only Eric Erlandson in the lineup. That is one of the reasons why *Live Through This* sounds so shockingly different from *Pretty on the Inside*, but the real reason is Love's desire to compete in the same commercial alternative-rock arena as her husband, Kurt Cobain. In fact, many rumors have claimed that Cobain ghost-wrote a substantial chunk of the album, and while that's unlikely, there's no denying that his patented stop-start dynamics, bare chords, and punk-pop melodies provide the blueprint for *Live Through This*. Love adds her signature rage and feminist rhetoric to the formula, but the lyrics that truly resonate are the ones that unintentionally predict Cobain's suicide. For all the raw pain of the lyrics, *Live Through This* rarely sounds raw because of the shiny production and the carefully considered dynamics. Despite this flaw, the album retains its power because it was one of the few records patterned on *Nevermind* that gets the formula right, with a set of gripping hooks and melodies that retain their power even if they follow the predictable grunge pattern. *—Stephen Thomas Erlewine*

My Body, the Hand Grenade / Oct. 28, 1997 / City Slang ♦♦♦♦
As Hole were dragging their heels working on the follow-up to *Live Through This*, their British label City Slang released *My Body, the Hand Grenade*, a collection of outtakes, live cuts, and rare tracks. Most of this material dates from the days of *Pretty on the Inside*, when Courtney Love was tagged as a riot grrrl, since she screamed over sludgy, heavy guitars, but there are also cuts from their anticlimatic *MTV Unplugged* appearance in 1995. While the rarity value of this music certainly makes it interesting, the music itself is pretty average, with the dreck outweighing the good stuff (including a rewrite of the Nirvana rarity "Old Age," for which none of the members of Nirvana are credited) by a wide margin. *—Stephen Thomas Erlewine*

Celebrity Skin / Sep. 8, 1998 / Geffen ♦♦♦
From the moment the *Pyromania* guitars herald open the title track on *Celebrity Skin*, it's clear Hole no longer is tortured. Gone are the roaring guitars and noise, the pain and the anguish that informed *Pretty on the Inside* and *Live Through This*. Some angst remains, but it's buried under a glaze of shiny guitars and hazy melodies, all intended to evoke the heyday of Californian pop in the late '70s. Conceptually, it's a bold move for a band that's nearly synonymous with grunge, but the makeover doesn't quite work. Part of the reason is that Hole's music was always compelling as nakedly cathartic spectacle—and that's exactly what has been excised on *Celebrity Skin*. In the past, Courtney Love pushed her emotions to the forefront, and the sheer forcefulness of her personality disguised the anonymity of her bandmates. A toned-down Love still may not be able to carry a tune, but there's little grit to her performance on *Celebrity Skin*, so she effortlessly blends with the faceless musical support—which is strange, considering her overpowering public image. Walking the line between soft rock and confessional grunge was a difficult task regardless, and to their credit, Hole—with the assistance of producer Michael Beinhorn and consultant Billy Corgan, who is credited with co-writing five songs and essentially pioneered the very sound of *Celebrity Skin* with his Smashing Pumpkins albums—has created an album that sounds like an arena-rock monster, but the hooks sink only halfway in, so it doesn't have much impact. It is a complete makeover, but instead of metamorphosing into a new band, Hole has unwittingly neutered itself. *—Stephen Thomas Erlewine*

The Hollies

f. 1962, Manchester, England

Pop/Rock, Merseybeat, British Invasion, Pop

One of the best and most commercially successful pop/rock acts of the British Invasion, when the Hollies began recording in 1963, they relied heavily upon the R&B/early rock & roll covers that provided the staple diet for countless British bands of the time. They quickly developed a more distinctive style of three-part harmonies (heavily influenced by the Everly Brothers), ringing guitars, and hook-happy material. The best early Hollies records evoke an infectious, melodic cheer similar to that of the early Beatles, although the Hollies were neither in their class (not an insult: nobody else was) nor demonstrated a similar capacity for artistic growth. They tried, though, easing into somewhat more sophisticated folk-rock and mildly psychedelic sounds as the decade wore on, especially on their albums. Although their first singles were R&B covers, the Hollies were much more at home with pop/rock material that provided a sympathetic complement to their glittering harmonies. They ran off an awesome series of hits in the U.K. in the '60s, making the Top 20 almost 20 times. Some of their best mid-'60s singles, like "Here I Go Again," "We're Through," and the British number one "I'm Alive," passed virtually unnoticed in the United States, where they couldn't make the Top 40 until early 1966, when "Look Through Any Window" did the trick. The Hollies really didn't break in America in a big way until "Bus Stop" (1966), their first Stateside Top Tenner; "On a Carousel," "Carrie Ann," and "Stop Stop Stop" were also big hits. Here the Hollies were providing something of a satisfying option for pop-oriented listeners that found the increasingly experimental outings of groups like the Beatles and Kinks too difficult to follow. At the same time, the production and harmonies were sophisticated enough to maintain a broader audience than more teen- and bubblegum-oriented British Invasion acts like Herman's Hermits. *—Richie Unterberger*

Stay With the Hollies / 1964 / BGO ♦♦

In the Hollies Style / 1964 / BGO ♦♦♦♦♦
Released only ten months after their debut album, *Stay With the Hollies*, their second album was a huge leap forward in every respect. Their famous airtight harmonies were now in place, and the sloppiness of the instrumental attack gone. Most important, the group developed enormously as songwriters. Eight of the 12 tracks were Hollies originals and quite skillful in their mastery of the British Invasion essentials of driving, catchy melodies and shining harmonies. A couple of the covers are duds, but the "Nitty Gritty/Something's Got a Hold of Me" medley is first-rate, and the version of "It's in His Kiss" (retitled "It's in Her Kiss") respectable. The Hollies weren't from Liverpool (though Manchester is fairly close), but this nonetheless ranks of one of the very best Merseybeat albums not released by the Beatles themselves. It doesn't include any British or American hits, but "Come On Home," "To You My Love," "Don't You Know," and "What Kind of Boy" (the last of which was written for them by one Big Dee Irwin) will appeal to any British Invasion fan. Surprisingly, none of the tracks were ever released in the United States, making the reissue all the more desirable an item for British Invasion collectors from U.S. shores, who most likely missed it entirely the first time around. *—Richie Unterberger*

The Hollies [BGO] / 1965 / BGO ♦♦♦
The Hollies' third album saw a band in the throes of transition between the Merseybeat and rock & roll with which they established themselves, and the folk-rock and soul music that was blowing the strongest winds of change in 1965. They clean up their backlog of cover staples with versions of tunes by Lloyd Price, Buddy Holly, and Roy Orbison, and delve into soul by taking on the Miracles' "Mickey's Monkey" and Curtis Mayfield's "You Must Believe Me." Their attempt at "Fortune Teller" won't make you forget the Rolling Stones' version; nor, for that matter, are any of the other covers impressive. That leaves five reasonably good originals, the best of which are the gorgeous "So Lonely" and the excellent Merseybeat knockoff "When I Come Home to You." They also sound Beatlesque on "I've Been Wrong," but "Too Many People" and their cover of Peter, Paul & Mary's "Very Last Day" hearken to a folk-rock direction. The album was issued in the U.S. as *Hear! Here!*, replacing "Mickey's Monkey" with their number one British hit "I'm Alive." *—Richie Unterberger*

For Certain Because / 1966 / BGO ♦♦♦
One gets the feeling that, as 1966 drew to a close amidst an incredible acceleration of innovations in the pop and rock world, the Hollies felt the need to prove themselves capable of artistic growth despite having established a very winning formula. *For Certain Because* was their first album entirely composed of original material, and it echoed pop's increased sophistication with fuller, more adventurous arrangements and more personal, folk-rock-influenced compositions. Such was the intense competition of the time that this record couldn't hope to take on *Revolver*, *Aftermath*, or *Face to Face*, but it nevertheless remains an admirable effort that may stand as the group's most accomplished album (greatest-hits packages excepted) of the '60s. The Hollies were very much a pop group and didn't let their somewhat more sober and introspective compositions stand in the way of their glittering harmonies and jangling guitars. Occasional brass, banjo, bells, and vibrating piano embellish their basic rock instrumentation on this pleasant, if hardly earth-shaking, work. The circus-like "Stop! Stop! Stop!," with its manic banjo, was a hit on both sides of the Atlantic; the good-natured "Pay You Back With Interest" a Top 30 hit in America; and the jazzy "Tell Me to My Face" was one of their best '60s album tracks. The LP was released as *Stop! Stop! Stop!* in the U.S. *—Richie Unterberger*

Would You Believe? / Jun. 1966 / EMI ♦♦♦
One of the less essential '60s albums by the Hollies, whose capabilities were arguably stretched by the two-album-a-year-pace-in-addition-to-three-hit-singles model established by the Beatles during this time. Their version of Paul Simon's "I Am a Rock" is nice, but the soul and early rock covers of Sam & Dave, Otis Redding, and Chuck Berry are pretty dispensable; the Hollies were not the Stones or the Animals, lacking their soul and interpretative imagination. Some of the originals are pretty ho-hum too (including the pathetic "Fifi the Flea," which was covered by the Everly Brothers). But every Hollies album of the '60s has some strong overlooked tracks. On this one, they're the surprisingly tough folk-rockers "Hard, Hard Year" and "I've Got a Way of My Own." The ultra-catchy "Don't You Even Care," written by Clint Ballard Jr. (also responsible for their number one British hit "I'm Alive," as well as "The Game of Love" and "You're No Good"), is the real obscure gem here and could have well been a hit under its own steam. The album's last song, "I Can't Let Go," was a big hit in Britain (and a small one in the U.S.) and one of the Hollies' best performances. The record was issued in America, in a slightly amended version, as *Beat Group!* *—Richie Unterberger*

Butterfly / 1967 / BGO ♦♦♦
This late 1967 album found the Hollies making some modest adjustments to the psychedelic era: occasionally trippy studio effects, a sitar on their most psychedelic track ("Maker"), songs that didn't always deal with boy-girl relationships. In fact, however, the

group's focus remained where it usually was: modest but pleasing, similar-sounding catchy tunes with high harmonies and strumming guitars. It's not remarkable or essential, but it's certainly pleasant enough, and a bit better than their earlier 1967 LP, *Evolution*, with some of their better album-only cuts ("Postcard," "Pegasus," "Butterfly," "Away Away Away"). With some track alterations, the record was issued in the U.S. as *Dear Eloise/King Midas in Reverse*; the U.K. edition, as collectors should note, has a few songs that were never released in the States ("Pegasus," "Elevated Observations?," "Try It"). *—Richie Unterberger*

Evolution / 1967 / Sundazed ✦✦

Words and Music by Bob Dylan / 1969 / Epic ✦✦✦
This is the most controversial album in the Hollies' entire output. Graham Nash claimed he quit over the decision to record it, and critics hated it. And on its face, this is all understandable—the Hollies' distinctive high harmony singing and British beat sound were not a natural fit with Bob Dylan's songs, with their mix of earthy sensibilities and raw musicality. With one possible exception, the songs here are not presented in their ideal forms, but that doesn't explain the hostility with which the album was greeted, until one remembers the reverence in which Dylan was held at the time and the Hollies' status as a pop/rock group; in many critics' eyes, the Hollies cutting an album of Dylan songs was only a step removed from Herman's Hermits recording one. The album has virtues, including Allan Clarke's powerful lead vocals and the soaring harmonies of Terry Sylvester and Tony Hicks, along with Hicks' lively and inventive guitar contributions to the album. The overblown, orchestrated version of "Blowin' in the Wind" may be the worst version of that song ever cut, though "Quit Your Lowdown Ways" is well sung and even better played, with some superb rockabilly-style acoustic guitar courtesy of Hicks. "All I Really Want to Do" has superb singing and a strange marimba accompaniment that somehow works. And then there is "My Back Pages," the best track on the album and the only one that sounds the way the Hollies of old would've done it, loose and flowing, with beautiful acoustic guitar at its center and a reed orchestra accompanying the band. A 1993 CD reissue of this album included two live cuts with Graham Nash in the band, doing Dylan songs from his final days in the band. *—Bruce Eder*

Hollies Sing Hollies / Nov. 1969 / Polydor ✦✦✦
Hollies Sing Hollies was the group's somewhat self-conscious follow-up to *Hollies Sing Dylan*—in the U.S., it formed the bulk of the *He Ain't Heavy He's My Brother* LP, with that smash single (totally unlike anything else on the album) overshadowing the rest of the record. If the Hollies began to lose credibility as a frontline rock group, the blame must rest with this album. The songwriting is generally melodic and very pleasant, but little of it is particularly memorable, and the arrangements mostly have a light rock/pop feel to them, closer to Gary Puckett & the Union Gap than to the Beatles. There are one or two very good songs, including "Please Let Me Please," with crisp rhythm guitars and slashing lead parts as well as a catchy central melody and an even better chorus. The group generates a heavier sound on "Do You Believe in Love," and it works, and Allan Clarke's "Soldiers Dilemma" is a rare foray into topical songwriting that's even more striking, heard in the context of the group's soaring harmonies. "Marigold"/"Gloria Swansong" is an ambitious attempt at a suite that doesn't sustain interest for its length, and "You Love 'Cos You Like It" is more lightweight pop, pleasant but not competitive with most of the group's surviving rivals. The weaknesses of this album are spotlighted by the bonus tracks from the 1996 CD reissue on France's Magic Records label—including the killer single sides "Sorry Suzanne," "Not That Way at All," and "He Ain't Heavy, He's My Brother," all of which show more confidence, invention, boldness, and clarity than the material it is supposed to augment on the original album. The French import is to be preferred as those bonus tracks significantly elevate the value of the original album. *—Bruce Eder*

He Ain't Heavy, He's My Brother / Dec. 1969 / Epic ✦✦✦
After delving into more "serious" music with the Dylan album, the Hollies return to their pop roots with this fine effort. All 11 selections are self-penned, and as usual, there is inconsistency in the quality of songwriting. However, even the most inconsequential tunes boast a good melody and solid musicianship. Three songs stand out: "Why Didn't You Believe" is contemporary white gospel at its best, with an intensity that befits the subject matter (though lyrics could have stood improvement); "He Ain't Heavy, He's My Brother" became one of their biggest hits, with Allan Clarke giving a heartfelt reading of the lyrics; and "My Life Is Over With You" is one Hollies song where music, lyrics and arrangement all fit together nearly perfectly. The orchestration is tasteful and restrained, Bobby Elliot's drumming is particularly strong, and lyrically there is a depth that is fitting and welcome. Even the songs that seem most lightweight, such as "Please Sign Your Letters" and "You Love 'Cos You Like It," have a bouncy quality that make them quite tolerable. Though the Hollies never gained a reputation as serious album artists, this is a good effort that maintains a balance between lightweight and serious pop material. *—Michael Ofjord*

Moving Finger / 1970 / Sundazed ✦✦

Confessions of the Mind / Dec. 1970 / BGO ✦✦✦
The group's first album of original material after Nash's departure was a competent but unremarkable affair. The harmonies and concise execution were still intact and the material still brightly pop-oriented, if increasingly serious in lyrical content and slightly more sophisticated in production. The Hollies were now becoming somewhat of an anachronism in a world of progressive album-oriented rock. Their considerable melodic strengths and professionalism ensured that their efforts were never embarrassing. But the hooks weren't as sharp as their vintage hits, and their content wasn't deep enough to establish them with an older rock audience. Most of the songs were originally issued in the U.S. on the Epic LP *Morning Finger*, which had a slightly different track lineup. *—Richie Unterberger*

Distant Light / Dec. 1971 / Epic ✦✦✦
The Hollies continued to tread water as the early '70s progressed. *Distant Light* offered nothing particularly new or unexpected, but the harmonies and songwriting remained at a high enough standard to refute any accusations of decline. Too pop for the album-oriented audience, and not light and frothy enough for the pop market, it would have been totally overlooked if not for the surprise success of the Creedence Clearwater Revival soundalike "Long Cool Woman in a Black Dress." Released in the States almost as an afterthought, it became (deservedly) their biggest American hit, reaching number two. It success inspired the return of Allan Clarke to the fold, after he had left the group to briefly pursue a solo career. *—Richie Unterberger*

Romany / 1972 / Epic ✦✦✦
The group's follow-up album to a pair of hit singles ("Long Cool Woman," "Long Dark Road") tries for the harder sound that sold those singles. *Romany*'s cover art deliberately recalls its immediate predecessor *Distant Light*, but otherwise the two albums are rather dissimilar. For starters, this is the album that the group cut during the short-lived tenure of Mikael Rickfors as lead singer—he's more of a weighty, David Clayton-Thomas type singer than Allan Clarke was, much more of a hard-rock crooner, as is evident on the version of David Ackles' "Down River" and the self-consciously heavy rocker "Slow Down." Tony Hicks and Terry Sylvester make a valiant effort to meld their harmonies into the familiar Hollies mode, and succeed on songs such as "Delaware Taggett and the Outlaw Boys" and "Jesus Was a Crossmaker," though apart from "Magic Woman Touch," most of this album's original first side lacks the memorable hooks, melodies, or tempos needed for hit material. There are tunes worth discovering, however, for anyone who has never heard this album. The title track, although it was too moody and arty to ever become a hit, could be the prettiest song to come from the group after the 1960s; the Tony Hicks co-authored "Blue in the Morning" has a hard-edged, crisp, economical guitar part reminiscent of "Long Dark Road"; and "Courage of Your Convictions" seems to be a conscious attempt at emulating the sound of "Long Cool Woman." The playing and singing are impressive, and these are solid album tracks, if not necessarily chart-topping material. *—Bruce Eder*

The Hollies' Greatest Hits / 1973 / Epic ✦✦✦✦✦
This compilation, whose release was sparked by the 1972 success of "Long Cool Woman in a Black Dress," the Hollies' most successful American single, contains 12 of their 14 biggest U.S. hits, 1964-1972, missing only "Jennifer Eccles" and "I Can't Let Go," for which it substitutes the slightly lower-charting, but perhaps more familiar "Dear Eloise" and "King Midas in Reverse." As such, it is very nearly as good a one-LP hits collection as there could be for the U.S. market at this time. *—William Ruhlmann*

The Hollies [1974] / 1974 / Epic ✦✦

What Goes Around / 1983 / Atlantic ✦✦✦
Graham Nash rejoined the Hollies for one album for the first time in 15 years, which certainly beefed up their harmonies. He also co-produced, but he didn't bring any songs along, which makes this something less than one might have hoped. The group did get its first U.S. hit in eight years and last so far with a remake of the Supremes' "Stop in the Name of Love." *—William Ruhlmann*

Not the Hits Again / Feb. 1986 / See For Miles ✦✦

The EP Collection / Apr. 1987 / See For Miles ✦✦✦
The British have an odd yen for album-length collections of tracks that appeared on EPs in the '60s, even if some or most of them also appeared on LPs and singles. The contents of this 22-song anthology of items from 1964-1966 Hollies EPs are pretty good, but almost everything is available on CD now, in the better context of album or greatest-hits reissues. Frustratingly, it does include two fine Merseyish originals from their debut 1964 EP, "What Kind of Love" and "When I'm Not There," that never made it onto LP otherwise. Except, that is, for the British 1978 LP compilation *The Best of the Hollies' EPs*, which duplicates the track listing of this disc almost exactly. *—Richie Unterberger*

● **Epic Anthology** / Jun. 15, 1990 / Epic ✦✦✦✦✦
A 20-track compilation that picks up when the Hollies signed with Epic in 1967 and presents their biggest hits plus select album tracks and rarities through 1975. Includes "Carrie-Anne," "He Ain't Heavy, He's My Brother," "Long Cool Woman (In a Black Dress)," and "The Air That I Breathe." *—William Ruhlmann*

● **All Time Greatest Hits** / Sep. 1990 / Curb ✦✦✦✦✦
A 12-track all-singles compilation that includes the Hollies' biggest U.S. hits on both Imperial ("Bus Stop," "Stop, Stop, Stop") and Epic Records from 1964 to 1975. *—William Ruhlmann*

Thirtieth Anniversary Collection 1963-1993 / 1993 / EMI America ✦✦✦✦✦
This three-CD, 57-track box set does a good if imperfect job of encapsulating the legacy of one of the British Invasion's better bands. This includes all of the Hollies' singles, A- and B-sides, from the '60s, as well as five previously unreleased tunes. The hits—"I'm Alive," "Bus Stop," "On a Carousel," and others—contain some of the finest beat harmonizing not done by the Beatles. The B-sides—many of them originals, some of them never before available in the United States—are often nearly equal in quality to the classic material. The compilation wisely touches upon only the essentials of their post-1970 singles ("Long Cool Woman" and "The Air That I Breathe"), and unwisely closes with three forgettable tracks from the early '90s. Don't be misled, however, that this box contains all of their best material—their early albums, though inconsistent, featured a fair number of strong original tunes which remain little known beyond collector circles. It's a good set, with an excellent booklet and thoroughly annotated discography, but not definitive. *—Richie Unterberger*

At Abbey Road 1966-1970 / 1997 / EMI ✦✦✦✦
With a few exceptions, the song lineup on this 24-track CD sounds familiar, but that's a misconception. The remastering job has been done so well that precious little on this CD sounds familiar, and it's all good. This collection picks up right where its predecessor left off, presenting a string of Hollies hits, B-sides, and notable album tracks, newly remastered in state-of-the-art sound off of original session masters. The results are frequently startling; rather than just enhancing the hits, the producers have applied the same care to their B-sides, and those are a deceptively fine group of songs in their own right. It rips the envelope altogether by throwing in the group's previously unissued recording of Graham Gouldman's "Schoolgirl," maybe the best unreleased track to come out of an EMI group this side of the Beatles' pounding version of "Leave My Kitten Alone." The remastering also makes the standard material sound more spacious and less compressed than ever before and opens up layers of sound on the guitars, percussion, and vocals that were previously obscured. Hollies fans may love this CD for a reason beyond the particular individual tracks or the dazzling sound textures; it's very much an affirmation of the peak that the band achieved in the late '60s, depicting their moves from British invasion-style rock & roll through psychedelia to pop/rock, all of it beautifully crafted and played. The notes by Bobby Elliott are highly entertaining as well as informative. —*Bruce Eder*

The Hollies [EMI] / Aug. 26, 1997 / EMI ✦✦✦
The Hollies' third album saw a band in the throes of transition between the Merseybeat and rock & roll with which they established themselves, and the folk-rock and soul music that was blowing the strongest winds of change in 1965. They clean up their backlog of cover staples with versions of tunes by Lloyd Price, Buddy Holly, and Roy Orbison, and delve into soul by taking on the Miracles' "Mickey's Monkey" and Curtis Mayfield's "You Must Believe Me." Their attempt at "Fortune Teller" won't make you forget the Rolling Stones' version; nor, for that matter, are any of the other covers impressive. That leaves five reasonably good originals, the best of which are the gorgeous "So Lonely" and the excellent Merseybeat knockoff "When I Come Home to You." They also sound Beatlesque on "I've Been Wrong," but "Too Many People" and their cover of Peter, Paul & Mary's "Very Last Day" hearken to a folk-rock direction. The album was issued in the U.S. as *Hear! Here!*, replacing "Mickey's Monkey" with their number one British hit "I'm Alive." [The album was reissued by British EMI in 1998 with both the stereo and mono mixes featured on a single CD.] —*Richie Unterberger*

Archive Alive! / Sep. 2, 1997 / Archive ✦✦✦
This 15-song concert recording made in September 1983 along the reunion tour with co-founder Graham Nash supplants the mid-1970s *Hollies Live.* The group recorded this show in 24-track, intending to release it as a live album, which never appeared in the wake of the financially abortive tour. Remastered in 24-bit digital from the original tapes, the CD captures the exquisite harmonies beautifully. The group performs the expected hits ("I Can't Let Go," "Just One Look," "Bus Stop," "On a Carousel," etc.) with some smoothing out, in keeping with the decade in which they were done. The keyboards (especially on a gorgeous rendition of "Just One Look") show the influence of synth-pop on some songs, but the band still rocks, especially on the jam to "Long Cool Woman," which uses "Shakin' All Over" as its jumping-off point. Among the surprises are the stripped-down "King Midas in Reverse" and the group's covers of "Wasted on the Way" and "Teach Your Children," which work well. And we get a live version of the then-current single, "Stop! In the Name of Love." —*Bruce Eder*

Mark Hollis

b. 1955, Tottenham, London, England
Post-Rock/Experimental, Alternative Pop/Rock, Singer/Songwriter, Adult Alternative Pop/Rock
The frontman of the influential new wave-era band Talk Talk, singer/songwriter Mark Hollis finally mounted his long-awaited solo career during the late 1990s. The younger brother of Ed Hollis, a disc jockey and producer who went on to manage bands such as Eddie and the Hot Rods, Hollis originally planned to become a child psychologist but in 1975 left university to relocate to London, eventually forming a band called the Reaction. In 1977, the Reaction recorded a demo for Island Records; among the tracks was a Hollis original titled "Talk Talk" which later surfaced on the Beggars Banquet punk compilation *Streets.* After just one single, 1978's "I Can't Resist," the Reaction disbanded, and through his brother, Hollis was first introduced to musicians Paul Webb, Lee Harris, and Simon Brenner, with whom he formed Talk Talk in 1981, soon signing to the EMI label.
With their 1982 debut *The Party's Over*, Talk Talk emerged as an archetype of new wave ideals, but with each successive record their sound grew more atmospheric and complex, moving further away from conventional pop structure. Records like 1986's *The Colour of Spring* and 1988's brilliant *Spirit of Eden* increasingly represented the vision of Hollis and producer Tim Friese-Green, who together steered away from the electronic pop of Talk Talk's early work towards a more organic, often acoustic sound textured by elements of jazz and ambient music. Despite lavish critical praise, relations with EMI disintegrated; personality conflicts within Talk Talk's ranks were growing as well, and after completing 1991's *Laughing Stock*, the group was essentially finished. Hollis then disappeared from sight for the next seven years; finally, in early 1998, he issued his self-titled solo debut, a beautiful continuation of the final Talk Talk records. *A/V Installation*, a collaboration with Phill Brown, was scheduled to follow. —*Jason Ankeny*

● **Mark Hollis** / 1998 / Polydor ✦✦✦✦✦
Achingly gorgeous and hauntingly stark, Mark Hollis' self-titled debut picks up where he left off with Talk Talk's *Laughing Stock* seven years earlier, re-emerging at the nexus point where jazz, ambient, and folk music collide. It's quite possibly the most quiet and intimate record ever made, each song cut to the bone for maximum emotional impact

and every note carrying enormous meaning—Hollis paints his music in fine, exquisite strokes, with an uncanny mastery of atmosphere that's frequently devastating. And if anything, his singularly resonant voice has grown even more plaintive with the passage of time, which combined with the understated artistry and minimalist beauty of tracks like "The Colour of Spring" and "Watershed" makes *Mark Hollis* a truly unique and indelible listening experience—his obvious understanding of the power of silence aside, one prays he doesn't again wait for the seven-year itch to strike before returning. —*Jason Ankeny*

Brenda Holloway

b. Jun. 21, 1946, Atascadero, CA
Vocals, Violin / Pop-Soul, Motown, Soul
This sultry '60s addition to the Motown roster waxed several memorable ballads for the firm. One of Motown's first Los Angeles signings, Holloway's Tamla debut, "Every Little Bit Hurts," was a soaring ballad that sailed up the pop charts in 1964, while Smokey Robinson wrote and produced Holloway's 1965 smash "When I'm Gone." The voluptuous vocalist opened several concerts for the Beatles on their 1965 U.S. tour, including their Shea Stadium show. In 1967 Holloway co-wrote and recorded the original version of "You've Made Me So Very Happy," later a gigantic hit for Blood, Sweat & Tears. —*Bill Dahl*

● **The Very Best of Brenda Holloway** / Feb. 23, 1999 / Motown ✦✦✦✦✦
This 15-track collection gathers up the very best of Holloway's recordings for Motown. A peripheral figure in the company's history, Brenda made the trek from Los Angeles to Detroit to record, working with producers Smokey Robinson, Mickey Stevenson, Henry Cosby, Frank Wilson, and label boss Berry Gordy. Holloway's big hits "Every Little Bit Hurts," "I'll Always Love You," and "When I'm Gone" are aboard, along with the original version of "You've Made Me So Very Happy," later appropriated by Blood, Sweat & Tears. Solid album material from the canceled Motown album *Hurtin' & Cryin'* makes up the majority of this collection, with "Hurt a Little Everyday," and "You Can Cry on My Shoulder" being two of the highlights. Two previously unreleased tracks, "You've Changed Me" and "Til Johnny Comes," round out the package. Holloway was a big-voiced gospel-style belter, and while not in the Motown front racks, this scintillating package makes a welcome addition to any soul collection. —*Cub Koda*

Buddy Holly

b. Sep. 7, 1936, Lubbock, TX, **d.** Feb. 3, 1959, Mason City, IA
Vocals, Guitar / Rockabilly, Rock & Roll
An enormously important and influential performer, Buddy Holly started in his native Texas doing country music, eventually adding R&B numbers to the set list after meeting Elvis Presley. He recorded early rockabilly sides in Nashville, resulting in the Decca singles "Blue Days, Black Nights" and "Modern Don Juan." But success didn't come until he formed the Crickets and recorded in Norman Petty's New Mexico studio, producing the number one hit "That'll Be the Day." Holly and Petty experimented in the studio, utilizing double-tracking ("Words of Love"), different forms of echo ("Peggy Sue," a second gold-selling Top Ten hit), and close-miking techniques, now commonplace in the industry. With the Crickets, he had the further chart hits "Oh, Boy!" (October 1957) (another Top Ten), "Maybe Baby" (February 1958), and "Think It Over"/"Fool's Paradise" (May 1958), while "Rave On" (April 1958) was a Holly "solo" hit. He went solo for real during 1958, however, marrying and relocating to New York. He charted with "Early in the Morning" and "Heartbeat," and released "It Doesn't Matter Anymore"/"Raining in My Heart" before embarking on the Winter Dance Party package tour, during which, on February 3, he, the Big Bopper, and Ritchie Valens were killed in an airplane crash. In England, where "It Doesn't Matter Anymore" went to number one in the wake of his death, Holly continued to score posthumous hits through the mid-'60s, and he exerted tremendous influence on the developing beat groups both for his music and for his self-contained approach to his work—writing his own songs, playing them with his own group. —*Cub Koda & William Ruhlmann*

☆ **The Chirping Crickets** / 1957 / MCA ✦✦✦✦✦
The debut album by the Crickets and the only one featuring Buddy Holly released during his lifetime, *The "Chirping" Crickets* contains the group's Number one single "That'll Be the Day" and its Top ten hit "Oh, Boy!" Other Crickets classics include "Not Fade Away," "Maybe Baby," and "I'm Looking for Someone to Love." The rest of the 12 tracks are not up to the standard set by those five, but those five are among the best rock & roll songs of the 1950s or ever, making this one of the most significant album debuts in rock & roll history, ranking with *Elvis Presley* and *Meet the Beatles.* —*William Ruhlmann*

☆ **The Complete Buddy Holly** / 1979 / MCA ✦✦✦✦✦
In the wake of the number one British ranking for *20 Golden Greats* in 1978 and the release of the feature film *The Buddy Holly Story*, MCA U.K. assembled this six-LP box set (which finally was released in the U.S. in February 1981). It traces Buddy Holly's career from his country & western duo with Bob Montgomery in 1954/1955 to his 1956 Nashville sessions for Decca Records; the Clovis, NM, recordings with the Crickets and producer Norman Petty that launched his career in 1957; the New York sessions of 1958; the final 1958 demo recordings; the various posthumously overdubbed versions of the demos; and other assorted rarities. In other words, all the material that Decca/MCA previously had spread across seven LPs—*The "Chirping" Crickets, Buddy Holly, That'll Be the Day, Reminiscing, Showcase, Holly in the Hills*, and *Giant*—between 1957 and 1969 (not counting the many compilations) was here, plus more. The box also contained an extensive scrapbook, lots of liner notes, and a detailed discography. It was, thus, the state of the art in box sets just prior to the CD era, and given Holly's importance in the history of rock & roll, an essential album for any serious collector. With the passing of the LP era,

it is out of print, and MCA claims to be gathering more unreleased material for some comparable box set, though years go by without its appearing. Meanwhile, if you needed one record album to demonstrate what the most popular music of the second half of the 20th century sounded like, this would be it. *—William Ruhlmann*

The Great Buddy Holly / 1982 / MCA ✦✦

For the First Time Anywhere / 1983 / MCA ✦✦✦✦✦
When this album was originally released in 1983, it was a major revelation in collector's circles. Here were the original, undubbed versions of eight songs that had appeared on posthumous Holly albums like *Reminiscing, Showcase* and others with overdubbed backing provided by the Fireballs and producer Norman Petty, along with two rarities to pad things out. And hearing the stripped-down Holly minus the audio cover-ups and beef-ups revealed strong (and sometimes superior) efforts all by themselves without the assistance. With future Cricket Jerry Allison on drums, a set of revolving bass players, and Sonny Curtis handling lead guitar chores on three tracks, Holly blasts through some bona fide Texas rockabilly here. Four of the eight tracks come from Buddy's pen, and these early efforts ("Rock-a-Bye Rock," "Because I Love You," "Changing All Those Changes," and "I'm Gonna Set My Foot Down") are sign pointers toward his later, more commercial style; in this case we get stripped-down, elemental pop tunes disguised as rockabilly ravers and country ballads. The collection is bookended with two more tracks, the original studio swipe of "Maybe Baby" and "That's My Desire," a ballad from the 1958 New York session that produced "Rave On." Although the overdubbing done to Holly's music made sense from a commercial standpoint at the time, this collection only whets your appetite to hear more of the real thing. *—Cub Koda*

☆ **From the Original Master Tapes** / 1985 / MCA ✦✦✦✦✦
MCA got serious about reissuing vintage music from its library in the 1980s, when it put the responsibility in the hands of producer Steve Hoffman, who was willing to spend the time and do the research required to find the right masters and also to propose doing right by them. One of the first results was *For the First Time Anywhere*, which unearthed a lot of previously unheard undubbed Holly demos, and Hoffman followed it up two years later with *From the Original Master Tapes*, the first Buddy Holly collection that was a revelation for its sound quality. Although it has been outdone in that department since, what with the advancement of digital technology and its uses, and there are compilations that take into account songs of his that became important in others' hands, this remains the best single-disc collection of Buddy Holly's music, featuring 20 of his biggest hits. The songs aren't presented in chronological order, but the disc flows well, running through every one of his hits and all of his best-known songs—"That'll Be the Day," "Peggy Sue," "Oh, Boy!," "Maybe Baby," "Rave On," "Think It Over," "Heartbeat," "It Doesn't Matter Anymore," "Everyday," "Not Fade Away," "Well . . . All Right," and many others. A few terrific songs are missing, but *From the Original Master Tapes* remains a first-rate introduction and a nearly definitive summary of the highlights of Holly's brief recording career. *—Bruce Eder & Stephen Thomas Erlewine*

☆ **The Buddy Holly Collection** / Sep. 28, 1993 / MCA ✦✦✦✦✦
The first comprehensive, remastered CD retrospective of Holly's work, including early tracks recorded in the Holly family garage, the Owen Bradley-produced singles, all the rockin' hits, orchestrated ballads, and tracks overdubbed with instrumentation after Holly's tragic death. Two discs, solid liner notes. *—Roch Parisien*

★ **Greatest Hits** / Sep. 24, 1996 / MCA ✦✦✦✦✦
MCA re-mastered 18 of Buddy Holly's best-known songs for 1996's *Greatest Hits* album. While the sound is fine, it isn't markedly better than that on *From the Original Master Tapes*, which also boasted a more complete track selection. Nevertheless, *Greatest Hits* is one of the most thorough single-disc collections ever assembled on Holly, and for audiophiles it may be worth the extra money. For most fans, *From the Original Master Tapes* remains the definitive single-disc set, with the double-disc *The Buddy Holly Collection* or the LP-only *The Complete Buddy Holly* providing better, more comprehensive overviews, which provide more value for your dollar than *Greatest Hits*. *—Stephen Thomas Erlewine*

☆ **The Chirping Crickets/Buddy Holly** / Jan. 30, 2001 / BGO ✦✦✦✦✦
Oh boy—that's the first reaction to seeing this British import turn up. RCA/BMG got around to remastering Elvis Presley's original albums at the end of the 1990s, but MCA/Universal, which owns Buddy Holly's legacy, has shown no such interest in the late Texas rock & roll legend's music. So, instead, it's fallen to Beat Goes On (BGO), the U.K. outfit. BGO combined the two albums that Buddy Holly saw released in his lifetime and slapped them onto one CD, remastered in 24-bit digital audio. Everyone who thinks they know this stuff should get ready for a shock when they hear what it sounds like on this disc—the listener can practically hear the action on Jerry Allison's drums, and when the guitar break on "Peggy Sue" comes in, it's like the instrument is in your face. And "Rave On" pretty much booms out the way it did onstage on a good night. What's more, the resolution on the tracks from both albums enhances the little details, such as the quality of the backup singing on "Send Me Some Lovin'." Also, there are excellent notes written from a uniquely British point of view and a thumbnail sketch of the history of each song. The disc is as essential to any collection as Elvis' Sun sides and his first two years at RCA, or the Beatles' first four years of music. *—Bruce Eder*

Hollywood Flames

f. 1949, Los Angeles, CA, **db.** 1967
Doo Wop, R&B
Long-lasting Los Angeles doo wop aggregation with a very fluid personnel roster. Bobby Day was one of the group's founders in 1950, and they recorded prolifically for Hollywood, Specialty, Lucky, Swingtime, Money, and other firms before cutting their one major hit, the rocking "Buzz Buzz Buzz," in 1957 for Ebb Records. Earl Nelson, who was later half of Bob and Earl, sang lead on the tune, and some of their subsequent Ebb 45s were rocking novelties. Day went on to solo success with "Rockin' Robin," and the group managed one more chart item, "Gee," for Chess in 1961 with Donald Height as lead. *—Bill Dahl*

● **The Hollywood Flames** / Aug. 3, 1992 / Specialty ✦✦✦✦✦
Though not in a class with the Moonglows, the Five Satins, or the Platters, the Hollywood Flames were a solid doo wop group that should have been much better known. The only song on this CD that was a major hit is the infectious "Buzz Buzz Buzz." Otherwise, listeners are treated to excellent material that fell through the cracks, which ranges from invigorating up-tempo songs like "Strollin' on the Beach," "A Little Bird," and "Crazy" to such engaging ballads as "Give Me Back My Heart," "A Star Fell," and "My Confession." While "Frankenstein's Den" shows that the Flames could be as much fun as the Coasters, the atypical and previously unreleased "This Heart of Mine" is as brooding as something Bobby "Blue" Bland would do. For doo wop aficionados who only know the Flames for "Buzz Buzz Buzz," this collection demonstrates that they had many other inspired moments. *—Alex Henderson*

Rupert Holmes

b. Feb. 24, 1947, Cheshire, England
Producer, Vocals, Keyboards, Songwriter / Soft Rock, Adult Contemporary, Singer/Songwriter
Singer, songwriter, and poet, Rupert Holmes has performed and written for various music legends. Although a reserved playwright and bookwriter, his contributions to the rock music industry and Broadway have been numerous. Holmes was born in England because of his father's involvement in USAF. After the family moved to New York, he developed an interest in music. He attended the Manhattan School of Music. It was after graduation that Holmes seriously began as a songwriter. A successful piano player, he played with the Cuff Links and the Buoys in the '70s. As an arranger and songwriter, he composed songs for Gene Pitney, the Platters, the Drifters, and the Partridge Family. At the age of 24, Holmes had a hit on both the American and U.K. charts, "Timothy" (1971). After this first hit, he decided on pursuing a singing career of his own. Composing for several popular '70s bands, he had no problem getting people to listen to him. He released his first album, *Widescreen*, in 1974. He then produced albums for such singing legends as Barbra Streisand, Sparks, and Sailors. A booming career was underway. He released several more albums in the '70s including *Rupert Holmes, The Singles*, and *Pursuit of Happiness*. The '80s took Holmes into a new realm of success. Although known as a singer and songwriter, he made international fame with "Escape (The Pina Colada Song)" and "Him," which placed on both the U.K. and American charts. It only added to the success of the albums *Partners in Crime, Adventure*, and *Full Circle*. Holmes is also an accomplished playwright. His 1986 Broadway musical, *The Mystery of Edwin Drood*, was the recipient of five Tony Awards. *—Kim Summers*

Widescreen / 1974 / Varese ✦✦✦
Holmes' debut betrayed the heavy influence of Brian Wilson and (to a lesser degree) Nilsson, but his self-professed cinematic brand of songwriting was far closer to adult contemporary and MOR Tin Pan Alley than either of those greats dared to tread. Barbra Streisand helped launch Holmes' career by covering two of the songs, "Widescreen" and "Letters in the Mail." The CD reissue adds two bonus tracks from his self-titled 1975 LP. *—Richie Unterberger*

● **Partners in Crime** / 1979 / Infinity ✦✦✦✦✦
Before the release of this successful 1979 album, Holmes released four albums that failed to capture him at his best. Shortly before this, Holmes made his mark as songwriter. He penned the kitschy cannibalism tale "Timothy" for the Buoys. From his 1976 effort *Singles* came "The Last of the Romantics" which was covered to great effect by Engelbert Humperdinck. *Partners in Crime* finds Holmes more focused with pop savvy and a great batch of songs. The effort's biggest hit, the ingratiating "Escape (The Pina Colada Song)," though skilled, is cutesy enough to make some people's eyes roll. Despite the nature of that track, Holmes was also willing to tackle more interesting issues. With the slightly disco-fied title track, he deftly examines the male/female dynamic as business deal. Throughout the song, Holmes is having a lot of fun with every salacious detail. "Nearsighted" has him going the power-pop route and all but wringing tears out of seeing "slightly out of focus." As *Partners in Crime* goes along, what becomes striking is some of the tracks' subtle use of R&B flourishes. "Him" depicts Holmes as the cuckold and has a beautiful string arrangement, a great hook, and strong, vivid lyrics. The album's best ballad, "The People That You Never Get to Love" has Holmes again giving a warm and confident vocal and is poignant rather than weepy. Although there are a few waste cuts, on the whole *Partners in Crime* is a thought-provoking and polished album. *—Jason Elias*

The Epoch Collection / Sep. 27, 1994 / Varese ✦✦✦✦✦
Before he liked pina coladas, Rupert Holmes was a singer/songwriter that attempted to blend Broadway traditions, Hollywood musicals, and soft-rock—not entirely dissimilar from Barry Manilow, in that respect. He was ambitious and interesting, and Varese's *Epoch Collection* contains the best of those ambitious, interesting, if not entirely successful, recordings. This is pretty showy stuff and Holmes' ambitions often get the better of him, but it's a rather fascinating curiosity for fans of Holmes and soft-rock for that very reason. *—Stephen Thomas Erlewine*

● **Greatest Hits** / Jul. 25, 2000 / Hip-O ✦✦✦✦✦
Rupert Holmes' swinging '70s sound only occupied a small portion of his career, as Hip-O's 18-track 2000 collection *Greatest Hits* illustrates. He had a yen to be a little bit more than a soft-rock craftsman—he drew heavily from Brill Building and Tin Pan Alley, plus Hollywood musicals, wryly obvious social commentary, and soft pop to create a dis-

tinctive blend. It's often overly ambitious—even his biggest hit, *Partners in Crime*, is a sociological portrait of me-era dating—and it can be a little fussy, particularly in the years after *Partners in Crime*, when his recordings gained the antiseptic cleanliness of '80s adult contemporary (even on his nostalgic theme song for "Remember WENN"). *Greatest Hits* contains all these aspects, perhaps downplaying the appealingly weird early '70s recordings a bit too much (those are collected on Varese's *Epoch Collection*), but giving a good idea of what Holmes' career was all about. And be forewarned—it's not just about Pina Coladas, and not a lot of these songs sound like that. —*Stephen Thomas Erlewine*

Holsapple-Stamey

f. 1991, North Carolina, db. 1992
Jangle Pop, Power Pop, College Rock
During the early '80s, guitarist/vocalist Chris Stamey and keyboardist/guitarist/vocalist Peter Holsapple led the dB's, one of the premier jangle-pop bands of the American pop underground. Stamey left the group in 1983, but Holsapple led the band until its final album, 1987's *The Sound of Music*. Four years after the dB's broke up, Holsapple and Stamey reunited to record an album that was in the vein of their previous collaborations. Released in 1991, *Mavericks*—the only album they ever released as a duo—received good reviews but didn't sell well. After the release of *Mavericks*, Stamey returned to his solo career and Holsapple formed the Continental Drifters with his wife Susan Cowsill. In 1994, Holsapple re-formed the dB's and the group released *Paris Avenue* later in the year. —*Stephen Thomas Erlewine*

Mavericks / 1991 / Rhino ✦✦✦✦
Eight years after Chris Stamey left the dB's (and three years after the group finally sputtered to a halt), he reunited with former bandmate Peter Holsapple (who became the group's *de facto* leader in Stamey's absence) for this duo album. *Mavericks* finds both Holsapple and Stamey sounding a bit older, quieter, and more pensive than they did in the old days; while one can see many flashes of the bright, angular power pop that dominated the dB's first two albums, most of the songs are dominated by acoustic instruments, somewhat slower tempos, and a more "mature" tone. The introspective overtones of "Angels," "I Know You Will," or "Close Your Eyes" mark a switch from what these guys were doing on *Repercussion* or *Stands for Decibels*, but if you're looking for clever and well-crafted pop tunes, both Holsapple and Stamey deliver the goods, and they do rock out a bit here and there (most notably on "Lovers Rock" and the wonderfully sardonic "I Want to Break Your Heart"). Both Chris and Peter are at the top of their form as vocalists and players, and they get plenty of welcome assistance from such Hoboken-scene notables as Dave Schramm, James MacMillan, and Jane Scarpantoni (fellow former dB Gene Holder even pops up on one cut). *Mavericks* often sounds like semi-acoustic post-new wave pop for grownups, but it's a good bit more fun (and less academic) than that description would suggest. —*Mark Deming*

Honey & the Bees

f. 1965, db. 1973
Soul
A minor but talented Philadelphia female soul quartet, Honey & the Bees made some relatively little-known records for the Arctic and Josie labels in the late '60s and early '70s with the aid of musicians that played on classic 1970s Gamble-Huff productions. These included Leon Huff himself on piano, and Ron Baker, Earl Young, Bobby Eli, and Norman Harris in the rhythm section; Harris and Thom Bell were among those who contributed to the songwriting. Honey & the Bees spent years on the club circuit, opening for bigger soul acts in Philadelphia and throughout the East Coast before disbanding in 1973. Group member Gwen Oliver married Fred Wesley of the JB's, whom she met when Honey & the Bees opened for James Brown in 1971. —*Richie Unterberger*

Dynamite / 1999 / Jamie ✦✦✦
This disc has 14 of their Arctic sides (four previously unreleased), nine of which are from 1966-69 singles. Lamentably, the liner notes do not include any dates or original release information. Although Honey & the Bees were more competent than distinctive as vocalists, the material and arrangements amount to some pretty decent Philadelphia soul from a time when the genre was starting to coalesce around the Gamble-Huff-Bell sound. What's here is not as slick or commercially successful as the Gamble-Huff-Bell blockbusters of the early and mid-1970s, which is fine, as it has an airiness that often escaped such blockbusters. The Gamble-Huff-Bell comparisons, however, are not gratuitous: Huff himself plays piano on some of the cuts, and the rhythm section includes Ron Baker, Earl Young, Bobby Eli, and Norman Harris, all of whom were present on many Philly soul smashes in later years. Honey and the Bees were versatile performers who could handle styles and songs ranging from emotional, melodic ballads ("Make You Mine") and midtempo dance tunes ("Why Do You Hurt the One Who Loves You") to harder, funkier outings betraying the influence of more progressive soul trends ("Love Addict," "Music (Makes You Want to Dance," "Baby, Do That Thing"). Fred Wesley of the JBs, who married group member Gwen Oliver, wrote the liner notes. —*Richie Unterberger*

Honey Cone

f. 1969, Los Angeles, CA, db. 1972
Soul
This female trio formed in Los Angeles in 1969. They were all experienced background vocalists. Carolyn Willis had been in the Girlfriends and Bob B. Soxx & the Blue Jeans,Edna Wright was Darlene Love's sister and had sung in the Blossoms and Bob B. Soxx & the Blue Jeans, and Shellie Clark had been an Ikette and regular on *The Jim Nabors Hour* in 1969 and 1970. They were signed by legendary songwriters Holland-Dozier-Holland to their Hot Wax label. They had their first major hit in 1969 with "Girls

It Ain't Easy," then garnered two consecutive R&B chart toppers in 1971 with "Want Ads" and "Stick-Up." "Want Ads" proved a '70s standard, also topping the pop charts. The Honey Cone scored two more R&B hits, "One Monkey Don't Show No Show" and "The Day I Found Myself" in 1971 and 1972, before things began to slow down. They continued on Hot Wax through 1972. Wright later recorded as a solo act. —*Ron Wynn*

● **Greatest Hits** / 1990 / Fantasy ✦✦✦✦✦
One of the finest girl groups of the early '70s, Honey Cone was often compared to Martha & the Vandellas for a number of reasons. The fact that the label they recorded for, Hot Wax/Invictus, was owned by former Motown producers/songwriters Holland/Dozier/Holland made it an obvious comparison. And also, the robust nature of Honey Cone's harmonies certainly bring the Vandellas to mind. On "Want Ads," "Stick Up," "One Monkey Don't Show No Show," and other hits included on this superb CD, the singers effectively combine sweetness and grit—pop sleekness and gospel-influenced soulfulness. To be sure, Honey Cone could pack quite a punch emotionally and harmonically. But as much potential as Honey Cone had, its success was short-lived—and the singers were gone from the charts by 1974. With its albums long out of print, *Greatest Hits* can serve as a fine introduction to Honey Cone's soul/pop legacy. —*Alex Henderson*

The Honeycombs

f. 1963, db. 1967
British Invasion, Early British Pop/Rock
Mostly renowned for their 1964 Top Five hit "Have I the Right," the Honeycombs were pretty much a front for producer Joe Meek and the songwriting-management team of Ken Howard and Alan Blaikley. With bee-sting guitar leads and lead singer Dennis O'Dell's wobbling vocals, which sounded like a Gene Pitney unable to hold notes, "Have I the Right" was a single that one either loved or hated, but couldn't forget. The relatively faceless group afforded Meek perhaps his fullest artistic expression in the studio; all the Honeycombs' singles and albums feature variable-speed vocals, ghostly organ, unpredictable runs, majestically thudding drums, and super-compressed sonics. The group managed a couple more minor American hits—"Is It Because" and "I Can't Stop," as well as another British Top 20 hit, "That's the Way"—and cut quite a few singles and two albums before Meek's death in early 1967 effectively finished the group as well. —*Richie Unterberger*

● **The Honeycombs** / 1964 / Repertoire ✦✦✦✦✦
Most famed for their 1964 one-shot British Invasion hit "Have I the Right" and for being the first rock band of any renown to feature a female drummer, the Honeycombs recorded a surprising amount of material in the mid-'60s. Even for collectors, this definitely falls into the "guilty pleasure" category. Lead singer Dennis O'Dell's wobbly voice sounds like a speeded-up Gene Pitney, and the material, though peppy and catchy, is exceedingly trite and innocuous. The group's chief asset, actually, was producer Joe Meek, who found the band to be a perfect vehicle for his eccentric production techniques. Meek used compression to the point of squashing, and used all manners of odd vari-speed vocals, bee-stinging guitars, tinny keyboards, and echo to achieve a sound that was quite otherworldly by 1964 standards. Besides "Have I the Right," this 1964 debut LP includes the British Top 20 hit "That's the Way" (featuring drummer Honey Lantree on vocals) and the ghostly ballads "Without You It Is Night" and "This Too Shall Pass Away," though most of the rest of the material is slight. This 1990 reissue adds seven bonus tracks from non-LP singles, including a German recording of "Have I the Right" and the manic, irresistible "I Can't Stop," which was a minor hit for the band in the U.S. —*Richie Unterberger*

All Systems Go / 1965 / Repertoire ✦✦✦
Despite downwardly spiraling commercial fortunes, the Honeycombs recorded a second album in 1965 that featured as many intriguing production flourishes and oddball British pop songs as their first effort. No hits were included on this LP—and be warned that the version of their minor hit single "I Can't Stop" (probably their best song) featured here is an inferior, drastically slower remake. This album also includes a mighty obscure ballad by Ray Davies, "Emptiness," that was never recorded by the Kinks (or any other artist but the Honeycombs, for that matter). It's not much of a song, but it's a find for Kinks fanatics. The record's highlights are the sparkling guitars of "Love in Tokyo" and the soulful ballad "Something I Got to Tell You" (featuring drummer Honey Lantree on vocals), which sounds like an honest-to-god hit-that-never-was. The CD reissue of the album adds six non-LP cuts from 1965-66 singles. The best of these are the tense, overwrought ballad "Should a Man Cry?" and the up-tempo "Can't Get Through to You," on which producer Joe Meek took his vari-speed vocals and neurotic rhythms to their farthest extremes. —*Richie Unterberger*

The Best of the Honeycombs / 1988 / PRT ✦✦✦
The German Repertoire label has reissued both of the Honeycombs' studio LPs with bonus tracks; oddly, they don't include quite a few of the group's A-sides. All six of those missing singles can be found on this reissue, along with most of their other best-known songs. Two of these A-sides are standouts: "Is It Because," a small hit in the U.K., is a driving number, and "Eyes" one of the spookiest productions from a man (Joe Meek) who specialized in them. If you pick this up thinking you'll forego the fanatically repackaged CDs for a 14-song greatest hits collection of this interesting but minor British Invasion band, be warned: the version of "I Can't Stop," the minor U.S. hit that was their best song, included here is not the original, but an inferior remake from their second album. —*Richie Unterberger*

The Honeydrippers

f. 1984
Rock & Roll
The Honeydrippers were an ad hoc group put together by ex-Led Zeppelin lead singer

Robert Plant and Atlantic Records executive Ahmet Ertegun to record a mini-album of '50s and '60s oldies in 1984. *—William Ruhlmann*

The Honeydrippers, Vol. 1 / 1984 / Es Paranza ✦✦✦✦✦
Five-song EP features Robert Plant singing such oldies as the hit remake of "Sea of Love," with a backup that includes Nile Rodgers, Jeff Beck, and Jimmy Page. *—William Ruhlmann*

The Honeys

f. 1961
Brill Building Pop, Girl Group, Surf, Pop
California girl group the Honeys was formed in 1961 by siblings Marilyn, Diane, and Barbara Rovell; originally dubbed the Rovell Sisters, the trio cut their teeth on the local amateur talent circuit, and in time Barbara was replaced by their cousin Sandra Glantz, who adopted the stage name Ginger Blake. Through producer Gary Usher, the Rovells were introduced to the Beach Boys' Brian Wilson, who agreed to produce the group; rechristened the Honeys—a nickname for female surfers—they reeled off a series of outstanding Capitol singles including "Shoot the Curl," "Pray for Surf," and the Phil Spector homage "The One You Can't Have," none of which made any kind of commercial impact. A move to Warner Bros. preceded 1964's superb "He's a Doll"; on December 7 of that year, Brian Wilson and Marilyn Rovell were also married. Despite their continuing lack of chart success, the Honeys remained sought-after backing vocalists on sessions for the Beach Boys and Jan & Dean; during the mid-1960s, the trio also recorded as Ginger and the Snaps, although by the time of their 1969 swan song "Goodnight My Love" the Honeys name had been restored. When Blake left the group to pursue a solo career, Marilyn and Diane worked under the name American Spring; in 1983, the Honeys reunited for a disappointing comeback record, *Ecstasy*. *—Jason Ankeny*

● **The Honeys Collection** / Oct. 31, 2000 / Collectors' Choice Music ✦✦✦
Fans of the Beach Boys will definitely be interested in this collection from the Honeys, a girl group trio including Brian Wilson's wife Marilyn, plus her sister Diane, and their cousin. Signed to Capitol, thanks to Wilson, most of the Honeys sessions were supervised by Wilson himself, occasionally with Capitol's in-house producer Nik Venet. *The Honeys Collection* brings together 26 tracks covering the group's early- to mid-'60s singles (and several backing vocal dates on records by other artists), plus two tracks from a 1983 comeback LP. The first phase of the Honeys was as a surf group ("honeys" was a term used either for female surfers or the girlfriends of male surfers), and their first single, "Surfin' Down the Swanee River," was produced by Brian Wilson from an idea for a novelty takeoff on the folk classic "Swanee River." Fortunately, the group soon moved on from surf novelties to embrace the classic girl group sound of Phil Spector—a big influence on Wilson professionally—and the bulk of the Honeys' best material is in this grandiose vein, high-drama songs like "Raindrops," "The One You Can't Have," and "He's a Doll." Besides the value for Beach Boys fans, the solid production muscle behind the trio results in some great examples of '60s girl group pop. The compilers also added several tracks with backing vocals by the Honeys, including the early Glen Campbell gem "Guess I'm Dumb," written and produced by Wilson himself. *—John Bush*

Hoodoo Gurus

f. 1981
College Rock, Aussie Rock, Power Pop, Alternative Pop/Rock
Like most bands, Australia's Hoodoo Gurus were largely the product of their influences; unlike most bands, however, the Hoodoos channelled their insipration from the vast entirety of the American pop cultural landscape, drawing on such disparate sources as B-movies, bad sitcoms, and junk food—in tandem with the usual suspects like garage rock, power pop, and surf—to create a distinctly kitschy and catchy sound. Formed in Sydney in 1981, Le Hoodoo Gurus (as they were originally dubbed) were led by singer/songwriter Dave Faulkner, whose infectious songs quickly earned them a record deal. In 1983, the Hoodoo Gurus recorded their excellent debut record *Stoneage Romeos*; dedicated to luminaries like *F-Troop's* Larry Storch and *Green Acres'* pig Arnold Ziffel, the album offered such trash-pop treats as the college radio fave "I Want You Back." Faulkner wrote an even stronger batch of tunes for 1985's *Mars Needs Guitars!*, an album highlighted by the superb single "Bitterweet" and marked by a widening scope which touched base with demented hillbilly humor ("Hayride to Hell") and crazed surf ("Like Wow—Wipeout"). With 1987's *Blow Your Cool*, the Hoodoos appeared poised for the big time; their tourmates, the Bangles, even contributed to the singles "What's My Scene" and "Good Times." However, the album failed to register beyond alternative radio. *—Jason Ankeny*

Stoneage Romeos / 1983 / A&M ✦✦✦✦✦
"Shake some action/Psychotic reaction/No satisfaction/Sky pilot, Sky Saxon/That's what I like/Blitzkrieg bop/To the jailhouse rock/Stop stop, at the hop/Do the bluejean bop/That's what I like!" In the first verse of "(Let's All) Turn On," Hoodoo Guru's frontman Dave Faulkner summed up the band's aesthetic so well that elaborating almost seems pointless, but while it's obvious that Faulkner and his friends had a healthy appreciation of rock & roll's past, one listen to their debut album, *Stoneage Romeos*, made clear they thought music was having a pretty good present, too. The Hoodoo Gurus played power pop with the force and enthusiasm of a full-bore rock band, and while they loved '60s garage rock (as if "(Let's All) Turn On" and "In the Echo Chamber" would permit any doubt on the subject), there was a lot more going on than that—check out the pop rock of "I Want You Back," the neo-exotica of "Zanzibar," the psychobilly of "Dig It Up," the heartbroken lament of "My Girl," and the straight-ahead rock of "I Was a Kamikaze Pilot." Faulkner, guitarist Brad Shepherd, bassist Clyde Bramley, and drummer James Baker loaded their songs with catchy melodies and killer pop hooks and played 'em with the sweaty enthusiasm of a crack rock & roll band that knew the value of a great tune. And *Stoneage Romeos* is funny as hell without sounding like the work of a joke band; the Gurus loved a good laugh, but they loved a good tune even more. *Stoneage Romeos* ranks with the most solid debut albums of the 1980s, and if you don't like the Hoodoo Gurus, I suspect you don't like rock & roll very much. *—Mark Deming*

● **Mars Needs Guitars** / 1985 / Elektra ✦✦✦✦✦
The Hoodoo Gurus followed the excellent *Stoneage Romeos* with the equally swell *Mars Needs Guitars!*, a second helping of Dave Faulkner's wonderfully skewed kitsch-pop confections. While the band's basic M.O. hasn't changed all that much in the interim—'60s-era pop, garage rock, and cowpunk remain their key musical reference points—Faulkner's skills as a songwriter have grown perceptibly: the opening "Bittersweet" is an absolute gem, with other highlights like "Death Defying" and "Show Some Emotion" trailing not far behind. Also commendable is the Gurus' sharp wit—from the hillbilly freakout of "Hayride to Hell" to the primitive B-movie stomp of the title track, their affection for the guilty pleasures of trash culture is infectious. Irresistible fun. *—Jason Ankeny*

Blow Your Cool! / 1987 / Elektra ✦✦✦✦✦
For the Hoodoo Gurus' third album, the group's American record label was hoping the band could come up with something a bit easier to market than the witty, '60s-obsessed pop/rock of *Stoneage Romeos* and *Mars Needs Guitars*, so they paired the group up with producer Mark Opitz, who had previously twisted the knobs for AC/DC, INXS, and the Divinyls. Opitz gave the band a smoother, slicker surface and a cracking, radio-friendly drum sound; he also weeded out the band's wackier material (nothing like "Dig It Up" or "Hayride to Hell" this time out) in favor of mega-hooky pop ("Out That Door" and "Good Times," the latter featuring the Bangles on backing vocals) and straight-ahead rock & roll ("Where Nowhere Is" and "Party Machine"). As a result, *Blow Your Cool!* is the least idiosyncratic album in the Hoodoo Gurus' catalog and doesn't reflect the sneaky wit or goofy charm that won them many of their early fans. But it also makes them sound like the great rock & roll band they always were and leaves little doubt that these guys didn't need to be funny to get over; Dave Faulkner even seems to enjoy having the opportunity to play it straight on the politically slanted "In the Middle of the Land," and the band rarely rocked as hard as they did on the tunes here where they throw the engine into fifth gear. *Blow Your Cool!* is in some respects a compromised Hoodoo Gurus album, but it's strong enough to prove that these guys could make a worthwhile album even while playing by someone else's rules. *—Mark Deming*

Magnum Cum Louder / Jun. 1989 / RCA ✦✦✦
1987's *Blow Your Cool!* found the Hoodoo Gurus adding a considerable amount of polish to their production and toning down their trademark humor in a bid for a wider audience. But in the United States, it didn't pay off; *Blow Your Cool!* opened few new doors for the Gurus, and they were dropped by Elektra Records. Thankfully, 1989's *Magnum Cum Louder* found them newly contracted to RCA Records and sounding like their loyal fans loved them to sound—loud, hooky, and rockin' out with a smile on their collective face. The album's opener, "Come Anytime," was the Gurus' most irresistible pop song since "Bittersweet," and "Another World," "All the Way," and "Baby Can Dance (Pts. II-IV)" proved they hadn't used up all their good hooks in one place. Meanwhile, those wanting something stronger got their fix with a handful of top-shelf rockers, most notably "Axegrinder," "Glamourpuss," "I Don't Know Anything," and "Death in the Afternoon." The high wackiness of Hoodoo Gurus classics like "Hayride to Hell" and "Dig It Up" is still missing from *Magnum Cum Louder*, but the overall tone is much more relaxed than *Blow Your Cool!*; Dave Faulkner seems to be having a fun with the songs here, especially the mock-pompous "Axegrinder," the smirking "Glamourpuss," and the baseball saga/music biz metaphor "Where's That Hit." The Hoodoo Gurus also went back to producing themselves, and the audio is full but uncluttered, with a roomy, natural sounding mix that flatters Brad Shepherd's guitars and Mark Kingsmill's drums more than the slicker, sterile sound of *Blow Your Cool! Magnum Cum Louder* proved that the Hoodoo Gurus knew better than anyone how to make a great Hoodoo Gurus album, and it marked a welcome return to form for the band. *—Mark Deming*

Kinky / Apr. 1991 / RCA ✦✦✦
1991's *Kinky* found the Hoodoo Gurus ready to crank up their amps and rock hard, and lo be it to me to find fault in anyone's desire to kick out the jams, especially one of the most enjoyable rock & roll outfits of their times. But the problem with *Kinky* is that it often rocks a bit *too* hard for its own good; while the Hoodoo Gurus always knew how to crank it up, they also knew *when* to crank it up, and Brad Shepherd's this-goes-to-11 guitar textures (boosted big time in Ed Stasium's boomy mix) on "Too Much Fun," "A Place in the Sun," and "Something's Coming" tended to drown out the band's poppier and more melodic inclinations, always one of their greatest virtues. And while the witty psychedelic pastiche of "Miss Freelove '69" marks the welcome return of two of Dave Faulkner's great obsessions— '60s rock at its cheesiest and musical parody that's both funny and fun to listen to—the band's touch is a bit too heavy to make the most of the material. Among the few songs where the band's dynamics are right on target are "1000 Miles Away," a surprisingly effective life-on-the-road ballad, and "Head in the Sand," an angry anti-addiction rant that makes the most of its own fury. And from a band that rarely had trouble coming up with memorable material, there are a few songs that simply sound like filler. There are more than a few pearly moments on *Kinky*, but it was a genuine letdown for the Hoodoo Gurus after the no-frills triumph of the album's immediate predecessor, *Magnum Cum Louder*. *—Mark Deming*

● **Electric Soup: The Singles Collection** / 1992 / RCA ✦✦✦✦✦
Electric Soup is a 19-track Australian-only collection of the band's best singles. And although the Hoodoo Gurus made several fine albums, this collection shows the band in

the best light, with their catchiest and best-loved songs. An excellent distillation and the best introduction to this sorely underrated brand of Aussie-pop. *—Chris Woodstra*

Gorilla Biscuit: The B-Sides and Rarities / 1993 / RCA ♦♦♦
Gorilla Biscuits, a companion to the singles collection *Electric Soup*, features another 20 songs, all B-sides and rarities. And though the songs are often not as instantly endearing as the singles, they're certainly not throwaways either, making it essential for hardcore fans and at least interesting for casual listeners. *—Chris Woodstra*

Crank / Sep. 13, 1994 / Zoo/Volcano ♦♦

Blue Cave / Aug. 1996 / Zoo/Volcano ♦♦♦
By the time the Hoodoo Gurus released their seventh album, *Blue Cave*, in 1996, the band had settled into a fairly predictable pattern for their records—namely, they hadn't changed their psychedelic, jangly guitar-pop much at all. Occasionally, they add louder guitars to the mix, but they are essentially the same band they were in 1986. That's not necessarily a bad thing—the Hoodoo Gurus have a way with crafting a solid hook. The problem with *Blue Cave* is that they just didn't come up with enough of them. A few songs stand out, but by and large the album is just a standard Hoodoo Gurus album, albeit an enjoyable one. *—Stephen Thomas Erlewine*

Bite the Bullet / Aug. 25, 1998 / Mushroom ♦♦♦♦♦
At first glance, *Bite the Bullet* is overwhelming: three CDs in a digipak so beautiful you almost don't want to play it—but then you see the track listing and the only question is, "Which first?" Included here is a live disc from the Gurus' farewell tour; a disc of Live at the Wireless Australian radio broadcasts; and a disc of B-sides, live stuff, and studio rarities. Disc one, recorded on Hoodoo Gurus' 52-date Australian farewell tour, is chock full o' rock. They played every room in the country, making sure no one missed a chance to catch the legendary band before they packed it in. No surprise, the live set rocks furiously: classics such as "What's My Scene," "Tojo," and "Like-Wow Wipeout" are mixed with previously unheard songs like "Dr. Rock" and back catalog cuts. The sound is full and raging—in concert, the ultra-loud Gurus, led by Mark Kingsmill's thunderous foot, have been known to regulate heartbeats, so if you are pregnant or a heart patient, avoid disc one. Disc two compiles their best performances on the Australian radio show Live at the Wireless, going back to 1983. Many surprises here, such as covers of the Zeros' "Wimp" and the Stooges' "I Got a Right," which will lay you to waste. Disc three moves further into obscurity, with seven B-sides that came after the *Gorilla Biscuits* B-side compilation (from *Crank* and *Blue Cave* sessions)—the only previously released tracks on the entire set. You have a medley of Ramones covers, unreleased demos, and several tracks dating back to the band's inception in 1981. Very cool, indeed. An essential for the band's fans, but beginners should start with the *Electric Soup* singles collection. *—Geoff Ginsberg*

Hootie & the Blowfish

f. 1989, Columbia, SC
Jam Bands, American Trad Rock, Adult Alternative Pop/Rock
Hootie & the Blowfish's mainstream pop variation of blues-rock brought the band to the top of the charts in 1995. Formed at the University of South Carolina, the group features lead vocalist/guitarist Darius Rucker, Mark Bryan, Dean Felber, and Jim "Soni" Sonefeld; the name refers to two friends of the band, not Rucker and the group itself. *Cracked Rear View*, the group's first album, was released in the fall of 1994 and a single, "Hold My Hand," worked its way into the Top Ten by the beginning of 1995. Its success propelled the album to number one, as well as launching a second hit, "Let Her Cry," which was quickly followed by "Only Wanna Be With You."

Cracked Rear View had become a massive success by the fall of 1995, going platinum several times over. By the time the group released their second album, *Fairweather Johnson*, in the spring of 1996, the debut had sold 13 million copies in the U.S. alone. *Fairweather Johnson* initially didn't replicate that success. It entered the charts at number one and sold two million copies within its first four months of release, but it didn't produce any hit singles on the level of the debut's "Hold My Hand" or "Let Her Cry." *Musical Chairs* followed in 1998. The album *Scattered, Smothered, and Covered* was issued two years later, featuring previously unreleased material, songs polled by the fans, and Hootie's own tribute to R.E.M. and the Smiths.*—Stephen Thomas Erlewine*

● **Cracked Rear View** / Jul. 5, 1994 / Atlantic ♦♦♦♦♦
Hootie and the Blowfish's debut album *Cracked Rear View* was *the* success story of 1994/1995, selling over 12 million copies. It's a startling large number, especially for a new band, but in some ways, the success of the record isn't that surprising. Although Hootie and the Blowfish aren't innovative, they deliver the goods, turning out an album of solid, rootsy folk-rock songs that have simple, powerful hooks. "Hold My Hand" has a sing-along chorus that epitomizes the band's good-times vibes. None of the tracks transcend their generic status, but they are strong songs for their genre, with crisp chords and bright melodies. Still, the songs wouldn't be convincing without the emotive vocals of Darius Rucker, whose gruff baritone has more grit than the actual songs. At their core, Hootie and the Blowfish is a bar band, but they managed to convince millions of listeners that they were the local bar band, and that's why *Cracked Rear View* was a major success. *—Stephen Thomas Erlewine*

Fairweather Johnson / Apr. 1996 / Atlantic ♦♦♦
Following up a debut as successful as *Cracked Rear View* would be intimidating for most groups, but it had to be especially daunting for such a direct, straightforward combo as Hootie & the Blowfish. What made *Cracked Rear View* such a success was its very unpretentiousness; how each song sounded like it was the crowd-pleaser from the local bar band. Hootie & the Blowfish haven't lost that universal appeal on their second album, *Fairweather Johnson*, but they have been able to add more weight to their music. While the essential formula of Hootie's music hasn't changed—Darius Rucker still belts out anthemic choruses over interweaving acoustic guitars—the band is stronger and more muscular, giving their simple, direct melodies powerful support. They also have learned how to shade their music with varying dynamics and subtle arrangements, which also adds depth to the band. And behind the bright, singalong melodies, Rucker has hidden some surprisingly introspective and searching lyrics, tackling everything from racism to heartbreak. Hootie & the Blowfish still have a bit of trouble coming up with a set of consistently engaging songs, but the weakest moments on *Fairweather Johnson* resonate more than those on *Cracked Rear View*, while the best moments eclipse those on the debut. It's a surprisingly assured and effective second album. *—Stephen Thomas Erlewine*

Musical Chairs / Sep. 15, 1998 / Atlantic ♦♦♦♦
Although Hootie & the Blowfish delivered a fine second album, they had no hope of matching the phenomenal success of their debut, *Cracked Rear View*, so *Fairweather Johnson* was perceived as a flop, even though it moved over two million copies. In a way, that perception of failure was the best thing that could have happened to the band. With the spotlight being shone somewhere else (Alanis Morissette, to be exact), Hootie & the Blowfish could return to what they loved best—playing music and being in a band. *Musical Chairs*, the group's third album, illustrates what a blessing it was for the group. Despite a couple of production flourishes, such as the occasional horn section and strings, it's no breakthrough or stylistic departure—it's simply a well-made album, filled with catchy tunes. In other words, it's exactly like their first two records, but the performances are more kinetic and fun than on *Fairweather Johnson*, and the songs are arguably as consistent as those on *Cracked Rear View*. That's why *Musical Chairs* feels a bit like a comeback, but it really shouldn't be viewed that way—it's just a consolidation of their talents and further proof that Hootie & the Blowfish are a fine mainstream pop-rock band. *—Stephen Thomas Erlewine*

Scattered, Smothered and Covered / Oct. 24, 2000 / Atlantic ♦♦♦
It's easy to make fun of Hootie & the Blowfish because they are what everyone says they are—a bar band made good. Since they were a bar band from the early '90s, it shouldn't come as a surprise that they knocked out Smiths and R.E.M. covers along with songs from the Led Zeppelin and Bill Withers songbooks—this was the music of the time, and they were a band of their time. All of this surfaces on their B-sides and rarities collection, *Scattered, Smothered and Covered*. As these 15 songs bounce between covers and tuneful originals slightly less memorable than their big hits, it occurs to you that this must be how Hootie & the Blowfish sounded in Southern college bars before they recorded *Cracked Rear View*—they're amiable, good-humored, earnest, and likable. Since the big hits are missing, the group sounds a bit like a local act, too—the kind of group that wrote sturdy songs but never found a transcendent hook—but that's not a bad thing, since that's always been part of their charm. And, the fact is, this band has real affection for jangle-pop-derived rock. They knew enough to dig out "I Go Blind," a good old 54-40 song, and place it on the *Friends* soundtrack at the height of the show's popularity, so they could make the guys some money. It's hard to hate a band that does that, and that lends a certain charm even to an album like *Scattered, Smothered and Covered*, which is as uneven as any rarities collection (and, of course, only necessary for the hardcore), but blessed with an unexpected charm, since it proves in the best possible way that Hootie & the Blowfish really were America's bar band of the '90s. *—Stephen Thomas Erlewine*

Hooverphonic

f. 1995, Brussels, Belgium
Ambient Pop, Adult Alternative Pop/Rock, Alternative Pop/Rock
The Belgian ambient pop band Hooverphonic featured vocalist Liesje Sadonius, guitarist/programmer Alex Callier, keyboardist Frank Duchêne, and guitarist Raymond Geerts. Known simply as Hoover across Europe, the group made their initial splash contributing the song "2Wicky" to the soundtrack of the 1996 Bernardo Bertolucci film *Stealing Beauty*, followed a year later by the full-length *New Stereophonic Sound Spectacular*. Sadonius left Hooverphonic a short time later, and was replaced by vocalist Geike Arnaert in time to record 1998's *Blue Wonder Power Milk*. *The Magnificent Tree* followed two years later. *—Jason Ankeny*

A New Stereophonic Sound Spectacular / Apr. 15, 1997 / Epic ♦♦♦
The Belgian trio Hooverphonic haphazardly tinkers around with ambient pop on its debut album, *A New Stereophonic Sound Spectacular*. Overall, it's a decent derivation of post-grunge and a healthy sampling of rising trip-hop and ambient electronica during the mid '90s, so perhaps it's all right for the album itself to experience floppy production. Lead singer Liesje Sadonius is sultry while defining Hooverphonic's signature shoegazer-like vocalics, with almost impressive electronic support from guitarists Alex Callier and Raymond Geerts and keyboardist Frank Duchêne. Debut single "2 Wicky" struts with a mysterious bass drop, and it's Sadonius' sexy vocal charm that fully ties it all together. Other tracks such as "Inhaler" and "Revolver" are moody but danceable, whereas "Nr. 9" blasts with hazy My Bloody Valentine -like distortion. The orchestration is tangled, but the artistic purpose of such musical beauty defines Hooverphonic's initial concept. *A New Stereophonic Sound Spectacular* depicts a glossy confidence, but not sheer enough for a fully enigmatic sound. But that's perfectly fine—Hooverphonic characterizes its own charm with experimental soundscapes of melodic disarray, but just barely. *—MacKenzie Wilson*

● **Blue Wonder Power Milk** / Aug. 11, 1998 / Epic ♦♦♦
Staying true to eclectic ambience through dramatic electronic music, Hooverphonic raise the pressure from their debut single "2Wicky" for a more passionate effort on their second album, *Blue Wonder Power Milk*. New vocalist Geike Arnaert captures an innocence that was practically blindsided on the first album by former lead singer Liesje Sadonius.

Blue Wonder Power Milk is intricately woven with string arrangements and pulsating dance club beats for a drowsy feel. Most songs featured on *Blue Wonder Power Milk* are guided by light strings, allowing Hooverphonic to gently fall into genres of indie pop, dream pop, and trip-hop, however each song does take on a life of its own—slowly. Album opener "Battersea" arrives with Arnaert's breathy vocals spiraling drum & bass track about self-indulgence. "Club Montepulciano," which received moderate airplay on college radio, and "Eden" both glide with an ethereal beauty whereas "Lung" thrives with heavy guitar licks and throbbing Depeche Mode-like synths. *Blue Wonder Power Milk* attempts a strong introduction, and while it is indeed enchanting, it's also slow to rise. It isn't until the latter part of the record where the music feels tight. Songs such as "Renaissance Affair" and "Tuna" both depict an artistical splendor. Both compose a naïveté, unlike "2Wicky" with personal lyrics and impersonal orchestral mystery. "Magenta" is pure symphonic bliss—raging keyboard hues are hard hitting with a delicate sensuality taking over the entire theme of the album. *Blue Wonder Power Milk* depicts what's yet to come from Hooverphonic, but also a sound that is unafraid to be young and wistful to be reworked in future albums. —*MacKenzie Wilson*

The Magnificent Tree / Sep. 26, 2000 / Epic ✦✦✦
Belgium's dream-pop trio Hooverphonic has seemed to creatively move beyond their icy smooth seascape found on 1998's *Blue Wonder Power Milk* and shift into a darkwave mood on their third full-length, *The Magnificent Tree*. Classic embryonic vocalic beauty from Geike Arnaert still carries the translucence of the band's signature ethereality, and she shines as hard as she did on the band's previous releases. However, musical composition on songs such as "Pink Fluffy Dinosaurs" and "Frosted Flake Wood" are more intricate and sonically defined. Chief songwriter and programmer Alex Callier and guitarist Raymond Geerts aim for abstract theatrics; multi-instrumentation is brooding and creeping, but Hooverphonic's distinct maturation cannot overshadow the gorgeous, flowing soundscapes they previously laid down. It's not disheartening by any means, for Hooverphonic does compose an attractive depiction of revamped new wave elements and twisted synth-pop in the face of new millennium teendom. They are far from manufactured label-conscious musical fascism, yet still are represented by a major label. But staying true to the Julee Cruise-like ambience, songs such as "Out of Sight" and "Mad About You" are thoroughly dramatic and make for an illustrious listen. *The Magnificent Tree* has not completely ignored the musical mystery, and the listener shouldn't forget such mastery while Hooverphonic's cultivation had to be perfectly split. —*MacKenzie Wilson*

Mary Hopkin

b. May 3, 1950, Pontardawe, Wales
Vocals, Guitar / Folk-Rock, Pop
It was the British supermodel Twiggy who alerted Paul McCartney to the Welsh singer Mary Hopkin when Apple Records was looking for talent in 1968. The waifish soprano scored a huge, worldwide smash with her first Apple single, the melancholy but rabble-rousing ballad "Those Were the Days," in late 1968; it actually knocked the Beatles' own "Hey Jude" out of the number one position in the U.K. Paul McCartney lent Hopkin a further hand by producing her first album and writing her second single, "Goodbye," which was also a hit. More comfortable with refined, precious ballads and folky pop than rock, Hopkin scored several more hit singles in the U.K., although she never entered the American Top 40 again. Her commercial success diminished as Apple's fortunes dwindled in the early '70s. —*Richie Unterberger*

● **Post Card** / 1969 / Apple ✦✦✦✦✦
Paul McCartney produced this debut album of twee but pretty, romantic pop-folk. Besides "Those Were the Days" (which actually originally appeared only on the British version, though it's on the CD reissue now available throughout the world), the highlights are Donovan's "Lord of the Reedy River" and "The Honeymoon Song," which McCartney himself had sung with the Beatles way back in 1963 on the BBC. If there's a fault to be found, it's that there's too high a percentage of pre-rock/pop standards à la "There's No Business Like Show Business." As it turns out this was more due to the leanings of McCartney than Hopkin, who preferred the more simply arranged folk numbers such as the Donovan covers and the Welsh "Y Blodyn Gwyn." Also on board is a rather nice composition, "The Game," by Beatles producer George Martin, who contributed some piano and orchestra conducting to the album. The CD reissue includes George Gershwin/Ira Gershwin's "Someone to Watch Over Me" (which was on the original U.K. version of the LP, but was taken off the American counterpart), as well as the "Those Were the Days" B-side "Turn! Turn! Turn!" and versions of "Those Were the Days" that Hopkin sang in Italian and Spanish. —*Richie Unterberger*

Earth Song, Ocean Song / 1971 / Apple ✦✦✦✦
More folk-oriented than her first effort, Mary Hopkin's lilting voice soothes the listener like hot tea with honey. Included in this set, which was produced by Tony Visconti, are her interpretations of Ralph McTell's "Streets of London," Cat Stevens' "The Wind" and Gallagher & Lyle's "International." —*James Chrispell*

Those Were the Days / 1972 / Apple ✦✦✦✦
It might amaze anyone who only knows her for "Those Were the Days" to realize that of the 17 songs on this imported CD, only four appeared on either of Mary Hopkin's albums, and that only "Those Were the Days" has been available elsewhere on CD since the mid-'90s. Who would have thought she'd released that much music in just three years? This collection is partly related to the similarly titled 11-song LP compilation of Hopkin's work that appeared during 1972. That release was premature, a result of Apple Records' thrashing about trying to generate revenue, but time has made the need for such a collection a little more clear. Hopkin ended up leaving behind a considerable number of singles that never made it onto albums, all of which are featured here along with most of their B-

sides; the latter are extremely important, because Hopkin usually preferred the B-sides, feeling they represented what she was really about as a singer far better than her A-sides. Almost all of the material is eminently listenable and much of it is extremely enjoyable. Hopkin may have regarded herself as a folksinger, but her intonation and articulation made her a very formidable pop talent as well, as revealed in her smoothly elegant version of "Que Sera Sera." Whether she was singing in Italian or English, or in a folk or pop idiom, Hopkin brought beguiling sensitivity and emotion to her recordings and is consistently interesting to hear for her finely nuanced diction. The sound here is state of the art circa the mid '90s, with a lot of warmth and detail, and the notes are reasonably thorough and accompanied by a detailed release history of each song. —*Bruce Eder*

Bruce Hornsby

b. Nov. 23, 1954, Williamsburg, VA
Vocals, Accordion, Piano / Heartland Rock, Adult Alternative Pop/Rock, Pop/Rock, Adult Contemporary
Bruce Hornsby and his band the Range signed to RCA in 1985. Their debut album, *The Way It Is*, eventually produced three Top 20 hits, the biggest of which was the socially conscious "The Way It Is," which featured Hornsby's characteristically melodic right-hand piano runs. The album stayed in the charts almost a year and a half and sold two million copies. Hornsby and the Range won the Best New Artist Grammy Award for 1986. Their second album, *Scenes From the Southside*, was not as successful as the debut, though it sold a million copies and produced the Top Ten single "The Valley Road." Hornsby also began to make his mark as a songwriter for others: Huey Lewis had a hit with his "Jacob's Ladder," as did Don Henley with "The End of the Innocence." Hornsby's third album, *A Night on the Town* (1990), found him trying to break out of his signature sound into other areas. It was less successful than its predecessors but, along with the pianist's extensive session work, it signaled his determination to tackle new musical challenges. Hornsby worked extensively as a producer and sideman in the early '90s, notably doing temporary duty in the Grateful Dead after their keyboardist, Brent Mydland, died in July 1990. —*William Ruhlmann*

● **The Way It Is** / Aug. 1986 / RCA ✦✦✦✦✦
One of the best collections of new songs released in the 1980s, performed to perfection by a versatile band led by a seasoned (if new to the listener) artist. The songs provide an American panorama, in terms of both landscape and social mores. This is smart, compassionate music for thinking adults…and you can dance to it, too. Includes "The Way It Is" and "Mandolin Rain." —*William Ruhlmann*

Scenes From the Southside / 1988 / RCA ✦✦✦✦
Although many bands feel pressure to record the follow-up to a successful debut, Bruce Hornsby is a seasoned musician who is comfortable in his own skin. For the most part, he and his band stick to the same formula that brought them success with *The Way It Is*. In other words, *Scenes From the Southside* is another strong set of piano-based pop with catchy melodies. While the other musicians are able, they just fill out the sound—this is Hornsby's gig. One of his greatest strengths is that, despite being an accomplished musician, he never shows off his chops at the expense of the song. The lyrics offer a slice of Americana; co-written with his brother, John Hornsby, the songs conjure up feelings of national pride ("Defenders of the Flag") as well as small-town nostalgia ("The Road Not Taken"). However the highlights of the album are the minor hits "Look Out Any Window" and "The Valley Road," with their sprawling, grandiose arrangements that rank among his finest work. While not quite as consistent as their debut, *Scenes From the Southside* is one of Hornsby's best efforts and a must-own for fans. —*Vik Iyengar*

A Night on the Town / Jul. 1990 / RCA ✦✦✦✦
Bruce Hornsby's hardest-rocking album, *A Night on the Town* announces that he is heading into a different direction in its first few notes. John Mellencamp's producer Don Gehman gives the sound, especially John Molo's drums, a feel reminiscent of Mellencamp's best work. The material here is among Hornsby's best, and guest players include Jerry Garcia, tenor saxman Wayne Shorter, banjo virtuoso Béla Fleck, vocalist Shawn Colvin (before she was known), and jazz bass legend Charlie Haden. The arrangements still include the mix of synthesized and real percussion, and the trademark piano licks are sprinkled abundantly throughout, but the overall feel is much more rock & roll than anything before or since. The songs are great, with a political edge to "Fire on the Cross" and "Barren Ground." The latter features Garcia's lead guitar, the former a fine Shorter sax solo. "Stander on the Mountain" is a perceptive reflection on a former BMOC, straight out of Hornsby's own attendance at a high school reunion, and "Lost Soul" is one of the most profound ballads he has composed, sung as a duet with Colvin. The single, "Across the River," is a powerful look at the pursuit of one's dreams in the face of local naysayers, and the subsequent return to one's hometown with the resultant "I-told-you-so's." With *A Night on the Town*, Bruce Hornsby achieves a mix of mostly up-tempo rock music, adult lyrical themes, and crisp production values that has seldom been matched by other popular musicians of his generation. Though it only peaked at number 20 (his first two albums had reached the Top Five), it is an artistic high point. —*Jim Newsom*

Harbor Lights / Apr. 6, 1993 / RCA ✦✦✦

Hot House / Jul. 18, 1995 / RCA ✦✦✦

Spirit Trail / Oct. 13, 1998 / RCA ✦✦✦

Here Come the Noise Makers / Oct. 24, 2000 / RCA ✦✦✦
Bruce Hornsby was 32 when "That's the Way It Is" hit number one and made him a star in the winter of 1986-1987, and he has used that stardom differently from the way a 22-year-old might have. You might say he's deliberately dismantled his popularity, gradually dispensing with the Range, the backing band he used to bill on his records, and with his

brother John, who used to write his lyrics, while making progressively less song-oriented records that have traced a steadily declining sales curve to the point that his sixth album, the 1998 double-CD *Spirit Trail*, spent only two weeks in the charts. Or you might say he's used his popularity, spending it on musical legitimacy by turning away from pop music, indulging in side projects such as his part-time membership in the Grateful Dead. *Here Come the Noise Makers*, a two-CD live album drawn from concerts in 1998-2000, is, he says, a gift to "our fans, our true fans," which is to say those who have stuck with him. His gift includes renditions of his biggest hits, "That's the Way It Is," "Mandolin Rain," and "The Valley Road," as well as hits he wrote, "Jacob's Ladder," and "The End of the Innocence," embedded in lengthy arrangements with lots of invocations of his musical influences—the Dead, George Gershwin, Samuel Barber, Bill Evans, Bud Powell, and Bob Dylan among them. Hornsby is determined to create a hybrid style that encompasses rock, jazz, and classical music within a jam-band mentality. If he doesn't succeed, it may be because there aren't enough "true fans" out there to follow him, or it may be because he is so impressed with his own showoff-ish virtuosity that he hasn't bothered to write music compelling enough to support his goals. — *William Ruhlmann*

Hot Chocolate

f. 1970, Brixton, London, England
Funk, Soul
An interracial English funk and soul group, Hot Chocolate scored a pair of huge hits in the '70s but were otherwise more enthusiastic than skilled. Lead singer Erroll Brown, guitarist Harvey Hinsley, keyboardist Larry Ferguson, bassist Tony Wilson, drummer Tony Connor, and conga player Patrick Olive were the original lineup. They recorded for Big Tree from 1975 to 1978, scoring a Top Ten R&B and pop hit with "You Sexy Thing" in 1975, which also was a gold single. They repeated the trick in 1978 with "Every 1's a Winner," once more earning a gold single in the process. No other Hot Chocolate song ever made it beyond number 40 on the R&B chart, and their albums never packed much commercial punch either. Wilson departed in 1975, and Olive switched to bass in his place. —*Ron Wynn*

● **Every 1's a Winner: The Very Best of Hot Chocolate** / 1987 / Capitol ✦✦✦✦✦
British soul band Hot Chocolate were known mainly by Americans for their huge 1975 hit "You Sexy Thing." But this 19-song anthology reveals that the band deserves more attention than they received. Lead singer Errol Brown was not only good with catchy dance tunes, but could deliver on romantic ballads, novelty tunes, inspirational material, or even message pieces such as "A Child's Prayer." The group was ahead of its time in other ways, having a racially mixed lineup in an era of increasing polarization, and also including reggae and rock elements in their production and sound. —*Ron Wynn*

Hot Tuna

f. Oct. 1970
Folk-Rock, Blues-Rock, Rock & Roll
Begun as an acoustic spin-off of the Jefferson Airplane, Hot Tuna eventually became the full-time focus of founding members Jack Casady and Jorma Kaukonen, emerging as a popular touring act of the 1970s. Originally dubbed Hot Shit, much to the chagrin of their label, RCA, their first performances were sandwiched between regular Airplane gigs. As a trio rounded out by harmonica player Will Scarlet, Hot Tuna debuted in 1970 with a low-key self-titled live LP of traditional blues and ragtime. By the following year's more rock-inspired *First Pull Up—Then Pull Down*, their roster included violinist Papa John Creach, concurrently a full-time member of the Airplane, and drummer Sammy Piazza. Minus Scarlet, a third album, *Burgers*, appeared in 1972. By the appearance of 1974's *The Phosphorous Rat*, both Casady and Kaukonen had officially exited Jefferson Airplane. Five studio albums followed for RCA before Hot Tuna announced their breakup in 1979. Both Kaukonen and Casady fronted new wave groups during the early '80s, then reformed Hot Tuna in 1986. In 1990, the pair released *Pair a Dice Found*, the first collection of new studio material in over a decade. —*Jason Ankeny*

Hot Tuna / May 1970 / RCA ✦✦✦✦
When Hot Tuna's self-titled debut album was released in May 1970, it seemed like the perfect spin-off project for a major rock group, Jefferson Airplane's lead guitarist and bass player indulging in a genre exercise by playing a set of old folk-blues tunes in a Berkeley coffeehouse. The music seemed as far removed from the Airplane's acid rock roar as it did from commercial prospects, and, thus it allowed these sometimes overlooked bandmembers to blow off some steam musically without threatening their day jobs. In retrospect, however, it's easy to hear that something more was going on. Friends since their teens, Jorma Kaukonen and Jack Casady had developed a musical rapport that anchored the Airplane sound but also existed independently of it, and shorn of the rock band arrangements and much of the electricity (Casady still played an electric bass), their interplay was all the more apparent. Kaukonen remained the accomplished fingerpicking stylist he had been before joining the Airplane, while Casady dispensed with the usual timekeeping duties of the bass in favor of extensive contrapuntal soloing, creating a musical conversation that was unique. It was put at the service of a batch of songs by the likes of the Reverend Gary Davis and Jelly Roll Morton with the occasional Kaukonen original thrown in, making for a distinct style. Kaukonen's wry singing showed an intense identification with the material that kept it from seeming repetitious despite the essential similarities of the tunes. (Harmonica player Will Scarlett also contributed to the mood.) The result was less an indulgence than a new direction. [The 1996 CD reissue added five tracks from the same set of shows, increasing the disc's running time by more than 45 percent. "Belly Shadow" was a lost Kaukonen instrumental. The others would become familiar numbers in Hot Tuna's repertoire.] —*William Ruhlmann*

First Pull Up, Then Pull Down / 1971 / RCA ✦✦✦
While the first Hot Tuna album had been an acoustic trio album featuring Jorma Kaukonen, Jack Casady, and Will Scarlet, this second album added violinist Papa John Creach and drummer Sammy Piazza, and most significant, it added electricity. Now, the sound was closer to Kaukonen's features in Jefferson Airplane. The highlight was the eight-minute "Keep Your Lamps Trimmed and Burning," although "Candy Man" also became a concert favorite. —*William Ruhlmann*

● **Burgers** / 1972 / RCA ✦✦✦✦
Burgers, Hot Tuna's third album, marked a crucial transition for the group. Until now, Hot Tuna had been viewed as a busman's holiday for Jefferson Airplane lead guitarist Jorma Kaukonen and bassist Jack Casady. Their first album was an acoustic set of folk-blues standards recorded in a coffeehouse, their second an electric version of the same that added violinist Papa John Creach (who also joined the Airplane) and drummer Sammy Piazza. Then the Airplane launched Grunt, its own vanity label, which encouraged all bandmembers to increase their participation in side projects. *Burgers*, originally released as the fourth Grunt album, sounded more like a full-fledged work than a satellite effort. It was Hot Tuna's first studio album, and Kaukonen wrote the bulk of the material, not all of it in the folk-blues style that had been the group's métier. "Sea Child," for example, employed his familiar acid-rock sound and would have fit seamlessly onto an Airplane album. And "Water Song," one of his most accomplished instrumentals, had a crystalline acoustic guitar part that really suggested the sound of rippling water. On the material that did recall the earlier albums, Hot Tuna split the difference between its acoustic and electric selves, sometimes, as on "True Religion," beginning in folky fingerpicking style only to add a rock band sound after the introduction. The result was more restrained than the second album, but not as free as the first, with the drums imposing steady rhythms that often kept Casady from soloing as much, though Creach's violin made for plenty of improvisation within the basic blues structures. All of which is to say that, not surprisingly, on its third album in as many years, Hot Tuna had evolved its own sound and music, and seemed less a diversion than its members' new top priority. —*William Ruhlmann*

The Phosphorescent Rat / 1973 / RCA ✦✦✦
Hot Tuna's first album made after the breakup of Jefferson Airplane found Jorma Kaukonen taking a firm hand: he's the author of nine out of ten songs. The walking tempos and familiar soaring, psychedelic guitar solos are in place, but much of the music is given over to Kaukonen's reflective lyrics, sung in his matter-of-fact voice, and there are strings on a couple of tracks. The group's fans, devoted as they were to its extended versions of blues standards, seem to have been unimpressed: the album was Hot Tuna's lowest-charting among those released during its 1970-1978 heyday. Probably a lack of enthusiasm at RCA, due to the demise of Jefferson Airplane, didn't help in the album's promotion, either. —*William Ruhlmann*

America's Choice / 1975 / RCA ✦✦✦
Hot Tuna returned to a heavier sound on their fifth album, which, although it again was dominated by Jorma Kaukonen's compositions, leaned more heavily on extended electric-guitar solos and even included a Robert Johnson classic, "Walkin' Blues." Drummer Bob Steeler replaced Sammy Piazza as of this release. The result was a modest recovery from the disappointing sales of *The Phosphorescent Rat*, although not a complete return to form. —*William Ruhlmann*

Yellow Fever / 1975 / RCA ✦✦✦
Hot Tuna's second album of 1975 began with a cover of Jimmy Reed's "Baby, What You Want Me to Do" rendered in the group's characteristic noisy electric-guitar style, an approach that was typical of this more-of-the-same album. By this point, Jorma Kaukonen seemed to have found a balance between his songwriting ambitions and the need to provide springboards for the group's boogie-all-night improvisations. Here, "Sunrise Dance With the Devil" and "Bar Room Crystal Ball" feature good lyrics and excellent hooks, yet still fit into Hot Tuna's heavy approach. —*William Ruhlmann*

Hoppkorv / 1976 / Grunt ✦✦✦
Unlike recent Hot Tuna albums, *Hoppkorv* found the group acting less as a mouthpiece for guitarist Jorma Kaukonen's compositions and more as a heavy rock cover band, handling such familiar material as Buddy Holly's "It's So Easy" and Chuck Berry's "Talkin' 'Bout You," although "Watch the North Wind Rise" was one of Kaukonen's better tunes. Even on the originals, the tempo had picked up, the arrangements were shorter; nothing here ran as long as five minutes, and the sound had been filled out by the occasional addition of keyboards, second guitar, and background vocals. So, *Hoppkorv* was closer to a straightforward pop-rock album than many Hot Tuna releases, and for that, predictably, it got higher marks from critics, who appreciated the variety, and lower marks from Tuna fans, who found less music to boogie to. —*William Ruhlmann*

Double Dose / 1978 / Grunt ✦✦✦

Splashdown / 1984 / Relix ✦✦✦

Historic Hot Tuna / 1985 / Relix ✦✦

Pair a Dice Found / Oct. 1990 / Epic ✦✦

Classic Hot Tuna Acoustic / Apr. 23, 1996 / Relix ✦✦✦
In 1985, Relix Records released the LP *Historic Hot Tuna*, which consisted of a side's worth of tracks recorded at KSAN-FM on April 30, 1971, with the band in an "acoustic" format (i.e., with Jorma Kaukonen on acoustic guitar), and a side's worth of tracks recorded at the closing of the Fillmore West on July 3, 1971, with the band in an "electric" format. Eleven years later, the label released more complete versions of the two performances on separate CDs. This one presents a 53-minute version of the April 1971 radio show. The material is drawn from the band's first two albums, *Hot Tuna* and *First Pull Up, Then Pull Down*, the differences being that the former was recorded without drum-

mer Sammy Piazza and violinist Papa John Creach and that the latter was recorded electric. For fans of the first Hot Tuna album, this will be an enjoyable, if inessential part two. — *William Ruhlmann*

Classic Hot Tuna Electric / Apr. 23, 1996 / Relix ✦✦✦

In 1985, Relix Records released the LP *Historic Hot Tuna*, which consisted of a side's worth of tracks recorded at KSAN-FM on April 30, 1971, with the band in an "acoustic" format, i.e., with Jorma Kaukonen on acoustic guitar, and a side's worth of tracks recorded at the closing of the Fillmore West on July 3, 1971, with the band in an "electric" format. Eleven years later, the label released more complete versions of the two performances on separate CDs. This one presents a 56-minute version of the July 1971 concert. The material is drawn from the band's first two albums, *Hot Tuna* and *First Pull Up, Then Pull Down*, the latter recorded only three months earlier. For fans of the first *First Pull Up, Then Pull Down*, this will be an enjoyable, if inessential alternate version. — *William Ruhlmann*

The Best of Hot Tuna / Jul. 28, 1998 / RCA ✦✦✦✦

This two-disc compilation of RCA recordings, made between 1969 and 1977, traces Hot Tuna's evolution from an acoustic folk-blues group to an electric blues-rock band, and then to a near-heavy-metal ensemble, and from a repertoire dominated by covers of songs by blues guitarists like the Reverend Gary Davis to one consisting largely of original material written by guitarist/singer Jorma Kaukonen. Actually, the transitions are not that dramatic, since Kaukonen continues to favor the same kinds of guitar figures whether he's playing acoustic or electric, and his own songs, albeit with more abstract lyrics, are steeped in the traditions that produced the cover material. The compilers might have pleased Hot Tuna fans by placing more emphasis on the group's jamming abilities, including more of its live material ("Death Don't Have No Mercy" is especially missed), and saved some of the Kaukonen compositions for a "best of Jorma" album. But that is not to say that the compilation isn't a balanced, representative condensation of Hot Tuna's career on RCA; it is. It's just that, like the Grateful Dead's, Hot Tuna's studio albums didn't necessarily reflect the best of the group as a performing unit. Note that the set includes a rare studio version of "Been So Long" originally released as a single and a previously unreleased 1977 live version of "Rock Me Baby." — *William Ruhlmann*

House of Freaks

f. 1986, **db.** 1992
Jangle Pop, Alternative Pop/Rock
House of Freaks were a completely original two-man act—Bryan Harvey and Johnny Hott—who played only guitar and drums, respectively, but achieved a full band sound. Formed in Richmond, VA in the late '80s, the Freaks specialized in Southern gothic, provided by Harvey's literary lyrics with references to regional culture. The band debuted on Rhino in 1987 with the *Bottom of the Ocean* EP and quickly followed with *Monkey on a Chain Gang* (Rhino 1987). The more cohesive follow-up, *Tantilla*, showcased their songwriting and unique style. An uneven EP, *To Our Friends*, followed in 1990 and finally gave way to a major-label deal with Giant and *Cakewalk* in 1991. House of Freaks eventually disbanded, but Harvey and Hott continued to work together, chiefly in Gutterball, a side project for them as well as Steve Wynn, formerly of Dream Syndicate, and Bob Rupe of the Silos, which has yielded two albums. —*Denise Sullivan*

Monkey on a Chain Gang / 1987 / Rhino ✦✦✦

Instantly likable pop, strong vocals, and beautiful melodies made it a wonder this two-man band didn't explode during the late '80s. Drummer Johnny Hott's style has a military beat, appropriate to the band's historical, Southern bent. Singer Bryan Harvey is incredibly original and confident. The record still sounds completely fresh. —*Denise Sullivan*

● Tantilla / 1989 / Rhino ✦✦✦✦✦

Folk and pop melodies drive this magnificent album from start to finish. The chorus to "Sun Gone Down" holds up against any great hook, from Nick Lowe to Tommy James. *Tantilla* is pure Southern gothic, as subjects from religion to the Civil War are addressed and set to a roots-music beat that is handy, tight pop/rock at the core. After so many years, this record has worn quite well. —*Denise Sullivan*

Cakewalk / Jan. 1991 / Giant/Reprise ✦✦✦

Still mining Southern gothic for inspiration and making modern roots music, House of Freaks were a bit early for the No Depression movement; "Rocking Chair" would sound just dandy beside anything by Wilco or Son Volt. Yet, on this record, the group tried to push the envelope of what their brand of folk and roots music was about and ended up sounding a little generic, perhaps due to producer Dennis Herring's Timbuk 3 touch. Nonetheless, the charming, Jules Shear-like "Honor Among Lovers" and the Waitsian drinking song "Remember Me Well" stand out. —*Denise Sullivan*

Invisible Jewel / 1994 / Brake Out ✦✦✦✦

Three years after their major-label debut, *Cakewalk*, House of Freaks' Bryan Harvey and Johnny Hott return to their indie roots with *Invisible Jewel*. The band's primitive-sounding yet expansive guitar and drum sound is still intact, taking in the usual mix of R.E.M. and Tom Waits-inspired folk-pop heard on earlier releases. And while many cuts feature a combination of jangly Americana and punk economy, the duo stretch out on the experimental blues "I'll Treat You Right Someday" and the garage rockin' "It's a Fucked Up World." The sound is both feedback-drenched and gothic in tone, with Southern-swamp madness and pop sweetness popping up throughout. Elsewhere, percussion exorcisms are let loose ("Fat Boy Tom") and John Lennon's primal scream bent is taken up with impressive results ("Hey, Hey, Hey, Hey"). The House of Freaks' faithful will not be disappointed. —*Stephen Cook*

The House of Love

f. 1986, London, England, **db.** 1994
Indie Pop, Alternative Pop/Rock, Noise Pop, College Rock
The post-Smiths guitar-pop of the House of Love was popular for a short time in the late '80s, as many college and alternative-rock fans became converts to their mixture of shiny ringing guitars, pseudo-psychedelic melodies, and bursts of noise. The British group formed in 1986; it featured Guy Chadwick (vocals, guitar), Terry Bickers (guitar), Andrea Heukamp (vocals, guitar), Pete Evans (drums), and Chris Groothuizen (bass). Their demo tape attracted the attention of Alan McGee, the head of Creation Records. McGee signed the band for a single, "Shine On," which was released in May of 1987 to some critical acclaim; it and its follow-up, "Real Animal," both sold poorly. Following a tour supporting the singles, Heukamp left the group. Instead of replacing her, the House of Love continued as a quartet, releasing their untitled debut album in the spring of 1988. Many U.K. critics called it one of the finest records of the year, and the band built up a cult audience.

The following year the band moved over to PhonoGram Records (PolyGram in the U.S.) and released two singles, "Never" and "I Don't Know Why I Love You," that failed to crack the British Top 40. By the end of 1989, Bickers left the group; he was replaced by Simon Walker. The House of Love's second untitled album (commonly called *Fontana*) was released in early 1990 to lukewarm sales and reviews; the band's revivalist guitar-pop didn't fit in with England's club-conscious pop scene, spearheaded by the Stone Roses and Happy Mondays. After the group's 1990 tour, Walker left the group and was replaced by Simon Mawby. The House of Love returned in early 1992 with *Babe Rainbow*, which received favorable reviews yet weak sales. The continuing lack of commercial success began to wear on the band, leading to their disbandment in 1994. —*Stephen Thomas Erlewine*

The House of Love [1988] / 1988 / Creation ✦✦✦✦✦

The missing link between the white-noise exploits of the Jesus & Mary Chain and the emergence of the shoegazer movement, the House of Love's self-titled debut LP is a dense, swirling collage of layered guitars underpinned by simple, three-chord pop songs. Opening with the droning brilliance of "Christine," frontman Guy Chadwick and lead guitarist Terry Bickers create a gauzy, atmospheric sound which blankets the entire album; tracks like "Hope," "Road" and "Love in a Car" shimmer with stately grace, deftly straddling the line between '60s-era psychedelia and contemporary noise-pop. A sparkling debut. —*Jason Ankeny*

The House of Love [1990] / 1990 / Fontana ✦✦✦

Following the combination of indie success and massive hype leading up to the band's first album proved to be too much for the original lineup, with Bickers leaving after a series of problems and pressures once the group signed to Fontana. Yet rarely has a fraught series of recording sessions resulted in something so flat-out stunning. The House of Love's second self-titled album in a row—third counting the German singles comp—remains something of a high-water mark in what can loosely be termed U.K. post-punk music, acting as an effective final statement before the onslaughts of Madchester, grunge, and Brit-pop. It's almost impossible to tell who is more responsible for what on the album, given its stitched-together nature, but whatever Bickers contributes matches Chadwick's cool but never cold performances note for note, and the result is deep blue rapture. Starting with the snaky crawl of "Hannah," sidling in over a series of echoed guitar notes, the 12-song collection does everything from revisiting past heights to scaling new ones. "Shine On" gets re-recorded in an arguably much more powerful performance, Evans' drums and Bickers pounding away out in front, while one early B-side, "The Hedonist," is turned from a light acoustic number into a evocative modern blues. Another, "Blind," is changed very little, its simple fragility still holding a soft sway. Everything else is new and quite often stunning, building on the combination of power and emotion from the first album perfectly. "I Don't Know Why I Love You" remains the group's definitive single, three and a half minutes of romantic angst matched by a fiery, perfectly arranged performance. "Beatles and the Stones," meanwhile, far from being a nostalgia piece, refers to the bands in question as "[making] it good to be alone," with a rich, melancholic acoustic performance to boot. Add in the fiery performances on songs like "32nd Floor" or "In a Room" and the result is a true lost classic. —*Ned Raggett*

Spy in the House of Love / 1990 / Fontana ✦✦✦

Chapter one: Label spends enough money on record to make a third-world country queasy. Chapter two: Record flops financially, despite its artistic triumphs. Chapter three: Label realizes financial failure of record and panics. Chapter four: Label raids band's vault and puts out hodgepodge collection cheap to help recuperate from newly incurred monetary woes. *A Spy in the House of Love* compiles a decent but scrapped single circa '88 ("Safe"), a handful of dolled-up tracks from the scrapped follow-up to their debut, and scraps from various ditched sessions. See a pattern? Though it sounds like a recipe for rotten cranapple pie, HOL despot Guy Chadwick was quick to toss off anything that wasn't top-rate, and occasionally his BS detector was a little off. In fact, "Marble," which comes from the initial sessions for the band's second album, was quality enough to find a spot on the band's best-of that came out eight years later. There are scattered bright spots ("Scratched Inside," "Ray") and moments where the band sounds like they're just plain bored ("Cut the Fool Down" and the appropriately titled "No Fire"). The "Love" songs (Parts II-V) peak through every other track on the second half. They veer from bluesy, stream-of-consciousness shreds to half-finished howlings and decent instrumentals. Certainly one of the least/last links in the House of Love chain, your time and money might be better spent hunting down one of their many wallet-sinking singles (like the one with a cover of the Chills' "Pink Frost" or another with a take on Cream's "Strange Brew"). A second volume of *Spy* is definitely called for, as the average House of Love fan's wallet sank deeper than Guy Chadwick's cheeks while scurrying for their three-part(!)

singles. (The U.S. version of *A Spy in the House of Love* bizarrely plugs the second album's version of "Shine On" betwixt "Cut the Fool Down" and "Ray.") —*Andy Kellman*

Babe Rainbow / Aug. 18, 1992 / Fontana ✦✦✦
Guy Chadwick had threatened to make a loud rock record, and by the middle of the opening "You Don't Understand" (which sounds a great deal like the Spencer Davis Group's "I'm a Man"), he had everyone duped. However, the gilded fragility of the following "Crush Me" and "Cruel" throw the listener for a loop, retreating to what made the House of Love the House of Love: well-crafted songs that seem out of time. They don't really sound wholly retro, modern, or futuristic—though there is something rather classicist about them. That's just one reason why *Babe Rainbow* went nowhere on the British charts, let alone dying a dustbin death in the States. Singles like "Feel" and "The Girl With the Loneliest Eyes" were simply too subtle to find a home on as many turntables as Nirvana or Pearl Jam at the time, and in the U.K. the flashy Brit-pop scene was just beginning to tighten its vice. In all seriousness, *Babe Rainbow* should be regarded as much as the band's prior albums. It's nearly as solid as both. It might not have the hazy glow of the debut or the slightly cinematic edge of the punchier follow-up, but the emotional range and level of songwriting still remain. Take this record at face value and see if it's not almost everything a guitar pop record should be. *Babe Rainbow* might not be a classic, but three-dollar used-bin stuffers don't get much better. —*Andy Kellman*

Audience With the Mind / 1994 / Fontana/Mercury ✦✦

Best Of / Sep. 1, 1998 / Fontana/Mercury/Chronicles ✦✦✦✦✦
With the House of Love's albums getting increasingly difficult to obtain, it was a pleasant surprise to see Mercury U.S. release *Best Of* in 1998. A gorgeous package with a debatable track selection, the label released it without much in the way of promotion, so it really wasn't treated any different from their proper albums in that respect. Unfortunately, the House of Love fell into a bit of a gray area with the music scenes in both the U.S. and their U.K. homeland. It would have been especially difficult for the band to break through in the States, with the late-'80s Billboard charts wanting nothing to do with gimmick-free songs with perfectionist craftsmanship. And once flannel, plaid, and distortion broke free in 1991, they were perfectly incapable of catering to the grunge scene's rebellious catharsis. Stubborn and eccentric, Guy Chadwick and company soldiered on to produce mostly quiet and invitingly personal pop singles, most of which are collected here ("Real Animal" is the lone outcast). The non-single picks are kind of odd. B-sides "Marble," "Let's Talk About You," and "Loneliness Is a Gun" are picked instead of early album highlights like "Love in a Car" and even better B-sides like "Purple Killer Rose." *Babe Rainbow* closer "Yer Eyes" is also chosen over arguably better material from that album. Despite these gripes, *Best Of* does its deed in representing all that was great about one of England's finest late-'80s/early-'90s bands. —*Andy Kellman*

● **1986-88: The Creation Recordings** / Jun. 25, 2001 / PLR ✦✦✦✦✦
Guitar pop—British or otherwise—was nearing wasteland status when the House of Love debuted with "Shine On" in the spring of 1987. The Smiths and Hüsker Dü were months away from their respective breakups, Echo & the Bunnymen were about to issue their less-than-great self-titled album, and the Go-Betweens were flirting with yuppiedom. Aside from the short-lived, often-gutless C-86 scene and the then brilliant Jesus & Mary Chain, the House of Love really didn't have that much competition. It's almost as if the bands that influenced them subconsciously faded to give them the much-deserved spotlight. Now that over a decade has passed since the release of the material collected here—everything they released on Creation, meaning 1988's self-titled debut and four singles racked with lithe greatness—those who claimed the band's popularity had to do with their existence during a dry era can finally be silenced. Why, you ask? Because most everything here smacks violently of timelessness. "Christine," the penultimate combination of gorgeously spectral pop and noise, still sounds every bit spectacular, as if the eras of acid house, shoegaze, grunge, Brit-pop, post-rock, etc., have done nothing to erode its effect. That song alone should be as well known as "Light My Fire" or, at the very least, "How Soon Is Now." Without a doubt, time has been extremely good to this era of the band, who, after 1988, was on the brink of leaving Creation for Fontana following a legendary bidding war. While Chadwick's boastfulness didn't help things, his band wasn't the group of underachievers many would like to say they were. Not a bit. If they were in fact underachievers, it was because not enough people bought their records when they were first released. Behold, for here is your penance. —*Andy Kellman*

House of Pain

f. 1990
Pop-Rap, Hardcore Rap, East Coast Rap, Hip-Hop
"Jump Around," an impossibly infectious and catchy single, instantly elevated House of Pain from an unknown white hip-hop group to near-stars when it became a massive crossover hit in 1992. Released on Tommy Boy Records, the group's eponymous debut was co-produced by DJ Muggs, who masterminded Cypress Hill's groundbreaking debut. Fronted by Irish-American rappers Everlast (b. Erik Schrody) and Danny Boy (b. Daniel O'Connor), along with Latvian-born DJ Lethal, House of Pain celebrated their heritage in a tongue-in-cheek fashion that quickly became schtick—wearing green, drinking prodigious amounts of beer, and swearing constantly. It certainly earned them attention at the outset, particularly when it was tied to a single like "Jump Around," but the bottom quickly fell out of their career, partially because of the band's self-consciously loutish behavior. Throughout their 1993 tour, the group ran into trouble with promoters and the law, culminating in Everlast's arrest for possessing an unregistered, unloaded pistol at Kennedy Airport. Like its predecessor, 1994's *Same As It Ever Was* was produced by DJ Muggs and was greeted with surprisingly strong reviews and sales—the latter of which, however, quickly slowed. Most of the next two years were spent in seclusion, and the group returned

in the fall of 1996 with *Truth Crushed to Earth Shall Rise Again*, a record that was ignored by both the press and the public. Everlast returned in 1998 as a solo act, and gained critical acclaim for his debut, *Whitey Ford Sings the Blues*. —*Stephen Thomas Erlewine*

● **House of Pain** / Jul. 21, 1992 / Tommy Boy ✦✦✦✦
It would be hard for nearly anyone to top the explosive, insanely catchy "Jump Around," so it's no great surprise to find that House of Pain isn't up to the task. At times, HOP comes close to duplicating the intoxicating power of their slamming single, but for the most part, their debut album is a repetitive circle of similar beats, misogyny, racism, and posturing lyrics. But the perfection of "Jump Around" almost makes up for the numerous faults. —*Stephen Thomas Erlewine*

Same As It Ever Was / Jun. 28, 1994 / Tommy Boy ✦✦✦✦
House of Pain's self-titled album had its moments, but on the whole, wasn't very memorable. However, the Irish-American group really blossomed on its far superior and much more hardcore second album, *Same As It Ever Was*. With this album, Everlast changed his style of rapping considerably and unveiled a much more distinctive and recognizable approach. Sounding twisted, damaged, and maniacal, Everlast grabs the listener's attention and refuses to let go on such wildly entertaining fare as "Back From the Dead," "Over There Shit," and "Runnin' Up on Ya." House of Pain's subject matter—namely, their superior rapping skills and the threat they pose to sucker MCs—is far from groundbreaking. But an abundance of strong, clever hooks and Everlast's psycho-like rapping make *Same As It Ever Was* consistently appealing. —*Alex Henderson*

Truth Crushed to Earth Shall Rise Again / Oct. 22, 1996 / Tommy Boy ✦✦✦
Having found its voice on *Same As It Ever Was*, House of Pain delivered an equally captivating effort with its third album, *Truth Crushed to Earth Shall Rise Again*. Being Anglo rappers in a genre that had grown increasingly hostile toward Whites, Everlast and Danny Boy encountered their share of racism and bigotry. And they responded by being unapologetically street and hardcore, while bragging about their Irish heritage. On the whole, the album's subject matter isn't very substantial—the group still spends too much time boasting. But as was also the case with *Same as It Ever Was*, the LP is impossible to resist thanks to House of Pain's insanely captivating hooks and Everlast's twisted style of rapping. —*Alex Henderson*

The Housemartins

f. 1984, Hull, England, **db.** Jun. 1988
College Rock, Jangle Pop, Alternative Pop/Rock
One of Britain's more popular indie guitar-pop groups of the late '80s, the Housemartins' post-Smiths guitar jangle and subtle updating of catchy, melodic British beat groups earned the Hull-based quartet a substantial critical and popular following within the U.K. Though the group never gained much more than a cult following in America, their balance of simple, memorable melodies and cutting sarcasm helped them rise into the British Top Ten, as well as earn consistently strong reviews. The Housemartins broke up in 1988, just before they fully broke into the mainstream. The group's lead songwriter, Paul Heaton, formed the Beautiful South the following year, and his new band capitalized on the success of the Housemartins to become one of the more popular U.K. groups of the early '90s.

Paul Heaton (vocals, guitar) formed the Housemartins with Ted Key (guitar), Stan Cullimore (bass), and Hugh Whitaker (drums) in 1984. From the outset, the group cultivated a distinctly English image, blending a cynical sense of humor with leftist political leanings and low-key, commonplace appearance. "Happy Hour," the Housemartins' third single, became the group's first hit in the summer of 1986, climbing all the way to number three. *London 0 Hull 4*, their debut album, followed shortly afterward. At the end of the year, the a cappella "Caravan of Love" became a number one hit. *The People Who Grinned Themselves to Death* followed in 1987, spawning the hit singles "Five Get Over Excited" and "Me and the Farmer." Though the Housemartins were developing into one of the most popular bands within Britain, they broke up in the summer of 1988. With drummer Hemmingway, Heaton formed the Beautiful South, which carried on the aesthetic of the Housemartins, but added more complex melodies and arrangements. Toward the end of 1988, a compilation of Housemartins singles and rarities called *Now That's What I Call Quite Good!* was released. —*Stephen Thomas Erlewine*

● **London 0 Hull 4** / 1986 / Go! Discs ✦✦✦✦✦
The Housemartins had a bouncy pop-rock sound that was reminiscent of the British beat groups of the mid-'60s. This album is full of catchy tunes, although the lyrics are sometimes more serious than the music might suggest. —*William Ruhlmann*

The People Who Grinned Themselves to Death / 1987 / Go! Discs ✦✦✦✦
Comparisons to the Smiths are essentially irrelevant by the point of the Housemartins' underrated sophomore effort—the melodies and arrangements move away from the upbeat guitar-pop shimmer of *London 0 Hull 4* to further explore the group's fascination with Motown and gospel, while P.d. Heaton's lyrics articulate a leftist anger and scathing social commentary the likes of which Morrissey's insularly personal lyrics only hint at. (Equally noteworthy is the defiantly British outlook of Heaton's songs–it's virtually impossible from an American standpoint to fully comprehend the sheer vitriol against the Queen espoused on the title cut, and lyrical snippets like "How come you wear Rupert Check when you think you're so hard?" and "Welcome to the new Scalextric's breed" are likely impenetrable to all but the hardiest Anglophiles.) There's some filler here–"We're Not Going Back" and "You Better Be Doubtful" simply go through the motions, and the instrumental "Pirate Aggro" seems at best an afterthought–but the peaks of *The People Who Grinned Themselves to Death* are glorious. In hindsight, however, it's obvious that the Housemartins had already run their course–with its alternating lead vocals from Heaton and drummer Dave Hemingway, the achingly lovely piano ballad closer "Build"

forecasts the twosome's continued collaboration in the Beautiful South, while the subtle yet soulful bass work of Norman Cook throughout the record anticipates the funk direction of his subsequent Beats International project. *—Jason Ankeny*

Now That's What I Call Quite Good! / 1988 / Go! Discs ✦✦✦✦✦
Gathering singles, B-sides, BBC sessions, and key album cuts from all chapters of the Housemartins' brief but brilliant career, the posthumous *Now That's What I Call Quite Good!* is both a glowing greatest-hits package and an odds-and-ends clearinghouse—a fitting epitaph for a band which thrived on contradictions in consistently pitting the personal versus the political and the secular versus the spiritual. Despite the uniform excellence of their two studio LPs, this release confirms once and for all that the Housemartins were first and foremost a singles band—even removed from their album context, highlights including "Bow Down," "Build," and "The Light Is Always Green" boast all the immediacy and infectiousness of classic pop radio fodder, even if their actual mainstream appeal was minimal at best. The previously uncollected material, meanwhile, reveals a warmth and intimacy often missing from Paul Heaton's most trenchant social commentaries—in particular, the "garage gospel" approach which distinguishes remarkable readings of Luther Ingram's "I'll Be Your Shelter" and the Isley Brothers' "Caravan of Love" (the latter the Housemartins' lone U.K. chart-topper) radiate an intensely humanistic empathy which underlines the utter conviction at the heart of all the group's work. *—Jason Ankeny*

Penelope Houston

Melodica, Vocals, Autoharp / Adult Alternative Pop/Rock, Alternative Pop/Rock, Singer/Songwriter

Penelope Houston is one of the most shocking reincarnations from the original punk era. She was the lead singer of the San Francisco band the Avengers, one of the very first full-out American punk acts, opening for the Sex Pistols on the last show of their legendary U.S. tour. After the group broke up in 1979, Houston worked for a time with Howard Devoto and released a 1986 single fronting the short-lived 30-, finally releasing her debut album in 1988. To the shock of those who remembered her work with the Avengers, Houston had transformed into a folk-rock singer/songwriter with alternative rock sensibilities. As a solo act, her material emphasized acoustic textures, haunting melodies, and her gentle soprano voice. Popular as a performing act in San Francisco, she had trouble finding recording deals. Her similar, somewhat more fully produced second album did not appear until 1993 (a couple cassette-only releases mixing live and studio material appeared in the interim); subsequent efforts include 1994's *Karmal Apple*, 1996's *Cut You*, 1999's *Tongue*, and 2000's *Once in a Blue Moon*. Fans of singer/songwriters like Suzanne Vega, Shawn Colvin, and Christine Lavin looking for something similar but darker would do well to check Houston out. *—Richie Unterberger*

● **Birdboys** / 1988 / Subterranean ✦✦✦✦✦
A moody, melodic debut that evokes the spirit of Nick Drake and Sandy Denny with its brooding images of loss. Mandolins, accordion, acoustic bass, and sparse percussion (usually tambourines and bells) almost qualify this as a contemporary folk album, but Houston's biting and somber approach draws from her punk and alternative-rock roots. The writing is inconsistent, and Houston's fragile voice is sometimes not as forceful as the material seems to demand, but overall this is one of the more underrated alternative music statements of the late 1980s. *—Richie Unterberger*

500 Lucky Pieces / 1992 / ID ✦✦✦
One of the tapes Houston released on her own label while she was without a recording contract. This professionally recorded set includes a number of songs that would be rerecorded for 1996's *Cut You*, including "Sweetheart," "White Out," "Fall Back," and "Glad I'm a Girl." A slightly folkier set than usual, it's good, but mostly of interest to serious fans, as much of the material is more widely available in similar versions on CD. If you're interested, though, the tape is available by contacting Id Records at PO Box 422163, San Francisco, CA 94142. *—Richie Unterberger*

The Whole World / Aug. 24, 1993 / Heyday ✦✦✦
Most old-school punk purists will never forgive Penelope Houston for giving up guitar-driven rock & roll for acoustic music (even if she did so several years before the "unplugged" phenomenon made such things fashionable). But anyone who has actually listened to *The Whole World* will notice that Houston's acoustic music is just as smart, feisty, and uncompromising as her work with the Avengers (it's not hard to imagine her old band cranking up "Glad I'm a Girl" or "On Borrowed Time"). And if her lyrics are less stridently political, they're also more intelligent and mature without sacrificing her opinions in the process (even her love songs reflect a refreshing warts-and-all realism). And while Penelope the Punk Goddess had a habit of wandering off-pitch with annoying frequency, Penelope the Singer/Songwriter is able to convey much of the same intensity with a lot more nuance and accuracy, and her band (anchored by Houston's husband and collaborator, Mel Peppas) makes up in resonance what they lack in volume. *The Whole World* is a strong and compelling album from a remarkably underrated artist; it's well worth a listen should it cross your path. *—Mark Deming*

Karmal Apple / 1994 / Normal ✦✦✦
One of Houston's more subdued efforts, with characteristically eclectic arrangements sprinkled with autoharp, melodica, mandolin, violin, and cello. There's a constant sense of uneasy suspicion, worry, failed romance, and vague dissatisfaction simmering underneath the pleasing modern folk-rock melodies. These elements alone imbue the set with a lot more interest than the average contemporary folk recording. It's not her best album, but it's a typically solid one, with an occasional light (only occasional, and very light) country touch. Still only available in Europe as of 1996. *—Richie Unterberger*

Cut You / Mar. 5, 1996 / Reprise ✦✦✦
A curious disc in that it's more of a career survey than a collection of newly minted material, although all of these tracks were recorded shortly before the album was issued, as is the standard for new releases. Many of the songs were released in different versions on previous albums, some as long ago as 1988. This could be because it's Houston's first effort to benefit from major-label distribution, meaning that it will mark the first time that many listeners outside of the San Francisco Bay Area will be exposed to her material. That may make it a disappointment for those who've followed her career and have the original versions. But it's a solid set of melodic and inventively arranged folk-rock, with arrangements that differ from the originals in interesting ways that avoid redundancy. It also offers proof that Houston helped pioneer the melodic-yet-hard-hitting alternative rock currently mined by such performers as Liz Phair and Aimee Mann. Ironically, because of the timing of the release, it may be perceived as being just the opposite. *—Richie Unterberger*

Tongue / Mar. 23, 1999 / Reprise ✦✦✦

Once in a Blue Moon / 2000 / Orchard ✦✦✦
Released on Houston's own label, this 15-song rarities collection combines six previously unreleased demos and outtakes with nine songs taken from the out-of-print European CDs *Silk Purse* (1993) and *Crazy Baby* (1994). Five of the newly issued items are songs demoed for her *Tongue* album in 1996, but never released, while "(Velvet) Things" was recorded in 1998 at her last Warner Bros. session. This wouldn't be considered among the more essential Houston and is probably not intended as such. It's just a decent, modest group of tunes that are hard to come by, particularly in the U.S. It also gives her the chance to release some compositions that she did not write, such as her cover of Alex Chilton's "Take Care" and a few songs by multi-instrumentalist, producer, and frequent Houston collaborator Pat Johnson. *Once in a Blue Moon* has her expected sturdy bittersweet folk-pop-rock, with little in the way of eye-opening surprises, but nothing that disgraces her discography either. Generally it's most interesting when it ventures a bit outside standard contemporary folk-rock arrangements, as on "Take Care," which puts her autoharp and swirling ghostly vocal harmonies to the fore; the uncommonly poppy and peppy "Black Eyed Peas"; and "Nina," with its traditional ballad-like tune and tasty mandolin. *—Richie Unterberger*

Whitney Houston

b. Aug. 9, 1963, Newark, NJ
Vocals / Club/Dance, Adult Contemporary, Urban, Dance-Pop

With pure pop music melded to stunning beauty, Whitney Houston's star shines bright whether she is singing ballads, up-tempo dance material, the national anthem, or cola commercials. Coming from a solid musical background, this daughter of soul singer Cissy Houston and cousin of Dionne Warwick debuted in 1985. Her first album, *Whitney Houston*, was the first in Billboard chart history by a woman to enter at number one, and with sales of 14 million copies, was the best-selling debut album of all time until Alanis Morrisette's *Jagged Little Pill*. She scored heavily on MTV with classy videos, helping to break the color barrier originally knocked down by Michael Jackson. Her second album, *Whitney*, was just as popular, scoring seven consecutive number ones in the U.S., shattering the previous record held by the Beatles.

After the disappointing performance of her third album, *I'm Your Baby Tonight*, Houston rocketed back to the top of the charts in late 1992 with the soundtrack from her first movie, *The Bodyguard*. The love theme from the movie, a version of Dolly Parton's "I Will Always Love You," broke all previous sales and airplay records, becoming the biggest single in pop music history; it also won her an almost innumerable amount of awards, including several Grammys.

Her work on the soundtracks to *Waiting to Exhale* and her second film, *The Preacher's Wife*, tided fans over until she returned with a new album of her own, *My Love Is Your Love*, in 1998. *—Cub Koda & Stephen Thomas Erlewine*

● **Whitney Houston** / 1985 / Arista ✦✦✦✦✦
The legend of Whitney Houston began with this self-titled album. It marked her shift away from the experimental songs she did with the group Material and a move into heavily produced, very slick urban contemporary and adult pop. Although Houston had learned her craft working in New York nightclubs and singing in a Baptist church in Newark, she was steered into radio-friendly ballads that emphasized style over substance. The album did yield an unprecedented string of number one hits, but "Saving All My Love for You" and "How Will I Know" created an impression of an incredibly talented vocalist using only a minimum of her skills. It also contained one of her few legitimate soul workouts in "The Greatest Love of All." *—Ron Wynn*

Whitney / 1987 / Arista ✦✦✦✦
Whitney Houston became an international star with this album. It sold more than ten million copies around the world, yielded a string of number one hit singles across the board like "I Wanna Dance With Somebody (Who Loves Me)," "Didn't We Almost Have It All" and "Love Will Save the Day," and established Houston as the era's top female star. She later went on to more than solidify that status, with other hit albums and a budding film career. While this is a far cry from soul, it's the ultimate in polished, super-produced urban contemporary material. *—Ron Wynn*

I'm Your Baby Tonight / 1990 / Arista ✦✦
While Houston's voice always provides some interesting listening, this is somewhat of a disappointing release, with very few memorable songs. While she attempts to make a larger foray into dance music, she fails to make the crossover impact of artists such as Mariah Carey and Taylor Dayne. The two high points she does reach on this album come in the form of ballads—the uplifting tale of another's love being enough to provide hap-

piness in "All the Man That I Need" and the powerful verses surrounding a love lost through one's own devices in "Miracle." —*Ashley S. Battel*

My Love Is Your Love / Nov. 17, 1998 / Arista ♦♦♦♦
For all intents and purposes, Whitney Houston retired from being a full-fledged recording artist after her third album, 1990s *I'm Your Baby Tonight*, choosing to be a Streisand-like celebrity who cultivated a career through movies, soundtrack contributions, and social appearances. She may have been content to continue in that direction for many years if Arista president Clive Davis didn't push her into recording *My Love Is Your Love*, her first album in eight years, which easily ranks among her best. Never before has Houston tried so many different sounds or tried so hard to be hip. It's one thing to work with Babyface, the standard-bearer of smooth soul in the '90s, but it's quite another to hire Wyclef Jean, Lauren Hill, Missy "Misdemeanor" Elliott, and Q-Tip—all cutting-edge artists (albeit on the accessible side of the cutting edge), the kind who never would have been associated with Houston in the late '80s. The gambit works. There is still a fair share of David Foster-produced adult contemporary ballads, but the true news is on the up-tempo and mid-tempo dance numbers. In fact, the songs that feel the stiffest are the big production numbers; tellingly, they're the songs that are the most reminiscent of old-school Houston. That's not to say she can no longer belt out ballads convincingly—in fact, the best ballads are where she restrains herself, delivering them with considerable nuance. Houston has never been quite so subtle before, nor has she ever shown this desire to branch out musically. That alone would be reason enough to rank *My Love Is Your Love* among her more interesting albums, but the fact that it works more often than not pushes it into the top rank of her recorded work. —*Stephen Thomas Erlewine*

The Greatest Hits / Apr. 18, 2000 / Arista ♦♦♦♦
Although *Whitney Houston's Greatest Hits* is a double-disc package, only the first disc actually contains original versions of Houston's hit singles; the second disc, *The Greatest Remixes*, collects remixes new and old for hardcore fans. Of course, it would be impossible to fit all of Houston's 20-plus chart singles onto one disc, but that format still could have produced a fantastic and near-definitive collection. That is, if Arista hadn't made the ridiculous choice not to include four number one hits: "How Will I Know," "So Emotional," "I Wanna Dance With Somebody (Who Loves Me)," and "I'm Your Baby Tonight." Granted, those songs are all present on *The Greatest Remixes*, but anyone wanting the original versions will have to purchase the *three* different albums they appeared on. That said, the compilation does do fans a few favors; there are three new tracks, including one duet apiece with Deborah Cox and Enrique Iglesias, and two hits make their first appearance on a Houston album: "One Moment in Time" (the 1988 Olympic theme) and "If You Say My Eyes Are Beautiful," a 1986 duet with Jermaine Jackson. Houston's Top 20 hit recording of "The Star-Spangled Banner," performed at Super Bowl XXV during the Gulf War, is tacked onto the remix disc as well. The *Greatest Hits* disc amply reinforces what a fine singles artist Houston has been for the entirety of her career. Overall, though, it's a frustrating package marred by record company greed—not only because of the glaring and intentional omissions, but also because casual fans won't appreciate paying double the money for a remix disc they probably aren't interested in owning. —*Steve Huey*

H.P. Lovecraft

f. 1967, **db.** 1969
Garage Rock, Psychedelic
Featuring two strong singers (who often sang dual leads), hauntingly hazy arrangements, and imaginative songwriting that drew from pop and folk influences, H.P. Lovecraft was one of the better psychedelic groups of the late '60s. The band was formed by ex-folky George Edwards in Chicago in 1967. Edwards and keyboardist Dave Michaels, a classically trained singer with a four-octave range, handled the vocals, which echoed Jefferson Airplane's in their depth and blend of high and low parts. Their self-titled 1967 LP was an impressive debut, featuring strong originals and covers of early compositions by Randy Newman and Fred Neil, as well as one of the first underground FM radio favorites, "White Ship." The band moved to California the following year; their second and last album, *H.P. Lovecraft II*, was a much more sprawling and unfocused work, despite some strong moments. A spin-off group, Lovecraft, released a couple LPs in the '70s that bore little relation to the first incarnation of the band. —*Richie Unterberger*

H.P. Lovecraft / 1967 / Philips ♦♦♦♦♦
With the exception of a couple of badly dated tracks, this is one of the best second-division psychedelic albums, with strong material that shows the immediately identifiable Edwards-Michaels vocal tandem at its best. According to the LP notes, the songs were largely inspired by novelist H.P. Lovecraft's "macabre tales and poems of Earth populated by another race." It's more haunting than gloomy, though, with deft touches of folk, jazz, and horns. —*Richie Unterberger*

H.P. Lovecraft II / 1968 / Philips ♦♦♦
Much more progressive than their first effort, the album also showed the band losing touch with some of their most obvious strengths, most notably their disciplined arrangements and incisive songwriting. The arrangements are more swirling and far denser on this follow-up. Unsurprisingly, the more concise, dual harmony numbers that bear the closest resemblance to the first album work best, especially "At the Mountains of Madness." —*Richie Unterberger*

At the Mountains of Madness / 1988 / Edsel ♦♦♦♦♦
A superb double-album package of all of their studio material. Includes both LPs, historical liner notes, and a 1967 non-LP single (released prior to their debut) that is much poppier than their albums. —*Richie Unterberger*

Live May 11, 1968 / 1991 / Sundazed ♦♦♦♦
Blessed with one of the best live recording qualities one can hear from '60s efforts—especially considering that H.P. Lovecraft was never a major success—*Live May 11, 1968* provides a reasonable alternate way for the curious to find out what the shouting was all about. Split almost evenly between first and second album material, and featuring then-new bassist Jeff Boyan (brought in to replace Jerry McGeorge), this release shows that the quintet certainly had something. If there are plenty of moments where the addictive blend of garage jamming and mindblown psychedelia seems on the verge of collapsing into noodling or bad Doors imitations, there's enough of H.P. Lovecraft's own particular approach to justify a listen by anyone into exploratory late-'60s rock. Certainly once or twice the band ends up sounding remarkably prescient—the opening of "Wayfaring Stranger" calls to mind the blend of propulsion and trance Can would shortly make its own in Germany, with Tegza's tight beats leading the way. Plenty of other examples can be noted, with the transferred tape itself further suggesting the European group's approach—check the midsection of "The Drifter," where only Michaels' keyboards steer away from the driving rhythm. Edwards and Michaels' lead vocals work great together live—their training and earlier studio experience showing well—and the whole band tackles the spirit of the times to a T. Two standout performances are the one-two punch of "The White Ship" and "At the Mountain of Madness," both of which also make for the perfect tribute to the original Lovecraft himself. Occasional introductory comments surface from Edwards, but otherwise the five just get it all together and take off—and do so quite well. —*Ned Raggett*

● **H.P. Lovecraft/H.P. Lovecraft II** / Sep. 12, 2000 / Collectors' Choice Music ♦♦♦♦♦

The Hudson Brothers

f. 1970
Power Pop
Those that remember the Hudson Brothers usually think of them as a bubblegum act of sorts, due to the fact that they hosted some comedy-variety TV shows in the mid-'70s. But they were in fact a real group, extremely Anglophile in orientation, with heavy debts to the Beatles and Beach Boys, and occasional hints of the Kinks. In these respects, as well as their harmonies and superficial vocal resemblances to Lennon and McCartney, they echoed other players in the sub-Beatle game, like Badfinger, the Move, and ELO. That might be raising your expectations too high: they weren't nearly as deep or clever as the Move, as infectious or energetic as Badfinger, or even as ambitious as ELO. During their brief mid-'70s vogue, they recorded a few albums for Elton John's Rocket label (some of which were produced by Elton's songwriting partner Bernie Taupin), and managed a few small hits, "So You Are a Star," "Lonely School Year," and "Rendezvous." —*Richie Unterberger*

● **So You Are a Star: The Best of the Hudson Brothers** / 1995 / Varese ♦♦♦♦
Radically different from the usual teen idol fare, the Hudson Brothers recorded classic pop in the style of the Beatles or the Beach Boys instead of emulating David Cassidy. As a result, the Hudson Brothers' recorded legacy is on a whole different plane from typical 1970s teen-idol sounds, and the best of this work is captured on *So You Are a Star: The Best of the Hudson Brothers*. Their sound combines an array of classic pop influences with a lush 1970s production style, and produced a pair of notable hits in "So You Are a Star" and "Rendezvous." Both songs show off their incredible gift to create original tunes that sound like their heroes: "So You Are a Star" stunningly recreates the woozy, psychedelic feel of "Strawberry Fields Forever," while "Rendezvous" is a perfect Beach Boys pastiche, right down to the boogie-woogie organ and doo wop vocal harmonies. Despite this gift for mimicry, other tracks on this collection show the Hudson Brothers were more than mere imitators. For instance, "Spinning the Wheel" is a piano-driven power- pop tune with melodic and harmonic twists worthy of the Raspberries, and "Lonely School Year" effectively contrasts a languid, lovely vocal melody with some frenetic rhythm guitar work to create a tune that is energetic and beautiful all at once. The group also throws in some new tracks for this compilation, the best being "Sweet Cindy," a rollicking mid-tempo track with a surprising country-rock feel to it. All in all, *So You Are a Star: The Best of the Hudson Brothers* is an extremely potent collection of pop tunes that is begging for rediscovery by 1970s power pop fanatics. Anyone who enjoys groups like the Raspberries or Badfinger will find plenty to enjoy on this disc. —*Donald A. Guarisco*

Hues Corporation

f. 1969, Los Angeles, CA, **db.** 1977
Philly Soul, Disco
A Los Angeles vocal trio that enjoyed two big hits in the mid '70s, notably "Rock the Boat" in 1974 for RCA. While it was lightweight, mainly pop work, it did take The Hues Corporation to number two on the R&B charts and get them their lone pop chart topper. The next single, "Rockin' Soul," peaked at number six on the R&B charts and number 18 on the pop charts. They had their final R&B hit the next year with "Love Corporation," which reached number 15, but it was evident that the audience was losing interest in their material. "I Caught Your Act" was the last release in 1977. H. Ann Kelley, Flemming Williams, and Bernard "St. Clair Lee" Henderson were the original lineup. Tom Brown replaced Williams in the wake of "Rock the Boat"'s success. He was then replaced by Karl Russell in 1975. —*Ron Wynn*

● **Rock the Boat: Golden Classics** / May 1993 / RCA ♦♦♦♦♦
Rock the Boat: Golden Classics may not have many songs as great as "Rock the Boat" (although it's nice to hear Allen Toussaint's "Freedom for the Stallion") but it summarizes the Hues Corporation's recordings well. It's frothy pop-soul and disco, with pleasing grooves—sometimes the grooves get a little repetitive, but nothing is outright bad here, either. Not really something to seek out, but not bad, all the same. —*Stephen Thomas Erlewine*

Hugo Largo

f. 1984, **db.** 1989
Dream Pop, Alternative Pop/Rock

In response to the wave of abrasive guitar dissonance then in vogue throughout the downtown New York music scene, ex-music critic Tim Sommer and performance artist Mimi Goese formed the ethereal Hugo Largo in 1984. Later rounded out by Hahn Rowe and Adam Peacock, the quartet turned heads with its unusual instrumental lineup, which bypassed guitars and drums in favor of two basses, a violin, and Goese's unique dive-bomber vocals. In 1988, R.E.M.'s Michael Stipe produced Hugo Largo's debut EP, *Drum*; fleshed out with additional new material, it was reissued on Brian Eno's fledgling Opal label a year later. After 1989's less experimental *Mettle*, the group disbanded; Sommer later became an executive at Atlantic Records, and Goese's long-planned solo debut, recorded with assistance from Rowe, was scheduled to appear in 1997. —*Jason Ankeny*

● **Drum** / 1988 / Opal ✦✦✦✦✦
Fronted by one of the most intriguing voices in rock (and one of the least heard), Hugo Largo's debut EP, reissued as a full album a short while after, is a mysterious blend of ambient acoustics and a New York art sensibility. Sparse, echo-laden instrumentation of bass, violin, and (despite the press release) some guitar and drums recall the work of the 4AD label and Roger Eno. Songs such as "Second Skin" and "Eskimo Song" highlight Mimi Goese's haunting, swooping vocals, at once ethereal, then diving down into a dark pit enclosed by clenched teeth. The altogether pleasantness of the instrumentation only serves to contrast Goese's talent even more. The beautiful cover of the Kinks' "Fancy" shows how they easily could have made any song their own, if they had ever chosen to do so. —*Ted Mills*

Mettle / 1989 / Opal ✦✦✦✦
Brian Eno's label Opal picked up Hugo Largo for its second album, and on one hand the songs are closer to pop (or a weird art school version thereof) yet on the other, the skill and emotional range of the band has broadened considerably. The menace of "Hot Day" abuts the beauty of "Jungle Jim" and the playfulness of "Turtle Song" (the one single from the album, bearing bonus tracks that should have been reissued). Goese draws out one word, then another, making musical loop-de-loops with the syllables, causing the listener to hang on every word for some sort of meaning. One wonders what could have come out if the group had continued, but *Mettle* is satisfying enough as an epitaph. —*Ted Mills*

Human League

f. 1977, Sheffield, Yorkshire, England
New Romantic, New Wave, Synth-Pop, Dance-Pop

Synth-pop's first international superstars, the Human League were among the earliest and most innovative bands to break into the pop mainstream on a wave of synthesizers and electronic rhythms, their marriage of infectious melodies and state-of-the-art technology proving enormously influential on countless acts following in their wake. Formed by synth players Martyn Ware and Ian Marsh with vocalist Philip Oakey and Adrian Wright, Human League released two albums before internal tensions forced Ware and Marsh to leave in 1980, at which time they formed the British Electric Foundation (and later Heaven 17). Oakey and Wright recruited a bassist and schoolgirls Susanne Sulley and Joanne Catherall to handle additional vocal duties, which paved the way for their breakthrough "Don't You Want Me," from the album *Dare!*; both topped their respective charts in England, and went on to become major hits in the U.S. as well. The much-anticipated follow-up *Hysteria* finally surfaced in 1984, but failed to match the massive success of *Dare!* To the surprise of many, the Human League resurfaced in 1986 with *Crash*, produced by the duo of Jam and Lewis; the plaintive lead single "Human" soon topped the U.S. charts, but the group failed to capitalize on its comeback success, disappearing from the charts for the remainder of the decade. The group's two 1990s albums, *Romantic?* and *Octopus*, both went largely unnoticed both at home and overseas. —*Jason Ankeny*

Reproduction / 1979 / Virgin ✦✦✦
Pop fans a bit put off by Human League's dispassionate vocals on their breakout hit "Don't You Want Me" would have been shocked by the degree of emotionlessness heard two years earlier on the band's 1979 debut. The trio of Marsh, Ware, and Oakey all handled vocals and synthesizers to create a set of grim, rigid tracks that revealed a greater lack of humanity than even Kraftwerk. It's a surprise that Human League hit the British charts at all (with the single "Empire State Human"), since this could well be the most detached synth-pop record ever released. —*John Bush*

Travelogue / 1980 / Virgin ✦✦✦
The Human League's second album, *Travelogue*, was its first to be released in the U.S. (Not that you would have noticed at the time, given the limited distribution; the album subsequently was picked up for reissue by Virgin/Atlantic in 1988.) It was also the last to feature the nearly original lineup of Martyn Ware, Ian Marsh, Philip Oakey, and Adrian Wright. Already, the band's synthesizer textures and Oakey's mannered voice were starting to lean in a pop direction, but much of this album retained the austere tone of earlier synthesizer groups such as Kraftwerk and Tangerine Dream. The conflicting musical directions led to a split in the band after this album, with Ware and Marsh forming Heaven 17 and Oakey and Wright reorganizing a new version of the Human League. Ironically, both ventures were more pop oriented than before. —*William Ruhlmann*

☆ **Dare** / 1981 / A&M ✦✦✦✦✦
Dare captures a moment in time perfectly—the moment post-punk's robotic fascination with synthesizers met a clinical Bowiesque infatuation with fashion and modern art, including pop culture, plus a healthy love of songcraft. Human League had shown much of this on their early singles, such as "Lebanon," but on *Dare* they simply gelled, as their style was supported by music and songs with emotional substance. That doesn't mean that the album isn't arty, since it certainly is, but that's part of its power—the self-conscious detachment enhances the postmodern sense of emotional isolation, obsession with form over content, and love of modernity for its own sake. That's why *Dare* struck a chord with listeners who didn't like synth-pop or the new romantics in 1981, and why it still sounds startlingly original decades after its original release—the technology may have dated, synths and drum machines may have become more advanced, but few have manipulated technology in such an emotionally effective way. Of course, that all wouldn't matter if the songs themselves didn't work smashingly, whether it's a mood piece as eerie as "Seconds," an anti-anthem like "The Things That Dreams Are Made Of," the danceclub glow of "Love Action (I Believe in Love)," or the utter genius of "Don't You Want Me," a devastating chronicle of a frayed romance wrapped in the greatest pop hooks and production of its year. The latter was a huge hit, so much so that it overshadowed the album in the minds of most listeners, yet, for all of its shining brilliance, it wasn't a pop supernova—it's simply the brightest star on this record, one of the defining records of its time. —*Stephen Thomas Erlewine*

Love and Dancing / 1982 / A&M ✦✦
Fascination! / 1983 / A&M ✦✦✦
Instead of following *Dare*, its internationally successful third album, with another full-length effort, the Human League re-emerged with this under-27-minute, six-track EP, which consists of the one new track on its *Love and Dancing* remix album, plus the A- and B-sides of its post-*Dare* singles "(Keep Feeling) Fascination" (in two versions) and "Mirror Man." Both those songs were hits in the pop-synthesizer style of *Dare*, but the group's failure to produce a new album after 19 months was an indication of the instability it would suffer for the rest of its career. —*William Ruhlmann*

Hysteria / 1984 / Virgin ✦✦✦
The Human League's two-and-a-half-year effort to come up with a follow-up to *Dare* resulted in *Hysteria*, which tinkered with the hit formula, demoting producer Martin Rushent to computer programmer on only a few cuts. It was probably a mistake to release the politically oriented "The Lebanon" as the first single, especially in the U.S., where the country is called merely "Lebanon" and where the band was known primarily for the romantic "Don't You Want Me." That song wasn't typical of the album, which featured a remake of the earlier hit ("Don't You Know I Want You"), but was mostly filled with nondescript synthesizer dance tracks that barely deserved to be called songs. *Hysteria* was the Human League's opportunity to consolidate their worldwide success with *Dare*; instead, they slumped slightly at home and put their career in jeopardy in America. —*William Ruhlmann*

Crash / 1986 / A&M ✦✦✦
The Human League turned to American R&B producers Jimmy Jam and Terry Lewis in the wake of their success with Janet Jackson's *Control*, and the combination brought the group its second number one hit with the Jam-Lewis composition "Human," which harked back to the earlier "Don't You Want Me," albeit with a gentler tone. The album's second single, the *Control*-soundalike "I Need Your Loving," was also a Jam-Lewis song (as was the U.K.-only third single, "Love Is All That Matters"), but the bulk of the album was made up of group-written songs with appealing backing tracks that maintained their dance appeal while eschewing the overtly synthesized sound of previous albums. That made *Crash* an improvement over the lackluster *Hysteria*, but still not on a par with *Dare*. —*William Ruhlmann*

Romantic? / Sep. 1990 / A&M ✦✦
Octopus / Jan. 27, 1995 / East West ✦✦✦
● **The Very Best of the Human League** / Jul. 14, 1998 / Ark 21 ✦✦✦✦✦
In the summer of 1998, the Human League set out on tour with the reunited Culture Club, both bands hoping to capitalize on the new wave nostalgia that was slowly sweeping the country. The tour naturally provided an ideal opportunity for a new hits collection, *The Very Best of the Human League*. Essentially, it's a slightly reworked version of *Greatest Hits*, sharing all the obvious tracks ("Don't You Want Me," "Love Action (I Believe in Love)," "Mirror Man," "Fascination (Keep Feeling)," "Human," "Being Boiled," "The Lebanon") and substituting earlier cuts like "The Sound of the Crowd" and "Open Your Heart" for middle-of-the-road '90s singles "Tell Me When," "Stay With Me Tonight," "Heart Like a Wheel," and "One Man in My Heart." Clearly, this collection is for fans who prefer *Crash* to *Dare*, and they'll likely be satisfied, since it's fairly consistent. That said, *Dare* fans should note that this album features a genuine rarity in "Together in Electric Dreams," Philip Oakey's collaboration with Giorgio Moroder for the 1984 film *Electric Dreams*. It doesn't pop up all that often on either Human League releases or various-artists collections, which means this is all the more valuable for collectors, who may also enjoy the "Audio Liner Notes" which feature the group retelling their history. The Snap remix of "Don't You Want Me," however, will be of little interest to either camp. —*Stephen Thomas Erlewine*

Secrets / Aug. 6, 2001 / Papillon ✦✦✦

Human Switchboard

f. 1976, **db.** 1982
Post-Punk, New Wave

Inspired by the Velvet Underground (especially lead vocalist Bob Pfeifer) and the angst-ridden post-punk of Joy Division, Human Switchboard debuted in 1977 with an EP produced by Pere Ubu's David Thomas. *Human Switchboard Live* was released by the band three years later (although it resembles a bootleg), after which the group released their only LP, *Who's Landing in My Hangar?* After yet another live album, *Coffee Break!*, this one consisting of radio broadcasts, the band promptly disintegrated. Pfeifer (who later landed an A&R position at Epic Records and went on to serve as president of Hollywood Records) released one solo album five years after the breakup, and keyboard player Myrna Marcarian later released an EP using only her first name. —*John Bush*

● **Who's Landing in My Hangar?** / 1981 / IRS ✦✦✦✦✦
Most music writers seemed incapable of discussing Human Switchboard without mentioning the Velvet Underground, and there's no getting around the fact Rob Pfeifer's melodic style and clipped vocal delivery bears a certain resemblance to what Lou Reed was doing back in his formative days. But there's an emotional tension and sexual paranoia in Pfeifer's work that sets him decidedly apart from the Velvets and their many followers, and songs like "This Town" and "Refrigerator Door" speak of a grim, landlocked existence that would likely not have occurred to anyone outside of the Midwest. And while Pfeifer's jagged guitar has a certain Velvets-like quality, the homey buzz of Myrna Marcarian's Farfisa organ makes it clear there's more than a little garage in this band's formula, and there's a weary wisdom to Marcarian's occasional vocals that's human and endearing. While Human Switchboard left behind a pair of live documents, *Who's Landing in My Hangar?* was their only studio album, and while the Spartan, low-budget production isn't always flattering to the band's sound, the cutting emotional clarity of these songs shines through; perhaps this isn't the ideal Human Switchboard album, but it leaves no doubt that they were a great, passionate band with plenty to say, and *Who's Landing in My Hangar* preserves ten of their best songs for the ages. A reissue is certainly in order. —*Mark Deming*

Humble Pie

f. 1968, Essex, England, **db.** 1975
Album Rock, Boogie Rock, British Blues, Arena Rock, Hard Rock, Blues-Rock
A showcase for former Small Faces frontman Steve Marriott and onetime Herd guitar virtuoso Peter Frampton, the hard-rock outfit Humble Pie formed in 1969. Signed to the Immediate label, Humble Pie soon issued their debut single "Natural Born Boogie," which hit the British Top Ten and paved the way for the group's premiere LP, *As Safe As Yesterday Is*. As Marriott directed the group towards a harder-edged, grittier sound far removed from the acoustic melodies favored by Frampton, his raw blues shouting began to dominate subsequent LPs like 1970's eponymous effort and 1971's *Rock On*; Frampton's role in the band he co-founded gradually diminished, and finally, after a highly charged U.S. tour which yielded 1971's commercial breakthrough *Performance—Rockin' the Fillmore*, the guitarist exited Humble Pie to embark on a solo career. The band grew even heavier for 1972's *Smokin'*, their most successful album to date. However, while 1973's ambitious double studio/live set *Eat It* fell just shy of the Top Ten, its 1974 follow-up *Thunderbox* failed to crack the Top 40. After 1975's *Street Rats* reached only number 100 before disappearing from the charts, Humble Pie disbanded, reforming in 1980. —*Jason Ankeny*

As Safe As Yesterday Is / Apr. 1969 / Immediate ✦✦✦✦
Humble Pie, known as boogie hammerheads, at least once achieved American popularity in the mid-'70s. Its origins were quite different, however, and its debut album, *As Safe As Yesterday Is*, was a visionary blend of hard blues, crushing rock, pastoral folk, and post-mod pop. It would be even more impressive if the group had written songs to support its sound, but it seemed to have overlooked that element of the equation. Still, there's no denying that the sound of the band isn't just good, it's quite engaging, as the band bring disparate elements together, letting them bump up against each other, forming a wildly rich blend of hippie folk and deeply sexy blues. Musically, this set a template for a lot of bands that followed later—Led Zeppelin seemed to directly lift parts of this, and Paul Weller would later rely heavily on this for his '90s comeback—and it's very intriguing, even rewarding, on that level. But it falls short of a genuine classic, even with its originality and influence, because the songwriting is rarely more than a structure for the playing and the album often sounds more like a period piece than an album that defined its times. —*Stephen Thomas Erlewine*

Town and Country / Aug. 1969 / Columbia ✦✦✦✦
Anyone who thinks of Humble Pie solely in terms of their latter-day boogie rock will be greatly surprised with this, the band's second release, for it is almost entirely acoustic. There is a gently rocking cover of Buddy Holly's "Heartbeat," and a couple of electrified Steve Marriott numbers, but the overall feel is definitely more of the country than the town or city. "The Sad Bag of Shaky Jake" is a typical Marriott country ditty, similar to those he would include almost as a token on each of the subsequent studio albums, and "Every Mother's Son" is structured as a folk tale. On "The Light of Love," Marriott even plays sitar. Peter Frampton's contributions here foreshadow the acoustic-based music he would make as a solo artist a few years later. As a whole, this is a crisp, cleanly recorded, attractive-sounding album, totally atypical of the Humble Pie catalog, but well worth a listen. —*Jim Newsom*

Humble Pie / 1970 / A&M ✦✦✦
Alternating hard-driving blues-rockers with country-folk numbers, *Humble Pie* neatly showcases the two sides of this band's personality on their first release for a major American label and third album overall. All of the elements are in place for the sound that would reach its studio peak with the next release, *Rock On*, and culminate with the classic *Live at the Fillmore* album. "Earth and Water Song" provides a blueprint for the acoustic guitar-based sound Peter Frampton would ride to multi-platinum success as a solo artist later in the decade. "One Eyed Trouser-Snake Rumba" and "Red Light Mama, Red Hot!" show the hard-rocking direction in which Steve Marriott would move the band after Frampton's departure the following year. —*Jim Newsom*

Performance: Rockin' the Fillmore / 1971 / A&M ✦✦✦

Rock On / 1971 / A&M ✦✦✦✦
On this, their second album, Humble Pie proved that they were not the "minor league Rolling Stones" as people often described them. Led by the soulful Steve Marriot, the Pie was a great *band* in every sense of the word. Although Peter Frampton elevated himself to superstar status in just a few years, this album proves what an excellent lead guitarist he was. The record has an undeniable live feel to it, due in part to Glyn Johns' humble yet precise recording, framing the group as if they were a boogie version of the Band. When all of these elements come together on songs such as "Sour Grain" and "Stone Cold Fever," it's an unbeatable combination. —*Matthew Greenwald*

Smokin' / 1972 / A&M ✦✦✦✦
After a couple of years of relentless touring, Humble Pie capitalized on their loyal U.S. following to capture the market with this, their third album. Although lead guitarist Peter Frampton was replaced by Clem Clemson—an excellent player—the band remained essentially the same. Led by singer-guitarist Steve Marriot's soulful wail, the group enjoyed a huge hit from this record, "30 Days in the Hole"—the track which defined the Pie's not-so-subtle appeal. The rest of the record is equally funky and intriguing. Stephen Still guests on "Road Runner 'G' Jam," playing some nasty Hammond organ fills. In the end though, the group defined themselves as the undisputed leaders of the boogie movement in the early 1970s, as a *band*. —*Matthew Greenwald*

Lost and Found / 1973 / A&M ✦✦✦✦✦
After the Top Ten success of *Smokin'*, A&M prepared *Lost and Found*, which collected Humble Pie's first two albums in one package. The marketing ploy was a success and the record charted in the Top 40. —*Stephen Thomas Erlewine*

Eat It / 1973 / A&M ✦✦✦

Thunderbox / 1974 / A&M ✦✦

Street Rats / 1975 / A&M ✦✦

On to Victory / 1980 / Atco ✦✦

Go for the Throat / 1981 / Atco ✦

● **Classics, Vol. 14** / 1987 / A&M ✦✦✦✦✦
Released in 1987, during the thick of the *Classics* series, this compilation winds up being one of the most successful of its brethren, containing almost all of Humble Pie's greatest hits, including "I Don't Need No Doctor," "Hot N Nasty," "Shine On," "30 Days in the Hole," and "C'Mon Everybody." This isn't a strict hits compilation, yet it summarizes the band's strengths better than most of its ilk and winds up being an effective introduction to the band. —*Stephen Thomas Erlewine*

Hot N' Nasty—The Anthology / Jun. 7, 1994 / A&M ✦✦✦✦
Album rock artists that never made great albums, Humble Pie are well served by *Hot N' Nasty*, a double-disc set that collects the hits and highlights from throughout their career. —*Stephen Thomas Erlewine*

● **Natural Born Bugie: The Immediate Anthology** / 2000 / ✦✦✦✦✦
Steve Marriott left the Small Faces behind because he wanted to boogie. He no longer wanted to deal with the precious minutia and English whimsy that proved to be the Small Faces' greatest legacy; he wanted to adopt American blues, rock, and folk for his own—a character trait not unique to Marriott, since not only his peers felt the same way, but also generations of British rockers who would decide to leave England behind for American roots music whenever they wanted to prove their authenticity. Humble Pie would later sink into heavy, obvious grandiosity, shooting for the cheap seats (and succeeding) in American stadiums, but the band's initial albums were fascinating amalgams of rustic folk, blues, and heavy rock with a slight progressive tinge, all underpinned by an earnest student's love for a form he doesn't quite intuitively understand. These were the records that Marriott made while Peter Frampton was still in the band, and the ex-Herd member proved to be pivotal to the group's success, since the group had two solid songwriters who fed off each other's energies. Not that they were perfect—far from it, actually, since they were both too earnest and too eager to delve into directionless jams—but the end result was fascinating, as Castle's excellent double-disc anthology *Natural Born Bugie* proves. Spanning two discs, this contains everything Humble Pie recorded for Immediate, including the band's debut single, *As Safe As Yesterday Is*, and *Town and Country*, plus no less than nine unreleased tracks and two songs only available on a German CD. This set makes a convincing argument that the group had a lot to offer in its early years, when country blues and folk were as prominent as driving bloozy boogie. So, there might not be any radio hits here, but this collection is often effective (and, at its worst, interesting) and easily the best way to hear the band at its peak. —*Stephen Thomas Erlewine*

20th Century Masters—The Millennium Collection: The Best of Humble Pie / Oct. 10, 2000 / Interscope ✦✦✦✦
20th Century Masters: The Millennium Collection may not be the perfect Humble Pie collection, but it's perfectly serviceable for most casual fans, since it does contain such staples as "Natural Born Woman," "Stone Cold Fever," "Shine On," "Hot N Nasty," and "I Don't Need No Doctor" among its 12 tracks. *The Best of Humble Pie* might remain a better, tighter listen, but this covers much of the same ground and has a more appetizing front cover, which makes it a good choice for budget-minded curious listeners. —*Stephen Thomas Erlewine*

Ian Hunter

b. Jun. 3, 1946, Shrewsbury, Shropshire, England
Vocals, Keyboards, Piano, Guitar / Album Rock, Proto-Punk, Hard Rock, Singer/Songwriter, Rock & Roll
With Mott the Hoople, guitarist/vocalist Ian Hunter established himself as one of the

toughest and most inventive hard-rock songwriters of the early '70s, setting the stage for punk rock with his edgy, intelligent songs. As a solo artist, Hunter never attained the commercial heights of Mott the Hoople but he cultivated a dedicated cult following. The teenaged Hunter joined a band called Silence in the early '60s. Silence released an album, but it received no attention. In 1968, he began playing bass with Freddie "Fingers" Lee and the duo played around Germany. Shortly afterward, Hunter became the vocalist for Mott the Hoople. During the next six years, Hunter sang and played piano and guitar with the band, becoming its lead songwriter within a few albums. Although few of their records sold, Mott the Hoople was one of the most popular live bands in England. In 1972, David Bowie produced their breakthrough album *All the Young Dudes*, and for the next two years, they had a consistent stream of hits in both the U.K. and the U.S. Hunter left the group in late 1974, taking along former Bowie guitarist Mick Ronson, who had just joined Mott. Hunter moved to New York, where he and Ronson began working on his solo debut. Released in 1975, *Ian Hunter* spawned "Once Bitten, Twice Shy," a Top 20 U.K. hit. Following its release, Hunter and Ronson embarked on a tour. After its completion, the pair parted ways, although they would reunite later in the '80s. *—Stephen Thomas Erlewine*

Ian Hunter / 1975 / Columbia ♦♦♦♦
After leaving Mott the Hoople in early 1975, Ian Hunter quickly threw himself into recording this eponymous solo debut. Not surprisingly, it contains a lot of the glam-rock charm of Hunter's old group: "The Truth, the Whole Truth, Nothing But the Truth" and "I Get So Excited" are fist-pumping tunes that combine punchy hard-rock riffs with intelligent lyrics in a manner similar to Mott the Hoople's finest moments. However, Ian Hunter pulls off this grandiose sound without the overtly ornate production that defined the final Mott the Hoople albums because Mick Ronson's cleverly crafted arrangements manage to create a big wall of sound without utilizing a huge amount of instruments or overdubs. As a result, Ian Hunter's lyrics shine through in each song and show off his totally personalized mixture of attitude and intelligence: the legendary and oft-covered "Once Bitten, Twice Shy" is a cheeky, clever exploration of rock & roll's ability to corrupt the innocent, and "Boy" is a critique of a rocker who has allowed his pretensions to overpower his heart (many say this tune was aimed at fellow star and onetime Mott the Hoople producer David Bowie). Another highlight is "It Ain't Easy When You Fall," a moving tribute to a fallen friend that gracefully builds from delicate verses into a soaring chorus. The end result is a memorable debut album that gives listeners their hard-rock fix and manages to engage their brains at the same time. Anyone interested in the finest moments of 1970s glam rock should give this classic a spin. *—Donald A. Guarisco*

All-American Alien Boy / 1976 / Columbia ♦♦♦
After the relative success of his debut, it would have been very easy for Ian Hunter to continue in the glam-inspired vein that made that album so successful. Instead, he twisted his sound in a jazz direction for *All American Alien Boy*, a partially successful attempt to open up his sound from its traditional rock & roll routes. Since Hunter couldn't utilize the producing and arranging skills of longtime cohort Mick Ronson because of a dispute with Ronson's manager, Hunter took the reins himself and invited a diverse cast of session musicians that included everyone from journeyman drummer Aynsley Dunbar to jazz bass wizard Jaco Pastorius. The resulting album mixture of conventional Mott the Hoople-style rock and sonic experiments never truly gels, but does contain some fine tracks. The experiments are hit and miss: the title track is a funky, sax-flavored exploration of Hunter's adjustment to life in America that works nicely, but the interesting lyrics of "Apathy 83" get buried in an uncharacteristically bland soft rock arrangement. The songs that work best are the more traditional-sounding numbers: "Irene Wilde" is a delicately crafted autobiographical ballad about the rejection that made Hunter decide to *"be somebody, someday,"* and "God—Take 1" is a stirring, Dylan-styled rocker featuring witty lyrics that illustrate a conversation with a weary and down-to-earth version of God. However, the true gem of the album is "You Nearly Did Me In," an elegant and emotional ballad about the emptiness that follows a romantic breakup. It also notable for the stirring backing vocals from guest stars Queen on its chorus. In the end, *All-American Alien Boy* lacks the consistency to fully succeed as an album but still offers enough stellar moments to make it worthwhile for Ian Hunter's fans. *—Donald A. Guarisco*

Overnight Angels / 1977 / Columbia ♦♦

Shades of Ian Hunter / 1979 / Chrysalis ♦♦♦♦♦
Shades of Ian Hunter may not be the most comprehensive of hits packages from this longtime rock & roller, but it does combine the best tracks from three of his most successful recordings. With 15 songs, this minor compilation pulls his best material from the outstanding *You're Never Alone With a Schizophrenic* album, as well as the off-the-wall *Short Back N' Sides* release from 1981 and the live *Welcome to the Club* offering from 1980. The first seven tunes from *Schizophrenic* include "Just Another Night" and the monumental "Cleveland Rocks," as well as the gorgeous "Ships." The next five are taken from *Short Back N' Sides*, highlighted by the haunting "Old Records Never Die." "Gun Control" rolls along firmly with its jittery pace, and the dissonance of "Central Park N' West grows with a strange appeal every time it's heard. The last three tracks that are taken from the live album include two of Mott the Hoople's biggest tunes in "All The Way From Memphis" and the teen rock anthem "All the Young Dudes." Ending the album with songs from his former band is an effective finish to this compilation, which makes for an abbreviated but pleasant listen. *—Mike DeGagne*

● **You're Never Alone With a Schizophrenic** / 1979 / Razor & Tie ♦♦♦♦♦
This classic album from 1979 is considered by many to be the high point of Ian Hunter's solo career. Although its sales never matched up to the enthusiastic critical reaction it received, this polished hard-rock gem has held up nicely through the years and is definitely deserving of its strong cult reputation. *You're Never Alone With a Schizophrenic* also marked the reunion of Hunter with his finest creative ally, Mick Ronson, who had been forced to sit out of Hunter's last few albums due to management problems. Together, the reunited duo put together an album that matches Hunter's literate lyrics to a set of catchy, finely crafted tunes brimming with rock & roll energy. Two of the finest tracks are "Cleveland Rocks," an affectionate, Mott the Hoople-styled tribute to an unsung rock & roll city that later became the theme for *The Drew Carey Show*, and "Ships," a heartrending ballad built on a spooky and ethereal keyboard-driven melody that was later covered with great success by Barry Manilow. Elsewhere, the album features plenty of tunes that soon became mainstays of Hunter's live show: "Just Another Night" is a rollicking rocker with an infectious, piano-pounding melody reminiscent of 1970s-era Rolling Stones, and "Bastard" is a pulsating rocker that features guest star John Cale contributing to its ominous hard-rock atmosphere. However, the unsung gem of the album is "When the Daylight Comes," a beautifully crafted mid-tempo rocker that balances a soulful, organ-driven melody with rousing guitar riffs and surprisingly vulnerable lyrics about romance. It should also be noted that *You're Never Alone With a Schizophrenic* benefits from a sterling mix by Bob Clearmountain, who gives the sound a muscular quality that makes it leap out of the stereo speakers. In the end, *You're Never Alone With a Schizophrenic* is not only Ian Hunter's finest and most consistent album but one of the true gems of late-'70s rock & roll. *—Donald A. Guarisco*

Ian Hunter Live/Welcome to the Club / 1980 / Chrysalis ♦♦♦
Recorded with guitarist Mick Ronson, *Ian Hunter Live / Welcome to the Club* is a tough, hard-rocking album that features material from both Ronson and Hunter. *—Stephen Thomas Erlewine*

Short Back and Sides / 1981 / Chrysalis ♦♦♦♦♦
Ian Hunter had been revitalized by punk rock, as *Short Back and Sides* shows. Featuring the Clash's Mick Jones on guitar, the music is a tougher and spikier take on Hunter's rock & roll, and his songwriting is at a near-peak. *—Stephen Thomas Erlewine*

All of the Good Ones Are Taken / 1983 / Columbia ♦♦♦

YUI Orta / 1990 / Mercury ♦♦♦♦

Artful Dodger / Mar. 1997 / Citadel ♦♦♦

Once Bitten Twice Shy / Aug. 8, 2000 / Columbia/Legacy ♦♦♦♦
Is this two-CD compilation a career retrospective (covering the years 1975-1996) or a rarities collection? Does it aim to present the best of Ian Hunter, or a selection of representative work from various phases of his solo career, or a combination of crowd-pleasing favorites and things that he or Columbia thinks should be heard? The answers are not clear from *Once Bitten Twice Shy*, which combines tracks from his solo albums with a dozen previously unreleased cuts and various hard to find items from singles and soundtracks. It has that feeling of a project that's designed to please everyone and ends up satisfying almost no one. While fans will relish some of the unreleased material, particularly a few outtakes and alternates from *Ian Hunter*, those otherwise unavailable songs are not that great, and it will not amuse many that two of the *Ian Hunter* outtakes have vocals recorded in 1999. Also, some of the rarities should have remained rare, such as an irrelevant live 1996 version of "All the Young Dudes" with Def Leppard. But the biggest problem with the material, outweighing collector concerns, is that the quality goes steadily downhill the later the years get, particularly from the early '80s onward. The decision to split the package into one "rockers" disc and one "ballads" disc isn't so astute, either. The "ballads" disc is the much inferior component, the production and songwriting venturing into crummy adult contemporary music on the tracks from the 1980s. One does wish it was otherwise, but really there's not much reason to hear Hunter's post-'70s solo work, and it's post-'70s material that comprises about half of this anthology. *—Richie Unterberger*

Rant / Apr. 24, 2001 / Varese ♦♦♦♦♦
The musical statement that is *Rant* includes textures and ideas that pick up where *Brain Capers* by Mott the Hoople left off. "Still Love Rock & Roll" ignites this set; it rocks with an authority that "All the Way From Memphis" only hinted at. As Dion DiMucci's *Shu Bop* album redefined the position of a '60s artist and delivered the goods, Ian Hunter's *Rant* reveals a '70s artist refining his philosophy. Rant he does, with eloquence and a new fire. Every track works, entertaining and enlightening, taking the listener through curves and turns, reaching the zenith in track ten, "Ripoff." From the "that's all you've got to live for" lyric to the song title itself, this song is a perfect pop tune, full of anger, passion, slashing guitar sounds, a condescending vocal, and hooks that are real magnetic grabbers. With production that is absolutely top-notch, Hunter bids adieu to his homeland. This album smartly moves sounds from guitar to keys, shifting moods, making a grand musical statement. *Rant* is a record that transcends so much of what was going on in music at the time, a record that is much too good for radio today. The Columbia/Legacy compilation *Once Bitten Twice Shy* delivered 38 Ian Hunter solo titles in the year 2000, giving the world a clear picture of his post-Hoople work and paving the way for this sensational recording. *—Joe Viglione*

Ivory Joe Hunter

b. Oct. 10, 1914, Kirbyville, TX, **d.** Nov. 8, 1974, Memphis, TN
Vocals, Songwriter, Piano / West Coast Blues, Piano Blues, R&B
Bespectacled and velvet-smooth in the vocal department, pianist Ivory Joe Hunter appeared too much mild-mannered to be a rock & roller. But when the rebellious music first crashed the American consciousness in the mid-'50s, there was Ivory Joe, deftly delivering his blues ballad "Since I Met You Baby" right alongside the wildest pioneers of the era. Hunter was already a grizzled R&B vet by that time who had first heard his voice on a 1933 Library of Congress cylinder recording made in Texas. He started his own label,

Ivory Records, to press up his "Blues at Sunrise" (with Johnny Moore's Three Blazers backing him), and it became a national hit when leased to Leon Rene's Exclusive imprint in 1945. Another Hunter enterprise, Pacific Records, hosted a major hit in 1948 when the pianist's "Pretty Mama Blues" topped the R&B charts for three weeks. At whatever logo Hunter paused from the mid-'40s through the late '50s, his platters sold like hotcakes. For Cincinnati-based King in 1948-49, he hit with "Don't Fall in Love With Me," "What Did You Do to Me," "Waiting in Vain," and "Guess Who." At MGM, he cut his immortal "I Almost Lost My Mind" (another R&B chart-topper in 1950), "I Need You So" (later covered by Elvis), and "It's a Sin." Signing with Atlantic in 1954, he hit big with "Since I Met You Baby" in 1956 and the two-sided smash "Empty Arms"/"Love's a Hurting Game" in 1957. —*Bill Dahl*

● **Since I Met You Baby: The Best of Ivory Joe Hunter** / Oct. 19, 1994 / Razor & Tie ✦✦✦✦✦

Bespectacled pianist Ivory Joe Hunter's crooning blues balladry made him a hot commodity from the late '40s through the late '50s, but he could rock reasonably convincingly hard too. He does both on this wonderful survey of his 1949-1958 MGM and Atlantic sides—"I Need You So," "I Almost Lost My Mind," and the title item are sophisticated and mellow, while "Rockin' Chair Boogie," "Love Is a Hurting Game," and "Shooty Booty" find the pianist in decidedly unsentimental moods. —*Bill Dahl*

Hunters & Collectors

f. 1981, **db.** 1998

Alternative Pop/Rock, College Rock, Aussie Rock

Ending up with the intensity and passion of a U2, Hunters and Collectors carved a unique path and place for themselves in Australian rock culture. The group was originally formed in post-punk 1981 in Melbourne as a collective rather than a band, an excursion into funk-rock rhythms and industrial Krautrock. The group's early performances are remembered as chaotic, with audience members encouraged to join in on the banging rubbish bin lids or fire extinguishers. The extended lineup included a massed horn section known as the Horns of Contempt. Inside all this was singer Mark Seymour, with an ear for a melody and a taste for lyrical poetry. The Hunters' reputation spread to Europe where a stripped-back band spent six months in 1983 recording a second album, *The Fireman's Curse*, in Germany with producer Conny Plank (Can, Kraftwerk). After a live album came *Human Frailty* where singer Mark Seymour's deep songs about alienation and sexual politics came to the fore. A newly recorded "Throw Your Arms Around Me" became one of the undisputed classic songs of Australian rock, and from then until their end Hunters and Collectors would remain one of Australian rock's favorite live attractions. While successive studio albums did their best to explore new themes and new sounds to varying degrees of success it was the live performances fans were waiting for, and with each new album it was the older material radio wanted to play. In the end Hunters and Collectors were strangled by their own legend. —*Ed Nimmervoll*

Hunters & Collectors / 1983 / Virgin ✦✦✦

Hunters & Collectors' self-titled debut is seething art funk comparable to a harder-edged Shriekback or less political Gang of Four. The latter two bands were built on the bedrock of Dave Allen's bass, and H&C's sound is likewise often dominated by formidable bassist John Archer. At this stage of H&C's career they were still working to develop an identity. The lyrics on *Hunters & Collectors* are stream-of-consciousness poetics that range from the merely incomprehensible to the downright silly, and singer Mark Seymour does not sound entirely comfortable delivering them. This would change in later years; *Hunters & Collectors*, meanwhile, is all about the muscular rhythms provided by Archer and drummer Doug Falconer. When they get hold of a good one, they motor right over the young band's shortcomings. This album's best moments are "Tow Truck," "Talking to a Stranger," and, especially, "Run Run Run," an epic song that begins on a relentless beat, then shifts midway through to a hypnotic groove that builds to a towering crescendo. —*Bill Cassel*

Fireman's Curse / 1983 / Virgin ✦✦

Jaws of Life / 1984 / Epic ✦✦✦✦

The Jaws of Life represented a breakthrough for Hunters & Collectors where their more ambitious artistic impulses were harnessed to melodic, concise, and structured songs. Less pretentious than *Hunters & Collectors* and less anarchic than *The Fireman's Curse*, *The Jaws of Life* took a strategic step toward accessibility without sacrificing any of the band's powerful intensity. While still predominantly dark, H&C's music in this period showed a growing humanity that could even be called soulful. Who would have guessed that they were capable of such a convincing take on Ray Charles' "I Believe in My Soul"? While Mark Seymour's words on *The Jaws of Life* can hardly be called linear or narrative, they are considerably less random and more evocative than on previous albums, and his vocals benefit from increased restraint. H&C's sound still rests squarely on the solid foundation of the Archer/Falconer rhythm section, with Seymour's slashing rhythm guitar and The Horns of Contempt working in and around the grooves. A couple of ballads—"Hayley's Doorstep" and "Carry Me"—and the anthemic "It's Early Days Yet" show off the band's increased range. On the whole, a superior and highly recommended record. —*Bill Cassel*

Way to Go Out / 1985 / White Label ✦✦

Human Frailty / 1986 / IRS ✦✦✦✦✦

Human Frailty is the sound of a band running on all cylinders. Though Hunters & Collectors had trouble melding their influences (funk, tribal rhythms, melodic hooks) into a cohesive sound in the past, on this 1986 album the band finally discovered their true strength; a balance of bass and drum-driven grooves set below punchy horns and counterpoint melody lines. "Is There Anybody in There?" is a particular standout with its un-

relenting rhythm section. The band uses their three-piece horn section to great effectiveness on "Everything's on Fire" and the loping, lazy swing of "Relief." *Human Frailty* is anything but and remains a great album to begin an association with the band's music. —*Steve Kurutz*

Fate / 1988 / IRS ✦✦✦✦✦

The finest moment of their later period, *Fate* is a cohesive and tightly produced album with an edge. "Back on the Breadline" received some attention through college and "Modern Rock" radio, making this the closest thing to an American breakthough the band has seen yet. —*Chris Woodstra*

Ghost Nation / Apr. 1990 / Atlantic ✦✦

● **Collected Works** / Aug. 1990 / IRS ✦✦✦

Hunters & Collectors began their career by playing the pub scene in Australia and from there the band slowly inflated into semi-stardom, mainly in their homeland. *Collected Works* takes the best tracks from the first ten years of the band's existence and lays them out in chronological order, resulting in a wonderful compilation. The 15 tracks come from their self-titled album, *The Jaws of Life*, *Human Frailty*, *Fate*, and *Ghost Nation*, with "Lumps of Lead" stemming from the 1982 *Pay Load* EP. H&C's dusty, basement dwelling sound shadows the band with character, presenting them with an element of low-key personality that sets them apart from other groups. Each song has a rough-edged savvy surrounding it, either by the gritty guitar playing or the mournful eagerness in Mark Seymour's vocals. "January Rain" carries a desolate aura that hovers above the entire tune, and "Carry Me" speaks volumes with its emanating bass riff and building guitar. What makes this band shine is the ghost-like air that drifts through their sound, which eventually becomes solidified by the strength of their instruments. With heavy emphasis on concrete guitar rhythms, balanced out by the creative application of horns, H&C's music heightens slightly throughout the duration of each of their songs. *Collected Works* doubles as a must-have for fans as well as a splendid intro into this underrated band. —*Mike DeGagne*

Cut / 1993 / Mushroom ✦✦✦

Every track on H&C's *Cut* album is brimming with high energy, explosive singing, and contagious hooks, making it one of this band's finest offerings. From the desperate sounding "Head Above Water" to the marching rhythm of "Holy Grail," a certain electricity is mustered from Mark Seymour's charged voice. Grinding guitar work coupled with the extensive flare of trumpets and a French horn set this band apart from other groups, offering a rough but flamboyant edge to their music. Like most Australian bands, Hunters & Collectors sustain a different sound than bands from Europe or the U.S., and it's this intangible contrast that gives them such an unrivaled flare. The bleakness in some of their songs is elevated by the instruments so that the conceptual message is understood, without the dismalness, making their music accessible both lyrically and musically. Some songs on this album harbor a slight whine from Seymour, but listeners soon get well accustomed to his style and welcome his honest wailing, as it sets a precedent for the music. Some of the best work from this group is spread across this 1992 release. —*Mike DeGagne*

Demon Flower / Jul. 18, 1995 / Shake ✦✦✦

Hüsker Dü

f. 1979, Minneapolis, MN, **db.** Dec. 17, 1987

College Rock, American Punk, Hardcore Punk, Alternative Pop/Rock, American Underground

Hüsker Dü and R.E.M. were the two American post-punk bands of the '80s that changed the direction of rock & roll. R.E.M. became superstars; Hüsker Dü never was more than a cult favorite. Nevertheless, their albums between 1981 and 1987 have proven remarkably influential; they provided the sonic blueprint for the roaring punk-pop hybrid that crossed over into the mainstream in the early '90s. Not only did they shape the sound of the music, they shaped the way independent bands made the transition to the major labels; they showed other bands that it was possible to record uncompromising music on a major label without losing any integrity or creative control. From the Replacements to Nirvana, the Pixies to Superchunk, nearly every major and minor band that appeared in the alternative underground in the late '80s and '90s owed a major debt to Hüsker Dü, whether they were aware of it or not. The band's two songwriters, guitarist Bob Mould and drummer Grant Hart, both had a knack for writing songs that essentially followed conventional pop structures, complete with memorable melodies, but were still punk songs. Hüsker Dü took the Buzzcocks' pioneering punk pop and made it harder, both musically and lyrically. Throughout their career, Hüsker Dü never lost their edge, never turned down their amplifiers, never compromised their music. While Hart and bassist Greg Norton were an unfailingly strong rhythm section, Mould would prove to be one of the most influential guitarists of the decade. With his slashing rhythms, distorted strumming, and blazing leads, he set the stage for the alternative guitar heroes of the late '80s and the '90s. —*Stephen Thomas Erlewine*

Land Speed Record / 1981 / SST ✦✦

A brief live EP, *Land Speed Record* races through its songs without regard for melody or riffs. As a sonic blitzkrieg, it's quite impressive, yet little of the record makes a lasting impression. —*Stephen Thomas Erlewine*

Everything Falls Apart / 1982 / Reflex ✦✦✦

On their first studio recording, *Everything Falls Apart*, Hüsker Dü demonstrates a sharper sense of purpose than on their live debut, *Land Speed Record*, but that doesn't necessarily make the album a breakthrough. Indeed, the trio demonstrates that they're capable of powerful noise, but not songcraft—the only song with a discernible hook is their thrashing cover of Donovan's "Sunshine Superman." Still, the band's hardcore is better than many of their contemporaries because their grasp of noise is superior. Even with the inconsistent songwriting, *Everything Falls Apart* rages with layers of blistering guitars and scorching rhythms which are exciting in their own right. *—Stephen Thomas Erlewine*

Metal Circus / 1983 / SST ♦♦♦
A five-song EP bristling with energy and pummeling guitars, *Metal Circus* is the first indication of Hüsker Dü's greatness. With these five songs, the band shows more invention, skill, and melody than they did over the course of a full album with *Everything Falls Apart*, and both Mould and Hart emerge as significant songwriters. While they both stay within hardcore conventions on *Metal Circus*, their songs illustrate that they would break free of its constrictions on their subsequent, masterful double album, *Zen Arcade*. *—Stephen Thomas Erlewine*

☆ **Zen Arcade** / 1984 / SST ♦♦♦♦♦
In many ways, it's impossible to overestimate the impact of Hüsker Dü's *Zen Arcade* on the American rock underground in the '80s. It's the record that exploded the limits of hardcore and what it could achieve. Hüsker Dü broke all of the rules with *Zen Arcade*. First and foremost, it's a sprawling concept album, even if the concept isn't immediately clear or comprehensible. More important are the individual songs. Both Bob Mould and Grant Hart abandoned the strict "fast, hard, loud" rules of hardcore punk with their songs for *Zen Arcade*. Without turning down the volume, Hüsker Dü tries everything—pop songs, tape experiments, acoustic songs, pianos, noisy psychedelia. Hüsker Dü willed themselves to make such a sprawling record—as the liner notes state, the album was recorded and mixed within 85 hours and consists almost entirely of first takes. That reckless, ridiculously single-minded approach does result in some weak moments—the sound is thin and the instrumentals drag on a bit too long—but it's also the key to the success of *Zen Arcade*. Hüsker Dü sounds phenomenally strong and possessed, as if they could do anything. The sonic experimentation is bolstered by Mould and Hart's increased sense of songcraft. Neither writer is afraid to let their pop influences show on *Zen Arcade*, which gives the songs—from the unrestrained rage of "Something I Learned Today" and the bitter, acoustic "Never Talking to You Again" to the eerie "Pink Turns to Blue" and anthemic "Turn On the News"—their weight. It's music that is informed by hardcore punk and indie-rock ideals without being limited by it. *—Stephen Thomas Erlewine*

★ **New Day Rising** / 1985 / SST ♦♦♦♦♦
For *New Day Rising*, the follow-up to their breakthrough double-album *Zen Arcade*, Hüsker Dü replaced concept with conciseness, concentrating on individual songs delivered as scalding post-hardcore pop. *New Day Rising* is not only a more vicious and relentless record than *Zen Arcade*, it's more melodic. Bob Mould and Grant Hart have written tightly crafted, melodic pop songs that don't compromise Hüsker's volcanic, unchecked power. Mould and Hart's songs owe a great deal to '60s pop, as the verses and choruses ebb and flow with immediately catchy hooks. Occasionally, the razor-thin production and waves of noise mean that it takes a little bit of effort to pick out the melodies, but more often the furious noise and melodies fuse together to create an overwhelming sonic force. It's possible to hear the rivalry between Mould and Hart on the album itself—each song is like a game of one-upmanship, as Mould responds to "The Girl Who Lives on Heaven Hill" with "Celebrated Summer." Neither songwriter slips—both turn in songs that are catchy, clever and alternately wracked with pain or teeming with humor. *New Day Rising* is a positively cathartic record and ranks as Hüsker Dü's most sustained moment of pure power. *—Stephen Thomas Erlewine*

☆ **Flip Your Wig** / 1985 / SST ♦♦♦♦♦
Spot—SST's house producer who manned the boards for *Zen Arcade* and *New Day Rising*—didn't produce *Flip Your Wig*, Hüsker Dü's second album of 1985, and the difference is immediately noticeable. Everything on *Flip Your Wig* is cleaner and brighter than on its two immediate predecessors, which is appropriate, considering that Bob Mould and Grant Hart have only increased their debt to '60s pop. The hooks and melodies are on the surface, right from the kick-start call-and-response of the title track. On paper, it might sound as if Hüsker Dü have watered down their hardcore ideals, but it doesn't play that way. *Flip Your Wig* is pop played as punk, as if this is the only time these songs could ever be heard. Which means Hart's love song "Green Eyes" and Mould's pure pop single "Makes No Sense at All" are delivered with the same rage and passion as Mould's blistering "Divide and Conquer" and Hart's "Keep Hanging On," or the pair of surging, neo-psychedelic and noise-wracked instrumentals that close the album. *Flip Your Wig* would be a remarkable record on its own terms, but the fact that it followed *New Day Rising* by a matter of months and *Zen Arcade* by just over a year is simply astonishing. *—Stephen Thomas Erlewine*

Candy Apple Grey / 1986 / Warner Brothers ♦♦♦
Moving to a major label doesn't affect Hüsker Dü's sound greatly—although the production is more full-bodied than Spot's razor-thin work, the Hüskers don't change their blazing attack at all. Much of *Candy Apple Grey* charges along on the same frenzied beat that propelled *New Day Rising* and *Flip Your Wig*, and both Mould and Hart are in fine form, spinning out fine punk-pop with "Sorry Somehow" and "Don't Want to Know If You Are Lonely." However, the sound is beginning to seem a bit tired, which is what makes Mould's two acoustic numbers, "Too Far Down" and "Hardly Getting Over It," so welcome. Demonstrating that punks can mature without losing their edge, Mould inverts the rules of conventional confessional singer/songwriter songs with these two haunting numbers, and in doing so, he illustrates the faults with the relatively staid post-hardcore punk that dominates the remainder of the record. *—Stephen Thomas Erlewine*

☆ **Warehouse: Songs & Stories** / 1987 / Warner Brothers ♦♦♦♦♦
It's cleaner and more produced than any of their records, which is one reason why many Hüsker Dü fans have never fully embraced their second double-album, *Warehouse: Songs and Stories*. Granted, *Warehouse* boasts a fuller production—complete with multi-tracked guitars and vocal, various percussion techniques, and endless studio effects—that would have seemed out of place a mere two years before its release. However, *Flip Your Wig* and *Candy Apple Grey* both *suggested* this full-fledged pop production and it's to Hüsker Dü's credit that they never sound like they are selling out with *Warehouse*. What they do sound like is breaking up. Although there was a schism apparent between Bob Mould and Grant Hart on *Candy Apple Grey*, they don't even sound like they are writing for the same band on *Warehouse*. But the individual songs on the album are powerhouses in their own right, as both songwriters exhibit a continuing sense of experimentation—Hart writes a sea shanty with "She Floated Away" and uses bubbling percussion on "Charity, Chastity, Prudence and Hope," while Mould nearly arrives at power pop with "Could You Be the One?" and touches on the singer/songwriter-styled folk rock with "No Reservations." *Warehouse* doesn't have the single-minded sense of purpose or eccentric sprawl of *Zen Arcade*, but as a collection of songs, it is of the first-order. Furthermore, its stylish production—which makes pop concessions without abandoning a punk ethos—pointed the way to the kind of "alternative" rock that dominated the mainstream in the early '90s. In all, it was a fine way for one of the most important bands of the '80s to call it a day. *—Stephen Thomas Erlewine*

Everything Falls Apart and More / 1993 / Rhino ♦♦♦
Rhino's reissue of Hüsker Dü's shattering first studio album includes a couple of rare singles, making it a must-have for the band's fans, as well as anyone interested in hardcore punk rock. Anyone unfamiliar with Hüsker Dü's early work should brace themselves for a breakneck force like no other. Not for the faint of heart. *—Stephen Thomas Erlewine*

The Living End / Oct. 1994 / Warner Brothers ♦♦♦
Recorded on their final tour, *The Living End* is an invigorating document of Hüsker Dü's blistering live power, highlighted by a couple unreleased songs and a manic cover of "Sheena Is a Punk Rocker." *—Stephen Thomas Erlewine*

Willie Hutch

b. 1946, Los Angeles, CA
Vocals, Guitar / Blaxploitation, R&B, Soul
Willie Hutch was a versatile figure at Motown, working with other artists as well as recording himself. Born Willie Hutchison in Los Angeles, he cut an album for RCA in 1969 before signing on with Berry Gordy's empire. Hutch first made his mark in 1973 by performing the soundtrack to a blaxploitation flick called "The Mack." In the mid-'70s, his "Love Power" and "Party Down" were solid hits. *—Bill Dahl*

The Mack / 1973 / Motown ♦♦♦♦♦
One of the great '70s soundtracks. An act called Sisters Love had a cameo in the blaxploitation film *The Mack*, and their manager suggested that Hutch do the soundtrack. The results included a pair of classic funk tunes, "Brothers Gonna Work It Out" and the title cut, and another score that far surpassed the quality of its film. *—Ron Wynn*

Foxy Brown / 1975 / Motown ♦♦♦
Willie Hutch is a multi-talented performer who never achieved fame or stardom. Despite some good moments, the sales here failed to meet or exceed the numbers of his previous soundtrack, *The Mack*. "Chase" borrows heavily from "Shaft," maybe too much. Hutch is full of fire on "The Theme of Foxy Brown," his distinctive tenor wringing the most from each note. "Give Me Some of That Good Old Love" had a foot-tapping groove, tough backing vocals from Maxine Williard, Julie Tilman, and Carol Willis, and all the elements of a hit record. Unfortunately, Motown only released "Foxy Brown" as a single, and nothing else. The vamping "Out There" and "Foxy Lady" are nasty and contagious. "You Sure Know How to Love Your Man" copies a bit of "Love Machine"'s bass line; it's Willie and the girls' most spirited performance, with Hutch showing that Wilson Pickett isn't the only person who can intersperse soulful screams between lyrics. The melodic "Ain't That (Mellow Mellow)" sounds like another single, but Motown wasn't hearing it; they were too busy concentrating on his *Love Power* LP, which also flopped. *—Andrew Hamilton*

● **The Very Best of Willie Hutch** / Aug. 25, 1998 / Motown ♦♦♦♦♦
One of the unsung heroes of 1970s soul, Willie Hutch was never the big name he deserved to be. The smooth singer/composer had a few major and moderate hits, but commercially, he didn't make it to the level of Marvin Gaye, Ronald Isley, and Curtis Mayfield (all of whom he inspires comparisons to). Released in late 1998, *The Very Best of Willie Hutch* spans 1972-1982 and reminds us how engaging a singer he was in his heyday. Hutch could get funky when he wanted to, and he does so with splendid results on "Get Ready for the Get Down" (a number 24 R&B hit), "Brothers Gonna Work It Out," and the theme from the 1973 blaxploitation film *Foxy Brown*. But for the most part, Hutch made his mark as a romantic crooner. It is Hutch's smooth, romantic side that prevails on "Sunshine Lady," "I Choose You," "What You Gonna Do After the Party," and his inspired makeover of Barbra Streisand's "The Way We Were." Appropriately, the CD opens with Hutch's biggest hit: the perky, feel-good anthem "Love Power," which went to number nine on the R&B singles charts. Full of gems that were recorded during Hutch's peak years, this CD is essential listening for lovers of 1970s soul. *—Alex Henderson*

Brian Hyland

b. Nov. 12, 1943, Woodhaven, NY
Vocals / Sunshine Pop, Teen Idol
Initially aiming his output at teens, Brian Hyland grew up fast and cut a serious cover of "Gypsy Woman," a hit by the Impressions that went gold in 1970. The Queens, NY, native enjoyed his biggest hit at the tender age of 16—the tongue-twisting "Itsy Bitsy Teenie

Weenie Yellow Polkadot Bikini," a cute ditty snapped up by Kapp Records after it was issued on the little Leader logo. Hyland moved to ABC-Paramount and already sounded more adult by the time "Sealed With a Kiss" hit in 1962. A string of solid sellers, including "The Joker Went Wild" in 1966, preceded his remake of "Gypsy Woman," produced by Del Shannon and released on Uni. —*Bill Dahl*

Greatest Hits / 1994 / Rhino ◆◆◆◆

Brian Hyland's "Itsy Bitsy Teenie Weenie Yellow Polka-Dot Bikini" is one of those songs that straddles the line between silly and annoying, but the public thought highly enough of it to make it a number one hit in 1960. Listeners expecting a full menu of similar novelties will be surprised by Hyland's *Greatest Hits*. Spanning the years 1960-1970, *Greatest Hits* consists mostly of Hyland's folk-pop from the mid- to late '60s, concluding with his 1970 hit version of the Impressions' "Gypsy Woman." Hyland's later singles seemed to aspire to "seriousness," although the aura of bubblegum pop remained regardless of the material. Most of these 18 tracks were charting hits although only three cracked the Billboard Top ten. —*Greg Adams*

● **The Very Best of Brian Hyland** / May 26, 1998 / Music Club ◆◆◆◆

Brian Hyland had more hits than you might think—it wasn't just 1960's "Itsy Bitsy Teenie Weenie Yellow Polkadot Bikini," 1962's "Sealed With a Kiss," and 1970's "Gypsy Woman," he hit the charts 19 other times between 1960 and 1971. Of course, only a handful of those other singles hit the Top 40, but that's still a very impressive run to keep hitting the lower reaches of the charts, and some of the singles that didn't make it that far deserved to—including the terrific "Warmed Over Kisses (Left Over Love)," "The Joker Went Wild," "Ginny Come Lately," and "I'll Never Stop Wanting You." All those are present on Music Club's *Very Best of Brian Hyland*, which contains 18 tracks, all of pretty consistent quality, from throughout the '60s. At 18 tracks, it might seem like it's a little long, but it's still missing a couple of moderate hits (such as "Run, Run Look and See") which could have been included. Nevertheless, what's here is pleasing, if a little dated, '60s pop that is a fine, representative overview of his career. —*Stephen Thomas Erlewine*

Ian & Sylvia

f. 1960, **db.** 1973

Folk Revival, Folk-Rock, Folk-Pop

One of the most popular acts of the early-'60s folk revival, Canadian duo of Ian and Sylvia Tyson made several fine albums that spotlighted their stirring harmonies on a mixture of traditional and contemporary material. While these recordings can seem a tad earnest and dated today, they were overlooked influences upon early folk-rockers such as the Jefferson Airplane, the Mamas and the Papas, and Fairport Convention, all of whom utilized similar blends of male/female lead/harmony vocals. They were also inspirations to fellow Canadian singer/songwriters such as Neil Young, Joni Mitchell, and Gordon Lightfoot. After moving from Toronto to New York in 1960, the duo released a self-titled debut (1962) that began a successful series of recordings for Vanguard, on which they helped expand the range of folk by adding bass. Ian & Sylvia were among the first to cover songs by Dylan, Lightfoot, Joni Mitchell, and Phil Ochs, and also began writing material of their own. By 1966, they began to use electric instruments, though their folk-rock generally lacked the focus and consistency of their acoustic recordings. In the late '60s, they would take stabs at country-rock and straight country music. The quality of their records and the size of their audience declined steadily after they ended their association with Vanguard in 1967. Both have since pursued separate solo careers. —*Richie Unterberger*

Ian & Sylvia [1962] / 1962 / Vanguard ✦✦✦

Ian & Sylvia's debut album is their most standard affair, and indeed a fairly typical folk recording for the era, with such traditional warhorses as "Rocks and Gravel" (also recorded, but not released, by Dylan during this time), "C.C. Rider," and "Handsome Molly." What made the pair immediately distinctive was their superb vocal dueting. Blended together, they canceled each other's weaknesses and gave the material great freshness and vigor. Ian's guitar and Sylvia's autoharp are backed by stellar playing from guitarist John Herald and string bassists Bill Lee (director Spike Lee's father) and Art Davis. —*Richie Unterberger*

Four Strong Winds / 1964 / Vanguard ✦✦✦✦✦

Ian & Sylvia hit their stride on their second LP, which features the first in a line of talented second guitarists (John Herald) they would use to augment their original guitar-autoharp-bass lineup. The album featured an assortment of largely traditional material that was unsurpassed in its time, encompassing bluegrass, spirituals, gospel, hillbilly, the French-Canadian standard "V'La L'bon Vent," a British prison song, and two tunes from the Cecil Sharp collection of Southern mountain folk songs of British origin. Two of the most impressive cuts, however, were contemporary compositions. One was their version of Bob Dylan's "Tomorrow Is a Long Time," one of the first obscure Dylan tunes to be committed to vinyl. The title cut, an Ian Tyson original, would prove to be the duo's first song to influence rock musicians, as the Searchers covered it shortly afterwards with a reverent version that was quite close to the original; Neil Young revived it in the late '70s. —*Richie Unterberger*

Northern Journey / 1964 / Vanguard ✦✦✦

The duo continue to fill out their sound on another collection of mostly traditional material, with John Herald (guitar), Monte Dunn (mandolin and guitar), and Eric Weissberg and Russ Savakus (bass) backing Ian & Sylvia's own guitar and autoharp. The few originals stand out much more than the traditional updates on this LP; Tyson's "Four Rode By" and "Some Day Soon" clearly point toward his future C&W/cowboy direction, and Fricker's "You Were on My Mind" remains their best (and best-known) song. —*Richie Unterberger*

Early Morning Rain / 1965 / Vanguard ✦✦✦

Side one of the original LP version of their fourth album continues in the eclectic folkie style of their earlier albums, containing only one original (Tyson's "Marlborough Street Blues"). The other cuts include the fine Gordon Lightfoot title track, a Johnny Cash cover ("Come in Stranger") that heralded their increasing interest in country and western music, one of their finest interpretations of a bona fide traditional warhorse ("Nancy Whiskey"), and "Darcy Farrow," a fine obscure composition that could pass for a traditional standard (written for the duo by an unknown Californian singer/songwriter pair). Side two, however, with the exception of one traditional tune and another Lightfoot cover, is composed entirely of originals. The most notable of these is Tyson's "Song for Canada" (written with Pete Gzowski). A bittersweet plea for greater communication between French- and English-speaking Canadians, it could just as well be heard as a comment on any sort of deteriorating relationship. —*Richie Unterberger*

Ian & Sylvia Play One More / 1966 / Vanguard ✦✦✦

Ian & Sylvia rely mostly on original material for the first time on this erratic record. For the first time, they employ full modern arrangements on four of the tracks, which some-

times works (their cover of Bacharach/David's "24 Hours From Tulsa") and sometimes doesn't (unfortunately for them, on one of their best compositions, "The French Girl"). They also cover songs by Phil Ochs and Scott McKenzie, and their own tunes range from solid numbers in their proven contemporary folk style ("Short Grass") to mediocre. Future Cream producer Felix Pappalardi plays bass. —*Richie Unterberger*

Lovin' Sound / 1967 / Polydor ✦✦✦

The Ian & Sylvia records bridging their folk phase and country-rock period were always uneven folk-rockish affairs, and this one, which remains one of their least-known 1960s efforts, was not an exception. Peg down your expectations a notch, though, and it isn't bad, and it's perhaps their most pop-oriented venture into the folk-rock waters. Paul Harris (keyboards and orchestral arrangements) and Harvey Brooks (bass), both among the most active session players on mid-'60s New York folk-rock records, were both in the band playing on this release. Largely forsaking the traditional folk material that had dominated their first albums, the set was split between original material and covers of contemporary songwriters Bob Dylan, Tim Hardin, and Johnny Cash (session guitarist David Rea contributed "Pilgrimage to Paradise"). Still, the duo never adapted to rock music as well as most of their ex-folkie peers, and the sound of *Lovin' Sound* is rather subdued and tentative. There are some good moody songs here, though, that grow on you, such as the title track (which would not have sounded unreasonable on AM radio) and "Trilogy." The covers of Hardin's "Hang on to a Dream" and "Reason to Believe," as well as Dylan's "I Don't Believe You," are well done as well. "Sunday," written as a CBC TV theme, is uncharacteristically happy-go-lucky, with a trumpet-mimicking vocal chorus that leaves one with the impression that they were making fun of California sunshine pop; "Where Did All the Love Go?" and Johnny Cash's "Big River" expressed their growing country leanings. As a lowlight, "National Hotel" was a cruddy goodtime-vaudevillian exercise that didn't suit the pair at all. —*Richie Unterberger*

So Much for Dreaming / 1967 / Vanguard ✦✦✦

Ian & Sylvia's adjustment to folk-rock was sometimes fine, sometimes awkward, and this was another inconsistent, though generally worthwhile, effort. Highlights include "Circle Game," one of the very first recorded covers of a Joni Mitchell composition. Tyson's "Wild Geese" and "Child Apart" count as some of their better unheralded tunes, and the occasional muted orchestration worked well on "Circle Game" and the melancholy title track. On the other hand, the attempts at blues were abominable, the traditional ballads anachronistic, and some of the material (especially Fricker's) undistinguished. —*Richie Unterberger*

The Best of Ian & Sylvia [Vanguard] / 1968 / Vanguard ✦✦✦

Best-of collections are not the best way to experience album-oriented artists like Ian & Sylvia. And this 12-song anthology of their '60s Vanguard work is not the most extensive retrospective of that era; *Greatest Hits* is considerably lengthier. It does include several of their best and most famous originals ("You Were on My Mind" and "Four String Winds") and covers ("24 Hours From Tulsa," "Early Morning Rain," "Changes"). —*Richie Unterberger*

Full Circle / 1968 / MGM ✦✦

● Greatest Hits / 1987 / Vanguard ✦✦✦✦✦

This compilation (CVSD 5/6) captures much of their best work. Do not confuse it with the identically titled Vanguard album 73114, which includes only half the material found on this set. —*William Ruhlmann*

Long Long Time / Oct. 25, 1994 / Vanguard ✦✦✦

After leaving Vanguard in 1967, Ian & Sylvia spent the next few years recording in a much more countrified style for MGM, Ampex (as figureheads of the band Great Speckled Bird), and Columbia. This compilation—ironically on Vanguard—draws from five albums they released between 1967 and 1971. While the duo's ambitions to expand their artistic horizons were admirable, the fact is that they were much more effective as eclectic folkies than country-pop-folk-rockers. The harmonies remained intact, but the material (mostly original) is often humdrum, the arrangements sometimes lackadaisical. A few cuts, like "Salmon in the Sea" and "Last Lonely Eagle," are reasonably strong; the highlights are the 1967 versions of "Hang on to a Dream" and "Reason to Believe," which were among the first Tim Hardin covers ever recorded. —*Richie Unterberger*

Live at Newport / Jun. 18, 1996 / Vanguard ✦✦✦

Divided about equally between material from their appearances at the 1963 and 1965 Newport Folk Festivals, these 14 tracks present concert versions of many of the duo's best songs, including "You Were on My Mind," "Someday Soon," "Song for Canada," and "Four Strong Winds." Eric Hord adds lead acoustic guitar on the 1963 cuts; Rick Turner does the same on the ones from 1965. Ian & Sylvia recorded studio versions of all of the songs on their '60s Vanguard albums, which makes this disc a sort of souvenir that's essential only for big fans, although the sound and performances are decent. *—Richie Unterberger*

The Best of the Vanguard Years / Aug. 11, 1998 / Vanguard ✦✦✦✦
The first upgrading of the Ian and Sylvia CD catalog is an improved version of *The Essential Ian & Sylvia*, with cleaner mastering and some songs added (most notably a pair of numbers—the best here—from the *Live at Newport* disc issued in the 1990s) for a total of 25. The sound is an improvement over the earlier CD versions, although the duo's music was so utterly underproduced—what annotator Ed Ward calls a hallmark of their sound—that this is represented by quieter background, rather than any astoundingly vivid textures. The obvious songs ("Four Strong Winds," "Some Day Soon," "You Were on My Mind," "The Circle Game," "Early Morning Rain," "Changes") are here, along with many less familiar numbers ("Mary Anne," "This Wheel's on Fire," "Satisfied Mind," "Keep on the Sunny Side," a live version of "The Greenwood Sidie"), although quite a few superb album tracks are still to be found exclusively on the duo's individual CDs. The main drawback is that the duo weren't always that interesting—both are surprisingly credible working in a blues idiom ("Rocks and Gravel," in a previously unissued alternate take), but when they cut with a full rock band, as on "When I Was a Cowboy," it's not always very inspired or effective; on the other hand, the harmonizing on "Play One More," amelded with the unobtrusive string and horn section, is breathtaking. *—Bruce Eder*

Janis Ian

b. Apr. 7, 1951, New York, NY
Vocals, Guitar / Contemporary Folk, Folk-Rock, Singer/Songwriter
A singer/songwriter both celebrated and decried for her pointed handling of taboo topics, Janis Ian enjoyed one of the more remarkable second acts in music history; after first finding success as a teen, her career slumped, only to enter a commercial resurgence almost a decade later. She wrote her first songs at the age of 12, and graduated to the New York folk circuit as a teenager. Her self-titled debut LP, which appeared when she was 15, contained "Society's Child (Baby I've Been Thinking)," a meditation on interracial romance. The single failed to attract much notice until conductor Leonard Bernstein invited its writer to perform the song on a television special; the ensuing publicity and furor over its subject matter pushed "Society's Child" into the upper rungs of the pop charts. In rapid succession, Ian recorded three more LPs but later took a temporary hiatus until 1971. With 1975's *Between the Lines*, she eclipsed all of her previous success; not only did the LP achieve platinum status, but the delicate single "At Seventeen" reached the Top Three and won a Grammy. While subsequent releases earned acclaim, they sold poorly. Ian spent 12 years without a contract before emerging in 1993 with *Breaking Silence*, which pulled no punches in tackling material like domestic violence, frank eroticism, and the Holocaust. Similarly, 1995's *Revenge* explored prostitution and homelessness. *—Jason Ankeny*

● **Between the Lines** / Mar. 1975 / Columbia ✦✦✦✦✦
"At Seventeen" is only one of a group of beautifully written, tastefully performed, and very moving songs. *— William Ruhlmann*

Society's Child: The Verve Recordings / Aug. 22, 1995 / Polydor ✦✦✦✦✦
The 41 songs on this double CD contain almost everything from the four albums that the singer/songwriter recorded for Verve in the late '60s. While it is true that Ian's early work may have been unduly savaged by unsympathetic rock critics, it's also true that the magnitude of her talent isn't large enough to merit a box set. As others have pointed out over the years, these compositions are often overly wordy, didactic, and self-absorbed, though these flaws are understandable (to a degree) given that Ian was in her mid- and late teens when they were recorded. At the same time, the grooves make a fairly strong case that Ian is underrated, if hardly a major figure; some of the songs are affecting, the arrangements (especially the early ones by Shangri-Las producer Shadow Morton) have a '60s-period charm, and she's a pretty strong singer. Although some Laura Nyro fans might find the comparison insulting, there's a similarity to be found in Ian's bluesier and more soulful vocals, especially on her later Verve records. So while this couldn't be classified as a milestone of the early singer/songwriter era, it's more enjoyable and impressive than a lot of listeners would expect, although two-and-a-half hours is too much to take at once. *—Richie Unterberger*

Ice Cube (O'Shea Jackson)

b. Jun. 15, 1969
Vocals / West Coast Rap, Hardcore Rap, G-Funk, Gangsta Rap, Golden Age
After leaving the seminal N.W.A., Ice Cube quickly established himself as one of hip-hop's best and most controversial artists. As a solo artist, his politics and social commentary sharpened substantially, and his first two records were equally praised and reviled; his lyrical stance was often violent, homophobic, and misogynist, yet it also happened to be considerably more articulate than many of his gangsta peers. Ice Cube (b. O'Shea Jackson) came from a surprisingly straight background, raised in South Central Los Angeles by parents who had jobs at UCLA. He formed the first incarnation of N.W.A. with Eazy-E and Dr. Dre in 1986; their debut album *Straight Outta Compton* became an underground hit over the course of 1989, but Cube's deep conflicts with N.W.A.'s management resulted in his departure late that year. Recorded with Public Enemy's production team, the Bomb Squad, his 1990 solo debut *AmeriKKKa's Most Wanted* was an instant hit; even amidst controversy over his lyrics, the album was hailed as a groundbreaking classic within hip-hop. His 1991 acting debut in John Singleton's acclaimed urban drama *Boyz 'N the Hood* was widely praised. Released later that year, *Death Certificate* was simultaneously more political and vulgar than *AmeriKKKa*, and several tracks provoked public condemnations of Cube as a racist himself; however, the furor didn't prevent it from reaching number two and going platinum. Following Cube's slot on the second Lollapalooza tour in 1992, *The Predator* became the first album to debut at number one on both the pop and R&B charts. However, with the rise of Dr. Dre's G-funk, his hold on the mass rap audience was beginning to slip. While 1993's *Lethal Injection* went platinum, its funkier sound wasn't well-received, and it was Cube's last official album for several years. He concentrated on producing and writing for other artists, and made amends with Dre on their 1995 duet "Natural Born Killaz"; he also appeared in the films *Higher Learning*, *Friday* (his screenwriting debut), and *Anaconda*. He returned to recording in 1998 with *War and Peace—The War Disc*; its sequel, *The Peace Disc*, followed two years later. *—Stephen Thomas Erlewine*

Kill at Will / 1990 / Profile ✦✦✦✦
Ice Cube's riveting debut album, *AmeriKKKa's Most Wanted* was still burning up the charts when Priority Records released this EP, which lacks that album's overall excellence but has its moments. With *Kill at Will*, Cube unveiled his engaging "The Product" and "Dead Homiez," a poignant lament for the victims of black-on-black crime that is among the best songs he's ever written. Enjoyable but not essential are remixes of "Endangered Species (Tales From the Darkside)" and the outrageous "Get Off My D*** and Tell Yo B**** to Come Here." Clearly, *Kill at Will* was intended for hardcore fans rather than casual listeners—who would do well to stick with *AmeriKKKa's Most Wanted* and *Death Certificate*. *—Alex Henderson*

☆ **AmeriKKKa's Most Wanted** / May 16, 1990 / Priority ✦✦✦✦✦
After leaving N.W.A. on anything but good terms with Dr. Dre and Eazy-E, Ice Cube launched his solo career with the hard-hitting and impressive *AmeriKKKa's Most Wanted*. While the Angelino continued to embrace gangster rap—a style in which MCs provide violent, graphic, first-person portrayals of thugs, gang members, drug dealers, etc.—there's a lot more to this riveting CD than that controversial approach. As much as Cube thrives on the shocking and the profane, it's clear that he isn't glamorizing the harsh urban realities he raps about, but rather, protesting them. "Once Upon a Time in the Projects" is about being arrested for being in the wrong place (a crack house) at the wrong time (during a drug bust), while "Endangered Species" (a duet with Public Enemy leader Chuck D) is a sobering reflection on the high mortality rate among young African-American males. On some of his subsequent recordings, Cube would, artistically speaking, become a victim of his own anger. But on *AmeriKKKa's Most Wanted*, a more lucid Cube quite effectively articulates just how bad things are in the America's inner cities—and how badly things need to change. *—Alex Henderson*

★ **Death Certificate** / Oct. 31, 1991 / Priority ✦✦✦✦✦
Death Certificate is even harder and angrier than *AmeriKKKa's Most Wanted*, which is both a good and a bad thing, depending on your politics. If you're inclined to see Ice Cube as a spokesman and social commentator, *Death Certificate* will support your claims—it continues the sharp insights and unflinching looks at contemporary urban lifestyles that his solo debut only hinted at; in short, its hardcore without any gangsta posturing. If you're inclined to see Ice Cube as a bigoted, misogynistic rabble-rouser, *Death Certificate* will also support your claims—"No Vaseline" contains explicit anti-semetic taunts directed at his former manager, there are homophobic slurs scattered throughout the album and women are frequently are either bitches or whores. However, if you look beyond the surface—no matter what political viewpoint you happen to have—you will find that Cube's rhymes do promote self-awareness and education. In short, they are some of the most incisive raps about life as a young black man since the advent of Public Enemy. Considering this, it's not surprising that *Death Certificate* bears the mark of Public Enemy's dense, abrasive soundscapes—it's a funkier, noisier and more musically effective album than *AmeriKKKa's Most Wanted*. Ice Cube had never before created a statement of purpose as coherent and incendiary as *Death Certificate* and, sadly, he never did again. *—Leo Stanley*

The Predator / Nov. 17, 1992 / Priority ✦✦✦
The Predator functions as the point in Cube's career where his albums started to become hit-and-miss collections of miscellaneous singles and filler rather than coherent body's of thematically connected work à la *Death Certificate* and *AmeriKKKa's Most Wanted*. So on the one hand, it's disappointing to find that Cube refrains from his formerly conceptual work in favor of seemingly radio-targeted efforts, yet, on the other hand, *The Predator* does prove successful as a collection of individual tracks, many of which stand as some of his most enthused work. Kicking off the album with force, "When Will They Shoot?" explodes with power, and then "Wicked" continues this aggressive tone. Things begin to falter a bit after that, though, both in terms of songwriting and lyrics as well as production. Of the remaining mediocre tracks, "It Was a Good Day" is an obvious highlight; quite similar in tone to Cube's previous crossover hit "Dead Homiez" and his subsequent crossover hit "You Know How We Do It," this song finds the rapper slowing down his tempo and trading anger and aggressive beats for modest contemplative indifference and relaxed G-funk production. The Muggs-produced tracks, "We Had to Tear This Motha—— Up" (the only blatant L.A. riot commentary) and "Check Yo Self," also stand out as some of the few bright moments on this otherwise mediocre album. *—Jason Birchmeier*

Lethal Injection / Dec. 7, 1993 / Scarface ✦✦
Lethal Injection signaled the point in Ice Cube's career when the once iconic rapper seemed suddenly unimportant as a rapper. His early work with N.W.A. and his early solo albums—*Amerikka's Most Wanted*, *Death Certificate*—had been innovative and important within the rap community due to Cube's knack for working with the genre's top producers and his poignant lyrics. But as foreshadowed on the suddenly shoddy *The Predator*, Cube suddenly seemed less focused with his music; coincidentally, this was around the same time that he began to earn acclaim for his role as an actor in films such as *Boyz*

'N the Hood and *Trespass*. The beginning-to-end disappointment of *Lethal Injection* only confirmed the fact that Cube seemed suddenly less interested in music as he was in cinema (his subsequent sabbatical from the rap world confirmed this). On this album, Cube seems suddenly out of important things to say. Granted, "You Know How We Do It" and "Bop Gun (One Nation)" were great songs and ultimately big hits for the artist, yet even these songs are fairly predictable exercises that don't really take any risks (with the former being a near rewrite of "It Was a Good Day"). Outside of these two standout tracks, there really isn't anything else here worth bothering with relative to Cube's earlier, more inspired work or his subsequent efforts on the ambitious *War & Peace* albums. *—Jason Birchmeier*

Bootlegs & B-Sides / Nov. 22, 1994 / Priority ✦✦

Featuring . . . Ice Cube / Dec. 16, 1997 / Priority ✦✦✦
Not necessarily intended as a greatest-hits album, *Featuring... Ice Cube* would end up functioning as one, since it collects a number of impressive songs from Cube's varied and often spotty 1990s discography. This album draws a few of the best moments from Cube's pre-*War & Peace* solo albums ["Bop Gun (One Nation)," "Check Yo Self," "Endangered Species," "It's a Man's World"], along with songs from other rappers' albums where he appeared as a guest star (most notably "Game Over" with Scarface and Dr. Dre) and also a few other random songs from various sources ("Natural Born Killaz," "Trespass," "Bend a Corner Wit Me"). The common thematic thread is the fact that Cube trades off verses with other rappers on each of the tracks. It's a bit of an untraditional concept for a compilation, but in the end it makes for a strong album. There are some problems with this concept, though, primarily the fact that many may mistake this for a greatest-hits album, and it's clearly not, missing many of Cube's best songs. It functions better as a sampler of Cube's non-solo album work, even if the few solo album tracks such as "Check Yo Self" may not fit into that category. For years, though, this album was the closest audiences could come to a proper greatest-hits collection. *—Jason Birchmeier*

War & Peace, Vol. 1 (The War Disc) / Nov. 17, 1998 / Priority ✦✦✦
Considering that he hadn't delivered a full-fledged solo album since 1993's disappointing *Lethal Injection*, maybe it shouldn't have been a surprise that Ice Cube returned hard in 1998 with *War & Peace, Vol. 1 (The War Disc)*, since five years is a long, long time to stay quiet. What was a surprise was how ambitious the album was. The first installment in a proposed double-disc set, *The War Disc* is a cacophonic, cluttered, impassioned record that nearly qualifies as a return to form. Designed as a hard-hitting record, it certainly takes no prisoners, as it moves from intense street-oriented jams to rap-metal fusions, such as the Korn-blessed "Fuck Dying," with its seething, distorted guitars. It's a head-spinning listen and, at first, it seems to be a forceful comeback. Upon closer inspection, *The War Disc* falters a bit. Not only does the relentless nature of the music wear a little thin, but Cube spends too much time trying to beat newcomers at their own game. His lyrical skills are still intact, but he spends way too much time boasting, particularly about material possessions, and his attempt to rechristen himself Don Mega, in a Wu-like move, simply seems awkward. Even so, the quality of the music—and the moments when he pulls it all together, such as "3 Strikes You In"—sustains *War* and makes it feel more cohesive than it actually is. The key is purpose—even if Cube doesn't always say exactly what he wants, he does have something to say. That alone makes *War & Peace*, with just one album completed, a more successful and rewarding listen than the typical double-disc hip-hop set of the late '90s. *—Stephen Thomas Erlewine*

War & Peace, Vol. 2 (The Peace Disc) / Feb. 29, 2000 / Priority ✦✦✦
The second volume of Ice Cube's *War & Peace* album finds the multi-talented veteran MC evolving beyond a mere gangsta rap artist. Of course, Ice Cube doesn't admit his maturity, starting the album off with "Hello," featuring MC Ren and Dr. Dre reinstating their thug stance. Yet for as much as Cube flexes about being hard, he has actually evolved into a wiser, more composed artist than the hate-fueled gangsta found on his early albums. Some of the songs on *War & Peace, Vol. 2* such as "Record Company Pimpin'" reflect the deep insight he is easily capable of injecting into his lyrics. Unfortunately, for every contemplative moment on this album, there are also plenty of songs such as "Can You Bounce?" and "Hello" that reduce themselves to simple, lucid attempts at hit singles. These songs are wonderful songs, rich in hooks and full of strong beats, but they don't really fit in with the rest of the album. The fact that Ice Cube churned out two albums of content during his lengthy absence from the rap world in the late '90s makes the two volumes of *War & Peace* overly eclectic. Cube's rapping sounds great with plenty of ideas that extend outside of simple gangsta motifs and slick rhymes full of wit; however, the constant changes in the album from hook-laden hits to denser, message-filled songs and from stark, minimal beats to up-tempo dance-rap make this a sometimes brilliant yet ultimately spotty, multidimensional album that needs more focus. *—Jason Birchmeier*

Ice-T (Tracy Morrow)

b. Feb. 14, 1959, Newark, NJ

Rap, Vocals, Leader / West Coast Rap, Hardcore Rap, Gangsta Rap, Golden Age

Ice-T (b. Tracy Morrow) has proven to be one of hip-hop's most articulate and intelligent stars, as well as one of its most frustrating. At his best, the rapper has written some of the best portraits of ghetto life and gangsters, as well as some of the best social commentary hip-hop has produced. Just as often, he can slip into sexism and gratuitous violence, and even then his rhymes are clever and biting. Ice-T's best recordings have always been made in conjunction with strong collaborators, whether it's the Bomb Squad or Jello Biafra. With his music, Ice-T has made a conscious effort to win the vast audience of white male adolescents, as his frequent excursions with his heavy metal band Body Count show. All the while, he has withstood a constant barrage of criticism and controversy to become a respected figure not only in the music press, but the mainstream media as well. *—Stephen Thomas Erlewine*

Rhyme Pays / 1987 / Sire ✦✦✦
Before Ice-T's ascension, L.A. rappers were known primarily for a synthesizer-dominated sound indebted to Kraftwerk's innovations as well as Africa Bambaataa's 1982 hit, "Planet Rock." While L.A. did have its share of hardcore rappers in the mid-1980s (including Toddy Tee, King Tee, and of course, Ice-T), hardcore rap was dominated by the East Coast. That begin to change in 1987, when Ice-T's debut album, *Rhyme Pays*, was released and sold several hundred thousand copies. Hard-hitting offerings like "409," "Make It Funky," and the title song (which samples Black Sabbath's "War Pigs" and underscores the L.A. resident's love of heavy metal) left no doubt that Ice had very little in common with the Egyptian Lover, the World Class Wreckin' Cru, or the L.A. Dream Team. The album doesn't contain as much gangsta rap as some of his subsequent releases, but it did have enough to stir some controversy. On "Squeeze the Trigger," "Pain," and a new version of "6 'N the Morning" (which had been the B-side of Ice's 1986 single "Doggin' the Wax" on Techno-Hop), Ice portrays ruthless felons and raps candidly about the horrors of the urban ghetto he'd been only too familiar with. With the release of *Rhyme Pays*, the West Coast was well on its way to becoming a crucial part of hip-hop. *—Alex Henderson*

Power / 1988 / Sire ✦✦✦✦✦
As riveting as *Rhyme Pays* was, Ice-T did hold back a little and avoided being too consistently sociopolitical. But with the outstanding *Power*, the gloves came all the way off, and Ice didn't hesitate to speak his mind about the harsh realities of inner-city life. On "Drama," "Soul On Ice" (an homage to his idol Iceberg Slim), "High Rollers" and other gangsta rap gems, Ice embraces a first-person format and raps with brutal honesty about the lives of gang members, players, and hustlers. Ice's detractors took the songs out of context, arguing that he was glorifying crime. But he countered that in fact, he was sending out an anti-crime message in a subliminal fashion and stressed that the criminals he portrayed ended up dead or behind bars. Another track that some misconstrued was "I'm Your Pusher," an interpretation of Curtis Mayfield's "Pusherman" that doesn't promoting the use of drugs, but uses double entendres to make an anti-drug statement. (Ice has always been vehemently outspoken in his opposition to drugs.) In the next few years, gangsta rap would degenerate into nothing more than cheap exploitation and empty cliches, but in Ice's hands, it was as informative as it was captivating. *—Alex Henderson*

☆ **The Iceberg/Freedom of Speech . . . Just Watch What You Say** / Oct. 1989 / Sire ✦✦✦✦✦
Ice-T threw listeners quite a curve ball with his riveting third album, *The Iceberg/Freedom of Speech... Just Watch What You Say*—arguably the closest hip-hop has come to George Orwell's *1984*. Instead of focusing heavily on gangster rap, Ice-T made First Amendment issues the CD's dominant theme. Setting the album's tone is the opener "Shut Up, Be Happy," which finds guest Jello Biafra (former leader of punk band Dead Kennedys) envisioning an Orwellian America in which the goverment controls and dominates every aspect of its citizens' lives. Though there are a few examples of first-rate gangster rap here—including "The Hunted Child" and the chilling "Peel Their Caps Back"—Ice's main concern this time is censorship and what he views as a widespread attack on free speech in the U.S. As angry and lyrically intense as most of *The Iceberg* is, Ice enjoys fun for its own sake on "My Word Is Bond" and "The Girl Tried to Kill Me"—an insanely funny rap/rock account of an encounter with a dominatrix. *—Alex Henderson*

★ **O.G. Original Gangster** / May 14, 1991 / Sire ✦✦✦✦✦
One of gangsta rap's defining albums, *O.G. Original Gangster* is a sprawling masterpiece that stands far and away as Ice-T's finest hour. Taken track by track, *O.G.* might not seem at first like the product of a unified vision; perspective-wise, it's all over the map. There's perceptive social analysis, chilling violence, psychological storytelling, hair-trigger rage, pleas for solutions to ghetto misery, cautionary morality tales, and cheerfully crude humor in the depictions of sex and defenses of street language. But with a few listens, it's possible to assimilate everything into a complex, detailed portrait of Ice-T's South Central L.A. roots—the album's contradictions reflect the complexities of real life. That's why the more intelligent, nuanced material isn't negated by the violence and sexism—both of which, incidentally, are held relatively in check, with the former having been reshaped into a terrifying but inescapable fact of life. That isn't to say that *O.G. Original Gangster* is designed to appeal to delicate intellectual sensibilities; it's still full of raw, street-level aggression that makes no apologies or concessions. That goes for the music as well as the lyrics. The beats are a little too hard-driving and jittery to really breathe like funk, which only adds to the dark, claustrophobic feel of the production. Ice smoothly keeps up with the music's furious pace and also debuts his soon-to-be-notorious metal band Body Count on one track. That kind of artistic ambition is all over the album, whether in the lean musical attack or the urgent rhymes. *O.G. Original Gangster* is a certifiable gangsta-rap classic, and arguably the most realistic, unvarnished representation of a world Ice-T was the first to chronicle on record. *—Steve Huey*

Body Count / 1992 / Sire ✦✦✦
Ice-T's excursion into heavy metal brought him a firestorm of controversy, but the album is actually a tepid collection of '80s-style arena metal that never sounds dangerous. Frequently, it's hard to tell if Ice takes this stuff seriously; tracks like "Body Count" and "Cop Killer" are invigorating stabs at social criticism, but most of the album is filled with stupid attempts at being threatening, like "KKK Bitch" and "Mama's Gotta Die Tonight." Maybe the humor was intentional, but too frequently the record sounded embarrassing. After "Cop Killer" was pulled from the album, it was replaced with a version of "The Iceberg" recorded with Jello Biafra. *—Stephen Thomas Erlewine*

Home Invasion / Mar. 23, 1993 / Priority ✦✦✦
Given the fact that most of *Home Invasion* was recorded during and after the "Cop Killer" media firestorm, it comes as no surprise that the album is an uneven, muddled affair, not the clean, focused attack of *O.G. Original Gangster*. Instead of producing an album that illustrates his confusion through the music (like Public Enemy's claustrophobic "Welcome to the Terrordome"), Ice-T made a confused album, unsure in its musical and lyrical direction. *Home Invasion* does have some flashes of brilliance (about a third of the album, particularly the tribute to the gang truce, "Gotta Lotta Love"), but it takes a little digging to find the best material. —*Stephen Thomas Erlewine*

The Classic Collection / May 4, 1993 / Rhino ✦✦
Ice-T's early sound was far different from the material that later earned him fame and controversy. His voice was higher, his cadence less assured, his commentary and ideas rough and evolving, and his backdrops less sophisticated, with straight scratches rather than multiple edits and song samples. While he did rap about social problems, Ice-T was then just as concerned with proving his manhood on the mike as many East Coast types, and had to overcome initial skepticism about a West Coast rapper not being inherently soft. This collection reissues formative Ice-T, including such seminal raps as "6 'N the Morning," "Killers," "Body Rock" and a 1992 autobiographical review of the old days, "Ice-A-Mix." It's also interesting to remember just how little furor there was in the mid-'80s over things that get people easy headlines in the 1990s. —*Ron Wynn*

VI: Return of the Real / Jun. 1996 / Priority ✦✦✦
As the title says, Ice-T returns to the street and the hardcore beats with his sixth album, *Return of the Real*. In fact, the return isn't just to hardcore—it's to hardcore that happened before gangsta rap, before the message and the music became diluted with endless B-boy posturing and loping P-Funk beats. In concept, the album is brilliant—Ice-T has always had an eye for lyrical detail and has always been a vocal supporter of hardcore, street-oriented hip-hop; at the very least, his rejection of G-funk/post-NWA gangsta rap is a bold political move. However, *Return of the Real* doesn't quite re-establish Ice-T as a force, mainly because the production sounds a bit dated. Sure, there are the occasional contemporary flourishes—usually in the guise of a Wu-Tang-style soundscape—but for the most part, Ice sounds like he's in his own world. Unfortunately, that doesn't mean that he has created a unique sonic world; it just means that he hasn't progressed far since 1991. Of course, there are a number of tracks that sound vibrant and alive, but *Return of the Real* can't help escape a creeping sense of stagnation that permeates through the entire album. —*Stephen Thomas Erlewine*

7th Deadly Sin / Oct. 12, 1999 / Coroner/Atomic Pop ✦✦✦
With artwork straight out of David Fincher's seminal 1995 serial killer flick *Seven*, Ice-T's seventh album *7th Deadly Sin* looks curiously out of place in 1999, and it has a sound to match. Ice-T doesn't really return to his classic sound of the late '80s/early '90s when he was a key player in the golden age of hip-hop, but he doesn't seem entirely concerned with staying current, either. The end result is a record that occasionally recalls *OG* or *Iceberg* while still having elements of everything from RZA's ominous, skeletal productions to the stripped-back Cali-rap of the late '90s. As a result, it straddles two extremes, which can actually be intriguing at times, especially since it is the sonic equivalent of Ice-T's place in hip-hop in 1999—a veteran that isn't washed up, but isn't quite in step with the times. Unfortunately, his lyrics don't really match the feel of the album, since he's decided to pretty much run through his traditional list of gangsta topics, even adding the now-cliched slow-jam tribute to Tupac and Biggie with "Valuable Game," a song based around En Vogue's "Don't Let Go" and easily the most embarrassing thing on the album. When he breaks from gangsta tradition or offers a twist on it, as he does on the title track or "Don't Hate the Playa," the songs have the opportunity to really take off, but they just highlight how most of the songs have lyrics that are simply too generic. But if *7th Deadly Sin* is taken on a purely musical level, it can be intriguing. Not always successful, but it at least offers a welcome change-up after a couple of undistinguished releases. —*Stephen Thomas Erlewine*

Greatest Hits: The Evidence / Aug. 8, 2000 / Atomic Pop ✦✦✦✦
Ice-T, the self-proclaimed "original gangster" of rap, is one of the few hip-hop artists who truly deserves a greatest-hits compilation. In a genre marked by overnight sensations, rapidly changing trends, and fans with short memories, he put together a long career marked by both consistency and innovation. This 16-track compilation, put together by Ice-T himself, covers 14 years, seven albums, and the title themes for two films (*Colors* and *New Jack City*), but fortunately concentrates primarily on the first five years of his career, when he was at his productive peak. Two more recent songs on this release were not previously domestically available, a U.K. remix of "The Lane," which doesn't add anything to the original, and the unreleased track "Money, Power, Women." Both are decent but should have been left off in favor of older, better classics. Fairly informative liner notes describe the creative process behind each song and each album from Ice-T's perspective. Most of the singles and recognizable songs are included here, with the mysterious exception of "Lifestyles of the Rich and Infamous" and "Gotta Lotta Love," which honored the gang truce in the wake of the L.A. riots. Also excluded are memorably risqué songs, such as "Girls L.G.B.N.A.F." and "Girl Tried to Kill Me," and some of Ice-T's more adventurous collaborations, including Body Count, the forerunner to Limp Bizkit and other rap-metal groups. These exceptions are peripheral, however, and the meat of his career is included here. —*Luke Forrest*

Icicle Works

f. 1980, db. 1990
Neo-Psychedelia, Post-Punk, New Wave
A product of the same Liverpool neo-psychedelic community which gave rise to Echo &

the Bunnymen and the Teardrop Explodes, the Icicle Works formed in 1980 from the ashes of local bands like City Limits and the Cherry Boys. A trio originally comprised of singer/guitarist Ian McNabb, bassist Chris Layhe, and drummer Chris Sharrock, the Icicle Works (who nicked their name from an obscure sci-fi novel) issued their debut single "Ascending" in 1981. After the success of subsequent efforts like 1982's "Nirvana," the band earned a deal with the Beggars Banquet label, and scored a U.K. Top 15 hit with "Love Is a Wonderful Colour."

The Icicle Works' self-titled debut appeared in 1984 and reached the U.S. Top 40 on the strength of the excellent single "Birds Fly (Whisper to a Scream)." The superior 1985 follow-up *The Small Price of a Bicycle* failed to match their earlier success, however, and neither the 1986 hits collection *Seven Singles Deep* nor 1987's *If You Want to Defeat Your Enemy Sing His Song* failed to generate much interest either.

Prior to recording 1988's *Blind*, both Layhe and Sharrock left the band, and were replaced by bassist Roy Corkhill and drummer Zak Starkey, the son of Ringo Starr. Minus Starkey, the Icicle Works (now rounded out by guitarist Mark Revell, keyboardist Dave Baldwin, and drummer Paul Burgess) completed one final album, *Permanent Damage*, before disbanding in 1990. McNabb continued on as a solo artist. —*Jason Ankeny*

Icicle Works / 1984 / Beggars Banquet ✦✦✦✦✦
The Icicle Works' self-titled debut as a whole is an excellent example of post-punk power and beauty. "Chop the Tree" alone is something of a lost classic, with Hugh Jones' note-perfect production, Sharrock's pounding, complex rhythm attack, and McNabb's exquisite singing providing one heck of a start. Indeed, McNabb here sounds like a clear precursor to singers like Neil Hannon of the Divine Comedy and the equal of the precise diction and passion of Edwyn Collins. When it comes to the hits, "Love Is a Wonderful Colour" is another prime vocal showcase, with a sparkling guitar/keyboard lead arrangement and a constantly shifting but never pointlessly show-off bass/drums pace. Frankly, the members of U2 must have wished they could be so emotional and so soaring at this point in their careers. As for "Birds Fly," the song stands as a joyous rave-up of quick drums and shimmering guitars with an inspiring, frenetic chorus tempered by a gentle, half-whispered conclusion. Further examples of the group's abilities crop up song for song: the amazing guitar break and serene conclusion of "Reaping the Rich Harvest," the clean crisp flow of "As the Dragonfly Flies" interrupted by a down and dirty guitar line, the soft pipe start to "Lovers' Day," and more. Concluding with the slow burn fire of "Nirvana," *The Icicle Works* is early-'80s U.K. rock at its considerable best. —*Ned Raggett*

Small Price of a Bicycle / 1985 / Beggars Banquet ✦✦✦✦✦

Understanding Jane / 1986 / Beggars Banquet ✦✦

Who Do You Want for Your Love? / 1986 / Beggars Banquet ✦✦

If You Want to Defeat Your Enemy Sing His Song / 1987 / Beggars Banquet ✦✦✦
The Ian Broudie-produced *Defeat Your Enemy* brought out the band's varying influences in different ways, resulting in a varied record touching on everything from funk to folk. But as successful as earlier works? Yes and no. Unquestionably, the band's knack for big, uplifting but not hollow performances was still in fine flower, as the smash single "Understanding Jane" showed. A quick, fierce rocker with an instantly catchy pop vibe and a brilliant chorus, it's a '50s tearjerker filtered through the Ramones with fantastic results. Another winner is the opening cut, "Evangeline," with a lovely chorus consisting of overdubbed vocals from the band and guest singer Alison Limerick and a quick, Motown-touched rhythm supporting McNabb's powerful singing. Then there's "Up Here in the North of England," a slow, string-touched waltz winningly sung while bitterly ripping into the political state of the nation line for line. McNabb's vocals throughout the album are deeper than before, but still with the same general sense of control and projection; if anything, he was doing a better David Bowie croon than Bowie himself could do at the time. However, elsewhere the elements are in place but the performance isn't quite there. Part of this can be laid at Broudie's feet as well as the various mixers on the record, who bring things to a too commercially ready punch and sheen. Consider the arena-level pound of Sharrock's drums on "Hope Springs Eternal," where earlier his performances wouldn't need such overamping to make their impact. It's not just a technical question, though; McNabb's guitar here aims for a classic rock style that the band doesn't really need. Other songs like "When You Were Mine" bury a good song and performance with technically accomplished but cold results. In the end, *Defeat Your Enemy* half defeats itself, but not without some blazingly brilliant results on the way. —*Ned Raggett*

Blind / 1988 / Beggars Banquet ✦✦

Permanent Damage / 1990 / Epic ✦✦✦

● **The Best of the Icicle Works** / 1995 / Beggars Banquet ✦✦✦✦✦
With individual song comments from McNabb, an appreciative essay, complete discography, and fine artwork, the Icicle Works collection provides an excellent overview of the group's heyday. If not quite as strong as the band's debut album as an experience due to the inclusion of less successful later numbers, all the hit singles and some fine album cuts appear, not to mention an interesting rarity or two. Beginning with the "long version" of the chiming drive of "Hollow Horse" from *The Small Price of a Bicycle*, this collection fully showcases McNabb's passionate, elegant quaver and driving songwriting, as well as the abilities of the fine Layhe/Sharrock rhythm section. The three biggest hits get pride of place near the start: "Love Is a Wonderful Colour," "Birds Fly" (with wry comments from McNabb on its stateside re-titling as "Whisper to a Scream"), and "Understanding Jane." This last one appears in a 1992 version via remixing and extra overdubs by McNabb, but it's still a perfect blast of just-sly-enough pop/punk. He does a similar remix job with *Small Price*'s gentler "When It All Comes Down," with equally fine results. "High Time," meanwhile, surfaces in its wonderful acoustic version from the "Kiss Off" single,

while an otherwise unreleased track, the brooding, dramatic "Firepower," was recorded shortly before the original lineup collapsed. —*Ned Raggett*

Ida

f. 1992, New York, NY
Sadcore, Indie Pop, Folk-Pop
Indie folk-pop band Ida formed in New York in 1992 around the core duo of singers/guitarists Daniel Littleton and Elizabeth Mitchell. Littleton emerged in 1985 as a member of the Annapolis, MD-based punk group the Hated; after their 1989 demise, he continued in a series of bands including Three Shades of Dirty, Choke and Slack, which also featured future Tsunami frontwoman Jenny Toomey. Mitchell, meanwhile, first began performing as one half of an acoustic duo with singer/songwriter (and fellow Brown University alum) Lisa Loeb; both Mitchell and Littleton later played on Loeb's breakthrough hit "Stay." After signing to Toomey's Simple Machines label, Ida debuted in 1994 with *Tales of Brave Ida*, a luminous collection of languid, minimalist pop songs; following the addition of Littleton's brother Michael (formerly of Baltimore's Hassassins) on drums, they returned in 1996 with the stunning *I Know About You*. The addition of Beekeeper bassist Karla Schickele preceded 1997's brilliant *Ten Small Paces*; the same lineup resurfaced a year later with an EP, *Losing True*. While a member of Ida, Dan Littleton also played in Liquorice with Toomey and His Name Is Alive's Trey Many; he and Mitchell were wed in late 1999, shortly after brother Michael's exit from the group. Following an ill-fated major label stay at Capitol, Ida finally released the full-length *Will You Find Me* on the Tiger Style imprint in the summer of 2000. A year later, the group returned with *The Braille Night*. —*Jason Ankeny*

Tales of Brave Ida / 1995 / Simple Machines ✦✦✦✦
The debut album by then-duo Dan Littleton and Elizabeth Mitchell is a beautiful and fragile piece of dreamy folk-pop. The spare yet clean production introduces a band whose vocal stylings and soft instrumentation help create a mood of uplifting contemplation. For a drumless effort, *Tales of Brave Ida* manages to fill the space with a rich, dynamic sound which appropriately revolves around the beautiful harmonizing of Mitchell and Littleton, whose quiet lyricism so perfectly mirrors the gentle strumming of acoustic and electric guitars. On songs like "Tempting" and "Slow Dance," Ida practice their own special brand of emotional reflection. The songs on this album focus mainly on the substance and importance of relationships.

Ida share a knack for illuminating the beauty of quietness with singers like Nick Drake and bands like Galaxie 500. *Tales of Brave Ida* is a bold and creative debut filled with folk-pop classics that will hopefully be rediscovered by a larger audience over the years. —*Marc Ruxin*

I Know About You / 1996 / Simple Machines ✦✦✦✦✦
The remarkable *I Know About You* benefits greatly from the addition of drummer Michael Littleton, whose spartan, pensive rhythms add a powerful new dynamic to Ida's quietly intense sound; at the same time, the harmonies and songs of Dan Littleton and Elizabeth Mitchell resonate with greater intellectual clarity and emotional depth than on *Tales of Brave Ida*—tracks like "Back Burner" and the centerpiece "Treasure Chest" are simply stunning. —*Jason Ankeny*

● **Ten Small Paces** / Sep. 23, 1997 / Simple Machines ✦✦✦✦✦
Continuing a tradition established on their previous album, *I Know About You*, Ida's ranks swell to include another new member on *Ten Small Paces*—bassist Karla Schickele, who also authors two of the recording's finest moments, "Fallen Arrow" and "Poor Dumb Bird." Continuing another Ida tradition, the record is even better than the one which preceded it: *Ten Small Paces* is unspeakably beautiful, a mesmerizing collection of songs marked by a rare intelligence and poignancy. Recorded at various points throughout the country, including His Name Is Alive mastermind Warren Defever's home studio in Michigan, the album maintains a loose, offhand feel perfectly suited to the warmth and intimacy of the group's material; strewn with covers—a superb reading of Neil Young's "Everybody Knows This Is Nowhere" refutes any notion that Ida can't rock out, while their rendition of Brian Eno's "Golden Hours" rejects the assumption that they possess no sense of humor—*Ten Small Paces* is both more understated and more dynamic than any of the band's previous work, stretching from the gentle opening instrumental opener "Hilot" to the bluesy revenge of Elizabeth Mitchell's razor-sharp "Purely Coincidental" with an absolute mastery of texture and mood. —*Jason Ankeny*

Will You Find Me / Jul. 11, 2000 / Tiger Style ✦✦✦✦
The first of two completed albums liberated from the clutches of Capitol in the wake of a recording deal gone bad, *Will You Find Me* projects all the confidence of the major label debut it was intended to be—Ida's most cohesive and haunting album to date, it's also their most direct, articulating the messy entanglements of desire and heartbreak with startling clarity. Although at least five of the album's 14 songs previously appeared on scattered singles and EPs, these new re-recordings benefit enormously from their improved production, uncluttered yet inventive arrangements, and the luminous vocal interplay of Elizabeth Mitchell, Daniel Littleton, and Karla Schickele; similarly, where in the past the group's lyrics sometimes strained too far for poetic resonance, the songs on *Will You Find Me* reveal a new honesty and simplicity—the rising and falling harmonies that conclude "Maybelle," arguably Ida's most singularly beautiful moment on record, communicate emotional depths that transcend language altogether. —*Jason Ankeny*

The Braille Night / Jun. 5, 2001 / Tiger Style ✦✦✦

Ides of March

f. Chicago, IL
Blue-Eyed Soul, Pop/Rock, Psychedelic, Hard Rock

Chicago's Ides of March burst onto the national scene in 1970 with the million-selling single "Vehicle," a tune that bore more than a passing resemblance to the then mega-selling Blood, Sweat & Tears. But the band's pedigree went back further than BS&T's, and with a much different origin. Formed in the mid-1960s in the Windy City, founding member Jim Peterik put the original Ides together as a teen band, strong on original material and British pop harmonies. Soon the band was recording for London's Parrot Records subsidiary, releasing five singles between 1966 and 1967, including the local hit "You Wouldn't Listen." By the late 1960s, however, Peterik had reconfigured the band to include a full horn section, and a new sound and style for the band was born. Ever the crafty commercial songwriter, Peterik fashioned a new single, "Vehicle," to showcase this sound, which mirrored the success of horn rock bands like Chase and Blood, Sweat & Tears. The record was a huge hit, spawning the soundalike follow-up "Superman." The other chart hit for the group (and a complete about-face from the horn-dominated sound of "Vehicle") was the wistful "L.A. Goodbye." Personnel problems and a label shift to RCA-Victor spelled the end of the band as Peterik eased into the 1980s in the role of producer/songwriter, penning several hits for the likes of .38 Special and others. The group re-formed in 1993 to record an album of new material and recuts of their hits going all the way back to "You Wouldn't Listen," and Peterik remains quite active both as a tunesmith and producer. —*Cub Koda*

● **Vehicle** / 1970 / Warner Brothers ✦✦✦✦
The band's first album (they had done five singles for Parrot when they were a Chicago teen band) finds them following the structure of their hit single with much of the music mirroring the then-fashionable horn rock sounds of Blood Sweat & Tears and fellow Windy City jazz rockers Chase. —*Cub Koda*

● **Ideology** / Mar. 28, 2000 / Sundazed ✦✦✦✦
This collection of 1965-1968 material, taken from rare regional singles along with a couple of previously unreleased tracks, is far removed from the Ides of March's horn-rock era (as heard on their 1970 hit "Vehicle"), both chronologically and stylistically. When they started, the Ides were a Chicago teen band, recording mostly original songs heavily influenced by folk-rock and the British Invasion, although a few of these cuts do use brass. In general that's good news (and preferable to the horn-rock of their later career), but the harmony-heavy pop/rock of this early work isn't too exciting. In common with several other groups from the Chicago and Midwest areas, the group favored a rather clean-cut, Americanized take on British Invasion bands like the Beatles and the Hollies, though the folk-rock of the Byrds is heard in the guitar arrangements especially. The local Chicago hits "You Wouldn't Listen" (which made Number 42 nationally) and "Roller Coaster" are here, but to be tough about it, there's not enough light and shade here to put the Ides on the level of good British Invasion bands, or even of good British Invasion-influenced bands from the same region, such as the New Colony Six. More to the point, there's too much light and not enough shade; although the harmonies are fairly impressive and the execution polished, the material is too often sunnily bland. The great exception to that is the riveting, raw folk-rocker "I'll Keep Searching," buried on a B-side, which has great bittersweet melodic hooks, melancholy harmonies, and dramatic stop-start tempos. The disc includes two 1965 songs that they recorded as the Shondels on a super-rare self-released 45, as well as the previously unreleased originals "One and One Does Not Make Three" and "I'll Take You Back." The latter of these, an uncommonly moody tune, is actually a highlight of the collection. —*Richie Unterberger*

The Idle Race

British Psychedelia, Prog-Rock/Art Rock, Psychedelic Pop, Psychedelic
In the history of 1960s British rock, Birmingham was a source of talent virtually in the same league with Liverpool. Although the city never produced a group as big as the Beatles, it was a seething cauldron of musical activity and home to literally hundreds of groups whose activities and memberships were in a constant state of ferment, yielding acts such as the Move, the Moody Blues, and the Electric Light Orchestra, whose influences extended well into the 1970s and beyond. Perhaps the most important of the Birmingham groups that didn't make it to the front rank was the Idle Race. The group occupies a strange focal point in the history of the city's music and, between 1960s and 1970s rock, as a link between Mike Sheridan & the Nightriders, the Move, the Electric Light Orchestra, and the Steve Gibbons Band. The Idle Race itself evolved out of one of the most promising of local early-'60s Birmingham bands, Mike Sheridan & the Nightriders. By the end of 1966, however, they'd begun evolving a new, more ornate sound, vaguely similar to some of the experimental tracks that the Beatles were putting on their albums, only more playful and straightforward; additionally, Jeff Lynne had become the dominant musical personality in the band. A name change seemed in order to go with their new sound, and the result was the Idle Race. In the wake of the group's continued struggle for success, Lynne finally jumped ship at the start of 1970 in favor of joining the Move. Most people, in speaking of the Idle Race, are referring to the group as it existed during the years 1966-1969 with Lynne in the lineup. —*Bruce Eder*

Birthday Party / 1968 / Sunset ✦✦✦✦✦
The debut album by this unjustly overlooked band is a piece of classic British psychedelia that transcends its origins. Most British bands trying to achieve a psychedelic sound in those days simply played softly and sang in a very effete and poetic manner—the Idle Race, by contrast, play hard here and don't sound effete so much as just cheerfully trippy, a lot like the Beatles of "Penny Lane" and "Strawberry Fields Forever." Jeff Lynne is the dominant personality here, as composer, guitarist, and singer, and, as one might expect given his presence, the music all has a Beatles-like quality of playfulness amid the musical invention. As demonstrated here, the Idle Race weren't quite as powerful a band as their rivals the Move—who also loved to cover American soul and folk-rock and, thus,

had a wider variety to their sound—but this album is steeped in beautiful melodies and even prettier embellishments in the singing and playing, yet never loses sight of its rock & roll underpinnings. Once in a while, as in "On With the Show," the sound effects are a little more prominent than one would like, and there's a certain music-hall ambience to a few songs (such as "Lucky Man") that is somewhat distracting—but those two numbers are followed by the joyous and pounding "Pie in the Sky," so it all balances, and overall, this album is very solid and a great deal of fun, as well as full of little surprises and signposts pointing toward Lynne's future. —*Bruce Eder*

Time Is / 1971 / Regal Zonophone ♦♦♦
Time Is is a mixed musical bag, but a surprisingly decent one for most of its length, coming from the remnants of the Idle Race after the departure of its most celebrated member. The post-Jeff Lynne version of the Idle Race is a very different animal from the earlier incarnation of the group—Mike Hopkins and Dave "Richie" Walker provide vocals far removed from Lynne's Lennon-esque stylings, very close in spirit, on "Sad O' Sad," to late acoustic Tyrannosaurus Rex (and, perhaps coincidentally, they were signed to the same label, Regal Zonophone, as that duo), and to Mungo Jerry at other times. Their flute embellishment on various songs gives them a vaguely progressive sound as well; coupled with their basic acoustic guitar sound and harmony singing, this version of the Idle Race and this album also recall the contemporary English act Prelude. Most of what's here is pleasant enough, until the group tries to get self-consciously heavy on "By the Sun," which sounds like a bad imitation of the Doors—the fuzzed out electric guitar may have been intended to draw progressive rock listeners, but it's all been heard before, and better, elsewhere, particularly on the Byrds' "Eight Miles High," which it threatens to imitate at certain points. "Alcatraz" is little better as a high-energy guitar rocker, but those two songs are surrounded by absolutely beautiful acoustic songs. Completists need not fear owning it, and even fans of Lynne's work may enjoy hearing what his bandmates got into after he left for greener musical pastures. —*Bruce Eder*

● **The Best of Idle Race** / 1990 / See For Miles ♦♦♦♦♦
See for Miles' 1990 compilation *The Best of Idle Race* contains a generous 25 tracks—just over half of what the Idle Race recorded. This means that it does have the great majority of the best material the band recorded, and it would satisfy everyone outside of the rabid collectors who need anything. The catch is, if you're into the Idle Race, you need everything, so this collection is essentially a stopgap until you can track down (or afford) EMI's 1996 complete collection, *Back to the Story.* Even then, this may be a little more listenable, since it boils the group's interesting but erratic career to its very best—which is obscure British psych at its best (in other words, it's for the collectors who will seek it out, not anyone else). —*Stephen Thomas Erlewine*

● **Back to the Story** / 1996 / EMI-Premier ♦♦♦♦♦
The Idle Race are a beloved band of British psychedelia collectors, because the music was rare, because the band was Jeff Lynne's first significant group, and because the music was, by and large, very good. There is a bit of a relative judgment there—this is not music that stands among the very best of British pop-psych of the '60s, since it's not as innovative or consistent as the Beatles, Pink Floyd, the Move, or even Tomorrow, but it's certainly among the best of the second tier, as singles like "Impostors of Life's Magazine," "Big Chief Wooly Bosher," and "Girl at the Window" illustrate. Since this band itself is a collectors item, it only makes sense for collectors to seek out EMI Premier's 1996 collection *Back to the Story,* which was only available for a brief period (possibly a matter of months) the year of its release. This is the complete Idle Race, containing the three albums (*Birthday Party, Idle Race, Time Is*), the ten non-album tracks, three previously unreleased alternate versions, and two songs from the Nightriders, Lynne's first band. This is a treasure trove for both British psych and ELO fanatics, and while the best of this is on See For Miles' *The Best of the Idle Race,* the hardcore are going to seek this out. But they will pay a price—just five years after its release, this was going for well over 120 dollars a pop on eBay. Is it worth it? If you have the cash and the inclination—the pure bloodlust to own this, damn the cost!—it probably is, but having that crazed collector mentality will is essentially to shelling out that price. But if it can be found at an affordable price, by all means get it. —*Stephen Thomas Erlewine*

Billy Idol

b. Nov. 30, 1955, Middlesex, England
Vocals / Album Rock, Pop/Rock, New Wave, Hard Rock
Billy Idol represents the bridge between punk rock and hard rock/metal, a logical enough connection that somehow seemed unlikely until he made the transition. Idol left Sussex University in 1976 to join the punk movement, specifically the group of rabid Sex Pistols fans called the Bromley Contingent. Many of the members formed their own bands, and Idol began Generation X with Tony James. Generation X became a moderate success during the punk heyday of the late '70s, especially in England, with Idol on snarling lead vocals.

When the band split in 1981, Idol went to New York and hooked up with manager Bill Aucoin (who had handled Kiss, among others). This resulted in Idol's grooming as more of a mainstream rock figure. His debut album, *Billy Idol,* came out in 1982 and spent two years on the charts as the result of such video hits as "White Wedding" and "Hot in the City." But it was Idol's second album, *Rebel Yell,* that was his big breakthrough, selling two million copies and spawning hits in the raucous title track and the ballad "Eyes Without a Face." Idol followed it up with *Whiplash Smile* in 1986 and *Charmed Life* in 1990.

Idol's first commercial failure came in 1993, with *Cyberpunk,* his stab at techno-influenced rock. —*William Ruhlmann*

Billy Idol / Jul. 1982 / Chrysalis ♦♦♦♦
Billy Idol's self-titled debut album was a snarling take on hard rock, injected with the spite and attitude of punk and new wave. While the record is spotty, Idol pulls it all together on the classic single "White Wedding." —*Stephen Thomas Erlewine*

Rebel Yell / 1983 / Chrysalis ♦♦♦♦
A slick, carefully crafted follow-up to his debut, *Rebel Yell* was Billy Idol's catchiest, most consistent fusion of synth-driven new wave pop and hard rock guitar pyrotechnics (courtesy of Steve Stevens). The eerie ballad "Eyes Without a Face" gave Idol his first U.S. Top Ten hit, while "Flesh for Fantasy" and the title track became MTV staples. Like much of Idol's solo output, it's all calculated for maximum appeal, but *Rebel Yell* also works too well not to be an infectiously guilty pleasure. —*Steve Huey*

Whiplash Smile / 1986 / Chrysalis ♦♦♦
While *Whiplash Smile* is Idol's most ambitious album, it only comes to life on hard-rocking pseudo-rockabilly like "To Be a Lover." Unfortunately, there aren't many songs that are as good as that single on this album. —*Stephen Thomas Erlewine*

Vital Idol / Sep. 1987 / Chrysalis ♦♦
Vital Idol is a sort of remixed greatest-hits collection, gathering some of Billy Idol's best tracks and extending them all past the five-minute mark. It doesn't really work as a hits collection, since it's missing key songs like "Rebel Yell" and "Eyes Without a Face," and most of the dance remixes are repetitious and uninteresting compared to the originals. It's most worthwhile for "Dancing With Myself" and the live hit version of "Mony Mony," both of which appeared in their original Idol versions on the *Don't Stop* EP. —*Steve Huey*

Charmed Life / 1990 / Chrysalis ♦♦♦♦
Like any Billy Idol album, *Charmed Life* is wildly inconsistent, but it has enough strong songs—like the gloriously tongue-in-cheek hard rock of "Cradle of Love"—to make most of the filler on the record forgivable. —*Stephen Thomas Erlewine*

Cyberpunk / Jun. 29, 1993 / Chrysalis ♦

● **Greatest Hits** / Mar. 27, 2001 / Capitol ♦♦♦♦
Billy Idol's recording career did such a fast fade in the early '90s that his beleaguered record label Chrysalis (since absorbed by Capitol) didn't even put out a best-of in the U.S. (*Idol Songs: 11 of the Best* was an interim report issued in Great Britain in 1988.) But the rise of the '80s rock radio format and Idol's own interest in a comeback make this belated hits collection timely. With one caveat, it is a well-chosen collection of the singer's most successful recordings. The exception, oddly enough, is his biggest hit, "Mony Mony," which is presented in a 1983 studio version rather than the 1987 live take that topped the charts. (The annotations claim "This version was never released as a single." Actually, it was—as Chrysalis 2543—but it flopped.) Otherwise, all of Idol's big hits are here, among them "Cradle of Love," "Eyes Without a Face," "To Be a Lover," "Rebel Yell," and "White Wedding," each of which reached the Top Ten on one side of the Atlantic or the other. Also included are an "unplugged" live version of "Rebel Yell" and a newly recorded cover of the 1985 Simple Minds hit "Don't You (Forget About Me)," which was co-written by Idol's producer, Keith Forsey. The only omitted chart singles are "Prodigal Blues," a track from Idol's unsuccessful 1993 album *Cyberpunk,* and "Speed," the title song from the 1994 film; both missed the American pop charts. In his day, Idol seemed to some a commercial sell-out of the punk ideal, having abandoned Generation X for a slicker image and sound. In retrospect, he seems more like a logical successor to the kind of portentous baritones who preceded him, particularly Jim Morrison and David Bowie, while Forsey's new wave/disco sound, anchored by guitarist Steve Stevens, holds up well. —*William Ruhlmann*

Natalie Imbruglia

b. Feb. 4, 1975, Sydney, Australia
Adult Alternative Pop/Rock
By mixing Lisa Loeb/Alanis Morissette-like singing with music that sounds similar to a more mainstream Portishead at times, Natalie Imbruglia has become one of the biggest pop sensations in Europe. Born in Sydney, Australia on February 4, 1975, Imbruglia was one of four sisters and grew up in a tiny beach town. After becoming a teen actress and landing a spot on the Australian soap opera *Neighbours,* Imbruglia decided that she would rather be a singer, and moved to London in 1996 to try her luck. It was a wise move, as she was soon signed to the RCA U.K. label. Deciding to release a single before her full-length debut, the track "Torn" was issued in 1997, and no one could have predicted its wild success. Produced and written by former Cure member Phil Thornalley, the single spent a total of 14 weeks at number one, sold over a millon copies, and broke the record for most airplay in U.K. history. Her debut album, *Left of the Middle,* was a major hit in Australia, the U.K., and the U.S. upon its release in early 1998. —*Greg Prato*

● **Left of the Middle** / Mar. 10, 1998 / RCA ♦♦♦♦
Expectations for Natalie Imbruglia's debut album *Left of the Middle* were high because of the runaway success of the pre-album single "Torn" during 1997-1998. Fans of the single will be pleased to hear that the album is quite similar in approach and sound to the breakthrough single: laid-back alterna-pop with sweetly melodic vocals. Admittedly, some of the material will be seen as pop fluff by certain listeners, but fans of popular latter-day female artists like Paula Cole, Sheryl Crow, and Meredith Brooks will find Imbruglia's debut most enjoyable. What separates Imbruglia from the aforementioned artists is her willingness to experiment with electronic sounds, no doubt courtesy of mixer Nigel Godrich (of Radiohead fame), which can be heard on such tracks as "Smoke." "Torn" proves to be the best song on the album, with its bouncy acoustic feel, but the pop/rocker "Big Mistake" is almost as good. Not all of the material on *Left of the Middle* fairs as well, however, such as the Alanis Morissette sound-alike "Intuition," but Natalie Imbruglia need not worry about being lumped into the copycat category; for the most part, she has a style all her own. —*Greg Prato*

The Impacts

f. 1961, **db.** 1966

Surf, Rock & Roll

Before beginning his career as a vocalist and songwriter, the multi-faceted Merrell Fankhauser was the lead guitarist of surf group the Impacts. He has repeatedly claimed in interviews that they recorded the original version of "Wipe Out," only to have the song and arrangement stolen by the Surfaris, who had a huge hit with it in 1963. The Impacts didn't get any hits themselves, but they did manage to release a respectable instrumental surf album on Del-Fi in 1962, as well as a few tracks on obscure compilation samplers issued in the early '60s. *—Richie Unterberger*

Wipe Out / 1962 / Del-Fi ♦♦♦

OK surf instrumentals, ranging from stompers to tropical-flavored slow tunes. Has some steel guitar, dirty sax, and the occasional hot lead (from Fankhauser), but nothing attains classic status. The version of "Wipe Out" is substantially different from (and not as good as) The Surfaris', featuring a saxophone and a raunchier feel. *—Richie Unterberger*

● **Desert Island Treasures** / Feb. 25, 1997 / Bacchus ♦♦♦♦♦

Desert Island Treasures collects the earliest recordings of veteran California guitarist Merrell Fankhauser with his surf band the Impacts and beat group Merrell and the Exiles. Both groups are excellent representatives of their given styles; the Impacts (circa 1963) were a tight surf unit with ripping sax and wild guitar, while the Exiles' material, recorded between 1964 and 1965, has a harder edge than many popular American groups attempting a British Invasion sound. Exiles guitarist Jeff Cotton would go on to play with Captain Beefheart before rejoining Fankhauser in the early-'70s band Mu. The music of Merrell Fankhauser is absolutely essential to any American '60s rock collection, be it these groups or his later psychedelic folk rock with Fapardokly and H.M.S. Bounty or progressive rock with Mu. *—Jim Powers*

Imperial Teen

Punk-Pop, Post-Grunge, Alternative Pop/Rock

Led by former Faith No More keyboardist Roddy Bottum, the alternative pop band Imperial Teen emerged from San Francisco in 1994; co-founded with drummer Lynn Perko, a veteran of Bay Area groups like the Dicks and Sister Double Happiness, the lineup was completed by former Wrecks bassist Jone Stebbings and vocalist Will Schwartz. Debuting in 1996 with the critical favorite *Seasick*, Imperial Teen resurfaced in early 1999 with *What Is Not to Love*. *—Jason Ankeny*

Seasick / 1996 / Slash/London ♦♦♦

Seasick, the first album from Faith No More keyboardist Roddy Bottum's side project Imperial Teen crosses the sexy groove of glam rock with fizzy pop melodies, slamming, noisy grunge, and off-kilter hooks. Imperial Teen's strongest attribute is the sleekness of their sound—though it's loud, it has style, which adds weight to the sometimes incomplete songs. Even with its weaknesses, *Seasick* is refreshing because it uses its dissonance with style and it works in gay lyrical themes without making homosexuality the end-all-be-all of their music, the way that queercore bands like Pansy Division do. *—Stephen Thomas Erlewine*

● **What Is Not to Love** / 1999 / Slash ♦♦♦♦

Imperial Teen's debut album, *Seasick*, was a very critically successful set of indie-pop, and it was an album that many felt would be hard to replicate. Replicate, however, is exactly what Imperial Teen does with their second album, *What Is Not to Love*. Every bit as strong as their debut, *What Is Not To Love* finds Imperial Teen avoiding a critical sophomore slump by sticking strongly to their formula and returning with a strong batch of songs. This time around the band has more pop emphasis and stronger tunes, for the most part, although there is a bit more of a dark, biting edge. The first single, "Yoo Hoo," may sound very similar to "You're One" (from *Seasick*) at first glance, but "Yoo Hoo" is much more tense, and the vocals have a much angrier, biting tone. This change in attitude is representative of much of *What Is Not to Love*, but it's far from a negative change. Other high points include the sarcastic gender bending pop gem "Lipstick," and the mellow, brooding "Crucible." *What Is Not to Love* shows that Imperial Teen is not merely a side project for former Faith No More keyboardist Roddy Bottum, but rather a notable band in their own right. *—Jason Damas*

The Impressions

f. 1958, Chicago, IL, **db.** 1983

Chicago Soul, Uptown Soul, Pop-Soul, Northern Soul, Soul

The first Impressions hit, "For Your Precious Love," was an anachronism when released in 1958. Jerry Butler's robust, yearning vocal was a throwback to deep-South gospel, and Curtis Mayfield's arrangement was decidedly barebones. But this song also precipitated the changes coming in R&B; you can hear the groundwork for soul music being laid, from the melisma of Butler's phrasing to Mayfield's skeletal guitar. The song literally flew in the face of then-popular doo wop formulas. Butler left the group in 1960, but the pared-down trio, led by Mayfield, cut a path that altered the R&B map. Mayfield's high falsetto and the trade-off vocals of Fred Cash and Sam Gooden framed a new kind of R&B: smooth and graceful, at times lilting, soaked in the history of gospel, and, thanks to Mayfield's lyrical examinations of racism and urban decay, the catalyst for the wave of socially aware black hits recorded in the '70s. The group's hits varied from supple statements of affirmation ("It's All Right," "People Get Ready") and romantic declarations ("Talking About My Baby," "I'm So Proud") to songs that were sociopolitical ("Choice of Colors," "This Is My Country") or mystical ("Gypsy Woman"). Their chart run ended by the late '60s, as did Mayfield's Midas touch; after recording the brilliant *Superfly* in 1972, his talents ran dry. Nonetheless, Mayfield's reputation as one of soul's supreme innovators cannot be exaggerated. *—John Floyd*

The Impressions / 1963 / Paramount ♦♦♦♦♦

A landmark soul date, one of The Impressions' finest albums. They showed once and for all that they would succeed as a trio, and also revealed to any who weren't aware Curtis Mayfield's brilliance as a composer. The hits came pouring out of Mayfield in the mid-'60s, and "It's All Right" was just the first of many gems he would write, produce, sing the lead vocals on, and arrange. A fabulous album. *—Ron Wynn*

Keep on Pushing / 1964 / Paramount ♦♦♦

Curtis Mayfield & the Impressions' "Keep on Pushing" came out during the height of the civil rights movement. The loping, beautiful classic perfectly captures the sense of the era in a straightforward, captivating way. It went to number ten R&B on Billboard's charts in summer 1964 and received airplay on pop and gospel stations. Similarly in theme and tone to "Keep on Pushing," and the group's 1965 hit "People Get Ready," Isley/Jasper/Isley's "Caravan of Love," topped the R&B charts in fall 1985, another testimony to Mayfield's influence. The follow-up was the catch "You Must Believe Me." Another inspiring hit to come from the *Keep on Pushing* LP was the group's rousing cover of "Amen." It was included in the movie *Lillies of the Field* starring Sidney Poitier for which the actor made history by being the first black man to win an Oscar. Its flip side was "Long, Long Winter," which perfectly captures the forlornness of being lonely during a winter in Chicago or anywhere else. Other standouts are the buoyant "Talking About My Baby," "I Thank Heaven," and delicious "I Love You (Yeah)," both of which received radio play as LP tracks; this was very usual in the '60s. Featuring arrangements by Johnny Pate, the *Keep on Pushing* LP was paired with the *People Get Ready* LP on the excellent 1996 single CD *Keep on Pushing/People Get Ready* from U.K. label Kent Records. *—Ed Hogan*

One by One / 1965 / Paramount ♦♦♦♦♦

The Impressions continued a great run of hit singles and fine albums with this outstanding release, one of three that were issued on ABC in 1965. The structure by now was both fixed and marvelous; songs revolved around Mayfield's leads, superb production and arrangements, guitar licks and riffs anchoring the backdrop, and Fred Cash and Sam Gooden interacting with Mayfield on the choruses, bridges, and turnarounds. *—Ron Wynn*

The Complete Vee-Jay Recordings / Nov. 22, 1993 / Vee-Jay ♦♦♦♦♦

The Impressions' early music has taken a back seat to what they did after Jerry Butler departed and Mayfield began doing the lead vocals, writing, producing, and arranging. This excellent 18-track disc helps put the early years into focus, with Butler showcased on seven cuts and Mayfield on eight. The Impressions weren't a bad five-member harmony unit; they just were not a great one in an era when you had to be fantastic simply to break out of the pack. These are mostly nice love songs, and they aren't lyrically different from thousands of similar tracks, but they did deserve a better fate than to be dropped from the Vee-Jay label in 1959. *—Ron Wynn*

Keep on Pushing/People Get Ready / Mar. 19, 1996 / Kent ♦♦♦♦♦

Two good Impressions albums from the mid-'60s, combined onto one CD, making them handier to collect in this fashion than hunting down good-quality copies of the rare original vinyl editions. As usual, the singles ("Keep on Pushing," "People Get Ready," "Amen," "I've Been Trying," "Woman's Got Soul," "You Must Believe Me") overshadow the LP-only cuts. But the Impressions made a higher standard of albums than most '60s soul groups, investing a lot of care in the songwriting and production, making this a decent pickup for those who want to go beyond the greatest-hits anthologies. *—Richie Unterberger*

This Is My Country/The Young Mods' Forgotten Story / Apr. 24, 1996 / Sequel ♦♦♦♦♦

Two fine late-'60s albums, combined onto one CD, including some hits and a wealth of good overlooked Mayfield compositions that touched on sensitive racial issues as well as romance. Offering excellent value, the CD is a recommended alternative to tracking down the hard-to-find original vinyl editions. *—Richie Unterberger*

Further Impressions / Jul. 1996 / Hip-O ♦♦♦♦

Featuring a selection of 14 songs making their compact disc debut, *Further Impressions: More Soulful Classics* fills in the gaps left by the single-disc MCA *Greatest Hits* collection and the more comprehensive double-disc anthology. Only four R&B hits are present, but the remaining ten songs are all first-rate album tracks that are nearly equal in quality. *Further Impressions* doesn't overlap at all with MCA's two previous Impressions sets, so it is a necessary addition to any fan's CD library. *—Stephen Thomas Erlewine*

Check Out Your Mind!/Times Have Changed / Dec. 17, 1996 / Sequel ♦♦♦

Sequel's *Check Out Your Mind/Times Have Changed* combines two albums the Impressions recorded for Curtom Records in 1970 and 1972, respectively. These albums have their moments and are quite attractive to fans of the smooth, funky sound of Philly soul in the early '70s, but they're too uneven to be recommended unconditionally. *—Stephen Thomas Erlewine*

★ **The Very Best of the Impressions** / Feb. 4, 1997 / Rhino ♦♦♦♦♦

A good 16-track anthology for the moderate Impressions fans, sticking to their most famous smashes—"Gypsy Woman," "It's All Right," "Keep on Pushing," "Amen," "People Get Ready," "We're a Winner," "Choice of Colors," "Check Out Your Mind," and so forth. Most of it's from the '60s, but it does end with three hits from the mid-'70s, after Mayfield's departure from the group. *—Richie Unterberger*

One by One/Ridin' High / Jun. 23, 1998 / Kent ♦♦♦

A two-for-one combination of two mid-1960s LPs on one compact disc. *One by One* is a misstep that was not uncommon among soul stars in the '60s: the record is dedicated almost entirely to standards such as "Twilight Time," "I Wanna Be Around," "Nature Boy," and "Mona Lisa." The strategy was to widen their appeal to a more adult pop audience, but supperclub ballads are not what you turn to the Impressions (or for that matter, any soul stars) for, and the album sounds mediocre decades later, with the expected syrupy big-band orchestration. Sam Gooden and Fred Cash take leads on one unmemorable song each; the three Curtis Mayfield-penned numbers, in bold contrast, are more soulful and understated, particularly the dramatically arranged "Just One Kiss From You." *Ridin' High* is a much more palatable kettle of fish, as Mayfield wrote almost all of the tunes and the production was back-to-business, straight-ahead Chicago soul. It's a bit of a treadmill affair as some of the songs had been previously recorded by Billy Butler, Major Lance, and Jerry Butler, but it's still quality ebullient music with fine leads and harmonies, exemplified by the small hit "I Need You." "Gotta Get Away," previously done by Billy Butler, and the sassy "Too Slow" are other highlights of a pretty solid album. *—Richie Unterberger*

Fabulous Impressions/We're a Winner / Sep. 29, 1998 / Kent ✦✦✦✦✦
A reissue that combines 1967's *The Fabulous Impressions* and 1968's *We're a Winner* onto one CD. Although *The Fabulous Impressions* was a solid enough soul record on its own merits, it's not one of the more notable entries in the Impressions' catalog. There aren't any big hits, although a couple cuts, "You Always Hurt Me" and "I Can't Stay Away From You," were modest R&B charters. At times it seemed that Mayfield was trying to follow in Motown's footsteps, as on "You Always Hurt Me" and "You Ought to Be in Heaven." "It's All Over" is the Impressions' version of a song that had already been a hit for Walter Jackson, and the cover of Gene McDaniels' "One Hundred Pounds of Clay" (the only selection not written by Mayfield) is filler. The above comments might lead you to believe this album is worse than it actually is; it's dependable, enjoyable, quality soul, with "Isle of Sirens" recalling earlier efforts like "Gypsy Woman" and "She Don't Love Me" offering a chunkier and tougher approach than their typical heartfelt optimism. While the title track of *We're a Winner* was one of Mayfield's classic civil rights-conscious anthems, most of this album was actually dedicated to standard romantic themes. Almost every cut was a quality Mayfield original, and the harmonies and vocal interplay among the group were outstanding. "Nothing Can Stop Me," which had been a hit in 1965 for Gene Chandler, was an up-tempo highlight, and "Little Brown Boy" showed more of the African-American pride that had been explored in "We're a Winner," albeit in a more tender ballad mode. The closing cover of "Up Up and Away" is misplaced, but overall this is one of the better Impressions albums to pick up if you want more than what's found on the greatest-hits collections. *—Richie Unterberger*

The ABC Rarities / Jun. 8, 1999 / Kent ✦✦✦
Twenty-six song compilation of non-LP singles, rarities that only showed up on obscure reissues and various-artists collections, and material (both released and unreleased) from their sessions for their late-'60s *The Versatile Impressions* album. As a listen it's a little uneven, due in large part to the over-preponderance of standards from *Versatile*. None of this is on level with the best '60s recordings by Mayfield and the Impressions. Much of it, though, is the fairly solid sort of stuff that fans who care enough about the act to go beyond greatest-hits compilations will like to have. Actually, some of these were not terribly obscure; "Never Could You Be" was a small R&B hit in the mid-'60s, and "We're Rolling On (Pts. 1 & 2)" was a small pop entry in 1968, as was the 1968 antiwar ballad "Don't Cry My Love" (written by Mayfield with jazz singer Oscar Brown Jr.). Oddities from the *Versatile* LP include the two lushly orchestrated songs they did for the *East of Java* soundtrack. However, much of the *Versatile* period is unsuitably pop in both material and production for the Impressions, although "Sermonette" and the previously unreleased "Devil in Your Soul" eschew that approach for some pretty gutsy, bluesy soul. *—Richie Unterberger*

● **Indelible Impressions** / Jun. 20, 2000 / Sequel ✦✦✦✦✦
This two-disc, 45-song CD represents the most comprehensive overview of the post-ABC/Paramount Records Impressions on the market. Curtom Records issued 24 Impressions singles from 1968 to 1976, and this double CD includes everything except their debut special product Yuletide single, "Merry Xmas, Happy New Year," and some B-sides omitted in favor of some album cuts. Tight productions, good songs, and an ever-changing lineup keep the listening appeal at a high level. The varying lineups were Curtis Mayfield, Sam Gooden, and Fred Cash; Leroy Hutson, Gooden, and Cash; Reggie Torian, Gooden, and Cash; Torian, Gooden, Cash, and Ralph Johnson; Torian, Gooden, Cash, and Nate Evans; and the final set, Cash, Gooden, and Torian. Checkered standouts include "Fool for You," "Check Out Your Mind," "I'm Loving Nothing," "Same Thing It Took," "Finally Got Myself Together," and "I Wish I'd Stayed in Bed." *—Andrew Hamilton*

The Incredible String Band

f. 1965, **db.** 1974
British Folk-Rock, British Folk, Folk-Rock, Psychedelic
The Incredible String Band were one of the most engaging groups to emerge from the esoteric '60s. Comprising the duo of Mike Heron and Robin Williamson, its sound was haunting Celtic folk melodies augmented by a variety of Middle Eastern and Asian instruments. After signing to the British wing of Elektra Records, the group's 1966 eponymous debut featured mostly original numbers enthusiastically played in American and Celtic folk styles. For the String Band's second album, *The 5000 Spirits or the Layers of the Onion*, exotic touches such as the Middle Eastern oud or Indian sitars and tambouras began to permeate the Incredibles' sound. Their next album *The Hangman's Beautiful Daughter* was the band's brief flirtation with stardom. Although the music was less commercial than its predecessor, it reached the Top Ten in the British album charts and was also the group's highest *Billboard* chart placing in America, reaching Number 161. An electrically amplified lineup performed at the Woodstock Festival in 1969, though the group began to lose its momentum in the early '70s. The band made the transition to electric rock & roll in 1972, but broke up in 1974, following the album *Hard Rope and Silken Twine*. Both founding members later began prolific solo careers, Heron's taking him in a rock direction, while Williamson explored his Celtic roots. *—Jim Powers*

The Incredible String Band / 1966 / Elektra ✦✦✦
As much a showcase for individual performances as group ones, the ISB's debut was their most traditional effort, though Williamson and Heron modernized traditional British Isles music with their whimsical songwriting and vari-pitch vocals. It also has minor contributions from guitarist Clive Palmer, who would leave the group after this album. *—Richie Unterberger*

5,000 Spirits or the Layers of The Onion / 1967 / Hannibal ✦✦✦✦✦
For their second album, the ISB officially reduced to the duo of Mike Heron and Robin Williamson. Lumped in with the psychedelic movement, that categorization was probably more due to the trippy cover graphics, the occasional Indian influences, and the whimsical, sometimes fantasy-ridden lyrical images than the music. It's more like a slightly cosmic version of traditional British folk than psychedelic rock. Although their next album, *The Hangman's Beautiful Daughter*, is usually considered their most adventurous, some listeners may find this to be the more accessible effort. It also featured what is probably Williamson's best-known song, "First Girl I Loved" (also familiar via Judy Collins' cover version, "First Boy I Loved"). *—Richie Unterberger*

● **Hangman's Beautiful Daughter** / 1968 / Hannibal ✦✦✦✦✦
The ISB's most ambitious album, with Williamson and Heron employing an arsenal of unusual instruments (sitar, gimbri, pan pipe, oud, chahanai, and more), and Dolly Collins adding a couple of the more dignified arrangements. It's usually considered their most important effort by critics, but there were also traces of the sprawling, occasionally grating lack of focus that would increasingly come to characterize their work. *—Richie Unterberger*

Relics of the Incredible String Band / 1970 / Elektra ✦✦✦✦✦
The ISB's prolific output makes a compilation a virtual necessity, and this two-record set selects wisely from the seven albums the group released in the U.S. between 1967 and 1970. From Robin Williamson's "First Girl I Loved" (covered by Judy Collins) and "Way Back in the 1960s" (recorded in 1967), to Mike Heron's "Air," and "This Moment," the ISB's eclectic, fanciful acoustic style is well portrayed. *— William Ruhlmann*

No Ruinous Feud / 1973 / Edsel ✦✦✦
The ISB began to change its approach in 1971, cutting back on its sometimes open-ended song structures and adding a rock rhythm section to selected tracks. But it wasn't until this album that everything came together, resulting in a delightful collection of songs that range from reggae to light pop, along with the traditional folk styles that had always been the group's strong suit. *— William Ruhlmann*

Wee Tam/The Big Huge / Oct. 18, 1994 / Hannibal ✦✦✦✦
Mixing English and American folk with what we now call "world music," the multi-instrumental Scottish duo of Robin Williamson and Mike Heron achieve a whimsical, delicate style that has never been duplicated. It reaches a peak here with such songs as "You Get Brighter." (*Wee Tam* is sometimes packaged with the simultaneously released *The Big Huge*, which is also recommended.) *— William Ruhlmann*

Chelsea Sessions 1967 / Oct. 7, 1997 / Resurgent ✦✦✦
These 13 demos were recorded in early 1967 shortly before the making of the ISB's second album, *The 5,000 Spirits or the Layers of the Onion* (though the liner notes speculate that "God Dog" might date from later than the other tracks). Only six of these actually showed up on *5,000 Spirits*, albeit in different, more produced versions; in fact, most of Robin Williamson's compositions on this release are performed solo by the writer. This gives fans a chance to hear the tracks (including their most famous song, "The First Girl I Loved") in acoustic, folkier incarnations, with slightly different lyrics on a couple of tunes. Of the remaining songs, "Lover Man" was recorded by Al Stewart on his debut album, "God Dog" by Shirley Collins in 1969, and "The Iron Stone" by ISB themselves on 1968's *Wee Tam and the Big Huge* album, while the others are unique to this disc. This unused material (the fidelity throughout is good, by the way) is both stylistically consistent and aesthetically up to par with what the ISB were recording on their early albums, and thus recommended to fans of the group. *—Richie Unterberger*

Indigo Girls

f. 1985, Decatur, GA
College Rock, Adult Alternative Pop/Rock, Singer/Songwriter
While they came into prominence as part of the late-'80s folky-singer/songwriter revival, the Indigo Girls have had staying power where other artists from the same era quickly faded. Their two-women-with-guitars formula may not seem very revolutionary on paper, but the combination of two distinct personalities and songwriting styles provides a tension and an interesting balance—Emily Saliers, hailing from the more traditional Joni Mitchell school, has the gentler sound, is more complex musically, and often leans toward the abstract and spiritual while Amy Ray draws heavily from the singer/songwriter aspects of punk rock for her more abrasive and direct approach. In more than a decade of recording, they have managed respectable mainstream success as well as keeping their rabid core following. Their eponymous national debut, released in 1989, gave them initial college radio credibility and the single "Closer to Fine" became a hit—the album eventually broke the Top 30 and earned a Grammy for Best Folk Recording that year. Though the follow-up, 1990's *Nomads Indians Saints*, didn't fare quite as well, the Indigo Girls made a comeback with 1992's *Rites of Passage*, which debuted at number 22 and went platinum by year's end. Almost exactly two years later, *Swamp Ophelia* was released and entered the charts at number nine. *—Chris Woodstra*

Strange Fire / 1987 / Epic/Legacy ✦✦✦

Strange Fire, the Indigo Girls' debut album, was re-released after their next album *Indigo Girls* hit big on college radio in 1989. The beautiful harmonies of college friends Amy Ray and Emily Saliers was immediately apparent on this album, the two-girls-with-guitars format felt like a breath of fresh air from a musical city (Athens, GA) known more for alternative acts such as the B-52's and R.E.M. Although most of the songs featured both women's voices complementing one another, it is clear that the songwriting came from two distinct sources. Emily Saliers, a talented guitarist, generally sings introspective songs in the tradition of folkies such as Joni Mitchell, whereas Amy Ray, whose influences include harder-edged acts such as Hüsker Dü, sings with a rare intensity only matched by the heavy strumming of her acoustic guitar. At this stage, the Indigo Girls are still developing and their lyrics suffer in comparison to their future efforts, which perhaps explains why the fiery, upbeat, and passionate songs of Amy Ray work better than the spare, mellow songs of Emily Saliers. They perform a cover of the Youngblood's "Get Together" that is every bit as good as the original, and their closing song "Land of Canaan" is a concert favorite. A must-own for fans, but casual listeners should start with their sophomore effort. — *Vik Iyengar*

● **Indigo Girls** / 1989 / Epic/Legacy ✦✦✦✦✦

With their first major label release, the Indigo Girls come on strong with an outstanding batch of tunes, watertight harmonies, impeccable musicianship, and flawless production. And entering the folk-rock music scene on the successful heels of R.E.M., Tracy Chapman, and 10,000 Maniacs pushed their sales over the million mark and earned the duo a Grammy for Best Folk Recording. The eponymous release kicks off with the upbeat jangle bounce of "Closer to Fine," a modest hit, all-time fan favorite written by Emily Saliers, and a tune the Girls still play at every concert. A particularly fascinating point is that the Indigo Girls never write songs together, but they compliment each other perfectly. The difference in styles becomes immediately apparent when the more dark and brooding Amy Ray steps up. Her remarkable contributions include "Secure Yourself," "Kid Fears," and "Blood and Fire," spiritual ruminations of life, love, pain, and faith which bury themselves deep inside your core whether invited or not. Weighting the opposite scales, Saliers offers a tender balance to Ray with two beautiful ballads, "Love's Recovery" and "History of Us." (Ray's "Land of Canaan" was once a ballad, but then she heard the Replacements and it became a bit of a rocker.) Chiming in with musical support are Hothouse Flowers, Luka Bloom, and fellow Georgians R.E.M. This self-titled release captures the passion of their youth with voices that are a little cloudy, untamed, and raw, but the power that surges through them suggests a maturity far beyond their years. The same can be said of the songwriting—sheer poetry. To attempt examinations of these songs would not do them justice, for the layers of meaning and emotion unfold best upon repeated listening. — *Kelly McCartney*

Nomads Indians Saints / Sep. 1990 / Epic ✦✦✦✦✦

Following the success of their 1989 debut and the reissue of the previously independent *Strange Fire*, the Indigo Girls answered with another Grammy-nominated offering. *Nomads Indians Saints* shows Emily Saliers and Amy Ray in fine form, delving a little deeper into the themes of love and faith that run through all of their work. Now that they've had the chance to travel around, see the world, and hear people's stories, their poetic vision has expanded somewhat to include a more global perspective, but without losing the intimacy that makes their songs so potent. The title of the record is lifted from "World Falls"—"I wish I was a nomad, an Indian, or a saint./Give me walking shoes, feathered arms, and a key to Heaven's gate"—Ray's exploration of the world's captivating beauty and her options in hopes of avoiding departure—aka the moment of death. Beguiling stuff this is. The catchy melodies allow you to sing along without thinking too much, but should you choose to dive in further they give you plenty to work with. The powerful metaphors of our individual and societal conditions Ray sets forth in "Pushing the Needle Too Far" should certainly not go unnoticed, nor should any of the songs on *Nomads Indians Saints*, including Saliers' "You and Me of the 10,000 Wars," a heart-wrenching examination of the pain and comfort of a relationship. One without the other is all but impossible to achieve and would feel almost hollow without its reflection. That's the way it is with the Indigo Girls—perfect harmony between the elements. — *Kelly McCartney*

Live: Back on the Bus Y'all / Jun. 4, 1991 / Epic ✦✦

Rites of Passage / Feb. 1992 / Epic ✦✦✦✦

Though not what you'd call polished or slick, *Rites of Passage* introduces a sound and structure that are a touch more refined than previous albums by Indigo Girls. Thanks to producer Peter Collins and a slew of amazing guests, including Jackson Browne, David Crosby, the Roches, and Lisa Germano, the added harmonies and diverse instrumentation put on a whole other spin. Heck, they even tossed in strings arranged and conducted by Michael Kamen. But lest you think otherwise, the songs themselves are pure Indigo Girls. One of the threads that runs through tunes by both Amy Ray and Emily Saliers seems to center around what it takes to be a good, kind person in this world, to do the right thing even in the face of danger or at all costs. Both women also express humility and reverence for a power greater than themselves, be it a cause, a god, a love, a fear, or a poet. Vocally, their harmonies have never been cleaner and clearer than on songs like Saliers' "Love Will Come to You" and "Virginia Woolf." And, naturally, Ray's fiery passion rears its head on "Jonas and Ezekial," "Joking," and "Chickenman." The Girls continue to be two of the most literate, engaging, and important songwriters in the folk-rock scene as they tackle issues ranging from Native American awareness to governmental misdoing. No misfires here, just a steady shot echoing forth. — *Kelly McCartney*

Swamp Ophelia / May 10, 1994 / Epic ✦✦✦

Amy Ray and Emily Saliers continue to hone their signature lush melodies on their sixth studio effort, *Swamp Ophelia*. Reflecting back to their pioneering singer/songwriting days of the late '80s and early '90s, this album is confident in the face of the male-dominated music industry and the Indigo Girls are no longer afraid to hit upon past relationships and personal emotion. Saliers and Ray's incredible harmonies are most stylish and songs such as "Language of the Kiss" and "Touch Me Fall" are illustriously romantic and serene. "Least Complicated" is vocally enchanting, layering bongos and percussion to make this cut an album standout. Their choir-like unison allows their vocal power to carry them through the entire record, but accompanying musicians, such as Lisa Germano (mandolin, violin), Canadian songstress Jane Siberry, and cellist Jane Scarpantoni, also make *Swamp Ophelia* more pleasurable. But the duo also move beyond the sweet and tender by dipping into darker realms, especially on "Dead Man's Hill." Their earthy voices creep along the haunting tom-toms to provoke another musical side. This album is another humanistic effort from the Indigo Girls' deep and indwelling passions and ideas. This release molds the beauty of what's yet to come. — *MacKenzie Wilson*

1200 Curfews / Oct. 24, 1995 / Epic ✦✦✦✦

1200 Curfews is a double live album recorded on the *Swamp Ophelia* tour from 1994 to 1995, covering the duo's best loved songs as well as some inspired covers of classics from Bob Dylan, Neil Young, and Joni Mitchell. And while this is obviously directed at the Indigo Girls' insatiable cult following, even casual fans will find the album engaging since the live performances are often more spirited and direct than the studio versions. — *Chris Woodstra*

Shaming of the Sun / Apr. 29, 1997 / Epic ✦✦✦

Shaming of the Sun isn't a great leap forward for the Indigo Girls, and in many ways, it raises more questions than any of their records. Retreating from the elaborate production of *Swamp Ophelia*, the Indigos rely on their trademark folky, singer-songwriter style, and while that certainly sounds pleasant, it's beginning to sound formulaic by this stage in the game. In fact, many of the songs come across as filler, albeit expertly performed filler. And that raises the question of whether the Indigo Girls have run out of ideas, or have merely hit a vicious slump. Unfortunately, *Shaming of the Sun* suggests the former. — *Thom Owens*

Come on Now Social / Sep. 28, 1999 / Epic ✦✦✦✦

Indigo Girls had sort of boxed themselves into the corner during the late '90s. They had become pop culture icons, as known for their politics as their music. Unfortunately, being in such a position meant their music had gotten a little stale, as the good but predictable *Shaming of the Sun* illustrated. The duo seized the opportunity to experiment and redefine their music with 1999's *Come on Now Social*. Amy Ray and Emily Saliers invited a host of guest musicians—including Sheryl Crow, Joan Osborne, Me'Shell Ndegeocello, Natacha Atlas, Sinéad O'Connor's backing band Ghostland, the Band's Garth Hudson, and Luscious Jackson's Kate Schellenbach—to contribute to their most eclectic set of songs to date. Yes, they had a full, even prog-rock sound on *Swamp Opheila*, but the Indigos tackle a number of different styles on *Come On Now*. "Go" opens the album in a roar, rocking harder than anything Indigo Girls have yet recorded, but it only sets the pace for the rest of the album in that it offers a departure. From that point on, the duo tries on other styles; they don't abandon the folk-rock that made their name, but they add straight-ahead rock & roll, old timey folk, modern country, and, in the case of the wonderful single "Peace Tonight," pop-soul. Not only are the different styles welcome, but the songwriting is strong and the performances revitalized. Indigo Girls never went away, but it's the highest compliment to be paid to *Come On Now Social* to say that it feels like a fully realized comeback. — *Stephen Thomas Erlewine*

● **Retrospective** / Oct. 3, 2000 / Epic/Legacy ✦✦✦✦✦

The Indigo Girls' 1999 album *Come on Now Social* was their first commercial failure after six consecutive gold or platinum albums. The appearance of the duo's first domestic compilation a year later is an unavoidably ominous sign, as their label takes its profits while it can. But that's no reason not to celebrate Amy Ray and Emily Saliers' remarkable run of high-quality recordings dating back to 1987's *Strange Fire*. Most of the songs with which they are most readily identified are included, among them the two chart singles "Closer to Fine" and "Galileo." (The only missing title that earned significant airplay is "Hammer and a Nail.") Feminist author Susan Faludi properly contextualizes the Indigo Girls in her liner notes as a group that created an assertive, independent female response to the Reagan-Bush era. But that aspect of their work was always framed by the music itself, dominated by their interweaving acoustic guitars and voices, and the commitment with which they sang. That combination of substance and fervor characterized the Indigo Girls' work, even when their songwriting flagged occasionally or their sound became repetitive. *Retrospective* captures the highlights of their work from 1987 to 1999, but proceeding chronologically, it also traces the changes that may have hurt the duo commercially by the end. Gradually, their politics became more explicit, which always tends to splinter an audience (though, of course, their views were not secret to their many fervent fans). And in their search for different sounds, they sometimes subverted their basic two-voices, two-acoustic-guitars identity. It remains possible that Indigo Girls will continue to score good, consistent sales, and the two new songs suggest that there's still creative fuel for this group to burn. But if they have crested, *Retrospective* confirms their status as one of the most accomplished recording units of their time. — *William Ruhlmann*

James Ingram

b. Feb. 16, 1956, Akron, OH

Vocals, Keyboards / Quiet Storm, Adult Contemporary, Urban

Ingram began performing with the band Revelation Funk in the early '70s, moving from Akron, OH, to Los Angeles in 1973. During the '70s, Ingram supported Ray Charles on the road with backup vocals and piano, played keyboards behind the Coasters on Dick Clark's oldies revues, and was Leon Haywood's musical director. After hearing a demo of him singing "Just Once," Quincy Jones asked Ingram to perform on his new album. Released in 1980 on *The Dude*, the number 17 "Just Once" was Ingram's first success, resulting in three Grammy nominations—Best New Artist, Best Pop Male Vocal, and Best R&B Vocal—winning in the two latter categories. Throughout the '80s, Ingram had steady popular success singing duets, but all of his solo albums failed to make a dent in the charts; in 1990 he scored his first solo hit, "I Don't Have the Heart." —*Stephen Thomas Erlewine*

● **The Greatest Hits: Power of Great Music** / Sep. 24, 1991 / Qwest ✦✦✦
James Ingram racked up a number of adult contemporary-styled R&B pop hits in the 1980s, many of them duets, and the bulk of those hits are collected on this 12-track 1991 compilation. His music may at times seem somewhat melodramatic, registering on the pop spectrum somewhere between Michael Bolton and Billy Ocean, but nonetheless exemplifies top-notch 1980s adult contemporary pop production at its zenith. This set includes his two hit duets with Patti Austin, those being "How Do You Keep the Music Playing" and their timeless chart-topper "Baby Come to Me." Also included is his monster duet with Linda Ronstadt, "Somewhere Out There," and his hit duet with Michael McDonald, the funky "Yah Mo B There" (definitely one of Ingram's coolest songs). A few rarities make an appearance, including "Where Did My Heart Go?" from the film *City Slickers*, and the BET theme "Remember the Dream." To round out the collection are his solo hits, among them the Grammy-winning "Just Once," "One Hundred Ways," and his only solo chart-topper, "I Don't Have the Heart." Buyer beware, however, because a more "extensive" hits collection, *Forever More*, was issued in 1999, with newly recorded (and inferior) versions of "Just Once," "One Hundred Ways," and "I Don't Have the Heart." To this date, however, this short set stands as the definitive James Ingram retrospective. —*Jose Promis*

● **Forever More (Love Songs, Hits & Duets)** / Apr. 13, 1999 / Private Music ✦✦✦
James Ingram never became a superstar, but he racked up a respectable number of adult contemporary and urban soul hits during the '80s and early '90s, many of which were duets. *Forever More: Best of James Ingram* collects 14 highlights from his career, including the hits "Just Once," "One Hundred Ways," "Baby, Come to Me," "Yah Mo Be There," "Somewhere Out There" and "I Don't Have the Heart." The remaining songs may not be as recognizable as the singles, but they're in the same vein and should please the casual fans that were lured in by the well-known hits. —*Stephen Thomas Erlewine*

Luther Ingram

b. Nov. 30, 1944, Jackson, TN
Vocals / Smooth Soul, Soul
This Jackson, TN, Southern-soul singer was one of the top artists at Stax during the early '70s. Hooking up with producer Johnny Baylor's tiny KoKo label, Ingram appeared regularly on the R&B charts after Baylor brought his firm into the Stax fold in 1969. Ingram's intimate vocal approach was well suited to ballads, and his 1970 hit revival of "Ain't That Loving You (For More Reasons than One)" set the stage for his R&B chart-topping classic "(If Loving You Is Wrong) I Don't Want to Be Right" two years later. Long after Stax had folded, Ingram was still releasing hit singles—clear into 1987. —*Bill Dahl*

● **Greatest Hits** / Apr. 1996 / The Right Stuff ✦✦✦✦✦
Managed and produced by the late and notorious Johnny Baylor, the guy many accused of causing Stax's demise, Luther Ingram had a rich, soulful tenor that dripped with soul. He recorded many classic deep soul sagas, hitting his pinnacle with "If Loving You Is Wrong (I Don't Want to Be Right)," a gripper that passionately justified infidelity, with a whining guitar underscoring Ingram's heartfelt testimonial to his outside woman. The soulful "Ain't That Loving You (For More Reasons Than One)" dropped before "If Loving You" and should have been Ingram's first monster. You'll have to search a bit to find a more endearing tribute from a man to his woman. The mid-tempo, good-time feeling "I'll Be Your Shelter," like the previous two tracks, was co-written by Homer Banks, a Southern soul songwriting fool. It did well on the charts and provided a break from the heavy ballads, which was likewise for the joyful "My Honey & Me." Other goodies include "Steal Away to the Hideaway," "Missing You" and a scrumptious remake of Sam Cooke's "You Were Made for Me." Ingram's adaptation to Stax surprised many; before Stax, he had recorded urban and Northern soul 45s for tiny companies that were little more than P.O. boxes. —*Andrew Hamilton*

The Ink Spots

f. 1938
Vocal Pop, R&B, Harmony Vocal Group
The Ink Spots played a large role in pioneering the black vocal group-harmony genre, helping to pave the way for the doo wop explosion of the '50s. The quavering high tenor of Bill Kenny presaged hundreds of street-corner leads to come, and the sweet harmonies of Charlie Fuqua, Deek Watson and bass Hoppy Jones (who died in 1944) backed him flawlessly.

Kenny's impeccable diction and Jones's deep drawl were both prominent on the Ink Spots' first smash on Decca in 1939, the sentimental "If I Didn't Care." From then through 1951, the group was seldom absent from the pop charts, topping the lists with "We Three (My Echo, My Shadow, and Me)" (1940), "I'm Making Believe" and "Into Each Life Some Rain Must Fall" (both in 1944), and "The Gypsy" and "To Each His Own" (both in 1946).

Watson eventually split to form his own group, the Brown Dots, and appeared in numerous low-budget film musicals, while Kenny attempted a solo career, notching a solo hit in 1951 with the uplifting "It Is No Secret." Countless groups masquerading as the Ink Spots have thrived across the nation since the '50s. —*Bill Dahl*

☆ **The Greatest Hits** / Oct. 26, 1989 / MCA ✦✦✦✦✦
Greatest Hits 1939-46 is a 15-track collection of the Ink Spots' hits for Decca Records. During this era, the vocal group was at the height of their popularity, and most of the group's best-known songs—"If I Didn't Care," "Whispering Grass," "Maybe," "Java Jive," "Street of Dreams," "Gypsy," "To Each His Own"—are collected on this excellent compilation. —*Stephen Thomas Erlewine*

★ **The Anthology** / Jun. 16, 1998 / MCA ✦✦✦✦✦
The Ink Spots are far more influential than people realize. The genetic-spliced brotherhood of their voices were the virtual blueprint for not only most of the doo wop groups, but groups like the Brothers Four, the Hi-Lo's, the Four Lads, and many others. This leads, ultimately, to even the Beach Boys. The Ink Spots had amazing harmony, really, really funny songs, and an incredible approach. This anthology, a double, is really the one thing that you need of theirs if you're interested in the group. Most of the songs sound the same, and are actually in the same key. But guess what? It doesn't matter. All of the tracks are extremely enjoyable, and aside from the historical significance, this is just a great listening experience. Listing tip: Listen to this on a warm, lazy afternoon with the libation of your choice. You can't miss. —*Matthew Greenwald*

20th Century Masters—The Millennium Collection: The Best of The Ink Spots / Oct. 5, 1999 / MCA ✦✦✦✦
MCA's *20th Century Masters: The Millennium Collection* is a good, basic collection of the Ink Spots' biggest hits—including "If I Didn't Care," "My Prayer," "Java Jive," "Don't Get Around Much Anymore," "I'm Making Believe," "The Gypsy," "I'm Beginning to See the Light," "Prisoner of Love," and "To Each His Own"—available at a budget price. Although there are a couple of hits and good songs missing, this has enough of the best-known tunes to make it worthwhile for casual listeners on a budget. —*Stephen Thomas Erlewine*

Inner City

f. 1988, Detroit, MI
Club/Dance, House, Dance-Pop
The group that took Detroit techno to the masses via the British charts and the world's dancefloors, Inner City was no crossover act—rather, an intense collaboration between a noted Chicago house vocalist and one of the most influential Detroit producers of the 1980s. Both Paris Grey and Kevin Saunderson were well-known for their contributions to the club music of their respective communities well before their 1989 debut album. Saunderson did more to advance techno than anyone except Juan Atkins and Derrick May; Grey recorded several house classics, including "Don't Make Me Jack." Between the two (and later addition Ann Saunderson, Kevin's wife), Inner City topped dance charts in America and Britain 11 times, hit Britain's Top 40 eight times, and sold over six million records. The group was formed in 1987 when Saunderson produced a track he felt needed lyrics. After Chicago vocalist Paris Grey was recommended by Chicago producer Terry Baldwin, the two collaborated on the single "Big Fun." It was finally released late in 1988 and hit the British charts, becoming a surprising crossover success. Signed to Virgin soon after, Saunderson and Grey hit again later that same year with the Top Ten single "Good Life." Their debut album *Paradise* (*Big Fun* on its American issue) reached the U.K. Top 20, though it largely failed to cross over on the American pop charts. *Paradise Remixed* followed in 1990 and later singles "Ain't Nobody Better," "Watcha Gonna Do With My Lovin'," and "That Man (He's Mine)" lit up dancefloors around the world, spreading the word about techno to thousands of mainstream clubbers familiar only with house music. After the popular single "Back Together Again" and third album *Praise*, the group went on a hiatus, as Saunderson returned to his more experimental roots. —*John Bush*

● **Big Fun** / 1989 / Virgin ✦✦✦✦✦
In the 1980s and '90s, a lot of dance music spotlighted female singers with thin, weak voices who seem on the verge of death. But house music has often been a home to expressive, big-voiced divas who can truly wail—a fine example being Paris Gray of the duo Inner City. Along with producer/composer Kevin Saunderson, Gray was responsible for some of the most rewarding dance music of the late '80s and early '90s. Inner City's debut album *Big Fun* (titled *Paradise* in the U.K.) is full of house gems that enjoyed extensive dance club exposure, including "Good Life," "Do You Love What You Feel," "Ain't Nobody Better," and the title song. While Saunderson's production is decidedly high-tech, Gray's warm, passionate singing is mindful of dance music's heritage and underscores its soul and gospel roots in a delightful way. Unfortunately, Inner City never crossed over to the R&B or pop markets as Virgin Records hoped—an irony considering that *Big Fun* is so much more individualistic and soulful than most of the generic efforts which dominated black radio in 1989. —*Alex Henderson*

Fire / 1990 / Virgin ✦✦✦
Inner City escaped the dreaded sophomore curse with its consistently enriching second album, *Fire*, which provides such inspired, gospel-influenced house music treasures as "My Heart's Not Here With You," "Lovelight," "What Does It Take" and "That Man (He's All Mine)." Like its predecessor, *Big Fun*, *Fire* shows Paris Gray to be a singer of depth and substance and Kevin Saunderson to be an inventive, distinctive producer. Inner City's vision remained positive, and "Hallelujah" and "Unity" are fine examples of the uplifting "love/peace/togetherness" theme that's common in house music. Though Saunderson liked to call Inner City's music "techno-house," both *Big Fun* and *Fire* are very melodic and accessible albums lacking the type of abrasiveness associated with techno. Once again, Inner City fared well in club and dance-music circles, but unfortunately, enjoyed little exposure in the R&B and pop markets. —*Alex Henderson*

Praise / 1992 / Virgin ✦✦✦

Inspiral Carpets

f. 1986, Manchester, England, **db.** 1994
Madchester, Alternative Pop/Rock
Of all of the Manchester bands of the early '90s, Inspiral Carpets were arguably the least interesting. They didn't explore the deep psychedelia of the rave scene as thoroughly as the Happy Mondays, nor did they have the classic pop skills of the Stone Roses. What the band did have was some massive organ hooks, courtesy of Clint Boon; the organ recalled the classic garage punk of the '60s. When the Inspiral Carpets could write a song that matched the sheer pleasure of their sound—and they managed at least two on each album, as well as their U.K. hit singles—the group made some wonderful pop gems; unfortunately, their hit-miss ratio was too low to make their albums consistent. When the Manchester fad passed, the Inspiral Carpets were still around and managed to keep scoring hits in the U.K. by losing some of the dated club beats and experimenting with their music slightly, including a collaboration with Mark E. Smith of the Fall on their 1994 album. —*Stephen Thomas Erlewine*

Life / Oct. 1990 / Elektra ◆◆◆◆
More rock-oriented than the other major Madchester bands, the Inspiral Carpets' debut draws heavily from 1960s British rock influences featuring Clint Boon's prominent use of the Hammond organ. Swirling around dense, fast-paced guitar, *Life* was less in debt to psychedelia than to the garage punk of the same period. Not only was their music grittier than their contemporaries, but the band's lyrics were darker and focused on observations of working-class life. As such, their slower pieces, including the hit "This Is How It Feels," were less often love songs than gutsy social testimonies. However, it is on the Hammond-driven tracks where the band really are at their best. "Weakness," with its quasi-surf guitar break, "Move," and "Commercial Rain" all feature intense organ grooves with soaring pop choruses. The stunning closer, "Sackville," brings together all the various elements of the band's sound in one powerful vision of poverty. Although the occasional homogeneity of the group's music stops the album from becoming a true classic, *Life* is a stunning piece of work. (Note: The British version of the album was different than the American pressing. "Commercial Rain," "Weakness," "Biggest Mountain," and "I'll Keep It in Mind" were cut. An additional cut, "Besides Me," was added.) —*Geoff Orens*

Beast Inside / May 7, 1991 / Elektra ◆◆
Revenge of the Goldfish / Oct. 13, 1992 / Elektra ◆◆◆
Inspiral Carpets continue to get further away from their club-oriented dance roots on their third album; fortunately, their pop songwriting continues to improve, which is why *Revenge of the Goldfish* never sounds like the work of a bunch of has-beens. —*Stephen Thomas Erlewine*

● **Singles** / Sep. 18, 1995 / Mute ◆◆◆◆◆
Inspiral Carpets couldn't really sustain their vision over the course of an entire album, yet they made a number of infectious Madchester singles, which became fairly big hits in England. The *Singles* collects all of the group's U.K. hits, from the swirling, sunny "Joe" to "I Want You," a duet with the Fall's Mark E. Smith that had previously been unavailable on album. Over the course of 17 tracks, nearly every one of the band's great moments ("This Is How It Feels," "Dragging Me Down," "She Comes in the Fall," "Saturn 5," "Uniform") is featured, making *Singles* a definitive overview of the laid-back baggy band's career. —*Stephen Thomas Erlewine*

The International Submarine Band

f. 1966, **db.** 1968
Country-Rock
The International Submarine Band is best remembered as country-rock pioneer Gram Parsons' first band, which isn't surprising since the group received almost no publicity when they were active in the late '60s. Though the band never quite realized their potential, their sole album, 1968's *Safe at Home*, suggests the path Parsons would later follow. Parsons formed the International Submarine band with guitarist John Nuese, bassist Ian Dunlop, and drummer Mickey Gauvin while he was studying theology at Harvard in the mid-'60s. Gram dropped out of college in 1966 and had the band move its operations to New York, where they began develop their synthesis of country and rock. By the end of the year, they had recorded two singles for Goldstar which were ignored. The group also recorded an album, which went unreleased; the tapes were later lost. Early in 1967, the band moved out to Los Angeles on the advice of former child actor Brandon de Wilde, who told the band he could get them into the movies. The International Submarine Band did indeed appear in a movie—Roger Corman's *The Trip*, which starred Peter Fonda. However, the group's music was erased, with the psychedelic blues of the Electric Flag overdubbed on the ISB's performance. Still, the band benefited from its performance in *The Trip*, since it increased their profile in the L.A. underground. By the end of 1967, the International Submarine Band had completed their debut album, *Safe at Home*. Although the group's fortunes were beginning to improve, Parsons left the band in February of 1968 to join the Byrds. Following Parsons' departure, the International Submarine Band attempted to replace the vocalist, but they couldn't find any possible candidates. —*Stephen Thomas Erlewine*

● **Safe at Home** / 1968 / Shiloh ◆◆◆◆◆
Safe at Home, Gram Parsons first full-length album (and the only LP he would record with The International Submarine Band), today sounds like a dry run for the country-rock he would later perfect with The Byrds and the Flying Burrito Brothers; it's also major changeup from the psychedelically shaded pop/rock of the ISB's impossible to find debut singles. In many ways, the album sounds more purely "country" than Parsons' best-known work; the Burritos' crucially important R&B edge had yet to make its presence felt in Gram's music, and on these sessions the rock influence is often more felt than

heard (probably due in part to the presence of Nashville session veterans who pitched in on piano and pedal steel). But Parsons considerable gifts as a songwriter were already evident on tunes like "Blue Eyes" and "Luxury Liner," and while there's a touch less grace in Gram's vocals than on his best work, his passion, understated wit, and deep love for country music are always in the forefront. And while Gram is the star of this show, his bandmates—John Nuese and Bob Buchanan on guitars, Jon Corneal on drums, and future Burrito Chris Ethridge on bass—are solid, soulful, and firmly in-the-pocket throughout. If *Safe at Home* sounds like a rough draft for Gram Parsons' later triumphs, it's also a fine record on its own terms, and leaves little doubt that the International Submarine Band's leader had something special right from the start. —*Mark Deming*

INXS

f. 1977, Sydney, Australia
College Rock, Album Rock, Alternative Dance, Post-Punk, Pop/Rock, New Wave
INXS hailed from the pubs of Australia, which is part of the reason they never comfortably fit in with new wave. Even when the band branched out into synth-pop on its early recordings, they were underpinned by a hard, Stonesy beat and lead singer Michael Hutchence's Jaggeresque strut. Ultimately, these were the very things that made INXS into international superstars in the late '80s. By that time, the group had harnessed their hard rock, dance and new wave influences into a sleek, stylish groove that made their 1987 album *Kick* into a multi-million-selling hit. While that sound was their key to stardom, it also proved to be their undoing; the group became boxed in by their Stonesy pop-funk in the early '90s, when their audience became entranced by harder-edged alternative rock. In spite of declining sales, INXS soldiered on, continuing to tour and record for a dedicated fan base into the late '90s, until Hutchence's tragic 1997 suicide cast the group's future in serious doubt. —*Stephen Thomas Erlewine*

INXS / 1980 / Atco ◆◆
Underneath the Colours / 1981 / Atco ◆◆◆
Shabooh Shoobah / 1982 / Atco ◆◆◆
On *Shabooh Shoobah*, INXS finally hit upon a smooth, stylish fusion of new wave synth-pop and rock & roll that drew equally from the Stones' dirty R&B-inspired rhythms and AC/DC's loud crunch. However, the group hits their stride only on a handful of tracks. The droning synth riff of "Don't Change" masks a hard, funky groove and "The One Thing" is an infectious, catchy pop single, yet most of the album lacks memorable songwriting. —*Stephen Thomas Erlewine*

The Swing / 1984 / Atco ◆◆◆
Consolidating the strengths of *Shabooh Shoobah*, *The Swing* is the first consistently impressive INXS album. With the Nile Rodgers-produced "Original Sin" acting as the centerpiece, *The Swing* retains the new wave pop sense and rock attack of their earlier albums, while adding a stronger emphasis on dance rhythms. At the same time, the group's songwriting had improved, with more than half of the album featuring memorable hooks. —*Stephen Thomas Erlewine*

Listen Like Thieves / 1985 / Atlantic ◆◆◆◆
INXS completes its transition into an excellent rock & roll singles band with this album. Unfortunately, the new configuration only works for three songs: "What You Need," "Listen Like Thieves," and "Kiss the Dirt (Falling Down the Mountain)." But these three songs are so strong that the album cannot be dismissed completely. The album is worth its price just for "What You Need," a strong Stones-y groove with Michael Hutchence singing more warmly than he ever has. —*Stephen Thomas Erlewine*

Kick / 1987 / Atlantic ◆◆◆◆◆
"What You Need" had taken INXS from college radio into the American Top Five, but there was little indication that the group would follow it with a multi-platinum blockbuster like *Kick*. Where the follow-ups to "What You Need" made barely a ripple on the pop charts, *Kick* spun off four Top Ten singles, including the band's only American number one, "Need You Tonight." *Kick* crystallized all of the band's influences—Stones-y rock & roll, pop, funk, contemporary dance-pop—into a cool, stylish dance/rock hybrid. It was perfectly suited to lead singer Michael Hutchence's feline sexuality, which certainly didn't hurt the band's already inventive videos. But it wasn't just image that provided their breakthrough. For the first (and really only) time, INXS made a consistently solid album that had no weak moments from top to bottom. More than that, really, *Kick* is an impeccably crafted pop *tour de force*, the band succeeding at everything they try. Every track has at least a subtly different feel from what came before it; INXS freely incorporates tense guitar riffs, rock & roll anthems, swing-tinged pop/rock, string-laden balladry, danceable pop-funk, horn-driven '60s soul, '80s R&B, and even a bit of the new wave-ish sound they'd started out with. More to the point, every song is catchy and memorable, branded with indelible hooks. Even without the band's sense of style, the flawless songcraft is intoxicating, and it's what makes *Kick* one of the best mainstream pop albums of the '80s. —*Steve Huey*

X / Sep. 1990 / Atlantic ◆◆◆
The seventh album from Australia's INXS basically sticks to the formula set up on *Kick*, mixing solid remixable dancefloor beats with slightly quirky production tricks, Michael Hutchence's rough-edged, bluesy vocals, and some good solid song hooks. The most immediate numbers are, of course, the two singles, "Suicide Blonde" and "Disappear," but other tracks stand out as potential hit material as well, including the anthemic "The Stairs." The biggest problems with the album are a tendency to play it safe, sticking to the tried and true—echoing a line in the thumping "Who Pays the Price," when Hutchence sings "it's all been felt before"—and the fact that there's very little in the way of subtlety on the entire album. All of the songs are designed for immediate radio contact—they don't

really give you a chance to grow into them, they just grab you by the throat and start shaking. "Know the Difference," as an example, threatens to be sneaky but immediately switches to an obvious assault instead. In the finish, the overwhelming lack of subtlety and sense of sameness overcomes the album as a whole. It's not that's it's a bad album. It's just nowhere near as good as it could—and should—have been. *—Steven McDonald*

Live Baby Live / 1991 / Atlantic ✦

Welcome to Wherever You Are / Aug. 4, 1992 / Atlantic ✦✦✦✦

Although INXS needed to experiment badly, their attempt at self-reinvention, *Welcome to Wherever You Are*, didn't even come close to gaining commercial or critical acceptance. From the start of the album, it's clear that INXS is out to confuse the standard perceptions of the band; the first instrument on the album is an Eastern-flavored horn. Special recording effects and exotic rhythms and sounds are abundant on the album. Evidently, the pop audience didn't care about INXS anymore, since nobody bought the album. And that is a shame, since it is one of their strongest. *—Stephen Thomas Erlewine*

Full Moon, Dirty Hearts / Nov. 2, 1993 / Atlantic ✦

Following the surprisingly adventurous and artistically successful *Welcome to Wherever You Are*, *Full Moon, Dirty Hearts* sounds tired and as calculated as *X*. While most of the exotic trappings of *Welcome* have been pared down, there is still the same sense of the band experimenting as a way to stay current. INXS sounds energetic throughout the album, but the experimentation is poorly executed and there is a serious lack of strong songs and singles, apart from two duets: "Please (You Got That . . .)" with Ray Charles and the title track, which features Chrissie Hynde. *—Stephen Thomas Erlewine*

● **The Greatest Hits** / 1994 / Atlantic ✦✦✦✦✦

While INXS have made a few consistent albums, singles are the best format for the group's stylish dance-rock. Throughout the '80s and early '90s, the group racked up nine Top 40 hits and seven of those singles hit the Top Ten. *Greatest Hits* collects all of those hits—including "Need You Tonight," "What You Need," "Devil Inside," "New Sensation," "Disappear," "Suicide Blonde," and "Never Tears Us Apart"—adding minor hits like "Original Sin" and "Listen Like Thieves," but curiously bypassing the pivotal "Don't Change" and excellent "Bitter Tears," which was a bigger hit than several songs on the record. Nevertheless, *Greatest Hits* lives up to its title and provides a fine introduction to the band. *—Stephen Thomas Erlewine*

Elegantly Wasted / Apr. 15, 1997 / Mercury ✦✦

INXS stumbled greatly in the early '90s, since their slick, professional fusion of disco and the Stones was singularly out of place in the grunge era. On the heels of U2's discovery of irony and the dance floor and Oasis' popularizing rock & roll hedonism again, INXS seemed to be better suited to the late '90s, but *Elegantly Wasted*, their first new studio album in four years, proves that theory wrong. The band does dabble in contemporary dance on *Elegantly Wasted*, but it all comes out sounding like the lite funk-n-roll of *Kick*, only without the energy. And without the tunes. Throughout *Elegantly Wasted*, INXS goes through the motions coming up with a record nearly as weak as *Full Moon, Dirty Hearts*. The really unfortunate thing is, it sounds like they were trying this time around. *—Stephen Thomas Erlewine*

Shine Like It Does: The Anthology (1979-1997) / Jun. 5, 2001 / Rhino ✦✦✦✦✦

From the vantage of 2001, the year Rhino released the double-disc retrospective *Shine Like It Does: The Anthology (1979-1997)*, it's a little hard to believe that this Australian sextet really rivaled U2 for popularity in 1987/1988, when *Kick* worked its way to multi-platinum global success. This, of course, means that they can still sound tied to the times, but that's leavened by their heritage as an Australian rock band—which means no matter how stylish they got, they could still rock really, really hard. Unfortunately, at the height of their popularity, they made records that camouflaged their raw talents with synthesized bass and drums, which is what rock bands did in the late '80s. And, throughout their career, INXS did tend to favor the sounds of the time. This can make *Shine Like It Does* sound a bit like a music travelogue of its time, especially because its 42 songs do have their fair share of songs that seem like filler, but what stands out when the collection is finished is how damn good INXS was when it all clicked. All the hits are here, along with some rarities, album tracks, quasi-rarities, and a number of remixes and single edits, giving this a reason to spread out over two discs. The problem is, even though there are more hits than misses, this doesn't quite justify its length for many listeners, even while it makes a convincing case that INXS has more than a disc worth of classics. Still, there's something to be said for this collection—it may not prove that INXS transcends their time like U2 or R.E.M., but it does prove that, at their best, they could turn out some of the best rock & roll of their time. *—Stephen Thomas Erlewine*

Donnie Iris

b. Beaver Falls, PA

Vocals, Guitar / Arena Rock, Pop/Rock, Power Pop, New Wave, Rock & Roll

He found fame as the lead singer of the Jaggerz (the one-hit wonder from 1970 responsible for the number-two hit "The Rapper"), but Donny Iris returned to the pop charts in the early '80s several times as a solo act. Born Dominic Ierace in Beaver Falls, PA, Iris began singing at weddings at age five and by eight was performing on local television and entering talent contests. When his voice changed, he took up the drums but later got back into singing while in high school. A self-taught guitarist, he formed Donnie & the Donnells while in college.

The Jaggerz, Iris' next band, were formed from the remains of several local bands. Though the band's big hit was "The Rapper," in actuality, the band began as an R&B revue. Outside of Pittsburgh, where songs like "Gotta Find My Way Back Home" and "(That's Why) Baby I Love You," (on Gambel Records) were radio favorites, this period did not bring much success to Iris or the band. Their next move was to Kama Sutra, where Iris's "The Rapper" was the first in a series of three hits the band enjoyed.

After the Jaggerz broke up, Iris toured with Wild Cherry, whose 1976 hit "Play That Funky Music" made them a hot property into the end of the decade. Unfortunately, Wild Cherry was another one-hit wonder, and Iris was out of a job by 1980.

That same year, Iris teamed up with keyboard player Mark Avsec (ex-Wild Cherry & Breathless) for the first in a series of good albums for MCA; the single "Ah! Leah!" hit number 29 that year, and six second-rank singles charted during the next five years. Avsec and Iris' collaboration proved to be a good thing in both the songwriting and artist/producer department during this time. By the time of 1993's *Footsoldier in the Moonlight*, though, Iris' talent as a songwriter had apparently dried up and he was relying entirely on Avsec originals *—Jim Worbois*

Back on the Streets / 1980 / Razor & Tie ✦✦✦✦

Donnie Iris emerged fronting his own band in the late '70s after stints with the Jaggerz and Wild Cherry. Hailing from Western Pennsylvania, Iris became a popular live draw before signing with RCA and releasing his debut record *Back on the Streets* (later reissued by Razor & Tie).

Working closely with Mark Avsec, who co-wrote, produced, and played keyboards, *Back on the Streets* is a blend of meat-and-potatoes rock and new wave, which succeeds due to its simple nature and some infectious hooks. The big hit was "Ah! Leah!" which, with its throbbing bassline and crunchy riffs, climbed to Number 29, but there's more here. Other choice cuts include the finger-snapping melody "I Can't Hear You" and the barroom love song "Agnes," which owes a debt to the Spencer Davis Group hit "Gimme Some Lovin'." *—Tom Demalon*

King Cool / 1981 / Razor & Tie ✦✦✦✦✦

The 1981 follow-up to Donnie Iris' debut, *King Cool* proved to be the commercial and critical peak for Iris and his band the Cruisers. The same cast returned from the first record with Mark Avsec again playing a pivotal role.

King Cool toned down some of the new wave leanings of *Back on the Streets* and concentrated more on a classic rock sound yielded rewarding results. Three singles charted from *King Cool* including the melodic "Sweet Merilee," which featured some lovely harmonies. Two songs managed to go Top 40; the rollicking, percussion-driven "Love Is Like a Rock" and "My Girl," their biggest hit reaching Number 25, which opted for a doo wop feel. Iris is a belter, vocally, and it worked to good effect on other infectious tracks like "The Promise," the punchy "Pretender," and the mid-tempo ballad "The Last to Know." *King Cool* managed to break no new ground, but served as a loving homage to crunchy, singalong rock. *—Tom Demalon*

The High and the Mighty / 1982 / MCA ✦✦✦

Fortune 410 / 1983 / MCA ✦✦✦✦

Donnie Iris is one of the classiest rock singers who deserved widespread stardom but never achieved it. At least the public and the radio had the good sense to embrace early-'80s hits "Ah! Leah!" and "Love Is Like a Rock." Iris and his solid backing band the Cruisers—keyboardist/producer Mark Avsec, guitarist Marty Lee, bass guitarist Albritton McClain, and drummer Kevin Valentine—maintained their high level of power pop and rock & roll quality on 1983's *Fortune 410*. *Fortune 410* does sound very much like a product of the 1980s due to tinges of new wave, particularly in Avsec's keyboard work. The perky "Human Evolution" has a bopping new wave beat; it's Devo-like, only with a better grasp of melody. Iris displays his wide vocal range on "Stagedoor Johnny." "Cry If You Want To" rolls along with a fine chorus in addition to McClain's infectiously supple bass lines and Lee's biting solo. Avsec's fast, sputtering synthesizer and Lee's gunfire-like fills propel "I Belong," but in some places it's hard to tell if Valentine is playing or if a drum machine is used. "She's So European" is fun, hyperactive pop/rock. During Donnie Iris and the Cruisers' 1980s prime, Avsec and Iris generally co-wrote the songs, although there was occasional input from the others. That's what makes the infectiously quirky, McClain-penned "Never Did I" such a pleasant surprise. *Fortune 410* closes with the astonishingly powerful and tuneful "Do You Compute?" As a single it reached the Top 60, but it deserved a much better fate. Avsec's sustained synthesizer chords and McClain's driving bass set the foundation for Lee's resonant, thundering power chords and Iris' unbelievable vocals. The chorus is amazing, and so are Iris' falsetto screams. Sadly, *Fortune 410* hadn't been reissued on CD as of 2000. *—Bret Adams*

Out of the Blue / Sep. 9, 1993 / Seathru ✦✦✦✦

Based on the quality of Donnie Iris' infectious power pop, he deserved to be a star, but things didn't quite work out that way. The Pennsylvania native (born Dominic Ierace) first hit it big with the Jaggerz's "The Rapper" in 1970 and another decade passed before Iris and his band the Cruisers signed with MCA Records and shot up the charts with the memorably catchy singles "Ah! Leah!" in 1980 and "Love Is Like a Rock" in 1981. However, the early 1980s marked the beginning of the youth-and-image-based MTV era, and it was not the best time to be a diminutive, bespectacled Italian guy pushing age 40, no matter how great your songs and voice were. Iris and keyboardist/producer Mark Avsec co-wrote most of the Donnie Iris and the Cruisers material, which was given a melodic crunch by guitarist Marty Lee. *Out of the Blue* is, in an odd sense, a best-of collection released by Seathru (part of Cleveland-area concert promotions giant Belkin Productions). It includes "Ah! Leah!," "Love Is Like a Rock," the minor hit "Injured in the Game of Love," and the superb *King Cool* track "That's the Way Love Ought to Be," which features Iris' unbelievable falsetto wail. Unfortunately, some other great minor hits such as "Tough World" and "Do You Compute?" are missing. Why? Iris said in a 1992 interview that MCA wanted too much money to license many of these other songs included on his four 1980-1983 albums for the label. Therefore, in addition to "Injured in the Game of Love" *Out of the Blue* includes "10th Street," "Ridin' Thunder," and "I Want You Back" from 1985's HME release *No Muss…No Fuss* and six newer songs, most notably "Love Whispers." —*Bret Adams*

● **20th Century Masters—The Millennium Collection: The Best of Donnie Iris** / Sep. 18, 2001 / MCA ✦✦✦✦
There are a lot of power poppers that traditionalist power pop fans don't like to give credit to. These are musicians that could craft a song and carve out a hook, but dressed these tunes in very commercial productions—and, even though these came at the height of power pop, that commercial production made these artists seem lesser than the dogged new wave of such artists as Tommy Keane or even Cheap Trick. In retrospect, the artists that had shiny productions and big, unstoppable hooks were every bit as power pop as their scruffier cousins, and Donnie Iris is one of them. His records often have the trappings of album rock in the early '80s, but the essence of his work is that of a geeky pop fan, turning out anthemic, melodic pop tunes, pumping them up with guitars filtered through Marshall amps. Sometimes, the end result was a little silly—the pounding "Love Is Like a Rock" is one of the goofiest songs ever recorded—but when it clicked, like on "Ah! Leah!," it clicked perfectly, illustrating that the gap between true power popsters and the supposed charlatans was simply a matter of style. And *20th Century Masters* does indeed capture Iris at his best, hitting all of his big, catchy pop tunes on one 12-track collection. Yeah, he does succumb to the sound of the times—which is endearing at times, especially when the production is as era-specific as that on "That's the Way Love Ought to Be" (it helps that the song works, too, of course)—but the best songs here will be irresistible to anyone with a serious power pop jones and no pop snobbery. —*Stephen Thomas Erlewine*

Iron Butterfly

f. 1966, San Diego, CA, **db.** 1971
Acid Rock, Heavy Metal, Psychedelic, Hard Rock
The heavy, psychedelic acid rock of Iron Butterfly may seem dated to some today, but the group was one of the first hard-rock bands to receive extensive radio airplay, and their best-known song, the 17-minute epic "In-A-Gadda-Da-Vida," established that more extended compositions were viable entries in the radio marketplace, paving the way for progressive AOR. *In-A-Gadda-Da-Vida* sold four million copies, spent over a year in the Top Ten, and was the first album to receive platinum certification after the RIAA instituted the award. (The title has been translated as "in the garden of Eden" or "in the garden of life.") A shortened version of the title track, which contained extended instrumental passages with loud guitars and classical/Eastern-influenced organ, plus a two-and-a-half-minute drum solo, reached number 30 on the singles charts. The follow-up, *Ball*, showed greater musical variety and went gold, but it also marked the beginning of the band's decline. Iron Butterfly broke up in 1971, reforming in the mid-'70s without success. —*Steve Huey*

Heavy / 1968 / Rhino ✦✦✦
Iron Butterfly's 1968 debut album *Heavy* established the band's trademark sound, relying on plodding, heavy guitar riffs and thundering drums. Most of the album was not particularly well written—the riffs *were* the songs, not their foundation—but the band's overwhelmingly loud sonic attack occasionally made up for the weakness in the material. —*Stephen Thomas Erlewine*

● **In-A-Gadda-Da-Vida** / 1968 / Atco ✦✦✦✦✦
With its endless, droning minor-key riff and mumbled vocals, "In-A-Gadda-Da-Vida" is arguably the most notorious song of the acid-rock era. According to legend, the group was so stoned when they recorded the track that they could neither pronounce the title "In the Garden of Eden" or end the track, so it rambles on for a full 17 minutes, which to some listeners sounds like eternity. But that's the essence of its appeal—it's the epitome of heavy psychedelic excess, encapsulating the most indulgent tendencies of the era. Iron Butterfly never matched the warped excesses of "In-A-Gadda-Da-Vida," either on their debut album of the same name or the rest of their catalog, yet they occasionally made some enjoyable fuzz-guitar-driven psychedelia that works as a period piece. The five tracks that share space with their magnum opus on *In-a-Gadda-Da-Vida* qualify as good artifacts, and the entire record still stands as the group's definitive album, especially since this is the only place the full-length title track is available. —*Stephen Thomas Erlewine*

Ball / 1969 / Collectors' Choice Music ✦✦✦
Following the huge success of their second record, *In-A-Gadda-Da-Vida*, Iron Butterfly scored a second straight Top Five album with *Ball*. While it didn't have any acid-rock freak-out to compare with the epic "In-A-Gadda-Da-Vida," *Ball* was a more ambitious album, as the group experimented with shorter, more melodic songs. Like any Iron Butterfly album, the quality of the material is wildly inconsistent, yet cut-for-cut, *Ball* is a more consistent album than their two previous records, as the group trimmed away some of the acid-rock excesses of their earlier records while retaining their brutally loud trademark heavy guitars. —*Stephen Thomas Erlewine*

Iron Butterfly Live / 1970 / Rhino ✦✦

Metamorphosis / 1970 / Rhino ✦✦✦
On *Ball*, Iron Butterfly began to expand their sound, attempting to write more concisely. On *Metamorphosis*, the group continued their musical explorations, adding a layered production to their sound. However, only keyboardist/vocalist Doug Ingle was enthusiastic about the band's new musical direction and most of the group refused to participate in the recording of the album, claiming it strayed too far from Iron Butterfly's signature sound. The truth of the matter is the rest of the band was right—under Ingle's direction, the group tries stylistic diversions that they do not have the ability to accomplish, including funk and acoustic ballads. Nevertheless, this ambition makes for an interesting listen, since Iron Butterfly's albums can be weighed down by their relentless heaviness.

Despite a handful of strong tracks—particularly the single "Easy Rider (Let the Wind Pay the Way)"—most of the album doesn't hold up on repeated plays. —*Stephen Thomas Erlewine*

Scorching Beauty / 1975 / Repertoire ✦✦

Sun and Steel / 1976 / Edsel ✦

Light and Heavy: The Best of Iron Butterfly / Jan. 19, 1993 / Rhino ✦✦✦✦
Although the compilation is quite generous, featuring 21 tracks on CD, *Light and Heavy: The Best of Iron Butterfly* isn't all that entertaining, due to Iron Butterfly's difficulties with producing compelling material. All of the group's highlights from 1968-1970 are included, although the career-making, 17-minute "In-A-Gadda-Da-Vida" is presented in its three-minute single edit. Since that is the only Iron Butterfly song most listeners know, the lack of the full-length version could potentially sink the album, but the fact of the matter is, "In-A-Gadda-Da-Vida" gets quite repetitive over the course of nearly 20 minutes. While the quality of the rest of *Light and Heavy* is spotty—ranging from heavy psychedelic rock to light psychedelic pop—it is a more intriguing listen than *In-A-Gadda-Da-Vida*, even if it doesn't have the period-piece charm of the original hit record. —*Stephen Thomas Erlewine*

Iron Maiden

f. 1976, London, England
New Wave of British Heavy Metal, British Metal, Heavy Metal
Known for such powerful hits as "Two Minutes to Midnight" and "The Trooper," Iron Maiden was and is one of the most influential bands of the heavy metal genre. The often-imitated band has existed for over 20 years, pumping out wild rock similar to Judas Priest. Iron Maiden has always been an underground attraction; although failing to ever obtain any real media attention in the U.S. (critics claimed them to be Satanists due to their dark musical themes and their use of grim mascot "Eddie"), they still became well known throughout the world and have remained consistently popular throughout their career. Iron Maiden was one of the first groups to be classified as "British Metal," and, along with Black Sabbath, Led Zeppelin and a host of other bands, set the style for the rock scene of the '80s. —*Barry Weber*

Iron Maiden / 1980 / Capitol ✦✦✦✦
Iron Maiden's 1980 self-titled album is certainly one of heavy metal's all-time best debuts. Surfacing from the underground along with a host of other New Wave of British Heavy Metal bands (e.g., Def Leppard, Motorhead), Maiden's debut proved to be incredibly influential for future metal bands—it was one of the first to merge heavy metal's power with punk's riffing and attitude, forging a blueprint for such genres as thrash, speed, death, and hardcore metal. While the band would branch out musically on future releases, *Iron Maiden* contains some of their most straight-ahead compositions, such as "Prowler," "Sanctuary," "Charlotte the Harlot" and the title track. The group's more-progressive direction is signaled by the 7 1/2 minute epic "Phantom of the Opera," as well as by the breakneck instrumental "Transylvania." Also featured was Maiden's first Top 40 U.K. single, the anthemic "Running Free," plus several calmer compositions like "Remember Tomorrow" and "Strange World," which showed that there was more to this young band than just bashing away. Bassist/leader Steve Harris proved to be the band's main songwriter/wordsmith early on, with lyrics that often proved thought-provoking—a sharp detour from the expected topic of sex, drugs, and rock & roll that most metal bands relied on, while vocalist Paul Di'Anno's oft-rough vocals were also a main ingredient. Add to it inspired performances by the other members (including second guitarist Dennis Stratton's sole album appearance with Maiden), and you have a promising, ultimately classic debut. (As with all of Iron Maiden's 1998 re-issues on Raw Power, a multimedia section is featured on the CD, which includes videos, band biographies, tour date history and photo galleries.) —*Greg Prato*

Killers / 1981 / Capitol ✦✦✦✦
Iron Maiden's sophomore effort, 1981's *Killers*, proved to be a more focused and developed affair than its predecessor. Contributing factors included the first appearance by new guitarist Adrian Smith, who helped develop Maiden's signature twin-guitar harmonies with original member Dave Murray, plus respected metal producer Martin "Deep Purple" Birch manning the controls for the first time (his first of ten albums with the band). *Killers* contains a much livelier sound than the debut, while bassist Steve Harris again played a prominent role in the songwriting, penning ten of the album's 11 tracks, while co-writing another. Chock full of classics, *Killers* is one consistent highlight—the homicidal tales of "Murders in the Rue Morgue" and the title track, the crushing instrumental "Genghis Khan," as well as such forgotten first-rate rockers as "Innocent Exile," "Purgatory," "Twilight Zone," and "Drifter." Inexplicably, the album's two best tracks—the shout-along anthem "Wrathchild" and the melodic "Prodigal Son"—were never issued as singles. Another hit album back home in England, *Killers* also gave the quintet their first taste of U.S. chart success, spurred on by their first stateside tour. *Killers* is another bona fide Maiden classic, but would also prove to be vocalist Paul Di'Anno's last with the group. (As with all of Iron Maiden's 1998 reissues on Raw Power, a multimedia section is featured on the CD, which includes videos, band biographies, tour date history, and photo galleries.) —*Greg Prato*

The Number of the Beast / 1982 / Capitol ✦✦✦✦✦
Even though Iron Maiden was on the brink of worldwide superstardom after their breakthrough sophomore effort, *Killers*, vocalist Paul Di'Anno left the band at the conclusion of their 1981 world tour. Many fans wondered if this would signal the end to one of metal's most promising new bands, but their worries were soon erased after hearing the 1982 masterpiece *The Number of the Beast*. Ex-Samson singer Bruce Dickinson replaced Di'Anno, and his strong, operatic vocals proved to be one of Maiden's most distinctive

trademarks. And while the music on their first albums contained elements of punk, *Beast* was a 100 percent true heavy metal album, as Maiden's songwriting and sound continued to solidify. Topping the charts in the U.K., and becoming their first U.S. Top 40 record, *Number of the Beast* spawned a pair of all-time classic metal anthems—"Run to the Hills" (which dealt with the plight of the American Indian) and the demonic title track (which caused controversy among religious groups, who wrongfully labeled the band Satan worshippers). But, like its predecessor, not a single weak track is included—"Invaders," "The Prisoner," "22 Acacia Avenue" (a follow-up to 1980's "Charlotte the Harlot"), and "Gangland" were all rocking highlights; the quieter "Children of the Damned" and "Hallowed Be Thy Name" were also featured. *The Number of the Beast* is quite simply one of the best heavy metal albums ever released. —*Greg Prato*

Piece of Mind / 1983 / Capitol ✦✦✦✦✦

By 1983's *Piece of Mind*, Iron Maiden was fast becoming one of the biggest metal bands on the planet, yet with each successive album, the group lost an original member. This time it would prove to be exit time for drummer Clive Burr, who was replaced by ex-Pat Travers skinsman Nicko McBrain, resulting in what many consider to be the quintessential Iron Maiden lineup (remaining intact until 1990). While all of the expected Maiden musical trademarks are again present (Harris' galloping bass lines, Dickinson's Herculean vocals, great guitar harmonies from Dave Murray/Adrian Smith), the sound is streamlined slightly, resulting in the band's most melodic and accessible album thus far. *Piece of Mind* also marked the first time that other members besides Steve Harris had a prominent say in the songwriting, resulting in such all-time metal standards as "Flight of the Icarus" and "The Trooper," while containing several musically ambitious compositions—"To Tame a Land" (based on the classic sci-fi novel *Dune* by Frank Herbert), "Still Life," and "Revelations." But Maiden never forgot that they were a metal band, as proven by "Die With Your Boots On," "Where Eagles Dare," and the aforementioned "Trooper." Although *Piece of Mind* was the first Maiden album to include filler ("Quest for Fire," "Sun and Steel"), it was overall another superb release, resulting in Iron Maiden's fourth classic in a row. (As with all of Iron Maiden's 1998 reissues on Raw Power, a multimedia section is featured on the CD, which includes videos, band biographies, tour date history, and photo galleries.) —*Greg Prato*

Powerslave / 1984 / Capitol ✦✦✦✦

Iron Maiden's music was evolving and growing with each successive release in the 80's; each album outsold its predecessor and widened their fan base. This was never more apparent than on 1984's *Powerslave*. It was the first Maiden album to feature the same lineup for more than a single record, and with a long tour under their belt, the playing on *Powerslave* was tight and inspired. While other popular metal bands of the day were busy conquering radio with accessible singles, Maiden decided to include several noncommercial extended pieces, a throwback of sorts to their '70s prog-rock influences (Jethro Tull, etc.). MTV embraced the album's two singles/videos, the rapid-fire "Aces High" and the complex antiwar tale "2 Minutes to Midnight," but what really made the album stand out as a true heavy metal achievement were the epic compositions. The second side only consists of three songs, including the superb and explosive title track, plus the long and winding 13 1/2 minute "Rime of the Ancient Mariner" (based on the famous Samuel Taylor Coleridge poem). Add to it perhaps Maiden's best instrumental, "Losfer Words (Big 'Orra)," and forgotten-yet-strong album cuts like "Flash of the Blade" and "The Duellists," and you have yet another highly recommended, essential Maiden classic. (As with all of Iron Maiden's 1998 reissues on Raw Power, a multimedia section is featured on the CD, which includes videos, band biographies, tour date history, and photo galleries.) —*Greg Prato*

Live After Death (The World Slavery Tour) / 1985 / Capitol ✦✦✦✦✦

Iron Maiden's World Slavery Tour was one of the longest and most extensive tours ever undertaken by a rock band. Lasting from August 9, 1984 to July 5, 1985 and visiting such countries as Poland, Austria, Hungry, Yugoslavia, Italy, France, Spain, Portugal, Scotland, England, Germany, Sweden, Canada, Japan, and the U.S., the show included a mammoth setup that replicated the intricate ancient Egyptian scenery of the *Powerslave* album cover. As a "thank you" to the hundreds of thousands of fans who packed arenas the world over, the double disc live set *Live After Death* was issued in 1985. Disc one is comprised of selections from a four-night stand at L.A.'s Long Beach Arena, with disc two comprised of performances from London's Hammersmith Odeon. The album is essentially a "best of" of sorts, since most of their singles released up to this point are featured in all of their high-decibel glory: "Aces High," "2 Minutes to Midnight," "The Trooper," "Flight of Icarus," "The Number of the Beast," "Run to the Hills," and "Running Free." Also included are such strong album tracks as "Wrathchild," "22 Acacia Avenue," "Children of the Damned," "Phantom of the Opera," "Hallowed Be Thy Name," "Iron Maiden," plus their two epics, "Powerslave" and "Rime of the Ancient Mariner," making it a near-complete overview. *Live After Death* is easily one of heavy metal's best live albums. (As with all of Iron Maiden's 1998 reissues on Raw Power, a multimedia section is featured on the CD, which includes videos, band biographies, tour date history, and photo galleries.) —*Greg Prato*

Somewhere in Time / 1986 / Capitol ✦✦

Seventh Son of a Seventh Son / 1988 / Capitol ✦✦✦✦✦

In 1988, harsh thrash metal and radio-friendly glam rock were the two chief heavy metal genres. Instead of aligning themselves to either camp, Iron Maiden stuck to their guns and issued a concept album, *Seventh Son of a Seventh Son.* Concept albums had spelled disaster for other metal bands in the past, but this proved not to be the case with Maiden, resulting in what many fans consider their last true classic album (and the last with guitarist Adrian Smith, until their late-'90s reunion). Although the songs are all lyrically tied together by the story of a prophet who tries (unsuccessfully) to warn a village of an impending holocaust, they don't have to be listened to in succession to be enjoyed—one of

the main reasons the album worked so well. A total of four singles were issued in the U.K. (all Top Tens)—"Can I Play With Madness?," "The Evil That Men Do," "The Clairvoyant," and "Infinite Dreams"—which all prove to be the album's best cuts. But like earlier Maiden albums, this is a complete album—while "Moonchild," "The Prophecy," "Only the Good Die Young," and the epic title track are not as well known as the singles, they are just as noteworthy. *Seventh Son of a Seventh Son* marked the end of a golden era for one of metal's all-time best bands. (Note: As with all of Iron Maiden's 1998 reissues on Raw Power, a multimedia section is featured on the CD, which includes videos, band biographies, tour date history, and photo galleries.) —*Greg Prato*

No Prayer for the Dying / 1990 / Epic ✦✦

Fear of the Dark / May 12, 1992 / Epic ✦✦

The X Factor / Oct. 10, 1995 / CMC International ✦✦

● **The Best of the Beast** / Sep. 24, 1996 / Raw Power ✦✦✦✦✦

Although Iron Maiden is known primarily in the U.S. as an album-oriented band, in their native England, the band has racked up many a hit single, most of which are featured on the 1996 "greatest-hits" collection, *Best of the Beast*. Available in two formats, either as a 16-track single disc (geared more toward the casual fan) or as a far more extensive 27-track double-disc set, complete with unreleased demos and aimed at the longtime fan. While the single disc contains many of Maiden's best-known songs—"The Number of the Beast," "The Trooper," "2 Minutes to Midnight," "Running Free (live)," "Wasted Years," "Can I Play With Madness"—several prime cuts are left off in favor of subpar Blaze Bayley-era material. It's incomprehensible that such fan favorites as "Flight of Icarus" and "Wrathchild" are left off in favor of "Virus" and "Man on the Edge," but more importantly, the single disc doesn't contain one track that features original vocalist Paul Di'Anno. The double disc is the better of the two, since it includes such non-single classics as "Rime of the Ancient Mariner (live)," "Phantom of the Opera," "Strange World (demo)," and "Where Eagles Dare" (while the two-CD does contain "Wrathchild," "Icarus" is still nowhere to be found). Serious fans are probably better off sticking with the full-length albums. —*Greg Prato*

Chris Isaak

b. Jun. 26, 1956, Stockton, CA

Vocals, Guitar / College Rock, Pop/Rock, Roots Rock

Chris Isaak clearly loves the reverb-laden rockabilly and country of Sun Studios. In particular, he transfers the sweeping melancholy of Roy Orbison's sweeping, classic melancholy Monument singles ("Crying," "Oh, Pretty Woman," "In Dreams") to the more stripped-down, rootsy sound of Sun. His stylized take on '50s and '60s rock & roll eventually made him into a star in the early '90s, thanks to the hit single "Wicked Game." Isaak released his first album, *Silvertone*, on Warner Bros. in 1985. It was critically well-received, yet it didn't sell. Two years later, he released *Chris Isaak* which managed to scrape into the Top 200 album charts. After its release, the singer began an acting career with a bit part in Jonathan Demme's 1988 film, *Married to the Mob*; he would later have parts in *Wild at Heart* and *The Silence of the Lambs*. Released in 1989, *Heart Shaped World* didn't manage to break big until late 1990, when "Wicked Game" was featured in David Lynch's *Wild at Heart*. Soon, the single became a Top Ten hit; the album also made it into the Top Ten and sold over a million copies. Both 1993's *San Francisco Days* and 1995's *Forever Blue* mine essentially the same vein as *Heart Shaped World*, yet both went gold and spawned a handful of hits. —*Stephen Thomas Erlewine*

Silvertone / 1985 / Warner Brothers ✦✦✦✦✦

Chris Isaak's debut album, *Silvertone*, named after his three-piece backup group, sets the pattern for his subsequent albums in its meticulously constructed retro sound. Isaak enters a time machine and emerges around 1960, when Roy Orbison is ruling the charts with his melodramatic ballads and Elvis Presley has just returned from the Army. Of course, what passed for a style 25 years before is in Isaak's hands stylization, and when he wails in an Orbison falsetto of romantic desperation, then does a flat, Presley-like recitation in the album-closing "Western Skies," it all seems over the top. But he is just about sincere enough to pull it off, and James Calvin Wilsey is a strong enough guitarist to keep the arrangements on track. So, to the extent that you can resist the "Is this guy kidding?" impression, the music is appealing. —*William Ruhlmann*

Chris Isaak / Dec. 1986 / Warner Brothers ✦✦✦

Chris Isaak moves up about five years from his usual stylistic focus by covering the Yardbirds' 1965 hit "Heart Full of Soul," but on his original tunes he remains in the Roy Orbison orbit, using his sob-filled voice and James Calvin Wilsey's Duane Eddy-like twangy guitar work to evoke the romantic angst of the early 1960s. Listening to him is still an oddly dislocating experience, but he does what he does so thoroughly it's hard not to go along if only for the running time of the record. —*William Ruhlmann*

● **Heart Shaped World** / Jun. 1989 / Reprise ✦✦✦✦✦

When filmmaker David Lynch backed a disquieting scene in *Blue Velvet* with Roy Orbison's "In Dreams," he demonstrated the eerie atmosphere behind its pre-'60s innocence. Orbison disciple Chris Isaak played those qualities to the hilt in his shimmering, spare "Wicked Game," so it was no surprise when Lynch included the ballad in *Wild at Heart*. What was surprising, given the fact that it sounded like nothing else on pop radio in 1990, was that "Wicked Game" became a breakout Top Ten hit, pushing Isaak's accompanying album *Heart Shaped World* to platinum status. Of course, there's more than that one moody masterpiece of a single to recommend *Heart Shaped World*. Isaak faithfully recreates his influences with production that's infinitely cleaner than Sun rock & roll, drawing more on its form than its attitude, but he's particularly suited to the sort of Orbison/Presley-style balladry that brought him a mass audience. His rich, sobbing croon is simply a gorgeous instrument, whether he's in a sonorous baritone or quavering falsetto. And he uses that instrument to tremendous effect here, coming across as a brooding romantic with a broken heart and swoon-inducing style. Of itself, *Heart Shaped World* is a pretty effective mood piece, showcasing Isaak doing a whole lot of what he does best. He does attempt a couple of rockers, but they never really *rock*—much like Orbison, it's clear that ballads are his true forte, and given the spirit Isaak wants to channel, the numbers feel much too tame. But aside from that flaw, the rest of *Heart Shaped World* is a supremely elegant late-night soundtrack, equally suited to steamy romance or solitary heartache. *—Steve Huey*

San Francisco Days / Apr. 13, 1993 / Reprise ✦✦✦✦
Chris Isaak's records are eerily out of time; the production is too clean and sterile to sound as if it was recorded at Sun Studios (a sound he clearly admires), but his music doesn't fit neatly into the sounds of contemporary radio. Accordingly, his sound is original yet familiar, appealing both to fans of early-'60s rock & roll and a modern audience. At times, Isaak tries too hard to emulate his idols—for instance, his strained Orbison-esque falsetto on "Two Hearts"—but when he doesn't try too hard, the results are often startling. *San Francisco Days* is Isaak's most musically diverse album yet. *—Stephen Thomas Erlewine*

Forever Blue / May 23, 1995 / Reprise ✦✦✦
Chris Isaak's albums all follow the same basic formula, yet he adds a grittier edge to *Forever Blue*. Kicking off with the bluesy stomp of "Baby Did a Bad Bad Thing," where Isaak tries to sound like John Lee Hooker, the album is another set of expertly crafted rock & roll, carefully designed to sound like the early '60s. It's enjoyable, yet it's never as consistent as *Heart Shaped World* or *San Francisco Days*. *—Stephen Thomas Erlewine*

Baja Sessions / Oct. 8, 1996 / Reprise ✦✦✦
The Baja Sessions is Chris Isaak's rootsiest record since *Silvertone*, alternating between loose versions of some of his earliest tracks and roughed-up, improved covers of recent hits like "Two Hearts." In addition to the older cuts, there are two new songs—"I Wonder" and "Return to Me"—which are fine additions to his catalog. *—Stephen Thomas Erlewine*

Wicked Ways: Anthology / Jun. 30, 1998 / Reprise ✦✦✦✦✦
Released in 1998, *Wicked Ways: Anthology* is not a greatest hits collection, nor is it a rarities collection. In fact, it's hard to tell what exactly it is, since it concentrates on a brief period of Isaak's career—the late '80s/early '90s—overlooks a lot of hits, contains oddities like a cover of "Heart Full of Soul" and an instrumental of "Wicked Game." This is not a representative selection of Isaak's music nor is it particularly listenable, and neither does it give a good selection of rarities for collections. In other words, it's an easy one to pass by. *—Stephen Thomas Erlewine*

Speak of the Devil / Sep. 22, 1998 / Reprise ✦✦✦✦
Speak of the Devil explores the same moody terrain as Isaak's previous records, though the songs are fleshed out with more contemporary touches. The leadoff track "Please" is unusually hard-hitting, with its acoustic/electric/soft/crash structure, Mellotron, and soundbite lyrics. "I'm Not Sleepy," is a roots-rock rave-up (wherein Isaak lyrically quotes Lennon's "Oh Yoko": "In the middle of the night I cry your name"); the title cut is an eerie celebration of love lost and found; "Talkin' 'Bout a Home" is the album's tour de force. Yet, some of the loungey vocal touches in "Flying" and the final instrumental track, "Super Magic 2000," would be right at home on an indie-rock record. And of course there's plenty of that thing Isaak does best: quintessential love's-gone-wrong 'n' let's-make-it-right songs, as on the loping, country-tinged "This Time" and the teary "Walk Slow." *—Denise Sullivan*

The Isley Brothers

f. 1954, Cincinnati, OH
Frat Rock, Quiet Storm, Urban, R&B, Funk, Soul
First formed in the early '50s, the Isley Brothers enjoyed one of the longest, most influential, and most diverse careers in the pantheon of popular music. In 1957, the siblings debuted with a string of failed doo wop singles. Their first effort for RCA, the call-and-response classic "Shout," failed to reach the pop Top 40 on its initial release, although it eventually became a frequently covered favorite. Still, success eluded the Isleys, and only after they left RCA in 1962 did they again have another hit, this time with their seminal cover of the Topnotes' "Twist and Shout." Like so many of the brothers' early R&B records, "Twist and Shout" earned greater commercial success when later rendered by a white group—in this case, the Beatles; other acts who notched hits by closely following the Isleys' blueprint were the Yardbirds ("Respectable," also covered by the Outsiders) and the Human Beinz ("Nobody But Me"). The Isleys signed to the Motown subsidiary Tamla in 1965, where they joined forces with the famed Holland-Dozier-Holland writing and production team. Their first single, the shimmering "This Old Heart of Mine," was their finest moment yet, and barely missed the pop Top Ten. The record was their only hit on Motown, however. The muscular and funky "It's Your Thing" hit Number Two on the U.S. charts in 1969, and became their most successful record. Spearheaded by Ernie Isley's hard-edged guitar leads, the group began incorporating more and more rock material into its repertoire as the 1970s dawned, and scored hits with covers of Stephen Stills' "Love the One You're With," Eric Burdon & War's "Spill the Wine," and Bob Dylan's "Lay Lady Lay." In 1973, the Isleys scored a massive hit with their rock-funk fusion cover of their own earlier single "Who's That Lady," retitled "That Lady (Part I)"; as the decade wore on, the group again altered its sound to fit into the booming disco market, and while their success on pop radio ran dry, they frequently topped the R&B charts. *—Jason Ankeny*

Twist & Shout! / 1962 / Sundazed ✦✦✦
On this album, The Isleys tried to mine the "Twist & Shout" groove for all it was worth. Produced by Bert Berns, over half the material was written or co-written by "Russell"; the same Russell who co-wrote "Twist And Shout," it was a pseudonym for Berns himself. Not that this was always necessarily a bad thing; "Twist And Shout" was a stone classic, and many of the other tunes do their best to emulate its groove with Latin rhythms and The Isleys' frayed, gospelish vocals. Some of the tracks, though, do little more than rework the basic riff, and even the ones that aren't blatant rewrites don't measure up to the hit. The ballad "Time After Time" is a nice change of pace, and the brothers are never less than energetic and entertaining, but this is really not that strong as a whole. The CD reissue on Sundazed includes three bonus tracks: the previously unreleased (and unremarkable) "Crazy Love" and the cool singles "Twistin' With Linda" and "Nobody But Me," which are easily available on Rhino's *Story* compilation. *—Richie Unterberger*

Get Into Something / 1970 / T Neck ✦✦✦
Another T-Neck release to receive reissue through Sony's Legacy division in the late '90s, *Get Into Something* boasts six Top 30 R&B chart hits. The first side serves up horn-inflected party jams, including the rousing title track and "Freedom," the latter of which sums up the record's overall uplifting theme of independence. The record isn't without its missteps—the sexist lyrics of "Take Inventory" are highly questionable: "Don't be so loyal and don't be so true/ 'cause if you are boy, they'll run over you." "Bless" is an obvious rewrite of "It's Your Thing"; the Isleys would have been better off leaving that classic alone. A trio of ballads are offered up on the flip, including "I Got to Find Me One." A song of devotion, it pleads for "one girl who believes in me and wants to marry me." Call me crazy, but wouldn't marriage render the taking of inventory an impossibility? Though not revolutionary or trailblazing, *Get Into Something* is every bit an excellent and vibrant funk/soul record. *—Andy Kellman*

Givin' It Back / 1971 / T Neck ✦✦✦
Containing two Stephen Stills selections, as well as CSNY's "Ohio," on the outside this album comes across like a tribute to the roots-rockers who once dubbed themselves the "Frozen Noses." Yet, the Isleys being the Isleys, they do a wonderful job reinterpreting the hit songs of CSNY and others, as their searing version of "Ohio," almost sensualizing violence in its crawling tempo, demonstrates. Also included is a great version of "Spill the Wine," as well as Bill Withers' "Cold Bologna." By no means a top priority for R&B fans, or even fans of the Isley Brothers, *Givin' It Back* is, nevertheless, an interesting album to hear if you can find it. *—Steve Kurutz*

The Isleys Live / 1973 / Rhino ✦✦✦✦✦
The 1973 Isley Brothers album *Isleys Live* received the makeover treatment in 1996 by Rhino Records, who remastered the whole disc and lengthened it with several extra selections not included on the original. The end result is one of the finest funk/soul live albums ever recorded. The first eight tracks come from club gigs in 1971 and '72, while the last three are from a 1969 show at Yankee Stadium. The group's biggest and most identifiable hit, "It's Your Thing," and is featured twice, each version extremely inspired. But the most interesting thing about *The Isleys Live* is the inclusion of several cover songs, such as Carole King's "It's Too Late," Neil Young's "Ohio," Bob Dylan's "Lay Lady Lay," and Stephen Stills' "Love the One You're With." The covers aren't straight-ahead rock readings, either; the Isleys inject their own funk 'n' soul into them, making the songs their own. The album is also a showcase for the talents of the woefully underrated guitarist Ernie Isley, who simply wails on a cover of Jimi Hendrix's "Machine Gun," and plays fantastically throughout. *—Greg Prato*

Brother, Brother, Brother / 1972 / T Neck ✦✦✦✦
With 1972's *Brother, Brother, Brother*, younger brothers Ernie and Marvin, along with in-law relative Chris Jasper, began to play major roles in the groups' sound. This also marked their first attempt to Isleyize classics made famous by others. Their rendition of Carole King's "It's Too Late" rivals the original, Ron Isley sings the tender ballad in a softer voice then he used on previous recordings. An update of Jackie Shannon's "Put a Little Love in Your Heart" is an uplifter. They didn't completely alienate fans of their harsher sound, the rocking, humorous "Pop That Thang" and "Lay Away" are fine examples of R&B/Rock. "Pop That Thang" has a sloopy beat and biting lyrics, while "Lay Away" takes off on the popular buying option before the advent of the credit card. The Isleys were big Carole King fans, in addition to "It's Too Late," they perform two other King songs, "Brother, Brother" and "Keep on Walkin'." The latter is coupled with "Sweet Season." Their own "Work to Do" is a stone rocker that has been recorded by many, including the Average White Band, who scored big with the cooker 30 years after its release, it remains one of the Isley Brothers' most requested songs. *—Andrew Hamilton*

☆ **3 + 3** / 1973 / T Neck ✦✦✦✦✦
Recorded in 1973, *3 + 3* was a major turning point for the Isley Brothers. With this album, the Isleys moved their T-Neck label from Buddah to Epic/CBS (which became Epic/Sony in the early '90s), and it was at Epic that they unveiled their new lineup. Lead singer Ronald Isley and his siblings O'Kelly and Rudolph remained, but the Isleys became a sextet instead of a trio when cousin Chris Jasper and younger brothers Ernie and Marvin were added. This new lineup was called 3 + 3, and the addition of Jasper on keyboards, Ernie on guitar, and Marvin on bass added exciting new elements to the Isleys' sound. One of finest R&B bassists of the 1970s, the ever-so-funky Marvin is in a class with heavyweights like Larry Graham and Louis Johnson—and Ernie is a stunning guitarist who is heavily influenced by Jimi Hendrix but has a distinctive style of his own. The Isleys had always been lovers of rock, but with the addition of Ernie, their sound became even more overtly rock-influenced. Nonetheless, the rock and pop elements didn't alienate R&B audiences, which ate this album up. The single "That Lady" (which is based on an Impressions-like gem they had recorded in 1964) was a major hit, and the Isleys are equally captivating on soul interpretations of Seals & Crofts' "Summer Breeze," James Taylor's "Don't Let Me Be Lonely Tonight," and the Doobie Brothers' "Listen to the Music." With this superb album, the Isley Brothers sounded better than ever—and they gained a lot of new fans without sacrificing the old ones. *—Alex Henderson*

The Heat Is On / 1975 / T Neck ✦✦✦✦✦

Live It Up / Jan. 1975 / T Neck ✦✦✦✦

Harvest for the World / 1976 / T Neck ✦✦✦✦

Go for Your Guns / 1977 / T Neck ✦✦✦✦

Showdown / 1978 / T Neck ✦✦✦✦

Winner Takes All / 1979 / T Neck ✦✦✦

Go All the Way / 1980 / T Neck ✦✦✦

Grand Slam / 1981 / T Neck ✦✦✦

Between the Sheets / 1983 / T Neck ✦✦✦

Greatest Hits & Rare Classics / Feb. 1991 / Motown ✦✦✦✦✦
Although the Isleys recorded some good stuff for Motown in the late '60s, it's generally true that the label's attempts to fit them into the standard Motown production line inhibited their creativity and individuality. This 22-track retrospective of their Motown days is dominated by material from in-house songwriters like Eddie Holland, Smokey Robinson, and Ivory Joe Hunter and doesn't rank among the Isleys' best work, though it's respectable enough. The best tracks—the Top Ten hit "This Old Heart of Mine," "Behind a Painted Smile," and "Take Some Time Out for Love"—are available on the Rhino best-of, but Isleys fans will find this a worthwhile summary of their brief Motown stay. Includes the original versions of two of their biggest hits cut for other labels, "Twist & Shout" and "It's Your Thing." —*Richie Unterberger*

It's Your Thing: The Story of the Isley Brothers / Aug. 24, 1999 / Epic/Legacy ✦✦✦✦✦
Divided into two volumes and spanning three discs, Rhino's 1991 compilation *The Isley Brothers Story* was the definitive retrospective of the groundbreaking R&B outfit, containing all of the hits plus key album tracks. Epic/Legacy's similarly titled *It's Your Thing: The Story of the Isley Brothers* attempts to best that record by offering a three-disc box set, filled with all the hits, plus an abundance of rarities. As a matter of fact, in order to differentiate this box from the previous retrospective, the compilers leaned a little too heavily on rarities, putting on alternate takes, live cuts, and outtakes with abandon, sequencing them between the hits and album tracks (at times, this even results in songs repeated back-to-back, as when "Shout" is followed by a live performance of the same song). All this is worthy material and will certainly be of interest to collectors. On the other hand, they weigh down the collection somewhat for less dedicated listeners. They hardly ruin the set, which is quite useful for anyone that wants a comprehensive hits and highlights collection, but compared to the earlier Rhino set, it isn't as engaging or exciting a listen. Ironically, by trying to outdo *The Isley Brothers Story* as a historical piece, it undercuts the band slightly—on the Rhino set, the Isleys always seem as if they're bursting vitality. That same music still sounds extraordinary here, but the context is somewhat a little too studied to replicate that same sense of dynamism. It's still a worthy set, but *It's Your Thing* nevertheless remains in the shadow of *The Isley Brothers Story.* —*Stephen Thomas Erlewine*

Shake It Up, Baby: Shout, Twist and Shout / Mar. 21, 2000 / Varese ✦✦✦✦
If you've been collecting Isley Brothers compilations over the years, you might not be enthused at the prospect of getting "Shout," "Twist and Shout," "Nobody but Me," "Respectable," and "Twistin' With Linda" for the second or third time. Indeed, 12 of these 16 cuts show up on Sundazed's reissue of the *Twist & Shout* album. That consideration aside, this is a good compilation of their early years, spanning the late 1950s to the early 1960s, and focusing mostly on the sides they cut for Wand. In fact, it's all from Wand, except for the key early RCA sides "Shout" and "Respectable"; there's nothing from their UA or T-Neck sessions. Overall, this collection represents the Isleys at their most untamed and gospel-R&B-informed, though it's definitely rock & roll, with a pop appeal added by New York production and outside songwriters like Bert Berns. As for the sides you might not have yet on CD if you're an Isley Brothers fan, the two to look out for are their nice cover of "Make It Easy on Yourself" (which wasn't released until it showed up on an Ace import in 1990) and the upbeat, so-so 1964 single "I'm Laughing to Keep From Crying." —*Richie Unterberger*

★ **The Ultimate Isley Brothers** / Oct. 17, 2000 / Epic/Legacy ✦✦✦✦✦
The Isley Brothers have had such a long and varied career that trying to sum up their highlights in a best-of package is bound to fall short of the mark. That hasn't, of course, kept people from trying to do so, in both single-disc and multi-disc sets. Every song on this 17-song, single-disc anthology was a hit. Yet it's so chronologically unbalanced, and so debatably chosen, as to be nothing more than a trek though some of their most commercially successful releases, entirely omitting many of their finest songs and severely short-changing their vital (and extensive) pre-1970 output. The pre-"It's Your Thing" era is represented by just two tracks, "Twist and Shout" and "Shout," omitting not just bona fide hits like "This Old Heart of Mine," but great cuts like "Nobody but Me" and "Testify." As a survey of their 1970s and early-1980s hits this does a more reasonable job. But still, few would agree that their cover of Seals & Crofts' "Summer Breeze," for instance, is among their best 17 songs, even if it did make number ten on the R&B listings in 1973. One good thing this collection *does* manage to do is include their cool 1971 cover of "Spill the Wine," which somehow did not make it onto the three-CD 1999 box set, *It's Your Thing: The Story of the Isley Brothers.* Other than "Spill the Wine," every song here appears on that box set, which is a recommended alternative if you can cough up a little more dough. Or better yet, try to find Rhino's two-volume, three-CD *Story* series, which not only has better selection and packaging than the Epic/Legacy collections, but sensibly divides the pre-"It's Your Thing" era and the post-"It's Your Thing" era into separate installments. —*Richie Unterberger*

Isotope 217

f. 1996, Chicago, IL
Experimental Rock, Indie Rock, Post-Rock/Experimental
The Chicago-based jazz-funk fusion ensemble Isotope 217 featured guitarist Jeff Parker along with percussionists John Herndon and Dan Bitney, all three better known for their work in Tortoise; the roster on the group's 1997 Thrill Jockey label debut *The Unstable Molecule* also includes trumpeter Rob Mazurek, bassist Matt Lux, and trombonist Sara P. Smith. *Utonian Automatic* followed in 1999, along with a split collaboration with Commander Mindfuck and Designer. A year later, *Who Stole the I Walkman* was released. —*Jason Ankeny*

● **The Unstable Molecule** / Nov. 4, 1997 / Thrill Jockey/New Beyond ✦✦✦✦
Isotope 217, one of Rob Mazurek's numerous Chicago jazz side projects, finds itself in a precarious position somewhere between post-rock and jazz. Isotope grew out of weekly jam sessions around the Chicago area and are put on record for the first time. Recruiting members of Tortoise (Dan Bitney, John Herndon, and Jeff Parker) for this effort, there is a pronounced lo-fi vibe, which is counteracted by Mazurek's jazz ambition. The end result is an album that is neither straight-ahead jazz or space-rock, but a quirky, funk-flavored, astute musical venture. Tracks like "Kryptonite Smokes the Red Line" and "La Jetee" explore mellow spaces and employ the uses of varied instrumentation including cello and other strings. "Audio Boxing" and "Beneath the Undertow" rely on catchy horn arrangements and precise construction, while providing a counterpoint to the subdued nature of the other tracks. *The Unstable Molecule* will satisfy anyone who has a taste for out of the ordinary jazz, and an inclination toward funk would not hurt either. It provides a consistent listen, but must be understood as a bridge between two genres. It is a serious effort to assimilate a post-rock sound with contemporary jazz, and it succeeds well. —*Marc Gilman*

Utonian Automatic / Aug. 10, 1999 / Thrill Jockey ✦✦✦✦
Isotope 217's second album *Utonian Automatic* contains more angular, extended fusion experiments like the jagged, noisy opener "Luh" and the quietly skewed "Rest for the Wicked." The group's percussive elements come to the fore on "Looking After Life on Mars," while "New Beyond"'s moody, murky keyboards settle the song into an uneasy lull. Over the course of *Utonian Automatic*'s seven tracks, Isotope 217 expand their experimental style, making it even more diverse and challenging. —*Heather Phares*

Who Stole the I Walkman? / Aug. 8, 2000 / Thrill Jockey ✦✦

The Iveys

f. 1968, **db.** 1969
Essentially the same as Badfinger, the Iveys landed on the Beatles' Apple label in late 1968 after the Beatles' personal assistant, Mal Evans, encouraged them to submit tapes to Paul McCartney. Their bright, melodic, and harmony-filled pop/rock sound immediately drew comparisons to the Beatles and to the work of McCartney in particular. Their sole album, *Maybe Tomorrow*, released in Europe in mid-1969, was an accomplished if somewhat lightweight collection of original material, reflecting the heavy influence of both McCartney and Ray Davies (indeed, the latter had expressed interest in producing the group before Apple picked them up). The LP gathered little attention, but after a name change to Badfinger, the replacement of bassist Ron Griffiths by Joey Molland, a commission to score the Peter Sellers/Ringo Starr film *The Magic Christian*, and a McCartney-penned hit single from the movie ("Come and Get It"), the group was on their way. A half-dozen of the tunes from *Maybe Tomorrow* ended up on Badfinger's first proper album, *Magic Christian Music.* —*Richie Unterberger*

Maybe Tomorrow / 1969 / Capitol ✦✦✦
Issued at long last in the U.S. in 1992, this is decent late-'60s British pop-rock, if somewhat less developed and more precious than Badfinger's prime efforts. Six of the better tracks were used on *Magic Christian*. The ones that got left behind are certainly not an embarrassment, with "Yesterday Ain't Coming Back," "Angelique," and "I've Been Waiting" (by far the album's hardest-rocking tune) ranking as the standouts. The CD reissue adds four rare cuts, two of them previously unreleased. —*Richie Unterberger*

Ivy

f. 1990
Indie Pop, Indie Rock, Alternative Pop/Rock
Less than a year after moving to New York from France in 1989, vocalist Dominique Durand formed the indie-pop band Ivy with guitarist Andy Chase. The two recorded a song together and when it clicked, they recruited bassist Adam Schlesinger (formerly with the Belltower) and signed with Seed Records. Ivy's first single, "Get Enough," was awarded Single of the Week by *NME*, and the 1994 EP *Lately* also drew praise from *Spin*. The group added guitarist Mike Viola and drummer Rafa Maciejak for the 1995 debut album *Realistic*, produced by Kurt Ralske. Two years later, Ivy switched labels and signed with Atlantic, releasing their second album, *Apartment Life*, in the fall of that year. —*John Bush*

Realistic / Feb. 14, 1995 / Seed ✦✦✦
Realistic isn't a great album on its own, but it hints strongly at Ivy's potential. A good deal of the songwriting comes from Academy Award-nominated Adam Schlesinger (also of Fountains of Wayne), who has an incredible ability to crank out pop songs—the writing on *Realistic* is occasionally marvelous, but bland. Overly slick production and a few lackadaisical songs keep the album from becoming very memorable. While French singer Dominique Durand's wispy, enchanting voice and several great pop songs ("Everyday," "Dying Star") make *Realistic* worthwhile, the band's later releases bring more life to Ivy's smooth and gentle style of pop. —*Nitsuh Abebe*

● **Apartment Life** / Oct. 7, 1997 / Atlantic ✦✦✦✦✦

Apartment Life, Ivy's second album, is an impressive leap forward for the trio, finding them consolidating their strengths while moving forward into new territory. Ivy has a lush sound that is derived equally from ethereal indie pop and classic '60s pop. Dominique Durand's voice is alternately haunting and beautiful, giving the songs an otherworldly quality, while Adam Schlesinger and Andy Chase's rhythm section keeps the music pinned down to earth. The result is a record that melodic, memorable and lovely—a rare late-'90s pop record that sounds utterly modern while evoking classic traditions. —*Stephen Thomas Erlewine*

Long Distance / Jul. 10, 2001 / Nettwerk America ✦✦✦

Long Distance adds some production tricks and subtle electronic flourishes to the polished pop Ivy perfected on *Apartment Life* but forgets the hooks and melodies that made their second album so delightful. Unfortunately, *Long Distance*'s airy songs breeze past without many distinguishing characteristics. The album's slick synths and trip-hop beats are dated—even trip-popsters like Morcheeba and Sneaker Pimps abandoned this sound years ago. "Lucy Doesn't Love You"'s sassy brass and lilting melody suggest a more sat-isfying song than it delivers, but the glossy, busy production smothers songs like "One More Last Kiss" and the seductive, bossa nova-tinged "Let's Stay Inside"; both need a more intimate approach. However, a handful of songs display some spirit and personality: "Disappointed"'s taut rhythm and slinky guitars provide a sleekly sexy backdrop for Dominique Durand's wistful vocals, and the shock of hearing some distorted guitars on "Blame it on Yourself" makes it memorable for that reason alone. Covering the Blow Monkeys' "Digging Your Scene" might have been an ironic move, but it's a highlight, due to its superior songwriting. Though "While We're in Love"'s poignant trip-hop actually works, the blasé, lovelorn lyrics —"We know it won't last forever/Because we're not meant to be together"—sound tired. *Long Distance*'s successful moments make its well-groomed monotony especially frustrating: Ivy polished these songs to a fare-thee-well and invited guests like James Iha and Eric Matthews to play on them, yet they couldn't give them more individuality or emotion. Ultimately, it's a "tasteful" album: vaguely hip background music for coffeehouses, soundtracks, and anyone else looking for a veneer of coolness. No one's asking Ivy to play lo-fi noise-rock, but *Long Distance* indicates that they're satisfied with trendy prettiness instead of looking for lasting beauty. —*Heather Phares*

J

Jackie & the Starlites

f. 1960, **db.** 1963
Doo Wop, R&B

Jackie and the Starlites were another one-hit wonder doo wop group—"Valerie," cut for Bobby Robinson's Fury label in 1960, being their one hit; it was cut at the tail end of the doo wop era and, indeed, may have been among the first songs in that style to appeal as an "oldie" in style. It barely brushed the national charts, but it was embraced by the community of doo wop singers as a standard.

Jackie La Rue originally started singing with an outfit called the Five Wings in the early 1950s, and cut a pair of singles with the group for King Records in 1955 before breaking up that year. Two of their members went on to form the Dubs, but La Rue wasn't heard from again in music until 1960, when the Starlites coalesced, consisting of Jackie Rue, as he was then known, Alton Thomas, John Felix, and Billy Montgomery. Rue was the star of the show as a superb acting singer, whose feigned weeping was apparently utterly convincing to onlookers and listeners. Their records following their successful debut were a mix of soul and upbeat ballads that failed to capture the imagination in the manner of "Valerie." By 1963, Fury Records was bankrupt, although the group managed to move on to Mascot Records in 1962 before disbanding sometime in the mid-'60s. Jackie Rue died of a drug overdose sometime in the late 1960s or early 1970s. —*Bruce Eder*

● **Jackie & the Starlites Meet the Bopchords: Golden Classics** / Apr. 19, 1990 / Collectables ♦♦♦♦♦

Valerie / 1991 / Relic ♦♦♦♦♦
This is one of the better doo wop collections one can buy, despite its coming out very late in the history of the form. Maybe the biggest surprise here is "I'm Comin' Home," and a track that anticipates the Rolling Stones' show-stopped "I'm Alright" with echoes of Smokey Robinson & the Miracles' "Way Over There," with a wailing, vocal cord-ripping performance by Rue. A lot of this stuff holds up well, even if Rue's weeping act gets a little predictable at times. "Don't Be Afraid," "Valerie," "Seven Day Fool," "I'm Coming Home," and a half dozen others put this collection over the top, and one nice bonus amid the singing is the surprisingly dexterous guitar backing on a lot of the material here. Proper master tapes seem to have been used, and some of this stuff appears here in stereo for the first time ever. —*Bruce Eder*

The Jackson 5

f. 1966, Gary, IN
Pop-Soul, Motown, Soul

The Jackson 5 was Motown's last great pop group and among the most successful singles acts of the '70s. The group consisted of five brothers—Jackie (b. May 4, 1951), Tito (b. Oct. 15, 1953), Jermaine (b. Dec. 11, 1954), Marlon (b. Mar. 12, 1957), and Michael Jackson (b. Aug. 29, 1958). They grew up in Gary, IN, and were first organized as a group by their father, Joe Jackson, in 1966. In essence, the group was a vocal ensemble centered on Michael, who, though the youngest, was clearly the most talented. The group came to the attention of Motown and was signed in 1969. Their first four singles, "I Want You Back," "ABC," "The Love You Save," and "I'll Be There," all hit number one in 1970; "Mama's Pearl" and "Never Can Say Goodbye" did almost as well in 1971.

In 1972, Motown launched both Michael Jackson and Jermaine Jackson as solo acts, and the group's efforts were gradually less successful in the following years, though "Dance Machine" was a big hit in 1974. In 1975, Jackie, Tito, Marlon, and Michael signed to Epic Records, adding brother Randy (b. Oct. 29, 1961) and became the Jacksons (the name the Jackson 5 was owned by Motown). (Although Jermaine stayed at Motown, he rejoined the group in 1984.) —*William Ruhlmann*

Diana Ross Presents the Jackson 5 / 1969 / Motown ♦♦♦♦♦
This Gary, IN family ensemble exploded onto the national scene with immediate and long-lasting impact in 1970. This album's combination of youthful exuberance and innocence, coupled with Motown production magic, yielded quick results, as "I Want You Back" topped both R&B and pop charts. Michael Jackson, the nine-year-old lead singer, became a national darling. Once they hit the big time, there was controversy over whether Diana Ross actually discovered them, but there was no question that Motown had unveiled another superstar act. —*Ron Wynn*

ABC / Apr. 1970 / Motown ♦♦♦♦♦
A fabulous album, arguably their best on Motown. While the debut album established the group's sound, this one cemented it and also made it clear that Michael was going to be a huge star for a long time. His blend of gentility, soul, and innocence sparkled on the title cut and throughout the album, while the songs, production, arrangement, and musical support were superb. —*Ron Wynn*

Third Album / Aug. 1970 / Motown ♦♦♦
The Jackson 5 solidified the audience they enjoyed with their first two albums by turning in a consistently produced and occasionally exciting third record. It included the fine ballad "I'll Be There" and another hit in "Mama's Pearl"; the group hadn't yet become hardened by Motown manipulation or troubled by internal dissension. Michael Jackson was still widely beloved and seen as the 1970s' Frankie Lymon, and this LP became their third Top Ten album in a row. —*Ron Wynn*

Maybe Tomorrow / 1971 / Motown ♦♦♦
Another fine album, with Michael Jackson displaying surprising conviction and earnestness on the title track. The group was rolling along with a strong mix of novelty/dance hits, ballads, and soul covers, scoring massive pop success and turning up all over the airwaves. —*Ron Wynn*

Looking Through the Windows / 1972 / Motown ♦♦♦
The Jackson 5 were still an engaging, delightful family unit when this album was released. They hadn't yet lost their innocent qualities and were also continuing to get first-rate material, production, and arrangements. They were three years away from the bitter fights that marred their exit from Motown, and Michael hadn't yet become a huge solo act. —*Ron Wynn*

Skywriter / 1973 / Motown ♦♦

Get It Together / 1973 / Motown ♦♦

Dancing Machine / 1974 / Motown ♦♦♦♦
For a brief time, it seemed as if the magic was back between Motown and the Jackson 5. The title track was their best up-tempo hit since "ABC," and put them back on top of the R&B charts for the first time in three years. It just missed topping the pop charts as well, peaking at number two. They even got a second chart hit from the album, and it restored their position within the pop and R&B communities. —*Ron Wynn*

The Jacksons / 1976 / Epic ♦♦♦
After the commercial reprieve from the innovative "Dancing Machine" and album of the same name, the successful five-year relationship with Motown and Berry Gordy ended. Their last Motown effort, *Moving Violation*, barely made a dent. After an acrimonious split, brother Jermaine Jackson stayed at Motown and Gordy fought and won, keeping the Jackson 5 moniker. *The Jacksons* isn't only an Epic label debut, it's the first album to feature youngest brother Randy Jackson. To ensure chart success, the group was teamed with Philadelphia producers Kenneth Gamble and Leon Huff, as well as their staff of writers and players. Despite the promise, *The Jacksons* was hampered by derivative tracks and a lack of knowing what to do with the group, particularly lead singer, Michael Jackson. The big hit here, the jerky, "Enjoy Yourself" perfectly captured Michael Jackson's late adolescence and newfound vocal tics and inflections. The song that best captures the Philly sound is "Show You the Way to Go" which has a pretty melody and a great vocal from Michael Jackson, but is essentially lyrically barren. The Dexter Wansel written and produced "Keep on Dancing" matches a substandard disco-fied track to Michael Jackson's singular vocals. The last track, the graceful "Blues Away" marks the writing debut of the group and is a great match between artists and producers. For the most part *The Jacksons* gives the guys by-the-numbers Philly tracks that could have been easily done by Lou Rawls. Despite the best songs, *The Jacksons* misses more than it hits. —*Jason Elias*

Goin' Places / 1977 / Epic ♦♦♦
The Jacksons' move to Epic regenerated their enthusiasm and spirit for several years. The Gamble/Huff team brought them fresh material and new production ideas, as well as better tracks and arrangements than they'd gotten in quite a while on Motown. This album got them R&B and pop hits and kept the family act in the spotlight for a little while longer. —*Ron Wynn*

Destiny / 1978 / Epic ♦♦♦♦♦
The Jacksons are finally turned loose to write and produce themselves, and the result is their best (non-hits collection) ever. The dance tracks still sound fresh; "Blame It on the Boogie," "Shake Your Body (Down to the Ground)"; and the ballads are heartfelt and smooth. This album is a dry run for Michael Jackson's adult solo career. —*William Ruhlmann*

Triumph / 1980 / Epic ♦♦♦♦♦
This album's predecessor *Destiny* was a high-selling album that featured the guys maturing and delving into self-production. In 1980, Michael Jackson's classic *Off the Wall* was still selling. This album has the group fleshing out their sound and songwriting abilities even more. The anthemic "Can't You Feel It" has enough hubris and undeniable craft to get this polished work started. But as *Triumph* plays, what's striking is that the songs don't immediately leap out at you but they all land on their feet. The blissful and funky

"Lovely One," with its effortless, punchy horns, has Michael Jackson with his quirky vocals and charisma. At it's best, this is a collaborative effort, not just super-hot Michael Jackson talking his brothers out for a spin. The Jackie Jackson-penned "Your Ways" creates the right mix of paranoia and uncertainty that meshed well with Michael Jackson's high-pitched and haunted lead. That certainly mixes well with *Triumph*'s best song, "Heartbreak Hotel." The track is an early instance of Michael Jackson's patented love as horror, kisses as doom ethos. The song's creepy aura and sound effects maximize the effect. The only ballad, "Time Waits for No One" has Michael Jackson getting weepy on the delicate and well-arranged track. The masterful "Walk Right Now" and "Give It Up" are two great examples of the group's chops in the studio and their grasp of the L.A. pop/funk sound. *Triumph* is a gorgeous effort and remains an absolute necessity for any comprehensive collection. *—Jason Elias*

Victory / 1984 / Epic ♦♦♦
Victory has the distinctions of being the only Jacksons album to feature all six brothers and the last Jacksons album to feature Michael Jackson. In the four years that had passed since the last Jacksons studio album, *Triumph*, Michael had become the biggest pop star in the world because of 1982's *Thriller*. He had little excuse other than family ties to work with his brothers again, but he agreed to a final album and tour. So, here one has the ludicrous situation of an album in which Marlon Jackson has as prominent a role as Michael Jackson. That's how it sounded to listeners in 1984, anyway, and they weren't fooled—"State of Shock," on which Michael shared vocals with Mick Jagger, was a gold Top Ten hit, and "Torture," which teamed Michael with Jermaine, made the Top 40, while the album went platinum. But the tracks by other group members went virtually ignored. In retrospect, *Victory* is a competent album of slick contemporary R&B, occasionally goosed toward greatness by the appearance of one of pop music's most identifiable voices. Which is the same thing you can say about nearly the entire Jackson 5/Jacksons catalog. *—William Ruhlmann*

2300 Jackson Street / 1989 / Epic ♦♦♦
This was the final gathering of the entire Jackson family, and it turned out to have both historical significance and some musical value. The team of L.A. and Babyface, then emerging as major producers, spearheaded the track "Nothin' Compares to U," and the title track was a nice autobiographical/family outing song. *—Ron Wynn*

Soulsation! / Jun. 27, 1995 / Motown ♦♦♦♦♦
Nineteen years after the release of *Anthology*, Motown finally tops that 33-track, three-LP compilation with this 82-track, four-and-a-half-hour, four-CD/cassette box set. The Jackson 5 were long overdue for box set treatment, and this one is well done. All the hits by the group as well as those by Michael and Jermaine Jackson are here (that is, from 1969-1975, the J5's tenure at Motown), along with a representative sampling of album cuts. The J5's albums were afterthoughts to their singles, but some of these songs are nevertheless interesting, whether the group is covering Sly and the Family Stone or Jackson Browne. An entire disc is given over to previously unreleased or rare tracks from the Motown vaults. Taken together, it may be more than all but the most die-hard fan wants to hear, which may be why Motown rushed out yet another single-disc hits collection, *The Ultimate Collection*, a couple of months later. But if you want the Jackson 5 on Motown, a big chunk of it is here. *—William Ruhlmann*

★ **The Ultimate Collection** / Aug. 15, 1995 / Motown ♦♦♦♦♦
Not quite as extensive as the 33-song *Anthology*, this 21-song single disc does include the group's biggest Motown hits, as well as early solo hits by Michael Jackson and Jermaine Jackson. *Anthology* is still the best way to go for those whose interest isn't deep enough to spring for the *Soulsation!* box. However, if you're on a budget, this does nail down most or all of the key cuts that most listeners want or need. *—Richie Unterberger*

Pre-History: The Lost Steeltown Recordings / Jun. 4, 1996 / Brunswick ♦♦♦
It sounds like Steeltown cut these 14 unpolished, pre-Motown Jackson 5 tracks in a garage, but that's the charm of this CD. Remakes of popular R&B songs rule this roost, and a couple originals had potential. Two tracks came out on a 45 credited to Ripples & Waves plus Michael. On "Let Me Carry Your Schoolbooks," shoddy production killed any possibilities it had; the vocals are practically knocked out by the horrible mix. "I Never Had a Girl," the best original ballad, features some serious crooning from Michael, Jackie, Tito, Jermaine, and Marlon. The "Monologue" and "Jam Session, Pt. 1 & 2" capture the youngsters in the studio unaware the tape was rolling. Motown liked the shuffling "You've Changed" so much they redid it and included it on the Jacksons' debut album. You'll enjoy their adolescent remakes of "My Girl," "Tracks of My Tears," "Under the Boardwalk," and "Saturday Night at the Movies." *—Andrew Hamilton*

20th Century Masters—The Millennium Collection: The Best of Jackson 5 / Oct. 26, 1999 / Motown ♦♦♦
The Jackson 5 installment of MCA's *20th Century Masters: The Millennium Collection* is a terrific, concise collection of the group's 11 biggest hits. There may be some smaller hits missing, but all the big tunes—"I Want You Back," "ABC," "The Love You Save," "I'll Be There," "Never Can Say Goodbye," "Dancing Machine"—are here, along with two solo Michael singles ("Got to Be There," "I Wanna Be Where You Are") and a solo cut from Jermaine ("Daddy's Home"). The end result is a budget-line disc ideal for budget-minded casual fans. *—Stephen Thomas Erlewine*

Anthology / Oct. 24, 2000 / Motown ♦♦♦♦♦
Newly remastered and recompiled for 2000, this version of the Jackson 5's *Anthology* takes the place of the original double-CD set, which was first issued on LP back in 1976. The main difference is that where the first *Anthology* featured some of Michael and Jermaine's earliest solo hits, this one is devoted exclusively to Jackson 5 material, with a little more detail added to the pictures of their early pop-soul years and their later, disco-influenced work. All of the group's charting singles are here, as well as important B-sides and album tracks, including several songs that have never previously appeared on CD. Later hits like "Dancing Machine" and "Hum Along and Dance" are also presented in their full-length LP versions. *—Steve Huey*

Chuck Jackson

b. Jun. 22, 1937, Latta, SC
Vocals / Uptown Soul, Pop-Soul, R&B, Soul
He's relatively forgotten today, and his brand of "uptown" soul is dismissed by the relatively vocal clique of critics who prefer their soul deep and down-home. But Chuck Jackson was a regular visitor to the R&B charts (and an occasional one to the pop listings) in the early '60s with such early pop-soul concoctions as "I Don't Want to Cry," "Any Day Now," and "Tell Him I'm Not Home." His records were very much of a piece with New York pop-rock-soul production, with cheeky brass, sweeping strings, and female backup vocalists. Spotted by Scepter Records while performing with Jackie Wilson's Revue, he started recording for the label in 1961. As was the case with labelmates Dionne Warwick and the Shirelles, Jackson's early-'60s arrangements blended pop, R&B, and New York session professionalism. Like Warwick, Jackson was one of the first singers to successfully record Bacharach-David material. Chuck had some success with some duets with Maxine Brown in the mid-'60s, but he left Wand in 1967 for Motown, at the urging of Smokey Robinson. Jackson was (perhaps understandably) lost in the shuffle during his four years at Motown, and he's barely been heard from since, although he remains a favorite on England's "Northern soul" scene. *—Richie Unterberger*

The Great Recordings: The Best of Chuck Jackson / 1995 / Tomato ♦♦♦♦♦
This 46-song, double-CD compilation of Wand-era recordings is the most extensive Jackson retrospective, though it doesn't include every last worthwhile track. It does contain his most important songs, as well as a few of his duets with Maxine Brown, but the programming leaves something to be desired, inserting some half-baked instrumentals, live cuts, and Elvis Presley covers among the prime stuff. *—Richie Unterberger*

Something You Got / Jun. 1996 / Soul Classics/Ichiban ♦♦♦♦♦
All 20 of the duet tracks that Jackson recorded with Maxine Brown for the Wand label between 1965 and 1967, comprising the entirety of their two albums for the company. It's reasonable pop/soul, but not nearly as memorable as the best male-female soul duets of the era (like the ones by Marvin Gaye and various Motown partners, or by Otis Redding and Carla Thomas). Highlights are the early compositions by the Jo Armstead-Nick Ashford-Valerie Simpson team, including a version of "Let's Go Get Stoned" that was recorded (though not released) before Ray Charles' more famous hit rendition. *—Richie Unterberger*

★ **The Very Best of Chuck Jackson 1961-1967** / Jun. 17, 1997 / Varese ♦♦♦♦♦
Varese's *The Very Best of Chuck Jackson* is a 16-track retrospective of his classic Wand recordings, featuring all of his biggest hits ("I Don't Want to Cry," "I Wake Up Crying," "Any Day Now," "Tell Him I'm Not Home," and the Maxine Brown duet "Something You Got") and several fine, lesser-known singles. Jackson's work was remarkably consistent, and there are many fine songs that didn't make the cut, but *The Very Best of Chuck Jackson* is the best single-disc overview of his greatest music yet assembled. *—Stephen Thomas Erlewine*

Smooth, Smooth Jackson / Jan. 27, 1998 / Sequel ♦♦♦♦
An import compilation of Chuck Jackson's All Platinum sides recorded in the '70s. Many are unaware Jackson recorded on the label that spawned the Moments, the Whatnauts, Sylvia, and Shirley Goodman before transforming into rap city with Sugar Hill Records. He only mustered two tiny hits: "Needing You, Wanting You" and "I've Got the Need," both written by Al Goodman, Harry Ray, and Walter Morris. The former features the Moments crooning delicately behind Jackson's smooth baritone; the latter is a duet with Sylvia Robinson that sounds like Al Goodman singing and not Jackson. The good stuff here includes "Cover Up or Get Ready," which is about as risqué as Jackson gets; he tells his lady "I've had a hard day but if you keep lying there like that you're gonna pay." "True Believer" and "Keep Ringing My Bell" are solid, as are Jacksons' updates of his own "I Don't Want to Cry" and "Any Day Now." He transforms chart busters—"And I Am Telling You," "It's Not Unusual," and "After the Loving"—into his personal toys. A worthy collection by an R&B legend. *—Andrew Hamilton*

I'll Never Get Over You / Dec. 1, 1998 / Varese ♦♦♦♦
Chuck Jackson's resonant baritone hardly gets untracked on this Charles Wallert production. Wallert's so laid-back on these 14 songs that the sound is closer to easy listening than soul. The only song he claims is an aching rendition of "Walk Away From Love," the David Ruffin hit (the beautiful female voices deserve bonuses), and two duets: "If I Let Myself Go" and "What Goes Around Comes Around." The title track is a rather mundane, lightweight track, and Wallert's "Reaching' for the Stars" is even flimsier. An older, mellower Jackson represents here; the stud who hit with "I Don't Wanna Cry" and "Any Day Now" is missing in action. *—Andrew Hamilton*

Freddie Jackson

b. Oct. 2, 1956, Harlem, New York City, NY
Vocals / Urban, Soul
Freddie Jackson ranks right behind Luther Vandross as the premier male vocalist of the '80s and early '90s in Urban Contemporary circles. He may in fact be a better pure soul singer, having had a solid gospel background. Jackson hasn't been able to duplicate Vandross' crossover appeal, however, although he's had a large number of R&B smashes. Since 1985, when his debut LP, *Rock Me Tonight*, was released on Capitol, Jackson has had many Top Ten R&B singles, and from 1985 until 1987, he had six number ones,

another number two, and two others at number eight and number nine respectively. He finally departed Capitol in 1994 for RCA, looking for a fresh start with *Here It Is*. After a long hiatus, Jackson resurfaced in early 2000 with *Life After 30*. *—Ron Wynn*

The Greatest Hits of Freddie Jackson / Jan. 25, 1994 / Capitol ♦♦♦♦♦
During his five-album stay at Capitol, Freddie Jackson repeatedly showed himself to be a soul man of unusual merit. Ranging from outstanding to decent, all five of his Capitol albums are worth owning. But if a listener is allotted only one Jackson CD, *The Greatest Hits of Freddie Jackson* is the logical choice. From "Rock Me Tonight," "Nice & Slow" and "Tasty Love" to "I Could Use a Little Love (Right Now)" and "Jam Tonight," all of the essential Jackson material is included. The CD does a fine job of summarizing Jackson's accomplishments at Capitol and proves that his extremely devoted following is well deserved. *—Alex Henderson*

● **For Old Times Sake: The Freddie Jackson Story** / Aug. 20, 1996 / EMI ♦♦♦♦
Although there's a fair amount of duplication between this and *Greatest Hits*, it's not exactly a greatest hits collection, divided as it is between high-charting singles and album tracks. It's perhaps more oriented toward his lover-man outings than *Greatest Hits*, which remains the first choice if you only want one Freddie Jackson disc. *—Richie Unterberger*

Anthology / Jun. 2, 1998 / Capitol ♦♦♦♦
Sliding over notes like satin sheets, you couldn't turn on a black radio station in the '80s without hearing Freddie Jackson's velvet vocals. From 1985 to 1992, the crooner racked up 17 Top Ten hits, making him one of the decade's biggest R&B stars. *Freddie Jackson Anthology* chronicles Jackson's sexy soul singing on two CDs that display his talent for conveying heartfelt emotions. With classics such as "Rock Me Tonight," "You Are My Lady" and "Love Me Down," this collection stylishly showcases the best of '80s R&B. *—Rosalind Cummings-Yeates*

J.J. Jackson (Jerome Louis Jackson)

b. Apr. 8, 1941, Brooklyn, NY
Vocals, Percussion / Pop-Soul, Soul
One of the most interesting obscure figures of '60s soul, Jackson scored a mammoth R&B hit in 1966 with one of the most infectious dance smashes of the decade, "But It's Alright." The New Yorker had worked as an arranger for Jack McDuff and Jimmy Witherspoon before his manager arranged for Jackson to come to England in 1966. Though "But It's Alright," with its classic stuttering guitar riff and sharp horn charts, sounded as authentic as any Stax/Volt single, it was actually recorded in the U.K. with British session musicians. Jackson—a mammoth, nearly 300-pound man who also played organ—was a grainy, good-natured belter in the mold of Otis Redding. A talented songwriter who penned much of his own material, he wrote the A-side of one of the Pretty Things' best mid-'60s R&B/raunch singles ("Come See Me"). Jackson never matched the success of "But It's Alright," but cut some singles which are highly valued by English Northern soul connoisseurs. His hard-to-find 1969 and 1970 albums found him exploring, in the manner of most other soul stars of the time, increased social consciousness in his songwriting and increasingly sophisticated horn and string arrangements. He later surfaced as a Los Angeles disc jockey, leading to a cameo appearance in the film *Car Wash* that has been sampled by numerous rappers. *—Richie Unterberger*

● **The Great J.J. Jackson** / 1966 / See for Miles ♦♦♦♦♦
A reissue of his 1966 album, recorded in England with British producer Miki Dallon. Includes "But It's Alright," his version of "Come See Me" (actually recorded after the Pretty Things' rendition), and the effervescent, boastful "I Dig Girls." Much more solid than the average '60s soul album, it shows Jackson as a fine songwriter and infectiously throaty vocalist on a mixture of up-tempo ravers and deep soul ballads. Somewhat similar to Otis Redding, but more pop-oriented, which is not necessarily a bad thing when you can make it work as well as J.J. does. *—Richie Unterberger*

Janet Jackson

b. May 16, 1966, Gary, IN
Vocals / Club/Dance, Adult Contemporary, Urban, Dance-Pop
Janet Jackson is the ninth and last child in the musically talented Jackson family that includes the Jackson 5, Michael Jackson, and Jermaine Jackson. Janet Jackson performed onstage with her brothers at the age of seven. At ten, she acted in the TV series *Good Times* and was later seen in *Diff'rent Strokes* and *Fame*. She released her first album, *Janet Jackson*, in 1982 and her second, *Dream Street*, in 1984, but neither of these records was notably successful. Then, in 1985, Jackson turned to the production team of Jimmy Jam and Terry Lewis (formerly of the Time) for the album *Control*, which, ironically, emphasized the artist's new maturity and independence, even though most of the songs were co-compositions of the three. *Control* was a massive hit: it topped the charts, selling more than four million copies, and spawned five Top Ten hits, including the Number One "When I Think of You." The follow-up, *Rhythm Nation 1814*, did even better, spawning seven Top Ten hits, among them the Number Ones "Miss You Much," "Escapade," and "Black Cat." In 1991, Jackson signed a new recording contract with Virgin Records for a reported $32 million. 1993's *janet.* proved to be as successful as her previous two releases, featuring a series of Top Ten singles including "If" and "That's the Way Love Goes." *—William Ruhlmann*

Janet Jackson / 1982 / A&M ♦♦

Dream Street / 1984 / A&M ♦♦

Control / 1986 / A&M ♦♦♦♦♦
Jam and Lewis tailor their contemporary dance-pop to the emerging personality of Jackson, who is attempting to take "Control" of her life on this record. In the course of that attempt, she comes across as an aggressive, independent woman, notably on "What Have You Done for Me Lately." But the album is primarily a production showcase; it may be tailored to Jackson's persona, but the real artists are Jam and Lewis. *—William Ruhlmann*

Rhythm Nation 1814 / 1989 / A&M ♦♦♦♦♦
After shocking the R&B world with 1986's *Control*—a gutsy, risk-taking triumph that was a radical departure from her first two albums—Michael and Jermaine Jackson's younger sister reached an even higher artistic plateau with the conceptual *Rhythm Nation 1814*. Once again, she enlists the help of Time graduates Jimmy Jam & Terry Lewis (one of the more soulful production/songwriting teams of 1980s and '90s R&B) with wildly successful results. In 1989, protest songs were common in rap, but rare in R&B—Jackson, following rap's lead, dares to address social and political topics on "The Knowledge," the disturbing "State of the World," and the poignant ballad "Living in a World" (which decries the reality of children being exposed to violence). Jackson's voice is wafer-thin, and she doesn't have much of a range—but she definitely has lots of soul and spirit and uses it to maximum advantage on those gems as well as non-political pieces ranging from the Prince-influenced funk/pop of "Miss You Much" and "Alright" to the caressing, silky ballads "Someday Is Tonight," "Alone," and "Come Back to Me" to the pop/rock smoker "Black Cat." For those purchasing their first Janet Jackson release, *Rhythm Nation* would be an even wiser investment than *Control*—and that's saying a lot. *—Alex Henderson*

janet / May 18, 1993 / Virgin ♦♦♦
After *Control* and *Rhythm Nation 1814*, Janet Jackson had quite a lot to live up to. Anyone who expected Jackson to top *Rhythm Nation*—her crowning achievement and an incredibly tough act to follow—was being unrealistic. But with *janet.*, she delivered a respectable offering that, although not as strong as either *Control* or *Nation*, has many strong points. As before, Jackson is joined by the prolific Jimmy Jam/Terry Lewis team, and their input is valuable on everything from the angry "This Time" and the hypnotic "That's the Way Love Goes" to the '60s-flavored "What'll I Do" and the sociopolitical "The New Agenda" (which features Public Enemy leader Chuck D). But perhaps the CD's most exciting track is "Funky Big Band," which samples jazz legend Lionel Hampton's 1938 big band classic "I'm In the Mood for Swing" with thrilling results. There are a few throwaways (including the lightweight ballad "Again"), but despite its shortcomings, *janet.* is a welcome addition to her catalog. *—Alex Henderson*

★ **Design of a Decade: 1986-1996** / Oct. 10, 1995 / A&M ♦♦♦♦♦
Design of a Decade: 1986/1996 is a misleading title. The bulk of Janet Jackson's greatest hits collection concentrates on *Control* and *Rhythm Nation 1814*, simply by contractual necessity. That is far from a fatal flaw. The hits from those two albums were state-of-the-art dance-pop productions at the time of their release, filled with bottomless beats and memorable, catchy hooks. None of the songs have lost any of their impact, from the funk of "Miss You Much" and "What Have You Done for Me Lately" to the ballads "Let's Wait Awhile" and "Come Back to Me." In addition to all 13 Top 40 hits from *Control* and *Rhythm Nation*—all but one went into the Top Five—*Design of a Decade* includes the biggest and best hit from *janet.*, the sultry "That's the Way Love Goes," and two new songs, "Runaway" and "Twenty Foreplay." It's a credit to Janet Jackson that the two new numbers feel like genuine hits, not tacked-on filler, and help make the album a compulsively listenable greatest hits collection. *—Stephen Thomas Erlewine*

The Velvet Rope / Oct. 7, 1997 / Virgin ♦♦♦
Where *janet.*, Ms. Jackson's third blockbuster album, implied sexuality with its teasing cover and seductive grooves, its sequel, *The Velvet Rope*, is sexually explicit, offering tales of bondage, body piercing, and bisexuality. Not that you'd necessarily know that from listening to *The Velvet Rope*, since the album sags with endless interludes, murmured vocals, and subdued urban grooves. Working with her mainstays Jimmy Jam and Terry Lewis, Jackson essentially reworks the hushed atmosphere of *janet.*, neglecting to put a new sonic spin on the material—for an album that wants to push the limits, it sounds surprisingly tame. Similarly, Jackson's attempts to broaden her sexual horizons frequently sound forced, whether it's the references to piercing or her recasting of Rod Stewart's "Tonight's the Night" as a lesbian anthem. Furthermore, the album is simply too long, which means the best moments sink into the murk. And that's unfortunate, because there are good moments on *The Velvet Rope*, but at its running time of 70+ minutes and 22 tracks, it's hard to work up the patience to find them. *—Stephen Thomas Erlewine*

All for You / Apr. 24, 2001 / Virgin ♦♦♦♦
The Velvet Rope was a fairly bold move on Janet Jackson's part, as she got seriously sexy—too serious, actually, since it had a fairly bitter tone, underscored by hints of perversity. Four years later, marked by one hidden marriage revealed through a divorce, Janet returned with *All for You*, an album that is as about sex as much as *The Velvet Rope*, yet there's a key difference—it feels sexy, not pornographic. With her trusty collaborators Jimmy Jam and Terry Lewis in tow, she's created a record that's luxurious and sensual, spreading leisurely over its 70 minutes, luring you in even when you know better. And there are certainly moments that make you wish you knew better. Though it's hardly as explicit as *The Velvet Rope*, this is her sexiest-sounding record, thanks to Jam and Lewis' silky groove and her breathy delivery, two things that make the record palatable throughout too many spoken interludes and songs that just don't quite click. Even if there is a fair share of filler, this is hardly as strained as *The Velvet Rope* (though in many respects, it's every bit as self-conscious), and there's an ease to its construction, topped off by such songs as "All for You" and "Doesn't Really Matter" that maintain Janet, Jam, and Lewis' reputation as the leading lights of contemporary urban soul. It'd be nicer if the album was leaner, concentrating on just the great songs, but indulgence is what this record encourages. Janet sprawls out throughout the album, indulging her whims, desires, and fantasies, but—fortunately for us—her indulgences are alluring in their self-absorption. Of

course, it helps to have Jam and Lewis on your side to articulate your indulgence. *—Stephen Thomas Erlewine*

Joe Jackson

b. Aug. 11, 1955, Burton-upon-Trent, England

Vocals, Keyboards, Piano / College Rock, Pop/Rock, New Wave, Singer/Songwriter

Of the three angry young men that emerged in the British new wave movement of the early '80s, Joe Jackson was perhaps the most idiosyncratic. Not content with being a pop songwriter, Jackson went to considerable lengths to prove himself as a composer—often, he even seemed to have contempt for pop music itself. Appearing a few years after Elvis Costello and Graham Parker, Joe Jackson was doomed to always live their shadow. Jackson was considerably more ambitious than Parker, rivaling Costello in his stylistic detours. After establishing himself as a gifted songwriter with a pair of edgy new wave pop records, he quickly set out to prove his eclecticism, recording album-length tributes to reggae, jump blues, traditional pop and jazz. While such diversity earned him critical praise and a cult following, it didn't result in widespread acclaim until 1982's *Night and Day*, which launched the jazzy hits "Steppin' Out" and "Always Something Breaking Us in Two." Once he had a taste of success, Jackson didn't become more accessible—he became weirder, crafting a number of self-consciously difficult records intended to push the boundaries of pop. Following his 1987 classical album *Will Power*, Jackson's audience began to decline, and by the early '90s, his cult was a fraction of its size a decade earlier. Despite his shrinking audience, Jackson was even less compromising in the '90s than he was in the '80s, eventually abandoning pop altogether. *—Stephen Thomas Erlewine*

★ **Look Sharp!** / Apr. 1979 / A&M ✦✦✦✦✦

A brilliant, accomplished debut, *Look Sharp!* established Joe Jackson as part of that camp of angry, intelligent young new wavers (i.e., Elvis Costello, Graham Parker) who approached pop music with the sardonic attitude and tense, aggressive energy of punk. Not as indebted to pub-rock as Parker and Costello, and much more lyrically straightforward than the latter, Jackson delivers a set of bristling, insanely catchy pop songs that seethe with energy and frustration. Several deal with the lack of thoughtful reflection in everyday life ("Sunday Papers," "Got the Time"), but many more concern the injuries and follies of romance. In the caustic yet charming witticisms of songs like the hit "Is She Really Going Out With Him?," "Happy Loving Couples," "Fools in Love," and "Pretty Girls," Jackson presents himself on the one hand as a man of integrity seeking genuine depth in love (and elsewhere), but leavens his stance with a wry, self-effacing humor, revealing his own vulnerability to loneliness and to purely physical attraction. *Look Sharp!* is the sound of a young man searching for substance in a superficial world—and it also happens to rock like hell. *—Steve Huey*

I'm the Man / Oct. 1979 / A&M ✦✦✦✦✦

Nearly a rewrite of *Look Sharp*, and capturing all of its brilliance, *I'm the Man* is pure power pop—hook filled, concise, and fun. Includes the wonderful "It's Different for Girls," a marginal hit in both the U.S. and U.K. *—Chris Woodstra*

Beat Crazy / 1980 / A&M ✦✦✦✦

Before exploring jump blues and early R&B on 1981's *Jumpin' Jive* and later jazz and Latin styles on 1982's *Night and Day*, Joe Jackson expanded his power pop and punk m.o. with this, his reggae-tinged third album. Jackson sticks with the short songs and punk feel of his first two releases, but strategically adds rocksteady and jazz elements here and there. A direct reggae influence is heard on such dub-style cuts like "In Every Dream Home," while more of a pastiche approach is evident on tracks like "Mad at You." Jackson even riffs off of Linton Kwesi Johnson's dub poetry sides with the dancefloor politics of "Battleground," while also laying down some straight ska on "Pretty Boys." One also gets intimations of the sophisticated jazz-pop songwriting of *Night and Day* with torching gems like "One to One." As is the case on most of his albums, Jackson covers a wide array of topics here, including modern relationships, feminism, club life, and the social fringe. A solid effort. *—Stephen Cook*

Jumpin' Jive / 1981 / A&M ✦✦✦✦✦

A delightful trip back to '40s and '50s jump blues and big-band swing. With faithful covers of Louis Jordan and Cab Calloway, Jackson appears to be having fun, while helping a new generation discover these classics. *—Chris Woodstra*

Night and Day / 1982 / A&M ✦✦✦✦✦

Like Elvis Costello, Joe Jackson managed some impressive genre jumping during the '80s. The man of "Look Sharp!" fame took in punk, new wave, ska, reggae, pop, and jump blues on his first four albums, managing to keep his fan base relatively intact in the process. Predating other sophisticated jazz-pop offerings from the likes of the Style Council and Everything But the Girl by a few years, Jackson released the mature and decidedly unpunk *Night and Day* in 1982. Evoking both the romanticism of Gershwin and Mercer's Tin Pan Alley Manhattan and the street-savvy sounds of barrio salsa and Latin jazz, Jackson concocts an original and very enjoyable adult contemporary release for the post-punk set. The first half covers the "night" side of things with electro-Latin numbers like "Chinatown" and "T.V. Age" and the hybrid pop gems "Another World" and "Steppin' Out." For the "day" side, Jackson turns classic songsmith ensconced in an Upper West Side apartment; while coming up with his own recasting of classic Broadway dramatics on "Breaking Us in Two" and "Real Men," Jackson provides progressive social commentary on relationships and sexual identity (things could have become mannered if it wasn't for Jackson's measured mix of idealization and originality). Maybe not the thing for moshing teddy boys, but certainly a fresh look for fans wary of another two-chord stomper. *—Stephen Cook*

Body & Soul / 1984 / A&M ✦✦✦

Continuing in his move away from pop music that began with *Night and Day*, Jackson shows his love of '50s jazz with detail best represented by the cover photo (nearly identical to the Sonny Rollins album of the same name). Features his last U.S. hit, "You Can't Get What You Want" and the beautiful "Be My Number Two." *—Chris Woodstra*

Big World / 1986 / A&M ✦✦✦

A brilliant collection of songs, running over an hour, finds Jackson as biting as ever as he surveys the world, but also tenderly reflective on "Home Town." *—William Ruhlmann*

Will Power / 1987 / A&M ✦✦

Live . . . 1980-1986 / 1988 / A&M ✦✦✦

A double-disc live collection, *Live . . . 1980-1986* manages to effectively trace the development of Joe Jackson's diverse career. Drawing from four different periods in the songwriter's career—with each period featuring a new backing band—*Live* captures Jackson with his original new wave trio, a 1983 quintet that was dominated by keyboards, a horn-driven group from 1984, and a 1986 quartet that specialized in straight-ahead rock & roll. The resulting album highlights his musical diversity, not his songwriting, which means the record is more intriguing as a historical document than as casual listening *—Stephen Thomas Erlewine*

Blaze of Glory / 1989 / A&M ✦✦✦

A loose concept album about a second-generation rock & roller struggling to come to terms with maturity, *Blaze of Glory* holds together fairly well, as the story takes a backseat to individual songs. While that does mean that the concept is never fleshed out, the approach results in a handful of brisk, stylish pop songs—including "Nineteen Forever" and "Down to London"—that are more compelling than the story itself. *—Stephen Thomas Erlewine*

Laughter & Lust / Apr. 30, 1991 / Virgin ✦✦✦

Night Music / Oct. 4, 1994 / Virgin ✦

Greatest Hits / May 7, 1996 / A&M ✦✦✦✦✦

A&M's 1996 collection *Greatest Hits* contains many of the basics in Joe Jackson's catalog, and that may be enough for some fans—after all, it has "Is She Really Going Out With Him?," "Look Sharp!," "Sunday Papers," "I'm the Man," "You Can't Get What You Want (Til You Know What You Want)," "Breaking Us in Two," "Steppin' Out" and "Nineteen Forever." The problem with the record is what lies around them. What's there isn't particularly bad, although inclusions like a live version of "Memphis" are fairly puzzling, but it isn't representative of Jackson's best, and it doesn't result in a great listen. It may satisfy those looking for just a handful of hits on one disc, but there are better Jackson compilations on the market. *—Stephen Thomas Erlewine*

This Is It! The A&M Years / Feb. 1997 / A&M ✦✦✦✦✦

This Is It! The A&M Years is a double-disc, 37-track collection covering Joe Jackson's commercial and creative heyday. Over the course of two discs, *This Is It!* runs through all of his biggest hits—"Is She Really Going Out With Him?," "It's Different for Girls," "Steppin' Out," "Breaking Us in Two," "You Can't Get What Want (Till You Know What You Want)"—plus a number of significant album tracks and lesser-known singles, making it a comprehensive retrospective of Jackson's pop-oriented work. While it's unfortunate that the compilation stops just short of his last pop album, 1991's *Laughter & Lust*, because it was released on Virgin Records, the great majority of his best work is here, making it a perfect choice for fans who want something more—and better assembled—than *Greatest Hits*, and those who don't want to dig as deep as the actual albums. *—Stephen Thomas Erlewine*

Heaven & Hell / Sep. 2, 1997 / Sony Classical ✦✦

Symphony No. 1 / Oct. 19, 1999 / Sony Classical ✦✦✦

No one who has been following Joe Jackson's more recent career will be surprised that he has produced *Symphony No. 1*, nor will they be surprised at its contents, especially if they have heard his previous instrumental works. In his liner notes, Jackson immediately defends himself against the charge that this cannot be a symphony since it is not being played by a symphony orchestra, but rather by a ten-piece ensemble featuring jazz trumpeter Terence Blanchard and rock guitarist Steve Vai. Certainly, the symphony form has been altered structurally in the 20th century, but one of the defining characteristics has remained that it is a work for a large group, and in that sense, Jackson's composition does not qualify, even though he multiplies the number of sounds through the use of electronic keyboards and computers. By "symphonic in structure," he seems to mean that it is a work in four parts in which various musical ideas are explored. Fair enough, and, in fact, in this sense *Symphony No. 1* is somewhat traditional, with its second, fast movement and its third, slow movement, which develop several themes, culminating in a last movement that draws them together. Jackson is unusual largely in the kinds of sounds he employs, sounds more familiar in rock and jazz. But leaving aside the question of whether or not *Symphony No. 1* is a real symphony, it does function, as Jackson says he intends it to, as program music, tracing a life from childhood to old age. One may or may not think of that narrative while listening, but one feels it, from the way the music slowly emerges in the first movement to the simplicity and confidence of the final one. In this sense, Jackson is both an optimist and a still-young composer; an older one might not have so hopeful a view of old age. *—William Ruhlmann*

Summer in the City: Live in New York / May 6, 2000 / Sony Classical ✦✦✦✦✦

The chameleonic Jackson is reunited with longtime bandmates Graham Maby (bass and vocals) and Gary Burke (drums) for this trio date, recorded live in August 1999. The opening "Summer in the City" promises much, and the album delivers. While the three don't always play to a song's strengths ("You Can't Get What You Want," for one, misses the full-band treatment), this release does showcase Jackson's piano and the group's interplay. The trio bounces through several Jackson originals, including "Fools in Love," "Down to

London," and a medley including "Be My Number Two" and "You Can't Get What You Want," as well as classics like "Mood Indigo," "Eleanor Rigby," and the title track. On this album, Jackson proves not only that he has not abandoned classic pop songs or his own pop hits, but that he is performing them better than ever. *—Ross Boissoneau*

Night and Day II / Oct. 24, 2000 / Sony Classical ♦♦♦
The first *Night and Day* album by Joe Jackson is an absolute pop music masterpiece. The "sequel," appropriately entitled *Night and Day II*, like the first, is an homage to New York City. The sequel musically quotes the lilting keyboard lines from Jackson's biggest hit, "Steppin' Out," several times, making one long to hear the original on *Night and Day*. Highlights included "Glamour and Pain" and "Happyland." Marianne Faithfull makes an interesting guest vocal appearance on "Love Got Lost." Jackson is still angry, but he's no longer a young man and as always his anger is tempered by a wry sense of humor. The songs on *Night and Day II* are not as easily accessible or memorable as the original, but this is still a great album and Joe Jackson is still the man. *—Tim Griggs*

● **Steppin' Out: The Very Best of Joe Jackson** / 2001 / A&M ♦♦♦♦♦
Spanning two discs and 38 songs, A&M's 2001 release *Steppin' Out: The Very Best of Joe Jackson* provides about as complete an overview of Joe Jackson's prime years as most listeners could want. Sure, this will not have everything that a hardcore fan loves, but it will have everything that a serious fan, who doesn't want to buy actual albums, needs: all the hits, plus most of the significant album tracks. For a while, Jackson was one of the most vital singer/songwriters around, testing his limits with each album and writing fine songs along the way. This album collects them all, proving that he was a formidable talent at the peak of his powers. *—Stephen Thomas Erlewine*

Michael Jackson

b. Aug. 29, 1958, Gary, IN
Vocals / New Jack Swing, Club/Dance, Pop/Rock, Motown, Urban, Funk, Dance-Pop, Soul
As part of the Jackson 5, a group made up of his brothers, Michael Jackson was among the most popular singing stars of the '70s. On his own, he was the biggest pop star of the '80s. Jackson was always the visual and vocal focus of the Jackson 5, who broke through to national success on the Motown label in 1970, when he was 11, with the first of four straight Number One hits, "I Want You Back." Jackson was also promoted as a solo artist, and he scored his first hit, "Got to Be There," in 1971. The Jackson 5's fortunes declined somewhat after the early '70s, and the group moved to Epic at mid-decade, with Michael temporarily abandoning his solo career and subsuming his group leadership to other members of what was now called the Jacksons. The group gradually built back its popularity by writing its own material. Jackson returned to solo work in 1979 with *Off the Wall*, a mature combination of driving dance songs ("Don't Stop 'til You Get Enough") and feelingly sung ballads ("She's Out of My Life") that outsold any previous group or solo effort, and spawned four Top Ten hits. Jackson again recorded and toured with the Jacksons, but his next album, *Thriller* (1982), became a musical phenomenon. It was the biggest-selling album of all time, moving 20 million copies in the U.S. alone and including seven Top Ten hits. His follow-up album, *Bad* (1987), accompanied by a solo world tour, sold six million copies domestically. Only six of its seven singles hit the Top Ten, but five in a row hit Number One. In late 1991, Jackson returned with *Dangerous*, which, by mid-1992, had sold four million copies and spawned the hits "Black and White," "Remember the Time," "In the Closet," and "Jam." *—William Ruhlmann*

☆ **Off the Wall** / 1979 / Epic ♦♦♦♦♦
Michael Jackson had recorded solo prior to the release of *Off the Wall* in 1979, but this was his breakthrough, the album that established him as an artist of astonishing talent and a bright star in his own right. This was a visionary album, a record that found a way to break disco wide open into a new world where the beat was undeniable, but not the primary focus—it was part of a colorful tapestry of lush ballads and strings, smooth soul and pop, soft rock, and alluring funk. Its roots hearken back to the Jacksons' huge mid-'70s hit "Dancing Machine," but this is an enormously fresh record, one that remains vibrant and giddily exciting years after its release. This is certainly due to Jackson's emergence as a blindingly gifted vocalist, equally skilled with overwrought ballads as "She's Out of My Life" as driving dancefloor shakers as "Working Day and Night" and "Get on the Floor," where his asides are as gripping as his delivery on the verses. It's also due to the brilliant songwriting, an intoxicating blend of strong melodies, rhythmic hooks, and indelible construction. Most of all, its success is due to the sound constructed by Jackson and producer Quincy Jones, a dazzling array of disco beats, funk guitars, clean mainstream pop, and unashamed (and therefore affecting) schmaltz that is utterly thrilling in its utter joy. This is highly professional, highly crafted music, and its details are evident, but the overall effect is nothing but pure pleasure. Jackson and Jones expanded this approach on the blockbuster *Thriller*, often with equally stunning results, but they never bettered it. *—Stephen Thomas Erlewine*

The Best of Michael Jackson / 1981 / Motown ♦♦♦
Michael Jackson's greatest hits, 1971-1975, emphasize his waiflike charm and youth (he was 13 when the first of these songs appeared) in ballads such as "Got to Be There," "Ben" (even if it is a love song to a rat), and "I Wanna Be Where You Are." The upbeat cover of "Rockin' Robin" is equally appealing. *—William Ruhlmann*

★ **Thriller** / 1982 / Epic ♦♦♦♦♦
Off the Wall was a massive success, spawning four Top Ten hits (two of them number ones), but nothing could have prepared Michael Jackson for *Thriller*. Nobody could have prepared anybody for the success of *Thriller*, since the magnitude of its success was simply unimaginable—an album that sold 40 million copies in its initial chart run, with *seven* of its nine tracks reaching the Top Ten. This was a record that had something for everybody, building on the basic blueprint of *Off the Wall* by adding harder funk, hard rock, softer ballads, and smoother soul—expanding the approach to have something for every audience. True, it wasn't as tight as *Off the Wall*—and the ridiculous, late-night house-of-horrors title track is the prime culprit, arriving in the middle of the record and sucking out its momentum—but those one or two cuts don't detract from a phenomenal set of music. It's calculated, to be sure, but the chutzpah of those calculations (before this, nobody would even have thought to bring in metal virtuoso Eddie Van Halen to play on a disco cut) is outdone by their success. And, although this is an undeniably fun record, the paranoia is already creeping in, manifesting itself in the record's two best songs: "Billie Jean," where a woman claims Michael is the father of her child, and the delirious "Wanna Be Startin' Something," the freshest funk on the album, but the most claustrophobic, scariest track Jackson ever recorded. These give the record its anchor and are part of the reason why the record is more than just a phenomenon. The other reason, of course, is that much of this is just simply great music. *—Stephen Thomas Erlewine*

Anthology / 1986 / Motown ♦♦♦♦♦
When a teenage Michael Jackson was known primarily for his membership in the Jackson 5, rock critics tended to dismiss him as bubblegum. But even at his most waifish, the pre-*Thriller*, pre-Quincy Jones Jackson could be soulful. Spanning 1971-1975, this two-CD set shows how inviting some of Jackson's early solo recordings were. Major hits like "Ben" (his oddly poignant ode to a rat), "I Wanna Be Where You Are," and "Got to Be There" are included, along with noteworthy album tracks like Bill Withers' "Ain't No Sunshine" and the standard "All the Things You Are." Anyone who doubted that he was a serious R&B/pop singer should have examined Jackson's moving version of the Philly soul classic "People Make the World Go Round" (which is heard with different lyrics than on the Stylistics' much better-known version). The package also contains a handful of Jackson 5 hits, including "Never Can Say Goodbye" and the infectious "Dancing Machine." To be sure, Jackson's solo albums of the early to mid-'70s had their share of filler, something this package isn't devoid of either. But thankfully, *Anthology* has a lot more pluses than minuses. For an introductory overview of Jackson's early accomplishments on his own, *Anthology* is the most logical choice. *—Alex Henderson*

Bad / 1987 / Epic ♦♦♦♦♦
The downside to a success like *Thriller* is that it's nearly impossible to follow, but Michael Jackson approached *Bad* much the same way he approached *Thriller*—take the basic formula of the predecessor, expand it slightly, and move it outward. This meant that he moved deeper into hard rock, deeper into schmaltzy adult contemporary, deeper into hard dance—essentially taking each portion of *Thriller* to an extreme, while increasing the quotient of immaculate studiocraft. He wound up with a sleeker, slicker *Thriller*, which isn't a bad thing, but it's not a rousing success, either. For one thing, the material just isn't as good. Look at the singles: only three can stand alongside album tracks from its predecessor ("Bad," "The Way You Make Me Feel," "I Just Can't Stop Loving You"), another is simply OK ("Smooth Criminal"), with the other two showcasing Jackson at his worst (the saccharine "Man in the Mirror," the misogynistic "Dirty Diana"). Then, there are the album tracks themselves, something that virtually didn't exist on *Thriller*. And they constitute a near-fatal dead spot on the record—songs three through six, from "Speed Demon" to "Another Part of Me," a sequence that's utterly faceless, lacking memorable hooks and melodies, even when Stevie Wonder steps in for "Just Good Friends," relying on nothing but studiocraft. Part of the joy of *Off the Wall* and *Thriller* was that craft was enhanced with tremendous songs, performances, and fresh, vivacious beats. For this dreadful stretch, everything is mechanical, and while the album rebounds with songs that prove mechanical can be tolerable if delivered with hooks and panache, it still makes *Bad* feel like an artifact of its time instead a piece of music that transcends it. *—Stephen Thomas Erlewine*

Dangerous / 1992 / Epic ♦♦♦
Despite the success of *Bad*, it was hard not to view it as a bit of a letdown, since it presented a cleaner, colder, calculated version of *Thriller*—something that delivered what it should on the surface, but wound up offering less in the long run. So, it was time for a change-up, something even a superstar as huge as Michael Jackson realized, so he left Quincy Jones behind, hired Guy mastermind Teddy Riley as the main producer, and worked with a variety of other producers, arrangers, and writers, most notably Bruce Swedien and Bill Bottrell. The end result of this is a much sharper, harder, riskier album than *Bad*, one that has its eyes on the street, even if its heart gets middle-class soft on "Heal the World." The shift in direction and change of collaborators has liberated Jackson, and he's written a set of songs that is considerably stronger than *Bad*, often approaching the consistency of *Off the Wall* and *Thriller*. If it is hardly as effervescent or joyous as either of those records, chalk it up to his suffocating stardom, which results in a set of songs without much real emotional center, either in their substance or performance. But, there's a lot to be said for professional craftsmanship at its peak, and *Dangerous* has plenty of that, not just on such fine singles as "In the Closet," "Remember the Time," or the blistering "Jam," but on album tracks like "Why You Wanna Trip on Me." *—Stephen Thomas Erlewine*

HIStory: Past, Present and Future, Book 1 / Jun. 20, 1995 / Epic ♦♦♦
Michael Jackson's double-disc *HIStory: Past, Present, and Future, Book I* is a monumental achievement of ego. Titled *HIStory Begins*, the first disc is a collection of his post-Motown hits, featuring some of the greatest music in pop history including "Billie Jean," "Don't Stop Til Ya Get Enough," "Beat It," and "Rock With You." It leaves some hits out—including the Number Ones "Say Say Say" and "Dirty Diana"—yet it's filled with enough prime material to be thoroughly intoxicating. That can't be said for the second disc, called *HIStory Continues* and consisting entirely of new material—which also happen to be the first songs he released since being accused of child molestation. *HIStory Continues* is easily the most personal album Jackson has recorded. References to the scandal permeate

almost every song, creating a thick atmosphere of paranoia. If Jackson's music had been the equal of *Thriller* or *Bad*, the nervous, vindicative lyrics wouldn't have been quite as overbearing. However, *HIStory Continues* reiterates musical ideas Jackson has been exploring since *Bad*. Jackson certainly tries to stay contemporary, yet he has a tendency to smooth out all of his rougher musical edges with show-biz schmaltz. Occasionally, Jackson produces some well-crafted pop that ranks with his best material: R. Kelly's "You Are Not Alone" is seductive, "Scream" improves on the slamming beats of his earlier single "Jam," and "Stranger in Moscow" is one of his most haunting ballads. Nevertheless, *HIStory Continues* stands as his weakest album since the mid-'70s. *—Stephen Thomas Erlewine*

Blood on the Dance Floor: History in the Mix / May 20, 1997 / Epic ✦✦

20th Century Masters—The Millennium Collection: The Best of Michael Jackson / Nov. 21, 2000 / Motown ✦✦✦✦
Michael Jackson's edition of *20th Century Masters—The Millennium Collection* concentrates entirely on his solo recordings from the early '70s, including such blockbusters as "Got to Be There," "Rockin' Robin," and "Ben." This doesn't contain every single one of his early solo hits, but it does contain the great majority of them, which means it might satisfy the tastes of many listeners who just want a sampling of the best of this era. *—Stephen Thomas Erlewine*

Invincible / Oct. 31, 2001 / Epic ✦✦✦

Walter Jackson

b. Mar. 19, 1938, Pensacola, FL, **d.** Jun. 20, 1983, Chicago, IL
Vocals / Chicago Soul, Northern Soul, R&B, Soul
Walter Jackson was '60s Chicago soul at its sweetest and, occasionally, most mainstream. In the mid-'60s, he had a brace of solid R&B hits—"Suddenly I'm All Alone," "It's an Uphill Climb (To the Bottom)," "Speak Her Name," "Welcome Home," "A Corner in the Sun"—without ever rising higher than the lower reaches of the Top 100. Recording for the OKeh stable, which was home to the top Chi-town soul talent, he benefited for a time from the production services of local masters Carl Davis and Curtis Mayfield, who handled the Impressions, Major Lance, Gene Chandler, and others. His sides employed similar punchy brass and strings, but in a smoother, more urbane fashion; Jackson was also comfortable with occasional outings into pure supper-club pop with nary a trace of R&B.

Jackson had already recorded for Columbia (and unsuccessfully auditioned for Motown) when OKeh A&R director Davis saw him at a Detroit piano bar in 1962. Stricken with polio as a young boy, Jackson had never let his disability get in the way of his musical ambitions, performing on crutches. Impressed with his commanding voice, Carl Davis thought of Walter as a Nat "King" Cole type of singer, and procured material for Jackson from Mayfield, Van McCoy, Chip Taylor, and other top-notch songwriters.

Despite the obvious pop crossover potential of Jackson's recordings, he remained obscure to white listeners. During the latter part of his stay with OKeh, he was reassigned from Davis' stable to producer Ted Cooper. Jackson had a few hits with Cooper, but there was little success after the late '60s, although he recorded for a few more labels before dying of a cerebral hemorrhage in 1983. *—Richie Unterberger*

● **The Best of Walter Jackson: Welcome Home, The Okeh Years** / Jun. 4, 1996 / Epic/Legacy ✦✦✦✦✦
Fifteen tracks from his artistic and commercial peak (1964-67), including his slew of R&B chart hits, highlights from LPs, and a flop single version of "My Ship Is Comin' In." Commercial pop/soul with elaborate production, reaching deeply enough into the gloss on occasion to rate as a vague precursor to the "quiet storm" music of subsequent decades. *—Richie Unterberger*

Wanda Jackson

b. Oct. 20, 1937, Maud, OK
Vocals / Country Gospel, Rockabilly, Traditional Country
Wanda Jackson was only halfway through high school when, in 1954, country singer Hank Thompson heard her on an Oklahoma City radio show and asked her to record with his band, the Brazos Valley Boys. By the end of the decade, Jackson had become one of America's first major female country and rockabilly singers. She had wanted to sign with Capitol, Thompson's label, but was turned down so she signed with Decca instead. Her mother made and helped design Wanda's stage outfits. "I was the first one to put some glamour in the country music—fringe dresses, high heels, long earrings," Jackson says of these outfits. When she first toured in 1955 and 1956, she was placed on a bill with none other than Elvis Presley, who encouraged her to sing rockabilly. In 1956, Jackson finally signed with Capitol, a relationship that lasted until the early '70s. Her recording career bounced back and forth between country and rockabilly; she did this by often putting one song in each style on either side of a single. Jackson cut the rockabilly hit "Fujiyama Mama" in 1958, which became a major success in Japan. Her version of "Let's Have a Party," which Elvis had cut earlier, was a U.S. Top 40 pop hit for her in 1960, after which she began calling her band the Party Timers. A year later, she was back in the country Top Ten with "Right or Wrong" and "In the Middle of a Heartache." In 1965, she topped the German charts with "Santa Domingo," sung in Dutch. In 1966, she hit the U.S. Top 20 with "The Box It Came In" and "Tears Will Be the Chaser for the Wine." Jackson's popularity continued through the end of the decade. *—Kurt Wolff*

There's a Party Goin' on / 1959 / Capitol ✦✦✦
While this doesn't have most of Wanda's best rockabilly sides (check the compilation *Rockin' With Wanda* for those), it's a pretty solid and energetic set. About half of it is taken up with retreads of the "Let's Have a Party" theme and covers of early rock hits like "Tweedlee Dee" and "Kansas City" which are, admittedly, well done. "Fallin'" and especially "Hard Headed Woman" are really fine cuts that rank among her best rock & roll performances. The real surprise of this album is the lightning-speed rockabilly riffing by Roy Clark; his playing on "Hard Headed Woman" is downright savage, almost enough to redeem all those horrible *Hee-Haw* programs. *—Richie Unterberger*

Rockin' with Wanda / 1960 / Capitol ✦✦✦✦✦
Absolutely the best collection of her rockabilly recordings, including her key 1956-60 singles—"Fujiyama Mama," "Mean Mean Man," "Hot Dog! That Made Him Mad," and others. A leading candidate for the best female rock & roll album of the 1950s. The British reissue adds four worthwhile bonus cuts, including the essential "Let's Have a Party." *—Richie Unterberger*

Rockin' in the Country: The Best of Wanda Jackson / Jun. 1990 / Rhino ✦✦✦✦✦
Perhaps the greatest of the rockabilly women, Wanda Jackson later turned to pure country. Rhino's *Best of Wanda Jackson—Rockin' in the Country* presents the best of both eras here on this 18-track collection. *—Jeff Tamarkin*

Right or Wrong [Box] / 1993 / Bear Family ✦✦✦✦
This four-CD set is like a photo album of Wanda Jackson growing up, from innocent adolescent to rockabilly star and the dominant female country singer of the early 1960s. Her complete recordings from the first Decca session in March 1954 until her Capitol session of November 2, 1962 constitute the part of her career that rock & roll and rockabilly fans most care about. Disc one covers those early years, the 15 songs she cut for Decca Records through 1955, when she was still treading a fine line in country music, seemingly trying to be the next Kitty Wells at least part of the time. The singing is glorious and the playing solid, although Jackson, working in this idiom, was like a racing thoroughbred being asked to canter around a track. Then comes "Baby Loves Him," a Jackson original that redefined her for the next few years as a rockabilly star. Disc two features Jackson treading that fine line between straight country and rock & roll, interspersed with slower, more traditional numbers. As late as 1961, disc three reveals, Jackson was still courting the rock & roll audience, although the main thrust of her career was moving back toward pure country, with forays into pop and country-pop. The country material on disc four had a serious edge to it by now, and the rock & roll was almost superfluous. By late 1962 and early 1963, however, her sides show the kind of opulent overproduction, complete with choruses and string sections, that would help give country-pop a bad name; her voice is as good as ever, but the material is a stretch after the hot rockin' sides. The booklet is more thorough than most from Bear Family. *—Bruce Eder*

Hits & Rarities / 1996 / Music Collection ✦✦✦
Since *Hits & Rarities* is a single-disc compilation that contains both well-known numbers like "Right and Wrong" and "Let's Have a Party," as well as several obscurities, the result is an entertaining collection, but one that's unsuited for both neophytes, who won't appreciate the rarities, and serious fans, who will find the inclusion of the familiar cuts extraneous. *—Thom Owens*

Vintage Collections Series / Jan. 23, 1996 / Capitol ✦✦✦✦✦
This 20-track anthology of Jackson's early work is roughly equal to Rhino's *Rockin' in the Country* in value. *Rockin' in the Country* offers a considerably wider range, chronologically speaking. *Vintage Collections*, on the other hand, focuses on 1956-61 recordings, affording greater depth for what is acknowledged as her most fertile period. Although it's issued on Capitol Nashville, it mixes rockabilly and straight country, including her biggest hits in each style ("Let's Have a Party," "Fujiyama Mama," "Right or Wrong") and some worthy obscurities. Those with an appetite for both rock & roll and country will find this the best compilation of her work; those who want just the rock & roll should look for the harder-to-find *Rockin' with Wanda* instead. *—Richie Unterberger*

● **Queen of Rockabilly** / Oct. 17, 2000 / Ace ✦✦✦✦✦
Ace's *Queen of Rockabilly* is the best overview of Wanda Jackson's raw, early rockabilly recordings yet assembled. Spanning 30 tracks and boasting fine liner notes and great sound, this is a terrific collection of exciting rockabilly. This is the best way to hear one the greatest rockabilly gals of the '50s. *—Stephen Thomas Erlewine*

Mick Jagger (Michael Philip Jagger)

b. Jul. 26, 1943, Dartford, Kent, England
Vocals, Keyboards, Harmonica, Guitar / Pop/Rock, Rock & Roll
As the lead singer for the Rolling Stones, Mick Jagger was one of the most popular and influential frontmen in the history of rock & roll. Jagger fronted the Rolling Stones for over 20 years before he began a solo career in 1985. During the early '80s, Jagger and Keith Richards conflicted over the musical direction of the band. Jagger wanted to move the band in a more pop- and dance-oriented direction while Richards wanted to stay true to the band's rock & roll and blues roots. By 1984, Jagger had begun recording a solo album where he pursued a more mainstream, dance-inflected pop direction. For the next few years, Jagger and Richards barely spoke to each other and sniped at the other in the press. During this time, Jagger tried to make his solo career as successful as the Rolling Stones, pouring all of his energy into his second solo album, 1987's *Primitive Cool*. Although the album received stronger reviews than *She's the Boss*, only one of the singles—"Let's Work"—scraped the bottom of the Top 40 and the record didn't go gold. Following the commercial failure of *Primitive Cool*, Jagger returned to the fold of the Rolling Stones in 1989, recording, releasing, and touring the *Steel Wheels* album. *Steel Wheels* was a massively successful venture and after the tour was completed, the Stones entered a slow period, where each of the members pursued solo projects. Jagger recorded his third solo album with Rick Rubin, who had previously worked with the Beastie Boys and Red Hot Chili Peppers. The resulting solo album, *Wandering Spirit*, was released in 1993 and received the strongest reviews of any of Jagger's solo efforts. *—Stephen Thomas Erlewine*

She's the Boss / 1985 / Atlantic ✦✦✦

Jagger employs a who's who including Herbie Hancock, Pete Townshend, and Jeff Beck for an album that replaces the familiar sound of the Stones with a more sophisticated but no less hard-rock sound. And the voice is familiar. Features the hit "Just Another Night." — *William Ruhlmann*

Primitive Cool / 1987 / Atlantic ✦✦✦

For his second solo album, Mick Jagger teamed up with producer Dave Stewart (Eurythmics), turning in a more adventurous and ambitious record. Of course, "adventurous" and "ambitious" are relative terms. In comparison to the carefully constructed, state-of-the-art pop/rock of *She's the Boss*, *Primitive Cool* sounds lively, as Jagger puts some genuine conviction behind the funky "Peace for the Wicked" and the country stylings of "Party Doll." Nevertheless, the album, like *She's the Boss* before it, is designed to establish Mick Jagger as a solo star in his own right, and *Primitive Cool* is filled with attempts at contemporary rock and dance-pop. The nadir of his stabs at modern pop is the appalling single "Let's Work," where the rock star tells his fans to get off their asses and start working, all to a bouncy, aerobicized beat. However, most of the album is more appealing than the single, even if Jagger's writing seems forced on the numbers designed with the Top 40 in mind ("Shoot Off Your Mouth," in particular). Not surprisingly, the best moments on *Primitive Cool* occur when he stops seeing the album as a way to jump-start his solo career and he concentrates on the music. While his emotionally unguarded songs ("War Baby" and "Party Doll") are the most affecting tracks on the record, songs like "Let's Work" are more indicative of Jagger's true feelings. — *Stephen Thomas Erlewine*

● **Wandering Spirit** / Feb. 9, 1993 / Atlantic ✦✦✦✦✦

Jagger doesn't show any signs of wear on his third—and by far best—solo album. If anything, his voice seems to have developed a deeper bottom end without sacrificing any of the highs. This is not always an advantage—the forced falsetto and rhythmic pulse of "Sweet Thing" causes a nightmarish flashback to the Stones' disco flirtations in the mid-'70s. But more times than not, this disc works. A lot of the credit goes to Jagger's backing band and producer Rick Rubin who keep things lean, mean, and simple. The economy of performance allows Jagger to remain credible on a wide variety of styles—he delivers a groovin', sultry version of Bill Withers' soul classic "Use Me," a passionate country ballad on "Evening Gown," and even pulls off an Irish traditional folk piece with "Handsome Molly." — *Roch Parisien*

Jags

f. 1978, **db.** 1982
Mod Revival, Power Pop, New Wave

The Jags are a fondly remembered one-hit wonder of the late-70s U.K. power-pop explosion. The quartet was formed in 1978 by the Yorkshire-based songwriting team of Nick Watkins (vocals) and John "Twink" Adler (guitar) with Steve Prudence (bass) and Alex Baird (drums). In July of 1978, they signed to Island Records and released a promising four-track EP. Their debut LP in 1980, *Evening Standards*, included the memorable, though highly derivative, "Back of My Hand," which reached the U.K. Top 20 the previous fall. The follow-up, "Woman's World" barely scraped its way on to the charts. Though *Evening Standards* featured a really solid set of punchy power pop songs, critics focussed instead on Watkins' Costello-like delivery, writing the band off as merely mimics. As steam ran out of the power-pop craze, the band attempted to change their sound a bit. 1981's *No Tie Like the Present*, featured a slightly new direction but it was generally overlooked. By 1982, the Jags had disbanded for good, though "Back of My Hand" had a revival of sorts in the '90s, appearing on several compilations. — *Chris Woodstra*

● **Evening Standard** / 1980 / Island ✦✦✦✦✦

The Jags made their debut with the classic "Back of My Hand," leaving high expectations for a full-length. *Evening Standards* featured a sharp set of similar sounding, bouncy pop songs in the vein of Elvis Costello and Nick Lowe. Though it can be faulted for being highly derivative and certainly more than a little repetitive, the set actually holds up better than most from the era. — *Chris Woodstra*

No Tie Like a Present / 1981 / Island ✦✦✦

The second album by the Jags is great, fun listening. Starting out with a cover of the Tremelos' "Here Comes My Baby," it rolls on through a series of very English-sounding pop tunes written by band members. Very reminiscent of the early '80s, it nevertheless has a lot of spunk—check out the surfer instrumental "Silver Birds" and you won't be disappointed. — *James Chrispell*

The Jam

f. 1975, Woking, Surrey, England, **db.** 1982
British Punk, Mod Revival, New Wave, Punk

The Jam were the most popular band to emerge from the initial wave of British punk rock in 1977; along with the Sex Pistols, the Clash, and the Buzzcocks, the Jam had the most impact on pop music. While they could barely get noticed in America, the trio became genuine superstars in Britain, with an impressive string of Top Ten singles in the late '70s and early '80s. The Jam could never have a hit in America because they were thoroughly and defiantly British. Under the direction of guitarist/vocalist/songwriter Paul Weller, the trio spearheaded a revival of mid-'60s mod groups, in the style of the Who and the Small Faces. Like the mod bands, the group dressed stylishly, worshipped American R&B, and played it loud and rough. By the time of the group's third album, Weller's songwriting had grown substantially, as he was beginning to write social commentaries and pop songs in the vein of the Kinks. Both his political songs and his romantic songs were steeped in British culture, filled with references and slang in the lyrics, as well as musical allusions. Furthermore, as the Jam grew more popular and musically

accessible, Weller became more insistent and stubborn about his beliefs, supporting leftist causes and adhering to the pop aesthetics of '60s British rock without ever succumbing to hippie values. Paradoxically, that meant even when their music became more pop than punk, they never abandoned the punk values—if anything, Weller stuck to the strident independent ethics of 1977 more than any other punk band just by simply refusing to change. — *Stephen Thomas Erlewine*

In the City / May 20, 1977 / Polydor ✦✦✦✦✦

On their debut, the Jam offered a good balance between the forward-looking, "destroy everything" aggression of punk with a certain reverence for '60s beat and R&B. In an era that preached attitude over musicianship, the Jam bettered the competition with good pop sense, strong melodies and plenty of hooks that compromised none of punk's ideals or energy, plus youth culture themes and an abrasive, ferocious attack. Even though the band would improve exponentially over the next couple of years, *In the City* is a remarkable debut and stands as one of the landmark punk albums. — *Chris Woodstra*

This Is the Modern World / Nov. 18, 1977 / Polydor ✦✦✦

As is so often the case for overnight successes, the Jam rush-recorded their sophomore effort during a hurried schedule to capitalize on the debut. This, combined with Weller's various personal distractions and temporary lack of interest, led to less than satisfying results, especially in comparison to *In the City*. *This Is the Modern World* can be faulted for borrowed Who licks, pale rewrites of the debut, somewhat cliched sloganeering, and unfinished ideas, but there were still some moments of inspiration, especially in more introspective Weller songs like "Life From a Window" and "I Need You (For Someone)"— both songs feature personal sentiments that the debut was clearly missing. *This Is the Modern World* is a flawed album by Jam standards, but it would certainly have received praise had it been released by another band. (The U.S. edition added the single "All Around the World" with a different track order.) — *Chris Woodstra*

☆ **All Mod Cons** / Nov. 3, 1978 / Polydor ✦✦✦✦✦

The band regrouped and refocused for *All Mod Cons*, an album that marked a great leap in songwriting maturity and sense of purpose. For the first time, Weller built, rather than fell back, upon his influences, carving a distinct voice all his own; he employed a story-style narrative with invented characters and vivid British imagery *a la* Ray Davies to make incisive social commentary—all in a musically irresistible package. The youthful perspective and impassioned delivery on *All Mod Cons* first earned Weller the "voice of a generation" tag, and it certainly captures a moment in time, but really, the feelings and sentiments expressed on the album just as easily speak to any future generation of young people. Terms like "classic" are often bandied about, but in the case of *All Mod Cons*, it is certainly deserved. — *Chris Woodstra*

☆ **Setting Sons** / Nov. 16, 1979 / Collector's Choice Music ✦✦✦✦✦

Setting Sons was originally planned as a concept album about three childhood friends who, upon meeting after some time apart, discover the different directions in which they've grown apart. Only about half of the songs ended up following the concept due to a rushed recording schedule, but where they do, Weller vividly depicts British life, male relationships, and coming to terms with entry into adulthood. Weller's observations of society are more pointed and pessimistic than ever, but at the same time, he's employed stronger melodies with a slicker production and comparatively fuller arrangements, even using heavy orchestration for a reworked version of Foxton's "Smithers-Jones." *Setting Sons* often reaches brilliance and stands among their best albums, but the inclusion of a number of throwaways and knock-offs (especially the out-of-place cover of "Heat Wave" which closes the album) mars an otherwise perfect album. — *Chris Woodstra*

☆ **Sound Affects** / Nov. 28, 1980 / Polydor ✦✦✦✦✦

Unhappy with the slicker approach of *Setting Sons*, the Jam got back to basics, using the direct, economic playing of *All Mod Cons* and "Going Underground," the simply brilliant single which preceded *Sound Affects* by a few months. Thematically, though, Weller explored a more indirect path, leaving behind (for the most part) the story-song narratives in favor of more abstract dealings in spirituality and perception—the approach stemming from his recent readings of Blake and Shelley (who was quoted on the sleeve), but more specifically Geoffrey Ash, whose *Camelot and the Vision of Albion* made a strong impression. Musically, Weller drew upon *Revolver*-era Beatles as a primary source (the bass line on "Start," which comes directly from "Taxman," being the most obvious occurrence), incorporating the occasional odd sound and echoed vocal, which implied psychedelia without succumbing to its excesses. From beginning to end, the songs are pure, clever, infectious pop—probably their catchiest—with "That's Entertainment" and the should-have-been-a-single "Man in the Corner Shop" standing out. — *Chris Woodstra*

The Gift / Mar. 12, 1982 / Polydor ✦✦✦

As good mods, the Jam always had a healthy respect for R&B and soul—even the first album featured the revved-up Northern soul of "Non-Stop Dancing." With *The Gift*, however, Weller seems to have become completely absorbed in it, and more specifically, in Stax-style soul with more than a hint of psychedelia *a la* "Psychedelic Shack." An uneven album marked by overindulgences like the instrumental "Circus" and unnecessarily long songs, *The Gift* still has no shortage of terrific songs, like the simply sublime "Ghost," "Town Called Malice" (the hit), and the funk workout of "Precious." Weller can obviously do "soulful"—his voice has never sounded better—but unfortunately, *The Gift*, with its excesses and marginal tracks, doesn't show his talents in the proper light. Points for ambition, but ultimately, this is their least consistent effort since *This Is the Modern World*. — *Chris Woodstra*

Dig the New Breed / Dec. 10, 1982 / Polydor ✦✦✦

A posthumous collection of live tracks from throughout their career, *Dig the New Breed* manages to chronicle the band's rapid progression quite nicely, from the aggressive early days through to the more polished last tour. Most notable for the inclusion of the non-LP cover of Eddie Floyd's "Big Bird," as well as a particularly moving reading of "Ghosts" which betters the album version, the collection shows what a terrific and consistent live act they were. —*Chris Woodstra*

★ **Snap!** / Oct. 14, 1983 / Polydor ♦♦♦♦♦
Snap! collects all of the Jam's singles, from "In the City" to "Beat Surrender," including several B-sides ("'A' Bomb in Wardour Street," "Dreams of Children") and a handful of rarities, like a demo of "That's Entertainment" and the rock version of "Smithers-Jones." For its compact disc release, several songs were trimmed, but *Snap!* remains a brilliant summation of why the Jam were one of the most important and beloved British bands of their era. The latter-day collection *Greatest Hits* covers much the same ground as *Snap!*, but the earlier compilation remains preferable because of sequencing and its inclusion of essential items like "'A' Bomb in Wardour Street" and "Dreams of Children." —*Stephen Thomas Erlewine*

Greatest Hits / Jul. 1, 1991 / Polydor ♦♦♦♦♦
Greatest Hits covers nearly the same ground as *Snap!*, with all the tracks but "Just Who Is the Five O'Clock Hero" included on the previous compilation. Granted, "That's Entertainment" is presented in the album version and "Funeral Pyre" in its original mix, but the album isn't quite as strong as *Snap!* Nevertheless, it has all of their hit singles, making it a thoroughly entertaining record, as well as an effective introduction to the group. —*Stephen Thomas Erlewine*

Extras: A Collection of Rarities / Apr. 6, 1992 / Polygram ♦♦♦♦♦
Extras offers 26 B-sides, rarities and unreleased tracks that, while far from complete (the wonderful "See Saw" is absent, for instance), is a fan's dream come true. This is a fans' album, to be sure, but for fans, the never-before-heard demos (like "Burning Sky" and "Thick As Thieves") have a certain spine-tingling effect, and the covers (like "So Sad About Us," "And Your Bird Can Sing," and "Disguises") are undeniably fun—often more so than the covers they chose to include on the proper albums. *Extras* is not a good introduction, to be sure, but for the converted, this is essential. —*Chris Woodstra*

Wasteland / Oct. 1992 / Pickwick ♦♦
Wasteland is a budget-line import which collects 16 tracks from throughout the Jam's career, mostly focusing on album tracks, but it also includes a couple of singles. Although they had no shortage of great material and the songs here are all great, the song selection (and order, for that matter) seems to have been carried out randomly. *Wasteland* is ultimately a waste of time. —*Chris Woodstra*

Beat Surrender / May 1993 / Karussell ♦♦
Just like *Wasteland*, the odd collection which preceded it by a year, *Beat Surrender* combines a couple of hits with poorly chosen album cuts for an incoherent and certainly far from comprehensive package. The Jam had a lot of great album tracks that were unfairly overshadowed by the singles, but *The Jam Collection* (released in 1996) offers better proof to that fact. —*Chris Woodstra*

Live Jam / Oct. 25, 1993 / Polydor ♦♦

Jam Collection / Oct. 22, 1996 / Polydor ♦♦♦
The Jam Collection is basically a purposeless compilation. Pulling a handful of album tracks from each of the group's records and throwing a few B-sides into the mix, it is neither a greatest hits nor rarities disc—it simply spotlights some tracks you might have missed. While that approach may seem logical on the surface, it actually falls apart under any scrutiny. The Jam were one of the definitive single bands, as collections like *Snap!*, *Greatest Hits*, and the B-sides comp *Extras* proved. *The Jam Collection* ignores those single completely for tracks that usually work better in their original album context, no matter how terrific they are as a song. Furthermore, it appears that the compilers didn't consider their selections carefully. While some songs like "English Rose," "Liza Radley," and "The Butterfly Collector" are obvious selections, the inclusion of several songs seems arbitrary. There are certainly a number of fine songs on *The Jam Collection*, but dedicated fans will have everything on here (or they should purchase the original albums) and casual fans are better served by *Snap!*, *Greatest Hits*, or even *All Mod Cons*, *Setting Sons*, and *Sound Affects*. *The Jam Collection*, then, simply has no purpose. —*Stephen Thomas Erlewine*

☆ **Direction Reaction Creation** / May 26, 1997 / Polydor ♦♦♦♦♦
Direction Reaction Creation is the ultimate Jam package, offering 117 tracks over five discs—essentially the band's complete studio recordings. With a strict adherence to chronological order, the box presents each single followed by its B-side(s) (six of which appear on CD for the first time, including the brilliant "See Saw"), followed by the proper album tracks—oddly, though, the album versions of the singles are chosen in most places. Unfortunately, this approach sometimes disrupts the flow of the albums, especially in the case of *All Mod Cons*, which loses three tracks to the treatment, and *Setting Sons*, which loses "Eton Rifles" to a separate disc. This is a small point for purists to debate—the difference is really unnoticeable in light of the truly great music found on the discs. In addition to the regular studio tracks, disc five offers over an hour of studio demos—22 previously unreleased tracks of considerably different takes of better-known material, a few never-before-heard Weller and Foxton originals, and some interesting covers like "Rain," "Dead End Street," and "Every Little Bit Hurts." A lavish 88-page booklet accompanies the set with great liner notes, an extensive band chronology and discography, and the band's complete gig list, along with plenty of rare photos and memorabilia. The Jam, simply put, were one the finest bands in rock & roll history, and *Direction Reaction Creation* offers the proof, showing both their remarkably rapid growth and their incredible consistency. —*Chris Woodstra*

James

f. 1982, Manchester, England
College Rock, Madchester, Adult Alternative Pop/Rock, Alternative Pop/Rock
As one of the first groups to be dubbed "the next Smiths," James became an institution on the British alternative music scene of the '80s and '90s with their pleasant folk-pop. Early in their career, James was blessed by praise from their idol Morrissey, which turned out to be both a blessing and a curse. The group was pegged as second-rate Smiths, yet continued to tour and record, eventually gaining a sizable following. In the late '80s, the group, like many of their British peers, became involved in the acid-house-inspired "baggy" scene and recorded the baggy-inspired "Sit Down," which became their breakthrough hit. Shortly after "Sit Down," James became more experimental, culminating in a collaboration with Brian Eno that resulted in their biggest American album, *Laid*, in 1993. James took four years to follow *Laid*, by which time their audience had returned to a cult following. —*Stephen Thomas Erlewine*

Stutter / 1986 / Blanco y Negro/Sire ♦♦♦
More of a manic fever rant than an album, *Stutter* is so grotesque and spasmodic that it rams you into a corner until you can do nothing but choke down its home-brewed indie-guitar arsenic. Thin, spiky, jagged folk music. Songs constructed like the Fire Engines having a few beers with Patti Smith as C.S. Lewis is screaming obscenities at small children. What's really at stake here is not the band's first attempts of Next Big Thing potential, but rather an extraordinary disaster of disagreement. As if a lunatic in his own home-built asylum, Tim Booth is a mere bystander to his wild vocals while the rest of the band watch Gavan Whelan have an absolute fit on—what sounds like—four drum kits at once. This is shoddy, shameless chaos. Nothing more than a terribly produced mess of tragic rock-star baiting and deliberate discordance. An amazing debut. —*Dean Carlson*

Strip-Mine / 1988 / Blanco y Negro/Sire ♦♦♦
Boasting a more detailed production than its predecessor, *Strip-Mine* accentuates James' more anthemic tendencies, but it's generally a stronger album than the first, featuring such charming folk-pop gems as "Stripmining." —*Stephen Thomas Erlewine*

One Man Clapping / 1989 / One Man/Rough Trade ♦♦♦
Released after James was dropped from Blanco Y Negro, *One Man Clapping* is a rather entertaining live album featuring highlights from the group's first two albums, but it's somewhat undone by Tim Booth's overly theatrical performance. —*Stephen Thomas Erlewine*

James / 1990 / Fontana ♦♦♦
Following the success of the revamped *Gold Mother* in England, the album was released as *James* in America. Although it contains one of their best singles in "Sit Down," that Madchester classic sits uneasily with the anthemic arena-rock that comprises the remainder of the album. —*Stephen Thomas Erlewine*

Gold Mother / Aug. 1990 / Fontana ♦♦♦♦
James completely revamped their lineup for *Gold Mother*, adding a violinist, a keyboardist, and a trumpeter to the band and attempting to write grand, ambitious arena-rock that recalled U2 and the Waterboys. Although a few of the tracks captured the sprawling, epic splendor that James wished to achieve, they have difficulty writing convincing material, and they aren't nearly as interesting as they were when they concentrated on jangling folk-pop. (*Gold Mother* was reissued in 1991 after a re-recorded version of "Sit Down" became a hit. "Sit Down" and "Lose Control" replaced "Crescendo" and "Hang On," but the baggy beats of the new songs sat uncomfortably with the sprawling, anthemic rock of *Gold Mother*.) —*Stephen Thomas Erlewine*

Seven / Mar. 17, 1992 / Fontana/Mercury ♦♦♦♦♦
Instead of following the Madchester leanings of "Sit Down," James carried on with the anthemic rock of *Gold Mother* on its follow-up, *Seven*. While *Seven* may indulge in the same arena-rock excesses as its predecessor, the group's writing and playing is controlled and textured, making a captivating exercise in grand, sprawling rock & roll. —*Stephen Thomas Erlewine*

Laid / Oct. 5, 1993 / Mercury ♦♦♦♦♦
Teaming up with producer Brian Eno had a considerable effect on James. Instead of pursuing the grandiose inclinations of *Gold Mother* and *Seven*, the group reduced their scale, choosing to explore texture in a dark, atmospheric and intimate setting. As a result, *Laid* is by far the most subdued album the band has ever made, and it benefits as a result—rarely have Tim Booth's vocal theatrics and poetics sounded so affecting. But what really makes *Laid* resonate is James' subtle, textured playing, which gives the record a quiet, graceful power. —*Stephen Thomas Erlewine*

Wah Wah / Oct. 1994 / Mercury ♦♦♦
Recorded during the *Laid* sessions but released a year later, *Wah-Wah* is a collaborative effort between James and producer Brian Eno. Where *Laid* concentrated on songs, *Wah-Wah* is about sound, and frequently it's fascinating, as its 23 songs float between ambient soundscapes, worldbeat, and pop songs. Although it's an atypical record for James, the band's music has rarely been as captivating as it is here. —*Stephen Thomas Erlewine*

Whiplash / Feb. 25, 1997 / Mercury ♦♦♦
Retreating from the experimental tendencies of *Laid* and *Wah-Wah*, James return to straight-forward anthemic folk-rock with *Whiplash*. Although the album isn't a retread of *Seven* or *Gold Mother*, it is considerably more rock-oriented than its two predecessors, particularly because the group has incorporated some elements of Brit-pop into their music. "She's a Star," the record's first single, soars on a slide guitar and heavy riff that falls somewhere between Suede and Oasis, as well as a distinctive falsetto from Tim Booth. It is a small song that aims big, which makes it surprisingly graceful, and it's a trick that

James only pulls off a couple more times on the album. While *Whiplash* does find them on more familiar territory, it doesn't have the layered sonics and consistently excellent songwriting that made *Laid* a breakthrough. In fact, is *Whiplash* is anything, it's a bit of a step backward—it's an album that will appeal to their cult, not a large audience. *—Stephen Thomas Erlewine*

• **The Best of James** / Jun. 30, 1998 / Fontana/Mercury ✦✦✦✦
An imperfect collection of a frustratingly uneven band, *The Best of James* is a tantalizing missed opportunity. James was always full of ambition and big ideas, from their early days as Smiths-like folk-rockers through their flirtation with baggy to their experimental dabbling with Brian Eno. Throughout it all, they hit as often as they missed, landing a handful of British hits and creating several more worthy album tracks. As album artists, however, they only occasionally were successful, as on 1993's terrific *Laid*. That's the reason why they are the perfect candidates for an 18-track retrospective like *The Best of*. Too bad the compilers botched this disc. It's not that the collection overlooks their first two albums for Sire—those had their moments, but they're not especially missed—it's that they gather most of the best Fontana material (plus "Hymn From a Village," one of their early singles for Factory, and two new tracks), then throw it all in the air, not caring where each song lands. Since James changed drastically from album to album, this really is a block-headed move; it's difficult to listen to these songs out of chronological order and the sequencing makes their achievements seem less impressive. That said, *The Best of* is nevertheless recommended as a starting point because no other James album accurately conveys their eclectism or their musical strengths; it's also nice to get all of these songs on one disc. Just be prepared to dig a little deeper—or at least learn how to program the CD player—if the collection sparks your interest. *—Stephen Thomas Erlewine*

Millionaires / Oct. 13, 1999 / Mercury ✦✦✦✦
Going from the folk skullduggery of *Stutter* to the lavish club steps of *Goldmother* to the introspective beauty of *Laid*, James have never been predictable. The band's progression has delivered a seemingly inconsistent but impressive body of work, and *Millionaires* is no exception. Crisp, shiny, accessible pop songs such as "Crash" (sounding, oddly, like 1990's manic "Come Home" and the bittersweet, *Laid*-era B-side "The Lake"), "I Know What I'm Here For," and "Afro Lover," seem designed to go for Top 40 gold. For a band like James, this is unusual—they've always seemed like the freaks and geeks of the school of popular and "credible" music. While it's not necessarily a bad thing for these outcasts to try to fit in, for at least half of the album it's exactly that: the flat, overproduced "Surprise" and the aimless "Dumb Jam" ignore the hook-laden nature of the band's past heights. Fortunately, the album's first half positively shines while taking this same populist approach. "Hello" succeeds with its hushed, electronic cries; "We're Going to Miss You" sounds like one of Midnight Oil's lost classics, simultaneously bitter and triumphant. Best of all, "Just Like Fred Astaire" somehow encapsulates every delirious high one feels when first falling in love. Essentially, the album two disparate halves: the former, an ecstatic stab of triumph and love, the latter, a mired, confused slab of dulling mediocrity. Indeed, *Millionaires* is as odd and unexpected as James' overall discography. With a little personal song programming, one can make it sound like the freaks and geeks knew what they were doing the entire time—they might be a bit lost at times, but they have the creative heart that the musical jocks, cheerleaders, and hooligans would never, ever, own themselves. *—Dean Carlson*

Pleased to Meet You / Jul. 17, 2001 / Mercury ✦✦✦✦✦
It's not so much that James weren't expected to make yet another good record; when 2001's *Pleased to Meet You* was released, they hadn't made a truly sub-par record since the late '80s. But it isn't just another *good* James record—it's their best. It's their tightest, freshest, most contemporary batch of songs, weatherproofed to stand the test of time. From the dizzily uplifting "Space," a Brian Eno-influenced and produced song (sure sounds like his voice is in the chorus, too), to the glacially sparse ballad "Alaskan Pipeline," the perfectly titled record is fresh-faced enough to sound like a band high on being in a studio together for the first time, but the material and the execution is too focused, too mature to sound like a rookie effort. As with the title track on 1993's *Laid*, an album highlight is buried near the end. This time it's "Getting Away With It," a song that represents the remainder of the album with a solid tune—with some of Tim Booth's finest, most meaningful lyrics that aren't necessarily preachy—and well-placed layers of synths and strings that accent an otherwise merely good James song. To wit, there's a power and a heft throughout that the band only hinted at previously. A band with a dusty best-of and nine previous studio albums isn't supposed to do this, unless they're the Rolling Stones. James' tenth makes you wonder what all the fuss over U2 and R.E.M.'s rebirths are about. And with this clutch of alternate reality top ten singles, strung together in the disguise of a flowing record, they're making the modern pop charts (in the U.K. and especially the U.S.) look hopelessly feeble. Songs of adulthood, parenthood, and addiction have rarely sounded this exciting. *—Andy Kellman*

James Gang

f. 1966, Cleveland, OH, **db.** 1976
Album Rock, Arena Rock, Hard Rock, Blues-Rock
For a brief period in the early '70s, the James Gang was one of the top hard-rock acts in America, thanks to the songwriting and inventive instrumental work of singer/guitarist Joe Walsh. The band was founded in Cleveland by drummer Jim Fox; its first lineup was fleshed out by bassist Tom Kriss and guitarist Glen Schwartz. The group toured the Midwest and built a name for itself, but Schwartz left the band in 1969. Walsh stepped in admirably, and word of the new guitar phenom spread quickly; the James Gang recorded its debut, *Yer Album*, later that year. The follow-up, *The James Gang Rides Again*, proved to be arguably the group's strongest and contained their best-known song, "Funk #49" (they never had a hit single). The album went gold, as did their next two, and hit the Top 20. James Gang fan Pete Townshend invited the group to open for the Who on a European tour in 1971; shortly thereafter, Walsh left the group, feeling constrained by the power-trio formula. He first formed Barnstorm; later, he recorded several solo albums and joined the Eagles for *Hotel California* and *The Long Run*. Dominic Troiano served as guitarist until 1973, when he joined the Guess Who; Tommy Bolin played on the *Bang* and *Miami* albums, but when he left to join Deep Purple, it essentially spelled the end of the James Gang, whose sales declined steadily following Walsh's departure. The James Gang finally broke up for good in 1976. *—Steve Huey*

Yer' Album / 1969 / One Way ✦✦✦✦
The James Gang's debut LP, *Yer' Album*, was very much a first record and very much a record of its time. The heavy rock scene of the period was given to extensive jamming, and four tracks ran more than six minutes each. The group had written some material, but they were still something of a cover band, and the disc included their extended workouts on Buffalo Springfield's "Bluebird" and the Yardbirds' "Lost Woman," the latter a nine-minute version complete with lengthy guitar, bass, and drum solos. But in addition to the blues rock there were also touches of pop and progressive rock, mostly from Walsh who displayed a nascent sense of melody, not to mention some of the taste for being a cutup that he would display in his solo career. Walsh's "Take a Look Around" must have made an impression on Pete Townshend during the period before the album's release when the James Gang was opening for the Who since Townshend borrowed it for the music he was writing for the abortive *Lifehouse* follow-up to *Tommy*. If "Wrapcity (i.e., Rhapsody) in English," a minute-long piano and strings interlude, seems incongruous in retrospect, recall that this was an eclectic era. But the otherwise promising "Fred," which followed, broke down into a pedestrian jazz routine, suggesting that the band was trying to cram too many influences onto one record and sometimes into one song. Nevertheless, they were talented improvisers, as the open-ended album closer, Jerry Ragavoy and Mort Shuman's "Stop," made clear. After ten minutes, Szymczyk faded the track out, but Walsh was still going strong. *Yer' Album* contained much to suggest that the James Gang, in particular its guitarist, had a great future, even if it was more an album of performances than compositions. *—William Ruhlmann*

Rides Again / 1970 / MCA ✦✦✦✦✦
With their second album *Rides Again*, the James Gang came into their own. Under the direction of guitarist Joe Walsh, the group—now featuring bassist Dale Peters—began incorporating keyboards into their hard rock, which helped open up their musical horizons. For much of the first side of *Rides Again*, the group tears through a bunch of boogie numbers, most notably the heavy groove of "Funk #49." On the second side, the James Gang departs from their trademark sound, adding keyboard flourishes and elements of country-rock to their hard rock. Walsh's songwriting had improved, giving the band solid support for their stylistic experiments. What ties the two sides of the record together is the strength of the band's musicianship, which burns brightly and powerfully on the hardest rockers, as well as on the sensitive ballads. *—Stephen Thomas Erlewine*

Thirds / 1971 / MCA ✦✦✦✦
The James Gang Rides Again set the stage for the group's third album to propel them to Top Ten, headliner status, but that didn't happen. The band was on its last legs, rent by dissension as Walsh became the focus of attention, and the appropriately titled *Thirds* reflected the conflict. Among the nine original songs, four were contributed by Walsh, two each by bass player Dale Peters and drummer Jim Fox, and one was a group composition. But it was Walsh's songs that stood out. His "Walk Away," was the first single, and it climbed into the Top 40 in at least one national chart, the group's only 45 to do that well. "Midnight Man," the follow-up single, was another Walsh tune, and it also made the charts. The Fox and Peters compositions were a step down in quality, particularly Peters'. But the problem wasn't just material, it was also musical approach. *James Gang Rides Again* had emphasized the band's hard rock sound, which was its strong suit. But they had never given up the idea of themselves as an eclectic unit, and *Thirds* was their most diverse effort yet, with pedal steel guitar, horn and string charts, and backup vocals by the Sweet Inspirations turning up on one track or another. At a time when Walsh was being hailed as a guitar hero to rank with the best rock had to offer, he was not only submerging himself in a group with inferiors, but also not playing much of the kind of lead guitar his supporters were raving about. As a result, though *Thirds* quickly earned a respectable chart position and eventually went gold, it was not the commercial breakthrough that might have been expected. *—William Ruhlmann*

Live in Concert / 1971 / One Way ✦✦✦
The James Gang earned a great number of fans through their live performances, so it made sense that they would release a live record within months of their successful third album. *Live in Concert* captures much of the energy of their live performances, with Joe Walsh's guitar solos catching fire on nearly every song. However, the record also makes it clear that he was beginning to outgrow the confines of the James Gang, as Fox and Peters struggled to keep up with his imaginative playing for most of the album. *—Stephen Thomas Erlewine*

Straight Shooter / 1972 / One Way ✦✦

Passin' Thru / 1972 / One Way ✦✦

Bang / 1973 / Atco ✦✦✦
Bang was the first record the James Gang recorded with Tommy Bolin, a former member of Zephyr. While the songs were still fairly undistinguished, Bolin's playing was imaginative and captivating, making the lack of interesting material forgivable. *—Stephen Thomas Erlewine*

The Best of the James Gang / 1973 / ABC ✦✦✦✦✦
A good collection of their innovative hard rock features "Walk Away" and "Funk 49." —*Dan Heilman*

Miami / 1974 / Atco ✦✦✦
Like *Bang* before it, *Miami* was a success solely because of the presence of guitarist Tommy Bolin. Bolin's energetic, muscular playing reinvigorated the James Gang, sparking the rest of the band into giving lively performances. Again, there was a noticeable lack of memorable songs, but *Miami* is worthwhile for guitar aficionados. —*Stephen Thomas Erlewine*

● **Greatest Hits** / May 2, 2000 / MCA ✦✦✦✦✦
Designed to supersede the previous MCA compilation *15 Greatest Hits*, this *Greatest Hits* features 16 James Gang tracks remastered for CD, plus detailed notes and commentary. The last two songs—"You're Gonna Need Me," and "The Ashes, the Rain, and I"—were recorded live, and there are also two tracks from the film *Zachariah* ("Laguna Salada" and "Country Fever") making their first appearances on a James Gang compilation. Another first-timer is the complete version of "The Bomber," an extended medley featuring an oft-edited bolero section that appears in full here. Thanks to the better sound and packaging, this one gets the nod over *15 Greatest Hits*—unless you're looking for specific songs on that one that don't appear here, or unless you're a more devoted fan, in which case you might prefer the double-disc Repertoire compilation *The Best of the James Gang*. —*Steve Huey*

Rick James

b. Feb. 1, 1952, Buffalo, NY
Vocals, Keyboards, Guitar, Bass / Quiet Storm, Urban, Funk
In the late '70s, when the fortunes of Motown Records seemed to be flagging, Rick James came along and rescued the company, providing funky hits that updated the label's style and saw it through into the mid-'80s. James had a journeyman's career playing bass in various groups before signing to Motown in 1978 as an artist, songwriter, and producer. His first two singles, "You and I" and "Mary Jane," did well on both the R&B and pop charts. James broke big with "Give It to Me Baby" and "Super Freak," two hits from his second album *Street Songs*. He turned his production attention to resuscitating the career of the Temptations, and also worked with Teena Marie and the Mary Jane Girls during the early '80s. He recorded a few more hits for Motown, including "Dance wit' Me" and "Sweet and Sexy Thing," before signing to Reprise. He charted briefly during the late '80s and gained attention in 1990 when MC Hammer scored a massive hit with a track containing significant portions of "Super Freak." Still, James has been plagued with drug and legal problems that have found him more frequently in court and in jail rather than in the recording studio. —*William Ruhlmann*

Bustin' Out: The Very Best of Rick James / May 17, 1994 / Motown ✦✦✦✦✦
In the late 1970s and early '80s, Rick James did more than anyone to challenge George Clinton's place on the funk throne. Eventually, his music would turn into a very tired cliche, but at his creative peak, James was among the most exciting and vital artists funk had to offer. Summarizing his Motown output from 1978-1986 and offering four new tracks from 1994 as well, this two-CD anthology reminds us just how great he once was, but it provides evidence of his artistic decline as well. Though some of the songs are mediocre, most are outstanding. Even the most casual funk fans owe it to themselves to savor such rowdy classics as "Super Freak," "You and I," "Love Gun," "Give It to Me, Baby" and "Ghetto Life." James was equally superb when it came to soul ballads—and anyone who thinks otherwise should give a serious listen to "Fire and Desire" (a stunning duet with Teena Marie), "Dream Maker," and "Ebony Eyes" (which features Smokey Robinson). Sadly, "Cold Blooded" and "17" illustrate how formulaic James' funk often sounded by the mid-1980s. Meanwhile, some of the new material (including an enjoyable remake of Norman Connors' "You Are My Starship") indicated that he had the potential make a comeback with the right guidance. Boasting many more pluses than minuses, this set is the best place for novices to start. —*Alex Henderson*

● **Ultimate Collection** / Mar. 25, 1997 / Motown ✦✦✦✦✦
This excellent overview of Rick James' Motown hits features seven Top Ten hits, including the seminal "Super Freak" as well as "Cold Blooded," "Give It to Me Baby," "You and I," "Mary Jane," "Dance Wit' Me" and "Bustin' Out." —*Jason Ankeny*

Tommy James & the Shondells

f. 1960, Dayton, OH, **db.** 1970
Brill Building Pop, Bubblegum, Pop/Rock, Soft Rock, Pop, Rock & Roll
Tommy James & the Shondells—the very mention of their name evokes images of dances and the fun that rock & roll represented, before it redefined itself on more serious terms. And between 1966 and 1969, the group enjoyed 14 Top 40 hits, most of which remain among the most eminently listenable examples of pop/rock. Because they weren't completely self-contained (they wrote some, but not all, of their hits) and weren't as rooted in rock & roll, it took decades for writers and pop historians to look with favor upon them. In 1960, with his family living in Niles, MI, 13-year-old Tommy James and a group of friends got together to play dances and parties. Their second release on the local Snap label, "Hanky Panky," became enormously popular in the area in 1963. The original Shondells broke up over the next two years, but suddenly, "Hanky Panky" broke out in Pittsburgh after a promoter found it in a used record bin. James recruited a new group of Shondells in the Raconteurs, a local Pittsburgh quintet, and the nationally re-released single topped the charts in 1966. Tommy James & the Shondells spent the next three and a half years trying to keep up with their own success. They were lucky enough to be making pop-oriented rock & roll while most of the rock world was trying to make more

serious records. The group did grab a piece of the prevailing style in late 1968 with the number one hit "Crimson and Clover," which utilized some creative sound distortion techniques. The end came simply from their desire to take a break in 1970—James was getting involved in other projects, including his own solo career, which saw some limited success. Though long regarded as a bubblegum act, the Shondells' music revealed its staying power during the '80s in fresh recordings by Joan Jett, Billy Idol, and Tiffany. —*Bruce Eder*

● **Anthology** / 1990 / Rhino ✦✦✦✦✦
James and his band had a remarkable string of hits from the mid-'60s to the early '70s, largely because of an uncanny ability to keep current with fast-changing pop trends, from their first garage-band hit, "Hanky Panky," to their psychedelicized songs like "Crimson and Clover." Even more remarkable, the music holds up entertainingly today, and this well-annotated, 27-track compilation contains all the hits and more. —*William Ruhlmann*

Crimson & Clover/Cellophane Symphony / Aug. 27, 1991 / Rhino ✦✦✦
One of the most flexible units in late '60s rock, Tommy James & the Shondells could go from teen-oriented power pop to way-out psychedelic experimentation without sounding derivative of anyone or allowing their own identity to become obscured. Generously combining two of their classic albums, *Cellophane Symphony* and *Crimson & Clover*, on a single CD, this reissue reminds us just how unpredictable the rockers could be. This was a band that managed to appeal to Beach Boys aficionados as well as the hippies who fancied Jefferson Airplane, the Doors, and Cream. Whether digging into psychedelic rock on "Crimson & Clover" (a major hit), "Cellophane Symphony" and the goofy "I Am a Tangerine," sugary power pop on "Do Something to Me," or smooth blue-eyed soul on "Crystal Blue Persuasion," the group consistently comes across as honest and true to itself. —*Alex Henderson*

The Very Best of Tommy James / Apr. 20, 1993 / Rhino ✦✦✦✦
A condensed version of Rhino's two Tommy James compilations combines solo tracks like "Draggin' the Line" with hits from The Shondells like "I Think We're Alone Now." Given its budget price, the selection is rather skimpy and leaves out several tracks. Most listeners will want the more comprehensive Shondells and solo James collections, but there is nothing wrong with the music here. —*AMG*

Hanky Panky/Mony Mony / Jan. 9, 1996 / Sequel ✦✦✦✦
Sequel's *Hanky Panky/Mony Mony* combines two early albums from Tommy James & the Shondells on one CD. The best moments on these albums were released as singles, which means that casual fans should stick to the hits collections. However, serious collectors might want to check out this disc, since it has a couple of strong album tracks and covers. They may not be as good as the hits, but they may satisfy fans of James' sound. —*Stephen Thomas Erlewine*

Tighter, Tighter / Apr. 4, 2000 / Varese ✦✦✦✦✦
Varese Sarabande's *Tighter, Tighter* chronicles Tommy James' work for Fantasy Records in the mid- to late '70s, plus a couple of MCA singles from the mid-'70s. During this time James had *no* hits whatsoever and he was even trying to cash in on the success *Alive & Kicking* had with "Tighter, Tighter" in 1971. James may have been shooting for big success, but also was taking advantage of the artistic freedom Fantasy allowed him. As he says in Kenneth Pobo's liner notes, he "loved it out at Fantasy (because) they gave me run of the place." Consequently, the music compiled on *Tighter, Tighter* has to be seen as some of James' most personal work and the results are pretty magnificent. Yes, everything here is firmly within the '70s soft-rock tradition—whether its ballads or surprisingly numerous covers of Gary Glitter glam-rock (let's face it, anything more than one qualifies as "numerous")—but it's all exceptionally well crafted and some cuts, like "Bobby Don't Leave Me Alone" the seven-minute tribute to James' friend Bobby Bloom, have a real emotional undercurrent. The rest of the compilation, which culls from the albums *In Touch* and *Midnight Rider*, may not have that pull, but it's still fantastically well-crafted soft-rock. The genre was rarely as well made and subtle as the 16 tracks on this compilation, both in terms of songcraft and production and, at least to these ears, it lends itself to repeat plays better than James' '60s work, which is, of course, just a matter of taste. But, if you're a big fan of the 1980 hit "Three Times in Love" or the softer side of James, this is the album you need to own. —*Stephen Thomas Erlewine*

Jamiroquai

f. 1992, London, England
Alternative Dance, Adult Alternative Pop/Rock, Trip-Hop, Club/Dance, Acid Jazz, Alternative Pop/Rock, Urban
An intriguing development in the '90s British club scene, Jamiroquai came together in 1992 with a blend of house rhythms and the influence of '70s soul, personified by vocalist Jason Kay, an occasional dead-ringer for Stevie Wonder. Also including drummer Derrick McKenzie, keyboard player Toby Smith, bassist Stuart Zender, and vibes player Wallis Buchanan, the group debuted in October 1992 with the single "When You Gonna Learn?" on Acid Jazz Records. Signed to Sony soon after, Jamiroquai released its debut album *Emergency on Planet Earth* in 1993. The album exploded in the U.K., hitting number one on the charts and going platinum. *The Return of the Space Cowboy* followed the first album into platinum territory upon its release in 1995, and though *Travelling Without Moving* had a slower start upon its release in 1996, it became the first Jamiroquai album to make moves across the Atlantic. The album hit gold and earned the group several MTV Video Music Awards. *Synkronized* followed in 1999. —*John Bush*

Emergency on Planet Earth / Aug. 10, 1993 / Columbia ✦✦✦✦
Jamiroquai made a large initial splash in 1993 with *Emergency on Planet Earth*, a psychedelic melange of tight funky rhythms, acid rock intimations, and '70s soul melodies.

Frontman Jay Kay introduces himself with an environmentally oriented manifesto inside the sleeve, and his lyrics smack of idealist save the planet revolution. But this revolution would be held on the dancefloor if the band's impressive rhythm section had anything to say about it. Horns, string arrangements, and a didgeridoo provide full texture on most of the album's tunes, and the socially aware party vibe raged into the U.K.'s number one album slot. For a debut, *Emergency* shows quite a range of diversity, from the up-tempo jazzy instrumental "Music of the Mind" to the stop-start funk of "Whatever It Is, I Just Can't Stop." *—Troy Carpenter*

● **The Return of the Space Cowboy** / 1995 / Columbia ✦✦✦✦✦
Jason Kay's dead-on Stevie Wonder impersonation drives the acid-jazz and funky R&B of Jamiroquai. He takes on social issues such as homelessness and Native Americans' rights. A good album, but constant tempo changes keep the groove from flowing. *—John Bush*

Travelling Without Moving / Sep. 9, 1996 / Work ✦✦✦✦
Travelling Without Moving deepens the acid-jazz and '70s soul fusions of *Return of the Space Cowboy*, yet it doesn't have the uniform consistency of its predecessor. Nevertheless, Jamiroquai's fusions sound more fully realized with each outing, which makes its patchy songwriting forgivable. *—Stephen Thomas Erlewine*

Synkronized / Jun. 8, 1999 / Work ✦✦✦✦
Three years after their breakout *Travelling Without Moving*, Jamiroquai returned with another album that charts Jay Kay's continuing fascination with club-bound music of the 1970s—from disco to jazz-funk to rare groove to later Motown—but also shows signs of maturity. Produced by Kay with Al Stone, who also collaborated on *Travelling Without Moving*, the album includes several tracks (like the single "Canned Heat") that work infectious acid jazz grooves, and Kay's hipster vocals give out feel-good vibes through a set of ambiguously good-time lyrics. Though other tracks show a bit of an electronica update to the affairs, each still spotlights how strong and tight the band is. It may not be a leap ahead in sound, but *Synkronized* is another solid Jamiroquai record. *—John Bush*

A Funk Odyssey / Sep. 11, 2001 / Epic ✦✦✦
Since the jarring reception of 1999's *Synkronized*, Jamiroquai constructs *A Funk Odyssey* for something more polished and slick inside their own brandish funky disco rock. Jason Kay and keyboardist/songwriter Toby Smith perfect a maturation that was left keyed in *Traveling Without Moving*, but left open-ended on *Synkronized* for a wide scope of musical delight. *A Funk Odyssey* taps into various illustrious grooves of the Latin world, classic rock, and mainstream club culture and Jamiroquai are tight and eager to make everyone shake their groove thing in their own light. First single "Little L" beams with Kanjagoogoo-like synths while warping into a funk-driven hue of orchestral whirlpools, but Jamiroquai allows the band's extroverted and unattached personality shine on the worldbeat tinged "Corner of the Earth." Jason Kay strips aside all disco humor and grandeur for something personally inviting, something that's heartfelt, too. *A Funk Odyssey* sparks classic enthusiasm, and it feels good. Dance music is not just a design, it's something far more tangible, and Jamiroquai surely captures a fierce desire to make it more emotional on the band's their own level. *—MacKenzie Wilson*

Jan & Dean

f. 1958, **db.** Apr. 1966
Folk-Rock, Doo Wop, Surf, Pop, Rock & Roll
Besides the Beach Boys, no other vocal group captured the sound of California surf music with as much success—both commercial and artistic—as Jan & Dean. When the Beach Boys began their climb to superstardom, Jan & Dean followed suit with a series of surf and hot rod hits that featured falsetto harmonies, chugging guitars, and Jan Berry's clean production. Brian Wilson himself sang backup vocals on their biggest hit (which he cowrote with Jan), "Surf City," in 1963. While they lacked the Beach Boys' depth and capacity for artistic growth, Jan & Dean's hits from 1963 and 1964—which also included "The Little Old Lady (From Pasadena)," "Drag City," "Honolulu Lulu," and the mini-soap opera "Dead Man's Curve"—are in the same class as the Beach Boys' early work in their infectious, energetic invocation of good times and California sunshine, adding an irresistibly reckless humor to the genre. The duo's success, already on the wane a bit, was tragically cut short by Jan Berry's near-fatal auto accident in April 1966, which had been eerily foreshadowed by the lyrics of "Dead Man's Curve." *—Richie Unterberger*

● **Surf City: The Best of Jan & Dean** / 1990 / EMI America ✦✦✦✦✦
Remembered mostly for their surfing hits, Jan & Dean had a bit more range than they're generally given credit for. Their roots were in doo wop, and after scoring surf and hot rod hits, they also cut some decent straight pop/rock songs and zany singles that verged on pop satire. *Surf City* includes just about all the material you'd want from the duo. The 22 songs include the big hits "Surf City," "Dead Man's Curve," and "The Little Old Lady (From Pasadena)," of course, but also feature nifty smaller successes like "Honolulu Lulu," "The New Girl in School," and "Ride the Wild Surf." The pair was second only to the Beach Boys in blending high, soaring harmonies with driving vocal surf and hot rod sounds. Of course, they weren't nearly as talented as Brian Wilson's group, but even their minor material has an irrepressible sense of fun and sparking L.A. pop/rock production and melodies. Other highlights include their rearrangement of the old standard "Linda" and the 1965 Top 40 hit "I Found a Girl," written by P.F. Sloan and Steve Barri. Sloan-Barri also penned their infectious theme for the classic rock film *The T.A.M.I. Show*, "(Here They Come) From All Over the World," which deserved to be a bigger hit than it was. The only major omissions of this well-packaged set are their early, heavily doo wop-influenced hits "Jennie Lee," "Baby Talk," and "Heart and Soul," which weren't recorded for EMI. *—Richie Unterberger*

Teen Suite 1958-1962 / Jul. 4, 1995 / Varese Sarabande ✦✦✦
When Jan & Dean hit it big with "Surf City," they'd actually already been active on the L.A. pop/rock scene for a good five years, recording numerous singles for small labels that owed much more to doo wop and teen-idol styles than surf music. This has over 20 tracks from the era, most taken from rare singles, including five from 1958 that were billed to Jan & Arnie (Jan's original partner was Arnie Ginsburg, who left shortly after their debut single and Top Ten hit, "Jennie Lee"). This is mawkish, primitively recorded stuff, but not without its charm and even importance. With their white doo wop harmonies, Jan & Dean's early records were a clear influence on the Beach Boys; the best of their energetically naive, fashion-conscious singles (which Jan Berry often helped write) were a vague, but definite, forerunner of garage rock and '60s California pop/rock; and even at this point, they had a zany and infectious sense of humor, especially on their go-for-broke doo wop updates of the standards "Clementine" and "Heart and Soul." Most listeners should stick with the EMI anthology, but more specialized tastes will find a lot of this enjoyable, the hits ("Baby Talk," "Jennie Lee," "Clementine") being the standouts, though songs like "Baggy Pants" and "Something a Little Bit Different" are surprisingly goofy and satirical for the era. *—Richie Unterberger*

● **All the Hits: From Surf City to Drag City** / Nov. 12, 1996 / EMI ✦✦✦✦✦
Two discs, each running over 70 minutes, of the duo's most celebrated performances from the late '50s through the mid-'60s. If you're stacking this up against the *Legendary Masters Series* compilation, the advantage of getting this one is that it adds their doo wop-influenced, pre-Liberty hits ("Baby Talk," "Heart and Soul," "A Sunday Kind of Love"), as well as the pre-Jan & Dean smash by Jan & Arnie ("Jennie Lee"). It also has a few good tunes not on the previous anthology, like "My Mighty G.T.O." and the original version of "Bucket 'T'" (covered by the Who in 1966). And it's stuffed with alternate takes of some of their most famous tunes, which could be viewed as either a boon or an irrelevance. Some of their flop singles were really cringe worthy: "The Universal Coward" is a stupid parody of "Universal Soldier," and "A Beginning From an End," a melodrama in which the singer's wife dies in childbirth (!) against a typically sunny Top 40 arrangement, is downright tasteless fare. Collectors will appreciate these bonuses mightily, but less intense fans, if they're not determined to have "Baby Talk" and "Jennie Lee," will probably be better off with the more focused and consistent *Legendary Masters Series* disc. *—Richie Unterberger*

Surf City: Very Best of Jan & Dean / Apr. 4, 2000 / EMI ✦✦✦
To call this set a "very best of" is laughable at best. Out of the 20 songs collected, only seven were actual hits, the rest being good to great cover material that was album ballast or B-sides. While hits like "Surf City," "Sidewalk Surfin'," "Ride the Wild Surf," and "Little Old Lady From Pasadena" are aboard, the set is padded out with filler like "Hang On Sloopy," "Norwegian Wood," "Memphis," a bad live version of "I Get Around," and even an instrumental used to fill up one of their old album sides. Early hits like "Linda" and "Heart and Soul" help to fill out the set and their version of "Surfin' Safari" (with backing from the Beach Boys) is a nice bonus, but this is a long way from the best or a very best. Nice clean transfers, but for completists only. *—Cub Koda*

Jane's Addiction

f. 1984, Los Angeles, CA, **db.** 1991
College Rock, Alternative Metal, Alternative Pop/Rock
Jane's Addiction were one of the most hotly pursued rock bands when they gained notice in Los Angeles in the mid-'80s, with record companies at their feet. Flamboyant frontman Perry Farrell, formerly of the band Psi Com, has an undeniable charisma and an interest in provocative art (he designed the band's album covers) and Jane's Addiction plays a hybrid of rock music—metal with strains of punk, folk, jazz, or you-name-it. Warner Bros. won the bidding war and released *Nothing Shocking* in 1988. The band's abrasive sound and aggressive attitude (typified by the nude sculpture on the cover) led to some resistance, but Jane's Addiction began to break through to an audience: the album spent 35 weeks in the charts. *Ritual de lo Habitual* followed in 1990 and was the band's commercial breakthrough, reaching the Top 20 and going gold. Farrell designed the travelling rock festival Lollapalooza as a farewell tour for Jane's Addiction—after the tour was completed at the end of the summer of 1991, the group split. *—William Ruhlmann*

Jane's Addiction / 1987 / Triple X ✦✦✦
When this live date was recorded at Hollywood's famous Sunset Strip club the Roxy in 1987, Jane's Addiction hadn't yet become the darlings of alternative-rock culture. The L.A. band's unorthodox fusion of Led Zeppelin-influenced hard rock, dark Velvet Underground-ish imagery and stream-of-consciousness art rock wasn't as focused or confident as it would be on the commanding *Ritual de Lo Habitual*. But even so, the band showed considerable potential. As erratic and self-indulgent as this set gets, many of the songs are quite memorable. Lead singer/composer Perry Farrell was always fascinated with the dark side of the human psyche, and that fascination serves him well on "Pigs in Zen," the twisted "Whores," and the alternative-rock favorite "Jane Says." And things get enjoyably trashy on covers of the Velvet Underground's "Rock & Roll" and the Rolling Stones' "Sympathy for the Devil." But while this CD will interest completists, more casual listeners should stick to *Ritual de Lo Habitual*. *—Alex Henderson*

Nothing's Shocking / 1988 / Warner Brothers ✦✦✦✦✦
Although Jane's Addiction's 1987 self-titled debut was an intriguing release (few alternative bands at the time had the courage to mix modern rock, prog rock, and heavy metal together), it paled in comparison to their now classic major-label release one year later, *Nothing's Shocking*. Produced by Dave Jerden and J.A.'s vocalist Perry Farrell, the album was more focused and packed more of a sonic wallop than it's predecessor; the fiery performances often create an amazing sense that it could all fall apart at any second, creating a fantastic musical tension. Such tracks as "Up the Beach," "Ocean Size," and one of alt-rock's greatest anthems, "Mountain Song," contain the spaciousness created by the

band's two biggest influences, Led Zeppelin and the Cure. Elsewhere, "Ted, Just Admit It" (about serial killer Ted Bundy) and the haunting yet gorgeous "Summertime Rolls" stretched to epic proportions, making great use of changing moods and dynamics (something most alt-rock bands of the time were oblivious to). An incredibly consistent and challenging album, other highlights included the rockers "Had a Dad" and "Pigs in Zen," the horn-driven "Idiots Rule," the jazz instrumental "Thank You Boys," and the up-tempo "Standing in the Shower... Thinking." Like most great bands, it was not a single member whose contribution was greater: Perry Farrell's unique voice and lyrics, Dave Navarro's guitar riffs and wailing leads, Eric Avery's sturdy bass lines, and one of rock's greatest and most powerful drummers, Stephen Perkins. *Nothing's Shocking* is a must-have for lovers of cutting-edge, influential, and timeless hard rock. *—Greg Prato*

★ **Ritual de lo Habitual** / Aug. 1990 / Warner Brothers ♦♦♦♦♦
1990's *Ritual de lo Habitual* served as Jane's Addiction's breakthrough to the mainstream (going gold and reaching the Top 20), and remains one of rock's all-time sprawling masterpieces. While it's predecessor, 1988's *Nothing's Shocking*, served as a fine introduction to the group, *Ritual de lo Habitual* proved to be even more daring; few (if any) alt-rock bands have composed a pair of epics that totaled nearly 20 minutes, let alone put them back to back for full dramatic effect. While the cheerful ditty "Been Caught Stealing" is the album's best known track, the opening "Stop!" is one of the band's best hard rock numbers, propelled by guitarist Dave Navarro's repetitive trashy funk riff, while "Ain't No Right" remains explosive in its defiant and vicious nature. Jane's Addiction always had a knack for penning beautiful ballads with a ghostly edge, again proven by the album closer, "Classic Girl." But it's the aforementioned epics that are the album's cornerstone: "Three Days" and "Then She Did...." Although Perry Farrell has never truly admitted what the two songs are about lyrically, they appear to be about an autobiographical romantic tryst between three lovers, as each composition twists and turns musically through every imaginable mood. And while the tracks "No One's Leaving," "Obvious," and "Of Course" may not be as renowned as other selections, they prove integral in the makeup of the album. Surprisingly, the band decided to call it a day just as *Ritual de lo Habitual* hit big, headlining the inaugural Lollapalooza tour (the brainchild of Farrell) in the summer of 1991 as their final road jaunt. Years later, it remains one of alt-rock's finest moments. *—Greg Prato*

Live and Rare / 1991 / Warner Brothers ♦♦

Kettle Whistle / Nov. 4, 1997 / Warner Brothers ♦♦♦
According to alterna-rock legend, Jane's Addiction was the band responsible for laying the groundwork of the alternative rock explosion in the early '90s, but like most legends, that's half true and half lie. Jane's was instrumental in making alternative rock accessible to the metal audience, mainly because they were essentially a metal band with neo-psychedelic, neo-prog pretensions—two genres that have always appealed to metal and hard rock audiences. Nothing confirms that fact like *Kettle Whistle*, an odds and ends collection of live tracks, demos, alternate takes, and new tracks recorded by a "relapsed" Jane's featuring all the original members minus Eric Avery, who is replaced by Flea. Unfortunately, *Kettle Whistle* isn't the best place to hear their achievements, whether you're a diehard or a curious fan. Simply put, nothing here needed to be released, and there are no revelations. If anything, cuts like the embarrassing "My Cat's Name Is Maceo" detract from the Jane's myth, and the reunited cuts sound like standard-issue Porno for Pyros. The demos and alternate takes are all unnecessary, sounding like miniature, emasculated versions of the finished product, with the exception of the swinging "Been Caught Stealing." The live tracks are another matter, capturing both the power and the transcendence of Jane's Addiction's live performances. That's still not enough to make *Kettle Whistle* a worthy release because there is no sense or logic to its sequencing, and only a few tracks capture the power of Jane's (and even those will be familiar to diehards through bootlegs). It's not a terrible record, but it isn't a very good one, and it's hard to picture *Kettle Whistle* as anything other than an attempt to cash in on their legend. *—Stephen Thomas Erlewine*

Japan

f. 1974, London, England
New Romantic, Post-Punk, New Wave, Prog Rock/Art Rock, Synth Pop
Japan's evolution from rather humble glam-rock beginnings into stylish synth-pop (and beyond) made the British group one of the more intriguing and successful artists of their era. In their primary incarnation, the group emulated the sound and image of glam-rockers like David Bowie and the New York Dolls; singer David Sylvian's over-the-top vocals, much in the vein of Bryan Ferry, also earned Japan frequent (if derisive) comparisons to Roxy Music. Japan signed to Germany's Ariola-Hansa Records in 1977 and debuted a year later with a pair of LPs, *Adolescent Sex* and *Obscure Alternatives*, which received little notice at home or in the U.S. but did find favor among Japanese audiences. With 1979's *Quiet Life*, Japan made a tremendous leap into more sophisticated stylistic and subtle territory; a subsequent hit single covering Smokey Robinson's "I Second That Emotion" further underscored the newfound soulfulness of their music. 1980's *Gentlemen Take Polaroids* continued to broaden Japan's scope, incorporating a variety of exotic influences into their increasingly atmospheric sound. With 1981's *Tin Drum*, the band peaked: tapping sources as diverse as funk and Middle Eastern rhythms, the album moved beyond pop confines into experimental tones and textures, and scored a U.K. smash with the single "Ghosts." However, *Tin Drum* also proved to be Japan's swan song; the individual members quickly forged ahead with solo projects, briefly re-teaming in 1989 under the name Rain Tree Crow. *—Jason Ankeny*

Adolescent Sex / 1978 / Caroline ♦♦♦♦♦
The debut album is vastly different from later work. *—Steve Aldrich*

Obscure Alternatives / 1978 / Caroline ♦♦♦
Continuing artsy glam-rock formula of debut. *—Steve Aldrich*

● **Quiet Life** / 1979 / Caroline ♦♦♦♦♦
Quiet Life is the album that transformed Japan from past-tense glam-rockers into futuristic synth-popsters, though they'd been leaning in that direction for awhile. It's also a solid proto-romantic synthesizer record, enhanced by Karn's superb fretless-bass work and Sylvian's smooth, sneering vocals spread over pop hits like the title track and "Fall in Love With Me." *—Keith Farley*

Gentlemen Take Polaroids / 1980 / Blue Plate ♦♦♦♦
The group's debut for Virgin, *Gentlemen Take Polaroids* is a bit slicker on the synthesizer side but less satisfying as an album; it sounds slightly more dated than other entries in the Japan discography. Still, it includes the hit title track, a few other solid tracks, and two pastoral synthesizer exercises named "The Art of Swimming" and "Taking Islands in Africa" (the latter recorded with Yellow Magic Orchestra's Ryuichi Sakamoto). *—Keith Farley*

Tin Drum / 1981 / Blue Plate ♦♦♦♦♦
On *Tin Drum*, Japan finally dropped their Bowie/Roxy fixations and began making their own music. The heavy Oriental influence, centered ironically more on China than Japan itself, is apparent from the cover shot (featuring a poster with the beatific face of Mao smiling down) to song titles like "Cantonese Boy" and "Visions of China" (the latter a medium-sized hit in Britain). Yet even beneath the surface, *Tin Drum* is a record indebted to Asian music. The synthesizer textures and percussion on the opener "Talking Drum" point to the Orient, and Sylvian uses his voice less like a rock star and more like another instrument in the mix, even on the Top Five hit "Ghosts." Karn's fretless bass, Barbieri's keyboards, Sylvian's voice—each sounds out similar ground and balances the others so perfectly that they frequently sound like one instrument. *—Keith Farley*

Assemblage / 1981 / Hansa ♦♦♦

Oil on Canvas / 1983 / Blue Plate ♦♦♦

Exorcising Ghosts / 1984 / Virgin ♦♦♦

Japancakes

Indie Rock, Post-Rock/Experimental
Improvisational drone-pop orchestra Japancakes was the brainchild of Athens, GA-based musician Eric Berg, who in 1997 had the idea of organizing a group of ten musicians to take the stage without any previous rehearsals all for the sake of playing a single "D" chord for 45 minutes. Fascinated by the subtle changes and imperfections which textured the performance, Berg began mounting other experiments within a similar conceptual framework; although the onstage lineup often expanded to as many as a dozen instrumentalists, other constants included Nick Bielli, Todd Kelly, Heather McIntosh, John Neff, and Scott Sosebee. The debut Japancakes album, *If I Could See Dallas*, followed on Kindercore in the autumn of 1999; an EP, *Down the Elements*, appeared in the spring, and the sophomore effort *Sleepy Strange* was issued in early 2001. *—Jason Ankeny*

● **If I Could See Dallas** / 1999 / Kindercore ♦♦♦♦♦
Japancakes' improvisational drone-pop symphonies defy easy classification, stretching a single chord to its breaking point and picking up the pieces to create dense but inviting soundscapes which somehow find the common ground between the soothing wash of ambient and the propulsive energy of rock. For *If I Could See Dallas*, group ringleader Eric Berg and engineer Andy Baker handcrafted the disc's 11 instrumentals from snatches of studio performances, giving the songs a form and shape their live set no doubt lacks, but the cumulative effect is no less hypnotic—for all of the record's cosmic glow, the recurring presence of steel guitar keeps the music rooted in terra firma, a paradox which makes the music that much more difficult to pinpoint in any single time or place. The evolutionary process which guides each song is almost imperceptibly subtle, their circular melodies shaded by analog synths and strings which bubble in and out of the mix—creating music which arrives without travelling, Japancakes is that rare experiment as fascinating in practice as it is in theory. *—Jason Ankeny*

Down the Elements / May 16, 2000 / Kindercore ♦♦♦♦
Eric Berg's heady instrumental visions maintain something of an unintentional defiance that suggests that the 21st century technology is still a far-off proposition. By focusing on cello strains, droning bass and guitar lines, and insistently groovy acoustic drum patterns, it appears that he and his other Athens, GA, cohorts don't recognize the cut-and-paste, sample-centric age that most rock is now generated in. This EP, which is sandwiched between two larger efforts of equally hypnotic textures, creates moods that are far more demanding of a listener's attention than much of the ambient music produced by the synthesists the world over. The wonderfully infectious riff that propels "A.W. Sonic" somehow manages to sustain its drawing power for the majority of the track's 11-minute lifespan. "Sputnik" and the title track are the disc's straight-ahead electronic fare, but they are so skillfully arranged it's as if they'd been secretly peering in the Orb's laboratory for years. As a lower-cost introduction to what Berg has begun to achieve from an experimental rock concept gone right (unlike most), *Down the Elements* is immensely satisfying. *—Joe Silva*

The Sleepy Strange / Feb. 13, 2001 / Kindercore ♦♦♦♦
Building on the accessible experimentation on *If I Could See Dallas* and the *Down the Elements* EP, Japancakes' aptly named second album, *The Sleepy Strange*, is both dreamy and earthy, complex and immediate, and challenging and soothing. Though their modus operandi—repeating melodic phrases for hours at a time to highlight the subtle shifts in tone and rhythm—remains the same, *The Sleepy Strange* is the band's most cohesive work to date, yet it keeps all of the spontaneous beauty of their previous releases. If any-

thing, the slightly more focused sound highlights the band's strong melodies and interplay, making it one of the warmest, most inviting post-rock albums since Jim O'Rourke's *Eureka*, which also featured a fair amount of Japancakes' secret weapon, the pedal steel guitar. Whether it takes the lead, as on the opening waltz "The Waiting," or adding to the weightless beauty of "Disconnect the Cables'" avant soft rock, the group's masterful use of the instrument gives the music a dreamy, strangely western-tinged timelessness. The surprisingly propulsive "Soft N EZ" adds naive-sounding analog synths to fiddles and pedal steel, highlighting the group's highly inventive (and somewhat startling) mix of styles and sounds within one track. This is also Japancakes' most varied album, both musically and emotionally; "This Year's Beat" subtly shifts from brooding to assuring, while the loopy, languid title track and the dark string- and keyboard-driven finale, "Vinyl Fever," couldn't be farther apart in sound or mood. Hypnotically beautiful, *The Sleepy Strange* is the best representation yet of Japancakes' exciting repetitions, and one of 2001's best albums. *—Heather Phares*

Jason & the Scorchers

f. 1981

College Rock, Heartland Rock, Cowpunk, Roots Rock

A country/hard-rock band formed by Illinois native Jason Ringenberg in 1981, Jason and the Scorchers came careening onto the indie-rock scene seemingly out of nowhere; their amalgam of speedy hard rock fused with Ringenberg's decidedly country twang—along with the band's ability to deftly negotiate between Rolling Stones-style stomps and quieter, more melodic acoustic country music—brought them critical acclaim and a cult following. Capitalizing quickly on the notoriety brought by their debut EP, the Scorchers kicked out two fine LPs (*Lost & Found* and *Still Standing*) that sounded perfect for radio, but not so slick as to sound manufactured. Despite their obvious talent, by the release of 1986's *Still Standing*, it seemed as though the band wasn't going anywhere. They had achieved a modicum of success but weren't able to break through to mass acclaim, partly because they came along just before the explosion of country radio in the late '80s/early '90s. Hence, rock radio was reluctant to play them because they sounded too country, and country radio thought they were too rock. Ringenberg re-formed the original Scorchers in 1994, and released a modest reunion record (*A Blazing Grace*) that sounded like the Scorchers of old. *—John Dougan*

Fervor EP / 1983 / EMI America ♦♦♦♦♦

Their debut EP has "Absolutely Sweet Marie" (which you'll play over and over and over), as well as some wonderful country-rock like "Hot Nights in Georgia." Ringenberg's twangy voice is a hoot to listen to, and Warner Hodges plays some great guitar. A wonderful, if too brief, record and a harbinger of some great rock & roll to come. R.E.M.'s Michael Stipe contributes a song ("Both Sides of the Line") and some backup vocals. *—John Dougan*

Lost & Found / 1985 / EMI America ♦♦♦♦♦

Of the Scorchers' three full-length LPs, this is by far the best. There is so much pent-up energy and excitement on this record, it sounds as if it will fly off your turntable (assuming you still have a turntable) at any moment. With Hodges (as usual) driving this machine, Ringenberg's wild-eyed country-punk persona is here in full fury, and the good times never let up. This should have been the album that made them stars, but it did solidify their audience and place them in larger concert venues, where they tore it up. *—John Dougan*

Still Standing / 1986 / Mammoth ♦♦♦

Produced by veteran hard rock producer Tom Werman, *Still Standing* is a fine record, but also shows subtle signs of the band in decline: the hard-rock is stiffer, Hodges' guitar is smoother and more akin to the anonymous hard-rock/heavy-metal guitar sound that defined AOR radio in the '80s. That notwithstanding, there are still songs like "Golden Ball and Chain," which sounds like an outtake from *Exile on Main Street* and, continuing with the Rolling Stones motif, a ripsnortin' cover of "19th Nervous Breakdown." A teensy bit disappointing in comparison to *Lost and Found*, but by no means a bad record or one to ignore. If you've liked the Scorchers up to this point, you'll want *Still Standing*. *—John Dougan*

Thunder & Fire / Dec. 1989 / A&M ♦♦♦

● **Essential, Vol. 1 (Are You Ready for the Country?)** / Oct. 20, 1992 / EMI America ♦♦♦♦♦

Essential, Vol. 1 (Are You Ready for the Country) compiles Jason & the Scorchers' first EP, *Fervor*, and their debut LP *Lost & Found*, adding four bonus tracks for good measure. It's an excellent way to acquire their best records, yet it was replaced four years later by the nearly identical *Both Sides of the Line*, which featured the EP and LP without the bonus tracks. *—Stephen Thomas Erlewine*

A Blazing Grace / Feb. 7, 1995 / Mammoth ♦♦♦

Both Sides of the Line / Sep. 1996 / EMI ♦♦♦♦♦

CD reissue combines the *Fervor* EP and *Lost & Found* album onto one disc, and thus offers the best way to collect their early material. *—Richie Unterberger*

Clear Impetuous Morning / Oct. 1996 / Mammoth ♦♦♦

Jawbox

f. 1989, Washington, DC, **db.** Apr. 17, 1997

Indie Rock, Post-Punk, Alternative Pop/Rock, Emo

In their eight-year existence, Jawbox released four studio albums of increasingly skillful post-punk, not necessarily carrying the torch of their Washington, D.C., elders (Minor Threat, Embrace, Rites of Spring), but instead building on the tradition of Chicago's thriving early-'80s scene (Big Black, Naked Raygun, Effigies). Highly and unfairly scrutinized for being the first act to leave über-indie Dischord Records, the band proved cynics wrong by releasing two excellent LPs for Atlantic that easily surpassed their Dischord output, all the while retaining their integrity and creative control. A phenomenal record, *For Your Own Special Sweetheart* easily stands as one of the best releases to come out of the fertile D.C. scene of the '80s and '90s. An onslaught of touring surrounded the release of *Sweetheart* (the band regularly toured eight months a year), exposing the band to its regular crowds and some new ones. Minimal MTV rotation for a couple videos introduced Jawbox to a select few, but the record went shamefully unnoticed outside of the usual indie community. A somewhat glossy sheen pervades their fourth LP, *Jawbox*, but the incessant touring gave way to a band capable of playing magically together in their sleep. Thankfully, the record is still the work of a vital, passionate band. The songs are nearly as good as those on *Sweetheart*, but the polished sound sacrifices some of the blood and sweat that likely went into the recording. If it was an attempt to be more accessible to radio, it didn't work; despite the customary critical approval, *Jawbox* went DOA in the shops with unfamiliar consumers. In April of 1997, the band decided to call it quits, a decision based on a culmination of several events. *—Andy Kellman*

Grippe / May 1991 / Dischord ♦♦♦

Essentially recorded after getting enough songs together to fill out a 12" chunk of vinyl, *Grippe's* achievement was obscured increasingly after each successive Jawbox LP. That doesn't prevent it from being an enjoyable, albeit introspectively brutal record. J. Robbins might address a "you" during "Paint Out the Light" and "Tools and Chrome," but a self-flagellating nature can be detected throughout. That's what initially separated the band from their post-hardcore peers; instead of railing against authority and other oppressors, Jawbox pointed the finger at themselves.

Musically it's their least distinct, marrying the earlier crunchy side of Joy Division with *Throb Throb*-era Naked Raygun. It's a pretty convincing synthesis, pulled off well by relative newcomers Kim Coletta (bass) and Adam Wade (drums), who sound well-honed enough for Robbins' effective Chicago-derived (NR, Effigies, etc.) guitar. Though most of the record doesn't require a skip button, the true highlight is a cover of Joy Division's "Something Must Break." Where Ian Curtis sounded typically cold and detached on the original, Robbins gradually boils over with each successive verse, draining any possible emotion from the song. As far as taking a song to another level, it rivals Hüsker Dü's explosive cover of the Byrds' "Eight Miles High." Overall, a promising debut. (The CD version adds the band's debut 7" EP, featuring two early versions of *Grippe* songs and another rackety self-browbeater, "Twister.") *—Andy Kellman*

Novelty / May 1992 / Dischord ♦♦♦♦

Novelty ushered in second guitarist and vocalist Bill Barbot, immediately bolstering Jawbox's might. Differing from the debut, the guitars are sharper and the riffs are more concise. Less straight-ahead, the record is also more dynamic, benefiting from more varied material. The only negative aspect is Iain Burgess' murky production. Normally an outstanding producer, Burgess gives *Novelty* a bizarre din that frustrates in places. Adam Wade's drums sound a bit canned, and J. Robbins' vocals sound too "from the depths" on occasion. It's still a marked improvement over *Grippe*, with Wade and bassist Kim Coletta sounding more in tune with each other; Barbot immediately proves to be the perfect foil for Robbins, engaging in some excellent guitar joust throughout.

Lyrically, Robbins gets more abstract. (He also screams a bit more, but in a well-controlled manner.) Less introspective perhaps, songs like the excellent "Static" (one of the band's finest moments) seem to tackle one-on-one issues. Otherwise, who knows exactly what Robbins is addressing? Definitely not cut-and-dry, the songs certainly leave themselves open to any form of interpretation, but how do you decode lines like "I've got this syllable sickness called the six second blues/No doubt quixotic talk has been subsumed"? Sounds neat, so go with it.

Novelty is transformed from a good record to a great one with the addition of the "Tongues" single. Full of dense swirls of swooping guitars, only to be ejected by a thick riff (the intro almost sounds like the Smiths' "How Soon Is Now"), the song separates the band from their D.C./Chicago roots while clinging to them at the same time. Call it My Bloody Minor Raygun. *—Andy Kellman*

● **For Your Own Special Sweetheart** / Jan. 1994 / Atlantic ♦♦♦♦♦

The screams of a thousand chain-wallet-clad indie purists could be heard across the nation once word spread of Jawbox's signing to Atlantic; no band had left the good ship Dischord for a major label prior to Jawbox, so it was seen by more closed-minded types as an unforgivable crime against D.I.Y. If they'd stuck around to hear the record that didn't bear the Dischord logo, they'd hear the band's best record, the one they had always wanted to make. And it wasn't just the label change that made *For Your Own Special Sweetheart* (a phrase taken from a Barbie product) a transitional record. Adam Wade left the band for art rockers Shudder to Think, and he was replaced on the traps by Zach Barocas.

Even more bristly and blaring than *Novelty*, Bill Barbot's and J. Robbins' guitars are about as tingly as a jump into a cactus. Their interplay reaches a zenith on *Sweetheart*. Imagine *two* Andy Gills in Gang of Four, and you'll see what they're getting at. Though not quite as jagged and dry as Gill, the guitars employ a little distortion to slightly round the edges out. Producer Ted Nicely knew just what to do with the rhythm section—Kim Coletta's bass is more prominent, and uber-drummer Barochas' complex tom shots run rampant. (He was more likely to emulate Jack DeJohnette than Topper Headon.)

Subject matter includes JG Ballard's *Concrete Insland*-inspired "Motorist," leaving Robbins wrecked in an ugly part of Chicago; "Savory" examines the objectification of the female species. Otherwise, you need your Jawbox decoder ring to decipher lyrical content. Sonically, the terrain is expansive. Though "Whitney Walks" is stuck at the end of the record, it's relative quietude deserves just as much attention as anything else. Otherwise it's a manic, thrilling ride, nothing short of brilliant. *—Andy Kellman*

Jawbox / Jul. 2, 1996 / Atlantic ♦♦♦♦
Aside from slicker production from John Agnello and more direct lyrics, not much separates Jawbox's only non-transitional record from *For Your Own Special Sweetheart.* It could be argued that the band could have gotten a little *too* comfortable playing together or just plain too damn skilled. At times it sounds so effortless that you wonder if they could have sleepwalked their way through the recording. Granted they never sound as if the passion isn't there, but the clean, dirt-free production might detract from that to a casual listener's ears.

The band's arrangements are just as strong as ever, perhaps more so. But another issue is an apparent too-worked-over nature. Were overdubbed acoustic guitars really needed? Were all those additional layers really necessary? They sound like a kid who breezes through an anatomy exam, finishing half an hour before anyone else—the kid decides to stay at his desk and scribble the internal organs of a nurse shark, rather than risk the embarrassment of looking like such a smarty-pants to the rest of the class.

More frustrating than anything else was that the slicker-sounding record left no impact on modern rock radio. But then again, just how many Top 40 hits deal with topics like all the B.S. and fake national pride U.S. students are fed in their history classes? And how many times do you hear a song with schizo time signatures and a chorus that goes something like "Take the big man down/Forktie/Chump crown"? It's no "Semi-Charmed Life," after all. Though this sadly ended up being the band's swan song, there really was no way for the band to top themselves. No point in going back to college when you graduated *magna cum laude. —Andy Kellman*

My Scrapbook of Fatal Accidents / Nov. 3, 1998 / DeSoto ♦♦♦♦
Ahh, riches! *My Scrapbook of Fatal Accidents* is a treasure trove for Jawbox fans, tying up just about every loose end in their complex discography. Most notable is an intense, kick-in-the-gut Peel session recorded three months after the release of *For Your Own Special Sweetheart.*. The collection also includes several compilation tracks, split single sides, a couple of fine outtakes, four tracks from their performance at Washington D.C.'s HFStival in 1996, and their impressive clutch of covers that appeared on a number of tribute albums (many of which had been out of print). The covers are always top-notch, ranging from the Buzzcocks to Cole Porter to a hilarious take on the Cure's "Meathook." This is a complete package that was put together in thanks to Jawbox fans for years of support. It comes with a booklet of photos spanning their career and another listing their extremely impressive touring history. The collector couldn't ask for more, and the merely curious will be intrigued enough to check out their other releases. *—Andy Kellman*

Jay & the Americans

f. 1961, New York, NY, **db.** 1971
Brill Building Pop, Pop/Rock
Though they had a bunch of hits in the 1960s, Jay & the Americans were a throwback to a previous era with their doo wop influenced vocals, neatly groomed, short-haired appearance, and mix of pop/rock with operatic schmaltz. Built around the neck-bulging upper-register vocals of Jay Black, their biggest hits—"She Cried," "Cara Mia," "Come a Little Bit Closer," and "Let's Lock the Door (And Throw Away the Key)"—came off as a sort of hit parade version of *West Side Story.* The group also relied on outside songwriters for their material, drifting into MOR covers of oldies by the end of the '60s, and were generally a sort of textbook of unhipness during a time when self-contained rock bands were becoming the norm. Now that there's no pressure to disparage them in favor of more authentic acts, you can appreciate them for what they were—purveyors, at their best, of enjoyable kitsch with little depth. Black wasn't even in the band when they got their first big hit, "She Cried," which went to number five in 1962. Produced by Leiber and Stoller, the booming percussion and soaring strings, as well as the sad melody, were reminiscent of their work with the Drifters, though in a much whiter mold. Black had replaced lead singer Jay Traynor by the time of their second hit in 1963, "Only in America." Out of the Top 40 for a few years after 1966, Jay and the boys resurfaced in 1969 and 1970 with smooth hit updates of the Drifters' "This Magic Moment" and the Ronettes' "Walkin' in the Rain" before heading to the oldies circuit. *—Richie Unterberger*

● **Come a Little Bit Closer: The Best of Jay & the Americans** / 1990 / United Artists ♦♦♦♦♦
Jay Black possesses one of the most remarkable voices in rock & roll. On *Come a Little Bit Closer—The Best of Jay & the Americans,* an exhaustive 28-song collection, you get all of the hits in superb fidelity, and plenty of bonuses. *—Jeff Tamarkin*

Jay-Z (Shawn Carter)

b. Dec. 4, 1970, Brooklyn, NY
Vocals / East Coast Rap, Gangsta Rap, Hip-Hop
It's hard to imagine a more perfect success story than Jay-Z's remarkable ascendance to the top of the rap game. After a challenging childhood in a rough Brooklyn neighborhood and some time on the streets as a hustler, the rapper otherwise known as Shawn Carter followed his confident instincts, starting his own record label, Roc-a-Fella, at a time when this practice simply wasn't done on such an ambitious scale. His debut album, *Reasonable Doubt,* became a critical favorite among those in the know and scored a gold single. But it wasn't until his third album, *Vol. 2: Hard Knock Life,* that Jay-Z transcended critically acclaimed status to widespread mainstream success thanks to a string of massive hits, most notably "Can I Get A..." Yet never one to be content, Jay-Z then embarked on a large-scale arena tour, elevating his popularity to even more astonishing heights. By the end of the '90s, he was arguably the most successful East Coast rapper, or at least the most recognized. By the time he dropped *The Dynasty* in late 2000, his success was just that—a dynasty on which he had leveraged a recognized label and a roster of burgeoning protégés, including Memphis Bleek and Beanie Sigel. *—Jason Birchmeier*

Reasonable Doubt / Jun. 25, 1996 / Roc-A-Fella/Priority ♦♦♦♦♦
Even if Jay-Z's debut album didn't have the polish, the superstar roster, or the hits of his subsequent late '90s albums, it retains an air of irreplaceability. No matter how many trendy producers or how many talented rappers Jay-Z would work with on later albums, he couldn't duplicate this one's naked sincerity and naive ambition. Having abandoned a life of hustling and secured a distribution deal with Priority for his own Roc-a-Fella label, he put everything he had at the time into this record. It's essentially an autobiographical album—as are his subsequent albums to a more self-conscious degree—exploring his enigmatic anti-thug hustler mentality. Where many rappers strike a sometimes contradictory and often hypocritical stance in hopes of impressing fans with their glamorized image, Jay-Z doesn't resort to excessive flossing, instead rapping with sincerity, even if it makes him a less ideal ghetto hero. It's this heartfelt sincerity that makes him so potent here; on subsequent albums he would try to recapture this confessional tone over and over, yet he has never sounded this committed. Furthermore, the album's two standout tracks—"Can't Knock the Hustle," featuring a beautiful chorus by Mary J. Blige, and "Dead Presidents II"—are downright masterpieces. So even if *Reasonable Doubt* isn't graced with a who's who roster of hip-hop talent, it's an unbelievably personal album, something Jay-Z has continually tried to duplicate unsuccessfully. *—Jason Birchmeier*

★ **In My Lifetime, Vol. 1** / Nov. 4, 1997 / Pay Day ♦♦♦♦♦
After the death of friend and compatriot the Notorious B.I.G. in early 1997, Jay-Z made his claim for the title of best rapper on the East Coast (or anywhere) with his sophomore shot, *In My Lifetime, Vol. 1.* Though the productions are just a bit flashier and more commercial than on his debut, Jay-Z remained the tough street rapper, and even improved a bit on his flow, already one of the best in the world of hip-hop. Still showing his roots in the Marcy projects (he's surrounded by a group of kids in a picture on the back cover), Jay-Z struts the line between project poet and up-and-coming player, and manages to have it both ways. He slings some of the most cutting rhymes heard in hip-hop, brushing off a legion of rappers riding his coattails on "Imaginary Player." But Jay-Z plays the ghetto celebrity equally well, and continues his slick, Cristal-sipping image with "I Know What Girls Like" (featuring Puff Daddy and Lil' Kim), "(Always Be My) Sunshine" (featuring Babyface and Foxy Brown), and "Lucky Me." Puff Daddy's Bad Boy stable is responsible for almost half the productions, and though they often verge far into pop territory, Jay-Z usually rescues them from a complete crossover. (Ironically, the most commercial production is actually from Teddy Riley on "The City Is Mine," with an unfortunate interpolation of Glenn Frey's "You Belong to the City.") Having one of the toughest producers around (Premier) as well as one of the slickest (Puff Daddy) sometimes creates a disconnect between who Jay-Z really is and who he wants to become, but he balances both personas with the best rapping heard in the rap game since the deaths of 2Pac and Notorious B.I.G. *—John Bush*

Vol. 2: Hard Knock Life / Sep. 29, 1998 / Def Jam ♦♦♦
Coming on the heels of two strong records which revealed the extent of Jay-Z's talents, *Vol. 2: Hard Knock Life* (it may be titled *Vol. 2,* but it's his third album, arguably his fourth if you count the *Streets Is Watching* soundtrack) is a little bit of a relative disappointment. Jay-Z had established himself as a savvy, street-smart rapper on those two records, but with *Hard Knock Life* he decided to shoot for crossover territory, for better and for worse. At his best, he shows no fear—witness how the title track shamelessly works a Broadway showstopper from *Annie* into a raging ghetto cry, yet keeps it smooth enough for radio. It's a stunning single, but unfortunately, it promises more than the rest of the album can deliver. Jay-Z remains a first-rate lyricist and MC, but too often his subjects are tired, especially since he winds up with no new revelations. Unfortunately, the same could be said for his music. For every "Hard Knock Life," there are a couple of standard post-gangsta jams that don't catch hold—and that's really too bad, because the best moments (including several tracks produced by such stars as Timbaland, Kid Capri, and Jermaine Dupri) are state-of-the-art, R&B-inflected mainstream hip-hop. And that's the problem—before, Jay-Z wasn't trying to play by the rules of the mainstream, but here he's trying to co-opt them. At times he does, but the times that fall flat have less strength or integrity than their predecessors, and that's what makes the entire record not quite as effective, despite its numerous high points. *—Stephen Thomas Erlewine*

Vol. 3: Life and Times of S. Carter / Dec. 28, 1999 / Def Jam ♦♦♦

The Dynasty Roc la Familia / Oct. 31, 2000 / Def Jam ♦♦♦
At the time of *The Dynasty Roc la Familia 2000's* release, Jay-Z's career had taken an odd turn for both the worst and for the best. On the one hand, he had begun co-opting mainstream crossover formulas on his *Vol. 2: Hard Knock Life,* and continued to do so on his *Vol. 3: Life and Times of S. Carter* album, employing a star-studded roster of producers and guest stars. This turn toward commercialism kick-started a growing backlash by critics and longtime fans who missed the earnest Jay-Z of *Reasonable Doubt.* Yet, on the other hand, the increasingly accessible tone of his albums also brought waves of new fans, the sort of mainstream listeners who don't normally venture too far into hip-hop culture. Here, he thankfully abandons the overt crossover tendencies of his previous albums, instead taking on the role of father figure, devoting over half of his album to the small cast of half-established rappers on his Roc-a-Fella label. It's pretty clear that Jay-Z is trying to build his dynasty by using his own album to relentlessly promote Beanie Sigel and Memphis Bleek, and to a lesser degree Amil and DJ Clue. As a result, it's a very standoffish album with an insular tone—Jay-Z goes out of his way to not let anyone overshadow his crew. Still, this doesn't resolve the problems that plagued his two previous albums. Since Jay-Z is undoubtedly one of the best East Coast MCs ever, you feel cheated when he of-

fers what ultimately functions as a group album. You do feel somewhat compensated, however, since there are some truly remarkable beat-driven songs, particularly "I Just Wanna Love U (Give It 2 Me)" (featuring the Neptunes on production), "Get Your Mind Right" (featuring Snoop Dogg), "Parking Lot Pimpin'," and "You, Me, Him and Her." While not one of Jay-Z's best albums, *The Dynasty* has enough bright moments and idiosyncracies to make it worth investigating, particularly if you're a fan of the Roc-a-Fella roster. —*Jason Birchmeier*

Jayhawks

f. 1985, Minneapolis, MN
Americana, Alternative Country-Rock
Led by the gifted songwriting, impeccable playing, and honeyed harmonies of vocalists/guitarists Mark Olson and Gary Louris, the Jayhawks' shimmering blend of country, folk and bar-band rock made them one of the most widely acclaimed artists to emerge from the alternative country scene. The group sprung up in 1985 out of the fertile Minneapolis music community, and drew on influences like Gram Parsons, the Louvin Brothers, Tim Hardin, and *Nashville Skyline*-era Bob Dylan for their eponymous debut in 1986. The Minneapolis independent label Twin/Tone issued an album of group demos titled *Blue Earth*, and the exposure gained the Jayhawks a contract with the major label American Records. With the help of producer George Drakoulias, the band recorded their breakthrough album *Hollywood Town Hall* in 1991. The fourth Jayhawks album, 1995's *Tomorrow the Green Grass*, was the group's finest, a beautiful collection of songs led off by the elegiac single "Blue," the recepient of significant airplay. Though Olson announced he was quitting the band, the Jayhawks released *Sound of Lies* in 1997. —*Jason Ankeny*

The Jayhawks / 1986 / Bunkhouse ✦✦✦

Blue Earth / 1989 / Twin/Tone ✦✦✦
The songs which make up *Blue Earth* originated as demos, and save for some minor studio tinkering, are presented here in their original embryonic state. As a consequence, the record lacks punch; spare and economical, the songs are simply too primitive to come to life in this setting. Nonetheless, the growth of the band's songwriting skills over their debut is substantial; while many of the themes—drifting, drinking, and lost love—remain the same, they're handled with greater insight and clarity than before, with a keen eye for detail and nuance. —*Jason Ankeny*

● **Hollywood Town Hall** / Sep. 15, 1992 / American ✦✦✦✦✦
Hollywood Town Hall is the Jayhawks' breakthrough record, a uniformly strong collection heralding a dramatic leap in maturity and depth over the band's earlier work. Benefitting greatly from the increased production values afforded by their newfound major label status, the group's songs—a handful of them redone from the earlier *Blue Earth*—shimmer like never before; the guitars crackle with energy, and Mark Olson and Gary Louris' harmonies lock together so organically that at times it's impossible to distinguish where one voice ends and the other begins. —*Jason Ankeny*

Tomorrow the Green Grass / Feb. 14, 1995 / American ✦✦✦✦
The Jayhawks' final record with singer/songwriter Mark Olson, *Tomorrow the Green Grass* is also the group's finest. While the band's earlier efforts perfected a more traditional brand of country-rock, their fourth record is marvelously eclectic, both musically and emotionally; never before had they rocked as hard as on "Real Light," dug as painfully deep as on "Two Hearts," or hit quite the same peaks of exuberance as on "Miss Williams' Guitar," a tribute to Olson's new wife, neo-folkie Victoria Williams. The addition of keyboardist Karen Grotberg brings rich new layers to the Jayhawks' sound, as does the inclusion of a string section on cuts like "Blue" and "I'd Run Away," a soaring pop song that's quite possibly the best thing the group ever recorded. A fitting legacy, indeed. —*Jason Ankeny*

Sound of Lies / Apr. 22, 1997 / American ✦✦✦
Following Mark Olson's amicable departure, the remaining Jayhawks reconvened under the direction of Gary Louris to record *Sound of Lies*, the band's most ambitious album to date. Like Wilco's *Being There*, *Sound of Lies* uses country-rock as a foundation and wanders off into a variety of different sonic territories, including surf-rock and Beatlesque pop, bringing the music closer to the sound of adult-alternative pop/rock. Although the surface of the album is pleasant and melodic, Louris has written a uniformly harrowing set of songs, inspired both by the dissolution of his partnership with Olson and a recent divorce. The lyrics have a naked, emotional honesty which would have been more affecting if the music echoed its sentiment, yet the record still has a subtle grace and power, proving that the Jayhawks remain a distinctive band without Olson. —*Thom Owens*

Smile / May 9, 2000 / American ✦✦✦
With *Smile*, the Jayhawks drop yet another sizable chunk of their alt-country sound by the roadside, adding in its place healthy doses of power pop and modern electronic music. Almost half of *Smile*'s songs feature looped percussion, overdubbed drum tracks, or flat-out, funky backbeats. Little blips of sound skitter underneath the mostly acoustic guitars on the wistful "What Led Me to This Town" and make "Queen of the World" a worthy candidate for a dance remix (if the Jayhawks were ever to consider such a thing). Their second record since the departure of founder and leader Mark Olson, *Smile* is meant as a direct reaction to the pessimism of *Sound of Lies*, their underappreciated, moody offering from 1997. Ironically, with the charismatic Gary Louris now fronting the group alone, they sound more like a band than ever before. Despite the modern touches, though, the fact remains that *Smile* retains just enough of a distinctly Americana feeling. On the warm and twangy "Better Days," one of Louris' best songs in years, he sings with genuine regret and heartache for the way he treated a long ago lover, and on "Break in the Clouds" he celebrates the comforts of domestic contentment, complete with pedal

steel and soaring harmonies that recall the band's landmark work *Hollywood Town Hall* from 1992. The general shift in direction may alienate a few long-term fans, but much like friends Wilco achieved with their adventurous *Summerteeth*, *Smile*'s modern touches may bring even more people into the band's orbit. What never changes on the Jayhawks' albums, it seems, are the blissful melodies and well-constructed tunes, and that may just be enough for even the toughest critics. —*John Duffy*

The J.B.'s

f. 1964
Soul-Jazz, Funk, Soul
Maceo Parker joined James Brown's fabled band in 1964, Alfred "Pee Wee" Ellis joined the fold two years later, and Fred Wesley came on board in 1968. Ellis co-wrote such classics as "Cold Sweat" and "Say It Loud—I'm Black and I'm Proud," and both he and Wesley at various points were musical director of the J.B.'s. Parker was immortalized in Brown's famous incantation "Maceo, come blow your horn." Ellis also served as musical director for Van Morrison, while Wesley and Parker were part of the Parliament/Funkadelic gang at their peak in the mid- and late '70s. The three of them have recorded in various permutations as Maceo and All the King's Men, Maceo and the Macks, the J.B.'s, Fred Wesley and the New J.B.'s, Fred Wesley and the Horny Horns, the John Book Horns, and simply under any one of their individual names. In the '80s and early '90s, with the resurgence of interest in James Brown and Parliament/Funkadelic, the three horn men have been involved in a plethora of recordings. (Note: All of the albums made by Parker, Ellis, and Wesley in their various permutations have been included here; the artist credited with the album appears at the end of the review.) —*Rob Bowman*

● **Funky Good Time: The Anthology** / Feb. 28, 1995 / Polydor/Chronicles ✦✦✦✦✦
The J.B.'s recorded under various billings in the early '70s, including the J.B.'s, Fred Wesley & the J.B.'s, Maceo & the Macks, the First Family, the Last Word, and others. This double CD gathers 30 of the prime tracks by all of the above configurations from the first half of the '70s, including all nine of their chart hits and quite a few rare singles and long versions. Often, James Brown himself chips in with incidental vocals (though this is mostly instrumental) and keyboards. The two-and-a-half hour program can start to sound monotonous if taken all at once, but it's prime, often riveting funk, jammed with lockstep grooves that vary between basic R&B vamps and imaginative, almost jazzy improvisation. —*Richie Unterberger*

Pass the Peas: The Best of the J.B.'s / Jun. 13, 2000 / Polydor ✦✦✦✦
Pass the Peas: The Best of the JBs collects all of the R&B chart hits from James Brown's backing group, including "Gimme Some More," "Damn Right I Am Somebody," and "The Grunt." "Hot Pants Road," "Doing It to Death," "Givin' up Food for Funk," and "(It's Not the Express) It's the J.B.'s Monaurail, Pts. 1 & 2" are some of the other highlights of this collection, which features Brown on keyboards and backing vocals on many of the songs. —*Heather Phares*

Wyclef Jean

b. Oct. 17, 1972
Producer, Vocals, Guitar / Contemporary R&B, East Coast Rap, Alternative Rap, Urban, Hip-Hop
The Haitian MC and producer who rocketed to fame along with the other two members of the Fugees (Pras and Lauryn Hill), Wyclef Jean was the first to embark on a solo side-project. Born in Haiti, though his family moved to South Florida while he was still a child, Jean grew up in Brooklyn, spending time with his cousin, Pras. After the two hooked up with Lauryn Hill, the Fugees were born and revealed as hip-hop superstars after their second album, 1996's *The Score*. The following year, he went out on his own for *The Carnival Featuring the Refugee All Stars*, though both of his bandmates made appearances. Thanks to the single "We Trying to Stay Alive" (and to the Bee Gees for the sample), the album hit the Top 20 and went gold. *Ecleftic: 2 Sides II a Book* followed in mid-2000. —*John Bush*

● **Presents the Carnival Featuring the Refugee All Stars** / Jun. 24, 1997 / Columbia ✦✦✦✦
The Score was one of those rare hip-hop albums that came out of nowhere and rewrote the rules. In the aftermath of its success, many pundits predicted that rap would move away from gangsta and toward a richer, more varied existence. Given such heady praise, perhaps it was reasonable that Wyclef Jean, the guitarist and male rapper for the Fugees, decided to follow *The Score* with a solo project. However, *Presents the Carnival* comes across like Jean presenting his case that he is the *true* genius in the Fugees. And he's partially right. He has the ambition and drive common to many great artists, but he lacks the skills to fulfill his vision. Of course, the very fact that he has an original vision makes Jean one of the more compelling figures of late-'90s hip-hop. Not content to rely solely on hip-hop, Jean adds all manners of influences to his music. You can hear reggae, soul, disco, Caribbean rhythms, worldbeat, and opera scattered throughout *The Carnival*, giving the record the riotous atmosphere of a title. Even so, Jean occasionally tries too hard, forcing disparate genres to mix and spending more time on production than songwriting. But even with all its faults, *The Carnival* delivers great thrills when operating at full strength, demonstrating that Jean is at least half a genius. —*Leo Stanley*

The Ecleftic: 2 Sides II a Book / Jul. 25, 2000 / Columbia ✦✦✦✦

Jefferson Airplane

f. 1965, San Francisco, CA, **db.** 1973
Album Rock, Folk-Rock, Psychedelic, Hard Rock
Jefferson Airplane was the first of the San Francisco psychedelic rock groups of the 1960s to achieve national recognition, and in its later configurations, billed as Jefferson Starship

or simply Starship, it remained a significant popular recording act well into the 1980s. The band was organized in the summer of 1965 by singer/songwriter Marty Balin (b. Jan. 30, 1943, Cincinnati), who recruited a band to play at the Matrix, a club he was planning to launch in San Francisco. RCA signed the Airplane and released their debut album, *Jefferson Airplane Takes Off* in 1966 to little commercial response. The group then invited in the lead singer of a rival group, Grace Slick of the Great Society. The new lineup released 1967's *Surrealistic Pillow*, a gold-selling Top Ten hit that spawned the Top Ten singles "Somebody to Love" and "White Rabbit." This success made Jefferson Airplane the top San Francisco group during the 1967 Summer of Love and helped touch off the national craze for psychedelic music, the hippie lifestyle, and youthful drug-taking. *After Bathing at Baxter's* was a more experimental effort that was less successful. But *Crown of Creation* was another gold-selling Top Ten hit, despite the lack of a successful single. *Bless Its Pointed Little Head* (Feb. 1969) was a live album, followed by *Volunteers* (Nov. 1969), another gold studio album. After a series of lineup changes, in 1974 the group name was changed to Jefferson Starship. — *William Ruhlmann*

Takes Off / Sep. 1966 / RCA ✦✦✦

The debut Jefferson Airplane album was dominated by singer Marty Balin, who wrote or co-wrote all the original material and sang most of the lead vocals in his heartbreaking tenor with Paul Kantner and Signe Anderson providing harmonies and backup. (Anderson's lead vocal on "Chauffeur Blues" indicated she was at least the equal of her successor, Grace Slick, as a belter.) The music consisted mostly of folk-rock love songs, the most memorable of which were "It's No Secret" and "Come Up the Years." (There was also a striking version of Dino Valente's "Get Together" recorded years before the Youngbloods' hit version.) Jorma Kaukonen already displayed a talent for mixing country, folk, and blues riffs in a rock context and Jack Casady already had a distinctive bass sound. But the Airplane of Balin-Kantner-Kaukonen-Anderson-Casady-Spence is to be distinguished from the Balin-Kantner-Kaukonen-Casady-Slick-Dryden version of the band that would emerge on record five months later chiefly by Balin's dominance. Later, Grace Slick would become the group's vocal and visual focal point. On *Takes Off*, the Airplane was Balin's group. (*Jefferson Airplane Takes Off* was released as RCA 3584 in September 1966. It was reissued as RCA 66797 on January 30, 1996, as a CD that contained both the stereo and mono versions and that added back the track "Runnin' 'Round This World," which had been deleted from all but initial copies due to the sexual and perceived drug references of the line "The nights I've spent with you have been fantastic trips." But the included version still eliminated the word "trips.") — *William Ruhlmann*

★ Surrealistic Pillow / Feb. 1967 / RCA ✦✦✦✦✦

Their groundbreaking folk-based psychedelic album hit like a shot heard round the world. From "White Rabbit" and "Somebody to Love" to the sublime "3/5 of a Mile in 10 Seconds," the sensibilities are fierce, the material is melodic, and the performances, sparked by new member Grace Slick on most of the lead vocals, are magnificent and inspired. The long-awaited remastered reissue (look for the 1996 release date on back of the CD jewel box) is a real treasure, featuring both the stereo and mono mixes of each song, which differed significantly in texture and focus. But the real beauty is the remastered sound, which captures the majesty of this album about as well as any '60s reissue yet heard—the 1996 reissue is the first CD version to sound better than original pressings of the LP, and it makes the album even more compelling. Every song is perfect, and the pity is that RCA didn't record any of the group's shows from this era for official release, apart from the all-too-brief set at Monterey the following summer, when this material made up the bulk of their repertory; and Grace Slick and Marty Balin (who never had a prettier song than "Today" from this album) shared the vocals and songwriting, and before politics and excessive experimentation, musical and chemical, began affecting the band's ability to do a straightforward song. The group never made a better album, and few artists from the era ever did. — *Bruce Eder*

After Bathing at Baxter's / Dec. 1967 / RCA ✦✦✦

Jefferson Airplane's third album was both a further exploration of the more unusual aspects of their second album, *Surrealistic Pillow*, and a reaction against that album's more conventional aspects and its commercial success. *After Bathing at Baxter's* was dominated by rhythm guitarist/singer Paul Kantner, who wrote or co-wrote six of the 11 selections, including the two singles "The Ballad of You & Me & Pooneil" and "Watch Her Ride." While Grace Slick wrote and sang the bizarre "rejoyce" (based on James Joyce's writings) and "Two Heads" (songs well to the left of the already-daring "White Rabbit"), the album also marked the emergence of the bass/guitar team of Jack Casady and Jorma Kaukonen, whose nine-minute instrumental "Spare Chaynge" foreshadowed their spinoff group Hot Tuna. *After Bathing at Baxter's* was the album on which the Airplane, touted as the leaders of the San Francisco acid-rock scene, actually tried to catch up to the movement. Unlike other psychedelic exponents, they had been primarily song-based rather than performance-based; despite the studio gimmicks and self-indulgence, they remained so. — *William Ruhlmann*

Crown of Creation / Sep. 1968 / RCA ✦✦✦✦

The group's fourth album, appearing ten months following *After Bathing at Baxter's*, isn't the same kind of leap forward that *Baxter's* represented from *Surrealistic Pillow*. Indeed, in many ways, *Crown of Creation* is a more conservative album stylistically, opening with "Lather," a Grace Slick original that was one of the group's very last forays (and certainly their last prominent one) into a folk idiom. Much of what follows is a lot more based in electric rock, as well as steeped in elements of science fiction (specifically author John Wyndham's book *The Chrysalids*) in several places, but *Crown of Creation* was still deliberately more accessible musically than its predecessor, even as the playing became more bold and daring within more traditional song structures. The overall album captured the group's rapidly evolving, very heavy live sound within the confines of some

fairly traditional song structures, and left ample room for Slick and Marty Balin to express themselves vocally, with Balin turning in one of his most heartfelt and moving performances on "If You Feel." "Ice Cream Phoenix" pulses with energy and "Greasy Heart" became a concert standard for the group—the studio original of the latter is notable for Slick's most powerful vocal performance since "Somebody to Love." And the album's big finish, "The House at Pooneil Corners," seemed to fire on all cylinders, a shattering finish to the album. *Crown of Creation* has been reissued on CD several times, including a Mobile Fidelity audiophile edition at the start of the '90s, but in 2001, RCA-BMG's European division released a remastered edition with two bonus tracks from the same sessions, the Spencer Dryden co-authored "Ribump Ba Bap Dum Dum" and the more accessible "Would You Like a Snack?" — *Bruce Eder*

Bless Its Pointed Little Head / Feb. 1969 / RCA ✦✦✦

Jefferson Airplane's first live album demonstrated the group's development as concert performers, taking a number of songs that had been performed in concise, pop-oriented versions on their early albums—"3/5's of a Mile in 10 Seconds," "Somebody to Love," "It's No Secret," "Plastic Fantastic Lover"—and rendering them in arrangements that were longer, harder rocking, and more densely textured, especially in terms of the guitar and bass lines constructed by Jorma Kaukonen and Jack Casady. The group's three-part vocal harmonizing and dueling was on display during such songs as a nearly seven-minute version of Fred Neil's folk-blues standard "The Other Side of This Life," here transformed into a swirling rocker. The album emphasized the talents of Kaukonen and singer Marty Balin over the team of Paul Kantner and Grace Slick, who had tended to dominate recent records: the blues song "Rock Me Baby" was a dry run for Hot Tuna, the band Kaukonen and Casady would form in two years, and Balin turned in powerful vocal performances on several of his own compositions, notably "It's No Secret." Jefferson Airplane was still at its best in concise, driving numbers, rather than in the jams on Donovan's "Fat Angel" (running 7:35) or the group improv "Bear Melt" (11:21); they were just too intense to stretch out comfortably. But *Bless Its Pointed Little Head* served an important function in the group's discography, demonstrating that their live work had a distinctly different focus and flavor from their studio recordings. — *William Ruhlmann*

Volunteers / Nov. 1969 / RCA ✦✦✦✦

Controversial at the time, delayed because of fights with the record company over lyrical content and the original title (*Volunteers of America*), *Volunteers* was a powerful release that neatly closed out and wrapped up the '60s. Here, the Jefferson Airplane presents itself in full revolutionary rhetoric, issuing a call to "tear down the walls" and "get it on together." "We Can Be Together" and "Volunteers" bookend the album, offering musical variations on the same chord progression and lyrical variations on the same theme. Between these politically charged rock anthems, the band offers a mix of words and music that reflect the competing ideals of simplicity and getting "back to the earth," and overthrowing greed and exploitation through political activism, adding a healthy dollop of psychedelic sci-fi for texture. Guitarist Jorma Kaukonen's beautiful arrangement of the traditional "Good Shepherd" is a standout here, and Jerry Garcia's pedal steel guitar gives "The Farm" an appropriately rural feel. The band's version of "Wooden Ships" is much more eerie than that released earlier in the year by Crosby, Stills & Nash. Oblique psychedelia is offered here via Grace Slick's "Hey Frederick" and ecologically tinged "Eskimo Blue Day." Drummer Spencer Dryden gives an inside look at the state of the band in the country singalong "A Song for All Seasons."

The musical arrangements here are quite potent. Nicky Hopkins' distinctive piano highlights a number of tracks, and Kaukonen's razor-toned lead guitar is the recording's unifying force, blazing through the mix, giving the album its distinctive sound. Although the political bent of the lyrics may seem dated to some, listening to *Volunteers* is like opening a time capsule on the end of an era, a time when young people still believed music had the power to change the world. — *Jim Newsom*

The Worst of Jefferson Airplane / Nov. 1970 / RCA ✦✦✦✦✦

Its smirky title notwithstanding, *The Worst of Jefferson Airplane* provides a fine recap of the band's first six albums. Released in 1970 shortly before Marty Balin's initial departure from the band, the album marked not only the end of the decade, but, unwittingly, the end of the group's most stable phase, membership-wise. The track selections are evenly divided among the first-generation albums; only the live *Bless Its Pointed Little Head* is represented by a single entry. Pains were also taken to include songs featuring lead vocalists Balin, Grace Slick, Paul Kantner, and guitarist Jorma Kaukonen. A few omissions are striking, most notably the chart single "Greasy Heart" and the signature Kantner track "Wooden Ships." Nevertheless, the songs chosen for this album accurately summarize the distinct feel of each Jefferson Airplane album of the '60s, and thus the disc represents an ideal way to introduce oneself to the band's early, most psychedelic material. — *Joseph McCombs*

Bark / Sep. 1971 / RCA ✦✦✦

By the time of *Bark*, personnel changes had gutted much of the original vision of the group, especially with the departure of Marty Balin. Paul Kantner and Grace Slick remained, but their compositions were growing increasingly ill-focused, and Jorma Kaukonen and new drummer Joey Covington were ill-equipped to pick up the songwriting slack. The result was an album that bore hallmarks of the classic Airplane sound, but lacked any classic Airplane songs. That said, the record isn't as bad as many reviewers have made it out to be. It's just mediocre, with little that sticks in the memory, despite occasional nice moments in cuts like Covington's "Pretty as You Feel" and Kantner's delicate "Third Week in the Chelsea." — *Richie Unterberger*

Long John Silver / Jul. 1972 / RCA ✦✦

Thirty Seconds Over Winterland / Apr. 1973 / RCA ✦✦

The Best of Jefferson Airplane / 1980 / RCA ♦♦♦♦
The Best of Jefferson Airplane is an imperfect but serviceable collection, featuring ten of the Airplane's best-known songs: "White Rabbit," "Somebody to Love," "Wild Tyme," "Won't You Try Saturday Afternoon," "Wooden Ships," "Third Week in the Chelsea Hotel" and "Long John Silver." This basic collection will be of use to a listener just looking for the hits, but more serious listeners will be better serviced by the more thorough compilations available, or the band's original albums. *—Stephen Thomas Erlewine*

2400 Fulton Street: An Anthology / Mar. 1987 / RCA ♦♦♦♦
This was the first serious effort to assemble the best and most interesting of the Jefferson Airplane's work from beginning to end. At the time, the group's catalog on CD was in a woeful state of disrepair, hastily mastered from LP production sources and sounding worse than original vinyl copies of many of the titles, and there was no comprehensive anthology, just the *Worst of Jefferson Airplane* compilation from 1970. *2400 Fulton Street* isn't ideal, jumping around a little too much, but provides a look for the uninitiated into the evolution of the group's sound from a mixed electric-acoustic folk rock ensemble, not too different from the Mugwumps et al., into a high-energy rock band and, for a time, one of the more daring psychedelic outfits. Additionally, even longtime fans will appreciate most of the jumps that are made, for all of the essentials are here—most of *Surrealistic Pillow*, along with highlights from the surrounding albums up through the end of the group's history (with a Levi's radio commercial featuring the band thrown in for good measure) and a few odd singles and B-sides that otherwise usually get overlooked. Moreover, the sound was a major improvement at the time (though it has since been outdone on the re-releases of the individual albums), and the notes contained what was, at the time, perhaps the best easily available account of the group's history. *—Bruce Eder*

Jefferson Airplane / Sep. 1989 / Epic ♦

Jefferson Airplane Loves You / Oct. 1992 / RCA ♦♦♦
A three-disc box set loaded with rarities, *Jefferson Airplane Loves You* is necessary for hardcore fans, but the double-disc *2400 Fulton Street* offers a better portrait of the band and is the essential purchase for casual fans. *—Stephen Thomas Erlewine*

● **Hits** / Sep. 29, 1998 / RCA ♦♦♦♦♦
There has been no dearth of greatest-hits and best-of albums devoted to Jefferson Airplane, Jefferson Starship, and Starship, but this is the first one combining tracks from all three editions of the group that started in San Francisco in the mid-'60s and ended its run in the early '90s with entirely different personnel. The band continued to maintain the same basic elements for most of its run, the constants being a soaring male tenor (either Marty Balin or Mickey Thomas) and a stinging lead guitar (either Jorma Kaukonen or Craig Chaquico), even if its best-remembered sound was the icy, stentorian contralto of on-again, off-again member Grace Slick. To say that the elements held constant is not to say that the band continued to sound the same, but if you listen to the chronologically sequenced album through, you can hear the transition clearly. True to its title, the 35-track *Hits* contains all of the band's most successful singles, omitting only two of its Top 40 entries. All the big hits are here, from "Somebody to Love" through "Miracles" to "We Built This City," accounting for 18 of the tracks. The rest of the album is filled out with less-successful singles and album tracks that became band standards. As this list indicates, compiler Paul Williams is more interested in Jefferson Airplane than Jefferson Starship and Starship, which are represented exclusively by singles, and a more balanced portrait of the later ensembles might have been provided by including illuminating album tracks. But this is the best two-disc summary of a group that, despite dizzying personnel changes, maintained its commercial acumen for over 20 years. *—William Ruhlmann*

The Roar of Jefferson Airplane / Jul. 10, 2001 / RCA ♦♦♦♦♦
The beauty of this collection is that it allows the listener to see the progression of Jefferson Airplane, from their first hit, "It's No Secret," onward, as they continued to produce hits. While the quality of their music remained constant into the late '60s, their sound changed moods, which is something that the listener feels during a playing of the album. The intensity jumps up and down, the use of instruments varies, and the vocals fluctuate. Due to this mixture, this album is one of the best ways to enjoy the band during one sitting. The album is highlighted by one of the band's most well-known hits, "Somebody to Love." However, it's placed midway through, giving a nice buildup; the album also includes perhaps Grace Slick's most powerful song, "Greasy Heart." This track best exhibits her tremendous vocal ability, which is both intense and soft as the track progresses. The only track that is missing from the collection is "White Rabbit," a Slick song that has been remembered since it debuted on *Surrealistic Pillow* in 1967. While this example of Slick's stunning vocals is left out, "Eat Starch Mom" isn't. She is at her best as she belts out a socially charged tune in which she, as Jeff Tamarkin writes in the liner notes, "takes digs at back-to-the-land hippie purists." In fact, what makes this album even more worthwhile is the brief insert by Tamarkin, which chronicles the beginnings of the band and speaks of each of the songs and their context in the history of Jefferson Airplane. *—Shawn Nicholls*

Jefferson Starship

f. 1974, **db.** 1984
Album Rock, Arena Rock, Pop/Rock, Hard Rock
With their 1974 metamorphosis into the Jefferson Starship, the group once known as the Jefferson Airplane underwent a radical facelift which resulted not only in a change of name but also a new lineup and a new musical identity. Formerly torch-bearers of the Haight-Ashbury counterculture, famed for psychedelic-era landmarks including *Surrealistic Pillow* and *Volunteers*, as the Starship the group reached even greater heights of success, forging a more mainstream sound and attitude which established them as one of the predominant hard rock units of their era. 1975's *Red Octopus*, became the Starship's most successful effort, topping the charts off and on throughout the year on the strength of the Top Three ballad "Miracles." Despite singer Grace Slick's protests that the music was growing too commercial, the band continued to hone a more mainstream identity on 1976's *Spitfire*, their first platinum-selling release, while 1978's *Earth* spawned the Top Ten hit "Count on Me." However, in the wake of the record's release Slick's long-standing drinking problem spun out of control, and she left the group during a European tour. Vocalist Marty Balin exited later in 1978, leaving the Starship without a lead singer; finally, in 1979 the remaining members recruited vocalist Mickey Thomas. Slick rejoined the group for 1982's *Winds of Change*. As simply Starship, they later scored the hits "We Built This City," "Sara" and "Nothing's Gonna Stop Us Now." *—Jason Ankeny*

Dragon Fly / 1974 / RCA ♦♦♦
Credited to "Grace Slick/Paul Kantner/Jefferson Starship," *Dragon Fly* was the transitional album between the various shifting aggregations Slick and Kantner had been recording with as Jefferson Airplane dissolved in the early 1970s and the new Jefferson Starship (which essentially was the Airplane with a new guitarist and bassist—Craig Chaquico and Pete Sears). But where such preceding efforts as *Sunfighter*, *Manhole*, and *Baron Von Tollbooth and the Chrome Nun* had suffered from indulgence and a lack of focus, *Dragon Fly*, from the first note of its rocking leadoff track, "Ride the Tiger" (a chart single), was a unified effort. Like much of the Airplane catalog and all of the Starship albums to follow, the album suffered from the band's communal approach to song selection (the eight tracks credited 12 writers, half of them band members), leading to an unevenness in the material. But unlike the recent Kantner/Slick/etc. albums, it sounded like the work of a seasoned band. (It didn't hurt that the album was cut just after a tour, instead of before one.) Especially notable was Chaquico, who on such tracks as "All Fly Away" and "Hyperdrive" demonstrated that he was a distinctive lead guitarist able to define the Starship sound just as the very different Jorma Kaukonen had the Airplane. But what turned *Dragon Fly* into an artistic and commercial triumph (it was the most popular album any of these people had been involved with in five years) was the return, for one song, of former Airplane singer Marty Balin, since that one song was the epic power ballad "Caroline," which became a radio favorite and remains one of the best songs the Airplane/Starship ever did. *—William Ruhlmann*

● **Red Octopus** / 1975 / RCA ♦♦♦♦♦
Technically speaking, *Red Octopus* was the first album credited to Jefferson Starship, though practically the same lineup made *Dragon Fly*, credited to Grace Slick/Paul Kantner/Jefferson Starship. The difference, however, was crucial: Marty Balin was once again a fully integrated band member, writing or co-writing five of the ten tracks. And there can be little doubt that it was Balin's irresistible ballad "Miracles," the biggest hit single in the Jefferson Whatever catalog, that propelled *Red Octopus* to the top of the charts, the only Jefferson album to chart that high and the best-selling album in their collective lives. This must have been sweet vindication for Balin, who founded Jefferson Airplane but then drifted away from the group as it veered away from his musical vision. Now, the collective was incorporating his taste without quite integrating it—"Miracles," with its strings and sax solo by nonband member Irv Cox, was hardly a characteristic Airplane/Starship track. But then, neither exactly was Papa John Creach's showcase, "Git Fiddler," or bassist Pete Sears' instrumental "Sandalphon," which sounded like something from an early Procol Harum album. Slick has three strong songs, among them the second single "Play on Love." Like *Dragon Fly*, *Red Octopus* reflected a multiplicity of musical tastes; there were ten credited songwriters, seven of whom were in the band. If there is any consistency in this material, it is in subject matter (love songs). The album is more ballad-heavy and melodic than the Airplane albums, which made it more accessible to the broader audience it reached, though "Sweeter Than Honey" is as tough a rocker as the band ever played. *—William Ruhlmann*

Spitfire / 1976 / RCA ♦♦♦
Trying to follow up the overwhelming success of their last record proved too much for the Starship. Nothing here can compare with the hit sound they had forged previously although they did get chart action with the song "With Your Love." Otherwise, a bad bump in the road for Jefferson Starship. *—James Chrispell*

Earth / 1978 / RCA ♦♦

Freedom at Point Zero / 1979 / RCA ♦♦♦
Freedom at Point Zero is not a great Jefferson Starship album; the wonder is that it is as good as it is. Since the band's previous album, the Top Ten, million-selling *Earth*, the group had lost its two lead singers, Grace Slick and Marty Balin, and they had been replaced by Mickey Thomas. "Jane," released as a single in advance of the album, displayed the result—even before Thomas' soaring tenor entered, it sounded like Foreigner. But it also made the Top 20, which helped the album into the Top Ten and to a gold record award. Reluctant leader Paul Kantner came back to the fore, and, at least on the energetic "Girl With the Hungry Eyes" (a chart single), that was a good thing, though the more typically discursive, rhythmically static songs like "Lightning Rose" and "Things to Come" (on which Thomas, through the magic of overdubbing, replaced Slick and Balin) slowed things down. Other songwriting contributors such as bassist Pete Sears and guitarist Craig Chaquico brought in generic arena rock bombast like "Awakening" and "Rock Music," making this a typically uneven effort. Although *Freedom at Point Zero* demonstrated that the group could soldier on, the band without its quirky individualists was ultimately too generic, which made Slick's return on the next album welcome. *—William Ruhlmann*

Gold / 1979 / RCA ♦♦♦♦
This 1979 compilation culls the hit singles and strongest album tracks from Jefferson Starship's four elemental-titled albums of the 1970s: 1974's *Dragon Fly* (evoking air), the 1975 number one smash *Red Octopus* (water), 1976's *Spitfire* (fire), and the more obvi-

ously titled *Earth* from 1978. These albums saw the Jefferson Starship hit-making machine at its peak, so this collection is a fine entrance for those new to the band's '70s material. It's a remarkably democratic set; tracks are selected evenly from *Dragon Fly* (three), *Red Octopus* (three), *Spitfire* (two), and *Earth* (three), and are divided fairly equitably among lead vocalists: Marty Balin (six), Grace Slick (four), and Paul Kantner/group (two). In the course of listening, it becomes obvious how strongly Balin's increasing MOR sensibilities were guiding the group's path as the decade progressed: By the end, he was singing all the radio hits. The Top 40 hits—"Miracles," "With Your Love," "Count on Me," and "Runaway"—are, of course, all included, as are a few of the group's more ambitious efforts: the sweeping soundscape "St. Charles," the heartfelt poetry of "Caroline," and the remarkable Grace Slick meditation on aging, "Hyperdrive." Unfortunately, owing to needless space considerations, some of the cuts are edited for length: "Miracles" is snipped from its seven-minute original to the 3:30 radio edit, and a minute is hacked from both "Runaway" and "Hyperdrive." The one unreleased track included, 1978's "Light the Sky on Fire," is an entirely forgettable Marty Balin vehicle with misplaced horns and a Pete Townsend-esque keyboard riff. *Gold*, as a compilation, doesn't adequately showcase the instrumental talents of lead guitarist Craig Chaquico, drummer John Barbata, fiddler Papa John Creach, or bassists/keyboardists Pete Sears and David Freiberg; nevertheless, it sits nicely as an overview of the group's multifaceted work in the second half of the decade. —*Joseph McCombs*

Modern Times / 1981 / RCA ✦✦✦
Slick comes back for one song, and "Find Your Way Back" becomes a hit. Also included is "Stairway to Cleveland," as gutsy a statement of purpose as any in rock. —*William Ruhlmann*

Winds of Change / 1982 / Grunt ✦✦

Nuclear Furniture / 1984 / RCA ✦✦

At Their Best / 1993 / RCA ✦✦✦✦
At Their Best is a ten-track, budget-priced collection that contains some of the Jefferson Starship's biggest hits—"Miracles," "Ride the Tiger," "Count on Me," "Jane," "Find Your Way Back"—plus five album tracks. As budget-line collections go, *At Their Best* isn't bad, especially since it contains the original versions of five hits, but better collections with better song selections are available for not much more money, which means this disc is unnecessary. —*Stephen Thomas Erlewine*

Windows of Heaven / Feb. 9, 1999 / CMC International ✦✦✦✦✦
Original Jefferson Starship band members Marty Balin, Jack Casady, and Paul Kantner are back with some songs about the millennium, protests, and life in general. Guest vocalist Grace Slick, who sings on one track, makes the album almost a full-scale reunion. New bandmates Prarie Prince (the Tubes) and T Lavitz (Dixie Dregs, Jazz Is Dead) add even more spice to the mix, as the offshoot of one of San Francisco's finest '60s psychedelic bands prepares itself for the 21st century. Vocalist Diana Mangano sounds remarkably similar to her predecessor, and helps to create a very Jefferson Airplane-ish vibe. This may not be the best album from the Starship/Airplane catalog, but it serves as a stunning reminder that much of the '60s psychedelic subculture is still alive and well and standing at the *Windows of Heaven*. —*Michael B. Smith*

Jellyfish
f. 1990, **db.** 1994
Pop Underground, Power Pop
Jellyfish seemingly had all the right ingredients for success—catchy, melodic pop songs squarely in the Beatles/Squeeze mold, plus strong kitsch appeal in its retro sound and wildly colorful, clashing wardrobe; thus far, however, popularity has been elusive. Founding members Andy Sturmer (drums, vocals) and Roger Manning (keyboards) previously played in the pop/rock quartet Beatnik Beatch; after that group called it quits, the Jellyfish lineup was rounded out with guitarist Jason Falkner and bassist Chris Manning, brother of Roger. *Bellybutton*, the group's well-received 1990 debut, produced a minor chart single in "Baby's Coming Back," but nothing made a major impact. The follow-up, *Spilt Milk*, followed the same style, adding more intricate arrangements and harmonies. —*Steve Huey*

Bellybutton / 1990 / Charisma ✦✦✦✦
Including lead singer/guitarist Andy Sturmer, bassist Jason Falkner, and keyboardist Roger Manning, the San Francisco band Jellyfish released their 1990 debut *Bellybutton* to critical raves. Despite the kudos and some play at video outlets, the album failed to make much of a commercial impact. It was truly unfortunate because *Bellybutton*, despite obvious influences, was a breath of fresh pop air. "The Man I Used to Be" kicks off the album as a catchy song about domestic failure wrapped in nautical metaphors. The single "The King Is Half-Undressed" is a slice of effervescent power pop whose melody runs counter to the lyrical theme of loneliness. In fact, behind the bounce and breeze of *Bellybutton*'s engaging songs is a recurring theme of melancholy and longing like "She Still Loves Him," with its stirring vocal harmonies and a blistering guitar solo, and the punchy "All I Want Is Everything." Better yet is the second chance the singer delights in on the joyous "Baby's Coming Back," which is accentuated with handclaps. Delightful. —*Tom Demalon*

• **Spilt Milk** / 1993 / Charisma ✦✦✦✦✦
For their second album, Jellyfish replaced the departed Jason Falkner with Tim Smith on bass. Jon Brion also came aboard with Lyle Workman to add to lead singer Andy Sturmer's guitar work. With Sturmer and keyboard player Roger Manning in place, however, Jellyfish managed to outdo their impressive debut with 1993's *Spilt Milk*. *Spilt Milk* expands on the sound of *Bellybutton* and is much more a studio creation than its prede-

cessor. Dreamy vocal harmonies, circus-like swirling organ passages, and crunchy guitars are layered in a manner that evokes the best of the Beatles and the Beach Boys. "Hush," the lead track, particularly recalls the Beach Boys with its luscious vocal harmonies, as does the pure pop of "The Ghost at Number One." And, as expected from this cast, the infectious, melt-in-your-ear melodies are accompanied with clever lyrics like those on the raucous "Joining a Fan Club" and the masturbation ode "He's My Best Friend." *Spilt Milk* is a flawless pop gem from start right through the unbridled optimism of the closing "Brighter Day." —*Tom Demalon*

Greatest / Jan. 19, 1999 / Charisma ✦✦✦

Jeru the Damaja (Kendrick Jeru Davis)
b. Brooklyn, NY
Producer, Lyricist / Hardcore Rap, East Coast Rap, Hip-Hop
Speaking out against what he saw as a decline in rap during the mid-'90s, Jeru the Damaja came to the fore as a self-proclaimed prophet and the savior of hip-hop, much as KRS-One had done almost ten years before. Jeru first appeared as a guest on Gang Starr's *Daily Operations* album, and his own deal with Payday/FFRR appeared soon after, resulting in 1994's *The Sun Rises in the East*. *Wrath of the Math* followed in 1996. Though he made few friends in the rap world—given his outspoken criticism of such popular figures as the Fugees and Sean "Puffy" Combs—he proved a vital force in the emergence of the new rap consciousness of the late '90s. —*John Bush*

• **The Sun Rises in the East** / Dec. 22, 1994 / Payday ✦✦✦✦
Resting halfway between the sultry swagger of gangsta and the classy tones of jazz-rap, Jeru began his career guesting for Guru on a few tracks. Although Gang Starr are listed as executive producers, *The Sun Rises in the East* has already established The Damaja as a unique voice in hip-hop. His inner-city lyrics on songs "You Can't Stop the Prophet" and "Ain't the Devil Happy," work well with his flowing sing-speak delivery. "Da Bichez" might offend some, even with the line: "I'm not talking about the queens, but the bitches." Nevertheless, *The Sun Rises in the East* is an amazing debut. —*John Bush*

Wrath of the Math / Oct. 1996 / Payday/London ✦✦✦✦
Wrath of the Math proved almost as effective as Jeru the Damaja's debut LP, even though little had changed—DJ Premier once again provides his customary scratchy, minimalist production and Jeru's lyrical themes focus either on hip-hop itself (as on "One Day") or the state of life on the streets ("Revenge of the Prophet"). *Wrath of the Math* just can't sustain the power of Jeru's message, however, since it includes five more tracks than on his debut. "Ya Playin' Yaself," "Not the Average" and "Me or the Papes" (which attempts to atone for the sins of "Da Bichez" from *The Sun Rises in the East*) are great songs, but the album just runs out of steam by the end. —*John Bush*

Heroz4hire / Sep. 7, 1999 / Knowsavage ✦✦✦
Just before the release of his third major-label album, Jeru the Damaja returned from a three-year absence with *Heroz4hire*, an independent albumreleased on his own Knowsavage label, featuring both production and mixing by Jeru himself. His rapping style, as dense and inventive as ever, entails listening to the album at least three or four times to understand the tongue-twisting rhymes. From his last album, Jeru continues his interrogation of women with more than love on their mind on "Bitchez Wit Dikz," and contributes an apocalyptic production to the historical saga "Renagade Slave." Jeru is surprisingly good as a producer, weaving scratchy, repetitious samples around tough, lo-fi beats—similar to DJ Premier's work on the first two Jeru LPs. Though the hooks here aren't quite as catchy as Premier's, the incredibly raw production suits the independent status of *Heroz4hire*. Jeru also shares the mic and the credits on several tracks; female rapper Mizmarvel appears on "Verbal Battle" and "Anotha Victim." The highlights are the hilarious New York exposé "Seinfeld" and the paternity case "Billie Jean (Safe Sex)." —*John Bush*

The Jesus & Mary Chain
f. 1984, Glasgow, **db.** 1998
College Rock, Noise Pop, Post-Punk, Alternative Pop/Rock
Like the Velvet Underground, their most obvious influence, the chart success of the Jesus & Mary Chain was virtually nonexistent, but their artistic impact was incalculable; quite simply, the British group made the world safe for white noise, orchestrating a sound dense in squalling feedback which served as an inspiration to everyone from My Bloody Valentine to Dinosaur Jr. Though the supporting players drifted in and out of focus, the heart of the Mary Chain remained vocalists and guitarists William and Jim Reid, Scottish-born brothers heavily influenced not only by underground legends like the Velvets and the Stooges but also by the sonic grandeur and pop savvy of Phil Spector and Brian Wilson. In the Jesus & Mary Chain, these two polarized aesthetics converged; equal parts bubblegum and formless guitar distortion, their sound both celebrated pop conventions and thoroughly subverted them. In late 1984, the band issued its seminal debut single, "Upside Down," a remarkable blast of livewire feedback anchored by a caveman-like drumbeat; the record made the Mary Chain an overnight sensation in the U.K., as did their nascent live shows, 20-minute sets of confrontational noise (performed with the band's members backs to the audience) which frequently ended in rioting. The follow-up, "You Trip Me Up," further perfected the formula, and led to their 1985 debut LP *Psychocandy*, which gift-wrapped sweet, simple pop songs in ribbons of droning guitar fuzz. After a two-year layoff, the Jesus & Mary Chain returned with *Darklands*, a dramatic shift in approach which stripped away the feedback to expose the skeletal guitar-pop at the music's core. —*Jason Ankeny*

★ **Psychocandy** / Nov. 1985 / Blanco y Negro/Warner Brothers ✦✦✦✦✦
The album that launched a thousand shoegazer bands, the visceral power of *Psy-*

chocandy has diminished not one whit in the years since it made its bow. Still far and away the Mary Chain's defining moment, standout cuts like "Just Like Honey," "The Hardest Walk" and "You Trip Me Up" represent the purest fusion of the Jeckyl-and-Hyde mindset that dominates the group—in subsequent years, they've been a noise band at times, while at others they've been a pop band, but here, they're both, and it's glorious. —*Jason Ankeny*

Darklands / Sep. 1987 / Blanco y Negro/Warner Brothers ✦✦✦✦✦
It's completely emblematic of the Mary Chain's perversity that they followed up the dissonant squalor of *Psychocandy* with the minimal, almost gentle guitar-pop of *Darklands*. Here, the melodies which the previous album's squalls of feedback threatened to rip open are left to their own devices; the results are quite stunning, with songs like "Deep One Perfect Morning," "Cherry Came Too" and the title track revealing unforeseen layers of beauty. —*Jason Ankeny*

Barbed Wire Kisses / Apr. 1988 / Blanco y Negro/Warner Brothers ✦✦✦
Despite the overall inconsistency of *Barbed Wire Kisses*, a collection of singles, B-sides, and other rarities, the record does contain more than enough superior moments to make it an essential purchase for all serious Mary Chain aficionados. Chief among them is "Upside Down," athe group's feedback-mad debut single and the purest distillation of their aesthetic they ever recorded. Other highlights include the menacing "Kill Surf City," a brutal deconstruction of "Surfin' U.S.A." and the sleek single "Sidewalking." —*Jason Ankeny*

Automatic / Oct. 1989 / Blanco y Negro/Warner Brothers ✦✦✦
Too much of *Automatic* is just that—formulaic, uninspired, and essentially rote music recorded with the aid of a drum machine. Splitting the difference between the feedback pyrotechnics of *Psychocandy* and the gentle pop of *Darklands*, the record sports a metallic, glossy guitar sheen which complements the synthetic beats all too well: robotic and processed, much of *Automatic* is simply lifeless. Even at their most lackluster, however, the Reid brothers can still spit out some terrific songs—both the menacing "Blues From a Gun" and "Head On" (later covered by the Pixies) are twisted, infectious gems. —*Jason Ankeny*

Honey's Dead / Mar. 1992 / Blanco y Negro/Def American ✦✦✦✦✦
A vast improvement over the preceding *Automatic*, *Honey's Dead* teams the Mary Chain with engineer/mixer Alan Moulder, who layers the album with a more organic and aggressive guitar sound than the Reid brothers have enjoyed in some time. The opening "Reverence," a live-wire feedback fever-dream stretched across a loping dance rhythm—quickly establishes the tone: *Honey's Dead* brings the noise, but it also emphasizes the group's unerring pop instincts, as further evidenced by such gems as "Far Gone and Out," "Rollercoaster" and "Sugar Ray." —*Jason Ankeny*

Stoned & Dethroned / Aug. 23, 1994 / Blanco y Negro/American ✦✦✦
More subdued than any of their previous records, the Jesus & Mary Chain explore a calmer, almost acoustic-oriented direction for part of *Stoned & Dethroned*. Apart from the hit duet with Mazzy Star's Hope Sandoval, "Sometimes Always," the fuzz-drenched pseudo-psychedelic pop that has become the group's trademark is more effective than any of the band's musical experiments. —*Stephen Thomas Erlewine*

The Jesus & Mary Chain Hate Rock & Roll / Sep. 26, 1995 / Blanco y Negro/American ✦✦
As befits an album bookended by tracks titled "I Love Rock & Roll" and "I Hate Rock & Roll," the Jesus & Mary Chain's Sub Pop label debut *Munki* is schizophrenic and impassioned, a record which both summarizes the band's career to date and cleans the slate for their future. Virtually each of the 17 tracks here echoes a prior moment in the Chain's existence, moving at breakneck pace from the volcanic noise of their earliest material to the bleak grace of *Darklands*, through to the sleek, supercharged pop of *Automatic*—even Mazzy Star's Hope Sandoval makes a cameo, as she did on *Stoned & Dethroned*. In a sense, it's an ideal primer to the Reid brothers' mercurial world, flirting with both brilliance and mediocrity; even after well over a decade, the Jesus & Mary Chain continue to thrill, irritate, and confound—they're a true love/hate obsession. —*Jason Ankeny*

Munki / Jun. 9, 1998 / Sub Pop ✦✦✦

Jesus Jones

f. Aug. 1988, **db.** 1994
Alternative Dance, Club/Dance, Alternative Pop/Rock, Dance-Pop

Jesus Jones' murky mix of samples, pop, dance tracks, and techno resulted in one huge international hit single, "Right Here, Right Now" (taken from their second album, *Doubt*), that pretty much sums up all of the band's virtues—a strong melody and hook, with a flair for making the dance club overtones mesh with the rock guitar. For their flaws, turn to their first album, which suffers from muddy beats, shapeless melodies, and intrusive samples, all of which plagued sections of *Doubt*. But when *Doubt* worked, as it did on "Right Here, Right Now," "International Bright Young Thing," and "Real, Real, Real," it showed that sample-driven dance club music could comfortably fit into pop music.

Based on the platinum success of *Doubt*, Jesus Jones' leader guitarist/vocalist Mike Edwards decided it was his mission to make techno palatable for the pop masses and recorded their follow-up album, 1993's *Perverse*, almost entirely on computer. The result was neither good pop music nor good techno; Jesus Jones' subsequent fall from the top of the U.S. and U.K. charts was as fast as their rise to the top. After a long layoff, they returned in the summer of 1997 with *Already*. Initially, the album was only released in the U.K.; it was released in the U.S. during the spring of 1998. —*Stephen Thomas Erlewine*

Liquidizer / 1989 / SBK ✦✦✦
Many cuts from original demos, including "Info Freako" and "Broken Bones" and lots of studio gizmos and harsh vocalizing. —*Bil Carpenter*

● **Doubt** / 1991 / SBK ✦✦✦✦
Jesus Jones' best album, *Doubt*, benefits greatly from Mike Edwards' improved songwriting, as well as a better idea of how to effectively fuse guitar-rock with samples and dance-club beats that hint at techno. There are slips in both areas—a few songs float past without ever making an impression, and some of the fusions sound rather forced and arbitrary. But those moments are outweighed by the ample portions of the album that do work; the album's title is belied by the giddy optimism of the catchy number two hit, and best song here, "Right Here, Right Now," and other singles like "Real, Real, Real," "International Bright Young Thing," and the B-side "I'm Burning" are nearly as good. Easily the high point of the band's career. —*Steve Huey*

Perverse / 1993 / SBK ✦✦✦✦
Perverse attempts to expand on the success Jesus Jones enjoyed with *Doubt*, not only commercially but artistically as well. The group made some history; this is the first album to be recorded entirely through a computer. Musically, *Perverse* is a synthesis of techno/rave dance music with traditional pop/rock songs and structures; it's an ambitious album that works sporadically. Bandleader Mike Edwards lost sight of most of the pop-song sensibility that made "Right Here, Right Now" an across-the-boards smash. Too often, the hooks are submerged beneath layers of computerized noise and aren't strong enough to pull themselves out. When *Perverse* clicks, Jesus Jones gives the listener an idea of how enjoyable a successful marriage of techno and rock could be. —*Stephen Thomas Erlewine*

Already / Aug. 18, 1997 / Food ✦✦
Jesus Jones were at the top of the world when they released their rock-techno fusion, *Perverse*, in 1993. Their second album, *Doubt*, had been an international success, which was rare for an English band in the early '90s, and they were tipped to be the next big thing. *Perverse*, however, was a massive bomb, sending the group into limbo. Over the next four years, leader Mike Edwards worked with various new lineups of Jesus Jones recording new material, which was all rejected by the label. In 1997, the band finally got *Already* approved and released. All that time didn't result in a flawless, polished production—it resulted in a tired, weary band that couldn't recapture the spark and energy of their early work. Edwards still works the same alternative pop/dance formula, and he occasionally comes up with a good hook, but they never amount to memorable songs, and the performances are too stilted to make *Already* a respectable comeback. —*Stephen Thomas Erlewine*

● **Greatest** / Sep. 28, 1999 / EMI ✦✦✦✦
This 20-track Japanese import contains pretty much everything of note that Jesus Jones recorded during their early '90s heyday, including "Info Freako," "Real, Real, Real," "International Bright Young Thing" and, of course, "Right Here, Right Now," in addition to an abundance of album tracks and lesser-known singles. Though this is a good collection, it's a little difficult to find (and, when it can be found, it's a little expensive), so it may best to wait for a collection that's more readily available. —*Stephen Thomas Erlewine*

The Jesus Lizard

f. 1987, Chicago, IL, **db.** Jul. 1, 1999
Noise-Rock, Alternative Metal, Indie Rock, Grunge, Alternative Pop/Rock, American Underground

Willfully abrasive and atonal, the Jesus Lizard emerged in the early '90s as a leading noise-rock band in the American independent underground. During the first part of the decade, the band turned out a series of independent records filled with scathing, disemboweling, guitar-driven pseudo-industrial noise, all of which received positive reviews in underground music publications and heavy college radio play. By the mid-'90s, the group's following had grown large enough to convince a major label, Capitol Records, to sign the band. The Jesus Lizard was formed by guitarist Duane Denison and vocalist David Yow and David Sims, two former members of the Austin-based post-hardcore noise group, Scratch Acid. Friend Steve Albini produced the group's debut album, 1990's *Head*. The following year, the group released their second album, *Goat*, which received positive reviews from mainstream music publications such as Spin magazine. By that time, the band had cultivated a large cult following among the American indie-rock underground, based on both the group's records and their notoriously reckless, occasionally violent and vulgar, live performances. In 1992, the band released their third album, *Liar*. Three years later, the group signed to Capitol and released *Shot*. *Blue* followed in 1998. —*Stephen Thomas Erlewine*

Pure / 1989 / Touch & Go ✦✦

Head / 1990 / Touch & Go ✦✦✦
Head, the Jesus Lizard's first full-length album, featured looser rhythms and a greater dynamic range than their debut EP, but that in no way diluted the impact of David Yow's manic vocals or the bracing force of Duane Denison's crushingly loud riffs. —*Stephen Thomas Erlewine*

Goat / 1991 / Touch & Go ✦✦✦✦✦
Building upon the intense, spirited noise-rock of their two previous records, *Goat* is the album where Jesus Lizard's twisted, post-hardcore punk comes into its own. Denison's acerbic guitar provides an appropriate setting for Yow's ranting tales of decadence and degradation. The Jesus Lizard never make a commentary about the urban filth they depict in their music—they're down in the grime because they like it there. —*Stephen Thomas Erlewine*

Liar / May 1992 / Touch & Go ✦✦✦✦✦
Jesus Lizard's third album, *Liar*, is their most focused set of bleak, grinding noise-rock, yet it lacks the wild abandon that made *Goat* so frightening. —*Stephen Thomas Erlewine*

Show / Apr. 1994 / Collision Arts/Giant ✦✦

Down / Oct. 1994 / Touch & Go ✦✦✦
While it was regarded as something of a disappointment when it was first released in 1994, in retrospect, *Down* stands as the last really vital album from the Jesus Lizard. It lacks the same degree of bone-crushing force and sweaty psychosis that made *Goat* and *Liar* instant classics (the band seems to be aiming for a slightly more subtle approach this time out), and most of the songs take a bit longer to sink in. But bassist David Sims and drummer Mac McNeilly were still capable of connecting like Mike Tyson against a speed bag on the heavy tunes, Duane Denison's sheets of chrome-plated guitar are as gloriously fragmented as ever, and there's never been a rock vocalist before or since quite like David Yow. It was also the last Jesus Lizard album to benefit from Steve Albini's spare, dry recording; if ever there was a band that didn't take to a more "hands-on," "user-friendly" production, it was the Jesus Lizard, and between Albini's decision not to work with the group again after they signed to Capitol Records and the departure of drummer McNeilly, this group was never the same in the studio again. *Liar* was the greatest recorded moment for the Jesus Lizard, but *Down* captured one of the most powerful American bands of the 1990s in their last gasp of twisted glory. —*Mark Deming*

Shot / Apr. 1996 / Capitol ✦✦

Blue / Apr. 21, 1998 / Capitol ✦✦✦
The first thing one notices about the Jesus Lizard's *Blue* is that finally you can hear enigmatic singer David Yow's vocals clearly. Without a lyric sheet, one didn't stand a chance of making out the majority of Yow's disturbed vocals on past releases, but thanks to producer Andy Gill (Red Hot Chili Peppers, ex-Gang of Four guitarist), it's no longer a necessity. It also marks the first recording appearance of new drummer Jim Kimball (with longtime guitarist Duane Denison and bassist David Sims rounding out the band), and shows that the band may be one of the most musically underrated rock bands today. Melody is also stressed more than ever (especially when compared to their noise-landslide first albums) on *Blue*, which heightens the band's unpredictability even further. And although the album proves to be a consistent full-length listen, some standout tracks include "I Can Learn," "Until the Rain," and "Post Coital Glow." The surprising "Until It Stopped to Die" shows the band laying down a killer jazz-like groove, with Yow adding his trademark eerie vocals on top of it. The Jesus Lizard's *Blue* proves that they're still one of the most challenging bands on the music scene today. —*Greg Prato*

● **Bang** / Jan. 18, 2000 / Touch & Go ✦✦✦✦

Jethro Tull

f. 1967, Blackpool, England, **db.** 1982
Album Rock, Arena Rock, Prog-Rock/Art Rock, Hard Rock
Jethro Tull was a unique phenomenon in popular music history. Their mix of hard rock, folk melodies, blues licks, surreal, impossibly dense lyrics, and overall profundity defied easy analysis, but that didn't dissuade fans from giving them 11 gold and five platinum albums. At the same time, critics rarely took them seriously, and they were off the cutting edge of popular music since the end of the 1970's. But no record store in the country would want to be without multiple copies of each of their most popular albums (*Benefit, Aqualung, Thick as a Brick, Living in the Past*), or their various "best-of" compilations, and few would knowingly ignore their newest releases. Of their contemporaries, only Yes could claim a similar degree of success, and Yes endured several major shifts in sound and membership in reaching the 1990s, while Tull remained remarkably stable over the same period. As co-founded and led by wildman-flautist-guitarist-singer-songwriter Ian Anderson, the group carved a place all its own in popular music. —*Bruce Eder*

This Was / 1968 / Chrysalis ✦✦✦
Jethro Tull was very much a blues band on their debut album, vaguely reminiscent of the Graham Bond Organization only more cohesive, and with greater commercial sense. The revelations about the group's roots on *This Was*—which was recorded during the summer of 1968—can be astonishing, even 30 years after the fact. Original lead guitarist Mick Abrahams contributed to the songwriting and the singing, and his presence as a serious bluesman is felt throughout, often for the better: "Some Day the Sun Won't Shine for You," an Ian Anderson original that could just as easily be credited to Big Bill Broonzy or Robert Johnson; "Cat's Squirrel," Abrahams' big showcase, where he ventures into Eric Clapton territory; and "It's Breaking Me Up," which also features some pretty hot guitar from Abrahams. Roland Kirk's "Serenade to a Cuckoo" (the first song Anderson learned to play on flute), their jazziest track ever, is one of the best parts of the album. The drum solo on "Dharma for One" now seems like a mistake, but is understandable in the context of the time in which it was done. The one number here that everybody knows, "A Song for Jeffrey," almost pales amid these surroundings, but at the time it was a superb example of commercial psychedelic blues. This would be the last album of its kind by the group, as Abrahams' departure and the lure of more fertile inspiration tugged them toward English folk music. Curiously, the audio mix here is better than that on their second album, with a much stronger, harder group sound overall. —*Bruce Eder*

Stand Up / Sep. 1969 / Chrysalis ✦✦✦
The group's second album, with Anderson (vocals, flute, acoustic guitars, keyboards, balalaika), Martin Barre (electric guitar, flute), Clive Bunker (drums), and Glen Cornick (bass), solidified the group's sound. There is still an element of blues, but except for "A New Day Yesterday," it is far more muted than on their first album, as Mick Abrahams' blues stylings are largely absent from Martin Barre's playing. The influence of folk music also began to manifest itself ("Look Into the Sun"). The instrumental "Bouree," which could've been an early Blood, Sweat & Tears track, became a favorite concert number, although at this point Anderson's flute playing on stage needed a lot of work; by his own admission, he just wasn't that good. Bassist Cornick would last only one more album, but

got his best moments here, on "Bouree." As a story-song with opaque lyrics and jarring tempo changes, "Back to the Family" is the forerunner to *Thick As a Brick*. The only major flaw in this album is the mix, which divides the electric and acoustic instruments and fails to find a solid center. The Mobile Fidelity audiophile CD, in addition to superior sound, recreates the original LP's "pop-up" jacket interior. —*Bruce Eder*

Benefit / Apr. 1970 / Chrysalis ✦✦✦
Benefit was the album on which the Tull sound solidified around folk music, abandoning blues as a major source. Beginning with the opening number, "With You There to Help Me," Anderson adopts his now-familiar slightly mournful folksinger/sage persona—his acoustic guitar carried the melody, joined by Martin Barre's electric instrument for the crescendos. This would be the model for much of the material on *Aqualung* and, especially, *Thick As a Brick*, although the acoustic/electric pairing would be executed more effectively on those albums. Most of the songs here display pleasant, delectably folk-like melodies, with Barre's guitar adding enough wattage to keep the rock listeners interested. "To Cry You a Song," "Son," and "For Michael Collins, Jeffrey and Me" all defined Tull's future sound: Barre's amp cranked up to ten (especially on "Son"), coming in above Anderson's acoustic strumming, a few unexpected changes in tempo, and Anderson spouting lyrics filled with dense, seemingly profound imagery and statements. As on *Stand Up*, the group was still officially a quartet, with future member John Evan appearing as a guest on keyboards. —*Bruce Eder*

● **Aqualung** / Apr. 1971 / Chrysalis ✦✦✦✦✦
Released at a time when a lot of bands were embracing pop-Christianity (*a la Jesus Christ Superstar*), *Aqualung* was a bold statement for a rock group, a pro-God anti-church tract that probably got lots of teenagers wrestling with these ideas for the first time in their lives. This was the album that made Jethro Tull a fixture on FM radio, with riff-heavy songs like "My God," "Hymn 43," "Locomotive Breath," "Cross-Eyed Mary," "Wind Up," and the title track. And from there, they became a major arena act, and a fixture at the top of the record charts for most of the 1970's. Mixing hard rock and folk melodies with Ian Anderson's dour musings on faith and religion (mostly how organized religion had restricted man's relationship with God), the record was extremely profound for a Number 7 chart hit, one of the most cerebral albums ever to reach millions of rock listeners. Indeed, from this point on, Anderson and company were compelled to stretch the lyrical envelope right to the breaking point. As a compact disc, *Aqualung* has gone through numerous editions, mostly owing to problems finding an original master tape when the CD boom began. When the album was issued by Chrysalis through Columbia Records in the mid-1980's, the source tape was an LP production master, and the first release was criticized for thin, tinny sound; Columbia remastered it sometime around 1987 or 1988, in a version with better sound. Chrysalis later switched distribution to Capitol-EMI, and they released a decent sounding CD that is currently available. Chrysalis also issued a 25th anniversary edition in 1996. —*Bruce Eder*

Thick As a Brick / Apr. 1972 / Chrysalis ✦✦✦✦✦
Jethro Tull's first LP-length epic is a masterpiece in the annals of progressive rock, and one of the few works of its kind that still holds up 25 years later. Mixing hard rock and English folk music with classical influences, set to stream-of-consciousness lyrics so dense with the imagery that one might spend weeks pondering their meaning—assuming one feels the need to do so—the group created a dazzling tour-de-force, at once playful, profound, and challenging, without overwhelming the listener. The original LP was the best sounding, best engineered record Tull had ever released, easily capturing the shifting dynamics between the soft all-acoustic passages and the electric rock crescendos surrounding them. The sound on the original Columbia Records CD (not identified as such, but recognizable by a "VK" prefix in its catalog number) was harsh and thin, and left a lot to be desired in terms of richness—the current Chrysalis disc is an improvement as well. —*Bruce Eder*

Living in the Past / Oct. 1972 / Chrysalis ✦✦✦✦✦
Listen to this 20-song collection, put together to capitalize on the explosive growth in the group's audience after *Aqualung*, and it is easy to understand just how fine a group Jethro Tull was in the early '70s. Most of the songs, apart from a few heavily played album tracks ("Song for Jeffrey" etc.) and a pair of live tracks from a 1970 Carnegie Hall show, came off of singles and EPs that, apart from the title song, were scarcely known in America, and it's all so solid that it needs no apology or explanation. Not only was Ian Anderson writing solid songs every time out, but the group's rhythm section was about the best in progressive rock's pop division. Along with any of the group's first five albums, this collection is seminal and essential to any Tull collection, and the only compilation by the group that is a must-own disc. —*Bruce Eder*

A Passion Play / Jul. 1973 / Chrysalis ✦✦✦✦
Jethro Tull's second album-length composition, *A Passion Play* is very different from—and not quite as successful as—*Thick As a Brick*. Ian Anderson utilizes reams of biblical (and biblical-sounding) references, interwoven with modern language, as a sort of rock equivalent to T.S. Eliot's The Wasteland. As with most progressive rock, the words seem important and profound, but their meaning is anyone's guess ("The ice-cream lady wet her drawers, to see you in the Passion Play…"), with Anderson as a dour but engaging singer/sage (who, at least at one point, seems to take on the role of a fallen angel). It helps to be aware of the framing story, about a newly deceased man called to review his life at the portals of heaven, who realizes that life on Earth is preferable to eternity in paradise. But the music puts it over successfully, a dazzling mix of old English folk and classical material, reshaped in electric rock terms. The band is at its peak form, sustaining the tension and anticipation of this album-length piece across 45 minutes, although the music runs out of inspiration about five minutes before it actually ends. The sound on the CD is significantly brighter than the LP, bringing out the full impact of the electric instru-

ments once the piece takes off, but also imparting more presence to the acoustic instruments (such as Anderson's guitar over the line "God of ages/Lord of time" and the sax part that follows). The only serious complaint about the compact disc is that it isn't indexed to separate the two halves of *A Passion Play* from the A.A. Milne-style interlude "The Story of the Hare That Lost His Spectacles," instead being treated as one long track. —*Bruce Eder*

War Child / Oct. 1974 / Chrysalis ◆◆◆

As a return to standard-length songs following two epic-length pieces (*Thick As a Brick* and *A Passion Play*), it was inevitable that the material on *War Child* would lack power. The music was no longer quite able to cover for the obscurity of Tull's lyrics: The title track is reasonably successful, but "Queen and Country" seems repetitive and pointless. "Ladies," by contrast, is one of Tull's folk-based pieces, and one of the prettiest songs on the record, beautifully sung and benefiting from some of Anderson's best flute playing to date. The band is very tight but doesn't get to really show its stuff until "Back-Door Angels," after which the album picks up: "Sealion" is one of Anderson's pseudo-philosophical musings on life, mixing full-out electric playing and restrained orchestral backing, while "Skating Away on the Thin Ice of a New Day" is a beautiful, largely acoustic number that was popular in concert. "Bungle in the Jungle," with a title that went over well, got most of the radio play. —*Bruce Eder*

Minstrel in the Gallery / Sep. 1975 / Chrysalis ◆◆◆◆

Minstrel in the Gallery was Tull's most artistically successful and elaborately produced album since *Thick As a Brick* and harkened back to that album with the inclusion of a 17-minute extended piece ("Baker Street Muse"). Although English folk elements abound, this is really a hard-rock showcase on a par with—and perhaps even more aggressive than—anything on *Aqualung*. The title track is a superb showcase for the group, freely mixing folk melodies, lilting flute passages, and archaic, pre-Elizabethan feel, and the fiercest electric rock in the group's history—parts of it do recall phrases from *A Passion Play*, but all of it is more successful than anything on *War Child*. Martin Barre's attack on the guitar is as ferocious as anything in the band's history, and John Evan's organ matches him amp for amp, while Barriemore Barlow and Jeffrey Hammond-Hammond hold things together in a furious performance. Anderson's flair for drama and melody come to the fore in "Cold Wind to Valhalla," and "Requiem" is the loveliest acoustic number in Tull's repertory, featuring nothing but Anderson's singing and acoustic guitar, Glascock's bass, and a small string orchestra backing them. "Nothing at All" isn't far behind for sheer, unabashed beauty, but "Black Satin Dancer" is a little too cacophonous for its own good. "Baker Street Muse" recalls *Thick As a Brick* and *A Passion Play*, not only in its structure but a few passages; at slightly under 17 minutes, it's a tad more manageable than either of its conceptual predecessors, and it has all of their virtues, freely overlapping hard rock and folk material, classical arrangements (some of the most tasteful string playing on a Tull recording), surprising tempo shifts, and complex stream-of-consciousness lyrics (some of which clearly veer into self-parody) into a compelling whole. —*Bruce Eder*

M.U.: The Best of Jethro Tull / Jan. 1976 / Chrysalis ◆◆◆◆

M.U. falls into the classic example of a compilation that is bound to irritate the dedicated yet will satisfy the needs of less devoted listeners. Since Jethro Tull is a prog-rock band that made cohesive concept albums, there will always be an audience that will believe it is impossible to assemble a coherent anthology, but the fact of the matter is, the group had a lot of songs that were staples on album-rock radio and *M.U.* simply compiles those tracks for listeners that don't want to invest in a series of concept records. Besides, the resulting compilation is an entertaining listen, thanks to such genre classics as "Aqualung," "Thick as a Brick," "Bungle in the Jungle," "Locomotive Breath," "Living in the Past" and "A Passion Play." These are the songs that define Tull for both hardcore and casual fans, and that's the reason why *M.U.* remains a popular and useful compilation, even if it isn't definitive. —*Stephen Thomas Erlewine*

Too Old to Rock & Roll: Too Young to Die! / May 1976 / Chrysalis ◆◆◆

This album was summarily dismissed by reviewers, who universally invoked their handbooks of hackneyed "critic speak." Cop-out terms like "indulgent" and "pretentious" were bandied about, employing the popular critic's method of simply discrediting an album due to its concurrent release with the arrival of punk-rock—as if that were an intellectually sound critique given the virtually unrelated style of Jethro Tull's music. The main knock on this album is the ill-conceived concept involving an aging rock star. That is a valid observation, but what rock concept albums are deserving of literary accolades? Precious few, if any. Lyrical themes notwithstanding, *Too Old to Rock & Roll* is a fine collection of independent rock songs that marked a return to the classic Tull style carved out on *Aqualung* and *Benefit*. Absent here are the muddled epic-length pieces synonymous with *Thick As a Brick* and *A Passion Play*, the pop leanings of *War Child*, and the complexity of *Minstrel in the Gallery*. So despite being the target of disparaging reviews, this album achieved modest chart success and boasted several quality rockers like "Quizz Kid," "Taxi Grab," and "Big Dipper." Martin Barre's unheralded lead guitar style remains a force, rescuing a couple of tracks from the doldrums. David Palmer's orchestral arrangements are, at times, a bit overblown but this album is far from the colossal disaster it's been portrayed as. Jethro Tull's third bassist John Glascock made his debut on this record, and Maddy Prior makes a guest appearance on the title track. —*Dave Sleger*

Songs From the Wood / Feb. 1977 / Chrysalis ◆◆◆◆

Far and away the prettiest record Tull has released at least since *Thick As a Brick* and a special treat for anyone with a fondness for the group's more folk-oriented material. Anderson had moved to the countryside sometime earlier, and it showed in his choice of source material. The band's aggressive rock interplay and Anderson's fascination with early British folk melodies produce a particularly appealing collection of songs—the se-

riousness with which the group took this effort can be discerned by the album's unofficial "full" title on the original LP: "Jethro Tull With Kitchen Prose, Gutter Rhymes, and Divers Songs from the Wood." The group's sound was never more carefully balanced between acoustic folk and hard rock—the result is an album that sounds a great deal like the work of Tull's Chrysalis Records labelmates Steeleye Span (though Nigel Pegrum never attacked his cymbals—or his entire drum kit—with Barriemore Barlow's ferocity). The harmonizing on "Songs From the Wood" fulfills the promise shown in some of the singing on *Thick As a Brick*, and the delicacy of much of the rest, including "Ring Out, Solstice Bells" (where the group plays full out, but with wonderful elegance), "Hunting Girl," and "Velvet Green," set a new standard for the group's sound. "Pibroch (Cap in Hand)," which is dominated by Martin Barre's electric guitar—in a stunning array of overlapping flourishes at full volume—is the only concession to the group's usual hard rock rave-ups, and even it has some lovely singing to counterbalance the bulk of the song. —*Bruce Eder*

Heavy Horses / Apr. 1978 / Chrysalis ◆◆◆◆

Jethro Tull's 11th studio album is one of their prettier records, a veritable celebration of English folk music chock full of gorgeous melodies, briskly played acoustic guitars and mandolins, and Anderson's flute lilting in the background, backed by the group in top form. This record is a fairly close cousin to 1977's *Songs From the Wood*, except that its songs are decidedly more passionate, sung with a rough, robust energy that much of Tull's work since *Thick As a Brick* had been missing, and surpassing even *Aqualung* in its lustiness. "No Lullaby" is the signature heavy riff song, a concert version of which opened *Live—Bursting Out*. Anderson sings it—and everything else here—as though it might be the last lines he ever gets to voice, with tremendous intensity. The band plays hard behind him throughout, with lead guitarist Martin Barre (most notably on "Weathercock") and bassist John Glascock showing up very well throughout. Anderson's production and Robin Black's engineering catch their every nuance without sacrificing the delicacy of his acoustic guitar and mandolin playing. "Acres Wild," "Rover," "One Brown Mouse," "Weathercock," and "Moths" (which makes this listener think of a folk version of Peter Gabriel's "Solsbury Hill"), the latter featuring some of David Palmer's most tasteful orchestral arrangements, are among the loveliest songs in the group's entire repertory. Curved Air's Darryl Way plays violin solo on the title track—a tribute to England's vanishing shire horses, which doesn't really take off until Way's instrument comes in on the break, with a marked tempo change—and on "Acres Wild." —*Bruce Eder*

Bursting Out: Jethro Tull Live / Oct. 1978 / Chrysalis ◆◆◆

Released just as punk was taking hold on the public's imagination in America and making groups like Tull seem like dinosaurs on their way to extinction, *Live—Bursting Out* became a seemingly perpetual denizen of the cutout bins for years afterward. However, it happened to be a good album, a more-than-decent capturing of a live Tull concert from Europe. The sound is remarkably good, given the group's arena-rock status at the time, and the repertoire is a solid representation of the group's history, going all the way back to "A New Day Yesterday" from their second album and up through 1977's *Songs From the Wood*, with stops along the way for "Bouree," "Aqualung," "Locomotive Breath," "Cross-Eyed Mary" and a compact reprise of *Thick As a Brick*. Some of these tracks work better than others—the tendency here is to play loud and hard, and sometimes that just doesn't translate well on record; seeing "Locomotive Breath" probably worked better than hearing it. —*Bruce Eder*

Stormwatch / Sep. 1979 / Chrysalis ◆◆

A / Sep. 1980 / Chrysalis ◆◆◆

Gone are the longtime Anderson images of the vagabond/sage (the group is clad in white jumpsuits on the cover)—also gone are the historical immersion of their music and anything resembling Dickensian, much less Elizabethan sensibilities. And nearly gone was Jethro Tull itself, for *A* started life as an Ian Anderson solo project but ended up as a Jethro Tull release, probably for commercial reasons. The difference is probably too subtle for most people to comprehend anyway. It is more reflective than Tull's usual work, but lacks the sudden, loud hard-rock explosions that punctuate most of the group's albums. The death of bassist John Glascock in late 1979, and the departure of Anderson's longtime friend John Evans after the release of *Stormwatch*, as well as the exit of arranger/keyboard player David Palmer, led to some major lineup shifts; Fairport Convention's Dave Pegg's taking over Glascock's spot and the addition of Eddie Jobson, ex-Roxy Music/King Crimson violinist/keyboardman all seem to have removed some of Anderson's impetus, at least for a time, for keeping the group going in the studio. What finally emerged is the first Tull record not to feature Anderson's acoustic guitar, yet it also has a more balanced sound than any of their prior records. Jobson's arrangements are leaner and more muscular than Palmer's, giving the music a stripped-down sound, a sort of *hard* folk-rock (reminiscent of Steeleye Span's *All Around My Hat*), augmented by synthesizer and electric violin; this somewhat updated Anderson's music and moved him into the art-rock category. Released in the midst of the punk/new wave boom in the United States, it didn't do too much for anyone's career, although it probably maintained Anderson's credibility better than any traditional Tull album would have. —*Bruce Eder*

The Broadsword and the Beast / Apr. 1982 / Chrysalis ◆

Under Wraps / Sep. 1984 / Chrysalis ◆

Crest of a Knave / Sep. 1987 / Chrysalis ◆◆◆

Ian Anderson and company seemed to make a conscious effort to update Jethro Tull's sound on this record. And, to the amazement (and distress) of many, it was voted the Grammy Award for Best Hard Rock/Heavy Metal Performance. Truth is, it isn't a bad album, with an opening track that qualifies as hard rock and pretty much shouts its credentials out in Martin Barre's screaming lead guitar line, present throughout. "Jump

Start" and "Raising Steam" also rock hard, and no one can complain of too much on this record being soft, apart from the acoustic "The Waking Edge," and "Budapest" and "Said She Was a Dancer," Anderson's two aging rock-star's-eye-view accounts of meeting women from around the world. The antiwar song "Mountain Men" is classic Tull-styled electric folk, all screaming electric guitars at a pretty high volume by its end. Overall this is a fairly successful album and arguably their best since 1978, even if it does seem a little insignificant in relation to, say, *Thick As a Brick*. By this time Tull was effectively a core trio of Anderson, Barre, and bassist Dave Pegg, augmented by whatever musicians (drummers Gerry Conway and Doane Perry, and Fairport Convention keyboard player Martin Allcock and violinist Ric Sanders) that they needed to fill out their sound. The result is a very lean-sounding group and a record probably as deserving of a Grammy as any other album of its year—in the cosmic scheme, it sort of made up for Tull's not winning one for *Thick As a Brick* or *Aqualung*, or for Dave Pegg's former band Fairport Convention never winning. *—Bruce Eder*

20 Years of Jethro Tull: Highlights / 1988 / Chrysalis ✦✦✦✦✦
A 21-track distillation of the four-disc Jethro Tull box set *20 Years of Jethro Tull*, this collection has a few rarities, yet its focus is on the songs every casual fan knows—album-rock hits and rarities, all assembled on one hits compilation. The more selective listener—and there are those among the casual listener (such is the character of art rock fans)—may find that this focuses too much on the accessible material, but anybody that learned to love the Tull through AM radio will find this a very good compilation overall, even if it's heavy on macho attitudes. *—Stephen Thomas Erlewine*

20 Years of Jethro Tull / Jul. 1988 / Chrysalis ✦✦✦
This four-disc box set is targeted at fans, containing more than its share of album tracks, rarities, live cuts, and interview segments. Though this is a pretty good academic overview, there aren't any great revelations here, and only hardcore fans need to invest in this multi-disc set. Even the curious fan that wants a bit more than *Aqualung* or hits will find this satisfactory. *—Stephen Thomas Erlewine*

Rock Island / Sep. 1989 / Chrysalis ✦✦

Catfish Rising / Sep. 10, 1991 / Chrysalis ✦✦✦
Jethro Tull's best album of the 1990's, a surging, hard-rocking monster (at least, compared to anything immediately before or since) that doesn't lose sight of good tunes or the folk sources that have served this band well. The lineup this time out is Anderson on acoustic and electric guitars, flute, and electric and acoustic mandolins, Martin Barre on electric guitar, Doane Perry on drums, Dave Pegg on bass, and Andrew Giddings on keyboards. The real difference between this and most of the group's output since the end of the 1970s lies in the songs, all of which are approached with serious energy and enthusiasm—the lyrics are completely forgettable, but for the first time since *War Child*, the band sounds like they're playing as though their lives depended on it. "Sparrow on the Schoolyard Wall" is at least as good a song as "Bungle in the Jungle" or "Skating Away on the Thin Ice of a New Day," and while that ain't exactly "My God," it's still better than most other recent Tull albums have done. "Still Loving You Tonight" and "Sleeping with the Dog" recall the group's blues roots, albeit not quite in bluesy enough fashion. There's still some dross, as there would almost have to be on an hour-long album, but overall this is the group's best album since the end of the 1970s. *—Bruce Eder*

The 25th Anniversary Boxed Set / Apr. 20, 1993 / Chrysalis ✦✦✦
Jethro Tull's four-CD celebration of their quarter of a century in the music business is only worth the time of hardcore Tull fans. Two discs are full-length live performances (both discs contain two of the same songs), one disc is full of alternate versions of their most famous tracks, and a final disc of new remixes of "classic" tracks (which includes the third appearance of "A Song for Jeffrey" on the four CDs). Casual fans are much better served by one of the smaller collections. *—Stephen Thomas Erlewine*

The Best of Jethro Tull: The Anniversary Collection / Jun. 29, 1993 / Chrysalis ✦✦✦✦✦
This double CD, containing about 150 minutes of music, was released around the same time as the 25th anniversary box and outclasses it in virtually every way possible. Instead of dwelling on rarities and live versions of songs, this collection simply assembles most of the best tracks on the group's records up through 1991. Of course, precisely what constitutes the "best" tracks is a matter of debate—the harder rocking numbers get picked in favor of the folkier, more lyrical tracks on most of the group's albums. The earlier songs are also remastered, giving them a sharper sound and, even more important, a better blended sound between the group's electric and acoustic instruments than the complete albums, which were remastered at an earlier date. For the truly dedicated, it is simpler just to buy them all—and certainly *This Was*, *Benefit*, *Aqualung*, *Thick As a Brick*, and *A Passion Play* are priority items, as should be, but for more casual listeners, this is the best overview of the group's work and infinitely superior to any of the prior "best of" or other anthologies of Tull's music. *—Bruce Eder*

Nightcap: The Unreleased Masters 1973-1991 / 1994 / Chrysalis ✦✦✦
This double CD is a true gift to hardcore fans, offering previously unseen glimpses of Jethro Tull when the group was at its absolute peak. Anyone else, however, may find the album rough going, for while the group was never tighter or more productive, the material isn't even second-rate. Essentially, *Nightcap* is Jethro Tull's version of the Beatles' *Anthology* releases. The first disc consists of tracks that the band started to record during 1973—the best parts of this material ended up being rewritten and incorporated into what became *A Passion Play*. These outtakes are pretty at times, but also unformed and distinctly unfinished—Anderson takes a gorgeous classical guitar solo on "First Post," but then the song drifts off, and "Tiger Toon" is an early version of the principal theme from "A Passion Play," not altered too much except in tempo. "Critique Oblique" offers material that made up the louder, later sections of "A Passion Play," with some impressive playing from Martin Barre on lead guitar and John Evan on organ—except that it goes nowhere for nine minutes; "Post Last" is an early version of the "Passion Play" finale. The 1974 outtakes and rare tracks that comprise the second disc are less problematic because they are less fragmentary. "Piece of Cake" is one of the best pieces of straight-ahead rock & roll that the band ever cut, so solid and straightforward that but for the presence of the flute it might not even sound like Jethro Tull. "Crew Nights," "The Curse," and "Hard Rider" aren't far behind, and there are other fine tracks here, more than compensating for the aimless noodling and pointless profundity that rear their heads elsewhere. And "Broadford Bazzar" is about the prettiest folk-style tune Anderson and company ever came up with. [British import.] *—Bruce Eder*

Roots to Branches / Sep. 12, 1995 / Chrysalis ✦✦

The Ultimate Set / Apr. 8, 1997 / Valley ✦✦

● **The Best of Jethro Tull** / Oct. 5, 1999 / Capitol ✦✦✦✦✦
Not only are there an awful lot of Jethro Tull compilations, there is a ton of comprehensive multi-disc collections in their catalog, so it's very easy to confuse the individual albums. For instance, the 1999 double-disc set *The Best of Jethro Tull* is billed as a digitally remastered album, which gives the impression that it is a remastered version of an older set, when it is actually a new collection culled from remastered tapes. Basically, this set is unnecessary for collectors, who will certainly have everything here, and any casual fan that already has a collection—whether it's the original *M.U.* or any of the many box sets—won't need this. But casual fans looking for a comprehensive yet fairly concise anthology should choose this *Best of* since it does have all the hits and key album tracks among its 36 songs, all presented in good remastered sound. It's not worth replacing an existing compilation in your collection, but if you need a Tull set, this is a good choice. *—Stephen Thomas Erlewine*

Very Best of Jethro Tull / Jun. 5, 2001 / Chrysalis ✦✦✦
How does one evaluate a best-of compilation by a legendary band who's released several such collections already? Frankly, most, if not all, of these selections have appeared on Jethro Tull hits collections and, in many cases, multiple times. And after decades of being critical of record companies capitalizing off artists by releasing one greatest-hits album after another, frontman Ian Anderson decided to choose the actual tracks for this album. The ironic thing is, this Tull collection is no different than those that preceded it, except that perhaps maximum disc space was utilized here, as it's comprised of 20 tracks and 78 minutes of music. There's nothing new here for avid Jethro Tull fans, and curious potential fans have at least a dozen other retrospectives to choose from. *—Dave Sleger*

The JetSet

f. 1979, **db.** 1988
Pop Underground, College Rock, Mod Revival
The Jet Set were one of the oddest footnotes in British pop music history. Loosely associated with the mod-revival of the late '70s, they not only recreated the sounds of '60s pop, but also attempted to mirror the careers and myths of their idols with a near-Rutles-esque media blitz, which included a proposed television series, Christmas greeting flexi-singles, comic strips, trading cards, and an array of fake Jet Set-related products. The band was formed in 1979 by teenage friends Paul Bevoir and Melvyn J. Taub. After recording a few demos with Secret Affair's Paul Bultitude, Bevoir and Taub pulled together a makeshift band for promotional photos. When record companies began to show interest, they enlisted keyboardist Angus Nanan and drummer Paul Bonin. Bultitude signed the band to his own label in 1983 and released their debut EP, *The Best of the Jet Set*, which began creating the Jet Set myth and concept. *There Goes the Neighborhood*, their first full-length album, was released in 1985 to a great deal of acclaim in the U.K. After 1986's *Go Bananas*, Bevoir retired from touring to concentrate on his songwriting and studio craft. In 1987, the band sought to create their own *Sgt. Pepper* with the lushly orchestrated and painstakingly produced *Vaudeville Park*, recreating not only the album's sound but also its packaging. True to form, they followed with reactionary back-to-basics recording sessions, in which Bevoir and Taub found they could no longer work together. The band was dissolved, and their final album, *Five*, was pieced together from the sessions. Bevoir formed Smalltown Parade in 1990 and resumed a solo career in 1994. *—Chris Woodstra*

The Best of the Jet Set / 1995 / Tangerine ✦✦✦✦✦
Best of the Jet Set gives a 27-track career overview of the band that wanted more than anything to be the Beatles. While their determination and ambition makes for fascinating story—detailed in the extensive booklet—their music had a naive charm and enough hooks to please any power pop aficionado. *—Chris Woodstra*

The Best of the Jet Set Too! / 1995 / Tangerine ✦✦✦✦✦
A companion disc to the first *Best of*, *Best of Too!* offers another 22 songs. In addition to the album tracks, a handful of rarities are included. Those who were won over by the first collection will undoubtedly need this one as well—the material is just as strong. *—Chris Woodstra*

● **Jetsetmania** / 2000 / Castle ✦✦✦✦✦
If you haven't heard the Jetset, nothing will prepare you for it. They are a group that seem like they didn't ever exist, as if they were created for a television show or movie decades later—sort of like the One-Ders in *That Thing You Do* or Mariah Carey in *Glitter*, when the groups don't play by the rules of history, they just float through it. But the Jetset were very real and they did appear on TV and they did have hits, at least on the U.K. indie charts, and they milked it for all it was worth, creating comics, trading cards, and the appearance of neo-Monkees/Beatles publicity stunts. All of this was to prop up a band, led by Paul Beauvoir, that turned out guitar pop and unabashedly worshipped '60s pop—not just the music, but the kitsch and culture. In short, they were an anachronism in the mid-

'80s, and they sound even more so years later, as the definitive 49-track, double-disc set *Jetsetmania!: The Ultimate Collection* illustrates. That doesn't mean this sounds bad, because it doesn't—it's cheerful, effervescent pop, sometimes catchy, sometimes not, always engaging in its own insulated sense of fun. Ultimately, this is pretty slight stuff, but its circumstances and surrounding story make it interesting. And, truth be told, its insulation, self-conscious reverence, and miniature pop tunes really are eerily prescient of the indie pop underground of the '90s. *—Stephen Thomas Erlewine*

Joan Jett (Joan Larkin)

b. Sep. 22, 1960, Philadelphia, PA

Vocals, Guitar / Album Rock, Arena Rock, Hard Rock

By playing pure and simple rock & roll without making an explicit issue of her gender, Joan Jett became a figurehead for several generations of female rockers. Jett's brand of rock & roll is loud and stripped down, yet with overpowering hooks—a combination of the Stones' tough, sinewy image and beat, AC/DC chords and glam-rock hooks. As the numerous covers she has recorded show, she adheres both to rock tradition and breaks with it—she plays classic three-chord rock & roll, yet she also loves the trashy elements (in particular, Gary Glitter) of it as well, and she plays with a defiant sneer. From her first band, the Runaways, through her hit-making days in the '80s with the Blackhearts right until her unexpected revival in the '90s, she hasn't changed her music, yet she's kept her quality control high, making one classic single ("I Love Rock-&-Roll") along the way. *—Stephen Thomas Erlewine*

Bad Reputation / 1981 / Blackheart ✦✦✦✦

Jett's debut album is an infectious romp through her influences, ranging from classic '50s and '60s rock & roll through glam-rock, three-chord loud'n'fast Ramones punk, and poppier new wave guitar-rock. Half the songs on the original album (not counting bonus tracks on the remastered reissue) are covers, but whether it's Lesley Gore's feminist girl-group anthem "You Don't Own Me" (featuring the Sex Pistols' Steve Jones and Paul Cook) or a roaring version of Gary Glitter's "Do You Wanna Touch Me (Oh Yeah)," Jett makes them all work. The production can be a little weak in spots, but Jett's exuberance and tough-girl attitude overcome most deficiencies. Plus, the title track is a classic. *—Steve Huey*

I Love Rock & Roll / 1981 / Blackheart ✦✦✦✦

I Love Rock & Roll, Joan Jett's first record with the Blackhearts, was a tougher, louder album than *Bad Reputation*, primarily because her new backing band gave her a more coherent sound. That dynamic, hard-rock crunch is what made the title track into an international hit, but it also gives the album dimension—not only can Jett and the Blackhearts tear up heavy glam-rockers, but they also pull off the mock psychedelia of Tommy James & the Shondells' "Crimson and Clover" with aplomb. On the whole, *I Love Rock & Roll* doesn't have as many strong songs as its predecessor, but the band's muscular, gritty sound makes the album just as good as *Bad Reputation*. *—Stephen Thomas Erlewine*

Album / 1983 / Blackheart ✦✦✦✦✦

Album is arguably Joan Jett's strongest non-compilation release, featuring a consistent, freewheelingly wide range of material (which the Blackhearts really tear into) and punchier, more detailed production. Once again, Jett delivers strong, enthusiastic performances, but this time, the quality of the material lends her equal support. The singles "Fake Friends" and "Everyday People" (the Sly and the Family Stone song) scraped the bottom of the Top 40 charts; other highlights include Jett's original "French Song," which details a ménage à trois. *—Steve Huey*

Glorious Results of a Misspent Youth / 1984 / Blackheart ✦✦✦✦

From her days with the all-girl band the Runaways through her work with her own band, Joan Jett has been a pioneer, if not an innovator. She has always paid loving tribute to the riffy rock music that she loves. On album number six, *Glorious Results of a Misspent Youth*, Jett, backed by her Blackhearts, churned out more of the same, but with some of the most satisfying and strongest material of her career. The album is an engaging collection that ranges from a glam-inflected update of the Runaways' classic "Cherry Bomb" to the swagger of the Gary Glitter hit "I Love You Love Me Love." Other songs include Jett's versions of "I Need Someone" and "New Orleans" and standout originals like the rocking "Frustrated," the full-tilt boogie of "Long Time," and a ballad, "Hold Me," that would sound mawkish coming from anyone else. Infectious choruses, crunchy melodies, and Jett's growling vocals make this album an excuse to turn the stereo up just a bit more. *—Tom Demalon*

Good Music / 1986 / Epic ✦✦✦

On *Good Music*, Joan Jett's hot streak showed signs of subsiding, with the production tending to weigh down some of the numbers and an overall weaker selection of material than her then-recent efforts. Still, the album did contain some fine moments, especially in the title track and the anthemic "Black Leather." *—Steve Huey*

Up Your Alley / 1988 / Epic ✦✦

The Hit List / 1990 / Epic ✦✦

Notorious / Aug. 20, 1991 / Epic ✦✦✦

Flashback / 1994 / Blackheart ✦✦✦✦✦

While it includes a healthy share of rarities, nothing on Joan Jett's career overview, *Flashback*, is second-rate. Even though she vascillated between punky hard rock and smoothed-out arena-rock for much of the '80s, the disc accentuates her rebellious nature, making *Flashback* an effective introduction to her career. Besides, it rocks like hell. *—Stephen Thomas Erlewine*

Pure and Simple / Jun. 14, 1994 / Warner Brothers ✦✦✦

A strong record showing that she has lost very little of her power, *Pure and Simple* contained contributions by several of Jett's fans, including members of L7 and Bikini Kill. *—Stephen Thomas Erlewine*

● **Fit to Be Tied: Great Hits by Joan Jett** / Nov. 18, 1997 / Mercury/Blackheart ✦✦✦✦✦

While it isn't a perfect collection, *Fit to Be Tied: Great Hits by Joan Jett & the Blackhearts* is a strong overview of Jett's career, featuring 15 of her biggest hits and best moments. Nearly all of her charting singles—"I Love Rock & Roll," "Crimson and Clover," "Do You Wanna Touch Me (Oh Yeah)," "Fake Friends," "Everyday People," "The Light of Day," "I Hate Myself for Loving You," "Little Liar"—are included, along with the Runaways staple "Cherry Bomb," several storming album cuts (including "Bad Reputation"), her cult cover of the *Mary Tyler Moore* theme "Love Is All Around" and the previously unreleased "World of Denial." Jett certainly made good albums, but the high points were almost always the singles, which is why *Fit to Be Tied* is such a successful, listenable collection. It should have been sequenced in chronological order, but it remains a first-rate summary of the peak of her career, as well as an excellent introduction to her straight-ahead style. *—Stephen Thomas Erlewine*

Fetish / Jun. 8, 1999 / Blackheart ✦✦✦

Freed from the constraints of a major label, Joan Jett & the Blackhearts assembled *Fetish*, a hodge-podge of previously released material, new songs, and live cuts, all about... sex, of course. Without question, there are some really great songs here, including the new tracks "Fetish" and "Baby Blue," but it's hard not to escape the feeling that this is filler, simply a recontextualization of the past passed off as the present. That's not to say that it isn't an enjoyable record, since most of this is rocks very hard (even with unnecessary covers of "Hanky Panky" and "Wooly Bully"), but it's hard to tell who it's for. Longtime fans will have the majority of the music here, while less dedicated listeners will prefer the hits collection, *Fit to Be Tied*. Nevertheless, hardcore fans will want the previously unreleased cuts, since they're all good, and they may find the recontextualizations interesting. *—Stephen Thomas Erlewine*

Jewel

b. May 23, 1974

Guitar, Vocals / Adult Alternative Pop/Rock, Singer/Songwriter

A contemporary folkie renowned for her expressive, crystalline voice, singer/songwriter Jewel was among the most successful of the many new female performers who dominated the pop charts throughout the 1990s. Raised in remote Homer, AK, she began her music career at the age of six, regularly performing alongside her singer/songwriter parents in local Eskimo villages and tourist attractions. While attending Michigan's Interlochen Fine Arts Academy, Jewel began writing her first songs; upon graduating, she moved into her van and began focusing on a career in music. After signing to Atlantic, in early 1995 Jewel issued her debut LP, *Pieces of You*; the record was a slow starter, not even breaking into the *Billboard* pop charts until some 14 months after its release, but eventually the single "Who Will Save Your Soul" became a major hit, and soon the album was a best-seller as well. Two other hits, "You Were Meant for Me" and "Foolish Games," followed. In 1998 Jewel returned with *Night Without Armor*, a collection of her spoken-word poetry; her hotly anticipated second album *Spirit* followed later that year. *—Jason Ankeny*

● **Pieces of You** / Feb. 28, 1995 / East West ✦✦✦✦

Pieces of You is a charming debut that is somewhat undone by its own naiveté. Jewel has a rich voice and an innocent, beguiling charm that makes "Who Will Save Your Soul?," "I'm Sensitive" and "You Were Meant for Me"—songs with slight, simple lyrics and catchy, sweet melodies—quite endearing; they sound like a high school diary brought to life. Songs this simple and sweet need clean, direct arrangements, but *Pieces of You* was largely recorded live, which means it often sounds ragged and rough. "Who Will Save Your Soul?," "You Were Meant for Me" and "Foolish Game" were all re-recorded before they became hit singles, and all three are superior in their single versions, since these live album cuts sound hurried. It's an unfortunate situation, since the slapdash production emphasizes the awkwardness of the lesser songs. Still, *Pieces of You* has enough charm to make it an ingratiating debut, even if the album doesn't quite fulfill Jewel's potential. *—Stephen Thomas Erlewine*

Spirit / Nov. 17, 1998 / Atlantic ✦✦✦✦

Alone among all the female singer/songwriters of the post-alternative '90s, Jewel appealed to sensitive female teenagers and preteen girls. Her pretty melodies, gentle folk-rock, and sweetly naïve lyrics were the sound of awkwardly creative adolescence, which made sense, since she was only a teenager at the time of her debut. That naïveté was the reason why *Pieces of You* was charming, even with its slapdash production. It wasn't until Jewel re-recorded the singles "Who Will Save Your Soul" and "You Were Meant for Me" that the album took off, because it was only then that the songs were given a proper polish. Realizing this, Jewel abandoned any pretenses of being just a girl with her guitar on her eagerly awaited second album, *Spirit*. Released nearly four years after *Pieces of You*, *Spirit* is a markedly different (but recognizable) album from its predecessor, due largely to Patrick Leonard's glossy, radio-ready production. Layered with gentle guitars and unobtrusive keyboards, every track feels as if it could be a hit single on adult alternative pop radio. If the production has changed, the basic sentiment behind the music has not—in essence, *Spirit* is the same record as *Pieces of You*, with the same sweet melodies and naïve poetry. Even if it doesn't have any standouts like "Who Will Save Your Soul," it is, song for song, a more consistent album, even if the lyrics are often startlingly naïve for a woman 24 years of age. But even if *Spirit* is a stronger, more listenable album than its predecessor, much of the awkward charm of *Pieces of You* has been removed—which means that even if she appeals to the same audience as before, some of her initial fans may find that she's now a bit too slick to truly connect. *—Stephen Thomas Erlewine*

Jilted John

New Wave

With its simple melodies and endearing silliness, Jilted John's song of the same name became one of the U.K.'s most popular punk/new wave novelty singles. Written and sung by actor Graham Fellows, "Jilted John" tells the story of an awkward teenager whose girlfriend Julie leaves him for Gordon, a better-looking guy with more money; John spends much of the song in a tantrum flinging insults at the pair ("Gordon is a moron!," etc.). When Manchester indie label Rabid released the song in 1978, demand was so overwhelming that EMI stepped in to handle its distribution. Fellows appeared on several television programs as the Jilted John character, which helped send the single to number four on the U.K. charts. "Jilted John" was followed by an album, *True Love Stories*, which failed to duplicate the success of its predecessor. Fellows returned to his acting career, which included a stint on the British soap *Coronation Street* and a biographical play about John Lennon. *—Steve Huey*

● **True Love Stories** / Nov. 1978 / Rabid ♦♦♦♦

If you know anything about Jilted John—whether you were a British pop kid in the late '70s, or a new wave fetishist—about all that you know is that he had one of the funniest one-off singles of the era, with the eponymous "Jilted John," the story of a boy who was left by his girlfriend for a guy called Gordon. It was a slice of sneering, self-deprecating genius, something that's shocking upon first listen, and remains funny on the 50th spin. Even those that cherished that single assumed that it was a spontaneous, unexpected burst of brilliance, something that Jilted John—otherwise known as Graham Fellows—couldn't have topped, since it was so good as it is. Certainly, the second- and third-generation listeners that became acquainted with the song through its presence on the seminal *DIY* series would think that way, since it wasn't even paired with its first-class flip, "Going Steady," which finds Jilted John in love with, and dating, Sharon. Even if they knew that, they couldn't be prepared for *True Love Stories*, which is one of the great lost albums of new wave. Firmly rooted in Blondie and Elvis Costello, Jilted John's magnum opus is still startlingly original in how it recycles pre-Beatles pop conventions with a punky defiance and a distinctly bent British humor—and, above it all, it tells a story, following Jilted John through his pubescent romantic trials. Throughout it all, the humor is as sharp as the songwriting is melodic, and the concept not only works, it captivates. And if none of the songs are as throat-grabbingly immediate as "Jilted John," there aren't any bombs—it's all catchy, clever (almost too clever, really), and giddily silly. *—Stephen Thomas Erlewine*

Jimmy Eat World

f. 1995

Emo, Post-Grunge, Alternative Pop/Rock

The Mesa, Arizona-based emo band Jimmy Eat World comprised singers/guitarists Jim Adkins and Tom Linton, bassist Rick Burch, and drummer Zach Lind, childhood friends who first collaborated in junior high school as a Metallica cover band. They issued their debut 7" on the Wooden Blue Records label in 1994, soon followed by a self-titled LP; after split singles with the likes of Christie Front Drive, Emery, and Blueprint, Jimmy Eat World signed to major label Capitol for their sophomore album, 1996's *Static Prevails*. A five-track EP issued on the Fueled by Ramen label heralded the subsequent release of their second Capitol effort, 1999's *Clarity*. *—Jason Ankeny*

Static Prevails / 1996 / Capitol ♦♦♦

With their third album *Clarity* being one of the most overlooked masterpieces of 1999, *Static Prevails* is Jimmy Eat World paying their dues in 1996. It could be the slight overproduction (a curse that has always haunted the band), being on a major label for the first time, or them trying to get a feel for pulling fancy studio tricks (i.e., numerous backing vocals, cellos, and Moog additions). Maybe it's all three, but what *Stactic Prevails* essentially lacks is the songwriting maturity that Jimmy Eat World could have perfected; but it's almost as if the studio heads at Capitol wouldn't let them so that there would be more room for radio-friendly pop songs. In the end, nobody won. However, tracks such as "Anderson Mesa," "Call It in the Air," and "Seventeen" don't cross that line of boring alternative rock but remain in that aggressive pop status. Nothing close to classic, but definitely a sign of better things to come. *—Mike DaRonco*

● **Clarity** / Feb. 23, 1999 / Big Wheel Recreation ♦♦♦♦

On the heels of their self-titled EP in late 1998, Jimmy Eat World released their breakthrough album, *Clarity*, in 1999 and took up the mantle of emo poster boys. Deftly produced by Mark Trombino and the band, *Clarity* mixes introspective balladry with power chord punk rock, elements of chamber pop, and subtle doses of electronica to create a remarkably unique album. Using string ensembles, drum loops, chimes, piano, vibraphones, and tight vocal harmonies to create intricately layered songs, *Clarity* alternates between hypnotic and hard rock, often in the same song. The snarl of "Blister" and "Crush" are counterbalanced by the understated beauty of "Table for Glasses" and "On a Sunday." However, most of the tracks mix both ends of the emotional spectrum with dramatic effects. The sweeping "Goodbye Sky Harbor," which clocks in at an epic 16 minutes 11 seconds, starts off as an up-tempo romp, but evolves into an expansive piece of dream pop that includes vocal loops, several layers of delicate electric guitars, bells, and a drum machine. Heartfelt, yearning vocals from Jim Adkins and Tom Linton tie the songs on *Clarity* together and set them apart from other post-grunge rock acts. Neither vocalist is afraid to wear his heart on his sleeve, but both pull it off without sounding wimpy or overly forlorn. They are also versatile enough to belt out the more aggressive tunes. Trombino also deserves praise for helping to brilliantly balance excellent songwriting and traditional rock elements with adventurous production and unique instrumentation. *—Mark Vanderhoff*

Singles / Aug. 8, 2000 / Big Wheel Recreation ♦♦♦♦

To buy some time during the two-year gap between their second and third full-length releases (1999's *Clarity* and 2001's *Bleed American*), Jimmy Eat World kept their fans satisfied by issuing a compilation of early singles from previous releases, titled simply *Singles*. Issued on the independent Big Wheel Recreation label, *Singles* serves as a fine career overview for this Arizona-based emo band, featuring a total of ten tracks, and including such highlights as "Opener," "H Model," and "Christmas Card." Although one of their official albums would be the best place to start discovering Jimmy Eat World (especially the aforementioned *Clarity*), *Singles* definitely serves its purpose. *—Greg Prato*

Bleed American / Jul. 17, 2001 / Grand Royal ♦♦♦♦

The last time Jimmy Eat World checked in with an all-new studio album, it was with their 1999 *tour de force*, *Clarity*. Since then, the band has issued the compilation *Singles* and jumped to a different record company—issuing their third full-length, *Bleed American*, on the Beastie Boys' Grand Royal label in 2001. The band has steadily built up a fanbase due to nonstop touring (Jimmy Eat World was enjoying a successful run on the Warped Tour upon the release of *Bleed American*, which could pay off big time with the release of one of their finest albums yet). Standout tracks include such melodic guitar-led emo rockers as the title track, "Get It Faster," and "Hear You Me," among others. *—Greg Prato*

The Jive Five

f. 1959, Brooklyn, NY

Doo Wop, R&B, Soul

Best known for the number one R&B hit "My True Story," the Jive Five were one of the few vocal groups to survive the transistion from the '50s to the '60s. In the process, they helped move the music itself forward, providing a key link between doo wop and '60s soul.

Formed in Brooklyn, NY, the group originally consisted of Eugene Pitt (lead), Jerome Hanna (tenor), Richard Harris (tenor), Billy Prophet (baritone), and Norman Johnson (bass). The Jive Five's first hit, "My True Story," was their biggest, peaking at number one on the R&B charts and number three on the pop charts in the summer of 1961. None of the band's subsequent singles—including the minor R&B hit, 1962's "These Golden Rings"—were as popular, but the group managed to keep performing and recording. Under the direction of Eugene Pitt and Norman Johnson, the Jive Five refashioned themselves as a soul band in 1964, forming a new lineup with Casey Spencer (tenor), Webster Harris (tenor), and Beatrice Best (baritone). This new incarnation of the band signed to United Artists Records. The group only had one hit on UA, 1965's "I'm a Happy Man."

In 1966, the Jive Five left United Artists and signed with Musicor, where they had the 1968 R&B hit "Sugar (Don't Take Away My Candy)." They changed labels again in 1970, signing with Decca. That same year, they changed their name to the Jyve Fyve, in order to appear more contemporary. The Jyve Fyve had only one minor R&B hit, 1970's "I Want You to Be My Baby."

The group continued to perform and record for a variety of small labels during the '70s, but they never had another hit. Throughout the '70s and '80s, the only constant member was Eugene Pitt. In 1975, Pitt changed the name of the group to Ebony, Ivory, and the Jades, but this new incarnation failed to gain much attention. In 1982, Pitt changed the name of the group back to the Jive Five and the band recorded two albums for the indie label, Ambient Sound. For the rest of the '80s and the '90s, the Jive Five were regulars on the oldies circuit. *—Stephen Thomas Erlewine*

● **The Jive Five** / 1989 / United Artists ♦♦♦♦♦

A superb 20-track collection, it features the Jive Five's finest material, recorded in the early '60s for Lescay/Belton; songs include "Rain," "My True Story," "No Not Again," "What Time Is It?," and "Hurry Back." *—AMG*

Greatest Hits / Apr. 18, 1990 / Collectables ♦♦♦

This contains all the Brooklynites' early hits and just-as-good B-sides, but omits later recordings, so it isn't definitive. Still, it doesn't get much better than "My True Story," "Begging You Please," "Hurry Back," "Never, Never," and "These Golden Rings," all heavyweight, doo wop-influenced ballads. The syncopated "Rain" has the same feel of "What Time Is It?" (also included); Eugene Pitt's masculine tenor hits all the right notes and high points on every tune. They sing of aliens from outer space on "People From Another World," displaying their immense, seemingly innate doo wop skills. A floating tenor is a feature on many tunes, including "No, Not Again." At 1:45, "Hully Gully Callin' Time" may be the briefest R&B hit in history, but it's magical, and filled the dance floors at early-'60s junior high school canteens and skating rinks every time it played. *—Andrew Hamilton*

The Complete United Artists Recordings . . . / Oct. 20, 1992 / Capitol ♦♦♦♦♦

A superior 21-track collection, it highlights the Jive Five's material for United Artists, recorded in the mid-'60s. *—AMG*

J.K. & Co.

f. 1967

Folk-Rock

The history of J.K. & Co. was little known, the details etched in admirably by Sundazed's CD reissue of their only album. The group was led by Jay Kaye, who was only 15 when he assembled J.K. & Co. in early 1968. With assistance from arranger Robert Buckley (also still in his teens), producer Robin Spurgin, and session musicians, he recorded a little-known album, *Suddenly One Summer*, for White Whale in Vancouver (to where he had briefly relocated from Las Vegas). His florid, melodic songwriting betrayed obvious debts to Donovan and George Harrison; his low-key vocals also recall George's late Beatle efforts. The sappier excesses of his lyrics haven't dated well, but his soothing arrangements (with low-key organs and saxes), beguiling melodies, and good-hearted, meditative ambience make him one of the worthier obscurities of the late '60s.

As a band, J.K. & Co. didn't really exist until after the album was completed, and Kaye formed a group to play the material live that included his cousin John Kaye on bass. Although the LP got a little bit of exposure on Californian underground radio stations, it was not well promoted and remains barely known, even by many psych-heads. Their career was not aided by the label's bizarre decision to pull a 36-second-long track, the instrumental introductory piece "Break of Dawn," as the single. While they did play live in California, they broke up around the end of the 1960s, without releasing any more recordings. The rare album was reissued on CD by Sundazed/BeatRocket in 2001. *—Richie Unterberger*

● **Suddenly One Summer** / 1969 / Beat Rocket ◆◆◆◆
This sounds like the solo album that George Harrison might have made before he left the Beatles, as several songs have that solemn, spiritual, forlorn quality Harrison perfected on cuts like "Long, Long, Long." With its languid guitars, organ, and somber mood, "Nobody" is so reminiscent of *All Things Must Pass* tracks like "Let It Roll" that one is surprised to find that this album was done well before the release of *All Things Must Pass* in the early '70s. Although the lyrics are blatantly hippie-ish, the music itself sets a dignified, almost stately mood with its intimacy and tasteful restraint. "Fly" and "Nobody" are genuine lost treasures of low-key late-'60s late psychedelia, and alone make the album worth investigating. But it's inspired and pleasurable the whole way through, down to the super-brief links and intros dotted throughout the record. *—Richie Unterberger*

Joan of Arc

f. Chicago, IL
Emo, Indie Rock, Alternative Pop/Rock
Based on their roots and their hometown, it's not surprising that Chicago's Joan of Arc blends post-rock's atmospherics and punk's volume and dynamics. Singer/guitarist Tim Kinsella, drummer Mike Kinsella, and bassist Sam Zurick came from the emocore band Cap'n Jazz; when that band broke up, the trio wanted to change their musical direction. They did just that when they started playing with keyboardist/guitarist Jeremy Boyle and guitarist Eric Bocek in the summer of 1996, removing the boundaries and structures of punk and including more experimental elements like tape loops and electronics.

Calling themselves Joan of Arc, the group went on tour with their friends, the Promise Ring (who also featured ex-Cap'n Jazz members), in August 1996. Joan of Arc's live set met with a strong, positive audience, just in time for their first 7", *Method & Sentiment*. After spending the fall of that year writing and recording, the band re-emerged in 1997 with *A Portable Model Of*, their full-length debut. The album continued Joan of Arc's evolution into an equally hard-hitting and progressive outfit that appealed to emo and post-rock fans alike. The following year they returned with *How Memory Works*, a more clearly stated version of their ambitious style. Joan of Arc rang in 1999 with the release of *Live in Chicago 1999*. *Gap* was released a year later. *—Heather Phares*

A Portable Model of Joan of Arc / Jun. 10, 1997 / Jade Tree ◆◆◆
From the ashes of the legendary Chicago emo band Cap'n Jazz came the Promise Rings boys and this highly experimental and very quirky pop-synth, whiny-soothing indie rock band Joan of Arc. This, their first release, consists mainly of interesting and calm instrumentation, odd sounds and effects, and the sometimes heavenly, sometimes over-the-edge vocals of Tim Kinsella. Most people will either fall in love immediately with this album, or find it hideous. But there is definitely something that stands out about this band—too bad no one can put a finger on just what that something is. *—Blake Butler*

● **How Memory Works** / May 12, 1998 / Jade Tree ◆◆◆
How Memory Works, Joan Of Arc's second album, displays perhaps the most creative use of electronics and composition within a rock framework since Analogue's stunning 1996 opus *AAD*. Like *AAD*, *How Memory Works* is woven together by bits of analog synth noise and short songs that never overstay their welcome. The band makes an emotional impact with varying speed. The faster songs bristle with a romantic, smile-inducing urgency, especially "This Life Cumulative," with its insistent beat, repeated major-key riffs, and quizzical lyrics. Tim Kinsella's vocals in "A Name" ebb and flow with stop-start rhythms, morphing into an awesome twin-guitar duel at song's middle. In the new wave-meets-prog "God Bless America," his brittle intonations crack under the strain of the song's clenched-fist chorus. Gastr Del Sol is a logical comparison for plaintive tracks such as "To've Had Two Of," with its acoustic guitar-and-vocal intro and gradual introduction of a cello and human voices. And while Kinsella's nonsensical lyrics and unpredictable pitch at times detract from the music's effectiveness, his performance on album closer "A Party Able Model Of" may unpredictably find the listener with moist eyes. *—Jonathan Cohen*

Live in Chicago 1999 / May 18, 1999 / Jade Tree ◆◆◆

The Gap / Sep. 19, 2000 / Jade Tree ◆◆

How Can Anything So Little Be Any More / May 15, 2001 / Jade Tree ◆◆◆
Joan of Arc's fifth record in as many years nearly accomplishes the impossible and overshadows the awful pomposity of their last release with even more pretension. The eight tracks included were left over from the extensive sessions that produced last year's expansive but wandering *The Gap*, and are, for the most part, difficult to stomach. It doesn't help that only half of the songs are even classifiable as songs, and the other four tracks are either ambient noise swells or children singing. Children singing in bad voices with weird nonsensical lyrics in fact. On a positive note, this posthumous release from the Chicago experimentalists does include some pretty good songs. Convulsive crooner Tim Kinsella sings about as well as he ever did, throwing away most of his twitchy phrasings for straightforward readings of his heavy-handed, double entendre-laden phrasings. Lyrics like "Jesus was so god…damn pretentious" show him still trying to make a point

of some sort and ruffle feathers, but any honesty or emotion he manages to expose is quickly destroyed by the record's hard-to-follow sequencing and those awful kids singing. The band does sounds great, and this record is much more reminiscent of their earlier and more relaxed acoustic-tinged music. For those who enjoyed the music made by Joan of Arc in their short career, this may be a nice farewell but, for those who were ever even a bit put off by the group, don't bother. *—Peter J. D'Angelo*

Jobriath (Bruce Campbell)

d. Jul. 1983
Glam Rock
Widely acclaimed today as the first ever openly (and genuinely) gay rock star, an iconic status which only seems to harden as time passes, Jobriath can also be described among the saddest casualties in modern musical history. The two albums he cut during 1973-1975 are collectors items today and deservedly so. But for at least two decades after their release, their maker's name was more likely to be evoked as an example of the dangers of hype than anything else, with the actual quality of both his music and his performance deeply buried beneath the avalanche of scorn which knowing critics still pour on his head. However, both Morrissey and the Pet Shop Boys have talked openly of their admiration for Jobriath, Jayne County has described him as America's premier glam-rock idol, and Mark Stewart is an unlikely, but equally loyal fan. So, too, are the generation of young glam-rock fans who were curious enough to look beyond the record company hype (and the music industry hatred) to investigate the intriguingly packaged, deliciously delivered records which bore the singer's name. Neither has been scarred by time, neither has been overtaken by age. In 1973-1975, Jobriath records were regarded as a waste of time. Today, they are simply timeless. *—Dave Thompson*

● **Jobriath** / 1973 / Elektra ◆◆◆◆
Grand, grandiose, obsessive, overbearing, precocious, pretentious—you could spend a lifetime browsing the thesaurus and still never put your finger on everything that makes Jobriath's debut the legend that it is. Of course it's rock, but it's so much more than that. Jobriath's voice falls somewhere between vaudeville over-elucidation and operatic emphasis; his lyrics ooze pierrots, aliens, and movie stars, and his arrangements make Queen sound like an underachieving garage band. A few years later, Meatloaf would take a similar grasp on the vastness of excess and make a million. Jobriath made a millstone, but the parallels are apparent all the same. Heartfelt ballad as medieval battering ram. The stars of the show are spotlit from the start. Eddie Kramer's production ranks among his most unrestrained ever, so that even the piano ballads are draped across the broadest of stages. Add the band to the brew, and you can hear the kitchen sinks flying in. But if *Jobriath* (like *Bat Out of Hell*) is awash in brain-charring overkill, the surfeit is by no means gratuitous—or rather, it is, but only because it needs to be. In any other surroundings, songs like "Movie Queen" and "Inside" would seem slight and trite. Here they are the shade that prefigures the light—the sun-bright blast of "Morning Starship," the *Rocky Horror* boogie of "Rock of Ages," the unfettered majesty of "Take Me I'm Yours." Jobriath's songs are big-screen Cinerama, the slightest motion ten feet tall, the tiniest whisper Sensurround sharp. Grand and grandiose, obsessive and overbearing, precocious, and pretentious—it's *Jobriath*. What else did you expect? *—Dave Thompson*

Creatures of the Street / 1974 / Elektra ◆◆
A rock opera with real operatics. A concept album with whatever concept you care to lay on it. A romantic comedy. Jobriath's second long-player spotlighted many of the same turns that made his debut so special—guitarist Peter Frampton, producer Eddie Kramer, vocalist Peggy Nestor—and reappraised many of the same lyrical icons and theatrical tricks as well. But if *Jobriath* caught our hero at least flirting with a rock & roll foundation, *Creatures of the Street* saw him writing soundtracks for every great movie that needed music to match, then mashing them together for the film that never was. We meet fallen stars and forgotten heroines, icicle icons and tragic auteurs and, if there's a hint of autobiography creeping into the frame, remember that *Creatures* was created on the back of a media denouement of almost unprecedented savagery. Last time out, Jobriath thought he had a chance and made an album that might sell. This time, he pulled down the shades and made the record he wanted. With just two exceptions, no song breaks the three-minute barrier, and most eschew the basics of pop hooks and choruses—it's a difficult, and occasionally choppy, approach that renders the entire album an exercise in incidental music and ensures that the disorientation never lets up. Snatches of it are immortal—the chorale "Dietrich/Fondyke" raises the curtain, the mandolin-folky "Scumbag" slobbers in the wings, the New York Dolls-y "Ooh La La" necks its neighbor in the back row. "Good Times" even looks back at *Jobriath* and pretends that the good times are still around the corner. But they're not, and the overall mood of *Creatures* is crushed and obstinate, saddening and saddened, the end of a dream that was too good to be true, too real to be a nightmare. Indeed, anybody approaching Jobriath for the first time would do well to place this album on a back burner somewhere, and get to grips with his debut first. Even dilettantism must sometimes be digestible. *—Dave Thompson*

Jodeci

f. 1990, Tiny Grove, NC
Club/Dance, Urban, R&B
If Boyz II Men are portrayed as a clean-cut, wholesome R&B vocal group, then Jodeci's wild, sexual, bad-boy image represents the other side of the coin. Made up of two sets of brothers, the group's name is a consolidation of three members' aliases: "JoJo" Hailey, Donald "DeVante Swing" DeGrate, and Cedric "K-Ci" Hailey; the group also includes Dalvin DeGrate. Natives of Charlotte, NC, all four members toured the South as young boys singing gospel music, even recording albums; both families belonged to the Pentecostal church, and the DeGrates' father was a minister. The boys were able to hear each

other's gospel songs played on the radio, and eventually were introduced through girlfriends as teenagers. However, when they did meet, K-Ci was with a girl Dalvin had been dating, and a fight nearly broke out. The Hailey brothers and DeVante started hanging out together, partying and talking about making R&B records together, coming up with the name Jodeci at this time. At age 16, DeVante ran away to Minneapolis to get a job in Prince's organization, but was refused. He returned to Charlotte, where he wrote a song and recorded JoJo singing it. The two planned on going to New York to shop the demo around by themselves, but both K-Ci and Dalvin decided to tag along at the last minute. By the time they got to New York, they had demo recordings of 29 songs, which they brought to the offices of Uptown Entertainment. They were almost rejected, but rapper Heavy D overheard the tape and talked Uptown president Andre Harrell into hearing the group. Harrell was impressed, and just like that, Jodeci signed a recording contract. In 1991, they recorded *Forever My Lady*, which featured the gold single "Come and Talk to Me" and went on to sell over three million copies. *—Steve Huey*

Forever My Lady / May 28, 1991 / Uptown/MCA ♦♦♦
A pair of brother acts combined forces to form Jodeci, a singing group with one foot in the future and the other squarely in the past. Dalvin and Devante Swing DeGrate teamed with Jo-Jo and K-Ci Hailey for a debut album that mixed vintage soul singing with New Jack production and bravado. But it wasn't the hip-hop-flavored songs that earned them popularity; instead, urban contemporary audiences embraced the love tunes "Come and Talk to Me" and the title track, signaling the beginnings of a move away from new jack swing that's become a full-fledged retreat. *—Ron Wynn*

● **Diary of a Mad Band** / 1993 / Uptown/MCA ♦♦♦♦♦
Jodeci juggles new jack swing and vintage soul on their second album, and wind up with a jarring, mismatched release. The disc's love songs, particularly "Cry for You," "What About Us" and "My Heart Belongs To You," are tender, passionately sung, sincere expressions of romance and love. But they diminish these with a string of innuendo-laden come-on numbers, complete with explicit language, tired raps and samples, and the kind of sentiments and appeals better suited to a *Penthouse Forum* entry than an album. *—Ron Wynn*

The Show, the After Party, the Hotel / Jul. 18, 1995 / Uptown/MCA ♦♦♦
Although their songs imply otherwise, the Hailey brothers had extensive careers in gospel before turning to secular music. The wails, shouts, and yells that accompany most of their hits reaffirm that tradition, and it's clearly audible often on their latest Uptown entry. Again they employ a running storyline/theme through the disc, this time incorporating audio vignettes about life on- and off-stage during a concert that are interspersed through the disc and help pad things out through what is a poorly edited and sequenced CD. Unlike many other urban and R&B groups, Jodeci doesn't really produce its material with singles in mind; there's not really one song here that works as a separate entity, even though several stations are playing edited cuts. Ironically, their refusal to emphasize radio hits, which in most cases would be deemed a sage creative ploy, frequently works against Jodeci. They let ballads drone on, uptempo tunes end awkwardly, and extend sections until they lose their impact. However Jodeci's earnestness and enthusiasm often helps them overcome cliched lyrics and melodramatic vocals, and there are enough good moments sprinkled throughout this disc to make it worthwhile for most urban contemporary listeners. *—Ron Wynn*

● **Greatest Hits** / Nov. 16, 1999 / MCA ♦♦♦♦
Although a *Greatest Hits* record from Jodeci would have been a wise, smart move, this planned album was never released. *—Stephen Thomas Erlewine*

Billy Joel

b. May 9, 1949, Hicksville, Long Island, NY
Vocals, Keyboards, Piano, Harmonica, Synthesizer, Organ / Album Rock, Pop/Rock, Soft Rock, Singer/Songwriter

Although Billy Joel never was a critic's favorite, the pianist emerged as one of the most popular singer/songwriters of the latter half of the '70s. Joel's music consistently demonstrates an affection for Beatlesque hooks and a flair for Tin Pan Alley and Broadway melodies. His fusion of two distinct eras made him a superstar in the late'70s and '80s, as he racked an impressive string of multi-platinum albums and hit singles.

As a teenager, Joel worked his way into the music industry by playing piano on several recordings produced by George "Shadow" Morton. He joined the Hassles in 1967, and the soul-inflected rock & roll band recorded two albums for United Artists that went nowhere. After the Hassles disbanded, Joel and the group's drummer formed the short-lived heavy metal organ-drum duo, Atilla. Joel struck out on a solo career in 1971, fashioning himself as a sensitive singer/songwriter with his debut album *Cold Spring Harbor.* The record went nowhere, so Joel hightailed it out to California, playing piano bars. The experience led to "Piano Man," the song that gave him his first hit in 1973. Two albums followed, neither of which were particularly successful, then Joel hooked up with producer Phil Ramone for his fifth album, *The Stranger.* Sleek, well-crafted, and unabashedly melodic, the record became a blockbuster, establishing Joel as a star. Throughout the late '70s and early '80s, Billy Joel was among the most popular rock & rollers, turning out a series of albums that sold millions of copies, spun off Top ten singles and won Grammys. His pace slowed in the second half of the '80s, as he retreated into the superstar pace of the '80s, releasing only two studio albums between 1985 and 1990 (both were huge successes). This was only the start of a slow-down—during the '90s, he released only one album, not counting compilations and live affairs. Despite the lack of new material, he remained a star, selling out stadiums on his concert tours.

Cold Spring Harbor / 1971 / Columbia ♦♦♦
A few short months after abandoning the heavy organ-and-drums duo Attila—partially because their sole record flopped, partially because he stole the drummer's wife—Billy Joel reinvented himself as a sensitive singer/songwriter. He had shown signs of McCartney-esque songcraft on *Hour of the Wolf,* the last Hassles album, but his debut album *Cold Spring Harbor* is where these talents blossomed. The record was uneven but very charming, boasting two of his finest songs—the lovely "She's Got a Way" and the bitterly cynical "Everybody Loves You Now"—and a score of flawed but nicely crafted songs that illustrated Joel's gift for melody, as well as his pretensions (the mock-gospel in "Tomorrow Is Today," a classical stab entitled "Nocturne"). In its own way, *Cold Spring Harbor* was a minor gem of the sensitive singer/songwriter era; Joel may have been in his formative stages as a craftsman, but his talents are apparent, and he never made an album as intimate and vulnerable ever again. Ironically, it didn't sound right upon its original release. Through a bizarre mastering error, the tapes were sped up—legend has it that upon hearing the completed album, he ripped it off the turntable, ran out of the house and threw it down the street. It wasn't until 1983 that Columbia released a corrected reissue. The speed wasn't the only thing changed—some songs were edited drastically ("You Can Make Me Free," one of the standouts, was chopped by nearly five minutes) and instruments and backing vocals were stripped away from numerous tracks. It may be a bastardization of the original release, but it's an acceptable one, since these changes only accentuate the intimacy and vulnerability of the recording. *—Stephen Thomas Erlewine*

Piano Man / Nov. 1973 / Columbia ♦♦♦♦
Embittered by legal disputes with his label and an endless tour to support a debut that was dead in the water, Billy Joel hunkered down in his adopted hometown of Los Angeles, spending six months as a lounge singer at a club. He didn't abandon his dreams—he continued to write songs, including "Piano Man," a fictionalized account of his weeks as a lounge singer. Through a combination of touring and constant hustling, he landed a contract with Columbia and recorded his second album in 1973. Clearly inspired by Elton John's *Tumbleweed Connection,* not only musically but lyrically, as well as James Taylor, Joel expands the vision and sound of *Cold Spring Harbor,* abandoning introspective numbers (apart from "You're My Home," a love letter to his wife) for character sketches and epics. Even the title track, a breakthrough hit based on his weeks as a saloon singer, focuses on the colorful patrons, not the singer. If his narratives are occasionally awkward or incomplete, he compensates with music that gives the songs a sweeping sense of purpose—they *feel* complete, thanks to his indelible melodies and savvy stylistic re-purposing. He may have borrowed his basic blueprint from *Tumbleweed Connection,* particularly with its Western imagery and bluesy gospel flourishes, but he makes it his own, largely due to his melodic flair, which is in greater evidence than on *Cold Spring Harbor. Piano Man* is where he suggests his potential as a musical craftsman. He may have weaknesses as a lyricist—such mishaps as the "instant pleasuredome" line in "You're My Home" illustrate that he doesn't have an ear for words—but *Piano Man* makes it clear that his skills as a melodicist can dazzle. *—Stephen Thomas Erlewine*

Streetlife Serenade / Oct. 1974 / Columbia ♦♦♦
Billy Joel hit a bit of a slump with *Streetlife Serenade,* his third album. Stylistically, it was a reiteration of its predecessor's *Tumbleweed Connection* obsessions, spiked with, of all things, *Rockford Files* synthesizers and ragtimes pulled from *The Sting.* That isn't a facetious reference, either—it's no coincidence that the record's single and best song, "The Entertainer," shares a title with the Scott Joplin rag that provided *The Sting* with a main theme. Joel is attempting a grand Americana lyrical vision, stretching from the Wild West through the Depression to "Los Angelenos" and "The Great Suburban Showdown." It doesn't work, not only because of his shortcomings as a writer, but because he didn't have the time to pull it all together. There are no less than two instrumentals, and even if "Root Beer Rag" (yet another sign of *The Sting*'s influence) is admittedly enjoyable, they're undeniably fillers, as is much of the second side. Since he has skills, he's able to turn out a few winners—"Roberta," a love song in the vein of *Cold Spring Harbor,* the mournful "Streetlife Serenader," and the stomping "Los Angelenos"—but it was the astonishingly bitter "The Entertainer," where he not only disparages his own role, but is filled with venom over "Piano Man" being released in a single edit, that made the subtext clear: he had enough with California, enough with the music industry, enough with being a sensitive singer-songwriter. It was time for Billy to say goodbye to Hollywood and head back home to New York. *—Stephen Thomas Erlewine*

Turnstiles / May 1976 / Columbia ♦♦♦♦♦
There's a reason *Turnstiles* begins with the Spector-esque epic "Say Goodbye to Hollywood." Shortly after *Streetlife Serenade,* Joel ditched California—and, by implication, sensitive Californian soft rock from sensitive singer/songwriters—for his hometown of New York. "Say Goodbye to Hollywood" was a celebration of his move, a repudiation of his past, a fanfare for a new beginning, which is exactly what *Turnstiles* was. He still was a singer/songwriter—indeed, "Summer, Highland Falls" was his best ballad to date, possibly his best ever—but he decided to run with his musical talents, turning the record into a whirlwind tour of pop styles, from Sinatra to Springsteen. There's little question that the cinematic sprawl of *Born to Run* had an effect on *Turnstiles,* since it has a similar wide screen feel, even if it clocks in at only eight songs. The key to the record's success is variety, the way the album whips from the bouncy, McCartney-esque "All You Wanna Do is Dance" to the saloon song "New York State of Mind"; the way the bitterly cynical "Angry Young Man" gives way to the beautiful "I've Loved These Days" and the surrealistic apocalyptic fantasy "Miami 2017 (Seen the Lights Go Out on Broadway)." No matter how much stylistic ground Joel covers, he's kept on track by his backing group. He fought to have his touring band support him on *Turnstiles,* going to the lengths of firing his original producer, and it was clearly the right move, since they lend the album a cohesive feel. It may not have been a hit, but it remains one of his most accomplished and satisfying

records, clearly paving the way to his twin peaks of the late '70s, *The Stranger* and *52nd Street*. —*Stephen Thomas Erlewine*

The Stranger / Sep. 1977 / Columbia ✦✦✦✦✦

Billy Joel teamed with Phil Ramone, a famed engineer who had just scored his first producing hits with Art Garfunkel's *Breakaway* and Paul Simon's *Still Crazy After All These Years* for *The Stranger*, his follow-up to *Turnstiles*. Joel still favored big, sweeping melodies but Ramone convinced him to streamline his arrangements and clean up the production. The results aren't necessarily revelatory, since he covered so much ground on *Turnstiles*, but the commercialism of *The Stranger* is a bit of a surprise. None of his ballads have been as sweet or slick as "Just the Way You Are"; he never had created a rocker as bouncy or infectious as "Only the Good Die Young"; and the glossy production of "She's Always a Woman" disguises its latent misogynist streak. Joel balanced such radio-ready material with a series of New York vignettes, seemingly inspired by Springsteen's working-class fables and clearly intended to be the artistic centerpieces of the album. They do provide *The Stranger* with the feel of a concept album, yet there is no true thematic connection between the pieces, and his lyrics are often vague or mean-spirited. His lyrical shortcomings are overshadowed by his musical strengths. Even if his melodies sound more Broadway than Beatles—the epic suite "Scenes From an Italian Restaurant" feels like a show-stopping closer—there's no denying that the melodies of each song on *The Stranger* are memorable, so much so that they strengthen the weaker portions of the album. Joel rarely wrote a set of songs better than those on *The Stranger*, nor did he often deliver an album as consistently listenable. —*Stephen Thomas Erlewine*

52nd Street / Oct. 1978 / Columbia ✦✦✦✦

Once *The Stranger* became a hit, Joel quickly re-entered the studio with producer Phil Ramone to record the follow-up, *52nd Street*. Instead of breaking from the sound of *The Stranger*, Joel chose to expand it, making it more sophisticated and somewhat jazzy. Often, his moves sounded as if they were responses to Steely Dan—indeed, his phrasing and melody for "Zanzibar" is a direct homage to Donald Fagen circa *The Royal Scam*, and it also boasts a solo from jazz great Freddie Hubbard, *a la* Steely Dan—but since Joel is a working-class populist, not an elitist college boy, he never shies away from big gestures and melodies. Consequently, *52nd Street* unintentionally embellishes the Broadway overtones of its predecessor, not only on a centerpiece like "Stiletto," but when he's rocking out on "Big Shot." That isn't necessarily bad, since Joel's strong suit turns out to be showmanship—he dazzles with his melodic skills and his enthusiastic performances. He also knows how to make a record. Song for song, *52nd Street* might not be as strong as *The Stranger*, but there are no weak songs—indeed, "Honesty," "My Life," "Until the Night" and the three mentioned above are among his best—and they all flow together smoothly, thanks to Ramone's seamless production and Joel's melodic craftsmanship. It's remarkable to think that in a matter of three records, Joel had hit upon a workable, marketable formula—one that not only made him one of the biggest-selling artists of his era, but one of the most enjoyable mainstream hit-makers. *52nd Street* is a testament to that achievement. —*Stephen Thomas Erlewine*

Glass Houses / Mar. 1980 / Columbia ✦✦✦✦✦

The back-to-back success of *The Stranger* and *52nd Street* may have brought Billy Joel fame and fortune, even a certain amount of self-satisfaction, but it didn't bring him critical respect, and it didn't dull his anger. If anything, being classified as a mainstream rocker—a soft-rocker—infuriated him, especially since a generation of punks and new wave kids were getting the praise that eluded him. He didn't take this lying down—he recorded *Glass Houses*. Comparatively a harder-rocking album than either of its predecessors, with a distinctly bitter edge, *Glass Houses* still displays the hallmarks of Billy Joel the pop craftsman and Phil Ramone the world-class hitmaker. Even its hardest songs—the terrifically paranoid "Sometimes a Fantasy," "Sleepin' with the Television On," "Close to the Borderline," the hit "You May Be Right"—have bold, direct melodies and clean arrangements, ideal for radio play. Instead of turning out to be a fiery rebuttal to his detractors, the album is a remarkable catalog of contemporary pop styles, from McCartneyesque whimsy ("Don't Ask Me Why") and arena-rock ("All for Leyna") to soft-rock ["C'etait Toi (You Were the One)"] and stylish new wave pop ("It's Still Rock & Roll to Me," which ironically is closer to new wave pop than rock). That's not a detriment; that's the album's strength. *The Stranger* and *52nd Street* were fine albums in their own right, but it's nice to hear Joel scale back his showman tendencies and deliver a solid pop-rock record. It may not be punk—then again, it may be his concept of punk—but *Glass Houses* is the closest Joel ever got to a pure rock album. —*Stephen Thomas Erlewine*

Songs in the Attic / Sep. 1981 / Columbia ✦✦✦✦

Having scored three multi-platinum hits in a row, Billy Joel took a breather, releasing his first live album, *Songs in the Attic*, as he worked on his ambitious follow-up to *Glass Houses*. Joel wisely decided to use the live album as an opportunity to draw attention to songs from his first four albums. Apart from "Piano Man," none of those songs had been heard by the large audience he had won with *The Stranger*. Furthermore, he now had a seasoned backing band that helped give his music a specific identity—in short, it was an opportunity to reclaim these songs, now that he had a signature sound. And Joel didn't botch the opportunity—*Songs in the Attic* is an excellent album, ranking among his very best work. With the possible exception of the *Turnstiles* material, every song is given a fuller, better arrangement that makes them all spring to life. "Los Angelenos" and "Everybody Loves You Now" hit harder in the live setting, while ballads like "She's Got a Way," "Summer, Highland Falls" and "I've Loved These Days" are richer and warmer in these versions. A few personal favorites from these albums may be missing, but what is here is impeccable, proving that even if Joel wasn't a celebrity in the early '70s, his best songs of the era rivaled his biggest hits. —*Stephen Thomas Erlewine*

The Nylon Curtain / Sep. 1982 / Columbia ✦✦✦

Billy Joel hit back as hard as he could with *Glass Houses*, his bid to prove that he could rock as hard as any of those new wave punks. He might not have proven himself a punk—for all of his claims of being a hard rocker, his work inevitably is pop because of his fondness for melody—but he proved to himself that he could still rock, even if the critics didn't give him any credit for it. It was now time to mature, to move pop/rock into the middle age and, in the process, earn critical respect. In short, *The Nylon Curtain* is where Billy Joel went serious, consciously crafting a song cycle about baby boomers in the Reagan era. Since this was an album about baby boomers, he chose to base his music almost entirely on the Beatles, the pivotal rock band for his generation. Joel is naturally inclined to write big melodies like McCartney, but he idolizes Lennon, which makes *The Nylon Curtain* a fascinating cross between ear candy and social commentary. His desire to record a grand concept album is admirable, but his ever-present lyrical shortcomings mean that the songs paint a picture without arriving at any insights. He occasionally gets lost in his own ambition, as on the waterlogged second side, but the first half of the song suite—"Allentown," "Laura," "Pressure," "Goodnight Saigon," "She's Right on Time"—are layered, successful, mature pop songs that bring Joel tantalizingly close to his ultimate goal of sophisticated pop/rock for mature audiences. —*Stephen Thomas Erlewine*

An Innocent Man / Aug. 1983 / Columbia ✦✦✦✦

Recording *The Nylon Curtain* exhausted Billy Joel, and even though it had a pair of major hits, it didn't rival its predecessors in terms of sales. Since he labored so hard at the record, he decided it was time for a break—it was time to record an album just for fun. And that's how his homage to pre-Beatles pop, *An Innocent Man*, was conceived: it was designed as a breezy romp through the music of his childhood. Joel's grasp on history isn't remarkably astute—the opener "Easy Money" is a slice of Stax/Volt pop-soul, via the Blues Brothers (quite possibly the inspiration for the album), and the label didn't break the pop charts until well after the British Invasion—but he's in top form as a craftsman throughout the record. Only once does he stumble on his own ambition ("This Night," which appropriates its chorus from Beethoven). For the rest of the record, he's effortlessly spinning out infectious, memorable melodies in a variety of styles, from the Four Seasons sendup "Uptown Girl" and the soulful "Tell Her About It" to a pair of doo wop tributes, "The Longest Time" and "Careless Talk." Joel has rarely sounded so carefree either in performance or writing, possibly due to "Christie Lee" Brinkley, a supermodel who became his new love prior to *An Innocent Man*. He can't stop writing about her throughout the album—only three songs, including the haunted title track, *aren't* about her in some form or fashion. That giddiness is infectious, helping make *An Innocent Man* an innocent delight that unwittingly closes Joel's classic period. —*Stephen Thomas Erlewine*

● Greatest Hits, Vols. 1 & 2 (1973-1985) / 1985 / Columbia ✦✦✦✦✦

Although it's missing a few important (not to mention big) hits, *Greatest Hits, Vols. 1 & 2* is an excellent retrospective of the first half of Billy Joel's career. Beginning with "Piano Man," the first disc runs through a number of early songs before arriving at the hit-making days of the late '70s; some of these songs, including "Captain Jack" and "New York State of Mind," weren't strictly hits, but were popular numbers within his stage show and became radio hits. Once the songs from *The Stranger* arrive halfway through the first disc, there's no stopping the hits (although "Scenes From an Italian Restaurant," an album track from *The Stranger*, manages its way onto the collection). In fact, over the next disc and a half, there's so many hits, it's inevitable that some are left off—to be specific, "Honesty," "Sometimes a Fantasy," "An Innocent Man," "Leave a Tender Moment," and "Keeping the Faith" aren't included. But all the other hits—including "Just the Way You Are," "Only the Good Die Young," "My Life," "You May Be Right," "It's Still Rock & Roll to Me," "Don't Ask Me Why," "Allentown," "Tell Her About It" and "Uptown Girl," among many others—*are* present and accounted for, as are two new songs ["You're Only Human (Second Wind)," "The Night Is Still Young"] that became hits as well. In short, *Greatest Hits, Vols. 1 & 2* does its job perfectly, encapsulating exactly why Billy Joel was one of the most popular singer/songwriters of the late '70s and early '80s. —*Stephen Thomas Erlewine*

The Bridge / Jul. 1986 / Columbia ✦✦✦

Riding high on the blockbuster *An Innocent Man* and with a new jet-setting bride at his side, Billy Joel took full advantage of the high life, as is clear from *The Bridge*, an album that unwittingly celebrates the excesses of the Reagan years. While he hasn't quite settled into middle age, Joel is ready to take advantage of his wealth and status, recruiting a hero (Ray Charles) and a new wave kid (Cyndi Lauper) for duets, turning to Sting for inspiration ("Running on Ice"), fronting a big band ("Big Man on Mulberry Street"), writing a song for a movie ("Modern Woman"), and picking up the guitar ("A Matter of Trust"), just for the hell of it. You could say that it's eclectic, but it's scattershot, because it's just Joel showing off his musical skills. He's done this before, to great effect on *Turnstiles*, but this is all about hubris, and, as such, it sounds exactly like its time. From its processed, distorted guitars to its hollow synthesizers, *The Bridge* sounds dated and it's his most uneven since *Streetlife Serenade*. Even on the hits, he sounds as if he's stretching—"This Is the Time" is labored compared to "Just the Way You Are" (not to mention considerably more vulgar); "A Matter of Trust" never hits upon a solid riff like "Sometimes a Fantasy"; "Modern Woman" is catchy but fluffy; "Baby Grand" is weighed down by Joel's vocal affectations. In context of the album, they're fairly enjoyable, but they hint at the dry spell that was just around the corner. Nevertheless, Joel still has enough panache and is riding on so much exuberance that *The Bridge* remains an entertaining listen, especially if it's viewed as a Reagan-era artifact. It just doesn't compare to what came before. —*Stephen Thomas Erlewine*

Kohuept (Live in Leningrad) / Oct. 1987 / Columbia ✦✦

Storm Front / Oct. 1989 / Columbia ✦✦
When he went for a masterpiece on *The Nylon Curtain*, Billy Joel worked with his band and producer Phil Ramone, crafting a Beatlesque song suite that was perfectly in step with *Turnstiles*. For *Storm Front*, he decided it was time to change things. He fired Ramone. He fired everyone in his band, save longtime drummer Liberty DeVito. He hired Mick Jones, the architect behind Foreigner's big AOR sound, to man the boards. He wrote a set of sober, somber songs, save "That's Not Her Style," a weirdly defensive song about his model wife, Christie Brinkley. He was left with an album that is singularly joyless. Joel makes no bones about his ambitions for *Storm Front*—when you lead with a history lesson as your first single (the monotonous chant "We Didn't Start the Fire"), it's clear that you're not interested in fun. That wouldn't have been a problem if his melodic skills weren't in decline. Joel packed all the strongest numbers into the first half of *Storm Front*, from the rocking "That's Not Her Style" and "I Go to Extremes" to the fisherman's plight "The Downeaster 'Alexa'" and the power ballad "Shameless," which Garth Brooks later made a standard. Compared to the murky second side, which perks up only mildly with "Leningrad" and "And So It Goes," it's upbeat, varied, melodic, and effective, but when it's compared to his catalog—not only such high-water marks as *The Stranger* or *Glass Houses*, but with a record as uneven as *The Bridge*—it pales musically and lyrically. The five singles ("Fire," "Style," "Extremes," "'Alexa'," "Goes") were catchy enough on the radio to propel the album to multi-platinum status, but in retrospect, *Storm Front* sounds like the beginning of the end. *—Stephen Thomas Erlewine*

River of Dreams / Aug. 10, 1993 / Columbia ✦✦
Billy Joel had never had taken as much time to record an album as he did with *River of Dreams*, and its troubled birth is clear upon the first listen. Never before had he recorded an album that sounded so labored, as if it was a struggle for him to write and record the songs. With *River of Dreams*, he's surrounded himself with ace studio musicians and star producer Danny Kortchmar, all of whom have the effect of deadening an already self-consciously serious set of songs. There are no light moments on the album, either lyrically or musically—all the songs are filled with middle-age dread, even the two best moments, the gospel-inflected title track and his song to his daughter, "Lullabye (Goodnight, My Angel)." Those two songs have the strongest melodies, but they're not as natural as his best material. Everywhere he tries too hard—the metaphors of "The Great Wall of China," the bizarre vocal intro to "Shades of Grey," minor-key melodies all over the place. He may be trying different things, but he doesn't sound comfortable with his detours, and by the end of the record, he sounds as exhausted as the listener feels. By that point, the closing track, "Famous Last Words," seems prophetic—*River of Dreams* feels like a sad close to an otherwise strong career, and from all indications he's given in the press, Joel claims it is indeed the last pop album he'll ever make. It's an unworthy way to depart. *—Stephen Thomas Erlewine*

Greatest Hits, Vol. 3 / Aug. 19, 1997 / Columbia ✦✦✦
Perhaps it was inevitable that Billy Joel's *Greatest Hits, Vol. 3* would pale next to its double-disc predecessor. *Greatest Hits, Vols. 1 & 2* covered nine albums (it ignored *Cold Spring Harbor*), a period during which Joel had 26 Top 100 hits. If it had picked up where the first collection left off, *Vol. 3* would have covered three studio albums, which produced 11 hits. That alone would have made a respectable hits collection, and it would have made sense, since *The Bridge* marked the beginning of a new phase of Joel's career. Instead, the 17-song *Vol. 3* begins with a pair of songs from *An Innocent Man* ("Keeping the Faith," "An Innocent Man") that sound entirely different from the material that follows, which finds Joel delving into mechanized, slickly produced adult contemporary pop. The remaining songs don't strictly adhere to his charting hits, substituting such album tracks as "Leningrad," "Shameless" and "Lullabye (Goodnight, My Angel)" for hits like "Modern Woman," "That's Not Her Style" and his non-LP cover of Elvis' "All Shook Up." Even with those missing hits, *Greatest Hits, Vol. 3* does summarize Joel's latter career quite well, culling most of his best songs from the time. However, the album ends on a down note, as it adds three new songs, all covers, that are limply produced and colorlessly played. Bob Dylan's "To Make You Feel My Love"—which Joel decided to perform as if it was a slow, sanitized *Blonde on Blonde* outtake—is the best of the trio, but none of them qualify as Joel classics, and they are an inauspicious way to end this chapter of his career. *—Stephen Thomas Erlewine*

2000 Years: The Millennium Concert / May 2, 2000 / Columbia ✦✦✦

David Johansen

b. Jan. 9, 1950, Staten Island, NY
Vocals, Harmonica / New York Punk, Hard Rock, Rock & Roll
Best known for his tenure fronting the hugely influential New York Dolls, David Johansen was a true chameleon; throughout the course of a career which saw him transform from a lipstick-smeared proto-punk hero into an urbane blue-eyed soul man and finally into a tuxedo-clad lounge lizard, he remained a rock & roll original, an unpredictable iconoclast and a true cultural innovator. The Dolls officially broke up in 1975, and Johansen entered the recording studio in 1977 with his support group, the Staten Island Boys, to cut his self-titled solo debut; while it sold no better than the Dolls' records, it did renew the critics' love affair with the singer and his gritty, soulful voice. With producer Mick Ronson, he returned in 1979 with the Motown-influenced *In Style*, followed in 1981 by the commercial-minded *Here Comes the Night*. While 1982's concert set *Live It Up* won some airplay for its medley of the Animals hits "We Gotta Get Out of This Place," "It's My Life," and "Don't Bring Me Down," Johansen was forced to reässess his career when 1984's dance-flavored *Sweet Revenge* tanked. At the end of 1984 he resurfaced in the pompadoured guise of Buster Poindexter, a supposed ethnomusicologist armed with an expansive knowledge of R&B chestnuts. As Poindexter's popularity grew, he began fronting a large band dubbed the Banshees in Blue and building a devoted following on the New York club circuit. In 1987, he issued an LP, *Buster Poindexter*, which featured the party classic "Hot Hot Hot," an effervescent cover of an obscure 1984 soca hit. In addition to reviving Johansen's career as a musical performer, Buster also renewed his long-dormant acting bug. *—Jason Ankeny*

● **From Pumps to Pompadour: The David Johansen Story** / Oct. 1995 / Rhino ✦✦✦✦✦
Drawing from all three phases of David Johansen's career, *From Pumps to Pompadours: The David Johansen Story* is a comprehensive of the hard rocker's career. Only three songs date from his influential days with The New York Dolls ("Trash," "Personality Crisis," "Babylon"), but that has been the most well-documented period of his career. While his biggest hits—in fact, his only hits—are the five Buster Poindexter tracks at the end of the disc, the middle portion of the album, which selects the highlights from his overlooked solo albums of the late '70s and early '80s, is where most of the best material lies. From the sleazy rush of "Funky but Chic" to the savage Animals medley "We Gotta Get out of This Place" / "Don't Bring Me Down" / "It's My Life," the 11 solo tracks make a case for Johansen being one of the finest hard rockers of his era. *—Stephen Thomas Erlewine*

John's Children

f. 1964, **db.** 1968
British Psychedelia, Psychedelic Pop, Mod, Psychedelic, British Invasion
Because Marc Bolan—soon to become T. Rex—was briefly a member, John's Children are perhaps accorded more reverence by '60s collectors and aficionados than they deserve. Still, they were an interesting, if minor, blip on the British mod and psychedelic scene during their relatively brief existence (1966-1968), although they were perhaps more notable for their flamboyant image and antics than their music. Yardbirds manager Simon Napier-Bell recalled that they were "positively the worst group I'd ever seen" when he chanced upon them in France in 1966, yet he was conned into taking them on as clients. Not proficient enough to be trusted to play on their own records, their first single, "Smashed Blocked"/"Strange Affair," was recorded with sessionmen in late 1966. This disorienting piece of musical mayhem, opening with a crescendo of swirling organs and an otherworldly over-reverbed vocal, was one of the first overtly psychedelic singles. Their improbable saga was launched when the single actually reached the bottom depths of the U.S. Top 100, cracking the Top Ten in some Florida and California markets. The group's U.S. company, White Whale, requested an album, which they shelved when it was received—an LP with the then-unthinkable title of *Orgasm*. Their second single, "Just What You Want, Just What You'll Get"/"But You're Mine," reached the British Top 40. At this point, Marc Bolan joined the group for a time as their principal singer and songwriter; details are hazy, but he recorded at least one single with the group, "Desdemona," as well as several unreleased cuts that have surfaced on reissues. Bolan departed in a squabble with Napier-Bell, and the group released a couple more flop singles before disbanding in 1968. Their half-dozen singles rank among the most collectible British '60s rock artifacts. *—Richie Unterberger*

Legendary Orgasm Album / 1982 / Cherry Red ✦✦✦
The first readily available edition of *Orgasm*. The skimpy, vaguely Who-ish songs are nearly buried under the mountainous overdubs of hysterical teenage screams, making this a true artifact—and nothing more—of an era. The reissue includes excellent liner notes and four bonus tracks—the fine psychedelic single "Smashed Blocked" and its decent follow-up, "Just What You Want—Just What You'll Get," the B-side of which ("But You're Mine") is an unabashed ripoff of The Who's "I Can't Explain." Be warned that the version of "Strange Affair" (the B-side of "Smashed Blocked") included here has, for some inexplicable reason, been presented backwards! *—Richie Unterberger*

Instant Action / 1985 / Hawkeye ✦✦✦
A hard-to-find collection of 18 rare and unreleased tracks by the band. It doesn't include three of the four songs on their first two singles, but it includes their ultra-rare follow-ups, as well as some rawer, unreleased versions of those later singles and some Andy Ellison solo 45s. The material borrows from the poppiest aspects of the Who and sprinkles in some campy British psychedelia; Bolan's songs and vocals are quite T. Rex-like, even at this early stage. They manage to get a bit tougher with "Jagged Time Lapse," with crashing drums and power chords aplenty. Ellison's solo singles are quite interesting, especially the oddball folk-psychedelic "Cornflake Zoo" and the bizarre lounge/soul version of the Beatles' "Help!" (unlisted on the sleeve). Includes voluminous liner notes. *—Richie Unterberger*

● **A Midsummer Night's Scene** / 1987 / Bam Caruso ✦✦✦✦✦
The A- and B-sides of all of their singles, plus the Andy Ellison solo number "It's Been a Long Time." It's missing some interesting material from *Instant Action*, but it's generally the best anthology available, as well as the only readily obtainable one. Comes with another set of fine, exhaustive liner notes—has a minor band ever been as well-documented by loving liner notes as John's Children has? *—Richie Unterberger*

A Midsummer Night's Scene [EP] / 1988 / Bam Caruso ✦✦✦
A four-song 12", with the title cut (a single from the Marc Bolan era that never made it past the test pressing stage) and three previously unreleased tracks: Ellison's nifty solo cuts "Help" and "Casbah Candy," and "Hippy Gumbo" (a Bolan composition with the whole group). One for the collectors. *—Richie Unterberger*

It's Child's Play / 1989 / Zonophone ✦✦✦
Yet more unreleased tracks. This four-song 7" EP is actually fairly worthwhile, capturing a somewhat rawer and more rock-oriented sound than the official singles. Includes the Bolan compositions "Hot Rod Mama" and "Perfumed Garden," as well as a cover of the R&B tune "Daddy Rolling Stone," which The Who had covered in a similar bashing power-chord style on the B-side of their second single. *—Richie Unterberger*

Elton John (Reginald Dwight)

b. Mar. 25, 1947, Pinner, Middlesex, England

Vocals, Keyboards, Piano / Album Rock, Pop/Rock, Soft Rock, Adult Contemporary, Singer/Songwriter, Rock & Roll

In terms of sales and lasting popularity, Elton John was the biggest pop superstar of the early '70s. Initially marketed as a singer/songwriter, John soon revealed he could craft Beatlesque pop and pound out rockers with equal aplomb. He could dip into soul, disco, and country, as well as classic pop balladry and even progressive rock. His versatility, combined with his effortless melodic skills, dynamic charisma, and flamboyant stage shows made him the most popular recording artist of the '70s. Unlike many pop stars, John was able to sustain his popularity, charting a Top 40 single every single year from 1970 to 1996. During that time, he had temporary slumps in creativity and sales, as he fell out of favor with critics, had fights with his lyricist Bernie Taupin, and battled various addictions and public scandals. But through it all, John remained a remarkably popular artist and many of his songs—including "Your Song," "Rocket Man," "Goodbye Yellow Brick Road," and "Don't Let the Sun Go Down on Me"—became contemporary pop standards. *—Stephen Thomas Erlewine*

Empty Sky / 1969 / Rocket/Island ♦♦

Although he had made a number of re-recordings of popular songs for a budget record label in the late '60s, *Empty Sky* was the first true solo album John recorded after leaving Bluesology; it also marked the beginning of his long and fruitful collaboration with lyricist Bernie Taupin. *Empty Sky* is quite indicative of the post-*Sgt. Pepper* era. With its ambitious arrangements and lyrics, it's clear that John and Taupin intended the album to be a major statement. Though it shows some signs of John's R&B roots, most of the album alternates between vaguely psychedelic rock and burgeoning pop songcraft, capped off by a bizarre reprise of brief moments of *all* of the songs on the record. There aren't any forgotten gems on *Empty Sky*, but it does suggest John's potential. (The CD reissue includes the bonus tracks "Lady Samantha," "All Across the Havens," "It's Me That You Need," and "Just Like Strange Rain.") *—Stephen Thomas Erlewine*

Elton John / Aug. 1970 / Rocket/Island ♦♦♦♦♦

Empty Sky was followed by *Elton John*, a more focused and realized record that deservedly became his first hit. John and Taupin's songwriting had become more immediate and successful; in particular, John's music had become sharper and more diverse, rescuing Taupin's frequently nebulous lyrics. "Take Me to the Pilot" might not make much sense lyrically, but John had the good sense to ground its willfully cryptic words with a catchy blues-based melody. Next to the increased sense of songcraft, the most noticeable change on *Elton John* is the addition of Paul Buckmaster's grandiose string arrangements. Buckmaster's orchestrations are never subtle, but they never overwhelm the vocalist, nor do they make the songs schmaltzy. Instead, they fit the ambitions of John and Taupin, as the instant standard "Your Song" illustrates. Even with the strings and choirs that dominate the sound of the album, John manages to rock out on a fair share of the record. Though there are a couple of underdeveloped songs, *Elton John* remains one of his best records. (The CD reissue includes the bonus tracks "Bad Side of the Moon," "Grey Seal," and "Rock & Roll Madonna.") *—Stephen Thomas Erlewine*

☆ **Tumbleweed Connection** / Jan. 1971 / Rocket/Island ♦♦♦♦♦

Instead of repeating the formula that made *Elton John* a success, John and Taupin attempted their most ambitious record to date for the follow-up to their breakthrough. A loose concept album about the American West, *Tumbleweed Connection* emphasized the pretentions that always lay beneath their songcraft. Half of the songs don't follow conventional pop song structures; instead, they flow between verses and vague choruses. These experiments are remarkably successful, primarily because Taupin's lyrics are evocative and John's melodic sense is at its best. As should be expected for a concept album about the Wild West, the music draws from country and blues in equal measures, ranging from the bluesy choruses of "Ballad of a Well-Known Gun" and the modified country of "Country Comfort" to the gospel-inflected "Burn Down the Mission" and the rolling, soulful "Amoreena." Paul Buckmaster manages to write dramatic but appropriate string arrangements that accentuate the cinematic feel of the album. (The CD reissue includes the bonus tracks "Into the Old Man's Shoes" and the original, stringless version of "Madman Across the Water.") *—Stephen Thomas Erlewine*

11-17-70 / Mar. 1971 / Rocket/Island ♦♦♦

The great thing about this early live record is its obscurity—not just that this isn't one of his better-known records, but that the set list is a fanboy's dream, heavy on album tracks, covers, and the kinds of song that make Elton John's early work so individual. It's not just that there are no hits here, but it's that these six (seven, on the CD reissue) songs emphasize the spare, hard-rocking bluesy singer/songwriter that may not have written his own words, but always sang them with conviction and melodies that made them seem like his own. This may be a minor effort in his catalog, but that's part of its pleasure—it's certainly a record from the time before Elton the superstar, as he tears through *Tumbleweed Connection* tracks prior to the record's release, does a phenomenal reworking of "Honky Tonk Women," hauls out B-sides like "Bad Side of the Moon," and gives a fierce, infectious performance. It's not essential for anyone but obsessives, but if you want any indication of what Elton sounded like prior to his big break, this is an excellent, even intoxicating, summary. *—Stephen Thomas Erlewine*

Madman Across the Water / Nov. 1971 / Rocket/Island ♦♦♦♦♦

Trading the cinematic aspirations of *Tumbleweed Connection* for a tentative stab at prog rock, Elton John and Bernie Taupin delivered another excellent collection of songs with *Madman Across the Water*. Like its two predecessors, *Madman Across the Water* is driven by the sweeping string arrangements of Paul Buckmaster, who gives the songs here a richly dark and haunting edge. And these are songs that benefit from grandiose treatments. With most songs clocking in around five minutes, the record feels like a major work, and in many ways it is. While it's not as adventurous as *Tumbleweed Connection*, the overall quality of the record is very high, particularly on character sketches "Levon" and "Razor Face," as well as the melodramatic "Tiny Dancer" and the paranoid title track. *Madman Across the Water* begins to fall apart toward the end, but the record remains an ambitious and rewarding work, and John never attained its darkly introspective atmosphere again. *—Stephen Thomas Erlewine*

☆ **Honky Chateau** / May 1972 / Rocket/Island ♦♦♦♦♦

Considerably lighter than *Madman Across the Water, Honky Chateau* is a rollicking collection of ballads, rockers, blues, country-rock, and soul songs. On paper, it reads like an eclectic mess, but it plays as the most focused and accomplished set of songs Elton John and Bernie Taupin ever wrote. The skittering boogie of "Honky Cat" and the light psychedelic pop of "Rocket Man" helped send *Honky Chateau* to the top of the charts, but what is truly impressive about the album is the depth of its material. From the surprisingly cynical and nasty "I Think I'm Gonna Kill Myself" to the moving ballad "Mona Lisas and Mad Hatters," John is at the top of his form, crafting immaculate pop songs with memorable melodies and powerful hooks. While Taupin's lyrics aren't much more comprehensible than before, John delivers them with skill and passion, making them feel more substantial than they are. But what makes *Honky Chateau* a classic is the songcraft, and the way John ties disparate strands of roots music into distinctive and idiosyncratic pop—it's one of the finest collections of mainstream singer/songwriter pop of the early '70s. *—Stephen Thomas Erlewine*

Don't Shoot Me I'm Only the Piano Player / Jan. 1973 / Rocket/Island ♦♦♦♦

Elton John became a true superstar with 1972's *Honky Chateau*. He followed that album with *Don't Shoot Me I'm Only the Piano Player*, his most direct, pop-oriented album to date. Designed as a pastiche of classic and contemporary pop styles, the album almost sounds like an attempt to demonstrate the diversity of the John/Taupin team. Though the hits are remarkable—"Daniel" is a moving ballad and "Crocodile Rock" is a sly take on '50s rock & roll—the album is slightly uneven. Several of the album tracks, particularly the knowing "I'm Gonna Be a Teenage Idol" and the rocking "Elderberry Wine," are as strong as anything John had recorded but there are too many melodies that simply don't catch hold. Nevertheless, the singles were strong enough to keep the album at the top of the charts and at its best, it is a very enjoyable piece of well-crafted pop/rock. (The CD reissue includes the bonus tracks "Screw You (Young Man's Blues)," "Jack Rabbit," "Whenever You're Ready (We'll Go Steady Again)," and the piano version of "Skyline Pigeon.") *—Stephen Thomas Erlewine*

Goodbye Yellow Brick Road / Oct. 1973 / Rocket/Island ♦♦♦♦♦

Goodbye Yellow Brick Road was where Elton John's personality began to gather more attention than his music, as it topped the American charts for eight straight weeks. In many ways, the double album was a recap of all the styles and sounds that made John a star. *Goodbye Yellow Brick Road* is all over the map, beginning with the prog-rock epic "Funeral for a Friend (Love Lies Bleeding)" and immediately careening into the balladry of "Candle in the Wind." For the rest of the album, John leaps between pop-craft ("Bennie and the Jets"), ballads ("Goodbye Yellow Brick Road"), hard rock ("Saturday Night's Alright for Fighting"), novelties ("Jamaica Jerk-Off"), Taupin's literary pretensions ("The Ballad of Danny Bailey"), and everything in between. Though its diversity is impressive, the album doesn't hold together very well. Even so, its individual moments are spectacular and the glitzy, crowd-pleasing showmanship that fuels the album pretty much defines what made Elton John a superstar in the early '70s. *—Stephen Thomas Erlewine*

Caribou / Jun. 1974 / Rocket/Island ♦♦♦

Glitzy showmanship is what fuels *Caribou*, the least successful collection to be reissued in this batch of albums. Though the shiny surface of the album is alluring, only a few tracks on the record rank among John's best work. "The Bitch Is Back" is one of his best hard-rock cuts and "Don't Let the Sun Go Down on Me" is one of his classic ballads, but the album tracks tend to be ridiculous filler on the order of "Solar Prestige a Gammon" or competent genre exercises like "You're So Static." There are a couple of exceptions—"Pinky" is a fine ballad and "Dixie Lily" is an endearing stab at country—but on the whole, *Caribou* is a disappointment. (The CD reissue includes the bonus tracks "Pinball Wizard," "Sick City," "Cold Highway," and "Step Into Christmas.") *—Stephen Thomas Erlewine*

★ **Greatest Hits** / Nov. 1974 / Polydor ♦♦♦♦♦

Rarely has a greatest hits collection been as effective as Elton John's first compilation of *Greatest Hits*. Released at the end of 1974, after *Goodbye Yellow Brick Road* and *Caribou* had effectively established him as a superstar, *Greatest Hits* is exactly what it says it is—it features every one of his Top ten singles ("Your Song," "Rocket Man," "Honky Cat," "Crocodile Rock," "Daniel," "Goodbye Yellow Brick Road," "Bennie and the Jets," "Don't Let the Sun Go Down on Me"), plus the number 12 "Saturday Night's Alright for Fighting" and radio and concert favorites "Border Song" and "Candle in the Wind." Despite the exclusion of a couple of lesser hits from this era, most notably "Levon" and "Tiny Dancer," *Greatest Hits* is a nearly flawless collection, offering a perfect introduction to Elton John and providing casual fans with almost all the hits they need. *—Stephen Thomas Erlewine*

☆ **Captain Fantastic & the Brown Dirt Cowboy** / May 1975 / Rocket/Island ♦♦♦♦♦

Sitting atop the charts in 1975, Elton John and Bernie Taupin recalled their rise to power in *Captain Fantastic & the Brown Dirt Cowboy*, their first explicitly conceptual effort since *Tumbleweed Connection*. It's no coincidence that it's their best album since then, showcasing each at the peak of their powers, as John crafts supple, elastic, versatile pop and Taupin's inscrutable wordplay is evocative, even moving. What's best about the record is that it works best of a piece—although it entered the charts at number one, this only had one huge hit in "Someone Saved My Life Tonight," which sounds even better here, since it tidily fits into the musical and lyrical themes. And although the musical skill on display here is dazzling, as it bounces between country and hard rock within the same song, this is certainly a grower. The album needs time to reveal its treasures, but once it does, it rivals *Tumbleweed* in terms of sheer consistency and eclipses it in scope, capturing John and Taupin at a pinnacle. They collapsed in hubris and excess not long afterward—*Rock of the Westies*, which followed just months later is as scattered as this is focused—but this remains one a testament to the strengths of their creative partnership. *—Stephen Thomas Erlewine*

Rock of the Westies / Oct. 1975 / Rocket/Island ✦✦
The title signals that this album is short on ballads and long on bouncers; the hit was "Island Girl," but the real key to this album's thinness is that it came a mere five months after its ambitious predecessor, and even for Elton and Bernie, that's a bit too soon to expect much quality. *—William Ruhlmann*

Here & There / May 1976 / Rocket/Island ✦✦✦
One side from a May 1974 London concert, one side from a November 1974 New York concert, released a year and a half later for the 1976 summer buying season when the artist didn't have a new studio recording ready, this second Elton John live album looks suspiciously like product and sounds like it, too. *—William Ruhlmann*

Blue Moves / Oct. 1976 / MCA ✦✦
An unprecedented year in the making, the two-record *Blue Moves* was Elton John's opening farewell, a dreary song cycle full of self-pity and recycled melodies by an artist who had finally run out of gas. The inevitable hit was "Sorry Seems to Be the Hardest Word," although "Tonight," the album's other memorable song, was just as indicative of the low emotional ebb of the John-Taupin team. As the Mamas and the Papas once said in an album title, "Farewell to the first golden era." *—William Ruhlmann*

A Single Man / Oct. 1978 / MCA ✦✦✦
It's not that Elton John was in need of a comeback in 1978, when he released *A Single Man*, because he was still one of pop's biggest stars. But he certainly had hit a creative drought with 1976's *Blue Moves*, a turgid double album that found Elton and his partner Bernie Taupin barely able to write a side's worth of memorable material. John took a couple of years off and reemerged with a new lyricist, name of Gary Osbourne, who was certainly more straightforward than Taupin, but not as inspired. Even if he lacked Bernie's endearing incomprehensibility, Osbourne kick-started John creatively, spurring him to write his strongest collection of songs since *Captain Fantastic*. Also, John left behind Gus Dudgeon, the other partner of his classic period, choosing to collaborate with Clive Franks. Now, this didn't result in a blockbuster of an album; even if it was a hit in both the U.K. and U.S., none of the songs, even hits like "Part-Time Love," are considered part of his basic canon, but this is easily one of his most underrated records, a tight collection of pop songs where the craft effortlessly shines. He does contemporary pop, elegant instrumentals like "Song for Guy," and even apes New Orleans R&B effectively on "Big Dipper." This, of course, is a testament to John's talents, especially because it didn't become a perennial in his catalog—for most artists, a record this skilled and sophisticated would be a highpoint. Here, it's simply Elton doing his job as best he can. [The 1998 reissue—which didn't appear in the U.S. until 2001—contains five bonus tracks, extensive liner notes, and restored artwork.] *—Stephen Thomas Erlewine*

Victim of Love / 1979 / MCA ✦
As he had in 1977 with Thom Bell, Elton John turned to German disco producer Pete Bellotte in 1979, acting only as the singer over Bellotte's tracks. It was a disaster: there were no hits, and *Victim of Love* was John's first new studio album not to go gold. This was the bottom of the decline John had been in artistically and commercially since 1976. *—William Ruhlmann*

21 at 33 / May 1980 / MCA ✦✦✦
An ambitious songwriting effort featuring Tom Robinson's collaboration on "Sartorial Eloquence" and Gary Osborne's on "Little Jeannie," although the best songs are by the returning Bernie Taupin: "Chasing the Crown" and "Two Rooms at the End of the World." *—William Ruhlmann*

The Fox / 1981 / MCA ✦✦
Sounding like it contained outtakes from the superior *21 at 33*, *The Fox* found Elton John still hedging his bets, writing four songs with Bernie Taupin, but still collaborating with Gary Osborne, Tom Robinson, and James Newton Howard. And the album's number 21 single, "Nobody Wins," was a Eurodisco cover. Altogether, a bump on the comeback road and not an auspicious beginning to John's tenure at Geffen Records. The album has since been acquired by MCA. *—William Ruhlmann*

Jump Up! / Apr. 1982 / MCA ✦✦✦
John began finding his greatest successes with ballads in the 1980s, and this album still finds him mixing collaborators, including Tim Rice (with whom he would write the 1994 soundtrack to *The Lion King*), this time to good effect: Gary Osborne contributes "Blue Eyes," while Bernie Taupin effectively eulogizes John Lennon in "Empty Garden." Originally on Geffen, this album has since been acquired by MCA. *—William Ruhlmann*

Too Low for Zero / May 1983 / MCA ✦✦✦✦✦
Elton John began inching back into the mainstream with *Jump Up*, an uneven but strong record highlighted by "Empty Garden." Its success set the stage for *Too Low for Zero*, a full-fledged reunion with his best collaborator, Bernie Taupin, and his classic touring band. Happily, this is a reunion that works like gangbusters, capturing everybody at a near-peak of their form. That means there aren't just hit singles, but there are album tracks, like the opener, "Cold As Christmas (In the Middle of the Year)," that strongly (and favorably) recall *Goodbye Yellow Brick Road*. John hadn't been this engaging in years, not since Gerald Ford was in office. Why does this work so well? Well, the question isn't just consistency, since records like *A Single Man* were strong, but it's because each cut here showcases John at a peak. He's rocking with a vengeance on "I'm Still Standing" and "Kiss the Bride," crafting a gorgeous romantic standard with "I Guess That's Why They Call It the Blues," while knocking songs as immaculately crafted as "Religion"—songs that anchor this album, giving the hits context. While this may not be as rich as his classic early period, it's a terrific record, an exemplary illustration of what a veteran artist could achieve in the early '80s. [The 1998 reissue—which didn't appear in the U.S. until 2001—contains one bonus track, full artwork, extensive liner notes, and remastered sound.] *—Stephen Thomas Erlewine*

Breaking Hearts / Jul. 1984 / MCA ✦✦✦
This album was paced by its number five big ballad hit, "Sad Songs (Say So Much)," one of Elton John's most memorable latter-day tunes. There were also two more Top 40 entries in "Who Wears These Shoes?" and "In Neon," but in retrospect, this is one of John's slighter albums of the '80s. *—William Ruhlmann*

Ice on Fire / Nov. 1985 / MCA ✦✦✦
Sandwiched between 1984's Top 20 hit *Breaking Hearts* and 1986's commercial disaster *Leather Jackets*, 1985's *Ice on Fire* is a forgotten Elton John effort. While it is hardly a masterpiece—it isn't even up to the standard of such '80s efforts as *Too Low for Zero*—it's still an enjoyable record, living proof of the power of professionalism. John was riding high on his comeback of the early '80s and ready to turn out another record. And that's what *Ice on Fire* is—another Elton John album, in the best possible sense. Sure, it does mark the reunion of John and lyricist Bernie Taupin with producer Gus Dudgeon, who helmed John's greatest recordings, but you'd never know it from the sound of the record. *Ice on Fire* is pure 1985, heavy on synthetic drums and keyboards—the kind of record where Davy Johnstone is credited with guitar, but it never sounds as if there's a guitar on the record, or any other "real" instrument, for that matter. That's not really a criticism, since John always made state-of-the-art records, so it should come as little surprise that this sounds like its time; it's sort of fun, in a way, since it instantly brings back its era. The biggest complaint is that much of the record never rises to the level of memorable. The two singles, the cold-war ballad "Nikita" and the George Michael-featured "Wrap Her Up," are the strongest items here, but even those are rather disposable. The rest of the album shares the same sparkling, canned production, and a few songs could have held their own on the Top 40, but much of it is just average Elton. *—Stephen Thomas Erlewine*

Leather Jackets / 1986 / MCA ✦✦

☆ **Greatest Hits, Vol. 2** / Apr. 28, 1986 / Polydor ✦✦✦✦✦
Greatest Hits, Vol. 2 rounds up the handful of singles that weren't included on Elton John's first *Greatest Hits* collection ("Levon," "Tiny Dancer") and adds the highlights from *Caribou*, *Captain Fantastic & the Brown Dirt Cowboy*, and *Rock of the Westies* ["The Bitch is Back," "Someone Saved My Life Tonight," "Island Girl," "Grow Some Funk of Your Own," "I Feel Like a Bullet (In the Gun of Robert Ford)"], plus two non-LP hit singles, ("Lucy in the Sky With Diamonds," "Philadelphia Freedom") and John's version of "Pinball Wizard," taken from the soundtrack to *Tommy*. In short, it's an excellent continuation of the first collection and taken together, they function as an ideal singles retrospective of the most successful singles artist of the early '70s. *—Stephen Thomas Erlewine*

Elton John Live in Australia (With the Melbourne Symphony Orchestra) / Jun. 1987 / MCA ✦✦

Live in Australia / Jun. 1987 / MCA ✦✦✦
Since this 1987 release is the album that brought "Candle in the Wind" to the charts for the first time—the song first released on *Goodbye Yellow Brick Road* and the song that John later reworked as a tribute to Princess Diana—it's easy to think of this as a fairly standard live album, even if it finds John and his band backed by an 88-piece orchestra. After all, that hit became so ubiquitous, and associated with this record, that it seems that it's just a hits record, but that couldn't be further from the truth. Yes, there are some perennials here—"Sorry Seems to Be the Hardest Word," "Tiny Dancer," "Your Song," "Don't Let the Sun Go Down on Me"—but this is a record that's tailored to the fanatic, leaning heavily on his sublime material from the early '70s. And since those records prominently featured Paul Buckmaster's lush string charts, these orchestral-graced versions never feel overly bombastic (although the horns may occupy more space than they should). That doesn't make *Live in Australia* necessary, of course, but it's far more interesting, even vital, than you might think, and far more vital than comparable live albums by his peers. In fact, hardcore fans who prefer *11-17-70* may be surprised how much they enjoy this record. [The 1998 reissue—which didn't appear in the U.S. until 2001—contains no bonus tracks, but has full artwork, extensive liner notes, and remastered sound.] *—Stephen Thomas Erlewine*

Greatest Hits, Vol. 3 (1979-1987) / Sep. 1987 / Geffen ✦✦✦✦✦
Greatest Hits, Vol. 3 (1979-1987) is a 12-track overview that compiles the bulk of Elton John's biggest hits from the '80s, including such classic tracks as "Little Jeannie," "I Guess That's Why They Call It the Blues," "Empty Garden," "Blue Eyes," "I'm Still Standing," and "Sad Songs (Say So Much)." It also includes the previously unreleased "Heartache All Over the World," a new single that failed to make the Top 40, as well as "Too Low for Zero," which never was a single. *Greatest Hits, Vol. 3* went out of print after John left Geffen for MCA, who issued a replacement package, *Greatest Hits 1976-1986*, which eliminates those two songs and adds "Sorry Seems to Be the Hardest Word," "Don't Go Breaking My Heart," and "Who Wears These Shoes?" to the remaining ten songs. *—Stephen Thomas Erlewine*

Reg Strikes Back / Jun. 1988 / MCA ✦✦
As Elton John's first album for MCA Records, *Reg Strikes Back* received a considerable amount of hype upon its release, but the results were considerably less inspired than his

early-'80s records for Geffen. It's always a bad sign when an artist re-records or reinterprets one of his classics, as John does here with "Mona Lisas and Mad Hatters, Pt. 2," but what really sinks *Reg Strikes Back* are the colorless tunes. Apart from the clenched dance-pop of "I Don't Wanna Go on With You Like That" and the simpy "A Word in Spanish," none of the melodies on the record are memorable, and even those aren't particularly strong. Instead of recharging his career, *Reg Strikes Back* began a dry spell that ran for nearly five years. *—Stephen Thomas Erlewine*

The Complete Thom Bell Sessions / 1989 / MCA ♦♦♦
Elton John released a three-song EP from his abortive 1977 sessions with Philadelphia International producer Thom Bell in 1979. Ten years later, he issued a six-song EP containing the initial three tracks and three more that are unremarkable. The things an artist will do for record collectors . . . *—William Ruhlmann*

Sleeping With the Past / Aug. 1989 / MCA ♦♦
The past Elton John has in mind is the era of soul music of the mid-1960s to the mid-1970s, and although all the songs are new, he recreates it well here. The album's most notable selection is the ballad "Sacrifice," which amazingly became his first-ever Number one hit in the U.K. *—William Ruhlmann*

To Be Continued . . . / 1990 / MCA ♦♦♦♦♦
The inevitable Elton John box set is a four-disc, 68-track affair covering 25 years of the biggest pop star since the Beatles. Hit after hit is heard, plus good album tracks and rarities. There's a big booklet with commentary by John and his lyricist, Bernie Taupin. In a pinch, you can get by with the two MCA and one Geffen greatest hits collections, but for a complete overview of Elton John's career, this is the place to come. *—William Ruhlmann*

The One / Jun. 23, 1992 / MCA ♦♦♦
Elton John once claimed that he could remember *The One* among his latter-day albums because it was the first he recorded without drugs or alcohol. If true—and there's no reason to doubt him—that could be the reason why this has more character than most of his albums since the early '80s, holding together well in its deliberately measured, mature songcraft by Elton and Bernie Taupin. There's less gloss than there has been on many of his late '80s records, and John gives a fairly convincing performance throughout this set of pretty good songs. If there's any real problem it's that the album just doesn't have many memorable songs. Though they're all reasonably melodic and well crafted, none of the songs have memorable musical or lyrical hooks and, if anything, Chris Thomas' production is too even-handed. Still, even if it isn't memorable, it does represent a meaningful move forward, just because it does sound warmer and considered than the records that immediately preceded it. [The 2001 reissue contains two bonus tracks, "Suit of Wolves" and "Fat Boys and Ugly Girls."] *—Stephen Thomas Erlewine*

Rare Masters / Oct. 20, 1992 / Polydor/Chronicles ♦♦♦♦
At the time *Rare Masters* was released in 1992, much of the selections on this 37-track double-disc compilation were indeed rare. They were issued on non-LP singles, B-sides, the *Friends* soundtrack, one-offs; some were buried on album tracks and some even stayed in the vault. Since then, Elton John's catalog has been remastered and reissued, with much of the best of this material appearing as bonus tracks, but the album still was worthwhile, since it not only has some songs that never appeared elsewhere on disc (such as "Step Into Christmas"'s B-side, "(Ho Ho Ho) Who'd Be A Turkey at Christmas"), but it also is a hell of a listen in its own right, showcasing great songs and forgotten gems from Elton's prime period. There aren't too many hits here, but the quality is startlingly high and consistent, showcasing John and Taupin's partnership at its peak—though they might not have hit the charts, "Bad Side of the Moon," "Rock & Roll Madonna," "Into the Old Man's Shoes," "Whenever You're Ready (We'll Go Steady Again)," "Screw You (Young Man's Blues)," and the radio staple "Madman Across the Water," plus "Grey Seal" (later re-recorded for *Goodbye Yellow Brick Road*) "are among the finest songs of the era, and they're the linchpins on a *rarities* on an obscurities collection, not a proper album. It doesn't quite keep that same high level throughout, largely due to the pleasant but forgettable instrumentals from *Friends*, but it's still an essential part of any Elton John collection. *—Stephen Thomas Erlewine*

Greatest Hits, 1976-1986 / Nov. 10, 1992 / MCA ♦♦♦♦♦
When Elton John left Geffen for MCA, *Greatest Hits, 1976-1986* replaced *Greatest Hits, Vol. 3 (1979-1987)*. The newer collection is a better collection than its predecessor, since it trims the failed single "Heartache All Over the World," which was added as an incentive for hardcore collectors, and "Too Low for Zero," replacing them with "Sorry Seems to Be the Hardest Word," "Don't Go Breaking My Heart" and "Who Wears These Shoes?." Those three cuts are added to ten songs that illustrate that John could still craft a killer pop single during the '80s. *—Stephen Thomas Erlewine*

Duets / Nov. 23, 1993 / MCA ♦♦
Unlike Frank Sinatra's album, John actually recorded in the studio with his duet partners, adding a spark to his album missing on Sinatra's *Duets*, even if his choices are nearly as bewildering. Some of the material doesn't work in the duet format, and his partners occasionally don't mesh with his current adult contemporary style. All of this makes *Duets* an ultimately disappointing record, even with the occasional successful track, like the kitschy number with drag queen RuPaul. *—Stephen Thomas Erlewine*

Chartbusters Go Pop! 20 Legendary Covers from 1969/70 as Sung by Elton John / 1994 / Cleopatra ♦♦
The title is no joke, but dead-on truth in advertising. Circa 1970, John helped pay the rent and gain studio expertise as a session vocalist for British quickie budget exploitation LPs that "re-created" the sound of current hit singles. John takes on such vintage AM mothballs as "In the Summertime," "Up Around the Bend," "My Baby Loves Lovin'," "Yellow River," and "Signed Sealed Delivered" here, along with a few songs that were only hits in the U.K. These records were never intended to be taken seriously as artistic statements, and one suspects that the studio players were having fun at someone else's expense on "In the Summertime," with farting raspberry noises and ridiculous orgiastic grunts by John during the instrumental break. Most of the time, though, he played it straight, his supple pipes proving to possess the necessary versatile anonymity required of such projects. This reissue, complete with scholarly liner notes, aspires to do nothing more than preserve this footnote in the budding superstar's career, of interest mostly to completists and novelty seekers. As far as unintentionally funny moments go, the highlight has to be John extolling, "To be young, gifted and black, that's where it's at!" on his cover of the Nina Simone classic. *—Richie Unterberger*

Made in England / Mar. 21, 1995 / Rocket/Island ♦♦♦
Made in England could as easily be the follow-up to Elton John's self-titled 1970 album as his first recording since the success of his songs for *The Lion King* soundtrack. John has brought back some of his old associates, including percussionist Ray Cooper, guitarist Davey Johnstone, and, particularly, orchestrator Paul Buckmaster, who gave the *Elton John* album its distinctive sound 25 years ago and contributes four string charts here. John remains a musical jukebox: "Please" has a twangy guitar riff that sounds like the Searchers, circa 1965, while guest organist Paul Carrack brings a soulful Booker T.-like feel to "Man." As usual, though, John's main vocal influence remains John Lennon, especially on the album's first single, "Believe," the lyrics to which also echo the tone of several of Lennon's solo ballads. Lyricist Bernie Taupin is unusually personal, writing mostly in short, simple, declarative sentences and giving his songs one-word titles ("House," "Cold," "Pain," etc.). His overall theme posits a positive conclusion ("Blessed") eventually triumphing over adversity ("Lies"). John never works up much feeling for this concept, though he does come off alternately angry and solemn as the lyrics seem to require, though without ever upsetting the melodic flow. It sounds, in other words, as if Taupin had a lot to get off his chest this time around, but his mouthpiece, as usual, was more interested in the sound of the words than in their meaning. Which, given the predictability of the message, seems to have been just as well. *—William Ruhlmann*

Love Songs / Sep. 24, 1996 / Mercury ♦♦♦
Not strictly a "greatest hits" collection, *Love Songs* contains Elton John's most famous ballads, from "Your Song" and "Don't Let the Sun Go Down on Me" to "Can You Feel the Love Tonight." Featuring two new songs, including the single "You Can Make History (Young Again)," *Love Songs* is designed for the casual John fan, who is familiar with his songs through adult contemporary radio. If you don't fall into that category, the compilation is bound to fall short of expectations, but the record nevertheless works well as a collection of ballads and soft rock. *—Stephen Thomas Erlewine*

Big Picture / Sep. 23, 1997 / Mercury ♦♦♦
The Big Picture finds Elton John in strong form, turning in a by-now-predictable collection of ballads and pop songs designed to appeal to the adult contemporary audience. The difference is inspiration. With *Made in England*, John and his collaborator Bernie Taupin showed signs of life, and they continue that winning streak here. There may be nothing new on *The Big Picture*, but it's well-crafted professional pop, demonstrating John's knack for catchy pop hooks and his way with a ballad. As with any latter-day John album, hits like "Something About the Way You Look Tonight" are balanced out by some filler, but the key to the album is how album tracks like "Recover Your Soul," "If the River Can Bend" and "The Big Picture" carry emotional and melodic weight. It's a solid effort from one of pop's most reliable artists. *—Stephen Thomas Erlewine*

Aida / Mar. 23, 1999 / Rocket/Island ♦♦♦

One Night Only / Nov. 21, 2000 / Universal ♦♦♦

Songs From the West Coast / Oct. 2, 2001 / Universal ♦♦♦♦
Throughout his songs for *The Road to El Dorado*, Elton John hinted at his classic sound of the early '70s, but it's still a refreshing surprise to find him largely returning to that sound on his 2001 album, *Songs From the West Coast*. It was easy to think that John wasn't interested in writing like this anymore, given not just his continued success, but the ease with which he was crafting pleasant adult contemporary records. There are still elements of that on *Songs From the West Coast*—a few of the ballads are a little too even-handed, and since this is a modern recording, it lacks the resonant warmth of such classics as *Honky Chateau* and *Tumbleweed Connection*. Still, this is the richest, best record he's released in a long time, an album where it feels like a hit single is secondary to the sheer pleasure of craft, whether it's crafting a song or an album. And this is an album that flows easily and naturally, setting the mood with the story sketch "The Emperor's New Clothes" and then heading in a number of scenic directions. Of these, "American Triangle," his elegy for Matthew Shepard, will likely receive the most attention, but the most interesting are songs like the bluesy "The Wasteland," "Ballad of the Boy in the Red Shoes," which recalls the *Tumbleweed* epics, the neo-*Captain Fantastic* tune "Dark Diamond," the soulful closer "This Train Don't Stop There Anymore," and "Birds," a terrific, spare, rolling country-rocker. His songwriting hasn't been this diverse or consistent since the early '80s, and he hasn't made a record better than this in years. No, *Songs From the West Coast* won't make you forget *Tumbleweed Connection*, but it often recalls those peaks, which, frankly, is enough. *—Stephen Thomas Erlewine*

Eric Johnson

b. Aug. 17, 1954, Texas
Guitar / Album Rock, Guitar Virtuoso, Fusion, Instrumental Rock
Grammy award winning guitar virtuoso Eric Johnson has long been a magazine cover favorite and live attraction, even without much radio airplay. Johnson was introduced to classic jazz and Elvis records by his father at a young age, and his own love for the Beatles and the Ventures helped to form his already maturing guitar style. By the time he

was 13, he was already a working musician in the Austin, TX, area which led to session work for artists like Cat Stevens, Carol King, and Christopher Cross. A 1984 appearance on Austin City Limits apparently caught the attention of Prince, who instructed his parent label, Warner Bros. Records, to sign the young musician. Within months, Johnson signed to Warner subsidiary Reprise Records and, in 1986, released his debut solo album *Tones*, featuring uncredited backing vocals by Prince collaborators Wendy and Lisa. His second release (on Capitol), *Ah Via Musicom*, contained the Grammy winning instrumental "Cliffs of Dover," which got some radio play and brought the guitarist to the public's attention. In the mid-'90s, Musician Magazine named Johnson among the 100 Greatest Guitarists of the 20th Century, he spent time collaborating with B.B. King, Chet Atkins, and Dweezil Zappa, and touring with Joe Satriani and Steve Vai under the name G3. The third album, *Venus Isle*, and playing with his side project Alien Love Child took up his attention in the late '90s, and the space blues recording *Live and Beyond* arrived in 2000. *—Zac Johnson*

Tones / 1986 / Reprise ♦♦♦♦
Tones, Eric Johnson's first solo album, is an exceptionally strong debut, and a record that is just as good as the guitarist's breakthrough 1990 release *Ah Via Musicom*. Grouped with longtime compatriots Roscoe Beck and Tommy Taylor, Johnson's trademark composing voice and so-sweet electric guitar are already on full display. True to the album's title, Johnson showcases many different guitar tones, from the violin-like sustain of his trademark distortion to the bell-like timbre of his clean-toned rhythm work. Johnson also sings on five of the nine songs on *Tones*, and his voice is as competently expressive as ever. The second half of this record is really where it moves from being simply "good" to "great." Emerging from Stephen Barber's almost new-agey Fairlight CMI vamp, "Trail of Tears" kicks into a driving groove punctuated by Johnson's chordal stabs and arpeggios and carried by one of the guitarist's best vocal melodies. The multi-tiered arrangement is also one of the high marks of Johnson's catalog. This track segues in turn into the wonderful "Bristol Shore." This song features Johnson making his guitar sound like a koto as well as throwing in some impossibly in-tune upper-register licks that are played so sweetly they seem to threaten to fly off into the stratosphere (pun intended). The lack of a "Cliffs of Dover," a catchy, driving instrumental showcase for Johnson's chops, does not cheapen *Tones* in any way. It is a beautiful and important album by one of the greatest electric guitarists ever to pick up the instrument. *—Daniel Gioffre*

● **Ah Via Musicom** / Feb. 1990 / Capitol ♦♦♦♦♦
After being overlooked on his debut, *Tones*, guitarist Eric Johnson burst onto the airwaves with the surprising hit "Cliffs of Dover." Armed with excellent chops and a clear tone, Johnson took a tired formula and made it sound fresh again. Despite his talents on the fret board, he plays with great restraint and chose to explore a variety of styles, including rock, pop, blues, country, and jazz. While his singing is not quite as interesting as his guitar playing, it is not obtrusive and is at times quite pleasing. This recording has reached near-classic proportions within the guitar community. *—Robert Taylor*

Venus Isle / Sep. 3, 1996 / Capitol ♦♦♦
Eric Johnson is notorious for his perfectionism, but the six-year wait between his breakthrough *Ah! Via Musicom* and its follow-up *Venus Isle* seems a little extravagant, especially considering the resulting album. In six years, it could be assumed that an artist would undergo a number of different phases, exploring several different musical genres and textures. Johnson didn't spend his six years exploring—he spent them refining. *Venus Isle* reveals no new insights about the guitarist, it only offers a new spin on the territory *Ah! Via Musicom* covered. In one respect, this isn't a bad thing. Johnson is a consummate guitarist, pulling out tones and licks from his instrument that no other musician can quite match. It is a joy to hear him play, but *Venus Isle* nevertheless seems like a lost opportunity because he never departs from his standard bag of tricks. There are the occasional jazzy grooves, a handful of blues, several fusion numbers, and a few stabs at prog rock—all of the things that distinguished the album's predecessor. With playing as stylish and distinctive as Johnson's, it may seem churlish to complain about the lack of innovation, but given the large span of time between albums, it should have been more adventurous and unique. *Venus Isle* would have been a perfect follow-up if it had been released in 1992 or 1993, but it has to rank as a disappointment, no matter how enjoyable portions of it are. *—Stephen Thomas Erlewine*

Seven Worlds / Sep. 22, 1998 / Ark 21 ♦♦♦♦♦
A rare find for fans of this acclaimed guitarist/songwriter, *Seven Worlds* is the long-lost solo debut from Eric Johnson. Cut in the late '70s, this album is far more than a promising collection of demos; it's a full length, fully-produced album that showcases all of Johnson's awesome talent—not only as a guitar virtuoso, but as a talented pop/rock songwriter. Tunes such as "Showdown" clearly indicate the talent that Johnson had, even at this early stage. A classy false start to a great career, and a must for fans of Eric Johnson. *—Matthew Greenwald*

Live and Beyond / Oct. 24, 2000 / Favored Nations ♦♦♦
The name may be a little misleading for fans expecting live versions of Eric Johnson's guitar hits, when in fact *Live and Beyond* is a collection of new songs recorded live on a three-date set in Austin with his band Alien Love Child. The album shifts from the spacy psychedelia of "Shape I'm In," through the jazz chords of "Rain," and into elaborate blues rock in songs like "The Boogie King," "World of Trouble," and "Last House on the Block." Accompanying the guitarist on these tracks is drummer Bill Marsh and longtime friend Chris Maresh on bass, while Storyville vocalist Malford Milligan adds his voice to "Once a Part of Me" and "Don't Cha Know." *Live and Beyond* showcases Johnson's ability to explode from one style to another, often within the same song, and still hold together a tight blues trio without resorting to the overplaying that many of his contemporaries can't seem to get out of their systems. *—Zac Johnson*

Daniel Johnston

b. Sacramento, CA
Vocals / Indie Rock, Alternative Pop/Rock, Singer/Songwriter
As with other talented but troubled artists such as Syd Barrett, Brian Wilson, and Roky Erickson, Daniel Johnston fights a daily battle with the chronic mental illness that has plagued him nearly his entire life. However, despite recurrent bouts of delusional behavior wherein he has physically endangered himself and others, Johnston has carved out a respectable, influential career as a singer/songwriter of extraordinary talent that has grown since his first crudely recorded cassette was released in 1980. He has become the singer/songwriter of choice of the alternative/underground rock scene, and at various times has had his work championed by members of Sonic Youth, Yo La Tengo, Butthole Surfers, Half Japanese, Nirvana (Kurt Cobain was often photographed wearing a Daniel Johnston T-shirt), and numerous others. For years, Johnston's recordings were basically homemade affairs, his plain voice accompanied by crude piano and guitar playing. His narrative concerns focused mainly on lost love, the pain of miscommunication, his love for the Beatles, and comic-book superhero Captain America. Johnston's music is unflinchingly direct, almost embarrassingly and painfully honest. In the late '80s, indie label Homestead issued some of Johnston's early recordings on vinyl and a full-blown appreciation of Johnston's work was well underway. Soon he was recording solo and with Half Japanese mastermind Jad Fair on the Shimmy Disc indie label, and with Butthole Surfer Paul Leary, who may well be the best producer/musical accompanist Johnston has ever had. Johnston, to the amazement of virtually everyone, went on to record for Atlantic and, despite occasional behavioral lapses, seemed more self-assured than ever. As a result, he recorded some of the best music of his career: smart, ebullient pop with ringing guitars, primitive keyboards, and a wonderfully naive way of looking at the world. *—John Dougan*

Yip/Jump Music / 1983 / Homestead ♦♦♦
As for his early music, this may be the best place to begin immersing yourself in the world of Daniel Johnston. Extremely primitively recorded with little instrumentation other than keyboards, Johnston's upbeat mood makes this a funny, sometimes moving exercise in obsessive behavior. Two things he thinks about a lot, the Beatles and Casper the Friendly Ghost, are the subject of songs, along with his usual examinations of unattainable love. Not the easiest record in the Johnston canon, but a rewarding one nonetheless. *—John Dougan*

Hi, How Are You / 1983 / Homestead ♦♦♦♦♦
As with *Yip/Jump Music*, *Hi, How Are You* was a reissue of a cassette recording Johnston made in 1983, and as such it reflects the most fertile period of his early development. Like its predecessor, this is a friendly record marked by his increasing skill as a pop songwriter and his increasingly comfortable singing. His mood here is good, especially during the defiant "Keep Punching Joe," which eschews bitterness for personal resolve. Another important release. *—John Dougan*

1990 / 1990 / Shimmy Disc ♦♦♦♦♦
Daniel Johnston's only Shimmy Disc release provides a nice showcase of the kind of spare and blunt material he excels at and contains plenty of his own brand of preaching. With his minimal guitar/piano accompaniment and childlike vocals, Johnston sounds at once bleak and innocent on nouveau church hymns like "Held the Hand" and "Lord Give Me Hope." He switches gears for some fire and brimstone, though, on the impassioned and painfully comic "Don't Play Cards With Satan" (one of three live numbers recorded at CBGB's). Johnston gets some help from Sonic Youth's Steve Shelley and Lee Ranaldo on the rousing, minor-key number "Spirit World Rising" and teams up with Jad Fair for the touching lament "Some Things Last a Long Time." The mood lightens a bit with a cover of the Beatles' "Got to Get You Into My Life," but with Johnston's gothic and chunky piano chords threatening to derail the song, the respite is brief. Johnston's battle with manic depression is well known and is made painfully explicit here when successive live cuts find him in tears at one moment ("Careless Love") and leading a singalong in the next ("Funeral Home"). In spite of the rough going, this Daniel Johnston release is still worth getting; It's certainly a must for his fans and not a bad purchase for the newcomer either. *—Stephen Cook*

● **Fun** / Sep. 13, 1994 / Atlantic ♦♦♦♦♦
Johnston's major label debut is, arguably, his finest moment. With considerable help from Butthole Surfer Paul Leary, Johnston has never sounded so self-assured or confident before. Some of the songs are more polished, but they're never slicked up to such a degree that this sounds like a user-friendly approximation of Johnston's style; in fact, there are plenty of tracks that return Johnston to the keyboards ("Delusion & Confusion" and "My Little Girl") for his freewheeling, primitive workouts. Exhibiting some of his strongest songwriting to date, *Fun* is a rewarding record that never loses its initial, visceral appeal. *—John Dougan*

Rejected Unknown / Oct. 9, 2001 / Gammon ♦♦♦
The title of *Rejected Unknown* might be aimed at Atlantic Records, who held Johnston in contractual limbo for years with little support or promotion after his major-label debut, 1994's *Fun*. Johnston was finally dropped by Atlantic, and the long since-completed *Rejected Unknown* finally emerged on Gammon Records in 2001 (after a planned Tim Kerr release was scrapped). While the music on *Rejected Unknown* can at first sound overly self-deprecating and even angry at times, Johnston is actually painting a much larger picture—a picture of endless longing for acceptance, hopeless romanticism, and unrequited love. On the rollicking piano-driven "I Lose," Johnston sings "Got left out of the 'in' crowd/I seen their type/A bunch of buttwipes that rule," at once as sarcastic as Randy Newman and with the endearing quality for which Johnston has become known. Plus, Johnston's musical contribution to the album is far greater than on *Fun*, adding piano, guitar, and even percussion to many tracks. As with most of Johnston's albums, there are

a few songs that just fall flat or come off as a little too coy, but overall, it's a quality addition to the catalog of one of songwriting's true originals. —*Jason Nickey*

Freedy Johnston

b. Kinsley, KS

Vocals, Guitar / Americana, Adult Alternative Pop/Rock, Singer/Songwriter

Pitting acute, evocative portraits of outsiders and beautiful losers against fragile, shimmering country-pop melodies, the acclaimed work of Freedy Johnston earned him a reputation as one of the brightest singer/songwriters to emerge in the 1990s. His debut LP, 1990's *The Trouble Tree*, attracted a cult following domestically while becoming a sizable hit abroad, especially in the Netherlands, where he became a star. However, Johnston remained a struggling musician at home, and in order to complete his 1992 sophomore effort *Can You Fly*, he was forced to sell the family farm, which he had inherited from his grandfather. The resulting recording, however, was a critical smash that ended up on a number of prominent year-end lists, and after another EP, *Unlucky*, he was signed to Elektra Records. His 1994 major-label debut, the Butch Vig-produced *This Perfect World*, proved to be Johnston's most satisfying release to date; its first single, "Bad Reputation," even earned him significant airplay on alternative formats. *Never Home* surfaced in early 1997. —*Jason Ankeny*

Trouble Tree / 1990 / Bar/None ✦✦✦✦

Johnston's debut, though not without its rough edges, firmly established him as a talent to be reckoned with—even his earliest songs are marked by great maturity and insight. —*Jason Ankeny*

Can You Fly / Apr. 14, 1992 / Bar/None ✦✦✦✦✦

A giant step forward from his likeable but ragged debut, Freedy Johnston's *Can You Fly* is a stunningly accomplished and coherent album that recalls the raw lyricism of such quintessentially American writers as Raymond Carver and Richard Hugo. Johnston sold his family's Kansas farm to finance the recording of *Can You Fly*, a fact that's cited in the record's opening line and reflected in several autobiographical songs about the guilty downside of pursuing a dream. Elsewhere, Johnston creates rich character studies of people who are vaguely aware that their lives have gone awry but aren't sure what to do about it. If Johnston's stories are bleak, however, the delicacy of his melodies and simple, clean production ensure that hearing them is downright exhilarating. Standouts include the wistful gambler's lament "The Lucky One," the tender "Mortician's Daughter" and especially the supernatural-tinged title track. Syd Straw contributes vocals on one track, the lovely duet "Down in Love." —*Kristi Coulter*

Unlucky / 1993 / Bar/None ✦✦✦

The six-song EP *Unlucky* features *Can You Fly*'s tale of Las Vegas woe, "The Lucky One," in both its completed and demo forms. In addition to three new Johnston originals, it also contains a terrific cover of Jimmy Webb's "Wichita Lineman." —*Jason Ankeny*

● **This Perfect World** / Jun. 28, 1994 / Elektra ✦✦✦✦

Freedy Johnston's major-label debut is less consistently stunning than its predecessor, 1992's *Can You Fly* but, taken on its own terms, it affirms his position as one of the best songwriters of his generation. Certainly no one paints more evocative portraits of lonely, disappointed people. The majority of these 12 tracks are about men who either know or strongly suspect that they've done something unforgivable, and such is Johnston's mastery as a lyricist that it's even subtly apparent when his narrators are lying to themselves. Johnston frames his bleak narratives with melodic, chiming folk-rock; if anything, the predominantly mid-tempo songs and radio-ready Butch Vig production are a little too smooth, robbing *This Perfect World* of the edge that made *Can You Fly* so piercing. The most memorable tracks are the sparsest ones, where Johnston's words and appealingly plain voice take center stage. In addition to the melancholy opener, "Bad Reputation," other highlights include "Can't Shake This Town" and the witty "Dolores"—few songwriters could pack so many *Lolita* allusions into three minutes of guitar pop without sounding too clever by half. Best of all is the mournful, eerie title track, which describes the possibly mortal sins of one man's past and the hopelessness of his future with the economy and punch of a good short story. —*Kristi Coulter*

Never Home / Feb. 25, 1997 / Elektra ✦✦✦✦✦

From the propulsive opener "On the Way Out" to the lilting closer "Something's Out There" (about, of all things, a UFO abduction), the sparkling *Never Home* is Johnston's most musically and emotionally expansive outing to date. Finding a sympathetic ear in producer and guitarist Danny Kortchmar, Johnston's songs transcend their dark themes to reveal unexpected and heretofore unseen moments of warmth and sentimentality; even edgy, Randy Newman-like character studies such as "He Wasn't Murdered" and "Gone to See the Fire" offer moments of tenderness which their subjects (suicide and arson, respectively) can't suppress. —*Jason Ankeny*

Blue Days Black Nights / Jul. 20, 1999 / Elektra ✦✦✦✦

The darkest, most understated Freedy Johnston record to date, *Blue Days Black Nights* is also the singer's most intimate effort, largely rejecting the quirky character studies of prior outings in favor of more plainly personal narratives, and revealing new shades of depth and honesty in the process. Co-producers T-Bone Burnett and Roger Moutenot cloak Johnston's songs in dusky atmospherics which underscore the music's spare beauty—far removed from the crackling pop flavor of the preceding *Never Home* or even the shimmering folk of *This Perfect World*, *Blue Days Black Nights* possesses a hushed gravity which insinuates itself only over repeated listens. At times the results are overly ponderous, but a handful of tracks—the opening "Underwater Life" and "Moving on a Holiday" included—rank among Johnston's finest. —*Jason Ankeny*

Right Between the Promises / Aug. 7, 2001 / Elektra ✦✦✦✦

Gloria Jones

b. Sep. 12, 1958, Long View, TX

Vocals (Background), Vocals / Pop-Soul, Northern Soul, Soul

When the name of Gloria Jones comes up in rocktalk, it's usually as a trivia question. Firstly, in the mid-'60s she recorded the original version of "Tainted Love," which was covered by Soft Cell for a huge international hit in 1982. She was also the girlfriend of British glam rocker Marc Bolan, in addition to singing and playing keyboards in his T. Rex band. Her considerable talent as as a soul singer gets lost in the shuffle, especially because few of her recordings are currently available.

Jones earns a spot in rock history on the merits of "Tainted Love" alone. This propulsive mid-'60s soul stomper, wholly dissimilar to Soft Cell's wimpy synth-pop cover, is one of the great '60s hits that never was. "Heartbeat" was another throbbing near-miss, recorded with, oddly enough, producer Ed Cobb, who was more renowned for his work with garage-pop groups like the Standells and the Chocolate Watch Band. Both "Heartbeat" and "Tainted Love" were written by Cobb as well, although Jones was not without songwriting talent, co-writing Marvin Gaye and Diana Ross' 1974 hit duet, "My Mistake." Jones never had more than regional success, and (like several other minor American soul singers) moved to Great Britain, where the cultish devotion of Northern Soul fans ensured regular work.

In 1974, Jones joined T. Rex (which by that time was fading rapidly) as a keyboardist and backing vocalist. Becoming romantically involved with the singer, she also helped sway him into a more soul/dance-oriented direction. Bolan in turn helped her out on her solo album *Vixen*, playing guitar and writing songs. After having a child, their time together came to a tragic end when Bolan was killed in a car accident in 1977, with Jones at the wheel. —*Richie Unterberger*

● **Come Go With Me** / 1966 / Uptown ✦✦✦✦

Competent but unexceptional commercial mid-'60s soul with a strong, brassy Motown flavor. Jones was clearly a powerhouse singer but wasn't getting the material her talents deserved. "Heartbeat," by far the best track on the album, was reissued in better company in Rhino's *Soul Shots* series. —*Richie Unterberger*

Howard Jones (John Howard Jones)

b. Feb. 23, 1955, Southampton, Hants, England

Vocals, Keyboards / Pop/Rock, New Wave, Synth Pop

One of the defining figures of mid-'80s synth-pop, Howard Jones merged the technology-intensive sound of new wave with the cheery optimism of hippies and late-'60s pop. After playing with jazz and funk bands after college, Jones began performing as a solo artist with only synthesizers and drum machines. By 1983, he had recorded his first single, the number three hit "New Song." "What Is Love" performed even better, prompting his debut album *Humans Lib* to top the charts in England. Jones' second album *Dream Into Action* went platinum in the U.S., and spawned hit singles like "Things Can Only Get Better," "Like to Get to Know You Well" and "Life in One Day." A new version of the album track "No One Is to Blame" became Jones' biggest U.S. hit, peaking at number four. In 1989, his "Everlasting Love" single became a Top 20 hit in America, though the album *Cross That Line* stalled on the charts. Jones returned three years later with the acoustic set titled *In the Running*, that failed to make the charts at all. Elektra dropped him in 1993, prompting Jones to hit the road, performing acoustic shows. He released *Working in the Backroom* on his own Dtox label, and followed in 1996 with *Live Acoustic America*. *People* followed two years later. —*Stephen Thomas Erlewine*

Human's Lib / 1984 / Elektra ✦✦✦✦✦

Human's Lib is fueled by the nonstop synth-pop hooks and brightly textured melodies that went on to be a trademark of Howard Jones. His brand of spirited keyboard-and-lyric exuberance lent itself to a large part of the mid-'80s, especially in Britain. The tracks on *Human's Lib* are energetic and colorful, coming to life the best on "New Song," a number 27 hit for Jones in the U.S., and on the finely structured "What Is Love?," which gave him the number 33 spot on the singles chart four months later. While both of these songs rested at the bottom end of Billboard's Top 40, they went to number three and number two, respectively, in the U.K., with the album going all the way to number one, proving that his techno-pop stylings were better-appreciated on his side of the Atlantic. Outside of the singles, the album still holds well, with efforts like "Hide and Seek," "Conditioning," and "Pearl in the Shell" following through with a buoyant but orderly techno-pop keenness mustered through his clean use of the synthesizer. Although 1985's *Dream Into Action* is tighter both musically and lyrically, *Human's Lib* acts as a well-grounded starting point for Jones' future success. —*Mike DeGagne*

Dream Into Action / 1985 / Elektra ✦✦✦✦

This album shows the synthesizer pop idol at the height of his creativity—*Dream Into Action* is definitely the most interesting of Jones' albums. It contains some of his best songs—"Things Can Only Get Better," "Life in One Day," and "No One Is to Blame." The CD includes two bonus tracks, "Bounce Right Back" and "Like to Get to Know You Well," both of which are worthwhile additions. —*Iotis Erlewine*

Action Replay / 1986 / Elektra ✦✦

One to One / 1986 / Elektra ✦✦

Cross That Line / 1989 / Elektra ✦✦✦

After a three-year wait, this album was a bit of a disappointment. Musically, it is his best yet, but it lacked a certain energy that the others had. The songs seemed to replace vivacity with length. The album didn't do very well on the charts; the number 13 single (U.S.), "Everlasting Love," was the biggest hit. Ironically, the best song on this album, "Out of Thin Air," does not use a single synthesizer but instead is a solo piano piece performed by Jones himself. After all those years of electronic music, a song featuring a real instrument is a welcome relief. —*Iotis Erlewine*

In the Running / Apr. 14, 1992 / Elektra ✦✦

● **The Best of Howard Jones** / Jun. 29, 1993 / Elektra ✦✦✦✦✦
The Best of Howard Jones compiles all the necessary material ever put forth by this pop synthesizer master and is overabundant with a hearty 18 tracks. Jones had a remarkable eight Top 40 singles throughout the course of the mid-1980s, churning out keyboard laden dance/pop songs that were bright and lively. His debut album, *Human's Lib*, was a blend of new wave shine and friendly pop, which harbored the uppity "New Song" and the Duran Duran sound-alike ballad "What Is Love?" Worthy of its number four mark on Billboard is the beautiful "No One Is to Blame," which was one of the prettiest songs from the era. His flair for catchy melodies comes alive on both "Things Can Only Get Better" and the synth spicy "Life in One Day." Other highlights include the rich textured "Everlasting Love" from 1989 and the vibrant elevated chorus of "Lift Me Up." illuminating Jones' surprising vocal range. Sounding similar to the British trio the Thompson Twins, who were popular at the same time, Howard Jones' music reflected the synth driven sound of the decade. This compilation gathers all of his hits and then some, making for a perfect one stop album. —*Mike DeGagne*

Live Acoustic America / Feb. 13, 1996 / Plump ✦✦✦
In 1992, coinciding with the release of his fifth album, *In The Running*, Howard Jones undertook a tour of the U.S. accompanying himself on acoustic piano with only a percussionist in support. The tour doesn't seem to have had the desired effect of successfully promoting his current album, which became his first to miss the charts in the U.S. and the U.K. (despite the hit "Lift Me Up") and ended his career as a major-label act. But it was artistically satisfying for an artist usually consigned to the synth-pop category, who could emphasize his melodies and hopeful lyrics, not to mention his instrumental virtuosity and elastic voice, in the format. This recording was made early in the tour, on April 28, at the Variety Arts Theater in Los Angeles. Jones plays all of his hits and a representative sampling of songs from his five albums. Jones' hits collection may make a better sampler, but this set demonstrates that he can generate his own electricity even when his machines are unplugged. —*William Ruhlmann*

Angels & Lovers / Aug. 1997 / Pony Canyon International ✦✦✦
By 1997, Howard Jones had disappeared from the spotlight. It had been five years since he had a major-label contract and eight since he had a hit, which meant that American labels weren't eager to release *Angels & Lovers*, his first studio album since 1992. It's easy to see why labels in the U.S. passed on the record, leaving it to the Japanese-based Pony Canyon label—there's not a hook to be heard on these 12 songs. Using a set of equipment that sounds like it hasn't been updated in ten years, Jones turns in a series of songs that have more to do with texture than melody. That's not to say *Angels & Lovers* is a New Age album, since each song has complete lyrics and melodies—it's just that the vocals blend into the washes of synthesizers. Only two songs, "You're the Buddha" and the title track, are up-tempo and danceable, while the other ten tracks are simple, featureless ballads. Lyrically, they are among his most introspective songs, but the listless, meditative music makes it difficult to pay attention to the words. Ultimately, *Angels & Lovers* is undone by Jones' allegiance to late '80s synthesizers. In simpler settings, these songs may have had some power, but in these polished, mechanized productions, they sound lifeless. —*Stephen Thomas Erlewine*

People / Jul. 14, 1998 / Ark 21 ✦✦✦
After spending most of the '90s without an American record contract, Howard Jones finally secured a deal with Ark 21 in 1998, issuing *People*, his first album of new material to be released in the U.S. since 1992's *In the Running*. Strictly speaking, it's not a brand-new album—it's a revamped version of *Angels & Lovers*, a 1997 Japanese-only release, minus two songs from that 12-track album and featuring three new tracks. Perhaps Jones or his label realized that *Angels & Lovers* was a moody record, devoid of hooks outside of the bouncy "You're the Buddha," and that's why they have front-loaded *People* with "Buddha" and the three new songs, all of which are catchy, polished, tuneful pop—it's a way to lure older fans into an album they'll likely find a little impenetrable, if their tastes haven't moved toward new age. That said, two of the new songs are fun—"Let the People Have Their Say" successfully revamps *Dream Into Action* with pulsating beats and a children's chorus, while "Tomorrow Is Now" offers something new: propulsive, infectious guitar pop. The other number, the faux-reggae "Everything," is weighed down by ridiculous wah-wah guitar, but at least has some spirit to it—the rest of the songs are simple, undistinguished ballads. They may be among his most introspective songs, but the listless, meditative music is too dull to justify close attention. Ultimately, *People*—like its cousin *Angels & Lovers*—is undone by Jones' portentous songs, which sound canned due to his unwavering allegiance to late-'80s synthesizers. In simpler settings, these songs may have had some power, but in these polished, mechanized productions, they sound lifeless. —*Stephen Thomas Erlewine*

Marti Jones

Vocals, Guitar / College Rock, Jangle Pop, Singer/Songwriter
Pop singer Marti Jones first emerged as the frontwoman of the group Color Me Gone before issuing her solo debut *Unsophisticated Time*—produced by future husband Don Dixon—in 1985. Though the recepient of widespread critical acclaim, Jones found little commercial success with LPs like 1986's *Match Game* (recorded with guests Mitch Easter, T-Bone Burnett, and Darlene Love) and 1988's *Used Guitars* (featuring contributions from Marshall Crenshaw and Janis Ian), and she was dropped by her label A&M. After signing to RCA for 1990's *Any Kind of Lie*, Jones disappeared from sight before signing

to Sugar Hill and returning in 1996 with a pair of new releases, *Live From Spirit Square* and *My Long-Haired Life*. —*Jason Ankeny*

Unsophisticated Time / 1985 / A&M ✦✦✦✦✦
Marti Jones' debut firmly establishes the winning formula of all her solo work—superb singing, excellent song selection (including compositions from the dBs and the Bongos), and tastefully simple musical backing and production (courtesy of future husband Don Dixon). —*Jason Ankeny*

Match Game / 1986 / A&M ✦✦✦
For the all-star *Match Game*, Marti Jones and producer Don Dixon are joined by guests including Marshall Crenshaw, Mitch Easter, T-Bone Burnett, Darlene Love, Richard Barone, and Paul Carrack; the song selection is similarly impressive, drawing from the pens of David Bowie ("Soul Love") and Free ("Soon I Will Be Gone") as well as Crenshaw, the dBs and the Bongos. Nonetheless, the album is Jones' show, and her rich, expressive performances never relinquish the spotlight. —*Jason Ankeny*

● **Used Guitars** / 1988 / A&M ✦✦✦✦✦
Marti Jones' best effort to date, *Used Guitars* expands on her folk-pop foundations to stretch into soul ("Twisted Vines") and piano ballads (the stunning "Ruby," co-written by Janis Ian). Again, the songs are astutely chosen and feature contributions from John Hiatt, Graham Parker and Jackie DeShannon; Jones' own compositions, penned with Don Dixon, are especially strong—the breezy opener "Tourist Town" is a stunner. —*Jason Ankeny*

Any Kind of Lie / Apr. 1990 / RCA ✦✦✦
With *Any Kind of Lie*, Marti Jones strives for autonomy; keeping the covers to a minimum (only Clive Gregson's "Second Choice" and Loudon Wainwright's "Old Friend" make the cut), she and Don Dixon write the nine remaining songs themselves. The results are mixed: while none of the couple's originals are weak, Jones' greatest strength as a performer is as an interpreter of other people's work—*Any Kind of Lie* is an impressive accomplishment, but it lacks the eclectic fun of her best efforts. —*Jason Ankeny*

Live at Spirit Square / Mar. 19, 1996 / Sugar Hill ✦✦✦
Appearing more than five and a half years after it was recorded, *Live at Spirit Square* chronicles a Marti Jones performance from August 29, 1990, made during her promotional tour for her fourth studio album, *Any Kind of Lie*. Not surprisingly, eight of the 17 songs in the set come from that album, with five from its predecessor, *Used Guitars*, and two each from *Match Game* and *Unsophisticated Time*. That means the album is not the perfect live compilation of Jones' best material, with the missing including such first-album favorites as "(If I Could) Walk Away" and "Lonely Is (As Lonely Does)." But you can't complain too loudly when the featured material is of the caliber of "I've Got Second Sight" and "Follow You All Over the World" (not to mention covers of songs by John Hiatt, Elvis Costello, and Loudon Wainwright III). Jones leads a five-piece band that is of course anchored by her husband, producer, co-songwriter, and comic foil Don Dixon. That means the pop/folk/rock is accomplished and infectious, and that the onstage patter and interplay give the album an engagingly comfortable feeling. Play this album back to back with Dixon's live one, *Chi-Town Budget Show*, and it'll be a fun evening. —*William Ruhlmann*

My Long-Haired Life / Oct. 15, 1996 / Sugar Hill ✦✦✦
Jones' first new studio effort in six years returns to the covers-heavy format of her earlier work, drawing from a wonderfully eclectic pool of material including Joe Tex's "You Got What It Takes," Squeeze's "Black Coffee in Bed," Joni Mitchell's "Songs to Aging Children Come" and Elvis Costello's "Sleep of the Just." —*Jason Ankeny*

Rickie Lee Jones

b. Nov. 8, 1954, Chicago, IL
Vocals, Keyboards, Guitar / Folk-Rock, Singer/Songwriter
Once touted as the natural successor to Joni Mitchell, singer/songwriter Rickie Lee Jones proved no less idiosyncratic or mercurial; like Mitchell, Jones experienced significant commercial success at the outset of her career, but a restless creative spirit—combined with a stubborn refusal to fit comfortably into any one musical niche—sealed her ultimate destiny as that of a highly-regarded cult heroine. She began performing around Los Angeles in the mid-'70s, honing her unique, Beat-influenced spoken-word monologues. Her first measure of success was as a songwriter, though she gained her own contract from Warner Bros. for her self-titled 1979 debut LP. Spurred by the success of the jazz-flavored hit single "Chuck E's in Love," *Rickie Lee Jones* became a smash both commercially and critically, earning praise for Jones' elastic vocals, vivid wordplay, and unique fusion of folk, jazz, and R&B. With 1981's follow-up *Pirates*, she began employing longer and more complex song structures. *The Magazine*, released in 1984, was her most slick, synth-driven outing to date. She was silent for most of the decade, finally resurfacing with 1989's sterling *Flying Cowboys*. For 1991's *Pop Pop*, Jones covered ballads ranging in origin from Tin Pan Alley to the Haight-Ashbury. After 1993's *Traffic From Paradise*, she embarked on an acoustic tour; *Naked Songs*, a document of those unplugged shows, followed in 1995. —*Jason Ankeny*

★ **Rickie Lee Jones** / Mar. 1979 / Warner Brothers ✦✦✦✦✦
One of the most impressive debuts for a singer/songwriter ever, this infectious mixture of styles not only features a strong collection of original songs (the hits are "Chuck E's in Love" and "Young Blood," but "Danny's All-Star Joint" and "Coolsville" are just as good) but also a singer with a savvy, distinctive voice that can be streetwise, childlike, and sophisticated, sometimes all in the same song. —*William Ruhlmann*

Pirates / Jul. 1981 / Warner Brothers ✦✦✦✦
After the critical (and commercial) success of her debut two years earlier, Rickie Lee Jones

had a lot riding on her sophomore album, *Pirates*. From the opening track, "We Belong Together," Jones served notice that she was willing to challenge herself and experiment with more unusual, complex song structures. Her unique phrasing and style reflect her interest in beat poets and the bohemian lifestyle, and on this album she relies on more obscure imagery than the direct, detailed observations on comrades used on her first album. There are a wide range of musical influences represented (rock, jazz, soul), but the acoustic arrangements are more piano-based than most of her other albums. While there is an undercurrent of reflection on failed romances, Jones also reveals her playful side with songs like "Woody and Dutch." The musical and lyrical variety on the album is best represented in the album's centerpiece, "Pirates (So Long Lonely Avenue)," where she moves through mood and tempo changes with ease. Although the songs may not immediately grab the listener, the lyrical and musical complexities ultimately make this album more rewarding with every listen. —*Vik Iyengar*

Girl at Her Volcano / 1983 / Warner Brothers ✦✦✦✦✦
This seven-song EP originally was released as a 10" record. It's a charming collection featuring Billy Strayhorn's standard "Lush Life," as well as the Left Banke bit "Walk Away Renee," which should give some sense of Jones' breadth. A minor, but enjoyable change of pace. —*William Ruhlmann*

The Magazine / Sep. 1984 / Warner Brothers ✦✦
The reason *The Magazine* was such a disappointment was that Jones had proven herself a major artist with her first two albums and turned into a self-conscious, pretentious, minor one on this, her third. Once, she made art by observing street people and describing them carefully; now she tried to make "Art" by navel-gazing. What a letdown. —*William Ruhlmann*

Flying Cowboys / Sep. 1989 / Geffen ✦✦✦✦
Five years after the disappointing *The Magazine*, Rickie Lee Jones returned to form with *Flying Cowboys*, which shared much of the playful, childlike charm of her debut, *Rickie Lee Jones*, and some of the musically diffuse, lyrically ambitious form of its follow-up, *Pirates*. From the opening track, "The Horses," which suggested a mother's delight with her child as much as a lover's devotion, Jones reintroduced the joyous tone of her early work as well as establishing the Western theme that would run through the album—cowboys, rodeos, horses, deserts—without adding up to an actual story line. The easy rhythms and lazy, flexible singing on the first few songs were reminiscent of Laura Nyro's work with Labelle on their *Gonna Take a Miracle* album, after which Jones branched out into reggae and folk-blues, coming up with an affectionate bluesman voice on "Ghost Train." "Satellites," the college radio hit, used the sprung rhythms and surprising choral parts familiar from her popular early songs. If Jones could be obscure and unfocused as a writer, that weakness was also her strength, since it was an expression of the imagination that also produced her most striking musical effects. Producer Walter Becker may have helped keep things from getting as grandiose as they had on *The Magazine*, but it was really the artist herself who managed to rein in from that album's self-importance. If what resulted was not as accomplished as *Pirates*, it was the most accessible and enjoyable music Jones had made since her debut. —*William Ruhlmann*

Pop Pop / Aug. 1991 / Geffen ✦✦✦
An eclectic collection of covers from one of jazz-pop's most eclectic performers, *Pop Pop* travels from the stage to tin pan alley through Jimi Hendrix's sky. Rickie Lee Jones cradles each of these songs with her pleading, gentle voice, backing them with subtle orchestration courtesy of notable performers including Robben Ford, Joe Henderson, and Charlie Haden. Although the album was produced by Don Was, it avoids some of the slick handling he has given to Paula Abdul and the B-52's, instead relying on Jones' honest, soulful interpretations.

Her attention to love songs of the '40s and '50s demonstrates almost a longing for simpler times and simpler love, and these qualities are echoed in the treatment of songs like "My One and Only Love" and "I'll Be Seeing You." Her subdued take on the psychedelic Jimi Hendrix screamer "Up From the Skies" is slowed to a bluesy acoustic number, while the bratty refrain from *Peter Pan*'s "I Won't Grow Up" seems blushingly sweet.

While fans of the folk styles she demonstrated with her 1979 self-titled debut might not see as much merit in these soulful jazz interpretations, it still demonstrates Jones' ability to evolve and her unwillingness to be pinned down into one category. —*Zac Johnson*

Traffic from Paradise / Sep. 14, 1993 / Geffen ✦✦

Naked Songs / Sep. 19, 1995 / Reprise ✦✦✦✦✦
Rickie Lee Jones "unplugged"—in fact, solo with an acoustic guitar or piano on all but a couple of tunes—*Naked Songs* is otherwise a retrospective concert album on which Jones cherrypicks songs from her five studio albums, including the hits "Chuck E's in Love" and "Young Blood," and others from her breakthrough debut record. The studio album arrangements always tried to support and augment Jones' idiosyncratic writing and playing style, which sounds less unusual when she is simply accompanying herself, and in many ways more effective. "Altar Boy," a previously unreleased song, strays into Leonard Cohen territory, mixing religion with eroticism. —*William Ruhlmann*

Ghostyhead / Jun. 17, 1997 / Warner Brothers ✦✦✦
Ghostyhead finds Rickie Lee Jones in the odd position of following a younger generation, as its languid trip-hop beats suggest that she has been listening to Portishead, Tricky, and Beth Orton. It is certainly a precarious situation, since she could seem out of touch and old-fashioned, but it is a makeover she pulls off surprisingly well. Jones tends to follow the trippy, free-form structures of trip-hop, which means the melodies occasionally meander and the lyrics are more impressionistic than usual, concentrating on the overall effect instead of the details. There are still more solidly constructed songs than atmospheric

instrumentals, which gives the album an anchor, making the electronic echoes and rolling beats all the more effective. Although the songs aren't among Jones' best, the musical adventurousness of *Ghostyhead*—which manages to be contemporary without sacrificing her style—makes the album a revitalization of sorts. —*Stephen Thomas Erlewine*

It's Like This / Sep. 12, 2000 / Artemis ✦✦✦
Not since Billie Holiday has there been a vocalist who so completely transforms a song into her own. On *It's Like This*, eclectic folkie Rickie Lee Jones envelops standards, showtunes, '70s soul, and even slick jazz-rock, interpreting them with her familiar childlike, breathy shouts. In a very similar vein as 1991's *Pop Pop*, Jones pulls together a collection of diverse songs from throughout the 20th century and gives them a sparse, fragile spin, kind of like Diana Krall and Bjork sharing coffee at an all-night diner.

Produced by Bruce Brody (who has also worked with Maria McKee and Bette Midler), this album is really a showcase for the dynamic vocalist—her voice pitching and yawing like a sloop far out at sea. Several notable artists scatter themselves unobtrusively throughout the album like Joe Jackson, Ben Folds, John Pizzarelli, and Taj Mahal; each lend a subtle bass line or harmony vocal, cautiously not stepping on any of Jones' delicate lines.

Her passionate, earthy version of Marvin Gaye's "blaxploitation" hit "Trouble Man" is as soulful as her cover of the Beatles' "For No One" is pleading, each reaching out to the listener like a whisper from an inch away. Jones' unmistakable style is unlike anyone else's, and that fact alone will turn away some potential listeners; however, for fans of gentle jazz-pop, *It's Like This* is an intimate, dreamy wander through the songbooks of the last century. —*Zac Johnson*

Tom Jones
b. Jun. 7, 1940, Pontypridd, South Wales
Vocals / Club/Dance, Vocal Pop, Pop, Country-Pop
Tom Jones became one of the most popular vocalists to emerge from the British Invasion. Since the mid-'60s, Jones has applied his full-throated, robust baritone to nearly every form of popular music, from pop, rock, and show tunes to country, dance, and techno. While performing, Jones always radiated a raw sexuality, which earned him a large following of devoted female fans who frequently threw underwear on stage. Jones' following never diminished over the decades; he was able to exploit trends, earning new fans while retaining his core following.

Born Thomas Jones Woodward, Tom Jones began singing professionally in 1963, and recorded his first single for Decca, "Chills and Fever," in late 1964. "Chills and Fever" didn't chart but "It's Not Unusual," released in early 1965, became a number one hit in the U.K. and a Top Ten hit in the U.S. A series of hits followed but Jones' popularity began to slip somewhat by the middle of 1966, causing Mills to redesign the singer's image into a more respectable, mature tuxedoed crooner. For the remainder of the '60s, he scored a consistent string of hits in both Britain and America. At the end of the decade, Jones relocated to America, where he hosted the television variety program, "This Is Tom Jones." Lucrative performances took up his time and he would not record again until the early '80s when he released a series of slick Nashville-styled country-pop albums that earned him a handful of hits.

Jones' next image makeover came in 1988, when he sang Prince's "Kiss" with the electronic dance outfit, the Art of Noise. In 1994, he was on the comeback trail again, releasing the alternative-dance-pop album *The Lead and How to Swing It*; the record was a moderate hit, gaining some play in dance clubs. —*Stephen Thomas Erlewine*

● **The Best of Tom Jones** / Jun. 2, 1998 / Polygram ✦✦✦✦✦
The Best of Tom Jones is a comprehensive collection of his greatest hits that supplants *The Complete Tom Jones* as being the definitive CD-era hits collection. Running 22 tracks where *The Complete* only featured 20, the disc contains everyone of Jones' classic singles, from "It's Not Unusual," "What's New Pussycat," "Thunderball," "Deliah" and "She's a Lady" to "Kiss." Even though this features the cream of the crop, there are a few weak moments here and there—Tom Jones wasn't exactly a consistent artist—but there's no denying that this is the pick for casual fans. —*Stephen Thomas Erlewine*

... Sings the Ballads / Jun. 22, 1999 / Music Club ✦✦✦
Tom Jones has never been known for his subtlety, which doesn't necessarily make him a prime candidate for a romantic ballad crooner. Nevertheless, like any showman, Jones gives the audience what they want, whether it's rock, country, blues, or ballads. In concert, this is certainly quite entertaining, but on record, it can be overbearing, as Music Club's *Tom... Sings the Ballads* illustrates. The collection contains 15 tracks Jones recorded in the early '70s, just after he stopped having big hits. The selection is divided between Vegas standards ("My Way," "The Impossible Dream," "Georgia On My Mind," "Brother Can You Spare a Dime," "Anniversary Song") and recent hits ["Tired of Being Alone," "Ebb Tide," "If," "If Loving You Is Wrong (I Don't Want to Be Right)," "You've Lost That Lovin' Feelin'," "You've Got a Friend"]. Jones sounds best on the Vegas numbers (not surprising for one of the quintessential Vegas showmen), and the other tunes veer toward kitsch, which may be of interest to some latter-day fans. Throughout both styles of songs, one thing remains the same—Jones' big brash voice. It's the kind of voice that was meant for the stage, and that's where it sounds best. On record, Jones tends to dominate his material, which is fine for up-tempo numbers, but it's a bit too much for slower songs. Nevertheless, some listeners find a certain gonzo charm to Jones' style, since it's all about him, not the song. And while this collection doesn't have any hits, it does capture what he is all about—glitzy, showbiz bombast. It's not top-shelf Jones, but it's a good collection of second-level Jones that delivers exactly what his fans expect. —*Stephen Thomas Erlewine*

20th Century Masters—The Millennium Collection: The Best of Tom Jones / Feb. 8, 2000 / Polygram ♦♦♦♦
Part of Universal's massive *20th Century Masters/The Millennium Collection*, this 12-song budget set draws on a dozen of Jones' best-known tunes. Highlights include "It's Not Unusual," "What's New Pussycat?," "Green Green Grass of Home," "I'll Never fall in Love Again," "Delilah," and "She's a Lady." A perfect, bare-bones introduction to this artist's early hits. *—Cub Koda*

Janis Joplin

b. Jan. 19, 1943, Port Arthur, TX, **d.** Oct. 4, 1970, Los Angeles, CA
Vocals / Album Rock, Hard Rock, Blues-Rock
The greatest white female rock singer of the 1960s, Janis Joplin was also a great blues singer, making her material her own with her wailing, raspy, supercharged emotional delivery. First rising to stardom as the frontwoman for San Francisco psychedelic band Big Brother & the Holding Company, she left the group in the late '60s for a brief and uneven (though commercially successful) career as a solo artist. Although she wasn't always supplied with the best material or most sympathetic musicians, her best recordings, with both Big Brother and on her own are some of the most exciting performances of her era. She also did much to redefine the role of women in rock with her assertive, sexually forthright persona and raunchy, electrifying onstage presence. Joplin was sometimes criticized for screeching at the expense of subtlety, but her final album *Pearl* was solid evidence of her growth as a mature, diverse stylist who could handle blues, soul, and folk-rock. "Mercedes Benz," "Get It While You Can," and Kris Kristofferson's "Me and Bobby McGee" are some of her very best tracks. Tragically, she died before the album's release, overdosing on heroin in a Hollywood hotel in October 1970. "Me and Bobby McGee" became a posthumous number one single in 1971, and thus the song with which she is most frequently identified. *—Richie Unterberger*

I Got Dem Ol' Kozmic Blues Again Mama! / 1969 / Columbia ♦♦♦
Joplin's solo debut was a letdown at the time of release, suffering in comparison with Big Brother's *Cheap Thrills* from the previous year, and shifting her style toward soul-rock in a way that disappointed some fans. Removed from that context, it sounds better today, though it's still flawed. Fronting the short-lived Kozmic Blues Band, the arrangements are horn heavy and the material soulful and bluesy. The band sounds a little stiff, though, and although Joplin's singing is good, she would sound more electrifying on various live versions of some of the songs that have come out over the years. The shortage of quality original compositions—indeed, there are only eight tracks total on the album—didn't help either, and the cover selections were erratic, particularly the Bee Gees' "To Love Somebody." On the other hand, "Try" is one of her best soul outings, and the reading of Rodgers-Hart's "Little Girl Blue" is inspired. The 1999 CD reissue adds three bonus tracks: a cover of Bob Dylan's "Dear Landlord" from the *Kozmic Blues* sessions that was first heard on the *Janis* box set and previously unreleased versions of "Summertime" and "Piece of My Heart" from the Woodstock Festival. "Summertime" is okay, but this "Piece of My Heart" really pales next to the Big Brother interpretation. *—Richie Unterberger*

☆ **Pearl** / Feb. 1971 / Columbia/Legacy ♦♦♦♦♦
Joplin's second masterpiece (after *Cheap Thrills*), *Pearl* was designed as a showcase for her powerhouse vocals, stripping down the arrangements that had often previously cluttered her music or threatened to drown her out. Thanks also to a more consistent set of songs, the results are magnificent—given room to breathe, Joplin's trademark rasp conveys an aching, desperate passion on funked-up, bluesy rockers, ballads both dramatic and tender, and her signature song, the posthumous number one hit "Me and Bobby McGee." The unfinished "Buried Alive in the Blues" features no Joplin vocals—she was scheduled to record them on the day after she was found dead. Its incompleteness mirrors Joplin's career; *Pearl*'s power leaves the listener to wonder what else Joplin could have accomplished, but few artists could ask for a better final statement. The 1999 CD reissue adds four previously unreleased live July 1970 recordings: "Tell Mama," "Little Girl Blue," "Try," and "Cry Baby." *—Steve Huey*

In Concert / May 1972 / Columbia ♦♦♦
About half of this two-record set features Janis Joplin with Big Brother & the Holding Company in 1968, performing songs like "Down on Me" and "Piece of My Heart." The rest, recorded in 1970, finds her with her backup group, Full Tilt Boogie, mostly performing songs from *I Got Dem Ol' Kozmic Blues Again Mama!* Joplin puts herself out onstage, both in terms of singing until her voice is raw and describing her life to her audiences. Parts of this album are moving, parts are heartbreaking, and the rest is just great rock & roll. *—William Ruhlmann*

• **Janis Joplin's Greatest Hits** / Jul. 1973 / Columbia/Legacy ♦♦♦♦♦
A solid, if skimpy, ten-track best-of that gathers the most important songs from Joplin's solo career, as well as her stint with Big Brother & the Holding Company. The compilation *18 Essential Songs* offers a wider selection, but does not include the original version of "Me and Bobby McGee," which makes *Greatest Hits* the better purchase for those who only want one Janis Joplin disc, even if it isn't definitive. The 1999 CD reissue adds two bonus tracks, "Maybe" and "Mercedes Benz." *—Steve Huey*

Farewell Song / 1983 / Columbia ♦♦♦
A ragtag collection of odds and ends, live and studio, from both the Big Brother and solo era. The best cuts are on the *Janis* box in different versions, but serious fans will find some interesting items here, especially the *Cheap Thrills*-era outtakes and live performances; "Misery 'N," "Farewell Song," and "Catch Me Daddy" were easily good enough to have qualified for inclusion on that album. *—Richie Unterberger*

Janis / Nov. 23, 1993 / Columbia/Legacy ♦♦♦♦♦
This three-CD box set is the most thorough and valuable retrospective of Janis Joplin's career. Besides including all of her most essential recordings with and without Big Brother & the Holding Company, this 49-song package features quite a few enticing rarities; 18 of the tracks were previously unissued. These include a 1962 home recording of the Joplin original "What Good Can Drinkin' Do," which marked the first time her singing was captured on tape; a pair of acoustic blues tunes from 1965 with backup guitar by future Jefferson Airplane star Jorma Kaukonen, an acoustic demo of "Me and Bobby McGee," a 1970 birthday song for John Lennon, and live performances from her appearance on "The Ed Sullivan Show" in 1969. The real showstopper is the previously unissued, eight-minute version of "Ball and Chain" from Big Brother's first set at the 1967 Monterey Pop Festival (the cut on the *Monterey Pop* box set is from their second set). The more forgettable tracks from her solo albums are wisely excised, as are the Big Brother songs which did not feature her vocals. This is the rare multidisc set of a major artist which manages to cover all the official milestones and present a bounty of worthwhile rarities at the same time. *—Richie Unterberger*

18 Essential Songs / Jan. 24, 1995 / Columbia/Legacy ♦♦♦♦♦
18 Essential Songs is a one-disc distillation of the triple-disc *Janis* box set. Running 70 minutes, it is a more extensive best-of than the ten-track 1973 *Janis Joplin's Greatest Hits* album. But it is denied "first pick" status because, unlike that album, it does not contain the hit version of Joplin's only number one single, "Me and Bobby McGee." (It does, however, contain an alternate demo version of that song.) *—William Ruhlmann*

Box of Pearls: The Janis Joplin Collection / Aug. 31, 1999 / Columbia/Legacy ♦♦♦♦♦
A limited-edition five-CD box set comprising both albums that Joplin made with Big Brother & the Holding Company (*Cheap Thrills* and *Big Brother & the Holding Company*), both of her solo albums (*I Got Dem Ol' Kozmic Blues Again Mama!* and *Pearl*), and a bonus EP with five previously unreleased recordings. Each of these four albums includes previously unreleased bonus tracks, and each is available separately with the same material. The tracks on the bonus EP aren't available anywhere else, and if you're devoted enough to consider laying out for this deluxe box, you're probably *most* interested in what's on that fifth disc. There are a couple of *Cheap Thrills* outtakes, "It's a Deal" and "Crazy Once You Know How," with a garagey feel and some typically scorching, uninhibited Big Brother lead guitar; it can be seen why they may not have been deemed strong enough for the album, but they're pretty cool to have. The live versions of "Maybe" (April 1969) and "Raise Your Hand" (October 1969) are okay, but not essential; of greater curiosity is the raw live charge through "Bo Diddley" (also October 1969). Note that this box does *not* include a good deal of material that has shown up on the *Janis* box, the *Janis* movie soundtrack, *In Concert*, and *Farewell Song*, so it's not a complete collection of Joplin's recordings. *—Richie Unterberger*

Journey

f. 1973, San Francisco, CA
Album Rock, Arena Rock, Pop/Rock, Soft Rock, Hard Rock
During its 14-year existence (1973-1987), Journey altered its musical approach and its personnel extensively while becoming a top touring and recording band. The only constant factor was guitarist Neal Schon, a music prodigy who had been a member of Santana in 1971-1972. The earliest lineup recorded *Journey* (1975), the first of three moderate-selling jazz-rock albums given over largely to instrumentals. By 1977, however, the group decided it needed a strong vocalist/frontman and hired Steve Perry. The results were immediately felt on the fourth album, *Infinity* (1978), which had sold a million copies by the end of the year. *Evolution* (1979) was similarly successful, as was *Departure*. After a live album, *Captured* (1981), Journey released *Escape*, which broke them through to the top ranks of pop groups by scoring three Top Ten hit singles, all ballads featuring Perry's smooth tenor: "Who's Crying Now," "Don't Stop Believin'," and "Open Arms." *Frontiers* (1983), featuring the hit "Separate Ways," was another big success, after which Perry released a successful solo album, *Street Talk* (1984). Following the *Raised on Radio* tour, Journey disbanded. *—William Ruhlmann*

Journey / Apr. 1975 / Columbia ♦♦
On its eponymous debut album, Journey was still trying to find its signature sound. They relied too much on prog rock, filling the album with meandering jazz-rock instrumentals that never quite catch fire. Furthermore, their pop songs are ill-formed and lack hooks—in short, they are too mainstream for the progressive audience and too unfocused for the pop audience. *—Stephen Thomas Erlewine*

Look Into the Future / Jan. 1976 / Columbia ♦♦

Next / Feb. 1977 / Columbia ♦♦
With *Next*, Journey began to break away from the jazzy, progressive-rock inclinations that dominated their first two albums, yet without a forceful lead vocalist like Steve Perry, the group lacks a focus and a pop sensibility, and their attempts at straight-ahead pop/rock suffer considerably as a result. *—Stephen Thomas Erlewine*

Infinity / May 1978 / Columbia ♦♦♦

Evolution / Apr. 1979 / Columbia ♦♦♦♦♦

Departure / Mar. 1980 / Columbia ♦♦♦
Featuring the driving "Any Way You Want It" and the Top 40 hit "Walks Like a Lady," *Departure* didn't mark a departure from Journey's successful pop/rock formula, but overall the record was a little weaker than their previous two albums. *—Stephen Thomas Erlewine*

Captured / Feb. 1981 / Columbia ♦♦♦
After spending the better half of the '70s as an ersatz prog band given to Neal Schon's noodling, never-ending solos, low record sales, and muddling about on the marginal rock circuit, the members of Journey certainly welcomed the phenomenal chart success and

arena tours that came their way in the late '70s. With *Captured*, a live double-disc from 1980, the newly crowned kings of AOR show off like a formerly fat girl at prom. "Separate Ways" and "Faithfully" were still a few years away, but the band had plenty of hits by this time and they blast through them all, including a blistering version of "Any Way You Want It." The band are in rare form and vocalist Steve Perry uses *Captured* as his coming out, while the thousands of diehards sweating in the blistering sun give the album an underlying hum of energy that tops even Perry's. —*Steve Kurutz*

Escape / Aug. 1981 / Columbia ✦✦✦✦✦
Escape was a groundbreaking album for San Francisco's Journey, charting three singles inside Billboard's Top Ten, with "Don't Stop Believing" reaching number nine, "Who's Crying Now" at number four, and "Open Arms" peaking at number two and holding there for six weeks. *Escape* flung Journey steadfastly into the AOR arena, combining Neil Schon's grand yet palatable guitar playing with Jonathan Cain's blatant keyboards. All this was topped off by the passionate, wide-ranged vocals of Steve Perry, who is the true lifeblood of this album, and this band. The songs on *Escape* deemed more rock flavored, with more hooks and a harder cadence compared to their former sound. "Who's Crying Now" spotlights the sweeping fervor of Perry's voice, whose theme about the ups and downs of a relationship was plentiful in Journey's repertoire. With "Don't Stop Believing," the whisper of Perry's ardor is crept up to with Schon's searing electric guitar work, making for a perfect rock song. One of rock's most beautiful ballads, "Open Arms" gleams with an honesty and feel only Steve Perry could muster. Outside of the singles, there is a certain electricity that circulates through the rest of the album. The songs are timeless, and as a whole, they have a way of rekindling the innocence of youthful romance and the rebelliousness of growing up, built from heartfelt songwriting and sturdy musicianship. —*Mike DeGagne*

Frontiers / Feb. 1983 / Columbia ✦✦✦✦
Frontiers managed to give Journey four Top 40 hits, with "After the Fall" and "Send Her My Love" both reaching number 23, "Faithfully" at number 12, and "Separate Ways" peaking at number eight—the same amount that 1981's *Escape* brandished. While they tried to use the same musical recipe as *Escape*, *Frontiers* comes up a little short, mainly because the keyboards seem to overtake both Schon's guitar playing and Steve Perry's strong singing. An overabundance of Jonathan Cain's synth work cloaks the quicker tunes and seeps into the ballads, slightly widening the strong partnership of Perry and Schon. "Faithfully" tried to match the powerful beauty of "Open Arms," and while it is a gorgeous ballad, it just comes inches away from conjuring up the same soft magic. "Separate Ways" grabs attention right off the bat with stinging synthesizer and a catchy guitar riff, and "Send Her My Love" emphasizes Perry's keen ability to pour his heart out. The rest of the songs on the album lack the warmth that Journey is famous for, especially in their mix of fervor and intimacy shown on this album's predecessor. —*Mike DeGagne*

Raised on Radio / May 1986 / Columbia ✦✦✦
Journey's ninth new studio album found the group reduced to a trio of guitarist Neal Schon, singer Steve Perry, and keyboard player Jonathan Cain. But even without their regular rhythm section, the group was able to re-create the accessible pop/rock sound perfected on earlier albums such as *Escape* and *Frontiers*. Schon's guitar still cut through the fat keyboard chords, and Perry's fluid tenor still gave the songs an airy, melodic appeal. All of that was good for sales of two million copies and five chart singles, four of which made the Top 40 and one of which, "Be Good to Yourself," reached the Top Ten. That didn't match the seven-million-selling number one *Escape*, but it confirmed that Journey's music had a large audience right to the (temporary) end of its career. —*William Ruhlmann*

● **Greatest Hits** / Nov. 15, 1988 / Columbia ✦✦✦✦✦
Greatest Hits is an excellent, thorough 14-track collection containing all of Journey's big hits, from 1978's "Wheel in the Sky" to 1986's "I'll Be Alright Without You." Although the songs aren't presented in chronological order and a handful of minor hits ("Suzanne," "Walks Like a Lady") aren't included, it doesn't matter, since every essential Journey single—"Only the Young," "Don't Stop Believin'," "Any Way You Want It," "Separate Ways," "Lovin', Touchin' Squeezin'," "Open Arms," "Send Her My Love"—is here, which means that it's all most casual fans will ever need. —*Stephen Thomas Erlewine*

Time 3 / Dec. 1, 1992 / Columbia ✦✦✦✦
Journey has given radio some of AOR's finest three-minute gems, both in hard rock and ballad form. *Time 3* strings together all their best songs, most of them popular and some not so well known, but all extremely enjoyable and laid out over the course of three discs. Set up chronologically, the first disc unleashes their raw sound, with the first eight songs being pre-Steve Perry. With tracks from *Infinity*, *Evolution*, and *Departure* rounding out disc one, a young Perry sets a musical precedent with his soaring voice. Even so, "Any Way You Want It" steals the show amidst all of their early material. Disc two is where this set truly shines, containing their biggest hits and covering the most entertaining and fruitful part of Journey's career. Seven of the songs here are from 1981's *Escape* album, including of course "Open Arms," "Don't Stop Believing," and "Who's Crying Now." The first half of the disc finishes off hits from the *Departure* album, and smoothly rolls into songs from the live *Captured*. The third disc starts off with the B-side "La Raza Del Sol," and follows with "Only Solutions" from the movie *Tron*. The best songs from *Frontiers* and *Raised on Radio* make up the next ten tracks, and finishes with wonderful live performances of "Girl Can't Help It" and "I'll Be Alright Without You." *Time 3*, which comes with a colorful booklet and informative liner notes about each song (released in this style when the set first hit shelves), is an extremely comprehensive overview. There is an overabundance of material here, but all of it is incredibly pleasing. —*Mike DeGagne*

Trial by Fire / Oct. 22, 1996 / Columbia ✦✦

Arrival / Apr. 3, 2001 / Columbia ✦✦✦
Journey was formed originally as a vehicle for Neal Schon's guitar pyrotechnics, but after five years the band sought out a lead singer to give them mainstream pop appeal, and Steve Perry did that, helping them to a string of seven consecutive multi-platinum albums before the band broke up in 1987. A 1996 reunion put them back in the winners' circle with *Trial by Fire*, but Perry then bowed out for health reasons, putting Journey in the sticky position of recruiting a new lead singer. (Drummer Steve Smith has also been replaced by Deen Castronovo formerly of Bad English.) They chose a soundalike, Steve Augeri, which suggests that they are more concerned with recreating their hits in concert than in making new music. A group of Journey's vintage always risks sounding like a copy band of itself, and *Arrival*, the first full-length album with Augeri, realizes that danger. The singer doesn't quite have Perry's smooth, flowing tenor, but he's close enough so that much of the time, especially in big arrangements, he can fool you, though at unadorned moments on ballads he sounds different. When he's not singing, the music is even more like Journey, with Schon's soaring leads supported by Jonathan Cain's bright keyboards in typical arena rock arrangements. It's hard to argue that the generalized romantic sentiments that make up the lyrics, here contributed by a variety of people including Augeri and Cain's wife, are any worse than Perry's, but Perry sang his words with more feeling than Augeri does. So, the new Journey turns out to be a half-step back to the old (make that the old, old Journey—pre-Perry, when Schon ruled). Odds are, that will be a more difficult sell at record stores, though Augeri's similarity to Perry means that the concert revenues shouldn't suffer. —*William Ruhlmann*

Joy Division
....

f. 1977, db. May 18, 1980
Post-Punk
Formed in the wake of the punk explosion in England, Joy Division became the first band in the post-punk movement by later emphasizing not anger and energy but mood and expression, pointing ahead to the rise of melancholy alternative music in the '80s. Though the group's raw initial sides fit the bill for any punk band, Joy Division later incorporated synthesizers (taboo in the low-tech world of '70s punk) and more haunting melodies, emphasized by the isolated, tortured lyrics of its lead vocalist, Ian Curtis. While the British punk movement shocked the world during the late '70s, Joy Division's quiet storm of musical restraint and emotive power proved to be just as important to independent music in the 1980s. Founded in 1977, the group signed to Manchester's Factory label and released *Unknown Pleasures* in 1979. The album enjoyed immense critical acclaim and a long stay on the UK's independent charts. During late 1979, Joy Division's manic live show gained many converts, partly due to rumors of Curtis' ill health. An epilepsy sufferer, he was prone to breakdowns and seizures while on stage—it soon grew difficult to distinguish the fits from his usual on-stage jerkiness and manic behavior. Just before their first U.S. tour, Curtis hung himself and the group quickly disbanded. Ironically, their final studio work, the single "Love Will Tear Us Apart" and the LP *Closer*, became big British hits. Early in 1981, the remaining trio formed New Order. —*John Bush*

☆ **Unknown Pleasures** / Jun. 1979 / Qwest ✦✦✦✦✦
Raw and vital, Joy Division's full-length debut juxtaposes the taut, visceral energy of the group's evolving sound with the ghostly presence of vocalist Ian Curtis, whose grasp on the corporeal world seems to diminish with each passing song. While as claustrophobic and remote as any of the band's records, *Unknown Pleasures* is informed by a sense of punk-influenced aggression absent from Joy Division's later work; the album's tangible tension derives from the efforts of the primal rhythm battery of Peter Hook and Stephen Morris to breathe life into the music at the same time that the vortex of Curtis' soul threatens to suck it all out. Remarkable. —*Jason Ankeny*

☆ **Closer** / Jul. 1980 / Qwest ✦✦✦✦✦
Released in the wake of Ian Curtis' suicide, *Closer* travels through the looking glass into a cold, hopeless world of menace and loss. The opener "Atrocity Exhibition" sets both the sonic and emotional tone of the record: brutal and distant, the music is stripped bare of its humanity, finding its foothold instead in metallic rhythms, damaged synth patterns, and jagged guitars. Looming over the proceedings are Curtis' disembodied vocals, which grip the songs from seemingly beyond the physical plane; while the singer dominates *Closer*, his presence is remote and ephemeral—while he can be felt at every moment, in truth he was already gone. —*Jason Ankeny*

Still / Oct. 1981 / Qwest ✦✦✦
Still collects outtakes and rarities along with a live set recorded on May 2, 1980, just over two weeks prior to Ian Curtis' death. In addition to the atmospheric "Glass" and the haunting funeral march "Dead Souls," the studio sides include four leftover tracks from the sessions for *Unknown Pleasures*, while the concert set includes performances of seminal tracks such as "Transmission," "Isolation" and "A Means to an End." Although neither as cogent nor as indispensible as the band's two studio records or the *Substance* compilation, *Still* is nonetheless a valuable chronicle of Joy Division's remarkable evolution, a growth charted by the inclusion of an early live cover of the Velvet Underground's "Sister Ray" to the only recorded version of the hypnotic "Ceremony," the ultimate Ian Curtis composition which later resurfaced as the first single from New Order. —*Jason Ankeny*

★ **Substance** / 1988 / Qwest ✦✦✦✦✦
Despite recording two of the greatest albums of the post-punk era (*Unknown Pleasures* and *Closer*, respectively), Joy Division was primarily a singles band, a legacy borne out by the stunning *Substance*. Beginning with the raw power of "Warsaw" and concluding with the classic "Love Will Tear Us Apart," the set collects the majority of the group's non-LP material, chronologically charting their monumental growth from visceral guitar noise to music of remarkable texture and emotional density; tracks like the oppressive

"Digital," the hypnotic "Transmission" and the self-explanatory "Atmosphere" (rescued from an obscure French flexi-disc) are simply stunning, unparalleled in their obsessive and haunting power. *—Jason Ankeny*

Permanent / Aug. 15, 1995 / Qwest/Warner Brothers ♦♦♦
Featuring selected highlights from *Unknown Pleasures* and *Closer*, *Permanent* contains some of Joy Division's best songs, but the compilation isn't as useful as *Substance*, which featured early demos and B-sides, nor is it as mesmerizing as the band's two original studio albums. Consequently, *Permanent* is not only useless for dedicated fans, it's an incomplete and misleading introduction for casual fans, even though it contains a wealth of brilliant music. *—Stephen Thomas Erlewine*

Heart & Soul / 1998 / London ♦♦♦♦♦
For serious fans, the four-disc box set *Heart and Soul* is the ultimate Joy Division collection, containing almost everything the quartet recorded, from the Warsaw demos to *Closer*, as well as a full disc of live material. Even if this lovingly assembled set (compiled by Jon Savage, with the assistence of Bernard Sumner and Peter Hook) does contain the bulk of everything the band recorded, it might be a little disconcerting to longtime fans to hear *Unknown Pleasures* and *Closer* surrounded by the EP tracks and B-sides, but the pleasures of this set outweigh that problem. Any Joy Division collector will have much of the previously unreleased material in some bootleg form, but they won't have it in such good fidelity. There are also several rarities, such as flexi-disc versions and alternate takes, that have been hard to find, and the live recordings, while not revelatory, are very strong. The end result is the rare box set that is actually succeeds as a full career retrospective that's equally appealing to dedicated fans and neophytes. *—Stephen Thomas Erlewine*

Judas Priest

f. 1970, Birmingham, England, **db.** 1996
New Wave of British Heavy Metal, Album Rock, British Metal, Heavy Metal, Hard Rock
Judas Priest was one of the most influential heavy metal bands of the '70s, spearheading the "new wave of British heavy metal" late in the decade. Decked out in leather and chains, the band fused the gothic doom of Black Sabbath with the riffs and speed of Led Zeppelin, adding a vicious two-lead guitar attack (by K.K. Downing and Glenn Tipton) to Rob Halford's dramatic vocals; in doing so, they set the pace for much popular heavy metal from 1975 until 1985, as well as laying the groundwork for the speed- and thrash-metal of the '80s. Judas Priest was formed in Birmingham, England in 1970, and recorded their debut, *Rocka Rolla*, for the independent U.K. label Gull in 1974. The follow-up, 1976's *Sad Wings of Destiny*, earned positive reviews and led to an international contract with CBS Records. *Sin After Sin* (1977) also received positive reviews, but 1978's *Stained Class* was the record that established them as an international force in metal. Along with 1979's *Hell Bent for Leather* (*Killing Machine* in the U.K.), *Stained Class* began the "new wave of British heavy metal" movement. A significant number of bands adapted Priest's leather-clad image and driving sound, making their music harder, faster, and louder. 1980's more mainstream *British Steel* entered the British charts at number three, and launched the hit singles "Breaking the Law" and "Living After Midnight"; *Point of Entry*, released the following year, was nearly as successful. Featuring the hit "You've Got Another Thing Comin'," *Screaming for Vengeance* (1982) marked the height of their popularity, peaking at number 17 in America and selling over a million copies. However, metal tastes were changing, and Judas Priest began to seem out of touch; as a result, their sales slipped in the latter half of the '80s. Following the creative return to form of 1990's *Painkiller*, Halford left to form his own thrash band, Fight. Judas Priest rebounded with singer Tim "Ripper" Owens and the album *Jugulator*, released in late 1997 to mostly poor reviews. *Demolition*, Owens' second studio recording with the band, was released in 2001. *—Stephen Thomas Erlewine*

Rocka Rolla / 1974 / Koch International ♦♦♦
A sketchy and underfocused debut, *Rocka Rolla* nonetheless begins to delineate the musical territory Judas Priest would explore over the remainder of the decade: frighteningly dark in its effect, tight in its grooves, and capable of expanding to epic song lengths. On the other hand, *Rocka Rolla* is also murkier, less precise, and powerful in its riff attack, and more blues-based; the stylistic debts to Black Sabbath and Deep Purple are obvious at this juncture, although they would become much less apparent on subsequent releases. The compositions alternate between short songs and extended suites; some are decent, but overall they don't establish a real direction and tend to plod aimlessly in many of the longer pieces. Mostly a curiosity for hardcore fans, *Rocka Rolla* definitely hints at Judas Priest's potential and originality, but doesn't always suggest the quantum leap in vision that would occur with their very next record. [Koch's 2000 CD reissue appends the version of "Diamonds and Rust" previously found on the compilation *Hero, Hero*.] *—Steve Huey*

Sad Wings of Destiny / 1976 / Koch International ♦♦♦♦
The groundbreaking *Sad Wings of Destiny* was the first great Judas Priest album, simultaneously taking the entire heavy metal genre to new depths of darkness and new heights of technical precision and musicality. *Sad Wings of Destiny* sounded like little else on the metal scene in 1976: it was heavy and chillingly bleak, in an almost unrelenting way that hadn't been seen since Black Sabbath's heyday, but its arrangements were much more intricately crafted, its sonic textures more varied, its grooves tight and menacing, yet tinged with a Gothic elegance under the raging torrent of guitar riffs. Just as importantly, the more prog-rock-influenced sections of *Rocka Rolla* have been brought under control, with the extended pieces displaying a newfound focus and direction, as well as complexity. Perhaps the only flaw lies in the album's pacing, which drags down some of the momentum towards the second half by keeping the slower pieces too close together (an effect not helped by the less-than-melodic rocker "Genocide"). However, virtually every other aspect of the album points to a stunning artistic leap forward. The opener, "Victim of Changes," was an instant metal classic, with Rob Halford delivering an electrifying performance; elsewhere, shorter songs like "The Ripper" and "Deceiver" come on like lightning-quick sneak attacks, ending before you know what's hit you. There are also two delicate, prog-style ballads, "Dreamer Deceiver" and the piano-based "Epitaph," demonstrating a compelling emotional range. Although neither as commercially successful nor as technically flashy as subsequent releases, *Sad Wings of Destiny* was an important milestone in the eventual development of the progressive metal subgenre, and established a standard of excellence to which Judas Priest would adhere through the remainder of the '70s. *—Steve Huey*

Sin After Sin / 1977 / Columbia ♦♦♦♦
Although *Sad Wings of Destiny* wasn't a huge seller, it did land Judas Priest a major-label deal with Columbia, for whom they debuted with the fearlessly experimental *Sin After Sin*. Retaining the progressive elements of its predecessor, *Sin After Sin* upped the levels of instrumental technique and melody while incorporating a greater variety of influences. It's possible to hear touches of Jimi Hendrix, Queen, Led Zeppelin, Pink Floyd, and Southern rock, not to mention one of the most effective left-field cover choices in metal history on the Joan Baez tune "Diamonds and Rust" (which became a minor hit in England). As a result, it isn't the most metallic or musically cohesive Priest album, but overall, it's extremely close to the same level of brilliance as most of their '70s output. Every track is worthwhile, although "Sinner" and "Dissident Aggressor" (later covered by Slayer, a real testament to its heaviness) are two particular highlights. *—Steve Huey*

Stained Class / Apr. 1978 / Columbia ♦♦♦♦♦
An indisputable metal masterpiece, *Stained Class* is the apex of '70s Judas Priest, a sinister, muscular collection that ties the disparate strands of their style together while jacking the adrenaline rush up to previously undreamed-of levels. Even the lone slow-tempo track, "Beyond the Realms of Death," has an exciting, visceral intensity, and the whole band is at the absolute peak of its powers in terms of technical execution. Lyrically, *Stained Class* is probably the darkest moment in a career filled with them; the whole second half of the record is positively obsessed with death, although the ridiculous 1989-90 court case alleging that the album provoked two Nevada teenagers' suicides was instead centered around the Gary Wright/Spooky Tooth cover "Better By You, Better Than Me," in which Rob Halford allegedly embedded the subliminal, backwards-recorded message, "Do it." At any rate, the air of malevolence about *Stained Class*, and the sheer power of its jackhammer guitar riffs, was unrivaled in heavy metal upon its release (even in Priest's own catalog), stamping the album an instant classic and solidifying Judas Priest's status as arguably the most original and musical metal band of its time. More than any other Priest album, the style of *Stained Class* also laid the groundwork for the thrash and speed metal that would rise to dominance in the mid- to late '80s, making it a defining moment for the "new wave of british heavy metal" movement and one of the genre's all-time landmarks. *—Steve Huey*

Hell Bent for Leather / Mar. 1979 / Columbia ♦♦♦♦♦
In 1979, Judas Priest was growing more and more influential. And as the 1980s progressed, it would become crystal clear that the British headbangers—who influenced everyone from Iron Maiden to Metallica to King Diamond—had every bit as great an impact as fellow British headbangers Black Sabbath. One of the Priest's strongest albums, *Hell Bent for Leather* cannot be described in anything less than glowing terms. Although gothic themes are present on such treasures as "The Green Manalishi (With the Two-Pronged Crown)"—originally recorded by Fleetwood Mac—"Evil Fantasies" and "Before the Dawn," the album generally isn't as dark or morbid as *Stained Class* or *Sin After Sin*. But musically, the band is as aggressive and brutally intense as ever. The two-guitar attack of Glenn Tipton and K. K. Downing is characteristically blistering, and lead singer Rob Halford never sounded more inspired. For those with even a casual interest in metal, *Hell Bent for Leather* is essential listening. *—Alex Henderson*

Unleashed in the East (Live in Japan) / Oct. 1979 / Columbia ♦♦♦♦
Judas Priest's first official live recording has always been met with equal amounts of acclaim and controversy: acclaim from those who consider it an excellent summation of the metal legend's 1970s output, and controversy from the critics and industry insiders who criticized what they believed to be a heavily over-dubbed and studio-enhanced performance, mockingly naming it "Unleashed in the Studio" at times. Before delving deeper into this issue, let it be said that except for a few unfortunate omissions ("Hell Bent for Leather," "Better By You, Better Than Me") the track listing here is quite impressive. Along with powerful versions of such storming anthems as "Exciter" and "Running Wild," the band delivers the definitive version of the prog-metallic "Sinner," and competent versions of their popular covers tunes, "Diamonds and Rust" and "The Green Manalishi (With the Two-Pronged Crown)." Interestingly, most of the tracks from the classic *Sad Wings of Destiny* fall short of their mark, however, perhaps because they forfeit heaviness at the expense of speed. As for the "live" dilemma, in the late '90s estranged singer Rob Halford would claim in interviews that, while the band's playing was indeed recorded entirely live, his vocals had been ruined in the original mix, forcing him to re-record them in one take in a concert-like setting. If this was the case, it would hardly be the first or most severe case of studio interference on a live recording, and fans seeking a concise, nearly flawless collection of Priest's 1970s hits will not be disappointed. *—Ed Rivadavia*

● **British Steel** / 1980 / Columbia/Legacy ♦♦♦♦♦
With *Hell Bent for Leather*, Judas Priest had begun the task of developing their image for increased mainstream attention, reveling in leather-and-motorcycle trappings while beginning to simplify and streamline their sound. *British Steel* brings that process full circle, offering the band's catchiest, most accessible set of tunes yet, while retaining the precision guitar assault and quasi-operatic vocals that had come to define their sound. It

was the simplest music Priest had yet attempted, but thanks to the (mostly) top-notch songwriting and AC/DC-like willingness to allow the songs' grooves room to breathe, the record is a smashing success overall, with maybe one or two subpar tracks. There are a couple of trends beginning here that would take their toll later on—the lyrics are a bit more juvenile, and the music seems to prize commercialism over complexity—but in this context, neither really matters, as Priest display a real penchant for stadium-ready anthems. "Breaking the Law" and "Living After Midnight" became genuine hit singles in the U.K., and deservedly so, while the album became their first to reach the U.S. Top 40, going platinum in the process. *—Steve Huey*

Point of Entry / 1981 / Columbia/Legacy ✦✦✦
Having reinvented themselves as an arena-metal act with the hugely successful *British Steel*, Judas Priest naturally opted to stay the course with *Point of Entry*, keeping things simple while adding a bluesy boogie in places, a sound they hadn't really attempted in quite some time. However, where *British Steel*'s simplicity was an effective reworking of the band's sound, *Point of Entry*'s songs aren't always up to par, making its less well-crafted tracks sound like lunkheaded, low-effort filler. When *Point of Entry* works, it works well—"Heading Out to the Highway," "Solar Angels," and "Desert Plains," for example, are great, driving hard-rock songs, but British rock-anthem hits "Don't Go" and "Hot Rockin'" seem oddly generic, given Priest's reputation for inventiveness. Even if *Point of Entry* is somewhat disappointing overall, though, it's partly because of the album's genre-transforming predecessors; it does have enough good moments to make it worthwhile to diehards and fans of the group's more commercial '80s output. *—Steve Huey*

Screaming for Vengeance / 1982 / Columbia/Legacy ✦✦✦✦
Following the under-written, erratic *Point of Entry*, *Screaming for Vengeance* returned Judas Priest to the top of the metal heap, boasting a much more consistent set of songs, highlighted by the monumental "You've Got Another Thing Comin'." Some of the bluesier elements of *Point of Entry* are still here, but the heavier moments tend to dominate the album's flavor (particularly the title track); plus, there are arena-ready headbanging anthems like "Electric Eye," "Bloodstone," and, of course, "You've Got Another Thing Comin'," the latter two proof that the band really knew how to work a mid-tempo rock groove. Although the sound is commercial, *Screaming for Vengeance* doesn't feel like it's pandering, as *Point of Entry* sometimes did; it's a catchy, accessible metal record in the best sense of the description, and it rivals *British Steel* as Priest's best album of the '80s. *—Steve Huey*

Defenders of the Faith / 1984 / Columbia/Legacy ✦✦✦
Having recaptured their heavyweight status with *Screaming for Vengeance*, Judas Priest stuck with their successful formula for the follow-up, *Defenders of the Faith*. Overall, it's a solidly constructed, unapologetically commercial metal record, and it doesn't feel underdeveloped as *Point of Entry* sometimes did. It isn't quite up to the level of *British Steel* or *Screaming for Vengeance*, partly because (unlike those two) it lacks a truly standout single, and partly because of a few lowest-common-denominator moments. Still, it's far from a bad entry in Priest's '80s arena-metal period, and it remains a favorite among many fans who prefer those recordings to the band's '70s work. *—Steve Huey*

Turbo / 1986 / Columbia ✦✦✦

Priest . . . Live! / 1987 / Columbia ✦✦

Ram It Down / 1988 / Columbia ✦✦

Painkiller / Aug. 1990 / Columbia ✦✦✦✦
From out of nowhere, Judas Priest suddenly revitalized themselves with *Painkiller*, in no small part because of new drummer Scott Travis, whose busy, virtuosic rhythmic base pushes Halford, Downing, and Tipton to their most energetic and impassioned performances in an extremely long time. Songs like the title track, "Leather Rebel," and "Metal Meltdown" thrash like mad; Halford's shrieking and growling is positively frightening, as he uses his incredible vocal range to an almost King Diamond-like effect. But it isn't just the rediscovered power that makes *Painkiller* the band's strongest musical effort in ages: the elegant "A Touch of Evil," for example, is reminiscent of the progressive, intricately arranged pieces of their '70s work. *Painkiller* is a qualified success—the album's Achilles heel is its lyrics, which rarely depart from standard-issue odes to heavy metal rebellion and comic book/fantasy themes that sometimes cross the line into cringe-inducing silliness; it almost seems like a deliberate avoidance of any substantive content. Still, if you can ignore the lyrics, the terrific, raging performances make *Painkiller* Judas Priest's first truly satisfying album since 1982's *Screaming for Vengeance*; unfortunately, it would also be their last with Rob Halford, taking some of the triumph away from their comeback. *—Steve Huey*

● **Metal Works '73-'93** / May 18, 1993 / Columbia ✦✦✦✦✦
Although the double-disc *Metal Works '73-'93* is an intoxicating listen, it isn't quite the definitive Judas Priest retrospective it could have been. Six of the band's 11 U.K. chart singles aren't here, and while "Johnny B. Goode" probably won't be missed, *Hell Bent for Leather*'s "Take on the World" and "Evening Star," *British Steel*'s "United," and *Point of Entry*'s "Don't Go" and "Hot Rockin'" ought to have been included, especially since they were released during the band's influential prime. One could also argue for more material from the *Stained Class* era and less from the weaker mid- to late-'80s albums. Plus, the songs aren't arranged in chronological order, which makes it difficult to piece together the band's evolution and (sometimes trend-following) stylistic shifts. But quibbles aside, the collection makes a strong case for Judas Priest's versatility, drawing from nearly all of their albums' material that encompasses dark, driving riff-rockers, melodic heavy metal, radio-ready commercial hard rock, the occasional ballad, and lyrics ranging from street-tough aggression and party anthems to sci-fi/fantasy themes and hints at Satanic posturing. The band's musicianship shines throughout; Priest's tightly controlled style was played with a sense of groove that allowed the music to breathe and kept it from sounding too tight-assed. In between the lesser-known tracks, which are often impressive, comes one metal classic after another—"Victim of Changes," "Living After Midnight," "Breaking the Law," "Hell Bent for Leather," "You've Got Another Thing Comin'," "Screaming for Vengeance," and more. Even if it isn't quite a definitive portrait of the band, it is an enjoyable one; many necessary items are here, and it rocks hard from start to finish. *—Steve Huey*

The Best of Judas Priest: Living After Midnight / Feb. 3, 1998 / Columbia/Legacy ✦✦✦✦✦
While the '80s may have been littered with many second-rate pop-metal knockoffs of little musical merit, Judas Priest, decked out in leather and studs, always stood tall above the pretenders as the genuine article of metal greatness. Along with Iron Maiden, they helped lead the way of the new wave of british heavy metal and are certainly one of the best and most influential metal bands ever. *Living After Midnight: The Best of Judas Priest* provides fans with a collection of late-'70s/early-'80s hard rocking classics by one of the best in the metal business. This collection focuses on the hits of Judas Priest's career, which came mostly during the early '80s, their artistic and commercial peak. Tracks like "Living After Midnight" and the MTV favorite "You've Got Another Thing Comin'" showcase one of the band's biggest strengths, which is the ability to be melodic without losing any of their intensity or edge. The band had the ability to make you sing along while they were bludgeoning you over the head with a heavy guitar attack. Live tracks like the fist pumping "Heading Out to the Highway" and "Tyrant" feature great performances by Rob Halford, who is one of the most gifted and distinct vocalists in heavy metal history. These tracks prove that Halford's soaring octave defying vocal range is no studio creation. The brutal "Metal Meltdown" and the epic "Victim of Changes" prominently display the twin guitar attack of K.K. Downing and Glen Tipton. Many of the guitar tracks laid down by this duo throughout their career helped provide a blueprint for many shredders that followed. In true metal form, this album rarely gives you a chance to come up for air, and despite the fact that some early classic cuts are missing from this album, *Living After Midnight: The Best Of Judas Priest* is a fine collection of top rate British heavy metal by one of the true masters. *—Paul Tinelli*

Phil Judd

b. Mar. 23, 1953
Guitar / New Wave
A founding member and early creative force behind New Zealand's Split Enz, Phil Judd quickly became disillusioned with the music industry and dropped out of the band in 1977. After rejoining Split Enz and leaving again, he spent a short time with two legendary New Zealand punk bands—Suburban Reptiles and Enemy—eventually setting up his own three-piece band, Swingers. Swingers had some minor success in their homeland (including a number one hit with the unforgettable "Counting the Beat") but fell apart by the early '80s. Judd released his first and only solo album in 1982, *Private Lives* (edited down to *The Swinger* EP in the U.S.). It was virtually ignored and Judd changed directions, focusing more on composing film music and pursuing art. In 1986, he joined with former Split Enz bandmates, Nigel Griggs and Noel Crombie along with guitarist Michael Den Elzen, to form Schnell Fenster. After two albums, the group broke up in 1992. Judd has since returned to film music along with rumored future solo projects in the works. Despite consistently producing some really terrific music, Judd's eccentric approach to pop music and skewed outlook have sadly been overlooked. *—Chris Woodstra*

The Swinger / 1983 / MCA ✦✦✦
A six-song EP drawn from the Australian *Private Lives* LP. *The Swinger* picks up where Judd's previous band, the Swingers, left off. Quirky pop songs with slightly odd subject matter are the focus but with a more polished, radio-ready production. Unfortunately overlooked, this is his only solo work to date. *—Chris Woodstra*

● **Private Lives** / 1983 / Mushroom ✦✦✦✦✦
Sadly Judd's only full-length album, *Private Lives* never saw release outside of Australia/New Zealand but fans of his work with Swingers or Split Enz should seek this one out rather than the inferior, edited version—*The Swinger*. *—Chris Woodstra*

Jules & the Polar Bears

f. 1978, **db.** 1980
New Wave
After the demise of the Funky Kings, singer/songwriter Jules Shear formed his own band consisting of Stephen Hague (keyboards and, later, a noted producer), Richard Bredice (guitar), David White (bass), and David Beebe (drums). They were signed to Columbia Records in 1978 solely on the basis of Shear's demos—at the time, the band had never played live together. They recorded their first LP, *Got No Breeding*, in 1978, which quickly found critical acclaim, drawing favorable comparisons to Jackson Browne, the Kinks, Bob Dylan, and Bruce Springsteen. Unfortunately, it failed to sell when Columbia tried to lump the band in with its new wave promotion. 1979's *Fenetiks*, another fine effort, went virtually unnoticed as well. A third LP, *Bad for Business*, was recorded, but Columbia decided to pass on it and the band folded. Shear moved on to a distinguished, though commercially unsuccessful, solo career, and Hague focused on production. The albums, especially *Got No Breeding*, remain cult favorites. *Bad for Business* was finally released in late '96 by Columbia/Legacy. *—Chris Woodstra*

● **Got No Breeding** / 1978 / Columbia/Legacy ✦✦✦✦✦
Though it is packed with memorable hooks and Jules Shear's subtle twist-of-phrase, *Got No Breeding* was virtually ignored upon release, due in part to Columbia Records mis-

marketing the band as part of the new wave. The Polar Bears were, in reality, just a good, hard-working rock band jamming with a sometimes overenthusiastic Shear. The songs are among Shear's finest and the album is one of his most consistently enjoyable. —*Chris Woodstra*

Phonetics/Fenetiks / 1979 / Columbia ✦✦✦
The second Polar Bears album follows much of the same formula as *Got No Breeding*, with less memorable results. The band still rocks in places but the overall production is slicker and a little more synthesizer heavy. Shear's songwriting is top-notch ranging from the pure pop of "Good Reason" to the beautiful ballad "Real Enough to Love." His delivery seems more restrained this time around. —*Chris Woodstra*

Bad for Business / Sep. 3, 1996 / Columbia/Legacy ✦✦✦
Deemed not commercially viable and a bit on the weird side by the powers that be at Columbia Records in 1980, *Bad for Business*, the third album from Jules and the Polar Bears, remained in the Columbia vaults for 16 years before being issued in 1996. *Bad for Business* still seems somewhat quirky after all these years, although not really much more than its predecessor *Fenetiks*, with which it shares a similar sound thanks to Stephen Hague's keyboards.

The real treat in Columbia's decision to release the record is its batch of hook-laden tunes and the frenetic spurts of lyrics from Jules Shear. Songs such as the driving pop of "In Love With the Ballet" and the sweet but edgy "Only a Motion" show Shear to be in fine form on *Bad for Business*. This is a chance to further discover a terrific songwriter and one of the criminally overlooked bands of the late '70s. —*Brett Hartenbach*

July

f. 1967, **db.** 1969
British Psychedelia, Psychedelic
July started out in the early 1960's as an Ealing-based skiffle act working under the name of the Playboys, and then metamorphosed into an R&B outfit known as the Thoughts and then the Tomcats, through which John "Speedy" Keen passed as a drummer. The final Tomcats lineup, which evolved out of an unrecorded band known as the Second Thoughts, found some success in Spain when they went to play a series of gigs in Madrid in 1966. They returned to England in 1968, the group's lineup consisting of Tony Duhig on guitar, John Field on flute and keyboards, Tom Newman on vocals, Alan Jamesplaying bass, and Chris Jackson on drums, and they changed their name to July. The band lasted barely a year, leaving behind one of the most sought-after LPs of the British psychedelic boom (on the Major Minor label in England, and Epic Records in the U.S. and Canada). Their sound was a mix of trippy, lugubrious psychedelic meanderings, eerie, trippy vignettes ("Dandelion Seeds," "My Clown"), and strange, bright electric-acoustic textured tracks ("Friendly Man"), with some dazzling guitar workouts ("Crying Is for Writers") for good measure, all spiced with some elements of world music, courtesy of Tony Duhig (who has since come to regard July as an embarrassing element in his resume). Their first single, "My Clown" backed with "Dandelion Seeds," has come to be considered a classic piece of psychedelia while the album is just plain collectable, despite some shortcomings. The band separated in 1969, with Duhig moving on to Jade Warrior, Newman becoming a well-respected engineer, with Mike Oldfield's *Tubular Bells* to his credit, and bassist Alan James later working with Cat Stevens and Kevin Coyne, among others. Of the various reissues, Bam-Caruso's 1987 *Dandelion Seeds* is the most accessible, with Essex's *The Second of July* consisting of previously unissued recordings from 1967. —*Bruce Eder & Steven McDonald*

● **July** / 1968 / Epic ✦✦✦✦
This album has come to be highly prized, mainly for the presence of "My Clown," which is considered to be one of the great psychedelic singles of all time. Tom Newman, who went on to glory as the engineer of choice for Mike Oldfield, handles the vocals for the majority of the album (the exception being Chris Jackson's "Crying Is for Writers"), as well as the majority of the songwriting. Tony Duhig, who later moved on to start Jade Warrior and Assegai, provides guitars and a strong sense of Indian music, although the greater part of his participation is via warbling and groaning guitars and a fortunately blazing solo in the midst of the otherwise painful "Crying Is for Writers." Very good psychedelia, for the most part, but a bit dated in places and heavily influenced by much of the music coming from the direction of San Francisco at that time. The first six cuts are perhaps the most essential, going by the original vinyl release—"My Clown" and "Dandelion Seeds" are delightful, while "Jolly Mary" is simply good fun. —*Steven McDonald*

June of 44

f. 1994
Math Rock, Experimental Rock, Noise-Rock, Indie Rock, Post-Rock/Experimental, Alternative Pop/Rock
Partially consisting of former members of Rodan (and sounding much like that band's hard indie rock), June of 44 includes Fred Erskine (bass), Sean Meadows (vocals, guitar), Doug Scharin (drums), and Jeff Mueller (vocals, guitar). Their debut, *Engine Takes to the Water*, was released in 1995; one of the underground's more prolific bands, they returned in 1996 with *Tropics and Meridians*, followed a year later by the *Anatomy of Sharks* EP. *Four Great Points*, June of 44's most experimental effort to date, was released in 1998. *Anahata* followed a year later, as did *Fish 6*.—*John Bush*

Engine Takes to the Water / 1995 / Quarterstick ✦✦✦
June of 44 play the same Midwest-based dark indie rock as Slint and Rodan, using complex arrangements and skewed rhythms to complement their great melodies. "June Miller" and "Have a Safe Trip, Dear" are the highlights. —*John Bush*

Tropics and Meridians / Jun. 18, 1996 / Quarterstick ✦✦✦✦
Featuring current and former members of slowcore icons Codeine and post-rock bands like Rodan, Rex, and the Sonora Pine, June of 44 is proof positive that a musically incestuous scene can sometimes be a good thing. With origins in the same Louisville scene that gave birth to obvious influences Squirrel Bait and Slint, this quartet sticks more toward the rock side of the instrumental music spectrum, but with more than enough dynamic compositional elements to give them a distinctive sound. *Tropics and Meridians*, their second LP, picks up right where their formidable debut left off, with a similarly broad spectrum of song structures. "Anisette" rides along on a menacing subterranean bass groove as Jeff Mueller delivers indecipherable howling that the Jesus Lizard would be proud of, while "Lawn Bowler" conjures up the spirit of Slint with its shifting moods and creepily dissonant harmonies. "June Leaf" is damn near danceable, with a freight-train-a-rollin' rhythm and a supple guitar line that caresses you oh-so-gently, then smacks you hard across the face for getting fresh. The album is just six tracks clocking in at just over 36 minutes, but it still offers plenty of bang for your 15 bucks. —*Bret Love*

● **Four Great Points** / Jan. 20, 1998 / Quarterstick ✦✦✦✦
June of 44's fourth full-length is their most experimental effort to date—fractured melodies and dub-like rhythms collide in a noisy atmosphere rich in detail, adorned with violins, trumpet, severe phasing effects, and even a typewriter. —*Jason Ankeny*

Anahata / Jun. 8, 1999 / Quarterstick ✦✦✦✦
Experimenting with jazz and funk influences takes June of 44 in a new direction on their fourth album, *Anahata*. The songs are atmospheric, mellow, and moody with more of a groove than previous albums. The band takes a rhythm-focused approach with bass player Fred Erskine and drummer Doug Scharin using piano loops, wah-wah bass, keyboards, vibraphones, and trumpet. Scharin's metronomic drumming propels each track and gives the songs a techno-like edge. Guitars take a backseat on this album and range from quiet, melodic meandering to calculated, explosive bursts. Erskine shares vocal duties with Sean Meadows and Jeff Mueller. However, Erskine's shaky, whiny vocals are weak; Meadows and Mueller's delicate, whispering vocals are far more accessible and effective. The track, "Wear Two Eyes (Boom)," also appears on the *Anatomy of Sharks* EP, but exists here in a different form with a major trumpet emphasis. "Cardiac Atlas" and "Five Dollars in My Pocket" epitomize the band's funkier moments with heavy bass and spoken vocal delivery. In contrast, "Equators to Bi-Polar" and "Southeast Boston," are lighter, more melodic songs with breathy vocals. *Anahata* can be a difficult listen, especially when expecting June of 44's earlier material, but the album is tight, well-executed, and ultimately intriguing. —*Tracy Frey*

Fish 6 / Oct. 19, 1999 / Touch & Go ✦✦✦

Jungle Brothers

f. 1986, New York, NY
Jazz-Rap, Alternative Rap, Hip-Hop, Political Rap, Golden Age
Although they predated the jazz-rap innovations of De La Soul, A Tribe Called Quest, and Digable Planets, the Jungle Brothers were never able to score with either rap fans or mainstream audiences, perhaps due to their embrace of a range of styles—including house music, Afrocentric philosophy, a James Brown fixation, and of course, the use of jazz samples—each of which has been the sole basis for the start-up of a rap act. Signed to a major label for 1989's *Done by the Forces of Nature*, the JBs failed to connect on that album, hailed by some as an ignored classic. Their Afrocentric slant gained the Jungle Brothers entry into the Native Tongue posse, a loose collective formed by hip-hop legend Afrikaa Bambaataa, including Queen Latifah (and, later, De La Soul and A Tribe Called Quest). The Jungle Brothers' chances of mainstream acceptance weren't helped at all by a four-year absence after the release of *Done by the Forces of Nature*, inspired mostly by Warner Bros. marketing strategies. Finally, in the summer of 1993, *J Beez Wit the Remedy* appeared, complete with a sizeable push from Warner Bros.; unfortunately, the large amount of promotion failed to carry the album. Obviously not learning from their earlier mistakes, Warner Bros. also delayed the release of the group's fourth album, *Raw Deluxe*, until mid-1997. —*John Bush*

● **Straight Out the Jungle** / 1988 / Warlock ✦✦✦✦✦
The trio's debut is powered by muscular funk riffs underpinned by an Afrocentric sensibility and a sharp sense of humor. —*John Floyd*

Done by the Forces of Nature / Nov. 1989 / Warner Brothers ✦✦✦✦✦
By injecting some vocal delicacy and some clever samples into their moderately militant message, they made a second album that elaborates on their own winning formula. —*John Floyd*

J. Beez Wit the Remedy / Jun. 22, 1993 / Warner Brothers ✦✦✦
Nearly four years after *Done by the Forces of Nature*, the Jungle Brothers return with a hazy, funky album, filled with their brand of literate hip-hop. Although they've made some stylistic progressions since the last record, it wasn't enough to be a completely groundbreaking release, nor was it commericial enough to break them out of their critically acclaimed/cult status. Instead, it was another solid, inventive album that didn't receive the attention it deserved. —*Stephen Thomas Erlewine*

Raw Deluxe / Jun. 3, 1997 / Gee Street ✦✦✦
The Jungle Brothers' career was plagued with delays and setbacks, which resulted in each of their albums being released several years after they were officially due. Their fourth effort, *Raw Deluxe*, is no different. The Jungle Brothers remain one of hip-hop's most inventive crews, crafting remarkably sophisticated, jazzy beats and rhyming with skill and intelligence, but they sound more as if they were aligned with late-'80s trends, not the styles of the late '90s. This isn't a bad thing, since they are musically and lyrically gifted,

but it also makes *Raw Deluxe* sound more like an artifact than a blazing comeback. —*Stephen Thomas Erlewine*

V.I.P. / Jan. 4, 2000 / V2 ✦✦✦✦

Even though the JBs originated the highly influential Native Tongues clique (De La Soul, A Tribe Called Quest), their ten-year run of musical mischief has been anything but native. Spearheaded by the acid beats of the Propellerheads' Alex Gifford, their latest foray, *V.I.P.*, is yet another experimental set, one that highlights the exquisite chemistry of group members Baby Bam and Mike G. While the JBs don't fit the traditional hip-hop image, that's part of their appeal, as their innocent, party-oriented raps hold one purpose—to get your back up off the wall. —*Matt Conaway*

Mickey Jupp

b. 1940

Vocals, Keyboards, Songwriter, Guitar / Pub Rock, Rock & Roll

Like Dave Edmunds, guitarist/pianist/vocalist Mickey Jupp was a champion of traditional rock & roll during the late '70s, a time when it had been all but discarded. Unlike Edmunds, Jupp wrote the majority of his own material, which updated '50s rock & roll with a tongue-in-cheek irony.

Jupp began his career with the Essex-based British R&B group theOrioles in the early '60s. The band earned a devoted local following in the early '60s, yet they were never had the opportunity to record. The Orioles broke up late in 1965, after Jupp was arrested for not making alimony payments to his wife. Three years later, he returned to music, forming Legend, who laid the groundwork for the English pub rock of the early '70s. Following the release of their third album in 1971, Legend disbanded and Jupp took another lengthy break from music. When he was coaxed back into performing in 1975 by Lee Brileaux, the lead singer of Dr. Feelgood, pub rock was in its last days, yet Jupp was well respected in the scene, since both Ducks Deluxe and Dr. Feelgood had recorded versions of his songs ("Cheque Book" and "Down at the Doctors," respectively).

Jupp released his first solo single, "Nature's Radio," on Arista Records in 1978. The single led to a contract with Stiff Records, who released the "Old Rock & Roller" single and the *Juppanese* album in 1978; the bulk of *Juppanese* was recorded and produced by Nick Lowe. Released the same year as his debut, *Mickey Jupp's Legend* featured material from his previous band. Following the release of *Juppanese*, Jupp joined Stiff's Rail Tour, although he left the lineup before it hit the U.S. because he was afraid of flying. Shortly afterward, he left Stiff Records and signed with Chrysalis in 1979. The same year he released *Long Distance Romancer*, which was produced by for 10cc members Kevin Godley and Lol Creme; like *Juppanese*, it failed to gain a large audience. Jupp moved over to A&M Records in 1982, releasing *Some People Can't Dance*. After releasing one more record on A&M, 1983's *Shampoo Haircut and Shave*, he was dropped from the label. Jupp spent the rest of the '80s and '90s touring the U.K., releasing the occasional album on independent labels. —*Stephen Thomas Erlewine*

● **Juppanese** / 1978 / Stiff ✦✦✦✦✦

Before he released his first solo album in 1978, Mickey Jupp's reputation as a songwriter had begun to grow, as pub rockers like Dr. Feelgood and Ducks Deluxe were covering his compositions. As a performer, Jupp didn't fare as well. The main problem with *Juppanese*, his first solo album, is his lifeless vocals. The first half of *Juppanese* was recorded with Rockpile, the rock & roll group fronted by guitarist Dave Edmunds and bassist Nick Lowe. Because Jupp's strength is standard three-chord rock & roll, the first side of the album works the best; while it never captures the joyous energy of Rockpile's best moments, it is considerably tighter and rawer than the slick second side, where Jupp's nondescript voice struggles to be heard amid the studio professionalism. Even though it features several of Jupp's finest songs, including "You'll Never Get Me up in One of Those" and "Old Rock & Roller," *Juppanese* doesn't include "Switchboard Susan," arguably his best song. Rockpile recorded the backing track for the album, yet Jupp refused to sing on it. Nick Lowe kept the tape, recording his own vocals for the song; his version is included on his 1979 album *Labour of Lust*. —*Stephen Thomas Erlewine*

Long Distance Romancer / 1979 / Chrysalis ✦✦✦

Long Distance Romancer, Jupp's first release for Chrysalis Records, continued the polished rock & roll of the second half of *Juppanese*, except it bettered it. Unlike Gary Brooker, producers Godley And Creme could exploit the slick, synth-based sound that Jupp was beginning to mine. However, the highly produced sound doesn't mesh with Jupp's main strength—direct, simple rock & roll. Instead of being powered by a driving beat, "Switchboard Susan" winds up sinking in the layers of keyboards and processed guitars. Yet the production does manage to save slight songs like "You Made a Fool out of Me," creating an album of pleasant pop/rock that never manges to really sink in. —*Stephen Thomas Erlewine*

Jurassic 5

f. 1993, Los Angeles, CA

Turntablism, Underground Rap, Alternative Rap, Hip-Hop

Though there's actually six of them, Jurassic 5 got everything else right on their self-titled debut EP. Part of the new rap underground of the late '90s (along with Company Flow, Mos Def, Doctor Octagon, and Sir Menelik), the sextet—rappers Marc 7even, Chali 2na, Zaakir, and Akil, plus producers Cut Chemist and DJ Nu-Mark—came together in 1993 at the Los Angeles cafe/venue named the Good Life. The six members were part of two different crews, Rebels of Rhythm and Unity Committee; after collaborating on a track, they combined into Jurassic 5 and debuted in 1995 with the "Unified Rebellion" single for TVT Records. At the tail end of 1997, the *Jurassic 5 EP* appeared and was hailed by critics as one of the freshest debuts of the year (if not the decade). Both Cut Chemist and Chali 2na are also part of the Latin-hop collective Ozomatli, while Chemist himself has recorded several mix-tapes plus the wide-issue album *Future Primitive Soundsession* (with Shortkut from Invisibl Skratch Piklz). The year 2000 found the group on tour with Fiona Apple and on the Warped Festival, just in time for the release of *Quality Control* that summer. —*John Bush*

● **Jurassic 5 EP** / Oct. 13, 1997 / Rumble/Pickininny ✦✦✦✦✦

Clocking in at just about one-third the running time of your average rap album circa 1997, Jurassic 5's debut was the most refreshing hip-hop release of the year, and not just because it abandoned the epic-length concepts of the rap mainstream. With old-school vibes to spare, excellent rhythmic raps, and the production genius of Cut Chemist and DJ Nu-Mark, *EP* finally delivered on all the diverse talents promised by the growing hip-hop underground. "Jayou" is a flute-loop classic, and "Concrete Schoolyard" has that nostalgic "can it all be so simple" vibe so rarely heard from hip-hop. —*John Bush*

Quality Control / Jun. 6, 2000 / Interscope ✦✦✦✦✦

In June 2000, almost seven years after their formation, underground rap's most lauded crew finally hit with a full-length. Great expectations aside, *Quality Control* hits all the same highs as Jurassic 5's excellent EP of three years earlier, stretching out their resume to nearly an hour with a few turntablist jaunts from resident beat-jugglers DJ Nu-Mark and Cut Chemist. The formula is very similar to the EP, with the group usually going through a couple of lines of five-man harmonics before splitting off for tongue-twister solos from Zaakir, Chali 2na, Akil, and Mark 7even. As expected, there are plenty of nods to old-school rap, from "LAUSD," with its brief tribute to hip-hop classic "The Bridge" by MC Shan, to "Monkey Bars," where the group claim inspiration (yet just a bit of distance) from their heroes: "Now you know us but it's not the Cold Crush, four MC's so it ain't the Furious / Not the Force MCs or the three from Treacherous, it's a blast from the past from the moment we bust." Where *Quality Control* really laps previous Jurassic 5 material is not only the lyrical material, though, but the themes and focus of the message tracks "Lausd," "World of Entertainment (Woe Is Me)," and "Contribution." The four-man crew take on major media and the responsibilities of adulthood with a degree of authority, eloquence, and compassion never before heard in rap music. (Just check out the lyrics to any of the above three at an online archive like www.ohhla.com). Though critics and uptight rap purists might fault them for not pushing the progression angle enough, Jurassic 5's rhymes are so devastating and the productions (by Nu-Mark and Cut Chemist) follow the raps so closely it certainly doesn't matter whether the group are old-school or not. —*John Bush*

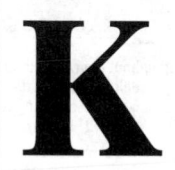

K-Ci & JoJo

f. 1997
Urban, Hip-Hop

K-Ci & JoJo, a solo project for one of the two brother teams which make up Jodeci, specifically Cedric "K-Ci" and Joel "JoJo" Hailey, followed up their group success with a 1997 album, *Love Always*. Emphasizing lush R&B ballads a bit more than on Jodeci records, the Haileys debuted as K-Ci & JoJo in mid-1996 on 2Pac's single "How Do U Want It," which spent two weeks at number one on the pop charts and sold over two million copies. Their first solo single was "How Could You," and "You Bring Me Up" hit the Top 40 in August 1997, just after the release of K-Ci & JoJo's debut album, *Love Always*. *It's Real* followed two years later and *X* was released in late 2000. —*John Bush*

● **Love Always** / Jun. 17, 1997 / MCA ◆◆◆

After becoming two of the best-known R&B singers of the 1990s as half of Jodeci, brothers K-Ci & JoJo Hailey formed a cohesive duo for *Love Always*. A definite surprise to Jodeci fans, the CD contains few traces of new jack swing and lacks the type of suggestive, R-rated lyrics the foursome had become known for. It was clear that the great soul music of the 1970s was very much on K-Ci & JoJo's minds when they made this album, an unpretentious collection of ballads and slow jams that isn't mind-blowing, but is definitely above average. In contrast to the homogenized nature of so much '90s R&B, things are refreshingly organic on such cuts as "Now and Forever," "Still Waiting" and "Baby Come Back." And an impressive cover of L.T.D.'s 1976 hit "Love Ballad" may very well be the best thing the Hailey brothers have ever done—inside or outside of Jodeci. —*Alex Henderson*

It's Real / Jun. 22, 1999 / MCA ◆◆◆

K-Ci & JoJo's first album *Love Always* established the Jodeci refugees as fine R&B vocalists, blending classic soul traditions with contemporary urban production and technique. Blessed with strong sales and good reviews, *Love Always* became a hit, setting up high expectations for the duo's second album, *It's Real*. For those expecting a flat-out masterpiece, *It's Real* will disappoint, primarily because it doesn't so much as expand on past glories as it simply replicates them. Since they're good singers with generally good material, this isn't a problem, even if it makes it all seem a little too pat and predictable. Occasionally, the Hailey brothers decide to rely a little bit too much on their impressive vocal technique, taking off on soaring glissanados that ultimately distract as much as they impress. That, combined with the stylistic similarity of the material, makes *It's Real* bog down a little bit, but the very best moments—"Makin' Me Say Goodbye," "I Wanna Get to Know You," "How Long Must I Cry," "Hello Darlin'," among others—are contemporary urban romantic soul at its finest, which is reason enough to hear the disc. —*Stephen Thomas Erlewine*

X / Dec. 5, 2000 / MCA ◆◆◆

X is the Roman numeral for ten, and this late-2000 release is titled *X* because it marks Cedric "K-Ci" Hailey and Joel "JoJo" Hailey's tenth anniversary in the recording business—first as two-thirds of the trio Jodeci, then as the duo K-Ci & JoJo. *X*, the duo's third album, isn't a radical departure from its two previous albums; like 1997's *Love Always* and 1999's double-platinum *It's Real*, this CD emphasizes romantic material and combines a high-tech urban contemporary production style with an appreciation of classic soul. K-Ci & JoJo were never a carbon copy of Jodeci, and *X* won't be mistaken for *Diary of a Mad Band*. Though *X* contains a few hip-hop-minded, up-tempo selections (including "Game Face" and "Thug N U Thug N Me"), romantic ballads and slow jams are dominant. A few of the tunes are retro-soul gems—especially "Wanna Do You Right" and the Bobby Womack-influenced "I Can't Find the Words"—although most of the time, *X* is merely decent urban contemporary. One thing that's never in doubt is the Hailey brothers' skills as vocalists; while a lot of urban contemporary artists get over on image alone, K-Ci & JoJo really do have impressive vocal ranges. *X* isn't a masterpiece, but unlike all of the urban artists who have nothing more than image and attitude going for them, the Hailey siblings bring some genuine talent to this generally pleasant, if predictable, CD. —*Alex Henderson*

Ernie K-Doe (Ernest Kador Jr.)

b. Feb. 22, 1936, New Orleans, LA, **d.** Jul. 5, 2001, New Orleans, LA
Vocals, Songwriter / New Orleans R&B, R&B

New Orleans vocalist Ernest Kador Jr., had one unforgettable R&B hit in 1961, aided by Benny Spellman's authoritative bass vocal. "Mother-In-Law" topped the charts for five weeks, and was recorded for Minit. K-Doe originally sang with The Blue Diamonds, who recorded for Savoy in 1954. Their ranks included Huey "Piano" Smith, Billy Tate, Frank Fields and Earl Palmer. "Te-Ta-Te-Ta-Ta" did reasonably well as a follow-up single, peaking at number 21. It would be six years before K-Doe would get another chart hit; the

singles "Later for Tomorrow" and a remake of "Until the Real Thing Comes Along" each gained only marginal success for Duke in 1967, his last releases to make any national noise. —*Ron Wynn*

● **Burn! K-Doe, Burn!** / 1989 / Charly ◆◆◆◆◆

This CD contains 24 Ernie K-Doe tracks recorded from 1960-1963. It includes Minit and Instant singles, plus Charly album tracks, and has two takes of "Mother-In-Law," plus "A Certain Girl" and others. The songs were produced by Allen Toussaint. —*Roundup Newsletter*

Kajagoogoo

f. 1982, **db.** 1985
New Romantic, New Wave, Synth Pop

Kajagoogoo's light synth-pop and pretty, photogenic look made the group an instant sensation in the early days of MTV. Led by vocalist Limahl (born Chris Hamill), the group also featured Steve Askew (guitar), Nick Beggs (vocals, bass), and Stuart Crawford (vocals, synthesizer). Produced by Duran Duran's Nick Rhodes, Kajagoogoo's debut single "Too Shy" hit number one in the U.K. in early 1983; it peaked at number five in the U.S. "Too Shy" and the following album *White Feathers* proved the band may have shared some similarities with Duran Duran and Naked Eyes—they were pretty and they played immediately accessible, polished pop—yet Kajagoogoo was essentially a synth-pop variation of a bubblegum group. Like a bubblegum group, they were destined to have only one big hit; "Ooh to Be Ah" and "Hang on Now" both were Top 15 U.K. hits, yet neither made an impact in the U.S. At the end of the 1983, Limahl left for a solo career. Kajagoogoo continued with Nick Beggs as the lead vocalist, releasing *Islands* in 1984; it disappeared from the charts quickly. Meanwhile, Limahl scored a hit with the theme song from *The Neverending Story*. Perhaps in an attempt to gain some credibility, the group shortened their name to Kaja and released *Crazy People's Right to Speak*. It was a sales disaster and the band broke up the following year. Limahl continued to record, albeit without much chart success; eventually, his records were not released in either the U.S. or the U.K.—his last album, 1992's *Love Is Blind*, was only released in Germany. —*Stephen Thomas Erlewine*

White Feathers / 1983 / One Way ◆◆◆◆

"Too Shy" was one of the flimsiest singles of the new wave era, a cloying and catchy bubblegum tune disguised as synth-pop. Kajagoogoo never quite matched those heights again—in fact, they rarely even came close. Their debut album *White Feathers* is filled with similarly lightweight synth-pop like "Magician Man," "Ooh to Be Ah," "Eronomics," "This Car Is Fast" and the theme song "Kajagoogoo." All of these are pleasantly danceable in a sub-Duran Duran fashion, but they are also frequently inane and ridiculous, and are of no use to anyone but hardcore new wave fetishists. —*Stephen Thomas Erlewine*

Islands / 1984 / EMI ◆◆◆

Limahl departed Kajagoogoo at the earliest opportunity, leaving the group to pursue the stardom that was destined to be his. Of course, fate decided that Limahl would be banished to obscurity after recording the theme for *The Never-Ending Story*, but his former band joined the ranks of the forgotten much sooner. Replacing Limahl with vocalist Nick Beggs, the group replicated the lightweight, danceable synth-pop of its debut on their second album, *Islands*, with one crucial difference—this time, there are no hooks. And without hooks or Limahl's campy, fey star appeal, Kajagoogoo's music just disappears into thin air. —*Stephen Thomas Erlewine*

● **Too Shy: The Singles . . . & More** / Sep. 7, 1993 / EMI ◆◆◆◆◆

As this collection proves, Kajagoogoo was a one-hit wonder. Only "Too Shy" stands out amidst the slick, bouncy new wave synth-pop that dominates the compilation, which covers material from all of the band's albums, as well as lead singer Limahl's solo career. Most of the music on the rest of the collection is pleasant, but none of it is memorable. However, "Too Shy" is one of the best pop singles of the new wave era, driven by layers of bubbly synths, an inanely catchy chorus and Limahl's thin, airy vocals. —*Stephen Thomas Erlewine*

Kaleidoscope

f. 1964, **db.** 1970
Psychedelic

No relation to the far better known American Kaleidoscope, though this British group was also psychedelic, and was active at almost exactly the same time in the late '60s. Highly esteemed by some collectors, Kaleidoscope epitomized certain of the more precious traits of British psychedelia with their fairytale lyrics and gentle, swirling folky sound. At times they sound like a far more melodic and accessible Incredible String Band. Their folky ballads have aged best, and although there's some period charm to be found throughout their two albums, it's all a bit too cloying to rank among the finest unknown psychedelia. Although they had a solid underground reputation in Britain, they never found wide success, and evolved into a similar group, Fairfield Parlour, by the end of the '60s. —*Richie Unterberger*

● **Tangerine Dream** / 1967 / Fontana ✦✦✦✦✦
Probably has the edge as the best of their two albums, but not by much. Includes several of their best songs: "Flight From Ashiya," "Dive Into Yesterday," "The Murder Of Lewis Tollani," and especially the fragile ballad "Please Excuse My Face." —*Richie Unterberger*

Faintly Blowing / 1969 / Fontana ✦✦✦
There's really not much difference between this and their debut album: if you like one, you'll like the other. It's perhaps more fully produced than their maiden effort, the stand-out being the ballad "Poem," which vies with "Please Excuse My Face" as their best composition. —*Richie Unterberger*

Kaleidoscope

f. 1966, **db.** 1970
Folk-Rock, Psychedelic, Blues-Rock
Kaleidoscope were arguably the most eclectic band of the psychedelic era, weaving together folk, blues, Middle Eastern, and acid more often and seamlessly than any other musicians. The California group were formed under the nucleus of multi-instrumentalists David Lindley and Chris Darrow in the mid-'60s. Adding fiddle, banjo, and various exotic string instruments such as the oud and saz to the traditional rock lineup, Kaleidoscope complemented their experimental sounds with taut and witty (if lyrically eccentric) songwriting. With the exception of their mawkish forays into old-timey music, Kaleidoscope's work holds up well. Their first three albums were their best, highlighted by the lengthy tracks "Taxim" and "Seven-Ate Sweet," which are groundbreaking fusions of Middle Eastern music and rock. Kaleidoscope were a popular live act, even incorporating some flamenco and belly dancers into their performances. But in commercial terms their very eclecticism probably worked against them. Hit singles, too, were a difficult proposition for such a versatile group to get to grips with, although several of their 45s were pretty good. —*Richie Unterberger*

Side Trips / Jun. 1967 / Epic ✦✦✦✦✦
This erratic but largely satisfying debut album unveiled a band capable of invigorating fusions of Middle Eastern music with touches of psychedelic and harmony pop, combining instruments such as the dulcimer, Dobro, mandolin, sax, and banjo in ways that had rarely been heard in either folk or rock. The end result was actually fairly psychedelic, and this record has some of their most worthy efforts, including "Egyptian Garden," "Please," and the spooky "Oh Death." Much less impressive were the old-time blues and jugband numbers such as "Minnie the Moocher." This LP would rate higher but for the presence of seven of the best ten tracks on the British *Bacon From Mars* compilation, a much better investment, and probably easier to find than the long out-of-print original Epic album. —*Richie Unterberger*

A Beacon from Mars / Jan. 1968 / Epic ✦✦✦
Kaleidoscope's second album is the best non-compilation showcase of their legendary eclecticism and versatility. It takes in a blues-rocking cover of Willie Cobbs' "You Don't Love Me"; Doug Kershaw's Cajun "Louisiana Man"; a scary old folk song ("Greenwood Sidee," about a woman who kills her two babies); a hilarious countryish indictment of marriage ("Baldheaded End of a Broom"); two good acid-folk originals ("Life Will Pass You By" and "I Found Out"); and two completely dissimilar 10-minute-plus originals: the Middle Eastern "Taxim" and the psychedelic workout "Beacon from Mars." Every one of these disparate styles is performed with authority and commitment, and the result still has the power to amaze. —*Stephen Raiteri*

The Incredible Kaleidoscope / Jun. 1969 / Epic ✦✦✦
Coming out of the San Francisco scene of the late '60s, Kaleidoscope melds rock, blues and middle eastern rhythms together to form a rather interesting kaleidoscope of sound. This first release includes a cover of Howlin' Wolf's "Killing Floor" along with what would become something of a highlight from this band called "Seven-Ate Sweet." Oh, and for those who are interested, Kaleidoscope boasts David Lindley as a member. Good, but now sounding dated, it is worth your while. —*James Chrispell*

Bacon from Mars / Aug. 1983 / Edsel ✦✦✦
A good compilation focusing on Kaleidoscope's best shorter tracks, including songs from their first three albums and three non-LP tracks. There's folk-rock, blues-rock, country, psychedelia, acid-folk, and Cajun- and Middle-Eastern-inspired music. The single "Nobody" finds the band backing R&B stars Larry Williams and Johnny "Guitar" Watson on a song also recorded by Three Dog Night; says Chris Darrow in the (extensive) liner notes, "too far out for the black stations, and too far out for the white stations." [This album has been superseded by *Blues from Baghdad: The Very Best of Kaleidoscope*, which contains *A Beacon from Mars* in its entirety.] —*Stephen Raiteri*

Rampe Rampe / Jun. 1984 / Edsel ✦✦✦
A compilation of the band's longer recordings, none of which were featured on Edsel's other Kaleidoscope collection *A Beacon from Mars*. All three—"Beacon From Mars" and "Taxim" from *A Beacon From Mars* and "Seven-Ate Sweet" from *Incredible Kaleidoscope*—are virtuoso displays. Also included are two other stray tracks, "Greenwood Sidee" (from *Beacon*) and the Middle Eastern instrumental B-side "Rampe Rampe." This collection (minus "Taxim") has been combined with Edsel's other Kaleidoscope compilation, *A Beacon From Mars*, on one CD, called *Blues From Baghdad: The Very Best of Kaleidoscope*. —*Stephen Raiteri*

Egyptian Candy (A Collection) / 1990 / Epic/Legacy ✦✦✦✦✦

An anthology from this most eclectic group of the 1960s, featuring some of the band's wildly diverse best moments alongside two rarities (the single version of "Why Try" and the rocking B-side "Elevator Man") and three previously unreleased tracks. Of the new songs, "Love Games" is as close to pop-psych as the band ever came; "Egyptian Candy" is almost as close, with a Middle Eastern touch; and "Sefan" is another in the band's line of Middle Eastern-inspired instrumentals. A worthwhile collection, but some good stuff is missing; see *Blues From Baghdad: The Very Best of Kaleidoscope* for a more extensive survey. —*Stephen Raiteri*

Blues from Baghdad: The Very Best of Kaleidoscope / Dec. 12, 1995 / Edsel ✦✦✦✦
This is a combination of Edsel's two previous Kaleidoscope compilations, *A Beacon From Mars* and *Rampe Rampe* (minus one track, the lengthy instrumental "Taxim"). At 78-plus minutes, it's the best and most extensive survey of Kaleidoscope's diverse work, encompassing traditional folk songs, folk-rock, country, acid-folk, blues-rock, psychedelic rock of several flavors, and Cajun and Middle Eastern music. Incredibly, the band did all of these things well, applying virtuosity on not only traditional rock band instruments, but also violin, banjo, harp guitar, oud, and others. A fascinating collection by a band that suffered in obscurity, but deserved much better. This was world music before the genre had a name. —*Stephen Raiteri*

● **Infinite Colours Infinite Patterns: The Best of Kaleidoscope** / Jul. 10, 2001 / Edsel ✦✦✦✦✦

Kalin Twins

b. Feb. 16, 1934, Port Jervis, NY
Close Harmony, Rock & Roll
Herbert and Harold Kalin, twin brother harmony singers, sang like a pop-focused version of the Everly Brothers, and they charted a few catchy records in 1958, including one Top Five hit. They represent one of the better acts to find a compromise between rock & roll and pop music, even if they weren't the Everlys by a long shot. Although Herbert and Harold Kalin were born in the same period as Elvis Presley, they came from more of a middle-class background, and from much further north as well. Not surprisingly, their musical preferences lay more with the pop music that preceded Elvis (so, to some degree, did Elvis' own taste), and their music was closer in spirit to that tamer third wave of rock & roll, exemplified by Bobby Darin, Paul Anka, and Dion DiMucci. The Kalins' first recording session took place in December of 1957, by which time the rock & roll boom was in full swing—the record company wanted them to compete for the teen market and insisted that they try something close in spirit and beat to the newer sounds. Their first session yielded a trio of songs that went nowhere, but they struck gold three months later with "When," a catchy romantic pop-rocker with a good beat (originally intended as a B-side) that rose to number five in the United States and number one in England. They appeared on *The Milt Grant Show*, Washington's answer to *American Bandstand*, and became nationally known, appearing on the typical package tours of the period. As the 1960s dawned, the Kalins moved away from teen-oriented numbers, preferring to perform more mature material. —*Bruce Eder*

● **When** / 1984 / Bear Family ✦✦✦✦✦
For once, Bear Family Records has compromised on a retrospective—the Kalin Twins left behind 38 songs, but only 30 of them are here, obviously to hold this to a single disc. Some of the stuff not present includes their covers of Gene Pitney's "Loneliness" and Jackie DeShannon's "Trouble," but there's some fascinating material in its place—the unreleased 1960 vintage "Make Love To Me" was a sincere attempt to give the duo a more mature sound, and their never-before-issued version of "Bye Bye Blackbird" has a surprise or two. "When" is the best known song here, and it's surrounded by some pleasant, lively teen pop ("Bubbles," "Schoolbell Dream"), but the country-rocker "Picture of You" is also very worthwhile. And "It's Only The Beginning" is one of the most unabashedly beautiful and achingly romantic pieces of pop-rock of the period that one is likely ever to hear. Some of this is too sappy for words ("True Love"), but it's still enjoyable overall. The order of the material is a bit haphazard, skipping around between years and sessions, but that can be fixed with some player programming. —*Bruce Eder*

Kansas

f. 1970, Topeka, KS
Album Rock, Arena Rock, Prog-Rock/Art Rock
Fusing the complexity of British prog-rock with an American heartland sound representative of their name, Kansas was among the most popular bands of the late 1970s; though typically dismissed by critics, many of the group's hits remain staples of AOR radio playlists to this day. Formed in Topeka in 1970, the founding members of the group—guitarist Kerry Livgren, bassist Dave Hope and drummer Phil Ehart—first played together while in high school; with the 1971 addition of violinist Robby Steinhardt, they changed their name to White Clover, reverting back to the Kansas moniker for good upon the 1972 arrivals of vocalist/keyboardist Steve Walsh and guitarist Richard Williams.

Kansas' self-titled debut LP appeared in 1974; their fan base grew to the point that their third effort, 1975's *Masque*, sold a quarter of a million copies. In 1976, *Leftoverture* truly catapulted Kansas to stardom. On the strength of the smash hit "Carry on Wayward Son," the album reached the Top Five and sold over three million copies. 1977's *Point of Know Return* was even more successful, spawning the monster hit "Dust in the Wind." *Monolith*, the band's first self-produced effort, also reached the Top Ten.

In the wake of 1980's *Audio-Visions*, Kansas began to splinter; Walsh soon quit to form a new band, Streets; the remaining members forged on without him, tapping vocalist John Elefante as his replacement. The group disbanded after only two albums, 1982's *Vinyl Confessions* and 1983's *Drastic Measures*. In 1986, however, Kansas re-formed around Ehart, Williams and Walsh; adding guitarist Steve Morse as well as bassist Billy Greer, the refurbished band debuted with the album *Power*. When the follow-up, 1988's In the Spirit of the Things, failed to hit, seven years passed before the release of their next effort, *Freaks of Nature*. *Always Never the Same* followed in 1998. Seeing the return of founder singer/songwriter Kerry Livgren, *Somewhere to Elsewhere* was released in 2000. *—Jason Ankeny*

Kansas / Mar. 1974 / Epic/Legacy ♦♦♦♦
Kansas stood apart from their peers, since they were an American band that dared play on the epic scale of such English art rockers as Genesis. Consequently, *Kansas* is a truly weird hybrid of British pomp, doggedly artistic concept, and arena-boogie, all served up with more violin than there is flute on a Jethro Tull album. It's hard not to admire their blatant ambition in one sense, since few bands try as hard as Kansas does here. Still, there are a lot of scales and arpeggios, galloping triplets, dramatic organ, and stately ballads that signify nothing and go nowhere. Since it's as grounded in boogie as it is in art, the group never gets as weird as their more interesting counterparts, but that reliance on arena rock does make them unique. But uniqueness isn't the same as good, or even interesting listening, even if *Kansas* remains a period piece like no other. *—Stephen Thomas Erlewine*

Song for America / Oct. 1974 / Kirshner ♦♦♦♦

Masque / Oct. 1975 / Columbia ♦♦♦
Kansas' third album, *Masque*, is a lyrically dark effort courtesy of guitarist/keyboardist Kerry Livgren's brooding songwriting. Musically, *Masque* foreshadows the tight melodies and instrumental interplay on the next two albums, *Leftoverture* and *Point of Know Return*, which together serve as the peak of Kansas' vision. The band deserves more respect than they get for incorporating British hard rock and progressive rock to become the only U.S. progressive-rock band of note during the genre's 1970s heyday. Robby Steinhardt's violin work certainly helped give Kansas a distinctive sound. The liner notes indicate *Masque* is a "concept album" thanks to the title's definition: "A disguise of reality created through a theatrical or musical performance." Vocalist/keyboardist Steve Walsh's "It Takes a Woman's Love (To Make a Man)" is the leadoff track, and it's atypical of the rest of the album. The song is a fairly basic, yet groovy, pop-rock tune about musicians' loneliness on the road, but it is spiced up with some saxophone lines. "Two Cents Worth" addresses guilt, misery, and spiritual longing—pretty heavy stuff for six guys who were only in their mid-20s. In "Icarus-Borne on Wings of Steel," Kansas' prog-rock ambitions show through the mythology-based lyrics and the densely arranged guitars and keyboards. Walsh and Steinhardt's "All the World" is largely a bleak examination of loneliness and death, although it does end with a glimmer of hope. "Child of Innocence" is a tough blast of hard rock with a soaring chorus. "Mysteries and Mayhem" rocks along, yet it's rich with haunting nightmare imagery and biblical references. The nine-and-a-half-minute epic "The Pinnacle" closes the album. [The 2001 CD reissue on Epic/Legacy adds previously unreleased demos of "Child of Innocence" and "It's You."] *—Bret Adams*

Leftoverture / Oct. 1976 / Epic/Legacy ♦♦♦♦♦
For any art rock band, the fourth album means it's time for a self-styled masterpiece—if you need proof, look at *Selling England By the Pound* or *Fragile*. So, with Kansas, the most determinedly arty of all American art rock bands, they composed and recorded *Leftoverture*, an impenetrable conundrum of significance that's capped off by nothing less than a five-part suite, appropriately titled "Magnum Opus," and featuring such promising movement titles as "Father Padilla Meets the Perfect Gnat" and "Release the Beavers." Of course, there's no telling whether this closing opus relates to the opener "Carry on Wayward Son," the greatest single Kansas every cut—a song that manages to be pompous, powerful, ridiculous, and catchy all at once. That they never manage to rival it anywhere on this record is as much a testament to their crippling ambition as their lack of skills. And it's unfair to say Kansas is unskilled, since they are certainly instrumentally proficient and they can craft songs or, rather, compositions that appear rather ambitious. Except these compositions aren't particularly complex, rhythmically or harmonically, and are in their own way as ambling as boogie rock, which still feels to be their foundation. It's not really fair to attack Kansas for a concept album with an impenetrable concept—it's possible to listen to *Lamb Lies Down on Broadway* hundreds of times and not know what the hell Rael is up to—but there's neither hooks or true grandiosity here to make it interesting. That said, this still may be Kansas' most consistent set, outside of *Point of Know Return*. Take that for what you will. [The 2001 CD reissue on Epic/Legacy adds a previously unreleased 1978 live version of "Carry on Wayward Son" and a previously unreleased 1977 live version of "Cheyenne Anthem."] *—Stephen Thomas Erlewine*

Point of Know Return / 1977 / Kirshner ♦♦♦♦
This is the definitive Kansas recording and includes their most famous tune, "Dust in the Wind." The band is in peak form and also churned out the single "Point Of Know Return," which is still played daily on classic rock stations. While their pop-oriented approach and standard rock guitar sound helped define the classic rock sound of the '70s, careful listening reveals that this band's talent goes beyond colleagues such as Bachman Turner Overdrive and Boston. Their arrangements and time signatures more accurately reflect the music of Yes and Emerson, Lake and Palmer. "Paradox" and "The Spider" are both excellent examples of their progressive approach. Unfortunately, the band always struggled to maintain a healthy balance of progression combined with pop. That made for such awkward moments here as "Portrait (He Knew)" and "Lightning's Hand." Yet despite the minor inconsistencies and a dated sound, their interplay and superior musicianship make this both an essential classic rock and progressive rock recording. *—Robert Taylor*

Two for the Show / 1978 / Kirshner ♦♦

Monolith / 1979 / Kirshner ♦

Audio-Visions / 1980 / Epic/Legacy ♦♦♦

Vinyl Confessions / 1982 / Epic/Legacy ♦♦♦

Drastic Measures / Jul. 1983 / Epic/Legacy ♦♦

Power / 1986 / MCA ♦♦♦

In the Spirit of Things / 1988 / MCA ♦♦♦
Kansas hired Bob Ezrin to tighten up their sound for 1988's *In the Spirit of Things*. In a strange way, the timing was opportune, since they had a hit in 1986's *Power*, and 1988 was welcome to veterans, thanks to the boom of classic rock radio stations and the rejuvenating power of the CD. And, give 'em credit—they wound up with an album that's arguably more focused than their '70s highlights. That doesn't mean it's on par, since they can't deliver a hit single as good as "Carry on Wayward Son" and "Point of Know Return," and whatever remnants of humor they had are gone, as this is doggedly somber. Still, they're musically more adept, thanks to Ezrin and guitarist Steve Morse, which is welcome. That doesn't mean it's an unqualified success, however, since the cavernous, DDD-wannabe production screams '88 even more than *Leftoverture* epitomizes 1976, and many of the songs in and of themselves. Nevertheless, *In the Spirit of Things* remains one of the group's more consistent albums and easily a latter-day highlight. [BTW: Brendan O'Brien, a superstar producer of the '90s, working with Pearl Jam and Stone Temple Pilots, recorded this record.] *—Stephen Thomas Erlewine*

Box Set / Jul. 12, 1994 / Epic/Legacy ♦♦♦♦
The Kansas Boxed Set is a double-disc, 26-track that contains all of the group's most popular songs—"Carry On Wayward Son," "Dust In the Wind," "Point of Know Return," "Hold On"—plus three previously unreleased live tracks, one demo and the newly recorded "Wheels." Collectors will certainly want those tracks, but they'll probably be frustrated by the album-rock staples that dominate the album. Conversely, most casual Kansas fans will be satisfied by the single-disc *Greatest Hits*, which contains all of the songs they know. The songs that they don't know—that is, the songs that form the bulk of this collection—may be among the best of the album tracks, but they still are weighed down by pomp and circumstance and are primarily of interest to hardcore fans, who will already have the original records. *—Stephen Thomas Erlewine*

• **The Best of Kansas [1999]** / Feb. 23, 1999 / Epic/Legacy ♦♦♦♦♦
Although it isn't perfect, *The Best of Kansas* is a solid 12-track collection that contains the bulk of the prog-rock group's greatest hits, including "Carry on Wayward Son," "Point of Know Return," "Dust in the Wind," "Hold On," "Play the Game Tonight" and "Fight Fire with Fire." A few fan favorites may be missing, but casual listeners will find that the best-known cuts are here. [The 1999 CD reissue adds three bonus tracks: "The Pinnacle," "The Devil Game," and "Closet Chronicles."] *—Stephen Thomas Erlewine*

Katrina and The Waves

f. 1981
Pop/Rock, New Wave
Led by ex-Soft Boy guitarist Kimberly Rew, Katrina and the Waves effortlessly evoked the irresistibly catchy guitar pop of the mid-'60s with their first three albums in the early '80s. Not only could Rew write songs that were instantly memorable ("Goin' Down to Liverpool" and "Walking on Sunshine"), but the band had a dynamic lead singer with the Kansas-born Katrina Leskanich, who could sound sweet or tough according to the material. After scoring a hit single with "Walking on Sunshine" in 1985, the band began to add a little bit of soul to their next album, *Waves*. While the experimentation was flawed, what really hurt the record was the fact that Rew only contributed two songs. *Waves* marked a downturn in their commercial fortunes that was fixed with 1989's *Break of Hearts*, when the band turned into indistinguishable commercial hacks; they were rewarded with a Top 20 hit, "That's the Way." Following *Break of Hearts*, Katrina and the Waves drifted for a number of years. In 1993, they began performing reunion gigs, but it wasn't until 1997 that the band bounced back, when they won that year's Euro-vision song contest. *—Stephen Thomas Erlewine*

• **Anthology** / Apr. 25, 1995 / One Way ♦♦♦♦
Fourteen songs that sum up the brief mid-1980s commercial peak of this spirited power pop quartet. As one would guess from the cover art, most of the material comes off of their self-titled Capitol album, which is here complete but with its tracks re-sequenced, augmented by four cuts thrown off of *Waves*. Strangely enough, "Sun Street," "Sleep on My Pillow," "Is That It?," and "Tears for Me," all good songs from the latter, are here, but Kimberley Rew's "Lovely Lindsey," one of the album's highlights, is missing. That's something of a puzzlement, as the group was only on Capitol Records for two albums, after all, so it would seem to be difficult to overlook a key track—like a 15th song would have killed the compilers. Intrinsically, there is nothing wrong with anything here, although even within the confines of this collection, there's a fall-off in quality from "Walking on Sunshine," "Going Down to Liverpool," "Do You Want Crying," and "Tears For Me," although everything here is good listening, if not all equally memorable. There are no notes, but the sound gives full play to the group's obvious virtues, especially Katrina Leskanich's lead vocals, Kimberley Rew's crunchy, melodic lead guitar (which sounds like it's in your lap), and Alex Cooper's drums. Overall, this is a decent if slightly slipshod attempt to compile the band's best work, which will do until Raven or some other enterprising foreign label takes up the task. *—Bruce Eder*

KC & The Sunshine Band

f. 1973, Miami, FL
Disco
In the early '70s, two white men, Harry "KC" Casey (b. Jan. 31, 1951) and Richard Finch

(b. Jan. 25, 1954), created a racially integrated disco band that based its music on various soul styles. They became one of the most commercially successful groups of the early disco era. KC & the Sunshine Band's disco was funky enough to be a staple in the clubs, while remaining melodic and sweet enough to be huge pop hits. The group continued to have hits until the early '80s; their last hit single, "Give It Up," was credited to KC in the U.S. *—Bil Carpenter*

● **The Best of KC & the Sunshine Band** / Jun. 1990 / Rhino ✦✦✦✦✦
A percussive mix of steel drums, whistle flutes, and funky group harmonies, this most soulful disco set includes all of their hits—"Get Down Tonight," "Please Don't Go," "That's the Way (I Like It)," "I'm Your Boogie Man," "(Shake, Shake, Shake) Shake Your Booty," and KC's solo hit, "Give It Up." *—Bil Carpenter*

25th Anniversary Edition / Jul. 20, 1999 / Rhino ✦✦✦
In 1999, Rhino celebrated the 25th anniversary of KC & the Sunshine Band's formation with this two-CD anthology. But technically, 1999 was their 26th anniversary—the soul/funk/disco band was formed in 1973, not 1974. For the casual listener and the budget-minded, a better and more concise choice would be Rhino's 1990 CD *The Best of KC & the Sunshine Band*, which summarizes their contributions with 16 tracks. But if your interest in KC goes beyond casual, *25th Anniversary Collection* isn't a bad release to have. The set contains all of the essential '70s hits offered on *The Best of KC & the Sunshine Band*, including "Get Down Tonight," "(Shake, Shake, Shake) Shake Your Booty," "That's The Way (I Like It)," "I'm Your Boogie Man," and "Keep It Comin' Love," as well as "Wrap Your Arms Around Me," "I Like To Do It," and the ballad "Please Don't Go." But *25th Anniversary Collection* also has its share of material that is enjoyable though less than essential—you need to be a seasoned, diehard KC fanatic to fully appreciate the Spanish-language version of "Please Don't Go" (titled "Por Favor, No Te Vayas"), Tom Moulton's 1994 remix of "Get Down Tonight," or KC and Teri DeSario's 1980 cover of Martha & the Vandellas' "Dancin' in the Streets." And if you're that much of a collector, you'll appreciate Brian Chin's comprehensive, informative liner notes—the writer has no problem articulating why KC's music was so popular in the '70s and why his classic grooves excited many hip-hop, dance-pop and house enthusiasts in the '90s. Rock critics might have dismissed KC in the '70s, but time has made it clear that KC's admirers—not the critics who gave him scathing reviews—were the smart ones. *—Alex Henderson*

Tommy Keene

b. Bethesda, MD
Vocals, Guitar / Pop Underground, College Rock, Jangle Pop, Pop/Rock, Power Pop, Alternative Pop/Rock
Tommy Keene is a guitarist/singer/songwriter who plays and writes melodic guitar-based pop/rock. In 1977, while attending the University of Maryland, Keene switched to guitar and formed the short-lived band the Rage with songwriter Richard X Heyman. Keene recorded two EPs for the tiny Dolphin label before being signed to Geffen, who released two full albums, *Songs From the Film* and *Based On Happy Times*, as well as *Run Now*, a six-song EP of previously recorded material, before dropping him from its roster. Keene inked a deal with Matador in the early '90s, recording the EP *Sleeping on a Roller Coaster* and a full-length album entitled *Ten Years After* in 1996. In addition to recording and touring behind his records, Tommy Keene spent some of the '90s as a guitar-for-hire, on the road with both Velvet Crush and Paul Westerberg. In 1998, he released a new studio album, *Isolation Party*. *—Jack Leaver*

Strange Alliance / 1982 / Avenue ✦✦
Strange Alliance was originally released in 1981, and then re-released the next year with a 7" single containing the song "Back to Zero." This bonus single was a smart move, as "Back to Zero" was a big jump forward in songwriting from most of what was on the album. *Strange Alliance* wasn't bad by any means, but there were fewer hooks and fewer memorable songs than on future Keene releases. Basically a power pop record with a raw garage—almost punkish—feel, it was better than most of what was being released in the same period. Overlooked then and now, the album is by no means a classic, but is definitely worth seeking out by Keene fans and those with an interest in music akin to Jules & the Polar Bears and early Greg Kihn. *—Rob Caldwell*

Songs from the Film / 1986 / Geffen ✦✦✦✦
In what seemed like an attempt by Geffen to make a "big" pop record and endear Keene to an audience wider than critics and a small cult of discerning record buyers, renowned producer Geoff Emerick (Elvis Costello, Beatles) only succeeded at rounding the edges, thus stealing the spark from Keene's performance. The drums are buried in the mix and Keene's distinctive vocals obscured behind a wash of studio processing, but fortunately, Keene's talent shines through in memorable songwriting and biting guitar solos. "In Our Lives" and "Goldtown" are classic Tommy Keene melodic power rockers, while "The Story Ends" stands among his best Beatlesque ballads. But the infectious "Places That Are Gone," which opens side one, sounds awkwardly sped up and doesn't come close to matching the quiet intensity of the version that appeared as the title track of the 1984 Dolphin EP. The story has it that Geffen rejected the original *Songs From the Film* sessions, produced by T-Bone Burnett and Don Dixon, to make this record, although the label at least momentarily came to their senses and released tracks from those sessions later that year on the excellent *Run Now* EP. [Geffen's 1998 CD reissue of *Songs from the Film* includes the *Run Now* EP, plus four previously unreleased songs: "Take Back Your Letters," "We're Two," an alternate full-band take of "Faith in Love" and a live cover of the Flamin' Groovies' "Teenage Head."] *—Jack Leaver*

Based on Happy Times / 1989 / Geffen ✦✦✦✦✦
Much like 1986's *Songs From the Film*, Geffen seemed bent on making Keene's music bigger than life with *Based on Happy Times*, but this time the overall production sounds less forced and truer to capturing the purity and aggressiveness of Keene's live sound. Recorded at Ardent Studios in Memphis with Joe Hardy and John Hampton at the helm, *Based on Happy Times* brought together the best elements of Keene's previous work, including excellently crafted pop songs, delicious guitar figures, and tight ensemble playing. Among the collection's strongest cuts: the sadly beautiful "This Could Be Fiction," which fades with a lovely string passage; the powerful "When Our Vows Break"; and the haunting album closer "A Way Out," featuring R.E.M.'s Peter Buck on mandolin. And as usual, Keene can pick interesting cover tunes, this time around doing a quirky and fun take on a Beach Boys obscurity, "Our Car Club," which also includes a guitar cameo by Buck. Perhaps if this superb record had been given the promotion it deserved, Tommy Keene would have the name recognition of the aforementioned artists. *—Jack Leaver*

● **Real Underground** / Aug. 2, 1993 / Alias ✦✦✦✦✦
A well-done and welcome retrospective of a talented guitarist/singer/songwriter, *The Real Underground* boasts 23 tracks, all of which are currently out of print in their original packaging or previously unreleased. Although this is a great collection, unfortunately it does not include anything from the two fine albums Keene made for Geffen, or the excellent tracks that company released on the *Run Now* EP. Regardless, fans will delight in having the outstanding Dolphin EP *Places That Are Gone* in its entirety, as well as singles and previously unreleased demos from 1982-92. Some of the fun in those unreleased tracks comes from great covers, such as the Who's "Tattoo" and the Flamin' Groovies' "Shake Some Action." *—Jack Leaver*

Driving into the Sun / 1995 / Alias ✦✦✦✦

Ten Years After / Feb. 13, 1996 / Matador ✦✦✦✦✦
The first full-length album since 1989's *Based on Happy Times*, *Ten Years After* comes closer to capturing the raw energy of a Tommy Keene live show than any of his previous studio recordings. Kicking off with a hard guitar assault in "Going Out Again," the intensity and emotion is sustained throughout the rest of this superb 12-song collection. Keene's voice has never sounded better, and his guitar lines are fluid and inspired. The strength of lyric and melody in songs such as "We Started Over Again" and "Turning On Blue" assure that Keene's songwriting craft is still in top form. *Ten Years After* contains a memorable hook at every turn, whether it's in the drive of the delicate acoustic guitar in the folky "Silent Town" or the thunderous eloquence of "Your Heart Beats Alone." And Keene's band is particularly impressive; bassist/vocalist Brad Quinn and drummer John Richardson rock hard, yet still provide the right rhythmic footing for each of the guitarists' musical detours—for example, the country flavoring of "You Can't Wait For Time." A must for longtime fans, as well as anyone who appreciates intelligent and well-crafted pop/rock that maintains a sharp edge. *—Jack Leaver*

Isolation Party / Feb. 24, 1998 / Matador ✦✦✦✦
Tommy Keene always sounded a bit smarter and edgier than the sizable majority of his pure pop brethren back in the early 1980s, and he was a much tougher guitarist than nearly any of his peers (check out his live take of Lou Reed's "Kill Your Sons" on the *Run Now* EP sometime and hear him blow a hole in Reed's original). Which might be why his best stuff hasn't dated much, and, 15 years after his debut album, he could still come up with an intelligent and razor sharp set of hard pop songs, with *Isolation Party* as the result. While the tunes may be a shade less catchy than the highlights from *Songs From the Film*, nothing here sounds like a dud, either, and Keene offers up plenty of committed rockers ("The World Outside," "Getting out From Under You," and "Long Time Missing") as well as hooky, lower-key pop numbers ("Tuesday Morning" and "Weak and Watered Down," the latter of which does not live up to its title). Also, recording for Matador, no one was likely to tell Keene to lighten up on his guitar parts, and the result is a harder and leaner set than he usually offered up in his earlier days (with a Mission of Burma cover for good measure), though the hallmarks of his style—moody but graceful melodies, a nimble and efficient rhythm section, and Keene's passionate vocals and subtly sublime guitar work—are still very much in evidence. In short, Tommy Keene has long been an underappreciated talent, and *Isolation Party* once again begs the question why someone this good isn't a major star (or at least a bigger cult figure). *—Mark Deming*

Kelis

Vocals / Contemporary R&B, Hardcore Rap, Alternative Rap, Urban, Hip-Hop
Harlem-bred hip-hop chanteuse Kelis is a strong woman. This singer/songwriter has the fire of Alanis Morissette, the sassiness of Queen Latifah, and a poise all her own. The daughter of a jazz musician and minister father, Kelis was encouraged to discover music by her mother. Whether it was singing with the Harlem Boys Choir, taking violin lessons, or worshipping the talents of her musician father, Kelis was practically destined to make music. She left home at 16 to pursue her own goals, and four years later Kelis had a deal with Virgin. In mid-1999, Kelis was beatboxing alongside rap troublemaker Ol' Dirty Bastard on his cut "Got Your Money" and her signature technicolor spiraled afro sparked critics' interests. Her brooding vocals blend sensible R&B additives, and the hip-hop layers are funky. Kelis captured feminist desires on her debut *Kaleidoscope*, released in December 1999. *—MacKenzie Wilson*

● **Kaleidoscope** / Dec. 7, 1999 / Virgin ✦✦✦✦
This release showcases the development of a great talent. The album's flaws stem from steps taken backward toward what one could call "mainstream" R&B. It's when Kelis and her production team create tracks that best fit her voice and uniqueness that the end results are outstanding. Although comparisons to Neneh Cherry are inevitable, she does carve out a niche for herself, armed with undeniable talent. *Kaleidoscope* starts out strongly enough with standouts such as "Caught out There," "Get Along with You," and "In the Morning." Sadly enough, the focus seems to lose its footing midway and from there on out, the remaining songs run from average to good. As an artist who could

become, with the proper guidance, a prominent figure for years to come, Kelis is one not to dismiss. *—Jaime Ikeda*

R. Kelly

Producer, Vocals, Keyboards / New Jack Swing, Urban

Urban R&B producer/vocalist/multi-instrumentalist/songwriter R. Kelly and his supporting band Public Announcement began recording in 1992 at the tail end of the new jack swing era, yet he was able to keep much of its sound alive while remaining commercially successful. While he's created a smooth, professional mixture of hip-hop beats, soul-man crooning, and funk, the most distinctive element of Kelly's music is its explicit carnality. Over the course of two albums, the singer has been able to make songs like "Sex Me," "Bump n' Grind," and "Your Body's Callin'" into hits because his production has been seductive enough to sell such blatant come-ons. *—Stephen Thomas Erlewine*

Born into the 90's / Jan. 14, 1992 / Jive ✦✦✦

One of the last popular new jack groups, this East Coast unit had some smash singles in 1992 doing both conventional R&B/soul and hip-hop/new jack tracks. They did both originals and covers, had an enthusiastic attitude, were well produced, and stayed on the urban contemporary outlets throughout the year. *—Ron Wynn*

● **12 Play** / Nov. 9, 1993 / Jive ✦✦✦✦✦

New jack swing may have been on its way out as a primary R&B sound, but R. Kelly didn't lose any points by employing it here. Kelly skillfully mixes '70s-style funk beats, '90s hip-hop production and his own raps, as well as those of Deandre Boykins and Carey Kelly. Sometimes things come perilously close to sounding corny and dated, but he manages to bring things off successfully. Kelly is a competent vocalist, but a master at striking and maintaining a heated mood, keeping a light touch no matter how explicit the language gets and giving this album distinction even as it mines territory that's essentially played out. *—Ron Wynn*

R. Kelly / Nov. 14, 1995 / Jive ✦✦✦✦✦

With the salacious *12 Play*, R. Kelly established himself as one of the top R&B hitmakers of the mid-'90s, rivalled only by Babyface and Dr. Dre for overall consistency. *12 Play* was marred by occasionally slight tunes which were obscured by the explicit sexuality of the lyrics. *R. Kelly* isn't hampered by those flaws, although it isn't a perfect record by any means. Throughout the album, Kelly relies on melody and grooves instead of overtly carnal imagery. But that doesn't mean he has cleaned up—Kelly remains a sly, seductive crooner, and his sexiness is more effective when it is suggestive. Nevertheless, his lyrics and music are never subtle—even on the ballads which dominate this album—which can make *R. Kelly* tiresome if taken as a whole. Taken as individual songs, the album works better than anything he has recorded to date. *—Stephen Thomas Erlewine*

R / Sep. 29, 1998 / Jive ✦✦✦

At the beginning of the '90s, R. Kelly was seen as a lewd, lascivious soulman. By the end of the decade, he had stripped those adjectives away and was seen as a contemporary equivalent of Marvin Gaye, thanks to the enormous success of "I Believe I Can Fly." Appropriately, *R*, the double-disc album that followed "I Believe I Can Fly"'s parent album, finds Kelly trying to live up to that legacy. He may be talented, but he has neither the vision or the depth to match such classic soulmen as Al Green, Stevie Wonder, Prince or Michael Jackson, all artists he emulates on *R*. Kelly's main strength is fusing contemporary material together into a slick, palatable, radio-ready record. Nobody else could have Jay-Z and Celine Dion on their album, and he's about the only one who could make it work, since he can work sensuous grooves as well as he can deliver a soaring ballad. To some, this may sound like nothing more than calculation—a big part of the reason why he doesn't instantly enter the hall of greats—because it's easy to see how he pieces it all together. When he's on, however, such calculation doesn't really matter, since it all flows, but such incidents only occur through about 40% of *R*. That's a major problem, considering the sheer length of the album. Clocking in at 29 long tracks, it takes real effort to sit through the record from beginning to end, especially since Kelly begins to repeat himself. If it was pruned a bit, the album would arguably be his best record. As it stands, *R* is an admirable effort, one that is among his better records even with all of its faults. *—Stephen Thomas Erlewine*

TP-2.Com / Nov. 7, 2000 / Jive ✦✦✦✦

For R. Kelly's follow-up to his epic double-disc *R* from 1998, the crooning lady's man scales back his artistic ambitions with *TP-2.Com*, an album harking back to his *12 Play* album from 1993. It's not so surprising that Kelly attempts to write a sequel to *12 Play*, a breakthrough album stacked with radio-friendly singles, rather than the overreaching scope of *R*, a disappointing album diluted by self-consciousness. This album's 19 songs may seem interchangeable at times in both lyrical and production terms, but Kelly manages to write some great songs that cut through the clutter. In particular, "I Wish" and the accompanying alternate version both stand out here as songs that break away from his usual romantic odes to sensuality. As he proves on nearly every song here, Kelly knows how to take proven formulas and funnel them through his own stylistic aesthetic, which usually means slowing down the tempo, laying on lush choruses of strings and background vocals, taming down the lyrics for radio, and catering his pitch primarily to wistful female listeners. *TP-2.Com* finds Kelly at his best as a pop artist, as he disregards the need to be "artistic" as he did on *R*, instead just focusing on giving the people precisely what they want: a consistent batch of well-crafted R&B odes to romance and sensuality, perfectly formatted for radio with plenty of hooks and the popular contemporary themes. *—Jason Birchmeier*

Chris Kenner

b. Dec. 25, 1929, Kenner, LA, **d.** Jan. 25, 1976, New Orleans, LA
Vocals / New Orleans R&B, R&B

Kenner wrote a number of enduring New Orleans R&B classics, although subsequent cover versions eclipsed all but "I Like It Like That," his Grammy-nominated greatest hit in 1961. Kenner co-wrote "Sick and Tired" with Fats Domino and charted with it in 1957 on Imperial, but Domino's version blew it out of the water. Signing with Joe Babashak's Instant label, Kenner's "I Like It Like That," "Land of 1000 Dances," and "Something You Got" sported Allen Toussaint's rolling piano behind Kenner's raw vocals. *—Bill Dahl*

Land of a Thousand Dances / 1966 / Atlantic ✦✦✦✦✦

● **I Like It Like That: Golden Classics** / 1987 / Collectables ✦✦✦✦✦

Vocalist Kenner's early-'60s sides for Instant, with Allen Toussaint laying down rolling piano behind him, represent New Orleans R&B at its most infectious. *—Bill Dahl*

Kenny

Glitter

One of the myriad bands thrust onto the British glam scene as it approached its end in the mid-'70s, Kenny was generally regarded, alongside the Bay City Rollers and Slik, as simply another in a long line of acts created by master songwriters Bill Martin and Phil Coulter. In fact, although the five-piece group's best-known material was indeed the work of that pair, Kenny's Rick Driscoll and Yan Stile were also very competent songwriters in their own right, as the group's final few releases proved. Indeed, the group had already existed for some three years before Martin and Coulter first encountered them. Under the name Chufff, the quartet were regulars on the free festival progressive rock circuit. They were discovered by Martin and Coulter in late 1974—according to legend, the band was rehearsing in a banana warehouse in the north London suburb of Enfield at the time and their initial response to the songwriters' overtures were disdainful. Martin and Coulter would not take no for an answer. Assured of stardom, Chufff agreed to become Kenny. In the event, stardom was to prove extremely fleeting. While "The Bump" made number three in early 1975, the group enjoyed just three further British hits, all penned by Martin-Coulter: the number four smash "Fancy Pants," "Baby I Love You OK" (number 12), and "Julie Ann" (number ten). The under-performance of Kenny's debut album furthered the band's desire to extricate themselves from their predicament and, in late 1976, Kenny went to court to free themselves from Martin-Coulter. They then signed to Polydor and recorded a new, all-original album, *Ricochet*, and the single "Hot Lips." Neither drew any attention whatsoever and when a serious road accident put Stile out of action, Kenny folded. *—Dave Thompson*

● **The Singles Collection Plus** / Sep. 26, 2000 / 7T's ✦✦✦

For a band whose hitmaking career ran to no more than 12 minutes worth of music, this is an awful lot of Kenny. Four tracks—"The Bump," "Fancy Pants," "Baby I Love You OK," and "Julie Ann"—round up all that history recalls as classic Kenny; respectively, they reached number three, number four, number 12, and number ten on the British chart during 1974-75, after which the band lapsed into an almost deafening commercial silence. But if *Collection* has one mission in mind, it is to prove that it wasn't strictly a fate they deserved. The band's *Sound of Super K* album, included in its entirety, indicates a pop sensibility which was at least on a par with the contemporary Mud and Rubettes, and, while that isn't necessarily a recommendation, it shouldn't have been a death sentence either. The problem, of course, was timing. By the time Kenny made their breakthrough, both the pop and glam veins which they were mining had hit on very hard times, indeed, while songwriters Bill Martin and Phil Coulter were still reeling from their dismissal from the Bay City Rollers camp. It would be another year before the pair truly regained their equilibrium, by which time they had already transferred their affections to another band entirely, the young Midge Ure's Slik. Indeed, Kenny's status as a kind of noble no-man's-land between those two giants is only reinforced by the two best cuts on this entire collection: "The Bump," which had already seen service on a Rollers B-side; and "Forever and Ever," which would become Slik's debut hit. For the remainder, *The Kenny Collection Plus* slips blithely between punchy glam pop and dreamy teen ballads, a few high-tempo dance floor crashers and a surprisingly mature rendition of "(Your Love Has Lifted Me) Higher and Higher." Nothing, however, is more memorable than it needs to be, and, ultimately, nothing is anything more than perfunctory. A greatest hits EP would probably have served Kenny far better. *—Dave Thompson*

Nik Kershaw

b. Mar. 1, 1958, Bristol, England
Vocals, Guitar / Pop/Rock, New Wave, Synth Pop

During the mid-'80s, Nik Kershaw managed to score a handful of pop hits and, in doing so, establish himself as a profitable commercial songwriter. Kershaw began his musical career by learning to play guitar when he was a teenager. In 1974, he joined his first band, Half Pint Hogg, which played nothing but Deep Purple covers. However, his musical ideas were not limited to heavy metal; after he left school, he joined a jazz-funk band called Fusion. Fusion released one album, *'Til I Hear from You*, in the late '70s. Once the group broke up, Kershaw signed to MCA Records with the help of Nine Below Zero's manager, Micky Modern.

Kershaw released his first solo single, "I Won't Let the Sun Go Down on Me," in 1983; it peaked at number 47 on the U.K. charts. His next single, "Wouldn't It Be Good," hit number five in the U.K. and charted at number 46 in the U.S. Its success led to stardom in Britain for Kershaw; "I Won't Let the Sun Go Down on Me" was re-released in summer of 1984 and charted at number two, leading to a series of hit singles. Released in 1986, his third album *Radio Musicola* wasn't as successful as his previous albums.

Kershaw subsequently retreated from performing and recording regularly. Although he released *The Works* in 1990, Kershaw's main musical contribution since the late '80s is as a songwriter; he's written several songs for other artists, including Chesney Hawke's hit single "The One and Only." After years of writing for others, Kershaw returned with his own *15 Minutes* for Pyramid Records. —*Stephen Thomas Erlewine*

Human Racing / 1983 / MCA ✦✦✦

His debut, although rough around the edges, showed talent and promise, and includes "Wouldn't It Be Good." —*Scott Bultman*

The Riddle / 1984 / MCA ✦✦✦✦✦

Kershaw's second album, containing a remixed "Wouldn't It Be Good," finally garnered some deserved attention. The rest is his unique style of well-crafted synth-pop. —*Scott Bultman*

Radio Musicola / 1986 / MCA ✦✦

The Works / 1990 / MCA ✦✦✦

The Best of Nik Kershaw / 1994 / Music Collection ✦✦✦✦

More comprehensive than the U.S. *Anthology*, the British *Best of Nick Kershaw* covers Kershaw's career from the beginning. Where it fails however, is in its exclusion of the single versions of some of the hits (including "Wouldn't It Be Good") in favor of 12-inch remixes. —*Chris Woodstra*

● **Anthology** / Jan. 31, 1995 / One Way ✦✦✦✦✦

Nik Kershaw's albums have always been somewhat spotty, which is what makes *Anthology* a welcome event. By concentrating only on the singer's best material and biggest hits, the disc is an entertaining listen and arguably the only album most casual fans will ever need. —*Sara Sytsma*

Chaka Khan

b. Mar. 23, 1953, Great Lakes, IL

Vocals / Quiet Storm, Club/Dance, Urban, Funk, Soul

Best known for her superb 1984 cover of Prince's "I Feel for You," R&B singer Chaka Khan enjoyed solo success as well as popularity as a member of the group Rufus. Raised on Chicago's South Side, she formed her first group at the age of 11 and later toured with Motown great Mary Wells as part of the Afro-Arts Theater. A few years later, she adopted the African name Chaka Khan while working on the Black Panthers' breakfast program. After quitting high school in 1969, Khan joined several unsuccessful bands, though her fortunes changed when she formed Rufus.

Distinguished by Khan's dynamic vocals, Rufus was among the preeminent funk groups of the decade and earned many gold or platinum albums before she went solo in 1978. *Chaka* proved to be a significant hit on the strength of the single "I'm Every Woman." Still, neither her sophomore album (1980's *Naughty*), nor its follow-up (*What 'Cha Gonna Do for Me*), was a hit. In 1982, Khan recorded *Echoes of an Era*, a collection of jazz standards. Her pop career was on shaky ground when she released 1984's *I Feel for You*, a platinum-seller launched by its title cut, a Grammy-winning, rap-inspired rendition of a fairly obscure Prince album track. Subsequent LPs kept Khan riding high on the R&B charts, though her standing in pop's mainstream again began to wane by the end of the 1980s. In 1990, she won her second Grammy for "I'll Be Good to You," a duet with Ray Charles. *Come 2 My House* appeared in 1998. —*Jason Ankeny*

● **Epiphany: The Best of Chaka Khan, Vol. 1** / Nov. 12, 1996 / Warner Brothers ✦✦✦✦✦

Epiphany: Best of Chaka Khan, Vol. 1 is a long-overdue collection of Khan's greatest hits, ranging from "Ain't Nobody" to "I'm Every Woman" with Rufus to "I Feel for You." Though Rufus' mid-'70s hits for ABC aren't included, all of her big hits for Warner are present. What nearly sinks the collection is the addition of no less than five new songs, including the Me'Shell Ndegeocello duet "Never Miss the Water," which aren't nearly as strong as the original hits. Even with the addition of the new cuts, *Epiphany* remains a fine compilation and is the best way to get caught up with Khan. —*Leo Stanley*

I'm Every Woman: The Best of Chaka Khan / Sep. 14, 1999 / Warner Brothers ✦✦✦✦

Kid Creole & the Coconuts

f. 1980, Montreal, Quebec, Canada

New Wave, Calypso, Novelty, Disco

In 1980, August Darnell became a staff producer at Ze Records and created the persona of Kid Creole with a backup group, the Coconuts, consisting of three female singers led by his wife Adriana ("Addy") Kaegi, and a band containing vibraphone player "Sugar-Coated" Andy Hernandez (aka Coati Mundi). Kid Creole was a deliberately comic figure, a Latinized Cab Calloway type in a zoot suit and broad-brimmed hat who sang songs like "Mister Softee" that found him decrying his impotence while being berated by the Coconuts. Ze made a deal with Sire Records, and the label released the second Kid Creole & the Coconuts album, *Fresh Fruit in Foreign Places*, in June 1981. It reached the charts briefly. *Fresh Fruit* was a concept album that found the Kid Creole character embarking on an *Odyssey*-like search for a character named Mimi, and it was given a stage production at the New York Public Theater. Darnell continued the story with his third album, which was released in the U.K. under the title *Tropical Gangsters* in May 1982. The band toured Britain for the first time to promote the album, and they broke big: the LP hit number three and three singles, "I'm a Wonderful Thing, Baby," "Stool Pigeon," and "Annie, I'm Not Your Daddy," made the Top Ten, with "Dear Addy" reaching the Top 40. In the U.S., where the album was retitled *Wise Guy*, the band remained cult favorites. Nevertheless, Kid Creole & the Coconuts remained a compelling live act with an imaginative visual style, which led to film and television opportunities. Kid Creole & the Coconuts

spent the 1990s touring internationally and releasing albums primarily outside the U.S. —*William Ruhlmann*

Off the Coast of Me / Aug. 1980 / Antilles ✦✦✦✦

Mixing disco, Caribbean music, and strains of big-band jazz, Kid Creole engages in a self-deprecating dialogue with his backup singers, The Coconuts, who dismiss him as "Mister Softee" and plead, "Can You Get Me Into Studio 54?" on this hilarious debut album. —*William Ruhlmann*

Fresh Fruit in Foreign Places / Jun. 1981 / ZE ✦✦✦✦

Musical gumbo of esoteric lilting, jazzy laidback disco, an acquired taste. —*Bil Carpenter*

Wise Guy / Jun. 1982 / Sire ✦✦✦✦✦

The ongoing adventures of Kid Creole continue on this bouncy collection that produced three British Top Ten hits, including "Annie, I'm Not Your Daddy" and "I'm a Wonderful Thing, Baby." —*William Ruhlmann*

Doppelganger / 1983 / ZE ✦✦✦

Armed with a fresh batch of tropical tales, August Darnell (a.k.a. Kid Creole) leads his band of eccentric vagabonds in another episode of the continuing saga of Mimi. Of course, it's not necessary to read the esoteric liner notes, nor is a knowledge of previous chapters required to enjoy the installment entitled *Doppelganger*. As usual, the only prerequisite is an acquired taste for the bizarre, often comical travelogues set to exotic pop which represent the essence of Kid Creole & the Coconuts. Darnell's infatuation with international environments results in a soundtrack characterized by ubiquitous percussion and spirited brass and woodwinds, although electric guitar also figures prominently in several songs. Much like Paul Simon's efforts on *Graceland*, Darnell incorporates world music elements to add a foreign flavor to pop postcards like "It's a Wonderful Life" and "There's Something Wrong in Paradise." Yet Darnell is rarely as serious as Simon, and only *Graceland's* lighthearted "You Can Call Me Al" could blend inconspicuously with the material on *Doppelganger*. A Caribbean-styled remake of Jimmy Soul's "If You Wanna Be Happy" is indicative of the album's affable nature. The song's obsession with appearances also reveals the thematic influence behind previous Kid Creole favorites such as "Annie, I'm Not Your Daddy" and "I'm a Wonderful Thing, Baby," both of which appear on their most popular album, *Wise Guy*. Nothing on *Doppelganger* can compare to those two British hits, yet nothing will fail to satisfy devoted fans either. For the uninitiated, *Doppelganger's* peculiar content presents a love-it or hate-it dilemma, but captivated listeners will probably enjoy discovering the rest of Kid Creole & the Coconuts' enchanting oeuvre. —*Vince Ripol*

In Praise of Older Women & Other Crimes / 1985 / Sire ✦✦

I, Too, Have Seen the Woods / 1987 / Sire ✦✦

Private Waters in the Great Divide / Mar. 1990 / Columbia ✦✦✦

You Shoulda Told Me You Were / Aug. 13, 1991 / Columbia ✦✦

● **Kid Creole Redux** / Mar. 17, 1992 / Sire ✦✦✦✦✦

Featuring the great majority of Kid Creole's singles, *Kid Creole Redux* is the perfect introduction to the eccentric dance-pop artist. —*Sara Sytsma*

To Travel Sideways / May 5, 1995 / Hot Productions ✦✦✦

After a four-year absence, Kid Creole & the Coconuts suddenly returned in 1995 (in Japan, anyway, with their efforts later made available in the U.S. and elsewhere), releasing two albums within two months. The first and less impressive one was *To Travel Sideways*. As ever, Kid Creole maintained his tropical dance sound (with forays into harder rock and disco) and his lyrical persona of a gigolo philosopher, warning, in "Baby, I'm Real," that the likelihood of his being faithful was slight and complaining, "You Shoulda Told Me You Were Catholic" before concluding "Life Is Always Good." But the album was padded with covers of the Beatles' "Things We Said Today," the hippie anthem "Get Together," and "The Anniversary Medley," which revisited old hits like "Annie I'm Not Your Daddy" and "Stool Pigeon." —*William Ruhlmann*

Kiss Me Before the Light Changes / Jun. 6, 1995 / Hot Productions ✦✦✦

After a four-year absence, Kid Creole & the Coconuts suddenly returned in 1995 (in Japan, anyway, with their efforts later made available in the U.S. and elsewhere), releasing two albums within two months. The second was *Kiss Me Before The Light Changes*, which found August "Kid Creole" Darnell reining in his previously outright comic persona in favor of heavily produced dance tracks that sometimes suggested a cross between Michael Jackson/Prince-style '80s pop-funk and his usual Caribbean influences. Of course, if you listened to the vocals that had been reduced in the mix, you heard some of Darnell's usual quirkiness, whether in "Heaven Knows," with its chorus, "Heaven knows that I love myself," the romantic distinctions of "Stop Sweatin' Me" (e.g., "Here's the difference between you and me / You like true romance and monogamy"), or the issues of race addressed in "To Travel Sideways" (a title song for the album that preceded this one, but did not appear on it). But there was little that measured up to the musical comedy material that had characterized the Kid Creole albums of the 1980s. —*William Ruhlmann*

Kid 'n Play

f. 1987, db. 1993

Party Rap, Pop-Rap, Old School Rap, Hip-Hop

Among the first groups to tame rap's hardcore mentality into a positive, message-oriented music suitable for teens and mass audiences, Kid 'n Play debuted in 1988 with the platinum album *2 Hype*, which the duo later spun into a deal involving films and a Saturday-morning cartoon show, the first involving a rap act. Though their recording activity became limited during the gangsta-dominated '90s—1991's *Face the Nation* was their last album—the group managed two sequels to their original *House Party* film, as well as the 1991 teen flick *Class Act*. Kid (b. Christopher Reid) and Play (b. Christopher Martin) first met while performing in rival high-school groups and initially teamed up as Fresh Force. Play's former bandmate, Hurby "Luv Bug" Azor, became the duo's manager and signed Kid 'n Play to Select Records in 1987. Despite the predominance of James Brown samples during the mid-'80s, Hurby "Luv Bug" Azor gave *2 Hype* a production job more rooted in disco and pop; thanks to the near Top Ten R&B hit "Rollin' with Kid 'n Play," the album eventually reached platinum status. *—John Bush*

- **2 Hype** / 1988 / Select ✦✦✦✦✦

Kid 'n Play's music height came on their debut album, *2 Hype*. This album rode up the charts with its tame take on late-'80s New York hip-hop and, more importantly, the group's image as teen-friendly, goofy dancers. This album's standout moment and largest hit, "Do This My Way," serves as a perfect summation of the duo's chemistry that proved so important to their commercial success; while these two are only modest rappers firing off many clichés on this song as well as others, they do it in such a conversational manner that it proved infectiously appealing to mainstream audiences in 1988. The duo also makes sure never to take the tough stance so prevalent in hip-hop at the time (LL Cool J, Rakim, KRS-One, Chuck D, Ice-T), instead reciting rhymes with a clean, carefree appeal often centering around innocent partying and girl chasing. Since this album's cover art is the only real insight to the group's most important assets—their fashion and their dancing (which made them MTV favorites)—it's somewhat hard to see what the appeal was with this album outside of its teen-friendly aim. Still, the album's simplicity and danceable beats still make it a bit infectious in a sugar-coated kind of way. Unfortunately, the group's image would quickly eclipse their music once they became Hollywood stars, making this their only worthwhile album. *—Jason Birchmeier*

Kid 'n Play's Funhouse / 1990 / Select ✦✦✦

One of two releases from the twosome in 1990, this one has new cuts with funkier, looser foundations and more ambitious adult lyrics and rapping style. *—Ron Wynn*

House Party [Original Soundtrack] / 1990 / Motown ✦✦✦

Not strictly, or even mainly, their album, it does contain the singles "Funhouse" and "Kid vs. Play (The Battle)." Its prime importance was as the soundtrack from an extremely successful film of the same name, which launched the duo into cinematic stardom. *—Ron Wynn*

Face the Nation / Sep. 24, 1991 / Select ✦✦

Kid Rock (Robert James Ritchie)

b. Jan. 17, 1971, Romeo, MI

Vocals / Rap-Rock, Rap-Metal, Alternative Metal, Heavy Metal, Hard Rock

One of the unlikeliest success stories in rock at the turn of the millennium, Detroit rap-rocker Kid Rock shot to superstardom with his fourth full-length album, 1998's *Devil Without a Cause*. What made it so shocking was that Rock had recorded his first demo a full decade before, been booted off major label Jive following his Beastie Boys-ish 1990 debut *Grits Sandwiches for Breakfast*, and toiled for most of the decade in obscurity, releasing albums to a small, mostly local fan base while earning his fair share of ridicule around his home state. Nevertheless, Rock persevered, and by the time rap-metal had begun to attract a substantial audience, he had perfected the outlandish, over-the-top white-trash persona that made *Devil Without a Cause* such an infectious party record. Rock briefly became notorious in 1990 when a New York college radio station aired *Grits Sandwiches*' profanity-laced ode to oral sex, "Yodelin' in the Valley," and was fined over $20,000 (a judgment later rescinded). After being dropped from Jive, Rock recorded two small-label albums on a shoestring budget; he also set about forming a backing band, dubbed Twisted Brown Trucker. Rapper Joe C. (b. Joseph Calleja) was one of the first to join, catching Rock's eye in 1994 because of his diminutive stature (due to a digestive condition known as celiac disease). As rap-metal acts began to dominate the hard rock landscape, Atlantic Records decided to take a chance on signing Rock. *Devil Without a Cause* didn't do much upon its initial release in August 1998, but a big promotional push helped make the second single and video, "Bawitdaba," a nationwide smash. The follow-up, "Cowboy," achieved similar success, and suddenly, after a decade of trying, Kid Rock was a superstar with a Top Five, seven-times-platinum album and a gig at Woodstock '99. Rock acquired the rights to his indie-label recordings and remixed or re-recorded the best material for 2000's *The History of Rock*. Sadly, a year after being forced to take a break from touring by his medical difficulties, Joe C. passed away in his sleep on November 16, 2000. *—Steve Huey*

- **Devil Without a Cause** / Aug. 18, 1998 / Lava/Atlantic ✦✦✦✦✦

I don't suspect that even Kid Rock believed he had an album as good as *Devil Without a Cause* in him. Nobody else believed it, that's for sure. But he didn't just find the perfect extention of his Beastie and Diamond Dave infatuations here, he came up with the great hard rock album of the late '90s—a fearlessly funny, bone-crunching record that manages to sustain its strength, not just until the end of its long running time, but through repeated plays. The key to its sucesss is that it's never trying to be a hip-hop record. It's simply a monster rock album, as Twisted Brown Trucker turns out thunderous, funky noise—and that's funky not just in the classic sense, but also in a Southern-fried, white trash sense, as he gives this as much foundation in country as he does hip-hop. But what really reigns supreme on *Devil Without a Cause* is a love of piledriving, classic hard rock, not just that of hometown hero Bob Seger, but Lynyrd Skynyrd, Van Halen, and faceless arena rock ballads. The Kid makes it all shine with rhymes so clever and irresistible that it's impossible not to quote them. For all its modernity—Rock's rapping, the titanic metallic guitars, Joe C's sideshow sidekick, the plea to "get in the pit and try to love someone"—this is firmly in the tradition of classic hard rock, and it's the best good-time hard rock album in years (certainly the best of the last three years of the '90s). *—Stephen Thomas Erlewine*

The History of Rock / May 30, 2000 / Lava/Atlantic ✦✦✦✦

Devil Without a Cause was so good it caused everybody to re-evaluate Kid Rock, including Rock himself. As he prepped a follow-up, he unleashed *The History of Rock*, a hodgepodge of new songs, unreleased tunes, demos, old cuts, and re-recordings. This not only bought the Kid time, it gave him a chance to revamp a past that was bordering on the seriously lame. According to *The History*, Rock always knew what he was doing. Anyone that's heard *The Polyfuze Method* knows that's not the case, but that's the beauty of *The History*, since the early stuff now sounds of a piece with *Devil*. It isn't nearly as good, but it has some of the same thrills since his band hits harder and funkier than any of its rap-rock peers and Rock now has a fully cultivated persona. Still, the songs just aren't here. Apart from the "Get out of Denver" rewrite "Born 2 B a Hick," "Early Mornin' Stoned Pimp," "3 Sheets to the Wind" and maybe the Skynyrd-aping "Prodigal Son," the older recordings are still clumsy, something the new song "American Bad Ass" is not. A shameless slab of self-mythology where the former Bob Ritchie calls out tag-lines from *Devil* and places himself in the company of Seger, the Beasties, and No-Show Jones, all to a sample of Metallica's "Sad But True," it's cool, more or less, but not as monumental as "Bawitdaba," which had true wit, original riffs, and a sense of purpose. But, once you've worn out *Devil* and you need a new fix, you're not going to find it on the older Kid Rock albums—you're going to find it here. It's not a great listen, but its swagger and white-trash style make it the second-best record in his catalog. *—Stephen Thomas Erlewine*

Johnny Kidd

b. Dec. 23, 1939, Willesden, London, **d.** Oct. 7, 1966, Radcliff

Vocals / Rock & Roll

One of England's top rock & roll outfits before the Beatles led the early-'60s beat boom, Johnny Kidd & the Pirates are best remembered today for one international rock classic ("Shakin' All Over") and as a seminal influence on several more famous groups, most notably the Who. The group cut their first record, the outstanding *Please Don't Touch*, in April 1959, highlighted by Fred Heath's menacing vocals. The group's subsequent records were an uneven mix of solid R&B-based rock juxtaposed with awkwardly covered "standards." In May of 1960, however, the band was in the studio to record one of those standards, "Yes Sir, That's My Baby," with an original B-side that they hadn't fully worked out. That B-side, a Heath original called "Shakin' All Over," became the A-side of a number one single that became the first original rock song in England to achieve the status of an international rock standard. Driven by Caddy's guitar and a mournful, ominous lead vocal by Heath, the song topped the charts and completely astonished everybody who heard it that such a track could have come from an English rock & roll band. Unfortunately, like every other British label of the era, EMI was never sure how best to deal with rock & roll success, and the group was made to record any amount of dross in the wake of this success, amid some superb follow-up numbers. The group was among the finest rock combos of the early '60s, with a wild stage act that had them playing in pirate regalia, but it never had enough consistent chart success to put it back in the top ranks of Britain's rock hierarchy, though they received a great deal of respect from the younger generation of rock & rollers. *—Bruce Eder*

Hits & Rarities / 1983 / See For Miles ✦✦✦✦✦

This collection is the best of three now available. It contains the strongest of Kidd's singles plus superb vault finds. Considered too rough for release in the '60s, they hold up splendidly. *—Bruce Eder*

- **Complete Johnny Kidd** / 1994 / EMI ✦✦✦✦✦

A double CD of everything this underrated band ever recorded, assembled chronologically and beautifully remastered and annotated (with great pictures, too). This is the collection to own, especially since it has been issued at mid-price. And fans of the Who or the Small Faces can double the priority of owning this collection. *—Bruce Eder*

Greg Kihn

b. 1952, Baltimore, MD

Vocals, Guitar / Pop/Rock, Power Pop, New Wave, Singer/Songwriter

Greg Kihn began his career in his hometown of Baltimore, MD, working in the singer/songwriter mold, but switched to straightforward rock & roll when he moved to San Francisco in 1974. The following year, he became one of the first artists signed to Matthew Kaufman's now legendary Beserkley Records, helping to carve the label's sound—melodic pop with a strong '60s-pop sensibility—a refreshing alternative to the bloated prog-rock of the time. In 1976, after his debut on the compilation *Beserkley Chartbusters*, he recorded his first album; through the '70s, he released an album each year and built a strong cult following through constant touring, becoming Beserkley's biggest seller. In 1981, he earned his first bonafide hit with the Top 20 single, "The Breakup Song (They Don't Write 'Em)," from the *Rockihnroll* album. He continued in a more commercial vein through the '80s with a series of pun-titled albums; *Kihntinued* (1982), *Kihnspiracy* (1983), *Kihntageous* (1984), and *Citizen Kihn* (1985). He scored his biggest hit with 1983's "Jeopardy" (number two) from the *Kihnspiracy* album. By the time *Love and Rock & Roll* was released in 1986, the puns had run out and so had the hits. Kihn kept a relatively low profile throughout the '90s, releasing *Mutiny* in 1994 and *Horror Show* in 1996. *—Chris Woodstra*

Greg Kihn / 1976 / Beserkley ✦✦✦

This record has it all: good songs (mostly written by Kihn) with strong vocals and tight harmonies. If you only know Kihn from the hits, you owe it to yourself to go back and track this record down. If you're only just discovering him, start here and grow with the band. —*Jim Worbois*

Greg Kihn Again / 1977 / Beserkley ✦✦✦✦
A fine follow-up to *Greg Kihn* as Kihn continues to grow as an artist and songwriter. His version of "For You" received some favorable comments from Springsteen as well as first dibs on an original Springsteen tune for a later album. —*Jim Worbois*

Next of Kihn / 1978 / Beserkley ✦✦✦
For the first time, Kihn has written all the songs and, with the first track, has adopted a harder edge to his sound, at least on that particular track. Overall, not a bad record but more of a lateral move as an artist than a step forward. —*Jim Worbois*

With the Naked Eye / 1979 / Beserkley ✦✦✦
The awaited Springsteen cover finally pops up on this record, as does a cover of label-mate Jonathan Richman's "Roadrunner." The former allows some of the Kihn magic to shine through but the latter is just a straight read with none of the fun of the original. In between are some pleasant songs but nothing really memorable. —*Jim Worbois*

Glass House Rock / 1980 / Beserkley ✦✦

Rockihnroll / 1981 / Beserkley ✦✦✦✦✦
With this album Kihn finally has the hit he long ago deserved ("Breakup Song"). He also manages to recapture some of what made the early records so enjoyable. Once again, with both the material and the performance, Kihn sounds as if he is enjoying himself. —*Jim Worbois*

Kihntinued / 1982 / Beserkley ✦✦✦✦✦
A couple of the tracks, like "Everyday/Saturday" and "Testify," are more memorable than nearly anything on the previous record, but still not up to the potential Kihn hinted at on his first couple albums. —*Jim Worbois*

Kihnspiracy / 1983 / Beserkley ✦✦

Kihntagious / 1984 / Beserkley ✦✦✦
Working on a well-worn formula could have spelled trouble for the Greg Kihn Band, but on *Kihntagious*, they've come through without so much as a scratch. Includes the hit "Re-united," along with eleven other good pop reasons to catch the Kihn fever. Well worth a listen. —*James Chrispell*

Citizen Kihn / 1985 / EMI America ✦✦

Love & Rock & Roll / 1986 / Beserkley ✦✦

● **Kihnsolidation: The Best of Greg Kihn** / Jul. 1989 / Rhino ✦✦✦✦✦
A fine sampling of Kihn's pop sensibility. Drawing from each of his albums, it includes the hits "The Breakup Song" and "Jeopardy" as well as his better album cuts. —*Chris Woodstra*

Unkihntrollable (Greg Kihn Live) / 1991 / Rhino ✦✦

Horror Show / Nov. 5, 1996 / Clean Cuts ✦✦✦
Horror Show is the title of Greg Kihn's first novel. Appropriately, the concept of the same name is a neo-collection of British Invasion pop-rock and folk-rock, complete with the occasional string and woodwind arrangements. Kihn doesn't limit himself to his own songs, working Ray Davies' "Waterloo Sunset" and the traditional "Come Back Baby" and "Trials, Troubles, Tribulations" into the concept. Though *Horror Show* never really tells a story, it is one of Kihn's most enjoyable latter-day albums, simply because of the variety of styles and its sense of purpose. —*Stephen Thomas Erlewine*

Killing Joke

f. 1978
Post-Punk, New Wave, Alternative Pop/Rock
Heavy and slow, Killing Joke (at least early in their career) was a quasi-metal band dancing to a tune of doom and gloom. They eventually became less heavy and more arty (the latter seems almost impossible)—more danceable even—but early on they made some urgent slabs of molten dynamite that oozed with the power of thick guitars, thudding drums and over-the-top singing. Formed in 1978 by vocalist Jaz Coleman and drummer Paul Ferguson, the duo then recruited bassist Youth and guitarist Geordie for their debut EP, *Turn to Red*. After signing with Island in 1979, Killing Joke moved to EG one year later and released their eponymous debut album in 1981. Despite controversial artwork and live shows, the group began amassing a following of both punk and disco fans with hard-edged but danceable singles like "Psyche," "Follow the Leader" and "Eighties." Though Youth left to form Brilliant, he was replaced by Paul Raven for 1983's *Fire Dances*, which demonstrated a calmer, more straightforward band than the one showcased on the group's earlier records. After 1988's *Outside the Gate*, the group broke up, only to reunite (with a new drummer, Martin Atkins) two years later for *Extremities, Dirt, & Various Repressed Emotions*. In 1994, Killing Joke re-formed as a trio with Coleman, Geordie, and Youth and the group released *Pandemonium*, a harder-edged, heavier album than their previous records. Two years later, the band released *Democracy*. —*Stephen Thomas Erlewine & John Dougan*

● **Killing Joke** / May 1981 / EG ✦✦✦✦✦
Since 1980, there have been a hundred bands who sound like this; but before Steve Albini and Al Jourgensen made it hip, the cold metallic throb of Killing Joke was exciting and fresh. The harshly sung vocals riding over the pulsating synth lines of the opener "Requiem" have a vigor and passion that few imitators have managed to match. The precise riffs and tight rhythms found in songs like "Wardance" would influence a generation of hardcore musicians; yet "The Wait," with its thrashing guitars and angry vocals, would find itself covered on a Metallica album only six years later. That such a bleak and furious

album could have such a widespread influence is a testament to its importance. Certain parts of the album have not dated well; the vocals and drums are mixed in such a way that they lose some of their effectiveness, and the fact that so many other bands have used this same formula does take some of the visceral feeling away. But this is an underground classic and deserves better than its relative unknown status. Fans of most kinds of heavy music will probably find something they like about this band, and this is as good a place as any to start the collection. —*Bradley Torreano*

What's THIS For . . . ! / Jul. 1981 / EG ✦✦✦
Killing Joke's second album, *What's THIS For . . . !* boasts much better production than the group's debut. However, the songs are cut from the same cloth; the stark, totalitarian imagery and sheer physical muscle of the group's incredible rhythm section is retained. Including several songs ("The Fall of Because," "Madness," and the single "Follow the Leaders") all lasting well in excess of five minutes, this release occasionally makes for daunting listening, but fans of malice and malcontent should accept no substitute. —*Alex Ogg*

Revelations / Jun. 1982 / EG ✦✦✦✦
The epitome of the difficult third-album syndrome. Using an outside producer (Conny Plank) for the first time only resulted, seemingly, in headaches and confusion. Recorded in Berlin, the location must have rubbed off on the band—witness the Teutonic undertones of "We Have Joy." The truth was that the original Killing Joke lineup was dissolving fast, and this manifests itself in the lack of cohesion and direction on the album. —*Alex Ogg*

Fire Dances / 1983 / EG ✦✦✦✦
After the difficult sessions leading up to *Revelations*, *Fire Dances* was Killing Joke's first album with new bass player Paul Raven. It saw them return, in part, to the primeval, tribal sound that they'd patented on their first two albums. "Song and Dance," "Feast of Blaze," and "Let's All Go to the Fire Dances" (all titular suggestions of the shamanic qualities of the songs themselves) are the standouts, yet the whole album is consistently strong. This stretching of the band's structure and texture, without abandoning their rhythmic power base, provided the blueprint which would be more fully realized on 1985's *Night Time*. At the time, though, this was a satisfying installment in their growing legacy. —*Alex Ogg*

Night Time / 1985 / EG ✦✦✦
An album in which Jaz Coleman abandoned the habit of a lifetime and attempted to sing. Popular critical belief has it that *Night Time* is one of the weakest albums in the Killing Joke canon—an ignoble attempt to weld pop luster to the denser elements of their sonic attack. Don't believe a word of it. In retrospect, this is the group's best album since *What's THIS For . . . !* Indeed, you could make a strong argument for saying that it's their finest work ever. The material is impassioned—sympathetically produced yet still hostile and alien. The career highpoint "Love Like Blood" gave them a deserved hit single, but there are plenty of other picks on the album, including "Kings and Queens" and "Eighties," the latter being a powerful indictment of a hollow decade. —*Alex Ogg*

Brighter Than a 1000 Suns / 1986 / EG ✦✦✦
The follow-up to 1985's commercial breakthrough *Night Time*, this solid effort is even more polished, as the trend of synthesizers replacing the guitar roar of old is further accelerated. There are significant concessions to contemporary dance rhythms this time around as well—even at their most bombastic, martial best, you could always dance to Killing Joke. While there are some excellent songs here, notably "Love of the Masses" and "Sanity," there is also a downside to the trade-off: The transition from gung-ho horsemen of the apocalypse to moody onlookers is not always an easy fit, and some of the band's edge is lost in the process. Jaz Coleman's lyrical obsessions with mysticism, it must be said, can also grate on the listener after a while. —*Alex Ogg*

Outside the Gate / 1988 / EG ✦✦

Extremities, Dirt & Various Repressed Emotions / 1990 / Noise ✦✦✦✦
This, Killing Joke's re-formation album, brings together the lineup of Coleman, Geordie, Raven, and Martin Atkins on a new label. A welcome return and easily the best of their official releases since *Night Time*, *Extremities* sees them work up a fair old sweat on "Money Is Not Our God" and "Age of Greed," the keynote tracks. The rhythm section, always the fulcrum of KJ's sound, is as fierce and unrelenting as listeners had come to expect, and Coleman is in fine voice. In this form, and to follow the album's capitalistic thread, Killing Joke are worth 20 of the bands who've openly imitated their sound in the last two decades. —*Alex Ogg*

Incomplete Collection 1980-1985 / 1990 / EG ✦✦✦✦
A box set limited to 4,000 colored vinyl copies of the band's first five albums for EG, this is one for the diehard collectors and vinyl loyalists, given that there's no CD equivalent to date. As of yet, fans await the definitive Killing Joke box set. —*Alex Ogg*

● **Laugh? I Nearly Bought One!** / Sep. 18, 1992 / Plan 9/Caroline ✦✦✦✦✦
Easily the best compilation available of Killing Joke's prime years with Virgin/EG. There is one major drawback, however: The "Wardance" B-side "Pssyche"—probably the greatest thing Killing Joke ever committed to vinyl—is only present in a live version. To date, the original studio cut still hasn't been reissued on a digital medium. The cover artwork for *Laugh? I Nearly Bought One*—a genuine photo of the Pope ranks of seig-heiling Nazis—is typically provocative, reminiscent of the picture of Fred Astaire dancing over the WWI trenches, which accompanied the original 7" issue of "Wardance"—a reminder that while goth bands in general were a colorless bunch, the blackest thing about Killing Joke was their sense of humor. —*Alex Ogg*

Pandemonium / Aug. 2, 1994 / Zoo ✦✦

Democracy / Apr. 1996 / Zoo ✦✦

No Way Out But Forward Go / May 22, 2001 / Pilot ✦✦✦

No Way Out But Forward Go is Killing Joke's first full-length release since 1996's *Democracy*, and the band's third live album. Taken from a 1985 concert on the *Night Time* tour, it's hardly a worthy substitute for a studio album, but it does showcase Killing Joke at their finest. The 17 tracks are split roughly equally between Youth-era and Paul Raven-era material, with most of the *Night Time* album being present. All of the early classics ("Wardance," "Requiem") are featured, as well as rarer songs such as "Pssyche." Live versions of two tracks from *Brighter Than a Thousand Suns* are also included, as is a full CD-ROM of the concert on some editions. Unfortunately, most of the show sounds as if it's been recorded in a rehearsal room, since the audience appears to be almost entirely lifeless. The band themselves give it their best effort, however, and throw themselves into the performance wholeheartedly. The only low point is "The Good Samaritan," which isn't really appropriate for a live setting. Other than that, it's a good representation of the band's bile-and-fire approach. *—Jim Harper*

Andy Kim (Andrew Joachim)

b. Dec. 5, 1946, Montreal, Quebec, Canada

Vocals, Songwriter / Brill Building Pop, Bubblegum, Pop/Rock

Born in Montreal in 1946, Andy Kim went to New York at the age of 16 to become a star. He soon returned home but then quit school and moved to New York to begin recording. He recorded several singles in 1963, but Kim remained unknown until he joined songwriters Jeff Barry and Ellie Greenwich, who helped out on the big late-'60s hits "How'd We Ever Get This Way," "So Good Together" and "Baby, I Love You" (a platinum-plus single). Andy Kim's albums of the period include *Rainbow Ride* (1969), *Baby I Love You* (1969), *Rock Me Gently* (1974) and his ... *Greatest Hits* (1974).

After his father died in 1976, Kim stopped recording, though he returned under the name Baron Longfellow with two albums: a self-titled LP in 1980 and *Prisoner by Design* in 1984. *—John Bush*

● **Baby I Love You: Greatest Hits** / Dec. 28, 1999 / EMI ✦✦✦✦

Andy Kim had many of his greatest songs and successes behind the scenes as a songwriter for such effervescent pop groups as the Monkees. He did have a solo career, however, that peaked with the terrific single "Rock Me Gently," a smash hit at the time and a staple of '70s compilations ever since. Of course, that's on *Baby I Love You: Greatest Hits*, which also includes smaller singles like the title track and "Shoot 'Em Up, Baby," along with oldies covers ("Be My Baby," "Oh Pretty Woman") and some fun originals by Kim. None of this strays too far from the sound etched out on "Rock Me Gently," even on the slower numbers, and while nothing is quite as good, it's enjoyable nevertheless, at least for fans of Kim and '70s AM pop. *—Stephen Thomas Erlewine*

King Crimson

f. 1969, England

Album Rock, Prog-Rock/Art Rock

If there is one group that embodies progressive rock, it is King Crimson. Led by guitar/Mellotron virtuoso Robert Fripp, during its first five years of existence the band stretched both the language and structure of rock into realms of jazz and classical music, all the while avoiding pop and psychedelic sensibilities. The absence of mainstream compromises and the lack of an overt sense of humor ultimately doomed the group to nothing more than a large cult following, but made their albums among the most enduring and respectable of the prog-rock era. Crimson's 1969 debut *In the Court of the Crimson King* was one of the most challenging albums of the entire fledgling progressive rock movement, but somehow it caught the public's collective ear at the right moment, becoming a hit in England and America. At the peak of the LP's success, the original band broke up; Fripp recorded albums with several other lineups through 1972, none of them stable. Later that year, however, Fripp put together a skilled new band; their debut album, *Larks' Tongues in Aspic*, made it all the way to the Top 20 in England in 1973. 1974's *Starless and Bible Black* made this the first lineup to remain intact for more than one American tour and more than one album. But, alas, even it had begun to splinter. One more album, *Red*, was completed that summer; Fripp disbanded the group on September 25, 1974, seemingly for the last time, and moved on to other projects. In 1981, Fripp formed a new group called Discipline; by the time their album was released that year, the group's name had been changed to King Crimson (the album was still titled *Discipline*, however). This band had a herky-jerky sound completely different from any of the other lineups to use that name; they splintered after two more albums, 1982's *Beat* and 1984's *Three of a Perfect Pair*. King Crimson remained silent until 1994, when Fripp reunited with an augmented version of the *Discipline*-era lineup, re-establishing Crimson as a viable touring and recording concern. *—Bruce Eder*

★ **In the Court of the Crimson King** / 1969 / EG ✦✦✦✦✦

The group's definitive album, and one of the most daring debut albums ever recorded by anybody. At the time, it blew all of the progressive/psychedelic competition (the Moody Blues, the Nice, etc.) out of the running, although it was almost too good for the band's own good—it took them nearly four years to come up with a record as strong or concise. Ian McDonald's Mellotron is the dominant instrument, along with his saxes and Fripp's guitar, making this a somewhat different-sounding record from everything else they ever did. And even though that Mellotron sound is muted and toned down compared to their concert work of the era (see *Epitaph*, below), it is still fierce and overpowering—coupled with some strong songwriting, most of it filled with dark and doom-laden visions, the strongest singing of Greg Lake's entire career, and Fripp's guitar playing (a strange mix of elegant classic, Hendrix-like rock explosions, and jazz noodling), the mix was overpowering. Fripp would be the only survivor on their subsequent records. Note: Be sure the CD you buy indicates it was made or distributed by Caroline Records—earlier versions sounded awful. *—Bruce Eder*

In the Wake of Poseidon / 1970 / EG ✦✦✦✦✦

King Crimson opened 1970 scarcely in existence as a band, having lost two key members (Ian McDonald and Michael Giles), with a third (Greg Lake) about to leave. Their second album—largely composed of Robert Fripp's songwriting and material salvaged from their stage repertory ("Pictures of a City" and "The Devil's Triangle")—is actually better produced and better sounding than their first. Surprisingly, Fripp's guitar is not the dominant instrument here: The Mellotron, taken over by Fripp after McDonald's departure—and played even better than before—still remains the band's signature. The record doesn't tread enough new ground to precisely rival *In the Court of the Crimson King*. Fripp, however, has made an impressive show of transmuting material that worked on stage ("Mars" aka "The Devil's Triangle") into viable studio creations, and "Cadence and Cascade" may be the prettiest song the group ever cut. "The Devil's Triangle," which is essentially an unauthorized adaptation of "Mars, Bringer of War" from Gustav Holst's *The Planets*, was later used in an eerie Bermuda Triangle documentary of the same name. In March of 2000, Caroline and Virgin released a 24-bit digitally remastered job that puts the two Mellotrons, Michael Giles' drums, Peter Giles' bass, and even Fripp's acoustic guitar and Keith Tippett's acoustic piano practically in the lap of the listener. *—Bruce Eder*

Lizard / 1970 / EG ✦✦✦

Lizard is very consciously jazz-oriented—the influence of Miles Davis (particularly *Sketches of Spain*) being especially prominent—and very progressive, even compared with the two preceding albums. The pieces are longer and have extensive developmental sections, reminiscent of classical music, and the lyrics are more ornate, while the subject matter is more exotic and rarified—epic, Ragnarok-like battles between good and evil that run cyclically. The doom-laden mood of the first two albums is just as strong, except that the music is prettier; the only thing missing is a sense of humor. Jon Anderson of Yes guests on one key number, "Prince Rupert Awakes" (which vocalist/bassist Gordon Haskell never completed), and the album is stronger for his presence. At the time of its release, some critics praised *Lizard* for finally breaking with the formula and structure that shaped the two preceding albums, but overall it's an acquired taste. *—Bruce Eder*

Islands / 1971 / EG ✦✦✦

The weakest Crimson studio album from their first era is only a real disappointment in relation to the extraordinarily high quality of the group's earlier efforts. The songs are somewhat uneven and draw from three years of inspiration. "The Letter" is an adaptation of "Drop In," a group composition that was featured in the early set of the original Crimson lineup from 1969, while "Song of the Gulls" goes back to the pre-King Crimson trio of Giles, Giles & Fripp for its source ("Suite No. 1"). There are also a few surprises, such as the Beatles-like harmonies on the raunchy "Ladies of the Road" and the extraordinary interweaving of electric guitar and Mellotron by Robert Fripp on "A Sailor's Tale, which is one of the highlights of the early- to mid-period group's output. Some of the music overstays its welcome—several of the six tracks are extended too far, out of the need to fill up an LP—but the virtuosity of the band picks up most of the slack on the composition side: Collins' saxes and Wallace's drums keep things much more than interesting in tandem with Fripp's guitar and Mellotron, and guest vocalist Paulina Lucas' keening accompaniment carries parts of "Formentera Lady" that might otherwise have dragged. After an unfotunate history of mediocre pressings, Virgin Records released a 24-bit digitally remastered CD that captured the original intact in March of 2000. *—Bruce Eder*

Earthbound / 1972 / Polydor ✦

Larks' Tongues in Aspic / 1973 / EG ✦✦✦✦✦

King Crimson reborn yet again—the newly configured band makes its debut with a violin (courtesy of David Cross) sharing center stage with Robert Fripp's guitars and his Mellotron, which is pushed into the background. The music is the most experimental of Fripp's career up to this time—though some of it actually dated (in embryonic form) back to the tail end of the Boz Burrell-Ian Wallace-Mel Collins lineup. And John Wetton was the group's strongest singer/bassist since Greg Lake's departure three years earlier. What's more, this lineup quickly established itself as a powerful performing unit working in a more purely experimental, less jazz-oriented vein than its immediate predecessor. "*Outer Limits* music" was how one reviewer referred to it, mixing Cross' demonic fiddling with shrieking electronics, Bill Bruford's astounding dexterity at the drum kit, Jamie Muir's melodic and usually understated percussion, Wetton's thundering (yet melodic) bass, and Fripp's guitar, which generated sounds ranging from traditional classical and soft pop-jazz licks to hair-curling electric flourishes. The remastered edition, which appeared in the summer of 2000 in Europe and slightly later in America, features beautifully remastered sound—among other advantages, it moves the finger cymbals opening the first section of the title track into sharp focus, with minimal hiss or noise to obscure them, exposes the multiple percussion instruments used on the opening of "Easy Money," and gives far more clarity to "The Talking Drum." This version is superior to any prior CD release of *Larks' Tongues in Aspic*, and contains a booklet reprinting period press clippings, session information, and production background on the album. *—Bruce Eder*

Starless and Bible Black / Mar. 1974 / EG ✦✦✦✦✦

Starless and Bible Black is even more powerful and daring than its predecessor, *Larks' Tongues in Aspic*, with jarring tempo shifts, explosive guitar riffs, and soaring, elegant, and delicate violin and Mellotron parts scattered throughout its 41 minutes, often all in the same songs. The album was on the outer fringes of accessible progressive rock, with enough musical ideas explored to make *Starless and Bible Black* more than background for tripping the way Emerson, Lake & Palmer's albums were used. "The Night Watch," a song about a Rembrandt painting, was, incredibly, a single release, although it was much more representative of the sound that Crimson was abandoning than where it was going in 1973-1974. More to that point were the contents of side two of the original LP, a pair of instrumentals that threw the group's hardest sounds right in the face of the listener, and gained some converts in the process. This album was remastered again for CD in the summer of 2000, in significantly improved sound that brought out the details (and surprising lyricism) of much of the material in far greater detail. The booklet included with the remastered version is not as impressive as some of the rest of the series entries in terms of information, but has great photos. —*Bruce Eder*

Red / Nov. 1974 / EG ◆◆◆◆

King Crimson falls apart once more, seemingly for the last time, as David Cross walks away during the making of this album. It became Robert Fripp's last thoughts on this version of the band, a bit noiser overall but with some surprising sounds featured, mostly out of the group's past—Mel Collins' and Ian McDonald's saxes, Marc Charig's cornet, and Robin Miller's oboe, thus providing a glimpse of what the 1972-era King Crimson might've sounded like handling the later group's repertory (which nearly happened). Indeed, Charig's cornet gets just about the best showcase it ever had on a King Crimson album, and the truth is that few intact groups could have gotten an album as good as *Red* together. The fact that it was put together by a band in its death throes makes it all the more impressive an achievement. Indeed, *Red* does improve in some respects on certain aspects of the previous album—including "Starless," a cousin to the prior album's title track—and only the lower quality of the vocal compositions keeps this from being as strongly recommended as its two predecessors. *Red* was reissued on CD in the summer of 2000 in a remastered edition that features killer sound and an excellent booklet, containing a good account of the circumstances surrounding the recording of this album. —*Bruce Eder*

USA / 1975 / Atlantic ◆◆◆

The group was disbanded, but at least two bootleg live albums (drawn from live FM radio broadcasts along their last tour) were circulating, and it was obvious there was some kind of audience, so *USA* was released. The performances are good, though *The Great Deceiver* box proved there was better material and there were better ways of treating these tapes. Eddie Jobson subs for David Cross on the violin on several of these cuts. —*Bruce Eder*

Young Person's Guide to King Crimson / 1976 / Island ◆◆◆◆◆

Two years after the group's breakup, Robert Fripp prepared this double-LP compilation, which included rare singles ("Groon"), Giles, Giles & Fripp-era outtakes ("I Talk to the Wind") and a booklet giving about the fullest account of the group's history ever done up to that point. Supplanted by later CD boxes, but this British import is as good a collection as one could have hoped for at the time. —*Bruce Eder*

Discipline / 1981 / EG ◆◆◆◆◆

When King Crimson leader Robert Fripp decided to assemble a new version of the band in the early '80s, prog-rock fans rejoiced, and most new wave fans frowned. But after hearing this new unit's first release, 1981's *Discipline*, all the elements that made other arty new wave rockers successful (i.e., Talking Heads, Pere Ubu, the Police, etc.) were evident. Combining the futuristic guitar of Adrian Belew with the textured guitar of Fripp doesn't sound like it would work on paper, but the pairing of these two originals worked out magically. Rounding out the quartet was bass wizard Tony Levin and ex-Yes drummer Bill Bruford. Belew's vocals fit the music perfectly, sounding like David Byrne at his most paranoid at times (the funk track "Thela Hun Ginjeet"). Some other highlights include the opening "Elephant Talk," driven by Tony Levin's "stick" (a strange bass-like instrument), the atmospheric "The Sheltering Sky," and the heavy rocker "Indiscipline." Many Crimson fans consider this album one of their best, right up there with *In the Court of the Crimson King*. It's easy to understand why after you hear the inspired performances by this hungry new version of the band. —*Greg Prato*

Beat / 1982 / EG ◆◆◆◆◆

Beat is not as good as its predecessor (1981's *Discipline*), but it's not too shabby, either. The '80s version of Crimson (Robert Fripp—guitar, Adrian Belew—vocals/guitar, Tony Levin—bass, and Bill Bruford—drums) retains the then-modern day new wave sound introduced on *Discipline*. The band's performances are still inspired, but the songwriting isn't as catchy or strong. The moody love song "Heartbeat" has become a concert favorite for the band, and contains a Jimi Hendrix-like backwards guitar solo. Other worthwhile tracks include "Waiting Man," which features world music sounds (thanks to some stunning bass/percussion interplay), and "Neurotica" does an excellent job of painting an unwavering picture of a large U.S. city, with its jerky rhythms and tense vocals. With lots of different guitar textures, bass explorations, and uncommon drum rhythms present, King Crimson's *Beat* will automatically appeal to other musicians. But since they're fantastic songwriters as well, you don't have to be a virtuoso to feel the passion of their music. —*Greg Prato*

3 of a Perfect Pair / Jul. 1984 / Warner Brothers ◆◆◆

Upon its release in 1984, *Three of a Perfect Pair* caused some unrest among fans of King Crimson. Most of their audience felt that the band had made a conscious and obvious decision to try to break through to a more mainstream pop audience. But in hindsight, this is hardly the case; it sounds unlike anything that was out at the time. Like 1982's *Beat*, *Three of a Perfect Pair* doesn't quite meet the high standards set by 1981's *Discipline*, but does contain a few Crimson treats. The opening title track contains an unrelenting groove that never seems to let up, while "Sleepless" starts off with Tony Levin laying down some funky bass until Adrian Belew's trademark paranoid vocals kick in and assure the listener that "it's alright to feel a little fear." Also included are the seven-minute instrumental soundscape "Industry" and the cautionary tale of a "Model Man." This would prove to be the new King Crimson's last release for nearly ten years; the group disbanded soon after

as its members concentrated on solo careers and other projects, until a mid-'90s reunion brought them all back together. —*Greg Prato*

Frame by Frame / 1991 / Caroline ◆◆◆◆

With its varying short-lived phases, King Crimson is well suited to the box set treatment, and overall, *Frame by Frame: The Essential King Crimson* doesn't disappoint. At four discs, it's perhaps a little hefty to serve as a comprehensive introduction for newcomers, even though it could work very well in that context; in the end, the box is more of a close-to-definitive package for fans who fall somewhere in between the realms of casual and devoted. The first three discs do an excellent job of summarizing King Crimson's extremely distinct prime-period lineups: the first disc concentrates on the often jazzy symphonic rock of 1969-1971 (including *almost* the entirety of *In the Court of the Crimson King*), the second covers the heavy, experimental soundscapes of 1973-1974, and the third features the off-kilter, new wave-influenced prog pop of 1981-1984. The fourth disc is a career-spanning sampler of live Crimson, and although the varying sound quality and musical styles make it a less cohesive listen than the other discs, it does give an excellent idea of the various lineups' extraordinary performing range. Bandleader/compiler Robert Fripp's selections are sometimes skewed toward particular albums, and devotees may cringe at the fact that some of the longer songs have been edited for time, but, in fact, all of this makes for a better, tighter listen; it's difficult to argue with what is here, and the edits often chop out less interesting sections of the pieces. Additionally, the remastering job and the liner notes are both excellent. So, in spite of its minor flaws, *Frame by Frame* is really everything one could want from a basic King Crimson box set. —*Steve Huey*

The Great Deceiver (Live 1973-1974) / Oct. 30, 1992 / Caroline ◆◆◆◆◆

Four CDs full of live King Crimson from 1973 and 1974, an era that many consider their best. Although some songs are repeated, they're never played the same way twice. If you're a King Crimson fan, that's enough of an incentive for purchase; if you're not, the musical expertise of the band might convert you, providing you have the money for a box set. —*Stephen Thomas Erlewine*

VROOOM / 1994 / Discipline ◆◆

THRAK / Apr. 1995 / Virgin ◆◆◆◆

The only progressive rock band from the '60s to be making new, vital, progressive music in the '90s, King Crimson returned from a ten-year exile in 1995 with *THRAK*, their first album since 1984's *3 of a Perfect Pair*. As with the '80s band, guitarist/ringleader Robert Fripp recruited singer/guitarist Adrian Belew, bassist Tony Levin, and drummer Bill Bruford for this incarnation of his classic band. However, he added to this familiar quartet two new members: Chapman Stick player Trey Gunn and ex-Mr. Mister drummer Pat Mastelotto. Effectively, Fripp created a "double trio," and the six musicians combine their instruments in extremely unique ways. The mix is very dense, overpoweringly so at times, but careful listens will reveal that each musician has his own place in each song; the denseness of the sound is by design, not the accidental result of too many cooks in the kitchen. Sometimes, as in "THRAK," the two trios are set against each other, in some sort of musical faux combat. In others, they just combine their respective sounds to massive effect. On "Dinosaur," perhaps the strongest track on the record, Mastelotto and Bruford set up an ominous tom-tom groove that supports an even more ominous guitar figure. The vocal, the musings of a long-dead sauropod, are vintage Belew, just as the freaky, falling-down-the-stairs solo in the middle is vintage Fripp. Other high points include the drum duet "B'Boom" and the two Belew/Fripp "Inner Garden" pieces. Allusions to earlier Crimson abounds, such as the form of "VROOM," for example, which is suspiciously reminiscent of "Red" (from the 1974 album of the same name), or the shout-out to "The Sheltering Sky" (from 1981's *Discipline*) in "Walking on Air." Thankfully, this never gets annoying, but instead acts as a subtle nudge and a wink to faithful fans. King Crimson came back in a major way with *THRAK*, and proved that, even in its fourth major incarnation, Fripp and company still had something to say. High-quality prog. —*Daniel Gioffre*

Thrakattak / Jun. 25, 1996 / DPL ◆◆◆

Thrakattak is a collection of live, improvised pieces the 1995 edition of King Crimson performed during their fall tour. Often, the group delves into dense, treacherous waters, heading into the unknown with reckless abandon. Sometimes, this results in soaring, majestic music, but occasionally it means that the band meanders directionlessly for far too long. And that means that even though this is filled with great, challenging music, there is simply too much mediocre material for anyone but diehard Crimson fans. —*Stephen Thomas Erlewine*

Epitaph / Apr. 15, 1997 / Discipline ◆◆◆◆

Double CD of live 1969 material from King Crimson's first and, ultimately, best-loved incarnation, featuring the same lineup that performed on the first album (Fripp, Lake, McDonald, and Giles). Other than four songs from BBC sessions, the entire set was drawn from shows from their late-'69 tour of the U.S. (after which the personnel was completely reorganized). The emphasis is on the three most famed songs from *In the Court of the Crimson King* (the title track, "Epitaph," and "21st Century Schizoid Man"), each of which is heard two or three times. Aside from some minor variations in the solos and lyrics, these are pretty similar to the studio versions, although they do show how adept the band were at re-creating the arrangements onstage. There are also a few numbers that the band never released as studio takes, although live versions of a few sneaked out on the *Frame by Frame* compilation: Donovan's druggy "Get Thy Bearings," an effectively bombastic take on Holst's "Mars" (two versions), the jazzy "Travel Weary Capricorn," and some rather shapeless improvisations. The fidelity is imperfect, but generally pretty good. It's not on the same level as the debut album, but it doesn't pretend to be—it's designed with the hardcore fan in mind (complete with 64 pages of liner notes). For that audience, it's a worthy supplement to this particular lineup's meager studio output. And if you crave yet more, two additional CDs of live '69 performances are available from Discipline via mail order only. *—Richie Unterberger*

King Curtis

b. Feb. 7, 1934, Fort Worth, TX, **d.** Aug. 14, 1971, New York, NY

Sax (Tenor) / Southern Soul, East Coast Blues, Soul-Jazz, Instrumental Rock, R&B

King Curtis was the last of the great R&B tenor sax giants. He came to prominence in the mid-'50s as a session musician in New York, recording, at one time or another, for most East Coast R&B labels. A long association with Atlantic/Atco began in 1958, especially on recordings by the Coasters. He recorded singles for many small labels in the '50s—his own Atco sessions (1958-1959), then Prestige/New Jazz and Prestige/TruSound for jazz and R&B albums (1960-1961). Curtis also had a #1 R&B single with "Soul Twist" on Enjoy Records (1962). He was signed by Capitol (1963-1964), where he cut mostly singles, including "Soul Serenade." Returning to Atlantic in 1965, he remained there for the rest of his life. He had solid R&B single success with "Memphis Soul Stew" and "Ode to Billie Joe" (1967). Beginning in 1967, Curtis started to take a more active studio role at Atlantic—leading and contracting sessions for other artists, producing with Jerry Wexler and later on his own. He also became the leader of Aretha Franklin's backing unit, the Kingpins. He compiled several albums of singles during this period. All aspects of his career were in full swing at the time he was murdered in 1971. *—Bob Porter*

● **Instant Soul: The Legendary King Curtis** / Oct. 19, 1994 / Razor & Tie ✦✦✦✦✦

Nice overview of Curtis' solo career, beginning with the breakthrough success of "Soul Twist" and "Soul Serenade" and moving through his later recordings for Atlantic. It's interesting to hear Curtis in both the Memphis and Muscle Shoals settings and how he adapts his horn to different grooves along the way. A solid collection of this artist's best, although points get shaved off for the inclusion of a later recut version of "Wiggle Wobble," rather than the original by Les Cooper that Curtis blew so magnificently on. *—Cub Koda*

Ben E. King (Benjamin Earl Nelson)

b. Sep. 23, 1938, Henderson, NC

Vocals / Pop-Soul, Brill Building Pop, Soul

Swirling strings, subtly shaded orchestrations, and Ben E. King's assured baritone were a blueprint for uptown soul success during the early '60s. King and his vocal group, the Five Crowns, were in the right place at the right time when, in 1959, the manager of the Drifters decided to sack his entire group and solicit replacements. As new lead singer for the Drifters, King crooned the soulful smashes "There Goes My Baby," "Save the Last Dance for Me," and "I Count the Tears" before heading out on his own in 1960. The vocalist's own Atco singles mirrored the sumptuous production of his Drifter sides, and "Spanish Harlem," "Don't Play That Song (You Lied)," and the R&B chart-topping "Stand by Me" were all huge successes. King remained with Atco through 1969, then triumphantly returned to Atlantic in 1975 with another #1 soul hit, "Supernatural Thing (Part 1)." With the re-release of "Stand by Me" as the theme to the 1986 film of the same title, King was in demand all over again, the stirring song improbably scaling the charts for a second time, despite being a quarter-century old. *—Bill Dahl*

Anthology / Apr. 20, 1993 / Rhino ✦✦✦✦✦

This two-disc, 50-song box set thoroughly documents the recordings that Ben E. King cut for Atlantic. Starting as the lead voice of the Drifters on such hits as "There Goes My Baby" and "Save the Last Dance for Me," King went on to a successful solo career with a string of singles that matched his smooth, sexy baritone with tastefully arranged string sections and Latin rhythms. All of those early hits—"Stand by Me" and "Spanish Harlem" were the biggest—are included here, along with non-hit 45s by the likes of Leiber/Stoller, Doc Pomus, Mort Shuman, Phil Spector, and Goffin/King that were nearly equal in worth. As the '60s progressed, King moved toward a more mainstream, heavier soul sound and less distinctive material, culminating in his parting from Atlantic in 1969. He returned to the label in the mid-'70s for a string of mainstream R&B successes. This compilation includes 16 non-LP singles from the '60s, which together with the hits constitute the definitive overview of this influential soul singer's work. *—Richie Unterberger*

● **Very Best of Ben E. King** / Feb. 3, 1998 / Rhino ✦✦✦✦✦

The Very Best of Ben E. King is an excellent 16-track collection that features his biggest hits from 1959-1975, including hits he had with the Drifters in addition to his solo smashes. Among the featured songs are "There Goes My Baby," "Dance With Me," "This Magic Moment," "Save the Last Dance for Me," "Spanish Harlem," "Stand By Me," "Amor," "Don't Play That Song (You Lied)," "How Can I Forget," "I (Who Have Nothing)" and "Supernatural Thing, Pt. 1." All of his best-known songs are available on this concise, affordable disc, which makes for an ideal introduction to this legendary R&B/soul vocalist. *—Stephen Thomas Erlewine*

Carole King

b. Feb. 9, 1942, Brooklyn, NY

Vocals, Keyboards, Piano, Guitar, Synthesizer / Brill Building Pop, Pop/Rock, Soft Rock, Pop, Adult Contemporary, Singer/Songwriter

While the landmark album *Tapestry* earned her superstar status, singer/songwriter Carole King had already firmly established herself as one of pop music's most gifted and successful composers, with work recorded by everyone from the Beatles to Aretha Franklin. With partner Gerry Goffin, whom she eventually married, King began writing under publishers Don Kirshner and Al Nevins in the famed pop songwriting house the Brill Building. In 1961, Goffin and King scored their first hit with the Shirelles' chart-topping "Will You Love Me Tomorrow"; their next effort, Bobby Vee's "Take Good Care of My Baby," also hit Number One, as did "The Locomotion," recorded by their baby-sitter, Little Eva. Together, the couple wrote over 100 chart hits in a vast range of styles, including the Chiffons' "One Fine Day," the Monkees' "Pleasant Valley Sunday," the Drifters' "Up on the Roof," the Cookies' "Chains" (later covered by the Beatles) and Aretha Franklin's "(You Make Me Feel) Like a Natural Woman." King also continued her attempts to mount a solo career, but scored only one hit, 1962's superb "It Might as Well Rain Until September." In 1971, however, she released *Tapestry*, which stayed on the charts for over six years and was the best-selling album of the era. A quiet, reflective work which proved seminal in the development of the singer/songwriter genre, *Tapestry* also scored a pair of hit singles, "So Far Away" and the chart-topping "It's Too Late," whose flip-side, "I Feel the Earth Move," garnered major airplay as well. 1971's *Music* also hit Number One, and generated the hit "Sweet Seasons"; 1972's *Rhymes and Reasons* reached Number Two on the charts, and 1974's *Wrap Around Joy*, which featured the hit "Jazzman," hit the Number One spot. *—Jason Ankeny*

Writer / 1970 / Epic/Legacy ✦✦✦

Writer, Carole King's solo debut, finds the legendary melodist searching for her voice. Stylistically, she dabbles with pop ("No Easy Way Down"), country ("To Love") and rock ("I Can't Hear You No More") with mixed results. While the political message of "Eventually" hasn't held up, neither have throwaways like "Raspberry Jam" and "Spaceship Races." Only on the yearning "Goin' Back" and a remake of "Up on the Roof" (backed by James Taylor's guitar and harmonies) does she settle into the living room intimacy that led to the landmark *Tapestry* album. *—J.P. Ollio*

★ **Tapestry** / Mar. 1971 / Epic/Legacy ✦✦✦✦✦

Carole King brought the fledgling singer/songwriter phenomenon to the masses with *Tapestry*, one of the most successful albums in pop music history. A remarkably expressive and intimate record, it's a work of consummate craftsmanship. Always a superior pop composer, King reaches even greater heights as a performer; new songs like the hits "It's Too Late" and "I Feel the Earth Move" rank solidly with past glories, while chestnuts like "You've Got a Friend," "Will You Still Love Me Tomorrow," and "(You Make Me Feel Like) A Natural Woman" take on added resonance when delivered in her own warm, compelling voice. With its reliance on pianos and gentle drumming, *Tapestry* is a light and airy work on its surface, occasionally skirting the boundaries of jazz, but it's also an intensely emotional record, the songs confessional and direct; in its time it connected with listeners like few records before it, and it remains an illuminating experience decades later. The 1999 CD reissue on Sony adds two bonus tracks: the previously unreleased outtake "Out in the Cold" and a previously unreleased live 1973 version (on solo piano) of "Smackwater Jack." *—Jason Ankeny*

Music / Dec. 1971 / Epic ✦✦✦✦

After years as one of the most prolific and successful songwriters in pop music, Carole King emerged in the '70s with *Tapestry*, an album that catapulted her to the forefront of the singer/songwriter movement. While she had mined her back catalog for that album, she relied more heavily on songs written with new collaborator Toni Stern for *Music*. Coming out on the heels of the classic *Tapestry*, it's hard not to feel like this album was a bit of a letdown. However, time has shown this album to be one of her finest. While these songs lyrically lack the simplistic beauty of Gerry Goffin-penned tunes, the melodies are very strong and Carole King adds some nice texture to her piano-based tunes with the tasteful percussion of Bobbye Hall. When King goes for grand statements, however, it doesn't always work. Her call for peace and brotherhood works on songs like the opening track, "Brother, Brother," but her voice is not strong enough and does not convey enough emotion to prevent uplifting tunes like "Carry Your Load" from sounding a bit hollow and preachy. But her songwriting is still in peak form, and there are many highlights including "It's Gonna Take Some Time" (also made into a hit by the Carpenters) and "Song of Long Ago" (with backing vocals by James Taylor). *—Vik Iyengar*

Rhymes & Reasons / Nov. 1972 / Epic/Legacy ✦✦✦

On her second follow-up to *Tapestry* and third new album in less than two years, King turned entirely to new compositions, most of them co-written with Toni Stern, rather than relying partly on songs from her back catalog. The result was a thinner collection than *Tapestry* or *Music*, although the album still went to number two and featured the Top 25 hit "Been to Canaan," as well as the warm love song "The First Day in August." *—William Ruhlmann*

Fantasy / Jun. 1973 / Epic ✦✦✦

Wrap Around Joy / Sep. 1974 / Epic ✦✦✦

More upbeat and rockin' than her last couple of efforts, *Wrap Around Joy* contains much of the jazz-tinged rock King was becoming known for. Here, she found chart action with "Jazzman" as well as the title track. A good, solid effort, as usual, from one of America's finest songwriters. *—James Chrispell*

Really Rosie / 1975 / Epic/Legacy ✦✦✦✦✦

The soundtrack to a television special originating from the pen of author Maurice Sendak, *Really Rosie* is that rare children's album with the wit and intelligence to capture the imaginations of adult listeners as well. Sendak's sharp, clever lyrics tell the story of young Brooklynite Rosie and a cast of vividly etched supporting characters including the apathetic Pierre and a boy named Chicken Soup; Carole King's melodies serve the material remarkably well, transforming even the most deliberately silly songs into catchy, piano-driven pop confections. In fact, it's in many ways her most fully realized record since *Tapestry*, with a sparkling charm and heartfelt sincerity that interim releases lacked. *—Jason Ankeny*

Thoroughbred / Jan. 1976 / Epic/Legacy ✦✦✦

Simple Things / Jul. 1977 / Capitol ✦✦

Welcome Home / 1978 / Capitol ✦✦

Her Greatest Hits: Songs of Long Ago / Mar. 1978 / Epic/Legacy ✦✦✦✦✦
This album was always sort of a joke among King's serious fans, containing 12 songs drawn from six albums, and liner notes that fail even to acknowledge the existence of *Writer*, her one pre-*Tapestry* solo LP. *A Natural Woman* supplanted it a few years ago, and the addition of two live cuts, "Eventually" and "(You Make Me Feel Like) A Natural Woman" from the Carnegie Hall concert on the 1999 reissue (Ode/Epic/Legacy 65846) doesn't extend the range or depth of the selection sufficiently. On the other hand, the 1999 remastering does improve the listening pleasure inherent in what is here—the material off of *Tapestry, Music, Rhymes & Reasons* and others is now very robust, with vivid instrumentation and a close, rich profile of King's voice. The selection of King's work is still only an inch deep, but it's a more rewarding inch. *—Bruce Eder*

Touch the Sky / 1979 / Capitol ✦✦

Pearls: Songs of Goffin and King / 1980 / Scarface ✦✦✦
Make no doubt about it, this is possibly Carole King's most important work since *Tapestry*, and why a similar album didn't follow *Tapestry* or its follow-up, *Music*, was a marketing blunder and a mystery. Missing here is Lou Adler's production, though King and her co-producer Mark Hallman are hardly inefficient. It's just that some songs get more attention than others. "Dancin With Tears in My Eyes" opens the collection, a pleasant new addition to their repertoire, but next to "Locomotion," "One Fine Day," "Chains," and "Snow Queen," its purpose is more to bring the album full circle than to try to compete with these classics. "One Fine Day," the song the Chiffons brought Top Five, was the hit, going Top 15 from this set 17 years later. The reworking of the Freddie Scott/Bobby Vee/Donny Osmond hit "Hey Girl" is breathtaking. Here Carole King is backed by lush production and a bluesy vocal that surpasses anything else on this record, as well as much of what was on the charts at this time. *Pearls: Songs of Goffin and King* is the set the artist's longtime fans craved when *Tapestry* made her more than a household name. This album deserves its place right next to *Tapestry*. *—Joe Viglione*

One to One / 1982 / Atlantic ✦✦

Speeding Time / 1983 / Atlantic ✦✦

City Streets / Apr. 1989 / Capitol ✦✦

Colour of Your Dreams / Mar. 16, 1993 / Rhythm Safari ✦✦

A Natural Woman: The Ode Collection (1968-1976) / Sep. 13, 1994 / Epic/Legacy ✦✦✦✦✦
Carole King had already written an enormous amount of pop classics by the time she began her solo career in earnest in the late '60s. With her second album, *Tapestry*, King became one of the most popular and artistically successful singer-songwriters of the early '70s. King never matched the consistent brilliance of *Tapestry*, yet managed to record many fine songs during the rest of the decade. *A Natural Woman* collects all of her finest moments over the course of two discs. *Tapestry* is included in its entirety, along with the highlights from her other albums, making *A Natural Woman* the one essential King album—apart from *Tapestry* itself, of course. *—Stephen Thomas Erlewine*

Carnegie Hall Concert: June 18 1971 / Oct. 29, 1996 / Epic/Legacy ✦✦✦✦✦
This 17-song set was recorded on June 18, 1971, just as *Tapestry* was topping the charts and making King a superstar. Featuring most of *Tapestry* and a few songs from *Writer* and *Music*, this is in a sense Carole King unplugged (although that terminology was not yet in use). King performs the first half-dozen songs alone at the piano; bassist Charles Larkey, guitarist Danny Kortchmar, and a string quartet back her (in varying combinations) throughout the rest of the program. *Tapestry* wasn't exactly a high-wattage affair to begin with, so these rearrangements aren't radical, but they're different enough from the studio versions to merit attention by serious King fans. James Taylor, then at the peak of his own popularity, joins King on vocals for a medley of some of her old Brill Building hits, "Will You Still Love Me Tomorrow"/"Some Kind of Wonderful"/"Up on the Roof." *—Richie Unterberger*

Evelyn "Champagne" King

b. Jun. 29, 1960, New York, NY [The Bronx]
Vocals / Quiet Storm, Club/Dance, Disco, House, Soul
Singer Evelyn "Champagne" King first came to fame with the million-selling '70s disco smashes "Shame" and "I Don't Know If It's Right." For a teenager, King's voice was quite mature; many at first thought she was a grown woman. Born in the Bronx, NY, she had a show biz lineage. Her uncle was actor/singer/dancer Avon Long and her father, Erik King, was a singer and often filled in or augmented the various singing groups that appeared at New York's Apollo Theater. By her teens, King had relocated to Philadelphia, PA, with her mother, Johnniea. To make ends meet, King and her mother became after-hours cleaning women. While working one night at Philadelphia International Records' recording base, Sigma Sound Studios producer T. Life overheard some tantalizing vocals coming from a washroom. There he discovered 16-year-old Evelyn King and her mother. Signing the singer to a production deal with Life's Galaxy Productions, he began gathering song material for the teenager with the grown woman's voice. Getting a deal with RCA Records, Life's first single with Evelyn "Champagne" King was "Dancin' Dancin' Dancin'," co-written by Life and Teddy Pendergrass. But it was a song written by John Fitch and Reuben Cross called "Shame" that gave her career-launching success. The extended 12" disco mix by New York club DJs-turned-record remixers Al Garrison and David Todd began gaining radio play. Eventually it went gold, hitting number seven R&B, number nine pop on Billboard's charts in spring 1978. The follow-up, "I Don't Know if It's Right," remixed by Garrison and Todd, also went gold also, peaking at number seven R&B, number 23 pop in fall 1978. Teaming with Kashif, she also had two number one R&B hits, "I'm in Love" and "Love Come Down." *—Ed Hogan*

Love Come Down: The Best of Evelyn "Champagne" King / Mar. 1993 / RCA ✦✦✦✦
Before the term "disco diva" was universally adopted, Evelyn "Champagne" King was hailed as dance music's reigning female vocalist. King was a sensation in disco's heyday, and she survived the backlash and prospered during the genre's evolution into dance music. She enjoyed a string of hits into the mid-'80s and was able to excel on rhythm-dominated material and sentimental ballads. This 15-track anthology includes her finest uptempo cuts ("Shame," "I'm In Love," and "Love Come Down," all done at the original hit length), plus underrated numbers such as "Don't Hide Our Love" and "Give Me One Reason." Those who remember King's hits will savor this collection, while others who missed her prime period will hear why she was so dominant. *—Ron Wynn*

● **Greatest Hits** / Feb. 20, 2001 / RCA ✦✦✦✦
Although its track listing is fairly similar to 1993's *Love Come Down* compilation (cutting a few numbers but featuring three more total), *Greatest Hits* gets the nod as the Evelyn "Champagne" King collection of choice, since it features the original 7" single versions, plus several rare, extended 12" mixes. Covering King's career from 1978's breakout hit "Shame" through 1986, *Greatest Hits* is as comprehensive a retrospective of her work as is ever likely to be released, capturing all the reasons she was a popular and important disco and R&B singer. *—Steve Huey*

The Kingsmen

f. 1957, Portland, OR, **db.** 1968
Frat Rock, Garage Rock, Rock & Roll
A rock & roll band from Portland, Oregon, the Kingsmen's one big hit "Louie, Louie" defined the garage-band style and became one of the all-time classics. After singer/guitarist Jack Ely had "incorrectly" taught the rest of the band the Wailers' version of Richard Berry's "Louie Louie" (thus altering the basic rhythm into the now famous duh-duh-duh, duh-duh, duh-duh-duh, duh-duh riff that has become the only way anyone has played it since), they recorded it for fifty dollars at a primitive local recording studio with only three mikes, Ely hollering the lyrics into an overhead boom mike suspended ten feet in the air. Released on a local label, the record went nowhere after Paul Revere & the Raiders quickly covered it in the Northwest market, although it had quickly become a standard for all teen bands in that area. In 1964, the record started to break nationally; though the song itself has been covered repeatedly, the version by Ely and the original lineup remains definitive. *—Cub Koda*

● **The Best of the Kingsmen** / 1989 / Rhino ✦✦✦✦✦
Although the Kingsmen's original albums are enjoyable as artifacts, they're unnecessary for anyone but hardcore collectors. For most listeners, Rhino's *The Best of the Kingsmen* will be all the Kingsmen they'll ever need to hear. Over the course of 18 tracks, all of the garage-rock band's greatest hits—not just "Louie Louie," but trashy gems like "Little Latin Lupe Lu," "Death of an Angel," "The Jolly Green Giant," "Annie Fanny," "Killer Joe" and "The Climb"—are featured, along with several fine album tracks which make this the definitive compilation. *—Stephen Thomas Erlewine*

The Very Best of the Kingsmen / Jun. 2, 1998 / Varese ✦✦✦✦✦
Far from being a "one hit wonder" group, the Kingsmen had more than their share of hit records and charting albums to go with it. This 18-track collection brings together all the tunes that enhance and extend their reputation as one of the all-time great party bands. Of course, "Louie Louie" is here, but so is its demonic flip, "Haunted Castle" along with "Jolly Green Giant," "Money," "Long Green," "Little Latin Lupe Lu" and "The Climb," chart entries all. Also along for the ride are album tracks like "Shake a Tail Feather," "Do You Love Me?," "Shout," "Twist and Shout" and "Killer Joe," making a strong case for the group as the ultimate in early to mid-'60s dance floor mania. Though other greatest hit packages exist on the band (and the original albums as well), this one does the best job of giving the full picture of what they really did and the transfers sound absolutely wonderful. Start your collection with this one. *—AMG*

The Kinks

f. 1963, London, England
Album Rock, Pop/Rock, British Invasion, Hard Rock, Rock & Roll
The Kinks were one of the most influential bands of the British Invasion. Like most groups of their era, they began as an R&B/blues outfit. Despite lead singer Ray Davies' fey, foppish manner, they rocked harder than their peers, thanks to the pulverizing guitar riffs of his brother, Dave. The Kinks' early singles ("You Really Got Me," "All Day and All of the Night") were brutal, three-chord ravers, popular in both the UK and US; they also paved the way toward punk and metal, while inspiring their peers (the Who's early singles aped the Kinks). Toward the mid-'60s, Davies came into his own as a songwriter, developing a wry wit and eye for social commentary and the Kinks' music changed subtly, becoming more subtle and melodic, culminating in *Face to Face* and *Something Else*. Just as every rock band embraced psychedelia, the Kinks retreated from turbulent changes in rock. Banned from touring America, due to a mishap with a musicians' union, Ray Davies turned inward and nostalgic, creating the defiantly quaint and English *Village Green Preservation Society*. The album flopped upon its 1968 release, yet it earned a devoted cult, proving quite influential over the years. Davies continued to pursue conceptual works with *Arthur* and *Lola*, the latter giving them their first genuine hit in five years. During the early '70s, the Kinks lost their audience in the UK while remaining a cult act in America, due to Davies' increasingly impenetrable concept albums. The Kinks refashioned themselves as a hard rock stadium act in the late '70s, which increased their American popularity, culminating in the Top 10 1979 hit, *Low Budget*. The Kinks

remained a popular concert attraction in the early '80s and they were MTV favorites as well, resulting in their late Top 10 hit, "Come Dancing." Their commercial fortunes declined in the second half of the '80s and by the time of 1993's *Phobia*, Ray and Dave were the only original members left. Following a live acoustic album in the mid-'90s, the Kinks faded away, as both brothers pursued solo projects. *—Stephen Thomas Erlewine*

Kinks / Oct. 1964 / Castle ♦♦♦

Although the best of the Kinks' early work is among the best British Invasion music, their initial pair of albums was far less consistent than those of the Beatles, Stones, and Who. Aside from the great "You Really Got Me," this was a scrabby, disappointing set with surprisingly thin production. As R&B cover artists, the Kinks weren't nearly as adept as the Stones and Yardbirds; Ray Davies' original tunes were, "You Really Got Me" aside, perfunctory Merseyish pastiches; and a couple of tunes that producer Shel Talmy penned for the group, "Bald Headed Woman" and "I've Been Driving On Bald Mountain," were simply abominable. The rave-up treatments of the R&B standards "Got Love If You Want It" and "Cadillac" were good, and the simple "Stop Your Sobbing" would eventually be covered by the Pretenders, but overall this is real patchy. The CD reissue, however, is a great improvement, adding a wealth of bonus tracks from early singles and their first EP, some excellent. The ferocious "All Day and All of the Night" was a classic hit whose razor-riffing outdid even "You Really Got Me," and the B-sides "It's Alright" and "I Gotta Move" are tremendous frenetic lost gems. There are also a couple of previously unissued cuts: an alternative take of "Too Much Monkey Business" and an early, Beatle-ish original, "I Don't Need You Any More." *—Richie Unterberger*

Kinda Kinks / Feb. 1965 / Castle ♦♦♦

The Kinks' second album (which, like their debut, now has a running order and track selection restored to the original British version) found the band relying more on original material, but had similarly threadbare production and songwriting for the most part. This sounded like a rush job in both composition and performance, largely devoted to unexceptional, even generic, British Invasion pop-rock. Aside from the great hit "Tired of Waiting for You" and its driving B-side "Come On Now," in fact, nothing here stood out, with the exception of the lovely ballad "Something Better Beginning." On the CD reissue, however, a fine clutch of bonus tracks help save the day. "Set Me Free" is a great cut with a minor melody reminiscent of the Zombies; "Everybody's Gonna Be Happy" is a peppy if unremarkable single; "See My Friends" is a super-cool excursion into Indian-influenced folk-rock, also showing Ray Davies start to flower into a lyricist of touching vulnerability and ambiguity; and "Well Respected Man" was his first blow of savage social satire. There's also a previously unissued, piano-dominated ballad, "I Go to Sleep," although this has been recorded by several artists, including the Pretenders. *—Richie Unterberger*

Kinkdom / 1965 / Rhino ♦♦♦

Kinkdom is the American version of the Kinks' third album, boasting an altered sequence, plus a few singles. The end result may be a little bit of a hodge-podge, but not notably so, since the Kinks weren't making deliberately cohesive albums at the time. And while a few of the songs are simply run-of-the-mill, there are some terrific numbers here—not just "A Well Respected Man" and "Dedicated Follower of Fashion," but the exuberant "Who'll Be the Next in Line" and "I Need You," the menacing "I'm Not Like Everybody Else" and the haunting "See My Friends." This results in a fine listen, but after Castle's 1998 revamping of the Kinks catalog, it's better to pick the music up on those reissues. *—Stephen Thomas Erlewine*

The Kink Kontroversy / 1965 / Castle ♦♦♦♦♦

The Kinks came into their own as album artists—and Ray Davies fully matured as a songwriter—with *Kontroversy*, which bridged their raw early British Invasion sound with more sophisticated lyrics and thoughtful production. There are still powerful ravers like the hit "Till the End of the Day" (utilizing yet another "You Really Got Me"-type riff) and the abrasive, Dave Davies-sung cover of "Milk Cow Blues," but tracks like the calypso pastiche "I'm On an Island," where Ray sings of isolation with a forlorn yet merry bite, were far more indicative of their future direction. Other great songs on this underrated album include the uneasy nostalgia of "Where Have All the Good Times Gone?," the plaintive, almost fatalistic ballads "Ring the Bells" and "The World Keeps Going Round," and the Dave Davies-sung declaration of independence, "I Am Free." Some mediocre filler detracts from the disc's overall punch, though the CD reissue adds the great swinging London satire hit "Dedicated Follower of Fashion," as well as previously unissued alternate takes of "When I See That Girl of Mine" and "Dedicated Follower of Fashion." *—Richie Unterberger*

☆ **Face to Face** / Oct. 28, 1966 / Castle ♦♦♦♦♦

The Kink Kontroversy was a considerable leap forward in terms of quality, but it pales next to *Face to Face*, one of the finest collections of pop songs released during the '60s. Conceived as a loose concept album, *Face to Face* sees Ray Davies' fascination with English class and social structures flourish, as he creates a number of vivid character portraits. Davies' growth as a lyricist has coincided with the Kinks' musical growth. *Face to Face* is filled with wonderful moments, whether it's the mocking Hawaiian guitars of the rocker "Holiday in Waikiki," the droning Eastern touches of "Fancy," the music-hall shuffle of "Dandy" or the lazily rolling "Sunny Afternoon." And that only scratches the surface of the riches of *Face to Face*, which offers other classics like "Rosy Won't You Please Come Home," "Party Line," "Too Much on My Mind," "Rainy Day in June" and "Most Exclusive Residence for Sale," making the record one of the most distinctive and accomplished albums of its time. [Castle Communication's 1998 CD reissue of *Face to Face* included six bonus tracks: the singles and B-sides "I'm Not Like Everybody Else," "Dead End Street," "Big Black Smoke," "Mister Pleasant" and "This Is Where I Belong," plus the previously unreleased "Mr. Reporter" and backing track "Little Women."] *—Stephen Thomas Erlewine*

☆ **Something Else by the Kinks** / 1967 / Castle ♦♦♦♦♦

Face to Face was a remarkable record, but its follow-up *Something Else* expands its accomplishments, offering 13 classic British pop songs. As Ray Davies' songwriting becomes more refined, he becomes more nostalgic and sentimental, retreating from the psychedelic and mod posturings that had dominated the rock world. Indeed, *Something Else* sounds like nothing else from 1967. The Kinks never rock very hard on the album, preferring acoustic ballads, music-hall numbers and tempered R&B to full-out guitar attacks. Part of the album's power lies in its calm music, since it provides an elegant support for Davies' character portraits and vignettes. From the martial stomp of "David Watts" to the lovely, shimmering "Waterloo Sunset," there's not a weak song on the record, and several—such as the allegorical "Two Sisters," the Noel Coward-esque "End of the Season," the rolling "Lazy Old Sun" and the wry "Situation Vacant"—are stunners. And just as impressive is the emergence of Dave Davies as a songwriter. His Dylanesque "Death of a Clown" and bluesy rocker "Love Me Til the Sun Shines" hold their own against Ray's masterpieces, and help make *Something Else* the endlessly fascinating album that it is. [Castle's 1998 CD reissue of *Something Else* contained eight bonus tracks: several A and B-sides from non-LP singles, from both the Kinks and Dave Davies as a solo act—"Act Nice and Gentle," "Autumn Almanac," "Susannah's Still Alive," "Wonderboy," "Polly," "Lincoln County," "There's No Life Without Love"—plus an alternate take of "Lazy Old Sun."] *—Stephen Thomas Erlewine*

Live at Kelvin Hall / Jan. 12, 1968 / Castle ♦♦♦

Recorded in Glasgow, Scotland while the Kinks were on tour in 1967, *Live at Kelvin Hall* has the distinction of being the only undoctored concert recording of a British Invasion band at the peak of their popularity. Like the Stones and the Beatles, the Kinks faced audiences filled with screaming, shrieking teenagers. Often, the noise was so loud that it drowned out the amps on stage and since the band couldn't hear each other, their performances were ragged and rough. The Kinks held together in Glasgow better than their peers, but *Live at Kelvin Hall* is still rough going. True, it does offer an audio document of the band in concert but the crowd is so damn noisy, it's hard to hear anything besides screaming. The band is buried under this cacophony, and while they turn out some energetic performances—not only of hits like "Till the End of the Day," "You Really Got Me" and the sing-along "Sunny Afternoon"—they're just sloppy enough to be a little tiring when combined with the roaring crowd. *Live at Kelvin Hall* may be interesting as an historical piece to some collectors, but it falls short of being pleasurable listening. [Castle's 1998 CD reissue of *Live At Kelvin Hall* contained both the mono and stereo versions of the album on a single disc.] *—Stephen Thomas Erlewine*

☆ **The Village Green Preservation Society** / Nov. 22, 1968 / Castle ♦♦♦♦♦

Ray Davies' sentimental, nostalgic streak emerged on *Something Else*, but it developed into a manifesto on *The Village Green Preservation Society*, a concept album lamenting the passing of old-fashioned English traditions. As the opening title song says, the Kinks—meaning Ray himself, in this case—were for preserving "draft beer and virginity," and throughout the rest of the album, he creates a series of stories, sketches and characters about a picturesque England that never really was. It's a lovely, gentle album, evoking a small British country town, and drawing the listener into its lazy rhythms and sensibilities. Although there is an undercurrent of regret running throughout the album, Davies' fondness for the past is warm, making the album feel like a sweet, hazy dream. And considering the subdued performances and the detailed instrumentations, it's not surprising that the record feels more like a Ray Davies solo project than a Kinks album. The bluesy shuffle of "Last of the Steam-Powered Trains" is the closest the album comes to rock & roll, and Dave's cameo on the menacing "Wicked Annabella" comes as surprise, since the album is so calm. But calm doesn't mean tame or bland—there are endless layers of musical and lyrical innovation on *The Village Green Preservation Society*, and its defiantly British sensibilities became the foundation of generations of British guitar-pop. [Castle's 1998 CD reissue of *Village Green Preservation* contained both the original 15-track mono version of the album, plus the 12-track stereo album that was initially planned for release in September 1968, but scrapped. The stereo album contains a slightly different running order and features two songs—"Days" and "Mr. Songbird"—that didn't make the final album. The CD also includes the mono single version of "Days" as a bonus track.] *—Stephen Thomas Erlewine*

☆ **Arthur (Or the Decline and Fall of the British Empire)** / Oct. 10, 1969 / Castle ♦♦♦♦♦

Arthur (Or the Decline and Fall of the British Empire) extends the British-oriented themes of *Village Green Preservation Society*, telling the story of a London man's decision to move to Australia during the aftermath of World War II. It's a detailed and loving song cycle, capturing the minutiae of suburban life, the numbing effect of bureaucracy and the horrors of war. On paper, *Arthur* sounds like a pretentious mess, but Ray Davies' lyrics and insights have rarely been so graceful or deftly executed, and the music is remarkable. An edgier and harder-rocking affair than *Village Green*, *Arthur* is as multi-layered musically as it is lyrically. "Shangri-La" evolves from English folk to hard rock, "Drivin'" has a lazy grace, "Young and Innocent Days" is a lovely, wistful ballad, "Some Mother's Son" is one of the most uncompromising anti-war songs ever recorded, while "Victoria" and "Arthur" rock with simple glee. The music makes the words cut deeper, and the songs never stray too far from the album's subject, making *Arthur* one of the most effective concept albums in rock history, as well as one of the best and most influential British pop records of its era. [Castle's 1998 CD reissue of *Arthur* contained 10 bonus tracks, including mono and stereo versions of the non-LP singles "Plastic Man," "Mindless Child of Motherhood" and "This Man He Weeps Tonight," mono versions of "Drivin'" and "She's

Bought a Hat Like Princess Marina," the B-side "King Kong" and the previously unreleased "Mr. Shoemakers Daugher."] *—Stephen Thomas Erlewine*

Lola vs. the Powerman & the Money-Go-Round, Pt. 1 / Nov. 27, 1970 / Castle ✦✦✦✦✦
"Lola" gave the Kinks an unexpected hit and its crisp, muscular sound, pitched halfway between acoustic folk and hard rock, provided a new style for the band. However, the song only hinted at what its accompanying album *Lola vs. the Powerman & the Moneygoround, Pt. 1* was all about. It didn't matter that Davies just had his first hit in years—he had suffered greatly at the hands of the music industry and he wanted to tell the story in song. Hence, *Lola*—a loose concept album about Ray Davies' own psychosis and bitter feelings toward the music industry. Davies never really delivers a cohesive story, but the record holds together because it's one of his strongest set of songs. Dave contributes the lovely "Strangers" and the appropriately paranoid "Rats," but this is truly Ray's show, as he lashes out at ex-managers (the boisterous vaudevillian "The Moneygoround"), publishers ("Denmark Street"), TV and music journalists (the hard-hitting "Top of the Pops"), label executives ("Powerman"), and, hell, just society in general ("Apeman," "Got to Be Free"). If his wit wasn't sharp, the entire project would be insufferable, but the album is as funny as it is angry. Furthermore, he balances his bile with three of his best melancholy ballads: "This Time Tomorrow," "A Long Way From Home," and the anti-welfare and union "Get Back in Line," which captures working-class angst better than any other rock song. These songs provide the spine for a wildly unfocused but nonetheless dazzling *tour de force* that reveals Davies' artistic strengths and endearing character flaws in equal measure. *—Stephen Thomas Erlewine*

Percy [Original Soundtrack] / Mar. 26, 1971 / Castle ✦✦

Muswell Hillbillies / Nov. 24, 1971 / Velvel ✦✦✦✦✦
How did the Kinks respond to the fresh start afforded by *Lola*? By delivering a skewed, distinctly British, cabaret take on Americana, all pinned down by Davies' loose autobiography and intense yearning to be anywhere else but here—or, as he says on the opening track, "I'm a 20th Century Man, but I don't want to be here." Unlike its predecessors, *Muswell Hillbillies* doesn't overtly seem like a concept album—there are no stories, as there are on *Lola*—but each song undoubtedly shares a similar theme, namely the lives of the working class. Cleverly, the music is a blend of American and British roots music, veering from rowdy blues to boozy vaudeville. There's as much good humor in the performances as there are in Davies' songs, which are among his savviest and funniest. They're also quite affectionate, a fact underpinned by the heartbreaking "Oklahoma USA," one of the starkest numbers Davies ever penned, seeming all the sadder surrounded by the careening country-rock and music hall. That's the key to *Muswell Hillbillies*—it mirrors the messy flow of life itself, rolling from love letters and laments to jokes and family reunions. Throughout it all, Davies' songwriting is at a peak, as are the Kinks themselves. There are a lot of subtle shifts in mood and genre on the album, and the band pulls it off effortlessly and joyously—but it's hard not to hear Dave Davies' backing vocals and have it not sound joyous. Regardless of its commercial fate, *Muswell Hillbillies* stands as one of the Kinks' best albums. *—Stephen Thomas Erlewine*

★ **The Kink Kronikles** / 1972 / Reprise ✦✦✦✦✦
Strictly speaking, the double-album compilation *The Kink Kronikles* isn't a greatest-hits collection. Covering the years 1966 through 1970, *The Kink Kronikles* may not be packed with hits—out of the album's 28 tracks, only nine were hits in the U.K. or the U.S.—yet it's a definitive overview of this era, which was one of Ray Davies' most productive (and influential) periods. Apart from the hits—the lazy, sardonic "Sunny Afternoon" and the gorgeous "Waterloo Sunset," and the 1970 comeback hits "Lola" and "Apeman"—there is a wealth of music that ranks among their very best material that isn't available on any other album. First off, non-LP British hit singles like the musichall raver "Dead End Street" and the wry "Autumn Almanac" are included, as are Dave Davies' two solo hits, "Death of a Clown" and "Suzannah's Still Alive." Then there are the wealth of non-LP singles and B-sides that *didn't* make the British charts, plus worthy unreleased songs, obscurities like "This Is Where I Belong" and "She's Got Everything," and album tracks that demonstrate another side of the Kinks' musical versatility and Davies' abilities. The key to the success of *The Kink Kronikles* is how the singles and rarities complement each other and, taken together, present a full portrait. It's the rare compilation that is equally valuable to the collector and to the neophyte fan. *—Stephen Thomas Erlewine*

Everybody's in Showbiz / Aug. 1972 / Velvel ✦✦✦
Everybody's in Showbiz is a double album with one record devoted to stories from the road and another devoted to songs from the road. It could be labeled "the drunkest album ever made," without a trace of hyperbole, since this is a charmingly loose, rowdy, silly record. It comes through strongest on the live record, of course, as it's filled with Ray's notoriously campy vaudevellian routine (dig the impromptu "Banana Boat Song" that leads into "Skin & Bone," or the rollicking "Baby Face"). Still, the live record is just a bonus, no matter how fun it is, since the travelogue of the first record is where the heart of *Everybody's in Showbiz* lies. Davies views the road as monotony—an endless stream of identical hotels, drunken sleep, anonymous towns, and really, really bad meals (at least three songs are about food, or have food metaphors). There's no sex on the album, at all, not even on Dave's contribution, "You Don't Know My Name." Some of this is quite funny—not just Ray's trademark wit, but musical jokes like the woozy beginning of "Unreal Reality" or the unbearably tongue-in-cheek "Look a Little on the Sunnyside"—but there's a real sense of melancholy running throughout the record, most notably on the album's one unqualified masterpiece, "Celluloid Heroes." By the time it gets there, anyone that's not a hardcore fan may have turned it off. Why? Because this album is where Ray Davies begins indulging his eccentricities, a move that only solidified their status as a cult act. There are enough quirks to alienate even fans of their late '60s masterpieces, but those very things make *Everybody's in Showbiz* an easy album for those cultists to hold dear to their hearts. *—Stephen Thomas Erlewine*

The Great Lost Kinks Album / 1973 / Reprise ✦✦✦✦✦
An aptly titled collection; out of print for many years, there are even some Kinks cultists who have never been able to hear this ragtag but worthy collection of late-'60s and early-'70s outtakes and rarities. Most of these were recorded around the same time as the 1968 LP *Village Green Preservation Society*; these low-key, wry, bouncy tunes would have fit in well with that record. Lyrically, they're on the whole slighter than much of their late-'60s work, perhaps accounting for why the group did not deign to release them at the time. Still, songs like "Rosemary Rose," "Misty Water," and "Mr. Songbird" would have hardly embarrassed the group, and rank as the highlights of this anthology. Besides 1969-era outtakes, it includes the single "Plastic Man," a couple of okay, way-obscure B-sides featuring Dave Davies, and some songs penned for long-forgotten film and television productions. It also has the dynamite 1966 B-side "I'm Not Like Everybody Else," though that's easily available on reissue these days. That's not the case for most of the rest of this album; Kinks fans will find it quite worthwhile, and should be on the lookout for it in the used bins. *—Richie Unterberger*

Preservation: Act 1 / 1973 / Velvel ✦✦✦
Preservation is Ray Davies' most ambitious project—a musical that used the quaint, small-town nostalgia of *Village Green* as a template to draw the entirety of society and how it works. Or, at least that's what the concept seems to be, since the storyline was so convoluted, it necessitated three separate LPs, spread over two albums, and it still didn't really make sense because the first album, *Preservation, Act 1*, acted more like an introduction to the characters, and all the story was condensed into the second album. Davies intended all of *Preservation* to stand as one double-album set, but he scrapped the first sessions for the album, which led to record company pressure to deliver an album before the end of 1973—hence, the appearance of *Preservation, Act 1* in mid-November. Stripped of much of the narrative, *Preservation* winds up playing like an explicitly theatrical *Village Green*, this time with specific characters—a bit like a novella instead of short stories. There are moments where everything clicks on *Preservation* and they're the ones that are closest to typical Davies—the stately "Daylight," the endearingly lazy "Sitting in the Midday Sun," the fairly rocking "Here Comes Flash," "Where Are They Now?," and the absolutely gorgeous "Sweet Lady Genevieve," a real candidate for Davies' forgotten masterpiece. Then, there's the rest of the record: unfocused attempts at story, showtunes, and characterizations, some of which are interesting, but the whole of it is rather tedious. *Preservation, Act 1* winds up as listenable due to the strength of those five songs, which form the core not only of this record, but the musical drama as a whole. The rest plays as artistic hubris, which is exactly what swallows *Preservation, Act 2* alive. *—Stephen Thomas Erlewine*

Preservation: Act 2 / 1974 / Velvel ✦✦
Ray Davies released the "song" songs from *Preservation*—the character sketches, the wry observations, the lovely ballads—on the first record (or "Act") of the musical drama, leaving the narrative for *Preservation, Act 2*, a double album released six months after its companion. Simply put, the record is a mess, an impenetrable jumble of story, theater, instrumentals, "announcements," unfinished ideas, guest singers, and, on occasion, a song or two. There may have been a workable theatrical production hidden somewhere in *Preservation*, but it was utterly lost on record (reportedly it was better live), due in no small part to how it was unevenly divided, a practice that revealed Davies' lack of realized songs for the project, *plus* his unfinished story. It was later revealed that Ray was at the end of his rope during the making of *Preservation*—he would have a breakdown during its supporting tour—so, perhaps it shouldn't be a surprise that the album doesn't work on its own. Nevertheless, it is remarkable that he was in such a fog, that he didn't realize that "Slum Kids," a staple in the *Preservation* shows and a concert favorite throughout the '70s, was the best rocker he penned for the project and left it off *both* records. Thankfully, it was added as a bonus track to VelVel's 1999 reissue of the album, improving the quality of the album considerably. [The single version of "Mirror of Love" was added as a second bonus track to that edition, as well.] *—Stephen Thomas Erlewine*

The Kinks Present a Soap Opera / 1975 / Velvel ✦✦
If there ever was a testament to Ray Davies' stubbornness and ornery perversity, it's *Soap Opera*. Released after the draining, two-part, hopelessly muddled rock opera *Preservation*, *Soap Opera* is the grandest concept album the Kinks ever made. Davies' tackled a topic that seemed manageable compared to *Preservation*—how "Ordinary People" escape the doldrums with dreams of stardom—but conceived the production as a bit of a radio play, with prominent guest vocalists and narration. Improbably, it *feels* larger, campier, more excessive than *Preservation*, even if it's considerably more focused and consistent. The main problem is, its presentation is so damn silly that it's hard to hear individual songs. Nothing here works as well as the best of *Preservation, Act 1*, but it holds together better as a record. Even so, *Soap Opera* winds up rather unsettling. Not only is it hard to get the gist of Davies' narrative but there's not enough, musically or lyrically, to make it compelling. Then, there's the nagging feeling that this isn't really a Kinks album, but rather a Ray Davies solo project in disguise; the songs are certainly Ray's, but there's little that sounds like the Kinks, largely due to that ludicrous production. This isn't just an outsider's suspicion, either—Dave Davies and Mick Avory both mention this unease in Peter Doggett's liner notes to the 1999 reissue of the album, but the true indication of the extent of Davies' *Soap Opera* indulgence is that he never was allowed to go this far over the top again. *—Stephen Thomas Erlewine*

The Kinks Present Schoolboys in Disgrace / 1975 / Velvel ✦✦
Ray Davies had indulged himself one time too often with *Soap Opera*, and his bandmates, namely brother Dave and founding member Mick Avory, revolted, insisting that

their sixth RCA album sound more like a Kinks album (certainly, that's something RCA wanted too). So, Davies designed their next album as a return to a simpler, band-oriented sound. Of course, he didn't jettison his love for conceptual works, so *Schoolboys in Disgrace* was born. Working under the presumption that a return to simple rock demanded a simple theme, Davies constructed the album as a nostalgic trip through childhood, reviving '50s rock & roll (including the occasional doo wop harmony) for the album's foundation, then turning the amps up high. There's no actual story per se—it's a series of vignettes, like a coming-of-age film. As such, it's intermittently successful, on both the hard rock ("Jack the Idiot Dunce") and ballads ("The First Time We Fall in Love"), but it's way too campy for anyone outside of the dedicated. And that campiness is all the stranger when married to thundering arena rock; at least with *Preservation*, the vaudeville made sense in context, but here, the Kinks are pulling in two separate ways, and *Schoolboys* winds up as one of their least satisfying albums as a result. —*Stephen Thomas Erlewine*

Sleepwalker / 1977 / Velvel ♦♦♦

Arista had made it clear they would not accept any concept albums from the Kinks, and *Sleepwalker*, their first effort for the label, makes good on the band's promise. Comprised entirely of glossy arena-rockers and power ballads, the album is more of a stylistic exercise than a collection of first-rate songs. Davies contributed a handful of fairly strong songs, highlighted by the exceptional "Juke Box Music," which sees Ray in a shockingly resigned frame of mind, claiming that rock & roll is just rock & roll, and nothing more. Unfortunately, he chose to illustrate that fact by loading the rest of *Sleepwalker* with competent but undistinguished mainstream rock. While that might have made the album a hit at the time, its processed sound and weak songs sound dated today, especially compared to the lively arena rock the Kinks later released. —*Stephen Thomas Erlewine*

Misfits / 1978 / Velvel ♦♦♦♦♦

The Kinks became arena rockers with *Sleepwalker*, and its follow-up, *Misfits*, follows in the same vein, but it's a considerable improvement on its predecessor. Ray Davies has learned how to write within the confines of the arena rock formula, and *Misfits* is one of rock & roll's great mid-life crisis albums, finding Davies considering whether he should even go on performing. "Misfits," a classic outsider rallying cry, and "Rock & Roll Fantasy" provide the two touchstones for the album—Davies admits that he and the Kinks will never be embraced by the rock & roll mainstream, but after Elvis' death, he's not even sure if rock & roll is something for mature adults to do. Over the course of *Misfits*, he finds answers to the question, both in his lyrics and through the band's muscular music. Eventually, he discovers that it is worth his time, but the search itself is superbly affecting—even songs like the music hall shuffle "Hay Fever," which appear as filler at first, have an idiosyncratic quirk that make them cut deeper. Although Ray would return to camp on their next album, *Misfits* is a moving record that manages to convey deep emotions while rocking hard. The Kinks hadn't made a record this good since *Muswell Hillbillies*. —*Stephen Thomas Erlewine*

Low Budget / 1979 / Velvel ♦♦♦♦

Low Budget doesn't have a narrative like *Preservation* or *Soap Opera*, but Ray Davies cleverly designed the album as a sly satire of the recession and oil crisis that gripped America in the late '70s—thereby satisfying his need to be a wry social commentator while giving American audiences a hook to identify with. It was a clever move that worked; not only did *Low Budget* become their highest-charting American album (not counting the 1966 *Greatest Hits* compilation), but it was also a fine set of arena-rock, one of the better mainstream hard rock albums of its time. And it certainly was of its time—so much so, that many of the concerns and production techniques have dated quite a bit in the decades since its initial release. Nevertheless, that gives the album a certain charm, since it now plays like a time capsule, a snapshot of what hard rock sounded like at the close of the '70s. Perhaps not so coincidentally, Davies' songwriting fluctuates throughout the album, since it's dictated as much by commercial as artistic concerns, but the moments when he manages to balance the two impulses—as on the disco-fueled "(Wish I Could Fly Like) Superman," the vaudevillian "Low Budget," "A Gallon of Gas," the roaring "Attitude" (possibly their best hard rocker of the era, by the way) and "Catch Me Now I'm Falling," where Ray takes on the persona of America itself—are irresistible. *Low Budget* may not have the depth of, say, *Arthur* or *Village Green*, but it's a terrifically entertaining testament to their skills as a professional rock band and Davies' savviness as a commercial songwriter. —*Stephen Thomas Erlewine*

Give the People What They Want / 1981 / Velvel ♦♦♦

Riding high on the success of *Low Budget*, the Kinks turned out another collection of hard-driving, arena-ready rock & roll with *Give the People What They Want*—in short, they delivered exactly what the title suggests. Throughout the record, the band kicks up a storm, rocking out with a surprising amount of precision, and although Ray Davies' writing isn't as strong as it was on the group's two previous albums, he has contributed a set of professional hard rock that is distinguished by solid hooks and a clever sense of humor. After all, there's a certain charm in hearing him rework "All Day and All of the Night" into the paranoid "Destroyer," or his pure cynicism on the title track. But the minor masterpiece of the album is "Better Things," a sweet piece of charming sentimentalism which is the only time Davies lets his guard down during the entire album. —*Stephen Thomas Erlewine*

State of Confusion / 1983 / Velvel ♦♦♦

State of Confusion had its share of glossy hard rock in the vein of "Low Budget" and "Destroyer," but the record came to life on the quieter numbers, whether it's the elegiac "Don't Forget to Dance," the wistful pop of "Long Distance," or the buoyant nostalgia of "Come Dancing," which became the group's biggest hit since "Tired of Waiting for You." —*Stephen Thomas Erlewine*

Word of Mouth / 1984 / Velvel ♦♦

State of Confusion gave the Kinks their biggest single in nearly 20 years, but they didn't try to replicate the music hall-tinged pop of "Come Dancing" on its follow-up *Word of Mouth*, preferring to concentrate on straightahead hard rock. Most of the material was well-crafted, but only a few songs were distinctive, particularly the circular, synth-spiked minor hit "Do It Again." —*Stephen Thomas Erlewine*

Think Visual / Dec. 1986 / MCA ♦♦

★ **Greatest Hits, Vol. 1** / 1989 / Rhino ♦♦♦♦♦

Featuring a total of 18 highlights from the Kinks' early career, Rhino's *Greatest Hits* is the definitive compilation of the group's hit singles from the mid-'60s. Beginning with "You Really Got Me" and ending with "Sunny Afternoon," all of the Kinks' essential garage-rockers and British Invasion singles are here—"All Day and All of the Night," "Till the End of the Day," "Tired of Waiting for You," "A Well Respected Man," "Stop Your Sobbing," "Dedicated Follower of Fashion," "I'm Not Like Everybody Else," "Where Have All the Good Times Gone." Only the ambitious, Indian-tinged British hit "See My Friends" is missing, but it isn't a major oversight, especially since the disc distills the group's uneven early albums into manageable form for many fans. While *Kinkdom*, *Kontroversy* and *Face to Face* have many excellent album tracks in their own right, *Greatest Hits* remains a terrific summation of the group's earliest, hardest-rocking work. —*Stephen Thomas Erlewine*

UK Jive / Sep. 1989 / MCA ♦♦

Even though the album was weighed down by its adherence to late-'80s state of the art studio techniques, *UK Jive* was a noticeable improvement over the lackluster *Think Visual*. Featuring only a handful of hard rockers—including the excellent, snarling "Aggravation"—the album was comprised of pop songs that painted an unfocused portrait of modern British life. Although many of Ray Davies' finest songs were based on a similar concept, his songwriting on *UK Jive* was frustratingly inconsistent, ranging from the infectious bop of the title track to the ham-fisted anthem "Down All Days (To 1992)." With the loping "Looney Balloon," Davies wrote one of his finest songs of the '80s, but the only track that equaled its conviction was his brother Dave's spiteful protest, "Dear Margaret." —*Stephen Thomas Erlewine*

Kinks Live: the Road / 1990 / MCA ♦♦

Lost & Found (1986-89) / Aug. 27, 1991 / MCA ♦♦

Phobia / Apr. 13, 1993 / Columbia ♦♦

Ray Davies continues to turn out three or four brilliant songs on albums that barely anyone will ever hear. For Kinks fans, that's enough to justify the purchase of any of their recent albums, and the harder-edged *Phobia* is no exception to that rule. —*AMG*

To the Bone [UK Single Disc] / Oct. 1994 / Grapevine ♦♦♦

Since the mid-'70s, The Kinks have not been able to stop themselves from attempting their own variations on pop music trends, taking stabs at everything from bombastic heavy metal to sleek disco-flavored pop. On *To the Bone*, the group became another one of the scores of veteran rock acts to record an acoustic, "unplugged" album. However, the group's American popularity was at an all-time low in the mid-'90s and the band wasn't able to score a major-label record deal, let alone land a spot on MTV's prime-time ratings bonanza, *Unplugged*. So, the group financed their acoustic greatest-hits record *To the Bone* themselves, releasing it on the U.K. independent label Grapevine. Naturally, Ray Davies' songs work well in such a stripped-back setting, but the album is nothing more than a pleasant diversion, featuring a lovely version of "Waterloo Sunset," possibly the most beautiful song of the rock & roll era. —*Stephen Thomas Erlewine*

Come Dancing With the Kinks: The Best of the Kinks 1977-1986 [2000] / 2000 / Velvel ♦♦♦

Although it closely resembles the 1986 Arista collection (and even boasts the same cover and title), this is not quite that album—it's a reinterpretation of that collection, spearheaded by Ray Davies. It restores "Catch Me Now I'm Falling," "Misfits," and "Sleepwalker" (the three songs dropped from the CD version of Arista's *Come Dancing*) and eliminates the excellent "Long Distance" along with "Heart of Gold" and the masterpiece "Juke Box Music," while adding "A Gallon of Gas," "Full Moon," and "Good Day," and shuffling the track order. Do all these monkeyshines result in a better album? No. It's close, but the subtle differences do make a difference, and the original still does reign supreme, since the running order on the original was simply superior. This new incarnation is still enjoyable—the substitutions are good, even if they don't match the originals—and it even remains an accurate introduction to this era. But anyone who can find the Arista issue of *Come Dancing* will find a better compilation than this Koch/Konk reworking. —*Stephen Thomas Erlewine*

The Songs We Sang for Auntie: BBC Sessions 1964-1977 / Mar. 6, 2001 / Sanctuary ♦♦♦

The Kinks' *BBC Sessions 1964-1977* is a non-essential, but highly enjoyable, addition to the band's discography. While most of the material has been released on studio albums, these sessions showcase a looser, rougher-edged approach. The collection also displays the evolution of the band: from the early R&B of "Cadillac" and "You Really Got Me" to the music hall retrospection of "Waterloo Sunset" and "Village Green Preservation Society" to the social criticism of "Money Talks" and "Celluloid Heroes." There are some rarities included: a Ray Davies song originally covered by Dave Berry, "This Strange Effect"; two songs Davies wrote for BBC television (and previously only available on the out-of-print *Great Lost Kinks Album*), "Did You See His Name" and "When I Turn Off the Living Room Lights"; and a Dave Davies rewrite of the John Koerner blues song "Good Luck Charm." The song introductions and interviews by unctuous BBC announcers are somewhat distracting but do provide period flavor. Highlights include raucous performances of "Till the End of the Day" and "Love Me Till the Sun Shines," as well as shimmering takes on "Waterloo Sunset" and "Days." —*Mary Grady*

Kiss

f. 1973, New York, NY

Album Rock, Arena Rock, Heavy Metal, Hard Rock, Pop-Metal

Rooted in the campy theatrics of Alice Cooper and the sleazy glam of the New York Dolls, Kiss became a favorite of American teenagers in the '70s. Decked out in outrageously flamboyant costumes and makeup, the band fashioned a captivating stage show featuring dry ice, smoke bombs, elaborate lighting, blood spitting and fire breathing. But Kiss' music shouldn't be dismissed—it was a commercially potent mix of anthemic, fist-pounding hard rock and ballads powered by loud guitars, cloying melodies and sweeping strings. Their sound laid the groundwork for both arena rock and the pop-metal that dominated rock in the late '80s. Kiss was the brainchild of Gene Simmons (bass, vocals) and Paul Stanley (rhythm guitar, vocals), who found drummer Peter Criss and guitarist Ace Frehley through ads. By April of 1975, the group had released three albums in just over a year, and built up a sizable fan base through constant touring. Culled from those numerous concerts, *Alive!* (released in the fall of 1975) made the band rock & roll superstars. The follow-up, *Destroyer*, became the group's first platinum album; it also featured their first Top Ten single, Peter Criss' power ballad "Beth." By 1977, Kiss was the most popular band in America; thousands of pieces of merchandise flooded the marketplace. Heralding a commercial slump, Criss left in 1980, as did Frehley in 1982. Sensing it was time for a change, Kiss dispensed with their makeup for the first time for 1983's *Lick It Up*; the publicity helped the album recapture their niche. For the next decade, Kiss turned out a series of best-selling albums with guitarist Bruce Kulick, culminating in the 1990 hit ballad "Forever," their biggest single since "Beth." In November 1991, drummer Eric Carr died at the age of 41 after a bout with cancer. In 1996, the original lineup of Kiss reunited to perform an international tour, complete with their notorious makeup and special effects. The tour was one of the most successful of 1996, and in 1998 the reunited group issued *Psycho Circus*. —*Stephen Thomas Erlewine*

Kiss / Apr. 1974 / Casablanca ✦✦✦✦✦

Kiss' 1974 self-titled debut is one of hard rock's all-time classic studio recordings. *Kiss* is chock full of their best and most renowned compositions, containing elements of Rolling Stones/New York Dolls party-hearty rock & roll, Beatles tunefulness, and Sabbath/Zep heavy metal, and wisely recorded primal and raw by producers Richie Wise and Kenny Kerner (of Gladys Knight fame). Main songwriters Stanley and Simmons each had a knack for coming up with killer melodies and riffs, as evidenced by "Nothin' to Lose" and "Deuce" (by Simmons), "Firehouse" and "Black Diamond" (by Stanley), as well as "Strutter" and "100,000 Years" (a collaboration by the two). Also included is the Ace Frehley alcohol anthem "Cold Gin," "Let Me Know" (a song that Stanley played for Simmons upon their very first meeting, then titled "Sunday Driver"), and one of Kiss' few instrumentals: the groovy "Love Theme From Kiss" (penned by the entire band). The only weak track is a tacky cover of the 1959 Bobby Rydell hit "Kissin' Time," which was added to subsequent pressings of the album to tie in with a "Kissing Contest" promotion the band was involved in at the time. Along with 1976's *Destroyer*, Kiss' self-titled debut is their finest studio album, and has only improved over the years. —*Greg Prato*

Hotter than Hell / Nov. 1974 / Casablanca ✦✦✦✦

Although Kiss' self-titled debut performed respectably on the charts, it was not the blockbuster they had hoped for. With the album fading on the charts in the summer of 1974, Kiss was summoned back into the studio to work on a follow-up. Producers Richie Wise and Kenny Kerner were on board again, and even though the sonics are muddier (and more filler is present composition-wise), *Hotter Than Hell* is another quintessential Kiss release. Many of the songs have been forgotten over the years (few are featured in concert anymore), but there are still more than a few gems to be found. It's unclear if the members of Kiss were having problems with their personal relationships at the time, but it's a common thread that runs through the songs. The plodding "Got to Choose" and the rapid-fire "Parasite" deal with love gone bad; the title track is about unobtainable love, while "Goin' Blind" is a disturbing tale of a 93-year-old having an affair with a 16-year-old. Also included are the early favorites "Let Me Go Rock & Roll" and "Watchin' You," as well as the original electric version of "Comin' Home" (an acoustic version was the opener of 1996's *Unplugged*), and "Strange Ways," which contains one of Ace Frehley's best guitar solos. Even though *Hotter Than Hell* actually fared worse on the charts than the debut, it has become a revered album among Kiss fans over the years—and rightfully so. —*Greg Prato*

Dressed to Kill / Apr. 1975 / Casablanca ✦✦✦✦✦

By the release of their third album, 1975's *Dressed To Kill*, Kiss was fast becoming America's top rock concert attraction, yet their record sales up to this point did not reflect their ticket sales. Casablanca label head Neil Bogart decided to take matters into his own hands, and produced the new record along with the band. The result is more vibrant-sounding than its predecessor, 1974's sludgefest *Hotter Than Hell*, and the songs have more of an obvious pop edge to them. The best-known song on the album by far is the party anthem "Rock & Roll All Nite," but it was the track "C'Mon and Love Me" that became a regional hit in the Detroit area, giving the band their first taste of radio success. Since the band was on the road for a year straight, songs such as "Room Service" and "Ladies In Waiting" deal with life on the road (i.e., groupies), and a pair of songs were reworked from Kiss' precursor band, Wicked Lester ("Love Her All I Can" and "She"). With *Dressed to Kill*'s Top 40 showing on the *Billboard* charts, the stage was now set for Kiss' big commercial breakthrough with their next release. —*Greg Prato*

● **Alive!** / Oct. 1975 / Casablanca ✦✦✦✦✦

Alive! was the album that catapulted Kiss from cult attraction to mega-superstars. It was their first Top Ten album, remaining on the charts for 110 weeks and eventually going quadruple platinum. Culled from shows in Detroit, New Jersey, Iowa, and Cleveland on the *Dressed to Kill* tour, producer Eddie Kramer did a masterful job of capturing the band's live performance on record. The band's youthful energy is contagious, and with positively electric versions of their best early material, it's no mystery why *Alive!* is widely regarded as one of the greatest live hard rock recordings of all time. "Rock & Roll All Nite" became a Top 20 smash and was the main reason for the album's success, but there are many other tracks that are just as strong—"Deuce," "Strutter," "Firehouse," "Parasite," "She," "100,000 Years," "Black Diamond," and "Cold Gin" all shine in a live setting. Although there's been some speculation of extensive overdubbing to correct mistakes, *Alive!* remains Kiss' greatest album ever. An essential addition to any rock collection. —*Greg Prato*

Destroyer / 1976 / Casablanca ✦✦✦✦✦

The pressure was on Kiss for their fifth release, and the band knew it. Their breakthrough, *Alive!*, was going to be hard to top, so instead of trying to recreate a concert setting in the studio, they went the opposite route. *Destroyer* is one of Kiss' most experimental studio albums, but also one of their strongest and most interesting. Alice Cooper/Pink Floyd producer Bob Ezrin was on hand, and he strongly encouraged the band to experiment—there's extensive use of sound effects (the album's untitled closing track), the appearance of a boy's choir ("Great Expectations"), and an orchestra-laden, heartfelt ballad ("Beth"). But there's plenty of Kiss' heavy thunder-rock to go around, such as the demonic "God of Thunder" and the sing-along anthems "Flaming Youth," "Shout It Out Loud," "King of the Night Time World," and "Detroit Rock City" (the latter a tale of a doomed concert-goer, complete with violent car crash sound effects). But it was the aforementioned Peter Criss ballad "Beth" that made *Destroyer* such a success; the song was a surprise Top Ten hit (it was originally released as a B-side to "Detroit Rock City"). Also included is a song that Nirvana would later cover ("Do You Love Me?"), as well as an ode to the pleasures of S&M, "Sweet Pain." *Destroyer* also marked the first time that a comic book illustration of the band appeared on the cover, confirming that the band was transforming from hard rockers to superheroes. —*Greg Prato*

Rock & Roll Over / 1976 / Casablanca ✦✦✦✦

With the massive success of their previous album, the experimental Bob Ezrin-produced *Destroyer* (which contained the surprise ballad hit "Beth"), Kiss could have taken the safe route and continued in that direction…or return to the raw hard rock of their first four albums. They chose the latter. Hooking back up with Eddie Kramer, the producer of their 1975 breakthrough release *Alive!* and their very first demo, Kiss rented out the Nanuet Star Theater in upstate New York to record their next album, *Rock & Roll Over*. With a more direct, in-your-face production, *Rock & Roll Over* is one of Kiss' most consistent records. Two of the album's best tracks became hit singles—the sleazy hard rocker "Calling Dr. Love," and an acoustic ballad that was originally intended for Rod Stewart, "Hard Luck Woman" (later covered by country star Garth Brooks). But like all other classic rock albums, the lesser-known material is often just as strong—"I Want You" and "Makin' Love" have become concert staples over the years, while "Mr. Speed" is one of Kiss' most underrated songs ever. Also included are the fan favorites "Take Me," "Ladies Room," "Love 'Em and Leave 'Em," and the original version of "See You In Your Dreams," which was later re-recorded for Gene Simmons' 1978 solo album. —*Greg Prato*

Love Gun / Jul. 1977 / Casablanca ✦✦✦✦✦

Love Gun was Kiss' fifth studio album in three years (and seventh release overall, peaking at #4 on Billboard), and proved to be the last release that the original line-up played on. By 1977, Kiss merchandising was flooding the marketplace (lunchboxes, makeup kits, comic books, etc.), and it would ultimately lead to a Kiss backlash in the '80s. But the band was still focused on their music for *Love Gun*, similar in sound and approach to their previous straight-ahead rock release, *Rock & Roll Over*. It included Ace Frehley's first lead vocal spot (the eventual concert staple "Shock Me"), as well as one of Kiss' best and most renowned hard rockers in the thunderous title track. The album's opener, "I Stole Your Love," also served as the opening number on Kiss' ensuing tour, while "Christine Sixteen" is one of the few Kiss tracks to contain piano prominently. "Almost Human" is an underrated rocker, and features a great Jimi Hendrix-esque guitar solo from Frehley (no doubt due to ex-Hendrix producer Eddie Kramer manning the boards again), while "Plaster Caster" is a tribute to the famous groupies of the same name. The only weak spots on an otherwise stellar album are an obvious "Rock & Roll All Nite" ripoff titled "Tomorrow and Tonight," and a pointless remake of the Phil Spector-penned classic "Then He Kissed Me" (reworked as "Then She Kissed Me"). —*Greg Prato*

Alive II / Nov. 1977 / Casablanca ✦✦✦✦

For Kiss' breakthrough 1975 release *Alive!*, the band had a total of three studio albums from which to select their in-concert repertoire. By mid-1977, Kiss had released another three studio recordings (*Destroyer*, *Rock & Roll Over*, and *Love Gun*), and with a new Kiss album needed for the holiday season, a second live album, *Alive II*, was assembled. Three sides were recorded live in concert at the Los Angeles Forum (with a few tracks recorded in Japan), while the fourth side featured five new studio recordings. Like its predecessor, there's been quite a lot of speculation concerning extensive overdubbing (the proof being that you can often hear several Paul Stanley voices singing backup simultaneously!), but *Alive II* shows that Kiss was still an exciting live band despite all the hype. Adrenaline-charged versions of "Detroit Rock City," "Love Gun," "Calling Dr. Love," "Shock Me," "God of Thunder," "I Want You," and "Shout It Out Loud" are all highlights. On the fourth side, Ace Frehley only plays on a single song (his self-penned classic "Rocket Ride") for reasons unknown, while Rick Derringer and session guitarist Bob Kulick filled in for the AWOL Frehley. Among the studio tracks is the made-for-the-stage anthem "Larger Than Life," which the band has surprisingly never performed live. —*Greg Prato*

Double Platinum / 1978 / Casablanca ✦✦✦✦✦
Double Platinum (Greatest Hits) is a double-album, 20-track collection that gathers all of Kiss' biggest hits ("Rock & Roll All Nite," "Beth," "Detroit Rock City," "Calling Dr. Love," "Love Gun"), but what makes it an essential retrospective and introduction is that it doesn't overlook key album tracks and concert favorites like "Cold Gin," "Deuce," "Black Diamond" and "She." If "Strutter" was represented by the original version, instead of a pointless 1978 remake—which was recorded only to entice collectors into buying an album of music they already owned—*Double Platinum* would have been a definitive collection, but as it stands, it's simply a very, very good overview. —*Stephen Thomas Erlewine*

Peter Criss / Oct. 1978 / Casablanca ✦✦✦
Although it's admirable that Peter Criss tried to explore different musical styles than the average '70s Kiss release on his 1978 solo album, the material (soul, classic rock & roll, ballads, etc.) ultimately falls flat without the input and/or backing of Simmons, Stanley, and Frehley. Due to Kiss' surprise 1976 smash ballad "Beth" (written and sung by Peter), Criss decided to include several similarly styled songs, but the material is completely limp—"Easy Thing," "Kiss the Girl Goodbye," "Don't You Let Me Down," and "I Can't Stop the Rain" are all bland and forgettable. '70s funk 'n' soul is touched upon with the tracks "That's the Kind of Sugar Papa Likes" and "You Matter To Me," as well as a fun cover of the rock & roll standard "Tossin' and Turnin'," but all are hardly substantial. The track "Hooked On Rock & Roll" tries to reaffirm that Criss is a diehard rocker at heart, but by the conclusion of *Peter Criss*, most rockers would have lost interest and tuned out. —*Greg Prato*

Ace Frehley / Oct. 1978 / Casablanca ✦✦✦✦✦
Of the four Kiss solo albums released simultaneously in 1978, the best of the bunch is guitarist Ace Frehley's. Similar in approach to Paul Stanley's album, Frehley did not stray far from the expected heavy Kiss sound (like Gene Simmons and Peter Criss did with their releases), but Ace was equipped with better compositions than Stanley. With future *Late Night With David Letterman* drummer Anton Fig helping out (as well as Letterman bassist Will Lee on three tracks), Ace Frehley proved once and for all that he was not simply a backup musician to Kiss head honchos Simmons and Stanley. All of the tracks are strong, such as the venomous opener "Rip It Out," as well as a few tracks that confirm that Frehley was indulging in alcohol and drugs a bit too much by the late '70s ("Snow Blind," "Ozone," and "Wiped Out"). You'll also find many underrated compositions ("Speedin' Back to My Baby," "What's On Your Mind?," "I'm In Need of Love"), a gorgeous instrumental ("Fractured Mirror"), and the Top 20 hit single "New York Groove." Unfortunately, when Ace left Kiss in 1982 (eventually forming Frehley's Comet), he never came close to topping this solid and inspired 1978 solo outing. —*Greg Prato*

Gene Simmons / Oct. 1978 / Casablanca ✦✦✦
Most Kiss fans associate Gene Simmons with the band's hardest-rocking compositions; after all, he's responsible for such heavies as "Watchin' You," "Calling Dr. Love," "Larger Than Life," and "Goin' Blind." So many Kiss fans must have been surprised when they heard Gene's diverse 1978 solo album, with songs that contained choirs and string arrangements, plus elements of Beatles pop, '70s funk/disco, and feel-good rock & roll. Granted, there are a few heavy rockers (such as the single "Radioactive," "Burning Up With Fever," and "See You In Your Dreams"), but Simmons was always a closet Beatles fan, as evidenced by "See You Tonite," "Always Near You," "Man of 1,000 Faces," and "Mr. Make Believe." The only real misstep is a preposterously embarrassing cover of the Disney classic "When You Wish Upon a Star" (complete with Disney-esque sound effects/music). But Simmons made sure that the top artists of the day lent a hand (Aerosmith's Joe Perry, Cheap Trick's Rick Nielsen, Donna Summer, Cher, Bob Seger, Jeff "Skunk" Baxter, Helen Reddy, and Janis Ian), which makes Gene's solo album an unpredictable, yet ultimately enjoyable release. —*Greg Prato*

Paul Stanley / Oct. 1978 / Casablanca ✦✦

Dynasty / 1979 / Casablanca ✦✦✦
Dynasty marked the first time that the original four members of Kiss did not all appear together for the entire album—session drummer Anton Fig subbed for Peter Criss due to the latter's erratic behavior and injuries sustained in a serious car crash. And even though it was a platinum-plus smash, *Dynasty* marked the beginning of Kiss' unfocused period, which would ultimately end in a nosedive of the band's popularity, as well as Criss and Frehley leaving the band by 1982. In latter-day interviews, the band has admitted that they started to listen to outsiders about what direction the music should go around the time of *Dynasty*. And since small children were a large part of Kiss' audience by 1979 (due to merchandising and the god-awful TV movie *Kiss Meets the Phantom*), the band began backing away from heavy metal and embracing pop. Included is their hit disco experiment "I Was Made for Loving You" (it was as good as any other disco song of the late '70s), as well as "Sure Know Something," a melodic pop rocker that should have also been a smash. Many other tracks would have been better if they weren't so glossed up (due to producer Vini Poncia), such as "Charisma," "Magic Touch," "Hard Times," and a great reworked cover of the Rolling Stones obscurity "2,000 Man." Not a horrible album (that distinction would go to 1981's *The Elder*), but certainly not on par with such classics as *Hotter Than Hell*, *Destroyer*, or *Love Gun*. —*Greg Prato*

Kiss Unmasked / Jun. 1980 / Casablanca ✦✦
Kiss Unmasked was the group's first album since *Destroyer* to not go platinum, and it's easy to see why. Driven by pedestrian riffs and melodies, none of the songs are memorable, and the group sounds uninspired throughout the record. Peter Criss left during the recording of the album; session drummer Anton Fig completed the record after Criss' departure. The change in drummers isn't evident in the music, but what the music does make clear is that it was time for Kiss to change their act. —*Stephen Thomas Erlewine*

Music From "The Elder" / 1981 / Casablanca ✦✦
By the end of 1980, Kiss knew that their next album had to be a strong one—a glorious return to hard rock *a la* their classic *Destroyer*. New drummer Eric Carr had refueled the band's desire to rock, and the quartet began working on a straight-ahead rock album in early 1981. Midway through, the band felt that they were rewriting past songs, and the sessions were aborted. Simmons and Stanley then came up with the idea of recording a concept album, based on a mythical original story by Simmons. *Destroyer* producer Bob Ezrin was back, and encouraged the band's concept album idea (against both Frehley and Carr's wishes). Simmons and Stanley had high hopes for *The Elder* (such as a movie, an elaborate tour, a follow-up record, etc.), but it completely bombed upon release. The reason? The music is totally uncharacteristic of Kiss—it resembles heavy prog-rock for the most part. Some of the songs could have been classics if the pompous and/or hard-to-decipher lyrics were replaced, such as "The Oath," "Only You," "I," and "Just a Boy." Only two tracks resemble the Kiss of old (Frehley's "Dark Light" and the instrumental "Escape From the Island"), while the rest is downright embarrassing ("Odyssey," "A World Without Heroes," "Under the Rose"). *The Elder* was the final straw for Frehley, who would leave the band in 1982. —*Greg Prato*

Creatures of the Night / Oct. 10, 1982 / Casablanca ✦✦✦✦
By 1982's *Creatures of the Night*, Kiss had finally ditched their plans of becoming "respectable artists" (starting with 1979's *Dynasty*), and had come to the realization that they were a loud, no-holds-barred heavy metal band. Easily their best since 1977's *Love Gun*, *Creatures of the Night* contains very little filler and sounds as if Kiss had been reborn (it also includes one of the heaviest drum sounds ever captured in the studio by any rock band). The band is inspired and enthusiastic throughout, especially on such rockers as the opening title track, "Killer," "War Machine," "Saint And Sinner," and one of their great anthems, "I Love It Loud." Also included is one of Kiss' better ballads, "I Still Love You" (later featured on 1996's *Unplugged* set), as well as "Rock & Roll Hell," a song written about Ace Frehley, who would soon officially make his resignation from the band public. Guitarist Vinnie Vincent (real name: Vinnie Cusano) handles guitar duties here, and was eventually named as Frehley's replacement, playing on the ensuing tour. Although *Creatures of the Night* deserved to be the album that put Kiss back on top of the charts, it performed below expectations (topping out at #45), as did its tour. Hence, the album is one of Kiss' most underrated. It didn't take a genius to figure out that the makeup had grown stale and was now getting in the way of their music. The time had finally come for the band to unmask. [Note: *Creatures of the Night* was later reissued in 1985 with a different cover (non-makeup) and remixed. But when all of Kiss' albums were remastered and re-released on CD in 1996, the original 1982 version was used.] —*Greg Prato*

Lick It Up / Sep. 18, 1983 / Mercury ✦✦✦✦
Due to the underachievement of their exceptional 1982 comeback album, *Creatures of the Night*, Kiss knew the time was right to drop the makeup, so in September 1983 the band shocked their fans by unmasking on MTV. Their first non-makeup album, *Lick It Up*, followed soon after, and successfully re-established the band amongst the heavy metal masses worldwide. Kiss also re-connected with their Stateside fans—*Lick It Up* was the band's first record to achieve gold status since 1980's *Unmasked*. The album's success was spurred by MTV's repeated airing of the imaginative video for the album's strong title track, and songs such as "Exciter," "Not for the Innocent," "A Million to One," and the rap-rocker "All Hell's Breaking Loose" confirmed that the band was back on the right track. Vinnie Vincent again proved to be a worthy replacement to original guitarist Ace Frehley, but would unfortunately leave the band after the completion of the *Lick It Up* worldwide tour (eventually resurfacing with the Vinnie Vincent Invasion in the late '80s). *Lick It Up* is undoubtedly Kiss' best non-makeup album. —*Greg Prato*

Animalize / Sep. 13, 1984 / Mercury ✦✦

Asylum / Sep. 16, 1985 / Mercury ✦

Crazy Nights / Sep. 18, 1987 / Mercury ✦

Smashes, Thrashes & Hits / 1988 / Mercury ✦✦✦✦
Smashes, Thrashes & Hits is a compilation of Kiss's greatest hits from their '80s career. Since there weren't enough chart-toppers from that period to fill an entire album, however, '70s classics from their more theatrical days are also included, such as "Love Gun," "Shout It Out Loud" and "Rock & Roll All Nite." (Peter Criss' power ballad, "Beth," is also featured on the album, but is a re-recorded version with then-drummer Eric Carr on vocals.) This combination of classic power rock and pop-metal is what makes the record entertaining, and the album's two new tracks, "Let's Put the X In Sex" and "(You Make Me) Rock Hard," continue to display Kiss' interesting melodies. Although necessary only to the avid Kiss fan, *Smashes, Thrashes & Hits* is an acceptable compilation and is another good introduction to the band. —*Barry Weber*

Hot in the Shade / Oct. 17, 1989 / Mercury ✦✦

Revenge / 1992 / Mercury ✦✦✦
Despite coming off a monster ballad with *Hot in the Shade*'s Michael Bolton-penned "Forever," Kiss was plagued by financial instability due to Simmons and Stanley's extravagance; worse, drummer Eric Carr succumbed to cancer in November 1991. But even with the grunge movement in full effect, Kiss was luckily recognized as a major influence on everyone from Trent Reznor to Lenny Kravitz—their '70s legacy intact despite the band's often dubious choices in the '80s. And even though they, too, were on the brink of commercial extinction, being savvy businessmen first and foremost, Gene Simmons and Paul Stanley fully understood the lay of the land. Not only did they need to make a definitive record, they needed to completely re-invent themselves, visually *and* sonically. The first step was to secure hard rock veteran Eric Singer to fill Carr's shoes; next, the band rekindled its relationship with producer Bob Ezrin. Again, never ones to ignore lucrative business opportunities, Simmons and Stanley swallowed their pride and rejoined forces with

former bandmate Vinnie Vincent. Together, they co-wrote *Revenge*'s three centerpieces—"Unholy," "I Just Wanna," and "Heart of Chrome." Bringing Vincent back to the Kiss fold ultimately proves to be the album's *coup de grâce*. Some of the cuts are excellent, delivered with conviction and panache, but for all the hype, the album is also tainted with filler. On the up tip, Ezrin's mongo-enormous production galvanizes the Kiss sound, making it fresh again. The band's promotional efforts would help propel the album's first-week sales sky high, culminating with a Top Ten Billboard chart entry, but indifference once again plagued the ensuing arena tour. *—John Franck*

Alive III / May 18, 1993 / Mercury ✦✦

MTV Unplugged / Mar. 12, 1996 / Mercury ✦✦✦
After sinking deep into this musical celebration, even the not-so-avid listener will sure know something about Kiss, a classic rock icon of the '70s roaring back in vibrant and passionate form. This recording of a session done expressly for the program *MTV Unplugged* in 1996 brought together a special group for quite a remarkable if unexpected reunion. Throughout this record, you can feel the support and raw adoration of the audience present, certainly a mixture of longtime fans and new admirers. Nearly rock & roll legends, Kiss exceeded expectations and, given their newfound energy, charisma, and love for the music, their performance provided the catalyst for the beginning of a quite successful world reunion tour. "Coming Home" delivers a feverish and electric opening that gets the crowd on its feet in a hurry. Soon the emotion and presence of this group are brought back with startling grace and wisdom on "Plaster Caster" and the beautiful acoustic medley "Goin' Blind." The decades of Kiss, their costumes, and their wild stadium shows roll back in a heartbeat through the crashing tune "Do You Love Me." "Beth" is the most heartwarming song of Kiss' power ballads: "Beth I know you're lonely/and I hope you'll be alright/'cause me and the boys will be playing all night." Finally, a Kiss show wouldn't be complete without the ultimate party song, "Rock & Roll All Night," a tune still electric without electric guitars. *—Shawn Haney*

You Wanted the Best You Got the Best / Jun. 25, 1996 / Polygram ✦

Greatest Kiss / Apr. 8, 1997 / Mercury ✦✦✦
Kiss has been the subject of numerous "best-of" compilations over the years, some released domestically (1978's *Double Platinum*, 1988's *Smashes, Thrashes, & Hits*), while others only in specified regions (1982's *Killers* in Europe, 1988's *Chikara* in Japan, etc.). The 1996 collection *Greatest Kiss* was originally intended to only be issued outside the U.S., but since it was selling well as an import stateside, it was eventually issued domestically one year later. There are four different versions of *Greatest Kiss*, each including a slightly different track listing: European/Australian, Japanese, Mexican, and U.S. Instead of focusing only on overlooked songs not included previously on their past "best-of" packages, *Greatest Kiss* is an extremely haphazardly assembled collection since the majority of the songs have been included on the aforementioned collections ("Rock & Roll All Nite," "Deuce," "Beth," "Detroit Rock City," etc.). Tracks making their first appearance on a Kiss anthology are "Sure Know Something," "Christine Sixteen," "Plaster Caster," "Flaming Youth," "Two Sides of the Coin," and a 1996 live version of "Shout It Out Loud." Instead of getting it right and focusing only on truly overlooked gems (such as "Magic Touch," "Larger Than Life," "Shock Me," "Parasite," "Talk to Me," "Rocket Ride," "Watchin' You," "Mr. Speed," "New York Groove," "I Stole Your Love," "King of the Night Time World," etc.), *Greatest Kiss* ultimately misses the mark. For the newcomer, stick with 1978's better-assembled *Double Platinum*. *—Greg Prato*

Psycho Circus / Sep. 22, 1998 / Mercury ✦✦

Klaatu

f. 1973, Toronto, Ontario, Canada, **db.** 1981
Album Rock, Psychedelic Pop, Pop/Rock, Prog-Rock/Art Rock
In August of 1976, the self-titled debut album by an unknown group called Klaatu was released on Capitol Records to little notice. The following February Steve Smith, a writer for the Providence Journal in Rhode Island, wrote an article titled "Could Klaatu Be the Beatles? Mystery Is a Magical Mystery Tour." The article began the rumor that Klaatu was "more than likely either in part or in whole the Beatles." These conjectures, fueled by a series of articles in trade magazines like *Billboard* created a huge amount of hype and Capitol did nothing to deny or confirm the rumors. Throughout 1977, record sales soared and radio stations ran "Is Klaatu the Beatles?" promotions. Reportedly, some of the "clues" as to whether or not Klaatu were the Beatles included backward messages, Morse code, references to the group's identities in the song lyrics, and the word "Beatles" hidden in various places on the record jacket. After several months of conjecture, the group's identity was revealed at the end of year—it wasn't the Beatles after all, it was Terry Draper (songwriter, vocalist, drummer), John Woloschuck, and Dee Long. Immediately, their record sales declined, and due to a backlash generated by the Beatles hoax their four subsequent albums failed to sell. The group broke up in 1981. *—Jim Powers*

Klaatu / 1976 / Capitol ✦✦✦✦
This album was a total enigma when it was first released in 1976. Each song had its own eccentric personality, and the entirety sounded like the concoction of some strange rock orchestra from the netherworld. The Beatles tag nailed to this band may have helped album sales, but in actuality only the song "Sub Rosa Subway" sounded anything like them (it's a convoluted "It's All Too Much" melody with McCartney-esque vocals). The rest of the tunes politely exploited surf music, '70s progressive rock, and children's novelty songs. "Calling Occupants of Interplanetary Craft" and "Little Neutrino" are the standout tracks besides "Subway." The former is the band's signature song, later covered by the Carpenters, while "Neutrino" utilizes phase-shifting and vocal effects to help jettison it into deep space. The overall impression left by this curio is that, no, the Fab Four weren't involved, but there was surely a spark of genius (other than George Martin) behind the myriad of instruments and sounds. *—Peter Kurtz*

Hope / 1977 / Capitol ✦✦✦
A somewhat disappointing follow-up to the promise left by the group's inspired debut, *Hope* was actually recorded just before the first album was released (and prior to the subsequent "Are Klaatu the Beatles?" rumors). The band opted for a more conceptual, rock opera sound, but they ended up sounding pretentious, and in some cases like a rip-off of Queen. If you're into LP sleeve art, though, this one is breathtaking. The artist, Ted Jones, did several of the band's striking album sleeves, but this is certainly the most beautiful. Drummer and band archivist Terry Draper later tried to retrieve the original oil painting from which the cover was shot, but discovered it had been pilfered by an unknown employee of Capitol. *—Peter Kurtz*

Sir Army Suit / 1978 / Capitol ✦✦✦
Sir Army Suit was Klaatu's attempt to make an album of straight pop songs and recover from the sophomore slump of *Hope*. There are some nifty pop numbers here, but the record received virtually no airplay, critics gave it a lukewarm response, and the group plunged further into obscurity. Once the Beatles rumor died, it appeared nobody wanted to accept Klaatu as Klaatu. In truth, the threesome still had difficulty establishing a sound and identity of their own, which wasn't helped by their continued anonymity (again, no photos or credits). The songs themselves hopped from '60s pop to heavy metal. On the most successful songs (the '60s pop), the titles are a giveaway: "A Routine Day," "Dear Christine," and "Tokeymore Field" can be heard as either glittering retro-pop at best, or at worst an unabashed plagiarism of the British Invasion. Top honor, though, must go to "Juicy Lucy," an exuberant splash of horn-inflected disco that at least brought them close to their own musical time and place. *—Peter Kurtz*

Endangered Species / 1980 / Capitol ✦✦

Magentalane / 1981 / Permanent Press ✦✦✦
Originally issued in 1981, Klaatu's fifth and final album *Magentalane* is highlighted by the elegiac ballad "December Dream," an homage to the recently-slain John Lennon which eerily mirrors the fallen Beatles' own late-period work. Even with the mystery of their idenities long ago solved, Klaatu still recalls the Fab Four with remarkable accuracy: "I Don't Wanna Go Home" conjures vintage McCartney, while "Mrs. Toad's Cookies" is like a *Yellow Submarine* track left on the cutting room floor. "A Million Miles Away" and "The Love of a Woman," on the other hand, bring to mind Electric Light Orchestra—inspiration once removed. *—Jason Ankeny*

Klaatu/Hope / Jan. 6, 1992 / Collectors' Choice Music ✦✦✦✦

● **Peaks** / 1993 / Attic ✦✦✦
Peaks fabulously outlines this mysterious band's short-lived career, and with all the Beatles comparisons aside, there really is some great music compiled on this set. Plucking the best tracks from all five of their albums, this hits collection reveals both the early, somewhat progressive sound of Klaatu as well as the better known sweet, polished material. Opening up with "Calling Occupants," a song that was later made famous by the Carpenters, and merging right into the Beatles-sounding tracks like "We're Off You Know" and "Sub Rosa Subway," their textured music and rich sound begins to take shape. Shards of *Sgt. Pepper* can be heard in songs like "Doctor Marvello" or "The Loneliest of Creatures," only making the likenesses more obvious, but entertainingly doing so. Great horn work, along with some ornate keyboard roundabouts make up the eight minute "Little Neutrino," as instruments imitate the sounds of atoms bumping into each other. Klaatu's plush love songs, like "Knee Deep in Love" or "I Can't Help It," were recurring tunes on Canadian radio throughout the early '80s, and can still hold their own today. Musicians John Woloschuk, Dee Long, and Terry Draper each contribute to the honeyed melodies and layered instrumentation equally, and while only a trio, they give Klaatu a much larger sound. *Peaks* is a better all-around package than its counterpart, *Klassic Klaatu*, since it contains six extra tracks and more detailed information. *—Mike DeGagne*

The KLF

f. 1987, Liverpool, England, **db.** May 5, 1992
Ambient House, Rave, Club/Dance, Newbeat, Acid House, House
More than any pop band in history, the KLF ripped off the music industry for a bucketful of loot and got away with it—as illustrated in their own guidebook to creating number one singles, *The Manual*. Bill Drummond and Jimi Cauty applied the tactics of punk shock-terrorism to late-'80s acid-house and became one of Britain's best-selling artists (recording also as the JAMS and the Timelords) just before their retirement in 1992. The duo then deleted their entire back catalogue—a potential loss in the millions of pounds—and declared they wouldn't release another record until peace was declared throughout the world. Debuting with a 1987 LP of rampant sonic piracy, the duo tempered the sampling only slightly for their big breakthrough, the arena anthem "Doctorin' the Tardis" by the Timelords. Even while the single was hitting number one on the charts though, the duo were playing a major part in the development of the '90s boom in ambient music, recording the classic *Chill Out* LP. The following year, Cauty and Drummond moved back to acid-house and earned the greatest success of their career with three Top Ten singles (including the chart-topper "3 A.M. Eternal") from the number one album *The White Room*. The popularity even carried over to American charts, though Cauty and Drummond retired in mid-1992 and refused to release any more material. They partially re-emerged in 1997 with the single "***k the Millennium," recorded as 2K. *—John Bush*

The History of the JAMS a.k.a. The Timelords / 1988 / TVT ✦✦✦✦
Interesting more for its sample-and-scatter philosophy than the thick Scottish brogue with which Drummond tries to emulate Run-D.M.C., *The History of the JAMs a.k.a. The*

Timelords takes no prisoners: Dave Brubeck's familiar saxophone riff from "Take Five" is looped onto the James Brown-style jam "Don't Take Five (Take What You Want)," Whitney Houston "guests" on the hilarious "Whitney Joins the JAMs" (a dry run for the later, actually *live*, appearance of Tammy Wynette), and assorted other stars of the past also make appearances (including the Beatles, MC5, Jimi Hendrix, and Petula Clark). Aside from the novelty tracks—which wear as thin as their production values—this is the only available KLF full-length containing "Doctorin' the Tardis," perhaps the most popular sports anthem ever recorded. —*John Bush*

● **Chill Out** / Jan. 1990 / Wax Trax! ✦✦✦✦✦
One of the initial works in the ambient house canon, *Chill Out* is the practically beatless soundtrack to a late-night journey along the Gulf Coast, and the track titles tell much of the story: "Six Hours to Louisiana, Black Coffee Going Cold," "3AM Somewhere Out of Beaumont," "Elvis on the Radio, Steel Guitar in My Soul." Recorded live by Drummond and Cauty (with much unintended help from sample victims Elvis Presley, Fleetwood Mac, and the throat singers of Tüva). *Chill Out* consists largely of fragmented, heavily reverbed steel guitar, environmental sounds (birds, trains), occasional synth, and an angelic vocal chorus repeating the KLF's own "Justified and Ancient" theme. Throughout, Drummond and Cauty display an instinctive talent for wallpaper music that's truly diverting, making *Chill Out* one of the essential ambient albums. —*John Bush*

The White Room / Mar. 1991 / Arista ✦✦✦✦✦
After the incredible success of their "Doctorin' the Tardis" single in 1988 (better known as that theme from *Dr. Who*), Drummond and Cauty had plenty of money to hire talented musicians (instead of merely sampling them, as on their early recordings). *The White Room* is the result, an album bursting with hit singles that nevertheless flows as well as any concept album. Often overlooked as a classic from the acid house era (mostly because of the KLF's retirement one year later), *The White Room* represents the commercial and artistic peak of late-'80s acid-house. —*John Bush*

KMFDM

f. 1984, **db.** Jan. 22, 1999
Alternative Pop/Rock, Industrial
KMFDM was one of Wax Trax's first industrial superstars, combining the corrosive scratching of their guitars with a hard, throbbing hip-hop-derived beat. In the late '80s, the German trio (originally a quartet) became an underground sensation not only in America but in much of Europe; clubs became devoted to playing their style of abrasive, distorted, guitar-driven dance music. KMFDM continued to be one of the major industrial bands of the '90s, with their recordings becoming even more aggressive, both musically and politically, as evidenced by releases including 1995's *Nihil* and *Juke-Joint Jezebel* as well as 1996's *XTORT*. A self-titled effort appeared in 1997, followed a year later by *Retro*. *Adios* was released in 1999, and KMFDM disbanded, with several members forming MDFMK. —*Stephen Thomas Erlewine*

Don't Blow Your Top / 1988 / Wax Trax! ✦✦

UAIOE / 1989 / Wax Trax! ✦✦✦

Naïve / 1990 / Wax Trax! ✦✦✦✦✦
KMFDM's fourth full-length album is one their strongest releases. It's a claustrophobic wall of noise, driven by a relentless jackhammer beat. —*Stephen Thomas Erlewine*

Money / 1992 / Wax Trax! ✦✦✦
Like Ministry, KMFDM has attracted listeners who aren't necessarily big fans of industrial music. Abrasive, noisy and dissonant, *Money!* hardly qualifies as easy listening. But compare this excellent CD to albums by Skinny Puppy and the seminal Throbbing Gristle, and you'll begin to see why *Money!* was considered to be much more accessible by comparison. The aggression of industrial noise is there, but so are elements of heavy metal, Eurodance music and hip-hop. And the overall results are as infectious as they are unpredictable. Club deejays found songs like "Vogue," "Bargeld" and "Sex on the Flag" hard to resist, as did the many dancers who discovered that a blistering metal guitar, distorted industrial vocals and a syncopated dance beat could indeed be united into a cohesive, exciting whole. —*Alex Henderson*

Angst / Oct. 13, 1993 / Wax Trax! ✦✦✦✦
KMFDM's unfocused industrial experiments of the late '80s finally blossomed on 1990's superb *Naïve* album, which displayed highly evolved production values and a cohesive blend of all the elements that have become the band's sonic trademarks: propulsive electro-industrial beats, shouted propaganda, and airtight heavy metal guitar riffing. The follow-up, 1992's inconsistent *Money*, continued in the same vein, but sounded uninspired, recycling many of the ideas on *Naïve*. On *Angst*, KMFDM finally reaches their full potential. Using unbridled aggression, boldfaced sloganeering, and constant self-reference (all imbued with a wonderful sense of humor) to make their points, KMFDM has created a singular voice in the often bland and cheerless genre of industrial music. Core members Sasha Konietzko and En Esch remain the band's central voices on *Angst* (both literally and ideologically), but the contributions of guitarist Mark Durante and vocalist Dorona Alberti are equally important to the group's sonic tapestry. "A Drug Against War" is the band's most over-the-top moment to date; racing along at about 320 beats per minute, it's got all the intensity of speed metal. And the hilarious "Sucks" ("our music is sampled/totally fake/it's done by machines 'coz they don't make mistakes") is a wonderfully irreverent blast of KMFDM's self-effacing sense of humor. Meanwhile, songs like "Move On" and "The Problem" (beautifully sung by Alberti) reflect the band's heartfelt political and social concerns. *Angst* is a great place for KMFDM newcomers to dig in. —*Andy Hinds*

Naïve/Hell to Go / 1994 / Wax Trax! ✦✦✦✦

Due to copyright problems with samples used on the original version of KMFDM's 1990 album *Naïve*, the album was taken out of circulation shortly after its release. It was reissued in 1994 as *Naïve/Hell to Go*, with the offending samples deleted and several of the tracks remixed. If you've got the original, with the orange cover art, you're lucky—it is rare and highly sought after. Even still, this version of *Naïve* (with green cover art) is worth having, thanks to its radical recasting of "Virus," "Godlike," and "Leibesleid." —*Andy Hinds*

Nihil / Apr. 4, 1995 / Wax Trax! ✦✦✦✦
KMFDM's seventh album, *Nihil*, finds the band sitting comfortably in the groove it started with 1990s *Naïve*. At this point, the German outfit has become an industrial musical collective, with various contributing vocalists and musicians coming in and out of the fold, while the nerve center of the group continues to be founders En Esch and Sasha Konietzko. Additionally, the group's ingenious marketing/merchandising skills (using the bold-faced KMFDM logo, idealistic sloganeering, and appropriately simplistic comic book artwork of Brute) have given the band a powerful, iconic image. The anthemic "Juke Joint Jezebel," with its disco-diva vocals (courtesy of Jennifer Ginsberg), remains the band's biggest "hit" to date; it is an enduring and indispensable dance floor favorite at goth/industrial clubs around the world. Other high points include the politically charged "Terror" and "Disobedience." Throughout the album, there is a core of intelligence which lifts KMFDM above many of their contemporaries. Significant contributions by growling vocalist Raymond Watts and super-tight guitarist Gunter Shulz add new colors to the KMFDM palette, and the overall production skills on *Nihil* are state of the art. While industrial music has a reputation for being abrasive, KMFDM's sound is actually quite polished and tight, with any real "noise" expertly airbrushed out of the mix. Which doesn't diminish the impact of the material; it merely streamlines the band's attack. —*Andy Hinds*

XTORT / Jun. 25, 1996 / Wax Trax! ✦✦✦
XTORT doesn't sound markedly different than KMFDM's other releases—there are still the bruising mechanical drum beats and numbingly drilling guitars, combined with barked vocals. What's noticeable about *XTORT*—their first album since industrial broke into the Top 40 with Nine Inch Nails' *The Downward Spiral*—is how the band made no concessions to the pop/rock mainstream whatsoever. They are still the same grimy, dank heavy dance band they were in the '80s. For some listeners, that means they're keeping the flame burning and, to a certain extent, they'd be right—KMFDM sounds as good as they ever have, and several tracks rank among their best. But, over a decade into their career, it would be nice to hear the band branch out and start to experiment a little bit more. —*Stephen Thomas Erlewine*

Symbols / Sep. 23, 1997 / Wax Trax! ✦✦✦
By 1997, KMFDM had become a dependable, prolific source for tightly produced, mostly top-notch heavy industrial music. To their great credit, the band never betrayed its countercultural ideals, becoming an independent empire without making any concessions to the mainstream. However, some of the band's ideas were getting a bit repetitive after nine albums. This self-titled effort (also known as *Symbols*, like Led Zeppelin's fourth album) was released during the "next big thing" hype of electronica, and finds the band peeling away some of its heavy guitars in favor of a more dance-oriented sound (which is where the band really started, anyway). And the programming skills here, admirably, have kept up with the times; some of this stuff sounds like it could have been produced by Prodigy. Luckily, KMFDM freshens its sound a bit with each album by bringing new contributing musicians into their collective; Tim Skold and ex-Skinny Puppy Ogre (with his unmistakably spooky growl) "sing" on a few tracks, while veteran industrial drummer William Reiflin adds live drums here and there. In all, this is as good as many of KMFDM's '90s albums, and is a fine place for newcomers to start. The clean, detailed production is of top quality, and many of the tunes—like "Megalomaniac" and "Anarchy"—are exceptional. But for those who have been following the band, *Symbols* offers few surprises. —*Andy Hinds*

● **Retro** / Nov. 17, 1998 / Wax Trax! ✦✦✦✦✦
KMFDM's greatest hits package is quite complete—it includes "Juke Joint Jezebel," "Rip the System!," the Ministry-ish "A Drug Against War," "Light," "Don't Blow Your Top" and "Godlike-Doglike." KMFDM's songs have always spoken about the unspeakable (something Nine Inch Nails and Tool would take even further), and their music and lyrics feed off of each other to create an energetic yet squeamish, invigorating but uncomfortable sound. To really get an idea how they evolved, though, start with the last track (from their first album) and work forward: their political and social commentary, as well as their emotional intensity, hasn't changed, although their energy level increased in the '90s as industrial exploded. At first, the band sounds like an annoyed Depeche Mode, but KMFDM had created their trademark gritty-yet-accessible sound by *Naïve*. Never known for their subtlety (lyrically or musically), their aural assaults and mostly danceable rhythms make this compilation a great overview of a band that pushed the limits of industrial music and changed it for the better. —*Gina Boldman*

Agogo / Nov. 17, 1998 / Wax Trax! ✦✦✦
This collection of rare and unreleased material is pretty good. Everything from the ultra heavy "Godlike" (featuring the late William Tucker, may he rest in peace) to the more dancey, funky numbers that old-school KMFDM are known for. This album plays like a greatest-hits, which is funny because all of the songs on this are over a decade old (all pre-*Angst*). While ultra old-school fans would definitely dig this CD, the new-school ones shouldn't be turned off by it, either; it's a very consistent and fun album and has a certain "polished" feel that one doesn't really expect from KMFDM's older material. "The Zip" (an unreleased track) is probably one of the funniest dance tracks ever heard. It has a man talking about how he is going to "get into the zip," the zip being the zipper on your

pants. The song "Godlike," on the other hand, is the highly political, ultra-heavy industrial rock that KMFDM have come to be known for since *Angst*. If you like KMFDM, this is a great addition to anyone's collection and should not be passed by. *—Alan Esher*

Adios / Apr. 20, 1999 / Wax Trax! ✦✦✦
KMFDM's final album starts out with a bitter goodbye on the title track, and the usual mechanical, sonic assault continues on tracks like "Witness," the Kraftwerk-inspired "R.U. OK?" and "Full Worm Garden." Some songs are more dance club than industrial; "Today" depicts a calmer eye before "Rubicon" and "Bereit" resume the high energy and aggressive stormy ambience that are the band's trademark. KMFDM sounds smoother yet maintains its emotive mayhem in all its glory. *—Gina Boldman*

The Knack

f. 1978, Los Angeles, CA, **db.** 1981
Power Pop, New Wave
Forming in Los Angeles in the late '70s, the Knack were neither punk nor rock, but pure simple pop, standing out amongst the musical dross that littered the Sunset Strip. Signing with Capitol after a feeding frenzy of label offers, they released their debut, *Get the Knack*, in 1979. With its leadoff single "My Sharona," the Knack climbed both the album and singles charts (eventually selling millions of copies around the globe), gained wide commercial acceptance, and regenerated the power-pop scene that had laid dormant for half a decade. The Knack's image, or lack thereof, was often unfavorably compared to the Beatles, but their music relied on the rough punchiness of the Kinks and the Who rather than the Fab Four. Their refusal to do interviews turned critics against them, and by the time they released their second album, … *But the Little Girls Understand*, less than a year after the debut, the backlash had already begun. *—Steven "Spaz" Schnee*

● **Get the Knack** / Apr. 1979 / Capitol ✦✦✦✦✦
The band attempted to update the Beatles sound for the new wave era on their debut. A good idea that was well executed, but critics cried "foul" when millions sold after Capitol's pre-release hype (it went gold in 13 days and eventually sold five million copies, making it one of the most successful debuts in history). *Get the Knack* is at once sleazy, sexist, hook-filled and endlessly catchy—above all, it's a guilty pleasure and an exercise in simple fun. When is power-pop *legitimate* anyway? Includes the unforgettable hits "My Sharona" and "Good Girls Don't." *—Chris Woodstra*

…But the Little Girls Understand / Dec. 1979 / Razor & Tie ✦✦✦
Mike Chapman summed it up best in the liner notes—"The songs are an assortment of feelings and emotions expressed redundantly as only the Knack can … This record is very dear to me and my bank manager." The self-deprecating title (which quotes Willie Dixon's "Back Door Man") isn't really an attempt to apologize but rather to let everyone know that they were in on the joke all along—and they're laughing all the way to the bank. This is essentially a rewrite of the debut, especially evident on the lead-off single "Baby Talks Dirty." It's not as good as *Get the Knack* and didn't sell nearly as well, but it *is* a good time for those who don't take rock & roll too seriously. *—Chris Woodstra*

Round Trip / 1981 / Capitol ✦✦
Serious Fun / Jan. 16, 1991 / Charisma ✦✦
The Retrospective: The Best of the Knack / Nov. 16, 1992 / Capitol ✦✦✦✦✦
For all but the most dedicated fans (and, if you're into power pop, chances are you're at least a little dedicated), the 17-track *Retrospective: The Best of the Knack* will be all the Knack you need, but even if your tastes run a little deeper, this will satisfy, and not because it contains collector bait like the demo version of "Rocket O' Love" and a cover of Springsteen's "Don't Look Back," but because its track selection is smart and infectious. That adds up to a fine collection of one of the great sleazy pleasures of the late '70s. *—Stephen Thomas Erlewine*

Very Best of the Knack / May 19, 1998 / Rhino ✦✦✦✦
Released to coincide with the group's 1998 reunion, Rhino's *The Very Best of the Knack* is designed to replace the 1992 compilation *Retrospective: The Best of the Knack*, and in many ways it does. Twelve of the 16 tracks are greatest hits, all but two of which were featured on *Retrospective*. Granted, "Rocket O' Love" appeared as a demo on the earlier compilation, and "Can't Put a Price on Love" is included here as a single edit, but it still contains all of the essentials—"My Sharona," "Baby Talks Dirty," "Good Girls Don't"—plus one strong song apiece from each of their first two albums ("That's What the Little Girls Do," "How Can Love Hurt So Much"), both of which probably should have been on the original compilation. Then again, *Retrospective* stretched to 17 songs, covering *Round Trip* and *Serious Fun* with some concentration, and *Retrospective* contains no less than four new songs: the solid original "She Says," a winning take on the infectious mock-Merseybeat "That Thing You Do!," and strong readings of two Nick Lowe tunes, "Teacher Teacher" and "I Knew the Bride (When She Used to Rock & Roll)." They're good songs and good performances, but they make the album feel less like a compilation, for better and for worse. *The Very Best of the Knack* remains a good choice for most casual fans, but listeners who want a compilation that concentrates on the body of the band's career might want to seek out *Retrospective*. *—Stephen Thomas Erlewine*

Zoom / Jul. 14, 1998 / Rhino ✦✦✦
Seven years after the failed comeback *Serious Fun*, the Knack reunited with new drummer Terry Bozzio in tow and recorded *Zoom*. Sounding like a re-energized and de-sleazed version of *Get the Knack*, *Zoom* is the best album the maligned power-pop band has recorded since their debut. Doug Fieger's songwriting is sharp and melodic and the band delivers the tunes with vigor. A few cuts are a little undistinguished, but there are more solid, memorable songs here than on most of their albums, and that alone makes it a successful comeback. *—Stephen Thomas Erlewine*

The Knickerbockers

f. 1964, Bergenfield, NJ, **db.** 1968
Frat Rock, Rock & Roll
In early 1966, the Knickerbockers hit the Top 20 with "Lies," the best and most accurate early Beatle imitation ever recorded; the lead vocals were a dead ringer for John Lennon and the whole production could have fit in snugly on the second side of *A Hard Day's Night*. Actually a frat rock band from New Jersey who didn't write much of their own material, they never made anything else as successful. A couple decent follow-ups—"One Track Mind" and the similarly mock-British Invasion "High on Love"—were small hits, but their albums were even blander than many of the era's other one-shot artists. Their three noteworthy singles were all featured in Rhino's *Nuggets* series. Drummer and singer Jimmy Walker briefly replaced Bill Medley in the Righteous Brothers. *—Richie Unterberger*

Jerk & Twine Time / 1965 / Sundazed ✦✦
Even if you're a dedicated collector, you should think twice about chasing down this album, which consists almost entirely of British Invasion and R&B covers in the frat-rock style, and not done especially well. The CD reissue has three bonus tracks, and an interview with a couple members of the band. *—Richie Unterberger*

Lies / 1965 / Sundazed ✦✦
● **The 20 Classic Tracks!** / 1988 / Sundazed ✦✦✦✦✦
The Great Lost Album / Sep. 27, 1994 / Sundazed ✦✦✦✦
Knickerbockerism!: Hits, Rarities, Unissued Cuts & More… / Feb. 24, 1997 / Sundazed ✦✦✦
Though its modern-day connotation means something quite the opposite in terms of flattery, the Knickerbockers in their heyday were the ultimate bar band. With a stripped-down lineup of guitar, bass, drums, and tenor saxophone and all four members singing, their repertoire truly "covered the waterfront." Their harmonies were gorgeous, fuller and sharper than your average self-contained band, and their collective ear for mimicry was unparalleled. When they recorded a deadly accurate Beatle sound-alike original, "Lies," for the tiny Challenge label, it started zooming up the charts, and the band seemed poised for multi-talented stardom. Alas, it was not to be, but certainly not for lack of talent. This definitive 36-track two-disc set documents—if not the best the group had to offer—at the very least, the best they were allowed to commit to magnetic tape, and spotlights their many strong points (impeccable harmonies, a solid-as-a-brick rhythm section, and a willingness to adapt to different types of material thrust upon them). We'll never really know what the Knickerbockers were ultimately capable of, but this collection shows that even when their rockin' locomotive was put on a single direction track, they still had much to contribute. A one-hit group, perhaps, but one with more talent than chart success, that much is obvious. *—Cub Koda*

Lies: The Very Best of the Knickerbockers / Jul. 28, 1998 / Collectables ✦✦✦✦
Despite its relatively shoddy packaging and remastering, Collectables' *Lies: The Very Best of the Knickerbockers* is a good collection of the band's best moments. All the hits are here ("Lies," "One Track Mind," "High on Love," "Jolly Green Giant"), along with 21 other album tracks, singles and B-sides. The Knickerbockers were a bit more than a one-hit wonder—they had a handful of good songs besides "Lies," and they could rock hard—but there's still enough filler here to test the patience of more casual fans. Then again, they may be better served by Sundazed's *The Fabulous Knickerbockers*, which is more concise and has a stronger song selection, even if it suffers from the same inconsistent material. Either way, Collectables' effort is admirable, even with its imperfections, and may suit the purposes of listeners who want to hear more than "Lies." *—Stephen Thomas Erlewine*

Gladys Knight

b. May 28, 1944, Atlanta, GA
Vocals / Smooth Soul, Pop-Soul, Quiet Storm, Motown, Soul, Urban
One of the great soul singers, Gladys Knight didn't hit her commercial stride until she moved to Motown in 1966. Steeped in the gospel tradition, like so many soul singers, Knight and backing group the Pips developed into one of Motown's most dependable acts, although they never quite scaled the commercial or artistic heights of fellow stars on the label like the Supremes, Marvin Gaye, and the Temptations. With Norman Whitfield providing the production and much of the songwriting, the Pips fit into the mainstream of Motown's machine well, scoring big hits with some rabble-rousers (like "Friendship Train" and the original version of "I Heard It Through the Grapevine"), mainstream mid-tempo soul ("It Should Have Been Me" and "The End of Our Road"), and smooth ballads like "If I Were Your Woman." In 1973, Knight had her biggest Motown hit with "Neither One of Us," which made number two; shortly afterwards, she and the Pips left Motown for Buddah. The group were briefly superstars in 1973-74, reeling off the smashes "Midnight Train to Georgia" (their only number one), "I've Got to Use My Imagination," and "Best Thing That Ever Happened to Me." This ranked as some of their best material, but Knight soon moved toward an easy listening, adult contemporary direction, one that she's maintained to this day. *—Richie Unterberger*

Anthology / 1974 / Motown ✦✦✦✦✦
Atlanta family-group Gladys Knight & the Pips had performed together for 14 years before signing with Motown in 1966. Earlier recordings for Huntom (the master recordings were later sold to Vee-Jay), Fury, and Maxx had generated five chart hits, including the Top Ten R&B smashes "Every Beat of My Heart" and "Letter Full of Tears," but it was on the Motown subsidiary Soul that Gladys Knight and company hit their stride. This compilation more than adequately covers this period of the Pips' career. Working primarily

with producer Norman Whitfield from 1967 through 1969, the group created such Motor City classics as "Everybody Needs Love," "I Heard It Through the Grapevine," "The End of Our Road," and "Friendship Train." From 1970 through 1973 the Pips worked with a variety of Motown producers, concentrating on ballads. Although they were perhaps a little less consistent, there was no shortage of hits, the most notable being 1970's "If I Were Your Woman" and 1973's "Neither One of Us (Wants to Be the First to Say Goodbye)." The updated double-CD version of *Anthology*, featuring digitally remastered sound, replaces about a dozen songs with different ones, though this 40-track collection still contains all of the essential hits and adds lengthy liner notes. Be aware that the three early-'60s hits that lead off the volume (on both versions of *Anthology*) are Motown re-recordings, not the originals. *—Rob Bowman*

Every Beat of My Heart / 1989 / Prime Cuts ♦♦♦
The best collection of Knight's pre-Motown sides, including both of their big early-'60s hits (the title track and "Letter Full of Tears"), but concentrating more heavily on their mid-'60s sessions. These were overseen by Van McCoy, who supplied the group with several of his own compositions as well. McCoy was one of the most melodically ambitious pop/soul composers of the era, and his songs on this compilation—"Either Way I Lose," "Why Don't You Love Me," "Lovers Always Forgive"—are achingly beautiful and rife with unexpected key changes. His "Stop and Get a Hold of Myself," on the other hand, is a more conventional (but equally first-rate) uptempo soul stomper. If there's any criticism of these sides, it's that Knight and the group don't establish a strong identity, handling doo wop-like ballads, girl-group-tinged pop, McCoy's idiosyncratic songs, and more modern pop-soul with chameleon-like skill. In the end, that doesn't detract from the strength of this CD, which is a collection of fine early to mid-'60s pop/soul. The major flaw is the inexplicable omission of the McCoy composition "Giving Up," a Top 40 hit for the group in 1964. *—Richie Unterberger*

Soul Survivors: The Best of Gladys Knight & the Pips 1973-1988 / Oct. 1990 / Rhino ♦♦♦♦♦
Soul Survivors—The Best of Gladys Knight & the Pips picks up where the Motown anthology left off, containing the most important singles that Gladys Knight And The Pips recorded for Buddah, Columbia, and MCA from the early '70s until the late '80s. The Buddah tracks, highlighted by the Jim Weatherly-written "Midnight Train to Georgia" and "Best Thing That Ever Happened to Me," contain some of Knight's most impassioned vocal performances. *—Rob Bowman*

Blue Lights in the Basement / Apr. 1996 / RCA ♦♦♦
Knight's stint for the Buddah label in the mid-'70s found her commercial success at its peak, landing hits like "Midnight Train to Georgia," "Best Thing That Ever Happened to Me," "Part Time Love," and "The Way We Were" (all included here). But this 17-track survey of 1973-78 material is not nearly as artistically satisfying as her Motown and Vee Jay recordings, finding her and the Pips easing into a middle-of-the-road sound that helped pave the way for mellow urban contemporary music. What's more, this compilation is not truly representative of the era, omitting the huge hit "I've Got to Use My Imagination," presumably because it's too uptempo to find a place on an anthology geared toward the "quiet storm" audience. *—Richie Unterberger*

The Ultimate Collection / Oct. 7, 1997 / Motown ♦♦♦♦♦
The Ultimate Collection nearly lives up to its billing, featuring 22 tracks on a single disc. Among the featured cuts are all of Gladys Knight & the Pips' Top Ten pop hits for Soul Records, including "Everybody Needs Love," "I Heard It Through the Grapevine," "The End of Our Road," "It Should Have Been Me," "The Nitty Gritty," "Friendship Train," "I Don't Want to Do Wrong," "If I Were Your Woman," and "Neither One of Us (Wants to Be the First to Say Goodbye)." For most casual fans, those who just want the hits, this will be the definitive collection of Knight's early career. *—Stephen Thomas Erlewine*

● **Essential Collection** / Sep. 28, 1999 / Hip-O ♦♦♦♦♦
There have been many Gladys Knight & the Pips collections over the years, yet few have drawn from all periods of their career. Hip-O's 1999 compilation *Essential Collection* does, beginning with their first hit for Vee-Jay, "Every Beat of My Heart," and ending with their last R&B number one, 1987's "Love Overboard." It doesn't feature every hit they ever had, but it does provide a good chronology of their career by featuring their biggest hits: "I Heard It Through the Grapevine," "If I Were Your Woman," "Neither One of Us (Wants to Be the First to Say Goodbye)," "Daddy Could Swear, I Declare," "Midnight Train to Georgia," "I've Got to Use My Imagination," "The Best Thing That Ever Happened to Me," "On and On," "Save the Overtime (For Me)," "Hero (Wind Beneath My Wings)." Anyone looking for a single disc covering the entire career of Gladys Knight & the Pips should turn here. *—Stephen Thomas Erlewine*

Buddy Knox

b. Jul. 20, 1933, Happy, TX, **d.** Feb. 14, 1999
Vocals, Guitar / Rockabilly, Rock & Roll
The brand of Texas rockabilly that Buddy Knox cooked up around 1957 wasn't quite as raw as that of his Memphis cohorts at Sun, but it was just as commercially potent. Knox sported a light, almost gentle vocal style, and his band, the Rhythm Orchids, obliged with upbeat backing that suited him well. Formed at West Texas State University, the Rhythm Orchids also included Jimmy Bowen on upright bass, and it was Bowen's equally light-hearted vocal on "I'm Stickin' with You" that originally graced the flip side of Knox's first smash, "Party Doll." Roulette Records astutely picked up the master from the tiny Triple-D logo, separated the sides, and the fledgling label enjoyed two giant hits for the price of one.

"Party Doll" soared to the very top of the pops, and Knox encored with the equally tuneful "Rock Your Little Baby to Sleep" and "Hula Love," which he performed in the 1957 rock flick *Jamboree*. Knox waxed the fine rockabilly-based "Swingin' Daddy," "Devil Woman," and a cover of Ruth Brown's "Somebody Touched Me" for Roulette before moving to Liberty and hitting with a pop-flavored rendition of the Clovers' song "Lovey Dovey" in 1960. Over three decades later, the Texas rocker remains a popular act on the oldies front. *—Bill Dahl*

● **The Best of Buddy Knox** / Jun. 1990 / Rhino ♦♦♦♦
Rhino's *The Best of Buddy Knox* is a definitive 18-track compilation featuring all of the hits the light rockabilly cat ever had, including "Party Doll," "Rock Your Little Baby to Sleep," "Hula Love," "Swingin' Daddy," "Somebody Touched Me," "Teasable, Pleasable You," "That's Why I Cry," "I Think I'm Gonna Kill Myself," "Lovey Dovey" and "Ling-Ting-Tong." *—Stephen Thomas Erlewine*

The Complete Roulette Recordings / May 7, 1996 / Sequel ♦♦♦
Knox only has one-half of this double CD; the second disc is devoted to tracks by his friend and contemporary, Jimmy Bowen. The approach isn't as odd as it seems: When Knox and Bowen began their recording careers, they were both part of the Rhythm Orchids, and a similar lineup of Orchids backs each solo singer on their respective recordings. Most listeners will be much better off with Rhino's briefer, more selective Knox best-of. Completists, however, will find all 30 of Knox's 1956-60 Roulette tracks on disc one of this two-pack. Including five previously unreleased songs, it's pleasant Tex-Mex rockabilly, tamer than Buddy Holly, but far gutsier than the Jimmy Bowen solo cuts that take up all of disc two. *—Richie Unterberger*

Chris Knox

b. Sep. 2, 1952, Invercargill, New Zealand
Vocals / New Zealand Rock, Indie Rock, Lo-Fi, Alternative Pop/Rock
Possibly the most important figure in New Zealand alternative/indie/post-punk rock, Chris Knox has been an integral figure of three of the country's more important rock bands (Tall Dwarfs, Toy Love, the Enemy), as well as recording prolifically as a solo artist. Although Knox has worked with guitarist Alec Bathgate on Tall Dwarfs records since the early '80s, he has also maintained a less active, but ongoing, solo career in which he writes, performs, and records without Bathgate's assistance. Knox has had an ample opportunity to work alone given that he and Bathgate, because of their different living circumstances, are usually only able to record together for short, infrequent bursts of time. Undoubtedly Knox's solo albums are more personal in nature than his group projects, yet in all honesty it can be difficult to find much difference between them and the Tall Dwarfs records. Working independently, Knox also staunchly adheres to a lo-fi, home recording ethic; he also favors songs which alternate between acoustic pop, post-psychedelia, and bursts of fuzzy garage noise, just as Tall Dwarfs do. Consequently, Tall Dwarfs fans will undoubtedly find Knox's records worth checking out, though on the whole the best of Tall Dwarfs is a better place to start investigating Knox's music. Within each Knox solo record there is a great deal of diversity, although it must be cautioned that there isn't a notable difference in approach from recording to recording. This can make his extensive discography less rewarding than those of pop auteurs who take greater care to vary their palette from release to release, such as England's Martin Newell. *—Richie Unterberger*

Not Given Lightly/Guppiplus / 1989 / Flying Nun ♦♦♦
Side one of this 12-inch plays at 45 RPM and is devoted solely to a song from the *Seizure* album, "Not Given Lightly," which is one of his most accessible (not to say Lennonesque) songs. Fans will be more concerned with the ten songs on side two, which plays at 33 RPM. Eight of the tracks are taken from his 1983 solo debut, *Songs for Cleaning Guppies*. These are more primitive and subdued than much of his later work, but just as experimental, and in some intangible way feel more personal. The disc is filled out with a couple of cuts from obscure New Zealand compilations. *—Richie Unterberger*

Seizure / 1989 / Flying Nun ♦♦♦
There's really little to distinguish this from a Tall Dwarfs record of the same period. Knox may be writing and playing everything, but it's very close in tone and tune to what he makes with Alec Bathgate—eclectic, psychedelic noise with lo-fi production values. If you need to differentiate, this seems to be somewhat cruder and more noise-oriented than the Tall Dwarfs projects; song titles like "The Woman Inside of Me" and "Rapist" are indication enough that the subjects stray just as far from the hit parade. If you like Tall Dwarfs well enough to pick up their albums every time you see one, you will want this as well, but if your interest is more casual, you'd be better off sticking with one or two Tall Dwarfs records. *—Richie Unterberger*

Polyfoto, Duck Shaped Pain & "Gum" / 1993 / Communion ♦♦♦
Recorded on a Walkman between 1990 and 1992, although you wouldn't really know from the quite listenable clarity of the results; fidelity-wise, it's no worse than other Knox/Tall Dwarfs product, and quite possibly better than some. More important is the content, a typically Knoxian journey through such varied topics as rape, Rodney King, distorted self-images, cosmetic surgery, and ruminations inspired by contemporary cultural theorists. The music is still pop/rock-experimentalism, sometimes approaching (as in "Trim Milk") his best melodies. It's not *so* outstanding, however, that the herky-jerky nature of the exploration can't start to get exhausting. With nearly 70 minutes, it may well have worked better in a somewhat edited fashion. *—Richie Unterberger*

Meat / Apr. 16, 1995 / Communion ♦♦♦

● **Songs of You & Me** / May 16, 1995 / Caroline ♦♦♦♦♦
Although this isn't a good deal different than his other work (both with the Tall Dwarfs and on his own), this may be Knox's best album, simply by virtue of the sheer amount of territory it covers over 21 songs. The fidelity is also somewhat better than most of his other releases, and although Knox has often championed the virtues of cheap home

recording, this is a considerable virtue. A bit of clarity, without coming at the expense of slickness, simply makes the stuff easier to listen to. The disc is also the strongest evidence of Knox's talents as one of the more interesting lyricists working in indie rock, examining psychological conflict with a complexity that takes several listenings to grip. —*Richie Unterberger*

Yes!! / Sep. 23, 1997 / Flying Nun ✦✦✦✦
Chris Knox's prolific output is so consistent in its quality and scope that it's often easy to forget just how good his records really are. While there's little to distinguish *Yes!!* from recent efforts like *Songs of You & Me* or *Meat*, that's hardly meant as a criticism—Knox's albums increasingly seem less like individual works than part of a much bigger picture that's still coming into focus, and compared to the erratic, anything-goes aesthetic which permeates the American lo-fi underground, it's refreshing to encounter an artist with such a firm grasp of his craft that he makes excellent albums seem almost automatic. —*Jason Ankeny*

Beat / Aug. 22, 2000 / Thirsty Ear ✦✦

Cub Koda

b. Oct. 1, 1948, Detroit, MI, **d.** Jul. 1, 2000
AMG Contributor, Liner Notes, Vocals, Harmonica, Guitar / Detroit Rock, Retro-Rock, Rockabilly, Blues-Rock, Electric Chicago Blues, Rock & Roll
Best known as the leader of Brownsville Station and composer of their hit, "Smokin' in the Boys Room," Cub Koda has proven that his roots went far deeper, both before the band's formation, during its days in the sun, and long after its demise. His high school band, the Del-Tinos, was dipping into blues and rockabilly as far back as 1963—not only pre-Butterfield, but pre-Beatles. Similarly, he recorded legendary home tapes during his off-hours from Brownsville, before the rockabilly revival had uttered its first hiccup, and later teamed with Hound Dog Taylor's former rhythm section, the Houserockers, to play the blues in the '80s. Along the way he cranked out a monthly column ("The Vinyl Junkie") and recorded a series of albums that kept roots music of all kinds alive without ever treating it like a museum piece. After a couple of bands in the late '60s that largely went unrecorded, Koda formed Brownsville Station in early 1969. The band debuted one year later, but it wasn't until 1973's number three hit "Smokin' in the Boys Room" that Brownsville gained a genuine hit. When Brownsville disbanded in 1979, Cub established himself as an expert record collector and critic through columns for *Goldmine* and *DISCoveries*. In 1980, Koda began working with Hound Dog Taylor's backing band, the Houserockers, and the trio ended up together for 15 years. Throughout the '80s and '90s, Koda has continued to divide his time equally between touring, recording, and writing. —*Stephen Thomas Erlewine*

Cub Koda & the Points / 1980 / Fan Club ✦✦✦✦
Koda's first solo album after Brownsville Station. Highlights include "Jail Bait" and "Welcome to My Job." —*Stephen Thomas Erlewine*

It's the Blues / 1981 / Fan Club ✦✦✦
The addition of bass and special guests Left Hand Frank and Lefty Dizz only distract from the chemistry between Cub and the Houserockers (even more obvious on their belated live follow-up), but this is a strong session, with the ex-stadium boogie boy sounding totally at home with these blues veterans. His vocal duet with Brewer Phillips on J.B. Lenoir's "Talk to Your Daughter" is a joy, and thankfully not every note is perfectly in place—or in the case of Brewer's guitar, in tune. Added treats: Koda's big-toned harp on "Rockin' This Joint Tonight" and humorous dialog with Frank on "Dirty Duck Blues." —*Dan Forte*

Cub Digs Chuck / 1989 / Garageland ✦✦✦
Koda's tribute album to Chuck Berry, featuring blistering versions of "Johnny B. Goode," "Maybellene," and others. —*Stephen Thomas Erlewine*

Live at B.L.U.E.S. 1982 / 1991 / Wolf ✦✦✦✦✦
What's wrong with this picture? The sawed-off bespectacled singer/guitarist from Brownsville Station fronting the late Hound Dog Taylor's ex-rhythm section, the Houserockers—blasphemy, you say? Get a life. Koda smokes like he's: 1) out to dispel any doubts about his legitimacy, and 2) having the time of his life. Opening with Howlin' Wolf's "Highway 49" (a rather tall order), the Cubmaster grabs the Chicago crowd by its collective neck and shakes it into submission. His guitar trade-offs with Brewer Phillips (no bass in this band) are a delight, and by "You Can't Sit Down" drummer Ted Harvey is blowing his police whistle—signalling that things be rockin'! Eddie Clearwater sits in on one tune, and Koda tips his hat to the guitarist with a stellar rendition of Eddie's "Hillbilly Blues." This is worthy of wider release, not to mention an encore. —*Dan Forte*

Cub Digs Bo / 1991 / Garageland ✦✦✦✦
Koda's tribute album to Bo Diddley, including powerhouse renditions of "Mumblin' Guitar," "Roadrunner," and "Background to a Music." —*Stephen Thomas Erlewine*

● **Welcome to My Job: The Cub Koda Collection 1963-93** / 1993 / Blue Wave ✦✦✦✦✦
Covering everything from his pre-Brownsville Station days to two brand-new songs, *Welcome to My Job* is the definitive collection of Cub Koda's versatile solo career. —*Stephen Thomas Erlewine*

Abba Dabba Dabba: A Bananza of Hits / Jul. 19, 1994 / Schoolkids ✦✦✦✦
Cub Koda's first album for Schoolkids' Records is his wildest, funniest, and simply best album in years. —*Stephen Thomas Erlewine*

The Joint Was Rockin' / 1996 / Deluge ✦✦✦✦
The Joint Was Rockin' is a raw, rowdy and deliriously fun record capturing Cub Koda live with the Houserockers in the early '80s. The Houserockers bash away like they were supporting Hound Dog Taylor and Cub proves that he can play the blues with true passion

and feeling. More than anything, however, *The Joint Was Rockin'* is a bracing jolt of energy and fun that's just as good as *Live at B.L.U.E.S. 1982*, his previous live set with the Houserockers. —*Stephen Thomas Erlewine*

Box Lunch / 1997 / J-Bird ✦✦✦✦
Cub Koda has tried a lot of different things in his long career, but he has never made anything close to *Box Lunch*. It's not just that the album consists of nothing but acoustic material; he has never been this open with his emotions. There are a few rockers—"Double Barrel Hell" is menacing and "Gimme Trash" is a tongue-in-cheek kitsch celebration—but the heart of the record is in the ballads, whether it's the nostalgic "We Were Crazy Back Then," the yearning "Runaway Heart," or the lovely "How Could Life Turn Out This Way," which evokes the spirit of Hank Williams. Cub has rarely been this naked with his feelings and the results are frequently moving. And, to cap it all off, he throws out "Susan Hayward's Diary," a charming finger-picked instrumental. Moments like this make you hope that it's not the last acoustic album Cub will make—*Box Lunch* is so good, you wish there were seconds. —*Stephen Thomas Erlewine*

Noise Monkeys / Mar. 2000 / J-Bird ✦✦✦✦
Arriving on the heels of the introspective, acoustic *Box Lunch*, *Noise Monkeys*—Cub Koda's reunion album with the Points, his first band after the demise of Brownsville Station—may come as a bit of a surprise. Make no mistake about it, the title of the record tells you what this album is all about: this is loud, dumb, fun, hard-driving rock & roll, the kind that sounds like it was cut by a bunch of noise monkeys. Some fans may have forgotten that Koda can rock hard when he wants to, and that's what he does with the Points on *Noise Monkeys*. The bulk of the album was recorded live in the studio in one day in June 1999; the final two songs were recorded live in concert, the following day. Not surprisingly, the album is a bracing, immediate, and above all, loud record, filled with guitars, guitars, and guitars. He hasn't rocked this hard or this intensely since the first Points album. But this record is a better one on many levels, due to the fact that the band members have matured as musicians. They can now knock off these songs in one take and sound totally convincing and energetic. But don't think that this is sophisticated music—this is dumb rock & roll, and proudly so—and it's all the better for it. Koda and the Points pound away, sounding stronger and better at the turn of the millennium than they did at the turn of the '70s. Sure, some of the songs are silly, but that's the point. The end result is a satisfying hard rock album with humor and character—something like that doesn't come along every day. —*Stephen Thomas Erlewine*

Komeda

f. 1991
Swedish Pop/Rock, Indie Pop, Indie Rock, Alternative Pop/Rock
Named in honor of Kryzstof Komeda, the late jazz musican/film composer best known for his work with Roman Polanski and Ingmar Bergman, the Swedish kitsch-pop outfit Komeda originated in 1991 as the pit band for a Buster Keaton festival. A series of other festival performances followed, with the quartet—comprised of vocalist Lena Karlsson, guitarist Mattias Nordlander, bassist Marcus Holmberg and Holmberg's brother Jonas on drums—often renaming themselves Projektor 7 for their cinema-related work. In 1993, they issued their debut album *Pop På Svenska*, which they followed with the *Plan 714 Till Komeda* EP two years later. The full-length *The Genius of Komeda* arrived in 1996, with *What Makes It Go?* appearing two years later. Komeda gained more acclaim with their appearance on 2000's *Heroes and Villains*, the soundtrack to Cartoon Network's popular *Powerpuff Girls* series, and the following year saw a burst of activity from the band, including reissues of *Pop På Svenska* and *Plan 714 Till Komeda* on Minty Fresh and a new album later in the year. —*Jason Ankeny*

Pop På Svenska / 1993 / North of No South ✦✦✦
Pop På Svenska certainly doesn't sound like a first album. This 1993 release (originally issued on Swedish label North of No South) has all of the catchy grooves, tight constructions, and all-around embraceable pop music as their later, English-language albums would show, with the addition of occasionally sweeping string arrangements. Yes, all of these songs are in Swedish; although the band had started out writing songs in English, and resumed doing so on the albums that followed, their first album is in their native language. But this won't be enough to keep most people from enjoying the happy intricacies of Komeda's upbeat moods, as heard on shining moments like "Ad Fontes" and "Feeling Fine." The band stretches out a bit at the end of the album with a hypnotic, extended jam, "Borgo," right before the quiet album closer. —*Joslyn Layne*

The Genius of Komeda / Sep. 24, 1996 / Minty Fresh ✦✦✦
A product of the same Swedish pop scene which spawned the equally effervescent Cardigans and Cloudberry Jam, *The Genius of Komeda* is another outstanding export, a bright and charmingly kitschy ode to space-age popcraft. Comparisons to Stereolab are certainly warranted, particularly on tracks like "Disko" and "Frolic" (with their "ba-ba-ba" backing vocals and futuristic effects), but Komeda's melodic smarts and cinematic aesthetic are all their own; tracks like the opening "More Is More" and "Rocket Plane (Music on the Moon)" are immediately ingratiating, and further buoying the album is the band's sharp, tongue-in-cheek wit—theirs is a joke well worth being in on. —*Jason Ankeny*

● **What Makes It Go?** / Apr. 20, 1998 / Minty Fresh ✦✦✦✦
Komeda are a Swedish quartet who give us quirky, danceable ditties with memorable melodies. Funky electronics, bass lines, and mesmerizing rhythms roll along by playing off one another. There exists a '60s flair with added horns, analog synths, and acoustic guitars that pound out rhythms. Maybe, a Stereolab reference could by placed with the synth/drums set up. Strings on every song are used to give the fun a twinge of sadness, a wonderful element. The vocals of Lena Karlsson are a deserving focus in the mix of *What Makes It Go?* Her phrasing and accenting make the words flow in these songs. She

is a sassy singer that sounds like an old blues/Dixieland singer set in the rock world. "Curious" seems to be the single, with a '60s Muzak feel highlighted by Stevie Wonder-sounding horns and organs. There is a nice flowing chorus chanting of the wonders of human nature. "Flabbergast" moves along playing with key, sounding a bit like the Cure. In parts, it sounds as if the Casio demonstration has stepped in alongside the amazing vocals of Karlsson. The chorus busts out of nowhere to step the song up levels. The lyrics are step-by-step directions for living. A nice outro of drone bells and strings creates a dramatic effect. Komeda always seem to keep the feeling light and fun. You cannot help smiling and nodding your head to *What Makes It Go?* —*David Serra*

Pop På Svenska + Plan 714 Till / Mar. 6, 2001 / Minty Fresh ✦✦✦✦
Finally Komeda's first album and following EP are widely available. Originally issued on Swedish label North of No South, *Pop På Svenska* (1993) and *Plan 714 Till* (1995) have since been available only as rare imports or at Komeda's shows, until supply finally trickled down to nothing. So, when fans (few of whom already owned these) were antsy for another Komeda album three years after 1998's *What Makes It Go?*, the Minty Fresh label smartly decided to reissue the band's unobtainable Swedish recordings as a two-fer. That's right, all of these songs are in Swedish; although the band had started out writing songs in English, and resumed doing so on the recordings following these, their first album and EP are in their native language. But this won't be enough to keep most people from enjoying the happy intricacies of Komeda's catchy, upbeat grooves and Lena Karlsson's pleasing voice—in fact, you just may learn a little Swedish while dancing along. And please don't expect to find an in-the-rough version of Komeda here, either—overall, the songs are just as tight and impressive as their later work, with the addition of a few interludes and more experimental moments. —*Joslyn Layne*

Koobas

Psychedelic, British Invasion, Prog-Rock/Art Rock, R&B
The Koobas were among the better failed rock bands in England during the mid-'60s. Their peers, among the most talented group of the early British beat boom never to make it, included the Roulettes, the Chants, and the Cheynes. Favorites of the press and popular for their live shows, they somehow never managed to chart a record despite a lot of breaks that came their way, including a tour opening for the Beatles, top management representation, and a contract on EMI/Columbia. They had a sound that was comparable to the Beatles, the Searchers, and the Mojos, as Liverpool exponents of American R&B with a strong yet lyrical attack on their guitars and convincing vocals, though the Koobas didn't start to blossom as songwriters until fairly late, which may have been part of their problem. They recorded good sounding and very entertaining songs, but somehow never connected with the right sound at the proper moment. By the middle of 1967, they'd altered their look and their sound, moving away from American-style R&B and toward psychedelia. The group members also began writing their own material, sometimes with help in the lyric department from manager Tony Stratton-Smith. Their singles still utilized outside songwriters, however, and the group's best crack at the chart came early in 1968 when they recorded Cat Stevens' "The First Cut Is the Deepest," complete with heavy fuzz-tone guitar. The group lasted just long enough to finish the album *Koobas*, a mix of topical songwriting, psychedelia, R&B, and nostalgia that might've found an audience if only there had been a Koobas still together to tour behind it and promote the record in early 1969. Instead, by 1970 the album was already in the cut-out bins. —*Bruce Eder*

The Koobas / Jul. 2000 / BGO ✦✦✦✦
The June 2000 reissue of the group's only album by Beat Goes On is significantly better than the original LP, expanded with the eight single sides they cut earlier for EMI/Columbia. Every one of the singles in question, A- or B-side, is superior to the majority of the album cuts that precede it on this CD. "Sweet Music" and its B-side "Face" display hard rippling attacks on the instruments and soaring, powerful vocals, all hooked around excellent songs. "Sally" and "Champagne & Caviar" are two exercises in nostalgia that work, in much the same manner as "Honey Pie" by the Beatles. Their plunge into psychedelia is also very energetic as represented here, and "The First Cut Is the Deepest," with its heavy fuzz-tone guitar, deserved more attention than it got. —*Bruce Eder*

Kool & The Gang

f. 1964, Jersey City, NJ
Urban, Funk, Soul
Formed as a jazz ensemble in the mid-'60s, Kool & the Gang became one of the most inspired and influential funk units during the '70s, and one of the most popular R&B groups of the '80s after their breakout hit "Celebration" in 1979. Just as funky as James Brown or Parliament (and sampled almost as frequently), Kool & the Gang relied on their jazz backgrounds and long friendship to form a tightly knit group with the interplay and improvisation of a jazz outfit, plus the energy and spark of a band with equal ties to soul, R&B and funk. Kool & the Gang became a quick success on the R&B charts, and with their sixth LP, *Wild and Peaceful*, they hit the big time. "Funky Stuff" became their first Top 40 hit at the end of 1973. Then both "Jungle Boogie" and "Hollywood Swinging" reached the pop Top Ten. In 1979, the group added two new vocalists, Earl Toon, Jr. and, more importantly, James "J.T." Taylor, a former Jersey nightclub singer. Kool & the Gang also began working with jazz fusion arranger Eumir Deodato, who produced their records from 1979 to 1982. The first such album, *Ladies Night*, was their biggest hit yet, the first of three consecutive platinum albums, with the Top Ten singles "Too Hot" and the title track. *Celebrate!*, released in 1980, spawned Kool & the Gang's only number one hit, "Celebration," an anthem favored by innumerable wedding receptions since. With Deodato, the group produced several more hits, including the singles "Take My Heart (You Can Have It If You Want It)," "Get Down on It" and "Big Fun," and the albums *Something Special* in 1981 and *As One* a year later. After Deodato left the fold in late 1982, Kool & the Gang proved their success wasn't solely due to him; they had two immense hits during 1984-85 ("Joanna" and "Cherish"), as well as two more Top Tens, "Misled" and "Fresh." —*John Bush*

• **The Very Best of Kool & the Gang** / Mar. 30, 1999 / Mercury ✦✦✦✦✦
The Very Best of Kool & the Gang describes this collection aptly: their early, funky beginnings are represented with songs like "Jungle Boogie," "Funky Stuff," and "Celebration," as well the smooth urban stylings the band developed later on, "Fresh" and "Cherish." Over 21 tracks, *The Very Best of Kool & the Gang* delivers exactly what the title promises. —*Heather Phares*

Kool Keith

Vocals, Producer / Underground Rap, Hip-Hop
After single-handedly redefining "warped" as the mind and mouth behind the Bronx-based Ultramagnetic MCs, "Kool" Keith Thornton—aka Rhythm X, aka Dr. Octagon, aka Dr. Dooom, aka Mr. Gerbik—headed for the outer reaches of the stratosphere with a variety of solo projects. A one-time psychiatric patient at Bellevue, Keith's lyrical thematics remained as free-flowing here as they ever were with the NY trio, connecting up complex meters with fierce, layers-deep metaphors and veiled criticisms of those who "water down the sound that comes from the ghetto." His own debut single, "Earth People" by Dr. Octagon, was quietly released in late 1995 on the San Francisco-based Bulk Recordings, and the track spread like wildfire through the hip-hop underground, as did the subsequent self-titled full-length released the following year. Featuring internationally renowned DJ Q-Bert (also of the Invisible Skratch Picklz) on turntables, as well as the Automator and DJ Shadow behind the boards, *Dr. Octagon*'s left-field fusion of sound collage, fierce turntable work, and bizarre, impressionistic rapping found audiences in the most unlikely of places, from hardcore hip-hop heads to jaded rock critics. Although a somewhat sophomoric preoccupation with body parts and scatology tended to dominate the album, Keith's complex weave of associations and shifting references is quite often amazing in its intricacy. The record found its way to the UK-based abstract hip-hop imprint Mo'Wax (for whom Shadow also records) in mid-1996, and was licensed by the label for European release [Mo'Wax also released a DJ-friendly instrumental version of the album titled, appropriately, *The Instrumentalyst (Octagon Beats)*]. The widespread popularity of the album eventually landed Keith at Geffen splinter Dreamworks in 1997; the label gave *Dr. Octagon* its third release mid-year, adding a number of bonus cuts. In early 1999 however, Keith's alter-ego Dr. Dooom unfortunately "killed off" Dr. Octagon on the opening track of the 1999 album *First Come, First Served* (released on Thornton's own Funky Ass label). Kool Keith signed to Ruffhouse/MCA for his second album under *that* alias, 1999's *Black Elvis/Lost in Space*. *Matthew* followed a year later. —*Sean Cooper*

Sex Style / Feb. 3, 1997 / Funky Ass ✦✦✦
It's not that Kool Keith's Dr. Octagon project (released less than a year before) completely avoided sex; in fact, it was the focus of several tracks. It's just that the first album to be released under his own name is completely obsessed with it. Besides the obviously X-rated tracks like "Regular Girl," "Little Girls," "Lovely Lady," and "In Your Face," Keith does address some of his previous themes—his status as an inter-planetary entity, and the mediocrity of the hip-hop world—but even on those songs, he brings up sex. Several songs are his most extreme ever, much closer to 2 Live Crew than his former band Ultramagnetic MC's, and though the production (by Kut Master Kurt) is just as excellent and eclectic as Dr. Octagon, the hardcore themes could be too much for listeners. —*John Bush*

• **Black Elvis/Lost in Space** / Aug. 10, 1999 / Ruffhouse ✦✦✦✦
After killing off his Dr. Octagon alias and resurrecting himself as an intergalactic Little Richard named Black Elvis (coiffured appropriately), Kool Keith returned in 1999 with his much-anticipated debut for Ruffhouse. Compared to the scatological bombast sprayed all over his *First Come, First Served* LP (released as Dr. Dooom on his own Funky Ass label earlier that year), *Black Elvis/Lost in Space* is remarkably tame. And despite jettisoning cohorts the Automator and DJ QBert, the results sound surprisingly similar to the *Dr. Octagon* album: sparse 808 beats, a few bizarre, faintly menacing organ lines for hooks, and a sample or two the likes of which have never been heard on a Dr. Dre record (like the odd banjo pickings on "Livin' Astro"). Also cropping up are a few of Keith's patented psychedelic nightmares (reminiscent of "Blue Flowers" and "Earth People"), including "Lost in Space," "Rockets on the Battlefield," and "I'm Seein' Robots." For "Supergalactic Lover," Keith injects a bit of stuttered Timbaland funk into the mix, though this tale of sexual prowess is appropriately schizoid. If *Black Elvis/Lost in Space* doesn't make quite the splash of 1996's *Dr. Octagon*, it's mostly because there's a distinct sense that Kool Keith is retreading familiar (through incredibly fun) territory. One thing's for sure, DJ QBert's scratching is definitely missed. —*John Bush*

Matthew / Jul. 25, 2000 / Funky Ass ✦✦

Spankmaster / Jun. 5, 2001 / TVT ✦✦✦
Kool Keith may not be one of the more popular MCs in the rap game, but he's surely proven himself to be one of the most creative. Particularly given the genre's commercial tendencies, Keith's limitless ability to engage with weird, perverse, and at times downright shocking music makes him stand out and merit special notice. Of course, anyone familiar with his past work—ranging from his old school days fronting the Ultramagnetic MCs to his celebrated Dr. Octagon collaboration—knows that Keith is far from generic. Here, he joins forces with Detroit's Esham and Santos for *Spankmaster*, and heads even further toward insanity than his preceding trilogy of albums for Funky Ass foreshadowed. It's fairly safe to presume that Esham's psychotic reputation has inspired Keith to take his own music to unexplored extremes that challenge the boundaries of sleaze, antagonism, and eccentricity. In regard to the lo-fi yet impressive production, the Spankmaster himself

actually crafted most of the 20 eclectic songs, with Esham and Santos taking the reins for the album's standout moments: "I Wanna Play," "Drugs," and "Spankmaster." The beats are nearly as untraditional as Keith's rhymes, culling their elements from a disparate concoction of sources, including quite a bit of live instrumentation. In the end, *Spankmaster* is no doubt an engaging listen, even if its budget quality level and lack of glitz and glimmer make it an album strictly for the underground. Recommended to the open-minded, particularly if you admire creativity, long for the uncanny, and secretly have a desire for perversity. Definitely not for the lighthearted. *—Jason Birchmeier*

Kool Moe Dee (Mohandas Dewese)

b. 1963, Harlem, NY

Vocals / Party Rap, Pop-Rap, Old School Rap, Golden Age

A member of one of the original hip-hop crews, the Treacherous 3, Kool Moe Dee later became a solo star in his own right in 1986 by teaming with a teenaged Teddy Riley (later famed as the king of new jack swing) on the crossover hit "Go See the Doctor." The single earned him a contract with Jive Records, for which he recorded three successful late-'80s albums, dominated by his skillful speed-raps. A long-running feud with LL Cool J—who stole his aggressive stance and rapping style, he claims—gained Kool Moe Dee headlines for awhile, but he began to fade by the early '90s. After several early street hits with the Treacherous 3 (including a few for Sugar Hill), Kool Moe Dee went solo with a 1986 debut album *I'm Kool Moe Dee* on Jive. With the following year's *How Ya Like Me Now,* Dee struck back at the brash young generation who had forsaken their forebears; the cover featured a red Kangol hat—the prominent trademark of LL Cool J—being crushed by the wheel of a Jeep. The album went platinum and was followed two years later by the gold-certified *Knowlege Is King,* for which Dee became the first rapper to perform at the Grammy Awards ceremonies. After his fourth album *Funke Funke Wisdom,* Jive/RCA dropped him, though he returned in 1994 with *Interlude.* *—John Bush*

★ **Greatest Hits** / 1989 / Jive ✦✦✦✦✦

As much as any single performer, Kool Moe Dee epitomized rap's rise from an East Coast underground genre to a national youth sound, and has been unceasing in his demands for respect and recognition. Dee was also among the first able to bring social significance to his material without being pedantic, and his songs (with the exception of "They Need Money") weren't littered with sexist and misogynistic rhetoric. This 15-song collection covers his biggest recordings, from novelty-type fare ("The Wild Wild West" and "Whosgotdaflava") to the safe sex number "Go See The Doctor," cultural battle cries like "Rise 'N' Shine" and "No Respect," and his "war" with L.L. Cool J that peaked with "Death Blow" and "How Ya Like Me Now." *—Ron Wynn*

Jive Collection Series, Vol. 2 / Jun. 27, 1995 / Jive ✦✦✦✦✦

Kool Moe Dee's installment of the *Jive Collection Series* contains all of the rapper's groundbreaking singles from the early '80s, plus a selection of lesser-known album tracks and singles. The album isn't as consistently entertaining as his previous *Greatest Hits* compilation but *Jive Collection Series* remains a good introduction to his pioneering career. *—Stephen Thomas Erlewine*

Korn

f. 1992, Bakersfield, CA

Alternative Metal, Post-Grunge, Heavy Metal

Korn's cathartic alternative funk-metal sound positioned the group among the most popular and provocative to emerge during the post-grunge era. Korn began its existence as the Bakersfield, California-based metal band LAPD, which included guitarists James "Munky" Shaffer and Brian "Head" Welch, bassist Reginald "Fieldy Snuts" Arvizu, and drummer David Silveria. After issuing an LP, the members of LAPD in 1993 crossed paths with Jonathan Davis, a mortuary science student moonlighting as the lead vocalist for the local group Sexart; they soon asked Davis to join the band, and upon his arrival, the quintet rechristened themselves Korn. After signing to Epic's Immortal imprint, they issued their debut album in late 1994; thanks to a relentless tour schedule that included stints opening for Ozzy Osbourne, Megadeth, Marilyn Manson and 311, the record slowly but steadily rose the charts, eventually going gold. Its 1996 follow-up, *Life Is Peachy,* was a more immediate smash, reaching the number three spot on the pop album charts. The following summer, they headlined Lollapalooza, but were forced to drop off the tour when Shaffer was diagnosed with viral meningitis. While recording their best-selling 1998 LP *Follow the Leader,* Korn made national headlines when a student in Zeeland, Michigan was suspended for wearing a T-shirt emblazoned with the group's logo; the school's principal later declared their music "indecent, vulgar and obscene," prompting the band to issue a cease-and-desist order. *Issues* followed in 1999. *—Jason Ankeny*

● **Korn** / Oct. 11, 1994 / Immortal/Epic ✦✦✦✦✦

With little publicity, radio play or MTV exposure, Korn took their eponymous 1995 debut to platinum status. Like all unexpected successes, it's easier to understand its popularity in retrospect. Although they disdain the "metal" label, there's no question that Korn is among the vanguard of post-grunge alt-metal outfits. Borrowing from Jane's Addiction, Rage Against The Machine, Pantera, Helmet, Faith No More, Anthrax, Public Enemy and N.W.A., Korn developed a testosterone-fueled, ultra-aggressive metal-rap hybrid. They're relentless, both in their musical attack and in lead singer Jonathan Davis' bleak, violent lyrics. Tales of abuse and alienation run rampant throughout the record. It's often disturbing and, to some ears, even offensive, but their music can have a cathartic effect that makes up for their vulgarity and questionable lapses in taste. It's a powerful sound and one that actually builds on the funk-metal innovations of the late '80s/early '90s instead of merely replicating them. *—Stephen Thomas Erlewine*

Life Is Peachy / Oct. 15, 1996 / Immortal/Epic ✦✦✦

With their second album *Life is Peachy,* Korn has enhanced their metallic influences, delving deeper into murky sonic textures and grinding, menacing rhythms straight out of underground black metal. Korn adds enough elements of alternative rock song structure to make the music accessible to the masses, and their songwriting has continued to improve. Nevertheless, the band's main strength is their raging, visceral sound which is far more memorable and effective than their songs. The riffs might not always catch hold, but the primal guitars and vocals always hit home. *—Stephen Thomas Erlewine*

Follow the Leader / Aug. 18, 1998 / Immortal/Epic ✦✦✦✦

More than anything, Korn is about sound. They write songs, but those wind up not being nearly as memorable as their lurching metallic hip-hop grind. They have yet to exhaust that sound, and that's why their third album *Follow the Leader* is an effective follow-up to their first two alt-metal landmarks. Not that it offers anything new—it's the same sound, offered in a more focused forum than *Life is Peachy,* but not sounding as fresh as *Korn.* In fact, it begins to wear a little thin toward the end of the album, but guitarists Head Welch and Munky Shaffer find enough tonal variations over the course of the album to keep it interesting, and vocalist Jonathan Davis nearly matches them with his cavalcade of voices. If the songs themselves don't leave much of an impression, it's because they're not supposed to—they're simply vehicles for the metallic grind, which provides all the visceral rush any Korn fan needs. *—Stephen Thomas Erlewine*

Issues / Nov. 16, 1999 / Immortal/Epic ✦✦✦✦

Released in the fall of 1999, when Korn was in danger of being overshadowed by such protégés as Limp Bizkit, *Issues* reaffirms the group's status as alt-metal leaders, illustrating that the true difference between Korn and their imitators is their mastery of sound. Korn is about nothing if not sound. Sure, Jonathan Davis doesn't merely toss off lyrics but in the end, it doesn't matter since voice and the various words that float to the surface simply enhance the mood. Similarly, the band doesn't really have any distinguished riffs or hooks—everything each member contributes adds to the overall sound—so, casual listeners can be forgiven if they think the songs sound the same, since not only do the tracks bleed into one other, the individual songs have no discernible high points. Each cut rises from the same dark sonic murk, occasionally surging forward with volume, power and aggression. It's mood music—songs don't matter, but the foreboding feeling and gloomy sounds do. To a certain extent, this has always been true of Korn albums, but it's particularly striking on *Issues* because they pull off a nifty trick of stripping their sound back to its bare essentials and expanding and rebuilding from that. They've decided to leave rap-metal to the likes of Limp Bizkit, since there is very little rapping or appropriation of hip-hop culture anywhere on *Issues.* By doing this, they have re-emphasized their skill as a band, and how they can find endless, often intriguing, variations on their core sound. *Issues* may not be the cathartic blast of anger their debut was, nor is it as adventurous as *Follow the Leader,* but it better showcases the sheer raw power of the band than either. *—Stephen Thomas Erlewine*

Kraftwerk

f. 1970, Düsseldorf, Germany

Experimental Rock, Proto-Punk, Kraut Rock, Club/Dance, Electronic

During the mid-'70s, Germany's Kraftwerk established the sonic blueprint followed by an extraordinary number of artists in the decades to come. From the British New Romantic movement to hip-hop to techno, the group's self-described "robot pop"—hypnotically minimal, obliquely rhythmic music performed solely via electronic means—resonates in virtually every new development to impact the contemporary pop scene of the late 20th century, and as pioneers of the electronic music form, their enduring influence cannot be overstated. Primary members Florian Schneider and Ralf Hütter first met as classical music students at the Düsseldorf Conservatory, and recorded one LP as Organisation before rechristening themselves Kraftwerk (German for "power station"). Immersing their music in the fledgling world of minimalist electronics, the pair made a surprising breakthrough into the pop market with their fourth album, 1974's *Autobahn*; an edited single version of the epic title track was a major hit at home and abroad. Subsequent albums *Radio-Activity, Trans-Europe Express* and *The Man Machine* explored futuristic technology concepts and increased the movement towards seeming musical mechanization. By this time, the members of Kraftwerk even publicly portrayed themselves as automatons, an image solidified by tracks like "We Are the Robots." The group disappeared from view during much of the '80s, releasing albums in 1981 (with the British chart-topping "Computer Love") and 1986. Except for a 1991 remixed best-of collection titled *The Mix* and an occasional live tour, they remained silent in the years to follow. *—Jason Ankeny*

Kraftwerk 1 / 1971 / Philips ✦✦✦✦

Leaving the free-form improvisation of their earlier group Organisation behind them, Ralf Hütter and Florian Schneider moved into the realm of disciplined electronic rhythms with *Kraftwerk 1,* and the rest was history. While not an artistic triumph comparable to the group's best work, their debut is nonetheless hypnotic and innovative, at times close in spirit to the work of Steve Reich or Terry Riley in its minimalist construction. *—Jason Ankeny*

Kraftwerk 2 / 1972 / Philips ✦✦✦

For their second Kraftwerk album, Ralf Hütter and Florian Schneider took the *sturm und drang* of the industrial revolution and implanted it into a musical core that consisted of electronic soundscapes and metronomic rhythmic pulsations, especially on the 17-minute opener "Klingklang." The future sound of industrial music was fashioned on this album and its predecessor. *—Archie Patterson*

Ralf and Florian / 1973 / Warner Brothers ✦✦✦

An extension of their improvisational live performances, Kraftwerk's third LP curbs their obsessive minimalism to achieve a more complete sound; a softer, smoother record largely dominated by electric piano and textured electronic percussion, it marks the duo's first true overtures toward melody and, by extension, dance music, setting the stage for the breakthroughs of *Autobahn* the following year. *—Jason Ankeny*

★ **Autobahn** / 1974 / Philips ✦✦✦✦✦
Although Kraftwerk's first three albums were groundbreaking in their own right, *Autobahn* is where the group's hypnotic electro-pulse genuinely came into its own. The main difference between *Autobahn* and its predecessors is how it develops an insistent, propulsive pulse which makes the repeated rhythms and riffs of the shimmering electronic keyboards and trance-like guitars all the more hypnotizing. The 22-minute title track, in a severely edited form, became an international hit single and remains the peak of the band's achievements—it encapsulates the band and why they are important within one track—but the rest of the album provides soundscapes equally as intriguing. Within *Autobahn*, the roots of electro-funk, ambient, and synth-pop are all evident—it's a pioneering album, even if its electronic trances might not capture the attention of all listeners. *—Stephen Thomas Erlewine*

Radio-Activity / 1975 / Capitol ✦✦✦
A concept album exploring themes of broadcast communications, *Radio-Activity* marked Kraftwerk's return to more obtuse territory, extensively utilizing static, oscillators, and even Cage-like moments of silence to approximate the sense of radio transmission; a pivotal record in the group's continuing development, the title track—the first they ever recorded in English—is their most fully realized electro-pop effort to date, while "The Voice of Energy" precipitates the robot voice so crucial to their subsequent work. *—Jason Ankeny*

☆ **Trans-Europe Express** / 1977 / Capitol ✦✦✦✦✦
Although *Autobahn* was a left-field masterpiece, *Trans-Europe Express* is often cited as perhaps the archetypal (and most accessible) Kraftwerk album. Melodic themes are repeated often and occasionally interwoven over deliberate, chugging beats, sometimes with manipulated vocals; the effect is mechanical yet hypnotic. Thematically, the record feels like parts of two different concept albums: one a meditation on the disparities between reality and image ("Hall of Mirrors" and "Showroom Dummies" share recurring images of glass, reflection, illusion and confused identities, as well as whimsical melodies), and the other the glorification of Europe. There is an impressive composition paying homage to "Franz Schubert," but the real meat of this approach is contained in the opening love letter, "Europe Endless," and the epic title track which shares themes and lyrics with the following track, "Metal on Metal." The song "Trans-Europe Express" is similar in concept to "Autobahn," as it mimics the swaying motion and insistent drive of a cross-continent train trip. What ultimately holds the album together, though, is the music, which is more consistently memorable even than that on *Autobahn*. Overall, *Trans-Europe Express* offers the best blend of minimalism, mechanized rhythms, and crafted, catchy melodies in the group's catalog; henceforth, their music would take on more danceable qualities only hinted at here (although the title cut provided the basis for Afrika Bambaataa's enormously important dancefloor smash "Planet Rock"). *—Steve Huey*

The Man Machine / 1978 / Capitol ✦✦✦✦✦
The Man Machine is closer to the sound and style that would define early new wave electro-pop—less minimalistic in its arrangements and more complex and danceable in its underlying rhythms. Like its predecessor, *Trans-Europe Express*, there is the feel of a divided concept album, with some songs devoted to science fiction-esque links between humans and technology, often with electronically processed vocals ("The Robots," "Spacelab," and the title track); others take the glamour of urbanization as their subject ("Neon Lights" and "Metropolis"). Plus, there's "The Model," a character sketch which falls under the latter category but takes a more cynical view of the title character's glamorous lifestyle. More pop-oriented than any of their previous work, the sound of *The Man Machine*—in particular among Kraftwerk's oeuvre—had a tremendous impact on the cold, robotic synth-pop of artists like Gary Numan, as well as Britain's later New Romantic movement. *—Steve Huey*

Computer World / 1981 / Warner Brothers ✦✦✦✦✦
The first of Kraftwerk's many extended periods of silence was broken with the release of *Computer World*, a record exploring the ramifications of living in a society dominated by technology. A tightly honed, starkly minimalist effort, its implementation of recent technological advances yields a brighter and sharper sound than ever before; the single "Pocket Calculator" typifies the group at their most playful, while "Home Computer" eerily presages the emergence of techno and house music later in the decade. *—Jason Ankeny*

Electric Cafe / 1986 / Elektra ✦✦✦

The Mix / Jun. 11, 1991 / Elektra ✦✦✦

Billy J. Kramer

b. Aug. 19, 1943, Bootle, England
Vocals / Merseybeat, British Invasion
One of the most popular Merseybeat singers, Billy J. Kramer was one of the most mild-mannered rockers of the entire British Invasion. He wasn't that noteworthy a singer, either, and more likely than not would have never been heard outside of northern England if he hadn't been gifted with several Lennon-McCartney songs in 1963 and 1964, including "Do You Want to Know a Secret," "I'll Keep You Satisfied" and "From a Window." That gave him his entrance into the charts on both sides of the Atlantic, but Kramer couldn't sustain his success after the supply of Lennon-McCartney tunes dried up. Significant? No. Enjoyable? Yes. Even tossing aside the considerable value of hearing otherwise unavailable Lennon-McCartney compositions, his best singles were enjoyably wimpy, melodic pop-rock, offering a guilty pleasure comparable to taking a break from Faulkner and diving into some superhero comics. Billy J. actually landed his biggest hit, the corny pop ballad "Little Children," without assistance from his benefactors; the single also broke him, briefly, as a star in the United States, where it and its flipside ("Bad to Me") both made the Top Ten. But after 1965's "Trains and Boats and Planes," the hits ceased. Kramer continued recording throughout the '60s, and has toured often on the oldies circuit. *—Richie Unterberger*

● **The Best of Billy J. Kramer** / Oct. 8, 1991 / EMI America ✦✦✦✦
A strong collection that presents all of his best—including a number of songs written by John Lennon and Paul McCartney—in excellent sound. *—Bruce Eder & Jeff Tamarkin*

Lenny Kravitz

b. May 26, 1964, New York, NY
Vocals, Drums, Guitar, Bass / Album Rock, American Trad Rock, Neo-Psychedelia, Pop/Rock
As a musician and a producer, Lenny Kravitz is unquestionably gifted. He can successfully recreate the sound and feeling of countless groups from the past; his music recalls everyone from Lennon, Hendrix, and Bowie to the Velvet Underground, Curtis Mayfield, and Prince. What Kravitz can't do is synthesize these influences into a distinctive style—every song on each of his albums sounds like it was recorded by a different artist. However, that's not entirely a bad thing, because Kravitz *can* reproduce the sound of his favorite artists exactly; "It Ain't Over 'Til It's Over" sounds like it was recorded in 1972, "Are You Gonna Go My Way" sounds like a forgotten track from 1968. His music might not be original, but it is quite enjoyable. Since his 1989 debut, *Let Love Rule*, Kravitz's songwriting and production skills have been consistently improving. His second album, *Mama Said*, gave him a number two hit with "It Ain't Over 'Til It's Over." *Are You Gonna Go My Way*, Kravitz's third album, was released in 1993; it was a stronger album than anything he had released in the past and was his most commercially successful record yet. 1995's *Circus*, however, was something of a letdown, and he did not resurface with his fifth effort—titled, appropriately enough, *5*—until mid-1998. *—Stephen Thomas Erlewine*

Let Love Rule / Sep. 1989 / Virgin ✦✦✦✦✦
In many ways, Lenny Kravitz's *Let Love Rule* is a thoroughly impressive debut. Like Prince, he plays nearly every instrument on the record, yet makes it sound organic and alive. Musically, it's a startlingly accurate replication of late-'60s psychedelia, crossed with a Princely groove and a heavy John Lennon fixation. Kravitz has no desire to move forward, he only wants to recreate classic rock, and as a result, *Let Love Rule* is an enormous, guilty pleasure. His songcraft may be derivative, but it's catchy—the title track has a lean groove and a colorful chorus, "Sittin' on Top of the World" and "Does Anybody Out There Even Care" have strong hooks, and while the stately psychedelia of "I Build This Garden for Us" can sound like a parody, it is quite effective. Kravitz stumbles when he gets preachy (the awkward "Mr. Cab Driver") or flowery ("Flower Child"), but that doesn't diminish the pleasures of *Let Love Rule*. *—Stephen Thomas Erlewine*

Mama Said / Apr. 2, 1991 / Virgin ✦✦✦
Moving forward a couple years from the psychedelic fixations of his debut, *Mama Said* finds Lenny Kravitz in the early '70s, trying to graft Curtis Mayfield and Jimi Hendrix influences to his Prince and Lennon obsessions. This time around, he synthesizes his influences better; it's essentially a seamless record, with all of its classic rock homages so carefully produced that it sounds as if it could have been released in 1972. Kravitz's songcraft has gotten better as well, with the swirling Philly soul of "It Ain't Over Till It's Over" and the rampaging Sly Stone-meets-Hendrix "Always on the Run" standing out as instantly addictive singles. Still, some of the joy that informed *Let Love Rule* has worn off, largely because it's more polished and studied than its predecessor. That, however, doesn't prevent *Mama Said* from being another thoroughly enjoyable guilty pleasure—its sweet soul and fuzzy hard rock are slyly seductive. Ironically for such an inviting record, *Mama Said* is Kravitz's divorce album, yet it never quite conveys any true pain or emotion, since he puts sound over substance. Essentially, the lyrics are afterthoughts, but with a record as immaculately produced and sonically pleasurable as *Mama Said*, it doesn't really matter that it's talking loud and saying nothing, because it sounds good while it's talking. *—Stephen Thomas Erlewine*

● **Are You Gonna Go My Way?** / Nov. 22, 1993 / Virgin ✦✦✦✦✦
The cover indicates that *Are You Gonna Go My Way?* is Lenny Kravitz's bid for rock stardom. Designed in the style of an early-'70s record, it features Kravitz in hippie clothing, apparently exposing himself to a photographer—in other words, he's a dangerously sexy counterculture rebel. That may have been true in 1970, but in 1993, he simply sounds like a weird sideshow exhibit, the man who never lived past 1973. Of course, it's easy to make such potshots, but Kravitz opens himself up to such attacks. No other artist, especially a successful one, has been quite so devoted to the past and ignorant of the present. Since he has considerable talent for songcraft and production, Kravitz isn't nearly as bad as could be, and *Are You Gonna Go My Way* is just as enjoyable and more accomplished than its predecessors. This time around, Hendrix is his chief influence, as evidenced by the roaring title track, and he does expand that with his traditional Lennon, Curtis Mayfield and Prince obsessions. Song for song, it's his most consistent album, although by the end of the record, his painstaking reproduction of classic rock sounds begins to appear a bit too studied, suggesting that Kravitz may have hit a creative wall. Nevertheless, that does nothing to diminish the enjoyment of this record. *—Stephen Thomas Erlewine*

Circus / Sep. 12, 1995 / Virgin ✦✦
After the fuzz-rock revivalism of *Are You Gonna Go My Way*, Lenny Kravitz seems to have

settled into a comfortable groove, alternating between early-'70s album rock and early-'70s soul, with the occasional Prince flourish thrown in for good measure. *Circus* is the weakest of Kravitz's albums, simply because he didn't change his style in a distinctive manner, replicating the sound of *Are You Gonna Go My Way* instead. To compound his problems, Kravitz kicks off the record with "Rock & Roll Is Dead," a workmanlike rewrite of "Are You Gonna Go My Way" that lacks hooks. However, after one more half-hearted rocker, *Circus* begins to open up, as Kravitz turns in a series of ballads and lightly psychedelic mid-tempo pop numbers, which prove to be his real strength. —*Stephen Thomas Erlewine*

5 / May 12, 1998 / Virgin ♦♦♦
Lenny Kravitz must have realized he bottomed out with the turgid *Circus*, so he decided to shake things up a bit on its follow-up, *5*. Like any veteran in the late '90s, he dabbled in electronica, adding a few trip-hop loops and analog synths to his bedrock rock n' soul. It's enough to make *5* sound relatively fresh, at least compared to the retro dead-end of *Circus*, yet it sounds like Kravitz *read* about the idea of electronica without actually listening to any music. Anemic synths and stilted drum loops (sampled from Kravitz's playing, not old records) are scattered throughout the record, along with vaguely distorted vocals. It's not enough to make Kravitz sound *hip*, especially since he still loves endless funk jams and electric sitars, but it does revitalize his sound. At least for a little while. By the end of the album, his songwriting sounds as tired and unmemorable as on *Circus*. Without hooks, melodies, and style, Kravitz's Sly, Mayfield, Hendrix, Lennon, and Prince pastiches are a bore. *5* has a few passable cuts, yet it falls short of the quirky hero worship and melodic smarts that made his first three records so enjoyable. —*Stephen Thomas Erlewine*

Greatest Hits / Oct. 24, 2000 / Virgin ♦♦♦♦♦
Lenny Kravitz's greatest gift is that he's a master synthesist, pulling together different sounds and styles from eras past to create a sound that wasn't necessarily blazingly original, but fresh due to his craft and sheer mastery of the studio. Since he was an unabashed classicist, he often suffered the brunt of nasty criticism, but, as records, they were often very good, particularly early in his career, before he indulged in the mannerisms of guitar-blasting stadium rock. Even if *Circus* and *5* were sunk by their own bloatedness, they still had good singles, as did those early albums, so the 2000 collection *Greatest Hits* album is a terrific encapsulation of Kravitz at the peak of his talents. Certainly, there are some fan favorites missing, and the non-chronological sequencing is maddening (two of his three worst singles are within the first three songs), but it does boast the magnificent new single "Again," along with such seminal Kravitz moments as "Are You Gonna Go My Way," "Mr. Cabdriver," "Stand By My Woman," "Always on the Run," "Believe," "Let Love Rule" and "It Ain't Over Till It's Over," which is enough to make this a first-class greatest hits. After all, it doesn't just have all the main songs, it also illustrates that he indeed is a master synthesizer. —*Stephen Thomas Erlewine*

Kursaal Flyers
f. 1975, **db.** 1977
Pub Rock, Power Pop, New Wave, Rock & Roll
The Kursaal Flyers bridged the gap between pub rock and power-pop, turning out a handful of fine albums and great singles in their brief two-year career. Comprised of Paul Shuttleworth (vocals), Graeme Douglas (guitar), Vic Collins (guitar, steel guitar, vocals), Riche Bull (bass, vocals), and Will Birch (drums), the band released their first album *Chocs Away* in 1975; it was followed soon afterward by *The Great Artiste*. Both records showed a grasp of country and roots-rock, as well as pure pop. They would begin to emphasize their pop elements with 1976's *Golden Mile*, released by CBS Records. The union with the major label helped the single "Little Does She Know" reach the British Top 20. Douglas left to join Eddie & the Hot Rods before the recording of their final album, *Five Live Kursaals* (1977); he was replaced by Barry Martin. The band broke up after the release of punk- and power-pop-injected *Five Live Kursaals*. Out of the members, only Will Birch and John Wicks stayed active—they formed the Records immediately after the Kursaal Flyers' disbandment. The Kursaal Flyers reunited in 1988, recording *A Former Tour de Force Is Forced to Tour*, which picks up right where they left off in 1977. —*Stephen Thomas Erlewine*

Chocs Away / 1975 / UK ♦♦

Great Artiste / 1975 / UK ♦♦♦

Golden Mile / 1976 / CBS ♦♦♦♦♦

Five Live Kursaals / 1977 / CBS ♦♦♦

● **In for a Spin** / 1985 / Edsel ♦♦♦♦♦
In for a Spin: The Best of the Kursaal Flyers is a comprehensive overview of the band's brief and underappreciated career, comprised of highlights from their three albums, plus the terrific non-LP single "Television Generation" and five previously unreleased tracks. —*Stephen Thomas Erlewine*

Kyuss
f. 1990, **db.** 1997
Stoner Metal, Alternative Metal, Heavy Metal, Hard Rock
Hailing from Palm Desert, California, Kyuss (pronounced "kai-uss") have become a heavy

metal Velvet Underground of sorts. Though they are widely acknowledged as pioneers of the booming underground "stoner rock" scene, the band enjoyed little commercial success during their brief existence. Still, their combination of sludgy, down-tuned guitars (often played through a bass amp for maximum earth-shaking intensity), galloping thrash metal rhythms, and organic drum sound has become the blueprint, often copied, but never replicated by countless underground metal bands.

Formed in 1990 by vocalist John Garcia, guitarist Josh Homme, bassist Nick Oliveri and drummer Brant Bjork, Kyuss began jamming at "desert parties," in and around the isolated towns of the southern California desert. The band eventually built a local following, signed with tiny independet label Dali Records, and released their first album *Wretch* in 1991. Underproduced and financed, the album failed to capture the band's live sound and went completely unnoticed, but constant touring earned them a reputation as a ferocious live unit as well as the respect of many fellow musicians. One of these, Masters of Reality singer/guitarist Chris Goss, decided to produce the band's next effort, 1992's stunning *Blues for the Red Sun*, eventually hailed as a landmark album by critics and fans alike. The Kyuss sound takes the heaviness of Black Sabbath, the feedback fuzzyness of Blue Cheer, and other '70s influences and infuses them with psychedelic flashes, massive grooves and a sensibility for '90s metal and thrash.

The band was signed to Elektra Records just as their label was about to go bankrupt, and despite the loss of bassist Oliveri (he was replaced by Scott Reeder), the band continued to build momentum. Also recorded under Goss' guidance, 1994's *Sky Valley* saw Kyuss taking the novel approach of grouping the songs into three extended suites, and nearly matched the brilliance of its predecessor. But despite their creative promise and growing fan-base, personal strife began tearing the band apart, and drummer Brant Bjork departed to let Alfredo Hernandez replace him on 1995's less inspired...*And the Circus Leave Town*, a final rift between Homme and Garcia finally brought the band to a halt. Homme, Reeder and Hernandez re-appeared as Queens of the Stone Age in 1998, and Garcia is currently a member of Unida. —*Ed Rivadavia*

Wretch / 1991 / Dali ♦♦♦

● **Blues for the Red Sun** / 1992 / Dali ♦♦♦♦♦
With Josh Homme's guitar tuned down two whole steps to C, and plugged into a bass amp for maximum distortion, stoner metal pioneers Kyuss achieve a major milestone in heavy music with their second album, 1992's *Blues for the Red Sun*. Producer Chris Goss masterfully captures the band's unique heavy/light formula, which becomes apparent as soon as the gentle but sinister intro melody gives way to the chugging main riff in the opener "Thumb." This segues immediately into the galloping "Green Machine," which pummels forward inexorably and even features that rarest rock & roll moment: a bass solo. "Thong Song" alternates rumbling guitar explosions with almost complete silence, and "Mondo Generator" plays like an extended acid trip. The slow-build of the epic "Freedom Run" and the driving "Allen's Wrench" are also highlights, and though the album is heavy on instrumentals, these actually provide a seamless transition from song to song. —*Ed Rivadavia*

Welcome to Sky Valley / Jun. 28, 1994 / Elektra ♦♦♦♦
After creating a classic with their second album, *Blues for the Red Sun*, desert metal gods Kyuss faced the unenviable task of delivering the goods once again for a new label, Elektra Records. And they almost pulled it off with 1994's stellar, *Sky Valley*. The album's 13 songs are divided into three "suites" which fully display the band's impressive creative range, from furious metal to psychedelic grooves, and anything in between. The first and most consistent of these suites starts with the huge guitar riff of "Gardenia" (which resembles molten lava flowing down the side of a volcano), continues into the moody space jam instrumental "Asteroid," and culminates in the strangely titled yet superbly diverse "Supa Scoopa and Mighty Scoop." Other highlights include the solid thrashing of "100 Degrees," the prog-rock instrumental "Whitewater," and the rather mellow (for Kyuss standards) "Demon Cleaner." But no song exemplifies the Kyuss sound as well as the aptly-titled "Odyssey," which opens suite number three and provides a veritable blue-print of the band's unique combination of ingredients. The track begins with a cryptic melody, explodes into a ferocious riff, glides into a psychedelic bridge, then returns to full-throttle for its conclusion. —*Ed Rivadavia*

...And the Circus Leaves Town / 1995 / Elektra ♦♦♦

Muchas Gracias: The Best of Kyuss / Nov. 28, 2000 / Elektra International ♦♦♦
Leave it to Kyuss—a sorely underappreciated band whose music was so ahead of its time that its huge influence became apparent only after its demise—to put out a best-of set that really isn't any such thing. In fact, *Muchas Gracias: The Best of Kyuss* is more of a collector's item, combining nine of the band's would-be hits (four of them in previously unreleased live versions) with no less than six album leftovers and B-sides. Predominantly instrumentals, few of these rarities actually approach the caliber of the band's incredible studio albums (the ultra-heavy "Shine," the frenetic "Flip the Phrase," and the epic "Sandpiper" come close) but Kyuss fanatics are bound to consider them a long-lost treasure nonetheless. For the first-time listener, however, *Muchas Gracias* paints an incomplete portrait that omits some of the cult heroes' best-known material, including the bludgeoning riffage of "Green Machine" and the space rock thrashing of "Odyssey." Neophytes are therefore advised to pick up either of the band's two best albums *Blues for the Red Sun* or *Sky Valley* instead. —*Ed Rivadavia*

L7

f. 1985, Los Angeles, CA
Riot Grrrl, Alternative Metal, Grunge, Alternative Pop/Rock
L7's heavy, punk-inflected, riff-oriented guitar grind—a mix of the Ramones, Motörhead, and Joan Jett—was what earned them a dedicated following of fans in the early '90s, not the fact that they were female. While the band is strongly feminist, they never let their rhetoric stand in the way of their roaring guitars. L7 always relies on the sheer sonic aggression of rock, not its lyrical power. When the group was on Sub Pop early in the '90s, the band sounded punkier and more abrasive; signing to a major label didn't cause them to lose that aggression—they just had better production, courtesy of Butch Vig (Nirvana, Smashing Pumpkins, Sonic Youth). Featuring "Pretend We're Dead," 1992's *Bricks Are Heavy* was a major alternative hit; their second major-label album, the coarse *Hungry for Stink*, was released right before L7 toured with 1994's Lollapalooza. The acclaimed *Beauty Process: Triple Platinum* followed in 1997, and a year later the group issued *Live—Omaha to Osaka*. 1999 saw the release of the L7 film documentary *The Beauty Process*, directed by former Nirvana bassist Krist Novoselic; a new studio LP, *Slap-Happy*, appeared later that same year. —*Stephen Thomas Erlewine*

L7 / 1990 / Epitaph ♦♦♦
L7's eponymous debut finds the band just beginning to get their sea legs; their trademark grungy fusion of punk and metal isn't quite fully formed yet, often skewing heavily toward one side of the equation or the other. That can sometimes give the album a schizophrenic feel: one minute they're sneering punk goddesses, the next they're offering hard-partying odes to rock & roll that could have been ripped from a Runaways record. But even if *L7* doesn't quite jell into a cohesive album, visceral moments like opener "Bite the Wax Tadpole" (the Chinese translation of "Coca Cola") make it worth investigating by devoted fans of the band's sludgy grind. —*Steve Huey*

Smell the Magic / Jul. 12, 1991 / Sub Pop ♦♦♦♦
On 1991's *Smell the Magic*, L7 begins to find the sense of melody to complement its distorted punk guitar assault. The band deserves ultimate praise for writing from a completely female perspective at all times, and the fabulous "Fast and Frightening" just might be the ultimate riot grrrrl anthem. "Shove" pleads the case for mosh pit etiquette, while "Just Like Me" demands equal rights (and vices) for male and female rock stars. The self-mocking "Broomstick" celebrates any "rock & roll hags" accusations with a sense of humor. "'Til the Wheels Fall Off" is another standout, thanks to it's relentless descending riff, and points the way toward the band's breakthrough album, *Bricks Are Heavy*. —*Ed Rivadavia*

● Bricks Are Heavy / Apr. 14, 1992 / Slash ♦♦♦♦♦
Though they hailed from sunny L.A., L7 became the poster girls for grunge, and more specifically the "riot grrrl" movement in 1992, with the meteoric success of their third album, *Bricks Are Heavy*. While their previous efforts had sounded sloppy and uneven, *Nevermind* producer Butch Vig helped the girls obtain a tight, compact sound on *Bricks*, pushing them to focus on their songwriting to boot. After all, great albums need great songs, and that's exactly what you have here. Mosh-pit anthem "Everglade" (sung by bassist Jennifer Finch) will simply knock you on your ass, and big single "Pretend We're Dead" is so good that its tough swagger harks back to seminal bad girl anthems like Joan Jett's "I Love Rock & Roll," Pat Benatar's "Hit Me With Your Best Shot," and even the Go-Go's—well, maybe not the Go-Go's. The sardonic "Diet Pill" tackles female compulsions with clever irony, and even when they let their mega-riffing take over on such full-throttle stomps as "Wargasm," "Mr. Integrity," and "Shitlist," L7 still manage to imbue their lyrics with humor and substance. Inevitably, a few songs (especially "Slide") tend to push the Nirvana envelope just a tad, but Vig's involvement aside, these four ladies had been doing this kind of thing for as long as the Seattle trio. L7's crowning achievement, *Bricks Are Heavy* sadly proved to be an impossible act to follow, and the band gradually faded into obscurity thereafter. —*Ed Rivadavia*

Hungry for Stink / Jul. 12, 1994 / Slash/Reprise ♦♦
While L7 sounds tremendous on *Hungry for Stink*, the band has neglected to write any songs. But when you're caught in the middle of a massive guitar grind this good, songs don't matter much. —*Stephen Thomas Erlewine*

The Beauty Process: Triple Platinum / Feb. 25, 1997 / Slash/Reprise ♦♦♦
Jennifer Finch left L7 after the completion of *The Beauty Process: Triple Platinum*, which is appropriate—the album feels like the end of an era. L7 still have enough attitude to make them underground rockers, but they continue to move closer to heavy metal biker territory with each record. *The Beauty Process* has a bigger, harder kick than *Hungry for Stink*, and it also has its fair share of hooks—they just don't play them for pop effect as they did on *Bricks Are Heavy*. Which means that *The Beauty Process* will appeal to old-

time fans and fans of Motörhead and AC/DC. In other words, it's a good hard-rock record, but it'll make some fans yearn for the days when L7 appeared revolutionary, not just keepers of the flame. —*Stephen Thomas Erlewine*

Live: Omaha to Osaka / Dec. 15, 1998 / Man's Ruin ♦♦♦
Until late 1998, bootlegs were the only place that L7 fans could go if they wanted to hear live recordings by the band. L7 wasn't bootlegged as extensively as Hole, but the alternative rockers certainly weren't ignored by them either. The first live L7 album that wasn't a bootleg came in December, 1998, when Man's Ruin put out *Live: Omaha to Osaka*. This generally excellent CD, which was recorded at clubs in Omaha, NE and Osaka, Japan, gets off to an amusing start when a high school marching band from Omaha performs a medley of L7 favorites. The high schoolers provide a good laugh, but the real fun comes when L7 takes the stage and tears into such punk-meets-metal gems as "Bad Things," "Death Wish," "Non-Existent Patricia" and "Slide." Unfortunately for L7, the Omaha gig came on a night when Megadeth was also playing that city. After a gutsy version of "Shitlist," the CD takes us to Osaka for five songs, including "Fast And Frightening," "Andres" and the goofy "Loranza, Giada, Allesandra." The sound quality isn't as sharp on the Osaka material as it is on the Omaha recordings, although L7 sounds equally inspired in the Japanese city. *Live: Omaha to Osaka* isn't perfect, but the disc's strengths by far outweigh its weaknesses—and it was nice to finally hear a live L7 album that wasn't a bootleg. —*Alex Henderson*

Slap-Happy / Aug. 24, 1999 / Bong Load ♦♦♦
Back on an indie label, after an initially successful but ultimately unfruitful run at a major, L7 turns out a respectable but predictable effort with *Slap-Happy*. It's not that the band was sapped of strength once Jennifer Finch left, since they still sound hard and raw, angry even. It's just that their sound has become a bit pat. It's a problem, since L7 is the kind of band that can't really expand their musical horizons without running the risk of being labeled a sellout, but after a while, churning out a series of similar albums makes it painfully clear the limitations of the band. That's not to say they're a bad band—after all, bands as great as the Ramones painted themselves into a similar corner—and that's not to say *Slap-Happy* isn't a good record. As a matter of fact, it's not bad, a few of the songs hit hard, and the band sounds energetic and muscular. As it's spinning, it's easy to get caught up in its momentum, but once it's finished, it's about as memorable as *The Beauty Process*—which means it leaves very little lasting impression. Certainly, it hits hard enough to be of interest to longtime followers, but it does raise the question of where do L7 go from here. —*Stephen Thomas Erlewine*

Best of L7: The Slash Years / May 2, 2000 / EMI ♦♦♦♦
L7 had the sound, style, and tough-grrrl attitude to hit it big in the aftermath of grunge's mainstream breakthrough, but unfortunately, the band was too often hampered by uneven songwriting. *The Best of L7: The Slash Years* collects four songs apiece from *Bricks Are Heavy*, *Hungry for Stink*, and *The Beauty Process: Triple Platinum* (although, as the title suggests, there's nothing from the fine Sub Pop album *Smell the Magic*). It's a pretty good distillation of the cream of those records, even if there are still a few tunes on *Bricks Are Heavy* that could have made the cut on a less mathematically selected best-of. In fact, as L7's most pop-oriented record, *Bricks Are Heavy* is still a slightly more accessible introduction, since following that album, the band tended to rely more on sheer power than melody. Nevertheless, *The Best of L7: The Slash Years* does encapsulate what the group was all about, and it's a great way to dig deeper into their catalog without having to buy all the individual albums. —*Steve Huey*

The La De Das

f. 1964, db. 1974
Garage Rock
Aside from Ray Columbus & the Invaders, the La De Das were New Zealand's most popular rock group of the '60s. As big fish in a very small pond, their work doesn't hold up to scrutiny in the company of the era's top American and English acts. But they did record some fine garage/pop numbers in the spirit of the Rolling Stones in the mid-'60s. A few of these ("How Is the Air Up There?" and "All Purpose Low") were big N.Z. hits, and they reached the Top Ten with covers of John Mayall's "On Top of the World" and a version of Bruce Channel's "Hey Baby." In 1968, they recorded a psychedelic-tinged children's concept LP, *The Happy Prince*, which bears resemblance to modern twee. After a failed attempt to crack the British market, the group soldiered on for quite some time with pedestrian hard rock that—like even the best of their early work—was very derivative of overseas trends. —*Richie Unterberger*

Rock & Roll Decade 1964-1974 / 1981 / EMI Australia ♦♦♦
A hefty double-album compilation, including most of their mid-'60s singles, the entire *The Happy Prince* LP, and a mixture of live and studio hard-rock material from the late

'60s and early '70s. Includes exhaustive liner notes from Australian rock authority Glenn A. Baker, and their rare fine 1965 punk debut 45 "Little Girl," but the final three sides of this two-fer are pretty tedious going. —*Richie Unterberger*

● **La De Das/Find Us a Way** / 1996 / CBS ✦✦✦✦✦
A double-LP reissue of their first two albums, covering their 1966-67 material, including nearly all of their best songs. Their debut (*La De Das*) is almost solely comprised of R&B covers, with the exception of the hit "How Is the Air up There?" *Find Us a Way* is better, with more original compositions and a more mature soulful rock approach, including the snarling singles "Find Us a Way" and "All Purpose Low." —*Richie Unterberger*

How Is the Air Up There? / 1999 / Zodiac ✦✦✦
This 29-track compilation collects pretty much all of the cover versions that the La De Das—one of New Zealand's most popular bands of all time—recorded as a group during their most productive two-year period. Most of these tunes were originally recorded by mod British groups, as well as hardline American R&B acts, appearing variously on 45s, an EP, and their first two albums. Their first hit—1966's "How Is the Air Up There?"—entered the then-recently started New Zealand Hit Parade, eventually peaking at number four. The song was picked up by Sydney radio stations and before long it was number one on the charts there. Their cover of John Mayall's "On Top of the World" (released in November 1966) made it to number two on the national charts. Afterwards, they began maintaining a residency at Auckland's hippest night club, the Galaxie, hitting again with a cover of Bruce Channel's "Hey Baby," which scored a number one position in March 1967. Other covers included here include: "Gimme Some Lovin'" (Spencer Davis Group), "My Little Red Book" (Love, the Standells), "Hey Girl," "What'cha Gonna Do About It," and "Shake" (the Small Faces), as well as the oft-covered blues/R&B chestnuts "Bright Lights, Big City" (Jimmy Reed), "I Put a Spell on You" (Screamin' Jay Hawkins), and "Land of a Thousand Dances" (Chris Kenner, Cannibal and the Headhunters). —*Bryan Thomas*

The La's
f. 1986
College Rock, Britpop, Alternative Pop/Rock
When the La's released their debut album in 1990, it made immediate waves in the British pop scene, as well as American college radio. Drawing from the hook-laden, ringing guitars of mid-'60s British pop as well as the post-punk pop of the Smiths, the La's self-titled first album—heralded by the hit single "There She Goes"—had a timeless, classic feel. It seemed like effortless music, yet that was not the case. From their inception in 1986 to the present day, lead singer/guitarist/songwriter Lee Mavers has been a perfectionist with a nearly obsessive eye for detail. Consequently, the La's were never able to totally fulfill their promise. —*Stephen Thomas Erlewine*

● **The La's** / 1990 / Go! Discs/London ✦✦✦✦✦
The La's were one of the few English alternative groups to keep traditional British guitar-pop alive during the late '80s and early '90s. Drawing heavily from the punchy British Invasion sound of early Beatles, the Hollies, the Searchers and Small Faces, the group's eponymous debut is a swirling array of ringing guitar hooks and strong, undeniable pop melodies. Throughout the record, chief songwriter Lee Mavers turns out small, well-crafted gems, highlighted by the hit single "There She Goes," whose jangling hooks and sighing melodies simply scratch the surface of the abundance of pleasures on the record. While Mavers claimed at the time that the label forced him to release *The La's*, it's hard to imagine the record being any more infectious. As it stands, *The La's* was a refreshing slice of classicist guitar-pop at the time of its release, and its charms have not faded over the years. —*Stephen Thomas Erlewine*

Breakloose: Lost La's 1984-1986 / 2000 / Viper ✦✦

LaBelle
f. 1962, db. 1976
Disco, Funk, Soul
A girl group from Philadelphia, LaBelle formed in 1962. Initially known as Blue-Belles, and then Patti LaBelle and the Blue Belles, the group's personnel consisted of Patti LaBelle, Cindy Birdsong, Sarah Dash, and Nona Hendryx. The quartet scored six R&B hits from 1962 through 1967 before Birdsong departed to join Diana Ross and the Supremes. Continuing as a trio, for the next seven years the group languished in obscurity. British manager Vicki Wickham remade their image in the early '70s and shortened the name to LaBelle. Decked out in ersatz futuristic garb, the threesome appeared as whirling dervishes delivering an explosive gospel/funk hybrid. Between late 1974 and late 1976, LaBelle enjoyed five R&B hits, the first, "Lady Marmalade," reaching the number one spot on the R&B and pop charts. Labelle split up in early 1977. —*Rob Bowman*

● **Lady Marmalade: The Best of Patti and LaBelle** / Feb. 28, 1995 / Epic/Legacy ✦✦✦✦
Lady Marmalade: The Best of LaBelle features eight of the group's best tracks—including their two hits, "Lady Marmalade" and "What Can I Do for You?"—as well as eight of Patti LaBelle's R&B hits from the late '70s, which were among the funkiest tracks she ever recorded. —*Stephen Thomas Erlewine*

Patti LaBelle
b. May 24, 1944, Philadelphia, PA
Vocals / Quiet Storm, Urban, Soul
Soul diva Patti LaBelle enjoyed one of the longest-lived careers in contemporary music, notching hits in a variety of sounds ranging from girl-group pop to space-age funk to lush ballads. Her first musical success came with the Blue Belles, who hit the Top 20 in 1962 with "I Sold My Heart to the Junkman." By the time they signed to Atlantic three years later, the quartet was known as Patti LaBelle and the Blue Belles. The group earned only

one minor hit until a change of direction in 1970—including a new name (LaBelle) and a more rock-oriented, funky sound—produced a hit, the chart-topping "Lady Marmalade." The group disbanded in the mid-'70s and its namesake mounted a solo career, issuing her eponymous debut in 1977. Upon signing with Philadelphia International, LaBelle scored a number one R&B hit with "If You Only Knew," from 1983's *I'm in Love Again*. Two years later, she reached the pop Top 20 with her *Beverly Hills Cop* soundtrack contribution "New Attitude." Her subsequent MCA debut, 1986's *The Winner in You*, went platinum on the strength of the Burt Bacharach-penned "On My Own," a duet with Michael McDonald. 1991's *Burnin'* earned a Grammy for Best Female R&B Performance. LaBelle recorded less and less frequently in the years to follow, however. —*Jason Ankeny*

Patti LaBelle / 1977 / Epic ✦✦✦

Winner in You / 1986 / MCA ✦✦✦

● **Greatest Hits** / 1996 / MCA ✦✦✦✦✦
The first Patti LaBelle compilation to span her work from the '60s to the '90s. It's weighted heavily toward her pop-R&B material from the '80s and '90s, with hits like "New Attitude," "On My Own," and "Feels Like Another One." It does lead off with the version of "Over the Rainbow" that she recorded with the Blue Belles in the '60s, and also has four LaBelle cuts, including the chart-topping "Lady Marmalade." —*Richie Unterberger*

You Are My Friend: The Ballads / Feb. 11, 1997 / Epic/Legacy ✦✦✦
You Are My Friend: Ballads collects 13 ballads Patti LaBelle and LaBelle recorded during the '70s, including "You Turn Me On," "Find the Love," "Quiet Time," "Isn't It A Shame," and "Come What May." Although the album sounds as if it is a greatest hits compilation, very few of these songs were hits, yet that doesn't detract from the disc's worth. It's designed for Patti LaBelle fans that want to dig a little deeper into her catalog without purchasing the actual albums, and they'll find several songs to cherish, even though the song selection is slightly uneven. —*Leo Stanley*

● **Something Silver** / Feb. 11, 1997 / Warner Brothers ✦✦✦✦
Most of the past LaBelle CD-era compilations have been poorly assembled, but this one is an exception. Whereas those other sets usually consist of a measly ten songs and some of their weaker commercial ventures, this set features their only major mainstream commercial hit, "Lady Marmalade," and fourteen underappreciated, stellar songs. Most of these songs were culled from the trio's two acclaimed Warner Brothers albums and a single RCA set in the 1971-73 period. Some of the selections demonstrate Nona Hendryx's flare for poignantly creative lyrics and intricate melodies on such confessionals as "Can I Speak To You Before You Go To Hollywood?" and "Sunday's News." However, the set also features their rock/funk-edged high-voltage covers of Aretha Franklin's "Runnin' Out of Fools," Cat Stevens' "Moonshadow" and the Rolling Stones' "Wild Horses," among others. This set more than any other honestly reveals what we lost when the group disbanded in 1976. —*Bill Carpenter*

The Best of the Early Years / Feb. 9, 1999 / Hip-O ✦✦✦✦
This album chronicles the recordings of Patti LaBelle and the Blue Belles from before their creation as a group—the Blue Belles' biggest hit, "I Sold My Heart To The Junkman," was actually recorded by a different group, and they were then assembled to promote it—to their departure from the small Philadelphia label for which they recorded in the mid-1960s. They scored a handful of minor hits with covers that were surprising for an R&B girl group, such as "You'll Never Walk Alone" and "Danny Boy," but their approach was similar to the gospel-influenced rhythmic sound of Motown, and lead singer Patti LaBelle was already showing off the pipes that would make her a major star in succeeding decades. It's hard to imagine how this material could have been handled better: the tracks are well-annotated, and Robert Pruter's liner notes tell the group's story concisely, yet completely. Tracks originally used on an artificially constructed "live" album have had the bogus audience sounds stripped off them for a more accurate sound. The material may be juvenilia and, at 37 minutes, there may not be much of it, but this is a textbook case of how to do a reissue. —*William Ruhlmann*

Labradford
f. 1992, Richmond, VA
Experimental Rock, Indie Rock, Post-Rock/Experimental
Consisting of bassist Robert Donne, guitarist/vocalist Mark Nelson, and Carter Brown on keyboards, Labradford are an experimental ambient/post-rock group from Richmond, Virginia. Incorporating electronics as well as non-traditional arrangement and production techniques, the group's soundtrack-y, effects-heavy sonic landscapes operate in a vein closely allied with groups such as Experimental Audio Research, Flying Saucer Attack, and Gastr del Sol, and have earned the group high praise among a diverse variety of different audiences. The trio have released material through American indies Merge and Kranky, as well as the Kiwi rock label Flying Nun and Stereolab's Duophonic imprint. Though occasionally incorporating vocal and rhythmic elements, the group rely most often on the drone aesthetic, mixing looping guitar effects and long keyboard passages with snippets of barely-audible voice and assorted found objects on records like 1994's *Prazision*, 1995's *Stable Reference*, 1996's self-titled effort and 1997's *Mi Media Naranja*. 1999 brought the release of a new album, *E Luxo So*, as well as a tour with Godspeed You Black Emperor! and their Festival Of Drifting series, which also featured appearances from Pole, Matmos and Papa M. The ultra-minimal *Fixed::Context* followed two years later. —*Sean Cooper*

Prazision / 1994 / Kranky ✦✦✦✦
As the premiere release on Kranky, which would become one of the nineties' most notable US indie labels for its series of adventurous releases, *Prazision* already holds a certain place in the history books. Regardless of who put it out, however, this excellent debut

would command attention for introducing Labradford and its marvelous drone/ambient sound to the world. Inspired by such cult-level titans of eighties drone as Spacemen 3 and Loop (whose ex-members almost immediately championed the band after *Prazision*'s appearance), the then duo's ability to create seemingly stark (but quite layered and complex the more you listened to it), echoed modern psychedelic masterpieces made itself apparent from the beginning. Notably, the band eschewed conventional percussion of any sort, relying on singer/guitarist Nelson's simple but effective guitar parts—usually consisting of a series of a few notes, repeated in sequence and given reverb—to carry the rhythm, while keyboards and organs explored all varieties of ambient and melodic approaches. Nelson's lyric delivery serves him best when simply reciting rather than singing, as on the beautifully chilling "Sliding Glass," and though the overall effect of his quiet, half-whispered vocals is very Spacemen 3-derivative, it certainly doesn't hurt the album any at all. The trump card here is "Gratitude," a keyboard-led piece which is in fact Labradford's own series of thank-yous to friends, family and labels for their support, delivered using a Vocoder. At once amusing and quite cool to listen to, it's a nicely unexpected touch on a solid first record. *—Ned Raggett*

A Stable Reference / 1995 / Kranky ♦♦♦♦

Having established their sound, Labradford took the admirable step on its sophomore release with extending it to further levels rather than simply refining what was already there, as well as adding bass player Robert Donne to the line-up. Whether various live appearances with Main in fact had an impact, Labradford here resembles that extremely avant-garde group in creating honest-to-goodness "post-rock" as originally defined by critic Simon Reynolds—music reliant on rock instruments but avoiding bluesy riffs and pop hooks in favor of sheer light and shade, very much at home in the studio. The biggest change on *Reference* has remained a near-constant ever since, namely the removal of lyrics and vocal parts from almost all tracks, outside of some extremely understated and intentionally buried in the mix bits scattered through the record. Other long-running motifs started to appear as well—astoundingly obscure cover art, short and/or nonsensical terms for song titles, such as "SEDR 77," and even more attention on mix complexity, with subtle yet important sonic elements and samples scattered through the songs. The middle track of the release remains the most noteworthy—"Eero," a long, doomy song consisting almost entirely of guitar reverb—without guitar—and dark keyboard drones echoing into the far distance. Songs like "Mas" and "Balanced on Its Own Flame" retain the greatest similarity to *Prazision* due to the echoed, deliberate guitar playing and general pace, yet in the end *Reference* already points to the increasingly more challenging albums in Labradford's near future. *—Ned Raggett*

Labradford / 1996 / Kranky ♦♦♦♦

On the band's self-titled third effort, rhythm in a traditional sense appears for the first time, with drum machines and other percussion patterns often mixed low but still notable. "Phantom Channel Crossing" starts the album on a wonderful note, with a clunky, machine-like sample carrying the track, before sliding into the equally fine "Midrange," combining many familiar elements from past efforts—whispered vocals, deliberate guitar pluckings, organ drones and otherwise, string accompaniment—into a drifting, mesmerizing whole. While not as notably a different step forward as *Reference*, Labradford here works its changes on a rather more low-key basis; the feeling is of refinement rather than sudden changes. It's also the band's shortest album yet—barely forty minutes long—but with only seven songs to share that time among the general feeling of relaxation mixed with understated tenseness remains as prominent as ever. Many of the most effective touches of the album don't call attention to themselves, but weave into the song to create the overall effect, such as the metronome pulse and intentionally discordant strings on "Scenic Recovery." Just when you think you have the band pegged, they tweak the recipe in new and surprising ways—the hallmark of the band's overall career. *—Ned Raggett*

● **Mi Media Naranja** / 1997 / Blast First! ♦♦♦♦♦

For all of the group's first three albums each being intriguing, engaging listens, there was no hint that *Media* would be as flat out amazing as it was. Yet it was, and remains Labradford's best album yet, an accomplished meshing of all the various elements to their sound over previous releases into one near-perfect sonic document. Making a specific benefit out of turning the minimal into something maximal always was the band's major ability, but it gets showcased here to a new, breathtaking extent. "S" sets the scene just right, with Mark Nelson's trademark deliberate echoed guitar plucking and all manner of ambient keyboard touches joined by gentle strings and, most notably of all, a crisp, dub-inflected rhythm, spare but forceful. Add to this an overlay near the start of the song of a high-frequency pitch—not annoying, but noticeable—and the end impression is of a band in full command of how to create detailed but not overly busy songs, compelling in their understated beauty. The album is packed with such high points and subtle sonic touches—the sample of a child and slight bossa-nova rhythm on "WR," the loops of running liquid and distant engines behind twinkly keyboard sounds—and then all that behind the usual guitar/organ interplay—on "I," along with cryptic found-sound man-on-the-street statements dropped in at various points to boot. Quietly fascinating and endlessly listenable, *Media* turns what had been a very good band indeed into a masterful one. *—Ned Raggett*

E Luxo So / May 10, 1999 / Kranky ♦♦♦♦

The underrated but present Labradford sense of humor turns up here in an amusing way—namely, the six song titles for the band's fifth record, which when read in order are in fact the album credits: recording studio, side players and so forth. Besides being entertainingly wry, this emphasizes even more than the one and two letter song titles from *Media* that Labradford are much more about musical than any lyrical intent—something always apparent, but even more so here, on the band's first full instrumental release. Compared with the low-key complexity of *Media*, *Luxo* is far more minimal and a bit less gripping as a result, though not by much. The keyboard (?)-provided rhythm on "with John Morand and assisted by Brian Hoffa" helps make it one of the quirkiest songs yet Labradford have done, while having piano instead of organ playing against the guitar makes it even more distinct. "Dulcimers played by Peter Neff. Strings played" actually verges on being modern classical, consisting almost solely of piano and a string quartet, with the exception of a sudden interruption of what sounds like a door opening and closing and various gears turning. "and Jonathan Morken. Photo provided by" has more of the in-depth sound layering expected of Labradford, with what sounds like a series of record pops helping to provide some of the rhythm beneath a piano/organ/guitar combination, but generally this is a more spacious sounding effort from the band, and not a bad one at all. *—Ned Raggett*

Fixed::Context / Feb. 20, 2001 / Kranky ♦♦♦♦

In the spirit of *Meddle*, *In-A-Gadda-Da-Vida*, and *Millions Now Living Will Never Die*, Labradford's sixth record features a side-length composition and a flip of shorter works. With *Fixed::Context*, they've built on the spatial qualities of *E Luxo So*, while making their most personal and intimate recording, despite it being completely vocal-less. Simple, subtle, and quite beautiful, the 37-minute album rewards during deep concentration and as use for background. It's just as scenic as Scenic and just as pleasantly dust-blown as Ry Cooder's score to *Paris, Texas*. Barely-there electronic rustling and an organ drone lead off the 18-minute-long "Twenty." Two spaghetti western-style guitars duel between the channels, both attentive to each other. Periodic skips and pops enter two-thirds through, fading away with the other carefully constructed layers as the side closes with a shrill tone. The twang slightly dissipates for "Up to Pizmo" and "David," where both guitars again gracefully lock horns. A pulsing stomp gradually comes into focus on the former, like a blues guitarist keeping the beat with his foot. On "David," an airy synth helps rid the track of gravitational pull, only to leave in favor of a furnace blast and more electrical surges. "Wien" is led by a reverberant synth melody, as the guitars play more of a supportive role. Not particularly maverick or innovative by any stretch, *Fixed::Context* loses none of its effect throughout a day's worth of rotation. The addition and subtraction of its graceful layers ebb and flow, shifting like harm-free plate tectonics. Like the best ambient music, it's solemn and deceptively melodic. If you found any of Labradford's earlier records to be too boring for your taste, this won't do anything to change your opinion. *—Andy Kellman*

Ladybug Transistor

f. 1994

Indie Pop, Chamber Pop

The indie-pop unit Ladybug Transistor was led by vocalist/guitarist Gary Olson, a one-time string stretcher and key inspector at his family's piano factory; the group debuted in 1996 with the LP *Marlborough Farms*, titled after Olson's Brooklyn-area home recording studio. After a line-up change which left only Olson and drummer Edward Powers remaining from Ladybug Transistor's original roster, Saturnine guitarist Jennifer Baron and her bassist brother Jeff were recruited prior to recording 1997's *Beverly Atonale*, issued on Merge. After completing the LP, Powers exited, and was replaced by Individual Fruit Pie drummer San Fadyl. The group's wonderful third album, *The Albemarle Sound*, followed in 1999. The indie kitsch stylings found on *Argyle Heir* were released in spring 2001. *—Jason Ankeny*

Marlborough Farms / Oct. 4, 1996 / Park N' Ride ♦♦♦

Beverley Atonale / Feb. 11, 1997 / Merge ♦♦♦♦

Ladybug Transistor makes delicate music. It's not that the band doesn't go uptempo, just that the sound remains gentle. If hard-rockers are most commonly found thrashing around a stage with a phallic guitar, then Transistor is the guy in the back of the room wearing a black beret and casually bobbing his head to the beat. On *Beverley Atonale*, Ladybug Transistor delivers a gorgeous suite of gentle, quiet pop music, infused with melody and hooks but never overtaking the listener. The lyrics are esoteric and often incomprehensible, but you gather quickly that words aren't really the point—the band aims to set a tone more with its sound than with witty wordplay. The album is heavily influenced by the past, by such artists as the Beach Boys and Burt Bacharach—"Windy" swipes its opening drum riff from Phil Spector and slides effortlessly into a trumpet-driven light pop tune with some great guitar riffs. The production is airy and full of space; though the sounds fit together, they also linger on their own far beyond each song's duration. On the whole, *Beverly Atonale* is the perfect driving music for a rainy summer day. *—Matthew Springer*

● **Albemarle Sound** / Mar. 23, 1999 / Merge ♦♦♦♦♦

With *The Albemarle Sound*, Ladybug Transistor finally achieves the pop grandeur their earlier records promised—from its lush arrangements and rich melodies right down to the perfectly retro cover art, the 1999 copyright date is the only telltale clue that the album wasn't actually released three decades earlier instead. As opposed to the like-minded bands of the Elephant 6 collective, whose similar nods in the direction of late-'60s popcraft butt heads with their concurrent desire to pursue more experimental paths, the Ladybugs aspire to exactly replicate the orchestral confections of obvious inspirations like Brian Wilson and Burt Bacharach; the baroque twists of songs like "Meadowport Arch" and "Today Knows" are realized with remarkable dexterity and flair, and even if it is occasionally off-putting to hear an album so completely out of touch with the times, *The Albemarle Sound* is so convincing and so affectionate that all reservations quickly disappear. *—Jason Ankeny*

Argyle Heir / May 22, 2001 / Merge ♦♦♦♦

Argyle Heir is a dreamy collection of orchestral pop songs set in the style of 1960s folk-rock. Gary Olson's lilting baritone vocals are comfortably cushioned in Joe McGinty's colorful string arrangements, which evoke the classic pop arrangements of Brian Wilson and George Martin; their ornate motifs complement the melodic structure of each track without obstructing the minimalist rhythm section. Though Olson handles the singing throughout, Jennifer Baron's rendering of "Catherine Elizabeth," an otherworldly Victorian folktale, recalls a young Marianne Faithfull. Filled with surrealistic lyrics, the crisp sounds of a plectrum stroking the bass and guitar lines, trumpet solos, expertly placed droplets of reverb, classical piano runs, instrumental vignettes, and seamless tempo changes, this collection displays a multi-textured cinematic veneer that's entirely unique, even though its origins lie somewhere in the back of Burt Bacharach's imagination. *—Tom Semioli*

Ladytron

Indie Pop, Electronica

Buzzy glam rock fashion plates Ladytron came together in a jet-set miracle in mid-1998. Daniel Hunt and Reuben Wu, who lurk in the background playing rhythm boxes and keyboards in the band, settled in Liverpool after a spate of DJ work in Japan and world travel, including a train trip in Bulgaria where they met vocalist Mira Aroyo. Helena Marnie, who also sings and plays keyboards for the group, also joined them and they began work on their first single, "He Took Her to a Movie," which was recorded for 50 pounds. The release brought a wave of critical attention with writers extending into jubilant metaphor to describe the band's unique sound, including one who wrote that they were "…a teasing glimpse of how Britney Spears might have sounded, had she been born in the GDR and a heroin addict."

Ladytron toured throughout the continent before beginning work on their debut EP, *Commodore Rock*, which was released in the summer of 2000, providing their fans another foray into the noisy world of early-'80s sound. The studio full-length *604* followed a year later. *—Stacia Proefrock*

● **604** / Feb. 6, 2001 / Emperor Norton ✦✦✦✦
On their debut full-length *604*, Ladytron prove how apt their name is: their sound mixes evocative vintage synths and plaintive female vocals as it references over two decades' worth of electronica, new wave, and rock (including Roxy Music, whose "Ladytron" is the group's namesake). Like the *Commodore Rock* EP, *604* balances Ladytron's experimental and pop sides. "Mu-Tron" and "Zmekya" reinterpret Add N to (X)'s noisy, dystopian soundscapes, and the shimmering "CSKA Sofia" sounds like Kraftwerk filtered through Broadcast. However, it's the tightly structured pop songs that set Ladytron apart. Helena Marnie is Ladytron's lovelorn heart and soul, a heartbroken disco diva singing through her tears on "Another Breakfast With You" and "Discotraxx" and a sadder but wiser confidante on "Playgirl." Meanwhile, Mira Aroya's deadpan singing and Bulgarian accent add a touch of Ninotchka-style wit and irony to "Paco!" which parodies a department store's fake cheeriness, and "I'm With the Pilots," a piece of Weimar Republic-era cabaret brought into the 21st century. Marnie and Aroya's vocals blend perfectly on songs like the brooding, witty single "He Took Her to a Movie." But Ladytron's mix of retro songwriting and modern themes is their most interesting, and distinctive, aspect. Set at the airport and the disco, "Jet Age" blends jealousy and sexual ambiguity, asking "Do you want to be her or don't you / Of course you do / But would she be you?" This subversive streak makes the album's synth-pop more progressive—and more satisfying—than its blatantly experimental moments, but either way, *604* is an exciting debut from a group capable of making overused influences sound fresh again. *—Heather Phares*

Laika

f. 1993, London, England

Ambient Pop, Dream Pop, Indie Rock, Post-Rock/Experimental

Like their namesake—the dog rocketed into orbit by the Soviets renowned as the first living creature to exit the earth's atmosphere—Laika travelled the spaceways, forging a distinct and wildly experimental fusion of hip-hop, jazz, electronica, dub and Krautrock without earthly precedent. A kind of Too Pure label all-star team comprised of former Moonshake vocalist/programmer Margaret Fiedler and bassist John Frenett, onetime PJ Harvey drummer Rob Ellis and noted producer Guy Fixsen as well as ex-God percussionist Lou Ciccotelli and saxophonist/flautist Louise Elliott, Laika formed in London during the autumn of 1993; their debut EP *Antenna* appeared the following summer. *Silver Apples of the Moon*, the group's acclaimed full-length debut, followed in early 1995; after a hiatus and the departure of Frenett, Laika resurfaced with *Sounds of the Satellites* in early 1997, garnering even greater critical praise. *Good Looking Blues* appeared in 2000. *—Jason Ankeny*

Silver Apples of the Moon / Mar. 28, 1995 / Too Pure ✦✦✦✦✦
A visionary debut, *Silver Apples of the Moon* channels the full scope of modern music: hip hop, dub, jungle, acid-jazz, electronica—you name it, it's here. Contradictions and ironies fuel the record: a feather-light surface sheen masks a dark, complex rhythmic undertow, while Margaret Fiedler's gentle, whispery vocals act as camouflage for the perversity and malice at the heart of highlights like "Marimba Song," "44 Robbers" and "Honey in Heat." *—Jason Ankeny*

● **Sounds of the Satellites** / Feb. 24, 1997 / Too Pure ✦✦✦✦✦
During the two years which passed between the release of *Silver Apples of the Moon* and its follow-up, *Sounds of the Satellites*, the dub, trip-hop and drum'n'bass sounds which made Laika so distinctive and original the first time out became commonplace; never given their proper due as pioneers of electronica anyway, their prospects for creating music of similar depth and invention appeared to grow dimmer and dimmer as time went on. Miraculously, *Sounds of the Satellites* is even better than its predecessor, a simulta-

neous expansion of the band's sonic palette and a brilliant refinement of their past innovations. The pivotal difference between Laika and other similarly inclined artists is their unparalleled sense of atmosphere: far removed from the pummeling insistence of groups like Prodigy or the Chemical Brothers, Laika also avoids the cinematic film-noir ambience of Portishead in favor of a subdued, dreamlike labyrinth of sound—the album is, by turns, claustrophobic ("Breather"), sexy ("Almost Sleeping") and menacing ("Shut Off/Curl Up"). Rarely is electronic music so suggestive, so fluid, or so human; *Sounds of the Satellites* exists in its own orbit, so far ahead of its contemporaries as to be off of the map. *—Jason Ankeny*

Good Looking Blues / Apr. 18, 2000 / Too Pure ✦✦✦✦
For a band that named itself after the first dog in outer space—and previous albums called *Sounds of the Satellites* and *Silver Apples of the Moon*—you'd think Laika would make spacey ambient music with a focus on quirky beats. And they do, sometimes. The emphasis, though, of *Good Looking Blues*, the London quartet's third album, is to give equal attention to Margaret Fiedler's smooth, somewhat gothic-and-soul-influenced vocals and the band's mixture of rock, slow electronic, and sit-on-your-couch dance music. Fiedler, who went to grade school with Liz Phair in Winnetka, Illinois and later played in a Smiths-sounding college band with Moby, speak-sings dark fictional stories about life's basic themes: love, sex, death, and work. But it's not quite that simple. For instance, on one of the album's standouts, "Black Cat Bone," she tells a story of a woman who kills her evil husband with voodoo: "Rocks for my pillow and sand for my bed/For better or worse, I left him for dead." Laika's talent is crafting a particular mood. This mood, however, is difficult to explain. With songs about nights of apologies on "Moccasin," a lover man leaving on "T Street," and working for the man until death do you part on "Widow's Weed" you can't deny that Laika is dealing with themes of depression and wallowing in sadness. And even though you wouldn't call the sound upbeat, it is indeed mesmerizing, tranquil, and head-bobbing. *—Amy Schroeder*

Lambchop

f. Nashville, TN

Chamber Pop, Alternative Country-Rock, Indie Rock

One of the hands-down weirdest groups to appear on the alternative scene in the mid-'90s, it's hard to tell whether Lambchop play alternative rock with a heavy Nashville country influence, straight country music with a heavy alternative rock influence, or whether the whole thing is just an ironic joke. The group are actually from Nashville, and number about ten members (although the lineup fluctuates). The chief of this zany crew, however, is singer/songwriter/guitarist Kurt Wagner, whose stream-of-consciousness laments are distinctly at odds with the (usually) comfortably normal-sounding country-pop arrangements. Musically, Lambchop can (and often does) offer a reasonable facsimile of the MOR Nashville country devised by producers such as Billy Sherrill (who handled Charlie Rich's most popular work, and worked with Tammy Wynette and Tanya Tucker in the '70s). Lambchop subverts the clichés of Nashville country with lyrics about suicide, bowling, and Theodore Dreiser-ish narratives about mundane everyday activities. There are also occasional interjections of post-punk guitar, thrash, clarinets, organ, and recorders that will not find a home in many trailer parks. This is not the solace that most listeners turn to country-pop for as a respite from their day-to-day activities; it *is* their day-to-day activities, rendered too unflinchingly for comfort. *—Richie Unterberger*

I Hope You're Sitting Down [aka Jack's Tulips] / Sep. 1994 / Merge ✦✦✦
A mix of post-modernism and straight (not roots) country music. The spooky organ fills, saxes, clarinets, and cello make this sound at times like the Art Ensemble of Chicago-as-country-band. Kurt Wagner's morose, resigned lyrics and dry, almost spoken delivery can get hard to take over the course of the hour-plus disc. "Soaker in the Pooper," a song about suicide in the bathroom, gave Wagner almost instant notoriety, and many of the other songs deal with similarly downbeat matters, although usually not as directly. *—Richie Unterberger*

Hank / 1996 / Merge ✦✦✦✦
In hindsight, the seven-track *Hank* EP would seem to herald the conclusion of Lambchop's "straight" country period—assuming, of course, that songs with titles like "Poor Bastard" and "I Sucked My Boss' Dick" could ever be considered pure country in the first place. The impossibly lush production which buoys tracks like "I'm a Stranger Here" and the gorgeous "Blame It on the Brunettes" screams Billy Sherrill, however, and the melancholia which permeates the disc is the stuff of which endless nights in smoky honky-tonks are made; ultimately, in their own singularly bizarre way, Lambchop has made what might just fly in under the radar as a classic country record, provided no one listens too closely. Of course, with the subsequent *Thriller*, they produced the most dissonant and difficult album of their career, kissing fame and fortune goodbye forever. Nashville's loss, not ours. *—Jason Ankeny*

● **How I Quit Smoking** / Jan. 30, 1996 / Merge ✦✦✦✦✦
Bonafide string arrangements give Lambchop's second album a much more "authentic" Nashville country feel than the first—meaning, ironically, that it sometimes sounds as gloppy, sentimental, and superficial as "real" Nashville country records. The arrangements are more inventive as well, mixing conventional country instruments like steel and acoustic guitars with saxes, clarinet, cornet, banjo, tin whistle, and more, along with the same kind of off-center organ featured on the first album. Wagner continues to mine the same offbeat lyrical territory, though unlike other audio verité talents like (say) Lou Reed, he doesn't bring much passion to his inner monologues. *—Richie Unterberger*

Thriller / Sep. 23, 1997 / Merge ✦✦✦✦
Following in the tradition of the brilliant "Cigaretiquette" single, which immediately preceded it, *Thriller* moves Lambchop sharply away from their signature alt-countrypolitan

sound, pushing instead toward a punchier, noisier aesthetic; borrowing its title from the best-selling album of all time and devoting no less than three of its eight tracks to East River Pipe covers, it's a strange, difficult record likely to baffle even the group's most devoted fans. Opening with the surreal doo wop of "My Face Your Ass" and then sliding into the oddly funky "Your Fucking Sunny Day," which comes complete with a Muscle Shoals-styled horn section, the record defies expectations at every turn; almost completely abandoning the string-laden, Nashville Sound-influenced approach of earlier efforts, *Thriller* is dark and dissonant, with an edgy, menacing lyrical slant to match. Not everything here works, but the album's sheer audacity alone makes it well worth a listen, again confirming Lambchop's status among the most consistently weird and fascinating bands around. —*Jason Ankeny*

What Another Man Spills / Sep. 8, 1998 / Merge ✦✦✦✦
It's a safe bet to expect the unexpected in regards to any new Lambchop effort, but the cryptically titled (and beautifully packaged) *What Another Man Spills* is the band's most consistently surprising and deliriously eclectic outing to date, with new twists around every corner. While it's their loveliest record since *How I Quit Smoking*, that album's countrypolitan gauze is largely a thing of the past, replaced here by a dreamy, jazz-like patina which proves a remarkably versatile backdrop not only for Kurt Wagner's originals but for a vast range of covers from Dump's "It's Not Alright" to Curtis Mayfield's "Give Me Your Love (Love Song)." The latter is easily the most jaw-dropping track on *What Another Man Spills*, with the group easily slipping into the song's soulful groove without a hint of irony, not even in Wagner's amazingly Prince-like falsetto; a later cover of the Frederick Knight smash "I've Been Lonely for So Long," while less surprising, is no less engaging, further solidifying Lambchop's growing debt to the Stax/Volt sound. Where the album's jumble of styles and offbeat covers might seem self-indulgent coming from any other band, Lambchop somehow makes it all work with their wit, style and intelligence intact—even five records in, they never cease to amaze. —*Jason Ankeny*

Nixon / 2000 / Merge ✦✦✦
As time went on, Lambchop got a little more musically accomplished, and Kurt Wagner more inclined to write songs that were a little less of a stream-of-consciousness jumble, and a little less random. This will still strike most as a mighty odd record, though. Ostensibly much of this record was inspired by former president Richard Nixon (there is even a suggested reading list of Nixon-related books on the sleeve). But there are no direct references to him, and even any indirect ones are so oblique that you'd never make the connection if the record had a different title (or contained no reading list). Wagner's songs are less of a laundry list of bringdown imagery and a tad more direct than in the past, but still suggestive of, well, the kind of voices and snatches of conversation a schizophrenic might hear and utter. The music? Yes, another incongruous clash of lush orchestrated countrypolitan music and alternative singer-songwriter rock, but the Philadelphia/'70s soul influences are pretty upfront on some tracks. Wagner even adopts a thin, breaking soul falsetto on "What Else Could It Be?" that sounds as much like a satire as an homage. There are some inventive, hard-to-identify, eerie reverberant effects on several tracks, adding a sense of atmosphere even if they're not particularly complementary to the songs or melodies. All of this contributes to the sensation of hearing a radio stuck between a 1990s alternative college station and a 1970s oldies one, without the static. There's still the sense that it's an in-joke outsiders will have a hard time puzzling through, even if it's more approachable than some of Lambchop's previous outings. —*Richie Unterberger*

Tools in the Dryer / Sep. 18, 2001 / Merge ✦✦✦
The Nashville-based Lambchop "is and has been" almost two dozen different members with a discography that boasts something like 23 cassettes, singles, EPs and full-lengths, as well as numerous one-off appearances on compilations, best-of collections, and the like. It's fairly safe to say, then, that *Tools In the Dryer*—unlike most odds 'n' ends collections—isn't entirely uncalled for. In fact, for fans of the prolific band, a collection of 16 "A-sides, B-sides, live tracks and remixes" is downright appreciated. Spanning 1987 to 2000 and compiled by member Jonathan Marx, the excellent *Tools In the Dryer* is a consistently enjoyable—though anything but comprehensive—collection that includes everything from the Vic Chesnutt-penned "Miss Prissy" to disorienting dance remixes and demos recorded before the band even officially formed. Newcomers to the quirky, countrified world of Lambchop should start with *Nixon* or *How I Quit Smoking*, but diehard fans should dive right into this trip through the band's memory lane of musical miscellanea. —*Jimmy Draper*

The Lambrettas
f. 1978, Brighton, England, **db.** 1981
Mod Revival, Power Pop, New Wave
The Lambrettas, featuring Jez Bird (guitar/vocals/keyboards), Doug Saunders (guitar), Mark Ellis (bass) and Paul Wincer (drums), jumped on the mod-revival bandwagon of the late '70s, dressing in matching mohair suits and naming themselves after one of the mod-favored motor scooters. Under the leadership of Bird's catchy songwriting, they proved to be more than just Jam sound-alikes, leaving behind mod-life arrogance/elitism in favor of a pure pop sensibility. The band signed to Elton John's Rocket Records in 1979 and after one failed single, "Go Steady," had a U.K. hit with their cover of Leiber and Stoller's "Poison Ivy." The follow-up singles "D-a-a-ance" and "Another Day (Another Girl)" also charted in the UK. The latter (originally titled "Page Three"), with its not-so-thinly veiled jabs at *The Sun* newspaper's practice of placing photos of topless women on page three, earned them some notoriety when the newspaper threatened legal action. *Beat Boys in the Jet Age*, their debut LP, released in 1980, collected the early singles and other similar-sounding originals. The mod-revival fad had pretty much run its course, however, and

subsequent singles and a second album, 1981's *Ambience*, were commercial flops despite efforts to break from the mod mold. The band called it quits in 1981 and faded quickly into obscurity, regrouping in the '90s. —*Chris Woodstra*

Beat Boys in the Jet Age / 1980 / Rocket ✦✦✦✦✦
The band's debut picks up on all of the elements that made the early Jam albums brilliant—a certain reverence for '60s pop with a youthful, forward-looking attitude, punk's high-charged energy and strong songwriting. *Beat Boys in the Jet Age* is an unfortunately forgotten album which features some of the era's best teen anthems and serves as a high-point of the often disappointing mod revival. The CD version adds three bonus tracks. —*Chris Woodstra*

Ambience / 1981 / Rocket ✦✦✦
As the mod revival was running out of steam, the band took a step away from the sound for a more mature and varied album. No longer is their main concern motor scooters, girls, and living for today as evident in the haunting "Good Times" and "Decent Town." Though it failed commercially, *Ambience* is a fine collection of Brit-pop worth seeking out. —*Chris Woodstra*

● **The Best of the Lambrettas: The Singles Collection** / 1995 / Dojo ✦✦✦✦
Like so many bands of the era, the Lambrettas are best represented by their singles; *Best of the Lambrettas* collects all of the A- and B-sides (as well as a newly recorded demo) in one place for the first time, providing the best introduction to the band. The songs are certainly of the time, but they've aged well, sounding as fresh as they did originally. —*Chris Woodstra*

● **The Definitive Collection/Beat Boys in the Jet Age** / 1998 / Castle Communications ✦✦✦✦✦
The Definitive Collection is probably a good name for this package, which combines the previously-available *The Singles Collection* and the classic first album in its entirety as a bonus (although four songs are duplicated as a result). This two disc collection remains an essential documentation of the brief mod revival as well as an excellent starting point for exploring the band. —*Chris Woodstra*

Major Lance
b. Apr. 4, 1941, Chicago, IL, d. Sep. 3, 1994, Decatur, GA
Vocals / Chicago Soul, Uptown Soul, Pop-Soul, Northern Soul, Soul
Blessed with a warm, sweet voice, Major Lance was one of the leading figures of Chicago soul during the '60s and the top-selling artist for OKeh Records during the decade. Lance not only had a lovely voice, but his material was excellent. During the height of his success, the majority of his songs were written by Curtis Mayfield and produced by Carl Davis, and the pair developed a smooth, Latin-flavored sound that was punctuated by brass and layered with vocal harmonies, usually from the Impressions. It was urban, uptown soul and while it was considerably less gritty than its Southern counterpart, its breezy rhythms and joyous melodies made songs like "The Monkey Time" and "Um, Um, Um, Um, Um, Um" some of the most popular good-time R&B of its era. Major Lance's career declined significantly after he parted ways with Mayfield and Davis in the late '60s, but his classic OKeh recordings remain some of the best-loved soul music of the decade. —*Stephen Thomas Erlewine*

● **Everybody Loves a Good Time!: The Best of Major Lance** / Feb. 28, 1995 / Epic/Legacy ✦✦✦✦✦
Delightful 40-song, double-CD compilation of Lance's best work for OKeh between 1962 and 1967, including all of the chart singles, quite a few misses and B-sides, five previously unreleased cuts, and some Curtis Mayfield songs from his debut LP. The later tracks, recorded after producer Carl Davis and songwriter Mayfield had moved on to other projects, suffer in comparison with Lance's 1963-65 output, as he tried to keep abreast of contemporary soul trends, especially Motown. For many listeners, a briefer best-of Lance compilation will suffice. But for soul fans, this is prime stuff, dominated by the classic Latin-influenced Chicago soul sound of the Davis-produced tracks. —*Richie Unterberger*

The Very Best of Major Lance / Sep. 5, 2000 / Epic/Legacy ✦✦✦✦✦
This 16-song, single-disc compilation concentrates on Lance's most well-known hits, including all of his highest-charting 45's: "Um, Um, Um, Um, Um, Um," "Hey Little Girl," "The Monkey Time," "Rhythm," and "The Matador." It's excellent Chicago '60s soul, but all of the cuts are also found on Epic/Legacy's 40-song, two-CD anthology *Everybody Loves a Good Time! The Best of Major Lance*. That compilation has a good number of decent non-hit tracks from the era (such as "Sweet Music") and remains the preferred alternative unless you're on a strict budget, or the type of listener who finds it hard to hear more than a single disc's worth of an artist that you like but don't love. That's not to say the selection for this best-of isn't good, with 11 of the 16 songs coming from the pen of Curtis Mayfield. —*Richie Unterberger*

Mark Lanegan
b. Nov. 25, 1964, Ellensburg, WA
Vocals, Guitar / Indie Rock, Alternative Pop/Rock, Singer/Songwriter
Mark Lanegan's solo albums are sufficiently dissimilar in tone from those of his regular group, Screaming Trees, to make listeners wonder where his true interests lie. His records often employ a much more acoustic tone, and address much more serious, personal concerns. Despite ample critical acclaim, Lanegan always kept the Screaming Trees his primary concern (that is, until their breakup). The original plan for Lanegan's first solo recording was to do an EP of blues songs with Nirvana's Kurt Cobain and Chris Novoselic, as well as Screaming Trees drummer Mark Pickerel. That didn't work out, and *The Winding Sheet* ended up being recorded with Pickerel, guitarist Mike Johnson (later bassist in Dinosaur Jr.), and noted producer Jack Endino on bass. Released in 1990, the album

included a cover of the Leadbelly folk number "Where Did You Sleep Last Night?" from the aborted sessions with Cobain and Novoselic; it became the basis for Nirvana's version on *MTV Unplugged.* Despite a good reception from the underground, it took until 1994 for Lanegan's brilliantly assured follow-up, *Whiskey for the Holy Ghost,* to surface, which again featured Johnson in a prominent role. Afterwards, Lanegan once again returned to Screaming Trees for what proved to be the band's final album, 1996's *Dust.* With the Trees on hiatus, Lanegan resumed his solo career with 1998's *Scraps at Midnight,* which followed in the vein of its predecessors. The follow-up appeared much more quickly this time; 1999's *I'll Take Care of You* was a quietly stunning covers album drawing on Lanegan's interest in roots music. Two years later, *Field Songs* arrived. —*Richie Unterberger & Steve Huey*

The Winding Sheet / 1990 / Sub Pop ✦✦✦✦

A dark side of this Screaming Trees vocalist. —*Robert Gordon*

● **Whiskey for the Holy Ghost** / Jan. 18, 1994 / Sub Pop ✦✦✦✦✦

Mark Lanegan's first solo album, 1990's *The Winding Sheet,* was a darker, quieter, and more emotionally troubling affair than what fans were accustomed to from his work as lead singer with the Screaming Trees. The follow-up album, 1994's *Whiskey for the Holy Ghost,* used *The Winding Sheet*'s sound and style as a starting point, with Lanegan and producer/instrumentalist Michael Johnson constructing resonant but low-key instrumental backdrops for the singer's tales of heartbreak, alcohol, and dashed hopes. While *The Winding Sheet* often sounded inspired but tentative, like the solo project from a member of an established band, *Whiskey for the Holy Ghost* speaks with a quiet but steely confidence of an artist emerging with his own distinct vision. The songs are more literate and better realized than on the debut, the arrangements are subtle and supportive (often eschewing electric guitars for keyboards and acoustic instruments), and Lanegan's voice, bathed in bourbon and nicotine, transforms the deep sorrow of the country blues (a clear inspiration for this music) into something new, compelling, and entirely his own. *Whiskey for the Holy Ghost* made it clear that Mark Lanegan had truly arrived as a solo artist, and it ranks alongside American Music Club's *Everclear* as one of the best "dark night of the soul" albums of the 1990s. —*Mark Deming*

Scraps at Midnight / Jul. 21, 1998 / Sub Pop ✦✦✦✦

With the Screaming Trees, Mark Lanegan is part of a dysfunctional family that can only pull its act together once in a while. As he's struggling to make the group work, he's taken away from his solo career, which has proven to be far more consistent than his band's. *Scraps at Midnight,* Lanegan's third solo effort (one arrives every four years or so), follows a similar path as his first two albums—it's a haunted, low-key affair steeped in blues, folk and country. The rustic setting allows Lanegan to spin some captivating tales, all delivered in his powerful, throaty growl. Although it's similar to its predecessor, *Scraps at Midnight* is arguably his most accomplished—it might just miss matching the excellence of *Whiskey for the Holy Ghost,* but with songs as uniformly strong and performances as passionate as these, it comes damn close. —*Stephen Thomas Erlewine*

I'll Take Care of You / Sep. 21, 1999 / Sub Pop ✦✦✦✦✦

By now, anyone who has heard one of Mark Lanegan's solo albums knows exactly what the others will sound like—Lanegan's weathered, smoky voice intones tales of quiet desperation over echoing electric guitar arpeggios, folky acoustic guitar work, and the occasional piano, organ, or violin embellishment. This approach has resulted in a compelling body of work, often possessed of remarkable depth, but it's also become something of a stylistic straitjacket over the course of several albums. And that's the only major knock against the otherwise brilliant *I'll Take Care of You,* Lanegan's fourth solo album, which marks the first time it hasn't taken him four years to deliver a follow-up. Perhaps that's because there's no original material here—*I'll Take Care of You* applies the drifting, elegiac qualities of its predecessors to a selection of well-chosen, mostly underexposed folk, country, and blues covers. It's a testament to Lanegan's interpretive skill that he's able to use his already well-established style so effectively yet again, as most of these versions range from stunning to merely excellent. Moreover, he never overplays the darker dirges, and the restrained arrangements help ensure that his melancholy never seems forced. As good as they are, there are parts of every Lanegan album that float off into the ether; however, the material on *I'll Take Care of You* helps keep him tethered, actually improving on his signature sound by tightening it up. So, even if you think you've heard it all from Lanegan before—and even if he'll have to open up his sound or risk diluting the qualities that make him compelling—*I'll Take Care of You* really is one of his most affecting, accessible recordings, if not *the* most. —*Steve Huey*

Field Songs / May 8, 2001 / Sub Pop ✦✦✦

Those looking for some stylistic shifts in Mark Lanegan's fifth solo outing might be a bit disappointed. Lanegan pours out blues- and gospel-tinged country-rock over ice and sips it for 42 and a half minutes—and that's precisely what he's been up to since 1990's *The Winding Sheet.* Why the heck not? He's damn good at it, and he proves it here on *Field Songs. Some* new things are abreast on this record as Ben Shepherd (Soundgarden) is present on most tracks lending his guitar and bass hands. Also present are Bill Rieflin (KMFDM, Lard, Ministry, etc.) and Duff McKagen (Guns & Roses) who each play on one track and are a part of Lanegan's touring band along with Shepherd. Mike Johnson (Dinosaur Jr.) has been on each of Lanegan's albums and continues to add much of the building blocks and the mortar necessary to pluck out these songs that are constructed much in the same vein as in the past but with some nuances and a greater color depth. Upon repeated listens, standout tracks such as "Miracle," "Kimiko's Dream House," and "Fix" become infectiously memorable as convincing tales about love gained and lost. All in all, every track is solid and worthy of numerous spins. —*Jack LV Isles*

Nicolette Larson

b. Jul. 17, 1952, Helena, MT, **d.** Dec. 16, 1997

Vocals, Percussion, Guitar / Urban Cowboy, Soft Rock, Country-Pop, Country-Rock

After working as a backup vocalist for several country-rock acts and serving as a member of Commander Cody's Lost Planet Airmen for several years during the mid-'70s, vocalist Nicolette Larson launched a solo career in the late '70s. Initially, Larson followed the sound of laid-back Californian country-rock, which resulted in a Top Ten pop hit in 1979 with "Lotta Love." In the years following the success of "Lotta Love," Larson continued to mine the soft rock California sound. Following one last attempt at pop success with 1982's *All Dressed Up and No Place to Go* and the single "I Only Want to Be With You," Larson retreated from the mainstream and starred in the country musical *Pump Boys and Dinettes.* Larson received positive reviews for her performance, which led to a record contract with MCA in 1983. On the basis of her performance, the Academy of Country Music named her the Best New Female Vocalist in 1984, even though she had yet to have any country hits. Larson finally released a country album in 1985 with ... *Say When,* but the record didn't live up to its hype. Though it was critically acclaimed, the album was far from a commercial success. Larson finally broke into the country charts in 1986 when "That's How You Know When Love's Right," a duet with Steve Wariner, climbed into the Top 10 and stayed in the charts for five months. The song was drawn from *Rose of My Heart,* which performed respectably. However, Larson didn't choose to follow the album up with another country record. In 1987, she recorded an album, *Shadows of Love,* in Italy and in the next year she began pursuing an acting career. —*Stephen Thomas Erlewine*

Nicolette / 1978 / Warner Brothers ✦✦✦✦

In the Nick of Time / 1979 / Warner Brothers ✦✦✦

Radioland / 1980 / Warner Brothers ✦✦✦

All Dressed Up & No Place To Go / 1982 / Warner Brothers ✦✦✦

● **The Very Best of Nicolette Larson** / Aug. 17, 1999 / Rhino ✦✦✦✦

Nicolette Larson was a staple of California pop and soft-rock in the '70s, not only as a solo artist, but as a backing vocalist for artists as diverse as Commander Cody's Lost Planet Airmen, the Nitty Gritty Dirt Band, Van Halen and Neil Young. As a matter of fact, Young gave Larson her breakthrough hit, "Lotta Love." The song turned out to be the peak of her popularity, climbing into the Top Ten in early 1979. She never had that kind of widespread popularity again, even if she had a few smaller pop hits to her credit, along with some success on the country charts. The charts may have changed, but the music really didn't—she always walked the line separating country-pop and Californian soft-rock. Throughout it all, her sweet voice was continually engaging, even when she worked with material that wasn't always convincing. That much is evident from Rhino's definitive retrospective, *The Very Best of Nicolette Larson.* Spanning her entire solo career, from her 1978 debut to her 1994 children's album, the 16-song collection contains all the major highlights, but its momentum sort of sags toward the end of the disc, as her material grew weaker and her productions became too clean. Nevertheless, this is an accurate portrait of her career. If *The Very Best of* isn't quite as cohesive as her first few albums, so be it— it charts the ups and downs of her career quite well, and in doing so, it offers a definitive, warts-and-all summary. —*Stephen Thomas Erlewine*

The Last Poets

f. May 16, 1969

Fusion, Political Rap, Poetry

With their politically charged raps, taut rhythms, and dedication to raising African-American consciousness, the Last Poets almost single-handedly laid the groundwork for the emergence of hip-hop. The group arose out of the prison experiences of Jalal Mansur Nuriddin, a U.S. Army paratrooper who chose jail as an alternative to fighting in Vietnam; while incarcerated, he converted to Islam, learned to "spiel" (an early form of rapping), and befriended fellow inmates Omar Ben Hassan and Abiodun Oyewole. Upon the trio's release from prison, they returned to the impoverished ghettos of Harlem, where they joined the East Wind poetry workshop and began performing their fusion of spiels and musical backing on neighborhood street corners. After a performance on a local television program, the group was signed by jazz producer Alan Douglas, who helmed their eye-opening eponymous debut LP in 1970. A collection condemning both white oppression ("White Man's Got a God Complex") and black stasis ("Niggas Are Scared of Revolution"), *The Last Poets* reached the U.S. Top Ten album chart. After the 1971 follow-up, *This Is Madness,* Jalal recruited former jazz drummer Suliaman El Hadi for 1972's *Chastisement,* which incorporated jazz-funk structures to create a sound the group dubbed "jazzoetry." Following the 1973 Jalal solo concept album *Hustler's Convention* (recorded under the alias Lightnin' Rod), the Last Poets issued 1974's *At Last,* a foray into free-form jazz; after its release, Nilajah exited, and with the exception of 1977's *Delights of the Garden,* the group kept a conspicuously low profile for the remainder of the decade. By the 1980s, however, the proliferation of rap—and the form's acknowledged debt to the Last Poets—made their early records sought-after collector's items; finally, in 1984 the group resurfaced with the LP *Oh, My People.* —*Jason Ankeny*

★ **The Last Poets** / 1970 / Metrotone ✦✦✦✦✦

If rap could be traced to one logical source point, this exceptional piece of vinyl would be it, without question. Though the strict adherence to syncopated rhythms and standard song structures are absent, all the elements that would later become the hallmarks of hip-hop by the early 1980s (and predictable fare by the 1990s) are here: vivid depictions of street level violence, vivid apocalyptic predictions of racial genocide. All that is missing are pointless party anthems. But running through all the songs on the Last Poets' debut is an urgent sense of the need for radical action in the nation as well as the black community. In addition to railing against the injustices perpetrated by white America, the Poets' comment on the economic and social devastation of drugs ("Jones Comin' Down," "Two Little Boys"), complacency in urban families ("Wake Up Niggers," "When the Revolution Comes"), the emotional release of sex ("Black Thighs"), and the weight of oppression that leads to hopelessness ("Surprises"). At the same time, they warn of the dangers of half-hearted commitment to revolutionary change: "don't talk about revolution until you are ready to eat rats." In the same manner that Marvin Gaye's landmark album *What's Goin' On* depicted the problems that doomed black culture, the Last Poets are now seen by many as prophets. But also like Gaye, the realization that the problems depicted on *The Last Poets* are now much worse marks the record as an unheeded warning, far more than just a piece of Black Power kitsch. In any event, a proper CD release is long overdue. —*John Duffy*

This Is Madness / 1971 / Metrotone ✦✦✦✦✦
A legendary set featuring a group of extremely controversial street poets. The Last Poets used offensive language brilliantly, talked in graphic detail about America's social and racial failures, and helped expose a wider audience to the sentiments of the '70s black nationalists. They were the forerunners of today's Afrocentric rappers, and also showed the way to a jazz/rap union now being explored on both sides of the Atlantic. This has been reissued on CD. —*Ron Wynn*

Delights in the Garden / 1977 / Charly ✦✦✦✦✦
Reactionist/revolutionist/humanist poets on fire. Highly recommended. With drummer Bernard Purdie. —*Michael G. Nastos*

Oh My People / 1984 / Celluloid ✦✦✦

Right On! / Dec. 28, 1990 / Collectables ✦✦✦✦

Retro Fit / 1992 / Ced ✦✦✦✦

Holy Terror / 1994 / Rykodisc ✦✦✦

The Legend: The Best of the Last Poets / Mar. 19, 1996 / M.I.L. Multimedia ✦✦✦✦✦
The Legend: The Best of the Last Poets is a 35-track, two-disc overview of the group's career. The first covers "The Beginnings," while the second's focus is "The Real Rap Masters." —*Jason Ankeny*

The Time Has Come / Apr. 15, 1997 / Mercury ✦✦✦✦
Picking up where *Holy Terror* and Omar Ben Hassan's solo album *Be Bop or Be Dead* left off, *The Time Has Come* is a scalding blend of avant-jazz, bebop and hip-hop, highlighted by cameos from Chuck D and Pharoah Sanders. These two guests may be impressive, but they don't steal the show—they merely demonstrate that the Last Poets are too diverse and way too smart to be pigeonholed into one particular category. Occasionally, the record may be a bit unfocused, and its relentless barrage of avant-poetry may be headache-inducing to some, but few records are as politically powerful and articulate as this. —*Leo Stanley*

Chastisement/Freedom Express / Sep. 30, 1997 / M.I.L. Multimedia ✦✦✦
Some 16 years separated the releases of *Chastisement* and *Freedom Express*, both found on this two-fer; the former, from 1972, is by far the stronger of the two—recorded with former drummer Suliaman El Hadi, it added jazz and funk to the group's fix to forge a new sound which they dubbed "jazzoetry." 1988's *Freedom Express* was the re-formed group's second comeback LP, and although it lacks the potency of their earlier work, it's still worth hearing. —*Jason Ankeny*

Latimore

b. Sep. 7, 1939, Charleston, TN
Vocals, Keyboards / Urban, Soul-Blues, Disco, Funk, Soul
Deep-voiced Latimore's sultry mid-'70s output for Miami's Glades label was a steamy marriage of soul and blues. Initially billed as Benny Latimore, the Tennessean began recording for Miami mogul Henry Stone in 1965, and his late-'60s Dade singles are solid deep-soul. Dropping his first name on Glades, Latimore finally found stardom in 1973 with a jazzy reading of T-Bone Walker's "Stormy Monday." He topped the soul lists in 1974 with the anguished "Let's Straighten It Out," a simmering soul/blues hybrid, and encored with the incendiary "Keep the Home Fires Burnin'" the next year. Most of Latimore's Glades sides were produced in Miami by Steve "Every Day I Have to Cry" Alaimo, and when he wasn't cutting his own hits, Latimore acted as a house pianist for parent TK Records. Latimore moved to Malaco during the '80s, his appeal undiminished. —*Bill Dahl*

● **Straighten It Out: The Best of Latimore** / Sep. 19, 1995 / Rhino ✦✦✦✦✦
All of Latimore's greatest hits are included on this 17-track collection *Straighten It Out: The Best of Latimore*, making the album the best overview of the seductive '70s soul balladeer's career. —*Stephen Thomas Erlewine*

Latin Playboys

f. 1994
Experimental Rock, Neo-Psychedelia, Tex-Mex
David Hidalgo and Louie Perez of Los Lobos hooked up with Tchad Blake and producer Mitchell Froom for this side project, a twisted and avant-garde take on roots music. Latin Playboys draw from blues, border music, experimental studio trickery, and cinematic sound textures on their ambitious self-titled 1994 album. All of the material was composed by Hidalgo and Perez, and shows a considerably more experimental direction than their work with Los Lobos. *Dose* followed in 1999. —*Richie Unterberger*

● **Latin Playboys** / Mar. 8, 1994 / Slash ✦✦✦
These are hardly "songs" in the conventional sense; more like eccentric sketches that create haunting moods. The players bounce back and forth between scratchy traditional

Latin music, free-associating blues numbers, and spaced-out honky-tonk. Grounded in roots music, the lyrics and song structures are almost impressionistic in tone, creating an effect similar to listening to your car radio as stations drift in and out of reach while you drive along the Mexican border. —*Richie Unterberger*

Dose / Mar. 2, 1999 / Atlantic ✦✦
This second album from the Latin Playboys continues the avant-roots explorations of their first record. Omnipresent on *Dose* is Mitchell Froom and Tchad Blake's signature production. The two are so good at what they do that they can make even an average song compelling due to the sonic wizardry of their recording techniques, and they utilize every trick in their lexicon here, from lo-fi vocals to distorted drums. David Hidalgo and Louie Perez do their part by conjuring up a wonderful variety of guitar tones, such as the exploding lead on the title track. However, the tunes here just aren't happening. Recording and production wizardry can only get one so far, and *Dose* is the result of technique trying to overcompensate for a temporary drop in imagination. This is not to say that there aren't some strong moments on this record. The smoldering "Lemon 'N Ice," featuring Jerry Marotta and Wendy & Lisa (of the Revolution fame), has almost a street-level Steely Dan vibe, and the opening instrumental, "Fiesta Erotica," features a heady dose of Irish and Middle Eastern tonalities. All in all, however, it is more likely to appeal to Froom/Blake fans than Los Lobos fans. Not a bad thing necessarily, but definitely a surprise for most who were expecting "La Bamba." —*Daniel Gioffre*

Cyndi Lauper

b. Jun. 20, 1953, Queens, NY
Vocals, Guitar / Pop/Rock, New Wave
Cyndi Lauper was one of the biggest stars of the early MTV era, selling five million copies of her debut album, *She's So Unusual*, as well as scoring a string of four Top Ten hits from the record, including the major hits "Girls Just Want to Have Fun" and "Time After Time." Lauper's thin, girlish voice and gleefully rag-tag appearance became one of the most distinctive images of the early '80s, which helped lead her not only to the top of the charts, but also to stardom. Throughout America, there were numbers of teenage girls dressing like Lauper and using "Girls Just Want to Have Fun" as an anthem, a call to arms for self-expression. At first, her music was a bright, colorful new wave fusion of a number of styles, including new wave, post-punk, reggae, pop, and funk. Both her music and her appearance helped popularize—and just as importantly, sanitize—the image of punk and new wave for America, making it an acceptable part of the pop landscape. Lauper didn't follow through on the success of *She's So Unusual*, choosing to turn toward middle-of-the-road balladry and mainstream pop, but her first album remains a benchmark of the early '80s. —*Stephen Thomas Erlewine*

● **She's So Unusual** / 1984 / Epic/Legacy ✦✦✦✦✦
One of the great new wave/early MTV records, *She's So Unusual* is a giddy mix of self-confidence, effervescent popcraft, unabashed sentimentality, subversiveness, and clever humor. In short, it's a multifaceted portrait of a multifaceted talent, an artist that's far more clever than her thin, deliberately girly voice would indicate. Then again, Lauper's voice suits her musical persona, since its chirpiness adds depth, or reconfigures the songs, whether it's the call to arms of "Girls Just Want to Have Fun" or the tearjerking "Time After Time." Lauper is at her very best on the first side, all of which were singles or received airplay, and this collection of songs—"Money Changes Everything," "Girls," "When You Were Mine," "Time," "She Bop," "All Through the Night"—is astonishing in its consistency, so strong that it makes the remaining tracks—all enjoyable, but rather pedestrian—charming by their association with songs so brilliantly alive. If Lauper couldn't maintain this level of consistency, it's because this captured her persona better than anyone could imagine—when a debut captures a personality so well, let alone a personality so tied to its time, the successive work can't help but pale in comparison. Still, when it's captured as brightly and brilliantly as it is here, it does result in a debut that retains its potency, long after its production seems a little dated. [The 2000 reissue contains three live bonus tracks, all enjoyable, all not really necessary.] —*Stephen Thomas Erlewine*

True Colors / 1986 / Portrait ✦✦✦
There were a few years in the mid-'80s when one couldn't go out for a cup of coffee without encountering Cyndi Lauper in one form or another. Her videos were playing constantly on MTV, her music was everywhere on the radio, and best of all, children were even dressing up as Cyndi for Halloween. In retrospect, it was a Lauperish time but it was all over quite quickly, in fact the period in the ultra-limelight didn't even span the period covered by two album releases, which means that this follow-up to her smash debut album was relegated to the also-ran pile, with sad results such as only one sort-of hit single the title track and nobody apparently interested in imitating the skirt she wore on the back cover photo, which seems like it is made of slashed up concert posters. Kind of a shame since so much love and attention went into this album. Guest stars and high dollar session musicians abound, including other '80s icons such as The Bangles and the manic Pee Wee Herman, who provides a great little answering machine bit at the end of "911." Lauper is a fantastic vocalist, meaning that any record producer worth hiring would be happy to dream up endless settings for her. This album is nothing if not ambitious, and some of the stretches really pay off, such as the ultimately endearing cover of Marvin Gaye's "What's Going On." Other aspects date badly. For example, highly reverberated and artificial sounding drums and keyboards were really popular at the time, but a vocalist with a clear voice such as Lauper sounds much better in the context of real instruments with their warmer sounds. When it comes to tunes such as the nice Cajun number "The Faraway Nearby," drums should have been turned way down and other instrumental colors brought up. Despite these sorts of problems, there really wasn't that much

music recorded by this artist during her most popular period, so fans will no doubt want to own it all. *—Eugene Chadbourne*

A Night to Remember / 1989 / Epic ✦✦

A Hat Full of Stars / 1992 / Epic ✦✦

Twelve Deadly Cyns / Jul. 18, 1995 / Epic ✦✦✦✦
Regrettably bypassing the Top Ten hit "The Goonies 'R' Good Enough," *12 Deady Cyns* features almost all of Cyndi Lauper's Top 40 hits, tacking on a handful of new tracks at the end, including "Hey Now (Girls Still Wanna Have Fun)," an updated version of her breakthrough hit single, "Girls Just Wanna Have Fun." As hits collections go, the album is fine, but with the exception of the ballad "True Colors" and the pop confection "Change of Heart," all of her finest songs and biggest hits were on *She's So Unusual*, which is a more consistent and entertaining album. *—Stephen Thomas Erlewine*

Sisters of Avalon / Apr. 1, 1997 / Epic ✦✦✦
Cyndi Lauper made a valient effort to jump-start her career with the varied and eclectic *Sisters of Avalon*. Working with producer Mark Saunders, Lauper attempts to work worldbeat, adult alternative and even trip-hop influences into her trademark adult-contemporary pop, and while the results aren't always successful, the record is the most intriguing and rewarding album she has made since *True Colors*. *—Stephen Thomas Erlewine*

Lazy Cowgirls

f. 1981

Indie Rock, Roots Rock, Alternative Pop/Rock, Punk

If the Ramones had been a road-tested biker gang instead of pop-obsessed cartoon speed merchants, they might have sounded something like the Lazy Cowgirls. Merging the buzzsaw roar of first-wave punk, the sneering attitude of '60s garage rock, the heart-on-your-sleeve honesty of honky tonk, and the self-assured swagger of the Rolling Stones, the Lazy Cowgirls play raw, sweaty outlaw rock & roll at its most furiously passionate and physically intense; like a Harley gunned up to 95 mph, the Lazy Cowgirls may not sound safe, but they sure are fun. Vocalist Pat Todd, guitarist D.D. Weekday (aka Doug Phillips), and bassist Keith Telligman left their hometown of Vincennes, IN, in 1981 to move to California, hoping to get a rock band off the ground. In 1983, they finally settled on fellow Indiana refugee Allen Clark as a drummer, and began hitting the L.A. club circuit as the Lazy Cowgirls. After countless shows playing to "no one, and people from work" (according to Todd), the band caught the ear of Chris Desjardins (aka Chris D.), former leader of art-punks the Flesh Eaters. Desjardins got the band a deal with Restless Records, and produced their self-titled debut LP in 1984. The band cut the near-definitive *How It Looks—How It Is* in 1990, but years of hard work with little commercial reward began to take their toll, and at the end of 1991 Telligman and Clark quit the group. The Cowgirls' rhythm section became something of a revolving door for the next few years, and while the Lazy Cowgirls cut a handful of singles and EPs for various small labels, conventional wisdom had it that the band had called it quits. But in 1995, the Cowgirls re-emerged with a new album, the superb *Ragged Soul*. *—Mark Deming*

Lazy Cowgirls / 1984 / Restless ✦✦✦

Tapping the Source / 1987 / Bomp! ✦✦✦✦
The Lazy Cowgirls' Chris D.-produced debut didn't quite capture what made them the best punk band to come out of L.A. after the SST explosion went bust, but 1987's *Tapping the Source* (with the band calling the shots alongside engineer Marc Mylar) was a major improvement that got their greasy roar onto plastic with something approaching the power it deserved. Like X and the New Bomb Turks, the Lazy Cowgirls are one of the few punk bands that understand rock & roll had a history prior to 1970, and alongside their top-fuel originals, which mix blamalama thrash with blues and country accents, the Cowgirls also cover two classic early rock sides (the Coasters' "Yakety Yak" and Larry Williams' "Justine") in their own inimitable style, and crank Jim Reeves' "Heartache" up to 90 mph without robbing it of its honky tonk pathos. Among the originals, "Goddamn Bottle" and "Mr. Screwdriver" are two songs about the perils of alcohol that, remarkably enough, don't sound preachy or annoyingly straight-edge, and actually rock hard. And no record collection can be considered complete without Pat Todd's full-bodied wail and D.D. Weekday's brilliantly sloppy guitar leads, and they're both in fine fettle here. *Tapping the Source* isn't the Lazy Cowgirls' best album, but it was their first great one, and if you've never checked out their road-tested genius, it's not a bad place to start. *—Mark Deming*

Radio Cowgirl / 1989 / Sympathy for the Record Industry ✦✦✦
The Lazy Cowgirls have made more than their share of brilliant records, but their real strength is as a live act, and this album, which preserves on plastic a typically high-powered live set the band played at KCSB-FM in Santa Barbara, California, offers all the evidence you need to encourage a right-minded rock fan to witness the Cowgirls experience up-close and in-person. A promo spot advertising the broadcast that kicks off this album proclaims that the Lazy Cowgirls will play "loud, fast, hard rock & roll music," and it's hard to disagree. There are a few sloppy moments here and there (be warned: this is real rock & roll, where not everything is supposed to be perfect), and the sound is a bit thin (like the unretouched two-track recording it is), but all four Cowgirls are clearly audible and pouring their heart and soul into every moment of the show (even on the joke cover of the theme from *Green Acres*). Besides, how many bands can cover the Ramones and the Saints alongside Larry Williams and Jim Reeves and actually do justice to all of 'em? *Radio Cowgirl* was the first release from Sympathy for the Record Industry, and it's difficult to think of many better ways to get into the music business; the CD edition is even better, tacking on eight hard-to-find studio tracks as a bonus. *—Mark Deming*

How It Looks, How It Is / 1990 / Sympathy for the Record Industry ✦✦✦✦✦
How It Looks, How It Is is a scorching hunk of speed raunch that works in the classic way that Ramones records work: it's unrepentant punk rock. Nuance is thrown out the window, and this is full-bore, head-on, manic guitar panic. Pat Todd, with a voice that sounds like a high-speed drill when he sings in his limited upper register, gives that slightly psycho edge that made the Cowgirls a fairly intimidating proposition. Some of the tracks sound half-assed, but most of this raunch and rumble (especially "D.I.E. in Indiana" and "When It All Comes Down") is prime (and primal) scorch. Enjoy. *—John Dougan*

● **Ragged Soul** / Oct. 24, 1995 / Crypt ✦✦✦✦✦
Ragged Soul was the first album in five years from the Lazy Cowgirls, and from the first blast of D.D. Weekday's guitar on "I Can't Be Satisfied" it's obvious that this band was ready to make up for lost time. Against all odds, *Ragged Soul* sounds like the band's best album ever; the twin-guitar punch of Weekday and Michael Leigh offers plenty of kick with no clutter, the rhythm section (Leonard Keringer on bass and Ed Huerta on drums) drives the songs forward without crowding anyone in the process, and Pat Todd proves he's one of the greatest unsung frontmen in rock, pouring out fire and passion on every cut. The material is top shelf, too, especially the bitterly anthemic "Frustration, Tragedy and Lies" and "Bought Your Lies." Tough, furious, loud and proud—*Ragged Soul* is roots-smart old-school punk at it's finest. *—Mark Deming*

A Little Sex & Death / Oct. 27, 1997 / Crypt ✦✦✦✦
Following up the Lazy Cowgirls' masterful *Ragged Soul* was no easy task, especially after long-time guitarist D.D. Weekday hung up his Les Paul causing *A Little Sex and Death* suffer a bit by comparison. New axeman Eric Chandler delivers solid work and suits the band's style quite well, but he lacks Weekday's undertow of sloppy genius, and while the songs on *Ragged Soul* were pure meat, this disc seems to have a bit of filler here and there. But if *Ragged Soul* was a great album, *A Little Sex and Death* is a very good one, and Pat Todd, always one of rock's great bellowers, never sounds less than thoroughly committed throughout. If it isn't quite as good as the album that immediately preceded it, *A Little Sex and Death* is still a far stronger and more committed work than nearly any other band covering their territory has made in ages—no small accomplishment after 14 years in the game. *—Mark Deming*

Broken Hearted on Valentines Day / Aug. 11, 1998 / Sympathy for the Record Industry ✦✦✦
The Lazy Cowgirls dropped this four-song EP during the interim between *A Little Sex and Death* and *Rank Outsider*, and if it's something less than essential, it packs a whole lot of wallop into just 12 minutes. With love gone wrong dominating the disc's four tunes, you get a hard-charging breakup tune ("Just the Last Goodbye"), two cranked-to-ten covers (Buddy Holly's "That Makes It Tough" and Johnny Cash's "Home of the Blues"), and the slower, blues-tinged title cut, which boasts a soulful vocal from Pat Todd and some superb guitar leads from Eric Chandler. While the excellent title song is the best reason to own this, *Broken Hearted on Valentines Day* has heart, soul, swagger, and energy to spare from first note to last—in short, it's a Lazy Cowgirls record, and every home should have one. *—Mark Deming*

Rank Outsider / Oct. 12, 1999 / Sympathy for the Record Industry ✦✦✦✦
The first of two albums the Lazy Cowgirls would drop within six months, *Rank Outsider* is a solid slice of meat-and-potatoes punk rock with plenty of rootsy side dishes included for variety. Returning guitarist Michael Leigh isn't quite up to the level of fuzzy genius of founding fret wrestler D.D. Weekday, but he certainly understands what these songs need and lays in plenty of high-impact downstroke with sweat and skill (and his parts feel better in context than what Eric Chandler brought to the picture on *A Little Sex and Death*). Singer Pat Todd is in superb, revved-up form here—if anything, the guy's vocals just get better and more confident with the passage of time—and while the presence of a few acoustic-based cuts is something new for this band, their loose, bluesy feel harkens back to *Exile On Main Street*-era Rolling Stones more than anyone in the *MTV Unplugged* crowd. Another great record from a band that knows how. *—Mark Deming*

Somewhere Down the Line / Apr. 18, 2000 / Sympathy for the Record Industry ✦✦✦✦
Something of a companion piece of 1999's *Rank Outsider* (the band considered releasing them as a double album, but opted for two separate albums released six months apart), *Somewhere Down the Line* finds the Lazy Cowgirls in a relatively calm and reflective mood. But the operative word is "relatively"—some numbers feature slower tempos (like the swaggering "Bittersweet Shit"), and the occasional acoustic tunes (such as "Stripper Blues" and "Leap of Faith") show off the band's taste for blues and honky-tonk styles. But if you're looking for the Lazy Cowgirls' traditional flat-out roots-punk wailing, cue up "Another Lost Cause" or "Back Down in the Basement" and you'll hear Pat Todd and the band rocking as hard as ever. One of the band's best albums, which in a burst of renewed activity bodes well for their future. *—Mark Deming*

Here and Now: (Live!) / Jul. 3, 2001 / Sympathy for the Record Industry ✦✦✦
The Lazy Cowgirls were extraordinarily prolific at the turn of the century, releasing two full-length albums within six months of each other that both boast songs that rival the quality of anything they've done in their lengthy career. This live-in-studio collection finds the band at a turning point, surveying a healthy portion of recent compositions, covers of favored influences and forgotten Cowgirl classics. While *Rank Outsider* and *Somewhere Down the Line* both featured acoustic tracks, the inclusion of non-electric selections on this live document seems to herald a serious interest in pursuing a more rural tone than the no-holds-barred punk rock that the band is known for. It's an appropriate direction, since leader Pat Todd's songs have always been informed as much by Hank Williams as the Ramones, and while the acoustic numbers don't match up to their original sources, they do pave the way for future country-flavored material that would serve the band well. "When It Comes to You I've Got No Dreams to Lose" is one of two new songs written for this project, and it's the highlight of the album, a tough-hearted number

with a far rootsier approach than the crash-and-burn of Cowgirls past. Even at a slower speed, though, the band expresses all of the reckless sentiment and hoarse honesty that fans have come to expect. The electric set unfortunately doesn't live up to the Lazy Cowgirls' full potential as a live band; the invited audience politely acknowledges each tune but the vibe is strangely sterile. *Here and Now: (Live!)* is best appreciated by long-time fans who will be excited to hear the reworked versions of older tunes and the spirited covers that pepper the set. —*Fred Beldin*

Le Tigre

f. 1999
Indie Rock, Alternative Pop/Rock
Riot grrrl Kathleen Hanna put Bikini Kill behind her before the dawn of the new millennium to create another brash female punk rock outlet, that of Le Tigre. Composed of Hanna, former international videomaker Sadie Benning, and zine creator Johanna Fateman, Le Tigre mold a healthy dose of sampled electronica, old-school garage rock, and moody instrumentals in there—feministic of course! They released their self-titled debut in late 1999. *From the Desk of Mr. Lady* followed in early 2001. —*MacKenzie Wilson*

● **Le Tigre** / Oct. 26, 1999 / Mr. Lady ✦✦✦✦✦
The debut effort from Le Tigre sounds like the best new wave album not to come from the 1980s. Here, frontwoman Kathleen Hanna expands on the lo-fi sounds she tinkered with on her debut solo album, *Julie Ruin*. Le Tigre melds punk, new wave and hip hop into a seemingly cute package. Each song is hummable, and Hanna's "valley girl intelligentsia" voice is perfectly deceptive. In "Deceptacon," a song loaded with the kind of simple contradictions that made Kurt Cobain's lyrics so effective, Hanna sings, "Let me hear you depoliticize my rhyme." "What's Yr Take on Cassavetes" is the best song about an auteur since King Missile's "Martin Scorsese." "My My Metrocard" and "Les and Ray," two of the best songs on the album, display a welcome sort of contradiction: both songs seem to be about escape and exploration ("Think I'll go a little/but then I go far"), but the catchy hooks of these tunes are inescapable. With Bikini Kill, Hanna's politics were as subtle as the Empire State Building. But with *Le Tigre*, as with the great Tom Tom Club song "Genius of Love," the listener is left not only humming and dancing, but exploring the wealth of reference material hidden within its confines. —*Brian Flota*

Feminist Sweepstakes / Oct. 16, 2001 / Mr. Lady ✦✦✦
On Le Tigre's second album Kathleen Hanna is no less radical, but her politically charged agenda sounds a bit callous and simple. And that's no accident: Hanna is simple. The concept behind Le Tigre, and the thing that differentiates it from her previous band, Bikini Kill, is that the drum machine rules. Each of *Feminist Sweepstakes*' 13 songs plinks along the rat-a-tat-tat beat of programmed percussion. The political outline is just a side effect. And Hanna straddles the line between cheeky and obnoxious throughout. It's certainly her lack of humor that makes this an arduous listen; it's her punk sensibilities that keep it at least interesting. She's fierce and committed in a way that hundreds of her rock-rap foes aren't. Hanna's enemies are bigger this time, and for a simple-minded gal, that's a huge step forward. —*Michael Gallucci*

Amanda Lear (Amanda Tapp)

b. 1941, Hong Kong
Vocals / Euro-Dance, Disco
Amanda Lear first surfaced in the early '70s as a fetishistically clothed album-cover model for Roxy Music. She was said to be a transsexual but, as she told *Interview* magazine, that was just a ruse dreamed up by her sponsor, David Bowie, to draw attention. Her importance to disco fans, however, began in 1977, when she recorded *I Am a Photograph* in Germany with production help from Tony Monn. *I Am a Photograph* is the first of six sleazy, hard-to-find albums in which she flaunts a voice so heavy with low notes it makes one wonder if she really isn't a man after all. But Lear's slow notes are simply an exaggeration of the whiskey-voiced sultriness created by Marlene Dietrich. That isn't to say, however, that Lear's lyrics—or the music's inverted proportions—don't exploit her mythology as a kinky concoction to the bursting point. —*Michael Freedberg*

I Am a Photograph / 1977 / Chrysalis ✦✦✦✦
Lear, previously known as a Roxy Music album cover model and a protégé of Salvador Dali, appears here as a cabaret countess. She enunciates sexually naughty suggestions in a smoke-and-velvet rasp. Her best subversions hit a dancer's most salacious fantasies dead on. Most of these songs support their studied lewdness with absurdly different music, creating tangible friction (e.g., "Alligator"—funk bottom, frothy violins on top) that makes Lear's tape-loop voice feel even naughtier. All of Lear's tempos assault disco norms, either as sleaze or ultra-fast high-energy. An album not to be missed. —*Michael Freedberg*

Sweet Revenge / 1978 / Chrysalis ✦✦✦✦
Producer Anthony Monn parades every effect known to Euro-dream imagery in support of Lear as disco vamp: whispers from inside a tunnel, rhythms that filter in subliminally, themes that scale up to soprano range, choirs of angels singing, guitar rhythm rock-ons, and, of course, Lear's voice. Lear's singing is perhaps Monn's greatest effect: androgynous, sultry, out of reach and horny at the same time, Lear works hard to pretend at playing the merciless siren. She can't properly sing even one note, but what's that got to do with anything? —*Michael Freedberg*

● **Super 20** / 1989 / Ariola ✦✦✦✦

The Leaves

f. 1965, San Fernando Valley, CA, **db.** 1967
Folk-Rock, Garage Rock

One of the first L.A. folk-rock groups to spring up in the wake of the Byrds in the mid-'60s, the Leaves are most remembered for recording the first—and one of the most successful—rock versions of "Hey Joe," which reached the Top 40 (and was a huge Californian hit) in 1966. None of their other releases approached this success (although "Too Many People" was a local hit), but the group recorded a fair number of strong covers and original songs during their brief existence. More explicitly Stones and Beatles-influenced than the Byrds, they didn't project as strong an identity as competitors like the Byrds or Love, despite displaying considerable talent for harmony rockers in both the folk-rock and British Invasion styles. After cutting some singles and an album for the tiny Mira label, they moved to Capitol and disbanded after a disappointing follow-up (*All the Good That's Happening,* 1967) that offered less distinguished material and a more diluted sound. Leaves bassist Jim Pons went on to join the Turtles for a while in the late '60s. —*Richie Unterberger*

Hey Joe / 1966 / One Way ✦✦✦
This is one hell of a debut album, especially for a group that only lasted for about a year after its release. The Leaves perform some superb folk-rock in a Byrds/Beatles vein ("Just a Moment," "Girl From the East"), excellent lyrical garage punk ("Words," "Tobacco Road"), and solid hard rock ("Hey Joe," "Too Many People"), and cross swords with the Rolling Stones ("You Better Move On," "Back On the Avenue"—the latter a ripoff of the Stones' "2120 South Michigan Avenue") and Bob Dylan ("Love Minus Zero"). The sound isn't exactly consistent, given the gamut of influences at work here, from Bo Diddley ("Dr. Stone") to primitive psychedelia ("War of Distortion"), but there isn't a bad song on the disc, and the CD reissue has about the best sound ever heard on this material, bringing out the guitars in a genuinely crisp and vivid fashion. Maybe the strangest and best track in that regard is their cover of "He Was a Friend of Mine," which incorporates elements of both the Searchers' "When You Walk In the Room" and the Byrds' "I'll Feel a Whole Lot Better" into its structure and beat—the guitars are a real kick there. The bonus tracks may have come from vinyl sources rather than tape, but they hold up very well for sound quality. Anyone who enjoyed the first two Byrds albums must own this disc. —*Bruce Eder & Richie Unterberger*

All the Good That's Happening / 1967 / One Way ✦✦
An uneven album, and understandably so because the group was disintegrating at the time it was made. The band's folk-rock sound is still its strongest side, and they play hard on numbers like "Twilight Sanctuary" and "With None Shoes," and give good accounts of Donovan's "To Try For the Sun" and Buffy St. Marie's "Codine." They get into a good dance groove on a cover of Jimmy Reed's "Let's Get Together" and the band original "Officer Shayne" (spoiled by a silly chorus), and achieve a sweet, languid spaciness on "On the Plane." Much of the rest is weak, however, and the group's psychedelic efforts here, "The Quieting of Oliver Tweak" and "Lemmon Princess," are embarrassingly fey compared with the psychedelic numbers on their prior album. Only Bobby Arlin was left at the finish of the sessions, and he padded the album out with the guitar-dominated, almost totally instrumental blues-oid "Flashback." The sound on the One Way CD is good and crisp. —*Bruce Eder*

1966 / 1982 / Fan Club ✦✦✦✦
Somewhat hard to find these days, this well-chosen best-of compilation includes the best cuts from the *Hey Joe* album and a clutch of fine rare and unreleased tracks. Highlights among these are the raw, original 45 version of "Too Many People," and the Beatlesque B-side "Funny Little World," a Byrds-like folk-rock cover of Dylan's "Love Minus Zero," and "Be with You," a superb ripoff of the Byrds' "All I Really Want to Do." Liner notes by Leaves member Jim Pons top off a fine package. —*Richie Unterberger*

● **Leaves Are Happening!** / 2000 / Sundazed ✦✦✦✦
At last, a legitimate and well-distributed reissue of everything the Leaves released on Mira between 1965 and 1966: the entire *Hey Joe* album, all of the non-LP songs from their singles, the single version of "Too Many People," and *three* versions of "Hey Joe" (from the hit single and two previous 45s which used slightly different arrangements). This is not the complete work of the Leaves, as it doesn't include anything from their 1967 Capitol LP *All the Good That's Happening,* but this is no loss, as that album was pretty lousy. (Two covers of unspecified origin from the compilation *1966* are also missing.) Although the Leaves were erratic, at their best they were a fine band who drew from the Byrds' folk-rock, the Beatles' melodicism, and the hard rock of the Rolling Stones, as best heard on "Hey Joe" and the less celebrated "Too Many People," "Be With You," "Just a Memory," "Dr. Stone," "Funny Little World," and "Words." The reissue is enhanced by the detailed history in the accompanying 16-page booklet. —*Richie Unterberger*

Led Zeppelin

f. Jul. 1968, England, **db.** Dec. 1980, London, England
Album Rock, British Blues, British Metal, Arena Rock, Heavy Metal, Hard Rock, Blues-Rock
Led Zeppelin was the definitive heavy metal band. It wasn't just their crushingly loud blues-rock, it was how they built upon that foundation, incorporated mythology, mysticism, and a variety of other genres (most notably world music and British folk).

Zeppelin refused to release popular songs from their albums as singles, thereby helping album-oriented rock grow in popularity during the '70s. As important as their music was their mystique. Led Zeppelin never granted interviews, letting legends arise around the band. Zeppelin had power and mystery, retaining both qualities after their 1980 disbandment.

Led Zeppelin had phenomenal success from the outset, as their 1969 debut was a surprise Top 10 hit in the UK and US. *Led Zeppelin II* also reached number one, spending more time on the charts; musically, its brutal blend of Chess blues and Sun rock & roll became the template for heavy metal. On its third album, Zeppelin laced English folk into its hard rock and while it wasn't as popular as its predecessors, it pointed toward 1971's untitled fourth album. *IV* was their highwater mark, selling millions of copies and remaining a hard rock perennial thanks to "Stairway to Heaven," "Black Dog" and "Rock & Roll." After this record, Led Zeppelin were the biggest band in the world and, since they gave almost no interviews, all sorts of myths surrounded the band, particularly rumors of occultism—rumors they played up with their next album, 1973's *Houses of the Holy.* That album, along with its double-album sequel *Physical Graffiti* (1975) and 1976's *Presence* were also blockbusters. Zeppelin's pace slowed in the second half of the '70s, as they dealt with a number of personal problems. They returned in 1979 with *In Through the Out Door,* which was an immediate massive success. As the group prepared for a world tour, drummer John Bonham died in an alcohol-related accident. Instead of continuing, Led Zeppelin disbanded, releasing the rarities and outtakes collection *Coda* in 1982. Although they were gone, Zeppelin's popularity didn't wane, and they continued to earn new generations of listeners over the next two decades. *—Stephen Thomas Erlewine*

☆ **Led Zeppelin [I]** / Jan. 12, 1969 / Atlantic ✦✦✦✦✦

Led Zeppelin had a fully formed, distinctive sound from the outset, as their eponymous debut illustrates. Taking the heavy, distorted electric blues of Jimi Hendrix, Jeff Beck, and Cream to an extreme, Zeppelin created a majestic, powerful brand of guitar rock constructed around simple, memorable riffs and lumbering rhythms. But the key to the group's attack was subtlety: It wasn't just an onslaught of guitar noise, it was shaded and textured, filled with alternating dynamics and tempos. As *Led Zeppelin* proves, the group was capable of such multi-layered music from the start. Although the extended psychedelic blues of "Dazed and Confused," "You Shook Me," and "I Can't Quit You Baby" often gather the most attention, the remainder of the album is a better indication of what would come later. "Babe I'm Gonna Leave You" shifts from folky verses to pummeling choruses; "Good Times Bad Times" and "How Many More Times" have groovy, bluesy shuffles; "Your Time Is Gonna Come" is an anthemic hard rocker; "Black Mountain Side" is pure English folk; and "Communication Breakdown" is a frenzied rocker with a nearly punkish attack. Although the album isn't as varied as some of their later efforts, it nevertheless marked a significant turning point in the evolution of hard rock and heavy metal. *—Stephen Thomas Erlewine*

☆ **Led Zeppelin II** / Oct. 22, 1969 / Atlantic ✦✦✦✦✦

Recorded quickly during Led Zeppelin's first American tours, *Led Zeppelin II* provided the blueprint for all the heavy metal bands that followed it. Since the group could only enter the studio for brief amounts of time, most of the songs that compose *II* are reworked blues and rock & roll standards that the band were performing onstage at the time. Not only did the short amount of time result in a lack of original material, it made the sound more direct. Jimmy Page still provided layers of guitar overdubs, but the overall sound of the album is heavy and hard, brutal and direct. "Whole Lotta Love," "The Lemon Song," and "Bring It on Home" are all based on classic blues songs—only, the riffs are simpler and louder and each song has an extended section for instrumental solos. Of the remaining six songs, two sport light acoustic touches ("Thank You," "Ramble On"), but the other four are straight-ahead heavy rock that follow the formula of the revamped blues songs. While *Led Zeppelin II* doesn't have the eclecticism of the group's debut, it's arguably more influential. After all, nearly every one of the hundreds of Zeppelin imitators used this record, with its lack of dynamics and its pummeling riffs, as a blueprint. *—Stephen Thomas Erlewine*

☆ **Led Zeppelin III** / Oct. 5, 1970 / Atlantic ✦✦✦✦✦

On their first two albums, Led Zeppelin unleashed a relentless barrage of heavy blues and rockabilly riffs, but *Led Zeppelin III* provided the band with the necessary room to grow musically. While there are still a handful of metallic rockers, *III* is built on a folky, acoustic foundation which gives the music extra depth. And even the rockers aren't as straightforward as before: The galloping "Immigrant Song" is powered by Plant's banshee wail, "Celebration Day" turns blues-rock inside out with a warped slide guitar riff, and "Out on the Tiles" lumbers along with a tricky, multi-part riff. Nevertheless, the heart of the album lies on the second side, when the band delve deeply into English folk. "Gallows Pole" updates a traditional tune with a menacing flair, and "Bron-Y-Aur Stomp" is an infectious acoustic romp, while "That's the Way" and "Tangerine" are shimmering songs with graceful country flourishes. The band haven't left the blues behind, but the twisted bottleneck blues of "Hats Off To (Roy) Harper" actually outstrips the epic "Since I've Been Loving You," which is the only time Zeppelin sound a bit set in their ways. *—Stephen Thomas Erlewine*

★ **Led Zeppelin IV** / Nov. 8, 1971 / Atlantic ✦✦✦✦✦

Encompassing heavy metal, folk, pure rock & roll, and blues, Led Zeppelin's untitled fourth album is a monolithic record, defining not only Led Zeppelin but the sound and style of '70s hard rock. Expanding on the breakthroughs of *III,* Zeppelin fuse their majestic hard rock with a mystical, rural English folk that gives the record an epic scope. Even at its most basic—the muscular, traditionalist "Rock & Roll"—the album has a grand sense of drama, which is only deepened by Plant's burgeoning obsession with mythology, religion, and the occult. Plant's mysticism comes to a head on the eerie folk ballad "The Ballad of Evermore," a mandolin-driven song with haunting vocals from Sandy Denny, and on the epic "Stairway to Heaven." Of all of Zeppelin's songs, "Stairway to Heaven" is the most famous, and not unjustly. Building from a simple fingerpicked acoustic guitar to a storming torrent of guitar riffs and solos, it encapsulates the entire album in one song. Which, of course, isn't discounting the rest of the album. "Going to California" is the group's best folk song, and the rockers are endlessly inventive, whether it's the complex, multi-layered "Black Dog," the pounding hippie satire "Misty Mountain Hop," or the funky riffs of "Four Sticks." But the closer, "When the Levee Breaks," is the one song truly equal to "Stairway," helping give *IV* the feeling of an epic. An apocalyptic slice of urban blues, "When the Levee Breaks" is as forceful and frightening as Zeppelin ever got, and its seismic rhythms and layered dynamics illustrate why none of their imitators could ever equal them. *—Stephen Thomas Erlewine*

☆ **Houses of the Holy** / Mar. 28, 1973 / Atlantic ✦✦✦✦✦

Houses of the Holy follows the same basic pattern as *Led Zeppelin IV,* but the approach is looser and more relaxed. Jimmy Page's riffs rely on ringing, folky hooks as much as they do on thundering blues-rock, giving the album a lighter, more open atmosphere. While the pseudo-reggae of "D'Yer Mak'er" and the affectionate James Brown send-up "The Crunge" suggest that the band were searching for material, they actually contribute to the musical diversity of the album. "The Rain Song" is one of Zep's finest moments, featuring a soaring string arrangement and a gentle, aching melody. "The Ocean" is just as good, starting with a heavy, funky guitar groove before slamming into an a cappella section and ending with a swinging, doo-wop-flavored rave-up. With the exception of the rampaging opening number, "The Song Remains the Same," the rest of *Houses of the Holy* is fairly straightforward, ranging from the foreboding "No Quarter" and the strutting hard rock of "Dancing Days" to the epic folk/metal fusion "Over the Hills and Far Away." Throughout the record, the band's playing is excellent, making the eclecticism of Page and Plant's songwriting sound coherent and natural. *—Stephen Thomas Erlewine*

☆ **Physical Graffiti** / Feb. 24, 1975 / Swan Song ✦✦✦✦✦

Led Zeppelin returned from a nearly two-year hiatus in 1975 with *Physical Graffiti,* a sprawling, ambitious double album. Zeppelin treats many of the songs on *Physical Graffiti* as forays into individual styles, only occasionally synthesizing sounds, notably on the tense, Eastern-influenced "Kashmir." With John Paul Jones' galloping keyboard, "Trampled Underfoot" ranks as their funkiest metallic grind, while "Houses of the Holy" is as effervescent as pre-Beatles pop and "Down By the Seaside" is the closest they've come to country. Even the heavier blues—the 11-minute "In My Time of Dying," the tightly wound "Custard Pie," and the monstrous epic "The Rover"—are subtly shaded, even if they're thunderously loud. Most of these heavy rockers are isolated on the first album, with the second half of *Physical Graffiti* sounding a little like a scrap-heap of experiments, jams, acoustic workouts, and neo-covers. This may not be as consistent as the first platter, but its quirks are entirely welcome, not just because they encompass the mean, decadent "Sick Again," but the heartbreaking "Ten Years Gone" and the utterly charming acoustic rock & roll of "Boogie With Stu" and "Black Country Woman." Yes, some of this could be labeled as filler, but like any great double album, its appeal lies in its great sprawl, since it captures elements of the band's personality rarely showcased elsewhere—and even at its worst, *Physical Graffiti* towers above its hard rock peers of the mid-'70s. *—Stephen Thomas Erlewine*

The Song Remains the Same / 1976 / Swan Song ✦✦

Led Zeppelin's initial popularity was based as much on their concerts as their albums, so it's strange that the group's only official live album is such an uninspired, boring affair. Released in conjunction with the pseudo-documentary film of the same name, *The Song Remains the Same* reproduces the very things that made Zeppelin concerts legendary—lengthy solos, intertwining interplay between Page and Plant, and ridiculously long songs ("Dazed and Confused" is nearly an entire half hour)—but the group's performance is not intoxicating, it's long-winded. As scores of bootlegs prove, Led Zeppelin could produce magic with the same formula, but *The Song Remains the Same* is excrutiatingly dull. *—Stephen Thomas Erlewine*

Presence / 1976 / Swan Song ✦✦✦

Presence scales back the size of *Physical Graffiti* to a single album, but it retains the grandiose scope of that double record. If anything, *Presence* has more majestic epics than its predecessor, opening with the surging, ten-minute "Achilles Last Stand" and closing with the meandering, nearly ten-minute "Tea for One." In between, Zeppelin add the lumbering blues workout "Nobody's Fault but Mine" and the terse, menacing "For Your Life," which is the best song on the album. These four tracks take up the bulk of the album, leaving three lighthearted throwaways to alleviate the foreboding atmosphere—and pretensions—of the epics. If all of the throwaways were as focused and funny as those on *Physical Graffiti* or *Houses of the Holy,* Zeppelin would have had another classic on their hands. However, the Crescent City love letter of "Royal Orleans" sags in the middle, and the ersatz rockabilly of "Candy Store Rock" doesn't muster up the loose, funky swagger of "Hots on for Nowhere," which it *should* in order to work. The three throwaways are also scattered haphazardly throughout the album, making it seem more ponderous than it actually is, and the result is the weakest album Zeppelin had yet recorded. *—Stephen Thomas Erlewine*

In Through the Out Door / 1979 / Swan Song ✦✦✦

Somewhere between *Presence* and *In Through the Out Door,* disco, punk, and new wave had overtaken rock & roll, and Led Zeppelin chose to tentatively embrace these pop revolutions, adding synthesizers to the mix and emphasizing John Bonham's inherent way with a groove. The album's opening number, "In the Evening," with its stomping rhythms and heavy, staggered riffs, suggests that the band haven't deviated from their course, but by the time the rolling shuffle of "South Bound Suarez" kicks into gear, it's apparent that they've regained their sense of humor. After "South Bound Suarez," the group try a variety of styles, whether it's an overdriven homage to Bakersfield County called "Hot Dog," the layered, Latin-tinged percussion and pianos of "Fool in the Rain," or the slickly seductive ballad "All My Love." "Carouselambra," a lurching, self-consciously ambitious synth-driven number, and the slow blues "I'm Gonna Crawl" aren't quite as impressive as the rest of the album, but the record was a graceful way to close to their career, even if it wasn't intended as the final chapter. *—Stephen Thomas Erlewine*

Coda / 1982 / Swan Song ♦♦♦
An odds-and-sods collection assembled after John Bonham's death, *Coda* is predictably a hit-or-miss affair. The best material comes from later in their career, including the ringing folk stomp of "Poor Tom," the jacked-up '50s rock & roll of "Ozone Baby," and their response to punk rock, the savage "Wearing and Tearing." The rest of the album—sadly including the Bonham showcase "Bonzo's Montreux"—is average, despite the presence of some stellar playing, especially on the early blues-rock blitzkrieg "I Can't Quit You Baby" and "We're Gonna Groove." *—Stephen Thomas Erlewine*

Led Zeppelin [Box Set] / Sep. 1990 / Swan Song ♦♦♦
Led Zeppelin's primary method of artistic expression was their albums. Although they had a handful of hit singles and selected album tracks were played endlessly on the radio, the true range of their music is only evident on the original albums, which were carefully sequenced and assembled. Consequently, the notion of a Led Zeppelin anthology is a bit strange—their records worked as individual pieces. Nevertheless, the four-disc box set *Led Zeppelin* includes most of their best and most famous material. Jimmy Page determined the set's running order, taking the songs out of their familiar contexts and placing them in a new, occasionally jarring, sequence, providing new insights to the band's music that dedicated fans will appreciate. *Led Zeppelin* is the only album in their catalog to include the classic B-side "Hey Hey What Can I Do," as well as their unreleased version of Robert Johnson's "Travelling Riverside Blues" and a live medley of Page's "White Summer/Black Mountain Side." Most fans will find these three tracks essential, but will balk at the price, especially since all of Zeppelin's albums have been re-mastered since the original release of the box set. While the box contains a wealth of brilliant music, all of it is better heard in its original incarnation. *—Stephen Thomas Erlewine*

Led Zeppelin Remasters / Feb. 21, 1992 / Swan Song ♦♦♦
A collection of most of Zeppelin's best-known tracks, this double-disc set only gives a slight idea of what the band accomplished in its career; stick with the original albums instead. *—Stephen Thomas Erlewine*

Led Zeppelin [Box Set 2] / Mar. 19, 1993 / Swan Song ♦♦♦
Rounding up all of the studio tracks that didn't appear on the first box (as well as the pleasant, but unremarkable, "Baby Come on Home"), *Boxed Set 2* is the perfect way to complete a Led Zeppelin library begun with the first box set. *—Stephen Thomas Erlewine*

Complete Studio Recordings / Sep. 24, 1993 / Swan Song ♦♦♦
Collecting all of Led Zeppelin's groundbreaking studio albums (as well as a reworked *Coda*) in one unattractive box, *The Complete Studio Recordings* is only necessary for hardcore fans wishing to replace their old records. Although the artwork inside the package is lavish, the box features no new material or remastering, making it completely irrelevant for those who already own the first two box sets. The music here is brilliant, but it's available in better, more attractive, and less expensive packages. *—Stephen Thomas Erlewine*

BBC Sessions / Nov. 11, 1997 / Atlantic ♦♦♦♦♦
Led Zeppelin's BBC sessions were among the most popular bootleg items of the rock & roll era, appearing on a myriad of illegal records and CDs. They were all the more popular because of the lack of official Led Zeppelin live albums, especially since *The Song Remains the Same* failed to capture the essence of the band. For anyone that hadn't heard the recordings, the mystique of Zeppelin's BBC Sessions was somewhat mystifying, but the official 1997 release of the double-disc *BBC Sessions* offered revelations for any fan who hadn't yet heard this music. While some collectors will be dismayed by the slight trimming on the "Whole Lotta Love Medley," almost all of the group's sessions are included here, and they prove why live Zeppelin was the stuff of legend. The 1969 sessions, recorded shortly after the release of the first album, are fiery and dynamic, outstripping the studio record for sheer power. Early versions of "You Shook Me," "Communication Breakdown," "What Is & What Should Never Be" and "Whole Lotta Love" hit harder than their recorded counterparts, while covers of Sleepy John Estes' "The Girl I Love She Got Long Black Wavy Hair," Robert Johnson's "Travelling Riverside Blues" and Eddie Cochran's "Something Else" are welcome additions to the Zeppelin catalog, confirming their folk, blues and rockabilly roots as well as their sense of vision. Zeppelin's grand vision comes into sharper relief on the second disc, which is comprised of their 1971 sessions. They still have their primal energy, but they're more adventurous, branching out into folk, twisted psychedelia, and weird blues-funk. Certainly, *BBC Sessions* is the kind of album that will only appeal to fans, but anyone who's ever doubted Zeppelin's power or vision will be set straight with this record. *—Stephen Thomas Erlewine*

Early Days: The Best of Led Zeppelin, Vol. 1 / Nov. 23, 1999 / Atlantic ♦♦♦♦
As legend has it, Led Zeppelin never played the singles game. That's not entirely true—"Whole Lotta Love" was a gold-selling, Top Five single, while "Immigrant Song," "Black Dog," and "D'yer Mak'er" all went Top 20. But since their reputation was built in part through album-rock radio, and since they never released "Stairway to Heaven" as a single, the impression that they were above hits and singles grew and grew. Zeppelin fostered it by refusing to issue compilations for years, forcing every fan to become familiar with the group on an album-by-album basis. Things began to change a bit in 1990, when Jimmy Page assembled the four-disc *Led Zeppelin* box, the group's first official compilation; it eventually opened the door for the 1999 release of *Early Days: The Best of Led Zeppelin, Volume One. Early Days* focuses on the first four Zeppelin albums, taking four songs from the first, just two apiece from the second and third, and the entire first side of *IV*, along with "When the Levee Breaks." And for the diehards, a video clip of Zeppelin performing "Communication Breakdown" on an English TV show is thrown onto the enhanced CD portion of the disc. It's basically the album longtime Zeppelin fans thought would never be released: a straight-up greatest-hits album. At one point, this may have been seen as sacrilege among devotees, but at this point, it's hard to imagine who would care about *Early Days* one way or another. Apart from the handful of casual fans who just want the radio staples on one disc—while not caring that other classics are absent—there really is no audience for this, since it doesn't recontextualize the catalog like the box sets. It's still pretty entertaining, yet *Early Days* feels unnecessary. Yet that cover photo is priceless. *—Stephen Thomas Erlewine*

Latter Days: The Best of Led Zeppelin, Vol. 2 / Mar. 21, 2000 / Atlantic ♦♦♦♦
Latter Days—The Best of Led Zeppelin, Vol. 2 offers ten highlights from *Houses of the Holy, Physical Graffiti, Presence,* and *In Through the Out Door.* While all fans can argue about missing album tracks—some may choose "The Rover" and "Over the Hills and Far Away" for should-have-beens, while others take "Custard Pie," "For Your Life" and "Hots on for Nowhere"—the only true staples missing are "Dancing Days" and the exquisite faux-Brazilian "Fool in the Rain." Thus, this is a pretty fine compilation for the casual fan, the kind who only wants the songs they hear on the radio all the time (such as "The Song Remains the Same," "No Quarter," "Trampled Underfoot," "Kashmir," "In the Evening"). Of course, any true Zeppelin enthusiast will want the full albums, but as a sampler of their last four records, *Latter Days* is just fine. *—Stephen Thomas Erlewine*

Laura Lee

b. Mar. 9, 1945, Detroit, MI
Vocals / Southern Soul, Soul
A tough '60s soul singer with a salty sense of humor (aimed mostly at the men in her life), Laura Lee recorded at Rick Hall's FAME studio in Muscle Shoals for the Chess label, and later for Hot Wax. In songs like "Wanted: Lover, No Experience Necessary," "A Man with Some Backbone," and the anthemic "Women's Love Rights," the female experience was brazenly discussed, debated, kicked around, and, finally, celebrated. Her music laid the groundwork for artists like Millie Jackson and Denise LaSalle to expand this proud, sexy, brash-talking corner of "women's" soul music. Lee had a country/soul, romantic side as well, as shown on her splended version of the Penn-Oldham classsic "Uptight Good Man." Lee is a fine, versatile, saucy singer whose work deserves more attention. *—Christine Ohlman*

That's How It Is: Chess Years / 1990 / Chess ♦♦♦♦♦
Laura Lee Rundless broke with her gospel roots in 1966 to wax a string of gritty, tough-talking country soul gems for Chess. Her recordings are very prized, and the best of them are included here. Songs like "Dirty Man," "Wanted: Lover, No Experience Necessary," "Uptight, Good Man" (written by Dan Penn and Spooner Oldham, not "Writer Unknown" as listed in the liner notes), and the beautiful, stately "Love More than Pride" celebrate, with a tell-it-like-it-is attitude, the joy and pain of the female experience in love. During the early '70s, Laura Lee continued to make records in the same vein at Hot Wax, but these earlier Chess sides are more satisfying. Soul music doesn't get any deeper or truer than this. *—Christine Ohlman, Roundup Newsletter*

● **Greatest Hits** / Jul. 1, 1991 / Fantasy ♦♦♦♦♦
Like the music of Honey Cone, Freda Payne, 100 Proof (Aged in Soul) and the Chairmen of the Board, Laura Lee's *Greatest Hits* underscores the fact that the demise of Holland/Dozier/Holland's Hot Wax label in 1974 wasn't due to a lack of strong material. Essentially, distribution problems killed the company, where former gospel singer turned brassy soul shouter Lee recorded some of her best work. The big-voiced Lee was best known for humorous yet biting songs encouraging women to demand respectful treatment in relationships—a theme that makes for powerful listening on such classics as "Wedlock Is a Padlock," "Crumbs Off the Table" and her best-known hits "Rip Off" and "Women's Love Rights." Lee's Hot Wax output has all of the trademarks of a Holland/Dozier/Holland project—tough, gospel-influenced belting is combined with a sleek production style. In fact, Lee's heartfelt singing is no less gritty than Carla Thomas' work at Stax; the main difference lies in the approach to production. But as talented as she was, Lee faded into obscurity after Hot Wax's demise. *—Alex Henderson*

The Left Banke

f. 1965, New York, NY, **db.** 1969
Sunshine Pop, Psychedelic Pop, Baroque Pop, Pop
This New York group pioneered "Baroque'n'Roll" in the '60s with their mix of pop/rock and grand, quasi-classical arrangements and melodies. Featuring teenage prodigy Michael Brown as keyboardist and chief songwriter, the group scored two quick hits with "Walk Away Renee" and "Pretty Ballerina." Chamber-like string arrangements, Steve Martin's soaring, near-falsetto lead vocals, and tight harmonies that borrowed from British Invasion bands like the Beatles and the Zombies were also key elements of the Left Banke sound. Unfortunately the group, which early on showed tremendous promise, was quickly torn asunder by dissension. Due to the nature of their music (which often employed session musicians), the Left Banke's sound was difficult to reproduce on the road, and one could sympathize with Brown's wishes to become a Brian Wilson-like figure, concentrating on writing and recording while the rest of the musicians took to the road. Most of the group's second and final album, *The Left Banke Too*, was recorded without Brown, who left in late 1967. While it still sported baroque arrangements and contained some fine moments, Brown's presence was sorely missed, and the record pales in comparison to their debut. Brown went on to form a Left Banke-styled group, Montage, which released a fine and underappreciated album in the late '60s. The original group, minus its key visionary Michael Brown, made an album's worth of ill-advised reunion recordings in 1978. *—Richie Unterberger*

● **There's Gonna Be a Storm: The Complete Recordings 1966-69** / 1992 / Mercury ♦♦♦♦♦
Though it's missing a few rarities—namely the Steve Martin single for Buddha that

reunited him with Michael Brown—this is the most definitive Left Banke compilation. It features the entirety of their two late-'60s albums, as well as a couple of singles that didn't make it onto LPs at the time (though they later appeared on Rhino's *History*) and a previously unissued cut, "Men Are Building Sand." Their debut 1967 LP, *Walk Away Renee/Pretty Ballerina*, is an underrated classic of the time, matching smart harmonies and pop hooks to baroque orchestration. Its brilliance casts a bit of a shadow over the rest of this collection. The group's 1968 album *Too* suffered from bloated production and, more importantly, the absence of chief songwriter/arranger Michael Brown. In turn, the 1967 single Brown cut under the Left Banke moniker with singer Bert Sommer suffers from the absence of lead vocalist Steve Martin. By the time Brown and Martin tenuously reunited for a late-1969 single, some of the spark had gone. All of the aforementioned highs and lows of this prodigiously talented but strife-ridden group are on this disc. *—Richie Unterberger*

The Lemon Pipers

f. 1967, Cincinnati, OH, **db.** 1969

Psychedelic Pop, Bubblegum, Psychedelic

The Lemon Pipers included singer Ivan Browne, guitarist William Bartlett, keyboardist R.G. Nave, bassist Steve Walmsley, and drummer William Albaugh. The group is best known for their number-one bubblegum hit "Green Tambourine" and several followups, all written by the team of Paul Leka and Shelley Pinz. The group actually wanted to play more psychedelic music; they only recorded "Green Tambourine" because their label would have dropped them had they refused. They eventually got the artistic control they wanted and ended up dropping off the charts for good with their first self-produced album. They broke up in 1969, with Bartlett joining Ram Jam. *—Steve Huey*

● **The Best of the Lemon Pipers: Green Tambourine** / Apr. 3, 2001 / Buddha ♦♦♦

This compilation is the first thorough domestic U.S. release gathering tracks from both out-of-print Lemon Pipers albums. Although known primarily for their international, ersatz, hippy bubblegum pop anthem "Green Tambourine," the quintet's formidable musical chops and material are displayed at the center of *The Best of the Lemon Pipers: Green Tambourine*. During their brief existence, the Lemon Pipers had two additional charting hits—"Rice Is Nice" and "Jelly Jungle (Of Orange Marmalade)"—for music mogul Neil Bogart's Kama Sutra label. Bogart was already hosting a number of successful bubblegum bands such as Ohio Express and 1910 Fruitgum Company. His hugely thriving production team featuring Jerry Kasenetz and Jeff Katz scouted Ivan and the Sabers—a local Oxford, OH, band. The band were self-contained instrumentally, but Bogart and company supplied the tunes. The team of producer/composer Paul Leka and lyricist Shelley Pinz provided the Lemon Pipers with a great deal of their material. When left to their own devices, the band ironically had very little in common with the sounds on the chart-topping "Green Tambourine." On the whole, the band falls somewhere between the over-the-top pseudo-psychedelia of the Strawberry Alarm Clock and the garage pop of the Blues Magoos. There are a few gems on *The Best of the Lemon Pipers: Green Tambourine*. The trippy "Catch Me Falling" takes on dimensions of Quicksilver Messenger Service, Buffalo Springfield, and the innovative fretwork of a Jorma Kaukonen-propelled Jefferson Airplane. "Dead End Street/Half Life"—the 11-minute epic that rounds out this compilation—recalls the indulgence of "In a Gadda Da Vida." However, variations in instrumentation as well as tempo are actually more akin to the Grateful Dead's "Cryptical Envelopment" suite. The sound on *The Best of the Lemon Pipers: Green Tambourine* is brilliant, leaving previous compilations and the European CD pressings sounding thin in comparison. *—Lindsay Planer*

The Lemonheads

f. 1984, Boston, MA

College Rock, Punk-Pop, Adult Alternative Pop/Rock, Hardcore Punk, Alternative Pop/Rock, American Underground

The Lemonheads' evolution from post-Hüsker Dü hardcore punk rockers to teenage heart-throbs is one of the strangest sagas in alternative music. Initially, the group was a punk-pop trio formed by three teenage Boston suburbanites, but over the years, the band became a vehicle for Evan Dando. Blessed with good looks and a warm, sweet voice, Dando became a teen-idol in the early '90s, when Nirvana's success made alternative bands commercially viable. While his simple, catchy songs were instantly accessible, they tended to hide the more subversive nature of his lyrics, as well as his gift for offbeat covers and devotion to country-rock father Gram Parsons. After developing his signature blend of pop, punk and country-rock on several independent records in the late '80s, Dando moved the Lemonheads to Atlantic Records in 1990. Two years later, *It's A Shame About Ray* made the group into media sensations, as Dando's face appeared on music and teen magazines across America and Britain. Though the Lemonheads were poised to become superstars, the band never quite found the right breakthrough single, and their popularity peaked in the early '90s. Around the same time, Dando descended into severe drug abuse that he curbed by the 1996 release of *Car Button Cloth*. However, he had missed his chance at stardom—though the group retained their cult, much of their audience had already slipped away. *—Stephen Thomas Erlewine*

Hate Your Friends / 1987 / Taang! ♦♦

The Lemonheads' debut album is a bit unfocused, spending most of its time thrashing around in post-Hüsker Dü hardcore punk, but its best moments ("Second Chance," "Fed Up") show that Evan Dando has a natural knack for pop hooks. *—Stephen Thomas Erlewine*

Creator / 1988 / Taang! ♦♦

Demonstrating an increased sense of pop, not only in their songwriting but also in their relatively measured performances, the Lemonheads turn in a winning second album with *Creator*. Although they still spend a little too much time mucking around with sub-hardcore noise, Evan Dando's gentler pop numbers are quite appealing, even when he treads a little too closely to dippy hippie cliches, and they certainly point the way to the engaging punk-pop of *Lick*. *—Stephen Thomas Erlewine*

Lick / 1989 / Taang! ♦♦♦♦

Although it's fairly incoherent, bouncing back and forth between punk-pop and folky pop, *Lick* is a thoroughly engaging record. The tensions between Evan Dando and Ben Deily are fairly evident throughout the album, especially since Dando's songs, with their immediate hooks and melodies, outshine his bandmates, but that unevenness makes the record endearingly messy. Also, the mess makes the group's best songs, including an inspired electric cover of Suzanne Vega's "Luka," shine all the more brightly. *—Stephen Thomas Erlewine*

Create Your Friends / 1989 / Taang! ♦♦♦

Create Your Friends combines the Lemonheads' first two albums for Taang!, *Hate Your Friends* and *Creator*, on one compact disc. While this material is fairly inconsistent, the hardcore numbers are enjoyable Hüsker Dü and Replacements ripoffs, and several of the songs illustrate Evan Dando's talent for simple pop hooks. *—Stephen Thomas Erlewine*

Lovey / 1990 / Atlantic ♦♦♦

Moving to a major label didn't affect the Lemonheads' sound as much as the departure of Ben Deily; without him, Evan Dando was free to let his sensitive side run wild, which is exactly what he does on *Lovey*. Dando never completely abandons punk-pop on *Lovey*, but he does balance it with excursions into jangle-pop and country-rock, many of which contain his best songwriting to date. By now, he has begun to develop a signature voice, a distinctly suburban and middle-class voice that embraces the mundane details of everyday life. That gives songs like "Stove" and "Lil' Seed" an off-kilter sensibility, which is made all the more appealing by his gift for simple hooks. Even though Dando has made significant strides forward, the most affecting moment on the record remains his stark and very pretty cover of Gram Parsons' "Brass Buttons." *—Stephen Thomas Erlewine*

● **It's a Shame About Ray** / Jun. 2, 1992 / Atlantic ♦♦♦♦♦

If *Lovey* captured Evan Dando as he found his signature blend of punk-pop, jangle-pop and folk-rock, *It's a Shame About Ray* is where he perfected that style. Breezing by in under half an hour, the album is a simple collection of sunny melodies and hooks, delivered with typical nonchalance by Dando. None of the songs are about anything major, nor do they have astonishingly original melodies, but that's part of their charm—they're immediately accessible and thoroughly catchy. Dando's laid-back observations of middle-class outcasts are minor gems. The heartbroken title track or "Confetti," the crushes of "Bit Part in Your Life," the love letter to substances "My Drug Buddy" or the wonderful "Alison's Starting to Happen," where a girl finds herself as she discovers punk rock, capture the laconic rhythms of suburbia, and his warm, friendly voice, which is offset by Juliana Hatfield's girlish harmonies, gives the songs an emotional resonance. [*It's a Shame About Ray* was later re-released with a competent punk-pop remake of Simon & Garfunkel's "Mrs. Robinson" added as a bonus track. As Dando approached stardom, the album was re-pressed again with the title of "My Drug Buddy" truncated to "Buddy." It was later restored to its original title.] *—Stephen Thomas Erlewine*

Come on Feel the Lemonheads / Oct. 12, 1993 / Atlantic ♦♦♦♦

Come on Feel the Lemonheads should have been the album that propelled the trio and Evan Dando to stardom, but instead of delivering a concise pop record in the vein of *It's a Shame About Ray*, they made a messy album that never quite found its focus. That's not to say that *Come On Feel* is without merit, because that's hardly the case. In many ways, it's the most interesting record that the Lemonheads have released, because it finds Dando confused about everything, particularly love, both for girls and drugs, and his burgeoning fame. There are moments of self-indulgence, whether it's the aimless piano instrumental "The Jello Fund" or two versions of the drug-obsessed "Style," yet they are as essential to the album's desperate tone as the heartbreaking acoustic ballad of "Favorite T." Between those two extremes are some of the finest power-pop and country-rock Dando has ever written. He still has a tendency to be too cutesy, as on the otherwise winning country-rock of "Being Around" and "Big Gay Heart," but the hooky rush of "The Great Big No," the bright "I'll Do It Anyway" and the lovely simplicity of "Into Your Arms" are irresistible. *Come On Feel* may not be as consistent or immediate as *It's a Shame About Ray*, but finding its pleasures is quite rewarding. *—Stephen Thomas Erlewine*

Car Button Cloth / Oct. 15, 1996 / Atlantic ♦♦♦

If *Come on Feel the Lemonheads* was a bit confused, *Car Button Cloth* is positively a mess, filled with perfect pop, stoned rock and rambling country-rock, which is alternately ingratiating and infuriating. Evan Dando may have (relatively) sobered up between the two records, but the sound of *Car Button Cloth* is even wearier than before—his voice is beginning to show signs of abuse, while the tempos often sag and lurch, occasionally becoming burdened with lead guitars that steal directly from J. Mascis. The turgid grunge that wears at the fringes of the record actually makes the gems all the more endearing. "If I Could Talk I'd Tell You" is one of Dando's finest three-chord sing-a-longs; the self-deprecating "The Outdoor Type" is excellent country-rock; the stop-start verses of "It's All True" are fleshed out by Dando's weary croak and the grunge interpretation of "Knoxville Girl" is actually very affecting. However, only dedicated fans will be willing to sort through the hubris to actually find these songs, which is unfortunate, because at its best, *Car Button Cloth* is as good as anything Dando has yet recorded. *—Stephen Thomas Erlewine*

The Best of the Lemonheads: The Atlantic Years / Jul. 14, 1998 / Atlantic ♦♦♦♦

Evan Dando—for all intents and purposes, he *is* the Lemonheads—is a sporadically brilliant songwriter. Every one of his albums contains as many flops as masterpieces, sometimes more. Hardcore fans have learned to live with this and even cherish his dopey detours, but there are many others who would prefer to have all the best bits on one disc. Which means, of course, that *The Best of the Lemonheads: The Atlantic Years* offered the perfect opportunity to achieve that goal. Unfortunately, it was bungled, at least in America (it was released in Europe and Japan with more tracks). With the exception of "Mrs. Robinson" (never a favorite of hardcore fans, but included for those nostalgic Gen-Xers), it's hard to argue with what's here, but it feels criminally brief at 12 tracks, especially since the songs are rarely over three minutes long. It's entertaining, to be sure, and it makes a convincing argument that Dando is a clever pop craftsman, but it leaves you wanting more—which isn't really what best-of albums should do. *—Stephen Thomas Erlewine*

LEN

f. 1991
Alternative Dance, Hip-Hop
The alternative pop/dance group LEN was formed in Toronto in 1991 by Marc "The Burger Pimp" Costanzo and his sister Sharon, initially to perform punk-pop-style music. However, an outside interest in hip-hop gradually crept into the group's style over the course of the EP and two full-length independent albums they issued from 1992-96 (including 1996's *Get Your Legs Broke*). As time passed, LEN picked up new members, including D Rock, DJ Moves, and Planet Pea. National exposure of the bright, laid-back pop single "Steal My Sunshine" on the soundtrack of the 1999 film *Go* set the stage for LEN's debut album, *You Can't Stop the Bum Rush*, later that year. *—Steve Huey*

● **You Can't Stop the Bum Rush** / May 25, 1999 / Work ✦✦✦✦
The debut by the Canadian four-piece LEN is a set of old-school tracks indebted to Sugar Hill Records and Afrika Bambaataa as well as more recent indie-rap agitators like the Beastie Boys. While the rapping is a bit stilted, the production is excellent and best heard on the first track, the monster hit "Steal My Sunshine," a bright slice of indie-pop with an old-school guitar loop and a suitably bumping bassline. For all of the great tracks here, it's difficult to escape the feeling that *You Can't Stop the Bum Rush* is a low-rent version of the Beastie Boys' 1998 album *Hello Nasty*—Biz Markie makes a few appearances as he did with the Beasties, and master turntablist Mr. Dibbs takes the role of Mix Master Mike with major contributions to one (very short) track. Still, the album's few derivative qualities never really get in the way of an enjoyable listen. *—John Bush*

John Lennon

b. Oct. 9, 1940, Liverpool, England, **d.** Dec. 8, 1980, New York, NY
Vocals, Keyboards, Guitar / Album Rock, Pop/Rock, Singer/Songwriter, Rock & Roll
Out of all the Beatles, John Lennon had the most interesting—and frustrating—solo career. Lennon was capable of inspired, brutally honest confessional songwriting and melodic songcraft; he also had a tendency to rest on his laurels, churning out straight-ahead rock & roll without much care. But the extremes, both in his music and his life, were what made him fascinating. Where Paul McCartney was content to be a rock star, Lennon dabbled in everything from revolutionary politics to the television talk-show circuit during the early '70s. After releasing a pair of acclaimed albums, *John Lennon/Plastic Ono Band* and *Imagine*, in the early '70s, Lennon sunk into an infamous "lost weekend" where his musical output was decidedly uneven and his public behavior was often embarassing. Halfway through the decade, he sobered up and retired from performing to become a house-husband and father. In 1980, he launched a comeback with his wife Yoko Ono, releasing the duet album *Double Fantasy* that fall. Just as his career was on an upswing, Lennon was tragically assassinated outside of his New York apartment building in December of 1980. He left behind an enormous legacy, not only as a musician, but as a writer, actor and activist. *—Stephen Thomas Erlewine*

Unfinished Music, No. 1: Two Virgins / Nov. 11, 1968 / Rykodisc ✦✦

Life with the Lions: Unfinished Music #2 / May 26, 1969 / Rykodisc ✦✦

Wedding Album / Oct. 20, 1969 / Rykodisc ✦✦

Live Peace in Toronto, 1969 / Dec. 12, 1969 / Capitol ✦✦✦
Although one of the world's best-kept secrets at the time, this was John Lennon's declaration of independence from the Beatles, the document of a concert appearance at Toronto's Rock & Roll Revival festival about a month after the conclusion of the Abbey Road sessions. Thrown together literally on the wing (they rehearsed only on the flight from England), the ad-hoc band consisting of Lennon, Yoko Ono, Eric Clapton on guitar, Klaus Voorman on bass and Alan White on drums hit the stage to the surprise and delight of the thousands who packed Varsity Stadium. "We're just going to do numbers we know, you know, because we've never played together before," confesses John, who was reportedly extremely nervous before going on. But the repertoire ought to have been a cakewalk for a quartet of seasoned rockers—blues-based oldies ("Blue Suede Shoes," "Money," "Dizzy Miss Lizzie") and basic recent Lennon numbers ("Yer Blues," "Cold Turkey," "Give Peace A Chance")—and they lay it down in a dignified, noisy, glorified garage band manner. Lennon is in fine vocal form, confident and funny despite his frequent apologias, while Yoko confines her caterwauling to "Cold Turkey." That was side one of the original LP. Side two, alas, was devoted entirely to Ono's wailing, pitchless, brainless, banshee vocalizing on "Don't Worry Kyoko" and "John John (Let's Hope For Peace)"—the former backed with plodding rock rhythms and the latter with feedback. No wonder you see many used copies of the LP with worn A-sides and clean, unplayed B-sides—and Yoko's "art" is just as irritating today as it was in 1969. But in those days, if you wanted John, you had to take the whole package. *—Richard S. Ginell*

☆ **John Lennon/Plastic Ono Band** / Dec. 11, 1970 / Capitol ✦✦✦✦✦
The cliché about singer-songwriters is that they sing confessionals direct from their heart, but John Lennon exploded the myth behind that cliché, as well as many others, on his first official solo record, *John Lennon/Plastic Ono Band*. Inspired by his primal scream therapy with Dr. Walter Janov, Lennon created a harrowing set of unflinchingly personal songs, laying out all of his fears and angers for everyone to hear. It was a revolutionary record—never before had a record been so explicitly introspective, and very few records made absolutely no concession to the audience's expectations, daring the listeners to meet all the artist's demands. Which isn't to say that the record is unlistenable. Lennon's songs range from tough rock & rollers to piano-based ballads and spare folk songs, and his melodies remain strong and memorable, which actually intensifies the pain and rage of the songs. Not much about *Plastic Ono Band* is hidden. Lennon presents everything on the surface, and the song titles—"Mother," "I Found Out," "Working Class Hero," "Isolation," "God," "My Mummy's Dead"—illustrate what each song is about, and charts his loss of faith in his parents, country, friends, fans and idols. It's an unflinching document of bare-bones despair and pain, but for all its nihlism, it is ultimately life-affiriming; it is unique not only in Lennon's catalog, but in all of popular music. Few albums are ever as harrowing, difficult, and rewarding as *John Lennon/Plastic Ono Band. —Stephen Thomas Erlewine*

☆ **Imagine** / Sep. 9, 1971 / Capitol ✦✦✦✦✦
After the harrowing *Plastic Ono Band*, Lennon returned to calmer, more conventional territory with *Imagine*. While the album had a softer surface, it was only marginally less confessional than its predecessor. Underneath the sweet strings of "Jealous Guy" lies a broken and scared man, the jaunty "Crippled Inside" is a mocking assault at an acquaintance, and "Imagine" is a paean for peace in a world with no Gods, possessions or classes, where everyone is equal. And Lennon doesn't shy away from the hard rockers—"How Do You Sleep" is a scathing attack on Paul McCartney, "I Don't Want to Be a Soldier" is a hypnotic anti-war song, and "Give Me Some Truth" is bitter hard rock. If *Imagine* doesn't have the thematic sweep of *Plastic Ono Band*, it is nevertheless a remarkable collection of songs that Lennon would never be able to better again. *—Stephen Thomas Erlewine*

Sometime in New York City/Live Jam / Jun. 12, 1972 / Capitol ✦✦
The first album co-billed to John Lennon and Yoko Ono to actually contain recognizable pop music, *Sometime in New York City* found the Lennons in an explicitly political phase, expounding on such topical subjects as the Attica prison riot and the treatment of activists John Sinclair and Angela Davis. Especially in the case of Lennon's songs, there is an appealing rock style to the material, even if the lyrics limit the record's appeal. *Sometime in New York City* was originally released with a free bonus disc that contained a live medley of Lennon's "Cold Turkey" and Ono's "Don't Worry Kyoko," and an appearance by the Lennons at a Mothers of Invention concert. This slight material now makes the album a two-CD set, and it is priced accordingly. *—William Ruhlmann*

Mind Games / Nov. 2, 1973 / Capitol ✦✦✦✦
After the hostile reaction to the politically charged *Sometime in New York City*, John Lennon moved away from explicit protest songs and returned to introspective songwriting with *Mind Games*. Lennon didn't leave politics behind—he just tempered his opinions with humor on songs like "Bring on the Lucie (Freda People)," which happened to undercut the intention of the song. It also indicated the confusion that lays at the heart of the album. Lennon doesn't know which way to go, so he tries everything. There are lovely ballads like "Out of the Blue" and "One Day (At A Time)," forced ham-fisted rockers like "Meat City" and "Tight As," sweeping Spectoresque pop on "Mind Games" and many midtempo, indistinguishable pop-rockers. While the best numbers are among Lennon's finest, there's only a handful of them, and the remainder of the record is simply pleasant. But compared to *Sometime in New York City*, as well as the subsequent *Walls and Bridges*, *Mind Games* sounded like a return to form. *—Stephen Thomas Erlewine*

Walls and Bridges / Sep. 26, 1974 / Capitol ✦✦✦
Walls and Bridges was recorded during John Lennon's infamous "lost weekend," as he exiled himself in California during a separation from Yoko Ono. Lennon's personal life was scattered, so it isn't surprising that *Walls and Bridges* is a mess itself, containing equal amounts of brilliance and nonsense. Falling between the two extremes was the bouncy Elton John duet "Whatever Gets You Thru the Night," which was Lennon's first solo number one hit. Its bright, sunny surface was replicated throughout the record, particularly on middling rockers like "What You Got" but also on enjoyable pop songs like "Old Dirt Road." However, the best moments on *Walls and Bridges* come when Lennon is more open with his emotions, like on "Going Down on Love," "Steel and Glass" and the beautiful, soaring "#9 Dream." Even with such fine moments, the album is decidedly uneven, containing too much mediocre material like "Beef Jerky" and "Ya Ya," which are weighed down by weak melodies and heavy overproduction. It wasn't a particularly graceful way to enter retirement. *—Stephen Thomas Erlewine*

Rock & Roll / Feb. 17, 1975 / Capitol ✦✦✦
It was a common practice in the early 1970s for artists to satisfy record companies' demands for frequent album releases by recording albums of cover songs (see the Band's *Moondog Matinee* and David Bowie's *Pinups* for other examples). The story of John Lennon's covers album is a little more complicated, but the result is the same, with the artist tackling songs from the '50s by many of his favorites, from Gene Vincent to Lloyd Price. Of course, these are the kinds of songs that turned up on early Beatles albums, and while Lennon doesn't reinvent them as strikingly as his old group did, he gives them an affectionate, knowing treatment. *—William Ruhlmann*

Shaved Fish / Oct. 24, 1975 / Capitol ✦✦✦✦
At the time of its release, *Shaved Fish* didn't attract as much attention as any compilation of John Lennon's work would have either a few years before or a few years after. Lennon had just issued the somewhat disappointing genre album, *Rock & Roll*, and was only a year from *Walls and Bridges*, not one of his strongest albums, and had also grown

somewhat stale as a public figure. Drawing on his singles up to that point in his career, it shows a punkier, more defiant vision of Lennon's work than subsequent compilations, which would dwell on a broader cross section of his output. "Happy Christmas" and "Imagine" are moments of peace in the company of artifacts from his political/agitprop ("Power to the People") and primal scream ("Mother") periods, and his attempts at topical songwriting ("Woman Is the Nigger of the World"), and "Whatever Gets You Through the Night," which was unique to this LP, was a better piece of mainstream rock & roll than any of the late-'50s numbers that he ground out for *Rock & Roll*. This collection, which was the last LP release to come from Lennon in any form until *Double Fantasy* five years later, was the only compilation of his work released in Lennon's own lifetime, and has since been supplanted by various posthumous assemblies of his music. *—Bruce Eder*

Double Fantasy / Nov. 17, 1980 / Capitol ✦✦✦✦
The most distinctive thing about *Double Fantasy*, the last album John Lennon released during his lifetime, is the very thing that keeps it from being a graceful return to form from the singer/songwriter, returning to active duty after five years of self-imposed exile. As legend has it, Lennon spent those years in domestic bliss, being a husband, raising a baby, and, of course, baking bread. *Double Fantasy* was designed as a window into that bliss and, to that extent, he decided to make it a joint album with Yoko Ono, to illustrate how complete there union was. For her part, Ono decided to take a stab at pop and while these are relatively tuneful for her, they nevertheless disrupt the feel and flow of Lennon's material, which has a consistent tone and theme. He's surprisingly sentimental, not just when he's expressing love for his wife ("Dear Yoko," "Woman") and child ("Beautiful Boy [Darling Boy]"), but when he's coming to terms with his quiet years ("Watching the Years," "Cleanup Time") and his return to creative life. These are really nice tunes, and what's special about them is their niceness—it's a sweet acceptance of middle age, which, of course, makes his assassination all the sadder. For that alone, *Double Fantasy* is noteworthy, yet it's hard not to think that it's a bit of a missed opportunity—primarily because its themes would be stronger without the Ono songs, but also because the production is just a little bit too slick and constrained, sounding very much of its time. Ultimately, these complaints fall by the wayside because Lennon's best songs here cement the last part of his legend, capturing him at peace and in love. According to some reports, that perception was a bit of a fantasy, but sometimes the fantasy means more than the reality, and that's certainly the case here. *—Stephen Thomas Erlewine*

● **The John Lennon Collection** / Nov. 10, 1982 / Capitol ✦✦✦✦✦
This 15-song collection (expanded to 19 in 1989 for the CD), released just short of two years after Lennon's death, provided a very generous overview of his solo career on a single LP, drawing on most of the major singles and also on songs that were widely covered, and from all periods of his career, from his late-Beatles-era solo political explorations up to the release of *Double Fantasy*. The producers, obviously working in collaboration with his widow and seeking to put the very best face on his career, and showcase his strongest and most memorable songs, pass right over *Sometime in New York* and much of the partly successful works that followed, which is sort of a shame—"Woman Is the Nigger of the World" may not quite rate alongside the stuff that is here, but it was a song that he did care about and played live more than once (significant in a career that included barely any scheduled concerts), and "John Sinclair" showed him playing blues with a ferocious passion. One also misses "Cold Turkey," which is as powerful a song as he wrote in his early solo career, but at the time of its release this was the broadest overview of Lennon's career to be found, and even included (on its CD version) the otherwise unanthologized B-side "Move Over Ms. L." *—Bruce Eder*

Milk & Honey / Jan. 27, 1984 / Polydor ✦✦✦
The sessions for 1980's *Double Fantasy* were supposed to yield two albums, the second to be released at a future time, but Lennon's assassination tragically halted the project in its tracks. A bit over three years later, Yoko Ono issued tapes of many of the songs planned for that album under the title *Milk And Honey*, laid out in the same John-Yoko-John-Yoko dialogue fashion as its predecessor. Not unexpectedly, it's a rougher, less polished product, lacking the finishing touches and additional takes that Lennon most likely would have called for. Nevertheless, Lennon's songs at this point in their development were often quite strong, tougher than those on *Double Fantasy* in general, and the ad libs and studio chatter that might not have made the final cut give us more of a glimpse of Lennon's delightfully quirky personality. "Nobody Told Me," the advance single off the album, is a rollicking, quizzical piece of work, maybe the best thing to come out of John's 1980 sessions despite the unfinished-sounding transition to the chorus. "Borrowed Time," another single, is a thoughtful, sparely-worded meditation on growing older attached to a Caribbean beat. Yoko's contributions, while not as strong as John's, are surprisingly listenable—the reggae-based "Don't Be Scared," in particular—and more current in texture, and her lyrics do tend to answer John's songs. As the album comes toward the close, the tone turns sentimental, culminating with one of John's loveliest tunes, "Grow Old With Me," as presented on a home-recorded cassette in lieu of a studio recording. The ironies of this song and some of the other Lennon material are obviously poignant in the light of the cruel events of Dec. 8, 1980; that and the fact that these songs haven't been as exposed as much as those on *Double Fantasy* lead some to prefer this sequel. *—Richard S. Ginell*

Live in New York City / Feb. 10, 1986 / Capitol ✦✦✦
John Lennon's concert appearances during his solo years were rare and scattered about, so any live document is worth hearing. Yet this one, the fabled One To One concert at Madison Square Garden, doesn't live up to its legend, however noble the cause (a benefit for the Willowbrook School For Children). Much of the problem, one suspects, is that Lennon concerts tended to be quick, casual one-offs; this material might have really rocked if John had broken the tunes in on the road first. Also, the Plastic Ono Elephants Memory Band is a fairly crude bunch of bashers, with Stan Bronstein's flailing sax and surprisingly poor drumming despite the support of Jim Keltner. So Lennon is pretty much left to his own devices. In the first few numbers, he sounds distracted, not in full command, even disconnected from the band. A core primal scream piece "Well Well Well" is given a perfunctory run through; "Instant Karma" sounds stiff, with embarrassing drum breaks ("We'll get it right next time," John says); and he makes only one reference to his Beatle past with a heavy-handed "Come Together." Things do improve later on when "Mother" and "Cold Turkey" work up a good lather, and "Hound Dog" is not bad, although the concluding "Give Peace A Chance" is limited to the brief excerpt included on *Shaved Fish*. Phil Spector was the original producer of the recording, and it's one of his murkier jobs, not nearly as focused as his work on *The Concert For Bangla Desh* in the very same arena the year before. More from the concert, including some of Yoko's numbers, can be found on the companion videocassette released at the same time. *—Richard S. Ginell*

Menlove Ave. / Nov. 3, 1986 / Capitol ✦✦✦
Following quickly on the heels of *Live In New York City*, a second posthumous Lennon release emerged from Yoko Ono's archives, with one side devoted to outtakes from the wild *Rock & Roll* sessions and the other to alternate takes from *Walls And Bridges*. The *Rock & Roll* side draws mostly from the first Phil Spector-produced sessions in Hollywood, which collapsed amidst storied incidents of '70s excess. There are two hitherto unreleased Lennon songs on board: "Here We Go Again" (co-written with Spector), a fairly uneventful song massively overproduced, and "Rock & Roll People," which has a more spartan production by Lennon and a nice kick to it. "Angel Baby," originally put out on the unauthorized *Roots* album, makes a raucous first official appearance here. "Since My Baby Left Me" sounds like a glorified party tape, giving us a taste of the madness of those sessions, and a lumbering rendition of Spector's chestnut "To Know Her Is to Love Her" closes the side. The *Walls And Bridges* alternates ("Steel And Glass," "Scared," "Old Dirt Road," "Nobody Loves You" and "Bless You") lack the orchestrations of the master takes, and they are better off for it; indeed "Steel And Glass" and "Scared" take on an especially starker power. By today's standards, this would be a pretty meager harvest of unheard Lennon, recommendable only to completists and the really dedicated fan. But in those pre-*Lost Lennon Tapes*/Lennon *Anthology* days, it was a tantalizing look into the vault. *—Richard S. Ginell*

Imagine: John Lennon [Original Soundtrack] / Oct. 10, 1988 / Capitol ✦✦✦✦
In 1988, the John Lennon estate released the documentary *Imagine: John Lennon*. A loving, airbrushed look at his life, the film offset the negative press generated by Albert Goldman's vicious unofficial bio *The Lives of John Lennon*, providing an unabashedly biased and entertaining chronicle of one of rock's greatest icons. Fanatics cherished the rare footage scattered throughout the documentary, and they also were thrilled by the first official release of "Real Love," a demo Lennon recorded at his Dakota apartment during the late '70s. (It would later be overdubbed and released as a Beatles track on *Anthology 2*.) Despite the inclusion of this and a rehearsal take of "Imagine," the soundtrack is geared toward casual fans. There's a brief roundup of nine major Beatles songs (including "Help!," "In My Life," "Strawberry Fields Forever," "A Day in the Life" and "The Ballad of John & Yoko"), then a summary of his solo works. *Imagine* may be a double album, but as it turns out, 21 tracks barely scratches the surface of a catalog as deep as Lennon's, especially if it attempts to cover both band and solo recordings. That means, of course, that many great songs—particularly early singles like "Cold Turkey" and "Instant Karma"—are missing. The featured songs emphasize Lennon's sensitive ballad side—it's all the idealistic dreamer, with Lennon the rocker or the social activist pushed to the side. Such an approach is bound to frustrate some fans, but the end result is an entirely listenable compilation and one that says a great deal about how Lennon was perceived at the conclusion of the '80s. *—Stephen Thomas Erlewine*

Lennon / 1990 / Capitol ✦✦✦✦✦
Two years after the first great Lennon revival—arriving in 1988, as an attempt to deflate Albert Goldman's trash-talking biography—Capitol released *Lennon*, a four-disc box set summary of his solo career. It does a remarkably good job, providing a thorough overview containing all the hits plus expertly chosen album tracks from his decidedly uneven records. The question is, is *Lennon* the one collection everybody needs? Not really. This may contain almost every great song Lennon recorded as a solo artist, yet the packaging is a little shoddy, and it could have been sequenced a little bit better. Still, as a summary, it's first-rate, rounding up the non-LP singles and condensing the records to their essence and thereby conveying the scope of Lennon's solo career very well. If you have the albums, plus a good singles collection, this isn't really necessary since it doesn't have anything too rare, but if you want one simple, albeit exhaustive, collection with everything you need, this fits the bill. *—Stephen Thomas Erlewine*

Lennon Legend: The Very Best of John Lennon / 1997 / Apple/Parlophone ✦✦✦✦✦
Lennon Legend was released in the fall of 1997 in England to replace the deleted *John Lennon Collection* and the 20-track collection is remarkably similar to its predecessor, replicating a full 16 tracks and deleting the relatively non-essential "I'm Losing You," "Dear Yoko" and "Move Over Ms. L." in favor of "Borrowed Time," "Mother," "Nobody Told Me" and "Working Class Hero." Even if the disc isn't sequenced in strict chronological order, the end result is the strongest single-disc Lennon collection yet. It might not offer everything of worth Lennon recorded—the *Plastic Ono Band* and *Imagine* albums remain essentials, and there's great-to-good songs scattered among his later solo records—but it does function as an excellent sampler and introduction to his solo career. *—Stephen Thomas Erlewine*

Anthology / Nov. 3, 1998 / Capitol ✦✦✦
During the great Lennon revival of the late '80s, Yoko Ono licensed to have the Westwood

One Radio Network air scores of unreleased home recordings and demos as the Lost Lennon Tapes radio show. At the time, there was endless speculation about when highlights would be released, likely as a box set. The proposed set never materialized, yet most of the material was heavily bootlegged, as the producers and Ono must have suspected. Despite the bootlegs, Ono didn't agree to an official collection of unreleased Lennon material until 1998, after the Beatles' *Anthology* series proved a critical and commercial success. Hence, the birth of Lennon's *Anthology*—a four-disc box set, comprised entirely of unreleased home recordings, demos and outtakes, many of which have never been previously bootlegged. As it's constructed, it's more of an aural biography than a music album. All the dialogue snippets, half-finished songs, throwaways and parodies ensure that it's never casual listening, yet that very approach creates an intriguing portrait of Lennon—a portrait of the man, not the artist. As such, there aren't really any forgotten treasures buried on the collection, even if many of these songs and takes are either completely unheard of or legendary among collecting circles. For every small pleasure, such as the Cheap Trick-backed version of "I'm Losing You," there is a small disappointment, such as how the Dylan diatribe, "Serve Yourself," doesn't quite live up to its legend. Ultimately, it doesn't matter if there are no major works or revelations, just a few good alternate tracks, because *Anthology* goes a long way toward capturing Lennon with all of his strengths and weaknesses. —*Stephen Thomas Erlewine*

Wonsaponatime / Nov. 3, 1998 / Capitol ✦✦✦
Released simultaneously with *Anthology*, *Wonsaponatime* condenses a four-disc box set into a digestable single-disc that feels more revelatory than its parent. That's because the compilers did an excellent job of selecting the highlights from the long-winded box, spotlighting the best alternate takes and unreleased songs. *Wonsaponatime* has a similar feel to *Anthology*, since it is culled from the same rough takes and studio rambling, but it's simply more accessible, letting less dedicated fans appreciate everything from the Cheap Trick-backed "I'm Losing You" and "God Save Oz," to alternates of "Working Class Hero," "God," "I Found Out" and "How Do You Sleep?" Again, these outtakes are not revelatory in the manner of Dylan's *Bootleg Series*, or even the Beatles' own *Anthology*, but they humanize Lennon, who has often been viewed as something of a saint in the years since his assassination. For that alone, *Wonsaponatime* is as welcome an addition to his catalog as the exhaustive *Anthology*. —*Stephen Thomas Erlewine*

Julian Lennon

b. Apr. 8, 1963, Liverpool, England
Vocals, Keyboards / Pop/Rock
The son of John Lennon and his first wife Cynthia, Julian Lennon parlayed a remarkable vocal similarity to his father into a moderately successful singing career during the 1980s. John Charles Julian Lennon was born on April 8, 1963 in Liverpool, and as a child inspired several Beatles compositions: "Lucy in the Sky with Diamonds" reportedly arose out of a drawing Julian made of a classmate, and following his parents' divorce, he became the subject of Paul McCartney's sympathetic "Hey Jude." Julian began playing guitar and drums at age ten, adding piano as a teenager; he appeared as a drummer on the track "Ya Ya" on the John Lennon album *Walls and Bridges*. Following his father's assassination, Lennon decided to pursue a singing career, although he worried that his vocal and stylistic similarity to his father would prove detrimental. He initially signed a contract to record an unreleased song stolen from John Lennon's vaults, but after thinking better of it, he enlisted Yoko Ono's help in buying out the contract.

Lennon signed with Atlantic and recorded his debut album, *Valotte*, at a French château of the same name. The album produced four chart singles, including the Top Tens "Valotte" and "Too Late for Goodbyes"; Lennon was nominated for a Grammy for Best New Artist. Success was accompanied by hedonistic indulgence, and the follow-up, 1986's underwritten *The Secret Value of Daydreaming*, perhaps suffered because of it. Lennon returned in 1989 with *Mr. Jordan*, an album that found him trying to break away from his John Lennon influences with a darker style reminiscent of David Bowie. However, the single "Now You're in Heaven" proved only a minor hit. Following 1991's *Help Yourself*, Lennon temporarily retired from the music industry and spent nearly seven years in seclusion. In the spring of 1998, he returned with *Photograph Smile*, an indie album initially issued only in Europe and Japan but given American release the following year. —*Steve Huey*

● **Valotte** / 1984 / Atlantic ✦✦✦✦
This strong debut showcases Julian's remarkable vocal resemblance to his father. —*Dan Heilman*

The Secret Value of Daydreaming / 1986 / Atlantic ✦✦✦
On *The Secret Value of Daydreaming*, the follow-up to his successful debut, Julian Lennon emphasizes his mainstream pop leanings by adding a tighter, more polished production which brings out the best in his songs. That is, it does when the songwriting is up to par. Lennon had some difficulty producing a consistent set of songs for his second album, with only a handful of tracks—including the hit "Stick Around"—standing out amidst the slick, immaculately-produced mateial. —*Stephen Thomas Erlewine*

Mr. Jordan / 1989 / Atlantic ✦✦
Julian Lennon did an about-face on *Mr. Jordan*, abandoning the polished mainstream pop of his first two albums for a darker, more rock-oriented sound. Lennon also changed his style of singing, choosing a deeper timbre that was eerily reminiscent of David Bowie—which was appropriate, because the thick gutiars that dominated the album were reminiscent of a kinder variation on Bowie's early '70s hard rock. Although Lennon's new sound was promising, he only came up with one song, the minor hit "Now You're in Heaven," that could support his musical visions. —*Stephen Thomas Erlewine*

Help Yourself / 1991 / Atlantic ✦✦✦

Following the flawed *Mr. Jordan*, Julian Lennon returned to straight-ahead pop with *Help Yourself*, which recalled the work of his father more than any of his other records. On *Help Yourself*, Lennon never seemed to be cannibalizing his father's songs; instead, he appeared to be learning from The Beatles, writing songs that were more carefully constructed than his previous work. Most of the record featured strong hooks and melodies, indicative of his songwriting progression, with the gorgeous "Saltwater" as the best evidence of his improved songwriting abilities. —*Stephen Thomas Erlewine*

Photograph Smile / Apr. 1998 / Varese ✦✦✦✦
Despite its moments of inspired songcraft, Julian Lennon's fourth album *Help Yourself* didn't find an audience in 1991. Shortly after its release, Lennon parted ways with Atlantic and entered a period of seclusion. By the time he returned to recording in 1998, the Beatles had already undergone one of their periodic "hip" phases, thanks to the hook-crazy Brit-pop crew. In many ways, bands like Oasis and Blur gave Lennon the go-ahead to return to the Beatles-esque songcraft of his debut *Valotte*, and that's exactly what he does on *Photograph Smile*, his first album in seven years. Much of the record is devoted to piano ballads similar to his big hit, "Valotte," with a couple of guitar-pop numbers thrown in for good measure. There's not much range on the album, but all the music is well-crafted and melodic—the kind of music that would receive greater praise if it wasn't made by the son of a Beatle. —*Stephen Thomas Erlewine*

● **VH1 Behind the Music: The Julian Lennon Collection** / Aug. 21, 2001 / Rhino ✦✦✦✦
Unlike some of the other discs in Rhino's *VH1 Behind the Music* series, Julian Lennon's edition is the first proper collection assembled about him, which may be why it succeeds so wildly. Every one of Lennon's hits is here, along with nearly every important album track, including latter-day selections like "Saltwater" and "Photograph Smile." These two songs prove that Julian Lennon grew stronger, more confident, as his career progressed, and they sound better than some of the earlier cuts that were stuck in the production of the late '80s (such as "This Is My Day," for instance). And while this doesn't make a case for Lennon as a consistent talent, it does have all the hits anybody could want, and "Valotte" and "Too Late for Goodbyes" hold up well, with "Say You're Wrong" and "Stick Around" making up the second tier. Then, there's the great "Now You're in Heaven," a wonderful Bowie rip-off that's not just among the best of its kind, it may be the best thing Lennon ever cut. But the unexpected thing about this collection is that the music gets better as it winds to a close, which almost never happens with an artist considered a one-hit wonder. And this does happen here, proving that while Julian Lennon's *Behind the Music* story was the most interesting in the '80s, his best work was done in the '90s. —*Stephen Thomas Erlewine*

Annie Lennox

b. Dec. 25, 1954, Aberdeen, Scotland
Vocals, Keyboards / Adult Alternative Pop/Rock, Club/Dance, Pop/Rock, Adult Contemporary
Following the disbandment of the Eurythmics in 1991, vocalist Annie Lennox began a solo career that rivaled her former group in terms of crossover popularity. During the early '80s, the sleek synth-pop of the Eurythmics became one of the most popular sounds of new wave, racking up a number of hits in both the U.S. and U.K., including "Sweet Dreams (Are Made of This)," "Love Is A Stranger," "Who's That Girl," and "Here Comes The Rain Again." *Diva*, Lennox's solo debut, arrived in 1992 and it showcased a calmer, more mature vocalist designed to crossover into the adult contemporary audience. On the strength of the singles "Walking on Broken Glass" and "Why," *Diva* sold over two million copies in the U.S. alone. Lennox delivered her second solo album, a covers collection entitled *Medusa*, in 1995. —*Stephen Thomas Erlewine*

● **Diva** / Apr. 28, 1992 / Arista ✦✦✦✦✦
Those expecting Annie Lennox to come out full guns blazing for her solo debut with the high energy Euro-electro-pop-meets-American-R&B of her Eurythmics work may have to wind their pacemakers down a notch. The enigmatic vocalist who made a career toying with different notions of gender now plays on the concept of fame—Lennox dressing up in the persona of a solitary *Diva* trapped by counterfeit glory. The framework offers an effective stage for Lennox's husky voice, showcasing her as much more of a chanteuse than in the past. But the music is strangely muted and understated. In fact, the album almost works best as one integrated mood-piece rather than a collection of individual songs. While Lennox succeeds in carving out a personality distinct from her Eurythmics days with *Diva*, one can't help but crave a shot of former partner Dave Stewart's musical muscle. —*Roch Parisien*

Medusa / Mar. 14, 1995 / Arista ✦✦

Let's Active

f. 1981, Chapel Hill, NC, **db.** 1988
College Rock, Jangle Pop, Power Pop
Mitch Easter carved his place in music history as a hip producer in the '80s, most notably for the early R.E.M. albums *Murmur* and *Reckoning*; unfortunately, these achievements often overshadowed and distracted him from giving his full commitment to his own recording career with Let's Active, a band that, between 1983 and 1988, released some of the finest Southern power-pop/jangle-pop of the decade. Easter set up his legendary Drive-In Studios in 1981 and formed Let's Active with bassist Faye Hunter and drummer Sara Romweber. The trio released a six-song EP, 1983's *Afoot*, on IRS Records. In 1984, the band released the more experimental *Cypress*. While the EP and album sold modestly, they found a strong following in the emerging alternative/"college rock" audience. Hunter and Romweber left shortly after the release, leaving Let's Active as essentially a solo project for Easter. 1986's *Big Plans For Everybody* was another critically praised yet

commercially undervalued album. The harder-edged *Every Dog Has His Day* was released in 1988. Following a small-scale promotional tour of college campuses, the band hung in limbo—no subsequent albums were recorded. Easter has continued producing into the '90s while infrequently playing with other bands, including Velvet Crush and Vinyl Devotion. —*Chris Woodstra*

Afoot / 1983 / IRS ✦✦✦✦
At the height of new wave-y synth pop, Let's Active managed to provide a breath of fresh air with its bright and bubbly sound. The guitar-based southern power pop band managed to capture new wave's quirkier elements with simplicity and classic pop craft. *Afoot*, essentially the demo that got them signed to IRS, does an excellent job of capturing the band's early period, when they were a tight trio centered around Mitch Easter's songwriting talents and production prowess. Their ability to pull off pop songs with economy and precision is especially evident on "Every Word Means No," an absolutely classic pop song by anyone's standards. —*Chris Woodstra*

Cypress / 1984 / IRS ✦✦✦✦✦
Cypress was the band's first recording made for release, as opposed to *Afoot* which was intended to be a demo. Some of its finest moments, such as "Easy Does" and "Waters Part," are in keeping with *Afoot* in terms of form, but the added care taken in its recording makes this album shine, and further illustrates Mitch Easter's talents as a producer; the more expansive arrangements (with a surprising amount of synthesizers) and subtle sonic explorations more fully illuminate the songs. Within a distinguished and consistent catalog, *Cypress* stands as the high-water mark for the band. —*Chris Woodstra*

Big Plans for Everybody / 1986 / IRS ✦✦✦
Let's Active sort of fell apart during the British tour for *Cypress* when Sara Romweber's unexpected exit disrupted the band and their "collective effort" feel. Rather than attempting to find a replacement, Mitch Easter opted to retreat into the studio and focus on music for the next record, and, from *Big Plans for Everybody* on, Let's Active became more or less a Mitch Easter studio project. This new definition didn't really hamper the record, but the changes were certainly noticeable. First of all, records made in 1986 sound very different from records made in 1984, and this is no exception. The new wave-ish flourishes and kinda-retro feel were removed in favor of a more straightforward, mainstream production. Easter's lyrics seem more universal while at the same time more personal and introspective than on previous records, though no less catchy. That, combined with the more organic arrangements, led to a highly rewarding album that, despite its many connections to the time, remains an album unfairly ignored. —*Chris Woodstra*

Every Dog Has His Day / Aug. 22, 1988 / IRS ✦✦✦
Every Dog Has His Day, the final Let's Active album, has a clearly different feel than the rest of their catalog. The album (especially the title track) has all the earmarks of a major bid for mainstream appeal, which it should have achieved. It sounds like an album of its time—it has *the* drum sound of 1988, and an overall heavier vibe, with the band rocking like never before, emphasizing a love of hard rock only briefly hinted at on earlier albums—and it's done very well. Some of the sonic changes may have been a result of the label's urging for the use of "name" producer John Leckie, a decision which is utterly confusing considering Mitch Easter's standing as a producer, not to mention his proven ability on previous Let's Active albums. At this album's peak moments, Easter's songs are top notch as always, though there seems to be a little less drive—often the songs seem like throwaways, albeit very good throwaways. —*Chris Woodstra*

● **Cypress/Afoot** / Jun. 1989 / IRS ✦✦✦✦✦
This excellent CD compilation of the *Afoot* EP and *Cypress* is now criminally out of print, but it does capture the prime early period of Let's Active. —*Chris Woodstra*

Level 42

f. 1980, Manchester, England
Pop/Rock, New Wave, Synth Pop
At the beginning of their career, Level 42 were a jazz-funk fusion band, following in the footsteps of such pioneers as Stanley Clarke. By the end of the '80s, they were a pop-R&B band with a number of hit singles to their credit. Featuring Mark King (bass, vocals), Phil Gould (drums), Boon Gould (guitar), and Mike Lindup (keyboards), the band formed in 1980. Before they released their first single, "Love Meeting Love," the band was pushed to add vocals to their music in order to give it a more commercial sound; they complied, with King becoming the lead singer. Released in 1981, their self-titled debut album was a slick soul-R&B collection that charted in the U.K. Top 20, resulting in the release of *The Early Tapes* by their former record label, Polydor. Level 42 had several minor hit singles before 1984's "The Sun Goes Down (Living It Up)" hit the British Top Ten. Released in late 1985, *World Machine* broke the band worldwide; "Lessons in Love" hit number one in Britain and "Something About You" hit number seven in America. Their next two records, *Running in the Family* (1987) and *Staring at the Sun* (1988), were a big success in the U.K., yet only made some headway in the U.S. Both of the Gould brothers left the band in late 1987; they were replaced by guitarist Alan Murphy and drummer Gary Husband. Murphy died of AIDS-related diseases in 1989; he was replaced by the renowned fusion guitarist Alan Holdsworth for 1991's *Guaranteed*. The band followed *Guaranteed* in 1995 with *Forever Now*. —*Stephen Thomas Erlewine*

● **Level Best** / 1989 / Polydor ✦✦✦✦✦
Polydor's *Level Best* is a thorough, successful overview of the smooth, jazzy British sophisti-pop outfit, containing all of their biggest hits and best material, including the sublime "Something About You." At 18 tracks, it may run a little long, but it still is as comprehensive a summary of Level 42's career as could be hoped. —*Stephen Thomas Erlewine*

LeVert

f. 1984, Ohio
Quiet Storm, Urban, Soul
As the official offspring of the O'Jays, LeVert is a trio from Philadelphia who combine the sweet harmonies that their fathers provided with the "rope-a-dope" style that will keep them in the spotlight in the '90s. Great music all around, and powerful vocals from Gerald LeVert, who also has his own solo album. —*John Book*

● **The Best of LeVert** / Mar. 20, 2001 / Rhino ✦✦✦✦✦
Best of LeVert highlights the exciting trio's blazing career. Not a complete overview but the best thing going 'til something more substantial comes along. Features the group's four R&B number one singles: "(Pop, Pop, Pop) Goes My Mind," "Casanova," "Addicted to You," and "Just Coolin'," featuring Heavy D. Their stunning debut, "I'm Still" (Tempre Records), is missing—maybe licensing was an issue, but its addition would have solidified this set. The exclusion of other singles, notably "Join in the Fun," "Sweet Sensation," "Pose," and "Fascination" keeps this enjoyable collection from being definitive. —*Andrew Hamilton*

Barbara Lewis

b. Feb. 9, 1943, South Lyon, MI
Vocals / Uptown Soul, Pop-Soul, Soul
Pop-soul doesn't get much better than Barbara Lewis, whose seductive, emotive croon took "Hello Stranger" to #3 in 1963. Lewis wrote all of the songs on her debut LP (including "Hello Stranger"), and confidently handled harmony soul numbers (some with backing by the Dells) and more pop-savvy tunes, some of which, like "Hello Stranger," were driven by an organ and a bossa nova-like beat. Follow-ups to "Hello Stranger" didn't sell nearly as well, and in the mid-'60s, she began doing some recordings in New York City, with assistance from producers like Bert Berns and Jerry Wexler, that employed more orchestral arrangements and pop-conscious material. The approach clicked, both commercially and artistically: "Baby I'm Yours" and "Make Me Your Baby" were both big hits, and both among the best mid-'60s girl-group style productions. Lewis cut an album in the late '60s for Stax (on the Enterprise subsidiary) that, as one would expect, gave her sound a grittier approach, without compromising the smooth and poppy elements integral to the singer's appeal. —*Richie Unterberger*

Many Grooves of Barbara Lewis / 1969 / Stax ✦✦✦
Although this late-'60s album isn't nearly as well known as her poppier mid-'60s hits, this is excellent sweet soul that avoids slickness. Still working with producer Ollie McLaughlin, Lewis recorded this set of strong soul-pop in Chicago. The slightly updated, gutsier tone of the arrangements did nothing to obscure her characteristically smooth and assured delivery. The CD reissue adds three bonus tracks from singles. —*Richie Unterberger*

★ **Hello Stranger: The Best of Barbara Lewis** / Jul. 19, 1994 / Rhino ✦✦✦✦✦
Some soul singers run hot, some run cool. Barbara Lewis ran cool, and thrillingly so. She was classy and sophisticated, even in the early to mid-'60s, a time where smooth pop-soul was the standard. Her voice was as soft as silk, and Atlantic gave her productions to match, resulting in an alluring body of work that still sounds seductive, yet comforting, years after their relief. During the mid-'60s, she hit the R&B charts steadily, crossing over to the pop charts with the number three "Hello Stranger," plus the Top 15 "Baby, I'm Yours," and "Make Me Your Baby." Those three, along with the bulk of her R&B hits, are all on Rhino's excellent compilation, *Hello Stranger: The Best of Barbara Lewis*. Since her work was so consistently good, there are inevitably some fan favorites missing, but everything here is excellent, representing her at her very best—and that means it's among the very best pop-soul of its time (or ever, for that matter). —*Stephen Thomas Erlewine*

Gary Lewis & the Playboys

b. Jun. 31, 1946, Manhattan, New York
Vocals, Drums, Guitar / Pop
The son of comedian Jerry Lewis formed this American rock group in 1964. After landing a gig at Disneyland, they were immediately signed to Liberty Records and handed over to pop production genius Snuff Garrett. Utilizing the best songwriters and studio players available, Garrett fashioned five Top Five hits in a matter of 18 months (15 in the Hot 100 by 1969) around Lewis's meager abilities, sometimes augmenting his voice in the studio with backup singers doubling his part. Lewis pretty well held his own against the British invasion, but the combination of his draft call in late 1966 and the rising tide of psychedelia put his days on the charts to an end. Still active on the oldies circuit, he fronts various backup bands under the name the Playboys. —*Cub Koda*

● **Legendary Masters Series** / 1990 / Capitol ✦✦✦✦✦
One of the most engaging pop acts of the mid-'60s, The Playboys benefited from strong songwriting (Al Kooper cowrote "This Diamond Ring") and studio personnel (courtesy of Leon Russell). It's still light, catchy pop with the enjoyable, unaffected vocals of Gary Lewis on top, and still fun. —*William Ruhlmann*

Greatest Hits / Apr. 5, 1994 / Curb ✦✦✦
Gary Lewis is not the kind of artist that inspires meticulous completism. Therefore, it's quite likely that many Lewis fans will not even notice the absence of some minor hits on this 10-song collection, which includes the biggest of the biggies ("This Diamond Ring," "She's Just My Style," "Everybody Loves a Clown"). The *Legendary Masters Series*, however, offers much more content, making this a much less desirable alternative. —*Richie Unterberger*

Everybody Loves a Clown/She's Just My Style / Jul. 28, 1998 / Collectables ✦✦✦✦✦
This two-LPs-on-one CD compilation from Collectables was previously available directly

from Capitol, and it's worth owning for the 12 tracks off of *She's Just My Style*, which was the best record that Gary Lewis & the Playboys ever cut. The digital remastering brings out the hard rocking sound on those cuts and especially on the guitars, and it is truly bracing. Apart from "Sha La La" and "Dreamin'," the first dozen tracks on this disc are pretty forgettable, if not downright dire—only hardcore Lewis fans need concern themselves with the other ten tracks off of *Everybody Loves a Clown*—but this is the easiest way to get those 12 hot rocking cuts off of *She's Just My Style*. Ideally, one starts the CD player at track ten and enjoys it from there on. —*Bruce Eder*

This Diamond Ring/A Session with Gary Lewis & the Playboys / Mar. 9, 1999 / Taragon ◆◆◆

Gary Lewis & the Playboys have never been taken too seriously by rock historians, which is somewhat a matter of prejudice, growing out of the idea (only partly true) that Lewis had a free ride, thanks to the help of his then superstar entertainer father—and their status as mid-'60s pop/rock entertainers, without a resident songwriter or a philosophy behind their work. They weren't great stylists, and the closest Lewis ever got to being a great drummer was getting a few pointers from his father's friend Buddy Rich. This two-albums-on-one-CD release shows the unfairness of that neglect. Apart from "This Diamond Ring," a song originally written with the Drifters in mind (who rejected it, as did Bobby Vee) which became a monster debut hit single, there's a lot of worthwhile, breezy pop/rock among the 16 tracks here. Lewis and company—Dave Walker, Dave Costell, Al Ramsay, and John R. West—do okay by covers of "Needles and Pins," "Sweet Little Rock & Roller," "All Day and All of the Night," "Dream Lover," "The Night Has a Thousand Eyes," "Concrete and Clay," etc. Two instrumental rarities, the original B-side off of "This Diamond Ring," "Hard to Find (Leroy's Tune)," and its replacement, "Tijuana Wedding"—a "La Bamba"/"Hang on Sloopy" piece of nonsense credited to Gary Lewis and producer and musical director Snuff Garrett and Leon Russell—fill out the CD, and are interesting for showing the band just jamming in the studio, rather than shooting for pop music perfection. The annotation is very thorough, and the sound, from 1998-era transfers, is excellent. —*Bruce Eder*

Huey Lewis (Hugh Anthony Cregg III)

b. Jul. 5, 1950, New York, NY

Vocals, Harmonica / Bar Band, Album Rock, Pop/Rock

With their straight-forward rock & roll, the San Francisco-based Huey Lewis & the News became one of America's most popular pop-rock bands of the mid-'80s. Inspired equally by British pub-rock (their previous incarnation, Clover, backed Elvis Costello on his debut album) and '60s R&B and rock & roll, the News had a driving, party-hearty spirit. At their core, the group were a working band, and they knew how to target their audience, writing odes to 9-to-5 jobs and sports. That much was clear on their first album, a simple bar-band record that earned some fans, but not widespread recognition. They had their first real taste of success with their second album, 1982's *Picture This*, thanks to a slicker production and a heavy dose of pop, evident on their first hit single, "Do You Believe in Love." This set the stage for *Sports*, one of the biggest blockbusters of the mid-'80s. Featuring the hits "I Want a New Drug," "Heart and Soul," "If This Is It" and "The Heart of Rock & Roll," its driving rock & roll appealed to blue-collar audiences, while their celebration of good times appealed to yuppies—the combination made the group stars. After reaching number one with "The Power of Love" from the soundtrack to *Back to the Future*, Lewis & the News returned in 1986 with *Fore!*, an album that emphasized their new-found slickness and mainstream appeal; as the single said, they now celebrated that it was "Hip to Be Square." *Fore!* was another smash success, but its sequel, 1988's *Small World*, found the group's popularity slipping as they experimented with roots music. They returned to basics with 1991's *Hard At Play*, but by that point, Huey Lewis & the News were off the pop mainstream radar. For the remainder of the '90s, the group worked sporadically, recording the occasional album and doing the occasional tour, where they remained a popular attraction. —*Stephen Thomas Erlewine*

Huey Lewis & the News / 1980 / Chrysalis ◆◆◆◆

On their eponymous debut, Huey Lewis & the News essentially act as a pub-rock band, turning out hard-driving covers and originals in a workmanlike fashion. While that usually makes for great club gigs, it only occasionally makes for great records, and the debut suffers from an uneven selection of material and a somewhat stiff prouction, mainly because the group can't quite reproduce their sound in the studio. Even with such flaws, the album shows signs of promise, particularly in the charging "Some of My Lies are True (Sooner or Later)." —*Stephen Thomas Erlewine*

Picture This / 1982 / Chrysalis ◆◆◆◆

Huey Lewis & the News sound considerably more focused on their second album, *Picture This*. By incorporating stronger elements of R&B and doo wop (their cover of "Buzz Buzz Buzz" is first-rate) and embracing pop to a much greater extent, the News find their own distinctive sound—clean-cut, steady middle-class rock & roll. They still suffer from uneven material, but "Do You Believe In Love?" is a stunner, a tight set of polished, anthemic hooks that is one of the best mainstream pop singles of the early '80s. —*Stephen Thomas Erlewine*

● **Sports** / 1983 / Chrysalis ◆◆◆◆◆

Picture This found Huey Lewis & the News developing a signature sound, but they truly came into their own on their third album, *Sports*. It's true that the record holds together better than its predecessors because it has a clear, professional production, but the real key is the songs. Where their previous albums were cluttered with generic filler, nearly every song on *Sports* has a huge hook. And even if the News aren't bothered by breaking new ground, there's no denying that the craftmanship on *Sports* is pretty infectious.

There's a reason why well over half of the album ("Heart of Rock & Roll," "Heart and Soul," "I Want a New Drug," "Walking on a Thin Line," "If This Is It") were huge American hit singles—they have instantly memorable hooks, driven home with economical precision by a tight bar band, who are given just enough polish to make them sound like superstars. And that's just what *Sports* made them. —*Stephen Thomas Erlewine*

Fore! / 1986 / Chrysalis ◆◆◆

Sports was one of the rare mainstream pop/rock albums where everything worked—the songs were catchy, and the sound was inviting, and it all sounded perfect on the radio. It would have been tough for Huey Lewis & the News to match its quality with its follow-up, *Fore!*, and it comes as little surprise that *Fore!* suffers from an overdose of the very things that made *Sports* nearly irresistible. Where the songs on *Sports* were so straightforward that they seemed inevitable, much of *Fore!* sounds labored, particularly when the News try to write a middle-class anthem. It's one thing to celebrate "The Heart of Rock & Roll," but it's quite another to proclaim it's "Hip to Be Square," especially if you're supported by a chorus of football players. And "Hip to Be Square," as well as "Stuck With You," where a married yuppie couple can't divorce because it would simply be too much hassle, makes Lewis' complacent tendencies all too clear. That wouldn't be a big problem if the songs were as catchy as "If This Is It" or "Heart and Soul," but they aren't, and the sound of the record is so sterile that the News no longer sound like a working band. *Fore!* is a reasonably enjoyable facsimile of the pleasures of *Sports*, yet it lacks the gleeful sense of fun that made that record, as well as portions of *Picture This*, so enjoyable. —*Stephen Thomas Erlewine*

Small World / 1988 / Chrysalis ◆◆

Small World was another platinum hit for Huey Lewis & the News, but the album was noticeably weaker than their previous three records. Lewis tries to position himself as a socially-conscious rocker—no less than three tracks have the word "world" in their title—writing songs about the perilous state of the environment and urging everybody to live together peacefully, since "there ain't no livin' in a perfect world." Such sanctimonious and simple lyrical platitudes would be acceptable if the band had written a set of catchy pop to support them. Instead, the group decided to stretch out, exploring rootsy American music like the zydeco of "Bobo Tempo" and the bluesy "Old Antone's." None of the musical diversions work as well as the bouncy Top Ten hit "Perfect World." However, "Perfect World" is the only song that ranks with the group's best material—as "Give Me the Keys (And I'll Drive You Crazy)" proves, the News had failed to come up with hooks that rivaled their earlier hits. —*Stephen Thomas Erlewine*

Hard at Play / Jan. 1991 / EMI America ◆◆◆

As the title indicates, *Hard at Play* is a return to the straightahead blues-inflected pop/rock that made Huey Lewis & the News superstars in the early '80s. While the material wasn't as consistently strong as *Sports* or *Picture This*, the band rocked with a renewed vigor and a handful of songs, including the anthemic hit "Couple Days Off," were as catchy as their older hits. —*Stephen Thomas Erlewine*

The Heart of Rock & Roll: The Best of Huey Lewis & the News / Nov. 18, 1992 / Chrysalis ◆◆◆◆◆

For four years, the U.K. compilation *The Heart of Rock & Roll: The Best of Huey Lewis & the News* was the only hits collection available on the San Franciscan bar band, and in some ways it's a better overview than the American retrospective, *Time Flies*. Although it does include a live version of "Workin' for a Livin'" and overlooks "Doing it All for My Baby" and "I Know What I Like," it contains several key tracks that aren't on *Time Flies*: "Hip to Be Square," "Back in Time" (which is only available on the *Back to the Future* soundtrack), "Jacob's Ladder," "Perfect World," the *We Are the World* track "Trouble in Paradise" and the terrific LP cut "Some of My Lies Are True." These tracks are added to the familiar hits to make *The Heart of Rock & Roll* a more thorough retrospective, and, in many ways, a better introduction than *Time Flies*. —*Stephen Thomas Erlewine*

Four Chords & Several Years Ago / Nov. 1, 1994 / Elektra ◆◆

Four Chords & Several Years Ago was a set of well-performed R&B covers by Huey Lewis & The News. While it lacked the polished energy of their *Sports*-era hits ("The Heart of Rock & Roll," "I Want a New Drug," "The Power of Love"), the album was filled with pleasant, professional performances that proved the band still knew how to construct a hit single—both "(She's) Some Kind of Wonderful" and "It's Alright" were minor hits. Even though it was a well-crafted record that managed to avoid the group's tendency for bombast, *Four Chords & Several Years Ago* never managed to be a compelling listen; it sounded better on the radio than it did on the stereo. —*Stephen Thomas Erlewine*

Time Flies: The Best of Huey Lewis & the News / Oct. 29, 1996 / Elektra ◆◆◆◆

Theoretically, it should be easy to assemble a greatest-hits collection from Huey Lewis & the News, since they spent most of the '80s in the Top Ten. *Time Flies… The Best of Huey Lewis & the News* proves that assumption false. Although many of the band's biggest hits are here—"Do You Believe in Love," "Workin' for a Livin'," "Heart and Soul," "I Want a New Drug," "The Heart of Rock & Roll," "If This Is It," "The Power of Love," "Stuck With You" and "Doing It All for My Baby"—the selection is remarkably uneven, bypassing many major hits from *Fore!* ("Hip to Be Square," "Jacob's Ladder," "I Know What I Like") and neglecting the latter-day hit singles "Perfect World" and "Couple Days Off" completely, both of which were the only things worth salvaging from their respective albums. In their place are four new songs, which are pleasant but unremarkable. Even though it is flawed, *Time Flies* remains a useful compilation, since it gathers all of the very best singles, particularly the ones from *Sports* and *Picture This*, in one place. However, the group could use an even better retrospective in the future. —*Stephen Thomas Erlewine*

Jerry Lee Lewis

b. Sep. 29, 1935, Ferriday, LA

Vocals, Piano / Honky Tonk, Rockabilly, Traditional Country, Rock & Roll

Is there an early rock & roller that has a crazier reputation than the Killer, Jerry Lee Lewis? His exploits as a piano-thumping egocentric wild man with an unquenchable thirst for living have become the fodder for numerous biographies, film documentaries, and a full-length Hollywood movie. Certainly few other artists came to the party with more ego and talent than he and lived to tell the tale. And certainly even fewer could successfully channel that energy into their music and prosper doing it as well as Jerry Lee. When he broke on the national scene in 1957 with his classic "Whole Lotta Shakin' Goin' On," he was every parents' worst nightmare perfectly realized: a long, blonde-haired Southerner who played the piano and sang with uncontrolled fury and abandon, while simultaneously reveling in his own sexuality. He was rock & roll's first great wild man and also rock & roll's first great eclectic. Ignoring all manner of musical boundaries is something that has not only allowed his music to have wide variety, but to survive the fads and fashions as well. Whether singing a melancholy country ballad, a lowdown blues or a blazing rocker, Lewis' wholesale commitment to the moment brings forth performances that are totally grounded in his personality and all singularly of one piece. Like the recordings of Hank Williams, Louis Armstrong and few others, Jerry Lee's early recorded work is one of the most amazing collections of American music in existence. *—Cub Koda*

Jerry Lee Lewis / 1957 / Rhino ♦♦♦♦♦

The Killer's original album for Sun Records makes the compact disc sweepstakes with his big hit, "Whole Lotta Shakin' Going On," appended to the original 12-track lineup. It's a curious mixture, as Sam Phillips pulled songs from all avenues of Jerry Lee's repertoire, everything from handkerchief weepers like "It All Depends," "Fools Like Me," and a staid "Goodnight Irene" to rockers like "Put Me Down," "Matchbox," "Ubangi Stomp," "Don't Be Cruel," and "High School Confidential." But Jerry Lee even rocks up stuff like Hank Williams' "Jambalaya" and "When the Saints Go Marching In," making this one terrific debut, even if a great deal of his best material was inexplicably left off. *—Cub Koda*

Jerry Lee's Greatest / 1961 / Rhino ♦♦♦

This was Jerry Lee's second album released on the Sun label and, with the exception of "Great Balls of Fire," it's all late-period Killer sides from his tenure at the label. While tracks like "Let's Talk About Us," "What'd I Say," and "As Long as I Live" have their own charm, this set simply isn't the place to start a Jerry Lee collection; stick with the Rhino single-disc best-of to fill that need. For original album freaks and completists only. *—Cub Koda*

The Greatest Live Show on Earth / 1964 / Bear Family ♦♦♦♦♦

Combining two live albums originally issued in the '60s, Lewis proves that the onslaught of the British Invasion hadn't lowered his rocking quotient one single bit. Blazing performances. *—Cub Koda*

☆ **Live at the Star Club** / 1980 / Bear Family ♦♦♦♦♦

The rock & roll landscape changed dramatically between the mid-1950s and 1964, when this five-star performance was recorded in Hamburg, Germany. The British Invasion was in full swing, and '50s icons like Chuck Berry, Little Richard, Elvis Presley and Bill Haley were no longer considered cutting-edge. Be that as it may, Lewis would continue to make live audiences sweat for decades to come. Amazingly, *Live at the Star Club* was only released in West Germany in the '60s and didn't come out in the U.S. until 1992. At 29, the Killer spares no passion whatsoever on frenzied versions of "Great Balls of Fire," "Whole Lotta Shakin' Goin' On," "Hound Dog" and other '50s classics. Though Lewis would record more and more country in the '60s, the only honky tonk treasure embraced here is Hank Williams' "Your Cheatin' Heart." For both hardcore Lewis devotees and more casual listeners, this stunning CD is essential. *—Alex Henderson*

★ **18 Original Sun Greatest Hits** / 1984 / Rhino ♦♦♦♦♦

This 18-song CD contains Jerry Lee Lewis' best rock & roll sides from the 240 or so tracks that he recorded for Sun Records. If that sounds like the very tiny tip of a very large iceberg—it is. But this 1984 compilation remains 40 of rock & roll's hottest minutes, revealing as much about Jerry Lee Lewis as it's possible to learn from watching the movie *Great Balls of Fire*! The hit singles and best B-sides are assembled around the core of his 1957 Sun album—a great, and instructive, musical decision. Lewis' rocking version of "Jambalaya" and his ivory-based rendition of "Matchbox," "Big Blon' Baby," "Big Legged Woman," and "It'll Be Me," are all prime examples of his fiercely sexual personality, pounding away on those keys and whooping and hollering like a white version of Piano Red. Equally important, "Crazy Arms" held what would prove to be the key to his professional salvation: a distinct way with a country song that didn't blow the song right apart and also didn't lose the rock & roll audience. A big hunk of this stuff is available on the Sun debut album, which should be heard at least once (assuming one can't afford the Bear Family label's *Classic* box with his whole Sun output), but this is the place to start. The mid-'80s digital transfer still sounds good; its quality proves that Rhino always gave good value to its customers. The guitars on "Put Me Down" and "Wild One"—yes, there is guitar on a lot of these sides—are nice and crunchy, even though they're buried under the piano. If there's a flaw here, it's the absence of any liner notes (not that much needs to be said about music like this). *—Bruce Eder*

Classic / 1989 / Bear Family ♦♦♦♦♦

At eight discs, including numerous alternate takes all presented in sequential order, Bear Family's thorough retrospective of Jerry Lee's Sun recordings on *Classic* is a monumental, even exhausting experience, even for those serious listeners prepared to immerse themselves in this music. Not that the music itself is taxing; it's among the very finest music of its time, probably of the 20th century. The key is the presentation—when these takes are strung together in the sequence of their recording (which can mean that the master is sandwiched between alternates), it may be possible to hear Lewis' approach develop, but the impact of his Sun recordings—the core mastertakes—becomes diffuse because it's impossible to hear those, as a body of work, without significant tweaking. Of course, this approach does enhance appreciation of Jerry Lee's music (there was serious craft behind it, as well as a staggering amount of raw talent), but it does make it the province of scholars and dedicated fans. Even with these problems—the fact that this does not make for easy listening—it's still an essential part of a comprehensive rock & roll, country or American music collection, because Jerry Lee's music is that good. As he said, he was one of the master stylists, and years later, that is more evident than ever. *—Stephen Thomas Erlewine*

★ **All Killer, No Filler: The Anthology** / May 18, 1993 / Rhino ♦♦♦♦♦

Out of all of the Jerry Lee Lewis compilations available on the market, only *All Killer, No Filler* contains material from all of the different labels he recorded for. Although there are twelve Sun tracks (including all of the major hits), the set doesn't draw enough from those early years; but then again, that's the intent. *All Killer, No Filler* is out to prove to an audience only familiar with his Sun singles that his country material is as brilliant as his rock & roll, and it succeeds. Stick with the *18 Original Sun Greatest Hits* if you only want rock & roll. If you want an idea of the scope of Lewis' talents and how consistently rich his music was throughout his career, you can't go wrong here. *—Stephen Thomas Erlewine*

The Locust Years . . . And the Return to the Promised Land / Nov. 29, 1994 / Bear Family ♦♦♦♦♦

Picking up where the eight-CD set *Classic* left off, the eight-CD box *The Locust Years . . . and the Return to the Promised Land* rivals its predecessor in musical quality. Tracing Jerry Lee Lewis' '60s career at Smash Records, the first two discs find the pianist trying to replicate his rock & roll success; while the performances were good, it was clear he was out of touch with the times. During the third disc, he begins to concentrate on country music. The fourth, fifth, and sixth discs match his Sun recordings for consistently brilliant performances; several of the songs became big hits on the country charts, establishing him as a country star. The seventh disc chronicles an exciting unreleased show, while the eighth disc is an unexceptional interview. For dedicated Jerry Lee Lewis fans, *The Locust Years* is every bit as essential as *Classic*. *—Stephen Thomas Erlewine*

Young Blood / May 23, 1995 / Sire ♦♦

25 All-Time Greatest Sun Recordings / Jun. 6, 2000 / Varese ♦♦♦♦♦

Just one of many of Jerry Lee's Sun best-ofs, this one largely sticks to the original single releases with a few strays like "Drinkin' Wine Spo-Dee-O-Dee" thrown in to fill things out. The transfers are as clean as it gets and although this doesn't replace Rhino's version of essentially the same material, it does offer a few stray tracks ("Love on Broadway," "Waitin' for a Train," "I Can't Seem fo Say Goodbye," "One Minute Past Eternity," "Invitation to Your Party") you might want or need if you don't feel like popping for Bear Family's exhaustive eight-disc box set. *—Cub Koda*

Mercury Smashes . . . and Rockin' Sessions / Dec. 13, 2000 / Bear Family ♦♦♦♦♦

The third installment of Bear Family's exhaustive reissue of Jerry Lee Lewis' complete recordings, *Mercury Smashes . . . and Rockin' Sessions*, covers the era that many listeners, even some fans, dismiss—his late-'60s and '70s recordings for Mercury. Conventional wisdom claims that the Killer was pretty much spent as a creative force during this time, since he had already made his near-triumphant comeback as a hard country singer on Mercury in the mid-'60s, and that he coasted on formula, except for the concentrated burst of the *Roots* album. Like most conventional wisdom, this one has a hint of truth, because his recordings did start to have a bit of formula and he did coast for a bit, but it ignores the fact that this was enjoyable formula and that Lewis remained an expert stylist, kicking out songs that may not have been first-rate, but were often given first-rate performances. This is why this set is enjoyable for the dedicated, even at its length of ten discs, because it's at a fairly consistent quality throughout; it also helps that the alternates are all stowed away on the final few discs, which means it's much easier to hear Lewis' main Mercury recordings and much easier to simply listen to, unlike either the *Classic* or *Locust Years* set. To be sure, this is for the dedicated, but if you're of the opinion that Lewis is one of the musical titans of the 20th century, this will enhance and deepen your love and respect instead of sully it. *—Stephen Thomas Erlewine*

Smiley Lewis

b. Jul. 5, 1913, DeQuincey, LA, **d.** Oct. 7, 1966, New Orleans, LA

Vocals, Piano, Guitar / New Orleans R&B, New Orleans Blues, Piano Blues, R&B

Dave Bartholomew has often been quoted to the effect that Smiley Lewis was a "bad luck singer," because he never sold more than 100,000 copies of his Imperial singles. In retrospect, Lewis was a lucky man in many respects—he enjoyed stellar support from New Orleans' ace sessioneers at Cosimo's, benefited from top-flight material and production (by Bartholomew), and left behind a legacy of marvelous Crescent City R&B. He began recording in 1947 and signed with Imperial three years later. As the New Orleans R&B sound developed rapidly during the early '50s, so did Lewis, rocking ever harder on "Lillie Mae," "Ain't Gonna Do It," and "Big Mamou." He scored his first national hit in 1952 with "The Bells Are Ringing," but enjoyed his biggest sales in 1955 with the exultant "I Hear You Knocking." (Pop chanteuse Gale Storm swiped his thunder for any pop crossover possibilities with her ludicrous whitewashed cover.) His blistering "Shame, Shame, Shame" found its way onto the soundtrack of the steamy Hollywood potboiler *Baby Doll* in 1957 but failed to find entry to the R&B charts. Lewis recorded one single each for OKeh, Dot and Loma in the '60s before dying in 1966, all but forgotten outside his New Orleans home base. *—Bill Dahl*

★ **The Best of Smiley Lewis** / Nov. 3, 1992 / Capitol ✦✦✦✦
Smiley Lewis made several fabulous singles, had a booming, terrific voice, and received the same great backing and support that defined the city's R&B sound. But Lewis' records seldom made it outside New Orleans, even though they were frequently brilliant. This great 24-track anthology contains the four that did make it to the charts, among them the signature song "I Hear You Knocking." It shows Lewis doing first-rate novelty tracks, ballads, weepers, up-tempo wailers, and blues, and making wonderful recordings. The set also includes a thorough discography and good notes and is superbly mastered. It's magnificent, exuberant R&B, and deserved a much better national fate than it enjoyed. —*Ron Wynn*

Shame, Shame, Shame / 1993 / Bear Family ✦✦✦✦✦
Exhaustive, multi-disc set comprising everything recorded by this New Orleans singer. With the songwriting talents of Dave Bartholomew aboard, utilizing the sound of the legendary J&M Studios, and the best Crescent City musicians available, this is truly New Orleans music at its very best. —*Cub Koda*

Gordon Lightfoot
b. Nov. 17, 1938, Orillia, Ontario, Canada
Vocals, Piano, Guitar / Folk-Rock, Soft Rock, Singer/Songwriter
Canadian Gordon Lightfoot first began to gain recognition in the mid-'60s as a songwriter when his compositions "For Lovin' Me" and "Early Morning Rain" became hits for Peter, Paul & Mary, and Marty Robbins topped the country charts with "Ribbon of Darkness." Lightfoot's own style was understated, his tasteful folk arrangements topped by a gentle burr of a voice. His albums began to appear in 1966, but it was not until the start of the '70s that he became a big success as a performer, scoring in 1970 with *Sit Down Young Stranger*, which contained his hit "If You Could Read My Mind," a song with a typically flowing melodic line and gently poetic lyrics.

Thereafter, the first half of the '70s were his. Lightfoot hit a peak in 1974 with *Sundown*, which went to number one, as did the title song when released on a single. Though he had developed a timeless style, Lightfoot was caught by the popular decline of folk-based music in the latter half of the 1970s, and has performed and recorded less frequently since, sometimes trying to conform to perceived commercial trends without success. But concert appearances in the early '90s confirmed that he remains an engaging performer and that his catalog of original songs is hard to match. *A Painter Passing Through* followed in 1998. —*William Ruhlmann*

Lightfoot! / Mar. 1966 / United Artists ✦✦✦✦✦
Lightfoot was already 27 at the time of his solo debut, which might have accounted in part for the unusually fully developed maturity and confidence on this recording, in both his songwriting and vocals. Contains some of his best compositions, including "Early Mornin' Rain," "I'm Not Sayin'," "The Way I Feel," "Lovin' Me," and "Ribbon of Darkness." At this point, Lightfoot was still including some covers in his repertoire, and he handles numbers by Phil Ochs ("Changes"), Ewan McColl ("The First Time Ever I Saw Your Face"), and Hamilton Camp ("Pride of Man") well. The whole album is included on *The United Artists Collection*. —*Richie Unterberger*

The Way I Feel / Apr. 1967 / United Artists ✦✦✦✦✦
Lightfoot had used additional guitar and bass on his debut, but for his second LP he went for a fuller band sound, using a couple of the noted Nashville sessionmen (Charlie McCoy and Ken Buttrey) who had played on Bob Dylan's *Blonde on Blonde*. The result was a brighter and more accessible sound, with the country elements more to the fore. The songs weren't quite as impressive as his first batch, but they were still very good, highlighted by the epic "Canadian Railroad Trilogy" and an electrified remake of "The Way I Feel." The whole album is included on *The United Artists Collection*. —*Richie Unterberger*

Did She Mention My Name / Jan. 1968 / United Artists ✦✦✦✦✦
Every '60s singer-songwriter of note expanded their instrumental approach as time went on, and Lightfoot was no exception. For his third album, he worked with John Simon (who would handle the Band and Big Brother), and occasionally used low-key orchestration. Though a tad more erratic than his earlier efforts, his songwriting remained remarkably consistent. His characteristically bright, uplifting outlook became more diverse as well, allowing for the chilling "Black Day in July" (written in response to the 1967 Detroit riots), the odd "Pussywillows, Cat-Tails" (an unusual and successful detour into baroque orchestral pop), and the ambiguous sobriety of "Does Your Mother Know." The whole album is included on *The United Artists Collection*. —*Richie Unterberger*

Back Here on Earth / Nov. 1968 / United Artists ✦✦✦
After the mild experimentation of *Did She Mention My Name?*, *Back Here on Earth* was a retrenchment of sorts, recorded in Nashville with a three-piece acoustic lineup and a more countrified approach. It's not quite as outstanding as his first three albums, lacking highlights on the order of "Early Mornin' Rain" or "Black Day in July." Lightfoot never offered weak material on his United Artists efforts, however, and *Back Here on Earth* is still a very solid set, certainly worth acquiring if you like his other LPs for this label. And all of the studio LPs for United Artists, of course, are available on the two-disc *The United Artists Collection*. —*Richie Unterberger*

Sunday Concert / 1969 / Capitol/EMI ✦✦✦
Recorded at a March 1969 concert in Toronto, this holds more interest than the usual live album because about half of the songs are Lightfoot compositions that had not been previously recorded in the studio. Accompanied by Red Shea on lead guitar and Rick Haynes on bass, he also mixed old favorites like "I'm Not Sayin'" and "Canadian Railroad Trilogy" with the new material on this set, which has good (though not outstanding) sound. These then-new songs aren't among his classics, but are up to the general high standard of his '60s work, with the socially conscious "The Lost Children" and the poetic "Leaves of Grass" standing out as lyrical highlights. This is the only one of Lightfoot's '60s United Artists albums that is not included on *The United Artists Collection*; EMI reissued it on CD in 1996. —*Richie Unterberger*

Sit Down Young Stranger / 1970 / Reprise ✦✦✦✦✦
Renamed *If You Could Read My Mind* after that track's Top Five success, *Sit Down Young Stranger* provided Gordon Lightfoot with his first commercial success as a performer. Augmenting his basic trio with musical luminaries and labelmates like Ry Cooder, John Sebastian and Van Dyke Parks, and with string arrangements by Nick DeCaro and Randy Newman, Lightfoot produced an album filled with attractive, folky melodies. The title track told the tale of a draft resister gone to Canada without resorting to polemics. The rest of Lightfoot's original lyrics were much more personal. The one non-original was the first cover of Kris Kristofferson's soon-to-be-classic "Me and Bobby McGee" to be issued. Meanwhile, "If You Could Read My Mind" was ubiquitous in the early months of 1971, launching Lightfoot on a six-year run of popularity. While future albums would begin to drift away from the folky acoustic timbres of this one (there are no drums to be found here), the beauty and simplicity of *Sit Down Young Stranger* make it a timeless recording. —*Jim Newsom*

Summer Side of Life / 1971 / Reprise ✦✦✦
This extraordinary release doesn't have big hits on it but contains some of his finest songwriting, from the political song "Miguel," to the wistful songs about divorce, "Same Old Loverman" and "Talking in Your Sleep," to the joyous "Cotton Jenny." This is highly recommended. —*Richard Meyer*

Don Quixote / 1972 / Reprise ✦✦✦
Perhaps one of his most Canadian releases, *Don Quixote* is a very pleasant folk sounding album. From "Alberta Bound" to "Christian Island" to "Ode to Big Blue," Lightfoot pays tribute to the many and varied places that make up his homeland. Also of note are such love songs as "Beautiful" and the lovely "Looking at the Rain." All in all, there's not a bad cut here. It's well worth your time. —*James Chrispell*

Sundown / 1974 / Reprise ✦✦✦✦✦
Lightfoot's commercial peak came with this album, which topped the U.S. charts, containing both the #1 title song and the Top 10 hit "Carefree Highway." But songs like "Somewhere U.S.A." and "High and Dry" are textured, catchy folk/rock on a par with the better known tunes. —*William Ruhlmann*

Gord's Gold / 1975 / Reprise ✦✦✦
Following the success of *Sundown*, Gordon Lightfoot continued his success by releasing a greatest-hits compilation. A double album (now a single CD), it contained his most popular songs from his Warner Bros. years on disc two and he re-recorded many of his early songs for side one of record one. Although not as good, perhaps, than the originals, this did bring them up to date with his current sound-style. Just about all the favorites are here. A good overview of a strong talent. —*James Chrispell*

Cold on the Shoulder / 1975 / Reprise ✦✦✦
Once you find a formula that works, why not try it again? That is just what Gordon Lightfoot does on *Cold On The Shoulder*. He doesn't vary from his success of the *Sundown* album by much, although some of these new tunes are a little more upbeat. Highlights include the hit "Rainy Day People" and the title track. Not another watermark, as it's sort of a holding pattern, but nothing bad about it either. —*James Chrispell*

Summertime Dream / 1976 / Reprise ✦✦✦✦✦
With *Summertime Dream*, Gordon Lightfoot produced one of his finest albums, and wrapped up a six-year period of popularity that he would not recapture. Propelled by his second biggest hit, "The Wreck of the Edmund Fitzgerald," *Summertime Dream* summed up the sound that had served Lightfoot so well in his post-"If You Could Read My Mind" days. This distinctive sound featured Lightfoot's strummed six- or 12-string guitar complemented by Terry Clements' electric guitar lines and Pee Wee Charles' pedal steel guitar accents. The material here is excellent, and the singer's voice is at its strongest. Mixing upbeat songs like "Race Among the Ruins," "I'd Do It Again" and the title track with beautiful ballads such as "I'm Not Supposed to Care" and "Spanish Moss," Lightfoot and his band deliver a tasty smorgasbord of intelligent, grown-up music. As for "Edmund Fitzgerald," its continued popularity more than 20 years after its release attests to the power of a well-told tale and a tasty guitar lick. —*Jim Newsom*

Early Morning Rain / 1976 / Sunset ✦✦✦
Early Morning Rain is a budget-line, 12-track sampler of Lightfoot's early recordings, featuring versions of "Early Morning Rain," "The Last Time I Saw Her," "I Want to Hear It from You," "The First Time Ever I Saw Your Face," "Did She Mention My Name," "The Way I Feel" and "Does Your Mother Know." There are better collections of this material, but this is still a fine selection. —*Stephen Thomas Erlewine*

Endless Wire / 1978 / Warner Brothers ✦✦

Shadows / 1982 / Warner Brothers ✦✦✦✦
A surprisingly strong collection from Gordon Lightfoot six years after the hits had stopped, *Shadows* finds him shedding his folk-singer image for that of an adult contemporary singer. There are keyboard textures here where previously there had been all stringed instruments. The change obviously reflected the performer's attempt to remain contemporary, and though *Shadows* found no radio airplay and little sales, the music on this disc is very good, mature and melodic. Songs like "In My Fashion" and "Heaven Help the Devil" sound like classic Lightfoot, built around folk song structures but more heavily orchestrated than in the '60s and '70s. "14 Karat Gold" sounds like a hit, while the title track and "All I'm After" are reminiscent of classic Lightfoot ballads like "Beautiful," with the acoustic guitar mixed upfront but augmented with tasteful keyboard colors. "She's Not the Same" borrows its introductory licks from "Down in the Boondocks," while

"Triangle" hearkens back to the singer's lyrical story tales of old. Throughout this fine disc, Lightfoot's attractive baritone voice sounds great. *Shadows* is a little-known recording well worth checking out. *—Jim Newsom*

If You Could Read My Mind / Mar. 2, 1987 / Reprise ✦✦✦✦✦
Originally released as *Sit Down Young Stranger* in the summer of 1970, this album was reissued under this name a few months later, as the song "If You Could Read My Mind" began its climb up the pop chart. The single peaked at number five, while the album reached number 12. It seemed as though "If You Could Read My Mind" was everywhere in the early months of 1971. Its appeal crossed genres and age groups, and its simplicity and acoustic arrangement fit in nicely with the burgeoning singer/songwriter scene then storming the airwaves and record stores. "If You Could Read My Mind" was not the first track released as a single from this album; Lightfoot's recording of Kris Kristofferson's soon-to-be-classic "Me and Bobby McGee," the only non-original in this collection, preceded it but barely dented the charts. The entire album is rich in the simple beauty of its folky melodies and personal lyrics. Lightfoot is accompanied here by his regular band of the time, Red Shea on guitar and Rick Haynes on bass. This trio is expanded on several cuts with Warner/Reprise labelmates Ry Cooder on bottleneck guitar and mandolin, John Sebastian on autoharp, harmonica and electric guitar, and Van Dyke Parks on harmonium. In addition, there are subtle string arrangements by Randy Newman on two tracks, Nick DeCaro on three. There are no drums to be found anywhere on this disc. This album fits in very well with the acoustic-based music being made at the turn of the '70s. Even so, the music here is timeless, still feeling and sounding great many years after its release. *—Jim Newsom*

Gord's Gold, Vol. 2 / Oct. 11, 1988 / Warner Brothers ✦✦

The Best of Gordon Lightfoot / Sep. 1, 1989 / Capitol/Curb ✦✦✦✦✦
A compilation of material Lightfoot recorded for United Artists in the '60s, and this features the best of that period, including Lightfoot standards such as "For Lovin' Me," "Early Morning Rain," and "Canadian Railroad Trilogy." *—William Ruhlmann*

Waiting for You / Apr. 13, 1993 / Reprise ✦✦✦
Anyone fearing that sobriety and serenity might dull Gordon Lightfoot's creative edge can rest at ease. Having apparently freed himself of several personal demons, *Waiting for You* delivers the most consistent Lightfoot to be heard since the late-'70s. While most tracks feature bass, drums, electric guitar, and/or keyboards (the synth washes sometimes overpower), for the most part the instrumentation is used sparingly, for color. The overwhelming feeling one derives from *Waiting for You* is of an intimate back-porch session soaking up the sounds of a rejuvenated Gordon Lightfoot and his guitar. *—Roch Parisien*

★ **The United Artists Collection** / Oct. 5, 1993 / EMI ✦✦✦✦✦
This double CD contains all four of the Toronto singer/songwriter's '60s studio albums (the live LP *Sunday Concert*, not included here, was also released in the '60s). On these records, his resonant vocals, lyrical ambition, and melodic strengths produced as close a rival to Bob Dylan as Canada ever fashioned during that decade, and foreshadowed work by other major Canadian singer/songwriters of the late '60s, such as Joni Mitchell, Neil Young, and Leonard Cohen. "Early Mornin' Rain" (covered by fellow Canadian folkies Ian & Sylvia), the folk-rock protest number "Black Day in July," the epic "Canadian Railroad Trilogy," and his cover of Ewan McColl's "The First Time Ever I Saw Your Face" are all present, and are among the most popular tracks Lightfoot has issued during his long career. Featuring both acoustic and folk-rock recordings, this neatly bundles Lightfoot's early work into a listenable and fairly inexpensive package. *—Richie Unterberger*

A Painter Passing Through / May 12, 1998 / Reprise ✦✦✦
With the release of *A Painter Passing Through*, Lightfoot appears to have found home and has turned in his best work in years. Gone are the uncertain arrangements of the past; in their place, there is a welcome return to the essence of the *Sundown* musical era. Full of pastoral points of view, *A Painter Passing Through* shows that Lightfoot has regained his voice and his ability to tell stories that enthrall the listener enough to keep them coming back for more. Of note are "Much to My Surprise," "On Yonge St.," and the title cut, which show a personal simplicity while also giving a great eye for detail. "I Used to Be a Country Singer" is an electric country-rock tune that is a joy to behold. If one can forget the past ten years or so of Lightfoot's career, get ahold of *A Painter Passing Through* and bask in the glow of one of music's premier storytellers. It's Gordon Lightfoot at his best in years. *—James Chrispell*

The Lightning Seeds

f. 1989, Liverpool, England
College Rock, Adult Alternative Pop/Rock, Britpop, Alternative Pop/Rock
The wispy pop outfit the Lightning Seeds were essentially the solo project of noted producer Ian Broudie, who first emerged as a member of Big in Japan, a product of the same Liverpudlian post-punk scene which gave rise to Echo & the Bunnymen, the Teardrop Explodes and Icicle Works. After Big in Japan split in 1979, Broudie followed a brief tenure in the Original Mirrors by producing the first two Bunnymen LPs, *Crocodiles* and *Heaven Up Here*, as well as work by the Fall, Wah! and Frazier Chorus. Seeking to return to performing, in 1982 he teamed with Wild Swans vocalist Paul Simpson under the name Care to release a series of shimmering singles which pointed in the direction Broudie followed in the Lightning Seeds, a one-man band backed by pop luminaries and session players. After scoring an international hit with the lush single "Pure," the Lightning Seeds issued their debut LP *Cloudcuckooland* in 1989. On 1992's *Sense*, Broudie made synth programmer Simon Rogers (formerly of the Fall) a full musical partner; for 1994's *Jollification*, he formed a touring band to play his first live shows since serving in the Original Mirrors over a decade ago. The British chart hits "Ready or Not" and "Three Lions on a Shirt" followed in 1996. *—Jason Ankeny*

Cloudcuckooland / 1989 / MCA ✦✦✦✦
Taking what he learned from his days in Big in Japan and his '80s production work with A-listers Echo & The Bunnymen, Ian Broudie created The Lightning Seeds project to better serve his cravings for shameless, lush pop. Even in these early days, with singles like "Pure" and "All I Want," you can hear why comparisons to a less burlesque Pet Shop Boys or a Matthew Sweet synth tribute band didn't have to be unpleasant criticisms. Ian Broudie has always had an evident love for freshly squeezed, exquisitely produced conservatism, but as in the decidedly odd "Control the Flame," not without the awareness of discovering it with well-constructed unsophistication. For some, Broudie destroyed his subsequent career by trying to recreate the gelatinous flavor of *Cloudcuckooland* without its flaws, relying too much on its John Hughes sonics, and mistaking his very strengths for hard and fast rules that would not and should not be deconstructed again. *—Dean Carlson*

Sense / Feb. 18, 1992 / MCA ✦✦✦
There's a certain school of distinctly British pop music characterized by a reserved, dignified demeanor and pretty, fragile melodies. The Lightning Seeds is one exponent of the genre that also includes such groups as Beautiful South and Trashcan Sinatras. The Seeds, mainly the one-man project of Liverpool artist-producer Ian Brodie, have more of a groove than their peers. Many of the songs tend to fall in the New Order camp, except that the vocals are more upfront than the rhythm tracks. *—Roch Parisien*

Jollification / Dec. 20, 1994 / Atlantic ✦✦✦✦
For the Lightning Seeds' third album, *Jollification*, Ian Broudie wrote his strongest batch of songs yet and managed to return to the top of the British charts. At ten tracks, *Jollification* is overly brief; eight of the ten tracks are genuine keepers and rank amongst the band's best work. "Lucky You," "Marvelous," "Perfect," and "Change" (which received some recognition in the U.S. due to its exposure in the movie *Clueless*), were all modern British pop gems that arrived at the height of Brit-pop. While the album is occasionally too produced—this is especially pronounced in the more synthesizer-driven songs—the melodies dominate despite their occasional stiffness. *Jollification* is Broudie's most cohesive and consistent album to date. *—Jason Damas*

Dizzy Heights / 1996 / Epic ✦✦✦✦
Released following the number-one success of "Three Lions"—the official song of the England football team's Euro 1996 campaign (written with alleged comedians Frank Skinner and David Baddiel)—*Dizzy Heights* was the product of an artist whose stock was running unnaturally high. As a result, it could boast three Top 20 singles: "What If...," "Sugar Coated Iceberg," and "You Showed Me." But guess what—this album sounds just like all of main man Ian Broudie's other creations; it has that same obsession with the perfect '60s melody, polite guitars, and saccharine vocals on an endless quest to rewrite "Unchained Melody" for the '90s. Too many plays will send you running to the dentist, or back to your Iggy albums at the very least. *—Alex Ogg*

● **Like You Do . . . Best of the Lightning Seeds** / 1997 / Epic ✦✦✦✦✦
Like You Do . . . Best of the Lightning Seeds is a splendid collection of Ian Broudie's finest moments, offering a definitive portrait of his appealingly sunny, catchy melodicism. Drawing from all four of the Lightning Seeds' first albums, the collection hits all of the high points—including "Three Lions" and a re-recorded "Waiting for Today to Happen"—and adds two new songs, "What You Say" and "Brain Drain," which are as engaging as the group's hit singles. In all, it's an ideal introduction to neophytes, and for longtime fans, it's a welcome reminder of Broudie's fine pop craftsmanship. *—Stephen Thomas Erlewine*

Tilt / Nov. 1999 / Epic ✦✦✦✦
Ian Broudie is probably one of the least likely people to embrace electronica, but on their fifth album *Tilt*, some of the Lightning Seeds' dancier undertones are brought to the forefront. The Seeds are no strangers to stiff, computerized beats; because the band was technically Broudie's solo act until 1996's stellar *Dizzy Heights*, he often used a drum machine to round out the sound. That's why *Tilt*, which is neither electronica nor rock, but merely danceable pop, is hardly a real reach for them. If anything, the album is a minor disappointment because it seems that just as the group began to sound like a live act (and enlisted Zak Starkey, Ringo Starr's son, as drummer) they reverted back to being a slick pop band. This is not to say that *Tilt* is a bad record, however; it's quite the opposite. Some of the lyrics here are Broudie's most affected yet, and some of the arrangements are very exciting. In a way, it's like a less-dated version of their debut *Cloudcuckooland*, released nearly ten years before this one. Highlights include the first single, the uptempo "Life's Too Short" and the techno-rocker "Crowdpleaser." Occasionally, the Lightning Seeds sound like a warmer version of the Pet Shop Boys, especially on "If Only" and "Happy Satellite." Furthermore, the second single, "Sweetest Soul Sensations," samples Al Green. Overall, however, the album gels into a cohesive statement that's sure to please both casual and die-hard fans of this excellent pop band. *—Jason Damas*

Lil' Kim

b. Jul. 11, 1975
Vocals / Hardcore Rap, East Coast Rap, Gangsta Rap, Hip-Hop
After making her presence known on Junior M.A.F.I.A.'s debut album *Conspiracy*, Lil' Kim launched a solo career in 1996 with the release of her first record, *Hard Core*. As the album's title implies, Lil' Kim was a raritiy among female rappers—one that not only concentrated on edgy, hardcore rap, but also explicit sexuality, two territories that had long been the province of male rappers. Of course, Lil' Kim's near-pornographic sexuality and hard-edged rhythms made her an anamoly within hip-hop, but *Hard Core* proved that she was no novelty, as it garnered positive reviews and strong sales. The first single from the album, "No Time," was a duet with Sean "Puffy" Combs, and became a number one rap single. *—Stephen Thomas Erlewine*

• **Hard Core** / Nov. 12, 1996 / Undeas/Big Beat ♦♦♦♦
After making her presence felt on Junior M.A.F.I.A.'s hit debut album, Lil' Kim broke out on her own, refashioning herself as a hardcore and defiantly sexy female rapper. Working with producers like Sean Combs and the Notorious B.I.G., Lil' Kim has developed a sleek but hard sound that is positively dripping with attitude and sex. When she slips into conventional, seductive R&B the record loses some steam, but her filthy, hard-driving tracks are stunning—it's hardcore in more than one sense of the word. *—Stephen Thomas Erlewine*

Notorious K.I.M. / Jun. 27, 2000 / Atlantic ♦♦♦
Four years after the death of close friend Notorious B.I.G. and after the critical downfall of collaborator Puff Daddy, Lil' Kim returns to the rap game with her glossy sophomore effort, *Notorious K.I.M.* Not much changed for Kim in those four years; she still balances delicately between being a proud female and a ho while constantly pleading her case to listeners about why she deserves respect. Kim still uses her emanating sexuality for its full potential, starting with the first musical track on the album, "Custom Make (Give It to You)." This particular song uses the orgasmic female moans from Lil' Louis' infamous house track "French Kiss" as its prime sample, instilling a sense of eroticism that cannot be ignored, often eclipsing Kim herself with the omnipresent sounds of sexual climax. By beginning the album with such a blatant aura of raw, sincere sexuality, Kim succeeds in her aim to get your attention in ways that male rappers simply cannot. But for as well as Kim uses subtle sexuality to keep listeners attentively elated, she really has little to say on her album. Every song features her cries for respect, which get a bit tiresome after a few songs, even if there are some catchy moments, some quality beats, and some interesting collaborations. Yes, she's sexy, attractive, strong, independent, and sly, but one wishes she would stop talking about herself after awhile. Her most valuable asset, her undeniable sexuality, also becomes her biggest weakness as she comes off as distastefully vain. *—Jason Birchmeier*

The Lilac Time

f. 1987, England, **db.** 1991
Indie Pop, Folk-Rock, Alternative Pop/Rock, College Rock, Adult Alternative Pop/Rock
Following a brief solo career under both his own name and the moniker Tin Tin, Stephen Duffy put together the Lilac Time, which traded in his former synth-pop excursions for pastoral, folky English pop strongly recalling *Skylarking*-era XTC. Joined by Mickey Harris, Nick Duffy, and Michael Giri, Duffy crafted several eclectic albums making use of traditional instruments, beginning with a self-titled debut in 1988. 1989's *Paradise Circus* offered a bit of country & western influence, which was largely abandoned on 1990's *... & Love For All*, partially produced by XTC's Andy Partridge. The Lilac Time's final album, 1991's *Astronauts*, began to return to the sound of Duffy's earlier solo career, so it was no surprise when the band broke up and Duffy resumed work as a solo artist. He reformed the group in 1999 to release *Looking for a Day in the Night*. *—Steve Huey*

The Lilac Time / 1987 / Mercury ♦♦♦♦
Charming, low-key tuneful, acoustic-based pop. Two tracks were added to the original U.K. edition. *—Steve Aldrich*

Paradise Circus / 1989 / Fontana ♦♦♦♦
Paradise Circus, the second album by Stephen Duffy's Lilac Time, delivers more of the great acoustic pop sounds heard on their first (self-titled) long player. Duffy possesses a truly unique writing style, mixing gorgeous melodies with lyrics that convey sensuality, lust, longing and melancholia. *—Robin Platts*

& Love for All / 1990 / Fontana ♦♦♦♦♦
The Lilac Time's third long player is packed with irresistible pop hooks. This is due in no small part to the appearance of XTC's Andy Partridge as producer on several tracks (the remainder are produced by John Leckie). There's plenty of Beatlesque pop, but Duffy retains his own musical identity throughout. If you're not familiar with Duffy's work, *& Love for All* is as good a place as any to be introduced to this perennially underrated artist. *—Robin Platts*

Astronauts / 1991 / Creation ♦♦♦♦
The last album by Stephen Duffy's underrated pop combo is, in many ways, their strongest. The group's gorgeous acoustic-based sound had been perfected by this point, and Duffy offers up his strongest batch of songs to date. From the sensual opener "In Iverna Gardens" to the exquisite closing ballad "Madresfield," this is a consistently great album. "Grey Skies and Work Things" is typical of the album's mood—quiet, sensual, melancholy and romantic. "Dreaming" is a slight return to the dance-oriented sound that typified Duffy's pre-Lilac Time solo work, but it still fits in well with the more subdued acoustic numbers. The Lilac Time's only release on Creation Records, *Astronauts* sold poorly, and the group split shortly thereafter. However, it remains—along with the solo follow-up *Music In Colors*—Duffy's strongest work, and a great introduction to his talents. *—Robin Platts*

Looking for a Day in the Night / Sep. 21, 1999 / spinART ♦♦♦♦
After eight years and several stunning solo CDs, Stephen Duffy resurrected The Lilac Time. And it is as if time stood still for them. *Looking For a Day in the Night* picks up where 1991's *Astronauts* stopped. This really is not a surprise, as Duffy has been flirting with folk music throughout his solo releases in the '90s. This is beautiful, quiet, acoustic focused contemporary folk music. Once again, Duffy has written some seemingly personal songs letting the world into his own struggles and confusion. The songs have several different layers, which are peeled away with each listening. The lyrics are pure poetry. A highlight is the wonderfully scathing "All Over Again," which addresses the music industry. Duffy does it in a style masking his bitterness with humor. Nick Duffy (brother to Stephen) contributes a great deal to this CD, writing the instrumental songs, with the achingly beautiful song "The Spirit Moves" a highlight. The CD is perfectly produced, and the musicianship is flawless. As usual, the vocals, with the tight harmonies, are always a highlight, and this CD is no exception. Duffy's voice is soft, gentle, and yet very emotional. This CD is a must for any fan of folk-rock (in the Simon and Garfunkel vein) and any Stephen Duffy or Lilac Time fan. This CD is just more evidence of Duffy's indescribable talent, which has been somewhat overlooked due to the immense success of "Kiss Me" which has had him labeled as an '80s "dance" artist. *—Aaron Badgley*

• **Compendium: The Fontana Trinity** / Jul. 24, 2001 / Fontana ♦♦♦♦♦
The very good news: *Compendium: The Fontana Trinity* crams selections from the Lilac Time's first three albums onto two CDs, in addition to scattering a rather thorough collection of stray tracks from singles released during the same period, between 1987 and 1990. An extremely attractive package, longtime fans will love to own most of the Lilac Time's Fontana output with updated sound. Each of the three records—1987's *The Lilac Time*, 1989's *Paradise Circus*, and 1990's *& Love for All*—are represented liberally, with over half of their songs included. Fans will also love to have strong non-album material that has been out of print for over a decade. *Compendium* also works as a great introduction for newcomers, as it does more than just offer a selection of the group's most accessible material. And by listening to this in its entirety, one gets a rather full picture of what the Lilac Time were about in their earliest and most productive stage. The somewhat irritating news: The key word is scatter. You'd think that the logical thing to do with a compilation like this would be to simply sequence the material in chronological fashion. This rationale wasn't applied—the sequence resembles what happens when you hit the shuffle button on your CD changer. Unless listeners want to go through the cumbersome task of programming their players, they won't get an idea of how the band developed throughout the four years covered here. Regardless of that problem, there's no doubting that the Lilac Time's complete ignorance of pop trends paid off in the long run; their tastefulness for classy pop runs much deeper than the Nick Drake-referencing band name. *—Andy Kellman*

Liliput

f. 1980, **db.** 1983
Post-Punk, Alternative Pop/Rock
During the punk rock era of the late '70s, there were three bands comprised of women who made some of the best, most adventurous, exhilarating, and most critically derided music of the time. Two were the English bands the Slits and the Raincoats, and the third band, from Switzerland, was Liliput. Fans of all three bands will argue ad infinitum as to who was the better, but one thing is for certain: Liliput was an amazing band that recorded amazing music. Formed in Zurich in 1978 by guitarist Marlene Marder and bassist/vocalist Klaudia Schiff, they began with the name Kleenex until the threat of a lawsuit by corporate giant Kimberly-Clark forced them to become Liliput in 1980. Recording for the great English indie label Rough Trade, the then-Kleenex produced jumpy, aggressive, clamorous punk-noise that featured Marder's scratchy, semi-melodic guitar and Schiff's yelping vocals. Not punk rock in the fast, loud, economical sense, Liliput were forging a different kind of punk, one that was gleefully anarchic, avant-garde, unrestrained, and suffused with a giddy, almost palpable sense of joy. By 1982, when they released their first LP, they seemed perfectly happy remaining in Switzerland, running the band as part of numerous other artistic projects (painting, writing, etc.) they pursued. By the end of 1983, Liliput had disbanded, and the music they had recorded quickly achieved legendary, but mostly unheard, status. As for the band, they seemed destined to be relegated to the status of feminist-inspired punk rock footnote. All of this changed in 1993, when the Swiss label Off Course released a double-disc, 46-track compilation of the entire recorded output of Kleenex/Liliput. Unfortunately, it went out of print shortly after its release, but Kill Rock Stars released it again in early 2001, making it more accessible than before. *—John Dougan*

Liliput / 1982 / Rough Trade ♦♦♦♦♦
You can bet that a karaoke version of Liliput's first full-length will never see the light of day. It's an exciting and ultimately accessible amalgam of crazy rhythms and impossible-to-replicate vocalisms. The recording found the band as a trio, having lost a drummer and a saxophonist. Only Astrid Spirit, Klaudia Schiff, and Marlene Marder remained, sharing all of the duties. Aside from the airy "Might Is Right" and the relatively forceful "Like or Lump It," there's hardly any prominent guitar. Otherwise, you probably wouldn't hear guitar unless you were specifically hunting for it in the mix, because it makes for just as much of a percussive element as the drums. Generally, they pound out a loping rhythm and chant unintelligible phrases, adding the occasional violin shriek or unidentifiable nuance. This method strikes gold with each attempt. "Do You Mind My Dream" snarls and swoops; the guitar is just as effectively plucky and trebly as the one found on Liquid Liquid's "Optimo" and Talking Heads' "I Zimbra." Spirit's squeaky vocals highlight "In a Mess" and "Tong Tong," both of which could be mistaken for New York funksters ESG. "Outburst" could be the best example of Liliput's greatness, with a jumpy bass line and the most animalistic of vocal gestures. Spirit "ugh"s in time with the one-two bass punch as if she were being karate chopped in the gut. At other points during the song, she alternates between "proper" singing and helium ingestion, breaking that up with hyena-like noises. *Liliput* actually gets more experimental than that. "Birdy" is a nails-on-chalkboard violin instrumental, gradually gathering steam until hitting overload. "Umamm," another instrumental, offers little more than tribal drums. Thanks to the similarly titled compilation, the album is available in its entirety. *—Andy Kellman*

Some Songs / 1983 / Rough Trade ♦♦♦
You can't really fault Liliput for a decline on *Some Songs*, because it's always tricky to follow up a great record with something just as wonderful or near it in quality. It is a minor

disappointment, though, because some of the nine tunes stitched together here are almost as innocuous and seemingly tossed-off as the album's title. They had long since established themselves as a top tier band, so that adds to the letdown factor. The trio featured on the debut returns, aided by a crew of pals on percussion, sax, and piano. Beat Schlatter (great name) reprises his role from an earlier incarnation of the group, providing, of course, drums. For the majority of the record, the gang works through material that sounds little more than half-realized. The seeds of good songs only show signs of sprouting on "Ring-A-Ding-Dong," "Terrified," and "A Silver Key Can Open an Iron Lock Somewhere," which never quite gets off the ground. "His Head All Read" positively echoes Young Marble Giants with its spare structure of tapping kick drum, rave-up guitar, and busy bass, but the vocals detract and sound patched on. It's missing the playful giddiness of the debut, but most importantly it's also missing the fun rhythms and carefree vocals. Nothing really breaks free from the mid-tempo tedium, which makes it far less engaging than the preceding LP and singles. The weaknesses of *Some Songs* are further magnified when listened to as part of the *Liliput* compilation, because much of it is eclipsed by the outtakes and unreleased material that preceded it. The first album undeniably dwarfs it. Maybe they were taking themselves too seriously, which is usually a problem. It quite possibly was a pitfall here. *—Andy Kellman*

• **Kleenex/Liliput** / 1993 / Off Course ✦✦✦✦✦
Switzerland's Off Course label was the first to issue this infamous double-disc set in 1993, which contains the entire recorded outputs of Kleenex and the following Liliput. It went out of print shortly after release, and since it was on a small label to begin with, not many were able to obtain it before its collector value shot through the roof. With the gradual, steady rise of female-dominated bands in the '80s and '90s who followed their path, this compilation became a holy grail. Thanks to some goading from journalist Jason Gross and involvement from the Kill Rock Stars label (who are paying a musical debt here), Kleenex and Liliput constant Marlene Marder saw to it that the compilation became available again. Aside from the two Liliput LPs (1982's *Liliput* and 1983's weaker *Some Songs*), the compilation includes four singles, one EP, and another LP's worth of intermittent outtakes and unreleased material. The Rough Trade singles differ greatly from one another, each holding a high level of quality. The unreleased material doesn't match the hot singles or great first LP, but it's enough to qualify as gravy. As to whether or not these recordings were worthy of hundreds of dollars, that can only be judged by those who paid such a sum. What's collected here certainly belongs in the same realm as the other great, pioneering, female-dominated bands of the time. Liliput were one of the finest in their field, male or female. From their punkier singles as Kleenex to their more avant-garde developments as Liliput, this compilation offers over two solid hours of great music that hasn't depreciated at all. In light of all the bands they've inspired, this stuff probably sounds even better than it did when it was first issued. *—Andy Kellman*

Lilys

f. Philadelphia, PA
Indie Pop, Dream Pop, Space Rock, Indie Rock, Shoegazing, Alternative Pop/Rock
The geographically and stylistically nomadic indie rock band Lilys was the vehicle of singer/songwriter Kurt Heasley, the group's founder and sole constant member. A Philadephia native, Heasley and the Lilys bowed with the 1991 single "February 14," a nod to My Bloody Valentine; while based in Washington, D.C., they recorded their 1992 debut LP *In the Presence of Nothing*, an even greater testament to their shoegazing fetish. A two-year silence followed as Heasley roamed the East Coast, finally resurfacing with 1994's *A Brief History of Amazing Letdowns* EP, on which the Lilys refashioned themselves as a guitar-pop band. The spare, minimalist *Eccsame the Photon Band* followed in 1995 before the now Boston-based Heasley delivered the next year's *Better Can't Make Your Life Better*, evidence of a strong British Invasion fixation. The *Services (For the Soon to Be Departed)* EP arrived in 1997; two years later, the Lilys resurfaced not only with the full-length *The 3-Way* but also *Lullabies*, their entry in Darla Records' continuing "Bliss Out" series. *—Jason Ankeny*

In the Presence of Nothing / 1992 / Slumberland ✦✦✦
Phase one of the Lilys' odyssey plunges Kurt Heasley and friends—among them members of Velocity Girl, the Ropers and Suddenly Tammy!—into the heart of the shoegazing phenomenon; *In the Presence of Nothing* is the quick follow-up to *Loveless* that My Bloody Valentine never made, with tracks like "There's No Such Thing as Black Orchids" and "The Way Snowflakes Fall" capturing the moment in vividly dreamy and atmospheric detail. A relic of its time, to be sure, but also a wonderful testament to shoegazing's brief but seminal moment in the sun. *—Jason Ankeny*

A Brief History of Amazing Letdowns / Mar. 25, 1994 / spinART ✦✦✦

• **Eccsame the Photon Band** / Jan. 31, 1995 / spinART ✦✦✦✦
The obscurely titled *Eccsame the Photon Band* is the Lilys' detour into spartan dream-pop, a guise they wear quite well. Kurt Heasley's soft, distanced voice is ideally suited to the coldly atmospheric textures of tracks like the langorous opener "High Writer at Home" and the narcotically catchy "The Hermit Crab," and while not everything works—too many of the ideas here are simply not realized to their fullest extent—the record is still one of the Lilys' best. It's a shame they shed this particular skin so quickly. *—Jason Ankeny*

Better Can't Make Your Life Better / 1996 / CHE ✦✦✦
Another new record, another new sound: on *Better Can't Make Your Life Better*, the Lilys hop into the time machine and travel back to the mid-'60s, immersing themselves in the style of the British Invasion. And while tracks like "Cambridge California," "Shovel Into Spade Kit" and "Can't Make Your Life Better" certainly bring to mind the timeless pleasures of early Kinks, Stones and Who, the record's easy appropriation of a 30-year-old sound underscores the Lilys' big problem—Kurt Heasley is a gifted chameleon, but until he comes up with an original identity all his own, his music will remain merely a pale imitation of its superior source material. *—Jason Ankeny*

The 3-Way / Apr. 20, 1999 / Sire ✦✦✦✦
Similar to the Brian Jonestown Massacre, the Lilys have made a career out of impersonating a British band circa 1966. Throughout their seven-year recording life they've moved from psychedelic to pop experimentalism and now, on *The 3-Way*, the group seems to be lifting generously from mod groups like the Small Faces and the Action. The fuzz guitar and farfisa organ of "Dimes Make Dollars" and the affected anglo singing of "Accepting Applications at University," for example, reek of the British invasion of the mid-'60s. Yet for all his posturing, the group's leader, Kurt Heasley, keeps his influences at bay enough to fill the album with songs that build on the sounds of the '60s rather than just aping them. "Leo Ryan (Our Pharaoh's Slave)," for instance, with its biting string section and saxophone noodlings, is as sophisticated as the very best U.K. pop. *—Steven Kurutz*

Zero Population Growth: Bliss Out 15 / Jul. 13, 1999 / Darla ✦✦

Limp Bizkit

f. 1994, Jacksonville, FL
Rap-Rock, Rap-Metal, Alternative Metal, Funk Metal
One of the most energetic groups in the fusion of metal, punk and hip-hop sometimes known as rapcore, Limp Bizkit was formed in Florida in 1994 by vocalist Fred Durst and his friend Sam Rivers on bass. Rivers' cousin John Otto soon joined on drums, and guitarist Wes Borland completed the original foursome (later supplemented by DJ Lethal). After Korn played the Jacksonville area in 1995, bassist Fieldy got several tattoos from Durst (a tattoo artist) and the two became friends. The next time Korn were in the area, they picked up Limp Bizkit's demo tape and were so impressed that they passed it on to their producer, Ross Robinson. Thanks mostly to word-of-mouth publicity, the band was chosen to tour with House of Pain and the Deftones. The label contracts came pouring in, and after signing with Flip/Interscope, Limp Bizkit released their debut album *Three Dollar Bill Y'All*. By mid-1998, Limp Bizkit had become one of the more hyped bands in underground rapcore, helped as well by more touring action—this time with Faith No More and later, Primus—as well as an appearance on MTV's Spring Break '98 fashion show. The biggest break, however, was a spot on that summer's Family Values Tour, which greatly raised the group's profile.

Limp Bizkit's much-anticipated second album, *Significant Other*, was released in June 1999, and it and the accompanying video for "Nookie" made the group superstars. *Significant Other* debuted at number one and had sold over four million copies by year's end, also helping push *Three Dollar Bill Y'All* past the platinum mark. Fred Durst, meanwhile, was tapped for a position as a senior vice president at Interscope Records in early July. However, in the midst of this massive success, controversy dogged the band following that summer's performance at Woodstock '99. In the wake of the riots and sexual assaults that proved to be the festival's unfortunate legacy, Durst was heavily criticized for egging on the already rowdy crowd and inciting them to "break stuff." Not only was at least one mosh-pit rape reported during the group's set (in addition to numerous other injuries), but the ensuing chaos forced festival organizers to pull the plug in the middle of their show. Even though Limp Bizkit's performance took place the day before the infamous festival-closing riots, the band was raked over the coals in the media, who blamed them for touching off the spark that inflamed a potentially volatile atmosphere. Undaunted, Limp Bizkit headlined that year's Family Values Tour, with the newly controversial Durst grabbing headlines for periodic clashes with Bizkit's tourmates. During the Napster flap of 2000, Durst became one of the most outspoken advocates of online music trading; that summer, Limp Bizkit embarked on a free, Napster-sponsored tour. All of this set the stage for the October release of the band's third album, *Chocolate Starfish and the Hot Dog Flavored Water*. *—John Bush*

Three Dollar Bill Y'All / Jul. 1, 1997 / Interscope ✦✦✦✦
With their major-label debut, *Three Dollar Bill Y'All*, Limp Bizkit quickly rose to the top of the alt-metal subgenre known as rapcore. Part of the reason the band stood out from their peers was their kinetic, frenzied energy. They might not have many original ideas—they are largely an outgrowth of Korn, Faith No More and the Chili Peppers—but they do the sound well. They have a powerful rhythm section and memorable hooks, most of which make up for the uneven songwriting. Then again, you're not looking for perfection on a debut—you're looking for a promising sound, and on that front, Limp Bizkit delivers. *—Stephen Thomas Erlewine*

• **Significant Other** / Jun. 22, 1999 / Interscope ✦✦✦✦
Limp Bizkit made their reputation through hard work, touring the hell out of their debut album *Three Dollar Bill Y'All* and thereby elevating themselves to the popularity status of their similarly rap-inflected, alt-metal mentors Korn. With their second album, *Significant Other*, they come close to reaching Korn's artistic level; at the very least, it's considerably more ambitious and multi-dimensional than *Three Dollar Bill*. Limp Bizkit, of course, hasn't abandoned their testosterone-overloaded signature sound, they've just built around it. There are flourishes of neo-psychedelia on pummeling metal numbers and there are swirls of strings, even crooning, at the most unexpected background. All of it simply enhances the force of their rap-metal attack, which can get a little tedious if it's unadorned. Not so coincidentally, the enlarged sonic palette also serves as emotional coloring for Fred Durst's lyrics. He broke up with his longtime girlfriend—his *Significant Other*, if you will—during the writing of the album, and his anguish is apparent throughout the record, as almost every song is infused with the guilt, anger, and regret that was churned up in the wake of separation. That, however, gives the impression that this is an alt-metal *Blood on the Tracks*. It's not. Nevertheless, it does have more emotional weight

than *Three Dollar Bill*, along with more effective, adventurous music. More importantly, it balances these new concerns with trace elements of their juvenile humor along with the overpowering aggro rap-metal that is their stock in trade. Which makes it a rare artistic leap forward that will still please audiences that just want more of the same. —*Stephen Thomas Erlewine*

Chocolate Starfish and the Hotdog Flavored Water / Oct. 17, 2000 / Interscope ♦♦
Let's start with the title, a title that's a winking acknowledgement that the group knows what their stereotype is. Limp Bizkit knows everybody believes they're juvenile vulgarians, so they're ready to prove 'em right. And how do they do that? With a title that's defiantly vulgar but, more revealingly, embarrassingly awkward. The scatological meaning of *Chocolate Starfish & the Hot Dog Flavored Water* is obvious to anyone that's graduated junior high, but it stumbles over its punch line, winding up as more bewildering than funny or offensive. But it doesn't stop there, or with the sickly cover art, since hot dogs and chocolate starfishes become lyrical themes on the album. Clearly, Limp leader Fred Durst takes some pride in his ass and dick joke, since he repeatedly uses it to illustrate the one theme of the album, namely how nobody understands him, especially in Limp Bizkit's year of success after 1999's *Significant Other*. And that's it. There's nothing else to the record. If the band supported him with sheets of noise, terrifying guitars, monstrous rhythms, or even a hook every now and then, Durst's narcissism may have been palatable, but the group pretty much churns out the same colorless heavy plod for each song. Combined, Durst's self-pitying and the monotonous music give away that the band bashed *Chocolate Starfish* out very quickly—it's the sound of a band determined to deliver a sequel in a finite amount of time. Since Bizkit has never relied on song or studiocraft, it shouldn't come as a surprise that neither is in evidence here, but the problem is they're fishing in a shallow pool. Previously, they had pent-up rage on their side, but here, the music sounds rote—when it gets louder, it signifies nothing, it just gets louder. —*Stephen Thomas Erlewine*

Bob Lind

b. Nov. 25, 1944, Baltimore, MD
Vocals, Songwriter / Folk-Rock, Pop, Singer/Songwriter
Bob Lind's "Elusive Butterfly" was one of the most successful one-shots of the mid-'60s folk-rock boom, reaching the Top Five in early 1966. He never came close to matching that early triumph, although other acts brought his songs to a wider audience with their covers of Lind compositions like "Cheryl's Going Home" (Blues Project), "Counting" (Marianne Faithfull), and "Mr. Zero" (Yardbirds' lead singer Keith Relf). The beauty of Jack Nitzsche's intricate production on Lind's two 1966 LPs, favoring acoustic guitars and pretty string arrangements, is admirable, but Lind himself hasn't worn that well. His songs are wordy and on the didactic side; his voice is nervous and lacks emotional range; his melodies are pretty, but not enormously so. —*Richie Unterberger*

● **The Best of Bob Lind: You Might Have Heard My Footsteps** / Jun. 29, 1993 / EMI ♦♦♦♦♦
This 25-song compilation includes the entire contents of his two 1966 LPs, as well as a 1967 single and two previously unreleased tracks. This period piece is highlighted by "Elusive Butterfly," the original versions of "Counting" and "Cheryl's Goin' Home," "Mr. Zero" (covered by Yardbird lead singer Keith Relf on a flop single), and the previously unreleased, gorgeous baroque rock song "English Afternoon." —*Richie Unterberger*

Lindisfarne

f. 1968, Newcastle-on-Tyne, England
British Folk-Rock, British Folk, Folk-Rock, Prog-Rock/Art Rock
Lindisfarne barely commands more than a footnote in most rock reference books. During the early '70s, however, Lindisfarne was one of the hottest folk-based rock bands in England, with chart placements on two of their albums that rivaled Jethro Tull, and had themselves proclaimed one of the most important groups of the decade. With a sound that mixed plaintive folk-like melodies, earthy but well-sung harmonies, and acoustic and electric textures, the group seemed poised for international success. Signed to Tony Stratten-Smith's Charisma Records, England's premiere progressive rock label, in 1970, they released their first (and best) album, *Nicely Out of Tune*, that same year. Their debut album captured the group's best attributes, a rollicking, upbeat, optimistic collection of hippie/folk music, somewhere midway between Fairport Convention and the early Grateful Dead, with a peculiarly urban, English working-class ambience. Their second album, *Fog on the Tyne*, released in 1971, marked their commercial breakthrough. That was when the media hype kicked in, raising expectations and aspirations for a group that, until four months earlier, had been a pleasant folk-rock outfit with a solid cult following. After a frantic period capitalizing on one massive success after another, the band released their third album, *Dingly Dell*, in 1972. The record had a very crisp sound, very upfront, and more of a mainstream hard rock sound than their previous two long-players. Unfortunately, this was not the move that the critics had wanted or expected of the band. Simon Cowe, Ray Laidlaw, and Rod Clements exited the band in early 1973 and formed a new group called Jack the Lad, which specialized in a harder, more basic pub rock sound, and went on to release three albums on Charisma. —*Bruce Eder*

Nicely Out of Tune / 1970 / Elektra ♦♦♦♦♦
Easily the best album the group ever recorded, *Nicely Out Of Tune* is one of the prettiest folk-rock albums of the late 1960s. If Lindisfarne had never recorded anything else, they'd be one of the most fondly remembered acts of their era just for this album. "Lady Eleanor" is a very pretty tune that manages to incorporate elegant mandolin over some heavy rock riffing. "Road To Kingdom Come" is closer in spirit to the group's usual pub-rock sound, a singalong-type number with lots of really crunchy harmonica, mandolin, and fiddle,

and a really catchy chorus—"Jackhammer Blues" is pretty nearly as good a rocker. But "Winter Song" is one of the gentlest, most haunting folk ballads of its period, almost too pretty to have come from a rock band, and "Alan In The River With Flowers" isn't far behind. The rest is in the same class and league, and as a bonus the CD contains two lost B-sides, "Knackers Yard Blues" and "Nothing But The Marvelous Is Beautiful"—they're not bad, either. —*Bruce Eder*

Fog on the Tyne / 1971 / Elektra ♦♦♦♦♦
The album that turned Lindisfarne into a chart-topping act, and made their tour of the United States a foregone conclusion. This is an earthier album, a piece of urban English folk-rock with a gentle, easygoing feel very different from the first album. "Meet Me on the Corner" has one of the most delectable singalong choruses of any rock song you'll ever hear. Additionally, the lyrics of this song, as well as those of "Together Forever" and "Fog on the Tyne," display a clarity, vivid imagery, and emotional subtlety just about worthy of Bob Dylan, and it is easy to see how "Meet Me on the Corner" could've reached the number four spot. "January Song" is nearly as pretty as "Winter Song" on the first album. And the record is worth the price just for the instrumental break on "Fog on the Tyne." —*Bruce Eder*

Dingly Dell / 1972 / Elektra ♦♦♦♦
Lindisfarne's third album, following two huge successes, was their make-or-break record, in terms of staying a major British act or achieving a major international following. It fell short of the mark, as far as the British rock press was concerned, and the group never recovered, splitting into two factions and breaking up soon after. Precisely what was wrong with *Dingly Dell* is unclear listening to the album today. The band's playing is spirited enough, and there are lots of enjoyable songs, even if they lack the cutting lyrical edge of "Meet Me on the Corner" or "Fog on the Tyne." Additionally, the sound here is excellent—"Mandolin King" lives up to its name, in terms of the glittering texture of that instrument, and the acoustic guitars, harmonium, fiddle, and so on are all cleanly presented in the mix (a surprise given the contortions that the group went through with producer Bob Johnston to get this album released). On the other hand, there was no equivalent to "Fog on the Tyne," and that was probably—along with the more overtly poetic "Meet Me on the Corner"—what the rock press was waiting for. When they didn't get it, and when principal songwriter Alan Hull suddenly revealed that he might be less than the Bob Dylan rival they'd presumed him to be, they savaged the album unfairly, and the group never recovered their lost momentum. The CD has new cover art and a fascinating Lindisfarne family tree inside the inlay card. —*Bruce Eder*

Lindisfarne Live / 1973 / Charisma ♦♦♦

Roll on Ruby / 1973 / Elektra ♦

Finest Hour / 1975 / Charisma ♦♦♦♦♦
A 16 song best-of, marking the end of the group's Charisma Records era. The CD equivalent *The Best of Lindisfarne: 16 Classic Tracks* is readily available. —*Bruce Eder*

Back and Fourth / 1979 / Atco ♦♦

Sleepless Nights / 1982 / LMP ♦♦

Peel Sessions / 1988 / Dutch East India ♦♦♦♦
Long before MTV's Unplugged sessions, deejay John Peel and the BBC would get acts on the air strumming away on acoustic or low-amplification electric instruments. Lindisfarne made the appearance at which the four cuts here ("Poor Old Ireland," "Mandolin King," "Lady Eleanor," "Road to Kingdom Come") were broadcast on May 8, 1972, when the group was still at its peak. The two songs off *Dingly Dell* fare pretty well, but the earlier numbers really shine. The sound is excellent, with really sharp resolution on the strummed guitars, and it's only a pity there wasn't more recorded, though what is here is fine, especially "Lady Eleanor." —*Bruce Eder*

● **The Best of Lindisfarne** / 1989 / Virgin ♦♦♦♦♦
The history is a little sketchy, but this collection does distill down the best of the group's first three Charisma Records albums. The only problem is that *Nicely Out of Tune* and *Fog On the Tyne* should be in any fan's collection complete, and also that later, post-Charisma hits like "Run For Home" are not here. This disc is a good introduction to the group, however, and an easy way for the neophyte to see if Lindisfarne is really for them. —*Bruce Eder*

Lindisfarne Live 1990 / Jul. 5, 1994 / Demon ♦♦♦

Caught in the Act / Oct. 13, 1994 / Castle ♦♦♦

Another Fine Mess / 1995 / Grapevine ♦♦♦♦

Run For Home: Lindisfarne Collected / Jun. 2, 1998 / Music Club ♦♦♦♦

David Lindley

b. 1944, San Marino, CA
Slide Guitar, Guitar (Steel), Arranger, Violin, Guitar, Fiddle / Bluegrass, Worldbeat, Tex-Mex, Blues-Rock, Rock & Roll
David Lindley is the consummate musician's musician. A much respected session player, Lindley has added his melodic string playing to albums by a lengthy list of artists including Bob Dylan and James Taylor. From 1971 until 1981, Lindley played a guiding role on Jackson Browne's recordings and concert performances. Lindley's eclectic approach provided the foundation for his own bands, Kaleidoscope (1967-1970) and El Rayo X (1981-1990). After playing with a series of traditional folk and bluegrass bands, Lindley joined a rock band, the Rodents. When the group disbanded, he formed his own group, Kaleidoscope, that blended traditional music with rock influences. Accepting an invitation to join Jackson Browne's band in 1971, Lindley remained with the singer/songwriter's group for a decade. When not touring or recording with Browne, he continued to explore

a variety of projects. In 1979, he began working with Ry Cooder, contributing heavily to Cooder's albums *Bop Till You Drop* and the soundtrack of the film *The Long Riders.* The collaboration continued, and in the early '90s, Lindley and Cooder toured as a duo. Lindley also found time to work on his own music. Shortly after releasing a solo album, *El Rayo X,* he formed a band of the same name. In 1990, Lindley began performing in a duo that he shared with Jordan-born percussionist Hani Naser. The two musicians continued to tour and record together until 1995. Lindley has collaborated with avant-garde guitarist and ethnomusicologist Henry Kaiser on several albums based on their field recordings. A two-week field recording expedition to Madagascar in 1991 yielded six albums of Malagasy music including the award-winning, two-volume set *A World Out of Time.* A trip to Norway in 1994 inspired two CDs, *Sweet Sunny North, Vol. One* and *Vol. Two.* —*Craig Harris*

• **El Rayo-X** / 1981 / Asylum ✦✦✦✦✦
By the time David Lindley made his move to a solo career, he was already a legend. Having toured and recorded with such names as Jackson Browne, Linda Ronstadt, and Crosby & Nash his reputation as a multi-instrumentalist (on almost any stringed instrument) was awesome. Lindley scored a contract with Elektra Records and put together an excellent band that was able to keep up with his eclectic vision. Combining blues, rock & roll, Cajun, Zydeco, Middle Eastern music, and other elements, his debut album is an absolute joy. Lindley's version of "Mercury Blues" became an FM radio staple, and his slide guitar performances on this track alone are easily some of the finest of the decade. There are some wonderfully skewed originals on the record as well, making *El Rayo-X* one of the greatest rock world music albums of its time. Fabulous. —*Matthew Greenwald*

Win This Record / 1982 / Elektra ✦✦✦✦
Following up their excellent debut and a season of intense touring, David Lindley and his crack band (now named El Rayo-X) recorded their second Elektra album. It turns out that they actually bettered the near perfection of the first. Opening with an excellent version of Etta James classic "Something's Got a Hold on Me," this track proves how tight the band had became. Lindley's slide guitar work is impressive as always. As an added bonus, the band's vocal harmonies are extremely tight and a welcome addition. A version of the Cajun classic "Brother John" held great significance at the time shortly after John Lennon's death—and again contains some of Lindley's best slide work to date. A rambling, fun record, *Win this Record* is one of the finest rock records of the 1980s. —*Matthew Greenwald*

El Rayo Live / 1983 / Asylum [Germany] ✦✦✦
David Lindley's American label, Elektra/Asylum Records, was not sufficiently impressed with the sales of his first two albums, *El Rayo-X* and *Win This Record,* to release this, his third album, domestically. But the international division of the company did find it worthy, so one has the unusual experience of having to dig around import bins to find a great album by an American artist recorded at several clubs in California, yet released only in Europe! (The same fate would befall Lindley's fourth album, *Mr. Dave,* in 1985.) Lindley, playing electric guitars, slide guitar, mellobar, and Hawaiian lap steel, is typically virtuosic and zany, opening the proceedings with "Wooly Bully" and taking it from there. The focus is on his string work, though the four-piece band is tight and Lindley's odd, reedy voice emphasizes the quirky nature of the material. Another triumph, and worth seeking out. —*William Ruhlmann*

Mr. Dave / 1985 / WEA ✦✦✦
A great album, don't know why it wasn't released in the U.S. —*Michael Katz*

Very Greasy / 1988 / Asylum ✦✦✦
The final El Rayo-X record, while lovely, does not exactly contain the power and fury of the first two. On this record, David Lindley and his cohorts explore a myriad of lighter, more Caribbean rhythms and textures, rendering a very pleasing album. Some great covers such as "Papa Was a Rolling Stone" and "Do You Wanna Dance" are pleasant enough, but the fact that hard rock warrior drummer Ian Wallace—who was such a big part of the power of their second record, *Win this Record*—is missing results in a weaker record. All in all, a very nice, eclectic slice, but not what this fine band was really about. —*Matthew Greenwald*

Lisa Lisa

f. 1985, **db.** 1991
Electro, Club/Dance, Disco, Dance-Pop, Freestyle
Based in Brooklyn, vocalist Lisa Lisa (born Lisa Velez) and her supporting band Cult Jam (Mike Hughes and Alex "Spanador" Mosley) were one of the most consistent pop-funk/R&B groups of the mid-'80s. Hughes and Mosley were also members of Full Force, the funk group that performed and produced the majority of Lisa Lisa & Cult Jam's albums.

Lisa Lisa & Cult Jam recorded their debut single, "I Wonder If I Take You Home," soon after forming in 1985, releasing it as an independent single. The group quickly signed to Columbia Records, which re-released the single; it climbed into the R&B Top Ten and the U.K. Top 20. The group amassed a number of hit songs throughout the '80s, yet by the end of the decade their success had begun to dry up; they disbanded after 1991's *Straight Outta Hell's Kitchen.* Lisa Lisa embarked on a solo career, releasing the commercially unsuccessful *LL 77* in 1993. —*Stephen Thomas Erlewine*

• **Past, Present and Future: The Best of Lisa Lisa & Cult Jam** / May 7, 1996 / Navarre ✦✦✦✦✦
Past, Present & Future stands as the most complete compilation of Lisa Lisa and Cult Jam's hits, assembling all eight of their U.S. Hot 100 hits, as well as three new songs and one new remix. The music still sounds fresh and innocent, bringing to mind old high school dances and romances, without sounding cliched or dated. What the album could use, however, is much more extensive liner notes and improved cover art. This album includes all of the bands hits, beginning with the early freestyle crossover jams "I Wonder If I Take You Home" and "Can You Feel The Beat" to the tragic high school romance ballad "All Cried Out," which resurfaced in the mid-1990s as a top ten hit for the vocal group Allure. The album's highlights, of course, are their two number one hits "Head To Toe" and "Lost In Emotion," which established them as one of the premier hit-making acts of the mid-to-late 1980s. To round out the hits are "Little Jackie Wants To Be A Star," an earthy and organic cautionary tale about success and its pitfalls, and their surprise 1991 house-dance smash "Let The Beat Hit 'Em," produced by then-ultra-hot Clivilles & Cole of C & C Music Factory fame. The new tracks on this set don't quite live up to their golden-era hits, but include a fun remake of Teena Marie's "I Need Your Lovin'" and a new hip-hop remix of "I Wonder If I Take You Home." All in all, a surprisingly great album, with the hits sounding just as fun and fresh as they did when they first hit the airwaves. —*Jose Promis*

Little Anthony & The Imperials

f. 1958, Brooklyn, NY, **db.** 1975
Doo Wop, R&B
Featuring the high-pitched vocals of Anthony Gourdine and a brace of solid material, Little Anthony & the Imperials had a much longer chart run than the majority of doo wop groups from the '50s. When the dust finally settled, the group clocked in with a total of ten entries in the Hot 100 between 1958 to 1974, including "Tears on My Pillow," "Two People in the World," "Wishful Thinking," "Oh Yeah," "So Much," "Shimmy Shimmy Ko Ko Bop" (not to be confused with the similarly titled "Shimmy Shimmy Ko Ko Wop" by the El Capris), "When You Wish Upon a Star," "Going Out of My Head," "Better Use Your Head," and "Hurt So Bad." The group was originally called the Chesters, but had their name changed to the Imperials by popular New York disc jockey Alan Freed. Gourdine's vocal similarities to the popular Frankie Lymon-inspired "kiddie group" sound, coupled with a tendency to chop up syllables and overstress lyrics, made theirs a style deceptively simple yet enduring. After revamping the group in 1964 down to a quartet, the sound changed from doo wop to a harder, more uptown R&B sound, best exemplified on hits like "I'm on the Outside Looking In." For many lovers of the genre, Little Anthony & the Imperials are simply New York-styled doo wop at its smoothest and finest. —*Cub Koda*

We Are the Imperials (Featuring Little Anthony) / 1959 / Collectables ✦✦✦
This is a straight-up reissue (no bonus tracks) of this '50s group's debut album on the End label. As such, it contains their first couple of big hits, "Two People in the World" and "Tears on My Pillow," along with album filler such as "Cha Cha Henry" and "Oh Yeah," as well as old standards like "When You Wish Upon a Star" and "Over the Rainbow." Almost worth having for the cover alone, this is one of the classics of '50s vocal-group harmony. —*Cub Koda*

• **The Best of Little Anthony & the Imperials [Rhino]** / Oct. 1989 / Rhino ✦✦✦✦✦
"Little" Anthony Gourdine's angst-ridden leads were ideal for tearjerkers and heartache ballads. Although this Brooklyn group began in the doo wop era, they were much more effective on soul songs, where group harmonies were low-key and Gourdine's voice was the major focus. This anthology includes "Hurt So Bad," "I'm on the Outside Looking In" and "Take Me Back," arguably their three finest hits, plus several others with equally theatrical vocals, but dissimilar chart performances. —*Ron Wynn*

The Best of Little Anthony & the Imperials [EMI] / May 28, 1996 / EMI ✦✦✦
Unlike the collection of the same name on Rhino, this focuses solely on their mid-to-late-'60s recordings for Veep and United Artists. That means you don't get any doo wop, but slickly arranged pop/soul that sometimes borders on easy listening, featuring string charts and Little Anthony's choked vocals (which could bring to mind an effeminate Johnny Mathis). The best and biggest of these cuts are also on the Rhino comp ("I'm on the Outside Looking In," "Goin' Out of My Head," "Hurt So Bad"), which gets the edge for its wider chronology. This is a satisfactory alternative, though, for those who prefer the Imperials' later phase, or want a more extensive sampler of their '60s stuff. —*Richie Unterberger*

We Are the Imperials/Shades of the 40's / Jun. 9, 1998 / West Side ✦✦✦✦
This Westside package features the first two albums by this influential and popular doo wop group of the 1950s. Their debut album from 1959, *We Are the Imperials,* brings together both sides of the group's first four singles (including their mega hit "Tears on My Pillow") plus four sides that were first issued on EPs in the late '50s. But the music on the disc is the group at their best and couldn't be bettered, boasting hits and turntable faves from one of the biggest stars to emerge from Goldner's doo wop stable of talent. The second album was the group's 1961 release, *Shades of the 40's,* a solid shot at moving the Imperials straight into the swank supper club market. The fare here is '40s standards done dead-straight with nary a rock & roll beat in sight, all designed to appeal to a more sophisticated adult audience. This can be heard to full effect on tracks such as "Loving You," "Glitter in Your Eyes," "Island of Love" (the group's debut disc), "Tragic" (heard here in two different single release forms: the original on Apex and its highly "echoed" reissue on Vee-Jay), "Come to Me," "Forgotten," "Elevator Operator," and "Give a Hug to Me." There's music on here so finely wrought and so heartfelt, certain passages of it will give you the cold chills by its sheer, unaffected beauty. This is much more than a dry history lesson; the Imperials made some mighty music that truly deserves a much wider hearing, and here's exactly where to start absorbing their genius. —*Cub Koda*

Little Eva

b. Jun. 29, 1943, Bellhaven, NC
Vocals / Brill Building Pop, Girl Group
Little Eva Narcissus Boyd was a babysitter for Carole King and Gerry Goffin when the

songwriting team was inspired to write "Locomotion," a song based on a dance that Eva would do around the house. Eva also got to sing on their demo, which impressed Don Kirshner enough to release it as it was. One of the greatest girl-group hits, "Locomotion," hit number one in 1962; the follow-up, "Keep Your Hands Off My Baby," was also written by Goffin-King. Almost as good as her debut, it reached the Top 20, and was even covered by the Beatles on stage in their early days (though they never recorded it in the studio). Unfortunately, Eva was then pigeonholed as a dance-craze singer and given inferior material. She never again reached the soulful heights of her first two singles; "Let's Turkey Trot" (1963) was her only other Top 20 hit. —*Richie Unterberger*

● **The Best of Little Eva** / 1988 / Collectables ✦✦✦✦✦
Fifteen songs, most cut for the Dimension label between 1962 and 1964. Includes all the hits and some pleasant girl-group flops in a more lightweight style than "Locomotion." —*Richie Unterberger*

The Loco-Motion / Feb. 27, 1996 / Rhino ✦✦✦
Some collectors will be glad to have some Little Eva available on CD domestically. At only ten cuts (and no liner notes), however, it's on the skimpy side, and "Let's Turkey Trot" is unexpectedly missing. The 15-song best-of on Murray Hill is considerably more extensive and well annotated (albeit getting harder to find). On the other hand, this Rhino comp does have seven songs not on the Murray Hill LP (including some obscure Goffin/King compositions), although some of these are covers of popular early '60s hits. —*Richie Unterberger*

Little Feat

f. 1969, Los Angeles, CA
Album Rock, Boogie Rock, Southern Rock, Hard Rock, Blues-Rock, Rock & Roll
Though they had all the trappings of a Southern-fried blues band, Little Feat were hardly conventional. Led by songwriter/guitarist Lowell George, Little Feat was a wildly eclectic band, bringing together strains of blues, R&B, country and rock & roll. The group was exceptionally gifted technically and their polished professionalism sat well with the slick sounds coming out of Southern California during the '70s. However, Little Feat were hardly slick—they had a surreal sensibility, as evidenced by George's idiosyncratic songwriting, which helped the band earn a cult following among critics and musicians. Though the band earned some success on album-oriented radio, the group was derailed after George's death in 1979. Little Feat re-formed in the late '80s, and while they were playing as well as ever, they lacked the skewed sensibility that made them cult favorites. Nevertheless, their albums and tours were successful, especially among American blues-rock fans. —*Stephen Thomas Erlewine*

☆ **Little Feat** / 1971 / Warner Brothers ✦✦✦✦✦
It sold poorly (around 11,000 copies) and the band never cut anything like it again, but Little Feat's eponymous debut isn't just one of their finest records, it's one of the great lost rock & roll albums. Even dedicated fans tend to overlook the album, largely because it's the polar opposite of the subtly intricate, funky rhythm & roll that made their reputation during the mid-'70s. *Little Feat* is a raw, hard-driving, funny and affectionate celebration of American weirdness, equal parts garage rock, roadhouse blues, post-Zappa bizarreness, post-Parsons country rock and slightly bent folk storytelling. Since it's grounded in roots rock, it feels familiar enough, but the vision of chief songwriter/guitarist/vocalist Lowell George is wholly unique and slightly off-center. He sees everything with a gently surreal sense of humor that remains affectionate, whether it's on an ode to a "Truck Stop Girl," the weary trucker's anthem "Willin'," or the goofy character sketch of the crusty old salt "Crazy Captain Gunboat Willie." That affection is balanced by gutsy slices of Americana like the careening travelogue "Strawberry Flats," the darkly humorous "Hamburger Midnight" and a jaw-dropping Howlin' Wolf medley guest-starring Ry Cooder, plus keyboardist Bill Payne's terrific opener "Snakes on Everything." The songwriting itself is remarkable enough, but the band is its equal—they're as loose, vibrant and alive as the Stones at their best. In most respects, this album has more in common with George's earlier band the Factory than the rest of the Little Feat catalog, but there's a deftness in the writing and performance that distinguishes it from either band's work, which makes it all the more remarkable. It's a pity that more people haven't heard the record, but that just means that anyone who owns it feels like they're in on a secret only they and a handful of others know. —*Stephen Thomas Erlewine*

☆ **Sailin' Shoes** / 1972 / Warner Brothers ✦✦✦✦✦
Little Feat's debut may have been a great album but it sold so poorly, they had to either broaden their audience or, in all likelihood, they'd be dropped from Warner. So, *Sailin' Shoes* is a consciously different record from its predecessor—less raw and bluesy, blessed with a varied production and catchier songs. That still doesn't make it a pop record, since Little Feat, particularly in its first incarnation, was simply too idiosyncratic, earthy and strange for that. It is, however, an utterly thrilling, individual blend of pop, rock, blues and country, due in no small part to a stellar set of songs from Lowell George. If anything, his quirks are all the more apparent here than they were on the debut, since Ted Templeman's production lends each song its own character, plus his pen was getting sharper. George truly finds his voice on this record, with each of his contributions sparkling with off-kilter humor, friendly surreal imagery and humanity, and he demonstrates he can authoritatively write anything from full-throttle rock & roll ("Teenage Nervous Breakdown"), sweet ballads ("Trouble," a sublimely reworked "Willin'"), skewered folk ("Sailin' Shoes"), paranoid rock ("Cold, Cold, Cold") and blues ("A Apolitical Blues") and, yes, even hooky mainstream rock ("Easy to Slip," which should have been the hit the band intended it to be). That's not to discount the contributions of the other members, particularly Bill Payne and Richie Hayward's "Tripe Face Boogie," which is justifiably one of the band's standards, but the thing that truly stuns on *Sailin' Shoes* is George's songwriting and how

the band brings it to a full, colorful life. Nobody could master the twists and turns within George's songs better than Little Feat, and both the songwriter and his band are in prime form here. —*Stephen Thomas Erlewine*

★ **Dixie Chicken** / 1973 / Warner Brothers ✦✦✦✦✦
Following Roy Estrada's departure during the supporting tour for *Sailin' Shoes*, Lowell George became infatuated with New Orleans R&B and mellow jamming, all of which came to a head on their third album, 1973's *Dixie Chicken*. Although George is firmly in charge—he dominates the record, writing or co-writing seven of the 10 songs—this is the point where Little Feat found its signature sound as a band, and no album they would cut from this point on was too different from this seductive, laid-back, funky record. But no album would be quite as good, either, since *Dixie Chicken* still had much of the charming lyrical eccentricities of the first two albums, plus what is arguably George's best-ever set of songs. Partially due to the New Orleans infatuation, the album holds together better than *Sailin' Shoes* and George takes full advantage of the band's increased musical palette, writing songs that sound easy but are quite sophisticated, such as the rolling "Two Trains," the gorgeous, shimmering "Juliette," the deeply soulful and funny "Fat Man in the Bathtub" and the country-funk of the title track, which was covered nearly as frequently as "Willin'." In addition to "Walkin' All Night," a loose bluesy jam by Barrere and Bill Payne, the band also hauls out two covers which fit George's vibe perfectly: Allan Toussaint's slow burner "On Your Way Down" and "Fool Yourself," which was written by Fred Tackett, who later joined a reunited Feat in the '80s. It all adds up to a nearly irresistible record, filled with great songwriting, sultry grooves and virtuosic performances that never are flashy. Little Feat, along with many jam bands that followed, tried to top this album, but they never managed to make a record this understated, appealing and fine. —*Stephen Thomas Erlewine*

Feats Don't Fail Me Now / 1974 / Warner Brothers ✦✦✦✦
If *Dixie Chicken* represented a pinnacle of Lowell George as a songwriter and band leader, its sequel *Feats Don't Fail Me Now* is the pinnacle of Little Feat as a group, showcasing each member at their finest. Not coincidentally, it's the moment where George begins to recede from the spotlight, leaving the band as a true democracy. These observations are only clear in hindsight, since if *Feats Don't Fail Me Now* is just taken as a record, it's nothing more than a damn good rock & roll record. That's not meant as a dismissal, either, since it's hard to make a rock & roll record as seemingly effortless and infectious as this. Though it effectively builds on the Southern-fried funkiness of *Dixie Chicken*, it's hardly as mellow as that record—there's a lot of grit, tougher rhythms, lots of guitar and organ. It's as supple as *Chicken*, though, which means that it's the sound of a touring band at their peak. As it happens, the band is on the top of their writing game, as well, with Bill Payne contributing the rollicking "Oh Atlanta" and Paul Barrere turning in one of his best songs, the jazzy funk of "Skin It Back." Each has a co-writing credit with George—Payne on the unreleased *Little Feat*-era nugget "The Fan" and Barrere (plus Fred Martin) on the infectious title track—who also has a couple of classics with "Rock & Roll Doctor" and the great "Spanish Moon." *Feats* peters out toward the end, as the group delves into a 10-minute medley of two *Sailin' Shoes* songs, but that doesn't hurt one of the best albums Little Feat ever cut. It's so good, the group used it as the template for the rest of their career. —*Stephen Thomas Erlewine*

The Last Record Album / 1975 / Warner Brothers ✦✦✦
The title of *The Last Record Album* isn't literally accurate, but it cuts a lot closer than the band intended, for this is really is the last album of the group's classic era. Starting with this album, leader Lowell George fades into the woodwork, and while the remainder of the group tries valiantly to keep the band afloat, the timing of friction was wrong and the amount of tension was too great. Musically, the group attempts to make *Feats Don't Fail Me Now, Pt. 2*, but the production from George is curiously flat, and, truth be told, the group just isn't inspired enough to make a satisfying album. For a very short album—only eight songs—too many of the cuts fall flat. Those that succeed, however, are quite good, particularly Paul Barrere and Bill Payne's gently propulsive "All That You Dream," Lowell George's beautiful "Long Distance Love," and the sublime "Mercenary Territory." Even these songs don't have the spark or character they would have had on the more organic *Feats*, due to George's exceedingly mellow So-Cal production, which is pleasant but doesn't provide Little Feat with enough room to breathe. There are enough signs of Little Feat's true character on *The Last Record Album*—the three previously mentioned songs are essential for any Feat fan—to make it fairly enjoyable, but it's clear that the band is beginning to run out of steam. [The CD reissue of *The Last Record Album* includes two bonus tracks, "Don't Bogart That Joint" and "A Apolitical Blues," that were originally included on the 1978 live album *Waiting for Columbus*. They were pulled from the CD reissue of that album due to time restrictions, and appeared here instead.] —*Stephen Thomas Erlewine*

Time Loves a Hero / 1977 / Warner Brothers ✦✦✦
When Little Feat headed into the studio to record *Time Loves a Hero*, tensions between the band members—more specifically, Lowell George and the rest of the band—were at a peak. George had not only succumbed to various addictions, but he was growing restless with the group's fondness for extending their jams into territory strikingly reminiscent of jazz fusion. The rest of the group brought in Ted Templeman, who previously worked on their debut and produced *Sailin' Shoes*, to mediate the sessions. George wasn't thrilled with that, but that's probably not the only reason why his presence isn't large on this release—all signs point to his frustration with the band, and he wasn't in great health, so he just didn't contribute to the record. He wrote one song, the pleasant but comparatively faceless "Rocket in My Pocket," and collaborated with Paul Barrere on "Keepin' Up With the Joneses." Barrere was responsible for the only bright moments on the album, the ingratiatingly silly "Old Folks' Boogie" and, along with Bill Payne and Ken Gradney,

the funky singalong title track. Elsewhere, Barrere and Payne come up dry, turning out generic pieces that are well-played but not as memorable as comparable Doobie Brothers' cuts from the same time. Then there's "Day at the Dog Races," a lengthy fusion jam that Templeman and everyone in the band loved—except for George, who, according to Bud Scoppa's liner notes in *Hotcakes & Outtakes*, disparagingly compared it to Weather Report. He was right—no matter how well Feat play on this track, it comes across as self-serving indulgence, and the clearest sign on this muddled album that they had indeed lost the plot. —*Stephen Thomas Erlewine*

Waiting for Columbus / 1978 / Warner Brothers ✦✦✦✦✦
Little Feat was one of the legendary live bands of the '70s, showered with praise by not only their small, fiercely dedicated cult of fans, but such fellow musicians like Bonnie Raitt, Robert Palmer and Jimmy Page. Given all that acclaim, it only made sense for the group to cut a live album. Unfortunately, they waited until 1977, when the group had entered its decline, but as the double-album *Waiting for Columbus* proves, Little Feat in its decline was still pretty great. Certainly, the group is far more inspired on stage than they were in the studio after 1975—just compare "All That You Dream," "Oh Atlanta," "Old Folks' Boogie," "Time Loves a Hero," and "Mercenary Territory" here to the cuts on *The Last Record Album* and *Time Loves a Hero*. The versions on *Waiting* are full-bodied and fully-realized, putting the studio cuts to shame. Early classics like "Fat Man in the Bathtub" and "Tripe Face Boogie" aren't as revelatory, but it's still a pleasure to hear a great band run through their best songs, stretching them out and finding new quirks within them. If there are any flaws with *Waiting for Columbus*, it's that the Feat do a little bit too much stretching, veering toward excessive jamming on occasion—and that mildly fuzzy focus is really the only way you'd be able to tell that this is a great live band recorded slightly after their prime. Even so, there's much to savor on *Waiting for Columbus*, one of the great live albums of its era, thanks to rich performances that prove Little Feat were one of the great live bands of their time. —*Stephen Thomas Erlewine*

Down on the Farm / 1979 / Warner Brothers ✦✦
As Little Feat were working on their seventh studio album, Lowell George was just marginally part of the group, spending much of his time completing his solo album, *Thanks I'll Eat It Here*. While he was touring in support of the record, he suffered a massive heart attack and died, leaving behind an uncompleted record with Little Feat. After mourning, the band regrouped and patched together *Down on the Farm*, the last album of the Lowell-led era. Since George was preoccupied during the recording, it's not surprising that he only makes himself heard on occasion on the album. It's also not surprising that the group was suffering, not just from the loss of a colleague, but from a lack of direction. They were drifting on *Time Loves a Hero*, after all, and while this is musically a little more straightforward than that fusion-flavored affair, it still is fairly uninspired. The surfaces are very slick, as should be expected with late-'70s Californian rock, which again doesn't let the group breathe, but the real problem is that the material is just not terribly memorable. Given the circumstances surrounding the completion of *Down on the Farm*, it's fairly easy to forgive the band this misstep, but it doesn't make the album any less disheartening. —*Stephen Thomas Erlewine*

Hoy-Hoy / 1981 / Warner Brothers ✦✦✦✦✦
Perhaps realizing that *Down on the Farm* wasn't the proper swan song for Little Feat, the group persuaded Warner Brothers to release a compilation of rarities and overlooked tracks as a swan song and farewell to fans. Filled with live performances, obscurities, album tracks, and a new song apiece from Bill Payne and Paul Barrere, *Hoy Hoy* is a bit scattered, a bit incoherent, a little bewildering, and wholly delightful—a perfect summation of a group filled with quirks, character, and funk, traits which were as much a blessing as they were a curse. *Hoy Hoy* is one of those rare albums that may be designed for diehards—who else really needs radio performances, early recordings from before the band was signed, and outtakes, especially if they're surrounded by early album tracks?—but still is a great introduction for novices. That doesn't mean it's as good as such masterpieces as *Sailin' Shoes*, *Dixie Chicken*, or *Waiting for Columbus*, but it does capture the group's careening, freewheeling spirit, humor, and musical versatility, arguably better than any single album. That's one of the nice things compilations like this can do—they can summarize what a band was all about in a way a straight studio album couldn't. So, that's why it may be a good gateway into the band for novices, even though it's missing such essentials as "Willin'" and "Fat Man in the Bathtub," but it's truly for the dedicated, who will not only love the rarities (and these live cuts are hotter, on whole, than *Columbus*) but will savor the context. —*Stephen Thomas Erlewine*

Let It Roll / Jul. 1988 / Warner Brothers ✦✦✦
When Little Feat reunited in 1988, they were embraced by some dedicated fans, but were spurned by nearly an equal number of cultists. That's because to certain diehards, Little Feat belonged to Lowell George and, without him, the group doesn't exist. While it is true that George was the main songwriter and visionary during the early years of the group, he had pulled away from the group in the last half of the '70s and only had a marginal impact on their final three albums of the '70s. Also, throughout their career, the band contributed significantly, co-writing songs with George, writing their own tunes and, of course, shaping the band's sound with their musicianship. Although George was gone, they still had the desire to perform, so it was understandable that they wanted to reunite, with Craig Fuller taking George's place. What's surprising about *Let It Roll* is not just that it works, but that it works smashingly. It sounds as if the group picked up after *The Last Record Album*, deciding to return to the sound of *Feats Don't Fail Me Now*. True, the songwriting might not have the idiosyncratic genius of George, but it's strong, catchy and memorable, from the fine singles "Hate to Lose Your Lovin'" and "Let it Roll" to album tracks. More importantly, the band sounds lively and playful—Little Feat hasn't sounded this good in the studio since *Feats*, so it's easy to see why the members wanted to regroup.

Yes, George is missed—it's hard not to miss such a gifted songwriter and musician—but *Let It Roll* isn't disrespectful of his memory, it keeps his music alive, which is the greatest compliment it can be paid. —*Stephen Thomas Erlewine*

Representing the Mambo / 1989 / Warner Brothers ✦✦

Shake Me Up / Sep. 24, 1991 / Morgan Creek ✦✦

● **The Best of Little Feat: As Time Goes By** / Feb. 10, 1994 / Warner Brothers ✦✦✦✦✦
As Time Goes By: The Best of Little Feat is an extraordinary collection that contains almost every essential Little Feat song from their '70s heyday with Lowell George, plus the two hits ("Let It Roll," "Hate to Lose Your Lovin'") from their late-'80s comeback. Most of the band's albums are worth hearing, but this is a great introduction for the curious and—since it features "Dixie Chicken," "Willin'," "Two Trains," "Fat Man in the Bathtub," "Sailin' Shoes," "Oh Atlanta" and "All That You Dream" in one place—it's a great summation of the group's achievements, and George's songwriting talent in particular. Unfortunately, *As Time Goes By* has only been released by the British division of Warner Brothers, but it's worth tracking down. —*Stephen Thomas Erlewine*

Ain't Had Enough Fun / Apr. 25, 1995 / Zoo ✦✦✦
The members of the group that has the legal right to call itself "Little Feat" perhaps are to be complemented for their realization, after three albums, that having Craig Fuller imitate the voice of the band's deceased founder, Lowell George, was ethically suspect. Or maybe they didn't realize; this album's liner notes say only that "mister fuller decided that the road life was not for him." In any case, the surviving "featsters" have cast against type, recruiting one Shaun Murphy, who can't imitate George but certainly can imitate longtime Feat booster Bonnie Raitt. The addition of a female voice allows for greater variety in lyric-writing and some entertaining call-and-response singing, however, and more important, it begins to free the group from the ghost of Lowell George. The featsters locate themselves more than ever in the mythology of New Orleans, alternating second-line rhythms with John Lee Hooker boogie. One may still wish they had found another name to distinguish themselves from George's group, but *Ain't Had Enough Fun* is a worthy addition to their catalog on its own terms. —*William Ruhlmann*

Live from Neon Park / Jun. 18, 1996 / Zoo ✦✦✦
Live from Neon Park is an exhaustive double-disc live set recorded on the tour supporting *Ain't Had Enough Fun*, the first Little Feat album that featured vocalist Shaun Murphy. The double-disc features all of the band's best-known material, from "Dixie Chicken" to "Let It Roll." The Feat have always been one of the best live rootsy rock bands, so they naturally give inspired performances, even if they occasionally sound like they've performed these songs one too many times. Still, dedicated Little Feat fans will find this to be an entertaining memento of the latter-day edition of the band. —*Thom Owens*

Under the Radar / Jun. 16, 1998 / CMC International ✦✦✦
Little Feat's first album for CMC International, *Under the Radar*, finds the group's new lineup fully assimilated, with Shaun Murphy sharing many of the lead vocals with mainstays Paul Barrere and Bill Payne. While the record is not as instantly accessible and spontaneous as the last record with Murphy, *Ain't Had Enough Fun*, there is a confidence that permeates every cut. Feat's slightly trippy Southern-fried music has made an amazing leap into the 1990s, and *Under the Radar* continues their rebirth. Tracks such as Barrere's "Home Ground" and "Loco-Motives" are good-time funky rockers, driven by Barrere's excellent slide guitar. Payne's title cut and "Eden's Wall" have a slightly dark hopefulness that has become a big part of the band's style. The final cut, "Calling the Children Home," is one of the group's greatest records, closing the album out in joyous New Orleans style. —*Matt Greenwald*

Chinese Work Songs / Jun. 20, 2000 / CMC International ✦✦✦
Some fans of Little Feat's classic 1970s recordings argue that the band should have lost the right to use that name when Lowell George died in 1979; as they see it, the band heard on 2000's *Chinese Work Songs* isn't really Little Feat. If this band can get away with calling itself Little Feat, the argument goes, why shouldn't Bob Weir assemble a band without the late Jerry Garcia and call it the Grateful Dead? You have no doubt heard those arguments, and while it's true that Little Feat recorded its best work in the 1970s, the lineup heard on *Chinese Work Songs* isn't half bad. In its 2000 incarnation, Little Feat's lineup ranges from 1970s members Bill Payne (keyboards), Richie Hayward (drums), Paul Barrere (guitar), Kenny Gradney (bass), and Sam Clayton (percussion) to more recent additions like guitarist Fred Tackett and female singer Shaun Murphy. The addition of Murphy in the 1990s proved to be a plus for the band, and her whiskey-voiced, Bonnie Raitt-influenced belting is a definite asset on this CD. *Chinese Work Songs* isn't in a class with 1973's *Dixie Chicken* or 1974's *Feats Don't Fail Me Now*, but it's a decent, if uneven, outing, and the 2000 lineup is faithful to the band's roots rock-Southern rock history on original material as well as covers of Bob Dylan's "It Takes a Lot to Laugh, It Takes a Train to Cry," the Band's "Rag Mama Rag," the Hooters' "Gimme a Stone," and Phish's "Sample in a Jar." Although not essential and not recommended to casual listeners—who would be better off with a collection of Little Feat's 1970s recordings for Warner Brothers—diehard Feat fans will find that *Chinese Work Songs*, despite its imperfections, is enjoyable more often than not. —*Alex Henderson*

Hotcakes and Outtakes: 30 Years of Little Feat / Sep. 19, 2000 / Rhino/Warner Archives ✦✦✦✦
Rhino's four-disc box set *Hotcakes & Outtakes* treats all of Little Feat's incarnations with equal respect. This even-handed approach has advantages, even if Lowell George dominates the proceedings. How could he not? He was a musician of immense talents, shaping the band's core sound while building an impressive body of songs. This set reveals that the rest of the band, while not writers of George's ilk, still wrote their share of great songs and, best of all, their fusion of funk, blues, country, rock and jazz still sounded

lively, even when they reunited a decade after his death. Yes, it was missing his unique brilliance and vision, yet the reunited Feat still carried the torch well, which this set proves. Still, the best thing about the box is the fourth disc, devoted to "Studio Artifacts," all dating from George's heyday with the band. Actually, it goes a little further than that, beginning with cuts from George and Roy Estrada's mid-'60s band the Factory and pre-Warner Bros recordings, plus a generous selection of outtakes and demos, including selections from George's solo album, *Thanks I'll Eat It Here*. It's a treasure trove for any Little Feat fan, filled with amazing cuts like the barn-storming "Rat Faced Dog"—tracks so good, it's hard to believe they haven't been released before. This fourth disc is reason for any devoted fan to pick up this set, but is this worthwhile for the curious? Well, yes, since this offers a great summary of their fascinating career, even if it duplicates some songs at the expense of album tracks like "A Apolitical Blues" which really should be here. Even with that flaw, *Hotcakes & Outtakes* performs its job well, proving that Little Feat is an American rock & roll band like no other. —*Stephen Thomas Erlewine*

Little Richard

b. Dec. 5, 1935, St. Louis, MO

Vocals, Piano / New Orleans R&B, Rock & Roll, R&B

One of the original rock & roll greats, Little Richard merged the fire of gospel with New Orleans R&B, pounding the piano and wailing with gleeful abandon. While numerous other R&B greats of the early 1950s had been moving in a similar direction, none of them matched the sheer electricity of Richard's vocals. With his bullet-speed deliveries, ecstatic trills, and the overjoyed force of personality in his singing, he was crucial in upping the voltage from high-powered R&B into the similar, yet different, guise of rock & roll. Although he was only a hitmaker for a couple of years or so, his influence upon both the soul and British Invasion stars of the 1960s was vast, and his early hits remain core classics of the rock repertoire. In 1955, at Lloyd Price's suggestion, Richard sent a demo tape to Specialty Records, who were impressed enough to sign him and arrange a session for him in New Orleans. That session, however, didn't get off the ground until Richard began fooling around with a slightly obscene ditty during a break. With slightly cleaned-up lyrics, "Tutti Frutti" was the record that gave birth to Little Richard as we know him—the gleeful "woo!"s, the furious piano playing, the sax-driven, pedal-to-the-metal rhythm section. In 1956 and 1957, Richard reeled off a string of classic hits—"Long Tall Sally," "Slippin' and Slidin'," "Jenny, Jenny," "Keep a Knockin'," "Good Golly, Miss Molly," "The Girl Can't Help It"—that remain the foundation of his fame. Little Richard was at the height of his commercial and artistic powers when he suddenly quit the business during an Australian tour in late 1957, enrolling in a bible college in Alabama shortly after returning to the States. By 1962, though, Richard had returned to rock & roll. At this point it's safe to assume that he never will get that much-hungered-for comeback hit, but he remains one of rock & roll's most colorful icons, still capable of turning on the charm and charisma well in his infrequent appearances in the limelight. —*Richie Unterberger*

☆ **18 Greatest Hits** / 1985 / Rhino ✦✦✦✦✦

18 Greatest Hits is the definitive single-disc collection of Little Richard's Specialty singles, especially for listeners who only want the hits. Every one of Richard's biggest hits—"Tutti Frutti," "Long Tall Sally," "Slippin' and Slidin'," "Rip It Up," "Ready Teddy," "The Girl Can't Help It," "Lucille," "Send Me Some Lovin'," "Keep A-Knockin'," "Good Golly Miss Molly"—are here, plus singles like "Heeby-Jeebies," "She's Got It," "Ooh! My Soul," "Miss Ann," "Kansas City/Hey Hey Hey," and "Bama Lama Bama Loo" that were bigger hits on the R&B charts than the pop charts. All of the singles are presented in chronological order, and the disc simply rips it up from beginning to end. It's a definitive collection. —*Stephen Thomas Erlewine*

The Specialty Box Set / 1989 / Specialty ✦✦✦✦✦

Dig it—a collection of all 73 songs that Little Richard cut for Specialty Records from 1955 through 1959, including early working versions of hits including "Long Tall Sally" and "Slippin' and Slidin'," may seem like overkill to the casual listener, but if you're thinking of buying this three-CD box, chances are you're not a casual listener. And if you're not thinking about it, then you should be. This set covers only four years in Little Richard's career, but manages to sum up virtually everything you need to know about him (his earlier sides, available on Bear Family, are an interesting appendix, but of his later stuff, only the early- and mid-'60s material, with Jimi Hendrix on guitar, hold any significance, mostly as a curiosity). Not only does the music make you want to get up and dance, but the notes—spread out on a lavishly illustrated booklet and the individual jewel boxes—tell the whole story of Specialty Records and the people behind it, including Art Rupe, Bumps Blackwell, Dave Bartholomew, and, of course, Richard Penniman himself. The session information alone could keep owners busy for a week. The sound is nothing less than breathtaking, loud and raunchy but razor sharp, and the price of this set—about $42 retail—makes it competitive with other Little Richard single-disc sets as well as more attractive than the price of boxes devoted to Elvis Presley and Chuck Berry. The only complaint—why couldn't the producers list the songs on the individual jewel boxes? —*Bruce Eder*

The Formative Years 1951-53 / Jul. 1989 / Bear Family ✦✦✦✦

Early Richard, pre-"Tutti Frutti." —*Cub Koda*

★ **The Georgia Peach** / Aug. 5, 1991 / Specialty ✦✦✦✦✦

Perhaps the greatest of Little Richard's greatest hits compilations, the 25-track *Georgia Peach* features all of his biggest hits in chronological order, as well as terrific singles that never were as big as "Tutti Frutti" and "Good Golly Miss Molly." On top of the sublime song selection and sound, the liner notes by compiler Billy Vera are splendid and insightful. —*Stephen Thomas Erlewine*

Shag on Down by the Union Hall / Feb. 13, 1996 / Specialty ✦✦✦✦✦

For those who want more classic Little Richard than a greatest-hits collection but aren't devoted enough to spring for the expensive box sets, this is an excellent anthology of 24 of his best lesser-known tracks. Most of it dates from his classic era at Specialty (1955-57), with alternate takes of a lot of his hits and some decent B-sides; there are also a few songs that he cut for the label during his 1964 comeback, including the minor hit "Bama Lama Bama Loo." —*Richie Unterberger*

Little River Band

f. Mar. 1975, Melbourne, Australia

Pop/Rock, Soft Rock, Adult Contemporary

One of Australia's most prominent musical exports of the 1970s, the Little River Band shot to fame on the strength of their glowing harmonies and mellow country-pop sound. After signing to Capitol, they issued their self-titled 1975 debut, scoring a Top 30 U.S. hit with the single "It's a Long Way There." In the States, the next Little River Band release—titled *Diamantina Cocktail*—compiled material from their first two Australian LPs; it proved to be their commercial breakthrough, launching the single "Help Is On Its Way" into the Top 20. Over the next two years, the band scored four Top Ten hits—"Reminiscing," "Lady," "Lonesome Loser" and "Cool Change"—and earned platinum status with their fifth album, *First Under the Wire*. The legendary George Martin produced the Little River Band's next studio effort, 1981's *Time Exposure*, scoring another pair of Top Ten smashes with "Take It Easy on Me" and "Night Owls." Another single, "Man on Your Mind," was also a success. 1983's *The Net* failed to match the popularity of the albums which preceded it, however, although the group continued recording into the 1990s. —*Jason Ankeny*

Reminiscing: The 20th Anniversary Collection / 1995 / Rhino ✦✦✦✦

An extremely comprehensive but equally enjoyable 34 tracks make up this two-CD set from Australia's Little River Band, including some infamous yet attractive add-ons. Every charted hit from LRB is here, along with some interesting rarities. A cover of Phil Everly's "When Will I Be Loved," never before issued in the U.S., is a real treat, as well as the potent "Long Jumping Jeweler," another single that was never released in America. A splendid cover of the Eagles' "Lyin' Eyes" and "Take It Easy" is performed live with Glenn Frey as a nifty little medley, and "Days on the Road" is a stark but attractive B-side addition. The real beauty of this album is uncovered in songs like "We Two," displaying all the vibrancy and flash exhibited by John Farnham, who took Shorrock's place in 1983. Farnham proves that he's just as fiery on "You're Driving Me Out of My Mind," with full-blown horns that overspill with dynamic flare. Wavy love songs like "Love Is the Bridge" and "It's Cold Out Tonight" display this band's multifaceted versatility, showing they can sing charming ballads with pristine honesty. Even though favorites like "The Night Owls" and "Reminiscing" cap off the solidness of this compilation, many other of their forgotten songs delightfully complete this hearty anthology. —*Mike DeGagne*

● **Greatest Hits [Expanded Edition]** / Jan. 25, 2000 / Capitol ✦✦✦✦✦

A group like Little River Band is the epitome of a fine singles act. It had two gold and two platinum albums in its late-'70s, early-'80s prime, but it's no surprise that its biggest seller is 1982's double-platinum *Greatest Hits*. In 2000, a 24-bit digitally remastered expanded edition was released and it's simply excellent. It adds six songs to the original's dozen, and these include the rest of LRB's charted singles. The 2000 version polishes the Australian band's smooth, irresistibly catchy brand of pop/rock. The sound quality is crisp and clean. All the instruments jump out. LRB—which featured an unusual-for-pop three-guitar lineup—was kind of faceless, so its many personnel changes didn't necessarily alienate fans. Glenn Shorrock sang most of the signature hits like "Lonesome Loser," "Reminiscing," "Cool Change," "Help Is on Its Way," "Take It Easy on Me," "Man on Your Mind," and "Happy Anniversary." Bassist Wayne Nelson sang "The Night Owls," one of LRB's most rock-oriented numbers. All the previously mentioned songs are included, of course, but the newly added ones help provide a clearer picture of the band's career. The most notable were LRB's last two Top 40 hits, "We Two" and the funky, horns-based "You're Driving Me Out of My Mind," both sung by Shorrock's replacement, John Farnham. Another Farnham track, "Playing to Win," is a surprising burst of hard rock with hyperactive synthesizer. The Shorrock-era extras are "I'll Always Call Your Name" and "It's Not a Wonder." The latter in particular is a welcome addition. 2000's *Greatest Hits*, which features a bare-bones essay by Simon Glickman, unquestionably supersedes its predecessor. It's a mid-line-priced gem for casual fans. Collectors should note that early copies of *Greatest Hits* mistakenly included alternate versions of some hits. —*Bret Adams*

Little Steven & the Disciples of Soul (Steve Van Zandt)

f. 1979, Boston, MA

Psychedelic, Prog-Rock/Art Rock, Hard Rock, Rock & Roll, Bar Band, Heartland Rock

Steven Van Zandt grew up in the same south New Jersey shore scene as Bruce Springsteen and Southside Johnny Lyon and was closely associated with them. He was a member of Springsteen's band Steel Mill in 1969-1970 and the Bruce Springsteen Band in 1971. He toured with the Dovells, then worked with Southside Johnny, helping him form the Asbury Jukes in 1974 and playing with the group, but he rejoined Springsteen in the E Street Band in early 1975. This group went on to massive success, and Van Zandt worked closely with Springsteen, co-producing *The River* (1980) and *Born in the U.S.A.* (1984) while also producing and writing material for Southside Johnny and Gary U.S. Bonds. In 1982, he organized Little Steven and the Disciples of Soul and released *Men Without Women* that year. He left the E Street Band on amicable terms in April 1984 and released the second Disciples of Soul album *Voice of America* that spring. His work as Little Steven found him taking an overt left-wing political stance, and in 1985 he organized Artists United Against Apartheid, recording the all-star Top 40 single "Sun City," which increased awareness about apartheid in South Africa and the part that musicians played in it by appearing at the country's Sun City entertainment complex. In 1987, having shed the Disciples of Soul, he released his third album, *Freedom—No Compromise. Revolution* followed in 1989. Though Van Zandt was without a record contract during the 1990s, he produced other artists and was involved in soundtrack work. In 1995, he rejoined the E Street Band for recordings and performances in connection with Springsteen's *Greatest Hits* album. He turned to acting in 1998, taking a featured role in the successful television series *The Sopranos*. In 1999, he again rejoined the E Street Band for its reunion tour, and he released a new album, *Born Again Savage*. *—William Ruhlmann & John Floyd*

Greatest Hits / Sep. 30, 1999 / EMI ✦✦✦✦✦
Compiler and annotator Sven Peterson notes that "Little Steven" Van Zandt was more successful in Europe than in his native U.S., with two of his albums reaching the Top Ten in Sweden, so it is appropriate that this compilation of his EMI recordings was assembled in Sweden and released in Europe, but not the U.S. Peterson has chosen five tracks each from Little Steven's three EMI albums, plus the non-LP single "Vote!," and sequenced them chronologically. Thus, it is possible to trace both the artist's musical development and, most strikingly, his increasing militancy. The songs from 1982's *Men Without Women* recall Van Zandt's writing for Southside Johnny and the Asbury Jukes and Gary U.S. Bonds; they are 1960s-style, R&B-tinged pop-rock informed by the wide-screen production sound Bruce Springsteen developed with Van Zandt's assistance, with lots of screaming lead guitar and horn charts. Starting with 1984's *Voice of America*, Van Zandt began to express his political opinions, and in the process to employ other musical styles, such as reggae. [Curiously, Peterson does not use "I Am a Patriot (And the River Opens for the Righteous)," a song widely performed by Jackson Browne that has become one of Van Zandt's better-known compositions, nor the 1985 Top 40 hit "Sun City," by Artists United Against Apartheid, an all-star group organized by Van Zandt.] By the time of 1987's *Freedom—No Compromise*, Van Zandt has incorporated everything from Latin rhythms to South African mbaqanga to mirror his political concerns, though he sounds most involved singing about the plight of Native Americans. Financially secure from his years with the E Street Band and his production work, Van Zandt made the kind of impassioned, high-quality music he wanted to—"freedom, no compromise" was his artistic motto as well as an album title. If that meant that his commercial prospects were limited, this compilation confirms that his recordings hold up as music and as statements of belief. *—William Ruhlmann*

Little Village

f. 1992, **db.** 1992
Rock & Roll
An early-'90s supergroup, Little Village is composed of string wizard Ry Cooder, tunesmith John Hiatt, English bassist Nick Lowe, and session drummer extraordinaire Jim Keltner. All four musicians originally played as a unit in 1987 on Hiatt's breakthrough album *Bring the Family*. In that context, all but Hiatt were sidemen. Four years later they collectively wrote and recorded their self-titled debut CD. Although the record was a bit of a disappointment, the live shows were superb. *—Rob Bowman*

Little Village / 1992 / Reprise ✦✦✦
Sometimes you just can't get lightning to strike in the same place twice, no matter how hard you try, and the sole album from Little Village serves as proof. In 1987, guitarist Ry Cooder, bassist Nick Lowe, and drummer Jim Keltner backed up singer and songwriter John Hiatt on his album *Bring the Family*; the album was hailed as an instant classic, but negotiations to reassemble the group for Hiatt's next album failed. Five years later, the four musicians were persuaded to give working together another try, but this time instead of backing Hiatt, they'd form a band called Little Village, with all the members writing collectively and Hiatt, Cooder, and Lowe trading off on vocals. The idea certainly sounded promising, and there's no denying that these guys play together brilliantly; *Little Village* rocks harder than *Bring the Family*, with Keltner and Lowe generating a bucketful of groove, and Cooder chiming in with a man-sized portion of his trademark funky guitar. But while the songs on *Bring the Family* were powerful, personal, and often deeply moving, here the band sounds like they're just looking to make a good-time party album, and while it is indeed a good time, the results just aren't as satisfying; bald spots and bad driving may be funny, but love and family are the kind of stuff that sticks with you. Also, while Little Village was supposed to be a democracy, it's significant that John Hiatt ended up with the lion's share of the vocals, and most of the songs sound like... well, like John Hiatt songs, which is by no means a bad thing, but with writers and vocalists of the caliber of Nick Lowe and Ry Cooder on board, it's a shame we don't hear more from them. After one album and one tour, Little Village called it a day, and while the album shows they knew how to work together, the finished product is just good fun, rather than the second instant classic they were shooting for. *—Mark Deming*

Little Willie John

b. Nov. 15, 1937, Cullendale, AK, **d.** May 26, 1968, Walla Walla, WA
Vocals / R&B, Soul
He's never received the accolades given to the likes of Sam Cooke, Clyde McPhatter, and James Brown, but Little Willie John ranks as one of R&B's most influential performers. His muscular high timbre and enormous technical and emotional range belied his young age (his first hit came when he was 18), but his mid-'50s work for Syd Nathan's King label would play a great part in the way soul music would sound. Everyone from Cooke, McPhatter, and Brown to Jackie Wilson, B.B. King, and Al Green has acknowledged his debt to this most overlooked of rock and soul pioneers. His debut recording, a smoking version of Titus Turner's "All around the World" from 1955, set the pattern for a remarkable string of hits: "Need Your Love So Bad," "Suffering with the Blues," "Fever," "Let Them Talk," and his last, "Sleep," from 1961. His version of "Fever" was copied note for note by Peggy Lee and Elvis Presley, both of whom had bigger hits with it; John's version, however, remains definitive. His second hit, "Need Your Love So Bad," contains one of the most intimate, tear-jerking vocals ever caught on tape. *—John Floyd*

● **Fever: The Best of Little Willie John** / Nov. 16, 1993 / Rhino ✦✦✦✦✦
Little Willie John had a commanding delivery, remarkable projection and a charismatic sound that was both instantly recognizable and unforgettable. His magical singles are all contained on this superb 20-track anthology, arguably the best single-disc set of John material available. It includes his best-known song, "Fever" (Peggy Lee's cover version became a huge smash), plus such marvelous numbers such as "Home at Last," "Heartbreak (It's Hurtin' Me)" and "You Hurt Me." While John was a dynamic heartache wailer, he could also do excellent dance/novelty and double-entendre tunes such as "Let's Rock While the Rockin's Good" and "Leave My Kitten Alone." This anthology demonstrates why he's still held in such high regard throughout the world of R&B and soul. *—Ron Wynn*

Live

f. 1988, York, PA
Post-Grunge, Alternative Pop/Rock
Live rose to chart success on the strength of its anthemic music and idealistic, overtly spiritual songwriting, two hallmarks which earned the group frequent comparisons to U2. The fledgling group played under a series of names before settling on Public Affection. After earning a rabid local following, in 1989 Public Affection released a cassette, *The Death of a Dictionary*, on their own Action Front label. Before drawing their new name out of a hat, Live recruited Talking Head Jerry Harrison to produce their 1991 debut, *Mental Jewelry*. A collection of songs based on the writings of Indian philosopher Jiddu Krishnamurti, the record made Live one of the key players in the post-Nirvana alternative music scene thanks to singles like "Operation Spirit (The Tyranny of Tradition)" and "Pain Lies on the Riverside." Three years later, Live returned with the muscular *Throwing Copper*, which lingered a number of months on the charts before pushing the group into the rock mainstream; after a series of popular singles like "Selling the Drama" and "I Alone," the album's slow build climaxed with the funereal "Lightning Crashes," which propelled the album to the top of the charts and paved the way for the hits "White, Discussion" and "All Over You." *—Jason Ankeny*

Mental Jewelry / Dec. 31, 1991 / Radioactive ✦✦✦
Live's debut album is full of Ed Kowalczyk's Eastern philosophical ideologies, based on Jiddu Krishnamurti (going as far as to name one track here after a Krishnamurti book, "You Are the World"). Considering the quartet were twentysomethings questioning their Christian upbringings at this time, it's understandable that they'd sing lines like "I have forever always tried/To stay clean and constantly baptized" and promote brotherhood, world peace, and self-awareness. But too soon *Mental Jewelry* sounds too idealistic, too preachy, and sometimes silly ("You've got ten fingers, two legs, one nose, like me, just like me," from "Brothers Unaware"). They hit the mark sometimes—like with the self-questioning "Mirror Song" and the U2-inspired "Pain Lies on the Riverside"—as well as the minor alt-radio and MTV hit "Operation Spirit (The Tyranny of Tradition)." But overall, *Mental Jewelry* is a reflection of a spiritually experimental Kowalczyk, and is not really meant for a larger audience. ["Good Pain," from *The Death of a Dictionary*, is revised here.] *—Gina Boldman*

● **Throwing Copper** / Apr. 19, 1994 / Radioactive ✦✦✦✦✦
On *Throwing Copper*, Live tightened their sound, added crashing crescendos for dramatic effect, and injected some anger into their sound and songwriting. They also eased up a bit on the Eastern philosophy; the result is a more cohesive, memorable record overall, and quite an improvement from the sometimes overly precious *Mental Jewelry*. And for all of *Mental Jewelry*'s ideologies, *Throwing Copper* is ultimately a more passionate and successful album, thanks to tracks like "I Alone," "Selling the Drama," and "All Over You," all of which received heavy radio play. The rebirth-themed "Lightning Crashes," the album's biggest hit, was written in memory of Barbara Lewis, a classmate who was killed by a drunk driver in 1993. Other standouts include the Kurt Cobain/Courtney Love-inspired "Stage," the apocalyptic "White, Discussion," the bass-driven, obsessive "Iris," and the dark "Dam at Otter Creek." Of course, Kowalczyk couldn't resist throwing in a song like "T.B.D." (for *Tibetan Book of the Dead*), based on Aldous Huxley's slow descent into death, aided by heroin. Its melodrama was a bit much, even for Live, and was just a sign of things to come on their next album, *Secret Samadhi*. But *Throwing Copper* is still a huge improvement from *Mental Jewelry*, and is the least overtly preachy Live album to date. *—Gina Boldman*

Secret Samadhi / Feb. 18, 1997 / Radioactive ✦✦✦
Throwing Copper made Live stars, but it didn't necessarily earn them respect. Evidently, the band thought that the problem lay with Jerry Harrison's crisp, commerical production, so they hired Jay Healey as a co-producer and set out to make a messy, hard-edged visionary statement. Unfortunately, *Secret Samadhi* fails like most self-conscious grand statements. Borrowing heavily from Jimmy Page's bag of tricks, Live spikes *Secret Samadhi* with Eastern-tinged strings, sitars and powerful, overdubbed guitars. However, Ed Kowalczyk's lyrics and singing remain indebted to early U2—he wants to say something big in a big way. The two approaches sit together uncomfortable, especially since Live's spirituality is ill-defined and the songs lack hooks. "Lakini's Juice" is propelled by a slide guitar riff out of *Physical Graffiti*, but there isn't a vocal melody, and that's symptomatic of the album's failure. While the scope of Live's ambition is admirable, the music falls flat in execution, especially when compared to the clear-headed, earnest arena-oriented alterna-rock of *Throwing Copper*. *—Stephen Thomas Erlewine*

The Distance to Here / Oct. 5, 1999 / Radioactive ✦✦✦

After the tepid reaction to the subdued, over-produced *Secret Samadhi*, Live took some time off to rethink their direction. For their fourth full-length studio album *The Distance to Here*, the band called on producer Jerry Harrison to recapture the raw energy and emotion that fueled *Mental Jewelry* and *Throwing Copper*. A self-conscious response to *Secret Samadhi* with plenty of guitar riffs, thunderous tempos and a mystical aura, *The Distance to Here* emerges from their last album's swirling, numbing stupor and regains some of *Throwing Copper*'s aggressive intensity. But Live doesn't just meld their last two albums for this release; it's a livelier, lighter collection. Though the group is slowly evolving their sound—Ed Kowalczyk's vulnerable-turned-angry vocals have become freer, more confident and more expressive, while Chad Taylor's background vocals add needed depth and harmony—they're retracing their steps before making any major changes. Live made its name by combining brutally honest, searching lyrics with equally intense and emotive music, but the fine line between genuine soul-searching and heavy-handed preaching is in the eye of the beholder. With *The Distance*, this line sways on individual songs: "Feel the Quiet River Rage," "Sparkle," "Meltdown," "Sun," and the title track—reflect Live's evolution, but the lumbering "Face and Ghost (The Children's Song)" and the gushy "Dance With Me," aim too high for their own good. This doesn't make for a failed or bad album, just an uneven one. Overall, Live continues to plunge into dramatic, emotional, and spiritual realms, but the band needs to be more adventurous musically to complement its ongoing spiritual journey. —*Gina Boldman*

V / Sep. 18, 2001 / MCA ✦✦✦

The Lively Ones
f. 1963

Surf

One of the best of the many instrumental surf bands working the Southern Californian region in 1963, the Lively Ones' recordings were built around storming, reverb-drenched Fender guitars, embellished by occasional raunchy sax breaks. Originality was not the Lively Ones' forte; over a period of about 12 months, they ground out about five albums, filled out with many covers or retitled numbers based on other rock and R&B compositions. They had a couple of hits in the L.A. area in 1963 ("Surf Rider" and "Rik-A-Tik"), but their best moment was probably "Goofy Foot," whose staccato gunfire of riffs deservedly propelled the track onto several modern best-of-surf anthologies. They ranged far and wide for source material, giving the surf treatment to "Telstar," "Exodus," "Rawhide," and Cole Porter's "Night and Day." Even the overdone standards are arranged and executed with panache. One best-of compilation is all you need, but anyone who likes Dick Dale will dig the Lively Ones' similar sleek arrangements and prototypically twangy, classy surf guitar leads. —*Richie Unterberger*

● **Hang Five!!! The Best of the Livelys** / Jan. 17, 1995 / Del-Fi ✦✦✦✦

A well-chosen 24-song retrospective, with six pages of informative liner notes by surf authority Domenic Priore. Includes "Goofy Foot," "Surf Rider," "Rik-A-Tik," and lots of other highlights from their Del-Fi releases, as well as a rare single they did for Smash. —*Richie Unterberger*

Heads Up: The Best of the Lively Ones, Vol. 2 / Apr. 20, 1999 / Del-Fi ✦✦✦

Taken together the two Lively Ones best-of volumes have 47 tracks, so this disc might more properly be titled "The Rest of the Lively Ones" rather than *The Best of the Lively Ones Vol. 2*. It's an inferior companion to the first volume, comprised mostly of covers of surf and instrumental standards by the Beach Boys, Dick Dale, Duane Eddy, and various one-shot hits. In no cases are these covers better than the originals, and while sometimes they're pretty well-done, at others they're distinctly weaker, especially on the instrumental versions of Beach Boys and Jan & Dean songs. —*Richie Unterberger*

Living Colour
f. 1984, New York, NY, db. 1995

College Rock, Album Rock, Alternative Metal, Alternative Pop/Rock, Hard Rock

During the 1980s, rock had become completely segregated and predictable—the complete opposite of the late '60s/early '70s, when such musically and ethnically varied artists as Jimi Hendrix, Sly & the Family Stone, and Santana ruled the earth. But bands such as New York's Living Colour helped break down the doors by the end of the decade, leading to a much more open-minded musical landscape that would eventually break down the doors for many future bands such as Rage Against the Machine. Although Living Colour's debut album, *Vivid*, was issued in the summer of 1988, it took a few months for momentum to build, and by the winter, the band's striking video for their anthem "Cult of Personality" was all over MTV—pushing *Vivid* to the upper reaches of the charts and to platinum certification. Living Colour also took home their first of several Grammy Awards as "Cult" won Best Hard Rock Performance at the 1989 ceremony. Starting with *Vivid* and continuing on future albums, the band showed that rock could still convey a message. The quartet regrouped a year later for their sophomore effort, *Time's Up*, an album that performed respectfully on the charts, but failed to live up to expectations of their smash debut. *Stain* was issued in 1993, the band's darkest and most challenging release yet. Although it failed to sell as well as its predecessors, it retained the band's large and dedicated following—as Living Colour appeared to be entering an interesting and groundbreaking new musical phase of their career. The band began writing the following year for what would be their fourth full-length, but an inability to settle on a single musical direction caused friction between the members, leading to Living Colour's demise in early 1995. —*Greg Prato*

Vivid / 1988 / Epic ✦✦✦✦✦

In 1988, few heavy metal bands were comprised of all black members, and fewer had the

talent or know-how to inject different musical forms into their hard rock sound (funk, punk, alternative, jazz, soul, rap)—but N.Y.C.'s Living Colour proved to be an exception. Unlike nearly all of the era's metal bands, the group's music has held up over time, thanks to its originality and execution. Living Colour leader/guitarist Vernon Reid spent years honing his six-string chops, and was one of the most respected guitarists in New York's underground scene. He couldn't have done a better job selecting members for his new rock band—singer Corey Glover, bassist Muzz Skillings, and drummer Will Calhoun—as their now-classic debut, *Vivid*, proves. Though the album was released in mid-1988, it picked up steam slowly, exploding at the year's end with the hit single/MTV anthem "Cult of Personality," which merged an instantly recognizable Reid guitar riff and lyrics that explored the dark side of world leaders past and present (and remains LC's best-known song). The album was also incredibly consistent, as proven by the rocker "Middle Man" (which contains lyrics from a note penned by Glover, in which he pondered suicide), the funky, anti-racist "Funny Vibe," the touching "Open Letter (To a Landlord)," plus the Caribbean rock of "Glamour Boys." Add to it an inspired reading of Talking Heads' "Memories Can't Wait," the Zeppelin-esque "Desperate People," and two complex love songs ("I Want to Know" and "Broken Hearts"), and you have one of the finest hard rock albums of the '80s—and for that matter, all time. —*Greg Prato*

Time's Up / Aug. 1990 / Epic ✦✦✦

Although Living Colour's second album, *Time's Up*, achieved gold certification shortly after its release and eventually won a Grammy award, it performed below expectations when compared to their debut, *Vivid*. It's not that it wasn't a strong album; in fact, in a lot of ways, it's just as good as its predecessor, but instead of merely copying a winning formula, *Time's Up* challenged the listener more—both musically and lyrically. A host of guest artists lent their hands to the proceedings, such as Little Richard, Queen Latifah, Maceo Parker, and Doug E. Fresh, which hints at just how all-encompassing *Time's Up* is. The few fans that were hoping that the band would streamline their sound and focus on their more pop-oriented material were bludgeoned with the hyperactive thrash title track (comparable to one of LC's biggest influences, Bad Brains). Other tracks, such as the jazz-rocker "Elvis Is Dead," the Zep-stomp of "Pride," and the gloriously pessimistic "Type" showed that success hadn't dulled the group's socially conscious attack. While heavy compositions were plentiful ("New Jack Theme," "Information Overload"), the band's more reflective side was evident by such outstanding tracks as "Fight the Fight," "Solace of You," and "This Is the Life," plus the love-torn ditty "Love Rears Its Ugly Head." *Time's Up* remains a convincing listen all these years later. —*Greg Prato*

Biscuits / Jul. 16, 1991 / Epic ✦✦✦

Released in conjunction with the inaugural Lollapalooza tour in 1991 (which Living Colour was part of, along with Jane's Addiction, Rollins Band, Ice T, etc.), the 6-track EP *Biscuits* was somewhat of a letdown. Coming off such a strong album as *Time's Up*, it was almost anti-climactic that a set of four so-so studio outtakes and a pair of live tracks was issued so shortly after their last release. While there's no denying that the ferocious reading of "Desperate People" from CBGB's in December of '89 is awesome, covers of James Brown's "Talkin' Loud and Sayin' Nothing" and Jimi Hendrix's "Burning of the Midnight Lamp" do not improve on the originals (as their cover of Talking Heads' "Memories Can't Wait" had, which is included here as a live version). Two outtakes from the *Time's Up* sessions, the metallic "Money Talks" and another cover, Al Green's "Love and Happiness," just don't measure up to the high quality of their 1990 album's other selections. *Biscuits* is recommended to hardcore fans only, newcomers should stick to any of their three full-length studio albums—*Vivid*, *Time's Up*, or *Stain*. —*Greg Prato*

Stain / Mar. 2, 1993 / Epic ✦✦✦

After wrapping up their stint with Lollapalooza '91, Living Colour took some time off to decide what to do next. Shortly after, bassist Muzz Skillings and the rest of the band decided to part company and was replaced by session-ace Doug Wimbish (whose credits included work with Jeff Beck, Madonna, Mick Jagger, etc.). Produced by Ron "Bad Brains" St. Germain, Living Colour's *Stain* showed the band's darker side even more, as samples were now added to the sonic mix. The tracks were more focused and streamlined when compared to the all-encompassing compositions on 1990's *Time's Up*, but were just as hard-hitting and thought provoking. The pessimistic viewpoint evidenced in such past tracks as "Type" can be found again in such tracks as "Go Away," "Ignorance Is Bliss," and "Never Satisfied," while "Postman" pulls no punches in its depiction of a deranged killer. The explosive "Auslander" was one of the album's best tracks, as was the melodic rocker "Leave It Alone," and the superb ballad "Nothingness," which deserved to be a hit. Although some of the songs miss the mark ("Bi," "This Little Pig," etc.), *Stain* was another engaging release from Living Colour. Although the album made the Top 40 and just missed going gold, the group would disband a year after the ensuing tour (citing "musical differences"). —*Greg Prato*

● **Pride** / Nov. 14, 1995 / Epic ✦✦✦✦✦

The same year that Living Colour announced its breakup, Epic issued a 17-track greatest-hits collection, *Pride*. As the collection proves, the band was ahead of their time and extremely influential—they were combining musical forms such as heavy metal and funk/rap/soul years before the musical form was commonplace (circa late '90s). But unlike the bands of the late '90s, Living Colour actually had thought-provoking messages in their music—racism, crooked landlords, the immortalization of celebrities/world leaders, etc.—as well as being superb musicians/songwriters. The best known of the bunch—"Cult of Personality," "Glamour Boys," "Funny Vibe," and "Type"—are obvious standouts, but the lesser known are just as strong. Living Colour was always about creating consistent albums from beginning to end, as such selections as the title track, "Time's Up," "Nothingness," "Solace of You," and "Open Letter (To a Landlord)" prove. Add to it several previously unreleased outtakes—"Release the Pressure," "Sacred Ground," "Visions," and a remix of "Love Rears Its Ugly Head"—and you have a near-definitive Living Colour collection that will appeal to both longtime fans and newcomers. —*Greg Prato*

LL Cool J (James Todd Smith)

b. Jan. 14, 1968, Bayshore, Long Island, NY

Rap, Vocals, Songwriter / Pop-Rap, East Coast Rap, Hip-Hop, Golden Age

Hip-hop is notorious for short-lived careers, but LL Cool J is the inevitable exception that proves the rule. Releasing his first single "I Can't Live Without My Radio" in 1985 when he was just 17 years old, LL Cool J initially was a hard-hitting, street-wise B-Boy with spare beats and ballistic rhymes. He quickly developed an alternate style, a romantic—and occasionally sappy—lover's rap epitomized by his mainstream breakthrough single, "I Need Love." LL's first two albums, *Radio* and *Bigger and Deffer*, made him a star, but he strived for pop stardom a little too much on 1989's *Walking With A Panther*. By 1990, his audience had declined somewhat, since his ballads and party raps were the opposite of the chaotic, edgy political hip-hop of Public Enemy or the gangsta rap of N.W.A., but he shot back to the top of the charts with *Mama Said Knock You Out*, which established him as one of hip-hop's genuine superstars. By the mid-'90s, he had starred in his own television sitcom, *In the House*, appeared in several films and had racked up two of his biggest singles with "Hey Lover" and "Doin' It." In short, he had proven that rappers could have long-term careers. —*Stephen Thomas Erlewine*

☆ **Radio** / 1985 / Def Jam/Columbia ✦✦✦✦✦

Run-D.M.C. was the first rap act to produce cohesive, fully realized albums, and LL Cool J was the first to follow in their footsteps. LL was a mere 17 years old when he recorded his classic debut album *Radio*, a brash, exuberant celebration of booming beats and B-boy attitude that launched not only the longest career in hip-hop, but also Rick Rubin's seminal Def Jam label. Rubin's back-cover credit ("Reduced by Rick Rubin") is an entirely apt description of his bare-bones production style. *Radio* is just as stripped-down and boisterously aggressive as any Run-D.M.C. album, sometimes even more so; the instrumentation is basically just a cranked-up beatbox, punctuated by DJ scratching. There are occasional brief samples, but few do anything more than emphasize a downbeat. The result is rap at its most skeletal, with a hard-hitting, street-level aggression that perfectly matches LL's cocksure teenage energy. Even the two ballads barely sound like ballads, since they're driven by the same slamming beats. Though they might sound a little squared-off to modern ears, LL's deft lyrics set new standards for MCs at the time; his clever disses and outrageous but playful boasts still hold up poetically. Although even LL himself would go on to more intricate rhyming, it isn't really necessary on such a loud, thumping adrenaline rush of a record. *Radio* was both an expansion of rap's artistic possibilities and a commercial success (for its time), helping attract new multiracial audiences to the music. While it may take a few listens for modern ears to adjust to the minimalist production, the fact that it hews so closely to rap's basic musical foundation means that it still possesses a surprisingly fresh energy, and isn't nearly as dated as many efforts that followed it (including, ironically, some of LL's own). —*Steve Huey*

Bigger and Deffer / 1987 / Def Jam ✦✦

Walking With a Panther / 1989 / Def Jam ✦✦✦✦

Walking With a Panther stands as a key turning point in LL Cool J's long career, when he soon found himself not quite as "bad!" as he once claimed. When he devoted a large portion of his first two albums, *Radio* (1985) and *Bigger and Deffer* (1987), to boasting about his talent in old-school fashion ("Rock the Bells," "I'm Bad"), he had justification—at that point in time he was arguably the undisputed MC of MCs. But by the time *Walking With a Panther* hit the streets in 1989, LL had a roster of contenders, most notably Kool Moe Dee and Ice T, who both ridiculed him on vinyl. It was clear to most that LL had to modify his approach, and, yes, he indeed modified his approach with *Walking With a Panther*, rapping over much more developed and dynamic production featuring a heavy use of samples as was the vogue at the time; furthermore, he started rapping about a host of topics besides himself. But besides "Going Back to Cali," one of LL's perennial moments, he's at his best here when he's rapping about women ("Big Ole Butt," "Jingling Baby"). Still, despite the variety and the improved production, this album never comes across as successfully as it should. While some tracks such as "Going Back to Cali" and "Jingling Baby" are successful, most aren't. At this point in his career, LL's limited—he can rap about himself and ladies but not much else. —*Jason Birchmeier*

Mama Said Knock You Out / Aug. 1990 / Def Jam ✦✦✦✦✦

Increasingly dismissed by hip-hop fans as an old-school relic and a slick pop sellout, LL Cool J rang in the '90s with *Mama Said Knock You Out*, a hard-edged artistic renaissance that became his biggest-selling album ever. Part of the credit is due to producer Marley Marl, whose thumping, bass-heavy sound helps LL reclaim the aggression of his early days. *Mama Said Knock You Out* isn't quite as hard as *Radio*, instead striking a balance between attitude and accessibility. But its greater variety and more layered arrangements make it LL's most listenable album, as well as keeping it in line with more contemporary sensibilities. Marl's productions on the slower tracks are smooth and soulful, but still funky; as a result, the ladies'-man side of LL's persona is the most convincing it's ever been, and his ballads don't feel sappy for arguably the first time on record. Even apart from the sympathetic musical settings, LL is at his most lyrically acrobatic, and the testosterone-fueled anthems are delivered with a force not often heard since his debut. The album's hits are a microcosm of its range—"The Boomin' System" is a nod to bass-loving b-boys with car stereos; "Around the Way Girl" is a lush, winning ballad; and the title cut is one of the most blistering statements of purpose in hip-hop. It leaves no doubt that *Mama Said Knock You Out* was intended to be a *tour de force*, to regain LL Cool J's credibility while proving that he was still one of rap's most singular talents. It succeeded

mightily, making him an across-the-board superstar and cementing his status as a rap icon beyond any doubt. —*Steve Huey*

14 Shots to the Dome / 1993 / Def Jam ✦✦

Mr. Smith / Nov. 1995 / Def Jam ✦✦✦

On the strength of the slow-burning Boyz II Men duet "Hey Lover," LL Cool J returned to the top of the charts with *Mr. Smith*, meaning the album is somewhat of a comeback for the veteran rapper. LL Cool J's skills had never deserted him, but his previous album, *14 Shots to the Dome*, was an exercise in hardcore that only worked in fits and spurts. There are a couple of hard moments on *Mr. Smith*, but the album is at its most successful when he concentrates on his seductive, romantic side. LL has gotten a bit dirtier since the teenage days of "I Need Love," but he never steps over into the explicit, lewd come-ons of R. Kelly, preferring to suggest everything with a series of double entendres, metaphors, and analogies. *Mr. Smith* isn't a perfect record—there's too many slack moments for it to qualify as one of his best—but it proves that LL Cool J remains vital a decade after his debut. —*Stephen Thomas Erlewine*

★ **All World: Greatest Hits** / Nov. 5, 1996 / Def Jam ✦✦✦✦✦

All World: Greatest Hits is an excellent compilation of LL Cool J's greatest hits, featuring 16 of his biggest and best singles, including "I Can't Live Without My Radio," "Rock the Bells," "I'm Bad," "I Need Love," "Going Back to Cali," "Jingling Baby," "The Boomin' System," "Mama Said Knock You Out," "Around the Way Girl" and "Hey Lover." It's the definitive retrospective of one of the greatest rappers to ever record, and if you doubt that statement's true, just take a listen to this collection. —*Stephen Thomas Erlewine*

Phenomenon / Sep. 23, 1997 / Def Jam ✦✦✦

Mr. Smith was the third comeback for LL Cool J, the third time he returned to commercial and creative strengths after being written off by many critics and fans. So, it shouldn't come as a surprise that its followup, *Phenomenon*, finds LL coasting—after all, after his two previous comeback albums, he allowed himself to slacken the pace a little bit and ride on his credentials. Fortunately, *Phenomenon* isn't nearly as weak as *14 Shots to the Dome* or *Bigger and Deffer*, but it simply doesn't have the power of masterpieces like *Radio* and *Mama Said Knock You Out*. Essentially, it's a retread of *Mr. Smith*, offering the same laid-back soul jams and rolling party beats. There's a couple of killer singles, a few dogs and a lot of filler—more so than on *Mr. Smith*, in fact. Still, *Phenomenon* sounds good when it's playing and even if it doesn't leave a lasting impression, it's a solid, professional effort that illustrates why LL is still in the game, 12 years after his first record. —*Stephen Thomas Erlewine*

G.O.A.T. Featuring James T. Smith: The Greatest of All Time / Sep. 12, 2000 / Def Jam ✦✦✦

Lisa Loeb

Vocals / Adult Alternative Pop/Rock, Singer/Songwriter

If she had never made another record, Lisa Loeb would still go down in the books as the first unsigned artist to top the American charts; her single "Stay"—from the soundtrack to 1994's *Reality Bites*—spent three weeks at number one soon after the film's release. Born in Dallas, Loeb studied piano as a child but later switched to guitar. At Brown University, she studied music theory and played as a duo with her roommate. After college, she attended Boston's Berklee School of Music for one semester, but then formed a full band in 1990, christened (in tribute to J.D. Salinger) Nine Stories: Tim Bright on guitar, Jonathan Feinberg on drums, and Joe Quigley on bass.

Lisa Loeb & Nine Stories began to gig around the Midwest, playing at Austin's South by Southwest seminar. Loeb then hooked up with producer Juan Patiño, and in early 1992 released the cassette-only *Purple Acoustic Tape*, which she sold at live shows. Several major labels showed interest in her, but Loeb remained unsigned by late 1993, when her friend Ethan Hawke asked her to contribute a song for his next picture. Director Ben Stiller decided that he liked one of Loeb's other songs even better, so "Stay" was inserted on the soundtrack. Released as a single in May 1994, it reached number one two months later and eventually sold over 750,000 copies worldwide. Loeb & Nine Stories received a Grammy nomination for Best Pop Performance by a Group, and won a Brit Award for Best International Newcomer. Geffen Records, which had shown interest in Loeb before "Stay," signed her later in 1994 and re-teamed her with Juan Patiño. Her debut album *Tails* was released just over a year after her signing, and proved successful with commercial radio as well. *Firecracker* appeared in 1997, scoring a hit with "I Do." —*John Bush*

● **Tails** / 1995 / Geffen ✦✦✦

Lisa Loeb is a rarity in the music industry. She released her first single—the gentle "Stay," taken from the *Reality Bites* soundtrack—before she was signed to any record label and saw it hit number one. Record companies were eager to sign her, and she eventually settled with Geffen. Instead of rushing out her debut album, she waited over a year, releasing *Tails* in the fall of 1995. Surprisingly, it didn't fade away, becoming a hit with adult alternative radio stations and listeners. That's because *Tails* delivers on the promise of "Stay." While the basic folk-rock elements of the song are present, much of the material on the record doesn't sound like her breakthrough hit; there are some distorted guitars here and there, and she even rocks out a little bit. Nothing on *Tails* is as good as "Stay," either; there are too many sophomoric lyrics and unfinished melodies, but it is a pleasant record and, in its own way, charming. There is an innocence and naiveté about Lisa Loeb that makes her music sweetly ingratiating, even when her ideas are underdeveloped. —*Stephen Thomas Erlewine*

Firecracker / Nov. 11, 1997 / Geffen ✦✦✦

Lisa Loeb's debut *Tails* failed to deliver on the promise of her first single "Stay," drifting into generic alterna-pop territory when it should have played up her lilting, melodic soft side. *Firecracker,* her second record, suffers from similar flaws, although in many ways it's a better album. For starters, it's considerably more eclectic, with a varied, textured production ranging from jangly folk-pop and pounding rockers to lush pop. However, variety isn't always the spice of life—instead of sounding accomplished, Loeb simply sounds unfocused. Still, there are a number of strong moments on the record that confirm Loeb is a talented melodicist when pushed—but if she wants to make a great record, she simply needs a little more direction. *—Stephen Thomas Erlewine*

Nils Lofgren

b. Jun. 21, 1951, Chicago, IL

Vocals, Keyboards, Guitar / Heartland Rock, Roots Rock, Rock & Roll

While singer/guitarist Nils Lofgren is better known for his work with Neil Young and Bruce Springsteen, his own solo career has produced a worthwhile, if inconsistent, body of work. Lofgren learned to play the accordion at age five and studied jazz and classical music as a child. He switched to rock guitar at 15 and formed the band Grin in 1969 with bassist Bob Gordon, drummer Bob Berberich, and later his brother Tom Lofgren on guitar. The group quickly built a reputation around Washington, D.C., and Neil Young and Crazy Horse guitarist Danny Whitten caught wind of them while touring in the area. Young invited Lofgren to play piano and sing on 1970's *After the Gold Rush,* and he also played on and wrote two songs for Crazy Horse's debut album the following year. Instead of remaining with Young, Lofgren used the resulting exposure to get Grin a record contract. The group recorded three albums from 1971 to 1972, garnering critical praise but no sales. A move to A&M produced the lackluster *Gone Crazy,* which proved to be Grin's swan song; Lofgren accepted an invitation from Young to tour in 1973 and play on his *Tonight's the Night* album. Grin officially disbanded in mid-1974 owing to lack of success and financial problems. Lofgren was rumored to be under consideration as a replacement for Mick Taylor in the Rolling Stones; instead, he signed to A&M as a solo artist. His first two solo efforts, *Nils Lofgren* and *Cry Tough,* were all-around successes, and Lofgren made a name for himself on supporting tours through stunts such as performing while jumping on a trampoline. Subsequent releases failed to develop Lofgren's sound any further, and he became more viable as a sideman than a solo performer. Following 1983's *Trans* tour with Young, Lofgren joined Bruce Springsteen's E Street Band, replacing Little Stevie Van Zandt in 1984, remaining there until the unit was dissolved in 1991. Lofgren returned to solo recording that year with *Silver Lining,* which featured guest appearances from Springsteen and members of Ringo Starr's band. *Acoustic Live* followed in 1998. *—Steve Huey*

● **Ultimate Collection** / Nov. 9, 1999 / Interscope ✦✦✦✦

Interscope's *Ultimate Collection* pretty much lives up to its billing by offering a generous 20 tracks from Nils Lofgren, including selections from his first band, Grin. Some fans will undoubtedly notice personal favorites missing, and it is true that there are some great songs missing, but this works well as both an introduction and as a solid sampler for casual fans. *—Stephen Thomas Erlewine*

Jack Logan

Indie Rock, Lo-Fi, Singer/Songwriter

Singer/songwriter Jack Logan was anything but the overnight success he appeared to be at first glance—a prolific and gifted talent, he spent over a decade as an unknown before emerging as a critic's darling with his 1994 debut *Bulk.* A native of southern Illinois, after high school Logan and his friend Kelly Keneipp relocated to Winder, Georgia, a small town located near Athens, a longtime musical hotbed home to acts ranging from R.E.M. to the B-52s. Logan garnered some underground notice during the mid-1980s for creating a comic book depicting R.E.M. guitarist Peter Buck as a superhero, but for the most part he languished in obscurity; while he and Keniepp spent their days working in a local motor-repair shop, their evenings were devoted to writing and recording songs with a shifting coterie of friends and drinking buddies. Eventually, Logan's home recordings made their way to Buck, who recommended them to Minneapolis-based producer Peter Jesperson, best known for his discovery of the Replacements. After contacting Logan, Jesperson requested a few tapes; he soon received some 600 songs, recorded over the course of more than ten years. Jesperson whittled the total down to 42 for release as *Bulk,* and after a 1995 EP, *Out of Whack,* Logan and guitarist/keyboardist Keneipp assembled a band dubbed Liquor Cabinet to enter the studio to record 1996's *Mood Elevator.* Two years later, he teamed with Weird Summer frontman Bob Kimbell for the Parasol label release *Little Private Angel; Tinker,* credited to Jack Logan's Compulsive Recorders, appeared in late 1998, followed by 1999's solo *Buzz Me In.* Yet another release, the *Bring Me the Head of Kelly Keneipp/Mature* EP, rounded out the year. *Monkey Paw* appeared in spring 2001. *—Jason Ankeny*

● **Bulk** / 1994 / Twin/Tone ✦✦✦✦✦

This album got a lot of notice when it was first released because it is a debut album containing 42 songs, essentially demo recordings, by Georgia songwriter Jack Logan. In his notes, Peter Jesperson of Twin Tone Records mentions coyly that he heard about Logan from "guitarist Peter Buck"—careful not to drop the R.E.M. association. Without this connection, one doubts that there would be a Logan album, and certainly not a 42-song debut. The songs are occasionally interesting but mostly derivative rock and R&B tunes. The lyrics are certainly not distinguished. If this were as auspicious a debut as is claimed by some of the sticker blurbs, then there must be a thousand unknown geniuses just waiting to burst forth. On the other hand, one song, "Chloroform," has twisted lyrics and a cool distorted track. *—Richard Meyer*

Mood Elevator / Jan. 16, 1996 / RE ✦✦✦✦

Jack Logan followed his critically acclaimed two-disc debut with *Mood Elevator,* a single disc collection recorded with his band Liquor Cabinet. *Mood Elevator* is a more direct record, accentuating the rootsy rock & roll undercurrents of his music. It may not be as impressive as *Bulk*—after all, the sheer number of good songs on the debut was stunning—but it is a tighter, more focused record and might be more accessible for neophytes. *—Stephen Thomas Erlewine*

Little Private Angel / June 1998 / Parasol ✦✦✦✦✦

An album-length collaboration between Jack Logan and Weird Summer frontman Bob Kimbell, *Little Private Angel* heralds a creative breakthrough for both participants, with each seemingly inspiring the other on to new musical heights. The joint venture proves so ideal because it plays to the strengths of both, with Kimbell contributing the tunes and Logan adding the lead vocals and lyrics; the latter's boozy croon and somber lyrics have never before been couched in such fully fleshed pop melodies, while the former's songs have never supported the kind of vocal and verbal gravity that are Logan's stock in trade. Even the right emotional balance is struck, navigating deftly between the lighthearted ("Frozen Rope" is an evocative baseball narrative, while a musical quote from "Leader of the Pack" distinguishes the title track) and the downcast (the pathos of the opening "Four Men in a Car" cuts with vivid intensity, and the desperation of "Nerves of Steel" is similarly palpable); equally noteworthy are Logan and Kimbell's harmonies, which make even the record's grittiest moments easy to swallow. Here's hoping their paths cross again soon. *—Jason Ankeny*

Tinker / Dec. 1998 / Backburner ✦✦✦✦✦

Singer/songwriter Jack Logan's half-serious moniker for his backing band this time out, the Compulsive Recorders, is more than an understatement. The former mechanic and all-around average Joe who brought us a 42-song debut opus (1994's *Bulk*) is nothing if not prolific. *Tinker,* short by Logan's standards at 11 tracks, showcases some mighty tasty material recorded with ex-Liquor Cabinet guitarist and long-time Logan crony Kelly Keneipp and a slew of similarly talented fellow Georgians. The album slams out of the gate with "Genius Boy," a blast of energy not heard on a (released) Logan recording since 1996's "When It All Comes Down" (from *Mood Elevator*). Logan's smart, self-deprecating lyrical gifts are in fine fettle, and Keneipp's crunchy, crotch-rattling axe work absolutely belongs behind these twisted story-songs. Like all of Logan's previous material, every track is a fascinating musical journey unto itself, and listeners will find a personal message in every one of them. *Tinker* may not boast the insolent overload of *Bulk,* the immediacy of *Mood Elevator* or the sublime mystery of *Little Private Angel,* but it's vintage Logan nonetheless; a plump, satisfying collection of tunes that rock the body and roll the cerebellum. *—Tom Hallett*

Bring Me the Head of Kelly Keneipp / Mar. 1999 / Backburner ✦✦✦

Buzz Me In / May 11, 1999 / Capricorn ✦✦✦

Jack Logan's sixth album *Buzz Me In* features more of his earthy songwriting. Reflective tracks like "I Brake for God," "Worldly Possessions," and "Melancholy Girl" show off his smoother, sweeter side, while rockers like "All Grown Up" sound slightly strained. Logan's more experimental pop dimension comes through on the album's best songs, like the bouncy "Metropolis" and "Glorious World," (which feature bright pianos), the couplet "Your Neck Smells Like Peppermint/C'mon Baby, Let Me Pay Your Rent," and "The Possibilities," a droning, laid-back number that remains accessible thanks to the album's shiny production. *—Heather Phares*

Monkey Paw / Apr. 10, 2001 / Backburner ✦✦✦✦✦

Monkey Paw is the seventh album by Georgia songwriter Jack Logan. This release proves yet again that, like the monkey paw referenced in the title, Logan seems to be charmed—compulsively recording songs at a Prince-like pace, yet persistently putting out excellent material. What distinguishes this release is the fact that it features music and lyrics written solely by Logan. Logan, who usually uses a collaborator to co-write the music, instead uses fellow Backburner label-mates, the Possibilities, solely as a backing band. This gives *Monkey Paw* a more cohesive sound than many of Logan's other, off-the-cuff recordings. In addition to being very prolific, Logan is extremely versatile. *Monkey Paw* flows easily between country ("I Wonder Where You Are"), Old-Timey blues ("It's Rare"), hard rock ("Scared of the Police"), and pure Logan originals ("Glass Eye Blues," and "Monkey Paw").Combining the sheen of *Buzz Me In* with the rougher sound of *Tinker, Monkey Paw* is Logan at his best—writing great rock songs about life's little moments. *Monkey Paw* stands as one of Logan's greatest and most accessible releases. *—Dan Lee*

Loggins & Messina

f. 1970, California, **db.** Jul. 1976

Pop/Rock, Folk-Rock, Soft Rock

Kenny Loggins and Jim Messina were the most successful pop/rock duo of the first half of the '70s. Loggins was a staff songwriter who had recently enjoyed success with a group of songs recorded by the Nitty Gritty Dirt Band when he came to the attention of Messina, a record producer and former member of Buffalo Springfield and Poco. Messina agreed to produce Loggins' first album, but somewhere along the way it became a duo effort that was released in 1972 under the title *Kenny Loggins with Jim Messina Sittin' In.* The album was a gold-seller that stayed in the charts more than two years.

In the next four years, Loggins & Messina released a series of gold or platinum albums, most of which hit the Top Ten. They were all played in a buoyant country-rock style with an accomplished band. *Loggins & Messina* (1972) featured the retro-rock hit "Your Mama Don't Dance." *Full Sail* (1973), *On Stage* (a double live album, 1974), and *Mother Lode* (1974) all hit the Top Ten. *So Fine* was an album of '50s cover songs. The pair's last new studio album, *Native Sons,* came out at the start of 1976.

Loggins & Messina split for two solo careers by the end of that year, their catalog completed by a greatest-hits album, *Best of Friends*, and a live record, *Finale*. *—William Ruhlmann*

Sittin' In / Jan. 1972 / Columbia ✦✦✦✦✦
This debut album was credited to "Kenny Loggins with Jim Messina" because the project had begun as a solo record by Loggins being produced by Messina. By the time it was finished, however, Messina had written or co-written six of the 11 songs, contributed "first guitar," and shared lead vocals on many tracks. Messina's "Nobody but You" and "Vahevala," co-written by Loggins' brother Dave, were the singles chart entries, but today everybody remembers the album for Loggins' "House at Pooh Corner," which had earned Loggins his record contract, and "Danny's Song," which Anne Murray took into the Top Ten the following year. The only thing wrong with this record is that it was too perfect—with their infectious blend of country, folk, rock and Caribbean music, L&M started out at the top of their game, and although they were able to match some of the material and performances on later records, the team never got any better than this. *—William Ruhlmann*

Loggins & Messina / Oct. 1972 / Columbia ✦✦✦✦✦
The first full-fledged L&M album found the duo in good form as songwriters, with Messina turning in the sparkling "Thinking Of You" and the two collaborating on the hit single "Your Mama Don't Dance" and "Angry Eyes." Their backup band was anchored by multi-instrumentalist Al Garth and also featured keyboardist Michael Omartian and Poco steel guitarist Rusty Young. *—William Ruhlmann*

Full Sail / Oct. 1973 / Columbia ✦✦✦
This is every inch a followup to *Loggins And Messina*, including a '50s rock & roll pastiche in the style of "Your Mama Don't Dance" called "My Music" that hit #16 as a single. Other notable material included Messina's island-rock anthem "Lahaina" and one of Loggins' sensitive-but-generic ballads, typically called "A Love Song." But then, the charm of L&M was that they could get away with something this sappy. Balance is the key to L&M albums, and it's the chief talent (among many) that producer Messina brings to them. Here, as on L&M's first two albums, he achieves a musical flow that's exhilarating, and the record is only denied a "finest" rating because the quality of the songwriting doesn't quite match those LPs. *—William Ruhlmann*

On Stage / Apr. 1974 / Columbia/Legacy ✦✦✦
Having assembled a strong backup band, L&M were at their best in concert, and this two-LP set catches all of their diverse talents, from the tight, intricate rockers devised by Messina to the sensitive ballad skills of Loggins and the band's ability to stretch out on the sidelong "Vahevala." [The 1998 CD reissue restored "Vahelva" to its full, uncut 20-minute running length and featured rare photos and 20-bit remastering.] *—William Ruhlmann*

Mother Lode / Oct. 1974 / Columbia ✦✦✦
From its brown-toned cover to its contents, Loggins & Messina's fourth studio album is a sober, low-key, reflective affair. The band's music, with its single flute, violin and horn lines, directed by Messina's intricate guitar and mandolin playing, serves a series of midtempo tunes expressing a lot of quiet dissatisfaction signalled by titles like "Be Free," "Changes," and "Move On." As usual in a Jim Messina production, all of this is elegantly, tastefully accomplished, but one could hardly come away from the record feeling that all was well in the L&M camp. *—William Ruhlmann*

Native Sons / Jan. 1976 / Columbia ✦✦✦
Loggins And Messina's fifth and last album of new studio material was also their least. No hit singles issued from a collection that featured a new backup band and extensive use of strings on a set of mediocre material. L&M's breakup at the end of the tour promoting this record seemed confirmation that they had exhausted the possibilities of their partnership. *—William Ruhlmann*

● **The Best of Friends** / Nov. 1976 / Columbia ✦✦✦✦✦
The Best of Friends contains ten of Loggins & Messina's best-known songs, not only including all of their big hits ("Vahevala," "Your Mama Don't Dance," "Thinking of You," "Watching the River Run"), but also key album tracks like "House at Pooh Corner," "Danny's Song," "Peace of Mind" and "Angry Eyes." *—Stephen Thomas Erlewine*

Finale / 1977 / Columbia ✦

Kenny Loggins

b. Jan. 7, 1948, Everett, WA
Vocals, Keyboards, Guitar / Pop/Rock, Soft Rock
Singer, songwriter, and guitarist Kenny Loggins was born in Everett, WA, and moved to Los Angeles in his teens. He got a job as a staff writer and wrote four songs used on a Nitty Gritty Dirt Band album in 1970, among them the hit "House at Pooh Corner." This brought him to the attention of former Poco member Jim Messina, now a staff producer at CBS, who intended to produce Loggins' debut album. The two ended up in a duo, however, and Loggins & Messina made a series of successful albums during the '70s.

Loggins & Messina broke up in 1976, and Loggins went on to solo stardom with such million-selling albums as *Celebrate Me Home*, *Nightwatch* (which included the hit "Whenever I Call You Friend"), and *Keep the Fire*, all in the cheerful, sensitive style he had displayed in Loggins & Messina. Loggins also became known as the king of the movie soundtrack song, scoring Top Ten hits with "I'm Alright" (from *Caddyshack*), "Footloose" (from *Footloose*), "Danger Zone" (from *Top Gun*), and "Nobody's Fool" (from *Caddyshack II*). His own albums sold less well (and came less frequently) throughout the '80s, with later efforts like 1991's *Leap of Faith*, 1997's *The Unimaginable Life* and 1998's *December* finding favor primarily in adult contemporary circles; in 1994, he also issued a children's album, *Return to Pooh Corner*, releasing its sequel *More Songs from Pooh Corner* in early 2000. *—William Ruhlmann*

Celebrate Me Home / Apr. 1977 / Columbia ✦✦✦✦
Freed from Loggins & Messina, Kenny Loggins retreats from that duo's folky conceits, turning to smooth, smooth soft rock, filled with leisurely paces, lush strings and electric pianos and easy attitude—so it's no surprise when you discover this is a co-production by Billy Joel's chief collaborator Phil Ramone and Bob James. There is a bit of surprise that this album doesn't really have any big hits to its credit, especially since Loggins would later have several Top Ten records, but this is a consistent record, maintaining its mellow mood even when the tempo picks up for the relatively insistent "I Believe in Love." Loggins is in good form throughout the record, and if even only the title track entered his readily-acknowledged canon, this has a fine, sustained mood: a soft late '70s vibe that makes it a nice artifact of its time, as well as one of his stronger records, as illustrated by its platinum status—something it achieved without any blockbuster singles. *—Stephen Thomas Erlewine*

Nightwatch / Jun. 1978 / Columbia ✦✦✦✦
Disregard the self-styled epic title track, a seven-and-half-minute indulgence that may be a bid for artistic credibility yet leads nowhere and doesn't have much to do with what follows. *Nightwatch* is, by and large, a more focused affair than his first. Granted, his first holds a mood better, a slice of great late '70s soft rock, but this has more pep and hooks, from the sprightly "Easy Drive" to a cover of Billy Joe Royal's "Down in the Boondocks" or, especially, the warm Stevie Nicks duet "Whenever I Call You Friend," which brought Loggins his first solo hit. These signal that this rocks a bit harder than its predecessor, which is true—while "Down 'N Dirty" may not be filthy, even with its harmonica, it does hit harder than anything on its predecessor (which, admittedly, is on a relative scale). This does wind up as one of his stronger records—and it was his biggest hit—but it also feels more like a collection of moments, moving from originals to covers and back again. Not necessarily a bad thing, since this is professional soft rock at its finest, but in comparison to the seductive *Celebrate Me Home* and the *tour de force* of *High Adventure*, *Nightwatch* pales slightly. (By the way, what led Loggins to credit himself as Ken Loggins throughout the album credits?) *—Stephen Thomas Erlewine*

Keep the Fire / Oct. 1979 / Columbia ✦✦✦
With a genuine hit to his credit, Kenny Loggins decided to stretch himself a bit on *Keep the Fire*, hiring Tom Dowd and toughening his sound slightly, adding a more flamboyant production in the process. He also decided to look like Doug Henning on the cover, which may be a surer sign that success had started to go to his head. All this resulted in a self-consciously tougher record than either of its predecessors, with a punchy sound, detailed production, and shades of boogie. Relying more on original material, this winds up being more uneven than *Nightwatch*, but it boasts more character, even if that means something as silly as "Mr. Night." Also, the record, though clearly presented as a relative band effort, complete with a photo of the supporting band on the back cover, winds up not being as unified as its two predecessors, even if it's more "band-like." Still, any complaints are erased by "This Is It," one of two pop classics Loggins recorded. Yes, the title track also became a hit, but the heart of this album is "This Is It," a mid-tempo charmer with lush, seductive verses, emphatic choruses, and great supporting vocals by Michael McDonald. This summarizes everything that's right about soft rock, and is enough of a masterwork to make the flaws and filler forgivable, since it lends this pleasant soft rock affair a real spine. *—Stephen Thomas Erlewine*

Kenny Loggins Alive / Sep. 1980 / Columbia ✦✦✦
Three albums into his solo career, and Kenny Loggins decides it's time for a double, live affair, appropriately titled *Kenny Loggins Alive*. Such are the perks of launching a career on the back of a successful group—you can borrow material to flesh out your solo works. This set, recorded between 1978 and 1980, still spends most of its time on Loggins' solo hits, including the non-LP hit "I'm Alright," originally featured on the *Caddyshack* soundtrack. Since Loggins didn't release a hits collection until 1997, this meant that the record was his *de facto* greatest hits for many a year, albeit a hits collection that was incomplete and a little padded. Nevertheless, this is a good, enjoyable live set that may not pack many revelations, but boasts solid performances and a good set list that will please casual and hardcore fans alike. *—Stephen Thomas Erlewine*

High Adventure / Sep. 1982 / Columbia ✦✦✦✦✦
Well, if Duran Duran decided to rip off *Raiders of the Lost Ark*, why not Kenny Loggins? After all, the swashbuckling cover to *High Adventure* fits this album, since it finds him relying equally on rockers and melodic pop/rock. The album kicks off with Loggins' hardest-rocking single, "Don't Fight It," a surging arena-rocker duet with Steve Perry. This signals that the rest of the record will be harder than his previous record and that's true to a certain extent, since this doesn't just rock on occasion, it also has his best ballads and mid-tempo charmers. In other words, it's his best album, showcasing all sides of his personality effectively. "Don't Fight It" is a great single, but the best moment here is "Heart to Heart," the second of two pop classics Loggins cut as a solo artist. Here, he has a great mid-tempo groove, a good lyric and an indelible melody that is soft rock at its finest. The rest of the album may not match this height—most of the genre didn't—but it's all strong (though it's awful strange that "Heartlight," a tribute to the children's foundation Heartlight, has the oddest melody he's ever written—an ominous march that just gets creepier when the children's choir pops up at the end). *Celebrate Me Home* may be more consistent, but this is the most diverse record he ever cut, blessed by fine studio craft and a nice reliance on pseudo-new wave production techniques. *—Stephen Thomas Erlewine*

Vox Humana / Mar. 1985 / Columbia ✦✦

Back to Avalon / 1988 / Columbia ✦✦✦

Leap of Faith / Sep. 10, 1991 / Columbia ✦✦

Outside: From the Redwoods / Aug. 10, 1993 / Columbia ✦✦✦

Return to Pooh Corner / 1994 / Sony Wonder ✦✦✦✦✦

● **Yesterday, Today, Tomorrow: The Greatest Hits** / Mar. 25, 1997 / Columbia ✦✦✦✦✦

Yesterday Today Tomorrow compiles Loggins' biggest solo hits, including the chart-topping "Footloose" theme, "Danger Zone" (from *Top Gun*) and "I'm Alright" (from the classic *Caddyshack*), along with the newly recorded single "For the First Time." —*Jason Ankeny*

The Unimaginable Life / Jul. 8, 1997 / Columbia ✦✦✦

Lone Justice

f. 1984, **db.** 1986

College Rock, Heartland Rock, Roots Rock

The roots-rock band Lone Justice was formed in Los Angeles by guitarist Ryan Hedgecock and singer Maria McKee, who first met while dabbling in the L.A. rockabilly scene. Their mutual affection for country music inspired them to found Lone Justice in 1982; initially, the group was strictly a cover band, but soon McKee began composing original material inspired by Dust Bowl-era balladry. Gradually, elements of rock began creeping into the group's sound as well, and soon the band became a local favorite. At the urging of Linda Ronstadt, they were awarded a contract with Geffen Records; their self-titled debut appeared in 1985, followed by a tour in support of U2. Still, despite good press and media hype, *Lone Justice* failed to sell; slickly produced by the band's manager Jimmy Iovine, it failed to connect with either country or rock audiences. All except McKee then exited the band prior to their second LP, *Shelter*. Shortly after the record's release, McKee broke up Lone Justice for good and went on to a solo career. —*Jason Ankeny*

● **Lone Justice** / 1985 / Geffen ✦✦✦✦

Few new bands receive the kind of critical buzz that Lone Justice generated prior to the release of their first album in 1985, and one senses the band (not to mention producer Jimmy Iovine and Geffen Records) wanted to deliver something special to merit the hype. Which was not necessarily a good thing; *Lone Justice* is an album that tries so hard to be great that it sometimes ends up tripping over its own ambitions. The record leaves no doubt that the first edition of Lone Justice was a very good band; on the best cuts, Maria McKee's voice sounds like a force of nature, bassist Marvin Etzioni and drummer Don Heffington are a strong and imaginative rhythm section whether they were playing souped-up country shuffles or fifth-gear rock & roll, and if guitarist Ryan Hedgecock isn't quite a virtuoso, he's solid and inspired when he gets to step to the forefront. But guest keyboardist Benmont Tench and the other high-priced help (including Little Steven, Mike Campbell, and an uncredited Annie Lennox) often overwhelm the group's personality, and while McKee's songs celebrating the heart and soul of rural America are unquestionably sincere, they don't always ring true, and they also seem to inspire Iovine's most bombastic production decisions. In the wake of the 1990s alt-country movement, in which dozens of bands mined similar musical territory with more satisfying results, *Lone Justice* sounds like an example of too many cooks spoiling the soup; there's enough good stuff to make it worth hearing, but it's hard not to wish Lone Justice had gotten the sort of sympathetic but hands-off production that allowed Wilco and the Jayhawks to do their best work. —*Mark Deming*

Shelter / 1986 / Geffen ✦✦✦

Shelter finds Lone Justice abandoning the cow-punk image of their debut in favor of a more polished '80s sound. What they came up with is rather a mishmash of material that only points the way for Maria McKee to don a solo outfit and carry on alone. *Shelter* falls into the trap of a record company dictating how and what a disc should sound like no matter what might happen to the group producing it. While there are strong cuts here, most notably "I Found Love" (a real '80s-sounding product), "Wheels," and "Dixie Storms" (which foretells Maria McKee's future in music), all have something to recommend them. The rest falls into the trap of songs produced to fulfill obligations. Lone Justice was a group not unlike Big Brother and the Holding Company, who had a great female lead singer and focal point along with competent sidemen. Once the record execs ventured to guess that Maria would sell more on her own, they urged her to jettison the band, which she did after *Shelter*. Such is life in the record biz. —*James Chrispell*

This World Is Not My Home / Jan. 12, 1999 / Geffen ✦✦✦

This hot elegy album for the dearly departed Lone Justice is sheer rockabilly road-trip, as well as an illuminating artifact by a smart (albeit frustrated) "crossover" band. Blends of hardcore old-country roots and fast modern originality can be iffy on the charts, but the efforts of post-Emmylou Harris drummer Don Heffington, Little Steven collaborator Ryan Hedgecock on guitar, and bassist Marvin "Mandolin Man" Etzioni are committed. In typical Justice fashion all songs are tagged by the distinct Kate Pierson-meets-Dolly Parton vocals of Maria McKee; in Emmylou-like "East of Eden" we hear great drums behind a rambly hand jive riff and lots of big-hair yelling. Highway rocker "Ways to Be Wicked" is all tambourines and banshee vibrato, and dramatic Maria gets talkative on stage with the lovestruck "Sweet Sweet Baby." A foot-stompin' good-time record. —*Becky Byrkit*

The Long Ryders

f. 1981, **db.** 1987

College Rock, Jangle Pop, Paisley Underground, Roots Rock

Although they played the same clubs as most of Los Angeles' "paisley underground" bands (i.e., Dream Syndicate, Rain Parade) and even featured Dream Syndicate leader Steve Wynn in an early lineup, the Long Ryders were actually more a roots-rock group strongly influenced by Gram Parsons. The group was founded by Kentucky native Sid Griffin, a Parsons devotee who moved to Los Angeles after hearing about that city's punk scene, with guitarist Stephen McCarthy, the only two members to remain throughout the group's tenure. The group's first rhythm section featured bassist Barry Shank and

drummer Matt Roberts; they, along with Griffin, had previously been members of the Unclaimed. The band's 1983 debut EP, *10-5-60*, was a blend of punk attitude, '60s rock, and traditional country (Griffin played steel guitar, autoharp, and mandolin). Their first full-length album, the following year's *Native Sons*, was also arguably their best, and featured guest vocals from former Byrd Gene Clark. Subsequent albums failed to find an audience, and unhappy with their label's promotional efforts but unable to secure a release from their contract, the Long Ryders called it quits in 1987. McCarthy formed Gutterball and, along with Griffin, contributed to the 1993 Gram Parsons tribute album *Commemorativo*. Griffin, meanwhile, moved to London and formed the Coal Porters; today he works as a music critic and writer, foreshadowed by his definitive 1985 biography of (who else?) Gram Parsons. —*Steve Huey*

10-5-60 EP / 1983 / PVC ✦✦✦

It didn't take a genius to figure out that Sid Griffin and his fellow Long Ryders loved the Byrds with all their hearts, but they rarely made their affection quite so obvious as on their debut EP, *10-5-60*. The photos on the front and back cover clearly echo old Byrds promo shots, and the opening cut, "Join My Gang," sounds like some long-lost outtake from *Turn! Turn! Turn!*, while "I Don't Care What's Right, I Don't Care What's Wrong" and "Born to Believe in You" wouldn't have been out of place on *The Notorious Byrd Brothers*. But if *10-5-60* doesn't always speak of a startlingly original vision, the truth is hardly anyone short of the Byrds did this kind of stuff quite so well, and they absorbed the trappings of mid-'60s folk-rock so completely that they sound less like a throwback than some vintage band who somehow passed through a wrinkle in time and ended up in 1983—they walk the walk *and* talk the talk. And Griffin was thankfully still getting the revved-up snottiness of his days with garage mavens the Unclaimed out of his system, because the rave-up title track (written with fellow Unclaimed vet Barry Shank) is one of the hardest rocking cuts the Long Ryders ever released, and it ranks among the most exciting performances to come out of the '80s garage revival. The Long Ryders would gain a lot in the way of depth and ambition by the time they next entered a studio, but *10-5-60* proved they already had the talent, vision, and energy that would make them one of the more memorable American bands of the 1980s. [*10-5-60* later appeared as a bonus on the CD release of the group's first fell-length album, *Native Sons*, with an outtake, "The Trip," added to the running order.] —*Mark Deming*

Native Sons / 1984 / Frontier ✦✦✦✦✦

Native Sons was the first full-length album by the Long Ryders and the one that established their eclectic mixture of Byrds/Clash/Flying Burrito Brothers' influences. The band wore those influences on their sleeve, literally, going so far as to recreate the cover of an unreleased Buffalo Springfield album, *Stampede*, for *Native Sons* and using the producer of the first two Flying Burrito Brothers albums, Henry Lewy. *Native Sons* lovingly captures the band's musical obsessions, while turning in an original sound that became the banner for both the paisley underground and cow punk styles in the mid-'80s. Highlights include several forays into country on "Final Wild Son," the Mel Tillis composition "Sweet Mental Revenge," "Fair Game," and the humorous "Never Got to Meet the Mom," complete with a raging down-home banjo break. "Ivory Tower," featuring the late ex-Byrd Gene Clark on vocals, remains the greatest song the Byrds never wrote and one of the most sincere tributes to that band's sound. The album's final track, "I Had a Dream," reveals the punk sensibility, cranking the jangling Rickenbackers up to ten, closing with cacophonous feedback. On *Native Sons*, the Long Ryders pioneered a musical design that future alternative roots rockers would use as a manual. *Native Sons* has been reissued on CD with the Long Ryders' initial EP, *10-5-60*. —*Al Campbell*

The State of Our Union / 1985 / Island ✦✦✦✦

The Long Ryders kicked off their major label debut, *State of Our Union*, with one of their most anthemic *and* most explicitly political songs, "Looking for Lewis and Clark," and that tune set the tone for the rest of the album—*State of Our Union* found The Long Ryders reaching for a larger audience at the same time that they were using their music to say a great deal more than they had in the past. Musically, plenty of roadwork had tightened the band's interplay to an even finer point than on *Native Sons* (Sid Griffin and Stephen McCarthy were both in superb voice, and their guitar work meshed perfectly), and Will Birch's production gave the songs a poppier sheen that still allowed the band's roots-conscious sound to shine through. Lyrically, *State of Our Union* took a long look at Reagan-era America as the gulf between the rich and the poor began to divide the nation, with "You Can't Ride the Boxcars Anymore," "Two Kinds of Love," and "Good Times Tomorrow, Hard Times Today" all exploring issues of economic injustice, and even the less obvious political songs often having a progressive subtext ("WDIA," a tribute to the great Memphis R&B radio station, deals with how the love of music brought together black and white listeners in the 1960s). *10-5-60* and *Native Sons* had already made it clear that the Long Ryders knew how to make great rock & roll, but *State of Our Union* suggested they had a lot else on their minds, and they were able to air their concerns while playing music that could move the masses…assuming that the masses ever heard them. (Ironically, a large portion of the audience for this very American album was in England, where the Long Ryders had become press favorites, and "Looking for Lewis and Clark" became a hit single.) [A deluxe edition, with bonus tracks, was issued in the mid-'90s by Griffin's label, Prima Records.] —*Mark Deming*

Two Fisted Tales / 1987 / Island ✦✦✦

This, *Two Fisted Tales*, the last album by the Long Ryders, pulls together all the various elements that had distinguished them from the rest of the jangly, '60s revisionist rock bands of the mid-'80s. The Long Ryders' sound was a unique blending of McGuinn-esque guitar figures with well-defined parameters that encompassed Gram Parsons' country rock sensibilities and the various tenants of traditional roots-rock. Highlights include, the kick-off track "Gunslinger Man," a powerful guitar assault that displays the band's ability to rock strong and hard. In contrast, "I Want You Bad," a Terry Adams-penned tune, also covered by Dave Edmunds, is a melodic song of long-distance desire. Here the vocal quality is particularly expressive and fitting to the song's message. On the other hand, formative years in the South are reflected on Sid Griffin's "Harriet Tubman's Gonna Carry Me Home." The overall instrumentation, which includes mandolin, autoharp, lap steel and a guest accordion by David Hidalgo from Los Lobos, reflects their allegiance to traditional Americana music. Unfortunately *Two Fisted Tales* was to be the Long Ryders swan song. However, in the '90s there are still those who recall the pioneering spirit of the Long Ryders. [In the mid-'90s a deluxe edition, with four bonus tracks, was issued by Griffin's label, Prima Records.] —*Jack Leaver*

Metallic B.O. / 1989 / Long Ryders Fan Club ◆◆◆
The Long Ryders were one of the finest retro/roots bands to emerge from the U.S. in the 1980s. Their recorded legacy on Island and Frontier easily bears this out. When the Ryders disbanded in 1988, they left behind miles (well, at least hundreds of yards) of unreleased tapes. This release, a fan-club-only compilation, illustrates the band's power and diversity, especially on cover tunes like "What Goes On" and "I Shall Be Released." The whole affair has been lovingly and intelligently put together, and is a nice tribute to one of the finest bands of the decade. —*Matthew Greenwald*

● **Looking for Lewis & Clark: Anthology** / Jul. 21, 1998 / Polygram Chronicles ◆◆◆◆
The Long Ryders were one of the greatest bands to come out of L.A. during the 1980s. The band combined rootsy influences such as Gram Parsons and Buffalo Springfield with an unlikely punk sensibility. They were refreshing, they cared about the songwriting, and they could rock. Coming from the long-lamented paisley underground scene, which included such bands as The Dream Syndicate, the Bangles and Rain Parade, the Ryders were easily the tightest, and well-deserving of their major record label deal with Island Records, following their brilliant debut for Frontier in 1984. Polygram Chronicles has neatly compiled all the above material, plus the early *10-5-60* EP, and loads of rare and unreleased tracks on The Long Ryders *Anthology*. It's an excellent collection from one of the most honest and genuinely gifted bands of the period. Tracks such as Ryders founder Sid Griffin's "Final Wild Son" and bassist Tom Stephens' "Years Long Ago" capture the essence of the band, which can almost be compared to a meeting of The Flying Burrito Brothers, Neil Young, and The Sex Pistols. Lead guitarist Stephen McCarthy's material has probably aged the best, with such polished tracks as "I Had a Dream" (one of the band's finest) and "Mason-Dixon Line" leaving you to wonder why we haven't heard a solo album from him. Individual praise, however, is not what The Long Ryders were about. They were a great *band*, and should be remembered as such. The Long Ryders *Anthology* accomplishes just that. —*Matt Greenwald*

Loop

f. 1986, London, England, **db.** 1990
Space Rock, Shoegazing, Alternative Pop/Rock
Discordant, elusive and utterly hypnotic, Loop conjured a dark, trance-like spell that contrasted sharply with the prevailing British pop music trends of their time. Equal parts the Stooges, Can and Hawkwind, in tandem with fellow travellers Spacemen 3 they resurrected the concept of space-rock for a new era, creating droning soundscapes of bleak beauty and harsh dissonance. Loop was formed in London in 1986 by vocalist/guitarist Robert Hampson, who at the time of the group's inception claimed to know only four chords; with wife Bex on drums and Glen Ray on bass, they debuted with the single "16 Dreams," its raw, feedback-powered sound offering clear evidence of a serious garage fixation. New drummer John Wills and bassist Neil MacKay were signed on a short time later, with their arrival heralding a more primal rhythmic foundation; the reconfigured Loop then issued its 1987 full-length debut *Heavens End*, winning acclaim for its densely distorted sound.

The World in Your Eyes, a collection of singles and B-sides, appeared in 1987; after signing to the Chapter 22 label, Loop resurfaced in 1988 with the 12-inch "Collision." In November of that same year the group also released their second full-length, the excellent *Fade Out*. Over a year passed before Loop returned to action with the "Arc-Lite" single, now sporting not only another new label, Situation Two, but also a second guitarist, Scott Dowson. After issuing their third and finest studio LP, 1990's *A Gilded Eternity*, Loop disbanded; a series of posthumous releases, among them the live *Dual* and the BBC sessions collection *Wolf Flow*, soon followed. In the wake of the band's demise, its four members split into two camps—while MacKay and Wills reunited in the Hair and Skin Trading Company, Hampson and Dowson went on to form the highly experimental Main. —*Jason Ankeny*

● **Heaven's End** / 1987 / Mute ◆◆◆◆◆
Had Loop been present at Woodstock, they probably would have hatched a plan to obtain all the brown acid that Wavy Gravy warned spectators not to take. After hearing his declaration that "The brown acid's a bummer, man!," Robert Hampson and his droogs would have likely gone incognito as security staff, offering to rid the concert goers of the bad trips waiting to be had. They would have preceded to ingest what they could and record something like *Heaven's End*, a filler-free release of warped senses and personal demons, self-contained blues, and psychotic dementia. It sounds like a vast toxic wasteland where all negativity is dumped by the soul. Simple, tense riffs repeat until a state of hypnosis and emotional emptiness remain. "Heaven's End" itself sounds like the soundtrack to a missing hallucination scene from *Easy Rider*, shifting and shuffling percussion and twisted vapor trails of guitar mutate into utter mush. Samples from *2001* pop up throughout the record, if the music itself wasn't enough to carry a prevailing sense of paranoia and claustrophobia. But all the late-'60s references become stifling in conveying what Loop did. Along the way, Loop gutted all the spiritual mysticism from Can, taking their

repetition. They also borrow Suicide's minimal charge and early PiL's wretched anguish, making something rather unique from their influences. Though *Heaven's End* demonstrates a crystal clear indebtedness to Detroit's high-energy mayhem of the late '60s, it's actually the gunmetal gray sound of the Stooges and MC5 filtered through decades of urban decay. —*Andy Kellman*

The World in Your Eyes / 1987 / Mute ◆◆◆◆
The World in Your Eyes compiles the entirety of Loop's "16 Dreams" and "Spinning" 12" singles and adds four extra songs. Their earlier phase tends to concentrate centrally on pounding a giant riff into submission with the least amount of backing necessary, with all the sunshine happiness of the most downered Stooges sub-blues imagined. Generally, *The World in Your Eyes* captures some of Loop's most straight-ahead material, and Robert Hampson's vocals are at their least-fiddled with, production-wise. Bex's Spartan drum patterns usually consist of "thwack," "thwack-thwack," or "thwack-thwack-pish"; she might not stand a chance in King Crimson, but she fits the bill perfectly on minimally stomping songs like "16 Dreams" and "Head On." The 10-minute "Burning World" and 13-minute extended version of "Burning Prisma" (how many other bands do extended versions of 10-minute songs?) both have the entrancing qualities of the best Spacemen 3; the lengthier version features some extended soloing that avoids flash and wank. "Brittle Head Girl"'s melancholia strikes upon third album Velvet Underground, bizarrely using shades of new wave synth. A brilliantly fevered cover of Suicide's "Rocket USA" (from a Peel Session) captures all the rush and frenzy of the original; Hampson's vocals do Alan Vega proud, evoking all the evacuated headspace required: "Gonna crash/Gonna die." A racing rhythm box drives it in the same manner of the original, but the stun guitars add something that the earlier version arguably lacks. —*Andy Kellman*

Fade Out / 1988 / Rough Trade ◆◆◆◆
Distinguishing one Loop record from another is nearly as tricky as doing the same for the Ramones or AC/DC. Since Loop more or less stuck to one thing, remaining consistently great and gradually developing an experimentalist streak throughout their brief lifespan, the actual sound of each record is what separates one from the next. Aside from increasing control over their instruments, there isn't a great deal of actual progress made, but this is no fault. Wrecking ball riffs that remain firmly balanced between lunkheaded and complex always play a major role; simple but effective rhythms propel; Robert Hampson's vocals generally play the role of additional instrument, doing little more than expressing the subject given in the titles. Like the remainder of their discography, the song titles themselves are ideally descriptive. "This Is Where You End" and "Torched" have some of Hampson's meanest vocals, contrasting with the wasted (or, well, faded) effect provided on "Fade Out." Repetitive stutter shuffles play throughout "Vision Stain." "Pulse" and "Black Sun" offer massive howling. The guitar leads sound ear-piercingly tinny and high in the mix on occasion, perhaps to distinguish further from the droning riffs. The Rough Trade CD adds five bonuses, including covers of the Pop Group and Can. Their version of the Pop Group's "Thief of Fire" slows the mania of the original down to a near-lumpen pace, still expressing all of Mark Stewart's exasperated vocals. Can's "Mother Sky" is more true to the original, clocking in at 11 minutes and containing the same trebly guitar buzz and tumble drums that the original thrives on. —*Andy Kellman*

Eternal—The Singles / 1989 / Chapter 22 ◆◆◆◆
Released by Chapter 22 on vinyl in 1989, *Eternal—The Singles* simply combines the "Collision" and "Black Sun" singles from the year prior, not adding anything as a bonus. Those who own the Rough Trade CD and the limited double-LP version of *Fade Out* gets everything located here as bonus tracks, except the accurately-titled "Circle Grave." Since "Circle Grave" isn't anything special, only diehard completists should seek it out. The band probably felt the same; otherwise it would have been included on the *Fade Out* CD. But those who insist on vinyl will definitely want to track this down for the excellent interpretations of the Pop Group's "Thief of Fire" and Can's storming "Mother Sky." —*Andy Kellman*

A Gilded Eternity / 1990 / Beggars Banquet ◆◆◆◆◆
There's a pervading din throughout Loop's last record, an unsettling feeling created by their guitars that slightly disturbs the senses in the way that Sonic Youth's guitars endlessly stir on *EVOL* and *Sister*. One hates to trot out the post-apocalyptic adjective, but if there are any ten songs that deserve that label, it's the batch strung together here. Deadened toms rattle throughout "Afterglow," while densely lurching guitars prod and peel back alternately between the left and right channels. "The Nail Will Burn" features yet another punishing Loop riff, giving the image of the heads of three longhairs bobbing up and down in unison on stage. "Breathe Into Me" and a remix of "Arc-Lite" also offer caveman subtlety and deeply penetrating repetition. But rather than simply drive a point home again and again hypnotically, there's a little more imagination running through the arrangements, making the record a little less direct than the ones predating it. Also, there's some great experimentation at hand, providing a taster for what Robert Hampson would soon be doing with Main. "Shot with a Diamond" (taking its name from a line in *Apocalypse Now*) sounds like a pendulum counting down to death. "Blood" features unidentified noises that cycle throughout, offering none of the riffs that typify the bulk of the band's material. Taken as a whole, it's Hawkwind minus the goofiness and Spacemen 3 minus the unnecessary tangents. Hampson broke the band up after this one, and it's easy to see why. He'd taken loud guitars as far as he could, and that experimentalist streak inside of him was obviously dying to be purged. Psychotic hypnotists they were. —*Andy Kellman*

Wolf Flow / 1991 / Reactor ◆◆◆◆
A compilation of the three Peel Sessions Loop recorded between 1987 and 1990, *Wolf Flow* presents a fine documentation or *de facto* "best of" for the Croydon band. As with most BBC recordings, the results are premium grade. Some might actually favor these

versions over their originals, given that Robert Hampson's vocals are less mired in production techniques. From the first session, "Soundhead" and a ten-minute "Straight to Your Heart" offer a little more clarity than their *Heaven's End* counterparts. Drums are given further presence, especially on the former. A seering version of "Rocket USA" (which also appears on *The World in Your Eyes*) could possibly be the definitive Suicide cover. The second session, predating the *Fade Out* sessions, features previews of "Pulse" and "This Is Where You End" that were changed little before entering the recording studio. The third session features a couple selections from the band's third and final record, *A Gilded Eternity*, as well as a B-side from the "Arc-Lite" single. The disorienting throb on "From Centre to Wave" is slightly sped up, adding further doom to the already creepy atmosphere. "Afterglow" kicks the distortion up a notch over the original and adds further force to the drums. "Sunburst," which probably holds the only non-indicative song title of Loop's career, drags slightly at nine minutes. Since Loop's three proper records and singles compilations vary little in quality, it's hard to recommend a starting point. But *Wolf Flow* shouldn't be turned down if given the chance to purchase. *—Andy Kellman*

Jennifer Lopez

b. Jul. 24, 1970
Club/Dance, Latin Pop, Urban, Dance-Pop
Actress/singer Jennifer Lopez was born in the Bronx, NY on July 24, 1970; after starting out in musical theater as a child, at age 16 she made her film debut in the little-seen *My Little Girl*, but her career then stalled until she was tapped to become one of the dancing "Fly Girls" on the television sketch comedy series *In Living Color*. A recurring role on the TV drama *Second Chances* followed before Lopez was thrust into the limelight co-starring with Wesley Snipes and Woody Harrelson in the 1995 feature film *Money Train*; smaller roles in pictures including *My Family/Mi Familia, Jack* and *Blood and Wine* followed before she landed the title role in 1997's *Selena*, portraying the slain Tejano singer. Co-starring opposite George Clooney in 1998's acclaimed *Out of Sight*, Lopez (the product of a Puerto Rican family) became the highest-paid Latina actress in Hollywood history; the following summer, she returned to her musical roots with her debut pop album *On the 6*, scoring a major hit with the infectious single "If You Had My Love." Lopez didn't waste time perfecting a sophomore effort, the appropriately titled *J. Lo*, which was issued in early 2001. *—Jason Ankeny*

● **On the 6** / Jun. 1, 1999 / Work ✦✦✦✦
Jennifer Lopez's debut album *On the 6* showcases the actress' sultry, versatile voice in a number of settings, including pop ballads, Latin pop, and R&B. Star producers like Sean "Puffy" Combs, Track Masters, and Emilio Estefan Jr. lend their talents to the album, making *On the 6* a perfectly polished and varied album, which features a musical blend Lopez calls "Latin soul."
   Smooth ballads such as "Should've Never," "Too Late," "Could This Be Love," and "No Me Ames," a duet with Latin superstar Marc Anthony, dominate the album's first half; while these songs show off the gentler side of Lopez's vocal gifts, they tend to sound too similar. It's on the R&B and Latin-tinged tracks where Lopez really shines. Along with the insistent first single "If You Had My Love," cuts like "Feelin' So Good" and "Let's Get Loud" have a fiery, soulful sound more in keeping with Lopez's public persona.
   On the 6's second half capitalizes on this spicy, upbeat side, particularly on "Waiting for Tonight" and "Open Off My Love," which draws inspiration from rap, R&B, and Latin styles with its sparse arrangement of horns, keyboards, and beats. The tropical remix of "No Me Ames" and "Una Noche Mas," the Spanish version of "Waiting for Tonight," emphasize Lopez's distinctive heritage, which elevates *On the 6* from a star's vanity project to an individual but accessible work of pop songcraft by a widely talented performer. *—Heather Phares*

J.Lo / Jan. 23, 2001 / Epic ✦✦✦
Most snickered when Jennifer Lopez made her pop move in 1999, figuring that it was no more than a one-off vanity project. As it turns out, she was as serious about her pop career as she was about acting, and even if she didn't possess a particularly distinguished voice, she was earnest and had some good mainstream pop singles, delivered with some seriously sexy videos. *On the Six* was big enough of a success to raise expectations for its sequel, *J-Lo*. Essentially, this is the same album as *On the Six*, only a little longer with a little less focus and not as many memorable songs. This lack of winning singles becomes a drag, since at over an hour, the record meanders much longer than it should. Yet, meander isn't really the right word, because the album sets its tone from the start, with the ingratiating "Love Don't Cost a Thing." From that point on, the tinny, skittering drum machines, smooth midrange, and alluringly thin vocals remain the same from song to song, with the occasional Latin cut thrown in to vary the rhythm somewhat. Lopez's strong suit remains dance tunes, not ballads, which tend to disappear in this reserved production and mannered vocals. So, *J-Lo* winds up as musically a mixed bag. Its longer running time makes it a little less appealing than its predecessor, yet it has just about the same number of strong songs, all of which sounding of a piece with *On the Six*, which makes it a success on a certain level. Still, there's this certain feeling of staid complacency and ordinariness that makes *J-Lo* feel less fun than her debut. *—Stephen Thomas Erlewine*

Mary Lou Lord

b. Salem, MA
Vocals, Guitar / Adult Alternative Pop/Rock, Indie Rock, Alternative Pop/Rock, Singer/Songwriter
Playing her way from the subways and streets of London and Boston, guitarist/vocalist/songwriter Mary Lou Lord broke into the indie-rock scene in 1994 on the Kill Rock Stars label. Lord released a self-titled EP in 1995 and a second EP, *Martian Saints*, in early 1997. *Got No Shadow*, her major-label debut with Sony Music's WORK Group, was

released in 1998. After a stint at Boston's Berklee School of Music, she moved to London and learned the art of busking in the subway. She moved back to Boston and continued to play mostly acoustic covers on city sidewalks and in subways. While most of Lord's live shows have been just her and her acoustic Martin guitar (even those beyond the subway), with the recording of *Got No Shadow*, she moved in the direction of electric pop-rock. *—Nick Kemper*

Mary Lou Lord [EP] / Jan. 6, 1995 / Kill Rock Stars ✦✦✦
By the time her self-titled debut EP was released in 1995, Mary Lou Lord was rather famous for someone whose only officially released recording had been a 7" indie single; in addition to having been the subject of a major-label bidding war, Lord incurred Courtney Love's jealous wrath over a rumored pre-Courtney fling with Kurt Cobain. It's tempting to examine *Mary Lou Lord* for veiled references to that incident, and it's not exactly a fruitless search. There's the vicious Matt Keating-written "That Kind of Girl," which contains several possible digs at Courtney, and Lord's own "The Bridge," a lament for a lover who has moved on to bigger and better things (rock superstardom?). But in the end, looking for clues about Lord's private life merely obscures the virtues of her music. Lord has a charmingly sweet, almost waifish voice, but thanks to her interpretive skill, it never becomes cloying or overbearingly naive. There is an air of wistfulness about some of the more upbeat songs—even on the only non-solo performance, an electric rock arrangement of Nick Saloman's "Lights Are Changing"—while the introspective songs are poignant and thoughtful, their intimacy comfortable and genuine. Yet there's more to Lord than just melancholy. The deadpan barbs of "That Kind of Girl" are actually more effective delivered in Lord's sweet voice, and the extensive indie rock catalog of "His Indie World" has a playful sense of humor. A charming debut on the surface, *Mary Lou Lord* only reveals more emotional depth with additional listening, and with covers outweighing originals, it's remarkable how well Lord ties it all together. *—Steve Huey*

Martian Saints [EP] / Jan. 28, 1997 / Kill Rock Stars ✦✦✦
Mary Lou Lord kicks off her second EP the same way she did the first—with a plugged-in, full-band reading of a song by the Bevis Frond's Nick Saloman, who guests on guitar. Yet there are subtle differences in her approach this time out—the intimacy of *Mary Lou Lord* seemed more personal, whereas *Martian Saints* is more about Lord's desire to simply spotlight some of her favorite songwriters. The smaller size of *Martian Saints* (five songs instead of eight) gives Lord less of a chance to develop a mood, but her impeccable taste in song selection comes through loud and clear. Just as impressive is her surprising range as an interpreter—she's equally at home with the playfulness of Saloman's title track and Pete Droge's "Sunspot Stopwatch" as she is on Elliott Smith's delicate "I Figured You Out" and Peter Laughner's gritty, urban Dylanesque epic "Cinderella Backstreet." And while Lord is not the most prolific songwriter herself, it says a lot about her abilities when her own "Salem '76" stands out as perhaps the best track on the EP, its sweet melody and clever turns of phrase masking themes of bitterness and betrayal. *Martian Saints* isn't as unified as its predecessor—these songs don't come off as different sides of her own personality in quite the same way—but if anything ties it all together, it's her infectious, fannish enthusiasm for the material, which is part of the reason she can do justice to such a wide range of songwriters. *—Steve Huey*

● **Got No Shadow** / Jan. 27, 1998 / Work ✦✦✦✦✦
For many years in the alternative revolution of the early '90s, Mary Lou Lord was touted as the next big thing by those in the know, but she never delivered a full-length album, preferring to turn out a series of indie EPs on Kill Rock Stars. It wasn't until 1998 that she released her full-length debut, *Got No Shadow*. While many of the titles on the album may be familiar to longtime fans—"Lights Are Changing," "Some Jingle Jangle Morning," "Western Union Desperate," "Subway"—the clean, polished sound of *Got No Shadow* might come as surprise. But the production actually does a nice job of opening up her sound, making it accessible like a Shawn Colvin record without losing integrity. Some critics may carp that Lord wrote or co-wrote seven of the 13 tracks of the record, with the rest of the songs devoted to covers of her longtime associate Nick Saloman (Bevis Frond), and one tune apiece from Elizabeth Cotton ("Shake Sugaree") and Freedy Johnston ("The Lucky One"), but that has the effect of strengthening the album, since there isn't a weak song here. Lord has a sweet, thin voice that is surprisingly versatile, and she delivers Saloman's songs as convincingly as her own. *Got No Shadow* is a little subdued, but Lord's charming performances, clever lyrics and catchy melodies prove remarkably resonant. It may not have the unvarnished appeal of the early EPs and tapes, but *Got No Shadow* was worth waiting for. *—Stephen Thomas Erlewine*

Los Bravos

f. 1965
In 1966, this Spanish quintet became one of the very few rock groups from a non-English speaking country to have an international smash with "Black Is Black," which got to number four in the U.S. and number two in the U.K. Lead singer Mike Kogel's overwrought, pinched vocals sounded so much like Gene Pitney that many listeners assumed that "Black Is Black" was a Pitney single, and the strong resemblance remained intact throughout Los Bravos' career, both in the singing and arrangements. Indeed, with their brassy pop/rock songs and production, which sounded about halfway between New York mid-'60s pop-soul and Jay & the Americans, Los Bravos sounded far more like a mainstream American pop/rock group than a Spanish or British one. Most of their records were sung in English, and although they never made the American Top 20 again, they were far more popular in Europe, even placing another single in the British Top 20 in late 1966 with "I Don't Care." *—Richie Unterberger*

● **All the Best** / 1993 / (no label) ✦✦✦✦✦
There's no label for this CD (though, oddly, it has the catalog #21670), but rest assured

that it's easily available in specialty shops and mail-order collector catalogs, and in fact is much easier to locate than their original LPs. Good value, with 30 songs (about 90% of them in English), including "Black Is Black" and "I Don't Care," and a host of little-known tunes that usually follow the melodramatic, elaborately produced pop/rock mold of their hits. Fairly strong stuff, if not especially compelling. *—Richie Unterberger*

Los Lobos

f. 1973, East Los Angeles, CA

College Rock, Heartland Rock, Americana, Adult Alternative Pop/Rock, Roots Rock, Tex-Mex

Los Lobos were one of America's most distinctive and original bands of the '80s. They may have had a hit with "La Bamba" in 1987, yet that cover barely scratches the surface of their talents. Los Lobos are eclectic in the best sense of the word. While they draw equally from rock, Tex-Mex, country, folk, R&B, blues, and traditional Spanish and Mexican music, their music never sounds forced or self-conscious. Instead, all of their influences became one graceful, gritty sound. From their very first recordings their rich musicality was apparent; on nearly every subsequent record they have found ways to redefine and expand their sound, without ever straying from the musical traditions that form the heart and soul of the band. *—Stephen Thomas Erlewine*

. . . And a Time to Dance / 1983 / Slash ♦♦♦

Only seven songs but they're a perfect summation of what the band does and why it's important. This perfectly seamless fusion of Tex-Mex, R&B, and rock & roll has powerhouse covers of the Ritchie Valens hit "Come on, Let's Go" and the norteño classic "A Te Dejo en San Antonio" thrown in for good measure. *—Kit Kiefer*

How Will the Wolf Survive? / 1984 / Slash/Warner Brothers ♦♦♦♦♦

Los Lobos spent years playing parties, wedding receptions, restaurants, bars, and anyplace else where someone might pay them for a gig before landing a deal with Slash Records, and their first full-length album for the label, *How Will the Wolf Survive?*, is the work of a band that had learned how to play something for everyone while still maintaining their own musical personality in the process. *How Will the Wolf Survive?* swings back and forth from straight-ahead rock ("Don't Worry Baby") and potent R&B grooves ("I Got Loaded") to country-accented blues ballads ("A Matter of Time") and Mexican traditional numbers ("Serenata Nortena"), with the band's exemplary taste, musical smarts, and road-tested maturity in evidence on every cut. While rarely flashy, even a casual listen offers all the proof you might need that Los Lobos was a band of world-class musicians, with David Hidalgo's guitar work especially impressive throughout. Just as importantly, *How Will the Wolf Survive?* was the first album where Los Lobos showed how much they had to say as songwriters, especially on "A Matter of Time" and the title cut, two songs that offered a moving and compassionate look at the lives of illegal aliens in America. On *. . . And a Time to Dance*, Los Lobos showed the world that they were a great dance band, but *How Will the Wolf Survive?* showed they were a great dance band, and a lot more besides. *—Mark Deming*

By the Light of the Moon / 1987 / Slash/Warner Brothers ♦♦♦♦

On *How Will the Wolf Survive?*, Los Lobos seemed to be feeling out the boundaries of how much they could say about the hard realities of life within the framework of good-time R&B-flavored rock & roll, and on their next album, 1987's *By the Light of the Moon*, the group gently shifted their focus to favor their more contemplative side. While the band certainly hadn't lost the ability to rock out (check out "My Baby's Gone" or "Shakin' Shakin' Shakes" for proof), most of the album displayed a lighter touch musically, with David Hidalgo's deft lead guitar and Cesar Rosas's precise rhythm chords fueling lean but smoky R&B numbers like "Is That All There Is?" and "All I Wanted to Do Was Dance" and understated musical snapshots like "One Time, One Night" and "River of Fools." Lyrically, *By the Light of the Moon* is dominated by the sad mysteries of life and the less-than-generous nature of fate, as ordinary people try to come to terms with death ("One Time, One Night"), disappointment ("Is That All There Is?"), love that's faded into the shadows ("The Hardest Time"), and the mingled comfort and uncertainties of faith ("Tears of God"). While the soundtrack album to the movie *La Bamba*, released the same year, captured Los Lobos at their most carefree and high-spirited as they called up the spirit of Ritchie Valens, *By the Light of the Moon* showed the other side of the coin as the group looked into the hearts and souls of themselves and the community around them, and if it's a harder album to enjoy than those that preceded it, its depth rewards repeated listenings. *—Mark Deming*

La Bamba [Original Soundtrack] / Jun. 1987 / Slash/Warner Brothers ♦♦♦

La Pistola y El Corazon / Sep. 1988 / Slash/Warner Brothers ♦♦♦

Los Lobos used the commercial breakthrough represented by *La Bamba* to turn to its first love, Mexican folk music, and recorded this excellent collection of norteño songs. If this is a band that seems to do too many things well, in a sense they are at their best when they narrow their focus, and they are certainly masters of their style here. *—William Ruhlmann*

The Neighborhood / Aug. 1990 / Slash/Warner Brothers ♦♦♦♦

Recharged by their set of Mexican music, Los Lobos return with arguably their finest straight rock & roll record. *The Neighborhood* effortlessly combines rock, R&B, blues, and country into a singular, powerful sound that manages to be as darkly funky as "I Walk Alone" and "Georgia Slop" and as gently moving as "Emily." *—Stephen Thomas Erlewine*

Kiko / May 1992 / Slash/Warner Brothers ♦♦♦♦

With its highly textured layers of sound, *Kiko* sounds like nothing else Los Lobos has done. Although their sound is still based in roots music of all kinds (rock, folk, Mexican, country), the band has shaped it into a dense, impressionistic wall of sound that intensifies the emotions behind such carefully constructed and moving songs as "Two Janes," "Angels with Dirty Faces," and "Kiko and the Lavender Moon." It's certainly their most ambitious album, and it's arguably their best. *—Stephen Thomas Erlewine*

• **Just Another Band from East L.A.: A Collection** / Aug. 31, 1993 / Warner Brothers ♦♦♦♦♦

By the time Los Lobos made their debut on record, they already had a half-decade of live gigs under their belt. That initial, independent release, *Del Este de Los Angeles*, went largely unrecognized however, and it wasn't until a half-decade later that the music business took notice. With the arrival of *. . . And a Time to Dance* however, they began to realize what many Southern California music fans had discovered years earlier. Here was a band that combined stunning instrumental chops with a flare for everything rootsy from '50s rock & roll and R&B to country twang and traditional norteño. They were a formidable live unit as well and the restaurants, weddings and parties that served as the group's initial circuit were soon replaced by gigs at the Olympic Auditorium (a defunct boxing arena where the group opened for P.I.L.) and the Whiskey a Go Go. *Just Another Band from East L.A.*, this two-disc, 41 song compilation of album cuts, soundtrack contributions, live tracks and unreleased material, celebrates the group's first fourteen years on record. It follows the band from their first recordings in the late '70s to 1992's visionary *Kiko*. Along the way, Los Lobos honed their blend of rock & roll and Tex Mex on a pair of T-Bone Burnett produced albums, returned to their roots for the traditional flavors of *La Pistola Y El Corazon*, and scored a number one hit with the title track to director Luis Valdez's film *La Bamba*. With each new full-length, the penmanship of David Hidalgo, Louie Perez and Cesar Rosas only seemed to improve and *Just Another Band* includes all of the songwriting highs. An excellent place to begin a journey into the music of Los Lobos. *—Nathan Bush*

Colossal Head / Mar. 19, 1996 / Warner Brothers ♦♦♦

Unlike most bands in their second decade of recording, Los Lobos gets more daring and diverse as they get older, creating sonic landscapes that are based in their justly celebrated roots-rock but twisting off into wild, unexpected directions. *Colossal Head* is their most adventerous work to date, building on the moody, atmospheric *Kiko* without losing sight of their gritty blues roots. While it certainly shows signs of David Hidalgo's lo-fi, experimental Latin Playboys project, the album isn't merely an exercise in sound. Los Lobos applies their broad musical pallete to a set of tightly-written, inventive songs that may not be as immediate as their past work, but is no less melodic and rewarding. Instead of running through a number of different genres on each individual song, they make a dream-like sonic collage that draws from jazz, funk, and avant garde as much as their traditional rock, R&B, Latin, and blues. What keeps *Colossal Head* from drifting off into space is Los Lobos' love of American musical traditions. Not only have they mastered their influences, they have fully assimilated them into their sound, creating their own, unique music. And that's far more interesting than simply regurgitating the same blues, rock, Mexican, and country licks. *—Stephen Thomas Erlewine*

This Time / Jul. 20, 1999 / Hollywood ♦♦♦

Given all the extracurricular projects members of Los Lobos pursued during the three years separating *Colossal Head* and its followup, it's not surprising that they've decided to show off what they've learned on *This Time*, resulting in a record that vacillates between songcraft and sonic sculptures. It could be said that *Kiko* and *Colassal Head* were like this as well, but the difference is that *This Time* has the structure of a straight-ahead rock & roll record, clocking in at 38 minutes with 11 short tracks. While that conciseness is welcome, it also points out the flaws in the post-Latin Playboys Los Lobos—Cesar Rosas' fine rockers are obscured by a layer of studio gauze, and David Hidalgo's songs can seem like excuses to run wild in the studio. If the production was truly evocative or innovative, that wouldn't be a problem, but *This Time* is another in a long line of murky, self-conscious productions from Froom, Blake, and Hidalgo, where creating sound is more important than making music. This is especially frustrating, since *This Time* has elements of a very good record—it's paced well and boasts strong moments from both Hidalgo ("This Time," "Turn Around") and Rosas ("Oh Yeah," "Cumbia Raza"). As it stands, it is Los Lobos' tightest record since *The Neighborhood*, but it's hard not to feel that it could have been better if Los Lobos saved the "explorations" for their side-projects. *—Stephen Thomas Erlewine*

Del Este de Los Angeles / Sep. 12, 2000 / Hollywood ♦♦♦

In 1978, when Los Lobos was paying their bills by playing weddings and Mexican restaurants in the greater Los Angeles area, they put out an independent album of their traditional Tex-Mex songs with a pumped-up rock & roll feel. The album, *Del Este de Los Angeles*, established their sound and gave them a jumping-off point for David Hidalgo and Louie Perez to start writing their own material. The LP has since been released by Hollywood Records on CD (not to be confused with their similarly titled box set *Just Another Band From East L.A.*) and is an interesting glimpse into the band on the verge of breaking away from their traditional roots and pushing into creating their own influential style. *—Zac Johnson*

El Cancionero: Mas y Mas / Nov. 7, 2000 / Rhino/Warner Archives ♦♦♦♦♦

A multi-disc, authoritative box set usually arrives toward the end of an artist's career, which is what made the appearance of Los Lobos' four-disc retrospective *El Cancionero: Mas Y Mas* in 2000 a little surprising. They weren't selling as many records, nor were they quite as hip as they were ten years earlier, yet they retained a devoted cult and critical following—they were still in the prime of their career, not ready to be enshrined. Fortunately, the band and Rhino went ahead and assembled a box, which winds up capturing a band at the height of its powers. The set smartly spends a lot of time on side projects, including the Latin Playboys, Los Super Seven, Houndog, and selections from Cesar Rosas' solo album, plus a healthy number of live songs, B-sides, tribute album tracks, and 11 previously unreleased tracks. These tracks deepen the already rich musical tapestry Los Lobos weaves, and the end result is pretty impressive. As the set winds from the authentic Mexican folk music of 1977 through the gutsy roots rock of 1987 and the dreamy soundscapes of 1992 to the daring music of the mid-'90s and then the consolidation of their strengths on 1999's *This Time*, it's hard not to be astonished not just by the band's range, but the fact that they do it all really well. This is the definitive portrait of Los Lobos, highlighting everything that they can do and containing almost all of their greatest songs; this is one of the rare times that a four-disc box set summarizes all of an artist's strengths, while telling a great musical story, as well. *—Stephen Thomas Erlewine*

Lothar & the Hand People

f. 1965, **db.** 1971

Psychedelic

One of the weirder psychedelic groups of the late '60s, the New York-based Lothar & the Hand People took special pride in augmenting many of their tunes with the theremin, a then-futuristic instrument most famous for its use in horror movies (as well as the Beach Boys' "Good Vibrations"). Playing eccentric satirical rock, good-time folk-rock, and experimental psychedelia, their material wasn't nearly strong enough to elevate them to the rank of innovators. Although their first album is their best, they are most fondly remembered for the trance-inducing "Space Hymn," an FM radio favorite for many years. *—Richie Unterberger*

● **Presenting . . . Lothar & The Hand People** / 1968 / Razor & Tie ✦✦✦

This group may be one of the more fondly remembered psychedelic cult bands of the late '60s, but their debut album hasn't dated that well. Their determinedly freaky material has some period charm, but the songwriting and singing really aren't all that hot. There are other problems: the frequent use of "Lothar," the group's theremin, sounds gimmicky rather than futuristic. They vacillate between good-time New York psychedelia in the style of The Youngbloods (who did it much better) and satirical shock-rock of The Mothers (who also did it much better), and the styles don't mix especially well. What sounded adventurous and far-out at the time can be a bit flat and embarrassing out of the context of the era. The saving grace of the CD reissue is the addition of six bonus cuts from their first three singles. Of variable quality, they nonetheless show The Hand People playing it straighter and, for the most part, the psychedelic folk-rock on these rare tracks was more effective and tuneful than the material on their LPs. The undoubted highlight is the fabulous "L-O-V-E (Ask For It By Name)," an explosive slice of pop-psychedelia that ranks as one of the best hit-singles-that-never-were of the late '60s. *—Richie Unterberger*

Lotion

f. 1992

Indie Rock, Alternative Pop/Rock

Lotion had released only two seven-inch singles ("Head" and "Tear," both on Kokopop) before the group recorded *Full Isaac* for spinArt in 1994. The album received glowing reviews from alternative outlets in America and England, including album of the year distinction from *The Village Voice*. The band—comprising vocalist Tony Zajkowski, guitarist Jim Ferguson, bassist Bill Ferguson and drummer Rob Youngberg—toured America and Europe (with Pavement, Throwing Muses and Mercury Rev), recorded a song for the Frank Sinatra tribute album *Chairman of the Board*, and released the EP *Juggernaut* on Big Cat. A second EP, *Agnew's Funeral*, followed in late 1995 before Lotion released *Nobody's Cool* early the following year. *The Telephone Album* followed in 1998. *—John Bush*

Full Isaac / 1994 / spinART ✦✦✦✦

Though their influences (Bob Mould, R.E.M., My Bloody Valentine) were a tad undigested at this early stage, Lotion's debut remains one of the most inventive and unusual rock albums of 1994. Pounding drums and thick, creative bass parts bolster a dizzying array of guitar textures: crashing, cascading, chiming, wailing—and that's just "Tear," the lead track and first single. Track two, "Dr. Link," showcases the band at its most adventurous. Twanging, almost country-ish guitar alternates with noisy thrash while an intricate bass pattern joins the bashing drums in groove-band-style synergy. The album begins to sag under the weight of its self-consciousness toward the end, but the anything-goes approach (tabla on "Long," cellos on "Around," courtesy of Rasputina) keeps things fresh most of the way through. Tony Zajkowski's high, plaintive vocals give an emotional charge to the songs, and the cryptic bits of lyrics that rise to the surface are never less than intriguing. The odd, cerebral song structures never settle into anything familiar, so each listen is like the first, an exploration of uncharted territory. This is the crux of *Full Isaac*'s achievement: It is an album of passionate, exciting rock music that does not become predictable for a single moment. *—Daniel Browne*

● **Nobody's Cool** / 1996 / Big Cat ✦✦✦✦✦

Nobody's Cool is perhaps the only album in rock history that is better known for its liner notes than for its music. Literary icon Thomas Pynchon is a Lotion fan, so he contributed a brief appreciative essay to this, their sophomore album. It is a testament to the group's talent and artistry that their songs hold up alongside Pynchon's hip, elaborate prose. *Nobody's Cool* retains the densely layered sound of their debut, but it's a tighter, more accessible set. For "Rock Chick," the band adds kitschy-loungey touches reminiscent of the Cardigans to a typically complex song structure, then tops it all off with an electric piano outro, proving that they have more than a few tricks left up their collective sleeve. "Precious Tiny" rides a glorious five-minute mess of a guitar solo into the post-modern sunset, with crashing drums, distant background vocals, and a plinking banjo for company. Throughout *Nobody's Cool*, lyrics yield meanings more readily than they do on 1994's *Full Isaac*. "Sandra," for instance, is narrated by a lovelorn stalker. The result is an album that is even more memorable and engaging than its predecessor, a veritable *tour de force*. Fans of Galaxie 500, Hüsker Dü, My Bloody Valentine, and R.E.M. can be grateful that Lotion is around to carry the torch for forward-thinking indie rock. *—Daniel Browne*

The Telephone Album / Mar. 10, 1998 / spinART ✦✦✦

Loud Family

f. 1991

Pop Underground, Indie Pop, Power Pop, Alternative Pop/Rock

After dissolving Game Theory, Scott Miller formed Loud Family, releasing their first album, *Plants and Birds and Rocks and Things*, in early 1992 on Alias Records. *Plants and Birds and Rocks and Things* received good reviews and maintained Miller's cult following, as did the subsequent EP, 1993's *Slouching Towards Liverpool*. In 1994, Loud Family released their second album, *The Tape of Only Linda*. The group's third album, *Interbabe Concern*, appeared in the late summer of 1996, followed two years later by *Days for Days*. Loud Family resurfaced in early 2000 with *Attractive Nuisance*. *—Stephen Thomas Erlewine*

● **Plants and Birds and Rocks and Things** / 1992 / Alias ✦✦✦✦✦

Scott Miller's final album with Game Theory suggested he was trying to iron out a few of the quirks in his musical personality, but five years later, the debut album from his new group the Loud Family found Miller's eccentricities taking center stage alongside his hooky and uniquely melodic pop songs. Anyone who loved Game Theory's Big Star-influenced smart pop will delight in *Plants and Birds and Rocks and Things*, as Miller's uncanny way with a hook remains unsurpassed, though Loud Family rocks harder than Game Theory and as players they're stronger than any of Game Theory's lineups. Those who loved the loopy montage of Game Theory's most ambitious album, *Lolita Nation*, will be pleased to note that Miller and producer Mitch Easter allow themselves plenty of room here for the incongruous, including the warped vocal samples of "Don't Thank Me All at Once," the darkly witty ranting of "Spot the Setup," and the bizarre split-channel effects of "Ballad of How You Can All Shut Up." And while Miller once called his songs with Game Theory "young-adult-hurt-feeling-athons," here hurt gets co-star billing with rage, anger, paranoia, and self-destructive angst; thematically, *Plants and Birds and Rocks and Things* slips into a lyrical darkness far deeper than Game Theory at its moodiest, making this pure pop for those who have a good time being unhappy. *Plants and Birds and Rocks and Things* was as strong as anything in Scott Miller's catalog, but it also made clear that Loud Family was going to push the outer edges of power pop harder than Game Theory; those who like their pop with a sharp citrus bite will find it highly refreshing, but those who prefer sweetness might want to program out a few cuts. *—Mark Deming*

The Tape of Only Linda / Oct. 25, 1994 / Alias ✦✦✦✦

Loud Family's first album, *Plants and Birds and Rocks and Things*, was obviously born of Scott Miller's fondness for the aural mix-and-match of the editing and mixing process. On the other hand, the group's follow-up, *The Tape of Only Linda*, reflects the work of a band that had spent some time on the road and came back playing tighter, harder, and louder than before. The sonic montage that dominated *Plants and Birds and Rocks and Things* is almost entirely absent; instead, this album goes for a live sound, with the group stretching out on longer tracks dominated by the guitar work of Miller and Zachary Smith, and while Miller's trademark melodic sense is very much in evidence, this is the closest thing to a straight-ahead rock album in his repertoire. (Even the album's semi-acoustic finale, "Ballet Hetero," has a surprisingly tough melodic undertow.) While Miller has traditionally dominated the songwriting process on his albums, *The Tape of Only Linda* reveals a greater sense of collaboration with his musicians; six of the ten tracks find him co-writing with other members of the band, and two songs are even sung by keyboard player Paul Wieneke (whose vocals don't fare quite as well as Miller's self-described "miserable whine"). Dark, heavy, and with more than a bit of sneering cynicism in its lyrics, this is the most atypical of Loud Family's albums; it's also one of their best. *—Mark Deming*

Interbabe Concern / Jul. 1996 / Alias ✦✦✦

Anyone who wondered where the fragmented songs and purposefully twisted aural montage went on Loud Family's second album, *The Tape of Only Linda*, will either be elated or annoyed to know they're back in force on the group's third full-length release, *Interbabe Concern*. While the edition of Loud Family that cut *The Tape of Only Linda* had been solidified by a solid dose of touring after the release of their first album, *Interbabe Concern* was cut with a new lineup in which Scott Miller handled all guitar duties and Kenny Kessel and Dawn Richardson took over on bass and drums (Paul Wieneke remained on keyboards and occasional lead vocals). This new Loud Family sounded more like Scott Miller's backing band than the group that made the first two albums, and without producer Mitch Easter on hand, Miller seems to have used *Interbabe Concern* as an opportunity to reacquaint himself with the cryptic side of his musical personality; there are a lot more short pseudo-tunes interspersed between the "real" songs, plenty of odd found noises and sound effects, and while Miller plays plenty of guitar here, there's a decidedly lower hard-and-heavy quotient than on the muscular *The Tape of Only Linda*. *Interbabe Concern* plays like a somewhat stranger version of Loud Family's debut, *Plants and Birds and Rocks and Things*, except that there are fewer memorable songs (there *are* memorable songs, of course, just not as many), the production has a lot less gloss, and Miller's fondness for chaos seems to outweigh his knack for perfect pop hooks. It's an inarguably interesting album, but one that demands a lot more work for the listener to ferret out the good stuff. In short, it's a lousy starting point for non-fans, and an acquired taste for the initiated. *—Mark Deming*

Days for Days / May 19, 1998 / Alias ✦✦✦

Scott Miller, leader of Loud Family, often seems to be torn between his gift for writing superb, intelligently hooky pop songs and his desire to send his work through the wildly fragmented grinder of his trademark editing process, which sometimes makes for a great album (*Plants and Birds and Rocks and Things*) and occasionally results in a puzzling semi-failure (*Interbabe Concern*). On *Days for Days*, Miller and his latest edition of Loud Family's attempt to have it both ways; the nine odd-numbered tracks are strange, untitled bits of studio weirdness, while the nine even-numbered cuts are full-fledged pop songs, and for the most part the "real" songs are a significant improvement over what he served up on *Interbabe Concern*, especially the spirited "Cortex the Killer," the sweetly sad "Way Too Helpful," and the moody "Sister Sleep." Miller also benefits from a far more *simpatico* group of musicians this time around; former Game Theory drummer Gil Ray has a sure but subtle touch that fits Miller's songs perfectly, Alison Faith Levy's keyboards and backing vocals work beautifully in this context, and their melodic contributions dovetail nicely with Miller's own. Skip half the tracks on *Days for Days* and you get one of Loud Family's finest albums—that, gentle readers, is why the good Lord gave us the programmable CD player. *—Mark Deming*

Attractive Nuisance / Feb. 22, 2000 / Alias ✦✦✦✦
While Scott Miller devoted a considerable amount of time on most of Loud Family's albums to slicing and reassembling his songs as if he were running them through some sort of smart-pop Veg-O-Matic, the group's fifth album, *Attractive Nuisance*, found Miller taking a step back and letting his songs play themselves out in real time for a change. *Attractive Nuisance* was Loud Family's most straightforward album since *The Tape of Only Linda*, and while that set found the group edging into a rock-oriented guitar-heavy attack that was something of a departure from Miller's best-known work, *Attractive Nuisance* was a wickedly arch slice of intelligent power pop whose alternately bracing and pensive melodies, angular guitar figures, and superb keyboard textures harked back to the best work of Miller's previous band, Game Theory. Anyone who longs for the smart, energetic hooks, and emotionally compelling melodies of *The Big Shot Chronicles* and *Lolita Nation* will be glad to know that they're very much in evidence on *Attractive Nuisance*, and the album found Miller and his band playing at the top of their form. Drummer Gil Ray and bassist Kenny Kessel are a subtle, solid, and inventive rhythm section, Alison Faith Levy's keyboard work fits these tunes perfectly (and she sounds great on the two lead vocals she contributes), and Miller's guitar work and singing are, as always, spot on. Stylistically, *Attractive Nuisance* does less to call attention to itself than anything in Loud Family's catalog, but in terms of presenting great songs played well, it may well be the strongest thing they've released since *Plants and Birds and Rocks and Things*. *—Mark Deming*

Love

f. 1965, Los Angeles, CA, **db.** 1974
Baroque Pop, Folk-Rock, Garage Rock, Psychedelic
One of the best West Coast folk-rock/psychedelic bands, Love may have also been the first widely acclaimed cult/underground group. During their brief heyday—lasting all of three albums—they drew from Byrdsish folk-rock, Stonesish hard rock, blues, jazz, flamenco, and even light orchestral pop to create a heady stew of their own. They were also one of the first integrated rock groups, led by genius singer/songwriter Arthur Lee, one of the most idiosyncratic and enigmatic talents of the 1960s. Stars in their native Los Angeles, and an early inspiration to the Doors, they perversely refused to tour until well past their peak. This ensured their failure to land a hit single or album, though in truth the band's vision may have been too elusive to attract mass success anyway. Their self-titled debut album (1966) introduced their marriage of the Byrds and the Stones on a set of mostly original material, and contained a small hit, their punkish adaptation of Bacharach-David's "My Little Red Book." 1967's *Da Capo* included their only Top 40 hit, the corkscrew-tempoed "7 and 7 Is." The first side was psychedelia at its best, with an eclectic palette encompassing furious jazz structures, gentle Spanish guitar interludes, and beautiful baroque pop with dream-like images ("She Comes in Colors"). It was also psychedelia at its most reckless, with the whole of side two taken up by a meandering 19-minute jam. One of the finest rock albums of all time, *Forever Changes* was an exceptionally strong set of material graced by captivating lyrics and glistening, unobtrusive horn and string arrangements; it was not a commercial hit in the U.S. (though it did pretty well in Britain), but remains an all-time favorite of many critics.*—Richie Unterberger*

Love / 1966 / Elektra ✦✦✦✦✦
Their debut is both their hardest-rocking early album, and their most Byrds-influenced. Lee's songwriting muse hadn't fully developed at this stage, and in comparison with their second and third efforts, this is the least striking of the LPs featuring their classic lineup, with some similar-sounding folk-rock compositions and stock riffs. A few of the tracks are great, though: their punky rendition of Bacharach/David's "My Little Red Book" was a minor hit, "Signed D.C." and "Mushroom Clouds" were superbly moody ballads, and Bryan Maclean's "Softly to Me" served notice that Lee wasn't the only songwriter of note in the band. *—Richie Unterberger*

☆ **Da Capo** / 1967 / Elektra ✦✦✦✦✦
Love broadened their scope into psychedelia on their sophomore effort, Lee's achingly melodic songwriting gifts reaching full flower. The six songs that comprised the first side of this album when it was first issued are a truly classic body of work, highlighted by the atomic blast of pre-punk rock "7 and 7 Is" (their only hit single), the manic jazz tempos of "Stephanie Knows Who," and the enchanting "She Comes in Colors," perhaps Lee's best composition (and reportedly the inspiration for the Rolling Stones' "She's a Rainbow"). It's only half a great album, though; the seventh and final track, "Revelation," is a tedious 19-minute jam which keeps *Da Capo* from attaining truly classic status. *—Richie Unterberger*

☆ **Forever Changes** / 1967 / Elektra ✦✦✦✦✦
It wasn't a hit, but *Forever Changes* continues to regularly appear on critics' lists of the top ten rock albums of all time, and it had an enormously far-reaching and durable influence that went way beyond chart listings. The best fusion of folk-rock and psychedelia, it features Lee's trembling vocals, beautiful melodies, haunting orchestral arrangements, and inscrutable but poetic lyrics, all of which sound nearly as fresh and intriguing upon repeated plays. One of rock's most organic, flowing masterpieces, every song has a lingering, shimmering beauty, including the two penned by the band's other talented songwriter/guitarist/singer, Bryan MacLean. [A 2001 expanded CD reissue on Rhino/Elektra adds lengthy historical liner notes and seven bonus tracks: the 1968 single "Your Mind and We Belong Together"/"Laughing Stock," the genuine *Forever Changes* outtake "Wonder People (I Do Wonder)," the demo "Hummingbirds" (essentially an instrumental version of "The Good Humor Man He Sees Everything Like This"), and alternate mixes of "Alone Again Or" and "You Set the Scene."] *—Richie Unterberger*

Four Sail / 1969 / Elektra ✦✦✦
Lee and Love started to lose focus by turning up the volume on this album. Hardly memorable. *—Jeff Tamarkin*

Out Here / 1969 / One Way ✦✦

False Start / 1970 / One Way ✦✦

★ **Love Story 1966-1972** / 1995 / Rhino/Elektra Traditions ✦✦✦✦✦
Double-CD box contains most of their classic first three albums (including the entirety of *Forever Changes*), all three non-LP tracks from their 1966-68 prime, and highlights of the post-Bryan Maclean albums from the late '60s and early '70s. Great booklet of liner notes and photos, but considering that all of those first three albums remain easy to find, and that the post-*Forever Changes* material is much inferior to the early recordings, it's not an essential purchase. The absence of "Revelation" from *Da Capo* is no big deal, but a few tracks from the debut are missing, including one of the better ones, "Mushroom Clouds." *—Richie Unterberger*

Love and Rockets

f. 1984, **db.** Apr. 29, 1999
College Rock, Goth Rock, Alternative Pop/Rock
Love and Rockets comprised guitarist/vocalist Daniel Ash, bassist/vocalist David J, and drummer Kevin Haskins, all former members of the pioneering goth band Bauhaus. However, the group didn't sound very similar to their first group. Instead, Love and Rockets emphasized the strains of psychedelia and glam rock that appeared underneath Bauhaus' gloomy drone, adding elements of pop songcraft, folk and R&B, as well as cryptic, self-important lyrics. For most of the late '80s, the group had a devoted cult following, resulting in a surprise Top Ten hit single, "So Alive," in 1989. During the early '90s, the group's audience steadily declined, although they still retained a number of loyal fans. *—Stephen Thomas Erlewine*

Seventh Dream of Teenage Heaven / 1985 / Beggars Banquet/RCA ✦✦✦
From behind the black shrouds and smoky din of Bauhaus—very much in contrast to their dark, gothic angst, very much like a nighttime liftoff—arises Love and Rockets. Their debut *Seventh Dream of Teenage Heaven*, a vast divergence from the Bauhaus sound, is marked by an ethereal quality, as much by the transcendental lyrics as the richly layered depth of the production; the atmosphere is one of reflection, yet all the while remaining enlightened, without the somber negativity often induced by such a journey into the mind. The title track sounds like a hot night under blue neon, and is totally addicting, as are many of the tracks; perhaps the most distinctive is the instrumental "Saudade," remarkable in its almost pastoral beauty. Another track, "Haunted When the Minutes Drag," starts deep in a funk, with overwhelming vocals pulling you into the song, yet shifts subtly to a feel of self-affirmation. Symbolizing the band's transition from gothic negativity to fields of thought and light, this is truly an album to attach memories to. *—Bob Sakomano*

Express / 1986 / Beggars Banquet/Big Time ✦✦✦✦✦
Rich in sonic detail, the neo-psychedelic *Express* offers a listening experience like no other album—guitars spiral to dizzying heights from beds of sound, arrangements swirl, songs change and mutate. "Kundalini Express" typifies Love and Rockets' approach, chugging along for several verses before breaking open and ascending into the heavens; Anglo-fied Eastern religious imagery and philosophy predominate lyrically, and in tandem with the psychedelic music, offer an almost quasi-religious experience. John A. Rivers (who also co-produced Love and Rockets' first album) outdoes himself with the sound on this disc, offering a huge, unique canvas for the band to paint its sound on: crystalline acoustic guitars cut through thick, distorted tones, and the bass is an equal player to the guitars and drums. "Yin & Yang the Flower Pot Man" is ecstatically upbeat, offering a propulsive rhythm, flailing guitars, and insistent bass—a compulsively danceable and bliss-inducing track. "An American Dream," meanwhile, is an anthem of sorts, with distinct sections setting apart the moods of hope, disillusionment and acceptance. *—Jonathan Ball*

● **Earth, Sun, Moon** / 1987 / Beggars Banquet/Big Time ✦✦✦✦✦
Earth, Sun, Moon reins in the rampant excesses of *Express* while remaining psychedelic; the near-white-out of the cover gives a clue to the music, as many of the songs emerge from a soup of white-noise guitar distortion. Much of the record addresses, in their nebulous fashion, hope and disappointment; the title track and "Youth" are two of their most simple, yet most affecting, songs. Not a "normal" pop record by any means, it is more straight-ahead than their previous work and includes the upbeat single "No New Tale to Tell," a college radio hit which set the stage for their popular breakthrough a year later. *—Jonathan Ball*

Love and Rockets / Apr. 1989 / Beggars Banquet/RCA ✦✦✦
As the band's breakthrough record in the U.S., riding high on the left-field success of the slinky T. Rex homage "So Alive," this album still divides the band's fans to the present. Charges of sell-out are incredibly curious, because aside from "So Alive," absolutely nothing here sounds like it would have gotten anywhere on the airwaves. While Ash and David J were clearly dividing their songwriting efforts, resulting in a rather schizophrenic album, what they were writing and performing were some of the best songs of their collected careers. David J gets to indulge rock & roll and blues traditionalism on a number of his tracks, beginning with the opening "**** (Jungle Law)," a radical reworking of the old "Signifying Monkey" standard with compressed production and an almost industrial beat from Haskins. Another redone oldie is "Bound for Hell," a tale of the Devil driving a train to down below; David J runs his vocals through crackly distortion, playing harmonica while Ash plays a huge, thrashy guitar line. Perhaps his best number is his most atypical: "Rock & Roll Babylon," a barbed study of fame with Ash's sax and a string quartet fleshing out the sound beautifully. Ash's songs do some roots revisiting as well, in their own ways. "No Big Deal" and especially "Motorcycle" show that the man's been listening to some Jesus and Mary Chain, but his wonderful vocal purr marks them as his own songs. An unexpected addition to everything is "The Purest Blue," a radical reworking of *Earth Sun Moon*'s "Waiting for the Flood" which leaves almost nothing of the original. *—Ned Raggett*

Hot Trip to Heaven / Sep. 27, 1994 / American ✦✦

Sweet F.A. / Mar. 19, 1996 / American ✦✦

Lift / Oct. 13, 1998 / Red Ant ✦✦✦
Lift was the follow-up to *Sweet F.A.*, Love and Rockets' poorly received return to guitar-based rock, but is more closely related to their previous album, the electronica-oriented *Hot Trip to Heaven*. But where *Hot Trip to Heaven*, though flawed, boasted strong songwriting and an intriguing mix of electronics and old-fashioned instruments, *Lift* suffers from a dearth of good material and an overreliance on techno clichés. Ash, J, and Haskins were doing their best to change with the times, but it's telling that the highlights of this album either sound like outtakes from earlier Love and Rockets albums ("Pink Flamingo," "Delicious Ocean") or invoke the memory of Bauhaus. "Party's Not Over" is a haunting and grandiose lament that would not have sounded out of place on *Burning From the Inside* and "Resurrection Hex" samples the Bauhaus songs "Stigmata Martyr" and "In the Night." Approaching the turn of the century, Love and Rockets sounded like a spent creative force, their best moments far behind them. *—Bill Cassel*

Love Sculpture

f. 1966, Cardiff, Wales, **db.** 1970
Prog-Rock/Art Rock, Blues-Rock
A British blues-rock band of the late '60s that, despite being very good, would normally be relegated to footnote status if it were not for the fact that the lead guitarist of this trio was the soon-to-be-famous Dave Edmunds. Like many similar bands of the times, Love Sculpture was really a showpiece for Edmunds' guitar playing talents (which on the first LP are considerable), and little else. The covers are well chosen, slightly revved-up, but mostly reverent versions of blues classics. They had a fluke hit in 1968 with a cover of the classical piece "Sabre Dance" rearranged for guitar. After two LPs, Love Sculpture split up in 1970. Edmunds went on to solo success ("I Hear You Knockin'") and a long, sometimes contentious relationship with ex-Brinsley Schwarz bassist Nick Lowe, which culminated in the great band Rockpile. Still, Love Sculpture, though slightly dated, is a hoot to listen to today. And Edmunds, full of youthful bravado and dazzling technique, certainly knows his way up and down a fretboard. *—John Dougan*

Blues Helping / 1968 / Rare Earth ✦✦✦✦✦
As hyperkinetic blues albums by White English kids go, this is a good one. Dave Edmunds, armed only with a 1959 Gibson 335 and a 100-watt Marshall stack, cranks through these recognizable blues covers (with one original instrumental) with reckless abandon and gobs of technique. Backup support is handled by bassist John Williams and drummer Congo Jones, who do their best to keep up and provide a rhythmic foundation for Edmunds to wail over. Edmunds also handled nearly all the vocals, and as blues singers go, he's merely serviceable, but what makes this album worthwhile is the revved-up guitar playing, especially when Edmunds shreds both Freddy King's "The Stumble" and Willie Dixon's "Wang Dang Doodle." *—John Dougan*

Forms & Feelings / 1969 / Parrot ✦✦✦
Forms & Feelings essentially replicates the high-voltage attack of *Blues Helping*, only with a notable lack of energy and an eye on the charts. It's no coincidence that the group chose to revamp L'Arlesienne's "Farandole," given that "Sabre Dance" was the only thing that distinguished Love Sculpture from the legions of British blues bands. But this time around, "Farandole" and all of *Forms & Feelings* sounded tired and redundant, with only a fraction of the passion that made the debut worthwhile. *—Stephen Thomas Erlewine*

● **Single's A's & B's** / 1980 / Harvest ✦✦✦✦✦
With 20 tracks Edmunds issued with Love Sculpture and Rockpile in the late '60s and early '70s, this import collection is certainly the best retrospective of his early years, if you can find it. Edmunds' image is that of a roots-rocker, and you'll find a lot of that here, ranging from the huge 1970 hit "I Hear You Knocking" to pedestrian oldies covers. Actually, though, he wasn't at all settled on this identity at the time, also cutting some psychedelia, folk-rock, and primitive art-rock. The magnificent Love Sculpture version of Khachaturian's "Sabre Dance," featuring faster-than-light riffs by Edmunds, was a British Top 10 hit; "Farandole" was an unsuccessful attempt to do the same for Bizet. Cuts like "Seagull," Tim Rose's oft-covered "Morning Dew," "In the Land of the Few," and the Moody Blues-like "River To Another Day" are uncharacteristically wistful reflections of late-'60s hippie rock. The album also includes the rare 1967 single by Edmunds' pre-Love Sculpture band, the Human Beans. *—Richie Unterberger*

Love Tractor

f. 1980
Jangle Pop, Alternative Pop/Rock, American Underground
Along with luminaries like R.E.M., the B-52's and Pylon, Love Tractor helped establish the college town of Athens, Georgia as a mecca of alternative music in the early '80s. Comprised of guitarist Michael Richmond, multi-instrumentalist Armistead Wellford, drummer Kit Schwartz and guitarist Mark Cline, the band's earliest material was instrumental, if for no other reason than that they could not afford a PA system. However, the approach set them clearly apart from other acts on the crowded Athens scene, and helped win them a deal with DB Records.

1982's *Love Tractor* documented their formative approach, which touched heavily on fusion and even cocktail music. By their 1983 follow-up *Around the Bend*, Richmond was taking the occasional stab at singing; after the 1984 EP *'Til the Cows Come Home*, Love Tractor resurfaced in 1987 with *This Ain't No Outerspace Ship*, a full vocal exercise which also found the group tackling a cover of the Gap Band's "Party Train."

The quartet enlisted Mitch Easter to produce 1989's *Themes From Venus*, which, while comprised largely of vocal tracks, did contain the instrumental "Nova Express," effectively bringing the Love Tractor story full circle. Accordingly, in 1991 the group decided to take a break from the music business; they reformed periodically, and began writing and performing new material for a projected album.

During their hiatus, Wellford played in Gutterball with Steve Wynn, Bob Rupe, Sparklehourse, and the House of Freaks. Cline travelled, studying Italian opera and ancient languages, while Richmond studied art history. After several failed attempts at completing their "comeback" album, Love Tractor returned in 2001 with *The Sky at Night* *—Jason Ankeny*

Love Tractor / 1982 / DB ✦✦✦

Around the Bend / 1983 / DB ✦✦✦
A gentle collection of songs with the distinctly Athens rural beat, in the mold cast by the B-52's and Pylon, and somehow related to surf music. Love Tractor augment their previously all-instrumental agenda with some obscured, tentative vocals. An acquired taste, to be sure. *—Denise Sullivan*

'Til the Cows Come Home / 1984 / DB ✦✦✦

Wheels of Pleasure / 1985 / DB ✦✦✦✦

This Ain't No Outer Space Ship / 1987 / Big Time ✦✦✦
On the basis of their first two albums, it was easy to peg Love Tractor as the artiest of the Athens, GA, jangle pop brigades, but anyone who saw them live knew that, like Pylon and R.E.M., they understood how to turn their quirks into potent party music when they took the stage in front of a lively crowd (too bad they never recorded their potent cover version of "You Dropped the Bomb on Me"). On *This Ain't No Outer Space Ship*, Love Tractor finally made their peace with the human voice after an initial reluctance to write lyrics; nearly all the tracks here are vocals, and their words on "Outside With Ma," "Night Club Scene," and "Small Town" are as sharply witty as their music. They also achieved a new approachability in their songs, never quite shedding their Feelies-like angularity, but letting a surer sense of rhythm give it a greater warmth, and the album has a stronger, funkier undertow as a result—this is smart music that you can actually dance to. And the goofy but potent cover of the Gap Band's "Party Train" is clever without a hint of irony. *This Ain't No Outer Space Ship* is Love Tractor's most purely pleasurable album, and proves that even smart people can throw a good party when they put their mind to it. The 2001 CD reissue tacks on two bonus tracks, including an amusingly idiosyncratic cover of Neil Young's "Ride My Llama." *—Mark Deming*

● **Themes From Venus** / 1989 / DB ✦✦✦✦✦
After the relative polish of *This Ain't No Outerspace Ship*—dominated by concise, hooky songs and plenty of vocals—Love Tractor took a bit of a step backwards on *Themes From Venus*, which would prove to be the band's final album (at least prior to their reunion in 2001). The tunes on *Themes From Venus* are longer and less structured than those on *Outerspace Ship*, the grooves are at once loopier and more prominent, and while most of the songs have vocals, the words take a definite back seat to the music. In a way, it sounds like a return to the good old days of *Around The Bend*, except that Love Tractor haven't given up anything they gained along the way—the band sounds a whole lot tighter and more muscular than they did in their earlier days, and when they hit a groove, they cover a lot of territory they never would have dreamed of exploring only a few years before. If *This Ain't No Outerspace Ship* made Love Tractor sound like the world's smartest party band, then *Themes From Venus* suggested they'd taken a few more classes and learned even more about groove. *Themes From Venus* closed the book on Love Tractor (at least for a while) with the group sounding louder and prouder than when they started, but just as willfully eccentric and charmingly witty—would that every band could manage such a feat. *—Mark Deming*

The Sky at Night / Mar. 6, 2001 / Razor & Tie ✦✦✦
After sitting out the whole of the 1990s (if only U2 had possessed such good judgment), Love Tractor made an unexpected and quite welcome return to recording in 2001 with *The Sky at Night*, their first album in 12 years. If you're an old fan wondering "Do they still sound like they used to?," the answer is "not exactly." On *The Sky at Night*, Mark Cline, Michael Richmond, and Armisted Wellford (drummer Andrew Carter opted not to return) have moved back to the primarily instrumental approach of their first two albums over the poppier, more song-oriented attack of *This Ain't No Outer Space Ship*;

while most of the songs have vocals, a significant minority do not, and as in their earlier work, literal meaning has taken a back seat to atmospherics. And the group's emphasis on the guitar has faded a bit; keyboards are more prominent than on any Love Tractor album of the past, with a slower, more measured sound taking the place of the more urgent attack dictated by rhythm guitars. But the band's intelligence, their understated wit, and their slightly skewed but irresistible, melodic approach have all survived unscathed, and while "Christ Among the Children" and "Balthus (The Old Clothesline)" recall the sound of Love Tractor's best-known work, "Bright," "Tree People," and "Antarctica" show them moving into a more ambient, impressionistic direction that suits them nicely. *The Sky at Night* suggests Love Tractor won't be covering any Gap Band tunes again any time soon, but they've also learned how to take the approach Brian Eno mapped out on *Music for Films* and make it both fun and emotionally expressive—no small thing. *—Mark Deming*

Darlene Love (Darlene Wright)

b. Jul. 26, 1938, Los Angeles, CA
Vocals / Girl Group, R&B

Amazingly, Darlene Love, a superb vocalist, hasn't had much of a track record as a solo singer, at least not in terms of hits. Love was a founding member of the Blossoms in 1957. They did several sessions and were resident singers on the television show *Shindig*. Love sang lead vocals on "He's a Rebel," which was credited to the Crystals, and "Zip-A-Dee-Doo-Dah," which was issued as Bob B. Soxx and the Bluejeans. She cut six singles for Spector's Phillies label, with "Wait Till My Bobby Gets Back Home" the most successful. Love became busy as an actress, but reunited with Spector for the 1977 single "Lord, If You're a Woman." Love appeared in all four *Lethal Weapon* films, and was also in the Royal Shakespeare Company's co-production of Stephen King's *Carrie*. Her 1990 LP, *Paint Another Picture*, failed to chart in America. Love later toured as a background vocalist with Cher. She appeared briefly on the soap opera *Another World* in 1993. *—Ron Wynn*

Masters / 1981 / Phil Spector International ✦✦✦

For a few years this collection of Spector-produced Darlene Love sides was one of the most coveted albums of rare Spector material. It's much easier to obtain in the 1990s, however, on ABKCO's *Best of* CD. *—Richie Unterberger*

● **The Best of Darlene Love** / Sep. 22, 1992 / ABKCO ✦✦✦✦✦

A terrific compilation of Love's Phil Spector-produced hits, it includes "(Today I Met) the Boy I'm Gonna Marry," "Wait Till My Bobby Gets Back Home" and the hits she sang for the Crystals, "He's a Rebel" and "He's Sure the Boy I Love." *—AMG*

Loverboy

f. 1980, Toronto, Canada
Album Rock, Arena Rock, Pop/Rock, Hard Rock

With a string of three multi-platinum albums, Loverboy was one of the most successful mainstream hard rock groups of the early '80s. The band formed in Toronto, Canada, in 1980 and immediately signed with CBS Records. Later that year, their Bruce Fairbairn-produced debut album appeared. Featuring the slick, hard-rocking singles "Turn Me Loose" and "The Kid Is Hot Tonite," the album went platinum in both Canada and America. Loverboy recorded the follow-up, *Get Lucky*, in 1981. Driven by the anthemic "Working for the Weekend," the Fairbairn-produced record was a major success in the U.S. and Canada, yet it failed to gain an audience anywhere in Europe. Nevertheless, the band was a staple on AOR stations across North America, as well as a popular concert attraction. The band's good fortunes continued with the 1983 album *Keep It Up*. Again, Loverboy worked with Fairbairn, who kept their melodic yet tough sound intact; the album featured the hit single "Hot Girls In Love." Loverboy's fortunes began to slip with 1985's *Lovin' Every Minute of It*—producer Tom Allom gave the band a harder edge which didn't prove as commercially successful as their past records. *—Stephen Thomas Erlewine*

Loverboy / 1980 / Columbia ✦✦✦✦✦

Although their later albums produced better-known hits, this debut offering from Loverboy is one of their best albums. Despite their later reputation as AOR hitmakers, Loverboy was marketed as a new wave group early on and this album makes it easy to see why: plenty of the songs feature the herky-jerky yet dance-friendly tempo associated with many new wave groups and sleek synthesizer textures form a central part of the group's sound. The most impressive songs are the ones that earned the band their early airplay: "The Kid Is Hot Tonite" is a radio-ready rocker that slickly balances midtempo guitar riffs with surging synthesizer lines and "Turn Me Loose" is a clever multi-genre hybrid that blends hard-rock guitar, a disco-ready beat, and new wave keyboard flourishes into a final product with across-the-board appeal. The remaining songs are just as interesting as the hits because they hop from genre to genre with style and energy: "Teenage Overdose" blends gritty heavy metal guitar riffs with snarling punk-style lyrics and a pop melody while "Little Girl" filters rockabilly through new-wave sonic techniques to create a retro-styled power pop tune worthy of Cheap Trick). These ambitious hybrids are performed with style and economy by the band and special note should also be taken of Mike Reno's vocals: whether he's paying tribute to Elvis Presley on "Little Girl" or hitting the peak of his falsetto range in "Turn Me Loose," he tackles every number with energy and verve. The end result may be kitschy, but it is undeniably well-crafted and makes perfect car stereo listening (the ultimate compliment for an AOR record). In short, Loverboy is a must for the group's fans and an excellent pick for anyone who enjoys the pop-rock of the 1980s. *—Donald A. Guarisco*

Get Lucky / 1981 / Columbia ✦✦✦✦

After making a promising start with their self-titled debut, Loverboy hit the big time in

1981 with *Get Lucky*. This canny combination of AOR hooks and new wave production gloss boasts some memorable radio-ready tunes but isn't as solid an album as its success might lead one to believe. The best tunes on *Get Lucky* were the songs that became its hit singles: "Working For The Weekend" is a party anthem that blends some gutsy hard-rock guitar riffs with a synthesizer-drenched new wave rhythm arrangement to become a huge hit while "The Lucky Ones" layers clever lyrics about the jealousy that success inspires in others over a song that mixes pomp-rock grandeur with a punchy AOR arrangement full of gutsy yet slick guitar riffs. Loverboy got additional airplay with "When It's Over," a moody power ballad that boasts a show-stoppingly emotional vocal performance from Mike Reno, and "Take Me To The Top," a sleek midtempo piece built on a hypnotic synthesizer arrangement. The rest of *Get Lucky* isn't as impressive as these hits because it relies on filler to pad the album out: "Gangs In The Street" is an overwrought song about street tensions whose lyrics are melodramatic to the point of being unintentionally funny and "Emotional" is a sloppy bar-band jam with annoyingly sexist lyrics and an awful vocal from Paul Dean. Due to this overabundance of less than stellar tracks, *Get Lucky* fails to be as consistent a listen as *Loverboy* or *Keep It Up* but offers enough solid tracks to please the group's fans and AOR fanatics. Other listeners may want to check out the album's highlights on a compilation before picking it up. *—Donald A. Guarisco*

Keep It Up / 1983 / Columbia ✦✦✦✦

After establishing themselves as a multi-platinum arena act with *Get Lucky*, Loverboy continued to crank out their unique new wave-tinged style of AOR on *Keep It Up*. Although this album's hits weren't as large or as indelible as those from *Get Lucky*, *Keep It Up* is actually a more consistent album. This time, the songs that hit the charts were "Hot Girls In Love" and "Queen Of The Broken Hearts." The former is an uptempo tune in the classic Loverboy style that dishes up a fist-pumping guitar rock tune fleshed out with slick synthesizer and organ textures. The latter song is a different, more complex animal: it's the surprisingly observant tale of a woman reluctant to fall in love that plays out over a hook-laden midtempo tune that plays off meditative guitar-laden verses against a synth-driven chorus that suddenly accelerates the tempo to a dance-pop level. Elsewhere, the album combines AOR hooks with lush instrumental treatments that approach prog-rock: "Prime Of Your Life" and "One Sided Love Affair" are built on stately, almost classical synthesizer riffs while "Danger Zone" boasts a complex arrangement that alternates moody electronics with dramatic guitar bombast. "Meltdown" is another tune in this artsy vein: it's a slow rocker that combines the heaviest guitar riffs on the album with layered synth parts reminiscent of Rush. None of the other tunes on *Keep It Up* are as instantly accessible as its hits, but everything is arranged and performed with care. As a result, the album doesn't suffer from the inconsistent songs that marred *Get Lucky* and succeeds as a fully-realized album of pop-rock. In short, *Keep It Up* is a worthwhile listen for Loverboy fans and anyone who is into 1980s AOR rock. *—Donald A. Guarisco*

Lovin' Every Minute of It / 1985 / Columbia ✦✦✦

While it was another platinum album, *Lovin' Every Minute of It*, was slightly weaker than Loverboy's first three records, due to a slip in songwriting quality. Although hits like "Lovin' Every Minute of It," "Dangerous," and "This Could Be the Night" were well-constructed arena-rock numbers, none of the album tracks were quite as catchy, resulting in the group's weakest record since their debut. *—Stephen Thomas Erlewine*

Wildside / 1987 / Columbia ✦✦

Big Ones / Oct. 1989 / Columbia ✦✦✦✦

Released the year that Loverboy decided to go their separate ways, *Big Ones* is about as thorough a hits compilation as one could expect from the group. There are a few singles missing—like "Queen of the Broken Hearts," "Dangerous" and "Lead a Double Life," as well as Mike Reno's duet with Ann Wilson, "Almost Paradise"—but the core hits are all here: "Turn Me Loose," "The Kid Is Hot Tonite," "Working for the Weekend," "When It's Over," "Hot Girls in Love," "Lovin' Every Minute of It," "This Could Be the Night," "Heaven in Your Eyes," "Notorious." Even though the subsequent *Loverboy Classics* covered more ground, *Big Ones* is a good, basic collection, ideal for any fan of the group. *—Stephen Thomas Erlewine*

● **Loverboy Classics: Their Greatest Hits** / Oct. 11, 1994 / Columbia ✦✦✦✦✦

The Toronto-based Loverboy, comprised of vocalist Mike Reno, guitarist Paul Dean, bassist Scott Smith, keyboardist Doug Johnson, and drummer Matthew Frenette, was never a big hit with critics, but the band members' blend of hard-edged pop won droves of fans and kept them at the forefront of pop/rock for most of the '80s. This album contains most of their hits (excepting some more minor cuts like "Queen of the Broken Hearts"), giving a broad overview of their work. Sex was always a hot topic for the band—think "Hot Girls in Love"—but there is more to Loverboy than just hormones. There are also party anthems, with "Working for the Weekend" and "Turn Me Loose" being iconic in the genre. What makes this all pay off for Loverboy is that, there being nothing wrong with some harmless monster rock, as sophomoric as it can oftentimes be, the band does it with tongue firmly implanted in cheek, which is much to their advantage. If they had had any pretensions, none of the material would have worked. But being able to sing "Little girl, don't you hesitate/'cause you're usin' live bait" with a straight face shows the band members are in on the joke. To spotlight their softer, more adult side, the band brings on "Heaven in Your Eyes" and, as a bonus, Reno's duet with Heart's Ann Wilson, "Almost Paradise," from the *Footloose* soundtrack, which is included, as Smith says in the liner notes, "as a way of selling more of this collection." Now who says they don't get the joke? *—Bryan Buss*

Loverboy VI / Sep. 30, 1997 / CMC International ✦✦✦

After a full decade off, Loverboy reunited in 1997 for *Six*. Like many of their peers, Loverboy wasn't able to secure a contract with a major label and decided to attach themselves to CMC International, an imprint specializing in veteran rockers. While the group certainly doesn't reach the heights of *Get Lucky*, they don't embarrass themselves. There certainly are some mediocre cuts scattered throughout the record, but the best moments make the record worthwhile for longtime Loverboy fans. *—Stephen Thomas Erlewine*

Live, Loud & Loose: 1982-1986 / Jun. 19, 2001 / Columbia/Legacy ♦♦♦
Loverboy was one of the most popular mainstream hard rock bands of the 1980s, and the Canadian quintet was one of the acts who laid the foundation for Bon Jovi and the "hair metal" movement at the end of the decade. Always a popular live act, 2001's 14-song *Live, Loud and Loose: 1982-1986* captures a boisterous period now sadly relegated to pop history: the prime time of fun-loving arena-rock. The very name Loverboy ensured the band was not going to be taken seriously by critics, but that didn't matter to the millions of fans who gobbled up albums like 1980's *Loverboy* and 1981's *Get Lucky*. Vocalist Mike Reno, guitarist Paul Dean, keyboardist Doug Johnson, bass guitarist Scott Smith and drummer Matt Frenette crafted wonderfully catchy hits, and virtually all of them are here including "Working for the Weekend," "Lady of the 80's," "Take Me to the Top," "When it's Over," "Lovin' Every Minute of It," "Hot Girls in Love," "Turn Me Loose" and "The Kid is Hot Tonight." The studio sheen is missing on these live tunes, but they still come across well in concert and Loverboy stretches a few of them out with a little jamming. Johnson's deceptively simple keyboard lines, Dean's mixture of power chords and catchy guitar licks and Smith's bass riffs bring Reno's dramatic vocals to life. Two minor hits in the Loverboy catalog, "Dangerous" and "Lead a Double Life," toss interesting twists and turns into the regular formula. The liner notes essay was written by MTV personality Nina Blackwood, who relates funny touring stories Loverboy told her over the years. Also featured in the liner notes is a touching tribute to Smith, who died in a boating accident in 2000. *Live, Loud and Loose: 1982-1986* is a nice souvenir of a lost era. *—Bret Adams*

Lyle Lovett

b. Nov. 1, 1957, Klein, TX
Vocals, Guitar / Alternative Country, Singer/Songwriter
Lyle Lovett was one of the most distincitve and original singer/songwriters to emerge during the '80s. Though he was initially labeled as a country singer, the tag never quite fit him. Lovett had more in common with '70s singer/songwriters like Guy Clark, Jesse Winchester, Randy Newman and Townes Van Zandt, combining a talent for incisive, witty lyrical detail with an eclectic array of music, ranging from country and folk to big-band swing and traditional pop. Lovett's literate, multi-layered songs stood out among the formulaic Nashville hit singles of the late '80s, as well as the new traditionalists that were beginning to take over country music. Drawing from alternative country and rock fans, Lovett quickly built up a cult following which began to spill over into the mainstream with his second album, 1987's *Pontiac*. Following *Pontiac*, his country audience declined but his reputation as a songwriter and musician continued to grow, and he sustained a dedicated cult following well into the '90s. *—Stephen Thomas Erlewine*

Lyle Lovett / 1986 / Curb ♦♦♦♦♦
With his eponymously titled debut LP, Lyle Lovett quickly established himself as the quirkiest, most gifted songwriter to emerge from Nashville in ages; like Steve Earle and Dwight Yoakam, who also issued debuts the same year, his music reflects a remarkably personal and unique vision—a breath of fresh air after so many years of cookie-cutter country-pop. Even from the outset, Lovett owes more to the likes of storytellers like Randy Newman and Tom Waits than to any of his country contemporaries; his songs are too wryly subversive and iconoclastic to fit within the Nashville straitjacket, whether acutely mocking stereotypes on "Cowboy Man," subverting cliches on "God Will" or delivering painterly narratives like "This Old Porch." More than simply a gifted lyricist, he's also a melodic, inventive and highly adaptable composer: "Closing Time" is a stately piano ballad, "You Can't Resist It" approaches anthemic rock territory, and the deliciously morbid "An Acceptable Level of Ecstasy (The Wedding Song)" introduces the rich, bluesy sound he would continue to explore in greater depth on subsequent outings. An outstanding debut. *—Jason Ankeny*

★ **Pontiac** / 1987 / Curb ♦♦♦♦♦
Greatly expanding upon the seemingly unlimited promise of his self-titled debut, Lyle Lovett returns with the exemplary *Pontiac*, which finds him sharpening his renowned songwriting skills while moving further away from traditional country without a single misstep. Opening with the arch "If I Had a Boat," Lovett proceeds to subvert the Nashville formula at every turn, next delivering "Give Back My Heart," a not-so-subtle dig at country's key demographic, and "L.A. County," which twists the classic revenge song to its ultimate extreme; in between he delivers a pair of stunning love songs, "I Loved You Yesterday" and the elegiac "Walk Through the Bottomland," the latter adorned by haunting vocal support from Emmylou Harris. Still, it's the second half of *Pontiac* where Lovett really spreads his wings, rejecting Nashville conventions to move headlong into jazz and blues territory; tipping his hand with the wonderfully snarky "She's No Lady," he quickly asserts himself as a jack of all musical trades, capable of mastering big band workouts like the slinky "Black and Blue" as well as beautifully mournful ballads like "Simple Song," *Pontiac*'s centerpiece and arguably Lovett's finest moment to date. *—Jason Ankeny*

Lyle Lovett & His Large Band / 1989 / Curb ♦♦♦♦♦
Lyle Lovett's excellent third album is his kiss-off to Nashville; here, for the last time, he compartmentalizes his music according to genre—country and non-country, essentially, although the lines are occasionally as blurred as the cover photo. Where on the previous *Pontiac* Lovett stuck all of his non-country material on the record's second half, here—clearly bristling from Nashville pigeonholing—he opens with a horn-powered instrumental, "The Blues Walk," before sliding into the absurdist narrative deadpan of "Here I Am"; as indicated by the title, big-band jazz is a crucial element of his ever-developing sound, as is his vocal interplay with the soulful Francine Reed, culminating in the wonderfully sassy duet "What Do You Do/The Glory of Love." Even when *Lyle Lovett and His Large Band* does turn its focus to country, the results are anything but ordinary, including a straightforward, albeit transgender, cover of the perennial "Stand by Your Man" as well as the haunting "Nobody Loves Me," one of the most deceptively simple and devastating cheating songs ever written. *—Jason Ankeny*

Joshua Judges Ruth / Mar. 31, 1992 / Curb ♦♦♦
Lyle Lovett goes folk-gospel. To be fair, the country tag was never a comfortable fit for Lovett's eclectic musings. *Joshua Judges Ruth* distances him from the category without firmly boxing him into any new ones. There is a southern-fried gospel feel throughout much of the album, even if it's sometimes irreverent. "Church" best displays Lovett's surreal, dry wit, recounting a hunger-driven church rebellion complete with full gospel backing vocals. "She's Leaving Me," featuring guest vocals from Emmylou Harris, is the one sop offered to traditional country. Overall, though, the mood is somber bordering on bleak. Like the album cover and insert photos, *Joshua* deals in shades of gray and themes of loneliness and death. What one misses the most on this release is the infrequent surfacing of Lovett's weird, playful sense of humor. *—Roch Parisien*

I Love Everybody / Sep. 27, 1994 / Curb ♦♦♦♦
A collection of odds and ends that Lyle Lovett has written over the years (some of the tunes date back to the late '70s), *I Love Everybody* doesn't have the self-conscious artistic importance of *Joshua Judges Ruth*, and it's all the better for it. Instead, Lovett offers a set of relaxed, casual songs, accentuating his infamous, off-kilter sense of humor ("Skinny Legs," "Penguins"). At the same time, the songs offer hints of Lovett's sly, subtle sense of menace, particularly "Creeps Like Me." *—Stephen Thomas Erlewine*

Road to Ensenada / Jun. 18, 1996 / Curb ♦♦♦♦♦
Since *Pontiac*, Lyle Lovett has been experimenting with different sounds, whether it was the big band posturing of *& His Large Band*, the gospel overtones of *Joshua Judges Ruth*, or the '70s singer/songwriter flourishes of *I Love Everybody*. With *The Road to Ensenada*, he hunkers down and produces his most straight forward album since *Pontiac*. As it happens, it is also his best record since that breakthrough album. Lovett strips the sound of the album down to the bare country essentials, allowing it to drift into western swing, country-rock, folk and honky tonk when necessary. He also decides to balance his weightier material ("Private Conversation," "Who Loves You Better," "It Ought to Be Easier," "I Can't Love You Anymore," "Christmas Morning") with fun, light-hearted numbers like "Don't Touch My Hat," "Fiona," and "That's Right (You're Not from Texas)," which are funny without being silly. In fact, *The Road to Ensenada* is the lightest album Lyle Lovett has ever made—the darkness that hung around the fringes of *Pontiac*, *Joshua Judges Ruth*, and *I Love Everybody* has drifted away, leaving his wry sense of humor and a newly found empathetic sentimentality. The combination of straightforward instrumentation and lean, catchy and incisive songwriting results in one of the best albums of his career—he's just as eclectic and off-handedly brilliant as he always has been, but on *The Road to Ensenada* he's more focused and less flashy about his own talent than he's ever been. *—Stephen Thomas Erlewine*

Step Inside This House / Sep. 22, 1998 / MCA ♦♦♦
Step Inside This House, in a way, is a perfect follow-up to *The Road to Ensenada*, his straightest country album since his debut, taking Lyle Lovett back to the very beginning, as he covers his favorite songwriters. He consciously avoids such obvious influences as Randy Newman and Jesse Winchester, choosing to concentrate almost solely on Texan singer/songwriters, resulting in a minor revelation. Lovett's place in Texas' progressive country tradition has always been evident, and his good taste has never been in question, but this not only confirms his strength as a performer, but also illustrates the origins of his clear, wry narratives. He not only sheds light on songwriters known better for their reputation than their actual recordings (Townes Van Zandt, Guy Clark, Walter Hyatt, Michael Martin Murphey, Robert Earl Keen), yet he carries a torch for obscure names like Eric Taylor, Vince Bell and Craig Calvert, David Rodriquez, and Steve Fromholz, who has no less than four songs on the album. For all the different writers, what's striking about *Step Inside This House* is how all the songs seem to spring from the same worldview. Few covers albums are as unified and Lovett's achievement is particularly noteworthy since none of the songs are standards. *—Stephen Thomas Erlewine*

Live in Texas / Jun. 29, 1999 / MCA ♦♦♦♦
In a way, Lyle Lovett has operated on two different levels since the beginning of his career. For many listeners, including critics, he's an exceptionally talented songwriter, revealing himself as the equal to such inspirations as Randy Newman. However, unlike most singer/songwriters, he's an entertainer, putting on one hell of a show every time he takes the stage. And that may be why *Live in Texas* is such a good album: For the first time, Lovett the entertainer has been captured on record. Not that his previous albums have been dry, but it's a pleasure to hear Lovett play with an audience (they love it, laughing at the punch lines in "Here I Am" and listening dead quiet to "North Dakota") and his songs, delivering vibrant, loose-limbed performances that confirm what a rich catalog he has. Recorded in Austin and San Antonio just prior to the release of his 1998 covers album *Step Inside This House*, *Live in Texas* is nearly a greatest-hits collection, graced with a couple of idiosyncratic choices (including a showcase for vocalist Francine Reed, "Wild Women Don't Get the Blues") that are nice additions to a uniformly excellent set of songs. Since Lovett never breaks from his recorded arrangements, what brings *Live in Texas* to life is the spirit of the performances, which not only rival the original recordings, but at times are more energetic or humorous. That doesn't necessarily make it a better album than any of his studio efforts—like most live albums, it plays better if you already know the material—but it's undeniably hard to resist. *—Stephen Thomas Erlewine*

Lene Lovich

b. Mar. 30, 1949, Detroit, MI
Vocals, Saxophone / New Wave

One of the more offbeat and memorable figures in new wave, Lene Lovich certainly drew much of her widely varied approach from her unconventional early experiences. Born of a Yugoslavian father and British mother, she spent much of her childhood in Detroit, MI. At age 13, she moved to Hull, England, with her mother. She ran away to London shortly thereafter, where she worked several odd jobs ranging from bingo caller to go-go dancer to street busker. Around this time, she developed an interest in art and theater, enrolling at the Central School of Art. She took up the saxophone and, after a brief stint in a soul-funk band (with future collaborator Les Chappell), Lovich wrote a string of songs for French disco star Cerrone. In 1978, Stiff Records signed her after hearing her first recording, a remake of "I Think We're Alone Now." She quickly became one of Stiff's brightest stars, headlining package tours and earning several U.K. hits over the next three years with the unforgettable "Lucky Number," "Say When," "Bird Song," and "New Toy." Unfortunately, her theatrical quirkiness didn't translate well into LP length and as new wave dissolved, she disappeared from the music scene. After an eight-year absence, she returned in 1990 with *March*. It failed to ignite any further interest and she again went into retirement. —*Chris Woodstra*

Stateless . . . Plus / 1979 / Rhino ✦✦✦✦✦
Stateless, her aptly titled 1978 debut, is a new wave cult classic. Featuring her offbeat vocals and quirky synth-heavy production, this is her finest moment. Includes the great single, "Lucky Number." Now reissued on CD as *Stateless . . . Plus* with five extra tracks and extensive liner notes. —*Chris Woodstra*

Flex . . . Plus / 1980 / Rhino ✦✦✦
Flex shows Lovich staying true to her unique sound, though it is somewhat watered down with super slick production. And while it doesn't quite match the debut, the new wave classic, "New Toy" (written by Thomas Dolby), makes it worthwhile. The CD reissue, *Flex . . . Plus*, offers six bonus tracks. —*Chris Woodstra*

No-Man's-Land / 1982 / Stiff ✦✦

March / 1990 / Pathfinder ✦✦

● **The Best of Lene Lovich** / Jun. 30, 1998 / Repertoire ✦✦✦✦✦

The Lovin' Spoonful

f. 1965, New York, NY, **db.** 1968
Folk-Rock, Pop

Right on the tails of the Beau Brummels and the Byrds, the Lovin' Spoonful were among the first American groups to challenge the domination of the British Invasion bands in the mid-'60s. Between mid-1965 and the end of 1967, the group was astonishingly successful, issuing one classic hit single after another, including "Do You Believe in Magic?," "You Didn't Have to Be So Nice," "Daydream" and "Summer in the City." Like most of the folk-rockers, the Lovin' Spoonful were more pop and rock than folk, which didn't detract from their music at all. Much more than the Byrds, and even more than the Mamas & the Papas, the group exhibited a brand of unabashedly melodic, cheery, and good-time music, though their best single, "Summer in the City," was uncharacteristically riff-driven and hard-driving. More influenced by blues and jug bands than other folk-rock acts, their albums were spotty and their covers at times downright weak. As glorious as their singles were, the group lacked the depth and innovation of the Byrds, their chief competitors for the crown of best folk-rock band, and their legacy hasn't been canonized with nearly as much reverence as their West Coast counterparts. —*Richie Unterberger*

☆ **Anthology** / Jan. 1990 / Rhino ✦✦✦✦✦
Unquestionably the finest collection of a major band that did much to launch American folk-rock in the mid-'60s. *Anthology* jams 26 cuts onto a single CD, including all of their hits and some of their strongest album tracks, drawing mostly from their 1965-66 prime. As for the more interesting non-smashes, these include the original version of John Sebastian's "Younger Girl," which was a hit in a more commercial version by the Critters; the minor 1967 hit "She Is Still a Mystery," a dreamily psychedelic number that holds its own with their other standards, but has somehow been forgotten by oldies radio; and "Good Time Music," recorded early in 1965 for an obscure Elektra sampler (and a small hit in a cover version by the Beau Brummels). The most overlooked find here is the instrumental "Lonely (Amy's Theme)," from the early Francis Ford Coppola film *You're a Big Boy Now*, a lushly orchestrated, melancholy tune featuring Sebastian's wistful harmonica. There are also little-known Sebastian originals, with vocals, from *You're a Big Boy Now* and Woody Allen's early screen venture *What's Up, Tiger Lily?* The accompanying booklet features comments from Sebastian himself about some of the group's most famous songs. —*Richie Unterberger*

★ **Greatest Hits** / Feb. 22, 2000 / Buddha ✦✦✦✦✦
Although it sports the same amount of tracks (26) as Rhino's 1993 *Anthology*, up to now the last word in comprehensive Spoonful compilations, the 2000 issue of the umpteenth collection from this short-lived '60s band gets the nod over all others. Taken from the original first-generation masters, apparently for the first time, the sound quality—with a crispness and definition previously unheard—and even track selection, is the finest yet. "On the Road Again," "Wild About My Lovin'," and "Darlin' Companion," all excellent tunes representative of the Spoonful's good-time folksy/jugband style that were omitted from the Rhino set, are included, further reinforcing this as the last word in single-disc anthologies from this legendary band. What's startling is how many great songs the group recorded in such a short time span. The majority of the tracks were released within a two-year period from 1965-1967, almost all springing from the pen of John Sebastian who also

took lead vocals on all the hits. The band was a textbook example of compressed quality, with only three tracks here breaking the three-minute barrier, and many clocking in at just under two. Which means there still could be an even more definitive compilation created by adding five more songs and extending the running time to the 77-minute CD maximum. Until then, this is the Lovin' Spoonful disc to own. —*Hal Horowitz*

Low

f. 1994, Duluth, MN
Sadcore, Slowcore, Dream Pop, Indie Rock, Alternative Pop/Rock, Christmas

Formed in Duluth, Minnesota in 1994, Low was perhaps the slowest of the so-called "slow-core" bands—delicate, austere and hypnotic, the trio's music rarely rose above a whisper, divining its dramatic tension in the unsettling open spaces created by the absence of sound. Initially comprising the husband-and-wife team of guitarist/vocalist Alan Sparhawk and drummer/vocalist Mimi Parker along with bassist John Nichols, Low began as an experimental reaction to the predominance of grunge; Shimmy Disc producer Kramer soon invited the group to record at his Noise N.J. studios, and the resulting demos earned them a deal with the Vernon Yard label.

After re-entering the studio with Kramer, Low emerged with their 1994 debut *I Could Live in Hope*, a beautiful set spotlighting the trio's hauntingly minimal aesthetic—even Parker's drum set consisted only of a snare and a hi-hat. Nichols exited the group prior to 1995's lovely *Long Division*, recorded with new bassist Zak Sally; a subsequent appearance on the Joy Division tribute *A Means to an End* was later expanded into the following year's *Transmission* EP, a five-track set also featuring a rendition of the Supreme Dicks' "Jack Smith." With new producer Steve Fisk, Low returned later in 1996 with *The Curtain Hits the Cast*. The *Songs for a Dead Pilot* EP followed in 1997 and marked their debut for Kranky, where they released such critically-acclaimed albums as 1999's *Secret Name* and 2001's *Things We Lost in the Fire*. The late '90s also saw them issue *Owl (Low Remixes)* and the *Christmas* mini-album, which featured a cover of "Little Drummer Boy" that became a minor hit when it was featured in the Gap's holiday season commercials in 2000. —*Jason Ankeny*

I Could Live in Hope / 1994 / Vernon Yard ✦✦✦✦
Like so many of their contemporaries, Low are repeatedly lumped into numerous derivative and nondescript headings intended to encompass slow-paced, instrument-driven music that maintains an indie aesthetic. Quite simply, no category can truly reveal the beauty and glory of Low's debut record *I Could Live in Hope*. Sad core? Not even close! *I Could Live in Hope* is an incredibly joyous journey of spirit and songwriting sensibility. The record remains patient and sparse throughout (just guitar, bass, high hat, and snare, and angelic vocals by the husband and wife team of Alan Sparhawk and Mimi Parker), but succeeds beautifully. Low truly behold the gift of understatement.

Working with long-time producer and New York underground mainstay Kramer, Low examine their own fears and haunting experiences, occasionally linking them with Biblical references, while consoling listeners with warm layers of ethereal vocals and waves of guitar reverberation. Tracks are simple one-word titles but that's all that they require—too much information would spoil the record's elegance. And that's probably why they open the record with "Words," a song about the overuse and misuse of language, that sets the tone for the entire album, right up to their plaintive and passionate cover of "You Are My Sunshine." Every small nuance of production is evident—Sparhawk's fingers not quite connecting on a chord change or sliding over a fret and echoing infinitely—making *I Could Live in Hope* a true testament to both Low and Kramer's penchant for capturing the lushest of soundscapes. —*Ken Taylor*

Long Division / 1995 / Vernon Yard/Virgin ✦✦✦✦✦
It's not just Kramer's production that gives Low the feel of snooze-rock champions Galaxie 500. The male vocals (provided by guitarist Alan) are lazy, wistful, and occasionally disappointed, alternately sounding like Dean Wareham and Michael Stipe. Red House Painters, the closest touchpoint for the minimalist accompaniment to *Long Division*, just can't compete with Low's bare, soul-searching oblivion. "Caroline" by itself is better than anything Galaxie 500 produced. —*John Bush*

The Curtain Hits the Cast / 1996 / Vernon Yard ✦✦✦✦
The Curtain Hits the Cast was Low's first "major" album, taking the indie buzz over their early work to a much larger audience. The band didn't lose anything in the process—the album shows them still firmly entrenched in the epically slow, lazy dirges that got them started. The only noticeable changes come in the form of more elaborate production, and a shift in the ratio of dark, creepy dirges to pretty, comforting ones (the latter winning out, as evidenced by the album's single, the beautiful "Over the Ocean"). Low is one of those rare bands who have created such a distinct musical world for themselves that even major changes can't distract them from it—just like every Cocteau Twins album is unmistakably theirs, and always good, listening to any Low recording involves revisiting a wonderful sound that can't be found anywhere else. *The Curtain Hits the Cast* is more accessible than much of the band's earlier work, but, since it's a Low album, it isn't really that much different—the album is probably the best introduction to Low's work. —*Nitsuh Abebe*

Secret Name / 1999 / Kranky ✦✦✦✦
This is unadulterated lo-fi/sadcore, semi-orchestrated pop/rock par excellence. The power trio is augmented by a string section, tympani and piano on this beautifully understated chamber-pop outing by a misunderstood Midwestern band. Mimi Parker's voice is stunning on "Weight of Water," which at times sounds like it might take flight, but naturally, it never does—and that's not a criticism. When Parker and Alan Sparhawk duet, as on "Missouri" or "Immune," the result is as chilling as anything Gram and Emmylou ever conspired on—though that's not to say it's country-tinged, just straight from the heart.

What Low do particularly well is stay grounded, close to the earth and real. The music is so warm it's a literal caress from the speakers—and that's no mean feat in their notoriously chilly genre. *—Denise Sullivan*

Christmas / 1999 / Kranky ✦✦✦✦
In their liner notes, Low hopes that their fans, "... will consider this our gift to you. Best wishes." Those who are already fans should be more than pleased with this little morsel. Throughout *Christmas* Low's trademark simplicity of instrumentation allows the listener to hear every nuance and crystalline detail. Beginning with "Just Like Christmas," we find the band at their poppiest with a drum sound and sleigh bells worthy of a restrained Phil Spector session. Mimi Parker's warm vibrato makes an irresistible mantra of the titular refrain. The album highlight "Blue Christmas" would have been doomed to a kitschy fate in most hands, but Mimi Parker's voice captures the broken-hearted melancholy of the original while eschewing any obvious Elvis references. The cover of "Silent Night" doesn't fare as well; the band fails to add anything of note to this holiday standard. *Christmas* also includes several songs that could alienate more secular listeners, especially "If You Were Born Today" which is chock-full of biblical references and paints an extremely despairing scenario on the fate of a contemporary Christ. Low does a rare thing in today's indie-rock milieu by refusing to survive on cynicism and worldliness alone. Whether or not one ascribes to their beliefs, the heartfelt and reverential beauty of their sound and lyrics are perfect for the holiday season. *Christmas* is a rich treat in a tiny package. *—Sanz Lashley*

In the Fishtank / 1999 / KonKurrent/Touch & Go ✦✦✦✦✦
In late 1999, the Dutch label KonKurrent invited Minneapolis band Low into an in-house studio to record one of the label's near-legendary *In the Fishtank* sessions; bands have two days to record between 20 to 30 minutes of all new material of their choosing. Also touring at the time were Low's pals, the Australian instrumental dynamos the Dirty Three. Low invited them in, and in the same collaborative spirit as another *In the Fishtank* session involving Tortoise and the Ex, this half-hour session is the document. What is truly amazing about this hookup is how natural these two bands sound playing with one another. Of the six songs recorded here, none is more successful that the nearly ten-minute cover of Neil Young's "Down by the River." The other five tracks are sensual Low originals full of longing and resplendent minimalism. The D3 hold their place in the Low mix, painting it out over a vaster, more colorful expanse, creating more space in their trademark suffocating mix. This is a studio collaboration that works. It's half an hour of music made from the heart of goodwill and the desire by six musicians to do nothing more than play together to see what happens. What resulted is some of the best material either unit has produced. *—Thom Jurek*

One More Reason to Forget / Feb. 1, 2000 / Bluesanct Musak ✦✦✦
Live albums have a tendency to be sterile, multi-tracked, overdubbed affairs that aren't a lot different than their studio equivalents. Low avoids that trap with *One More Reason to Forget*, which was recorded in a church using room microphones, thereby capturing the sound not only of the band but of the room—an old church—as well. *One More Reason*'s track listing is a testament to Low's ability to change gears during a set. Sure, most of the songs are quite slow and pretty, but based on these seven tracks, they can hardly be called samey. From the purely pretty ("Venus") to the outright experimental and intense (the 17-minute "Do You Know How to Waltz?"), the band proves that it can more than make up for lack of tempo changes with a group of lovely, vibrant songs performed to perfection. *—Josh Modell*

Over the Ocean / Jul. 27, 2000 / Vernon Yard ✦✦✦
One of Low's trademark songs, "Over the Ocean" helped to bring the ascetic band to the attention of a larger audience; like most Low compositions, it is uniquely beautiful and instantly recognizable. "Violence," a track from their previous Vernon Yard record *Long Division*, and an early, even more reserved version of *Songs for a Dead Pilot*'s austere "Be There" are also included. *—Bryan Carroll*

● **Things We Lost in the Fire** / Jan. 22, 2001 / Kranky ✦✦✦✦✦
Over the course of their career, Low's glacially beautiful music has gradually melted into something much more accessible and intimate. The thaw culminates on *Things We Lost in the Fire*; despite its brooding title, it's the group's loveliest, most approachable collection of songs yet. Voluptuous strings, softly fuzzy guitars, and propulsive percussion suffuse songs like the sweetly melancholy opener "Sunflower" and the slo-mo pop of "Dinosaur Act" and "July" with a warmth and direction that Low's best work has always hinted at. Even the album's darkest moments, such as the tense, implosive "Whitetail," have more emotional urgency, heightened by Alan and Mimi's close, brooding harmonies. Yet Mimi's airy solo on the spare, undulating "Laser Beam" is equally spine tingling. *Things We Lost in the Fire* also features more of Low's understated stylistic experiments: "Medicine Magazines"'s slightly jazzy harmonies and tempo add a bit of swing to the group's usually steady rhythms, while "Kind of Girl" delves into earthy yet ethereal chamber folk. Breathtakingly gorgeous moments, such as "Like a Forest"'s pealing strings and poignant melody, and "Whore"'s build from delicate harmonies into a gently triumphant swell of guitars, vocals, and sparkling percussion reaffirm that Low have perfected and refined their sound. The finale, "In Metal," evolves from a melancholy ballad into one of the group's sunniest, most kinetic songs, mirroring the overall transformation of their music. A perfect match for its late-winter release date, *Things We Lost in the Fire*'s slowly rising warmth and subtly hopeful tone not only make this Low's most cohesive, compelling collection, but one of 2001's best albums. *—Heather Phares*

Nick Lowe

b. Mar. 25, 1949, Woodchurch, Suffolk, England
Producer, Vocals, Songwriter, Bass / Pub Rock, Pop/Rock, Power Pop, New Wave, Roots Rock, Country-Rock, Rock & Roll
As the leader of the seminal pub rockers Brinsley Schwarz, a producer and a solo artist, Nick Lowe held considerable influence over the development of punk rock. With the Brinsleys, Lowe began a back-to-basics movement that flowered into punk rock in the late '70s. As the house producer for Stiff, he recorded many seminal records by the likes of the Damned, Elvis Costello and the Pretenders. His rough, ragged production style earned him the nickname "Basher," and also established the amateurish, D.I.Y. aesthetics of punk. Despite his massive influence on punk rock, Lowe never really was a punk rocker. Lowe was concerned with bringing back the tradition of three-minute pop singles and hard-driving rock & roll, but he subverted his melodic songcraft with a nasty sense of humor. His early solo singles and albums *Jesus of Cool* and *Labour of Lust* overflowed with hooks, bizzare jokes and an infectious energy that made them some of the most acclaimed pop records of the New Wave era. As New Wave began to fade away in the early '80s, Lowe began to explore roots-rock, eventually becoming a full-fledged country-rocker in the '90s. While he never had another hit after 1980's "Cruel to Be Kind," his records found a devoted cult audience, and often were critically praised. *—Stephen Thomas Erlewine*

Bowi [EP] / May 1977 / Stiff ✦✦✦✦✦

★ **Jesus of Cool** / 1978 / Demon ✦✦✦✦✦
For his first solo album, *Pure Pop for Now People*, Nick Lowe completely abandoned the rootsy underpinnings of his work with Brinsley Schwarz and refashioned himself as a pop craftsman—or, as the original British title put it, the *Jesus of Cool*. Lowe tries anything and everything on the record, from the sweet pop of "Tonight" to the blinding rock of "Heart of the City." It's a veritable tour de force of his songwriting talent, as well as his wit. Not only does he turn in a set of wildly eclectic pop songs, he writes lyrics that slyly and gleefully subvert and pervert rock & roll tradition. *Pure Pop for Now People* sounds like '60s pop from an alternate universe, where hit singles are about actresses who are eaten by their pet dogs, castrating Castro, and grown men who write odes to teen idols. He also writes about the sleaziness of the music business itself with unrestrained joy. If Lowe's sense of humor wasn't so sharp and his melodies weren't so catchy, the amalgam of pop music and pop culture wouldn't have been so successful. However, he not only can write pop songs, he knows how to record them—each song sounds like an individual single, and the cheap production means that the album sounds like it's coming out of tinny radio speakers. And that also means that it doesn't matter what sequence these songs are put in—the album is like a jukebox, where different musical styles can follow each other and all make perfect sense. *—Stephen Thomas Erlewine*

☆ **Labour of Lust** / 1979 / Demon ✦✦✦✦✦
Jesus of Cool was a jukebox, spinning out a series of perfectly crafted—and decidedly quirky and subversive—pop singles. In contrast, Nick Lowe's second album *Labour of Lust* is the work of a bar band, in this case Rockpile, playing the hell out of the same type of songs. Naturally, the result is a more coherent sound that may be a little less free-wheelingly eclectic, but it is no less brilliant. Recorded simultaneously with Dave Edmunds' *Repeat When Necessary*, *Labour of Lust* benefits from the muscular support of Rockpile, who make Lowe's songs crackle with vitality. Working primarily in the roots-rock vein of Brinsley Schwarz, but energizing his traditionalist tendencies with strong pop melodies, a sense of humor and an edgy new wave sensibility, Lowe comes up with one of his best sets of songs. Not only is his only hit, the propulsively hook-laden "Cruel to Be Kind," here, but so are the rampaging outsider anthem "Born Fighter," the tongue-in-cheek, Chuck Berry-style "Love So Fine," the wonderful pure pop of "Dose of You," the haunting "Endless Grey Ribbon," the druggy "Big Kick, Plain Scrap!," and the terrific "Cracking Up," as well as his definitive version of Mickey Jupp's "Switchboard Susan." It's an exceptional collection of inventive pop songs, delivered with vigor and energy, making it one of the great records of the new wave. *—Stephen Thomas Erlewine*

Nick the Knife / 1982 / Demon ✦✦✦
Following the dissolution of Rockpile, Nick Lowe recorded *Nick the Knife* with the group's guitarist Billy Bremner and drummer Terry Williams, accentuating the real reason behind the band's split—the difference between Dave Edmunds' rigid roots-rock and Lowe's carefree, funny revisionism. *Nick the Knife* may work in the conventions of classic rock & roll and pop, but it never sounds enslaved to his roots—any record with a song as infectiously ridiculous as "Ba Doom" can't take itself too seriously, and that's the charm of the album. While the songs aren't as consistently strong as those on *Labour of Lust*, Lowe contributes a handful of classics, including "Heart," "Stick It Where the Sun Don't Shine," "Too Many Teardrops," "Burning," "Queen of Sheba," "Couldn't Love You (Any More Than I Do)" and the silly "Zulu Kiss." And even in its weakest moments, *Nick the Knife* has a sunny, relaxed charm that makes the album a thoroughly enjoyable listen. *—Stephen Thomas Erlewine*

The Abominable Showman / 1983 / Demon ✦✦
Caught between the desire for another big pop hit and his burgeoning re-interest in country music, Nick Lowe made the most confused album in his career with *The Abominable Showman*. Although Lowe's craftsmanship hasn't abandoned him, he isn't particularly inspired on *Abominable Showman*. Furthermore, much of the album is hampered by stiff, dated new wave production, which makes amiable throwaways like "Saint Beneath the Paint" irritating. Still, Lowe manages to break through the tedium with charming, clever pop-rockers like "We Want Action," "Time Wounds All Heels," "(For Every Woman Who Ever Made a Fool of a Man There's a Woman Who Made A) Man of the Fool," and the silly doo wop of "Tanque-Rae." But a song as sharp as "Ragin' Eyes," with its wryly observed lyrics and infectious melody, make it clear that the rest of the album is lacking. *—Stephen Thomas Erlewine*

Nick Lowe & His Cowboy Outfit / 1984 / Demon ✦✦✦
The title isn't entirely in jest—*Nick Lowe & His Cowboy Outfit* does represent Lowe's reinvention as a roots-rocker, as he delves into Tex-Mex, country-rock, garage rock and, of course, pop. After the muddled *The Abominable Showman*, *Cowboy Outfit* sounds

positively vibrant, thanks in no small part to Lowe's backing band, comprised largely of veteran pub-rockers. The songs are also more consistently memorable, from the Farfisa-driven "Half a Boy and Half a Man" to the sublime covers of Mickey Jupp's "You'll Never Get Me Up In One of Those" and Sandie Shaw's "Breakaway." The rest of the album's pleasures, however, are subtle. "Maureen" and "God's Gift to Women" are charming yet slight, and the songs become increasingly lightweight as the album approaches its close. Even with the uneven songs, the Cowboy Outfit make the material appealing, and Lowe certainly sounds more appealing—and comfortable—as a roots-rocker than as an aging new wave popster. —*Stephen Thomas Erlewine*

The Rose of England / 1985 / Demon ✦✦✦✦✦
Following through on the roots-rock leanings of *Cowboy Outfit*, Nick Lowe delivered the delightful *The Rose of England*. While some of the material is still rather lightweight—"Lucky Dog" and "Bo Bo Skediddle" are defiant and thoroughly entertaining throwaways—much of the record is clever and charming, delivered with laidback confidence from the Cowboy Outfit. "Darlin' Angel Eyes" and "The Rose of England" are minor classics in the Lowe canon, while his cover of John Hiatt's "She Don't Love Nobody" and the revival of the rockabilly standard "7 Nights to Rock" keep the album moving. Still, it's his stark take on Elvis Costello's lovely "Indoor Fireworks" that gives the album an anchor, and it's a performance so affecting that it makes the neutered reworking of "I Knew the Bride" completely forgivable. —*Stephen Thomas Erlewine*

Pinker and Prouder Than Previous / 1988 / Demon ✦✦✦
Abandoning the Cowboy Outfit but not roots-rock, Nick Lowe followed the winning *The Rose of England* with the amiable but muddled *Pinker and Prouder Than Previous*. Working with the same blend of classic pop, rock & roll, and country-rock, Lowe gets thing off to a roaring start with the driving "(You're My) Wildest Dream," but the record quickly bogs down in mediocre material. Many of the songs are certainly not bad, yet they rarely distinguish themselves from each other—only "Lover's Jamboree," John Hiatt's "Love Gets Strange" and Graham Parker's "Black Lincoln Continental" stand out, and they would have been second-string songs on *The Rose of England*. That doesn't necessarily make *Pinker and Prouder Than Previous* a bad record; it's just not particularly memorable. —*Stephen Thomas Erlewine*

● Basher: The Best of Nick Lowe / Sep. 1989 / Columbia ✦✦✦✦✦
Containing no less than 25 tracks, *Basher: The Best of Nick Lowe* is an excellent overview of Lowe's solo career, detailing how he evolved from a quirky, innovative new wave pop craftsman to a fine roots-rocker. All of Lowe's absolutely essential songs—from "So It Goes" and "Heart of the City" through "Cracking Up," "Born Fighter," and "Cruel to Be Kind" to "American Squirm," "The Rose of England" "Half a Boy and Half a Man" and "Raging Eyes"—are here, and while *Jesus of Cool* and *Labour of Lust* are essential in their own right, *Basher* is a terrific introduction to his body of work. —*Stephen Thomas Erlewine*

Party of One / 1990 / Upstart ✦✦
Nick Lowe settled a long-standing feud with Dave Edmunds with *Party of One*, hiring his former Rockpile mate to produce the album. Edmunds gives Lowe a sharper sound than before, keeping a tight reign on the performances and the songs—for the first time, there are no covers on a Nick Lowe album. Theoretically, that wouldn't be a problem, but Lowe was in a songwriting slump at the time of *Party of One*. "All Men Are Liars," with its weird jab at dance-pop idol Rick Astley, is symptomatic of the record's flaws—ingratiating melodies are undercut by forced humor and bland support. Even the best moments—"(I Want To Build a) Jumbo Ark," "What's Shakin' on the Hill," "I Don't Know Why You Keep Me On"—are undercut by stiff, colorless performances. For an artist who is defined by his relaxed charm, the stilted *Party of One* comes as an unwelcome surprise. —*Stephen Thomas Erlewine*

The Wilderness Years / 1991 / Demon ✦✦✦✦✦
Between the disbanding of Brinsley Schwarz in 1974 and the formation of Rockpile in 1977, Nick Lowe recorded a lot, attempting to settle on a sound. Simultaneously, he became the house producer at Stiff Records, where he became notorious for his raw, quickly produced records. That attitude shines through on *The Wilderness Years*, a compilation of singles, outtakes, covers, rarities and demos Lowe recorded during this year. With the exception of *Pure Pop/Jesus of Cool*, no other record captures Lowe's sense of humor or love of pop music quite as well. Divided equally between gems and glorious throwaways, *The Wilderness Years* is all over the place, but that's its charm. It has the notorious songs Lowe wrote to break his contract with United Artists ("Bay City Rollers We Love You," "Let's Go to the Disco," "Rollers Show"), both sides of his first Stiff single ("So It Goes," "Heart of the City"), his "erstwhile Stiff advertising jingle" "I Love My Label," terrific covers of "Halfway to Paradise" and Sandy Posey's "Born a Woman," plus forgotten gems like the demo for "Endless Sleep" and "Heart," "Fool Too Long" (which was written for Dr. Feelgood), and "I Got a Job," a song Nick claims he doesn't remember writing or recording. In fact, Nick doesn't think much of any of this material, but an artist isn't always the best judge of his own work—he rarely got any better than he did here. —*Stephen Thomas Erlewine*

The Impossible Bird / Nov. 29, 1994 / Upstart ✦✦✦✦✦
Nick Lowe's best records have always been full of clever lyrics and undeniable pop craftsmanship; the exception is *The Impossible Bird*. For most of the 1980s, Lowe had been appropriating country and R&B influences, but *The Impossible Bird* is where he fully incorporates those styles into his songwriting. Lowe doesn't abandon his gift for melody; "Soulful Wind" and "12-Step Program (To Quit You Babe)" are as catchy as anything he's ever written. The difference is haunting songs like "The Beast in Me" and "Withered on the Vine," two rich, sad, introspective numbers that Lowe would never have put on previous albums. And that's what makes *The Impossible Bird* his best album since *Labour of Lust*—it's the most focused, mature, personal music of his career, without a single throwaway. —*Stephen Thomas Erlewine*

Dig My Mood / Jan. 26, 1998 / Upstart ✦✦✦✦
The Impossible Bird revitalized Nick Lowe's career, finding him in a rare moment of reflection and focus, resulting in one of the very best records of his career. Its follow-up, *Dig My Mood*, doesn't reach the same peaks, but it matches the same high standard, offering 12 songs with no filler or novelties. The dark, torchy opener "Faithless Lover" may come as a bit of a surprise, especially since it's followed a song later by "You Inspire Me," another torch number, this time in the vein of k.d. lang. These two songs actually are a good indicator of the tone of *Dig My Mood*, since the country-rock that dominated *The Impossible Bird* actually fades into the background over the course of the album, popping up most directly on the funny Johnny Cash homage "Man That I've Become" and "I Must Be Getting Over You." The rest of the record is a skillful, laidback hybrid of torchy pop, R&B and country that is subtle in its execution. Lowe's voice is in the forefront, but it's gentle and unassuming, blending perfectly with the guitars, pianos and accordions. His songs are quietly ambitious, exploring new territory lyrically and musically, without leaving his signature style. As always, his taste in covers is impeccable, finding Henry McCullough's little-known "Failed Christian" and the wonderful, overlooked Ivory Joe Hunter gem "The Cold Grey Light of Dawn." They are the final, irresistible grace notes to an album that finds Lowe at his best. —*Stephen Thomas Erlewine*

The Doings / Jul. 27, 1999 / Demon ✦✦✦✦
The subtitle of the four-disc box set *The Doings* is *The Solo Years*, and the 86-track compilation never once strays from that edict. Disc one kicks off with Nick Lowe's seminal single "So It Goes," bypassing his early work with Brinsley Schwarz. By the end of that first disc, the compilation is already at *Nick the Knife*, his first album after the disbandment of Rockpile, and none of that group's official recordings are here. As it stands, *The Doings* falls just below the definitive mark, mainly because of those omissions. It's still a worthwhile set, though, playing much like an expanded version of *Basher*. It could be argued that it moves a little too quickly through Lowe's '70s and '80s material, especially since the third disc contains almost all of his '90s albums *Impossible Bird* and *Dig My Mood*. Then again, those two records really are among the best music he's ever made, so they deserve such an elevated position. Still, such decisions help point out what's missing from *The Doings*, and there are some great songs not included, but that's nit-picking. What's here is excellent, tracing a good history of Nick's solo career, perfect for casual fans wanting a comprehensive anthology. But *The Doings* is really for obsessive fans, and they'll be pleased by the rarities. Not only is the original fast version of "Cruel to Be Kind" here, but there's a full disc of live recordings, demos, and home recordings, all of high quality. Not only does *The Doings* do a good job of collecting obscurities, it does an even better job of drawing a portrait of Lowe's solo recordings. Ultimately, that's what makes *The Doings* a success. —*Stephen Thomas Erlewine*

The Convincer / Oct. 11, 2001 / Yep Roc ✦✦✦✦
The Convincer is the last installment in a trilogy begun with *The Impossible Bird* and musically it falls between that record's country-rock and the torch songs of 1997's *Dig My Mood*. No surprises then, but that's fine, because Lowe hasn't delivered three records this consistent in a very long time, if ever. All three records are warm, intimate affairs, yet they all have a different mood. *Bird* was a quintessential breakup record, *Mood* was the soundtrack to a late-night seduction, while *The Convincer* is a laid-back record that simply feels good. It's a smooth affair, whether Lowe is crooning a cover of Johnny Rivers' "Poor Side of Town" or "Homewrecker," where it's clear that he still loves the title seductress, even if she turned his life upside down. And that's the key to the record—there's a real sense of joy from Lowe, a sense that he knows he's been in a creative renaissance and that he's enjoying every second of it, and that spills over to the record itself. It's a record comprised of little triumphs—the relaxed rockabilly of "Has She Got a Friend?," the telling details of "Lately I've Let Things Slide," and the wry ballad "I'm a Mess." At the end of the record, when he's convincing his sweetheart "Let's Stay in and Make Love," the listener is as smitten as the object of his affection. That may not be earth-shaking, but it's thoroughly charming all the same. —*Stephen Thomas Erlewine*

L.T.D.

f. 1968, Greensboro, NC, **db.** 1981
Urban, Funk

Long-running funk outfit L.T.D.—Love, Togetherness and Devotion—was formed in Greensboro, NC in 1968 by keyboardist Jimmie "J.D." Davis and bassist Abraham "Onion" Miller, both former backing musicians for the great Sam and Dave. Upon relocating to New York City, the twosome recruited guitarist Johnny McGhee, horn player Carle Vickers, saxophonists Arthur "Lorenzo" Carnegie, Toby Wynn and Abraham Miller, and trombonist Jake Riley Jr. Vocalist/drummer Jeffrey Osborne also signed on before the group settled in Los Angeles, where Osborne's brother, keyboardist Billy Osborne joined the lineup as well. L.T.D. signed with the A&M label to issue their 1974 debut *Love, Togetherness and Devotion*. On their third LP, 1976's *Love to the World*, the group scored their first Top 20 pop hit, "Love Ballad." The follow-up, 1977's *Something to Love*, included the Top Five smash "(Every Time I Turn Around) Back in Love Again," and four years later L.T.D. returned to the Top 40 once again with "Shine On." However, Osborne then exited to pursue a solo career, and despite the additions of vocalists Leslie Wilson and Andre Ray, the band's commercial fortunes dimmed. In the wake of 1981's *Love Magic*, L.T.D. disbanded, but during the early '90s McGhee reformed the group, with 1999's *Marry You* featuring vocalists Greg Henneghan, Nakeisha Turner and Ronnie Henson, bassist Terry Gamble, keyboardist Ryan Cooper, drummer Jay Nichols and percussionist Mamadi Nyasuma. —*Jason Ankeny*

● Greatest Hits / Jun. 18, 1996 / A&M ✦✦✦✦✦
All of LTD's biggest singles—including "Never Get Enough of Your Love," "Share My

Love," "Holding On (When Love Is Gone)," "Where Did We Go Wrong," "Kickin' Back," "Love Ballad," and "(Every Time I Turn Around) Back in Love Again"—are included on this single-disc collection, making it the definitve retrospective of the late '70s smooth soul band. *—Stephen Thomas Erlewine*

Lulu

b. Nov. 3, 1948, Lennox Castle, Glasgow

Vocals / Girl Group, British Invasion, Pop

Most Americans first heard of Lulu when she soared to the top of the charts with the pop ballad "To Sir with Love," the theme to the film of the same name, in 1967. Actually, the Scottish singer—born Marie McDonald McLaughlin Lawrie—had been a star in Britain since 1964, when she hit the Top Ten with a raucous version of "Shout." Lulu's mid-'60s recordings (which included a version of "Here Comes the Night" that preceded Them's hit rendition) were often surprisingly rowdy and R&B-influenced. Although she didn't match Dusty Springfield, her Brenda Lee-like rasp could be quite gutsy and soulful. Her career was headed in a determinedly middle-of-the-road direction by the late '60s, which saw her hosting a British variety show and marrying Bee Gee Maurice Gibb (they have since divorced). Recording intermittently ever since, she raised a few eyebrows by traveling to Muscle Shoals studios to record her 1970 album *New Routes*, and releasing a single of David Bowie tunes (which Bowie also played on and co-produced) in 1973. *—Richie Unterberger*

● **From Crayons to Perfume: The Best of Lulu** / Nov. 15, 1994 / Rhino ✦✦✦✦✦

By far the most wide-ranging retrospective of a singer who never found the consistently good material that her considerable talents deserved. Starting with her 1964 British hit cover of "Shout," it also includes the number one single "To Sir with Love" and a few of her other British Top Ten hits from the '60s, including the nice '65 soul ballad "Leave a Little Love" and the chirpy 1967 Neil Diamond tune "The Boat That I Row" (the flipside of "To Sir with Love," which wasn't a hit at all in the U.K.). Unfortunately, it gives short shift to the raunchy R&B she recorded in the mid-'60s, but it does include the sadly neglected, moody "Dreary Nights and Rows" (penned by "To Sir with Love" author Mark London) and the Top 40 orchestrated ballad "Best of Both Worlds," co-arranged by future Led Zepper John Paul Jones. You also get nifty covers of Tim Rose's "Morning Dew" and Nilsson's "Without Him," along with a few songs she recorded with Atlantic (some with the Dixie Flyers) that gave her more sympathetic soul material than she was accustomed to, including the hit "Oh Me Oh My." There's also her semi-legendary 1974 single "Watch That Man"/"The Man Who Sold the World," a double-sided 45 of David Bowie covers produced by Bowie himself, and the theme song to the James Bond film *The Man with the Golden Gun*. This 20-song compilation doesn't gather together all her fine material by any means, but it's the only one to cover most of her career. *—Richie Unterberger*

Luna

f. 1991

Indie Pop, Dream Pop, Alternative Pop/Rock

In the wake of the rather acrimonious breakup of his previous band, Galaxie 500, singer/guitarist Dean Wareham issued a 1991 solo EP, *Anaesthesia*, and appeared on the brilliant Mercury Rev single "Car Wash Hair" before announcing the formation of a new band, dubbed Luna, in 1992. Originally named Luna 2, the trio was a kind of alternative-pop supergroup which also included former Chills bassist Justin Harewood and ex-Feelies drummer Stanley Demeski; after signing with Elektra, they debuted with the LP *Lunapark*, which earned comparison to Wareham's Galaxie 500 output for his continued reliance on laconic, Lou Reed/Tom Verlaine-inspired vocals and minimalist songcraft. In truth, however, Luna employed more uptempo rhythms and sharper melodies than its predecessor, a point further driven home by the 1994 masterpiece *Bewitched*; featuring new second guitarist Sean Eden, the LP also included a guest appearance from the Velvet Underground's legendary Sterling Morrison, who added his distinctive guitar presence to tracks like "Friendly Advice" and "Great Jones Street." Another guest, Stereolab's Laetitia Sadier, turned up to duet with Wareham on a cover of the Serge Gainsbourg/Brigitte Bardot classic "Bonnie and Clyde" for the follow-up, 1995's *Penthouse*; minus Demeski, Luna resurfaced in 1997 with *Pup Tent*. Just prior to releasing their fifth full-length, *The Days of Our Nights*, Elektra dropped the band; eventually landing at the Jericho label, Luna finally issued the album in the U.S. in the fall of 1999. The new millennium saw many changes for the band again. Founding bassist Justin Harwood left the band, moving back to his native New Zealand to spend time raising his baby girl. Ben Lee/Ultrababyfat bassist Brita Phillips replaced Harwood after touring with Luna during a spring 2000 tour. The first concert album, *Luna Live!*, recorded at the 9:30 Club in Washington, D.C. in December 1999 and the Knitting Factory in New York in July 2000, was issued in early 2001. *—Jason Ankeny*

Lunapark / Aug. 18, 1992 / Elektra ✦✦✦

Luna's first album doesn't sound that different from Galaxie 500, except that Dean Wareham's pop sensibilites come to the forefront with his new band, which makes *Lunapark* more enjoyable than most of his old band's albums. *—Stephen Thomas Erlewine*

● **Bewitched** / Mar. 1, 1994 / Elektra ✦✦✦✦✦

While it doesn't sound all that much different than their debut, Luna's second album is a stronger record, featuring improved playing and songwriting. *—Stephen Thomas Erlewine*

Penthouse / Aug. 8, 1995 / Elektra ✦✦✦✦

Penthouse isn't as entrancing as *Bewitched*, since Dean Wareham is suffering a slight songwriting slump, yet the group's lush, droning guitars remain enchanting, and they're effectively fleshed out by primitive keyboards and strings. None of the songs are that dissimilar from each other, yet the washes of airy melodies and guitars make *Penthouse* quite listenable. And the album does feature one terrific bonus track with "Bonnie and Clyde," a cover of a Serge Gainsbourg and Brigitte Bardot song performed in French by Wareham and Laetitia Sadier of Stereolab. *—Stephen Thomas Erlewine*

Pup Tent / Jul. 29, 1997 / Elektra ✦✦✦

Pup Tent finds Luna breaking away from their signature dreamy pop ever so slightly, adding the occasional brass flourish and waves of loud guitar. The expansion isn't entirely successful, since it often seems forced and de-emphasizes the hazy melodic qualities that are the hallmark of Luna's best music. Even with the weaker moments, there are a number of fine songs on *Pup Tent*. It just takes a little effort to dig them out. *—Stephen Thomas Erlewine*

The Days of Our Nights / Oct. 26, 1999 / Jericho ✦✦✦

Fans of the late great Galaxie 500 would hope that a new Luna release proves as captivating as Dean Wareham's first band. In the case of *The Days of Our Nights*, however, old grounds have not been revisited. Instrumentally the album is wonderful—filled with nicely toasted guitars, lovely melody lines, crispy drums, and a myriad of ear-candy touches in the production. One can take several tracks and proclaim them to be diamantes of pop craft, yet the lack of emotional nuance in the vocals becomes apparent as the disc wears on. The vocals certainly weren't phoned in, because they are nicely performed and recorded, but feeling seems absent. Wareham is a much better singer than he was ten years ago upon the release of Galaxie 500's *On Fire*, but some might miss the raw and nasal reediness of yore. *—Sanz Lashley*

Luscious Jackson

f. 1991, New York, NY, **db.** 2000

Indie Pop, Alternative Pop/Rock

With their dark hip-hop-influenced alternative rock, Luscious Jackson recreates the dense, multicultural bohemian world of New York in a collage of sound, where Spanish guitars, jazzy keyboards, funky beats, and breathy, sing-song vocals combine into one. Like the Beastie Boys, Luscious Jackson's eclectism doesn't acknowledge boundaries; instead, it takes freely from every kind of music. The group's first two recordings, 1992's *In Search of Manny* and 1994's *Natural Ingredients*, earned them a cult following and positive critical reviews. The core of Luscious Jackson—Kate Schellenbach (drums), Jill Cunniff (vocals, bass), and Gabby Glaser (vocals, guitar)—all met as teenagers on the New York post-punk scene of the early '80s. In 1991, Cunniff and Glaser began writing songs and recruited Schellenbach plus friend Vivian Trimble. The group's debut EP, *In Search of Manny*, appeared on the Beastie Boys' record label, Grand Royal. Luscious Jackson's debut album *Natural Ingredients* earned favorable reviews. Working with producer Daniel Lanois, the group released *Fever In Fever Out* in 1996, and gained a breakout single with "Naked Eye." Trimble left the band in 1998, and the trio returned in 1999 with *Electric Honey*. *—Stephen Thomas Erlewine*

● **In Search of Manny** / 1992 / Grand Royal/Capitol ✦✦✦✦✦

A darkly funky, atmospheric EP where hip-hop is used as a basis for the folk-tinged songs, which paint detailed, textured portraits of the New York bohemian slacker scene. An impressive debut from this New York quartet. *—Stephen Thomas Erlewine*

Natural Ingredients / Aug. 23, 1994 / Grand Royal/Capitol ✦✦✦✦

Luscious Jackson's first full-length album, *Natural Ingredients*, features a brighter, more open sound than *In Search of Manny*, without losing the funky, organic feel of the EP. Musically, the band continue to refine their hip-hop influenced pop, adding stronger hooks and denser grooves. *Natural Ingredients* isn't as consistent or edgy as *In Search of Manny*, but the record fulfills their initial promise. *—Stephen Thomas Erlewine*.

Fever In Fever Out / Oct. 29, 1996 / Grand Royal/Capitol ✦✦✦

For all of its sunny eclecticism, *Natural Ingredients* lacked the darkly funky urban soundscapes that made *In Search of Manny* so engaging. *Fever In Fever Out* brings that dark funkiness while keeping the pop hooks that made *Natural Ingredients* a step forward. Producer Daniel Lanois keeps his ambient tendencies to a minimum, providing just enough atmosphere to make songs as catchy as the jazzy, intricate "Naked Eye" surprisingly haunting. But what really impresses is the sense of forward motion Luscious Jackson displays on *Fever In Fever Out*, how their eclecticism is becoming more seamless as their songs grow stronger. *—Stephen Thomas Erlewine*

Electric Honey / Jun. 29, 1999 / Grand Royal/Capitol ✦✦✦

Reversing course from the kaleidoscopic pop of *Fever in Fever Out*, *Electric Honey* finds Luscious Jackson narrowing their focus, concentrating more on groove and texture than full-fledged songs. This isn't necessarily a bad thing, since their albums always had strong rhythm, but *Electric Honey* tends to float away. Somewhere along the way, Luscious Jackson smoothed out all their quirks and grit, shaping their sound into an appealingly funky, multilayered, post-alternative pop groove. On the surface, or as background music, it's quite pleasing, but it's never really compelling, especially since many of the songs are never really about anything—which is especially frustrating since the opening pair of "Nervous Breakthrough" and "Ladyfingers" are terrific continuations of *Fever In*. After that opening, *Electric Honey* doesn't begin to unravel as much as it settles into its own mire, recycling sounds familiar from its two predecessors, while offering slight songs about "Summer Daze," "Sexy Hypnotist"s, "Friends," "Alien Lover"s, and "Space Diva"s. The fluffiness of the songs wouldn't matter if each song had its own distinct feel. Instead, the entire album is variations on a groove—breezy and enjoyable, to be sure, but nevertheless a little too lightweight to really take hold. Lightweight songwriting also suggests that Luscious Jackson may be running out of ideas, and it's hard to shake the impression that no matter how enjoyable certain parts of *Electric Honey* are, it finds the band treading water, not breaking new ground. *—Stephen Thomas Erlewine*

Lush

f. Oct. 1988, London, England, **db.** Feb. 23, 1998

Dream Pop, Britpop, Shoegazing, Alternative Pop/Rock, Noise Pop

Meshing dreamy, feedback-drenched guitars with airy, catchy melodies, Lush were one of the most prominent shoegazing bands of the early '90s. Led by guitarists Miki Berenyi and Emma Anderson, the British band earned a cult following within the British and American undergrounds with their first EPs, yet they never quite attained the critical respect given to their peers My Bloody Valentine and Ride. Even so, the group lasted longer than any other of their contemporaries (with the exception of the Boo Radleys), developing sharp pop skills as their career progressed. By the time of their final album, 1996's *Lovelife*, the band had converted themselves into a power-pop band with dream-pop overtones, which resulted in the greatest chart success of their career. Their success was dealt a blow when drummer Chris Acland committed suicide in the fall of 1996, effectively bringing the band to an end. *—Stephen Thomas Erlewine*

Gala / Dec. 1990 / 4AD/Reprise ✦✦✦✦

Serving as an introduction to the U.S. market, *Gala* compiles the band's first three EPs and adds a couple outtakes. One thing that went overlooked about Lush was their ability to veer from violent and edgy noise breaks to pop effervescence. They were *always* capable of spewing out Saturday morning glow and Sunday evening doom from song to song. Their early reliance on sheets of distortion, buried vocals, and production issues didn't help this situation. As a result, their out-the-gate raw talent went rather unnoticed, evidenced on their earliest works. *Scar* demonstrated their under-appreciated diversity immediately. "Thoughtforms" is an example of their heavenly pop greatness, with the vocals sweeter and lighter than angel food cake. The haunting, atmospheric vocals and jittery tempos on the doomy "Second Sight" would end up laying the foundation for Chapterhouse's early material. Not a bad start. Guthrie and his beard hopped on board for the *Mad Love* EP, immediately chucking the guitars through the Guthrie-izer(tm). Most criticism of the EP pointed at the Cocteau Twin himself, who was accused of heavy-handedness. The guitars do sound a bit like Guthrie's own, but in a more assaultive, jabbing manner. A bad thing? No. All four tracks are goodies, from the cascading and shimmering walls of "De-Luxe" to the darker and heavier middle tracks. Production was an issue again on the *Sweetness and Light* EP. Tim Friese-Greene kind of polarizes the band's extreme ends, separating the noise and pop just a little too much. Despite a patched-on noise break during the title track, it's still one of the band's career highlights. "Sunbathing" is left in the sun too long, muffling the guitars and shrinking the sparse percussion. "Breeze" wafts by gracefully. *—Andy Kellman*

Spooky / Jan. 1992 / 4AD/Reprise ✦✦✦

For Lush's first proper full-length, the band opted to work again with Robin Guthrie. Though generally delightful, *Spooky* suffers from being bottlenecked into a dream-drift haze that isn't as convincing as the ones concocted by the likes of My Bloody Valentine and A.R. Kane. On paper the Guthrie/Lush collaboration seems like a match made in heaven; however, this lacks a punch and balance that begins to frustrate by the latter half. Whatever dynamics Lush appear to be capable of are rendered limp by Guthrie's sonic razing. Saving the record from being buried is a batch of quality songs. Despite its faults, it's more hit than miss. It's easy to criticize the lack of drive, but the drifting nature *is* rapturous in spots. Regardless, the draftiness is relied upon too often.

The three singles released from the LP ("Nothing Natural," "For Love," and "Superblast!") showcase the aggressive side, if only through a relative nature. As with much of the band's early material, guitars dart and veer all over hell's half acre—just as you hear a gentle strum in one ear, another guitar whisks by like an overhead jet, only to be grounded to a halt by a swollen jolt from some netherworld. If stripped of its myriad effects, "For Love" would sound like a top-rate Go-Betweens song, filled with lovely jangles and smart songwriting. Closer "Monochrome" is a melancholy ballad whose cousin is Catherine Wheel's "Black Metallic." Beneath all the swooning and swaying, it almost suckers you into missing the cheesy "dum-dum-dum" drum lead-in to the choruses, airlifted out of your least favorite Top 40 schlock ballad circa '86. Those devils! *—Andy Kellman*

● **Split** / Jun. 1994 / 4AD/Reprise ✦✦✦✦✦

Entire albums spent exploring the depths of the various nasty things surrounding romantic relationships were nothing new by the mid-'90s, but the vaguely cinematic and slightly conceptual *Split* is something more. Perhaps it's the manner in which each distinctive song manages to melt into the next. Or maybe it's the across-the-board improvements over *Spooky*. Most knew they were capable of more after the decent but flawed record, but it's doubtful many could have predicted something this thoroughly wonderful and varied. Throughout, Lush sounds confident and downright muscular, as opposed to the feathery wisps of earlier material that could be knocked down with the slightest of breezes. Miki Berenyi's high-heaven vocals have increased range, power, and presence. Chris Acland's drums propel the proceedings more than before, perhaps pushed into better realms by new bassist Phil King. Producer Mike Hedges knows just what to do with the band's elements, adding grace and balance that no other could previously achieve. Kudos as well to a bang-up job by mixmaster Alan Moulder.

It's an ardent roller coaster ride, centered around the lengthy mourners "Desire Lines" (oddly a single) and "Never-Never," which clock in at eight minutes apiece. Berenyi effectively conveys the resigned and soul-deadened nature of the lyrics. "Blackout" and "Hypocrite" prove the band's ability to be more assaultive, laying the foundation for their sound on *Lovelife*. Through breezy pop ("Lit Up"), brief shards of electrocuting dread ("Invisible Man"), and tales of obsessive voyeurism ("Starlust"), *Split* touches on most forms of emotional turbulence. Not necessarily a comeback but certainly a legitimizing stunner, the record prevented the band from being lost amidst the bunker of form-over-function dream pop bands. *Split* shattered every negative aspect of those failed acts with flying colors. A fantastic record within any realm. *—Andy Kellman*

Lovelife / Mar. 5, 1996 / 4AD/Reprise ✦✦✦✦✦

Lovelife represents a major shift in style for Lush. Nearly abandoning the trancy melodies and droning guitars that were their trademark, the band has crafted an album full of sharp hooks and melodies, one that owes a great deal to the Britpop mania of 1995. From the circular melody of the opening "Ladykillers," it's clear that Lush had been influenced by the direct, jagged pop of Elastica, but they also have reached back into '60s pop. All of the ballads on *Lovelife* are rooted in the hazy dream-pop of the early '90s, but they are given stylish, mod arrangements complete with muted brass. Even more startling is the Nancy Sinatra/Lee Hazlewood pastiche of "Ciao!," an irresistible duet between Miki Berenyi and Pulp's Jarvis Cocker. *Lovelife* would have simply been an embarrassing attempt to seem fashionable if Lush hadn't succeeded in updating their sound. However, they have been able to recreate themselves as a pop band and the result is their most direct—and arguably their most rewarding—album. *—Stephen Thomas Erlewine*

Topolino / May 26, 1998 / 4AD ✦✦✦

Despite lacking two songs included on its Japanese counterpart, the Canadian version of *Topolino* is the better one, thanks to a lengthier track listing and a couple minor highlights not found on the other. Like its sister, this version is mainly for completists. With rare occasion, the material isn't on a par with *Lovelife*, which is expected with all extras collections. It's no *Hatful of Hollow*, but what is? It shares seven of the same songs with the other *Topolino*, including the brilliant "Ex," the sunny and chirpy "I Wanna Be Your Girlfriend," and the Stephin Merritt cover "I Have the Moon." Amongst the tracks exclusive to this version are an outstanding cover of Zounds' "Demystification," retaining all the defiant spirit of the original while building on its singalong catchiness. Otherwise, Emma Anderson's somber acoustic tunes "Shut Up" and "Outside World" along with the pleasant lounge jazz of "Cul de Sac" and equally lighthearted "Tinkerbell" set this apart from the Japanese version. One major grumble is that similar compilations didn't crop up after the releases of *Spooky* and *Split*. But such compilations didn't come into fruition at the time because *Lovelife* brought Lush more popularity outside its native Britain, thus upping the demand for a collection like *Topolino*. The band's morph into more straight-ahead pop appealed to more ears. Lush increased its focus on the songs more than the sounds; burying the vocals and adding layers of distortion would cause this material to sound just like the band's earlier material. Perhaps Lush's later songs weren't as unique, but the group did show a level of confidence and ability to not get set in its ways. More importantly, there's nothing wrong with well-done, three-minute pop songs. *—Andy Kellman*

Ciao! 1989-1996 / Mar. 19, 2001 / 4AD ✦✦✦✦✦

In what could have been a means to deflect a slow release schedule, 4AD started rolling out compilations of some of their deep catalog bands in 2000 and 2001. The Cocteau Twins were first, followed by Heidi Berry and Modern English. In early 2001, 4AD released *Ciao! 1989-1996*, a collection of Lush's finest moments. Evenly taking four to five songs from each of the band's three proper studio records and their early EPs compilation (*Gala*), *Ciao* is a decent summary of the band's eight-year existence, collecting most of their singles, several album cuts, and one of their better B-sides (a cover of the Gist's "Love at First Sight"). The tracks run in reverse chronology, starting with the confident, no frills, straight-ahead pop of "Ladykillers" and ending with the wispy haze of "Etheriel." Pop songs were always at the heart of Lush's songs, but the distortion, buried vocals, and general trickery gradually weathered away with each of their successive releases. So listening to *Ciao* uninterrupted plays like a photograph slowly going out of focus. A long-time fan's general preference might find a bone or two to pick with the selection, but that's always a hazard in picking a portable introduction. Those who go on to check out the band's studio albums on the strength of *Ciao* will be happy to discover several strong songs, so *Ciao* hardly drains the pool. Reeling in a newbie shouldn't be too difficult. Lush seemingly had a couple fine records left in them when drummer Chris Acland took his life, but one listen to *Ciao* paints a complete picture. *—Andy Kellman*

Frankie Lymon

b. Sep. 30, 1942, Harlem, NY, **d.** Feb. 28, 1968, Harlem, New York City, NY

Vocals / Doo Wop, R&B

Frankie Lymon (1942-1968) & the Teenagers were a New York doo-wop group consisting of Joe Negroni, Herman Santiago, Jimmy Merchant, and Sherman Garnes but centered around the extraordinary talents of their lead singer, thirteen-year-old Frankie Lymon. Lymon was credited with their first big hit, "Why Do Fools Fall in Love" (In the early-'90s, a federal judge ruled after a lengthy trial that Lymon hadn't written "Why Do Fools Fall in Love"—another member of the Teenagers had). His wise-beyond-his-years vocal and performing abilities not only made the Teenagers a group several notches above the competition but made Lymon the first Black teenage pop star. Though only together for a brief 18-month period, Lymon & the Teenagers exerted an enormous influence, spawning several "kid" vocal groups and providing initial inspiration to Berry Gordy to model his entire Motown production approach around Lymon's original vocal style. Inexplicably, the group split into two factions at the height of their success, and neither had a hit again. Lymon died from a drug overdose at age 26. Diana Ross, Smokey Robinson, Len Barry, and his principal protégé, Michael Jackson (whose early recordings with the Jackson 5 are virtual re-creations of the early Lymon sound, merely updated) all show the influence of Frankie Lymon & the Teenagers's groundbreaking work. *—Cub Koda*

The Complete Recordings / Jul. 15, 1994 / Bear Family ✦✦✦

This five-CD set contains more Frankie Lymon & the Teenagers than any casual fan has likely ever thought of listening to, much less owning. Only one of its five CDs is less than satisfying, yet only a portion of this collection contains music that is actually important to the history of rock & roll. The first disc contains everything that Lymon and the Teenagers recorded together for official release. By the second disc, we're already into the Teenagers' recordings without Lymon, as well as live performances by Lymon and the Teenagers from *The Ed Sullivan Show* and various Alan Freed concert events. The final three discs are made up entirely of Lymon's solo sides from 1957 through 1968. From the 20 or so familiar early songs, one hears them "progress" to the later numbers, where their vocalizing became more sophisticated and subtle, but less cohesive. Disc three opens the Frankie Lymon solo material, and with all due respect to his memory, it's a disaster. His early solo sides, from 1957 through early 1958, tried to appeal strictly to pop listeners, with results that had no beat or any other serious appeal. Disc four finds him back on track, featuring 30 entertaining and engaging rock & roll songs that show Lymon in extraordinarily good voice. Disc five continues with Lymon's recordings for Columbia in 1964 to his final records in 1968. The sad and surprising part is that a lot of it isn't bad at all. Lymon's voice matured into a fairly nondescript instrument, but he could still put a good song over, as many of these later tracks show. *—Bruce Eder*

Essential Recordings 1955-1961 / May 6, 1997 / Sequel ♦♦♦♦
This two-CD compilation stands midway between Rhino's perfectly good Teenagers collection and Bear Family's monster box of every extant note of music that Lymon and company ever left behind. It's mid-priced, which is an advantage, and it has very detailed notes that explain the origins of a number of songs whose histories haven't always been clear, but it may be more Frankie Lymon than most need. But it is fun—the first 14 songs on disc one include the entire *Teenagers* album, a staple of rock & roll collections (and the Roulette catalog) for decades, an album that Larry Lazell's notes remind you made it to number 19 on the charts, a major sales success for a 1950s rock & roll album. The first 23 songs of 32 on disc one are the quintet's complete recordings together, in the order in which they were done—they reveal a thriving enterprise, a vocal group that could do relatively little wrong within the context of their era, most of their material solid romantic doo wop-style vocal rock. The new remasterings reveal more detail than Rhino's late-'80s work, and have a brighter sound, but they're not quite ideal, revealing some flaws (especially harshness) in the surviving masters ("Share") that detract from the listening experience. Lazell's notes are informative, and the booklet recreates various period trade ads for the group's releases. Still, most fans will likely opt for the Rhino CD, although this release does make the Bear Family and Collectables collections less desirable. *—Bruce Eder*

★ **The Very Best of Frankie Lymon & the Teenagers** / Oct. 6, 1998 / Rhino ♦♦♦♦♦
Although finally getting their due in the last few years of the 20th century, Frankie Lymon & The Teenagers have nonetheless been the subjects of several best-of packages, even including multi-album and CD box sets on Bear Family and Murray Hill. This 16-track very-best-of comes almost ten years after Rhino's release of an excellent 20-track best-of, and like that single-disc collection, all the big hits are here: "Why Do Fools Fall In Love," "ABC's of Love," "I Want You to Be My Girl," "I Promise to Remember," "I'm Not a Juvenile Delinquent," and later sides like "Goody Goody" and his last solo hit, "Little Bitty Pretty One." In fact, this new reissue even appropriates most of Bob Hyde's excellent notes from the 1989 package, trackwise only differing in the leaving off of later tracks like "Thumb Thumb," "Portable On My Shoulder," "Creation of Love" and the Teenagers' rocking "Love Is a Clown." The perfect entry-level compilation for digging this groundbreaking vocal group. *—Cub Koda*

Barbara Lynn

b. Jan. 16, 1942, Beaumont, TX
Vocals, Guitar / Northern Soul, New Orleans R&B, Blues-Rock, R&B, Soul
A bluesy southpaw guitarist from Beaumont, TX, Barbara Lynn Ozen wrote her own ticket to hitdom with the 1962 smash "You'll Lose a Good Thing," an R&B chart-topper. Texas producer Huey Meaux brought Lynn to Cosimo's studio in New Orleans to cut the atmospheric downbeat tune, her debut single on the Jamie label. Follow-ups included the bouncy "Oh! Baby (We Got a Good Thing Goin')"—better remembered through the Rolling Stones' faithful cover—and her minor 1966 hit on the often-covered "You Left the Water Running." Barbara Lynn resurfaced again in 1994, this time recording for Bullseye Blues. Her CD *So Good* included a new version of "This Is the Thanks I Get," but no reprise of "You'll Lose a Good Thing." Lynn remains active, currently recording for Antone's. *—Bill Dahl*

The Best of Barbara Lynn: The Atlantic Years / Nov. 22, 1994 / Ichiban/Soul Classics ♦♦♦
This 20-track collection gathers most of Lynn's output for Atlantic between 1968 and 1973, including most of her 1968 *Here Is Barbara Lynn* album and several non-LP singles. Commercially, Lynn's stay at Atlantic was not fruitful, yielding only a couple moderate R&B hits, the self-penned "This Is the Thanks I Get" and "Until Then, I'll Suffer" (both included). Artistically, this is fairly solid period soul, but a bit faceless. It seems as though Atlantic tried to fit Lynn into current soul trends; many of the 1968 tracks are quite derivative of Motown, and many of the later sides take a Memphis/Muscle Shoals approach. Those are fine influences, of course, but Lynn's strengths were her original songwriting and bluesy Southern phrasing. The most outstanding tracks are from her first Atlantic single, "This Is the Thanks I Get" and "Ring Telephone Ring," when much of her original relaxed Texas/New Orleans R&B style was still in evidence. The version of "You'll Lose a Good Thing" here, incidentally, is a remake, not the original 1962 hit. *—Richie Unterberger*

• **You'll Lose a Good Thing** / 1997 / Bear Family ♦♦♦♦♦
Single-disc, 28-track compilation of her best early sides from 1962-65, including a half-dozen previously unreleased cuts. Although the material is a bit uneven, it's worthy, idiosyncratic stuff with a bluesier, swampier feel than most any other soul being made during the time. New Orleans-styled horns, bluesy organ, and some gutsy guitar licks usually decorate the arrangements, while Lynn puts the tunes across with an assured reserve. The prize obscurity here is the original version of "Oh Baby (We Got a Good Thing Goin')" (which Lynn wrote), covered by the Rolling Stones in 1965, though it must be said that the Stones' more assertive, guitar-driven version outclasses Lynn's less forceful presentation. The documentation is unusually incomplete by Bear Family standards—there's no indication, for instance, of when the unreleased material was recorded. But at any rate, it's good overlooked soul, usually upbeat, sometimes with a downcast feel that verges on the morose, as on "Dedicate the Blues to Me" and "Ring Telephone Ring." Another oddity is "Can't Buy My Love," on which it sounds like producer Huey Meaux was trying to replicate the organ-colored polka-rock he'd just crafted for the Sir Douglas Quintet. *—Richie Unterberger*

Lynyrd Skynyrd

f. 1965, Jacksonville, FL
Album Rock, Boogie Rock, Arena Rock, Southern Rock, Hard Rock, Blues-Rock
Lynyrd Skynyrd was the definitive Southern Rock band, fusing the overdriven power of blues-rock with a rebellious, Southern image and a hard-rock swagger. Skynyrd never relied on the jazzy improvisations of the Allman Brothers. Instead, they were a hard-living, hard-driving rock & roll band—they may have jammed endlessly on stage, but their music remained firmly entrenched in blues, rock and country. For many, Lynyrd Skynyrd's redneck image tended to obscure the songwriting skills of its leader, Ronnie VanZant. Throughout the band's early records, VanZant demonstrated a knack for lyrical detail and a down-to-earth honesty that had more in common with country than rock & roll. During the height of Skynyrd's popularity in the mid-'70s, however, VanZant's talents were overshadowed by the group's gritty, greasy blues-rock. Sadly, it wasn't until he was killed in a tragic plane crash in 1977 along with two other band members that many listeners began to realize his talents. Skynyrd split up after the plane crash, but they reunited a decade later, becoming a popular concert act during the early '90s. *—Stephen Thomas Erlewine*

☆ **Pronounced Leh-Nerd Skin-Nerd** / Sep. 1973 / MCA ♦♦♦♦♦
The Allman Brothers came first, but Lynyrd Skynyrd epitomized Southern rock. The Allmans were exceptionally gifted musicians, as much bluesmen as rockers. Skynyrd was nothing but rockers, and they were Southern rockers to the bone. This didn't just mean that they were rednecks, but that they brought it all together—the blues, country, garage rock, Southern poetry—in a way that sounded more like the South than even the Allmans. And a large portion of that derives from their hard, lean edge, which was nowhere more apparent than on their debut album, *Pronounced Leh-Nerd Skin-Nerd*. Produced by Al Kooper, there are few records that sound this raw and uncompromising, especially records by debut bands. Then again, few bands sound this confident and fully formed with their first record. Perhaps the record is stronger because it's only eight songs, so there isn't a wasted moment, but that doesn't discount the sheer strength of each song. Consider the opening juxtaposition of the rollicking "I Ain't the One" with the heartbreaking "Tuesday's Gone." Two songs couldn't be more opposed, yet Skynyrd sounds equally convincing on both. If that's all the record did, it would still be fondly regarded, but it wouldn't have been influential. The genius of Skynyrd is that it unselfconsciously blended album-oriented hard rock, blues, country, and garage rock, turning it all into a distinctive sound that sounds familiar but thoroughly unique. On top of that, there's the highly individual voice of Ronnie VanZant, a songwriter that isn't afraid to be nakedly sentimental, spin tales of the South, or to twist macho conventions with humor. And, lest we forget, while he does this, the band rocks like a motherfucker. It's the birth of a great band who birthed an entire genre with this album. *—Stephen Thomas Erlewine*

☆ **Second Helping** / Apr. 1974 / MCA ♦♦♦♦♦
Lynyrd Skynyrd wrote the book on Southern rock with their first album, so it only made sense that they followed it for their second album, aptly titled *Second Helping*. Sticking with producer Al Kooper (who, after all, discovered them), the group turned out a record that replicated all the strengths of the original, but was a little tighter and a little more professional. But it also revealed that the band, under the direction of songwriter Ronnie VanZant, was developing a truly original voice. Of course, the band had already developed their own musical voice, but it was enhanced considerably by VanZant's writing, which was at turns plainly poetic, surprisingly clever, and always revealing. Though *Second Helping* isn't as hard a rock record as *Pronounced*, it is the songs that make the record. "Sweet Home Alabama" became ubiquitous, yet it's rivaled by such terrific songs as the snide, punkish "Workin' for MCA," the Southern groove "Don't Ask Me No Questions," the affecting "The Ballad of Curtis Loew," and "The Needle and the Spoon," a drug tale as affecting as their rival Neil Young's "Needle and the Damage Done," but much harder rocking. This is the part of Skynyrd that most people forget—they were a great band, but they were indelible because that was married to great writing. And nowhere was that more evident than on *Second Helping*. *—Stephen Thomas Erlewine*

Nuthin' Fancy / Mar. 1975 / MCA ♦♦♦
Second Helping brought Lynyrd Skynyrd mass success and for the follow-up they offered *Nuthin' Fancy*. It was a self-deprecating title for a record that may have offered more of the same, at least on the surface, but was still nearly peerless as a Southern rock record. The biggest difference with this record is that the band, through touring, has become heavier and harder, fitting right in with the heavy album rock bands of the mid-'70s. The second notable difference is that Ronnie VanZant may have been pressed for material, since there are several songs here that are just good generic rockers. But, he and Skynyrd prove that what makes a great band great is how they treat generic material, and Skynyrd makes the whole of *Nothin' Fancy* feel every bit as convincing as their first two records.

For one, the record has a rawer edge than *Second Helping*, which helps make the slight preponderance of predictable (but not bad) material easy to accept, since it all sounds so good. Then, there's the fact that many of these eight songs still showcase VanZant at the top of his game, whether it's the storming opener "Saturday Night Special," "Railroad Song," "On the Hunt," or the rollicking "Whiskey Rock-A-Roller." Yes, this does pale in comparison with its predecessors, but most hard rock bands would give their left arm for a record that swaggers and hits as hard as *Nuthin' Fancy*. —*Stephen Thomas Erlewine*

Gimme Back My Bullets / Feb. 1976 / MCA ♦♦♦

Lynyrd Skynyrd begins to show signs of wear on their third album, *Gimme Back My Bullets*. The band had switched producers, hiring Tom Dowd, the producer that served Atlantic's roster so well during the label's heyday. Unfortunately, he wasn't perfectly suited for Skynyrd, at least at this point in their history. The group had toured regularly since the release of their debut and it showed, not just in their performance, but in the songwriting of Ronnie VanZant, who had been so consistent through their first three albums. Not to say that he was spent—the title track was defiant as "All I Can Do Is Write About It" was affecting, while "Searching" was a good ballad and "Double Trouble" was a good rocker. These songs, however, were surrounded by songs that leaned to the dull side of generic (unlike those on *Nuthin' Fancy*) and Dowd's production didn't inject energy into the group's performances. This doesn't mean *Gimme Back My Bullets* is a bad record, since the group was still in fairly good shape and they had some fine songs, but coming after three dynamite albums, it was undoubtedly a disappointment—so much so that it still sounds like a disappointment years later, even though it's one of only a handful of records by the original band. —*Stephen Thomas Erlewine*

One More from the Road / Sep. 1976 / MCA ♦♦♦

Double live albums were commonplace during the '70s, even for bands that weren't particularly good in concert. As a travelin' band, Lynyrd Skynyrd made their fame and fortune by being good in concert, so it made sense that they released a double-live, entitled *One More From the Road*, in 1976, months after the release of their fourth album, *Gimme Back My Bullets*. That might have been rather quick for a live album—only three years separated this record from the group's debut—but it was enthusiastically embraced, entering the Top Ten (it would become one of their best-selling albums, as well). It's easy to see why it was welcomed since this album demonstrates what a phenomenal catalog of songs they accumulated. *Street Survivors*, which appeared the following year, added "That Smell" and "You Got That Right" to the canon, but this pretty much has everything else, sometimes extended into jams as long as the Allmans on this record, but always much rawer, nearly dangerous. That catalog, as much as the strong performances, makes *One More From the Road* worth hearing. Heard here, on one record, the consistency of Skynyrd's work falls into relief, and they not only clearly tower above their peers based on what's here, the cover of "T for Texas" illustrates that they're carrying on the Southern tradition, not starting a new one. Like most live albums, this is not necessarily essential, but if you're a fan, it's damn hard to take this album off after it starts. —*Stephen Thomas Erlewine*

Street Survivors / Oct. 1977 / MCA ♦♦♦♦♦

Street Survivors appeared in stores just days before Lynyrd Skynyrd's touring plane crashed, tragically killing many members of the band, including lead singer and songwriter Ronnie VanZant. Consequently, it's hard to see *Street Survivors* outside of the tragedy, especially since the best-known song here, "That Smell," reeks of death and foreboding. If the band had lived, however, *Street Survivors* would have been seen as an unqualified triumph, a record that firmly re-established Skynyrd's status as the great Southern rock band. As it stands, it's a triumph tinged with a hint of sadness, sadness that's projected onto it from listeners aware of what happened to the band after recording. Viewed as merely a record, it's a hell of an album. The band springs back to life with the addition of guitarist Steve Gaines, and VanZant used the time off the road to write a strong set of songs, highlighted by "That Smell," "You Got That Right," and the relentless boogie "I Know a Little." It's tighter than any record since *Second Helping* and as raw as *Nuthin' Fancy*. If the original band was fated to leave after this record, at least they left with a record that serves as a testament to Skynyrd's unique greatness. —*Stephen Thomas Erlewine*

Skynyrd's First and ... Last / Sep. 1978 / MCA ♦♦♦

So named because this consists of Skynyrd's earliest recordings and was released after the tragic plane crash, thereby seeming to close the door on the band's career, *Skynyrd's First and ... Last* is more than a simple historic curiosity, but not too much more. This music is more notable for being interesting—in how it's possible to hear Ronnie VanZant coming into his own as a writer, or hearing future Blackfoot leader Ricky Medlocke's early songs—than it is for being good, which it certainly is. Taken on its own, separated from the rest of the group's catalog, this would likely be seen as a great forgotten hard rock album from an obscure Southern outfit, but since Skynyrd went on to greater things, this winds up as a footnote—enjoyable, yes, but not quite necessary. —*Stephen Thomas Erlewine*

★ Gold & Platinum / Dec. 1979 / MCA ♦♦♦♦♦

Gold and Platinum was compiled by Gary Rossington and Allen Collins, the two surviving members of Lynyrd Skynyrd, after the band's tragic plane crash of 1977. Though many years have elapsed since its 1979 release, the double-record set remains the best, most concise compilation of the ground-breaking southern rock band. Over the course of two albums, all of Skynyrd's hits—"Sweet Home Alabama," "Free Bird," "Saturday Night Special," "What's Your Name," "You Got That Right"—are featured, as well as essential album tracks like "That Smell," "Down South Jukin'," "Gimme Three Steps," "I Know A Little," and "Tuesday's Gone." Some great songs like "Working for MCA" are missing, and the four-disc box set may be more comprehensive, but it's hard to imagine a better, more concise greatest hits collection than *Gold & Platinum*. —*Stephen Thomas Erlewine*

Southern By the Grace of God: Lynyrd Skynyrd Tribute Tour, Vol. 1 / Apr. 1988 / MCA ♦♦♦♦♦

For its first live album since the fatal 1977 plane crash, Lynyrd Skynyrd drafted a few friends to sit in as guest artists, including former Dixie Dregs guitarist Steve Morse, fiddle wizard Charlie Daniels, and former Marshall Tucker Band guitarist Toy Caldwell, who contributes some of his unique thumb-picking guitar work to the J.J. Cale tune "Call Me the Breeze." Johnny VanZant, younger brother of the late Ronnie VanZant, steps forward as lead singer, and even pulls in his other brother Donnie of .38 Special to sing along, and Artimus Pyle proves that he still has what it takes to provide the backbeat for one of the South's most enduring legends. While *Southern By the Grace of God* may not match the intensity of *One More From the Road*, it still delivers some excellent Southern jamming, pairing a few of the South's best-loved musicians with one of the world's legendary rock & roll bands. —*Michael B. Smith*

Lynyrd Skynyrd 1991 / Jun. 11, 1991 / Atlantic ♦♦

Lynyrd Skynyrd [Box Set] / Nov. 12, 1991 / MCA ♦♦♦♦♦

It was only fitting that the ultimate Southern rock institution Lynyrd Skynyrd—certainly one of the more tragic stories in rock & roll history—should be one of the first bands to benefit from a comprehensive box set. Following the format of the highly successful Led Zeppelin box set, this three-disc, 47-song anthology provides a near-perfect career retrospective, complete with a carefully researched booklet with meticulous historical essays and rare photos for the new and rabid fan alike. The latter will probably be most interested in disc one, which features a number of early demos dating back as early as 1970 and not featured in prior collections, as well as an embryonic demo of "Freebird" minus its extended-jam coda. The nine-minute version from the band's milestone debut, *Pronounced ...* is also featured here, of course, as is most of the material from the group's next album, *Second Helping*, generally regarded as their career peak. Disc two alone could serve as a greatest-hits set, as classic after classic is rattled off in mind-blowing succession. And even when the creative fires finally begin to wane somewhat as the set approaches the *Nuthin' Fancy* and *Gimme Back My Bullets* material (recorded at a time when the band was plagued by overwork and escalating drug abuse), the set wisely offers alternate versions and live renditions to keep things interesting. The first half of disc three alternates never-before-heard concert performances with other, equally inspired live versions. Its second half is dominated by the unintentional swan song *Street Survivors*. Released only three days before the fateful plane crash, the album saw a re-energized Skynyrd achieving a new level of maturity, power, and purpose. Although most box sets tend to be a bit too much for the casual fan to swallow, this one feels just right. —*Ed Rivadavia*

The Last Rebel / Feb. 16, 1993 / Atlantic ♦♦

Endangered Species / Aug. 9, 1994 / Capricorn ♦♦♦♦

Okay, it's the latter-day band with lots of replacement members, but this is a great record, and this time out there are no repertory problems. This is Skynyrd's "unplugged" album, with the band performing most of its best-known songs without amplification, on an array of instruments that includes mandolin. The songs come off very strong and surprisingly natural in this setting, and it's all good enough and different enough to make *Endangered Species* a necessary addition to the collection of any fan of the original band. —*Bruce Eder*

Freebird: The Movie / Aug. 13, 1996 / MCA ♦♦♦

Despite its title, *Freebird: The Movie* does *not* contain a series of variations on the title song (granted, only four versions of "Freebird" could have fit on a standard-play compact disc). Instead, it captures a number of highlights from the soundtrack of *Freebird: The Movie*, a documentary about Lynyrd Skynyrd's final tour. In addition to a dynamite version of "Freebird," the album contains a number of rare Skynyrd live cuts, including the first released live takes of "What's Your Name" and "That Smell." For dedicated fans, it's a live momento worth seeking out and cherishing. —*Stephen Thomas Erlewine*

Twenty / Apr. 29, 1997 / CMC International ♦♦

The Essential Lynyrd Skynyrd / Aug. 25, 1998 / MCA ♦♦♦

Putting together the definitive Lynyrd Skynyrd retrospective would be a daunting prospect to all but the most callous of critics who still deny the group their place at the table of rock & roll heroes and innovators. This two-disc, 25-track (!!) anthology makes the perfect introductory set to this Southern rock institution and one great career overview for longtime fans. All the hits like "Sweet Home Alabama," "Gimme Three Steps," "Saturday Night Special," and "That Smell" are aboard, along with "What's Your Name," "Workin' for MCA," "I Know a Little" and "Free Bird" in both live and original studio versions. Other highlights include great album tracks like "The Ballad of Curtis Loew," "Call Me the Breeze" and "You Got That Right," an acoustic version of "All I Can Do Is Write About It," and early demo versions of "Four Walls of Raiford" and "Comin' Home." If you're planning on only making one Lynyrd Skynyrd entry into your collection, this is certainly the one to get. —*Cub Koda*

Skynyrd's First: Complete Muscle Shoals / Nov. 17, 1998 / MCA ♦♦♦♦♦

This may be the greatest unissued first album ever to surface from a major band. The story behind the 78 minutes of music on this CD, cut two years before their official debut album, could fill a chapter of a book. Cut primarily during late June and late July of 1971, with a quintet of 1972-vintage tracks added, they constitute the group's complete studio recordings from the period when they were still trying to get signed. Seven of the songs were released on the 1978 album *Skynyrd's First and ... Last*, and three others appear on the 1991 boxed set, while "Comin' Home" turned up on *The Essential Lynyrd Skynyrd* earlier that same year, but this is the first time this potent body of work has been assembled properly, in one place. And, additionally, one previously unissued track justifies the price of this disc by itself—the original demo version of "Free Bird," on which the soaring harmonies, Billy Powell's beautiful piano, and the Collins-Rossington guitar duo plays with startling fire and lyricism. Several of the tracks do contain overdubs laid on in the mid-'70s (mostly Ed King's bass and some guitar, and even a Mellotron on "White Dove"), but this is still the band at its most raw and unaffected, in terms of what the core members are playing. Ronnie VanZant's singing was not only powerful, but beautiful at this stage of his career, and the group's playing—especially the Rossington-Collins double lead-guitar attack—is filled with a fresh spirit of experimentation and adventure that makes these tracks essential listening for anyone who has ever enjoyed this band's work. —*Bruce Eder*

Solo Flytes / Oct. 12, 1999 / MCA ✦✦✦
Lynyrd Skynyrd wisely disbanded after the tragic 1977 plane crash that killed its leader, Ronnie VanZant. The band later reunited, another wise move, but at that point in time, the members needed time to grieve and move on by pursuing other projects. And that's exactly what they did. Guitarists Gary Rossington and Allen Collins formed the Rossington-Collins Band, which featured various other Skynyrd members. A little while later, drummer Artimus Pyle formed his own band. Both groups were active in the early '80s, with Collins releasing his own album in 1983, but tragedy struck again in 1986 when Collins suffered a car accident that left him paralyzed. Rossington carried on briefly, before re-forming Skynyrd. Highlights from these three post-Skynyrd bands, plus a solo cut by Steve Gaines, the guitarist who joined Skynyrd for the *Street Survivors* album, are compiled on 1999's *Solo Flytes*, a 17-track collection that tells everything that needs to be told about this period in the band's history. Neither the Rossington-Collins Band (which dominates this disc with 11 songs), the Artimus Pyle Band, nor the Allen Collins Band made any classics, but they were entertaining Southern rock outfits. By and large, the music on *Solo Flytes* is generic material in the best sense—meaning that it typifies its genre—but it suffers from songwriting that is not only weaker than Ronnie VaZant's, but not as good as that of .38 Special, the most popular Southern rock band of the early '80s. That said, dedicated fans of Lynyrd Skynyrd will likely find this interesting and, by and large, pretty enjoyable. It fills in some gaps nicely, pulling the best songs from records that were well-done but uneven. —*Stephen Thomas Erlewine*

All Time Greatest Hits / Mar. 14, 2000 / MCA ✦✦✦✦
Lynyrd Skynyrd's 2000 compilation *All Time Greatest Hits* suffers from the same ailments that plague many compilations of its time, but there is one problem in particular that hurts it: instead of offering all of the "all time greatest hits" on one disc, the compilers pulled their punches, overlooking a few big songs while occasionally substituting live or acoustic versions for the original studio versions. That means that this is a Skynyrd compilation without the famed original version of "Free Bird"—a live version is here instead. It doesn't really matter that it's a good version, taken from 1976's *One More From the Road*, or that the live version actually charted in the Top 40; nor does it matter that "All I Can Do Is Write About It" is a good acoustic version originally released on the eponymous 1991 box set, because this is a collection made for a general audience. It should, therefore, have the versions that a general audience knows best. Apart from that, and the usual nitpicking over songs which should have been included ("Workin' for MCA," "Don't Ask Me No Questions," etc.), this remains a solid collection, containing most of the Skynyrd material that a casual follower could want. If the double-album *Silver & Gold* remains the greater compilation, that's because it captures the essence of the band better. This includes most of the best-known songs on one disc, and that's noteworthy in its own right; it may even be preferable for some listeners. —*Stephen Thomas Erlewine*

Skynyrd Collectybles / Nov. 21, 2000 / MCA ✦✦✦✦
Skynyrd Collectybles is a set for the devoted, a collection of rarities from Lynyrd Skynyrd's prime period—namely, when Ronnie VanZant led the band. The great thing about this is that it doesn't play as something *just* for the devoted—it's quite enjoyable for anyone who's a fan of Skynyrd's classic work. This does have some historically significant material, namely the inclusion of the early, pre-Skynyrd "Shade Tree Recordings," cut between 1968 and 1970, and the "Quinvy Recordings" from 1970. There are also outtakes from *Second Helping* and *Street Survivors*, and a full album's worth of live material recorded either at the Fox Theater in 1976 or on WMC-FM in 1973. Nothing is particularly revelatory, even the early recording of "Free Bird," but it's all of high quality and anything that adds to classic Skynyrd's body of work is welcome indeed. —*Stephen Thomas Erlewine*

The Lyres
f. 1979, Boston, MA
American Punk, Garage Rock Revival, Indie Rock, Punk
Few bands in Boston rock & roll history have lasted as long, and made as much good music, as the Lyres. Led by garage-rock obsessive, record collector, Farfisa organ king, and world-class megalomaniac Jeff "Monoman" Conolly, the Lyres rose from the ashes of Conolly's first band, DMZ. Sporting a similar high-energy trash-rock sound indebted to the Seeds, ? and the Mysterians, the Stooges, and the early British Invasion (especially early

Kinks), the Lyres, for a brief, shining moment, were the kingpins of Boston's punk rock scene. Resembling venerable British blues-rockers Savoy Brown because of a constantly changing lineup (something like 40 musicians have passed through the ranks), the Lyres (or more specifically, Monoman) gleefully party on, oblivious of trends or the assorted vagaries of the alternative rock marketplace. A dinosaur in his own right? Perhaps, but as long as Jeff Conolly has his organ, a few guys behind him and a place to play, the simple joy that can only be had through rock & roll will exist in this world—hipness be damned! —*John Dougan*

AHS: 1005 / 1981 / Ace of Hearts ✦✦✦✦✦

On Fyre / 1984 / Ace of Hearts ✦✦✦✦✦
Of the dozens of bands that emerged in the 1980s garage rock revival, the Lyres were one of the few that seemed to realize that the point wasn't about how much paisley clothing you could wear or finding the right vintage effects pedals (i.e., wallowing in nostalgia for an era you were too young to have actually witnessed—the musical equivalent of living in an episode of *Happy Days*), but about playing cool stripped-down rock & roll. Jeff "Monoman" Conolly understood that the Sonics and the Ramones were traveling in the same direction, but merely using a different path to get there, and, as a result, the Lyres' recordings have an energy and passion that's stood the test of time far better than most of their contemporaries; their debut LP, *On Fyre*, may well be their best. The Lyres divide their time equally between covers and originals here, and Conolly's songs are strong enough to stand proudly beside those of his heroes; truth to tell, the album's two most exciting songs, "Don't Give It Up Now" and "Help You Ann," came from his pen. While Conolly's Vox Continental organ keeps his 1960s obsessions up-front throughout, the rest of the band is capable of generating a hard-driving groove, and the performances capture what was exciting and soulful about 1960s punk without drowning in a sea of "retro." If *On Fyre* has a flaw, it's pacing; the best songs appear on side one, rendering the second half just a bit anticlimactic. But there's good stuff throughout the album, and anyone who digs rock of all eras will find something to shake to on *On Fyre*. —*Mark Deming*

Lyres Lyres / 1986 / New Rose ✦✦✦
More emotionally complex and reflective than *On Fyre*, this could well be one of the most mature garage rock records ever recorded. That doesn't mean that energy and excitement are sacrificed for dour introspection—far from it. This is a total joy from start to finish, and a great place to hang out after a thousand or so spins of *On Fyre*. —*John Dougan*

A Promise Is a Promise / 1988 / Ace of Hearts ✦✦✦
A Promise is a Promise combines old, new, studio, and live material—both original and covers—from Boston's legendary garage-rock combo. Tracks 1-12 were recorded in New York City, tracks 13-15 were recorded live at VPRO in Holland (before a radio audience), and track 16 was recorded live in Rennes, France. Despite the crazy quilt impression, it all hangs together surprisingly well as the performances are universally tight and energetic. Interestingly, there are two versions, both live and studio, of "She's Got Eyes That Tell Lies" by Him & the Others (there is no duplication otherwise). Other notable covers: "You'll Never Do It Baby" (the Pretty Things), "Running Through the Night" (the Mystic Tide), "Jagged Time Lapse" (John's Children, Marc Bolan's pre-T-Rex outfit), "Touch" (the Bristols) with Wally Tax, and "Witch" (the Sonics). Also worth noting: Stiv Bators (the Dead Boys) guests on the opening track, "Here's a Heart."

The original Ace of Hearts CD and cassette editions drop "We Sell Soul" (from Roky Erickson's pre-Thirteenth Floor Elevators group, the Spades) and add "Jezebel" (Frankie Laine), "Go-Go-Girl" (Bolan), "Help You Ann" (from *On Fyre*), "Don't Give It Up Now" (from *Lyres Lyres*), and "Cinderella" (the Sonics). "Help You Ann" and "Don't Give It Up Now" are the only live versions that don't quite work: the former sounds rushed—maybe they were already tired of playing it by this point—and the latter is marred by a homophobic comment (about AIDS) from lead singer/keyboard player, Jeff "Monoman" Conolly. Thankfully, he sticks to the original lyrics for most of the rest of the live material.

A Promise is a Promise isn't the best starting point for the Lyres neophyte, but for those who already know and love *On Fyre* and *Lyres Lyres*, it's a worthy addition to their collection. —*Kathleen C. Fennessy*

The Lyres Live 1983: Let's Have a Party!! / 1989 / Pryct ✦✦✦
Recorded live in the studio for Emerson College's great Boston music show Metrowave, these 13 slices of reckless abandon get about as close as one can to the "majesticity" (according to the guy introducing them) of a typical Lyres gig. Includes great versions of "Never Met a Girl Like You" and "Gonna Find a New Love." BYOB and crank it up! —*John Dougan*

● Some Lyres / Mar. 11, 1994 / Taang! ✦✦✦✦✦
An excellent, if brief (12 tracks) part-career retrospective, part-collection of oddities that includes their 1979 debut single "How Do You Know" b/w "Don't Give it Up Now." Packaged as a parody of the Rolling Stones' controversial *Some Girls*, *Some Lyres* proves to be a valuable introduction. —*John Dougan*

M

f. 1978, England
New Wave

Known to the world as the new wave one-hit wonder M, Robin Scott scored one of the first commercially successful electro-pop/dance singles with 1979's international number one smash "Pop Muzik." Scott attended Croydon Art College in the late 1960s, where his classmates included Malcolm McLaren, and began performing topical folk songs in area clubs. This led to the release of an early LP, *Woman From the Green Grass*, on Head Records, which quickly went bankrupt. Scott worked on a variety of musical projects during the early '70s, hoping to break through. He eventually became manager and producer for the pub-rock band Roogalator, producing their "Cincinnati Fatback," one of the first singles released by the pioneering U.K. indie Stiff Records. Scott's label, Do-It, also released the first Adam and the Ants LP, *Dirk Wears White Sox*. Scott moved to Paris in 1978, where he produced the all-female punk rock band the Slits, and a previously recorded single was issued under the name Comic Romance. Around the same time, Scott christened himself M and recorded the single "Moderne Man," which flopped. However, M's next release, "Pop Muzik," was an instant classic; it featured support from Roogalator bassist Julian Scott (Robin's brother), keyboardist Wally Badarou, programmer John Lewis, and vocalist Brigit Novik, Scott's wife. Demand for an LP was met by *New York-London-Paris-Munich*, which added woodwind player Gary Barnacles and drummer Phil Gould to M's backing band. The follow-ups to "Pop Muzik," "Moonlight and Muzak" and "That's the Way the Money Goes," were minor hits in the U.K., although Scott had seen the last of his singles chart successes in the U.S. *The Official Secrets Act* (1980) was less commercially successful, a trend continued on 1982's *Famous Last Words*, which Scott's U.K. label MCA refused to release. In the meantime, Scott worked with Yellow Magic Orchestra keyboardist and budding solo artist Ryuichi Sakamoto. Scott later dabbled in African music collaborations, especially Kenyan music, but most of the material languished in the vaults as Scott faded from sight as a solo artist. — *Steve Huey*

● **New York-London-Paris-Munich** / 1979 / Sire ✦✦✦✦✦
Of course, "Pop Muzik" was the only song on M's debut album *New York-London-Paris-Munich* to become a big hit ("Moonlight and Muzak" and "That's the Way the Money Goes" were minor chart entries in the U.K.), but there's actually quite a bit of entertaining music on the record. Granted, the sound of the record is more entertaining than the songwriting, but with its synthesized, danceable beats, big, catchy hooks, and glossy "futuristic" production, it's a terrific new wave artifact. — *Stephen Thomas Erlewine*

Official Secrets Act / 1980 / Sire ✦✦

Famous Last Words / 1982 / Sire ✦✦

● **Pop Muzik: The Very Best of M** / 1996 / Music Club ✦✦✦✦✦

Pop Muzik / Jan. 5, 1998 / Collectables ✦✦✦✦✦
Collectables' *Pop Muzik* is a retitled reissue of M's debut album, *New York-London-Paris-Munich*. Of course, "Pop Muzik" was the only song to become a big hit ("Moonlight and Muzak" and "That's the Way the Money Goes" were minor chart entries in the U.K.), but there's actually quite a bit of entertaining music on the record. Granted, the sound of the record is more entertaining than the songwriting, but with its synthesized, danceable beats, big, catchy hooks, and glossy "futuristic" production, it's a terrific new wave artifact. — *Stephen Thomas Erlewine*

Kirsty MacColl

b. Oct. 10, 1959, Croydon, England, **d.** Dec. 18, 2000, Cozumel, Mexico
Vocals, Guitar / College Rock, Adult Alternative Pop/Rock, Folk-Rock, Singer/Songwriter

Kirsty MacColl, daughter of folk singer/songwriter Ewan MacColl, began her own musical career while still in her teens, singing in a band called the Addix, and eventually signed to the legendary Stiff Records. Her first single, the modern girl-group gem, "They Don't Know," was released in 1979. Though it failed in the charts, it was later a major hit for Tracey Ullman. She switched to Polydor in the '80s and landed a U.K. Top 20 hit with the novelty song "There's a Guy Works Down the Chip Shop (Swears He's Elvis)." She followed the single with her first LP, *Desperate Character*, in 1981. In 1984, she married producer Steve Lillywhite and put her solo career on hold, raising their two children and working as a backup singer. MacColl returned in 1989 with a more mature effort, *Kite*, which reached the U.K. Top 20. Two more albums, *Electric Landlady* (1991) and *Titanic Days* (1993), displayed great talent and diversity and, above all, good pop sensibilities; after a lengthy hiatus, MacColl resurfaced in 2000 with *Tropical Brainstorm*. Shortly after, on December 18, 2000, MacColl was killed by a speedboat while swimming off the coast of Mexico. — *Chris Woodstra*

Desperate Character / 1981 / Polydor ✦✦✦

Kite / 1989 / Capitol ✦✦✦
After nearly a decade's absence as solo performer, MacColl released the low-key *Kite*, a decidedly more mature effort. Her literate and sharp vocals are perfectly matched with lush, textured folk-pop arrangements. Johnny Marr contributes his distinctive guitar playing on several tracks. — *Chris Woodstra*

Electric Landlady / Jun. 25, 1991 / Capitol ✦✦✦✦
MacColl is in peak form on the more experimental *Electric Landlady*. Playing with a different band on nearly every track, she effortlessly moves from the hip-hop of "Walking Down Madison," to the Latin-tinged "My Affair," to the Smiths' sound-alike "Children of the Revolution" (co-written by Smiths guitarist Johnny Marr). Overall, she builds on the folk-pop of her previous effort with much stronger material. Her lyrics have become more personal, mainly focusing on her relationship with and the recent death of her father. — *Chris Woodstra*

The Essential Collection / 1993 / Stiff ✦✦✦✦✦
A fine collection of Kirsty MacColl's early singles for Stiff Records in the late '70s. She wrote effortlessly melodic three-minute pop singles that managed to recast the classic girl-group sound of the '60s into a style that was contemporary and timeless, much like how Rockpile energetically recast '50s and '60s rock & roll. Not only were these singles some of the best she's ever written, the singles were among the best pop songs of the era, including the original version of Tracey Ullman's hit "They Don't Know" and the infectious "There's a Guy Works Down the Chip Shop (Swears He's Elvis)." — *Chris Woodstra*

Titanic Days / Oct. 5, 1993 / IRS ✦✦✦
MacColl delivers another brilliant album with 1993's *Titanic Days*. The arrangements have become more ambitious, as evident in the jazzy "Bad" and the heavily orchestrated "Soho Square." The lyrics are still sharp with biting commentary, this time backed by a more dance-oriented pop. — *Chris Woodstra*

● **Galore** / Jan. 24, 1995 / Virgin ✦✦✦✦✦
Eighteen-track compilation. The strength of these collected forces may just be sufficient to overcome Kirsty MacColl's two fatal commercial "flaws": she spreads herself all over the musical map, and she writes intelligent, often drily humorous lyrics about life and relationships that never pander to chart sentimentality. MacColl oozes a pure, fresh-scrubbed, girl-next-door quality that belies the sophistication of her songwriting without ever resorting to vacant innocence. — *Roch Parisien*

What Do Pretty Girls Do? / Jun. 16, 1998 / Hux ✦✦✦✦✦
What Do Pretty Girls Do? is a collection of four performances Kirsty MacColl did for BBC radio from 1989 to 1995—15 tracks in all. Aside from the obvious album tracks from each period (this was for promotion afterall), MacColl pulls out some old favorites from the early days—a country take on "There's a Guy Works Down the Chip Shop (Swears He's Elvis)," "A New England" (a duet with the song's writer, Billy Bragg), and "He's on the Beach"—as well as a couple of well-chosen covers like "Walk Right Back" and the charming "Darling, Let's Have Another Baby" (also a duet with Billy Bragg). BBC sets are always fun for fans, but for an artist like MacColl, who has always shyed away from live performance and whose albums have always been so meticulously produced, with multi-layered vocals and carefully conceived arrangements, this one is particularly revealing. She sounds relaxed—there's no doubt that she's genuinely having a good time—and, the sheer quality of the songs (and her voice) is made even more apparent in this straightforward, no-frills setting. — *Chris Woodstra*

Tropical Brainstorm / Apr. 25, 2000 / V2 International ✦✦✦✦

The One and Only / Aug. 28, 2001 / Metro ✦✦✦✦
A rather eccentric compilation, this focuses mostly on MacColl's work for Stiff, adding a few tracks by other artists on which she guested. It includes some of her more notable singles, such as "A New England" and "They Don't Know," as well as B-sides like "Turn My Motor On," "Please Go to Sleep," and "Quietly Alone." Also on board are some selections that aren't exactly proper MacColl performances. She sang backup vocals on Billy Bragg's "Greeting to the New Brunette" from Bragg's *Victim of Geography* album and Ewan MacColl's "The Manchester Rambler" (from 1983); "Libertango," meanwhile, is taken from Irish accordionist Sharon Shannon's *Each Little Thing* album. 12" mixes of "Terry" and "A New England" also count among tracks that might be sought by collectors, but wouldn't be judged by many as among her best work. MacColl's *The Essential Collection* remains the superior anthology, particularly as that includes her non-Stiff British hit "There's a Guy Works Down the Chip Shop (Swears He's Elvis)." *The One and Only* is still a collection of above-average (mostly) '80s pop/rock, but would it have been that hard to include specific dates of release for the otherwise well-annotated tracks? — *Richie Unterberger*

Madness

f. 1978, Camden, London, England, **db.** 1986
Pop/Rock, Ska Revival, New Wave
Along with the Specials, Madness were one of the leading bands of the ska-revival of the late '70s and early '80s. As their career progressed, Madness expanded their trademark "nutty sound," incorporating elements of Motown, soul, and British pop. They were one of the most beloved bands Britain produced during the '80s, yet they influenced bands on both sides of the Atlantic.

Taking their name from a Prince Buster song, Madness' first single was "The Prince." Released on Two-Tone in 1978, it was a surprise success. After it reached the Top 20, Madness signed with Stiff, quickly releasing "One Step Beyond," their first Top Ten hit, which was followed by an album of the same name. Over the next three years, Madness had a virtually uninterrupted run of 13 Top Ten singles, making them one of the most popular bands in the U.K., rivaling only the Jam in widespread popularity. Where the Jam appealed to teenagers and young adults, Madness had a broad fan base, reaching from children to the elderly. Despite their phenomenal success in the U.K., they made little headway in the U.S. Madness began to expand their sound with their 1982 album, *The Rise and Fall,* a pop-oriented, Kinksian album. This record featured "Our House," the single that gave them their first American hit, but just as the group had broken into the U.S., lead songwriter Mike Barson left the group. Their popularity immediately started to slide. They managed to stay in the British Top Ten with 1984's *Keep Moving,* but their next album didn't capture a sizable audience. The group disbanded in 1986, only to return two years later as *the* Madness, in a comeback bid that didn't go anywhere. Their days as hitmakers may have been over, but in the '90s, Madness had successful reunion tours. Lead singer Suggs released a solo album in 1995, yet he returned for more reunion shows during the late '90s. *—Stephen Thomas Erlewine*

One Step Beyond / 1979 / Sire ✦✦✦✦✦
Madness made a name for themselves early on with a silly image and irresistible novelty-dance numbers like "One Step Beyond" and the similar-sounding "Night Boat to Cairo." They did that extremely well on their debut—certainly these singles are among the finest of the era—but what made *One Step Beyond* such a remarkable record was not only the fun-time music they created, but also the diversity they displayed. Combining ska with distinctly British flavors of music-hall and '60s pop along with soul and even a hint of punk, Madness created a unique sound that, while very much a part of the 2-Tone ska-revival, also managed to transcend it. *One Step Beyond* is a charming album packed with some terrific songs, and it arguably stands as the high point of their distinguished career. *—Chris Woodstra*

Absolutely / Oct. 1980 / Sire ✦✦✦
For their second album, Madness continued the bright and bouncy fun of their debut. *Absolutely* placed slightly more emphasis on their novelty aspect, creating something of a fun-house atmosphere with stray sounds, exaggerated accents, faster tempos, and often unintelligible lyrics rattled off by Suggs at breakneck speed. Although the album shows a dip in quality control and much less diversity than *One Step Beyond,* it is nevertheless a charming romp with its share of inspired moments, like the classic singles "Baggy Trousers" and "Embarrasment." *—Chris Woodstra*

Seven / Sep. 1981 / Stiff ✦✦✦
Their "nutty sound" seems to fall to the background somewhat on this move toward more mature songwriting. Expanding beyond the limited scope of ska, this is a fine pop effort at times dabbling in more experimental sounds such as sitars and Arabic rhythms. Includes the splendid single "It Must Be Love." *—Chris Woodstra*

Rise and Fall / 1982 / Stiff ✦✦✦✦✦
Madness Present the Rise and Fall marks the band's most mature effort and artistic statement. Completely devoid of their early ska influence, they paint a picture of British life in the spirit of the Kinks' *Village Green Preservation Society.* Though it was never released in the U.S., several tracks were later placed on the compilation *Madness,* including "Our House," their biggest Stateside hit. *—Chris Woodstra*

☆ **Complete Madness** / 1982 / Stiff ✦✦✦✦✦
The 16-track compilation *The Complete Madness* compiles all of the group's early singles—from "The Prince" to "House of Fun"—and adds a handful of classic album tracks and concert favorites like "In the City," "Bed and Breakfast Man," and "Madness." It's thorough and a thoroughly entertaining collection, encapsulating exactly why Madness were significant and, more importantly, how much fun their "nutty sound" was. Furthermore, *The Complete Madness* isn't just an introduction—since it contains a wealth of non-LP singles like "Cardiac Arrest" and "House of Fun," it's essential for any Madness collectors. The compilation is definitive proof that Madness were one of the great singles acts of their era. *—Stephen Thomas Erlewine*

Madness / 1983 / Geffen ✦✦✦✦✦
Madness is a U.S. compilation released to capitalize on the success of "Our House." Aside from handful of earlier singles like "Night Boat to Cairo," "It Must Be Love," "Cardiac Arrest," and "House of Fun," the collection's real focus is on material from the previous year's *Madness Present the Rise and Fall,* which wasn't released in America. The collection suffers from a mixture of two distinct periods in the band's career and some glaring omissions, but there is no shortage of great material, making for a pretty good, though far from perfect, introduction. *—Chris Woodstra*

Keep Moving / 1984 / Geffen ✦✦
By 1986, the Clive Langer/Alan Winstanley production team had become synonymous with an all-too-slick approach. And despite their previous, well-tempered work with the band, *Keep Moving* falls into the same formulaic pitfalls of the period, incorporating the overused Afrodiziak and TKO horns, as well as a full gospel choir and even a cameo from Michael Caine. Overbearing production aside, this is well-crafted Brit-pop that explores a brighter, though decidedly less memorable side than the previous album. [The American issue replaces the lesser "Waltz Into Mischief" with the stray singles "Wings of a Dove" and "The Sun and the Rain," along with "Prospects" and "Samantha," making it the preferable version of the album.] *—Chris Woodstra*

Mad Not Mad / 1985 / Geffen ✦✦✦
This ironically peppy set of '80s pop would prove to be Madness' final studio album, and the band was clearly not in the best of moods while they recorded it. Their previous album had suffered the weakest chart showing of the band's career, and they had recently lost their founding father figure (keyboardist Mike Barson). They had left their record company, setting up their own "Zarjazz" label. Like the Beatles' *Let It Be,* this record has "One Last Stab" written all over it. The album opens with a bitingly overt declaration of the band's determination to hang on in the cynically mercurial music business ("I'll Compete") and concludes with one of many images of an inevitably approaching ending ("shivering to a halt…no one wants to speak too soon, although we all knew"). Several songs dwell on themes of transience and aging ("Time," "Yesterday's Men"), and the title track openly broods over the sting of Barson's departure. The album almost seems to fortell its own lack of success. Its ultimate failure to reignite the group's popularity might be blamed on the slickly synthetic over-production. Clive Langer and Alan Wistanley occasionally strike an inspired balance between soulful pop and subtle reggae rythyms, but more often they replace the warmth of Barson's pianos with a cold emphasis on drum machines and synthesizers. Some of the songwriting, however, is on par with the band's most mature work, and the lively melodies lend a perfect irony to the band's wry social commentary and personal brooding. *—Darryl Cater*

Utter Madness / 1986 / Zarjazz ✦✦✦
Picking up where *Complete Madness* left off, this collection includes all of the key singles from 1982 to 1986. A good collection, though listeners will probably be better served by simply sticking to *Rise and Fall* for a representation of this period. *—Chris Woodstra*

It's Madness—16 Greatest Hits / Jul. 1, 1991 / EMI ✦
It's Madness is the first part of an awkwardly sequenced two-disc collection that contains all of the singles and most of the B-sides from the first album in 1978 through the departure of pianist Mike Barson in 1984. Oddly enough, this first CD covers a patchy sampling of the middle of that period, beginning with the January, 1980 release of "My Girl" and running through the 1983 single "Wings of a Dove." While it does offer a thorough history of the chart performances of each single, *It's Madness* and its separately sold companion piece, *It's Madness, Too,* have been antiquated by the subsequent release of the box set *The Business.* That compilation offers several B-sides that didn't make the *It's Madness* discs, and it also covers the post-Barson era. *—Evan Cater*

The Business / 1992 / Virgin ✦✦✦
The Business is not the comprehensive, one-stop shopping solution for Madness that it appears to be based on the track listing. The three-disc box does contain all of the singles and B-sides, but the inclusion of spoken bits between and overlapping into the songs makes for an awkward listen. Certainly the goal of this package was to tell the story of the band, but both the band and listener would be better served by letting the music speak for itself. *—Chris Woodstra*

It's Madness Too / 1992 / Phantom ✦
It's Madness, Too is the second part of an awkwardly sequenced two-disc collection that contains all of the singles and most of the B-sides from the first album in 1978 through the departure of pianist Mike Barson in 1984. *It's Madness, Too* spans a broader range of Madness history than the first disc, running from the first single in 1979, "The Prince" through the last single from 1984's *Keep Moving,* "Michael Caine." It also includes material from the middle period of 1980-1983 that was missing from *It's Madness.* While *It's Madness, Too* does offer a thorough history of the chart performances of each single, the album and its companion piece, *It's Madness,* have been antiquated by the subsequent release of the box set *The Business.* That compilation offers several B-sides that didn't make the *It's Madness* discs, and it also covers the post-Barson era. *—Evan Cater*

Divine Madness / 1992 / Virgin ✦✦✦✦✦
This U.K.-only collection attempts to condense the band's career onto a single disc—from the early singles to 1985's *Mad Not Mad.* Though the two distinct periods lead to a somewhat disjointed listen, the chronological sequencing works as an adequate career survey, and the offering of the non-LP tracks "Driving in My Car" and "(Waiting) For the Ghost Train" are a nice touch. *Complete Madness* is still the best collection, but this one isn't bad either, despite a few omissions. *—Chris Woodstra*

Total Madness: The Very Best of Madness / Sep. 9, 1997 / Geffen ✦✦✦
Since Geffen doesn't possess the rights to the bulk of Madness's best, most influential work, *Total Madness: The Very Best of Madness* isn't the definitive compilation it could have been. Instead of drawing heavily on their early ska singles, *Total Madness* relies on the latter-day albums *Keep Moving* and *Mad Not Mad,* as well as adding three cuts from the 1983 compilation *Madness,* which means that only four songs—"Our House," "It Must Be Love," "Tomorrow's Just Another Day," "One Step Beyond"—are genuine classics. There are several hits here—such as "Michael Caine," "Wings of a Dove," "Yesterday's Men," and "One Better Day"—but they aren't nearly as vital as "House of Fun," "Night Boat to Cairo," or "Cardiac Arrest," three hit singles which were on *Madness.* As a result, *Total Madness* winds up being an overview of Madness in their decline, with a couple of earlier hits thrown in for good measure. On that level, it isn't bad, but it certainly doesn't capture the essence of the band, and both dedicated fans and curious listeners would be better served by *Complete Madness* or *Madness.* *—Stephen Thomas Erlewine*

Wonderful / Dec. 14, 1999 / EMI ✦✦✦✦
Madness officially disbanded in 1986, but the members never seemed content to call it quits. Finally, after 13 years, six singles collections, five "Madstock" reunion concerts, three ill-fated spin-off attempts, two live CDs, and two box sets, the boys worked up enough courage to celebrate their 20th anniversary with their first new album since *Mad Not Mad*. Pianist Mike Barson was back, of course, but the real returning heroes were producers Clive Langer and Alan Wistanley, whose sure-handed pop sensibility is all over the record. Though these '70s ska pioneers might have benefited from the success of '90s ska bands like Blur, No Doubt, the Mighty Mighty Bosstones, and Smashmouth, *Wonderful* is not really a ska record. "The Communicator" and "Drip Drop Fred" (which features guest vocals from fellow Stiff Records alum Ian Dury, to whom the record is dedicated) are the only songs that seek to approximate the old, nutty sound. The rest harken back to the slickly orchestrated pop of early-'80s albums like *Keep Moving* and *The Rise and Fall*. If tracks three through 11 don't quite live up to the promise established by the two irresistible singles "Lovestruck" and "Johnny the Horse," they don't embarrass either. Among the best are "4am," a slightly more expensive version of one of the better songs from Suggs' solo career, and the typically self-referential "Saturday Night, Sunday Morning," which likens the band to "thieves returning to the scene of the crime." On the whole, it's a pretty successful return. Some fans might find the bombastic production somewhat cloying, but it undoubtedly delighted Virgin Records, which seemed sure to jump at the chance to release a few more greatest hits compilations. *—Evan Cater*

★ **Ultimate Collection** / Nov. 14, 2000 / Hip-O ✦✦✦✦✦
The Madness volume of Hip-O's *Ultimate Collection* series is one of the few entries that actually lives up to its title. The 19-track disc is about the most complete single-disc collection of Madness' British and American hits yet, containing everything from "One Step Beyond" and "My Girl" to "Michael Caine" and "Wings of a Dove." The quality of the music does drop off a bit in the post-*Rise and Fall* years, but it's hard not to listen to this collection and not be impressed by the depth and strength of Madness as a single act. And there's no better place to be seduced by Madness' infectious, nutty sound than this single-disc set. *—Stephen Thomas Erlewine*

Madonna (Madonna Louise Veronica Ciccone)

b. Aug. 16, 1958, Rochester, MI
Vocals / Club/Dance, Pop/Rock, Adult Contemporary, Dance-Pop
Madonna's celebrity tends to overshadow her music, and in some ways, her mastery of image and marketing seems greater than her recordings. Nevertheless, she wouldn't have been able to sustain superstardom for two decades if she didn't also deliver musically, and her albums have usually been fascinating, creative affairs that brought underground dance-club trends into the mainstream.

Madonna first made an impression with her 1982 with club hit, "Everybody." She released her debut album the following year; thanks to the Top 40 "Holiday," it became a hit. Madonna's star rose during 1984, as "Borderline" and "Lucky Star" reached the Top Ten. Her second album *Like a Virgin* arrived late that year, with her first film *Desperately Seeking Susan* following that next summer. With these two projects, Madonna rocketed to international superstardom. "Like a Virgin" and "Material Girl" were defining anthems, teenage girls started dressing like her and she became a favorite of tabloids, thanks in no small part to her own past—nude photos from 1977 were published in both Playboy and Penthouse, yet this simply added to her mystique. *True Blue* (1986) was more complex than her previous work, earning critical acclaim as well as hits in "Papa Don't Preach" and "Open Your Heart." After two film flops, (*Shanghai Surprise, Who's That Girl*), she returned with *Like a Prayer* in 1989; it was her most ambitious and acclaimed album to date, sparking both hits and controversy. Soon, that controversy began to overwhelm the music, as her video for "Justify My Love" was banned by MTV. Following her tour documentary *Truth or Dare*, Madonna released a soft-core photo book called *Sex* in 1992. Her new album, the well-reviewed *Erotica*, was released simultaneously, but *Sex* was a disaster, hurting the album's sales. *Bedtime Stories*, released two years later, was a more subdued affair than *Erotica*, and it spawned her biggest hit, "Take a Bow." Following her starring role in the 1995 film adaptation of Andrew Lloyd Webber's *Evita*, Madonna returned in 1998 with the electronica-inspired *Ray of Light*, which restored her critical and popular cache as a trailblazer. She followed through on its success with 2000's *Music*, a glitzy dance album. *—Stephen Thomas Erlewine*

Madonna / 1983 / Sire ✦✦✦✦✦
Although she never left it behind, it's been easy to overlook that Madonna began her career as a disco diva in an era that didn't have disco divas. It was an era where disco was anathema to the mainstream pop, and she had a huge role in popularizing dance music as a popular music again, crashing through the door Michael Jackson opened with *Thriller*. Certainly, her undeniable charisma, chutzpah, and sex appeal had a lot to do with that—it always did, throughout her career—but she wouldn't have broken through if the music wasn't so good. And her eponymous debut isn't simply good, it set the standard for dance-pop for the next 20 years. Why did it do so? Because it cleverly incorporated great pop songs with stylish, state-of-the-art beats, and it shrewdly walked a line between being a rush of sound and a showcase for a dynamic lead singer. This is music where all of the elements may not particularly impressive on their own—the arrangement, synth, and drum programming are fairly rudimentary; Madonna's singing isn't particularly strong; the songs, while hooky and memorable, couldn't necessarily hold up on their own without the production—but taken together, it's utterly irresistible. And that's the hallmark of dance-pop: every element blends together into an intoxicating sound, where the hooks and rhythms are so hooky, the shallowness is something to celebrate. And there are some great songs here, whether it's the effervescent "Lucky Star," "Borderline," and "Holiday" or the darker, carnal urgency of "Burning Up" and "Physical Attraction." And if Madonna would later sing better, she illustrates here that a good voice is secondary to dance-pop. What's really necessary is personality, since that sells a song where there are no instruments that sound real. Here, Madonna is on fire, and that's the reason why it launched her career, launched dance-pop, and remains a terrific, nearly timeless, listen. *—Stephen Thomas Erlewine*

Like a Virgin / 1984 / Sire ✦✦✦✦✦
Madonna had hits with her first album, even reaching the Top Ten twice with "Borderline" and "Lucky Star," but she didn't become a superstar, an icon, until her second album, *Like a Virgin*. She saw the opening for this kind of explosion and seized it, bringing in former Chic guitarist Nile Rodgers in as a producer, to help her expand her sound, and then carefully constructed her image as an ironic, ferociously sexy Boy Toy; the Steven Meisel-shot cover, capturing her as a buxom bride with a Boy Toy belt buckle on the front, and dressing after a night of passion, was as key to her reinvention as the music itself. Yet, there's no discounting the best songs on the record, the moments when her grand concepts are married to music that transcends the mere classification of dance-pop. These, of course, are "Material Girl" and "Like a Virgin," the two songs that made her an icon, and the two songs that remain definitive statements. They overshadow the rest of the record, not just because they are a perfect match of theme and sound, but because the rest of the album vacillates wildly in terms of quality. The other two singles, "Angel" and "Dress You Up," are excellent standard-issue dance-pop, and there are other moments that work well ("Over and Over," "Stay," the earnest cover of Rose Royce's "Love Don't Live Here"), but overall, it adds up to less than the sum of its parts—partially because the singles are so good, but also because on the first album, she stunned with style and a certain joy. Here, the calculation is apparent, and while that's part of Madonna's essence—even something that makes her fun—it throws the record's balance off a little too much for it to be consistent, even if it justifiably made her a star. *—Stephen Thomas Erlewine*

True Blue / 1986 / Sire ✦✦✦✦✦
True Blue is the album where Madonna truly became Madonna the Superstar—the endlessly ambitious, fearlessly provocative entertainer that knew how to outrage, spark debates, get good reviews... and make good music while she's at it. To complain that *True Blue* is calculated is to not get Madonna—that's a large part of what she does, and she is exceptional at it, but she also makes fine music. What's brilliant about *True Blue* is that she does both here, using the music to hook in critics just as she's baiting a mass audience with such masterstrokes as "Papa Don't Preach," where she defiantly states she's keeping her baby. It's easy to position anti-abortionism as feminism, but what's tricky is to transcend your status as a dance-pop diva by consciously recalling classic girl-group pop ("True Blue," "Jimmy Jimmy") to snag the critics, while deepening the dance grooves ("Open Your Heart," "Where's the Party"), touching on Latin rhythms ("La Isla Bonita"), making a plea for world peace ("Love Makes the World Go Round"), and delivering a tremendous ballad that rewrites the rules of adult contemporary crossover ("Live to Tell"). It's even harder to have the entire album play as an organic, cohesive work. Certainly, there's some calculation behind the entire thing, but what matters is the end result, one of the great dance-pop albums, a record that demonstrates Madonna's true skills as a songwriter, record-maker, provocateur, and entertainer through its wide reach, accomplishment, and sheer sense of fun. *—Stephen Thomas Erlewine*

You Can Dance / 1987 / Sire ✦✦✦
Released in 1987 as a stop-gap, the remix album *You Can Dance* reworks material from Madonna's first three albums. Actually, it keeps the spotlight on her first record, adding non-LP singles like "Into the Groove" for good measure, along with a bonus track of "Where's the Party." Since it's a dance album, it doesn't matter that "Holiday" and "Into the Groove" are here twice, once each in dub versions, because the essential grooves and music are quite different in each incarnation. It is true that some of this now sounds dated—these are quite clearly extended mixes from the mid-'80s—but that's part of its charm, and it all holds together quite well. Not essential, but fun. *—Stephen Thomas Erlewine*

Who's That Girl / Jul. 21, 1987 / Sire ✦✦

☆ **Like a Prayer** / 1989 / Sire ✦✦✦✦✦
Out of all of Madonna's albums, *Like a Prayer* is her most explicit attempt at a major artistic statement. Even though it is apparent that she is trying to make a "serious" album, the kaleidoscopic variety of pop styles on *Like a Prayer* is quite dazzling. Ranging from the deep funk of "Express Yourself" and "Keep It Together," to the haunting "Oh Father" and "Like a Prayer," Madonna displays a commanding sense of songcraft, making this her best and most consistent album. *—Stephen Thomas Erlewine*

★ **The Immaculate Collection** / 1990 / Sire ✦✦✦✦✦
On the surface, the single-disc hits compilation *The Immaculate Collection* appears to be a definitive retrospective of Madonna's heyday in the '80s. After all, it features 17 of Madonna's greatest hits, from "Holiday" and "Like a Virgin" to "Like a Prayer" and "Vogue." However, looks can be deceiving. It's true that *The Immaculate Collection* contains the bulk of Madonna's hits, but there are several big hits that aren't present, including "Angel," "Dress You Up," "True Blue," "Who's That Girl," and "Causing a Commotion." The songs that are included are frequently altered. Everything on the collection is remastered in Q-sound, which gives an exaggerated sense of stereo separation that often distorts the original intent of the recordings. Furthermore, several songs are faster than their original versions and some are faded out earlier than either their single or album versions, while others are segued together. In other words, while all the hits are present, they're simply not in their correct versions. Nevertheless, *The Immaculate Collection* remains a necessary purchase, because it captures everything Madonna is about and it proves that she was one of the finest singles artists of the '80s. Until the original single

versions are compiled on another album, *The Immaculate Collection* is the closest thing to a definitive retrospective. *—Stephen Thomas Erlewine*

Dick Tracy: "I'm Breathless" (Music from & Inspired by the Film) / May 1990 / Sire ✦✦

Erotica / Oct. 20, 1992 / Maverick ✦✦✦

While it didn't set the charts on fire like her previous albums, the ambitious *Erotica* contains some of Madonna's best and most accomplished music (including the hit singles "Deeper and Deeper" and "Rain"), even if it runs a bit long. *—Stephen Thomas Erlewine*

Bedtime Stories / Oct. 25, 1994 / Maverick ✦✦✦✦

Perhaps Madonna correctly guessed that the public overdosed on the raw carnality of her book *Sex*. Perhaps she wanted to offer a more optimistic take on sex than the distant *Erotica*. Either way, *Bedtime Stories* is a warm album, with deep, gently pulsating grooves; the album's title isn't totally tongue-in-cheek. The best songs on the album ("Secret," "Inside of Me," "Sanctuary," "Bedtime Story," "Take a Bow") slowly work their melodies into the subconscious as the bass pulses. In that sense, it does offer an antidote to *Erotica*, which was filled with deep but cold grooves. The entire production of *Bedtime Stories* suggests that she wants listeners to acknowledge that her music isn't one-dimensional. She has succeeded with that goal, since *Bedtime Stories* offers her most humane and open music; it's even seductive. *—Stephen Thomas Erlewine*

Something to Remember / Nov. 7, 1995 / Maverick ✦✦✦✦✦

Something to Remember is Madonna's second greatest hits collection, compiling a selection of the singer's ballads. Several of her biggest hits are included, including the number ones "Crazy for You," "Live to Tell," "This Used to Be My Playground," and "Take a Bow," as well as a handful of first-rate album tracks (a remixed "Love Don't Live Here Anymore," "Something to Remember," "Oh Father"), and three new tracks, most notably a version of Marvin Gaye's "I Want You" recorded with the British trip-hop group Massive Attack. Only two tracks on the album overlap with *The Immaculate Collection*, and the disc also marks the first appearance of "This Used to Be My Playground" and "I'll Remember" on one of Madonna's albums. Throughout the album, Madonna proves that she's a terrific singer whose voice has improved over the years. Not one of the tracks is second-rate, and the best songs on *Something to Remember* rank among the best pop music of the '80s and '90s. *—Stephen Thomas Erlewine*

Selections from Evita / Jul. 29, 1997 / Warner Brothers ✦✦✦

Selections from Evita boils the original double-disc soundtrack to a single, 77-minute disc of highlights, featuring such songs as "You Must Love Me," "Don't Cry for Me Argentina," and "Another Suitcase." For fans that liked the hit singles and familiar items from *Evita* but didn't want the entire soundtrack, *Selections* is an excellent purchase. *—Stephen Thomas Erlewine*

Ray of Light / Mar. 3, 1998 / Maverick ✦✦✦✦

Returning to pop after a four-year hiatus, Madonna enlisted respected techno producer William Orbit as her collaborator for *Ray of Light*, a self-conscious effort to stay abreast of contemporary trends. Unlike other veteran artists who attempted to come to terms with electronica, Madonna was always a dance artist, so it's no real shock to hear her sing over breakbeats, pulsating electronics, and blunted trip-hop beats. Still, it's mildly surprising that it works as well as it does, largely due to Madonna and Orbit's subtle attack. They've reigned in the beats, tamed electronica's eccentricities, and retained her flair for pop melodies, creating the first mainstream pop album that successfully embraces techno. Sonically, it's the most adventurous record she has made, but it's far from inaccessible, since the textures are alluring and the songs have a strong melodic foundation, whether it's the swirling title track, the meditative opener, "Substitute for Love," or the ballad "Frozen." For all of its attributes, there's a certain distance to *Ray of Light*, born of the carefully constructed productions and Madonna's newly mannered, technically precise singing. It all results in her most mature and restrained album, which is an easy achievement to admire, yet not necessarily an easy one to love. *—Stephen Thomas Erlewine*

Music / Sep. 19, 2000 / Maverick ✦✦✦✦

Filled with vocoders, stylish neo-electro beats, dalliances with trip-hop, and, occasionally, eerie synthesized atmospherics, *Music* blows by in a kaleidoscopic rush of color, technique, style, and substance. It has so many layers that it's easily as self-aware and earnest as *Ray of Light*, where her studiousness complimented a record heavy on spirituality and reflection. Here, she mines that territory occasionally, especially as the record winds toward its conclusion, but she applies her new tricks toward celebrations of music itself. That's not only true of the full-throttle dance numbers but also for ballads like "I Deserve It" and "Nobody's Perfect," where the sentiments are couched in electronic effects and lolling, rolling beats. Ultimately, that results in the least introspective or revealing record Madonna has made since *Like a Prayer*, yet that doesn't mean she doesn't invest herself in the record. Working with a stable of producers, she has created an album that is her most explicitly musical and restlessly creative since, well, *Like a Prayer*. She may have sacrificed some cohesion for that willful creativity but it's hard to begrudge her that, since so much of the album works. If, apart from the haunting closer "Gone," the Orbit collaborations fail to equal *Ray of Light* or "Beautiful Stranger," they're still sleekly admirable, and they're offset by the terrific Guy Sigsworth/Mark "Spike" Stent mid-tempo cut "What It Feels Like for a Girl" and Madonna's thriving partnership with Mirwais. This team is responsible for the heart of the record, with such stunners as the intricate, sensual, folk-psych "Don't Tell Me," the eerily seductive "Paradise (Not for Me)," and the thumping title track, which sounds funkier, denser, sexier with each spin. Whenever she works with Mirwais, *Music* truly comes alive with the spark and style. *—Stephen Thomas Erlewine*

Johnny Maestro

b. May 7, 1939, New York, NY

Vocals / Doo Wop

After making a name for himself as lead singer of the Crests, vocalist Johnny Maestro formed Brooklyn Bridge in 1967 and scored a gold record the next year on Buddah with a cover of the Fifth Dimension's heartbroken "Worst That Could Happen." Brooklyn Bridge was an amalgam of Maestro, the Del Satins (the vocal group that backed Dion on many of his early- '60s solo hits), and a brassy outfit called the Rhythm Method. Brooklyn Bridge enjoyed several more hits in 1969 and 1970, and Maestro still performs on the oldies circuit. *—Bill Dahl*

The Best of the Rest of Johnny Maestro & the Crests / Dec. 20, 1993 / Ace (UK) ✦✦✦✦

A veritable treasure trove for the true doo wop fan, this brings together 29 rarities and a slew of unreleased material in one delightful collection. In addition to unreleased gems like "Learning 'Bout Love," "Let Me Be the One," "Let True Love Begin," and "Strange Love," there are great alternate takes of "Six Nights a Week," "Step by Step," and "The Angels Listened In." Far from being bottom-of-the-barrel leftovers, these tunes deserve a much wider hearing. *—Cub Koda*

Magazine

f. 1977, **db.** 1981

Post-Punk

After leaving the Buzzcocks in 1977, vocalist Howard Devoto formed Magazine; one of the first post-punk bands, they kept the edgy, nervous energy of punk, adding elements of art rock, particularly with their theatrical live shows and shards of keyboards. Devoto's lyrics were combinations of social commentary and poetic fragments, while the band alternated between cold, jagged chords and gloomy, atmospheric sonic landscapes. Magazine's first single, "Shot by Both Sides," appeared in early 1978, gathering good reviews on both sides of the Atlantic and charting in the U.K. at number 41. *Real Life*, released later in 1978, continued the confrontational, arty pop-punk of "Shot by Both Sides." *Secondhand Daylight* was somewhat of a departure from the debut, featuring more keyboards, smoother rhythms, and streamlined lyrics from Devoto. Despite its ambitiousness, the record was poorly received by the press. In the summer of 1980, Magazine released "Sweetheart Contract," which became their second and last British chart hit, peaking at number 54. *Magic, Murder and the Weather* was released in the spring of 1981; it proved to be Magazine's last album. Devoto left the group in May of 1981 to pursue a solo career and the band broke up shortly afterward. *—Stephen Thomas Erlewine*

Real Life / Apr. 1978 / Blue Plate ✦✦✦✦✦

Magazine's *Real Life* is post-punk ground zero. Singer/lyricist Howard Devoto split from Buzzcocks to be less musically direct and therefore more adventurous with his new outfit. Taking the groundwork laid by his previous band and applying the artsy abstractions given to the basic rock formula pioneered by the likes of Roxy Music, David Bowie, and the Krautrock style, Devoto chose his new partners well—partners who were talented musicians, not afraid to display their skills. (Well, actually, the flat-drumming Martin Jackson would be gone after this, replaced by the much better John Doyle.) Magazine were never about finding a riff, bashing out a knuckle-dragging rhythm, screaming about everyday young-adult angst and taking a break after every two minutes. The arrangements and structures here—as on each successive Magazine recording—are herkyjerky, tightly wound, unpredictable, and sometimes funky (for one great example of the latter, check the onset of the breakdown just before the three minute mark of the opening "Definitive Gaze"), perfectly suited for Devoto's swoopy, livewire vocal tendencies. Even the most punk-sounding song here, "Recoil," sounds a little bizarre when compared to most of Magazine's contemporaries. And then there's the more daring aspects, like the spacey keyboard passages (some of which haven't aged too well, though they're hardly Asiatic) and Devoto's lyrics, a how-to manual for many songwriters that followed, from Momus to Thom Yorke. Often cryptic and very open to interpretation, his wordplay is always enough to retain interest and provoke analysis. It might be up for debate as to what the best Magazine record is, but *Real Life* is an undeniably terrific debut, thanks in no small part to the Devoto/Shelley-penned "Shot by Both Sides" and the thumping, triumphant "The Light Pours Out of Me." Everything else is gravy. *—Andy Kellman*

Secondhand Daylight / 1979 / Blue Plate ✦✦✦✦

Secondhand Daylight must have been committed in the cold. You can practically see the steam coming out of Howard Devoto as he sneeringly spews out lines like "Today I bumped into you again/I have no idea what you want" in "Permafrost." You can picture Dave Formula swiping frost off his keys and Barry Adamson blowing on his hands during the intro to "Feed the Enemy," while Johns McGeoch and Doyle zip up their parkas. More than anything, *Daylight* is a showcase for Formula's chilly but expressive keyboard work; he appears to release as many demons as Devoto does throughout the course of the dark album. Detached tales of relationships damaged beyond repair dominate the album, and it's not nearly as bouncy as *Real Life* or *The Correct Use of Soap*—the only real chugger is "Rhythm of Cruelty." Despite the sub-zero climate and lack of dance numbers, it isn't a completely impenetrable record. It's not as immediately satisfying as their first and third albums, but it deserves just as much recognition as Magazine's other stellar works. *—Andy Kellman*

The Correct Use of Soap / 1980 / Blue Plate ✦✦✦✦✦

The Correct Use of Soap is a bit of a return to more standard operational form for Magazine, who thawed out after the recording of *Secondhand Daylight* to throw this bouncy batch of rhythmically intricate and colorful songs together, which is something of a surprise when considering that they enlisted Martin Hannett (Joy Division), master of the gray hues, as producer. A poppier and funkier record than its predecessors—and not just apparent from a faithful cover of Sly & the Family Stone's "Thank You"—it features the rhythm section of John Doyle and Barry Adamson at their non-showy best and guitarist John McGeoch at his most cunningly percussive; save for the called-for razzle-dazzle on "Sweetheart Contract," keyboardist Dave Formula takes more of a back seat, using piano more frequently and no longer driving the songs to the point of detracting from the greatness of his mates, as the biggest complaint of *Secondhand Daylight* goes. Howard Devoto's lyrics are also a little less depressive, though they're no less biting. The closing "A Song From Under the Floorboards" includes Devoto zingers like "My irritability keeps me alive and kicking" and "I know the meaning of life, it doesn't help me a bit." His themes of distrust and romantic turbulence remain focal, evident in "You Never Knew Me" ("Do you want the truth or do you want your sanity?") and "I Want to Burn Again" ("I met your lover yesterday / Wearing some things I left at your place / Singing a song that means a lot to me"). Finally, let it be said that "Look what fear's done to body," from the opening "Because You're Frightened," is a paranoiac's slogan for the ages. Not that the entire record isn't post-punk for the ages. *—Andy Kellman*

Play. / 1980 / EMI ✦✦

Magic, Murder, and the Weather / Sep. 1981 / EMI ✦✦✦
Magazine's final studio album, *Magic, Murder, and the Weather,* finds Dave Formula's washes of cold, brittle keyboards dominating the bitter and cynical music. Occasionally, Howard Devoto's weary lyrics surface through the icy mix, but it's clear that Devoto and Magazine have both had better days. It's not a graceful way to bow out, but the album has enough strong moments to prevent it from being an embarrassment as well. *—Stephen Thomas Erlewine*

After the Fact / 1982 / IRS ✦✦✦
Released after Magazine disbanded in 1981, *After the Fact* was designed as a career overview for its British release, collecting the group's singles and selected highlights from their four albums. In its American incarnation, *After the Fact* was radically different. Instead of functioning as an overview, it collected several B-sides, augmenting them with album tracks, and only a few of those overlapped with its U.K. counterpart. So, the British version (which has a green cover) is for the neophyte, and the American version (red cover) is for the collector, which is a strange state of affairs for this distinctly British post-punk band. *—Stephen Thomas Erlewine*

Rays & Hail: 1978-81 / 1987 / Virgin ✦✦✦✦
A comprehensive compilation that samples from all of the band's albums, as well as including the original single version of "Shot by Both Sides." *—Stephen Thomas Erlewine*

Scree / Mar. 8, 1991 / Blue Plate ✦✦✦
Scree: Rarities 1978-1981 is a thorough assemblage of A-sides and B-sides that essentially can't be found on any of Magazine's studio records. Even in the event of title duplication ("Rhythm of Cruelty," "The Light Pours Out of Me"), the disc offers alternative mixes. The strength of the disc isn't merely due to the excellence of non-album A-sides like "Touch and Go," "Give Me Everything," and "Upside Down"; in most cases, the B-sides rival the A-sides or, at the very least, would have made fine album material. The opening "My Mind Ain't So Open," which was the B-side to Magazine's debut single "Shot by Both Sides," is a hyperactive tune with bleating saxophones and screaming guitars, the most straight-ahead punk song the band recorded; unlike the remainder of the band's material, the structure is relatively traditional and doesn't feature the prominent keyboards that became integral to their sound. Covers of Captain Beefheart's "I Love You You Big Dummy" and John Barry's "Goldfinger" are as good as you'd expect (see Buzzcocks' *Time's Up* for a more faithful version of the former, recorded before Howard Devoto's defection to form this band), and a trio of live cuts from the *Sweetheart Contract* 12" ("Feed the Enemy," "Twenty Years Ago," "Shot by Both Sides") add icing to the cake. Altogether, the collection is just as essential as the band's first three studio albums. Apart from the live material on this disc, most of the tracks became available again in 2000 on the *Maybe It's Right to Be Nervous Now* box set. *—Andy Kellman*

• **Where the Power Is** / Sep. 25, 2000 / Virgin ✦✦✦✦✦
An accurate title, *Where the Power Is* successfully trots out the bouncier, assaultive side of Magazine. They were one of the best in the early era of post-punk, rarely doing anything mediocre. Released simultaneously with the triple-disc *Maybe It's Right to Be Nervous Now,* it oddly duplicates much of 1987's *Rays and Hail* compilation. So why not keep *Rays and Hail* in print and just reissue it with additional liner notes or something? Well, the answer's commerce. A new title means new sales, and even completists will apprehensively shell out again for the same batch of songs. Literally—there's only a handful of songs here that aren't on *Rays and Hail.* Though some of the versions may differ (album version versus single version), only compulsive completists give a toss about such things. Confusingly, *Rays and Hail did remain in print* when this was issued, even getting a re-pressing! Did someone in Virgin's catalog department fall asleep? Fine as an isolated release for the newbie, *Where the Power Is* just makes things quite confusing for the rest, basically a baffler amongst the rest of Magazine's discography. Not a great deal can be debated as far as it being representative is concerned, so in that manner it succeeds. *—Andy Kellman*

Maybe It's Right to Be Nervous Now / Sep. 25, 2000 / Virgin ✦✦✦✦
Magazine's three-disc box set is a mess. Breaking the group's history down to two eras spread across the first two-thirds of the box and adding a fantastic and well-needed third disc dedicated solely to Peel Sessions, it's yet another multi-disc package that half-pleases both fan and neophyte. Only *four* of the 45 tracks come directly from the band's four studio LPs. Oddly enough, seven-tenths of the decent live album *Play* is strewn across the first two discs. Why include the majority of a live album that caters to diehards, therefore leaving out the better studio versions? Eight B-sides are scattered throughout, most of which were previously available on *Scree.* Four "alternative mixes" add further frustration, including a sub-standard (demo?) "Shot by Both Sides." That could be the biggest gripe. Not including the definitive version of "Shot by Both Sides," which is to post-punk what "Anarchy in the U.K." is to punk, would be similar to leaving "Love Is the Drug" off of a Roxy Music collection. So aside from the Peel Sessions, a fan is getting hardly anything new. The neophyte would be better off picking up the single-disc *Where the Power Is,* which draws from this and obviously costs less. The Peel Sessions disc is the real meat. Four sessions yield 15 thoroughly exciting songs. Everything is delivered with excellence, although Howard Devoto might have wanted to impair keyboardist Dave Formula's busy hands. Some versions might be preferable to their album counterparts, including the furious take on the Devoto/Pete Shelley-penned "Boredom." Despite the numerous complications with this box, the high rating is deserved. Many would argue that it could have been done better, but the material is undoubtedly strong. The package itself is a treat, containing the results of Devoto's personal archive ransacking. *—Andy Kellman*

The Magicians

Folk-Rock, Psychedelic

Although they're rather mistakenly thought of a '60s garage band due to the inclusion of their fine 1965 single, "An Invitation to Cry," on the original *Nuggets* compilation, the Magicians were an all-around pop/rock group that also drew from folk-rock, blues, and soul. They had a pretty intricate history for a short-lived act that only managed to put out four Columbia singles between 1965 and 1967. Drummer and songwriter Alan Gordon was playing in Tex & the Chex in Greenwich Village when they were discovered by record producers Bob Wyld and Art Polhemus. Gordon had written "An Invitation to Cry" with Jimmy Woods, which he recorded with Tex & the Chex. The producers wanted a better singer and enlisted Garry Bonner to do the vocals. The resulting recording, "An Invitation to Cry," was superb moody pop/rock with a touch of blue-eyed soul, enhanced by an imaginative production highlighting ominous distorted guitar riffs, graceful tempo shifts, accomplished vocal harmonies, and Bonner's anguished lead vocal. The group, renamed the Magicians, got a deal with Columbia and gained a following in New York. They never did come up with another song on the order of "An Invitation to Cry," though, on their two 1966 Columbia singles, which showed an eclectic group conversant with both folk-rock and sophisticated pop/rock. They did some unissued recordings in 1966, but the band never did put out an LP, although one subsequent flop single did appear on Columbia in early 1967. Bonner and Gordon were at this time becoming successful pop/rock songwriters for other artists, particularly the Turtles, for whom they composed "Happy Together," "She'd Rather Be With Me," "You Know What I Mean," and "She's My Girl." A Magicians CD, containing the four singles and some unissued demos and outtakes, appeared in 1999. *—Richie Unterberger*

• **An Invitation to Cry** / Feb. 8, 1999 / Sundazed ✦✦✦✦
Both sides of their four 1965-67 singles on Columbia, plus five previously unissued tracks from the same period. The possibility of an album's worth of Magicians' material has long intrigued collectors of '60s music, most of whom are only familiar with their "An Invitation to Cry" single from *Nuggets.* The rest of the material is okay, but a bit of a letdown, lacking any standout numbers on the order of "An Invitation to Cry." Too, the Magicians didn't seem to have the time to solidify a special sound. At times it's Lovin' Spoonful-like folk-rock (they cover two songs from the debut album by minor Greenwich Village folk-rocker David Blue); sometimes it's Young Rascals-ish soul-rock, with a poppier bent; sometimes it's journeyman blues-rock (covers of "Back Door Man" and "Who Do You Love"); sometimes it's fair period 1966 pop/rock. The Gordon-Bonner songwriting collaboration had not yet been cemented; in fact there are only two Gordon-Bonner compositions here, although on some of the other tracks one or the other wrote with other partners. In retrospect it's unfortunate that the Magicians didn't hold together longer, until the Gordon-Bonner team had matured, but fate plays its own cards. *—Richie Unterberger*

Magnetic Fields

f. 1990, Boston, MA

Indie Pop, Indie Rock, Lo-Fi

The Magnetic Fields are a bona fide band, but in most essential respects they are the project of studio wunderkind Stephin Merritt, who writes, produces, and (lately) sings all of their material, as well as plays many of the instruments, concocting a sort of indie-pop synth-rock. While the Magnetic Fields may draw upon the electronic textures of vintage acts like ABBA, Kraftwerk, Roxy Music with Eno, Joy Division, and Gary Numan, Merritt's vision is far more pointed toward the alternative rock underground. His songs are also far warmer and more pure pop-oriented than the above reference points might lead you to believe, sounding at times like late-20th century equivalents to Phil Spector or Brian Wilson, with an emphasis on pop hooks and eccentric, romantically reflective lyrics rather than the bedrock synthetic rhythms and textures. In addition to his work with Magnetic Fields, Merritt has involved himself in several side projects, the most notable being the 6ths' all-star *Wasps Nests* album. *—Richie Unterberger*

Distant Plastic Trees / 1990 / Red Flame ✦✦✦
The Magnetic Fields' debut unveiled an unusually skilled indie-rock auteur in Stephin Merritt, aided by the sometimes overlooked contributions of the other band members on cello, horns, vocals, and percussion. Although not quite as polished as later Magnetic Fields releases, it's a decent set of tunes guided by Merritt's inventive pop melodies and unexpectedly imaginative facility with cheap synthesizers. Merge has combined this album and its successor, *The Wayward Bus,* onto one disc with its CD reissue. *—Richie Unterberger*

The Wayward Bus / 1991 / Feel Good All Over ♦♦♦♦
The last of the two Magnetic Fields albums to feature Susan Amway as lead singer, this has Merritt's most gorgeous melodies and most pop-friendly production, strongly recalling Phil Spector in particular (more than one of the songs quotes the opening "Be My Baby" rhythms). Merge has combined this album and its predecessor, *Distant Plastic Trees*, onto one disc with its CD reissue. *—Richie Unterberger*

Holiday / 1994 / Merge ♦♦♦♦
Starting with this album, Merritt, who had never sung on previous Magnetic Fields discs, took over the vocal chores with the departure of Susan Amway. His low and somewhat sober tones are less accessible, and the music began to move in a more percolating electro-pop direction as well. This is probably the most enjoyable of their Merritt-sung efforts, though, with a couple of real standouts in "The Trouble I've Been Looking For" and "In My Car." *—Richie Unterberger*

The Charm of the Highway Strip / 1994 / Merge ♦♦♦♦
Merritt took more of a narrative approach than usual on this album, which was in part inspired (as the title indicates) by on-the-road experiences and exhibited a (very slight) country influence. Not as good as *Holiday*, although it has characteristically agile songwriting and production. *—Richie Unterberger*

The Wayward Bus/Distant Plastic Trees / Jan. 23, 1995 / Merge ♦♦♦♦
Both of the group's debut albums are combined onto one CD for this reissue, which effectively summarizes the period in which all of the Magnetic Fields' material was sung by Susan Amway rather than Stephin Merritt. There are reservations attached to recommending this as the first purchase, since the subsequent albums on which Merritt handles all of the vocals are obviously a more accurate reflection of his auteurist vision. The fact is, however, that the Amway-sung albums are more immediately attractive to most listeners, especially *The Wayward Bus*. *—Richie Unterberger*

Get Lost / Oct. 24, 1995 / Merge ♦♦♦
Merritt's homespun (although not carelessly lo-fi) approach to electronic pop is a big part of the Magnetic Fields' charm, but he may be starting to stretch it to the limit with *Get Lost*. The most electro-oriented of their releases to date, it's also perhaps their least engaging, although the brooding ballad "Don't Look Away" is one of their best songs. They may want to start thinking about varying their synthetic percussions and patterns more, as these are starting too sound a little too boxy and similar for comfort. *—Richie Unterberger*

● **69 Love Songs [Limited Edition]** / Sep. 7, 1999 / Merge ♦♦♦♦♦
As the sprawling magnitude of its cheeky title suggests, *69 Love Songs* is Stephin Merritt's most ambitious as well as fully realized work to date, a three-disc epic of classically chiseled pop songs that explore both the promise and pitfalls of modern romance through the jaundiced eye of an irredeemable misanthrope. A true A-to-Z catalog of touchingly bittersweet love songs that runs the gamut from tender ballads to pithy folk tunes to bluesy vamps, the sheer scope of the record allows all of Merritt's musical personas to converge: the regular use of guest vocalists recalls his work as the 6ths, the romantic fatalism suggests the Gothic Archies project, and the stately melodies evoke the Future Bible Heroes. The whole is much greater than the sum of its parts, however; for all of Merritt's scathing wit and icy detachment, there's a depth and sensitivity to these songs largely absent from his past work, and each one of these 69 tracks approaches *l'amour* from refreshing angles, galvanizing the love song form with rare sophistication and elegance. Naturally, given a project of this size there's the occasional bit of filler, but all in all, *69 Love Songs* maintains a remarkable consistency throughout, and the highlights ("I Don't Believe in the Sun," "All My Little Words," "Asleep and Dreaming," "Busby Berkeley Dreams," and "Acoustic Guitar," to name just a few) are jaw-droppingly superb. Also available as three individual releases, *69 Love Songs* was nevertheless conceived as a whole and is best absorbed as such, with all of its twists and turns taken in stride; despite its three-hour length, the music boasts the craftsmanship and economy that remain the hallmarks of classic American pop songwriting, a tradition Merritt upholds even as he subverts the formula in new and brilliant ways. *—Jason Ankeny*

The Main Ingredient

f. 1966, Harlem, NY
Soul
Originally formed in 1964 as the Poets, this New York soul group (Donald McPherson, Luther Simmons Jr., and Tony Sylvester) recorded for Red Bird before changing their name in 1966. After McPherson's death in 1971, Cuba Gooding became the lead singer, and the band scored three Top 40 hits, including "Everybody Plays the Fool," which went to number three.

The Main Ingredient tried it again in 1986, with Cuba Gooding returning to his lead spot. They recorded for Zakia, but didn't get much response to "Do Me Right." They kept trying, cutting a song on Polydor in 1989. Longtime group member Luther Simmons, who had left in 1975 to become a stockbroker and then come back in 1980, returned to Wall Street and was replaced for this session by Jerome Jackson. *—Bil Carpenter & Stephen Thomas Erlewine*

● **The All-Time Greatest Hits** / Oct. 25, 1990 / RCA ♦♦♦♦
It wasn't until 1971 that the Main Ingredient's fortunes changed; when Cuba Gooding replaced Donald McPherson, his engaging voice helped make them part of the "sweet" soul trend. Gooding's leads made "Spinning Around (I Must Be Falling in Love)" and "Everybody Plays the Fool" huge hits, as well as "Just Don't Want to Be Lonely" and "Happiness Is Just Around the Bend." These and several other hits are featured on this anthology covering their prime years on RCA. *—Ron Wynn*

A Quiet Storm / Apr. 1996 / RCA ♦♦♦♦
Be cautioned that this 20-track retrospective of material spanning the late '60s to the mid-'70s is not a best-of, although it does include some of their biggest hits ("Just Don't Want to Be Lonely," "Everybody Plays the Fool"). As the title indicates, this focuses on the mellow and romantic side of the group. As the Main Ingredient largely specialized in mellow and romantic songs, this ends up being close to something of a best-of anyway. The relentless soft-pillow ambience of the tracks can become wearisome; in this context, the easygoing "Everybody Plays the Fool" sounds more like a blitzkrieg than a "quiet storm." *—Richie Unterberger*

Make-Up

f. 1995, Washington, DC
Indie Rock
Indie-punk subversives the Make-Up emerged from the ashes of the seminal Washington, D.C. outfit Nation of Ulysses, reuniting vocalist Ian Svenonious, guitarist James Canty, and drummer Steve Gamboa (who together also previously teamed in the short-lived Cupid Car Club, M.P. as well as the T.A.M.I. Show). Completing the lineup with bassist Michelle Mae, the Make-Up surfaced in early 1995 with their debut single "Blue Is Beautiful," the first call-to-arms to spring from their self-styled liberation theology 'Gospel Yeh-Yeh,' a belief system advocating the oppressed masses to "get theirs" and "off the pigs in all their forms." Split singles with the Meta-Matics and Slant 6 followed, and in the wake of the "R.U.A. Believer" single the group returned in early 1996 with their first LP, the Dischord label release *Destination: Love LIVE! at Cold Rice*. In February 1997, the quartet launched their second album, *The Make-Up After Dark*; a third full-length, *Sound Verite*, appeared on K Records just a month later. The subject of James Schneider's 1997 tour film *Blue Is Beautiful*, the Make-Up rounded out the year with "Free Arthur Lee," recorded in tribute to the imprisoned leader of the legendary psychedelic-era band Love; upon completing their 1998 LP *In Mass Mind*, the band toured Brazil, returning to the U.S. to issue the singles "Wade in the Water" and "Untouchable Sound." The brilliant *Save Yourself* followed in the fall of 1999. *—Jason Ankeny*

Destination: Live at Cold Rice / 1996 / Dischord ♦♦♦♦♦
The Make-Up's debut album *Destination: Live At Cold Rice* was recorded in concert, which is appropriate. Where most bands focus on writing tight songs or ambitious musical interludes, the Make-Up create music where the style is the substance. They're about sex, energy, and the underground, and all of those gel into a dynamic record on *Destination: Live at Cold Rice*. Since the band concentrates on sound, not songs, there are several tuneless, total throwaways on the record, but the group's kinetic performance glosses over such shortcomings, because what matters with the Make-Up is the total package. And on *Destination: Live at Cold Rice*, they have arrived fully formed. *—Stephen Thomas Erlewine*

Make-Up After Dark / Feb. 3, 1997 / Dischord ♦♦♦
After Dark follows the same basic formula as Make-Up's debut, capturing the group in their element: in concert. But where *Destination Love: Live at Cold Rice* was mostly successful with a few slow moments, *After Dark*'s muddier sound and longer, drawn-out songs make it an occasionally engaging but less cohesive album. The slow, expanded version of "We Can't Be Contained" drags down the momentum, and while songs like "(Here Comes) the Judge" and "Don't Mind the Mind" are still enjoyable, they were better performed on the debut album. However, "Blue Is Beautiful," "We're Having a Baby," and "Make Up Is: Lies" add the dynamic edge that most of *After Dark* lacks. Though the album finds Make-Up exploring the slower, quieter aspects of their style, *After Dark*'s live format doesn't do justice to the group's experiments. *—Heather Phares*

Sound Verite / Feb. 7, 1997 / K ♦♦♦♦
For their first studio album, the Make-Up brought in producer Calvin Johnson, one of the leaders of the International Pop Underground the Make-Up is identified with. Johnson keeps the sound raw and ragged, which suits the band's kinetic, half-ironic, and totally sincere blend of indie-rock and the Stones. Songwriting isn't one of the Make-Up's specialties—very few of the individual songs stand out—yet their overall sound is frighteningly energetic. The brittle production makes *Sound Verite* sound as if it would break in two at any moment, especially since the band keeps pushing themselves forward at a blinding speed. On the whole, the record isn't as a complete an experience as *Destination: Live at Cold Rice*, but it comes damn close to reaching those peaks. *—Stephen Thomas Erlewine*

In Mass Mind / Apr. 7, 1998 / Dischord ♦♦♦♦♦
For 1998's *In Mass Mind*, their second studio album and fourth long-player overall, Make-Up recruited Adam & Eve—a.k.a. Royal Trux's Neil Hagerty and Jennifer Herrema—for production duties. As evidenced by the album's warm, detailed sound, the collaboration is a perfect fit, bringing just enough polish and focus to Make-Up's music to make it even more powerful. "Black Wire Pt. 1," "Drop the Needle," and "The Joy of Sound" show off the group's dynamic, theatrical side, while "Earth Worm," "Do You Like Gospel Music," "Time Machine," and "Caught Up in the Rapture" are atmospheric and soulful, further explorations into the band's widening sonic territory. *—Heather Phares*

● **I Want Some** / Mar. 23, 1999 / K ♦♦♦♦♦
Lazy journalists and cynics have at times given the Make-Up a classification that falls somewhere between Jon Spencer Blues Explosion meets Prince and the New Power Generation. Even if this is a slightly accurate but unfair account of their sound, what these people fail to recognize is their ability to fuse punk with Motown soul, garage rock, funk, and gospel. On top of Ian Svenonius' preacher-esque vocals, high-pitched squeals help layer the Make-Up's self-proclaimed, trademark "gospel ya-ya" sound. And the word is being spread not only as a live band, but also in part of their countless singles all

conveniently packaged on *I Want Some.* Twenty-three songs total from all their split singles and 7"s previously released on vinyl. Living proof that they are one of the hardest working bands in show business; and they're doing it all for the kids! *—Mike DaRonco*

Save Yourself / Oct. 26, 1999 / K ♦♦♦♦♦
Save Yourself, the Make-Up's sixth album in just over three years, reflects not only the group's prolific nature but the corresponding growth spurt in their sound as well. Though it's not as eclectic as their singles compilation *I Want Some, Save Yourself*'s nine tracks include rave-ups like "White Belts" and moody, psychedelic pieces like the title track and "I Am Pentagon." Brendan Canty's clean production and the songs' intricate arrangements make this album the most accomplished and limber blend of punk, gospel, psychedelia, and soul from the Make-Up—that is, until their next album. *—Heather Phares*

Stephen Malkmus

b. May 30, 1966, Santa Monica, CA
Vocals, Guitar / Indie Rock, Singer/Songwriter
After Pavement announced they were going on hiatus at the end of 1999, the status of one of America's finest indie rock bands was a mystery for the first half of 2000. It became clearer that summer, however, when it was revealed that both singers/songwriters/guitarists Stephen Malkmus and Scott Kannberg were preparing solo albums. Malkmus was particularly busy during that time, performing new songs with Kim's Bedroom—a one-off group that also included Sonic Youth's Kim Gordon and Jim O'Rourke—that spring in Holland and recording them at studios near his hometown of Portland, OR. Working with him were the Jicks, a.k.a. Portland indie rock veterans drummer/percussionist John Moen and bassist Joanna Bolme. Moen had played with the Fastbacks, the Dharma Bums, and his own group, the Maroons; Bolme played with the Minders and worked as an engineer at Jackpot Studios, where Pavement's *Terror Twilight* was demoed and parts of Malkmus' new project were recorded. Initially, Malkmus intended to release the album on his own or through a local label, but when his old label Matador received a copy, they agreed to release it. By the time Malkmus officially confirmed Pavement's breakup in the November 2000 issue of Spin magazine, Matador announced it was releasing the album—originally titled *Swedish Reggae* and then changed to *Stephen Malkmus*—in February 2001. That January, the single "Discretion Grove" arrived and Stephen Malkmus and the Jicks made their live debut at New York's Bowery Ballroom. They embarked on a tour of the U.K. that winter and toured the U.S. in the spring, including a gig at South by Southwest with labelmates Mogwai and the reunited Soft Boys. Former Pavement percussionist Bob Nastanovich acted as the Jicks' tour manager and Elastica leader Justine Frischmann—another friend of Malkmus'—joined the band as a guitarist for selected dates. *—Heather Phares*

● **Stephen Malkmus** / Feb. 13, 2001 / Matador ♦♦♦♦♦
Much like the Pixies' *Trompe Le Monde,* Pavement's swan song, *Terror Twilight,* sounded a lot like a disguised solo album from the group's chief singer/songwriter, Stephen Malkmus. The album's polished production and earnest, ambitious songwriting—not to mention lack of Scott Kannberg songs—sounded miles away from the playful, slightly chaotic rock that made albums like *Slanted & Enchanted* and *Crooked Rain, Crooked Rain* so exciting. Yet Malkmus' actual solo debut, aptly named *Stephen Malkmus,* reclaims some of the energetic creativity of Pavement's best albums. In fact, it sounds like the most fun he's had in a studio since *Wowee Zowee.* This may be because he didn't have to deal with the confines and expectations of a new Pavement album; Malkmus didn't originally plan to release the album through Matador, which possibly removed some of the pressure to make a "statement" with this collection. Which is good, because instantly catchy, zany songs like "Troubbble" might not have made it to the album. Though placing most of the zippy, instantly catchy songs near the top of the album works against it somewhat, as a whole it's refreshingly free of the typical solo debut's gravity and earnestness. By keeping things light, *Stephen Malkmus*—the album and, very likely, the person—defies heavy analysis from critics and fans. No, it's not quite the same as another Pavement album, but its literate, funny eclecticism is almost as irresistible. *—Heather Phares*

The Mamas & the Papas

f. 1964, New York, NY, **db.** 1972
Sunshine Pop, Folk-Rock, Pop
The leading California-based vocal group of the '60s, the Mamas & the Papas epitomized the ethos of mid- to late-'60s pop culture: live free, play free, and love free. Their music, built around radiant harmonies and a solid electric-folk foundation, was gorgeous on its own terms, but a major part of its appeal lay in the easygoing Southern California lifestyle it endorsed.

Founder and leader John Phillips came out of early rock roots and a partly successful folk career, as did Cass Elliott and Denny Doherty, while Phillips' wife Michelle was an ex-model who also sang. They got together out of several failed folk groups just as the music was going electric, pulled up stakes in New York and headed west, where they signed with Lou Adler and wowed the world with a song called "California Dreamin'."

Phillips was a pop poet with a commercial edge, and a good arranger. The group had enviable chart success, lived well, and indulged themselves lavishly yet retained credibility with the counterculture. But it all came apart in a couple of years, as the quartet's intertwining romantic entanglements, coupled with their chemical excesses (detailed in separate books by John and Michelle Phillips), strangled their ability to work. By 1971 they were a fond memory, although a reconstituted version of the quartet has done well on the oldies circuit in the late '80s and early '90s. *—Bruce Eder*

If You Can Believe Your Eyes and Ears / Mar. 1966 / MCA ♦♦♦♦♦
In the spring of 1966, *If You Can Believe Your Eyes and Ears* represented a genuinely new sound, as fresh to listeners as the songs on *Meet the Beatles* had seemed two years earlier. Released just as "California Dreaming" was ascending the charts by leaps and bounds, it was the product of months of rehearsal in the Virgin Islands and John Phillips' discovery of what one could do to build a polished recorded sound in the studio—it embraced folk-rock, pop/rock, pop, and soul, and also reflected the kind of care that acts like the Beatles were putting into their records at the time. "Monday, Monday" and "California Dreamin'" are familiar enough to anyone who's ever listened to the radio, and "Go Where You Wanna Go" isn't far behind, in this version or the very similar rendition by the Fifth Dimension. But the rest is mighty compelling even to casual listeners, including the ethereal "Got a Feelin'," the rocking "Straight Shooter" and "Somebody Groovy," the jaunty, torch song-style version of "I Call Your Name," and the prettiest versions of "Do You Wanna Dance" and "Spanish Harlem" that anyone ever recorded.

If the material here has a certain glow that the Mamas & the Papas' subsequent LPs lacked, that may be due in part to the extensive rehearsal and the exhilaration of their first experience in the studio, but also a result of the fact that it was recorded before the members' personal conflicts began interfering with their ability to work together. The work was all spontaneous and unforced here, as opposed to the emotional complications that had to be overcome before their next sessions. *—Bruce Eder*

The Mamas & the Papas / Sep. 1966 / Dunhill ♦♦♦♦
This, the second album by the Mamas & the Papas, was recorded and released during the precise high point in their brief career, and, not surprisingly, one of their most tumultuous times. During the recording of the album, Michelle Phillips (temporarily estranged from husband John Phillips) was unceremoniously booted out of the band. Replacement Jill Gibson filled in for a brief period before Michelle was finally brought back into the band. (It's uncertain weather Gibson is on the album, however.) The end result—while not *quite* as striking as a whole as their debut—is still magnificent. Aside from the hits "I Saw Her Again," which was possibly the hardest-rocking track the group ever recorded, and "Words of Love" (featuring Cass Elliot), the rest of the album has numerous highlights. Most notably, "My Heart Stood Still" (written by Rodgers and Hart) and "Once Was a Time I Thought" are perhaps the finest recordings that the group ever cut. *—Matthew Greenwald*

Deliver / 1967 / MCA ♦♦♦♦
By the time the Mamas and the Papas recorded and released their third album, the group was continuing, in the words of singer Denny Doherty, "on its own momentum." Acrimonious personnel changes, rock stardom, fame, money, and drugs (among other factors) were taking their toll on the group's chemistry. Fortunately, this momentum is precisely the reason that the album succeeds. Buttressed by the singles "Creeque Alley" (the sometimes hilarious story of how the group came together), "Look Through My Window," and the stupendous remake of "Dedicated to the One I Love," the album has some exquisite moments. "Look Through My Window" also is one of the group's most realized recordings, and the cover of "Twist and Shout" is an absolute killer. Much of the record, frankly, doesn't sound too different than the group's first two albums, but with the songwriting, vocal, and production excellence, why tamper with genius? The group felt so too, which is why this album is Michelle Phillips' personal favorite. It's not too hard to see why. *—Matthew Greenwald*

Farewell to the First Golden Era / 1967 / MCA ♦♦♦♦♦
At the time of its release in October 1967, *Farewell to the First Golden Era* was great for what it was, but ominous for what it foreshadowed, with both of those characteristics apparent in the album title. It was, as the term "Golden Era" indicated, a greatest-hits album, its 12 tracks including all nine of the Mamas & the Papas' chart singles up to that time: the gold-selling number one "Monday, Monday"; the gold-selling Top Ten "California Dreamin'"; the Top Tens "I Saw Her Again Last Night," "Words of Love," "Dedicated to the One I Love," and "Creeque Alley"; the Top 40s "Look Through My Window" and "Twelve Thirty (Young Girls Are Coming to the Canyon)"; and the chart entry "Dancing in the Street." But this wasn't just the first golden era, it was the only one, and with a lone Top 40 hit (a cover of Rodgers & Hart's "Glad to Be Unhappy") left and one half-hearted album (*The Papas & the Mamas,* April 1968) to come before the group's breakup, this really was farewell. [Originally released in October 1967 by Dunhill Records as Dunhill 50025, *Farewell to the First Golden Era* was reissued by MCA Records as MCA 709.] *— William Ruhlmann*

Papas & Mamas / 1968 / MCA ♦♦♦
An often misunderstood album, this album (aside from the 1971 "reunion" album) was the final record by the Mamas and the Papas. As time goes by, it has held up incredibly well, and sounds better today than when it was released in mid-1968. The centerpiece of the album is "Dream a Little Dream," which very well may be the finest cover version that the group ever recorded, and in the end, was a very nice way to end the group's short but incredible career. The album also contains some excellent John Phillips material such as "12:30" (a minor hit), "Rooms," and "Too Late." These three tracks form a mini-medley in the middle of the second side, and add a lot of dimension to the record. Cut at the Phillips' home studio, the album has a simple sound, but when the vocal majesty cuts through on such tracks as "Mansions" (one of the band's lost masterpieces), it's faultless. *—Matthew Greenwald*

16 Greatest Hits / 1970 / MCA ♦♦♦♦
A great overview of the music from this group, one of the founders of the California sound in the late '60s. This is a good collection of their unforgettable electric folk-pop songs, including "Monday, Monday" and "California Dreamin'." [Originally released in August 1969 by Dunhill Records, *16 of Their Greatest Hits,* it was reissued on CD by MCA Records in 1986.] *—AMG*

People Like Us / 1971 / MCA Special Products ✦✦

Monterey International Pop Festival / 1971 / One Way ✦✦

Creeque Alley / Mar. 12, 1991 / MCA ✦✦✦✦✦
They weren't the most important folk-rock group of the mid-'60s; the Byrds and others produced more enduring music. Yet the Mamas & the Papas were undoubtedly the most commercially successful folk-rock group of their time, racking up an astonishing nine Top 30 hits in little more than a year and a half. This 43-song double CD is by far the most comprehensive document of their legacy. It draws most heavily from their two 1966 albums (nine songs originate from their debut album *If You Can Believe Your Eyes and Ears* alone), when John Phillips' songwriting talent had yet to exhaust itself. Beyond the hits, the material is variable. Quite a few album tracks—especially "Got a Feelin'," "Straight Shooter," "Go Where You Wanna Go," "Once Was a Time I Thought," and their cover of Lennon/McCartney's "I Call Your Name"—were strong enough to have been hits under their own steam. Their slowed-down, California-ized versions of rock oldies were more problematic. And there's no doubt that their later material is less spirited and memorable than their initial burst of glory. The set includes various late-'60s and '70s solo recordings by each of the group's members (including small hit singles by John Phillips and Cass Elliott). Perhaps the most intriguing rarities are from the members' pre-Mamas days. These include commercial folk by the Big Three (featuring Cass Elliott) and primitive pop-folk-rock by the Mugwumps (including Elliott, Denny Doherty, and future Lovin' Spoonful member Zal Yanovsky). —*Richie Unterberger*

● **Greatest Hits** / Mar. 10, 1998 / MCA ✦✦✦✦✦
Not to be confused with earlier hits compilations, the catalog number on this 20-song collection is MCAD-11740. This is the single-CD successor to *Creeque Alley*, the double-disc career retrospective issued in the early 1990s. All of the hits from "California Dreamin'" to "Dream a Little Dream of Me" are here, along with their more celebrated album tracks, and the notes by Joseph Laredo provide a decent overview of the group's formation and history. The stuff has been remastered yet again, although the level of improvement over *Creeque Alley* seems modest (*Creeque Alley* sounded really good) compared with that double disc's improvement over the earlier, wholly inadequate masters from the 1980s. For someone who doesn't have a lot of money to spend on the band, this is the place to start, superseding all other single-disc hits collections. —*Bruce Eder*

The Before They Were the Mamas & the Papas . . . the Magic Circle / Mar. 9, 1999 / Varese ✦✦✦
Before the Mamas & the Papas formed, the four members were in various commercial folk-pop groups, including the Smoothies, the New Journeymen, the Halifax Three, the Big Three, and the Mugwumps. To make matters confusing for discographers (though more interesting for listeners), there are several unreleased studio tracks by *ad hoc* aggregations with members of the Mugwumps and Big Three. As for the music, this could be a more comprehensive overview of the Mamas & the Papas' roots, but it does illustrate the various forms of pop, folk, and rock that members were playing around with before the whole shebang coalesced with "California Dreamin'." There is Four Freshmen-influenced folk with choral vocals on the 1960 single by the Smoothies; lively pop-folk by the Big Three; and corny satire ("The Man Who Wouldn't Sing Along With Mitch") by the Halifax Three. "Oh Suzanna" and "Tom Dooley" by the temporary lineups mentioned above, come damn close to folk-rock, and serve as more evidence that various musicians were toying with the form a good year or so before the Byrds' "Mr. Tambourine Man." Speaking of which, there are three previously unreleased 1965 demos by the New Journeymen that also have a tentative folk-rock sound, including a version of "Mr. Tambourine Man"; it was probably recorded after the Byrds' rendition, but it indicates that some folk-rockers could have been playing around with similar ideas before the form's commercial breakthrough. There are a couple of actual Mamas & Papas hits ("California Dreamin'" and "Creeque Alley") that almost everyone who picks up this compilation will have already, and the selection is sometimes questionable (the absence of the Mugwumps' "Here It Is Another Day," co-written by Elliot and perhaps their best song, is unfortunate). Still, it's a fascinating and at times musically fine document of the Mamas & Papas' tangled roots. —*Richie Unterberger*

Man or Astro-Man?

f. 1992
Surf Revival, Indie Rock, Instrumental Rock
Man or Astro-man? are four college kids from Auburn who play some of the most pristinely crafted surf instrumentals since the 1960s. Formed by CoCo the Electronic Monkey Wizard on alternate universe bass, Birdstuff on traps, Star Crunch on guitar, and Dr. Delecto & his Invisible Vaportron on bass, the group released their first full-length album, *Is it . . . Man or Astro-man?*, in 1993. The band found time to put out a new 45 record practically every other week in addition to full-length releases like 1994's *Destroy All Astromen!*, 1996's *Experiment Zero*, and 1997's *Live Transmissions from Uranus*. The themes of the tunes usually run the gamut from spies to sci-fi. Dexter X later replaced Dr. Delecto, and Starcrunch left the band as well. The collection, *Beyond the Black Hole*, was issued in summer 2001. It also featured three brand new tracks. —*Matt Carlson*

● **Is It . . . Man or Astro-Man?** / 1993 / Estrus ✦✦✦✦
Though the kitschy samples from cartoon programs and B-movies don't have an incredibly long shelf life, the infectious surf stomp on songs like "Sadie Hawkins Atom Bomb," "Eric Estrotica," and "Invasion of the Dragonmen" saves *Is It . . . Man or Astro-Man?* from wearing out before its welcome. —*John Bush*

Destroy All Astromen!! / 1994 / Estrus ✦✦✦
Only Man or Astro-man? could incorporate NASA samples into their music and make them sound exciting, with their hypnotic surf-rock and infatuation with cheesy, low-grade

sci-fi flicks. With *Destroy All Astromen*, their plans of eventually conquering Earth are carried through with this live recording that not only pays tribute to the aforementioned influences, but also to their musical inspirations. Covers of Dick Dale, the Rezillos, and even the *Mystery Science 3000* theme song can be found on this full-length. Not as experimental or "out there" in comparison to their material on Touch and Go Records, but it still holds true to the Man or Astro-man? ethics of being ahead of their time in the surf genre. —*Mike DaRonco*

Project Infinity / 1995 / Estrus ✦✦✦

Intravenous Television Continuum / 1995 / One Louder ✦✦✦✦
Intravenous Television Continuum doesn't deviate from Man or Astro-man?'s spacy surf-rock at all, but it delivers one of the most consistent batches of songs and sonics in their catalog. —*Stephen Thomas Erlewine*

Experiment Zero / Apr. 1996 / Touch & Go ✦✦✦
How do they do it? After what seems like a million EPs and a number of full-lengths under their belt, one would think that Man or Astro-man? would either run out of material or at least develop a severe case of carpal-tunnel syndrome. But with *Experiment Zero*, they prove that a band can stay one step ahead of everyone as long as they're not shy about covering new ground. Sure, this could have been another surf record that mimics the style of the Ventures or Dick Dale, but Man or Astro-man? always add their own unique brand of wacked-out science fiction and off-the-wall playfulness. With that mentality, Man or Astro-man? continue to manage to stray away from adjectives such as "generic" or "carbon copy" with *Experiment Zero*. —*Mike DaRonco*

What Remains Inside a Black Hole / Jan. 28, 1997 / Au-Go-Go ✦✦✦

Made From Technetium / Sep. 1997 / Touch & Go ✦✦✦
Cutting away some of their kitsch tendencies, Man or Astro-man? turned in a tough, muscular ninth album with *Made From Technetium*. The surf and spy influences have been de-emphasized in favor of a harder approach that still reverberates with pop-culture references. The difference results in a record that remains raw and invigorating, even when the group runs out of memorable riffs. —*Stephen Thomas Erlewine*

EEVIAC: Operational Index and Reference Guide / Apr. 20, 1999 / Touch & Go ✦✦✦✦
Coming up with one of their tightest and most listenable albums to date, Man or Astro-Man? apply their hard-driving, sci-fi surf-rock to something of a concept album on *EEVIAC* (full title: *EEVIAC: Operational Index and Reference Guide, Including Other Modern Computational Devices*). The exact nature of that concept is difficult to decipher—something about an alien supercomputer and an obsession with technical jargon—but what matters more is that the group has continued to expand its sound, using more electronic effects and de-emphasizing kitschy samples in favor of their own, electronically altered vocals. There are even a few numbers that recall the punky, amphetamine-fueled guitar-pop of early British new wave; the jams—although still providing a few meandering moments—generally create fleshed-out soundscapes. One of the group's better albums. —*Steve Huey*

A Spectrum of Infinite Scale / Sep. 5, 2000 / Touch & Go ✦✦✦
Another mix of spaced-out surf and instrumental tracks. The usual goodness from the boys here, with plenty of bad sci-fi flick samples to start the songs, which all have the requisite clever song titles. The album begins and ends with a wall-of-sound mix of feedback and drums, with washes of ambient synthesizer added for texture.
One track, in particular, stands out. "Simple Text File," is exactly that; a recording of a dot-matrix printer in operation. The fact that tonal variations can result in a possible melody being developed is quite interesting, and used for novel effect here.
Overall, this is another very good collection of tight playing and propulsive instrumentals. —*Jeremy Salmon*

Beyond the Black Hole / Jul. 17, 2001 / Estrus ✦✦✦

Melissa Manchester

b. Feb. 15, 1951, New York, NY [The Bronx]
Vocals, Keyboards / AM Pop, Soft Rock, Adult Contemporary
MOR singer-songwriter Melissa Manchester, whose father was a bassoonist for the New York Metropolitan Opera, began singing commercial jingles at age 15 and went on to become a staff writer for Chappell Music while attending the High School of Performing Arts. After taking a songwriting class at New York University taught by Paul Simon, Manchester took her talents to the Manhattan club scene, where she was discovered by Bette Midler and Barry Manilow; the two hired her as a backup singer in 1971. She recorded her debut album, *Home to Myself*, in 1973, co-writing many of the songs with Carole Bayer Sager. 1975's *Melissa* produced her first Top Ten hit, "Midnight Blue," and set the tone for most of her career with its direct, slickly produced MOR pop sound. She and Kenny Loggins co-wrote the latter's 1978 duet hit with Stevie Nicks, "Whenever I Call You Friend," and the following year, Manchester returned to the Top Ten with "Don't Cry Out Loud." 1980 saw Manchester become the first singer to have two movie themes nominated for Academy Awards (*Ice Castles* and *The Promise*); two years later she achieved her highest *Billboard* singles chart placing with the number five hit "You Should Hear How She Talks About You," which won a Grammy for Best Female Vocal Performance. Through the '80s and '90s, Manchester has alternated occasional recording with scriptwriting and acting, appearing with Bette Midler in *For the Boys* and on the television series *Blossom* as the title character's birth mother. —*Steve Huey*

● **The Essence of Melissa Manchester** / May 20, 1997 / Arista ✦✦✦✦✦
The Essence of Melissa Manchester is a comprehensive overview of her decade's worth of recordings for Arista. During her stint at the label, she was at the peak of her popularity, racking up a string of adult contemporary hits including "Midnight Blue," "Just Too

Many People," "Just You and I," "Don't Cry Out Loud," "Pretty Girls," the Peabo Bryson duet "Lovers After All" and "You Should Hear How She Talks About You." All of those hits, plus several lesser-known gems like "Whenever I Call You Friend," are included on this terrific compilation, which is a definitive retrospective of her finest recordings. *—Stephen Thomas Erlewine*

The Manhattans

f. 1962, Jersey City, NJ

Northern Soul, Quiet Storm, Doo Wop, Urban, Soul

A venerable soul quintet from New Jersey, whose career has spanned the dawn of soul and the death of disco, although they have steadfastly preferred ballads over the years. Led initially by George Smith, who died in 1970, the Manhattans first charted in 1965 with "I Wanna Be (Your Everything)." After a string of solid R&B sellers on Carnival and DeLuxe, Gerald Alston replaced the late Smith and the group moved to Columbia. In 1976 they struck pay dirt with the elegant platinum-selling ballad "Kiss and Say Goodbye," which topped both the pop and soul lists. Several more huge R&B hits preceded their uplifting 1980 gold record "Shining Star," and still more followed. *—Bill Dahl*

For You and Yours: Golden Carnival Classics, Pt. 2 / Apr. 24, 1990 / Collectables ♦♦♦♦♦

For many Manhattans fans, their earliest singles for Carnival were their greatest. These featured the wondrous George "Smitty" Smith, a young Blue Lovett, and some classic heartbreak and anguished soul singles, such as the divine "I Wanna Be (Your Everything)." These haven't been available on anthologies very often, and haven't been available anywhere since the early days of the Solid Smoke series. While Collectables' reissues sometimes leave a lot to be desired in the sound category, these songs are so good and so rare that any anthology featuring them has to get the highest recommendation, regardless of technical merit. This is the second of two volumes covering this era. *—Ron Wynn*

• **Dedicated to You: Golden Carnival Classics, Pt. 1** / Apr. 24, 1990 / Collectables ♦♦♦♦♦

The first of two superb volumes covering the Manhattans' early years on the Carnival label, the period many regard as their greatest. While they didn't come close to equaling the crossover/pop success they would enjoy with Columbia in their second incarnation, these were the pure soul works. The group featured both a glorious George "Smitty" Smith and young Blue Lovett, and their songs were produced solely with soul/R&B audiences in mind. There was little of the slick, polished orchestrations or smooth arrangements that were the hallmark of the Columbia hits. Instead, Smith's aching, soaring leads and the group's alternately mellow and frenzied harmonies were the high points. No matter what the sound quality, both this album and its counterpart are essential purchases for soul fans. *—Ron Wynn*

• **Kiss and Say Goodbye: The Best of the Manhattans:** / Oct. 31, 1995 / Columbia/Legacy ♦♦♦♦♦

The Best of the Manhattans: Kiss and Say Goodbye is a terrific, 19-song overview of the Manhattans' recordings for Columbia in the '70s. All but two of the group's Top Ten R&B hits for the label are featured—there's no "We Never Danced to a Love Song" or "Crazy," but "There's No Me Without You," "Don't Take Your Love," "Hurt," "Kiss and Say Goodbye," "I Kinda Miss You," "It Feels So Good to Be Loved So Bad," "Am I Losing You" and "Shining Star" are all present—and several fine lesser-known singles and album tracks are added for good measure. Although the collection might be a bit too extensive for casual fans, it's the definitive overview of the Manhattans' time as a smooth soul group, illustrating how they helped develop the quiet storm subgenre. *—Stephen Thomas Erlewine*

Love Songs / Jan. 18, 2000 / Columbia/Legacy ♦♦♦

Like Sony's other *Love Songs* compilations, this one runs the risk of overlapping too much with greatest-hits discs for some consumers' tastes. Seven of the 13 tracks here are on *The Best of the Manhattans: Kiss and Say Goodbye*, which, like *Love Songs*, surveys their recordings from the 1970s and early 1980s for Columbia. Still, this collection does retrieve three R&B chart singles that eluded *The Best of the Manhattans*...: "We Never Danced to a Love Song," "Girl of My Dream," and "The Way We Were/Memories." The disc is filled out by a couple of album tracks and their 1972 single "A Million to One," which was actually on the Deluxe label. *—Richie Unterberger*

Manic Street Preachers

f. 1991

Brit-pop, Alternative Pop/Rock

Dressed in glam clothing, wearing heavy eyeliner and shouting political rhetoric, the Manic Street Preachers emerged from their hometown of Blackwood, Wales in 1991 as self-styled "Generation Terrorists." Fashioning themselves after the Clash and the Sex Pistols, the Manics were on a mission, intending to restore revolution to rock & roll at a time when Britain was dominated by trancy shoegazers and faceless, trippy acid-house. Their self-consciously dangerous image, leftist leanings, crunching hard rock, and outsider status made them favorites of the British music press and helped them build a rabidly dedicated following. For much of the band's early career, it was impossible to separate the rhetoric from the music and even from the members themselves—the group's image was forever associated with lyricist/guitarist Richey James carving the words "4 Real" into his arm during an early interview. As the British pop music climate shifted toward Brit-pop in the wake of Suede, the Manics didn't achieve fame, but they had notoriety. Legions of followers emerged, including many bands that formed the core of the short-lived "new wave of new wave" movement. But as the group climbed toward stardom, the story didn't get simpler—it got weirder. James' behavior became increasingly bizarre, culminating on the group's harrowing 1994 album, *The Holy Bible*. Early in 1995, James disappeared, leaving no trace of his whereabouts. The remaining trio carried on with 1996's *Everything Must Go*, the album that established them as superstars in England, yet that came at the expense of the arrogant, renegade gender-bending and revolutionary rhetoric that earned them their initial fan base. *—Stephen Thomas Erlewine*

Generation Terrorists / Feb. 1992 / Columbia ♦♦♦♦

Debut albums rarely come as ambitious as the Manic Street Preachers' *Generation Terrorists*. Released in England as a double album (it was trimmed to the length of a single record in America), the album teemed with slogans, political rhetoric, and scarily inarticulate angst. Since the Manics deliver these charged lyrics as heavy guitar-rockers, the music doesn't always hit quite as forcefully as intended. The relatively polished production and big guitar sound occasionally sell the music short, especially the lesser songs, yet the Manics' passion is undeniable, even on the weaker cuts. While the album is loaded with a little bit too much unrealized material in retrospect, its best moments—the fiery "Slash N' Burn," "Little Baby Nothing," the incendiary "Stay Beautiful," the sardonic "You Love Us," and the haunting "Motorcycle Emptiness"—capture the Manics in all their raging glory. *—Stephen Thomas Erlewine*

Gold Against the Soul / Jun. 1993 / Columbia ♦♦♦

Taking the hard rock inclinations of *Generation Terrorists* to an extreme, the Manic Street Preachers delivered a flawed but intriguing second album with *Gold Against the Soul*. Inspired by Guns & Roses, the Manics decided to rework their working-class angst as heavy arena rock; they seize upon the latent politicism of Guns & Roses' tortured white-trash metal, interpreting it as a call to arms. Since the Manics are more intellectual and revolutionary than the Gunners, *Gold Against the Soul* burns with inspired, if confused, rhetoric. The Manics, however, aren't quite as gifted with hooks at this stage—their power derives from their self-belief, which they can't quite translate into songs. They are given a bigger, louder production on *Gold Against the Soul*, which makes the album a more visceral listen than *Generation Terrorists*, but the songs aren't as consistently compelling as those on the debut. "From Despair to Where" is a vibrant anthem, and "Drug Drug Druggy," "Roses in the Hospital," "Yourself," and "Sleepflower" all have a similar energy, but the peaks don't arrive quite as frequently as before. Nevertheless, the rage is more articulate and the sound is stronger, making *Gold Against the Soul* a flawed but worthy step forward. *—Stephen Thomas Erlewine*

The Holy Bible / Aug. 1994 / Epic ♦♦♦♦♦

It's difficult not to look at *The Holy Bible* as Richey James' last will and testament, yet that only makes the record all the more powerful. A remarkable step forward from the Manic Street Preachers' first two records, *The Holy Bible* is a tense, harrowing collection of tortured, cryptic declarations of depression—the diary of anorexia "4st 7lb" is one of the most chilling songs in rock & roll. James' lyrics, which are punctuated by Nicky Wire's political tirades, are unflinching in their bleakness. Every song has a passage frightening in its imagery. Although the music itself isn't as scarily intense, its tight, terse hard rock and glam hooks accentuate the paranoia behind the songs, making the lyrics cut deeper. *—Stephen Thomas Erlewine*

• **Everything Must Go** / May 1996 / Epic ♦♦♦♦♦

Months after the release of the harrowing *The Holy Bible*, Manic Street Preachers guitarist Richey James disappeared, leaving no trace of his whereabouts or his well-being. Ultimately, the remaining trio decided to carry on, releasing their fourth album *Everything Must Go* in 1996. Considering the tragic circumstances that surrounded it, *Everything Must Go* is the strongest, most focused, and certainly the most optimistic album the Manics ever released. Five of the songs feature lyrics Richey left behind before his disappearance, and while offering no motivation for his actions, they do hint at the depths of his despair. Nicky Wire wrote the remaining lyrics, and his songs give the record its weight and balance, confronting the issue of Richey's disappearance in a roundabout way, never explicitly mentioning the topic but offering a gritty dose of realistic optimism offering the hope that things *will* get better; after the nihilism of *The Holy Bible*, the outlook is all the more inspiring. Furthermore, the Manics' musical attack has become leaner; their music still rages, but it's channeled into concise, anthemic rock songs that soar on their own belief. Above all, *Everything Must Go* is a cathartic experience—it is genuinely moving to hear the Manics offering hope without sinking to mawkish sentimentality or collapsing under the weight of their situation. *—Stephen Thomas Erlewine*

This Is My Truth Tell Me Yours / Aug. 25, 1998 / Virgin ♦♦♦♦

If *Everything Must Go* found Manic Street Preachers coping with Richey James' sudden, unexplained disappearance, its follow-up, *This Is My Truth, Tell Me Yours*, finds them putting the tragedy behind them and flourishing as a trio. Wisely, the group builds on the grand sound of *Everything Must Go*, creating a strangely effective fusion of string-drenched, sweeping arena rock and impassioned, brutally honest punk. Since the band never writes about anything less than major issues, whether it be political or personal, it's appropriate that their music sounds as majestic and overpowering as their pretensions. Given that the first single was titled "If You Tolerate This, Then Your Children Will Be Next," calling the Manics pretentious is fair game, but they make their pretensions work through a blend of intelligence, passion, and sheer musicality. *This Is My Truth* sports more musical variety than its predecessors, which means it can meander a bit, particularly toward the end. Nevertheless, these misgivings disappear with repeated listens, as each song logically flows into the next. If the album ultimately isn't as raw or shattering as *The Holy Bible* or emotionally wrenching as *Everything Must Go*, it's because the ghost of Richey has been put behind them. That doesn't mean that *This Is My Truth* is light, easygoing listening—the portentous, murky closer "SYMM" guarantees that—but it's not as torturous as its immediate predecessors. But what it shares with them is a searing passion and intelligence that is unmatched among their peers on either side of the ocean—and, in doing so, it emphasizes the Manics' uniqueness as one of the few bands of the '90s that can deliver albums as bracing intellectually as they are sonically. *—Stephen Thomas Erlewine*

Know Your Enemy / Mar. 19, 2001 / Virgin ♦♦♦

The massive success of the Manics' post-Richey James albums put them in an awkward position. They were always known for their agit-prop and political posturing, which sometimes enhanced their music, sometimes distracted from it, sometimes saved it. But, as their star began to rise and Nicky Wire became the group's chief writer, they lost some of their bile and bite—just as their music turned into lush arena rock. So, even if the sales and reviews were good, it was time to strike back with a harsh, political record—hence, *Know Your Enemy.* This is the album where the Manics tie all their disparate strands together, up the political ante, try new things, all in an attempt to prove they're still vital. When it works, this can be pretty invigorating, but when it doesn't, it's utterly maddening. The push and pull of the ridiculous and the passionate have always made the Manics a fascinating band, but here, it teeters precariously between sublime and silly. The Manics sound the most convincing when they return to raging rockers, or on their sweeping mid-tempo arena ballads. When they stretch, they fall on their face. Now, the Manics, under James and Wire alike, have always walked this line (particularly on *The Holy Bible,* where it worked because of the intense rage of the lyrics and music), but here the targets seem a little lazy and obvious, and since they pour out over the course of a record that runs an interminable 74 minutes, they no longer seem like quirks, they seem like crutches. They severely harm a record that rocks harder, sounds better, than anything since James disappeared—but lacks the sense of craft that made *Everything Must Go* a minor masterpiece. *—Stephen Thomas Erlewine*

Barry Manilow (Barry Alan Pincus)

b. Jun. 17, 1946, Brooklyn, NY

Vocals, Piano / Soft Rock, Adult Contemporary

Although he has never earned the respect of critics or much of the public, Barry Manilow was one of the most successful recording artists of the '70s. Manilow began his pop music career by writing advertising jingles in the '60s; during this time, the Juilliard-trained musician honed his pop instincts, as evidenced by the sheer number of successful advertisements he wrote. In 1971, he began accompanying Bette Midler on piano as she performed in New York City's gay bathhouses. Manilow arranged her first two albums, which helped him earn a record contract with Bell. His self-titled first album was a flop, yet his second featured the number one ballad "Mandy."

"Mandy" began a decade's worth of polished MOR hits for Manilow, which included the number one singles "I Write the Songs" and "Looks Like We Made It," as well as Top Tens "Could It Be Magic," "Copacabana (At the Copa)," and "I Made It Through the Rain." Manilow also became a popular live act during this time. By the mid-'80s, he decided to broaden his musical horizons by making records of jazz and pop standards. At the end of the decade, the widow of Johnny Mercer invited him to set music to a number of the great songwriter's unpublished lyrics. Manilow continued in a similar vein on the records *Singin' With the Big Bands* (1994) and *Another Life* (1995), before he made the nostalgia-drenched *Summer of '78* in 1996. *Sings Sinatra* followed two years later. *—Stephen Thomas Erlewine*

Live / May 1977 / Arista ♦♦♦♦

Live was Barry Manilow's only number one album, selling over three million copies, and aside from his greatest-hits collections, it was also his most consistent. In fact, *Live* was pretty close to a greatest-hits collection itself, covering most of Manilow's biggest chart successes up to 1977 and including a few of his stronger album cuts as well (primarily from *This One's for You*). The real treats for fans are a couple of medleys: one a jazz/boogie workout culminating in the theme from *American Bandstand* and the other a series of the high-profile advertising jingles Manilow penned before getting his big break as a solo performer (for products like Dr. Pepper, Kentucky Fried Chicken, State Farm, McDonald's, and others). Manilow delivers tight, professional, totally unselfconscious performances, maintaining his energy all through the double-LP set. It's arguably his strongest effort. *—Steve Huey*

● **Greatest Hits, Vol. 1** / Nov. 1978 / Arista ♦♦♦♦

The first half of the 1978 two-record set *Greatest Hits,* the CD issue of *Greatest Hits, Vol. 1* contains ten tracks from Manilow's '70s prime; however, since it's incomplete without the material on *Vol. 2,* those looking for a more or less definitive overview will need both volumes. For those who want more, the rest of this period's worthwhile songs not on these two volumes can be found on *Live.* *—Steve Huey*

Greatest Hits, Vol. 2 / Nov. 1983 / Arista ♦♦♦♦

The second half of the 1978 two-record set *Greatest Hits,* the CD issue of *Greatest Hits, Vol. 2* contains nine tracks from Manilow's '70s prime; however, since it's incomplete without the material on *Vol. 1,* those looking for a more or less definitive overview will need both volumes. For those who want more, the rest of this period's worthwhile songs not found on these two volumes can be heard on *Live.* *—Steve Huey*

Greatest Hits, Vol. 3 / 1989 / Arista ♦♦♦♦

Manilow's third volume of *Greatest Hits* is less essential than the first two, covering mostly selections from his less successful post-'70s career (*One Voice* onward). This isn't his most popular or memorable material, but it is a handy overview of his more uneven early-'80s career for fans who want to dig a little deeper but don't want to search out those albums. *—Steve Huey*

Aimee Mann

b. Aug. 9, 1960

Vocals, Guitar, Bass / Pop Underground, Adult Alternative Pop/Rock, Singer/Songwriter

During the '80s, Aimee Man led the post-new wave pop group, Til Tuesday. After releasing three albums with the group, Mann broke up the band and embarked on a solo career. Her first solo album, *Whatever,* was a more introspective, folk-tinged effort than Til Tuesday's albums and received uniformly positive reviews upon its release in the summer of 1993. Early in 1995, Mann had a modest hit with "That's Just What You Are," a song included on the soundtrack to the television series, *Melrose Place.* After her long dispute with former label Imago was finally settled, she signed with DGC Records. Mann's second album, *I'm With Stupid,* was released in England in the late fall of 1995 and in January of 1996 in America. Again, it was greeted to positive reviews, but weak sales. *—Stephen Thomas Erlewine*

Whatever / May 11, 1993 / Geffen ♦♦♦♦♦

On her solo debut *Whatever,* the former vocalist for Til Tuesday cements her position as a center-stage artist and top-notch songwriter, and Aimee Mann's blend of wit, smarts, cynicism, and downright humability make for a wonderfully pleasing collection of catchy songs. Musically, the jangle-pop feel of *Whatever* harkens back to the Beatles and the Byrds but without forsaking its contemporary origin. Lyrically, it is often hard to know whether Mann is spilling her guts out over a love or a deal gone bad. In fact, it is often a combination. But the seamless ease with which she tells the tales, moving from her head to her heart and back again, exposes her mighty talent. Teaming with some of her former bandmates, including longtime collaborator Jon Brion, gives Mann a comfort and a sure footing from which to climb and stretch, which she does with certainty. "I Should've Known," "Could've Been Anyone," and "Say Anything" get the heads bobbing, while the more somber "4th of July" and "Stupid Thing" will beckon forth even the loneliest of hankies. And how many artists pay tribute to Charles Dickens? (Witness "Jacob Marley's Chain.") Talk about literate songwriters and you have to speak of Aimee Mann. The dismissive tone of the title belies the time that was put into this album, for even after its recording, it took Mann quite a long while to find a home. Initially released on Imago Records, *Whatever* was later reissued by Geffen Records. *—Kelly McCartney*

I'm With Stupid / Nov. 1995 / Geffen ♦♦♦

From the opening of "Long Shot," with its rolling hip-hop-derived beat and its nonchalant profanity, it's clear that Aimee Mann is trying to appeal to a wider audience with her second solo album, *I'm With Stupid.* Taking her cues from Liz Phair and Beck, she adds alternative rock flourishes to her music but she never abandons her love of the basic, three-minute pop single. Mann builds from the more pop-oriented songs on *Whatever,* incorporating her confessional singer/songwriter instincts into the pop songs while working with a more adventerous production and instrumentation. Occasionally, the fusion is a bit awkward, but the best moments on *I'm With Stupid*—the sighing "Choice in the Matter," the nearly perfect "That's Just What You Are," featuring backing vocals by Glenn Tilbrook, and the Bernard Butler collaboration "Sugarcoated"—surpass even the best moments on *Whatever.* However, *I'm With Stupid* falls short of matching Mann's debut for consistent song quality—there are several tracks that are pleasant but simply don't lead anywhere. Nevertheless, the album confirms that she is a distinctive, talented songwriter. At her best, she is as capable of melding melody with intelligent lyrics as her idols Elvis Costello, Difford/Tilbrook, and Ray Davies. *—Stephen Thomas Erlewine*

● **Bachelor No. 2** / May 2, 2000 / Superego ♦♦♦♦♦

It's no shock that *Bachelor No. 2, or the last remains of the dodo* sounds identical to her songs for Paul Thomas Anderson's *Magnolia,* since it was written and recorded at roughly the same time (the two records share four songs). Yet *Bachelor No. 2* is hardly a retread, having its own identity and flow; it's more intimate, a little more fragile, a little more craftmanslike—more like an Aimee Mann record, really. That, of course, is not a bad thing, especially since Mann has never sounded as assured as she does here, nor has she ever had a better set of songs. Surprisingly, this cohesive album was produced by a handful of different producers and Mann collaborated with three songwriters (Jon Brion being the most noteworthy of both categories). It sounds like the work of one writer and one production team, which is testament to the fact that Mann has finally found the ideal sound to match her literate, mildly self-deprecating, clever, melancholy, melodic style. *Bachelor No. 2* is crisp, clear, and direct, but deceptive. It's hardly a guitar-and-voice record, there are layers of details in the arrangements, particularly in how the various guitars and keyboards weave seamlessly together. There has never been a better sound for her songs, and she's never been more consistently compelling as a writer either. To call *Bachelor No. 2* a masterpiece may be overstating the matter somewhat, since an album this unassuming (but not unconfident) is too intimate to be labeled as such, yet it isn't hyperbole to call it the finest record Mann has made to date. *—Stephen Thomas Erlewine*

Ultimate Collection / Sep. 12, 2000 / Hip-O ♦♦♦♦♦

Unable to get an album released between 1995 and 1999, Aimee Mann suddenly had three on the market within 12 months, including this September 2000 compilation. There is, of course, a certain irony that the current configuration of a record company that gave her so much trouble (demanding changes to her third album, refusing to release it, dropping her, and then forcing her to buy back the album's master tapes) is now attempting to cash in on the exposure she received due to her 1999 Academy Award nomination for "Save Me" from *Magnolia.* Mann's music is catchy, guitar-based pop/rock, which *sounds* like it should be at the top of the charts. But since Mann has reached the Top 40 only twice in 15 years, she has largely been subject to standard operating procedure in the major-label record business. Journalists have howled largely on critical grounds, and *Ultimate Collection* should give them more ammunition despite its limits. One of her two hits, "What About Love," is not included, and only three tracks have been licensed from her most popular period. Two regular albums doesn't seem like much material to choose from for a best-of, so to make up for the limited choice of material, compilation producer Rhonda Shields has pulled a variety of stray tracks, turning this into a virtual rarities album. Several songs were contributed to movie soundtracks, and five tracks are drawn from the non-LP B-sides of singles. Thus, even those who have copies of *Whatever* and *I'm With Stupid* will need this album, and they will find that the rarities are some of her better performances. Aimee Mann is unquestionably one of the most impressive singer/songwriters of her time, but her lyrics of bitter romantic complaint may destine her to a limited audience. *—William Ruhlmann*

Manfred Mann (Manfred Lubowitz)

b. Oct. 21, 1940, Johannesburg, South Africa

Vocals, Keyboards / Jazz-Rock, Pop/Rock, British Invasion, Prog-Rock/Art Rock

The scion of a wealthy South African family, Manfred Lubowitz recognized while still a teenager that his real interests lay far from Johannesburg and its white-dominated culture—rather, he wanted to play jazz and blues. To do this, he ultimately had to leave South Africa for England, where he picked up a new stage name, Manfred Manne (the last name borrowed from Shelly Manne), later Manfred Mann. He also found a friend and collaborator in one Mike Hugg, a drummer with whom he formed a band that—against his wishes—was ultimately christened Manfred Mann. The various incarnations of Manfred Mann, playing jazz and R&B-based rock and later pop-rock and progressive rock, lasted until 1971, when the man took back his name. Future group names, mostly designated Manfred Mann's Earth Band, would have an apostrophe attached to his name, as Mann also embarked on a career as a producer and songwriter. He has also released recordings designated as solo projects, usually under the title "Manfred Mann's Plain Music." *—Bruce Eder*

☆ **The Five Faces of Manfred Mann** / Sep. 11, 1964 / EMI ♦♦♦♦♦

The debut album by Manfred Mann holds up even better 40 years on than it did in 1964. It's also one of the longest LPs of its era, clocking in at 39 minutes, and there's not a wasted note or a song extended too far among its 14 tracks. The Manfreds never had the reputation that the Rolling Stones enjoyed, which is a shame, because *The Five Faces of Manfred Mann* is one of the great blues-based British invasion albums; it's a hot, rocking record that benefits from some virtuoso playing as well, and some of the best singing of its era, courtesy of Paul Jones, who blew most of his rivals out of the competition with his magnificently impassioned, soulful performance on "Untie Me," and his simmering, lusty renditions of "Smokestack Lightning" and "Bring It to Jerome." The stereo mix of the album, which never surfaced officially in England until this 1997 EMI anniversary reissue (remastered in 24-bit digital sound), holds up very nicely, with sharp separation between the channels yet—apart from a few moments on "Untie Me"—few moments of artificiality. *—Bruce Eder*

The Manfred Mann Album / 1964 / Ascot ♦♦♦

Manfred Mann's debut full-length U.S. platter was probably their strongest, and indeed one of the stronger British Invasion albums of the very competitive year of 1964. Besides the smash "Do Wah Diddy Diddy," it contained a number of fine soul and R&B covers. Standouts were the versions of "Untie Me" and Ike & Tina Turner's "It's Gonna Work Out Fine," as well as the strong pounding Paul Jones original, "Without You." *—Richie Unterberger*

My Little Red Book of Winners / 1965 / Ascot ♦♦♦♦

One of Manfred Mann's finest early records, *My Little Red Book of Winners* was, aside from being a fine album that captured the band's early sensibility, a highly influential record. The hit song "My Little Red Book," an excellent arrangement of the Bacharah/David masterpiece, was included in the hit movie *What's New Pussycat*. It was there that Love's lead singer Arthur Lee first heard it, and then arranged it for his band. Lee also aped a sense of style and phrasing from Mann's lead singer Paul Jones, and did so to great effect. The rest of this record is equally brilliant in spots. "The One in the Middle," an excellent mid-tempo blues from Jones, proved what a fine and witty songwriter he was. Other covers on the album include "Oh No, Not My Baby" and "With God on Our Side," which illustrate how efffectively the band could capture any style and make it their own. *—Matthew Greenwald*

Mann Made / 1965 / HMV ♦♦♦♦♦

The group's second British album, released just as the original lineup was entering a state of collapse with the impending departure of two key members, shows some of the changes that can happen in a year as they move away from Chess Records' brand of blues as their bass line. Instead, they produce a sound that slightly smoother and a lot more soulful. A handful of originals, mostly by Mike Vickers and Mike Hugg with one Paul Jones-authored number thrown in, are scattered amid covers of songs originated by the Temptations, the Skyliners, and T-Bone Walker. If it isn't as fierce, bold, or daringly ambitious as the Manfreds' debut long-player, *Mann Made* is just as much a virtuoso effort, and a surprisingly cohesive one considering that it was released immediately after Mike Vickers and Paul Jones announced their respective departures from the band. The 1997 EMI 100th Anniversary series edition features 24-bit digital EMI CD remastering that is as sharp and clean as one could possibly hope for. *—Bruce Eder*

Soul of Mann / 1967 / See For Miles ♦♦♦

Amidst their pop/rock, blues, and folk-rock, Manfred Mann peppered their early recordings with jazzy instrumentals that faintly suggested a jazz-rock direction. *Soul of Mann* is a compilation which EMI put together in the wake of the group's departure from the label for Fontana Records. It is made up of most of these early instrumental efforts, which originally appeared scattered about on various singles, EPs, and LPs between 1963 and 1966 (though one song, "L.S.D.," is actually a blues-rocker with a Paul Jones vocal). This collection is more interesting than you might think, despite the presence of a lot of repeated material; *Soul of Mann* is not only a very good album, but also the group's single most jazz-oriented release. No one would put Manfred Mann on the level of genuine American jazz acts like Oscar Peterson, but these cuts are executed with a surprising amount of style and wit. The Manfreds were nothing if not eclectic, producing downright strange instrumental takes on "Satisfaction," "I Got You Babe," and "My Generation." There are straighter (but still imaginative) versions of songs by the Yardbirds and Cannonball Adderley, as well as their own originals (the bluesy stomper "Mr. Anello," featuring Tom McGuinness on lead guitar, is a standout). Mike Vickers, Mike Hugg, and Manfred Mann also show their particular indebtedness to Milt Jackson and the Modern Jazz Quartet on several of these sides. Manfred Mann fans will find this worth picking up, especially given that several of the tracks never came out in the U.S., such as the aforementioned "Mr. Anello" and all of the pop covers they did for the 1966 EP *Instrumental Asylum*. The 1999 EMI reissue includes both the mono and stereo mixes of the album, remastered in 24-bit digital sound. (British import) *—Richie Unterberger & Bruce Eder*

Chapter Three, Vol. 1 / 1969 / Polydor ♦♦♦♦

It's light years from the airy pop of "Do Wah Diddy Diddy," recorded by the hit-making first group formed by South African Manfred Mann and Mike Hugg in 1963. This is as much jazz as rock. There's hardly any guitar, but a swaggering horn section compensates. Imagine a darker, moodier Traffic with Mann manning the organ instead of Steve Winwood. Hugg's raspy vocals are featured on the first album recorded with the new band. The standout tracks are the album-opening "Travelling Lady" and "Time," but they are hardly the only strong ones. *—Mark Allan*

The Roaring Silence / 1976 / Warner Brothers ♦♦♦♦♦

A later edition of Mann's band, which had a '70s hit with Bruce Springsteen's "Blinded by the Light" (on this album). *—William Ruhlmann*

The R&B Years / 1982 / See For Miles ♦♦♦♦♦

The Manfreds always took great pains to point out that their true love was R&B and jazz, not the pop/rock they sang on their hit singles, although they should have realized that their fans dug both approaches. Anyway, this 20-song compilation is a good taste of their purer sounds, taken from LPs, EPs, and singles cut by the band during the Paul Jones era (1963-66). Look to EMI's fine *Best of Manfred Mann* CD for the big hits; this has covers of R&B and soul cuts by the likes of Willie Dixon, Muddy Waters, and Screamin' Jay Hawkins, as well as some more-than-competent group originals in the same vein. "I'm Your Kingpin," "Without You," and "Hubble Bubble (Toil and Trouble)" rank among the better early self-penned British R&B, and their cover of Ben E. King's "Groovin'" is a stormer. Although Manfred Mann weren't quite as fine R&B interpreters as fellow British Invaders the Stones, Yardbirds, and Animals, they were quite respectable, and this is a good complement to the more wide-ranging EMI anthology. *—Richie Unterberger*

● **The Best of Manfred Mann: The Definitive Collection** / Jun. 2, 1992 / EMI America ♦♦♦♦♦

This is one of nearly a dozen anthologies of Manfred Mann's music that cover their EMI period, and the 25 songs here make it the biggest of them. Additionally, there is an 11-minute interview with the band here, dating from December of 1964, that has never before appeared on record in the United States. The hits are all here, sometimes in more than one version, along with a cross-section of album tracks and B-sides, and it all sounds very good, though EMI's recent 24-bit remasterings of the band's original British LPs are much more impressive. But this CD misses being "definitive" because it leaves out some key B-sides to their early singles and overlooks the contents of several top-selling British EPs. The truth be told, no single CD, even one 73 minutes long, would be adequate to the task of defining this group's history or sound, even just covering the years 1963-66. As it is, the presence here of numbers like "She" and "The One in the Middle" (both written by Paul Jones) and their version of "My Little Red Book" (not a favorite of the band members, incidentally), makes this an essential part of any collection of the band's work, but one should also own *The Singles Plus* to get access to numbers like "Groovin'" and "Brother Jack," and the individual U.K. albums have enough merit to make them every bit as essential. In fairness, *The Definitive Collection* is the most thoroughly annotated compilation of the group's work to surface as of the year 2000, and the group interview, though superficial and awkward, makes it unique. *—Bruce Eder*

Chapter Two: The Best of the Fontana Years / Oct. 11, 1994 / Fontana ♦♦♦

The departure of Paul Jones for a solo career in 1966 spelled major reorganization for Manfred and his troops, who recruited lead vocalist Mike D'Abo and bassist (and Beatle chum) Klaus Voormann. To the surprise of many, the new lineup rattled off seven Top Ten British hits in the next three years in a far less R&B-oriented style. Emphasizing harmonies and Manfred Mann's inventiveness as arranger and keyboardist (often employing the then-futuristic Mellotron), this represented the group's most commercial phase, with an upbeat approach that bordered on downright chipper. These 20 tracks include all the key singles from this time, as well as a few LP cuts. Frankly, this rather lightweight, prototypically cheery late-'60s British pop—sounding rather like a more commercial version of the *Odessey & Oracle*-era Zombies—hasn't aged nearly as well as their far gutsier Paul Jones-era recordings. Only one of these songs was a hit in the U.S., but it was a big one—their great 1968 arrangement of the then-unreleased Bob Dylan song "The Mighty Quinn." *—Richie Unterberger*

The Best of Manfred Mann's Earth Band / 1996 / Warner Archives ♦♦♦

Groovin' with the Manfreds (The Manfred Mann R&B Album) / 1996 / EMI ♦♦♦♦

The 26 songs here represent a slightly better investment than the See For Miles Records R&B collection by the Manfreds, as well as newer remasterings (by 14 years) of the same material. The notes by Paul Jones also provide an inside perspective, as well as a funny account of his entry into the band (and offer an incidental defense of Bo Diddley's underrated complexity as a writer and influence on the Manfreds). Songs include "Smokestack Lightning," "Hoochie Coochie Man," "Got My Mojo Working," "Groovin'," "Watermelon Man," "I Put a Spell on You," and a bunch of other standards and originals. The only frustration is the presence of a shot of the band playing at the Marquee, which makes one wish all the more that somebody had recorded one of their shows at the time. The group's command of R&B and blues improved as they went on—it was always little strange hearing an outfit as non-guitar-dominated as the Manfreds do some of this stuff, with lots of vibraphone and organ, not to mention sax—all of which, along with their jazz roots, separated them from the Stones, Yardbirds, et al. But by the time of "Down the Road Apiece," they were making it work close to 100 percent of the time. —*Bruce Eder*

- **The Best of the EMI Years** / Jan. 23, 1996 / Griffin ♦♦♦♦♦
This double-CD replaces EMI's *Best Of* anthology (1992) as the collection of choice for their British Invasion years due to its slightly more extensive length (34 tracks), including most of the tracks on the previous compilation. It has all of the British and American hits, as well as some standout B-sides and album tracks, some of which have been quite hard to come by on reissues. Classic British Invasion music by one of the most versatile bands of the era, comfortable with both straight pop/rock and jazz-tinged R&B. —*Richie Unterberger*

Manfred Mann Album/Five Faces of Manfred Mann / Feb. 20, 1996 / EMI ♦♦♦♦♦
A CD reissue of their first two albums, with a few bonus tracks, most notably a previously unreleased version of "Sticks and Stones" and the instrumental "Mr. Anello," which was included on their U.K. debut LP, but left off its stateside counterpart. Very good British Invasion music, though most of the best songs are available on Griffin's *The Best of the EMI Years.* —*Richie Unterberger*

BBC Sessions / Nov. 3, 1998 / EMI ♦♦♦
This 24-song collection of tracks recorded for the BBC from 1964-66 sounds very good, thanks to the Paul Jones-fronted lineup (although a few of the songs are instrumentals). Of most interest are four tunes the band never released in the 1960s, including a version of "Parchman Farm" that features only Jones and his harmonica, and the obscure, mediocre Barry-Greenwich composition "That's the Way I Feel." More unexpected are a couple of Jones originals the band never did in the studio, the bluesy and derivative "I Need You" and "It Took a Little While." There's no "Doo Wah Diddy Diddy," but most of the other big mid-'60s hits are played ("Sha La La," "Come Tomorrow," "Pretty Flamingo," "If You Gotta Go, Go Now"), as well as some of their better LP and EP cuts. This is recommended a little above the usual BBC archive compilation, because Manfred Mann played extremely well live, and because there are actually some notable changes from the familiar studio arrangements from time to time. That's especially evident on "Machines," which is decisively better than the studio version; this take, powered by a great bass riff, even sounds strong enough to have been an off-the-wall hit single. —*Richie Unterberger*

Barbara Manning

b. San Diego, CA
Vocals, Guitar / Indie Rock, Alternative Pop/Rock, Singer/Songwriter
On her solo albums and work for SF Seals, Manning has proved herself an important voice in indie-rock. Based in San Francisco, she first proved herself on 1988's *Lately I Keep Scissors*, and released *One Perfect Green Blanket* in 1992. Other solo efforts include 1995's *Barbara Manning Sings with the Original Artists*, 1997's *1212*, 1998's *In New Zealand*, and 2000's *Homeless Is Where the Heart Is.* —*John Bush*

- **Lately I Keep Scissors** / 1988 / Heyday ♦♦♦♦♦
Her first full-length solo release features some of Barbara Manning's catchiest compositions, the most infectious of which include the poignant "Every Pretty Girl" and propulsive "Something You've Got (isn't good)." The bittersweet title track, "Scissors," features the sound of scissors opening and closing as part of the rhythm track (producing a lulling, metronome-like effect). Another notable track, "Mark E. Smith & Brix," is an ode to the leader of the Fall and his ex-wife/sometime collaborator. It's performed in the distinctively minimalist style of the Young Marble Giants and features another unique rhythmic touch—"sampler of coins crashing." —*Kathleen C. Fennessy*

Barbara Manning Sings With the Original Artists / 1995 / Feel Good All Over/Bar/None/Koch ♦♦♦♦
Barbara Manning Sings With the Original Artists is a somewhat slight but wholly enjoyable release from a short-lived "supergroup" consisting of vocalist Barbara Manning and members of Young Marble Giants (Stuart Moxham), the Mekons (Jon Langford), and others. The music has more of a retro/lounge feel than the folk-tinged pop with which Manning is usually associated. Further, she is only credited with one song ("Optimism Is Its Own Reward"), while Moxham and Langford penned the rest of the originals. "Cry Me a River" is a faithful, non-ironic cover of the Julie London classic (much like Grenadine's "I Only Have Eyes for You"), while "Martian Man" is a lovely Lora Logic (X-Ray Spex, Essential Logic) cover embellished with brass and sitar. As a whole, the recording evokes the same sort of insouciant ambience fellow lounge lizards Grenadine, Combustible Edison, and Friends of Dean Martinez were making around the same time (the mid-'90s). Similarly, the approach is more sincere than campy. Moxham's garage-y "Daddy Bully" breaks the mold—but not the mood—to some extent by taking as its inspiration Sam the Sham & the Pharoahs' '60s nugget "Wooly Bully." —*Kathleen C. Fennessy*

1212 / Jun. 10, 1997 / Matador ♦♦♦♦♦
For all of her past recorded output, Barbara Manning has never been the most prolific of composers, her many albums relying instead on her gifts as an interpreter of other writers' songs; the achievement of *1212* isn't simply that it's made up largely of Manning orig-

inals, but that chief among them is her most ambitious creation to date, a stunning four-part mini-rock opera known collectively as "The Arsonist Story." The chilling tale of a young firestarter told from a series of narrative angles, it's a major triumph both lyrically and musically, expanding upon the folk-pop basics of Manning's previous records to conjure a truly haunting and complex story of abuse and destruction. The other originals are excellent as well, and the covers are particularly well-chosen, especially a rendition of Richard Thompson's "End of the Rainbow" which makes for a fittingly bleak coda to "The Arsonist Story." —*Jason Ankeny*

Homeless Is Where the Heart Is / Jan. 18, 2000 / Naiv ♦♦♦♦

Under One Roof: Singles and Oddities / 2000 / Interstate ♦♦♦♦
Decent as an introduction, but probably better suited for the devoted fan, this 18-song, career-spanning set showcases the impressive eclecticism of Barbara Manning. From the Celtic-tinged cover of Paul McCartney's "Don't Let It Bring You Down" to the driving grunge pop of "Damned Lucky," Manning's talents as both a songwriter and song interpreter are in evidence. Culled from 7"s, compilations, previously unreleased tracks, and off-the-cuff outtakes, the collection may lack cohesiveness but ultimately triumphs by virtue of Manning's sincerity. Sure, a few too many tracks might fall firmly into the "oddity" category, such as a hilariously out-of-tune duet with Mad V. Dog on Hank Williams' "Baby We're Really in Love," but the general quality of these tracks prove that not all the great female songwriters of the '90s were in the Lilith Fair camp. —*Matt Fink*

You Should Know by Now / May 22, 2001 / Innerstate ♦♦♦
With this release, Barbara Manning made her debut recording with the Go-Luckys!, one of several groups she's fronted or been a part of since beginning her career. It was superior punk-poppish indie rock, with a harder rocking edge than some of her folkier recordings have employed. Her songs (often co-written with others, or, in the case of the instrumental "Boston Song," wholly written by Go-Luckys! Fabrizio and Flavio Steinbach) were wary negotiations of romance and the trials of coping with loneliness and pressure. They differed from many other indie rockers combing the same territory in that they remained open to better times and better situations, rather than reveling in or retreating into alienated postures. She was actually most effective when she got more specific and direct about her frustrations, as on "Never Made Love" and "Incapable," which had the best tunes of any of the songs on the record as well. Jeff Palmer's musical saw added occasionally goofy ambience that was rather at odds with the mostly somber outlook of the album. —*Jimmy James*

Mansun

f. 1995
Brit-pop, Neo-Prog
Arriving in the aftermath of Brit-pop, Mansun was one of the first British guitar bands to depart from the prevailing styles of the mid-'90s, leaving both light, Beatlesque pop and studied trad rock behind. Mansun had more in common with early-'90s bands like Suede and the Manic Street Preachers, groups that stood defiantly outside of the pop spotlight, yet managed to cultivate a devoted fan base. By combining a dark, grandiose vision with the driving intensity of hard rock and the stylish swagger of new romanticism, Mansun didn't sound a thing like their contemporaries. Led by guitarist/vocalist Paul Draper, Mansun formed in Chester, England, in the mid-'90s. Draper met Stove King (bass) at Wrexham Art College. The pair, who worked at a photo laboratory together, met Dominic Chad (lead guitar) at a local pub he was managing. The trio began playing, supported by a series of drummers. Early in 1996, the group released the limited-edition single "Take It Easy Chicken" on their own Sci Fi Hi Fi label, and it entered the play list for Radio 1. Initially, the U.K. music weeklies tagged Mansun as one of the crowd of post-Oasis, lad rock bands. Over the course of the year, the band released a series of singles, each more ambitious than the one before. By the end of the year, they had earned their first Melody Maker cover. In February of 1997, Mansun released their debut album, *Attack of the Grey Lantern*, on Parlophone Records. It unexpectedly entered the charts at number one, earning enthusiastic reviews in the process. By that time, Mansun had been hailed as one of the best new bands of the year, and the record was praised throughout the U.K. music press. —*Stephen Thomas Erlewine*

- **Attack of the Grey Lantern** / 1997 / Epic ♦♦♦♦♦
Opening with the swirling, cinematic strings of "The Chad Who Loved Me," Mansun's debut album *Attack of the Grey Lantern* is anything but a conventional Brit-pop record. Few debut records are this assured, especially when a group is developing such an idiosyncratic, individual style. Mansun recalls many artists—Suede, Manic Street Preachers, Tears for Fears, David Bowie, ABC, Blur, Prince—without sounding exactly like any of them. *Attack of the Grey Lantern* is a grandiose, darkly seductive blend of new wave and '90s indie rock, filled with phased guitars, drum machines, and subversive, off-kilter song structures, many of which wind past five minutes. No song is ever quite what it seems—"Mansun's Only Love Song" balances between soul and fractured pop, "Stripper Vicar" has new wave backing vocals and hard-rock chords, while "Taxloss" marries Suede's dark glam rock with uneasy psychedelia. It's an ambitious, even pretentious, record, but Mansun has enough confidence and skill to make it an astonishingly original debut. [The American edition of *Attack of the Grey Lantern*, however, is a bit of a different story. For some reason, the sequencing has been completely scrambled and "Stripper Vicar" has been replaced by the inferior early single "Take It Easy, Chicken." Since almost all of the songs were segued together and the album worked as a series of shifting sonic textures and moods, the re-sequenced album is simply a disaster, ludicrously robbing a fine concept album of its concept.] —*Stephen Thomas Erlewine*

Six / Apr. 20, 1999 / Epic ♦♦♦
Since Mansun's debut album *Attack of the Grey Lantern* was some sort of convoluted

song cycle, it shouldn't have been surprising that their second album, *Six*, felt like the second coming of prog rock. What was a surprise was the extent to which Mansun pushed the limits forward on the album. From the garish Marillion-styled artwork to the endlessly shifting, segued songs, *Six* fits into the grand tradition of prog rock, and it does tell some kind of a story, even if it's impossible to tell what that story may be. In fact, it's difficult to get into the music itself, even as it dazzles with its twists, turns, appropriations and recontextualizations. And, make no mistakes, *Six* is frequently dazzling, since Mansun skillfully melds classic prog and pop styles with contemporary ideas, including a healthy portion of electronica. It's a head-spinning listen, especially the first time through when it's impossible to tell where it's going or where it's going to end. That feeling doesn't quite let up on repeated listens, either, mainly because the record is so dense with impenetrable ideas—ideas that are confounding even when you think you understand where Paul Draper is going with the entire thing. On one scale, that's an impressive achievement, but it's diminished somewhat when you take into account that *Six* isn't particularly rewarding once you get a handle on it. Since it never reveals its secrets, or even its clues, it's hard to embrace the record, even for all of its many attributes. Still, *Six* is clearly the work of ambitious, gifted musicians who aren't willing to stay still, which is reason enough to try to come to terms with it. —*Stephen Thomas Erlewine*

Little Kix / Aug. 14, 2000 / Parlophone ♦♦♦

Mansun's *Little Kix* is an album of the joke being on them. *Attack of the Grey Lantern* brazenly screamed its melodies amidst the pomp and circumstance, *Six* showed that Marillion-like "concept" albums even had their place in the post-Britpop landscape, and on both attempts, the more Mansun seemed out of touch with the masses, the better off they were. Here, the band simply seems out of touch with themselves. As leadoff single "I Can Only Disappoint U" croons in with over-accented curls and turns, one notices that the band's characteristic over-production is turned down to outline the band's actual songwriting chops. Which is laudable. Yet, in "Soundtrack 4 2 Lovers" (spelled the New Edition way) or "Electric Man" (the most significant nod to Suede's "The Chemistry Between Us" in ages), a new, lovelorn Mansun is shown stripped of their highly divisive costuming of old—and their bare bodies are ugly. It's this album's simpler approach that shows them naked and floppy without their previous new romantic/prog-rock garments to hide their failings. With oafish lyrics carrying these semi-tunes along like "Video games, we have lost our souls/Bulldozer head 'cos we're stoned," there's a feeling that Mansun is grasping toward just about anything new for a sense of perspective. Admittedly, the band's commendable, urgent rises of orchestration still remain, which is a strong selling point. It's the feeling of a mistaken step that feels the most damaging. With future work with Paul Oakenfold, one hopes that *Little Kix* will merely be seen as a pause between superior albums. Indeed, as in the George Michael clap-along "Until the Next Life," Draper sings: "We were always acting out some drama." If he is to be believed, it's a fine time for them to get out of intermission and to start making plans for some new kind of pageant play. —*Dean Carlson*

Mantronix

f. 1984, New York, NY, **db.** 1991

Old School Rap, Electro, Club/Dance, House, Hip-Hop, Golden Age

Over and above their standing as one of the best and most innovative groups from hip-hop's golden age, Mantronix provided rap music with its first man-machine, Kurtis Mantronik. A turntable master who incorporated synthesizers and samplers into the rhythmatic mix instead of succumbing to the popular use of samples simply as pop hooks, Mantronik exploited technology with a quintessentially old-school attitude which had little use for instruction manuals and accepted use. After the hip-hop world began to catch up with Mantronik's developments, he moved from hardcore hip-hop to skirt the leading edge of club music, from electro to ragga, techno and house—boundaries increasingly fragile due to his pioneering efforts. With MC Tee on vocals, Mantronix debuted in 1985 with the single "Fresh Is the Word," a street and club hit around New York. The full-length *Mantronix: The Album* followed in 1986, paced by "Ladies" and "Basslines" a pair of crossovers that joined the first wave of hip-hop chartmakers in Britain. The increasing popularity of hip-hop gave Mantronix a chance at a major-label contract, and in 1988 the duo released their first album for Capitol, *In Full Effect*. Two additional albums followed, but Mantronix had effectively disbanded by 1991. Kurtis Mantronik began producing other acts, but returned later in the decade with a solo LP. —*John Bush*

★ **Mantronix: The Album** / 1985 / Sleeping Bag ♦♦♦♦♦

Curtis "Mantronik" Khaleel was often quoted as saying that his mission was to "take rap a step beyond the streets," and the innovative producer/mixmaster accomplished that goal on Mantronix's debut album, *Mantronix: The Album*. This excellent 1985 LP was way ahead of its time; while the rapping of Mantronix's partner MC Tee is pure mid-'80s New York hip-hop, the production is anything but conventional. On gems like "Needle to the Groove," "Bassline," and the hit "Fresh Is the Word," you can hear the parallels between Tee's rhyming and the East Coast b-boy rhymes that Run-D.M.C., L.L. Cool J, and the Fat Boys were providing in 1985. But *Mantronix: The Album*'s high-tech, futuristic production sets it apart from other New York hip-hop of the mid-'80s, and even though one of the LP's tracks is titled "Hardcore Hip-Hop," Mantronix had a hard time appealing to hip-hop's hardcore. *Mantronix: The Album* actually fared better in dance music, electro-funk, and club circles than it did among hardcore b-boys. But this is definitely a hip-hop record, and it is also Mantronix's most essential release. —*Alex Henderson*

Music Madness / 1986 / Sleeping Bag ♦♦♦♦♦

Many Mantronix fans will tell you that the group provided its best and most essential work when it was signed to the small Sleeping Bag label and MC Tee was still on board. Listening to *Music Madness*, it's hard to argue with that. This 1986 LP, which was Mantronix's second album and its last album before leaving Sleeping Bag for Capitol, is proof of how fresh-sounding and creative Mantronix was in the beginning. The futuristic outlook that defines "Scream," the single "Who Is It," and other tracks set *Music Madness* apart from other hip-hop albums that came from New York in 1986; Tee's rapping is very much in the 1980s b-boy tradition, but the club-minded producing and mixing of Curtis "Mantronik" Khaleel is unlike anything you would have heard on a Run-D.M.C. or L.L. Cool J album back then. And that fact wasn't lost on hip-hop's hardcore, which felt that *Music Madness* wasn't street enough. Mantronik was fond of saying that his goal was to "take rap a step beyond the streets," and this album tended to attract dance music and electro-funk lovers and club hounds more than hardcore hip-hoppers. *The Album* remains Mantronix's best album, but this excellent LP runs a close second. —*Alex Henderson*

In Full Effect / 1988 / Capitol ♦♦♦

This Should Move Ya / 1990 / Capitol ♦♦♦

The Incredible Sound Machine / Mar. 18, 1991 / Capitol ♦♦

The Best of Mantronix 1985-1999 / Mar. 15, 1999 / Virgin ♦♦♦♦♦

A solid Mantronix compilation (though U.K. only) for all those unable to find the out-of-print originals, *The Best of 1985-1999* includes undeniable hip-hop classics like "Bassline," "Ladies" and "King of the Beats" as well as a new single, "Push Yer Hands Up" (which had first appeared on Mantronik's 1998 solo album). —*John Bush*

The Mar-Keys

f. 1958, Memphis, TN

Southern Soul, Instrumental Rock, Soul

Despite scoring only one national hit, the 1961 instrumental smash "Last Night," the Mar-Keys remain one of the most important groups ever to emerge from the Memphis music scene. As the first house band for the legendary Stax label, they appeared on some of the greatest records in soul history, with their ranks also producing such renowned musicians as guitarist Steve Cropper and bassist Donald "Duck" Dunn. The Mar-Keys formed in 1958 and included drummer Terry Johnson, pianist Jerry Lee "Smoochie" Smith, saxophonists Don Nix and Charles Axton, and trumpeter Wayne Jackson in addition to Cropper and Dunn. Originally dubbed the Royal Spades, in 1960 the group joined the staff at Axton's mother Estelle's Satellite label, backing artists that included Rufus Thomas and his daughter Carla. A year later, the Mar-Keys headlined the Chips Moman-penned "Last Night," which reached the number three spot in the summer of 1961. When Satellite changed its name to Stax, the Mar-Keys remained on board, laying the foundation for the classic Memphis soul sound through with their funky, sophisticated grooves; concurrently they recorded a series of singles including "Pop-Eye Stroll," "The Morning After," and "Philly Dog," although none repeated the commercial success of "Last Night." In 1962 Cropper and Dunn left the lineup to co-found the famed Booker T. and the MG's. Other personnel changes followed, although the Mar-Keys continued on for several more years before the name was eventually dropped. Jackson then formed another top-notch session group, the Memphis Horns, while Axton led the Packers, scoring a 1965 hit with "Hole in the Wall." Nix, meanwhile, mounted a solo career, also producing records for artists including Freddie King, Jeff Beck, and Furry Lewis. —*Jason Ankeny*

The Mar-Keys / 1961 / Atlantic ♦♦♦

Do the Pop-Eye / 1962 / Atlantic ♦♦♦

Back to Back / 1967 / Atlantic ♦♦♦♦♦

Recorded live at Paris in 1967, when the Stax-Volt Revue was touring Europe. This is just about exactly what you'd expect: solid, straight-ahead live versions of the instrumental group's best-known tunes, in good sound. Booker T. & the MG's take seven of album's ten tracks, including their hits "Green Onions" and "Hip Hug-Her"; the Mar-Keys do "Last Night" and a couple of other numbers. —*Richie Unterberger*

Damifiknow! / 1969 / Stax ♦♦♦

For this session, the Mar-Keys were basically Booker T. & the MG's, augmented by trumpeter Wayne Jackson and tenor saxophonist Andrew Love (who would soon become the Memphis Horns). It's not quite fair to call this laid-back set easy listening, but it's certainly not much more than background listening as they wind their way through a mix of originals and covers of shopworn '60s tunes like "Mustang Sally," "Soul Man," and "Daydream." It's pleasant and executed with the expected precision, but it has to rate among the musicians' more secondary efforts, whether they're calling themselves the MG's or something else. The album was combined with the 1971 Mar-Keys LP *Memphis Experience* onto a single-CD reissue in 1994. —*Richie Unterberger*

Memphis Experience / 1971 / Stax ♦♦

● **Damifiknow!/Memphis Experience** / May 20, 1994 / Stax ♦♦♦♦

A two-for-one disc combining a couple strange releases, neither of which were truly the Mar-Keys. *Damnifiknow!* was played by Booker T. & the MG's, supplemented by a horn section that would become the Memphis Horns; *Memphis Experience* combined Mar-Keys outtakes with instrumentals by Memphis musicians with no connection to prior Mar-Keys lineups. It's a convenient way for major Stax/soul collectors to pick up two of the group's odder records, but it's not a representative reflection of the Mar-Keys. Nor is the music especially noteworthy: *Damifiknow!* is easygoing, rather humdrum soul instrumentals that don't pack nearly the punch of the MG's at their best, while *Memphis Experience* is average wordless early '70s soul-funk with occasional psychedelic/hard rock tinges. —*Richie Unterberger*

The Marcels

f. Pittsburgh, PA

Doo Wop, R&B

This Pittsburgh ensemble deserved a much better fate than being known primarily for a novelty-tinged cover of "Blue Moon." Baritone vocalist Richard F. Knauss teamed with Fred Johnson, Gene J. Bricker, Ron Mundy, and lead vocalist Cornelius Harp, an integrated ensemble. They named themselves after Harp's hairstyle, the marcel. The group did a string of covers as demo tapes that were sent to Colpix. The label's A&R director had them cut several oldies at RCA's New York studios in 1961, one of them being "Blue Moon." They used the bass intro arrangement from the Cadillacs' "Zoom" and the results were a huge hit. It eventually topped both the pop and R&B charts, and also was an international smash. The group eventually appeared in the film *Twist Around the Clock* with Dion and Chubby Checker. They eventually recorded an 18-cut LP for Colpix. Alan Johnson and Walt Maddox later replaced Knauss and Gene Bricker, making them an all-black unit. The group did score another Top Ten pop single with "Heartaches," another cover of a pre-rock single. This peaked at number seven pop and number 19 R&B in 1961. They continued recording on Kyra, Queen Bee, St. Clair, Rocky, and Monogram with varying lineups, but never again equaled their past success. *—Ron Wynn*

● **The Best of the Marcels** / Apr. 1990 / Rhino ♦♦♦♦♦

An outstanding vocal ensemble that is exceptional on nonsense/novelty tunes like "Blue Moon." *—Ron Wynn*

Summertime / 1992 / Relic ♦♦♦♦♦

Fans of this extraordinary doo wop outfit will have to own this CD, containing 24 demo tracks including "Zoom," and the number that ultimately evolved into their celebrated cover of Rodgers & Hart's "Blue Moon." Also on hand are "A Sunday Kind of Love," "Over the Rainbow," "I Could Have Danced All Night," "Spanish Harlem," "Save the Last Dance for Me," "Got a Job," "Stormy Weather," and "That Lucky Old Sun" (two different versions), among others, rounded out with a quartet of completed numbers from much later in their history. The notes are entertaining and surprisingly honest in their admission of lack of information on certain tracks and their histories. *—Bruce Eder*

Complete Colpix Sessions / Apr. 16, 1995 / Castle ♦♦♦♦

Marillion

f. 1978, Aylesbury, England

Album Rock, Neo-Prog, Prog Rock/Art Rock

Marillion emerged from the short-lived progressive rock revival of the early '80s to become one of the most enduring cult acts of the era. Soon after forming in 1978, the group recruited vocalist Fish (born Derek Dick) and found a hit with their second album, 1984's *Fugazi*, which streamlined the intricacies of the group's prog-rock debut in favor of a more straight-ahead hard rock identity. The singles "Assassin" and "Punch and Judy" both became British hits. With 1985's *Misplaced Childhood*, Marillion earned its greatest success to date; the lush ballad "Kayleigh" reached the number two position on the U.K. charts, and became a hit in the U.S. as well. After 1987's *Clutching at Straws*, however, Fish left the band for a solo career. The group then added vocalist Steve Hogarth, intending 1991's *Holidays in Eden* as a more mainstream rock album; it failed to attract a wider audience. Marillion returned to standard prog-rock with *Brave* and *Afraid of Sunlight*, though they changed their style again to a softer sound for 1997's *This Strange Engine*. One year later, the band returned to the studio to record their tenth album, *Radiation*. Again changing styles, the effort showed the influences of the Beatles and Radiohead, specifically *OK Computer*. *—Jason Ankeny & Dale Jensen*

● **Script for a Jester's Tear** / 1983 / Never ♦♦♦♦♦

At the time, Marillion's remarkable, full-fledged 1983 debut *Script for a Jester's Tear* was considered an odd bird: replete with Peter Gabriel face paint and lengthy, technical compositions, Marillion ushered in a new generation of prog rock that bound them forever to the heroics of early day Genesis. Intricate, complex, and theatrical almost to a fault, *Script for a Jester's Tear* remains the band's best and sets the bar for their later work. Filled with extraordinary songs that remained staples in the band's live gigs, the album begins with the poignant title track, on which Fish leads his band of merry men on a broken-hearted *tour de force* that culminates with the singer decrying that "...the game is over." "He Knows You Know," a song sprinkled with drug paranoia and guilt; as the song veers to its chorus, Fish announces, "Fast feed, crystal fever, swarming through a fractured mind." If "The Web" hints at a grain of commercialism, "Garden Party" is a joyous anthem that showcases Marillion at the peak of its powers. Bogged down by some hilariously over-the-top British poetry, "Chelsea Monday" may be one of the album's lesser moments (if there are any), but the magical "Forgotten Sons" concludes the opus magnificently. Luckily for Marillion fans, EMI released a remastered version of *Script* with two different versions of "Market Square Heroes," "Three Boats Down From the Candy," "Grendel," "Chelsea Monday," the demo of "He Knows You Know," and an alternate track titled "Charting the Single." A vital piece for any Marillion head and an essential work for any self-respecting first- or second-generation prog rock fan. *—John Franck*

Fugazi / 1984 / Never ♦♦♦♦

At the conclusion of the *Script for a Jester's Tear* tour, Marillion decided to give drummer Mick Pointer his marching orders, replacing him momentarily with Camel's Andy Ward and later by American studio whiz, Jonathan Mover. Mover's recruitment proved to be short lived as Fish ushered in Steve Hackett's drummer/percussionist, Ian Mosley, whose spot-on drumming was the perfect foil for Marillion's meticulous musicianship. With Mosley, the band set out to record its sophomore effort. The first track to emerge from the *Fugazi* sessions would be "Punch and Judy" (which EMI released as the album's first single). In hindsight, this wasn't a smart move—the single quickly vanished into chart oblivion. As the sessions turned into a grueling, and at times, exasperating multi-studio juggling act (ten different studios were used for the tracking/mixing of the record) *Fugazi* proved to be a somewhat disjointed follow-up to the classic *Script for a Jester's Tear*. Despite its superlative arrangements, the album lacked its predecessor's cohesion and focus, but all was not lost: buried in the album's murky mix are three Marillion classics. "Assassing," "Incubus" and, especially, the album's title track showcase the band at its melodramatic best. The cryptic "Fugazi" was a highlight of the band's live set for many years to follow. In 1998, EMI issued a remastered version of *Fugazi* featuring a bonus disc full of oddities and demos including "Three Boats Down From the Candy," a 12" version of "Cinderella Search" and four of the album's original demos. The remastered version goes a long way toward restoring the album's original sonic aesthetic (lost somewhere along the way in initial vinyl and CD pressings). *—John Franck*

● **Misplaced Childhood** / 1985 / Never ♦♦♦♦♦

After the album-tour-album cycle of *Script for Jester's Tear*, *Fugazi*, and the subsequent Euro-only release of *Real to Reel*, Marillion retreated to Berlin's Hansa Ton Studios with Rolling Stones producer Chris Kimsey to work on their next opus. Armed with a handful of lyrics born out of a self-confessed acid trip, Fish came up with the elaborate concept for 1985's *Misplaced Childhood*. Touching upon his early childhood experiences and his inability to deal with a slew of bad breakups exacerbated by a never-ending series of rock-star-type "indulgences," *Misplaced Childhood* would prove to be not only the band's most accomplished release to date, but also its most streamlined. Initial record company skepticism over the band's decision to forge ahead with a '70s-style prog rock opus split into two halves (side one and two) quickly evaporated as Marillion delivered its two most commercial singles ever: "Kayleigh" and "Lavender." With its lush production and punchy mix, the album went on to become the band's greatest commercial triumph, especially in Europe where they would rise from theater attraction to bona fide stadium royalty. The subsequent U.S. success of "Kayleigh" would also see Marillion returning to the States for a difficult tour as Rush's support act. In 1999, EMI/Sanctuary re-released a remastered version of the album featuring a bonus disc of oddities including live fave "Freaks," the previously unreleased "Blue Angel," alternate takes of "Kayleigh," and "Heart of Lothian" as well as *Misplaced Childhood*'s actual demos. *—John Franck*

Clutching at Straws / Jun. 19, 1987 / Sanctuary ♦♦♦

The follow-up to *Misplaced Childhood* is even more personal and often disturbing with its ruminations on alcohol abuse and self-betrayal. *—Michael P. Dawson*

The Thieving Magpie (La Gazza Ladra) / 1988 / Capitol ♦♦♦

1988's *The Thieving Magpie* is a sprawling double-disc live set which manages to tie up virtually all the loose ends from Marillion's years with charismatic frontman Fish. Like 1984's *Real to Reel* mini live album, *Magpie* offers mostly sterling performances packed with both feeling and technical precision, which often times manage to better their studio counterparts thanks to their road-worthy fluidity. But unlike that seamlessly assembled mini live album, it does suffer from the occasional silence between tracks, or even noticeable variations in sound quality, crowd noise, and general ambiance. Sure, most listeners won't give a hoot about such details when faced with the sheer creative breadth (some would say absurdity) of such Marillion magnum opuses as "Fugazi," "Script for a Jester's Tear," and "Chelsea Monday" to name but a few. First-time listeners should be advised against starting their Marillion collection with this challenging release (or risk their brains exploding like water balloons); but with the inclusion of a complete performance of the band's greatest masterpiece, *Misplaced Childhood*, *Magpie* becomes a real treat for serious fans. *—Ed Rivadavia*

Season's End / 1989 / Never ♦♦♦♦♦

After Fish's departure, Marillion teetered on the brink of collapse: the frontman's distinct voice and poetic prose made him the defining member of the band. One can only imagine how record executives held their collective breath as Steve Hogarth was brought in to take the reins. His first outing with band, 1989's *Season's End*, removed all doubts about the band's future. Hogarth's unique, expressive voice fit Marillion perfectly; on the full throttle rock assault of "The Uninvited Guest," or the emotional "After You," Hogarth's singularity is unmistakable. The heartfelt "Easter," with its imaginative electric-acoustic arrangement, is another showcase for Hogarth's talents. Marillion's ability to write music whose ideals live and breathe in the listener continues on *Seasons End*, particularly on the inspiring "Holloway Girl," which dissects the injustice of incarcerating mentally ill female inmates (at England's Holloway Prison) instead of placing them in appropriate psychiatric facilities. The beautiful "Easter" is the band's plea for peace in Ireland, while "The King of Sunset Town" has its lyrical roots in the massacre at Tiananmen Square. Hogarth's flexible range and beautiful phrasing shines on the entire album. In 1999 Marillion released a remastered version of *Seasons End*, including a bonus disc of outtakes and alternate versions as well as the previously unreleased "The Bell in the Sea," and "The Release." Both are strong tracks and are welcome additions to the Marillion catalogue. While 1995's *Afraid of Sunlight* is the peak of Marillion's growing, impressive body of work, *Season's End* shouldn't be missed either. *—Jeri Montesano*

Holidays in Eden / 1991 / EMI ♦♦♦

Six of One, Half-Dozen of the Other / Jul. 14, 1992 / IRS ♦♦♦♦

Few band's careers are as clearly divided into two separate eras as Marillion, whose four mid-'80s albums with exuberant vocalist Fish briefly resurrected progressive rock in all its extravagance, only to be followed by an even longer stretch of years and albums with the comparatively mainstream Steve Hogarth fronting the band in a generally more consumer-friendly, adult-oriented rock guise. Without even attempting to enter into a lengthy discussion over each singer's merits, let it be said that a continuous listen through *Six of One, Half-Dozen of the Other* is tantamount to a wild ride through the mind of a band suffering from multiple personality disorder—of which Fish, admittedly owns nine out of ten. The disc opens with the two most accomplished radio entries from each of the group's two phases, namely the beautiful "Cover My Eyes (Pain & Heaven)" from the second phase and the captivating "Kayleigh" from the first. But from here on out, similarly melodic gems like "Dry Land" and "No One Can" begin to rub shoulders uneasily with such preposterous prog rock epics as "Assassing" and "Garden Party." Ironically, it is the Fish-era material that sounds most uniform—if only for its outlandish diversity—when compared to the often clumsy experiments (see the ill-advised pop metal of "Hooks in You" and "Uninvited Guest") of the band's second incarnation. A less democratic but gentler approach would have been to sequence these tracks in chronological order, but truth be told, Marillion is the kind of band that simply defies greatest-hits packages. Dedicated progressive rock fans would be better suited to just shell out for the recently remastered and repackaged original albums. *—Ed Rivadavia*

Brave / Feb. 8, 1994 / IRS ♦♦♦
Rebounding from the inconsistent *Holidays in Eden*, Marillion retreated to the studio for 15 months to write and record the concept album *Brave*. Telling the story of an abused girl wandering on Severn Bridge, the album is a solid mix of symphonic tracks with a pronounced rock edge. A band known for trilogies, the final set of "The Great Escape," "The Last of You," and "Falling From the Moon" form one of the most dynamic showcases for vocalist Steve Hogarth and guitarist Steve Rothery. *Brave* remains the most complex Marillion release to date, with layers and layers of sound. A full-length movie of *Brave*, directed by Richard Stanley, was released in Europe in conjunction with the album. *—Dale Jensen*

Afraid of Sunlight / 1995 / Sanctuary ♦♦♦♦
Afraid of Sunlight was Marillion's first real progressive album since Fish had left the band. While it does not rank as high as classics like *Script for a Jester's Tear* or *Fugazi*, it still has some very strong moments. "Cannibal Surf Babe" is a tribute to the '60s (sort of). It starts off like the Beach Boys' "California Girls" before turning into the nightmarish tale of a cannibal woman! But the best moments are in the second half of the album, with tracks such as "Out of This World," "Afraid of Sunlight," and "King." As usual with Marillion, the keyboards stand out the most. There are some very beautiful melodic moments and perhaps a better mix between calm and agressive melodies than on previous albums made with Steve Hogarth. *—Alex S. Garcia*

This Strange Engine / Jul. 22, 1997 / Castle ♦♦♦

Radiation / Oct. 27, 1998 / Velvel ♦♦♦

Marillion.Com / Nov. 9, 1999 / Never ♦♦♦

Marilyn Manson

f. 1989
Industrial Metal, Alternative Metal, Heavy Metal
Love him or hate him, the self-proclaimed "Antichrist Superstar" Marilyn Manson was indisputably among the most notorious and controversial entertainers of the 1990s. Celebrated by supporters as a crusader for free speech and denounced by detractors as little more than a poor man's Alice Cooper, he was the latest in a long line of shock rockers. Widely dismissed by critics, Manson was a major draw with the youth market as a mainstream anti-hero, much to the chagrin of conservative politicians and concerned parents. Born Brian Warner, he formed the band in the late '80s with guitarist Scott Mitchell; by 1992 their gothic stage show made them a popular act in the South Florida area. In 1993, Nine Inch Nails' Trent Reznor came calling and the group's debut LP, *Portrait of an American Family*, was released in 1994 on Reznor's Nothing label. Manson's notoriety began to soar—he ripped apart a copy of the Book of Mormon while onstage in Salt Lake City and was bestowed the title of "Reverend" by the Church of Satan's founder Anton LaVey. His cult following—comprised almost entirely of disaffected white suburban teens—continued to swell, and 1996's *Antichrist Superstar* debuted at number three on the album charts. As Manson's popularity grew, so did the furor surrounding him—his performances and albums were the subject of widespread attacks from the right-wing and religious fronts. The glam-inspired *Mechanical Animals* followed in 1998. *—Jason Ankeny*

Portrait of an American Family / Jul. 12, 1994 / Nothing/Interscope ♦♦♦
Coming up screaming from the depths of Florida—there being no scarier state in the union—Marilyn Manson cannily positioned themselves as a goth-industrial hybrid on their debut album, *Portrait of an American Family*. At this stage in their evolution, Marilyn Manson was clearly a band, not just the project of Brian Warner a.k.a. Mr. Manson, who would later simply adopt his band's name as his own. Also, horror-show schlock was a bigger factor than it would be later on, when he wanted to be the Antichrist Superstar for the world at large. In other words, it's Manson at his silliest, singing about "My Monkey" and "Snake Eyes and Sissies." Beneath all the camp shock, there are signs of Warner's unerring eye for genuine outrage and musical talent, particularly on the trio of "Cake and Sodomy," "Lunch Box," and "Dope Hat." But even a few years on from its 1994 release, *Portrait of an American Family* has begun to sound a little dated, especially since its Nine Inch Nails-meets-WASP-meets-Alice Cooper formula was fully realized on Manson's follow-up album, *Antichrist Superstar*. Here, it's in sketch form, and by the end of the album it's clear that Warner, Manson, whatever you want to call him, needs a full canvas to truly wreak havoc. *—Stephen Thomas Erlewine*

Smells Like Children / Oct. 24, 1995 / Nothing/Interscope ♦♦♦
A year on from *Portrait of an American Family*, Marilyn Manson released the stopgap EP *Smells Like Children*. Where the full-length debut showed sparks of character and invention beneath industrial-metal sludge, *Smells Like Children* is a smartly crafted horrorshow, filled with vulgarity, ugliness, goth freaks, and sideshow scares. Manson wisely chose to heighten his cartoonish personality with the EP. Most of the record is devoted to spoken words and samples, all designed to push to the outrage buttons of middle America. Between those sonic collages arrives one new song, retitled remixes of *Portrait* songs—"Kiddie Grinder," "Everlasting Cocksucker," "Dance of the Dope Hats," "White Trash"—and three covers ("Sweet Dreams," "I Put a Spell on You," "Rock & Roll Nigger"), all given a trademark spooky makeover. Musically, it may not amount to much—it's goth-metal-industrial, as good as the "Dope Hat," "Lunch Box," and "Cake and Sodomy" trilogy that distinguished the debut—but as a sonic sculpture, as an *objet d'art*, it's effective and wickedly fascinating. It's exactly what Brian Warner needed to do to establish Marilyn Manson as America's boogeyman for the late '90s. [And it also helped enhance his myth for his fans. *Smells Like Children* originally was released promotionally, complete with unauthorized *Willy Wonka & the Chocolate Factory* samples and other unapproved sound bites. It was pulled, censored, and re-edited ("Abuse (pt. 1)" and "Abuse (pt. 2)" were removed from the EP) before it was offically released in October 1995, and the original promo copies became valuable collectibles and the most bootlegged item in the Manson catalog.] *—Stephen Thomas Erlewine*

● **Antichrist Superstar** / Sep. 8, 1996 / Nothing/Interscope ♦♦♦♦♦
Boasting a fuller sound and a more focused sense of purpose, *Antichrist Superstar* is a substantial improvement on Marilyn Manson's debut album, *Portrait of an American Family*. The band draws equally from schlock-metal, progressive metal, new wave, goth-rock, and industrial rock, and with the help of producers Trent Reznor and Dave Ogilvie, the group creates a boiling, mockingly satanic mess of guitars, synthesizers, and ridiculously "scary" vocals. Though the sonic details make *Anitchrist Superstar* an intriguing listen, it's not as extreme as it could have been—in particular, the guitars are surprisingly anemic, sounding like buzzing vacuums instead of unwieldy chainsaws. Even with that considered, *Antichrist Superstar* is an unexpectedly cohesive album from a silly shock-metal band and will stand as Marilyn Manson's definitive statement. *—Stephen Thomas Erlewine*

Mechanical Animals / Sep. 15, 1998 / Nothing/Interscope ♦♦♦♦
Antichrist Superstar performed its intended purpose—it made Marilyn Manson internationally famous, a living realization of his fictional "antichrist superstar." He had gained the attention of not only rock fans, but the public at large; however, many critics bestowed their praise not on the former Brian Warner, but on Trent Reznor, Manson's mentor and producer. Surely angered by the attention being focused elsewhere, he decided to break from Reznor and industrial metal with his third album, *Mechanical Animals*. Taking his image and musical cues from Bowie, Warner reworked Marilyn Manson into a sleek, androgynous space alien named Omega, *a la* Ziggy Stardust, and constructed a glammy variation of his trademark goth-metal. With pal Billy Corgan as an unofficial consultant and Soundgarden producer Michael Beinhorn manning the boards, Manson turns *Mechanical Animals* into a big, clean rock record—the kind that stands in direct opposition to the dark, twisted industrial nightmares he painted with his first two albums. It can make for a welcome change of pace, since his glammed-up goth is more tuneful than his clattering industrial cacophony, but it lacks the cartoonish menace that distinguished his prior music. And without that, Marilyn Manson seems a little ordinary, believe it or not—more like a '90s version of Alice Cooper than ever before. True, *Mechanical Animals* is the group's most accessible effort, but Manson should have remembered one thing—demons are never that scary in the light. *—Stephen Thomas Erlewine*

The Last Tour on Earth / Nov. 16, 1999 / Nothing/Interscope ♦♦♦
The Last Tour on Earth, the live souvenir from the ill-fated *Mechanical Animals* tour, is an aural document of a primarily visual experience. Marilyn Manson's records are extremely well-crafted, filled with revealing sonic details, but in concert he concentrates on spectacle, preferring dazzling visuals to new arrangements. That's not a bad thing—Manson is an agent provocateur and his shows *should* be an overwhelming visual experience. There's no need for reinvented versions of "The Beautiful People" or "Irresponsible Hate Anthem," since they serve as the soundtrack for the sights. So, even if it's a good selection of Manson favorites performed by a tight band, it's hard to see the purpose of *The Last Tour on Earth*. Apart from rougher vocals and slightly more immediate sound, there are no true differences between the stage and studio version of these songs. Unlike many live albums, there isn't much visceral energy, because the music had to be fairly regimented to coincide with the visuals. Based on the music, it's hard to tell that this is a live album, except for stray crowd noises and Manson's onstage ramblings, which are more interesting than the music. It's fascinating to hear him act like a sober Jim Morrison, trying to get his audience to yell "motherfucker" and winding up with an incoherent "Maoohahfuer," or relating his spellbinding vision of a dreamworld, where the land is made of drugs, cops give Mr. Manson head, and God is spelled "D-R-U-G-S," especially since these rants are delivered, by name, to the midwestern off-markets of Grand Rapids, Michigan and Cedar Rapids, Iowa. This may be the best moment of the record, but it doesn't change the fact that it's not necessary for anyone but diehards. *—Stephen Thomas Erlewine*

Holy Wood (In the Shadow of the Valley of Death) / Nov. 14, 2000 / Nothing/Interscope ♦♦♦♦♦
In 2000, he not only was recovering from his fans' rejection of *Mechanical Animals*, he was scarred from Columbine and, worst of all, he was no longer America's demon dog. What was Brian Warner to do, standing on such uneasy ground? As a smart man and savvy marketer, he knew that it was time to consolidate his strengths, blend Omega with the Antichrist Superstar, and return with a harsh, controversial, operatic epic: a vulgar concept album to seduce his core audiences of alienated teens and cultural cops. The resulting album, *Holy Wood (In the Shadow of the Valley of Death)*, is intended as the third part of the trilogy beginning with *Antichrist Superstar*, and its convoluted story line is fairly autobiographical, but the amazing thing isn't the story—it's that he figured out to

meld the hooks and subtle sonic shading of *Mechanical Animals* with the ugly, neo-industrial metallicisms of *Antichrist*. Consequently, it's easy to see this as the definitive Marilyn Manson album since it's tuneful *and* abrasive. Then again, much of its charm lies in Manson trying so hard, perfecting details in the concept, lyrics, themes, production, sequencing, the tarot card parodies in the liner notes, the self-theft, the self-consciously blasphemous cover art. There's so much effort, *Holy Wood* winds up a stronger and more consistent album than any of his other work. If there's any problem, it's that Manson's shock rock seems a little quaint in 2000. Eminem's vibrant, surrealistic white-trash fantasias were the sound of 2000, while Marilyn Manson's rock operas, religious baiting, and goth gear are from an era passed. It's to Warner's credit as, yes, an artist, that *Holy Wood* works anyway. *—Stephen Thomas Erlewine*

The Marshall Tucker Band

f. 1971, Spartanburg, SC

Boogie Rock, Southern Rock, Country-Rock

One of the major Southern-rock bands of the '70s, the Marshall Tucker Band combined rock, country, and jazz, and featured extended instrumental passages on which lead guitarist Toy Caldwell shone. The band was signed to Capricorn Records and released its debut album, *The Marshall Tucker Band*, in 1973. They gained recognition through a tour with the Allman Brothers Band and found significant success during the course of the '70s, with most of their albums going gold. Their peak came with the million-selling album *Carolina Dreams* and its Top 15 single "Heard It in a Love Song" in 1977. The band was slowed down by the death of bassist Tommy Caldwell in a car accident in 1980, and it faded from the album charts after 1982. Toy Caldwell left for a solo career soon after, but by 1998, the band was enjoying a resurgence of popularity, with an all-new album and a substantial fan base. *—William Ruhlmann & Michael B. Smith*

Greatest Hits / 1978 / AJK ✦✦✦✦✦

Fusing country-rock with bits of loose-structured jazz that popped up here and there, the Marshall Tucker Band found themselves alongside bands like Little Feat and Pure Prairie League in the middle of the mid-'70s Southern rock explosion. While maybe not as prominent as other bands in their field, the addition of saxophone and flute in their music gave them an edge that was a distinguishing attribute to their music. Lead guitarist Toy Caldwell, with brother Tommy on bass, churned out some appealing jamboree-flavored rock as well some charming slow material. Only eight tracks make up this sparse hits collection, and even though it includes their two biggest singles with "Fire on the Mountain" and the beautiful "Heard It in a Love Song," it's not enough to truly represent this band's music. The album kicks off with "Can't You See," made famous by country superstar Waylon Jennings in 1976, as well as FM radio staples "24 Hours at a Time" and "Searchin' for a Rainbow." With over 13 albums under their belt, the spirited mix of traditional country and electrified rock that exists in the Marshall Tucker Band's repertoire is impossible to appreciate within the radius of only eight songs. *—Mike DeGagne*

● **The Best of the Marshall Tucker Band: The Capricorn Years** / 1995 / ERA ✦✦✦✦✦

Although *Greatest Hits* is certainly a fine introduction to the music of the Marshall Tucker Band, *The Capricorn Years* is much better. The 29 tracks herein are representative of seven fine record albums, all of which were recorded on the Capricorn Records label during the 1970s. Not only are the hits included, but also classic MTB cuts like "Virginia," "Bob Away My Blues," and "Desert Skies." There are two versions of the band's best-known song, "Can't You See," both the live and studio takes, and full-length live cuts of "Ramblin'" and "24 Hours at a Time," making this the definitive introductory package, as well as a keepsake for all MTB fans. The package also includes a nice liner note booklet, with lots of previously unreleased photographs. *—Michael B. Smith*

Marshmallow Coast

Noise Pop, Indie Pop, Lo-Fi

Yet another branch of the Elephant 6 collective family tree, the Marshmallow Coast was the alias of avant-popster Andy Gonzalez, also a satellite member of both Of Montreal and the Music Tapes. Outside of an EP, *The Scent of Credibility*, and a split single with Midget and Hairs, the Marshmallow Coast was little-known prior to the 1999 release of their Kindercore label debut LP *Seniors and Juniors*. Their sophomore, self-titled effort followed a year later. *—Jason Ankeny*

Seniors and Juniors / 1999 / Kindercore ✦✦✦✦

Much of what's fascinating about the continued growth of the Elephant 6 sphere is that each new project to emerge from the collective seems to shed new light on the records which preceded it, establishing connections and filling in gaps to further expand the concept of a unified musical universe. *Seniors and Juniors* exists in the space separating the guileless pop euphoria of Of Montreal and the chaotic fantasias of the Music Tapes, the two bands which housed Andy Gonzalez prior to his adoption of the Marshmallow Coast alias. Fractured and eccentric yet strangely affecting, the surface simplicity of these home recordings belies an emotional immediacy which reveals itself further with each listen—the album is so obviously a labor of love that its more awkward moments aren't just forgivable, they're absolutely endearing. *—Jason Ankeny*

● **Marshmallow Coasting** / Sep. 26, 2000 / Kindercore ✦✦✦✦

Little in the charmingly off-key simplicity of the Marshmallow Coast's *Seniors and Juniors* anticipated the quantum leap forward made by the follow-up, *Marshmallow Coasting*. Recorded with the aid of Andy Gonzales' Of Montreal mates, the disc often suggests a mutated clone of that band's classic *Gay Parade* album, lacking its conceptual density (at least superficially) but achieving a similar balance between childlike wonderment and skewed pop brilliance that's both defiantly retro and proudly postmodern. Gonzales' fractured melodies benefit enormously from the collaborative model: *Marshmallow Coasting* thrives on the kinds of bright harmonies and complex arrangements absent from his earlier solo efforts, and although it's something of a self-inflicted knock against the incestuousness of the Elephant 6 aesthetic that Gonzales sounds exactly like Of Montreal's Kevin Barnes on tracks like "Lonliest (sic) Heart in Texas"—maybe it is Barnes, who knows?—its also a tribute to the collective's unique and unified spirit. *—Jason Ankeny*

Martha & the Vandellas

f. 1963, Detroit, MI, **db.** 1972

Pop-Soul, Girl Group, Motown, Soul

Along with the Supremes, Martha & the Vandellas defined the distaff side of the Motown Sound in the 1960s; their biggest hits, including "Heat Wave," "Dancing in the Street" and "Nowhere to Run," remain among the most potent and enduring dance records of the era. The Top 30 success of the 1963 ballad "Come and Get These Memories" first brought the group to the attention of Motown's hit-making production team of Holland-Dozier-Holland, who crafted their next smash, the galvanizing Top Five classic "Heat Wave," which perfected the mix of impassioned call-and-response vocals, pulsing rhythms, and full-bodied horns that became the trio's trademark. After singer Kim Weston turned down the Marvin Gaye/Ivy Jo Hunter/Mickey Stevenson composition "Dancing in the Street," the song was shuttled to Martha & the Vandellas; refashioned by Holland-Dozier-Holland to fit the group's formula, the anthem became their biggest hit and definitive statement, reaching Number Two in the summer of 1964. A year later, they returned with another smash, the savage "Nowhere to Run," followed by "I'm Ready for Love." 1967's "Jimmy Mack" and "Honey Chile" were the last records overseen by the Holland-Dozier-Holland team before their defection from Motown and were also the final significant Vandellas hits; the trio continued unsuccessfully for a few more years before breaking up in the wake of a December, 1972 farewell performance at Detroit's Cobo Hall. *—Jason Ankeny*

☆ **Live Wire! The Singles (1962-1972)** / Sep. 7, 1993 / Motown ✦✦✦✦✦

This two-CD box set includes all of the top singles and many of the flipsides that Martha Reeves & the Vandellas cut for Motown. All the hits are here, of course; the collector will be especially interested in the B-sides and non-hit singles, many of which employed the songwriting talents of Motown regulars like Holland-Dozier-Holland and Mickey Stevenson. There's also the rare single (featuring Gloria Williamson on lead vocals) cut by the Vells in 1962, before Reeves took top billing and the group changed their name. Eight of these cuts have never been released on album before. Among the non-hits, there isn't anything to match "Heat Wave" or "Dancing in the Street," but Reeves' astonishingly powerful voice never falters. She was arguably Motown's most talented female singer, but the label's investment in her seemed to flag as the decade progressed. The later material lacks the distinction of her classic period, though the 1970 album track "I Should Be Proud" is a little-known (if somewhat heavy-handed) protest against the Vietnam War. *—Richie Unterberger*

★ **The Ultimate Collection** / Feb. 10, 1998 / Motown ✦✦✦✦✦

Motown is notorious for recycling their catalog as endless hit collections, but *The Ultimate Collection* is one of the finest series of greatest-hits CDs they have ever assembled. Each disc contains all of the major hits from an artist, plus important B-sides, album tracks, and minor hits. Martha & the Vandellas' entry in the series is no exception to the rule, boasting all their Top Ten pop and R&B hits—"Come and Get These Memories," "Heat Wave," "Quicksand," "Dancing in the Street," "Nowhere to Run," "My Baby Loves Me," "I'm Ready for Love," "Jimmy Mack"—plus smaller hits and B-sides, resulting in a total of 25 tracks. For anyone who wants a definitive hits collection but is hesitant to invest in the double-disc *Live Wire!*, *The Ultimate Collection* is an ideal choice. *—Stephen Thomas Erlewine*

The Marvelettes

f. 1960, Inkster, MI

Pop-Soul, Girl Group, Motown, Soul

Probably the most pop-oriented of Motown's major female acts, the Marvelettes didn't project as strong an identity as the Supremes, Mary Wells, or Martha Reeves, but recorded quite a few hits, including Motown's first number one single, "Please Mr. Postman" (1961). "Postman," as well as other chirpy early '60s hits like "Playboy," "Twistin' Postman," and "Beechwood 4-5789," were the label's purest girl-group efforts. After a few years, they moved from girl-group sounds to up-tempo and mid-tempo numbers that were more characteristic of Motown's production line. They received no small help from Smokey Robinson, who produced and wrote many of their singles; Holland-Dozier-Holland, Berry Gordy, Mickey Stevenson, Marvin Gaye, and Ashford-Simpson also got involved with the songwriting and production at various points. While the Marvelettes didn't cut as many monster smashes as most of their Motown peers after the early '60s, they did periodically surface with classic hits like "Too Many Fish in the Sea," "Don't Mess with Bill," and "The Hunter Gets Captured by the Game." There were also plenty of fine minor hits and misses, like 1965's "I'll Keep Holding On," which is just as memorable as the well-known Motown chart-toppers of the era. *—Richie Unterberger*

Deliver: The Singles (1961-1971) / Sep. 7, 1993 / Motown ✦✦✦✦✦

Forty-one songs, featuring most of both the A-sides and B-sides, nine of which had never been issued on album before. The ace Motown songwriting and production stable was involved in virtually every one of these tracks, making for a surprisingly strong and consistent collection. Includes all the chart hits, as well as rarities like the Phil Spector-style single they released in 1963 as the Darnells. *—Richie Unterberger*

● **The Ultimate Collection** / Feb. 10, 1998 / Motown ✦✦✦✦✦

Motown is notorious for recycling their catalog as endless hit collections, but *The Ultimate Collection* is one of the finest series of greatest-hits CDs they have ever assembled.

Each disc contains all of the major hits from an artist, plus important B-sides, album tracks, and minor hits. The Marvelettes' entry in the series is no exception to the rule, boasting all their Top Ten pop and R&B hits, not only from their early-'60s heyday but also their late-'60s comeback: "Please Mr. Postman," "Playboy," "Beechwood 4-5789," "Someday, Someway," "Strange I Know," "Don't Mess with Bill," "My Baby Must Be a Magician," "The Hunter Gets Captured By the Game," "When You're Young and in Love." The disc also features a number of smaller hits and B-sides, resulting in a total of 25 tracks. For anyone who wants a definitive hits collection but is hesitant to invest in the double-disc *Deliver, The Ultimate Collection* is an ideal choice. *—Stephen Thomas Erlewine*

20th Century Masters—The Millennium Collection: The Best of the Marvelettes / Aug. 15, 2000 / Motown ✦✦✦✦

A brief 11-song CD that contains the hits and only the hits from the Marvelettes; these are all A-sides that did some damage on the charts, and no B-sides or album cuts are included. Everything from the early, raucous five-lady "Please Mr. Postman" to "My Baby Must Be a Magician," which featured Wanda Young-Rogers, session singers, and Melvin Franklin's bass intro. This front-runner special includes the conga-driven "Too Many Fish in the Sea"; "I'll Keep Holding On," cut in New York City by Mickey Stevenson; and Smokey's "Don't Mess With Bill," digitally remastered and enhanced. *—Andrew Hamilton*

Marvin & Johnny

f. 1953
R&B

One of the first notable rhythm and blues duos, Marvin & Johnny weren't so much a permanent act as Marvin Phillips (b. Oct. 23, 1931) and several partners that he would name "Johnny." Although Emory Perry was the most frequent of these, Phillips also duetted with Jesse Belvin, making number two in the R&B chart (as Jesse & Marvin) with "Dream Girl," Carl Green, and others, though Phillips called Perry "my main Johnny." Whoever was singing, Marvin & Johnny were significant, if not major, figures in the transition from West Coast jump blues to hotter sax-driven R&B sides that began to approach rock & roll; they were also forerunners of doo wop with their appealingly grainy harmonies and occasional sly sense of humor. Recording for Specialty and Modern, they had a couple of Top Ten R&B hits, "Baby Doll" (1953) and "Tick Tock"/"Cherry Pie" (1954), and also issued several other strong singles, sometimes in a sort of updated Louis Jordan style. They faded after the mid-'50s, although they would also record for Aladdin and several other small Los Angeles labels. *—Richie Unterberger*

● **Flipped Out** / 1992 / Specialty ✦✦✦✦✦

Twenty-five early- to-mid-'50s tracks cut for the Specialty label, some previously unissued, varying between loose up-tempo grooves and ballads. "Baby Doll" was the hit, but the pounding boogie of "Wine Woogie" and the sassy duetting on "Boy Loves Girl" are other highlights of a pretty strong set of early-'50s R&B. But it doesn't have material they recorded during the same era for Modern, including their most famous single, "Tick Tock"/"Cherry Pie." *—Richie Unterberger*

Richard Marx

b. Sep. 16, 1963, Chicago, IL
Vocals, Piano, Guitar / Pop/Rock, Adult Contemporary

Before he released his first album, Richard Marx sang on commercials and was a backing vocalist for Lionel Richie. It was here that he learned the commercial pop skills that made him an adult contemporary radio star in the late '80s. Marx shot to the top of the charts upon the release of his eponymous debut in 1987. Marx's first hit was the California rocker "Don't Mean Nothing," but his real strength lay with ballads like "Right Here Waiting," which became an adult contemporary staple in the late '80s. *Richard Marx* and 1989's *Repeat Offender* generated a string of three consecutive number one hits in America—"Hold on to the Nights," "Satisfied," and "Right Here Waiting." With the release of *Rush Street* in 1991, his commercial fortunes started to slip somewhat as the mainstream shifted away from the slick, well-constructed songs that are his forte. Despite the Top Ten hit single "Now and Forever," 1994's *Paid Vacation* fell from the charts quickly, and Marx entered a period of seclusion, returning in the spring of 1997 with *Flesh & Bone*, an album tailored toward the adult contemporary market. *Days in Avalon* was quietly issued in fall 2000. *—Stephen Thomas Erlewine*

● **Greatest Hits** / Nov. 4, 1997 / Capitol ✦✦✦✦✦

Richard Marx's *Greatest Hits* performs a valuable service for his fans, collecting all of his hit singles—"Don't Mean Nothing," "Should've Known Better," "Endless Summer Nights," "Hold on to the Nights," "Satisfied," "Right Here Waiting," "Angela," "Children of the Night," "Keep Coming Back," "Hazard," "Take This Heart," "Now and Forever"—on one disc. For both the casual and the longtime fan, this is a blessing, since Marx's albums were usually uneven, featuring a few strong cuts surrounded by filler. *Greatest Hits* cuts away the chaff, leaving behind the best cuts, resulting in an ideal career summary of this popular MOR pop-rocker. *—Stephen Thomas Erlewine*

Barbara Mason

b. 1949, Philadelphia, PA
Vocals, Songwriter / Pop-Soul, Soul

An interesting minor soul performer, Mason initially focused on songwriting when she entered the music business in her teens. As a performer, though, she had a huge hit in 1965 with her self-penned "Yes, I'm Ready" (number five pop, number two R&B), a fetching soul-pop confection that spotlighted her high, girlish vocals. One of the first examples of the sweet, lush sound that came to be called Philly soul, she had modest success

throughout the rest of the decade on the small Arctic label, reaching the pop Top 40 again in 1965 with "Sad, Sad Girl."

In the early and mid-'70s, Mason toughened her persona considerably, singing about sexual love and infidelity with a frankness that was uncommon for a female soul singer in songs like "Bed and Board," "From His Woman to You," and "Shackin' Up." Sweet soul continued to be her groove, and she continued to write some of her material. But the production, as it was throughout soul in the '70s, was more funk-oriented, and at times Mason would interrupt her singing to deliver some straight-talkin' raps about romance. Curtis Mayfield produced her on a cover of Mayfield's "Give Me Your Love," which restored her to the pop Top 40 and R&B Top Ten in 1973; "From His Woman to You" and "Shackin' Up" were also solid soul sellers in the mid-'70s. After leaving Buddah Records in 1975, she only dented the charts periodically, with "I Am Your Woman, She Is Your Wife" (1978), "Another Man" (1984), and a couple of other singles. *—Richie Unterberger*

Yes, I'm Ready / 1965 / Arctic ✦✦✦✦

Barbara Mason was very much a teenager when "Yes, I'm Ready" climbed the charts and this endearing debut LP was released. "Ready" is a captivating ballad that has been remade by many. Her first hit single, "Girls Have Feelings Too," shows the sweet innocence of youth. "Sad, Sad Girl," another self-written Mason ballad, drips with hurt as she explains how blue her world has become since she lost her fellow. Mason wrote most of her singles and has said they're based on real life experiences; she often could be seen visibly crying on stage while delivering one of her songs. Other than the B-sides, the rest of the album consists of remakes like "Something You Got," "Moon River," and "Misty." Mason wasn't at her best redoing the material of others; the efforts seem lackluster compared to her recordings of original compositions. *—Andrew Hamilton*

Oh How It Hurts / 1968 / Arctic ✦✦✦✦

Barbara Mason's second and final LP for Arctic Records was released three years after her first. The Arctic label waxed 60 records before folding; 14 were Mason releases. Jimmy Bishop, a Philadelphia DJ, owned the label and included "Yes, I'm Ready" on this collection to bolster sales, since all of Mason's Arctic hits except the title track are on her debut. Incidentally, that's Kenny Gamble crooning backing vocals on "Ready"; Gamble also recorded for Arctic and wrote some sides for Mason before going on to form Gamble, Neptune, and Philadelphia International Records. Only "Oh How It Hurts" sold well from this collection, and deservedly so; the sad ballad touches the heart every time you hear it. Mason sings with pain and the lyrics hit home. The excellent "Is It Me, or Is It Her" makes this a must collection. You won't find this jewel on any other compilation to date; it's even missing from the excellent 27-track Bear Family anthology of her Arctic years. The rest of the tracks are misses and flip sides. Mason always covered songs; her first LP had six remakes but there are only a few here, the best being "You Can Depend on Me," a nifty reworking of the Miracles song. Mason has yet to receive the credit she deserves for being an innovator of the sweet Philly sound; all the other sweet Philly singers—Brenda & the Tabulations, the Delfonics, Blue Magic, the Stylistics, and others—came after Mason. The rhythm section of M.F.S.B. played on Mason's recordings long before gaining recognition on the Philadelphia International label. *—Andrew Hamilton*

● **The Very Best of Barbara Mason** / May 7, 1996 / Sequel ✦✦✦✦✦

Most of this 15-track compilation deals with her 1972-75 stint on Buddah, ending with a few tracks from the late '70s and early '80s. Those who prefer '60s soul to '70s soul will prefer her early work, but at the time of its release this was the best CD compilation of her material available, including the hits "Give Me Your Love," "From His Woman to You," and "Shackin' Up." The version of "Yes, I'm Ready" here, by the way, is not the 1965 original, but an early-'70s remake. *—Richie Unterberger*

Yes, I'm Ready / Nov. 1, 1997 / Bear Family ✦✦✦✦✦

These are Barbara's early sides for Arctic Records; it's not complete, but the rest of her Arctic stuff appears on *Oh How It Hurts*, also on Bear Family. Buy both and you should have everything she recorded at Arctic. She cut as many remakes as originals, some were standards, which suggests Arctic had hopes of crossing her over to the pop market, which never happened to any significant degree. The remakes run the gamut from Archie Bell's "Tighten Up" to Barbara Lynn's "You'll Lose a Good Thing," a perfectly suited vehicle for Mason's innocent, sweet, aching voice. *—Andrew Hamilton*

The Best of the Buddha Years / Jul. 10, 2001 / Buddha ✦✦✦

Barbara Mason's Buddha years spanned from 1971 to 1975 and represented a growth period from a wet-eyed soprano to a mature, throaty singing, bodacious woman. While not as arresting to some as her teary breakout Arctic Records sides, these were stellar waxings by a talented singer who had a unique way of phrasing lyrics, and who never hesitated to reveal the fragility of her mental being or an often-bruised heart. The 14 tracks include an update of "Yes I'm Ready," complete with monologue, the scandalous (for the times) "Shackin' Up," and a bourbon/gin special "You Can Be With the One You Don't Love," cause it'll have you reaching for a bottle. There's a fair share of he-say, she-say dramas: "Betty Crutcher" and Lester Snell's "From His Woman to You," Norma Toney's "So He Is Yours Now," a long salty version of Billy Paul's "Me and Mrs. Jones" revised as "Me and Mr. Jones," and Mason's self-written dilemma "Caught in the Middle." *—Andrew Hamilton*

Dave Mason

b. May 10, 1944, Worcester, England
Vocals, Guitar / Pop/Rock, Soft Rock, Prog Rock/Art Rock

After serving as road manager for the Spencer Davis Group and meeting Steve Winwood, singer/guitarist Dave Mason found fame as one of the founding members of the jazz/rock/pop fusion group Traffic. However, conflicts between Winwood and Mason over the group's direction led to the latter's departure in 1969 after three albums. Mason moved to Los Angeles and joined Delaney and Bonnie before beginning his solo career. His 1970 solo debut, *Alone Together*, went gold and has proven to be arguably his best album. Mason next collaborated with Mama Cass Elliot for *Dave Mason & Cass Elliot*, but its reception was lukewarm at best. Mason settled permanently in America in 1973 and signed a long-term contract with CBS, recording a series of moderately successful, often inconsistent pop/rock albums featuring originals and a sprinkling of covers. Mason scored his biggest solo hit in 1977 with "We Just Disagree," which reached number 12. New Mason material was scarce in the 1980s, except for a beer commercial; Mason continued to tour, though, and joined Fleetwood Mac in 1994; 1999 saw the release of *Live: 40,000 Headmen Tour*, which also featured Jim Capaldi. *It's Like You Never Left* followed a year later. —*Steve Huey*

Alone Together / 1970 / MCA ✦✦✦✦✦
Dave Mason's first solo album was one of several recordings to come out of the Leon Russell/Delaney & Bonnie Bramlett axis in 1970. (Other notables included Eric Clapton's solo debut and Joe Cocker's *Mad Dogs and Englishmen*.) *Alone Together* contains an excellent batch of melodically pleasing songs, built on a fat bed of strumming acoustic guitars with tasteful electric guitar accents and leads. Mason's vocals are embellished with harmonies from Rita Coolidge, Claudia Lennear, and Delaney & Bonnie Bramlett. Besides the well-known semi-hit "Only You Know and I Know," and which was also a number 20 hit for the Bramletts, highlights include the bouncy gospel-inflected "Waitin' on You," and the banjo-bejeweled "Just a Song." "Look at You Look at Me" and the wonderfully wah-wahed "Shouldn't Have Took More Than You Gave" are reminiscent of Mason's former band, Traffic, whose drummer, Jim Capaldi is among the all-star cast assembled here.

    Alone Together represents Dave Mason at his peak. Later releases would betray lyrical shallowness, forced rhymes, and cliched guitar licks. But here, everything comes together perfectly. The original vinyl release of *Alone Together* was also noteworthy for the marble grain of the record itself—as the record played on the turntable, the tonearm appeared to be floating through the clouds. —*Jim Newsom*

Long Lost Friend: The Best of Dave Mason / Jun. 6, 1995 / Columbia/Legacy ✦✦✦✦
The Best of Dave Mason at Columbia would be a more accurate title, as this doesn't include work from his early-'70s LPs for Blue Thumb. The 19 tracks spotlight selections from seven albums that he recorded for Columbia. Including the hits "We Just Disagree," "Let It Go, Let It Flow," and "Will You Still Love Me Tomorrow," it charts his move from easygoing early-'70s FM rock to a more mainstream AOR pop sound. —*Richie Unterberger*

● **Ultimate Collection** / Sep. 21, 1999 / Hip-O ✦✦✦✦
Even Dave Mason will tell you that his songs have been rehashed and repackaged more times than he can (or cares to) remember. "Feelin' Alright" alone has been covered nearly 50 times and has even been denigrated to the level of car commercials (Nissan, no less!). This latest, however, may in fact be the greatest. Though it only spans 20 years of Mason's self-taught and self-(mis)directed career, this "ultimate" Dave Mason collection includes most of his best-known songs and a number of rarer gems, giving a solid introduction to this oft-misunderstood musician. This compilation shows many sides of Mason: the opening hippie bounce of "You Can All Join In"; the grammatically questionable Delaney and Bonnie-d roots chug of "Only You Know and I Know" (produced by Tommy Li Puma and featuring the likes of Leon Russell, Rita Coolidge, and fellow gridlocker Jim Capaldi); the easy dedication and advice of "Can't Stop Worrying, Can't Stop Loving," "Shouldn't Have Took More Than You Gave," and "To Be Free"; the rhythmic undertones of "Look at You Look at Me"; the cowbell-driven shuffle of "Let It Go, Let It Flow"; and the quick jangle of "Satin Red and Black Velvet Woman." Though licensing litigation probably prevented inclusion of Mason's collaborations with Eric Clapton, Carlos Santana, Bob Dylan, George Harrison, and Paul McCartney, the album does include the puzzlingly productive pairing with Cass Elliott ("Walk to the Point") and his 1987 bi-studio pop reunion with Steve Winwood ("Two Hearts"). And what Dave Mason compilation would be complete without his highest-charting hit "We Just Disagree"? Certainly not this one. After all, it is the "ultimate." —*Matthew Robinson*

Massive Attack

f. 1987, Bristol, England
Electronica, Alternative Dance, Trip-Hop, Club/Dance, Alternative Pop/Rock
The pioneering force behind the rise of trip-hop, Massive Attack was among the most innovative and influential groups of their generation; their hypnotic sound—a darkly sensual and cinematic fusion of hip-hop rhythms, soulful melodies, dub grooves, and choice samples—set the pace for much of the dance music to emerge throughout the 1990s, paving the way for such acclaimed artists as Portishead, Sneaker Pimps, Beth Orton, and Tricky, himself a Massive Attack alumnus. The group was formed by Mushroom and Daddy G., two members of a successful Bristol soundsystem named the Wild Bunch, plus grafitti artists 3D. Two other Wild Bunch alums, Nellee Hooper and Tricky, also spent time in the new group. After several classic singles, including "Unfinished Sympathy" and "Safe From Harm," Massive Attack issued their LP debut *Blue Lines* in 1991. While by no means a huge commercial success, the record was met with major critical praise, and was dubbed an instant classic in many quarters. Shara Nelson, featured on many of the album's most memorable tracks, left for a solo career soon after, and a three-year layoff preceded their second album, *Protection*, another commercial and critical hit. Soon after its release, both Hooper and Tricky made formal exits to work as independent producers. The third full-length Massive Attack effort, *Mezzanine*, appeared in 1998. —*Jason Ankeny*

★ **Blue Lines** / Aug. 6, 1991 / Virgin ✦✦✦✦✦
The first masterpiece of what was only termed trip-hop much later, *Blue Lines* filtered American hip-hop through the lens of British club culture, a stylish, nocturnal sense of scene that encompassed music from rare groove to dub to dance. The album balances dark, diva-led club jams along the lines of Soul II Soul with some of the best British rap (vocals and production) heard up to that point, occasionally on the same track. The opener "Safe From Harm" is the best example, with diva vocalist Shara Nelson trading off lines with the group's own monotone (yet effective) rapping. Even more than hip-hop or dance, however, dub is the big touchstone on *Blue Lines*. Most of the productions aren't quite as earthy as you'd expect, but the influence is palpable in the atmospherics of the songs, like the faraway electric piano on "One Love" (with beautiful vocals from the near-legendary Horace Andy). One track, "Five Man Army," makes the dub inspiration explicit, with a clattering percussion line, moderate reverb on the guitar and drums, and Andy's exquisite falsetto flitting over the chorus. *Blue Lines* isn't all darkness, either—"Be Thankful for What You've Got" is quite close to the smooth soul tune conjured by its title, and "Unfinished Sympathy"—the group's first classic production—is a tremendously moving fusion of up-tempo hip-hop and dancefloor jam with slow-moving, syrupy strings. Flaunting both their range and their tremendously evocative productions, Massive Attack recorded one of the best dance albums of all time. —*John Bush*

Protection / 1994 / Virgin ✦✦✦✦
Massive Attack's sophomore effort could never be as stunning as *Blue Lines*, and a slight drop in production and songwriting quality made the comparisons easy. Still, from the first two songs *Protection* sounds worthy of their debut. The opening title track is pure excellence, with melancholy keyboards, throbbing acid lines, and fragmented beats perfectly complementing the transcendent vocals of Tracey Thorn (an inspired choice to replace the departed Shara Nelson as their muse). Tricky, another soon-to-be-solo performer, makes his breakout on this record, with blunted performances on "Karmacoma," another highlight, as well as "Eurochild." But even though the production is just as intriguing as on *Blue Lines*, there's a bit lacking here—Massive Attack don't summon quite the emotional power they did previously. Guest Craig Armstrong's piano work on the aimless tracks "Weather Storm" and "Heat Miser" leans uncomfortably close to Muzak, and his arrangement and conducting for "Sly" isn't much better (vocals by Nicolette save the track somewhat). Though it's still miles ahead of the growing raft of trip-hop making the rounds in the mid-'90s, *Protection* is rather a disappointment. —*John Bush*

No Protection: Massive Attack Vs. Mad Professor / 1995 / Gyroscope ✦✦✦✦
Protection was widely considered a disappointing follow-up to Massive Attack's groundbreaking debut, *Blue Lines*. Where their debut bent all of the conventional hip-hop, dub reggae, and soul rules, *Protection* essentially delivered more of the same. Perhaps that's the reason why Mad Professor's remix of the album, *No Protection*, was welcomed with open arms by both Massive Attack fans and critics. Mad Professor has returned the group to their experimental, cut-and-paste dub reggae and hip-hop roots. He has gutted the songs—twisting and reassembling the vocal tracks, giving the songs deeper, fuller grooves and an eerily seductive atmosphere. In other words, he has made *Protection* into a more daring and fulfilling album with his remixes. —*Stephen Thomas Erlewine*

☆ **Mezzanine** / Apr. 27, 1998 / Virgin ✦✦✦✦✦
Increasingly ignored amidst the exploding trip-hop scene, Massive Attack finally returned in 1998 with *Mezzanine*, a record immediately announcing not only that the group was back, but that they'd recorded a set of songs just as singular and revelatory as on their debut, almost a decade back. It all begins with a stunning one-two-three-four punch: "Angel," "Risingson," "Teardrop," and "Inertia Creeps." Augmenting their samples and keyboards with a studio band, Massive Attack open with "Angel," a stark production featuring pointed beats and a distorted bass line that frames the vocal (by group regular Horace Andy) and a two-minute flame-out with raging guitars. "Risingson" is a dense, dark feature for Massive Attack themselves (on production as well as vocals), with a kitchen sink's worth of dubby effects and reverb. "Teardrop" introduces another genius collaboration—with Elizabeth Fraser from Cocteau Twins—from a production unit with a knack for recruiting gifted performers. The blend of earthy with ethereal shouldn't work at all, but Massive Attack pull it off in fine fashion. "Inertia Creeps" could well be the highlight, another feature for just the core threesome. With eerie atmospherics, fuzz-tone guitars, and a wealth of effects, the song could well be the best production from the best team of producers the electronic world had ever seen.

    Obviously, the rest of the album can't compete, but there's certainly no sign of the side-two slump (heard on *Protection*), as both Andy and Fraser return for excellent, mid-tempo tracks ("Man Next Door" and "Black Milk," respectively). —*John Bush*

Singles 90/98 / Dec. 15, 1998 / Virgin ✦✦✦

Master P (Percy Miller)

b. Apr. 29, 1970, New Orleans, LA
Vocals, Producer / Southern Rap, Hardcore Rap, Gangsta Rap, Hip-Hop
Master P created a hip-hop empire without registering on any mainstream radar. For several years, he operated solely in the rap underground, eventually surfacing in the mid-'90s as a recording artist and producer who knew exactly what his audience wanted. And what they wanted was gangsta rap. With his independent label No Limit, Master P gave them gangsta rap at its most basic—violent, vulgar lyrics, hard-edged beats, whiny synthesizers, and blunted bass. He wasn't a great rapper, and neither was anyone on No Limit; occasionally, the No Limit rappers were even talentless and clumsy. But in a time when major labels were running away from the controversy that gangsta rap caused and Dr. Dre, the father of the genre, was proclaiming it dead, Master P stayed on course, delivering album after album of unadulterated gangsta. It was recorded cheaply and packaged cheaply, and almost all of the records on No Limit were interchangeable, but that didn't matter, because Master P kept making money and getting paid. —*Stephen Thomas Erlewine*

Get Away Clean / 1991 / In-A-Minute/No Limit ♦

Mama's Bad Boy / 1992 / In-A-Minute/No Limit ♦

Ghetto's Tryin' to Kill Me! / Jul. 15, 1994 / No Limit/Priority ♦♦♦

99 Ways to Die / 1995 / No Limit/Priority ♦♦

Ice Cream Man / Apr. 1996 / No Limit/Priority ♦♦♦

● **Ghetto D** / Sep. 2, 1997 / No Limit/Priority ♦♦♦♦♦
On the surface, *Ghetto D* may look like another piece of product from Master P's No Limit empire, and there's a certain amount of truth to that. Master P is a master marketer and he knows how to create demand for his product, which means informing the public that it is out there. He spreads the word about future No Limit releases throughout *Ghetto D*: artwork for forthcoming albums forms 90 percent of the album's artwork, and No Limit artists rap on the record as much as Master P himself. As a result, *Ghetto D* plays much like one of the *West Coast Bad Boyz* discs—it sounds like a various-artists sampler. And not only does it sound like a various-artists record, it also sounds like a virtual catalog of '90s rap styles, from wimpy Bone Thugs-N-Harmony ballads ("1 Miss My Homies") to Wu-Tang craziness ("Let's Get 'Em) to G-funk ("Weed & Money"). Master P is a consummate ripoff artist, capable of copying any number of popular records and styles with flair. He's done this on almost all of No Limit's records, but what makes *Ghetto D* different is the ease of the whole thing. Master P is using better equipment this time around, which helps him make better, more seamless records, thereby making his facsimiles sound similar to the originals. The shameless ripoffs make *Ghetto D* an entertaining listen—it's fun to guess who the No Limit crew is ripping off now—yet it's hampered by its ridiculous 80-minute running time. Theoretically, it gives you more bang for your buck, but by the ninth song, "Captain Kirk," the album seems endless. However, that overindulgence is a hallmark of Master P and No Limit, and that's what makes *Ghetto D* his definitive statement. —*Stephen Thomas Erlewine*

MP Da Last Don / Jun. 2, 1998 / No Limit/Priority ♦♦♦

Only God Can Judge Me / Oct. 26, 1999 / No Limit/Priority ♦♦

Ghetto Postage / Nov. 28, 2000 / No Limit/Priority ♦♦♦♦
It's hard to attribute musical quality to Master P's success in the late '90s, but primarily based upon the quality of *Ghetto Postage* rather than marketing gimmicks or musical trends, the rapper has come close to rivaling his best album of the 1990s, *Ghetto D*. Like that breakthrough album, *Ghetto Postage* is a simplistic *tour de force* through a myriad of proven gangsta rap motifs. Beginning with the standard "I'm Bout It" variation, this time titled "Bout Dat," Master P and his post-Beats By the Pound production team—primarily Carlos Stephens, XL, Ke-Noe, Myke Diesel, and Suga Bear—move through the motifs without making them seem too clichéd and, more importantly, performing with an aura of confidence and poise, two attributes sorely lacking on *Only God Can Judge Me,* this album's clumsy predecessor. So while *Ghetto Postage* doesn't win any awards for finesse or craft, even if it is one of the best No Limit albums, it does deserve acclaim for not surrendering to the trite stunnin'-bling-bling-flossfest clichés littering rap at the end of 2000 and for at least being a blatant motif exercise with integrity—thug farce or not, Master P is actually a rather *likable* guy here. And more than anything, he does what he does best here: He gives his fans exactly what they want—ultra-simple, call-and-response gangsta rap with charisma—without any self-serving, egocentric attempts to be an "artist." —*Jason Birchmeier*

The Master's Apprentices
f. 1965, db. 1972
One could easily make the case for designating the Master's Apprentices as the best Australian rock band of the '60s. Featuring singer Jim Keays and songwriter/rhythm guitarist Mick Bower, the band's earliest recordings combined the gritty R&B/rock of Brits like the Pretty Things with the minor-key melodies of the Yardbirds. The compelling "Wars or Hands of Time" and the dreamy psychedelia of "Living in a Child's Dream" were undiscovered classics, although the latter was a Top Ten hit in Australia. Bower left the group after suffering a nervous breakdown in late 1967, and the Masters grew steadily less interesting, moving from flower pop and hard rock to progressive and acoustic sounds. Plagued by instability (undergoing eight personnel changes between 1966 and 1968), the group moved to England in the early '70s, achieving some cult success with progressive rock albums before breaking up in 1972. —*Richie Unterberger*

The Master's Apprentices / 1967 / Regal Zonophone ♦♦♦
Debut mixes sloppy covers of popular '60s rock and soul tunes with some fine originals, most of which were reissued on the much more widely available best-of *Hands of Time.* Collectors will find this of most interest for the fairly strong original track "Theme for a Social Climber," which somehow didn't make it onto that compilation. The German CD reissue also includes their second album, *Masterpiece.* —*Richie Unterberger*

● **Hands of Time** / 1980 / Raven ♦♦♦♦♦
Twenty-four-song compilation covering the group's most popular recordings from 1965-72. The eight Mick Bower-penned cuts from 1965-67 are the clear highlights; most of the rest, like much of the Australian rock of the time, is extremely derivative of British progressive rock trends. Includes excellent detailed history by renowned Australian rock archivist Glenn A. Baker. —*Richie Unterberger*

Jam It Up! / 1986 / Raven ♦♦

Masterpiece / 1991 / TRC ♦♦♦
The group had changed a lot in both personnel and style by the time they issued their second LP, two and a half years after their first. It's a respectable but oddly schizophrenic effort, finding them searching for an identity with competent forays into hard rock, early

progressive rock, and poppy folk-rock, with orchestral instrumental links between many of the tracks adding to the confusion (as there's no concept driving the LP). "A Dog, a Siren and Memories" ranks as the most accurate Simon & Garfunkel imitation ever. The German CD reissue also includes their first, self-titled album. —*Richie Unterberger*

Masters of Reality
f. 1986
Stoner Metal, Progressive Metal, Heavy Metal, Hard Rock
Led by singer/guitarist Chris Goss, Masters of Reality were something of an anomaly on the late-'80s/early-'90s rock scene, playing a strongly Cream- and Zeppelin-influenced brand of hard rock with modern touches. Their original members included bassist Googe, guitarist Tim Harrington, and drummer Vinnie Ludovico. Goss broke up the band shortly after their well-received, self-titled debut album in 1989; he reformed the group as a trio a few years later with Googe and legendary ex-Cream drummer Ginger Baker. This lineup recorded 1993's *Sunrise on the Sufferbus,* which slightly altered the group's sound but again received enthusiastic reviews. However, Masters of Reality never quite fit into prevailing hard rock trends, and they remained a well-kept secret to most of the listening public. In hindsight, their retro obsessions and warm, spacious guitar sound set a clear precedent for the '90s stoner-rock movement; while the Masters' less metallic sound wouldn't have been a perfect stylistic fit, the link was reinforced by Goss' acclaimed production work on three of the four Kyuss albums. Those records helped pave the way for a new career in production for Goss, and Masters of Reality went on hiatus for several years. Goss reunited with Googe in 1997, adding guitarist Brendan McNichol and drummer Victor Indrizzo for a series of live dates that resulted in the album *How High the Moon: Live at the Viper Room.* An all-new studio album titled *Welcome to the Western Lodge* was released in Europe in 1999, but did not appear on American shores until Spitfire licensed it in early 2001. —*Steve Huey*

Masters of Reality / 1988 / Delicious Vinyl ♦♦♦♦
Because the Los Angeles-based Masters of Reality took their name from the title of a scorching Black Sabbath album, some assumed they were a heavy metal band. But in fact, their forte is a bluesy approach with a late-1960s/early-'70s type of appeal. Though subtle traces of Sabbath can occasionally be heard on a few of their songs, their sound owes a lot more to Ten Years After and the Doors. First released by Def American in 1989 and reissued by Delicious Vinyl in 1990, this impressive offering was produced by Rick Rubin and has the markings of a Rubin production. The thing that makes Rubin so great a producer is his willingness to follow his gut instincts, an approach that has served him well whether producing Slayer, Johnny Cash, or L.L. Cool J, and one that clearly works to the Masters' advantage on such pearls as "Domino," "Gettin' High," and "The Eyes of Texas." Rubin is the type of producer who knows how to step aside when appropriate and let artists be themselves. Under his direction, the material sounds well produced, but never over-produced. —*Alex Henderson*

● **Sunrise on the Sufferbus** / 1993 / Chrysalis ♦♦♦♦♦
Although they were short-lived, the Masters of Reality were indeed one of the finest bands to emerge from the early '90s. Obviously, having Ginger Baker on drums was enough to ensure them some publicity. Baker's playing on the album is striking, to say the least. But it's Chris Goss' songwriting and singing, which brilliantly wed British blues and the more whimsical style of Ray Davies, that really surprise. One of the decade's true lost classics. —*Matthew Greenwald*

How High the Moon: Live at the Viper Room / Jun. 10, 1997 / Malicious Vinyl ♦♦♦♦
Even though they play hard rock, the Masters of Reality's sensibilities have always been more in line with the improvisatory nature of late-'60s blues-rock than the plodding chords of late-'70s arena-rock. Consequently, it shouldn't be a surprise that *How High the Moon: Live at the Viper Room* captures the band at their best, running through several of their staples plus a handful of new songs. What really matters is the group's musical interplay and the ideas they trade throughout the concert. There's a genuine spark and excitement to their exchanges, which makes *How High the Moon* one of their most successful records. —*Stephen Thomas Erlewine*

Welcome to the Western Lodge / 1999 / Spitfire ♦♦

Matchbox Twenty
f. 1996
Adult Alternative Pop/Rock, Post-Grunge, Pop/Rock
Upon the release of their debut album *Yourself or Someone Like You* in the fall of 1996, Matchbox Twenty was pigeonholed as one of the legions of post-grunge guitar-bands that roamed the American pop scene in the middle of the '90s. As their breakthrough single, "Push," climbed the charts, it was widely assumed that they were a one-hit wonder, but *Yourself or Someone Like You* continued to spin off singles well into 1998. By then, the Orlando-based group made up of Rob Thomas, Brian Yale, Paul Doucette, Adam Gaynor, and Kyle Cook had managed to make their mix of '70s arena rock and early '90s American alterna-rock the sound of mainstream American rock.

Matchbox Twenty reserved 1999 as the year to record their eagerly anticipated second album, but they didn't disappear from the spotlight due to the unexpected success of "Smooth," a Santana song co-written and sung by Rob Thomas. Throughout the second half of 1999, "Smooth" was inescapable, as it and *Supernatural* sat on the top of the pop charts. Its success brought more attention to Matchbox Twenty, and sales of *Yourself or Someone Like You* rocketed to over ten million copies.

All of this success happened as Matchbox Twenty was recording its second album. The success raised expectations for the new album, entitled *Mad Season,* which was released in May, 2000. The album, while as polished and radio-friendly as their debut release, nevertheless failed to make the outstanding commercial impact that *Yourself of Someone Like You* had achieved. —*Stephen Thomas Erlewine*

● **Yourself or Someone Like You** / Oct. 1, 1996 / Atlantic ✦✦✦

Yourself or Someone Like You turned out to be the standard-bearer for post-alternative rock because it has a '90s sheen in its production, but, for all the world, its core sounds like classic rock. Lead singer/songwriter Rob Thomas adopted some of Eddie Vedder's vocal mannerisms, but they were smoothed out, lacking the angst and pain that were Vedder's hallmark. Matchbox Twenty functioned much the same way, picking up at Pearl Jam's fascination for album rock, but deciding to stick to the classic blueprint instead of personalizing it. All of this resulted in a record that is much more straightforward than most alt-rock albums, even if it follows the pattern of a classic '90s album—not just in its production dynamics, but down to the acoustic-based slow number that closes the record. It blends the most familiar elements of the two golden eras of album-oriented rock, finding a balance that is comfortable for mainstream fans of either side. Other bands with similar sounds that could have done the same thing, yet matchbox twenty distanced themselves from the pack with sturdy songs and fairly strong hooks, all delivered forcefully with Thomas' distinctive bravado. Their music is not flashy, nor is it as ingratiating as Third Eye Blind's pop instincts. It is, however, solid, American rock, reminiscent of a blend of Petty and Pearl Jam. So, it shouldn't have been surprising when the album found a wide audience. For many observers it was still unexpected, because the sound seemed a little plain. What they didn't realize was that *Yourself or Someone Like You* wound up being the point where mainstream American rock stopped being willfully eccentric and returned to being unassuming and kind of ordinary. —*Stephen Thomas Erlewine*

Mad Season / May 23, 2000 / Atlantic ✦✦✦✦

On *Yourself or Someone Like You*, Matchbox Twenty's ability to craft sturdy, mainstream rock was overshadowed by their reliance on loud guitars, colorless production, and bombastic vocalizing. They trade that sound for a varied, accomplished, smooth production on their second album, *Mad Season*. Throughout this record, Matchbox Twenty seem unashamed that they sound their best when they're simply a mainstream rock band. They exploit this strength by expanding the production, adding horns and layers of keyboards to their sound, opening up the mix, and emphasizing their melodies. That shift in direction may disarm some fans of the debut, which was pretty much just guitars, but the band winds up with a big, bright, shiny album that's livelier than its predecessor. That alone makes *Mad Season* more engaging than the debut, but the real surprise is the group's growth as craftsmen and Rob Thomas' progression as a songwriter and singer. Prior to this album, Thomas had a tendency to oversell his songs, not just in the delivery but in the writing, and the band followed him along. Here, they tone down their performances and while the end result is heavily produced, the overall feel is more relaxed and welcoming than the debut. Of course, it also helps that they have a solid set of songs—a set that eclipses their previous effort, even if there are a few dull moments here and there. Even with those occasional missteps, the end result is a strong, unabashedly mainstream record that finds the band coming into their own. —*Stephen Thomas Erlewine*

Matching Mole

f. 1971, **db.** 1972

Canterbury Scene, Prog Rock/Art Rock

Between his departure from the Soft Machine and the proper beginning of his solo career, Robert Wyatt steered Matching Mole, an outfit which bore much similarity to his later work with Soft Machine. Indeed, the name Matching Mole was chosen as a subtle pun on Soft Machine (the sound of the English words "matching mole" are very similar to the French translation of "soft machine," *machine molle*). However, Matching Mole didn't measure up to either his best Soft Machine work or his best solo outings. Although Wyatt occasionally let his vocal charm and humor shine, in the main Matching Mole were an outlet for the improvisational talents of the band, which often veered from inspiration into dated fusionoid noodling.

The first lineup of Matching Mole also included former Caravan member Dave Sinclair on keyboards, Phil Miller on guitar, and Bill MacCormick. Wyatt wrote most of the material on the 1972 self-titled debut. By the follow-up, *Little Red Book* (also 1972), Sinclair had been replaced by David MacRae, and the group had become a more democratic enterprise, with all the members contributing material more or less equally. Robert Fripp produced the second LP, and Eno guested on synthesizer on one track, though neither celebrity dramatically affected or improved the band's sound. Never destined to be a commercial enterprise, Matching Mole had folded by the end of 1972; Wyatt began his lengthy solo career, and Phil Miller went on to two other Canterbury art-rock bands, Hatfield & the North and National Health. —*Richie Unterberger*

● **Matching Mole** / 1972 / BGO ✦✦✦✦

The opening track, "O Caroline," is indicative of Wyatt at his best: art rock with a human face, a playful vocal, and soul. Much of the record is instrumental improvisation, though, with the humor largely confined to the song titles ("Instant Pussy," "Dedicated to Hugh, But You Weren't Listening"). For every nifty passage (the extended melancholy Mellotron solo on "Immediate Curtain," the goofy scat vocals on "Signed Curtain"), there's equal or greater instrumental patter. Some art-rock devotees really get behind this album, but it doesn't count among the more enduring statements by the Canterbury crowd. —*Richie Unterberger*

Little Red Record / 1972 / BGO ✦✦

Maybe it's because Wyatt relinquished his firm upper hand on the songwriting (everybody in the band pens material) and production (Robert Fripp takes over), but this is a distinct comedown from Matching Mole's debut. The fusion rock chops assert themselves much more strongly on this largely instrumental set, though not to any great effect or

purpose. It's not just difficult listening, but a bit of a bore, which is probably not what they intended. Another great song title, though, in "Starting in the Middle of the Day We Can Drink Our Politics Away." —*Richie Unterberger*

Smoke Signals / May 22, 2001 / Cuneiform ✦✦✦

Recorded at various European performances from the spring of 1972, this is a substantial addition to the catalog of a band that only put out two studio albums. The sound is good, and the performances almost wholly instrumental art jazz-rock, not far removed from those heard in the early 1970s by the Soft Machine, drummer/singer Robert Wyatt's previous band. It's electric pianist Bill McRae who wrote most of the material on this disc, and it's the sort of cerebral, intricate, serious fusion-y stuff that might appeal as much, or more, to jazzheads as to prog rockers. Wyatt goes off into some wordless scats at one point, but these aren't conventional rock-songs-with-lyrics at all. There is an admirable variety of textures with some distortion and buzzing, cooked up by McRae and guitarist Phil Miller, but it doesn't boast very accessible melodic ideas, preferring to furrow into angular and at times ominous progressions. The eerie, electronically treated vocal scatting on Wyatt's mischievously titled "Instant Pussy" is a highlight. Five of the nine songs, incidentally, do not appear on the band's studio albums. —*Richie Unterberger*

Material Issue

f. 1986, Chicago, IL, **db.** 1972

Power Pop, Alternative Pop/Rock

Material Issue's music is a return to the classic power-pop formula: catchy, melodic songs driven by loud, jangly guitars and usually paying tribute to girls and teenage love. The inevitable Beatles/Big Star/Cheap Trick/Tom Petty comparisons sparked intense interest in the band from power-pop fans and critics, and the group's musical allegiances were further underscored when ex-Shoes member Jeff Murphy produced their first two records, and Cheap Trick's Rick Nielsen guested on 1994's *Freak City Soundtrack*. The group was formed in Chicago by vocalist/guitarist Jim Ellison, an early member of Green, and his friend Ted Ansani (bass); they located drummer Mike Zelenko through a want ad. They released a self-titled EP in 1987 and attracted some local attention through a 1989 single. Their 1991 debut for Mercury, *International Pop Overthrow*, was hailed as pure power-pop in all its glory and earned the group a fan base; several songs became hits on modern-rock radio. *Destination Universe* tended to follow an identical formula and was not as well received. *Freak City Soundtrack* utilized a more streamlined,'70s hard rock production and consolidated the group's standing as critics' darlings, but when the album failed to sell, Mercury dropped the group. Sadly, Ellison committed suicide on June 20, 1996, suffocating himself in his garage with carbon monoxide fumes from his moped. —*Steve Huey*

● **International Pop Overthrow** / Feb. 5, 1991 / Mercury ✦✦✦✦✦

A title like *International Pop Overthrow* suggests a far more revolutionary and ambitious approach than what Material Issue actually served up on their first album—Jim Ellison doesn't sound like he wants to take over the world so much as he wants (a) a girl to like him, and (b) three-minute pop songs to regain their rightful place on the radio (which, come to think of it, was a fairly revolutionary notion in 1991). Singer/guitarist/songwriter Ellison and his partners Ted Ansani on bass and Mike Zelenko on drums sound like power-pop classicists, worshiping at the altar of Big Star, the Raspberries, and the Scruffs, though Ellison's melodies are leaner and more direct than those of his obvious inspirations, and his willingness to turn up the tempos and let the guitars distort reminds us all that punk influenced good pop as much as pop influenced good punk. ("Trouble" and the title cut also confirm that Ellison occasionally thought about subjects other than girls.) The production by Jeff Murphy (whose band, Shoes, were doubtless another key influence on MI's sound) is clean and uncluttered, but maybe a bit too much so—while nothing gets in the band's way, the group rarely displays as much power as they deserve, and the boomy sound could stand to be balanced with a bit more top-end crunch (especially on the hard-driving title track, which does feature the album's best line—"I don't need a girlfriend, I need an accomplice"). But anyone who was looking for the future of power pop in 1991 might well have imagined these guys were it, and now without reason—*International Pop Overthrow* is smart, hooky, and not afraid to sound edgy or let the amps go into the red. —*Mark Deming*

Destination Universe / Mar. 1992 / Mercury ✦✦✦

Led by frontman Jim Ellison, Material Issue produced some of the '90s most memorable power-pop moments by combining the best elements of Cheap Trick and Shoes. *Destination Universe*, the band's sophomore effort, showcases their talent for punching out three-minute sonic bursts of energy. Each song packs irresistible hooks, crunchy pop guitars, and soaring vocals into brief odes to love both lost "Ballad of a Lonely Man" and found "Next Big Thing." There's not a whole lot of variation here, but when the formula works, on tracks such as "What Girls Want," "The Loneliest Heart," and "Don't You Think I Know," it's difficult to argue. Though not their most commercially successful release, *Destination Universe* may be Material Issue's most consistently satisfying album. —*Michael Frey*

Freak City Soundtrack / Mar. 8, 1994 / Mercury ✦✦✦

If anyone knows power pop, it's Mike Chapman. Having produced everyone from Blondie and the Knack to Sweet and Scandal, Chapman is an undisputed master when it comes to uniting guitar-powered rock aggression and pop infectiousness. Chapman did exactly that when he produced Material Issue's third album, the superb *Freak City Soundtrack*. From "Ordinary Girl" and "Funny Feeling" to the clever single "Kim the Waitress," Chapman brings out the best in the melodic yet hard-rockin' band. Issue never fails to rock any more than it fails to employ irresistible hooks and a striking harmonic sense. One can pinpoint a variety of influences from the 1960s and '70s—Cheap Trick, Sweet, and Thin Lizzy as well as the Byrds and the Beatles—but there's no question that Material Issue was a fine band in its own right. Sadly, this CD wasn't the big commercial breakthrough Issue's followers were hoping it would be. *—Alex Henderson*

Telecommando Americano / May 20, 1997 / Rykodisc ♦♦♦

It's hard not to listen to *Telecommando Americano* and feel a sense of loss, given that guitarist/songwriter Jim Ellison commited suicide shortly after completing the recording of these 11 songs. Technically, the record would have been demos for Material Issue's fourth album, but they are all that he left behind, and they demonstrate that he had a gift for both jangly and fuzzy power-pop hooks. No matter how good these are, there's a sense that Ellison took his life before he reached his full potential, and that's really what makes *Telecommando Americano* so sad—he had the gift, but he hadn't completely mastered it yet. [*Telecommando Americano* also features the trio's eponymous 1987 debut EP, which is the first time the record has been available on compact disc.] *—Stephen Thomas Erlewine*

Dave Matthews

b. Jan. 9, 1967, Johannesburg, South Africa

Vocals, Guitar / Jam Bands, American Trad Rock, Adult Alternative Pop/Rock

The South African vocalist/guitarist Dave Matthews formed his namesake band in Virginia in the early '90s. The group's music presents a more pop-oriented version of The Grateful Dead, crossed with the worldbeat explorations of Paul Simon and Sting. The band built up a strong word-of-mouth following in the early '90s by touring the country constantly, concentrating on college campuses. In addition to amassing a sizable following, their self-released album *Remember Two Things* sold well for an independent release; soon, they were attracting the attention of majors. Signing with RCA, the Dave Matthews Band released their major-label debut, *Under the Table & Dreaming*, in the fall of 1994. By spring of 1995, the record had launched the hit single "What Would You Say" and sold over a million copies. A year and a half after its release, the record had sold over four million copies in the U.S. alone. In April of 1996, the Dave Matthews Band released *Crash*, which entered the charts at number two and quickly went platinum. *—Stephen Thomas Erlewine*

Remember Two Things / 1993 / RCA ♦♦♦

Although the Dave Matthews Band's debut album *Remember Two Things* is hindered by a number of long-winded jams and an unfocused production, the record is an impressive showcase for their instrumental prowess. *—Stephen Thomas Erlewine*

Recently / 1994 / RCA ♦♦♦♦

A captivating and enthralling release, the Dave Matthews Band put forth a strong effort to produce a record that identifies their personality. *Recently* was initially sold only to fan club members. Led by lead singer/guitarist Dave Matthews, the five-some blends a mix of soulful grooves and eclectic percussive rhythms to create a majestic portrait of musical art they can claim as their own. Each member of this group seems to be a gifted virtuoso at his instrument. Leroi Moore, educated in the art of jazz, lights up the beauty and richness of the sax. Carter Beauford deepens the band's texture with an overwhelming but alluring presence of rhythms. Boyd Tinsley is both elegant and colorful on violin. Stefan Lessard jams with shimmering brilliance on bass. The title track, "Recently," is delicate and smooth, with the polished percussive jamming of Matthews on acoustic guitar. Friend and accomplished guitarist/arranger extraordinaire Tim Reynolds shares the spotlight in the tune "Dancing Nancies." Most importantly, this record grants the listeners an early look at the Dave Matthews Band live in concert. A mysterious and haunting Bob Dylan tune "All Along the Watchtower" is performed with startling power. The track, along with the equally frightening "Halloween," was recorded live at Trax, in Charlottesville, VA, in February of 1994. *—Shawn Haney*

● **Under the Table & Dreaming** / Apr. 1994 / RCA ♦♦♦♦♦

On their major-label debut, *Under the Table & Dreaming*, the Dave Matthews Band is helped by the lean production of Steve Lillywhite, who manages to rein in the group's tendency to meander. The result is a set of eclectic pop/rock that is accentuated by bursts of instrumental virtuosity instead of being ruled by it. That also means that the Dave Matthews Band is capable of turning out pop songs, and as the hit single "What Would You Say" and "Ants Marching" illustrate, they have a flair for catchy hooks. *—Stephen Thomas Erlewine*

Crash / Apr. 1996 / RCA ♦♦♦

Under the Table & Dreaming, the Dave Matthews Band's first major label album, was their popular breakthrough, bringing their mildly eclectic sound to a mass audience. Although the group appeals to the same audience as Blues Traveler, Hootie & the Blowfish, and the Spin Doctors, the Dave Matthews Band has more influences than their peers. Fusing together folk-rock, worldbeat, jazz, and pop, the band is arguably the most musically adept of all their contemporaries. However, they have trouble coming up with engaging hooks, as their third album, *Crash*, proves. Although the band continues to get better—their musical cross-breeding is effortless and seamless—they often don't have an attractive frame for their skills. Strangely, the lack of memorable melodies doesn't particularly hurt the album—it actually emphasizes the band's instrumental talents. Nevertheless, since there's a lack of strong pop hooks, *Crash* is an album that will please fans, but not novices. *—Stephen Thomas Erlewine*

Live at Red Rocks 8.15.95 / Oct. 28, 1997 / Bama Rags/RCA ♦♦♦♦

No other band in rock's history went to such great lengths to shut down bootleggers as the Dave Matthews Band. They shut down stores that sold live boots of Matthews concerts, and they shut down labels that pressed the bootlegs, essentially crippling the underground industry. That didn't stop the boots completely, however, and Matthews finally retalliated in the fall of 1997 with the double-disc *Live at Red Rocks 8.15.95*, the first in a series of official live albums from the band. To the outsider, this series might seem a little odd, since the group doesn't have an explicitly fanatical following like those of the Grateful Dead or Phish, but like those two bands, the Dave Matthews Band has a similar fondness for improvisation, which makes their live recordings desirable for dedicated fans. *Live at Red Rocks 8.15.95* shouldn't disappoint fans already familiar with the band's loose-limbed, jazzy live show, but it should come as a revelation to listeners unacquainted with that aspect of Matthews. In fact, the record often sounds livelier and more energetic than its studio counterparts, and that alone makes it a necessary purchase for dedicated fans. *—Stephen Thomas Erlewine*

Before These Crowded Streets / Apr. 28, 1998 / RCA ♦♦♦♦

The Dave Matthews Band made their reputation through touring, spending endless nights on the road improvising. Often, their records hinted at the eclecticism and adventure inherent in those improvisation, but *Before These Crowded Streets* is the first album to fully capture that adventurous spirit. Not coincidentally, it's their least accessible record, even if it's more of a consolidation than it is a step forward. Early Dave Matthews albums were devoted to the worldbeat fusions of *Graceland* and Sting, but his RCA efforts incorporated these influences into a smoother, pop-oriented style. Here, everything hangs out. Old trademarks, like jittery acoustic grooves and jazzy chords, are here, augmented by complex polyrhythms, Mideastern dirges and, on two tracks, the slashing strings of the Kronos Quartet. Some fans may find the new, darker textures a little disarming at first, but they're a logical extension of the group's work, and in many ways, this sonic daring results in the most rewarding album they've yet recorded. The Dave Matthews Band hasn't completely vanquished their demons, however—songwriting remains a problem, especially since relying on grooves, improvisation, and texture allows them to skimp on melody, and Matthews' lyrics can be awkward and embarrassing, especially if he's writing about sex. Still, these are minor flaws on an album that relies on tone and improvisation, both of which are in ample supply on *Before These Crowded Streets*. *—Stephen Thomas Erlewine*

Live at Luther College / Jan. 19, 1999 / RCA ♦♦♦♦

After the bootleg industry was revolutionized by CDs in the late '80s, it seemed that every contemporary recording artist had at least one bootleg on the market. It wasn't that studio outtakes were suddenly available—it was that it was easier than ever to record, press, and distribute live concerts. Rock bands who jammed, whether they were hard rockers like Pearl Jam or noodlers like Phish, were in particular demand since, as the adage goes, no two shows were exactly alike. Given this inastiable appetite for new live records, it's a wonder that more artists didn't make like Dave Matthews and launch a series of official releases of notable live shows. It especially makes sense in Matthews' case, since his band sounds better and is more adventurous in a live setting than they are in the studio, as the first installment, *Live at Red Rocks Rocks* illustrated. Its follow-up, *Live at Luther College*, takes a different tactic. Instead of featuring the band, it's Matthews alone acoustically, supported by his friend, session guitarist Tim Reynolds. The double-disc album was culled from the duo's 1996 tour and, not surprisingly, the bulk of the material focuses on Matthews' first two albums for RCA. What is surprising is that the songs arguably sound better in this setting, since all of the group improvisations are stripped away, leaving the songs to speak for themselves. Accordingly, Matthews isn't nearly as eccentric in his vocal tics, letting the music flow simply and engagingly. The results are quite entertaining, and even if the album was intended just for fans, it's the rare specialty item that could win new listeners. *—Stephen Thomas Erlewine*

Listener Supported / Nov. 23, 1999 / RCA ♦♦♦

With the release of the double-disc *Listener Supported* in 1999, the Dave Matthews Band now had four live albums to their credit (including their self-released debut *Remember Two Things* and Matthews' solo set *Live at Luther College*). Bootleggers had discovered that certain bands had voracious audiences who would listen to anything by the group. Once Dave Matthews discovered he had one of those bands and that he had scores of unofficial discs on the market, he decided to release official live albums on a regular basis. A good business decision, but it has the effect of diluting his discography somewhat, especially when the end result is as ordinary as *Listener Supported*. Unlike audience tapes and bootlegged shows—which, in an ideal world, capture a band loose and unaware—the concert on *Listener Supported* was recorded for a PBS television show, *In the Spotlight*. This may have affected their performance somewhat, since there just isn't much energy to the recording. Part of the problem is that DMB don't really explore new musical territory through improvisations—they just settle into a groove and ride it. Not that there's anything wrong with that, but it does mean that there's not as much identity to an individual DMB show as there is in, say, a Phish show. When the band nails the groove live, they can be more engaging than they are on record. But if they just float on by, as they do on *Listener Supported*, the songs and jams are flatter and never really go anywhere. If you're already a fan—a very devoted fan—that's fine, but otherwise, listening to these two discs nonstop will be a little dull. DMB are capable of more than this; *Listener Supported* just captures them on an off night. *—Stephen Thomas Erlewine*

Everyday / Feb. 27, 2001 / RCA ♦♦♦

The fourth proper studio album by the Dave Matthews Band had a rough birth, as the group jettisoned a set of sessions recorded with their longtime producer Steve Lillywhite, starting afresh with Glen Ballard, the mastermind behind Alanis Morissette's *Jagged Little Pill*. Ballard has a tremendous influence on the resulting record, collaborating with Matthews on every track and changing the direction of their sound. To a certain extent, the change is welcome, since *Before These Crowded Streets* suggested that the group was running out of steam, but the sudden shift toward measured maturation and slickness is jarring all the same, since it emphasizes Matthews' melodies and leadership over the group interplay that is the group's calling card. It's not that the music is now simplistic, since there are still some tricky rhythms and shifts in tone, but the group doesn't have much room to stretch in Ballard's precise arrangements. In a sense, they sort of benefit from this increased focus, since the group's instrumental excursions can be a little flabby, but it still robs them of much of their character. Also, *Everyday* sounds like it was the product of a difficult birth and wouldn't have gelled if Ballard hadn't been involved, pushing Matthews toward completion. It does result in a record that's more cohesive than its predecessor, but it's far less engagingly loose-limbed than DMB at its peak. Perhaps that's just a byproduct of maturation, but *Everyday* feels like forced maturation, a record that suppresses the group's best attributes in favor of a moderate, self-consciously classy stab at adult pop. That it works pretty well at that level is a testament to Ballard's skills, but it feels more like a weirdly abortive solo project by Matthews than a full-fledged DMB effort. —*Stephen Thomas Erlewine*

Eric Matthews

b. 1969, Compton, California

Vocals, Trumpet, Organ / Indie Pop, Chamber Pop, Indie Rock, Singer/Songwriter

The work of Eric Matthews was a direct reaction to the lo-fi recording practices so prevalent throughout the alternative music scene of the 1990s; while many of the decade's artists trafficked in a defiantly ragged, do-it-yourself aesthetic, Matthews' records grew out of orchestral theories and practices and revelled in the stately elegance of warm harmonies and lush arrangements. Matthews fell in love with the symphonic pop of the Beach Boys, Burt Bacharach, and the Bee Gees at an early age; John Williams' score for *Star Wars* steered him into orchestral music, and he picked up his first instrument, the trumpet, while in elementary school. With Richard Davies, an Australian-born singer/songwriter best known for fronting the cult band the Moles, he formed the duo Cardinal, a forum for Davies' wry songwriting and Matthews' arranging skills and instrumental talents (which now included a mastery of piano, organ, harpsichord, and marimba). Internal difficulties resulted in Cardinal's brief lifespan, however, and Matthews soon resurfaced as a solo artist. In 1995, he issued his debut, *It's Heavy in Here*, an ornate, complex collection highlighting his emerging vocal and composing skills. The excellent *Lateness of the Hour* followed in 1997. —*Jason Ankeny*

● **It's Heavy in Here** / Sep. 26, 1995 / Sub Pop ✦✦✦✦✦

Sounding like Lou Barlow singing Nick Drake songs, Eric Matthews constructs an impressive debut with *It's Heavy in Here*, and construct is the right word. Matthews composes and arranges his songs, using string sections, arpeggiated guitars, trumpets, and whispered vocals—it's orchestral pop for the post-Nirvana generation. *It's Heavy in Here* works both as a mood piece and as individual songs—the individual tracks balance each other, providing different shades, textures, and variations on one theme. Matthews' sighing melodies reflect beautiful melancholy, not a haunting despair, and that's why *It's Heavy in Here* is such a refreshing debut. —*Stephen Thomas Erlewine*

The Lateness of the Hour / Aug. 26, 1997 / Sub Pop ✦✦✦✦✦

Displaying an increased sense of songcraft and sharper arrangements, *The Lateness of the Hour* takes the virtues of Eric Matthews' debut, *It's Heavy in Here*, and amplifies them, resulting in a richer, fuller album. Where its predecessor only made a passing acknowledgment of rock, there's more guitar on *The Lateness of the Hour*, and it has a less orchestral feel—the strings and horns are used as coloring, accentuating the songs in the style of swinging '60s pop. Matthews still has a problem with writing provocative lyrics, but his melodicism is at a peak. Each song has a memorable melody which is surrounded by rolling guitars, lush strings, and sweet brass. The best songs have an effortless grace, while even the weaker moments are enjoyable because of the lavish arrangements. For some listeners, Matthews might be too precious—his voice is almost inhumanly fey and breathy—but on the basis of *The Lateness of the Hour* there's little denying that he is developing into a first-rate songwriter and arranger. —*Stephen Thomas Erlewine*

Ian Matthews (Ian Matthews MacDonald)

b. Jun. 1946, Lincolnshire, England

Vocals, Guitar, Guitar (Acoustic) / British Folk-Rock, British Folk, Folk-Rock, Singer/ Songwriter

Ian Matthews (now spelled Iain to reflect his Celtic roots) has had a widely varied and complex recording career. He began as the lead singer for Fairport Convention, but during their 1969 *Unhalfbricking* sessions, he decided to leave due to growing musical differences with the band. After making his first solo album, *Matthews Southern Comfort*, he released two albums with a band of the same name. They had a hit with a version of "Woodstock." Matthews left in 1971 for a second chance at a solo career, releasing two fine folk-rock albums for Vertigo. He then formed Plainsong while finishing the contractual obligation album, *Journey From Gospel Oak*—one of his finest recorded moments despite the conditions. Plainsong released one critically acclaimed album on Elektra and then disbanded while recording the second. His stay at Elektra ended after two more acclaimed yet overlooked country-folk albums—*Valley Hi* (1973) and *Some Days You Eat the Bear and Some Days the Bear Eats You* (1974). He began experimenting in different styles for the rest of the '70s, often with uninspired and unsuccessful results. He did, however, have a U.S. Top Ten hit in 1978 with "Shake It" from the *Stealin Home* album. The '90s have found him reviving his solo career, signing to Watermelon Records and returning to his folk-rock roots. —*Chris Woodstra*

Matthews Southern Comfort / 1969 / Decca ✦✦✦✦

This is a transitional album for Matthews. Having recently exited Fairport Convention, this record pays tribute to that period of his career in both material ("A Castle Far") and in the choice of musicians who back him (many of them from Fairport Convention). At

the same time, songs like "A Commercial Proposition" indicate where Matthews is headed on 1971's *Later That Same Year*. —*Jim Worbois*

Second Spring / 1969 / Line ✦✦✦

With this album, Matthews' Southern Comfort is a real band and, in addition to Matthews, also includes Roger Swallow (ex-Marmalade) and Marc Griffiths (ex-Spooky Tooth). Though there is really nothing that makes this a memorable record, it's still quite a nice record overall. If you already know his work on Elektra, Mooncrest, or even *Later That Same Year*, it would be well worth your while to search this record out. —*Jim Worbois*

1 2 3 Too Good / 1970 / MCA ✦✦

Later That Same Year / Dec. 1970 / Line ✦✦✦

Best known for the hit "Woodstock," this is really the album on which Matthews first finds his direction. A nice mix of covers and originals, this record has held up nicely over the years. —*Jim Worbois*

If You Saw Thro' My Eyes / Jan. 1971 / Vertigo ✦✦✦✦✦

In late 1970, shortly after his band Matthews Southern Comfort hit number one in Great Britain with its version of Joni Mitchell's "Woodstock," Ian Matthews decided that he needed more creative freedom and left for a solo career. The subsequent album, *If You Saw Thro' My Eyes*, his fourth and best release since leaving Fairport Convention in 1969, was recorded and released within the next few months. It also reunited him with former Fairport bandmates Sandy Denny, who had left the band in late 1969, and Richard Thompson, who would depart by the time of this album's release. Both would bring their distinctive personalities to the proceedings without ever overwhelming Matthews' own vision. As a bandleader and songwriter, Matthews' growth is quite evident here, guiding a stellar cast through seven excellent new originals and three well-chosen covers. Throughout, Matthews' sweet yet evocative tenor is perfect for the material, which succeeds in its blend of British and American folk, rock, and pop. Furthermore, he once again shows a keen eye for the work of others, while also proving his prowess as a first-rate interpretive singer. But it's the beautiful, prayer-like title track that is the record's crowning moment. Joined simply by Denny's piano and breathtaking second vocal, along with a tasteful backwards guitar interlude by Renwick, Matthews' quiet plea for guidance is as moving and personal a song as he's ever recorded. A number of other highlights make *If You Saw Thro' My Eyes* one of the best efforts by a Fairport alumnus. —*Brett Hartenbach*

Tigers Will Survive / Nov. 1971 / Vertigo ✦✦✦✦

Tigers Will Survive, Ian Matthews' second release of 1971, and fifth in less than three years, continues the Anglo-American folk-rock that he began in 1968 with Fairport Convention. Following his departure from the band in early 1969, Matthews' style quickly veered from the British traditional direction that Fairport was headed, gravitating more toward the American singer/songwriter scene that was the source for much of the group's material in their early days, keeping him closer to the mid-Atlantic mix of *What We Did on Our Holidays* (his last record with the band). *If You Saw Thro' My Eyes*, his previous album, reunited him with members of his old band, as well as others from the revolving Fairport/Fotheringay cast, but this time out, with the exception of Richard Thompson's accordion on a couple of tunes (credited as Woolfe J. Flywheel), he opts for the backing of the English rock band Quiver. And while it may lack some of the cohesive personality of its predecessor, *Tigers Will Survive* still shares its primarily acoustic sound, augmented by a strong rhythm section and touches of electric guitar. Also, as was the case with that album, the toughest moment is courtesy of Richard Farina, whose "House of Unamerican Blues Activity Dream" brings an edginess and anger to Matthews' characteristically pretty and reflective tone, though his self-penned title track is close behind. Elsewhere, the beautiful "Morning Song" and Phil Spector's "Da Do Ron Ron" (without a change in gender) are high points for Ian Matthews, the songwriter and interpreter, respectively. The former is among the two or three best songs he'd written, while the latter, a wonderful a cappella rendition of the Crystals' classic, bolstered only by hand claps, brings a lightness and energy to the record. *Tigers Will Survive*, though just a rung below *If You Saw Thro' My Eyes*, is another fine effort for Matthews. The two recordings were later teamed together on one CD. —*Brett Hartenbach*

Journeys From Gospel Oak / 1972 / Mooncrest ✦✦✦✦✦

Billed as a contractual obligation record by the artist, *Journeys From Gospel Oak* is easily as good as Matthews' best work. It is most assuredly a companion piece to Plainsong's *In Search of Amelia Earhart* (an album loosely based on the disappearance of Amelia Earhart), this time loosely based around the night Hank Williams died. This album includes such solid tracks as Gene Clark's "Polly," "Bride 1945" by Paul Siebel, and the haunting Jimmy Webb tune, "Met Her on a Plane." A strong (but often overlooked record) and well worth the effort it takes to find a copy. —*Jim Worbois*

Valley Hi / 1973 / Elektra ✦✦✦✦

With ex-Monkee Michael Nesmith at the helm and an array of C&W sidemen on hand, Ian Matthews recorded what is probably his most overtly country album to date, 1973's *Valley Hi*. The record opens with a pair of tracks—his own "Keep on Sailing" and the traditional "Old Man at the Mill"—that had been scheduled to appear on the second release by his former band Plainsong, which Elektra chose to shelve. Matthews then proceeds to cover rarities by Randy Newman and Richard Thompson, whose "Shady Lies" had only surfaced before on an obscure 1969 recording by Fairport crony Marc Ellington, as well as chestnuts by Jackson Browne and country legend Don Gibson. Elsewhere, he delivers terrific versions of Nesmith's tale of friendship turned to love, "Propinquity," and Steve Young's now classic "7 Bridges Road." Matthews' excellent rendition of the latter set the standard for the song, which became a hit in the early '80s for the Eagles, using an identical arrangement. He also added one new original, along with two (including "Keep on

Sailing" and "Save Your Sorrows") from the aborted Plainsong release, all three of which rank with his best. Though he has since stated his dissatisfaction with the album, *Valley Hi* nonetheless remains among Ian Matthews' finest. *—Brett Hartenbach*

Some Days You Eat the Bear and Some Days the Bear Eats You / 1974 / Elektra ✦✦✦
Ian Matthews' fifth solo effort since leaving Matthews' Southern Comfort, *Some Days You Eat the Bear and Some Days the Bear Eats You* continues the country-rock of its predecessor, the Michael Nesmith-produced *Valley Hi*, but with more emphasis on the L.A. singer/songwriter sound and less on straightforward country. Though both records were recorded in Southern California, Nesmith brought a distinct Nashville flavor to *Valley Hi*, utilizing such country greats as steel guitarist Red Rhodes and fiddler Byron Berline. Here, Matthews (who handles the production duties) draws from the vast pool of L.A. session regulars, including Jackson Browne sideman David Lindley, Jeff "Skunk" Baxter from Steely Dan, and America's rhythm section. This—along with the occasional saxophone and double-tracked lead vocal—accentuates the pop sense evident just below the surface in Matthews' past work, giving *Some Days You Eat the Bear* a slightly more polished, commercial feel. For material, he once again borrows from the catalogs of favorites such as Jesse Winchester and Gene Clark (whose "Tried So Hard" seems to be a leftover from the *Valley Hi* sessions), as well as covering now-classic tunes by the likes of Steely Dan, Danny Whitten, and Tom Waits, all of which suit his warm, emotive tenor nicely. There's also the usual peppering of fine originals, which at their best hold their own next to his choice of covers. Matthews' best song here is also one of his most enduring, the Hank Williams tribute "A Wailing Goodbye," in which he imagines himself attending the funeral of the country & western legend. A solid final album for Elektra, *Some Days You Eat the Bear* seems to serve as the bridge between his folk and country-rock days of the late '60s and early '70s and the more pop and rock direction that would dominate the next decade of his career. *—Brett Hartenbach*

Go for Broke / 1975 / Columbia ✦✦

Hit and Run / 1976 / Columbia ✦✦

Stealin' Home / 1978 / Line ✦✦✦

Discreet Repeat / 1978 / Rockburgh ✦✦✦
This is a nice cross-label compilation which features some of his best work (stuff recorded for Vertigo, Elektra, and Mooncrest) as well as some of his least interesting work. If you are a fan of Matthews, you likely own all these records already. If not, this compilation will help you decide which areas of his career you will need to concentrate on in order to build your Ian Matthews collection. *—Jim Worbois*

Siamese Friends / 1979 / Line ✦✦

Spot of Interference / 1980 / Rockburgh ✦✦✦
With his previous outing, the overly polished *Siamese Friends* (1979), Ian Matthews failed to capitalize on the Top 20 success of "Shake It," from his 1978 release, *Stealin' Home*. He quickly returned the following year with a new U.S. label, a new direction, and a new album, *Spot of Interference*. His third straight record produced by Sandy Roberton, *Spot of Interference* leaves behind the MOR feel that had dominated his last four or five years, in favor of a power pop and new wave sound that fits him curiously well. Aside from pairing once again with Roberton, he also continues his work with *Siamese Friends* songwriting collaborators and musicians Bob Metzger and Mark Griffiths. These teamings yield some fine moments and performances, but it's covers like the frenetic pop/rock of "I Survived the '70s" and Jules Shear's "Driftwood From Disaster" that push Matthews, as well as his ordinarily sweet tenor, to the limit. And though this may seem a bit out of character, he never comes off like a misplaced folkie. Other highlights include former bandmate Richard Thompson's social rant, "Civilisation," as well as an updated version of the Left Banke's "She May Call You Up Tonight," which sounds as fresh here as it did in 1967. His one and only release for RSO Records, *Spot of Interference* was Matthews' best album since *Some Days You Eat the Bear and Some Days the Bear Eats You* in 1974. *—Brett Hartenbach*

Moods for Mallards / 1983 / Shanghai ✦✦

Shook / 1983 / Line ✦✦

Walking a Changing Line / 1988 / Windham Hill ✦✦✦
When PolyGram refused to release his 1983 record *Shook* in either the U.S. or England, Iain Matthews became disillusioned and decided to put his career on hold indefinitely. He returned in 1988 with an album dedicated solely to the songs of Jules Shear. Issued by Windham Hill, *Walking a Changing Line* was the label's first vocal release, though it still retained touches of the label's trademark new age sound throughout. Matthews' voice has rarely sounded better, and his choice of songs is inspired, showcasing both the depth and beauty of Shear's writing while staying away from obvious choices. Over half of the compositions were either rare or unknown at the time—even to many Shear aficionados—including two songs from a hard-to-find Jules and the Polar Bears EP and two tracks from their then-unreleased *Bad for Business* album. One of the previously unheard tunes, the reflective, a cappella "On Squirrel Hill," written about the Pittsburgh suburb where Shear grew up, couldn't be more ideally suited to Matthews' expressive tenor and style, and is not only one of the best moments on the record, but also of his career. Often, dated keyboard sounds and soporific synth preludes do become intrusive, not to mention indulgent, but it's a credit to Matthews' skill as an interpreter and Shear's brilliant songs that things never degenerate into new age mush. Still, with what seems to be the perfect pairing of singer and songwriter, along with demos and live versions—sans synthesizers—which surfaced in the succeeding years, one can't help but see *Walking a Changing Line* as a missed opportunity by Matthews to create not only a very good album, but a truly great one. *—Brett Hartenbach*

Pure & Crooked / Aug. 1990 / Watermelon ✦✦✦
On his second recording following a self-imposed, five-year hiatus, and his first featuring any original material, Iain Matthews (he changed the spelling of his first name to its original Gaelic form) returned with a songwriting vengeance, penning eight of the 11 tunes for *Pure & Crooked*, his 14th solo record. By no means prolific throughout most of his career—the majority of his albums contained maybe three or four originals—his output here had been prior to this, equaled only by the 1971 release *If You Saw Thro' My Eyes*. And while his previous recording, *Walking a Changing Line* showed him in fine form beneath its new age trappings, *Pure & Crooked* is as natural and assured as Matthews has sounded in quite awhile. Once again employing the the help of producer Mark Hallman, Matthews, with cuts such as "Like Dominoes," which opens the album, and the vitriolic "New Shirt," delivers some of the most convincing folk-rock of his career. Elsewhere, "Busby's Babes," a touching memory of his boyhood idols' untimely deaths; the reflective "Rains of '62," and the Charlie Parker inspired "Bridge of Cherokee," rank with his best songs. In the past, Matthews had always had a knack for finding great material from outside sources, and his trio of choices here are good enough, though only Peter Gabriel's "Mercy Street" truly stands out. Originally released on the now defunct Gold Castle label in 1990, *Pure & Crooked* was rereleased four years later on the Austin, TX-based Watermelon Records with five extra songs, including the a cappella tunes "Drive" and "O'Connell Street," and a terrific, live solo version of Danny Whitten's "I Don't Wanna Talk About It." *—Brett Hartenbach*

● **The Best of Matthews' Southern Comfort** / Mar. 10, 1992 / MCA ✦✦✦✦✦
A fine 16-track collection drawing from Matthews' first solo effort and the two Matthews' Southern Comfort albums. Includes the band's hit version of "Woodstock." *—Chris Woodstra*

Orphans & Outcasts, Vol. 1: Collection of Demos, 1969-1979 / 1993 / Dirty Linen ✦✦✦
Iain Matthews left Fairport Convention in 1969 and wasted no time in getting his own career started, releasing his first solo record within a few months of his departure. The decade that followed proved to be quite a productive one for him, including two bands and 13 albums, and by evidence of this 20-song collection, much more. These various outtakes, demos, radio broadcasts, and live recordings—taken primarily from his first five post-Fairport years—remained in the vault until 1991 with the release of *Orphans and Outcasts, Vol. 1*. Going back to a handful of 1969 Matthews Southern Comfort recordings, which are every bit as strong as what eventually ended up on the respective records, the bulk of *Orphans and Outcasts* is of an unusually high caliber for a compilation of this sort. Of the highlights, many come from BBC radio broadcasts, including Plainsong's 1973 recordings of Gene Clark's "Spanish Guitar" and Paul Siebel's "Any Day Woman," which are real finds. Other BBC sessions include Matthews leading a terrific band which featured Richard Thompson and Andy Roberts on guitars, through four tunes, including Dylan's "It Takes a Lot to Laugh, It Takes a Train to Cry" and his own "Hearts." Elsewhere, his demos for the disappointing *Go for Broke*, recorded in Emitt Rhodes' garage, possess a spark that was sadly missing from the finished album. The consistently high quality of the material here makes *Orphans and Outcasts, Vol. 1* an excellent addendum to Iain Matthews' early work. *—Brett Hartenbach*

If You Saw Thro' My Eyes/Tigers Will Survive / 1993 / Vertigo ✦✦✦✦✦
Vertigo combined Ian Matthews' two 1971 albums, *If You Saw Thro' My Eyes* and *Tigers Will Survive*, on one CD. After leaving Southern Comfort, Matthews reunited with Fairport Convention members Richard Thompson and Sandy Denny and made one of his finest albums with *If You Saw Thro' My Eyes*. Though the material and playing is superior to his previous work, it was unfortunately overlooked at the time. Recorded during two different periods of time broken up by a U.S. tour, *Tigers Will Survive*, his follow-up to *If You Saw Through My Eyes*, lacks the focus of its predecessor. Still worthwhile if only for "Morning Star," one of Matthews' most beautiful originals. *—Chris Woodstra*

● **The Soul of Many Places** / May 11, 1993 / Elektra ✦✦✦✦✦
The Soul of Many Places compiles the best moments from Matthews' recording high point for Elektra (1972-1974). Featuring selections from *Valley Hi*, *Some Days You Eat the Bear...*, and Plainsong's *The Search for Amelia Earhart*, this is the best introduction to Matthews' finest work. The inclusion of non-LP tracks makes this essential for fans as well. *—Chris Woodstra*

Skeleton Keys / May 18, 1993 / Rhino ✦✦✦
Since the early days of his career, Ian Matthews has been pigeonholed as a folk or country-rock artist—more than likely because of his voice and emphasis on songwriting (original and borrowed)—when in reality he spent a good portion of the '70s and '80s dabbling in various styles, from new wave, synth- and jazz-inflected pop to a new age-influenced record for Windham Hill. Released in 1993, *Skeleton Keys* may be what most would expect from Matthews, but it's actually more of a return to an acoustic sound that hadn't really dominated his albums since the first half of the '70s. In fact, *Skeleton Keys* is probably the most acoustic-oriented studio recording he's made to date, featuring acoustic guitar, acoustic bass, dobro, accordion, mandolin, and fiddle, with only subtle touches of electric guitar. As a writer, Matthews has always included at least a handful of original gems with each record, while also showing a good ear for the songs of others, but *Skeleton Keys* is his first comprised of all his own material. There are a number of highlights here, though most seem to come from the most melancholy moments, including the moving Miles Davis tribute "God's Empty Chair," the autobiographical analogy of "Compass and Chart," the touching "Every Crushing Blow," and the dark, imagistic "Living in Reverse." Elsewhere, cuts such as "Cover Girl," "The Ties We Break," "A Cross to Bear," and the folk-rap "Back of the Bus" are not without their own certain charms, though one can't help but think that replacing some of the lesser tunes with a couple of well-chosen covers

may have done a lot for the record as a whole. Still, *Skeleton Keys* continues a strong and steady comeback for Ian Matthews. *—Brett Hartenbach*

Orphans & Outcasts, Vol. 2: Collection of Demos, 1981-1989 / 1994 / Dirty Linen ✦✦✦

The second in Iain Matthews' series of demos, outtakes, etc., *Orphans & Outcasts, Vol. 2* concentrates on his 1980s output, relating to the years that bookend his self-imposed hiatus between 1983 and 1987. The pre-1983 cuts, along with one recording from 1984, were taken from his techno and new wave dabblings with the Seattle-based Hi-Fi, and to a greater degree, his *Shook*-era demos. And while many fans of Matthews' '70s work had trouble warming up to this phase of his career, which takes up nearly half of the collection, there are some memorable moments, as there were with the various records of this time. Still, the inclusion of early (quite different) versions of "Perfect Timing" and "Voices" from 1990's *Pure & Crooked* ("Voices" was added to the 1994 *Pure & Crooked* reissue) should be of interest, even if only as a curiosity, to those put off by this period. The second half of *Orphans & Outcasts, Vol. 2* begins with the album's true highlights—six Jules Shear songs which were demoed for *Walking a Changing Line*. None of the tunes appeared on the record, and only "Steady" had, at this point, been issued on one of Shear's own releases. Sparsely arranged, with acoustic guitar, vocals, and the occasional programmed rhythms, these demos actually benefit from the absence of the final album's new age veneer. Of the remaining tracks, only "We Don't Talk Anymore," which seems to have been picked for parts of *Pure & Crooked*'s "Rains of '62," is of any real interest. *Orphans & Outcasts, Vol. 2* doesn't quite meet the standard set by its predecessor, but the *Walking a Changing Line* demos alone make it essential for fans. *—Brett Hartenbach*

Dark Ride / Jun. 7, 1994 / Watermelon ✦✦✦

God Looked Down / Aug. 13, 1996 / Watermelon ✦✦✦

In the wake of his 1988 comeback—an entire record dedicated to the work of Jules Shear—Iain Matthews seemed to gain confidence and momentum as a writer, beginning with 1990's *Pure & Crooked*. Of the three albums that followed, two of them, including *God Looked Down*, are made up solely of his own material (although the basic melody of "So Many Eyes" was taken from the traditional "Nottamun Town," from his Fairport Convention days). And while Matthews' work has always been quite personal and individualistic even when covering other people's tunes, there's something about *God Looked Down* that hits a little closer to the bone. One of the album's best tracks, "Power of Blue," is maybe his most intimate and telling song since "If You Saw Thro' My Eyes," while elsewhere there are touches of hope, fear, wonder, and inadequacy—both personal and societal. Musically, Matthews and longtime producer Mark Hallman create a more rock-based folk sound than his previous couple of outings, cloaking his acoustic-based tunes in bass, drums, and dark shades of organ and electric guitar. There also seems to be a freedom gained over the years from the fact that Matthews accepts and appreciates his "borderline career," settling nicely into his cult status, and the record benefits from this. Like his past couple of releases, *God Looked Down* may lack the consistency of his best records, but it still delivers some successful, introspective folk-rock. *—Brett Hartenbach*

Seattle Years 1978-1984 / Oct. 8, 1996 / Varese ✦✦✦✦

Between 1978 and 1984, Ian Matthews relocated to Seattle, shed the acoustic folkiness and introspection he had become known for in favor of a more contemporary, commercial sound; *The Seattle Years* collects the highlights from the four solo albums he recorded during this period—*Stealin' Home*, *Siamese Friends*, *Spot of Interference*, and *Shook* (unfortunately, the one album he did with Hi-Fi in the same period is sadly unrepresented). Though Matthews is best remembered for his work just prior to this period, the collection presents the high points into a highly listenable fashion and, in retrospect, his take on ultra-slick soft-rock stands up against the best of the genre. Included is his biggest hit, "Shake It," as well as lesser-known but well-executed album tracks like a new wave/power-pop reading of the Left Banke classic "She May Call You Up Tonight" and Jona Lewie's "The Baby She's on the Street." *—Chris Woodstra*

Nights in Manhattan (and Points West) / Aug. 5, 1997 / DCC ✦✦✦

Originally released in the late '80s as a mail-order-only cassette entitled *Ian Matthews Live* (he changed the spelling of his first name shortly thereafter), *Nights in Manhattan* (recorded in New York City in May of 1988) was reissued in 1997 with four added tracks that were recorded live two and a half years later in California (hence the "and Points West"). Matthews, along with Mark Hallman (acoustic guitar, vocals), Craig Negoescu (keyboards, vocals), and David Hayes (acoustic bass), though concentrating on material from *Walking a Changing Line*, touches on various points in his extensive career—including his days with Fairport Convention ("Meet on the Ledge"), Matthews' Southern Comfort ("Woodstock"), and Plainsong ("Even the Guiding Light"), as well as a smattering of tunes from his solo years. The performances here are engaging, and Matthews' excellent voice is strong and clear throughout, though the sporadic use of electronic keyboards and sequenced drums is, on occasion, superfluous, and dates a couple of the tracks. A few of the highlights include a stirring, a cappella version of "Woodstock," the Youngbloods' classic "Darkness, Darkness," and a beautiful reading of Jules Shear's "This Fabrication." *—Brett Hartenbach*

Orphans & Outcasts, Vol. 3 / 1999 / Perfect Pitch ✦✦✦

With *Orphans & Outcasts, Vol. 3*, Iain Matthews once again digs into his seemingly endless vault of unreleased recordings for another collection of oddments from his 30-plus year career. *Vol. 3* runs the gamut from his first recorded lead vocal (a scratchy 1965 recording by Pyramid) to the live, previously unreleased "Sing Sister Sing," a song scheduled to appear on his next solo record. In between, we get outtakes, live recordings, radio broadcasts, and an assortment of demos (ranging from a 1969 recording of "Woodstock" to "Jaques and Tambo" from 1996). Unlike the first two collections, not much here is necessarily essential, though a number of cuts would fit nicely on the corresponding Iain Matthews album and should be of interest to fans. Highlights include three tracks ("Hearts," "Home," and "Never Ending") from a 1970 BBC broadcast featuring backing by Andy Roberts and Richard Thompson, Plainsong's beautiful a capella arrangement of "I'll Fly Away," and the demos for Jules Shear's "This Fabrication" and "Except for a Tear," sans synthesizers. *—Brett Hartenbach*

Maxwell

b. 1973

Vocals / Contemporary R&B, Urban

To the legions of R&B listeners during the mid-'90s, Maxwell presented a new option: the tenderness of true romance, instead of the fleeting joy of sex. With his debut album, *Maxwell's Urban Hang Suite*, Maxwell united the psycho-sexual funk of Prince with Marvin Gaye's idea of the romance concept album. Born in Brooklyn in 1973 of West Indian-Puerto Rican heritage, Maxwell first began playing music at the age of 17 when a friend gave him a battered Casio keyboard. He started to compose music and soon became a staple on the New York club circuit. Signed to Columbia in 1994, Maxwell recorded his debut album that same year, with accompaniment from guitarist Wah Wah Watson, saxophonist Stuart Matthewman, and songwriter Leon Ware—who had previously collaborated on Gaye's thematic classic *I Want You*. A series of label shake-ups prevented the album's release for almost two years, but *Maxwell's Urban Hang Suite* finally appeared in March 1996. Though the album wasn't successful upon its release, a second single, "Ascension (Never Wonder)," made the Top 40 late that year, pushing the album into gold territory. *Embrya* followed in 1998, and Maxwell scored again with the hit "Fortunate" from the *Life* soundtrack. *—John Bush*

● **Maxwell's Urban Hang Suite** / Feb. 27, 1996 / Columbia ✦✦✦✦✦

Maxwell's debut offers up a sophisticated and stylized take on late-'60s and early-'70 soul. Sam Cooke, Marvin Gaye, Al Green, and the like are subtly referenced over the course of these 11 tracks of wide-screen soul. Mixing sensual funk with ballad sincerity, Maxwell coolly sings through highlights like "Welcome," "...Til the Cops Come Knockin'," and "Ascension (Don't Ever Wonder)." The atmospheric, cool-breeze soundscape comes courtesy of Maxwell and Sade cohort Stuart Mathewman. More expansive and airy sounding than the deep groove and gospel sides by fellow retro-soulster D'Angelo, *Urban Hang Suite* is destined to become a classic contemporary R&B disc. *—Stephen Cook*

Embrya / Jun. 23, 1998 / Columbia ✦✦✦

Maxwell's ambition was one of the appealing qualities of his debut, *Urban Hang Suite*, especially since very few of his contemporaries were attempting to expand the boundaries of contemporary R&B. However, blessings can be curses, and that very ambition gets the better of Maxwell on his second album, *Embrya*. Loaded with pretentious song titles ("Gestation: Mythos," "Arroz con Pollo," "Luxury: Cococure"), the album bogs down in its own sophistication and his desire to make deep, serious music. Like Terence Trent D'Arby—whose *Neither Fish Nor Flesh* offers a frightening parallel to *Embrya*—Maxwell wants to be so much more than another soul crooner, but his gifts become obscured the more he pushes them forward. To be sure, *Embrya* is far from a wash-out. Maxwell does have a remarkable voice and he can write really good modern soul songs—it's just that he has a tendency to think that's not enough and then he over-stuffs his songs with ideas that lead nowhere. With a little more focus, *Embrya* could have been an impressive second step. As it stands, it's a bit of a sophomore stumble, albeit one with promising moments. *—Stephen Thomas Erlewine*

Now / Aug. 14, 2001 / Columbia ✦✦✦✦

Maxwell is a gifted record-maker, which isn't necessarily the same thing as a gifted songwriter. He has a nice, sweet voice, a healthy love for classic soul from Marvin to Prince, an appealing arty streak largely missing from contemporary R&B, and he can arrange his self-recorded productions quite alluringly, balancing the guitars, synths, drum machines, and horns nimbly, often coming up with fresh songs. If only his songs were as memorable as his sounds! True, *Now* is more song-centric than his previous releases, barring possibly his debut, but this is still well-crafted mood music where the overall seductive sound matters more than what he's saying specifically. That's part of the reason why his cover of Kate Bush's "This Woman's Work" (revived here after being debuted on his *MTV Unplugged*) is so startling—it's not just that he's picked an unlikely source for a great cover, but it's the one time that he marries his sumptuous sound to a song with substance. That's not to say that *Now* is a bad record—it's hard to call anything that sounds this good a bad album—but it's held back by Maxwell's emphasis on sound over song. If he were just making mood music, that would be acceptable, but he's trying to live up to the tradition of Marvin and Prince, and while his productions often live up to that legacy, he has yet to write songs memorable enough to truly justify those comparisons. *—Stephen Thomas Erlewine*

John Mayall

b. Nov. 29, 1933, Macclesfield, Cheshire, England

Vocals, Ukulele, Tambourine, Leader, Keyboards, Harpsichord, Harmonium, Piano, Harmonica, Guitar, Organ / Blues Revival, British Blues, Electric Harmonica Blues, Blues-Rock

The elder statesman of British blues, it is John Mayall's lot to be more renowned as a bandleader and mentor than as a performer in his own right. Throughout the '60s, his band, the Bluesbreakers, acted as a finishing school for the leading British blues-rock musicians of the era. Guitarists Eric Clapton, Peter Green, and Mick Taylor joined his band in a remarkable succession in the mid-'60s, honing their chops with Mayall before going on to join Cream, Fleetwood Mac, and the Rolling Stones, respectively. John McVie and Mick Fleetwood, Jack Bruce, Aynsley Dunbar, Dick Heckstall-Smith, Andy Fraser (of

Free), John Almond, and Jon Mark also played and recorded with Mayall for varying lengths of times in the '60s. Mayall's personnel has tended to overshadow his own considerable abilities. Only an adequate singer, the multi-instrumentalist was adept in bringing out the best in his younger charges (Mayall himself was in his thirties by the time the Bluesbreakers began to make a name for themselves). Doing his best to provide a context in which they could play Chicago-style electric blues, Mayall was never complacent, writing most of his own material (which ranged from good to humdrum), revamping his lineup with unnerving regularity, and constantly experimenting within his basic blues format. Some of these experiments (with jazz-rock and an album on which he played all the instruments except drums) were forgettable; others, like his foray into acoustic music in the late '60s, were quite successful. Mayall's output has caught some flak from critics for paling next to the real African-American deal, but much of his vintage work—if weeded out selectively—is quite strong, especially his legendary 1966 LP with Eric Clapton, which both launched Clapton into stardom and kick-started the blues boom into full gear in England. —*Richie Unterberger*

John Mayall Plays John Mayall / Mar. 26, 1965 / Decca ✦✦✦
Recorded live at the British club Klooks Kleek in late 1964 before Clapton joined (Roger Dean plays lead guitar), this is a fine set of early British R&B with a more pronounced rock feel (akin to the Rolling Stones) than Mayall's other '60s work. Mayall wrote all but one of the songs on this overlooked but driving, highly enjoyable LP that is recommended to connisseurs of early British blues-rock. —*Richie Unterberger*

★ **Bluesbreakers With Eric Clapton** / Jul. 1966 / Deram ✦✦✦✦✦
Bluesbreakers With Eric Clapton was Eric Clapton's first fully realized album as a blues guitarist—more than that, it was a seminal blues album of the 1960s, perhaps the best British blues album ever cut, and the best LP ever recorded by John Mayall's Bluesbreakers. Standing midway between Clapton's stint with the Yardbirds and the formation of Cream, this album featured the new guitar hero on a series of stripped-down blues standards, Mayall pieces, and one Mayall/Clapton composition, all of which had him stretching out in the idiom for the first time in the studio. This album was the culmination of a very successful year of playing with John Mayall, a fully realized blues creation, featuring sounds very close to the group's stage performances, and with no compromises. Credit has to go to producer Mike Vernon for the purity and simplicity of the record; most British producers of that era wouldn't have been able to get it recorded this way, much less released. One can hear the very direct influence of Buddy Guy and a handful of other American bluesmen in the playing. And lest anyone forget the rest of the quartet: future pop-rock superstar John McVie and drummer Hughie Flint provide a rock-hard rhythm section, and Mayall's organ playing, vocalizing, and second guitar are all of a piece with Clapton's work. His guitar naturally dominates most of this record, and he can also be heard taking his first lead vocal, but McVie and Flint are just as intense and give the tracks an extra level of steel-strung tension and power, none of which have diminished across four decades. In 1998, Polygram Records issued a remastered version of this album on CD, featuring both the stereo and mono mixes of the original tracks and new notes. —*Bruce Eder*

Raw Blues / Jan. 1967 / Deram ✦✦
A Hard Road / Feb. 17, 1967 / Deram ✦✦✦✦
Eric Clapton is usually thought of as Mayall's most important righthand man, but the case could also be made for his successor, Peter Green. The future Fleetwood Mac founder leaves a strong stamp on his only album with the Bluesbreakers, singing a few tracks and writing a couple, including the devastating instrumental "Supernatural." Green's use of thick sustain on this track clearly pointed the way to his use of this feature on Fleetwood Mac's hits "Albatross" and "Black Magic Woman," as well as providing a blueprint for Carlos Santana's style. Mayall acquits himself fairly well on this mostly original set (with occasional guest horns), though some of the material is fairly mundane. Highlights include the uncharacteristically rambunctious "Leaping Christine" and the cover of Freddie King's "Someday After a While (You'll Be Sorry)." —*Richie Unterberger*

Crusade / Sep. 1, 1967 / London ✦✦✦✦✦
The personnel changes in John Mayall's Bluesbreakers continued on his fourth album, and although Mayall had vowed not to, he had added two permanent horn players. Perhaps because he was putting out his second album within a year, Mayall wasn't able to fill up the record with his own compositions and turned to blues standards, which certainly didn't hurt the record overall. Mayall's heroes included Buddy Guy, Otis Rush, Freddie King, and Sonny Boy Williamson, and he did them proud. The album became his third straight U.K. Top Ten and, following the Bluesbreakers' first U.S. tour in the summer of 1967, his first charting album in America. —*William Ruhlmann*

The Blues Alone / Nov. 1967 / Deram ✦✦✦
The Blues Alone was the first Mayall "solo" album (without the Bluesbreakers). Mayall played and overdubbed all instruments except drums, which were handled by Bluesbreaker Keef Hartley. The album also tried to serve notice that, despite his band being a spawning ground for several British stars by now, the real star of the group was its leader. But it didn't quite prove that, since Mayall, while certainly competent on harmonica, keyboards, and guitars, doesn't display the flair of an Eric Clapton or Peter Green, and the overdubbing, as is so often the case, robs the recording of any real sense of interplay. —*William Ruhlmann*

Blues From Laurel Canyon / 1968 / Deram ✦✦✦✦✦
Mayall's first post-Bluesbreakers album saw the man returning to his roots after the jazz/blues fusion that was *Bare Wires*. *Blues From Laurel Canyon* is a blues album, through and through. Testimony to this is the fact that there's a guitar solo only 50 seconds into the opening track. Indeed, Mayall dispersed the entire brass section for *Blues*

From Laurel Canyon, and instead chose the solid but relatively limited backing of Mick Taylor (guitar), Colin Allen (drums), and Stephen Thompson (bass). Instantly, it is apparent that John Mayall hasn't lost his touch with the blues. "Vacation," the album's opener, reminds one exactly why this artist is so celebrated for his songwriting ability. The staggering Mick Taylor (here still in his teens) truly proves his worth as a blues guitarist, while Stephen Thompson (also in his late teens) works superbly with one of the genre's most interesting drummers, Colin Allen. *Blues From Laurel Canyon* is as unerring as *Bluesbreakers With Eric Clapton*, and equally as musically interesting. Not only is this one of the finest John Mayall albums, it is also a highlight in the blues genus. —*Ben Davies*

Bare Wires / Jun. 21, 1968 / Deram ✦✦✦
Bare Wires was the first Bluesbreakers album of new studio material since *A Hard Road*, released 16 months before. In that time, the band had turned over entirely, expanding to become a septet. Mayall's musical conception had also expanded—the album began with a 23-minute "Bare Wires Suite," which included more jazz influences than usual and featured introspective lyrics. In retrospect, all of this is a bit indulgent, but at the time it helped Mayall out of what had come to seem a blues straitjacket (although he would eventually return to a strict blues approach). It isn't surprising that he dropped the "Bluesbreakers" name after this release. [The album was Mayall's most successful ever in the U.K., hitting number three.] —*William Ruhlmann*

Looking Back / Aug. 1969 / Deram ✦✦✦
Reasonably interesting collection of non-LP singles from 1964 to 1968, featuring almost all of the notable musicians that passed through the Bluesbreakers throughout the decade. "Sitting in the Rain" (with Peter Green) showcases fine fingerpicking, the haunting "Jenny" is one of Mayall's best originals, and "Stormy Monday" is one of the few cuts from 1966 that briefly featured both Eric Clapton and Jack Bruce. The rest is largely passably pleasant and doesn't rank among Mayall's finest work. —*Richie Unterberger*

The Turning Point / 1969 / Deram ✦✦✦✦✦
Recorded just after Mick Taylor departed for the Stones, Mayall eliminated drums entirely on this live recording. With mostly acoustic guitars and John Almond on flutes and sax, Mayall and his band, as his typically overblown liner notes state, "explore seldom-used areas within the framework of low volume music." But it does work. The all-original material is flowing and melodic, with long jazzy grooves that don't lose sight of their bluesy underpinnings. Lyrically, Mayall stretches out a bit into social comment on "The Laws Must Change" on this fine, meditative mood album. —*Richie Unterberger*

Thru the Years / 1971 / Deram ✦✦✦✦✦
A grab bag of rare tracks from the '60s, some of which stand among Mayall's finest. His debut 1964 single "Crawling up a Hill" is one of his best originals; this comp also includes a couple of 1964-65 flipsides that were never otherwise issued in the U.S. The eight songs featuring Peter Green include some top-notch material that outpaces much of the only album recorded by the Green lineup (*A Hard Road*), particularly the Green originals "Missing You" and "Out of Reach," a great B-side with devastating, icy guitar lines and downbeat lyrics that ranks as one of the great lost blues-rock cuts of the '60s. The set is filled out with a few songs from the Mick Taylor era, the highlight being the vicious instrumental "Knockers Step Forward." Look for the CD reissue and not the early-'70s double U.S. album of the same name, which includes a lot of superfluous material and omits the three 1964-65 songs from British 45s. —*Richie Unterberger*

Latest Edition / 1974 / Polydor ✦✦✦
The title makes a virtue of necessity, as John Mayall introduces another all-new lineup (actually, bassist Larry Taylor is returning from an older edition). Two guitarists, Hightide Harris and Randy Resnick, lead the band in more of an up-tempo R&B style than has been used in much of Mayall's music during the past several years, starting with the timely "Gasoline Blues" (1974 was the year of the gas lines, remember?) and going on to "Troubled Times" (which advises impeaching President Nixon). Still, this was a lackluster set, which is only appropriate since it was Mayall's swan song with Polydor, and the album became his first to miss the charts in the U.S. since 1967. —*William Ruhlmann*

A Sense of Place / Mar. 1990 / Island ✦✦✦
London Blues (1964-1969) / Oct. 20, 1992 / Deram ✦✦✦✦✦
Featuring 40 tracks over two discs, *London Blues* is an excellent collection of most of the best moments from Mayall and the Bluesbreakers' early recordings, a time when Eric Clapton, Peter Green, and Mick Taylor all passed through the band. —*Stephen Thomas Erlewine*

Room to Move (1969-1974) / Oct. 20, 1992 / Polydor ✦✦✦✦✦
The majority of Mayall and the Bluesbreakers' best material from the early '70s is collected on this 29-track, double-disc set. Although Clapton appears on a couple of songs, the playing on *Room to Move* isn't as universally breathtaking as it is on *London Blues*, but the collection is thoroughly listenable, and it does feature many fine musicians. —*Stephen Thomas Erlewine*

Wake Up Call / Apr. 6, 1993 / Jive/Novus ✦✦✦
As It All Began: The Best of John Mayall & the Bluesbreakers 1964-1969 / Jan. 27, 1998 / Polydor ✦✦✦✦✦
As It All Began: The Best of John Mayall & the Bluesbreakers 1964-1968 is an excellent 20-track retrospective, capturing Mayall's band at their peak. The Bluesbreakers went through several different lineups during those four years, with musicians the caliber of Eric Clapton, Mick Taylor, Paul Butterfield, Mick Fleetwood, John McVie, and Peter Green floating through the group. Hardcore fans of any of those musicians, or of British blues, will naturally want to familiarize themselves with the original albums, but *As It All Began* is a fine sampler for the casual fan, featuring such staples as "Lonely Years," "Bernard

Jenkins," "All Your Love," "Parchman Farm," "Double Trouble," "The Death of J.B. Lenoir," and "Miss James." Even at 20 tracks, there are a number of fine moments missing from this collection, but *As It All Began* remains the best available single-disc overview of the Bluesbreakers' prime period. *—Stephen Thomas Erlewine*

Drivin' On: The ABC Years (1975-1982) / Sep. 22, 1998 / MCA ✦✦✦✦
This two-disc, 32-track compilation brings together highlights from Mayall's output for ABC Records in the 1970s. Pulled from the albums *New Year, New Band, New Company, Notice to Appear, Lots of People; A Banquet of Blues; A Hard Core Package;* and *Last of the British Blues*, these cherry-picked tracks also do a nice job of highlighting Mayall's estimable writing skills as well. Highlights include "Seven Days Too Long," "Old Time Blues," "You Can't Put Me Down," "Sitting on the Outside," "My Train Time" and the title track. As a special bonus, there's the second disc inclusion of four live tracks from a 1982 Bluesbreaker reunion gig featuring John McVie back at his original post on bass and Mick Taylor on lead guitar providing the fireworks. *—Cub Koda*

Silver Tones: The Best of John Mayall & the Bluesbreakers / Nov. 10, 1998 / Jive ✦✦✦

Curtis Mayfield

b. Jun. 3, 1942, Chicago, IL, **d.** Dec. 26, 1999
Vocals, Guitar (Electric), Guitar / Blaxploitation, Chicago Soul, Uptown Soul, Quiet Storm, R&B, Funk, Soul

Perhaps because he didn't cross over to the pop audience as heavily as Motown's stars, it may be that the scope of Curtis Mayfield's talents and contributions have yet to be fully recognized. Judged merely by his records alone, the man's legacy is enormous. As the leader of the Impressions, he recorded some of the finest soul vocal group music of the 1960s. As a solo artist in the 1970s, he helped pioneer funk and helped introduce hard-hitting urban commentary into soul music. "Gypsy Woman," "It's All Right," "People Get Ready," "Freddie's Dead," and "Superfly" are merely the most famous of his many hit records. But Curtis Mayfield isn't just a singer. He wrote most of his material at a time when that was not the norm for soul performers. He was among the first—if not the very first—to speak openly about African-American pride and community struggle in his compositions. As a songwriter and a producer, he was a key architect of Chicago soul, penning material and working on sessions by notable Windy City soulsters like Gene Chandler, Jerry Butler, Major Lance, and Billy Butler. In this sense, he can be compared to Smokey Robinson, who also managed to find time to write and produce many classics for other soul stars. Mayfield was also an excellent guitarist, and his rolling, Latin-influenced lines were highlights of the Impressions' recordings in the '60s. During the next decade, he would toughen up his guitar work and production, incorporating some of the best features of psychedelic rock and funk. *—Richie Unterberger*

☆ **Curtis** / Sep. 1970 / Rhino ✦✦✦✦✦
The first solo album by the former leader of the Impressions, *Curtis* represented a musical apotheosis for Curtis Mayfield—indeed, it was practically the "*Sgt. Pepper's*" album of '70s soul, helping with its content and its success to open the whole genre to much bigger, richer musical canvases than artists had previously worked with. All of Mayfield's years of experience of life, music, and people were pulled together into a rich, powerful, topical musical statement that reflected not only the most up-to-date soul sounds of its period, finely produced by Mayfield himself, and the immediacy of the times and their political and social concerns, but also embraced the most elegant R&B sounds out of the past. As a producer, Mayfield embraced the most progressive soul sounds of the era, stretching them out compellingly on numbers like "Move on Up," but also drew on orchestral sounds (especially harps), to achieve some striking musical timbres (check out "Wild and Free"), and wove all of these influences, plus the topical nature of the songs, into a neat, amazingly lean whole. There was only one hit single off of this record, "(Don't Worry) If There's a Hell Down Below We're All Going to Go," which made number three, but the album as a whole was a single entity and really had to be heard that way. In the fall of 2000, Rhino Records reissued *Curtis* with upgraded sound and nine bonus tracks that extended its running time to over 70 minutes. All but one are demos, including "Miss Black America" and "The Making of You," but mostly consist of tracks that he completed for subsequent albums; they're fascinating to hear, representing very different, much more jagged and stripped-down sounds. The upgraded CD concludes with the single version of "(Don't Worry) If There's a Hell Below We're All Going to Go." *—Bruce Eder*

Curtis/Live! / 1971 / Rhino ✦✦✦✦
Recorded and released at one of the high points of Curtis Mayfield's career, this live album provides several reasons why the late Mayfield is regarded as the black Bob Dylan. The performances contained herein represent the high-water mark of social consciousness. Newer numbers such as "Stone Junkie" and "Superfly" (from the soundtrack of the same name), along with classics like "People Get Ready," are enough to give credence to Mayfield's stature. Awesome. *—Matthew Greenwald*

Roots / 1971 / Rhino ✦✦✦✦✦
Curtis Mayfield's visionary album, a landmark creation every bit as compelling and as far-reaching in its musical and extra-musical goals as Marvin Gaye's contemporary *What's Goin' On.* Opening on the hit "Get Down," the album soars on some of the sweetest and most eloquent—yet driving—soul sounds heard up to that time. Mayfield's growing musical ambitions, first manifested on the *Curtis* album, and his more sophisticated political sensibilities, presented with a lot of raw power on *Curtis Live!*, are pulled together here in a new, richer studio language, embodied in extended song structures ("Underground"), idealistic yet lyrically dazzling anthems ("We Got to Have Peace," "Keep On Keeping On," and, best of all, the soaring "Beautiful Brother of Mine"), and impassioned blues ("Now You're Gone"). The music is even bolder than the material on the *Curtis* album, with Mayfield expanding his instrumental range to the level of a veritable soul orchestra; and the recording is better realized, as Mayfield, with that album and a behind him, shows a degree of confidence that only a handful of soul artists of thi could have mustered. Charly Records had this album out on CD in the 1980s, but Rhi acquisition of the Curtom catalog in 1996 led to a remastered and expanded reissu 1999 with superior sound, detailed annotation, and the addition of four bonus trac Apart from a slow, funky, stripped-down but eminently listenable demo of "Unde ground" (which reveals just how sophisticated Mayfield's conceptions—forget the finishe versions—of his songs were), the latter consist of the single edits of "Get Down," "We Go to Have Peace," and "Beautiful Brother of Mine." They seem redundant after the album versions, though they don't detract at all from the extraordinary value of this mid-priced CD. *—Bruce Eder*

☆ **Superfly** / Jul. 1972 / Curtom ✦✦✦✦✦
A post-Impressions Curtis Mayfield recorded one dynamic solo project after another in the 1970s, but if a listener could own only one of them, *Superfly* would be the ideal choice. The sleek yet earthy soundtrack to one of the '70s' most celebrated blaxploitation films, *Superfly* is full of riveting, sometimes chilling sociopolitical commentary reflecting on the drugs, violence, and crime plaguing the inner city. Unlike so many soundtracks, this outstanding CD can be fully appreciated whether or not one has seen the film. From the infectious title song to "Freddie's Dead" (a reflection on a junkie's tragic life as troubling as it is poignant) to the hard-hitting "Pusherman" (brilliantly interpreted by rapper Ice-T in 1988), *Superfly* is clearly Mayfield's finest hour. *—Alex Henderson*

Curtis in Chicago / 1973 / Curtom ✦✦✦✦✦
In the midst of a great run of superb albums, Curtis Mayfield cranked out a fine live set displaying how penetrating his music was in concert. He headed a fine combo, performed extended versions of several hits, sang with authority, earnestness, and conviction, and got an equally intense response from the audience. *—Ron Wynn*

Back to the World / May 1973 / Curtom ✦✦✦✦✦
Another stirring album by Curtis Mayfield, now in a groove on his own label. Mayfield's works issued challenges across the board, urging everyone to examine his or her prejudices and then seek a solution. While he always included one or two wonderful love songs for balance, these albums were largely examinations of American issues in the 1970s. He scored three R&B chart hits, with "Future Shock" just missing the Top Ten, but that was icing on the cake. Mayfield's music had far more importance than simply getting hits. *—Ron Wynn*

Got to Find a Way / 1974 / Curtom ✦✦✦
Curtis Mayfield continued his run of excellent albums in the '70s with this follow-up to the huge hit *Superfly* soundtrack. This album had more love songs than some of his earlier material, although he didn't tone down his searing attacks on American injustice and hyprocisy. His vocals continued to be alternately poignant, urgent, and accusatory, while his lyrics, production, and arrangements were once again magnificent. *—Ron Wynn*

Sweet Exorcist / 1974 / Curtom ✦✦✦
Curtis Mayfield hit a stride during the '70s that was unparalleled among R&B/soul performers from an album standpoint. He was writing, producing, arranging, and performing on great album after great album, then distributing them on his own label as well. This one included the big hit "Kung Fu," plus the title song, and once more perfectly blended rigorous message tracks and steamy love songs. Sadly, it hasn't been reissued on CD and isn't on the list to be at this time. *—Ron Wynn*

There's No Place Like America Today / 1975 / Curtom ✦✦✦✦✦
Curtis Mayfield continued his string of powerful, assertive message albums with this mid-'70s release, but, as luck would have it, the only hit the album scored came with a love tune, "Only You, Babe." Still, the title tune, "Hard Times," "When Seasons Change" and "Blue Monday People" were unrelenting, unapologetic statements of frustration and anger. Mayfield also included "So in Love" and "Love to the People" to balance the menu, but the finest cuts addressed the inequities and injustices he saw being ignored. *—Ron Wynn*

Give Get Take Have / 1976 / Ichiban ✦✦✦
Less sociopolitical than previous efforts, *Give Get Take Have* offers "Mr. Welfare Man" as its sole attempt to enlighten and enhance. Mayfield was obviously experiencing the joys of new love when he cut "Only You Babe" and "This Love Is Sweet," and the tear-jerking numbers "In Your Arms Again" and "Party Night." His aching falsetto coos and purrs, but sounds weakened on this LP. Overall, the album falls short of Mayfield's former releases, but even great artists don't always achieve their usual high standards. This was originally released on Curtom Records in the mid-'70s. *—Andrew Hamilton*

Never Say You Can't Survive / 1977 / Ichiban ✦✦

Do It All Night / 1978 / Curtom ✦✦✦
Curtis Mayfield's astrological sign is Gemini, and *Do It All Night*—originally released on Curtom Records in 1978—reflects the sign's duality trait. On half of the six songs (all of side one on the original vinyl album) Mayfield's collaborates with Gil Askey, the guy behind the emergence of disco diva Linda Clifford. The title track, "No Goodbyes," and "Party Party" are all disco length and dominated by percussions, rhythms, and swirling strings—not really Mayfield, but the times called for disco and he delivered as best he could. "Keeps Me Loving You" and "In Love, in Love, in Love" are typical Mayfield ballads done to perfection in his delicate falsetto. The only tune that made noise is the engaging "You Are, You Are," a minor R&B hit that Linda Clifford recorded earlier. If you're looking for songs with a message or positive social themes look elsewhere; this set's about dancin' and love. *—Andrew Hamilton*

Live in Europe / Jul. 1987 / Curtom ✦✦✦
Although Curtis Mayfield's album sales had decreased significantly by the late '70s, the

veteran remained a popular live attraction well into the '80s. Audi- ...ear both gems from his years with the influential Impressions and ...nd he gives them exactly what they want on this album (released as ...nd a two-CD set). Mayfield reminds us just how great the Impressions ... versions of such '60s classics as "Gypsy Woman" (which greatly influ- ...Brothers), "It's Alright" and the inspirational "People Get Ready," and is ...ating on incisive, early-'70s sociopolitical hits like "Pusherman," "Freddie's ...f There's a Hell Below." *Live in Europe*'s main flaw isn't Mayfield's perform- ... band that, although decent, just doesn't go that extra mile or do this superb ...istice. Horns, a main ingredient of many of his hits, are sorely missed—espe- ..."Move on Up"—and Buzz Amato's keyboards simply can't take their place. ...*Henderson*

...Time: Classic Collection / 1990 / Curtom ✦✦✦✦✦
...anthology spotlights Curtis Mayfield's biggest hits as a solo star since 1970. It in- ...des his first hit as a lead artist, "(Don't Worry) If There's a Hell Below We're All Gonna ...," plus "Superfly," "Freddie's Dead," "So in Love" and many other classics recorded for ...is Curtom label. Mayfield penned many masterful sociopolitical and protest tunes, but could also write poignant, expressive love songs. *—Ron Wynn*

Take It to the Streets / Feb. 1990 / Curtom ✦✦✦
In the 1980s and '90s, some soul veterans turned to high-tech urban-contemporary sounds in an effort to appeal to black radio. Curtis Mayfield, however, continued to deliver rewarding albums by remaining true to himself and sticking with the type of classic soul approach that put him on the map. *Take It to the Streets* falls short of the unmitigated excellence of *Superfly* or *Sweet Exorcist*, but is a respectable effort demonstrating that he could still pack a punch as a vocalist, composer, and producer. There's much to savor and admire here, including "Homeless" (which makes it clear that Mayfield hadn't lost his touch when it came to biting sociopolitical commentary), "He's a Fly Guy," the charismatic "Who Was That Lady," and an engaging remake of "On and On" (a gem he wrote for Gladys Knight & the Pips in 1973). With the re-emergence of hard-hitting "blaxploitation" (black exploitation) films in the late '80s, the gritty imagery of "I'm Gonna Get You Sucka" and the haunting "He's A Fly Guy" proved quite timely. While this material could have used some horns, Mayfield generally employs technology in a soulful way—employing "real instruments" along with keyboards and drum machines, and never letting his production sound stiff, unnatural, or forced. *—Alex Henderson*

★ **The Anthology 1961-1977** / Dec. 8, 1992 / MCA ✦✦✦✦✦
MCA's double-disc *The Anthology 1961-1977* is the definitive overview of Curtis Mayfield's career, as the only compilation to draw from both his solo work and the best of his output with the Impressions. In fact, even discounting the four Curtom tracks that spill over onto disc two, the first disc's 26 selections constitute far and away the most extensive Impressions best-of on the market. Toss in ten of the most essential Mayfield solo tracks, and the result is breathtaking in its progression from romantic soul, often informed by doo wop and gospel, to expansive, ambitiously arranged funk jams. It's also fascinating to hear Mayfield's social conscience emerging as the '60s progress, since he was among the very first R&B artists to explore political issues in his music, paving the way for countless others to do so during the '70s. If you're only interested in Mayfield's funkier solo work, Rhino's *The Very Best of Curtis Mayfield* features all but one of the solo tracks included here, plus several more. But in order to fully grasp Mayfield's impact on R&B and his talent as a singer, songwriter, musician, and producer, *The Anthology 1961-1977* is absolutely essential. *—Steve Huey*

Living Legend / Aug. 1, 1995 / Curtom ✦✦✦
Living Legend is a double-disc collection of some of Curtis Mayfield's finest solo material from the '70s, but it contains too much mediocre material to function as an effective introduction to the soul great. *—Stephen Thomas Erlewine*

People Get Ready: The Curtis Mayfield Story / Feb. 27, 1996 / Rhino ✦✦✦✦✦
Like most large box sets, this three-CD, 51-song production is too extensive for the casual fan and sacrifices consistency in an attempt to span an entire career. The focus is on Mayfield's solo work; much of the first disc is devoted to his most popular work with the Impressions, but the remainder of the compilation surveys his solo output, from 1970 to 1990. The Impressions tracks are uniformly excellent, but the Mayfield-only cuts are more problematic. The best of these—the *Superfly* highlights, of course, and early '70s singles like "(Don't Worry) If There's a Hell Below We're All Going to Go" and "Beautiful Brother of Mine"—are as good as everything he ever did. But even in the early '70s, he was erratic, and after *Superfly* (his career summit), nothing he did smacked of brilliance. Some of the post-*Superfly* stuff is okay, but considering that this period takes up half of disc two and all of disc three, it means you're in for a pretty swift downhill slide over the last half of the box. Mayfield never lost his vocal abilities, or his production skills, but after the late '70s his material was simply unimpressive, getting into pedestrian dance music and romantic urban contemporary. For a Mayfield retrospective, you're much better off with MCA's two-disc *Anthology*, which goes into the Impressions period with much greater depth, and includes the cream of his '70s solo recordings. *—Richie Unterberger*

The Very Best of Curtis Mayfield / Mar. 10, 1996 / Rhino ✦✦✦✦✦
Rhino's *The Very Best of Curtis Mayfield* is devoted to material the legendary soul man recorded after leaving the Impressions, focusing particularly on his classic songs from the early '70s. There are more comprehensive compilations on the market, namely the sublime double-disc *Anthology* and the flawed but worthwhile box *People Get Ready*, but this is the best bet for anyone wanting a concise sampler of Mayfield's groundbreaking funk-soul, since it contains all of the bare-bone essentials: "(Don't Worry) If There's a Hell Below, We're All Going to Go"; "Move on Up"; "We Got to Have Peace"; "Freddie's Dead"; "Superfly"; "Pusherman"; "Future Shock"; and "Kung Fu." Yes, Mayfield also made cohesive, frequently stunning albums during this era and his work with the Impressions was just as influential, but this disc benefits from its narrow focus, since the end result is a collection ideal for the curious and the novice, while also providing a great listen for anyone who already knows the records. *—Stephen Thomas Erlewine*

New World Order / Oct. 1, 1996 / Warner Brothers ✦✦✦
New World Order is a touching, moving comeback from Curtis Mayfield. As the first new music Mayfield has recorded since he was paralyzed in 1990, the album engenders a lot of goodwill—it's undeniably affecting to hear him sing again, especially with the knowledge that his performances had to be recorded line-by-line, due to his paralysis. The joy of hearing him sing makes the inconsistency of the album forgivable, especially since he is in good voice. Narada Michael Walden, Daryle Simmons, and Organized have all contributed productions where are sensitive but strong, which gives the album added weight. The songs are hit-and-miss, but the main strength of the record is that it illustrates that Mayfield can make music that is still vital. *—Leo Stanley*

Superfly: Deluxe 25th Anniversary Edition / Nov. 11, 1997 / Rhino ✦✦✦
This expanded version of the classic album adds so much material that it really needs to be reviewed separately from the original article. The first disc of the two-CD set presents the entire album as it was originally sequenced, with the addition of the single mixes of "Freddie's Dead" and "Superfly." It's disc two that's really of interest to collectors, assembling about 40 minutes of different material from the same era, all but two tracks previously unissued (and those two were not released in the U.S.). In some cases this is fairly extraneous, as in the alternate mix of "Pusherman," but there's some interesting, even gripping stuff as well. Especially good is "Ghetto Child," which served as the harder, sparser demo of the song that eventually became "Little Child Runnin' Wild," and the 1970 demo "The Underground," whose hard-hitting lyrics and heavy guitar riffs are obvious prototypes for the *Superfly* approach. The full-length take of the instrumental "Junkie Chase," as well as instrumental versions of a couple of songs that had vocals on the original album, are atmospheric if not as essential; there are also a couple of radio spots and a seven-minute 1995 interview with Mayfield about the record. The second disc is good listening, though probably not of much interest to fans who aren't curious about the music's history. It makes a great bonus if you're upgrading to CD, however, as does an accompanying booklet with detailed text about the songs. *—Richie Unterberger*

Give It Up: The Best of the Curtom Years 1970-1977 / 1998 / Empire Music ✦✦✦✦
Give It Up illustrates the sociopolitical side of Curtis Mayfield. The pulsating, horn-driven "Move On Up" has all the social significance of his early positive songs with the Impressions, and "We the People Who Are Darker Than Blue" showed the world that Mayfield was possessed of unique insight. "Back to the World" speaks of soldiers returning from Vietnam, while "Billy Jack" and "Superfly" are apt depictions of inner-city characters. This also contains motivators like "We Got to Have Peace," "Keep On Keeping On," "People Get Ready," and "Mighty, Mighty Spade and Whitey." *—Andrew Hamilton*

Gospel / Jan. 19, 1999 / Rhino ✦✦✦
This enjoyable (yet somewhat questionable) compilation gathers together many of the religious songs that Curtis Mayfield penned and performed, both with the Impressions in the '60s and as a solo artist in the '70s. As a songwriter, Mayfield was astounding. In addition to the well-known lyrics of "Amen" and "People Get Ready," there are several songs that are open to interpretation; while Mayfield may have been addressing God in "You Ought to Be in Heaven" and "When We're Alone," they work equally well as conventional love songs. The older material, performed with the Impressions, doesn't sound dated in the least. Some of the later songs, however, are prone to excesses not uncommon in '70s music (excessive overdubbing, and the obligatory string section.) One may wonder why Rhino would release this compilation of readily available material (excluding one unnecessary unreleased live track), but it is lively, enjoyable and in some cases essential music. [No Mayfield collection is complete without "People Get Ready," but newcomers will be better served in purchasing one of his many "Best Of" compilations.] *—Steve McMullen*

Move on Up: The Singles Anthology / May 16, 2000 / Sequel ✦✦✦✦✦
Curtis Mayfield is inarguably one of the giants of soul, turning out work equally great with the Impressions and as a solo artist alike—and making great singles and albums simultaneously. There are so many great moments in his catalog that it's easy to make a good collection of highlights, which Sequel's *Move On Up: The Singles Anthology* most certainly is. That doesn't mean it's the perfect collection. At two discs and 39 tracks, it actually suffers from over-length and evenhandedness, offering a bit too much of the late-'70s work that simply isn't as good as the music from the early '70s. Nevertheless, this is a thorough overview of Curtis' Curtom singles, and for some listeners, that may be a selling point, even though MCA's 1992 *Anthology 1961-1977* provides a better overview of his peak work. *—Stephen Thomas Erlewine*

20th Century Masters—The Millennium Collection: The Best of Curtis Mayfield / Jun. 6, 2000 / MCA ✦✦✦✦
The Millennium Collection: The Best of Curtis Mayfield & the Impressions collects some of the best songs Mayfield recorded with the Impressions and on his own, including "Gypsy Woman," "People Get Ready," "Freddie's Dead," "Superfly," "Woman's Got Soul," and "Choice of Colors." Though a thorough look at Mayfield's talents and innovations is beyond the scope of this album, *The Millennium Collection* does provide enough of his definitive tracks to make it a worthwhile overview of his work. *—Heather Phares*

Percy Mayfield

b. Aug. 12, 1920, Minden, LA, **d.** Aug. 11, 1984, Los Angeles, CA
Vocals, Songwriter, Piano / Urban Blues, West Coast Blues, Piano Blues, R&B, Soul
A masterful songwriter whose touching blues ballad "Please Send Me Someone to Love,"

a multi-layered universal lament, was a number one R&B hit in 1950, Percy Mayfield had the world by the tail until a horrific 1952 auto wreck left him facially disfigured. That didn't stop the poet laureate of the blues from writing in prolific fashion, though. As Ray Charles's favorite scribe during the '60s, he handed the Genius such gems as "Hit the Road Jack" and "At the Club." Art Rupe's Specialty logo signed Mayfield in 1950 and he scored a solid string of R&B smashes over the next couple of years. "Please Send Me Someone to Love" and its equally potent flip "Strange Things Happening" were followed in the charts by "Lost Love," "What a Fool I Was," "Prayin' for Your Return," "Cry Baby," and "Big Question," cementing Mayfield's reputation as a blues balladeer of the highest order. Mayfield's lyrics were usually as insightfully downbeat as his tempos; he was a true master at expressing his innermost feelings, laced with vulnerability and pathos (his "Life Is Suicide" and "The River's Invitation" are two prime examples). *—Bill Dahl*

★ **Poet of the Blues** / 1990 / Specialty ✦✦✦✦✦
The insightful songwriting skills of this West Coaster were matched by his wry, plaintive vocal delivery (Mayfield was usually his own best interpreter). The 25 sides here date from his hit-laden 1950-1954 stay at Art Rupe's Specialty logo and include his univesal lament "Please Send Me Someone to Love," and the resolutely downbeat "Strange Things Happening" and "Lost Love," and an ironic "The River's Invitation." Saxman Maxwell Davis led the horn-powered combos providing sympathetic support behind Mayfield. *—Bill Dahl*

Percy Mayfield Live / 1992 / Winner ✦✦✦
Although the first-ever release of live Mayfield material is culled from performances between 1981 and 1983, the twilight of the singer's blues career, he remains in fine, laid-back voice throughout. The selections draw on all periods of his three decades as a songwriter, and include "Please Send Me Someone to Love," "The River's Invitation" and "Don't Start Lying to Me." Founding Paul Butterfield Blues Band pianist Mark Naftalin backs Mayfield throughout the collection; he also served as the set's producer. *—Jason Ankeny*

Memory Pain / Sep. 17, 1992 / Specialty ✦✦✦✦✦
Ranging from major hits to alternate takes and rarities, this CD (released in 1992) illustrates the prolific nature of Percy Mayfield's Specialty Records output during the 1950s. Though not everything on *Memory Pain* is essential, the collection of early R&B and 12-bar blues is consistently satisfying. The best known song here is the number one hit of 1950, "Please Send Me Someone to Love," and many listeners will also be familiar with such gems as "Strange Things Happening" and the title song. A singer who was flexible as well as charismatic, Mayfield is as convincing on a rare version of the mournful, jazz-tinged "Nightless Lovers" as he is on 12-bar numbers like "My Blues" and "The Big Question." The CD ends on an interesting note with a demo of "Hit the Road Jack" (which became a major hit for Ray Charles). Highly recommended. *—Alex Henderson*

Maze Featuring Frankie Beverly

f. 1976
Urban, Funk
Frankie Beverly & Maze may be the ultimate Urban Contemporary group, though they're much more soulful and funky than many of their counterparts. They began in Philadelphia as the Butlers, and later became Raw Soul. They moved to San Francisco in the mid-'70s, and switched identities again to Maze. The lineup was lead singer Frankie Beverly, Wayne Thomas, Sam Porter, Robin Duke, Roame Lowry, McKinley Williams, and Joe Provost. Ahaguna G. Sun later replaced Provost, and Sun was subsequently replaced by Billy "Shoes" Johnson. Ron Smith replaced Thomas, and Phillip Woo was added on keyboards in 1980. Though they've had only one number one R&B hit in their long tenure ("Back in Stride" in 1985), Maze's popularity is unquestioned, especially as a live act. They recorded for Capitol from 1977 until 1989, when they moved to Warner Brothers and issued another smash LP in *Silky Soul*. Other releases include 1993's *Back to Basics* and 1996's *Southern Girl. —Ron Wynn*

Maze Featuring Frankie Beverly / 1977 / Capitol ✦✦✦✦✦
At a time when disco reigned supreme, Maze & Frankie Beverly took the R&B charts by storm with a smooth yet gritty soul/funk approach that rejected the disco beat entirely. Growing up in the soul hotbed of Philadelphia had a definite impact on Maze's distinctive sound, which owed as much to Marvin Gaye as it did to Philly soul. Classics like "While I'm Alone," "Lady of Magic," "You," and the hit "Happy Feelins" earned Maze an intensely devoted bunch of followers, who will tell you in a minute that the charismatic Beverly is the very essence of a soul singer. Though it wasn't a single, one of the best offerings on the album is "Colorblind," a jewel expressing Beverly's frustration over the racial polarization that plagued the U.S. in 1977 and remained alive and well years later. This outstanding debut album didn't do much in the pop market, but thanks to enthusiastic support from the R&B market, it went gold. *—Alex Henderson*

Live in New Orleans / 1981 / Capitol ✦✦✦✦
A superb live album, one of the finest soul/funk concert dates ever released. Frankie Beverly and Maze managed to capture on this two-album set the energy, spontaneity, and nonstop excitement of their concerts, which have always been among the finest on the R&B/soul/funk circuit. The set functioned as both a greatest hits work and a wonderful introduction to people who'd never seen their live show. The album version of "Joy and Pain" became an international hit, and led to other singles being pulled and re-released in extended versions. *—Ron Wynn*

Maze / 1982 / Capitol ✦✦✦

Silky Soul / Sep. 1989 / Warner Brothers ✦✦✦

The Greatest Hits of Maze . . . Lifelines, Vol. 1 / Nov. 8, 1989 / Capitol ✦✦✦✦

When the Philadelphia band Raw Soul moved to San Francisco in the mid-'70s, they changed their name to Maze and made Frankie Beverly their lead singer. Beverly's personality and exuberance and their evolution into one of the tightest bands on the soul scene turned Maze into an institution. This collects formative hits from their years on Capitol, including "Golden Time of Day" and "Joy and Pain." It shows that they were both an enjoyable up-tempo and funk band and a convincing ballad and love song ensemble. *—Ron Wynn*

● **Anthology** / Jan. 23, 1996 / Capitol ✦✦✦✦
Maze has been a fan favorite since the mid-'70s; while they've received little critical notice or adulation except among soul and R&B scribes, Maze has seldom been out of the charts since making their debut on Capitol. Lead singer Frankie Beverly's roots extend back to classic doo wop and East Coast soul; although he made the transition to funk, then urban material, Beverly always had plenty of soul and passion in his vocals. Maze also blazed their own musical trail; when such competitors as Earth, Wind & Fire, the Bar-Kays, Con Funk Shun, and Slave were featuring surging horn sections and jazz-tinged arrangements with heavy bass lines, Beverly and company favored rock-influenced guitar parts juxtaposed against soulful organ riffs or synthesizer riffs and just a trace of reggae and/or Latin rhythm. Beverly enjoyed several hits on Capitol but became unsatisfied with their inability to break the group beyond the R&B/funk market. They departed Capitol in the late '80s, and resurfaced on Warner Bros., where they continued making strong, distinctive releases. *Anthology* gathers the best (at least most of the best) singles the band did for Capitol, among them classics like "Southern Girl," "Before I Let Go," the complete "Joy and Pain" and "Happy Feeling." Despite being only an 18-cut, single-disc release, there's a completeness not often available in a single CD set. British journalist David Nathan's notes are comprehensive, and nicely combine anecdotal and discographical references. While it would be good if Capitol and Warner Bros. could combine on a multi-disc set, until (or if) that happens, here's a fine tribute to one of R&B's most underrated and consistently enjoyable bands. *—Ron Wynn*

Mazzy Star

f. 1989
Dream Pop, Adult Alternative Pop/Rock, Alternative Pop/Rock
If psychedelic music has a voice in '90s post-punk, Mazzy Star may be its strongest reincarnation. That doesn't necessarily mean that fans of the Jefferson Airplane and the Grateful Dead will find the band to their liking, however. Mazzy Star much prefer the dark side of psychedelia, as exemplified by the most distended tracks of the Doors and the Velvet Underground. Their fuzzy guitar workouts and plaintive folky compositions are often suffused in a dissociative ennui that is very much of the 1990s, however much their textures may recall the drug-induced states of vintage psychedelia. Their second album, 1993's *Tonight That I Might See*, had been around for about a year before it suddenly got hot, reaching the Top 40, and spinning off a small hit single, "Fade Into You." *—Richie Unterberger*

She Hangs Brightly / 1990 / Capitol ✦✦✦
Mazzy Star's debut *She Hangs Brightly* picks up where Opal's *Happy Nightmare Baby* left off; merely exchanging Kendra Smith's langorous vocals for the more sultry presence of Hope Sandoval, David Roback continues chasing the neo-psychedelic holy grail he's pursued since his days with the Rain Parade, albeit with mixed success here. After opening with a pair of standouts, the dreamy "Halah" and the garage-inspired "Blue Flower," the album quickly loses focus, and even the group's solid grasp of atmosphere and texture can't overcome the songs' distinctly unmemorable melodies. *—Jason Ankeny*

● **So Tonight That I Might See** / Sep. 27, 1993 / Capitol ✦✦✦✦✦
Treading a similar path as their debut, Mazzy Star generally succeed in their efforts to create an otherworldly, dream-state-like buzz with their lulling songs and layers of droning guitars. The duo offers a considerably warmer and more authentic persona on the pretty, acoustic-dominated songs than the droning trance-rock exercises. With its socially detached self-absorption, this CD is like a definitive soundtrack for the slacker elements of Generation X. *—Richie Unterberger*

Among My Swan / Oct. 29, 1996 / Capitol ✦✦✦✦
The similarity between *Among My Swan* and *So Tonight I Might See* is all the more mind-boggling when considering the four years it took to record the album. Stylistically, there is no difference between the records—it is still the same crawling, trancey acoustic-folk—but that's not necessarily a bad thing. Mazzy Star has a pleasant sound and their songwriting is always consistent, making their records enjoyable. However, *Among My Swan* lacks any standouts on the level of "Fade Into You," which makes it a less compelling listen, especially on repeated plays. In other words, it's a holding pattern, which should appeal to the converted, without making any new fans. *—Stephen Thomas Erlewine*

MC5

f. 1964, Lincoln Park, MI, **db.** 1972
Detroit Rock, Proto-Punk, Hard Rock
Alongside their Detroit-area brethren the Stooges, the MC5 essentially laid the foundations for the emergence of punk—deafeningly loud and uncompromisingly intense, the group's politics were ultimately as crucial as their music, their revolutionary sloganeering and anti-establishment outrage crystallizing the counterculture movement at its most volatile and threatening. The MC5 celebrated the holy trinity of sex, drugs, and rock & roll, their incendiary live sets offering a defiantly bacchanalian counterpoint to the peace-and-love reveries of their hippie contemporaries. Although corporate censorship, label interference, and legal hassles combined to cripple the band's hopes of mainstream

notoriety, both their sound and their sensibility remain seminal influences on successive generations of artists.

The Motor City Five was formed in 1964 by vocalist Rob Tyner plus guitarists Fred "Sonic" Smith and Wayne Kramer, later adding bassist Michael Davis and drummer Dennis Thompson. In 1966, the MC5 landed a regular gig at the famed Detroit venue the Grande Ballroom, building a fanatical local fanbase on the strength of their increasingly anarchic live appearances. Their debut album, the classic *Kick Out the Jams*, reached the national Top 30, though retailers refused to carry copies due to its inclusion of Tyner's trademark battle cry of "Kick out the jams, motherfuckers!" Dropped by Elektra, they signed to Atlantic and released 1970's *Back in the USA*. The political stance and feedback-driven fury were gone, however, dividing fans and critics. When the 1971 follow-up *High Time* failed to even reach the charts Atlantic released the MC5 from their contract. In 1972, both Tyner and Thompson announced their retirement from active touring.

As the years went by, however, the MC5's influence expanded—punk, hard rock, and power pop all clearly reflected the band's impact. Following the band's demise its members pursued new projects: Tyner released several solo records before suffering a fatal heart attack in 1991. Smith, meanwhile, formed Sonic's Rendezvous, and in 1980 he wed Patti Smith, dying of heart failure in 1994. Kramer resurfaced in 1995 with a blistering solo album, *The Hard Stuff*, the first of several new efforts for punk label Epitaph. *—Jason Ankeny*

☆ **Kick out the Jams** / 1969 / Elektra ✦✦✦✦✦
Rather than try to capture their legendary onstage energy in a studio, MC5 opted to record their first album during a live concert at their home base, Detroit's Grande Ballroom, and while some folks who were there have quibbled that *Kick out the Jams* isn't the most accurate representation of the band's sound, it's certainly the best of the band's three original albums, and easily beats the many semi-authorized live recordings of MC5 that have emerged in recent years, if only for the clarity of Bruce Botnick's recording. From Brother J.C. Crawford's rabble-rousing introduction to the final wash on feedback on "Starship," *Kick out the Jams* is one of the most powerfully energetic live albums ever made; Wayne Kramer and Fred "Sonic" Smith were a lethal combination on tightly interlocked guitars, bassist Michael Smith and drummer Dennis Thompson were as strong a rhythm section as Detroit ever produced, and Rob Tyner's vocals could actually match the soulful fire-power of the musicians, no small accomplishment. Even on the relatively subdued numbers (such as the blues workout "Motor City Is Burning"), the band sounds like they're locked in tight and cooking with gas, while the full-blown rockers (pretty much all of side one) are as gloriously thunderous as anything ever committed to tape; this is an album that refuses to be played quietly. For many years, Detroit was considered the High Energy Rock & Roll Capital of the World, and *Kick out the Jams* provided all the evidence anyone might need for the city to hold on to the title. *—Mark Deming*

Back in the U.S.A. / 1970 / Rhino ✦✦✦✦✦
While lacking the monumental impact of *Kick out the Jams*, the MC5's second album is in many regards their best and most influential, its lean, edgy sound anticipating the emergence of both the punk and power-pop movements to follow later in the decade. Bookended by a pair of telling covers—Little Richard's "Tutti Frutti" and Chuck Berry's "Back in the USA"—the disc is as much a look back at rock & roll's origins as it is a push forward into the music's future; given the Five's vaunted revolutionary leanings, for instance, it's both surprising and refreshing to discover the record's emotional centerpiece is a doo wop-inspired ballad, "Let Me Try," that's the most lovely and gentle song in their catalog. The recurring theme which drives *Back in the USA* is adolescence, its reminiscences alternately fond and embittered—while cuts like "Tonight," "Teenage Lust," "High School" and "Shakin' Street" celebrate youth in all its rebellious glory, others like "The American Ruse" and "The Human Being Lawnmower" condemn a system which eats its young, filling their heads with lies before sending them off to war. Equally gripping is the record's singular sound—produced by Jon Landau with an almost complete disregard for the bottom end, *Back in the USA* captures a live-wire intensity 180 degrees removed from the group's live sound yet perfectly suited to the material at hand, resulting in music which not only salutes the power of rock & roll but also reaffirms it. *—Jason Ankeny*

High Time / 1971 / Rhino ✦✦✦✦
MC5 was nearing the end of their long and bumpy trail when they cut *High Time* in 1971, and it was widely ignored upon initial release. While it lacks the flame-thrower energy and "Off the man!" politics of *Kick out the Jams* or the frantic pace and "AM Radio of the People" sound of *Back in the USA*, heard in 2000, *High Time* sounds like MC5's relative equivalent to the Velvet Underground's *Loaded*, their last and most accessible album, but still highly idiosyncratic and full of well-written, solidly played tunes. Fred Smith's "Sister Anne" and "Skunk (Sonically Speaking)" bookend the album with a pair of smart, solidly performed hard rockers (bolstered by fine horn charts), and Wayne Kramer's "Poison" ranks with the best songs he brought to the band (he later revived it for his solo album *The Hard Stuff*). For a group that was apparently on the verge of collapse, MC5 approaches this material with no small amount of skill and enthusiasm, and Geoffrey Haslam's production gives the band a big, punchy sound that suits them better than the lean, trebly tone of *Back in the USA*. It's interesting to imagine what MC5's history might have been like if *High Time* had been their first or second album rather than their last; while less stridently political than their other work, musically it's as uncompromising as anything they ever put to wax and would have given them much greater opportunities to subvert America's youth if the kids had ever had the chance to hear it. *—Mark Deming*

Babes in Arms / 1983 / ROIR ✦✦✦
Wayne Kramer assembled this collection of 15 rare MC5 tracks, and while trying to cover the career of a band who helped give birth to punk rock AND made it onto Spiro Agnew's enemies list might seem like a near-impossible task in less than an hour, *Babes in Arms* does a pretty respectable job of capturing what the MC5 were all about in one convenient package. Most of the cuts on *Babes in Arms* are alternate versions of songs from the band's three studio albums, but while the most of the tracks appear in variant mixes or longer edits, the differences are minimal enough that they can pass for the originals in a pinch (one crucial exception: a great acoustic version of Fred "Sonic" Smith's "Shakin' Street"), making *Babes in Arms* a solid "Best of the MC5" collection. Even more importantly, the set also includes several excellent and hard-to-find early single sides, including the amusing garage-protest nugget "One of the Guys" and a primal, in-the-red rave-up on "Looking at You" that leaves the version on *Back in the U.S.A.* in the dust. The one previously unreleased song, "Gold," is an unfocused jam that doesn't really go anywhere, and the sound quality of the source materials isn't all that hot (especially on the CD version), but otherwise *Babes in Arms* is a howling, furious blast of what made the MC5 one of the finest (and most dangerous) American rock bands of the 1960s. Crank it up loud—the guys would want it that way. *—Mark Deming*

American Ruse / 1994 / Total Energy ✦✦

Teenage Lust / Apr. 1996 / Alive ✦✦✦
The existence of an early board tape captures the MC5 in all their rocking glory, recorded live at the Saginaw Civic Center, January 1st, 1970. This show falls in between the two studio releases for Atlantic (*Back in the U.S.A.* and *High Time*), finding the band restyling themselves for mass consumption while remaining a very potent force as a live act. The set list reflects this, combining tunes from their live album ("Ramblin' Rose," "Rama Lama Fa Fa Fa," and a medley of "Starship" and "Kick out The Jams") with harder takes of songs from *Back in the U.S.A.* than what appear on the studio release. Although this has been around for a number of years as a bootleg release with dubious fidelity, this is its first official release. *—Cub Koda*

★ **The Big Bang: The Best of the MC5** / Feb. 15, 2000 / Rhino ✦✦✦✦✦
A best-of for a group who only made three albums might be considered an inessential addition to their discography, particularly as all three of those albums remain available on CD. However, if you only want one MC5 album, this compilation makes more sense than if might appear at first. It draws judiciously from each of the three records; adds three somewhat rare tracks from pre-*Kick out the Jams* singles; and finishes with a live 1972 cut, "Thunder Express," recorded for French TV and previously available on a Skydog CD. In somewhat of a surprise, it leans most heavily on *Back in the USA* (with eight tracks), and not so much on the album that most would view as their most significant effort, *Kick out the Jams* (only four tracks). That decision works out better than you might think. The three tracks from 1967-68 singles are fairly similar to the *Kick out the Jams* vibe anyway, and if you don't own *Kick out the Jams* already, you may well be ready for something a little cleaner-sounding and less assaultive by the time seven songs have gone by. It's unfortunate, nonetheless, that the two remaining pre-*Kick out the Jams* tracks from non-LP 45s, "One of the Guys" and a different version of *Kick out the Jams*' "Borderline," were not included. *Kick out the Jams* itself would get most people's nod as the first and most essential MC5 purchase, but this is a close second, its value enhanced by detailed historical liner notes. *—Richie Unterberger*

MC Hammer (Stanley Kirk Burrell)

b. Mar. 30, 1962, Oakland, CA
Vocals / Pop-Rap, West Coast Rap, Hip-Hop
Considered either the ultimate success story or consummate fraud, Oakland's MC Hammer, a one-time jack-of-all-trades for the Oakland Athletics baseball team, dominated the charts in 1990 with *Please Hammer Don't Hurt 'Em*. The single "U Can't Touch This," despite a rather feeble rap and recycle job on Rick James's single "Superfreak," was an enormous crossover smash. Hammer live puts on a fine show as far as dancing, sound, light effects, production, and such. But from a technical standpoint, everything, from his rhymes to his enunciation, qualifies as the ultimate in "wack" (weak) performance. He does have great taste in cover songs, picking choice items from Marvin Gaye, B.B. King, The Chi-Lites, and Prince, among others. He's since dropped the MC from his name.

After staying in the limelight as a racehorse owner and Evander Holyfield's promoter, Hammer returned to the rap wars in 1994 with *The Funky Headhunter*. It featured a leaner, harder sound, with assistance and material provided by gangsta-rap producers, and featured Hammer sporting a more street look. He previewed the new style on Arsenio Hall's show early in the year, then issued the CD in March. It debuted at number two on Billboard's R&B charts, then dipped the next week to six. Skeptics voiced their doubts about the new Hammer, especially in the hip-hop press. *—Ron Wynn*

Let's Get It Started / 1988 / Capitol ✦✦✦
MC Hammer's debut effort established him as a hip-hop superstar, with energetic dance tracks under its pop-tinged choruses, highlighted by the single "Turn This Mutha Out." *—Stephen Thomas Erlewine*

Please Hammer, Don't Hurt 'Em / Jan. 1990 / Capitol ✦✦✦✦
A remarkable commercial success for its time, MC Hammer's *Please Hammer, Don't Hurt 'Em* proved that rap had enormous commercial potential if packaged and marketed correctly. And few albums with the exception of Vanilla Ice's *To the Extreme* were as well-packaged and well-marketed as this album. To contemporary ears (and to seasoned ears at the time), it's pretty apparent that Hammer isn't that talented of a rapper. He's essentially reveling in cliché here, sugar-coating the rhymes of his street-orientated (and therefore less commercial) predecessors such as Rakim, L.L. Cool J, and Slick Rick. With the aid of some blatant sample-driven beats and his recycling of rap's greatest clichés, this is a fairly conservative album musically, never wandering far from proven pop formula. Though contemporary listeners don't get the chance to relish it, Hammer's image was of vital importance to this album's appeal, more so than the music. Without his eccentric

attire, his manic dancing, and his choreographed videos (which received tremendous play on MTV), this album is pretty predictable. Sure, moments such as "U Can't Touch This" are undeniably infectious with their familiar samples and proven songwriting techniques, but it's hard to have much respect for this album as an artistic statement—it's the quintessential co-opting of hip-hop for commerce. If you simply enjoy the album as diluted hip-hop, or if you can enjoy the admittedly brilliant co-opting of proven clichés, then this is a great album. But this album's true importance lies in being one of the first moments when hip-hop's commercial potential become strikingly apparent. *—Jason Birchmeier*

Too Legit to Quit / Oct. 21, 1991 / EMI-Capitol Special Markets ✦✦✦
With his third album, *Too Legit to Quit*, Hammer dropped the "MC" from his name, but didn't undergo any major changes musically. Indeed, *Legit* provided a heavy dose of the thing that made *Please Hammer, Don't Hurt Em* so successful: likeable, fun pop/rap that appealed to mainstream Top 40 audiences more than the hood. For a few years, Hammer almost seemed to be the Michael Jackson of rap. Although it fell short of *Please Hammer's* artistic and commercial success, *Legit* definitely had its share of inviting hits, including "This Is the Way We Roll" and the title song. While Hammer hasn't always been the most challenging artist in the world, the Oakland native has some noteworthy social commentary in "Living in a World Like This" and "Brothers Hang On"—both of which are disturbing commentaries on the harsh realities of ghetto life. *—Alex Henderson*

The Funky Headhunter / Mar. 1, 1994 / Giant ✦✦✦
The former M.C. Hammer resurfaced with a new musical identity and rap approach on this 1994 album. Getting help from new-school producers and debuting a video on *The Arsenio Hall Show*, Hammer's sound was leaner, his rapping tougher and more fluid, and his subject matter harder and less humorous. The results seemed to have worked; *Funky Headhunter* peaked at number two on the R&B list, went gold, and remained in the Top 30 midway through the year. *—Ron Wynn*

Inside Out / Sep. 12, 1995 / Giant ✦✦

● **Greatest Hits** / Oct. 1, 1996 / Capitol ✦✦✦✦✦
Despite being one of the best-selling rappers of all-time, none of MC Hammer's albums were very consistent—the singles stood out like a sore thumb among the filler on each record, which is why *Greatest Hits* is such a good bargain. *Greatest Hits* compiles 12 of Hammer's biggest hits for Capitol Records, including "U Can't Touch This," "Pump It Up," "Turn This Mutha Out," "They Put Me in the Mix," "Have You Seen Her," "Pray," "Here Comes the Hammer," "2 Legit 2 Quit," "Do Not Pass Me By," and "Addams Groove." It's not only an excellent introduction to MC Hammer, it's the best album in his entire catalog. *—Stephen Thomas Erlewine*

McAlmont & Butler

f. 1995, **db.** 1996
After Bernard Butler left Suede following the group's second LP, *Dog Man Star*, the guitarist joined forces with the British soul star David McAlmont. In 1996, the duo released the album *The Sound of McAlmont & Butler*, while it was a huge hit in the U.K., the two acrimoniously dissolved their partnership before they could record a follow-up. *—Jason Ankeny*

● **The Sound of . . McAlmont & Butler** / Jan. 1996 / Hut ✦✦✦✦
The complete works of David McAlmont and Bernard Butler's stormy, short-lived collaboration are collected on *The Sound of McAlmont & Butler*. Featuring the all the songs from their two singles, "Yes" and "You Do," the disc illustrates why the collaboration didn't last more than a few months in 1995. Both of the musicians are extremely talented—McAlmont's voice soars like few other contemporary soul and pop singers, while Butler has a talent for grandiose, majestic songs and arrangements that his contemporaries generally disdain—but both are prone to indulgence, which is exactly what happened. Instead of achieving the dark, theatrical beauty of *Dog Man Star*, his last album with Suede, Butler throws literally everything into the mix—all of his songs sound like extensions of his magnum opus with Suede, "Stay Together," without the precise vision of Brett Anderson to temper his more outlandish tendencies. That's because McAlmont has a tendency for the outlandish too—he's just as likely to collapse into vocal histrionics as he is to reach new sonic heights. Consequently, the songs on *The Sound of McAlmont & Butler* are about *sound*, not about melody. There are selected highlights—the duo fulfills their ambitions on the gorgeous "Yes"—but for the most part, the album is disappointingly tedious and frustratingly unengaging. In short, a wasted opportunity. *—Stephen Thomas Erlewine*

Paul McCartney

b. Jun. 18, 1942, Liverpool, England
Vocals, Keyboards, Guitar (Electric), Piano, Guitar, Bass, Guitar (Acoustic) / Album Rock, Pop/Rock, Soft Rock, Adult Contemporary, Rock & Roll
Out of all the former Beatles, Paul McCartney by far had the most successful solo career, maintaining a constant presence in the British and American charts during the '70s and '80s. In America alone, he had nine number one singles and seven number one albums during the first 12 years of his solo career. Although he sold records, McCartney never attained much critical respect, especially when compared to his former partner John Lennon. Then again, he pursued a different path than Lennon, deciding early on that he wanted to be in a rock band. Within a year after the Beatles' breakup, McCartney had formed Wings with his wife Linda, and the group remained active for the next ten years, racking up a string of hit albums, singles, and tours in the meantime. By the late '70s, many critics were taking pot shots at McCartney's effortlessly melodic songcraft, but that didn't stop the public from buying his records. His sales didn't slow considerably until the late '80s, and he retalliated with his first full-scale tour since the '70s, which was a considerable success. During the '90s, McCartney recorded less frequently, concentrating on projects like his first classical recording, a techno album and the Beatles' *Anthology*. *—Stephen Thomas Erlewine*

McCartney / Apr. 20, 1970 / Capitol ✦✦✦✦
Paul McCartney retreated from the spotlight of the Beatles by recording his first solo album at his home studio, performing nearly all of the instruments himself. Appropriately, *McCartney* has an endearingly ragged, homemade quality that makes even its filler—and there is quite a bit of filler—rather ingratiating. Only a handful of songs rank as full-fledged McCartney classics, but those songs—the light folk-pop of "That Would Be Something," the sweet, gentle "Every Night," the ramshackle Beatles leftover "Teddy Boy" and the staggering "Maybe I'm Amazed" (not coincidentally the only rocker on the album)—are full of all the easy melodic charm that is McCartney's trademark. The rest of the album is charmingly slight, especially if it is read as a way to bring Paul back to earth after the heights of the Beatles. At the time the throwaway nature of much of the material was a shock, but it has become charming in retrospect. Unfortunately, in retrospect it also appears as a harbinger of the nagging mediocrity that would plague McCartney's entire solo career. *—Stephen Thomas Erlewine*

☆ **Ram** / May 17, 1971 / Capitol ✦✦✦✦✦
Compared to *McCartney*, Paul McCartney's second solo album *Ram*—which was credited as a collaboration with his wife Linda—is a more substantial and produced effort, yet it has much of the same homemade charm as its predecessor. Divided between simple pop-rockers and cleverly constructed mini-suites like "Uncle Albert/Admiral Halsey" and "Back Seat of My Car," *Ram* doesn't gel into any major statement, but it has many pleasurable detours. McCartney layers the ramshackle rhythm tracks with odd sound effects and off-kilter arrangements. While the production might not always work, it does make for pleasant ear candy, not only on lovely songs like "Heart of the Country," but also on throwaway numbers like the hard-rocking "Smile Away" and "Monkberry Moon Delight." Unfortunately, most of *Ram* is comprised of filler, and while it's *enjoyable* filler, it prevents the record from being much more than pleasurable diversion. *—Stephen Thomas Erlewine*

Wild Life / Dec. 7, 1971 / Capitol ✦✦✦
The irony of the first Wings album is that it seems more domesticated than *Ram*, feeling more like a Paul 'n' Linda effort than that record. Perhaps it's because this album is filled with music that's defiantly lightweight—not just the cloying cover of "Love Is Strange" but two versions *apiece* of songs called "Mumbo" and "Bip Bop." If this is a great musician bringing his band up to speed, so be it, but it never seems that way—it feels like one step removed from coasting, which is wanking. It's easy to get irritated by the upfront cutesiness, since it's married to music that's featherweight at best. Then again, that's what makes this record bizarrely fascinating—it's hard to imagine a record with less substance, especially from an artist who's not just among the most influential of the 20th century, but from one known for precise song and studiocraft. Here, he's thrown it all to the wind, trying to make a record that sounds as pastoral and relaxed as the album's cover photo. He makes something that sounds easy—easy enough that you and a couple of neighbors who you don't know very well could knock it out in your garage on a lazy Saturday afternoon—and that's what's frustrating and amazing about it. Yeah, it's possible to call this a terrible record, but it's so strange in its domestic bent and feigned ordinariness that it winds up being a pop album like no other. *—Stephen Thomas Erlewine*

Red Rose Speedway / Apr. 30, 1973 / Capitol ✦✦✦✦
All right, he's made a record with his wife and a record with his pickup band where democracy is allegedly the conceit even if it never sounds that way, so he returns to a solo effort, making the most disjointed album he ever cut. There's a certain fascination to its fragmented nature, not just because it's decidedly on the softer side of things, but because his desire for homegrown eccentricity has been fused with his inclination for bombastic art rock à la *Abbey Road*. Consequently, *Red Rose Speedway* winds up being a really strange record, one that veers toward the schmaltzy AOR MOR (especially on the hit single "My Love"), yet is thoroughly twisted in its own desire toward domestic art. As a result, this is every bit as insular as the lo-fi records of the early '90s, but considerably more artful, since it was, after all, designed by one of the great pop composers of the century. Yes, the greatest songs here are slight—"Big Barn Bed," "One More Kiss," and "When the Night"—but this is a deliberately slight record (slight in the way a snapshot album is important to a family yet glazes the eyes of any outside observer). Work your way into the inner circle, and McCartney's little flourishes are intoxicating—not just the melodies, but the facile production and offhand invention. If these are miniscule steps forward, consider this: if Brian Wilson can be praised for his half-assed ideas and execution, then why not McCartney, who has more character here than the Beach Boys did on their Brother records? Truthfully. *—Stephen Thomas Erlewine*

Band on the Run / Dec. 5, 1973 / Capitol ✦✦✦✦✦
Neither the dippy, rustic *Wild Life* nor the slick AOR flourishes of *Red Rose Speedway* earned McCartney much respect, so he made the selfconsciously ambitious *Band on the Run* to rebuke his critics. On the surface, *Band on the Run* appears to be constructed as a song cycle in the vein of *Abbey Road*, but subsequent listens reveal that the only similarities the two albums share are simply superficial. McCartney's talent for songcraft and nuanced arrangements is in ample display throughout the record, which makes many of the songs—including the nonsensical title track—sound more substantial than they actually are. While a handful of the songs are excellent—the surging, inspired surrealism of "Jet" is by far one of his best solo recordings, "Bluebird" is sunny acoustic pop, and "Helen Wheels" captures McCartney rocking with abandon—most of the songs are more style than substance. Yet McCartney's melodies are more consistent than any of his previous solo records, and there are no throwaways; the songs just happen to be not very good.

Still, the record is enjoyable, whether it's the minor-key "Mrs. Vanderbilt" or "Let Me Roll It," a silly response to John Lennon's "How Do You Sleep," which does make *Band on the Run* one of McCartney's finest solo efforts. However, there's little of real substance on the record. No matter how elaborate the production is, or how cleverly his mini-suites are constructed, *Band on the Run* is nothing more than a triumph of showmanship. *—Stephen Thomas Erlewine*

Venus and Mars / May 27, 1975 / Capitol ✦✦✦
Band on the Run was a commercial success, but even if it was billed as a Wings effort, it was primarily recorded by Paul, Linda, and Denny Laine. So, it was time to once again turn Wings into a genuine band, adding Joe English and Jimmy McCulloch to the lineup and even letting the latter contribute a song. This faux-democracy isn't what signals that this is a band effort—it's the attitude, construction, and pacing, which McCartney acknowledges as much, opening with an acoustic title track that's a salute to arena rock, leading to a genuine arena rock anthem, "Rock Show." From that, it's pretty much rocking pop tunes, paced with a couple of ballads and a little whimsy, all graced with a little of the production flair that distinguished *Band on the Run*. But where that record was clearly a studio creation and consciously elaborate, this is a straightforward affair where the sonic details are simply window dressing. McCartney doesn't really try anything new, but the songs are a little more varied than the uniform, glossy production would suggest; he dips into soft-shoe music hall shuffle on "You Gave Me the Answer," gets a little psychedelic with "Spirits of Ancient Egypt," kicks out a '50s rock & roll groove with "Magento and Titanium Man," and unveils a typically sweet and lovely melody on "Listen to What the Man Said." These are a slight shifts on an album that certainly feels like the overture for the arena rock tour that it was, which makes it one of McCartney's more consistent listens, even though it's possible to scan the song listing after several listens and not recognize any song outside of "Listen to What the Man Said" and the opening medley by title. *—Stephen Thomas Erlewine*

Wings at the Speed of Sound / Mar. 25, 1976 / Capitol ✦✦
If *Venus and Mars* had the façade of being an album by a band, *At the Speed of Sound* really is a full-band effort, where everybody gets a chance to sing, even contribute a song. This, ironically, winds up as considerably less cohesive than its predecessor despite these efforts for community, not because Wings was not a band in the proper sense, but because nobody else in the band pulsed as much weight as McCartney, who was resting on his laurels here. Consider this: The two hits "Let 'Em In" and "Silly Love Songs" are so lightweight that their lack of substance seems nearly defiant. They have sweet, nice melodies and are well crafted, but as songs they're nonexistent, working primarily as effervescent popcraft of their time. And that's the case for most of *At the Speed of Sound*, as tracks like "She's My Baby" play like the hits, only without memorable hooks. There is a bit of charm to the record, arriving in Linda's awkwardly sung "Cook of the House," the mellow "Must Do Something About It," and especially "Beware My Love," the best-written song here that effortlessly moves from sun-drenched harmonies to hard rock. Apart from the latter, these are modest pleasures buried on an album that may have been a chart-topping blockbuster, but now seems like one of McCartney's most transient works. [The CD reissue contains three bonus tracks, including the trad jazz instrumental "Walking in the Park With Eloise," which his father wrote, and the charming laid-back country "Sally G," which is better than most of the songs on *Speed*.] *—Stephen Thomas Erlewine*

Wings Over America / Dec. 11, 1976 / Capitol ✦✦✦
Basically, there are two things that rock bands do—they make an album and they go on tour. Since Paul McCartney fervently wanted to believe Wings were a real rock band, he had them record an album or two (*Venus and Mars, At the Speed of Sound*) and then took the group on the road. So, in March of 1976 he released *At the Speed of Sound* and launched his first solo tour of America. At the end of the hugely successful, heavily hyped tour, he released *Wings Over America*, a triple-album set (later reissued as a two-CD set) that re-created an entire concert from various shows performed on the tour. It was a massive set list, running over two hours and featuring 30 songs, and it was well received at the time, partially because he revived some Beatles tunes and partially because it wasn't the disaster some naysayers expected. Wings were never a particularly gifted band and nowhere is that more evident than on *Wings Over America*. Matters aren't really helped by the fact that the large set list gives McCartney full opportunity to show off his vast array of affected voices, from crooner to rocker to bluesman. Also, the songs, in retrospect, rely too heavily on the recent Wings albums, which weren't really loaded with great tunes. (It's also hard to believe that there were two Denny Laine vocals so early in the program, or that the concert ended with the plodding rocker "Soily," which was never released on any other McCartney album.) In the end, the combination of workmanlike performances and pedestrian songs diminishes the appeal of such small pleasures as the acoustic Beatles set or the storming "Hi Hi Hi" and leaves *Wings Over America* as a souvenir for hardcore fans. *—Stephen Thomas Erlewine*

London Town / Mar. 31, 1978 / Capitol ✦✦✦✦
Reduced to the core trio of McCartney, McCartney, and Laine after the successful *Speed of Sound* tour, *London Town* finds Wings dropping the band façade slightly, turning in their most song-oriented effort since *Band on the Run*—which, not coincidentally, was recorded with this very trio. And although its high points don't shine as brightly as those on its two immediate predecessors, it's certainly stronger than *Speed* and, in its own way, as satisfying as *Venus and Mars*. What *London Town* has in its favor is Wings' (or, more likely, McCartney's) decision to settle into slick soft rock, relying on glossy, synth-heavy productions as he ratchets up the melodic quotient. This gives the album a distinctly European flavor, a feeling that intensifies when the lyrics are taken into the equation, and this gives *London Town* a different flavor than almost any other record in his catalog. And if its best moments aren't as strong as McCartney at his best they, along with the album tracks, find him skillfully crafting engagingly light, tuneful songs that charm with their offhanded craft, domesticity, and unapologetic sweetness. McCartney's humor is in evidence here, too, with the terrific "Famous Groupies," which means there's a little of everything he does here, outside of flat-out rocking. It's a laid-back, almost effortless collection of professional pop and, as such, it's one of his strongest albums. *—Stephen Thomas Erlewine*

Wings Greatest / Nov. 22, 1978 / Capitol ✦✦✦✦✦
Released in 1978 after *London Town* gave McCartney another huge hit, *Wings Greatest* rounds up McCartney's greatest hits from 1971 to 1978—which means it skips "Maybe I'm Amazed" but touches on *Ram*. The main strength of this collection is that it contains many hits that never appeared on any album, and these are among McCartney's very best solo singles: the eccentric domesticity of "Another Day," the choogling rocker "Junior's Farm," the Bond anthem "Live and Let Die," the piledriving "Hi Hi Hi," and "Mull of Kintyre," a Scottish-styled folk ballad that was his biggest hit in England. And yes, it's fair to peg these as McCartney successes, since some of them were billed as McCartney, not Wings, and as such, this record is a great overview of McCartney's first decade of solo recording, containing many of his very best solo tunes. One consumer warning: Much of this overlaps with 1988's *All the Best* (both the U.S. and U.K. editions), which is more comprehensive for the listener looking for a more complete retrospective. *—Stephen Thomas Erlewine*

Back to the Egg / May 24, 1979 / Capitol ✦✦
Back to the Egg was Paul McCartney's attempt to get back to rock & roll after the soft-rock of *London Town*. Assembling a new lineup of Wings, McCartney led the group through a set of his most undistinguished songs, ranging from the forced arena-rock of "Old Siam Sir" to the formulaic adult contemporary pap of "Arrow Through Me"—and those are two of the more memorable cuts on the record. Part of the problem is the weak sound of the record and Wings' faceless performances, but the true problem is the songs, which have no spark whatsoever. On the basis of *Back to the Egg*, it's no wonder that McCartney returned to solo recordings after its relative failure. *—Stephen Thomas Erlewine*

McCartney II / May 21, 1980 / Capitol ✦✦✦
Entitled *McCartney II* because its one-man band approach mirrors that of his first solo album, McCartney's first record since the breakup of Wings was greeted upon its release as a return to form, especially since its synth-heavy arrangements seemed to represent his acceptance of new wave. In retrospect, the record is muddled and confused, nowhere more so than on the frazzled sequencing of "Temporary Secretary," where McCartney spits out ridiculous lyrics with a self-consciously atonal melody over gurgling synths. Things rarely get worse than that, and occasionally, as in the effortless hooks of "Coming Up," the record is quite enjoyable. Nevertheless, the majority of *McCartney II* is forced, and its lack of memorable melodies is accentuated by the stiff electronics, which were not innovative at the time and are even more awkward in the present. At least *McCartney II* finds Paul in an adventurous state of mind, which is a relief after years of formulaic pop. In some ways, the fact that he was trying was more relevant than the fact that the experiments failed. *—Stephen Thomas Erlewine*

Tug of War / Apr. 26, 1982 / Capitol ✦✦✦✦✦
Reuniting with producer George Martin was a bit of a masterstroke on the part of Paul McCartney, since it guaranteed that *Tug of War* would receive a large, attentive audience. Martin does help McCartney focus, but it's hard to give all the credit to *Tug of War*, since McCartney was showing signs of creative rebirth on *McCartney II*, a homemade collection of synth-based tunes. This lush, ambitious, sprawling album couldn't be further from that record. That was deliberately experimental and intimate, while this is nothing less than a grand gesture, playing as McCartney's attempt to summarize everything he can do on one record. There's majestic balladry, folky guitars, unabashed whimsy, unashamed sentimentality, clever jokes, silliness, hints of reggae, a rockabilly duet with Carl Perkins, two collaborations with Stevie Wonder, and, of course, lots of great tunes. If anything, McCartney's trying a bit too hard here, and there are times that the music sags with its own ambition (or slightly dated production, as on the smash single "Ebony and Ivory"). But, at its best—the surging title track, the giddy "Take It Away," the vaudevillian stomp "Ballroom Dancing," the Lennon tribute "Here Today," the wonderful "Wanderlust"—it's as good as McCartney gets. *—Stephen Thomas Erlewine*

Pipes of Peace / Nov. 1983 / Capitol ✦✦✦
Perhaps it isn't surprising that McCartney's grip on the pop charts started to slip with *Pipes of Peace*, since it was released after his 40th birthday—and most rockers do not mature particularly gracefully. Although it's rather fascinating that the album didn't reach the Top Ten, despite a blockbuster duet with Michael Jackson in "Say Say Say," *Pipes of Peace* bewilders in other ways, particularly in its allusions to *Tug of War*. It often seems as if this album was constructed as a deliberate mirror image of its predecessor; it is also produced by George Martin, also contains two duets with an African-American superstar (Jackson here, Stevie Wonder there), also acknowledges an old bandmate (a Lennon tribute there, a Ringo cameo here), and even contains "Tug of Peace," a deliberate answer song to its predecessor. If only it were nearly as adventurous as *Tug of War*! Instead of dabbling in all his myriad musical personas, McCartney settles back into a soft rock groove, tempered somewhat by a desire to be contemporary (which means a heavy reliance on drum machines and synthesizers). Instead of sounding modern, McCartney winds up sounding like an aging rocker desperately trying to keep up with the time. Still, at its best, *Pipes of Peace* is ingratiating soft rock. In particular, the first side is close to irresistible. Not enough to add up to a latter-day triumph from McCartney, but it still contains better songs than its blockbuster mid-'70s counterparts, and even if it's a little lightweight, it has more flair in its craft and more style in its sound than other McCartney

albums, which is enough to make it a minor musical success, despite its disappointing chart performance. *—Stephen Thomas Erlewine*

Give My Regards to Broad Street / Oct. 1984 / Capitol ✦✦

There's no justifying, let alone explaining, Macca's disastrous 1984 film *Give My Regards to Broad Street*—a nearly impenetrable "farce" involving stolen tapes, ghosts, and funny moustaches—and the soundtrack, if anything, is even messier. With just a few exceptions, this relies on older McCartney material from *Revolver* to *Tug of War*, with one significant touch—everything has been re-recorded. And that doesn't just mean that "Yesterday" has a new solo McCartney version, it means that he's *recut* songs as recent as "Ballroom Dancing" and *Pipes of Peace*'s "So Bad." Perhaps if he reinterpreted them, this would at least be interesting, but he replicates the original recordings, down to the same solos. This would be an unmitigated disaster if it wasn't for "No More Lonely Nights," an absolutely lovely mid-tempo tune graced by a terrific David Gilmour guitar solo. Of course, he has to diminish that tune by including three versions of it (*five* on the CD reissue), which means that it's a much better bet to pick that up on *All the Best* instead of here. *—Stephen Thomas Erlewine*

Press to Play / Sep. 19, 1986 / Capitol ✦✦✦

At the time, *Press to Play* was occasionally promoted as Macca's response to punk—which we all better hope is not true, since that means he was responding ten years after the fact, signaling just how out of touch he was. But McCartney wasn't that disconnected from reality (he did talk about punk in interviews from the late '70s), so a more accurate view of *Press to Play* is to see it as McCartney trying to reconnect with his classic strengths, from orchestral pop and whimsy to driving rockers and sweet love songs. All this is apparent on the record, often in pretty charming fashion. "Stranglehold" has an offhand charm, "Good Times Coming/Feel the Sun" feels like a forgotten *Red Rose Speedway* medley, "Move Over Busker" has a brisk gait (better than its cousin, "Angry," anyway), and "Press" is a terrific mid-'80s drum machine-driven slice of synth-pop, utterly featherweight in the best possible way. Each of these captures a different side of McCartney, and that's the overriding impression of *Press to Play*—McCartney is dabbling in each of his strengths, just to see what works. It doesn't wind up as one of his stronger albums, but it's more interesting than some of his more consistent ones, and those aforementioned cuts demonstrate that he could still cut effective pop records when he put his mind to it. *—Stephen Thomas Erlewine*

All the Best / 1987 / Capitol ✦✦✦✦✦

Technically, *All the Best* was the first compilation of McCartney's solo material, since *Wings Greatest* covered songs released under the Wings aegis. Well, there is considerable overlap between the two records—no less than *ten* of that album's 12 songs are here, yet only the hard-rocking "Hi Hi Hi" is truly missed—although the seven new songs do give this album a different character, for better or worse. With the U.S. version of *All the Best*, which has four different songs than its British counterpart, the balance shifts toward the positive, since it simply boasts a better selection of songs. Yes, "Once Upon a Long Ago," the single offered as bait on the British *All the Best*, isn't here, but it's not missed since two of the four songs exclusive to the American version are among McCartney's best solo singles ("Junior's Farm," "Uncle Albert/Admiral Halsey") and the other two are good adult contemporary easy listening (the previously non-LP "Goodnight Tonight," "With a Little Luck"). These songs add to the retrospective, although it's still not perfect—such highlights as "Maybe I'm Amazed" and "Take It Away" really should have been included. However, as a cross section of McCartney's solo singles, this is very, very good. It may be a little heavy on the schmaltz at times, yet this is still mainstream pop craft of the highest order. *—Stephen Thomas Erlewine*

Flowers in the Dirt / May 1989 / Capitol ✦✦✦

McCartney must not only have been conscious of his slipping commercial fortunes, he must have realized that his records hadn't been treated seriously for years, so he decided to make a full-fledged comeback effort with *Flowers in the Dirt*. His most significant move was to write a series of songs with Elvis Costello, some of which appeared on Costello's own *Spike* and many of which surfaced here. These may not be epochal songs, the way many wished them to be, but McCartney and Costello turn out to be successful collaborators, spurring each other toward interesting work. And, in McCartney's case, that carried over to the album as a whole, as he aimed for more ambitious lyrics, themes, sounds, and productions for *Flowers in the Dirt*. This didn't necessarily result in a more successful album than its predecessors, but it had more heart, ambition, and nerve, which was certainly welcome. And the moments that did work were pretty terrific. Many of these were McCartney/McManus collaborations, from the moderate hit "My Brave Face" to the duet "You Want Her Too" and "That Day Is Done," but McCartney also demonstrates considerable muscle on his own, from the domestic journal "We Got Married" to the lovely "This One." This increased ambition also means McCartney meanders a bit, writing songs that are more notable for what they try to achieve than what they do, and at times the production is too fussy and inextricably tied to its time, but as a self-styled comeback affair, *Flowers in the Dirt* works very well. *—Stephen Thomas Erlewine*

Tripping the Live Fantastic / Oct. 1990 / Capitol ✦✦

Liverpool Oratorio / 1991 / Angel ✦✦

Unplugged (The Official Bootleg) / May 1991 / Capitol ✦✦✦✦

Released after the studied, meticulous *Flowers in the Dirt*, the live acoustic concert album *Unplugged* was a breath of fresh air, and it remains one of the most enjoyable records in McCartney's catalog. Running through a selection of oldies—not only his own, but Beatles and rock & roll chestnuts—McCartney is carefree and charming, making songs like "Be-Bop-a-Lula" and "Blue Moon of Kentucky" (which finds Paul melding Bill Monroe with Elvis) sound fresh. But the real revelations of the record are the songs McCartney hauls out from his debut—"That Would Be Something," "Every Night," and "Junk"—which sound lovely and timeless, restoring them to their proper place in his canon. They help make *Unplugged* into a thoroughly enjoyable minor gem. *—Stephen Thomas Erlewine*

Choba B CCCP / Oct. 28, 1991 / Capitol ✦✦

This album of rock & roll oldies—"Lucille," "Twenty Flight Rock," and others—was recorded in two days in July, 1987, and released exclusively in the Soviet Union in 1988. It finally saw release in the U.S. in 1991 with one extra track, "I'm in Love Again," added. McCartney gives a spirited reading to the songs, which, it may be noted, are in some cases ("Ain't That a Shame," "Just Because") the same ones chosen by John Lennon for his similar *Rock & Roll* album. But McCartney is characteristically more eclectic, including such ringers as "Summertime" and "Don't Get Around Much Anymore." *—William Ruhlmann*

Off the Ground / Feb. 1993 / Capitol ✦✦

Flowers in the Dirt did earn good reviews but perhaps more important was its accompanying tour, McCartney's first full-fledged world tour in years. Given the tour's enthusiastic reception, McCartney could wait until 1993 to deliver the album's proper sequel, *Off the Ground*. Though it isn't as consciously ambitious, *Off the Ground* certainly picks up where *Flowers* left off, as McCartney feels no shame in making an album that doesn't aim for the charts (though success would certainly be welcomed), yet is still classy, professional, and ambitious. Two key differences appear: It's a leaner production (making the mid-tempo numbers seem less cloying and giving the rockers real kick), and McCartney's social conscience dominates the record (which is easily his most politically active, as he rails against animal testing and pleads for world peace several times). He doesn't leave love or whimsy behind ("Biker Like an Icon" is easily his worst, most studied stab at whimsy), and he still has a pair of fine McCartney/McManus songs ("Mistress and Maid," "The Lovers That Never Were") to pull out. This all results in a record that has its virtues—it's clean and direct, where many of his solo albums are diffuse and meandering, and it's serious-minded where many rely on cutesiness—but, overall, *Off the Ground* feels like less than the sum of its parts, possibly because the seriousness is too studied, perhaps because the approach is a bit too stodgy. Nevertheless, this has nearly as many successful moments as *Flowers in the Dirt*, standing as a deliberately serious comeback record by an artist who spent too much time relying on his natural charm, and who feels no shame in overcompensating at this stage of the game. *—Stephen Thomas Erlewine*

Paul Is Live / Nov. 16, 1993 / Capitol ✦✦

Flaming Pie / May 27, 1997 / Capitol ✦✦✦✦✦

According to McCartney, working on the Beatles *Anthology* project inspired him to record an album that was stripped-back, immediate, and fun, one less studied and produced than most of his recent work. In many ways, *Flaming Pie* fulfills those goals. A largely acoustic collection of simple songs, *Flaming Pie* is direct and unassuming, and at its best, it recalls the homely charm of *McCartney* and *Ram*. McCartney still has a tendency to wallow in trite sentiment, and his more ambitious numbers, like the string-drenched epic "Beautiful Night" or the silly Beatlesque psychedelia of "Flaming Pie," tend to fall flat. But when he works on a small scale, as on the waltzing "The Song We Were Singing," "Calico Skies," "Great Day" and "Little Willow," the's gently affecting, and the moderately rocking pop of "The World Tonight" and "Young Boy" is more ingratiating than the pair of aimless bluesy jams with Steve Miller. Even with the filler, which should be expected on any McCartney album, *Flaming Pie* is one of his most successful latter-day efforts, mainly because McCartney is at his best when he doesn't try so hard and lets his effortless melodic gifts rise to the surface. *—Stephen Thomas Erlewine*

Standing Stone / Sep. 23, 1997 / Angel ✦✦✦

Paul McCartney's second classical work, following six years after his first, the *Liverpool Oratorio*, is a 75-minute "symphonic poem" which, along with an actual poem printed in the CD booklet, tries "to describe the way Celtic man might have wondered about the origins of life and the mystery of existence," as an explanatory note puts it. This musical description is for the most part surprisingly somber and, not so surprisingly, episodic. As a composer, even with the resources of the London Symphony Orchestra at his disposal, McCartney assembles his music as though he were constructing an album of pop songs, presenting a series of moods and melodies more notable for their contrasts and discrete effects than for any unity. The composer remains a facile melodist, which is an important quality in classical as well as pop music, and there are aural pleasures here and there. But the musical ideas are merely presented without being woven effectively together or developed. Ambitious as McCartney's organizing principle may have been, it's no wonder that in his note he puts the word "story" in quotation marks. *—William Tilland*

Run Devil Run / Oct. 5, 1999 / EMI ✦✦✦✦

When Paul McCartney returned to the studio a year after his wife Linda's death, he wanted to cut loose and have a good time. He gathered a bunch of friends, most notably guitarist David Gilmour, with the intention of cutting a collection of rock & roll oldies with minimal rehearsal and a handful of takes. On the surface, that makes *Run Devil Run* like *Choba B CCCP*, but there are subtle differences that make *Devil* a far superior effort. This time around, there's a real freshness to the performances. Gilmour, in particular, amazes, turning in some of his finest playing in years. Similarly, McCartney is invigorated, leaving behind his vocal schtick, laying back and rocking out with a set of fairly unfamiliar oldies. Only three songs—"All Shook Up," "Lonesome Town," and "Brown Eyed Handsome Man"—are radio staples; and while "I Got Stung," "Blue Jean Bop," "She Said Yeah," "Honey Hush," and "Movie Magg" are known by aficionados, they're not ubiquitous standards. This leaves room for a few more obscure numbers, such as Little Richard's "Shake a Hand," the Vipers' "No Other Baby," and the Fats Domino B-side "Coquette," plus three terrific new songs from McCartney: "Run Devil Run," a fantastic Chuck Berry-styled narrative; "Try Not to Cry," a strong bluesy pop number; and "What It Is," a catchy up-tempo shuffle. Best of all, McCartney and co-producer Chris Thomas create an appealingly out-of-time production—heavily compressed sound, yes, but cleaner than '50s recordings and livelier, grittier than most '90s albums. It all adds up to a dynamic, loose, carefree, and utterly infectious record, one of his best solo albums. *—Stephen Thomas Erlewine*

Liverpool Sound Collage / Sep. 5, 2000 / Capitol ♦♦♦
The hype mill, stoked in part by McCartney himself, promoted this CD as nothing less than a posthumous chapter in the Beatles' saga ("a new little piece of Beatles," in Paul's words). Nonsense, for this is really just the latest of McCartney's excursions into electronica, an interest of his that dates back to the Beatles' boundary-shredding experiments with musique concrete and the Moog synthesizer in the 1960s. It is a series of five electronic collages, with occasional eruptions of a new tune called "Free Now" (actually a catchy repetitive riff, no more or less), sounds of the auto tunnel under the Mersey, pieces of strange off-the-cuff interviews conducted by Paul on the Liverpool streets (he asks, disingenuously, "What do you think of the Beatles?"), snippets of a chorale from his Liverpool Oratorio—and yes, some Beatle talk from the 1965 sessions for "Think for Yourself." All of the tracks are given separately distributed credits to McCartney, the Beatles, the group Super Furry Animals, and Youth—his collaborator in previous electronica projects—but in fact, the whole hour-long CD is of a single piece. The most effective segment is the one credited solely to Youth (bearing the unwieldy title "Real Gone Dub Made in Manifest in the Vortex of the Eternal Now"), where the pitchless electronic sounds are at their wildest and the disembodied Beatles voices and ghostly choruses are hauntingly adrift in a high-tech netherworld. As a listening experience, it is at least as casually absorbing as McCartney's two *Fireman* albums—and it grows on you, provided that you drop any expectations of this being a long-lost Beatles album. *—Richard Ginell*

★ **Wingspan** / May 8, 2001 / Capitol ♦♦♦♦♦
Paul McCartney always got the short end of the stick when he was in the Beatles and again in the '70s, as he and his erstwhile partner John Lennon pursued solo careers. McCartney was attacked for his virtues—for his melodicism and his domesticity, along with his desire to form a real touring band following the Beatles. None of these were celebrated at the time, but he moved many, many records and sold countless concert tickets, which only hardened opposition toward him. But, in retrospect, McCartney's albums make for the most fascinating body of work among any of the ex-Beatles, and really among any of his peers. Yes, there were pitfalls among the heights, but that's part of what makes his career so fascinating—each record is distinctive, and even if the songs themselves are shallow, at least lyrically, the melodic skill and studio savvy behind each are hard not to admire. This may require a bit of conversion, and if you're not up to trudging through his individual works, even such masterworks as *Ram* (truly the roots of home-made pop), the double-disc set *Wingspan* is ideal. McCartney has had a number of career overviews before, including such seemingly comprehensive discs as *All the Best*, but those were plagued by vaguely haphazard sequencing. This is nearly perfectly executed, dividing McCartney's career between the "hits" and "history," with the latter being devoted to album tracks that are acknowledged classics, yet never were singles. Now, it's true that this isn't completely comprehensive, but nothing has come as close to capturing the quirky brilliance of McCartney's solo career, how it balanced whimsical pop with unabashedly sentimental romantic ballads, piledriving rockers, and anything in between. *—Stephen Thomas Erlewine*

The McCoys

f. 1962, Union City, IN, **db.** 1969
Pop, Pop/Rock, Psychedelic
This Indiana group were still in high school when they were tapped by the Strangeloves' production team of Feldman-Goldstein-Gottehrer as a vehicle for their material in 1965. Their first effort, "Hang on Sloopy," was a monster number one smash, built around a riff and chorus that ranks with "Louie Louie" and "La Bamba" as a garage band perennial with its compelling, elemental simplicity. Featuring the lead vocals and lead guitar of a young Rick Derringer, they went on to cut a lot of similar chunky, innocuous pop/rock over the next couple years with fair success. The "Hang on Sloopy" soundalike "Fever" was their only other Top Ten entry, and the Ritchie Valens cover "C'Mon Let's Go" their only other Top 40 hit.

The McCoys recorded very little original material during their early years at Bang Records; most of it was supplied by the Feldman-Goldstein-Gottehrer production team, much of which consisted of unexceptional derivations of the "Hang on Sloopy" prototype. Notable exceptions were the folky "Sorrow," covered for a Top Ten hit by the Merseys in Great Britain (and covered by David Bowie on *Pin Ups* a decade later), and the adventurous Middle Eastern-tinged garage psychedelia of "Don't Worry Mother," their best cut besides "Hang on Sloopy." The McCoys proved unusually durable after their career as a teen pop band; in the late '60s, they broke from their Bang producers to record psychedelic and progressive rock for Mercury. Most of the group joined Johnny Winter's backup band in the early '70s, and in 1973 Rick Derringer joined the Edgar Winter group as lead guitarist and vocalist, after which he had a successful hard rock solo career. *—Richie Unterberger*

Psychedelic Years / 1994 / One Way ♦♦
Some rock & roll acts slid easily into the psychedelic era, and did well with it—the Beatles, the Pretty Things, the Who, the Rolling Stones (overlooking *Satanic Majesties*), even the Rascals (sort of). Unfortunately, the McCoys weren't one of them—the band that turned "Hang on Sloopy" into a teen anthem just wasn't that good mixing psychedelic rock, blues, country, and jazz, with brass and saxes in their instrumental mix. This CD combines all but two songs off of the 1968 vintage *Infinite McCoys* and *Human Ball* albums. There is some good playing by Rick Zehringer (aka Derringer) and keyboard man Robert Peterson, and some interesting jazzy moments too ("Resurrection"), where it is just them, but you've got to be patient to get to them and listen to some really pretentious crap in the meantime, not to mention ignore the trumpets, trombones, and saxes (arranged by Fred Lipsius) that get you there. There is a near-absence of decent tunes ("Open Your Eyes" is an exception), or memorable hooks, and the best piece of blues here ("Stormy Monday Blues") isn't worth the wait to get to. For completists only. *—Bruce Eder*

● **Hang on Sloopy: The Best of the McCoys** / Jun. 6, 1995 / Epic/Legacy ♦♦♦♦♦
22-track compilation of their best mid-'60s material, including all the hits and tracks from their two Bang LPs, non-album singles, and a couple of previously unissued cuts. Much of this is rather forgettable if inoffensive, other than "Hang on Sloopy," "Fever," "Sorrow," and "Don't Worry Mother." *—Richie Unterberger*

Michael McDonald

b. 1952, St. Louis, MO
Vocals, Keyboards / Blue-Eyed Soul, Pop/Rock, Soft Rock, Adult Contemporary
With his husky, soulful baritone, Michael McDonald became one of the most distinctive and popular vocalists—both as a lead singer, and as a harmony singer for the likes of Steely Dan, Kenny Loggins, Toto, Christopher Cross, and Robbie Dupree—to emerge from the laid-back California pop/rock scene of the late '70s. McDonald found the middle ground between blue-eyed soul and smooth soft rock, a sound which made him a star. He initially essayed his signature style with the Doobie Brothers, ushering in the group's most popular period with hits like "What a Fool Believes" and "Taking It to the Streets." McDonald disbanded the group in 1982 to pursue a solo career. Initially, his solo career was quite successful, as his first album generated the Top Ten hit "I Keep Forgettin' (Every Time You're Near)," which also reached the R&B Top Ten, plus the James Ingram duet "Yah Mo B There." He lost some momentum with his second album, 1985's *No Lookin' Back*, but that was followed by a chart-topping duet with Patti LaBelle, "On My Own," plus the Top Ten hit, "Sweet Freedom." By the end of the decade, his popularity had faded away, since he was reluctant to work regularly and hesitant to update his sound to suit shifting popular tastes. In the '90s, he reunited with the Doobies on occasion and he was featured on Donald Fagen's 1994 New York Rock and Soul Revue. His recording career was hampered by conflicts with his label, Reprise, which delayed his 1997 album by three years—it finally appeared in 2000 on an independent label. *—Stephen Thomas Erlewine*

● **The Very Best of Michael McDonald** / 2001 / Rhino ♦♦♦♦♦
For too long, there wasn't a Michael McDonald compilation available domestically. Rhino/Warner Archives' 2001 release *The Very Best of Michael McDonald* corrects that situation, offering a generous 16 tracks, including duets and a previous unreleased version of *Higher Ground*. The collection concentrates solely on his solo recordings for Warner/Reprise, which means it ends in 1993 and doesn't include anything from his long-delayed 2000 album. This isn't necessarily a bad thing, because McDonald stopped having hits in the late '80s, so there's nothing missing (even though casual fans can be forgiven for wondering why latter-day Doobie Brothers singles aren't here; at a certain point, those became indistinguishable from McDonald's solo work). At its best—which would be "No Lookin' Back," "I Keep Forgettin' (Every Time You're Near)," "Yah Mo Be There," "On My Own," and "Sweet Freedom"—this captures everything that's good about laid-back, West Coast, soul-tinged soft rock. At its worst, it's professional, well constructed, and listenable, lacking only songs that work their way underneath your skin. In a way, the length works against the compilation, since the merely pleasant feels like padding, but McDonald's greatest hits remain sterling examples of finely made, soft blue-eyed soul. *—Stephen Thomas Erlewine*

Barry McGuire

b. Oct. 15, 1935, Oklahoma City, OK
Vocals, Songwriter, Guitar / Folk-Rock, Singer/Songwriter
Barry McGuire achieved one-hit wonder status for the 1965 folk-rock protest song "Eve of Destruction," which topped the charts. He began his career in folk music earlier in the decade and had been a member of the New Christy Minstrels, for whom he co-wrote the hit "Green, Green." McGuire was unable to follow up "Eve of Destruction" despite several subsequent releases, but he found success in the Christian music field in the 1970s. He now devotes his time to a charity that sponsors poor children in Third World countries. *—William Ruhlmann*

● **Anthology** / 1994 / One Way ♦♦♦♦♦
Although the packaging leaves something to be desired, all of Barry McGuire's hits, including "Eve of Destruction" and many similar-sounding protest folk-rockers, are featured on *Anthology*. *—Stephen Thomas Erlewine*

Maria McKee

b. Aug. 17, 1964, Los Angeles, CA
Vocals, Guitar / College Rock, Americana, Alternative Country-Rock, Roots Rock, Alternative Pop/Rock
While she was with Lone Justice, Maria McKee always showed promise; her gritty, soulful mix of R&B, rock, and country helped distinguish the band from the multitude of '80s roots rockers. When she released her first solo album in the late '80s, it suffered from the same problem as Lone Justice—lots of potential, but no delivery. However, 1993's *You Gotta Sin to Get Saved* showed McKee making good on her promise, with an album of impassioned rockers and ballads. Three years later, McKee released her third solo album, *Life Is Sweet*, an album that marked a depature from her roots rock roots and a movement toward alternative and art rock. *—Stephen Thomas Erlewine*

Maria McKee / Jun. 1989 / Geffen ♦♦♦
Three years after Lone Justice's last album, Maria McKee released her self-titled debut,

which showed that her skills as a songwriter had grown considerably since her first band. Not only were her songs better, but McKee's singing had improved; while it was still a little thin, her voice had grown grittier and more soulful, which made her songs all the more convincing. Unfortunately, most of McKee's musical growth was obscured by Mitchell Froom's mushy overproduction. *—Stephen Thomas Erlewine*

You Gotta Sin to Get Saved / Jun. 22, 1993 / Geffen ✦✦✦✦
A few years after an underappreciated solo album, former Lone Justice leader Maria McKee returns with *You Gotta Sin to Get Saved*, her best album yet. With Black Crowes and Jayhawks producer George Drakoulias at the helm, *You Gotta Sin to Get Saved* evokes the country-rock vibe of the early '70s (much like the aforementioned groups) without sounding like a studied replica. McKee sings a dynamic mix of originals and covers with genuine conviction, making *You Gotta Sin to Get Saved* an album that demands repeated plays. *—Stephen Thomas Erlewine*

Life Is Sweet / Mar. 26, 1996 / Geffen ✦✦✦
For most of her career, Maria McKee has never deviated from country-rock, but *Life Is Sweet* is a bold departure from her trademark sound, taking her into new sonic territories. Although the loud, distorted guitars are the first noticeable change, it soon becomes apparent that the thing that makes the album sound so different is its latent progressive-rock influences. Throughout the album, McKee weaves complex, layered arrangements that interweave strings, guitars, and keyboards. Appropriately, her melodies are more convoluted than ever before, yet they never become too obtuse. Lyrically, she has become more cryptic and angry, but that is all part of the plan—*Life Is Sweet* is McKee's bid to be taken seriously as an artist. For some reason, that means she has constructed a hybrid of the prog-rock arrangements that dominate the first half of the album and the confessional songwriting that is prominent on the second. Fortunately, the results sound better than they read, primarily because beneath all of the bombastic arrangements, McKee has retained her keen sense of songcraft. Still, with its art-rock tendencies and naked ambition, *Life Is Sweet* may not appeal to fans that have become attached to McKee's country-rock. For those willing to accept her pretensions, it is a frustrating but rewarding album. *—Stephen Thomas Erlewine*

● **Ultimate Collection** / Aug. 22, 2000 / Hip-O ✦✦✦✦
The Ultimate Collection collects Maria McKee's definitive moments with Lone Justice and as a solo artist. Her sensual yet down-to-earth vocals and gritty songwriting stand out on Lone Justice tracks like "Don't Toss Us Away," "Shelter," and "Ways to Be Wicked"; her growth as both a singer and a writer is reflected on solo songs such as "Absolutely Barking Stars," "Breathe," and "What Else You Wanna Know." The collection also includes some interesting bonuses, including Lone Justice's live version of "Sweet Jane," an acoustic demo of "Show Me Heaven," and "If Love Is a Red Dress," which originally appeared on the *Pulp Fiction* soundtrack. At 17 tracks long, *This One Is for the Girl* comes pretty close to being an ultimate collection of McKee's body of work. *—Heather Phares*

Sarah McLachlan

b. Jan. 28, 1968, Halifax, Nova Scotia, Canada
Vocals, Piano, Guitar / Adult Alternative Pop/Rock, Alternative Pop/Rock, Singer/Songwriter

Sincer her debut in 1988, Sarah McLachlan's atmospheric folk-pop has gained a devoted following of fans not only in Canada, where she has established star status, but also in the U.S. and U.K. Each album has shown her growing both as a musician and songwriter, continually redefining herself and emerging as a major voice in the growing Adult Alternative Pop format. On the strength of her debut, 1988's *Touch*, she was signed to Arista for international distribution. The album eventually reached gold status in Canada and was reissued worldwide in 1989. In 1991, she followed up with *Solace*, an impressive collection that showed a great leap in songcraft and built a strong cult following in the U.S. *Fumbling Toward Ecstasy*, her strongest and most personal effort to date, was released in late 1993. The album peaked in the U.S. charts at number 50 and by the end of 1994, it reached platinum status after 62 weeks on the chart. "Possession," the single from the album, broke the Top 100 and received considerable airplay, especially on modern rock radio, where it reached number 14. "Good Enough" also found a home in that format, reaching number 16. In 1997, McLachlan began work on her fourth album, the enormously successful *Surfacing*, which debuted at number two on the pop albums chart. In addition to her own albums, she organized the successful Lilith Fair tour, a package tour focusing on emerging women singer/songwriters. *—Chris Woodstra*

Touch / 1988 / Arista ✦✦✦
On her debut effort, McLachlan sets the stage for future greatness. While only in her early twenties, she shows insights beyond her years with highly personal and introspective lyrics. *—Chris Woodstra*

Solace / Sep. 10, 1991 / Arista ✦✦✦✦✦
Solace is at once comforting, mysterious, expansive, timeless, and familiar. The sophomore jinx was certainly eluded here, as McLachlan sets forth a superior collection of songs and performances with the help of longtime producer Pierre Marchand. The opening track, "Drawn to the Rhythm," serves its title well and does the job of luring you in. Intelligent, intriguing lyrics and lilting melodies abound, whether amidst the pulsing rhythms of "Into the Fire" and "Back Door Man" or the quietly profound stories of "Home" and "Shelter." Although pretty much all of the tunes will grab you at one point or another, "The Path of Thorns (Terms)" and "I Will Not Forget You" are especially memorable, the latter not to be confused with McLachlan's "I Will Remember You," which appears on the 1995 soundtrack for *The Brothers McMullen. Solace* is a wonderful record that offers a glimpse of the astounding talent of a young Sarah McLachlan. *—Kelly McCartney*

● **Fumbling Towards Ecstasy** / Oct. 22, 1993 / Arista ✦✦✦✦✦
Fumbling Towards Ecstasy finds Sarah McLachlan racing toward success as she re-teams with producer Pierre Marchand on her breakthrough release and finest offering to date. Stretching her lyrical wings and experimenting a bit more instrumentally, the radiance of her work has somehow solidified here. Ecstasy is certainly attained, though not by fumbling, for McLachlan has far too much finesse to be so awkward as that. "Possession," the track that caught people's attention and began her pop-chart ascension, is a twisted tale of love as told through the mind and heart of a stalker, although as voiced by McLachlan, many would wish to have such a problem. Two versions of "Possession" are included: the first is a fully produced, upbeat, drum-looped groove that comes off as all but happy; the second is a minimalist hidden track with just McLachlan and her piano sketching the story in a much more haunting, almost eerie fashion. From the light-hearted comparisons of love's sweetness in "Ice Cream" to the more somber experience of the impending death of a loved one in "Hold On," McLachlan never flinches, never takes the easy route of cliché and formula. This care and attention given to her art allows each song to stand strong individually, making the whole an extraordinary collection. *—Kelly McCartney*

The Freedom Sessions / Mar. 28, 1995 / Arista ✦✦✦
A nice companion piece to *Fumbling Towards Ecstasy, The Freedom Sessions* offers seven early versions of songs from that album in a more stripped-down form. Also included is a cover of Tom Waits' "Ol' 55." *—Chris Woodstra*

Rarities, B-Sides, and Other Stuff / 1996 / Nettwerk ✦✦✦
In the time it took her to release her first three proper albums, Sarah McLachlan has put out nearly as much music as B-sides singles, or as stray tracks for compilations and soundtracks, leaving no easy job for fans wanting her entire output. *Rarities, B-Sides, and Other Stuff* collects 13 of these non-album tracks, including "I Will Remember You" from the *Brother McMullen* soundtrack, "Dear God," the song she contributed to an XTC tribute album, a cover of Joni Mitchell's "Blue," and several remixes. While this by no means empties the vaults or even collects all the necessary B-sides (her spot-on version of Peter Gabriel's "Solsbury Hill," for instance, is not included), *Rarities* focus on remixes *does*, in the end, provide an interesting and highly listenable alternate view of the artist. *—Chris Woodstra*

Surfacing / Jul. 15, 1997 / Arista ✦✦✦
Surfacing was released as the first Lilith Fair tour hit the road, and Sarah McLachlan benefited enormously from the timing. As the organizer of Lilith Fair, McLachlan was on the cover of magazines across America and Canada, which helped *Surfacing* debut at number two on the U.S. charts—a particularly remarkable feat, since its predecessor, *Fumbling Towards Ecstasy*, peaked at number 50. All the commercial success and media hype disguised the fact that *Surfacing* not only didn't offer anything new from McLachlan, but it wasn't a particularly strong consolidation of her talents. That it isn't to say it's a bad record, because it certainly isn't—there are several fine songs on the album, including the single "Building a Mystery"—but it doesn't offer anything new, and the songs aren't as consistently captivating as they were on *Fumbling Towards Ecstasy*. And that suggests that even though McLachlan is at the height of her popularity, she may beginning to run out of ideas. *—Stephen Thomas Erlewine*

Mirrorball / Jun. 15, 1999 / Arista ✦✦✦
Released at the front end of what might be Lilith Fair's last hurrah, *Mirrorball* is a take-home sampler of the live performances that have catapulted McLachlan into the modern rock stratosphere. Over half of the album's 14 songs are radio hits (including four of the first five), proving McLachlan's worth as a pop songstress bar none, but also hinting at an underlying stagnation in her recent musical output. Though fans of McLachlan and folks who missed her Lilith performances will likely enjoy *Mirrorball*, it's a little too by-the-book to win any converts or please critical listeners. There is few dialogue between songs, for example, and the sound quality is so pristine that if it weren't for the occasional hoot and holler from the audience one would never know it's a live album. *—Steve Kurutz*

Don McLean

b. Oct. 2, 1945, New Rochelle, NY
Vocals, Guitar / Folk-Rock, Soft Rock, Singer/Songwriter

Famed for—and ultimately defined by—his perennial "American Pie," singer/songwriter Don McLean was born October 2, 1945 in New Rochelle, NY. After getting his start in the folk clubs of New York City during the mid-'60s, McLean built a small following through his work with Pete Seeger on the Clearwater, a sloop which sailed up and down the eastern seaboard to promote environmental causes.

Still, McLean was primarily singing in elementary schools and the like when in 1970 he issued his debut album, *Tapestry*. The album fared poorly, but he returned in 1971 with *American Pie*; the title track, an elegiac eight-and-a-half-minute folk-pop epic inspired by the tragic death of Buddy Holly, became a number one hit, and the LP soon reached the top of the charts as well.

Subsequent records like 1972's self-titled effort and 1974's *Playin' Favorites* deliberately avoided any attempts to recreate the "American Pie" flavor; not surprisingly, his sales plummeted. After 1974's *Homeless Brother* and 1976's *Solo*, United Artists dropped McLean from his contract; he resurfaced on Arista the next year with *Prime Time*, but when it too fared poorly, he spent the next several years without a label.

McLean enjoyed a renaissance of sorts with 1980's *Chain Lightning*, his first Top 30 LP in close to a decade. However, 1981's *Believers* failed to sustain the comeback, and after 1983's *Dominion* he was again left without benefit of label support. McLean spent the remainder of his career primarily on the road, grudglingly restoring "American Pie" to his set list and drawing inspiration from the country market; he also returned to the studio for projects like 1990's *For the Memories* and 1995's *River of Love*. —*Jason Ankeny*

American Pie / Oct. 1971 / BGO ♦♦♦♦♦
The album that made McLean famous. The title track is the only real rocker, but the rest is intelligently produced and at times quite haunting, if a little angst-ridden. —*Bruce Eder*

● **Greatest Hits Then & Now** / 1987 / EMI America ♦♦♦♦♦
For most fans, the single-disc *Greatest Hits Then & Now* will be all the Don McLean they need, since it compiles all of his hits and best-known songs on one concise disc. —*Stephen Thomas Erlewine*

Favorites & Rarities / 1992 / EMI America ♦♦♦♦
Spanning two discs and 42 tracks, *Favorites & Rarities* really is directed toward diehards, not casual fans looking for a thorough overview. Although all his biggest hits are here, they're surrounded by material that will delight only the dedicated, including alternate versions and no less than 18 previously unreleased tracks. This material, while interesting to the converted (there is a question to just how interesting it actually is, though), makes this a rather tedious listen for anybody that's just looking for "American Pie" and "Vincent," plus a couple other tunes in the same vein. Not an unnecessary compilation, since it's filled with rarities, but not definitive, either. —*Stephen Thomas Erlewine*

Clyde McPhatter

b. Nov. 15, 1932, Durham, NC, **d.** Jun. 13, 1972, Teaneck, NJ
Vocals / R&B
As the lead singer for Billy Ward & His Dominoes and the Drifters, Clyde McPhatter was one of the most important R&B vocalists of the '50s. His high, passionate vocals were charged with gospel inflections, as well as blues—his fusion of the sacred and the secular was crucial in the develpoment of R&B and soul. While his recordings with Ward and the Drifters were his most influential, McPhatter's solo records were equally excellent, as well as popular—his first nine solo singles were all Top Ten R&B hits, and three of those—"Treasure of Love," "Long Lonely Nights," "A Lover's Question"—were number one. However, his career began to slide in the '60s as he became increasingly depedent on alcohol. His abuse eventually led to his early death in 1972, yet Clyde McPhatter's legacy could be heard throughout the soul and R&B of the '60s and '70s, particularly in the seductive smooth soul of Al Green and the Spinners. —*Stephen Thomas Erlewine*

★ **Deep Sea Ball: The Best of Clyde McPhatter** / Oct. 1, 1991 / Atlantic ♦♦♦♦♦
This is about as perfect a summary of Clyde McPhatter's solo years with Atlantic as there is to buy, in the absence of a box of his complete output for the label or a Sequel Records reissue of his Atlantic LPs. Those who are most familiar with McPhatter's singing from his days with the Drifters will be pleased by all 19 songs here, which represent a more mature voice and embody musical ambitions that carried McPhatter toward the same kind of expansive, pop-oriented R&B that Sam Cooke also started working toward (and would hit bigger with) a couple of years later. He could still rock out, as on the title track, but he also had a sense of the dramatic in his singing and used it to powerful effect on songs like "Without Love," "Treasure of Love," and "A Lover's Question" may be McPhatter's best remembered solo hits, but even the non-chart sides here, like "I Can't Stand Up Alone" (which harkens back to McPhatter's roots as a gospel singer) and the big-band R&B of "I'm Lonely Tonight," are gorgeous pieces of music that demand to be heard. The only drawback is that the material isn't in chronological order, which wouldn't be a problem at all if the recording dates had been listed next to the tracks in the notes. But it sounds fine and the music is so compelling that it holds up regardless of the programming decisions. —*Bruce Eder*

★ **The Forgotten Angel** / Sep. 29, 1998 / 32 Jazz ♦♦♦♦♦
Finally, a definitive compilation of Clyde McPhatter! This two-disc collection chronicles McPhatter's hits (and some tunes that should have been hits) from the early '50s through the early '60s. It begins with over a dozen selections of Drifters material from mid-1953 to late 1954, including "Lucille" and "Money Honey." After these come classics from McPhatter's solo career (the recordings here pick up in 1955), including "Without Love (There Is Nothing)," "Lover Please," "Thirty Days," "Lovey Dovey," "I Can't Stand Up Alone," and the oldies-radio regular "A Lover's Question." With this collection, which has relatively excellent sound quality (except the few live cuts), the 32 label has done fans of early R&B vocals a great service, for McPhatter is one of the undisputed greats (Smokey Robinson and Jackie Wilson were *his* fans). *The Forgotten Angel* will stand up to a lifetime of listening. —*Joslyn Layne*

A Shot of Rhythm and Blues / Jul. 18, 2000 / Sundazed ♦♦♦
McPhatter was dropping out of sight commercially when he recorded for Amy from 1965 to 1967. This compilation of both sides of his five 1965-1967 Amy singles (augmented by four previously unreleased alternate takes) demonstrates that although his voice was still in decent shape, there was really no compelling reason to think that he should have had been worthy of attention during this period. It's middling mid-'60s soul, and although McPhatter was able to record material by some name players—such as Joe Tex, Rick Hall, Billy Sherrill, and Van McCoy—he wasn't coming across great songs. And the truth was, McPhatter's voice wasn't as well suited to 1960s soul with full-bodied production as it was to doo wop and 1950s R&B. There's nothing that objectionable about these tracks, yet nothing too memorable, either, with McPhatter and his producers trying various settings, usually slick uptown soul ones. It hasn't been too easy to hear this stuff, and this reissue thus does have its value to big McPhatter fans, with Sundazed's typical thorough liner notes and documentation. —*Richie Unterberger*

Meat Loaf (Marvin Lee Aday)

b. Jan. 22, 1946, Dallas, TX
Vocals / Album Rock, Arena Rock, Pop/Rock, Hard Rock
Marvin Lee Aday was a singer and occasional actor who, for reasons never definitively answered, recorded under the name Meat Loaf. In all likelihood a childhood nickname, the tag stuck, and many puns followed as the performer—who tipped the scales at well over 300 pounds—became one of the biggest chart acts of the 1970s before enjoying a commercial renaissance two decades later. A member of several touring musicals and off-Broadway productions, Meat Loaf gained the help of classically trained pianist/composer Jim Steinman and producer Todd Rundgren to record 1977's *Bat Out of Hell*, a teen rock opera which spawned three Top 40 singles—"Two Out of Three Ain't Bad," "Paradise by the Dashboard Light," and "You Took the Words Right out of My Mouth"—on its way to becoming one of the best-selling albums of the decade. After Meat Loaf and Steinman had a falling out, solo records like 1984's *Bad Attitude* and 1986's *Blind Before I Stop* bombed. Several years were spent in relative obscurity, though the pair reunited in 1993 for *Bat Out of Hell II: Back into Hell*, which continued the original's storyline, duplicated its thunderous sound and proved almost as successful, selling over five million copies. Without Steinman, Meat Loaf returned in 1995 with *Welcome to the Neighborhood*. —*Jason Ankeny*

● **Bat Out of Hell** / 1977 / Epic/Legacy ♦♦♦♦♦
There is no other album like *Bat out of Hell*, unless you want to count the sequel. This is grand guginol pop—epic, gothic, operatic, and silly, and it's appealing because of all of this. Jim Steinman was a composer without peer, simply because nobody else wanted to make mini-epics like this. And there never could have been a singer more suited for his compositions than Meat Loaf, a singer partial to bombast, albeit shaded bombast. The compositions are staggeringly ridiculous, yet Meat Loaf finds the emotional core in each song, bringing true heartbreak to "Two out of Three Ain't Bad" and sly humor to "Paradise by the Dashboard Light." There's no discounting the production of Todd Rundgren, either, who gives Steinman's self-styled grandiosity a production that's staggeringly big, but never overwhelming and always alluring. While the sentiments are deliberately adolescent and filled with jokes and exaggerated clichés, there's real (albeit silly) wit behind these compositions, not just in the lyrics but in the music, which is a savvy blend of oldies pastiche, show tunes, prog rock, Springsteen-esque narratives, and blistering hard rock (thereby sounding a bit like an extension of *Rocky Horror Picture Show*, which brought Meat Loaf to the national stage). It may be easy to dismiss this as ridiculous, but there's real style and craft here and its kitsch is intentional. It may elevate adolescent passion to operatic dimensions, and that's certainly silly, but it's hard not to marvel at the skill behind this grandly silly, irresistible album. —*Stephen Thomas Erlewine*

Meatloaf (Featuring Stoney) / 1979 / Prodigal ♦♦

Dead Ringer / 1981 / Epic ♦♦♦
Although it took Meat Loaf and composer Jim Steinman another 12 years to come up with the marketing gimmick of positioning an album as a deliberate follow-up to the multi-platinum *Bat out of Hell*, *Dead Ringer* was the *real Bat II*. Once again, Steinman wrote extended, operatic songs with hyperbolic lyrics ("I'll Kill You If You Don't Come Back" was one title) and organized a backup band anchored by E Street Band members Max Weinberg (drums) and Roy Bittan (keyboards), while Meat Loaf sang with a passion all the more compelling for its hint of the ridiculous. In the U.S., with four years separating *Bat* and *Dead Ringer*, nobody cared much. But in the U.K., where *Bat* was still going strong, *Dead Ringer* topped the charts, and the title track, featuring a perfectly cast Cher as duet singer, went Top Ten. In retrospect, the missing ingredient in the album is Todd Rundgren's pop sensibility as producer; he was the one who knew how long the compositions could go for maximum dramatic impact without becoming exhausting. It was Rundgren who made *Bat out of Hell* a fiery listening experience—producing himself, Meat Loaf often sounded only warmed over. —*William Ruhlmann*

Midnight at the Lost and Found / 1983 / Epic ♦♦
Singer Meat Loaf and composer Jim Steinman tried to do without producer Todd Rundgren, who had handled their masterpiece, *Bat out of Hell*, on its follow-up, *Dead Ringer*, and they managed okay. But then Meat Loaf tried to do without Steinman on the third album, *Midnight at the Lost and Found*, didn't even come close. Meat Loaf was in typically impassioned form, but the material just didn't scale the heights of Steinman's incredible hubris. The U.S. had long since lost interest, but even in the U.K., where Meat Loaf was loved, the album was a step down commercially. —*William Ruhlmann*

Hits Out of Hell / 1984 / Epic ♦♦♦
Since Meat Loaf's *Bat out of Hell* album is vastly better than its follow-ups, *Dead Ringer* and *Midnight at the Lost and Found*, the idea of doing a hits compilation culling familiar tracks from the three albums is not really a good one. But the second and third albums did feature U.K. hits, and *Hits* does contain the four key tracks from *Bat*—the title track, "Two out of Three Ain't Bad," "You Took the Words Right out of My Mouth," and "Paradise by the Dashboard Light." A few tracks from *Dead Ringer*, notably "Read 'Em and Weep" and "I'm Gonna Love Her for Both of Us," are in the same spirit, but the songs from *Midnight* are simply inferior. —*William Ruhlmann*

Bad Attitude / 1984 / RCA ♦♦♦
Meat Loaf collects a couple of Jim Steinman songs and he, Paul Jacobs, and Mack work at recreating the Todd Rundgren production sound for an album of high-voltage rock. [Originally released on Arista Records in the U.K. in October 1984, *Bad Attitude* was released in the U.S. on RCA Records in April 1985.] —*William Ruhlmann*

Blind Before I Stop / 1986 / Atlantic ♦♦

Bat out of Hell II: Back Into Hell / 1993 / MCA ♦♦♦♦♦
Although Meat Loaf has made several albums since *Bat out of Hell* (most of them never released in the U.S.), *Bat out of Hell II: Back Into Hell* is an explicit sequel to that milestone of '70s pop culture. Reprising the formula of the original nearly to the letter, *Back Into Hell* is bombastic and has too much detail, thanks to the pseudo-operatic splendor of Jim Steinman's grandly cinematic songs. From the arrangements to the length of the tracks, everything on the album is overstated; even the album version of the hit single, "I Would Do Anything for Love (But I Won't Do That)," is 12 minutes long. Yet that's precisely the point of this album and is also why it works so well. No other rock & roller besides Meat Loaf could pull off the humor and theatricality of *Back Into Hell* and make it seem real. In that sense, it's a worthy successor to the original. *—Stephen Thomas Erlewine*

Welcome to the Neighbourhood / Nov. 14, 1995 / Virgin ♦♦♦
After having scored a surprising commercial comeback with 1993's *Bat out of Hell II: Back Into Hell*, his reunion with songwriter Jim Steinman, Meat Loaf tried to make it on his own, just as he had from 1983 to 1993, and with similarly disappointing results. As with albums like *Bad Attitude*, a couple of Steinman songs were tossed in, in this case the minor "Original Sin" (copyright 1989) and "Left in the Dark" (copyright 1980), a song previously cut by Barbra Streisand. But most of the album's songwriting was provided by a team of people, including pop songwriter Diane Warren, Van Halen lead singer Sammy Hagar, and ex-E Streeter Steven Van Zandt, plus producer Ron Nevison, trying to clone the flamboyant Steinman style and failing to do so. Especially the Warren material (which sounded more like the kind of thing she tends to write for Michael Bolton) lacked Steinman's gothic excess, sly humor, and lyrical reach. Meat Loaf, as usual, sang like his life depended on it, while a band that was less distinctive than it should have been given such notable participants as Kenny Aronoff and Kasim Sulton churned out sub-metal riffs. The resulting sales fall-off was not as great as it had been before, but it remained true that Meat without Steinman was only half a loaf. *—William Ruhlmann*

Live Around the World / 1996 / Tommy Boy ♦♦♦♦♦

The Very Best of Meatloaf / Nov. 10, 1998 / Epic ♦♦♦♦
Unlike previous collections Epic has assembled, the double-disc *The Very Best of Meat Loaf* draws not only from his recordings for the label, but it also licenses his '90s comeback recordings for MCA. Which means, of course, that the 20-track collection is indeed the "very best" of Meat Loaf. Not all of his charting hits are here—"What You See Is What You Get," his 1971 single with Stoney, is absent, as is "I'm Gonna Love Her for the Both of Us," the only hit he had between the two *Bat out of Hell* albums—but all of the key album tracks from the two blockbusters are here, along with highlights from the sequels to the sequel, which means everything that anyone but a diehard Meat Loaf fan could want is on this collection ("Paradise by the Dashboard Light," "Two out of Three Ain't Bad," "You Took the Words Right out of My Mouth," "Bat out of Hell," "I'd Do Anything for Love (But I Won't Do That)," "Rock & Roll Dreams Come True," "Objects in the Rear View Mirror May Appear Closer Than They Are," a remix of "Life is a Lemon and I Want My Money Back"). That said, it is true that either *Bat out of Hell* is a more cohesive listen than this set, simply because they were designed as complete albums. Consquently, casual fans may be just as happy to purchase those two discs, which will set them back about as much as *The Very Best of Meat Loaf*, but anyone who wants all the hits on one set should pick this up. *—Stephen Thomas Erlewine*

Meat Puppets

f. 1980

College Rock, American Punk, Cowpunk, Hardcore Punk, Alternative Pop/Rock, American Underground

Out of all of the bands that made SST Records a towering force in the American underground during the mid-'80s, the Meat Puppets lasted the longest, surviving where other bands fell apart. The Meat Puppets never had the dedicated following of Hüsker Dü or the Minutemen—two fellow SST bands that played the same circuit as the Puppets—but they were able to carve out a long career where other hardcore bands could not because they always drew from conventional hard rock as well as punk. Not only did they play hard, loud, and fast, but they also had elements of the blues-rock of ZZ Top, the ambling folk-rock of the Grateful Dead, and Neil Young's country-rock and hard rock. As they grew older, the band matured musically, developing an accomplished instrumental technique and moving closer to the traditional hard rock that was always underneath their punk; but they never quite abandoned their punk roots, even when they briefly broke into the mainstream in the early '90s. *—Stephen Thomas Erlewine*

Meat Puppets / 1982 / Rykodisc ♦♦♦
Although the Meat Puppets would later become best known for their intriguing blend of country, punk, rock, folk, psychedelia, and whatever else they could toss in their musical blender, the trio's 1982 self-titled full-length debut was a furious hardcore album. Totally ferocious and red hot, the album rarely lets up on its full-throttle attack—Curt Kirkwood's vocals bear little resemblance to the wasted, off-key country-rock warbling on such seminal releases as *Meat Puppets II* and *Up on the Sun*; instead, the singing style consists of larynx-shredding screaming that renders the lyrics incomprehensible. Still, there's something special about such slop-rockers as "Love Offering," "Blue-Green God," "Saturday Morning," and "Our Friends." And as a sign of things to come, for a few brief fleeting moments, the band attempts to conquer country (on covers of "Walking Boss" and "Tumblin' Tumbleweeds"). The 1999 Rykodisc reissue more than doubled the original album's track listing, including their early *In a Car* EP and a total of 12 outtakes/demos, the best of the bunch being covers of the Stooges' "I Got a Right," Neil Young's "I Am a Child," and the Grateful Dead's "Franklin's Tower." *—Greg Prato*

★ **Meat Puppets II** / 1983 / Rykodisc ♦♦♦♦♦
The Meat Puppets' second album, 1984's appropriately titled *Meat Puppets II*, has since gone down in the rock history books as an all-time classic, and rightfully so. The Meat Puppets were one of the first punk acts to inject different musical styles into their sound, something that was an absolute no-no at the time—especially the sparkling sounds of country. The trio resembles a more conventional band than on their white-noise self-titled debut; the songwriting had improved dramatically, and you could even clearly decipher the playing and singing this time around. As many '90s alt-rock fans know, *Meat Puppets II* reached a whole new generation of fans when Nirvana covered the album's three best tracks on their *MTV Unplugged* special from 1994—"Plateau," "Lake of Fire," and "Oh, Me." But this was an incredibly consistent recording from beginning to end; other highlights included the instrumentals "Magic Toy Missing," "Aurora Borealis," and "I'm a Mindless Idiot," the rockers "Split Myself in Two" and "New Gods," plus such mellower fare as "Lost," "We're Here," "Climbing," and "The Whistling Song." The 1999 Rykodisc reissue contained seven additional tracks, including the contrasting two-part epic "Teenager(s)," as well as "What to Do" and "100% of Nothing." An essential recording that sounds as fresh and inviting as the day it was released. *—Greg Prato*

Up on the Sun / 1985 / Rykodisc ♦♦♦♦♦
What does a band do when they're trying to follow up a masterpiece? Release another masterpiece, of course. That's exactly what the Meat Puppets did with 1985's *Up on the Sun*. Issued one year after *Meat Puppets II*, the songwriting had become more focused, the performances were tighter, and Curt Kirkwood's vocals had progressed from a high-pitched warbling to a soothing monotone. *Up on the Sun* catches the Arizona trio in a relaxed mood, for the most part; the tunes aren't wound up as tightly as its predecessor, with the album-opening title track, the instrumental "Seal Whales," and "Hot Pink" being fine examples. Other highlights include "Maiden's Milk," which contains some great instrumental interplay between the band members, as well as the upbeat "Away," the funky "Buckethead," the psychedelic "Two Rivers," and the furious "Enchanted Porkfist." As with the other 1999 Meat Puppets reissues on Rykodisc, rarities and demos are included as bonus tracks, including a haunting demo of the album's title track. *—Greg Prato*

Huevos / 1987 / Rykodisc ♦♦♦♦
Recorded and released just a few months after the experimental *Mirage*, 1987's *Huevos* was a return to the Meat Puppets' earlier, more straight-ahead direction. The band (guitarist/singer Curt Kirkwood in particular) had always voiced their admiration of ZZ Top, and *Huevos* contained Billy Gibbons & Co.'s influence more than any other Puppets release. But don't be misled—it wasn't a ripoff, the trio simply incorporated ZZ's sound into their energetic, unpredictable rock. It also didn't hurt that *Huevos* contained the band's best set of songs since 1985's classic *Up on the Sun*, comprised almost entirely of heavy rockers ("Paradise," "Look at the Rain," "Crazy," "Fruit," "Automatic Mojo," "Dry Rain," etc.). Another major improvement of *Huevos* over *Mirage* was that Derrick Bostrom's drums no longer sounded metronome-perfect and robotic, giving the performances a much livelier edge. The bonus tracks included on the '99 Ryko reissue included several demos of *Huevos* tunes, including a lengthier and much more laid-back version of "Sexy Music," as well as a medley of "I Can't Be Counted On" and Jimmy Reed's "Baby What You Want Me to Do." *—Greg Prato*

Mirage / 1987 / Rykodisc ♦♦♦
As many Meat Puppets fans had realized by 1987's *Mirage*, the trio would change gears and broaden their sound with each successive album. This was never more apparent than on their fourth full-length release. Synthesizers were used to add textures to the tunes, while the drums sounded metronome-perfect, almost as if a drum machine was supplying the patterns. Strangely, although *Mirage* was the trio's most experimental album, it also turned out to be one of their most psychedelia-based works. The groovy little ditty "Get on Down" turned out to be one of the band's first videos aired on MTV, while the title track, the melodic "Leaves," the country rocker "Confusion Fog," the unrelenting "Beauty," and the album-closing punk freak-out "Liquified" are all standouts. Several previously unreleased demos were included on the 1999 Rykodisc reissue, as well as a solo Curt Kirkwood original, "Grand Intro." *—Greg Prato*

Monsters / 1989 / Rykodisc ♦♦♦
The Meat Puppets' final release for SST, 1989's *Monsters* is best described as a cross between their experimental *Mirage* and the more in-your-face *Huevos* (both released only a few months apart in 1987). Several major labels had been hotly pursuing the trio, but when negotiations slowed to a snail's pace, they decided to issue another album on SST in the meantime. Curt Kirkwood's crunchy guitar riffs are spotlighted throughout the album, but some of the songs are hindered by synth textures and the fact that the songs were recorded one instrument at a time, which mutes any excitement of the trio playing live in a room together (which was what made *Huevos* such a success). Still, several highlights were included—the vicious album-opening "Attacked by Monsters," the melodic "Light," the tough rocker "The Void," the rollicking instrumental "Flight of the Fire Weasel," the warped love song "Strings on Your Heart," and the sleepy album closer, "Almost Like Being Alive." Three bonus tracks were added to the 1999 Rykodisc reissue: the previously unheard original "Wish Upon a Storm" and two radically different versions of "Flight of the Fire Weasel." *—Greg Prato*

No Strings Attached / 1990 / SST ♦♦♦
An extremely well-thought-out two-LP sampler of the Pups from their SST days. Tracks go up to and include material from *Monsters*. SST released this after the band left the venerable indie label for London in 1990. An excellent anthology. *—John Dougan*

Forbidden Places / Jul. 9, 1991 / London ♦♦♦
Veteran independent rockers the Meat Puppets finally took the plunge and signed with a major label in the early '90s, London Records, the first home of one of their favorite bands,

ZZ Top. Judging from their previous release (1989's *Monsters*), it appeared as though the trio was going in a more experimental direction, away from the raw and direct approach of their early works. But the Puppets surprised their fans by going back to their live-in-the-room feel, resulting in one of their finest albums, 1991's *Forbidden Places*. Unfortunately, it became yet another criminally overlooked release for the band, getting lost in the shuffle since it was released just prior to the Seattle explosion in the fall of 1991. The turbo-charged album opener, "Sam," is a razor-sharp rocker that features a humorous, lightning-fast vocal delivery from the Kirkwood brothers; other standouts include the bluesy "Nail It Down," the tranquil "This Day" and "No Longer Gone," and such ragers as "Open Wide," "Popskull," and the title track. And what Meat Puppets album would be complete without a few country ditties? The lonesome "That's How It Goes" and the breakneck album-closing instrumental "Six Gallon Pie" showed off the trio's cowboy roots splendidly. *—Greg Prato*

Too High to Die / Jan. 25, 1994 / London ♦♦♦♦
Although the Meat Puppets' previous album, 1991's *Forbidden Places*, was one of the Arizona trio's finest, the band wasn't completely happy with the album's sound, courtesy of longtime Dwight Yoakam producer Pete Anderson. So on their second album for London Records, 1994's *Too High To Die*, the trio hooked up with Butthole Surfer Paul Leary to put them back on track. Not only did they succeed, but they scored a big radio hit with the melodic rocker "Backwater," and the release became their first to be certified gold. The electrified album opener "Violet Eyes" kicks things off, and immediately thereafter, the trio takes you on a wild musical rollercoaster ride. Hard rock ("We Don't Exist," "Station," an unlisted remake of "Lake of Fire"), blues rock ("Roof With a Hole"), ballads ("Shine," "Why?"), country ("Comin' Down"), and demented pop rock ("Never to Be Found," "Severed Goddess Hand," "Flaming Heart," "Things") help make up perhaps the band's most musically varied album. *—Greg Prato*

No Joke! / Oct. 3, 1995 / London ♦♦

Live in Montana / Feb. 23, 1999 / Rykodisc ♦♦♦
Although the Meat Puppets were considered one of the most exciting and exhilarating alt-punk bands, the original lineup never got around to issuing a live album during their tenure from 1982-1996. Just prior to the re-release of all their '80s SST albums in 1999 on Rykodisc, the band's first live album ever, *Live in Montana*, was issued. Recorded on December 7-8, 1988 (at the Sundance and Top Hat clubs) while on tour supporting their *Huevos* album, several tracks from their forthcoming *Monsters* release are included as well—the album-opening "Touchdown King," "Attacked by Monsters," and "Party 'Til the World Obeys." Also featured are versions of such classics as "Plateau," "Maiden's Milk," "Lake of Fire," and "Liquified," as well as surprise covers like "Cotton Candy Land," "Dough Rey Mi," "S.W.A.T. (Get Down)," "Blue Bayou," and a crunchy album-closing medley of "The Small Hours/Paranoid/Sweet Leaf." Although the trio often goes for feel over precision with the playing and singing (even more so than on their already loose early albums), the spontaneous electricity captured on *Live in Montana* is contagious. *—Greg Prato*

Golden Lies / Sep. 26, 2000 / Atlantic ♦♦♦
With all the turmoil and tragedy surrounding his family, it's no wonder Meat Puppets leader Curt Kirkwood fled Arizona to make a fresh start in Austin, TX. Breaking with the past, Kirkwood assembled a new quartet version of the Meat Puppets, featuring two former members of the Austin band Pariah. As presented on *Golden Lies*, the new Puppets are a surprisingly heavy, hard-rocking outfit, turning in one of the loudest records in the group's catalog. It's also one of the best-produced, boasting a thick, full, shiny sound. Some of the quirkier, more freewheeling edges of the old Puppets have been sanded off—there's very little of Kirkwood's vaunted country influence here, and the record sometimes feels a little too uniform when the inevitable comparisons to the Pups of yesteryear are made. But really, many individual moments work very well, and it's encouraging to hear Kirkwood returning to form. Songs like "I Quit," "You Love Me," and "Endless Wave" have that classic airy Pups feel, but with an added jolt of intensity supplied by the new band. Not everything on the record works; some of the lyrics try a little too hard for the trippy surrealism that's become Kirkwood's hallmark, and a few songs feature a sort of half-rapped speak-sing that comes off as awkward. *Golden Lies* doesn't quite recapture the glory of the Puppets' SST years, or the pop breakthrough of *Too High to Die*, but its very existence is a triumphant achievement. *—Steve Huey*

Joe Meek

b. 1929, Glouster, England, **d.** Feb. 3, 1967
Producer / Early British Pop/Rock, Pop, Instrumental Rock
Not an artist in the traditional sense of the term—he couldn't play or sing at all—producer Joe Meek has nonetheless been belatedly recognized as an important, even inimitable, figure of early British rock & roll. Like Phil Spector, Meek developed idiosyncratic production techniques that, much more than the artists he worked with, stamped a vision of mad genius on his recordings. In Meek's case, this usually amounted to super-compressed sound, wavering sped-up vocals, ghostly backing violins and choruses, spooky echo and reverb, ticky-tack varispeed piano, and all manners of Halloween and outer-space sound effects. The recordings were all the more remarkable for being produced not in a state-of-the-art studio, but in Meek's own bedroom-sized facility, located over a shop within the flat he rented. Meek couldn't rightly be compared to Phil Spector—he favored gawky, dippy teen-idol fare for gawky, dippy teen idols, not the gutsy soul and R&B-infused Wall of Sound. But he was a trailblazer in his own right—even before Spector, he set up shop as rock & roll's very first independent producer of note, making recordings on his own terms and leasing them to labels for distribution. *—Richie Unterberger*

Joe Meek Story, Vol. 1 / 1991 / Line ♦♦♦
Although one can hear the genesis of some of Meek's unique methods on this 20-track collection of 1960 releases, the material and performances are fairly insufferable, exhibit A in the lameness of much pre-Beatle British rock. Includes the super-rare (and silly) science fiction EP about intelligent life in outer space that he created with then-futuristic sound effects and tape manipulation under the moniker "The Blue Men." *—Richie Unterberger*

Joe Meek Story: The Pye Years / 1991 / Sequel ♦♦♦
48-track double CD of Meek productions released on the British Pye label between 1960 and 1966 give a surprisingly scattershot and fragmented overview of his work, with an overabundance of weak early '60s-type teen idol and instrumental fare, despite some strong tracks by the Honeycombs, Riot Squad, and Glenda Collins. *—Richie Unterberger*

I Hear a New World: An Outer Space Music Fantasy / 1991 / RPM ♦♦♦
In 1960, Joe Meek—already thinking in terms that couldn't be constrained by the limits of the day's technologies and marketing strategies—devised a "concept LP" of sorts that speculated about the nature of life on the moon (this was almost ten years before Apollo 11). Working with a group of musicians he dubbed the Blue Men, this "outer space music fantasy" tried to conjure the mood of the cosmos with the clavioline, a Hawaiian guitar, a rinky-dink piano, and then-futuristic electronic noises and sound effects. Listening today, the largely instrumental work sounds futuristic in a very dated way, especially the Chipmunks-like, electronically sped-up voices that were meant to simulate those little green men. As *Monty Python's Flying Circus* would say, it all sounds a bit silly, but it's an interesting insight into his unique production techniques—the sounds he sculpted for "Magnetic Field," for instance, are a clear forerunner of the electronic pulses that open and close "Telstar." Only four tracks from the opus were released at the time, on a super-rare EP; 30 years later, the RPM CD *I Hear a New World* presented the full work to the public for the first time. The 2001 RPM "Special Edition" release of *I Hear a New World* adds a 35-minute spoken monologue from 1962 in which Meek talks about his life, career, recording equipment, and production/working methods. The fidelity is hissy and scratchy (although quite comprehensible) and it gets dull as Meek takes a detailed tour of his studio sans visuals, but if you're enough of a Meek fan to seek out *I Hear a New World* in the first place, it's likely you'll find this a significant bonus. There's also an enhanced CD track with a three-minute 1964 TV interview clip of Meek, though it's playable only on PCs, not Macs. *—Richie Unterberger*

Work in Progress: The Triumph Sessions / 1994 / RPM ♦♦
Twenty-seven outtakes, demos, and previously unissued tracks that Meek recorded at his Triumph label in 1959 and 1960. Most of these are unfinished (sometimes they're not close to finished); the West Five and the Fabulous Flee-Rakkers get about half the tracks, and such fellow no-names as Chick Lewis, Ricky Wayne, Yolanda, Lee Sutton, and Eve Boswell fill out the compilation (John Leyton, who did eventually get some hits, has one track). Stylistically it's all over the board, from instrumental '50s rock to rockabilly to pop ballads and awful lounge piano singing, as well as a couple of demos featuring Meek's own off-key vocals. It's been assembled not for the general listener, but for the Meek scholar, who knows full well that the quality of both the audio and the actual songs isn't up to what you'll find on most CDs, by Meek or anybody else. It's patchy, sometimes embarrassingly so, but it does provide insights into the man's methods at a time when he was just spreading his wings. Sometimes it's kinda cool, especially when Meek plays around with echo and odd effects/arrangements. Mostly, though, it's only of use to the Joe Meek fan club, which is no slur upon the label that compiled the disc—that's exactly the kind of audience for which it was intended. *—Richie Unterberger*

★ **It's Hard to Believe: The Amazing World of Joe Meek** / Oct. 1995 / Razor & Tie ♦♦♦♦♦
Twenty of Meek's most notable hit singles and misses from 1960 to 1966. Includes his biggest hit productions (the Tornados' "Telstar," the Honeycombs' "Have I the Right," Heinz' "Just like Eddie," Mike Berry's "Tribute to Buddy Holly," John Leyton's "Johnny Remember Me"). Just as intriguing, though, are the more obscure items, some of which are hard or impossible to find on other compilations. Among these are the wild horror-rock of Screaming Lord Sutch's "'Til the Following Night," the super-creepy Moontrekkers instrumental "Night of the Vampire," the soul-pop of the Riot Squad (with Mitch Mitchell on drums), brassy femme pop by Glenda Collins, and a couple of excerpts from *I Hear a New World*, his bizarre outer-space opus. There are many other interesting Meek discs out there for those who want to go further, but this is an excellent introduction. *—Richie Unterberger*

Let's Go! Joe Meek's Girls / 1996 / RPM ♦♦♦
When you take the plunge into a Joe Meek rarity CD, you have fair warning that you're not going to encounter many lost masterworks. This compilation of 29 tracks by female singers he worked with in the early and mid-'60s, though, is one of the better ones on the market. None of these—by the likes of Jenny Moss, Gunilla Thorn, Kim Roberts, and Yolanda—were hits (ten tracks weren't even previously released), and frankly they didn't deserve to be, due to the extremely innocuous and slight nature of the material. That's not, however, what Meek connoisseurs are seeking with these archival releases. You want examples of Meek's inimitable outer space bathroom production techniques, whether highly polished or in progress, and you get them here, via the Casper-the-ghost strings, compressed percussion, and spooky keyboards. Which makes it a not half-bad document if you've got the Meek bug, even if the songs themselves are completely overshadowed by their embellishments, although the odd tune (Jenny Moss' "Hobbies," Pamela Blue's "Hey There Stranger," and especially Glenda Collins' dramatic "Baby It Hurts") carried some hit potential. *—Richie Unterberger*

Megadeth

f. 1983, Los Angeles, CA
Speed Metal, Heavy Metal, Thrash
After he left Metallica in 1983, guitarist/vocalist Dave Mustaine formed the thrash metal

quartet Megadeth. Though Megadeth followed the basic blueprint of Metallica's relentless attack, Mustaine's group distinguished themselves from his earlier band by lessening the progressive-rock influences, adding an emphasis on instrumental skills, speeding the tempo up slightly and making the instrumental attack harsher. By streamlining the classic thrash-metal approach and making the music more threatening, as well as making the lyrics more nihilistic, Megadeth became one of the leading bands of the genre during the mid- to late '80s. Each album they released went at least gold, and they continually sold out arenas across America, in addition to developing a strong following overseas. By the early '90s, they had toned their music down slightly, yet that simply increased their following—all of their proper '90s albums debuted in the Top Ten. *—Stephen Thomas Erlewine*

Killing Is My Business . . . And Business Is Good! / 1985 / Combat ✦✦✦
After his exit from Metallica, Dave Mustaine regrouped with his own band on this debut album, accentuating his own chaotic, driving rhythm guitar work and careening, lightning-fast solos. The music here is as raw as Megadeth gets, and that can be both good and bad—Megadeth's later precise, complex riffing and composition aren't completely developed, but the music is performed with a great deal of energy, while Mustaine's vocals (never his strong point) are amateurish at best. Highlights include a retooled version of Nancy Sinatra's "Boots" and "Mechanix," a Mustaine composition written with Metallica which turned into the latter's "The Four Horsemen." *—Steve Huey*

• **Peace Sells . . . But Who's Buying?** / 1986 / Capitol ✦✦✦✦✦
Arguably Megadeth's strongest effort and a classic of early thrash, *Peace Sells* combines a punkish political awareness with a dark, threatening, typically heavy-metal worldview, preoccupied with evil, the occult, and the like. The anthemic title track and "Wake Up Dead" are the two major standouts, and there is also a cover of Willie Dixon's "I Ain't Superstitious," which takes on an air of supernaturally induced paranoia in the album's context. The lines between hell and earth are blurred throughout the album, and the crashing, complex music backs up Mustaine's apocalyptic vision of life as damnation—his limited vocal style is used to great effect, growling and snarling in a barely intelligible fashion under all the complicated guitar work. Vital, necessary thrash. *—Steve Huey*

So Far, So Good . . . So What! / 1988 / Capitol ✦✦✦
A largely uninspired effort recorded with a new guitarist and drummer, *So Far, So Good . . . So What!* lacks the conceptual unity and musical bite of *Peace Sells*, which helps push much of its lyrical material into the realm of self-parody, as Mustaine rants about the P.M.R.C., the apocalypse, ex-girlfriends, and other people he is angry with, while hinting at the depth of his substance abuse problem with "502," a paean to driving drunk. The album wants to sound threatening but mostly comes off as forced and somewhat juvenile; typical is the embarrassing cover of "Anarchy in the U.K.," which is played in Megadeth's tightly controlled riffing style and without the looseness of the original, making it sound stilted and stiff—and Mustaine doesn't even get the lyrics right. This one is for diehards only. *—Steve Huey*

Rust in Peace / Sep. 24, 1990 / Capitol ✦✦✦✦✦
A sobered-up Mustaine returns with yet another lineup, this one featuring ex-Cacophony guitar virtuoso Marty Friedman and drummer Nick Menza, for what is easily Megadeth's strongest musical effort. As Metallica was then doing, Mustaine accentuates the progressive tendencies of his compositions, producing rhythmically complex, technically challenging thrash suites that he and Friedman burn through with impeccable execution and jaw-dropping skill. Thanks to Mustaine's focus on the music rather than his sometimes clumsy lyrics, *Rust in Peace* arguably holds up better than any other Megadeth release, even for listeners who think they've outgrown heavy metal. While the whole album is consistently impressive, the obvious highlight is the epic, Eastern-tinged "Hangar 18." *—Steve Huey*

Countdown to Extinction / Jul. 14, 1992 / Capitol ✦✦✦✦
Megadeth guns for arena-thrash success and gets it on *Countdown to Extinction*. Following the lead of 1991's *Metallica*, Megadeth trades in their lengthy, progressive compositions for streamlined, tightly written and played songs more conducive to radio and MTV airplay. Cries of "sellout" seem pointless when the results are artistically (as well as commercially) successful; songs like the mega-hit "Symphony of Destruction," "Skin O' My Teeth," "Foreclosure of a Dream," and "Sweating Bullets" are among the band's best. *—Steve Huey*

Youthanasia / Nov. 1, 1994 / Capitol ✦✦✦
Megadeth's follow-up to the hit *Countdown to Extinction* lacks the focus of its predecessor, but *Youthanasia* makes up the difference with more accessible, radio-friendly production and tighter riffs. Unfortunately, they have abandoned some of the more experimental, progressive elements in their music, but those are hardly missed in the jackhammer riffs of tracks like "Train of Consequences." *—Stephen Thomas Erlewine*

Hidden Treasures / Jul. 18, 1995 / Capitol ✦✦

Cryptic Writings / Jun. 17, 1997 / Capitol ✦✦✦

Risk / Aug. 31, 1999 / Capitol ✦✦✦

Capitol Punishment: The Megadeth Years / Oct. 24, 2000 / Capitol ✦✦✦✦
A 14-track career retrospective featuring two new songs, *Capitol Punishment: The Megadeth Years* attempts to distill the output of a primarily album-oriented band into a set of their best-known (among audiences in 2000) work. Most immediately obvious to fans of old-school Megadeth is that there's hardly anything from the thrash years: one track apiece from *Peace Sells . . . But Who's Buying?* and *So Far, So Good . . . So What!* and two from *Rust in Peace*. Instead, *Capitol Punishment* concentrates on their more recent, radio-oriented sound—about two-thirds of its tracks date from *Countdown to Extinction* on. And it doesn't even cover that territory very well; two of the four singles from *Countdown* ("Skin O' My Teeth" and "Foreclosure of a Dream") are missing, as are the movie-soundtrack contributions collected on *Hidden Treasures* ("Go to Hell," "99 Ways to Die," "Angry Again") that helped build their popular audience in between albums. It's hard to fault what *was* chosen, because the tracks here do represent some of Megadeth's most memorable recordings. It's also arranged in reverse chronological order, which, to the collection's credit, allows listeners only familiar with the band's recent albums to trace their development back to its roots. That's only to a certain extent, though, since those roots are portrayed so sketchily here. A best-of compilation for any group with as large a discography as Megadeth's is bound to omit at least a couple fan favorites, but *Capitol Punishment* is far too incomplete to qualify as an essential retrospective and too scattershot to make for a cohesive listen; instead, it's more of a sampler for casual fans who simply want one disc with some of the group's most popular songs. *—Steve Huey*

The World Needs a Hero / May 15, 2001 / Sanctuary ✦✦✦

The Mekons

f. 1976, Leeds, England

College Rock, Post-Punk, Alternative Pop/Rock

More than any band that came out of late-'70s England, the Mekons have perhaps the most devoted fans of any band even remotely connected to punk rock. And why not? After over two decades together, this band, with an ever-shifting lineup (only Jon Langford and Tom Greenhaigh remain from the original lineup), has produced some of the best rock & roll on the planet, from amateurish rock-noise to cool synth-driven pop to guitar rave-ups to post-modern country. The group's early singles were exceedingly low-fi, fun, challenging and anarchic—principles to which the band has clung, musical genre notwithstanding, since their inception. With their debut album, the Mekons turned into a slightly more accomplished post-punk band who wielded trebly guitars and shouted vocals over semi-funky rhythms tracks. In 1985, they released the startling *Fear and Whiskey*, a ragged country album influenced by the ghosts of Hank Williams and Gram Parsons. Thus began the second coming of the Mekons, who finally began to reach an underground/alternative rock audience that had missed them the first time around. Since the mid-'80s, the group has continually reinvented itself: sodden country band, wiseass folk-rock band, cranked-up guitar band, troublemaking punk band; whatever the scenario, what has remained consistent throughout the Mekons' existence has been great, great music. *—John Dougan*

The Quality of Mercy Is Not Strnen / 1979 / Caroline ✦✦✦
Here's where it all began. Not the best Mekons album available, but *Quality*, along with their second album, *Devils, Rats and Piggies*, and a *A Special Message from Godzilla* (Red Rhino, 1980, now out of print) shows off the Mekons' noisy, avant-garde side. It's abrasive and not as user-friendly as their later records, but this was an exciting time for British punk-rock, and this music, as dense and difficult as it may be, reflects punk's seemingly limitless possibilities. Issued by Blue Plate on CD in 1990. *—John Dougan*

Fear and Whiskey / 1985 / Sin ✦✦✦✦✦
A startling, unexpected record that sounds as wonderful now as it did when it was released. *Fear and Whiskey* uses American country music as its foundation, and the Mekons (ever the playful band) screw around with the genre, alternating between an honest-to-God reverence and flat-out parody. Don't expect sharply executed singing and playing; that's never been the Mekons' style. Instead, plan on a rambling, sodden opus of cowpunk with Hank Williams' ghost lurking in the shadows. In 1989, *Fear and Whiskey* was issued on CD by the Minneapolis-based indie label Twin/Tone with extra material and retitled *Original Sin*. *—John Dougan*

Edge of the World / 1986 / Sin ✦✦✦✦✦
Hot on the heels of *Fear* came this terrific follow-up that mined the same cowpunk terrain as its predecessor. The new members (Timms, et al.) sound fully integrated into the lineup, and the manic intensity doesn't let up for an instant. It's a party, but a very weird one indeed. *—John Dougan*

Honky Tonkin' / 1987 / Twin/Tone ✦✦✦✦
Finally, nearly a decade after the first Mekons release and after years of purchasing high-priced English imports, one of America's coolest indie labels manages to unleash the mighty Mekons domestically. The wonderful *Honky Tonkin'* marks the Mekons' last overt country/cowpunk record as they slowly shifted into more guitar-oriented rock. Its title taken from the classic Hank Williams song, this is slightly less essential than *Fear* or *Edge*, but with songs as great as "If They Hang You" and the goofy "Sympathy for the Mekons," you most certainly need it as you build your Mekons collection. *—John Dougan*

New York / 1987 / Combat ✦✦✦✦✦
You know a band is great when they release odds and ends that are better than most other bands' painstakingly rendered studio efforts. *New York* is a shambling ode to life on the road that features live tracks, band commentary (including snoring), and a ratty version of the Band's "The Shape I'm In." Upon its release, I thought *New York* the province of Mekons fanatics, that the casual fan or curious would tire of its casual attitude, lack of focus, and its audio-verité documentary approach. Now I think that if you like the Mekons, there is no good reason not to possess this recording. Originally released on cassette, *New York* was reissued on CD by ROIR/Important in 1990. *—John Dougan*

So Good It Hurts / 1988 / Twin/Tone ✦✦✦
The second release for Twin/Tone showed the Mekons putting a bit of reggae and Latin rhythms into the more-folk-than-country mix. *So Good* sounds a tad subdued in comparison to earlier records, but that does not indicate a lackadaisical attitude or a softening

of the band after nearly a decade of recorded work. In fact, its best moments ("Sometime I Feel Like Fletcher Christian") live up to the album's title. —*John Dougan*

● **The Mekons Rock & Roll** / Sep. 1989 / Collector's Choice Music ✦✦✦✦✦
Asking a Mekons fan to select a favorite Mekons record is crazy—there isn't one; there are many. But, if the situation were such that a choice had to be made, this might be the record. Loud, unruly guitars, pissed-off vocals—the Mekons have made an unregenerate, unapologetic punk rock record. This is a dark record, one that comfortably negotiates the dark recesses of rock & roll. They rip the messianic aspirations of U2's Bono ("Blow Your Tuneless Trumpet"), sing a tale of substance abuse that is both cautionary and parodic ("Cocaine Lil"), all the while cranking up a sonic tar pit of guitar noise. Bands this far on in a career, generally speaking, don't make records this good. But *The Mekons Rock & Roll* is one of those cathartic records that only righteously indignant, justifiably pissed-off, grizzled veterans could make. Sadly, and perhaps unsurprisingly, it sold next to nothing and precipitated the band's departure from A&M, who didn't want to release another record like this one. —*John Dougan*

Curse of the Mekons / 1991 / Blast First ✦✦✦✦✦
It's amazing that as down and out as the Mekons were at this point, they could manage to summon up the emotional wherewithal to make a record as excellent as *Curse*, but they did. The title most definitely reflects the band's mindset at this time, but this is not the music of self-pity and despair ("We're right in all we distrust," yelps Greenhaigh on the title track); in fact, if it weren't for *The Mekons Rock & Roll*, this might be the Mekons' finest moment. Politically charged songs despairing about communism and capitalism, a return to C&W (Sally Timms' passionate reading of John Anderson's "Wild and Blue"), and a dig at America's status as the world's only post-Cold War superpower ("100% Song"). Heady stuff, and not all happy, but remarkably assured and very rewarding. —*John Dougan*

It Falleth Like Gentle Rain From Heaven: The Mekons Story / 1993 / CNT ✦✦

I Love Mekons / Oct. 18, 1993 / Quarterstick ✦✦✦✦✦
A series of rancorous disagreements with the high and mighty at Warner Bros. subsidiary Loud forced the Mekons into an unanticipated two years of silence that nearly scuttled this record and ended the band's career. Eventually, Warner relented (they had maintained the record was not good enough to release), and the increasingly restless Mekons fans were able to judge for themselves that this was another terrific Mekons record. More traditionally rock-oriented and less prone to stylistic leaps than before, *I Love Mekons* is a strong, confident record that should have placed the Mekons at the forefront of the growing alternative rock market. It didn't, but often there's no accounting for taste. —*John Dougan*

Retreat From Memphis / May 2, 1994 / Quarterstick ✦✦✦
The Mekons were still dealing with the legal battle to free themselves from their ill-advised deal with Loud Records (a short-lived, Warner-distributed "alternative" imprint, not to be confused with the hip-hop label that signed Wu-Tang Clan) and get *I Love Mekons* released when they wrote and recorded *Retreat From Memphis*, and the strain shows in the music. *Retreat From Memphis* is direct, straightforward, and angry in a way the Mekons had not been for quite a while; with Suzie Honeyman and her fiddle making only a few cameo appearances, the twangy undertow of *Fear and Whiskey* and *Honky Tonkin'* was gone, and the dub-wise studio experimentation of *F.U.N. '90* and *Curse of the Mekons* was put on hold in favor of a more traditional guitars/bass/drums/ranting approach. And, being the punks at heart that they will always be, the Mekons make the most of their anger; if the band sounds a bit battle weary at times on *Retreat From Memphis*, they're also possessed of a righteous wrath, as if they were convinced this could be their last time around and they were determined to go down swinging. *Retreat From Memphis* was the most straightforward Mekons album since *The Mekons Rock & Roll*, and anyone who loves that great album's blend of into-the-wind defiance and brave fatalism will find plenty to shout along with here. —*Mark Deming*

United / Aug. 28, 1995 / Quarterstick ✦✦✦
Included as part of the Mekons' book of the same name, *United* offers a fine soundtrack to the various chunks of fiction, tour stories, and beautiful artwork included in the small tome. Fans of the Mekons should enjoy the diverse, often intentionally ramshackle disc, which has more in common with the band's art-school roots than it does with its rock material. The exceptions, however, are quite notable. "Orpheus," later re-recorded on *I Have Been to Heaven and Back: Hen's Teeth and Other Lost Fragments of Unpopular Culture Vol. 1*, is as fine a song as the band has composed, and elsewhere the found sound experiments and excursions into dubby electronica sample liberally from the Mekons' back catalog. —*Joshua Klein*

Pussy, King of the Pirates / Jan. 30, 1996 / Quarterstick ✦✦

Me / May 19, 1998 / Quarterstick ✦✦✦
After a four-year hiatus—not counting the many solo projects, collaborations, and other odd detours that filled the gap—the Mekons return to action with *Me*, another sterling addition to their catalog. Jon Langford's boozy adventures with the Waco Brothers and the Pine Valley Cosmonauts have clearly influenced tracks like "Gin & It" and "Whisky Sex Shack," while "Tourettes" and "Belly to Belly" are just as snotty as anything the band unleashed two decades earlier; indeed, while *Me* doesn't really add anything new to the Mekons canon, it also doesn't take anything away—even going on the two-decade mark, they remain the truest representation of the punk spirit around. —*Jason Ankeny*

I Have Been to Heaven and Back ...., Vol. 1 / Apr. 20, 1999 / Quarterstick ✦✦✦✦
Mekons' heaven is one of ethical socialism, something they idealize but feel has never been realized. The reality is a thin, barely held together level of entropy that is on the verge of the cataclysmic. The Mekons' live shows exude that frantic urgency. Every perfor-

mance has the sudden importance of apocalyptic religion. The Mekons destruct onstage in a last-ditch effort to save you with guitars and charged lyrics. The cover of this live rarities collection is a photograph of just such a charged moment. Guitarist and vocalist Jon Langford (Bloodshot Records, Waco Brothers, Three Johns, etc.) is lifted from the stage and twisted around by a power chord he just launched. Vocalist Sally Timms beams with an electric, revival-like ecstasy, tambourine overhead. Another Mekon caught up in his fallen shorts, crashes to the floor. Smugly, accordion player Rico Bell smiles over all. Outtakes from sessions for previous albums are jumbled in with unexpected covers (English children's rhyme "Oranges and Lemons" and Rod Stewart's "You Wear it Well"), audience tapings, and more rarities. Called *Vol. 1*, Mekons actually first rewarded their fans with such a detailed hodgepodge in 1982 with *The Mekons Story* and in 1987 on *New York*. These originally English post-punk rockers deliver a fair amount of Americana in their ragged anthems and every line is a closely held belief or personal revelation. On "This Funeral Is for the Wrong Corpse" (never before available in its full length), Langford espouses his political ideals. In "The Ballad of Sally," Timms shares her own insecurity. Mekons offers their fans powerful, Americanized post-punk British rock that is a channel for beliefs on fire and active honesty. —*Tom Schulte*

Where Were You?: Hens Teeth and Other Lost Fragments of Popular Culture, Vol. 2 / Sep. 7, 1999 / Quarterstick ✦✦✦✦
The Mekons' *Where Were You?: Hens Teeth and Other Lost Fragments of Popular Culture, Vol. 2* is the second volume of rare and unreleased tracks from the group's archives. Covers, outtakes, radio sessions, and B-sides make up the body of this collection and document the Mekons' fearless sonic experimentation. Reworkings of Ray Davies' "Fancy," Johnny Cash's "Folsom Prison Blues," and the Ex's "Crap Rap" hint at the album's diversity, reflecting the group's British rock roots, their fascination with country music, and their ties with the experimental underground. Famed rock writer Lester Bangs sings and plays guitar on the trippy "One Horse Dub," thanks to a cassette recording made nine years before the song was completed in 1990. The group's bracing mix of proletarian punk and sparkling, eclectic pop enlivens every track, from "Mekons Rock & Roll" (an alternate version of "Memphis Egypt") to the countrified new wave instrumental "Darkness." Subversively gentle protest songs, like the live version of "My Song at Night" (from the Kathy Acker collaboration *Pussy King of the Pirates*) and the demo "Nice Julie (Waltz)" and noisy, abstract pieces like "Hashish in Marseilles" and "Polaroid (I Don't Own, I Only Dote)" further the Mekons' reputation as politically and musically progressive. Though *Where Were You* is a must for fans, newcomers to the band will also find plenty to enjoy. —*Heather Phares*

Journey to the End of the Night / Mar. 7, 2000 / Quarterstick ✦✦✦✦
The Mekons have always thrived on musical contradiction, reveling in their clashes instead of diluting their collective influences, realizing that it's less interesting to play it safe. However, there is little evidence of this inclination on *Journey to the End of the Night*, perhaps their most straightforward album. Long-time fans looking for the fire of their most impassioned music may be suspicious: for once the Mekons sound like a band getting older, but this isn't a bad thing. On *Journey*, they avoid the sort of jarring juxtapositions that made previous collections more difficult to digest, but they don't stick to a uniform sound; instead, "Tina"'s light reggae rhythms, chugging guitar line, and melodica coexist peacefully with the low-budget electro of "The Flood."
The more reserved songcraft results in one of the group's most sensitive sets of songs. "Ordinary Night" effectively communicates a touching story of love fumbled by a familiar, tragic character in two verses. The duet "Last Weeks of the War" uses truly ominous language in its tale of a broken relationship: "Little black book/Full of little white lies/The straightjacket has arrived/I'll try it on for size," Jon Langford sings, while Timms is both strong and sympathetic ("I'm not ruined but I need repair"). On *Journey to the End of the Night*, the Mekons have crafted a collection of rich, musically agreeable settings for sympathetic character sketches like these. —*Nathan Bush*

Mel & Tim

Chicago Soul, Pop-Soul, Disco, Soul
Mississippi cousins Mel Hardin and Tim McPherson had two tremendous hits in the late '60s and early '70s, one a classic novelty tune, the other a great slow wailer. They were signed to Gene Chandler's Bamboo label and their song "Backfield in Motion" remains a soul staple. It was both a Top Ten pop hit and number three R&B single. The follow-up was a decent effort, "Good Guys Only Win in the Movies," which made the R&B Top 20. But they were back in the hunt in a big way in 1972, as "Starting All Over Again" peaked at number four R&B and number 19 pop. It was the duo's only Stax hit, although they continued recording for the company through the mid-'70s and were even in the film *Wattstax*, doing "I May Not Be What You Want." —*Ron Wynn*

Good Guys Only Win in the Movies / 1969 / Sundazed ✦✦✦✦✦
Mel & Tim's debut album featured both of their smashes, "Backfield in Motion" and "Good Guys Only Win in the Movies." As full-length soul records of the era go, it's a bit above average, if only because the duo wrote a high percentage of their own material. It's sweet Chicago pop/soul circa 1969-70 at its most centrist: not too slick, not terribly earthy, and not as distinctive as the Impressions or Gene Chandler, although the sound bears general similarities. The CD reissue has five extra bonus tracks from singles that were issued around the same era. —*Richie Unterberger*

● **Starting All Over Again** / 1972 / Stax ✦✦✦✦✦
Originally released on vinyl in 1972, these 14 tracks made up the first Stax Records album for cousins Mel Hardin and Tim McPherson. They scored with "Backfield in Motion" (not included here) on Gene Chandler's Bamboo Records prior to Stax. This album

features the moving "Starting All Over Again," a scrumptious remake of Don & Juan's "What's Your Name," as well as other un-panned nuggets. *—Andrew Hamilton*

Melanie

b. Feb. 3, 1947, Queens, NY

Singer, Vocals, Guitar / AM Pop, Jesus Rock, Folk-Rock, Pop, Singer/Songwriter, Folk-Pop

No talent who came out of Woodstock and was actively performing more than a quarter century later remained as closely associated with '60s flower power than Melanie. Born Melanie Safka in Astoria, Queens in 1947, she mounted a singing career in college, and in 1969 chanced to meet producer Peter Schekeryk. Her first album, *Born to Be*, was released by Buddah later that same year. On August 16, Melanie took the stage at Woodstock; her commercial breakthrough came 11 months later with "Lay Down (Candles in the Rain)," recorded with the Edwin Hawkins Singers. The song rose to number six, while the accompanying LP *Candles in the Rain* reached the Top 20. In January 1971, Melanie's version of "What Have They Done to My Song, Ma" charted in Britain, where she emerged as a major star. Around this time, Melanie rebelled against her contract with Buddah; with help from Schekeryk, whom she had married, she organized her own label, Neighborhood Records, during the summer. Her first subsequent single, "Brand New Key," hit number one in the U.S. on its way to becoming a million-seller, thanks to its not-so-subtle sexual undertones. The accompanying album, *Gather Me*, was the best-produced long-player she had ever released and reached a chart position of Number 15. However, faced with declining sales for the follow-ups, Melanie withdrew from the stage and devoted her time to more personal and domestic concerns; Neighborhood Records was closed down in the mid-'70s. In 1982, Melanie cut a comeback album, *Arabesque*; a year later, her single "Every Breath of the Way" hit the British charts. At the end of the '80s, she re-emerged with her theme music for the television series *Beauty and the Beast*. She appeared at one of the Woodstock 20th anniversary events and continued to perform and record periodically. *—Bruce Eder*

The Best of Melanie / 1990 / Rhino ✦✦✦✦✦

Eighteen songs from her 1968-1974 heyday, including all six of her Top 40 hit singles, and her unexpectedly passionate cover of the Rolling Stones' "Ruby Tuesday." *—Richie Unterberger*

• **Beautiful People: The Greatest Hits of Melanie** / Jul. 13, 1999 / Buddha ✦✦✦✦✦

Beautiful People: The Greatest Hits of Melanie gets the nod over the 1990 Rhino compilation *The Best of Melanie* as the best compilation of the singer's work. Containing 19 tracks where the earlier album contained 18, it could hardly be longer and fit on one CD. The songs have been mastered from their original master tapes for the first time by Robert Fripp (!) and David Singleton, so the sound quality is the best yet. The set contains the original LP version of Melanie's Top Ten hit "Lay Down (Candles in the Rain)," running just over seven minutes, as opposed to the nearly four-minute single edit. Also featured are two recent songs, "Summer of Love II" and "I Will Get Over." That's all on the credit side. On the debit side, it is not in chronological order and the selection leaves off several of Melanie's singles chart entries, notably "Bitter Bad," which made the Top 40 (and is included in the Rhino compilation). Nevertheless, this must be counted as the best Melanie compilation yet, featuring her number-one hit "Brand New Key," as well as standards like "Beautiful People" and "What Have They Done to My Song, Ma?." *—William Ruhlmann*

John Cougar Mellencamp

b. Oct. 7, 1951, Seymour, IN

Vocals, Guitar / Bar Band, Heartland Rock, Pop/Rock, Roots Rock, Hard Rock, Album Rock

Throughout his career, John Mellencamp has had to fight, whether it was for the right to record under his own name or for respect as an artist. Of course, he never made it easily on himself. Mellencamp began his career in the late '70s as a Bruce Springsteen clone called Johnny Cougar. As his career progressed, his music became more distinctive, developing into a Stonesy blend of hard-rock and folk-rock. His musical development coincided with his growth in popularity—by the time "Hurts So Good" and "Jack and Diane" became hits in 1982, Mellencamp had created his own variation of the heartland rock of Springsteen, Tom Petty, and Bob Seger. While he had the record sales, it took several years before rock critics took him seriously. For some artists, this would be easy to ignore, but Mellencamp had the desire to be a serious social commentator, chronicling the times and trials of Midwestern baby boomers. *Scarecrow*, released in 1985, fulfilled his wish of being taken serious, and every record he released after it was greeted warmly by critics. Furthermore, he sustained his popularity into the late '90s, only occasionally experiencing dips in record sales. *—Stephen Thomas Erlewine*

Chestnut Street Incident / 1976 / Original Masters ✦

John Mellencamp began his career as Johnny Cougar, on the advice of his manager Tony DeFries. Cougar's debut, *Chestnut Street Incident*, was released in 1976 in a whirlwind of hype, which the album simply didn't deserve. At best, the record is a competent collection of Stonesy rockers, infused with a blue-collar Bruce Springsteen/Bob Seger attitude, but Cougar's music and lyrics aren't memorable and are often laughable. *—Stephen Thomas Erlewine*

The Kid Inside / 1977 / Original Masters ✦

A Biography / 1978 / Riva ✦

John Cougar / 1979 / Riva ✦

Once "I Need a Lover" became an Australian hit, Riva in America decided to release John Cougar's eponymous fourth album, adding the song to the record as well. Essentially, *John Cougar* is sonically similar to *A Biography*, but apart from the tacked-on "I Need a Lover," none of the songs hit the mark. *—Stephen Thomas Erlewine*

Nothin' Matters and What if It Did / 1980 / Riva ✦✦✦

American Fool / 1982 / Mercury ✦✦✦✦

John Cougar's first albums were so bereft of strong material that the lean swagger of *American Fool* came as a shock. The difference is evident from the opening song "Hurts So Good," a hard, Stonesy rocker with an irresistibly sleazy hook. Cougar never wrote anything as catchy as this before, nor had his romantic vision of small-town America resonated like it did on "Jack & Diane," a minor and remarkably affecting sketch of dead-end romance. These two songs are the only true keepers on *American Fool*, but the rest of the record works better than his previous material because his band is tighter than ever before, making his weaker moments convincing. Besides, songs like "Hand to Hold On to" and "China Girl," for all their faults, do indicate that his sense of craft is improving considerably. *—Stephen Thomas Erlewine*

Uh-Huh / 1983 / Mercury ✦✦✦✦✦

Since *American Fool* illustrated that John Cougar was becoming an actual songwriter, it's only proper that he reclaimed his actual last name, Mellencamp, for the follow-up, *Uh-Huh*. After all, now that he had success, he wanted to be taken seriously, and *Uh-Huh* reflects that in its portraits of broken-hearted life in the Midwest and its rumbling undercurrent of despair. Although his lyrics still had the tendency to be a little too vague, they were more effective than ever before, as was his music; he might not have changed his style at all—it was still a fusion of the Stones and Springsteen—except that he now knew how to make it his own. *Uh-Huh* runs out of steam toward the end, but the first half—with the dynamic rocker "Crumblin' Down," this best protest song, "Pink Houses," the punky "Authority Song," the melancholy "Warmer Place to Sleep," and the garage-rocker "Play Guitar"—makes the record his first terrific album. *—Stephen Thomas Erlewine*

• **Scarecrow** / 1985 / Mercury ✦✦✦✦✦

Uh-Huh found John Mellencamp coming into his own, but he perfected his Heartland rock with *Scarecrow*. A loose concept album about lost innocence and the crumbling of small-town America, *Scarecrow* says as much with its tough rock and gentle folk-rock as it does with its lyrics, which remain a weak point for Mellencamp. Nevertheless, his writing has never been more powerful: "Rain on the Scarecrow" and "Small Town" capture the hopes and fears of middle America, while "Lonely Ol' Night" and "Rumbleseat" effortlessly convey the desperate loneliness of being stuck in a dead-end life. Those four songs form the core of the album, and while the rest of the album isn't quite as strong, that's only a relative term, since it's filled with lean hooks and powerful, economical playing that make *Scarecrow* one of the definitive blue-collar rock albums of the mid-'80s. *—Stephen Thomas Erlewine*

The Lonesome Jubilee / 1987 / Mercury ✦✦✦✦✦

John Mellencamp's fascination with the American heartland came into full flower on *Scarecrow*, but with its follow-up *The Lonesome Jubilee*, he began exploring American folk musics, adding fiddle, accordions, and acoustic guitars to his band, which allowed him to explore folk and country. The expansion of his band coincided with his continuing growth as a songwriter. Song for song, *The Lonesome Jubilee* is Mellencamp's strongest album, the record where he captured his romantic, if decidedly melancholy, vision of working-class America. He may recycle the same lyrical ideas as before, but he captures them better than ever, and his music is richer, which gives the album resonance. Again, there are a few moments where Mellencamp's reach exceeds his grasp, but "Paper in Fire," "Check It Out," "Cherry Bomb," "Empty Hands," and "Hard Times for an Honest Man" make the record his best. *—Stephen Thomas Erlewine*

Big Daddy / May 1989 / Mercury ✦✦✦

Continuing with the folk inclinations of *The Lonesome Jubilee*, John Mellencamp recorded his most ambitious and serious-minded album with *Big Daddy*. Mellencamp produced the record himself, giving the album a concise and stripped-down sound, which help give his songs the appearance of being gritty statements of truth. Unfortunately, Mellencamp isn't saying nearly as much as he believes he is, since his lyrics tend to be cliched and half-baked, making much of the album feel pompous and self-serving. This is only reinforced by the lack of rockers on *Big Daddy*, since he saves the most carefree moment—a ripping cover of the Hombres' "Let It Out (Let It All Hang Out)"—for an unlisted bonus track. Still, when he does hit his target, like on the gentle "Jackie Brown," the stuttering, fiddle-driven "Sometimes a Great Notion," and even the self-pitying "Pop Singer," Mellencamp proves that his talents haven't abandoned him. *—Stephen Thomas Erlewine*

Whenever We Wanted / Oct. 8, 1991 / Mercury ✦✦✦

Mellencamp took his signature blend of Stonesy rock and folk as far as it could go on *Big Daddy*, so he wisely returned to straight-ahead rock & roll with *Whenever We Wanted*. *Uh-Huh* was the last record he made that rocked as hard and consistently as this, and his songwriting had improved considerably in the years since that breakthrough release. Which means, of course, that *Whenever We Wanted* is more consistent than the earlier record, but it never reaches the highs of *Uh-Huh*. Even its best moments ("Love and Happiness," "Get a Leg Up," "Whenever We Wanted," "Again Tonight") shine because of their craftmenship, failing to achieve the kinetic energy of his earlier work. *Whenever We Wanted* remains a solid record, but it's one that feels like a holding pattern. *—Stephen Thomas Erlewine*

Human Wheels / Sep. 7, 1993 / Mercury ✦✦✦✦

Following the stripped-down rock & roll of *Whenever We Wanted*, the somber *Human Wheels* comes as a bit of shock. Throughout his mid-'80s peak, Mellencamp infused his best work with despair, but he never has sounded as beaten and broken as he does on *Human Wheels*. It's not just that the record sounds murky and bleak, but his singing is weary and the lyrics are filled with resignation. Consequently, *Human Wheels* isn't a particularly easy listen, even though it doesn't depart from his signature sound, but it is a rewarding one, and the record is arguably his most affecting. *—Stephen Thomas Erlewine*

Dance Naked / Jun. 21, 1994 / Mercury ♦♦♦
A short, stripped-down collection of basic rock & roll, *Dance Naked* isn't quite as powerful as *Human Wheels*, but it has more good songs in its 30 minutes than most 70-minute albums. *—Stephen Thomas Erlewine*

Mr. Happy Go Lucky / Sep. 10, 1996 / Mercury ♦♦♦
John Mellencamp responded to his massive heart attack and close-call with death with *Mr. Happy Go Lucky*, the most overtly ambitious album in his career. Mellencamp has always been a bit of a fatalist, so it isn't any great surprise that there is an undercurrent of dark mortality running through most of his songs. What is a surprise is his musical approach. Although he hasn't abandoned the essential elements of his music—the rootsy instrumentation, the violins, the simple song structures, the gritty folk-rock—he has augmented it with the help of Junior Vasquez, a noted dance producer. Vasquez doesn't push Mellencamp into dance, but he adds certain dynamics and techniques from club music to *Mr. Happy Go Lucky* which ocasionally gives the album a greater depth. It's a gentle change, not a forceful one—nothing sounds like dance music, but there are deeper rhythms and bass throughout the album, which breathes life into well-crafted songs like "Key West Intermezzo." Since he doesn't pursue dance completely on *Mr. Happy Go Lucky*, Mellencamp doesn't end up alienating his fans, but the reluctance to give himself over to dance makes the album uneven. Ironically, the tracks that exhibit Vasquez's influence the least are the least successful—they simply sound like Mellencamp is going through the motions. Nevertheless, *Mr. Happy Go Lucky* proves that Mellencamp has more surprises in him than many listeners would have expected and suggests that he is in the process of revitalizing his career. *—Stephen Thomas Erlewine*

● **The Best That I Could Do (1978-1988)** / Nov. 18, 1997 / Mercury ♦♦♦♦♦
The Best That I Could Do is an appropriately self-deprecating title for John Mellencamp's greatest-hits collection, considering that the heartland rocker never seemed too convinced of his own worth. Of course, he had to struggle to get any respect after he was saddled with the stage name Johnny Cougar early in his career, but this 14-track collection proves that he was one of the best unabashed, straight-ahead rockers of the '80s. Fourteen tracks actually turns out to be a little too short to contain all of his great singles—songs like "Rain on the Scarecrow," "Rumbleseat," "Pop Singer," "Again Tonight" and "What If I Came Knocking" are left off the collection (there's nothing from 1988's *Big Daddy* at all)—but it's hard to argue with what's here. Over the course of 14 tracks, such classic rock hits as "I Need a Lover," "Hurts So Good," "Jack and Diane," "Crumblin' Down," "Pink Houses," "Lonely Ol' Night," "Small Town," "Paper in Fire," "Cherry Bomb," "Check It Out," "Get a Leg Up," and "Wild Night" are chronicled, with a new cover of Terry Reid's "Without Expression" added for good measure. It may fall short of being definitive, but only by a small margin, and it remains an excellent overview and introduction to Mellencamp's remarkably consistent body of work. *—Stephen Thomas Erlewine*

John Mellencamp / Oct. 6, 1998 / Columbia ♦♦♦
Although Mercury Records had delivered five consecutive platinum albums for John Mellencamp, he left the label in 1997, complaining about its inability to break hit singles for him anymore, and signed to Columbia Records. His self-titled label debut, issued the day before his 47th birthday, seemed intended to mark a new beginning for an artist who had managed more than one career rebirth. Commercially, it did not fulfill that ambition, becoming his worst seller in 19 years. Artistically, it represented not so much a new Mellencamp as another Mellencamp album. The musical style remained firmly rooted in 1966 pop/rock (you had to figure the man's personal jukebox included songs like Los Bravos' "Black Is Black," Donovan's "Sunshine Superman," and the Rolling Stones' "19th Nervous Breakdown"), despite a few interludes of unusual instrumentation (like what Brian Jones used to bring to the Stones). Lyrically, Mellencamp continued to preach an unearned pessimism that he seemed to hope would be mistaken for thoughtfulness. Still obsessed with being taken seriously, he continued to think that the best way to achieve that was to sound serious, and he did, on Biblical treatises like "Fruit Trader" and "Eden Is Burning" and simple-minded philosophical statements like "Your Life Is Now." But the album's best material was found in songs he probably thought of as throwaways, the catchy Caribbean rhythm number "I'm Not Running Anymore" (which could have been a hit single) and the best of the romantic tunes, "Miss Missy," songs that were actually about something. If he really wanted to reinvent himself again (and ignite his record sales), he would have been better advised to invest his music with more of this sense of fun—dare we say it?—to put a little Johnny Cougar back into John Mellencamp. *—William Ruhlmann*

Rough Harvest / Aug. 17, 1999 / Mercury ♦♦♦
When John Mellencamp left Mercury Records for Columbia in 1997, he owed his long-time label two more albums—one was a hits collection (*The Best That I Could Do*), the other was *Rough Harvest*. Not quite a rarities collection, not quite a live album, *Rough Harvest* offers a selection of acoustic arrangements of Mellencamp's personal favorites (which happen to lean toward album tracks from the '90s), plus several covers, recorded live at his studio, Belmont Mall, in 1997. On paper, this may seem like it's nothing more than a toss-off, just a way to fulfill contractual obligations, but it doesn't play that way. There's a warm feeling to the performances, a nice loose off-the-cuff feeling that enhances the emotions in these low-key, subtlely crafted songs. The newer songs benefit from this setting, as do familiar hits like "Rain on the Scarecrow" and "Jackie Brown," and the covers of "In My Time of Dying," "Farewell Angelina," "Under the Boardwalk," and "Wild Night." This may be a gentle difference that only devoted fans will notice, but that's who this album was made for, and they'll undoubtedly enjoy this intimate record. *—Stephen Thomas Erlewine*

Harold Melvin

b. Jun. 25, 1939, Philadelphia, PA, **d.** Mar. 24, 1997, Philadelphia, PA
Vocals / Philly Soul, Doo Wop, Soul, Smooth Soul
Starting out in 1954 in Philadelphia as a doo wop group with Harold Melvin as lead singer, the Blue Notes first recorded for the New York-based Josie label two years later. They debuted on the R&B charts in 1960 on the Value label with "My Hero," but it was not until 1972, when drummer Teddy Pendergrass took over lead vocal chores and the group came under the wing of producers Kenny Gamble and Leon Huff and their Philadelphia International label, that Harold Melvin & the Blue Notes became consistent chart-makers. Pendergrass' vocals smoldered with sensuality. Combined with the smooth group harmonies that had always been a Blue Note trademark, Gamble and Huff's superior writing, and lush productions, the superb TSOP house band records such as "I Miss You," "If You Don't Know Me by Now," and "The Love I Lost" were staples on both black and white radio from 1972 to 1975. Pendergrass went solo in 1975 and the Blue Notes' glory days came to an end. *—Rob Bowman*

★ **Collector's Item** / 1976 / Philadelphia International ♦♦♦♦♦
It rounds up such hits as "Wake Up Everybody," "Bad Luck," "If You Don't Know Me by Now," and "The Love I Lost," all benchmarks of an era. *—John Floyd*

☆ **If You Don't Know Me by Now: The Best of Harold Melvin & the Blue Notes** / Feb. 28, 1995 / Epic/Legacy ♦♦♦♦♦
Although the ten-track disc is criminally brief, *The Best of Harold Melvin & the Bluenotes* contains most of their biggest hits and offers a good portrait of one of the finest soul groups of the '70s. *—Stephen Thomas Erlewine*

★ **The Ultimate Blue Notes [Expanded]** / Aug. 21, 2001 / Epic/Legacy ♦♦♦♦♦
Actually the ultimate Blue Notes with Teddy Pendergrass, this collection covers their Philadelphia International years from 1972-1975 as in-depth and representative of the band's talents as a single disc can get. Not to split too many hairs, but the vocal soul group did have a handful of good songs past this period, although none that match the majestic sweep of this material. Boasting dance beats, swirling strings, smooth crooning storytelling, and Pendergrass' booming baritone, this is some of the best as well as most representative R&B of the '70s, and this 15-track compilation is all you'll need to hear why. Practically double the amount of songs as *Collectors Item* and over twice as long, this anthology adds such often ignored gems as the almost eight minute "Yesterday I Had the Blues" and the original version of "Don't Leave Me This Way" before Thelma Houston took it Top Ten which itself clocks in at another six minutes. An updating of Legacy's 1995 *If You Don't Know Me by Now: The Best of Harold Melvin & the Blue Notes*, this 2001 disc features improved sound, new liner notes with full chart documentation for pop and R&B positions, slightly different track selection, all full-length album versions and a snazzier looking package. Sequenced for most appropriate musical flow (as opposed to chronologically), the disc mixes upbeat tracks with softer ballads for a more consistent listening experience, helped by the coherent Gamble & Huff production team. If you need one album from the legendary soul vocal group, this is certainly the one to choose. *—Hal Horowitz*

Members

f. 1977, **db.** 1984
Ska Revival, New Wave
The Members were among the new wave of British bands jumping on the punk bandwagon. The band—composed of Nicky Tesco (vocals), Jean-Marie Caroll (guitar), Gary Baker (guitar), Adrian Lillywhite (drums), and Chris Payne (bass)—was among the first to successfully blend reggae rhythms with punk's attitude and aggression. Stiff Records saw some promise in the band and signed them early in 1978, releasing their first single, "Solitary Confinement." Their Virgin debut single, 1979's "Sound of the Suburbs," made it into the British Top 20 but subsequent singles failed to match its success. They soon recorded their first LP, *Live at the Chelsea Nightclub*, which also made a brief appearance in the lower reaches of the U.K. charts. Around this time, the Two-Tone movement was stealing much of their limelight and their popularity began to fade. After one more album for Virgin in 1980, *1980 The Choice Is Yours*, they were dropped by the label. After a brief layoff, they returned in 1982 with *Uprhythm, Downbeat* (released in 1983 in the U.K. as *Going West*) broadening their sound with horns and a more serious attitude. "Working Girl" from the album became a cult classic in the U.S. through MTV exposure but mainsteam acceptance eluded them on both sides of the Atlantic. The band called it quits the following year. *—Chris Woodstra*

At the 1980 Chelsea Night Club / 1979 / Caroline ♦♦♦♦♦
The only Members album worth owning, *Chelsea Nightclub* plays into the band's strengths and is loaded with their strongest songwriting (e.g., "Stand Up and Spit," "Off-Shore Banking Business"). *—John Dougan*

1980 the Choice Is Yours / 1980 / Virgin ♦♦

Uprhythm, Downbeat / 1982 / Arista ♦♦♦
After the flop of *1980 the Choice Is Yours*, the band took two years off to regroup and change strategies; the resulting *Uprhythm, Downbeat* (retitled *Going West* and released a year later in the U.K.) shows a more serious band (now a seven-piece with a horn section) with a fuller sound. Their punk edges have been smoothed over, leaving a slick reggae-funk-pop sound. While it fit nicely with the new wave era, it hasn't dated very well. Only the classic "Working Girl" leaves a lasting impression. *—Chris Woodstra*

● **Sound of the Suburbs: A Collection of the Members' Finest Moments** / Apr. 18, 1995 / Caroline ♦♦♦♦♦
True to its subtitle, this 18-track collection compiles the finest moments of the band's

two-year stay at Virgin Records (1979-1980). While this period was the strongest for the band, it would have been nice to include a track or two from their final album, *Uprhythm, Downbeat,* such as the near-hit "Working Girl." *—Chris Woodstra*

Men at Work

f. 1979, Melbourne, Australia, **db.** 1985

Pop/Rock, New Wave

One of the new wave era's more surprising success stories, Men at Work rocketed out of Melbourne, Australia in 1982, becoming the year's most successful group. Transplanted Scot, Colin Hay (lead vocals, guitar) formed the group as an acoustic duo with Ron Strykert (guitar, vocals) in 1979, but they soon expanded, adding John Rees (bass), Greg Ham (saxophone, flute, keyboards), and Jerry Speiser (drums). Favorites on Australia's pub circuit, they became the country's highest-paid unsigned band; by 1981, they landed a contract with Australian Columbia and released "Who Can It Be Now?" It became a huge hit, as did their 1982 debut album, *Business as Usual*; its Police-styled rhythms, catchy guitar hooks, wailing saxophones, and off-kilter sense of humor made it an international blockbuster, topping the Australian charts for ten weeks and America's for 15. Funny, irreverent videos for "Who Can It Be Now" and "Down Under" helped send both singles to number one. After winning a Grammy for 1982's Best New Artist, the band's momentum continued with 1983's *Cargo*, which reached number three in the U.S. and generated the Top Ten singles "Overkill" and "It's a Mistake." But soon, the bottom fell out of the band's popularity. After an extensive tour that included dates with the Clash and the Stray Cats, the band took an extended break; after releasing 1985's *Two Hearts*, which failed to generate one Top 40 single, they broke up. Hay pursued a solo career, but neither of his two American solo albums—1987's *Looking for Jack* and 1990's *Wayfaring Sons* (1990)—were successes. In the '90s, Hay continued to release albums in Australia and began an acting career. He and Ham re-formed Men at Work in 1998, issuing the live hits collection *Brazil*. *—Stephen Thomas Erlewine*

Business as Usual / 1982 / CBS ✦✦✦✦✦

Business as Usual became a surprise international hit on the basis "Who Can It Be Now?" and "Down Under," two excellent singles that merged straight-ahead pop-rock hooks with a quirky new wave production and an offbeat sense of humor. Colin Hay's keening vocals uncannily recall Sting, and the band's rhythmic pulse and phased guitars also bring to mind a bar-band version of the Police. And that helps make the remainder of *Business as Usual* enjoyable. There's a fair amount of filler on the record, but "Be Good Johnny," "I Can See It In Your Eyes," and "Down by the Sea" are all fine new wave pop songs, making *Business as Usual* one of the more enjoyable mainstream-oriented efforts of the era. *—Stephen Thomas Erlewine*

Cargo / 1983 / CBS ✦✦✦✦✦

Cargo was bashed out fairly quickly, but it its release was delayed because of the success of Men at Work's debut, *Business as Usual*. Though it was recorded on the road, *Cargo* is considerably more diverse—but not necessarily more ambitious—than its predecessor. Again, the album is anchored by two extraordinary singles. Fortunately, the soaring ballad "Overkill" and the satiric, anti-nuclear "It's a Mistake" aren't rewrites of "Who Can It Be Now?" and "Down Under," demonstrating more depth than anything on the debut. Despite this growth, the remainder of *Cargo* is weighed down by filler. "Doctor Heckyll and Mr. Jive" might be goofy fun and "High Wire" and "Blue for You" are tight pop songs, but the rest are simply pleasant, ocassionally embarassing ("I Like To," "Settle Down My Boy"), new wave pop. *—Stephen Thomas Erlewine*

Two Hearts / 1985 / Columbia ✦✦

By the time of their third album, Men at Work's music had become a bland, synthesized variation on mainstream pop, featuring none of the melodic sensibilities or subtle humor of their first two albums. Although the album went gold, it featured no Top 40 singles. The commercial performance of *Two Hearts* was a considerable disappointment after their first two multi-platinum records and the band broke up shortly after its release. *—Stephen Thomas Erlewine*

● **Contraband: The Best of Men at Work** / Mar. 26, 1996 / Columbia/Legacy ✦✦✦✦

Men at Work's records were always somewhat uneven affairs. Certainly, the singles were the highlights, but they had a handful of first-rate album tracks that made the records necessary for dedicated fans, even if the overall album was inconsistent. *Contraband: The Best of Men at Work* does a terrific job of consolidating all of their highlights onto one disc. From hits like "Who Can It Be Now?," "Down Under," "Overkill," and "It's a Mistake" to slightly neglected album tracks like "Be Good Johnny," *Contraband* has every great track from the Australian new wave band. For most fans, it will be the only disc they need. *—Stephen Thomas Erlewine*

Men Without Hats

f. 1980, Montreal, Quebec, Canada, **db.** 1991

New Wave, Synth Pop

The new wave synth pop collective Men Without Hats was formed in 1980 by brothers Ivan and Stefan Doroschuk. The group independently released their debut EP, *Folk of the 80's*, in 1980; it was reissued the following year by Stiff in Britain. Taken from their 1982 debut *Rhythm of Youth*, the single "The Safety Dance" became a major hit, peaking on the American charts at number three in 1983. Driven by an insistent three-chord synthesizer riff, the song was one of the biggest synth-pop hits of the new wave era. The group wasn't able to exploit its success, however. *Folk of the '80s (Part III)* stalled at number 127 on the charts in America and made even less of an impact in other parts of the world. Thanks to the minor hit title track, 1987's *Pop Goes the World* was a bigger success, yet it didn't recapture the audience their first album had gained. Released two years later, *The Adventures of Women & Men Without Hate in the 21st Century* failed to chart, as did its follow-up, 1991's *Sideways*. The two albums' lack of success effectively put an end to Men Without Hats' career. *—Stephen Thomas Erlewine*

Rhythm of Youth / 1982 / MCA ✦✦✦✦✦

Men Without Hats' debut album *Rhythm of Youth* was a set of catchy, appealing synth-pop. Although the material on the album was wildly inconsistent, the group's energy was infectious, making up for the weaker songs. And when the band managed to write a solid melody—such as the hit single "The Safety Dance"—the results were quite memorable. *—Stephen Thomas Erlewine*

Folk of the '80s (Part III) / 1984 / MCA ✦✦✦

Men Without Hats' follow-up to their successful first album repeated the same formula as the debut with essentially the same results. Though *Folk of the '80s (Part III)* has its share of tedious material, the best songs on the album are as fun and charming as the finest moments from the debut. However, the band's audience had declined since the release of the first record, and *Folk of the '80s (Part III)* stiffed. *—Stephen Thomas Erlewine*

Pop Goes the World / 1987 / Mercury ✦✦✦✦

Men Without Hats broke big with their 1982 debut, *Rhythm of Youth*. Though they never maintained that level of success, their third album *Pop Goes the World* was a smart, well-crafted, woefully underrated offering. The album chronicles the quest for and backlash of fame on songs like the title track, on which Ivan sings "Johnny and Jenny had a crazy dream/see their pictures in a magazine." Perhaps it was a way of dealing with the band's sudden success failure, particularly on "Lose My Way" and "The Real World." Thankfully, a wild sense of humor and a heartbreaking poignancy keeps the album from becoming too serious. Additionally, each song is vastly different: there are some lullabies ("Moonbeam"), some anthems ("Jenny Wore Black"), and some dirges ("Bright Side of the Sun"—which is criminally short, adding to its power). Cartoonish but dark, this album marries wide-eyed innocence with cynicism in its recurring themes (celebrity, loss, rejuvenation, the vastness of our world) and characters (Jenny and Johnny, who are credited with bass and guitar, respectively). It takes a few listens to fully absorb the stories and lessons interwoven in *Pop Goes the World*'s synthesizer-driven, somewhat goofy, sometimes somber cuts. Though there are some quirky aspects to the album (from the intro with a beckoning voice like that of Newcleus's helium-driven "Jam on It" to an intro to "Walk on Water" that sounds like a faraway voice on a hissing vinyl album) nothing seems gimmicky. Overall, the album is solid, smart, haunting, and complete. *—Bryan Buss*

The Adventures of Women & Men Without Hate in the 21st Century. / Oct. 1989 / Mercury ✦✦

Following the success of 1987's *Pop Goes the World* LP, Men Without Hats pursued a similar stylistic direction with 1989's *Adventures of Women & Men Without Hate in the 21st Century*. Aside from its unwieldy title, the album was also hampered by a lack of strong material. The *Pop Goes the World* album had been the Hats' most consistent effort in terms of songwriting, and *Adventures* . . . suffered by comparison. Singer/songwriter Ivan was increasingly focusing on themes such as environmentalism (before it became trendy) and feminism, but sometimes the message seemed to take precedence over the song. A perfect example was the album's first single, the Canadian hit "Hey Men." The song's pro-woman message was admirable, but the song itself was a dull rocker, particularly ill-suited to Ivan's voice and the Hats' style. The result was tepid, and much of the album was similarly disappointing. There were moments that echoed the greatness of the *Pop Goes the World* LP, but there weren't enough of them. (This album is noteworthy for being the first Men Without Hats record to include a cover version—of Abba's "S.O.S."!) *—Robin Platts*

Sideways / 1991 / Mercury ✦✦

Just when you thought you'd heard everything . . . Here we have an album of guitar-driven alt-rock from Montreal electro-pop ensemble Men Without Hats. Apparently, the Hats' lead singer/songwriter Ivan Doroschuk had taken to hanging out with Montreal scenesters like the Doughboys, who encouraged him to pursue his predilection for loud guitars. He had made a brief foray in this direction in 1985, but record company disinterest in the idea had pushed him back to electro-pop. Now that grungy guitars and alternative rock were all the rage, the idea seemed more viable to all concerned. Overall, it must be said, the Hats weren't as well-suited to this sound. Still, the record had its moments, with Ivan's distinctive voice and way with a melody helping to retain a little of the earlier Hats sound. Having covered Abba's "S.O.S." on their previous album, the Hats now delivered a guitar-driven cover of the Beatles' "I Am the Walrus." Not their strongest record by any means, but they gave it their best shot, and the title track got plenty of exposure in Canada (the album wasn't released in the U.S.). *—Robin Platts*

● **Collection** / Feb. 20, 1996 / Oglio ✦✦✦✦✦

Men Without Hats were never an album-oriented band, so *Collection* does the casual fan a favor by compiling all of their hits—namely "The Safety Dance" (included in its original single mix) and "Pop Goes the World"—onto one disc. While many of the songs aren't as strong as those two singles, they are enjoyable new wave artifacts, making the compilation a fun nostalgia trip. Still, some casual fans will be disappointed that there aren't any lost classics on *Collection*, but less-discerning listeners will be pleased. *—Stephen Thomas Erlewine*

Mendoza Line

f. 1995, Athens, GA

Indie Pop, Indie Rock

Athens, GA indie-pop outfit the Mendoza Line was formed during the summer of 1995 by singers/guitarists Timothy Bracy and Peter Hoffman, longtime friends born and raised in McLean, VA alongside future bandmates Paul Deppler and Margaret Maurice. Andres

Galdames and Lori Carrier completed the original lineup, so named in tribute to ex-major league slugger Mario Mendoza, whose .215 lifetime batting average remains the absolute minimum any self-respecting ballplayer can maintain without banishment to the minors; formed from the remnants of Athens band the Incompetones, the Mendoza Line signed to local label Kindercore to issue their 1997 debut *Poems to a Pawnshop*, which favored a more kinetic indie-rock approach than the subtly pastoral sound introduced on the follow-up EP, *Like Someone in Love*. Shannon McArdle signed on prior to 1999's *I Like You When You're Not Around*, released concurrently with the group's relocation from Georgia to Brooklyn, NY; the superb *We're All in This Alone*, the Mendoza Line's first effort for new label Bar/None, followed in the spring of 2000. *—Jason Ankeny*

Poems to a Pawnshop / 1997 / Kindercore ♦♦♦

I Like You When You're Not Around / 1999 / Kindercore ♦♦♦♦

● **We're All in This Alone** / Mar. 28, 2000 / Bar/None ♦♦♦♦♦
The Mendoza Line has for so long made charmingly homespun if ultimately insignificant pop records that the woozy beauty and emotional depth of *We're All in This Alone* is nothing short of revelatory; the product of the band's near breakup and relocation from their native Georgia to Brooklyn (all crowding into the same apartment, no less), the album channels their interpersonal turmoil into a gorgeously understated examination of the sexual dynamics that divide and conquer men and women alike. The songs proceed in point/counterpoint fashion, with Margaret Maurice and Shannon McArdle contributing the distaff perspective while Timothy Bracy and Peter Hoffman refute the charges; the debate culminates with the record's centerpiece, the lovely "Where You'll Land," in which both sides at the very least agree that it will all end in tears, regardless of where the blame lies. The wise-ass bite of the lyrics and the ramshackle radiance of the band's spaciously jangly melodies mask the bitter truths at the heart of *We're All in This Alone*; in outlining the essential differences that separate the sexes, the Mendoza Line's songs feed on resignation and recrimination. The irony, of course, is that the same things that hold the band's music together drive the band's members (and their respective genders) farther apart. *—Jason Ankeny*

Like Someone in Love / Mar. 28, 2000 / Kindercore ♦♦♦
The Mendoza Line's *Like Someone in Love* collects ten more fine specimens of their strummy, sensitive, country-inflected indie pop. Songs like "The Aragon & Trianon," "I Know I Will Not Find the Words," "Running With an Older Crowd," and "Casey at the Bar" showcase the band's increasingly adept blend of fuzzy guitars, honky tonk pianos, soft harmonies, and wry lyrics. Sunny and sad at the same time, *Like Someone in Love* proves that the Mendoza Line's gentleness is their greatest strength. *—Heather Phares*

Menswear

f. 1994, London, England

Neo-Glam, Indie Pop, Brit-pop, Alternative Pop/Rock

Menswear signed a record contract before they played more than five gigs. That alone tells you everything you need to know about the band. Menswear were an outgrowth of the post-Blur pop scene in London, England, a group of charming, handsome young men that wanted to be in a pop group more than they wanted to play music. Consequently, they received their fair share of detractors, but the band weathered the storm, becoming one of the most popular Brit-pop bands of 1995.

The members of Menswear—vocalist Johnny Dean (b. December 12, 1971), guitarist Simon White, guitarist Chris Gentry (b. February 23, 1977), bassist Stuart Black, and drummer Matt Everett—told everyone around Camden, London that they were in a band before they had actually rehearsed. Toward the end of 1994, they decided to actually start playing music, choosing the name Menswear and writing Elastica and Blur-inspired pop songs.

The group's first single, "I'll Manage Somehow," received good notices in the *NME* and *Melody Maker*, and their second single, "Daydreamer," peaked at number 14. *—Stephen Thomas Erlewine*

● **Nuisance** / Oct. 24, 1995 / Laurel ♦♦♦♦♦
Perhaps Menswear was always destined to be a footnote in pop history, a product of the heady good times of London in 1994 and 1995. Reportedly signed after only three shows, the band was never given the chance to fully develop before they recorded their debut album, *Nuisance*. At the time of their first single, they appropriated the sound of Blur and the style of Pulp; by the time *Nuisance* was released, they also incorporated the sound of Elastica and Oasis, making the band a virtual Cliff Notes of Brit-pop. Naturally, Menswear doesn't quite have the skills or panache of any of their idols, but that doesn't mean they are lacking in charm. Like Oasis and Blur, Menswear appropriates sections of pop history, claiming them as their own. However, they aren't half the songwriters that Noel Gallagher and Damon Albarn are, which means many of their ideas are never developed. Nevertheless, when they assimilate them fully—like the intoxicating rush of "Around You Again" or the sweeping ballad "Being Brave," which lifts the intro to Pink Floyd's "Comfortably Numb"—the band is an undeniable guilty pleasure. When pressed, the 'swear can come up with irresistably infectious pop gems, from the frazzled Monkees pop of "Sleeping In" to the flat-out great single "Daydreamer," which sounds more like Wire than Elastica, only funnier, even if it may be unintentional. Even funnier are Johnny Dean's lyrics, from the groupie saga of "125 West 3rd Street" to "Stardust," a silly attack on Primal Scream's Bobby Gillespie. In all, *Nuisance* is the perfect product from a band that is better known for being seen than being heard. *—Stephen Thomas Erlewine*

We Love You / Aug. 1996 / London ♦♦
Menswear's debut, *Nuisance*, was an energy-filled song cycle that arrived at the height of the Brit-pop movement as popularized by Blur, Oasis, Suede, and Elastica, but as witnessed by the band's lack of an immediate follow-up (and the decline of Brit-pop), Menswear soon ran out of ideas. *We Love You* is essentially a nine-track compilation of the band's non-LP double-single, "We Love You," released in the summer of 1996, and all of the B-sides from those discs. While the title track is an excellent piece of Beatlesque pop, much of the rest of the EP is filled with bad ideas. "Crash" and "People I'm Hooch" recall the glory days of Menswear, but the three bland live tracks, which includes the awful instrumental "Phat Kid Music," indicates that the band was in trouble. Subsequently, they were dropped by London, indefinitely shelving their second LP. *—Jason Damas*

Hay Tiempo! / Oct. 1998 / Polydor ♦♦♦
To most, Menswear's 1996 one-off single *We Love You* was the band's swan song. However, despite being dropped by their record company in every country but Japan, Menswear still managed to release their second album, *Hay Tiempo*, in that country. This record, however, was hardly what anyone would expect from them. More or less abandoning their stylized, loud pop formula, *Hay Tiempo* is much more rooted in trad rock, with no less than three five-minute plus opuses in the middle of a ten-song cycle. The disc is a textbook sophomore slump; Menswear was essentially a singles band, yet there are not many standout tracks here. The more aggressive songs, for the most part, sound bland and uninspired, with the sole exception of "Waiting for the Sun," which evokes some of the joys found in their debut. The songs that do stand out are mostly the ballads, like the orchestral opener "Every Sound's a Melody" and the excellent "Coming Home," essentially a rewrite of the previous album's "Being Brave." "Coming Home" is not only the best track on the album, but was unfortunately also the band's subtle wave goodbye; shortly after the release of *Hay Tiempo* they permanently disbanded. This disc does have a few virtues, however, the most notable being that it does, surprisingly, hold up better upon repeat listens. This alone makes it a worthwhile buy for hardcore fans of the band, even though the price and relative obscurity of each copy is a sizeable obstacle. *Hay Tiempo* may not have been the best way for Menswear to say goodbye, but it is a set of ten songs that may please die-hard fans. *—Jason Damas*

Mental As Anything

New Wave

Formed on a whim by a group of bored art students in search of free drinks, Australia's prankish Mental As Anything went on to forge a career spanning across several decades, their tongues remaining planted firmly in cheek throughout the duration of their existence. Debuting in 1978, the Sydney-based group quickly earned enough of a cult following to record a single, 1979's "The Nips Are Getting Bigger"; it was a Top 20 hit down under, and when their debut LP, *Get Wet*, achieved similar success, the group was off and running. Mental As Anything resurfaced in 1980 with *Espresso Bongo*, which generated two more hit singles, "Come Around" and "(Just Like) Romeo and Juliet." After 1982's *Cats and Dogs* achieved platinum status, Mental As Anything began attracting worldwide notice, and in 1982, they mounted their first tour of the United States. Fan Elvis Costello produced the single "I Didn't Mean to Be Mean," issued later that same year, and in 1983 the group issued their fourth LP *Creatures of Leisure*. In 1985 they returned with *Fundamental As Anything*, their biggest hit to date; the single "Live It Up" was a smash throughout much of the globe. After 1989's *Cyclone Raymond*, they mounted a touring art exhibition which traveled across the country, but for the most part, the quintet was out of the limelight for the early part of the next decade. A Mental As Anything B-sides collection, *Chemical Travel*, appeared in 1993, and in 1995 the band's first new studio LP in six years, *Liar Liar Pants on Fire*, returned them to the Top 40 on the strength of the hit "Mr. Natural." In 1997, Mental As Anything celebrated their 20-year anniversary with the original lineup still intact; the LP *Garage* appeared the following year. *—Jason Ankeny*

Get Wet / 1979 / Regular ♦♦♦♦
The Mentals' debut album, predated by the single (and opening track) "The Nips Are Getting Bigger," is a terrific grab bag of influences melded together by five artistic heads, creating a unique and original sound that also sounds comforting and familiar. Blending classic rock & roll (from Elvis to the Beatles) with a new wave outlook, the Mentals end up sounding like a heavenly mix of Rockpile and Squeeze. Martin Plaza's warm and inviting vocals dominate the album, both on his songs and his bandmates' tracks as well, although guitarist Reg Mombassa and keyboardist Greedy Smith have their chance to shine (bassist Peter O'Doherty weighs in with two tracks, though he only sings lead on "Love Is Not a Gift"). Cameron Allan's stiff production tends to hide a bit of the band's playfulness, but the band's energy does filter out in the songs. "The Nips Are Getting Bigger" is a fantastic opener, full of witty wordplay and great band dynamics. "Business and Pleasure," "Talk to Baby Jesus," "Fringe Benefits," "Insurance Man," and "Egypt" are all classic Mentals tracks that never loose their charm. Though the album isn't perfect, there isn't a terrible song in the bunch. If you're looking for great chops, catchy songs, and a bucketful of charm, you needn't look any further than Mental As Anything. *—Stephen SPAZ Schnee*

Espresso Bongo / 1980 / Regular ♦♦
After such a fantastic debut, you'd expect the Mentals to fall on their face for their sophomore release, and they almost did. Sounding like it consists of songs leftover from the sessions for their debut, *Espresso Bongo* does no one any favors, although it is not a bad album. Cameron Allan's production is even flatter than before, sucking almost all the excitement out of what could have been an exciting album. Martin Plaza, who dominated the first album, is buried on this one, only writing three of its 12 tracks. Slide guitarist Reg Mombassa, a great writer and original vocalist in his own right, dominates the proceedings this time out. "Troop Movements in the Ukraine," "Semitrailer," "Harmonic Visions," and the single "Come Around" are standouts on the album, though bassist Peter O'Doherty's "Away" and "The Girl" are the weakest cuts here (which he made up for on later albums by penning some of the band's finest tracks). Keyboardist Greedy Smith, like

Plaza, is sorely missed with only two tracks to his credit. Still, the band doesn't fail dismally, and their natural talents are hard to miss. If only they'd get rid of that lousy producer. *—Stephen SPAZ Schnee*

Cats and Dogs / 1981 / Regular ✦✦✦✦✦
With a great debut and a so-so sophomore effort behind them, it was make-or-break time for the Mentals when they went in to record this, their third effort. With sympathetic production from Bruce Brown and Russell Dunlop, the Mentals created their first true "classic" album, which takes the best elements from their debut album and betters them by leaps and bounds. Greedy Smith's bouncy "Too Many Times" leads off the album like a gunshot starting a race, but there are only winners from here on out. "If You Leave Me, Can I Come Too?," a huge single that made them superstars in Australia, is a fantastic blend of pop smarts and roots rock. "Let's Cook" is more fun than the Galloping Gourmet could ever hope to be. "Walking on Rails," "Got Hit," and "Looking for Bird" are meat-and-potatoes rock & roll with hooks aplenty. "Chemical Travel" is an absolute treat with a driving beat. Everyone in the band shines on this album, from Martin Plaza's warm drawl to Reg Mombassa's amazing slide fretwork and Greedy Smith's confident and playful keyboards. O'Doherty and Delisle are the backbone of the album, one of pop music's finest rhythm sections. All in all, a fantastic album that bears repeated listenings. *—Stephen SPAZ Schnee*

● **Creatures of Leisure** / 1983 / A&M ✦✦✦✦✦
Following up their biggest album yet, the Mentals rose to the occasion on this, their fourth full-length release. Though it may seem to be the little brother to 1981's *Cats and Dogs*, *Creatures of Leisure* is actually an even better album than it's predecessor. With producers Bruce Brown and Russell Dunlop again spinning the knobs, the Mentals serve up a batch of incredible songs, making the Rockpile-meets-Squeeze comparisons more accurate than ever. There's not a bad track in the bunch, with many of them already confirmed Mentals classics, including "Brain Brain" (a radio staple on U.S. college stations in '83), "Spirit Got Lost," "Bitter to Swallow," "Kissing of Her Lips," and "Close Again." Martin Plaza's already warm voice was more sincere and emotional this time out, while Greedy Smith's songwriting had matured ten-fold since the band's debut four years earlier. Reg Mombassa and Peter O'Doherty's songs were their best yet, with O'Doherty's "Red to Green" being an album standout (on an album of standouts). The Mentals' best album to date, it is a must have for pure pop fans, new wave fans, rock & roll fans, and Aussie rock fans. *—Stephen SPAZ Schnee*

Fundamental As Anything / Mar. 1985 / Columbia ✦✦✦✦
Though not as fabulous as their previous effort, *Creatures of Leisure, Fundamental As Anything* comes awfully close. With legendary producer Richard Gottehrer (Blondie, Yachts, etc.) at the controls, the Mentals' fifth album was their most commercial yet. Though Wayne Delisle's sure and steady drumming is muddled in fake drum sounds, the band is still on fire and serving up oodles of great songs. This time, keyboardist Greedy Smith dominates with some of the band's biggest hits, including "You're So Strong," "Date With Destiny," and the perfect pop of "Live It Up." Martin Plaza lights up the album by penning "Big Wheel," "Bus Ride," and "Good Friday" and lends his awesome pipes to Peter O'Doherty's "Hold On" and Reg Mombassa's "Splashing." O'Doherty and Mombassa handle a few of their own songs as well, making this another showcase for all five talented members. Though it has the most "dated" production of all their albums, *Fundamental* is an apt title to say the least. Another great album from one of Australia's finest outfits. *—Stephen SPAZ Schnee*

Mouth to Mouth / 1988 / Columbia ✦✦✦✦

Cyclone Raymond / 1989 / Columbia ✦✦✦✦✦

Liar Liar Pants on Fire / 1995 / BMG Ariola ✦✦✦✦✦
With their first album of new material in six years, Mental As Anything came out with all guns blazing. Dropping the slick production that turned off many of their fans during the late '80s, the Mentals returned to the basic sound of their first two albums, sounding more raw than ever before. With renewed vigor, the band let the songs speak (sing?) for themselves, keeping everything as basic as possible. "Mr. Natural," the first single, leads the album off in the right direction with a thumping, glam-like beat and a basic, albeit catchy, melody courtesy of Martin Plaza. Reg Mombassa's "Nigel" is up next and features one of the best, if not most morbid, opening lines in recent Mentals history ("Oh, by the way, Nigel died yesterday!"). "Surfer Joe Revisited" updates the tale and finds the legendary Surfer Joe trading in his old life and spending more time surfing the Internet ("He had a moptop/Now, he's got a laptop"). "Marianne" is about the legendary Marianne Faithfull. Greedy Smith's breezy acoustic-based "To the Mountains" is one of the best things he's written yet. "Too Down to Cry" is the song Chris Isaak has been trying to write for years. The band even finds time to do a cover of Wreckless Eric's "Whole Wide World." A fantastic return to form by this rock monster with five heads and a whole lot of talent. *—Stephen "Spaz" Schnee*

Chemical Travel / Aug. 25, 1998 / Flying Nun ✦✦✦
While the band was on indefinite sabbatical while pursuing side projects, there had been no new Mentals product for nearly four years. Knowing that too much time away could hurt any band no matter how big or small, the Mentals new management company and their label decided to issue this collection of B-sides and album tracks as a companion to their greatest hits package released seven years earlier. Beginning with "C.Y.O. Dance," a track from their debut EP (released prior to their first full-length, *Get Wet*), this collection features all the classic Mentals trademarks: expert musicianship, top notch songs, and unbridled energy. Though there is not a hit single in the bunch, *Chemical Travel* is every bit as fun and enjoyable as any of their albums. Rarities like "Assault and Flattery," "L'Amour No More," and "Wouldn't Try to Explain" sound great next to key album tracks like "Fiona," "Some Feelings," "Talk to Baby Jesus," and "Not Enough." *—Stephen SPAZ Schnee*

Garage / Aug. 25, 1998 / Mushroom ✦✦✦
Celebrating their 21st anniversary, the Mentals continue to please with this follow-up to their 1995 comeback album, *Liar Liar Pants on Fire*. Though not as pleasing as that album, *Garage* is still a fine celebration of 21 years of the same five guys playing music together. "Just My Luck," the leadoff track and first single, is prime Martin Plaza. "Calling Colin," written and sung by Peter O'Doherty, was the second single taken from the album and should have been a huge success worldwide, being one of the catchiest pop songs released during the '90s. Besides the two singles, there are some great songs on *Garage* ("Does She," "Lemon Peel," "Up & Down," "Money," and "Complaining" are all worthy of mentioning), but the album is weighed down by a few too many meat-and-potatoes rockers that make the toes tap but don't inspire the listener to get involved as deeply as they would like. Initial Australian copies included a bonus anniversary disc featuring six tracks from their back catalog (though nothing rare or unreleased). *—Stephen SPAZ Schnee*

Best Of Mental As Anything / 1999 / Festival ✦✦✦✦✦
Containing every track from *Greatest Hits, Vol. 1* (but this time, in chronological order) and adding ten more Mentals gems, this is the ultimate introduction to one of Australia's finest pop/rock outfits. Fans of Squeeze and Nick Lowe's side of Rockpile will be foaming at the mouth after hearing this very fine collection of Mentals classics. Yes, all the hits are here, including "Live It Up," "You're So Strong," "The Nips Are Getting Bigger," and "If You Leave Me, Can I Come Too?." Though the track listing is perfect, why choose the non-single "Dorothy Parker's Hair" from the album *Garage* over singles like "Calling Colin" or "Just My Luck"? Then again, that's a minor point. Twenty-four tracks in all. *—Stephen "Spaz" Schnee*

Beetroot Stains / 2001 / Universal ✦✦✦
After 25 years of making music together, the boys in Mental As Anything made some serious career decisions. Bassist Peter O'Doherty decided to leave the band and concentrate on his family and art. Guitarist Reg Mombassa (O'Doherty's brother) followed, leaving two vacancies in the band. Enter guitarist Murray Cook and bassist/guitarist Duck Barraclough. With the lineup change came a shift in musical direction as well. Martin Plaza's solo recordings have always embraced dance rhythms, and for the first time, he's brought some of them with him onto a Mentals album. "Fine Line," the first single and opening track, introduces this new sound immediately with its loopy rhythm and speak-sung verses. More like a B-side than an A-side, this semi-instrumental track is interesting at best. "Special Filter" is classic Mentals, though a bit more sophisticated rhythmically. Imagine "Big Wheel" from *Fundamental* with a groovy dance beat. "Stretchmarks" and "The Ballad of Narell, Pts. One and Two" are Barraclough-led tracks and rock harder (with less melodic flair) then any previous Mentals release. "Davy Jones Got the Part" takes a humorous look at Charles Manson being passed over after auditioning for a part in the Monkees. Greedy Smith, usually the trusty pop tunesmith of the band, serves up three fine tracks that recall the Mentals of old: "Holiday Away From My Head," "Different Girls," and "$25 More." For listeners unfamiliar with the Mentals, this may be an appealing introduction to the talents of the band. Even as a collection of solo offshoots, this would have been a treat. For longtime fans, though, perhaps they should have changed the band's name to Experimental As Anything. *—Stephen "Spaz" Schnee*

Natalie Merchant

b. Oct. 26, 1963
Vocals, Piano / Adult Alternative Pop/Rock, Singer/Songwriter
First rising to fame at the helm of the popular folk-rock band 10,000 Maniacs, Natalie Merchant subsequently enjoyed even greater success as a solo performer as her plaintive vocals and literate, socially conscious songs established her among the preeminent female performers in contemporary pop. Born October 26, 1963 in Jamestown, NY, Merchant joined 10,000 Maniacs at the age of 17, quickly becoming the band's driving artistic force; after a pair of successful independent releases, they signed to Elektra in 1985, and in the years to follow emerged among the most popular acts in alternative rock, shooting into the Top 40 with 1987's superb *In My Tribe*. However, around the time of recording 1992's *Our Time in Eden*, Merchant gave her bandmates two years notice, and after the release of 1994's *MTV Unplugged* publicly announced she was leaving their ranks. Her 1995 solo debut, *Tigerlily*, debuted just shy of the Top Ten, scoring a hit with the single "Carnival"; it was followed in 1998 by *Ophelia*. *Live in Concert*, recorded at New York's Neil Simon Theatre, appeared a year later. A prominent social activist, Merchant also regularly campaigned in the name of such hot-button issues as animal rights, domestic violence, and homelessness. *—Jason Ankeny*

● **Tigerlily** / Jun. 20, 1995 / Elektra ✦✦✦✦✦
Tigerlily, Natalie Merchant's first solo record, does sound different than 10,000 Maniacs. Instead of relying strictly on jangly folk-rock, Merchant continues opening her music up as she did on *Our Time in Eden*, her last album with the Maniacs. From the understated groove of "Carnival" to the rolling "San Andreas Fault," the added emphasis on rhythmic texture works, creating an intimate but not exclusive atmosphere that holds throughout the record, even when her occasionally sophomoric, sentimental poetry threatens to sink the album in the weight of its own preciousness (as in "River," her tribute to the late actor River Phoenix). *—Stephen Thomas Erlewine*

Ophelia / May 19, 1998 / Elektra ✦✦✦
Tigerlily established that Natalie Merchant could survive outside of 10,000 Maniacs, both commercially and artistically. Its follow-up album, *Ophelia*, is a bit more problematic. Initially, the album appears to be conceptual, tracing the Ophelia character through modern

times. That concept quickly falls away, leaving studied, if somewhat elliptical, lyrical portraits. Like *Tigerlily*, the songs on *Ophelia* have hushed, layered arrangements that are outgrowths, not replicas, of 10,000's jangly folk-rock. However, *Ophelia* lacks the subtle sonic textures and graceful hooks that made Merchant's debut so charming. Instead, all of the subdued songs—only "Kind & Generous" has a clear-cut, singalong hook—blend together, which makes the album decidedly less accessible. Unfortunately, it doesn't always reward the close listening it demands. A few songs reveal hidden layers and meanings upon repeated listens, but on the whole *Ophelia* sounds too insular and similar to make a large impression. —*Stephen Thomas Erlewine*

Live in Concert / Nov. 9, 1999 / Elektra ♦♦♦

Mercury Rev

f. Buffalo, NY

Noise Pop, Dream Pop, Neo-Psychedelia, Indie Rock, Alternative Pop/Rock

Not so much a band as a long, strange trip, the chaotic avant-pop pranksters Mercury Rev formed in Buffalo, NY in the late '80s. Always rife with personality conflicts, group members interacted with one another infrequently, and their first recordings evolved simply as a means of creating soundtracks for their experimental student films. Encouraged to further their music by academic mentor Tony Conrad, the loosely connected aggregate dubbed Mercury Rev (a name whose inspiration was variously attributed to an imaginary Russian ballet dancer, a sharp rise in temperature, or a revved-up auto) began to emerge, and eventually the group recorded a demo onto a reel of 35mm magnetic film. The demo tape somehow made its way to the British offices of the Rough Trade label, which contacted singer David Baker about signing the group. Soon, the band convened to record their debut *Yerself Is Steam*, a brilliantly melodic and free-form set highlighted by distorted art-pop epics like "Chasing a Bee," "Coney Island Cyclone," and "Frittering," *Yerself Is Steam* was issued to widespread acclaim in 1991; however, within weeks of the LP's release Rough Trade's American branch declared bankruptcy, aborting any hopes of proper distribution or promotion. Mercury Rev then set up studio space in a barn to craft their second album, *Boces*; after completing the principal recording sessions, the group collected samples from sites as far-ranging as Times Square and NASA's Cape Canaveral to flesh out the music's dense, prismatic sound. After relations soured to the point where Baker was travelling to gigs apart from his bandmates, he was dismissed from Mercury Rev's ranks; 1995's shimmering *See You on the Other Side* found the group—newly freed of Baker's darker impulses—exploring increasingly diverse stylistic territory with newfound emotional depth. The lovely *Deserter's Songs* followed in the fall of 1998. —*Jason Ankeny*

Yerself Is Steam / 1991 / Columbia ♦♦♦♦♦

Music dictated not by logic but by intuition, *Yerself Is Steam* is an album at war with itself, split by its desire to achieve both melodic pop bliss and white-noise transcendence within the same space; it succeeds brilliantly, avant-bubblegum fuel injected by fits and flourishes of prismatic chaos. From the comic malevolence of David Baker's mad-scientist creations to Jonathan Donahue's opiate lullabies, *Yerself Is Steam* is vividly cinematic—between the roller coaster feedback of "Coney Island Cyclone" and the narcoleptic ebb and flow of the climactic "Very Sleepy Rivers," the songs perfectly evoke their titular aspirations; likewise, from the album title (say it out loud) onward, the lyrics revel in the quirks and idiosyncrasies of language, buoyed by a homophonous prankishness and dada rhyme schemes, which, in their own odd way, suggest a kind of poetry. A near-perfect debut from a band that would only get better from here on out. [The American edition appends the superb single "Car Wash Hair," while some foreign releases include the bonus disc *Lego My Ego*, a crazy quilt knitted together from unlikely covers (Sly Stone's "If You Want Me to Stay," Miles Davis' "Shhh"), *Peel Sessions* highlights, and wonderfully loopy studio chatter.] —*Jason Ankeny*

● **Boces** / Jun. 1, 1993 / Columbia ♦♦♦♦♦

With *Boces*, Mercury Rev took everything that made *Yerself Is Steam* such an impressive debut and made their second album even more so. Over the course of ten minutes, opening epic "Meth of a Rockette's Kick" moves from dreamy musing to guitar-fueled crests—and throws in flutes, harps, a brass section, and a choir for good measure—announcing that the group is at the height of its powers. Thrashy freakouts like "Trickle Down" sound even more explosive and stand in sharper contrast to the Technicolor pop of "Something for Joey" and "Hi Speed Boats," while the sweetly lovelorn "Bronx Cheer" and "Downs Are Feminine Balloons" (key lyric: "If there's one thing I can't stand, it's up") reveal the vulnerability beneath the group's jet-powered guitars. But *Boces* doesn't just perfect the sound Mercury Rev pioneered on *Yerself Is Steam*, it expands it in predictably unpredictable ways. The Cheshire cat jazz-pop of "Boys Peel Out," the sleepwalking speed metal of "Snorry Mouth," and the spooky, smoky finale "Girlfren," though very different from each other, are equally captivating examples of the band's witty, innovative modus operandi. Mercury Rev never released another album as joyfully, unselfconsciously creative as *Boces*; after chief weirdo David Baker departed, the band pursued other fascinating directions, but this album remains one of the highest points of its career. —*Heather Phares*

See You on the Other Side / Sep. 19, 1995 / Work ♦♦♦♦

After David Baker left the group for weirder pastures, the rest of Mercury Rev returned with *See You on the Other Side*, an album very much in the group's expansive, experimental tradition, yet distinct from its work with Baker. The sprawling compositions, elaborate arrangements, and jazzy leanings Mercury Rev perfected on *Boces* return on *See You on the Other Side*, as exemplified by the opening track, "Empire State (Son House in Excelsis)." But without Baker's merry prankster vocals, the album feels a bit unbalanced, as though the group was still adjusting to making music without him when the album

was recorded. The lean, tense "Young Man's Stride" could've had even more impact had Baker sung it but, for the most part, Jonathan Donahue handles all the vocal duties ably, swinging the group toward its gently whimsical side in the process. The brilliant single "Everlasting Arm" sweetly deconstructs *Pet Sounds*-style pop years before that became one of indie rock's dominant styles, while "A Kiss From an Old Flame (A Trip to the Moon)" lives up to its title with giddy, swirling flutes and otherworldly backing vocals. Dreamy, yearning songs like "Sudden Ray of Hope" and "Racing the Tide" revel in the unabashed prettiness that Mercury Rev used to hide under layers of freaked-out guitars, and "Peaceful Night," the group's quirky take on Tin Pan Alley songwriting, proves that they weren't getting less inventive as time went on, they were just getting subtler about it. *See You on the Other Side*'s relatively short length adds to its rather unfair middle-child status, but it pointed the way toward Mercury Rev's breakthrough with *Deserter's Songs*, and is a completely charming—if underrated—album in its own right. —*Heather Phares*

Deserter's Songs / Sep. 29, 1998 / V2 ♦♦♦♦♦

Four albums in and Mercury Rev remains as surprising and daring as ever—exchanging the volcanic noise and twisted sensibilities of earlier releases for ornate arrangements and ethereal strings, *Deserter's Songs* unlocks the beauty always hidden just below the band's surface, its lush harmonics and soothing textures bathing in an almost unearthly light. Standouts including the exquisitely waltz-like "Tonite It Shows" and the celestial "Endlessly" are like lullabies, their music-box melodies gentle and narcotic; even the most pop-oriented moments like "Opus 40" and "Hudson Line" share a symphonic, candy-colored majesty far removed from conventional rock idioms. Complete with its fractured instrumental interludes and odd effects, *Deserter's Songs* sounds like no other album—for that matter, it doesn't even sound like Mercury Rev, yet there's no mistaking the record's brilliance for anyone else. —*Jason Ankeny*

All Is Dream / Sep. 11, 2001 / V2 ♦♦♦♦

Moody, majestic, and unpredictable, *All Is Dream* plays like *Deserter's Songs*' evil twin, polarizing that album's gently trippy, symphonic pop into paranoid and exuberant extremes that range from the eerie lullaby "Lincoln's Eyes" to the giddy show-tune-in-search-of-a-musical "A Drop in Time." Starting with the symphonic grandeur of "The Dark Is Rising," the album's ambitious, self-indulgent vibe recalls '60s and '70s psych and prog rock concept albums as well as the band's own expansive body of work. The first half of *All Is Dream* journeys through the band's dark side with songs like the brooding "Tides of the Moon," which pits Jonathan Donahue's spooked, singsong vocals against appropriately unearthly theremins, glockenspiels, and organs, while the second half's "Nite and Fog" and "Little Rhymes" sound twice as sunny compared to the preceding weirdness. The contrast between the album's halves is so sharp that it seems designed for vinyl; flipping this record over would be immensely satisfying. Though nothing on *All Is Dream* is as immediate as *Deserter's Songs*' "Goddess on a Hiway" or "Delta Sun Bottleneck Stomp," this album may be stronger as a whole, moving gracefully from singer/songwriter ballads like the beautiful "Spiders and Flies" to guitar-driven epics like "You're My Queen" and "Hercules." An unfashionably self-indulgent and earnest album, *All Is Dream* certainly isn't for everyone, and may not even be for some Mercury Rev fans, but in its own personal, insular way, it's another triumph for the band. —*Heather Phares*

The Merry-Go-Round

db. 1969

Baroque Pop, Pop

Like the Left Banke, the Merry-Go-Round were teen pop/rock prodigies who combined British Invasion pop melodies with Baroque pop studio polish. The L.A. group, dominated by singer/songwriter Emmitt Rhodes, had a couple huge local hits—"Live" and "You're a Very Lovely Woman"—but achieved little national success before disbanding in 1969. A Paul McCartney sound-alike and lookalike, Rhodes was blatantly influenced by McCartney's *Magical Mystery Tour*-era compositions, as one listen to "Pardon Me" (a ringer for "Fool on the Hill") will attest. Rhodes achieved modest commercial and critical recognition with his solo recordings in the early '70s. —*Richie Unterberger*

● **The Best of the Merry-Go-Round** / 1985 / Rhino ♦♦♦♦♦

A 14-song compilation of songs from their sole album, plus a few rare singles. Highlights include "Live," "Come Ride," "Time Will Show the Wiser" (covered by Fairport Convention on their first album), and especially the gorgeous, haunting string ballad "You're a Very Lovely Woman." Solid, melodic late-'60s pop-rock with sophisticated arrangements, though it's sometimes lightweight. —*Richie Unterberger*

The Merseybeats

f. 1963, **db.** 1966

Merseybeat, British Invasion

The Merseybeats were one of the better Liverpool bands of the British Invasion, scoring several large and minor hits in the U.K., although they made no impact whatsoever in America. Friends of the Who (with whom they shared management for a time) and the Beatles, the band leaned toward mid-tempo harmony numbers, with the occasional ballads and ravers thrown in. Not nearly as distinguished as top-line British Invasion pop-rockers like the Hollies and the Searchers, the Merseybeats did have classy taste in cover material, recording the original version of Bacharach/David's "Wishin' and Hopin'" (a hit in the U.S. for Dusty Springfield), reaching the U.K. Top 40 with "I Stand Accused" (covered by Elvis Costello), and releasing covers of "Mr. Moonlight" and "Fortune Teller" before the Beatles and the Stones recorded their more famous versions. Like many of the original Liverpool bands, they were crippled by a lack of songwriting talent. After breaking up in 1966, members Tony Crane and Billy Kinsley formed the Merseys, who landed a huge British hit with "Sorrow" (covered by David Bowie on *Pin Ups*) the same year. *—Richie Unterberger*

The Merseybeats / 1964 / Fontana ✦✦✦
A very well-programmed 18-song collection representing the band's good and bad sides. The former includes crisp pop/rock ditties like "Don't Turn Around," "Last Night," and "It's Love That Really Counts," while the latter is mostly an over-reliance on show tunes. *—Bruce Eder*

● **Beat & Ballads** / 1982 / Edsel ✦✦✦✦✦
All of their British hits, and indeed most of the A- and B-sides they cut between 1963 and 1965—"I Think of You," "Don't Turn Around," "Wishin 'N' Hopin'," "I Stand Accused." Also includes the 1964 single "Last Night," which flopped, but is one of the best obscure British invasion pop-rockers. *—Richie Unterberger*

● **The Very Best of the Merseybeats** / 1998 / Spectrum ✦✦✦
Spectrum's *The Very Best of the Merseybeats* is a good budget-line U.K. collection featuring all of the group's Top 30 hits, plus a selection of good lesser-known singles and album tracks that often equal the originals. If you can't find *Beat & Ballads* this is a good alternative. *—Stephen Thomas Erlewine*

The Merton Parkas

f. 1978, **db.** 1980
Mod Revival, Power Pop, New Wave
The Merton Parkas, taking their name from their home in South London (Merton) and the classic mod-wear (the parka) are another footnote in the British mod-revival of the late '70s (which itself was merely a footnote in music history). Formed by brothers Mick Talbot (keyboards) and Danny Talbot (vocals) along with Neil Wurrel (bass) and Simon Smith (drums) in 1978, they became one of the first third-wave mod-revivalists to release an album, *Face in the Crowd*, which featured the hit single "You Need Wheels." While many of the movement's followers took a more serious approach, the Merton Parkas tapped into the novelty side of the genre, becoming something of a mod version of Madness, though less innovative (and less interesting). Mick Talbot later teamed up with Paul Weller to form the Style Council in 1983. *—Chris Woodstra*

● **Face in the Crowd** / 1979 / Beggars Banquet ✦✦✦✦✦
The band's sole LP, while certainly flawed, offers a lightweight, novelty approach to the Jam-inspired mod-revival. A little too derivative to be taken seriously, but there are some fun songs nonetheless such as the U.K. hit "You Need Wheels," "Plastic Smile," and the title track. *—Chris Woodstra*

The Complete Mod Collection / 1997 / Anagram ✦✦✦✦✦

Metallica

f. 1981, Los Angeles, CA
Speed Metal, Heavy Metal, Thrash, Hard Rock
Metallica was easily the best, most influential heavy metal band of the '80s, responsible for bringing the music back to earth. Instead of playing the usual rock star games of metal stars of the early '80s, the band looked and talked like they were from the street. Metallica expanded the limits of thrash, using speed and volume not for their own sake, but to enhance their intricately structured compositions. The release of 1983's *Kill 'Em All* marked the beginning of the legitimization of heavy metal's underground, bringing new complexity and depth to thrash metal. With each album, the band's playing and writing improved; James Hetfield developed a signature rhythm playing that matched his growl, while lead guitarist Kirk Hammett became one of the most copied guitarists in metal. Lars Ulrich's thunderous, yet complex, drumming clicked in perfectly with Cliff Burton's innovative bass playing. After releasing their masterpiece *Master of Puppets* in 1986, tragedy struck the band when their tour bus crashed while traveling in Sweden, killing Burton. Jason Newsted was his replacement; two years later, the band released the conceptually ambitious *... And Justice for All*, which hit the Top Ten without any radio play and very little support from MTV. But Metallica completely crossed over into the mainstream with 1991's *Metallica*, which found the band trading in their long compositions for more concise song structures; it resulted in a number one album that sold over seven million copies in the U.S. alone. By the '90s, Metallica had changed the rules for all heavy metal bands; they were the leaders of the genre, respected not only by headbangers, but by mainstream record buyers and critics. No other heavy metal band has ever been able to pull off such a trick. *—Stephen Thomas Erlewine*

☆ **Kill 'Em All** / 1983 / Elektra ✦✦✦✦✦
The true birth of thrash. On *Kill 'Em All*, Metallica fuses the intricate riffing of New Wave of British Heavy Metal bands like Judas Priest, Iron Maiden, and Diamond Head with the velocity of Motorhead and hardcore punk. James Hetfield's highly technical rhythm guitar style drives most of the album, setting new standards of power, precision, and stamina. But really, the rest of the band is just as dexterous, playing with tightly controlled fury even at the most ridiculously fast tempos. There are already several extended, multi-sectioned compositions foreshadowing the band's later progressive epics, though these are driven by adrenaline, not texture. A few tributes to heavy metal itself are a bit dated lyrically; like Diamond Head, the band's biggest influence, *Kill 'Em All*'s most effective tone is one of supernatural malevolence—as pure sound, the record is already straight from the pits of hell. Ex-member Dave Mustaine co-wrote four of the original ten tracks, but the material all sounds of a piece. And actually, anyone who worked backwards through the band's catalog might not fully appreciate the impact of *Kill 'Em All* when it first appeared—unlike later releases, there simply isn't much musical variation (apart from a lyrical bass solo from Cliff Burton). The band's musical ambition also grew rapidly, so today, *Kill 'Em All* sounds more like the foundation for greater things to come. But that doesn't take anything away from how fresh it sounded upon first release, and time hasn't dulled the giddy rush of excitement in these performances. Frightening, awe-inspiring, and absolutely relentless, *Kill 'Em All* is pure destructive power, executed with jaw-dropping levels of scientific precision. An Elektra reissue added the cover songs "Blitzkrieg" and "Am I Evil?" from the European *Creeping Death* EP, which were deleted and later included on *Garage, Inc.* *—Steve Huey*

Ride the Lightning / 1984 / Elektra ✦✦✦✦✦
Kill 'Em All may have revitalized heavy metal's underground, but *Ride the Lightning* was even more stunning, exhibiting staggering musical growth and boldly charting new directions that would affect heavy metal for years to come. Incredibly ambitious for a one-year-later sophomore effort, *Ride the Lightning* finds Metallica aggressively expanding their compositional technique and range of expression. Every track tries something new, and every musical experiment succeeds mightily. The lyrics push into new territory as well—more personal, more socially conscious, less metal posturing. But the true heart of *Ride the Lightning* lies in its rich musical imagination. There are extended, progressive epics; tight, concise groove-rockers; thrashers that blow anything on *Kill 'Em All* out of the water, both in their urgency and the barest hints of melody that have been added to the choruses. Some innovations are flourishes that add important bits of color, like the lilting, pseudo-classical intro to the furious "Fight Fire With Fire," or the harmonized leads that pop up on several tracks. Others are major reinventions of Metallica's sound, like the nine-minute, album-closing instrumental "The Call of Ktulu," or the haunting suicide lament "Fade to Black." The latter is an all-time metal classic; it begins as an acoustic-driven, minor-key ballad, then gets slashed open by electric guitars playing a wordless chorus, and ends in a wrenching guitar solo over a thrashy yet lyrical rhythm figure. Basically, in a nutshell, Metallica sounded like it could do anything. Heavy metal hadn't seen this kind of ambition since Judas Priest's late-'70s classics, and *Ride the Lightning* effectively rewrote the rule book for a generation of thrashers. If *Kill 'Em All* was the manifesto, *Ride the Lightning* was the revolution itself. *—Steve Huey*

★ **Master of Puppets** / 1986 / Elektra ✦✦✦✦✦
Even though *Master of Puppets* didn't take as gigantic a leap forward as *Ride the Lightning*, it was the band's greatest achievement, hailed as a masterpiece by critics far outside heavy metal's core audience. It was also a substantial hit, reaching the Top 30 and selling three million copies despite absolutely nonexistent airplay. Instead of a radical reinvention, *Master of Puppets* is a refinement of past innovations. In fact, it's possible to compare *Ride the Lightning* and *Master of Puppets* song for song and note striking similarities between corresponding track positions on each record (although *Lightning*'s closing instrumental has been bumped up to next-to-last in *Master*'s running order). That hint of conservatism is really the only conceivable flaw here. Though it isn't as startling as *Ride the Lightning*, *Master of Puppets* feels more unified, both thematically and musically. Everything about it feels blown up to epic proportions (indeed, the songs are much longer on average), and the band feels more in control of its direction. You'd never know it by the lyrics, though—in one way or another, nearly every song on *Master of Puppets* deals with the fear of powerlessness. Sometimes they're about hypocritical authority (military and religious leaders), sometimes primal, uncontrollable human urges (drugs, insanity, rage), and, in true H.P. Lovecraft fashion, sometimes monsters. Yet by bookending the album with two slices of thrash mayhem ("Battery" and "Damage, Inc."), the band reigns triumphant through sheer force—of sound, of will, of malice. The arrangements are thick and muscular, and the material varies enough in texture and tempo to hold interest through all its twists and turns. Some critics have called *Master of Puppets* the best heavy metal album ever recorded; if it isn't, it certainly comes close. *—Steve Huey*

Garage Days Re-Revisited / 1987 / Elektra ✦✦✦
Following Cliff Burton's death, Metallica took some time off and initiated new bassist Jason Newsted with a raw, unpolished EP of covers originally recorded by Diamond Head, Holocaust, Killing Joke, Budgie, and the Misfits. Most fit the band's style quite well; only "Last Caress" sounds out of place, as the original seemed looser and more dangerous. As a showcase for some strong metal riffs and material by mostly underground bands, the EP works quite well. *—Steve Huey*

... And Justice for All / 1988 / Elektra ✦✦✦✦✦
The most immediately noticeable aspect of *... And Justice for All* isn't Metallica's still-growing compositional sophistication or the apocalyptic lyrical portrait of a society in decay. It's the weird, bone-dry production. The guitars buzz thinly, the drums click more than pound, and Jason Newsted's bass is nearly inaudible. It's a shame that the cold, flat sound obscures some of the sonic details, because *... And Justice for All* is Metallica's most complex, ambitious work; every song is an expanded suite, with only two of the nine tracks clocking in at under six minutes. It takes a while to sink in, but given time, *... And Justice for All* reveals some of Metallica's best material. It also reveals the band's determination to pull out all the compositional stops, throwing in extra sections, odd-numbered time signatures, and dense webs of guitar arpeggios and harmonized leads. At times, it seems like they're doing it simply because they can; parts of the album lack direction, and probably should have been trimmed for momentum's sake. Pacing-wise, the album again loosely follows the blueprint of *Ride the Lightning*, though not as closely as *Master of Puppets*. This time around, the fourth song—once again a ballad with a thrashy chorus and outro—gave the band one of the unlikeliest Top 40 singles in history; "One" was an instant metal classic, based on Dalton Trumbo's anti-war novel *Johnny Got His Gun* and climaxing with a pulverizing machine-gun imitation. As a whole, opinions on *... And Justice for All* remain somewhat divided: some think it's a slightly flawed masterpiece and the pinnacle of Metallica's progressive years; others see it as bloated and overambitious. Either interpretation can be readily supported, but the band had clearly

taken this direction as far as it could. The difficulty of reproducing these songs in concert eventually convinced Metallica that it was time for an overhaul. *—Steve Huey*

Metallica / Aug. 1991 / Elektra ✦✦✦✦✦
After the muddled production and ultra-complicated song structures of *…And Justice For All*, Metallica decided that they had taken the progressive elements of their music as far as they could and that a simplification and streamlining of their sound was in order. While the assessment made sense from a musical standpoint, it also presented an opportunity to commercialize their music, and *Metallica* accomplishes both goals. The best songs are more melodic and immediate, the crushing, stripped-down grooves of "Enter Sandman," "Sad But True," and "Wherever I May Roam" sticking to traditional structures and using the same main riffs throughout; the crisp, professional production by Bob Rock adds to their accessibility. "The Unforgiven" and "Nothing Else Matters" avoid the slash-and-burn guitar riffs that had always punctuated the band's ballads; the latter is a full-fledged love song complete with string section, which works much better than might be imagined. The song- and riff-writing slips here and there, a rare occurrence for Metallica, which some longtime fans interpreted as filler next to a batch of singles calculated for commercial success. The objections were often more to the idea that Metallica was doing *anything* explicitly commercial, but millions more disagreed. In fact, the band's popularity exploded so much that most of their back catalog found mainstream acceptance in its own right, while other progressively inclined speed-metal bands copied the move toward simplification. In retrospect, *Metallica* is a good, but not quite great, album, one whose best moments deservedly captured the heavy metal crown, but whose approach also foreshadowed a creative decline. *—Steve Huey*

Live Shit: Binge and Purge / Nov. 23, 1993 / Elektra ✦✦✦
Weighing in at three CDs and three videos, plus a bunch of tour memorabilia, the sheer bulk of *Live Shit…Binge and Purge* scares off anyone but the most devoted fans, which is too bad. Although it is exhausting, this box provides ample proof of the brutal power of Metallica in concert—the entire program of a Mexico City concert is included, and it is awe-inspiring. For hardcore fans, *Live Shit* is a godsend. *—Stephen Thomas Erlewine*

Load / Jun. 4, 1996 / Elektra ✦✦✦
Delivered five years after their eponymous "black" album in 1991, *Load* captures Metallica settling into an uneasy period of maturation. Under the guidance of producer Bob Rock, Metallica have streamlined their sound, cutting away most of the twisting, unpredictable time signatures and the mind-numbingly fast riffs. What's left is polished—and disappointingly straightforward—heavy metal. Metallica's attempts at expanding their sonic palette have made them seem more conventional than they ever have before. They add in Southern boogie rock, country-rock, and power ballads to their bag of tricks, which make them sound like '70s arena rock holdovers. Metallica's idea of opening up their sound is to concentrate on relentless mid-tempo boogie—over half the album is dedicated to songs that are meant to groove, but they simply don't swing. Metallica sounds tight, but with the material they've written, they should sound loose. That becomes apparent as the songs drag out over the album's nearly 80-minute running time—there are only so many times that a band can work the same tempo *exactly the same way* before it becomes tedious. It isn't surprising to hear Metallica get stodgier and more conservative as they get older, but it is nonetheless depressing. *—Stephen Thomas Erlewine*

Re-Load / Nov. 18, 1997 / Elektra ✦✦✦
Metallica recorded so much material for *Load*—their first album in five years—that they had to leave many songs unfinished, otherwise they would have missed their deadline. During the supporting tour for *Load*, they continued to work on the unfinished material, as well as write new songs, and they soon had enough material for a new album, *Re-Load*. The title suggests that *Re-Load* simply is a retread of its predecessor, and in many ways that's correct—there's still too much bone-headed, heavy southern rock for it to be anything other than the sequel to *Load*—but there's enough left curves to make it a better record. Marianne Faithfull's backing vocals on "The Memory Remains" complements the weird, uneasy melody and "Where the Wild Things Are" has a eerie menace that Metallica never achieved on *Load*. There are also a couple of ballads and country-rockers that don't work quite so well (it's never a good idea to have an explicit sequel, as on "The Unforgiven II"), and that, along with a few plodding Metallica-by-numbers, is what keeps *Re-Load* from being a full success. Still, the towering closer "Fixxxer," along with handful of cuts that successfully push the outer edges of Metallica's sound, make the record worthwhile. *—Stephen Thomas Erlewine*

Garage Inc. / Nov. 24, 1998 / Elektra ✦✦✦✦
For many years, Metallica's 1987 EP *Garage Days Re-Revisited* was the most sought-after item in their catalog; it was constantly bootlegged in the '90s, and often supplemented by a host of covers Metallica had released on singles and compilations throughout the years. By 1998, the band had understandably grown frustrated with this situation and decided to confront the problem head-on by reissuing all these rarities. Savvy businessmen that they are, they also realized they needed to give hardcore fans who already owned all the covers a reason to purchase the new set—hence, the expansion of the *Garage Days* EP to the double-disc blowout *Garage Inc*. The second disc's rarities are balanced by the first disc's new covers, the bulk of which were recorded following the *Re-Load* tour. It shouldn't come as a surprise that these covers recall the blaze'n'boogie heavy rock of the *Loads*, but what is a surprise is that Metallica seems to have found their footing in this style through other people's songs. Whether it's Bob Seger, Blue Öyster Cult, Thin Lizzy, Nick Cave, or the all-star jam on Lynyrd Skynyrd's "Tuesday's Gone," the band effortlessly makes the songs seem like their own, through a bizarre mix of respect and ballsy irreverence. Sure, it may not be nearly as raw as early Metallica, but it is a better listen than either of the *Load* records. And if raw is what you want, the equally diverse disc two provides all the thrills you could hope for. At one time, it might have seemed a little odd that Metallica would cover Budgie, Diamond Head, the Misfits, and Queen, but if *Garage Inc.* proves anything, it's that the group's musical instincts, risks, and sense of humor have made them the greatest metal band of the '80s and '90s. *—Stephen Thomas Erlewine*

S&M / Nov. 23, 1999 / Elektra ✦✦✦
After 1988's *…And Justice for All*, Metallica pared down its progressive, heavy metal sound. During the '90s, the band's studio releases grew slicker and more produced, resulting in mostly radio-friendly, good ol' boy metal. By the end of the decade, Metallica was established as the pioneer of modern metal, but the band hadn't done anything innovative, arguably, in ten years. In April 1999, the group performed two concerts with the San Francisco Symphony, and the result was *S&M*, a two-disc collection of the concerts. Overall, the album successfully pairs violin strings with guitar strings, but it's no surprise that the best tracks here are the older songs; their multi-layered, compositional style works well with symphonic arrangements. "Master of Puppets," "Call of the Ktulu," "One," and "For Whom the Bell Tolls" sound richer and fuller with violin, trumpet, clarinet, harp, trombone, and flute accompaniments, but "Sad but True," "Devil's Dance," and especially "Of Wolf and Man" range from haphazard and melodramatic to uninspired. *S&M* definitely has its moments, and not just with the pre-*Black Album* material: "Fuel" surpasses the furious pumping energy of the studio version, "Hero of the Day" stays poignant throughout, and "Until It Sleeps" has a wonderfully sinister feel. James Hetfield maintains his madman persona from beginning to end, laughing maniacally and grunting and growling at all the right moments. Overall, the symphony adds a macabre, ghoulish atmosphere—it all sounds like a Broadway freak show or a revved-up Danny Elfman nightmare. Which is exactly what a Metallica album should sound like, even if every song isn't the best (or most appropriate) in the band's catalog. *—Gina Boldman*

The Meters

f. 1966, New Orleans, LA, **db.** 1977
New Orleans R&B, R&B, Funk, Soul
The Meters defined New Orleans funk, not only on their own recordings, but also as the backing band for numerous artists, including many produced by Allen Toussaint. Where the funk of Sly Stone and James Brown was wild, careening, and determinedly urban, the Meters were down-home and earthy. Nearly all of their own recordings were instrumentals, putting the emphasis on the organic and complex rhythms. The syncopated, layered percussion intertwined with the gritty grooves of the guitar and organ, creating a distinctive sound that earned a small, devoted cult during the '70s, including musicians like Paul McCartney and Robert Palmer, both of whom used the group as a backing band for recording. Despite their reputation as an extraordinary live band, the Meters never broke into the mainstream, but their sound provided the basis for much of the funk and hip-hop of the '80s and '90s. *—Stephen Thomas Erlewine*

The Meters / 1969 / Sundazed ✦✦✦
This seminal New Orleans funk group's debut album features the semi-hit "Cissy Strut" and its follow-up, "Sophisticated Sissy." This 1999 reissue also offers two previously unreleased bonus tracks, "The Look of Love" and "Soul Machine." Other highlights include "Here Comes the Meter Man," "Live Wire," and "Sehorn's Farm." *—Cub Koda*

Struttin' / 1970 / Sundazed ✦✦✦
As the third full-length album released by the Meters, *Struttin'* may not appear to be drastically different than its predecessors, at least not on the surface. After all, the title of the lead single "Chicken Strut" intentionally recalls their previous biggest "Cissy Strut," and it has the same basic Meters groove. And if the essential sound remains unchanged, that's because that organic, earthy funk is the Meters' signature. Other groups have tried to replicate it, but nobody ever played it better. Because of that, *Struttin* is an enjoyable record, even if it never quite feels like anything more focused than a series of jam sessions; after all, that's what it was. This time around, however, the Meters did make a conscious decision to emphasize vocals, and not just with shout-alongs on the chorus ("Chicken Strut," "Same Old Thing"), but with Art Neville's leads on covers of Ty Hunter's soulful uptown shuffle "Darling, Darling, Darling," Jimmy Webb's groovy ballad "Wichita Lineman," and Lee Dorsey's "Ride Your Pony" (the Meters provided support on the original recording). This gives the album a bit more diversity than its predecessors, which is welcome, even for devotees of the group's admittedly addictive sound. But the real difference is how the band seems willing to expand their signature sound. "Hand Clapping Song" is a spare, syncopated breakdown without an obvious through-line, while "Joog" turns the group's groove inside out. These variations are entertaining—as entertaining as the vocals—and the songs that are solidly in the Meters tradition are also fun. The results are pretty terrific, though given the fact that *Struttin'* never really pulls itself into a coherent album, it may be the kind of first-rate record only aficionados of the band will need to seek out. *—Stephen Thomas Erlewine*

Look-Ka Py Py / Jan. 1970 / Sundazed ✦✦✦✦
The second album by Art Neville's band continues the sound that made them New Orleans legends. In addition to the title track, there's plenty of funk aboard in songs like like "Pungee," "9 'Til 5," "Rigor Mortis," "Funky Miracle," and "Yeah, You're Right." This 1999 reissue also features two previously unreleased bonus tracks, "Grass" and "Borro." *—Cub Koda*

Cabbage Alley / 1972 / Sundazed ✦✦✦✦
Leaving Josie for Reprise did change the Meters, even if the change wasn't necessarily for the better. They became slicker, jammier, and, in the conventional sense, funkier, even if the grit seemed to start to dissipate. So, even if this is just the Meters' fourth album, *Cabbage Alley* does mark a sea-change in their outlook, bringing them fully into the '70s and finding them sacrificing feel for texture, even if that's a very subtle transition. Part of the problem is that the group doesn't really have any good songs to hang their sounds onto,

but, if you're looking just for sounds and groove, *Cabbage Alley* doesn't disappoint. The Meters' overall feel might have gotten a little softer than necessary, but they still are a remarkably sympathetic, supple group and it's a pleasure to hear them play. Still, there's not much here outside of hearing them play, and while that's pretty great, it's hard not to wish that there were songs, even when they delve into smooth soul like "Birds" or when the group simply jams on mid-tempo grooves, that stood out from the pack. [Sundazed's 2000 reissue contains two bonus tracks—both parts of "Chug Chug Chug-A-Lug (Push and Shove)."] —*Stephen Thomas Erlewine*

Cissy Strut / 1974 / Island ✦✦✦✦✦
The Meters made their anthemic funk cuts on Josie in the late '60s. The New Orleans crew backed Fats Domino, Lee Dorsey, and Aaron Neville before they started jamming on their own in the late '60s. Island issued this anthology of Josie material in the mid-'70s. It came out in the U.S. too. Rounder has since reissued some of this material. —*Ron Wynn*

Rejuvenation / 1974 / Sundazed ✦✦✦✦✦
The title is a tip-off, as is the garish, blaxploitation-chic photo on the cover—*Rejuvenation*, the Meters' second album for Reprise, should be seen as a bit of a new beginning for the quintessential New Orleans funk group. It's not a clean beginning, since they were pointing in this direction on *Cabbage Alley*, but this is where their glistening, clear production, crisp performances, rock influences, and hard-edged funk coalesce into a sound distinct from their Josie recordings—not better, just different. As such, this is the definitive Reprise album from the Meters, not just because the material is stronger (which admittedly is true), but because the performances are continually inspired and the production is professional but hits at a gut level, resulting in a first-class funk album. [Sundazed's 2000 reissue contains the single versions of "People Say" and "Hey Pocky-A-Way" as bonus tracks.] —*Stephen Thomas Erlewine*

Fire on the Bayou / 1975 / Sundazed ✦✦✦✦✦
The Meters' third album for Reprise, *Fire on the Bayou*, is their best record for the label for a variety of reasons, not least of which is the high quality of material throughout the record and a focus from the band that keeps the music simmering, even if it never quite reaches a boil. That's not a bad thing, because the music IS simmering, always hot and enticing, never lukewarm or too cool. There's not anything that comes out and grabs your throat, the way that "Hey Pocky Way" does, but there never seems to be a concession to mainstream funk, the way *Cabbage Alley* or *Rejuvenation* seemed to be. This just keeps things rolling, nice and smooth. There's not anything that separates itself from its partners—something that's unfortunately true of all of the Reprise albums—but the overall feel is better than the Meters' other Reprise albums, since it has more grit and presence than its compatriots. [Sundazed's 2000 reissue contains one bonus track, a "long version" of "Running Fast."] —*Stephen Thomas Erlewine*

The Best of the Meters / 1975 / Virgo ✦✦✦
A good collection of this quintessential New Orleans funk group's best '70s singles for the Reprise label. Of course they did their finest cuts for Josie, but turned in some reasonably good work on Reprise in a more rock/funk direction. "Hey, Pokey-A-Way" was probably the closest Reprise cut to matching the superb Josie singles. But these are the songs that got them gigs with the Rolling Stones and work with Paul McCartney and Robert Palmer, so they did have some value. —*Ron Wynn*

Trick Bag / 1976 / Sundazed ✦✦

New Directions / 1977 / Sundazed ✦✦✦

Uptown Rulers: The Meters Live on the Queen Mary / 1992 / Rhino ✦✦✦✦✦
At long last, a live Meters album. In the studio, they were raw but precise. Live, things get a little more raggedy and a lot more energetic. New Orleans chestnuts (some of them Meters originals—"Fire on the Bayou," "Africa,"—and some not—"Rockin' Pneumonia," "I Know," etc.) predominate, but some unforgivable dreck worms its way in, too ("Love the One You're With," "Make It With You"). None of which matters: if you're a fool for a Meters groove, you'll want this, and you won't even notice the tunes—it's what they do with them that counts. It was recorded live on the Queen Mary in 1975 at a party hosted by Paul and Linda McCartney (the same party that Professor Longhair's *Live on the Queen Mary* album came from). —*Roundup Newsletter*

☆ **Funkify Your Life** / Feb. 28, 1995 / Rhino ✦✦✦✦✦
Two discs of the Meters is a lot to ask of most casual fans, yet for the devoted few, *Funkify Your Life* is essential. Featuring tracks from both their Josie and Warner years, the double-disc set captures some of the rawest New Orleans funk recorded in the Crescent City. —*Stephen Thomas Erlewine*

★ **The Very Best of the Meters** / Jun. 10, 1997 / Rhino ✦✦✦✦✦
In keeping with the drift of Rhino's *Very Best of* volumes, this 16-track disc provides a more concise, budget-minded retrospective for listeners who might not want a set that offers twice as much or more (in this case, Rhino's own two-disc *Funkify Your Life* anthology). That's not necessarily a criticism—funk grooves can get tiring over the course of two hours if you're not a rhythm fiend. Should you want to keep your Meters to the one-sitting level, this smartly chosen, well-annotated set is fine, including all of the cuts ("Cissy Strut," "Sophisticated Cissy," "Look-Ka Py Py," "Hey Pocky A-Way," "Fire on the Bayou") you'd expect to find on a greatest-hits set. —*Richie Unterberger*

Kickback / Feb. 2001 / Sundazed ✦✦✦
Not for one minute will you mistake this collection of unreleased recordings as a proper album. It isn't just the preponderance of covers, it's the subtle shifts in production and tone, lending a general unevenness to this record, even if it's culled just from 1975 and 1976 (meaning they're leftovers from *Fire on the Bayou* and *Trick Bag*). That doesn't mean it's a bad listen by any stretch, since even if *Kickback* is second-rate and leftover Meters, they're still an incredibly supple, engaging band that can take such bad choice of material like Neil Young's "Down by the River" and turn it into something listenable. Such cover choices as that, the Beatles' "Come Together," and Stephen Stills' "Love the One You're With" all sound intriguing, particularly to the record geek that's this album's core audience, but apart from the latter (and a fine, surprisingly hard-rocking alternate version of "Honky Tonk Women"), these kind of choices play better in theory than in actuality. The rest of the record may not have as distinctive a calling card, but they're better, finding the band laying back and doing what they do best, which is laying down a solid, irresistible groove. No, there's not much here that's essential, but it's fine second-tier stuff that will satisfy the dedicated. And, truth be told, second-tier Meters still sounds pretty good to the unconverted, too. —*Stephen Thomas Erlewine*

Method Man (Clifford Smith)

b. Apr. 2, 1971, Alexandria, VA

Vocals / Hardcore Rap, East Coast Rap, Hip-Hop

Born Clifford Smith on Staten Island, Method Man and his mush-mouthed rapping style electrified the 1993 debut album by the hip-hop collective Wu-Tang Clan. The incredibly dark, raw sound of *Enter the Wu-Tang (36 Chambers)* influenced many rappers, and the album eventually reached gold status. As part of the Wu-Tang Clan's contract, each member had the authority to sign separate solo contracts, so Method Man moved to Def Jam for his solo debut *Tical*. The single "Bring the Pain" just missed the Top 40 in 1994, but the following year "I'll Be There for You/You're All I Need to Get By" (his duet with Mary J. Blige) reached number three in the charts. His second duet, "How High" featuring Redman, hit the Top 15 in August 1995. A single with Wu-Tang mates Raekwon and Ghost Face Killer breached the Top 40 later that year. *Tical 2: Judgment Day* followed in 1998, and a year later Method Man resurfaced with *Blackout!*, his long-awaited collaboration with Redman. —*John Bush*

● **Tical** / 1994 / Def Jam ✦✦✦✦✦
As a quick follow-up to Wu-Tang Clan's debut album *Enter the Wu-Tang*, Method Man's solo debut confirms the rapper's status as the group's undeniable superstar. Never short on charisma, Method Man accentuates his lucid lyrical flow with ample personality on *Tical*; on each song, you listen attentively, forever engaged with the rapper's witty rhymes. Furthermore, RZA shines as a producer here, proving not only that *Enter the Wu-Tang* wasn't a novelty record but also that he can shape his beats and soundscapes to each member's personality. In the case of Method Man, RZA chooses to craft short, up-tempo tracks driven by aggressive beats, particularly on raging songs such as "Bring the Pain" and "Release Yo' Delf." Furthermore, besides these rambunctious moments, the album's other noteworthy moment comes on "All I Need," a similarly thunderous song that uncannily functions as a love ballad, delivered with plenty of wit. Yet Method Man's superstar antics, his one-man showmanship, and RZA's accompanying beats also prevent this album from being as well-crafted as successive Wu-Tang solo albums such as Raekwon's *Only Built 4 Cuban Linx*, the Genius' *Liquid Swords*, and Ghostface Killah's *Ironman*. Where those albums find RZA stepping into the spotlight with highly cinematic production and also find a greater abundance of Wu-Tang guest appearances, resulting in conceptual albums, *Tical* comes off sounding like a collection of radio-aimed singles. Still, even if this album isn't as all-around poetic as the other aforementioned early Wu-Tang solo albums, Method Man is still the group's best MC, and *Tical* succinctly summarizes why. Furthermore, the album's consistent production style makes it a more accessible listen than succeeding albums such as *Tical 2000: Judgement Day*. —*Jason Birchmeier*

Tical 2000: Judgement Day / Nov. 10, 1998 / Def Jam ✦✦✦✦
After attaining superstar status with the short, simple, and to-the-point accessibility of *Tical* (and heavily aided by RZA's rousing production), Method Man took a drastically different approach with *Tical 2000: Judgement Day*, making an epic album full of twisting story lines, countless guest stars, and a revolving roster of producers. So looking at the quite opposite approach Method Man chose for his sophomore album, it's a bit difficult to comparatively rate the two since they have so little in common. On the one hand, where *Tical* suffered a bit with its one-sidedness, *Tical 2000* manages to bring an exceeding amount of variety: an abundance of skits, numerous non-Wu-Tang guest rappers, and a revolving ensemble of producers. Yet on the other hand, where *Tical* was driven by effective consistency, *Tical 2000* is weighed down and ultimately diluted by its far-reaching scope. And the latter of these two views seems the more important attribute to note with this particular album. In his aim to improve upon *Tical*'s few minor weaknesses, Method Man simply went too far; there are just way too many skits here and too many guest appearances to make this a beginning to end, satisfying listen—with variety comes inconsistency. So even if tracks such as the album-concluding "Judgment Day" are magnificent, it's often a chore to get there without skipping tracks. —*Jason Birchmeier*

Blackout! / Sep. 28, 1999 / Def Jam ✦✦✦✦
Hip-hop fans have known for years that Method Man and Redman are two of the top MCs in the field, and their tour together not only proved the fact, but also showed they rap incredibly well together. Their deliveries are similar and the flow never falters, but the hint of gravel in Meth's voice makes them easily distinguishable. Now, with *Blackout!*, the duo's first album together (though both guested on each other's 1998 LPs), listeners have the proof on wax. Skating on top of spare, hard-hitting productions by Erick Sermon, Wu-Tang's RZA, Mathematics, and Redman himself—under his Reggie Noble alias—Meth and Redman trade off on hardcore rhymes and freestyle over each other. There's barely room for breath, but the rhymes are tight and inventive throughout. There are only two guest appearances (for Ja Rule & L.L. Cool J on "4 Seasons" and Ghostface and Street on the hilarious *Blair Witch Project* send-off "Run 4 Cover"), and the focus on just Meth and Redman makes for an even tighter, more combustible LP. Even with the high expectations

that come along with a project of this magnitude *Blackout!* rarely disappoints. *—John Bush*

MFSB

f. 1971, Philadelphia, PA, **db.** 1981

Philly Soul, Instrumental Rock, Soul

This instrumental ensemble punctuated many hits produced by the duo of Kenny Gamble and Leon Huff in the '70s. They were a blend of string, horn, and rhythm players. The roster included bassist Larry Moore; keyboardist Lenny Pakula; guitarists Norman Harris, James Herb Smith, and Roland Chambers; drummer Earl Young; and percussionists/drummers Miguel Fuentes and Quinton Joseph. Gamble, Huff, Don Renaldo, Dexter Wansel, and Vince Montana all took turns conducting the orchestra. While backing the O'Jays, Harold Melvin & the Blue Notes, the Intruders, and many others, MFSB also cut several LPs as performers from 1973 through 1980. "TSOP (The Sound of Philadelphia)," with the Three Degrees, was *Soul Train's* theme song in 1974 and also topped the R&B and pop charts. They earned another hit in 1975 with "T.L.C. (Tender Lovin' Care)," which made it to Number Two. The title track of their final LP, "Mysteries of the World," was a big hit in England in 1980. They also did sessions with Melba Moore, the Stylistics, Spinners, and others outside the Philadelphia International umbrella. *—Ron Wynn*

● **The Best of MFSB: Love Is the Message** / Oct. 31, 1995 / Epic Associated/Legacy ♦♦♦♦♦

The Best of MFSB: Love Is the Message is a comprehensive 16-track collection that features all of MFSB's big hits—"TSOP (The Sound of Philadelphia)," "Love is the Message," "Sexy"—plus a selection of highlights from the group's records, thereby resulting in a nearly definitive overview of the Philly soul/disco group's career. *—Stephen Thomas Erlewine*

Deep Grooves / Apr. 6, 1999 / Epic Associated/Legacy ♦♦♦♦

While the previous *The Best of MFSB: Love Is the Message* remains the best introduction to the genre-defining sound of the Philadelphia International label's ace house band, the aptly titled *Deep Grooves* is even more of a funk primer, plunging further into the thick, bad-ass soul aesthetic that distinguished its era. Always a study in contrasts—impeccably tight yet possessed of a loose-cannon edge, elegant and sophisticated yet down-and-dirty—MFSB's music remains electrifying, boasting a timelessness that has eluded the work of many of their contemporaries; their instrumental renditions of classics like "Back Stabbers," "Family Affair," and "Freddie's Dead" expand on the funk potential of the originals, pushing the groove to cavernous new extremes. *—Jason Ankeny*

George Michael

b. Jun. 25, 1963, Bushey, England

Vocals, Guitar / Pop/Rock, Adult Contemporary, Urban, Dance-Pop

Yorgos Kyriatou Panayioutou (George Michael) achieved fame in the duo Wham! in his native U.K. in 1982. Through 1986, he and his partner, Andrew Ridgeley, scored hit after hit in a variety of styles from rap to up-tempo pop to slow ballads. As songwriter and lead singer, Michael gradually overshadowed the group, and by the time they split, he was ready for a massively successful solo career. This began with the 1987 album *Faith*, which featured a series of chart-topping hit singles and sold more than seven million copies. That Michael had not achieved a similar critical success was evident from the title of his follow-up album, *Listen Without Prejudice—Vol. 1*, which, though it sold a million copies, included two Top Ten hits, and hit number two, must be considered a major commercial disappointment. After the failure of *Listen Without Prejudice*, Michael engaged in a bitter legal battle with his record company, eventually buying his way out his Columbia contract and signing with Dreamworks. In 1996, he released *Older*, its sales clearly hampered by his long hiatus away from performing. In 1998, Michael made tabloid headlines when he was arrested for lewd conduct in a men's public restroom at a park near his Beverly Hills home; following the incident, he appeared on CNN and publicly revealed his homosexuality. *—William Ruhlmann*

★ **Faith** / 1987 / Columbia ♦♦♦♦♦

A superbly crafted mainstream pop/rock masterpiece, *Faith* made George Michael an international solo star, selling over ten million copies in the U.S. alone as of 2000. Perhaps even more impressively, it also made him the first white solo artist to hit number one on the R&B album charts. Michael had already proven the soulful power of his pipes by singing a duet with Aretha Franklin on the 1987 smash "I Knew You Were Waiting (For Me)," but he went even farther when it came to crafting his own material, using sophisticated '70s soul as an indispensable part of his foundation. Of course, it's only a part. *Faith's* ingenuity lies in the way it straddles pop, adult contemporary, R&B, and dance music as though there were no distinctions between them. In addition to his basic repertoire of funky dance-pop and airy, shimmering ballads, Michael appropriates the Bo Diddley beat for the rockabilly-tinged title track, and proves himself a better-than-decent torch singer on the cocktail jazz of "Kissing a Fool." Michael arranged and produced the album himself, and the familiarity of many of these songs can obscure his skills in those departments—close listening reveals his knack for shifting elements in and out of the mix and adding subtle embellishments when a little emphasis or variety is needed. Though *Faith* couldn't completely shake Michael's bubblegum image in some quarters, the album's themes were decidedly adult. "I Want Your Sex" was the most notorious example, of course, but even the love songs were strikingly personal and mature, grappling with complex adult desires and scarred by past heartbreak. All of it adds up to one of the finest pop albums of the '80s, setting a high-water mark that Michael has only been able to reach in isolated moments since. *—Steve Huey*

Listen Without Prejudice, Vol. 1 / Aug. 1990 / Columbia ♦♦♦♦

Michael's follow-up to the massive success of *Faith* found him turning inward, trying to gain critical acclaim as well as sales. *Listen Without Prejudice* is not an entirely successful effort; Michael has cut back on the effortless hooks and melodies that crammed not only *Faith* but also his singles with Wham!, and his socially conscious lyrics tend to be heavy-handed. But the highlights—the light, Beatlesque harmonies of "Heal the Pain," and the plodding number one "Praying for Time," "Waiting for That Day," and the Top Ten "Freedom '90"—make a case for his talents as a pop craftsman. *—Stephen Thomas Erlewine*

Older / Apr. 1996 / DreamWorks ♦♦♦

Older is the album that many observers initially believed *Listen Without Prejudice, Vol. 1* to be—a relentlessly serious affair, George Michael's bid for artistic credibility. It's an album that makes *Listen Without Prejudice* sound like *Faith*. Michael has dispensed with the catchy, frothy dance-pop numbers that brought him fame, concentrating on stately, pretentious ballads—even "Fastlove," the album's one dance track, lacks the carefree spark of his earlier work. Although Michael's skills as a pop craftsman still shine through—several songs are well-constructed ballads that rank with his best material—his earnestness sinks the album. It is one thing to be mature and another to be boring. Too often, Michael mistakes slight melodies for mature craftsmanship and *Older* never quite recovers. When melodies do pop up, he doesn't deliver them with enough force to make an impact, and the album slowly disappears as a result. *—Stephen Thomas Erlewine*

Ladies & Gentlemen: The Best of George Michael / Nov. 10, 1998 / Columbia ♦♦♦♦♦

When George Michael was riding high on the charts, only a handful of critics acknowledged that he was a brilliant mainstream pop singer/songwriter who, at his best, rivaled his idol Elton John in crafting state-of-the-art pop songs and productions. For nearly a full decade, he was a superstar in his native U.K. and the U.S., and even when *Older* failed to win an American audience, he retained his stranglehold on the British and European charts. As a solo male hitmaker, virtually nobody could touch him between 1984 and 1994, and even when his grasp began to slip, he still made compelling music. All of this is proven by his first hits compilation, *Ladies & Gentlemen: The Best of George Michael*. Spanning two discs, 28 songs, and two distinctive halves—one "For the Heart" (ballads), one "For the Feet" (dance tunes)—the collection is a monster, as impressive for its size as it is for its achievements. To some casual listeners, the sheer scope of the collection may seem overwhelming, since it doesn't just have the hits, but also rarities, compilation tracks, lesser-known singles, and duets. Of course, that's precisely what makes it worthwhile for anyone who owns all the albums. (They'll also be interested that many of the mixes sound slightly different—as if the masters were run through the antiquated "Q Sound" process that marred Madonna's similar *Immaculate Collection*.) And some skeptics may be swayed after listening to the individual discs, which are surprisingly consistent works that reveal forgotten gems, and thereby the true depth of his talent. It is true that listening to both discs in a row is a little exhausting, but there's little question that *Ladies & Gentlemen* comes close to being definitive. *—Stephen Thomas Erlewine*

Songs From the Last Century / Dec. 14, 1999 / Virgin ♦♦♦

Unlike many covers albums, *Songs From the Last Century* is a cohesive, enjoyable diversion. With the help of co-producer Phil Ramone, George Michael has crafted a warm, intimate album built around a small combo of piano, guitar, bass, and drums. Orchestras, big bands, harps, and, on one occasion, a rock band, augment the basic combo, yet the flourishes never change the essential, close-knit nature of the group. For the first time ever, Michael sounds relaxed. He's laying back, singing songs he loves, not worrying about chart success, and the end result is quite fetching, even if it isn't perfect. The main flaw with *Songs From the Last Century* is that it's so smooth, it's occasionally a little sleepy, a trait that's emphasized by Michael's fairly predictable taste in covers—"Brother Can You Spare a Dime," "My Baby Just Cares for Me," and "The First Time Ever I Saw Your Face," among others. Nevertheless, he does bring style and sophistication to these standards, even such often-covered yet still difficult tunes as "Wild As the Wind." When his selections are idiosyncratic—whether it's a jazzy reading of "Roxanne," the brassy "Secret Love," the little-remembered "I Remember You," or a revelatory reading of "Miss Sarajevo," a song commonly dismissed as a U2 side project—the album is delightful. Certainly, *Songs From the Last Century* isn't a major work; it's a way for Michael to decompress and have some fun, and the diehards that stuck with him through the turbulent '90s are likely to be charmed. *—Stephen Thomas Erlewine*

Lee Michaels

b. Nov. 24, 1945, Los Angeles, CA

Vocals, Keyboards, Piano, Bass / AM Pop, Psychedelic Pop, Blue-Eyed Soul, Pop/Rock, Psychedelic

One of the most interesting second-division California psychedelic musicians, keyboardist Lee Michaels was one of the most soulful white vocalists of the late '60s and early '70s. Between 1968 and 1972, he released half a dozen accomplished albums on A&M that encompassed baroque psychedelic pop and gritty white, sometimes gospelish R&B with equal facility. A capable songwriter, Michaels was blessed with an astonishing upper range, occasionally letting loose some thrilling funky wails. In 1971, he landed a surprise Top Ten single with "Do You Know What I Mean," one of the best and funkiest AM hits of the early '70s. Michaels was unusual for a San Francisco act in that he relied mostly on an organ-based sound, especially after the first pair of albums, when for a time he played, live and in the studio, with the mammoth drummer "Frosty" as his only accompanist. His albums in the mid-'70s for Columbia, however, were both critical and commercial disappointments. *—Richie Unterberger*

Carnival of Life / 1968 / One Way ♦♦♦

Lee Michaels, a veteran of the Los Angeles and San Francisco bar-band scene in the mid-'60s, struck out on his own in 1967 after fronting bands with such illustrious alumni as Joel Scott Hill, Bob Mosley, and John Barbata. Michaels' music was characterized by his soulful vocals and equally soulful organ playing. These awesome talents would be polished on his second and third albums, but his debut, while interesting, falls a bit short. The main problem is that A&M saw Michaels as sort of a psychedelic singer/songwriter/rocker. In reality, he was sort of a California version of Steve Winwood. *Carnival of Life* has some excellent performances by Michaels and especially drummer Eddie Hoh. Both rock hard on the album's nine cuts, but the material is a bit dated and tends to end up in some hard-rock clichés of the period. Still, it's a promising if quirky start of what would be a fine career. *—Matthew Greenwald*

Recital / 1968 / One Way ♦♦♦

After a somewhat uneven debut album, Lee Michaels found his footing on this record. Michaels, a keen student of R&B as well as classical music, was obviously able to wrangle a bit more artistic control at A&M, and it shows. Overdubs of piano, harpsichord, and organ by Michaels created a wonderful sonic depth, and along with John Barbata's solid drumming, the result is staggering. Michaels was not exactly a singer/songwriter, but on this record, songs such as "Blind" and "Fell in Love Today" find a real voice for his R&B leanings. The record also contains the fabulous single "If I Lose You," which should have been a Top 40 hit. In the end, *Recital* is a very funky pop album that was ahead of its time. *—Matthew Greenwald*

Lee Michaels / 1969 / One Way ♦♦♦♦♦

One of the masterpieces of the period, *Lee Michaels* was essentially recorded live in the studio by only Michaels (organ/bass pedals) and Frosty on drums. It's a fabulous performance and one of the finest R&B/rock sets of the period. The first side is comprised of a medley of soulful workouts that come out sounding not unlike Led Zeppelin. Here, Michaels pulls out all the stops (literally) and showcases the organ as a bona fide rock instrument. Despite the lengthy drum solo, it's one of the finest sides of Los Angeles rock & roll. Michaels also reprises "My Friends,"a song from his first album, to great effect. *Lee Michaels* is also home to the good-time, pro-drug anthem "Highty Hi," as well as an awesome cover of "Stormy Monday." A true party platter. *—Matthew Greenwald*

Fifth / 1971 / One Way ♦♦♦

Following the success of his third album, Lee Michaels continued the path of a solo artist—solo meaning that most of the sounds on the record were primarily recorded by Lee alone. Organ (Hammond and pipe), piano, harpsichord, and organ bass create a heavy, dense foundation. Michaels had a unique sound, and along with his larynx-shredding vocals, the results are staggering. Aided by Joel Larson on drums, Michaels does a lot of covers on this record—including "Willie and the Hand Jive," "Ya Ya," and "Can I Get a Witness." Michaels renders them all in an infectious, gospel style. There are only a few originals on the album, and one, "Do You Know What I Mean" (which really *sounded* like a cover), was a monstrous hit and cemented Lee Michaels as one of the best white blues performers of the period, along with Joe Cocker and Steve Winwood. *—Matthew Greenwald*

• **The Collection** / Jul. 14, 1992 / Rhino ♦♦♦♦♦

Good 18-track overview of his A&M work, drawing from all six of the albums he released between 1968 and 1972. Includes "Do You Know What I Mean," "Stormy Monday," "Heighty Hi," "Hello," "The War," and "Carnival of Life," as well as the 1969 non-LP B-side "Goodbye, Goodbye," and his only Top 40 single besides "Do You Know What I Mean," a cover of "Can I Get a Witness." *—Richie Unterberger*

Best of Lee Michaels / Aug. 26, 1997 / One Way ♦♦♦

Mickey & Sylvia

f. 1956, **db.** 1965

Rock & Roll, R&B

Although this duo is primarily remembered as a one-hit act—for "Love Is Strange," which reached number 11 in 1957—they actually recorded quite a few exciting hybrids of R&B and rock & roll in the mid- and late '50s. Playing on countless '50s sessions for various labels (especially Atlantic and OKeh), Mickey Baker was one of the greatest guitar players of early rock & roll. With his partner (and former guitar student) Sylvia Robinson, he got to stretch out a bit from his usual role, with some trailblazing, piercing, lean, and bluesy leads. Vocally, Mickey & Sylvia had an engagingly playful, occasionally sly and sassy repartee that makes up in charm what it might lack in smoke and firepower. Their recordings were inconsistent, but at their best they offered a fetching blend of blues, Bo Diddley, calypso, and doo wop.

After "Love Is Strange," whose devastating licks inspired countless guitarists, the duo notched a couple more substantial R&B hits. But although they recorded as late as 1965, they never approached the Top 20 again. Mickey Baker recorded as a solo artist and enjoyed a fairly successful career as an expatriate sessionman in France. Sylvia Robinson unexpectedly re-emerged with the number three pre-disco hit "Pillow Talk" in 1973, and co-founded the pioneering rap label Sugar Hill in the late '70s. *—Richie Unterberger*

Love Is Strange / 1990 / Bear Family ♦♦♦

This two-CD, 60-song (!) set includes many alternate takes and a fair amount of previously unreleased material, spanning 1955 to 1964. A lot of the obscurities are in the close harmony, doo wop vein and are disappointingly short on verbal sparring and scorching Baker guitar. Lovingly packaged, but everyone except hardcore specialists should stick with the RCA compilation. *—Richie Unterberger*

• **"Love Is Strange" & Other Hits** / Mar. 1990 / RCA ♦♦♦♦♦

Unless you're a major R&B collector, it's likely you've never heard anything by this duo besides "Love Is Strange," their only major hit (and a great one). With 20 cuts from 1956-1960, this disc reissues the bulk of their most interesting work. "Love Is Strange" will remain their most memorable tune after you've heard this, but on the whole, this is way-above-average '50s R&B/rock. If you're hungering for more great solos like the ones in "Love Is Strange," you'll find some here, especially in "There Oughta Be a Law" and the instrumental "Shake It Up," although Baker's virtuosity doesn't dominate most of the songs. Some of these tunes are routine doo wop, but a little over half the material is pretty strong, ranging from the calypso-rock they're best remembered for to ballads to straight-ahead R&B shouters, with King Curtis on sax. *—Richie Unterberger*

The Willow Sessions / 1995 / Sequel ♦♦♦

Mickey & Sylvia are properly thought of as '50s rock & rollers, but they actually did a good deal of recording in the '60s, though without much notable commercial success. Most of this 19-track CD was recorded in the early '60s for their own label, Willow; only one song, "Baby You're So Fine," was a hit, making the R&B Top 30. The album doesn't have the fire of their best sides for RCA in the '50s, but it's not bad, usually purveying a groove similar to their early work, though tamer. Occasionally Mickey brandishes blues-rock chops to show that he can still cut deep with his axe, especially on "Darling (I Miss You So)" and the previously unissued instrumentals "Sylvia's Blues" and "Mickey's Blues." There are also a few curious (but fairly respectable) cuts dating from the late '60s that Sylvia recorded for the All Platinum label in a much more contemporary soul vein. *—Richie Unterberger*

• **Love Is Strange: A Golden Classics Edition** / Apr. 22, 1997 / Collectables ♦♦♦♦♦

Although the packaging and sound are a little below par, *Golden Classics Edition* contains 18 tracks from Mickey & Sylvia's prime period—not just "Love Is Strange," but a wealth of strong, lesser-known singles—making it a good overview of the underrated R&B duo. *—Stephen Thomas Erlewine*

Midnight Oil

f. 1975, Sydney, Australia

College Rock, Aussie Rock, Album Rock, Alternative Pop/Rock

Australia's Midnight Oil brought a new sense of political and social immediacy to pop music: not only did incendiary hits like "Beds Are Burning" and "Blue Sky Mine" bring global attention to the plight of, respectively, aboriginal settlers and impoverished workers, but the group also put its money where its mouth was—in addition to mounting benefit performances for groups like Greenpeace and Save the Whales, frontman Peter Garrett even ran for the Australian Senate on the Nuclear Disarmament Party ticket. Christened Midnight Oil just after Garrett joined in 1975, the group formed the label Powderworks to issue their self-titled debut—a taut, impassioned collection of guitar rock which quickly established the group's sound—in 1978. With their 1979 sophomore effort *Head Injuries*, the band scored their first hit single, "Cold Cold Change." Third album *Place Without a Postcard* achieved platinum status on the strength of the smash "Armistice Day," which won the group an American deal with Columbia Records. Their follow-up, 1983's *10, 9, 8, 7, 6, 5, 4, 3, 2, 1*, spent over two years in the Australian Top 40. The Australian aborigines' plight came to the fore on 1987's *Diesel and Dust*, the Oils' breakthrough record: sparked by the hit single "Beds Are Burning," the album reached the U.S. Top 20 and made the band a household commodity. *—Jason Ankeny*

Midnight Oil / 1978 / Columbia ♦♦♦

From early on, Midnight Oil earned their sound the way many great bands do—playing wherever and whenever they could, and their eponymous debut shows the influence of their days immersed in Sydney's pub rock scene. Though they hadn't quite hit on a signature sound, the raw, punkish energy of their guitar-driven debut is exciting, resulting in some excellent songs, especially the powerful opening track "Powderworks." But as great as the songs are, the attitude propelling them is equally important. Setting them apart from similar bands of this era was their spiking of hard rock (with its decidedly non-punk fetish for wailing guitar solos) with the amateurish zeal of punk, both leavened by an impressive yet subtle command of dynamics. Peter Garrett's voice bounces between a soaring falsetto and a strong, baritone bellow, Jim Moginie and Martin Rotsey trade licks (Moginie switches often between guitar and organ), while Andrew James and Rob Hirst anchor the proceedings. Because of this, the album shifts moods frequently, but the transitions don't sound awkward because the band is firmly in control. The brevity of the album's length enhances this feeling—from the roaring "Used and Abused" to the moody "Surfing With a Spoon" and from the rapid-fire "Run by Night" to the down-tempo prog rock of "Nothing Ventured, Nothing Gained," the album is a pretty short ride, but an interesting one for the fan already acquainted with *10, 9, 8, 7, 6, 5, 4, 3, 2, 1, Diesel and Dust, and Blue Sky Mining*, and is curious about the band's beginnings. *—James Haag*

Head Injuries / 1979 / Columbia ♦♦♦♦♦

Fortunately the same was not true on their second release, *Head Injuries* (great title). From start to finish this is a stoked and smokin' piece of punk-inspired hard rock with Garrett wailing away as though his life depended on it. Furious, relentless, chocked to the brim with solid songs and fierce playing, *Head Injuries* is hands-down the best of the Oil's early output. *—John Dougan*

Bird Noises / 1980 / Columbia ♦♦♦

On this four-song EP, Midnight Oil tried some musical variations after two albums of hard rock. "Let's rock," declared Peter Garrett at the outset of "No Time for Games" (a lament for the loss of childhood in the modern world), but the music in fact was restrained, and the group tried acoustic instruments and a moody instrumental, for an intriguing change-of-pace from their usual style. [Originally released in November 1980 in Australia on Powderworks Records, *Bird Noises* was released in 1990 in the U.S. on Columbia Records as Columbia 46136.] *—William Ruhlmann*

Place Without a Postcard / 1981 / Columbia ✦✦✦
Place Without a Postcard, produced by the usually reliable Glyn Johns, is so-so, but a real letdown after the intensity of *Head Injuries*. The songs are very good and at its best, it hints at the consistency that was to mark the rest of their recorded work, but it never coalesces into a whole. Even after repeated plays, *Place Without a Postcard* is too much of a mess to recommend unequivocally. *—John Dougan*

10, 9, 8, 7, 6, 5, 4, 3, 2, 1 / 1983 / Columbia ✦✦✦✦✦
Midnight Oil were already one of Australia's most popular bands when they made their American debut with *10, 9, 8, 7, 6, 5, 4, 3, 2, 1*, and while some knowledge of the intelligent but physical hard rock of the group's first three albums might have made it a bit easier for U.S. audiences to swallow, *10, 9, 8…* was a daunting first listen even for loyal fans. Blending an art rocker's sense of adventure and fondness for odd textures, a hard rocker's muscular force and love of power chords, and a peace punk's passion for an intelligent rant, Midnight Oil bore small resemblance to anyone on *10, 9, 8…*, running from the dreamy but ominous "Outside World" and "Maralinga" to the bone-crushing fury of "Only the Strong" and "Somebody's Trying to Tell Me Something" while making a number of stops in between. Nick Launay's deliberately eccentric production made the most of the band's dramatically oddball approach (dig that panning! check out that drum sound!), and for an album that so often goes for the purposeful left turn, it's remarkably listenable and catchy, offering up one passionate anthem after another. The band's politics are both well considered and unapologetically upfront throughout, which probably didn't help much with sales in the United States, where dance singles traditionally don't feature the chant "Better to die on your feet than to live on your knees," and questioning American foreign policy is uncommon on Top Ten albums (the album stayed on the Aussie charts for over two years, and "Power and the Passion" was a major success on the singles chart). As catchy as the Easybeats, as sweaty and hard-hitting as Rose Tattoo, and lots smarter than either, Midnight Oil were among the finest bands to emerge from Australia during the 1980s, and *10, 9, 8, 7, 6, 5, 4, 3, 2, 1* was their first undeniably great album and still ranks with their very best. *—Mark Deming*

Red Sails in the Sunset / 1984 / Columbia ✦✦✦✦✦
Midnight Oil's second international release found them ambitiously taking on a variety of lyrical causes in a variety of musical styles. Their basic approach, with its martial rhythms, chanted vocals, and guitar textures, served as a jumping-off place, but they always sounded more assured when they stuck to that, rather than trying other things. And the unrelentingly judgmental tone of the lyrics, sung with dead seriousness by Peter Garrett, tended to douse the album's potential enjoyment, too. It's hard to dance when you're being lectured to. It wasn't much of a surprise when Garrett decided to run for the Australian Senate shortly after this album's release. [Originally released on CBS Records Australia in 1984, *Red Sails in the Sunset* was released on Columbia Records in the U.S. in July 1985.] *—William Ruhlmann*

Species Deceases / 1985 / Columbia ✦✦✦
Midnight Oil marked the 40th anniversary of the dropping of the atomic bomb on Hiroshima by cutting this four-song EP of driving rock & roll songs on international political themes. "Some say it's progress, I say it's cruel," Peter Garrett sang in "Progress," a song that disparaged "third world infanticide" and "junk in the stratosphere." Environmentalism gave way to war protest on "Blossom and Blood," which referred specifically to Hiroshima. *Species Deceases* efficiently presented Midnight Oil's usual lyric concerns and musical style in miniature form, and at an EP price, it made a good short sampler of the group. [Originally released by CBS Records Australia in 1985, *Species Deceases* was released by Columbia Records in the U.S. in 1990.] *—William Ruhlmann*

● **Diesel and Dust** / Aug. 1987 / Columbia ✦✦✦✦✦
Midnight Oil frontman Peter Garrett has long been active in elective politics in Australia, and like any good politician, he knows that sometimes the most important thing is to get your message out to the masses, even it means speaking with a bit less force than might be your custom. While the hard edges and challenging angles of *10, 9, 8, 7, 6, 5, 4, 3, 2, 1* and *Red Sails in the Sunset* made *Midnight Oil* bona fide superstars in Australia, they were little more than a rumor in most of the rest of the world, and for their sixth album, *Diesel and Dust*, the band made some changes in their approach. On *Diesel and Dust*, there's less in the way of bruising hard rock like "Best of Both Worlds," nothing as eccentric as "Outside World," and very little as esoterically regional as "Jimmy Sharman's Boxers," while the production favors the tuneful side of the band's songwriting (which, truth to tell, was always there) and buffs away some of the band's harsher edges. As a result, *Diesel and Dust* isn't an album for hardcore Oils fans, but as a bid for a larger audience, it was both shrewd and well executed—it was the group's first real worldwide success, going platinum in America and spawning a massive hit single, "Beds Are Burning." *Diesel and Dust* is that rarity, a bid for the larger audience that's also an artistic success and a triumph for leftist politics—even the Clash never managed that hat trick this well. *—Mark Deming*

Blue Sky Mining / Feb. 1990 / Columbia ✦✦✦✦
Success hadn't changed Midnight Oil with its 1990 album *Blue Sky Mining*. The Australian band had finally broken through with its previous record, *Diesel and Dust*, but chart accomplishments didn't temper the group. *Blue Sky Mining* found lead singer Peter Garrett and the boys singing about familiar themes with their usual passion. The songs aren't quite on par with those from *Diesel and Dust*, but there's still enough here to make it a worthy follow-up. The lead track, "Blue Sky Mine," dealt with the oppression of the lower working class within the context of a mining company. The immediately catchy cut managed to find mid-chart success. Other notable tracks are the driving "Forgotten Years," which also managed a bit of airplay, and the menacing "Mountains of Burma." The band stumbles only once, on the clumsy love song "Shakers and Movers." *—Tom Demalon*

Scream in Blue Live / May 5, 1992 / Columbia ✦✦

Earth and Sun and Moon / Apr. 1993 / Columbia ✦✦✦✦✦
If *Earth and Sun and Moon* isn't Midnight Oil's best effort, it's certainly close. The band still sticks to themes that are close to its heart—the environment, native peoples, and other social causes—but rarely has it managed to fashion an albumful of songs that are as musically intoxicating as on this 1993 release. "My Country" is full of jangling guitars and keyboards; the punchy title track has an infectious singalong harmony; and "Bushfire" adds some mean wah-wah guitar. The Oils managed to score some radio play on AOR and modern rock stations with the bracing "Truganini," the dramatic, piano-tinged rocker "Drums of Heaven," and the grinding shuffle of "Outbreak of Love." A satisfying release for longtime fans and new converts alike. *—Tom Demalon*

Breathe / Oct. 15, 1996 / Columbia ✦✦✦
Breathe strips away some of the big, detailed production of *Earth and Sun and Moon*, replacing it with a more direct sound while keeping the anthemic melodicism of the group's more recent records intact. The result is an album that is less ambitious than its predecessor, yet also more forceful, and Midnight Oil sounds enlivened in this less constricted setting. *Breathe* may not have the overall impact of *Diesel and Dust* and *Earth and Sun and Moon*, but it remains one of the group's best latter-day records. *—Stephen Thomas Erlewine*

20,000 Watt R.S.L.: Greatest Hits / Nov. 4, 1997 / Columbia ✦✦✦
As Midnight Oil's first compilation, *20,000 Watt R.S.L.: Greatest Hits* isn't all it could have been. Most of the group's late '80s/early '90s hits are here—"Beds Are Burning," "The Dead Heart," "Dreamworld," "Blue Sky Mine," "Forgotten Years," "King of the Mountain," "Truganini"—and many highlights from the group's early albums ("Power and the Passion," "Koscluszko," "US Forces," "Best of Both Worlds," "Back on the Borderline," "Don't Wanna Be the One") are also present. However, the music is not sequenced chronologically—it flips between the two periods of the group's career with no rhyme or reason, adding two new tracks ("What Goes On," "White Skin Black Heart") from the group's forthcoming 1998 album, *Redneck Wonderland*. The result is a jumble that doesn't give a good sense of Midnight Oil's career, but provides enough of their highlights to make it worthwhile for casual fans. However, anyone wanting a true sense of the band's progression will have to wait for another compilation. *—Stephen Thomas Erlewine*

Redneck Wonderland / Nov. 3, 1998 / Columbia ✦✦✦
For this, its 12th full-length album, Midnight Oil re-hired producer Warne Livesey, who had worked with them on their biggest international successes, *Diesel and Dust* and *Blue Sky Mining*. He helped them to achieve a sound that was a virtual compendium of familiar late-'60s rock styles—Led Zeppelin on the title track, the Beatles on "Safety Chain Blues," the Who on "Blot," the Beach Boys on "Drop in the Ocean." At least, that was true musically; the vocals were sometimes so compressed they sounded like they were coming out of a bullhorn. Given the lyrics, that was appropriate, since the album was, as the band's press bio put it, "written and recorded in response to the rise of anti-Asia MP Pauline Hanson and her far-right One Nation Party." Outside of Australia, that could make the songs difficult to understand completely, although, for example, the environmentalist sense of "Concrete" and "Seeing Is Believing" were unmistakable, and the group's anger fueled its performances. Still, lines like "triumphalism gotta be a curse or even worse" probably sent more fans to the dictionary than the barricades. In Australia, the album went Top Ten, though it failed to chart in the U.S., which is less an indication of its local focus than of the group and/or its record company's diminished interest in the international market. *—William Ruhlmann*

The Real Thing / Jul. 17, 2000 / Columbia ✦✦✦✦
With Midnight Oil's live album (*Scream in Blue*) and their first "greatest-hits" collection (*20,000 Watt R.S.L.*), it might seem strange to learn of the band releasing yet another concert album of past favorites. However, there are a few important distinctions. First, *The Real Thing* has four new songs straight from the studio. Second, all these live songs are from the band's more subtle acoustic performances. And third, it is one of the most definitive collections the band has ever recorded. "The Dead Heart" sounds utterly magnificent, injecting restrained aboriginal majesty into one of the band's most over-played songs. However, "In the Valley" (taken from the band's *MTV Unplugged* show) is the most telling: Completely subverted into a piano-led solo instead of the original's searing peaks, Peter Garrett vocalizes the loss of the recent death of a loved one with such vulnerability it is nothing less than astonishing. So with this in mind, are the new studio tracks even worthwhile or just distractions? Well, both "Say Your Prayers" and "The Last of the Diggers" retain the renewed vitriol of albums like *Redneck Wonderland*, yet more with the natural tones of *Earth and Sun and Moon* this time around. One may feel that *The Real Thing* as a whole might lack the sheer onslaught of a more varied, "plugged" Midnight Oil, but even an embittered listener would have to admit that the band is first and foremost a live group. Because to showcase such strengths in this enormously rewarding collection of acoustic live selections is a welcome open door for a casual listener as well as a blowing kiss to longtime, loyal fans. *—Dean Carlson*

Mighty Baby

f. 1965, **db.** 1971

Psychedelic, Prog Rock/Art Rock

The British psychedelic band Mighty Baby grew out of the Action, the Liverpool-based R&B outfit signed to Parlophone by George Martin in 1965. Long considered one of Martin's best discoveries this side of the Beatles, the Action consisted of Reggie King (vocals), Alan King (guitar), Pete Watson (guitar), Mike Evans (bass), and Roger Powell (drums). After Watson left in 1967, he was succeeded by keyboardist Ian Whiteman and blues guitarist Martin Stone. This new lineup evolved beyond the R&B/soul sound that the original Action had played and into a top-flight experimental group, incorporating the kinds of long jams and folk/blues influences that the West Coast bands were starting to export around the world. Reggie King was gone by early 1968, and the remaining members went through a number of name changes. In 1968, they hooked up with the managers who represented Pink Floyd and T. Rex and cut a new series of demo recordings, featuring Whiteman (who wrote most of the songs) and Alan King on lead vocals. The president of the band's new record label, Head Records, for reasons best known to himself, chose "Mighty Baby" as the group's new name. The self-titled album that followed was a masterpiece of late psychedelic rock, with long, fluid guitar lines and radiant harmonies; still, *Mighty Baby* didn't sell very well, although the group continued to play live shows to enthusiastic audiences. Their record label folded in 1970, and the group eventually signed to the Blue Horizon label, where they released a respectable if not wholly successful second album, *A Jug of Love*. It was clear by then, however, that their moment had passed, both personally and professionally. Mighty Baby broke up in 1971, although several of the members periodically played together on various projects. *—Bruce Eder*

Egyptian Tomb / 1968 / Psycho ✦✦✦
Some collectors rate this group highly, but it's difficult to hear why on this album of fairly generic late-'60s British rock. Things pick up a bit on the final two cuts, "I'm From the Country" and "At a Point Between Fate and Destiny, " which have a tuneful, melancholy appeal largely absent from the other tracks. *—Richie Unterberger*

● **Mighty Baby** / 1969 / Head ✦✦✦✦✦
This hour-long CD is one of the best bodies of British psychedelia ever released. It contains the complete *Mighty Baby* album from Head Records, expanded to 13 tracks with the addition of five tracks cut by the Action during its 1967 transition period. The opening number, "Egyptian Tomb," sets the tone for the entire album—in terms of content, structure, and beat, it sounds like the early Allman Brothers, or maybe the Grateful Dead in one of their harder-rocking moments, jamming with Crosby, Stills, Nash & Young on an impromptu version of CSN's "Pre-Road Downs." The beauty of the original *Mighty Baby* album tracks is that they're psychedelia with a solid beat, none of that noodle-rock that drugged-up Brits usually engaged in. "A Friend You Know But Never See" might have passed muster on the Byrds' *Notorious Byrd Brothers* album. Other songs noodle around too much, but overall this is some of the most energetic psychedelia to come out of England, and anyone who enjoys psychedelic guitar will love Martin Stone's and Alan King's work on this album. The bonus tracks, all "lost" demos, are even better; highly rhythmic, driving rock (check out "Understanding Love") with lots of spacy guitar and tougher-than-normal flower-power introspective lyrics, with some gorgeous harmonies dressing it all up—a near perfect meld of garage rock and psychedelic sensibilities. *—Bruce Eder*

The Mighty Mighty Bosstones

f. 1985
Ska-Punk, Third Wave Ska Revival, Alternative Pop/Rock
A great deal of the groundwork for the mid- to late-'90s explosion of ska and ska-metal was laid by the Mighty Mighty Bosstones, who were one of the first bands to cross high-energy ska with hardcore punk and heavy metal and also helped shift its tone toward testosterone-filled party music. The Bosstones built up a devoted cult following throughout their career, but even in spite of their 1997 radio smash "The Impression That I Get," their level of commercial success has not yet matched that of more pop-oriented third-wave ska bands, like No Doubt and Sublime, who followed in their wake. After a few misstarts, the Bosstones recorded their debut album, *Devil's Night Out*, in 1989. The follow-up, 1992's *More Noise and Other Disturbances*, earned the group a major-label deal with Mercury for *Don't Know How to Party*. One year after 1994's *Question the Answers* (one of their finest efforts), the Mighty Mighty Bosstones appeared in the film *Clueless*, performing "Where'd You Go" and "Someday I Suppose," two of their most popular numbers. They also landed a main-stage slot on that summer's Lollapalooza tour. In 1997, thanks to the breakthrough of ska-pop bands like No Doubt and Sublime, *Let's Face It* became the band's biggest-selling album yet, buoyed by the modern-rock radio smash "The Impression That I Get." *Live From the Middle East* followed in 1998. *—Steve Huey*

Devils Night Out / 1990 / Taang! ✦✦✦✦
The Bosstones' debut is an energetic, skankin' party album fusing ska with punk and hard rock, with more of an emphasis on ska than the band would show on later records. The band shifts freely between styles, making *Devils Night Out* their most spirited, free-wheeling collection of ska-core. Highlights include the humorous "Hope I Never Lose My Wallet," "A Little Bit Ugly," and "The Bartender's Song." *—Steve Huey*

More Noise and Other Disturbances / 1992 / Taang! ✦✦✦
As the title indicates, the Bosstones' second album begins to downplay their ska influences in favor of punk and hard rock. The songwriting slipped a bit, a problem that would plague the band throughout its early career, when they concentrated more on touring than crafting records in the studio. Nevertheless, there are enough good moments here to make it worthwhile for fans of the group's party-hearty, so-called "plaid" sound. *—Steve Huey*

Where'd You Go? / 1992 / Taang! ✦✦✦
Never officially titled, this EP is also referred to as simply *Mighty Mighty Bosstones*. Two originals, including the title track, are present, as well as several punked-out hard rock covers—Aerosmith's "Sweet Emotion," Metallica's "Enter Sandman," and Van Halen's "Ain't Talkin' 'Bout Love." Logically, this one emphasizes the punk/metal components of the Bosstones' sound over their ska influence. *—Steve Huey*

Don't Know How to Party / Mar. 1993 / Mercury ✦✦✦

Ska-Core, The Devil & More / Mar. 8, 1994 / Mercury ✦✦✦
This mini-album contains the definitive version of the Bosstones' signature song, "Someday I Suppose," plus covers of early Bob Marley ("Simmer Down") and hardcore bands like Minor Threat, Angry Samoans, and SSD. Aside from the jazzy Marley cover and the well-crafted fusion of "Someday I Suppose," most of the songs—true to the title—essentially sound like thrashy hardcore with horn breaks. *—Steve Huey*

Question the Answers / Oct. 4, 1994 / Mercury ✦✦✦✦✦
A skanking return to form for the Bosstones, sporting probably the band's best songwriting since its debut album. Their ska, funk, punk, and metal influences blend together in seamless, exciting ways, using the horn section in unexpected places, and the melodies are undeniably strong. Highlights include "Pictures to Prove It," "Bronzing the Garbage," "Toxic Toast," and "Hell of a Hat." *—Steve Huey*

● **Let's Face It** / Mar. 11, 1997 / Mercury ✦✦✦✦✦
With No Doubt and Sublime having dominated the pop airwaves in 1996, it wasn't too much of a stretch for the Mighty Mighty Bosstones to hope for similar success, even if their sound was louder and heavier overall—after all, they had been arguably the best-known ska band in the American underground for some time and had laid much of the groundwork for the style's commercial success. So the Bosstones took their time with *Let's Face It*, crafting a catchy, solidly written record with accessible mainstream production courtesy of longtime collaborator Paul Q. Kolderie and Sean Slade. The results paid immediate dividends, with "The Impression That I Get" becoming a runaway smash on modern-rock radio and pushing the album into the Top 30 (it eventually went platinum). Some longtime fans complained that the band had toned down their manic metal tendencies too much in their push for mainstream acceptance, but really, *Let's Face It* simply draws more upon other influences the band had had all along. It's the Bosstones album most inspired by the British Two-Tone movement of the early '80s, when pop melodies and pleas for tolerance and equality were often as important as the grooves—and that's certainly the case here, as the band turns in probably their most substantive set of lyrics to date. There are a few punky hard rock numbers, too, and even if they don't quite have the hard-partying energy of past efforts in that vein, they are well-constructed songs that keep the album's momentum flowing. Even if the production is a tiny bit slick, and the playing time is rather short (a little over half an hour), it's still difficult to view *Let's Face It* as anything but a rousing success and easily one of the band's best albums. *—Steve Huey*

Pay Attention / May 2, 2000 / Island Def Jam ✦✦✦✦
The Mighty Mighty Bosstones' newfound willingness to take their time working out material paid off with *Let's Face It*, and thus, *Pay Attention* didn't appear until three years later. Even if ska's commercial momentum had slowed, the album was still worth the wait. Thanks to the band's tight quality control, the tunes here are catchy, but not quite as immediately poppy as much of *Let's Face It*—there's more punk and hard rock, with ska rhythms more integral to some tracks than others. The party anthems of yesteryear are pretty much gone, but in their place is a tone of reflective maturity; personal and social concerns are given an equal airing, and the band's sense of humor is still very much in evidence. Moreover, the Bosstones are still trying new musical approaches, as evidenced by the summery island feel of "She Just Happened" and the surprising Irish turn of "Riot on Broad Street." Other highlights include the alternately swinging and skanking opener "Let Me Be," the hard-rocking lead single "So Sad to Say," the bouncy sing-along "Where You Come From," the up-tempo "The Skeleton Song," and the poignant (yet not overly sentimental) album closer "The Day He Didn't Die." A few weaker numbers could have been trimmed without making the album seem short; also, a fairly large percentage of the songs would simply sound like catchy hard rock if the horn section was removed. Then again, it's not the first time the Bosstones have recorded material like that, and in the end, it's hard to see *Pay Attention* as anything less than the band's third high-quality album in a row. *—Steve Huey*

Mike + the Mechanics

f. 1985, **db.** 1995
Pop/Rock, Adult Contemporary
While Phil Collins was pursuing his solo career in 1985, Genesis bassist/guitarist Mike Rutherford formed the pop/rock band Mike + the Mechanics. Featuring Rutherford (bass), former Ace and Squeeze member Paul Carrack (vocals, keyboards), ex-Sad Cafe member Paul Young (vocals), keyboardist Adrian Lee, and drummer Peter Van Hooke, the group released their self-titled first album late in 1985. The record produced two Top Ten hit singles, "Silent Running (On Dangerous Ground)" and "All I Need Is a Miracle," which both peaked on the charts in early 1986. During 1986, Rutherford returned to Genesis and Carrack revived his solo career. Mike + the Mechanics didn't release another album until 1988's *The Living Years*. The record was a greater success than the first album, spawning the Number One hit single "The Living Years." After its release, the group was inactive for another few years; they returned in 1991 with *Word of Mouth*, which failed to duplicate the success of their first two records. Four years later, Mike + the Mechanics released their fourth record, *Beggar on a Beach of Gold*, which was a moderate hit in the U.K. In the spring of 1996, Mike + the Mechanics released the greatest-hits collection *Hits* in Britain; *M6* followed four years later. Young died of a heart attack on July 15, 2000. *—Stephen Thomas Erlewine*

Mike + the Mechanics [1985] / 1985 / Atlantic ✦✦✦✦
After little success with a solo career, Genesis founder Mike Rutherford put together this offshoot band and struck gold. The very anthemic "Silent Running" was a huge hit, as was its follow-up "All I Need Is a Miracle." The rest of the disc falls in between these two

styles with enjoyable results. Included are vocals courtesy of Paul Carrack and Paul Young. —*James Chrispell*

The Living Years / 1988 / Atlantic ◆◆◆◆
Propelled by their first success and a stagnant period in Genesis' output, *Living Years* continued the winning ways of Mike + the Mechanics. The touching anthem "The Living Years" steamed up the charts, and while nothing else struck gold, everything here can be recommended. —*James Chrispell*

Word of Mouth / 1991 / Atlantic ◆◆◆
Atlantic Records had reason to think they had a sure thing on their hands in the 1991 release of Mike + the Mechanics' third album, *Word of Mouth*. Here was a band with solid Top 40 pedigree, led by a guitarist/bassist with Genesis credentials (Mike Rutherford) and featuring not one but *two* vocalists with dozens of successful songs under their belts (Paul Carrack and Paul Young). The band had already recorded two hit albums and even scored a number one hit in "The Living Years." The new record led off with two killer pop songs—the opening "Get Up," with its adrenaline-inducing piano runs and catchy chorus, and the rousing singalong title track. But within a few months of its release, *Word of Mouth* had already been banished to the discount racks and budget bins of nearly every record store in the English-speaking world. So what happened? It may be that music consumers had caught wind of the mediocre keyboard-based pop ballads that filled out the rest of the album. Songs like "A Time and Place," "Everybody Gets a Second Chance," and "Let's Pretend It Didn't Happen" are anemic lite-rock anthems that even Phil Collins would have passed on. Chances are, fans stayed away from this one because the word of mouth just wasn't good. —*Evan Cater*

Beggar on a Beach of Gold / Feb. 28, 1995 / Virgin ◆◆◆◆
Mike + the Mechanics found themselves with faltering sales for *Word of Mouth* and for good reason, too; much of the album was filled with formulaic ballads and mediocre writing. With *Beggar on a Beach of Gold*, Mike Rutherford helped confront this problem by extending the songwriting duties, writing with Paul Carrack and producer Christopher Neil, as well as continuing his collaboration with B.A. Robertson. Thus, songs such as the upbeat numbers "Over My Shoulder" and "Another Cup of Coffee" effectively push past the band's formula with the musicians sounding looser than on previous records. "Plain and Simple" even has some loud guitars. Lyrically, the band has extended themselves as well. "The Ghost of Sex and You" and "Someone Always Hates Someone" approach serious questions about life and relationships without succumbing to adult contemporary clichés. The production has also nicely updated Mike and the Mechanics' sound with electronic loops and keyboard effects, adding a spring to the band's step. While such safe nods to electronica will not impress many younger fans, it should excite the group's core audience, which is a bit older. In the end, although the band does not completely avoid bland material here, this is a surprisingly nice creative turn in the road for a group many counted out. —*Geoff Orens*

● **Hits** / Mar. 1996 / Virgin ◆◆◆◆
All of Mike + the Mechanics' biggest hits are included on the 13-track collection, *Hits*. Though there are a fair share of non-hits and mediocre albums tracks, *Hits* is a first-rate compilation, giving the casual fan all of the essential Mike + the Mechanics tracks, from "Silent Running (On Dangerous Ground)" and "All I Need Is a Miracle" to "The Silent Years." —*Stephen Thomas Erlewine*

Mike + the Mechanics [1999] / May 31, 1999 / Virgin ◆◆◆

Milla

Vocals / Adult Alternative Pop/Rock, Dance-Pop
Milla Jovovich is an ex-teen supermodel/actress who recorded an unexpectedly interesting debut album, *The Divine Comedy*, in 1994. Far from the trite dance-pop released by most models angling for a music career, Jovovich's debut is largely acoustic, rooted equally in philosophy and her Slavic background, and surprisingly thoughtful and well crafted. In 1998, Milla returned with *Peopletree Sessions*, a mail-order only release. —*Heather Phares*

● **The Divine Comedy** / Apr. 5, 1994 / SBK ◆◆◆◆
Milla is supermodel and actress Milla Jovovich, and 1994's *The Divine Comedy* was her debut release. While it's now common for models and actors to try their hand at music, the good results of *The Divine Comedy* are *not* as common. Produced by Rupert Hine, the album is a low-key, laid-back affair featuring guest appearances by Eric Bazilian and Martha Davis. Milla has a pleasant voice and above-average songwriting ability, and the songs are organic, light, airy concoctions that work well in their understated settings. The jaunty, folk-inflected "Gentlemen Who Fell" was an alternative rock hit. Other noteworthy cuts include the otherworldly "The Alien Song (For Those Who Listen)" and the medieval "Charlie." —*Tom Demalon*

The Peopletree Sessions / 1998 / Peopletree ◆◆◆
Milla Jovovich's 1994 debut *The Divine Comedy* was an engaging Euro-folk-pop album replete with traditional instruments like dulcimer, fiddle, harmonium, and mandolin. It showcased Jovovich's acute sense of melody and intelligent lyrics and was slickly produced by Rupert Hine; comparisons to Sally Oldfield and Laurie Anderson's more commercial moments were accurate. While Peopletree Records specializes in "electronic folk," *The Peopletree Sessions* stylistically marks a 180-degree turnaround for Jovovich. "Efolk" has nothing to do with the implementation of traditional instruments commonly associated with folk music, nor with the "electrified" nature of folk-rock, but everything to do with the do-it-yourself, in-home approach as it relates to the project's overall production—home studios versus corporate studios. *The Peopletree Sessions* is a dark, electro-urban, dadaistic recording that lacks melody and dynamics and relies almost exclusively on

electronic gadgetry. Any of its monotonous and dirge-like tracks would make for an appropriate music track for a contemporary, black and white, stream-of-consciousness video or film. —*Dave Sleger*

The Millennium

f. 1968
Sunshine Pop, Psychedelic Pop, Baroque Pop, Soft Rock, Psychedelic, Pop
Influenced by psychedelia and California rock, pop/rock producer Curt Boettcher (the Association) decided to assemble a studio supergroup who would explore progressive sounds in 1968. Millennium's resultant album would find no commercial success and only half-baked artistic success, but nonetheless retains some period charm. Influenced in roughly equal measures by the Association, the Mamas and the Papas, the *Smile*-era Beach Boys, Nilsson, the Left Banke, and the Fifth Dimension, Boettcher and his friends came up with a hybrid that was at once too unabashedly commercial for underground FM radio and too weird for the AM dial. It would have fit in better on the AM airwaves, though; the almost too-cheerful sunshine harmonies and catchy melodies dominate the suite-like, diverse set of elaborately produced '60s pop/rock tunes. —*Richie Unterberger*

● **Begin** / 1968 / Columbia ◆◆◆◆◆
This record can truly be described as a bona fide lost classic. The brainchild of producers Curt Boettcher and Gary Usher, the group was formed out of the remnants of their previous studio project, Sagittarius, which was preceded by yet another aggregation, the Ballroom. On *The Millennium Begin*, hard rock, breezy ballads, and psychedelia all merge into an absolutely air-tight concept album, easily on the level of other, more widely popular albums from the era such as *The Notorious Byrd Brothers*, which share not only Usher's production skills, but similarities in concept and construction. The songwriting, mostly by Joey Stec and Curt Boettcher, is sterling and innovative, and yet never strays into the area of psychedelic overindulgence which marred so many records from this era. "It's You," for example, by Stec, is as powerful and fully realized as you'll ever hear from the era, easily on par with songs by the Beach Boys and the Byrds, and, yes, even the Beatles. *Begin* was at the time the most expensive album Columbia ever produced, and it sounds like it. An absolute necessity for any fan of late-'60s psychedelia and a wonderful rediscovery that sounds as vital today as it did the day it was released. [Disc three of the 2001 Sundazed three-CD release *Magic Time: The Millennium/Ballroom Recordings* includes everything from the *Begin* album, as well as the unreleased "Blight"/"Just About the Same" single that was added to the 1990 *Begin reissue*, and the single versions of "It's You," "I Just Want to Be Your Friend," "5 A.M.," "Prelude," "To Claudia on Thursday," and "There Is Nothing More to Say." The other two CDs have tracks from other acts Boettcher was involved with during the late 1960s (most of them by his prior group, the Ballroom), as well as previously unreleased instrumental versions of three songs from the *Begin* album: "It Won't Always Be the Same," "There Is Nothing More to Say," and "To Claudia on Thursday."] —*Matthew Greenwald*

The Second Millennium / 2000 / Archives ◆◆◆
If you need further proof of what an amazing group the Millennium were, then this Japanese import is just for you. Collectors of the band may find some overlap, but this collection from 2000 has a handful of tracks that were not made available on either of the 2001 compilations put out by Poptones and Sundazed. For the most part, what you'll find here mainly comprises rough demos from the band's classic 1968 LP, *Begin*. Tracks like "It's You" and "It Won't Always Be the Same" may lose their colorful, produced luster, but it's also apparent how strong the tracks are at the core. The band often seem to walk the line between being a brilliant, perfect sunshine pop band and just a run-of-the-mill folk-rock band. While some of their mid-paced country-rock experiments are not successful, this collection proves what great pop songwriters the combination of Joey Stec and Michael Fennelly could be. "The Ways I Love You" and "Sometime or Another" were sparkling and relaxed. Rewarding moments like these abound on the record with the ultra-melodic bubblegum of "I Just Don't Know How to Say Goodbye" and the sugary, addictive feel of "Baby, It's Real." The track "Suspended Animation"—with its brushed drums and detached, spaced vocals about androids and new worlds—provides more than just a guilty pleasure. In fact, the track is probably the best on the collection and gives hope that the band would have drifted off and made the first sci-fi summer pop record. Of course, fans will never know, but quality collections like this should keep imaginations at work for years. —*Jon Pruett*

The Millennium Continues / 2000 / Trattoria Family Club ◆◆◆

Again / Oct. 23, 2000 / Poptones ◆◆◆◆
Shortly after releasing *Begin*—in retrospect arguably the finest soft kaleidoscopic pop album to surface during the entire 1960s—the Millennium split up while attempting to translate the group's studio expertise into an actual touring combo. However, during its mid- to late-'60s stint, the loose group of itinerant friends made a veritable wealth of unreleased tapes both as the Millennium and under various other guises (Ballroom, Sagittarius, solo efforts). Thirty-odd years after the release of *Begin*, British label Poptones was given unlimited access to that treasure trove of recordings, and *Again* is the first album culled from the vaults.
Again collects pre-production demos for *Begin* as well as other material that has never been released previously; in fact, some of the songs were intended for the band's never-recorded second album and are thankfully issued for the first time here. When compared with the landmark *Begin*, the album is rough-cut and, understandably, does not sparkle with exactly the same brilliance. It is, however, a valuable artifact that offers a fascinating glimpse into the recording methods of Curt Boettcher and company. Even more than *Begin*, the album displays Boettcher's production genius and the band's consistently sensational songwriting and playing. Evidence lies not only in the presence of the

pre-production tracks for "Claudia on Thursday," "It Won't Always Be the Same," and "It's You," but also in the previously unreleased "Love at Last," a jazz-meets-Rolling Stones gem. Lost is some of the translucent dreaminess that pervades the band's official release, but that does not render *Again* any less magical. This album should be a godsend to fans of the band. *—Stanton Swihart*

Magic Time: The Millennium/Ballroom Sessions / May 29, 2001 / Sundazed ✦✦✦
Pay attention here, because although this release contains a lot of material by the Millennium, it's not exactly a Millennium album and not exactly an expanded edition of the *Begin* album, although everything from that record is here. This three-CD package is really a roundup of numerous Curt Boettcher-affiliated recordings from 1965-1968, focusing mostly on tracks by the Millennium and his prior band, the Ballroom. Disc three is *all* Millennium, featuring not only the *Begin* album, but the unreleased "Blight"/"Just About the Same" single that was added to the 1990 *Begin* reissue, and the single versions of "It's You," "I Just Want to Be Your Friend," "5 A.M.," "Prelude," "To Claudia on Thursday," and "There Is Nothing More to Say." Disc two has the original versions, as done by the Ballroom, of three songs that would be redone on the Millennium's *Begin* album ("5 A.M.," "Karmic Dream Sequence #1," "The Island"). There's lot's more on this anthology, though, including the scarce 1967 Warner Bros. single by the Ballroom that represented their sole release; the entire album's worth of stuff, unreleased at the time, done by the Ballroom in late 1966; yet more unreleased Ballroom songs and instrumental backing tracks; and odds and ends from other projects Boettcher worked on in the mid- to late '60s. The Ballroom tracks, and most of the other non-Millennium cuts, are inventive but fluffy sunshine pop, with intricate, multi-layered helium-high harmonies, and lyrics that often dive into a never-never land of psych-pop romance. In general, they're more lightweight than the Millennium record, so those new to Boettcher's work should start with *Begin* itself before deciding whether to take such a deep plunge. For someone heavily into the Boettcher clan, though, it's a valuable archive release, with a thorough 24-page booklet. *—Richie Unterberger*

Steve Miller

b. Oct. 5, 1943, Milwaukee, WI

Vocals, Keyboards, Songwriter, Guitar / Album Rock, Arena Rock, Pop/Rock, Psychedelic, Blues-Rock

Steve Miller's career has encompassed two distinct stages: one of the top San Francisco blues-rockers during the late '60s and early '70s, and one of the top-selling pop/rock acts of the mid- to-late '70s and early '80s. Miller moved to Chicago in 1964 to get involved in the local blues scene, teaming with Barry Goldberg for two years. He then moved to San Francisco and formed the first incarnation of the Steve Miller Blues Band. Capitol signed the group following the Monterey Pop Festival, and they flew to London to record *Children of the Future*, which was praised by critics and received some airplay on FM radio. It established Miller's early style as a blues-rocker influenced but not overpowered by psychedelia. The follow-up, *Sailor*, has been hailed as perhaps Miller's best early effort. A series of high-quality albums followed; while Miller remained a popular artist, pop radio failed to pick up on any of his material at this time, even though tracks like "Space Cowboy" and "Brave New World" had become FM rock staples. Things looked bad for Miller when he broke his neck in a car accident and subsequently developed hepatitis, which put him out of commission for most of 1972 and early 1973. He spent his recuperation time reinventing himself as a blues-influenced pop-rocker, writing compact, melodic, catchy songs. This approach was introduced on his 1973 LP *The Joker* and was an instant success, with the album going platinum and the title track hitting number one on the pop charts. *Fly Like an Eagle* was released in 1976 and eclipsed its predecessor in terms of quality and sales. The title track from 1982's *Abracadbra* gave him his third number one single and proved to be his last major commercial success. *—Steve Huey*

Children of the Future / 1968 / Capitol ✦✦✦✦
Steve Miller Band's debut *Children of the Future* is certainly an album of its time, awash in studio effects and lyrical conceits. The odd thing is, it's a record that's part English and part San Franciscan, draping its blues-rock in spacey sound effects usually heard on U.K. psych. This results in a bit of a dichotomy, but a pleasant one, since the group has a lazy, relaxed way with a groove, an ingratiating singer in Miller, and a very good singer/songwriter in Boz Scaggs, whose "Baby's Callin' Me Home" and "Steppin' Stone" are certainly highlights. Still, this is a record that's about surface as much as it is about substance, and essays a fairly intriguing space blues that, like many hippie records, meanders a bit too long for its own good. Still, *Children of the Future* is a fairly satisfying psych-blues relic and a promising start for SMB. *—Stephen Thomas Erlewine*

Sailor / 1968 / Capitol ✦✦✦✦✦
Sailor, the second album from the Steve Miller Band, follows the same pattern as its predecessor, yet improves on it considerably, thanks to a better selection of material, sharper production, and less meandering. The band hasn't lost its identity as space blues merchants, but it has married it to focused performances and tight, catchy songs, highlighted by "Living in the USA," the lovely "Quicksilver Girl," and Boz Scaggs' "Overdrive" and "Dime-a-Dance Romance," plus a fine cover choice in "Gangster of Love." Sonically, this still may be a little bit too dated for some listeners, evoking 1968 just a bit too strongly, but it is a welcome step forward for the SMB. *—Stephen Thomas Erlewine*

Your Saving Grace / 1969 / Capitol ✦✦✦
Your Saving Grace tends to fall through the cracks in some Steve Miller retrospectives, perhaps understandably, since it was the fourth record his band released in two years. Sonically, it's pretty much of a piece with *Sailor* and *Brave New World*, and if it doesn't have as much memorable material, chalk that up to constant work, which does tend to dry the creative well. Still, this is a fairly enjoyable record, particularly for fans of SMB's early work, getting by more on sound than substance, but the trippy version of "Motherless Children" remains a highlight from this era. *—Stephen Thomas Erlewine*

Brave New World / 1969 / Capitol ✦✦✦✦✦
Blasting out of stereo speakers in the summer of 1969, *Brave New World* was more fully realized, and rocked harder, than the Steve Miller Band's first two albums. From the opening storm of the uplifting title track to the final scorcher, "My Dark Hour," featuring Paul McCartney (credited as "Paul Ramon"), this recording was the strongest project before Miller's *Fly Like an Eagle* days. "Celebration Song" has a sliding bass line, while "LT's Midnight Dream" features Miller's slide guitar. "Can't You Hear Your Daddy's Heartbeat" sounds like it was lifted right off of Jimi Hendrix's *Are You Experienced*, and "Got Love 'Cause You Need It" also has a Hendrix-ian feel. "Kow Kow" is a wonderfully oblique song featuring Nicky Hopkins' distinctive piano style. Hopkins' piano coda on that song alone is worth the price of this album. "Space Cowboy," one of several songs co-written with Ben Sidran, defined one of Miller's many personas. "Seasons," another Sidran collaboration, is a beautifully atmospheric, slow-tempo piece. Steve Miller's guitar playing is the star of this album, blazing across the whole affair more prominently than on any other release in his lengthy career; many of the songs have a power trio feel. In addition to the fine guitar work, Miller's vocals are stronger here, and during this era in general, than they would be in his hitmaking days in the mid-'70s, when he was much more laid-back and overdubbed. Ever the borrower, adapter, and integrator, Steve Miller shapes the blues, psychedelia, sound effects, sweet multi-tracked vocal harmonies, and guitar-driven hard rock into one cohesive musical statement with this release. *—Jim Newsom*

Number 5 / 1970 / Capitol ✦✦✦✦
Released in the summer of 1970, *Number 5* was the fifth LP by the Steve Miller Band in just over two years. While it compares favorably to its immediate predecessor, *Your Saving Grace*, it is not quite up to the consistent excellence of the potent *Brave New World* from the previous summer. However, it does have a fair share of delights, especially the opening triumvirate of "Good Morning," "I Love You," and "Going to the Country." These selections, and all of side one, have a distinctly more rural feel than did previous recordings, due perhaps to the fact that the tracks were recorded in Nashville. Charlie McCoy contributes harmonica to several of these cuts, and Buddy Spicher plays fiddle on "Going to the Country," while Bobby Thompson adds banjo to "Tokin's." Side two is more uneven, with the leadoff mid-tempo rocker, "Going to Mexico," serving as a conclusion to the first side's thematic coherence, and the closing "Never Kill Another Man" a string-laden ballad. Sandwiched between them are three experimental-sounding pieces, seasoned with sound effects, buried vocals, and semi-political themes. Although it couldn't have been predicted at the time, *Number 5* represented the end of an era for Steve Miller and bandmates, and subsequent albums would sound nothing like this first batch of great recordings. *—Jim Newsom*

Rock Love / 1971 / Capitol ✦
What a disappointing surprise. A full year had elapsed since the release of *Number 5*, completing a string of excellent albums by the Steve Miller Band. The unsuspecting record buyer had every right to expect another quality product. What he got instead was this travesty of generic white-boy bluesisms, recorded live but sounding dead. In retrospect, the title track can be heard as a precursor to "The Joker," but there is no reason to own this album except to wonder if the Steve Miller Band was really this boring in concert, and if so, why it was documented. *—Jim Newsom*

Anthology / 1972 / Capitol ✦✦✦✦✦
Released in 1972, *Anthology* provides a 16-track summary of the Steve Miller Band's first five albums, distilling their uneven space blues into a tight, effective collection of highlights. These songs are hardly as tuneful or effortlessly catchy as the songs on 1978's *Greatest Hits*—apart from "Living in the USA," "Space Cowboy," and "Going to Mexico," there's nothing particularly immediate here—but they're first-rate period pieces, capturing Miller's space blues at its most effectively spacey. *—Stephen Thomas Erlewine*

Recall the Beginning: A Journey From Eden / 1972 / Capitol ✦✦✦

The Joker / 1973 / Capitol ✦✦✦
With *The Joker*, Steve Miller reached new heights of popularity and commercial success but sank to a level of musical and lyrical banality from which he would not soon recover. This is not to say this is a terrible album, but measured against his classic first five albums, *The Joker* is very disappointing. While the title track is a catchy piece of fluff that hit the number one spot on the singles charts, most of the tracks on this recording sound like filler. "Mary Lou" is a cover of an old Ronnie Hawkins song; "Your Cash Ain't Nothin' but Trash" is a '50s doo wop song by the Clovers, and "Come on in My Kitchen" is the oft-recorded Robert Johnson blues song, credited here to Woody Payne (the same songwriting credit given by John Renbourn on his *Faro Annie* album a year earlier). Even the originals here are based on borrowed ideas. "Sugar Babe" and "Shu Ba Da Du Ma Ma Ma Ma" are pleasant diversions, but as the titles suggest, of very little substance. The album sounds at times like it was recorded in a cave, with the drums sounding like cardboard boxes. This recording reached number two on the album charts on the strength of the single, but for those familiar with Steve Miller's music from 1968-1970, *The Joker* was little more than trash. *—Jim Newsom*

Fly Like an Eagle / 1976 / Capitol ✦✦✦✦✦
Steve Miller had started to essay his classic sound with *The Joker*, but 1976's *Fly Like an Eagle* is where he took flight, creating his definitive slice of space blues. The key is focus, even on an album as stylishly, self-consciously trippy as this, since the focus brings about his strongest set of songs (both originals and covers), plus a detailed atmospheric production where everything fits. It still can sound fairly dated—those whooshing keyboards and cavernous echoes are certainly of their time—but its essence hasn't aged, as "Fly Like

an Eagle" drifts like a cool breeze, while "Take the Money and Run" and "Rock & Me" are fiendishly hooky, friendly rockers. The rest of the album may not be quite up to those standards, but there aren't any duds, either, as "Wild Mountain Honey" and "Mercury Blues" give this a comfortable backdrop, thanks to Miller's offhand, lazy charm. Though it may not quite transcend its time, it certainly is an album rock landmark of the mid-'70s and its best moments (namely, the aforementioned singles) are classics of the idiom. —*Stephen Thomas Erlewine*

Book of Dreams / 1977 / Capitol ✦✦✦✦
Unless the Black Crowes dress up in NASA drag or Garth Brooks takes his glam-industrial doppelganger Chris Gaines into Mothership terrain, Steve Miller should retain his monopoly on the "Space Cowboy" moniker for many years to come. And it is here, on this 1977 blockbuster, that Miller shored up his cosmic persona: From the winged horse on the album cover to a judicious smattering of synthesizers in the music, *Book of Dreams* bridged the gap between blues-rock and the indulgences of prog rock. Things do go awry when Renaissance Faire whimsy takes over clunkers like "Wish Upon a Star" and "Babes in the Wood," but luckily the balance of the record offers a satisfying blend of meaty blues and country riffs and tasteful atmospherics. The well-known suspects include "Swingtown," "Wintertime," and "Threshold," with relatively straightforward rock & boogie highlights coming by way of "True Fine Love," "Jet Airliner," and "Jungle Love." The non-hit cuts, "Sacrifice" and "My Own Space," do stand up to these FM favorites but fall short of making the album something the casual fan should consider with Miller's *Greatest Hits 1974-1978* in hand (that collection includes seven tracks off of *Book of Dreams*, plus all the hits from *The Joker* and *Fly Like an Eagle*). Still, this is a highlight of the '70s classic rock era and one of Miller's finest releases. —*Stephen Cook*

● **Greatest Hits 1974-1978** / 1978 / Capitol ✦✦✦✦✦
Greatest Hits 1974-1978 collects the majority of Steve Miller's biggest hits—"The Joker," "Take the Money and Run," "Rock'n Me," "Fly Like an Eagle," "Jet Airliner," "Jungle Love," "Swingtown"—and seven album tracks that received a fair amount of airplay on album rock radio. The collection only covers a total of three albums—*The Joker, Fly Like an Eagle, Book of Dreams*—with the latter two providing the bulk of the material. Because of this, "Living in the USA," one of Miller's biggest hits of the late '60s/early '70s, isn't included but it isn't missed, since all of his other hits of the '70s are included. The thoroughness of *Greatest Hits 1974-1978* makes it an excellent introduction to Miller and for many casual fans, it also means that they can contain their Steve Miller collection to one disc. —*Stephen Thomas Erlewine*

Circle of Love / 1981 / Capitol ✦✦✦
Divided in half, with one side of catchy pop tunes and one side devoted to a 16-minute space blues workout called "Macho City," the design of *Circle of Love* feels like a throwback to 1971, when people truly paid attention to the flow of an album. In 1981, it was a bit of anachronism, but its old-fashioned feel (and its tedious "Macho City") are saved by the mini-album of pop/rock that might not have produced any undeniable classics, but includes tuneful, well-crafted numbers that serve as worthy follow-ups to *Fly Like an Eagle* and *Book of Dreams*. —*Stephen Thomas Erlewine*

Abracadabra / 1982 / Capitol ✦✦✦
Steve Miller was always catchy and tuneful, but he never turned out an unabashed pop album until 1982's *Abracadabra*. This isn't just pop in construction, it's pop in attitude, filled with effervescent melodies and deeply silly lyrics, perhaps none more noteworthy than the immortal couplet "Abra-Abracadabra/I wanna reach out and grab ya." Those words graced the title track, which turned out to be one of his biggest hits, and if nothing else is quite as irresistibly goofy as that song, there still is a surplus of engagingly tuneful material, all dressed up in psuedo-new wave production so favored by AOR veterans in the early '80s. All of that may not make this one of Miller's definitive albums, especially in the view of hardcore space blues heads, but it's pretty damn irresistible for listeners who find "Abracadabra" one of the highlights of faux-new wave AOR. —*Stephen Thomas Erlewine*

Steve Miller Band: Live! / 1983 / Capitol ✦✦

Italian X Rays / 1984 / Capitol ✦✦

Living in the 20th Century / Dec. 15, 1987 / Capitol ✦✦

Born 2B Blue / 1988 / Capitol ✦✦✦

The Best of Steve Miller (1968-1973) / 1990 / Capitol ✦✦✦✦✦
The Best of 1968-1973 is a solid collection that features many of the highlights from Steve Miller's first five years of recording, including "The Joker," "Living in the U.S.A.," "Space Cowboy," and "Gangster of Love." This compilation isn't as consistently thrilling as *Greatest Hits 1974-1978*, which also features "The Joker," and it's not as sharply assembled as 1972's *Anthology*, but it remains an adequate overview of Miller's early records, especially for fans only familiar with *Greatest Hits*. —*Stephen Thomas Erlewine*

Wide River / Jun. 8, 1993 / Polydor ✦✦

Steve Miller Band [Box Set] / Jul. 26, 1994 / Capitol ✦✦✦✦✦
Close to definitive is the best way to describe the three-disc box *Steve Miller Band*. That, or missed opportunity. The set is divided pretty well, with the first disc being devoted to the early years, the second to the hitmaking era, and the third to the blues. Now, this isn't a hard-and-fast breakdown, since there's no one on God's green earth who would call "Abracadabra" a blues, but it's a pretty good template for a box. The problem is the execution, particularly as the box gets off the ground. The historical childhood recordings that kick off the first disc are interesting, but they're alienating for anyone outside of hardcore fans. Then, much of the early work is present in oddly edited versions, which aren't particularly welcome. Still, this does round up nearly all of the highlights from throughout Miller's career, which does make it valuable for fans who want a pretty exhaustive, but not definitive, compilation. Nevertheless, *Anthology* and *Greatest Hits*, especially, remain the best way to hear Miller at his peak. —*Stephen Thomas Erlewine*

Milli Vanilli

f. Germany
Euro-Dance, Dance-Pop
The most notorious group of the '80s, bar none. Eurodisco producer Frank Farian (who created Boney M and Far Corporation) recruited two handsome, talentless dweebs to lip-sync to his pre-fab dance-pop ditties, such as "Girl You Know It's True" and "Blame It on the Rain." The group was an instant smash, selling millions of albums and winning a Best New Group Grammy. Farian later spilled the beans that the group didn't even sing on their records, creating an uproar that made them the enemies of scorned fans and critics; their Grammy was quickly revoked and the group ceased its existence. One half of the duo, Rob Pilatus, died April 2, 1998 after overdosing on drugs and alcohol; he was just 32 years old. —*John Floyd*

All or Nothing / Nov. 14, 1988 / Hansa ✦✦✦
Trivia time. Milli Vanilli's first album was never released in its original incarnation in America. That album was called *All or Nothing*, and the bulk of it was used as the basis for the smash-hit American album *Girl You Know It's True*. Its title was also used for the 1990 effort *The Remix Album*, which went gold in the U.S.—proof positive that Milli Vanilli was really a phenomenon. So, there was a bit of confusion, since both *All or Nothing* and *Girl You Know It's True* looked like variations on the same album, which was kind of true and kind of not. Either way, *Girl* was a stronger album, better sequenced and boasting a better set of songs. *All or Nothing* does have four of the big hits—"Baby Don't Forget My Number," "Girl You Know It's True," "I'm Gonna Miss You," and, of course, the title track (all Top Five U.S. singles, by the way)—but it's missing the fine Diane Warren ballad "Blame It on the Rain," which was the key ingredient that sent this set of trashy Euro-disco into the American stratosphere. The album cuts here tend to emphasize that Euro-trash side of the group, which may have given away the game if included on the American effort. All of this makes *All or Nothing* a more interesting and funnier set than its U.S. counterpart, but it's not as much fun, since it indulges in the worse tendencies of Europop. So, no, it's not as good an album as the reshuffled and restructured *Girl You Know It's True*, but this is where you can hear the roots of the scandal that later toppled frontmen Rob and Fab. —*Stephen Thomas Erlewine*

● **Girl You Know It's True** / 1989 / Arista ✦✦✦
As soon as the news spread, America was shocked—shocked, I tell you, shocked!—that the pretty German boys in Milli Vanilli weren't actually soulfully singing in flawless English on this album's impeccably constructed dance tracks. The fact is, with dance-pop (especially Euro-dance!), artificiality is the name of the game, and that's what is *good* about it. It's the distinguishing characteristic, its identity, the core of its being. On that level, it's hard not to listen to *Girl You Know It's True* and marvel at the level of producer/songwriter/musician/all-around mastermind and mad genius Frank Farian's studiocraft, since it doesn't even sound like he programmed a computer to make this music; it sounds like something the machine wrote on its own accord. There are no natural sounds or human emotions on this record, just a bunch of shiny hooks and big beats, all processed and precisely assembled to be totally irresistible to a mass audience. This isn't just music that's all surface, this is music that gives the impression of having a surface, then not delivering on that. Years after the lip-synching hubbub, it's hard to imagine why there was such a fuss about an album so transparent, lightweight, and intentionally disposable. Then again, listening to it now, you can't believe that anyone thought Rob and Fab were really singing, since not only don't the voices not match the picture on the cover, but they don't match any picture at all. But when it comes down to it, this music is so manufactured, it doesn't sound like *anyone* is really singing. And that's what's sort of cool about it. —*Stephen Thomas Erlewine*

Moment of Truth / May 13, 1991 / Hansa/BMG ✦✦

Garnet Mimms

b. Nov. 16, 1933, Ashland, VA
Vocals, Piano / Deep Soul, Southern Soul, Northern Soul, R&B, Soul
With his backing band the Enchanters in the early '60s, Garnet Mimms cut several fine, underrated R&B singles, including the hit "Cry Baby." After the Enchanters fell apart in 1964, Mimms pursued a solo career that merged a sophisticated R&B backing with his gospel-influenced singing. He made many terrific records that never hit the charts; it wasn't until 1977 that he had another hit, "What It Is." But in the '60s, Mimms made many records that should have been hits; they remain criminally unheard, but fans of '60s soul and R&B should seek them out. —*Stephen Thomas Erlewine*

Cry Baby / Sep. 20, 1963 / United Artists ✦✦✦✦✦
Mimms' debut album was a well-above-average effort for soul LPs of the era. Besides the title smash, it featured solid material that married Garnet's gospel feel with uptown New York soul production; "Anytime You Want Me," "Wanting You," and "Baby Don't You Weep" were some of his finest songs. It's been reissued in its entirety, along with 14 other cuts, on the British CD *Cry Baby/Warm & Soulful*; most of the songs are on the domestic compilation *The Best of Garnet Mimms*. —*Richie Unterberger*

● **The Best of Garnet Mimms: Cry Baby** / 1993 / EMI ✦✦✦✦✦
Excellent compilation of this early soul singer, whose influence extended beyond his one big hit, the 1963 title track. Emerging from a gospel background and obscure doo wop groups, Mimms invested the increasingly sophisticated R&B sound of the mid-'60s with both emotion and supple pipes. He never hit the Top Ten after "Cry Baby," but rang off a

string of minor hits like "Baby Don't You Weep," "For Your Precious Love," "It Was Easier to Hurt Her," and "I'll Take Good Care of You." Grittier than Motown, but not as down-home as Stax, Mimms married his vocals to the uptown production values and pop songwriting savvy of his producer, Jerry Ragavoy, to produce some of the more memorable early soul recordings. This 25-track anthology, covering his recordings for United Artists between 1963 and 1966, is unerringly consistent. It features all of his hit singles, highlights from the three albums he released during this period, and the original versions of "My Baby" (later one of Janis Joplin's signature tunes) and "Anytime You Want Me" (covered by the Who on a B-side in 1965). —*Richie Unterberger*

Cry Baby/Warm & Soulful / 1995 / BGO ♦♦♦♦♦
This 26-track compilation of Mimms' work between 1963 and 1966 (including his entire '63 debut LP) is roughly equal in merit to the U.S. *The Best of Garnet Mimms* compilation. Each focuses upon the singer's prime; each largely duplicates the other's track selection; and each has some songs that are not on the other. The most notable item here that isn't on the American compilation is "It Won't Hurt (Half as Much)," which was also recorded by Them in the mid-'60s. The U.S. anthology, however, rates a slight edge: it's easier to locate (in North America, that is), and has the crucial track "My Baby" (covered by Janis Joplin), which is missing from this British comp. —*Richie Unterberger*

Ministry

f. 1981, Chicago, IL
Industrial Dance, Industrial Metal, Alternative Metal, Alternative Pop/Rock, Industrial
Until Nine Inch Nails crossed over to the mainstream, Ministry did more than any other band to popularize industrial music, injecting large doses of punky, over-the-top aggression and roaring heavy metal guitar riffs that helped their music find favor with metal and alternative audiences outside of industrial's cult fan base. That's not to say Ministry had a commercial or generally accessible sound: they were unremittingly intense, abrasive, pounding, and repetitive, and not always guitar-oriented (samples, synthesizers, and tape effects were a primary focus just as often as guitars and distorted vocals). However, both live and in the studio, they achieved a huge, crushing sound that put most of their contemporaries in aggressive musical genres to shame. Plus, founder and frontman Al Jourgensen gave the group a greater aura of style and theater than other industrial bands, who seemed rather faceless when compared with Jourgensen's leather-clad cowboy/biker look and the edgy shock tactics of such videos as "N.W.O." and "Just One Fix." Jourgensen formed Ministry in 1981 as a synth-pop group, eventually giving the band a complete overhaul in 1987 with the addition of bassist/co-producer Paul Barker and a loose aggregation of supporting musicians. 1988's *The Land of Rape and Honey* proved to be Ministry's stylistic breakthrough, a taut, explosive fusion of heavy metal, industrial dance beats and samples, and punk aggression. After 1989's *The Mind Is a Terrible Thing to Taste* built on its predecessor's artistic success, Jourgensen embarked on a flurry of side projects, the most prominent being Revolting Cocks. The 1991 single "Jesus Built My Hotrod" and its accompanying album *Psalm 69* (issued in 1992) represented the peak of Ministry's popularity, helping earn them a spot on the inaugural Lollapalooza tour. However, their recorded output subsequently dwindled, partially because of the myriad side projects and partially due to heroin abuse within the band. Ministry did resurface periodically during the '90s, but their albums didn't match prior critical or commercial success. —*Steve Huey*

With Sympathy / 1983 / Arista ♦♦♦
Rather than the trademark bone-munching industrial metal of later years, *With Sympathy* is panto-goth new wave synth-pop that sounds less like the band chewing your pancreas and more like Human League's surly little brother. Great stuff, then, for those who allied themselves with Ally Sheedy's character in *The Breakfast Club*. "Here We Go" grinds all over some electronic horns, "Work for Love" stop-starts and shouts about like "Walk This Way" without all that scary rap, and the whole record becomes a secret weapon against the contrived snarls of the albums to follow. Surely, Al Jourgensen must be more insecure about his past than a superstar linebacker over childhood courses in ballet. —*Dean Carlson*

Twelve Inch Singles (1981-1984) / 1985 / Wax Trax! ♦♦♦
Included are all of their best-known hits and great songs before they got signed by a major label (Sire). Early techno-industrial music from the early '80s. —*John Book*

Twitch / 1986 / Sire ♦♦♦
The name Ministry brings to mind images of big, dumb guitars and arena rock sensibility. But before they created their influential third album, *The Land of Rape and Honey*, there was *Twitch*. And this album probably owes more to Front 242 than anything. The only thing remotely resembling their later music is the use of psychotic sampling that Al Jourgensen and Paul Barker will always be known for. A good example being "Like You," the first track on the album. Other differences include Patty Jourgensen singing on the song "The Angel" and Al Jourgensen actually trying to sound unaggravated at times. It's interesting though repetitive at times ("Crash and Burn"), and if you care to listen to Mr. Jourgensen's rants, he really does have something to say. "Isle of Man" tells the story of the arrival of Columbus and how the persecution of the Indians will be revisited on the offenders in time. Make no mistake: This sounds nothing like any of Ministry's other albums; listeners may hear how they became what they did. —*Alan Esher*

- **The Land of Rape and Honey** / 1988 / Sire ♦♦♦♦♦
The Land of Rape and Honey represented Ministry's stylistic breakthrough, combining assaultive percussion, samples, synths, and (sometimes) crunching guitars with distorted, barking vocals. For all the emphasis on the group's metal/industrial fusion, it's really only the first three (and best) tracks on *Rape and Honey*—"Stigmata," "The Missing," and "Deity"—that employ guitars extensively. The remainder of the album merely suggests heavy

metal aggression through its electronic and sampled elements; it is far more industrial in feel, even though it's just as dark. Ministry was the industrial band that, more than any other, appealed to metal fans, and it was *The Land of Rape and Honey* that began to lay claim to that status. —*Steve Huey*

The Mind Is a Terrible Thing to Taste / Nov. 1989 / Sire ♦♦♦♦
In what many consider to be Ministry's peak, the band creates another wonderful album to follow *The Land of Rape and Honey*. Fusing thrash guitars with excellent synth and percussion work, Ministry lay the foundation for even more followers of the band's music. But what makes the album even more commendable is the unique flair and the avoidance of cliché elements that have brought down the guitar-heavy industrial-rock genre. Purists might argue that Ministry has given up these roots; but it's plain to see that the roots remain, and are only revamped by the necessary progression of a band that has been around for so many years. The sound is Ministry's, most definitely. —*Marc van der Pol*

In Case You Didn't Feel Like Showing Up (Live) / Sep. 4, 1990 / Sire ♦♦♦♦
It's not often that a live album can display the precision of a studio recording, as well as capture the mood of a live show. *In Case You Didn't Feel Like Showing Up* does both of these things, as well as containing some of the standout tracks from two of Ministry's best albums (*The Land of Rape and Honey* and *The Mind is a Terrible Thing to Taste*). A great place for a newbie to start out, as well as a hardcore fan to rehear some of his favorite tracks in an intense and superbly recorded live setting. Fantastic. —*Marc van der Pol*

Psalm 69: The Way to Succeed & The Way to Suck Eggs / Jul. 14, 1992 / Sire ♦♦♦♦
Although this is Ministry's most accessible album, it is not a sellout. Al Jourgensen and company never let the intensity up, with the machine-like grind of the rhythm section constantly driving the same 16th-note rhythms again and again. "Just One Fix" is the best track on a remarkable, intense album, which also includes the single "Jesus Built My Hotrod." —*Stephen Thomas Erlewine*

Filth Pig / 1995 / Sire ♦♦

The Dark Side of the Spoon / Jun. 8, 1999 / Warner Brothers ♦♦♦
Having struggled back to their feet, Ministry ambitiously attempts to broaden their signature sound with *Dark Side of the Spoon*. While it is a better record than *Filth Pig*, that's largely because of a few strong moments propping up a number of surprisingly bland attempts at aggression. Tunefulness was never Ministry's strong point, and several songs are built on extremely rudimentary vocal melodies. While it's admirable that the group is trying new things this far into its career, it never quite settles on a definite approach. Besides, not everything they're trying is new; a few parts are reminiscent of their earliest, synth-oriented days, while some of the dark humor that used to fill Revolting Cocks albums pops up here and there. The problem with the latter is that instead of being performed as though the band might snap at any second (as in the past), it sounds a little dopey and ineffectual. It would be a mistake to say that the album is a complete failure; "Supermanic Soul" and "Bad Blood" integrate some of the noisiness of *Filth Pig* with sound effects and classic Ministry riffs, while the otherwise dull "Eureka Pile" successfully works in some Eastern-tinged female vocals. But it does become apparent—especially over the second half—that the band simply doesn't sound as fearsome; so, *Dark Side of the Spoon* can't be considered the successful expansion of their sound that would bode well for the future. —*Steve Huey*

Greatest Fits / Jun. 19, 2001 / Warner Brothers ♦♦♦♦♦
You can almost see Ministry straining against releasing a compilation, not just because it's called *Greatest Fits* but because they're not featured on the front and obscured on the back cover. And it's also true that the selection isn't quite as lean as it could have been, and it's hurt by non-chronological sequencing, opening with the *AI* soundtrack contribution "What About Us?" (ignored by listeners—sadly reminiscent of the film itself—yet one of their best singles in years), and careening through their history without any real roadmap. That does result in some unwelcome, unexpected detours, but the basic journey isn't just good, it proves that Ministry's stature as industrial giants isn't just warranted, but that few other bands could be as powerful as they were at their peak. And, in a way, the inclusion of such missteps as "Lay Lady Lay" (which really would have been better suited for a Revolting Cocks album) illustrates just how terrific "Stigmata," "The Land of Rape and Honey," "N.W.O.," "Just One Fix," and "Jesus Built My Hot Rod" are. And, for those that just want a concentrated blast of prime Ministry, this is as good as you'll get. —*Stephen Thomas Erlewine*

Kylie Minogue

b. May 28, 1968, Melbourne, Australia
Vocals / Club/Dance, Euro-Dance, Europop, Adult Contemporary, Dance-Pop
Although she's only managed one hit in the U.S. since her arrival as a singer in 1987, Kylie Minogue is both Australia and Europe's biggest selling female pop singer over that period and a pop culture icon in those areas. Her image on the cover of magazines is guaranteed to produce extra sales. But a singing career was never what Minogue had in mind for herself. In 1979, she began her acting career in the Australian TV drama series *Skyways*, before achieving national fame in the five-days-a-week soap opera *Neighbours*. Around the time Minogue joined, *Neighbours* also started airing in the U.K. A major celebrity on the basis of her *Neighbours* popularity, Minogue had agreed to give a charity performance in the company of other personalities, choosing to sing Little Eva's "Loco-Motion." Someone hit on the idea of submitting a tape of the performance to local record company, Mushroom, who didn't think much of the demo but saw the potential in releasing a single by the extremely popular young TV star. In their wildest dreams no one imagined a national number one record with the recorded version of "Loco-Motion" (July 1987). In Australia, the U.K., and Europe, Minogue was scoring hit after hit and quickly

left *Neighbours* to meet the demand on her. Without anything approaching Madonna's musical strength, like Madonna, Minogue has ensured her survival with imaginative videos and by keeping fans guessing and intrigued with consistent changes of personal image. She has also appeared in a number of movies over the years. *—Ed Nimmervoll*

Kylie / Dec. 1988 / David Geffen Co. ✦✦✦
While the production values on Kylie's debut are dated at best and the tunes are nothing but standard late-'80s Stock-Aitken-Waterman bubblegum, there are some rather endearing qualities to it. Firstly, she shows a lot more personality than the other Stock, et al. frontperson, Rick Astley. Secondly, her cuteness makes these rather vapid tracks bearable. Her cover of "Loco-Motion" made only small waves in the U.S., but this was the album that launched her career as both pop star and icon in Europe. *—Chris True*

Enjoy Yourself / 1989 / David Geffen Co. ✦✦✦
Given that it's the same team that put together her first LP, it's no surprise that *Enjoy Yourself* sounds very similar to her debut. Which is fine if you take into consideration that at the time this formula was pure gold. Europe went mad for the diminutive Australian, and this simple dance-pop is catchy stuff. Stock-Aitken-Waterman knew what they had and they crafted songs that kept Kylie in the public eye. All in all, a good companion to her debut. *—Chris True*

Rhythm of Love / 1990 / Mushroom ✦✦✦
Yes, it's still simple Stock-Aitken-Waterman dance-pop, but *Rhythm of Love* is leaps and bounds more mature than Kylie's first two releases. The songwriting is stronger, the production dynamic, and Kylie seems more confident vocally. And while *Kylie* and *Enjoy Yourself* were collections of songs to back up singles, this is a more complete album, with many of the tracks—"Things Can Only Get Better" a prime example—single worthy. Definitely her best work from the Stock-Aitken-Waterman era. *—Chris True*

Let's Get to It / 1991 / Mushroom ✦✦✦
While it's certainly as danceable as *Rhythm of Love*, *Let's Get to It* seems to try too hard. By this point in her career, Kylie had transformed from her innocent dance-pop image to what the press dubbed "SexKylie." Obviously, this wasn't accidental on her part. From the title to the heavy breathing effects to the kind of creepy cover pic, this is Kylie as a self-made sex kitten. What makes this album interesting musically is that she has taken creative control of her career as well as image control. She co-wrote much of the record, and while there are some noticeable missteps (the stadium keyboard part that lays the foundation of "I Guess I Like It Like That," for example), she shows potential. Not her most solid release, but fans of her early work will enjoy it. *—Chris True*

● **Greatest Hits [1994]** / 1994 / Mushroom ✦✦✦✦✦
An excellent overview of the first half of Minogue's career, this 1994 collection is the place to start. Lifting the singles and better album tracks from her first four albums, this is chock-full of the light dance-pop that made Minogue one of the biggest European pop stars of the late '80s/early '90s. With tracks like "Loco-Motion," "Better the Devil You Know," and "What Do I Have to Do?," it's absolutely perfect for the unknowing. *—Chris True*

Kylie Minogue / 1994 / Deconstruction ✦✦✦✦
Meant as a statement of her new direction, Kylie Minogue's fifth album no longer featured the Stock-Aitken-Waterman production gloss and found the diminutive singer working with hip dance producers like David Seaman. From the first notes of the opener "Confide in Me," you know this is not the teen pop queen of old. Kylie Minogue (also note the use of her last name on the cover) wanted to sound grown up, and she pulls it off with ease. While it is still dance-pop, there's atmosphere and style in the songs that wasn't there on *Let's Get to It*. Definitely the start of the second phase of her career. *—Chris True*

Impossible Princess / 1997 / Deconstruction ✦✦✦✦
By 1997, much of the pop music landscape had changed. The music papers were declaring the "Techno Revolution" was on, Oasis and Manic Street Preachers were ruling the charts, and simple dance-pop seemed to be the domain of teenage girls. So what does the dance-pop diva of the '90s do? She recruits Manic Street Preachers' James Dean Bradfield, Sean Moore, and Nicky Wire, starts writing unaided, and completely changes musical direction. Enter Kylie Minogue's *Impossible Princess* (the title was changed to *Kylie Minogue* after the death of Princess Diana). From the trippy cover art to the abundance of guitars and experimental vocal tracks, this was her "great leap forward." The move got her in the papers, but, unfortunately, critical acclaim was lacking. So were sales. Critics called it a mistake, and the public was less than impressed. Which is sad, because this is a pretty damn good record. Unlike her early work, this album sounds stronger and has a more natural feel. Her songwriting abilities have come a long way, and *Impossible Princess* actually flows together as an album. Worth another look. *—Chris True*

Intimate & Live / Feb. 2, 1999 / Mushroom ✦✦✦
This two-disc set was recorded during Kylie's *Impossible Princess* tour. While most of the newer tracks are solid and sound close to the album versions, her soft dance-pop version of the Clash's "Should I Stay or Should I Go?" is downright awful. Mainly for diehard collectors, less familiar fans will want to check out a greatest hits compilation or her 1997 album *Impossible Princess*. *—Chris True*

Light Years / Sep. 25, 2000 / Parlophone ✦✦✦✦✦
In 1998, Kylie Minogue was dropped by dance label DeConstruction, and some thought she had committed career suicide. Obviously the backlash of 1997's *Impossible Princess* taught the diminutive Aussie one important lesson. Sometimes you have to just go with, what you know—go back to basics. And that's just what Minogue has done with 2000's *Light Years*. Symbolically dropping her last name from the cover, she re-enters the territory that made her great. Granted, with the teen pop movement at its strongest, one could say she just has good timing, but this work is leaps and bounds better than her Stock-Aitken-Waterman work. *Light Years* is not just another Minogue dance-pop record, but a great collection of disco stylings and Europop kitsch. "Spinning Around" is a fun and string-laden declaration that she may have made a mistake back in 1997, and the Robbie Williams-/Guy Chambers-penned "Your Disco Needs You" is probably one of the best dance songs of the last ten years. Arguably one of the best disco records since the '70s, *Light Years* is Minogue comfortable with who she is and what she's good at. *—Chris True*

Minor Threat

f. 1980, Washington, DC, **db.** 1983
Straight-Edge, American Punk, Hardcore Punk, American Underground
Minor Threat was the definitive Washington, D.C. hardcore punk band, setting the style for the straight-edge punk movement of the early '80s. Led by vocalist Ian MacKaye, the band was staunchly independent and fiercely sober. Through their songs, the group rejected drugs and alcohol, espoused anti-establishment politics, and led a call for self-awareness. Every song was fast, sharp, and lethal, often clocking in at just around a minute. Their speed and fury often hid their fairly catchy melodies, but the band's main function was to vent rage. Over the course of three years, Minor Threat released two EPs, one album and several singles, all of which were quite popular in the American punk underground. Their records and concerts helped spawn straight-edge, an American punk lifestyle based on the group's intense, clean-living ideology.

The origins of Minor Threat lie in the Teen Idles, Ian MacKaye's first band. MacKaye formed the Teen Idles while still in high school and founded the Dischord label to put out his group's records. Shortly after graduation, the Teen Idles had broken up and MacKaye had formed Minor Threat with former Idles drummer Jeff Nelson, bassist Brian Baker, and guitarist Lyle Preslar. During 1980-81, Minor Threat released several singles and EPs and played many concerts along the East Coast. In 1982, bassist Baker had left and was replaced by Steve Hansen. With Hansen on board, the group recorded their only full-length album, *Out of Step*. Upon its 1983 release, the album became popular within the underground and Minor Threat were becoming alternative stars, which didn't sit well with MacKaye. By the end of the year he broke up the band. MacKaye and Nelson continued to run Dischord, which thrived well into the '90s. MacKaye later played in Egg Hunt (with Nelson), Embrace, Skewbald, and Pailhead before forming Fugazi, who carried on the aesthetic, if not the sound, of Minor Threat. *—Stephen Thomas Erlewine*

★ **Complete Discography** / 1988 / Dischord ✦✦✦✦✦
Complete Discography compiles Minor Threat's entire body of recordings on a single compact disc. Hardcore, as a rule, wasn't particularly musically diverse, but Minor Threat were one of the genre's groundbreaking acts and their music has held up better than most of their contemporaries. As the de-facto leaders of the Washington, D.C. hardcore scene, the band pioneered the straight-edge mentality by emphasizing impossibly fast tempos, brief songs, political lyrics, and a drug and alcohol-free lifestyle. Besides setting the precedent for several generations of punk rockers with their music and ideals, Minor Threat were simply a better band than most hardcore groups. They had a tight, distinctive sound that wasn't as heavy as their Californian counterparts and, therefore, was often more bracing and effective. Although some of the music on *Complete Discography*, like much of hardcore in general, hasn't aged particularly well—with its cheap production, rigid song structures, and political concerns, it is very much a piece of the early '80s—the sound remains invigorating; the band possessed a visceral energy matched by only a handful of their peers. *Complete Discography*, in fact, is not only one of the cornerstones of any hardcore collection, it's not a bad way to become acquainted with hardcore. *—Stephen Thomas Erlewine*

Minutemen

f. 1980, San Pedro, CA, **db.** 1986
College Rock, Post-Punk, Hardcore Punk, Alternative Pop/Rock, American Underground
More than any other hardcore band, the Minutemen epitomized the free-thinking independent ideals that formed the core of punk/alternative music. Wildy eclectic and politically revolutionary, the Minutemen never stayed in one place too long—they moved from punk to free jazz to funk to folk at a blinding speed. And they toured and recorded at blinding speed—during the early '80s, they were constantly on the road, turning out records whenever they had a chance. Like their peers Black Flag, Hüsker Dü, R.E.M., Sonic Youth, and the Meat Puppets, the Minutemen built a large, dedicated cult following throughout the United States through their relentless touring. Like their fellow American indie bands, the trio was poised to break into the world of major labels in 1986, and they would have if it wasn't for the tragic death of guitarist/vocalist D. Boon in December of 1985. Even though bassist Mike Watt and drummer George Hurley carried on with fIREHOSE in the late '80s, the legacy of the Minutemen overshadowed the new band in the late '80s and early '90s, as the San Pedro trio influenced several generations of musicians. *—Stephen Thomas Erlewine*

Paranoid Time / 1980 / SST ✦✦✦
The Minutemen's debut EP *Paranoid Time* is a startlingly coherent set of primal minimalism—a cross between Californian hardcore punk and the succinct experimentalism of Wire. It speeds by too quickly for any particular song to stand out, but the band's terse, frenetic energy is invigorating, as are their imaginative ideas. *—Stephen Thomas Erlewine*

The Punch Line / 1981 / SST ✦✦✦
The Minutemen may have come out of the same California hardcore scene that produced Black Flag, Circle Jerks, and Fear, but they not only bore little resemblance to their West Coast contemporaries, they didn't sound much like anyone else in American rock at that time. *The Punch Line* was the band's first album, packing 18 tunes into less than 25 minutes, and if the music shares hardcore's lust for speed and assaultive rhythmic

punch, their sharp, fragmented melodies, complex tempos, and overtly poetic and political lyrics made clear they were rugged individuals; imagine James Blood Ulmer teaching Wire how to get funky and you start to get an idea of what *The Punch Line* sounds like. It wasn't until the band began to slow down a bit on *What Makes a Man Start Fires?* that the strength of the group's individual songs became clear, and *The Punch Line* works better as a unified sonic assault than as a collection of tunes, but moments do stand out, especially "Tension," "Fanatics," and the title cut, which certainly lends a new perspective to Native American history. *The Punch Line* was as wildly inventive as anything spawned by American punk, and the band would only get better on subsequent releases. *—Mark Deming*

Buzz or Howl Under the Influence of Heat / 1983 / SST ♦♦♦♦♦
What Makes a Man Start Fires? marked a real step forward for the Minutemen, and while *Double Nickels on the Dime* was where the group would reach their peak, there were plenty of signs pointing to that album's diverse brilliance on this eight-song EP. While "Dreams Are Free, Motherfucker!" and "The Toe Jam" are goofy, noisy throwaways (hey, this *was* a EP sandwiched between albums), the rest of the songs found the band consolidating their strengths and growing even tighter and more confident. "I Felt Like a Gringo" and "Cut" merge funky rhythms with a punk rocker's sense of concision, "Self Referenced" and "The Product" reveal how far this band's writing had progressed since *The Punch Line*, and "Little Man With a Gun in His Hand" showed the Minutemen could reduce the tempo and the volume and still create stunning music. It's hard to think of a stronger rhythm section in an independent band in the 1980s than Mike Watt and George Hurley, and D. Boon was by any standards a superb guitarist, with smarts, style, and a keen sense of how to edit himself. *Buzz or Howl Under the Influence of Heat* remains a superb record from a band just edging into greatness. *—Mark Deming*

What Makes a Man Start Fires? / 1983 / SST ♦♦♦♦♦
The Minutemen had already come up with a sound as distinctive as anything to come out of the American punk underground—lean, fractured, and urgent—with their debut album, 1981's *The Punch Line*. But on their second (relatively) long-player, *What Makes a Man Start Fires?*, the three dudes from Pedro opted to slow down their tempos a bit, and something remarkable happened—the Minutemen revealed that they were writing really great songs, with a remarkable degree of stylistic diversity. If you were looking for three-chord blast, the Minutemen were still capable of delivering, as the opening cut proved (the hyper-anthemic "Bob Dylan Wrote Propaganda Songs"), but there was just as much churning, minimalistic funk as punk bile in their sound (bassist Mike Watt and drummer George Hurley were already a strikingly powerful and imaginative rhythm section), and D. Boon's guitar solos were the work of a man who could say a lot musically in a very short space of time. Leaping with confidence and agility between loud rants ("Split Red"), troubled meditations ("Plight"), and plainspoken addresses on the state of the world ("Mutiny in Jonestown"), the Minutemen were showing a maturity of vision that far outstripped most of their contemporaries and a musical intelligence that blended a startling sophistication with a street kid's passion for fast-and-loud. It says a lot about the Minutemen's growth that *The Punch Line* sounded like a great punk album, but a year later *What Makes a Man Start Fires?* sounded like a great album—period. *—Mark Deming*

The Politics of Time / 1984 / SST ♦♦♦
The Minutemen had as high a batting average as any band that came out of the California punk scene, releasing a number of superb records that confirmed their status as one of the finest, most intelligent, most forward-thinking, and most individual bands of their time. However, there isn't an awful lot of that on *The Politics of Time*; this compilation ties together a bagful of studio outtakes, rehearsal recordings, and live tapes of highly variable quality (one of which is thoroughly inaudible; it's a joke, but not necessarily a funny one). The album leads off well enough with seven tunes the band recorded for an unreleased album. Stylistically, the songs fit comfortably between the ambitious *What Makes a Man Start Fires?* and the magnum opus *Double Nickels on the Dime*; on their own, they would have made for a superb EP, and "Working Men Are Pissed" and "Shit You Hear at Parties" are excellent. But side two is bogged down with far too many unfocused, lo-fi live tapes, and while the selections by the Reactionaries (an embryonic version of the Minutemen) are historically interesting, ultimately they're little more than juvenilia from a band destined to create much stronger music. The Minutemen were far too gifted to make an album that wasn't worth hearing, and completists will be more than willing to forgive the duff tracks to get at the handful of great songs here, but ultimately *The Politics of Time* is the band's least essential release. *—Mark Deming*

★ **Double Nickels on the Dime** / 1984 / SST ♦♦♦♦♦
If *What Makes a Man Start Fires?* was a remarkable step forward from the Minutemen's promising debut album, *The Punch Line*, then *Double Nickels on the Dime* was a quantum leap into greatness, a sprawling 44-song set that was as impressive as it was ambitious. While punk rock was obviously the starting point for the Minutemen's musical journey (which they celebrated on the funny and moving "History Lesson Part II"), by this point the group seemed up for almost anything—D. Boon's guitar work suggested the adventurous melodic sense of jazz tempered with the bite and concision of punk rock, while Mike Watt's full-bodied bass was the perfect foil for Boon's leads and drummer George Hurley possessed a snap and swing that would be the envy of nearly any band. In the course of *Double Nickels on the Dime*'s four sides, the band tackles leftist punk ("Political Song for Michael Jackson to Sing"), Spanish guitar workouts ("Cohesion"), neo-Nortena polka ("Corona"), blues-based laments ("Jesus and Tequila"), avant-garde exercises ("Mr. Robot's Holy Orders"), and even a stripped-to-the-frame Van Halen cover ("Ain't Talkin' 'Bout Love"). From start to finish, the Minutemen play and sing with an estimable intelligence and unshakable conviction, and the album is full of striking moments that cohere into a truly remarkable whole; all three members write with smarts, good humor, and an eye for the adventurous, and they hit pay dirt with startling frequency. And if Ethan James' production is a bit Spartan, it's also efficient, cleaner than their work with Spot, and captures the performances with clarity (and without intruding upon the band's ideas). Simply put, *Double Nickels on the Dime* was the finest album of the Minutemen's career, and one of the very best American rock albums of the 1980s. *—Mark Deming*

My First Bells / 1985 / SST ♦♦♦♦♦
A superb collection of all Minutemen recordings from their first EP (*Paranoid Time*) up to and including *What Makes a Man Start Fires*. Rather than going crazy looking for those hard-to-find bits of vinyl, here's the whole shootin' match from 1980-83 in one spot. Cheap at twice the price. *—John Dougan*

Project Mersh / 1985 / SST ♦♦♦♦♦
"I got it! We'll have them write hit songs!" some nameless record company executive says in the cover painting to the Minutemen's 1985 EP *Project Mersh*, and that joke covers about half of the record's formula. While the Minutemen had been writing more melodic and approachable songs with each release, the massive barrage of 90-to-180-second songs on the epic *Double Nickels on the Dime* was at once an embarrassment of riches and a bit much for a casual listener to chew on. So for this tongue-in-cheek experiment in making a "commercial" (or "mersh") recording, D. Boon and Mike Watt wrote a few actual three-minute-plus rock tunes, complete with verses and choruses and melodic hooks. On top of that, the band made a game stab at cleaning up their act in the studio; while hardly on the level of something Bob Ezrin or Richard Perry would come up with, *Project Mersh* boasts a good bit more polish than anything the band had released up to that point and even featured horn overdubs and keyboards on a few tracks. But the punch line was that the Minutemen had used all this fancy window dressing on songs that weren't all that different from what they'd been doing all along—"The Cheerleaders" and "King of the Hill" are typically intelligent, clear-eyed polemics from Boon, and Watt's "Tour-Spiel" is one punker's bitterly funny ode to life on the road (it stands comfortably beside their cover of Steppenwolf's variation on the same theme, "Hey Lawdy Mama"). While the Minutemen were a band that followed their own creative path from the beginning to the end, *Project Mersh* made clear they could have followed a more easily traveled road and still made good music with plenty to say. *—Mark Deming*

3-Way Tie for Last / Oct. 1985 / SST ♦♦♦♦♦
D. Boon's death in December 1985 was one of rock's most tragic occurrences. And, a decade later, I find that it still affects the way I listen to this, the "final" Minutemen record. Boon was hitting his stride here; the songs were emphatic, smart, and marked by his increasing sociopolitical awareness. Boon did not suffer fools gladly, and this record (as does the best of the Minutemen) retains a strong sense of moral indignation (listen to "The Price of Paradise" and "The Big Stick"). One fact that shouldn't be lost in eulogizing over Boon was the significant role Mike Watt was playing in the band. This hadn't happened overnight, but with each successive record Watt's confidence as a bass player and songwriter was growing, and by the time of *3-Way Tie*, his skills were in full flower—so much so that one side of the record is called Side D., the other Side Mike. Dense and driving, this is a bittersweet moment closing an excellent band's career. *—John Dougan*

Ballot Result / 1987 / SST ♦♦♦♦
Before they had even released *3-Way Tie for Last* in the fall of 1985, the Minutemen had blocked out plans for their next album, which was to be a sprawling three-LP set featuring three sides of studio material and three sides of live recordings. Initial pressings of *3-Way Tie* included a ballot so fans could vote for the songs to be included on the live half of the upcoming album; the tragic death of D. Boon meant the Minutemen would never make another studio album, but Mike Watt and George Hurley compiled the ballots sent in by fans and used the results as the basis for this album, which uses radio broadcasts, studio outtakes, rehearsal tapes, and audience recordings to assemble a final tribute to their fallen comrade. As you might expect, the quality of the sound varies quite a bit from track to track (though there's nothing as awful as the stuff on side two of *The Politics of Time*), and there are a few items here that were outtakes for a good reason (like the overlong version of "Mr. Robot's Holy Orders" or the spontaneous soundtrack improvisation "Hell"). But for the most part, *Ballot Result* is a fitting memorial that makes clear the Minutemen were just as strong onstage as they were in the studio and that their songs were smart, provocative, adventurous, and stand up well to the test of time. The fiery first side of material from the WREK-FM broadcast previously bootlegged on *Just a Minute, Men* alone makes this album well worth owning, and there are plenty of other gems scattered through the rest of the set. *Ballot Result* is hardly the ideal Minutemen live album, but it offers tangible evidence that they were one of the greatest American bands of their time, and that's not an accomplishment to be sneezed at. *—Mark Deming*

Post-Mersh, Vol. 1 / 1987 / SST ♦♦♦♦♦
The Minutemen's *Post-Mersh* is a valuable series, collecting all of the group's official discography, with the exception of *Double Nickels on the Dime*, *3-Way Tie For Last*, and *Ballot Result*, over the course of three discs. *Post-Mersh, Vol. 1* starts at the beginning, combining the trio's first two albums, *The Punch Line* (1981) and *What Makes A Man Start Fires?* (1983) on one disc. *—Stephen Thomas Erlewine*

Post-Mersh, Vol. 2 / 1987 / SST ♦♦♦♦♦
Picking up where the first volume left off, *Post-Mersh, Vol. 2* contains the Minutemen's 1983 *Buzz or Howl Under the Influence of Heat* LP and the 1985 *Project Mersh* EP. *—Stephen Thomas Erlewine*

Post-Mersh, Vol. 3 / 1989 / SST ♦♦♦♦♦
The third and final volume of *Post-Mersh* crams an extraordinary amount of music on one-disc, compiling the EPs *Paranoid Time* (1980), *Bean-Spill* (1982), and *Tour-Spiel*

(1985), the 1981 "Joy" single, and the 1984 rarities and outtakes collection *The Politics of Time*. *—Stephen Thomas Erlewine*

Introducing the Minutemen / Jul. 28, 1998 / SST ✦✦✦✦✦
Along with such bands as Black Flag, Minor Threat, and the Circle Jerks, the Minutemen were one of the prominent underground punk bands of the early '80s, who helped pave the way for countless other bands who would soon follow. Although only a trio (the late, great D. Boon on vocals/guitar, bassist Mike Watt, and drummer George Hurley), the Minutemen were capable of creating quite an enjoyable racket, as evidenced from any one of the 35 tracks that comprise the 1998 career overview, *Introducing the Minutemen*. Although the band has ceased to exist since late 1985, after Boon died in an auto accident, they continue to be name-checked by new punk bands as a major influence. The majority of the tracks don't stretch past the two-minute mark (several not even past a minute), as the group specialized in succinct blasts of energetic punk—"Definitions," "Fanatics," "Search," and so on. But toward the end of their career, the trio began to branch out musically—"Corona" (which became the theme song for MTV's *Jackass* program), the surprisingly melodic "Price of Paradise," "This Ain't No Picnic," and "I Felt Like a Gringo." As the title suggests, *Introducing the Minutemen* serves as a perfect introduction to this notable '80s band. *—Greg Prato*

The Misfits

f. 1977, **db.** 1983
Hardcore Punk, American Underground
Genuinely shocking or tasteless, campy fun? It was sometimes hard to tell which way the Misfits wanted to be taken, and the immense cult following that has grown up in the years after their actual existence (1977-1983) seems divided in its own assessment. It certainly wasn't the Misfits' musicianship—which was as crude as the recording quality of most of their oeuvre—that endeared them to so many, although Glenn Danzig possessed one of the most distinctive and tuneful bellows in hardcore punk. Rather, it was Danzig's penchant for catchy, anthemic melodies, often delivered at warp speed, and his lyrical obsession with grade-B horror films and splatter imagery that helped the Misfits build a rabid posthumous following. Namedrops and covers by metal bands like Metallica and Guns & Roses kept the Misfits' songs circulating during the mid- to late '80s, when their tangled discography remained only sporadically in print—reissues were maddeningly incomplete, and much of the band's prime material was confined to rare singles and EPs. The mid-'90s saw a spate of CD reissues that, while not quite presenting all of the Misfits' songs in the most concise, collectible format, at least succeeded in getting them all back into print, allowing those who missed the band the first time around to hear why they've enjoyed such enduring cult popularity. *—Steve Huey*

Walk Among Us / 1982 / Slash/Rhino ✦✦✦✦✦
With imagery lifted from sci-fi flicks and gory horror films, Glenn Danzig and Co. sound all revved up and ready to go on their debut record. With Ramones-influenced punk that occasionally veers into speedy, unintelligible hardcore, this is a ferocious, relentless record that makes no apologies for its capacity to alienate listeners. Ugly, unrepentantly nasty, and essential. Issued on CD in 1988. *—John Dougan*

Earth A.D./Wolfsblood / 1983 / Plan 9/Caroline ✦✦✦✦✦
With their second album, the incredibly short *Earth A.D./Wolfsblood*, the Misfits speed up the tempo even more, which combines with their amateurish musicianship to produce a wall of thrashy sonic murk. Additionally, *Earth A.D.* doesn't have the same catchy melodies that made previous Misfits records so exciting; however, the CD reissue appends the "Die Die My Darling" single, which injects a burst of melodicism that makes the set more listenable. Dedicated fans will certainly want this album; others might be more inclined to hear it broken up over the two CD compilations, which contain all of its tracks. *—Steve Huey*

Legacy of Brutality / 1985 / Plan 9/Caroline ✦✦✦
Legacy of Brutality compiles a variety of Misfits rarities and outtakes, including the entire unreleased portion of the band's unreleased 1978 debut, *Static Age* (several of its tracks that appeared on early EPs are not included here). Also present are the A-sides of the non-LP singles "Halloween" and "Who Killed Marilyn?," the latter actually a Glenn Danzig solo record. As an entity unto itself, the compilation plays a little inconsistently, and with the various reissues in recent years, it's not quite invaluable any longer, but it's arguably a better way to hear this material than the *Static Age* reissue, especially since a couple of *Legacy*'s better songs are not on any of the other single-disc compilations. *—Steve Huey*

● **Misfits** / 1986 / Plan 9/Caroline ✦✦✦✦✦
Purists may disagree, but for the benighted, this is the best place to start—a 20-track anthology that gives you the most Misfits for your money. Everything that made the Misfits great is here, including the odd remix, alternate take, and re-edited version. The band is loud and defiant, as is Danzig, whose considerable vocal chops are well displayed here. The perfect music for an evening of headbanging or watching gore films. Collectors who don't want to invest in the box set should note that this is also the only place to get "London Dungeon" and "Ghouls' Night Out," the B-sides of the "Night of the Living Dead" single. *—John Dougan*

Die Die My Darling / 1987 / Plan 9/Caroline ✦✦✦

Collection II / 1995 / Caroline ✦✦✦✦
Collection II picks up where the *Misfits* collection left off, making widely available for the first time many of the band's legendary early tracks, including "Attitude," "Last Caress," "We Are 138," and several other non-LP singles. There are also a selection of tracks from *Walk Among Us* not covered by the first compilation, as well as the remainder of the *Earth A.D.* album. If you began your Misfits collection with the first compilation, *Collection II* makes an excellent supplement, and the two put together are close to being definitive. *—Steve Huey*

Static Age / Oct. 31, 1995 / Caroline ✦✦✦
Static Age was to be the Misfits' debut album; it was recorded in 1978 and rejected by every record company the group brought it to. Thanks to the resurgence of interest in the Misfits, *Static Age* was finally released for the first time in 1997 by Caroline. Some of the material, in remixed form, was included on the band's early EPs and, later, on the two *Collection* releases; the remainder, also remixed, had been collected on the *Legacy of Brutality* compilation, which also offers a few rarities not available elsewhere. Since the entirety of *Static Age* is available elsewhere, Misfits fanatics probably already have the material; it's interesting to hear the LP as it was originally intended, but those who can do without that experience should probably stick to the other compilations. *—Steve Huey*

Box Set / Feb. 27, 1996 / Caroline ✦✦✦✦✦
The Misfits' self-titled box set is designed for the collector, not the casual fan. Featuring a selection of tracks from their five official albums, the set is full of rarities, including the entire *Static Age* album, which has never been released, plus 30 other rarities, ranging from outtakes to alternate takes. Of course, this means that *The Misfits* won't be of interest to anyone but the diehard fans, but for those fans, it's an indispensable, rare treasure. *—Stephen Thomas Erlewine*

American Psycho / May 13, 1997 / Geffen ✦✦✦
The Misfits were always the most ridiculous of all hardcore bands, but age has only made them sillier, as the reunion album *American Psycho* proves. Without Glenn Danzig, the group loses much of their menace and new vocalist Michale Graves helps the band turn into a kitschy goth-punk outfit that relies more on metal than hardcore. Since they have trouble writing catchy riffs, the Misfits rely on their campy persona to make the album listenable, and on occasion—such as "Hate the Living, Love the Dead," "Abominable Dr. Phibes," "Dig Up Her Bones," and "Don't Open Til Doomsday"—they are so over-the-top they're funny. However, the majority of *American Psycho* is simply labored and uninvolving and, in that respect, it's no different than most reunion albums. *—Stephen Thomas Erlewine*

Famous Monsters / Oct. 5, 1999 / Roadrunner ✦✦

The Missing Links

f. 1964, **db.** 1966
Garage Rock
One of the best Australian bands of the '60s, though they weren't even stars in their home country, the Missing Links started as a very raw, Kinks-like combo, gaining a number two hit in New Zealand with "We 2 Should Live"/"Untrue." The first lineup folded in 1965, and a second, with entirely different personnel, took the name. This aggregation cut the rawest Australian garage/punk of the era, and indeed some of the best from anywhere, sounding at their best like a fusion of the Troggs and the early Who, letting loose at times with wild feedback that was quite ahead of its time. They didn't find commercial success, and split after several singles, an EP, and an album. Various members turned up in other Australian groups like Running Jumping Standing Still and Python Lee Jackson; the most notable of these was guitarist Doug Ford, who joined Running Jumping Standing Still and then graduated to the Master's Apprentices, the best Australian band of the '60s other than the Easybeats. *—Richie Unterberger*

The Missing Links / 1984 / Raven ✦✦✦✦
Their lone album is an uneven affair. The best cuts, "Wild About You," "Some Kinda Fun," "You're Drivin' Me Insane," "Mama Keep Your Big Mouth Shut," and "Speak No Evil," are tremendous '60s punk, with blistering, feedback-ridden guitar and cord-shredding vocals. The rest is rather ordinary group originals and covers, save "H'Tuom Tuhs," a nearly-six-minute backwards version of "Mama Keep Your Big Mouth Shut" that was quite experimental for 1966, if not terribly listenable. *—Richie Unterberger*

The Missing Links . . . Unchained! / 1984 / Phillips ✦✦
This four-song EP is worth tracking down if you're into the group, and if you can find it, but inessential otherwise. Contains rough-hewn covers of "Wooly Bully," James Brown's "I'll Go Crazy," and Them's "One More Time"; the best track, "Don't Give Me No Friction," is available on the compilation *Raven EP-LP, Vol. 1*. *—Richie Unterberger*

● **Driving You Insane** / 1999 / Half a Cow ✦✦✦✦
In addition to assembling all two-dozen cuts known to exist by both the first and second lineup of the Missing Links, this exemplary reissue adds three songs by the Showmen (whose rhythm section joined the second lineup) and a live 1966 TV version of "Diddy Wah Diddy" by Running Jumping Standing Still (founded by a couple of ex-Missing Links). It's quite a package, consisting in the main of everything from their sole LP, *The Missing Links*; the non-LP B-side "Somethin' Else"; all four songs from their 1966 EP *The Links Unchained*; "We 2 Should Live"/"Untrue," the only single (and only official release) of the first Missing Links lineup; and five tracks recorded by the first lineup that were unreleased at the time. Not everything here is boss, but the best of it establishes the Missing Links as the best Australian '60s garage/punk band, and one of the better ones from anywhere on the globe. Note that although, confusingly, not one of the Missing Links in the first lineup was in the second one that recorded, the recordings by the first lineup are engagingly raw R&B/British Invasion pop-style numbers, even if they lack the manic frenzy and feedback experimentation of the second lineup's best moments, such as "Speak No Evil," "Don't Give Me No Friction," and "You're Drivin' Me Insane." Another significant plus is the detailed 40-page booklet, which gives as comprehensive a lowdown on this mysterious cult band as is likely to ever appear. *—Richie Unterberger*

Missing Persons

f. 1980, Los Angeles, CA, **db.** 1986
Pop/Rock, New Wave

Famed as much for their video-ready space-age image as for their music, the Los Angeles-based New Wave outfit Missing Persons formed in 1980, a year after the marriage of singer Dale Bozzio and her drummer husband Terry. A onetime member of Frank Zappa's backing band, Terry Bozzio met the former Dale Consalvi (an ex-Playboy Bunny) at a Hollywood recording studio; after founding Missing Persons—initially dubbed U.S. Drag—the couple recruited fellow Zappa alumni Warren Cuccurullo on guitar and Patrick O'Hearn on bass, and with classically trained keyboardist Chuck Wild in tow, they began playing area clubs.

In 1981, the band released its self-titled debut EP; after signing to Capitol, the label reissued the record in 1982, and the singles "Words" and "Destination Unknown" both nearly hit the Top 40. Their videos also helped Missing Persons find success on the fledgling MTV network, where Dale Bozzio's hiccuping voice and campy look (comprised of shocking-pink hair and sci-fi outfits capped off with Plexiglass bras) combined with the group's synth-driven songs to make them naturals for heavy rotation. Later in 1982, the group issued its first full-length album, *Spring Session M* (an anagram of their name), which launched the underground smash "Walking in L.A."

After 1984's *Rhyme and Reason* notched only a minor hit with the single "Give," Missing Persons enlisted Chic's Bernard Edwards to produce 1986's dance-pop effort *Color in Your Life*; the album stiffed, however, and both the band and the Bozzios themselves broke up. While Dale Bozzio issued one solo album on Prince's Paisley Park label, Terry Bozzio went on to work with Jeff Beck; Cuccurullo, meanwhile, joined Duran Duran, O'Hearn recorded several instrumental new age albums, and Wild composed music for films and television. —*Jason Ankeny*

Missing Persons / 1982 / Capitol ♦♦♦
Built around the core of husband-and-wife team Dale and Terry Bozzio—the latter being a former member of Frank Zappa's band—Missing Persons debuted in 1982 with this attempt to package the avant-garde for your average mall customer. The hybrid wasn't nearly as crummy as that description sounds, and on tracks like "Destination Unknown" (on the Capitol version, the label that picked it up after it was originally released independently by producer Ken Scott) there's a kernel of real musical ambition and zest. —*Alex Ogg*

Spring Session M / 1982 / One Way ♦♦♦♦♦
In 1982, Missing Persons established themselves on the new wave pop scene by loading up their hair with shocking pink dye and enough hairspray to tear a hole in the ozone layer big enough to poke a small parking garage through, programming a few synthesizers to play hyper dance-pop, scrambling their band name into *Spring Session M*, and scrawling those words across the jacket of their first full length record. The band scored one hit single from the album, "Walking in L.A.," which is the catchiest effort on the record. The two singles from their self-titled debut EP, "Destination Unknown" and "Words," are both tolerable. But the rest of *Spring Session M* is somewhat overwhelmed by the Cyndi Lauper screechiness of lead singer Dale Bozzio's vocals, Warren Cuccurullo's wailing guitars, and the relentless chirpiness of the keyboards and synthesizers, of which there are so many that it took three band members (Terry Bozzio, Chuck Wild, and Patrick O'Hearn) to manage them all. —*Evan Cater*

Rhyme & Reason / 1984 / One Way ♦♦♦
Though some consider this to be Missing Persons' best album, it is, in essence, a catalog of flawed ambition and missed opportunities. For other, more sober critics, the band's moment had passed and they were in serious danger of outstaying their welcome. Trite rock songs such as "Surrender Your Heart" did little to assuage that opinion. The one clawback is "Give," the least obvious and least expansive track on a record that singularly fails to adhere to those values elsewhere. —*Alex Ogg*

Color in Your Life / 1986 / One Way ♦♦
Produced by Bernard Edwards (of Chic fame), *Color in Your Life* saw Missing Persons apply further cosmetic surgery to their already highly commercial sound. Funk was a touchstone currency of the new romantic movement, and Missing Persons accommodated it with more dexterity than some, but that's not saying much. Dale Bozzio's voice flounders in this unsympathetic environment, and the band play like they know the game is up—and it was. Dale, who had long-since romantically disentangled herself from husband Terry Bozzio, moved on to release a solo record on Prince's Paisley Park label. —*Alex Ogg*

● **The Best of Missing Persons** / 1987 / Capitol ♦♦♦♦♦
The two main qualities of this band, heard on this compilation taken from their three albums and one EP, are the untutored singing of Dale Bozzio and the technical facility of the musicians, expressed in the inventive guitar and keyboard arrangements. High-quality '80s rock. —*William Ruhlmann*

The Mission UK

f. 1986, Leeds, England
College Rock, Goth Rock, Alternative Pop/Rock

Derided by critics as pompous, melodramatic, and bombastic, the Mission, as they were known in their native U.K. (their name had to be changed in America owing to a Philadelphia R&B band with the same moniker), nonetheless attracted a core audience of goth-rock fans and continues to record today. The Mission was formed in 1986 by guitarist/singer Wayne Hussey and bassist Craig Adams, who both left the Sisters of Mercy to do so. (Hussey had also played with the Walkie Talkies and Dead or Alive.) The two recruited Artery guitarist Simon Hinkler and former Red Lorry Yellow Lorry drummer Mick Brown and called themselves the Sisterhood, to which Sisters of Mercy leader

Andrew Eldritch objected strenuously. The Mission released two successful independent singles in the U.K. and signed to Mercury in 1986. The group soon completed its debut album, *God's Own Medicine*, which critics lambasted as ponderous and derivative of Led Zeppelin and Yes, but the album produced several U.K. hits anyway. The band toured extensively in the U.K. and America; Adams had to return home from the latter after suffering from exhaustion. Produced by Led Zeppelin bassist John Paul Jones, *Children* widened the band's audience, reaching number two on the U.K. album charts. 1990's *Carved in Sand* shed some of the Mission's Zep fascination for more refined songwriting. Hinkler left the band midway through the supporting tour and was eventually replaced permanently by Paul Etchells. Meanwhile, several Mission members backed Slade members Noddy Holder and Jim Lea on the Christmas charity single "Merry Xmas Everybody." By 1992, Hussey was the only original member left; following the 1994 *Sum and Substance* retrospective, he recorded the 1995 album *Neverland* with a new Mission lineup. *Blue* followed a year later, with the greatest hits retrospective *Ressurection* appearing in fall 1999. —*Steve Huey*

God's Own Medicine / 1986 / Mercury ♦♦♦♦♦
Goth-pop was defined by the Mission, who took the heavy goth sounds of the Sisters of Mercy and mixed it with better melody and Led Zeppelin-style arrangements. This album is where it all took off. The independent singles that the Mission released were the perfect warm-up for the bombastic and shimmering songs on *God's Own Medicine*. The opener "Wasteland" is the perfect example of the formula that Wayne Hussey and company used to take over the U.K. in the late '80s, while the album's ballads, "Let Sleeping Dogs Lie" and "Love Me to Death," stand up well next to rockers like "Sacrilege" and the stunning single "Severina." This album marks an important chapter in the history of both goth and British rock. —*Chris True*

The First Chapter / 1987 / Mercury ♦♦♦♦
Featuring covers and singles from the pre-*God's Own Medicine* era, *The First Chapter* can at times reinforce the critics' view that the Mission were nothing but a pompous goth band intent on dredging up rock's past. The opener, a shoddy cover of the Beatles' "Tomorrow Never Knows," is a perfect example of that, proving that at times Wayne and his mates should have left well enough alone. Fortunately, this collection includes some of the Mission's finer moments. Cover versions of Free's "Wishing Well" and Patti Smith's "Dancing Barefoot" manage to merge classic rock tracks with the Mission's glossy and dramatic approach with ease. The best moments of *The First Chapter* are found in the Mission's own compositions, especially the single "Serpents Kiss" and "The Crystal Ocean," both of which shimmer with Hussey's signature 12-string sound, and one of the best non-drum machine rhythm sections that came out of the English goth rock scene. —*Chris True*

Children / 1988 / Mercury ♦♦♦♦
It is hard to remember that at one time goth rock was actually taken (sort of) seriously. When the Mission's *Children* came out in 1988, the English goth movement was immense. While American audiences were force-fed the gleaming production and banal lyrics of hair metal, Brits were dealing with gleaming production and pastoral lyrics worshipped by kids dressed in black. Critics lambasted goth, calling it pompous, derivative, and lacking in imagination. Critics don't buy records, however (they get them for free), and the public made it a movement. The Mission's *Children* was perfectly timed, spent time at the upper reaches of the U.K. charts, and was the band's first, albeit cultish, success in the U.S. *Children* is the Mission's big statement. Besides the fact that it was a prolific seller, *Children* was a well-done and accessible album—at times. Songs like the single "Heaven on Earth" are lush, shimmering affairs that are almost dreamlike in their delivery, while tracks like "Black Mountain Mist" and "Breathe" are short interludes that are reminiscent of Led Zeppelin. Of course, that may be all due to the fact that Led Zeppelin bassist and arranger John Paul Jones produced and played on the album. Musically, the Mission were at their best and most dramatic on *Children*. But there are moments that firmly place this album in the cement of goth in 1988, and there's no way out. The goth movement could at times be silly and overblown, but it produced some strong music, and the Mission's *Children* is a perfect example that sometimes you shouldn't read too much into everything. —*Chris True*

Carved in Sand / Feb. 1990 / Mercury ♦♦♦♦
The much delayed and highly anticipated *Carved in Sand* was even more popular than its predecessor, *Children*. The last album recorded by the Mission in their original lineup, *Carved in Sand* spawned three U.K. hit singles, a massive European tour, and unrelenting media attention from the English music press. *Carved in Sand* pretty much picks up where *Children* left off; with grandiose, shimmering arena rock-style songs like "Deliverance," only this time Wayne Hussey tries to extend his lyrical ability to encompass social issues. Songs like "Into the Blue," which has a light environmental theme, and "Amelia" (touching on the issue of child abuse and molestation) are two of the strongest tracks, musically speaking. Hussey almost pulls off the role of social commentator, but his dramatics get in the way. The rest of the album is a typical Mission album: great music, great production, mediocre lyrics. Hussey had said that at the time the band was about nothing but dramatics. Even though *Carved in Sand* proves his point, it's still a great album. —*Chris True*

Grains of Sand / Nov. 1990 / Mercury ♦♦♦♦
An interesting collection, *Grains of Sand* is not a Mission album proper, but rather a chance for the listener to hear the other songs that were recorded for *Carved in Sand*. The single "Hands Across the Ocean" is a nugget of pop brilliance that hints at what came next for Wayne Hussey. Most of the tracks are solid, but covers of "Love," and "Mr. Pleasant" are better off as B-sides. The strength of songs like "Hands…," "Divided We Fall,"

and "Mercenary" are good arguments that the sessions for *Carved in Sand* produced what could have been one hell of a double album. *—Chris True*

Masque / Dec. 1991 / Mercury ♦♦♦
While *Children* and *Carved in Sand* were bona fide, arena-rock powerhouses, *Masque* was a 180 degree turnaround. The end product of an aborted Wayne Hussey solo album, as well as the first Mission U.K. album not to feature original lead guitarist Simon Hinkler, *Masque* is a dancy, electronic step forward for the Mission. Unfortunately for the band, their fans weren't impressed, which is sad because *Masque* isn't really that off-putting. Critics, likewise, were harsh regarding the change—ironic, due to the fact that they had spent a lot of time and money giving the band a hard time for following a "formula." The production of *Masque* is near perfect and the songs are roughly similar to previous Mission releases, but the dominance of keyboards and (oddly) fiddles drove a lot of casual fans away. The opener, "Never Again'" is in the same vein as early tunes like "Wasteland" and "Deliverance," while "Like a Child Again" revisits the melodic pop of "Hands Across the Ocean." This is an album of varying styles and experiments that is worth another look. *—Chris True*

● **Sum and Substance** / May 17, 1994 / Mercury ♦♦♦♦♦
A solid collection of the Mission's best from their years at Mercury (1986-1994), featuring excellent remixes of "Beyond the Pale" and "Like a Child Again." The only thing lacking here are the stellar tracks from their Chapter 22 Records days—"Serpents Kiss," "Crystal Ocean," and "Garden of Delight"—which leaves the more devoted fan wishing for a more sizable collection. This is a fine overview, however, and it's nice to have all of the great singles in one place. *—Chris True*

Resurrection: The Greatest Hits / Nov. 2, 1999 / Cleopatra ♦♦♦♦
Leave it to Wayne Hussey to come back in a unique way. Instead of releasing a collection of old songs in a new package, he reworked some of the best of the Mission's back catalog, bringing the past into the present. The songs are as majestic as ever, this time combined with the keyboard-enhanced sound which first appeared on albums like *Masque*. While it may take some time getting used to the reworked sound on classics like "Wasteland" and "Deliverance," the new production gives them new life. This is a must-have for longtime fans, who will be pleased that Hussey seems comfortable with the past—resurrection indeed. *—Chris True*

Mission of Burma

f. 1980, Boston, MA, **db.** 1983
American Punk, Post-Punk, Punk
Of all the punk-inspired bands that came out of Boston in the early '80s, none were better than Mission of Burma. Arty without being too pretentious, capable of writing gripping songs and playing with ferocious intensity, the group galvanized Boston's alternative rock scene, and despite a too-short existence, set a standard for excellence that has rarely been equalled. Burma's music is vintage early-'80s post-punk: jittery rhythms, odd shifts in time, declamatory vocals; an aural assault similarly employed by bands such as the Gang of Four, Mekons, and Pere Ubu. Also, conspicuously present in the mix was the proto-punk of the Stooges and Velvet Underground, bands that inspired Burma's darker songwriting impulses and tendencies toward longish, repetitive jams capable of boring holes into your skull. What Burma added was a sonic texture through the use of extreme volume. After debuting with the explosive single "Academy Fight Song," Burma released the full-length *Vs.* Unbeknownst to fans, this was the beginning of the end. After a bittersweet farewell tour in 1983, the shows were released as a live LP entitled *The Horrible Truth About Burma*, an occasionally thrilling example of their considerable stage prowess. Frontman Roger Miller went on to a career as a solo artist and with his non-touring band Birdsongs of the Mesozoic. *—John Dougan*

Vs. / 1982 / Rykodisc ♦♦♦♦♦
The EP *Signals, Calls and Marches* suggested that Mission of Burma had the talent and vision to become one of America's great rock bands; the subsequent album *Vs.* proved beyond a doubt that the group had arrived and was fully realizing its potential. MOB's blend of punk rock fury and post-collegiate musical smarts had been honed to a razor-sharp point by the time *Vs.* was recorded, and they had fully worked through the British influences that occasionally surfaced on *Signals, Calls and Marches*, maturing into a band whose sound was as distinctive as anyone of its generation. Roger Miller's guitar work had gained greater depth and confidence in the year since *Signals*, the rhythm section of Clint Conley and Peter Prescott epitomized both strength and intelligence, and MOB was exploring trickier structures and more dramatic use of dynamics this time out; the subtle tension of "Trem Two" and the powerful mid-tempo angst of "Einstein's Day" were a genuine step forward in the group's development, while "The Ballad of Johnny Burma," "Fun World," and "That's How I Escaped My Certain Fate" made it clear that the band had lost none of its rib-cracking impact along the way. It's daunting to imagine just how far Mission of Burma could have taken its music had Roger Miller's hearing problems not caused the band to break up the following year, but regardless of lost potential, very few American bands from the 1980s released an album as ambitious or as powerful as *Vs.*, and it still sounds like a classic. Rykodisc's remastered 1997 reissue sounds terrific and adds four solid bonus tracks. *—Mark Deming*

The Horrible Truth About Burma / 1985 / Rykodisc ♦♦♦
Signals, Calls and Marches and *Vs.* proved that Mission of Burma were one of the best American bands to emerge in the wake of punk's first wave (and before the rise of indie rock), and no one who saw them live seems willing to dispute that they were a powerhouse onstage. So it doesn't make much sense that the group's posthumous live album, *The Horrible Truth About Burma*, recorded during five dates of their final tour, isn't nearly as strong as their studio recordings, but the band's choice of material for their final gesture lets them down. Mission of Burma chose to fill *The Horrible Truth* with previously unrecorded songs, which was a fine idea on paper, since the band had already announced their upcoming breakup when they played these shows and wanted to preserve tunes that might otherwise be lost to the ages. But while there's isn't a bad song to be found, there also isn't anything that scales the peaks of "That's When I Reach for My Revolver," "Einstein's Day," or "Fun World," though "Peking Spring" comes close, and the curious might wonder if Steve Albini was listening when they played this album's take of "Dumbells" in Chicago. It seems significant that two of the strongest cuts are covers: the Stooges' "1970" and "Heart of Darkness" by Pere Ubu. And while Mission of Burma are in strong, hard-hitting form throughout, much of the time they lack the fierce precision that made *Vs.* so memorable. *The Horrible Truth About Burma* is a fine souvenir for fans but not much of an intro for beginners; the home video release *Live at the Bradford*, shot at the band's final concert, does a superior job of capturing what made this group so compelling. *—Mark Deming*

Mission of Burma [EP] / 1987 / Taang! ♦♦♦
Here's the first of two table scrap releases from Mission of Burma, post-breakup. The thing is, these table scraps make for a fine feast, as there's little filler to be found here. Though starting off with an inferior, rough-sounding version of "This Is Not a Photograph," your money is worth it alone for the track that follows, Clint Conley's "Peking Spring," which nears "That's When I Reach for My Revolver" in catchiness and immediacy. The rambunctious, rumbling "Blackboard" is another furious gem. When drummer Peter Prescott exclaims, "You have done these awful deeds / Now you have to pay," you almost want to turn off the stereo and hide under your bed. *—Andy Kellman*

Forget / 1987 / Taang! ♦♦♦
One of the reasons Mission of Burma's small recorded oeuvre is so impressive is because it's so consistent—they released two singles, a six-cut EP, and a 12-song album in a four-year recording career, and there's not a song among them that isn't worth hearing. One of the band's secrets was a matter of strict quality control, and if you need any proof, just give a spin to *Forget*, a 12-song collection of demos and outtakes recorded between 1979 and 1982. While this disc isn't bad by any stretch of the imagination, it's not up to the standards of *Signals, Calls and Marches* or *Vs.*; the songs often seem to be repeating themes Mission of Burma explored elsewhere, and the performances (as well as the recording) lack the resonance of the band's studio work. (Superior versions of two of the songs, "Progress" and "Forget," appear as bonus tracks on the CD reissue of *Vs.*, as if to offer further proof *Forget* doesn't capture the band at their peak.) But it's worth pointing out that Mission of Burma were among the best American bands of the 1980s, and the material on *Forget* would hardly convince anyone otherwise; the edges may be rough, but the intense and intelligent heart of Mission of Burma beats strong and clear on this disc, and given how little MOB material is available, practically anything is a welcome addition to the pantheon. If you loved *Vs.* or *Signals, Calls and Marches*, don't expect something on quite the same level, and if you've never heard Mission of Burma, you should pick up those records first. But anyone who is already familiar with this band's achievement will be happy to have *Forget* in their collection. *—Mark Deming*

● **Mission of Burma** / 1988 / Rykodisc ♦♦♦♦♦
Mission of Burma were one of the most important and influential American bands of their time, but they also rocked hard with intelligence and a unique personal vision, and their records still sound fresh and exciting nearly two decades after they were recorded. The 1988 compilation *Mission of Burma* marked the first attempt to upgrade the band's back catalog to compact disc, and as an introduction to their music you could hardly do better. *Mission Of Burma* features the superb *Signals, Calls and Marches* EP and the masterful *Vs.* album in their entirety, as well as the A-side to their first single (the justifiably legendary "Academy Fight Song"), three fine *Vs.*-era unreleased tracks, and two cuts from the posthumous live album *The Horrible Truth About Burma*. With the band's three 12" releases now available on individual compact discs (with superior remastering and bonus tracks), *Mission Of Burma* isn't as essential as it was in 1988, but it still contains the lion's share of the band's catalog, and if you want a crash course in one of the first and greatest bands of the 80's indie-rock revolution, this disc is just what you've been looking for. *—Mark Deming*

Let There Be Burma / 1990 / Taang! ♦♦♦
With so little material available, it's common for outtakes and assorted ephemera to be released to a ravenous horde of uncritical fans. These are interesting but non-essential releases. The Rykodisc release serves as the most exhaustive and authoritative document. Caveat Emptor: *Let There Be Burma* is a re-release of *Mission of Burma* (not to be confused with the Rykodisc release) and *Forget* on one disc. *—John Dougan*

Mr. Bungle

f. 1985, Eureka, CA
Experimental Rock, Alternative Metal, Funk Metal, Alternative Pop/Rock
Mr. Bungle's sound and approach is a unique mix of the experimental, the abstract, and the absurd. It all began in 1985, in the town of Eureka, CA; the group met while in high school and took their moniker from a children's educational film regarding bad habits (it was featured in a Pee Wee Herman HBO special). The group's first demo, *The Raging Wrath of the Easter Bunny*, was recorded around this time; with each new demo, their sound became progressively more mutated, until musical boundaries began to melt (metal, funk, experimental, jazz, ska, techno, etc.). Mike Patton landed the lead vocalist slot with Faith No More in 1988 (it was in fact a Mr. Bungle demo that got Patton the job), and instead of breaking up Mr. Bungle, Patton decided to keep both bands going simultaneously. Due to FNM's success, Mr. Bungle was signed to Warner Bros., who released their self-titled debut in 1991 (with almost all the members going by obscure aliases). The

band built a large and loyal cult following on the subsequent tour, as they performed in masks to hide their identities, and played unlikely covers during their set. When the tour wrapped up in 1992, Patton returned to Faith No More, while the rest of the group focused on side projects; guitarist Trey Spruance briefly joined Patton in FNM for 1995's *King for a Day.* It took the band four long years to follow up their debut with 1995's superb *Disco Volante.* An extensive world tour followed, with the group widening their fan base. Mr. Bungle quickly regrouped in early 1997 to record an album of their eclectic cover songs, which was eventually put on hold before completion as Patton began a tour with Faith No More and the others returned to their additional projects. The group reconvened in 1999 for the release of *California.* —*Greg Prato*

Mr. Bungle / 1991 / Warner Brothers ✦✦✦✦✦
When Mr. Bungle's debut album was released in the summer of 1991, the band was wrongly given the title of "Mike Patton's side project." In reality, Patton (listed as "Vlad Drac" on the album) was in Mr. Bungle before joining Faith No More. While there are a few similarities to FNM (airy keyboards, crunchy guitar riffs, Patton's unmistakable vocals, etc.), they are really two completely different bands. Although Faith No More's music can be quite daring, their songs are rooted in conventional song structures, whereas Mr. Bungle's music is a bit more eccentric. Their debut would turn out to be not as focused and fully realized as their next album (1995's *Disco Volante*), but the groundwork would be laid for their future triumph. The musical ideas are all over the place on such tracks as the John Travolta/Patrick Swayze tribute "Quote Unquote" (originally titled "Travolta," then quickly renamed when the lawyers came around), the rubbery funk and ska of "Carousel," and the uncomfortable anger of "My Ass Is on Fire." The group's unique sense of humor sometimes works well ("Egg"), while floundering at other times (the one-dimensional "The Girls of Porn"). The outlandish John Zorn co-produced the record with the band, encouraging Mr. Bungle to indulge in all of their demented fantasies. It's a good thing he did. —*Greg Prato*

● **Disco Volante** / Oct. 10, 1995 / Warner Brothers ✦✦✦✦✦
Mr. Bungle is the musical equivalent of a David Lynch movie. On their uncompromising second release, *Disco Volante,* the group focuses their sound a bit more than on their 1991 self-titled debut but still keeps things unruly and completely unpredictable. This is a band whose sole purpose is to break all the pre-existing rules of music and doesn't think twice about taking chances. What they've created in the process is a totally original and new musical style and an album that sounds like nothing which currently exists. The group, whose members go by aliases, may be the most talented rock instrumentalists today, as they skip musical genres effortlessly, while Mike Patton illustrates why many consider him to be the best singer in rock. The group tackles plodding death metal ("Everyone I Went to High School With Is Dead"), deranged children's songs ("After School Special"), and a Middle Eastern techno number that has to be heard to be believed ("Desert Search for Techno Allah"). Many of the songs radically change genres mid-song, encompassing the sounds of Ennio Morricone, John Zorn, Frank Zappa, and other heretofore un-thought-of musical mutations. Not music to unwind to after a hard day, but it will challenge your mind when the right mood hits. —*Greg Prato*

California / Jul. 13, 1999 / Warner Brothers ✦✦✦✦
Four years after *Disco Volante,* Mr. Bungle returns with *California,* which immediately distinguishes itself from its predecessors—it's probably their most heavily orchestrated record to date and their most melodic overall, as well as the least dependent on rock styles. That's certainly not to imply that this is a tame or immediately accessible record, nor that Mr. Bungle has suddenly gone sane. There is a stronger lounge-music orientation to the group's trademark rapid-fire genre-hopping; we hear more pop, swing, rockabilly, country & western, bossa nova, Hawaiian and Middle Eastern music, jazz, Zappa-esque doo wop, arty funk, post-rock, space-age pop, spaghetti-Western music, warped circus melodies, and even dramatic pseudo-new age, plus just a smidgen of heavy metal. Sure, some of those sounds have appeared on Mr. Bungle records past, but the difference this time is the focus with which the band deploys its arsenal. *California* is their most concise album to date, clocking in at around 45 minutes; plus, while the song structures are far from traditional, they're edging more in that direction and that greatly helps the listener in making sense of the often random-sounding juxtapositions of musical genres (assuming, of course, that you're supposed to even try to make sense of them). As with any Mr. Bungle album, *California* requires at least a few listens to pull together, but its particular brand of schizophrenia isn't nearly as impenetrable as that of *Disco Volante,* even if it will still make you marvel at the fact that such a defiantly odd, uncommercial band records for Warner Brothers. —*Steve Huey*

Mr. Mister

f. 1982, **db.** 1988
Pop/Rock, Adult Contemporary
Mr. Mister was formed in 1982 by session musicians Richard Page (bass, vocals) and Steve George (keyboards), both of whom had played on hits for REO Speedwagon and John Parr and wanted to taste success under their own identities. The lineup was rounded out by guitarist Steve Farris and drummer Pat Mastelotto, and Mr. Mister recorded its debut album, *I Wear a Face,* in 1984. *Welcome to the Real World* was the band's big break, however; "Broken Wings" and "Kyrie" both hit number one and were followed by the Top Ten "Is This Love." After one more album, *Go On,* which produced only the minor hit "Something Real (Inside Me/Inside You)," Farris left the band, which has not been heard from since. Page turned down offers to join Toto and Chicago. —*Steve Huey*

I Wear the Face / 1984 / RCA ✦✦✦
An uneven, but impressive debut comes from these L.A. songwriters/session musicians with already significant credentials. —*AMG*

Welcome to the Real World / 1985 / RCA ✦✦✦✦
Here are the major pop hits "Broken Wings," "Kyrie," and "Is It Love" from this band of session musicians and songwriters. —*Kenneth M. Cassidy*

● **The Best of Mr. Mister** / Apr. 17, 2001 / Buddha ✦✦✦✦
Buddha's *Best of Mr. Mister* may only clock in at 12 tracks, but it's a succinct, accurate summary of the group's career, containing not only hits like "Broken Wings" and "Kyrie," but also a good cross section of their album tracks. Certainly, some hardcore followers will notice particular favorites missing, but for most listeners, this will contain all the Mr. Mister they'll need. —*Stephen Thomas Erlewine*

The Misunderstood

f. 1963, **db.** 1969
Garage Rock, Psychedelic
Of the thousands of U.S. garage bands that struggled in the 1960s without achieving international success, the Misunderstood were not only among the very best, but among the very few to progress beyond basic garage sounds to music that has been (belatedly) recognized as nearly as accomplished and innovative as that of the British Invasion bands that touched off the garage explosion in the first place. Formed in Riverside, CA, in 1963, the group began as a basic R&B/rock combo in the tradition of the Stones and Animals but rapidly moved toward a proto-psychedelic sound with guitar feedback, sustain, Middle Eastern influences, and exploratory song structures that strongly echoed the Yardbirds. The band moved to England in 1966 in an attempt to find a sympathetic audience, cutting six songs that found them anticipating the early innovations of groups like Pink Floyd and Jimi Hendrix. The group were praised by the British press and up-and-coming acts like Pink Floyd and the Move, but were hounded by U.S. draft authorities and internal problems, and disbanded in confusion around early 1967. —*Richie Unterberger*

● **Before the Dream Faded** / 1982 / Cherry Red ✦✦✦✦✦
One of the great lost '60s albums. Side one includes all six of the tracks they recorded in England in 1966, with magnificent guitar work and nervy, ambitious (if a bit overtly cosmic) songwriting that combines some of the best aspects of the Jeff Beck-era Yardbirds and Syd Barrett's Pink Floyd. Remember that Pink Floyd and Hendrix had yet to record when these sides were waxed; they aren't derivations, but genuinely innovative and groundbreaking performances. Side two contains seven pre-psychedelic demos from their U.S. garage days in the mid-'60s that, while not nearly as important as their 1966 work, are solid, crunching R&B-soaked rock in the tradition of their chief British influences. —*Richie Unterberger*

Golden Glass / 1984 / Cherry Red ✦✦✦
Only Glenn Campbell remains from the original lineup on this album of 1969 material. Competent blues-rock, with some commendable steel guitar work by Campbell, it's nonetheless a pale shadow of the group's psychedelic recordings. Instead of picking this up, be on the lookout for a three-song EP (also called *Golden Glass*) that includes wild psychedelic covers of "Shake Your Money Maker" and "I'm Not Talkin'" by the original lineup in early 1966, and the eight-minute 1969 track "Golden Glass," which is probably the best cut from the last version of the band. —*Richie Unterberger*

The Legendary Goldstar Album/Golden Glass / 1997 / Cherry Red ✦✦✦
In early 1966, with John Peel as producer, the Misunderstood went into Gold Star studio in Los Angeles to make some demos. Although the tapes have disappeared, an acetate of some of the songs still exists, from which eight tracks (two of which had previously been released) were rescued for reissue on the first disc of this double CD. Judged against their magnificent recordings in Britain in late 1966 (with slightly different personnel), it's a bit of a letdown. The group at this point were a competent but not extraordinary blues-rock act, offering competent renditions of standards by Howlin' Wolf, Muddy Waters, Jimmy Reed, and the like that only hinted at the originality that would blossom on their U.K. sessions. Indeed, the two tracks that have previously been available ("Shake Your Money Maker" and a wild, extended "I'm Not Talkin'" with ferocious distorted guitar breaks) are by far the best in the set. The second disc is just a straight reissue of the long-available *Golden Glass* album, recorded by a later lineup of the Misunderstood, in which steel guitarist Glenn Campbell was the only remaining member from the glory days. *Before the Dream Faded* is the essential Misunderstood compilation, but this double disc does compile all of their known remaining recordings for the collectors who want everything by the group. —*Richie Unterberger*

Joni Mitchell

b. Nov. 7, 1943, Fort McLeod, Alberta, Canada
Vocals, Keyboards, Piano, Guitar / Album Rock, Vocal Jazz, Jazz-Rock, Folk-Rock, Singer/Songwriter, Folk-Jazz
When the dust settles, Joni Mitchell may stand as the most important and influential female recording artist of the late 20th century. Uncompromising and iconoclastic, Mitchell confounded expectations at every turn; restlessly innovative, her music evolved from deeply-personal folk stylings into pop, jazz, avant-garde, and even world music, presaging the multi-cultural experimentation of the 1980s and 1990s by over a decade. Fiercely independent, her work steadfastly resisted the whims of both mainstream audiences and the male-dominated recording industry—while Mitchell's records never sold in the same numbers enjoyed by contemporaries like Carole King, Janis Joplin, or Aretha Franklin, none experimented so recklessly with their artistic identities or so bravely explored territory outside of the accepted confines of pop music. The commercial and critical approval awarded her landmark 1971 record *Blue* was unprecedented: a luminous, starkly confessional set, it firmly established Mitchell as one of pop music's most remarkable and insightful talents. Predictably, she turned away from *Blue*'s incandescent folk with 1972's

For the Roses, the first of the many major stylistic turns she would take over the course of her daring career. Backed by rock-jazz performer Tom Scott, Mitchell's music began moving into more pop-oriented territory, a change typified by the single "You Turn Me On (I'm a Radio)," her first significant hit. The follow-up, 1974's classic *Court and Spark*, was her most commercially successful outing: a sparkling, jazz-accented set, it reached the number two spot on the U.S. album charts and launched three hit singles—"Help Me," "Free Man in Paris," and "Raised on Robbery." 1975's *The Hissing of Summer Lawns* was a bold, almost avant-garde record which housed her increasingly complex songs in experimental, jazz-inspired settings; "The Jungle Line" introduced the rhythms of African Burundi drums, placing her far ahead of the pop world's mid-1980s fascination with world music. *—Jason Ankeny*

Joni Mitchell (aka Song to a Seagull) / Mar. 1968 / Reprise ✦✦✦

Joni Mitchell's debut release is a concept album. Side one, subtitled "I Came to the City," generally exhibits songs about urban subjects that are often dour or repressed in some way. "Out of the City and Down to the Seaside," by contrast, is a celebration of nature and countryside, mostly containing selections of a charming, positive, or more outgoing nature. What sets this release apart from those of other confession-style singer/songwriters of the time is the craft, subtlety, and evocative power of Mitchell's lyrics and harmonic style. Numbers such as "Marcie," "Michael From Mountains," "The Dawntreader," and "The Pirate of Penance" effectively utilize sophisticated chord progressions rarely found in this genre. Verses are substantive and highly charged, exhibiting careful workmanship. "Song to a Seagull" has graceful and vivid lyrics about the joys of freedom set to a haunting, wide-ranging vocal line. Conversely, "Cactus Tree" explores the downside of a no-strings-attached approach to life, the fear of committing to a relationship (ironically wedding these words to a hopeful melody and pulsating guitar texture). "Marcie" utilizes poignant, twisting music set to desolately lonely lyrics about a jilted woman; the recurrent use of red and green imagery in the verses is especially clever. Character studies such as "I Had a King" and "Nathan La Franeer" are painfully bleak in contrast to the lithe domestic scene of "Sisotowbell Lane" and the winsomely reserved love song "Michael From Mountains." Unusual in her oeuvre are the overlapping dialogue prose manner of "The Pirate of Penance" and the jaunty honky-tonk stylings of "Night in the City." Mitchell sings in a light, gossamer, at times diffident manner; vocal harmony is sparingly employed here. David Crosby's production is simple and effective. This excellent debut is well worth hearing. *—David Cleary*

Clouds / May 1969 / Reprise ✦✦✦

Clouds is a stark stunner, a great leap forward for Joni Mitchell. Vocals here are more forthright and assured than on her debut and exhibit a remarkable level of subtle expressiveness. Guitar alone is used in accompaniment, and the variety of playing approaches and sounds gotten here is most impressive. "The Fiddle and the Drum," a protest song that imaginatively compares the Vietnam-era warmongering U.S. government to a bitter friend, dispenses with instrumental accompaniment altogether. The sketches presented of lovers by turns depressive ("Tin Angel"), roguish ("That Song About the Midway"), and faithless ("The Gallery") are vividly memorable. Forthright lyrics about the unsureness of new love ("I Don't Know Where I Stand"), misuse of the occult ("Roses Blue"), and mental illness ("I Think I Understand") are very striking. Mitchell's classic singer/songwriter standards "Chelsea Morning" and "Both Sides Now" respectively receive energetically vibrant and warmly thoughtful performances. Imaginatively unusual and subtle harmonies abound here, never more so in her body of work than on the remarkable "Songs to Aging Children Come," which sets floridly impressionistic lyrics to a lovely tune that is supported by perhaps the most remarkably sophisticated chord sequence in all of pop music. Mitchell's riveting self-portrait on the album's cover is a further asset. This essential release is a must-listen. *—David Cleary*

Ladies of the Canyon / Apr. 1970 / Reprise ✦✦✦✦✦

This wonderfully varied release shows a number of new tendencies in Joni Mitchell's work, some of which would come to fuller fruition on subsequent albums. "The Arrangement," "Rainy Night House," and "Woodstock" contain lengthy instrumental sections, presaging the extensive non-vocal stretches in later selections such as "Down to You" from *Court and Spark*. Jazz elements are noticeable in the wind solos of "For Free" and "Conversation," exhibiting an important influence that would extend as late as *Mingus*. The unusually poignant desolation of "The Arrangement" would surface more strongly in *Blue*. A number of the selections here ("Willy" and "Blue Boy") use piano rather than guitar accompaniment; arrangements here are often more colorful and complex than before, utilizing cello, clarinet, flute, saxophone, and percussion. Mitchell sings more clearly and expressively than on prior albums, most strikingly so on "Woodstock," her celebration of the pivotal 1960s New York rock festival. This number, given a haunting electric piano accompaniment, is sung in a gutsy, raw, soulful manner; the selection proves amply that pop music anthems don't all have to be loud production numbers. Songs here take many moods, ranging from the sunny, easygoing "Morning Morgantown" (a charming small-town portrait) to the nervously energetic "Conversation" (about a love triangle in the making) to the cryptically spooky "The Priest" (presenting the speaker's love for a Spartan man) to the sweetly sentimental classic "The Circle Game" (denoting the passage of time in touching terms) to the bouncy and vibrant single "Big Yellow Taxi" (with humorous lyrics on ecological matters) to the plummy, sumptuous title track (a celebration of creativity in all its manifestations). This album is yet another essential listen in Mitchell's recorded canon. *—David Cleary*

☆ **Blue** / Jun. 1971 / Reprise ✦✦✦✦✦

Sad, spare, and beautiful, *Blue* is the quintessential confessional singer/songwriter album. Forthright and poetic, Mitchell's songs are raw nerves, tales of love and loss (two words with relative meaning here) etched with stunning complexity; even tracks like "All I Want," "My Old Man," and "Carey"—the brightest, most hopeful moments on the record—are darkened by bittersweet moments of sorrow and loneliness. At the same time that songs like "Little Green" (about a child given up for adoption) and the title cut (a hymn to salvation supposedly penned for James Taylor) raise the stakes of confessional folk-pop to new levels of honesty and openness, Mitchell's music moves beyond the constraints of acoustic folk into more intricate and diverse territory, setting the stage for the experimentation of her later work. Unrivaled in its intensity and insight, *Blue* remains a watershed. *—Jason Ankeny*

For the Roses / Nov. 1972 / Asylum ✦✦✦✦✦

On *For the Roses*, Joni Mitchell began to explore jazz and other influences in earnest. As one might expect from a transitional album, there is a lot of stylistic ground explored, including straight folk selections using guitar ("For the Roses") and piano ("Banquet," "See You Sometime," "Lesson in Survival"), overtly jazzy numbers ("Barangrill," "Cold Blue Steel and Sweet Fire"), and hybrids that cross the two ("Let the Wind Carry Me," "Electricity," "Woman of Heart and Mind," "Judgment of the Moon and Stars"). "Blonde In the Bleachers" grafts a rock & roll band coda onto a piano-based singer/songwriter main body. The hit single "You Turn Me on I'm a Radio" is an unusual essay into country-tinged pop, sporting a Dylanesque harmonica solo played by Graham Nash and lush backing vocals. Arrangements here build solidly upon the tentative expansion of scoring first seen in *Ladies of the Canyon*. "Judgment of the Moon and Stars" and "Let the Wind Carry Me" present lengthy instrumental interludes. Lyrics here are among Mitchell's best, continuing in the vein of gripping honesty and heartfelt depth exhibited on *Blue*. As always, there are selections about relationship problems, such as "Lesson in Survival," "See You Sometime," and perhaps the best of all her songs in this genre, "Woman of Heart and Mind." "Cold Blue Steel and Sweet Fire" presents a gritty inner-city survival scene, while "Barangrill" winsomely extols the uncomplicated virtues of a roadside truck stop. More than a bridge between great albums, this excellent disc is a top-notch listen in its own right. *—David Cleary*

★ **Court and Spark** / Jan. 1974 / Asylum ✦✦✦✦✦

Mitchell reached her commercial high point with *Court and Spark*, a remarkably deft fusion of folk, pop, and jazz which stands as her best-selling work to date. While as unified and insightful as *Blue*, the album—a concept record exploring the roles of honesty and trust in relationships, romantic and otherwise—moves away from confessional songwriting into evocative character studies: the hit "Free Man in Paris," written about David Geffen, is a not-so-subtle dig at the machinations of the music industry, while "Raised on Robbery" offers an acutely funny look at the predatory environment of the singles bar scene. Much of *Court and Spark* is devoted to wary love songs: both the title cut and "Help Me," the record's most successful single, carefully measure the risks of romance, while "People's Parties" and "The Same Situation" are fraught with worry and self-doubt (standing in direct opposition to the music, which is smart, smooth, and assured from the first note to the last). *—Jason Ankeny*

Miles of Aisles / Nov. 1974 / Asylum ✦✦✦

Like most live albums, this two-record set was a profit-taking release on which the artist re-presented many of her old songs for a new acceptance now that she had a larger pop audience. Backed by the pop-jazz ensemble the L.A. Express Mitchell reprised the best from her first five albums, pointedly ignoring *Court and Spark*, and including two new cuts, "Love or Money" and "Jericho." *—William Ruhlmann*

The Hissing of Summer Lawns / Nov. 1975 / Asylum ✦✦✦✦✦

Mitchell evolved from the smooth jazz-pop of *Court and Spark* to the radical *The Hissing of Summer Lawns*, an adventurous work which remains among her most difficult records. After opening with the graceful "In France They Kiss on Main Street," the album veers sharply into "The Jungle Line," an odd, Moog-driven piece backed by the rhythms of the warrior drums of Burundi—a move into multiculturalism which beat the likes of Paul Simon, Peter Gabriel, and Sting to the punch by a decade. While not as prescient, songs like "Edith and the Kingpin" and "Harry's House—Centerpiece" are no less complex or idiosyncratic, employing minor-key melodies and richly detailed lyrics to arrive at a strange and beautiful fusion of jazz and shimmering avant-pop. *—Jason Ankeny*

Hejira / Nov. 1976 / Asylum ✦✦✦

Joni Mitchell's *Hejira* would be the last in an astonishingly long run of top-notch studio albums dating back to her debut. Some vestiges of her old style remain here; "Song for Sharon" utilizes the static, pithy vocal harmonies from *Ladies of the Canyon*'s "Woodstock," "Refuge of the Roads" features woodwind touches reminiscent of those in "Barangrill" from *For the Roses*, and "Coyote" is a fast guitar-strummed number that has precedents as far back as *Clouds*' "Chelsea Morning." But by and large, this release is the most overtly jazz-oriented of her career up to this point—hip and cool, but never smug or icy. "Blue Motel Room" in particular is a prototypic slow jazz-club combo number, appropriately smooth, smoky, and languorous. "Coyote," "Black Crow," and the title track are by contrast energetically restless fast-tempo selections. The rest of the songs here cleverly explore variants on mid- to slow-tempo approaches. None of these cuts are traditionally tuneful in the manner of Mitchell's older folk efforts; the effect here is one of subtle rolls and ridges on a green meadow rather than the outgoing beauty of a flower garden. Mitchell's verses, many concerned with character portraits, are among the most polished of her career; the most striking of these studies are that of the decrepit Delta crooner of "Furry Sings the Blues" and the ambivalent speaker of "Song to Sharon," who has difficulty choosing between commitment and freedom. Arrangements are sparse, yet surprisingly varied, the most striking of which is the kaleidoscopically pointillistic one used on "Amelia." Performances are excellent, with special kudos reserved for Jaco Pastorius' melodic bass playing on "Refuge of the Roads" and the title cut. This excellent album is a rewarding listen. *—David Cleary*

Don Juan's Reckless Daughter / Dec. 1977 / Asylum ✦✦

Mingus / Jun. 1979 / Asylum ✦✦✦
Mitchell sets lyrics to Charles Mingus' last melodies in collaboration with the composer and a who's who of prominent jazz musicians. *—William Ruhlmann*

Shadows and Light / Sep. 1980 / Asylum ✦✦✦
Shadows and Light is Joni Mitchell's second live album, and it serves as a good retrospective of her more jazzy period from 1975-1979. As expected, she assembles a group of all-star musicians including Pat Metheny (guitar), Jaco Pastorius (bass), Lyle Mays (keyboards), and Michael Brecker (saxophone) that give these compositions more energy than on the studio recordings. The musicians are given room to jam, and they sound terrific on up-tempo songs such as "Coyote" and "In France They Kiss on Main Street." If there is a general theme of these songs, it's about growing older and maturing after the failed idealism of the late '60s (the album opens with audio clips from the movie *Rebel Without a Cause*"). Although this album is pleasing, the live arrangements are not different enough from the studio versions to warrant higher marks. In fact, Joni Mitchell has always been an album artist who recorded studio albums that had a sound and feel all their own. While *Shadows and Light* provides a nice summary of her experimental period for casual fans, interested listeners should start with *Hejira* or *Hissing of Summer Lawns*. *—Vik Iyengar*

Wild Things Run Fast / Oct. 1982 / Geffen ✦✦✦
On her first new studio album of original material in five years and her debut for Geffen Records, Joni Mitchell achieved more of a balance between her pop abilities and her jazz aspirations, meanwhile rediscovering a more direct, emotional lyric approach. The result was her best album since the mid-'70s. *—William Ruhlmann*

Dog Eat Dog / Oct. 1985 / Geffen ✦✦

Chalk Mark in a Rain Storm / Mar. 1988 / Geffen ✦✦✦
Long before Frank Sinatra made his *Duets* album, Joni Mitchell cast a variety of name singers in prominent roles for the songs on *Chalk Mark in a Rain Storm*. Peter Gabriel sings with her on the leadoff track, "My Secret Place," and Don Henley is heard on "Lakota" and "Snakes and Ladders," Billy Idol and Tom Petty have roles in "Dancin' Clown," and Willie Nelson brings his dry phrasing to "Cool Water," while ex-Cars singer Benjamin Orr and ex-Prince associates Wendy Melvoin and Lisa Coleman also have backup parts. Mitchell uses the vocal firepower over spare tracks heavy on percussion (by Manu Katche) and programming to tell stories and comment on social issues. "Lakota" deals with Native American and environmental matters, "Cool Water" (a Mitchell rewrite of the Bob Nolan original) discusses water pollution, "The Tea Leaf Prophecy (Lay Down Your Arms)" and "The Beat of Black Wings" tell war-related tales. But Mitchell's main theme, which encompasses those topics, concerns the evils of contemporary culture in which one struggles to be "Number One," rises and falls like a game of "Snakes and Ladders," and suffers "The Reoccurring Dream" brought on by advertising. *Chalk Mark in a Rain Storm* rarely makes these points personally enough to stir the listener, and the trendy percussion sound (popular with artists like Gabriel and Kate Bush in the '80s) is already beginning to sound dated. But the songwriting and Mitchell's voice remain impressive, especially when she recalls her past with a revised version of "Corrina, Corrina" at the end. *—William Ruhlmann*

Night Ride Home / Feb. 19, 1991 / Geffen ✦✦✦
Cutting back on the guest musicians of her previous effort and paring down to a basic small group of musicians helps add immediacy to *Night Ride Home*. While this release features several of Joni Mitchell's favorites, nothing here would become a hit, as Joni tended to buck trends and follow her own beat. Very involved and a rather tough listen, but well worth the attention, this would be her last for Geffen, where she languished unnoticed while the label went heavy metal crazy. *—James Chrispell*

Turbulent Indigo / Oct. 25, 1994 / Reprise ✦✦✦
Joni Mitchell returned to the relatively spare style of albums like *Hejira* and her early folk collections on *Turbulent Indigo*, emphasizing her acoustic guitar strumming and singing on a series of songs that detail the political and social discontent she had previously explored on *Dog Eat Dog* and *Chalk Mark in a Rain Storm*. In the brief opener, "Sunny Sunday," a woman tries to shoot out a streetlight with a pistol and misses every night, a metaphor for the individual's futile struggle against civilization, and Mitchell repeats much the same message in songs like "Sex Kills," a generalized criticism of everything from lawyers to the hole in the ozone layer; "Turbulent Indigo," which describes the inability of people to understand artists; "Last Chance Lost," which treats romantic disappointment, and "Not to Blame," about spousal abuse. The low-key music and restrained vocals stand in contrast to the lyrics—over and over, Mitchell's imagery refers to guns and violence. *Turbulent Indigo* provides a disturbing view of modern life made all the more compelling by its calm presentation. *—William Ruhlmann*

Hits / Oct. 29, 1996 / Reprise ✦✦✦✦✦
The album is a long overdue anthology of one of Canada's most celebrated ex-pats, Joni Mitchell. She sanctioned the release only on the condition that she be allowed to compile companion album *Misses*. While the 15-strong *Hits* focuses on the her earlier folk-pop crossover successes, many made famous initially by others ("Both Sides Now," "Woodstock," "The Circle Game"), *Misses* is a personal cross-section of her more challenging early material and more recent recordings—the riveting "The Wolf That Lives in Lindsey" from *Mingus* is especially enlightening. One should not pick up one disc without the other. With the flood of box sets released in recent years for far less deserving artists, it's odd that Reprise didn't go all out and make this a more elaborate tribute. *—Roch Parisien*

Misses / Oct. 29, 1996 / Reprise ✦✦✦
Misses intends to round up the best of Joni Mitchell's failed singles and forgotten album tracks, which is a daunting task, to be sure. In a career as acclaimed, idiosyncratic, and prolific as Mitchell's, it's problematic to boil all the forgotten favorites down to one disc, but the task is made all the more difficult by the fact that the songwriter herself compiled the collection and she has an agenda. Mitchell is out to prove that her neglected Geffen recordings during the '80s were as consistent as her classic '70s albums for Reprise. Although she is correct in her assessment that the albums should be given more respect, her execution could have been better. The bulk of *Misses* is comprised of the Geffen recordings, which were frequently difficult to appreciate, and in this presentation, they aren't any easier to digest. "A Case of You," which probably should have been on *Hits*, is added as bait, but casual fans of that song won't find the rest of *Misses* as illuminating as *Blue*. In fact, only the converted will be willing to make an effort with the bulk of *Misses*, and they'll probably find the individual albums more rewarding. So, the record doesn't appeal to its intended audience, leaving it without one *—Stephen Thomas Erlewine*

Taming the Tiger / Sep. 29, 1998 / Reprise ✦✦✦
This latest disc from Joni Mitchell harkens back to the days when she heard the hissing of summer lawns and the jazzier essays of her *Hejira* days. The only difference between then and now is her use of a guitar synthesizer for her aural textures and melody templates. Always employing the best of musicians to help her out, Mitchell takes off on a trip through "Harlem in Havana" and ending up with "Tiger Bones" to show for it. Along the way, she puts forth "No Apologies" and rocks things up with "Lead Balloon," which will remind one of "Big Yellow Taxi" and holds one of her best opening one-liners ever. With "Taming the Tiger" dedicated to her newfound daughter and grandson, "Stay in Touch" could be about them, or almost anyone Joni's been close to. Either way, it's a great tune. *Taming the Tiger* is her most pleasing and consistent disc since the mid-'70s; even after all these years, Joni Mitchell continues to expand her music while keeping her integrity intact. This is definitely one of her best. *—James Chrispell*

Both Sides Now / Feb. 8, 2000 / Reprise ✦✦✦
Ex-husband Larry Klein, who serves as co-producer and musical director, explains in his liner notes that Joni Mitchell intended to tell the story of a "modern" romantic relationship in the songs, most of which come from the '30s and '40s. If so, her concept of a modern relationship is very troubled—most of the selections are unhappy love songs. Vince Mendoza's arrangements—a third of them played by a gigantic 71-piece orchestra, a third by a regular-size orchestra, and a third by a swing-style big band—often suggest the oceanic sweep and serious, melancholy tone of film noir movie music. They also do a lot of Mitchell's work for her. As a singer, she has never had much projection or power, but she is a master of phrasing and tone. Mitchell often sounds like an alternate Billie Holiday, with the breathiness and note decay characteristic of later Holiday, if none of her delayed timing. *Both Sides Now* is not revelatory in a musical sense, but it does achieve its intention of reconceiving Joni Mitchell as an interpretive singer. *—William Ruhlmann*

Mobb Deep

f. 1992, Queensbridge, NY
Hardcore Rap, East Coast Rap, Gangsta Rap, Hip-Hop
While most hardcore gangsta rappers and rap groups are quickly written off by seasoned rap fans and critics as lowbrow exploitation, Mobb Deep quickly overcame this initial stereotype in the late '90s, becoming one of the few gangsta rap groups to garner unanimous acclaim from all sides of the rap community. Mobb Deep members Prodigy and Havoc originally met while both attending the prestigious Graphic Arts High School in Manhattan as teenagers. Still in their late teens, the duo released their debut album in 1993, *Juvenile Hell*, on the 4th & Broadway label. Though the album wasn't that successful from either a financial or critical standpoint, it did serve as a fitting platform for the duo to launch their careers. Their brutally honest reality rapping and complimentary self-produced melancholy beats landed them a deal with the up-and-coming Loud label in 1995, resulting in their first major-label release, *The Infamous*. Propelled to awareness partially by fellow Queens rapper Nas, who took a similar approach lyrically on his championed *Illmatic* album from 1994, Mobb Deep suddenly found themselves developing a quickly growing cult following. Even critics championed their poetic depiction of New York street life and also their trademark production, the bleak aural equivalent of their sullen rhymes. By the end of the decade, Mobb Deep's *Murda Muzik* debuted at number three on Soundscan before quickly going platinum, exemplifying exactly how far they had come within less than a decade without compromising their harsh approach. *—Jason Birchmeier*

Juvenile Hell / Apr. 13, 1993 / 4th & Broadway ✦✦

The Infamous / Apr. 25, 1995 / Loud ✦✦✦✦
Where Mobb Deep's debut album *Juvenile Hell* garnered the young duo a healthy cult following and scored them a record deal with *Loud Records*, it seems merely an omen of what the Queensbridge rappers would achieve on *The Infamous*. At the time of this album's release, they were relatively unknown. Luckily for them, though, another Queensbridge rapper with a similar poetic style of reality rapping, Nas, had won tremendous acclaim with his debut, *Illmatic*. So when this release hit the streets, the public was hungry for more of what Nas had delivered in such harsh terms; *The Infamous* didn't disappoint. Undeniably even more bleak than *Illmatic*, it functioned as a cinematic portrait of Hellish New York City, the ghetto lifestyle that hadn't yet made its way into East Coast rap in the early 1990s. And with the help of two potent singles that were boosted by substantial radio play—"Shook Ones, Pt. 2" and "Survival of the Fittest"—*The Infamous* eventually made its way into the hands of critics and hip-hop heads outside of New York. As a result, this album set the stage for the breakthrough success of the group's successive album, *Hell on Earth*. Yet where this next album featured a polished, more developed version of *Havoc*'s trademark sullen production—chilling piano notes, shimmering

melancholy strings, dusty crackling ambience, emotive cries of sadness—*The Infamous'* production was less polished and incredibly raw, making this album what many fans consider to be their finest, as the group slowly ascended to mass-catering commercial popularity. —*Jason Birchmeier*

● **Hell on Earth** / Nov. 19, 1996 / Loud ✦✦✦✦✦
When it came time for Mobb Deep to follow up the duo's acclaimed *The Infamous* album, Havoc and Prodigy chose not to depart from their formula for success, crafting yet another album of foreboding beats, eerie soundscapes, and grim lyrics. Since Havoc handles most of the group's production, duplicating his patented aesthetic—the sound of harsh urban darkness set to symphonic beats—wasn't a problem; similarly, he and his partner, Prodigy, didn't seem short on disturbing reality-based rhymes about the side of street life no one likes to think about. *Hell on Earth* remains Mobb Deep's best '90s album, surpassing the oft-hailed *Infamous* album with its aesthetics. Yes, Havoc and Prodigy are repeating themselves here in terms of both production and MCing, but they polish their style, crafting more evocative soundscapes and reciting more horrifying rhymes. The album's highlights—most notably "Hell on Earth" and "G.O.D., Pt. 3"—prove this, surpassing even *The Infamous'* best moment, "Shook Ones, Pt. 2." Of course, it's debatable whether or not the group's succeeding album, *Murda Musik*, tops this album. That album's shining moment, "Quiet Storm," is Mobb Deep's best moment of the decade, but *Murda Muzik* finds the duo trying to expand by incorporating guest rappers and experimenting with new styles; it is this experimentation, though, that prevents *Murda Muzik* from surpassing *Hell on Earth*, a perfect summation from beginning to end of the group's trademark aesthetic. —*Jason Birchmeier*

Murda Muzik / Apr. 27, 1999 / Loud ✦✦✦✦
After a three-year hiatus and numerous release date pushbacks, Mobb Deep got on their job once again with the punishing release of *Murda Muzik*. The duo, well-known for their lethal realism both in their infinitely dark yet moving beats and their stark and ruthless crime-rhyme lyrics, continued their grim odyssey with this, their fourth effort. Released amidst so much watered-down product, *Murda Muzik* is an arguable masterpiece in the Puffy and Master P era. Mobb Deep once described their music as the sound of hypnotic thug life. An accurate description, for their music is more than just guns and herb smoking, it taps into the collective sense of fear and horror, the evil in men's hearts, and the struggle for good in the gardens of waste. Mobb music can make you cry, can make you scared, can amplify your inner rage; its depth allows for the gamut of emotional reactions.

On this album, primary producer Havoc reached a high level of mastery in his production efforts, a truly signature style of deep bass grooves, piercing organs, ice-cold snare pops, melodic samples, and haunting orchestral snippets. Each song creates its own mood whether it be a call to stop the violence on "Spread Love" or a call for full throttle livin' on "I'm Goin' Out." Guest appearances by Raekwon, Lil' Kim, Lil Cease, Cormega, Kool G. Rap, Eightball, and Infamous Mobb add texture to already bangin' tracks. The album overall can best be described as pure ear- and mind-twisting pleasure and pain. The album will affect you, get under your skin, make you rash up, and then salve you. *Murda Muzik* is a complete album and a renewal of the truly hardcore movement. —*Michael Di Bella*

Moby (Richard Melville Hall)

b. Sep. 11, 1965, Darien, CT
Mixing, DJ, Producer, Vocals / Electronica, Ambient Techno, Trance, Club/Dance, Techno, Alternative Pop/Rock, House
Moby was one of the most controversial figures in techno music, alternately praised for bringing a face to the notoriously anonymous electronic genre, as well as being scorned by hordes of techno artists and fans for diluting and trivalizing the form. In either case, Moby was one of the most important dance music figures of the early '90s, helping bring the music to a mainstream audience both in England and in America. Moby fused rapid disco beats with heavy distorted guitars, punk rhythms, and detailed productions that drew equally from pop, dance, and movie soundtracks. Not only did his music differ from both the cool surface textures of ambient music and the hedonistic world of house music, but so did his lifestyle—Moby was infamous for his devout, radical Christian beliefs, as well as his environmental and vegan activism. "Go" became a British Top Ten hit in 1991, establishing him as one of the premier techno producers. By the time he came to the attention of American record critics with 1995's *Everything Is Wrong*, his following from the early '90s had begun to erode, particularly in Britain. Nevertheless, he remained one of the most recognizable figures within techno; after he abandoned the music for guitar-rock with 1996's *Animal Rights*, he returned to a heavy electronic base with 1997's *I Like to Score* and 1999's *Play*, the latter of which made him a genuine breakout pop star. —*Stephen Thomas Erlewine*

★ **Moby** / 1992 / Instinct ✦✦✦✦✦
After recording a string of dance classics culminating with the pop hit "Go," Moby released his full-length debut balancing those songs with a few decidedly inventive album tracks. Moby's melodic sense developed much quicker than other early techno producers; despite the criticisms leveled at his later direction (or lack thereof), his first album is a masterpiece of challenging, unrepetitive, beautifully programmed rave-techno. Though the familiar tracks "Drop a Beat," "Next Is the E," and "Go" are the highlights here, the final two tracks, "Slight Return" and "Stream," are fine examples of early chill-out techno. —*John Bush*

Early Underground / Apr. 28, 1993 / Instinct ✦✦✦✦
A 15-track compilation of Moby's early career, collected from seven releases, this album fails to show the diversity that makes his self-titled LP such a joy. The tracks here are acceptable early rave-techno, but they won't appeal to those who think repetition is a sign

of artistic deficiency. Most of the vocal samples are typical fare for the early '90s, but "Go (Original)" is more than worthy. —*John Bush*

Ambient / Aug. 17, 1993 / Instinct ✦✦✦
Hoping to cash in on the ambient-house craze in 1993, Instinct Records released a collection of Moby's softer tracks (which, to his credit, had been recorded long before). Tracks like "My Beautiful Blue Sky," "Piano and Strings," and "Myopia" showcase his talent for majestic orchestral sounds and melodic synth layered over slower beats and percussion. —*John Bush*

Mixmag Live!, Vol. 7 / 1995 / Mixmag ✦✦✦✦
Moby and Slam's Orde Mekle mixed this seventh volume (cassette only) in *Mixmag*'s series of DJ compilations. —*John Bush*

Everything Is Wrong / Mar. 14, 1995 / Elektra ✦✦✦✦✦
For his first major-label album, Moby pulled out all the stops, trying to fit as many different styles as possible into 50 minutes. From fast breakbeats to pseudo-industrial thrash, ambient trance to dance-pop, Moby tries it all. It's not quite a statement of genius—for all the bluster, there really isn't that much difference between his songs, which are nearly all standard three-chord progressions; it's all in the production. What ties everything together is Moby's understanding of the beat. The pulse holds steady throughout the record, making it sound like a very good night at a club. —*Stephen Thomas Erlewine*

Animal Rights / Feb. 11, 1996 / Elektra ✦✦

Rare: Collected B-Sides / Aug. 1996 / Instinct ✦✦✦
Rare: Collected B-sides isn't just for the die-hard Moby fan. Compiling a number of B-sides and non-LP singles on a single disc, *Rare* features a few run-of-the mill remixes, but usually these alternate versions offer a significantly new spin on the songs. More importantly, tracks like the notorious "Thousand"—which zips by at the impossibly fast speed of a thousand beats per minute—are included, making it a necessary listen for any dedicated fan of Moby. —*Stephen Thomas Erlewine*

I Like to Score / Aug. 26, 1997 / Elektra ✦✦✦
Considering that Moby's music is most effective in small doses, perhaps it shouldn't be a surprise that the compilation *I Like to Score* is a strong record. However, it does come as a surprise, since Moby's music usually sounds too insular for the kind of shifting, provocative atmospherics needed for effective film music. Here, on this collection of cinematic instrumental work, Moby demonstrates that he can capture the mood and feeling of a film while retaining his musical identity. Nothing here is particularly complex, and not all of it works—his reworking of John Barry's "James Bond Theme" sounds like a major studio's idea of what the kids are listening to these days—but by and large, *I Like to Score* is every bit as effective as Moby's official releases. —*Stephen Thomas Erlewine*

● **Play** / Jun. 1, 1999 / V2 ✦✦✦✦✦
Following a notorious flirtation with alternative rock, Moby returned to the electronic dance mainstream on the 1997 album *I Like to Score*. With 1999's *Play*, he made yet another leap back toward the electronica base that had passed him by during the mid-'90s. The first two tracks, "Honey" and "Find My Baby," weave short blues or gospel vocal samples around rather disinterested breakbeat techno. This version of blues-meets-electronica is undoubtedly intriguing to the all-important NPR crowd, but it is more than just a bit gimmicky to any techno fans who know their Carl Craig from Carl Cox. Fortunately, Moby redeems himself in a big way over the rest of the album with a spate of tracks that return him to the evocative, melancholy techno that's been a specialty since his early days. The tinkly piano line and warped string samples on "Porcelain" frame a meaningful, devastatingly understated vocal from the man himself, while "South Side" is just another pop song by someone who shouldn't be singing—that is, until the transcendent chorus redeems everything. Surprisingly, many of Moby's vocal tracks are highlights; he has an unerring sense of how to frame his fragile vocals with sympathetic productions. Occasionally, the similarities to contemporary dance superstars like Fatboy Slim and Chemical Brothers are just a bit too close for comfort, as on the stale big-beat anthem "Bodyrock." Still, Moby shows himself back in the groove after a long hiatus, balancing his sublime early sound with the breakbeat techno evolution of the '90s. —*John Bush*

Songs 1993-1998 / Jul. 11, 2000 / Elektra ✦✦✦
When *Play* became a breakout hit in 1999, Elektra readied a basic trainer for listeners new to Moby's practically trademarked style of down-tempo house baroque. Ranging from the *Move EP*, his major-label debut, to the soundtrack-inspired *I Like to Score*, *Songs 1993-1998* trawls the back catalog to pluck tracks on the same atmospheric level as *Play* classics like "Porcelain" or "South Side." Many of these tracks—especially ones from *Everything Is Wrong* and *Animal Rights*—sound much better in this format, divorced from the rock flame-outs that often surrounded them on the original albums. And though the version of his classic "Go" is actually a re-recording from 1998, it's a solid update that retains much of the original but never sounds like a pointless remake. *Songs 1993-1998* also spotlights Moby's continuing excellence in a number of genres, including a few of his Hi-NRG house singles from the mid-'90s ("Feeling So Real," "Move"), as well as his frequently beautiful ambient excursions ("God Moving Over the Face of the Waters," "The Rain Falls and the Sky Shudders"). It's a shame that the compilation completely skips his seminal early productions ("Drop a Beat," "Next Is the E") and a few rarities would've been nice for collectors, but *Songs 1993-1998* will satisfy fans of *Play* waiting for a new album. —*John Bush*

Moby Grape

f. Sep. 1966, San Francisco, CA
Folk-Rock, Psychedelic, Country-Rock
One of the best '60s San Francisco bands, Moby Grape were also one of the most versatile.

Although they are most often identified with the psychedelic scene, their specialty was combining all sorts of roots music—folk, blues, country, and classic rock & roll—with some Summer of Love vibes and multilayered, triple-guitar arrangements. All of those elements only truly coalesced, however, for their 1967 debut LP. Although subsequent albums had more good moments than many listeners are aware of, a combination of personal problems and bad management effectively killed off the group by the end of the 1960s. Matthew Katz, who managed the Jefferson Airplane in their early days, helped put together Moby Grape around Skip Spence, a legendarily colorful Canadian native who played drums in the Airplane's first lineup. Their 1967 self-titled debut remains their signature statement, though the folk-rock and country-rock worked better than the boogies; "Omaha," "Sittin' by the Window," "Changes," and "Lazy Me" are some of their best songs. Moby Grape's follow-up, the double LP *Wow*, was one of the most disappointing records of the '60s, in light of the high expectations fostered by the debut. The studio half of the package had much more erratic songwriting than the first recording, and the group members didn't blend their instrumental and vocal skills nearly as well. *—Richie Unterberger*

★ **Moby Grape (1967)** / Jun. 1967 / San Francisco Sound ♦♦♦♦♦
Moby Grape's career was a long, sad series of minor disasters, in which nearly anything that could have gone wrong did, but their self-titled debut album was their one moment of unqualified triumph. *Moby Grape* is one of the finest (perhaps *the* finest) album to come out of the San Francisco psychedelic scene, brimming with great songs and fresh ideas while blessedly avoiding the pitfalls that pock marked the work of their contemporaries—no long, unfocused jams, no self-indulgent philosophy, and no attempts to sonically recreate the sound of an acid trip. Instead, Moby Grape built their sound around the brilliantly interwoven guitar work of Jerry Miller, Peter Lewis, and Skip Spence, and the clear, bright harmonies of all five members. As songwriters, the group blended straight-ahead rock & roll, smart pop, blues, country, and folk accents into a flavorful brew that was all their own, with a clever melodic sense that reflected the lysergic energy surrounding them without drowning in it. And producer David Rubinson got it all on tape in a manner which captured the band's infectious energy and soaring melodies with uncluttered clarity, while subtly exploring the possibilities of the stereo mixing process. "Omaha," "Fall on You," "Hey Grandma," and "8:05" sound like obvious hits (and might have been if Columbia hadn't released them as singles all at once), but the truth is there isn't a dud track to be found here, and time has been extremely kind to this record. *Moby Grape* is as refreshing today as it was upon first release, and if fate prevented the group from making a follow-up that was as consistently strong, for one brief shining moment Moby Grape proved to the world they were one of America's great bands. While history remembers the Grateful Dead and Jefferson Airplane as being more important, the truth is neither group ever made an album quite this good. *—Mark Deming*

Grape Jam / 1968 / Columbia ♦♦

Wow / 1968 / Columbia ♦♦

Truly Fine Citizen / 1969 / Columbia ♦♦

Moby Grape '69 / Jan. 30, 1969 / Columbia ♦♦♦
After the unfortunate departure of Skip Spence, Moby Grape continued as a four-piece band. They still had the power, songwriting, and talent, but Spence's exit was something that robbed the band of an indefinable magic. Nevertheless, *'69* is a good and very real album. Sounding like it was cut from a variety of sessions at different times, this album isn't exactly what you would call cohesive, but it is still excellent, in places. Bob Mosley shines on the rocker "Hoochie" and the gorgeous pop/folk ballad "It's a Beautiful Day Today," which is underscored by some brilliant fingerpicking guitar from Peter Lewis. Lewis also has some excellent country-oriented songs here, notably "I Am Not Willing" and "If You Can't Learn From My Mistakes," the latter of which still graces his solo performances. The record concludes with "Seeing." Recorded (partially) before his exit, it remains one of Spence's finest songs, easily one of Moby Grape's most glorious (and disturbing) achievements, and a good reason to get this record as well. *—Matthew Greenwald*

20 Granite Creek / 1971 / Reprise ♦♦♦♦♦

Moby Grape '84 / 1984 / San Francisco Sound ♦♦♦

● **Vintage: The Very Best of Moby Grape** / May 11, 1993 / Columbia/Legacy ♦♦♦♦♦
It's hard to imagine a better-produced package of Moby Grape's work than this two-disc, 48-track condensation of their best late-'60s recordings. The first disc of this set centers around their entire 1967 self-titled debut LP (included in its entirety), which mixed blues, country, and folk influences with hard-charging psychedelic rock & roll. The result was one of the Summer of Love's more enduring works. The second disc boils their wildly inconsistent 1968-69 material down to a fairly strong and coherent selection. While it doesn't match the peak of the group's initial burst, it features some strong folk and country-rock originals that wear much better in the absence of the bloated jams and half-baked hard rock that could make their albums a chore to sit through. Each disc includes interesting demos, outtakes, and live performances that round out the legacy of this prodigiously talented but ill-fated band, which was overcome by internal strife and label/management difficulties after their promising debut. *—Richie Unterberger*

Los Mockers

Garage Rock
The best group that South America produced during the 1960s, and not merely a novelty item. Formed in Montevideo, Uruguay, in the mid-'60s, the group relocated to Argentina in 1966 after winning a contract with EMI Argentina. Their sole LP and a few singles show the group to possess an uncanny ability to imitate early Rolling Stones songs without being that obvious about it. Almost all of their material was original, sung in English by Polo Pereira, who (with a slight accent) emulates Mick Jagger's early snarl more accurately than anyone else from the time. You can detect apparent reference points to early Jagger/Richard tunes like "Off the Hook," and more sophisticated works like *Aftermath* ("Empty Harem" is complete with a "Paint It Black"-like guitar). The original lineup of Los Mockers disbanded in 1967, although other configurations using the name recorded a few more discs in the late '60s. In the '80s and '90s, Los Mockers reached a much greater international audience than they did in their heyday via internationally distributed reissues of their mid-'60s work and are widely respected by collectors as one of the best '60s garage groups. *—Richie Unterberger*

● **Los Mockers** / 1994 / Get Hip ♦♦♦♦♦
The best and most easily available of the several Los Mockers reissues that have appeared, built around their 1966 LP, with additional tracks from the '65-'67 era. No, of course, it's not nearly as good as the Rolling Stones. But it's fun, and much better than much of the (frequently inept) Stones-inspired U.S. garage music of the same era. *—Richie Unterberger*

Modern English

f. 1979, **db.** 1991
New Wave
British punk quintet from Colchester formed in 1979 and featuring singer and guitarist Robbie Grey, guitarist Gary McDowell, bassist Mick Conroy, keyboard player Stephen Walker, and drummer Richard Brown. By 1990, personnel changes had left the group a trio of Grey and Conroy, with keyboardist, guitarist, and singer Aaron Davidson. Modern English disbanded one year later, then re-formed in 1996 for a live tour. *—William Ruhlmann*

Mesh & Lace / 1981 / 4AD ♦♦♦
The debut album by this overlooked 4AD outfit from Colchester in Essex. In many ways, Modern English helped to define the sound and image of that pioneering label; while admittedly pretentious at times, they were also sharp-edged, intellectual, and obsessed with aestheticism. The standouts here are the title-track, "Smiles and Laughter," and "Gathering Dust," an epic post-punk exercise in aural dynamics. The keyboard rush that they employ is one of the punkiest uses of Stephen Walker's synthesizer imaginable—at least prior to the development of the industrial movement. *—Alex Ogg*

● **After the Snow** / 1982 / 4AD ♦♦♦♦
British quintet Modern English released its second album, *After the Snow*, in 1982. Produced by Hugh Jones, *After the Snow* contained "I Melt With You," one of the most enduring songs of the new wave era. Although the propulsive, hook-laden track didn't climb very high on the charts, it became an instantly recognizable song through heavy club play, and remains so today. The rest of the album doesn't come close to such heights, although there are some engaging moments. "Someone's Calling" alternates chiming guitars and moody synthesizer with stutter-step drumming to good effect, and "Life in the Gladhouse" has a tumbling, percussive beat and jittery melody. Featuring one minor classic and a handful of solid cuts, *After the Snow* is highly listenable and contains some of the better music of its time. *—Tom Demalon*

Ricochet Days / 1984 / Sire ♦♦♦♦♦
Leaving behind the artistic adventures of their first two albums (particularly impressive was 1982's *After the Snow*), *Ricochet Days* begins Modern English's slow decline toward the status of just another synth band. The material, though beautifully produced by the reliable Hugh Jones and boasting some pliable hooks, lacks the conviction and attack of old. "Hands Across the Sea" and "Spinning Me Round" are serviceable but hardly vital additions to the band's songbook. *—Alex Ogg*

Stop Start / 1986 / Sire ♦♦♦
Picked up by Sire Records, Modern English found it difficult to break free from perceptions of them as a *de facto* 4AD band (a situation which also occurred with the Cocteau Twins). So they made this rather regrettable, overtly commercial album which impressed no one. Songs such as "Night Train" and "Love Breaks Down" were all sheen and polish rather than substance. Others, like "The Greatest Show," simply meander endlessly. An interesting footnote is that ex-Rubinoo Tommy Dunbar co-wrote "Ink and Paper." *—Alex Ogg*

Pillow Lips / May 1990 / TVT ♦♦♦
This was the group's first album after re-forming around original members Robbie Grey (vocals), Mick Conroy (bass), and ex-March Violets member Aaron Davidson (guitar/keyboards), who had joined in 1986 only to see the current lineup at that time disintegrate. The trio moved to the U.S. and conjured a minor hit single with a remixed version of the portentous "I Melt With You." Older fans of the band despaired of their new, slicker variant. Despite their modest breakthrough, the group broke up again in 1991. *—Alex Ogg*

Life in the Gladhouse, 1980-1984: Best of Modern English / Mar. 20, 2001 / 4AD ♦♦♦
Few bands have been quite as misrepresented by their hit songs as Modern English was by its 1983 smash "I Melt With You." An exquisite pop confection celebrating the joy of youthful romance (and a huge American video hit in the early days of MTV), "I Melt With You" was something of an anomaly for this moody and experimental crew, whose songs generally tended to have titles like "Black Houses" and "Swans on Glass" and whose sound owed as much to Joy Division as it did to fellow new romantics like Duran Duran. Really, there's nothing much like "I Melt With You" anywhere else on this retrospective compilation. The program opens with the strange and desolate "16 Days," and stays roughly in that vein through songs that all seem to thud along at the same 120-bpm tempo and all seem to mine the same vein of post-punk socio-romantic angst. Imagine a slightly more melodic but enervated Gang of Four (especially on "Black Houses") or a

really gloomy Flock of Seagulls ("Rainbows End"). It's not bad stuff, but the only really noteworthy song here is the hit single, and one of the most noteworthy things about it is its dissimilarity to the rest of the band's oeuvre. —*Rick Anderson*

Modest Mouse

f. 1993

Noise Pop, Emo, Indie Rock, Lo-Fi, Alternative Pop/Rock

Issaquah, WA indie-rock trio Modest Mouse was formed in 1993 by vocalist/guitarist Isaac Brock, bassist Eric Judy, and drummer Jeremiah Green. After honing their muscular sound in "The Shed"—a makeshift practice space built by Brock on the land next to his mother's trailer—Modest Mouse entered Calvin Johnson's Dub Narcotic Studios to cut their 1994 self-titled debut single, released on Johnson's K Records label. Following a move to the Up label, the trio issued two 1996 LPs, *This Is a Long Drive for Someone With Nothing to Think About* and *Interstate 8.* After returning to K, Modest Mouse released *The Fruit That Ate Itself* in 1997; their follow-up later that year, *The Lonesome Crowded West,* was the band's breakthrough, and in the wake of a major-label bidding war they signed to Sony. The rarities collection *Building Nothing Out of Something* appeared on Up in early 2000, followed later that year by their long-awaited Epic debut *The Moon & Antarctica.* —*Jason Ankeny*

This Is a Long Drive for Someone With Nothing to Think About / Feb. 27, 1996 / Up ✦✦✦✦

Expanding upon the themes of emotional and geographic isolation found in the band's previous work, *This Is a Long Drive for Someone With Nothing to Think About* finds Modest Mouse mixing slow, brooding numbers such as "Custom Concern" and "Talking Shit About a Pretty Sunset" with thrashing guitar workouts like "Breakthrough" and "Head South." The general mood here is one of loneliness and desperation, eloquently expressed through both the lyrics and the rhythmic, sprawling instrumentation. "Dramamine," for instance, with its driving, mid-tempo beat and ricocheting guitar line, sums up the hopelessness of a doomed relationship, while the frantic "Head South" deals with the feeling of "being ashamed of your old space." The mandolin, slide guitar, and cello featured throughout the album give the songs a certain degree of depth that makes them stand out from average indie rock fare. In general, *This Is a Long Drive for Someone With Nothing to Think About* is a fine album of guitar-based rock, and Modest Mouse distinguishes itself here with songs whose meanings are simultaneously universal and painfully personal. —*Brandon Gentry*

The Fruit That Ate Itself / 1997 / K ✦✦✦

Produced by Calvin Johnson, *The Fruit That Ate Itself* possesses a leaner and meaner sound than earlier Modest Mouse releases—the emphasis here is less on noise than groove, and the spare, edgy approach of cuts like "Dirty Fingernails" and the title track recalls the goofy indie-funk of Dub Narcotic Sound System and other like-minded Johnson-helmed projects. —*Jason Ankeny*

Lonesome Crowded West / Oct. 7, 1997 / Up ✦✦✦✦✦

Talk about original, this band has something for just about everyone. They can do quiet, brooding acoustics like "Bankrupt on Selling," dark and pounding thrashers like "Cowboy Dan," funky jump-around emo like "Jesus Christ Was an Only Child"—just about anything. Throughout the whole album is a white-trash feeling and a sort of down-to-earth analysis of the state of the world, without sounding pretentious. Give this album a listen and you can be sure that you will be singing the rambling, catchy, almost whiny vocals in no time. If you dig indie-rock at its very best, go pick this album up. —*Blake Butler*

Building Nothing Out of Something / Jan. 18, 2000 / Up ✦✦✦✦✦

Building Nothing Out of Something collects Modest Mouse singles and rare tracks from the group's indie-label years, including the studio tracks from the *Interstate 8* EP and their contributions to the Sub Pop Singles Club. Despite the songs' motley origins, *Building Nothing Out of Something* works well as an album, balancing the group's quirky and often poignant pop songs with their more abrasive rock side. The wonderfully dreamy, off-kilter "Interstate 8" and "Workin' on Leavin' the Livin'" (which cleverly quotes *Eraserhead*'s "Lady in the Radiator Song") are two shining examples of the group's elastic, loopy guitar pop, while "All Nite Diner," "A Life of Arctic Sounds," and "Other People's Lives" define their high-strung rock sound. Slower songs like "Grey Ice Water" and the Santo & Johnny homage "Sleepwalkin'" round out this look at Modest Mouse's diverse but consistently worthwhile indie output. —*Heather Phares*

● The Moon & Antarctica / Jun. 13, 2000 / Sony ✦✦✦✦✦

Modest Mouse's Epic debut *The Moon & Antarctica* finds them strangely subdued, focusing on mortality as well as the moody, acoustic side of their music and downplaying the edgy, spastic rock that helped make them indie stars. Not that their first major-label release sounds like a sellout—actually, the slight sheen of Brian Deck's production enhances the album's introspective tone—but occasionally *The Moon & Antarctica*'s melancholy becomes ponderous.

Unfortunately, the album's middle stretch contains three such songs, "The Cold Part," "Alone Down There," and "The Stars Are Projectors," which tend to blur together into one 17-minute long piece that bogs down the album's momentum. Individually, each of these songs is sweeping and haunting in its own right, but grouping them together blunts their impact. However, this trilogy does provide a sharp contrast to, as well as a bridge across, *The Moon & Antarctica*'s more vibrant beginning and end. Though it explores death and the afterlife, *The Moon & Antarctica*'s liveliest moments are its most effective. "3rd Planet"'s simple, ramshackle melody and strange, moving lyrics ("Your heart felt good"), the elastic guitars on "Gravity Rides Everything" and the angular, jumpy "Tiny Cities Made of Ashes" and "A Different City" get the album off to a strong start, while the fresh, unaffected "Wild Packs of Family Dogs," "Paper Thin Walls," and "Lives" bring it to an

atmospheric, affecting peak before "What People Are Made Of" closes the album with a climactic burst of noise. Their most cohesive collection of songs to date, *The Moon & Antarctica* is an impressive, if flawed, map of Modest Mouse's ambitions and fears. —*Heather Phares*

Sad Sappy Sucker / Apr. 24, 2001 / K ✦✦✦

Sad Sappy Sucker is Modest Mouse's "lost album." It was recorded by K Records' Calvin Johnson in 1994 and was supposed to be the band's debut, but delays shelved the record and it disappeared. The 2001 release of *Sad Sappy Sucker* gives fans an opportunity to see the humble beginnings of one of the Pacific Northwest's most original bands. All 12 songs recorded during the Dub Narcotic Studio sessions are on the album, including the impossible to find "Worms vs. Birds 7." As a bonus treat, there are nine songs from Isaac Brock's Dial-a-Song project. These were on his answering machine everyday and could only be heard by calling in. The thick textures, crazy drawl vocals, and grand flair of later Modest Mouse albums such as *The Lonesome Crowded West* and *The Moon & Antarctica* are not fully realized on *Sad Sappy Sucker.* But Modest Mouse's future suburban sprawl is evident in the chug-chug of "From Point A to Point B" and the slow/fast groove of "Race Car Grin You Ain't No Landmark." On the latter, Brock sings, "Looks like accounting's not accountable for anything or anyone at all." But *Sad Sappy Sucker* is no case of a "reissue, repackage, repackage" revenue scheme, this album is a gift for die-hard fans, put out by a label that probably loves Modest Mouse as much as the fans do. —*Charles Spano*

Mogwai

f. 1996, Glasgow, Scotland

Experimental Rock, Space Rock, Indie Rock, Post-Rock/Experimental

The cosmic post-rock band Mogwai was formed in Glasgow, Scotland in 1996 by guitarist/vocalist Stuart Braithwaite, guitarist Dominic Aitchison, and drummer Martin Bulloch, longtime friends with the goal of creating "serious guitar music." Toward that end they added another guitarist, John Cummings, before debuting in March 1996 with the single "Tuner," a rarity in the Mogwai discography for its prominent vocals; the follow-up, a split single with Dweeb titled "Angels vs. Aliens," landed in the Top Ten on the British indie charts. Following appearances on a series of compilations, Mogwai returned later in the year with the 7" "Summer"; after another early 1997 single, "New Paths to Helicon," the group issued *Ten Rapid,* a collection of their earliest material. Around the time of recording the superb 1997 EP *4 Satin,* former Teenage Fanclub and Telstar Ponies member Brendan O'Hare joined the lineup in time to record their debut studio LP *Mogwai Young Team,* exiting a short time later to return to his primary projects Macrocosmica and Fiend 1. Again a quartet, Mogwai next issued 1998's *Kicking a Dead Pig,* a two-disc remix collection; the *No Education No Future (Fuck the Curfew)* EP appeared a few months later. In 1999, they released *Come on Die Young.* *Rock Action* arrived in early 2001. —*Jason Ankeny*

Ten Rapid (Collected Recordings 1996-1997) / Jul. 4, 1997 / Jetset ✦✦✦✦

Ten Rapid compiles the bulk of the singles Mogwai released between 1995 and 1997, but the tone of the music is so consistent, it could have all come from the same session. Like a post-rock band, Mogwai is about subtle, shifting sonics and repetition, but they are hardly as precious or cerebral as any post-rock group. Each of their songs sounds as if it goes around in a circle, surrounding itself in interlocking, mathematical patterns. While there are waves of feedback washing over the album, the music itself sounds like it's in the distance. Their habit of burying vocals (which aren't featured that often in the first place) also keeps Mogwai from reach, and nothing on *Ten Rapid* is immediately engaging, even though it is intriguing. With repeated listens, the album reveals its hidden layers, and the music becomes hypnotic in its gradual, deliberate pace and interwoven guitars. —*Stephen Thomas Erlewine*

● Young Team / Oct. 27, 1997 / Jetset ✦✦✦✦✦

Young Team, Mogwai's first full-length album fulfills the promise of their early singles and EPs, offering a complex, intertwining set of crawling instrumentals, shimmering soundscapes, and shards of noise. Picking up where *Ten Rapid* left off, Mogwai use the sheer length of an album to their advantage, recording a series of songs that meld together—it's easy to forget where one song begins and the other ends. The record itself takes its time to begin, as the sound of chiming processed guitars and murmured sampled vocals floats to the surface. Throughout the album, the sound of the band keeps shifting, and it's not just through explosions of noise—Mogwai isn't merely jamming, they have a planned vision, subtly texturing their music with small, telling details. When the epic "Mogwai Fears Satan" draws the album to a close, it becomes clear that the band has expanded the horizons of post-rock, creating a record of sonic invention and emotional force that sounds unlike anything their guitar-based contemporaries have created. —*Stephen Thomas Erlewine*

Kicking a Dead Pig: Mogwai Songs Remixed + Fear Satan Remixes / May 18, 1998 / Jetset ✦✦

Come on Die Young / Apr. 6, 1999 / Matador ✦✦✦

"Too much, too soon" is a tattered rock & roll cliché, but it continues to tell the tale of many young bands, such as Glasgow's acclaimed post-rock collective Mogwai. Usually, the phrase is hauled out to describe an intoxicated downward spiral by bands that had too much success all at once, but Mogwai suffered too much praise—too many accolades from critics, too much reverence from underground hipsters. The singles compilation *Ten Rapid* and the debut *Young Team* deserved all the acclaim they earned, but a funny thing happened while Mogwai was recording their much-anticipated second album, ironically titled *Come on Die Young*—the band went stale, producing a lethargic trawl through post-Slint and Sonic Youth territory. Where their free-form noise improvisations were utterly enthralling on their earlier records, the ebb and flow is entirely too familiar throughout *Come on Die Young*, largely because they follow the same pattern on each song. And each cut blends into the next, creating the impression of one endless track that teeters between deliberately dreamy crawls and random bursts of noise. Granted, that was the blueprint for *Young Team*, but there is little dynamism anywhere on *Come on Die Young*. Mogwai repeat the same riffs with the same inflection, never pushing themselves toward new sonic territory, yet never hitting a mesmerizing trance. It feels like a degraded photocopy of their earlier records—it's possible to discern the initial spark that made them fascinating, but this current incarnation is too smudged and muddy to hold attention on its own terms. Perhaps *Come on Die Young* wouldn't have seemed as disappointing if it hadn't arrived on the wave of hype and expectation, but the truth is, it pales in comparison to their own work. *—Stephen Thomas Erlewine*

Rock Action / Apr. 24, 2001 / Matador ♦♦♦
Their most impressive work since *Young Team*, Mogwai's third album, *Rock Action*, boasts an ironic title as well as an ironically successful new direction. By stripping away much of the noodling and noise of their earlier work in favor of tighter structures, more immediate melodies, and vocals, they've recaptured the excitement that surrounded their first releases. Like so many groups stuck with the post-rock tag, Mogwai needed a way to expand beyond the term without changing their sound completely, and aided by guests like producer Dave Fridmann and Super Furry Animals' Gruff Rhys, they've found it. *Rock Action* incorporates bristling distortion, propulsive drums, and electronic textures similar to Tortoise's *Standards*—particularly on the opening track "Sine Wave"—but the album's most remarkable moments revisit and reinvent more traditional sounds. Buoyed by lush string arrangements and Fridmann's detailed, warm production, the brooding ballads "Take Me Somewhere Nice" and "Dial: Revenge" couldn't be further from "rock action," but they display the album's refreshing restraint and immediacy. In particular, "Dial: Revenge"—so named because "dial" is the Welsh word for "revenge"—benefits from Rhys' emotive yet cryptic vocals in his mother tongue, but the general emphasis on vocals adds to the album's organic, emotive feel. Nowhere is this more evident than the nine-minute epic "2 Rights Make One Wrong": With its lush layers of brass, strings, banjo, guitars, and vocals, it sounds like the rock-oriented cousin of Jim O'Rourke's pocket symphonies. Meanwhile, "You Don't Know Jesus" uses its eight-minute length to reaffirm that the group is still at the top of its game when it comes to guitar-driven catharsis. "Secret Pint" sends the album out on a serene note, proving that in the proper hands, the quietest ballad is just as commanding as the loudest rock action; *Rock Action* shows that Mogwai have mastered both styles. *—Heather Phares*

Essra Mohawk (Elayne Hurvitz)

b. Philadelphia, PA
Song Credits, Vocals, Keyboards, Songwriter / Prog Rock/Art Rock, Alternative Pop/Rock
Singer/songwriter Essra Mohawk (b. Sandra Elayne Hurvitz, Philadelphia, PA) is one of those unfortunate artists whose work is celebrated by critics and a small group of ardent admirers, but never by the public at large. In the course of a bumpy career she has made eight albums, each for different record labels. As a songwriter, she has enjoyed some measure of success, but over 30 years into her career she still remains a well-kept secret. Mohawk's first single was "The Boy With the Way"/B-side "Memory of Your Voice" on Liberty records in 1964. She declined several offers of staff writerships, although the Shangri-Las and Vanilla Fudge began recording her material. In 1967, Mohawk met Frank Zappa, eventually joining the Mothers of Invention, where she reluctantly assumed the moniker Uncle Meat. Frank Zappa signed her to his Bizarre label (a Verve subsidiary) and her first album *Sandy's Album is Here at Last* appeared soon after.

In 1969 Sandra Hurvitz became Essra Mohawk and recorded her second album, *Primordial Lovers*, hailed as one of the best 25 albums ever made by Rolling Stone magazine. The album missed out on wider publicity and never charted. During her tenure with David Geffen, Mohawk languished unjustly in the shadows of Laura Nyro and Joni Mitchell.

In 1974 Mohawk moved to the Asylum label, where she released *Essra Mohawk*. Again, critical acclaim was abundant, but proper promotion and healthy sales were not. Two years later, the same fate greeted her fourth album *Essra*, which appeared on Private Stock. Further albums, *Burnin' Shinin'* and *E-Turn* fared no better, but in 1986 Mohawk enjoyed a huge hit as the songwriter of Cyndi Lauper's Billboard Number Three hit, "Change of Heart," and later in that decade Tina Turner recorded "Stronger Than the Wind," again penned by Mohawk. Since then, she has recorded further albums *Raindance* and *Essie Mae Hawk Meets the Killer Groove Band*, to the rapturous applause of her ever-loyal following. *—Charles Donovan*

• **Primordial Lovers MM** / 2000 / Rhino Handmade ♦♦♦♦
This single-disc release compiles two out-of-print recordings from one of America's rarest treasures—Essra Mohawk. Ever since its release in March of 1970, *Primordial Lovers* has been globally lauded and hailed by journalists, enthusiasts, as well as musical peers. Mohawk indeed delivers a uniquely grounded and earthy folk masterpiece. With sparse, yet effective, accompaniment, the tales woven by Mohawk are hypnotically sweet and tinged with the tangible pleasures of humanity. Her vibe is notably more organic than artists such as Joni Mitchell—whose immense shadow ultimately became a dark cloud over the recognition that Mohawk rightfully deserved. Mohawk's eponymous release from 1975 is no less intense than her previous long-player. It is much more elaborately structured, which makes listening all the more interesting. The lighter arrangements have turned inward and the music has taken on a slightly more rock and less folk approach and feel. Lyrically, the album is more sensual ("You Make Me Come to Pieces" and "Openin' My Love's Doors") than her previous effort. The sound quality on *Primordial Lovers MM* is flawless, although some might go further, declaring it breathtaking—especially those comparing worn vinyl copies to this disc. All the warm nuances and acoustic overtones are immaculately reproduced, creating a vitally fresh listening experience. The full-color 24-page liner notes booklet reproduces every aspect of the original LP releases, including the contents of the lyrics booklet that accompanied initial pressings of *Primordial Lovers*. An enormous bonus is the page upon page of notes Mohawk penned for this project. Her recollections and memoirs go beyond the imagery and into the artist's mindset. *—Lindsay Planer*

Mojave 3

f. England
Indie Pop, Dream Pop, Alternative Pop/Rock, Sadcore
Between the recording and release of Slowdive's ambient *Pygmalion*, Neil Halstead began writing more song-based tunes to occupy down time. Weeks after being dropped by Creation, Halstead and the remaining members of Slowdive (Rachel Goswell and Ian McCutcheon) recorded six demos within three days, much of it live without overdubs. Their manager brought the tape to 4AD head Ivo Watts-Russell, who immediately gave the trio money to record more material. Feeling that the direction was too removed to retain the Slowdive moniker, they christened themselves Mojave, only to add "3" later for legal purposes. Signed to 4AD, the six demos and three later-recorded songs made up 1996's *Ask Me Tomorrow*. Subtle, sparse, and somber, the record drew likenesses to Mazzy Star and the Cowboy Junkies, along with some debatable country references. Not necessarily country, it sounded like unplugged Slowdive with a slight twang. The band gigged for several months, including a package 4AD tour in the U.S. with Scheer and Lush, dubbed "The Shaving the Pavement Tour."

The shift away from Slowdive was completed with 1998's *Out of Tune*. More upbeat in nature, it also featured more involved arrangements. Former Chapterhouse guitarist Simon Rowe was officially added as a member, as well as Alan Forrester on keys. Their full-time presence helped round out the band's sound. At this point, Mojave 3—and Halstead's classicist songwriting in particular—began to earn favorable comparisons to Bob Dylan, Nick Drake, and Neil Young. *Excuses for Travellers* followed two years later, continuing in similar fashion as something of a hybrid of their first two LPs. *—Andy Kellman*

• **Ask Me Tomorrow** / 1996 / 4AD ♦♦♦♦♦
Much like Mazzy Star but with less Western ambience, Mojave 3 plays a slightly countrified version of Galaxie 500. The band is just as dreamy as Dean Wareham and company, but all the edges are shaved off to be compatible with the trademark 4AD sound. *—John Bush*

Out of Tune / 1998 / Sire ♦♦♦♦♦
A record informed by all of the sun-baked ambience and arid beauty that the band's name implies, with *Out of Tune* Mojave 3 severs all remaining ties to their shoegazing past—textured by flourishes of pedal steel, trumpet, and Hammond organ, Neil Halstead's songs have become surprisingly traditional in both form and shape, yet in many regards rank among the best music he's produced to date. Even more countrified than the preceding *Ask Me Tomorrow*, the album possesses a dusty melancholia that's truly affecting—no longer hiding behind an impenetrable wall of noise, Halstead has blossomed into a superb writer, and the best songs on *Out of Tune* ("Who Do You Love" and "Some Kinda Angel" among them) achieve a luminous austerity recalling nothing so much as *Blonde on Blonde*-era Dylan. Not so innovative or ambitious as Halstead's work in Slowdive, to be certain, Mojave 3's music nevertheless claims a timelessness its already dated forerunner sadly lacks, with an honesty and grace that never go out of fashion. *—Jason Ankeny*

Excuses for Travellers / May 15, 2000 / 4AD ♦♦♦♦
Quickly becoming one of the most consistently excellent bands of the late '90s and early '00s, Mojave 3 have crafted their third timeless gem. Progression obviously isn't priority number one on their list of things to do—the prime directive remains a humble stab at the notion of "Why, shucks—we just wanna make nice records." Neil Halstead again handles the bulk of songwriting, and his craft continues to be finely stitched like a blanket that provides warmth for decades. *Excuses for Travellers* finds a midpoint between *Ask Me Tomorrow* and *Out of Tune*—it's not as peppy as the latter, but it's not as hushed as the former. There are some subtle differences from the two other records, like the shadings of banjo that appear from time to time and the further presence of horns. Halstead's voice sounds a little gruff on occasion, but it's no detracting factor. Most notable is a Rachel Goswell-sung track, "Bringin' Me Home," which surprisingly adds a subtle touch of synth, presumably courtesy of producer/associate Mark Van Hoen (Locust). Hearing Goswell take lead vocals is like hearing from a long-lost friend. Certainly her gorgeous voice—which sounds relatively toughened on the song—has been the band's secret weapon. Why she hasn't stepped out more is anyone's guess. No offense to Halstead's vocals, but will there ever be a Mojave 3 record dominated by her voice? One can only hope. Few can fault Mojave 3 for hanging their hat on the same rung for a while, as long as they keep cranking out pearls like they have every two years. There might be little variance, but each of their records to date are utterly classicist *and* fresh. *—Andy Kellman*

The Mojo Men

f. 1965, **db.** 1969
Garage Rock, Psychedelic
One of the earliest San Francisco rock bands, the Mojo Men had local hits on the Autumn label with "Dance With Me," "She's My Baby," and a cover of the Rolling Stones' "Off the Hook" in the mid-'60s. Their early sides displayed a raunchy but thin approach taken from the mold of British Invasion groups like the Stones and Them. In 1966, after female drummer Jan Errico joined from the San Francisco folk-rock group the Vejtables, they

moved to Reprise and pursued folky psychedelic pop directions, and had a Top 40 hit with a Baroque arrangement of Buffalo Springfield's "Sit Down I Think I Love You" in 1967. In their later days, they developed more intricate arrangements and harmonies that reflected the influence of the Mamas & the Papas and Jefferson Airplane, although they weren't in the same league as those groups. Their many singles never fully displayed the band's considerable songwriting and vocal talents, and after changing their name to the Mojo and finally just Mojo, they disbanded in the late '60s. —*Richie Unterberger*

Dance With Me / 1984 / Eva ✦✦✦

A ragtag collection, drawn from their first seven singles and a few unreleased tracks. The later tracks, featuring Errico, are much more ornate productions that sound like a somewhat less refined Mamas & the Papas. A wealth of unreleased material (much of it original) that has circulated among collectors shows them to be a much more interesting group than this album would indicate; unfortunately, this anthology (the only one available) focuses on their more simplistic and derivative numbers. —*Richie Unterberger*

Whys Ain't Supposed to Be / 1995 / Sundazed ✦✦✦

This 21-track disc covers the Mojo Men's first incarnation, when they were a pop-garage group, not the pop-folk-rock act they would evolve into when Jan Errico joined. "She's My Baby" and "Dance With Me" made some noise regionally, "Dance With Me" making the middle of the national charts, but Autumn Records folded before the group got the chance to do any albums. Assembled from a handful of Autumn 45s and many previously unissued recordings, this could be considered the Mojo Men's lost album. But it's really not worth getting excited about, even if you're a garage fan. The thumping, monotonous drums and rinky-dink organ patterns can grate, and worse, the material is often so thin as to be puerile. Juvenile lyrics are a mainstay of many garage recordings, but the Mojo Men's compositions could be downright annoying. Their emulations of the Rolling Stones, the Kinks, and the Animals were pale, though some promise could be heard in a few moodier, folk-rock influenced cuts. —*Richie Unterberger*

● **Sit Down . . . It's the Mojo Men** / Nov. 14, 1995 / Sundazed ✦✦✦✦✦

An 18-song compilation of material from their 1966-68 hitch with Reprise, combining several singles with five tracks from an unreleased album. This fully documents the second phase of the band, when they added drummer Jan Errico and changed from a secondrate garage band into a better (but not fully first-rate) pop/folk-rock group. This isn't half bad for the genre, but you can see why they never really distinguished themselves from the San Francisco crowd. It's way too pop to be associated with the Haight-Ashbury scene, a little too weird to be compared to, say, the Association (with the occasional sudden blasts of psychedelic fuzz guitar and baroque production), not as accomplished as the Mamas & the Papas, and gussied up with too many conventional pop string arrangements. Van Dyke Parks arranged a few of the singles, including their lone hit, "Sit Down I Think I Love You" (which is here). Most of the material was written by Errico and bassist Jim Alaimo, and although it's a pleasantly worthwhile archival collection, it's not a major find. —*Richie Unterberger*

Molly Hatchet

f. 1975, Jacksonville, FL, db. 1989
Boogie Rock, Southern Rock, Hard Rock
Named after a legendary Southern prostitute who allegedly beheaded and mutilated her clients, Jacksonville's Molly Hatchet melded loud hard-rock boogie with guitar jam-oriented Southern rock. Formed in 1975, the group's lineup featured three guitarists—Dave Hlubek, Steve Holland, and Duane Roland—plus vocalist Danny Joe Brown, bassist Banner Thomas, and drummer Bruce Crump. The group recorded a self-titled debut album in 1978, which quickly went platinum; the follow-up, *Flirtin' With Disaster*, was even more successful, selling over two million copies. Brown left the group in 1980 after the constant touring became too tiresome; he was replaced by Jimmy Farrar for *Beatin' the Odds*, but Farrar's voice was less immediately identifiable, and Molly Hatchet's commercial appeal began a slow decline. The band experimented with horns on *Take No Prisoners*, but Farrar left for a solo career soon afterwards. Brown rejoined the band in 1982, but the ensuing album, *No Guts . . . No Glory*, flopped, and guitarist Hlubek insisted on revamping Molly Hatchet's sound. After *The Deed is Done*, a straightforward pop/rock album, the group took some time off in 1985 while its *Double Trouble Live* album, a collection of some of its best-known songs, was released. Molly Hatchet returned in 1989 without Hlubek for an album of straight, polished AOR, *Lightning Strikes Twice*. Not even the group's fan base bought the record, and they disbanded shortly afterward. Molly Hatchet reunited in the mid-'90s as an active touring outfit, releasing *Devil's Canyon*, their first record since *Lightning Strikes Twice*, in 1996. Continuing to recapture the style of their glory days, *Silent Reign of Heroes* followed in 1998, and *Kingdom of XII* appeared in early 2001. —*Steve Huey*

● **Greatest Hits** / 1985 / Epic ✦✦✦✦✦

Nice collection of their best-known tunes. Some of Southern rock's finest moments. —*Cub Koda*

Moloko

f. 1993, Sheffield, Yorkshire, England
Electronica, Trip-Hop, Club/Dance, House
The Sheffield-based dance-pop duo Moloko is the end result of Irish-born singer Roisin Murphy's attempt to pick up mixer/producer Mark Brydon at a 1994 party with the come-on, "Do you like my tight sweater? See how it fits my body." Brydon saw musical potential in her attitude, and the two formed a creative and romantic partnership.
Murphy, who never sang outside of the shower before, was a newcomer to the music business. However, Brydon had many years of experience with U.K. house music acts

House Arrest and Cloud 9, helped found Sheffield's Fon studios, and remixed artists like Eric B & Rakim and Psychic TV. Soon after forming Moloko, they released their debut single, "Where Is the What If the What Is in the Why?," and signed to Echo Records.

The band's full-length debut, inevitably named *Do You Like My Tight Sweater?*, came out in 1995 and was an equal mix of Murphy's slinky attitude and Brydon's musical prowess. The album combined dance, funk, and trip-hop elements in an approach similar to Portishead or Massive Attack but with a sense of humor and sass unique to Moloko. Though the album's U.S. release occurred nearly a year later, the single "Fun for Me" was featured prominently on the *Batman & Robin* soundtrack and received some radio airplay.

Moloko toured with kindred musical spirits such as Pulp, built a home studio, and recorded the follow-up to *Do You Like My Tight Sweater?*, titled *I Am Not a Doctor*. Released in 1998 (and late 1999 in the U.S.), the album continued in Moloko's witty, funky tradition. The group's third album, *Things to Make and Do*, was issued in the U.K. in the spring of 2000. —*Heather Phares*

● **Do You Like My Tight Sweater?** / Nov. 1995 / Echo ✦✦✦✦✦

The aptly named *Do You Like My Tight Sweater?* slinks and bounces on a funky backbone of fat basslines and innovative beats that support singer Roisin Murphy's sly, theatrical vocals and lyrics. Part catwoman, part roid, her singing ranges from a knowing purr to an androgynous growl and creates characters like party weirdos, dominatrixes, killer bunnies, and ghosts.

As dramatic as her vocals are, however, Murphy is an anti-diva; her musical surroundings equal her singing in importance. The other half of *Do You Like My Tight Sweater?*'s individuality comes from Mark Brydon's arrangements, which combine fluid tempos, sudden breakbeats, witty sound effects, and unearthly keyboards in sci-fi grooves that appeal to the brain and body.

Standout tracks like "Fun for Me," "I Can't Help Myself," "Lotus Eaters," and "Party Weirdo" mix sensuality, technology, funk, and electronica in a unique and stylish blend. While some of the sillier songs like "On My Horsey" and "Dirty Monkey" disrupt the flow of *Do You Like My Tight Sweater?*, the danceable creativity of Moloko's debut overrides its quirks. —*Heather Phares*

I Am Not a Doctor / Aug. 24, 1998 / Echo ✦✦✦✦

I Am Not a Doctor could have been called "Moloko 2.0." A better integration of tech appeal and sex appeal than the group's debut *Do You Like My Tight Sweater?*, Moloko's singing, writing, and musical reach are all upgraded on *I Am Not a Doctor*. The result is a more entertaining and less self-conscious album.

Songs like "The Flipside," "Blink," and "Pretty Bridges" offer a stylized, pop take on jungle, while the ballads "Downsized," "Caught in a Whisper," and "Should've Been Could've Been" mix pathos with the band's dry wit. The deadpan new wave of "Sorry," the cyberfunky "The Id," and the techno torch-song "Sing It Back" show off Moloko's expanded range.

Musically and vocally, Roisin Murphy and Mark Brydon blend their talents more smoothly on *I Am Not a Doctor*. Murphy's voice melds with the horns, strings, and keyboards backing her, while real and electronic drums punctuate each song expressively. A balance of contradictions, Moloko keeps inventiveness and listenability high on their second album. —*Heather Phares*

Things to Make and Do / Oct. 31, 2000 / Roadrunner International ✦✦✦✦

The Moments

f. 1968, Hackensack, NJ, db. 1978
Pop-Soul, Quiet Storm, R&B, Soul
One of the most consistent R&B aggregations of the '70s, the Moments enjoyed a string of major hits throughout the decade. The Hackensack, NJ, trio introduced themselves and the Stang label with "Not on the Outside" in 1968, and topped the R&B charts in 1970 with the gold-plated "Love on a Two-Way Street," produced by Sylvia Robinson (one half of Mickey & Sylvia). Other major soul smashes by the Moments included "If I Didn't Care" and "All I Have" in 1970, "Sexy Mama" in 1973, and another Number One R&B item, "Look at Me (I'm in Love)," in 1975. Members Harry Ray, Al Goodman, and William Brown changed their billing to Ray, Goodman & Brown in 1978 and topped the soul lists the next year with the slickly harmonized "Special Lady" on Polydor. The renamed trio remained potent soul hitmakers through the '80s. —*Bill Dahl*

● **Love on a Two Way Street: The Best of the Moments** / Jul. 15, 1996 / Rhino ✦✦✦✦✦

The Moments charted regularly on the R&B charts and copped the Number Three position on the pop charts with "Love on a Two-Way Street." This CD chronicles a group that underwent some changes before Billy Brown, Al Goodman, and Harry Ray meshed and made the Moments a popular R&B entity. Diehard fans will notice two omissions: "Girl I'm Going to Miss You," a floater sung by Brown in an aching falsetto and "Somebody Loves You Baby," the B-side of "Sunday." The inclusion of "I'm Willing" by Harry Ray (one of his solo releases) and an extended version of "Sexy Mama" softens the oversights. Incidentally, Billy Brown sings all the parts on "I Do"—the lead, the background, and the spoken parts. Essential listening; don't hesitate to add this one to your shopping cart. —*Andrew Hamilton*

Momus (Nicholas Currie)

b. 1960, Paisley, Scotland
Producer / Shibuya-Kei, Indie Pop, Chamber Pop, Alternative Dance, Indie Rock, Alternative Pop/Rock, Singer/Songwriter, Synth Pop
Momus was the alias of Nick Currie, a Scottish-born singer, songwriter, and provocateur

whose music careened from acoustic ballads to electro-pop to acid house and back again. Born in 1960, Currie spent time living in Greece and Canada before returning to Scotland to attend university. In 1981, he dropped out of school and played in the Happy Family before moving to London. *Circus Maximus*, released in 1986, was the first offering recorded under the Momus name. The album spotlighted Currie's rich baritone and fascination with themes of psycho-sexuality and cultural crises, recurring motifs throughout his extensive catalog of work.

A move to Creation Records preceded the release of 1987's melancholy *The Poison Boyfriend*, followed by 1988's homoerotic *Tender Pervert*. With 1991's *Hippopotamomus*—dedicated to the late Serge Gainsbourg—Momus came under attack; the album, dubbed "a record about sex for children," drew fire from feminists. In 1994, Currie made tabloid headlines for his marriage to 17-year-old Shazna Nessa, the daughter of a Bangladesh-born restauranteur. Currie and Nessa first met when she was just 14; though she was sent back to Bangladesh by her parents to enter into an arranged marriage, she escaped to return to marry Currie, forcing the couple to go underground for fear that Nessa's family would kidnap her. Currie, now living in exile in Paris, resurfaced in 1995 with *The Philosophy of Momus*. He also found sudden success in Japan writing and producing for the Lolita-pop songstress Kahimi Karie, with whom he notched a string of five consecutive Top Five hits. *20 Vodka Jellies*, a collection of demos performed by Momus and intended for Karie, appeared in 1997. He issued *Ping Pong* in 1997, returning a year later with *The Little Red Songbook*. 1999's *Stars Forever* was arguably Momus' most controversial and provocative artistic statement yet—mounted to help defray massive legal costs facing Currie's U.S. label Le Grand Magistery, each of its songs was "commissioned" for $1000 apiece and written to the various "patrons'" specifications. —*Jason Ankeny*

Circus Maximus / Jan. 1986 / el-Cherry Red ✦✦✦

The Poison Boyfriend / 1987 / Creation ✦✦✦

● **Tender Pervert** / 1988 / Creation ✦✦✦✦✦
Tender Pervert is the first great Momus album, thanks to a newfound affinity for synth-pop and songcraft, not to mention his sudden discovery of irony. It's hard to say which is more important to the overall effect. The lush, electro-acoustic arrangements provide a platform for Momus' increasing production acumen, and the rambling song-poems of albums past are either condensed into melodic, verse-chorus structures, or held together by focused storytelling (as with the Yukio Mishima-influenced epic "Bishonen"). What's more, the wry humor hinted at on *The Poison Boyfriend* blossoms into a signature worldview here, complete with a nasty, cold-blooded edge in which Momus takes obvious pleasure. Paradoxically, when he's writing with a bit of ironic distance, Momus seems freed up to discuss more personal matters, perhaps because he's not trying so excruciatingly hard to present himself as thoughtful. A few stories are appropriated, but regardless of the source, they all seem to have more emotional resonance for their author; as such, it's the first time he's really found the humanity of his subjects, instead of simply using them to illustrate ideas. Overseen by a god who gets his kicks watching humanity inflict pain on itself, the characters on *Tender Pervert* live confusing, duplicitous lives, putting up a front to deal with the world's expectations while carefully hiding their true selves and goals. Yet no matter how dark their desires might get, they're quite often sympathetic, imbued with charm and elegance by Momus' faux-New Romantic backing tracks. And that's to say nothing of the singer's own lyrical wit, which flourishes on "I Was a Maoist Intellectual," "The Homosexual," and "A Complete History of Sexual Jealousy, Parts 17-24" in particular. All in all, *Tender Pervert* is easily one of Momus' most impressive albums, striking just the right balance between his earlier and later work. —*Steve Huey*

Don't Stop the Night / 1989 / Creation ✦✦✦✦

Monsters of Love: Singles 1985-90 / 1990 / Creation ✦✦✦✦

Hippopotamomus / 1991 / Creation ✦✦✦✦✦

The Ultraconformist / 1992 / Richmond ✦✦✦✦

Timelord / 1993 / Creation ✦✦

Philosophy of Momus / 1995 / Cherry Red ✦✦✦

20 Vodka Jellies / 1997 / Cherry Red ✦✦✦✦✦
Although *20 Vodka Jellies* is, as the cover says, "an assortment of curiosities and rarities," it also turns out to be one of Momus' strongest and most accessible efforts. Most of this material consists of well-produced demos (many recorded by other artists), plus a few new songs and some B-sides and outtakes that hadn't made it onto an official Momus release. This sort of collection usually doesn't reward anyone besides an artist's most devoted fans, but *20 Vodka Jellies* is actually an effective showcase for Momus' ample skill as a pop songwriter, as well as his musical versatility. "The End of History" and "Nobody" were recorded by Japanese singer Noriko "The Poison Girlfriend" Sekiguchi on her *Shyness* album, while the first five songs on the album were written for Shibuya-kei star Kahimi Karie; there's also the Momus version of Karie's Japanese Top Five hit "Good Morning World," originally commissioned for a cosmetics advertisement. Aside from being some of his most compulsively listenable material, these songs fit right into the Shibuya-kei movement's diverse, often kitschy tastes, neatly demonstrating Momus' own eclecticism. Also present are four "grunge demos," made when the prospect of a collaboration with Nirvana producer Butch Vig seemed likely; aside from the use of distorted electric guitars, they aren't a tremendous musical departure, but they are solidly written, humorously quirky pop songs. Still, even if he can't quite pull off hard rock, Momus can travel as far afield as crooning a trip-hop/lounge version of the Buzzcocks' "Orgasm Addict," which works surprisingly well once you get past the bizarreness of the concept. In general, the lyrical sensibilities on *20 Vodka Jellies* aren't as overtly twisted or perverse as his other late-'90s releases (although several moments certainly are), but the music is

impressive and extremely well crafted, and the lyrics are still literate and playful. —*Steve Huey*

Ping Pong / 1997 / Bungalow/Setanta ✦✦✦
The second Momus album issued in America by Le Grand Magistery, *Ping Pong* marks the flowering of the so-called "analog baroque" style that would be further developed on *The Little Red Songbook* (although there had been hints of it even in the early synth-pop days). The themes and obsessions are typical of latter-day Momus—misanthropic wit, sexual mischief, intellectual esoterica, Japanese culture—and are scattered around the album in an occasionally cohesive fashion. As usual, Momus' stylistic range is impressive: baroque chamber pop, of course, but also waltzes, disco, delicate ballads, Shibuya-kei pop, mock Russian dances, Serge Gainsbourg/Jacques Brel-style French pop, bossa nova, and extended rambling narratives, to cover the majority of it. Although the album is somewhat uneven, highlights are plentiful: the snarky loathing of "His Majesty the Baby," the angel/devil dichotomy in "My Pervert Doppelganger" (a recurring theme in Momus' work), the cleverly constructed wordplay of "I Want You, But I Don't Need You" and "My Kindly Friend the Censor," and Momus' own version of "Lolitapop Dollhouse," the young-feminist anthem he penned for Kahimi Karie. Unfortunately, there are times when *Ping Pong* bogs down in unfocused, overly long songs that stall the momentum built up by the best material. With some more editing, *Ping Pong* might have been one of Momus' best efforts; as it is, it's simply a fine album, uneven but featuring too much top-notch material for most fans to pass up. —*Steve Huey*

Little Red Songbook / Oct. 13, 1998 / Le Grand Magistery ✦✦✦✦
The record that best defines Momus' self-described "analog baroque" phase, *The Little Red Songbook* plays up his longstanding obsession with Serge Gainsbourg's dark humor and lascivious persona, placing it in a bed of lilting, unpredictable, and classically influenced melodies. The instrumentation is minimalist, usually employing only harpsichord, analog synth, bass sampled from a Nintendo GameBoy, and drum tracks from a cheap keyboard—an odd blend of classicism and kitschy futurism. The arrangements are often more layered than they sound at first, thanks to Momus' skill as a producer, but the resulting Vivaldi-meets-Kraftwerk sound still has an artificial, inorganic, low-budget feel. Not only is that intentional, but it perfectly fits the wry detachment of many of the album's tales of sexual manipulation; while some songs' observations are cultural rather than sexual, *The Little Red Songbook* is overall one of Momus' most explicitly vulgar records. However, its bluntness doesn't mean that the concise lyrical vignettes aren't clever—the list of "Everyone I Have Ever Slept With" turns into a rambling awards show speech, and "Coming in a Girl's Mouth" spends most of its time pondering the symbolic meaning of that act, not just its physical realities. In fact, the subject matter's clash with Momus' "cultured" chamber-pop appropriations makes for a compelling tension. It's equally possible to hear this as sophisticated pop with a conscious affectation of elegant, high-class decadence, or as an intentionally trashy, dirty way of subverting the pomposity of music and literature regarded as "high art," skillfully using its own forms against it. Either way, it's unabashedly self-referential, morally dubious, and scathingly funny—in other words, everything a great latter-day Momus album should be. The album ends with instrumental "karaoke versions" of nine of its songs, which were used in a record-your-own-Momus-parody contest (the winning entries appeared on *Stars Forever*). [Note: Legal objections forced the removal of one of the album's songs; when *The Little Red Songbook* was reissued sans the offending track, there were three short new songs included as a substitute.] —*Steve Huey*

● **Stars Forever** / Aug. 24, 1999 / Le Grand Magistery ✦✦✦✦✦
Grand artistic statement or money-grubbing sham? Befitting Momus' standing as contemporary pop's most eminent provocateur, *Stars Forever* is both—a double-disc collection of analog-baroque cameos commissioned for $1000 each in the name of saving the singer's label from the ravages of legal fees, it's a frequently brilliant treatise on the never-ending battle between art and commerce, rising to the heights of the former as often as it succumbs to the depths of the latter. The idea behind *Stars Forever* is simple—30 "patrons" (among them everyone from modern artist Jeff Koons to hip NYC record store Other Music to the crazy kids who contribute to the online Indiepop List service) fork over a grand each for the honor of being eternally immortalized in a Momus song—but the long-term ramifications of the project are complex and unsettling, and the paradoxes and questions it provokes are myriad. After all, who among us is truly fit to judge Momus' actions and intents? Should we respect the honesty of his "patronage pop" or deplore its capitalist shamelessness? Do these songs rob his music of the perversely personal bent which makes him special, or do they lift him out of the rut of self-obsession and offer an entirely new creative path? And what if the profits went not to a struggling indie label but to Sony? Furthermore, I'm getting paid to write this review—how hypocritical is that? Perhaps the greatest value of *Stars Forever* is as a litmus test which forces each listener to answer these questions and countless others for themselves—admire the record or despise it, it might just change your perception of pop music and the business that drives it forever. —*Jason Ankeny*

Folktronic / Feb. 27, 2001 / Analogue Baroque ✦✦✦
In 1952, anthropologist/ethnomusicologist/filmmaker/collector of curiosities/polymath Harry Smith released his *Anthology of American Folk Music* on Folkways. The brilliance of the six LP collection of pre-WWII music was in Harry Smith's ability to see connections between dark ballads, rollicking social music, and geographically disparate songs. His collection defined the music in the context of American culture and created a dramatically novel worldview.

Scottish-born eccentric Nick Currie, aka Momus, is a Harry Smith for the age of information. Not only does he continue to put out wonderfully odd albums, but he has a newspaper column of cultural criticism, is a rabid Japanophile and pop culture addict, a magazine junkie, uses his website to address whatever touches his fancy, and comments on everything from art to history to literature to philosophy to mass media. Momus always attaches a character or concept to his albums, and *Folktronic* is his anthology of fake folk. It takes a warped mind to connect mountain music and electronica, but this is just the kind of thing that has gained Momus his cult following. All the humor, jesting, parody, and sexual cruelty that we've come to love him for are here. Songs like "Finnegan the Folk Hero" pop and bleep as digital technology meets tomorrow's shanties. "Little Apples" is about science, Momus' G4 computer, and his digital camera. "The Penis Song" is a brave new ballad that tells the hapless tale of the hero's meeting with rock groupie turned artist, Cynthia Plaster Caster. You must hear it to believe it. Though *The Little Red Songbook* and *Stars Forever* would be better introductions to the wonderful world of baroque pop, *Folktronic* is a must-have for Momus fanatics. The artist formerly known as Maoist Intellectual, Futuristic Vaudevillian, and Audio Portraitist always seems to do something new and unexpected, and this time the space-age folkie molds traditional ballads and Appalachian ditties out of plastic and silicon. —*Charles Spano*

Eddie Money

b. Mar. 2, 1949, Brooklyn, NY

Vocals, Saxophone, Keyboards / Album Rock, Arena Rock, Pop/Rock

Arriving at the height of album-rock's popularity in the late '70s, Eddie Money didn't have a remarkable voice, but he did have a knack for catchy, blue-collar rock & roll, which he delivered with a surprising amount of polished, radio-friendly finesse. The son of a Brooklyn cop, Eddie Mahoney initially followed in his father's footsteps and attended the New York Police Academy during the early '70s, but at night, he sang in rock bands under the name Eddie Money. He decided to pursue music full-time: quitting the Academy, he moved to Berkeley, CA, and became a regular at Bay Area clubs. Thanks to legendary promoter Bill Graham, Money signed a contract with Columbia Records and released his eponymous debut in 1977. During the late '70s, he had a handful of album-rock and Top 40 "Baby Hold On" and "Maybe I'm a Fool." He survived the early MTV era with clever videos for songs like "Shakin'" and "Think I'm In Love," but he couldn't resist the temptations of a rock & roll lifestyle: his popularity dipped as he struggled with various addictions in the mid-'80s. A few years later, Money was sober again and made a remarkable comeback with Top Ten singles like 1986's "Take Me Home Tonight" and 1988's "Walk on Water." 1990's "Peace in Our Time," which reached Number 11, was Money's last big hit—during the early '90s, his popularity faded and he retired to the oldies circuit. He returned with a new album, *Ready Eddie*, in 1999. —*Stephen Thomas Erlewine*

● **The Best of Eddie Money** / Jul. 24, 2001 / Columbia/Legacy ✦✦✦✦✦

Columbia/Legacy's 2001 release *The Best of Eddie Money* supplants the earlier 1989 collection *Greatest Hits: The Sound of Money* as the best overview of Money's career. Again, it's not sequenced chronologically, nor is it as tight as it should have been (Money is somebody that would really sound terrific on an eight or ten-song collection), but it's very good all the same, containing all of his big hits, plus live versions of "Rock & Roll the Place" and "No Control" previously only available on a promo EP. So, even if it's not perfect, it will still satisfy the needs of most Money fans. —*Stephen Thomas Erlewine*

The Monkees

f. 1965, Los Angeles, CA, db. 1969

Sunshine Pop, Psychedelic Pop, Bubblegum, Pop/Rock, Pop

Formed primarily for the purpose of starring in a television series, the Monkees were on one hand a cynically manufactured group, devised to cash in on the early Beatles' success by applying the most superficial aspects of the British Invasion formula to capture a preteen audience. On the other hand, they weren't devoid of musical talent, and at their best managed to craft some enduring pop/rock hits. "I'm a Believer," "Last Train to Clarksville," "A Little Bit Me, a Little Bit You," "Pleasant Valley Sunday," "Stepping Stone," "Take a Giant Step," "Valleri," "Words"—all were pleasantly jangling, harmony rock numbers with hooks big enough for a meat locker, and all were huge hits in 1966-68. Scorned at their peak by hipsters for not playing on many of their own records, the group gained some belated critical respect for their catchy, good-time brand of pop. It would be foolish to pretend, however, that they were a band of serious significance, despite the occasional genuinely serious artistic aspirations of the members. From the outset, it was made clear that the Monkees were hired to be television actors first and musicians a distant second. There would be original material generated for them to sing in the series, mostly by professional songwriters like Tommy Boyce, Bobby Hart, Carole King, Gerry Goffin, and Neil Diamond. There would be records, as well—had to be, with that kind of weekly exposure, to promote the tunes—but the group wouldn't do much more than sing, although the series would give the impression that they played their own instruments. —*Richie Unterberger*

The Monkees / Oct. 1966 / Rhino ✦✦✦✦

The Monkees did virtually nothing besides sing lead vocals on their full-length debut; poor Peter Tork didn't even get to do that, his contribution being limited to one of the six guitar parts on "Papa Gene's Blues." Given that it wasn't a project of high integrity, it wasn't bad—in fact, much of this is reasonably gutsy pop/rock, including their TV theme song, the hits "Last Train to Clarksville" and "Take a Giant Step," and various decent songs by top Brill Building tunesmiths like Goffin/King, Boyce/Hart, and David Gates. Nesmith was allowed one composition ("Papa Gene's Blues") that indicated his country-rock direction. The CD reissue includes unremarkable bonus tracks of alternate versions of the Monkees theme and a couple of songs that would turn up on subsequent LPs. —*Richie Unterberger*

More of the Monkees / Jan. 10, 1967 / Rhino ✦✦✦✦

Second album, same as the first, virtually: a huge single ("I'm a Believer"/"Steppin' Stone"), a couple of token Mike Nesmith songs (including "Mary, Mary," previously recorded by the Paul Butterfield Blues Band and a rap hit for Run-D.M.C. in 1988), tunes by Boyce/Hart, Goffin/King, Neil Diamond, Jeff Barry, Neil Sedaka, and Carole Bayer; no participation from the group other than lead vocals. The band was quite upset at their lack of input at the time, but it's relatively decent (if quite harmless) pop/rock, featuring one of their best album tracks, "She." Like all of the Rhino CD reissues, it adds marginally interesting bonus tracks of unreleased alternate versions, including an early take of "I'm a Believer." —*Richie Unterberger*

Headquarters / May 22, 1967 / Rhino ✦✦✦✦✦

For their third album, the Monkees were determined to wrest control of the creative process, and with producer Chip Douglas functioning as frequent bassist and auxiliary member, they were indeed able to play most of the instruments and write much of the material. It would be nice to report that the result far exceeded previous efforts and established the group as visionary artists, but in fact this was, again, pleasantly inoffensive pop/rock. There was more of a country flavor and a sense of personal involvement, though the group still tapped songwriting pros like Boyce/Hart and Mann/Weil for about half the songs. Standouts included Nesmith's "You Just May Be the One," one of his best Monkee tunes, and Tork's "For Pete's Sake," which became the show's closing theme. The CD reissue includes six unreleased tracks and alternate takes, a couple of which (Nilsson's "All of Your Toys" and Nesmith's "The Girl I Knew Somewhere") rank among their finest. —*Richie Unterberger*

Pisces, Aquarius, Capricorn & Jones Ltd. / Nov. 14, 1967 / Rhino ✦✦✦✦✦

One of their better efforts, featuring the double-sided hit "Pleasant Valley Sunday"/ "Words," and some of their best album tracks, like "She Hangs Out," "Star Collector," and "Cuddly Toy," the last of which was one of the first Nilsson songs to be covered by a major artist. As usual, some of the country-rockers and half-baked psychedelic tunes are tedious, though a couple tracks are notable for featuring some of the first uses of a Moog synthesizer on a rock record. The CD reissue adds some previously unissued alternate mixes, as well as the killer soulful B-side "Goin' Down," which ranks as one of their very best tracks despite its obscurity. —*Richie Unterberger*

The Birds, the Bees & the Monkees / Apr. 22, 1968 / Rhino ✦✦✦

Not one of their better efforts, dominated almost wholly by session musicians (with the occasional songwriting and instrumental contribution by Mike Nesmith) and containing too many sickly sweet Davy Jones-sung numbers. It does have the hits "Daydream Believer" and "Valleri," as well as Nesmith's "Tapioca Tundra," which just inched into the Top 40, but overall the material is pretty weak. The CD adds some previously unissued songs and alternate takes, the only one of interest being Peter Tork's "Lady's Baby," which sounds like a Buffalo Springfield outtake with its laid-back country/folk/rock flavor. —*Richie Unterberger*

Head / Dec. 1, 1968 / Rhino ✦✦✦

Like the film from which it came, the soundtrack to *Head* was far from a masterpiece, but had some inspired moments. These include the spacy "Porpoise Song," written by Gerry Goffin and Carole King; the tough-rocking "Circle Sky," probably the best song Mike Nesmith wrote for the group; "Can You Dig It," one of Peter Tork's best contributions; and "As We Go Along" and "Daddy's Song," little-known songs by Carole King and Nilsson, respectively. As a listening experience, it's made more difficult by the juxtaposition of music and dialogue from the film. The CD reissue adds bonus unissued jingles and alternate takes, highlighted by a live version of "Circle Sky." —*Richie Unterberger*

Instant Replay / Feb. 15, 1969 / Rhino ✦✦✦

By 1969's *Instant Replay*, it was all over but the funeral. Peter Tork had already left the fold and the songs were little more than disjointed solo vehicles for the remaining three, combined with older unreleased tracks from the vaults. This afforded far too much rope for schmaltzy Jones ballads, although Nesmith salvages the day once again with tasty country inflections on the wistful "Don't Wait for Me" and "While I Cry." This otherwise slight collection—for intensive Monkees fans only—is at least beefed up by some interesting previously unreleased songs, rather than just alternate mixes. —*Roch Parisien*

The Monkees Present / Oct. 1969 / Rhino ✦✦✦

Like *Instant Replay*, *The Monkees Present* was an incoherent collection of pop and country-rock. Although most of the album was well produced but bland, Mike Nesmith's contributions, particularly "Listen to the Band," indicated that he was continuing to grow as a songwriter. However, his handful of songs couldn't save the album from being a rather desultory affair. After the record's release, Nesmith left the band to pursue a solo career. —*Stephen Thomas Erlewine*

Changes / Jun. 1970 / Rhino ✦✦

For most intents and purposes, the Monkees had broken up before the recording of *Changes*, their final record. Peter Tork and Mike Nesmith had left the band, leaving only Micky Dolenz and Davy Jones. Although Dolenz was a relatively accomplished songwriter, he only contributed one song to *Changes*, which meant both he and Jones were vehicles for a variety of professional songwriters, particularly Jeff Barry, who also produced the majority of the album. Most of the material was bland pop, featuring a couple of R&B and soul inflections to liven up the sound. Neither Dolenz or Jones sounds inspired by the material, which isn't surprising—out of the 12 songs, only Boyce and Hart's "I Never Though It Peculiar" makes any sort of impression. The lack of worthwhile material and the slick, passionless production easily make *Changes* the weakest record The Monkees released. Until they reunited for *Pool It*, that is. —*Stephen Thomas Erlewine*

Pool It! / 1986 / Rhino ✦

Missing Links / 1987 / Rhino ✦✦✦
A fine selection of rarities and oddities that every Monkee maniac with more than a passing interest should own. *—Jeff Tamarkin*

Missing Links, Vol. 2 / 1990 / Rhino ✦✦✦
Nineteen rare and unreleased tracks that, like the rest of the Monkees' output, ranges from excellent to insufferable, with plenty of mediocre material between. The highlights are the sprightly pop-rocker "All the King's Horses" (a 1966 Mike Nesmith original) and alternate versions of two of the group's best singles, "Words" and "Valleri." These alternate takes aren't exactly better, but they are definitely different and less elaborately produced. Most of the rest is either lightweight 1966 pop-rock or weedy 1968 Mike Nesmith country-rock tunes that foreshadow his solo work; several cuts are alternate versions of songs that were hardly notable efforts in the first place. An exception is the live 1968 recording of the unusually forceful Nesmith original "Circle Sky," which was featured in their movie *Head* (although a studio version was substituted on the actual soundtrack album). Odds and ends like an instrumental banjo piece by Peter Tork and a Spanish Christmas carol are pleasant but inessential. A thoughtfully compiled CD, it nonetheless really gives this group more respect than they're due by treating these artifacts with such importance. *—Richie Unterberger*

Listen to the Band / Sep. 24, 1991 / Rhino ✦✦✦✦✦
The very idea of a Monkees box set would have seemed inconceivable at any time before the 1990s, and probably still would to any label other than Rhino Records. Yet, this four-CD, 83-song compilation manages to justify itself very nicely, despite the existence of heavily expanded editions of most of the group's albums on CD, and the *Missing Links* volumes. Those individual CDs gathered together are for the true musical completists, whereas this is the documentary overview for the fan who wants five hours of fun and adventure. The song selection is a mix of important released material, essential outtakes that have shown up on *Missing Links*, and a handful of yet more unissued songs that slipped past the programming of those discs. Surprisingly, not a track is wasted, showing how deep one could go into the group's output and still come up with gold. Disc four is the weak link—the group was breaking down, its prospects were fading by the week once the series was cancelled in 1968, and yet the individual members were carrying on in their music-making, using the Monkees name and the commercial doors it still opened. Little of the music sounded like "the Monkees" although there are some superb tracks by Michael Nesmith and some decent pop/rock numbers by Mickey Dolenz and Davy Jones. The sound is excellent throughout, and the accompanying booklet would easily be worth the price of another CD, containing as it does a detailed history of each song in the set, how it came to be written and recorded, and the personal and business events connected with the group and coinciding with the recordings. It's all fun and musically very informative as well, and a great capper to the label's cycle of Monkees music releases.
—Bruce Eder

★ **Greatest Hits** / Nov. 1995 / Rhino ✦✦✦✦✦
Twenty-song collection includes all of their big chart hits, as well as key album tracks like "(Theme From) the Monkees" and "Mary, Mary," and the ace B-side "Goin' Down." The slightly more extensive Arista anthology still has the edge, due to the inclusion of two good cuts ("Take a Giant Step" and "She") that are somehow omitted from this Rhino compilation. On the other hand, if you're still in the market for just one Monkees album, this will do just fine. Good, extensive liner notes, though the last two songs (from 1987 singles that only featured Dolenz and Tork) are a waste. *—Richie Unterberger*

Missing Links, Vol. 3 / Mar. 26, 1996 / Rhino ✦✦✦
Rhino treats the Monkees catalog with a seriousness akin to the Beatles' *Anthology* series, but it's nonsense to pretend that the group's outtakes/rarities are deserving of such fanatical scrutiny. There are a lot more than anyone suspected, though, and volume three of the *Missing Links* presents 24 more, again proving that the bottom of the Monkees' barrel has the same mixture of fun and boredom as hiding in a barrel as a stowaway. There are too many trivial cuts here from the late '60s—that goes for both the slight pop/rockers and Nesmith's less slight country-rockers. On the other hand, there are some good 'uns, like the Dolenz-sung acoustic 1967 demo "She'll Be There," and which recalls early British Invasion acts like Peter & Gordon; different/rare mixes/takes of "Circle Sky" (one of Nesmith's best compositions), Jeff Barry's "She Hangs Out," and Neil Diamond's "Love to Love"; "How Insensitive," Nesmith's imaginative country rearrangement of an Antonio Carlos Jobim (!) standard; and "Merry Go Round" and "Zor and Zam," insanely experimental outings for a teenybopper group. Thrown into the mix are novelties like commercials and an Italian version of the Monkees' theme, icing the cake on an inconsistency that makes the nearby presence of a CD remote button a necessity. *—Richie Unterberger*

Justus / Oct. 15, 1996 / Rhino ✦✦✦
As the final reunion album from the Monkees—and the first one featuring Mike Nesmith, who produced the record—*Justus* isn't bad. Nesmith occasionally steers the group toward country-rock, but the record is largely comprised of nondescript pop/rock that is neither remarkable nor unpleasant. Frequently, the Monkees show their age with strained vocals, but *Justus* is far from the disaster of *Pool It*, and it may stir warm, nostalgic memories from many long-term fans—if they're willing to sift through the mediocre songs that form the bulk of the album. *—Stephen Thomas Erlewine*

Anthology / Apr. 21, 1998 / Rhino ✦✦✦✦
Rhino's *Listen to the Band* box set was for the collectors, and their terrific 20-song *Greatest Hits* was for the casual fans. Their third attempt at a Monkees compilation, the double-disc *Anthology*, falls somewhere in between. Over the course of an exhausting 56 tracks, all of the group's hits are hauled out again, with such fine album tracks as "She," "Take a Giant Step," "Your Auntie Grizelda," "You Just May Be the One" and "What Am I Doing Hangin' Round" added for good measure. On the surface of things, this seems like a good thing, but the set is padded out with lesser album cuts and latter-day tracks from their three reunion albums that makes *Anthology* more of a chore than a pleasure. Since there are no genuine rarities here, it won't quite appeal to collectors, and since *Greatest Hits* suits the purposes of the average fans, it remains a mystery just who this set is for, even if it is loaded with good music. *—Stephen Thomas Erlewine*

Headquarters Sessions / Sep. 21, 2000 / Rhino Handmade ✦✦✦✦
Like many Rhino Handmade releases (available only via Internet), the Monkees' *Headquarters Sessions* is marketed for fanatics. Indeed, this set—which contains over three discs filled with all the outtakes and studio chatter you could ever hope for or need—is essentially the Holy Grail of Monkees material. Informal versions of "Cripple Creek," "Don't Be Cruel," "Nine Times Blue," "The Story of Rock & Roll" (made into a modest hit by the Turtles), and "She's So Far Out, She's In" are only a handful of the set's rarites. On the tracks that would become the *Headquarters* album, it becomes obvious this was an amateur band struggling to get through a simple take. However, you can feel the camaraderie (even though Davy Jones is absent from most of this) between musicians Mike Nesmith and Peter Tork, while actor Mickey Dolenz is heard numerous times throughout apologizing for yet another drum flub. In this potentially volatile scenario, there is a sense of friendship and lack of studio ego, which is exactly why this package is so charming. These are mainly actors, struggling to prove their musicianship, maintaining their cool, while finding out the hard way how difficult the recording process actually is (and how good Don Kirshner's studio musicians were). After *Headquarters*, the Monkees would never attempt to go into the studio again depending wholly on themselves. Their individual musical direction, especially in Nesmith's case, would be required from then on, with the final results being mixed at best. Along with the mainly unreleased instrumental versions of these tracks, studio flubs and conversations is the scrapped mono version of *Headquarters* with a completely different song sequence that included Nesmith's "The Girl I Knew Somewhere." *—Al Campbell*

Music Box / Feb. 20, 2001 / Rhino ✦✦✦✦✦
It's hard not to wonder why the four-disc *Music Box* even exists. After all, Rhino has not only released definitive reissues of all of the Monkees' studio albums, complete with bonus tracks, but the label has a series devoted to rarities (*Missing Links*), a single-disc greatest hits album, a double-disc anthology, and *another* four-disc box, *Listen to the Band*, which is excellent. So where does that leave *Music Box*? Well, it is "reconfigured" into a booklike box, which must appeal to somebody, but more importantly, it tries to pull off a nifty trick—providing an exhaustive overview for the casual listener, while filling in the holes for those serious fans who only have the proper reissued albums. On both counts, this works well. Let's get the basics out of the way: This *sounds* great, and Andrew Sandoval's liner notes are terrific, particularly the song-by-song breakdown that not only includes the Monkees' reflections, but also those of various producers and songwriters. Then, there's the song selection, which is impeccable for the first three discs, which devote a year each to 1966, 1967, and 1968, blending hits with rarities, album versions, and alternate takes, never once seeming like a sop to collectors. The fourth disc is a little more problematic, just because it spans from 1969 to 1996, containing reunion tracks that some fans may rather not hear, but it still has more than enough minor gems that will please the dedicated. And, when it gets right down to it, *Music Box* succeeds on two counts: Everyone who needs to plug in gaps will be satisfied with this (plus they'll like the fine flow of the songs) and, more importantly, this is a wonderful choice for anyone looking for a good, thorough overview of the Monkees' best, delving far deeper than the hits. It doesn't really trump *Listen to the Band*, but it's nearly an equal. *—Stephen Thomas Erlewine*

Summer 1967: The Complete U.S. Concert Recordings / May 18, 2001 / Rhino HandMade ✦✦✦
This four-disc package gathers the only known professionally documented concerts by the Monkees on their 1967 summer tour. Each of the four discs contains a complete performance—hence the repetition of material. Disc one contains a monophonic demo recording made by crew member/photographer Winton Teel. The results of which were the criterion in whether or not it would be feasible to send a crew and equipment to sonically capture later dates on the tour. It becomes obvious that the results, while favorable, were far from optimal. The set list and stage antics were similar on every stop of the Monkees '67 tour. The "Theme From 'The Monkees'" would blare from the PA system and the lads would bound out of two mock Vox audio speaker cabinets. The self-contained quartet would then churn through hit singles as well as a few choice album cuts. Each band member is likewise featured in a spotlight performance; "Cripple Creek" being the most solo of them all, as Peter Tork was usually accompanied by nothing more than his own banjo. Backing up the other three soloists is the five-piece pop combo the Sundowners. They are particularly effective on Michael Nesmith's cover of Willie Dixon's "You Can't Judge a Book (By Looking at the Cover)." The show wraps up with the return of the self-contained quartet grinding through garage rock renditions of hits such as "I'm a Believer" and "(I'm Not Your) Steppin' Stone." The recordings are an engineering nightmare. Buzzes, pops, and musicians performing into microphones that don't work all together ... seemingly everything that could, does go wrong at some point. However, the massive transfer of energy between audience and performer—especially under the circumstances—can't be buried in the mix. Spontaneity and reinvention night after night likewise can't be faked. *Summer 1967: The Complete U.S. Concert Recordings* is a vital pop/rock relic available in a limited edition of 3500 from Rhino HandMade. *—Lindsay Planer*

The Monks

f. 1964, **db.** 1967

Garage Rock, Rock & Roll

One of the strangest stories in rock history, the Monks were formed in the early '60s by American G.I.s stationed in Germany. After their discharge, the group stayed on in Germany as the Torquays, a fairly standard "beat" band. After changing their name to the Monks in the mid-'60s, they also changed their music, attitude, and appearance radically. Gone were standard oldie covers, replaced by furious, minimalistic original material that anticipated the blunt, harsh commentary of the punk era. Their insistent rhythms recalled martial beats and polkas as much as garage rock, and the weirdness quotient was heightened by electric banjo, berserk organ runs, and occasional bursts of feedback guitar. To prove that they meant business, the Monks shaved the top of their heads and performed their songs—crude diatribes about the Vietnam war, dehumanized society, and love/hate affairs with girls—in actual monks' clothing. This was pretty strong stuff for 1966 Germany, and their shocking repertoire and attire were received with more confusion than hostility or warm praise. They disbanded in confusion around 1967, but their sole album—one of the most oddball constructions in all of rock—gained a hardcore cult following among collectors, and has ironically made them much more popular and influential on an international level than they were during their lifetime. *—Richie Unterberger*

● **Black Monk Time** / 1966 / Infinite Zero/American ✦✦✦✦✦

The Monks' only album is packed with angst anthems on the order of "Shut Up," "I Hate You," "Complication," and "Drunken Maria." One of the strangest recordings of all time, it's now finally available in the U.S. as a 1997 CD reissue on Infinite Zero. The repackage is made all the more appealing with the inclusion of their two later non-LP singles, the live 1966 "Monk Chant," and a couple of 1965 demos, making it the definitive document of the Monks' recorded legacy. *—Richie Unterberger*

Five Upstart Americans / Nov. 2, 1999 / Omplatten ✦✦✦

Rawer than their primordial opus, *Black Monk Time*, *Five Upstart Americans* is a collection of demos by proto-punks the Monks (recorded when they were still known as the Torquays). While most demonstration recordings are, by nature, more primitive than the finished product, these sessions could be seen as even more representative of the Monks primal vision. Here their "over-beat" songs of love/hate, confusion, and frustration are stripped to their bare essentials, with minimal lyrics and overdubs. Taped in a single day in 1965, most of these performances remained unreleased for 34 years ("I Hate You" and "Oh, How to Do Now" were included as bonus tracks on Infinite Zero's reissue of *Black Monk Time* in 1997). Though essential listening for Monk converts, the uninitiated should bless themselves with *Black Monk Time* before proceeding further. *Five Upstart Americans* also includes their first 45 (as Five Torquays), which only hints at what was to come. *—Bart Bealmear*

Let's Start a Beat: Live From Cavestomp! / Oct. 31, 2000 / Varese ✦✦✦

In November 1999, the Monks reunited to play their first shows in 32 years at the Cavestomp festivals in New York. (In fact, these were their first shows ever in the United States, although the band were comprised entirely of Americans.) Considering the long layoff, they were in pretty good shape, running their most of their repertoire with a decidedly un-mellow verve. And considering that they recorded just one album and a few non-LP singles and demos, of course, it wasn't that hard to run through most of that repertoire in a single gig. This disc has live versions of most of the songs from their 1966 *Black Monk Time* album and a few of those stray non-LP odds and ends, as well as a couple of jams. Non-Monk Mike Fornatale helped out a bit on backup vocals (and takes one lead, on "Boys Are Boys"), but otherwise it's the actual original quintet you hear here. The arrangements are fairly close to those heard on the original '60s cuts, but a little more straight-ahead rock in flavor, with some more space given to jams. So, is this as good as, or as sufficient a sampling of their limited oeuvre, as the original *Black Monk Time* record? No; as rock reunions go, that would be a downright singular achievement. It's a surprisingly respectable document, however. *—Richie Unterberger*

The Monochrome Set

f. 1978

New Wave, Alternative Pop/Rock

When the British art-school punk band the B-Sides changed their name and direction to become Adam & the Ants, guitarist/vocalist Bid and guitarist Lester Square opted out to form their own group, the Monochrome Set. Founded in London in 1978, the band (also comprised of ex-Gloria Mundi and Mean Street bassist Jeremy Harrington and former Art Attacks drummer J.D. Crowe) was quickly snapped up by the Rough Trade label, and during 1979 issued three singles—"He's Frank," "Eine Symphonie des Grauens," and their signature number, "Monochrome Set"—all completely different in content and stylistic approach.

After former B-Sides bassist Andy Warren grew tired of life in Adam & the Ants, he rejoined bandmates Bid and Square, replacing Harrington. In 1980 the Monochrome Set released their debut album, the cabaret-flavored *Strange Boutique*, followed later that year by the singles "405 Lines" and "Apocalypso" as well as another, more accessible full-length effort, *Love Zombies*. Complete with new guitarist Foz, keyboardist Caroline Booth, and drummer Nick Wesolowski, they returned in 1982 with a cleaner, more melodic sound on the LP *Eligible Bachelors*; "The Jet Set Junta," a satiric jab at the Falklands Islands conflict, became a significant hit the next year.

Following the depatrure of Square, the Monochrome Set veered even closer to light pop fare on singles like 1985's "Jacob's Ladder"; the sound subsquently crystallized on the nostalgically-themed LP *The Lost Weekend*. When the record met with dismal commercial response, the group disbanded, only to reform in 1989 around the nucleus of Bid, Square and Warren along with new keyboaridst Orson Presence. The 1990 album *Dante's Casino* did little to raise the Monochrome Set's chart visibility, but the band soldiered on, releasing *Charade* in 1993, *Misere* in 1994 and *Trinity Road* in 1995. *—Jason Ankeny*

Strange Boutique / 1980 / Dindisc ✦✦✦

Monochrome Set's debut album for Virgin followed the indie success of their singles "Alphaville," "Eine Symphonie Des Grauens," and "The Monochrome Set." By the time it was scheduled, Andy Warren (ex-Adam & the Ants) had replaced Jeremy Harrington on bass, and the lineup was completed by guitarist Lester Square (also ex-Ants), Indian-born vocalist/guitarist Bid, and former Art Attacks drummer J.D. Haney. Although it can't quite match *Eligible Bachelors* for songwriting, there are a number of superb, non-single album tracks that make this an essential purchase for fans—especially "Ici les Enfants," "The Puerto Rican Fence Climber," and "The Lighter Side of Dating." Amid the austerity of post-punk England, and before we became awash with irony and archness, we needed a band who could raise their eyebrows and smirk at it all without ever being condescending (or maybe only a *little* bit condescending). *—Alex Ogg*

Love Zombies / 1981 / Dindisc ✦✦✦✦✦

The group's second album (and last for Virgin subsidiary Dindisc), *Love Zombies* features more accomplished songwriting from main man Bid—especially the title track and the playful "The Man With the Black Moustache." Fans—BBC Radio DJ John Peel among them—had long since recognized the Monochrome Set's supreme compositional agility. This is amply demonstrated by *Love Zombies*, which switches from sweet pop to wry ballads to a kind of alt-rock rumba with disarming ease. "The Weird, Wild and Wonderful World of Tony Potts," incidentally, is a tribute to the band's visual designer and "fifth member." And isn't "In Love, Cancer?" one of the all-time great song titles? *—Alex Ogg*

Eligible Bachelors / 1982 / Cherry Red ✦✦✦

One of the classic, undiscovered albums of the early '80s, *Eligible Bachelors* is a *tour de force* of wit and musical imagination. It features some of the funniest songs ever committed to vinyl, kicking off with "Jet Set Junta," which, alongside bookend song "The Ruling Class," pillories the neuroses of the wealthy. "The Mating Game" is also deeply amusing as a cad's cynical guide to the opposite sex, with lyrics like, "Blond, brunette or redhead, black, yellow or white/They taste the same, in the mating game." But it's not all jokes. "The Midas Touch" is an exquisite slice of whimsy riding a near-perfect guitar riff, with an emotional reach that shames most peers of songwriter Bid. Whether or not the rear cover testimonial from Andy Warhol is genuine, the Monochrome Set had released an age-defining record here. It's a shame nobody else knew about it. *—Alex Ogg*

Volume! Brilliance! Contrast! / 1983 / Cherry Red ✦✦✦✦✦

This is another compilation, but back in 1983 this hugely rewarding record acted as a roundup of the group's career to date and was of immeasurable value to fans. It's aged well, too, and worth hunting down for some (quite radically different) radio versions of songs, oddities, and jocular moments, including John Peel introducing "Fat Fun" and thinking aloud that those Monochrome boys might be having a pop at him. The fact that it includes a wish list of the band's best songs (with the possible exception of "The Midas Touch" and "The Mating Game") to this point in their career is another reason to recommend it. *—Alex Ogg*

The Lost Weekend / 1985 / Blanco y Negro ✦✦✦

The Monochrome Set's curtain call before Bid launched a haphazard solo career, *Lost Weekend* offers "Jacob's Ladder," which was almost a hit single (heck, there was even a video). It was not to be, however, despite the move to Warners' subsidiary Blanco y Negro. The irony of the Monochrome Set was that they were always a small-budget band working on the most regal material. Still, there are several more great songs here, the best including "Letter from Viola," "Cargo," and "Wallflower" (also a single). *—Alex Ogg*

Fin / 1986 / el/Cherry Red ✦✦

Colour Transmission / 1988 / Virgin ✦✦✦✦

Westminster Affair / 1988 / Cherry Red ✦✦✦

Presented as a soundtrack to a French film, though nobody can remember seeing it, *Westminster Affair* is another workman-like and, frankly, unnecessary compilation of Monochrome Set material. Four cuts from *Volume! Contrast! Brilliance!* reappear, and there are a few singles, a big chunk of *Eligible Bachelors*, and a song from *The Lost Weekend*. Again, it's a decent running order, and these are undoubtedly great songs, but they're all available elsewhere. *—Alex Ogg*

Dante's Casino / 1990 / Vinyl Japan ✦✦

B & W Minstrels / 1995 / Cherry Red ✦✦✦

As a document of this ever-inventive band's earliest material dating from 1975 to 1979—before they signed with Virgin—*B&W Minstrels* encompasses the Monochrome Set singles for Rough Trade and Disques Bleu, as well as previously unheard demos. This marks an engaging period in their development, though to some extent, the group seemed to be born fully formed anyway. Most bands at this stage in their career haven't a clue as to what they want to sound like. For spoiled kids the Monochrome Set, however, the problem seemed to be one of choosing from their innumerable options; here's a band who could settle happily in any style they wanted, from straight pop to ballroom or cabaret. *B&W Minstrels* provides an entertaining run through their early repertoire, and it saves you from having to hunt down those singles. *—Alex Ogg*

● **Tomorrow Will Be Too Long: The Best of the Monocrome Set** / Apr. 25, 1995 / Caroline ✦✦✦✦✦

Its title taken from the closing track on their debut album, this is yet another Monochrome Set compilation. This one includes picks from the group's two-album spell with Virgin. While the material is uniformly good, listeners should skip this in preference to a more thorough retrospective (either Cherry Red's *History: 1978-1996* or Snapper's *Chaps*). —*Alex Ogg*

Monster Magnet

f. 1990

Stoner Metal, Alternative Metal, Heavy Metal, Hard Rock

Throughout most of the 1990s, Monster Magnet struggled against the prejudices imposed upon image and sound by alternative rock fashion nazis. However, thanks to that movement's decline and the band's dogged persistence, their fourth album, *Powertrip*, catapulted to gold sales status with the help of its massive hard rock hit "Space Lord." They also became one of the most successful and influential bands of the burgeoning underground '70s-influenced metal scene, frequently called stoner rock. New Jersey native Dave Wyndorf was already a rock & roll veteran by the time he formed Monster Magnet in 1989, having cut his teeth with little-known punk band Shrapnel in the late '70s. After a few years of relative silence, Wyndorf began assembling Monster Magnet. Fusing their punk, space rock, and psychedelic influences, the band developed a sludgy, feedback-heavy hard rock sound. Monster Magnet eventually caught the attention of independent label Caroline Records and entered the studio in 1992 to record their first full-length album—the impressive and highly original *Spine of God*. 1993's *Superjudge* proved to be a stellar major-label debut and though the band chose to sacrifice some of their trademark feedback, it only served to accentuate their muscular metal riffs. Unfortunately, the group's classic rock sound and attitude was highly unfashionable at the time, arriving at the height of the post-Nirvana alternative boom, and the album sold poorly. Under mounting pressure to deliver a more commercial follow-up, Monster Magnet delivered a decidedly sleeker—though no less space rock drenched—effort with 1995's *Dopes to Infinity*. Still, the album sold only slightly better than its predecessor. Mentally and physically exhausted, Wyndorf exiled himself to Las Vegas to begin composing the tracks which would shape 1998's breakthrough release *Powertrip*. —*Ed Rivadavia*

● **Spine of God** / Feb. 28, 1992 / Caroline ◆◆◆◆◆
The metal album for people who hate metal albums. A glorious and unapologetic celebration of pure indulgence, *Spine of God* is the ultimate stoner goof, a brilliant satire of headbanger culture so pitch-perfect that it's almost tempting to take it at face value. Bearing the warning "It's a satanic drug thing...you wouldn't understand," the record is a complete mind-fuck—the production is positively viscous, a hallucinatory sludge of echo-drenched vocals, bone-rattling drums, and reverbed guitars which seem to stretch on into infinity; frontman Dave Wyndorf is like a shamanic idiot-savant floating in a sea of bong-water, growling proclamations like "If Satan lived in Heaven, he'd be me" in the midst of deadpan fantasy freakouts which name-check every teenage metalhead staple from Led Zep to *Playboy* to whippets. (There's even a toweringly psychedelic ode to everyone's favorite room deodorizer, "Ozium.") Monster Magnet's genius is that their music speaks directly to the audience it's poking fun at—*Spine of God*'s sheer sonic intensity is brain-warping stuff even without chemical additives, and its themes of sex, drugs, and evil are so hilariously over-the-top that it's impossible not to be charmed by the absolute mindlessness of it all. No matter what, proof positive that the road of excess leads anywhere but the palace of wisdom. —*Jason Ankeny*

Superjudge / 1993 / A&M ◆◆◆
The group originates from the early-'70s Motor City madness sound that gave us such badass buzzsaw groups as MC5 and the Stooges. You get echoes of psychedelic space-rock ("Dinosaur Vacume"), shards of grunge, and wiffs of industrial noise, but for the most part, "Superjudge" is just plain, dirty, blinding power rock. They is mean, these Monster Magnet types. In fact, the song "Evil (Is Going On)" is simply the scariest tune married to the most awesome hard rock riff so far this year. Then, just as they have you reaching for the earplugs, the group pulls out an acoustic guitar for the quasi-mystical "Cage Around the Sun" and sitar for the raga-tinged "Black Balloon." This group defines what is meant by the expression "lock up your daughters." —*Roch Parisien*

Tab / 1993 / Caroline ◆◆

Dopes to Infinity / 1995 / A&M ◆◆◆◆◆
It is quite apparent that Monster Magnet attempted to slightly tone things down for their second major label release, 1995's *Dopes to Infinity*. By sacrificing some guitar distortion and feedback, the band's space rock tendencies gained more prominence, making this perhaps the definitive space rock album of the 90's. "Negasonic Teenage Warhead" was a moderately successful single, though the complicated title probably didn't help. "Look to Your Orb for the Warning" builds on an irresistibly slow groove before descending into a psychedelic jam. Leader Dave Wyndorf also proves he is capable of composing both the chunkiest riffs on the driving "King of Mars," as well as the odd sweet melody on "Dead Christmas." And though the band cuts loose on "I Control, I Fly" and "Third Alternative," due to its different studio approach this is probably the most "different" album of Monster Magnet's career. —*Ed Rivadavia*

Powertrip / Jun. 16, 1998 / A&M ◆◆◆◆
Turning down the neo-psychedelic white-trash vibe that ran through their best albums, *Superjudge* and *Dopes to Infinity*, Monster Magnet winds up with their most conventional record in *Powertrip*. This time around, the group churns out a heavy, metallic grind that sounds something like an unholy hybrid of the Stooges, Soundgarden, and Sabbath (of course, any hybrid of those three groups is unlikely to be holy). They still have a tendency to concentrate more on sound than songs, but they have a powerful, unvarnished roar and a knack for memorable riffs, and that's enough to keep *Powertrip* interesting, even if it lacks the more intriguing sonic flourishes that distinguished their earlier records. —*Stephen Thomas Erlewine*

God Says No / Apr. 10, 2001 / A&M ◆◆◆
Like other bands credited with pioneering the stoner metal scene in the early '90s, Monster Magnet continue to drift further and further from the trademark sonic characteristics (distortion, psychedelics, space rock) of the genre they helped create. And after stripping down their sound to a no-frills, streamlined attack on 1998's breakthrough album *Powertrip*, band leader Dave Wyndorf refused to sit on his laurels when it came time to devise Magnet's fifth album, *God Says No*. Instead, in a display of massive creative "cojones" and/or utter commercial suicide, Wyndorf leads the group into unexplored territory. The result being that while *Powertrip*'s single-minded urgency and unbridled power seemed to trap the listener behind the wheel of a drag racer on the verge of flaming out, *God Says No* is arguably the band's mellowest set yet, and certainly their most diverse. With their laid-back grooves and unexpected use of triggered electronic drumbeats, the title track and "Queen of You" are the best examples of this turn of events. And even when they do pick up the pace a bit, tracks like "Silver Future" and the amphetamine surf rock of "Kiss of the Scorpion" never quite lose control on the scale of *Powertrip*'s Stooges-fueled recklessness. Older fans and recent converts alike may prefer the album's second half, where at least some of Magnet's lo-fi, fuzzed-out past and *Powertrip*'s raw, unyielding sonic attack finally surface. But new converts will get to savor all the band's flavors, including space rock anthems like "Melt" and "Cry," which hearken back to 1995's *Dopes to Infinity* with their familiar-sounding hypnotic riffs. In the end, some may be disappointed by *God Says No*'s all-around sense of restraint, but open-minded fans will have to acknowledge Wyndorf's courageous insistence on breaking new ground with his continually inspired songwriting. —*Ed Rivadavia*

Chris Montez

b. Jan. 17, 1943, Los Angeles, CA

Vocals / Rock & Roll

One of the leading rockers in the Los Angeles Hispanic community after the tragic death of Ritchie Valens, Chris Montez later mellowed out under the tutelage of Herb Alpert and tallied several MOR-style hits. His first smash was on Monogram in 1962, "Let's Dance." It was a grinding rocker with roller-rink organ. Montez changed his attitude after signing with A&M. With Alpert producing, Montez adopted an easygoing approach on "Call Me," "The More I See You," and "Time After Time," all solid sellers in 1966. The formula quickly faded, however, and his final chart entry came the following year with "Because of You." —*Bill Dahl*

● **All-Time Greatest Hits** / 1991 / DCC ◆◆◆◆◆
Montez began as a Ritchie Valens-style rocker and reemerged as a crooner of pop ballads in the mid-'60s. He excelled at both styles, each of which is amply documented here. —*Jeff Tamarkin*

Montrose

f. 1972, California, db. 1977

Arena Rock, Heavy Metal, Hard Rock

After leaving the Edgar Winter Group in 1972, guitarist Ronnie Montrose decided to form his own band, so he called a young singer by the name of Sammy Hagar to join his new project. Hagar left in 1975 to do his own solo project, but the band continued with other singers and various lineups before splitting up in 1977. Ronnie Montrose now performs as a solo artist and does session work from time to time. —*John Book*

Montrose / 1973 / Warner Brothers ◆◆◆◆
The '70s gave us a slew of classic hard rock albums—the likes of which may never be equaled—and though it hasn't had the lasting influence of, say, Boston's or Ted Nugent's first albums, Montrose's eponymous debut proved equally influential and important in its day. Released in 1973, the record also introduced a young Sammy Hagar to the world, but the explosive aggression of Ronnie Montrose's biting guitar left no doubt as to why it was his name gracing the cover. A rock-solid rhythm section featuring drummer Denny Carmassi and bassist Bill Church certainly didn't hurt, either, and unstoppable anthems such as "Rock the Nation" and "Good Rockin' Tonight" would lay the ground rules for an entire generation of late-'70s California bands, most notably Van Halen. Admittedly, tracks like "Make It Last" and "I Don't Want It" sound rather dated by today's sonic standards (no thanks to their ultra-silly lyrics), but no amount of time can dim the sheer euphoria of "Bad Motor Scooter," the adolescent nastiness of "Rock Candy," and the simply gargantuan main riff of the phenomenal "Space Station #5." A welcome addition to any respectable '70s hard rock collection. —*Ed Rivadavia*

Paper Money / 1974 / Warner Brothers ◆◆◆
The second album from Montrose with Hagar as vocalist is just as good as their self-titled debut, with a great collection of songs. —*John Book*

Warner Brothers Presents...Montrose / 1975 / Warner Brothers ◆◆◆◆
Some of the best guitar work Ronnie Montrose has ever done appears here, with Bob James on vocals. It contains such songs as "Matriarch," "Black Train," "All I Need," and "Twenty Flight Rock." —*John Book*

Jump on It / 1976 / Warner Brothers ◆◆◆

● **The Very Best of Montrose** / Oct. 17, 2000 / Rhino ◆◆◆◆
Except for a few ill-advised power ballads, Montrose was a hard-driving, head-butting, riff-rattling, nonstop rock machine whose best qualities—creative guitar playing, hooky melodies, and smart production—were arguably the blueprint for Van Halen and any number of other similar crunch proto-metalers. As the only compilation of this under-recognized band, *The Very Best Of* captures 15 highlights from four Warner Bros. albums spanning 1973-1976, and tacks on three difficult-to-find cuts from 1987's reunion disc on Enigma. With track by track annotation from the guitarist/songwriter/producer (and on

one track, singer), remastered sound, well-documented liner notes, as well as full credits, there's little that Rhino could have improved on here. Although the first eight tunes that cover the Sammy Hagar years (*Montrose* and *Paper Money*) are the best known, there's plenty of solid rocking on the other ten tracks. Singer Bob James (not the jazz fusion pianist) wasn't nearly as magnetic as his better-known predecessor, but his Lou Gramm-styled range suited the material just fine, and the band, whose members changed on almost every album, were always solid, if unremarkable professionals. Tough piledrivers like "Rock Candy," "I Got the Fire," "Let's Go," and "Dancin' Feet," with their chunky, thunderous riffs and lighter-raising yet forgettable lyrics, can get any biker party started, and hearing them all together for the first time makes you wonder why Montrose isn't more highly regarded as an early influence on countless hot guitar rockers. No matter, because this is 76 minutes of undiluted, rugged guitar rock at its finest. Leave your brain cells at home and just enjoy. *—Hal Horowitz*

The Moody Blues

f. 1964, Birmingham, England
British Psychedelia, Album Rock, Pop/Rock, British Invasion, Prog Rock/Art Rock
Although they're best known today for their lush, lyrically and musically profound (some would say bombastic) psychedelic-era albums and singles, the Moody Blues started out as one of the better R&B-based combos of the British Invasion. The group's first single, 1964 "Steal Your Heart Away," didn't touch the British charts, but the follow-up "Go Now" fulfilled every expectation and more, reaching number one in England. Despite their fledgling songwriting efforts and the access they had to American demos, this version of the group never came up with another single success, and in late 1966, after the addition of vocalist Justin Hayward, the reconstituted Moody Blues scored their big break when Deram Records decided that it needed a long-playing record to promote its new "Deramic Stereo." The Moody Blues were picked for the proposed project, a rock version of Dvorak's *New World Symphony*, and immediately convinced the staff producer and the engineer to abandon the source material and permit the group to use a series of its own compositions that depicted an archetypal "day," from morning to night. Using the tracks laid down by the band, and orchestrated by conductor Peter Knight, the resulting album *Days of Future Passed* became a landmark in the band's history. The mix of rock and classical sounds was new, and at first puzzled the record company, but eventually the record was issued. This album, and its singles "Nights in White Satin" and "Tuesday Afternoon," hooked directly into the musical sides of the Summer of Love and its aftermath. *In Search of the Lost Chord* (1968) abandoned the orchestra in favor of the Mellotron, which quickly became a part of their signature sound. Beginning with *A Question of Balance* (1970), the group made the decision to record albums that they could play in concert, reducing their reliance on overdubbing and toughening up their sound. *—Bruce Eder*

Go Now/Moody Blues #1 / 1965 / London ✦✦✦
The first and only U.S. album by the first, rhythm-and-blues-inspired incarnation of the Moody Blues led by Denny Laine, is an okay compilation of early singles and B-sides, but has long since been supplanted by better collections. The title song and "From the Bottom of My Heart" are killer tracks, however. *—Bruce Eder*

The Magnificent Moodies / 1965 / Repertoire ✦✦✦✦
In 1988, Polydor Records reissued the 1966 LP *The Magnificent Moodies* on CD with 25 songs, the original 12 album sides and the complete single and EP-output of the pre-Justin Hayward/John Lodge lineup of the group. The sound is excellent (except on "Go Now," which still sounds a bit tinny) and the inclusion of such single sides as "From the Bottom of My Heart" and their version of "Time Is on My Side," plus Denny Laine's soulful "It's Easy Child," make this an eye-opening experience for anyone who thinks that "Go Now" was as far as the original group got in the excellence department—indeed, "From the Bottom of My Heart" is still one of the greatest British invasion singles ever released, even if it barely made the bottom of the charts in America. The last six songs on the Polydor CD, including "Everyday," "This Is My House," "He Can Win," and "Boulevard De La Madelaine," come from the transitional phase in the group's history and show a move toward a more opulent and more pop-oriented sound. In 1992, Repertoire Records re-released this compilation on CD with the identical title and cover art, but containing only the first 19 songs from the Polydor disc, basically limited to the original album and the early R&B single sides. *—Bruce Eder*

Days of Future Passed / 1967 / Polydor ✦✦✦✦✦
The 1997 remastered reissue (check the catalog number) of the reconstituted Moody Blues' first album, complete with significantly improved sound and new notes, featuring interview material with the band members about the songs, the album, and its evolution. New members Justin Hayward and John Lodge established themselves on guitar, bass, and vocals, and the band begins its venture into progressive rock territory with the London Festival Orchestra. The material, highlighted by the presence of Hayward's "Tuesday Afternoon" and "Nights In White Satin," has an air of pretentiousness, but it really rocks fairly hard, especially as heard here, and the orchestral interludes, courtesy of the late Peter Knight, have an epic sweep that is enhanced on the 1997 reissues. In 1967, a lot of people hungry for something to put on the turntable after *Sgt. Pepper* turned to this, and made it into an international hit. *—Bruce Eder*

In Search of the Lost Chord / 1968 / Polydor ✦✦✦
This 1997 remastered edition of the group's second progressive album was long overdue (the original release from the '80s had an audible crack in the sound on one song). The sound is significantly better than the old PolyGram version, so close that you can actually hear the action on many of the instruments, and even displays somewhat better resolution than the Mobile Fidelity gold-plated audiophile disc. The original credits and interior gatefold art are gone, but in their place are new notes by the band members, which provide some insights into the making of the album, on which the Moody Blues discovered drugs and mysticism as a basis for songwriting and came up with a compelling psychedelic creation, filled with songs about Timothy Leary and the astral plane, and other psychedelic-era concerns. They dumped the orchestra this time out in favor of Mike Pinder's Mellotron, which was a more than adequate substitute, and the rest of the band joined in with flutes, sitar, tablas, and cellos, the playing of which was mostly learned on the spot. The whole album was one big experiment to see how far the group could go with any instruments they could find, thus making this album a rather close cousin to the Beatles' records of the same era. It is all beautiful and elegant, and "Legend of a Mind's" chorus about "Timothy Leary's dead/Oh, no—he's outside, looking in" ended up anticipating reality; upon his death in 1996, Leary was cremated and launched into space on a privately owned satellite, with the remains of *Star Trek* creator Gene Roddenberry (another '60s pop-culture icon), and other well-heeled clients. *—Bruce Eder*

On the Threshold of a Dream / 1969 / Polydor ✦✦✦✦✦
The 1997 remastered edition of this album can be considered definitive, superior in sonic detail to either the original PolyGram CD or the Mobile Fidelity audiophile disc, though the latter has some appeal, recreating the original LP's elaborate libretto. The new notes reveal something of the creative process that the band used in devising its albums and preparing its songs. The group abandoned the Oriental and Indian influences from the prior album in favor of more traditional Western melody, as well as science fiction and religious imagery. Similarly, the sitars and tablas disappear, replaced by much heavier use of the Mellotron and the grand piano, among other Western instruments. Both keyboards come to the fore in the album's centerpiece, "Have You Heard/The Voyage," a Mike Pinder *tour de force* and a wonderful piece of progressive psychedelia. The songs also rock much harder in spots than their previous records—"To Share Our Love" has a much harder sound than ever before, capturing the master's true sound better than any prior release, CD or vinyl. *—Bruce Eder*

To Our Children's Children's Children / 1969 / Polydor ✦✦✦
The 1997 remastering of this disc somewhat improves the sound on the band's most personal album, although the difference is less dramatic than in the other classic seven albums, and fans may miss the lyrics that were formerly included. Oddly enough, this was also the group's poorest-selling album of their psychedelic era, taking a lot longer to go gold—for all of their presumed connection to their audience, the band was perhaps stretching that link a little thinner than usual here. The material dwells mostly on time and what its passage means, and there is a peculiar feeling of loneliness and isolation to many of the songs. This was also the last of the group's big "studio" sound productions, built up in layer upon layer of overdubbed instruments—the sound is very lush and rich, but proved impossible to recreate properly on stage, and after this they would restrict themselves to recording songs that the five of them could play in concert. There are no extended suites on this album, but Hayward's "Watching and Waiting" and "Gypsy" have proved to be among the most popular songs in the group's history. The notes in the new edition also give a good account of how and why the group founded their own Threshold label with *Children's Children* and their growing estrangement from Decca Records. *—Bruce Eder*

Question of Balance / 1970 / Polydor ✦✦✦
The group's first real attempt at a harder rock sound still has some psychedelic elements, but they're achieved with an overall leaner studio sound. The group was tryng to take stock of itself at this time, and came up with some surprisingly strong, lean numbers (Pinder's Mellotron is surprisingly restrained until the final number, "The Balance"), which also embraced politics for the first time ("Question" seemed to display the dislocation that a lot of younger listeners were feeling during Vietnam). The surprisingly jagged opening track, "Question," recorded several months earlier, became a popular concert number as well as a number two (or number one, depending upon whose chart one looks at) single. Graeme Edge's "Don't You Feel Small" and Justin Hayward's "It's Up to You" both had a great beat, but the real highlight here is John Lodge's "Tortoise and the Hare," a fast-paced number that the band used to rip through in concert with some searing guitar solos by Hayward. Ray Thomas' "And the Tide Rushes In" (written in the wake of a fight with his wife) is one of the prettiest psychedelic songs ever written, a sweetly languid piece with some gorgeous shimmering instrumental effects. The 1997 remastered edition brings out the guitar sound with amazing force and clarity, and the notes tell a lot about the turmoil the band was starting to feel after three years of whirlwind success. The only loss is the absence of the lyrics included in earlier editions. *—Bruce Eder*

● **Every Good Boy Deserves Favour** / 1971 / Polydor ✦✦✦✦✦
The best realized of the group's classic albums finally comes into its own in this beautifully remastered edition from 1997. The lush melodies and the sound of Michael Pinder's mellotron was never richer, and the guitar pyrotechnics on pieces like "The Story in Your Eyes" were never more vivid. "Emily's Song," "Nice to Be Here," and "My Song" are among the best work the group has ever done, and "The Story in Your Eyes" is the best rock number they ever cut, with a bracing beat and the kind of lyrical complexity one more expected out of George Harrison at the time—the sound here is so crisp that the sustain on the feedback over the opening is now clearly audible well into the number. *—Bruce Eder*

Seventh Sojourn / 1972 / Polydor ✦✦✦
The 1997 remastered version of this final classic-era album, which closed out the group's psychedelic era, brings out more detail than the original issue. The really interesting element, however, is the notes, where the band members recall their almost universal unhappiness during the recording and the stresses that were threatening to break them up. The album contains the group's hardest-rocking body of songs, and shows the sudden emergence of John Lodge, who had never been a writing mainstay of the band before, as

a major songwriter with "Isn't Life Strange" and "I'm Just a Singer in a Rock & Roll Band" (which reflected some of the strain of the group members), both of which became hits. Lodge's and Graeme Edge's driving rhythm section comes through, as does the improved keyboard device called the Chamberlain, which supplanted the Mellotron here with a much stronger sound (especially on stage). Justin Hayward's "New Horizons" was the most romantic number since "Nights in White Satin." —*Bruce Eder*

Caught Live + 5 / 1977 / Polydor ✦✦✦✦
The Moody Blues put out this collection, a live concert augmented by some previously unreleased studio cuts, once they'd decided to re-form at the end of the 1970s, to get some product out. They never liked the concert much as a document (the unofficial word is that several of the group members were under the influence of controlled substances during the show, and, thus, less sharp than they might otherwise have been), which is one reason why they didn't authorize its release on CD until 1996. The 1969 Royal Albert Hall show sounds a lot better than it did on the LP, with a closeness that was never evident before—Justin Hayward's guitar and Michael Pinder's various Mellotrons, in particular, sound really close, and the singing comes out with more detail. The songs come primarily from *Days of Future Passed, Lost Chord,* and *Threshold of a Dream;* they rock hard on "Legend of a Mind" and "Ride My See-Saw," and "Tuesday Afternoon" is a highlight as well. As for the studio cuts, they're salvaged from failed album sessions in 1967 and 1968—not bad, but definitely filler. —*Bruce Eder*

Octave / 1978 / Polydor ✦✦✦
The group's first post-reunion album is uneven in spots, but Justin Hayward's songwriting and singing maintains its haunting romantic edge, and John Lodge shows a newly prominent and energetic voice as a composer. Keyboard player Mike Pinder exited after finishing this album, leaving behind one song on the record. —*Bruce Eder*

Long Distance Voyager / 1981 / Polydor ✦✦✦
The group's biggest-selling album of the '80s also marked a turning point in their fortunes, where they began losing even the mainstream critics. The music has drive, and is extremely well played and produced (this was the only album the band ever got to do at their own, custom-designed Threshold Studios), but also seemed very dated in its time, with a '60s sensibility that was out of place. —*Bruce Eder*

The Present / 1983 / Polydor ✦✦
The Other Side of Life / 1986 / Polydor ✦✦✦
The group's best album in several years benefitted mostly from the presence of the Top Ten single "Your Wildest Dreams," which managed to turn their status as dinosaurs from the '60s psychedelic era into a plus, with a great beat to boot and a very entertaining video featuring young British psychedelic rockers the Mood Six playing the young Moody Blues. The rest was fairly routine, alas, but the single was strong enough on its own terms to revive interest in the group one more time out. —*Bruce Eder*

Prelude / 1987 / Polydor ✦✦✦
A collection of little known "transitional" period tracks in the group's history, dating from the period after guitarist/vocalist Denny Laine exited and after Justin Hayward and John Lodge replaced them, but before the band had fully hit upon a new sound. Some of the stuff is surprisingly Beatlesque, and "Love and Beauty" marks the group's first use of the Mellotron and the layered vocals that would define their later psychedelic-era sound. And all of this is rounded out by the presence of the late-'60s studio tracks that filled out their 1978 compilation *Caught Live + 5.* This disc, out of print in America, is worth tracking down for fans as an import. —*Bruce Eder*

Sur La Mer / 1988 / Polydor ✦✦
Keys of the Kingdom / Jun. 25, 1991 / Polydor ✦
Disappointing studio album from the band—now reduced officially to a quartet with the departure of Patrick Moraz from the keyboard spot. The melodies lack freshness and invention, the lyrics are predictable in the worst possible way, and the band fails to generate any excitement or interest on this record. —*Bruce Eder*

A Night at Red Rocks with the Colorado . . . / 1993 / Polydor ✦✦✦
Having succeeded in the '80s by drawing on '60s nostalgia with a song ("Your Wildest Dreams") and video, the Moody Blues in the '90s began tailoring entire shows to recapture their '60s glory days—and they succeeded. Performing on tour with a series of regional orchestras, they brought the majesty of their old studio sound onto the stage for the first time on songs like "Nights in White Satin" and "Tuesday Afternoon," and audiences reponded by turning them into one of the top concert draws of the decade. This album and the accompanying video is beautifully recorded (and the video looks gorgeous, too) and performed, and the group—caught amid the splendor of one of the prettiest outdoor concert venues in the West (Stevie Nicks has also done a video there) and with the orchestra backing them up on half the numbers, rise to the occasion with a drive and eloquence that they haven't shown on-stage in many years. An essential recording and video for any fan of the group. —*Bruce Eder*

Time Traveller / Sep. 27, 1994 / Polydor ✦✦✦✦✦
When the Moody Blues were due for the box set treatment, it would have been uncharacteristic for the production to be lacking in overstated grandiosity. On that count, this four-CD retrospective does not disappoint, including the bulk of their most famous work (from their 1967-72 albums), lots from their later records and side projects, and a few rarities. There's not a great deal of reason for anyone but fanatics to fork out for this package; the albums (which were specifically programmed to work as separate entities) remain readily available, there's too much late stuff and Hayward/Blue Jays tracks, and there's nothing from the Denny Laine era. The three non-LP 1967 cuts that open the set are available on the double import LP *A Dream,* an album that also has the additional 1967 B-side "Really Haven't Got the Time," which somehow doesn't make it onto *Time*

Traveller. As consolation, the liner notes are pretty good and extensive, and the first printings of the box include a bonus disc of a 1992 concert with the Colorado Symphony Orchestra. —*Richie Unterberger*

● **The Best of the Moody Blues** / Jan. 28, 1997 / Polydor ✦✦✦✦✦
The 17-track *The Best of the Moody Blues* contains all of the group's biggest hits, from 1964's "Go Now" to 1988's "I Know You're Out There Somewhere." Between those two songs, all of the Moodies' best-known songs are featured, including "Nights in White Satin," "Tuesday Afternoon," "Ride My See-Saw," "Story in Your Eyes," and "Your Wildest Dreams," making the compilation an excellent choice for casual fans. —*Stephen Thomas Erlewine*

Strange Times / Aug. 1999 / Universal ✦✦✦
A lot of people will laugh at the idea of a new Moody Blues album, eight years after their last new release and 35 years after the original band started in the business. The fact is, though, that this is about the liveliest and leanest that the group has sounded in more than 20 years. Among this collection of 14 songs, ten have very pleasing melodies, unpretentious lyrics, and generally attractive performances. That puts *Strange Times* several steps above the last few of the group's albums. In contrast to their previous album, *Keys of the Kingdom,* the vast majority of songs here are steeped in romance rather than pop mysticism—nothing here is quite as catchy as "In Your Wildest Dreams," but several come close. Moreover, the group has built its sound on *Strange Times* around acoustic and electric guitars. The electronic keyboards are embellishment, nothing more, making for an unexpectedly lean and melodic album, less symphonic than anything they've done in decades. There are a few unfortunate digressions into the mystical side of the band's persona, but most of what's here are unpretentious love songs. *Strange Times* is still their most attractive album since *Octave,* and boasts their best album opener ("English Sunset") since "You and Me" from *Seventh Sojourn.* Not everything works that well, but even some of the heavy-handed work here, such as "The One," which has some pretty vocal flourishes. "The Swallow" is one of Hayward's prettier slow numbers and worth its five-minute running time. There are still some mistakes, to be sure, including the pretentious title song and Graeme Edge's album-closing recital, "Nothing Changes," but *Strange Times* is still about as good an album as the Moody Blues have cut since the '70s. —*Bruce Eder*

The Moonglows

f. 1951, Louisville, KY
Doo Wop, R&B
Among the most seminal R&B and doo wop groups of all time, the Moonglows' lineup featured some of the genre's greatest pure singers. The original lineup from Louisville included Bobby Lester, Harvey Fuqua, Alexander Graves, and Prentiss Barnes, with guitarist Billy Johnson. They were originally called the Crazy Sounds, but were renamed by disc jockey Alan Freed as the Moonglows. The group also cut some recordings as the Moonlighters. Their first major hit was the number one R&B gem "Sincerely" for Chess in 1954, which reached number 20 on the pop charts. They enjoyed five more Top Ten R&B hits on Chess from 1955 to 1958, among them "Most of All," "We Go Together," "See Saw," and "Please Send Me Someone to Love," as well as "Ten Commandments of Love." Fuqua, the nephew of Charlie Fuqua of the Ink Spots, left in 1958. He recorded "Ten Commandments of Love" as Harvey & the Moonglows with Marvin Gaye, Reese Palmner, James Knowland, and Chester Simmons before founding his own label, Tri-Phi. Fuqua created and produced the Spinners in 1961 and wrote and produced for Motown until the early '70s. The Moonglows disbanded in the '60s, then reunited in 1972 with Fuqua, Lester, Graves, Doc Williams, and Chuck Lewis. They recorded for RCA and a reworked version of "Sincerely" eventually charted, but wasn't a major hit. —*Ron Wynn*

Blue Velvet: The Ultimate Collection / Dec. 7, 1993 / Chess ✦✦✦✦✦
Few rivaled the Moonglows in musical sophistication, inventiveness or flair. They could sing gorgeous heartache ballads, rollicking up-tempo rhythm tunes, creditable period-piece novelty numbers, wonderful pop covers or shattering originals. This two-disc set contains 44 outstanding numbers, with every major Moonglows anthem and several others that weren't big hits but deserved to be, such as "Penny Arcade" and "Love Is a River." This collection updates and expands the *Greatest Sides* single LP release briefly available when Sugar Hill had the Chess catalog in the 1970s. It wisely restricts material to the era when they were at their best, the 1950s, and includes an excellent booklet. —*Ron Wynn*

● **Their Greatest Hits** / May 20, 1997 / Chess/MCA ✦✦✦✦
At 16 tracks, *Their Greatest Hits* isn't nearly as comprehensive as the two-CD *Blue Velvet,* which has 44 songs. But for someone who wants just the highlights, as opposed to just about everything, *Their Greatest Hits* is the better buy, including their most celebrated tunes ("Ten Commandments of Love," "Sincerely," "Blue Velvet"). The only selection not on *Blue Velvet* is a different take of "Over and Over Again," presented in its "fast version." It does not, however, include "Mama Loocie," which featured Marvin Gaye's first recorded lead vocal. —*Richie Unterberger*

Mandy Moore

b. Apr. 10, 1984, Nashua, NH
Teen Pop, Adult Contemporary, Dance-Pop
Teen dance-pop singer Mandy Moore was born in Nashua, NH on April 10, 1984 but raised in Orlando, FL; determined to be an entertainer from the age of six onward, she was later known throughout the Orlando area as the "National Anthem Girl" for her regular performances of "The Star Spangled Banner" at local sporting events. Breaking into the recording industry via voiceovers and commercials, in 1999 Moore became the latest Orlando teen to sign a record contract after landing at Sony; her debut album *So Real* appeared late that year. The album spawned a hit with "Candy, a remix of which also

appeared on her 2000 release *I Wanna Be With You.* A self-titled sophomore effort appeared in summer 2001. She has three cats: Milo, Zoe, and Chloe. *—Jason Ankeny*

So Real / Dec. 7, 1999 / Epic/550 Music ♦♦♦
Fifteen-year-old Mandy Moore's debut album sounded like it was inspired almost entirely by listening to recent hit albums by 'N Sync, the Backstreet Boys, and Britney Spears. Tracks like "So Real" and "Let Me Be the One" clearly echoed "Backstreet's Back," and Moore's occasional growls were straight out of "...Baby One More Time." But the singer seemed to have aimed at a slightly younger demographic: Her initial single, "Candy," pointedly described love in terms of sugar treats, as if she weren't sure whether she wanted to be at lovers' lane or a snack bar. Naturally, all of the songs adhered to the second-person form of address, in which the singer was continually exhorting "you" and "boy" to do something of a romantic nature ("Walk Me Home," "Lock Me in Your Heart," "Quit Breaking My Heart," "Let Me Be the One"). But things always remained chaste, whether she was declaring, "My innocence won't be denied" in "So Real" or suggesting the "uncharted territory we'll discover" before quickly adding, "You'll always be my dream lover," in "Lock Me in Your Heart." Meanwhile, of course, the downbeats, as high in the mix as those of any disco track, slavishly propelled the songs to mid-tempo rhythms. Moore can carry a tune, but with no particular distinction, and since the songs were generic expressions of the type, the real questions seemed to be, could she dance, would her videos be good, and how would she be marketed? As *So Real* was being released, "Candy" was moving up the charts purely on sales points, since radio had become resistant to adding more teen queens, while MTV had yet to bite. All of that had more to do with whether Mandy Moore would succeed than did the music, which was mediocre, but typical. *—William Ruhlmann*

I Wanna Be With You / May 9, 2000 / Epic/550 Music ♦♦♦
Pop quiz. So, the album that you planned to be a teen-pop blockbuster to rival BMG's massive success with Britney Spears and Christina Aguilera flops with nary a trace. What do you do? Well, if you're 550/Epic, faced with the flailing Mandy Moore debut, you shuffle the order of the songs, remix a couple of tracks, and shoot a new, sexy glamour shot of your underage diva so she looks shockingly like Britney. A crass marketing move, to be sure, but hey, tough times call for drastic measures like that. The thing is, the revamped, puzzlingly titled *I Wanna Be With You (Special Edition)* (thereby giving the impression that this is an extended EP release or that there's a "regular" edition of *I Wanna Be With You,* which there's not) works a lot better than its predecessor. Why? Because it's trashier, flashier, gaudier, and altogether more disposable: all essential ingredients for a good teen-pop album, since it should be something that is of the moment, not designed for the ages. *I Wanna Be With You* is definitely, almost defiantly of the moment, and while there's more than its fair share of filler (let's face it, there was a reason why the album needed to be reworked), that filler glitters here where it was simply dull on the predecessor. And, most of all, it's pretty fun, whether it's on ballads or dance numbers. Moore still isn't as good as Britney or Christina, since she just doesn't have a comparable persona or material, but with this she vaults above Jessica Simpson and maybe, just maybe, captures the bronze for female teen-pop divas in 2000 (Hoku being disqualified because she is pitched at a younger crowd). *—Stephen Thomas Erlewine*

• **Mandy Moore** / Jun. 19, 2001 / Epic ♦♦♦♦♦
Never let it be said that Mandy Moore, her label, and team of producers didn't work it. Once *So Real* failed to make headway, they retooled it as the "special edition" *I Wanna Be With You,* which wasn't a real hit, but it was a step in the right direction. Then, with her official second album, they finally got the formula right. *Mandy Moore* manages to pack more hooks, melody, beats, clever production flourishes, and fun into its 13 tracks than nearly all of its peers—remarkably, it's a stronger album, through and through, than either of Britney's first two albums or Christina's record. That doesn't mean that it has singles as strong as those albums; even if the surging "In My Pocket," the faux-sitar spiked "You Remind Me," and hip-hop ballad "Saturate Me" are all fine tunes, meant to be played on the radio, they aren't as distinctive as "...Baby One More Time" or "Genie in a Bottle." Also, although Moore isn't a bad singer, she's not particularly charismatic, and the production team isn't as gaudily, enjoyably crass as Max Martin. So, why is *Mandy Moore* such a good record? Because of consistency. This may not hit tremendous heights, yet everybody involved is working so hard that they've managed to come up with a record that's consistently satisfying. It doesn't stretch the teen pop formula much, just enough to give the record character, and Moore delivers the songs sturdily, never taking the forefront, but blending into the lush, layered production, so the music just rolls forth as a whole. And that whole sounds great—immaculately crafted, precisely polished, exactly what a teen pop album should be. Of course, it would have been greater if a couple of the songs were genuine knockouts, but usually this genre sacrifices consistency for dizzying peaks and it's refreshing to hear a teen pop record that plays like a record, instead of singles-n-filler. *—Stephen Thomas Erlewine*

Melba Moore (Melba Hill)

b. Oct. 29, 1945, New York, NY
Vocals / Quiet Storm, Soul
There were early signs that Melba Moore would become an entertainer. The most obvious motivation was her mother Bonnie Davis, who was also a successful singer. Witnessing the success that her mother endured, Moore knew the entertainment industry would not escape her. Her stepfather, also a musician, gave her invaluable advice and guidance. He sensed his stepdaughter's irresistible urge to be in the entertainment industry, so he began to show her the ropes. The results landed Moore jobs singing jingles and background vocals. She hit it big when she joined the cast of the Broadway musical *Hair.* Moore accepted and eventually won the lead role. It was the first time in history that a black actress replaced a white actress (Diane Keaton) for the lead role on Broadway. In 1975, she married Charles Huggins. The two formed Hush Productions and began seeking out R&B artists that they could manage and produce, the most famous being Freddie Jackson. In the same year, "I Am His Lady" was released on Buddah; it was Moore's first single to hit the charts. It would be seven years and 12 singles later before she would claim her first Top Ten single, 1982's dance/club track "Love's Comin' at Ya." Moore's next ten releases spawned four Top 20 and two Top Ten singles: "Livin' for Your Love" and "Love the One I'm With." The single to follow the latter was "A Little Bit More." The year was 1986, and it was Moore's first number one song but not her last. Also released in the same year, "Falling" claimed the top spot on the charts. Thereafter, Moore released seven more singles. Two were Top 20 hits and three were Top Ten hits, including the black national anthem "Lift Every Voice and Sing." *—Craig Lytle*

The This Is It: The Best of Melba Moore / 1995 / Razor & Tie ♦♦♦♦
This Is It: The Best of Melba Moore is an excellent overview of Moore's peak years, containing all of the hits she had in the '80s on EMI America and Capitol Records. Over the course of 18 tracks, all of her Top Ten R&B hits from the decade—"Love's Comin' at Ya," "Livin' for Your Love," "Love the One I'm With (A Lot of Love)," "A Little Bit More," "Falling," "It's Been So Long"—are featured, along with some good minor hits and album tracks. Some casual fans might find 18 tracks a bit much, but there's no question that this is the definitive summation of Moore's hitmaking years. *—Stephen Thomas Erlewine*

• **Little Bit Moore: The Magic of Melba Moore** / Jan. 28, 1997 / EMI ♦♦♦♦
A selection of 14 tracks from her 1980s albums, usually sticking to a mainstream urban contemporary vein. Includes the hits "Falling," "I'm in Love," "Underlove," "Livin' for Your Love," "A Little Bit More," and "I Can't Complain," the last two of which are duets with Freddie Jackson. *—Richie Unterberger*

Moose

f. 1990
Dream Pop, Shoegazing, Alternative Pop/Rock
Not so much underrated as unheard, Moose grew up in Britain's distortion-heavy shoegazing movement of the early '90s but soon shed the fuzzy wash of their compatriots to embrace a clean, acoustic-based style—inspired by '60s icons Burt Bacharach and Tim Buckley as well as jangle merchants like the Byrds and R.E.M.—that still relied on the intense guitar effects which characterized the band's early works. Moose was formed in early 1990 by the songwriting team of Kevin (K.J.) McKillop and Russell Yates (Yates had appeared in an early incarnation of Stereolab), plus drummer Damien Warburton and bassist Jeremy Tishler. The group signed to Hut Records (also the British home of Smashing Pumpkins and the Verve) in 1990, and began recording with producer Guy Fixsen (later of Laika).

After the release of three EPs during 1991, both Warburton and Tishler left the band; Moose then added drummer Richard Thomas and the brothers Fong, Lincoln on bass and Russell on guitar and sometime production. Hut Records had just formed an alliance with the major label Virgin, which condensed Moose's past material onto a seven-track EP, *Sonny and Sam.* (It served as an American primer for the band, but proved to be their only stateside release.) Hut financed a full-length album, *...XYZ,* in 1992 and recruited Mitch Easter for production and Dolores O'Riordon of the Cranberries for harmony vocals on one track. The album sold poorly, however, and Hut dropped the band by early 1993. Not fazed in the least, Moose came back with the *Liquid Make Up* EP for their own Cool Badge label. Its leadoff track, "I Wanted to See You to See If I Wanted You," was a charming piece of pop, their best single yet. Signed to Belgium's Play It Again Sam Records, the band released their second album, *Honey Bee,* in early 1994. It wisely included a different version of "I Wanted to See You to See If I Wanted You," but Moose appeared to be verging on overkill with yet another carbon-copy version included on the *Bang Bang* EP several months later. Perhaps signalling a stall in creativity, third album *Live a Little, Love a Lot* was released with no attaching single, though the Cocteau Twins' Liz Fraser did lend her vocals to one track. *—John Bush*

Sonny and Sam [EP] / Jan. 1992 / Virgin ♦♦♦
An out-of-print American EP, it summarizes Moose's first three EPs for the British label Hut. The band's shoegazing roots are easily seen on blissed-out tracks such as "This River Will Never Run Dry" and "Do You Remember?" *—John Bush*

• **...Xyz** / Sep. 1992 / Hut ♦♦♦♦♦
Showcasing a new sound for Moose after the hazy guitar-effects experimentation of their first three EPs, *...Xyz* focused on the pop whimsy that had only been hinted at previously. Songs like "The Whistling Song" and the leadoff single "Little Bird" are, by and large, acoustic pop songs with effects serving only as texture. It was a formula that worked very well, guided by the steady hand of producer Mitch Easter (R.E.M., Let's Active). Dolores O'Riordan of the Cranberries makes an appearance singing harmony vocal on "Soon Is Never Soon Enough." The compact-disc issue includes a bonus live version of "This River Is Nearly Dry," while a limited vinyl pressing includes an extra 7" single. *—John Bush*

Honey Bee / Jan. 1994 / Play It Again Sam ♦♦♦♦
Moose's second album showed the band moving toward pure pop, though much of the acoustic jangle which Mitch Easter had encouraged on their debut album was abandoned. In its place, Moose returned to the skewed song structures and guitar effects which had characterized their first three EPs. "I Wanted to See You to See If I Wanted You" is the band's best single period, and though the album sounds disjointed (being the band's first in-house production credit), there are many pleasing moments, like the first single "Uptown Invisible" and "Joe Courtesy." A limited-edition vinyl pressing of *Honey Bee* includes a bonus 7" single. *—John Bush*

Live a Little, Love a Lot / Feb. 1996 / Play It Again Sam ♦♦♦♦
A fair criticism of the early '90s shoegaze scene was that most of the bands really didn't know how to play or sing. They could write good melodies, but what good are melodies when the vocalist has a short range? And just how many sets of ears prefer a wash of distortion to a tricky chord change? Since Moose were tagged as shoegazers for their first EPs, they immediately lost a good number of potential ears. That's really too bad, because any of the negative attributes associated with that style of band were never an issue with Moose to begin with. Just as important, *Live a Little Love a Lot* is where they truly came into their own, playing a variation of classic pop that any fan of the Byrds or Lee Hazlewood—hell, the Byrds or Lee Hazlewood *themselves*—can appreciate. With some new tricks up their sleeves like further use of strings and horns, along with reverential nods to the past (witness the sly "hoo-ha"s in "Poor Man," no doubt a wink to Ennio Morricone's spaghetti western film scores), Moose blow through 11 breezy acoustic pop songs. Easygoing and graceful but not lightweight or hollow, the only true fault with the record is the latter half's inability to break free from a slight case of apathy. It could have used a song with the pep of the opening "Play God" (featuring the Cocteau Twins' Liz Fraser), or maybe some balance would have been achieved by placing the lively "Rubdown" (Handclaps? Horns? Bonus.) near the end of the sequence. So here's yet another fine band's third record, chucked mercilessly into the oldfart dustbin by the record store clerk and sniffed at. "Shoegaze. Feh." Little does that clerk realize how great this record will sound in 2020. *—Andy Kellman*

High Ball Me! / Apr. 2000 / Nickel and Dimes ♦♦♦♦♦
How how *how* can bands as excellent as Moose get passed over? *High Ball Me* was on the shelf for no less than a couple years before finding a label to release it, with four years passing since their last full-length. And guess what? It's another dazzling, fearless pop record—everything the House of Love wanted to do but couldn't—with a sense of humor, no less. Following a mood-setting curveball intro, the driving "I Can't Get Enough of You" is the most straight-ahead thing they've done to date. Not simple by any means and still certifiably Moose, chase-scene bongos and an almost Mould-like guitar line carry along, with a spaghetti western/Dick Dale-style second guitar to offset it. There are enough neat production flourishes to provide newly discovered nuances after many plays: handclaps here, a violin there, a well-placed shading of synth every now and then. The rich, soothing voice of Russell Yates is the icing on the cake, like Guy Chadwick without the bitterness. Yates and K.J. McKillop have reached dizzied heights as a songwriting duo here, stringing together a varied deck that hangs together as their easiest flowing 40 minutes. The country influences appear to be phased out in favor of more nods to the likes of Hazlewood and Nilsson, but Moose is smart enough to not be too obvious about it. Nurse Ratched's droll intonation of "medication time" at the onset of the record's intro is fitting—*High Ball Me* is sweeter than a teaspoon of orange Triaminic. It's truly a backwards time in music when golden records like this have difficulty finding a way to be released. *—Andy Kellman*

Alanis Morissette

b. Jun. 1, 1974, Ottawa, Ontario, Canada
Vocals / Adult Alternative Pop/Rock, Post-Grunge, Pop/Rock, Alternative Pop/Rock, Singer/Songwriter
Alanis Morissette was one of the most unlikely stars of the mid-'90s. A former child actress turned dance-pop diva, Morissette transformed herself into a confessional alternative singer/songwriter, in the vein of Liz Phair and Tori Amos. However, she added enough pop sensibility, slight hip-hop flourishes, and marketing savvy to that formula to become a superstar with her third album, *Jagged Little Pill*. A former castmember of *You Can't Do That on Television*, a children's television program, in 1991 she released her debut album, *Alanis*, a collection of pop-oriented dance numbers and ballads that was successful in Canada, selling over 100,000 copies. Following the release of 1992's *Now Is the Time*, Morissette relocated to Los Angeles, where she met writer/producer Glen Ballard in early 1994. Despite the duo's mainstream pop pedigree, they decided to pursue an edgier, alternative rock-oriented direction. The result was *Jagged Little Pill*, which on the strength of the single "You Oughta Know" rocketed into the Top Ten and multi-platinum status. The second and third singles from *Jagged Little Pill*, "Hand in My Pocket" and "All I Really Want," kept the album in the Top Ten. Her fourth single, "Ironic," which proved to be her biggest crossover success. Morissette won several Grammy awards in 1996, including Album of the Year and Song of the Year. Her much-anticipated follow-up, *Supposed Former Infatuation Junkie*, was released in the autumn of 1998.*—Stephen Thomas Erlewine*

● **Jagged Little Pill** / Jun. 13, 1995 / Maverick/Reprise ♦♦♦♦♦
It's remarkable that Alanis Morissette's *Jagged Little Pill* struck a sympathetic chord with millions of listeners, because it's so doggedly, determinedly insular. This, after all, plays like an emotional purging, prompted by a bitter relationship—and, according to all the lyrical hints, that's likely a record executive who took advantage of a young Alanis. She never disguises her outright rage and disgust, whether it's the vengeful wrath of "You Oughta Know" or asking him "you scan the credits for your name and wonder why it's not there." This is such insider information that it's hard to believe that millions of listeners not just bought it, but embraced it, turning Alanis Morisette into a mid-'90s phenomenon. Perhaps it was the individuality that made it appealing, since its specificity lent it genuineness—and, even if this is clearly an attempt to embrace the "women in rock" movement in alterna-rock, Morissette's intentions are genuine. Often, it seems like Glen Ballard's pop inclinations fight against Alanis' exorcisms, as her bitter diary entries are given a pop gloss that gives them entry to the pop charts. What's all the more remarkable is that Alanis isn't a particularly good singer, stretching the limits of pitch and credibility with her octave-skipping caterwauling. At its core, this is the work of an ambitious but sophomoric 19-year-old, once burned by love, but still willing to open her heart a second time. All of this adds up to a record that's surprisingly effective, an utterly fascinating exploration of a young woman's psyche. As slick as the music is, the lyrics are unvarnished and Morissette unflinchingly explores emotions so common, most people would be ashamed to articulate them. This doesn't make *Jagged Little Pill* great, but it does make it a fascinating record, a phenomenon that's intensely personal. *—Stephen Thomas Erlewine*

Supposed Former Infatuation Junkie / Nov. 3, 1998 / Maverick/Reprise ♦♦♦♦
While it's not a repudiation of her blockbuster, *Supposed Former Infatuation Junkie* is a clear step forward, teeming with ambition and filled with new musical ideas and different sonic textures. Morissette's voice still sears, but she has more control over her singing, rarely reaching the piercing heights that occasionally made *Pill* jarring. Also, she has clearly spent some time crafting her lyrics; not only do they never sound like straight diary entries, she no longer is trying to fit too many syllables into a phrase. These two differences are subtle—the brooding, Eastern-styled music that dominates *Supposed* is not. There are numerous extensions of the vague hip-hop and pop fusions that made "Hand in Pocket" and "All I Really Want" huge hits ("Front Row," "UR," "Thank U," "So Pure"), but much of the album is devoted to moody ballads and mid-tempo pop, where the textured production functions as a backdrop for Morissette's crypticly introspective lyrics. Far from being alienating, this approach works surprisingly well—not only do the pop tunes sound catchier, but the ballads, with their winding melodies and dark colors, sound strong and brave. If anything, the record is more coherent album than its predecessor and even if it isn't as accessible or as compulsively listenable, it's a richer record. That said, it won't win any new fans—for all of her success, Morissette is a weird acquired taste, due to her idiosyncratic vocals and doggedly convoluted confessionals—but it certainly confirms that she doesn't quite sound like anyone else, either. *—Stephen Thomas Erlewine*

Alanis Unplugged / Nov. 9, 1999 / Maverick ♦♦♦
Often, artists embrace *Unplugged* as an opportunity to stroll through their back catalog. Not Alanis Morissette. Instead of concentrating on the familiar (only four songs from *Jagged Little Pill* are here, and neither of its sequel's hits, "Thank U" and "So Pure," are performed), Morissette uses *Unplugged* as a way to reintroduce *Supposed Former Infatuation Junkie* to an audience that largely ignored it the first time around. It's easy to see why Morissette is so intent on selling these songs. Although their meaning may be elusive at times, they're extremely personal songs, which benefit from the stripped-down arrangements and intimate surroundings. Even so, the songs require close, careful listening before they truly catch hold, and even then, they're often easier to admire than love. By closing the performance with the non-LP soundtrack contribution "Uninvited," Morissette unwittingly highlights the reason why *Supposed* failed to gain a large audience. Like much of that album, "Uninvited is also heavy on mood and cryptic lyrics, but the song is blessed with an indelible melody and haunting atmosphere. Compared with that song, the *Supposed* tunes, plus the three previously unreleased songs (including "No Pressure Over Cappucinio" and "Princess Familiar"), are all intriguing but never as compelling, largely because they demand that the listener meet them on their own terms. Here, they're a bit more accessible, but it makes *Unplugged* just slightly less elusive than *Supposed* itself. *—Stephen Thomas Erlewine*

Morphine

f. 1990, **db.** 1999
Indie Rock, Alternative Pop/Rock
Morphine is a rarity—bluesy, bare-bones rock & roll without any guitars. Instead of guitar riffs, the trio relies on sliding two-string bass lines, raucous saxophones, and wry, ironically detached vocals. During the mid-'90s, Morphine gained a sizable cult following in America, primarily due to good word of mouth, heavy college airplay, and positive reviews. The group released their debut album, *Good*, on the independent Accurate-Distortion in 1991; its positive reception set the stage for 1993's *Cure for Pain*, which received good reviews from a variety of music and mainstream publications. Morphine supported *Cure for Pain* with an extensive American and European tour that lasted throughout 1994, which helped the album sell over 300,000 copies—an impressive feat for an independent release. In late 1996, Dreamworks bought out the majority share of Morphine's contract from Rykodisc. *Like Swimming*, the group's debut for Dreamworks, was released in the spring of 1997 to generally favorable reviews, yet it failed to break the band out of cult status. On June 3, 1999, frontman Mark Sandman died after suffering a heart attack during a gig in Rome. *—Stephen Thomas Erlewine*

Good / Sep. 8, 1992 / Rykodisc ♦♦♦
While it may not be as stellar as their future releases would be, Morphine's debut album, 1992's *Good*, did a splendid job of introducing the Boston trio's highly original sound. While it was the alternative crowd who immediately latched onto Morphine, their music was geared more toward the jazz scene—a wailing saxophone, lead bass (played with a slide), and lyrics influenced by '50s beat poetry were all-important ingredients. The opening title track remains one of the band's darkest, while other selections are a bit more upbeat—"Have a Lucky Day" and the inappropriately titled "The Saddest Song"; all the while, the band excels at creating different moods with each successive track. Other highlights include the mid-paced "Claire" and "The Only One," the slight salsa feel of "You Speak My Language," the frantic "Test-Tube Baby/Shoot'm Down," and the more calm and sultry "You Look Like Rain." On their next release, *Cure for Pain*, Morphine would improve further on the strength of their songwriting and cutting-edge sound, but *Good* still contains more than a few standouts. *—Greg Prato*

● **Cure for Pain** / Sep. 1993 / Rykodisc ♦♦♦♦♦
With their cult following growing, Morphine expanded their audience even further with

their exceptional 1994 sophomore effort, *Cure for Pain*. Whereas their debut, *Good*, was intriguing yet not entirely consistent, *Cure for Pain* more than delivered. The songwriting was stronger and more succinct this time around, while new drummer Billy Conway made his recording debut with the trio (replacing Jerome Deupree). Like the debut, most of the material shifts between depressed and upbeat, with a few cacophonic rockers thrown in between. Such selections as "Buena," "I'm Free Now," "All Wrong," "Candy," "Thursday," "In Spite of Me" (one of the few tracks to contain six-string guitar), "Let's Take a Trip Together," "Sheila," and the title track are all certifiable Morphine classics. And again, Mark Sandman's two-string slide bass and Dana Colley's sax work help create impressive atmospherics throughout the album. *Cure for Pain* was unquestionably one of the best and most cutting-edge rock releases of the '90s. *—Greg Prato*

Yes / Mar. 1995 / Rykodisc ♦♦♦♦♦
On their third release, 1995's *Yes*, Morphine shied away from the more accessible direction they laid down on 1994's superb *Cure for Pain*, going for a more challenging (but just as rewarding) direction. While the singles/videos "Honey White" and "Super Sex" did contain a pop edge (and were the album's best), other tracks, such as "The Jury" and "Sharks" pushed the envelope by containing lyrics that sound as if they're stream-of-consciousness. Like its predecessor, it's a highly consistent album—even the lesser-known tracks are integral to the album's overall makeup. "Scratch," "All Your Way," "I Had My Chance," "Free Love," and "Gone for Good" all sound like the observations of a broken-down man, steeped in despair. But the mood lightens up on such selections as "Radar" and the title track, plus the aforementioned singles. With nearly all alt-rock bands sounding identical and bashing angrily away at their instruments in 1995, Morphine proved to be in a league all by themselves. *Yes* is perhaps just a shade less spectacular than *Cure for Pain*, but certainly not by much. *—Greg Prato*

Like Swimming / Mar. 11, 1997 / DreamWorks ♦♦♦
After three highly acclaimed releases on Rykodisc, 1997's *Like Swimming* was Morphine's first recording for Dreamworks, which put the trio on the verge of a major commercial breakthrough (their last album, *Yes*, reached the middle of Billboard's Hot 100 album chart). And although the album contained its share of highlights, it turned out to not be as strong as its predecessors were and failed to break the band through to the big time. Some of the material doesn't sound fully developed, almost as if the Boston trio was rushed to complete the album. Still, the trio nails down the unmistakable Morphine sound on such great tracks as "Early to Bed," "Eleven O'Clock," "Swing It Low," and the title track. Other selections, such as "Potion," "I Know You (Pt. III)," "Wishing Well," "French Fries w/Pepper," and "Hanging on a Curtain," are all notable, but not as gripping or memorable as the material that made *Cure for Pain* and *Yes* such exceptional releases. Again, *Like Swimming* is not a total washout, but it is a disappointment when compared to the above-mentioned classic albums. *—Greg Prato*

B-Sides & Otherwise / Sep. 23, 1997 / Rykodisc ♦♦♦
Perhaps as a contractual obligation, only a few months after *Like Swimming* appeared in record stores, a collection of B-sides and soundtrack-only material titled *B-Sides and Otherwise* was issued by Morphine's original label, Rykodisc. While the trio always used unconventionality to their advantage, their acute pop sensibilities appealed to a wider audience; however, the material here is more challenging and abstract than your average Morphine release. Some songs, such as the eight-minute soundscape "Down Love's Tributaries," test the listener's patience, while others, such as live radio broadcasts of two tracks ("Have a Lucky Day" and "All Wrong"), are thoroughly enjoyable. Other highlights include a beautiful acoustic guitar instrumental from the movie *Get Shorty* entitled "Bo's Veranda," plus "Shame," "Kerouac," "Pulled Over the Car," "Mail," the charged-up "Mile High," and the humorous "My Brain." An interesting collection of oddities that will appeal to the dedicated fan, *B-Sides and Otherwise* captures the band at their most experimental. *—Greg Prato*

The Night / Feb. 1, 2000 / DreamWorks ♦♦♦
Morphine's fourth studio release, 1997's *Like Swimming*, was a bit of a disappointment when compared to such stellar earlier releases as *Cure for Pain* and *Yes*. After singer/two-string bassist Mark Sandman died of a heart attack on-stage in 1999, many Morphine fans assumed that *Like Swimming* would be the band's swansong—thankfully, it wasn't. The Boston trio completed their fifth album just prior to Sandman's untimely passing, entitled *The Night*, and it's definitely an improvement over its predecessor. Whereas many of the songs on their previous album sounded unfinished and rushed, *The Night* sounds like a fully realized work. In fact, the band took time to focus on expanding their minimalist sound to include other instruments (cello, violin, upright bass, oud, organ) and new approaches (female backup singers, string arrangements), while Sandman produced the album himself. Highlights include the ghostly "Souvenir," the Middle Eastern sounds of "Rope on Fire," the sultry album-opening title track, and the up-tempo (by Morphine standards, anyway) "Top Floor, Bottom Buzzer." *The Night* shows that Morphine was just entering a new phase of their career, and it's a shame that Mark Sandman is no longer with us to follow through on this promising new direction. *—Greg Prato*

Bootleg Detroit / Sep. 26, 2000 / Rykodisc ♦♦♦
The odd title of this final sanctioned release by Morphine before Mark Sandman's untimely death comes from its origin—a tape made by an audience member at a Detroit show during Morphine's *Cure for Pain* tour. While the tapes were mastered by Sandman shortly before his demise, the original quality of the recording cannot be overcome. Still, this is a good document of Morphine's excellent live show and displays the energy and passion that they played with during the tour that supported their breakthrough album. Some short tracks featuring banter probably could have been sacrificed in favor of more songs, but on the whole the album stands as a loving tribute to an innovative band. *—Stacia Proefrock*

Van Morrison

b. Aug. 31, 1945, Belfast, Northern Ireland
Vocals, Saxophone, Leader, Keyboards, Songwriter, Harmonica, Guitar / Celtic Rock, Album Rock, Jazz-Rock, Blue-Eyed Soul, Pop/Rock, Folk-Rock, Soft Rock, Adult Contemporary, Singer/Songwriter

Equal parts blue-eyed soul shouter and wild-eyed poet-sorcerer, Van Morrison was among popular music's true innovators, a restless seeker whose alchemical fusion of R&B, jazz, blues, and Celtic folk produced perhaps the most spiritually transcendent body of work in the rock & roll canon. Morrison enjoyed a massive cult following which grew exponentially throughout the course of his lengthy and prolific career; his recordings cover extraordinary stylistic ground yet retain a consistency and purity virtually unmatched among his contemporaries.

George Ivan Morrison was born in Belfast, Northern Ireland on August 31, 1945. At 15 he quit school to join the local R&B band the Monarchs, touring military bases throughout Europe before returning home to form his own group, Them. The band enjoyed modest success after their debut in 1964; Morrison left the band following a 1966 tour of the U.S.

Morrison's first solo sessions produced arguably his most familiar hit, the jubilant "Brown-Eyed Girl." 1968's *Astral Weeks* remains not only Morrison's masterpiece, but one of the greatest records ever made—a haunting, deeply personal collection of impressionistic folk-styled epics. The follow-up, 1970's *Moondance*, was every bit as brilliant—buoyant and optimistic where *Astral Weeks* was dark and anguished, it cracked the Top 40, generating the perennials "Caravan" and "Into the Mystic."

The first half of the 1970s was the most fertile creative period of Morrison's career—after *His Band and the Street Choir* yielded his biggest chart hit, "Domino," Morrison released 1971's *Tupelo Honey* and 1974's stunning *Veedon Fleece*.

Into the Music, released in 1979, was first in a series of albums which dealt with spiritual themes. 1989's *Avalon Sunset* heralded a commercial rebirth of sorts—"Whenever God Shines His Light," a duet with Cliff Richard, became Morrison's first U.K. Top 20 hit in over two decades.

1991's ambitious double set *Hymns to the Silence*, was widely hailed as his most impressive outing in years. Throughout the '90s, and into the new century, Morrison continued alternating between new studio albums and collections of rare and live material, including the surprising *The Skiffle Sessions: Live in Belfast* which was released in 2000. *—Jason Ankeny*

Blowin' Your Mind! / 1967 / Epic/Legacy ♦♦♦
Although his first solo album is remembered for containing the immortal pop hit "Brown Eyed Girl," *Blowin' Your Mind!* is actually a dry run for Van Morrison's masterpiece, *Astral Weeks*. Songs like "Who Drove the Red Sports Car" look to that song cycle, even as "Midnight Special" nods to Morrison's R&B past. But it is the agonizing "T.B. Sheets"—all nine-and-three-quarters minutes of it—that dominates this record and belies its trendy title and pop association. "T.B. Sheets" takes the blues and reinvents it as noble tragedy and humiliating mortality. It is where Van Morrison emerges as an artist. [*Blowin' Your Mind!* was superseded by *Bang Masters*, which contains all of its tracks except "He Ain't Give You None," presented in an alternate take, plus Morrison's other recordings for Bang, in 1991.] *—William Ruhlmann*

☆ **Astral Weeks** / Nov. 1968 / Warner Brothers ♦♦♦♦♦
Astral Weeks is generally considered one of the best albums in pop music history. For all that renown, *Astral Weeks* is anything but an archetypal rock & roll album: In fact, it isn't a rock & roll album at all. Employing a mixture of folk, blues, jazz, and classical music, Van Morrison spins out a series of extended ruminations on his Belfast upbringing, including the remarkable character "Madame George" and the climactic epiphany experienced on "Cyprus Avenue." Accompanying himself on acoustic guitar, Morrison sings in his elastic, bluesy voice, accompanied by a jazz rhythm section (Jay Berliner, guitar, Richard Davis, bass, Connie Kay, drums), plus reeds (John Payne) and vibes (Warren Smith Jr.), with a string quartet overdubbed. An emotional outpouring cast in delicate musical structures, *Astral Weeks* has a unique musical power. Unlike any record before or since, it nevertheless encompasses the passion and tenderness that have always mixed in the best postwar popular music, easily justifying the critics' raves. *—William Ruhlmann*

☆ **Moondance** / Feb. 1970 / Warner Brothers ♦♦♦♦♦
The yang to *Astral Weeks*' yin, the brilliant *Moondance* is every bit as much a classic as its predecessor; Morrison's first commercially successful solo effort, it retains the previous album's deeply spiritual thrust but transcends its bleak, cathartic intensity to instead explore themes of renewal and redemption. Light, soulful, and jazzy, *Moondance* opens with the sweetly nostalgic "And It Stoned Me," the song's pastoral imagery establishing the dominant lyrical motif recurring throughout the album—virtually every track exults in natural wonder, whether it's the nocturnal magic celebrated by the title cut or the unlimited promise offered in "Brand New Day." At the heart of the record is "Caravan," an incantatory ode to the power of radio; equally stirring is the majestic "Into the Mystic," a song of such elemental beauty and grace as to stand as arguably the quintessential Morrison moment. *—Jason Ankeny*

His Band and the Street Choir / Oct. 1970 / Warner Brothers ♦♦♦♦♦
After the brilliant one-two punch of *Astral Weeks* and *Moondance*, *His Band and the Street Choir* brings Morrison back down to earth, both literally and figuratively. While neither as innovative nor as edgy as its predecessors, *His Band and the Street Choir* also lacks their overt mysticism; at heart, the album is simply Morrison's valentine to the rhythm and blues that inspired him, resulting in the muscular and joyous tribute "Domino" as well as the bouncy "Blue Money" and "Call Me Up in Dreamland." *—Jason Ankeny*

Tupelo Honey / Oct. 1971 / Mercury ♦♦♦♦♦
Tupelo Honey is typical of Morrison's early-1970s work in both sound and structure; after dispensing with the requisite hit—here, the buoyant, R&B-inflected "Wild Night"—he truly gets down to business, settling into a luminously pastoral drift typified by the nostalgic "Old Old Woodstock." At the heart of the record are a pair of stunning love songs, "You're My Woman" and the hymn-like title cut, one of Morrison's most enduring and transcendent compositions. *—Jason Ankeny*

Saint Dominic's Preview / 1972 / Mercury ♦♦♦♦♦
While less thematically and sonically cohesive than Morrison's prior albums, *Saint Dominic's Preview* nonetheless hangs together on the strength of its songs, an intriguingly diverse collection which draws together the disparate threads of the singer's recent work into one sterling package. The opener, "Jackie Wilson Said (I'm in Heaven When You Smile)" is pure R&B jubilation, while the title cut, although essentially a rewrite of "Tupelo Honey," is stunning gospel-pop; both "Listen to the Lion" and "Almost Independence Day," meanwhile, mark a return to the epic mystical explorations of Morrison's earlier work and offer a pair of his most primal performances. *—Jason Ankeny*

Hard Nose the Highway / Aug. 1973 / Mercury ♦♦♦
Although it marks a decline from the astonishing run of five great albums Van Morrison had made from 1968 through 1972, *Hard Nose the Highway* is still a respectable, if uneven, effort, notably containing "Snow in San Anselmo" (which features the Oakland Symphony Chamber Chorus) and "Warm Love." Nevertheless, it marked the end of Morrison's greatest period of creativity and accomplishment. *—William Ruhlmann*

It's Too Late to Stop Now / Jan. 1974 / Mercury ♦♦♦♦♦
While Morrison is, to be kind, an erratic and temperamental live performer, he's in stellar form throughout the double album *It's Too Late to Stop Now*, a superb concert set which neatly summarizes his career from his days with Them (represented by scorching renditions of "Gloria" and "Here Comes the Night") through 1973's *Hard Nose the Highway* ("Warm Love," "Wild Children"). In addition to the hits, including "Caravan," "Domino" and "Into the Mystic" (the final line of which gives the album its title), Morrison even pulls out a handful of R&B chestnuts ("Bring It on Home to Me," "Ain't Nothin' You Can Do") before capping off the collection with a show-stopping rendition of *Astral Weeks'* "Cyprus Avenue." An engaging, warm portrait of the Man at the peak of his powers. *—Jason Ankeny*

Veedon Fleece / Feb. 1974 / Mercury ♦♦♦♦♦
The final album of Morrison's remarkably prolific and innovative 1968-1974 period (followed by three years of silence), *Veedon Fleece* brings the singer full circle, returning him to the introspection and poignancy of *Astral Weeks*. Composed following his sudden divorce from wife Janet Planet and subsequent retreat from the U.S., the songs are subtle and spartan, the performances deeply felt; though less tortured and cathartic than *Astral Weeks*, it's a record fraught with emotional upheaval, as evidenced by such superior moments as "Linden Arden Stole the Highlights," "Who Was That Masked Man," and "You Don't Pull No Punches, But You Don't Push the River." *—Jason Ankeny*

A Period of Transition / 1977 / Mercury ♦♦♦
Titles rarely come as explicit as *A Period of Transition*, a record Van Morrison released three years after *Veedon Fleece*, an uncommonly long period of inactivity for this prolific artist. It was his longest rest, before or since, and in many ways, he emerges from a cocoon here, leaving behind the lushly dark introspection of *Veedon Fleece* for a mellow, good-natured R&B-flavored singer/songwriter sound that may turn introspective, it never feels dark—it's warm, welcoming, infused with spirituality and humor. Still, like any period of transition, this is somewhat tentative and uneven, with its best moments being, at best, minor masterpieces. Yet there's a charm to the album Morrison and co-producer Mac Rebennack have made, a laid-back organic feel that may not be exciting, but it's inviting—all the more so when it's seen as the transitional effort it is. *—Stephen Thomas Erlewine*

Wavelength / 1978 / Mercury ♦♦♦♦
Wavelength essentially picks up where *A Period of Transition* left off, offering a focused, full-bodied alternative to that record's warmly fuzzy lack of direction. Like that album, it's hardly a major entry in his catalog, but there are signs that Morrison is finding his footing for his latter-day voice. Again, the primary appeal of this record is its atmosphere, a charmingly relaxed outing, high on mildly swinging mid-tempo numbers and round, welcoming ballads. Surely, an album of subtle pleasures like this is primarily for the converted, but once you're there, it's hard not to resist *Wavelength*. *—Stephen Thomas Erlewine*

Into the Music / 1979 / Warner Brothers ♦♦♦♦♦
Into the Music may not seem like a great Van Morrison record, one of his very best, upon first listen, especially if you're trying to compare it to such masterpieces as *Astral Weeks* and *Moondance*, or even *Tupelo Honey*. Yet this is certainly one of his best records, one that is quietly winning and thoroughly ingratiating, sounding stronger, even irresistible, with each new spin. In a sense, this is the definitive post-classic era Morrison, since it summarizes all of his attributes while showcasing each at a peak. Musically, this is a little harder and rootsier than its two predecessors, but only a little; this is still remarkably relaxed music, where the charm is in its ease of delivery and compositions. The difference, there's more grit in the performances, more substance in the songs, letting Van the craftsman shine through along with his spirituality and grace. There may be no masterworks on the level of his early-'70s records, but these are deft, subtle songs that are full-bodied songs, unlike their counterparts on this album's immediate predecessors or successors. There's little question that this is not a knock-out record, and some could even be excused if they find its charms elusive—but once you've entered Van's sizeable cult, few records sound as much like Morrison as this, a record that served as culmination of where he was coming from and served as blueprint for where he was going. *—Stephen Thomas Erlewine*

Common One / 1980 / Warner Brothers ♦♦♦
Morrison was working through one of his greatest yet least-appreciated creative periods when he made this album, one that burrows deeply into an introspective jazz-rooted spiritual groove. With Mark Isham's lonely muted trumpet up front, we're in the jazz world immediately with "Haunts of Ancient Peace," merging perfectly with the Van's idiosyncratic vocal style. A low-pressure soul-jazz organ riff lays down the base of the most easily assimilated track, "Satisfied," as Morrison's lyric indicates that he has reached a state of internal peace. "Wild Honey" has R&B horn riffs over Philly-sound strings, while "Spirit" mostly pursues a self-fulfillment path similar to that of "Satisfied." Ultimately, the record stands or falls upon two remarkable, gigantic 15-minute pieces, "Summertime in England" and "When Heart Is Open." "Summertime's" propulsive opening drops names of Morrison's favorite poets and authors; the track teeters upon indulgence but you are drawn in by the Van's obsessions with lines and phrases like "common one" and "let your red robe go," his voice becoming a twin brother of arranger Pee Wee Ellis's riffing sax. Lonely horns over the hilltops open "When Heart Is Open," and it begins to resemble a sequel to Miles Davis' treatment of "In a Silent Way," setting a peaceful, mesmerizing mood that carries you through its enormous length to the end of the record. No wonder the rock critics of the time didn't get it; this is music outside the pop mainstream, and even the Van's own earlier musical territory. But it retains its trance-like power to this day. *—Richard S. Ginell*

Beautiful Vision / 1982 / Warner Brothers ♦♦♦
Beautiful Vision shares much sonically with its predecessor, *Common One*, being heavy on long, winding song-poems, moderate tempos, dense lyricism, and dated production. Still, this winds up being a stronger articulation of what Morrison was attempting to do on *Common One*—much like how *Wavelength* got *A Period of Transition* right. That doesn't mean that this is a particularly easy album to warm to, since Morrison seems to be consciously creating an insular world here, only of interest to those willing to delve deeply into his own world, letting his elliptical melodies charm instead of frustrate, to let the leisurely pace seduce rather than lull. Once you do that, the record reveals such charming moments as "She Gives Me Religion," "Beautiful Vision," and "Cleaning Windows," a skipping light R&B tune that became one of his latter-day standards. Too much of *Beautiful Vision* is the product of a willfully idiosyncratic, yet oddly measured vision to make it essential for anyone other than diehards, but moments such as that make it worth a listen. *—Stephen Thomas Erlewine*

The Inarticulate Speech of the Heart / Mar. 1983 / Warner Brothers ♦♦♦♦
Almost a forgotten album, Inarticulate Speech of the Heart takes us to the deepest, most inward areas of Van Morrison's renegade Irish soul, the culmination of his spiritual jazz period—and also, perhaps not coincidentally, the last record he made for Warner Bros. Four of the 11 tracks are moody instrumentals—which might partly explain the indifference of many rock critics toward the album, although the album's very title gives a clue to their presence. The mood is predominately mellow but never flaccid or complacent; there is a radiance that glows throughout. "Higher Than the World" is simply one of the most beautiful recordings Morrison ever made, with Mark Isham's choir-like synthesizer laying down the lovely backdrop. The instrumental "Connswater" is the most Irish-flavored piece the Van had made up to that point—and would continue to be until he recorded with the Chieftains in 1988. "Rave On, John Donne"—in part a recitation invoking a roster of writers over a supple two-chord vamp—seems to have had the longest afterlife, reappearing in the Van's live shows and greatest hits compilations. "The Street Only Knew Your Name" is the only piece that could be classified as a rocker, tempered even here by the synthesizer overlays. The record sold poorly, but many of those who bought it consider it one of the most cherished items in their Van Morrison collections. *—Richard S. Ginell*

A Sense of Wonder / 1985 / Mercury ♦♦♦
Van Morrison's U.S. label debut with PolyGram (which had issued his *Live at the Opera House Belfast* album in England earlier) is a strong effort, mixing some of his familiar influences—R&B, poetry, mysticism—on such characteristic tracks as "Tore Down a La Rimbaud." It might be fair to say that, by now, Morrison's fans had heard what he had to say and the rest was just repetition, but he continued to write and perform at a high level at this mature stage in his career. *—William Ruhlmann*

Live at the Grand Opera House Belfast / 1985 / Mercury ♦♦♦
Van Morrison is a legendary live performer, capable of invigorating, incendiary performances that can be utterly hypnotic, as the near-classic 1974 set *It's Too Late to Stop Now* illustrates. Released ten years later, *Live at the Grand Opera House Belfast* may not be as gripping, but Van wasn't as gripping a decade later, either. That's not to say he was past his prime, since he was still turning out fearless idiosyncratic records (and this, to be sure, fits right into that category). Still, he had become settled into a signature sound that may have been warm and filled with life, but it was so subtly shaded that it was primarily of interest only for the devoted. And that's what this record is—an album for devoted fans, finding Van turning out passionate versions of latter-day tunes from "Full Force Gale" to "Cleaning Windows." Nothing particularly revelatory, yet it's a nice listen for those dedicated fans. *—Stephen Thomas Erlewine*

No Guru, No Method, No Teacher / Jul. 1986 / Mercury ♦♦♦
With "Ivory Tower," Van Morrison produced another excellent rocker in his familiar style, while "In the Garden" took him to one of his more spiritual, religious spaces. *—William Ruhlmann*

Poetic Champions Compose / 1987 / Mercury ✦✦✦✦

If the title didn't tip you off, the opening five-minute jazz instrumental "Spanish Steps" certainly reveals that *Poetic Champions Compose* is an art record. Of course, Morrison has been making art records since at least *Inarticulate Speech of the Heart*, perhaps *Common One*, so that shouldn't come as a surprise. What is a bit of a shock is that Morrison begins to shake off his self-conscious straitjacket here, letting a little more grit into the music, even if the record still is firmly ensconced in mid-tempos and ballads, with only Van's voice (soulful, yet not histrionic), to pull you in. Much of this tends to float by, with only the occasional song ("I Forgot That Love Existed," "Did Ye Get Healed?") distinguishing themselves. The overly mellow atmosphere and Van's arch artiness may not make it universally appealing, yet this record is warmer, stronger than many of its predecessors, one of his highlights from the '80s. —*Stephen Thomas Erlewine*

Irish Heartbeat / 1988 / Mercury ✦✦✦✦✦

Although still purposeful, Van Morrison's '80s albums were becoming repetitive when he took a break for this collaboration with the Chieftains on traditional Irish songs. The result takes him back to his earliest days and finds him singing with renewed conviction. This album should appeal to all fans of Irish music as well as Morrison lovers. —*William Ruhlmann*

Avalon Sunset / Jun. 1989 / Mercury ✦✦✦✦✦

Van Morrison scored one of his biggest commercial successes with *Avalon Sunset*, a record highlighted by the gorgeous "Have I Told You Lately," one of his most heartfelt love songs and a major radio hit which helped introduce his music to a new generation of listeners. Not a consistently strong LP, *Avalon Sunset* is nevertheless the work of a master craftsman, its lush orchestration and atmospheric production casting an irresistibly elegant spell; a deeply spiritual record, it also includes the standout opener "Whenever God Shines His Light," a collaboration with Cliff Richard. —*Jason Ankeny*

★ **The Best of Van Morrison** / Jan. 1990 / Mercury ✦✦✦✦✦

For an artist that's doggedly album-oriented, plus a songwriter who revels in subtlety, Van Morrison doesn't seem like a logical candidate for a successful greatest-hits compilation. Nevertheless, *The Best of Van Morrison* is a cracker-jack compilation, tracing Van the Man from his days with Them, through his best-known tunes ("Brown-Eyed Girl," "Moondance," "Blue Money," "Wild Night"), to highlights from the '70s and '80s cult efforts, topped off by "Wonderful Remark," a song first heard on the *King of Comedy* soundtrack. This collection makes Morrison's work seem a little more immediate and accessible than it usually is, but that's a blessing, since it provides a great summary of his hits and a nice introduction for the curious. Yes, it could have dug deeper into the catalog, but as a sampler, it can't be faulted. —*Stephen Thomas Erlewine*

Enlightenment / Feb. 1990 / Mercury ✦✦✦

Essentially the same album as *Avalon Sunset*, *Enlightenment* is an immaculately produced collection of spiritually infused R&B and mid-tempo singer/songwriter fare. If *Avalon Sunset* has the edge over these two sets, it's because the sound was a little fresher there and that it, overall, had a stronger set of songs. *Enlightenment* dips down after a strong opening pair ("Real Real Gone," "Enlightenment"), settling into a pleasant sound that never winds up turning out a particularly notable song. Certainly not a bad record and livelier than those he was making a decade before, but still not particularly engaging, either. —*Stephen Thomas Erlewine*

The Bang Masters / Feb. 26, 1991 / Epic ✦✦✦✦✦

During the period between his departure from Them and his masterpiece *Astral Weeks*, Van Morrison tenured with Bert Berns' Bang label, notching his biggest solo hit with the classic single "Brown Eyed Girl" and laying the groundwork for the transcendent material to follow. *The Bang Masters* compiles the best of his recordings for the label, and although a good part of it is negligible in comparison to Morrison's greatest work, it's still necessary listening for fans. The remarkable "T.B. Sheets" captures Morrison at his most emotionally shattering, while early attempts at "Beside You" and "Madame George" hint at the genius just around the corner. —*Jason Ankeny*

Hymns to the Silence / Sep. 24, 1991 / Mercury ✦✦✦

Morrison's best album of the '90s still casually hangs out in the spiritual world that served as his home for most of his '80s material, but the mystical touches are at least kept in check for a good deal of the time. Better still is that Morrison sings with a passion that had crawled into laziness during big, and crucial, chunks of his career (most prominently the early to mid-'80s). The songs, or more accurately (as the title makes very clear) hymns, combine the elements that have guided Morrison's best albums—R&B, folk, pop, Celtic, rock, even gospel—for a satisfying journey through the mystic and the real. Its double-disc length, however, is a bit off-putting; a spirited rewrite of his last album (1990's *Enlightenment*) really doesn't need this much space to make its point. But his rambling musings (like the soulfully suave "Why Must I Always Explain") retain a compelling power. —*Michael Gallucci*

The Best of Van Morrison, Vol. 2 / Mar. 9, 1993 / Mercury ✦✦✦✦✦

No big hit singles are here, or even familiar songs for that matter. Van Morrison compiled *The Best Of, Volume 2* himself, leaning heavily toward his recent work. As an anthology, it doesn't completely work, since it's uneven and lacking a sense of scope; what makes the album fascinating is to see how Morrison views himself. Although there are many good (even great) songs here, *The Best Of, Volume 2* only works as an introduction to Morrison's idiosyncratic recent work instead of his entire career. —*Stephen Thomas Erlewine*

Too Long in Exile / Jun. 8, 1993 / Mercury ✦✦

Too Long in Exile marks a welcome return to the earthy secular world, an embrace of rootsy R&B and smoky jazz, a street album that ranks with Morrison's best. He weaves

a kind of magic with a funky "Good Morning Little Schoolgirl" and the confessional blues of "Bigtime Operator," a story-song recounting some harrowing early experiences within the music industry. Instrumentally, the album is driven by a smooth horn section, Van's harmonica, and British vet Georgie Fame's virtuoso Hammond B-3. The proceedings stall briefly toward the end with a pair of vapid jazz pieces and noodling instrumental backing that does little justice to a W.B. Yeats text, but the searing closer "Tell Me What You Want" moves things right back into club territory. —*Roch Parisien*

A Night in San Francisco / May 17, 1994 / Mercury ✦✦✦

Van Morrison's third commercially released live album takes a show format that frequently spotlights the backup band, led by organist/singer Georgie Fame and featuring singers Brian Kennedy and James Hunter, as well as saxophonist Candy Dulfer and blues singers John Lee Hooker, Junior Wells, and Jimmy Witherspoon. Even Morrison's daughter Shana comes on to sing his "Beautiful Vision." The material is not limited to Morrison compositions, either. In fact, it isn't so much that Morrison & Co. cover a variety of rock, pop, blues, R&B, and jazz standards as that many pieces are medleys that contain complete songs and quotes from others, rather in the way that a jazz soloist will suddenly throw in a few bars of a familiar tune. Those who want to see Morrison as an esoteric singer/songwriter rather than a showman may find this album a mongrel creation, but it's undeniably lively, and that's the first requirement of a live album. —*William Ruhlmann*

Payin' Dues / Nov. 1, 1994 / Charly ✦✦✦

A most fascinating double disc. The first contains the tracks found on *Bang Masters*; the bonus CD contains 31 previously unreleased acoustic ditties. The word ditties is a description, not a value judgment. According to one account, Morrison cut these purely out of necessity to fulfill his Bang contract, delivering the most unusable material possible. All of the cuts are between 45 and 90 seconds, divided between the inane (numerous nonsensical variations on "La Bamba," "Twist and Shout," and "Hang on Sloopy") and the viciously uncommercial ("The Big Royalty Check," "Ring Worm," "Blow in Your Nose"), along with a few silly variations on "Madame George." Along with Lou Reed's *Metal Machine Music*, this ranks as the least commercial music ever recorded by a major rock artist, and the nastiest spit in the eye of commercial expectations and contractual obligations. It's much more listenable than *Metal Machine Music*, though, and funnier. If you haven't picked up the *Bang Masters* collection, the addition of this off-the-wall material (which may never find release in the U.S.) makes *Payin' Dues* a recommended alternative. —*Richie Unterberger*

Days Like This / Jun. 20, 1995 / Mercury ✦✦

Van Morrison is a songwriter. He's paid to write about romance. We know this because he tells us on "Songwriter." A list of clichés, presumably intended to be ironic, the song unintentionally reveals the real problem with *Days like This*—Van Morrison is going through the motions. *Days like This* smooths over the rougher edges of the R&B-dominated *Too Long in Exile* without returning to the meditative, jazzy explorations of his '80s works. Instead, the ensuing album is a completely competent yet completely uninspired pop-R&B workout, with Van sounding as if he couldn't care less about the words leaving his mouth. And that, in a way, explains the empty rhymes of "Songwriter"—it's just a job and Van will get paid no matter what he turns out. —*Stephen Thomas Erlewine*

How Long Has This Been Going On / Feb. 1996 / Verve ✦✦

Songs of Mose Allison: Tell Me Something / Oct. 8, 1996 / Verve ✦✦✦

Songs of Mose Allison: Tell Me Something is a tribute record to Mose Allison coordinated by Van Morrison, who brought in his longtime sidemen, Georgie Fame, Ben Sidran, and Allison himself to record a selection of Mose's best songs. That doesn't necessarily mean his most famous, even though many of his best-known songs are here. Instead, the musicians are interested in capturing the laid-back, idiosyncratic spirit of Allison's music by combining famous numbers with lesser-known tunes and performing them a warm, relaxed manner. By and large, the approach works, and it is a better, jazzier record than Morrison's previous album, *How Long Has This Been Going On*. —*Stephen Thomas Erlewine*

The Healing Game / Mar. 4, 1997 / Mercury ✦✦✦

Van Morrison's 23rd studio album of original material in 30 years follows two jazz-oriented side projects, during which he was able to indulge his affection for the works of others, especially those of Mose Allison. Returning to his own work, Morrison seems to want to come to terms with the bitterness sometimes expressed in more recent original albums like *Too Long in Exile* and *Days Like This*. That bitterness has not dissipated by any means, as he demonstrates most clearly in "This Weight" and "It Once Was My Life," but now he is at pains to make clear that he became a musician because of a pure, simple joy in music-making. But that joy has been reduced by the demands of celebrity, and if this makes him the Greta Garbo of rock, so be it. His fear is that he will be reduced to being merely an entertainer. When he isn't complaining, Morrison presents the same kind of material he has been giving us for decades now, mid-tempo tunes paced by warm, graceful horn charts in which he evokes passion and spirituality largely through the use of nature imagery and rhythmic repetition. In his attempt to get back to his original inspiration, however, he gives "It Once Was My Life" and especially "If You Love Me" a doo wop sound, which seems to achieve the desired effect, such that in the album-closing title track he declares success: "Here I am again/back on the corner again/back where I belong." And with his return to "those ancient streets," his career comes full circle. —*William Ruhlmann*

The Philosopher's Stone / Jun. 16, 1998 / Polydor ✦✦✦

Van Morrison has always been a prolific artist, releasing nearly an album a year for 30 years. All the while, he had a stockpile of unreleased material in the vaults, many of which became legendary among collectors. A selection of this material was planned for inclusion on a box set, but when he realized the sheer amount of worthy material, he decided to separate the unreleased cuts and release them as the double-disc set *The Philosopher's Stone*. Certainly, the collection is for fans, but not just hardcore fans—there are a number of great songs here, from "Madame Joy" and "Naked in the Jungle" to "Crazy Jane on Gold" and "The Street Only Knew Your Name." A full 26 of the 30 tracks on the album have never been released in any form, while the remaining four—"Wonderful Remark," "Real Real Gone," "Flamingoes Fly," "Bright Side of the Road"—are present in alternate takes. In all, *The Philosopher's Stone* is a welcome addition to Van Morrison's official catalog—some of these songs are so good, it would have been a shame if they had stayed locked in the vaults. *—Stephen Thomas Erlewine*

The Skiffle Sessions: Live in Belfast 1998 / Jan. 18, 2000 / Pointblank ✦✦✦✦
Van Morrison probably chose to give a pair of skiffle concerts in November, 1998 not because he was nostalgic, but because he has genuine love for this music. At least, that's the impression *The Skiffle Sessions* gives. It's a cheerfully old-fashioned yet curiously fresh album. By skipping "Rock Island Line," the style's best-known tune, and emphasizing the music's foundation in American folk, blues, and jazz, they wind up revitalizing skiffle while paying homage to it. Yes, this may be corny at times, yet it's a clever, diverse record. They delve into blues, letting Barber have a Dixieland trombone solo on "Frankie and Johnny," invite Dr. John to play some New Orleans on "Goin' Home" and "Good Morning Blues," haul out Jimmie Rodgers' "Muleskinner Blues" and Leadbelly's "Goodnight Irene," paying tribute to both country and folk. Only "Don't You Rock Me Daddio" fits the clichés of skiffle, and here it's only one side of a rich, generous collection of roots music. Some might say that this multifaceted approach to skiffle is revisionism, but it isn't; skiffle itself was a hybrid, drawing from all sorts of American roots music but given an endearing twist by idealist British musicians, who loved the American myth as much as the music. *The Skiffle Sessions* captures this love of myth and music, while being a hell of a good listen. Morrison's career has been idiosyncratic and unpredictable, but nothing has been quite as surprising as this. Really, there's no reason why a skiffle album released in 2000 should be as irresistible as this, but Morrison, Donegan, and Barber bring such heart and love to this music that it's hard not to be charmed. *—Stephen Thomas Erlewine*

You Win Again / Oct. 3, 2000 / Virgin ✦✦✦
Van Morrison has always been eccentric, but as he grows older, he seems to get more comfortable with his eccentricities and doesn't strain as hard to be distinctive. That's why it seems natural to have two albums in one year be as willfully individual as *The Skiffle Sessions* and *You Win Again*, a duet album with Linda Gail Lewis. In all honesty, in 2000, nobody but Jerry Lee Lewis fanatics really remembered that his sister Linda Gail is a talent in her own right, but Morrison had a soft spot for her and decided to record a full album with her. It's a modest affair, sporting only one Morrison original ("No Way Pedro") and relying heavily on Jerry Lee's catalog, opening with four songs inextricably associated with his Sun recordings. But, if this is a tribute album, it's only because this music is in the same spirit as those great recordings. Not everything here is associated with Jerry Lee, but Linda Gail's piano is reminiscent of her sibling, and both she and Morrison have the same fearless spirit as the Killer, easily making these songs fit their voices and blur the distinctions between R&B, blues, country, and rock & roll. Best of all, this is never a conscious decision; they're just pounding out a bunch of songs they love. *You Win Again* sounds like it was knocked off in one afternoon by a bar band that knows each other so well, they can anticipate each other's next move. It wasn't, of course, but that's the highest compliment it can be paid. No, it's not a major work in Van's catalog, but it's hard not to smile when listening to it, just like *The Skiffle Sessions*. It's a roots effort that never sounds studied—just easy, welcoming, and thoroughly enjoyable. *—Stephen Thomas Erlewine*

Morrissey

b. May 22, 1959, Manchester, England
Vocals / College Rock, Alternative Pop/Rock
With the Smiths, singer/songwriter Morrissey established himself as a post-punk hero, becoming the spokesman for millions of disaffected teenagers and young adults with his literate, biting, and sensitive lyrics and dramatic vocals. After the band broke up in 1987, he pursued a solo career, releasing his first album the following year. While he released several excellent singles in the late '80s, he ultimately began to sink into his persona without producing enough quality songs. After 1991's self-absorbed *Kill Uncle*, many critics considered him as a has-been, with his best work in the past. Thanks to the explosive, Mick Ronson-produced *Your Arsenal*, Morrissey regained his credibility; it was almost universally acclaimed as one of the best albums of the year and many said it was his best work since the Smiths' masterpiece *The Queen Is Dead*. His fan base continued to grow, both in size and devotion. With 1994's *Vauxhall and I*, he even had a hit single ("The More You Ignore Me, the Closer I Get") scrape the Top 50 singles chart in America, which would have been unthinkable when "Hand in Glove" was released a decade earlier. However, 1997's *Maladjusted* was a commercial failure; the compilation *My Early Burglary Years* followed a year later. *—Stephen Thomas Erlewine*

Viva Hate / Mar. 22, 1988 / Sire ✦✦✦✦✦
Following the breakup of the Smiths, Morrissey needed to prove that he was a viable artist without Johnny Marr, and *Viva Hate* fulfilled that goal with grace. Working with producer Stephen Street and guitarist Vini Reilly (of the Durutti Column), Morrissey doesn't drastically depart from the sound of *Strangeways, Here We Come*, offering a selection of 12 jangling guitar-pop sounds. One major concession is the presence of synthesizers—which is ironic, considering the Smiths' adamant opposition to keyboards—but neither the sound, nor Morrissey's wit, is diluted. And while the music is occasionally pedestrian, Morrissey compensates with a superb batch of lyrics, ranging from his conventional despair ("Little Man, What Now?," "I Don't Mind If You Forget Me") to the savage political tirade of "Margaret on a Guillotine." Nevertheless, the two master strokes on the album—the gorgeous "Everyday is Like Sunday" and the infectious "Suedehead"—were previously singles, and both are on the compilation, *Bona Drag*. *—Stephen Thomas Erlewine*

Bona Drag / Oct. 8, 1990 / Sire ✦✦✦✦✦
As he was toiling on *Kill Uncle*, Morrissey released *Bona Drag*, a compilation of singles and B-sides, including "Everyday is Like Sunday" and "Suedehead" from *Viva Hate*. While the record conveniently overlooks some rarities, the selections on *Bona Drag* are uniformly first-rate and many of the songs—"Picadilly Palare," "Interesting Drug," "November Spawned a Monster," "The Last of the Famous International Playboys," "Lucky Lisp," "Disappointed," "He Knows I'd Love to See Him," and "Ouija Board, Ouija Board"—are Morrissey classics, arguably making *Bona Drag* a more consistent and entertaining record than *Viva Hate*. *—Stephen Thomas Erlewine*

Kill Uncle / Mar. 5, 1991 / Sire ✦✦
With *Kill Uncle*, Morrissey descended into the ranks of self-parody, churning out a series of pleasant but tired alternative jangle-pop songs that had neither melody nor much wit to distinguish them. Part of the problem lies with his choice of collaborators. Producers Clive Langer and Alan Winstanley don't provide the appropriately sympathetic backdrop for Morrissey's sly humor, while guitarist Mark E. Nevin is incapable of developing hooks. A few cuts, such as "(I'm) The End of the Family Line" and "There's a Place in Hell for Me and My Friends," stand out, but *Kill Uncle* is Morrissey's least distinguished record. *—Stephen Thomas Erlewine*

● **Your Arsenal** / Jul. 28, 1992 / Sire ✦✦✦✦✦
Morrissey bounced back from the lackluster *Kill Uncle* with the terrific *Your Arsenal*. A dynamic, invigorating fusion of glam rock and rockabilly, *Your Arsenal* rocks harder than any other record Morrissey ever made. Guitarist Alan Whyte's riffs swagger with a self-absorbed arrogance, and producer Mick Ronson gives the music a tough, stylish sheen—it may be a break from Morrissey's jangle pop, but the music is sharper than at has been since the Smiths, and so is Morrissey's pen. Running through his trademark litany of emotional, social, and personal observations, Morrissey is viciously clever and occasionally moving. And the songs—whether it's the rush of "You're Gonna Need Someone on Your Side," the menacing "We'll Let You Know," the spare rockabilly bop of "Certain People I Know," the gospel-tinged "I Know It's Gonna Happen Someday" or "Tomorrow"—are uniformly excellent, forming the core of Morrissey's finest solo record and his best work since *The Queen Is Dead*. *—Stephen Thomas Erlewine*

Beethoven Was Deaf / May 10, 1993 / EMI ✦✦✦
Recorded on the English *Your Arsenal* tour, the 16-track album *Beethoven Was Deaf* is an effective argument for Morrissey's capabilities as a live performer. Although none of the songs, which are all drawn from his solo career, are drastically different than their original studio incarnation, they are performed with skill by Morrissey's pseudo-rockabilly band, giving the singer ample opportunity to flaunt his charisma. But it's not just charisma—Morrissey is a powerful, if unconventional vocalist, capable of squeezing out all the wit and exaggerated emotion from each song. While many of his great solo songs are here ("Suedehead," "Certain People I Know," "Sister I'm a Poet"), it relies a little too heavily on *Your Arsenal* to be a good career overview, yet it remains a fine souvenir for hardcore fans. *—Stephen Thomas Erlewine*

Vauxhall and I / Mar. 22, 1994 / Sire ✦✦✦✦✦
While it isn't a gutsy rock & roll record like *Your Arsenal*, *Vauxhall and I* is equally impressive. Filled with carefully constructed guitar-pop gems, the album contains some of Morrissey's best material since the Smiths. Out of all of his solo albums, *Vauxhall and I* sounds the most like his former band, yet the textured, ringing guitar on this record is an extension of his past, not a replication of it. In fact, with songs like "Now My Heart Is Full" and "Hold on to Your Friends," Morrissey sounds more comfortable and peaceful than he ever has. And "The More You Ignore Me, the Closer I Get," "Speedway," and "Spring-Heeled Jim" prove that he hasn't lost his vicious wit. *—Stephen Thomas Erlewine*

World of Morrissey / Feb. 21, 1995 / Sire ✦✦✦
Released to coincide with Morrissey's brief winter tour of England in 1995, *World of Morrissey* follows none of the accepted rules for compilations. It's not a hits collection, nor is it a best-of—the disc is filled with album cuts, live tracks, a couple of B-sides and a new single, all of which dedicated Morrissey fans already own. However, the choice of songs does mean something—the choice of the vaguely threatening "Spring-Heeled Jim" over "Now My Heart Is Full" and the sad "Billy Budd" over "The More You Ignore Me, the Closer I Get" makes the calm *Vauxhall and I* seem darker than it is. But that melancholy is cut by the sly taunt of "Have-a-Go Merchant" and the perennial "Last of the Famous International Playboys," as well as a long, bizarre crawl through "Moon River." Only hardcore fans will notice such subtle matters as running orders; for them, *World of Morrissey* is a mix tape. *—Stephen Thomas Erlewine*

Southpaw Grammar / Aug. 28, 1995 / Reprise ✦✦
If *Vauxhall and I* represented a more mature Morrissey, *Southpaw Grammar* superficially presents a more rough & tumble version of the singer. As his previous single, "Boxers," indicated, Morrissey's fascination with boxing and violence has reached full fruition. The music appropriately reflects this, with growling, distorted guitars and martial rhythms. But *Southpaw Grammar* doesn't rock as hard or with as much style as the rockabilly-inflected *Your Arsenal*—instead, it's his art-rock album, complete with strings, drum solos, and two ten-minute songs. Of these, the winding, menacing "The Teachers Are Afraid of the Pupils" works the best, and it represents a significant change in Morrissey's outlook; instead of the children being outsiders, the teachers are. Throughout *Southpaw*

Grammar, the privileged are oppressed by their fortunes, while working-class toughs are celebrated for their violence. However, there is no cohesive glue to the record. "The Teachers" uses its 11 minutes effectively, but "Southpaw" is merely ponderous. "Reader Meet Author" and "Dangenham Dave" are classic three-minute pop songs, but "Do Your Best and Don't Worry" is strictly by the books. Nevertheless, there is plenty of enjoyable music on the record, even if the concept is flawed. *—Stephen Thomas Erlewine*

Maladjusted / Aug. 12, 1997 / Mercury ✦✦✦
In theory, *Maladjusted* should have been a readjustment to standard indie rock territory for Morrissey after the prog rock detour of *Southpaw Grammar*, but Morrissey isn't that simple. From the opening title track, with its menacing, swirling paranoia, it's clear that *Maladjusted* isn't a simple return to form. That isn't to say that the album is devoid of the jangly, maudlin pop songs that are Morrissey's trademark—in fact, the lead single, "Alma Matters," ais a quietly catchy tune that ranks as vintage Morrissey. Nevertheless, it's a little misleading, because *Maladjusted* isn't strictly by the book. Morrissey has incorporated his newfound fascination with prog rock into his trademark sound much better than he did on *Southpaw Grammar*, as the lumbering beat of "Papa Jack" and sawing strings of "Ambitious Outsiders" illustrate, but that fascination signals how insular Morrissey's world has become. Things are rarely more insular—or weirder—than "Sorrow Will Come in the End," a spoken-word, neo-classical rant about his loss to Mike Joyce in a Smiths royalty suit (the song was pulled from the British version of the album, due to legal reasons), but "Roy's Keen," an ode to a keen window cleaner, isn't far behind. The remainder of the album—particularly the lovely "Wide to Receive," "He Cried" and "Trouble Love Me"—may be similarly self-obsessed, yet the music is warm and welcoming, thanks to strong craftsmanship and fine performances. They're charming songs, but they're subtle charms, offering the kind of pleasures only longtime Morrissey followers will find irresistible. *—Stephen Thomas Erlewine*

• **Suedehead: The Best of Morrissey** / Sep. 8, 1997 / EMI ✦✦✦✦✦
Morrissey has always favored compilations, releasing such hodgepodges of singles, B-sides, and album tracks as *Bona Drag* and *World of Morrissey*, but the 19-track *Suedehead: The Best of Morrissey* is the first official "hits" collection he has released in his solo career. Spanning his years at EMI—from 1988's *Viva Hate* to 1994's *Vauxhall and I*, with the 1995 single "Sunny" added as a bonus—*Suedehead* is an imperfect collection, especially since it's sequenced out of chronological order, but it's pretty great all the same, featuring a basic selection of singles such as "Suedehead," "Everyday Is Like Sunday," "Tomorrow," "Interesting Drug," "Our Frank," "Piccadilly Palare," "We Hate It When Our Friends Become Successful," "The Last of the Famous International Playboys," "Boxers" and "The More You Ignore Me, the Closer I Get." There's also a handful of rarities, such as the extended version of "Interlude" and his cover of the Jam's "That's Entertainment," but at its core, this disc is a solid collection that may convince skeptics that Morrissey's solo records did indeed have a lot to offer. *—Stephen Thomas Erlewine*

My Early Burglary Years / Sep. 15, 1998 / Reprise ✦✦✦
Possibly left without a record contract, working without a manager, living in self-imposed exile, Morrissey returned to what he knew best in the fall of 1998—recycling his own material. *My Early Burglary Years* was released under the pretense of offering American audiences songs, such as "Sunny," previously unavailable on their shores—which is kind of ridiculous, since anyone still buying Morrissey records in 1998 likely buys every single, regardless of their country of origin. That leaves *My Early Burglary Years* as another odd collection of rarities, singles, and album tracks. There are undoubtedly some fans who haven't bought every single, but this disc won't necessarily help them, since the rarities are mixed in with familiar material. That said, *My Early Burglary Years* is a better bit for lapsed collectors looking to pick up some rare songs than *World of Morrissey*, since it has such non-LP items as the entire "Sunny" single and "Cosmic Dancer" (which is a previously released version, contrary to the cover sticker's claims), which have never appeared on a comp or as bonus tracks. It's not quite enough to excuse the repeat appearances of the seemingly ubiquitous "Sister I'm a Poet" and "Jack the Ripper" (as well as album tracks from *Southpaw Grammar*), or the lack of a comprehensive B-sides and rarities collection, but at least it's a step in the right direction. *—Stephen Thomas Erlewine*

Mos Def (Dante Beze)

Vocals / East Coast Rap, Hip-Hop, Political Rap, Underground Rap
One of the best in the '90s new school of Native Tongue rappers (alongside Common and the Bush Babees), Mos Def guested with old-school Native Tongues De La Soul and recorded for Rawkus Records, the home of independent-minded rap of the 1990s. Born Dante Beze, he began rhyming at the age of nine and formed his first group, Urban Thermo Dynamics (UTD), with his brother and sister. Invited to join the Native Tongues family founded by Afrika Bambaataa and including A Tribe Called Quest and De La Soul among its members, Mos Def agreed and appeared on the fourth De La Soul LP, *Stakes Is High*. He also contributed a verse on the second Bush Babees album, then released his first single "The Universal Magnetic," for the seminal rap independent Rawkus; A Tribe Called Quest's Q-Tip appeared on his second single, "Body Rock." Mos Def began recording for his debut album (with Talib Kweli), *Black Star*, released in September 1998. *Black on Both Sides* followed in the fall of 1999. *—John Bush*

• **Black Star** / Aug. 26, 1998 / Priority ✦✦✦✦✦
While Puff Daddy and his followers continued to dictate the direction hip-hop would take into the millennium, Mos Def and Talib Kweli surfaced from the underground to pull the sounds in the opposite direction. Their 13 rhyme-fests on this superior debut show that old-school rap still sounds surprisingly fresh in the sea of overblown vanity productions. There's no slack evident in the tight wordplays of Def and Kweli as they twist and turn through sparse, jazz-rooted rhythms calling out for awareness and freedom of the mind. Their viewpoints stem directly from the teachings of Marcus Garvey, the legendary activist who fought for the rights of blacks all around the world in the first half of the 20th century. Def and Kweli's ideals are sure lofty; not only are they out to preach Garvey's words, but they also hope to purge rap music of its negativity and violence. For the most part, it works. Their wisdom-first philosophy hits hard when played off their lyrical intensity, a bass-first production and stellar scratching. While these MCs don't have all of the vocal pizzazz of A Tribe Called Quest's Phife and Q-Tip at their best, flawless tracks like the cool bop of "K.O.S. (Determination)" and "Definition" hint that *Black Star* is only the first of many brilliantly executed positive statements for these two street poets. *—Jason Kaufman*

Black on Both Sides / Oct. 12, 1999 / Rawkus ✦✦✦✦✦
Mos Def's partnership with Talib Kweli produced one of the most important hip-hop albums of the late '90s, 1997's brilliant *Black Star*. Consciously designed as a return to rap's musical foundations and a manifesto for reclaiming the art form from gangsta/playa domination, it succeeded mightily on both counts, raising expectations sky-high for Mos Def's solo debut. He met them all with *Black on Both Sides*, a record every bit as dazzling and visionary as *Black Star*. *Black on Both Sides* strives to not only refine but expand the scope of Mos Def's talents, turning the solo spotlight on his intricate wordplay and nimble rhythmic skills—but also his increasing eclecticism. The main reference points are pretty much the same—old-school rap, which allows for a sense of playfulness as well as history, and the Native Tongues posse's fascination with jazz, both for its sophistication and cultural heritage. But they're supported by a rich depth that comes from forays into reggae (as well as its aura of spiritual conscience), pop, soul, funk, and even hardcore punk (that on the album's centerpiece, "Rock & Roll," a dissection of white America's history of appropriating black musical innovations). In keeping with his goal of restoring hip-hop's sociopolitical consciousness, Def's lyrics are as intelligent and thoughtfully crafted as one would expect, but he doesn't stop there—he sings quite passably on several tracks, plays live instruments on others (including bass, drums, congas, vibraphone, and keyboards), and even collaborates on a string arrangement. In short, *Black on Both Sides* is a *tour de force* by an artist out to prove he can do it all. Its ambition and execution rank it as one of the best albums of 1999, and it consolidates Mos Def's position as one of hip-hop's brightest hopes entering the 21st century. *—Steve Huey*

The Motels

f. 1973, Berkeley, CA, **db.** 1987
American Punk, L.A. Punk, Pop/Rock, New Wave
Led by the charismatic Martha Davis, the Motels were one of the most successful and acclaimed bands to emerge from the fertile Los Angeles new wave scene, reaching the Top Ten in 1982 with their biggest hit, "Only the Lonely." Davis formed the group in 1972 while living in Berkeley, CA, recruiting guitarist Dean Chamberlain and bassist Richard D'Andrea; originally dubbed the Warfield Foxes, they became the Motels upon relocating to L.A., but despite interest from a number of record labels the group suffered through endless lineup changes, finally disbanding in 1976. Davis soon formed a new Motels roster with guitarist Jeff Jourard, his saxophonist/keyboardist brother Marty, bassist Michael Goodroe, and drummer Brian Glascock; signing to Capitol, in 1979 the group issued their self-titled debut LP, scoring a minor hit with the ballad "Total Control." Guitarist Tim McGovern, formerly of the Pop!, replaced Jeff Jourard prior to the release of the 1980 sophomore effort *Careful*. After Capitol rejected the Motels' third album, *All Four One*, McGovern exited, and the group re-recorded the album with guitarist Guy Perry and assorted session musicians. This time the label relented, releasing *All Four One* in 1982; the album eventually went gold on the strength of the atmospheric "Only the Lonely," which ascended to the number nine spot. The evocative "Suddenly Last Summer," the lead single from the Motels' 1983 follow-up, *Little Robbers*, reached number nine as well a year later, yielding the Top 40 entry "Remember the Nights." 1985's *Shock* generated the band's final hit, "Shame." A cancer scare prompted Davis to dissolve the Motels in 1987, the year she made her solo debut with *Policy*. In mid-1998 she reformed the group, touring under the name the Motels Featuring Martha Davis. A collection entitled *Anthologyland* followed in early 2001. *—Jason Ankeny*

The Motels / 1979 / Capitol ✦✦✦
1979's self-titled debut release from the California band the Motels comes across as what a less pretentious Doors might have sounded like had they emerged during the new wave era. *The Motels* is a fairly cold, almost robotic affair which trades in lyrics that explore the darker side of life in Los Angeles. There are a few tracks that bear repeated listens like the frantic "Kix" and "Celia," a warning to a woman involved with the wrong guy. "Total Control," a big hit for the band in Australia and later covered by Tina Turner, is the album's standout with its menacing lyrics of possession delivered by Martha Davis. She is the one consistently redeeming attraction of this dated record. Although she tends to over-sing at times, Davis is a riveting and sensual vocalists and her vocals hint at the potential in the band. *—Tom Demalon*

Careful / 1980 / Capitol ✦✦✦✦
With their second release, the Motels make steps toward a more seamless style of new wave-inflected pop. *Careful* kicks off with the perky, sax-driven "Danger," and there are more hits than misses. The lyrics still lean toward the darker side as on the moody, watercolor melody of the title track, but there are also moments that are pop gems like the Europop-styled "Bonjour Baby," the mid-tempo rock of "Days Are O.K. (But the Nights Were Made for Love)," which features the album's catchiest hook, and the up-tempo "Cry Baby." Martha Davis, with her distinctive vocals, is still the band's trump card, but this time around the band gives her a little more backing. *—Tom Demalon*

All 4 One / 1982 / One Way ✦✦✦✦✦
The Motels' third album *All 4 One* finds the group working the fine line between

mainstream arena-rock and quirky new wave pop. Their roots lie in the sleek, polished Californian hard rock that dominated late-'70s and early-'80s album-oriented radio, but *All 4 One* has a shiny new wave production, complete with keyboards and processed guitars. Still, it plays like arena rock, especially since Martha Davis oversings each track, but its best moments—"Take the L" (out of lover and it's over) and the single "Only the Lonely"—are embarrassingly catchy guilty pleasures that make the album an entertaining nostalgia piece. One Way's CD reissue is even more attractive, since it adds the group's two other big singles, "Suddenly Last Summer" and "Shame," as bonus tracks. —*Stephen Thomas Erlewine*

Little Robbers / 1983 / One Way ✦✦✦✦✦
Little Robbers, the follow-up to the Motels' commercial breakthrough *All 4 One*, is nearly as consistent as its predecessor, finding the perfect balance between mainstream rock conventions and quirky new wave flourishes. Again, the singles are the best parts of the record, with the hazy "Suddenly Last Summer" deservedly reaching the Top Ten and "Remember the Nights" being a fine AOR workout, but the remainder of the album suffers from undistinguished material and a distinct lack of hooks. —*Stephen Thomas Erlewine*

Shock / 1985 / Capitol ✦✦

Policy / 1987 / Capitol ✦✦

● **No Vacancy: The Best of the Motels** / 1990 / Capitol ✦✦✦✦✦
All five of the Motels' albums are well worth acquiring—even 1985's more commercial *Shock*. But for an introductory overview of the often dark and unsettling band's legacy, *No Vacancy* is highly recommended. This superb CD boasts all of the songs the Motels were best known for, including the dreamy "Suddenly Last Summer," the clever "Little Robbers," and the melancholy hits "Only the Lonely" and "Take the L." But as *No Vacancy* illustrates, they had many more artistic triumphs than those hits. Often compared to the Doors, the Motels didn't sound very much like Jim Morrison and company—but paralleled that fellow L.A. band in that they were experts when it came to depicting Hollywood's darker side. Classics like "So L.A.," "Apocalypso," and the troubling "Celia" brilliantly capture the type of emotional desperation that's prevalent in Tinseltown. Meanwhile, Pat Benatar is a valid comparison on "Cries and Whispers" and "Shame," both examples of the slicker, more commercial direction the Motels were taking in the end. But even at her most commercial, the charismatic Martha Davis sounds soulful and inspired. —*Alex Henderson*

Anthologyland / Oct. 17, 2000 / Oglio ✦✦✦
Designed as a supplement to (not a replacement for) the *No Vacancy* best-of, *Anthologyland* is a double-disc compilation of Motels demos, outtakes, live cuts, and other rarities. Prepared with the help of Martha Davis, *Anthologyland* effectively works as a hidden history of the band, featuring alternate versions of most of their key songs, plus obscurities like their demo of "Take My Breath Away," the *Top Gun* love theme that ended up assigned to Berlin instead. Casual fans won't find this all that necessary, but for devotees, *Anthologyland* is a treasure trove. —*Steve Huey*

Mother Love Bone
f. 1988, db. 1990
Grunge, Heavy Metal, Hard Rock
When other Seattle bands were releasing singles and EPs of hard garage grunge, Mother Love Bone had their sights set on the arenas, making a grandiose heavy metal that recalled Zeppelin and Aerosmith with a slight punk fervor; in a sense, the band was a response to Guns & Roses' sleazy guitar boogie. Considering that guitarist Stone Gossard and bassist Jeff Ament formed the rhythmic core of the Stooges-soaked Green River, it was a little strange that the band played it so safe, but that was mainly due to the lead vocalist, Andrew Wood. Wood was a modern-day hippie, preaching love and understanding, as well as a healthy dose of sex. Most of the hooks came from Gossard and Ament, but Wood was the focal point. The band was set to make their stab at the big time with 1990's *Apple*, but Wood died of a heroin overdose before it was released; the *Temple of the Dog* album, featuring Gossard, Ament, Soundgarden's Matt Cameron and Chris Cornell, and vocalist Eddie Vedder, was released as a tribute to him.

Gossard and Ament went on to form Pearl Jam, which took many of the hard rock elements of Mother Love Bone, except it was rawer and more honest. Also, Pearl Jam had a distinctive lead vocalist and lyricist in Eddie Vedder, who easily eclipsed the macho posturings of Wood. —*Stephen Thomas Erlewine*

● **Stardog Champion** / 1990 / Stardog ✦✦✦✦✦
Released after the phenomenal success of Pearl Jam, *Mother Love Bone* collects everything Mother Love Bone ever released. Their resurrection of the epic hard rock of the 1970s was quite good, but also derivative. While Wood was a fine singer, he wasn't a very original vocalist and often sounded very similar to Robert Plant. *Mother Love Bone* is the definitive collection of the band and worth the time of fans of Pearl Jam and the Seattle scene. —*Stephen Thomas Erlewine*

Mötley Crüe
f. 1981
Pop-Metal, Album Rock, Hair Metal, Heavy Metal, Hard Rock
Known for having more "sex, drugs, and rock & roll" than any other band in rock history, Mötley Crüe's infamous reputation left them a force to be reckoned with in the '80s, and that reputation evolved into the '90s as the band continued to retain massive record sales. Some know them best for their controversial approaches to metal; others might remember them as the performers of such songs as "Wild Side" and "Dr. Feelgood," but no one knows the Crüe better than the bands they have influenced, from Lita Ford to Ratt to Guns & Roses to Marilyn Manson. These four high school dropouts who seemed rejected by the rest of the world—singer Vince Neil, guitarist Mick Mars, bassist Nikki Sixx, and drummer Tommy Lee—eventually became one of the biggest metal bands of all time, but their road to success was anything but easy. —*Barry Weber*

Too Fast for Love / 1981 / Motley/Beyond ✦✦✦✦
On their debut album, Mötley Crüe essentially comes across as a bash-'em-out bar band, making up in enthusiasm what they lack in technical skill. Yet that's part of the appeal of *Too Fast for Love*, a chance to hear the band without the glossy production of their later, most popular work, showcasing their down-and-dirty roots. The fact that pop-metal songwriting was not really a consideration helps the album come off as more genuinely trashy and sleazy, celebrating its own grime with exuberant zest. This is the Crüe playing it lean and mean, effortlessly capturing the tough swagger that often came off a bit more calculated in later years, and it's one of their most invigorating records. [In 1999, the Crüe remastered and reissued *Too Fast for Love* on their own Motley/Beyond label with four bonus tracks: three interesting previously unreleased songs and a version of the title track with a different intro.] —*Steve Huey*

Shout at the Devil / 1983 / Motley/Beyond ✦✦✦✦✦
Shout at the Devil displays Mötley Crüe's sleazy, notorious (yet quite entertaining) metal at its best. When compared to its predecessor, *Too Fast for Love*, one can see that the band's musical range has certainly widened over the course of these two albums; the record features catchy, hard-rocking songs, but also includes an instrumental ("God Bless the Children of the Beast") and a powerful cover of the Beatles' "Helter Skelter." While such later albums as *Dr. Feelgood* would achieve a higher amount of critical acclaim, no present Mötley Crüe album surpasses the quality of *Shout at the Devil*. [In 1999, the Crüe remastered and reissued *Shout at the Devil* on their own Motley/Beyond label with four bonus tracks: three demos, including versions of the title track and "Looks That Kill," and a previously unreleased song.] —*Barry Weber*

Theater of Pain / 1985 / Motley/Beyond ✦✦✦✦
Backing away from the mild pseudo-Satanic posturing on parts of *Shout at the Devil* in favor of a more glammed-up image, Mötley Crüe really began to hit their commercial stride with *Theatre of Pain*, which broke them on MTV with the power ballad "Home Sweet Home" and a remake of Brownsville Station's "Smokin' in the Boys Room"; the latter also landed them on the Top 40 singles chart for the first time. Overall, the guitar riffing sounds less *heavy* metal and more pop-metal; similarly, the sound of the record is slicker and more arranged, polished for mainstream acceptance and airplay. A higher percentage of dull filler has crept into the songwriting, but there are still enough high points to rescue the album's momentum. [In 1999, the Crüe remastered and reissued *Theatre of Pain* on their own Motley/Beyond label with five bonus tracks: demos of "Home Sweet Home," "Keep Your Eye on the Money," and "City Boy Blues," plus rough mixes of "Smokin' in the Boys Room" and "Home Sweet Home" (the latter an instrumental).] —*Steve Huey*

Girls, Girls, Girls / 1987 / Motley/Beyond ✦✦✦✦
Girls, Girls, Girls continued Mötley Crüe's commercial hot streak, eventually going quadruple-platinum as its predecessor *Theatre of Pain* had; meanwhile, the title track brought them their second Top 20 single, and "Wild Side" became a popular MTV item. In general, the Crüe really plays up the sleaze factor on this album, trying to recapture some of the street-tough grittiness that fueled *Too Fast for Love*—even appearing on the cover astride motorcycles and wearing leather; this time around, the influence of Aerosmith is felt to a much greater degree. The production is too polished to really give the record a raw, dirty feel, but the raunchiness comes through all the same. Again, there's a bit of filler, as though the band knew they didn't have to make a *completely* consistent record to maintain their popularity, but there are enough high points along the way to make *Girls, Girls, Girls* an entertaining party-metal platter. (In 1999, the Crüe remastered and reissued *Girls, Girls, Girls* on their own Motley/Beyond label with four bonus tracks: instrumental mixes of three selections, plus the previously unreleased song "Rodeo.") —*Steve Huey*

Dr. Feelgood / Sep. 1989 / Motley/Beyond ✦✦✦✦✦
Mötley Crüe's albums were a lot like episodes of *Married With Children* in the sense that they may not be great works of art, but can be darn entertaining. With Bob Rock serving as producer, the L.A. headbangers savor the joys of trashy, unapologetically decadent fun on *Dr. Feelgood*—an album that makes no pretense at being anything else. While nothing here is quite as commanding as "Shout at the Devil," "Wild Side," or "Live Wire," such hook-oriented MTV smashes as "Kickstart My Heart," the amusing "Don't Go Away Mad (Just Go Away)" and the title song are infectious and hard to resist, and helped make this the best-selling Mötley Crüe album ever, as well as providing their first Top Ten singles. Unfortunately, the album would be lead singer Vince Neil's last album with the band. Neil's departure—and pop/metal's decline in popularity in the mid-'90s—proved to be severe blows to Mötley Crüe. [In 1999, the Crüe remastered and reissued *Dr. Feelgood* on their own Motley/Beyond label with bonus tracks.] —*Alex Henderson*

Decade of Decadence / 1991 / Elektra ✦✦✦✦✦
Elektra Entertainment drew on the five albums Mötley Crüe had recorded in the 1980s and threw in a few new songs as well when assembling the best-of collection *Decade of Decadence*. The title couldn't be more appropriate—whether the subject matter is strippers ("Girls, Girls, Girls") or the occult ("Shout at the Devil"), Crüe delights in some of rock's sleaziest decadence since Kiss and Sweet. Die-hard aficionados will already be more than familiar with such headbanger classics as "Looks That Kill," "Wild Side," and "Piece of Your Action," but for those new to the band's metal and hard rock, the album isn't a bad introduction at all. The previously unreleased material includes a live version of "Kickstart My Heart" and an ironic cover of the Sex Pistols' "Anarchy in the U.K." In the

'70s, the punk and metal audiences were hardly the best of friends; but in the '80s, it became downright fashionable for headbangers to embrace punk. *—Alex Henderson*

Mötley Crüe / Mar. 15, 1994 / Motley/Beyond ✦✦

Generation Swine / Jun. 24, 1997 / Motley/Beyond ✦✦

● **Greatest Hits** / Oct. 27, 1998 / Motley/Beyond ✦✦✦✦✦
Mötley Crüe parted ways with Elektra in the spring of 1998, releasing their second compilation, *Greatest Hits*, on their own label that fall. Weighing in at 17 tracks, including two pedestrian new songs, *Greatest Hits* duplicates much of *Decade of Decadence* featuring no less than eight songs—"Looks That Kill," "Home Sweet Home" (original, not the *Decade* version), "Smokin' in the Boys' Room," "Girls, Girls, Girls," "Wild Side," "Dr. Feelgood," "Kickstart My Heart" (original, not the live version that was on *Decade*), "Primal Scream"—that were on the previous collection. Considering all that overlap, you can be forgiven for thinking that the two compilations are interchangeable, but *Greatest Hits* actually has the edge, not just because it doesn't feature the silly "Anarchy in the U.K." cover, but because it features a greater selection of hits from their masterpiece, *Dr. Feelgood*, including "Without You," "Don't Go Away Mad (Just Go Away)," and "Same Ol' Situation (S.O.S.)," all of which weren't on *Decade*. It has its flaws, to be sure—the sequencing is illogical, the newer songs are lame, and the original "Shout at the Devil" should have been featured instead of the atrocious *Generation Swine* re-recording—but it's still the best overview yet assembled. *—Stephen Thomas Erlewine*

Supersonic and Demonic Relics / Jun. 29, 1999 / Motley/Beyond ✦✦

New Tattoo / Jun. 20, 2000 / Motley/Beyond ✦✦✦
Forget the stylistic dabbling and forced attempts to fit the '90s rock market that plagued Mötley Crüe throughout the decade. *New Tattoo* is a full-fledged return to their trademark sound: sleazy hard rock with a slight glam tinge (although not quite as much as before). And it's *really* sleazy, the band apparently having decided to return to their bread and butter with a vengeance. In spite of a couple of sentimental ballads, odes to prostitutes, S&M, erotic-cabaret stars, glue-sniffing trailer-park teenage girls, and even a corny nod to Internet porn dominate the record. It seems like a conscious determination on the band's part to outdo themselves in the lewdness department, perhaps because they've realized that making concessions to '90s trends isn't really their forte, or perhaps as a pointed reaction against the lack of hedonism in the vast majority of '90s rock. There's more than a hint of bitterness about all of that on "1st Band on the Moon" and "Fake"; the former is more playful, lamenting the disappearance of party-hearty arena rock and horny groupies, while the latter is an angry, unfocused rant against greedy record-industry hypocrites (ironically, "Fake" seems dissatisfied with the rock & roll lifestyle the band spends the rest of the album singing about). The songwriting is occasionally somewhat lackluster, but never as erratic as *Generation Swine*, and even if there aren't any classic singles here on the level of the band's best work in the '80s, the material overall is pretty consistently melodic. By this point, anyone who still follows Mötley Crüe is likely to be a rabid diehard, and that (actually rather substantial) fan base will be ecstatic over *New Tattoo*. *—Steve Huey*

Motörhead

f. 1975, London, England, **db.** 1982
New Wave of British Heavy Metal, British Metal, Speed Metal, Heavy Metal, Thrash, Hard Rock
Motörhead's overwhelmingly loud and fast style of heavy metal was one of the most groundbreaking styles the genre had to offer in the late '70s. Though the group's leader Lemmy Kilminster had his roots in the hard-rocking space-rock band Hawkwind, Motörhead didn't bother with his old group's progressive tendencies, choosing to amplify the heavy biker-rock elements of Hawkwind with the speed of punk rock. Motörhead wasn't punk rock—they formed before the Sex Pistols and they loved the hell-for-leather imagery of bikers too much to conform with the safety-pinned, ripped T-shirts of punk—but they were the first metal band to harness that energy and, in the process, they created speed-metal and thrash-metal. Unlike many of their contemporaries, Motörhead continued performing well into the '90s. Although the band changed its lineup many, many times—Lemmy was its only consistent member—they never changed their raging sound. *—Stephen Thomas Erlewine*

Motörhead / 1977 / Roadrunner ✦✦✦
Before forming Motörhead, Ian Kilmister (aka Lemmy) could boast of having been a member of space-rock cowboys Hawkwind and a career in horsebreaking (that's horsebreaking, not housebreaking). He was also, to top it all, the son of a vicar. Having been expelled from his former employers after a disagreement with border guards over the contents of his luggage, he took the name for his new band from the final song he'd written for Hawkwind. Together with Larry Wallis of the Pink Fairies and drummer Philthy Animal Taylor, Motörhead recorded a debut album that was rejected by United Artists (you can just imagine the face of the poor guy who got the short straw and had to *tell* Lemmy), though it was eventually released as *On Parole* in 1979. As a result, the group expanded with the addition of "Fast" Eddie Clarke on guitar. Wallis then left after just one rehearsal, leaving the classic Motörhead lineup in shape for their debut proper. Rock & roll had never heard the like. Though only a minor chart success, *Motörhead* patented the group's style: Lemmy's rasping vocal over a speeding juggernaut of guitar, bass, and drums. The lyrical theme was "Don't mess with us" instead of "Don't mess with our hair." Before this, hard rock was about musicianship and exhibitionism. Motörhead, conversely, returned mainstream rock to its most brutal base elements—no wonder the punks liked them. *—Alex Ogg*

Overkill / 1979 / Castle Music America ✦✦✦✦✦
While Motörhead's self-titled debut had performed respectfully on the British charts, it was their second release, 1979's *Overkill*, that went Top 30, selling 100,000 units in Europe (all the while without proper distribution in the U.S.). Produced by ex-Rolling Stones main man Jimmy Miller (*Sticky Fingers, Exile on Main Street*), *Overkill* can be pinpointed as the album that finally focused the Motörhead sound—part metal, part punk, and part good old rock & roll. While several tracks would become cornerstones for their superb 1981 live album *No Sleep 'Til Hammersmith* (such as the title track, "Stay Clean," "Capricorn," "No Class," and "Metropolis"), other lesser-known tracks are just as exceptional—"(I Won't) Pay Your Price," "Damage Case," "Limb From Limb," etc. Included on the 1999 Castle reissue were five bonus tracks, including such B-sides as "Too Late, Too Late" and "Like a Nightmare," as well as a fun cover of the party standard "Louie Louie." *—Greg Prato*

Bomber / 1979 / Castle ✦✦✦✦
Sensing that the commercial tides were changing for them by mid-1979 (thanks to the surprise chart success of *Overkill*), the mighty Motörhead returned to studio to issue their second release of the year, *Bomber*. Again behind the boards was longtime Rolling Stones producer Jimmy Miller, and while it was another solid outing, with hindsight it was a shade less exceptional as its predecessor was or its successor (1980's *Ace of Spades*) would be. Still, the trio of Lemmy, "Fast" Eddie Clarke, and "Philthy Animal" Taylor are in fine form, cranking out another slab of prime metallic punk. "Stone Dead Forever" and the album-closing title track proved to be the best-known selections, while other standouts include "Dead Men Tell No Tales," "Stone Dead Forever," and "Poison." *Bomber* proved that its predecessor's success was no fluke, becoming the band's first to crack the U.K. Top 20, and reaching Number 12 on the album chart. Included on the 1999 Castle reissue was the B-side "Over the Top," as well as the four-track live EP *The Golden Years*. *—Greg Prato*

Ace of Spades / 1980 / Castle Music America ✦✦✦✦✦
1980's *Ace of Spades* was the album that put Motörhead on the top of the heavy metal heap, albeit for a brief length of time. The band's raw sound was still in place, but the anthemic title track broke the band through to a broader audience; the single reached the British Top 20, while the album peaked at number four on the charts. The trio couldn't have picked a better time to issue their best studio album yet, as England was in the midst of a massive heavy metal movement—bands such as Australia's AC/DC and Judas Priest had released big albums, while newcomers such as Iron Maiden and Def Leppard were making a big splash as well. As with 1979's *Overkill*, Lemmy & Co. had issued another extremely consistent album—while tracks such as "(We Are) The Road Crew" and "The Hammer" would become instant concert standards, such lesser-known titles as "Shoot You in the Back," "Jailbait," and the brief "Bite the Bullet" are all standouts as well. Unfortunately, *Ace of Spades* would prove to be original lineup's last classic studio album; Lemmy would be the only original member remaining by 1984. The 1999 Castle reissue included three bonus tracks, including the B-side "Dirty Love" and a Top Five collaboration with the U.K. all-female metal band Girlschool, "Please Don't Touch." *—Greg Prato*

No Sleep 'Til Hammersmith / 1981 / Castle Music America ✦✦✦✦✦
If you had to pinpoint an album that gave birth to thrash metal, many metalheads would agree it was Motörhead's classic 1981 live album *No Sleep 'Til Hammersmith*. The original lineup of Motörhead was sheer electricity and excitement in concert, and the live set captures the trio at their peak. Nearly all of the best tracks from their first four studio albums are featured here (1977's self-titled debut, 1979's *Overkill* and *Bomber*, and 1980's *Ace of Spades*), but the live versions often prove to be even better than the originals. Such all-time metal anthems as "Ace of Spades," "Stay Clean," "(We Are) The Road Crew," "Overkill," "Bomber," and "Motörhead" are featured in all their eardrum-shattering glory, as is the mini-epic "Metropolis," "Iron Horse," and "No Class." Originally released on Bronze, the 1999 Castle reissue included excellent remastered sound, as well as three bonus tracks not on the original release—"Over the Top," "Capricorn (Alternative Version)," and a cover of the Yardbirds' blues-rock classic "Train Kept A-Rollin'." If you could only own a single Motörhead disc, *No Sleep 'Til Hammersmith* might be your best bet. *—Greg Prato*

Iron Fist / 1982 / Castle Music America ✦✦✦✦
Five years after its self-titled debut album, Motörhead wasn't compromising or softening its approach one iota. *Iron Fist* is state-of-the-art Motörhead—bombastic, abrasive, and thoroughly captivating. Having done more than its part to define the emerging thrash metal genre, Motörhead was known for taking no prisoners. And songs like "Speedfreak" (which could be considered a Motörhead manifesto), "Go to Hell," and the title song made it clear that it wasn't about to stop. The last album by the Lemmy/Fast Eddie Clarke/Philthy Animal Taylor edition of the band, *Fist* was reissued on CD in 1990 with the obscure "Remember Me, I'm Gone" added. *—Alex Henderson*

★ **No Remorse** / 1984 / Castle Music America ✦✦✦✦✦
1984's *No Remorse* is an awesome double-disc anthology of nothing but Motörhead's very best tracks. The 1999 reissue on Castle expanded the track listing to a meaty 29 selections, five of which weren't included on the original. While it doesn't come with a leather cover as the original limited-edition vinyl version did, the music still holds up as some of the most lethal, high-voltage heavy metal ever. Easily one of the most important and influential bands to come out of the late-'70s/early-'80s New Wave of British Heavy Metal movement (just listen to Metallica and Megadeth), *No Remorse* is the ultimate purchase for the newcomer just discovering this great outfit. Mixing studio with live material, highlights include the album-opening "Ace of Spades," "Stay Clean," "Iron Fist," "Overkill," "(We Are) The Road Crew," as well as a few interesting collaborations with Girlschool ("Please Don't Touch") and Wendy O. Williams ("No Class" and "Stand By Your Man"). There is no better Motörhead collection than *No Remorse*. *—Greg Prato*

Orgasmatron / 1986 / Castle Music America ✦✦✦
On the surface, Motörhead appear to be trying something new with *Orgasmatron*, bringing in producer Bill Laswell to put a slightly different slant on their signature sound. Laswell does beef up the mix with added sonic detail, which works to particularly good effect on the title track—the densely layered production helps transform the song and its simple riff into a chugging psychedelic noisefest. Elsewhere, the production sometimes has the effect of muting the band's energy, sounding oddly processed and lacking the raw bite of past work (which foreshadows their decline over the next few years). It doesn't help that the songwriting is somewhat inconsistent, with "Deaf Forever" and "Built for Speed" standing out amongst a batch of tunes that sometimes sound as though Motörhead was trying a little too self-consciously to do what people expected from a Motörhead album. Still, in Motörhead's case, that distinction is easily lost, so even if *Orgasmatron* is somewhat erratic, most fans will find a hidden favorite or two. [In 1999, Castle remastered and reissued *Orgasmatron* with three bonus tracks: live versions of "On the Road" and "Steal Your Face," taken from the "Deaf Forever" 12" single, and an alternate take of "Claw."] —*Steve Huey*

Rock & Roll / 1987 / Castle Music America ✦✦✦

1916 / Feb. 26, 1991 / WTG ✦✦✦✦✦
Lemmy Kilmister had been leading Motörhead for 16 years by the time *1916* was recorded in 1991. Over the years, Motörhead had experienced more than its share of personnel changes—and in fact, Kilmister was its only remaining original member. But the band's sound hadn't changed much, and time hadn't made its sledgehammer approach any less appealing. As sobering as his reflections on the horrors of World War I are on the title song, he's unapologetically amusing on "Going to Brazil," "Angel City" (an ode to the "beautiful" party people of L.A.), and "Ramones" (which salutes the New York punk band). Whether the subject matter is humorously fun or more serious, Motörhead is as inspired as ever on *1916*. —*Alex Henderson*

March or Die / Jul. 14, 1992 / WTG ✦✦
All the Aces: The Best of Motörhead / 1993 / Roadrunner ✦✦✦✦
Although it isn't as extensive as *No Remorse*, *All the Aces: The Best of Motörhead* does gather the best of the best of that collection, as well as the cream of the uneven, Bill Laswell-produced *Orgasmatron* (although the "Ace of Spades" remix which closes the original track listing could have been left off in favor of another, more necessary item). There's plenty of quality material from Motörhead's early-'80s heyday that didn't make the cut here, so it's better to think of *All the Aces* as a concise survey rather than a definitive encapsulation. But it is a very good concise survey. [In 1999, Castle reissued *All the Aces* with two live bonus tracks and a separate bonus disc titled *The Muggers Tapes*, a live recording of a side project called the Muggers featuring Eddie Clarke, Phil Taylor, John "Speedy" Keen, and Billy Wrath. It's closer to heavy pub rock than metal, and it's designed to entice the Motörhead rarities collector who already has the material here; it pales in comparison to the power of the Motörhead songs, and non-collectors probably won't find it all that crucial.] —*Steve Huey*

Overnight Sensation / Oct. 15, 1996 / CMC International ✦✦✦✦
Following the extremely thrashy *Sacrifice*, Motörhead returned to their typical three-chord rock & roll onslaught with 1996's *Overnight Sensation*. Also the band's most eclectic in years, its tracks range from pedal to the metal stompers like "Civil War" and "Eat the Gun" to mid-paced groovers like "Listen to Your Heart" (featuring acoustic guitars—shock!) and the classy "I Don't Believe a Word." Always a great lyricist, vocalist/bassist Lemmy takes it up a notch with the highly ironic title track and what is quite possibly the band's greatest song of the decade, the exceptionally funny "Crazy Like a Fox." Despite its terrifying cover (featuring the trio's ugly mugs instead of the band's trademark iron monster), this wonderfully raw and honest record is guaranteed to please, especially older fans. —*Ed Rivadavia*

Motors
f. 1977, **db.** 1980
Pub Rock, Power Pop, New Wave
After several years in England's pub rock scene, ex-Duck Deluxe members Nick Garvey and Andy McMaster formed the Motors in 1977 with vocalist Bram Tchaikovsky and drummer Ricky Slaughter. Their first album was a splendid piece of guitar-driven pop/rock highlighted by the single "Dancing the Night Away." *Approved By* was the album that earned them the U.K. hits "Airport" and "Forget About You"; the record saw the band's songwriting improving with forceful melodies and invigorating performances. After that record, the Motors split up; Garvey and McMaster used the band's name for the 1980 album *Tenement Steps*, which didn't equal the spark of their first two records. —*Stephen Thomas Erlewine*

Motors 1 / 1977 / Virgin ✦✦✦
Their debut features a reworked version of pub rock with an edgier punk feel. Includes the catchy single "Dancing the Night Away," the high point of the album. —*Chris Woodstra*

Approved by the Motors / 1978 / Virgin ✦✦✦✦✦
Their second album shows a marked improvement over the debut, with a stronger melodic base and catchier songs including the British hits "Airport" and "Forget About You." The CD version adds three bonus tracks. —*Chris Woodstra*

Tenement Steps / 1980 / Virgin ✦✦
The band, now reduced to Nick Garvey and Andy McMaster, is a little too ambitious and overproduced. While not their best album, it does include one of their finest songs, "Love

and Loneliness," making it worthwhile for those who liked the first two albums. Essential for collectors if only for the uniquely shaped sleeve. —*Chris Woodstra*

● **Airport: The Motors' Greatest Hits** / Apr. 25, 1995 / Caroline ✦✦✦✦✦
A solid collection of the band's best moments, *Airport* provides a good introduction for the uninitiated, drawing from the brilliant first two albums and the lesser *Tenement Steps*. —*Chris Woodstra*

Mott the Hoople
f. 1969, **db.** 1976
Album Rock, Proto-Punk, Glam Rock, Hard Rock
Mott the Hoople are one of the great also-rans in the history of rock & roll. Though the band scored a number of album-rock hits in the early '70s, they never quite broke through into the mainstream. Nevertheless, their nasty fusion of heavy metal, glam rock, and Bob Dylan's sneering hipster cynicism provided the groundwork for many British punk bands, most notably the Clash. At the center of Mott the Hoople was lead vocalist/pianist Ian Hunter, a late addition to the band who developed into its focal point as his songwriting grew. Hunter was able to subvert rock & roll conventions with his lyrics and the band, led by guitarist Mick Ralphs, had a tough, muscular sound that kept the band firmly in hard-rock territory, even when they flirted with homosexual imagery and glammy makeup. However, the group's lack of success meant that they inevitably splintered apart in the '70s, with Ralphs forming Bad Company and Hunter launching a cult solo career. —*Stephen Thomas Erlewine*

Mott the Hoople / 1969 / Atlantic ✦✦✦✦
Enough works on Mott the Hoople's eponymous debut album, and enough is so imaginatively freewheeling, that it's easier to think of the record as a bit more successful than it actually is. After all, their combination of Stonesy swagger, Kinksian crunch, and Dylanesque cynicism is one of the great blueprints for hard rock, and its potential is apparent the moment their monumental instrumental "You Really Got Me" kicks off the record. This is followed by two covers, Doug Sahm's "At the Crossroads" and Sonny Bono's "Laugh at Me," that demonstrate their musicality more than their depth, since all three of these songs sound like they derive from the same vantage point. Then, to cap it off, Ian Hunter turns in "Backsliding Fearlessly" and Mick Ralphs gives Mott their first anthem with the pile-driving "Rock & Roll Queen." Up to this point, the album is wildly imaginative and invigorating, and that's enough to make this a fine debut, even if it falls off the tracks during the second side. The first side and those two originals reveal a band whose rowdy power is matched by sly humor, clever twists, and fierce intelligence—all qualities they built a career on, and this blueprint still stands the test of time. —*Stephen Thomas Erlewine*

Mad Shadows / 1970 / Atlantic ✦✦
Brain Capers / 1971 / Atlantic ✦✦✦✦✦
Re-teaming with producer Guy Stevens, Mott the Hoople delivered the great forgotten British hard rock album with their fourth album, *Brain Capers*. Stevens was a legendary rock & roll wild man and he kept Mott careening through their performances; they sound harder than ever, even dangerous at times. This fortunately coincided with Ian Hunter's emergence as a fantastic songwriter, as tuneful and clever as any of his peers. All these changes are evident from the moment *Brain Capers* kicks in with the monumental "Death May Be Your Santa Claus," a phenomenally pile-driving number that just seems *inevitable*. As it gives way to a cover of Dion's "Your Own Backyard," it becomes clear that Mott has pulled off the trick of being sensitive while still rocking. And that's not the end of it—they ride an epic wave on the nine-minute "The Journey," pull off a love song on "Sweet Angeline," and generally rock like hell throughout the record. The most amazing thing about the album is that none of the songs really change character—it's all straightforward hard rock, graced with Dylanesque organ—but there are all sorts of variations on that basic sound, proving how versatile they are. It's a fantastic album, the culmination of their early years. When a record this confident and tremendous stiffed, it's little wonder they thought about chucking it all in; and it isn't a surprise that, when they decided to continue, it was with a change in sound. They couldn't have topped this if they tried. —*Stephen Thomas Erlewine*

Wildlife / 1971 / Atlantic ✦✦✦✦
Since they had little success and seemed to be going off the tracks, Mott the Hoople was encouraged to produce their third album with anyone that wasn't Guy Stevens. Eventually, they chose themselves, creating a record that is bright and punchy, standing in direct contrast to *Mad Shadow*'s enveloping fog. They wound up with *Wildlife*, a record that still seems a little transitional, yet is considerably more confident, unified, and enjoyable. Ironically, even if this is a much better record, few songs are as immediately gripping as "Walkin' With a Mountain," but both Mick Ralphs and Ian Hunter turn out some fine rockers, while driving the group toward some interesting territory, like the string-drenched "Waterlow," the country-tinged "It Must Be Love," and the ambling "Original Mixed-Up Kid," or even the surprisingly straight and faithful reading of Melanie's "Lay Down." These give the record a slightly rural feel, lending credence to the title, and the album is unique in Mott's decidedly urban body of work for that very reason—it's lighter, quirkier, more friendly than the rest. Of course, it didn't widen their audience, and they returned to brutal rock with *Brain Capers*, but in retrospect it's a charming anomaly in their catalog. —*Stephen Thomas Erlewine*

☆ **All the Young Dudes** / 1972 / Columbia ✦✦✦✦✦
Just at the moment they were calling it a day, David Bowie swooped in and convinced them to stick around. Bowie spearheaded an image makeover, urging them to glam themselves up. He gave them a surefire hit with "All the Young Dudes," had them cover his idol's "Sweet Jane," and produced *All the Young Dudes*, the album that was designed to

make them stars. Lo and behold, it did, which is as much a testament to Bowie's popularity as it is to his studio skill. Not to discount his assistance, since his production results in one of the most satisfying glam records and the title track is one of the all-time great rock songs, but the album wouldn't have worked if Mott hadn't already found its voice on *Brain Capers*. True, *Dudes* isn't nearly as wild as its predecessor, but the band's swagger is unmistakable underneath the flair and Hunter remains on a songwriting roll, with "Momma's Little Jewel," "Sucker," and "One of the Boys" standing among his best. Take a close look at the credits, though—these were all co-written by his bandmates, and the other highlight, "Ready for Love/After Lights," is penned entirely by Mick Ralphs who would later revive the first section with Bad Company. The entire band was on a roll here, turning out great performances and writing with vigor. They may not be as sexy as either Bowie or Bolan, but they make up for it with knowing humor, huge riffs, and terrific tunes, dressed up with style by Ziggy himself. No wonder it's not just a great Mott record—it's one of the defining glam platters. *—Stephen Thomas Erlewine*

☆ **Mott** / 1973 / Columbia ✦✦✦✦✦
All the Young Dudes actually brought Mott the Hoople success, but you wouldn't know that from its sequel, *Mott*. Ian Hunter's songs are a set of road tales fraught with exhaustion, disillusionment, and dashed dreams, all told with a wry sense of humor so evident on Mott's earlier work. So, this is no ordinary road album, where a band whines about the perils of traveling—it's more of a wry commentary on rock & roll itself, which, as Hunter notes, is a "loser's game." *Mott* doesn't sound that way, though—it's as winning and infectious as rock & roll gets. Even with the undercurrents of ironic despair and restrained hostility, this is a fun record (partially *because* of that despair and hostility, of course). This sounds better, looser, than *All the Young Dudes*, as the band jives through "All the Way From Memphis" and "Honaloochie Boogie," beats the living hell outta "Violence," swaggers on "Whizz Kid," and simply drives it home on "Drivin' Sister." Apart from the New York Dolls (who, after all, were in a league of their own), glam never sounds as *rock* as it does here. To top it all off, Hunter writes the best lament for rock ever with "Ballad of Mott the Hoople," a song that conveys just how heartbreaking rock & roll is for the average band. If that wasn't enough, he *trumps* that song with the closer "I Wish I Was Your Mother," a peerless breakup song that still surprises, even after it's familiar. It's a graceful, unexpected way to close a record that stands as one of the best of its era. *—Stephen Thomas Erlewine*

The Hoople / 1974 / Columbia ✦✦✦✦✦
Mott was so good that the sequel, appropriately named *The Hoople*, has been unfairly dismissed as not living up to the group's promise. Yes, it doesn't compare to its predecessor, but most records don't. The bigger problem is that Mick Ralphs chose to leave during the supporting tour for *Mott*, leaving Ian Hunter as the undisputed leader of the group and subtly changing the character of the band's sound. Even with Hunter as the band's main songwriter, Ralphs helped shape their musical direction, so without a collaborator in hand, Hunter was left without a center. So, it isn't surprising that the record seems a little uneven, both in terms of songwriting and sound, but it's hardly without merit. "Roll Away the Stone," a leftover from *Mott*, is first-rate; "Crash Street Kidds" rocks viciously; "The Golden Age of Rock & Roll" is a pleasant spin on Bowie-esque nostalgia (think "Drive-In Saturday"); and Overend Watts follows through on that theme with "Born Late '58," a perfectly credible rocker. This all makes *The Hoople* an entertaining listen, even if it doesn't compare to Mott's earlier masterpieces. *—Stephen Thomas Erlewine*

Mott the Hoople Live / 1974 / Columbia ✦✦✦
By 1974, Mott the Hoople was quite possibly the greatest concert band in the world, a blur of high-energy rock, high content poetics, and high camp costuming—Ian Hunter the tough guy in leather and shades; Ariel Bender the street kid, all satin hat flash; Overend Watts, the freakoid in skyscraper thigh boots; and a live show which out-dressed the lot of them. If any band deserved a live album, it was Mott. And if any live album failed to deliver, it was this one. Two shows recorded five months and two continents apart (London's Hammersmith Odeon in December 1973; New York's Uris Theater in May 1974) are highlighted by just seven songs and one medley. The hits "All the Young Dudes" and "All the Way From Memphis," of course, are present, but the remainder of the track list is bizarre to say the least—the ballads "Rest in Peace" and "Rose" were British B-sides only, while "Sucker," "Walking With a Mountain," and "Sweet Angeline" were never much more than filler on their own original albums. It is a great album in its own way, the band are in terrific form, and Bender plays the guitar hero better than anyone else of his entire generation. But Mott gigs, like their albums, were about more than simple snapshots—that was what made the band so important, that's what made their music so memorable. And that's what the fearfully episodic *Live* completely overlooks. *—Dave Thompson*

Drive On / 1975 / Columbia ✦✦

Greatest Hits / 1975 / Columbia ✦✦✦
A petty little package this is, and no mistake. It was no secret, of course, that the end of Mott the Hoople was a rancorous, bitter affair. But while former frontman Ian Hunter was igniting his solo career with an album of songs which could have been Mott's, did his erstwhile bandmates truly have nothing better to occupy their time with than compiling a collection which not only skews all that they really achieved during three years of hits, but also undermines those who played on them as well? True, guitarist Mick Ronson was a member of the band for a mere matter of months before he split for a new band with Hunter; true, too, that his contributions to Mott's recorded catalog amounted to just one minor hit single, the spookily valedictory "Saturday Gigs." But to see his name in the same tiny print reserved for the session players who appear elsewhere revises history with semi-Stalinist zeal—or at least, spitefulness. Oh, the politics of pop, how important they all seemed at the time. Today, of course, *Greatest Hits* exists as a mere prelude to the flood of Mott compilations which have since hit the shelves, and one whose ten-song contents seem impossibly skimpy—you can be in and out of the album in under 40 minutes. But, in fairness, that was all that was demanded of it. Each of the band's U.K. hits is here, including two ("Foxy Foxy" and the aforementioned "Saturday Gigs") which, at the time, had yet to appear on LP, while two slabs of unabashedly autobiography from the *Mott* album and one more from *The Hoople* basically appear as bonus tracks. Sharp and to the point—would that all compilations could make their mark so unerringly! *—Dave Thompson*

Shouting and Pointing / 1976 / Columbia ✦

★ **The Ballad of Mott: A Retrospective** / Jun. 15, 1993 / Columbia/Legacy ✦✦✦✦✦
Although it was subsequently rendered academic by the release of the *All the Young Dudes* box set, *Ballad of Mott* would stand proud as the finest *Mott the Hoople* collection on the market for close to five years—and, in many ways, it remains so. The emphasis is on the band's years at the top, the 1972-74 period when they machine gunned out hit singles, at the same time as operating a virtual revolving door for guitarists. Mick Ralphs, Ariel Bender, and Mick Ronson all filed through the band during that period, and all three left some startling classics behind them—the tasteful effervescence of "All the Young Dudes," "Violence," and "Whizz Kid" (Ralphs); the playful flash of "Roll Away the Stone," "Crash Street Kids," and "Golden Age of Rock & Roll" (Bender); the majestic sobriety of "Saturday Gigs" and "Lounge Lizard"—both present here in previously unreleased form (Ronson). Of course all the hit singles are aboard, together with four well-chosen cuts from the band's years with Island/Atlantic in the days before fame came knocking. There's also some meaty rarities above and beyond the aforementioned—the jokey "Henry & the H Bombs," recorded during the *Dudes* sessions with producer David Bowie, a version of *The Hoople's* masterful "Through the Looking Glass," which dissolves midway through into an utterly unexpected barrage of invective; and the opening verse of Don McLean's "American Pie," with which Mott introduced their 1974 era tours. Add a clutch of U.K. B-sides (nothing spectacular, but nice to have), and a generous dose of primo album cuts and, while *The Ballad of Mott* did draw some criticism from a Mott fanbase which was hoping for even more vault-exhuming lovelies, in terms of truly telling the story, it's a peerless collection. Yes, even more so than the box set. *—Dave Thompson*

Backsliding Fearlessly: The Early Years / Apr. 19, 1994 / Rhino ✦✦✦✦✦
A compilation of 16 songs from their first four albums, covering their strongest material from the records pre-dating their *All the Young Dudes* breakthrough. This shows the band casting about, sometimes wildly, for an identity. The earliest tunes (including a cover of Sonny Bono's "Laugh at Me") are perhaps the most blatant imitations of Dylan's *Blonde on Blonde* period ever attempted. Subsequent efforts found them getting into boogie and hard rock, with a few Stones riffs copped here and there. The gut-stomping "Death May Be Your Santa Claus" is a highlight, and Ian Hunter's piano-based ballad "When My Mind's Gone" hints at the more complex psychological territory he'd explore during Mott's prime. This isn't bad and is often interesting, but it is neither very similar to Mott's best work, nor nearly as good as Mott's best stuff. Weirdest cut: a cover of Melanie's "Lay Down." But where is their instrumental version of "You Really Got Me"? *—Richie Unterberger*

Bob Mould

b. 1961, Malone, NY
Vocals, Guitar / College Rock, Indie Rock, Alternative Pop/Rock, Singer/Songwriter, American Underground
Guitarist/singer/songwriter Bob Mould was initially a member of Hüsker Dü, one of the most influential American bands of the '80s. Hüsker Dü was a post-hardcore punk band that helped define the sound and ideals of alternative rock. After Hüsker Dü broke up, Bob Mould signed a solo contract with Virgin in 1988 and released his first solo album, *Workbook*, one year later. A major shift in sonic direction, the album was an introspective collection, featuring keyboards, acoustic guitars, and even strings. Mould returned to loud, guitar-driven rock on his second solo album, 1990's *Black Sheets of Rain*. In 1992, he formed a new group named Sugar. Their debut album, *Copper Blue*, became Mould's most successful project to date. The second Sugar album, 1994's *File Under: Easy Listening*, received good reviews but didn't match the performance of *Copper Blue*. By 1995, Mould had broken up the band and begun to work on a third album entirely by himself. Mould played all of the instruments on his self-titled third album, which was released in the spring of 1996. *The Last Dog and Pony Show* followed in 1998. *—Stephen Thomas Erlewine*

● **Workbook** / Apr. 1989 / Virgin ✦✦✦✦✦
Arriving after years of sonic bombast in Hüsker Dü, the reflective, acoustic nature of Bob Mould's first solo album, *Workbook*, was a bold statement of renewal. Like all of Mould's work, it's an intensely introspective record, finding him purging demons left over from the dissolution of Hüsker Dü. Instead of relying on raging guitars, Mould explores a wide variety of styles, from pure pop ("See a Little Light") to reflective folk laced with cellos. It's an astonishing array of styles, and the songs are among Mould's finest. For many observers, the record established him as a major songwriter, but it also established a way for underground post-punk artists to mature—echoes of *Workbook* could be heard throughout the '90s, from R.E.M.'s elegiac *Automatic for the People* to Nirvana's use of cellos on *In Utero* and *Unplugged*. But *Workbook* remains a stunning work of individuality, marrying a distinctive body of songs with an original musical vision. Occasionally, the production is a little too pristine, but the power of the songs cannot be diminished. *—Stephen Thomas Erlewine*

Black Sheets of Rain / May 1990 / Virgin ✦✦✦
A scalding, monolithic collection of soul-baring lyrics and primal guitars, *Black Sheets of*

Rain is extremely powerful musically, but is also slightly monotonous. Nevertheless, the record features several inspired songs from Mould, including the catchy single "It's Too Late." *—Stephen Thomas Erlewine*

Poison Years / Jul. 26, 1994 / Virgin ✦✦✦
Drawing heavily from *Black Sheets of Rain*, this anthology of Mould's time at Virgin doesn't give enough space to the brilliant *Workbook*, but it does have several fiery live tracks, including a harrowing version of Richard Thompson's "Shoot Out the Lights." *—Stephen Thomas Erlewine*

Bob Mould / Apr. 30, 1996 / Rykodisc ✦✦✦✦✦
As he was promoting the last Sugar album, *File Under: Easy Listening*, Bob Mould hinted that he was tired of working with a band and was fascinated by the simple, four-track recordings of Sebadoh and Guided by Voices. So, it didn't come as a complete surprise when he disbanded Sugar a year after the release of *FU:EL* and began working on a record by himself. *Bob Mould*, his third solo album, was recorded entirely by Mould, but it doesn't sound like a lo-fi project—it doesn't have the professional production of Sugar's records, but it has all their sonic detail. What has changed is the details themselves. *Bob Mould* may not surge on waves of loud guitars like Hüsker Dü or Sugar, but Mould is reaching into new territory, using distortion as a coloring device and exploring trancier melodies. And Mould sounds revitalized throughout the album—although it is clear that this isn't a collection of first-takes, his obsession with making the album entirely on his own makes the music fierce and alive. Mould may be heading further into singer/songwriter territory with each album he releases, but he keeps his music away from stodginess by continually changing his approach and delving into new sonic territories. It also doesn't hurt that his increasingly bitter lyrics are gut-wrenchingly provocative and his melodies are consistently engaging. *—Stephen Thomas Erlewine*

The Last Dog and Pony Show / Aug. 25, 1998 / Rykodisc ✦✦✦✦
Just before *The Last Dog and Pony Show* hit the streets, Bob Mould announced that his supporting tour would be the last time he hit the road with a full electric band. From this point on, he would be challenging himself, finding different musical avenues to explore and leaving his trademark tower of guitars behind. Presumably, this also meant that *The Last Dog and Pony Show* would be the recorded farewell to this sound, and it is indeed an excellent consolidation of all of his musical quirks and signatures. *The Last Dog and Pony Show* is the work of a craftsman, not a nakedly emotional confessional like *Workbook* or *Bob Mould*. That's not to say the album is lightweight, since seriousness is one of Mould's signatures, but there is a sense of humor that hasn't been heard since Sugar, and he, overall, sounds more relaxed than he has in years. He's so relaxed, in fact, that he lets down his guard on the cheerfully ridiculous pseudo-rap "Megamanic," the only track on *Show* that offers a musical departure from Mould's past. The rest of the record is clearly a Mould album, from the rushing rockers to the impassioned acoustic ballads, but the craft in both the songwriting and the production guarantees that the music never sounds like a retread, even if it does sound familiar. And that's not a bad way to draw to a close the first part of his career, if Mould does indeed turn his back on his signature sound. *—Stephen Thomas Erlewine*

Mountain

f. 1969, Long Island, NY, **db.** 1972
Hard Rock
Hard-rock band Mountain was formed in 1969 by guitarist Leslie West and bassist and former Cream producer Felix Pappalardi. The two met while West was a member of Long Island R&B band the Vagrants, local heroes who never broke nationally; when West left to record the solo album *Leslie West—Mountain*, Pappalardi produced for him. The results were satisfying enough for the two to form a partnership, and Mountain's first lineup included drummer N.D. Smart and keyboardist Steve Knight. The group played its fourth live performance ever at Woodstock, after which Smart was replaced by Corky Laing. Their debut album, 1970's *Mountain Climbing*, went gold, thanks in part to the hard rock classic "Mississippi Queen." *Nantucket Sleighride* was equally successful, but the group failed to progress with its next album, and after *Mountain Live* in 1972, the group broke up. Pappalardi, whose hearing had been damaged by Mountain's excessive in-concert volume, returned to production, while West and Laing teamed up with ex-Cream bassist Jack Bruce under the name West, Bruce and Laing. A brief reunion featuring West and Pappalardi from the group's original lineup took place in 1974. In subsequent years, West and Laing revived the group for live shows, sometimes joined by Pappalardi; West also performed with his own Leslie West Band. Pappalardi was shot and killed by his wife in 1983. Two years later, West and Laing regrouped with Mark Clarke on bass and recorded an album before once again calling it quits. Laing has served as PolyGram's A&R vice president since 1989. *—Steve Huey*

Over the Top / Apr. 11, 1995 / Columbia/Legacy ✦✦✦✦✦
Over the Top is right. Two discs of Mountain, complete with all the AOR hits, unreleased tracks, two newly recorded songs, a nearly six-minute guitar solo and a 20-minute jam is a bit much for anyone but the most devoted Leslie West fans, yet the number of rarities and classy packaging make the set a necessary item for the dedicated. *—Stephen Thomas Erlewine*

Mouse & the Traps

Folk-Rock, Garage Rock, Psychedelic
This Tyler, TX, group from the mid-'60s is most known for their uncanny imitation of *Highway 61*-era Dylan, "A Public Execution." Featured on the *Nuggets* compilation, it is to Dylan what the Knickerbockers' "Lies" is to the Beatles: one of the few rip-offs so utterly accurate that it could easily fool listeners into mistaking it for the original article. Spearheaded by singer/songwriter Ronnie Weiss, the group actually recorded quite a few decent singles between 1965 and 1969 without approaching any sort of national recognition. "Mouse" never got as explicitly Dylanesque again, but there's no doubt that Weiss often recalled a non-atonal Dylan with his nasal delivery, and several of their singles were a much more melodic, pop-oriented extension of Dylan's mid-'60s sound. Recording almost exclusively original material, they were one of the better regional groups of the time, and also waxed some capable Texas punk-psychedelia and good-time pop-rockers. *—Richie Unterberger*

Public Execution / 1982 / Eva ✦✦✦✦✦
Nineteen-song compilation includes most of their '60s singles, as well as the 1966 single they recorded under the name Positively 13 O'Clock with singer Jimmy Rabbit. Most of the songs are original material of a pretty high standard; a good buy for '60s specialists. *—Richie Unterberger*

● **Fraternity Years** / Jun. 24, 1997 / Big Beat ✦✦✦✦✦
The first Mouse & the Traps compilation of a truly official nature, taken right from the master tapes. The 25 tracks do miss a few of their least essential cuts—the awful country novelty "Would You Believe," their mediocre final single for Bell, and the "Psychotic Reaction" single they recorded under the pseudonym of Positively 13 O'Clock. But everything else is here, with the neat bonuses of a 1967 single credited to *another* pseudonym (Chris St. John) and seven interesting previously unreleased sides, including the moving folk-rock-protest number "Nobody Cares" and a you-gotta-hear-it-to-believe-it cover of "You Are My Sunshine" (set to the arrangement of James Brown's "I Got You"!). The lengthy liner notes present the best history of the group ever written, capping an excellent reissue of a fine band who was probably too chameleon-like to find their niche in the national market. *—Richie Unterberger*

Mouse on Mars

f. 1993, Düsseldorf, Germany
IDM, Experimental Ambient, Experimental Techno, Electronica, Ambient Techno, Post-Rock/Experimental
German post-techno duo Mouse on Mars are among a growing number of electronic music groups dabbling in complex, heavily hybridized forms that include everything from ambient, techno, and dub to rock, jazz, and jungle. The combined efforts of Andi Toma and Jan St. Werner, MoM formed in 1993; working from Werner's studio, the pair fused an admiration for the early experiments of Krautrock outfits like Can, Neu!, Kluster, and Kraftwerk into an offbeat update including influences from the burgeoning German techno and ambient scenes. MoM's first single, "Frosch," was released by the Too Pure label soon after, and was also included on the debut album, *Vulvaland*. Immediately hailed for its beguiling, inventive edge that seemed to resist all efforts at easy "schublade" (an even less flattering approximation of the English "pigeonhole"). More upbeat and varied than their debut, *Iaora Tahiti* made some inroads into the American marketplace, but the group's somewhat challenging complexity and steadfast refusal to pander make widespread popularity unlikely. Werner also records as Microstoria with Oval's Markus Popp. *—Sean Cooper*

Vulvaland / 1994 / Too Pure/American ✦✦✦✦
A wibbly, barely digital match of ambient texturology with experimental strains of techno, dub, and Krautrock. While the flip relies too heavily on four-on-the-floor ambient house cliches, the A-side is a prize, cultivating a weird, electronics-based avant-pop vibe as successful as it is unique. *—Sean Cooper*

● **Iaora Tahiti** / Oct. 3, 1995 / Too Pure/American ✦✦✦✦✦
More upbeat and with far greater detail than the debut, *Iaora Tahiti* proves Werner and Toma haven't stood still. The pair's fondness for all things lo-fi follows them here, but just as evident is a depth and punch lacking in their earlier material. Jungle-style programming pops up on the first single, "Bib," as well as elements of dub, funk, industrial, film soundtracks, and musique concrete. *—Sean Cooper*

Cache Coeur Naif EP / 1997 / Too Pure ✦✦✦✦
In 1997, while American bands were struggling to incorporate the trendy gadgetry of electronica into their acts and major labels were running around trying to sign their own private Chemical Brothers, many of the European scene's more stalwart experimentalists (Aphex Twin, Warp Records, Mark Van Hoen, Witchman) were drawing on the catchiness of the pop tradition by adding vocalists, quoting '70s soul and jazz in their music, and/or (in Warp's case) signing jazz-funk (Jimi Tenor, Red Snapper) and rock (Broadcast) acts to their rosters. Mouse on Mars make their bid on the former with "Cache Coeur Naif," a 4-track EP (and the group's first release under their own name in more than two years) featuring Stereolab vocalists Mary Hansen and Laetitia Sadier. While only one of the songs features vocals in anything like a "pop" sense (verse-chorus-etc.), each incorporates at least a Hansen whisper or a Sadier purr (en Francaise, natch) wrapped around gloriously off-kilter, bleached-out dub-electro rhythms and the usual, Mars-bound assortment of wheezy bleeps, whirrs, and crackles. An excellent return. *—Sean Cooper*

Autoditacker / Aug. 18, 1997 / Too Pure ✦✦✦✦✦
Autoditacker finds Mouse on Mars continuing to grow and improve, adding textures and detail to their dense, electronic soundscapes without compromising their sound. They still are indebted to Krautrock and dub, but they continue to add new sounds and styles to their music, including long ambient stretches and flirtations with drum'n'bass. There are no silent moments on *Autoditacker*—every inch of the tape is filled with rhythms, keyboards, and electronic squiggles. Each listen reveals new layers of the group's intricate arrangements, and the shifting instrumentation and themes recall the best adventurous jazz in terms of unpredictability. It's another stunning record in a distinguished, inventive catalog. *—Stephen Thomas Erlewine*

Instrumentals / Oct. 13, 1997 / Thrill Jockey ✦✦✦✦✦

While previous releases such as *Vulvaland* and *Iaora Tahiti* had more or less their share of remarkable moments, *Instrumentals* was the closest thing yet to the sort of album the best of those moments suggested Mouse on Mars was capable of. Unlike the jittery pop-electronica of MoM's only months-previously issued *Autoditacker*, *Instrumentals* (released on their newly launched Sonig label) profiled the group's more relaxed, experimental side, working tracks up out of a mush of warm, sputtery electronics and vaguely bouncing rhythms. The album is only about 70 percent new material (it includes MoM's contributions to two Sub Rosa compilations dedicated to the work of philosopher Gilles Deleuze), but the placement of the two recycled tracks in the context of an album of which the rest matches them in both quality and atmosphere makes *Instrumentals* undoubtedly MoM's most enjoyable and consistent effort. —*Sean Cooper*

Glam / Jul. 20, 1998 / Sonig ✦✦✦✦✦

This LP of warm, grubby electronica was originally recorded as the soundtrack to an American film staring Tony "*Who's the Boss?*" Danza, and finally saw general (if somewhat limited) release in 1998, after it became clear the film would never be completed. Despite the passage of time, however (most of these tracks date from 1993 and 1994), *Glam* contains some of Toma and Werner's most compelling material to date, and listens like a sort of combined laboratory/proving ground for the dauby, impressionistic abstraction later pursued on the 1997 MoM LP *Instrumentals* and by Werner side project Lithops. The least "genrefied" of MoM's already exceptionally itinerant discography, *Glam* is also wonderfully diverse, mixing tracks containing clamorous, sometimes goofy rhythms with introspective cuts consisting of little more than patterned clicks and raspy, absorbing organ drones. —*Sean Cooper*

Niun Niggung / Feb. 8, 2000 / Thrill Jockey ✦✦✦✦

From the first few seconds of Mouse on Mars' sixth full-length, it appeared that Germany's most inventive duo had deserted the bubble'n'squeak electronica they'd trademarked and instead gone the way of instrument-driven post-rockers like Tortoise or Kreidler. There's a chamber quartet in attendance and a hushed air that sounds almost mature. After a minute of suspense though, things go all wibbly and electronic fans will find themselves back in the happy preserves of prime Mouse on Mars. The duo's vision of techno on *Niun Niggung* is impeccably perfectionist but texturally messy and surprisingly organic: it's electronic dance as produced by robotic hill-people. The highlight is "Super Sonig Fadeout," a propulsive track that begins with several moments of metallic distortion. Slowly, ingeniously, the noise organizes itself into a loping, incredibly funky beat that drives the rest of the track. The music on *Niun Niggung* is far too much fun to provoke the question of whether Toma and St. Werner have progressed or not (which is always a matter for serious analysis in electronic circles), but the album does occasionally sound more like an attempt to duplicate the Mouse on Mars formula than the real thing. [The American release of *Niun Niggung* included a radically different configuration from the British and German release, plus several bonus tracks.] —*John Bush*

Idiology / Apr. 24, 2001 / Thrill Jockey ✦✦✦✦✦

While their peers in the field of electronic music continued to either overshoot experimentally (resulting in radical, unlistenable work) or make the same records over and over again, German duo Mouse on Mars pumped out radical, intriguing work by the bucketful. *Idiology*, the duo's seventh full LP in as many years, is a more immediate album than its predecessor (*Niun Niggung*), not quite as reliant on the hyper-programming and content to simply chug along with crunchy beats and the usual roster of push-the-envelope effects. The opener (and single) "Actionist Respoke" sets the agenda immediately, with a red-line vocal sample shimmying its way through a crunchy breakbeat production. It's probably the most traditional track on the album though, as the pair throws away the MoM rulebook for much of the rest of *Idiology*. "Subsequence" works its way around a dabbling piano line soon taken up by clarinet and strings as well, with all manner of effects/samples chirping away in the background. Tracks three and four comprise ten minutes of practically beatless, chaotic bliss, introduced by a fetchingly over-enunciated vocal from drummer Dodo Nkishi. The next, "Catching Butterflies With Hands," lurches along like an obviously dysfunctional toy from some Disney cartoon, struggling to perform its duties and, in an odd way no one could've expected, succeeding. Hidden within *Idiology* are at least half-a-dozen mini-masterpieces of neo-electronic composition, and as many tracks of flat-out electro-funk. Most significant of all when considering Mouse on Mars is that, in the notoriously coattails-riding electronic scene, no one's been able to duplicate what MoM do so often, so consistently, and so well. —*John Bush*

The Move

f. 1966, db. 1972

British Psychedelia, Psychedelic Pop, Psychedelic, British Invasion, Prog Rock/Art Rock, Rock & Roll

The Move were the best and most important British group of the late '60s that never made a significant dent in the American market. Through the band's several phases (which were sometimes dictated more by image than musical direction), their chief asset was guitarist and songwriter Roy Wood, who combined a knack for Beatlesque pop with a peculiarly British, and occasionally morbid, sense of humor. On their final albums (with considerable input from Jeff Lynne), the band became artier and more ambitious, hinting at the orchestral rock that Wood and Lynne would devise for the Electric Light Orchestra. The Move, however, always placed more emphasis on the pop than the art, and never lost sight of their hardcore rock & roll roots.

Formed from several established Birmingham groups, the band moved to London and crafted an explosive live act with early singles heavily influenced by mod pop in their chunky chords and oddball character sketches. With Wood handling all of the writing, the

group's first four singles ("Night of Fear," "I Can Hear the Grass Grow," "Flowers in the Rain," and "Fire Brigade") all made the British Top Ten in 1967-68. They topped the British charts for the only time in 1969 with one of their best songs, "Blackberry Way," a kind of black-humored flipside to "Penny Lane." The group's second album, *Shazam* (1970), was one of their best, allowing them to stretch out in more progressive and experimental directions than they could within the format of hit singles. A rapid succession of personnel changes made the Move, if anything, a more interesting group in the early '70s. This was due primarily to the addition of Jeff Lynne, whose cheerier pop inclinations would effectively counterpoint Wood's darker and more ironic compositions for the later albums *Looking On* (1971) and *Message From the Country* (1972). As a result of their increasing fascination with orchestral rock, Wood and Lynne discontinued the Move in the early '70s to form the Electric Light Orchestra. Wood left ELO in 1972 to pursue a career as a leader of Wizzard and as a solo artist. —*Richie Unterberger*

The Move / 1968 / Repertoire ✦✦✦✦✦

The Move's debut album was a solid effort of mod-pop-psychedelia, boasting a number of fine Roy Wood compositions: the British hits "Flowers in the Rain" and "Flower Brigade," the original version of "Cherry Blossom Clinic," and the lesser-known but equally worthy "Yellow Rainbow" and "Walk Upon the Water." The three routine covers (of Eddie Cochran, the Coasters, and Moby Grape) that pad the album dilute it only slightly. The German CD reissue adds seven bonus tracks from late-'60s singles, but if you can live with vinyl, you should still seek out the A&M double-LP compilation *The Best of the Move*, which has the entire debut album and even more of their late-'60s and early-'70s 45s. —*Richie Unterberger*

Something Else From the Move / 1968 / Regal Zonophone ✦✦✦

When the Move were reaching the peak of their popularity after a burst of fine psychedelic-tinged power pop singles, they issued this rather odd live five-song 12" EP consisting entirely of covers. If nothing else, it proves the Move were a dynamic live act with an eclectic range, to say the least, as they cover tunes by the Byrds, Love, Eddie Cochran, Jerry Lee Lewis, and Spooky Tooth on this set. They really burn it up, in fact, on the Byrds' "So You Want to Be a Rock & Roll Star" and Love's "Stephanie Knows Who," with spinning and frenetic guitar work. The rest of the set is more routine, coming off more as a tribute to some of their idiosyncratic favorites. —*Richie Unterberger*

☆ **Shazam** / 1970 / Repertoire ✦✦✦✦✦

The single most accomplished album to be recorded by any of the Birmingham rock bands (which include the Moody Blues), *Shazam* is sort of *Sgt. Pepper* with an attitude, a mixture of expansive progressive rock worthy of the Beatles and high energy music honed by years of playing loud on-stage. The rendition of Tom Paxton's "The Last Thing on My Mind" pushes these guys simultaneously into Byrds and Jimi Hendrix territory, while "Beautiful Daughter" is one of the most unabashedly pretty records of this era, and "Cherry Blossom Clinic Revisited" is defiantly strange. The album only exists as an import from Japan, paired up on one CD with the earlier *Flowers in the Rain* album (all songs in print domestically or a better German version filled out with five live tracks from London's Marquee Club, off of the super-rare *Something Else* EP). —*Bruce Eder*

Looking On / 1971 / Repertoire ✦✦✦

Probably their weakest album, finding the group trying to blend progressive elements with lumpy hard rock boogie on obscure, extended tracks. The songs do look forward to the Electric Light Orchestra, for good or ill, in the helium-like high harmonies and the wide palette of instruments. Most of the multi-instrumentation is provided by Roy Wood, who picks up oboe, sitar, slide guitar, cello, and saxophone in addition to his usual guitar chores. Includes the British Top Ten single "Brontosaurus." —*Richie Unterberger*

Message From the Country / 1971 / BGO ✦✦✦✦✦

The group's last good album, weaker than *Shazam* but pleasant enough in its sub-*White Album* way. —*Bruce Eder*

Split Ends / 1972 / United Artists ✦✦✦✦✦

Basically an improved version of *Message From the Country*, replacing that album's weakest tracks with some fine British singles, especially "Tonight," "Chinatown," and "Do Ya." With the release of all of these tracks and the entire *Message From the Country* album on the 1994 reissue *Great Move!*, fans no longer have to seek out this package. —*Richie Unterberger*

Black Country Rock / 1993 / Gold Standard ✦✦✦

This quasi-legal compilation of 26 BBC performances from the late 1960s, in reasonable to excellent fidelity, shows the Move's astonishing versatility and range of influences. Ten of these are live-in-the-studio run-throughs of original material, including most of their early British hits—"Night of Fear," "Fire Brigade," "Flowers in the Rain," "I Can Hear the Grass Grow," and "Blackberry Way." More interesting from a historical perspective are the 16 covers, showing an eclectic range that must have been the equal of any major group of the time—the Byrds, Simon & Garfunkel, Tim Rose, Love, Jerry Lee Lewis, Eddie Cochran, Neil Diamond, Jackie Wilson, Janis Joplin, Johnny Cash, Moby Grape, and the Beach Boys all come in for the Move's accomplished chunky rock, harmony-laden treatment. The covers of the Byrds' "Goin' Back" and Paul Simon's "Sounds of Silence" are particularly nifty. It's not recommended to anyone except serious fans, but that small audience could hardly wish for a better collection of rarities from the group's salad days. —*Richie Unterberger*

BBC Sessions / 1994 / Band of Joy ✦✦✦

This is exactly the same (in content and fidelity) as the quasi-legal *Black Country Rock* compilation on Gold Standard, with the notable omission of one of the best songs, a cover of Simon & Garfunkel's "The Sounds of Silence." Otherwise, this anthology of 25 BBC performances from the late '60s, in reasonable to excellent fidelity, shows the Move's astonishing versatility and range of influences. Ten of these are live-in-the-studio run-throughs of original material, including most of their early British hits—"Night of Fear," "Fire Brigade," "Flowers in the Rain," "I Can Hear the Grass Grow," and "Blackberry Way." More interesting from a historical perspective are the 16 covers, showing an eclectic range that must have been the equal of any major group of the time—the Byrds, Tim Rose, Love, Jerry Lee Lewis, Eddie Cochran, Neil Diamond, Jackie Wilson, Janis Joplin, Johnny Cash, Moby Grape, and the Beach Boys all come in for the Move's accomplished chunky rock, harmony-laden treatment. The cover of the Byrds' "Goin' Back" is particularly nifty. It's not recommended to anyone except serious fans, but that small audience could hardly wish for a better collection of rarities from the group's salad days. *—Richie Unterberger*

★ **Great Move! The Best of the Move** / Jun. 15, 1994 / EMI America ✦✦✦✦✦
The title is really a misnomer; it includes much of the best of the Move, but can hardly stake a claim as a definitive collection, as it only covers their final years in the early '70s. Which isn't to say it isn't good. This is basically a spruced-up version of their final album, *Message From the Country* (1971), with the addition of five bonus tracks from early-'70s singles. *Message From the Country* itself was an erratic affair, alternating between lumbering forays into hard rock, revivalist roots rock, and country, and some of Roy Wood and Jeff Lynne's most inspired Beatlesque progressive compositions. The singles, most of which were previously issued on the *Split Ends* compilation, include some of their most memorable moments. "Tonight" (a British hit) is Roy Wood at his most tuneful, wistful, and folk-rockish; "Chinatown," though not quite as good (and not quite as big a British hit), is in much the same vein; and "Do Ya," redone with much more success by ELO, is one of their catchiest all-out rockers. Wood also gets into heavy sounds on the Top Ten British hit "California Man." Includes informative liner notes by respected rock critic Ira Robbins. *—Richie Unterberger*

Movements / 1997 / West Side ✦✦✦✦✦
This may be more Move than the casual fan wants, but it's not just another rehashed collection. From the remastered sound to the presence of various outtakes (including lost live tracks), the 30th anniversary triple-disc *Movements* is as definitive a set as we'll ever have on this band, containing everything except for the *Message From the Country* album. Disc one consists of the group's early singles plus *The Move* album and one outtake ("Disturbance"), all sounding really clear and tough, the loudest pop psychedelic music you'll ever hear out of England. Disc two contains the complete *Shazam* album, as well as alternate stereo or undubbed mixes of such songs as "Cherry Blossom Clinic," "(Here We Go Round) The Lemon Tree," "Fire Brigade," and an Italian-sung version of "Something." The sound is okay, with brilliant delineation on the guitars and basses, but not quite the revelation that one would hope (20-bit remastering would have been a real treat on *Shazam*). "Wild Tiger Woman Blues" is worth the price of this disc by itself, and the early version of "Curly" is lots of fun, while the undubbed "Fire Brigade" is raw and punkish. Disc three starts off with the complete *Looking On* album, which still lacks some presence, but is the best version yet heard. The real deal here, however, is the first-ever CD version of the live *Something Else* EP remastered from the original live tapes. The notes by John Platt are pretty cool, too, and coupled with the remastered *Message From the Country*, this set pretty well closes the books on the Move, as far as reissues of fully authorized stuff goes. *—Bruce Eder*

★ **The Best of the Move** / 1997 / Repertoire ✦✦✦✦✦
One has the marvel at the recent activity surrounding the Move—from a ten-year period in which the legendary band was scarcely represented on vinyl, we're now at a point where practically every note they ever recorded for release is in print on CD, and there's even a collection of BBC performances as well as a few bootlegs circulating. This 24-song collection concentrates on their single A- and B-sides for Regal Zonophone, Deram, Harvest, Fly, and Ariola. The first 15 songs, from "Night of Fear" to "California Man," are arranged in A-side release order, and tracks 17-23 are devoted to the most relevant of their B-sides. This probably isn't the wisest way to have programmed the disc, since it means sliding through a multitude of styles and sounds across a five-year period twice, with a previously unissued Italian version of "Something" tagged on as the 24th song. Additionally, whether or not this is actually "the best of the Move" is a matter of contention—one could make a case for a compilation of that name that would draw on a few of their album tracks as well. It also has competition from *Omnibus*, a double-CD set containing all of their single A- and B-sides, albeit at a heftier price. On the whole, however, this disc is a good compromise, assuming one doesn't mind the separation of the single sides—the sound is very bright and almost startling in its clarity, to the point that even the mix on "Brontosaurus" is crisp, and acoustic guitar-based numbers like "Tonight" are glorious. *—Bruce Eder*

● **Omnibus: The 60's Singles As and Bs** / Aug. 24, 1999 / Edsel ✦✦✦✦✦
Subtitled "The 60s Singles As and Bs," here's almost all the Move you'll ever need. If you're a fan of '60s British pop with alternating heavy dashes of psychedelia and '50s retro-rock thrown in, the Move were the perfect embodiment of that odd blend. For newcomers, this is the group that Jeff Lynne later joined which permutated into the Electric Light Orchestra after scoring one last hit as the Move with the two-sided killer "Do Ya" b/w "California Man," both outside the timeline of this package, thus making it sadly incomplete. But the 20 tracks aboard are the original group with Carl Wayne and deliver all the other hits, B-sides, and even include two bonus tracks, an Italian version of "Something" and the withdrawn B-side "Vote for Me." Fans of the early Who will go bonkers for this one, solid Brit-pop all the way. *—Cub Koda*

Movietone

Ambient Pop, Slowcore, Dream Pop, Space Rock, Indie Rock, Post-Rock/Experimental
Formed in Bristol, England in 1994, Movietone displayed its quiet, sensual songs on a number of releases in the mid '90s for the Planet, Domino, and Drag City labels. Band members Florence Lovegrove, Matt Elliott, Rachel Brook, Kate Wright, and Matt Jones issued two 7"s with Planet before their self-titled full-length debut came out in 1996—two more 7's would follow before their Drag City debut, *Day and Night*, in 1997. The band then went on a three-year hiatus before producing their next full-length, *The Blossom Filled Streets*, in the summer of 2000. Like their previous releases, *The Blossom Filled Streets* is gentle and complex, with a light touch that shows how much the band has grown. *—Stacia Proefrock*

Day & Night / Dec. 9, 1997 / Drag City ✦✦✦✦

● **The Blossom Filled Streets** / Jul. 10, 2000 / Drag City ✦✦✦✦
Introspective, delicate, and atmospheric, the music of Movietone envelops the listener like a warm bath. Vocalist Kate Wright's poetic lyrics offer up vignettes that twist themselves inextricably amongst the layers of sound, surfacing occasionally to bloom in honey tones. The richness of the band's composition and instrumentation make this music almost impossible to categorize. They use strings and prepared piano like art rock auteurs, cruise sonic landscapes like Bluetile Lounge or Galaxie 500, and the ends of their songs often tumble into extended improvisations that rival free jazz. It may be overly simplistic to say that a band called Movietone makes music that sounds like the soundtrack to melancholy film scenes under gaslight and stars, but they do make that music, and its filmic richness makes this album a most unique treat. *—Stacia Proefrock*

The Moving Sidewalks

Garage Rock, Psychedelic
Before forming ZZ Top, Billy Gibbons was the lead guitarist of this Houston, TX, group, who released one album and a few singles in the late '60s. Their single "99th Floor" became one of the most famous vintage garage 45s after its inclusion on *Pebbles, Vol. 2*, but the Sidewalks actually leaned much more heavily toward psychedelic and blues-rock. In fact, the group supported Jimi Hendrix at one of his early U.S. gigs and Gibbons became one of Hendrix's first boosters on U.S. shores; strange as it may seem, Hendrix was quite impressed with Gibbons himself, even at this early juncture. The Moving Sidewalks never developed into anything more than a regional act, and are known primarily as a starting point for Gibbons. *—Richie Unterberger*

● **Flash** / 1968 / Tantara ✦✦✦✦
The sole album by the Moving Sidewalks is as fascinating as it is unremarkable. As the birthing ground for legendary blues-rock guitarist Billy Gibbons, one would expect at least a taste of what would later make ZZ Top one of the best touring and recording bands on the planet; sadly, the album offers little in the way of revelation in its 15 tracks. Admittedly, at the time of ZZ Top's 1970 debut, Gibbons' transformation from a journeyman bandleader into a boogie blues demigod was still not fully realized, but his chops were miles away from what is heard here. Part of that lies in the fact that ZZ Top was less about psychedelia than straight blues; whatever psychedelic touches made their way onto the studio albums were largely an accessory. (They would eventually fully integrate on 1979's *Deguello*.) The Moving Sidewalks, on the other hand, were psychedelic rockers whose songs hinted at the blues without fully diving in. The songs show little of Gibbons' future promise, and in fact are so thoroughly mediocre (both in writing and playing) that it's amazing to think he was only a few years away from international success. "Pluto-Sept. 31st" shows a clear Hendrix influence (the two guitarists openly admired each other), and as a bonus, Akarma's reissue includes five bonus singles that are some of the strongest material on the album, especially "Need Me," "I Want to Hold Your Hand," and the legendary single "99th Floor." *—Jim Smith*

99th Floor / 1982 / Eva ✦✦✦✦
All 15 songs recorded by the group, including their entire album (*Flash*) and three singles. "Every Night a New Surprise" is the only psych-punk number besides "99th Floor" on this LP of extremely Hendrix-influenced originals, with a bit of Stevie Winwood-like soul here and there, as well as an unusual heavy psychedelic treatment of "I Want to Hold Your Hand." *—Richie Unterberger*

Mu

f. 1971, **db.** 1974
Psychedelic, Prog Rock/Art Rock
This intriguing early-'70s Southern Californian group featured the talents of singer/songwriter Merrell Fankhauser (who was also at the helm of cult classics in the '60s by Fapardokly and HMS Bounty) and Jeff Cotton, previously slide guitarist with Captain Beefheart. Their sole album (from 1971) is a gem of the late hippie era, combining the fractured blues-based tangents of Beefheart with the loose flow and stoned lyricism of bands like the late-'60s Grateful Dead. After a couple more singles, Mu moved to Maui and cut a fair amount of unreleased material before breaking up around 1974. Their eponymous album, as well as a lot of their unreleased material, was reissued in the '80s. *—Richie Unterberger*

Mu / 1971 / RTV ✦✦✦✦✦
One of the best overlooked albums of the early '70s. Daring rhythms and song structures that build off the blues without following the standard three-chord/12-bar progressions, occasional modal jazzy sax by Cotton, and great slide guitar combine to form one of the most unclassifiable recordings of the time, with a high-spirited lightness that avoids the heavy excesses that sometimes burdened late-period psychedelia. *—Richie Unterberger*

End of an Era / 1988 / Reckless ✦✦✦
Seventeen songs recorded after their relocation to Maui in 1974. More subdued and acoustic than the *Mu* LP, but still worthwhile, with Crosby, Stills, & Nash-like harmonies,

melancholy melodies, and almost prototypically hippie-ish lyrics about visitations from other planets, searches for lost lands, mystical love, and the like. *—Richie Unterberger*

- **Mu Compilation** / 1997 / Sundazed ♦♦♦♦♦

The definitive Mu collection. Besides including all of the 1971 *Mu* album, this double CD also includes all of the 1974 Mu material that surfaced on the Reckless *End of an Era* compilation, as well as the four 1974 Mu tracks that were included on Merrell Fankhauser's *The Maui Album* (also originally on Reckless). Don't worry about sorting out the discographical details; what you need to know is that this has everything in its best-ever sound quality, as well as one song ("You've Been There Before") that never came out on the Reckless LPs. The 1974 cuts aren't on the same level as the songs from the 1971 LP, but at its best, this is still cosmic folk-blues-rock in the best sense of the term. *—Richie Unterberger*

µ-Ziq (Michael Paradinas)

b. 1971, Wimbledon, London, England

Remixing, Producer / IDM, Experimental Techno, Electronica, Ambient Techno, Jungle/Drum 'N Bass, Techno

One of the premiere names in the field of electronic home-listening music, Mike Paradinas' recordings retained the abrasive flavor of early techno pioneers and explored the periphery of experimental electronica even while coddling to his unusual ear for melody, the occasional piece of vintage synthesizer, and distorted beat-box rhythms. While his side-projects—including Diesel M, Jake Slazenger, Gary Moscheles, Kid Spatula, and Tusken Raiders—have often emphasized (or satired) his debts to jazz, funk, and electro, Paradinas reserved his most original and exciting work for major album releases as µ-Ziq. Early µ-Ziq LPs were based around the most ear-splitting buzz-saw percussion ever heard (in a musical environment or otherwise), with fast-moving though deceptively fragile synthesizer melodies running over the top. As Paradinas began weaving his various influences into a convincing whole, his work became more fully developed (though possibly not as exciting), a fluid blend of breakbeat hip-hop and drum'n'bass with industrial effects and the same brittle melodies from his earlier work. *—John Bush*

Tango N' Vectif / Nov. 1993 / EFA ♦♦♦♦♦

This album immediately paired the young bedroom rat as a contemporary of Richard "Aphex Twin" James, on whose label it appeared. The offbeat envelope-pushing themes and occasionally heavily distorted percussion sees the comparison through, but that's where the similarity ends. His only full-length work with former bandmate Francis Naughton. *—Sean Cooper*

Bluff Limbo / May 1994 / Rephlex ♦♦♦

µ-Ziq Vs. The Auteurs / Oct. 1994 / Hut/Astralwerks ♦♦♦

In Pine Effect / Oct. 31, 1995 / Astralwerks ♦♦♦♦

His most stylistically developed album under the µ-Ziq name to date. Although Paradinas is big on insisting his music isn't for dancing, most of the tracks here feature a familiar dancefloor pulse, with alternately arresting and sidesplitting melodies floating above signature percussion and some interesting brass work. "Phiesope" even samples Kristen Hersh! *—Sean Cooper*

Urmur Bile Trax, Vols. 1 & 2 / Feb. 4, 1997 / Astralwerks ♦♦♦

- **Lunatic Harness** / Jun. 30, 1997 / Astralwerks ♦♦♦♦♦

Mike Paradinas' first success story from the frontlines of ambient/electro/drum'n'bass experimentation comes via his second attempt, *Lunatic Harness*. Following the brief but for the most part uninteresting toybox chop-up of 1996's *Urmur Bile Trax*, the album escapes the mire of noncommittal cheekiness (an affectation that also damaged some of his Jake Slazenger work) by returning to early releases such as *Tango 'N Vectif* and *Bluff Limbo* for inspiration, fusing pretty, affecting melodies and dynamic ambient atmospheres with beats that manage a tight balance between structured groove and complete chaos. *—Sean Cooper*

Royal Astronomy / Jul. 27, 1999 / Astralwerks ♦♦♦♦

After the drum'n'bass updates on his previous full-length, *Royal Astronomy* in large part returns Mike Paradinas to the green pastures of his youth—electro-slanted melodic techno and post-rave ambience with an eye on classics of his early career like *Tango 'N Vectif*. From the cinematic opener "Scaling" and the simple melodies of the single "The Fear" (with vocals by a Japanese-born, British-based author named Kazumi), Paradinas keeps it simple throughout. Indeed, the pendulum bass and synth-strings on "Gruber's Mandolin" could have been taken stock-and-barrel from either of his first two Rephlex albums. Still, there are breakbeats all over this record—and on two of the best tracks, the gorgeous production titled "Carpet Muncher" and "Autumn Acid," a song slightly reminiscent of Aphex Twin's "Windowlicker." There's also plenty of hip-hop attitude on other tracks, from the Gang Starr sample on "The Motorbike Track" to the turntable spinbacks on "The Hwicci Song." For the most part, it's obvious that Paradinas' sampler has moved on and gained for it. *—John Bush*

Mud

f. 1966, **db.** 1980

Glitter, Glam Rock, Hard Rock, Rock & Roll

Mention the name Mud to most Americans—even those neck-deep in the '70s revival—and the likely result will be a blank stare. In England, however, between 1974 and 1976, Mud were one of the hottest rock & roll acts there was, charting a series of monster hit singles and recording a pair of delightful oldies-oriented albums. They were never a profoundly philosophical band, and never pretended to be—the group played music to have a good time, and merely asked that others join in, which millions of Britons did for a few years. After some Chinn/Chapman-penned hit singles, the group's debut album, *Mud Rock*, sold well, and the band might've gone on perfectly well this way, cutting hit singles and doing an LP once a year, but for a problem that came up late in 1974, when Mud was persuaded to sign a contract with the new Private Stock label despite still being under contract with producer Mickie Most. They ultimately did get a succession of hit singles out on Private Stock, and for another year Mud were a fixture on the U.K. charts (and nonexistent as a presence in America), before their appeal faded. Glam rock faded as punk and disco came to dominate the airwaves and the charts. They continued to record for Private Stock and RCA-U.K. until 1980, but nothing they did ever sold in numbers resembling their past glories. Mud's ride at the top was a short one, not even three years from start to finish before they disappeared from the charts, but they never intended to have a long or lasting impact on music, just help people have a good time. *—Bruce Eder*

- **The Gold Collection** / 1996 / EMI Gold ♦♦♦♦

The Singles '67-'78 / 1997 / Repertoire ♦♦♦

Although countless Mud compilations have been released over the years, none of them managed to cover every phase of the group's career. This was remedied in 1997 with the release of *The Singles '67-'78*. This overwhelmingly generous collection spans two discs and includes the A- and B-sides of each single the group released. Of course, the most impressive tracks are the hits from the group's stint at RAK Records: the combination of pop hooks and guitar firepower utilized for stomping glam classics like "Tiger Feet" and "Dynamite" still sound fresh and exciting today. However, this set also unearths some surprisingly good tracks from the group's oft-overlooked periods at Private Stock and RCA Records: "L'L'Lucy" is a full-throttle rock tune built on a smile-inducing vocal stutter hook and the languid yet catchy "Slow Talking Boy" is unlike anything else in the Mud catalog. Unfortunately, this generous array of material means the listener has to sit through more than one dud along the way, like the pleasant but inconsequential covers of "Lean on Me" and "Drift Away." Even hardcore Mud fans may be tempted to scan through filler tracks like these. That said, *The Singles '67-'78* remains the definitive way for any glam fan to explore the full history of this underrated group and it further enhances its value with a nice set of liner notes that include track-by-track commentary from lead vocalist Les Gray. Casual listeners will probably be better off with a single-disc compilation, but *The Singles '67-'78* is the collection of choice for Mud enthusiasts. *—Donald A. Guarisco*

Mud Rock/Mud Rock, Vol. 2 / Nov. 25, 1998 / BGO ♦♦♦

The two albums represented on this one CD slot in so perfectly alongside one another, that—but for the silly narration—it's hard to tell where one ends and the other begins. The 20 songs, either vintage tunes ("The End of the World," "Let's Have a Party," "Tobacco Road," "Diana," "Tallahassee Lassie," "Living Doll") or numbers done in a retro-style, are all attractively done, not in a burlesque manner or in a slavish, deadening authentic style. "The Secrets That You Keep" was a huge hit for the group, but it's such an beautiful song, that the authors could probably have brought it to Elvis himself—though by 1975, it's unlikely he would've done as much with it as Les Gray and Mud did. All of the group's major RAK hits are present in one form or another, the sound is excellent, and the notes are reasonably extensive and informative. *—Bruce Eder*

Best of the 70's / Nov. 28, 2000 / Disky ♦♦♦

This generous budget-line compilation covers glam rock favorites Mud. Although often shrugged off by the music press as puppets for producers Nicky Chinn and Mike Chapman, this collection shows that the band's music has held up nicely. They had an edge on many glam groups because they incorporated a solid knowledge of (and obvious love for) classic 1950s and 1960s rock & roll into their guitar-heavy glam sound. Indeed, hits like "Rocket" and "The Cat Crept In" sound like rockabilly tracks from Sun Records played in a heavy 1970s style. This set also includes plenty of amped-up covers of favorites like "One Night" and "Blue Moon." One of the most inventive covers is the group's hit reinterpretation of the Buddy Holly classic "Oh Boy," which starts as an a cappella tune and builds into a sultry, slow rocker. This aspect of their style lends a classic touch to their music that keeps engaging long after the glam rock trend has passed. Other highlights include "The Secrets That You Keep," a retro-styled ballad that features a nifty Elvis Presley impression from vocalist Les Gray, and "Dyna-Mite," a hard-rocking tale of a beautiful woman; this song's exciting arrangement builds from suspenseful, guitar-strummed verses to a triumphant, percussion-driven chorus. The downside of this collection is that it ignores some successful singles from Mud's post-RAK Records period and includes a few too many covers when it might have been nice to see some B-sides or other rarities. Despite these quibbles, *Best of the 70's* is a fine introduction to the retro-glam sound of Mud. *—Donald A. Guarisco*

Mudhoney

f. 1988, Seattle, WA

Garage Punk, Grunge, Alternative Pop/Rock, American Underground

With their fuzzed-out guitars and Mark Arm's straining vocals, Mudhoney defined '80s and '90s grunge rock. In fact, their 1988 debut single "Touch Me, I'm Sick" is the definitive grunge song—an obnoxious, dirty song driven by massively distorted guitars and a screaming vocal. It was a terrific, invigorating song that the band rewrote on each album that followed, but that's alright because Mudhoney only has one other song—a slow, sludgy Stooges grind. But their limitations are ultimately endearing; the band is a punk band, not like a '70s or '80s group, but like a '60s garage band, kicking out the same three chords with an unbridled enthusiasm. Leave the serious themes to Nirvana, Pearl Jam, Soundgarden, and Alice in Chains—Mudhoney takes the same themes but makes them sleazy and trashy, like the Russ Meyer film they named themselves after. Their records are inconsistent but when they are good, they are great. *—Stephen Thomas Erlewine*

Mudhoney / Jul. 1989 / Sub Pop ♦♦♦
Mudhoney's first full-length album cut away the acid-rock excesses of their debut EP, concentrating on a tighter, punkier sound, highlighted by the raging "You Got It (Keep It Out of My Face)." *—Stephen Thomas Erlewine*

Superfuzz Bigmuff (Plus Early Singles) / Oct. 25, 1990 / Sub Pop ♦♦♦♦♦
Named after the band's favorite distortion pedal, *Superfuzz Bigmuff* was actually Mudhoney's first EP; the *Superfuzz Bigmuff (Plus Early Singles)* package collects that recording, as well as the A- and B-sides of their first two 45s and two covers (of the Dicks and Sonic Youth), all released in 1988-89. Taken as a whole, this output makes a case for Mudhoney as the first true grunge band; due to the time constraints of the forms in which this material was originally released, it also makes for their best, most consistent album, as the band largely refrains from the sort of aimless, grinding Stooges updates that slow the momentum of most of their records. Instead, *Superfuzz Bigmuff* has all the best attributes of Mudhoney's Stooges fixation—whether slow or fast, this music is grimy, raucous, and violently enthusiastic, with a stronger melodic sensibility than Iggy's band possessed. Mudhoney's dominant traits are simple chord progressions and a filthy-sounding, ultra-distorted guitar racket, punctuated by Mark Arm's snarling, demonic howls. It isn't the most original approach to rock & roll, but when it all comes into focus—as on their (and Sub Pop's) debut single, the ultimate grunge anthem "Touch Me I'm Sick"—Mudhoney's power is absolutely throttling. "Touch Me I'm Sick" would be essential listening for anyone even remotely interested in the genesis of the Seattle scene, but the album is full of menacing, vital rock & roll, plus sharp songwriting that elevates several other songs to classic status. Mudhoney's musical range may be quite limited, but as *Superfuzz Bigmuff* proves, they can be amazing at what they *can* do. This is the birth of grunge, and a reminder of exactly why the music was christened with a word meaning "dirt." *—Steve Huey*

Every Good Boy Deserves Fudge / Jul. 26, 1991 / Sub Pop ♦♦♦♦
It's no great stylistic breakthrough, but what Mudhoney record is? Instead, it's another solid album of fuzzed-out three-chord garage rockers. There's nothing as great as "Touch Me, I'm Sick" or "In 'N' Out of Grace," but song for song, it's their most consistent album. *—Stephen Thomas Erlewine*

Piece of Cake / Oct. 1992 / Reprise ♦♦♦
By 1992, grunge was becoming rock's new Flavor of the Month, and Mudhoney, being the naturally contrary types that they were, seemed to be getting a bit bored with it; besides, after several years of roadwork, the band had gained enough speed and precision to allow the garage rock and old-school punk flavors to rise to the surface of their aural cocktail (or, more appropriately, their aural Trash Can Punch). *Piece of Cake* was the band's major-label debut, but you wouldn't have guessed that by listening to it; Conrad Uno's production is as no-frills as ever, and the short bursts of goofy noise and techno parodies that punctuate the album make it clear Mudhoney were taking themselves (and their career) no more seriously than they ever had. If those looking for the big shaggy sloppiness of "Touch Me I'm Sick" or "You Got It" might feel a bit let down by *Piece of Cake*, there's a snot-nosed fury to "No End in Sight" and "Suck You Dry" that makes it clear these guys were always a punk band at heart (albeit a punk band who *really* liked Blue Cheer), and if you're looking for heaviness, "Ritzville" and "I'm Spun" will convince you they hadn't forgotten how to drop that D tuning. Faster and fiercer than ever, but no less fuzzy or messed-up, *Piece of Cake* proved Mudhoney's palate was a few shades broader than some folks might have expected, but without turning their backs on the glorious ugliness that was always their stock-in-trade. *—Mark Deming*

Five Dollar Bob's Mock Cooter Stew / Oct. 26, 1993 / Reprise ♦♦♦
A stopgap EP that sounds like it was recorded in a garage, *Five Dollar Bob's Mock Cooter Stew* has some of Mudhoney's rawest and best rock & roll. *—Stephen Thomas Erlewine*

My Brother the Cow / Mar. 28, 1995 / Reprise ♦♦♦♦
Mudhoney didn't invent grunge, but they were one of the first bands to truly define the style, and thanks to the bizarro-world logic that has defined their career, they seemed to loose interest in the stuff once you could actually make serious money playing it, ensuring that they wouldn't have to deal with the mainstream adulation that made followers like Nirvana, Pearl Jam, and Soundgarden into multi-platinum cash cows. By 1995, grunge's brief fling on the charts was pretty much over ... just in time for Mudhoney to decide they liked the stuff again, and make the finest album of their career, *My Brother the Cow*. On *My Brother the Cow*, Mudhoney finally found a noisy middle ground where their fondness for Billy Childish and Blue Cheer could peacefully coexist, and the songs are less sludgy and more driving than their early classics, but with enough cheap stompbox thunder to remind you of who's playing. A few years on the road had made Mudhoney a much stronger and tighter band, able to fully grasp the hard rock guitar figures they dearly loved to mock, but without falling into big rock pomp. And they came up with a dozen tunes that gave them plenty of room to sneer brilliantly (one of their greatest gifts), especially "Generation Spokesmodel," "F.D.K. (Fearless Doctor Killers)," and "Into Yer Shtik" (in which some nameless rock scene figure is advised to "blow your brains out too"). And as icing on the cake, the CD has the greatest hidden bonus track of all time. For better or worse, Mudhoney always played their game their own way, and they never played it better than on *My Brother the Cow*. *—Mark Deming*

Tomorrow Hit Today / Sep. 22, 1998 / Reprise ♦♦♦♦
On their fourth release for Reprise and seventh overall, Mudhoney shows that they have absolutely no plans to mellow out in their old age. On *Tomorrow Hit Today*, the influential Seattle outfit harness their attack more than the full-throttle previous release, *My Brother the Cow*. Mark Arm still sings with all the attitude he can muster, while the others gleefully bash away at their instruments, creating tunes comparable to the enjoyable racket that the New York Dolls and Stooges laid down earlier. And it's very impressive that Mudhoney can still deliver true garage rock all these years later—"I Have to Laugh" and the opening "A Thousand Forms of Mind" are classic Mudhoney stompers, and they mix it up with '60s surf ("Night of the Hunted"), and blues-rock ("Move With the Wind"). Along with the Melvins, Mudhoney are one of the few remaining Seattle originals, and *Tomorrow Hit Today* is one of their finest and most focused. *—Greg Prato*

● **March to Fuzz** / Jan. 18, 2000 / Sub Pop ♦♦♦♦♦
Mudhoney was most convincing when the 7" recording format limited their more indulgent tendencies. In general (especially early on), their albums were always peppered with great songs—usually variations on the band's trademark scuzzy sound and sneering attitude—but rarely sustained momentum all the way through, thanks in part to the band's weakness for ponderous jams. The sorely needed, two-disc best-of *March to Fuzz* attempts to have it both ways: the first disc is a generous, 22-track overview of their recordings from 1988-1998, while the second compiles 30 rarities for the devotees. It's a tactic that's been used before, and it's usually maddening, giving both casual and die-hard fans an entire disc they don't want. But *March to Fuzz* actually works very well. For one, it's not priced as a double-disc set, and for another, both discs are actually very strong. Mudhoney's sound didn't change very much over the course of their career, which means that even though disc one isn't arranged chronologically, everything is pretty much of a piece. It's also very well-chosen, even if the surprisingly strong latter-day albums *My Brother the Cow* and *Tomorrow Hit Today* aren't heavily represented. But the disc makes a convincing case that Mudhoney never stopped making bruising, vital rock & roll, or writing great (albeit samey) songs. The rarities disc is surprisingly entertaining, featuring plenty of cover versions, cranky goofs, and songs that were certainly better than some of their album tracks, but were relegated to B-sides or indie compilations. Their '60s garage and surf roots are actually summed up very effectively here, as well as their love of early-'80s hardcore. *March to Fuzz* might be a little hard to handle all in one sitting, but it's hard to imagine a better overview of Mudhoney's career. *—Steve Huey*

Here Comes Sickness: Best of BBC Recordings / Sep. 26, 2000 / Varese ♦♦♦♦
Divided up into three different encounters with the BBC, *Here Comes Sickness* exhibits Mudhoney in their youth for a 1989 in-studio appearance on *The John Peel Show*, in their later years for a 1995 in-studio show for *Evening Session*, and a live concert set from 1995's Reading Festival for *the John Peel Show*. As far as the live, in-studio programs, Mudhoney is fairly tight. The production of the in-studio tracks from 1989 and 1995 are louder and cleaner sounding than the album versions of the songs. A perfect example is the opening number and title track "Here Comes Sickness." The band plays at a much more frantic pace filled with more emotion than the version from their 1989 self-titled album. Mark Arm's vocals slur and hiss, Steve Turner's lead guitar work stings with a vengeance, Matt Lukin's bass chugs along, and Dan Peters' drums are well-miked, adding to the overall strength of the tracks. Some of the songs are also sketches for their studio albums. The edition of "Poisoned Water Poisons the Mind," which later evolved into "Poisoned Water" on 1998's *Tomorrow Hit Today*, is shorter due to the absence of its guitar solo and outro. "Judgement, Rage, Retribution and Thyme," which turned up on 1995's *My Brother the Cow*, is more stripped down and less chintzy than that record's version, which included a corny marimba line. Flaws begin to appear in the Reading set though, but it's mainly due to how the instruments are mixed. Arm's vocals vary from being some of his best, projecting the feeling that he's going to rip someone's head off ("Into Yer Schtik"), to sounding his weakest, fighting to be heard over the loud guitars ("Judgement, Rage, Retribution and Thyme"). Lukin's bass is also nearly inaudible throughout the majority of the Reading set, and Peters' drums seem to fade in and out. *—Stephen Howell*

The Mumps

American Punk, New York Punk, New Wave, Punk

The Mumps were one of the most obscure, but distinctive, New York bands of the late '70s, performing an absurdly theatrical fusion of pop, punk, and glam rock. Led by vocalist Lance Loud, the group's music was an affectionate satire of '70s kitsch culture, predating the similar obsessions of the B-52's by a number of years. The Mumps rocked as hard as the New York Dolls, while writing clever pop hooks the updated trashy garage and bubblegum singles of the '70s.

Although they never even earned a large underground following, the group was a favorite of many punk rockers of the era (including the Ramones, Blondie, the New York Dolls, X, Television, the Cramps, Devo, and the Go-Go's), as well as '80s alternative rockers like R.E.M., Game Theory, and Sparks.

In addition to Lance Loud, the core lineup of the Mumps also featured keyboardist Kristiann Hoffman, guitarist Rob Duprey, bassist Kevin Kiely, and drummer Paul Rutner. Over the years, the lineup changed slightly, with Loud, Hoffman, and Duprey remaining the constant members in each incarnation of the band. The Mumps only released two singles while they were active in the late '70s, but in 1994 Eggbert Records released a CD called *Fatal Charms* that compiled everything the band ever recorded, including outtakes, alternate takes, and live rehearsals. *Fatal Charms* proves that the Mumps' music remains vibrant, creative, and intoxicatingly bizzare nearly 20 years after it was recorded. *—Stephen Thomas Erlewine*

Fatal Charm / 1994 / Eggbert ♦♦♦♦♦
Fatal Charm compiles essentially the complete recorded works of the quirky New York band, including the simply wonderful "Crocodile Tears," as well as some equally spirited outtakes and live rehearsals. Though very little of the Mumps' music was released during their five years together as a band, their live shows were legendary, influencing many of the next generation of new wave and alternative rockers; *Fatal Charm* helps explain why bands continue to namedrop them 20 years later. *—Chris Woodstra*

Mungo Jerry

f. 1970

AM Pop, Album Rock, Jug Band, Folk-Rock, Rockabilly, Skiffle

Mungo Jerry is one of rock's great one-hit successes. Outside of England, they're known for exactly one song, but that song, "In the Summertime," is a seasonal anthem known by listeners who weren't even born when it was released. Mungo Jerry was a solid blues outfit as well—in fact, one suspects they were the kind of blues band that purists Alexis Korner and Cyril Davies would have loved, had they ever intersected—and knew how to get the most out of their jug band sound, which has helped them survive for three decades. The quartet had a pleasing, low-key jug band sound, folk-like but also bluesy, which was unusual in 1969, a time when most British bands that were into blues were shooting for high-wattage virtuosity. They sounded less like the Cream or Blind Faith and a lot more like Jesse Fuller or Tampa Red, or even Piano Red (aka Dr. Feelgood). Mungo Jerry became one of the very first acts placed on the Pye label's new Dawn Records imprint, a progressive label that was intended to update Pye's image. The membership of Mungo Jerry began coming apart almost from the outset of their success. Mike Cole, who was replaced by John Godfrey, was followed out of the lineup by Paul King and Colin Earl, although their exit was somewhat more acrimonious—they attempted to take the name Mungo Jerry, but Ray Dorset, as the singer, guitarist, and songwriter, held onto the name. Instead, King and Earl cut solo albums for Pye and went on the road as the Earl King Boogie Band with former bandmate Joe Rush in the lineup. —*Bruce Eder*

● **The Best of Mungo Jerry** / Jun. 2, 1998 / Music Club ✦✦✦✦

Mungo Jerry may seem like an ultimate one-hit wonder, since their big hit "In the Summertime" seems like the very definition of a novelty one-off, but the post-hippie, British jug band actually had a pretty varied, interesting body of work. Music Club's 20-track collection *Best of Mungo Jerry* collects much of the very best of that work, and while there are some notable songs missing (such as "Motherfucker Boogie"), this is a consistently entertaining collection that will satisfy the needs of most listeners. —*Stephen Thomas Erlewine*

Anthology / Mar. 7, 2000 / Castle Music America ✦✦✦✦

Castle's double-disc set *Anthology* may be quite long at 39 tracks, but Mungo Jerry actually warrants that kind of in-depth look—provided that you're already converted to the peculiar joys of this almost electric jug band. They had a lot more to offer outside of "In the Summertime," although that shuffling boogie is a terrific definition of a one-hit wonder, but you have to already like that sound to want to dig into this set. If you do, there are a lot of offbeat gems to hear, from old-timey folk and blues songs to originals. It is a lot of Mungo Jerry, and it's not for everybody, but for collectors who want an exhaustive overview, this satisfies. —*Stephen Thomas Erlewine*

Peter Murphy

b. Jul. 11, 1957, Northampton, England

Vocals / College Rock, Post-Punk, Goth Rock, Alternative Pop/Rock

Despite having a successful solo career as a cult artist, vocalist Peter Murphy remains best known as the lead vocalist for Bauhaus, the pioneering post-punk goth-rock band of the early '80s. After disbanding Bauhaus in 1983, Murphy formed Dali's Car with former Japan member, Mick Karn. Dali's Car only released one album, *The Waking Hour*, in 1984. Following its release, the duo broke up and Murphy hesitatingly began a solo career with a cover of Magazine's "The Light Pours Out of Me." In 1986, he released his first full-fledged solo album, *Should the World Fail to Fall Apart*; two years later, Murphy released his second solo album, *Love Hysteria*. Like its predecessor, *Love Hysteria* received lukewarm reviews but sold well to his dedicated fan base. With 1990's *Deep*, Murphy had a surprise hit—the first single from the record, the Bowie-esque "Cuts You Up," became the American modern rock hit of the year, spending seven weeks at the top of the U.S. charts and crossing over to AOR radio and the pop charts, where it peaked at number 55. Murphy wasn't able to sustain that success with his next album, 1992's *Holy Smoke*. —*Stephen Thomas Erlewine*

Should the World Fail to Fall Apart / 1986 / Beggars Banquet ✦✦✦✦

Following the collapse of Dali's Car, Murphy embarked on a solo career in earnest, fortuitously hooking up with Howard Hughes, who had been working with fellow cult artists the Associates. With 4AD label head Ivo Watts-Russell drafted in to produce and guest musicians popping in as desired, Murphy and Hughes created a slightly fragmentary but still intriguing record. Caught between his recent past (the use of fretless bass on "Canvas Beauty" was a dead giveaway that he missed working with Mick Karn) and his eventual solo successes, Murphy concentrates here mostly on breaking free of the goth stereotype in which he had found himself trapped. His vocal passion isn't diminished in the slightest, but this time the music over which he sings is generally lighter and freer in tone; he himself handles drum programming, core guitar parts, and keyboard lines while Hughes takes care of the rest. The quietly anthemic title track and "God Sends" stand out as thorough successes on these lines. Two covers also crop up, both worthy of note: A solid run-through of Magazine's "The Light Pours Out of Me" with that band's guitarist John McGeoch; more noteworthy is a fierce rip on Pere Ubu's "Final Solution." The ghosts of Bauhaus do crop up at points, most notably "Never Man," with haunting backing vocals and a generally creepy feeling. Meanwhile, "The Answer Is Clear" has a more direct connection, with none other than Bauhaus guitarist Daniel Ash contributing some fine feedback squalls. Ironically enough, the song itself is a pointed response to Ash's own recent Tones on Tail song "The Movement of Fear," which Murphy took as an attack on himself! —*Ned Raggett*

Love Hysteria / 1988 / Beggars Banquet ✦✦✦

Having assembled, for touring purposes, what would soon be his formal backing band, the Hundred Men, and more specifically, having found a new key songwriting collaborator in ex-B. Movie keyboardist Paul Statham, Murphy created his most elegant post-Bauhaus effort to date. *Love Hysteria* had definite Bowie echoes, though the feeling was more late-'70s Berlin-era than *Ziggy* glam. That said, with his band turning in a variety of bright, lively performances and with sympathetic production from ex-Fall member/ arranger Simon Rogers, Murphy matched the music with flair, his voice even more of a passionate croon than a powerful howl. Lead single "All Night Long" was something of an American breakthrough hit; its upbeat rock drive and lush keyboards are a perfect bed for Murphy's performance. Other moments, such as the ringing acoustic/electric guitar combinations on "Indigo Eyes" and "Dragnet Eyes," take Murphy even further away from Bauhaus' shadow, though "His Circle and Hers Meet" and "Blind Sublime" have a brusquer energy. The definite highlights of the album are two majestic ballads: "Time Has Got Nothing to Do With It," with a fine Statham synth line matching Murphy's soaring vocals; and "My Last Two Weeks," a simply wonderful romantic sentiment. If his lyrics now sometimes have the feeling of formal philosophical pronouncements, the sense of style with which he sings them saves the performances more often than not. Closing with a fun romp through Iggy Pop's "Funtime," saluting another one of Murphy's old heroes with an appropriately strong vocal and amusing horror-movie samples, *Love Hysteria* shows Murphy fully coming into his own as a performer. —*Ned Raggett*

Deep / 1990 / Beggars Banquet ✦✦✦✦✦

Perhaps the stars were right, or perhaps his American company, flush from the unexpected success of Murphy's former bandmates in Love and Rockets, just decided to give Murphy a well-deserved publicity push. Whatever it was, with *Deep* Murphy scored an honest to goodness American radio/MTV hit thanks to the tender, lively "Cuts You Up," a love song with solid energy and an inspired vocal. It was a perfect calling card for the album as a whole, with Murphy in excelsis throughout and his Hundred Men providing everything from the lush, acoustic guitar wash of "Marlene Dietrich's Favorite Poem" to the stripped-down Arabic-tinged funk/hip-hop punch of the commanding "Roll Call." Through it all, Murphy simply sounds like he's having the time of his life, singing both for the sheer joy of it and for the dramatic power of his commanding voice. He's even comfortable enough to do an open rewrite of Bauhaus' "In the Flat Field," renamed "The Line Between the Devil's Teeth"; it has almost the same verse structure, definitely some of the same lyrics, but still, it's something he could have only done in his solo days. Quite why nothing else on the album connected with the public as strongly as "Cuts You Up" is a mystery; its follow-up single, "A Strange Kind of Love," was a striking love song, with acoustic guitar and plaintive Statham keyboards supporting one of Murphy's strongest lyrics and performances. Regardless, *Deep* showed Murphy balancing mass appeal and his own distinct art with perfection. —*Ned Raggett*

Holy Smoke / Apr. 14, 1992 / Beggars Banquet ✦✦✦

Hopes for another surprise American success from Peter Murphy with *Deep*'s follow-up went unfulfilled, as success proved not to be the case; released in the initial craze of the grunge/alternative mega-crossover, *Smoke*'s elegant ballads and angular, arty rockers simply didn't fit in. Taken on its own merits, though, *Smoke* is quite a strong release, avoiding any cloning of *Deep* or "Cuts You Up" in favor of a different approach meant to bring out the band's live power more directly. Producer Mike Thorne gets some great performances out of them and Murphy both, giving the album a crisp, solid punch throughout, even during its quieter moments. The album is like *Deep* in one important respect—variety, which is showcased successfully throughout. "Low Room" was an especially powerful blast, the band firing out a choppy, strong rhythm as Murphy almost barks his lyrics; similar, if not as totally successful, energy appeared with "Kill the Hate" and "Dream Gone By." On the quieter tip, "Let Me Love You," the understated drive of "Our Secret Garden," and the lovely opener "Keep Me From Harm" are all fine showcases for Murphy at his most love-drunk. "The Sweetest Drop" was the lead single, but better choices would have been "You're So Close," with an anthemic, stunning chorus and a flat-out brilliant vocal, and the cleverly titled "Hit Song." Murphy's dramatic singing, concluding in a duet with guest singer Alison Limerick's lovely falsetto, makes it all the more enjoyable. —*Ned Raggett*

Cascade / Apr. 11, 1995 / Beggars Banquet ✦✦✦✦

Following the *Holy Smoke* tour, the Hundred Men disbanded, with only Statham remaining as Murphy's main songwriting partner. Along with the help of producer Pascal Gabriel and some good session players, including extra "infinite guitar" from cult musician Michael Brook, Murphy created the marvelous *Cascade*. Another step further up in Murphy's continuing embrace of generally positive, inspiring work, *Cascade* shows him once again not repeating himself, aside perhaps from the sprightly, acoustic guitar-led "The Scarlet Thing in You." Otherwise, the music this time is generally lush and electronic, emphasizing Statham's atmospherics and melodies to their fullest. "Subway" is a good example, with Statham's synth strings creating a striking air for both the band's performance and Murphy's own passionate vocals, which cheekily quote the old Petula Clark hit "Don't Sleep in the Subway." "Gliding Like a While," which immediately follows it, is just as vast and powerful, a strong guitar/electronics arrangement giving Murphy the opportunity to deliver an equally compelling lyric and chorus. More upfront rockers haven't been left out of the equation: "Disappearing" builds a slow crunch reminiscent of his cover of "The Light Pours Out of Me," while "Wild Birds Flock to Me" has a good charge to it, accentuated by some fine backing vocals. Arguably Murphy's best song yet appears smack dab at the album's center: "I'll Fall With Your Knife." With a slightly quirky Statham keyboard loop starting things out, it develops from a minimal vocal/electric guitar combination into a huge, skybound declaration of love and devotion. It's Murphy at his most commanding and passionate, and the band's brilliant performance doesn't let up a jot. —*Ned Raggett*

• **Wild Birds 1985-1995: The Best of the Beggars Banquet Years** / Feb. 22, 2000 / Beggars Banquet ♦♦♦♦♦
Compiled by Murphy himself, *Wild Birds* is a well-timed collection spanning the five albums he recorded for Beggars Banquet between 1985 and 1995. Quite naturally, it begins with his biggest hit, "Cuts You Up," and includes alternative standards like "All Night Long," "Indigo Eyes," and "Deep Ocean, Vast Sea." Murphy weights the compilation toward his most recent work—four songs are taken from 1995's *Cascade*, as many as from his best album, 1990's *Deep*—and unfortunately shunts his underrated debut, *Should the World Fail to Fall Apart*. Despite this small caveat, *Wild Birds* is an excellent compilation; though Murphy usually focused on making conceptual statements with his albums, the individual singles released from them were remarkably infectious, especially given the sublime nature of his musical style. *—John Bush*

Alive Just for Love / Jul. 31, 2001 / Metropolis ♦♦♦
After the monumental Bauhaus reunion tour in late 1998, Peter Murphy quickly jumped back into his solo work, making around the U.S. during the new millennium. He didn't have a label or industry support, just the love of his fans. And in celebration of their dedication, Murphy issued a best-of collection on Beggars Banquet and took to the stage. Two successful legs surprised Murphy, and his expanding fan base as well. For everyone instantly took to his new musical boundaries of Middle Eastern authenticities while forever appreciating his solo hits. To thank his loyal fans, Murphy issued his eighth album *Alive Just for Love* in summer 2001. Now with a new record deal (Metropolis), and a fresh fervor, this double-disc reflects the intimate evening captured at the El Rey Theatre in Los Angeles.The songs were stripped and delicately approached while Murphy's harkening vocals never sounded so lush. Accompanied by Peter DiStefano (Porno for Pyros) on guitar and violin virtuoso Hugh Marsh, *Alive Just for Love* highlights personal appeal and intricate acoustic beauty on favorites like "All Night Long" and "Marlene Dietrich's Favourite Poem," however new song "Cool Cool Breeze" exudes a sweet airiness to Murphy's approach to songwriting. "Keep Me From Harm" from 1994's *Holy Smoke* glitters with Marsh's violin plucking composing a new-fangled sneakiness to the song itself. "Cuts You Up" slides fragile bow guitar licks with Murphy's hushing vocals, bringing the most cheers of adoration from the crowd. Disc two is short with a rare performance by Bauhaus mate David J. on "Who Killed Mr. Moonlight" and "All We Ever Wanted Was Everything." Humble and enjoying his cult-like status, Peter Murphy appears grateful for what he does for a living. He's a perfectionist, but with added humility. *Alive Just for Love* personifies that exact thing. *—MacKenzie Wilson*

Music Explosion

f. Mansfield, OH
Frat Rock, Bubblegum
One-hit-wonder Ohio garage band that reached number two in 1967 with "Little Bit O'Soul," a great gutsy pop/rock number with a classic bass-organ riff. Whatever personality they may have had was coated in the studio by producers Jeffrey Katz and Jerry Kasenetz, who would soon help create bubblegum with acts like the 1910 Fruitgum Co. and the Ohio Express. The Music Explosion didn't have nearly as juvenile a sound as those groups, but they never latched onto another piece of material nearly as attention-grabbing as "Little Bit O'Soul," entering the Top 100 only once more with the tiny hit "Sunshine Games." *—Richie Unterberger*

Little Bit O' Soul / 1986 / Performance ♦♦♦
Fourteen tracks taken from their sole album and several non-hit singles. Nothing comes close to matching the ultra-catchy "Little Bit O' Soul," and in fact, on the whole it's quite mediocre and unmemorable. *—Richie Unterberger*

• **Anthology** / Apr. 25, 1995 / One Way ♦♦♦♦♦
Although it could have been packaged and sequenced with more care, One Way's 21-track *Anthology* provides all the material a hardcore fan could want from a Music Explosion collection, and far more than the average listener needs. While "Little Bit O' Soul" is an incredible single, the remainder of the group's songs are generally undistinguished, ranging between competent garage covers and pleasant, but unmemorable, '60s pop/rock, making *Anthology* unnecessary for anyone but dedicated '60s collectors. *—Stephen Thomas Erlewine*

The Music Machine

Garage Rock, Psychedelic
Most famous for "Talk Talk," a Top 20 single from 1966 that was one of the most manic '60s garage-punk hits, the Music Machine had much more depth and songwriting talent than the typical one-hit wonders of the day. Lead singer and songwriter Sean Bonniwell's strangled lyrics and dark, verbose vision paced the group's wiry psychedelic guitar lines and ominous, minor-key Farfisa organ. Only one album was released with the original lineup, and the group's ferocious energy was diluted on subsequent recordings. Despite chalking up only one more minor hit single ("The People in Me"), the Music Machine recorded quite a few excellent, imaginatively produced singles and album tracks that found them exploring the darker side of psychedelia with compelling intensity and imagination. *—Richie Unterberger*

(Turn On) The Music Machine / 1966 / Original Sound ♦♦♦
The Music Machine's debut would have been a lot better if they'd let Sean Bonniwell write all of the songs. Yer it was, as was often the case at the time, divided between fine Bonniwell originals and dispensable covers of current rock hits. Which means that, side by side with excellent Bonniwell originals like "Talk Talk," "The People in Me," and "Trouble," you'll find lukewarm covers of Neil Diamond's "Cherry Cherry," the Beatles' "Taxman," and "96 Tears" (though the slow, moody reading of "Hey Joe" is nice). Most of the Bonniwell songs were issued in much better company on the Rhino anthology, although one good one, the typically tortuous "Wrong," is only available on this album. *—Richie Unterberger*

Bonniwell's Music Machine / 1967 / Warner Brothers ♦♦♦
The Music Machine were renamed the Bonniwell Music Machine when they went to Warner Bros., as the original lineup disbanded at some point, leaving only chief singer and songwriter Sean Bonniwell. Much of the material on Warner, however, was recorded by the original group, and this album was pasted together from some singles (some of which had appeared on Original Sound in 1967) and other tracks, both by the original incarnation and a second outfit that was pretty much a Sean Bonniwell solo vehicle. Accordingly, the tone of the album is pretty uneven, but much of the material is excellent. In fact, some of the songs rate among their best; a few are also found on the Rhino anthology, but other first-rate tunes ("Bottom of the Soul," "Talk Me Down," "The Trap") are not. Some of the cuts (presumably those recorded after the first lineup broke up) find Bonniwell branching out from psych-punk into a poppier and more eclectic direction, sometimes with very good results, sometimes not. Long out of print and difficult to find, the entire album is included on the Sundazed CD reissue *Beyond the Garage*, meaning that it's no longer necessary to search for an original copy. *—Richie Unterberger*

• **The Best of the Music Machine** / 1984 / Rhino ♦♦♦♦♦
Besides "Talk Talk" and "The People in Me," this features the best cuts from their first LP, some fine non-LP singles that rank among the best obscure gems of the psychedelic era, and some decent previously unissued cuts. The package is enhanced by detailed liner notes by Sean Bonniwell. *—Richie Unterberger*

Beyond the Garage / Nov. 14, 1995 / Sundazed ♦♦♦♦♦
Although the material the Music Machine recorded for Warner Bros. (released under the name Bonniwell Music Machine) is little known, it's almost up to the high standards of their Original Sound sides. It's also been extremely hard to find, until this excellent 20-track reissue. This contains the entire contents of the 1968 *Bonniwell Music Machine* album (some of which had actually been released on the Music Machine's 1967 singles for Original Sound), plus various rare singles and a couple of unreleased tunes. Though a bit erratic, the best of this is thrilling stuff, as exciting as experimental garage rock ever got. "Bottom of the Soul," "The Eagle Never Hunts the Fly," "Talk Me Down," and "Double Yellow Line" all count among their toughest pop-psych punkers. Tracks like "Tin Can Beach," "The Trap," and "Discrepancy" also show songwriter and lead singer Sean Bonniwell expanding from the pounding guitar-organ prototype into more eclectic, but equally compelling, directions with touches of folk and orchestration. Inventive studio arrangements and lyrical wordplay are constants throughout. You won't find Bonniwell's name mentioned in many standard rock reference books, but this CD further bolsters his credentials as one of the most underappreciated innovators of late-'60s rock. *—Richie Unterberger*

Turn On: The Best of the Music Machine / Mar. 23, 1999 / Collectables ♦♦♦♦♦
This album contains all 12 tracks from the Music Machine's 1966 debut album, *(Turn On) The Music Machine* (Original Sound 5015), including their two chart singles, "Talk Talk" and "The People in Me," plus both sides of both of their third and fourth singles, "Double Yellow Line"/"Absolutely Positive" and "I've Loved You"/"The Eagle Never Hunts the Fly." This is the group's entire output for Original Sound Records; they switched to Warner Bros. in 1967 and changed their personnel and their name to Bonniwell's Music Machine. Singer/guitarist/songwriter Sean Bonniwell dominates the proceedings with his sonorous voice, whether the band is playing originals like the unforgettable garage rock classic "Talk Talk" or such covers as the Beatles' "Taxman" and fellow garage dwellers ? and the Mysterians' "96 Tears." The playing is rudimentary, but more disciplined than that of many of the rock bands that came into existence in the mid-'60s, and Bonniwell's songwriting is sufficiently varied that it is regrettable the group didn't get much of a chance beyond its initial hit. *—William Ruhlmann*

Ignition / Jun. 27, 2000 / Sundazed ♦♦♦
As this has a mixture of rare singles and unreleased tracks from 1965-1969, it's primarily for converted Music Machine fans, not for those who want just one album by the group or a place to start investigation. That said, it's a pretty interesting assortment of odds and ends, a few of which are among the band's best efforts. Foremost among them is the explosive (and quite innovative for its time) 1966 number "Point of No Return" with its unusual mixture of folk-rock and pre-acid guitar work, as well as a magnificent anguished, subtly anti-war vocal by singer and songwriter Sean Bonniwell. The moody, building-from-a-smolder-to-a-roar "Dark White," a 1969 outtake, was already heard on the out-of-print Rhino best-of LP. It's also one of Bonniwell's better creations, as well as one of the best lyrical meditations upon the ambiguous tension of sexual desire that you're likely to hear. "Advise and Consent" is a decent obscure flop single, though not one of the group's greatest. As for the previously unveiled outings, the 1965 demos by the Ragamuffins (the trio of future Music Machine members Bonniwell, drummer Ron Edgar, and bassist Keith Olsen) are especially interesting, catching them in their tentative transition from folk-pop to garage psychedelia. "Citizen Fear," one of the latest tracks (from 1969), has the careering sonics and intriguing sociometaphysical (if that's a word) words typical of Bonniwell's better songs. Much of the rest, though, is simply not up to the caliber of the band's best stuff. Still, it's a worthy complement to the *(Turn On) The Music Machine* album and Sundazed's previous collection of lesser-known material, *Beyond the Garage*. *—Richie Unterberger*

Os Mutantes

f. 1965, São Paulo, Brazil
Obscuro, Foreign Language Rock, Brazilian Pop, MPB, Tropicalia
A seminal rock band in Brazil, Os Mutantes used their solid musical background to take

major pop/rock contributions from the Beatles and American bands and mix everything with deep electronics knowledge, Brazilian music, '60s psychedelia, and irreverent attitude, creating a result which can be discerned in today's Brazilian pop.

Brothers Arnaldo and Sérgio Dias Baptista formed Mutantes with Rita Lee Jones in 1965. The bizarre outfit was backed by competence and inventiveness, such as insecticide cans which were perfect to simulate cymbals—and were used effectively in recording sessions. It was evident that their path was linked to tropicália—which had the same ideals proposed by Os Mutantes, in its salad of philosophy, cultural industry, and pop culture. Gilberto Gil was immediately attracted by their anarchic attitude, and invited them to back him and record their single "O Relógio." In 1968, they performed in the album-manifesto *Tropicália ou Panis et Circensis*, with Gil, Caetano Veloso, Gal Costa, and Tom Zé. Soon after, they recorded their first LP (*Os Mutantes*), an unexpected translation of *Sgt. Pepper's* to the Brazilian idiom. In 1969, they recorded their second album, also self-titled. Among the band's own hits, they shamelessly included in that album the jingle "Algo Mais," which they had written for Shell Combustibles. The LP *A Divina Comédia* appeared in 1970, and ^O Jardim Elétrico the next.

Though Rita departed from the group not long after, the duo continued to play together, and advanced a progressive rock direction with *A E o Z*. In 1975, Os Mutantes recorded *Tudo Foi Feito Pelo Sol*. In the '90s, David Byrne began promoting their old recordings, which provoked a revival movement with plenty of reissuing of their albums. *—Alvaro Neder*

Os Mutantes / 1968 / Omplatten ✦✦✦✦✦

The band's debut album, *Os Mutantes*, is far and away their best—a wildly inventive trip that assimilates orchestral-pop, whimsical psychedelia, *musique concrète*, found-sound environments—and that's just the first song! Elsewhere there are nods to Carnaval, albeit with distinct hippie sensibilities, incorporating fuzz-tone guitars and go-go basslines. Two tracks, "O Relogio" and "Le Premier Bonheur du Jour," work through pastoral French pop, sounding closer to the Swingle Singers than Gilberto Gil. Though not all of the experimentation succeeds—the languid Brazilian blues of "Baby" is rather cumbersome—and pop/rock listeners may have a hard time finding the hooks, Os Mutantes' first album is an astonishing listen. It's far more experimental than any of the albums produced by the era's first-rate psychedelic bands of Britain or America. *—John Bush*

Mutantes / 1969 / Omplatten ✦✦✦✦

One album into their career in 1969, *Mutantes* showed few signs of musical burnout after turning in one of the oddest LPs released in the '60s. Similar to its predecessor, *Mutantes* relies on an atmosphere of experimentation and continual musical collisions, walking a fine line between innovation and pointless genre exercises. The lead track ("Dom Quixote") has the same focus on stylistic cut-and-paste as their debut LP's first track ("Panis et Circenses"). Among the band's musical contemporaries, *Mutantes* sounds similar only to songs like the Who's miniature suite "A Quick One While He's Away"—though done in three minutes instead of nine, and much more confusing given the language barrier. The album highlights ("Nao Va Se Perder por Ai") and ("Dois Mil e Um") come with what sounds like a typically twisted take on roots music (both Brazilian and American), complete with banjo, accordion, and twangy vocals. Though there are several other enjoyable tracks, including "Magica" and a slap-happy stomp called "Rita Lee," there's a palpable sense that the experimentation here isn't serving much more than its own ends. If the first album's relentless eclecticism did in fact occasionally resulted in dry passages, it's especially true here. *—John Bush*

Divina Comedia Ou Ando Meio Desligado / 1970 / Omplatten ✦✦✦✦

Three Brazilian teenagers start a garage band. They know nothing of music theory, have no equipment (they built their own guitar pedals and used tin cans as cymbals), but lots and lots of cannabis. Though the existence of Os Mutantes is in itself unremarkable, what is mind-blowing is the top-notch quality of the music. These three teens, Rita Lee (vocals), Sergio Baptista (guitar), and Arnaldo Baptista (drums), while attempting to mimic their heroes in the states, were able to surpass them. This was due to their inability to adequately imitate (due to their geographic isolation), and the band's unfettered creativity. For these reasons, their meld of otherworldly guitar noise, crisp harmonies, and propulsive drumming found no equal among American counterparts like the 13th Floor Elevators and the Electric Prunes. While these bands just picked up where *Sgt. Pepper's* left off, Os Mutantes made music that had no point of reference until almost 30 years later. This album is one of their best, and it showcases the band's ability to morph genres into their own warped originality. The opener "Ando Meio Desligado" beats American psychedelic rock at its own game, combining a great hook with untamed guitar theatrics and sound effects. On "Meu Refrigerador Neo Funciona," Rita Lee does Janis Joplin while Sergio overdubs his patented weirdness. "Desculpe, Baby" is a deceptively simple but intricate ballad, while "Hey Boy" turns doo wop on its head, contorting it into a whole new form. With each listen, *A Divina Comedia on Ando Meio Desligado* unveils new secrets, making it well worth the price of admission—lower than ever now that it's been reissued stateside. *—Ari Wiznitzer*

E Seus Cometas No Pais Do Baurets / 1972 / Polydor ✦✦✦✦✦

The fifth album from Os Mutantes was officially their last, although they would record another one in the same year, released as Rita Lee's solo album. There was little sound technology available, so they had to invent their own wah-wah, flanger, and phaser pedals, sound systems, and more. The second track is an acoustic ballad where the innocent voice of Rita Lee presents the love declaration of a bitch to her dog, backed by a bumbo leguero (typical instrument of South American countries and a trademark of protesters against dictatorship). It is no surprise that they were hated by the government: censorship delayed the release of the album, due to the title and the lyrics of "Cabeludo Patriota" ("Hairy Patriot"). Os Mutantes changed it to "A Hora E A Vez Do Cabelo Nascer" and added some noise over the censored lyrics. That leads you to think that their debauchery, irreverence, and utmost ignorance and alienation in relation to the grave happenings of the time produced some serious awareness. On the properly musical side, they show uncanny virtuosity in several different styles (rock, funk, ballad, jazz-rock) in tracks longer than the usual, filled with improvisation and beautiful and challenging solos. After so much effort to not be taken seriously, "Balada Do Louco" ("Ballad of the Insane") may pass unperceived. Its deep existential meaning, dealing with the feeling of rejection by society for not conforming to its standards, is an important song that may provide with some understanding for Arnaldo's mysterious suicide attempt in the '80s, at the same time serving as the key for understanding their concept: "I swear that it is better to not be the normal/If I can think that God is me." *—Alvaro Neder*

Personalidade / 1998 / Polydor ✦✦✦✦

Os Mutantes' greatest-hits collection *Personalidade* provides a remarkably balanced look at the group's career, especially compared with the American collection *Everything Is Possible*. The album includes seven tracks from the group's first two years (1968-69) and seven from their later years (1970-72). If there is a focus, it's on tracks from the band's first two albums, including "Panis et Circenses," "Baby," "Rita Lee," "Não Vá Se Perder Por Aí," "Caminhante Noturno," "Banho de Lua," and "Dois Mil e Um." Still, there are plenty of great later tracks, like "Jardim Elétrico" and "Meu Refrigerador Não Funciona." *—John Bush*

● **Everything Is Possible: The Best of Os Mutantes** / Jun. 8, 1999 / Luaka Bop ✦✦✦✦✦

The first major-label release of Mutantes material was this 1999 compilation, put together by longtime Brazilian fan David Byrne through his Luaka Bop label. Including tracks from the band's late-'60s and early-'70s LPs (available separately through Omplatten), *Everything Is Possible* is a solid collection that only includes 14 tracks but does spotlight Mutantes' tremendous diversity. From the birth of tropicalia on their first album from 1968 (wildly experimental pop songs like "Panis Et Circenses" and "Bat Macumba") plus their later, more straight-ahead incarnations, the album gives beginners a solid place to start. The inclusion of both versions of the rather tiresome Janis Joplin retread "Baby" is a bit regrettable, but all around, *Everything Is Possible* gets it right better than could be hoped from a domestic compilation. *—John Bush*

Tecnicolor / 2000 / Universal ✦✦✦

In 1970, Os Mutantes re-recorded in English a full LP's worth of their best songs, apparently hoping to crack the American and European market. (Brazilian expiates Caetano Veloso and Gilberto Gil would make the same move, for political reasons, one year later.) If ever, the late flowering of the psychedelic era was the perfect time for a Mutantes breakthrough, considering the trio's zany songwriting sense and even more anarchic production methods. And though the album never saw release until the next century—Western audiences proved far more understanding of Sergio Mendes' easy-pop version of Brazilian music forms anyway—*Tecnicolor* acquired a new lease on life when it was finally reissued in 2000. By no means did Mutantes commercialize their sound. The tape-music experimentation and freak-out guitar lines are, if anything, farther out than the first few Mutantes LPs. Though a few of the tracks—"Panis Et Circenses" especially—lose much of their cache with the addition of English lyrics, for the most part these versions equal or even better the originals. *—John Bush*

My Bloody Valentine

f. 1984, Dublin, Ireland

Dream Pop, Shoegazing, Alternative Pop/Rock, Noise Pop

Like the Velvet Underground, Sonic Youth, and the Jesus & Mary Chain before them, My Bloody Valentine redefined what noise meant within the context of pop songwriting. Led by guitarist Kevin Shields, the group released several EPs in the mid-'80s before recording the era-defining *Isn't Anything* in 1988, a record that merged lilting, ethereal melodies of the Cocteau Twins with crushingly loud, shimmering distortion. Though My Bloody Valentine rejected rock & roll conventions, it didn't subscribe to the precious tendencies of anti-rock art-pop bands. Instead, it rode crashing waves of white noise to unpredictable conclusions, particularly since their noise wasn't paralyzing like the typical avant-garde noise-rock band: It was translucent, glimmering, and beautiful. Shields was a perfectionist, especially when it came to recording, as much of My Bloody Valentine's sound was conceived within the studio itself. Nevertheless, the band was known as a formidible live act, even though they rarely moved, or even looked at the audience, while they were onstage. Their notorious lack of movement was branded "shoegazing" by the British music press, and soon there were legions of other shoegazers—Ride, Lush, the Boo Radleys, Chapterhouse, Slowdive—that, along with the rolling dance-influenced Madchester scene, dominated British indie-rock of the late '80s and early '90s. As shoegazing reached its peak in 1991, My Bloody Valentine released *Loveless*, which broke new sonic ground and was hailed as a masterpiece. Though the band was poised for a popular breakthrough, they disappeared into the studio and didn't emerge over the next five years, leaving behind a legacy that proved profoundly influential in the direction of '90s alternative rock. *—Stephen Thomas Erlewine*

This is Your Bloody Valentine / 1985 / Tycoon ✦✦

Isn't Anything / 1988 / Creation/Sire ✦✦✦✦✦

Though it's often seen as just a precursor to their magnum opus *Loveless*, in its own way, My Bloody Valentine's *Isn't Anything* is nearly as groundbreaking as their 1991 masterpiece. Not only was it the most lucid, expansive articulation yet of the group's sound, it virtually created the shoegazing scene and spawned legions of followers. The album's tightly structured songs still bore traces of My Bloody Valentine's previous incarnation as jangly indie-popsters, but Kevin Shields and company crafted wide-ranging experiments within those confines. "Feed Me With Your Kiss"'s mix of bruising guitars, drums, and sensual boy-girl vocals define My Bloody Valentine's signature sound, while "All I Need"'s weightless guitars and vocal melodies melt into a heady haze. Shields' unique tunings, tremolo, and micing techniques stand out on "You Never Should" and "Nothing Much to Lose," but Deb Googe's surprisingly funky bass line on "Soft As Snow (But Warm Inside)" reaffirms that all of the Valentines contributed to their innovative sound. Indeed, many of *Isn't Anything*'s disturbingly beautiful highlights come from Blinda Butcher. On the wrenching "No More Sorry," she sings abstractly pained lyrics like "Your septic heart and deadly hand/Loved me black and blue," barely audible over a swarm of fragile yet menacing guitars, while on "Several Girls Galore," she's sexy, yet dazed and distant; it sounds like she's whispering in your ear outside of a blaring nightclub. The Valentines' dark side is especially prominent on the album, particularly on "Sueisfine," where the chorus slyly morphs from "Sue is fine" to "Suicide." *Isn't Anything* captures My Bloody Valentine's revolutionary style in its infancy and points the way to *Loveless*, but it's far more than just a dress rehearsal for the band's moment of greatness. *—Heather Phares*

Ecstasy & Wine / 1989 / Lazy ✦✦✦✦
Before Kevin Shields was a guitar god, before *Isn't Anything* and *Loveless* became seminal classics, My Bloody Valentine was a struggling goth band trying to find their place in the music scene. When they disposed of their original singer, they started moving toward Cocteau Twins territory, using guitarist Bilinda Butcher's airy voice to redefine their image. *Ecstasy & Wine*, which combines the two EPs that came before *Isn't Anything*, is the sound of a band discovering their unique voice. "Strawberry Wine" is a gorgeous pop gem, with Shields and Butcher exploring the guitar landscapes that would later become their trademark. Both "Can I Touch You" and "Clair" are rare examples of My Bloody Valentine's talent for making swaggering hard rock ditties. Although a few of the songs lean toward the pop/rock of the Jesus and Mary Chain, it is quite amazing how even at this stage they seemed to understand the sound that would make them unique. Fans of the band will find this album essential, and even curious onlookers may find themselves drawn in by the gorgeous sound of one of the most unique bands in rock history. *—Bradley Torreano*

Glider [EP] / 1989 / Sire ✦✦✦✦
The *Glider* EP finds My Bloody Valentine exploring the different harmonics in their dissonances and distortion, creating floating layers of sound that are hypnotic in their ebb and flow. The first song, "Soon," is one of the group's greatest sound paintings, filled with evocative textures and eerie, disembodied rhythms, while the title track is nearly as fascinating, making *Glider* an essential addition to a My Bloody Valentine library. *—Stephen Thomas Erlewine*

★ **Loveless** / Nov. 5, 1991 / Sire ✦✦✦✦✦
Isn't Anything was good enough to inspire an entire scene of My Bloody Valentine soundalikes, but *Loveless*' greatness proved that the band was inimitable. After two painstaking years in the studio and nearly bankrupting their label Creation in the process, the group emerged with their masterpiece, which fulfilled all of the promise of their previous albums. If *Isn't Anything* was the Valentines' sonic blueprint, then *Loveless* saw those plans fleshed out, in the most literal sense: "Loomer," "What You Want," and "To Here Knows When"'s arrangements are so lush, they're practically tangible. With its voluptuous yet ethereal melodies and arrangements, *Loveless* intimates sensuality and sexuality instead of instead of stating them explicitly; Kevin Shields and Blinda Butcher's vocals meld perfectly with the trippy sonics around them, suggesting druggy sex or sexy drugs. From the commanding "Only Shallow" and "Come in Alone" to breathy reflections like "Sometimes" and "Blown a Wish," the album balances complexity and immediately memorable pop melodies with remarkable self-assurance, given its difficult creation. But *Loveless* doesn't just perfect the group's approach, it also hints at their continuing growth: "Soon" fuses the Valentines' roaring guitars with a dance-inspired beat, while the symphonic interlude "Touched" suggests an updated take on Fripp and Eno's pioneering guitar/electronics experiments. These glimpses into the band's evolution make Shields' difficulty in delivering a follow-up to *Loveless* even more frustrating, but completely understandable—the album's perfection sounded shoegazing's death-knell and raised expectations for the next My Bloody Valentine album to unreasonably high levels. Though Shields' collaborations with Yo La Tengo, Primal Scream, J. Mascis, and others were often rewarding, they were no match for *Loveless*. However, as My Bloody Valentine fans—and, apparently, Shields himself—will attest, nothing is. *—Heather Phares*

My Life Story

f. 1990

Chamber Pop, Brit-pop, Alternative Pop/Rock

My Life Story was one of many orchestral British pop groups that appeared in the wake of Pulp and Suede. Led by Jake Shillingford, who comes across as a low-rent Neil Hannon (the Divine Comedy), the group never won the critical respect of its influences—or even contemporaries like the Divine Comedy—but they won a hardcore following of die-hard Anglophiles. Playing concerts in underground London clubs, the band slowly built a small following, self-releasing their indie debut EP, *Big*, at the end of 1990. By 1992, the band consisted of a total of 11 musicians. During 1993, My Life Story's profile began to rise considerably, as they contributed strings to the Wonder Stuff's "Welcome to the Cheap Seats." That fall, they signed to Mother Tongue Records, releasing the single "Girl A, Girl B, Boy C" by the end of the year. The record was named Single of the Week by both Melody Maker and NME, and My Life Story opened for both Blur and Pulp during the winter of 1994. *Melody Maker* named the group's 1995 debut album, *Mornington Crescent*, one the year's best albums, but the record didn't sell in large numbers. As they recorded their major-label debut during the spring and summer of 1996, My Life Story played a series of high-profile gigs that increased their profile substantially. *The Golden Mile*, My Life Story's long-delayed major-label debut, was finally released in March of 1997. Although the band's audience was larger than ever, a critical backlash had begun, and the reviews for *The Golden Mile* were frequently harsh—Select labeled the record as "the worst album ever made." *—Stephen Thomas Erlewine*

Mornington Crescent / Feb. 6, 1995 / Mother Tongue ✦✦✦
My Life Story's debut album *Mornington Crescent* is a fitfully engaging collection of grandiose, orchestral pop. Jake Shillingford sounds like a bizarre cross between Martin Fry and Scott Walker, and while he occasionally has the wit and melodic skills to make his grand ambitions work—"Girl A, Girl B, Boy C" soars with its strings and wry lyrical observations—he too often relies on style, not substance, ultimately making *Mornington Crescent* a frustrating debut. *—Stephen Thomas Erlewine*

● **The Golden Mile** / Mar. 10, 1997 / Parlophone ✦✦✦
With a bigger budget to support his delusions of grandeur, Jake Shillingford takes My Life Story completely over the top with their major-label debut, *The Golden Mile*. Shillingford hasn't grown much as a lyricist—if anything, his witticisms and asides are cutesier and more banal than before—but his sense of melody has sharpened, making the single "12 Reasons Why I Love Her" and "Sparkle" shimmer. Unfortunately, these are the exceptions, not the rule. Too often, the music is weighed down by Shillingford's preciousness and its own pretentiousness, which has the effect of making the weakest moments on the record—"You Can't Uneat the Apple," "Mr. Boyd," the matching "April 1st" and "November 5th," and the ludicrous "The King of Kissingdom"—seem positively comical. Even so, the lush, glossy production helps make such flaws more tolerable than the half-baked music of *Mornington Crescent*, and *The Golden Mile* consequently sounds like a qualified step forward for the band. *—Stephen Thomas Erlewine*

Joined Up Talking / Feb. 21, 2000 / IT ✦✦✦

My Life With the Thrill Kill Kult

f. 1987, Chicago, IL

Alternative Dance, Alternative Pop/Rock, Industrial, House

Most house-based dance music is either completely devoid of content or has a fairly serious political consciousness. Not so with My Life With the Thrill Kill Kult. With their schlocky mix of samples, synths, beats, Satan, and sex, the group is a hyped-up, stylized psychedelic/industrial dance troupe who revels in bad taste of all kinds. And the sheer tastelessness of their records gained a large cult following in the early '90s, culminating in their 1991 *Sexplosion* album and its single, "Sex on Wheels." Though albums like *13 Above the Night*, *Blue Buddha*, and *A Crime for All Seasons* didn't achieve the same prominence as *Sexplosion*, the group cranked out their sleazy sounds for the better part of the '90s. *—Stephen Thomas Erlewine*

I See Good Spirits & I See Bad Spirits / 1988 / Wax Trax! ✦✦✦

Kooler Than Jesus / 1990 / Wax Trax! ✦✦✦✦
My Life with the Thrill Kill Kult's Industrial blend of B-movie samples, house beats, and kitschy apocalyptic pretense coheres nicely on *Kooler Than Jesus*. The 1990 EP on Wax Trax/TVT Records features two original tracks ("Kooler Than Jesus" and "Devil Bunnies") along with the combined material from the Chicago group's first two 12" vinyl-only single releases *My Life with the Thrill Kill Kult* and *Some Have to Dance, Some Have to Kill*. Highlights like "Devil Bunnies" and "Resisting the Spirit" feature an atmospheric range and programming prowess that makes this offering one of the outfit's best. While lacking the continuity and psycho/sexual excesses featured in *Confessions of a Knife* or *Sexpolosion*, *Kooler Than Jesus* has more than enough conceptual strength and inspired production of its own, making it one of the industrial genre's significant early '90s releases. *—Vincent Jeffries*

Confessions of a Knife / 1990 / Wax Trax! ✦✦✦
On *Confessions of a Knife*, Groovie Mann and company mix up a healthy dose of funky and organic instrumentation to create industrial music that's more extreme disco than house. A pulsing bass guitar propels the 1990 release, adding a rhythmic and textural depth to the group's sample-and-synth laden sound. Highlight tracks include "A Daisy Chain 4 Satan (Acid and Flowers Mix)" and "The Days of Swine and Roses." Each of the disc's first six cuts posses a fine balance of nihilistic intensity and structural finesse. The momentum fades as "Rivers of Blood, Years of Darkness," a below average remix of "Kooler Than Jesus" and "Burning Out" languish in a repetitiveness that the record fails to break out of. Despite its less-than-stellar second half, *Confessions of a Knife* is a significant offering that fans of My Life With the Thrill Kill Kult should definitely acquaint themselves with. *—Vincent Jeffries*

● **Sexplosion!** / 1991 / Interscope ✦✦✦✦
Though My Life With the Thrill Kill Kult has fared well among supporters of underground industrial and gothic music, the fairly accessible *Sexplosion!* consists of, for the most part, what is essentially melodic, high-energy Euro-dance music—but with quite a difference. Loaded with soundbites and references to S&M, bondage, and sexual misadventures, *Sexplosion!* is deliberately outrageous and over-the-top. With song titles like "Leathersex," "The International Sin Set," and "Sex on Wheels," it's clear that the Thrill Kill Kult loves shock value. But this highly cinematic and often amusing CD is so tongue-in-cheek and self-consciously erotic that it's hard to regard the unique, distinctive Thrill Kill Kult as genuinely subversive. Rather, *Sexplosion!*'s main aim is to have fun and entertain—and on that level, it's quite sucessful. *—Alex Henderson*

13 Above the Night / 1994 / Interscope ✦✦✦

Hit & Run Holiday / Aug. 22, 1995 / Rykodisc ✦✦✦✦
Thrill Kill Kult's take on sleazy excess is comparable to that of John Waters—which is to say that the band celebrates the inherent kitsch value of sex, drugs, and Satan. *Hit & Run*

Holiday contains such gems as the surf rock romp "Glamour Is a Rocky Road" (with its lipstick-smeared drama overdoses and cheap tricks), the supercharged "Hot Blood Risin'" ("Just a holiday chaser in search of my destiny/Come on, get in!"), and the blissed-out instrumental outro piece, "The Last Ride Out." Sunnier than some of TKK's earlier work, *Hit & Run Holiday*'s vibe is closer to a '50s B-movie beach party than an after-hours S&M club. —*Andy Hinds*

Crime for All Seasons / Jun. 10, 1997 / Rykodisc ✦✦✦
By the time My Life With the Thrill Kill Kult released *Crime for All Seasons* in 1997, they had spent too much time away from the spotlight and their audience, and the industrial/rave audience had declined sharply. So, the album was generally ignored, but this doesn't necessarily mean that the album was terrible. In fact, it isn't that much weaker than their other albums, which were similarly inconsistent, and it offers enough fine moments to keep fans happy, even though it does raise questions of whether the group has run out of ideas. —*Stephen Thomas Erlewine*

Dirty Little Secrets / Oct. 26, 1999 / Rykodisc ✦✦✦

The Mystic Tide

f. 1965, **db.** 1967
Garage Rock, Psychedelic
Of the many garage bands who released unrecognized and obscure singles in the mid-'60s, the Mystic Tide were one of the very best. The Long Island group released four singles on their own labels in 1966 and 1967, mostly for distribution at their own gigs (and apparently they didn't sell too well there, either). While the production on these is fairly raw, the group had genuine original talent, pursuing a dark, psychedelic vision with overloaded distorted guitar breaks. Their tunes (all written by guitarist Joe Docko) combined the minor-key melodies of British Invasion groups like the Zombies with the raunch of acts like Them. Unlike most other American groups following this path, however, they added a mysterioso (at times vaguely Middle Eastern) element that echoed the innovations of groups like the Doors, the Velvet Underground, and the very early Pink Floyd and Soft Machine, though the Mystic Tide most likely didn't hear any of these groups. Their sound and outlook were perhaps too foreboding for even local success, and the group disbanded in 1967, ironically finding a much greater audience when their singles were reissued for psych/garage collectors in the '80s. —*Richie Unterberger*

● **Solid Ground** / 1994 / Distortions ✦✦✦✦✦
Both sides of their four singles, plus three earlier demos in a lighter, more Zombies-like style. The grinding "Frustration" and the ominous "Running Through the Night," featuring Docko's prickly psychedelic guitar, are garage classics; the lengthy instrumental "Psychedelic Journey" anticipates Pink Floyd's "Interstellar Overdrive"; and "I Search for a New Love" has delightful interweaving harmonies. The final seven tracks on this 18-cut

disc were recorded by Docko over two decades later, with a lumbering sub-Hendrix approach (including two Mystic Tide remakes). Fortunately, their placement at the end of the CD means that they can be ignored with ease by discriminating listeners. —*Richie Unterberger*

The Mystics

f. 1958, Brooklyn, NY
Brill Building Pop, Doo Wop
Formed in Brooklyn, NY, in the late '50s, this white doo wop group, consisting of Al Contrera, Al Cracolici, Phil Cracolici, George Galfo, and Bob Ferrante, scored their one and only major national hit in 1959 with the Doc Pomus/Mort Shuman-authored "Hushabye." Released in May of 1959, the song spent nine weeks of that spring and summer on the charts, rising to number 20. It is one of those "perfect" records, exemplifying a musical genre—the soaring, radiant harmonies were astonishing in their purity, which was matched by the innocence of the song itself; the gentle support of Bucky Pizzarelli's and Al Caiolla's clean, crisp guitars, and Panama Francis' understated drumming meshed with the singing in ways that simply couldn't be improved. The song was later covered by such harmony-oriented groups as Jay & the Americans and the Beach Boys, and has become a rock & roll standard, but the original has never been equaled. The group attempted a follow-up in the fall of 1959 with "Don't Take the Stars," a livelier, even more ambitious number showing off gorgeous multi-layered harmonies and resplendent in an achingly catchy melody, but somehow the song missed. By that time, the group's manager and record label were bringing in other talents to augment the Mystics' sound. The beauty of "Hushabye," however, coupled with the quality of their subsequent work—even though none of it ever reached a wide audience—left an impression among doo wop enthusiasts that lingered for decades, leading to a comeback in the early '80s. —*Bruce Eder*

● **The Mystics Meet the Jarmels** / 1990 / Ace ✦✦✦✦
All surviving 16 tracks recorded by the Mystics for Laurie Records, in impeccable sound. The only drawback to the excellence of this package (which also includes 14 songs by the Laurie group the Jarmels) is the slightly sketchy notes, which don't do full justice to the group or its influence. The fidelity here is astonishing, almost like being in the studio with the singers, and it puts to shame many domestic reissues of the same period. "Hushabye" is only one of the gems here, and anyone who hasn't heard "Don't Take the Stars" should make it his or her business to hear it on this collection. Amid the expected glowing harmony ballads are a few hard-rocking jump numbers like "Goodbye Mr. Blues," featuring new member Eddie Shotz on lead vocals, which came near the end of their time at Laurie, in 1961. Among the other treasures is an originally unreleased version of Ernie Maresca's "Let Me Steal Your Heart Away," with Paul Simon on lead vocal. (British import) —*Bruce Eder*

*N Sync

Teen Pop, Euro-Dance, Adult Contemporary, Dance-Pop

Like the Backstreet Boys before them, the teenage male vocal group *N Sync emerged from Orlando, FL; though formed in 1996, their roots trace back much earlier to singers J.C. Chasez and Justin Timberlake, who together previously co-starred on the Disney Channel's *The Mickey Mouse Club* before later relocating to Nashville, where they worked on solo projects with the same vocal coach and songwriters. Timberlake soon returned to Orlando, where he befriended Chris Kirkpatrick and Joey Fatone; with Chasez, the four agreed to form a band, and with the addition of bass James Lance Bass, *N Sync was complete. Hooking up with a series of producers including Denniz Pop, the group recorded their self-titled debut LP, initially released on BMG Ariola Munich; *N Sync soon became an overnight success throughout much of Europe, with the singles "I Want You Back" and "Tearing Up My Heart" both becoming major hits. The album was released in the U.S. in the spring of 1998, and—accompanied by a tour of the nation's roller rinks—it became an American hit as well; *Home for Christmas* followed later that same year, and in the spring of 2000, the group broke sales records with *No Strings Attached*, which sold close to 2.5 million copies in its first week of release. The kitschy-pop third album, *Celebrity*, appeared in summer 2001. —*Jason Ankeny*

'N Sync / Mar. 24, 1998 / RCA ♦♦♦

Riding the wave of post-Spice Girls dance-pop groups and sounding suspiciously like a low-rent, American Take That, the Orlando, FL-based 'N Sync came bursting out of roller rinks across the U.S. in the spring of 1998 with their eponymous debut. The group hired a number of producers, including the Backstreet Boys' Kristian Lundin and Denniz Pop & Max Martin, the team behind Robyn and Ace of Base, who help turn the album into a pleasing piece of ear candy. They don't have the charisma or tunes of the Spice Girls or All Saints, nor do they have a visionary like Gary Barlow or a sex symbol like Robbie Williams in the group. The only thing the five boys of *N Sync have is good looks, good producers, and a couple of catchy singles, like "I Want You Back." That's enough for a hit, and not quite enough for an album. Even so, the filler is well made and competently performed, which means their teen fans will enjoy the album while it's hot. Whether they return to it again—either out of affection or kitsch—is another matter entirely. —*Stephen Thomas Erlewine*

No Strings Attached / Mar. 21, 2000 / Jive ♦♦♦♦

Prior to the release of their second album, *N Sync split from their manager in a bitter dispute and signed with Jive, the kings of teen pop. For *N Sync, the move provided them with an opportunity to, in the immortal words of George W. Bush, "define themselves," to prove that they were an independent unit—hence the title *No Strings Attached*. To cynical critics, they very well might sound the same as ever, yet this really blows away their previous record. That much is clear from the storming lead single "Bye Bye Bye," a pile-driving dance number with the catchiest chorus they've ever sang. However, the album isn't really just singles-n-filler, it actually is well sequenced and fairly balanced, much like the Backstreet Boys' *Millennium* or Christina Aguilera's album. Like those records, *No Strings Attached* pulls away from the standard dance-pop formula, strengthening it with harder street beats, electronica flourishes, ballads with some grit, and well-crafted pop tunes. Nobody is going to mistake this for Fatboy Slim, Beck, or TLC—it's still lightweight teen pop. Yet, it's very good teen pop, managing to not only work well within its limitations, but to push it slightly while retaining its breezy, hooky identity. *N Sync still can seem a little ordinary, lacking a truly charismatic punch ala Britney or Christina, yet they do deserve credit for shaking things up a little bit, since it's resulted in an effervescent, ingratiatingly cheerful album that's a vast improvement on the debut. —*Stephen Thomas Erlewine*

● **Celebrity** / Jul. 24, 2001 / Jive ♦♦♦♦♦

*N Sync is nothing if not literal. Last time around, they freed themselves from their manager and titled the record *No Strings Attached*. This time around, after that album moved millions of copies, they've released an album called *Celebrity*, none too subtly drawing attention to the fact that they're stars. That's right—this is a trials-n-tribulations of fame album, in the grand tradition of *Bad*, *Use Your Illusion*, and *In Utero*. The difference is, of course, that the boys have been thirsting for this attention since they were children, so they're entirely comfortable with their position as kings of teen pop, and they celebrate their celebrity. And that signals what is so right about the record too—'N Sync is self-aware, not just of their position in the pop world, but how to consolidate their strengths while pushing forward. Since time immemorial (or at least since 1987), any pop group rounds up hot producers before making a new record, but *N Sync has found producers that accentuate different sides of their music, from Brian McKnight smoothly delivering J.C. Chasez's "Selfish" to the Neptunes' subtle harpsichord groove on "Girlfriend." Nobody sticks around for too long and that's a blessing, since it keeps the album moving. As soon

as BT's "Pop" wraps up, we're in Rodney Jerkins territory for the skittering title track and, not long afterward, Max Martin returns with "Tell Me, Tell Me...Baby," just in case old-school fans are missing Martin's patented Euro-schtick. All this means, on at least a superficial level, is that it's the group's most varied album yet, but the emergence of Timberlake and Chasez as credible soulful singers and, yes, songwriters makes it their best album yet, and one of the best of the teen pop boom of 1999-2001. —*Stephen Thomas Erlewine*

Naked Eyes

f. 1981, **db.** 1984

New Romantic, New Wave, Synth-Pop

A key presence in the synth pop movement of the early '80s, the New Romantic duo Naked Eyes formed in Britain in 1981. Comprised of former schoolmates Pete Byrne (vocals) and Rob Fisher (keyboards), Naked Eyes debuted in March 1983 with the LP *Burning Bridges*, reissued in the U.S. a month later (minus several tracks) as a self-titled effort. The lead single, a majestic cover of the Burt Bacharach-Hal David perennial "Always Something There to Remind Me," emerged as a hit on both sides of the Atlantic, reaching the U.S. Top Ten on the strength of its video, which received heavy airplay on the fledgling MTV network. The American follow-up "Promises, Promises" (not the Bacharach/ David composition) was also a major hit, and Naked Eyes' future looked bright; however, 1984's *Fuel for the Fire* fared poorly, its lone single "(What) In the Name of Love" barely scraping into the Top 40. The duo disbanded soon after, and in 1988 Fisher resurfaced as one half of the pop duo Climie Fisher. He died August 25, 1999 of complications following stomach surgery. —*Jason Ankeny*

Naked Eyes / 1983 / EMI America ♦♦♦♦

Naked Eyes were in peak form for their debut, showing a highly likable, warmer side to the often cold and detached synth-duo form. The songs they're best known for, "Always Something There to Remind Me," "Promises, Promises" and "When the Lights Go Down," are all included here, though the album can also be found in its entirety (save for one track) on the more readily available *Promises, Promises: The Very Best of Naked Eyes*. [For some reason, Naked Eyes' debut was released in slightly different forms on either side of the Atlantic. *Naked Eyes*, released a month after its British counterpart, *Burning Bridges*, was given new artwork and dropped two tracks. Both tracks were reinstated for the *Very Best Of* collection.] —*Chris Woodstra*

Fuel for the Fire / 1984 / EMI America ♦♦

By late 1984, most synth pop acts attempted to redefine themselves rather than be trapped by the genre's limited scope. Naked Eyes, however, didn't give up the fight, instead opting to recreate the formula of their debut. The results were predictably less interesting the first outing, but *Fuel for Fire* did manage to recapture the magic at least once with "(What) In the Name of Love." All but two tracks were compiled on *Promises, Promises: The Very Best of Naked Eyes*. —*Chris Woodstra*

The Best of Naked Eyes / Apr. 31, 1991 / EMI America ♦♦♦♦♦

Best of Naked Eyes offers 15 tracks of the synth pop duo's best moments from their two U.S. albums, 1983's *Naked Eyes* and 1984's *Burning Bridges*. The collection is surpassed by the more extensive *Very Best Of* from 1994, but is notable for the inclusion of one track, "Could Be," which the second collection excluded. —*Chris Woodstra*

● **Promises, Promises: The Very Best of Naked Eyes** / Apr. 19, 1994 / EMI America ♦♦♦♦♦

It seems odd that a group which really only released two albums' worth of material in the span of about 18 months should warrant two best-of collections released only three years apart. Nevertheless, *Promises, Promises: The Very Best of Naked Eyes* beats the competition by offering 20 tracks, including all four of the hits, most of the album tracks, a few B-sides, and two versions of "Promises, Promises"—nearly the all of the duo's recorded output. And while anything more than four songs is probably overkill for all but the new wave-obsessed, it is nice to have it all available in one package. —*Chris Woodstra*

Nas (Nasir Jones)

b. Long Island, NY

Vocals / East Coast Rap, Hip-Hop, Gangsta Rap

Rumors began to circulate during the early '90s in New York about a prodigious youth capable of challenging Rakim, the legend who had set a new standard for MCing in the late '80s. For years, no one dared to even draw a comparison to Rakim—it was blasphemous to do so. Yet when Nas debuted in 1991 on Main Source's "Live at the Barbeque" and then dropped his first solo single, "Half Time," a year later, the comparison to Rakim was made. So when Nas finally released his debut album *Illmatic* in 1994, it was perhaps no surprise when unprecedented fanfare ensued. New York's hip-hop community championed Nas as the second coming, and justifiably so. After all, *Illmatic* was and will forever remain a masterpiece; Nas had not only a flawless rhyming technique but, more importantly, the lyrics of a street poet. Two years later Nas returned with *It Was Written*, another startling performance that brought him commercial success in addition to the admiration he had already won with *Illmatic*. When he then returned after a long three-year hiatus with not one but two albums in 1999, expectations were high to say the least—and for the most part, they went unfulfilled. The hip-hop diehards who had originally championed Nas back in the early '90s criticized his new mass-market approach and arguably irreverent attitude. The passion for the streets that had fueled his early work was displaced by a passion for money and fame. Nas had gone from street icon to international icon—by the end of the '90 most called him a superstar, some called him a sellout, few called him a poet. *—Jason Birchmeier*

● **Illmatic** / Apr. 19, 1994 / Columbia ✦✦✦✦✦
Nas unexpectedly burst onto the rap scene with little foreshadowing in early 1994, convincingly declaring himself—and subsequently being critically declared—a rap prodigy. Showered with critical acclaim yet modest commercial success, *Illmatic* stands as a near masterpiece, particularly since Nas quickly moved toward an occasionally diluted, dumbed-down commercial approach with subsequent albums. Yet the ghetto-superstar tendencies of Nas' late-'90s work are nowhere to be found here, as the young rapper focuses exclusively on MCing and literate lyrics rather than catchy choruses or pop interpolations. Songs such as "N.Y. State of Mind" and "The World Is Yours" feature staggering lyrics rich in enabling Utopian ghetto ideology and equally rich in a prophetic sense. Based on lyrics such as these and Nas' lucid delivery, it's no surprise the rap community instantly championed the young rapper, quickly propelling his ego toward pomposity. Yet in addition to Nas' lyrics and delivery, *Illmatic*'s production team—most notably, DJ Premier and Pete Rock—deserves recognition for making this album so engaging; their production here resembled few others at the time of this album's release in the early to mid-'90s. Yet as championed as this album has become, it still isn't quite the masterpiece most claim it to be. First of all, it's rather brief at only ten tracks, sounding almost like an EP. Furthermore, some of the tracks suffer from second-rate guest appearances (Q-Tip's amazing contribution stands out, though), and some of the tracks such as "One Time 4 Your Mind" aren't quite on par with the album's better moments ("One Love," "Life's a Bitch," "N.Y. State of Mind," "The World Is Yours"). Despite these minor complaints, though, most Nas fans will cherish this album as the only 1990s album by the artist that isn't hampered by blatant radio-crossover attempts ("Street Dreams," "Hate Me Now," "Nastradamus"). *—Jason Birchmeier*

It Was Written / Jul. 2, 1996 / Columbia ✦✦✦✦
For his second album, *It Was Written*, Nas hired a bunch of hip-hop's biggest producers—including Dr. Dre, DJ Premier, Stretch, and Trackmasters—to help him create the musical bed for his daring, groundbreaking rhymes. Although that rhyme style isn't as startling on *It Was Written* as it was one his debut, *Illmatic*, Nas has deepened his talents, creating a complex series of rhymes that not only flow, but manage to tell coherent stories as well. Furthermore, Nas often concentrates on creating vignettes about life in the ghetto that never are apolitical or ambivalent. This time around, the production is more detailed and elaborate, which gives the music a wider appeal. Sometimes this is a detriment—Nas sounds better when he tries to keep it at street-level—but usually, Nas' lyrical force cuts through the commercial sheen. Combined with the spare but deep grooves, his rhymes have a resonance unmatched by most of his mid-'90s contemporaries. Because, no matter how deep his lyrics are, his grooves are just as deep and that bottomless funk and spare beats is what makes *It Was Written* so compulsively listenable. *—Leo Stanley*

I Am . . . The Autobiography / Apr. 6, 1999 / Columbia ✦✦✦
I Am . . . is the third album and fourth stage in the evolution of Queensbridge's living legend Nasir Jones, from Nasty Nas to Nas to Nas Escobar to Nastradamus, the soothsaying mega-thug poet. This third installment is an introspective work from one of hip-hop's made men. Always billed as a hip-hop messiah, Nas rose through the ranks of hip-hop on the strength of powerful poetry. Contrary to the album's title, the scope of the work extends beyond the autobiography as Nas takes on politics, the state of hip-hop, Y2K, race, and religion with his own unique perspective. While *Illmatic* was Nas at his rawest and *It Was Written* was Nas' attempt to reconcile his underground leanings with his new-found fame, acclaim, and wealth, the Nas of *I Am . . .* is honest about his elevated status yet still feels the tension of no longer being ravenous on the mic. Musically, *I Am* is somewhat unimaginative by Nas' stratospheric standards. Tried and true producers, the Trackmasters stamp the album with their signature catchy grooves and samples, but some of these tracks lack the sonic depth to do justice to the prophecies of the pharaoh, Nas. Superproducer Premier comes to save the day on two outstanding tracks: "NY State of Mind, Pt. II" and "Nas Is Like." These two cuts are nothing short of *Illmatic* perfection. "Nas Is Like"'s symphonic composition is the perfect complement for an MC of Nas' supreme vocal quality and precise lyrics. Despite some of the blandness on the production end, Nas still shines as the old soul storyteller and crime-rhyme chronicler on cuts like "We Will Survive," a dirge for fallen rappers. Nas also experiments stylistically on "Big Things," sporting a Midwest cadence, and on "You Won't See Me Tonight," a Timbaland-produced duet with R&B songstress Aaliyah. *—Michael Di Bella*

Nastradamus / Nov. 23, 1999 / Columbia ✦✦✦
From boy to man to king to prophet, Nas re-emerged six months after his third album with *Nastradamus*, a pre-millenial statement touching on the future, spirituality, and family—issues that Nas has broached before, though never with this much devotion. It could have been an intriguing concept album, but *Nastradamus* is continually compromised by tracks that don't contribute to the theme. For every emotional track like "Some of Us Have Angels" or "God Love Us," there are the same old street-life anthems you'd expect to hear, like "Shoot 'em Up," "Come Get Me," "You Owe Me." They sound OK (thanks to production from L.E.S., DJ Premier, and Timbaland), but the result is yet another drawn out hip-hop album that wanders aimlessly and never really says anything. Nas' rapping is superb as usual, but for the most part it's a wasted effort. *—Keith Farley*

Johnny Nash

b. Aug. 19, 1940, Houston, TX
Vocals / Pop-Soul, Reggae-Pop, Soul
Though by no means an artistic innovator on par with contemporaries such as Bob Marley or Jimmy Cliff, singer Johnny Nash nevertheless proved a pivotal force behind the mainstream acceptance of reggae with the international success of his 1972 chart-topper "I Can See Clearly Now." Born in Houston, TX, on August 19, 1940, Nash signed to ABC-Paramount to release his 1957 debut single "A Teenager Sings the Blues," scoring his first chart hit early the following year with a rendition of Doris Day's "A Very Special Love." Marketed as a rival to Johnny Mathis, he even began a film career with 1959's *Take a Giant Step* before his career flagged with a series of little-noticed singles for Warner Bros., Groove, and Argo. Nash returned to prominence in 1965 when the ballad "Let's Move and Groove Together" reached the R&B Top Five; more importantly, the record became a major hit in Jamaica, where he traveled in 1967 on a promotional tour. During a return trip, he cut the ska-influenced single "Hold Me Tight" at Byron Lee's Federal Studios—a Top Five pop hit on both sides of the Atlantic, the record was issued on his own JAD label, which in early 1970 scored a Top 40 hit with a reggaefied rendition of Sam Cooke's "Cupid" as well. The following year Nash scored a major British hit with his reading of the Bob Marley perennial "Stir It Up"; while living in Britain, he signed to Epic, which in 1972 released his biggest hit, "I Can See Clearly Now," which sat atop the American pop charts for four weeks. Although his popularity at home again dimmed, Nash returned to the U.K. charts in 1975 with his number one cover of the Little Anthony classic "Tears on My Pillow." *—Jason Ankeny*

I Can See Clearly Now / 1972 / Epic ✦✦✦✦
Singer/songwriter/producer Johnny Nash's million-seller "I Can See Clearly Now" did more to bring the reggae music sound into the mainstream than any other single record up to that point. To be sure, there were previous reggae hits (Millie Small's "My Boy Lollipop," Desmond Dekker & the Aces's 1969 hit "Israelites"), but Nash's buoyant, breezy, optimistic classic proved to be a phenomenal record holding the number one pop position for four weeks and going to number one adult contemporary on Billboard's charts in fall 1972. Houston,TX-native Nash had been recording in Jamaica for some years before having his biggest hit. On the *I Can See Clearly Now* album, Nash used members of Bob Marley and the Wailers and recorded several Marley songs: "Stir It Up," the follow-up single, "Comma Comma," the smooth "Guava Jelly," and the Nash/Marley co-written ballad, "You Poured Sugar on Me." The tender album track "(It Was) So Nice While It Lasted" received radio play. Other standouts are the punchy horns-flavored "Ooh Baby You've Been Good to Me" and the lullaby-ish ballad "There Are More Questions Than Answers." It's a tribute to its high quality that *I Can See Clearly Now* was in print almost three decades after its original release. *—Ed Hogan*

● **The Reggae Collection** / Sep. 21, 1993 / Epic ✦✦✦✦
Nash was the first American singer to incorporate reggae rhythms, and as such deserves a lot of credit for paving the way for the acceptance of bona fide Jamaican performers. His own pop-soul-reggae concoctions, though, were often rather watery in comparison to the real thing. This brings together 20 of the reggae-style tracks he cut between 1968 and the mid-'70s, including his hits "Hold Me Tight," "Cupid," and "Stir It Up"; the version of "I Can See Clearly Now" is an alternate take. This leans too heavily on his 1972-75 Epic material without enough of his late-'60s work; the small hit "You Got Soul" is missing, and the delightfully light and soaring "Hold Me Tight" towers over most everything else here. Almost half the tracks were previously unreleased or previously unavailable in the U.S. *—Richie Unterberger*

The Best of Johnny Nash / 1996 / Columbia ✦✦✦✦
The Best of Johnny Nash is a terrific collection of Johnny Nash's early-'70s pop-reggae crossover hits, highlighted by "Stir It Up" and "I Can See Clearly Now." *—Stephen Thomas Erlewine*

The Nashville Teens

f. 1962, Weybridge, Surrey, England
British Invasion, Rock & Roll
The Nashville Teens were one of a brace of British acts competing for attention in the booming days of the early British Invasion and its early purely English phenomenon, the British beat boom. They were distinguished from most of the others by scoring a memorable and serious hit released in the summer of 1964, "Tobacco Road," which charted high on both sides of the Atlantic. The group's rock & roll credentials were as solid as that of any English band, as was demonstrated by the number of gigs that they played backing visiting American stars. What they lacked, however (apart from solid in-house songwriting talent), was one (or more) interesting personalities in their ranks that could be put before the public and a collective personality that could be defined, musically or any other way. Additionally, they were musically flexible to a fault, literally, capable of playing boogie-style rock & roll in the best Jerry Lee Lewis style or slightly bluesier and more folk-influenced songs, and even dabbled in doo wop, but they never had a sound, beyond the crunching attack on "Tobacco Road," that could be identified. As early as 1965, more than sheer enthusiasm for the music was needed to attract listeners, and after a few minor Top 40 British entries, the Nashville Teens followed the route of acts like the Swingin' Blue Jeans and the original Moody Blues to smaller venues and less prestigious opening

act spots. By 1968, not even a hard, slashing cover of Bob Dylan's "All Along the Watchtower" could get them noticed. By the early '80s, however, they'd achieved a certain degree of respect among collectors of British Invasion material, even in America where only "Tobacco Road" had ever made any impression. *—Bruce Eder*

Tobacco Road / 1964 / One Way ✦✦✦✦
The Nashville Teens were a truly kick-ass rock & roll band from London. Their main claim to fame was providing the kamikaze backup behind Jerry Lee Lewis on his *Live at the Star Club* LP and recording the massive hit "Tobacco Road." This disc reissues that entire 1964 album and adds another 14 bonus tracks to it, getting us all the way to 1971 in the group's recorded output. Hot versions Of "Mona," "I Like It Like That," "La Bamba," and "Too Much" are the album's high points, and while the later tracks are a nice touch, they don't quite measure to the group's halcyon days. *—Cub Koda*

Nashville Teens / 1974 / New World ✦✦✦
A mid-'70s reissue with some hard-to-find tracks that are actually superior to much of the released tracks from the 1960s. Probably the best single album by this band. *—Bruce Eder*

● **Best of the Nashville Teens** / 1993 / EMI ✦✦✦✦✦
The group recorded a fair amount of material in the '60s, almost all of which is included on this 24-track anthology, which contains their sole album (from 1964) and several singles. They had no songwriting talent (only two of these tunes are originals); and they drifted rather aimlessly in search of an identity or style, stabbing at straight pop, folk-rock, and hard rock. Some Shel Talmy-produced numbers from 1966 are of mild interest, as are some nicely arranged folk-pop tunes from 1965 (which suffer from mediocre vocals), but even British Invasion completists will be unimpressed by this collection. As a final insult, the mix of "Tobacco Road" which leads off this set is notably inferior to the familiar hit vinyl version. *—Richie Unterberger*

Nation of Ulysses

f. 1988, **db.** 1992
Emo, Indie Rock, Alternative Pop/Rock, American Underground
Whether a fiercely polemical punk band with liner notes full of anarchist propaganda or a parody of same, Nation of Ulysses formed in early 1988 around vocalist Ian Svenonius, guitarists Steve Kroner and Tim Green, bassist Steve Gamboa, and drummer James Canty (brother of Fugazi's Brendan Canty). The band recorded only two albums—with an EP on Dischord between—and subsequently split in late 1992, with Svenonius, Gamboa, and Canty re-forming as Cupid Car Club and later Make-Up while Green appeared with the Fakes, the Young Ginns, and Kicking Giant. *—John Bush*

13 Point Program to Destroy America / 1991 / Dischord ✦✦✦✦✦
A raging collection of songs preaching an ideology of insomnia, teenage rebellion, and sharp dressing, the Nation of Ulysses' *13-Point Program to Destroy America* comes across as a blueprint for the complete overthrow of adult society in favor of one ruled entirely by the cool kids. Nearly every track on the album is played at breakneck speed, and the overall message is one of uprising. "A Kid Who Tells on Another Kid Is a Dead Kid" and "Cool Senior High School (Fight Song)" extol the virtues of kids sticking together to exclude those not fit for the glorious new society, namely grown-ups and squares. All the songs are punk gems, and after a couple of listens the revolutionary rhetoric starts to sounds pretty damn exciting, maybe because it's not entirely clear whether or not the Nation of Ulysses is serious or just playing a joke on all the indie-rock hipsters. Either way, it's hard for anyone to not enjoy songs like "Look Out! Soul Is Back" and "Today I Met the Girl I'm Going to Marry." The revolution might not be here quite yet, but when it comes, be sure to have this album as proof to your worthiness. *—Brandon Gentry*

● **Plays Pretty for Baby** / 1992 / Dischord ✦✦✦✦✦
This is genius. This is a revolution, of both thought and sound. The Nation of Ulysses is unmatchable by any band ever; they have created a dialectic, a movement, and a youthful assault of the mind and senses. Like Greek to a Caucasian child, most will never understand even partially the spirit that lurks in these movements for it is about something higher than mere music. There is something that moves beyond the lingoes of "The Aspirin Kid" Ian Svenonious, the complicated scriptures that fill the liner notes, the infamous reputations of insane and overwhelming live performance. A warped hybrid synthesis of trashy garage rock, spastic jazz, and creative freedoms. Languages created and swallowed amidst the words and discordant melodies. Full of fervor, anger, wit, and remorse. Solid spastic percussion, swirling distorted guitars, droning bass, and swollen horns. Rambling exploding vocals spitting words of animosity and love, of rebellion and unity, of awakening and medicine. The Nation of Ulysses must prevail." *—Blake Butler*

The Embassy Tapes / 2000 / Dischord ✦✦✦✦
The Nation of Ulysses were seminal in a modern way, transcending easy definition. They obviously affected many bands, both in their body-shattering live performance reputation (mimicked by acts such as At the Drive-In and XBXRX) and in their rambling sonic attacks and flawless revolutionary songwriting. Nothing can touch the unending spout of energy and passion contained within their movements, as their cacophonous passion was put into the ridiculous, the childish, the pure. The Nation of Ulysses disbanded in 1992 after a short career that produced two full-length albums, and many people continued to romanticize the band, creating an underground cult following that has continued to spread partially via post-NOU projects of the band members, most notably the Make-Up and the Fucking Champs. Fortunately for listeners, a few of the NOU's later tracks written after their last album, *Plays Pretty for Baby*, were recorded inside the comfort of the Embassy, the band's group home. Although their second guitarist, Steve Kroner, was absent, these tapes still contained the everlasting youthful explosion of the NOU, including arguably some of their most well-written songs, such as "A.P.E. Embassy" and "Hex-Proof," and some reworked versions of their older songs, including "Shakedown" and "Last Train to Cool." Although the tape quality was quite low due to the volume of the music and the subpar recording process, *The Embassy Tapes* still commands an obvious value, a remaining trace of the much-loved, much-adorned Nation of Ulysses. *—Blake Butler*

Naughty By Nature

f. 1991, East Orange, NJ
Pop-Rap, Hardcore Rap, East Coast Rap, Golden Age
One of the finest '90s rap posses received some help from Queen Latifah on their 1991 debut and landed a huge hit with the naggingly incessant "O.P.P." Naughty By Nature scored another huge hit with their next release. *19 Naughty III* featured "Hip Hip Hooray," which rivaled "O.P.P." as a crossover smash and national catchphrase in 1993. They followed with *Poverty's Paradise* in 1995 and *Nature's Fury* in 1999. *—John Floyd*

Naughty By Nature / Sep. 3, 1991 / Tommy Boy ✦✦✦✦✦
This leering trio's first single, "O.P.P.," dominated the airwaves in the fall of 1991 on the strength of its home-truth bedroom message and its butt-hugging beat. Fans of the single will find plenty more in NBN's rollicking debut album. *—John Floyd*

19 Naughty III / Feb. 23, 1993 / Tommy Boy ✦✦✦✦
With its slamming beats and infectious hooks (exemplified by the hit single "Hip Hop Hooray"), *19 Naughty III*, Naughty By Nature's second album, proves that they're not a one-hit-wonder group. Although the music is terrific, the lyrical posturing and misogyny can grow tiresome. *—Stephen Thomas Erlewine*

Poverty's Paradise / May 2, 1995 / Tommy Boy ✦✦✦
For their third album, Naughty By Nature do little to truly change their style. Some of the beats are little slower and funkier, some of the rhymes are more dexterous, some of the rhythms are a little more complex—yet nothing distinguishes *Poverty's Paradise* from the group's two previous, and superior, records. *—Stephen Thomas Erlewine*

● **Nature's Finest: Naughty By Nature's Greatest Hits** / Mar. 9, 1999 / Tommy Boy ✦✦✦✦✦
Essential stuff for both diehards and casual fans alike, *Nature's Finest* is an excellent overview of Naughty By Nature's work to date—the blockbusters "O.P.P." and "Hip Hop Hooray" are here of course, as is their poignant tribute to Tupac Shakur ("Mourn You 'til I Join You"), along with hard-to-find remixes and soundtrack contributions. Even the most devoted fan might be put off by the entirely unnecessary megamix of the group's biggest hits, however. *—Chuck Donkers*

19 Naughty Nine: Nature's Fury / Apr. 27, 1999 / Arista ✦✦✦
Longevity is a rare for hip-hop artists, since audiences place a priority on new sounds. It's difficult for veteran acts to continue to cultivate new sounds, and many have fallen by the wayside as they've tried to keep up with the times—but not Naughty By Nature. They've never really changed their core sound, which is an alluring fusion of hardcore sentiments, pop hooks, and funky rhythms. But by not changing, they've managed to retain an audience, since they're reliable—each Naughty By Nature record sounds essentially the same, but it's a satisfying sound that balances catchy hooks and clever, literate rhymes. Few artists are ever able to establish a track record like that, and it's amazing that *19 Naughty Nine: Nature's Fury*—the group's fourth album and first for Arista Records—maintains the high quality. True, some listeners may wish NBN tried out different sounds and styles, but for the most part, the album delivers what any fan of the group could want: several killer party jams, a couple of slow numbers, and a handful of amiable filler. Nothing stands out as an outright classic in the vein of "O.P.P." or "Hip Hop Hooray," but there's genuine grit to the rhythms and rhymes and the music remains accessible and catchy—in short, the best of *Nature's Fury* proves that it's possible to be melodic and hardcore at the same time, to have both hooks and substance. It might not break new ground, but the album proves that Vinnie and Treach have developed their own signature sound and have found ways to keep it fresh and exciting nearly a decade into their career. *—Stephen Thomas Erlewine*

Nazareth

f. 1968, Dunfermline, Scotland
Album Rock, Hard Rock
The Scottish hard rock quartet Nazareth had a handful of hard-rock hits in the late '70s, including the proto-power ballad, "Love Hurts." Formed in 1968, the band featured vocalist Dan McCafferty, guitarist Manny Charlton, bassist Pete Agnew, and drummer Darrell Sweet. The band had relocated to London by 1970, and they released their self-titled debut album in 1971. Both *Nazareth* and 1972's *Exercises* received favorable attention by British hard rockers, but it was 1973's *Razamanaz* that moved them into the U.K. Top Ten (both "Broken Down Angel" and "Bad Bad Boy" were hit singles). *Loud N' Proud* and *Rampant* (both 1974) followed the same formula, yet were slightly less successful.

Released the following year, *Hair of the Dog* established Nazareth as an internationally popular hard-rock band. Featuring their revamped version of the Everly Brothers' "Love Hurts," the album sold over a million copies in the U.S. Until the end of the '70s, the band continued successfully as a quartet, releasing a series of Top 100 albums. In 1979, they added former Sensational Alex Harvey Band guitarist Zal Cleminson to their lineup; he left after recording two albums—1979's *No Mean City* and 1980's *Malice in Wonderland*—and was replaced by former Spirit keyboardist John Locke. Following the live 1981 album *'Snaz*, guitarist Bill Rankin also joined the group; Locke left soon after his addition and Rankin switched to keyboards.

By this time, their commercial appeal had dwindled across both the U.K. and the U.S. By the mid-'80s, Nazareth was left without a record contract, so the band was put on hiatus for a few years. They returned in 1992 with *No Jive*, which failed to gain an audience in America and Europe. In 1999, Nazareth resurfaced yet again with *Boogaloo. —Stephen Thomas Erlewine*

● **Hair of the Dog** / 1975 / A&M ✦✦✦✦✦

After slowly but surely building a fanbase around the world with albums like *Razamanaz* and *Loud & Proud*, Nazareth finally hit the big time in 1975 with *Hair of the Dog*. The title-track sets the mood for this stark album of hard rock with its combination of relentless guitar riffs, a throbbing, cowbell-driven beat, and an angry vocal from Dan McCafferty that denounces a "heart-breaker, soul-shaker." The end result is a memorably ferocious rocker that has become a staple of hard rock radio stations. The remainder of the album divides its time between similarly pulverizing hard rock fare and some intriguing experiments with the group's sound. In the rocker category, notable tracks include "Miss Misery," a bad romance lament driven by a doomy riff worthy of Black Sabbath, and "Changin' Times," a throbbing hard rock tune driven by a hypnotic, circular-sounding guitar riff. In the experimental category, the big highlight is "Please Don't Judas Me," an epic tune about paranoia that trades heavy metal riffs for a spooky, synthesizer-dominated atmosphere that is further enhanced by some light, Pink Floyd-styled slide guitar work. The American edition of this album also included a surprise hit for the group with their power ballad reinterpretation of the Everly Brothers classic "Love Hurts." However, the album's surprise highlight is a song that bridges the gap between the straight hard rock and experimental songs, "Beggars Day/Rose in Heather"; it starts out as a stomping rocker but smoothly transforms itself midway through into a gentle and spacey instrumental where soaring synthesizer lines support some moody guitar work. All in all, *Hair of the Dog* is the finest album in the Nazareth catalog. It is a necessity for both the group's fans and anyone who loves 1970s hard rock. *—Donald A. Guarisco*

The Nazz

f. 1967, Philadelphia, PA, **db.** 1969

Power Pop, Psychedelic

Inspired by a variety of British Invasion groups, from the omnipresent Beatles to the cult favorites the Move, Todd Rundgren and his Woody's Truck Stop colleague Carson Van Osten formed the Nazz in 1967. Taking their name from an obscure Yardbirds song, the Nazz were arguably the first Anglophiles in rock history. There had been many groups that drew inspiration from the Beatles and the Stones, but none had been so self-consciously reverent as the Nazz. One of their first singles, "Open My Eyes," twisted the riff from the Who's "I Can't Explain," and much of their music felt like homages to Brit-rock from the Kinks to Cream, thereby setting a precedent that was followed by scores of North American guitar-pop bands from the Raspberries to Sloan. *—Stephen Thomas Erlewine*

● **Nazz** / 1968 / Rhino ✦✦✦✦

Though many of their American peers interpreted the sounds of the British Invasion in different ways, the Nazz's take on jangly guitar pop and nascent heavy psychedelia turned into a blueprint for the American Anglophile power pop guitar bands that followed in the '70s. Which is why the Nazz's eponymous debut album is still a fascinating listen, even if portions of the record haven't dated particularly well. Ironically, one of the songs that hasn't aged well is "Hello, It's Me," a ballad that Todd Rundgren later turned into a contemporary standard. It fails here because its dirgey arrangement meanders—something that can't be said for the rest of *Nazz*. That's not to say that the band knows exactly where they're going, since it often seems like they don't; they just like to try a lot of different styles, cross-breeding their favorite bands in a blatant act of fanboy worship. At their best, the results of this approach are flat-out stunning, as on the lead cut "Open My Eyes," which twists the Who's "I Can't Explain" around until it winds up in Roy Wood territory. While that may be the only undisputed classic on the record, almost everything else on the album will be interesting to listeners that are as obsessive about '60s Brit-rock as the Nazz themselves. It's great to hear Rundgren and lead vocalist Stewkey approximate the high-pitched harmonies of Cream on "Back of Your Mind," or hearing them swing through London on "See What You Can Be." It's possible that some pure pop fans will hear too much Cream and Hendrix on the record, but they're exceptional showpieces for Rundgren's fine guitar. And that's what shines through on *Nazz*—even when the record gets muddled, it's possible to hear the first flowering of Rundgren's talents. *—Stephen Thomas Erlewine*

Nazz Nazz / 1969 / Rhino ✦✦✦✦

Originally intended as a double album titled *Fungo Bat*, *Nazz Nazz* is at once as equally diverse and more cohesive than the Nazz's eponymous debut. It's a weird trick, but the group pulls it off, largely due to the rapidly maturing talents of Rundgren, their main songwriter and producer. Throughout the Nazz's first record, he proved that he was a gifted mimic and a savvy melodicist, yet he never quite landed upon a signature style outside of their debut single "Hello It's Me"/"Open My Eyes." Not coincidentally, these were the two songs on the record that the Nazz produced themselves, and they followed that lead on *Nazz Nazz*, fusing their sundry influences into a distinctive psych-pop sound. Sonically, it's certainly more ambitious than it's predecessor and, apart from the odd forays into soul and blues (filtered through Cream, naturally) on "Featherbedding Lover" and "Kiddie Boy," it's more consistent. In many ways, that makes *Nazz Nazz* a better listen than its predecessor, even if it doesn't have a knockout punch like "Open My Eyes." That's because Rundgren's songs exhibit a stronger sense of identity, as ballads like "Letters Don't Count" and snarky pop-rockers like "Hang on Paul" point the way toward his solo career. There are a few embarassing detours, such as the hippie-dippy "Meridian Leeward," but the second Nazz record rivals the first because it offers a progression. It shows that the band, or at least Rundgren, have figured out how to blend their influences into something original. The Nazz may never have delivered a follow-up to this—*Nazz III* consists of the remaining sessions from the abandoned double album—but this is certainly ground zero for Rundgren's fascinating solo career. *—Stephen Thomas Erlewine*

Nazz III / 1970 / Rhino ✦✦✦

Fungo Bat was scrapped for a variety of reasons, among them Todd Rundgren's insistence on singing lead vocals on his newer songs. *Nazz Nazz* was released instead, leaving the second half of the proposed LP temporarily in the vaults. Rundgren left the group before it was released. Taking hold of uncontested leadership of the group, lead vocalist Robert "Stewkey" Antoni erased Rundgren's lead vocals, replacing them with his own, releasing the entire project as *Nazz III*. This is, at the very least, sour grapes, but the situation is made all the more peculiar since much of the material finds Rundgren's songwriting moving toward the signature pop style that dominated his first solo records. Stewkey has publicly stated his distaste for Rundgren's Laura Nyro infatuation, so it's a little odd to hear him sing such finely crafted songs as "Only One Winner" and "Some People." That aside, *Nazz III* is an impressive effort that, if taken in conjunction, would have resulted in a very good double record. Sure, there's some clutter, but such detours as "Loosen Up," a po-faced parody of Archie Bell & the Drells' "Tighten Up," reveal the snotty side of Rundgren's humor. More importantly, the bulk of the record indicates how rapidly he was developing as a songwriter and a producer. Where he proved himself as a gifted mimick on *Nazz*, the group's second two albums found him assimilating those influences and developing a signature style. If anything, *Nazz III* demonstrates that better than its predecessor, which often seemed a little disjointed. There still isn't anything as immediate and indelible as "Open My Eyes," yet the best moments easily provide the road map for Rundgren's solo career. Even if he doesn't sing on it. *—Stephen Thomas Erlewine*

The Best of Nazz / 1983 / Rhino ✦✦✦✦✦

Contains good examples of the band's powerful up-tempo material ("Open My Eyes"), the kind of Rundgren ballad material that defined the group to its pop audience ("Hello, It's Me"), and some interesting covers ("Kicks," a previously unreleased "Train Kept A-Rollin'"). *—William Ruhlmann*

Nazz From Philadelphia / 1997 / Distortions ✦✦

This compilation of late-'60s demos and alternate takes should not be viewed as being on the same level as their three albums. But when a cult band such as the Nazz only made three LPs, followers hunger for more, and this delivers the goods to satisfy the tastes and curiosities of specialists. A late-'67 demo of "Hello It's Me," close to the released version but less fully produced (particularly in regard to the backing vocals), is the highlight. Otherwise there's another song from the same late-'67 tape ("Crowded"), a mid-'68 demo of "Lemming Song" (a different version of which appeared on their debut album), alternate versions of "Kicks" and "Some People," radio commercials, a slightly different take of "Open My Eyes" (no phase on the guitar), and some alternates of songs from their second and third albums. The differences between these versions and the official ones are not radical, and if listened to for musical value alone rather than historical purposes, the tracks reflect (as does all their work) a confused band. They gravitated between soul-tinged ballads, power pop, and harder psychedelia and blues-rock, rarely coming up with tunes in the same league as their debut "Hello It's Me"/"Open My Eyes" single. If you've gotten this far, you'll also want the "Sydney's Lunchbox"/"It Must Be Everywhere" 45 (also on Distortions), which unearths two previously unheard songs from the late '60s. *—Richie Unterberger*

13th & Pine / 1998 / Distortions ✦✦✦

A collection of odds and sods, rarities and obscurities, Distortions' *13th & Pine* is designed for the obsessive Todd Rundgren collectors out there, and, in that sense, it satisfies, since there is a lot of weird, unheard music here. Still, this is a collection primarily of small pleasures, lacking revelations or forgotten gems—it's just simply a way to dig deeper. That's not a bad thing, but it does mean that it's inconsequential for anybody outside of the obsessives (and even they may find it a little marginal). *—Stephen Thomas Erlewine*

Me'Shell NdegéOcello

Vocals, Bass / Contemporary R&B, Club/Dance, M-Base, Alternative Pop/Rock, Singer/Songwriter

Me'Shell NdegéOcello blurs sexual conventions as much as any artist since Prince; more importantly, she blurs musical boundaries, too, creating a funky rock & roll that can veer off into sweet pop or dance-club bliss. Her 1993 debut, *Plantation Lullabies*, was critically acclaimed and scored a minor hit with "If That's Your Boyfriend (He Wasn't Last Night)," but she really began to receive mainstream attention with her hit 1994 duet with John Mellencamp, "Wild Night." Her follow-up, *Peace Beyond Passion*, appeared in 1996, and in 1999 she returned with *Bitter*. *—Stephen Thomas Erlewine*

Plantation Lullabies / 1993 / Maverick ✦✦✦✦

Me'Shell NdegéOcello's debut album twists and turns through so many genres—R&B, pop, jazz, hip-hop—that it's hard to put a finger on just where she wants to take its 13 songs. That she also spins conventional racial and sexual identity here makes *Plantation Lullabies* an occasionally overwhelming—as well as a vibrantly sophisticated—listen. NdegéOcello defies labels throughout, tagging her slinking and crawling songs with a rubbery flow that's just as rooted in '70s funky soul as it is in '90s hip-hop culture. The best songs here—"If That's Your Boyfriend (He Wasn't Last Night)," "Dred Loc," and "Outside Your Door"—work their way into their grooves with a seamless, and almost uniform, bounce. It can be a bit derivative (for all of NdegéOcello's genre-crossing, she always seems to go back to the same musical blueprint), but most of the time it's just about as boundary-busting and as affecting as '90s R&B gets. *—Michael Gallucci*

Me'shell NdegéOcello / 1994 / Maverick ✦✦✦

● **Peace Beyond Passion** / Jun. 25, 1996 / Warner Brothers ✦✦✦✦✦

There are times on Me'Shell NdegéOcello's second album where the funky hybrid of R&B

and alterna-pop that she laid down on her 1993 debut *Plantation Lullabies* actually seems to take on an ethereal quality. Beats and grooves float effortlessly out of the fluid rhythms, and NdegéOcello herself sings with a soothing reserve that was a little too deliberate on her previous work. And it's a better album because of it. *Peace Beyond Passion* is built around a triumvirate of songs addressing man's inhumanity toward man throughout the ages (with such heavy-handed titles as "Deuteronomy: Niggerman" and "Leviticus: Faggot"), but the real highlights of the set are a wry take on Bill Withers' "Who Is He and What Is He to You" and the ultra-smooth, slow-burning "Stay." It's new-age soul that's as spiritually purifying as it is musically sophisticated. *—Michael Gallucci*

Bitter / Aug. 24, 1999 / Warner Brothers ✦✦✦✦
Bitter is an appropriate title for Me'Shell NdegéOcello's third album. Inspired by a torturous romantic relationship, *Bitter* surges with emotions, and most of them are shaded with regret, remorse, or bitterness. Undoubtedly, the relationship was painful, but it has given NdegéOcello an artistic focus missing on her two previous albums. It provides a sorrowful, meditative emotional template that she matches with moody, slow songs that flow into each other. It's the kind of album that demands close listening, otherwise it has the tendency to fade into the background. For some listeners, concentrated listening may be a little difficult, given the bleak emotions of the music, but NdegéOcello's subtle songcraft truly reveals itself upon close inspection. And, with repeated plays, *Bitter* reveals itself as the most personal—and in many ways, most rewarding—album of her career. *—Stephen Thomas Erlewine*

Ned's Atomic Dustbin

f. Nov. 1987, Stourbridge, West Midlands, England
Alternative Pop/Rock, Dance-Pop
Ned's Atomic Dustbin's stylish fusion of punk and funk earned them a fair number of fans in the early '90s, just as England's Stone Roses-inspired "Madchester" scene was drawing to a close. Comprised of Jonn Penney (vocals), Rat (guitar), Matt Cheslin (bass), Alex Griffin (bass), and Dan Warton (drums), the group began as a neo-goth-rock outfit in the late '80s. By the beginning of the '90s, the band had developed a dense, assaultive sound that was distinguished by their thundering two-bass attack. Ned's released their first single, "Kill Your Television," in 1990; on the back of a slick, sloganeering marketing attack (epitomized by the 86 T-shirts the band had designed in their first three years), the single reached the U.K. Top 50 and led to a record contract with Sony Music. The band released their debut album, *God Fodder*, in 1991; it entered the charts at number four. For the rest of the year, the group toured the world and released singles drawn from *God Fodder*. Though they remained popular in the U.K., they weren't able to gather anything larger than a cult following in America. Released in 1992, *Are You Normal?* also failed to expand their following. For 1995's *Brainbloodvolume*, Ned's decided to expand their trademark sound by experimenting with techno music, yet the album proved a commercial failure. *—Stephen Thomas Erlewine*

● **Godfodder** / 1991 / Columbia ✦✦✦✦
Ned's Atomic Dustbin may be one of Britain's most overlooked bands, which is surprising, considering that while their releases may not be groundbreaking, each one is certainly solid. The band emerged in the early '90s, and was quickly grouped (along with bands like Pop Will Eat Itself and Carter U.S.M.) into the English "grebo" scene: punk-influenced, electronica-informed, hyper, lighthearted rock. *Godfodder*, their first major release, is arguably their best. Featuring college-radio hits like "Kill Your Television" and "Grey Cell Green," it's a consistently satisfying blend of frenzied, melodic rock, with the occasional touch of quirkiness; the band's use of two basses (one playing "normal" basslines, the other scratching out harmonic riffs) keeps their sound light and hooky enough to put quite a distance between their oeuvre and that of the average grebo or punk band. *—Nitsuh Abebe*

Bite / 1991 / Chapter 22 ✦✦✦

Are You Normal? / Nov. 3, 1992 / Chaos/Columbia ✦✦✦
Godfodder, Ned's Atomic Dustbin's first U.S. release, focused on the hyper punk aspect of England's "grebo" movement, relying on insanely catchy hooks and the band's dual-bass sound to keep things interesting. On *Are You Normal?*, they've managed to back down a bit and let the dynamics of the basses soak through the rush of power chords that dominate their early work. The result is an almost bouncy, bright album, full of great hooks and lyrical cleverness. It's less immediately gratifying than the speedy pop of *Godfodder*, but less disposable as well; a few songs seem like they've gone awry, somewhere, but there are enough tracks like "Not Sleeping Around" (the lodge-in-your-head single) to give fans of the early work something to hang onto. In the larger history of the band, *Are You Normal?* stands as the point at which the group began to develop their true sound, laying off on the exuberant punk-pop and working with the sampling, electronics, and ultramodern production that would mark their next album, *Brainbloodvolume*. There are, of course, a few missteps, but when the sound works, it puts quite a few of Ned's contemporaries to shame. *—Nitsuh Abebe*

Brainbloodvolume / 1995 / Work/Furtive ✦✦✦
In an attempt to get their career back on track, Ned's Atomic Dustbin shake up their sound on their third album, *Brainbloodvolume*. Some of the songs feature a meatier guitar. *—Stephen Thomas Erlewine*

522 / 1995 / Furtive ✦✦✦
One could write off *522* as a largely useless collection, and with reason—some of its tracks aren't exactly necessary, especially "dance" remixes of "Intact" and "Kill Your Televison" that sound positively childish compared to the wave of electronica which followed them in the late 1990s. On the other hand, quite a bit of the 22-song compilation is just as appealing (and sometimes more) than the band's album work, including: their cover of the Bay City Rollers' "Saturday Night" (from the *So I Married an Axe Murderer* soundtrack), a few songs from their first album, *Bite* (which is difficult to find in the U.S.), and a smattering of wonderful rarities ("Flexiblehead," "Twenty Three Hour Toothache.") Even with the slack trimmed away, there's more than an album's worth of decent work here—and this is not the sort of side work that differs immensely from the band's major releases. Definitely a good addition for hardcore fans, and just as useful for casual ones. *—Nitsuh Abebe*

Intact / 1998 / Song Square/Sony ✦✦✦

Fred Neil

b. Jan. 1, 1936, St. Petersburg, FL, **d.** Jul. 7, 2001, Summerland Key, FL
Vocals, Guitar / Folk-Rock, Singer/Songwriter
Moody, bluesy, and melodic, Fred Neil was one of the most compelling folk-rockers to emerge from Greenwich Village in the mid-'60s. His albums showcased his extraordinarily low, rich voice on intensely personal and reflective compositions, sounding like a cross between Tim Buckley and Tim Hardin. His influence was subtle but significant; before forming the Lovin' Spoonful, John Sebastian played harmonica on Neil's first album, which also featured guitarist Felix Pappalardi, who went on to produce Cream. The Jefferson Airplane featured Neil's "Other Side of This Life" prominently in their concerts, and dedicated a couple of songs ("Ballad of You and Me and Pooneil" and "House at Pooneil Corner") to him. On the B-side of "Crying" is Neil's "Candy Man," one of Roy Orbison's bluesiest efforts. Stephen Stills has mentioned Neil as an influence on his guitar playing. Most famously, Nilsson took Fred's "Everybody's Talkin'" into the Top Ten as the theme to the movie *Midnight Cowboy*. For all his tangential influence, Neil himself has remained an enigmatic, mysterious figure. His recorded output was formidable but sparse. Always a recluse, he retreated to his home in Coconut Grove, FL, after achieving cult success, and hasn't released anything since a live album in 1971. *—Richie Unterberger*

Hootenanny Live at the Bitter End / 1964 / FM ✦✦
This is a rare compilation of live folk performances from the Bitter End in New York circa 1963, with three tracks apiece by Fred Neil, Len Chandler, Jo Mapes, and Bob Carey. The Neil material stands leagues above the rest of the LP and includes two songs that he would not record on his solo albums for Elektra and Capitol, as well as one ("That's the Bag I'm In") that he would redo on *Fred Neil*. These tunes find his rich folk-blues fusion fully formed and are highly recommended to Neil fans. All of the other performers sing sincere, twee coffeehouse folk that illustrates (if only in retrospect) just how necessary it was for gutsier artists like Neil to come along and blow them out of the water. *—Richie Unterberger*

Bleecker & MacDougal / 1964 / Elektra ✦✦✦✦✦
Neil's Greenwich village coffeehouse roots are in strongest evidence on this album (later retitled *Little Bit of Rain*). The drummerless (but not entirely acoustic) album is also his bluesiest recording. The uniformly strong tracks include "Other Side of This Life" and "Candy Man." *—Richie Unterberger*

Tear Down the Walls / 1965 / Elektra ✦✦✦
Before establishing himself as a solo singer/songwriter, Neil briefly played and recorded as a duo with Vince Martin in the mid-1960s, resulting in one rare Elektra LP, *Tear Down the Walls*. Far more based in early-'60s troubadour/coffeehouse folk than Neil's solo efforts, this is divided pretty evenly between the artist's originals and trad folk covers, although there is one Martin original. Neil's earthy, bluesy vocal style is already fully formed but somewhat compromised by the higher, sweeter, and more conventional tones of Martin, who duets with Neil on most of the tunes. Neil's bluesy, laconic persona does come to the fore on "Weary Blues," "Baby" (which has a tinge of Indian raga), and especially "Wild Child in a World of Trouble," which Neil sings by himself. Even the more standard-style numbers are at the least pleasant, including a good version of "Morning Dew." *—Richie Unterberger*

Everybody's Talkin' / 1966 / Capitol ✦✦✦✦✦
Originally released in early 1967 as simply *Fred Neil* and re-released as *Everybody's Talkin'* in 1969 after Harry Nilsson had a huge international hit from the soundtrack of "Midnight Cowboy," this album is one of the greatest progressive folk albums to date. At the time of its recording, Neil was a well-known figure in the folk world and an influential hero to such up-and-coming future legends as David Crosby, Tim Buckley, John Sebastian, Stephen Stills, and many others. The reasons for this are all on this record. Every track on this superb album is marked by Neil's wholly original approach, combining folk, blues, gospel, and jazz (among other things) to create a synthesis that is beguiling to both the ear and the heart. Neil's baritone reaches its lowest, honey-soaked depths on cuts like "Faretheewell," "That's the Bag I'm In," the title track, and many more. Folk music (and music in general) doesn't get much better than this. *—Matthew Greenwald*

Fred Neil / 1967 / Capitol ✦✦✦✦✦
Neil's second album was his best, fully completing his transition to electric folk-rock. "Everybody's Talkin'," "The Dolphins," and "That's the Bag I'm In" are all among his best (and most frequently covered) compositions. Currently hard to find, all of its tracks reappeared on the British mid-'80s *The Very Best of Fred Neil* compilation, although that LP is itself hard to locate these days. *—Richie Unterberger*

Sessions / 1967 / Capitol ✦✦✦
Sessions was a peculiar record that seemed to find Neil losing his focus to some degree, even as he increased his appetite for experimentation with arrangements and songwriting. The loose, informal feel of most of the cuts suggested that the performances were rehearsals or jams, rather than finely honed finished products; indeed, the take number of

each track was appended onto the songs' actual titles. This meant that the virtues of compositions like "Fools Are a Long Time Coming," which would have been quite good if edited down, were a bit obscured by the swirling layers of guitars and casual execution. Others, like "Merry Go Round," "Roll On Rosie," and the interminable "Look Over Yonder," meandered for minutes on end in search of a definite groove or tempo, dallying with raga-type improvisations at times. Neil's vocal genius, however, remained intact, and the best two cuts were the most straight-ahead: "Felicity" is a nice oblique meditation-cum-love song, and the cover of Percy Mayfield's "Please Send Me Somebody to Love" is effective. *—Richie Unterberger*

Other Side of This Life / 1971 / Capitol ♦♦♦
Neil's final album was an odd, stitched-together affair matching one LP side of live, acoustic material with a side of studio leftovers. The live half (on which Neil is assisted by second guitarist Monte Dunn) does not provide any revelations when compared to the studio prototypes, but he does deliver decent versions of several of his best songs, including "The Dolphins," "Everybody's Talkin'," and "Other Side of This Life." Side two has OK, but not remarkably interesting, alternates of "Badi-Da" and "Felicity," as well as a fair version of the soul standard "You Don't Miss Your Water" and a traditional blues, "Come Back Baby," with Les McCann on piano. *—Richie Unterberger*

The Very Best of Fred Neil / 1986 / See For Miles ♦♦♦♦♦
It doesn't include any of his Elektra tracks, but this is a good compilation of his Capitol work, including all of the 1967 album *Fred Neil* (which featured Stephen Stills) and four tracks from his follow-up LP *Sessions*. Contains "Everybody's Talkin'," "Green Rocky Road," and the beautiful "The Dolphins." *—Richie Unterberger*

★ **The Many Sides of Fred Neil** / 1998 / Collectors' Choice Music ♦♦♦♦♦
For many, the name Fred Neil will be familiar only as that belonging to the songwriter of the modern classic "Everybody's Talkin'," or perhaps "Candyman," "The Dolphins," or "Other Side of This Life," songs that Roy Orbison, Tim Buckley, and the Jefferson Airplane, respectively, recorded. However, Neil's influence extends much farther. John Sebastian, David Crosby, Stephen Stills, and Bob Dylan all claimed him as an influence, since he blended traditional and contemporary folk, blues, rock, gospel, Indian, and pop influences into a distinctive, idiosyncratic style. His music was not only influential, it was quite rich on its own terms and some of the best music of its era. Unfortunately, since Neil chose a life of seclusion in 1971, disappearing from both recording and performing, his work was neglected. Remedying the situation, *The Many Sides* bypasses his Elektra material, instead offering a complete summary of his Capitol recordings, including his three albums for the label (*Fred Neil*, *Sessions*, *Other Side of This Life*), both sides of a non-LP single with the Nashville Street Singers, and six unreleased cuts. It's a long overdue compilation and one that certainly stands as a definitive portrait of an influential and criminally underappreciated folk-rock figure. After listening to *The Many Sides of Fred Neil*, it makes sense that Neil turned into a recluse—this is moody, haunting music, unlike much of the work of his contemporaries. In particular, his eponymous album boasts challenging, innovative arrangments that remain fresh and startling to this day. The rest of his work may be a little uneven in comparison, but it's frequently compelling and often matches its heights. Most importantly, *The Many Sides of Fred Neil* grants Neil his proper place in folk-rock history, confirming his unique vision and talent. *—Stephen Thomas Erlewine*

Rick Nelson

b. May 8, 1940, Teaneck, NJ, **d.** Dec. 31, 1985, Dallas, TX
Vocals, Guitar / Teen Idol, Rockabilly, Country-Rock, Rock & Roll
Rick Nelson was one of the very biggest of the '50s teen idols, so it took a while for him to attain the same level of critical respectability as other early rock greats. Yet now the consensus is that he made some of the finest pop/rock recordings of his era. Sure, he had more promotional push than any other rock musician of the '50s; no, he wasn't the greatest singer; and yes, others rocked harder. But Nelson was extraordinarily consistent during the first five years of his recording career, crafting pleasant pop-rockabilly hybrids with ace session players and projecting an archetype of the sensitive, reticent young adult with his accomplished vocals. He also played a somewhat underestimated role in rock & roll's absorption into mainstream America—how bad could rock be if it was featured on one of America's favorite family situation comedies on a weekly basis? Ricky could rock pretty hard when he wanted to, as on "Be-Bop Baby" and "Stood Up," though in a polished fashion that wasn't quite as wild and threatening as rockabilly's Southern originators. Nelson really hit his stride, though, with mid-tempo numbers and ballads that provided a more secure niche for his calm vocals and narrow range. From 1957 to 1962, he was about the highest-selling singer in the U.S. except for Elvis, making the Top 40 about 30 times. "Poor Little Fool" and "Lonesome Town" (1958) were early indications of his ballad style; in the early '60s, "Travelin' Man," "Young World," "Teen Age Idol," and other hits pointed to a more countrified, mature style as he honed in on his 21st birthday (by which time he would shorten his billing from "Ricky" to "Rick"). Nelson had a strong country feel to much of his material from the beginning, and by the late '60s it was becoming dominant. He formed one of the earliest country-rock groups, the Stone Canyon Band, and though a cover of Bob Dylan's "She Belongs to Me" made the Top 40 in 1970, his country-rock outings attracted more critical acclaim than commercial success, until 1972's "Garden Party." A rare self-composed number, based around the frosty reception granted his contemporary material at a rock & roll oldies show, it became his last Top Ten hit. *—Richie Unterberger*

Rick Sings Nelson / 1970 / MCA ♦♦♦

Rudy the Fifth / 1971 / MCA ♦♦♦

Garden Party / 1972 / MCA ♦♦♦♦♦
This comeback introduced Nelson to a new generation. *—Bill Dahl*

Rick Nelson Country / 1973 / MCA ♦♦♦

Windfall / 1974 / MCA ♦♦♦♦

Playing to Win / 1981 / Capitol ♦♦♦♦
Playing to Win was an album of beginnings and endings for Rick Nelson. It was his first LP in more than three years, marking the start of his fifth label affiliation, this one with Capitol Records, and, though it was released just short of five years before his death, it was his last album of new, original material to be released during his lifetime, followed only by 1985's *All My Best*, a collection of re-recordings of his hits marketed on television. In his bid for yet another commercial comeback, Nelson updated his rock & roll sound to take into consideration the heartland rock of artists like Bruce Springsteen, Bob Seger, and Tom Petty, as well as punk/new wave. As always, he had great taste, which allowed him to pick great material: John Fogerty's forgotten 1975 song "Almost Saturday Night"; "Back to Schooldays" from Graham Parker's 1976 debut album *Howlin' Wind*; John Hiatt's "It Hasn't Happened Yet," which would become a country hit for Rosanne Cash in 1983; and Ry Cooder's lilting "Do the Best You Can." He also contributed two of his own compositions, both of which seemed to have bitter personal meanings: "The Loser Babe Is You," a romantic kiss-off perhaps directed at his soon-to-be-ex-wife, and "Call It What You Want," likely addressed to his last label, Epic Records. He never intended the result to be his final statement, but it will serve. The 2001 CD reissue adds six tracks, including the 1982 one-off single "No Fair Falling in Love"/"Give 'Em My Number"; three tracks that first appeared on the *Legacy* box set, among them a convincing version of Buddy Holly's "Rave On" and the previously unreleased John Hiatt song "Radio Girl." That makes three Hiatt songs on the disc, and Nelson should have done even more of them. *—William Ruhlmann*

Hey Pretty Baby / 1986 / Rockstar ♦♦♦
If you're looking for Imperial-era material that's not on the EMI best-of compilation CDs, this 16-track British import offers a good selection. Much of this is not present on those domestic CDs, and the collection emphasizes his more rocking side, with James Burton frequently contributing his tasty licks. But it doesn't compare with the best of his vintage material, though it's pleasant enough (and quite innocuous); most listeners will be content to pick up the greatest-hits comps and leave it at that. *—Richie Unterberger*

★ **Legendary Masters** / 1990 / EMI America ♦♦♦♦♦
Legendary Masters compiles all of the hits Ricky Nelson released for Imperial Records in the late '50s, including "Be-Bop Baby," "Stood Up," "Lonesome Town," "It's Late," "Poor Little Fool," "Sweeter Than You," "Just a Little Too Much," "Never Be Anyone Else but You," and "Believe What You Say." A few essential items are missing—such as the Verve sides "A Teenager's Romance" and "I'm Walking"—and it would have been nice if the disc had extended into the early '60s, so songs like "Travelin' Man" and "Mary Lou" could have been included, but *Legendary Masters* remains a vital collection from one of the most undervalued early rock & rollers. *—Stephen Thomas Erlewine*

Best of 1963-1975 / 1990 / MCA ♦♦♦
No longer Rockin' Ricky, but Responsible Rick, his Decca output was wildly inconsistent. The early efforts like "Fools Rush In" and "String Along" still feature guitarist James Burton prominently. *—Bill Dahl*

The Best of Rick Nelson, Vol. 2 / Mar. 18, 1991 / EMI America ♦♦♦♦♦
Focusing primarily on Rick's early-'60s material for Imperial, this 27-cut disc is not quite as rocking as *Volume One*, but still offers plenty of worthy moments. It includes all of his massive, mid-tempo teen idol ballad hits of the era: "Young World," "A Wonder Like You," "Teenage Idol," "It's Up to You," and the number one hit "Travelin' Man." Teen ballads they might have been, but James Burton's masterful guitar licks and Nelson's assured, committed delivery placed them leagues above other teen-idol hits of the period. Of more interest to serious fans are the inclusion of several minor hit singles and covers of R&B tunes. And of course, there's the first-class rockabilly hit "Hello Mary Lou" (penned by Gene Pitney), perhaps his best recording of the decade. His surprisingly raucous cover of "Summertime" features, amazingly, the same bass line used as a hook on the Blues Magoos' psych-pop-garage hit "We Ain't Got Anything Yet" years later. The pleasures of this CD are modest but consistent. *—Richie Unterberger*

Stay Young: The Epic Recordings / Aug. 31, 1993 / Epic ♦♦♦♦
Stay Young is an entertaining overview of Rick Nelson's country-tinged years at Epic, proving that he recorded plenty of worthwhile material in the '70s. *—Stephen Thomas Erlewine*

Rockin' With Ricky / 1996 / Ace ♦♦♦♦♦
Originally released as an LP in 1984, the CD version of this collection of Nelson's hardest-rocking early material doubles in length to include a whopping 32 tracks (on one disc) from the late '50s and early '60s. This has most of his up-tempo smashes, à la "Be-Bop Baby," "Waitin' in School," and "Believe What You Say," with a host of LP tracks, many of them covers of songs made famous by Elvis, Carl Perkins, Roy Orbison, and the like. The two volumes of greatest hits on EMI are more well-rounded, and on the whole, better retrospectives of his classic era. This is pretty good proof that he could rock respectably, though, with some good cuts that are hard to find on reissues, like "You're So Fine" and "Poor Loser." *—Richie Unterberger*

The Best of the Later Years (1963-1975) / 1997 / Ace ♦♦♦
On the surface, this would appear to have the advantage over its American counterpart (MCA's *Best of 1963-75* compilation). It's got far more material, for one thing: 26 songs, which is 11 more than the domestic retrospective. There are a couple of significant omissions of tracks that appear on the U.S. set, though, most notably the moody Billy

Vera-penned "Mean Old World." Its absence from this anthology is inexcusable, as it was his best mid-'60s recording. Judgment calls aside, this does have the hits Nelson managed to squeeze in on Decca before the rise of the Beatles ("For You" and the great "Fools Rush In"), along with some rocking obscurities like "I Got a Woman" and "Gypsy Woman"; the ballads "The Very Thought of You," "I Wonder," and "There's Nothing I Can Say" are also quite good. After 1964 he slid into early country-rock, which veered from decent to dispensable. "Garden Party" is here, of course, but the additional late-'60s and early-'70s cuts not present on MCA's disc really don't add much. *—Richie Unterberger*

For Your Sweet Love/Sings for You / 1997 / Ace ✦✦✦
This combines Nelson's first two Decca albums (each originally released in 1963) into one CD. Although "Gypsy Woman," "I Got a Woman," and "Fools Rush In" stand up to the best of his early-'60s hits, the rest of the material is too average, and the execution too low-energy, to merit attention from anyone except fervid Nelson fans. It's nonetheless among the best stuff that Nelson would record for the label. Some of the best tracks are also on the anthologies covering the singer's Decca's work, which are recommended alternatives for those not seeking a complete Nelson discography. *—Richie Unterberger*

Very Thought of You/Spotlight on Rick / Dec. 9, 1997 / Ace ✦✦✦
Two 1964 albums are combined onto one CD on this reissue, which adds historical liner notes. Nelson's mid-'60s albums would have seemed like far more respectable efforts had they been able to escape comparison with a fast-changing rock scene. As it was, the innovations of the British Invasion, Beach Boys, Phil Spector, and much more made his records, as professional and pleasant as they were, seem hopelessly outdated. *The Very Thought of You* was passable, mostly medium-tempo pop-rock that did little to either embarrass the singer or raise the listener's temperature. The title track was a Top 40 hit, and his last, it turned out, for six years. There are obscure songs by Mann-Weil ("I Don't Wanna Love You") and Charlie Rich ("Just a Little Bit Sweet"), but it all sounds like pleasant throwaway filler, the best cut being his cover of the great lost Drifters-like tune "I Wonder" (a small hit in 1961 for the Pentagons). Nelson continued to tread water on *Spotlight on Rick*, which had some average contributions by above-average writers like Baker Knight and Jerry Fuller. An energetic stab at Chuck Berry's "I'm Talking About You" and a nice tune from the pen of ex-Cricket Sonny Curtis ("Don't Breathe a Word"), were mild highlights. *—Richie Unterberger*

Best Always/Love and Kisses / Mar. 10, 1998 / Ace ✦✦✦
A two-fer CD reissue combining two 1965 LPs onto one disc. *Best Always* isn't bad, although there's little to distinguish it from the other easygoing pop-rock albums he made during the period, except for the slightly higher quality of the material. "Mean Old World," both more forceful and moodier than anything else he cut in 1964-65, is by far the best song, but there are some OK numbers from the pens of Johnny Burnette and Jerry Fuller; Jimmy Seals and Dash Crofts also contribute to a couple of tunes, "Only the Young" (written by Seals and Charles Eugene) boasting a quite good pop melody. Rick stretches his vocal range on the cover of the Skyliners' "Since I Don't Have You" and gives a taste of his upcoming move into country with a version of "You Don't Know Me." Even by the modest standards of Nelson's early Decca albums, *Love and Kisses* is a tepid, stagnant collection. Some of the cuts sound vaguely updated with harder-edged guitars than unusual, and there's a hint of his future country direction with the cover of Roger Miller's "I Catch Myself Crying." But had the album never appeared, it wouldn't have added to or subtracted a whit from the total sum of his legacy. Three of the numbers were featured in Nelson's forgotten *Love and Kisses* film, including the embarrassing single "Come Out Dancin'." *—Richie Unterberger*

Bright Lights & Country Music/Country Fever / Jun. 23, 1998 / Ace ✦✦✦
This is a reissue of the two albums—1966's *Bright Lights & Country Music*, and 1967's *Country Fever*—on which Nelson plunged for the first time into country music whole hog. On *Bright Lights* he still used his regular band, but augmented them with Glen Campbell and future Byrd Clarence White, and regular guitarist James Burton played dobro. It wasn't country-rock, but straight country without any Nashville gloss in the production, emphasizing covers of songs by Willie Nelson, Merle Travis, Bill Anderson, and Doug Kershaw. Nelson sounded more engaged with the material than he had in years and the album was a decent effort, but as it relied so heavily on songs that had already been made famous by others, it wasn't going to make him stand out as an innovator. Nelson acquitted himself well with his one original, "You Just Can't Quit," and Campbell contributed "Here I Am," yet the best cut was the fastest: "Night Train to Memphis." *Country Fever* was similarly weighted toward interpretations of country classics. Hank Williams, Jimmie Rodgers, and Acuff-Rose all get covered, and his sensitive reading of Willie Nelson's "Funny How Time Slips Away" was a standout. There's no denying, though, that the best cut is the one that gets closest to rockabilly (a cover of "Mystery Train"). Nelson's two original compositions weren't much, but on the other hand there was an obscure Bob Dylan tune that the composer had not released ("Walkin' Down the Line"), and "Things You Gave Me," with its steady beat and harmonies sounded more like a foreshadowing of late-'60s California country-rock than anything else Nelson had recorded up to this point. *—Richie Unterberger*

Another Side of Rick/Perspective / Sep. 29, 1998 / Ace ✦✦✦
A reissue that combines 1967's *Another Side of Rick* and 1968's *Perspective* onto one CD. By 1967, Nelson's records were no longer selling, and were out of step with contemporary trends. So, why not, someone must have reasoned, try to put Nelson in step with contemporary trends on *Another Side of Rick*? It was about as good a strategy as any, considering that his tried-and-true rockaballad format wasn't working. But giving him fruity psychedelic baroque production was not the answer, indeed yielding rather embarrassing results. Nelson showed good taste by covering three Tim Hardin songs, but producer John Boylan's five songs not only weren't that good, but weren't a good match for the vocalist. Nelson wasn't totally blameless, penning one of the album's crummiest songs, the overdone pop psychedelic "Marshmallow Skies," with James Burton. At one point during the cover of "Georgia on My Mind," the musicians suddenly slip into double-time, as if they can't wait to get the album over with. Although released in August 1968, *Perspective* had actually been recorded 16 months earlier, an indication that Decca wasn't exactly eager to keep Nelson in the forefront of the market in the late '60s. Like *Another Side of Rick*, this found him making ill-advised efforts to modernize his sound with a more orchestrated production that often verged on the rococo. Nelson did have good taste in selecting material, covering songs by Paul Simon, Richie Havens, and Harry Nilsson, plus five by Randy Newman to end the album. Producer John Boylan added most of the remaining tunes, including the odd "Hello to the Wind (Bonjour Le Vent)" (co-written with Nelson), which, with its Burt Bacharach-type piano-based melody and brief interlude of spoken female French narration, might find a comfortable home on some lounge music reissue. *—Richie Unterberger*

Legacy / Nov. 21, 2000 / Capitol ✦✦✦✦✦
As a four-CD set spanning Rick Nelson's entire career, this will likely stand as the most thorough overview of the singer's music ever issued. This doesn't mean, though, that it's the best anthology of his work, unless you subscribe to the viewpoint that his post-mid-'60s records were about as good as his pre-mid-'60s ones, since a full two discs (or half) of this package is devoted to that post-mid-'60s output. Basically, it illustrates his trajectory in phases: disc one, as a good-to-great pop-rockabilly singer; disc two, as a still-good but not quite as vital teen idol in the late '50s and early '60s; disc three, as a fair but not great country-rocker; and disc four, as a has-been playing out the string with uninspired adult contemporary and revival tracks during his final years. The album is an impressive feat of cross-licensing, though, starting with three songs from his first singles (for Verve, and never easy to find on reissues), drawing a lot from his creative peak at Imperial, and then from his spottier efforts for Decca and other labels. All of his Top 40 hits are here, along with a dozen or so previously unreleased tracks, none too remarkable, as well as the 45-single versions of a few early hits. The song selection is very good, but not infallible: The absence of the moody "Mean Old World," which was about the best thing he did in the mid-'60s, is inexplicable. If you are a big fan and do like Nelson's country-rock phase, this is a reasonable investment, but if you don't, you should stick to those collections that focus on his 1957-1965 recordings. *—Richie Unterberger*

Ricky/Ricky Nelson / Jun. 19, 2001 / Capitol ✦✦✦✦
Ricky Nelson's first two albums and assorted singles, recorded when he was 17 years old, are triumphs of taste over experience. As chronicled in James Ritz's liner notes, Nelson turned to music more or less on a dare, and while he could carry a tune, he had little personality as a singer when he started, relying for his popularity more on his familiarity as a television star and his good looks. The sound of the day was Elvis Presley-styled rockabilly and the even wilder sounds of Jerry Lee Lewis and black R&B performers, but unlike such pale imitators as Pat Boone, Nelson didn't have to be talked into awkwardly appropriating such material; clearly, he really liked it. Especially on the earliest cuts here he was barely competent, completely draining "Whole Lotta Shakin' Goin' On" of its sexual threat, for example. But he learned fast; by the time of recording the material for his second album, *Ricky Nelson* (tracks 16-27), he had vastly improved, and his band, led by guitarist James Burton, was first-class, so that, for example, "There's Good Rockin' Tonight" sounded like it could have been made at Sun Studio in Memphis instead of Master Recorders in Los Angeles. Of course, all that meant was that he was still an imitator, albeit a good one, but everyone starts out imitating, and his choices of what to copy, along with his enthusiasm, marked him as a promising new artist. The onrush of pop celebrity tended to obscure that at the time *Ricky* made him the youngest recording artist ever to have a number one LP—but more than four decades later it's much easier to appreciate Nelson's early efforts as a teen rocker. *—William Ruhlmann*

Ricky Sings Again/Songs By Ricky / Jun. 19, 2001 / Capitol ✦✦✦✦
The second of four discs containing Rick Nelson's complete recordings for Imperial Records, *Ricky Sings Again/Songs By Ricky* combines the singer's third and fourth albums, both released initially in 1959, with alternate takes and a few other stray tracks. By this point in his career, Nelson, who turned 19 that year, had begun to distinguish himself from the rockabilly legends he admired, at least to the extent of retaining his own songwriters to pen original (if derivative) material, notably brothers Dorsey and Johnny Burnette, who handled the more rocking tunes, and Baker Knight, who wrote ballads and some light rhythm numbers; between them, they contributed 15 of the 27 different songs heard here. It's easy to tell what they were listening to—"It's Late" is reminiscent of the Everly Brothers' "Wake Up Little Susie," "You'll Never Know What You're Missing" is a rewrite of Elvis Presley's "Treat Me Nice," and "A Long Vacation" apes Buddy Holly's "Not Fade Away." The similarity to Presley's records is accentuated by the use of the Jordanaires, who also sang backup for him, but Nelson's band is distinctive, particularly lead guitarist James Burton, and the singer himself had grown in confidence since his early recordings. As such, this is the peak of Nelson's early career, a time when he was scoring hit after hit with his singles (six of the songs on the disc made the Top Ten) and even assaulted the LP charts (according to Cash Box, *Ricky Sings Again* hit number one and *Songs By Ricky* made the Top Ten, though Billboard's rankings were much lower). Also featured are Hank Williams and Johnny Cash covers that anticipate Nelson's turn toward country music, as well as the bizarre reading of Billie Holiday's suicide ballad "Gloomy Sunday" that first turned up on the *Legacy* box set. *—William Ruhlmann*

Album Seven By Rick/Rick Sings Spirituals / Jun. 19, 2001 / Capitol ✦✦✦✦
The fourth and final disc reissuing the complete recordings of Ricky Nelson on Imperial Records (1957-1962) contains his final newly recorded album for the label, *Album Seven By Rick*, four non-LP singles originally released in 1961 and 1962, and, to round things

out, a long-out-of-print four-song gospel EP, *Ricky Sings Spirituals*. The bulk of the material comes from the point in Nelson's career when he had re-established himself with "Travelin' Man" after the fade-out of his early teen idol success. Not surprisingly, he turned again to "Travelin' Man" songwriter Jerry Fuller, who provides a full third of the tracks on this disc, among them the hits "A Wonder Like You," "Young World," and "It's Up to You." Other frequently heard songwriters are Dave Burgess (five cuts, three of them with Fuller), Baker Knight (four cuts), and Dorsey Burnette (two cuts). Having such writers shape material for him was a boon to Nelson, and if nothing here quite rises to the level of his biggest hits, there is much good early-'60s pop/rock. The covers of "Summertime" and "I Can't Stop Loving You" are effective, and Nelson and his band turn in believable renditions of some original gospel songs. There's even "Teenage Idol," which comments on his early career and became yet another hit. The recordings he was making in the early '60s suggested Nelson had made the transition from the earnest, derivative music he performed at the start of his career to a stream of high-quality material that would seem to assure him a place near the top of the pop heap, which is probably why at this point Decca made him an unprecedented offer and spirited him away from Imperial. Who could have known that his hitmaking days were just about over? *—William Ruhlmann*

More Songs by Ricky/Rick Is 21 / Jun. 19, 2001 / Capitol ♦♦♦♦
The third in a series of four CD reissues containing the complete Imperial Records recordings of Rick Nelson combines his fifth and sixth albums with his five singles from the same period, November 1959 to May 1961. The story told here is one of musical exploration, as Nelson's early success as a teen heartthrob who liked to play Sun Records-style rockabilly faded and he began casting around for other approaches to maintain his popularity. After the relatively disappointing performance of a pair of singles, "I Wanna Be Loved" and "Young Emotions," ballads that peaked only in the Top 20, he made *More Songs by Ricky*, an album that found him attempting to update decades-old standards like "Time After Time" and come up with brass-heavy production numbers in emulation of then-popular Lloyd Price. As annotator James Ritz writes, the best way to appreciate the results is to "take everything he had already done musically and throw it out the window," but even if you do, you are still left with an artist who sounds comfortable only when he gets back to rocking, notably on the Dorsey Burnette composition "Hey Pretty Baby." Amazingly, however, he pulled out of this tailspin, artistically and commercially, with his sixth album, *Rick Is 21*, on which he developed a new pop/rock sound that contained echoes of his rockabilly past but also made its peace with early-'60s pop, especially on the double-sided hit "Travelin' Man"/"Hello Mary Lou," and also on other custom-written songs by Dave Burgess, Jerry Fuller, Gene Pitney, and Johnny Rivers. As a result, the collection might be subtitled "The Fall and Rise of Rick Nelson," and if the going gets rough early on, the tale has a happy ending. [*More Songs by Ricky* is presented for the first time in true stereo here.] *–William Ruhlmann*

The Neon Philharmonic

f. 1967, **db.** 1975
Obscuro, Psychedelic Pop, Baroque Pop, Psychedelic
Such was the influence of psychedelic music in the late '60s that even pop-based acts like the Fifth Dimension, Kenny Rogers, and the Association felt obliged to put in their two cents' worth. Such was the case with the Neon Philharmonic, which was primarily a vehicle for songwriter/arranger/keyboardist Tupper Saussy. Also featuring singer Don Gant, the group had an easygoing, not-too-memorable Top 20 pop hit in mid-1969, "Morning Girl." Their debut album, *The Moth Confesses*, was a much stranger piece of work, sounding something like Jimmy Webb on acid. For all of its ambitious orchestral arrangements and operatic lyrical reach, it has dated in the most embarrassing and silly of fashions, sounding like the aural equivalent of the middle-class accountant who decides to take acid with his kids in a misguided attempt to get with it. Though the bloated arrangements, Gant's white-bread vocals, and the overwrought, sentimental lyrics came closer to Rod McKuen than Van Dyke Parks, the NH did manage another album, as well as a few singles, and were active as late as 1975. Saussy then became an anti-tax activist, going underground to avoid Federal authorities in the 1980s. *—Richie Unterberger*

● **The Moth Confesses** / 1969 / Sundazed ♦♦♦♦
A timepiece in the less impressive sense of the term, seeking to fuse the conceptual ambition and sophisticated production of *Pet Sounds* and *Song Cycle* with MOR pop. It doesn't work that well, particularly since songwriter Tupper Saussy is clearly more well versed in (and comfortable with) MOR pop. The collision of grandoise romantic songs, rococo string arrangements, and a touch of psychedelic experimentation is so bizarre that it exerts a strange fascination, but it doesn't make for durable music. The album included the hit single, "Morning Girl"; the CD reissue adds six bonus cuts from non-LP singles that are more straightforward than the bulk of *The Moth Confesses*. *—Richie Unterberger*

The Nerves

f. 1975, **db.** 1978
Power Pop, New Wave
They could've been contenders had they stayed together long enough, but the Nerves, despite their brief existence, were one of the most exciting bands in power pop. Formed by Jack Lee, Peter Case, and Paul Collins in 1975, their career was over by 1978, but they produced a great EP that featured the power-pop classic "Hanging on the Telephone," which was later recorded (and wonderfully so) by Blondie. Ultimately, having three talented songwriters in one band hurried the demise of the Nerves, and all three principals found greater happiness and success with their new bands, although Jack Lee (arguably the most talented songwriter of the three) had the shortest career and eventually dropped out of sight after a fine solo record (*Jack Lee's Greatest Hits, Vol. 1*) in 1981. Case went on to form the Plimsouls, who recorded two good records and a transcendent pop song, "A Million Miles Away." After breaking up in 1984, Case recorded as a roots-rock solo act for the rest of the decade and into the '90s, although there is a rumor he's put the Plimsouls back together. Collins formed the Beat (later Paul Collins' Beat), who were merely OK, and has done little since the mid-'80s. *—John Dougan*

● **Nerves [EP]** / 1976 / Nerves ♦♦♦♦♦
There was only one EP; it had four songs, and each one is great. Although I'm sure this record has vanished from the face of the earth, if you run across it, snatch it up; it's wonderful. Best song: Paul Collins' "Working Too Hard." There is a French import release from 1986 that includes outtakes and some related ephemera. But, sadly, this EP stands as the sum total of a great band. *—John Dougan*

Michael Nesmith

b. Dec. 30, 1942, Houston, TX
Vocals, Guitar / Folk-Rock, Singer/Songwriter, Country-Rock
The comparatively level-headed member of '60s teen sensation the Monkees, Michael Nesmith was the most proficient instrumentalist in the group and wrote their best in-house songs, rootsy pop numbers like "Papa Gene's Blues," "You Told Me," "You Just May Be the One" and "Tapioca Tundra." In fact, he had written many songs before even joining the group, and one of his compositions, "Different Drum," was a hit for Linda Ronstadt and the Stone Poneys in 1968. After he left the Monkees one year later, it wasn't a surprise that he became the only one of his bandmates to sustain a solo career; in fact, his dozen (or so) '70s LPs were among the most groundbreaking country-rock recordings of the era. Throughout the 1970s and into the '80s, Nesmith continued to record sporadically, though his communications company Pacific Arts began taking up more of his time by the early '80s. Pacific Arts proved to be an important pioneer in the development of music video, the concept he had furthered in the rough-and-tumble pace of the Monkees' TV show. *—John Bush*

Wichita Train Whistle Songs / 1968 / Dot ♦♦♦
This is a record with an interesting history. In 1967, the Monkees phenomenon had reached its zenith. Michael Nesmith, of course, being a member of the group as well as author of several songs on some *extremely* well-selling albums, had, to put it mildly, a very nice amount of change in the bank. As 1967 began to close out, Nesmith was faced with an interesting dilemma (i.e., a rather large tax bill forthcoming). In order to solve this problem, as well as further his musical curiosity, he came up with a novel idea. Armed with a solo contract from Dot Records (Nesmith has since retained the rights), a series of *huge* recording sessions were booked in November of 1967 with a cast of over 50 of the best session players of the day. Booked over a weekend ("golden time" for the union musicians), and catered by Chasen's Silver Service (easily one of the most expensive restaurants in Beverly Hills), it was one hell of a write-off. Musically, it was ambitious and successful, too. The arrangements on the ten Nesmith originals (instrumentals of complete songs) are daunting and elaborate as well. The fusion of symphonic music, country, and rock is positively original and spectacular at the same time. This record has stood the test of time well and is very worthwhile to even the most casual listener. *—Matthew Greenwald*

Magnetic South / Jul. 1970 / Pacific Arts ♦♦♦♦♦
Anyone who'd been listening closely to the songs Michael Nesmith wrote while a member of the Monkees (or heard his hard to find 1968 solo debut for Dot) already knew that Nesmith had a soft spot for country music. But when Nesmith left the pre-Fab Four to form the First National Band, he dove head first into the twangy stuff, and if he wasn't the first guy to merge country and rock (Gram Parsons easily beat him to the punch on that), he was certainly doing it well before country-rock became the next big thing, and *Magnetic South* made it clear he had his own distinct way of bringing the two genres together. Nesmith put together a top-flight band who sound at once relaxed and thoroughly committed, whether easing through a laid-back number like "Joanne" or kicking up some dust on "Mama Nantucket"; O.J. "Red" Rhodes' pedal steel work is superb throughout, while bassist John London and drummer John Ware offer strong, unobtrusive support (the great Earl P. Hall also sits in on piano). And though the phrase "cosmic cowboy" wasn't coined for Nesmith, it could have been; here, he indulges himself in a consciously poetic and philosophical lyrical style that's a good bit more abstract than one would expect from a former Monkee, though Nesmith's dry sense of humor is always lurking around the corner, ready to rescue him when he slips too deep into pretension. Mixing a country sound with a rocker's instincts, and blending airy thoughts on the nature of life and love with iconography of life in the West that brought together the old and the new, Michael Nesmith reveled in contradictions on *Magnetic South* and made them sound as comfortable as well-worn cowboy boots and as fun as a Saturday night barn dance. It's a minor masterpiece of country-rock, and while the Eagles may have sold more records, Nesmith yodels a hell of a lot better than any of them. *—Mark Deming*

Loose Salute / Nov. 1970 / Pacific Arts ♦♦♦♦
After reinventing himself as an engagingly spacey cowboy on the splendid *Magnetic South*, Michael Nesmith took a slightly more eclectic approach on his second album with the First National Band, *Loose Salute*. While country flavors still dominate the album (and Red Rhodes' pedal steel work was even stronger this time out), the up-tempo numbers swing a bit harder (especially the rollicking "Dedicated Friend"), there's a funky R&B undertow to "Bye, Bye, Bye," the rhythm guitars on "Silver Moon" suggest Nesmith had heard a bit of reggae, and "Tengo Amore" brings a Latin influence into the mix. But Nesmith's love of old-school country still rings clear on every cut (especially the steel-dominated remake of the Monkees' "Listen to the Band"), and after letting the world know about his deeper side on *Magnetic South*, *Loose Salute* found Nesmith writing

about more direct and organic themes (love, faith, ditching work, leaving the Monkees). Nesmith also took over as producer, and he gets a tougher and tighter sound from the band than Felton Jarvis managed on *Magnetic South. Loose Salute* doesn't cohere quite as well as *Magnetic South*, but the material is strong, the band sounds great, and Michael Nesmith offered even more surprises than he had in his first turn at bat; it's one of the strongest records in his catalog as a solo artist. —*Mark Deming*

Nevada Fighter / 1971 / Pacific Arts ✦✦✦

Nevada Fighter kicks off with the witty and loose-limbed "The Grand Ennui," and for a moment it sounds like the album will pick up where Michael Nesmith's previous album with the First National Band, *Loose Salute*, left off. But before long, the album shifts gears, and it becomes obvious that Nesmith had something different in mind this time. Except for the rollicking side-closer, "Nevada Fighter," most of the material on side one suggests the more introspective moments of *Magnetic South* but without the same balance of charm and dry humor that made that album so appealing (though "Propinquity (I've Just Begun to Care)" is a fine love song that's a good bit more approachable than its title would lead you to expect). Side two is turned over to material by other songwriters, and while this shifts the album's lyrical tone rather dramatically, Nesmith reveals himself to be a fine interpretive vocalist, and "Texas Morning" and "The Rainmaker" are splendid songs that would merit anyone's attention. The First National Band were also augmented by a number of session musicians on *Nevada Fighter* (including James Burton and Ronn Tutt from Elvis Presley's band), and the arrangements have a decidedly different flavor than on Nesmith's previous two albums, especially in the second half (though Red Rhodes' pedal steel is predictably splendid throughout). *Nevada Fighter* is a fine album, but it's also the weakest of the three Nesmith would cut with the First National Band, and it's not hard to imagine that Nesmith was starting to look for new pastures while he was recording this set. —*Mark Deming*

Tantamount to Treason / 1972 / Pacific Arts ✦✦✦

Tantamount to Treason has a lazy feel to it, perhaps inspired by the beer recipe Papa Nes includes in the album's liner notes. That laziness is the reason the album is not as listenable as the previous three records, since you almost need to be "in the mood" to put this one on. That said, it's still quite a nice album and is worth tracking down. —*Jim Worbois*

And the Hits Just Keep on Comin' / 1972 / Pacific Arts ✦✦✦✦✦

In 1972, Michael Nesmith had released four albums for RCA Records that didn't sell especially well, and he had parted ways with his band, with only pedal steel guitarist Red Rhodes interested in working on Nesmith's next project. RCA gave Nesmith a limited window of time to make his next album for them, so it was necessity rather than design that led Nesmith to cut *And the Hits Just Keep on Comin'* with just himself on acoustic guitar and Rhodes on pedal steel. But the results were truly inspired; Nesmith and Rhodes use the album's spare instrumentation to their advantage, with the performances both empathetic and intimate, and Rhodes' masterful steel gives these songs a graceful resonance few full bands could muster. And while the ten songs find Nesmith in one of his more introspective phases, here he manages to keep one foot planted firmly in the real world while the other traipses the cosmos (even the trippiest song here, "The Candidate," manages a certain tongue-in-cheek wit that keeps it on *terra firma*, and "Keep On" offers neo-hippie philosophy rooted in good ol' Texas horse sense). He also offers up a superb folk-styled remake of "Different Drum" that has a bluesy lope missing from Linda Ronstadt's better-known version. *And the Hits Just Keep on Comin'* is modest in approach but very satisfying in execution, practically defining the phrase "happy accident." —*Mark Deming*

Pretty Much Your Standard Ranch Stash / 1973 / Pacific Arts ✦✦✦✦✦

After hitting a groove with *And the Hits Just Keep on Comin'*, which Michael Nesmith recorded with just pedal steel guitarist Red Rhodes for accompaniment, Nesmith beefed his sound up again with a full band on *Pretty Much Your Standard Ranch Stash*. But the previous album seems to have reminded Nesmith about the virtues of restraint, and while he had a six-piece band at his disposal this time out, the arrangements are tight and efficient, offering the warmth and immediacy of his *First National Band* sessions (and sometimes even beating them for subtle, understated swing). Red Rhodes, as always, is the star soloist here, but the rest of the band also shines, in particular the guitars of Jay Lacy and Dr. Robert Warford and the solid drumming of Danny Lane. Nesmith wrote one of his best and purest country songs for this set, "Winonah," and offered up a solid remake of the Monkees obscurity "Some of Shelly's Blues," while dipping into bluegrass for the lovely acoustic medley "Back Porch and a Fruit Jar Full of Iced Tea." *Pretty Much Your Standard Ranch Stash* was Michael Nesmith's final album for RCA Records, and if it didn't fare especially well in the marketplace, from a musical standpoint he certainly left the House That Nipper Built on a high note—it was hardly your standard '70s country-rock album. —*Mark Deming*

The Prison / 1974 / Pacific Arts ✦✦

From a Radio Engine to the Photon Wing / 1977 / Pacific Arts ✦✦

Live at Palais / 1978 / Pacific Arts ✦✦✦✦

Live at Palais is one of the rare concert recordings released by Michael "Papa Nez" Nesmith. In the early '90s, when the rest of his back catalog was being issued on CD, Nez refused to allow the disc to be included in overhaul—citing dissatisfaction with the performance. Due to the demand of enthusiasts worldwide, consent was granted to not only reissue the disc, but also to compliment the package with nearly a half-hour of additional music. The material covered here is primarily derived from the half-dozen albums Nez did on RCA Records in the early '70s. A majority of the tracks are refugees from one of Nesmith's most fertile creative periods in the late '60s, just prior to leaving the Monkees. On *Live at Palais*, Nesmith's folk-tinged originals are replaced by electric and decidedly

more emotive renderings. While much of the folksy spirit remains, songs such as "Calico Girlfriend" and "Some of Shelly's Blues" have matured—featuring the essence of the Southwest Americana that Nesmith's music so aptly depicts. The bonus material is as strong as—if not arguably more potent than—the Palais performance. From a 1981 show at the Armadillo World Headquarters in Austin, TX, comes another, albeit heavier, version of "Grand Ennui" as well as the only live version of the previously mentioned "Capsule." The other pair of bonus tracks is from a concert sponsored by Gretsch Guitars in 1995. Incidentally, Nesmith owned one of only three electric 12-string Gretsch guitars manufactured in the mid- to late '60s. His affinity is obvious and translates into some outstanding music ranging from the tender "Crippled Lion" to the raucous "Listen to the Band." —*Lindsay Planer*

Infinite Rider on the Big Dogma / 1979 / Pacific Arts ✦✦✦

This is easily Nesmith's most interesting record from the '70s Pacific Arts material, and the one that most often calls for repeated listenings. By this time, he was getting heavily into video, so a number of these tracks were also turned into music videos (check out the Grammy-winning *Elephant Parts*). While not a must, it's still a record worth searching out. —*Jim Worbois*

Newer Stuff / 1989 / Rhino ✦✦✦

This compilation of later solo material is often glossy and overreaching but still quite impressive. —*Jeff Tamarkin*

The Older Stuff: Best of Michael Nesmith (1970-1973) / 1991 / Rhino ✦✦✦✦✦

Post-Monkees country-oriented material is proof that at least one member of the "pre-fab four" possessed genuine musical talent. —*Jeff Tamarkin*

Tropical Campfires / Oct. 27, 1992 / Pacific Arts ✦✦✦✦

Along with Lindsay Buckingham's *Out of the Cradle* this album may be one of the finest and most underrated albums of the 1990s. Nesmith and his crack band run through 12 of the most delicious slices of Americana to be put on record in ages. The mood of the album is a cross between Bahamian, tropical, country, and other forms, all forging a unique synthesis of pop that might be very hard to match. Nesmith's songs and vocals are wholly original and personal, and tunes such as "I Am Not That" and "Laugh Kills Lonesome" bear the indefinable Nesmith stamp of humor with a compact and irresistible force. In addition to the excellent originals, Nesmith and his band cover two classic Cole Porter songs with excellent results, and both ("In the Still of the Night" and "Begin the Beguine") fit the menu perfectly. Absolutely delectable. —*Matthew Greenwald*

● Complete / Sep. 28, 1993 / Pacific Arts ✦✦✦✦✦

This two-CD set brings together the three albums Michael Nesmith recorded with his group the First National Band in 1971 and 1972, *Magnetic South, Loose Salute*, and *Nevada Fighter*. In his liner notes to this set, Nesmith says that he never intended the three First National Band albums to be a trilogy, and while the individual albums do have subtle but distinct personalities of their own, they also play well as a set, with the laidback *Magnetic South* easing comfortably into the slightly more rock-oriented *Loose Salute* and *Nevada Fighter*'s addition of sessionmen and a handful of covers leading the group into the sunset. Nesmith's notes also declare his status as "one of the pioneers of country-rock" to be "nonsense," and while anyone whose listened to these albums might think Nez protests too much on this point, it's certainly true that his fusion of country's sound and rock & roll's soul was decidedly his own and bore little resemblance to that of anyone else working in the same direction. (He also was fortunate to have one of the best pedal steel players alive, Red Rhodes, in his band, and his playing alone would make these discs worth your time.) The First National Band albums were among the finest music of Michael Nesmith's solo career, and anyone interested in his body of work (or in country-rock and its best and most intelligent) would do well to pick up *Complete*. —*Mark Deming*

The Garden / 1994 / Rio Royal ✦✦

16 Original Classics / Sep. 28, 1999 / Collectables ✦✦✦

16 Original Classics is actually the 1970 Mike Nesmith album *Magnetic South* with five extra bonus tracks tacked on. This was one of the highlights from any of the post-Monkee recording careers, confirming Nesmith as a pioneer of the country-rock genre with an incredible vocal range, proven talent as a songwriter, and the ability to arrange a group of top-notch country pickers. The First National Band featured longtime Nesmith cohorts, petal steel guitarist Red Rhodes, bassist John London, and drummer John Ware. The moderate success of the single "Joanne" (included on this package) made Nesmith the first ex-Monkee to put a solo record on the charts. —*Al Campbell*

Neu!
....

f. 1971, Düsseldorf, Germany, **db.** 1975
Proto-Punk, Kraut Rock, Prog-Rock/Art Rock, Electronic

While little-known and relatively unheralded during their brief existence, the Krautrock duo Neu! cast a large shadow over later generations of musicians and served as a major influence on artists as diverse as David Bowie, Sonic Youth, Pere Ubu, Julian Cope, and Stereolab.

Neu! formed in Düsseldorf, Germany in 1971 after multi-instrumentalists Michael Rother and Klaus Dinger both split from Kraftwerk. Recorded in the space of four days with Can producer Conrad Plank, the duo's self-titled debut appeared early in 1972 and quickly established their affection for minimalist melodies and lock-groove rhythms. While virtually ignored throughout the rest of the world, the album sold extremely well in West Germany, resulting in a tour with support from Guru Guru's Uli Trepte and Eberhard Krahnemann.

Rother and Dinger returned to the studio in 1973 for *Neu! 2*, where a shortfall of cash allowed the duo to complete only two songs, "Super" and "Neueschnee," which they subsequently remixed at varying and disorienting speeds in order to flesh out a full-length album. After the record's release, Rother joined Dieter Moebius and Joachim Roedelius of Cluster to form Harmonia, but Neu! officially reunited in 1975 to record *Neu! 75*. After its release, they again disbanded; Rother continued on as a solo performer, while Dinger and drummer Hans Lampe formed La Dusseldorf. In the mid-'80s, Rother and Dinger reformed yet again, although the recording sessions, titled *Neu! 4*, did not officially surface until 1996. —*Jason Ankeny*

● **Neu!** / 1972 / Billingsgate ✦✦✦✦✦
Fresh after leaving Kraftwerk in the fall of 1971 for what they perceived to be a lack of vision, guitarist Michael Rother and drummer Klaus Dinger formed their own unit and changed the face of German rock forever—eventually influencing their former employer, Florian Schneider of Kraftwerk. The 1974 album *Autobahn* was a genteel reconsideration of the music played here. Neu! created a sound that was literally made for cruising in an automobile. Dinger's mechanical, cut-time drumming and Rother's two-note bass runs adorned with cleverly manipulated and dreamy guitar riffs and fills were the hallmarks of the "motorik" sound that would become the band's trademark. All hell breaks loose on Dinger's "Negativeland" as an industrial soundscape eventually gives way to a bass and guitar squall as darkly enticing as anything on Joy Division's *Unknown Pleasures*. It's really obvious now how the Joy Division sound was influenced by this simply and darkly delicious brew of noise, bass throb, percussive hypnosis, and oddly placed, strangely under-mixed guitar. Rother's style had as much to do with not playing as it did with virtuosity, and his fills of open chords, stuttered cadences, and broken syntax provided a much needed diversion for the metronymic regularity of the rhythm section. Rother didn't riff; he painted a mix with whatever was necessary to get the point across. His mannerisms here are not to draw attention to himself, but rather to that numbing, incessant rhythm provided wondrously by Dinger. Neu!'s debut album was driving music for the apocalypse in 1971. Oddly enough, after a millennial change, a constant stream of samples being taken from it, and its influence saturating both the rock and electronica scenes, the album still sounds ahead of its time. —*Thom Jurek*

Neu! 2 / 1973 / United Artists ✦✦✦✦
After the considerable success of their self-titled debut album, Klaus Dinger and Michael Rother set out ambitiously to record a follow-up. Virtually everything went wrong. The first of the artistic and personal differences that existed between them not only began to surface, but to flourish in the face of a nearly impossible studio deadline and overly tight budget. While the basic Neu! sound was not an issue, how to augment it was. As both a guitarist and a composer, Rother had already begun moving in the direction he would end up in with Dieter Moebius and Hans-Joachim Roedelius in Harmonia, and on his later solo recordings: a more unified, melodic, airy, and soaring sound that was full of light and yearning. Dinger, on the other hand, was looking for more anarchy, more chaos, and rock & roll dynamics. He wanted a music that was as dramatic and confrontational as he was. It's amazing this album turned out as well as it did. On top of all this, Neu! ran out of money in the middle of the project. Their plight was met by total indifference from the record company, who wouldn't advance them another mark. So they did what any normal self-respecting band would do: They simply re-edited and remixed two singles off the album and put them on side two to fill up the time. The end result is a perverse and controversial album, one that gives the middle finger to the label, and perhaps to the record-buying public as well. That said, the disc is a very worthy one as a whole; it's a beautiful bridge between the start repetition of the debut and the lush melodic textures of *Neu! 75*. —*Thom Jurek*

Neu! 75 / 1975 / United Artists ✦✦✦✦✦
After a two-year break, Neu! members Klaus Dinger and Michael Rother buried their differences temporarily, and reunited for another go at the "motorik" sound they had developed with their debut in 1972. The strange tension and presentation of *Neu! 2* and the emergence of their former band, Kraftwerk, may have precipitated the reunion, but whatever the reason, the end result proved worth the time, effort, and bickering it took to crank this one out. One thing that is noticeably different on *Neu! 75* is the presence of synthesizers and the preference of them, it seems, over Rother's guitar. The ten-minute "E-Musick" becomes Neu!'s signature track for this disc, however. With distorted percussion—courtesy of a synth and sequencer, as well as a drum kit put through a phase shifter—Rother's melodic synth lines are free to roam, wide and far, foreshadowing his guitar solos a few minutes later. These long screaming lines, reminiscent of Steve Hillage at his best, with Dinger's wonderful rhythm backing and treatments of the instruments, provides a definitive statement on the Neu! "motorik" sound. This is music not only for traveling from one place to the next, but also for disappearance into the ether at a steady pace. This may have been Neu!'s final statement—at least in the studio; Dinger issued (without Rother's permission) an inferior live 1972 album—but at least they went out on a much higher note than *Neu! 2*, and in a place where their innovations are still being not only recognized, but utilized. —*Thom Jurek*

72 Live! / 1996 / Captain Trip ✦✦✦

Neu! 4 / 1996 / Captain Trip ✦✦✦
Recorded sometime in the mid-'80s but not released until over a decade later, *Neu! 4* picks up where the duo left off in 1975, exploring the extremes of both white noise and ambient beauty. Like *Neu! 2*, the album fills out with remixes of the basic tracks, but where the earlier effort simply varied playback speeds, the material on *Neu! 4* undergoes radical, even alien transformations. Much of the record predates 1990s electronic music with remarkable foresight: "Fly Dutch II" is a spacy techno loop which stakes out territory later claimed by Mouse on Mars, "Danzing" is a brutal electro experiment, and "86 Commer-

cial Trash" is constructed around samples from German television advertisements. —*Jason Ankeny*

Neutral Milk Hotel

f. 1989
Neo-Prog, Neo-Psychedelia, Indie Rock, Lo-Fi, Alternative Pop/Rock
The self-described "fuzz-folk" project Neutral Milk Hotel was one of the primary outgrowths of the Elephant 6 Recording Company collective, a coterie of like-minded, lo-fi indie groups—including the Apples (in stereo), the Olivia Tremor Control, and Secret Square—who shared musicians, ideas, and sensibilities. While ranging in sound and concept from solo acoustic work to full band performances, Neutral Milk Hotel essentially remained the work of Jeff Mangum, a singer/songwriter from the remote town of Ruston, LA. Ruston was also home to Robert Schneider (later of the Apples), as well as William Cullen Hart and Bill Doss (who formed the Olivia Tremor Control); throughout high school, the aspiring musicians—all influenced by the likes of the Beatles, the Beach Boys, the Zombies, Pink Floyd, and Sonic Youth—exchanged home recordings and played in each other's bands.

Neutral Milk Hotel first took shape in 1989 as a noise-rock trio which played its debut gig at a local laundromat; a year later Mangum, Hart, and Doss moved to Athens, GA, to form the group Cranberry Life Cycle, which later became Synthetic Flying Machine (and ultimately the Olivia Tremor Control) after Mangum's departure. In 1993, he and Schneider relocated to Denver, CO, where Schneider soon founded the Apples (in stereo). Eventually, Mangum gravitated to New York and resumed recording under the Neutral Milk Hotel aegis. After a series of singles and privately released cassettes including *Invent Yourself a Shortcake, Beauty*, and *Hype City*, Mangum travelled back to Denver to record the critically acclaimed 1996 album *On Avery Island* on Schneider's four-track machine; in the the spring of 1997 he again returned to Colorado to begin work on the follow-up, the brilliant *In the Aeroplane Over the Sea*. —*Jason Ankeny*

On Avery Island / Mar. 26, 1996 / Merge ✦✦✦✦
Like their Elephant 6 labelmates and kindred spirits Olivia Tremor Control's *Music From the Unrealized Film Script 'Dusk at Cubist Castle,'* Neutral Milk Hotel's debut *On Avery Island* is an inscrutable concept album, a chronicle of an insular world told in a remarkably universal language. A fuzzy masterpiece of experimental lo-fi recording, the album wraps its ragged pop songs in ribbons of loops, marching-band squawks, and Casio noodling; the opener "Song Against Sex" is as much a manifesto as a kick-off, a self-propelled marvel hopped up on rapid-fire wordplay and a stunningly ramshackle melody punctuated by bloated trombone moans. Throughout the record, Jeff Mangum's wheels threaten to fly off at any time—his songs are cryptic and crazed, his ideas fast and furious, and together they force the home-recording concept out of the basement and into a brave new world. —*Jason Ankeny*

● **In the Aeroplane Over the Sea** / Feb. 10, 1998 / Merge ✦✦✦✦
Perhaps best likened to a marching band on an acid trip, Neutral Milk Hotel's second album is another quixotic sonic parade; lo-fi yet lush, impenetrable yet wholly accessible, *In the Aeroplane Over the Sea* is either the work of a genius or an utter crackpot, with the truth probably falling somewhere in between. Again teaming with producer Robert Schneider, Jeff Mangum invests the material here with new maturity and clarity; while the songs run continuously together, as they did on the previous *On Avery Island*, there is a much clearer sense of shifting dynamics from track to track, with a greater emphasis on structure and texture. Mangum's vocals are far more emotive as well; whether caught in the rush of spiritual epiphany ("The King of Carrot Flowers Pts. Two and Three") or in the grip of sexual anxiety ("Two-Headed Boy"), he sings with a new fervor, composed in equal measure of ecstasy and anguish. However, as his musical concepts continue to come into sharper focus, one hopes his stream-of-consciousness lyrical ideas soon begin to do the same; while Mangum spins his words with the rapid-fire intensity of a young Dylan, the songs are far too cryptic and abstract to fully sink in—*In the Aeroplane Over the Sea* is undoubtedly a major statement, but just what it's saying is anyone's guess. —*Jason Ankeny*

The Neville Brothers

f. 1977, New Orleans, LA
New Orleans R&B, R&B, Funk, Soul
Throughout their long careers as both solo performers and as members of the group which bore their family name, the Neville Brothers proudly carried the torch of their native New Orleans' rich R&B legacy. Although the four siblings—Arthur, Charles, Aaron, and Cyril—did not officially unite under the Neville Brothers aegis until 1977, all had crossed musical paths in the past, while also enjoying success with other unrelated projects. Eldest brother Art was the first to tackle a recording career, when in 1954 his high school band the Hawketts cut "Mardi Gras Mambo," a song which later became the annual carnival's unofficial anthem. In 1960, Aaron scored his first solo hit, "Over You"; in 1966, he notched a pop smash with the classic "Tell It Like It Is," a lush ballad showcasing his gossamer vocals. In 1977 the siblings offically banded together as the Neville Brothers. Despite their gift for intricate four-part harmonies, their self-titled 1978 debut unsuccessfully cast the vocal quartet as a disco band, and following a dismal response they were dropped by their label, Capitol. The Nevilles spent the following three years without a contract, but after signing with A&M, fan Bette Midler helped secure the services of producer Joel Dorn for 1981's superior *Fiyo on the Bayou*. Despite widespread critical acclaim, the album sold poorly, and again the Nevilles were cut loose from their contract. In 1989, they re-signed to A&M and recruited the services of famed New Orleans producer Daniel Lanois; the atmospheric *Yellow Moon*, the group's finest hour, finally earned them success on the charts, thanks in part to the anthemic single "Sister Rosa."

1990's *Brother's Keeper* fared even better, no doubt spurred by Aaron's concurrent success with Linda Ronstadt on the smash duet "Don't Know Much." *—Jason Ankeny*

Fiyo on the Bayou / Apr. 1981 / A&M ✦✦✦✦✦

A brilliant updating of the New Orleans R&B sound to include strains of Cajun, rock, and reggae on standards ranging from "Hey Pocky Way" to "The Ten Commandments of Love" and "Sitting in Limbo." *—William Ruhlmann*

Neville-Ization / Jun. 1984 / Diablo ✦✦✦

It took Black Top Records two years to put this record out after the Neville Brothers recorded it live at Tipitina's in New Orleans in September, 1982, and one reason may be that it presents a mediocre, going-through-the-motions set. At their best, the Nevilles achieve a transcendent musical mixture, and even at the level of mere professionalism they're an impressive unit, but this just isn't the live album of which they are capable. *—William Ruhlmann*

★ **Treacherous: A History of the Neville Brothers** / 1986 / Rhino ✦✦✦✦✦

The music of the Neville Brothers was more a matter of rumor than documentation to most record buyers outside the New Orleans area until 1986, when Rhino Records finally gathered together their various solo and group records dating back 30 years and presented their story coherently on this two-disc set. Suddenly, it all makes sense, and the Nevilles' mixture of styles emerges as a singular American genre unto itself. This record is a revelation. *—William Ruhlmann*

Uptown / Mar. 1987 / EMI America ✦✦

Yellow Moon / 1989 / A&M ✦✦✦✦

The Neville Brothers made a bid for pop/rock stardom with this well-produced album for A&M, their first under a new pact with the label inked in the late '80s. It was certainly as solid as any they cut for A&M; the vocals were both nicely arranged and expertly performed, the arrangements were basically solid, and the selections were intelligently picked and sequenced. The album charted and remained there for many weeks, while the Nevilles toured and generated lots of interest. It didn't become a hit, but it did respectably and represents perhaps their finest overall pop LP. *—Ron Wynn*

Brother's Keeper / Jul. 1990 / A&M ✦✦✦

Why doesn't more R&B sound like this? Although hampered by a poor mix, *Brother's Keeper* is nevertheless a classic example of what makes the Neville Brothers so good... and so frustrating. Tracks like the booty-shaking funk of "Brother Jake" or the gospel-tinged "Steer Me Right" are full of soulful vocals and wonderful harmonies. Aaron Neville's timeless voice is displayed beautifully on "Fearless," where he is joined by Linda Ronstadt for one of the strongest tracks on the record. The Neville Brothers ecumenical spirituality permeates every second of *Brother's Keeper*, making for a few awkward moments (like the head-scratching opener "Brother Blood," for example) but a few moments of true sublimity (as when Art Neville spits "Pro choice-no choice/We're sending our sons and daughters to their slaughter" on "Sons and Daughters"). The pop material on *Brother's Keeper*, such as Link Wray's "Fallin' Rain," works well, but other tracks, like "River of Life," seem forced. If the Neville Brothers showed a little discretion with regard to their lyrics and cut a couple tracks, they would have had a much stronger album, which in a way is as good a statement as one could make about their entire career. *—Daniel Gioffre*

Treacherous Too: A History of the Neville Brothers, Vol. 2 (1955-1987) / Feb. 1, 1991 / Rhino ✦✦✦✦✦

Okay, there's no such thing as secondhand revelation, but the Neville Brothers had more than enough stray tracks from their decades of local music-making around New Orleans to justify this second, single-disc follow-up to Rhino's first Nevilles history. There's more of an emphasis on novelty material here, but once again you can hear the roots of the Nevilles' cross-genre appeal in pop, R&B, and soul music dating back to the 1950s. Since most of these songs were recorded as singles, they have an immediate surface appeal, but repeated listenings also bring out the sounds of the tight session bands (including members of the Meters) who backed the Nevilles up. Actually, it's only the five 1980s tracks from just-OK albums like *Neville-ization* and *Uptown* that keep this collection from classic status, not the older stuff. *—William Ruhlmann*

Live on Planet Earth / Apr. 19, 1994 / A&M ✦✦✦

Mitakuye Oyasin Oyasin/All My Relations / May 14, 1996 / A&M ✦✦✦

● **The Very Best of the Neville Brothers** / Jan. 14, 1997 / Rhino ✦✦✦✦✦

Sixteen-track compilation focusing almost exclusively on the period spanning the late '70s to the late '80s. A couple of Aaron Neville's big '60s hits ("Tell It like It Is" and "Over You") are thrown in as well, as are a couple of cuts from the Wild Tchoupitoulas' 1976 album. Some may argue that the Nevilles' sprawling output is too difficult to condense into a single disc. On the other hand, given how often they're criticized for underachieving on record, this is a pretty suitable purchase for someone whose interest only runs deep enough for one anthology. *—Richie Unterberger*

Live at Tipitina's 1982 / Aug. 18, 1998 / Rhino ✦✦✦✦✦

Valence Street / Feb. 16, 1999 / Columbia ✦✦✦✦

Uptown Rulin': The Best Of / Aug. 24, 1999 / Interscope ✦✦✦✦

The Neville Brothers had always been critic's favorites, but never more so than during their tenure at A&M Records during the late '80s and early '90s. They released their first album, *Yellow Moon*, for the label in 1989, a few years after the acclaimed Rhino compilation *Treacherous: A History of the Neville Brothers* appeared on the shelves. *Treacherous* contained selections from all the Neville Brothers—not just group recordings but side-projects and solo cuts—and helped cement their reputation among record collectors and critics, which in turn set the stage for the enthusiastic reception of *Yellow Moon*. That

enthusiasm failed to wane over the next few years, as each subsequent album was greeted by critics with open arms. The problem was, each record was pretty much the same. With producer Daniel Lanois, the Nevilles attempted to create grand, mythical albums, heavy with import and meaning. Lanois didn't abandon his trademark hazy, murkily mysterious production—a style that wasn't necessarily suited for the organic Nevilles, even if it did result in some evocative sonic hybrids. Consequently, each of the A&M albums functioned best as a series of moments, even if they were designed to work as individual albums (the prototype, *Yellow Moon*, unsurprisingly standing as the lone exception to the rule). That's why *Uptown Rulin'* is a solid addition to their catalog. By collecting highlights from the A&M albums, it offers fans a good summary of these intriguing but mixed years. It isn't on the same level as *Treacherous* or its sequel, but it's a nice addendum to fans of that groundbreaking compilation. *—Stephen Thomas Erlewine*

Aaron Neville

b. Jan. 24, 1941, New Orleans, LA

Vocals / Pop-Soul, New Orleans R&B, Adult Contemporary, R&B, Soul

Although Neville is often compared to singer Sam Cooke in terms of sheer vocal refinement, he has a voice and style uniquely his own. Today he is well known as part of the New Orleans sound of the Neville Brothers. Yet, aside from the 1967 number one R&B hit "Tell It Like It Is," few have heard his incredible early solo recordings. Many of the first recordings of Aaron Neville, in the early and mid-'60s, were arranged, produced, and often written by the brilliant Allen Toussaint—another talent only now being really appreciated. Most of these sides were cut for the Minit (and later) Parlo labels. Songs like "She Took You for a Ride" and "You Think You're So Smart" on Parlo are masterpieces. While his more recent work, including that with Linda Ronstadt, makes for pleasant listening, it lacks the sheer persuasion of his early songs. Aaron has re-recorded his early work often, and it is important to hear the originals. The early sides of Aaron Neville are just waiting to be heard. *—Michael Erlewine and Ron Wynn*

Greatest Hits / 1957 / Curb ✦✦✦

Early New Orleans soul from velvet-voiced Aaron Neville, including the smooth, aching "Tell It Like It Is" and the gutsy, declarative "Over You," a shuffling R&B number. The eight other selections, especially "Jail House," "Hard Nut to Crack," and "Since You're Gone," offers an insightful overview of the golden tenor whose vocal abilities get more amazing with time. *—Andrew Hamilton*

Tell It Like It Is / 1967 / Collectables ✦✦✦✦

Eleven of Neville's best Parlo cuts, including those mentioned above, are included on one CD. His biggest solo smash from 1966, plus more songs in the same style. Sublime stuff. *—Bill Dahl*

Orchid in the Storm / Dec. 1986 / Rhino ✦✦✦✦✦

Aaron Neville's wondrous singing on this poorly distributed EP was overlooked by many still unaware of his stunning falsetto. But Neville covered doo wop, soul, and even country on this project, singing with a soaring conviction and poignancy that made it a delightful, though short, set. Rhino has thankfully reissued it on CD. It's actually closer to representing Neville's real style than his recent much-hyped, overproduced pop records. *—Ron Wynn*

● **Tell It Like It Is: Golden Classics** / 1989 / Collectables ✦✦✦✦✦

One of many collections covering Aaron Neville's superb early R&B and soul classics. The burly Neville, whose delicate, feathery voice stands in vivid contrast to his muscular body, made great heartache ballads, up-tempo wailers, and brilliantly sung originals for tiny New Orleans labels, often not even getting widespread soul airplay. Now that's he's hot property, the domestic anthologies are coming out left and right. This one is as good as any other, although for my money the import labels have still done a better job on early Neville than the American companies. *—Ron Wynn*

My Greatest Gift / 1991 / Rounder ✦✦✦

The songs that made Neville famous among soul and R&B fans were done years before he became a recognized star, for tiny Southern labels. The 12 tracks on this anthology were recorded in the late '60s, when Neville's soaring falsetto, emphatic delivery, and gut-wrenching treatments were locked out of the pop mainstream. Although this isn't the definitive version of "Tell It Like It Is," it's far from a throwaway. On "Love Letters," "Hercules," "Mojo Hannah," and "Where Is My Baby," Aaron Neville tackled the soul mountain and conquered it. *—Ron Wynn*

Warm Your Heart / Jun. 11, 1991 / A&M ✦✦✦

When Aaron Neville signed with A&M in the early 1990s, optimists were hoping for some five-star soul gems along the lines of his classic '60s recordings. Instead, his first A&M date, *Warm Your Heart*, found the veteran New Orleans singer taking a much more pop-minded approach, with generally decent results. While Neville didn't abandon soul music, this CD made it clear that A&M was intent on making him a major hit in the pop market (which had been exposed to him in 1989 thanks to his duets with Linda Ronstadt). Though hardly in a class with such classics as "Tell It Like It Is" and "She Took You for a Ride," tracks like the haunting "That's the Way She Loves," the gritty "Angola Bound," and a remake of the Main Ingredient's "Everybody Plays the Fool" showed that Neville still had plenty of warmth and charisma. But although this is far from a bad album, it must be stressed that a collection of his '60s classics would be a much wiser investment. *—Alex Henderson*

The Very Best of Aaron Neville / Jan. 11, 2000 / A&M ✦✦✦✦

In some ways, *The Very Best of Aaron Neville* is a very welcome addition to his catalog, since it's the first collection to touch on all areas of Neville's long career. However, it winds up being a bit unsatisfying, not just because it only has one cut from the Neville Brothers, but because his New Orleans R&B and down-home soul just don't fit that well with his smooth, cleanly produced latter-day work. Then again, the compilers didn't spend too much time with the early recordings, since the collection contains only a handful of R&B nuggets (including, of course, "Tell It Like It Is," plus "Over You") before settling into the '80s and '90s albums. It's not a bad summary of those albums, actually, containing such hits as "Don't Know Much" and "Everybody Plays the Fool," plus a good cross-section of album tracks and lesser-known cuts, such as his version of "Stardust" with Rob Wasserman. As such, *The Very Best of Aaron Neville* is recommended primarily to fans of his later recordings. Listeners who prefer the early R&B work or the Neville Brothers should look to compilations of that material, since they won't be satiated by this disc. *—Stephen Thomas Erlewine*

● **Ultimate Collection** / Aug. 21, 2001 / Hip-O ✦✦✦✦✦
Although it not surprisingly shares a whopping nine tracks with 2000's *The Very Best of Aaron Neville*, 2001's *Ultimate Collection* cherry picks from a far wider range of years (1960-1997) than the A&M period which was used almost exclusively for the former anthology. As such, it's a considerably broader and ultimately a better representation of the Neville Brothers' famed muscular singer with the impossibly angelic falsetto voice. The compilation gradually shifts moods and years, smartly bunching most of the upbeat '60s selections (including some interesting obscurities like "Why Worry," the original B-side of "Tell It Like It Is") toward the middle. The collection also rescues a pair of gorgeous R&B covers ("Pledging My Love" and "For Your Precious Love") from an obscure 1985 Joel Dorn-produced EP, as well as "The 10 Commandments of Love," included in the difficult-to-find Neville Brothers 1981 release, *Fiyo on the Bayou*. It smartly plays down the rest of their music which is easily available elsewhere, but does include Neville's dramatic rendition of Sam Cooke's "A Change Is Gonna Come," one of his most stirring performances from *Yellow Moon*. Thankfully the album doesn't get bogged down in some of the slick and sappy concoctions Neville often gravitates to. While the rather forced rock & roll of Chuck Berry's "You Never Can Tell" doesn't quite fit the predominantly languorous mood, and the track list strangely omits Neville's version of George Jones' "The Grand Tour" or Skylark's "Wildflower"—both of which remain concert staples—this is a stunning and consistently enjoyable representation of one of the most distinctive and memorable voices in American music. *—Hal Horowitz*

New Colony Six

f. 1964, Chicago, IL
Garage Rock, Rock & Roll
Chicago's New Colony Six originally emerged as a tough, British Invasion-styled outfit prominently featuring Farfisa organ and a novel (at the time) Lesley guitar. Scoring a huge local hit with "I Confess," their early recordings—exemplified by their 1966 debut album, *Breakthrough*—featured first-class original material that gave the sound of Them and the Yardbirds a more commercial, American garage-based, vocal harmony approach. The rest of the '60s saw the band gradually abandoning their roots for middle-of-the-road pop with horns and strings. Continuing to rack up major local hits and minor national ones, they finally cracked the U.S. Top 30 with "Love You So Much" (1968) and "Things I'd Like to Say" (1969). *—Richie Unterberger*

Breakthrough / 1966 / Sentar ✦✦✦✦✦
Breakthrough was one of the very finest American garage LPs, fusing Midwestern guitar-organ pop with the raunch of British Invasion groups and stressing well-written original material. It is also extremely rare and extremely expensive should you locate an original copy. But take heart—ten of the 12 tracks have been reissued on Sundazed's *At the River's Edge* CD. The two other songs are routine, dispensable covers of the Yardbirds' "Mr. You're a Better Man than I" and the McCoys' "Hang On Sloopy," so you shouldn't fret about their absence from your collection. *—Richie Unterberger*

● **At the River's Edge** / 1993 / Sundazed ✦✦✦✦✦
Twenty-two tracks, including all of the worthwhile songs from their classic *Breakthrough* album, a non-LP single, and most of their second album, *Colonization*. The only New Colony Six package worth owning. *—Richie Unterberger*

Colonized! The Best of New Colony Six / Apr. 6, 1993 / Rhino ✦✦

New Edition

f. 1982, Boston, MA
Teen Pop, New Jack Swing, Urban, Hip-Hop
When Maurice Starr assembled New Edition in the early '80s, he never could have guessed that the group would produce some of the biggest, most influential urban R&B stars of the following decade. At the time of their first record, Bobby Brown, Ralph Tresvant, Ricky Bell, Mike Bivins, and Ronnie DeVoe were barely in their teens, yet they had impressive voices and a natural charisma that sent them to the charts with their first single, "Candy Girl." Their second album was even bigger, featuring the number two single "Cool It Now." New Edition's songs were either light funk or sweet ballads, yet they followed their formula well, even if much of it seems quaint now, especially compared to their groundbreaking solo work.

Brown left the band after their third album, being replaced by Johnny Gill. The band released two more albums before splitting. After the group was finished, they each became successful as solo artists in the late '80s. New Edition reunited in 1996, releasing a new album titled *Home Again* in the fall of that year. The *Lost in Love: The Best of Slow Jams* collection appeared in 1998. *—Stephen Thomas Erlewine*

● **Greatest Hits, Vol. 1** / Oct. 1, 1991 / MCA ✦✦✦✦✦
For anyone who missed New Edition in either its Jackson 5 imitation phase or final days as a funkier, more aggressive urban contemporary vocal group with a slight dance

influence, this collection contains examples of both incarnations. Kiddie-pop hits such as "Candy Girl," "Cool It Now," and "Mr. Telephone Man" are included, along with their final hits "If It Isn't Love," "Can You Stand the Rain," and the appropriately titled "Is This the End." This anthology shows how dominant New Edition was during the 1980s and early '90s. *—Ron Wynn*

New Edition Solo Hits / Dec. 3, 1996 / MCA ✦✦✦
A 12-track compilation of four tracks each by spin-off acts of New Edition seems like a strange way to pick up their work, to say the least. Still, if you want some hits by Bobby Brown, Bell Biv DeVoe, and Ralph Tresvant, and are for some reason uninterested in scoping out their albums or waiting for their one-artist-only greatest-hits collections, this is a succinct mini-primer of one of the most successful clans in urban contemporary music. *—Richie Unterberger*

All the Number Ones / May 9, 2000 / Hip-O ✦✦✦✦✦
An excellent idea that might be slightly disappointing in the execution, *All the Number Ones* collects 18 singles that topped *Billboard* magazine's R&B charts, all performed either by New Edition or its members in their various outside projects. That results in a terrific, endlessly playable collection of urban pop-soul and new jack swing, but it also means that several of the collective's best-known songs are left off simply because they didn't top the R&B charts. Missing in action are Bobby Brown's "Roni" and "Rock Wit'cha," Bell Biv DeVoe's "Do Me!," Johnny Gill's "Fairweather Friend," and Ralph Tresvant's "Stone Cold Gentleman" and "Do What I Gotta Do," plus a bevy of New Edition hits. In fact, it might have been an even better idea to gather the biggest hits by the various New Edition spin-offs and leave the parent group's output alone; such an approach would have erased the contrast between the early New Edition bubblegum singles that lead off this collection and the grittier, funkier new jack hits that follow. Still, at least these omissions are due to the compilation's stated intent (collecting *All the Number Ones* and nothing else), rather than a record-company marketing tactic. Even casual fans will undoubtedly miss at least a couple of the aforementioned hits, but really, what *is* here makes for a great listen and a fine introduction to one of the most influential R&B family trees of the '80s and early '90s. *—Steve Huey*

New Kids on the Block

f. 1984, Boston, MA
Teen Pop, Urban, Dance-Pop
After his success with New Edition, producer Maurice Starr decided to replicate the group, substituting the young black teenagers for suburban white kids. The result was New Kids on the Block, which quickly eclipsed the popularity of Starr's previous group. Comprising Boston area singers Donnie Wahlberg, Jordan Knight, Jon Knight, Danny Wood, and Joe McIntyre, the new Kids were awkward and enthusiastic on their 1986 debut, which wasn't surprising considering that the oldest members were barely 16 years old. With their next album, 1988's *Hangin' Tough*, the group's image had toughened up and they had the material to support it. From the saccharine ballad "I'll Be Loving You Forever" to the title track's stab at funk, the band had a seemingly endless streak of hits in 1988 and 1989; their Christmas album even went double platinum. New Kid mania continued with 1990's *Step by Step*, but that was the end of the road for their short time in the sun. *—Stephen Thomas Erlewine*

New Kids on the Block / 1986 / Columbia ✦✦✦
Debut with "Be My Girl." *—Bil Carpenter*

Hangin' Tough / 1988 / Columbia ✦✦✦✦
Good songs collected by New Kids mastermind Maurice Starr highlight this smash, including "I'll Be Loving You (Forever)," "You Got It (The Right Stuff)," "Please Don't Go Girl," and the title track. Tight, warm, even soulful harmony on the ballads. *—Dan Heilman & Bil Carpenter*

Step by Step / May 15, 1990 / Columbia ✦✦✦
In an attempt for some respect, the group wrote some cuts on *Step by Step*, a more serious, harder-sounding album. Although the title track was number one for three weeks and the followup, "Tonight," went Top Ten, they couldn't replicate the success of *Hangin' Tough*. *—Bil Carpenter*

Face the Music / Jan. 25, 1994 / Columbia ✦✦✦
The New Kids return after much ridicule and doubt with the defensive *Face the Music*, and, surprise!—it isn't bad at all. Sure, they've changed their style a bit—their new jack R&B is a bit rougher, the lyrics are a touch nastier, and their hip-hop sounds a little more *real*—but none of it sounds fake, and the best tracks on the album might impress even the most jaded listener. *—Stephen Thomas Erlewine*

● **Greatest Hits** / Feb. 16, 1999 / Columbia ✦✦✦✦
If *Greatest Hits* doesn't seem as fun as it should be, that's because the New Kids on the Block's material has dated, even though it, in many ways, set the template for the teen pop of the late '90s/early 2000s. Max Martin used Maurice Starr's formula, but he writes better songs—only "I'll Be Loving You (Forever)" and "You Got It (The Right Stuff)" stand the test of time as good pop singles, but the rest are pretty much triumphs of recording and the form. Also, the sequencing doesn't play to their strengths, failing to gain much momentum as it plays. This still is recommended as the first pick, since it does have all of NKOTB's hits on one disc, but it's still sort of a shock that this doesn't play as trashy fun, the way it does in memory—or the way Milli Vanilli's music now does. *—Stephen Thomas Erlewine*

New Order

f. 1980, Manchester, England

College Rock, Alternative Dance, Club/Dance, Post-Punk, Alternative Pop/Rock, Synth Pop, House

Rising from the ashes of the legendary British post-punk unit Joy Division, the enigmatic New Order triumphed over tragedy to emerge as one of the most influential and acclaimed bands of the 1980s; embracing the electronic textures and disco rhythms of the underground club culture many years in advance of their contemporaries, the group's pioneering fusion of new wave aesthetics and dance music successfully bridged the gap between the two worlds, creating a distinctively thoughtful and oblique brand of synth pop appealing equally to the mind, body, and soul. After completing sessions for Joy Division's sophomore effort, *Closer*, frontman Ian Curtis hanged himself on May 18, 1980; devastated, the remaining trio re-formed a few months later as New Order. With the single "Everything's Gone Green," the group first began adorning their sound with synthesizers and sequencers, inspired by the music of Kraftwerk as well as the electro beats coming up from the New York underground; 1982's "Temptation" continued the trend, and like its predecessor was a major favorite among clubgoers. After a year-long hiatus, New Order resurfaced in 1983 with their breakthrough hit "Blue Monday"; packaged in a provocative sleeve designed to recall a computer disk, with virtually no information about the band itself—a hallmark of their mysterious, distant image—it perfectly married singer Bernard Sumner's plaintive yet cold vocals and abstract lyrics with cutting-edge drum-machine rhythms ideal for club consumption. "Blue Monday" went on to become the best-selling 12" release of all time, moving over three million copies worldwide. In 1987 they issued *Substance*, a much-needed collection of singles and remixes; it was New Order's American breakthrough, cracking the Top 40 on the strength of the newly recorded single "True Faith," which itself reached number 32 on the U.S. pop charts. —*Jason Ankeny*

Movement / 1981 / Qwest ♦♦♦

New Order's debut album *Movement* bridges the gap between the synthesizer-heavy music the group would later develop and Joy Division's languid, morbid drone. *Movement* pointed the way toward New Order's future by featuring more synthesizers than any of Joy Division's records, as well as more accessible hooks and melodies. —*Stephen Thomas Erlewine*

Power, Corruption & Lies / 1983 / Qwest ♦♦♦♦♦

New Order's second album was their giant step out of the looming shadow of Joy Division, clearly establishing their own unique and innovative musical identity. Seamlessly incorporating Gillian Gilbert's lush synth patterns into the mix, *Power, Corruption & Lies* springs from the propulsive, almost liquid bass of Peter Hook and the increasingly strong compositional skills of Bernard Sumner to firmly install the group as a cutting-edge electronic dance unit, one with unsurpassed reserves of humanity and depth—tracks like "Age of Consent" and the shimmering "Your Silent Face" speak to the mind and the body in equal measure. The U.S. release also appended their breakthrough club hit "Blue Monday," a masterpiece of the genre. —*Jason Ankeny*

Low-life / 1985 / Qwest ♦♦♦♦♦

New Order's evolution from post-punk survivors to state of the art electronic unit became complete with the superb *Low-life*, the first of their albums to receive a proper American release. Tracks like "Sub-Culture" and "The Perfect Kiss" represent dance-pop at its very finest—propulsive, smart, and edgy, they combine lush synth patterns and programmed beats with a level of emotional investment seemingly at odds with its environs, creating a tension which keeps the music fresh and involving where other club hits from the era now seem dated and vacuous. In spite of their new technological mastery, the group remains as eccentric and unpredictable as ever—"Elegia" is a delicate instrumental piece, while the opening "Love Vigilantes" is quite nearly a folk song, complete with a squawking harmonica intro, and is utterly unlike anything else in the New Order catalog; still, it succeeds brilliantly, the work of a band at the very top of its game. —*Jason Ankeny*

Brotherhood / 1986 / Qwest ♦♦♦♦

One of the least-synthesized albums in New Order's discography, *Brotherhood* offers the simultaneous peak of the group's hook-filled songwriting (not just on the single "Bizarre Love Triangle") and Peter Hook's trademark bass work, which takes a plaintive, upper-register lead on highlights like "Weirdo" and "Broken Promise." As usual, the lines dividing organic and electronic are quite fuzzy, resulting in stark drum-machine lines for the tender ballad "All Day Long." Sumner's fondness for bizarre, enigmatic lyrics continues apace with songs like the closer ("Every second counts, when I am with you/I think you are a pig, you should be in a zoo"). —*John Bush*

☆ **Substance** / 1987 / Qwest ♦♦♦♦♦

Substance is a double-disc set collecting New Order's singles, including several songs that were never available on the group's albums, at least in these versions. While there are a couple of re-recordings of earlier singles, most of *Substance* consists of 12" single mixes designed for danceclub play. Arguably, these 12" mixes represent New Order's most groundbreaking and successful work, since they expanded the notion of what a rock & roll band, particularly an indie rock band, could do. *Substance* collects the best of their remixes, and in the process it showcases not only the group's musical innovations, but also their songwriting prowess—"Temptation," "Blue Monday," "Bizarre Love Triangle," and "True Faith" are some of the finest pop songs of the '80s. Although it is a double-disc set, *Substance* isn't overly long. Instead it offers a perfect introduction to New Order, while providing collectors with an invaluable collection of singles. —*Stephen Thomas Erlewine*

Technique / 1989 / Qwest ♦♦♦♦♦

The first post-acid house masterpiece of British pop, *Technique* presents New Order doing what they'd done best for close to a decade—writing brilliant left-field pop songs and consistently blurring the line between electronic dance and alternative pop. From the driving singles "Fine Time," "Run," and "Round & Round," it would appear that *Technique* was the band's most dance-slanted record yet, though rockier album tracks like "Love Less" and "All the Way" reveal the band having it both ways. "Mr. Disco" proves that the group's baffling sense of humor is still intact. —*John Bush*

Republic / May 11, 1993 / Qwest ♦♦♦♦

Pulling back slightly from the raw, dance-oriented *Technique*, New Order took a break for four years and then crafted another slice of prime guitar pop. In keeping with previous work, *Republic* simply borrows elements of contemporary innovations in club music to frame a set of effortlessly enjoyable alternative pop songs. As on *Technique*, the singles ("World," "Spooky") are the most danceable on the record, while lyrical concerns are among the most direct of the group's career, including "Ruined in a Day" and "Times Change," sure signs of the demise of Factory Records. —*John Bush*

The Rest of New Order / 1995 / London ♦♦♦

★ **The Best of New Order** / Mar. 14, 1995 / Qwest ♦♦♦♦♦

Instead of presenting New Order as a progressive dance band as *Substance* did, *The Best of New Order* showcases New Order the pop band, condensing most of their hit singles onto one disc. A couple of remixes are thrown in (Shep Pettibone takes over "Blue Monday"), and several classics, including "Temptation" and "Ceremony" are missing, but it is still a concise explanation of why the group was one of the most important dance groups of the '80s. —*Stephen Thomas Erlewine*

The New Radicals

f. 1997, db. 1999

Pop Underground, Adult Alternative Pop/Rock, Alternative Pop/Rock

A pop-rock group that was formed in the late 1990s but was heavily influenced by the rock and soul of the 1970s, the New Radicals are the creation of singer/producer/songwriter Gregg Alexander—a native of Grosse Point, MI (near Detroit). Growing up in Michigan, Alexander started listening to both rock and R&B extensively as a child and was only 12 when he acquired his first electric guitar. After high school, he traveled around the U.S. and lived in both New York and Los Angeles. It was in L.A. that he formed the New Radicals, which signed with MCA in 1997 and soon got to work on *Maybe You've Been Brainwashed Too*—a 1970s-minded CD that came out in October 1998. Alexander did all of the producing and arranging and most of the songwriting on the promising album, which was the group's sole release—after scoring the hit "You Get What You Give," he disbanded the New Radicals to focus on production work. —*Alex Henderson*

● **Maybe You've Been Brainwashed Too** / Oct. 20, 1998 / MCA ♦♦♦♦

The more things change in music, the more they stay the same. The alternative rockers of the 1990s may have caused so-called corporate rockers like Poison and Bon Jovi to become less visible, but at the same time, the worship of 1970s baby boomer culture was alive and well among post-baby boomers. In 1998, one of the most memorable examples of 1970s-flavored music came from the New Radicals. Although Radicals singer/leader Gregg Alexander was quick to espouse a left-wing point of view, *Maybe You've Been Brainwashed Too* doesn't beat listeners over the head with a sociopolitical agenda. Nor is the CD an exercise in angry 1990s angst-rock. Rather, Alexander's band is a congenial and highly melodic throwback to the rock and blue-eyed soul of the early to mid-1970s. Alexander's vocals have a very Mick Jagger-ish quality, but while the Rolling Stones were a rock & roll band that occasionally dabbled in soul and funk, the Radicals favor pop-rock that is consistently mindful of classic Northern soul. Hook-happy offerings like "Jehovah Made This Whole Joint for You," "Flowers," and "Mother We Just Can't Get Enough" give the impression that Alexander holds the Stones and the artists of Motown Records in equally high regard. Without question, *Brainwashed* was among the more promising releases of late 1998. —*Alex Henderson*

New York City

f. 1972, New York, NY

Smooth Soul, Soul, Philly Soul

New York City scored the first time out with "I'm Doing Fine Now," so on the surface New York City may have seemed like just a bunch of guys who got together, had a hit, and disbanded. Members John Brown and Claude Johnson had illustrious histories in music. Brown sang with the Five Satins, the Cadillacs, and filled in with the Moonglows when founder and member Harvey Fuqua called. Johnson sang with the Genies and was Don of Don & Juan. Tim McQueen (lead singer) and Eddie Schell, like Brown and Johnson, had sung in countless groups around New York City.

Before New York City, the four had recorded and gigged under the name Tri-Boro Exchange—a city bridge that links three boroughs (it was suggested by producer Wes Farrell). One single was released on Buddah Records. Farrell convinced Philly legend Thom Bell to produce some tracks for the group, including "I'm Doing Fine Now," written by Sherman Marshall and Bell—it went to number 17 pop in 1973.

On the strength of the hit they started making personal appearances. Backing them on the road was the Big Apple Band, whose members included the late Bernard Edwards and Nile Rogers, who later formed Chic. None of the follow-ups came close to repeating their initial success. "Make Me Twice the Man," written by McQueen, stalled at number 93, while "Quick, Fast, in a Hurry" peaked at number 79. Chicago's Notations remade the McQueen song, a ballad that suggested their deep doo wop roots. The Chelsea label released two albums and a handful of singles, and then it was all over for New York City. *—Andrew Hamilton*

- **I'm Doin' Fine Now** / Aug. 5, 1993 / Collectables ♦♦♦♦
This CD contains tracks from New York City's debut Chelsea Records LP. The Thom Bell productions mimic the sides he was creating for the Spinners and others. Bell uses female backing like he did with the Spinners, at times making them more prominent in the mix than the group members. New York City's lead singer Tim McQueen has an expressive voice suitable for pop and sounds comfortable with Bell's orchestrations. The group's roots, however, were heavy in doo wop, as member John Brown sang with the Five Satins. The other members were Tim McQueen, Ed Shell, and Claude Johnson. "I'm Doing Fine Now" invaded the pop Top 20, nesting at number 17. Thom Bell and Linda Creed's "Quick, Fast, in a Hurry" sounds too formulaic; its chart progress halted at number 79. McQueen wrote their third release, "Make Me Twice the Man" which fared worse at number 97; yet this was more New York City's sound than Bell Productions'. Both of the above pop flops reached higher rungs on Billboard's R&B chart. "Uncle James" has to be a Spinners reject. The song has Philippe Wynne written all over it; all it's missing is a Wynne-type testifying sermon. *—Andrew Hamilton*

- **The Best of New York City: I'm Doin' Fine Now** / 1999 / Sequel ♦♦♦♦♦
Best of New York City: I'm Doin' Fine Now is the final word on this unfairly underrated band, who, despite their name and place of origin, created some of the finest Philly soul of the era. The opening number "I'm Doin' Fine Now" certainly stands as one of the great forgotten singles of the genre (and the '70s in general). Both of the band's albums—1973's *I'm Doing Fine Now* and 1974's *Soulful Road*—are included in their entirety and the liner notes give a good overview of the band's career. Although nothing really can compete with the absolute brilliance of "I'm Doin' Fine Now," New York City's material was surprisingly strong on both albums, with standouts like "Make Me Twice the Man" and "Quick, Fast, in a Hurry." This collection is absolutely essential for any fan of '70s soul. *—Chris Woodstra*

The New York Dolls

f. 1971, New York, NY, **db.** 1977
New York Punk, Album Rock, Proto-Punk, Glam Rock, Hard Rock
The New York Dolls created punk rock before there was a term for it. Building on the Rolling Stones' dirty rock & roll, Mick Jagger's androgyny, girl-group pop, the glam rock of David Bowie and T. Rex, and the Stooges' anarchic noise, the New York Dolls created a new form of hard rock that presaged both punk rock and heavy metal. Their drug-fueled, shambolic performances influenced a generation of musicians in New York and London, who all went on to form punk bands. And although they self-destructed quickly, the band's two albums remained two of the most popular cult records in rock & roll history.

After generating considerable buzz in New York and England, the New York Dolls signed with Mercury Records in late 1972. Their eponymous 1973 debut, produced by Todd Rundgren, received overwhelmingly positive reviews, but it didn't stir the interest of the general public, stalling at 116 on the U.S. charts. The band's follow-up, 1974's *Too Much Too Soon*, was produced by the legendary girl-group producer George "Shadow" Morton. Although the sound of the record was relatively streamlined, the album was another commercial failure. Mercury dropped the band soon afterward, then the group hooked up with manager Malcolm McLaren, who used the Dolls as a test ground for the provocative promotions that would later bring the Sex Pistols notoriety. Every strategy he tried with the Dolls backfired, chief amongst those his idea to give the group a communist chic makeover, dressing them in red leather and having them perform in front of the USSR's flag. This tactic didn't stir interest and soon the group began to splinter, with guitarist Johnny Thunders leaving in 1975. Vocalist David Johansen and guitarist Syl Sylvain fired McLaren and worked with a variety of lineups before disbanding in 1977. *—Stephen Thomas Erlewine*

★ **The New York Dolls** / 1973 / Mercury ♦♦♦♦♦
There are hints of girl-group pop and more than a hint of the Rolling Stones, but *The New York Dolls* doesn't really sound like anything that came before it. It's hard rock with a self-conscious wit, a celebration of camp and kitsch that retains a menacing, malevolent edge. The New York Dolls play as if they can barely keep the music from falling apart and David Johansen sings and screams like a man possessed. *The New York Dolls* is a noisy, reckless album that rocks and rolls with a vengance. The Dolls rework old Chuck Berry and Stones riffs, playing them with a sloppy, violent glee. "Personality Crisis," "Looking for a Kiss," and "Trash" strut with confidence, while "Vietnamese Baby" and "Frankenstein" sound otherworldly, working the same frightening drone over and over again. *The New York Dolls* was the definitive proto-punk album, even more than anything the Stooges released. It plunders history while celebrating it, creating a sleazy urban mythology along the way. *—Stephen Thomas Erlewine*

☆ **Too Much Too Soon** / 1974 / Mercury ♦♦♦♦♦
After the clatter of their first album failed to bring them a wide audience, the New York Dolls hired producer Shadow Morton to work on the follow-up, *Too Much Too Soon*. The differences are apparent right from the start of the ferocious opener, "Babylon." Not only are the guitars cleaner, but the mix is dominated by waves of studio sound effects and female backing vocals. Ironically, instead of making the Dolls sound safer, all the added frills emphasize their gleeful sleaziness and reckless sound. The Dolls sound on the verge of falling apart throughout the album, as Johnny Thunders and Syl Sylvain relentlessly trade buzz-saw riffs while David Johansen sings, shouts, and sashays on top of the racket. Band originals—including the bluesy raver "It's Too Late," the noisy girl-group pop of "Puss N' Boots," and the Thunders showcase "Chatterbox"—are rounded out by obscure R&B and rock & roll covers tailor-made for the group. Johansen vamps throughout Leiber & Stoller's "Bad Detective," Archie Bell's "(There's Gonna Be A) Showdown," the Cadets "Stranded in the Jungle," and Sonny Boy Williamson's "Don't Start Me Talkin'," yet it's with grit and affection—he really means it, man! The whole record collapses with the scathing "Human Being," on which a bunch of cross-dressing misfits defiantly declare that it's OK that they want too many things, 'cause they're human beings, just like you and me. Three years later, the Sex Pistols failed to come up with anything as musically visceral and dangerous. Perhaps that's why the Dolls never found their audience in the early '70s: Not only were they punk rock before punk rock was cool, but they remained weirder and more idiosyncratic than any of the bands that followed. And they rocked harder, too. *—Stephen Thomas Erlewine*

Rock & Roll / Oct. 18, 1994 / Mercury ♦♦♦♦♦
Rock & Roll contains all of the original material from the Dolls' two classic albums and adds a couple of outtakes and rarities. So why isn't it as much fun as *New York Dolls* or *Too Much Too Soon?* For starters, the Dolls' versions of "Pills," "Stranded in the Jungle," "Don't Start Me Talkin," and "(There's Gonna Be A) Showdown" weren't filler, they were essential to the overall feeling of the albums. And that brings us to the main problem of *Rock & Roll*—it isn't sequenced in an inviting manner. Instead of showcasing the New York Dolls in all of their trashy glory, the disc manages to make them sound rather tedious, which is something their proper albums certainly aren't. Nevertheless, there's plenty of fine music here, and hardcore fans will want the rarities. But the original albums remain the best way to hear the Dolls. *—Stephen Thomas Erlewine*

Hard Night's Day / Aug. 15, 2000 / Norton ♦♦♦
This collection of 1973 studio demos includes just about everything in the Dolls' repertoire at the time (21 songs) and was recorded just prior to their entering the studio with producer Todd Rundgren to lay down their first album. While the takes aren't drastically different, they are rawer. Rundgren added a sheen to the album that just isn't here (which makes David Johansen's off-key singing and Johnny Thunders' missed guitar notes all the more obvious). A fine fan souvenir, but no replacement for the official studio work. *—Michael Gallucci*

Newcleus

f. 1979, Brooklyn, NY
Old School Rap, Electro
Although they recorded only two albums, Newcleus contributed one true electro classic in "Jam on Revenge (The Wikki-Wikki Song)," which has been immortalized on hundreds of hip-hop mix tapes and often included in even techno DJ's sets. The origins of Newcleus lay in a 1977 Brooklyn DJ collective known as Jam-On Productions, including Ben "Cozmo D" Cenac, his cousin Monique Angevin, and her brother Pete (all teenagers and still in high school). Many members—MCs as well as DJs—came and went as the group played block parties all over the borough, and by 1979, the group centered around Cenac, his future wife Yvette "Lady E" Cook, Monique Angevin, and *her* future husband, Bob "Chilly B" Crafton. (The foursome named their group Newcleus as a result of the coming together of their families.)

By this time, Cenac had begun to accumulate a collection of electronic recording equipment, and the quartet recorded a demo tape of material. With several minutes left at the end of the tape, Newcleus recorded a favorite from their block parties, with each member's vocals sped up to resemble the Chipmunks. The track, "Jam-On's Revenge," impressed producer Joe Webb more than the other Newcleus material, and it became the group's first single, released in 1983 on Mayhew Records. A huge street success, the track became known unofficially as "the Wikki-Wikki song" (after the refrain); when it was re-released later that year on Sunnyview Records, it had become "Jam on Revenge (The Wikki-Wikki Song)."

The single hit Top 40 on the R&B charts in 1983, and its follow-up "Jam on It" did well on even the pop charts. "Computer Age (Push the Button)" was a more mature single, with accomplished rapping and better synthesizer effects, and it also hit the R&B Top 40. The first Newcleus LP, *Jam on Revenge*, was a bit of a disappointment, and their second album, *Space Is the Place*, did even more poorly upon release in 1984. Without a single as noteworthy as "Jam on Revenge" or "Computer Age," and with the advent of Run-D.M.C.'s organic, rock-influenced approach to rap music, Newcleus faded quickly. Though the Cenacs and the Craftons continued to record sporadically until 1989, they didn't hit the R&B charts after 1986. *—John Bush*

- **Jam on This!: The Best of Newcleus** / Jul. 22, 1997 / Rhino ♦♦♦
Newcleus deserve mention in any history of electro/hip-hop of the early '80s because of two certifiable classics: "Jam on Revenge (The Wikki-Wikki Song)" and "Computer Age (Push the Button)." Two tracks hardly fill a major compilation album, and at first glance, the group wouldn't appear to deserve their own best-of set; however, the compilers at Rhino did a good job of selecting tracks from the group's two albums, 1984's *Jam on Revenge* and the following year's *Space Is the Place* (a reference to jazz mystic Sun Ra). Other than the obvious hits, great album tracks include "Auto-Man," "I Wanna Be a B-Boy," and "Let's Jam." *—John Bush*

Martin Newell

Alternative Pop/Rock
One of the great eccentrics of modern English pop/rock, Martin Newell's songs are recommended listening for anyone who enjoys the peculiarly British eccentricities of Ray Davies, Andy Partridge, Syd Barrett, and the like. His grasp of the pop hook has been second to few throughout the 1980s and '90s; his arrangements favor a guitar jangle but are usually infused with a whimsical eclecticism full of goofy sound effects and unusual

garnishes of unexpected percussion and string instruments. His voice is winningly quizzical, but his chief assets are his compositions, which reflect contemporary English life with a wry combination of affection and cynicism.

For most of the 1980s, Newell was the mainstay of Cleaners From Venus, who recorded most of their albums at home for cassette-only self-release, although they eventually put out some vinyl product. After a short stint as head of the similar Brotherhood of Lizards, Martin started a solo career in the 1990s that was essentially a continuation of the territory he'd explored in the 1980s; sometimes he re-recorded songs from the previous decade. The difference, if any, was that he was concentrating on the proper official album market instead of the cassette underground, with somewhat higher (though not slick) production values.

Newell's most acclaimed album was 1993's *The Greatest Living Englishman*, which was produced by Andy Partridge of XTC. *The Off White Album* (1995) was a bit more baroque in approach, with occasional string arrangements. *Spirit Cage* was issued in fall 2000. Newell has co-written material with Captain Sensible and is a poet/humorist of some renown in Britain, publishing his own prose with a good deal of success and writing humorous pieces for the *Independent* newspaper. Ironically, his music is virtually unknown on his home turf, although he enjoys a considerable cult following in Germany, Japan, France, and on certain American college radio stations. *—Richie Unterberger*

● **The Greatest Living Englishman** / Nov. 1993 / Pipeline ♦♦♦♦♦
As it was produced by XTC's Andy Partridge (who also plays most of the drums), this was Newell's first project to receive any semblance of mainstream media attention in the U.S. What he was presenting, however, differed little in essence from what he'd been doing since Cleaners From Venus started in the early '80s: tuneful pop with heart and clever lyrics that could be joyfully optimistic, whimsically satirical, or dourly cynical. In fact, a few of these songs are remakes of things that Newell had done in the Cleaners days, such as "Home Counties Boy" and the very Kinks-like "A Street Called Prospect" and "Christmas in Suburbia." The production was more in line with state-of-the-art standards, but really the results were no worse or better than on Newell's '80s recordings: less idiosyncratically homespun, perhaps, but more accessible to a wider audience. Playing, as always, like a snapshot of English life, it's the most suitable introduction to Newell's work, not in the least because it's one of his few albums that's reasonably obtainable without a major effort. *—Richie Unterberger*

The Off White Album / 1995 / Humbug ♦♦♦
Newell's second widely distributed album (he self-released some tapes under his own name in the 1980s) is a bit more precious and ornate than *The Greatest Living Englishman*, particularly when the songs employ string arrangements. At these times especially, this sounds a bit like Elvis Costello's unplugged/string quartet releases. Newell's phrasing, too, is getting more deliberate in a way that also faintly recalls Costello, though Martin doesn't sound as calcluated in his delivery. As far as the songs go, it's largely more of the same: witty, affecting vignettes about British characters, simultaneously evoking a glorious past and a somewhat unsettling, frustrating present. It's not his best record, but it's still more inventive, intelligent British pop than what you hear from most other such artists that try to carry this kind of thing off. *—Richie Unterberger*

Martin Newell's Box of Old Humbug / 1996 / Humbug ♦♦♦♦♦
A three-CD box set containing *The Greatest Living Englishman*, *The Off White Album*, and the four-song CD single *Let's Kiosk!* The single, which is available separately, has "The Jangling Man" (from *The Greatest Living Englishman*) and three otherwise unavailable tracks which are quite up to the standards of his albums, although they wouldn't be standouts on them. If you're interested enough in Newell in the first place to find *any* of his work, you're more likely than not devoted enough to check out *anything* he's done. So if you haven't gotten any of this stuff yet, it makes sense to splurge and get the whole danged package at once. Here's as good a place as any to mention that Newell uses incidental noises of schoolchildren and birds as well as anybody in rock; the best track on the single, "I Will Haunt Your Room," is an outstanding example of this. *—Richie Unterberger*

The Wayward Genius of Martin Newell / Sep. 7, 1999 / Cherry Red ♦♦♦♦
Newell's catalog is so big that nothing less than a box set could serve as an adequate retrospective. This 21-song compilation, though, is pretty good, with 11 songs from his Cleaners From Venus days, three by his separate group project the Brotherhood of Lizards, and seven solo cuts. Whatever the source, his songs are consistently pleasurable, melodic, and lyrically witty and insightful—which is not the most common combination in pop music. And these songs *are* pop, of the very British variety, rather than singer/songwriter stuff, arty experimentation, or some such things. Drawbacks? Well, none of the original release dates or sources from which these were taken are listed, and even committed Newell fans might have a hard time placing where and when these songs originally appeared, although the booklet does include a very large discography. In addition, sometimes inferior versions of songs are used in cases where better ones appeared on his cassette-only releases. Still, it's a good collection, including some of his very best songs, such as "Living With Victoria Grey" and "Mercury Girl." *—Richie Unterberger*

The Spirit Cage / Nov. 21, 2000 / Cherry Red ♦♦♦
It's true enough that *The Spirit Cage* is more of the same from middle-aged Newell. But sometimes more of the same is good, and sometimes—not that often, actually—middle-aged is not synonymous with artistic decline or burnout. On this album, he offers a dozen perky, melodic songs that are witty without playing for laughs. It's not as lo-fi as his numerous cassette-only releases, but it's not overly slick either, and quite heavy on the jangly reverb guitar that he uses well. Songwise it sounds like it could have just as well been written and recorded by him in 1987 or 1995, as 2000, but there is a somewhat more low-key and less sardonic vibe than he's flashed at some points in the past. If you're looking for slight deviations from his standard melodic guitar pop, "Sugarcane" has a Spanish-Mediterranean feel to the guitars and rhythms, and there are a couple of piano-dominated ballads (at which his occasional resemblance to Elvis Costello becomes more prominent). "My Old School" revisits familiar Newell Brit-pop territory with its bouncy yet bittersweet nostalgia. Less successfully, "Days Like These" gets into a rustic blues-folk mode, recalling all those '70s records when various past and present Faces/Small Faces would go acoustic. That track isn't downright bad, though, and the album is pretty consistent melodic, thoughtful pop/rock. *—Richie Unterberger*

Randy Newman

b. Nov. 28, 1943, New Orleans, LA
Vocals, Conductor, Composer, Arranger, Piano / Album Rock, Original Score, Film Music, Soundtracks, Brill Building Pop, Pop/Rock, Pop, Singer/Songwriter
Randy Newman was an anomaly among early '70s singer/songwriters. Though he was slightly influenced by Bob Dylan, his music owed more to New Orleans R&B and traditional pop than folk. Newman developed an idiosyncratic style that alternated between sweeping, cinematic pop and rolling R&B, which were tied together by his nasty sense of humor. Where his peers concentrated on confessional songwriting, Newman drew characters, creating a world filled with misfits, outcasts, charlatans, and con-men. Though he occasionally showed sympathy for his characters, he became well known for his biting sense of satire, highlighted by his fluke 1978 hit "Short People" and his parody of '80s yuppies, "I Love L.A." While Newman's records consistently received strongly positive reviews, he made his money through composing film scores for films like *Ragtime* and *The Natural*. His albums may never have sold in large amounts, but his work influenced several generations of songwriters, including Lyle Lovett and Mark Knopfler. *—Stephen Thomas Erlewine*

Randy Newman / 1968 / Reprise ♦♦♦♦♦
"Randy Newman creates something new under the sun," read the banner on the back of Newman's debut album, but it wasn't so much that as that in keeping with the intended irony of the statement, Newman was intent upon taking clichés and using them to satirize social conventions, a popular parlor game in the late '60s. Thus, we have "Love Story" (predating the sappy book/movie of the same title), in which the lovers retire to Florida and pass away, "So Long Dad," in which a son squares things with his old man, and "Davy the Fat Boy," in which an affectionate friend exploits the title character. But there were also songs like "Living Without You" and "I Think It's Gonna Rain Today," which were so painfully lonely you wished they weren't so sincere. Taken together, this was an audacious first album by a major, if extremely quirky, talent. *—William Ruhlmann*

★ **12 Songs** / 1970 / Reprise ♦♦♦♦♦
On his debut album, Randy Newman sounded as if he was still getting used to the notion of performing his own songs in the studio (despite years of cutting songwriting demos), but apparently he was a pretty quick study, and his second long-player, *12 Songs*, was a striking step forward for Newman as a recording artist. While much of *Randy Newman* was heavily orchestrated, *12 Songs* was cut with a small combo (Ry Cooder and Clarence White take turns on guitar), leaving a lot more room for Newman's Fats Domino-gone-cynical piano and the bluesier side of his vocal style, and Randy sounds far more confident and comfortable in this context. And Newman's second batch of songs were even stronger than his first (no small accomplishment), rocking more and grooving harder but losing none of their intelligence and careful craft in the process. "Have You Seen My Baby?" and "Mama Told Me Not to Come" are a pair of sly, updated New Orleans-style rockers (both of which would be much-covered in the coming years); "Let's Burn Down the Cornfield" and "Suzanne" are subtly ominous tales of love and sex; "Yellow Man" was an early meditation on one of Newman's favorite themes, the absurdity of racial prejudice (which he would also glance at in his straight-but-twisted cover of "Underneath the Harlem Moon"); and "My Old Kentucky Home" is a hilarious and quite uncharitable look at life in the deep South (another theme that would pop up in his later work). Newman's humor started getting more acidic with *12 Songs*, but here even his most mordant character studies boast a recognizable humanity, which often make his subjects both pitiable and all the more loathsome. Superb material brilliantly executed, *12 Songs* was Randy Newman's first great album, and is still one of his finest moments on record. *—Mark Deming*

Randy Newman Live / 1971 / Reprise ♦♦♦
Looking like a bootleg and sounding like the radio-promo item it was intended to be, *Randy Newman Live* is as straightforward as live albums get: a clean but unexceptional recording of Randy Newman alone at his piano, running through nine tunes from his first two albums and five new numbers (three of which would pop up on later studio albums, though the unremarkable "Tickle Me" and "Maybe I'm Doing It Wrong" remain exclusive to this release). At less than 30 minutes, the album is a bit light on material (especially since three shows were recorded for this set), and while Newman's performance is witty and engaging, the studio versions of these songs are preferable, though the solo performance of "Davy the Fat Boy" has a certain stark resonance the original lacks, and his vocals are a good bit stronger than on his first album. *Randy Newman Live* is OK for completists and fun for rabid fans, but most anyone else would be better served hearing these songs elsewhere. *—Mark Deming*

☆ **Sail Away** / 1972 / Reprise ♦♦♦♦♦
On his third studio album, Randy Newman found a middle ground between the heavily orchestrated pop of his debut and the more stripped-down, rock-oriented approach of *12 Songs*, and managed to bring new strength to both sides of his musical personality in the process. The title track, which Newman has described as a sort of commercial jingle written for slave traders looking to recruit naïve Africans, and "Old Man," in which an elderly man is rejected with feigned compassion by his son, were set to Newman's

most evocative arrangements to date and rank with the most intelligent and effective use of a large ensemble by anyone in pop music. On the other end of the scale, "Last Night I Had a Dream" and "You Can Leave Your Hat On" are lean, potent mid-tempo rock tunes, the former featuring some slashing and ominous slide guitar from Ry Cooder, and the latter a witty and willfully perverse bit of erotic absurdity that later became a hit for Joe Cocker (who sounded as if he took the joke at face value). Elsewhere, Newman cynically ponders the perils of a stardom he would never achieve ("Lonely at the Top," originally written for Frank Sinatra), offers a broad and amusing bit of political satire ("Political Science"), and concludes with one of the most bitter rants against religion that anyone committed to vinyl prior to the punk era ["God's Song (That's Why I Love Mankind")]. Whether he's writing for three pieces or 30, Newman makes superb use of the sounds available to him, and his vocals are the model of making the most of a limited instrument. Overall, *Sail Away* is one of Newman's finest works, musically adventurous and displaying a lyrical subtlety that would begin to fade in his subsequent works. *—Mark Deming*

☆ **Good Old Boys** / 1974 / Reprise ✦✦✦✦✦

Randy Newman's songwriting often walks a narrow line between intelligent satire and willful cruelty, and that line was never finer than on the album *Good Old Boys*. Newman had long displayed a fascination with the American South, and *Good Old Boys* was a song cycle where he gave free reign to his most imaginative (and venomous) thoughts on the subject. The album's scabrous opening cut, "Rednecks," is guaranteed to offend practically anyone with it's tale of a slow-witted, willfully (and proudly) ignorant Southerner obsessed with "keeping the n——s down." "A Wedding in Cherokee County" is more polite but hardly less mean-spirited, in which an impotent hick marries a circus freak; if the song's melody and arrangement weren't so skillful, it would be hard to imagine anyone bothering with this musical geek show. But elsewhere, *Good Old Boys* displays a very real compassion for the blighted history of the South, leavened with a knowing wit. "Birmingham" is a funny but humane tale of working class Alabamians, "Louisiana 1927" and "Kingfish" are intelligent and powerfully evocative tales of the deep South in the depths of the Great Depression, and "Rollin'" is cheerful on the surface and troubling to anyone willing to look beneath it. Musically, Newman dives deep into his influences in Southern soul and also adds potent country accents (with the help of Al Perkins pedal-steel guitar) while dressing up his songs in typically expert string and horn arrangements. And Newman assumes each character, either brave or foolish, with the skill of a gifted actor, giving even his most loathsome characters enough depth that they're human beings, despite their flaws. *Good Old Boys* is one of Newman's finest albums; it's also one of his most provocative and infuriating, and that's probably just the way he wanted it. *—Mark Deming*

Little Criminals / 1977 / Reprise ✦✦✦

After *Good Old Boys*, one of the most ambitious and thematically unified albums of his career, Randy Newman seemed to beat a willful retreat for his next project, 1977's *Little Criminals*. For the most part abandoning the carefully structured orchestral arrangements that dominated *Good Old Boys* and *Sail Away*, Newman cut *Little Criminals* with a handful of pop-friendly session musicians and L.A. Mellow Mafia regulars (including most of the Eagles), and his arch, cutting satire gave way to a lighter but less thoughtful tone, with the humor becoming less mean-spirited (though becoming much *more* venomous than "Rednecks" might have been difficult). Newman even revisited one of his favorite themes, the pointlessness of racial prejudice, with a metaphor so silly no one could fail to understand it. Or at least that's what he thought when he wrote "Short People"; the song unexpectedly took off as a novelty hit, and the vertically challenged across the country began attacking Newman for what they saw as an affront to their dignity and well-being. As a result, *Little Criminals* became Newman's first (and only) gold album in the United States, but this set wasn't an especially good way to introduce the average record buyer to his work. *Little Criminals* lacks the scope of Newman's best work, the music is skillful but bland, and several of the songs sound like padding (especially "You Can't Fool the Fat Man" and "Jolly Coppers on Parade"). While the title tune, "Rider in the Rain," "In Germany Before the War," and "Sigmund Freud's Impersonation of Albert Einstein in America" (which was written for the movie *Ragtime* but not used) are fine songs, much of *Little Criminals* sounds like Newman was treading water; it's not his worst album, but it sounds like the work of a man figuring out what his next move should be. *—Mark Deming*

Born Again / 1979 / Reprise ✦✦✦

After the song "Short People" finally earned Randy Newman the hit single he claimed he always wanted (and in perhaps the worst way possible), Newman told reporters that for his next album he was preparing "a larger insult." And sure enough, *Born Again* was packed full of losers and misfits for whom Newman's contempt was unmistakable; from a man who had found some measure of understanding in his tales of thugs, stalkers, and slave traders on previous releases, the unmistakable bile Newman summoned up on "Half a Man," "Mr. Sheep," and "Pretty Boy" seems little short of perverse. And while Newman indulges in his usual passion for social satire here, "They Just Got Married" and "It's Money That I Love" are so stunningly unsubtle you have a hard time believing they came from the same man who wrote "Sail Away" or "Kingfish" (though "It's Money That I Love" has a piano line that would do Fats Domino proud). "The Story of a Rock & Roll Band" is a hilarious and deadly accurate parody of Electric Light Orchestra (admittedly an easy target, but still beautifully executed), and the all-too-brief "William Brown" is a lovely vignette that wouldn't have been out of place on *12 Songs* or *Sail Away*, but otherwise *Born Again* is the weakest non-soundtrack album of Randy Newman's career. *—Mark Deming*

Trouble in Paradise / 1983 / Reprise ✦✦✦✦✦

Randy Newman began the slow process of transforming himself into a polished L.A. songcrafter on the album *Little Criminals*, and with *Trouble in Paradise* the metamorphosis was complete; by this time, Newman could make a record just as ear-pleasing as anything Paul Simon, Don Henley, or Lindsey Buckingham could come up with, and proved it by persuading all three to appear on the sessions. But no matter how polished the arrangements and smooth the production, Newman's songs don't sound like they're ready for radio, and he's too bright not to understand that songs about apartheid, self-pitying white bluesmen, and arrogant yuppies are poor prospects for the pop charts. *Trouble in Paradise* marked the high point of Newman's struggle between pop sheen and his satiric impulses, and the album is a significant improvement over *Little Criminals* and *Born Again*. The targets of Newman's satirical gaze are easy to skewer, and his pen is hardly subtle, but the overall tone is more respectful than on *Born Again* and the results are stronger. The bitter Afrikaner in "Christmas in Capetown" and the egocentric blowhard in "My Life Is Good" have at least *earned* Newman's disgust, and while many of the character studies ("Mikey," "I'm Different") and vignettes ("Miami," "Take Me Back") take a less than charitable view of their protagonists, like the losers and half-wits that populate *Good Old Boys*, they're human beings whose flaws reveal a hint of tragedy. And the closing number, "Song for the Dead," is a stunner in which a soldier explains to the bodies he's burying the purpose behind the war that took their lives. While too slick for Newman's core audience, *Trouble in Paradise* was his most intelligent and best realized work since *Good Old Boys*, and his finest album of the 1980s. *—Mark Deming*

Land of Dreams / 1988 / Reprise ✦✦✦✦

Unlike his contemporaries in the singer/songwriter community, Randy Newman has displayed little interest in writing about himself, with nearly every song in his repertoire set in the voice of some imagined character. So 1988's *Land of Dreams* was startling because its first three songs formed a triptych about Newman's childhood; for the first time on one of his albums, Newman was clearly writing about his own life, and the results were extraordinary. "Dixie Flyer" tells how Newman and his mother came to move from Los Angeles to New Orleans during World War II; "New Orleans Wins the War," introduces young Newman to the issues of race in the Deep South as he ponders the odd realities of life in "The City That Care Forgot"; and in "Four Eyes," cross-eyed Newman is forced to confront responsibility (and cruelty) for the first time on his first day in school. But while *Land of Dreams* begins as an unusually strong and compelling concept album, Newman apparently lost interest in writing about himself, and from track four onward, *Land of Dreams* is content to pick up where *Trouble in Paradise* left off. Themes of race and class in America dominate the second half of the album, most potently on "Roll With the Punches" and "I Want You to Hurt Like I Do," two "responses" to the grandstanding compassion of "We Are the World." *Land of Dreams* is a strong piece of work from Randy Newman, but if he'd had the courage to follow what he'd started with the first three songs, he might have had a masterpiece. *—Mark Deming*

Faust / Sep. 19, 1995 / Warner Brothers ✦✦

Guilty: 30 Years of Randy Newman / Nov. 3, 1998 / Rhino ✦✦✦✦

There was no Randy Newman compilation available in America until Rhino released the four-disc box set *Guilty: 30 Years of Randy Newman* in the fall of 1998. Boasting two discs of album highlights, a disc of rarities, and a disc devoted to "Film Music," *Guilty* attempts to be a definitive artistic portrait, yet it winds up a little frustrating. Dedicated fans don't have much need for the first two discs; even if they provide an excellent summary, they're designed for casual listeners, who won't have much interest in the other two discs. "Odds & Ends," the third disc, is the jewel in this crown for longtime fans, since it contains a wealth of rarities, including the excellent "Gone Dead Train" from *Performance*, a weird Pat Boone-produced single from 1961 ("Golden Gridiron Boy"), a selection of 1968 songwriting demos, a host of working tracks for films, and a revelatory "Masterman and Baby J," which contains no rapping. "Film Music," the fourth disc, is another welcome addition to his catalog. Newman is a sensitive, accomplished film composer in the classic Hollywood style, and not only are his scores are rewarding on their own merits (as are the excerpts here), he's written a handful of great songs, such as "I Love to See You Smile" (*Parenthood*) and "You've Got a Friend in Me" (*Toy Story*), which have not appeared on a Newman album until now. These final discs are valuable for serious fans, yet they may not want to purchase the entire box in order to acquire the rarities. And that's the problem with *Guilty*—the package is lovely and the execution first-rate, but both casual and dedicated fans would have been better served if the set had been divided into two different compilations. *—Stephen Thomas Erlewine*

Bad Love / Jun. 1, 1999 / DreamWorks ✦✦✦

Newman's first collection of pop songs since 1988's *Land of Dreams* finds him as satirically biting as ever, yet unafraid to tackle personal and heartfelt concerns. Few are out of harm's way when Newman's at the keyboard: Old rock stars get it in "I'm Dead (But I Don't Know It)," dirty old men in "Shame" and "The World Isn't Fair," and cultural imperialism in "The Great Nations of Europe." In addition, there's perhaps one of his most beautiful and personal songs yet, "I Miss You," and even a schmaltzy one, "Every Time It Rains." The production team of Mitchell Froom and Tchad Blake ensure that there are no missteps by maintaining a timeless, orchestrated sound with original instrumentation. Doubters who thought Newman lost his edge after dozens of blockbuster movies needn't worry anymore—few of these songs would find their way onto the smiley soundtracks, yet all of them should rest comfortably alongside his other four-star offerings. *—Denise Sullivan*

Olivia Newton-John

b. Sep. 26, 1948, Cambridge, England

Vocals / Soft Rock, Adult Contemporary, Country-Pop

Olivia Newton-John skillfully made the transition from popular country-pop singer to popular mainstream soft-rock singer, becoming one of the most successful vocalists of the

'70s in the process. The transition itself wasn't much of a stretch—her early '70s hits "I Honestly Love You" and "Have You Never Been Mellow" were country only in the loosest sense—yet the extent of her success in both fields was remarkable. As a country singer, her first five charting singles all went Top Ten in the US; as a pop singer, she had no lest than 15 Top Ten hits, including five number one singles, highlighted by "Physical," which spent ten weeks at number one in 1981-82. Newton-John's sweet voice suited both country-pop and soft-rock perfectly, which is what kept her at the top of the charts until the mid-'80s. After 1984, she was no longer able to reach the Top 40, partially because of shifting musical tastes and partially because she was unable to successfully record sexy dance-pop, no matter how hard she tried. Nevertheless, her '70s and '80s hits remained soft-rock and adult contemporary staples into the '90s, when she was no longer recording frequently. —*Stephen Thomas Erlewine*

Back to Basics / Jun. 9, 1992 / Geffen ✦✦✦✦

An artist well-defined by her hit singles, Olivia Newton-John has had a stylistically varied career, as is illustrated on *Back to Basics: The Essential Collection 1971-1992*, a set that ranges from her teary ballad "I Honestly Love You" to that bouncy paean to getting horizontal, "Physical." Fans may quibble that such hits as "Let Me Be There" and "Make a Move on Me" are not included, but Newton-John's two greatest-hits albums are out of print, and this is the only collection to combine both her good-girl and bad-girl personae. —*William Ruhlmann*

● **Magic: The Best of Olivia Newton-John** / Sep. 11, 2001 / UTV Records ✦✦✦✦✦

UTV Records' *Magic: The Very Best of Olivia Newton-John* is the best compilation ever assembled on Newton-John's career, largely because it does cover her entire career, hitting every major point from her early-'70s soft country-pop hits, like "I Honestly Love You," through her star-making turn in *Grease*, selections from *Xanadu*, up to the *Physical* era and its fallout. That takes a total of 20 tracks, plus the bonus track of "The Grease Megamix," and that gives a listener nearly everything they need from Olivia. When the biggest complaint is that the collection sequences "You're the One That I Want" before "Summer Nights," it means that this is certainly a collection that can be called definitive. —*Stephen Thomas Erlewine*

The Nice

f. 1967, **db.** 1970

British Psychedelia, Prog Rock/Art Rock

One of the first art-rock bands to experiment with classical forms and fusion, the Nice was an early vehicle for the talents of keyboard virtuoso Keith Emerson, who plundered Mozart, Sibelius, and Tchaikovsky for his extended rock instrumental forays. The group began as the backing band for British soul singer P.P. Arnold and also featured guitarist David O'List, drummer Brian "Blinky" Davison, and bassist Lee Jackson. In October 1967, only two months after formation, the group split from Arnold, christened itself the Nice, and released a single called "The Thoughts of Emerlist Davjack," which became the title track of their 1968 debut album. The Nice quickly built a reputation as an exciting, theatrical live band thanks to Emerson, who dressed in gold lame, hurled knives into his Hammond organ to produce strange sounds, and mimed masturbation onstage. Emerson's antics spawned controversy with *Ars Longa Vita Brevis*, which contained a cover of Leonard Bernstein's *West Side Story* song "America." The Nice performed it at the Royal Albert Hall while burning an American flag, and Bernstein subsequently attempted to stop the song's release in the U.S. Emerson had emerged as the star of the group, both in terms of instrumental skill and showmanship, and the fed-up O'List had departed the group by the time of the album's release to join Roxy Music. *Nice* and *Five Bridges Suite* became big hit albums in Britain, but the group never broke through in America. In 1969, Emerson met Greg Lake, then with King Crimson, on a U.S. tour, and broke up the Nice in frustration in 1970 due to its lack of success. He, Lake, and drummer Carl Palmer formed the much more popular Emerson, Lake and Palmer, which expanded on Emerson's innovations with the Nice. The remaining Nice members went on to several short and/or unsuccessful stints with other groups before fading away. —*Steve Huey*

Here Come the Nice: The Immediate Anthology 3 CD Set / 2000 / Castle ✦✦✦✦

There have been so many reissues and recompilations of the music that the Nice did for Immediate Records that it's difficult even for people who worked on those reissues to tell some of them apart without a scorecard. However, this set stands out, not only for its comprehensive nature but also for its sound quality, which is exceptional. The vexing aspect of working with the Nice's Immediate catalog was the lack of first-generation master tapes—the record company's holdings were scattered to the four winds when it went bankrupt at the dawn of the 1970s. Castle Communications, however, has finally found what sounds like the real thing, and it makes a world of difference: no background noise, minimal tape hiss, each instrument loud and up-front, and all of the playing sharply delineated even in the busiest passages of the group's most complex works. What's more, the stereo separation is now sharp enough to enhance the music in a serious way—the divided string section in the "Brandenburger" section of "Ars Longa Vita Brevis," for example, adds to the appeal of the band's playing in ways that were difficult to discern on earlier CD releases, as well as on most of the LP issues. And the live cuts from the Fillmore East from the third album are now transcendent. Just as important as the research that went into locating the first-generation tapes is the producers' success in finding the group's complete alternate takes; every odd outtake that ever surfaced in the band's history is present on disc three of this set, along with a quartet of previously unreleased live tracks recorded in concert during 1968 and 1969. —*Bruce Eder*

Billy Nicholls

British Psychedelia, Psychedelic Pop, Psychedelic, British Invasion

While still in his teens, Billy Nicholls recorded one of the more sought-after rarities of British psychedelic pop, *Would You Believe*. Nicholls was one of the most Beach Boys-influenced British singer/songwriters, and *Would You Believe* often recalled the *Pet Sounds*/*Smile* period in its melodic construction and ornate production. The album understandably betrayed greater traces of late-'60s British psychedelia than the Beach Boys' efforts did, and it would be foolish to put Nicholls on the same level as Brian Wilson, as *Would You Believe* ultimately displayed more promise than pure genius. Nonetheless, that promise was considerable, and it is a shame that the album was essentially unreleased after it was finished in 1968 (although a few dozen promotional copies went out). This short-circuited Nicholls' career, and although he did some recording in later years, he's mostly known by mainstream rock fans (if at all) for his peripheral role in some group and individual member projects by the Who. He co-wrote, played, and sang on "Forever's No Time at All" on Pete Townshend's debut solo album, *Who Came First*. He wrote singles for Roger Daltrey and Leo Sayer and did some backing vocals on the Who's *Who Are You* album, as well as the *Tommy* film soundtrack. In the post-Keith Moon years he did some work as the Who's musical director. The *Would You Believe* album, which sold for astronomical prices on the collectors' market due to its rarity, was finally reissued on CD in 1999. —*Richie Unterberger*

● **Would You Believe** / 1968 / Immediate ✦✦✦

Nicholls' stillborn 1968 album does indeed recall the Beach Boys' 1966-67 era, not just due to Billy's melodies and high, versatile vocals, but also the production of Andrew Oldham, an avowed fan of Phil Spector and *Pet Sounds*. Although very attractive, however, the songs and production do not have the depth and emotional resonance of *Pet Sounds*. This is not a knock; Nicholls was very young at the time, after all, and it's hard to match Brian Wilson, though Oldham pulled out a bunch of tricks with baroque keyboards, tasteful brass, and airy multi-part harmonies. As with the Oldham-produced cuts done by Del Shannon in the same era, the deftly elaborate L.A.-meets-London semi-Wall of Sound is more impressive than the pretty but often rather slight material. It's still a pleasurable listen, with the more acoustic and darker "Come Again" slightly foreshadowing the kind of sound Pete Townshend would employ on much of *Who Came First*, and "Girl from New York" (with Steve Marriott on lead guitar) going for a gutsier British rock vibe. The CD reissue (on the Immediate imprint, but actually put out by the British reissue label Sequel) includes mono single versions of "Would You Believe?" and "Daytime Girl" as bonus tracks. —*Richie Unterberger*

Stevie Nicks

b. May 26, 1948, Phoenix, AZ

Vocals / Album Rock, Pop/Rock, Soft Rock

Famed for her mystical chanteuse image, singer/songwriter Stevie Nicks enjoyed phenomenal success not only as a solo artist but also as a key member of Fleetwood Mac. During high school, Nicks met fellow student Lindsey Buckingham, with whom she formed the band Fritz. Even after the group disbanded, Buckingham remained her partner and soon became her lover as well. After moving to Los Angeles, the duo recorded their 1973 debut LP, *Buckingham-Nicks*. Though the album flopped, it caught the attention of the members of Fleetwood Mac, who invited Buckingham and Nicks to join their ranks in 1974. In quick time, the revitalized group achieved unparalled success with 1975's *Fleetwood Mac* and 1977's *Rumours*. Major hit singles like "Dreams" and "Rhiannon" made Nicks a focal point of Fleetwood Mac, and in 1981 she took time off from the group to record her solo debut, *Bella Donna*, which hit number one. In 1983, Nicks released her second solo effort, *The Wild Heart*, highlighted by the Top Five smash "Stand Back." *Rock a Little* appeared in 1985, and was followed by *The Other Side of the Mirror* in 1989. She left Fleetwood Mac in 1993, and issued *Street Angel* a year later. In 1997, she rejoined Fleetwood Mac for the tour album *The Dance*. A Nicks solo box set, *Enchanted*, followed in 1998. —*Jason Ankeny*

Bella Donna / 1981 / Modern ✦✦✦✦

Stevie Nicks' solo career was off to an impressive, if overdue, start with *Bella Donna*, which left no doubt that she could function quite well without the input of her colleagues in Fleetwood Mac (a band she would remain a member of until 1993). The album yielded a number of hits that seemed omnipresent in the '80s, including the moving "Leather and Lace" (which unites Nicks with Don Henley), the poetic "Edge of Seventeen," and her rootsy duet with Tom Petty, "Stop Draggin' My Heart Around." But equally engaging are less exposed tracks like the haunting "After the Glitter Fades." Hit producer Jimmy Iovine wisely avoids overproducing, and keeps things sounding organic on this striking debut. —*Alex Henderson*

The Wild Heart / 1983 / Modern ✦✦✦

Stevie Nicks was following both her debut solo album, *Bella Donna* (1981), which had topped the charts, sold over a million copies (now over four million), and spawned four Top 40 hits, and Fleetwood Mac's *Mirage* (1982), which had topped the charts, sold over a million copies (now over two million), and spawned three Top 40 hits (including her "Gypsy"), when she released her second solo album, *The Wild Heart*. She was the most successful American female pop singer of the time. Not surprisingly, she played it safe: *The Wild Heart* contained nothing that would disturb fans of her previous work and much that echoed it. As on *Bella Donna*, producer Jimmy Iovine took a simpler, more conventional pop/rock approach to the arrangements than Fleetwood Mac's inventive Lindsey Buckingham did on Nicks's songs, which meant the music was more straightforward than her typically elliptical lyrics. Iovine did get a Mac-like sound on "Nightbird," in which Nicks repeated her invocation to "the white winged dove" from *Bella Donna*'s

"Edge of Seventeen," and on "Sable on Blond," a "Gypsy" soundalike. His most daring effort was the album's leadoff single, "Stand Back," which boasted a disco tempo. Elsewhere, the songs were largely interchangeable with those on *Bella Donna*, even down to the obligatory duet with Tom Petty. Nicks seemed to know what she was up to—one song was called, "Nothing Ever Changes." As, a result, *The Wild Heart* sold to the faithful—it made the Top Ten, sold over a million copies, and spawned three Top 40 hits ("Stand Back," "Nightbird," and "If Anyone Falls"). And that was appropriate: If you loved *Bella Donna*, you would like *The Wild Heart* very much. *—William Ruhlmann*

Rock a Little / 1985 / Modern ✦✦✦✦✦
In contrast to the earthy, rootsy qualities of *Bella Donna*, Stevie Nicks took a slicker, more high-tech approach on her third solo album, *Rock a Little*. But for all its glossiness, this pop-rock CD comes across as sincere and heartfelt rather than formulaic or contrived. From the catchy "I Can't Wait" to the intense "No Spoken Word" to the dark "The Nightmare," everything on *Rock a Little* is as honest as it is memorable. Assisting Jimmy Iovine and Rick Nowels with the production, Nicks wisely sees to it that technology adds to her songs instead of smothering or overpowering them. *—Alex Henderson*

The Other Side of the Mirror / May 1989 / Modern ✦✦✦
Stevie Nicks' fourth solo album received more than its share of negative reviews from rock critics, who seemed to mistake her poetic and not always terribly discernable lyrics for pretentiousness. Although not as strong as Nicks' three previous solo dates, *The Other Side of the Mirror* is a decent CD that has many more pluses than minuses. While there are a few less than memorable moments, some of the songs—including "Long Way to Go," "Ghosts" and "Whole Lotta Trouble"—are fairly strong. Nicks' more devoted followers will want this album, which should be purchased only if one already has *Bella Donna*, *The Wild Heart*, and *Rock a Little*. *—Alex Henderson*

● **Timespace: The Best of Stevie Nicks** / Sep. 3, 1991 / Modern ✦✦✦✦✦
With material produced by names such as Jon Bon Jovi, Danny Kortchmar, and Jimmy Iovine, Stevie Nicks' solo work singled her out as a prominent artist outside of her glory days with Fleetwood Mac. With a remarkable 11 Top 40 singles that spawned from only four solo albums, not including 1994's *Street Angel*, Nicks proved that her sometimes fragile, sometimes pleasingly sharp voice could stand up well without the backing of Lindsay Buckingham's revered guitar work. *Timespace* groups together her biggest songs and makes for a favorable compilation of her material. Only a few of her charted singles are left off *Timespace*, like 1982's "After the Glitter Fades" and "Needles and Pins," the other duet with Tom Petty. The beautiful "Leather and Lace," sung with Don Henley from her first album *Bella Donna*, is an obvious inclusion here, as is her highest charting single "Stop Draggin' My Heart Around," taken from the same debut release. Nicks' surging vocal range thunders through "Stand Back," and even more so alongside the guitar thrust of "Edge of Seventeen," her most rock-induced single. *Timespace* captures the softer side of Nicks as well, best heard within the lushness of "Beauty and the Beast" and the wholehearted approach put forth on "Has Anyone Ever Written Anything for You." Capped off with her last big hit of the '80s in "Rooms on Fire" from the otherwise substandard *The Other Side of the Mirror*, this compilation is a splendid representation of her lone material. *—Mike DeGagne*

Maybe Love Will Change Your Mind / May 26, 1994 / Atlantic ✦✦✦

Street Angel / June 7, 1994 / Modern ✦✦

Enchanted: The Works of Stevie Nicks / Apr. 7, 1998 / Atlantic ✦✦✦
Stevie Nicks certainly was a major star in the '70s and early '80s, both as a key member of Fleetwood Mac and as a solo artist. She had a long string of hit singles with the group and alone, enough to justify a double-disc set, but the three-disc box set *Enchanted* is a case of overkill for anyone but hardcore fans. *Enchanted* is devoted entirely to Nicks' solo career, contianing no Mac hits whatsoever. All of her hits—"Bella Donna," "Stop Draggin' My Heart Around," "Edge of Seventeen," "Leather and Lace," "Stand Back," "Talk to Me," "I Can't Wait"—are here, as are minor singles and album cuts, plus non-LP B-sides, soundtrack cuts, unreleased items, demos and live tracks. All of those rarities are interesting only to hardcore collectors and tend to weigh down the listenability of the set. Still, there are enough rarities (and enough good rarities) to make this box necessary for collectors. It's just that less dedicated fans—and that includes fans who are only familiar with her Fleetwood Mac work—should probably stick to the greatest-hits collection or *Bella Donna*. *—Stephen Thomas Erlewine*

Trouble in Shangri-La / May 1, 2001 / Warner Brothers ✦✦✦✦
Stevie Nicks calls in a few friends on this one. *Trouble in Shangri-La* enlists some of music's most popular females, including Macy Gray, Sarah McLachlan, and Dixie Chick Natalie Maines. If Nicks hadn't been doing it for years, this might feel like a calculated attempt to follow the trend set by Santana's *Supernatural*. Her liner notes have always been star-studded. Over the years she's gotten help from the likes of Don Henley, Don Felder, Bruce Hornsby, Mike Campbell, and Tom Petty. Most prominent on this album is Sheryl Crow, who co-produced five of the album's 13 tracks. Her signature guitar sound shines through on many of the songs. Maines performs the album's only true duet on "Too Far From Texas." The other guests are noticeable, but act mostly as backup voices and musicians. Make no mistake about it—this is a Nicks album from beginning to end, and she's at the top of her game here. It's not a departure, but a renewed energy makes this her best work since 1985's *Rock a Little*. Titles like "Sorcerer" and "Bombay Sapphires" preserve her mystical persona, and despite their mythical sound, they touch on human and very personal subject matter. Her deliberate lyrics sometimes feel a bit more like prose than verse, but the conviction in her voice adds legitimacy to her words. While Nicks' voice has matured, it is just as strong as it ever was. She shows great range, from the heartbroken tenderness of "Love Changes" to the aggressive rock of "Fall From Grace." *Trouble in Shangri-La* not only reminds listeners what Nicks has meant to music, but it finds her a place in modern-day pop. *—Brad Kohlenstein*

Nico

b. Oct. 16, 1938, Cologne, Germany, **d.** Jul. 18, 1988
Vocals / Proto-Punk, Experimental, Prog Rock/Art Rock
One of the most fascinating figures of rock's fringes, Nico hobnobbed, worked, and was romantically linked with an incredible assortment of the most legendary entertainers of the 1960s. The paradox of her career was that she herself never attained the fame of her peers, pursuing a distinctly individualistic and uncompromising musical career that was uncommercial, but wholly admirable and influential. Nico first rose to fame as a European supermodel before moving to New York, where Andy Warhol installed her as a vestigial presence and occasional lead singer for the Velvet Underground. After contributing unforgettable deadpan vocals to three of the songs on their classic 1967 debut album, Nico embarked on a solo career, recording folk-rock flavored songs for her debut *Chelsea Girl* album with assistance from Jackson Browne, Lou Reed, and John Cale. Her 1969 follow-up, *The Marble Index*, was a dramatic departure that unveiled her doom-laden, gothic persona, produced by Cale and prominently featuring her deep vocals, impenetrable lyrics, and ghostly harmonium. Her career fell into disarray during the rest of the '70s and the '80s, as she struggled with a massive drug habit and tangled personal life. The original goth-rocker, Nico's albums are demanding and bleak, but map a unique and starkly powerful vision that has become more influential with age. *—Richie Unterberger*

● **Chelsea Girl** / 1967 / Polydor ✦✦✦✦✦
Nico's distanced, German-accented voice is presented over austere strings and, in one case, electric guitar on a series of songs reminiscent of her work with the Velvet Underground and written by Velvets John Cale and Lou Reed. Other songs (some unrecorded elsewhere) were written by a young Jackson Browne. *—William Ruhlmann*

The Marble Index / 1969 / Elektra ✦✦✦
The quirky, orchestrated folk-rock of Nico's 1968 debut album *Chelsea Girl* in no way prepared listeners for the stark, almost avant-garde flavor of her 1969 follow-up, *The Marble Index*. Produced by former Velvet Underground partner John Cale, the chanteuse presented an uncompromisingly bleak, gothic soundscape on her second album. Dominated by spare harmonium and Nico's deep, brooding vocals, this album unveiled her singularly morose songwriting (her first record featured none of her compositions). Owing more to European classical and folk music than rock, it found little favor with 1969 audiences. But like the work of the Velvet Underground, it proved to be quite influential in the long run on a future generation of black-clad goth-rockers. The 1991 reissue of this recording adds two previously unreleased songs, "Roses in the Snow" and "Nibelungen." *—Richie Unterberger*

Desert Shore / 1970 / Reprise ✦✦✦✦✦
While Nico was the member of the Velvet Underground who had had the least experience in music prior to joining the group (while she had recorded a pop single in England, she'd never been a member of a working band before Andy Warhol introduced her to the Velvets), she was also the one who strayed farthest from traditional rock & roll after her brief tenure with the band, and by the time she recorded *Desertshore*, her work had little (if anything) to do with traditional Western pop. John Cale, who produced and arranged *Desertshore*, once described the music as having more to do with 20th century classical music than anything else, and while that may be going a bit far to make a point, even compared to the avant-rock frenzy of the Velvet Underground's early material, *Desertshore* is challenging stuff. Nico's dour Teutonic monotone is a compelling but hardly welcoming vocal presence, and the songs, centered around the steady drone of her harmonium, are often grim meditations on fate that are crafted and performed with inarguable skill and intelligence, but are also a bit samey, and the album's downbeat tone gets to be rough sledding by the end of side two. Cale's arrangements are superb throughout, and "My Only Child," "Afraid," and "The Falconer" are quite beautiful in their own ascetic way, but like the bulk of Nico's repertoire, *Desertshore* is an album practically designed to polarize its listeners; you'll either embrace it's darkness or give up on it before the end of side one. Then again, given the thoroughly uncompromising nature of her career as a musician, that's probably just what Nico had in mind. *—Mark Deming*

The End / 1974 / Island ✦✦✦✦✦
It is one of the most entrenched visions in the rock critic's vocabulary; Nico as doomed Valkyrie, droning death-like through a harsh gothic monotone, a drained beauty pumping dirges from her harmonium while a voice as old as dirt hangs cobwebs round the chords. In fact she only made one album which remotely fit that bill—this one—and it's a symbol of its significance that even the cliché emerges as a thing of stunning beauty. Her first album following three years of rumor and speculation, *The End* was consciously designed to highlight the Nico of already pertinent myth. Stark, dark, bare, and frightening, the harmonium dominant even amid the splendor of Eno's synthesized menace, John Cale's childlike piano, and Phil Manzanera's scratchy, effects-whipped guitar, it is the howling wind upon wuthering heights, deathless secrets in airless dungeons, ancient mysteries in the guise of modern icons. Former lover Jim Morrison haunts the stately "You Forgot to Answer," a song written about the last time Nico saw him, in a hired limousine on the day of his death; of course he reappears in the title track, an epic recounting of the Doors' own "The End," but blacker than even they envisioned it, an echoing maze of torch-lit corridors and spectral children, and so intense that, by the time Nico reaches the "mother... father" passage, she is too weary even to scream. The cracked groan which emerges instead is all the more chilling for its understatement, and the musicians were as affected as the listener. But to dwell on the fear is to overlook the beauty—

The End, first and foremost, is an album of intimate simplicity and deceptive depths. —*Dave Thompson*

Drama of Exile / 1981 / Aura ✦✦✦
It was a shock at the time and today the thrill still lingers. Almost 15 years after she quit the Velvet Underground, and with four stunningly stubborn solo albums under her belt, Nico was finally ready to return to rock & roll, with a conventional band and a clutch of great songs which proved that, whatever else she'd lost during a career spent on the bleakest fringe of the idiom, the arts of composition and interpretation were not part of it. As a member of the Velvets, she'd performed two songs, the stately "All Tomorrow's Parties" and the fragile "Femme Fatale." Now she added a third to her bow, a relentless "Waiting for the Man" which took its lead from composer Lou Reed's own recent revisions of the song but never lost sight of the trademark primitivism which gave it its original power—that's not Maureen Tucker on drums, but close your eyes and it could be. Elsewhere, David Bowie's "Heroes" was given an almost militaristic going over, the chopping guitars, rolling drums, and a triumphant Davey Payne sax solo conspiring to prove that while Bowie had written about what he saw in Berlin, Nico sang of what she knew. It was stirring stuff and, again, all the more surprising for who was behind it. Nico reveled in the confusion. Across her own compositions, *Drama of Exile* explored the faces and places Nico witnessed during her own dramatic exile. The haunting, almost Indian-sounding "Orly Flight," the rattled funk of "The Sphinx," and the droning/hypnotic "Purple Lips" all suggested adventures which never made the newspapers, while "One More Chance" made it obvious that she didn't regret one of them. Nor, once this album was assimilated by the world at large, would she ever need to. —*Dave Thompson*

Do or Die / 1982 / ROIR ✦✦✦

Camera Obscura / 1985 / Beggars Banquet ✦✦

Peel Sessions / 1988 / Dutch East India ✦✦✦
In February 1971, Nico recorded a four-song session for the BBC that included songs from three of her solo albums. "No One Is There" and "Frozen Warnings" had appeared on 1969's *The Marble Index*, and "Janitor of Lunacy" on 1970's *Desert Shore*; "Secret Side" would appear on 1974's *The End*. Frequently bootlegged over the years, this official release presents the performance at the right speed in pristine sound. These renditions are about as bare-boned as they come, with no accompaniment save Nico's own harmonium. In both material and performance, she leans toward the more wistful and gothic of her numbers. They don't differ drastically from the LP versions, but it's an interesting addition to fans' collections. —*Richie Unterberger*

Hanging Gardens / 1990 / Restless ✦✦✦

Heroine / 1995 / Anagram ✦✦

Icon / Apr. 1996 / Cleopatra ✦✦✦
A hodge-podge of recordings from the early 1980s, including the "Saeta"/"Vegas" single along with live material, outtakes, and interviews, released on the heels of the acclaimed 1995 documentary *Nico/Icon*. —*Jason Ankeny*

The Classic Years / Sep. 15, 1998 / Island ✦✦✦✦
The Classic Years is an excellent, portable introduction to the challenging and singular work of Nico. It's questionable as to why Chronicles opted to include her three vocal contributions to *The Velvet Underground and Nico*, however. What are the odds of someone *not* owning that record prior to checking out the ice queen's solo material? Nonetheless, the tracks certainly don't sound out of place. A handful of songs are taken from each of her first four (and best) albums, including her debut single for Immediate from 1965. —*Andy Kellman*

Night Ranger

f. 1981, **db.** 1989
Arena Rock, Heavy Metal, Pop/Rock, Hard Rock, Pop-Metal
Featuring ex-Ozzy Osbourne guitarist Brad Gillis and former Montrose keyboardist Alan Fitzgerald, Night Ranger was one of the most popular mainstream hard rock bands of the mid-'80s. The group formed in the early '80s in San Francisco; in addition to Gillis and Fitzgerald, the members included Jack Blades (vocals, bass), Jeff Watson (guitar), and Kelly Keagy (drums). After a few local gigs, promoter Bill Graham managed to get them supporting slots on Judas Priest, Santana, and Doobie Brothers concerts. Night Ranger's first album, *Dawn Patrol* (1982), reached number 38 on the U.S. charts, yet it was 1983's *Midnight Madness* that established the band as a commercial force. Featuring the AOR hit "(You Can Still) Rock in America" and the number five single "Sister Christian," the record peaked at number 15 and sold over a million copies. 1985's *7 Wishes* was just as successful, reaching number ten on the charts. Night Ranger's audience began to diminish after 1987's *Big Life*. Fitzgerald left the following year and the band released their last album, *Man in Motion*, which failed to go gold or spawn any Top 40 singles. Night Ranger broke up the next year. Jack Blades joined the supergroup Damn Yankees, which also featured Ted Nugent and Tommy Shaw. A reunited Night Ranger returned in 1998 with *Seven*. —*Stephen Thomas Erlewine*

Dawn Patrol / 1982 / Camel ✦✦✦✦
Unlike many of their pop-metal contemporaries, Night Ranger's early work has aged quite well, and this excellent 1982 debut is a well-kept secret of the genre. Dripping with hooks and irresistible choruses, "Don't Tell Me You Love Me," "Sing Me Away," and "Young Girl in Love" are simply outstanding songs. Anyone doubting the band's ability to rock out need only listen to the vicious bursts of "Eddie's Comin' Out Tonight" and "Play Rough." And despite offering the mandatory power ballad in "Call My Name" (which is actually quite good), the band rarely allow the album's intensity level to lag. —*Ed Rivadavia*

Midnight Madness / 1983 / Camel ✦✦✦✦
Night Ranger's second album *Midnight Madness* may not have been as consistent as their debut, but it did spawn the band's biggest hit, "Sister Christian." While it served as their commercial breakthrough, the infamous power ballad also relegated the group to "one-hit wonder" status while fueling their reputation as being "too soft" for a metal band. But as can be seen by the album's frenetic opener "(You can Still) Rock in America," Night Ranger actually rocked as hard as any of their pop-metal contemporaries, and *Midnight Madness* offers a number of memorable melodic rockers like "Rumours in the Air," "When You close Your Eyes," and "Why does Love Have to Change" as well. —*Ed Rivadavia*

● **Night Ranger's Greatest Hits** / Jun. 1989 / Camel ✦✦✦✦
Similar to AOR rockers Styx, Journey, and REO Speedwagon, Night Ranger yielded the same electric guitar wallop via Jeff Watson and Brad Gillis and sported a high-powered lead singer in the likes of Jack Blades. Since their albums only contained a small amount of strong material, *Night Ranger's Greatest Hits* is the essential one-stop for all of this band's best work. With half of these songs finding their way to Billboard's Top 40, it's evident that Night Ranger did produce some likeable rock & roll. Highlighted by "Sister Christian," the band's one-part-ballad, two-parts-guitar-throttle claim-to-fame, along with the amusing pretentiousness of "Sentimental Street," this compilation does have its moments. The bouncy rock tempo of "Goodbye" towed along by some skillful electric guitar playing makes this an avid standout. Even the Sammy Hagar-sounding "Don't Tell Me You Love Me" still holds up, as does the glossy melody that maneuvers its way through "When You Close Your Eyes." "Four in the Morning" follows suit with its systematic chords and rollicking chorus, and Blades pulls no punches on "The Secret to My Success" from the movie of the same name. This is truly the only Night Ranger album one will ever need. —*Mike DeGagne*

20th Century Masters—The Millennium Collection: The Best of Night Ranger / Jul. 18, 2000 / MCA ✦✦✦✦
The Best of Night Ranger: The Millennium Collection delivers 11 of the group's pop-metal and power-ballad hits, including the Top Ten singles "Sister Christian" and "Sentimental Street" and the Top 20 hits "Goodbye," "Four in the Morning," and "When You Close Your Eyes." Album rock radio staples like "Eddie's Comin' Out Tonight," "(You Can Still) Rock in America," and "I Did it For Love" round out this solid, entertaining collection from one of the '80s most popular hard rock bands. —*Heather Phares*

Harry Nilsson

b. Jun. 15, 1941, Brooklyn, NY, **d.** Jan. 15, 1994, Agoura Hills, CA
Vocals, Piano / Album Rock, Psychedelic Pop, Baroque Pop, Brill Building Pop, Pop/Rock, Soft Rock, Pop, Singer/Songwriter
Although he synthesized disparate elements of both rock and pop traditions, singer/songwriter Harry Nilsson was at heart a maverick whose allegiance belonged to neither. His initial series of albums in the late '60s made him a personal favorite of the Beatles, who found a natural affinity with his knack for catchy melodies, witty lyrics, and extraordinary vocal range. Thought of as a songwriter first and a performer second, he became a pop star himself in the late '60s and early '70s with "Everybody's Talking" and "Without You."

Nilsson had been struggling to make inroads into the music business for over five years before his critically acclaimed 1967 album, *Pandemonium Shadow Show*. Three Dog Night took Harry's "One" into the Top Ten in 1969, and Nilsson's second LP, *Aerial Ballet*, continued the ambitious pop-rock direction of his debut. When one of its songs, "Everybody's Talkin'," was used as the theme for the *Midnight Cowboy* film, Nilsson had his first Top Ten hit. The irony was that, although Nilsson was primarily identified as a singer/songwriter, the song was a cover of a composition by folk-rocker Fred Neil.

Nilsson would never be content to be pigeonholed into definite categories, as demonstrated by his two 1970 albums. One was devoted entirely to covers of songs by Randy Newman; another was his soundtrack to an animated children's special, *The Point*. And it was another cover (of a Badfinger album track) that gave him his biggest single, the number one smash "Without You." Yet Nilsson didn't cash in on his stardom in a conventional manner; he never performed in concert (there were occasional television appearances), preferring to craft his artistry in the studio.

During the first half of the 1970s, he broadened his range from the well-crafted, peppy, sensitive tunes that had dotted his early releases, cutting some tougher, more sour work. Much of Nilsson's notoriety stems from a period in the mid-1970s when he was a drinking buddy of John Lennon in Los Angeles. Lennon produced *Pussycats*, his last album to make the Top 100. After a few rather unsuccessful late '70s album, Nilsson withdrew from the studio into family life. In failing health in the 1990s, diagnosed with diabetes and suffering a massive heart attack, he died in early 1994, just after finishing the vocal tracks for a new album. —*Richie Unterberger*

Pandemonium Shadow Show / 1967 / RCA ✦✦✦✦✦
Harry Nilsson's debut album *Pandemonium Shadow Show* was notoriously loved by the Beatles, and it's easy to see why. This is the only record of its time that feels akin to *Sgt. Pepper* and, in some ways, it's every bit as impressive. Nilsson works on a much smaller scale, leaning heavily on whimsy yet cutting it with sardonic humor and embellishing it with remarkable song and studiocraft; it's as if McCartney and Lennon were fused into the same body. *Pandemonium* can't help but feel like a cheeky show of strength by a remarkably gifted imp, spinning out psychedelic fantasias and jokes and trumping his idols by turning out a cover of "She's Leaving Home" (recorded ten days after *Sgt. Pepper*'s release) that rivals the original. Beneath all the light playful melodies ("There Will Never Be" is swinging London, L.A. style) or glorious laments (he rarely equaled "Sleep Late,

My Lady Friend"), there are serious strains: the lyrics of "Cuddly Toy" are as unsettling as the melody catchy, the circus-stomp "Ten Little Indians" is a darkly addictive retelling of the Ten Commandments, and "1941" is quietly heartbreaking beneath its jaunty cabaret. Throughout it all, Nilsson impresses with his humor, cleverness and, above all, how his songwriting blossoms under his shockingly inventive studiocraft. Psychedelic-pop albums rarely came better than this, and it remains a thorough delight. *—Stephen Thomas Erlewine*

Skidoo / 1968 / RCA/Victor ✦✦
Harry Nilsson's soundtrack to Otto Preminger's cheerfully "anti-establishment" film *Skidoo* is more memorable than the film itself, but that's a bit of a relative statement. The film has been almost entirely forgotten, and the soundtrack is remembered only by Nilsson cultists, primarily for the absolutely brilliant opener, "The Cast and Crew," where all the credits are *sung*, with a really nifty tune on top of that. Nothing tops that, even though "I Will Take You There" is nice, "Garbage Can Ballet" feels like a pleasant holdover from *Aerial Ballet*, and the main theme slips and slides memorably. The remainder of the record is pretty good, brass-heavy soundtrack work, quite clearly of its time yet relatively charming because of it. It's not all that striking—it's just agreeable background music—except for the end, when Carol Channing sings "Skidoo," a moment that's utterly jarring after nearly a half hour of lulling mood music. And not in a good way. *—Stephen Thomas Erlewine*

Aerial Ballet / 1968 / RCA ✦✦✦✦✦
As "Daddy's Song" opens *Aerial Ballet* with a cheeky saunter, it's clear that Harry Nilsson decided to pick up where he left off with his debut, offering another round of effervescent, devilishly clever pop, equal parts lite psychedelia, pretty ballads, and music hall cabaret. It's not a carbon copy, however. In one sense, he entrenches himself a little bit, emphasizing his lighter edges and humor, writing songs so cheerfully lightweight—a love song about his mom and dad, an ode to his favorite desk, an address or two to a "Little Cowboy"—that it may be a little too cloying for some tastes, even for fans of *Pandemonium Shadow Show*. Those are balanced by a couple major steps forward, namely "Everybody's Talkin'" and "One." The former finds Nilsson adopting a rolling folk-pop backing for a Fred Neil song, making it into an instant, Grammy-winning classic. The latter was the greatest song he had written to date, a haunting tale of loneliness reminiscent of McCartney, yet with its own voice. These are the songs anchoring an album that may be a little lightweight, but it's engagingly, deliberately lightweight. If it's a bit dated, it wears its old charms well. *—Stephen Thomas Erlewine*

Harry / 1969 / RCA ✦✦✦✦
Ironically, *Harry* is where Harry Nilsson began to become *Nilsson*, an immensely gifted singer/songwriter/musician with a warped sense of humor that tended to slightly overwhelm his skills, at least to those who aren't quite operating on the same level. This aspect of his personality surfaces partially because the record is a crazy quilt of originals, covers, bizarre Americana, quiet ballads, show tunes, and soft-shoe shuffles. It doesn't really hold together, per se, due to its lack of focus (which, if you're a cultist, is naturally the reason why it's charming). Due to the sheer number of shuffling nostalgia trips, it seems as if Nilsson is attempting to sell the entire album on personality and, to anyone who isn't converted to his unique perspective, these may the moments that make *Harry* a little difficult to take, even with songs as expertly constructed as the delightful "Nobody Cares About the Railroads Anymore," an attempt to ape Randy Newman's Tin Pan Alley style. Then, there are the songs that really work, such as the sardonically cute "The Puppy Song," the gentle "Mournin' Glory Story," and "I Guess the Lord Must Be in New York City," a thoroughly winning folk-rock song he wrote for *Midnight Cowboy* but was rejected in favor of "Everybody's Talkin'." These are the moments that deliver on the promise of his first two records, while the rest suggests where he would go next, whether in the immediate future (a cover of Newman's "Simon Smith and the Amazing Dancing Bear") or several years later (the weird in-jokes and insularity of portions of the album, which would become his modus operandi as of *Nilsson Schmilsson*). *—Stephen Thomas Erlewine*

The Point! / 1970 / RCA ✦✦✦✦
The Point! is the soundtrack to a cartoon feature originally aired on ABC TV in 1971. Especially at this stage of his career, Harry Nilsson was uniquely suited for writing and recording children's music, given his sweet melodicism and love of whimsy. As it happens, *The Point!* worked out better than anyone could have expected, not just because "Everything's Got 'Em," "Me and My Arrow," "Think About Your Troubles," and "Are You Sleeping?" are songs strong enough to have been on a proper Nilsson record. There's also an intangible quality to this record, a warmth and generosity that really wasn't on any of his other albums, quite possibly because his humor is never sardonic or reliant on in-jokes. It's gentle and loving, as is the music. The tale is fantastical enough to be of interest to children (and the moral is strong enough to reassure them and their parents), but the songs and music are so strong that the album continues to be a source of wonder, even as those children become adults. *—Stephen Thomas Erlewine*

Nilsson Sings Newman / Feb. 1970 / Buddha ✦✦✦✦✦
Named Stereo Review's album of the year (and, really, can you ask for a better endorsement than that?) upon its release and generally regarded as the album that introduced Randy Newman the songwriter to a wide audience, *Nilsson Sings Newman* has gained a reputation of being an minor masterwork. This, in a way, is misguiding, since this isn't an obvious record, where the songs are delivered simply and directly. It's deliberately an album of subtle pleasures, crafted, as the liner notes state, line-by-line in the studio. As such, the preponderance of quiet piano-and-voice tracks (featuring Newman himself on piano, Nilsson on vocals) means the record can slip away upon the first few listens, especially for anyone expecting an undeniable masterpiece. Yet, a masterpiece is what this is, albeit a subtle, graceful masterpiece where the pleasure is in the grace notes, small gestures, and in-jokes. Not to say that this is devoid of emotion, it's just that the emotion is subdued, whether it's on a straightforward love song ("Caroline") or a tongue-in-cheek tale like "Love Story." For an album that introduced a songwriter as idiosyncratic as Newman, it's only appropriate that Nilsson's interpretations are every bit as original as the songs. His clear intonation and sweet, high voice are more palatable than Randy's slurred, bluesy growl, but the wild thing is, these versions demand that the listeners surrender to Nilsson's own terms. He's created gentle, intricate arrangements of tuneful yet clever songs and, as such, the album may be as much an acquired taste as Newman. Once you've acquired that taste, this is as sweet as honey. *—Stephen Thomas Erlewine*

Aerial Pandemonium Ballet / 1971 / Buddha ✦✦✦✦
What is hubris? It is *Aerial Pandemonium Ballet*, a folly Harry Nilsson crafted after winning a Grammy for "Everybody's Talkin'." Riding upon the goodwill generated by the award, he decided to compress and edit his first two (quite brilliant) albums into one record. He remixed tracks, erased old vocals, over-sang some new ones, edited sections out of certain songs, and slowed others down. Apart from the intros and outros, there are no brand-new items, just old tunes presented in slightly new, slightly off-putting ways. If you're not familiar with the debut, this will be pretty enchanting since the two records weren't that far apart stylistically and, let's face it, he was working with pretty terrific source material. Still, it's no substitute for the originals, and if you have a chance (and you do, with Britain's RCA Camden reissue), pick up the originals. *—Stephen Thomas Erlewine*

Nilsson Schmilsson / Nov. 1971 / RCA ✦✦✦✦✦
Nilsson had a hit, a Grammy, and critical success, yet he still didn't have a genuine blockbuster to his name when it came time to finally deliver a full-fledged follow-up to *Nilsson Sings Newman*, so he decided it was time to make that unabashed, mainstream pop/rock album. Hiring Streisand's producer Richard Perry as a collaborator, Nilsson made a streamlined, slightly domesticated, unashamed set of mature pop/rock, with a slight twist. This is an album, after all, that begins by pining for the reckless days of youth, then segues into a snapshot of suburban disconnectedness before winding through a salute to and covers of old R&B tunes ("Early in the Morning" and "Let the Good Times Roll," respectively), druggie humor ("Coconut"), and surging hard rock ("Jump Into the Fire"). There are certainly hints of the Nilsson of old, particularly in his fondness for Tin Pan Alley and McCartney melodicism—as well as his impish wit—yet he hadn't made a record as cohesive as this since his first time out, nor had he ever made something as shiny and appealing as this. It may be more accessible than before, yet it's anchored by his mischievous humor and wonderful idiosyncracies. Chances are that those lured in by the grandly melodramatic "Without You" will not be prepared for either the subtle charms of "The Moonbeam Song" or the off-kilter sensibility that makes even his breeziest pop slightly strange. In short, it's a near-perfect summary of everything Nilsson could do; he could be craftier and stranger, but never did he achieve the perfect balance as he did here. *—Stephen Thomas Erlewine*

Son of Schmilsson / Jul. 1972 / RCA ✦✦✦✦✦
Emboldened by a huge hit and hanging with Lennon and Ringo, Harry Nilsson was ready to let it all go when it came time to record a follow-up to *Nilsson Schmilsson*. The very title of *Son of Schmilsson* implies that it's a de facto sequel to its smash predecessor but, as always with Nilsson, don't take everything at face value. Yes, he's back with producer Richard Perry and he's working from the same gleefully melodic, polished pop/rock territory as before, but this is an incredibly schizoid record, an album by an enormously gifted musician deciding that, since he's already going unhinged, he might as well *indulge* himself while he's at it. And, wow, are the results ever worth it. Opening with a song to a groupie—he sang his balls off, baby, he nearly broke the microphone—and ending with an ode to "The Most Beautiful World in the World," this record careens all over the place, bouncing from one idea to another, punctuated with B-horror movie sound effects, bizarre humor, profanity, and belches. There are song parodies, seemingly straight piano ballads, vulgar hard rock, lovely love songs, and a cheerful singalong with retirees at an old folks home who all proclaim, "I'd rather be dead than wet my bed." The sheer perversity of it all would be fascinating, yet if that's all it had to offer, it'd merely be a curiosity, the way his post-*Pussy Cats* records are. Instead, this is all married to a fantastic set of songs that illustrate what a skilled, versatile songsmith Nilsson was. No, it may not be the easiest album to warm to—and it's just about the weirdest record to reach number 12 and go gold—but if you appreciate Nilsson's musicality and weirdo humor, he never got any better. *—Stephen Thomas Erlewine*

A Little Touch of Schmilsson in the Night / 1973 / RCA ✦✦
Nilsson was nearly a decade ahead of Linda Ronstadt and other nouveau crooners in hiring a conductor/arranger of the pre-rock era (in this case Gordon Jenkins) and recording an album of standards before a full orchestra. And he did it better than most, proving to be a marvelous interpreter of songs like "What'll I Do?" and "Makin' Whoopee!" His version of "As Time Goes By" became a minor hit. *—William Ruhlmann*

Son of Dracula / Apr. 1, 1974 / RCA ✦✦

Pussy Cats / Aug. 19, 1974 / Buddha ✦✦✦
The relationship between Nilsson and Lennon is legendary. They were notorious boozehounds and carousers, getting kicked out of clubs for misbehavior and generally terrorizing L.A. during Lennon's "Lost Weekend" of 1974. They wanted to make an album together—hell, anyone working at such a peak *would*—and the result was *Pussy Cats*, a Nilsson album produced by Lennon. Almost immediately, Nilsson got sick, resulting in a ruptured vocal cord. Not wanting Lennon to stop the sessions, Nilsson never told his friend, stubbornly working his way through the sessions until he lost his voice entirely. These are the sessions that make up *Pussy Cats*, an utterly bewildering record that's more

baffling than entertaining. Like many superstar projects of its time, this is studded with contributions from friends and studio musicians, all intent on having a good time in the studio—which usually means hammering out rock & roll oldies. In this case, it meant both Dylan's "Subterranean Homesick Blues" and the childrens song "Loop De Loop," which gives a good idea where Nilsson was at. Through its messiness, *Pussy Cats* winds up showing how he and Lennon violently careened between hedonism and self-loathing. Of the new songs, the inadvertently revealing "All My Life" is the strongest, followed by the sweet "Don't Forget Me," yet this is more about tone than substance. It's about hearing Nilsson's voice getting progressively harsher, as the backing remains appealingly professional and slick. It doesn't quite jibe, and it's certainly incoherent, but that's it's charm. It may not be as wild as the Lost Weekend itself, but it couldn't have been recorded at any other time and remains a fascinating aural snapshot of the early days of 1974. *—Stephen Thomas Erlewine*

Duit on Mon Dei / 1975 / RCA ✦✦✦

More tongue-in-cheek wordplay from Harry Nilsson. The album was originally titled *God's Greatest Hits*, but powers that be persuaded Nilsson to change it. His voice as well as his talent for writing catchy tunes was wearing thin here, and as with previous efforts, nothing stands out like his earlier material. *Duit On Mon Dei* is an artist on the wane. *—James Chrispell*

Sandman / 1975 / RCA ✦✦✦

Nilsson started going off the tracks at *Pussy Cats*, but his descent into sheer, unhinged lunacy became apparent with *Sandman*, his second album of 1975. It was easy to view *Duit on Mi Dei* as transitory, but this proves that it was a transition to craziness and cultdom. At this point, he was abandoned by Lennon, left alone in L.A. and Nilsson just didn't care. He continued to roam, rampage, and record, ensconcing himself in his own world of in-jokes, Tin Pan Alley melodies, soft rock, clever wit, and sheer drunkenness. Check the cover—on the front, he has a bottle of wine between his legs, on the back he's overcome by a sandcrab. On the album itself, he repudiates rock & roll, realizes "Pretty Soon There'll Be Nothing Left for Everybody," has a drunken conversation with himself (so extreme that he's thrown out of the bar), explains why he did not go to work today, writes an ode to flying saucers, offers cheekily literal instructions on how to write a song and then covers a song from the last album. Melodically, he's still strong, but the gleeful craziness overwhelms the pretty music and accessible production, resulting in an album that makes *Son of Schmilsson* and *Pussy Cats* seem normal, which may only signal just how far away from the mainstream Nilsson was at this point. But, in a way, he was still brilliant—these are exceptional recordings, and his warped sense of humor is funnier than its ever been. That's not to say that *Sandman* is an easy record—you have to not only accept Nilsson's quirks, but embrace them more than his talents to love this album—but if your head is properly calibrated, this is one to treasure. *—Stephen Thomas Erlewine*

That's the Way It Is / 1976 / RCA ✦✦

Well, what do you expect from an artist who's reading Penthouse, surrounded by liquor bottles and cigarettes, on the cover of his album? Perfection? Accessibility? Sanity? Well, you ain't gonna get that from Nilsson, a man who left sanity behind shortly after he entered the mainstream with *Nilsson Schmilsson*. Instead, you get a record from an artist who's *just* at the fringe of popular culture, not really caring if he has a hit, but not really wanting to be so weird that he's just a cult. Realizing all of this, the artist also knows that he doesn't need to try so hard—he can be as lazy as he looks on the cover. So, that means *That's the Way It Is* is essentially a covers record, with songs ranging from material penned by longtime favorite Randy Newman ("Sail Away") to longtime fan George Harrison ("That Is All") to oldies ("Just One Look/Baby I'm Yours") to obscurities ("She Sits Down on Me" and "Zombie Jamboree"). Only two original songs then: the faux-reggae "Moonshine Bandit" and "Daylight Has Caught Me," co-written by Dr. John. Everything's given a rather lush, but not particularly sleek, treatment placing it closer to soft rock than to the unabashed cult rock that Nilsson was producing at this point. So, this winds up being an album that's not as gleefully weird and funny as its predecessors and yet is stranger because of that. Because, for chrissakes, who wants this album? It doesn't have enough perversity or indulgence for those who treasure his weirdness, but it's way too idiosyncratic and odd for anyone who might like the L.A.-style vibe. Not a bad record, really, but certainly not a very good one, even by latter-day Nilsson standards. *—Stephen Thomas Erlewine*

Knnillssonn / 1977 / RCA ✦✦✦

Realizing that he had nothing left to lose when he got to the end of his RCA contract, Nilsson wound up recording his best, most distinctive record since *Pussy Cats*, maybe *Son of Schmilsson*. Abandoning the very idea of a mainstream pop album is just the beginning of his conceptual coup here. Recording almost all of the sounds with keyboards and guitars, Nilsson also decided to drive the guitars into the background. In some ways, this may make it similar to *A Little Touch of Schmilsson in the Night*, but instead of being a standards record, this is all new material, written in a classical pop style and delivered in a slightly modernistic fashion. The result is an album that's out of step with its time and with the era's music in general. With its old-fashioned pop sensibility and weirdly out of sync production, plus Nilsson's trademark clever songsmithery and impish humor, *Knnillssonn* is a pop album like no other. It has his best set of songs in many a year, and the production is fascinating, yet at times it sounds like he's trying a little too hard. Still, there are brilliant moments, whether it's a tune as seductive as "All I Think About Is You" or the Agatha Christie murder mystery salute "Who Done It?" For all the cultists who struggled with, and at times embraced, his years of uneven records, this is their reward: an album that may only appeal to a small audience, but that satisfies their every desire about what an album from their favorite artist should be. *—Stephen Thomas Erlewine*

● **All-Time Greatest Hits** / 1978 / RCA ✦✦✦✦✦

Nilsson's albums tended to hang together well, but that didn't keep him from throwing off singles, at least in the late '60s and early '70s. This collection contains all ten of his chart singles (including "Everybody's Talkin'"), plus his version of his song "One," which was a hit for Three Dog Night. *—William Ruhlmann*

Nilsson '62: The Debut Sessions / 1995 / RPM ✦

Harry Nilsson does indeed sing on these 21 tracks, recorded at one fell swoop during a 1962 demo session. But it could not be considered either a proper Nilsson album or a stellar moment in the singer/songwriter's career. The somewhat complicated story is this: in 1962, unknown Los Angeles guitarist and songwriter Scott Turner met Nilsson. Impressed with his voice, he arranged to have Harry demo many of his tunes. Harry helped write a couple of the songs, but this was Turner's show. The material, some written with John Marascalco (who had penned some stuff for Little Richard) or actor Audie Murphy (!), was bland, wimpy early '60s pop. At its worst, it recalled such insufferable teen idols as Mark Dinning ("Teen Angel"). This in itself was bad enough, but Turner compounded the damage by overdubbing most of the original demos with hack Nashville country backing in 1977 and 1994. This strategy never leads to positive results, and although Harry does indeed sing well, the tunes and overdubs are so poor as to make listening painful, of interest only for purely historical reasons. Seven of the songs were spared the Nashville treatment; five were overdubbed in 1962 by L.A. session aces like James Burton, Leon Russell, Herb Alpert, and Hal Blaine, and just two were left untouched. These tracks may have higher "integrity," such as it is, but still there's not a single thing here worth hearing unless you're a Nilsson scholar. *—Richie Unterberger*

Personal Best: The Harry Nilsson Anthology / Feb. 28, 1995 / RCA ✦✦✦✦✦

Spanning two discs, *Personal Best: The Harry Nilsson Anthology* is a comprehensive overview of Nilsson's varied career, including all of the hits and many significant album tracks, yet it offers too much material for the casual fan, who would be better served by *All-Time Greatest Hits*. *—Stephen Thomas Erlewine*

Nine Inch Nails

f. 1989, Cleveland, OH

Industrial Metal, Alternative Metal, Alternative Pop/Rock, Industrial

Nine Inch Nails, the one-man band of Trent Reznor, brought industrial music to the masses with 1989's *Pretty Hate Machine*. With its electronic rush, incessant beats, and distorted guitars, the album appeared to be like much industrial music on the surface, yet Reznor wrote pop songs, not the soundtrack to a personal horror movie. NIN's scarred, harsh soundscapes were bleak enough, yet Reznor's lyrics raise the despair and self-loathing to new heights; at times, his relentless darkness can veer dangerously close to self-parody. *Pretty Hate Machine* wasn't a hit when it was released, but by the time Reznor assembled a band for the first Lollapalooza tour in 1991, the group had a sizable following that only grew with NIN's ferocious performances on the tour. Legal troubles with his record company delayed the release of a second album. In 1992, he released a stop-gap EP, *Broken*, that was harder and more abrasive than the debut, yet still conformed to conventional song structures; it debuted in the Billboard Top Ten. With their second full-length album, Reznor showed his true roots—'70s progressive rock. *The Downward Spiral* was promoted as a concept album, a cohesive piece of work; it also featured ex-King Crimson guitarist Adrian Belew. Still, NIN is able to straddle two seemingly opposing genres easily, gaining alternative and mainstream hard rock fans alike; whether he likes it or not, Trent Reznor is the man that made industrial palatable for pop fans. *—Stephen Thomas Erlewine*

★ **Pretty Hate Machine** / Nov. 1989 / TVT ✦✦✦✦✦

Virtually ignored upon its 1989 release, *Pretty Hate Machine* gradually became a word-of-mouth cult favorite; despite frequent critical bashings, its stature and historical importance only grew in hindsight. In addition to its stealthy rise to prominence, part of the album's legend was that budding auteur Trent Reznor took advantage of his low-level job at a Cleveland studio to begin recording it. Reznor had a background in synth pop, and the vast majority of *Pretty Hate Machine* was electronic. Synths voiced all the main riffs, driven by pounding drum machines; distorted guitars were an important textural element, but not the primary focus. *Pretty Hate Machine* was something unique in industrial music—certainly no one else was attempting the balladry of "Something I Can Never Have," but the crucial difference was even simpler. Instead of numbing the listener with mechanical repetition, *Pretty Hate Machine*'s bleak electronics were subordinate to catchy riffs and verse-chorus song structures, which was why it built such a rabid following with so little publicity. That innovation was the most important step in bringing industrial music to a wide audience, as proven by the frequency with which late-'90s alternative metal bands copied NIN's interwoven guitar/synth textures. It was a new soundtrack for adolescent angst—noisily aggressive and coldly detached, tied together by a dominant personality. Reznor's tortured confusion and self-obsession gave industrial music a human voice, a point of connection. His lyrics were filled with betrayal, whether by lovers, society, or God; it was essentially the sound of childhood illusions shattering, and Reznor was not taking it lying down. Plus, the absolute dichotomies in his world—there was either purity and perfection, *or* depravity and worthlessness—made for smashing melodrama. Perhaps the greatest achievement of *Pretty Hate Machine* was that it brought emotional extravagance to a genre whose main theme had nearly always been dehumanization. *—Steve Huey*

Broken / Sep. 22, 1992 / Nothing/Interscope ✦✦✦✦✦

During the time that *Pretty Hate Machine* was becoming an underground sensation, Trent Reznor became embroiled in legal difficulties with his label that prevented the release of any new Nine Inch Nails material. But the three-year wait actually helped—most of NIN's fans were relatively recent converts, and they eagerly snapped up 1992's *Broken*, which afforded the already angst-ridden Reznor the opportunity to vent his ample frustration over the imbroglio. Where *Pretty Hate Machine* had a few moments of reflection and sardonic humor, *Broken* is a concentrated blast of caustic, naked rage. Given how draining it is, a full-length album in its style would unquestionably have been wearisome, even self-parodic. So, *Broken* is the rare EP that's conceptually focused and complete unto itself. Production-wise, it's also a step up from *Pretty Hate Machine*, and a showcase for Reznor's flowering studio acumen. While *Pretty Hate Machine* was primarily electronic, *Broken* is loaded with heavy, jagged guitars, processed through a veritable meat grinder of effects into a massive wall of distortion. Each song one-ups the viciousness of its predecessor; even the two relatively subdued instrumental interludes are full of abrasive textures. There are two hidden bonus cuts at the end of the CD (early pressings had them on a separate disc); they're neither as produced nor as intense, and thus separated conceptually as well as physically. The cover of Adam Ant's "(You're So) Physical" was something of a revelation—not just demonstrating Reznor's fondness for new wave, but serving as a touchstone for his self-conscious, glammed-up sense of style. That—and his skills as a producer and arranger—would reach their fullest realization on *The Downward Spiral*, but *Broken*'s tight focus and frothing intensity make it a major work in its own right. —*Steve Huey*

Fixed / Nov. 1992 / Nothing/Interscope ✦✦✦

The companion piece to Trent Reznor's explosive industrial rock / metal opus *Broken*, *Fixed* sees the songs twisted through an intense remix process that makes them even darker than the original doom rock creations they began as. With contributions from noted studio experts like Jim Thirlwell, Coil, Butch Vig, and Reznor himself, the more industrial versions of these guitar themed tracks appear in a completely new light. The mixes range from sinisterly quiet to more beat- and drum-oriented, but they also retain the awesome power of the core compositions. The remix of the Grammy winning "Wish" for instance features a lengthy saturated drum intro, which only gives it more credence when it erupts into the original buzz saw guitar riff that dominates the track. Other mixes incorporate backwards tapes and difficult-to-pinpoint noise manipulations, but rather than building the songs to the point where things grow tedious, they tend to completely tear them apart while adding to the apocalyptic vision that enveloped the original disc. Even though Nine Inch Nails was thrust into the mainstream spotlight, this record shows the group returning to its roots and creating a daring new translation of songs that were pummeling from the start. Alongside "Wish," both "Gave Up" and "Happiness in Slavery" are given a few new readings, and while they are nowhere near as direct as the vicious attack of *Broken*, *Fixed* is still an impressive feat and a necessary counterpoint to an important record. —*Peter J. D'Angelo*

The Downward Spiral / Mar. 8, 1994 / Nothing/Interscope ✦✦✦✦

The Downward Spiral positioned Trent Reznor as industrial's own Phil Spector, painting detailed, layered soundscapes from a wide tonal palette. Not only did he fully integrated the crashing metal guitars of *Broken*, but several newfound elements—expanded song structures, odd time signatures, shifting arrangements filled with novel sounds, tremendous textural variety—can be traced to the influence of progressive rock. So can the painstaking attention devoted to pacing and contrast—*The Downward Spiral* is full of striking sonic juxtapositions and sudden about-faces in tone, which make for a fascinating listen. More important than craft in turning Reznor into a full-fledged rock star, however, was his brooding persona. Grunge had the mainstream salivating over melodramatic angst, which had always been Reznor's stock in trade. The left-field hit "Closer" made him a postmodern shaman for the '90s, obsessed with exposing the dark side he saw behind even the most innocuous façades. In fact, his theatrics on *The Downward Spiral*—all the preening self-absorption and serpentine sexuality—seemed directly descended from Jim Morrison. Yet Reznor's nihilism often seemed like a reaction against some repressively extreme standard of purity, so the depravity he wallowed in didn't necessarily seem that depraved. That's part of the reason why, in spite of its many virtues, *The Downward Spiral* falls just short of being the masterpiece it wants to be. For one thing, fascination with texture occasionally dissolves the hooky songwriting that fueled *Pretty Hate Machine*. But more than that, Reznor's unflinching bleakness was beginning to seem like a carefully calibrated posture; his increasing musical sophistication points up the lyrical holding pattern. Having said that, the album ends on an affecting emotional peak—"Hurt" mingles drama and introspection in a way Reznor had never quite managed before. It's evidence of depth behind the charisma that deservedly made him a star. —*Steve Huey*

Further Down the Spiral / May 30, 1995 / Island/TVT ✦✦

The Fragile / Sep. 21, 1999 / Nothing/Interscope ✦✦✦

As the double-disc *The Fragile* unfurls, all of Nine Inch Nails' trademarks—gargantuan, processed guitars, ominous electro rhythms, near-ambient keyboards, Trent Reznor's shredded vocals and tortured words—are unveiled, all sounding pretty much how they did on *The Downward Spiral*. Upon closer inspection, there are new frills, yet these aren't apparent without digging—and what's on the surface isn't necessarily inviting, either. There is nothing as rhythmic or catchy as "Closer," nothing as jarring as the piano chorus of "March of the Pigs," no ballad as naked as "Hurt." When Reznor does try for something immediate and visceral, he sounds recycled. Fortunately, *The Fragile* lives up to its title once the first disc is over. There are some detours into noisy bluster (some, like the Marilyn Manson dis "Starfuckers, Inc.," work quite well) but they're surrounded by long, evocative instrumental sections that highlight Reznor's gifts for arrangement. Whenever Reznor crafts delicate, alternately haunting and pretty soundscapes or interesting sonic juxtapositions, *The Fragile* is compelling. Since they provide a change of pace, the bursts of industrial noise assist the flow of the album, which never feels indulgent, even though it runs over 100 minutes. Still, *The Fragile* is ultimately a letdown. There's no denying that it's often gripping, offering odd and interesting variations on NIN themes, but that's the problem—they're just variations, not progressions. Considering that it arrives five years after *Spiral*, that is a disappointment. It's easy to tell where the time went—Reznor's music is immaculately crafted and arranged, with every note and nuance gliding into the next—but he spent more time constructing surfaces than songs. Those surfaces can be enticing but since it's just surface, *The Fragile* winds up being vaguely unsatisfying. —*Stephen Thomas Erlewine*

1910 Fruitgum Company

f. 1967, **db.** 1969

Bubblegum

The prototypical bubblegum group, the 1910 Fruitgum Company was the brainchild of Buddah Records house producers Jerry Kasenetz and Jeff Katz, also the masterminds behind such phenoms as the Ohio Express and the Music Explosion. The Kasenetz-Katz formula was a simple one: they enlisted anonymous studio musicians (in this case, vocalistsMark Gutkowski and Joey Levine—also the singer in the Ohio Express—along with guitarists Frank Jeckell, Pat Karwan, and Chuck Travis, horn player Larry Ripley, and drummers Rusty Oppenheimer and Floyd Marcus) and prolifically recorded lightweight, fluffy pop songs which found an eager audience in fans looking for an alternative to the edgier rock music of the late 1960s. With the 1910 Fruitgum Company, the Kasenetz-Katz team scored their first major hit, the 1968 Top Five smash "Simon Says," launching the bubblegum craze; that same year they also scored with the singles "1, 2, 3 Red Light" and "Goody Goody Gumdrops," all three issued as title tracks from the group's first trio of LPs. 1969's "Indian Giver," the title cut from the Fruitgum Company's fourth album, was their last Top Five hit, and after one last LP, *Hard Ride*, the group was disbanded; some of its members later resurfaced in the Kasenetz-Katz Singing Orchestral Circus. —*Jason Ankeny*

● **The Best of the 1910 Fruitgum Company: Simon Says** / Apr. 3, 2001 / Buddha ✦✦✦✦

The Best of the 1910 Fruitgum Company: Simon Says is the only thorough CD compilation available domestically—although their first four long-players have been issued on compact disc in either Japan or Europe. The appeal of the 1910 Fruitgum Company lies primarily in their effective ability to marry undemanding rhythms to equally puerile premises—as evidenced in their Top Five hits "Simon Says," "1, 2, 3, Red Light," and "Indian Giver." There were many configurations of musicians under the 1910 Fruitgum Company moniker. The band actually began as a discovery by bubblegum pop music moguls Jerry Kasenetz and Jeff Katz of a Central Ohio group named Jeckell & the Hydes. Before one can say "Bazooka Joe," Kasenetz and Katz had again struck gold, issuing their first farfisa-driven hit, "Simon Says," in late 1967. While the band might have been marketed primarily toward a gradeschool audience, their sly and otherwise innocuous lyrical double entendre gave their older brothers and sisters something else to think about. Musically, 1910's churning beat-laden rhythms accompanied by the undeniably catchy abandon of Mark Gutowski's lead vocals gave the band a feel of prepubescent garage pop. As was often the case at the time, actual membership within the group fluctuated wildly. Initial recordings did, however, feature members of Jeckell & the Hydes with professional studio musicians augmenting when necessary. By the time of their fifth release, *Hard Ride*, there was an entirely different set of musicians behind the microphones. The only personnel to remain were creators Kasenetz and Katz. In addition to the hits *The Best of the 1910 Fruitgum Company: Simon Says* features, it also includes tracks from the not-as-successful incarnations of the band—including the ersatz heavy metal/psychedelic "The Train" from *Hard Ride*. —*Lindsay Planer*

Nirvana

f. 1987, Aberdeen, WA, **db.** 1994

Grunge, Alternative Pop/Rock

Prior to Nirvana, alternative music was consigned to specialty sections of record stores and major labels considered it to be, at the very most, a tax write-off. After the band's second album, 1991's *Nevermind*, nothing was ever quite the same, for better and for worse. Nirvana popularized punk, post-punk, and indie-rock, unintentionally bringing it into the American mainstream like no other band before it. While its sound was equal parts Black Sabbath (as learned by fellow Washington underground rockers, the Melvins) and Cheap Trick, Nirvana's aesthetics were strictly indie-rock. They covered Vaselines songs, they revived new wave cuts by Devo, and leader Kurt Cobain relentlessly pushed his favorite bands—whether it was art-punk of the Raincoats or the country-fried hardcore of the Meat Puppets—as if his favorite records were always more important than his own music. While Nirvana's ideology was indie-rock and their melodies were pop, the sonic rush of their records and live shows merged the post-industrial white noise with heavy metal grind. And that's what made the group an unprecedented multi-platinum sensation. Jane's Addiction and Soundgarden may have proven to the vast American heavy metal audience that alternative could rock, and the Pixies may have merged pop sensibilities with indie-rock white noise, but Nirvana pulled at all together, creating a sound that was both fiery and melodic. Since Nirvana was rooted in the indie aesthetic but loved pop music, they fought their stardom while courting it, becoming some of the most notorious anti-rock stars in history. The result was a conscious attempt to shed their audience with the abrasive *In Utero*, which only partially fulfilled the band's goal. But by that point, the fate of the band and Kurt Cobain had been sealed. Suffering from drug addiction and manic depression, Cobain had become destructive and suicidal, though his management and label were able to hide the extent of his problems from the public until April 8, 1994, when he was found dead of a self-inflicted shotgun wound. Cobain may not have been able to weather Nirvana's success, but the band's legacy stands as one of the most influential in rock & roll history. —*Stephen Thomas Erlewine*

Bleach / 1989 / Sub Pop ♦♦♦
This is one case where the legend really precedes the record itself. Cut for about 600 dollars in Jack Endino's studio over just a matter of days, this captures Nirvana at a formative stage, still indebted to the murk that became known as grunge, yet not quite finding their voice as songwriters. Which isn't to say that they were devoid of original material, since even at this stage Kurt Cobain illustrated signs of his considerable songcraft, particularly on the minor-key ballad "About a Girl" and the dense churn of "Blew." A few songs come close to that level, but that's more a triumph of sound than structure, as "Negative Creep" and "School" get by on attitude and churn, while the cover of "Love Buzz" winds up being one of the highlights because this gives a true menace to their sound, thanks to its menacing melody. The rest of it sinks into the sludge, as the group itself winds up succumbing to grinding sub-metallic riffing that has little power, due to lack of riffs and lack of a good drummer. *Bleach* is more than a historical curiosity since it does have its share of great songs, but it isn't a lost classic—it's a debut from a band that shows potential but haven't yet achieved it. *—Stephen Thomas Erlewine*

★ **Nevermind** / Sep. 24, 1991 / DGC ♦♦♦♦♦
Nevermind was never meant to change the world, but you can never predict when the zeitgeist will hit, and Nirvana's second album turned out to be the place where alternative rock crashed into the mainstream. This wasn't entirely an accident, either, since Nirvana did sign with a major label, and they did release a record with a shiny surface, no matter how humongous the guitars sounded. And, yes, *Nevermind* is probably a little shinier than it should be, positively glistening with echo and fuzz-box distortion, especially when compared with the black-and-white murk of *Bleach*. This doesn't discount the record, since it's not only much harder than any mainstream rock of 1991, its character isn't on the surface, it's in the exhilaratingly raw music and haunting songs. Kurt Cobain's personal problems and subsequent suicide naturally deepens the dark undercurrents, but no matter how much anguish there is on *Nevermind*, it's bracing because he exorcises those demons through his evocative wordplay and mangled screams—and because the band has a tremendous, unbridled power that transcends the pain, turning into pure catharsis. And, that's as key to the record's success as Cobain's songwriting, since Krist Novoselic and Dave Grohl help turn this into music that is gripping, powerful, and even fun (and, really, there's no other way to characterize "Territorial Pissings" or the surging "Breed"). In retrospect, *Nevermind* may seem a little too unassuming for its mythic status—it's simply a great modern punk record—but even though it may no longer seem life-changing, it is certainly life-affirming, which may just be better. *—Stephen Thomas Erlewine*

Incesticide / Dec. 1992 / DGC ♦♦♦♦♦
Buying time and thwarting bootleggers, Nirvana and DGC released the rarities compilation *Incesticide* toward the end of 1992. Like any odds 'n sods collection, this is uneven, but that's its charm since this captures Nirvana's character better than any official album. After all, this was a band that was born equally from '70s sludge metal, bubblegum pop, post-punk artiness, and indie rock inclusiveness, each of which are apparent on this collection. There are some non-entities here, particularly on the second side, but the plodding sub-metallic grind was part of their identity, one part of their multi-faceted character. Nirvana meant everything to everyone, from the jangle pop veterans to the garage rock ravers that worshipped the Stooges to stoner metal fetishes and indie rock bed-sits that adopted Sebadoh just as they outgrew Morrissey—everybody LOVED Nirvana, and there's something for every kind fan here, thanks to murky sludge, Devo and Vaseline covers, BBC sessions, instrumentals, and limited-edition singles, plus sub-Melvins goop, everything visceral where *Bleach* was tame. *Nevermind* doesn't capture this freewheeling indie spirit but *Incesticide* does, piling on some essentials in the meantime—the pummeling "Dive," the childhood snapshot "Sliver," the terrific forgotten indie pop tune "Been a Son," and "Aneurysm," perhaps the greatest single song the group ever recorded. Yeah, there's some filler here, but *this* is the sound of what Nirvana were actually like. *—Stephen Thomas Erlewine*

☆ **In Utero** / Sep. 21, 1993 / DGC ♦♦♦♦♦
Nirvana probably hired Steve Albini to produce *In Utero* with the hopes of creating their own *Surfer Rosa*, or at least shoring up their indie cred after becoming a pop phenomenon with a glossy punk record. *In Utero*, of course, turned out to be their last record, and it's hard not to hear it as Kurt Cobain's suicide note, since Albini's stark, uncompromising sound provides the perfect setting for Cobain's bleak, even nihilistic, lyrics. Even if the album wasn't a literal suicide note, it was certainly a conscious attempt to shed their audience—an attempt that worked, by the way, since the record had lost its momentum when Cobain died in the spring of 1994. Even though the band tempered some of Albini's extreme tactics in a remix, the record remains a deliberately alienating experience, front-loaded with many of its strongest songs, then descending into a series of brief, dissonant squalls before concluding with "All Apologies," which only gets sadder with each passing year. Throughout it all, Cobain's songwriting is typically haunting, and its best moments rank among his finest work, but the over-amped dynamicism of the recording seems like a way to camouflage his dispiritedness—as does the fact that he consigned such great songs as "Verse Chorus Verse" and "I Hate Myself and Want to Die" to compilations, when they would have fit, even illuminated the themes of *In Utero*. Even without those songs, *In Utero* remains a shattering listen, whether it's viewed as Cobain's farewell letter or self-styled audience alienation. Few other records are as willfully difficult as this. *—Stephen Thomas Erlewine*

☆ **MTV Unplugged in New York** / Nov. 1, 1994 / DGC ♦♦♦♦♦
If *In Utero* is a suicide note, *MTV Unplugged in New York* is a message from beyond the grave, a summation of Kurt Cobain's talents and pain so fascinating, it's hard to listen to repeatedly. Is it the choice of material or the spare surroundings that make it so effective? Well, it's certainly a combination of both, how the version of the Vaselines' "Jesus Doesn't Want Me for a Sunbeam" or the three covers of *Meat Puppets II* songs mean as much as "All Apologies" or "Something in the Way." This, in many senses, isn't just an abnormal Nirvana record, capturing them in their sincerest desire to be R.E.M. circa *Automatic for the People*, it's the Nirvana record that nobody, especially Kurt, wanted revealed. It's a nakedly emotional record, unintentionally so, as the subtext means more than the main themes of how Nirvana wanted to prove its worth and diversity, showcasing the depth of their songwriting. As it turns out, it accomplishes its goals rather too well; this is a band, and songwriter, on the verge of discovering a new sound and style. Then, there's the subtexts, as Kurt's hurt and suicidal impulses bubble to the surface even as he's trying to suppress them. Few records are as unblinkingly bare and naked as this, especially albums recorded by their peers. No other band could have offered covers of David Bowie's "The Man Who Sold the World" and the folk standard "Where Did You Sleep Last Night" on the same record, turning in chilling performances of both—performances that reveal as much as their original songs. *—Stephen Thomas Erlewine*

From the Muddy Banks of the Wishkah / Oct. 1, 1996 / Geffen ♦♦♦♦
From the Muddy Banks of the Wishkah is the second posthumous Nirvana record, an attempt to capture Nirvana at the peak of its powers on stage. That doesn't necessarily mean all the band's best-known songs are here—"Come As You Are," "All Apologies," and "About a Girl" are all absent—but it does mean that this is the closest representation to what Nirvana sounded like on-stage. It may not be perfect and it's a little scattershot due to its varied source material (the tapes were recorded anywhere between 1989 and 1994), but it's still a terrific record, thanks to a sharp selection of performances and a set list that relies on B-sides, album tracks, and album favorites, highlighting the group at its best. It's not necessary, but it still finds a great band in top form. *—Stephen Thomas Erlewine*

No Doubt

f. 1987

Ska-Punk, Adult Alternative Pop/Rock, Third Wave Ska Revival, Post-Grunge, Alternative Pop/Rock

With the return of the punks in the mid-'90s came a resurgence of their slightly more commercial rivals, new wave bands. No Doubt found a niche as a new wave/ska band, on the strength of vocalist Gwen Stefani's persona—alternately an embrace of little-girl-lost innocence and riot grrl feminism—exemplified on the band's breakout single, "Just a Girl." When No Doubt's live act began to attract regional interest, Interscope Records signed them in 1991. The band's debut a year later, an odd fusion of '80s pop and ska, sank without a trace in the wake of the grunge movement. As a result, Interscope refused to support No Doubt's tour or further recordings. The band responded by recording on their own during 1993-94; the result was the self-released *The Beacon Street Collection*, much rawer and more punk-inspired than the debut. By late 1994, Interscope allowed recordings to resume, and *Tragic Kingdom* was released in October 1995. The album served as a document of the breakup of Stefani and bassist Tony Kanal, whose relationship had lasted seven years. Thanks to constant touring and the appearance of "Just a Girl" and "Spiderwebs" on MTV's Buzz Bin, the album hit the Top Ten in 1996. By the end of the year, *Tragic Kingdom* hit number one on the album charts, almost a year after its first release. *—John Bush*

No Doubt / Mar. 17, 1992 / Interscope ♦♦♦
Despite No Doubt's punk influences, they weren't included in the grunge boom of the early '90s. Much of the cause is due to the band's debut album, a work of polished production inspired more by '80s synth than No Doubt's heritage. Compared to Southern California's accepted ska/punk fusion, the album is overly pop-oriented, with new wave keyboards and punchy brass proving a foil to the basically ska framework. Stefani's extroverted vocals rescue the affair, however. *—John Bush*

Beacon Street Collection / Mar. 1995 / Beacon Street/Interscope ♦♦♦♦
When No Doubt's debut album proved a disappointment to Interscope executives, the label withdrew support from the band and refused to release them from their contract. The group's self-produced reply, recorded during several sessions from 1993 to early 1995, is their finest album. The synth and new wave influences of the debut are pushed to the background and replaced by a raw sound inspired more by punk. *—John Bush*

● **Tragic Kingdom** / Oct. 10, 1995 / Trauma/Interscope ♦♦♦♦
Led by the infectious, pseudo-new wave single "Just a Girl," No Doubt's major-label debut *Tragic Kingdom* straddles the line between '90s punk, third-wave ska, and pop sensibility. The record was produced by Matthew Wilder, the auteur behind "Break My Stride"—a clever mainstream co-opting of new wave quirkiness, and, as such, an ideal pairing. Wilder kept his production lean and accessible, accentuating No Doubt's appealing mix of new wave melodicism, post-grunge rock, and West Coast sunshine. Even though the band isn't always able to fuse their edgy energy with pop melodies, the combination worked far better than anyone could have hoped. When everything does click, the record is pure fun, even if some of the album makes you wish they could sustain that energy throughout the record. *Tragic Kingdom* might not have made much of an impact upon its initial release in late 1995, but throughout 1996 "Just a Girl" and "Spiderwebs" positively ruled the airwaves, both alternative and mainstream, and in 1997 they cemented their cross-generational appeal with the ballad hit "Don't Speak." *—Stephen Thomas Erlewine*

Return of Saturn / Apr. 11, 2000 / Interscope ♦♦♦♦♦
Return to Saturn is an almost defiantly mature record about two things: Stefani's exploration of a troubled romance and her own romantic ideals, plus a serious attempt by the group to not only keep new wave alive, but to make that adolescent music relevant to an older audience. It's a high concept, but *Return to Saturn* is filled with satisfying

contradictions. It's melodic, but deceptively complex; it can seem frothy, but it's never frivolous. No Doubt's desire to expand the emotional template of new wave is the perfect match for Stefani's themes—she may be writing about love, but she's not writing adolescent love songs. Fragments of her teenaged romantic fantasies remain, but she's writing as a woman in her late 20s. She's tired of being another "ex-girlfriend"—she wants to fall in love, get married, and have a family. It's a subject that's surprisingly uncommon in pop music, which would alone make *Return to Saturn* an interesting album. What makes it a successful one is that the band delivers an aural equivalent of Stefani's lyrical themes. They also begin with their adolescent musical ideals, adding depth and detail to their pop-ska foundation. They've balance their non-ironic love of new wave with contemporary production and a sensibility borrowed from classic rock: that albums are greater than the sum of their parts. Surprisingly, they pull it off—it's a far stronger record than *Tragic Kingdom*, even if the catchiest numbers don't have the same swagger and punch as their previous hit singles. So be it. With *Return to Saturn*, No Doubt have made a terrific, layered record that exceeds any expectations set by *Tragic Kingdom*. Not only have they found their voice, they know what to do with it. —*Stephen Thomas Erlewine*

NOFX

f. 1983

Skatepunk, Punk-Pop, Punk Revival, Alternative Pop/Rock, Punk
Formed in Berkeley in 1983 and relocating to Los Angeles not long afterwards, NOFX has steered clear of major labels and commercial exposure over the course of their career, recording an impressive number of full-lengths plus an assortment of EPs and singles. The band started out as a trio comprising vocalist/bassist Fat Mike, guitarist Eric Melvin, and drummer Erik Sandin. NOFX recorded two 7" EPs for the Mystic label in 1985, *No F-X* and *So What If We're on Mystic?* The EP *The PMRC Can Suck on This* was released on Fat Mike's own Fat Wreck Chords label in 1987, and NOFX's first full-length, *S&M Airlines*, was released on the legendary punk label Epitaph in 1989; the band has remained there ever since, despite the release of several albums and EPs on Fat Wreck Chords, which gradually grew into a premier stable of punk revival artists. Following 1990's *Ribbed* and 1991's *Liberal Animation*, Aaron Abeyta became the permanent second guitarist (as well as trumpeter), adopting the nickname El Hefe. Dragged into the mainstream spotlight by the mid-'90s success of labelmates Bad Religion and the Offspring, NOFX compensated with albums like 1992's *White Trash, Two Heebs and a Bean* that were even closer to the anti-commercial extreme. The El Hefe-anchored lineup continued to blossom with 1994's *Punk in Drublic*, often regarded as the band's best. Releases on Fat Wreck Chords continued throughout the '90s, as did the full-length Epitaph albums, like 1996's grungier, less up-tempo *Heavy Petting Zoo*, 1997's punkier *So Long and Thanks for All the Shoes*, and 2000's *Pump Up the Valuum* and *Bottles to the Ground*; the latter album followed an experimental Fat Wreck Chords EP titled *The Decline*, which consisted entirely of the 18-minute title track. —*John Bush & Steve Huey*

S&M Airlines / 1989 / Epitaph ✦✦

Ribbed / 1990 / Epitaph ✦✦

Liberal Animation / 1991 / Epitaph ✦

White Trash, Two Heebs & a Bean / Nov. 5, 1992 / Epitaph ✦✦✦✦
The title of NOFX's *White Trash, Two Heebs and a Bean* is a pretty fair indicator of what's going on in the grooves—specifically, tongue-in-cheek, politcally-incorrect forays into America's pan-cultural society. A SoCal punk band which recalls both the eclecticism and attitude of Camper Van Beethoven, NOFX rips through much more than standard-issue thrash; they transform Minor Threat's "Straight Edge" into a blues song with fake B.B. King vocals, go ska for the wry character study "Bob," and examine lesbian lifestyles with surprising maturity on "Liza and Louise." Not quite so understanding is "Johnny Appleseed," which pokes fun at the very concept of cultural diversity and is sung in a Hispanic accent by guitarist El Hefe. —*Jason Ankeny*

● **Punk in Drublic** / 1994 / Epitaph ✦✦✦✦✦
With their 1994 album *Punk in Drublic*, NOFX truly hit their stride. The quartet didn't change their approach at all—at their core, they remain a heavy, speed-addled, hook-conscious post-hardcore punk group—but their songwriting has improved, as has their attack. Prior to this record, they merely showed promise, but with *Punk in Drublic* they fulfilled their potential. —*Stephen Thomas Erlewine*

Heavy Petting Zoo / Jan. 30, 1996 / Epitaph ✦✦✦
The mildly offensive album art—essentially, it's a play on the album's title—disguises the fact that NOFX's punk rock is hardly breaking new ground. Taking the heavy guitar attack of the Sex Pistols and melding it with the us-against-them mentality of mid-'80s American hardcore, NOFX winds up sounding like a conservative punk band with metal leanings. Some of the songs are standouts, but most of the album blends together. As an expression of adolescent rage, *Heavy Petting Zoo* serves its purpose—it's basically just a barrage of heavy riffs and gut-busting bellowing—but it doesn't hold up on repeated listens. —*Stephen Thomas Erlewine*

So Long & Thanks for All the Shoes / Oct. 21, 1997 / Epitaph ✦✦

Pump up the Valuum / Jun. 13, 2000 / Epitaph ✦✦✦✦
Longtime fans of independent punk giants NOFX will be happy that for *Pump up the Valuum* the band changed absolutely nothing about their sound. All the songs follow the group's now standard three-chord punk style with witty songs that rip on the world around them. The most notable tracks are those that take aim at the music business. "Dinosaurs Will Die" is about the impending change in the music industry with the MP3 explosion. "Stanger Than Fishin'" (an obvious knock on former label mates Bad Religion's song "Stranger Than Fiction") goes after industry phonies. The album also contains some

of the band's signature gross-out tunes "Lousie" and "My Vaginia." While not as good as *Punk in Drublic* or *The Longest Line*, it should satisfy most punk fans' cravings. —*Curtis Zimmermann*

Naz Nomad & the Nightmares

Punk
Better known as legendary U.K. punk/pop combo the Damned, the Nightmares was a fun one-off side project that enabled the 1984-era lineup of that band to let down their hair, paying tribute to any number of '60s garage/psych forebears. The Nightmares' sole album, *Give Daddy the Knife Cindy*, captures their success at doing just that. —*Ned Raggett*

Give Daddy the Knife Cindy / 1984 / Big Beat ✦✦✦✦
Cleverly packaged as a soundtrack to a fictitious late-'60s rock exploitation flick, *Cindy* gives the Nightmares the opportunity to showcase their love of the trashy punk of the era. Armed with appropriate pseudonyms—Dave Vanian becomes Mr. Nomad, while Captain Sensible turns into Sphinx Svenson, and Rat Scabies into Nick Detroit—the combo merrily run through a well-chosen set of psychedelic nuggets, some well known and others utterly obscure. Leading off with the Isley Brothers' "Nobody but Me" (as reimagined by the Human Beinz), the Nightmares sound like they were indeed recorded at the time and place. Vanian gets to apply his dark croon and joyful shouting in spades, while the rest of the band fire on all cylinders. Standout covers include the Seeds' underrated love song "The Wind Blows Your Hair," given a great Vanian vocal, and fun run-throughs of Paul Revere & the Raiders' "Kicks" and the Electric Prunes' "I Had Too Much to Dream (Last Night)." Kim Fowley's notorious pseudopsych "The Trip" gets a brief revisit as well, while whoever wrote "She Lied" and "I Can't Stand This Love, Goodbye" are equally well served. Not wanting to stay completely out of the fun, the Nightmares wrap things up with two originals: the period piece "Do You Know (I Know)" and "Just Call Me Sky," a hilarious fake live track in which Nomad introduces each of his bandmates to wild applause and cheering as they each do a quick solo turn. Sure, the originals are what need to be heard, but *Cindy* is a great romp that stands on its own. —*Ned Raggett*

Klaus Nomi (Klaus Sperber)

b. 1945, Bavarian Alps, Germany, d. Aug. 6, 1983, New York, NY
Vocals / Club/Dance, Experimental, New Wave, Synth Pop, Disco
One of the first prominent persons to die of AIDS, Klaus Nomi mixed rock and disco stylings with a classical and operatic repertoire. He was born Klaus Sperber in Berlin in 1945, but moved to New York in the mid-'70s, working as a pastry chef and nightclub singer. One of his sets impressed David Bowie, and Nomi soon found himself backing the star on *Saturday Night Live*. He began touring Europe and the U.S. as a cabaret act and signed to RCA in 1980. His first single was a cover of Elvis Presley's "Can't Help Falling in Love," and his 1982 debut album included compositions from Chubby Checker alongside Charles Camille Saint-Saëns. Nomi later worked with famed electro producer Man Parrish, but covered baroque composer Henry Purcell as well as Donna Summer. He died on August 6, 1983, after which several compilations were released plus a live date in America. —*John Bush*

● **Eclipsed: The Best Of Klaus Nomi** / Aug. 24, 1999 / Razor & Tie ✦✦✦✦✦
To use a well-worn cliche, Klaus Nomi is an acquired taste. Granted, if your tastes run toward Euro-dance, art-schlock, disco kitsch, or new wave weirdness, it may not be all that difficult to acquire since Nomi fused all of those, plus a genuine taste for opera, into a distinctive synthesized post-modernist melange. Razor & Tie's *Eclipsed: The Best of Klaus Nomi* gathers 15 of his best moments onto one definitive collection. It's hard to tell which songs here were meant seriously and which were meant as an avantprank—probably the covers of Lou Christie's "Lightning Strikes," Elvis' "Can't Help Falling in Love," Barbra Lewis' "Just One Look," and "Ding Dong (The Witch is Dead)" were all pranks—but it's all strangely engaging, even with Nomi's high operatic voice and chilly Germanic demeanor. It's not for everybody, but anyone with an affection for the quirkiest side of new wave should give *Eclipsed* at least one spin. —*Stephen Thomas Erlewine*

The Notorious B.I.G. (Christopher Wallace)

b. May 21, 1972, d. Mar. 9, 1997
Vocals / Pop-Rap, Hardcore Rap, East Coast Rap, Gangsta Rap, Club/Dance, Hip-Hop
The Brooklyn-born rapper the Notorious B.I.G. (born Chris Wallace) first gained attention for his work on Mary J. Blige's "What's the 411?" When he delivered his debut album, *Ready to Die*, in 1994, it became one of the most popular hip-hop releases of the year. In June of 1995, his single "One More Chance" debuted at number five in the pop singles chart, tying Michael Jackson's "Scream" as the highest-debuting single of all time; *Ready to Die* eventually sold two million copies. With its success, the Notorious B.I.G. became the most visible figue in East Coast hip-hop, and he became a target in the heated feud between the two coasts; especially, he and Tupac Shakur, a former ally, became vicious rivals. As the Notorious B.I.G. was preparing his second album, Shakur was shot and killed in Las Vegas. Many in the media speculated that Biggie's camp was responsible for the shooting, accusations that he and his producer, Sean "Puffy" Combs, vehemently denied. Early on the morning of March 9, the Notorious B.I.G. was returning to his hotel in Los Angeles when another car pulled up aside his car and opened fire, killing him instantly. Shakur had been killed just six months earlier. The Notorious B.I.G.'s second album, the double-disc *Life After Death*, was released three weeks later, debuting at number one on the charts. —*Stephen Thomas Erlewine*

★ **Ready to Die** / Sep. 13, 1994 / Bad Boy ✦✦✦✦✦
Upon considering how realized and mature this album sounds from beginning to end, with literally no lulls or second-rate moments, also keep in mind that this was the

Notorious B.I.G.'s debut album. There isn't a moment on this album when Biggie doesn't sound sure of himself; his gangsta tales never seem overly dramatic and his boasts never seem like macho bragging—it all sounds sincere, almost too sincere. No matter whether Biggie was really the man he claimed to be or whether he simply understood the makings of an alluring persona, he crafts for himself one of the most powerful characterizations that rap has ever seen. From the harsh thug posing of "Gimme the Loot" to the grim reality of "Ready to Die" to the glamorous pimpery of "Big Poppa," Biggie never sounds ordinary and transcends any hint of cliché. His mammoth persona is ultimately the most enduring attribute of this beginning-to-end masterpiece, but Puff Daddy's role as producer also should be noted, as he seems nearly as responsible as Biggie for this album's perfection. Granted, *Ready to Die* isn't as epic or as grandiose as the follow-up double album, *Life After Death*, yet it is a bit more accessible and a better starting point for newcomers. *—Jason Birchmeier*

Life After Death / Mar. 25, 1997 / Bad Boy ✦✦✦✦✦

With the Notorious B.I.G.'s debut masterpiece, *Ready to Die*, the gangsta rapper found himself crowned the king of the East Coast. So when it came time to succeed his instant classic, Biggie and executive producer Puff Daddy decided to release the epic 24-track *Life After Death*, figuring that if they couldn't surpass the near-perfect quality of *Ready to Die*, they would at least surpass it in terms of quantity. The result was, and still is, staggering. Often compared to 2Pac's similarly epic *All Eyez on Me* for obvious reasons, *Life After Death* finds Biggie never short on rhymes and never stumbling, as he moves swiftly from one motif to another, forever retaining his sense of gangsta suave. It is this uncanny marriage of urbane sophistication and ruthless aggression that makes Biggie so engaging—he finds a perfect balance. As expected with an album of this scope featuring this high-profile of a rapper, there are numerous collaborators besides fellow Bad Boy Puff Daddy: Bone Thugs-N-Harmony, Lil' Kim, Mase, the L.O.X., Too Short, R. Kelly, Jay-Z, and DMC, along with producers such as Havoc, RZA, and DJ Premier. Furthermore, there are a handful of tracks here such as "Hypnotize" and "Mo Money Mo Problems" that stand as perennial anthems. The only thing that may hold this album back from being an undeniable masterpiece is its bloated size; at 24 tracks and two discs, *Life After Death* is a daunting listen, and some moments are undoubtedly better than others. *—Jason Birchmeier*

Born Again / Dec. 7, 1999 / Bad Boy ✦✦✦

Considering it was released almost three years after his death, it'd be easy to dismiss the Notorious B.I.G.'s third album as a cash-in or merely a tribute album, similar to Puff Daddy's *No Way Out*. Fact is, *Born Again* includes a lot of previously unheard material from Biggie, and guest spots from Busta Rhymes, Redman & Method Man, Missy Elliott, Ice Cube, and Snoop Dogg work better than could be expected. It's difficult to say where all this material came from, but it's probable that the productions were simply arranged around old rhymes from Biggie himself. On most tracks, he takes a spotlight and then the guest rapper comes in. Thanks to executive producer Puff Daddy, it'd be easy to fool those not into hip-hop that Notorious B.I.G. was still alive. The outro, a spoken-word reminiscence by Voletta Wallace (his mother) is a bit touching but also a bit ghoulish. For B.I.G. fans, this is another must-have, but for anyone that thinks the rap industry routinely goes too far in pursuit of the almighty dollar, *Born Again* is yet further proof. *—Keith Farley*

Aldo Nova

b. Montreal, Quebec, Canada

Vocals, Guitar / Heavy Metal, Hard Rock

Born in Montreal, Aldo Nova (aka Aldo Scarporuscio) released three solo albums during the '80s (*Fantasy* in 1982, *Subject* one year later, and *Twitch* in 1985), but then took a long break. In 1990, he contributed his guitar work to Jon Bon Jovi's "Blaze of Glory" and, after signing to Bon Jovi's JAMBCO Records, Nova released *Blood on the Bricks* in 1991. *—John Bush*

Aldo Nova / 1981 / Portrait ✦✦✦✦✦

Canadian rock singer/songwriter Aldo Nova doesn't get enough credit (some cynics would say blame) for helping invent the 1980s pop-metal genre, which focused equally on hard rocking anthems and soaring power ballads. *Aldo Nova* appeared in 1982 complete with irresistible melodies and choruses, explosive guitar licks, and huge-sounding drums. It was a full year or more before Def Leppard, Night Ranger, Bon Jovi, and others would latch on to this formula and rocket to stardom. Nova wrote, produced, arranged, and performed his double-platinum debut album by himself, except for drums and some bass guitar and piano parts. Nova is quite proficient on guitar, but his secret weapon is his keyboard and synthesizer prowess. The hit single (and early MTV favorite) "Fantasy" cannot be denied; it's loaded with guitar and keyboard hooks as well as a catchy chorus. "Foolin' Yourself" has a more straightforward pop feel and it was a minor hit. "Ball and Chain" is the best-known power ballad on *Aldo Nova*, but the hypnotic "You're My Love" is better. "Hot Love" is propelled by several guitar solo bursts. "Heart to Heart" and "See the Light" are fast, energetic songs with crisp guitar riffs and swirling synthesizer lines. *Aldo Nova* is a minor classic. *—Bret Adams*

Subject . . . Aldo Nova / 1983 / Portrait ✦✦✦

After the huge success of his self-titled debut album, Aldo Nova defied his record company, which basically wanted a carbon copy for the sophomore follow-up, and made a very loose concept album touching on themes such as dreams, imagination, and paradise. *Subject: Aldo Nova* still featured hooks and melodies galore (and an emphasis on keyboards and synthesizers), but the format was different. Perhaps this style curve confused listeners, and as a result, *Subject: Aldo Nova* sold much less than its predecessor and only went gold. (Nova also claimed Portrait didn't promote the album properly.) Three impressively spasmodic synthesizer segments—"Subject's Theme," "Armageddon (Race Cars)," and "Armageddon"—open *Subject: Aldo Nova* and lead into its highlight, "Monkey on Your Back." This disturbing anti-heroin song features a mid-tempo, menacing throb thanks to relentlessly roaring drums, bass guitar, and rhythm guitar and slow, sustained lead guitar fills. "Hey Operator" and "Cry Baby Cry" are carried by infectious choruses. "Victim of a Broken Heart" is the album's obligatory power ballad. *Subject: Aldo Nova* isn't as good as *Aldo Nova*, but Nova had the courage to try something a little bit different. *—Bret Adams*

Twitch / 1985 / Portrait ✦✦

Blood on the Bricks / 1991 / Jambco ✦✦

● **A Portrait of Aldo Nova** / 1992 / Epic ✦✦✦✦✦

At 18 tracks, this is a lot of Aldo Nova, especially since Nova is pretty much the province of early '80s hard rock fetishists. Still, there's a reason why Nova has fans, and it's because his music was trippier and stranger than that of his peers, whether it was Billy Squier or Accept. As such, it has dated a little bit, but in a good way, since this has more character than a lot of early '80s arena-metal. That doesn't mean that this will satisfy listeners just looking for "Fantasy" but for those that like to dig a little deeper into this era, this is definitely worth a spin. *—Stephen Thomas Erlewine*

Nova's Dream / Nov. 18, 1997 / BMG Canada ✦✦✦

On his first album in five years, Nova returns to his signature hard rock sound for efforts including "Are You Inexperienced?," "Excuse Me While I Scream!!!," and "The Pressure's Killing Me." *—Jason Ankeny*

NRBQ

f. 1967, Miami, FL

Bar Band, Roots Rock, Rock & Roll, Novelty

NRBQ (the New Rhythm and Blues Quartet) have amassed a fanatical cult following over more than two decades of recording and touring with their incredibly versatile eclecticism; their music might veer from country to rockabilly to pop to bar-band R&B to blues to free jazz, all in the same album. The group's wacky, sometimes corny sense of humor and in-concert unpredictability (sometimes vowing to play whatever song audience members request) have endeared them to fans, even if some find them a bit precious. Formed in 1967, NRBQ attracted immediate attention with their wide-ranging musicianship and were signed to Columbia. On their 1969 self-titled debut, the band covered rockabilly and Sun Ra on one record and pulled it off; not surprisingly, rave reviews followed. NRBQ followed it with *Boppin' the Blues*, a collaboration with rockabilly singer Carl Perkins; it too received critical praise, but Columbia was unhappy with the group's sales and dropped it. After a series of short-lived label stays, in 1989 the band got another one-album major-label deal with Virgin, which resulted in *Wild Weekend*, their first album to make the charts since the debut record. *—Steve Huey*

NRBQ [1969] / 1969 / Columbia ✦✦✦

The Q's debut is as succinct a summation of what this band was about than perhaps anything they've released since. After opening the record with a storming version of Eddie Cochran's "C'mon Everybody," they take a breath and leap headlong into a raucous version of Sun Ra's "Number 9." Add to that a songwriting collaboration between Terry Adams and jazz composer Carla Bley, and the great guitar playing of Steve Ferguson (really great on "Stomp"), and you've got the makings of a tremendously important record by a furiously eclectic and always wonderful band. *—John Dougan*

Scraps / 1972 / Rounder ✦✦✦✦

For the uninitiated, NRBQ is an oddity. How does one, for instance, approach a band who sings a song like "Howard Johnson's Got His Ho-Jo Working?" The answer may be, "not very seriously," but then another problem reveals itself: the songs are so catchy. "Who Put the Garlic in the Glue?" and "Magnet" bounce along like an early-'70s version of Ben Folds Five. Together, pianist Terry Adams, bassist Joey Spampinato, guitarist Al Anderson, drummer Tom Staley, and vocalist Frank Gadler find a bigger sound than the sum of their parts. *Scraps* is filled with pop music that manages the duel feat of making the listener feel good while remaining intelligent. The songs, with a couple of exceptions, are only two to three minutes long; that equals out to 14 cuts from the original album, which was a lot of tracks in 1972. Three bonus tracks have been added and the entire album has been remastered. There is also a great deal of breadth in Spampinato and Adams' songwriting, from the rocking "Don't You Knock at My Door" to the instrumental "Tragic Magic" to the gentle "Only You." Spampinato, who had written very little on previous albums, wrote several gentle ballads, including "Boys in the City" and "It's Not So Hard." John DeAngelis' liner notes keeps tabs on the NRBQ's evolving lineup and provides good information on the context of the recording. *Scraps'* appeal sneaks up on the listener, reminding them that some music is just meant to be enjoyed. *—Ronnie Lankford, Jr.*

Workshop / 1973 / Kama Sutra ✦✦✦

All Hopped Up / 1977 / Rounder ✦✦✦✦

NRBQ's fourth album (and first with drummer Tom Ardolino, solidifying a lineup that would last for close to 20 years) plays down the band's goofier tendencies in favor of a set that shows off their considerable chops as both players and songwriters. The more introspective side of the band's jazz leanings come to the forefront on "Doctor's Wind" and "Queen Talk"; Terry Adams contributes a strong, vaguely Beatlesque tune called "It Feels Good" and the lovely "Things to You," Joey Spampinato turns in a pair of subtle pop gems, "That's Alright" and "Still in School"; and can anyone explain why Al Anderson's wonderful and engagingly heart-tugging "Riding in My Car" wasn't a hit single? *All Hopped Up* also features a handful of stellar covers, including a jumped-up take on "I Got a Rocket in My Pocket" (Adams' barrelhouse piano truly shines), a swinging version of "Cecilia," and a rollicking ride through Big Joe Turner's "Honey Hush," and the band's loosely tight communication is a fine thing to hear on all cuts. And even the album's token weird one from Adams, "Call Him Off, Roger," could pass for a serious pop tune if you didn't pay too much attention to the lyrics (about a dog with designs on Adams' arm). Just in case you thought NRBQ had gotten all normal on us, though, the album closes with the most extraordinary version of the theme from "Bonanza" you will ever hear. It's hard to say why anyone would want an entirely serious album from NRBQ, but *All Hopped Up* is closer than most, and proves their charm and their talent is what makes them great, not their idiosyncratic sense of humor. *—Mark Deming*

NRBQ at Yankee Stadium / 1978 / Mercury ✦✦✦✦✦
More than just NRBQ's best record, but one of the great records of the '70s (maybe ever!). This album contains the strongest batch of new Q songs on one record, many of them the best and most memorable songs in the band's long and storied career. Starting with Terry Adams' herky-jerky "Green Lights" to the rollicking "I Want You Bad," the band has rarely sounded better. The record's gem, however, is an Al Anderson song left over from their previous record (*All Hopped Up on Red Rooster*), "Ridin' in My Car." A song about lost love and blown chances, it has Anderson's characteristic wry sensibility and (non-fatal) heartache, all wrapped up in a ebullient pop package driven by Terry Adams' melodic keyboard riffing and Tom Ardolino's amazingly assertive drumming. *Yankee Stadium* should have been a huge album, but Mercury booted it and never capitalized on the band's fanatical support base. Caveat emptor: When this record was issued by Mercury on CD just a couple of years back, they inexplicably left off "Ridin' in My Car." *—John Dougan*

Kick Me Hard / 1979 / Rounder ✦✦✦✦✦
NRBQ's short-lived alliance with Mercury Records resulted in one of the tightest and most consistently rockin' albums of their career, *NRBQ at Yankee Stadium*, but a year later they found themselves back on their own Red Rooster label, where the band relaxed and let their characteristic wit come to the forefront on 1979's *Kick Me Hard*. Opening with a musical look at America's drug laws as only NRBQ could interpret them ("Wacky Tobacky"), *Kick Me Hard* finds the Q indulging their fondness for goofiness on tunes like "It Was an Accident" (romance is complicated by unplanned pregnancy), "Things We Like to Do" (a rewrite of an old Ross Bagdasarian number in which the guys declare their fondness for miniskirts and the TV show *CHiPs*), and "Chores" (in which someone seems to enjoy doing their pig imitation just a bit *too much*). But as always, NRBQ also provides an equal amount of evidence that they're one of the most solid, soulful, and eclectic bands on the planet, running from barrelhouse R&B ("All Night Long"), rootsy rockabilly ("This Old House"), cool jazz ("Tenderly"), and other stuff that simply exists in a world all its own ("Electric Train"), with the band displaying sharp chops and tremendous charm throughout (especially guitarist Al Anderson and keyboard wizard Terry Adams). And as a bonus, you get perhaps the most remarkable version of "North to Alaska" ever captured by modern recording equipment! How can you go wrong? [The 1989 CD reissue of the album tacks on eight bonus cuts, including the free jazz workout "Welcome to Orlando" and "What Can I Say," later covered by Yo La Tengo.] *—Mark Deming*

Tiddlywinks / 1980 / Rounder ✦✦✦✦✦
After being unceremoniously dumped by Mercury after *Yankee Stadium*, NRBQ returned to the warm embrace of Rounder and recorded a string of fine records that started with *Kick Me Hard*. This lineup was to remain intact for nearly 20 years, but here, fairly early on, the synchronicity among the quartet was apparent; it was if they'd been playing together forever, and the music excelled as a result. The songwriting was getting better too: Al, Terry, and Joey were dividing the chores but never losing the group's cohesiveness. At times, Terry's songs would be a little too goofy, and Joey's heartfelt pop might dip into saccharine sweetness now and again, but never so much that it becomes a huge problem. Of these two excellent records, *Kick Me Hard* lives up to its title, especially during the bluesy organ workout "Don't You Know" and the riff-happy "All Night Long" (great solo by Al). *Tiddlywinks* is carried by "Me and the Boys" (later to be recorded by Bonnie Raitt) and Anderson's beautiful "Never Take the Place of You." *—John Dougan*

Grooves in Orbit / 1983 / Bearsville/Rhino ✦✦✦
Back to a major label, NRBQ came up with a solid record that, again, didn't significantly increase their audience, even though many musicians (Elvis Costello, Bonnie Raitt) were singing their praises. Although very good, *Grooves* is not significantly better (actually it's not any better) than *Kick Me Hard* or *Tiddlywinks*. Both sides end with a whimper rather than a bang, and it seems that the band was developing an overreliance on recycling material (their cover of Johnny Cash's "Get Rhythm" shows up on *Yankee Stadium*). Still, the crucial stuff ("Rain at the Drive-In" and "Smackeroo") fit the bill. *—John Dougan*

Tap Dancin' Bats / 1983 / Rounder ✦✦✦
While the Q was recording *Grooves* for Bearsville, Rounder released this bizarre chunk of odds and sods that featured the band's experimental side. Ask anyone who's ever gone to an NRBQ gig and they'll tell you that the Q are as likely to play Sun Ra as they are Carl Perkins, or sometimes fuse the two. *Tapdancin' Bats* has such supremely strange moments: their paean to wrestler/actor Lou Albano, "Captain Lou," a crazy novelty song from the '50s, "Rats in My Room," some straightahead (but slightly skewed) rock & roll, and the title track, a dissonant jazz blurt that sounds like Ornette Coleman. Truly inspiring stuff. *—John Dougan*

She Sings, They Play / 1985 / Rounder ✦✦✦
During the mid-'80s, bassist Joey Spampinato married country music legend Skeeter Davis, and what better way to celebrate than with a record that featured Skeeter's great voice with the Q backing her up. To those who have little patience for classic country performers and who simply want to hear NRBQ rock, this is probably a minor work. But, for the rest of us, it's an unfettered joy. *—John Dougan*

RC Cola & a Moon Pie / 1986 / Rounder ✦✦

Lou and the Q / 1986 / Rounder ✦✦

God Bless Us All / 1987 / Rounder ✦✦✦
Go figure this: Rounder decides to release two live recordings in succession. Granted, NRBQ had long been known for great live shows, but these records, while certainly enjoyable, seem a little perfunctory and only hint at the kind of excitement the band was capable of generating live. Still, on *God Bless Us All*, Al tears through an inspired "Crazy Like a Fox" and the whole band cranks on "Shake, Rattle and Roll." *Diggin'* has a pounding "It Comes to Me Naturally" and the country standard "Scarlet Ribbons." Both records are fun, but neither is essential unless you're a completist. *—John Dougan*

Diggin' Uncle Q (Live) / 1988 / Rounder ✦✦

Wild Weekend / Sep. 1989 / Virgin ✦✦

● **Peek-A-Boo: The Best of NRBQ (1969-1989)** / Oct. 1990 / Rhino ✦✦✦✦✦
A two-CD set that does a great job of hitting the band's high spots without sacrificing any of the freewheeling stylistic leaps or engaging lunacy that has made NRBQ one of America's longest-lived bands. If you're interested in a career overview and little more, this is the ideal release. However, it is my considered opinion that anyone who loves this stuff (and to emphatically use a double negative, there's nothing not to love) will have their appetite whetted for more. Not a slow spot, ill-chosen track, or bad decision among the 35 songs, this is as great a statement for NRBQ as one of the best rock bands America has ever produced. Few bands, genre notwithstanding, have been able to effortlessly recombine styles, be so defiantly off-the-wall, and rock like all get-out for so long and still sound so good. God bless them all. *—John Dougan*

Honest Dollar / Jul. 10, 1992 / Rykodisc ✦✦

Stay With We: The Best of NRBQ / May 11, 1993 / Columbia/Legacy ✦✦✦
Featuring 24 songs including eight unreleased tracks, *Stay With We* is the definitive compilation of NRBQ's early years at Columbia. *—Stephen Thomas Erlewine*

Message for the Mess Age / Feb. 22, 1994 / Forward/Rhino ✦✦✦
Sadly, the last record with Al on guitar (he's since been replaced by Joey's brother Johnny, ex-guitar slinger for the Incredible Casuals and Four Star Combo) isn't a knockout, but the material is strong and makes one optimistic for the Q's next 25 years. Al does contribute another achingly beautiful song, "A Better Word for Love," and even the goofy moments ("Girl Scout Cookies" and the spell-my-name-right-anthem "Spampinato") don't sound nearly as forced as they occasionally have in the past. We're lucky to still have 'em around. *—John Dougan*

Tokyo: Recorded Live at on Air West Tokyo / Feb. 11, 1997 / Rounder ✦✦✦

You're Nice People You Are / Jul. 8, 1997 / Rounder ✦✦✦

Riding in My Car / Apr. 6, 1999 / Rounder ✦✦✦✦

NRBQ [1999] / Sep. 14, 1999 / Rounder ✦✦✦
Thirty years after they began their professional recording career, NRBQ was still rolling on, and in order to commemorate their anniversary they released another album called *NRBQ*—which happens to be the title of their first album from 1969. More significantly for longtime Q fans, 1999's *NRBQ* is their first proper studio album (meaning, not a children's album or live album or reissue) in five years, since 1994's confused *Message for the Mess Age*. *NRBQ* does improve on that effort, largely because the band has gotten comfortable with Al Anderson's replacement, Johnny Spampinato, which makes it sound better than its predecessor; in retrospect, that record suffers from Anderson's desire to be elsewhere. Here, they hit upon a comfortable, earthy groove early on, and they ride it throughout the album. Sure, they get too cutesy—"Puddin' Truck," "CM Pups," and "I Want My Mommy" being prime suspects—but it wouldn't be a Q album without that. And it also wouldn't be a Q album if the musicianship wasn't so thoroughly impressive and rich that it makes up for the other flaws, whether it's cutesiness or underdeveloped material. At its core, *NRBQ* the 1999 version isn't much different than most of their studio LPs, but it's a solid and entertaining one, and considering that it arrives on their 30th anniversary, that alone is an accomplishment of sorts. *—Stephen Thomas Erlewine*

Ted Nugent

b. Dec. 13, 1948, Detroit, MI
Vocals, Leader, Percussion, Guitar, Bass / Detroit Rock, Album Rock, Arena Rock, Heavy Metal, Hard Rock
Throughout his lengthy career, guitar wildman Ted Nugent has reveled in the controversy and criticism that always seem to follow in his path. While there's no denying his exceptional talent on the six-string, his knack for penning arena rock anthems, or his standing as one of rock's top live acts, it's his non-musical endeavors that have caused the most condemnation from his detractors (his pro-right wing beliefs, pro-gun advocacy, appreciation of hunting animals, and so on). But by the same token, Nugent is a family man and one of the few hard rockers who has admirably stuck by his lifelong anti-drugs and -drink stance throughout his career. Born on December 13, 1948, in Detroit, MI, Nugent became interested in rock & roll early in the game. In the '60s, Nugent formed his first bands, but it wasn't until the formation of the Amboy Dukes that the Nuge got his first taste of stardom. By the mid-'70s, Nugent decided to finally ditch the Amboy Dukes name and set out on his own. By the release of 1977's *Cat Scratch Fever*, Nugent and his band were one of the top rock bands in the U.S. Nugent continued to tour and crank out forgettable albums throughout the '80s. By the end of the decade, Nugent joined the rock supergroup Damn Yankees, resulting in the quartet's self-titled debut in 1990, which became a surprise hit. But ultimately, the union proved to be short-lived and the band called it quits. Nugent returned to his solo career, issuing his best album in over a decade, 1995's back-to-basics

Spirit of the Wild, while several archival releases turned up throughout the '90s. —*Greg Prato*

Journey to the Center of the Mind / Jun. 1968 / Repertoire ✦✦✦
Long before Ted Nugent made his name as a mighty crossbow hunter, there was this heavy Detroit band in which he was content to play lead guitar, something he does very well and with much less threat to the Midwest's deer population. The Nuge shouldn't try to take all the credit for this band, because the other members such as vocalist John Drake and rhythm guitarist Steve Farmer contributed with great aplomb, the latter writing much of the material on the second side's ambitious suite as well as co-writing the title hit with Nugent. This is some hard-hitting, well-done psychedelic music, recorded with taste by a producer known much more for his work with mainstream jazz artists, Bob Shad. One thing that made the Amboy Dukes special was the amount of power and drive in their playing, something lacking in other psychedelic outfits that take a more airy-fairy approach. The Nuge's guitar sound is recorded as if this was a mainstream jazz album by Harold Land, and it helps. —*Eugene Chadbourne*

Ted Nugent / Nov. 1975 / Epic ✦✦✦
After disintegrating the Amboy Dukes in the early '70s, Ted Nugent finally decided to strike out on his own as a solo star. Even without a recording contract, Nugent toured constantly, built up a fervent following, and created a smoking hard rock quartet with the help of singer/guitarist Derek St. Holmes, bassist Rob Grange, and drummer Cliff Davies. The band's first release, 1975's *Ted Nugent*, is a prime slice of testosterone-heavy, raging, unapologetic rock & roll, and along with the band's 1977 release *Cat Scratch Fever*, it is Nugent's best solo studio album. While the grinding opening track "Stranglehold" stretches beyond eight minutes and contains several extended, fiery hot guitar leads, it does not come off as your typical '70s overindulgent fare—every single note counts as Nugent wails away as if his life depended on it. Other Nuge classics include "Motor City Madhouse," plus the St. Holmes-sung "Hey Baby" and "Just What the Doctor Ordered," all eventually becoming arena staples and making the band one of the late-'70s top concert draws. Additional highlights are the unexpected breezy jazz ballad "You Make Me Feel Right at Home," plus the untamed rockers "Stormtroopin'" and "Queen of the Forest." Nugent himself hails *Ted Nugent* as his best work, and with good reason. It's an essential hard rock classic. [Note: As with Nugent's other 1999 reissues, an insightful essay on this Nugent-era by journalist Gary Graff is included, plus bonus tracks.] —*Greg Prato*

Free-for-All / 1976 / Epic ✦✦✦✦✦
While Ted Nugent's second solo album, 1976's *Free-for-All*, was another raging slab of rock & roll, it wasn't quite as consistent as his self-titled debut. The main reason was due to singer/rhythm guitarist Derek St. Holmes' departure from the band just as recording of the album began (due to constant grappling with the Nuge about certain musical issues). To solve the problem, producer Tom Werman convinced a then unknown singer by the name of Meat Loaf to handle the vocal chores on the songs Derek was going to sing. While it seems like a mismatch in theory, the results were not catastrophic—such rockers as "Writing on the Wall" (a virtual rewrite of "Stranglehold"), "Street Rats," and "Hammerdown" are classic Nuge stompers. But they would have been stronger with St. Holmes' contributions, as evidenced by a bonus outtake of "Street Rats" with St. Holmes on vocals and the turbo-charged "Turn It Up." But still, the title track is one of Ted's all-time best (featuring a downright vicious groove), as is the rocking tale about the 1967 Detroit riots, "Dog Eat Dog." Despite St. Holmes' absence (he would return in time for the album's subsequent tour), *Free-for-All* solidified Ted's commercial success, reaching the Top 25. [Note: As with Nugent's other 1999 reissues, an insightful essay on this Ted era by journalist Gary Graff is included, plus bonus tracks.] —*Greg Prato*

Cat Scratch Fever / 1977 / Epic ✦✦✦✦✦
Despite becoming one of the rock's biggest concert attractions, Ted Nugent needed that one album and single that would break through in a big way, and the 1977 album and single of the same name, *Cat Scratch Fever*, did the trick. *Cat Scratch Fever* matched the focused ferocity of Nugent's excellent 1975 debut (due to singer Derek St. Holmes' re-entry into the band), featuring another first-rate set of brash hard rockers. While the title track is a certified classic anthem (the only solo-Nugent single to crack the Top 30), other tracks are just as delightful, such as the oh-so-subtle "Wang Dang Sweet Poontang." Further standouts include such underrated compositions as "Live It Up," "Workin' Hard, Playin' Hard," and "Out of Control," plus the exquisitely melodic instrumental "Home Bound," which the Beastie Boys would sample on their 1992 mega-hit album *Check Your Head* (the track "The Biz vs. the Nuge"). A Top 20 release, *Cat Scratch Fever* was the last Nugent release to feature his original solo band, (St. Holmes, along with bassist Rob Grange, left for good in 1978). And while he enjoyed further chart success with such titles as *Weekend Warriors* and *Double Live Gonzo*, many consider *Cat Scratch Fever* to be Ted Nugent's finest hour. [Note: As with Nugent's other 1999 reissues, an insightful essay on this Nugent era by journalist Gary Graff is included, plus bonus tracks.] —*Greg Prato*

Weekend Warriors / 1978 / Epic ✦✦✦
Weekend Warriors, Nugent's follow-up to the career peaks of *Cat Scratch Fever* and *Double Live Gonzos!*, isn't quite as strong as his two previous albums, but it remains one of his better albums, featuring a handful of prime hard rockers. —*Stephen Thomas Erlewine*

Double Live Gonzo / 1978 / Epic ✦✦✦✦✦
As exciting as they were, Ted Nugent's first three albums lacked the sonic punch-in-the-gut of his outrageous live performances, something readily proved by 1978's classic *Double Live Gonzo!* Both Nugent and his band are in top form, yielding a fierce performance of their numerous mid-'70s classics. Mega hit "Cat Scratch Fever" makes an obligatory appearance, but it's the songs from Nugent's self-titled debut which truly stand out.

"Just What the Doctor Ordered" is damn near perfect and the band really clicks on extended jams through "Motor City Madhouse" and the fantastic "Stranglehold." A consummate showman, Nugent also unleashes a number of hilarious, motormouth stage raps on "Baby Please Don't Go" and "Wang Dang Sweet Poontang" before offering the definitive version of his early classic "Great White Buffalo." In the year of the live album (1978), this one's about as good as they come. —*Ed Rivadavia*

● **Great Gonzos!: The Best of Ted Nugent** / 1981 / Epic/Legacy ✦✦✦✦
When originally released in 1981, the ten-track *Great Gonzos!: The Best of Ted Nugent* was an expertly selected collection of Ted Nugent's best-known material. But with the advent of the CD, the length of albums can now be stretched out, such is the case with the 1999 reissue of *Great Gonzos!* All of the previous ten tracks are remastered and featured in all of their ferocious glory, as well as three extra tracks not included on the original: the exceptional instrumental from 1977, "Home Bound," plus the explosive rockers "Yank Me, Crank Me" and "Give Me Just a Little." While the Nuge is known primarily for his shorter compositions that are still classic rock radio favorites ("Cat Scratch Fever," "Just What the Doctor Ordered," "Free-For-All," "Dog Eat Dog"), his longer tracks are just as gripping ("Stranglehold," "Wango Tango," "Wang Dang Sweet Poontang"). The selections are taken mostly from Nugent's first three albums (his best work), but *Great Gonzos!* still neglects several standouts, such as "Hey Baby," "Live It Up," and "Out of Control." Still, *Great Gonzos!: The Best of Ted Nugent* remains an essential purchase for admirers of fine '70s-era hard rock/heavy metal. —*Greg Prato*

Nugent / 1982 / Atlantic ✦✦

Penetrator / 1984 / Atlantic ✦

Little Miss Dangerous / Mar. 1986 / Atlantic ✦

If You Can't Lick 'Em . . . Lick 'Em / 1988 / Atlantic ✦✦

Out of Control / Jun. 22, 1993 / Epic/Legacy ✦✦✦✦✦
Out of Control is a comprehensive double-disc set that contains 34 songs from all stages of Nugent's career, tracing his rise from the Amboy Dukes to the arena-rock "madman" of the '70s. Along the way, all of his most popular songs are heard: "Journey to the Center of Your Mind," "Call of the Wild," "Great White Buffalo," "Stranglehold," "Cat Scratch Fever," "Wango Tango." There are a couple of unreleased songs and alternate takes to entice collectors, but for most listeners, this—or *Double Live Gonzo*—will be all the Nuge they need. —*Stephen Thomas Erlewine*

Spirit of the Wild / May 2, 1995 / Atlantic ✦✦✦✦✦
Spirit of the Wild ranks as one of Ted Nugent's finest moments because it cuts away the filler and keeps the wildman's tendency for indulgence in check. A fair amount of the material does concern itself with the wilderness, which fits right in with his '90s reinvention as a conservative family-values spokesman. That doesn't mean that it's a tame record—it means that Nugent sounds committed again, since that passion for hunting and family flows throughout his performance. —*Stephen Thomas Erlewine*

Loaded for Bear: The Best of Ted Nugent & Amboy Dukes / Jun. 22, 1999 / Epic/Legacy ✦✦✦✦
As many Nugent fans know, before reaching fame in the '70s with his gonzoid rock, Ted got started with the Detroit-based Amboy Dukes. While the band released several albums from the '60s through the '70s, many consider their early work to be their best, and their formative years are featured on the 18-track compilation *Loaded for Bear: The Best of Ted Nugent & the Amboy Dukes*. The band is best remembered for the Top 20 hit/drug anthem "Journey to the Center of the Mind" (the outspoken anti-substance Ted swears he didn't know it was a pro-drug song at the time), but *Loaded for Bear* shows they had other standouts in their repertoire. The music is more akin to the Stones and Yardbirds than *Cat Scratch Fever*, as evidenced by a cover of "Baby Please Don't Go," "Dr. Slingshot," and "You Talk Sunshine, I Breathe Fire," plus the lengthy compositions "Prodigal Man" and "Migration." [Note: As with Nugent's other 1999 reissues, an insightful essay on this Ted era by journalist Gary Graff is included.] —*Greg Prato*

Gary Numan (Gary Anthony James Webb)
b. Mar. 8, 1958, Hammersmith, London, England
Vocals, Keyboards, Synthesizer / New Romantic, New Wave, Electronic, Synth Pop
Gary Numan managed to incorporate the electronic innovations of Kraftwerk, Brian Eno, and David Bowie into pop music, creating some of the first synth pop hits of the new wave era. Numan originally performed under the name Tubeway Army, which had a chart-topping British single with "Are 'Friends' Electric?" The first record he released under his own name, 1979's *Pleasure Principle*, featured the international hit "Cars"; the single hit number one in the U.K. and reached the U.S. Top Ten. Throughout the early '80s, Numan was one of the most popular artists in the U.K., amassing several Top Ten hits and two number one albums. Around 1983, his career began to slip, as each record became indistinguishable from the other. Even as he fell out of the Top Ten, Numan held on to his die-hard fans. He continued to record into the '90s, releasing *Fury* in 1998 and *Dramatis Project* and *Pure* in 2000. Early 2001 saw the release of *Live at Labatt's Hammersmith Apollo.* —*Stephen Thomas Erlewine*

Tubeway Army / Nov. 1978 / Beggars Banquet ✦✦✦✦
The classic, long-out-of-print self-titled debut by Gary Numan's Tubeway Army was finally reissued by Beggars Banquet, who have done a masterful job remastering the tracks and adding a live set from 1978 as a bonus. In the past, many have felt that Numan's debut disc didn't measure up to his later triumphs (1979's *Replicas*, 1980's *Telekon*, etc.), but listening to it today, you discover that it's the most underrated of all his early albums. Numan & the Tubeway Army were one of the first new wave/punk bands (along with Kraftwerk and Devo) to successfully fuse robotic synthesizers with rock & roll. Gary

Numan's guitar riffing is more prominent here than on any other of his albums, which gives the tunes a splendid *Ziggy Stardust* feel at times. Kicking things off with several strong compositions—"Listen to the Sirens," "The Life Machine," and "Friends"—the album sags momentarily in the middle ("My Love Is Liquid"), but soon returns to its high standards with "Are You Real?" and "Jo the Waiter." The reissue of *Tubeway Army* wraps up with the 13-track *Living Ornaments '78: Live at the Roxy* set, which was previously released only as a bootleg. Although lo-fi, it's an audience recording containing songs that didn't make it to the debut. [Note: In addition to bonus tracks, all of the Gary Numan/Begggars Banquet re-releases contain classic photographs and informative liner notes by Numan biographer Steve Malins.] *—Greg Prato*

Replicas / Apr. 1979 / Beggars Banquet ♦♦♦♦
By the release of their second album, *Replicas*, Gary Numan was the undisputed focal point and leader of icy electro-punkers Tubeway Army. And the move proved to be massively successful back home in the U.K., where both the album and the single "Are 'Friends' Electric?" topped the charts. The band had made a conscious effort to streamline the sound heard on their 1978 self-titled debut—the distorted guitar riffs were played on Moog synthesizers instead, and Numan had perfected his faux-space-age persona. And the paranoia that is very evident in the lyrics and vocals on Numan's next release, *The Pleasure Principle*, can be detected on *Replicas*. Another near-perfect album by the band, highlights are many—"Me! I Disconnect From You," "The Machman," "You Are in My Vision," and one of the most underrated new wave/synth-driven compositions of the whole era, the chilling ballad "Down in the Park." And out of all the Gary Numan/Beggars Banquet reissues, *Replicas* contains the strongest bonus tracks, such as never heard outtakes from the recording sessions, including "The Crazies," "Only a Downstat," and the B-side to the original "Are 'Friends' Electric?" single, "We Are So Fragile." [Note: In addition to bonus tracks, all of the Gary Numan/Begggars Banquet re-releases contain classic photographs and informative liner notes by Numan biographer Steve Malins.] *—Greg Prato*

The Pleasure Principle / Sep. 1979 / Beggars Banquet ♦♦♦♦♦
The most popular of all the Gary Numan albums is undeniably 1979's *The Pleasure Principle*. The reasons are simple—there is not a single weak moment on the disc, it contains his sole U.S. (number one worldwide) hit, "Cars," and new drummer Cedric Sharpley adds a whole new dimension with his powerful percussion work. *The Pleasure Principle* is also one of the first Gary Numan albums to feature true ensemble playing, especially heard within the airtight, killer groove of "Metal" (one of Numan's all-time best tracks). Starting things off with the atmospheric instrumental "Airlane," the quality of the songs get stronger and stronger as the album progresses—"Films," "M.E.," "Observer," "Conversation," the aforementioned "Cars," and the U.K. Top Ten hit "Complex" all show Numan in top form. The 1998 reissue contains three unreleased instrumentals (one the B-side to the "Cars" single, "Asylum"), as well as four live tracks. If you had to own just one Gary Numan album, *The Pleasure Principle* would be it. [Note: In addition to bonus tracks, all of the Gary Numan/Begggars Banquet re-releases contain classic photographs and informative liner notes by Numan biographer Steve Malins.] *—Greg Prato*

Telekon / 1980 / Beggars Banquet ♦♦♦
Gary Numan's follow-up to the flawless *The Pleasure Principle* was 1980's *Telekon*. Although it was another mega-hit back home in England (his third consecutive number one album), Numan could not follow up his massive new wave hit "Cars" in the United States, where he was unjustly slapped with the one-hit-wonder tag. *Telekon* would also turn out to be the last true classic Numan album, as monetary problems and an unfocused attempt to try different musical forms (as well as a short-lived retirement) would steer him away from his original vision. Although *Telekon* was indeed a strong album, it could have been even stronger if it included the U.K. Top Ten singles "I Die: You Die" and "We Are Glass" (both were recorded during the *Telekon* sessions). Numan experimented with funk for the first time in his career ("Remind Me to Smile"), but there were still plenty of chilling synth excursions to keep the Numan faithful satisfied—"This Wreckage," "The Aircrash Bureau," "I'm an Agent," and "I Dream of Wires" are all choice cuts. The 1998 Beggars Banquet re-release eventually did include both the U.K. singles, as well as several other rarities, including a bare "piano version" of "Down in the Park." [Note: In addition to bonus tracks, all of the Gary Numan/Beggars Banquet re-releases contain classic photographs and informative liner notes by Numan biographer Steve Malins.] *—Greg Prato*

Dance / Sep. 1981 / Atco ♦♦
A transition album of sorts, *Dance* saw Numan departing from the jerky machine music of his synth pop prime to embrace a (bit) warmer sound that is less robotic and more free form. The subject matter on highlights like "She's Got Claws," "Slowcar to China," "Cry the Clock Said," and "Crash" are quintessentially Numan, but their musical frameworks are quite far removed from early hits like "Are 'Friends' Electric?" and "Cars." Undoubtedly a shock to fans, *Dance* hasn't aged very well, either. The music is just a bit too far removed from the subjects to make much sense. *—John Bush*

I, Assassin / 1982 / Arista ♦♦♦
Although it showcases his trademark sound to a fine effect, the repetitive, formulaic songwriting of *I, Assassin* suggests that Gary Numan had hit a brick wall with his robotic, synthesized pop. *—Stephen Thomas Erlewine*

Warriors / 1983 / Beggars Banquet ♦♦
Former Be-Bop Deluxe leader Bill Nelson was brought in to produce this album and provide some soaring lead guitar work, but the collaboration with Numan was beset by difficulties involving Numan's ego and approach to recording. While Nelson's production is evident on many tracks and his guitar is heard in several places, much of this is business as usual (a B-side, "Poetry and Power," features more Nelson and has gone on to a great deal of popularity, especially with the Gravity Kills cover on *Random*). The science fiction influences here are Robert A. Heinlein's *The Moon Is a Harsh Mistress* and Harlan Ellison's *"'Repent, Harlequin!' Cried the Tick-Tock Man."* While there is some evidence of confusion as to his direction, the music and songwriting has more energy than anything on the predecessor, *I, Assassin*, with some genuinely engaging moments along the way. *—Steven McDonald*

Berserker / 1984 / Numa ♦♦♦
Originally released in 1984 on his own Numa label, *Berserker* is one of the most synthesizer-heavy albums from Numan's mid-'80s period, with tracks like "My Dying Machine," the title track and "A Child With the Ghost," written in tribute to longtime friend and bass player Paul Gardiner. *—John Bush*

Isolate: The Numa Years / 1992 / Numa ♦♦♦♦
A hefty five-disc package that paints in the birth, death, and rebirth of Gary Numan's own record label—licensed, at the time of this release, to Eagle Records in the U.K. and Cleopatra in the U.S. The release of *The Numa Years* along with *Exile* was supposed to signal the dramatic return of Numan to the forefront, riding the crest of a wave of renewed interest and reference from the late-'90s electronica crowd, but this seems to have fizzled in a rather boring manner, with nothing much coming of *Exile* and this box set seeming to receive only lukewarm attention at best. This box set being overlooked is something of a shame, however. Despite the presence of the limp pseudo-Prince *Machine and Soul*, *The Numa Years* manages to pack in some fine examples of Numan at his best, filling out the original albums with B-sides from the period (a big plus in themselves) though the various single remixes are overlooked here. On offer in this set are *Berserker*, *The Fury*, *Strange Charm*, *Machine and Soul*, and *Sacrifice*, the last finding Numan in a monumentally black mood. There is a definite and severe stylistic shift between *Strange Charm* and *Machine and Soul*, resulting from Numan's three-album stint with the I.R.S. label and his move to a full home-based studio. Demonstrated very well during the course of this set, and reinforced by the booklet notes (which draw from Numan's autobiography, *Praying to the Aliens*), is a single notion: that Numan committed one of the cardinal sins of the music business—falling prey to panic as market trends swept new batches of short-term frontrunners past him, and subsequently setting out to chase the market as best he could, rather than capitalizing on everything he had. *—Steven McDonald*

● **Premier Hits** / Mar. 25, 1997 / Beggars Banquet ♦♦♦♦♦
In the U.S., Gary Numan is remembered as a one-hit-wonder, while back home in his native England, he continued to crank out hit after hit and became a superstar in the process. His icy space-age persona and sound may be forever associated with early-80's British new wave (Flock of Seagulls, early Duran Duran, etc.), but he was the originator, and today seems pretty darned original. Numan was a scholar of the David Bowie *Ziggy Stardust*-era, and used Bowie's space alien approach as a starting point. While retaining his futuristic lyrics, Gary stripped *Ziggy's* sound free of the distorted guitar riffing and posturing, and replaced it with clinical synthesizers and a standoffish stage persona. His music also gives off a paranoid vibe at times, as evidenced on the hits "I Die: You Die" and "Are 'Friends' Electric?" But Numan's songs can also sedate you ("Down in the Park"), while other times sneak up on you (the unexpected punk rocker "Bombers"). And of course there's his sole U.S. hit, "Cars," which sounds like a not so distant ancestor to fellow futuristic weirdos Devo. *—Greg Prato*

Remodulate: The Numa Chronicles / Aug. 4, 1998 / Cleopatra ♦♦♦♦
Remodulate: The Numa Chronicles is a two-CD retrospective covering Gary Numan's output for his own Numa label from 1984-1995; however, fans looking for a concise overview of that period should be warned that the second CD consists of live material from throughout Numan's career. Also, some fans will appreciate the fact that some singles on the first disc are included in their extended versions, while others might find that they detract from the overall playability. [Note: the vinyl release of *Remodulate* contains two bonus tracks.] *—Steve Huey*

N.W.A.

f. 1986, **db.** 1991
West Coast Rap, Hardcore Rap, Gangsta Rap, Golden Age
N.W.A., the unapologetically violent and sexist pioneers of gangsta rap, is in many ways the most notorious group in the history of rap. Emerging in the late '80s, when Public Enemy had rewritten the rules of hardcore rap by proving that it could be intelligent, revolutionary, and socially aware, N.W.A. capitalized on PE's sonic breakthroughs while ignoring their message. Instead, the five-piece crew celebrated the violence and hedonism of the criminal life, capturing it all in blunt, harsh language. Initially, the group's relentless attack appeared to be serious, vital commentary, and it even provoked the FBI to caution N.W.A.'s record company, but following Ice Cube's departure late 1989, the group began to turn to self-parody. With his high-pitched whine, Eazy-E's urban nightmares now seemed like comic book fantasies, but ones that fulfilled the fantasies of the teenage, white suburbanites that had become their core audience, and the group became more popular than ever. Nevertheless, clashing egos prevented the band from recording a third album, and they fell apart once producer Dr. Dre left for a solo career in 1992. Although the group was no longer active, their influence—from their funky, bass-driven beats to their exaggerated lyrics—was evident throughout the '90s. *—Stephen Thomas Erlewine*

N.W.A. and the Posse / 1987 / Ruthless/Priority ♦♦

★ **Straight Outta Compton** / 1988 / Ruthless/Priority ♦♦♦♦♦
Straight Outta Compton wasn't quite the first gangsta rap album, but it was the first one to find a popular audience, and its sensibility virtually defined the genre from its 1988 release on. It established gangsta rap—and, moreover, West Coast rap in general—as a commercial force, going platinum with no airplay and crossing over with shock-hungry white teenagers. Unlike Ice-T, there's little social criticism or reflection on the gangsta lifestyle;

most of the record is about raising hell—harassing women, driving drunk, shooting it out with cops and partygoers. All of that directionless rebellion and rage produces some of the most frightening, visceral moments in all of rap, especially the amazing opening trio of songs, which threaten to dwarf everything that follows. Given the album's sheer force, the production is surprisingly spare, even a little low-budget—mostly DJ scratches and a drum machine, plus a few sampled horn blasts and bits of funk guitar. Although they were as much a reaction against pop-friendly rap, *Straight Outta Compton*'s insistent claims of reality ring a little hollow today, since it hardly ever depicts consequences. But despite all the romanticized invincibility, the force and detail of Ice Cube's writing makes the exaggerations resonate. Although Cube wrote some of his bandmates' raps, including nearly all of Eazy-E's, each member has a distinct delivery and character, and the energy of their individual personalities puts their generic imitators to shame. But although *Straight Outta Compton* has its own share of posturing, it still sounds refreshingly uncalculated because of its irreverent, gonzo sense of humor, still unfortunately rare in hardcore rap. There are several undistinguished misfires during the second half, but they aren't nearly enough to detract from the overall magnitude. It's impossible to overstate the enduring impact of *Straight Outta Compton*; as polarizing as its outlook may be, it remains an essential landmark, one of hip-hop's all-time greatest. *—Steve Huey*

100 Miles and Runnin' / Aug. 1990 / Ruthless/Priority ✦✦✦
Released almost two years after the seminal *Straight Outta Compton* and a little less than a year before the flawed *Niggaz4life*, *100 Miles and Runnin'* effectively accomplishes what an EP should. It both built upon the lingering hype that had surrounded *Straight Outta Compton*-era N.W.A. and foreshadowed the *Niggaz4life*-era N.W.A., a group that had grown increasingly dissident, yet also much wiser after experiencing seemingly endless controversy. This EP's title track remains one of their best moments—if not their best—and with the accompanying video picturing them fleeing from police, it was a fitting song for them to release at the time; furthermore, the song's thick, heavy production showcases rather brilliantly the fact that Dr. Dre had furthered his production talents immensely. Though hard to stomach, "Just Don't Bite It" is anything but forgettable as well, with Eazy-E and MC Ren's prerogatives transcending farce into much more potent territory, making this their most amusing (in a perverse juvenile sense) yet also their most effectively disturbing venture into misogynistic/pornographic rap. As great as *Straight Outta Compton* was, Dre's beats were still a bit primitive there, and Eazy-E was nowhere near the rapper he is here; furthermore, while *Niggaz4life* finds the group at their most realized, that album's tone often proves far too distasteful. Succinct yet poignant with a heavy use of cinematic skits, this EP showcases N.W.A.'s keys to success flawlessly, making it their most perfect release, balancing their strengths perfectly across five songs, each representing different aspects of the group's tainted ideology. *—Jason Birchmeier*

Niggaz4life / May 30, 1991 / Ruthless/Priority ✦✦✦✦
It couldn't have been easy for N.W.A. to follow up *Straight Outta Compton*, a undoubtedly landmark moment in rap history. So after three years of enormous controversy, inner strife, and anticipation, it wasn't exactly a surprise when the group's follow-up, *Niggaz4life*, found N.W.A. a much different group. They weren't out to rouse people anymore à la "Fuck the Police"; they were out to literally shock! By, for the most part, devoting the first half of this album to minority-orientated aggressive revelation and the second half to merciless misogyny, N.W.A. succeeded in making a truly disturbing if not horrifying album. Unfortunately, in their effort to create what stands as one of the most malicious albums ever, the group eclipsed their talent. For instance, some of Dre's most ominous productions ever lie buried beneath near-inaccessible lyrics; only the most carefree individuals will be able to wade through songs such as "To Kill a Hooker" to hear them. Occasionally, such as in "Automobile" or "I'd Rather Fuck You," Eazy-E does manage to at least integrate some ill-advised humor, but, for the most part, there's just no excuse for this album's blatantly irresponsible lyrics. In the end, N.W.A. dilutes their talent with sharp and thick profanity, exemplifying just how distraught they were with each other and with the world and why their collaborations would quickly come to an end. They had taken their music as far as it could go with this album—too far for it's own good, in fact. *—Jason Birchmeier*

Greatest Hits / Jul. 1996 / Ruthless/Priority ✦✦✦✦✦
N.W.A.'s career isn't necessarily one that lends itself well to anthologies. Though they had important singles, especially in the underground hip-hop community in the late '80s, they never received any support from radio or MTV, which meant they never had any official "hits." Instead, their albums were more important, popular and influential than singles, even if individual tracks—"Fuck tha Police," "Straight Outta Compton," "Gangsta Gangsta," "Express Yourself"—became the focus of attention. And, if you notice, all those songs were from *Straight Outta Compton*, the only good album the group ever made. *Greatest Hits* does include all of the high points from that album (the title track is present in a previously unavailable remix), plus a scatter-shot sampling of raw early singles and the highlights from *100 Miles & Runnin'* and *Niggaz4Life*. It's nice to have the good tracks isolated from the group's latter-day efforts, but *Greatest Hits* is unnecessary—all you need is *Straight Outta Compton*. *—Stephen Thomas Erlewine*

The NWA Legacy, Vol. 1: 1988-1998 / Mar. 22, 1999 / Ruthless/Priority ✦✦✦✦

Laura Nyro

b. Oct. 18, 1947, New York, NY (The Bronx), d. Apr. 9, 1997
Vocals, Piano, Guitar / Singer/Songwriter, Pop
Laura Nyro was one of pop music's true originals: a brilliant and innovative composer, her songs found greater commercial success in the hands of other performers, but her own records—intricate, haunting works highlighting her singularly powerful vocal phrasing, evocative lyrics, and alchemical fusion of gospel, soul, folk, and jazz structures—

remain her definitive artistic legacy. Her first LP, 1966's *More Than a New Discovery*, was commercially unsuccessful though it proved a treasure trove of material for artists like the Fifth Dimension, Barbra Streisand, and Blood, Sweat & Tears. After an appearance at 1967's Monterey Pop Festival, Nyro gained a fan in David Geffen, who became her manager. He also won Nyro a contract with Columbia, and in 1968 she returned with the extraordinary *Eli and the Thirteenth Confession*, which earned vast critical acclaim. At the age of 24 however, Nyro announced her retirement; she married and severed her industry connections. However, the marriage ended in divorce, and in 1975 she resurfaced with *Smile*. However, the long layoff derailed whatever chart momentum her music had accrued, and after the dismal sales of 1978's *Nested*, she again retreated from the music business. When Nyro finally returned from her self-imposed exile in 1984 with *Mother's Spiritual*, her music had grown more reserved and introspective. *Walk the Dog and Light the Light*, her first collection of new material in nearly a decade, followed in 1993. Nyro died of ovarian cancer in 1997. *—Jason Ankeny*

More Than a New Discovery / 1966 / Verve/Forecast ✦✦✦
A collection given over to the more conventional, if high-quality, early Nyro songs that later became hits (and standards) in the hands of other performers. The album includes "Wedding Bell Blues," "Stoney End," and "And When I Die." [Also released under the title *The First Songs* and reissued on Columbia Records in 1973.] *—William Ruhlmann*

● **Eli and the Thirteenth Confession** / 1968 / Columbia ✦✦✦✦✦
The hits (for others) keep coming—"Sweet Blindness," "Eli's Comin'," and "Stoned Soul Picnic" are all here, sung by their author—but Nyro not only proves herself a powerful singer in her own right, comfortable in styles from jazz to gospel/R&B to stark balladry, she also begins to turn to a more introspective, personal writing and singing which no one will be able to replicate. *—William Ruhlmann*

New York Tendaberry / 1969 / Columbia ✦✦✦✦✦
A stunning musical journey through love, loss, religion, and eroticism, by turns passionate, inspired, and suicidal, this is Nyro's most accomplished, most idiosyncratic record, and one of the greatest singer/songwriter works ever made. Using a wide vocal range and her often delicate piano work with deftly added instrumental touches, Nyro creates an aural landscape that spans the extremes of human emotion. It's not listed as her "pick" album only because it's not the place to start; rather, it's the logical conclusion of her musical development. *—William Ruhlmann*

Gonna Take a Miracle / 1971 / Columbia ✦✦✦✦✦
A joyous change of pace, this album presents inspired readings of pop/R&B hits of the '60s, songs like "Jimmy Mack" and "Nowhere to Run," produced by creamy-smooth soul producers Gamble & Huff and sung rapturously by Nyro, with gorgeous backing by Patti LaBelle, Sarah Dash, and Nona Hendryx. *—William Ruhlmann*

The First Songs / 1973 / Columbia ✦✦✦
Columbia Records acquired Laura Nyro's 1967 debut album from Verve Forecast and reissued it in 1973, by which time such songs as "Wedding Bell Blues," "Stoney End," and "And When I Die" had become enormously successful copyrights for Nyro. *—William Ruhlmann*

Smile / 1976 / Columbia ✦✦✦
This warm comeback album is Laura Nyro's *Double Fantasy*, a return to action by a mature artist, who retains her emotional power but has worked through her problems and beaten back her demons to emerge as a "Sexy Mama." *—William Ruhlmann*

Season of Lights . . . Laura Nyro in Concert / 1977 / Columbia ✦✦

Nested / 1978 / Columbia ✦✦✦✦
A typically strong outing but short of the best by this intelligent, provocative, intensely personal singer/songwriter. As the title implies, she seems more relaxed than on earlier albums. On "Rhythm and Blues," she almost sounds like she's having fun, not one of her trademarks. Nyro wrote all the songs as usual, added organ and guitar to her familiar piano playing, and also co-produced the album. John Sebastian and Felix Cavaliere add coloring to the sound provided by crack studio vets, including guitarist John Tropea. *—Mark Allan*

Mother's Spiritual / 1984 / Columbia ✦✦

Live at the Bottom Line / 1990 / A&M ✦✦✦

Walk the Dog & Light the Light (Run the Dog Darling Light Delight) / Aug. 17, 1993 / Columbia ✦✦✦✦

Stoned Soul Picnic: The Best of Laura Nyro / Feb. 18, 1997 / Columbia/Legacy ✦✦✦✦✦
A double-CD, career-spanning retrospective that offers little in the way of surprises: it's a tastefully selected overview of her career highlights, heaviest (and justifiably so) on her late '60s albums. There's the inevitable feeling of letdown as disc two progresses; her post-early '70s material is far less interesting than her earliest work, even if it's inoffensive. All of the first five albums (through 1971's *Gonna Take a Miracle*) are now on CD, so this is most suitable for the fan who isn't passionate enough to be a completist. Includes a couple of previously unreleased live tracks from the 1990s; the version of "Sweet Blindness," unfortunately, is not the original late-'60s recording, but from a late-'70s live album. *—Richie Unterberger*

● **Time and Love: The Essential Masters** / Oct. 10, 2000 / Columbia/Legacy ✦✦✦✦✦
As a 16-song, single-disc best-of, this does the job very nicely for those who want Nyro's best and most famous songs in one place. Only nine tracks into the CD you've already heard "Sweet Blindness," "Wedding Bell Blues," "And When I Die," "Blowin' Away," "Eli's Comin'," "Stoney End," and "Stoned Soul Picnic," which should be enough to convince anyone that Nyro was a major singer/songwriter. An argument could be made that, as an album-oriented performer whose career spanned about three decades, this is too brief a sampling of her discography, and too lopsided, as just one of the songs was recorded after

1970 (at which point she had yet to reach her 25th birthday). Still, the hard facts are that Nyro's best recordings and compositions were those from the beginning of her career. If you want greater breadth, there's the two-CD *Stoned Soul Picnic: The Best of Laura Nyro* compilation. But if a best-of's all you want, you don't lose much by springing for *Time and Love* instead, as disc two of *Stoned Soul Picnic* really isn't that good. Another good reason to consider this the first choice: *Time and Love* uses the original 1968 studio version of "Sweet Blindness" (a 1976 live rendition was used on *Stoned Soul Picnic*). —*Richie Unterberger*

Angel in the Dark / Mar. 6, 2001 / Rounder ♦♦♦♦
Angel in the Dark is a lovely recording featuring the graceful vocals and finely crafted songs that everyone expects from Laura Nyro. These sessions were completed in the summer of 1995 and represent the last music Nyro recorded. The title cut and "Sweet Dream Fade" mine the same soul terrain as her late '60s recordings, featuring horns and under-lined by heavy guitar riffs. These upbeat pieces perfectly integrate voice, arrangements, and lyrics to create an organic whole, and are two of the best cuts on the album. Slower, piano-based songs like "Triple Goddess Twilight," "He Was Too Good to Me," and "Serious Playground" are mixed in between these songs. These pieces are quieter and intro-spective, with Nyro's voice more intimate. It is almost as though she was sitting at the pi-ano, late at night, and singing to herself. There are also several covers including "Will You Still Love Me Tomorrow" and "Let It Be Me." The first of these is over five minutes and has been slowed down so much that it drags. In fact, she slows down all of the covers as if to convert them into heartfelt ballads. This works best on "Ooh Baby, Baby," partly be-cause the arrangement is fuller and more dynamic. One other standout is the upbeat "Gardenia Talk," filled with lively percussion and a sensual vocal. *Angel in the Dark* is a fine coda, perfect for late-night listening, and a perfect companion to Nyro's other record-ings. —*Ronnie Lankford, Jr.*

Oasis

f. 1993, Manchester, England
British Trad Rock, Britpop, Pop/Rock, Alternative Pop/Rock, Hard Rock

Oasis shot from obscurity to stardom in 1994, becoming one of Britain's most popular and critically acclaimed bands of the decade; along with Blur and Suede, they are responsible for returning British guitar-pop to the top of the charts. Led by guitarist/songwriter Noel Gallagher and his vocalist brother Liam, the Manchester quintet adopts the rough, thuggish image of the Stones and the Who, crosses it with Beatlesque melodies and hooks, distinctly British lyrical themes and song structures like the Jam and the Kinks, and ties it all together with a massive, loud guitar roar, as well as a defiant sneer that draws equally from the Sex Pistols' rebelliousness and the Stone Roses' cocksure arrogance. Gallagher's songs frequently rework previous hits from T. Rex ("Cigarettes and Alcohol" borrows the riff from "Bang a Gong") to Wham! ("Fade Away" takes the melody from "Freedom"), yet the group always puts the hooks in different settings, updating past hits for a new era. —*Stephen Thomas Erlewine*

● **Definitely Maybe** / Aug. 1994 / Epic ♦♦♦♦

Definitely Maybe manages to encapsulate much of the best of British rock & roll—from the Beatles to the Stone Roses—in the space of 11 songs. Their sound is louder and more guitar-oriented than any British band since the Sex Pistols, and the band are blessed with the excellent songwriting of Noel Gallagher. Gallagher writes perfect pop songs, offering a platform for his brother Liam's brash, snarling vocals. Not only does the band have melodies, but they have the capability to work a groove with more dexterity than most post-punk groups. But what makes *Definitely Maybe* so intoxicating is that it already resembles a greatest-hits album. From the swirling rush of "Rock & Roll Star," through the sinewy "Shakermaker," to the heartbreaking "Live Forever," each song sounds like an instant classic. —*Stephen Thomas Erlewine*

(What's the Story) Morning Glory? / Oct. 3, 1995 / Epic ♦♦♦♦♦

If *Definitely Maybe* was an unintentional concept album about wanting to be a rock & roll star, *(What's the Story) Morning Glory?* is what happens after the dreams come true. Oasis turns in a relatively introspective second record, filled with big, gorgeous ballads instead of ripping rockers. Unlike *Definitely Maybe*, the production on *Morning Glory* is varied enough to handle the range in emotions; instead of drowning everything with amplifiers turned up to 12, there are strings, keyboards, and harmonicas. This expanded production helps give Noel Gallagher's sweeping melodies an emotional resonance that he occasionally can't convey lyrically. However, that is far from a fatal flaw; Gallagher's lyrics work best in fragments, where the images catch in your mind and grow, thanks to the music. Gallagher may be guilty of some borrowing, or even plagiarism, but he uses the familiar riffs as building blocks. This is where his genius lies: He's a thief and doesn't have many original thoughts, but as a pop/rock melodicist he's pretty much without peer. Likewise, as musicians, Oasis are hardly innovators, yet they have a majestic grandeur in their sound that makes ballads like "Wonderwall" or rockers like "Some Might Say" positively transcendent. Alan White does add authority to the rhythm section, but the most noticeable change is in Liam Gallagher. His voice sneered throughout *Definitely Maybe*, but on *Morning Glory* his singing has become more textured and skillful. He gives the lyric in the raging title track a hint of regret, is sympathetic on "Wonderwall," defiant on "Some Might Say," and humorous on "She's Electric," a bawdy rewrite of "Digsy's Diner." It might not have the immediate impact of *Definitely Maybe*, but *Morning Glory* is just as exciting and compulsively listenable. —*Stephen Thomas Erlewine*

Be Here Now / Aug. 26, 1997 / Epic ♦♦♦♦

Arriving with the force of a hurricane, Oasis' third album, *Be Here Now*, is a bright, bold, colorful tour de force that simply steamrolls over any criticism. The key to Oasis' sound is its inevitability—they are unwavering in their confidence, which means that even the hardest rockers are slow, steady, and heavy, not fast. And that self-possessed confidence, that belief in their greatness, makes *Be Here Now* intensely enjoyable, even though it offers no real songwriting breakthroughs. Noel Gallagher remains a remarkably talented synthesist, bringing together disparate strands—"D'You Know What I Mean" has an N.W.A. drum loop, a Zeppelinesque wall of guitars, electronica gurgles, and lyrical allusions to the Beatles and Dylan—to create impossibly catchy songs that sound fresh, no matter how many older songs he references. He may be working familiar territory throughout *Be Here Now*, but it doesn't matter because the craftsmanship is good. "The Girl In the Dirty Shirt" is irresistible pop, and epics like "Magic Pie" and "All Around the World" simply soar, while the rockers "My Big Mouth," "It's Getting Better (Man!!!)" and "Be Here Now" attack with a bone-crunching force. Noel is smart enough to balance his classicist tendencies with spacious, open production, filling the album with found sounds, layers of guitars, keyboards and strings, giving the record its humungous, immediate feel. The sprawling sound and huge melodic hooks would be enough to make *Be Here Now* a

winner, but Liam Gallagher's vocals give the album emotional resonance. Singing better than ever, Liam injects venom into the rockers, but he also delivers the nakedly emotional lyrics of "Don't Go Away" with affecting vulnerability. That combination of violence and sensitivity gives Oasis an emotional core, and makes *Be Here Now* a triumphant album. —*Stephen Thomas Erlewine*

The Masterplan / Nov. 3, 1998 / Epic ♦♦♦♦♦

For American audiences, the phenomenal worldwide success of Oasis was a little puzzling. That's because they only had part of the picture—unless they were hardcore fans, they didn't hear nearly three albums of material released on B-sides and non-LP singles. Critics and fans alike claimed that the best of these B-sides were as strong as the best moments on the albums, and they were right. None of the albums had a song that rocked as hard as "Fade Away" (cleverly built on a stolen melody from Wham's "Freedom"), "Headshrinker" or "Acquiesce." There was nothing as charming as the lite psychedelic pastiche "Underneath the Sky" or the Bacharach tribute "Going Nowhere"; there was nothing as affecting as Noel Gallagher's acoustic plea "Talk Tonight" or the minor-key, McCartneyesque "Rockin' Chair," nothing as epic as "The Masterplan." Most bands wouldn't throw songs of this caliber away on B-sides, but Noel Gallagher followed the example of his heroes the Jam and the Smiths, who released singles where the B-sides rivaled the A-sides. This meant many American fans missed these songs, so to remedy this situation, Oasis released the B-sides compilation *The Masterplan*. Oasis unfortunately chose to opt for a single disc of highlights instead of a complete double-disc set, which means a wealth of great songs—"Take Me Away," "Whatever," "D'Yer Wanna Be a Spaceman?," "Round Are Way," "It's Better People," "Step Out," a raging cover of "Cum on Feel the Noize"—are missing. But *The Masterplan* winds up quite enjoyable anyway. Apart from the sludgy instrumental "The Swamp Song," there isn't a weak track here, and the brilliant moments are essential not only for Oasis fans, but any casual follower of Britpop or post-grunge rock & roll. —*Stephen Thomas Erlewine*

Standing on the Shoulder of Giants / Feb. 29, 2000 / Epic ♦♦♦

Since Noel Gallagher plays most of the parts on the album, *Standing on the Shoulder of Giants* isn't really the debut of the new, post-Guigsy/Bonehead lineup, but it is clearly the beginning of a new Oasis, Mark II. Such a grandiose statement may imply that it's a clear break from Oasis' past, yet that's hardly the case, since many signatures are still in place—strummed acoustic guitars, big hooks, undeveloped lyrics, familiar rhymes, and a gigantic wall of sound. The arrangements are every bit as detailed as *Be Here Now*, but they're clearer and better focused, since Oasis' brains weren't clouded with excess and hubris. Ironically, this is also their most overtly druggy, psychedelic release to date—Gallagher and Mark "Spike" Stent spent endless hours adding mellotrons, swirling guitars, and vague dance floor ideas borrowed from the Chemical Brothers and the Charlatans UK, while Noel's melodies invariably follow the minor-key patterns typical of '60s psychedelic pop. Yet for all of its heavy psychedelic influence, *Standing on the Shoulder of Giants* is really a self-consciously mature departure from the group's usual ebullience, a deliberately mellow, midtempo album spiked with hints of big beat and electronica to prove that they're with it. This may result in the most cohesive Oasis record since *Definitely Maybe*, but that cohesion has come at a price. Few songs are as bracing as Noel's best work from the first three albums; not even the rockers have the giddy rush or alluring sparkle of classic Oasis. Yes, this flows well, but it's the work of a self-consciously older band and it's hard not to miss the hard rock, pure attitude, and gigantic hooks that made the group's reputation in the first place. —*Stephen Thomas Erlewine*

Familiar to Millions / Nov. 21, 2000 / Epic ♦♦♦

It's stunning just how quickly Oasis lost the plot. Sure, they always indulged themselves, but that was part of their charm, yet all their excess and hubris led to the ugly implosion on the Be Here Now tour. Once they lost momentum, it was inevitable that the group would start to splinter, with Bonehead and Guigsy leaving for saner territory prior to the release of their fourth album. Now, the Gallaghers ruled the roost by themselves and, like any insecure megalomaniacs, they surrounded themselves with average musicians—musicians that were technically better than the Mancunian mooks they replaced, but had less character. And that may be the reason why the double-live *Familiar to Millions*, documenting Oasis' Wembley Stadium show in the summer of 2000, is satisfying without being transcendent, the way they were at their 1995/96 peak—it finds the group just after they firmly entrenched themselves as professionals. Well, almost all of them. God bless Liam, who remains unbelievably obnoxious, slurring and swearing incomprehensibly, picking fights with audiences, exhorting the gals to get their tits out, and, above all, singing like a bastard. He does his best to keep the music alive, trying to make it something more than solid hard rock. Occasionally, he pulls it off, but he's constrained by the dogged professionalism of the others, plus the group's insistence on playing the 2000 set list, from the off-stage intro of "Fucking in the Bushes" to the encore covers. Yeah, it's pretty good but it ain't great, either. It's fun, but it's cheap fun—and, at their best, Oasis gave great fun. —*Stephen Thomas Erlewine*

Ocean Colour Scene

f. 1989

British Trad Rock, Britpop, Alternative Pop/Rock

Falling between the energetic pop/rock of mod revival and the psychedelic experimentations of Traffic, Ocean Colour Scene came to be one of the leading bands of the traditionalist, post-Oasis British rock of the mid-'90s. Although they had formed in the late '80s and had several hits during the height of "Madchester" in the early '90s, the band didn't earn a large following until 1996, when their second album *Moseley Shoals* became a multi-platinum success story in the UK. Their ascent was greatly aided by Paul Weller and Oasis' Noel Gallagher, who both publicly praised Ocean Colour Scene for keeping the flame of real rock & roll burning during the '90s. And, according to one specific definition, they were right, since Ocean Colour Scene was nothing if not rock & roll traditionalists, drawing heavily from British Invasion pop, psychedelia, soul, R&B and blues-rock to create a reverential homage to classic rock. Their devotion to trad-rock may have earned them decidedly mixed-reviews, but that was the very thing that earned them a sizable following. —*Stephen Thomas Erlewine*

Ocean Colour Scene / Sep. 8, 1992 / Fontana ✦✦✦

Ocean Colour Scene's eponymous debut album suffered from botched production that smoothed all the edges out of the group's fusion of classic rock, R&B and Madchester grooves. Occasionally, the band's personality peeks through the polished sound, such as on the terrific single "Sway," but the record is stifled by radio-friendly production, which prevents the group from stretching out musically, as well as wildly inconsistent songwriting. —*Stephen Thomas Erlewine*

● **Moseley Shoals** / Apr. 1996 / MCA ✦✦✦✦✦

By the time Ocean Colour Scene released their debut album in 1992, they were already considered has-beens. The band had formed during the height of Madchester, but they never released their first album until the scene was already dead, which left them without a following. But between their debut and their second album, 1996's *Moseley Shoals,* a strange thing happened—the band was taken under the wings of two of Britain's biggest pop stars, Paul Weller and Noel Gallagher. The band suddenly catapulted back into the spotlight because of their superstar connections, but the music actually deserved the attention. Ocean Colour Scene had spent the time between their two albums improving their sound. On *Moseley Shoals,* they are looser, funkier, and have a strong, organic R&B vibe that was inherited from the Small Faces and Weller's solo recordings. They sprinkle Beatlesque and Stonesy flourishes throughout the album, as well as the odd prog-rock flair, adding an even more eclectic flavor to their traditionalist pop/rock. Ocean Colour Scene is still developing their songwriting skills—the sound is more impressive than the songs throughout *Moseley Shoals*—but their second album is an unexpectedly enjoyable record. —*Stephen Thomas Erlewine*

B-Sides: Seaside & Freerides / Mar. 1997 / MCA ✦✦✦✦

Rounding up all the B-sides, demos and rarities Ocean Colour Scene released over the course of 1996, when the band was riding the crest of their popularity, *B-Sides: Seaside & Freerides,* for all its inconsistency, illustrates the depth of their ambition, as well as their flaws. Primarily comprised of acoustic material, including a demo of "The Circle" and a fine, stripped-down version of "The Day We Caught the Train," the 16 tracks on *B-Sides* can tend to sound a little samey, but when the group branches out to the neo-prog-rock of the very English "Huckleberry Grove" or to the funky instrumental "Chicken Bones and Stones," they sound better than ever, and a couple of early songs by the pre-Ocean Colour Scene band the Fanatics are interesting. Still, about half of the songs suggest that OCS may be a little too reverent in their appreciation for late-'60s rock, since they come across as only stylistic exercise, not full songs. And their live cover of "Day Tripper," featuring Noel Gallagher on guitar and Liam Gallagher on vocals, is an embarrassment, simply because Liam's restrained vocals slay Simon Fowler's bellowing. But this is an isolated moment on *B-Sides: Seaside & Freerides,* since it contains enough first-rate material to make it necessary for dedicated fans. —*Stephen Thomas Erlewine*

Marchin' Already / Sep. 1997 / MCA ✦✦✦✦✦

Ocean Colour Scene reinvented themselves as trad rock journeymen with their second album, *Moseley Shoals,* a record indebted to late-'60s blues-rock, mod pop, psychedelia, and prog rock. Surprisingly, the album became a blockbuster in the U.K., so it isn't entirely surprising that its successor, *Marchin' Already,* is essentially *Moseley Shoals, Pt. 2* with a bigger budget. Despite a few production flourishes—heavily panned, distorted psychedelic guitars, trombone solos, and two P.P. Arnold backing vocals—Ocean Colour Scene doesn't sound at all different on *Marchin' Already,* and their songwriting shows no noticeable improvement. But the album isn't a retreat; it's a continuation of everything that made *Moseley Shoals* such an entertaining record, and it's nearly as good as its predecessor. *Marchin' Already* is equally balanced between soulful stompers ("Travellers Tune"), rockers ("Hundred Mile High City"), and prog-inflected ballads ("Better Day," "Besides Yourself"), all delivered with almost too much passion. But the key to Ocean Colour Scene is that they are fervently committed to trad rock, which means they pour themselves into predictable songs that turn out to be quite satisfying, even if they are guilty pleasures. And if that's the case, *Marchin' Already* is a great guilty pleasure. —*Stephen Thomas Erlewine*

One From the Modern / Sep. 13, 1999 / Island ✦✦✦✦

Mechanical Wonder / May 1, 2001 / Ark 21 ✦✦✦

It's sort of fitting that the first album Ocean Colour Scene released in the U.S. since their breakthrough and masterpiece *Moseley Shoals* was 2001's *Mechanical Wonder,* their

weakest since *Moseley Shoals.* It's not that the record is a failure, since it hardly is. It's just—kind of predictable, really, offering no new spin or variation on OCS's patented blend of mod, early Humble Pie and latter-day Paul Weller. That's not entirely a bad thing, since Ocean Colour Scene does this sound not just better than their peers (admittedly, in 2001, there weren't that many bands attempting this sound anymore; it's a long way from 1996), but holds its own with the bands they pattern themselves after. The problem is that the songwriting has gotten a little mannered, a little undistinguished, and the performances, while sturdy, tend to be slightly flat. This wouldn't be noticeable if everything on the record was at the same level, since it would then seem to be just a solid, mildly satisfying album by a sturdy group. It's that the band can still hit it out of the ballpark, no more notably than on the opener "Up on the Downside," a swirling, sexy song that is easily one of their greatest songs. There are other moments that click—the rampaging "Can't Get Back to the Baseline" or the mildly insistent shuffle of "Give Me a Letter"—but the first song is so good, it overshadows the rest of the record, which is simply good, average OSC. But, *One From the Modern* explored more territory with better songwriting, and that disappointment is compounded by that lone great single "Up on the Downside," which illustrates that they can still deliver songs as enthralling as "One Hundred Mile City." —*Stephen Thomas Erlewine*

Billy Ocean

b. Jan. 21, 1950, Trinidad, West Indies

Vocals / Quiet Storm, Adult Contemporary, Urban, Dance-Pop

Born in Trinidad, Billy Ocean emigrated to the U.K. as a child. He worked as a tailor while pursuing music on the side in the '60s, then broke through with the Motown-flavored "Love Really Hurts without You," which hit number three in the U.K. in 1976. Ocean continued to have U.K. hits through the end of the '70s but didn't achieve mass success in the U.S. until 1984, when "Caribbean Queen (No More Love on the Run)" became a number one hit, the first of seven Top Ten hits over the next four years. —*William Ruhlmann*

Nights (Feel Like Getting Down) / 1981 / Epic ✦✦✦

Billy Ocean was on his way to superstardom with this album, his first big hit release on Epic. The title song was his first R&B Top 10 record, and he got another couple of chart singles before beginning his run of R&B and pop hits. It also demonstrated his equal ability doing exuberant uptempo dance tunes and convincing, if at times oversung and vapid, ballads. Epic was later left red-faced when an act they developed moved over to Jive/RCA and went platinum. —*Ron Wynn*

Inner Feelings / 1982 / Epic ✦✦

Suddenly / 1984 / Jive ✦✦✦✦

Billy Ocean vaulted into international stardom with this album in 1984. The album peaked at number nine, was on the charts for over a year and a half, and yielded three R&B hits that were all also pop smashes. Ocean would sing on the soundtrack for the film *The Jewel Of The Nile,* make sellout appearances around the world, and appear regularly on television and videos. At this point he was a bigger pop star than R&B artist, as two of his three hits did better as crossover vehicles than R&B tunes. —*Ron Wynn*

Love Zone / 1986 / Jive ✦✦✦✦

Billy Ocean was riding atop the charts when he issued this album in '86. The title track contained both a fine arrangement and Ocean's emphatic lead vocal, and was a huge hit. He topped the R&B charts twice that year with both "Love Zone" and "There'll Be Sad Songs (To Make You Cry)," each of which was also a huge pop smash, the latter topping the pop chart. This was arguably his finest album, and was certainly his most successful. —*Ron Wynn*

Tear Down These Walls / 1988 / Jive ✦✦✦

● **Greatest Hits** / Oct. 1989 / Jive ✦✦✦✦✦

Contains his cool '80s disco hits "Caribbean Queen" and "Get outta My Dreams, Get into My Car" and piano-based ballads like "There'll Be Sad Songs to Make You Cry." —*Bil Carpenter*

Phil Ochs

b. Dec. 19, 1940, El Paso, TX, d. Apr. 9, 1976, Far Rockaway, NY

Vocals, Guitar / Folk-Rock, Singer/Songwriter, Political Folk

Singer/songwriter Phil Ochs was a self-coined "singing journalist" when he began performing in New York in the early '60s. Like Bob Dylan, the rival who always outpaced him, Ochs made his reputation singing topical protest songs. He stayed with them much longer than Dylan (and indeed would never really abandon them), but eventually he too would follow Dylan into electric music and more personal, abstract, and romantic compositions. Ochs came off as a perennial second-best to critics during his heyday. It was only after his tragic tailspin and eventual death that he was properly appreciated as one of the most sincere and humane songwriters of his day, whether detailing political atrocities or more poetic concerns. More melodic than Dylan (if not as lyrically innovative), his music's strident accusations were tempered by a warm delivery and underlying compassion, addressing all manner of anti-war, civil rights, labor, and social justice issues. —*Richie Unterberger*

All the News That's Fit to Sing / 1964 / Hannibal ✦✦✦

Early on in his career, someone described Phil Ochs as a "singing journalist," and his first album, *All The News That's Fit To Sing,* represented the state of the art in topical songs in 1964. Which presents a bit of a problem when listening to it today; Ochs's debut is so much a product of its time and place that it just sounds perplexing a few decades on. Remember Lou Marsh? Or William Worthy? Well, if you don't (and I'll bet you have lots of company), the songs about them on this album may not mean much to you, and while the facts behind the Vietnam War, the Cuban Missile Crisis, and the Civil Rights Movement are doubtless clearer in your mind, that only gives them a perversely nostalgic quality that hardly becomes them. And past the issue of topicality, *All The News That's Fit To Sing* captures Phil Ochs when he was still young and a bit green; his vocals are sometimes hesitant, his material is often a bit obvious, and the spare two-guitar accompaniment (Danny Kalb plays the flashier licks) is a bit too generically folkie for its own good. But Ochs' remarkable talent is still apparent, despite the album's flaws; "One More Parade" and "Power and the Glory" are as striking now as the day they were written, "Too Many Martyrs" and "Celia" summon an emotional power that has outlived their topicality, and his adaptation of Edgar Allan Poe's "The Bells" proves his musical instincts were as keen as his lyrical ones. A flawed but engaging debut which points to the stronger work Ochs would soon put to wax. *—Mark Deming*

I Ain't Marching Anymore / 1965 / Hannibal ✦✦✦✦✦
What a difference a year made for Phil Ochs—his 1964 debut *All The News That's Fit To Sing* gained him a reputation as the most promising songwriter to come out of the Greenwich Village folk scene since Bob Dylan, and 1965's *I Ain't Marching Anymore* proved he was every bit as good as his press clippings said. Ochs had grown by leaps and bounds as a performer in the space between the two albums, and where Phil sometimes sounded a bit clumsy and uncertain on his first LP, here he brims with confidence, and his guitar work—simple but forceful and efficient—didn't require another musician's sweetening as it did on *All The News*. Most importantly, while Ochs' songwriting was uneven but compelling in his first collection, *I Ain't Marching Anymore* finds him in consistently strong form throughout. The craft and the emotional weight of the material makes even the most dated material ("Draft Dodger Rag" and "Here's To The State Of Mississippi") effective today, and a surprising number of the songs remain as potent (and sadly timely) today as in 1965, especially "Iron Maiden" and "That's What I Want To Hear." And if there are fewer jokes on this set, "Draft Dodger Rag" is funnier than anything on Phil's first album, and his cover of Ewan MacColl's "Ballad Of The Carpenter" (as well as his adaptation of Alfred Noyes' "The Highwayman") revealed what a strong interpretive performer he could be. (His liner notes are pretty good, too; it's a shame he didn't write more prose.) Literally dozens of singer/songwriters jumped on the protest bandwagon after the success of Bob Dylan and Joan Baez, but one would be hard pressed to name one who made an album that works as well almost four decades later as *I Ain't Marching Anymore*. *—Mark Deming*

Phil Ochs in Concert / 1966 / Elektra ✦✦✦✦✦
It's since been revealed that some or all of these tracks were not "in concert" at all, but recorded in the studio, with audience noise dubbed on afterwards. Nevertheless, this is Ochs' finest acoustic album. As a lyricist, he was moving from the singing journalist mode to more abstract symbolism, but still attacked U.S. imperialism, knock-kneed bleeding hearts, and even organized religion with an uncompromising sensitivity. Some haunting, wistful ballads transcended topical concerns entirely, including the beautiful love song "Changes" and "There But for Fortune" (a British hit for Joan Baez). *—Richie Unterberger*

★ **Pleasures of the Harbor** / 1967 / A&M ✦✦✦✦✦
Going into the studio after Dylan's move into rock accompaniment and *Sgt. Pepper*'s vast expansion of pop music, Ochs wanted to make a record that reflected all these trends, and he hired producer Larry Marks, arranger Ian Freebairn-Smith, and pianist Lincoln Mayorga—all of whom had classical backgrounds—to help him realize his vision. The result was *Pleasures of the Harbor*, his most musically varied and ambitious album, one routinely cited as his greatest accomplishment. Though the lyrics were usually not directly political, they continued to reflect his established points of view. His social criticisms here were complex, and they went largely unnoticed on a long album full of long songs, many of which did not support the literal interpretations they nevertheless received. The album was consistently imbued with images of mortality, and it all came together on the abstract, electronic-tinged final track, "The Crucifixion." Usually taken to be about John F. Kennedy, it concerns the emergence of a hero in a corrupt world and his inevitable downfall through betrayal. Ochs offers no satisfying resolution; the goals cannot be compromised, and they will not be fulfilled. It was anything but easy listening, but it was an effective conclusion to a brilliant album that anticipated the devastating and tragic turn of the late '60s, as well as its maker's own eventual decline and demise. *—William Ruhlmann*

Tape From California / Jul. 1968 / A&M ✦✦✦
On his fourth album, *Pleasures of the Harbor*, Phil Ochs broke from both his topical songwriting style and his acoustic folk music approach for an album of long, poetic songs set to elaborate, eclectic arrangements. For its follow-up, *Tape From California*, he combined his earlier and more recent styles, addressing such issues as war and union organizing along with more discursive efforts, and including a few more complicated arrangements mixed in with simple guitar accompaniments. There were some directly political efforts, but in the more poetic songs, Ochs seemed to be painting a portrait of a desperate, debased society and his own sense of personal decline. For example, the marathon "When in Rome" conflated images from slavery, the Nuremberg trials, and ancient Rome to compile a compendium of evil and decadence through the centuries, clearly implying that the present day was another such era. Ochs imbued his lyrics with his characteristic sense of irony, and the arrangements by producer Larry Marks, Bob Thompson, and Ian Freebairn-Smith complemented the songs wittily. But released in the middle of 1968, the most tumultuous year of the tumultuous '60s, *Tape from California* was often hard to listen to, because it was such a frighteningly accurate portrait of its times, eerily mirroring the point at which passionate argument over the direction of the country spilled over into violence and a widespread sense of absurdity. *—William Ruhlmann*

Rehearsals for Retirement / 1969 / A&M ✦✦✦
On *Rehearsals for Retirement*, Ochs retained his poetic sense, but his songs were imbued with the conflicts of the times. The leadoff track, "Pretty Smart on My Part," the hardest-rocking number Ochs had yet recorded, is sung in the persona of a violent right-wing extremist who fantasizes about running over hitchhikers, whipping women, and finally assassinating the president and taking over the government. Similarly, "I Kill Therefore I Am," a twangy rocker, is sung in the voice of a policeman who hates long-hairs, blacks, students, and homosexuals and plans to spray them with mace, beat them, and shoot them. Specifically combining the poetical with the political, the gentle waltz-time piano ballad "William Butler Yeats Visits Lincoln Park and Escapes Unscathed" is a haunting depiction of the confrontation between demonstrators and police in Chicago, quickly followed by a dancehall ditty that sends up its somber reflections without relieving the tragic tone. The result of the convention and the subsequent election of Richard Nixon as president represents, in the songwriter's judgment, the dawn of "Another Age," and a terrible one. That declaration is as positive as things get on *Rehearsals for Retirement*. For much of the album, Ochs expresses despair rather than anger. "My Life," another attractive piano ballad laced with strings, traces his personal disillusionment, while "The Scorpion Departs but Never Returns," actually a topical song about a nuclear submarine that sank in 1968, evokes familiar Ochs references to sailors, who, here, all drown. The plaintive "Doesn't Lenny Live Here Anymore" concerns the drug overdose death of comedian Lenny Bruce. In retrospect, especially because of Ochs' suicide seven years later, it is impossible not to see the evidence of the songwriter's personal anguish in *Rehearsals for Retirement*. *—William Ruhlmann*

Phil Ochs's Greatest Hits / 1970 / Edsel ✦✦✦
Not really his greatest hits (the title was intended as irony). This is his final, troubled studio album, and a good companion to *Gunfight at Carnegie Hall* *—Bruce Eder*

Gunfight at Carnegie Hall / 1975 / A&M ✦✦✦✦✦
On the cover of *Greatest Hits*, Phil Ochs had appeared in a gold lamé suit like the one Elvis Presley wore on the cover of the 1959 album *50,000,000 Elvis Fans Can't Be Wrong: Elvis' Gold Records, Vol. 2*. On the back cover was the legend, "50 Phil Ochs fans can't be wrong!" The suit and the *Greatest Hits* title were part of a concept Ochs, who had recently seen Presley perform in Las Vegas, was pursuing at the time. Always a student of popular culture, he harked back to the rebellious tone of 1950s rock & roll and wedded it to the revolutionary fervor of the late '60s—or at least that was the idea for *Gunfight at Carnegie Hall*. Beginning a tour the month that *Greatest Hits* was released, he wore the suit onstage and for the first time used a backing band, mixing his own new and old songs with medleys of songs associated with Presley and Buddy Holly, as well as a version of "Mona Lisa," and even Merle Haggard's recent anti-hippie anthem "Okie From Muskogee." His two Carnegie Hall shows on the nights of March 27th and 28th, 1970, were marred by various incidents recounted on the back cover of the album. *Gunfight at Carnegie Hall*, containing 46-and-a-half minutes of the reported three-hour second show, focuses on the singer's attempt to explain his concept to a skeptical audience, which he does with a certain cockeyed wit, if without complete success, at least in front of these listeners. Ochs lobbied long for A&M to release an album drawn from the embattled show, which the label belatedly did, but only briefly and in Canada. *Gunfight at Carnegie Hall* was eventually reissued as part of a Collector's Choice two-fer, paired with *Rehearsals for Retirement*. *—William Ruhlmann*

Chords of Fame / 1976 / A&M ✦✦✦✦✦
Compiled by noted music archivist Michael Ochs (who was also Phil Ochs' brother and manager), *Chords of Fame* is a peerless overview of Phil Ochs career in music, from his early days as a "singing journalist" penning topical numbers like "Draft Dodger Rag" and "I Ain't Marchin' Anymore" to the deeply personal introspection of his later work, as typified by "No More Songs" and "Jim Dean of Indiana." The first (and still one of the only) Phil Ochs compilations that covers material from his albums for both Elektra and A&M, *Chords of Fame* includes most of Ochs' best known songs (including "There But For Fortune" and "Outside of a Small Circle of Friends") as well as a handful of rare and otherwise unavailable cuts, such as an absorbing live take of "Crucifixion" and a version of "I Ain't Marchin' Anymore" recorded with an electric rock band. Featuring a superb liner essay by poet and musician Ed Sanders, *Chords of Fame* was an obvious labor of love released only a few months after Ochs' suicide in 1976; sadly, it's fallen out of print and has never been reissued on CD, but anyone interested in Phil Ochs who runs across it at a library or used record store is well advised to pick it up and introduce themselves to one of the finest songwriters of his generation. *—Mark Deming*

A Toast to Those Who Are Gone / 1987 / Rhino ✦✦✦
14 previously unreleased demos, all of excellent fidelity; while no dates or sources are given for these sessions, an educated guess would put them in his earliest, most topical period, circa 1964-65. Most of these feature just Phil and acoustic guitar, and sound as strong as the material officially released on his first Elektra LPs. The other, equally fine cuts seem to date from a later period, and show him delving into intensely personal, nonpolitical concerns. *—Richie Unterberger*

The War Is Over: The Best of Phil Ochs / 1988 / A&M ✦✦✦
This single disc compilation was never the "best of" that it claimed to be, and wasn't even a reasonably definitive representation of Ochs' music for very long (the *Vancouver* live album showed up two years later and took that honor away). Now, with the release of Rhino's triple-CD *Farewells & Fantasies* and the European A&M double disc *American Troubadour*, this disc's indifferent sound and huge holes in its song line-up render it useless even for the casual fan. Indeed, it may even be harmful to Ochs' reputation, missing pieces like "Crucifixion" (which is like leaving "Imagine" or "Mother" off of a John Lennon portrait). Save up your money if you have to, but go with the Rhino set or the A&M import, or both. *—Bruce Eder*

The Broadside Tapes 1 / 1989 / Smithsonian/Folkways ✦✦✦

Phil Ochs left behind dozens of demos, primarily songs that he put down on tape at the West 104th Street Manhattan offices of *Broadside* magazine. These aren't really "demos" in the sense of showcasing the songs for possible recording; he was recording these so that *Broadside's* editors could print the lyrics. Thus, there are choruses left out, and there's a lot of noise on some of them (these were done in what was essentially a newspaper office), all in the name of getting the words down, as Ochs strums his guitar and runs through the songs in a semi-formal fashion. The material is classic Ochs, earnest and topical, yet also weirdly funny and eclectic—doing songs not only dealing with racism and workers' rights, but also about blacklist victim John Henry Faulk and the then-current controversy surrounding a memorial to Alfred Packer, a mountain guide who was convicted of eating five people to survive in a blizzard. Some of the material is surprisingly lighthearted in its tone and execution, such as "Spaceman" and "Christine Keeler." Among the serious songs, "Remember Me" is one of the best pieces he ever wrote. The strangest moment here is Ochs' cover, in a duet with Eric Andersen, of the Beatles' song "I Should've Known Better," recorded in 1964 at New York's Village Gate. Like most other rock & roll bands of the time, the Beatles were anathema to the folk audience, and Ochs' willingness to do the song, even in a spirit of fun, is startling. Perhaps the most revealing performances here, however, are "The Passing of My Life" and "That's the Way It's Gonna Be," which betray feelings of deep melancholy that might have hinted at the self-destructive suicidal tendencies that ultimately ended Ochs' life. —*Bruce Eder*

There But for Fortune / 1989 / Elektra ✦✦✦✦✦

The best of his early sides, covering his first three albums, though weighted heavily toward the third, *Phil Ochs in Concert*, probably because it's the only one not reissued by Hannibal-Carthage. —*Bruce Eder & William Ruhlmann*

There and Now: Live in Vancouver / 1990 / Rhino ✦✦✦✦✦

This is the definitive Phil Ochs live album, found in a search of tape vaults 21 years after the fact. A "lost" 1968 concert, with poet Allen Ginsberg playing the bells on (you guessed it!) "The Bells," and featuring the best parts of his concert repertory, old and new, from "The Highwayman" through "William Butler Yeats Visits Lincoln Park And Escapes Unscathed," with stops along the way for "Outside of a Small Circle of Friends" and other underground calls-to-arms and reality checks. —*Bruce Eder*

Live at Newport / Mar. 12, 1996 / Vanguard ✦✦✦✦

A dozen songs from Ochs' performances at the 1963, 1964, and 1966 Newport Folk Festivals. Four of these cuts were previously available on the *Newport Broadside* and *Evening Concerts, Vol. 1* anthologies, but the rest were previously unreleased. While all of these songs are available on his studio albums, Ochs was in good form for these shows, so these are good supplementary versions. Especially noteworthy are the 1966 tracks; four of the five songs would appear in far more elaborately produced arrangements on his *Pleasures of the Harbor* and *Tape from California* albums. These solo acoustic performances are interesting contrasts, putting the voice and the lyrics at the forefront, in the best unplugged tradition.

Ochs' singing on "Cross My Heart" is painfully flat, but the sincerity of the words and their importance to him carry the performance. Additionally, the version of "Half A Century High" (sung as "Half A Century Wise") included here runs over seven minutes, and contains several verses that never made it into the official studio recording of this song. The differences point up the tragic side of Ochs' career, in that he sacrificed chunks of his message and his art, and one of his best and most personal songs, in pursuit of commercial success and stardom. —*Richie Unterberger & Bruce Eder*

Farewells & Fantasies / Aug. 19, 1997 / Rhino ✦✦✦✦✦

This 53-song triple-CD set is the most comprehensive collection of Ochs' career that anyone with the cash is likely to see. This set largely supplants Ochs' Elektra discs. The 21-song first disc, steeped in the defiant, leftist politics of the early '60s—sort of a political time capsule—sums up his early career as a singing activist/journalist, filled with a mixture of seething outrage and youthful optimism, and sparked by the more than occasional turn of phrase and inventive topical allusion. In addition to expected tracks like "I Ain't Marchin' Anymore," "The Bells," "The Power and the Glory," "Bound for Glory," and "The Highwayman" (from the Vancouver show), listeners get a pair of previously unreleased tracks, including "Morning," one of the very first songs Ochs wrote in New York. The second disc takes a more poetic turn and shows the first signs of maturation, as well the deepening despair and resignation that would ultimately destroy Ochs. Its 16 songs merge his later A&M material with the transitional songs present on his 1966 Elektra "live" album, along with a pair of 1964-vintage demos. And the third disc sums up Ochs in his most daring musical guise, holding audiences spellbound with live performances of "Crucifixion" and his other epic compositions; venturing successfully into art rock with "Pleasures of the Harbor;" parodying his own style as he satirizes the country's foibles in "Outside of a Small Circle of Friends;" performing obituaries to his life ("Chords of Fame") and its purpose ("No More Songs"); and generally challenging even those who thought they knew and understood him. The 98-page booklet is richly annotated and impressively illustrated, and the sound is uniformly excellent. —*Bruce Eder*

The Early Years / Jun. 20, 2000 / Vanguard ✦✦✦✦

This is actually an expanded version of the Vanguard CD *Live at Newport*, although it isn't billed as such. It includes all 13 songs from that album, prefacing them with seven studio tracks that Ochs did for the 1964 Vanguard compilation LP *The Original New Folks, Vol. 2.* Even if you think you own everything by Ochs, you'll need this if you're a completist, because only five of those Vanguard studio tracks actually made it onto *The Original New Folks, Vol. 2.* The other two, "How Long" and "Davey Moore," were recorded at the same sessions, but were previously unreleased. Although these seven studio cuts still find Ochs a ways from hitting his mid-1960s peak, they're worth hearing as good, if

sometimes didactic, topical/protest tunes. The version of "There But for Fortune," one of his most famous compositions, has much more of a hasty troubadour gallop than the more renowned take on *Phil Ochs in Concert*. In addition, the songs "Talking Airplane Disaster," "How Long," and "Davey Moore" (yes, about the same fatal boxing incident that inspired the similarly obscure Bob Dylan song "Who Killed Davey Moore?") are not available in any other versions. The live material was taken from Ochs' performances at the 1963, 1964, and 1966 Newport Folk Festivals. While all of the tunes are available in studio versions, these are worthwhile supplements, particularly the five 1966 songs, as four of them would appear in far more elaborately produced arrangements on his *Pleasures of the Harbor* and *Tape from California* albums. These solo acoustic performances are interesting contrasts, putting the voice and the lyrics at the forefront, in the best unplugged tradition. —*Richie Unterberger*

Sinéad O'Connor

b. Dec. 8, 1966, Dublin, Ireland

Vocals, Keyboards, Guitar / College Rock, Adult Alternative Pop/Rock, Alternative Pop/Rock, Singer/Songwriter

Sinéad O'Connor ranked among the most distinctive and controversial pop music stars of the 1990s, the first and in many ways the most influential of the numerous female performers whose music dominated airwaves throughout the decade. Brash and outspoken, with her shaven head, angry visage and shapeless wardrobe a direct challenge to the popular culture's long-prevailing notions of femininity and sexuality, O'Connor irrevocably altered the image of women in rock; railing against long-standing stereotypes simply by asserting herself not as a sex object but as a serious artist, she kick-started a revolt which led the way for performers ranging from Liz Phair to Courtney Love to Alanis Morissette. *The Lion and the Cobra* was one of the most acclaimed debut records of 1987, with a pair of alternative radio hits in the singles "Mandinka" and "Troy." However, O'Connor remained a cult figure prior to the release of 1990's chart-topping *I Do Not Want What I Haven't Got*, a harrowing masterpiece sparked by the recent dissolution of her marriage to drummer John Reynolds. Boosted by the single and video "Nothing Compares 2 U," the album established her as a major star, but controversy dogged her—she refused to perform in New Jersey if "The Star Spangled Banner" was played prior to her appearance, a move which brought public criticism from no less than Frank Sinatra, who threatened to "kick her ass." Guesting on *Saturday Night Live* in 1992, O'Connor ended her performance by ripping up a photo of Pope John Paul II, resulting in a wave of condemnation unlike any she'd previously encountered. Two weeks after the *SNL* performance, she appeared at a Bob Dylan tribute concert at Madison Square Garden, and was promptly booed off the stage. Now a virtual pariah, O'Connor kept a low profile for the next several years; 1994's *Universal Mother*, despite good reviews, failed to relaunch her to superstar status. —*Jason Ankeny*

The Lion and the Cobra / 1987 / Ensign/Chrysalis ✦✦✦✦✦

Sinéad O'Connor's debut *The Lion and the Cobra* was a sensation upon its 1987 release, and it remains a distinctive record, finding a major talent striving to achieve her own voice. Like many debuts, it's entirely possible to hear her influences, from Peter Gabriel to Prince and contemporary rap, but what's striking about the record is how she synthesizes these into her own sound—an eerie, expansive sound heavy on atmosphere and tortured passion. If the album occasionally sinks into its own atmospheric murk a little too often, she pulls everything back into focus with songs as bracing as the hard-rocking "Mandinka" or the sexy hip-hop of "I Want Your (Hands on Me)." Still, those ethereal soundscapes are every bit as enticing as the direct material, since "Troy," "Jackie," and "Jerusalem" are compelling because of their hushed, quiet intensity. It's not a perfect album, since it can succumb to uneven pacing, but it's a thoroughly impressive debut—and it's all the more impressive when you realize she only topped it with its immediate successor, before losing all focus. —*Stephen Thomas Erlewine*

● **I Do Not Want What I Haven't Got** / Mar. 1990 / Ensign/Chrysalis ✦✦✦✦✦

I Do Not Want What I Haven't Got became Sinéad O'Connor's popular breakthrough on the strength of the stunning Prince cover "Nothing Compares 2 U," which topped the pop charts for a month. But even its remarkable intimacy wasn't adequate preparation for the harrowing confessionals that composed the majority of the album. Informed by her stormy relationship with drummer John Reynolds, who fathered O'Connor's first child before the couple broke up, *I Do Not Want What I Haven't Got* lays the singer's psyche startlingly and sometimes uncomfortably bare. The songs mostly address relationships with parents, children, and (especially) lovers, through which O'Connor weaves a stubborn refusal to be defined by anyone but herself. In fact, the album is almost *too* personal and cathartic to draw the listener in close, since O'Connor projects such turmoil and offers such specific detail. Her confrontational openness makes it easy to overlook O'Connor's musical versatility. Granted, not all of the music is as brilliantly audacious as "I Am Stretched on Your Grave," which marries a Frank O'Connor poem to eerie Celtic melodies and a James Brown "Funky Drummer" sample. But the album plays like a *tour de force* in its demonstration of everything O'Connor can do: dramatic orchestral ballads, intimate confessionals, catchy pop/rock, driving guitar rock, and protest folk, not to mention the nearly six-minute a cappella title track. What's consistent throughout is the frighteningly strong emotion O'Connor brings to bear on the material, while remaining sensitive to each piece's individual demands. Aside from being a brilliant album in its own right, *I Do Not Want What I Haven't Got* foreshadowed the rise of deeply introspective female singer/songwriters like Tori Amos and Sarah McLachlan, who were more traditionally feminine and connected with a wider audience. Which takes nothing away from anyone; if anything, it's evidence that, when on top of her game, O'Connor was a singular talent. —*Steve Huey*

Am I Not Your Girl? / Sep. 22, 1992 / Ensign/Chrysalis ✦✦

Universal Mother / Sep. 13, 1994 / Ensign/Chrysalis ✦✦✦
O'Connor's first album of original material since her breakthrough *I Do Not Want What I Haven't Got* is nearly as confused as her big-band album, *Am I Not Your Girl?* O'Connor has lost her sense of conceptual unity, which makes her most extreme moments quite embarrassing ("Red Football" and the white hip-hop of "Famine"). Every so often, she manages to pull off a number that shows why her first two albums were so startling and captivating, but through most of *Universal Mother*, O'Connor sounds lost and confused. *—Stephen Thomas Erlewine*

So Far . . . The Best of Sinéad O'Connor / Nov. 18, 1997 / Chrysalis ✦✦✦
So Far . . . The Best of Sinéad O'Connor is a missed opportunity, failing to deliver a comprehensive overview of the first part of O'Connor's career, or an adequate hits collection. Part of the problem is the fact that O'Connor is an album artist that happens to deliver great singles as well, which means there will be essential tracks missing from a collection, even if it relies solely on the singles. *So Far* decides to circumvent this problem by combining album tracks with singles, but that doesn't work, since it gives the patchy *Universal Mother* preference over the excellent *The Lion and the Cobra* and omits such singles as "Three Babies." Things are further muddled by the inclusion of the non-LP rarities "Heroine," "You Made Me the Thief of Your Heart," and "Empire." All three songs are worthy, but they would make more sense on a rarities collection, which could also feature B-sides and non-LP singles like "Silent Night" and "My Special Child," which have never appeared on an album. Their inclusion was designed to convince hardcore fans into buying this album, but they make the collection less appealing to casual fans. In a way, that's not a bad thing, since *So Far* doesn't provide a good introduction to O'Connor, even if it does contain such essential songs as "Mandinka," "Troy," "Nothing Compares 2 U," "I Want Your (Hands on Me)," "I Am Stretched on Your Grave," and "The Emperor's New Clothes." However, those moments of brilliance sound awkward when put in a collection as poorly conceived as this. Only extremely casual fans, those that just want the hits on one disc, need this, since most listeners with a passing interest in O'Connor are much better served by the original albums. *—Stephen Thomas Erlewine*

Faith and Courage / Jun. 13, 2000 / Atlantic ✦✦✦
Sinéad O'Connor will not be taken in the midst of headlining controversy. She was ordained a Catholic priest in 1998, soon after her traumatic scenes of attempted suicide and custody battles over her daughter, Roisin. Former colleague and friend, ex-Pogues frontman Shane McGowan lashed back at O'Connor after she publicly criticized his wild drinking behavior. She should be down and out, ill-fated from making her signature political accusations and illustriously raw life songs, but O'Connor will not be tested. Her fifth studio release of original material since 1994's *Universal Mother, Faith and Courage* is obviously O'Connor's umpteenth disposition of reclaiming self-definition.

She sounds lonely and afraid in songs like "Jealous" and "Dancing Lessons," yet her fierce confidence overpowers such insecurity on the pinch-hitting "No Man's Woman." Don't be too fooled, for O'Connor only lasts so long, regardless of her insisting nature to be on top of her game. She is a sensitive person and her most honest work shines on the sorrowful "Hold Back the Night" and on Celtic-rock "The Lamb's Book of Life," a brandish slap against her native Ireland. Emotionally spiritual and artistic, *Faith and Courage* tries so hard to take control as Sinéad O'Connor refrains from being taken, but her bitterness prevails. *—MacKenzie Wilson*

Of Montreal

f. Athens, GA
Indie Pop, Lo-Fi
The brainchild of singer/guitarist Kevin Barnes, euphoric indie-popsters Of Montreal were among the second wave of bands to emerge from the sprawling Elephant 6 collective. A native of Athens, GA, Barnes was inspired to form the group in the wake of a broken romance with a woman from Montreal; signing to Bar/None while living in Florida, he subsequently moved to Cleveland and Minneapolis in search of compatible bandmates, finally returning home to collaborate with bassist Bryan Helium (also a member of Athens' Elf Power) and drummer Derek Almstead. Of Montreal's debut album *Cherry Peel* appeared in mid-1997, followed that autumn by an EP, *The Bird Who Continues to Eat the Rabbit's Flower.* After Helium left to focus on Elf Power full-time, Almstead assumed bass duties, and keyboardist Dottie Alexander and drummer Jamey Huggins joined the lineup; still, the second Of Montreal full-length, 1998's *The Bedside Drama: A Petite Tragedy*, was recorded primarily as a Barnes solo project. Multi-instrumentalist A.C. Forrester signed on for 1999's sublime *The Gay Parade*; the singles retrospective *Horse and Elephant Eatery* followed in the spring of 2000. *—Jason Ankeny*

Cherry Peel / Jul. 15, 1997 / Bar/None ✦✦✦✦
Hailing from the '90s-resurgent Athens, GA, scene, unofficial homebase to the Elephant 6 collective, Of Montreal is perhaps the least publicized band in the Elephant 6 stable but not because they make the least-worthy music. To the contrary, *Cherry Peel* is one of the most unabashedly pretty releases from that group, and, in fact, stands apart from most everything in the pop scene due to its simple, unassuming innocence. The vocals of songwriter Kevin Barnes are achingly heartfelt and puppyish, and his songs seem to spring directly out of childhood, or at least seem touched by a childlike yearning, so much so that you can't help feeling all fuzzy inside and perhaps desirous of hugging someone, maybe your mom, after hearing them. And the songs are uniformly expert: "In Dreams I Dance With You" comes across like a cupid-struck Pinocchio's sweet longing; "Montreal" is a wasteland ballad worthy of Neil Young; and "Don't Ask Me to Explain" will make your heart palpitate and bubble up into your throat it is so unpretentiously euphonic. The gorgeous lushness of *Cherry Peel* conceals the bedroom-bred genesis of the entire undertaking. And though it would be easy to dismiss the whole album as so much cuteness, Of Montreal never hint at irony. The band is not mocking pop, it loves the form and the chance to express that joy; and that joy is on full display on *Cherry Peel* like no band since the early Beatles. *—Stanton Swihart*

The Bird Who Continues to Eat the Rabbit's Flower / 1997 / Kindercore ✦✦✦
Of Montreal's 1997 mini-album, *The Bird Who Continues to Eat the Rabbit's Flower*, stands alone as the Of Montreal album that seems not to be built around a unifying concept of some sort. That makes it seem like a throwaway of sorts when compared to the rest of the Of Montreal catalog, but *The Bird Who Continues to Eat the Rabbit's Flower* contains some standout moments. The Kevin Barnes original "On the Drive Home" and the covers of the Who's "Disguises" and Elf Power's "Secret Ocean" are the highlights, played with joyful earnestness and not a shred of irony. Before distinguishing themselves from the rest of the Elephant 6 collective by releasing several eccentric, unapologetically bright, concept albums, Of Montreal were just another band essentially copying the early Beatles formula with a lo-fi twist. This is not such a bad thing, but those looking to capture what makes Of Montreal such a unique and ambitious pop group will not find that here. This is a starting point for Of Montreal, worthy in and of itself, but merely the building blocks for stellar albums to come. *—Scott Sepich*

The Bedside Drama: A Petite Tragedy / 1998 / Kindercore/Elephant 6 ✦✦✦✦
A continuation and maturation of the playfulness exhibited on earlier releases, Of Montreal create the brand of theatrical psychedelic pop that many of their '60s predecessors hinted at but only few achieved. Overall less overtly rock-influenced than either *Cherry Peel* or *Horse and Elephant Eatery*, Kevin Barnes continues to change chords with nearly every word, twirling Vaudevillian melodies that incredibly bring to life all the whimsy and melancholy of the characters he carefully orchestrates. Though these characters don't yet take on the florid personalities that would be found in later Of Montreal albums, Barnes nonetheless proved himself an adept illustrator, as he charted the dizzying highs of infatuation, the leveling off of emotion, and the devastating collapse of a relationship with a picturesque precision. Still sweetly naïve with the swinging skiffle pop of "One of a Very Few of a Kind" and the gorgeously complex melodies of "Happy Yellow Bumblebee," the latter finding the narrator becoming a bee, befriending beetles and centipedes, avoiding spiders, and getting lonely because his parents are dead and his brothers and sisters are nowhere to be found, the absurdity of the songwriting never grows tiresome. Even so, understated gloominess creeps into tracks with the dark piano strikes of "Panda Bear" and the sprightly "It's Easy to Sleep When You're Dead," although the narrator escapes with the conclusion that life is a better choice in the end. Overall, an album that marked a crucial stage in the evolution from the lo-fi garage pop of *Cherry Peel* to the ambitious rock carnival of *The Gay Parade* and cemented Of Montreal's status as one of the most creatively relevant groups of the late '90s. *—Matt Fink*

● **The Gay Parade** / Feb. 16, 1999 / Bar/None ✦✦✦✦✦
The Gay Parade is indie-pop's very own *Sgt. Pepper*, a richly detailed, grandly ambitious concept record which forgoes the ponderous pretensions the phrase implies to instead exult in the simple joys of everyday life. Kevin Barnes' songs radiate a childlike wonder and boundless enthusiasm, discovering beauty in the most unlikely of places; his lyrics suggest psychedelic nursery rhymes, populated by absurdist characters (each and every one depicted on the jacket art) sketched in Crayola across a series of majestic melodies and ornate arrangements which belie the record's surface naiveté. For all of *The Gay Parade*'s effervescence and whimsy, there's also a melancholy which pervades songs like "Jacques Lamure," "The Autobiographical Grandpa" and "My Friend Will Be Me," recalling the lovelorn hues of the previous Of Montreal record, *The Bedside Drama: A Petite Tragedy*; far from deflating the euphoria, however, these moments simply acknowledge the necessity of sadness and loss to the human experience, and deem them worthy of celebration as well. These are songs in the key of life, Zen-like expressions of simplicity and innocence resonating with remarkable complexity and wisdom. *—Jason Ankeny*

Horse & Elephant Eatery (No Elephants Allowed): The Singles & Songles Album / Mar. 28, 2000 / Bar/None ✦✦✦✦
Where previous Of Montreal records evoked children's picture books in their grand narrative scope, off-the-wall characters, and candy-colored hues, *Horse & Elephant Eatery (No Elephants Allowed)*—a compilation of "singles and songles" (i.e., material previously released in a variety of non-album formats)—is more akin to a schoolboy's collage assembled from cut-out photos, construction paper, and paste, a composite of random ideas and far-flung images that together form a charmingly chaotic whole. While the disc of course lacks the thematic unity common to the group's previous conceptual efforts, the songs nevertheless hang together on the strength of their shared warmth and effervescence—perhaps no other contemporary group makes pop music so utterly guileless and unashamedly rapturous, articulating an innocence remarkably free of irony and calculation. Much of *Horse & Elephant Eatery* recalls the carnival-esque character studies of its brilliant predecessor *The Gay Parade*—repaying his obvious debt to Ray Davies with a fine cover of the Kinks' "The World Keeps Going 'Round," Of Montreal mastermind Kevin Barnes strikes a perfect balance between fairy-tale whimsy and slice-of-life reality on moments like "The Problem With April," "Nicki Lighthouse," and "Ira's Brief Life As a Spider," creating a kaleidoscopic fantasy world even as his songs capture moments of heartbreakingly human poignance. Silly, sappy, and sentimental, to be sure, *Horse & Elephant Eatery* is just as often sublime. *—Jason Ankeny*

The Early Four Track Recordings / Jan. 16, 2001 / Kindercore ✦✦
Of Montreal's *The Early Four Track Recordings* collects unreleased, lo-fi material from the archives of the band's vibrant and dynamic frontman, Kevin Barnes. With songs predating Of Montreal's inception as a full band, the collection is playfully (re)named as a song-by-song series of goofy events involving Dustin Hoffman, although the tracks are clearly

drawn together from several different recording sessions. The stripped-down indie pop tunes vary in tempo and mood, indicative of the musical and lyrical flexibility that Barnes would develop with his bandmates in the albums to come. Tracks such as "Dustin Hoffman Gets a Bath" and "Dustin Hoffman Scrubs Too Hard and Loses Soap" feature the Beatlesque, slightly off-kilter chord progressions and lyrics established in Of Montreal's charming debut album, *Cherry Peel*, while later in the collection "Dustin Hoffman's Wife Makes a Sarcastic Remark..." hints at the sweet, wacky instrumentation and subject matter that brought popular and critical success to the band's fourth album, *The Gay Parade*. At other moments, however, the collection is bogged down by the dull, monotone meanderings of "Dustin Hoffman Feigns Ignorance of Missing Bathtub" and "Dustin Hoffman's Children Don't Enter the Bathroom." To committed fans, the insight into Barnes' early development as an innovative songwriter is generous, but on the whole, *The Early Four-Track Recordings* does not add tremendous value to Of Montreal's discography. The collection works well enough as a stand-alone release of lo-fi pop, but to get a more accurate sense of Of Montreal's zealous and adept sound in a non-album form, listeners would be better advised to seek out the singles collection *Horse and Elephant Eatery (No Elephants Allowed)*. *—Michelle Cross*

Coquelicot Asleep in the Poppies: A Variety of Whimsical Verse / Apr. 23, 2001 / Kindercore ✦✦✦✦✦
Of Montreal's major voice Kevin Barnes has unparalleled talent to write lyrics that double as relatable adult situations and children's fable. This trend continues on *Coquelicot Asleep in the Poppies*. While there are come similarities to their previous efforts *Bedside Drama* and *The Gay Parade*, *Coquelicot* is more ambitious in its concept, arrangements, lyrics, and even artwork. As with other Of Montreal albums, this one works as a concept, but the songs also stand on their own, which is even more impressive. The songs are awash in melodies and harmony, a trademark of Of Montreal's previous work as well as other Elephant 6 related bands. Barnes continues to write amazingly creative lyrics full of imagery, even including interludes of story on "Lecithin's Tale of a DNA Experiment That Went Terribly Awry" and "The Events Leading Up to the Collapse of Detective Dullight." "Let's Do Everything for the First Time" is classic Of Montreal, while "Penelope" has a Syd Barrett feel to it. Strings are the main feature of mellow and beautiful "It's a Very Starry Night," and "It's Just So" could have been lifted right off of *Bedside Drama*. The band also incorporates a wide variety of instruments such as cello and violin to accordion and theremin. *Coquelicot* builds perfectly upon *The Gay Parade* and shows the progression of a great band. *—Tyson Bjorge*

Offspring

f. 1985, Garden Grove, CA
Punk-Pop, Post-Grunge, Punk Revival, Alternative Pop/Rock
Offspring's metal-inflected punk became a popular sensation in 1994, selling over four million copies on an independent record label. While the group's credentials and approach follow the indie-rock tradition of the '80s, sonically they sound more like an edgy, hard-driving heavy metal band, with their precise, pulsing power chords and Dexter Holland's flat vocals. The Offspring released their second album, *Ignition*, in 1993. It was an underground hit, setting the stage for the across-the-board success of 1994's *Smash*. The Nirvana-soundalike "Come out and Play," the first single from the album, became a hit in the summer of 1994 as the band was played on both alternative and album rock stations, confirming their broad-based appeal. "Self Esteem," the second single, followed the same soft verse/loud chorus formula and stayed on the charts nearly twice as long as "Come out and Play." Following a prolonged bidding war and much soul-searching, the Offspring decided to leave Epitaph Records in 1996 for Columbia Records. The move was particularly controversial within the punk community. After much delay, the Offspring finally released their Columbia debut, *Ixnay on the Hombre*, in February of 1997. Expectation for the record was high and it did receive good reviews, but failed to become a crossover hit on the level of *Smash*, and the group also lost a significant portion of their hardcore punk audience, due to the album's major-label status. *Americana* followed in 1998, scoring the hit "Pretty Fly (For a White Guy)." *—Stephen Thomas Erlewine*

Offspring / 1989 / Epitaph ✦✦✦
The Offspring's self-titled debut album is a rawer, harder-edged collection than their breakthrough set *Smash*, but that doesn't necessarily mean it's a better record. Although it makes a more convincing argument for the band's punk credibility—the record lacks the metal guitar crunch that dominated *Smash*—*The Offspring* doesn't have any songs driven by hooks as catchy as "Keep 'Em Separated" or "Self Esteem," nor does it have the consistency of *Smash*. A handful of tracks make a lasting impression, but most of *The Offspring* is notable for its surface style, not its substance. *—Stephen Thomas Erlewine*

Ignition / Mar. 8, 1993 / Epitaph ✦✦✦✦

● **Smash** / Aug. 23, 1994 / Epitaph ✦✦✦✦✦
The Offspring's second album for Epitaph did the impossible: it landed in the Top Five, unheard of for independent records. The Offspring crossed over due to the raucous, Eastern-tinged single "Come out and Play (Keep 'Em Separated)," which stopped and started just like Nirvana, only without the Seattle trio's recklessness. The record stayed in the charts because The Offspring sounded relentlessly heavy, no matter how much the band claimed to be punk. Their tempos are slower than traditional hardcore, and their attack is as heavy as Metallica. But they acted like they were punk, with odes to no "Self Esteem" and singing about fighting in school. Nothing on the album matches the incessant catchiness of the singles, but *Smash* is a solid record, filled with enough heavy riffs to keep most teenagers happy. *—Stephen Thomas Erlewine*

Ixnay on the Hombre / Feb. 4, 1997 / Columbia ✦✦✦
The Offspring may have been a product of the Southern California hardcore scene, but their instincts have always been more metal than punk. Their guitars plod along with a heavy backbeat, and even their speedier numbers are weighed down by clumsy riffs, which is evident on *Ixnay on the Hombre*, the follow-up to the group's unexpected hit *Smash*. Despite Jello Biafra's opening assertation of the Offspring's punk credentials, *Ixnay on the Hombre* sounds like a competent hard-rock band trying to hitch themselves to the post-grunge bandwagon. The riffs don't have hooks, and Dexter Holland yelps his vocals tunelessly. Of course, much hardcore followed this formula, but it got by on its self-rightousness and visceral forward force. Since Offspring *slows down the tempo* of hardcore, it doesn't have either the undiluted rage of hardcore, or the four-on-the-floor groove of hard rock. Also, they haven't come up with a ridiculous hook on the level of "Come Out and Play (Keep 'Em Separated)" or "Self Esteem," which leaves *Ixnay on the Hombre* as a tedious, turgid mess of anemic punk-metal. *—Stephen Thomas Erlewine*

Americana / Nov. 10, 1998 / Columbia ✦✦✦
With integrity intact and a hearty combination of poppy punk and wit throughout, the Offspring's fifth album is a raucous ride through America as seen through the eyes of a weary, but still optimistic, young kid. Riffs on political correctness, '70s radio fodder, and suburban disquiet are spread thick on *Americana*. If the band's targets seem a bit simple and predictable, its music rarely is. The SoCal roots aren't played to a fault, the blend of salsa and alterna-rock sounds natural, and the Offspring pretty much laugh at their culture, as well as themselves, the entire time. Best track is "Pretty Fly (For a White Guy)," which manages to bridge Def Leppard and Latin hip-hop (and the musical timeline they represent) and, in the process, disrobes Middle America's average white teen's quick fascination with and instant disposability of a once-regional heritage. With *Americana*, the Offspring are merely contributing their part. *—Michael Gallucci*

Conspiracy of One / Nov. 14, 2000 / Columbia ✦✦✦
Contrary to the popular belief of music critics, listeners and artists alike, a band that doesn't deviate from its genre on its albums isn't musically limited. There are many layers to any given genre of music, and growing into it is just as much of an accomplishment as, say, experimenting with several different categories. What's wrong with sounding the same if you get better and better at it with each album?

On *Conspiracy of One*, the Offspring do just that, resulting in their most musically mature collection to date. The tight arrangements, vocal interplay and refined guitar work on "Original Prankster," "Want You Bad," and "Million Miles Away" sound like Offspring songs, but don't all sound the same. The band departs from its SoCal punk roots at times—a ballad called "Denial, Revisited" provides one of the album's slower instances. They also inject elements of hip-hop, rap-metal, and Nirvana-like grunge into a few songs, giving *Conspiracy of One* some musical diversity, but it's subtle; the album remains firmly planted in the world of punk. Each song features Dexter Holland's lead vocals and Noodles and Holland's crafty guitar playing, the group's two defining factors. The album also features some smart lyrics, though the Offspring do have some sophomoric fun on the party anthem "One Fine Day." *Conspiracy of One* is a solid and well-crafted recording and offers a fine progression from a band that has no qualms about doing what they do best. *—Liana Jonas*

Mary Margaret O'Hara

Vocals / Singer/Songwriter
Though the subject of great critical acclaim, to date singer/songwriter Mary Margaret O'Hara has issued only one LP. The sister of comedienne Catherine O'Hara (best known for her work in the groundbreaking sketch comedy series *SCTV* and the *Home Alone* movies), she was born in Toronto; after graduating from the Ontario Art College, she joined her first band, the soul-pop outfit Dollars. In 1976 O'Hara signed on with the group Songship—soon renamed the Go Deo Chorus—and began writing much of the group's material.

She left the band in 1983, but not before recording the demos which subsequently earned her a contract with Virgin Records. After a series of delays and label battles, in 1988 O'Hara finally issued her lone full-length album, *Miss America*, which she co-produced with the innovative guitarist Michael Brook; a four-song holiday release, *The Christmas EP*, followed in 1991. O'Hara subsequently appeared with a diverse range of artists, contributing vocals to recordings from Morrissey, Gary Lucas, the Henrys, This Mortal Coil and John & Mary. In 1996, she also contributed a song to the benefit album *Sweet Relief II: The Gravity of the Situation: The Songs of Vic Chestnutt*. An occasional actress, she appeared in the films *The Hunter* (1980), *Candy Mountain* (1987) and *The Events Leading Up to My Death* (1992). *—Jason Ankeny*

● **Miss America** / 1988 / Virgin ✦✦✦✦✦
Originally recorded in 1984 and not released until 1988, *Miss America* still sounds light years ahead of its time: Mary Margaret O'Hara is a force of nature, a remarkable singer and composer whose crystal-clear soprano acrobatics and hypnotic songs defy accepted conventions. Flirting intermittently with country ("Anew Day," "Dear Darling") and jazz ("Keeping You in Mind"), O'Hara works primarily with pop dynamics, but deconstructs and reassembles the form according to her own blueprint: "Year in Song" is jaggedly intense, "To Cry About" is gorgeously ambient, and "Body's in Trouble" is delicately gripping, yet none conform easily to such facile assessments, with hairpin turns in mood and atmosphere which blindside expectations. Following instead its own abstract internal logic, *Miss America* is a work of mad-scientist genius, and it remains a singular experience. *—Jason Ankeny*

Ohio Express

f. 1968, Mansfield, OH, **db.** 1969
AM Pop, Bubblegum
Ohio Express and the 1910 Fruitgum Co. were two of the leading late-'60s bubblegum

rock groups. Under the aegis of producers Jerry Kasenetz and Jeff Katz, both of these rather anonymous bands surfaced repeatedly on the late-'60s pop charts for Buddah Records, spearheading the bubblegum rock craze. With Joey Levine taking the vocals on their early hits, The Ohio Express roared up in 1968 with "Yummy Yummy Yummy" and "Chewy Chewy," a pair of million-sellers. Future 10CC leader Graham Gouldman fronted the Express on their final chart bow in 1969, "Sausalito (Is the Place to Go)."

At the same time, another Kasenetz-Katz discovery, New Jersey's 1910 Fruitgum Co., was bubbling over with the obnoxiously catchy "Simon Says," "1, 2, 3, Red Light," and "Indian Giver," another gold record triumvirate. Like their labelmates, their mercurial chart run was history before 1969 was over. *—Bill Dahl*

• **The Best of the Ohio Express: Yummy, Yummy, Yummy** / Apr. 3, 2001 / Buddha ♦♦♦♦
The Best of the Ohio Express: Yummy Yummy Yummy serves up 14 jaw-aching tracks from the chewy, chewy center of the late '60s synthesized pop music otherwise known as bubblegum pop. The efforts of the revolving-door stream of musicians who performed and recorded under the Ohio Express moniker is the focus of this succinct compilation that clocks in at shortly over a half hour. The Buckeye-based Ohio Express were originally called Sir Timothy & the Royals—a teenage garage band working locally for weekend gigs such as parties, school proms, and so on. They were scouted by producers Jerry Kasenetz and Jeff Katz. Their unwillingness to take their cues from the hitmaking Kasenetz and Katz assured that any future autonomy would be doubtful. As had become the tradition with their labelmates and chart rivals the 1910 Fruitgum Company and the Lemon Pipers, recordings were issued by a band using the same Ohio Express name. Kasenetz and Katz released these records with little or no regard for the band formerly known as Sir Timothy & the Royals back in Ohio—who were now also known as the Ohio Express. Confused yet? Their biggest hit, "Yummy Yummy Yummy," had first been offered to—and rejected by—Jay and the Techniques, who were searching for a follow up to "Apple, Peaches, Pumpkin Pie." The session musician and lead vocalist on the track so impressed the label, he was deemed the Ohio Express' lead singer. Other charting hits for the band included on this collection include: "Chewy Chewy," "Sweeter Than Sugar," and "Mercy." Nearing the end of Kasenetz and Katz's run with the Ohio Express was the country-rock flavor heard on "Sausalito (Is the Place to Go)." The backing group would eventually become the core of 10cc on this seminal Graham Gouldman composition. *—Lindsay Planer*

The Ohio Players

f. 1959, Dayton, OH
Funk, Soul

With their slinky, horn-powered grooves, impeccable musicianship and eye-popping album covers, the Ohio Players were among the top funk bands of the mid-1970s. Emerging from the musical hotbed of Dayton in 1959, their debut "Trespassin'" hit the R&B charts in early 1968. Although the Players' trademark bottom-heavy, horn-driven sound was already blossoming, their follow-up, "It's a Cryin' Shame" flopped; increasingly influenced by the groundbreaking funk of Sly and the Family Stone, their single "Pain" reached the R&B Top 40 in late 1971. A year later, *Pleasure* launched the absurdist smash "Funky Worm." At Mercury, the Ohio Players enjoyed their greateat success; not only did their sound coalesce, but they became notorious for their sexually provocative LP covers, a tradition begun during their Westbound tenure. Their 1974 Mercury debut *Skin Tight* was their first unequivocal classic, launching the hit title track as well as "Jive Turkey." Its follow-up, *Fire*, remains the Players' masterpiece, topping the pop charts on the strength of its bone-rattling title cut, itself a number one hit; "I Want to Be Free," one of the band's few attempts at social commentary, was also highly successful. 1975's *Honey*—which featured perhaps the Players' most controversial and erotic cover to date—was another monster, generating the chart-topping masterpiece "Love Rollercoaster" in addition to the hits "Sweet Sticky Thing" and "Fopp." The insistent "Who'd She Coo?," from 1976's *Contradiction*, was the Players' last number one R&B hit, and as the 1970s drew to a close, the band's fortunes continued to decline. *—Jason Ankeny*

Pain / 1971 / Westbound ♦♦♦♦
Creatively, commercially, and conceptually, *Pain* was a major step forward for the Ohio Players. This 1971 album was quite a departure from their previous work—in the late-'60s, the Midwesterners' forte had been raw, hard-edged Southern-style soul along the lines of Sam & Dave, Rufus Thomas, and Wilson Picket. But with *Pain*, they became a lot more experimental and unveiled an interesting, distinctive brand of funk that incorporated elements of jazz and blues as well as rock. The jazz influence is especially strong on "Never Had a Dream," "Singing in the Morning," and the hit title song, while "The Reds" is a progressive blues number that draws on jazz as well as psychedelic rock. It was with *Pain*, the Players' first album for Westbound, that they unveiled their goofy Granny character, which the funksters continued to have fun with on their subsequent Westbound releases but discontinued when they moved to Mercury with 1974's *Skin Tight*. And it was with *Pain* that they became famous (some would say infamous) for their erotic LP covers. Employing S&M/bondage imagery, *Pain*'s front cover was considered shocking in 1971. Although the Velvet Underground had written songs about S&M, and the British spy thriller *The Avengers* frequently hinted at kinky sex—Diana Rigg's Emma Peel character often dressed like a dominatrix—S&M and fetishism were very taboo subjects for Middle America in 1971. And not surprisingly, some retailers refused to carry *Pain*. But the album, although not huge, was a decent seller. With *Pain*, the Ohio Players' Westbound period was off to an impressive and creative start. *—Alex Henderson*

Pleasure / 1972 / Westbound ♦♦♦♦
When the Ohio Players recorded their second Westbound album, *Pleasure*, in 1972, they weren't as big as they would be from 1974-1976. But their popularity was growing—slowly but surely—and those who were hip to the band recognized it as one of the most cutting-edge acts in the funk field. A lot of bands were providing funk in 1972, but not many of them used jazz progressions as creatively as the Players use them on "Laid It," "Walked Away From You," and *Pleasure*'s title song. Those tracks are gems, and the Players are equally captivating on the sweet soul ballad "Varee Is Love." But the best known tune on the album is the goofy "Funky Worm," which employed the Players' amusing Granny character and was, in 1972, their biggest hit to date. Long after the band's popularity faded, "Funky Worm" would live on in the 1980s and 1990s thanks to the various hip-hoppers who sampled its irresistible bass line. Like *Pain* in 1971, *Pleasure* had a kinky cover that generated some controversy—the same bald woman who brandished a bullwhip and wore dominatrix attire on the front cover of *Pain* was chained up on the cover of *Pleasure*. Some folks found the Players' kinky LP covers intriguing, while others were shocked and offended. And the Players, having struggled in the 1960s, were happy to be noticed. But ultimately, it is the quality of the music—not the bondage-minded cover—that makes *Pleasure* a funk classic. *—Alex Henderson*

Ecstacy / 1973 / Westbound ♦♦♦
Throughout the 1970s, the Ohio Players were famous (or infamous) for their erotic album covers. But there are major differences between the covers of Mercury albums like *Skin Tight, Fire, Honey*, and *Contradiction* and the covers of such Westbound releases as *Pleasure* and *Pain*. At Mercury, the Players' album covers favored softcore erotica à la Playboy or Penthouse, whereas the covers of their Westbound LPs were more bizarre and offered kinky bondage/S&M imagery. Those covers came under attack from different parts of the political spectrum; some of the more radical feminists accused the Players of objectifying women, while Republicans and Christian fundamentalists accused them of promoting moral decline. And the Players were laughing all the way to the bank—at least from 1974 on. When their third Westbound album, *Ecstasy*, came out in 1973, they were still a year away from signing with Mercury and becoming really huge. But they did have a small cult following, which found that *Ecstasy* fell short of the excellence of *Pain* and *Pleasure*. Nonetheless, the material is respectable and generally decent. Serious Players fans will find sweaty funk items like "Spinning," "Black Cat," and the title song to be enjoyable even though they aren't among the band's essential recordings. While *Ecstasy* isn't recommended to casual listeners, it isn't a bad album to have in your collection if you fancy yourself a hardcore Players addict. *—Alex Henderson*

Climax / 1974 / Westbound ♦♦♦
By the time Westbound released *Climax* in 1974, the Ohio Players had left the Detroit-based label and signed with Mercury, where they would soon explode commercially with the superb *Skin Tight*. But Westbound still had enough material in the can to put together a few more Players LPs, including *Climax* and the 1975 release *Rattlesnake*. This collection contains a few songs that had already come out on previous Players albums—"Players Balling" first appeared on 1971's *Pain*, while "Sleep Talk" and the instrumental "Food Stamps, Y'all" had been heard on 1973's *Ecstasy*. But most of the tunes were previously unreleased, including the title song (a soul-jazz instrumental) and covers of "Proud Mary" and Marvin Gaye's "What's Going On." Except for "Players Balling," this collection is unremarkable—generally competent, but not remarkable or mind-blowing. *Climax* is enjoyable and interesting if you're a serious Ohio Players collector, although more casual listeners would do well to skip this album and spend their money on *Fire, Skin Tight*, or *Honey* instead. *—Alex Henderson*

Skin Tight / 1974 / Mercury ♦♦♦♦♦
Skin Tight was a major turning point for the Ohio Players, who had enjoyed several hits on Black radio (including "Pain," "Funky Worm," "Varee Is Love" and "I Wanna Hear from You"), but hadn't been huge. Switching from Westbound to Mercury, the Dayton funksters became exactly that—huge—and went from enjoying a cult following to being one of the most celebrated funk bands of the 1970s. With *Skin Tight*, the band's erotic album covers went from employing bizarre S&M/bondage imagery to being more *Playboy*-ish, and its music became less abstract (but remained quite risk-taking and unpredictable). The title song and "Jive Turkey" are down and dirty funk classics, and the jazz-influenced "Heaven Must Be like This" illustrates the fact that the Players could also be captivatingly romantic. *—Alex Henderson*

Rattlesnake / 1975 / Westbound ♦♦♦
When the Ohio Players' Mercury smashes were burning up the charts in the mid-'70s, Westbound no doubt regretted letting the funksters get away and wished that it had been the label that released "Fire," "Love Rollercoaster," and "I Want to Be Free." But since Westbound no longer had the Players under contract, it tried to cash in on their popularity by putting out material that it had in the can. Released in 1975 but recorded from 1972-1973—when the Players were still signed to Westbound—*Rattlesnake* is a collection that only a hardcore Players fan would find of interest. Not that the material is bad; most of it is decent, if less than remarkable. Though *Rattlesnake* contains a few songs that had already come out on 1972's *Pleasure* or 1973's *Ecstacy* (including the funky "Spinning," the infectious "Laid It," and the sentimental ballad "Varee Is Love"), its main focus is previously unreleased material. And the material that Westbound pulls from its vaults ranges from the funky title song and the disco-ish instrumental "Hollywood Hump" (which would have been at home on a KC & the Sunshine Band album) to the jazz instrumental "Gone Forever." Meanwhile, "Rooster Poot" is a mildly amusing funk tune that features the Players' Granny character, which they retired for good after signing with Mercury. Although far from essential and not recommended to casual listeners, *Rattlesnake* is an interesting listen if you're a seasoned collector. *—Alex Henderson*

Fire / 1975 / Mercury ♦♦♦♦♦
After greatly increasing its visibility with *Skin Tight*, the Ohio Players became even more

visible with *Fire*—an unpredictable masterpiece that boasted such explosive horn-driven funk jewels as "Smoke" and the wildly addictive title song. The Players were always best known for their hard-edged funk, but in fact, there was much more to their legacy. "I Want to Be Free," the almost innocent "Together" and the remorseful "It's All Over" demonstrate that their ballads and slower material could be first-rate soul treasures. The influence of gospel imagery and the Black church experience had asserted itself on *Skin Tight*'s "Is Anybody Gonna Be Saved," and does so once again on the intense "What the Hell" and the hit "Runnin' from the Devil." Without question, *Fire* was one of the Ohio Players' greatest triumphs—both commercially and artistically. *—Alex Henderson*

Honey / 1975 / Mercury ✦✦✦✦✦
Honey may have had the most controversial LP cover of 1975. Its erotic cover, which depicted a nude model covered in honey, was protested by feminists when it was alleged that the model had become stuck to the floor during the photo shoot. Some retailers, in fact, refused to carry it. All the controversy certainly didn't hurt the album commercially. In 1975, the Ohio Players were one of R&B's most successful acts, and were inescapable for anyone who listened to Black radio at the time. The album kept the band's commercial momentum going thanks to such hard-driving funk as "Love Rollercoaster" (a song that was sampled to death by rappers in the 1980s and '90s and covered by the Red Hot Chili Peppers in 1996), "Fopp," and the playfully jazz-influenced hit "Sweet Sticky Thing." While the Players' outstanding contributions to funk would continue to have an enormous impact long after the band's popularity faded, it's important to stress that only about half of *Honey* falls into the funk category. In fact, lead singer Sugarfoot's moving performance on the remorseful "Alone" makes one wish that the Players' ballads were discussed more often. *—Alex Henderson*

Contradiction / 1976 / Mercury ✦✦✦✦
Upon the release of this album, the Ohio Players were at the pinnacle of their long music careers, which date back to the late 1950s. This album produced the number one Billboard R&B single "Who'd She Coo." The rhythm arrangement and jazzy horn arrangement are complemented by a titillating guitar, colorful vocals and a suggestive lyric. While the title is "Who'd She Coo," the chant is actually "oochie coo" but was modified due to its racy content. The ballad "My Life," with its rolling rhythm and frigid background vocals, shines with Leroy Bonner's agile baritone. Still on a somber note, "Bi-Centennial" sends a social message to the masses, and the title track is a direct reflection of life. Some of these compositions stray from course with instrumental interludes, but that can be understood considering the group was initially assembled as an instrumental band. "Who'd She Coo" was the funk ensemble's last number one hit, but they would return to the top ten on their album *Angel* with "O-H-I-O." Though there were competitive groups emerging, internal strife facilitated the demise of this pioneering funk band. *—Craig Lytle*

★ **Ohio Players Gold** / 1976 / Mercury ✦✦✦✦✦
When it gets right down to it, the Ohio Players' albums were as memorable for their risque album covers as they were for their music. Sure, there were some seriously funky individual tracks, but the Players couldn't keep the momentum up throughout the course of an entire album. And that's why *Ohio Players Gold* is such a useful collection, even in light of more comprehensive latter-day collections. *Ohio Players Gold* has the good stuff and absolutely no filler. From the scorching "Fire" and the wild "Love Rollercoaster" to the sly "Jive Turkey" and "Who'd She Coo?," nearly every one of the group's finest songs is present and accounted for on *Gold*. Naturally, there are some omissions—"Funky Worm" really should have been on the collection, especially since it was their first number one R&B hit—but this album should satisfy most listeners that just want the hits. If you want to dig a little deeper into their catalog without sampling their albums, try *Funk on Fire: The Mercury Anthology* but otherwise, stick with the *Gold* and you'll reap its rewards. *—Leo Stanley*

Angel / 1977 / Mercury ✦✦✦
There are three elements that can always be found on the Ohio Players' albums that were released during their heyday: funky tracks, hyped ballads and sexually suggestive album covers. This LP is no different, featuring three releases in "Body Vibes," "O-H-I-O" and "Merry Go Round." The first and last peaked at 19 and 77 respectively on the Billboard R&B charts. The second of the three is an uptempo cut, in which the song's title is the only lyric; it is repeated in a whispery chant in the verse and the word itself is sung throughout the chorus. This formula proved successful as the single cracked the Top Ten at number nine inside of 18 weeks. It was also the last Top Ten single for the Dayton, Ohio funk aggregate.

"Angel," the title track, and "Can You Still Love Me" were not released, but are classic Ohio Players' compositions. "Angel" is a mid-tempo number honed with danced rhythms and piercing horns which Leroy "Sugarfoot" Bonner shrouds with his trademark baritone, complemented by superb background vocals. Bonner maintains that same vocal appeal on "Can You Still Love Me," leaving room for falsetto-flavored background vocals that are creatively arranged. *—Craig Lytle*

Mr. Mean / 1977 / Mercury ✦

Jass-Ay-La-Dee / 1978 / Mercury ✦

Tenderness / 1981 / Boardwalk ✦✦✦

Funk on Fire: The Mercury Anthology / Jun. 6, 1995 / Mercury Funk Essentials ✦✦✦✦✦
One hour, 54 minutes and 12 seconds of innovative funk on two discs is nothing to sneeze at, particularly when the tracks are prime Ohio Players cuts. Mercury adroitly chronicles their chart-blazing career with full-length, unedited versions of winners and album treats. From the bluesy, strutting "Jive Turkey" to "More Than Love," the group displays their superb musicianship and ingenuity on 28 slabs of funk and soul. The guys proved they can slow-jam with anyone on "Together" and the super-lush "Honey." The Ohio Players were affectionately known as Sugarfoot, Billy, Pee Wee, Merv, Diamond, Jones, and Satch, all of whom contributed collectively in the writing and production of all the songs. Everyone is familiar with the hits, and most of their fans already have them; it's unsung pearls like "Good Luck Charm," and the convenience of having these smokin' grooves in one sweet package, that makes *Funk on Fire* a must. *—Andrew Hamilton*

Orgasm: The Very Best of the Westbound Years / Jun. 30, 1998 / Southbound ✦✦✦✦✦
The majority of music fans are familiar with the legendary Ohio Players through such mid- to late-'70s pop-funk hits as "Love Rollercoaster," "Fire," and "Fopp." What many don't realize is that the band had been around since the '60s, and released a trilogy of hard funk records from 1972-1973 on the Westbound label—*Pain*, *Pleasure*, and *Ecstasy*—that were easily comparable to the early-'70s classics by their rival Westbound labelmates, Funkadelic. And since the albums have been out-of-print for some time, the European import *Orgasm: The Very Best of the Westbound Years* is a solid collection of tracks from this era. Included is the 1972 novelty hit "Funky Worm," as well as all the sizzling title tracks from the three albums. A pair of songs from outside the trilogy is added, "Climax" (one of the collection's best tracks) and a cover of Marvin Gaye's "What's Going On," both from 1974. A previously unissued track, "Ain't That Lovin' You (For More Reasons Than One)," is tacked on the end, making *Orgasm* an excellent anthology of the Ohio Players' early years, before they achieved mass mainstream success. *—Greg Prato*

20th Century Masters—The Millennium Collection: The Best of The Ohio Players / Feb. 1, 2000 / Mercury ✦✦✦
If the Ohio Players' *Funk On Fire* CD is too much material for you, then this dozen from Dayton, Ohio's most famous band should set you right. Includes their two number one pop hits "Love Rollercoaster" and "Fire," along with "Skin Tight," "Jive Turkey," and their anthem "O-H-I-O." Mellow down with three soothing ballads: the jazz-flavored "Sweet Sticky Thing," the ultimate floater "Heaven Must Be Like This," and guitarist/vocalist Sugarfoot's favorite tune "I Wanna Be Free." The compilers tripped by including "Happy Holidays" and "Let's Do It"—"Honey" and "Together" would have made this package far stronger and practically critic-proof. *—Andrew Hamilton*

Oingo Boingo

f. 1977, **db.** 1996
New Wave, Alternative Pop/Rock
Led by the wide-ranging musical talent of Danny Elfman (who would go on to score film and TV projects ranging from *Batman* to *The Simpsons*), Los Angeles' Oingo Boingo carved out a respectable reputation among the new wave set with a quirky pop style that owed a heavy debt to bands like XTC. In 1994, Oingo Boingo reemerged as Boingo, releasing a new album that didn't attract much attention; the self-expanatory *Farewell* followed two years later. *—Dan Heilman*

● **Best O' Boingo** / 1992 / MCA ✦✦✦✦
It captures their peculiar-yet-catchy style well. *—Dan Heilman*

● **Anthology** / Nov. 2, 1999 / Hip-O ✦✦✦✦
Oingo Boingo's two-disc *Anthology* collects some of the finest examples of their eclectic sound, including "Weird Science" and the Halloween anthem "Dead Man's Party." Tracks like "Only A Lad," "Grey Matter" and "Cinderella Undercover" define their cerebral-yet-catchy style, and live versions of "Tender Lumpkins," "Whole Day Off" and "Insects" hint at the group's theatrical concerts. The most complete of the Oingo Boingo collections, *Anthology* picks up where *Best O' Boingo* left off, making it a good starting point for those new to the group's quirky pop. *—Heather Phares*

The O'Jays

f. 1958, Canton, OH
Pop-Soul, Quiet Storm, Philly Soul, Urban, Soul
Perhaps the reigning vocal group of the '70s and '80s, the O'Jays began in Canton as the Triumphs in 1958. The original lineup was Eddie Levert, Walter Williams, William Powell, Bobby Massey, and Bill Isles. They recorded as the Mascots for King in 1961 and were renamed by Cleveland disc jockey Eddie O'Jay. Isles departed in 1965 and Massey left in 1971 to become a producer, making the group a trio. They got their first chart single in 1963 for Imperial, for whom they recorded until 1967. The O'Jays' first major hit was "I'll Be Sweeter Tomorrow (Than I Was Today)" for Bell in 1967, which reached number eight on the R&B charts. They continued on Bell and Neptune until they attained stardom in 1972 on Philadelphia International. "Back Stabbers" was the first of eight number one R&B hits they would get on the label from 1972-1987. Others included "Love Train," "Give the People What They Want," "I Love Music," "Livin' for the Weekend," "Message to Our Music," "Use Ta Be My Girl," "Darlin' Darlin' Baby (Sweet, Tender, Love)" and "Lovin' You." They also had eight other Top Ten R&B hits and four other Top Ten pop smashes, while "Love Train" also topped the pop charts in 1973. They moved to EMI in 1987 and continued recording. *—Ron Wynn*

Comin' Through / 1965 / Imperial ✦✦✦
The O'Jays were a fledgling five-member outfit when they issued their debut album in 1965. They generated a little attention with the dance/novelty tune "Do the Wiggle," and also issued a pair of good ballads in "Lonely Drifter" and "Lipstick Traces." None of these songs were as masterfully produced or arranged as the epic Gamble/Huff material, but it did reveal the potential they had for R&B stardom. This album has been out of print for years, although some of the songs have surfaced on anthologies. *—Ron Wynn*

Back on Top / 1968 / Bell ✦✦✦

The O'Jays in Philadelphia / 1969 / Epic Associated/Legacy ✦✦✦✦✦
Contrary to what its title suggests, *The O'Jays in Philadelphia* isn't a live album. Rather,

the title of this studio date refers to the beginning of their association with Philly's R&B scene and producers/songwriters Kenny Gamble & Leon Huff. What they didn't know in 1969 was just how long and fruitful that association would end up being. This album wasn't the major hit that *Back Stabbers* would be, but not for lack of strong material. From "One Night Affair" to "Let Me In Your World," this superb album is quintessential Philly soul. While Eddie Levert's gospel-influenced belting is as gritty as anything that came from Stax Records, the production is as notably sleek. A few years later, Gamble & Huff would produce a longer, heavily syncopated version of "Affair" for Jerry Butler that some soul historians exalt as the first disco single. The main problem with the CD configuration of this classic is its skimpiness—Legacy could have easily added at least another half hour of material. *—Alex Henderson*

☆ **Back Stabbers** / 1972 / Epic Associated/Legacy ♦♦♦♦♦
Although you could lean toward *Ship Ahoy*, it would be hard to argue with the general assessment that *Back Stabbers* is the O'Jays' greatest album. Certainly, no other single in 1973 was as transcendent and definitive as "Love Train," without question their greatest track. "Back Stabbers" isn't far behind it; the message, harmonies, Eddie Levert's lead, and the group's refrains are all testimonies to soul's glory, and Gamble and Huff were in peak form. There were other good songs on the record, like "Listen to the Clock on the Wall" and "Shiftless, Shady, Jealous Kind of People," and three other hit singles, "992 Arguments," "Time to Get Down," and "Sunshine," but they were completely blown away by "Love Train" and "Back Stabbers." (Originally released in August 1972 as Philadelphia International 31712, *Back Stabbers* was reissued on March 12, 1996, as Epic Associated/Legacy 661Jl3, as part of Legacy's *Rhythm & Soul* Series, with liner notes by David Ritz.) *—Ron Wynn & William Ruhlmann*

Ship Ahoy / 1973 / Philadelphia International ♦♦♦♦♦
The "other" O'Jays album masterpiece, *Ship Ahoy* combined shattering message tracks and stunning love songs in a fashion matched only by Curtis Mayfield's finest material. From the album cover showing a slave ship to the memorable title song and incredible "For the Love of Money," Gamble and Huff addressed every social ill from envy to racism and greed. Eddie Levert's leads were consistently magnificent, as were the harmonies, production and arrangements. "Put Your Hands Together" and "You Got Your Hooks In Me" would be good album cuts, but on *Ship Ahoy* they were merely icing on the cake. *—Ron Wynn*

Survival / 1975 / Epic Associated/Legacy ♦♦♦♦♦
The O'Jays followed the spectacular *Backstabbers* and *Ship Ahoy* with the good, but not on the same level, *Survival*. It was unrealistic to expect masterpieces every time out, and the LP included many strong ballads and good message tracks. But while it may not have been as epic in its performances and compositions, it was certainly the other albums' equal in sales strength. The group had two number one R&B hits in 1975, "Give The People What They Want" and "I Love Music (Part 1)." In addition, the title track made the charts as the B-side to "Let Me Make Love To You," another rousing ballad. *—Ron Wynn*

Family Reunion / 1975 / Philadelphia International ♦♦♦
In the 1970s, Philadelphia International Records could seemingly do no wrong where the O'Jays were concerned. The Cleveland trio recorded one gem after another under Gamble & Huff's direction, and *Family Reunion* was no exception. Nothing on this CD has the angry bite of "Back Stabbers," "Don't Call Me Brother" or "Rich Get Richer," and the mood is upbeat and optimistic on everything from the uplifting "Unity" to the ballad "Stairway to Heaven" (not to be confused with the Led Zeppelin song) to the escapist party anthem "Livin' for the Weekend." With the intoxicating "I Love Music," the O'Jays stressed the soul side of disco and provided one of the most appealing hits of the disco era. From start to finish, *Family Reunion* was a valuable addition to a catalogue that already had its share of treasures. *—Alex Henderson*

Message in Our Music / 1976 / The Right Stuff ♦♦♦
The O'Jays' vocals are stellar throughout this lively eight-song collection. Political and social lyrics weigh heavy but don't overburden this set. "Darlin' Darlin' Baby" is a killer midtempo love romp with equally effective leads by Eddie Levert and Walter Williams. "Paradise" was overlooked, with Walter Williams doing his falsetto "doo dah"s on the breaks and the trio spitting out Gamble & Huff's lyrics at breakneck speed. "Make a Joyful Noise" finds Eddie wailing like a Baptist preacher on a song that's more gospel than R&B; the title track is a typical message song made extraordinary by a great production and sensational vocals. The harmonies on "I Swear I Love No One But You" will blow you away. Another good slice of soul from the Canton, OH natives. *—Andrew Hamilton*

★ **Collector's Item** / 1977 / Philadelphia International ♦♦♦♦♦
After enjoying an impressive string of gold and platinum albums, The O'Jays had this collection of their biggest hits on Philadelphia International released in 1978. There was no way to lose with such songs as "Back Stabbers," "Love Train," "For the Love of Money" and "I Love Music." Unfortunately, Philadelphia International haphazardly sequenced the collection, ignoring chronological and stylistic considerations and just sticking tracks on the two sides without any attention to pacing. That gaffe aside, it's a worthy anthology for the casual listener, although the hardcore fan should look elsewhere. *—Ron Wynn*

So Full of Love / 1978 / The Right Stuff ♦♦♦
None of the albums the O'Jays recorded for Philadelphia International in the 1970s were weak or disappointing, although some were stronger than others. *So Full of Love*, which The Right Stuff reissued on CD in 1993, isn't quite essential, and isn't in a class with *Back Stabbers*, *Ship Ahoy* or *Family Reunion*. But the platinum album does have a lot going for it, including the major hit "Use Ta Be My Girl," and the heartfelt ballads "Cry Together" and "Brandy," and the captivating "This Time Baby," which would become a hit for soul/disco diva Jackie Moore in 1979. A funk treasure that should have been a major hit was the intense "Strokety Stroke." Once again, the O'Jays worked with Philly's best—not only Gamble & Huff, but also Thom Bell and Bunny Sigler. *Love* was a departure from their previous Philly International offerings in that it contained no social or political commentary whatsoever—with the disco era in full swing, Eddie Levert felt that the market for R&B message songs had dried up. *—Alex Henderson*

Love Train: The Best of the O'Jays / Aug. 9, 1994 / Epic Associated/Legacy ♦♦♦♦♦
All of the band's monster 1972-76 Philadelphia International hits are here, as well as a couple of small ones. The essay by Robert Palmer is good, but at a mere ten tracks, the selection is unaccountably skimpy. *—Richie Unterberger*

Let Me Make Love to You / Jan. 24, 1995 / Epic Associated/Legacy ♦♦♦
Like *Give the People What They Want*, *Let Me Make Love To You* is a concept compilation, collecting 10 of The O'Jays' most under-appreciated love ballads, including the title track, which was a minor hit, "Stairway to Heaven," and "Listen to the Clock on the Wall." Again, the disc is not a hits collection, but a sampling of some of the group's finest album tracks and forgotten singles, and in that context, it's very enjoyable. *—Stephen Thomas Erlewine*

Give the People What They Want / Feb. 28, 1995 / Epic Associated/Legacy ♦♦♦
In addition to liner notes, a major problem with the first CD configurations of the classic O'Jays albums like *Ship Ahoy* and *Family Reunion* was their brevity. By LP standards, roughly 35-40 minutes was generous; but for CDs, it's undeniably skimpy. In 1995, Sony's reissue-oriented Legacy label was fairly generous when assembling *Give the People What They Want*, a CD containing material from those gems as well as *Back Stabbers* and *Survival*. Everything here is first rate—from the angry socio-political commentary of "Give the People What They Want" and "Rich Get Richer" to the romantic optimism of "(They Call Me) Mr. Lucky," the CD reminds us how consistently superb the O'Jays were during the '70s. It also reminds us of another important fact: under Gamble & Huff, the group's albums tended to contain very little, if any, filler. Most of these pearls—including the moving "How Time Flies" and the biting "Shiftless, Shady, Jealous Kind of People"—weren't even released as singles. *—Alex Henderson*

The Ultimate Collection / 1999 / Marginal ♦♦♦♦♦
This collection contains most of the O'Jays' Imperial/Minit Records sides, one, "I'll Be Sweeter Tomorrow" from their Bell Records stint, and "Miracles," an early recording on Dayco Records. Collectors go crazy over these highly sought after pre-Philadelphia International tracks. The biggest pop record was "Lipstick Traces" led by Walter Williams. The others were awesome in Northeast Ohio, including "How Does It Feel," "Lonely Drifter," "Crack Up Laughing," and "Stand in for Love." Two falsetto-led chillers by William Powell ("Oh How You Hurt Me," and "Working on Your Case,") along with the occasional lead from Williams add diversity to Eddie Levert's frequent leads. While this is not definitive—that would take another CD—it is essential. *—Andrew Hamilton*

The Best of the O'Jays: 1976-1991 / Feb. 9, 1999 / The Right Stuff ♦♦♦♦♦
O'Jays fans may find the time period contained in this compilation odd. In 1976, the O'Jays were in the middle of their hitmaking period with CBS-distributed Philadelphia International Records (PIR). In 1985, PIR switched distribution to EMI, the catalog for which is owned by Capitol Records, for which The Right Stuff serves as the reissue arm. The group signed directly to EMI in 1985, remaining until 1993. Though they scored 14 R&B chart hits between 1985 and 1993, The Right Stuff must have felt that there were not enough big hits to justify a compilation of that period. So, the label has licensed ten of the 17 tracks here from PIR, dating back to the 1976 number one R&B hit "Message in Our Music." From there on, most of the group's R&B Top 40 hits over the next 15 years are included, among them chart-toppers "Darlin' Darlin' Baby (Sweet, Tender, Love)," "Use Ta Be My Girl," "Lovin' You," and "Have You Had Your Love Today," though three of their Top 20 hits are missing. With their gruff vocals contrasted by the creamy production style of Kenny Gamble and Leon Huff, the O'Jays on these (and their earlier '70s recordings) proved a valid successor to the pop-soul style pioneered by Motown in the '60s. Their pop crossover appeal was always fitful, and, in fact, only one song here, the gold-selling "Use Ta Be My Girl," made the pop Top Ten. But their work was remarkably consistent and, toward the end of this period, even surprisingly diverse, as when they recorded Bob Dylan's "Emotionally Yours" in a gospel style and took it into the R&B Top Ten in 1991. *—William Ruhlmann*

Ol' Dirty Bastard (Russell Jones)

Vocals / Hardcore Rap, East Coast Rap, Hip-Hop

A member of the Brooklyn hip-hop congregation the Wu-Tang Clan, Ol' Dirty Bastard released his first solo album in the spring of 1995, after the Clan imploded. Produced by fellow Wu-Tang member Prince Rakeem, Ol' Dirty Bastard's *Return to the 36 Chambers* sounds identical to the Clan's 1993 debut album, *Enter the Wu-Tang (36 Chambers)*. The colorful ODB, who also began calling himself Big Baby Jesus, made any number of headlines in the years to follow for his regular run-ins with the law; he finally released his second solo effort, *Nigga Please*, in 1999. True to form, he was unable to shake the mighty arm of the law, and in July of 2001, Ol' Dirty was sentenced to two to four years in the state penitentiary for charges stemming from crack cocaine possesion. All of which set the stage for the August 2001 greatest hits package, *Free Dirty*. *—Stephen Thomas Erlewine*

● **Return to the 36 Chambers** / Mar. 28, 1995 / Elektra ♦♦♦♦♦
As a member of the Wu-Tang Clan, Ol' Dirty Bastard's bizarre, free-form rants added both comic relief and a dangerous unpredictability to the group's chemistry. ODB's RZA-produced solo debut *Return to the 36 Chambers* stretches his schtick over a full album, which if anything makes him sound even more unbalanced. Long before the album ends, it's

clear that ODB has emptied his bag of tricks—loose, off-the-beat raps that sometimes don't even rhyme, unbelievably graphic vulgarity, gonzo off-key warbling (which sounds a little like Biz Markie as a mental patient), and general goofing off. Yet within that role as hardcore rap's clown prince of psychosis, ODB is pretty damned entertaining. His leaps in association are often as disturbing as they are funny, whether they're couched in scatological detail or not; they certainly don't make his widely publicized erratic behavior seem at all surprising. And, despite the unstructured feel dominating most of the album, there are a fair share of hooks, and two absolutely killer singles in "Shimmy Shimmy Ya" and "Brooklyn Zoo." Certainly, there's no reason for the album to be as long as it is, considering the dull filler toward the end. But, even though *Return to the 36 Chambers* might not be the most earth-shattering piece of the Wu-Tang puzzle, it's an infectious party record which proves that, despite his limitations, Ol' Dirty Bastard has the charisma to carry an album on his own. *—Steve Huey*

Nigga Please / Sep. 14, 1999 / Elektra ✦✦✦✦
Hollywood may have Austin Powers, but hip-hop has it's own international man of mystery; his name is the Ol' Dirty Bastard. ODB lives and suffers with the adage that any publicity is good publicity, as he has not spent the greater part of the last two years gaining widespread notoriety for the music he makes. Rather, he has spent a majority of that time turning up on local crime blotters from coast to coast, trying to raise bail money, recuperating from gunshot wounds, rescuing a kid who was struck by a car, and hijacking the 1998 Grammy awards. With that in mind, it should be obvious by now that personalities of ODB's magnitude come around once in a lifetime. And even though he is repetitiously contradictory with his neurotic ramblings, who cares? That's half of his appeal, as there is an irrefutable attraction to ODB's carefree and inebriated outlook on life. With rhymes frequently so garbled that they are barely decipherable, calling ODB a quintessential lyricist would surely insult the intelligence of any hip-hop purist. Yet the dirt dog is indubitably a distinguished emcee and a uniquely abrasive one at that, as he turns an array of voice cracking/bloodcurdling hooks into grisly masterpieces. Examples include the nonsensical crooning of his Rick James interpolations "Cold Blooded" and "You Don't Want to Fuck With Me," and the ridiculously addictive "Rollin Wit You." Despite that ODB's production chores are handled admirably by the Neptunes, Irv Gotti and RZA, the backing acoustics are hardly needed; ODB rarely stays on beat and there is little, or no structure to his rhyme sequences. Safely nestled away in his own little world, there is no containing ODB's free-spirited outlook on life. His is a world that is heavy on shock value, yet undeniably entertaining. *—Matt Conaway*

Free Dirty: Best of Ol' Dirty Bastard / Aug. 28, 2001 / Rhino ✦✦✦✦✦

Old 97's

f. 1993

Americana, Alternative Country-Rock, Indie Pop

The Dallas, Texas alt-country quartet the Old 97's formed in 1993, led by singer and guitarist Rhett Miller. Along with bassist Murry Hammond and second guitarist Ken Bethea, the group cut their initial demos at Austin's famed Cedar Creek Recording. Following the addition of drummer Philip Peeples, the Old 97's issued *Wreck Your Life* in 1995. *Fight Songs* was issued in 1999; the same year, the early 1994 recording *Hitchhike to Rhome* was reissued on CD, and the mini-album *Early Tracks* delivered more of the same in 2000. Critical press hailed the unit in early 2001 with the release of *Satellite Rides*. *—Jason Ankeny*

Hitchhike to Rhome / 1994 / Big Iron ✦✦✦
Many bands blend country and rock, but few brew this concoction as well as the Old 97's on *Hitchhike to Rhome*. Energetic frontman Rhett Miller commands attention as a charismatic vocalist and clever songwriter on tracks such as "St. Ignatius" and "If My Heart Was a Car." On the album's highlight "Stoned," he even manages to successfully infuse the adjectives "dope" and "fly" into a country song. Bass player Murry Hammond supplies smooth harmonies throughout the album, in addition to lead vocals on the excellent Merle Haggard cover "Mama Tried." Musically, the Old 97's are capable of shifting comfortably between bluegrassy honky tonk ("Doreen") and the occasional serene ballad ("Dancing With Tears.") Ken Bethea's guitar leads the band throughout their rowdy ride while Philip Peeples' steady drumming manages to somehow hold everything together. Other standouts include "Drowning in the Days," "Hands Off," and "504." Further demonstrating their country roots, there is even a secret hidden version of Webb Pierce's "Tupelo County Jail" after the last listed track. Though their debut sounds more sparse and simplified than their subsequent releases, *Hitchhike to Rhome* showcases the spark of a truly original band with endless potential. *—Michael Frey*

Wreck Your Life / Oct. 3, 1995 / Bloodshot ✦✦✦
While Old 97's second album, 1995's *Wreck Your Life*, continues the forlorn West Texas twang-a-billy that they pioneered with their debut, the sharp songwriting of vocalist Rhett Miller steps out to the forefront this time 'round. He weeps through the lovesick romp "Doreen" and chunks through longtime favorite "Big Brown Eyes" with a newfound poetic touch to the age-old traumas of love ("I'm callin' time and temperature just for some company," "You made a big impression for a girl of your size"). At the same time, it's hard to believe the barroom ballad "W-I-F-E" wasn't written by George Jones back in the late '50s. Supporting Miller's keening vocals is bassist and yodeler Murry Hammond, whose musical accents are understated, but without them many a song would fall flat. Well-chosen covers, including the Tex-Mex standard "You Belong to My Heart" and a stomp through "My Sweet Blue-Eyed Darlin'" that would do Bill Monroe proud round out the album, although a few songs near the end seem to lose steam. Nevertheless, *Wreck Your Life* contains some killer tracks and the band exudes an honest energy that would only improve on future releases. *—Zac Johnson*

● **Too Far to Care** / Jun. 17, 1997 / Elektra/Asylum ✦✦✦✦✦
Serving as the ideal apex between the Old 97's Texas twang and smart pop fascinations, *Too Far to Care* is instantly catchy and endearing; heartbreaking desert soul and punk-fueled swagger all at the same time. Chief songwriter Rhett Miller turns a phrase like a doorknob and opens doors to dusty barrooms and tattered bedrooms, both containing the same boozy characters in various states of emotional undress. The initial blast of "Timebomb" carries through the first three songs, relenting finally in the breathy croon of "Salome," accented warmly by bassist Murry Hammond's light harmonies and guitarist Ken Bethea's airy tremolo-heavy guitar. Other highlights include the high-speed chase of "Melt Show," the reckless surge of "House That Used to Be," and their confident re-recording of "Big Brown Eyes" (originally appearing on their 1995 album *Wreck Your Life*). Throughout the album, Miller's swooning howl aches with too many miles on the road and too many lonely nights, familiar topics to be sure but he still manages to tackle them like he invented heartache. The curse of Old 97's may be that country fans consider it too rock & roll, and rock fans can't get past the twang, but for those who dip both feet into these streams, it really doesn't get any better than this band and this album. *—Zac Johnson*

Fight Songs / Apr. 27, 1999 / Elektra/Asylum ✦✦✦
Texas troubadours Old 97's moved farther away from their traditional C&W sound on their 1999 release, *Fight Songs*, instead incorporating warmly distorted guitars and crunchy rhythms into their brash pop songs. Thankfully for fans of the band, the terrific songwriting is still there, but the sound is a little more polished than the twang-a-billy bombast of their previous album, *Too Far to Care*. The heavy grit of the lead track, "Jagged," is augmented by Rhett Miller and Murray Hammond's bright vocals, whereas the rhumba stylings of "What We Talk About" slinks along like two strangers locked in a tango. Songs seem more thoroughly constructed this time around, relying less on pure bravado and more on structure. That works well for the most part, but there's something lacking that was unrelenting and instantly likable in their previous release. That being said, *Fight Songs* is still a bright and worthwhile album with as many strong songs as any of their releases. *—Zac Johnson*

Early Tracks / May 23, 2000 / Bloodshot ✦✦✦
A collection of out-of-print seven-inch singles and previously unreleased tracks, *Early Tracks* exhibits the Old 97's uncanny ability to play witty, memorable, country-rock that chugs along at a freight train's pace. Despite the fact that this EP has been pieced together from spare parts, the material is surprisingly strong. With its unrelenting twang and Rhett Miller's nimble wordplay, "Ray Charles" would have fit perfectly into place on *Wreck Your Life*, while "Cryin' Drunk," a swaggering track that is stylistically similar to "Just Like California," would find *Too Far to Care* to be a better fit. Bassist Murry Hammond makes strong contributions, handling lead vocals on "Sound of Running," "Harold's Super Service," and a cover of Johnny Cash's "Let the Train Blow the Whistle." Also present are the dynamic "Por Favor," a swaying, breezy version of "W-I-F-E," and the devilish "Eyes For You." *Early Tracks* is sure to please fans pleading for a return to the days before the pop sheen of *Fight Songs*, as well as those who just can't get enough of this truly arresting and irresistible quartet. *—Michael Frey*

Satellite Rides / Mar. 20, 2001 / Elektra/Asylum ✦✦✦✦
Moving even further away from their alt-country roots, the Old 97's fifth effort is a consistently engaging and unpretentious strummy power pop nugget. Bits of the effortless hook-driven approach of Marshall Crenshaw and Nick Lowe mesh with winning melodies that stick in your skull after the first spin. Hints of Brit Invasion Beatles/Badfinger-styled harmonies also infiltrate these songs, bringing a crisp vocal attack to play, especially in bassist Murray Hammond's subtle backing work. Guitarist/singer/songwriter Rhett Miller has honed his composing and arrangement skills to a fine edge, cramming these compact cuts (nothing runs over four minutes, most clock in around three) with smart lyrics and sharp, unaffected playing. There's still a little twang remaining from the old days in the driving double-time "Am I Too Late," and even a solo acoustic guitar ballad in "Question," but the band seems most comfortable pounding out crafty, infectious instant singles like "Rollerskate Skinny." Miller's voice is perfect for these songs, mixing just the right amount of pride, innocence, and youthful exuberance into the predominantly upbeat lyrics. But just as importantly, there's a presence and immediacy to *Satellite Rides*, partially due to the expert touch of mixer Tchad Blake, that makes it jump out of the speakers like the locomotive that provides the band with its name. Deftly incorporating their Texas roots with yodeling and a snappy punch makes "Up the Devil's Pay" one of the disc's most successful tracks, but there really isn't a lackluster performance here. The six-song live bonus EP that came free with early pressings proves how skillful the quartet is in concert, and that their biting, cohesive style is no studio-concocted fluke. The Old 97's sound is organic and natural, and on *Satellite Rides* they find the perfect balance between their roots in rugged country and pure chiming pop. *—Hal Horowitz*

Will Oldham

Vocals, Guitar / Alternative Country, Indie Rock, Lo-Fi, Singer/Songwriter

For most of the '90s, Will Oldham was the mastermind of Palace Music, a shambling, country-tinged indie-rock group that recorded under a variety of names. The only constant in Palace was Oldham, and he would often record as a solo artist under the Palace name. That fact made his decision to retire the Palace name in 1997 somewhat baffling, since for all intents and purposes, he was the band. Nevertheless, *Joya*, Oldham's first album as a solo artist, was slightly different than Palace, boasting a slightly darker and somber tone. Like all the Palace records, *Joya* was released on Drag City to positive critical notices and a moderately successful cult following. Although the subsequent *I See a*

Darkness was attributed to Bonnie Prince Billy, Oldham continued using his given name for releases including *Ode Music* and *Guarapero: Lost Blues 2*. The second Bonnie Prince Billy album, *Ease Down the Road*, arrived in early 2001 and featured collaborators including David Pajo, Catherine Irwin, Mike Fellows and Harmony Korine. *—Stephen Thomas Erlewine*

Joya / Oct. 21, 1997 / Drag City ♦♦♦♦
Retiring the Palace moniker for no reason other than a whim, Will Oldham doesn't necessarily explore new territory on his first official solo album, *Joya*. Oldham sticks to the simple, slow acoustic country-folk songs that dominated the latter-day Palace albums, and like before, the songs teeter between apparent sincerity and inscrutible irony. The hushed dynamics of the music and his whispered vocals suggest that Oldham means what he's saying, but his appropriation of American folk imagery and impenetrable wordplay suggest otherwise. As always, there are a few songs that have a quiet power (including "Antagonism" and a collaboration with the Silver Jews' Dave Berman), but the overall effect of *Joya* is a familiar one—it's a promising, ultimately unfulfilling record that doesn't quite prove whether Oldham is a songwriter of pretense or genuine talent. *—Stephen Thomas Erlewine*

Western Music / Mar. 24, 1998 / Acuarela Ovni ♦♦♦
Keeping up to date with Will Oldham's complete output can be an arduous task—he has always exploited the shorter formats of the 7" and EP, producing a healthy amount of material in between his full-length releases. However, seeking out the 7" and EP formats can be rewarding, as the material often matches—and occasionally surpasses—the quality of his albums. The genesis of *Western Music* (released by the combined forces of two obscure labels for *The Affliction Series*) is typical, coming from a variety of sessions. Two tracks are solo Oldham, while Mick Turner and Jim White of the Dirty Three and former Gastr del Sol member David Grubbs play anonymous roles elsewhere. On nearly every song, Oldham approaches the level of his best work although, ultimately, each has its shortcomings. "Always Bathing in the Evening" relishes in its simple language. "Wade in/ Wade in," he sings, as voices in the distance chime in with "Blowing/Jump in/Waiting/ Jump in." While there is little lyrical matter to speak of, it sounds fantastic. *Western Music*'s most complete song is "Jump In Jump In, Come In Come In," though even this, with its plodding tempo, feels more like a rehearsal on disc. Inspiration only seems to strike with the final verse. Only on "Three Photographs" (an oddity in a career full of them) does Oldham manage to throw us yet another curve. It's an intriguing, fragmentary story told through pictures. Over the most rudimentary, lo-fi guitar strum, Oldham's voice is sped up slightly, producing a humorous, Paul Simon effect. *Western Music* came during a particularly prolific time for Oldham, though *Joya*, his full-length album from the period, is more consistent. *—Nathan Bush*

• **I See A Darkness** / 1999 / Palace ♦♦♦♦♦
Bonnie Prince Billy's album, *I See a Darkness*, seems to pick up where Oldham's 1997 album, *Joya*, left off; a more melodic style than the veteran Palace listener might be used to. Oldham definitely hasn't abandoned his foundation of mordant lyrics and minimalist arrangements, but he has built a variety of different layers that make this album an emotional and pleasurable listening experience.

In "Nomadic Revery," Oldham draws upon his classic Appalachian sound; it's the kind of song that begs you to join in. Oldham has always given the kind of energy to his character's voices that most people are afraid to relate to. This is all too evident in "Death to Everyone," Oldham punches out his bitter poetry in his most somber voice. The album takes its most surprising turn on "Madeleine-Mary," a Celtic-style folk song set to a Rastafarian guitar sound. "Today I Was an Evil One" introduces a horn section that drives home his morbid words in a strangely elegant manner. The album closes with a short and rare love song called "Raining in Darling"; Oldham stretches his voice to its most impressive limits, and the number is touching and hopeful. *—Gregg Rounds*

Get on Jolly / 2000 / Palace ♦♦♦
Credited to Marquis de Tren and Bonny Billy, *Get on Jolly* is performed by Will Oldham along with Dirty Three member and Tren Brother Mick Turner. With words adapted from *Gitanjali* by Rabindranath Tagore (1861-1941), a Nobel Prize-winning poet from India, Oldham sings in a somber, yet expressive mode, giving an air of sacredness to the effort. Turner's low-key accompaniment, meanwhile, provides a loose, meandering minor-key backdrop. Though a pleasant enough listen, *Get on Jolly* is by no means an essential release for either artist; only ardent fans will find it worth their while. *—Jason Nickey*

Guarapero: Lost Blues 2 / Feb. 22, 2000 / Drag City ♦♦♦
Guarapero/Lost Blues 2 gathers seven years' worth of rarities from Will Oldham, including an unusual reading of D.H. Lawrence's poem *The Risen Lord*, with a clunky, cheesy drum machine in the background, as well as a radical reworking of Lynyrd Skynyrd's "Every Mother's Son." Several of these songs come from BBC sessions, but the sound quality on tracks like "Gezundheit" and "Let the Wires Ring" suggests they were recorded on wax cylinder and transmitted by a crystal set, which, of course, only amplifies the songs' sparse, timeless feel. "The Spider's Dude Is Often There" and "For the Mekons Et Al" are among the most exuberant Palace songs on *Guarapero*, while Oldham tracks like "No More Rides" and "Sugarcane Juice Drinker" trace his development as a performer and songwriter. Due to the time span it covers, it's natural that *Guarapero/Lost Blues 2* is a bit disjointed; nevertheless, it fills in the gaps for Oldham completists and is an entertaining, if scattered, look at some of his musical sketches over the years. *—Heather Phares*

The Olivia Tremor Control

f. 1992
Experimental Rock, Neo-Psychedelia, Indie Rock, Lo-Fi
As much a concept as a band, the Olivia Tremor Control was one of the most visible and innovative members of the Elephant 6 Recording Company collective, a coterie of like-minded, lo-fi indie groups—including the Apples (in stereo), Neutral Milk Hotel and Secret Square—who shared musicians, ideas and sensibilities. In 1995, the OTC debuted with the EP *California Demise*, the first chapter in an ongoing series of high-concept recordings built around the surreal plot of an imaginary film conceived by singers/ songwriters/multi-instrumentalists William Cullen Hart and Bill Doss. The follow-up seven-inch, "The Giant Day," led directly into the group's 1996 debut double-LP, *Music from the Unrealized Film Script "Dusk at Cubist Castle,"* a sprawling collection of Beatlesque psychedelia, popcraft and tape loops culled from some 200 unrecorded songs. The first few thousand copies of the album also included a bonus disc of ambient "dream sequences." *Black Foliage: Animation Music By The Olivia Tremor Control* followed in 1999. *—Jason Ankeny*

• **Dusk at Cubist Castle** / Aug. 1996 / Flydaddy ♦♦♦♦♦
Not the Beatles, but an incredible facsimile: on their sprawling 27-song debut opus *Music From the Unrealized Film Script "Dusk at Cubist Castle,"* the Olivia Tremor Control manage to summon not only the sound of the *White Album*-era Fab Four, but also the unfettered creativity. The soundtrack to an as-yet unmade film about a pair of women named Olivia and Jacqueline and a massive earthquake dubbed the California Demise, the album incorporates a slew of influences and textures (including Beach Boys-flavored pop, psychedelia, Krautrock, noise, and folk-rock) and synthesizes them into a distinct homebrew of shimmering harmonies, guitar drones, backwards tape loops and inventive effects. As an added bonus, the first few thousand copies come with a bonus CD of ambient "dream sequences"—titled *Explanation II*—which, when played simultaneously with the first disc, realizes true quadraphonic sound. Amazing. *—Jason Ankeny*

Black Foliage: Animation Music / 1999 / Flydaddy ♦♦♦♦
If the preceding *Dusk at Cubist Castle* was the Olivia Tremor Control's very own *White Album*, then the labyrinthine *Black Foliage* is their *Smile*—it's an imploding masterpiece, a work teetering on the cliff's edge between genius and madness. Torn at the seams between pop transcendence and noise radicalism, the group attempts to have it both ways, meaning teenage symphonies to God like "A New Day" rest uneasily alongside musique concrete-styled tape pastiches such as "Combinations" (which, along with the similarly styled, multi-part title track, is one of the many sonic motifs snaking its way throughout the record); there are at least enough ideas for five albums here, which is both *Black Foliage's* strength and its weakness—it's impossible not to get lost inside of the OTC's swirling schizophrenia, and too often snatches of brilliance flash by too quickly to savor the moment. Moreover, with songs like "California Demise 3" continuing the oblique narrative running through previous the OTC records, the artistic statement the record is making (and there undoubtedly is one) is impenetrable at best; still, with each of the band's successive releases seeming like just part of a much bigger picture only now beginning to come into focus, maybe that's the point—ultimately, *Black Foliage* just might be an end-of-the-millennium appeal which speaks directly and solely to the unconscious. *—Jason Ankeny*

Singles and Beyond / Aug. 8, 2000 / Emperor Norton ♦♦♦
Singles and Beyond, as the title suggests, collects most of the material the Olivia Tremor Control released before their first full-length, *Dusk at Cubist Castle*. Although the "band sound" is still coalescing, apparently all the ingredients were in place even from the start. Sure, there's plenty of solid guitar pop/psych in store, but many of the more experimental aspects of the band (that are often released under other names like Black Swan Network or Frosted Ambassador) are also in place. Also in place is a vague "concept," of sorts, that not only links these tunes to their later, full-length recordings but provides a sense of cohesion that often lacks in singles compilations. These guys are true masters of home recording; most of these tracks were recorded at their various abodes, on four-track machines. Whether it's the tastefully bizarre production touches at the end of "Fireplace" or the Burroughs-ian cut up technique of "Christmas With William S.," the Olivia Tremor Control not only knows what they want, but they know how to achieve it as well; no small feat for home recorders. Since Elephant 6 bands tend to release material on a variety of labels with a variety of formats, *Singles and Beyond* is a welcome addition for folks who missed out the first time around. *—Sean Westergaard*

The Olympics

f. 1958, Los Angeles, CA, **db.** 1966
R&B, Brown-Eyed Soul
The Olympics were one of the great L.A.-based acts who managed to score regional hits on the West Coast by balancing upbeat and often humorous novelty R&B tunes with those about popular dances of the day. They are perhaps best remembered for "Western Movies." The Coasters-type novelty number caught on quickly, right around the same time that all of America was preoccupied with western-themed movies and TV shows. The single climbed to number eight pop and number seven R&B in 1958. The Olympics then moved over to the Arvee label in 1959. For their numerous A-sides, the Olympics preferred to issue inner-city generated dance ditties, including the Smith/Goldsmith-penned "(Baby) Hully Gully," "The Philly Dog," "The Slop," and "The Duck." The group only occasionally performed ballads, like the doo wop-inspired "Stay Where You Are," and a few rockers like "Shimmy Like Kate" and "Dance By the Light of the Moon." Mostly, the Olympics attempted to duplicate their hit status with novelty songs along the lines of "Western Movies." Their biggest success in the novelty realm was their remake of "Big Boy Pete," written and first recorded by Don & Dewey for Specialty. Other regional hits included "Little Pedro," "Little Dooley," and "Big Chief Little Foot." Others, like the humorous "Dodge City" and "(I Wanna) Dance With the Teacher" sound like teenage West Coast Americana at its most innocent. After the Olympics left Arvee, they

scored a couple of hits in 1963 on the L.A.-based Tri-Disc label: the rollicking dance ditty "The Bounce" and "Dancin' Holiday." Both were produced by Fred Smith. —*Bryan Thomas*

● **All-Time Greatest Hits!** / 1991 / Sandstone Music ✦✦✦✦

During their heyday and long after their breakup, the Olympics found themselves being compared to the Coasters more than anyone. While they had their own sound and were far from clones, the Olympics had a lighthearted, fun approach that made comparisons to the Coasters inevitable. Those adjectives certainly describe most of the 26 songs included on *All Time Greatest Hits!*, one of the more comprehensive and thoughtfully assembled Olympics collections available. In retrospect, humorous songs like "Dodge City," "(I Wanna) Dance With the Teacher," "Big Chief, Little Foot" and the 1958 hit "Western Movies" sound like teenage Americana at its most innocent (though at the time, extremist church groups saw nothing innocent in this material). Another high point of this CD (released by DCC Compact Classics in 1991) is the original version of "Good Lovin'," which would become a major hit for the Rascals. Thoroughly entertaining, *All Time Greatest Hits!* is definitely worth acquiring. —*Alex Henderson*

Doin' the Hully Gully/Dance by the Light of the Moon/Party Time / Mar. 1, 1994 / Ace ✦✦✦✦✦

Featuring 26 tracks, this single-disc contains three complete Olympics albums—*Doin' the Hully Gully*, *Dancy By the Light of the Moon*, and *Party Time*. For any serious fan, it's indispensable, and even casual fans will be well-served by the collection. —*Stephen Thomas Erlewine*

100 Proof (Aged in Soul)

f. 1969, Detroit, MI
Funk, Soul

100 Proof (Aged in Soul) teamed Detroit area vocalists Steve Mancha (born Clyde Wilson), Eddie Holiday (Eddie Anderson) and Joe Stubbs (the brother of the Four Tops' Levi Stubbs and an alumnus of the Contours and the Falcons). The trio was assembled by the famed writing and producing team of Brian Holland, Lamont Dozier and Eddie Holland, who in 1967 left the Motown label to set up their own record companies, Invictus and Hot Wax; they signed 100 Proof to the latter, and in 1969 issued the group's debut single, "Too Many Cooks (Spoil the Soup)." The follow-up, "Somebody's Been Sleeping," cracked the pop Top Ten in the fall of 1970; boasting a gritty, earthy approach closer in spirit to southern soul than the Motor City's trademark sound, the group issued a pair of LPs—*Somebody's Been Sleeping in My Bed* and the 1972 effort *Deliciously Yours*—but never again recaptured the commercial momentum of their first hit, finally dissolving in 1973. The 100 Proof (Aged in Soul) name was briefly resurrected, albeit with an all-new lineup, in 1977. —*Jason Ankeny*

● **Greatest Hits** / 1990 / Fantasy ✦✦✦✦✦

If one of Stax's artists had gone to Motown and received Eddie Holland's input, it might have sounded something like 100 Proof (Aged In Soul)—a jewel of a group that wasn't nearly as well known as it should have been. For Hot Wax/Invictus, 100 Proof wasn't as commercially successful as Honey Cone, the Chairmen of the Board or Freda Payne. But it certainly wasn't due to a lack of strong material. Full of gems, this collection shows how rewarding things could be when a group with an obvious love of Stax and Memphis soul embraced Holland's sleeker, more elaborate production style. The gritty "Somebody's Been Sleeping In My Bed" was a major hit, but surprisingly, jewels like "Driveway," "90 Day Freeze" and "Too Many Cooks (Spoil the Soup)" were only medium-size hits. "One Man's Leftovers (Is Another Man's Feast)" sounds like a poor person's "Somebody's Been Sleeping In My Bed," but on the whole, this CD shows how exciting things could be when Southern and Northern soul elements were combined. —*Alex Henderson*

The 101'ers

f. May 1974, **db.** Jun. 1976
Pub Rock, New Wave

Primarily known as the band Joe Strummer was in before he joined the Clash, the 101'ers were part of the last wave of British pub rock bands of the mid-'70s. The group never released any recordings while they were together, yet they were among the important transitional figures in the metamorphosis of pub rock into punk rock.

Joe Strummer formed the 101'ers in May of 1974, recruiting guitarist Clive Timperley, bassist Dan Kelleher and drummer Richard Dudanski; according to legend, the group either named themselves after the torture room in George Orwell's *1984* or the building where they lived. By the end of the summer, the group had performed their first concert, playing Brixton's Telegraph pub. For the next year and a half, the 101'ers worked the pub rock circuit. During 1975 and early 1976, the group laid down some demos. In the first half of 1976, the 101'ers had been opening for the Sex Pistols on selected dates. Inspired by the Pistols and the burgeoning punk movement, Strummer decided to quit the 101'ers in June 1976 and form the Clash. Within a month, the group's only single, "Keys to Your Heart," was released on Chiswick Records.

Following the demise of the 101'ers, Dudanski played with the Raincoats and, later, Public Image Limited; Timperley joined the Passions and Kelleher became a member of the Derelicts. In 1981, after the Clash had become stars, Strummer allowed a 101'ers compilation called *Elgin Avenue Breakdown* to be released. —*Stephen Thomas Erlewine*

● **Elgin Avenue Breakdown** / 1981 / Andalucia ✦✦✦✦

The 101'ers never released a proper album while they were together, only turning out one single, a terrific pub rocker called "Keys to Your Heart." They probably would have remained a pub rock footnote for much longer if it hadn't been for lead singer Joe

Strummer, whose massive success with the Clash led to an independent release (spearheaded by Strummer and the 101'ers drummer Snake Hips Dudanski) of *Elgin Avenue Breakdown* in 1981. It's not really correct to call this an album proper, since it contains the remnants of three demo sessions, including one recorded at the BBC, and a live audience tape, all shuffled and spit out seemingly at random. So, it's an utterly chaotic mess, with wildly varying sound quality, but that's part of its charm, since this is, after all, a collection of artifacts from a band that never got a chance to make an album, so you take whatever you can find. And, yes, this is good enough to hear even if you're not a Clash maniac, but you probably have to be a rock & roll fiend to really dig this. This is firmly within the tradition of such high-energy, ballsy pub groups as Ducks Deluxe, Eddie & the Hot Rods, and Dr. Feelgood, which means there's a lot of Stones-n-R&B-fueled rockers, spiked with a liberal amount of covers. These covers are tremendously spirited, even wild, and the originals follow suit, particularly the standouts "Letsagetabitarockin'" and "Keys to Your Heart" (included in an alternate version from the single). Make no mistake, this is a record only for die-hard collectors and rockers, but for that group, it's worth the search. —*Stephen Thomas Erlewine*

The Only Ones

f. 1977, **db.** 1981
Power Pop, New Wave, Punk

Led by the raffish and slightly scuzzy romance-obsessed Peter Perrett, the Only Ones were one of the punk era's most underrated bands. Not as confrontational as the Sex Pistols, as politically indulgent as the Clash, or as stripped-down as the Ramones, the Only Ones played not-so-fast guitar rock that sounded deeply indebted to the New York Dolls and other mid-'70s proto-punks. Singing his intelligently crafted pop songs in a semi-tuneful whine of a voice and backed by a band that effectively combined youthful exuberance with gracefully aging veterans, Perrett was an astute chronicler of the vagaries of modern, dysfunctional love. Despite a career that lasted from 1978-1981 and one certifiable "hit" song to their credit (the brilliant "Another Girl, Another Planet") the Only Ones became the archetypal contenders that never broke big, despite assurances from fans and critics that they couldn't miss. —*John Dougan*

The Only Ones / Apr. 1978 / Columbia ✦✦✦✦✦

"Another Girl, Another Planet" is here, but then again, it surfaces on a number of Only Ones records. The best of their studio releases, this record is a tuneful anomaly of mid-'70s rock that stands in stark contrast to the prevailing punk zeitgeist. Still, the band (even the old guys) play with an infectious enthusiasm, and Perrett, despite his tendency toward adenoidal Dylanesque vocals, is particularly winning. —*John Dougan*

Even Serpents Shine / 1979 / CBS ✦✦✦✦

● **Special View** / 1979 / Epic ✦✦✦✦✦

In America, Epic couldn't decide whether or not to release any Only Ones recordings, so they came up with this half-way measure: a sampler. *Special View* took the strongest tracks from their debut, added tracks from their so-so second album, *Even Serpents Shine*, and the result was (surprise) a great record. All these years later, *Special View* is as good a sampler of early Only Ones as anyone could have hoped for and should be considered an important purchase, although I think it's no longer in print. —*John Dougan*

Baby's Got a Gun / Jun. 1980 / Epic ✦✦✦

Remains / 1984 / Closer ✦✦

Peel Sessions / 1989 / Strange Fruit ✦✦✦✦✦

Frankly, one could argue an eloquent case either way as to why *Special View* or the *Peel Sessions* are the most important Only Ones recordings. I tend to recommend the *Peel Sessions*, because it's rougher, a little meaner, and The Only Ones were in the midst of their 15 minutes of fame as a rock band; plus, there's a swagger here that's missing on other recordings. —*John Dougan*

Onyx

f. 1990, Queens, NY
Hardcore Rap, East Coast Rap, Hip-Hop

The hip-hop trio Onyx ushered in a new development in 1993; rap in the mosh pit. Their shouting, in-your-face brand of high volume rapping didn't sit well with everyone, but their debut CD, *Bacdafucup*, included a huge crossover smash with "Slam." The follow-up *All We Got Iz Us* appeared in 1995; after signing to Def Jam, Onyx returned three years later with *Shut 'Em Down*. —*Ron Wynn*

● **Bacdafucup** / 1993 / Def Jam ✦✦✦✦

At the time that *Bacdafucup* hit the record racks and airwaves, Onyx seemed to be inventing a genre all their own: heavy metal rap. Of course, on closer inspection, it is not at all surprising stylistically, given their link to Def Jam and Run DMC, the record company and crew that introduced heavy guitar riffs into hip-hop. Onyx, though, seemed far more threateningly hardcore than Run DMC ever were, and each song on their debut album seems like a quick-triggered, menacing chip set squarely on the shoulders of MCs Big DS, Suavé, Fredro, and Sticky Fingaz. That the entire album from beginning to end circumvents almost any backlash by being so brilliantly catchy as well, is a sterling tribute to how strong a quartet Onyx truly is on this first effort. The group gives the impression that they wanted to spotlight the sort of cartoonish, directionless anger that existed in a lot of hardcore rap, and then funnel that sort of energy into songs full of singalong choruses and joyous, chanted hooks that lend a certain feeling of camaraderie to the whole album. The release is mostly co-produced by Run DMC's Jam Master Jay and newcomer Chyskillz, and its music has a tense, wired edge that amplifies the vividness of the threatening lyrics. Sonically, it has a hardcore East Coast/New York City cast, full of throbbing bass and screeching siren-like effects. The grimy urban vibe is matched by Onyx's narrative thuggery, discharged straight from the streets like pumped-up news dispatches and predating the roughneck rap trend by several years. It's hard to imagine, given the gritty content of the album, that Onyx was aiming for airplay with *Bacdafucup*; nevertheless, almost in spite of itself, it was so good that it earned just that. *—Stanton Swihart*

All We Got Iz Us / Nov. 1995 / Def Jam ✦✦✦
The second offering from Queens' Onyx is another fix of dark and psychotic microphone marauding. Unlike their debut album *Bacdafucup*, the trio's 1995 sophomore project contains no MTV-friendly cuts like "Slam." Rather, *All We Got Iz Us* is strictly the dark side, espousing basically one emotion: rage. This is a primal album of raucous wailing over sparse, rumbling beats. It is the sound of what slithers under the streets of New York. Sticky Fingaz asserts himself as the lyricist of the crew, sounding off like a powder keg ready to blow while Fredro Starr provides the solid but simplistic beats. Onyx cares little about solutions to the problems that have riled them up, they're simply reacting to them by letting out a guttural roar of anger and violence. Perhaps the forerunners of hardcore artists such as DMX, they in many ways authored the grimy, lowdown flow. In spite of their talents, without the benefit of airplay *All We Got Iz Us* fizzled. Regardless, Onyx maintained their "right to remain violent" and for what they do, they do it very well on this album. The standout cuts include: "Last Dayz," "Live Niguz," "Walk In New York," "Shout," and "Geto Mentalitee," featuring All City. *—Michael Di Bella*

Shut 'Em Down / Jun. 2, 1998 / Def Jam ✦✦✦
Shut 'Em Down is officially the followup to *All We Got Iz Us*, but since that second album was largely forgotten, the record might as well have been a followup to *Bacdafucup*, the debut that briefly made Onyx a hip-hop sensation. Onyx haven't changed that much since then; their hardcore rhythms still hit hard, their lyrics are still profane and they still shout their lyrics as often as they rap. In short, they still make the oversized, near-parodic hardcore rap that made "Slam" a smash hit. Unfortunately, there isn't anything on *Shut 'Em Down* nearly as good as "Slam." There's nothing that's flat-out bad, on the other hand, but there's no denying that the horrorcore schtick wears a bit thin. At first, it sounds good to have Onyx back, but it soon becomes clear that they need to develop a new sonic direction, otherwise they will have shut themselves down. *—Stephen Thomas Erlewine*

Opal
f. 1984, **db.** 1988
Dream Pop, Neo-Psychedelia, Alternative Pop/Rock
The neo-psychedelic group Opal formed in the mid-'80s, featuring former Rain Parade guitarist David Roback and former Dream Syndicate bassist Kendra Smith. Initially, the group was called Clay Allison, but the group dropped the name after one single; Roback, Smith, and drummer Keith Mitchell released the remaining Clay Allison tracks under their own name in 1984, on the *Fell from the Sun* EP. After its release, the group adopted the name Opal and released an EP, *Northern Line*, in 1985. *Happy Nightmare Baby*, their first full-length album, followed in 1987. Smith left the group during the *Happy Nightmare* tour, effectively putting an end to the band. Roback continued with vocalist Hope Sandoval; the group then metamorphosed into Mazzy Star. *—Stephen Thomas Erlewine*

● **Happy Nightmare Baby** / 1987 / SST ✦✦✦✦✦
Transcending the limitations of its psychedelic-era inspirations, Opal's one and only album goes beyond nostalgia to forge its own distinct and swirling tapestry of moody drones and guitar washes. Edgier and darker than the group's earlier singles, *Happy Nightmare Baby* is also considerably more rock-oriented; the opening "Rocket Machine" recalls T. Rex, while the keyboard textures bear the influence of another mind-expanding L.A. band, the Doors. Still, the record has an ambience all its own—Kendra Smith is a singularly evocative vocalist, and David Roback's guitar work is powerful and expressive. *—Jason Ankeny*

Early Recordings / 1989 / Rough Trade ✦✦✦✦✦
While Opal's *Happy Nightmare Baby* is more representative of the group's richly textured brand of neo-psychedelia, the stripped-down *Early Recordings* compilation is an even better example of David Roback and Kendra Smith's remarkable songcraft. Released in the wake of the group's breakup, the album collects the majority of tracks from the *Fell From the Sun* and *Northern Line* EPs, along with a handful of outtakes and unreleased cuts, all spotlighting Opal's more subdued, acoustic-folk side. Peeling away the mystical haze which enshrouded *Happy Nightmare Baby*, the songs are plaintive and stark, exposing the emotional complexity at the band's core—the wistful "Empty Box Blues" and the haunting "Harriet Brown," both previously unissued, are unmatched in their beauty and grace. *—Jason Ankeny*

Operation Ivy
f. May 1987, **db.** May 1989
Ska-Punk, Third Wave Ska Revival, Alternative Pop/Rock
Mixing hardcore punk with ska music inspired by the Specials, Operation Ivy formed in May 1987 from the ashes of a handful of Bay Area bands. Comprising vocalist Jesse Michaels, guitarist/vocalist Lint (Tim Armstrong), bassist Matt McCall (Freeman), and drummer Dave Mello with saxophone player Paul Bae, the band recorded the "Vulnerability" single for Lookout! Records in 1987. The *Hectic* EP followed later that year, but Operation Ivy broke up in May 1989, just before the release of debut album *Energy*. Michaels later joined Big Rig, while McCall and Armstrong played in Downfall before forming Rancid in the early '90s. *—John Bush*

Energy / 1990 / Lookout ✦✦✦✦

● **Operation Ivy** / 1991 / Lookout ✦✦✦✦✦
After Operation Ivy called it quits at the end of the '80s, Lookout put together this compilation of all of the recorded studio material ever released by the group. Much like Minor Threat's *Complete Discography*, this follows the recorded history of a band that burnt out quickly and had a relentlessly creative view of punk music. The underground classics are all here: "Take Warning," "Unity," "Freeze Up," "Junkie's Runnin' Dry," and 23 other prime tracks. Being one of the first bands to pursue the ska punk sound in California, Operation Ivy was a trailblazer in a genre that quickly became generic due to a glut of like-minded artists. But this should not be held against the group because they made fantastic music for the short time they existed. The CD comes complete with the lyrics to all of the songs, and several good pictures of the band. Countless bands would ape this sound without any creative improvement throughout the '90s, and two of the members would go on to lead the more punk-influenced Rancid. This might be the best ska punk collection by a single band committed to disc, and anyone with even a passing interest in the genre should do themselves a favor and buy this album right away. *—Bradley Torreano*

Seedy / 1993 / KarmaKredit ✦✦

Orange Juice
f. 1976, Glasgow, Scotland, **db.** 1984
Indie Pop, Post-Punk, New Wave
The leaders of the Scottish neo-pop uprising, Orange Juice formed in Glasgow in late 1976. Originally dubbed the Nu-Sonics, the group comprised vocalist/guitarist Edwyn Collins, guitarist James Kirk, bassist David McClymont, and drummer Steven Daly; following the formation of the Postcard label by Collins protégé Alan Horne, the quartet renamed itself Orange Juice in 1979, adopting the new moniker as well as an aura of romantic innocence as a direct reaction to the increasingly macho aggression of punk; as Postcard's flagship band, Orange Juice quickly distinguished the label as a leading proponent of independent pop music; their 1980 debut single, "Falling and Laughing," garnered massive critical acclaim, and subsequent releases like "Blueboy" and "Poor Old Soul" further established the group as a major new talent. Soon, sessions began for a full-length album; however, in the midst of recording, Orange Juice left Postcard to sign to Polydor, which funded the LP's completion. After the 1982 release of the album, titled *You Can't Hide Your Love Forever*, ex-Josef K guitarist Malcolm Ross joined the group, hastening the exit of Kirk and Daly and paving the way for Zimbabwe-born drummer Zeke Manyika. Manyika's addition gave Collins the new capability of exploring a more complex fusion of pop and blue-eyed soul; consequently, 1982's *Rip It Up* was a more ambitious affair than its predecessor, veering from the buoyant Motown tribute "I Can't Help Myself" to the energetic pop of the title track, Orange Juice's lone Top Ten single. However, subsequent releases failed to chart, and relations between the group and Polydor began to disintegrate; amid these tensions, both Ross and McClymont quit. After a makeshift tour, Collins and Manyika returned to the studio to record a dark, ambitious full-length effort; released in 1984, neither *The Orange Juice* nor its singles charted. *—Jason Ankeny*

You Can't Hide Your Love Forever / 1982 / Polydor ✦✦✦✦
With the sort of bold title that recalled the optimism of the '60s (and, of course, echoes the Beatles' "You've Got to Hide Your Love Away"), Orange Juice's long-playing debut announced a band with a considerable repertoire of musical ideas and some endearingly honest songs about romantic dysfunction and rejection. For some, their purist vision was too near to sentiment and too knowingly coy, but that's a cynic's view. There are some lovely songs here, especially the previous Postcard release "Falling and Laughing" and the single "L.O.V.E. Love." And, in contrast to their reputation, these fey Glaswegians could rock out when the moment demanded it, too. *—Alex Ogg*

Rip It Up / 1982 / Polydor ✦✦✦✦
Joined by Malcom Ross (ex-Josef K) and sublime percussionist Zeke Manyika, Edwyn Collins moved further away from the pure pop sound of old and further into cross-rhythms and skinny-white-boy funk on this, Orange Juice's second album. That the band was not wholly submerged or embarrassed by this bold move is a tribute to Collins' skill as a songwriter as much as their musicianship. In truth, his worldview was still dominated by romance and relationships, or the lack thereof, but he was finding ever more appealing avenues of expression to document his disappointments. The title track is the standout—it gave Collins a fleeting glimpse of the U.K. Top Ten when it was released as a single—but "I Can't Help Myself" is another thoroughbred effort. *—Alex Ogg*

The Orange Juice / 1984 / Polydor ✦✦✦
1984's *The Orange Juice* album is comprised of semi-gloomy descending tones, except for the first song entitled "Lean Period." As Edwyn Collins' last hurrah with the band, it seems his involvement is lackluster as his creativity and impact is barely present. Unlike *You Can't Hide Your Love Forever* or *Rip It Up*, *The Orange Juice* contains a pace that is crawling and, at times, stagnant, with a few bright spots emerging from some rich-textured keyboards and a minute amount of quirky guitar. "The Artisan" is kept alive by some lively organ and a poignant Collins, and "What Presence" contains some admirable guitar twang, but aside from these songs the rest of the album is short of any gloss in both flow and bounce. A repetitive undercurrent runs through all of the songs, and the starry, romantic feel that is usually prevalent sounds a tad empty, like on "Get While the Getting's Good." As suave as Edwyn Collins is, it still helps to have a few catchy rhythms or melodies tucked away somewhere to hold interest. Three or four of this album's songs are average sounding, but earlier work from Orange Juice presents the band in a much more upbeat atmosphere. *—Mike DeGagne*

In a Nutshell / 1985 / Polydor ✦✦✦
The *original* Orange Juice compilation album, the vinyl issue came with a free flexidisc

of the band's masterful "Felicity," a song so wonderful, you really need it in a more robust format. Rush-released in the wake of the band's collapse, it has since been supplanted by the superior *The Very Best of Orange Juice*, aka *The Esteemed Orange Juice*. However, the compilers of *In a Nutshell* did take the time to licence the group's early Postcard singles—"Falling and Laughing" and "Poor Old Soul"—which is a major bonus. —*Alex Ogg*

● **The Very Best of Orange Juice** / Oct. 1995 / Polydor ✦✦✦✦✦
Released in the wake of Edwyn Collins' surprise success with "A Girl Like You," *The Very Best of Orange Juice* contains all of the Scottish pop group's biggest hit singles, offering an excellent introduction to their career, as well as rounding up all the highlights from their often incoherent records. —*Stephen Thomas Erlewine*

The Orb

f. 1989, London, England
Ambient House, Electronica, Ambient Techno, Ambient Dub, IDM
The Orb virtually invented the electronic genre known as ambient-house, resurrecting slower, more soulful rhythms and providing a soundtrack for early-morning ravers once the clubs closed their doors. The group popularized the genre as well, by appearing on the British chart show *Top of the Pops* and hitting number one in the U.K. with the 1992 album *U.F.Orb*. Frontman Dr. Alex Paterson's formula was quite simple: he slowed down the rhythms of classic Chicago house and added synthwork and effects inspired by '70s ambient pioneers Brian Eno and Tangerine Dream. The Orb's breakout singles, 1989's "A Huge Ever Growing Pulsating Brain That Rules from the Centre of the Ultraworld" and 1990's "Little Fluffy Clouds," hit the U.K. charts upon release and sparked their debut album, 1991's *The Orb's Adventures Beyond the Ultraworld*. Second album *U.F.Orb* reached number one in Britain during 1992, thanks to the Top Ten single "Blue Room." Contract troubles delayed for three years their third studio LP, *Orbus Terrarum*, and the distance resulted in a collection of dense rhythms far removed from previous material. The Orb returned to the great beyond with the spacey sounds of 1997's *Orblivion*. —*John Bush*

★ **The Orb's Adventures Beyond the Ultraworld** / Aug. 1991 / Big Life/Island Red ✦✦✦✦✦
Much like the early Orb-related project recorded as Space, *Adventures Beyond the Ultraworld* simulates a journey through the outer realms—progressing from the soaring ambient-pop of "Little Fluffy Clouds" and the stoned "Back Side of the Moon" (a veiled Pink Floyd reference) to "Into the Fourth Dimension" and ending (after more than two hours) with the glorious live mix of "A Huge Ever Growing Pulsating Brain." A varied cast of samples (*Flash Gordon*, space broadcasts, foreign-language whispers) and warm synthesizer tones provide a convincing bed for the mid-tempo house beats and occasionally dub-inflected ambience. With a clever balance of BBC Radiophonics Workshop soundtracks, '70s ambient meister-works by Eno, Hillage, and Floyd, plus the steady influence of Larry Heard's sublime Chicago house, *Adventures Beyond the Ultraworld* is the album that defined the ambient-house movement. —*John Bush*

☆ **U.F.Orb** / Mar. 1992 / Big Life/Island Red ✦✦✦✦✦
The commercial and artistic peak of the ambient-house movement, *U.F.Orb* strides past the debut with more periods of free-form ambience and less reliance on a standard 4/4 beat. From the opener "O.O.B.E." through the bass-heavy gait of "Blue Room" and "Towers of Dub," the flow is more natural and ranges farther than most would have expected. The bevy of contributors (including Steve Hillage, Jah Wobble, Youth, Thomas Fehlmann, and Slam) never threaten to overload the proceedings, though the minimalist sampling of *Ultraworld* is replaced by a production focus much more dense and busy, especially on the rain-forest-on-Saturn ethno-ambience of "Close Encounters." Elsewhere, Paterson maintains his fascination with the earthy dub bass lines of Mad Professor and Lee Perry, even while he's indulging in flights of fancy indebted to Sun Ra. —*John Bush*

Live 93 / Nov. 22, 1993 / Island Red ✦✦✦✦
Although the thought of an Orb live album may raise some eyebrows, the resulting two-CD set is amazing, a complete representation of the group in concert and living proof that techno is indeed a live, as well as recorded, art form. Besides, the consistent Pink Floyd jokes on the record (as well as the brilliant cover art) are hilarious. —*Stephen Thomas Erlewine*

Pomme Fritz / Jun. 13, 1994 / Island Red ✦✦✦

Orbus Terrarum / Apr. 4, 1995 / Island ✦✦✦✦
The perfect response to a music-scene swamped by what Paterson himself called "lame ambient noodling for seventy minutes," *Orbus Terrarum* brings the mothership back to earth for a collision with some surprisingly harsh percussion and noisy synth. The melodies and dub lines of previous Orb recordings are still in the mix, and the esoteric bent of *Pomme Fritz* is muted somewhat. *Orbus Terrarum* is definitely not the place to start, but it's still a worthy successor to *U.F.Orb*. The final track "Slug Dub" is an ambient epic with vocal samples taken from a children's story. —*John Bush*

Auntie Aubrey's Excursions Beyond the Call of Duty, Pt. 1 / Jul. 15, 1996 / Deviant ✦✦✦✦
A double-disc compilation of over two and a half hours of remixes, *Excursions* includes Orb reworkings of well-known bands (Primal Scream, Erasure, Depeche Mode, Killing Joke) and more obscure acts (Keiichi Suzuki, Love Kittens). Several mixes sound a bit dated and the scattershot quality of the set can distract listeners, but the inclusion of several epiphanous moments (Material's "Praying Mantra," Primal Scream's "Higher than the Sun" and Sun Electric's "O'Locco") makes the album worthwhile for fans. Included is a thick book including colorful discographies and an interesting essay. —*John Bush*

Orblivion / Feb. 24, 1997 / Island ✦✦✦✦✦

If the Orb's 1995 release *Orbvs Terrarum* was an extended meditation on the earthbound, the band's follow-up in *Orblivion* rises from the muck of primordial ectoplasm for a guided tour of late-20th century Western culture's more paranoid face. From the Cold War (the album kicks off with Joseph McCarthy's intoning of the immortal invective "Are you now, or have you ever been…") to the pre-millennial ranting of David Thewlis' warped, apocalyptic monologue from Mike Leigh's *Naked* ("The bar code! The ubiquitous bar code!"), *Orblivion* does for post-industrial, turn-of-the-century mania what earlier albums such as *The Orb's Adventures Beyond the Ultraworld* and *U.F.Orb* did for aliens and flying saucers. Like the previous record—an effusive mix of sprawling environmental textures; clanging, treated percussion; and humorous, trainspottery samples—*Orblivion* brings with it another adjustment in mood, combining elements of downbeat, electro, and drum'n'bass with dense, soupy amalgams of treated electronics and shimmering rhythms. *Orblivion* also evidences a renewed interest in the more immediately engaging, upbeat pop of "Perpetual Dawn"- and "Little Fluffy Clouds"-era Orb, with a deeper, more embellished sound marked, in all likelihood, by the first full-time contributions from former engineer Andy Hughes (who replaced Kris Weston after the latter's departure in 1994). Dub is still the organizing principle of the Orb's music, however, and whatever one's opinion of the actual album (reactions are likely to range from "genius" to "aimless") the production is undeniably amazing. —*Sean Cooper*

U.F.Off: The Best of Orb / Oct. 5, 1998 / Island ✦✦✦✦
A brief, twelve-track trip through the Orb's singles archive, *U.F.Off* includes mixes of just about every single from "A Huge Evergrowing Pulsating Brain" through "Toxygene" (though not in strictly chronological order). Singles compilations for electronic artists hardly ever fit the bill for long-time listeners or neophytes, yet this one is put together well and remains a solid addition to any collection. The double-disc version includes additional remixes plus a few unreleased tracks ("Mickey Mars," "Pi"). —*Keith Farley*

Cydonia / Feb. 27, 2001 / MCA ✦✦✦

Auntie Aubrey's Excursions Beyond the Call of Duty, Pt. 2 / Sep. 4, 2001 / Ultra ✦✦✦✦

Roy Orbison

b. Apr. 23, 1936, Vernon, TX, d. Dec. 6, 1988, Madison, TN
Vocals, Guitar / Pop/Rock, Pop, Rockabilly, Rock & Roll
Although he shared the same rockabilly roots as Carl Perkins, Johnny Cash, and Elvis Presley, Roy Orbison went on to pioneer an entirely different brand of country/pop-based rock & roll in the early '60s. What he lacked in charisma and photogenic looks, Orbison made up for in spades with his quavering operatic voice and melodramatic narratives of unrequited love and yearning. In the process, he established rock & roll archetypes of the underdog and the hopelessly romantic loser. Orbison made his first widely distributed recordings for Sun Records in 1956. Roy was a capable rockabilly singer, and had a small national hit with his first Sun single, "Ooby Dooby." But even then, he was far more comfortable as a ballad singer than as a hepped-up rockabilly jive cat. He finally found his voice with Monument Records, scoring a number two hit in 1960 with "Only the Lonely." This established the Roy Orbison persona for good: a brooding rockaballad of failed love with a sweet, haunting melody, enhanced by his Caruso-like vocal trills at the song's emotional climax. These and his subsequent Monument hits also boasted innovative, quasi-symphonic production, with Roy's voice and guitar backed by surging strings, ominous drum rolls, and heavenly choirs of backup vocalists. Between 1960 and 1965, Orbison would have 15 Top 40 hits for Monument, including such nail-biting mini-dramas as "Running Scared," "Crying," "In Dreams," and "It's Over." Not just a singer of tear-jerking ballads, he was also capable of effecting a tough, bluesy swagger on "Dream Baby," "Candy Man," and "Mean Woman Blues." In fact, his biggest and best hit was also his hardest-rocking: "Oh, Pretty Woman" soared to number one in late 1964, at the peak of the British Invasion. —*Richie Unterberger*

Crying / 1962 / Columbia ✦✦

There Is Only One / 1965 / MGM ✦✦
Orbison explains in the liner notes that MGM will allow him "a new climate of freedom" as an artist, but the results of his first album for the label were unimpressive. He forsakes much of the rock & roll foundation of his classic early-'60s hits for Nashville country & western on most of the LP, complete with barroom piano. The material (mostly written by Orbison with various collaborators) doesn't approach the magnificence of his best work, and his version of his composition "Claudette" isn't nearly as good as the Everly Brothers' hit rendition from 1958. The highlight is the strange, almost rambling minor hit single, "Ride Away." —*Richie Unterberger*

The Fastest Guitar Alive / 1968 / Columbia ✦✦
Orbison's one bid for film stardom, *The Fastest Guitar Alive*, was an unqualified flop. The soundtrack fares slightly better, but only slightly. With ten songs clocking in at a mere 27 minutes, most of the tunes—which Roy composed with longtime collaborator Bill Dees—borrow from the cheesiest elements of cowboy music, with quasi-Mexican guitar riffs, silly Indian chants, and uneasy spaghetti-Western pathos. For all its ill-conceived failure, it includes what may be his best obscure tune, the little-anthologized "Whirlwind." With its galloping rhythm, emotive operatic vocals, swirling strings, and ghostly backing vocals, it recalls the best uptempo ballads that he recorded during his early-'60s heyday at the Monument label. In 1968, of course, few listeners were interested. —*Richie Unterberger*

The All-Time Greatest Hits of Roy Orbison / 1976 / Monument ✦✦✦✦✦
The All-Time Greatest Hits of Roy Orbison is an essential collection. It rounds up 20 of the Big O's best '60s recordings, with some fine album tracks thrown in. —*John Floyd*

★ **For the Lonely: 18 Greatest Hits** / 1988 / Rhino ♦♦♦♦♦
Appearing as it did just a few months before Roy Orbison's death, this single CD best-of was incredibly fortuitous for Rhino Records. It was the first compilation to include both Orbison's early successes on Sun Records along with his early-'60s hits for Monument Records and, thus, was as definitive as most casual fans needed it to be. The sound is impeccable, as is the choice of material (which was not difficult to assemble). One gets only a somewhat sketchy overview of Orbison's developing talent, ignoring the years between his Sun and Monument recordings, but that's usually the purpose of a greatest hits collection anyway. For those who want more, *The Legendary Roy Orbison* gives a better overall account, but as a four-CD set is a lot more expensive; *All-Time Greatest Hits* gives a somewhat fuller account of the Monument years (and all of his Monument albums were available individually as well); and the out-of-print MGM best-of covers the music from the years following his departure from Monument. (The best of the latter doesn't sound that different from the Monument material—Orbison's post-Monument songs just never caught the public's ear or managed to become hit records.) But *For the Lonely* is the best account of the music that everyone already recognizes and knows. *—Bruce Eder*

The Legendary Roy Orbison / 1988 / Columbia ♦♦♦♦♦
Tracing Roy Orbison's career from its beginnings at Sun through his big hits at Monument to his largely forgotten late-'60s recordings for MGM, the four-disc set is an exhaustive, definitive history of Orbison's peak years. Yes, his late-'80s comeback is missing (this was released a year before *Mystery Girl*, after all), but this is still as exhaustive as most serious listeners will likely need, since it contains nearly every crucial track, plus such rarities as non-LP soundtrack contributions (including the title song to the Orbison-starrer *Fastest Guitar Alive*). It does lose momentum toward the end, since Orbison's material starts to dip in quality, but there still are some hidden gems to be discovered. Hardcore fans will probably be better off with Bear Family's exhaustive *Orbison*, which has all the Sun and Monument recordings, and wait for the inevitable MGM sequel. Those that want a comprehensive, but not complete, overview will be more than satisfied with this set. *—Stephen Thomas Erlewine*

The Classic Roy Orbison (1965-1968) / 1989 / Rhino ♦♦♦
The hits dried up when Orbison left the Monument label for MGM in 1965. The 14 recordings here, taken from singles and LP tracks, feature arrangements and production not far removed from his classic Monument era. The singing is wonderful, but stacked up against his classic hits, a lot is missing. Lacking the ace songwriting of his best work, there's lots of midtempo, melodramatic rock balladry here, but somehow nothing nearly as gripping as his best compositions. *—Richie Unterberger*

Our Love Song / 1989 / Monument ♦♦
Skimpily assembled package of a dozen obscurities, most from the early and mid-'60s Monument era. "(I Get So) Sentimental" and "Born On The Wind" count as some of his better unknown tunes from that time, but on the whole it's a poor and haphazard collection. *—Richie Unterberger*

Sun Years / 1989 / Rhino ♦♦♦♦♦
20-track compilation of Orbison's Sun sides, including both sides of all four of his official Sun 45s, and a dozen tracks he recorded for the label that remained unissued at the time. Orbison at this point was a decent but somewhat also-ran rockabilly singer, and not nearly as suited for the style as fellow Sun artists Elvis Presley, Jerry Lee Lewis, and Carl Perkins. He also had yet to find his songwriting or singing voice with balladeering pop-rock material, so this collection may disappoint those who expect something along the lines of Roy's famous Monument hits. It's not at all bad, though, with standout cuts such as "Ooby Dooby," "Rock House," and "Devil Doll"; it's just not Orbison at either his best or his most comfortable. *—Richie Unterberger*

Mystery Girl / 1989 / Virgin ♦♦♦♦
Although it had been years since his last recording, Roy Orbison was inducted into the Rock & Roll Hall of Fame in 1987. Perhaps as a result of the newfound interest in his music, he was invited to record with the supergroup the Traveling Wilburys. Roy Orbison had a renewed sense of purpose, and also began recording material for a new solo album. Collaborating with Jeff Lynne and Tom Petty, Roy Orbison recreates the feel of his old recordings while sounding modern. His voice sounds as strong as ever, and he is still able to hit the high notes that convey a sad, lonely ache. The highlight of the album is "She's a Mystery to Me," a haunting ballad penned by U2's Bono and the Edge that perfectly plays to all of Orbison's strengths as a singer. Released in the months after his death, *Mystery Girl* was the highest-charting album of his career and spawned the hit "You Got It"—it is a shame that Orbison was not around to experience his success. This comeback album represents Roy Orbison at his best. *—Vik Iyengar*

The Sun Years 1956-58 / Apr. 1989 / Bear Family ♦♦♦♦♦
Roy Orbison wasn't among the great rockabilly cats, as his voice was a little too rich and his performances a little too mannered to truly rock with abandon. Nevertheless, he did cut a pair of terrific rockabilly singles for Sun with "Ooby Dooby" and "Domino." He never quite reached those heights again while on Sun, as Bear Family's single-disc collection *The Sun Years 1956-58* illustrates. Containing every track he recorded for the label, including alternate takes and undubbed mixes, the collection suffers from too much similar-sounding material. Apart from the previously mentioned singles, Orbison only made a handful of songs that really rocked, and they tend lose their impact when mixed in among the mediocre songs and minutely different alternate takes. For hardcore Orbison and rockabilly collectors, the very comprehensiveness of *The Sun Years 1956-58* makes the disc necessary, but most fans—especially those enamored with his grandiose, theatrical ballads—will find that this collection is overkill. *—Stephen Thomas Erlewine*

Singles Collection / Oct. 1990 / Polygram ♦♦♦
Overlooked at the time of its issue, as it was almost simultaneously released with Rhino's *The Classic Roy Orbison (1965-1968)*, this offers a more comprehensive look at his post-Monument recordings. That doesn't mean that it's better. Most of the 1965-1968 cuts on this album are also on the Rhino one, though "She" and "Heartache," which are only on *Singles Collection*, are a couple of his better late-'60s songs. The post-1968 tracks that take up the rest of the anthology are a waste, an embarrassment at worst, as Orbison failed to either successfully incorporate contemporary influences or offer quality variations on his tested formula. Stick with the cheaper, more succinct, and easier to find *The Classic Roy Orbison* for an overview of this era. *—Richie Unterberger*

King of Hearts / Oct. 20, 1992 / Virgin ♦♦♦
The posthumously released *King of Hearts* collects a handful of Orbison's final vocal tracks along with a few demos and non-LP singles, including the Jeff Lynne-produced "Heartbreak Radio." The highlight, however, is an amazing duet of "Crying" recorded with k.d. lang. *—Jason Ankeny*

16 Biggest Hits / Feb. 2, 1999 / Monument/Legacy ♦♦♦♦♦
Roy Orbison scored 20 consecutive Top 40 hits between 1960 and 1965, all but the last of them on the Monument Records label. This compilation presents 16 of the first 17 of those hits (missing is the 1963 Christmas song "Pretty Paper"), from the 1960 gold-seller "Only the Lonely" to the 1964 chart-topper "Oh, Pretty Woman," with Orbison's seven other Top Ten hits of the era in between. Technically, a few of Orbison's singles of 1965 and 1966 did a little better in the charts than a few of the ones here, and, of course, he scored a final, posthumous Top Ten hit with "You Got It" on Virgin Records in 1989. But this collection presents the music from the hottest part of his career in chronological order, with standards like "Crying" sharing space with lesser, but still worthy songs like "I'm Hurtin'." Aficionados know Orbison's Sun works, and his later recordings earned him a new audience, but the Monument hit singles of the early '60s are what he is best remembered for, and they're all here. *—William Ruhlmann*

Roy Orbison: Authorized Bootleg Collection / Oct. 26, 1999 / Orbison ♦♦♦
Orbison's widow, Barbara, organized the release of these four live concert recordings taken from various points in Orbison's career. The set list doesn't vary much from show to show; an artist like Orbison would be hidebound to sing his hits, and the audience certainly lets him know which ones they want to hear throughout this four-disc collection. Regarding sound quality, these are soundboard tapes cleaned up as much as possible; don't expect them to sound awful and they won't, but don't expect them to sound like a record either, because they fall quite short. However, you don't come to a Roy Orbison concert, tap your foot, and say, "Nice mix on the bass player." No, you come to hear Orbison, and here's one time when a vocal-heavy board tape has the spotlight falling on the right set of shoulders. If you're going to subject yourself to listening to four hours of one person singing louder then the entire band track put together, it might as well be somebody great like Roy Orbison. He never falters once in these shows, presiding over all of them with a laid-back, good-natured stage personality that perfectly fits the music. For completists and hardcore fans only, perhaps, but here's one of rock & roll's greatest singers tearing it up in four hit-packed concerts; it doesn't get much better than that, sound quality be damned. *—Cub Koda*

Orbison / May 8, 2001 / Bear Family ♦♦♦♦♦
The German label Bear Family issued this seven-CD Roy Orbison retrospective from 1955 to 1965; it collects virtually every known Orbison recording from what has been tagged his "golden decade." And when the folks at Bear Family say "every known recording," they mean it. There are oodles of unissued alternates takes, unreleased demos—including Orbison's original versions of songs written for Buddy Holly ("An Empty Cup") and the Every Brothers ("Claudette" as well as "Love Hurts"). There is an entire CD dedicated to the complete recordings of the material recorded by the Teen Kings—a first for any Orbison collection. In addition, the latter third of the last disc offers all of Orbison's Coca Cola commercials as a cap off (no pun intended) to the golden decade. Reissue producers Howard Cockburn, Richard Weize, and John Beecher (for the Teen Kings material) looked under every rock and found tracks believed lost or erased from the period—including the Wink Westerners material (most likely the Teen Kings under another name)—and have assembled the most complete Roy Orbison collection of the period ever. This one is definitive. This set completely leaves the travesty that is the Columbia box released in 1988 in the dust. This Orbison box has pristine sound in most cases, and where it doesn't, it is certainly far superior to any other collection on the market and far better than any of the semi-legal pirates. *—Thom Jurek*

Orbital

f. 1987, Sevenoaks, Kent, England
Electronica, Ambient Techno, Techno
Orbital became one of the biggest names in techno during the mid-'90s by solving the irreconcilable differences previously inherent in the genre: to stay true to the dance underground and, at the same time, force entry into the rock arena, where an album functions as an artistic statement—not a collection of singles—and a band's prowess is demonstrated by the actual performance of live music. Though Phil and Paul Hartnoll first charted with a single, they later became known for critically praised albums that sold well with a surprising amount of rock fans as well as electronic listeners. The duo's first single, 1989's "Chime," was an unusually sublime rave anthem that hit the British Top 20 and gained the duo a full-length release, a self-titled 1991 album. Orbital's second LP, also untitled but nicknamed the "brown" album, unified the disjointed feel of its predecessor. An American tour plus appearances at Woodstock 2 and the Glastonbury Festival confirmed the duo's status as one of the premier live acts in electronic music. Following in 1994,

Snivilization became Orbital's biggest hit, reaching number four in the British album charts. The Hartnolls' fifth album, 1996's *In Sides*, became their most acclaimed album, with many excellent reviews in publications that had never covered electronic music. Still, it was over three years before the release of Orbital's next album, 1999's *Middle of Nowhere*. *—John Bush*

Orbital / Oct. 1991 / ffrr ✦✦✦✦
The U.S. version of Orbital's debut album serves as a good primer to the group's early history, including standard versions of the early singles "Chime," "Omen," "Satan" and "Midnight," in addition to two B-sides which showed Phil and Paul's first stab at varying their Kraftwerk-inspired sound. "Belfast" (from the "Satan" single) is a warm, mid-tempo synth track inspired by Depeche Mode; "Choice," at the other extreme, is an aggro-house piece with vocal samples (e.g., "Wake Up!") that recall socially e.g., conscious punks like Crass. *—John Bush*

● **Orbital 2** / 1992 / ffrr ✦✦✦✦✦
Opening with a looped *Star Trek* sample, Orbital's second album progresses through eight tracks of warm, unrepetitive techno in what sounds more like a DJ mix album than an LP, with no bows to mainstream sensibilities. Here, the duo's acknowledged inspiration from Kraftwerk, present before but always in the background, came to the fore. The brilliant manner in which the Hartnolls weave several synth lines, samples, sung vocals, and percussion—mathematically precise but still beautifully orchestrated—updated Kraftwerk's mastery of minimalist electronic music. One of the highlight of the '90s techno movement, the "brown" album is still Orbital's most exciting work. *—John Bush*

Snivilisation / Aug. 23, 1994 / ffrr ✦✦✦✦
The political commentary inherent in 1994's *Snivilization* extended even to the Top 30 single "Are We Here?," whose criminal justice bill mix voiced Phil and Paul's concern over what the bill might lead to—silence. Musically, the album delivers on the diverse promises of early B-sides "Choice" and "Belfast," with more harbingers to their thrash background—especially on "Quality Seconds"—and the addition of a third member, vocalist Alison Goldfrapp, on two songs. The shuffling, quasi-Eastern jungle rhythms of "Are We Here?," a beautiful piano run to begin "Kein Trink Wasser," and the glorious ambient climax "Attached" also reflect the fact that *Snivilization* is Orbital's most varied LP. *—John Bush*

In Sides / Mar. 1996 / ffrr/London ✦✦✦✦✦
In Sides isn't Orbital's best album, or the most accomplished, but it is the most definitive. It pulses with the energy of the debut, the lush flow of the second, and the conceptual theme of *Snivilisation*. The focus this time, though, is ecology. "The Girl with the Sun in Her Head" was recorded on a Greenpeace bus using only solar power, and "Dwr Budr" (Welsh for "dirty water") also criticizes the misuse of natural resources. Phil and Paul's respect for the jungle/drum 'n bass movement showed in the moderate breakbeat rhythms on several tracks. *—John Bush*

Middle of Nowhere / Jun. 8, 1999 / ffrr/London ✦✦✦✦
Electronica routinely covers more ground, more quickly, than any style of music on the planet; the hottest new sound in January is old hat by March and downright foolish to even mention in June. Orbital, however, is the great constant in the world of techno. Every few years, the brothers Hartnoll manage to turn in excellent albums that occasionally reference the latest sound but rarely vary from the chord-heavy melodics of their debut single, "Chime." Though it took a bit longer to release, *Middle of Nowhere* is another typically excellent Orbital album. Experiments with breakbeats and other styles of music made interesting mixers of their previous two albums, *Snivilisation* and *In Sides*, and this fifth album includes nods to big beat-techno ("I Don't Know You People") and soundtrack composers. The latter is hardly a surprise, considering the Hartnolls' sideline gig as score composers (*Event Horizon*, *The Saint*). The opener, "Way Out," adds trumpet solos and a symphonic grandeur—reminiscent of John Barry's scores for the *James Bond* films—to the quintessential Orbital sound. Even considering the lack of real progression in sound, *Middle of Nowhere* reflects the pair once again making all the right moves and not slowing down a bit. *—John Bush*

The Altogether / May 22, 2001 / ffrr/London ✦✦
Growing farther away from both the electronica mainstream as well as its experimental underground with each release, the sixth full album by Orbital finds the Hartnoll brothers very tired indeed, recycling sounds and styles they'd pioneered ten years earlier. Sampling arch-metal heroes Tool and the fratboy staple "Surfin' Bird" (not even the *original* "Surfin' Bird"!) for a pair of aggro-thrash tracks doesn't exactly bode well for *The Altogether*, and even when the duo work in more familiar territory, it's far *too* familiar. "Funny Break (One Is Enough)" is a return to the majestic, trademarked Orbital sound of their debut "Chime," but this isn't even the first time they've gone back to their staple. "Oi!" is another solid production, but incredibly it also borrows heavily from the repertoire, with the hazy female siren-calls from past Orbital classics like "Halcyon + On + On" and "The Girl With the Sun in Her Hair." And the Hartnolls' one concession to the currents of electronica circa 2001, a vocalist collaboration ("Illuminate," featuring David Gray), is a totally misguided crossover and one of the blandest tracks they've ever been associated with. Their cover of the *Dr. Who* theme may sound a little risqué to fans of the ancient sci-fi series (especially those most middle-aged and curmudgeonly), but the track is obvious and unintentionally hilarious. It's genuinely surprising to find a consistent act like Orbital slipping to such depths, but *The Altogether* is a poor album and by far a low point in Orbital's career. *—John Bush*

Orchestral Manoeuvres in the Dark

f. 1978, Liverpool, England
Alternative Dance, New Romantic, Post-Punk, New Wave, Synth Pop

Featuring the core members Paul Humphreys and Andy McCluskey, the Liverpudlian synth-pop group Orchestral Manoeuvers in the Dark formed in the late '70s. They released their first single "Electricity" on Factory Records; the record led to a contract with Virgin's subsidiary DinDisc, and in 1980, the group released their self-titled debut album. *Organisation* appeared the same year, which featured the U.K. Top Ten single "Enola Gay." OMD's next few albums—*Architecture and Morality* (1981), *Dazzle Ships* (1983), *Junk Culture* (1984)—found the band experimenting with their sound, resulting in several U.K. hit singles. Recorded with two new members, Graham and Neil Weir, *Crush*, their most pop-oriented album, found more success in America than in Britain, as the single "So in Love" hit number 26 on the charts. "If You Leave," taken from the *Pretty in Pink*, soundtrack was their biggest American hit, climbing to number four in 1986. *The Pacific Age* was released the same year, yet America was the only country where it was popular. *—Stephen Thomas Erlewine*

Orchestral Manoeuvres in the Dark / Feb. 22, 1980 / Virgin ✦✦✦
OMD's first full album won as much attention for its brilliant die-cut cover—another example of Peter Saville's cutting-edge way around design—as for its music, and its music is wonderful. For all that, this is a young band, working for just about the last time with original percussionist Winston; there's both a variety and ambition present that never overreaches itself. The influences are perfectly clear throughout, but McCluskey and Humphreys would have been the last people to deny how Kraftwerk, Sparks, and other avatars of post-guitar pop touched them. What's undeniably thrilling, though, is how quickly the two synthesized their own style. Consider "Almost," with its dramatic keyboard opening suddenly shifting into a collage of wheezing sound beats and McCluskey's precise bass and heartfelt, lovelorn singing and lyrics. The chilly keyboard base of "The Messerschmitt Twins" gets offset by McCluskey's steadily stronger vocal, while the swooping, slightly hollow singing on "Mystereality" slips around a quietly quirky arrangement, helped just enough by Cooper's at-the-time guest sax. Even the fairly goofy "Dancing" has a weird atmosphere at play in the metallic vocals and groaning tones. In terms of sheer immediacy, there's little doubt what the two highlights are—the re-recorded and arguably better version of "Electricity" is pure zeitgeist, a celebration of synth pop's incipient reign with fast beats and even faster singing. "Messages," though it would later benefit from a far more stunning reworking, still wears the emotion of its lyrics on its sleeve, with a killer opening line—"It worries me, this kind of thing, how you hope to live alone and occupy your waking hours"—and a melody both propulsive and fragile. The mysterious chimes and spy-movie dramatics of "Red Frame/White Light" (inspired by a phone box) are almost as striking. *Orchestral Manoeuvres in the Dark* is just like the band that made it—perfectly of its time and easily transcending it. *—Ned Raggett*

Organisation / Oct. 24, 1980 / Virgin ✦✦✦✦
If OMD's debut album showed the band could succeed just as well on full-length efforts as singles, *Organisation* upped the ante even further, situating the band in the enviable position of at once being creative innovators and radio-friendly pop giants. That was shown as much by the astounding lead track and sole single from the album, "Enola Gay." Not merely a great showcase for new member Holmes, whose live-wire drumming took the core electronic beat as a launching point and easily outdid it, "Enola Gay" is a flat-out pop classic—clever, heartfelt, thrilling, and confident, not to mention catchy and arranged brilliantly. The outrageous use of the atomic bomb scenario—especially striking given the era's nuclear war fears—informs the seemingly giddy song with a cut-to-the-quick fear and melancholy, and the result is captivating. Far from being a one-hit wonder, though, *Organisation* is packed with a number of gems, showing the band's reach and ability continuing to increase. Holmes slots into the band's efforts perfectly, steering away from straightforward time structures while never losing the core dance drive, able to play both powerfully and subtly. McCluskey's singing, his own brand of sweetly wounded soul for a different age and approach, is simply wonderful—the clattering industrial paranoia of "The Misunderstanding" results in wrenching wails, a moody cover of "The More I See You" results in a deeper-voiced passion. Everything from the winsome claustrophobia of "VCL XI" and the gentle, cool flow on "Statues" to the quirky boulevardier swing of "Motion and Heart" has a part to play. Meanwhile, album closer "Stanlow," inspired by the power plant where McCluskey's father worked, concluded things on a haunting note, murky mechanical beats and a slow, mournful melody leading the beautiful way. *—Ned Raggett*

Architecture & Morality / Nov. 8, 1981 / Virgin ✦✦✦✦✦
If there was a clear high point for OMD in terms of balancing relentless experimentation and seemingly unstoppable mainstream success in the U.K., *Architecture & Morality* is it. Again combining everything from design and presentation to even the title into an overall artistic effort, this album showed that OMD was arguably the first Liverpool band since the later Beatles to make such a sweeping, all-bases-covered achievement—more so because OMD owed nothing to the Fab Four. All it takes is a consideration of the three smash singles from the album to see the group in full flower. "Souvenir," featuring Humphreys in a quiet but still warm and beautiful lead role, eases in on haunting semi-vocal sighs before settling into its gentle, sparkling melody. The mid-song instrumental break, with its shifted tempos and further wordless calls, is especially inspired. "Joan of Arc," meanwhile, takes the drama of "Enola Gay" to new heights; again, wordless vocals provide the intro and backing, while an initially quiet melody develops into a towering heartbreaker, with McCluskey and band in full flight. If that wasn't enough, the scenario was continued and made even more epic with "Maid of Orleans," starting with a quick-cut series of melancholic drones and shades before a punchy, then rolling martial beat kicks in, with Holmes and technology in perfect combination. With another bravura McCluskey lead and a mock-bagpipe lead that's easily more entrancing than the real

thing, it's a wrenching ballad like no other before it and little since. Any number of other high points can be named, such as the opening, "The New Stone Age," with McCluskey's emotional fear palpable over a rough combination of nervous electronic pulses, piercing keyboard parts, and slightly distorted guitar. "She's Leaving" achieves its own polished pop perfection–it would have made an inspired choice for a fourth single if one had been forthcoming–while the heartbreaking "Sealand" and "Georgia" hint at where OMD would go next, with *Dazzle Ships*. —*Ned Raggett*

Dazzle Ships / Mar. 4, 1983 / Virgin ✦✦✦✦

OMD's glistening run of top-flight singles and chart domination came to a temporary but dramatic halt with *Dazzle Ships*, the point where the band's pushing of boundaries reached their furthest limit. McCluskey, Humphreys, and company couldn't take many listeners with them, though, and it's little surprise why–a couple of moments aside, *Dazzle Ships* is pop of the most fragmented kind, a concept album released in an era that had nothing to do with such conceits. On its own merits, though, it is dazzling indeed, a *Kid A* of its time that never received a comparative level of contemporary attention and appreciation. Indeed, Radiohead's own plunge into abstract electronics and meditations on biological and technological advances seems to be echoing the themes and construction of *Dazzle Ships*. What else can be said when hearing the album's lead single, the soaring "Genetic Engineering," with its Speak & Spell toy vocals and an opening sequence that also sounds like the inspiration for "Fitter, Happier," for instance? Why it wasn't a hit remains a mystery, but it and the equally enjoyable, energetic "Telegraph" and "Radio Waves" are definitely the poppiest moments on the album. Conceived around visions of cryptic Cold War tension, the rise of computers in everyday life, and European and global reference points–time zone recordings and snippets of shortwave broadcasts–*Dazzle Ships* beats Kraftwerk at their own game, science and the future turned into surprisingly warm, evocative songs or sudden stop-start instrumental fragments. "Dazzle Ships (Parts II, III, and VII)" itself captures the alien feeling of the album best, with its distanced, echoing noises and curious rhythms, sliding into the lovely "The Romance of the Telescope." "This Is Helena" works in everything from what sounds like heavily treated and flanged string arrangements to radio announcer samples, while "Silent Running" becomes another in the line of emotional, breathtaking OMD ballads, McCluskey's voice the gripping centerpiece. —*Ned Raggett*

Junk Culture / Apr. 30, 1984 / A&M ✦✦✦✦

Smarting from *Dazzle Ships'* commercial failure, the band had a bit of a rethink when it came to their fifth album–happily, the end result showed that the group was still firing on all fours. While very much a pop-oriented album and a clear retreat from the exploratory reaches of previous work, *Junk Culture* was no sacrifice of ideals in pursuit of cash. In comparison to the group's late-'80s work, when it seemed commercial success was all that mattered, *Junk Culture* exhibits all the best qualities of OMD at their most accessible–instantly memorable melodies and McCluskey's distinct singing voice, clever but emotional lyrics, and fine playing all around. A string of winning singles didn't hurt, to be sure; indeed, opening number "Tesla Girls" is easily the group's high point when it comes to sheer sprightly pop, as perfect a tribute to obvious OMD inspirational source Sparks as any–witty lines about science and romance wedded to a great melody (prefaced by a brilliant, hyperactive intro). "Locomotion" takes a slightly slower but equally entertaining turn, sneaking in a bit of steel drum to the appropriately chugging rhythm and letting the guest horn section take a prominent role, its sunny blasts offsetting the deceptively downcast lines McCluskey sings. Meanwhile, "Talking Loud and Clear" ends the record on a reflective note–Cooper's intra-verse sax lines and mock harp snaking through the quiet groove of the song. As for the remainder of the album, if there are hints here and there of the less-successful late-'80s period, at other points the more adventurous side of the band steps up. The instrumental title track smoothly blends reggae rhythms with the haunting mock choirs familiar from earlier efforts, while the elegiac, Humphreys-sung "Never No More" and McCluskey's "Hard Day" both make for lower-key highlights. —*Ned Raggett*

Crush / Jun. 17, 1985 / A&M ✦✦✦✦✦

Following through on the pop inclinations of *Junk Culture*, OMD recorded a full-fledged mainstream pop album with *Crush*. Considerably calmer and more accessible than their previous records, the album may be less adventurous than their earlier work, but the breezy melodic charm of dance-pop singles like "So In Love" make *Crush* a thoroughly winning album. —*Stephen Thomas Erlewine*

The Pacific Age / Sep. 29, 1986 / A&M ✦✦

Sugar Tax / Jun. 11, 1991 / Virgin ✦✦

With the split between McCluskey and the rest of the band resolved by the former's decision to carry on with the band's name on his own, the question before *Sugar Tax's* appearance was whether the change would spark a new era of success for someone who clearly could balance artistic and commercial impulses in a winning fashion. The answer, based on the album–not entirely. The era of *Architecture and Morality* wouldn't be revisited anyway, for better or for worse, but instead of delightful confections with subtle heft like "Enola Gay" and "Tesla Girls," on *Sugar Tax* McCluskey is comfortably settled into a less-spectacular range of songs that only occasionally connect. Like fellow refugees from the early '80s such as Billy Mackenzie and Marc Almond, McCluskey found himself bedeviled in the early '90s with an artistic block that resulted in his fine singing style surrounded by pedestrian arrangements and indifferent songs. There was one definite redeeming number at the start: "Sailing on the Seven Seas," with glam-styled beats underpinning a giddy, playful romp that showed McCluskey still hadn't lost his touch entirely, and which became OMD's biggest single at home since "Souvenir." Beyond that, though, the album can best be described as pleasant instead of memorable, an exploration by McCluskey into calmer waters recorded entirely by himself outside of some guitar from

Stuart Boyle. Without his longtime bandmates to help him, the results lack an essential spark (Holmes' drumming creativity being especially missed). In a tip of the hat to a clear source of inspiration, *Sugar Tax* includes a pleasant cover of Kraftwerk's "Neon Lights," with guest vocals by Christine Mellor, while "Apollo XI" uses *Dazzle Ships*-styled sample collages made up of moon-landing broadcasts, though the song itself isn't much. Even at its most active–"Call My Name" and "Pandora's Box"–*Sugar Tax* is for the most part just there. —*Ned Raggett*

Liberator / Jun. 29, 1993 / Virgin ✦✦

Universal / 1996 / Virgin ✦✦

● The Singles / Nov. 17, 1998 / Virgin ✦✦✦✦✦

Looking back on 20 years of creative growth since the electro-pop band's inception, *The OMD Singles* is logically and chronologically arranged. The earliest recordings, 1980's "Electricity" and "Messages," prove electric messages were being channeled from such German pioneers as Kraftwerk and Neu. These English boys were enamored of melody, though, and it was not long before such dulcet, song-like structure became self-evident, as in 1984's "Tesla Girls." From then on, it is a steady climb in coherence, with synth rhythms downplayed in order to bring the melodic theme to the front. The pinnacle of this progression is OMD's memorable "So in Love" (1985) and "If You Leave" (from 1986's *Pretty in Pink*). The album closes with their last hit, 1996's glam-influenced autobiography "Walking on the Milky Way." Last original member, Andy McCluskey, has blessed this greatest-hits package as the final swan song for the long-lived group. Originating in post-punk synth experimentation and closing in dated, but still strong, pop productions, *The OMD Singles* is an excellent timeline of the band whose sound covered in a single career that same territory explored by the Human League, Erasure, Yaz, New Order, and beyond. —*Thomas Schulte*

The Original Brothers and Sisters of Love

Alternative Folk, Appalachian Folk, Sea Shanties, Folk-Rock, Neo-Prog

The Original Brothers and Sisters of Love started out in Brighton, MI, in the mid-'90s as a duo of brothers Jamie and Tim Monger, dubbed the Original Brothers of Love. Each had played in other bands, and Tim performed solo, but, with the exception of recording their friend, the Gok (who, incidentally, also named their band), this was the first time the brothers worked together. The two singer/songwriter guitarists added various instruments to their repertoire over the years, including mandolin and harmonica.

The duo was joined by four more musicians in as many years, resulting in the Original Brothers and Sisters of Love: Tim and Jamie Monger, guitarist/vocalist Greg McIntosh, New Zealand violinist and vocalist Liz Auchinvole, bassist Scott McClintock, and percussionist Martin Juarez. Fall of 1999 brought the release of TOBASOL's debut CD, *The Legende of Jeb Minor*, on Detroit area label Planet Ant. By the time of the album's release, however, drummer Martin Juarez had left the band. His role was filled by area musician Josh Tillinghast (of Larval) until the band enlisted a permanent drummer, Fido Kennington.

In April 2000, TOBASOL's debut album was reissued nationally on their new label, The Telegraph Company. A year later, the band wrapped up recording their follow-up, *H.O.M.E.S., Vol. 1*, and headed down to Texas to perform at the annual festival South By Southwest. The second album was released in August 2001, while the band toured the U.S. for two months. The album is the first in a two-part series of recordings that draw upon the locales and experiences of living in Michigan. From the title–an acronym schoolkids are taught to help remember the names of the surrounding Great Lakes (Huron, Ontario, Michigan, Erie, and Superior)–to songs about Michigan winters and the demise of Detroit's Tiger Stadium, the Original Brothers and Sisters of Love tell personal tales with an imagination and passion that have universal appeal. —*Joslyn Layne*

The Legende of Jeb Minor / 1999 / Telegraph Company ✦✦✦✦

The most remarkable thing about the Original Brothers and Sisters of Love's debut album *The Legende of Jeb Minor* is that it sounds entirely out of time. If anything, it sounds like a great unreleased album from the vaults of Harvest Records, since its blend of folk, psychedelia, prog-rock, and sea shanties is of piece with the legendary British label's willfully eccentric bent. Still, such a compliment may seem backhanded, a way to dismiss the record as a self-conscious attempt to recreate the '70s. That's not the case at all. *The Legende of Jeb Minor* may recall classic progressive albums, but that's only because the Brothers and Sisters have the inclination to follow their ideas past their logical conclusion, resulting in fresh configurations of familiar sounds. *The Legende* is firmly rooted in folk traditions–most of the songs are built on acoustic guitars, there are whistles and accordions peppered throughout the mix, the backing vocals are a blend of sea shanties and campfire singalongs–but it isn't a folk album because the band's sensibilities are somewhat post-modern. They don't see any boundaries between musical styles or genres, or even lyrical subject; there are songs that play as fables and others that sound like myths. They never renounce the past–they build on it, creating an album that is gently mesmerizing as it sways from tranquil to surging folk-prog anthems. The best thing about it all is that the music always feels familiar, as if you've heard the songs hundreds of times before, yet it simultaneously feels fresh and unpredictable–in other words, a little out of time, drawing from the past and set in the present, but belonging to neither. It's a neat trick to pull off, and the fact that *The Legende of Jeb Minor* is a debut effort makes it all the more impressive. —*Stephen Thomas Erlewine*

● H.O.M.E.S., Vol. 1 / Aug. 14, 2001 / Telegraph Company ✦✦✦✦

There's no denying the sheer artiness of the Original Brothers and Sisters of Love, even if their second album, *H.O.M.E.S.*, is positively streamlined and muscular compared to their endearingly precious debut, *The Legende of Jeb Minor*. Here, TOBASOL strengthen their sound, retaining their enticing ethereal feel, yet making it more direct with a clean, direct production and melodies that delve into tuneful psychedelia as often as they seem like forgotten folk songs. In retrospect, it's a logical outgrowth of their first album, yet the punchy, live production comes as a bit of a shock at first. While this sound isn't as dreamy as *Jeb Minor*, it's enhances the group's essential character. The Brothers and Sisters still don't sound like anybody else, as they blend the past and present, not just in their music, but in their very lyrics. If their debut hung suspended in time, this record has a clear sense of place—namely, Michigan, particularly Michigan's past. Like a folky, American XTC, they reconstruct the past for the present, borrowing folk inflections for pop songs and vice versa. And make no mistake—even with neo-folk tales like the stomping "Foreman of the Mill," there's a heavier pop element here, evidenced by both the skipping "Michigan and Trumbull," the dissonant-specked "Beautiful Night," even the lovely "Silent Apologies." Although *H.O.M.E.S.* is constructed like a classic record, flowing easily and filled with warm, little sonic details, TOBASOL have created a record that's nevertheless new. It's easy to get caught up in their thrill of discovery as they craft a delightfully eccentric record that consolidates their strengths while pushing into new territory. *—Stephen Thomas Erlewine*

The Originals

f. 1966, Detroit, MI

Motown, Urban, Disco, Soul

Detroit soul vocal group. Led by Freddie Gorman, the Originals took the R&B world by storm in 1969, although they had worked at Motown for years as invaluable background vocalists. Gorman recorded as a solo for Berry Gordy in 1961 and co-wrote "Please Mr. Postman" for the Marvelettes, and the Originals cut a version of Leadbelly's "Goodnight Irene" for Gordy's Soul subsidiary in '66 with ex-Falcon Joe Stubbs as lead. But Stubbs had split to form 100 Proof (Aged in Soul) by the time the quartet waxed the beautiful doo wop throwback "Baby I'm for Real," an R&B chart-topper in '69 that was co-written and lushly produced by Marvin Gaye. The same combination also produced "The Bells," another major hit in 1970. Former solo act Ty Hunter joined the group in 1971, and the Originals continued to chart into the next decade. *—Bill Dahl*

● **Motown Superstar Series, Vol. 10** / 1976 / Motown ✦✦✦✦✦
The Detroit-based Originals began singing in 1966, with tenor vocalists Crathman Spencer and Henry Dixon, bassist Freddie Gorman and baritone Walter Gaines. Marvin Gaye helped bring them to Motown and later wrote or co-wrote three of their singles, including the anthemic "Baby, I'm For Real." That single, their other major hit, "The Bells," and the third Gaye single, "We Can Make It Baby," are among the tunes on this anthology. They weren't a great group, but their two hits are as gripping and wonderfully produced and arranged as any Motown material. *—Ron Wynn*

The Very Best of the Originals / Mar. 23, 1999 / Motown ✦✦✦✦
Their hits from the late '60s through the mid '70s, along with some LP cuts, B-sides, and unreleased tracks. The first six songs were produced or co-produced by Marvin Gaye in 1969-70 (including the hits "Baby I'm for Real" and "The Bells"). These have been sometimes cited as forerunners to his *What's Going On* album, but it would be wrong to view them as a *What's Going On* supplement. They're in much more of a lush, group vocal, sweet soul style, although some traces of ideas Gaye would play with in the early '70s are present, particularly in the way the background voices weave around each other. The one previously unreleased Gaye production, "Just to Keep You Satisfied," would be reworked, with the same backing track and backing vocals but a different lead vocal and lyrics, on Gaye's *Let's Get It On* album. The rest of the tracks are largely in a competent sweet soul mold, also including a previously unreleased Holland-Dozier-Holland number from 1966 ("Suspicion") with a more uptempo sound, a Stevie Wonder-composed and -produced cut from 1974, "Game Called Love," and the 1976 disco smash, "Down to Love Town." *—Richie Unterberger*

The Orioles

f. 1948, Baltimore, MD, **db.** 1954

Doo Wop, R&B

Led by Sonny Til, the Orioles were the first Black vocal group to sing music directly for a Black audience. Through their early recordings—which were made in the late '40s and early '50s—the band laid the groundwork for R&B vocal groups and doo wop. The Orioles fused traditional pop songs with gospel sensibilities and arranged blues and gospel material with smooth harmonies, designed to appeal to the broadest audience possible. In 1948, their debut "It's Too Soon to Know" became a number one R&B hit and crossed over to number 13 on the pop charts. At the time of its release, no Black group had managed to cross over to the pop charts with what was then-known as a "race" record. The Orioles immediately followed the success of their debut single with the seasonal "(It's Gonna Be A) Lonely Christmas," which reached the R&B Top Ten at the end of 1948. "Tell Me So" became the Orioles' second number one R&B hit in the spring of 1949, beginning a streak of hit R&B singles that year. In addition to "Tell Me So," the group charted with "A Kiss and a Rose," "I Challenge Your Kiss" and "Forgive and Forget." Following their peak year of 1949, the group ran into tragedy in 1950 when guitarist Tommy Gaither was killed in an automobile accident that also injured two other members. The Orioles scored their next hit in 1952, when "Baby Please Don't Go" reached number eight on the R&B charts. The following year, the group had their biggest hit with "Crying in the Chapel," which spent five weeks on the R&B charts and reached number 11 on the pop charts, eventually going gold; Elvis Presley had a hit with the song 12 years later. Toward the end of the year, the group had another Top Ten R&B hit with "In the Mission of St. Augustine." The single would turn out to be their last hit. *—Stephen Thomas Erlewine*

★ **Sing Their Greatest Hits** / Nov. 25, 1991 / Collectables ✦✦✦✦✦
This Orioles hit package is about equal to any other that's available, but pales next to the Bear Family boxed set. The now defunct Murray Hill also had a great Orioles box several years ago. Save your money and grab the Bear Family if you really want the real story on The Orioles. *—Ron Wynn*

Jubilee Sides / 1993 / Bear Family ✦✦✦✦✦
Six CDs, covering 1948 through 1960, and in that 400+ minutes you get an overview of the transition of postwar rhythm & blues from the black community to the heart of mainstream popular music. Disc one opens with their earliest sides from July 1948, when the quintet was still very heavily influenced by the Ink Spots. The group's music during this period grew rapidly in sophistication; their second session shows a startling level of confidence, the group embellishing the melody and harmony of their songs and transforming them into something new. The sound quality of some of the material on this disc is less than perfect, due to the state of the best available masters. Things get very interesting on disc two, with the first recordings to feature a string section (their first conscious effort at crossing over into the pop market. On disc three, they continued to record in their trademark sophisticated sound, although some songs also capture them at their bluesiest. Disc four catches the group moving into a fully mainstream R&B vogue, as well as Sonny Til's superb duets with Edna McGriff. Disc five covers the period of their biggest hit, "Crying In the Chapel"—by 1953-54, the Orioles were generally working in a kind of big-band R&B mode, and most of this material, in keeping with their success of the era, did get out. Disc six covers the tail end of the group's original period with Jubilee and then picks up for a coda in the 1960s. This material is a little less focused than much of what has come before, for the Orioles were competing in a crowded new arena of R&B-turned-rock & roll. The notes are fascinating, and the sound, apart from the bulk of disc one, is excellent, improving as the recording dates advance. *—Bruce Eder*

Orlando

f. 1994

New Romantic, Britpop

Orlando was the most successful and visible band to emerge from the extremely brief romo movement of the mid-'90s. Led by songwriter/keyboardist Dickon Edwards, Orlando combined the stylish, synthesized dance-pop of the early '80s with Pulp's sense of purpose, the Manic Street Preachers' sense of outrage, Morrissey's sense of humor and a lyrical stance that bordered on the explicitly gay. Thanks to journalist Simon Price, the duo became a sensation on the pages of Melody Maker, who grouped Orlando with bands like Plastic Fantastic, DexDexter, and Hollywood as Romo bands—i.e., bands that revived the stylistic sensibilities of new romantics and crossed it with modernist art. Despite a huge push within the media, romo failed miserably, with Melody Maker's package tour playing to audiences of less than 100 in early 1996. Most of the bands crashed and burned following the tour, but Orlando persevered, becoming one of only three romo bands to actually release singles. In the summer of 1996, Orlando released their first EP, *Just for a Second*, which received decidedly mixed reviews, ranging from Price's enthusiastic praise to several other publications who panned it. *The Magic EP* followed in the fall, and it received similar reviews. "Nature's Hated," the group's third single, was scheduled for spring release in 1997. Orlando finally delivered their full-length debut, *Passive Soul*, in September 1997. It was greeted with indifference and generally lukewarm reviews. The label barely supported the album and the group failed to launch a full-scale English tour. Within a month of its release, *Passive Soul* had disappeared. By the end of the year, group founder Dickon unleashed a shocker—he was leaving the band to start the harder-edged Fosca. *—Stephen Thomas Erlewine*

Just for a Second / 1996 / Blanco Y Negro ✦✦✦
Not quite the auspicious debut that it wants to be, "Just for a Second" crosses awkward, lite-funk similar to latter-day Duran Duran with a synthesized symphonic, disco sweep, straight out of Euro-pop. Try as it may, it never quite develops a melody, especially since Tim Chipping's thin, quivering voice can't carry a tune, yet it still manages to make a definitive stylistic statement. Political statements are reserved for the piano-driven ballad "Something to Write Home About," one of the more explicitly gay anthems of the '90s, or "The Trouble With You," which consists of classical music in one channel, and an interview stating Orlando's modus operandi on the other. *—Stephen Thomas Erlewine*

Magic EP / 1996 / Blanco Y Negro ✦✦✦✦✦
A more diverse, but not necessarily more accomplished, affair than *Just for a Second*, *The Magic EP* is the definitive Orlando recording, capturing the awkward gap between their pretensions and their achievements. "Don't Kill My Rage" is a boisterous disco number that has a tight arrangement, but is undercut by Tim's chirping, wavering and tuneless falsetto. "Fatal" is a downright bizarre attempt to fuse Euro-disco with G-Funk that actually features Tim's best vocal. "Contained" is a spare, Northern Soul-styled R&B track, highlighted by percolating horns, and "Up Against It" is a grand, theatrical piano ballad much like "Something to Write Home About." Throughout it all, Dickon really tries to say something, usually to no avail. However, his botched imagery and poetry are endearing, and are perfectly suited for Tim's non-voice. *—Stephen Thomas Erlewine*

● **Passive Soul** / Sep. 1997 / Blanco Y Negro ✦✦✦✦✦
Nobody wanted romo, but the music industry didn't realize that until it was too late. It wasn't until Melody Maker's Fiddling When Romo Burns tour went up in flames that the industry and journalists realized that Simon Price and Taylor Parkes' grand folly wasn't going to work. Just about 100 people attended the tour throughout the entire nation in 1996, but a few recordings were stuck in the pipeline. Mostly, they were singles, but there was one full-length record ready to be unleashed—Orlando's brilliant *Passive Soul*. Even if there had been competition within the romo world—in other words, if other romo

bands had been allowed to release a full-length album—*Passive Soul* would still stand as the movement's *Sgt. Pepper* since it is so fully realized and accomplished. After all, Orlando had a broader reach than their peers, digging back to the past to draw on Motown, Northern Soul and Philly Soul, all crossed with an ironic detachment borrowed from Bowie and Brian Ferry, of course, but also pitched at the intimate scale and deliberate introspection so reminiscent of the Sarah Records roster. So, yes, this album masterminded by Tim and Dickon is clearly studied and careful, but that earnestness of ambition is endearing, especially since it's tempered by the bedsit fascinations and obsessions of these effete misfits. That means there are some bewildering moments on *Passive Moments*—the "Oh Tennenbaum" introduction to the album, the crooning of Tim, Dickon's weirdly personal confessions, such as "a brown carpet will hide all stains"—but it's ultimately a triumph of unabashed style and shyness, filled with lively hooks and impassionedly fey sentiment. Yes, it is all too precious—even Sebadoh fans will find this entirely too sensitive—but that's its charm, since Orlando is about being delicate outsiders who find life within pop music, especially when it's awkward, geeky and just waiting to bloom. This album captures that outsider sentiment as well as any other pop album, which means that its not just the Best Romo Album Ever (and it still would have been the best, even if another romo group would have had the chance to record), but it's one of the best indie pop records of its time. *—Stephen Thomas Erlewine*

Tony Orlando (Michael Anthony Orlando Cassivitis)

b. Apr. 3, 1944, New York, NY [Manhattan]

Vocals / Brill Building Pop, Teen Idol, Soft Rock, Pop

In conjunction with his backing duo Dawn, singer Tony Orlando was one of the biggest pop stars of the early '70s, best remembered for the mammoth hit "Tie a Yellow Ribbon 'Round the Ole Oak Tree." Orlando's first hit, 1961's "Halfway to Paradise," was written for him by Carole King, who also authored the Top 20 follow-up, "Bless You." However, after scoring a minor chart entry with "Happy Times (Are Here to Stay)," his career ground to a halt. In early 1970, Orlando received a call from Bell Records producer Hank Medress requesting that he lay down a lead vocal over a demo recorded by a Detroit-based act called Dawn, consisting of vocalists Telma Hopkins and Joyce Vincent. The record, "Candida," became a massive hit, rising to number three on the singles charts. Orlando quickly agreed to cut another record with Dawn; titled "Knock Three Times," the single topped the charts in early 1971, and finally he returned to music full-time, signing with Bell and going on tour with Hopkins and Vincent under the banner of Dawn, Featuring Tony Orlando. Released in 1973, "Tie a Yellow Ribbon" became Orlando's biggest hit yet, and was named the top-selling single of the year. Long after its original success, the song re-entered the public consciousness with renewed force in 1981, becoming something of anthem during the Iranian hostage crisis as American citizens regularly tied yellow ribbons around trees as a symbol of their hopes and prayers for the hostages' safe return. By that time, Tony Orlando and Dawn had long since dissolved after scoring subsequent Top Ten hits with 1973's "Say, Has Anybody Seen My Sweet Gypsy Rose?," 1974's "Steppin' Out (Gonna Boogie Tonight)," and 1975's chart-topping "He Don't Love You (Like I Love You)." *—Jason Ankeny*

Definitive Collection / Oct. 27, 1998 / Arista ♦♦♦♦

True to its title, the 18-track *The Definitive Collection* gathers all of the Tony Orlando and Dawn you possibly could ever want. Starting at the very beginning of the '70s and carrying on strong for a good half-decade, the schlocky-pop-meets-vaudeville trio managed three number one singles before the Top 40 rolled them out for good. All of the huge hits are here—"Candida," "Knock Three Times," "Tie a Yellow Ribbon Round the Ole Oak Tree," "Say, Has Anybody Seen My Sweet Gypsy Rose," "He Don't Love You Like I Love You"—along with handful of lesser tunes [like "Steppin' Out (Gonna Boogie Tonight)"] and one misplaced album cut. So, if you're in need of some of the '70s' most insipid, wince-inducing songs, this is your one and only stop for Orlando's contribution to the annals. *—Michael Gallucci*

Orleans

f. 1972, New York, NY

AM Pop, Pop/Rock, Soft Rock

Best known for their hits "Still the One" and "Dance With Me," Orleans was founded in New York in 1972 by John Hall, Larry Hoppen and Wells Kelly. Hoppen's brother Lance joined before the group signed with ABC Records in 1973; working with producers Barry Beckett and Roger Hawkins at Muscle Shoals Studios, they released their self-titled debut later that year. In 1974 Orleans recorded a self-produced album in New York's Bearsville Studio, but ABC didn't like it and dropped the group from the label, leaving Asylum to release the album *Let There Be Magic* in 1974, spurring the group's first big hit, 1975's "Dance with Me."

Their album *Waking and Dreaming* contained the hit "Still the One," which ABC-TV used as a theme song for that year. In 1977, Hall, who wrote many of the groups hits with his wife Johanna, left the group to pursue a solo career. He recorded two solo albums after signing with Elektra Records, and became something of a spokesman for the anti-nuclear power movement, helping to organize a group called MUSE (Musicians United for Safe Energy). Hall eventually worked with Jackson Browne, Graham Nash and Bonnie Raitt to organize the No Nukes concerts at Madison Square Garden in 1979.

Without Hall, Orleans went through several other personnel changes before it had a number 11 hit with "Love Takes Time," from the album *Forever.* Though MCA's Infinity label went bankrupt in 1980, the group persevered, performing together in clubs and releasing the album *One of a Kind* in 1982. In 1984 Kelly died in London of a heroin overdose, and by the early '90s, Hall ditched his solo career and returned to performing with Orleans. After the group released 1994's *Orleans Live, Vol. 1*, and 1995's *Analog Men* on its own Major Record Label, Hall and the Hoppen brothers continued to tour as an acoustic trio. *—Richard Skelly*

● **We're Still Having Fun: The Best of Orleans** / Jun. 24, 1997 / Rhino ♦♦♦♦♦

We're Still Having Fun: The Best of Orleans is a comprehensive overview of the soft-rock band's career, featuring no less than 20 tracks. Not only are all of their hits included ("Let There Be Music," "Dance With Me," "Still the One," "Reach," "Love Takes Time"), but so are overlooked singles and album tracks. Although it may contain too much music for casual listeners—many of Orleans' lesser tracks tended to sound similar—it's hard to imagine a compilation more thorough than this. *—Stephen Thomas Erlewine*

Jim O'Rourke

b. 1969, Chicago, IL

Producer, Multi Instruments, Guitar / Experimental Rock, Indie Rock, Post-Rock/ Experimental

American post-classical composer Jim O'Rourke has been a key component in the increasing overlap of the American and European experimental music avant-garde, working in everything from jazz and rock to ambient and electro-acoustic and building many a bridge in between. A Chicago native, his work has found equal truck with experimental jazz and noise fanatics, chill room denizens, and bedroom experimentalists, and has had the resultant effect of cross-polinating many otherwise isolated compositional communities. Dealing most often with prepared guitar in improvisational group settings, O'Rourke has also released a fair bit of material as a soloist, althought more often in the electro-acoustic/musique concrete vein. He's collaborated with such contemporary improv heroes as Derek Bailey, Henry Kaiser, Eddie Prevost and Keith Rowe (of English improv group AMM), KK Null, David Jackman (Organum), and early Krautrock experimentalists Faust. O'Rourke was also engaged in an ongoing exploration of experimental rock as a member of Gastr Del Sol, who released albums through the Teen Beat and Table of the Elements labels. *—Sean Cooper*

Terminal Pharmacy / 1995 / Tzadik ♦♦♦♦

With *Terminal Pharmacy*, Jim O'Rourke creates a soundscape so calm and minimal that some people, lacking patience for the seeming formlessness, could do entirely without it, while others will find themselves repeatedly putting it in their CD player at home, work, or wherever they need warmth dispersed throughout the air. Seeping steadily from the edge of silence comes crackles, thin fuzz, and extended string tones. Less narrative than what "electro-acoustic" usually refers to, "Cede" hums at the back of your mind. Given almost a minute of silence in between, the second piece then begins; sounding like a very quiet improvisation, the instruments whisper bowed rounds, a conversation in tininess that grows bolder at moments. *—Joslyn Layne*

Bad Timing / Aug. 25, 1997 / Drag City ♦♦♦♦♦

With *Bad Timing*, O'Rourke attempts a return to the organic atmosphere of acoustic guitar from his explorations in electronica. The album consists of four songs clocking in at roughly ten minutes each, and is characterized by O'Rourke's ambient acoustic exploration. Three of the tracks enlist various instruments from cello to trumpet and even drums. The songs are highly textured and require patience, as they slowly evolve from abstract riffs into clear melodies. The album encompasses a rich dynamic range despite the seeming limitations that acoustic guitar could impose. There is a fair amount of splicing and mixing, which attests to the fact that O'Rourke has not completely dispensed with his passion for electronic music, but these interludes often provide a unique perspective. The highlight of the album is the final track, "Happy Trails," which begins with distorted acoustic noise, followed by an upbeat country rhythm provided by Tortoise's John McEntire. In sum, *Bad Timing* is a consistent effort and well worth a listen, especially during the mellow early morning hours. *—Marc Gilman*

● **Eureka** / Feb. 16, 1999 / Drag City ♦♦♦♦♦

It's a good bet to expect the unexpected with Jim O'Rourke—no matter which hat he's wearing (solo artist, bandmate, producer, remixer, etc.), each of the endlessly prolific projects that bears his name takes on a shape and identity all its own while retaining the originality and ingenuity that have become the hallmarks of his singular body of work. *Eureka* is perhaps his most stunning and surprising detour yet, a full-blown excursion into lush, melodic pop; granted, there's something inherently perverse about the very notion of O'Rourke and Chicago underground cronies like trombonist Jeb Bishop and cornetist Rob Mazurek tackling such classicist stuff, but instead the album is short on irony and long on affection—in fact, its most subversive dimension is its very real mainstream appeal. What's most fascinating about *Eureka* is that its big, bright pop is actually the perfect showcase for O'Rourke's mastery of sound—highlights like the epic opener "Women of the World" and a joyously schmaltzy cover of the Bacharach/David chestnut "Something Big" are crafted with remarkable care and depth, the former in particular building and blooming in truly majestic fashion. On a conceptual level, of course, it's easy to view *Eureka* as another in a long line of deconstructionist experiments, a reading more overtly avant songs like "Movie on the Way Down" and "Through the Night Softly" certainly bears out; on a deeper level, however, it's a true labor of love, and its sheer exuberance and creativity go further in re-shaping the pop aesthetic than any pure intellectual exercise ever could. *—Jason Ankeny*

Halfway to a Threeway [EP] / Jan. 20, 2000 / Drag City ♦♦♦♦

Jim O'Rourke's *Halfway to a Threeway* comes across as a portable, stripped-down version of *Eureka*'s lush fusion of symphonic pop, folk, jazz, and soft rock. Though it's not quite as elaborate as the album, the EP's four songs also show that O'Rourke is both a skilled instrumentalist and polished songwriter. "The Workplace" is a witty tale of androgyny and cross-dressing that features vocals from the Sea and Cake's Archer Prewitt and Sam Prekop, while the charming instrumental "Not Sport, Martial Art" mixes loping, slightly jazzy guitars, syncopated percussion, and snazzy cornet flourishes. "Fuzzy Sun" is the kissing cousin of *Eureka*'s "Ghost Ship in a Storm," yet it has its own melancholy charm. Best of all, though, is the epic title track; lyrically and musically, it's as darkly humorous and moving as anything O'Rourke produced for Smog. He makes lyrics like "Can't wipe this smile off my face/As you strut by in your leg brace" seem poignant, thanks to the song's beautiful, spooky harmonies and delicate guitar work. On its smaller scale, *Halfway to a Threeway* is just as successful as *Eureka* at showcasing Jim O'Rourke's musical innovation, warmth, and humor. —*Heather Phares*

Orpheus

f. 1967, Boston, MA, **db.** 1971
Sunshine Pop, Soft Rock, Psychedelic Pop, Psychedelic

Boston's Orpheus made four albums in the late '60s and early '70s that were something of an antecedent to soft rock. Although some of the members had roots in the folk scene, and although they were lumped in with the heavier and more psychedelic bands that comprised the short-lived "Bosstown Sound," Orpheus was in fact much closer to the "sunshine pop" of the late '60s heard on AM radio. Producer Alan Lorber (the key generator of the Bosstown Sound hype, who also produced Ultimate Spinach and other local bands) gave their light harmony pop tunes elaborate orchestrated arrangements that, even as they hinted at baroque classical music, also betrayed his extensive experience working on television commercials.

Jack McKenes and Eric Gulliksen of Orpheus had played together in a pop-folk group, the Minutemen, and McKenes and Bruce Arnold formed the pop-folk duo the Villagers, before the three of them plus drummer Harry Sandler linked up to form Orpheus. Relying largely on original material, mostly written by Arnold and Gulliksen, Orpheus cut three LPs for MGM (the primary home of Bosstown sound bands) in the late 1960s. Despite the marketing of the Bosstown sound as a hip and album-oriented phenomenon, the group's harmonies and songwriting were in fact more similar to singles groups such as the Fifth Dimension and the Association, even with echoes of the Lettermen in places. There might have been some traces of folk and psychedelic music on some tracks, but the light, sometimes precious, love songs were forerunners of adult contemporary music. Sometimes, for instance, the albums sound rather like the songs (although not the arrangements) played by Chicago at their most unabashedly pop. Orpheus, however, were ordinary if ambitious songwriters, lacking the grand melodies to either get them national popularity in their lifetime, or retroactive cult status.

When Orpheus made their fourth and final album for Bell in 1971, only Arnold was left from the original band, although the LP had songwriting and vocals from Steve Martin (not the same as the Steve Martin who sang lead for the Left Banke), who had written some material on Orpheus' MGM recording. The double-CD Big Beat compilation *The Best of Orpheus* has almost everything from the MGM LPs, as well as a couple of songs from the Bell LP and some previously unreleased material. —*Richie Unterberger*

Orpheus / Dec. 1967 / MGM ✦✦✦

Orpheus' self-titled debut album, released at the end of 1967 (and not to be confused with their fourth LP, which was also self-titled, but was released in 1971 on Bell), is a curious piece mixing lightweight pop with heavyweight ambition. Although Orpheus was pegged as part of the Bosstown sound, which largely consisted of psychedelic or heavy rock bands, and although some of the members were ex-folkies, they were sentimental pop songwriters at heart. There's nothing wrong with that, but producer Alan Lorber dressed up the arrangements with quasi-classical orchestration that sound, unfortunately, like television commercial jingles trying to be more important. The material is somewhat like sunshine pop, somewhat like mainstream harmony pop bands of the era such as the Association and the Fifth Dimension, and slightly tinged with flower-power lyricism. Although the melodies are unusual, they're not memorable, and the whole combination is such an odd mixture of second-tier AM radio melodies and arty pretension that it's sometimes (unintentionally, no doubt) faintly laughable. Sitars come in for part of "Never in My Life," a track which goes through various phases of varispeed at the end for a further psychedelic touch; "The Dream," one of the better cuts, has the sort of downbeat dreaminess typical of Dino Valenti's cult 1968 album, with more ornate production. However, it's hard to imagine psychedelic enthusiasts going for this froth in a big way, and it lacks the hooks that would grab less adventurous pop listeners. The entire LP, with the exception of "Lesley's World," is available on Big Beat's double-CD compilation *Best of Orpheus.* —*Richie Unterberger*

Ascending / 1968 / MGM ✦✦✦

On this, their second album, Orpheus has created more rococo, orchestrated sunshine pop. It's different from their debut only in the virtual absence of the occasional psychedelic flourishes. This release is also distinguishable from the first by some uncharacteristic departures into good-time folk-rock ("Borneo") and straightforward, late-'60s rock (the cover of "She's Not There"). Otherwise, it offers harmony and sunshine pop with lyrics and arrangements suggestive of a fairyland where lovers perpetually walk on air, best heard on "I'll Fly," which sounds a bit like a Jimmy Webb outtake that missed out on getting onto a Fifth Dimension LP. The group and producer Alan Lorber often seem to be trying to create elegant chamber rock, but the music could use a lot more guts and realism. The melodies prove that Orpheus is no Left Banke, although they give "Walk Away Renee" a try, launching their cover with harmonies ripped off from the Association's "Never My Love." With the exception of "Don't Be So Serious," all of the album's tracks are included on the double-CD Big Beat compilation *The Best of Orpheus.* —*Richie Unterberger*

Joyful / 1969 / MGM ✦✦

Orpheus' final MGM album is softer and poppier than the other LPs the group had done

for the label, but not *that* much softer and poppier, as Orpheus were already pretty piffling at the outset. Like their other albums, it's full of lushly orchestrated original material that strives to be grand and important, but is much closer to mushy, sunshine pop than art. The feel-good bounciness of the harmonies and lyrics is incessant. It's one thing to be airy, another to be airheaded, and the group often treads perilously close to the latter trait. In order for pop/rock this light and romantic to work, the melodies have to be damn good; on this album, however, they're not close to being good enough, though the disc might find favor with sunshine pop cultists after something with a little more pretension than is common in the style. All of the songs are included on the Big Beat double-CD compilation *The Best of Orpheus.* —*Richie Unterberger*

The Best of Orpheus / 1995 / Big Beat ✦✦✦✦

This double-CD compilation includes almost all of the tracks from their first three albums, as well as a couple from the one they did in 1971 for Bell (by which time Bruce Arnold was the only remaining original member). Over the course of two discs the group is given a more comprehensive and respectful retrospective than they deserve; the lushness turns to mushiness for all but the most rabid sunshine pop fans. Despite the volume of material, the packaging isn't so hot either. Stray tracks are missing from the first two LPs, and although some of the material is apparently rare and unreleased (as it doesn't appear on the albums), details are not given in the extensive, typically self-aggrandizing liner notes by producer Alan Lorber; in fact, a few tracks are identified as coming from specific albums when in fact they did not appear on those discs. Those tracks include an alternate version of "Can't Find the Time to Tell You"; the peculiar "Anatomy of I've Never Seen Love Like This" (in which Lorber and Arnold, with narration, illustrate how they layered and produced an Orpheus track); and a live version of "Just a Little Bit" (redone on the second LP) by the Villagers, the pre-Orpheus folk duo that included future Orpheus members Bruce Arnold and Jack McKenes. The booklet manages to include a lot of information about the band without coming close to conveying a cohesive chronological history. —*Richie Unterberger*

● **The Very Best of Orpheus** / May 15, 2001 / Varese ✦✦✦✦

Varese's 2001 collection *The Very Best of Orpheus* is the best overview of the Boston psychedelic band's career assembled. There may be others that are more comprehensive, but this collects the very best of their four albums, including a couple of rare single sides to boot. —*Stephen Thomas Erlewine*

Beth Orton

b. Dec. 1970, Norwich, England
Vocals, Guitar / Alternative Folk, Adult Alternative Pop/Rock, Trip-Hop, Singer/Songwriter

Singer/songwriter Beth Orton combined the passionate beauty of the acoustic folk tradition with the electronic beats of trip-hop to create a fresh, distinct fusion of roots and rhythm. Born in Norwich, England in December 1970, Orton debuted as one half of the duo Spill, a one-off project with William Orbit which released a cover of John Martyn's "Don't Wanna Know About Evil." She continued working with Orbit on his 1993 LP *Strange Cargo 3*, co-writing and singing the track "Water from a Vine Leaf" before appearing with the group Red Snapper on their first singles "Snapper" and "In Deep." In 1995 Orton teamed with the Chemical Brothers for "Alive: Alone," the ultimate track on their *Exit Planet Dust* LP. After assembling a backing band comprised of double bassist Ali Friend, guitarist Ted Barnes, keyboardist Lee Spencer and drummer Wildcat Will, she finally issued her 1996 debut EP *She Cries Your Name*; her stunning full-length bow *Trailer Park*, produced in part by Andrew Weatherall, followed later in the year. In 1997, Orton released the superb *Best Bit* EP, a move towards a more organic, soulful sound highlighted by a pair of duets with folk-jazz legend Terry Callier; the full-length *Central Reservation* followed in 1999. —*Jason Ankeny*

Trailer Park / 1996 / Dedicated ✦✦✦✦✦

A folkie for the electronica age, Beth Orton brilliantly bridges the gap between acoustic songcraft and digital dance beats with her extraordinary debut album, *Trailer Park.* Fusing the plaintive emotional power of the singer/songwriter tradition with the distanced cool of trip-hop rhythms, Orton creates a fresh, distinct, and surprisingly organic sound without obvious precedent; blessed with a warm, ethereal voice capable of adapting comfortably to Spartan folk ("Whenever," a touching cover of the Spector/Greenwich/Barry-penned "I Wish I Never Saw the Sunshine"), buoyant pop ("Live As We Dream," "How Far"), and spacey, densely layered electronica ("Tangent," "Touch Me With Your Love"), she shifts gears with remarkable ease, the depth and clarity of her unique perspective connecting even the most disparate tracks together into a unified whole. Simply put, *Trailer Park* is one of the most promising and innovative debuts of its era. —*Jason Ankeny*

Best Bit EP / 1997 / Heavenly ✦✦✦✦

Best Bit is a masterpiece in miniature, a four-track EP of stunning vision and depth; Orton's first substantial release since her groundbreaking debut album *Trailer Park*, it moves away from the electronic textures of her previous work to forge a more organic compound of folk, dance-pop and jazz. The title track, with its loose, swinging trip-hop rhythms and treated background vocals, is closest in spirit to the album, but by the second cut, the evocative "Skimming Stone," Orton is in uncharted territory, juxtaposing moody piano-jazz with spaced-out guitar textures. The revelation of *Best Bit*, however, is the record's second half, a pair of breathtaking duets with singer Terry Callier: the first, a cover of Fred Neil's "Dolphins," represents folk-jazz fusion at its finest and most eccentric, with Orton's ethereal presence matching perfectly with Callier's warm, soulful croon. No less wonderful or touching is the closing "Lean on Me," a Callier original featuring Orton's most impassioned vocal turn to date—proof positive that under her remote electronic rhythms there beats a fragile human heart. —*Jason Ankeny*

● **Central Reservation** / Mar. 9, 1999 / Arista ✦✦✦✦

On her stunning sophomore album, *Central Reservation*, Beth Orton slips free of the electronic textures that colored her acclaimed 1996 debut, *Trailer Park*, stripping her music down to its raw essentials to produce a work of stark simplicity and rare poignancy. With the exception of a pair of Ben Watt-produced tracks ("Stars All Seem to Weep" and a remix of the title cut), *Central Reservation* rejects synthetic sounds and beats altogether in favor of an organic atmosphere somewhere between folk, jazz, and the blues; the focal point is instead Orton's evocatively soulful voice, which invests songs like "Sweetest Decline" and "Feel to Believe" with remarkable warmth and honesty. It's a risky move creatively as well as commercially—after all, the club culture was the first to champion Orton's talents—but it pays off handsomely; for all its brilliance, elements of *Trailer Park* already feel dated, but the new material possesses a timelessness that recalls the best of Nick Drake or Sandy Denny, with a haunting beauty to match. And while much has been made of the melancholy that pervades her music, ultimately *Central Reservation* is first and foremost a record about hope and survival; its emotional centerpiece, the seven-minute "Pass in Time" (a spine-tingling duet with legendary folk-jazz mystic Terry Callier), grapples with the death of Orton's mother, but its underlying message of healing and perseverance is powerfully life-affirming—her music hasn't merely discovered the light at the end of the tunnel, it's now bathing in it. *—Jason Ankeny*

Jeffrey Osborne

b. Mar. 9, 1948, Providence, RI
Vocals / Urban, Funk, Soul

Jeffrey Osborne began his professional singing career in 1969 with a popular funk and soul group called Love Men Ltd. The band moved to Los Angeles in 1970 and changed its name to L.T.D. Osborne was originally brought on as the drummer and eventually became the lead vocalist. After more than ten years with the band, he decided to pursue a solo career, which produced such Top 40 hits as "Don't You Get So Mad," "Stay With Me Tonight" and "Love Power," which he performed with Dionne Warwick.

Born in Providence, Rhode Island, Jeffrey Osborne was the youngest of 12 children and was constantly bombarded with music as he was growing up. He had five brothers and six sisters, some of whom went on to have music careers. His father, Clarence "Legs" Osborne, was a popular trumpeter who played with Lionel Hampton, Count Basie and Duke Ellington, and died when Jeffrey was only 13. His mother, Wanita, is ancestored by a Pequot Indian sachem. His oldest brother, Clay Osborne, is a singer and pianist, and Billy, another brother, is a songwriter and producer in Los Angeles. But Osborne's father had the greatest influence on his musical career; Clarence "Legs" Osborne turned down many top band offers during his career to be with his family. It was only after receiving his mother's encouragement that Jeffrey left for Los Angeles to play with L.T.D. At the age of 15, he sat in with the O'Jays when the drummer was too tired to play, and went on to play with them for two weeks. It was at a Providence nightclub that fate brought him together with the band Love Men Ltd. in 1969.

Osborne's solo career has brought him five gold and platinum albums, including *Stay With Me Tonight*, *Aymuk* and *Only Human*. He also recorded an album of duets with popular singer James Ingram, and scored an international hit with "On the Wings of Love" in 1982. Osborne's touring and recording continue to keep him busy much of the time, but he also devotes some of his time to charity work. *—Kim Summers*

● **Jeffrey Osborne** / 1982 / A&M ✦✦✦✦

As vocalist for the group L.T.D., Osborne's booming voice led hits like "Love Ballad," "Where Did We Go Wrong," and "Shine On." The group enjoyed constant success and offered a catalog of well-executed and classic albums including 1977's *Something to Love* and *Togetherness* from 1978. In 1982 it came as a complete shock when Osborne made his solo bid. Unlike countless other acts who did the same thing, his self-titled release proves that it was a great decision. Producer George Duke offered Osborne an up-to-the-minute sound with a collection of great studio players ranging from drummer Steve Ferrone to bassist Louis Johnson. That being said, a few of the tracks here don't play to Osborne's strengths as a committed and slightly quirky vocalist. "New Love" and "Eeenie Meenie" are so proficient yet by the numbers anyone could have sung them. The best tracks on this album give him the needed challenges that make him soar. The first single, the moody and rhythmic "Really Don't Need No Light," co-written by Osborne and David "Hawk" Wolinski, benefits from a string arrangement from George Del Barrio. The ballad "You Were Made to Love" not only perfectly captures Duke's uncluttered and precise production style, it also plays to Osborne's emotionality. The last track, "Congratulations," is a great tearjerker that has Osborne's reserve and intellect making it that much better. This is an impressive solo debut from one of R&B and pop's best vocalists. *—Jason Elias*

● **Ultimate Collection** / Sep. 7, 1999 / Hip-O ✦✦✦✦✦

At 17 tracks, containing all of his solo smashes plus selections from L.T.D. where he sang lead, Hip-O's *Ultimate Collection* fulfills the promise of its title, since it does feature all the best-known songs associated with Osborne. *—Stephen Thomas Erlewine*

More of My Best / Jul. 18, 2000 / Hip-O ✦✦✦✦

More of My Best gathers the highlights from Jeffrey Osborne's A&M, Arista, and Capitol releases, including L.T.D. hits like "Never Get Enough of Your Love," "Where Did We Go Wrong," and "Stranger." Top 40 solo hits such as "Soweto," "Room With a View," "In Your Eyes," and his collaborations with Dionne Warwick ("Take Good Care of You & Me") and Najee ("Loving Every Moment") make this collection worthwhile for fans looking to dig deeper into Osborne's work. *—Heather Phares*

Love Songs / Feb. 6, 2001 / Hip-O ✦✦✦✦

Jeffrey Osborne was always known as a romantic crooner, so it makes sense that a collection of his "love songs" would work quite well, and *Love Songs* does. Spanning 18

tracks, including four cuts from his first band L.T.D., this isn't strictly a hits collection, although it does have such charting items as "On the Wings of Love," "Eenie Meenie," "We're Going All the Way," and "You Should Be Mine (The Woo Woo Song)." This is heavy on album tracks, which may not make it the choice of some casual fans. Nevertheless, anyone looking for a romantic mood music album from Osborne is likely to be quite satisfied by this. *—Stephen Thomas Erlewine*

Joan Osborne

Vocals / American Trad Rock, Adult Alternative Pop/Rock

Born in Anchorage, KY, Joan Osborne sang occasionally as a child, but had given up on her voice after going to NYU's film school. At a bar on open-mic night, she decided to try a Billie Holiday song and eventually became a regular at the club's open-mic jam sessions. Osborne formed a band from the players, and began touring around the New York area. Forming her own Womanly Hips label, she released the live album *Soul Show* in 1992. After the 1994 EP *Blue Million Miles*, she signed a contract with Mercury. Released in 1995, Osborne's major-label debut *Relish* hit the Top Ten and achieved triple-platinum status. She was awarded with the album of the year by *Entertainment Weekly*, appeared on the cover of *Rolling Stone* and gained seven Grammy nominations in 1996. Five years after the breakthrough release of *Relish*, Osborne hooked up with Mitchell Froom (Suzanne Vega, Crowded House, Los Lobos) to issue *Righteous Love*. *—John Bush*

● **Relish** / 1995 / Blue Gorilla/Mercury ✦✦✦✦✦

"Relish" can be a sharp, bittersweet condiment; it can also suggest a determined gusto to live to the fullest. Combined, these two images provide a good taste of Joan Osborne's major-label debut (the live *Soul Show* was self-released in 1992). Grounded in blues, soul and gospel, the Kentucky native wields her gritty voice with personality and forceful presence, kind of Melissa Etheridge meets Sophie B. Hawkins with a splash of Jann Arden. Osborne's passion for life oozes from the grooves. There's an uplifting fervor to her material and delivery, as if every second, every note was being individually savored. Key track "One of Us" sets the disc's optimistic tone. It's a simple, direct statement of faith, honest and unadorned, one framed in a near-perfect chorus and delectable Neil Youngish guitar riff. This isn't one of those sugary, superficial, goody-two-shoes Amy Grant kind of deals. "Right Hand Man" and "Let's Just Get Naked" confirm that Osborne's earthy, enlightened spirituality shares the same bed with sensuality and sexuality. Well-rounded both lyrically and musically, there's also no contradiction in this universe between "Lumina"'s thoughtful balladry and the wailing harp and acoustic slide bursting the seams of "Help Me." *—Roch Parisien*

Early Recordings / Nov. 5, 1996 / Mercury ✦✦

Righteous Love / Sep. 12, 2000 / Interscope ✦✦✦

Five years after scoring with the mega hit "One of Us" and becoming the topic of more than a few religious conservatives' tirades, Joan Osborne returns with *Righteous Love*, sporting a more polished feel than on her debut, *Relish*. Producer Mitchell Froom brings along a few of his Los Lobos/Latin Playboys pals (Steve Berlin, Louie Perez) and adds some taut muscle to Osborne's songs, but at times comes close to overshadowing her work. Mitchell ropes in the loud blues and soul leanings that made her previous album so much fun, and the singer herself emotes in a much more restrained pop vein. An awkward cover of Gary Wright's "Love Is Alive" seems like a bit of a misstep, and Osborne manages to squeeze the last remaining bits of emotion out of Bob Dylan's "To Make You Feel My Love," a tune that even Billy Joel or Garth Brooks' adult-contemporary stabs couldn't ruin. Her reading is by far the best of the three. Don't expect a blockbuster hit on the level of "One of Us," but *Righteous Love*, for all its woes, holds enough treasures of its own. *—John Duffy*

Ozzy Osbourne

b. Dec. 3, 1948, Birmingham, England
Vocals, Leader / Album Rock, British Metal, Heavy Metal, Hard Rock, Neo-Classical Metal

Though many bands have succeeded in earning the hatred of parents and media worldwide throughout the past few decades, arguably only such acts as Alice Cooper, Judas Priest and Marilyn Manson have tied the controversial record of Ozzy Osbourne. The former Black Sabbath frontman has been ridiculed over his career, mostly due to rumors denouncing him as a psychopath and Satanist. Despite his outlandish reputation, however, one cannot deny that Osbourne has had an immeasurable effect on heavy metal. While he doesn't possess a great voice (it's thin and doesn't have much range), he makes up for it with his good ear and dramatic flair. As a showman, his instincts are nearly as impeccable; his live shows have been overwrought spectacles of gore and glitz that have endeared him to adolescents around the world. Indeed, Osbourne has managed to establish himself as an international superstar, capable of selling millions of records with each album and packing arenas across the globe, capturing new fans with each record. *—Barry Weber*

Blizzard of Ozz / 1980 / Jet ✦✦✦✦✦

Ozzy Osbourne's 1981 solo debut *Blizzard of Ozz* was a masterpiece of neo-classical metal that, along with Van Halen's first album, became a cornerstone of '80s metal guitar. Upon its release, there was considerable doubt that Ozzy could become a viable solo attraction. *Blizzard of Ozz* demonstrated not only his ear for melody, but also an unfailing instinct for assembling top-notch backing bands. Onetime Quiet Riot guitarist Randy Rhoads was a startling discovery, arriving here as a unique, fully formed talent. Rhoads was just as responsible as Osbourne—perhaps even more so—for the album's musical direction, and his application of classical-guitar techniques and scales rewrote the rulebook just as radically as Eddie Van Halen had. Rhoads could hold his own as a flashy soloist, but his detailed, ambitious compositions and arrangements revealed his true depth, as well as creating a sense of doomy, sinister elegance built on Ritchie Blackmore's minor-key innovations. All of this may seem to downplay the importance of Ozzy himself, which shouldn't be the case at all. The music is a thoroughly convincing match for his lyrical obsession with the dark side (which was never an embrace, as many conservative watch-dogs assumed); so, despite its collaborative nature, it's unequivocally stamped with Ozzy's personality. What's more, the band is far more versatile and subtle than Sabbath, freeing Ozzy from his habit of singing in unison with the guitar (and proving that he had an excellent grasp of how to frame his limited voice). Nothing short of revelatory, *Blizzard of Ozz* deservedly made Ozzy a star, and it set new standards for musical virtuosity in the realm of heavy metal. *—Steve Huey*

Diary of a Madman / 1981 / Jet ✦✦✦✦✦
The follow-up to the masterful *Blizzard of Ozz, Diary of a Madman* was rushed into existence by a band desperate to finish its next album before an upcoming tour. As a result, it doesn't feel quite as fully realized—a couple of the ballads are overly long and slow the momentum, and Randy Rhoads' guide solo on "Little Dolls" was never replaced with a version intended for the public. Yet despite the fact that some songs could have used a longer gestation period, there are numerous moments of brilliance on *Diary of a Madman*—at least half of it stands up to anything on *Blizzard*, and the title track is a jaw-droppingly intricate epic that represents the most classically influenced work of Rhoads' all-too-brief career. But even if parts of the album don't quite live up to the band's previous (and incredibly high) standards, they're by no means bad; moreover, the production is fuller, and the instruments better recorded this time around. It's not uncommon to find fans who prefer *Diary* to *Blizzard*, since it sets an even more mystical, eerie mood, and since Rhoads' playing is progressing to an even higher level. One can only wonder what the Osbourne/Rhoads collaboration might have produced in the future, had Rhoads not been killed in a bizarre and sadly avoidable plane crash. *—Steve Huey*

Speak of the Devil / 1982 / Jet ✦✦✦
Immediately following the death of Ozzy Osbourne's dear friend and collaborator Randy Rhoads, tentative plans for a live recording from the Rhoads tours were quickly scrapped. Instead, the deeply troubled singer opted for a pair of one-offs at New York City's Ritz club. No one had any idea what Ozzy would do, and an evening of Black Sabbath covers was the furthest thing from everyone's mind. Ozzy had been portrayed as a washed-up, vocally challenged frontman by his ex-bandmates, and the perception was that Ozzy could no longer sing the original Sabbath material. Hiring metal producer Max Norman to man the boards, Ozzy enlisted Night Ranger guitarist Brad Gillis to play the role of Tony Iommi for the evening. The show itself took on an ominous tone with a chair visibly propped up on the edge of the stage; upon it rested a spiral notebook containing the lyrics to all the Sabbath songs of the evening, from which Ozzy read throughout the show. Still, *Speak of the Devil* is strengthened by the classic combo of Rudy Sarzo and Tommy Aldridge on bass and drums, undoubtedly one the best rhythm sections of Ozzy's solo career. And immediately, it becomes obvious that Brad Gillis was the right man for the gig. Playing Iommi to a tee, Gillis effortlessly leads the band through some of the best of the Sabbath catalog; *Speak of the Devil* ends up solid throughout, if somewhat unremarkable at times. Listening to the remastered version, there's no doubt that the vocals feature some heavily doctored patch-ups, but regardless, Ozzy proved his point to his ex-bandmates. Following the recording, due to the uncertainty surrounding the Ozzy camp, Gillis would jump ship and rejoin the ranks of Night Ranger. *—John Franck*

Bark at the Moon / 1983 / Epic ✦✦✦
Osbourne finds a permanent replacement for Rhoads in Jake E. Lee, a more standard metal guitarist without Rhoads' neo-classical compositional ability or stylistic flair. Still, Osbourne and his band turn in a competent, workmanlike set of heavy metal featuring the crunching title track, whose video (featuring Osbourne dressed as a werewolf) became popular on MTV. Unfortunately, substance abuse problems would help prevent Osbourne from releasing another record up to the standards of *Bark at the Moon* for nearly the rest of the decade. *—Steve Huey*

The Ultimate Sin / 1986 / Epic ✦✦

Tribute / 1987 / Epic ✦✦✦✦✦
This live double album, released five years after Randy Rhoads' death, showcases a hard rock guitarist whose all-around ability was arguably second only to Eddie Van Halen. Osbourne leads his best band lineup through the entire *Blizzard* repertoire, plus a few *Diary* and Sabbath numbers. Of special note are Rhoads' unaccompanied solos, leaving no doubts about his virtuosity, and the studio outtakes of his short solo piece, "Dee." Rhoads' entire output is absolutely essential for guitar freaks, but he sounds even better live than in the studio. *—Steve Huey*

No Rest for the Wicked / 1989 / Epic ✦✦✦✦
Things start to improve here, as Zakk Wylde replaces Jake E. Lee on guitar and Osbourne comes up with his best set since 1983. Again, it's not quite up to the level of excellence his *Blizzard of Ozz* band achieved, but Osbourne sounds somewhat rejuvenated, and Wylde is a more consistently interesting guitarist than Lee. Highlights include "Miracle Man" (in which Ozzy gloats about the downfall of the TV preachers who had long attacked him as an agent of Satan) and the MTV hits "Crazy Babies" and "Breaking All the Rules." *—Steve Huey*

Just Say Ozzy / Jan. 1990 / Epic ✦✦

No More Tears / Sep. 17, 1991 / Epic ✦✦✦✦
Around the time that *No More Tears* was in pre-production, Ozzy Osbourne must have noticed that there was a sudden change in the rock genre—music that he had been placing on his previous '80s albums was growing stale, and the public seemed to show more interest in heavy metal rather than hard rock. With that in mind, Osbourne brought in Motörhead singer Lemmy Kilmister to aid in writing the songs for *No More Tears*, which contribute to making the album one of his best ever. The record, like *No Rest for the Wicked*, uses a heavier, tighter sound when compared to the likes of *Diary of a Madman*, but at the same time manages to maintain catchy melodies and innovative lyrics. While Ozzy's songwriting has definitely matured a bit through the years (evident through the power ballads "Time After Time" and "Mama, I'm Coming Home"), parents will still find plenty of obnoxious material on this album to complain about ("I Don't Want to Change the World" and "Desire"). *No More Tears* documents Osbourne's shift into the '90s quite effectively, and proves to be his best studio effort since 1981's *Blizzard of Ozz*. *—Barry Weber*

Ozzmosis / Oct. 24, 1995 / Epic ✦✦

OzzFest, Vol. 1: Live / Apr. 29, 1997 / Red Ant ✦✦✦

● **The Ozzman Cometh: Greatest Hits** / Nov. 11, 1997 / Epic ✦✦✦✦✦
Theoretically, a greatest-hits collection should be an easy job for someone like Ozzy Osbourne, whose career always thrived on singles. However, this is not the case, as *Ozzman Cometh* proves. While the compilation does boast some of his biggest hits, including "Crazy Train," "Goodbye to Romance" and "Shot In the Dark," some of his most memorable songs, such as "I Don't Know," "Flying High Again," and "Miracle Man," are surprisingly missing. Instead of extra tracks from his 15-year career, listeners aren't even given definitive Ozzy—the album is unfortunately overshadowed with Black Sabbath basement tapes, including "Fairies Wear Boots" and "War Pigs." Although Osbourne never failed to put Sabbath hits into his live shows and albums, the idea that re-recorded material from his former band replaces some of his best songs is a little depressing. The album also includes one new track, "Back on Earth," which continues the musical setting similar to *Ozzmosis* (where Osbourne counts on synthesizers instead of guitars). Despite its flaws, however, *Ozzman Cometh* certainly delivers a good collection of hits, making it and *Tribute* the only necessary Ozzy albums for casual fans. *—Barry Weber*

Gilbert O'Sullivan

b. Dec. 1, 1946, Waterford, Ireland
Vocals / AM Pop, Pop/Rock, Soft Rock, Pop, Singer/Songwriter
Singer/songwriter Gilbert O'Sullivan successfully combined a flair for Beatlesque popcraft with an old-fashioned musichall sensibility to emerge as one of the most distinctive and popular new performers of the early 1970s. The wit and craft of O'Sullivan's music aside, much of his early success was predicated on his unusual image—at the peak of the hippie movement, he resembled nothing so much as a Depression-era street urchin, complete with pudding-bowl haircut, short pants and flat cap. This helped make "We Will" and "No Matter How I Try" British hits, and in 1971 O'Sullivan issued his debut LP, *Himself*; a year later, he finally broke through to the American market with the ballad "Alone Again (Naturally)," which topped the U.S. pop charts. Around this time, the singer jettisoned his so-called "Bisto Kid" image in favor of an endless series of collegiate-styled sweaters embossed with the letter "G." In late 1972, O'Sullivan scored his first British number one with "Clair," falling just shy of topping charts on the other side of the Atlantic; the follow-up, "Get Down," reached number one at home as well, as did the LP *Back to Front*. As quickly as O'Sullivan ascended to fame, however, his star began to fall—although singles like "Ooh Baby" and "Happiness Is Me and You" continued to chart, they sold increasingly fewer copies, and after 1973 his overseas popularity essentially ceased altogether. At home, he notched his final Top 20 hit with 1975's "I Don't Love You But I Think I Like You," subsequently leaving his label MAM; returning to CBS, albums like 1977's *Southpaw* and 1980's *Off Centre* failed to find an audience, and outside of the minor hit "What's in a Kiss?" O'Sullivan disappeared from the charts. *—Jason Ankeny*

● **The Best of Gilbert O'Sullivan** / 1991 / Rhino ✦✦✦✦✦
Gilbert O'Sullivan's lengthy but erratic career is nicely summarized on this well-assembled 20-track retrospective. Best remembered in the U.S. for the coy, McCartney-esque pop of hits like "Alone Again (Naturally)" and "Clair," O'Sullivan was actually a major star in his native Britain, notching a series of smashes which also included "Nothing Rhymed," "Underneath the Blanket Go" and "What's in a Kiss"; although at times his material can be insufferably cute, at its peak the music also possesses an undeniable charm as well as a playfulness that makes even the most saccharine moments tough to actively dislike. *—Jason Ankeny*

Shuggie Otis (Johnny Otis, Jr.)

b. Nov. 30, 1953, Los Angeles, CA
Harmonica, Guitar, Bass / Album Rock, Neo-Psychedelia, Soul
Shuggie Otis may not be a household name, but his "Strawberry Letter 23" is in the record collections of millions of households. The Brothers Johnson's cover of "Strawberry Letter 23" has sold over a million copies. It was on their LP, *Right On Time*, which went platinum, selling over a million copies, holding the number one R&B spot for three weeks and making it to number 13 pop in spring 1977. Otis wrote "Strawberry Letter 23" for his girlfriend, who used strawberry scented paper for her letters to him. Another Otis favorite, "Inspiration Information" received substantial airplay in Chicago and other markets, charting #56 R&B in early 1975.

Born Johnny Otis, Jr. on November 30, 1953, in Los Angeles, CA, Otis' formidable musical talents appeared at an early age. He began his professional career around 1965, when he was in his early teens. He played a guitar solo on his bandleader father Johnny Otis' 1969 R&B hit, "Country Girl."

Signing with CBS Records, Otis began recording virtuoso guitar-laced R&B/West Coast Blues sides. His first LP was *Al Kooper Introduces Shuggie Otis*, followed by 1970's

Here Comes Shuggie Otis, which was issued on the CBS imprint, Epic Records. Otis' *Freedom Flight* was issued in September 1971 and included the original version of "Strawberry Letter 23," the heart-tugging "Someone's Always Singing," "Ice Cold Daydream" and the bluesy "Me and My Woman."

His LP, *Inspiration Information* was issued in October 1974 with Otis playing all of the instruments on jazzy and Latin-tinged R&B numbers. The LP was one of the first releases to showcase the electronic rhythm box then found usually on organs.

Later on in the '90s, Otis played with his own band around northern California and toured extensively. *—Ed Hogan*

• **Inspiration Information** / 1974 / Luaka Bop ✦✦✦✦✦
Ignored upon its release in 1975 and celebrated upon its reissue in 2001, Shuggie Otis' fourth and last album, *Inspiration Information*, exists out of time—a record that was of its time, but didn't belong of it; a record that was idiosyncratic but not necessarily visionary. It was psychedelic soul that was released far too late to be part of any zeitgeist and it was buried at the time. Otis crafted all of this essentially alone, playing each instrument himself, and it's quite clearly a reflection of his inner psyche, and no matter how much it floats and skates upon its own sound, it's a welcoming, inviting sound. But, no matter how much the partisans claim—and their effusive praise is plastered all over the liner notes—this isn't revolutionary, even if it's delightfully idiosyncratic. So, don't fall for the hyperbole. This isn't an album that knocks your head off—it's subtle, intricate music that's equal parts head music and elegant funk, a record that slowly works its way under your skin. Part of the reason it sounds so intriguing in 2001 is that there just aren't that many musicians that doggedly pursue their individual vision while retaining a sense of focus. But it isn't a record without precedent, nor is it startling. It's a record for people that have heard a lot of music, maybe too much, and are looking for a new musical romance. [Luaka Bop's reissue contains four fine bonus tracks. The reissue also replaces the original cover with a "hip," self-consciously retro cover.] *—Stephen Thomas Erlewine*

Shuggie's Boogie: Shuggie Otis Plays the Blues / 1994 / Epic/Legacy ✦✦✦✦✦
Culled from four albums, except for one previously unreleased track, this tour de force is all the more remarkable because the prodigy who produced it was so young. In fact, he recalls during a boyish spoken intro in "Shuggie's Boogie" how he used to wear dark glasses and paint a mustache to look older than his 14 or 15 years when he played in bars in the band of his legendary father Johnny Otis. During the same intro he effortlessly throws off guitar impersonations of T-Bone Walker, B.B. King and Elmore James. This compilation has a few rousing, uptempo numbers, but the highlights are the slow, soulful tunes. One unfortunate omission is the seven-minute "Oxford Gray" from his 1970 album *Here Comes Shuggie Otis*. *—Mark Allan*

The Outfield

Pop/Rock

Ironically, given their obsession with America's favorite pastime, the Outfield got their start in London's East End. Playing under the name, The Baseball Boys, the trio of bassist/singer Tony Lewis, guitarist/keyboardist John Spinks and drummer Alan Jackman played around London and recorded some early demos, attracting the attention of Columbia/CBS Records. They were signed shortly thereafter and began working on their debut album, *Play Deep*, which was released in 1985. The album was a smash success, going triple platinum, reaching #9 on the album charts, and producing their biggest song, "Your Love," which was a top ten hit. To support the album, they launched an international tour, opening for Journey and Starship. They began recording their second album in 1986 and in 1987 issued *Bangin'*. While not duplicating the huge commercial success of their debut, it did produce two hit singles, "Since You've Been Gone" and "No Surrender." The band's third album featured a bit of a stylistic shift, and was more meticulously produced than their previous efforts. *Voices of Babylon*, released in 1988, produced a single of the same name, but the band's commercial success was slipping. Jackman left the band after it was recorded and they hired Paul Reed to step in as drummer for the Voices tour.

Spinks and Lewis, now officially a duo, switched labels and began recording *Diamond Days* for MCA. A new session drummer, Simon Dawson, joined them and helped add an electronic edge to their sound. *Diamond Days* produced one of their biggest singles, "For You." They followed up with 1992's *Rockeye*. Its single, "Winning It All" became a feature at sporting events and was on the *Mighty Ducks* soundtrack. Simon Dawson had become increasingly involved in the shaping of the band's sound and became an official member of the band at this time. They went on hiatus for much of the mid-'90s, returning to record an exclusive release for their fan club entitled *It Ain't Over*, then embarking on a kind of '80s revival tour. In 1998 they released *Extra Innings*, which was a compilation of several songs they wrote during the '90s, and also featured four new songs written in 1998. *—Stacia Proefrock*

• **Big Innings: The Best of the Outfield** / Sep. 3, 1996 / Sony Legacy ✦✦✦✦
The Outfield's brisk pop sound gave them five Top 40 singles within the span of five years. Their sound is comprised of remnants of classic rock which is soothed by the fluidness of Tony Lewis' voice, and a front-line guitar attack driven by John Spinks. *Big Innings* is a generous sixteen track compilation made up of The Outfield's hits as well as their unreleased and B-side material, offering a delightful roam through their short lived stint. With "Your Love," "All The Love In The World," and "Voices Of Babylon" representing some of their greatest chart successes, the rest of the collection still houses many other pleasing contributions. The effectively encumbered guitar charge of "Since You've Been Gone" from 1987's *Bangin'* stands out, as does the sheer charm of "For You" off of 1990's *Diamond Days*. Although acoustic tracks such as "Alone With You" and "Through The Years" appear in mono, they are welcomed just the same. The disappointing *Rockeye* album contributes it's two best efforts in "Closer To Me" and "Winning It All" while "One Hot Country" from the *If Looks Could Kill* soundtrack is the set's weakest contribution, sounding glitzy and overly-effusive even for the nineties. Still, with only one or two feeble tracks, *Big Innings* is a more-than-sufficient hits package. *—Mike DeGagne*

• **Super Hits** / Jul. 21, 1998 / Columbia/Legacy ✦✦✦✦
Since the ten-track budget-line collection *Super Hits* offers all the basics from the Outfield's handful of hitmaking years—"Your Love," "All the Love in the World," "Everytime You Cry," "Since You've Been Gone," "Voices of Babylon"—it may be preferable for casual fans that find the 16-track anthology *Big Innings* a little too large. The songs on *Super Hits* may not be sequenced in chronological order, but all the hits are here without as much filler, which makes it a better choice for most listeners. *—Stephen Thomas Erlewine*

OutKast

f. 1992, Atlanta, GA

Dirty South, Southern Rap, Alternative Rap, Hip-Hop

OutKast's blend of gritty Southern soul, fluid raps, and the rolling G-funk of their Organized Noize production crew epitomized the Atlanta wing of hip-hop's rising force, the Dirty South, during the late '90s. Along with Goodie Mob, OutKast took Southern hip-hop in bold, innovative new directions: less reliance on aggression, more positivity and melody, thicker arrangements, and intricate lyrics. After Dre and Big Boi hit number one on the rap charts with their first single, "Player's Ball," the duo embarked on a run of platinum albums spiked with several hit singles, enjoying numerous critical accolades in addition to their commercial success.

Andre Benjamin (Dre) and Antwan Patton (Big Boi) attended the same high school in the Atlanta borough of East Point, and several lyrical battles made each gain respect for the other's skills. They formed OutKast, and were pursued by Organized Noize Productions, hitmakers for TLC and Xscape. Signed to the local LaFace label just after high school, OutKast recorded and released "Player's Ball," then watched the single rise to number one on the rap charts. It slipped from the top spot only after six weeks, was certified gold, and created a buzz for a full-length release. That album, *Southernplayalisticadillacmuzik*, hit the Top 20 in 1994 and was certified platinum by the end of the year. Dre and Big Boi also won Best New Rap Group of the Year at the 1995 Source Awards. OutKast returned with a new album in 1996, releasing *ATLiens* that August; it hit number two and went platinum with help from the gold-selling single "Elevators (Me & You)" (number 12 pop, number one rap), as well as the Top 40 title track. *Aquemini* followed in 1998, also hitting number two and going double-platinum. There were no huge hit singles this time around, but critics lavishly praised the album's unified, progressive vision, hailing it as a great leap forward and including it on many year-end polls. Unfortunately, in a somewhat bizarre turn of events, OutKast was sued over the album's lead single "Rosa Parks" by none other than the civil rights pioneer herself, who claimed that the group had unlawfully appropriated her name to promote their music, also objecting to some of the song's language. The initial court decision dismissed the suit in late 1999. Dre modified his name to Andre 3000 before the group issued its hotly anticipated fourth album, *Stankonia*, in late 2000. Riding the momentum of uniformly excellent reviews and the stellar singles "B.O.B." and "Ms. Jackson," *Stankonia* debuted at number two and went triple platinum in just a few months; meanwhile, "Ms. Jackson" became their first number one pop single the following February. *—John Bush*

Southernplayalisticadillacmuzik / Apr. 26, 1994 / La Face ✦✦✦✦
It is on the OutKast's debut album that the fledgling production team Organized Noize began forging one of the most distinctive production sounds in popular music in the '90s: part hip-hop; part live, Southern-fried guitar licks and booty-thick bass runs; and part lazy, early-'70s soul. The album was not only artistically successful but also thrived commercially, leaping into the Top 20 album chart on the back of the outstanding hit single "Player's Ball" and eventually going platinum. Although a little bit too dependent on overly simplistic and programmed snare beats, the music is unconditionally excellent, with languid, mellow melodies sliding atop rapid, mechanical drums. Organized Noize already had their distinguishing sound figured out, down to the last twanged, wah-wahed note. But what makes *Southernplayalisticadillacmuzick* such a wonderful album has even more to do with the presence of its rappers, Dre and Big Boi. No one sounded like OutKast in 1994—a mixture of lyrical acuity, goofball humor, Southern drawl, funky timing, and legitimate offbeat personalities. Few rappers of the '90s have displayed such an inventive sense of rhyme flow either, and few rap artists in general have ears as attuned to creating such catchy melodic and vocal hooks. Almost every song has some sort of tuneful chant or repetitive hook that marks it as instantly memorable. There are occasional dull and mediocre spots, such as "Call of Da Wild" and the overlong "Funky Ride," that can't even be elevated by a head-nodding bass line or a tricky rhyme. Such low points, however, are far outshined by the brilliant moments. Already an extremely strong showing, OutKast would continue to develop into one of the finest, most consistently challenging (not to mention booty-shaking) rap groups of the decade. *—Stanton Swihart*

ATLiens / Aug. 27, 1996 / La Face ✦✦✦✦✦
Though they were likely lost on casual hip-hop fans, *Southernplayalisticadillacmuzik* was full of subtle indications that OutKast were a lot more inventive than your average Southern playas. Their idiosyncrasies bubbled to the surface on their sophomore effort, *ATLiens*, an album of spacy sci-fi funk performed on live instruments. Largely abandoning the hard-partying playa characters of their debut, Dre and Big Boi develop a startlingly fresh, original sound to go along with their futuristic new personas. George Clinton's space obsessions might seem to make P-Funk obvious musical source material, but *ATLiens* ignores the hard funk in favor of a smooth, laid-back vibe that perfectly suits the duo's sense of melody. The album's chief musical foundation is still soul, especially the

early-'70s variety, but other influences begin to pop up as well. Some tracks have a spiritual, almost gospel feel (though only in tone, not lyrical content), and the Organized Noize production team frequently employs the spacious mixes and echo effects of dub reggae in creating the album's alien soundscapes. In addition to the striking musical leap forward, Dre and Big Boi continue to grow as rappers; their flows are getting more tongue-twistingly complex, and their lyrics more free-associative. Despite a couple of overly sleepy moments during the second half, *ATLiens* is overall a smashing success thanks to its highly distinctive style, and stands as probably OutKast's most focused work (though it isn't as wildly varied as subsequent efforts). The album may have alienated (pun recognized, but not intended) the more conservative wing of the group's fans, but it broke new ground for Southern hip-hop and marked OutKast as one of the most creatively restless and ambitious hip-hop groups of the '90s. *—Steve Huey*

☆ **Aquemini** / Sep. 29, 1998 / La Face ✦✦✦✦✦
Even compared to their already excellent and forward-looking catalog, OutKast's sprawling third album *Aquemini* was a stroke of brilliance. The chilled-out space-funk of *ATLiens* had already thrown some fans for a loop, and *Aquemini* made it clear that its predecessor was no detour, but a stepping stone for even greater ambitions. Some of *ATLiens*' ethereal futurism is still present, but more often *Aquemini* plants its feet on the ground for a surprisingly down-home flavor. The music draws from a vastly eclectic palette of sources, and the live instrumentation is fuller-sounding than *ATLiens*. Most importantly, producers Organized Noize imbue their tracks with a Southern earthiness and simultaneous spirituality that come across regardless of what Dre and Big Boi are rapping about. Not that they shy away from rougher subject matter, but their perspective is grounded and responsible, intentionally avoiding hardcore clichés. Their distinctive vocal deliveries are now fully mature, with a recognizably Southern rhythmic bounce but loads more technique than their territorial peers. Those flows grace some of the richest and most inventive hip-hop tracks of the decade. The airy lead single "Rosa Parks" juxtaposes porch-front acoustic guitar with DJ scratches and a stomping harmonica break that could have come from nowhere but the South. Unexpected touches like that are all over the record: the live orchestra on "Return of the 'G'," the electronic, George Clinton-guested "Synthesizer," the reggae horns and dub-style echo of "SpottieOttieDopaliscious," the hard-rocking wah-wah guitar of "Chonkyfire," and on and on. What's most impressive is the way everything comes together to justify the full-CD running time, something few hip-hop epics of this scope ever accomplish. After a few listens, not even the meditative jams on the second half of the album feel all that excessive. *Aquemini* fulfills all its ambitions, covering more than enough territory to qualify it as a virtuosic masterpiece, and a landmark hip-hop album of the late '90s. *—Steve Huey*

★ **Stankonia** / Oct. 31, 2000 / La Face ✦✦✦✦✦
Stankonia was OutKast's second straight masterstroke, an album just as ambitious, just as all-over-the-map, and even hookier than its predecessor. With producers Organized Noize playing a diminished role, *Stankonia* reclaims the duo's futuristic bent. Keyboardist/producer Earthtone III helms most of the backing tracks, and while the live-performance approach is still present, there's more reliance on programmed percussion, otherworldly synthesizers, and surreal sound effects. Yet the results are surprisingly warm and soulful, a trippy sort of techno-psychedelic funk. Every repeat listen seems to uncover some new element in the mix, but most of the songs have such memorable hooks that it's easy to stay diverted. The immediate dividends include two of 2000's best singles: "B.O.B." is the fastest of several tracks built on jittery drum'n'bass rhythms, but Andre and Big Boi keep up with awe-inspiring effortlessness. "Ms. Jackson," meanwhile, is an anguished plea directed at the mother of the mother of an out-of-wedlock child, tinged with regret, bitterness, and affection. Its sensitivity and social awareness are echoed in varying proportions elsewhere, from the Public Enemy-style rant "Gasoline Dreams" to the heartbreaking suicide tale "Toilet Tisha." But the group also returns to its roots for some of the most testosterone-drenched material since their debut. Then again, OutKast doesn't take its posturing too seriously, which is why they can portray women holding their own, or make bizarre boasts about being "So Fresh, So Clean." Given the variety of moods, it helps that the album is broken up by brief, usually humorous interludes, which serve as a sort of reset button. It takes a few listens to pull everything together, but given the immense scope, it's striking how few weak tracks there are. It's no wonder *Stankonia* consolidated OutKast's status as critics' darlings, and began attracting broad new audiences: its across-the-board appeal and ambition overshadowed nearly every other pop album released in 2000. *—Steve Huey*

The Outlaws

f. 1972, Tampa, FL
Southern Rock
Southern rock unit the Outlaws was formed in Tampa, FL in 1972 by singers/guitarists Hughie Thomasson and Henry Paul, bassist Frank O'Keefe, and drummer Monte Yoho. With the 1973 addition of guitarist Billy Jones, the lineup was complete, and after a year of intense touring the band became the first act signed to Arista under Clive Davis; the Outlaws' self-titled 1975 album spotlighted their Eagles-influenced harmonies and Allman Brothers-like guitar attack, yielding the Top 40 hit "There Goes Another Love Song." In the wake of 1977's Bill Szymczyk-produced *Hurry Sundown*, both Paul and O'Keefe exited, with guitarist Freddie Salem, bassist Harvey Dalton Arnold, and second drummer David Dix signing on for the 1978 concert set *Bring It Back Alive* and the studio effort *Playin' to Win*. Salem was the next to go, and the lineup shuffles continued when Arnold announced his departure following 1979's *In the Eye of the Storm*, with bassist Rick Cua recruited for the next year's *Ghost Riders in the Sky*, which netted a Top 40 entry with its title track, a rendition of the Vaughn Monroe favorite. Yoho left to rejoin Henry Paul soon after, and with the subsequent exit of Jones, only Thomasson remained from the original Outlaws roster—not surprisingly, the group disbanded upon completing 1982's *Los Hombres Malo*. A year later Thomasson and Paul formed a new Outlaws lineup, adding guitarist Chris Hicks, bassist Barry Borden, and drummer Jeff Howell; after issuing 1986's *Soldiers of Fortune*, Paul again quit the band, with the remaining quartet returning in 1993 with *Hittin' the Road*. While Paul resurfaced in 1994 in the chart-topping contemporary country band Blackhawk, Thomasson later toured with the reformed Lynyrd Skynyrd while continuing to lead the Outlaws, releasing *So-Low* in 2000. Sadly, Jones and O'Keefe died within three weeks of one another in early 1985. *—Jason Ankeny*

● **The Best of the Outlaws: Green Grass and High Tides** / Oct. 1, 1996 / Arista ✦✦✦✦✦
The Best of the Outlaws: Green Grass and High Tides is a comprehensive, 16-track overview of the '70s southern rock band, featuring all their hits—"There Goes Another Love Song," "Breaker-Breaker," "Hurry Sundown" and "(Ghost) Riders in the Sky"—plus liner notes by the band's founding members, Henry Paul and Hughie Thomasson. *—Stephen Thomas Erlewine*

Outrageous Cherry

f. 1992, Detroit, MI
Indie Pop, Alternative Pop/Rock
Named after a brilliant red hair dye, Detroit's Outrageous Cherry explores the sunnier side of droning, fuzzy indie rock.

The band started as a recording project in 1992 but blossomed into a full-fledged group when singer/guitarist/producer Matthew Smith, bassist Chad Gilchrist, guitarist Larry Ray and drummer Deb Agnolli began performing live in 1993.

Outrageous Cherry's wistful noise-pop debuted with a limited-edition 7" of "Pale, Frail Lovely One" on the local Third Gear label. The song's deceptively simple, garagey sound formed the template for the group's style: on albums like 1994's *Outrageous Cherry* and 1997's *Nothing's Gonna Cheer You Up*, Smith and Ray's alternately jangly and feedback-laced guitars and Agnolli's minimalist, floor tom-and-snare drumming combine with sweet vocals for a sound that falls between nostalgic and experimental.

Along with his duties in Outrageous Cherry, Smith also performs in the country-tinged Volebeats and often collaborates with His Name Is Alive's Warren Defever on producing and recording projects, as does Gilchrist, doubling as Outrageous Cherry and His Name is Alive's bassist. In 1999, Aran Ruth replaced Gilchrist on bass, and the group released their first album for Del-Fi's new music imprint, DF2K, *Out There In The Dark*. The group also contributed a version of "Keep Everything Under Your Hat" for that year's Skip Spence tribute *More Oar*. *—Heather Phares*

Outrageous Cherry / 1994 / BarNone ✦✦✦✦
Outrageous Cherry's self-titled debut is an entertaining introduction to their retro-experimental sound. Their first single, "Pale Frail Lovely One," remains one of the band's finest moments, encapsulating the light and shadows of their sound. The sunny "Til I Run Out" and extended, noisy guitar bursts of "The Stare" and "Ace 100" demonstrate Matthew Smith's writing and playing versatility and Deb Agnolli's effective, minimalist drumming. *—Heather Phares*

Stereo Action Rent Party / Jun. 25, 1996 / Third Gear ✦✦✦
Most times that a group records an album comprised of nothing but cover tunes, the finished product falls short of expectations. And it's not always the band's fault; it can be hard to top the originals, and even harder for the listener to not compare the two versions. Artists can either take the approach of David Bowie's *Pin-Ups*, which included strictly well-known songs, or Metallica's *Garage Days Revisited* albums, comprised of interesting obscurities. Outrageous Cherry uses the latter's approach on their *Stereo Action Rent Party* album, recording a full-length of mostly obscure covers (the most well-known of the bunch are still pretty obscure—Television's "Days" and the MC5's "Miss X"). By not including any list of who recorded the original versions anywhere inside the CD booklet, the group makes each song completely their own. "Sign of the Times" kicks things off on a carefree note, the already mentioned "Days" stresses the original's beautiful guitar interplay, while "Ring Around the Moon" contains lots of rock & roll attitude. The band recorded the whole album at a friend's house, with the album's low-tech cover artwork fitting O.C.'s approach to the project perfectly. *—Greg Prato*

Nothing's Gonna Cheer You Up / Jun. 17, 1997 / Third Gear ✦✦✦✦✦
The third release by Outrageous Cherry, *Nothing's Gonna Cheer You Up*, shows the band filtering classic sounds of the past—the jangle-rock of the Byrds, Big Star, and early R.E.M., and the dark minimalism of the Velvet Underground—through '90s lo-fi technology. The band has a very talented songwriter in guitarist/singer (and producer) Matthew Smith—if he was writing songs like the ones on *N.G.C.Y.U.* back in the '60s, he'd have several hits on his hands. The opening track, "I've Never Seen Your World," sets the tone for the rest of the album, and is a perfect example of what to expect from the other cuts (cleanly strummed guitars, echoey and distant vocals, primitive drumming *a la* V.U.'s Moe Tucker, etc.). Many of the tracks contain strong melodic hooks that create a comforting sense of familiarity, which is the ultimate sign of great songwriting. Other standout tracks include "Panavision 70," "Genevieve," and the title track. This is definitely Outrageous Cherry's best and most accomplished album yet, a guaranteed delight for fans of fuzzed-out, sticky-sweet '60s pop. *—Greg Prato*

● **Out There in the Dark** / 1999 / Del-Fi ✦✦✦✦✦
Outrageous Cherry's 4th album *Out There In The Dark* is their first for DF2K, the contemporary sister label of Del-Fi, one of the classic labels of the '50s and '60s. The group's jangly, bubblegum-noise aesthetic fits DF2K's retro-contemporary pop agenda to a tee; *Out There In The Dark* is not only one of Outrageous Cherry's finest albums, but also a fine choice for one of DF2K's first releases.

Though the band's bittersweet-yet-tough sound hasn't changed much since their early singles, singer/songwriter Matt Smith's songwriting has refined over the years, and the group's arrangements have expanded to include violins, cellos and trumpets. *Out There In The Dark* is also the group's most diverse album, with bouncy pop numbers like "Tracy," "Corruptable" and the made-for-AM radio "Where Do I Go When You Dream" balancing moodier songs like the album's slow-dance centerpiece, "Easy Come, Uneasy Glow." Their trippy side comes to the front on the excellent, backwards guitar-driven "Only The Easy Way Down" and in the title track's drifting guitars and shifting tempos. Smith's ultra-faithful, vintage production style sparkles on "A Bad Movie," and the album closer "There's No Escape From The Infinite" is one of the group's extended, trance-inducing noise workouts—and a further display of the range Outrageous Cherry finds in updating the styles of the past.

While their sound evokes a host of garage-psych bands, from '60s originators to '80s revivalists, Outrageous Cherry's affection for this kind of music and their experimental touches make their albums a bit like a jukebox full of forgotten hits, and a bit like a time machine with its controls set for the past and the future. And as always, *Out There In The Dark* is an enjoyable, entertaining ride. —*Heather Phares*

The Outsiders

f. 1964
Psychedelic Pop
The Outsiders started in Cleveland, OH, as a garden-variety bar band led by guitarist and songwriter Tom King. The addition of vocalist Sonny Geraci infused the band with new life. Signed to Capitol Records in 1967, the group scored big with the single "Time Won't Let Me," their finest moment.

Personnel changes and management conflicts stalled the band's career but not before they had racked up several hits. —*Cub Koda*

● **Capitol Collectors Series** / 1991 / Capitol ✦✦✦✦
All their best in one neat little package. Includes "Time Won't Let Me," "Respectable," and "Girl in Love." —*Cub Koda*

The Outsiders

f. 1964, db. 1970
Garage Rock, Psychedelic
Not to be confused with the Cleveland pop/rock group who had a Top Ten hit in 1966 with "Time Won't Let Me," these Outsiders (from Amsterdam, Holland) could issue a serious claim for consideration as the finest rock band of the '60s to hail from a non-English-speaking nation. Led by singer/songwriter Wally Tax, the group was quite comparable to England's Pretty Things in their fine raw, punky R&B/pop with basic but riveting hooks. Like the Pretty Things, the Outsiders (who sang entirely in English) made similar psychedelic/progressive ventures in the late '60s that cut loose from their R&B roots without losing sight of them entirely. Recording several albums of material (consisting wholly of original compositions) between 1965 and 1969, the group tempered their punky, almost proto-hardcore ravers with melancholy, pensive folk-rockers and unpredictable production touches ranging from Baroque mandolins and harpsichords to found radio static. The Outsiders' music was fraught with tension, the punkish rhythms playing against the melodic tunes, the R&B sensibilities against the pop hooks, often within the same song. They were unknown on an international level to all but the most fervent '60s collectors. Wally Tax moved to the U.S. in the early '70s, where he recorded one album as the leader of the band Tax Free. —*Richie Unterberger*

The Outsiders / 1967 / Pseudonym ✦✦✦✦✦
Their super-raw debut album, a few songs of which were recorded live. Some of this is too melodically primitive and clumsy to survive the ages, but tracks like "Filthy Rich," "Won't You Listen," and "If You Don't Treat Me Right" are comparable to little else of the era with their savage, Pretty Things-on-speed mood and hyper-fast tempos. The CD reissue adds several bonus tracks. —*Richie Unterberger*

C.Q. / 1968 / Polydor ✦✦✦✦✦
Their final LP (now available on CD) is one of the finer unsung psychedelic records of the late '60s. Heavy echoes of Syd Barrett-era Pink Floyd, Hendrix, and psychedelic-era Pretty Things, with adroit shifts from crunching rock and soft, almost folky passages to spacy phase-shift bits and just plain dementia. The album has an ominous and creepy, but rocking, ambience that still cuts deep. —*Richie Unterberger*

● **The Best of the Outsiders** / 1979 / MFP ✦✦✦✦✦
16-song compilation collects most of their singles, ranging from raunchy cuts like "Touch" and "I'm Only Trying To Prove Myself" to tuneful, forceful folk-rockish cuts like "I've Been Loving You So Long" and "Summer Is Here." Very consistent and strong, only a couple clunkers. —*Richie Unterberger*

C.Q. Sessions / 1994 / Pseudonym ✦✦✦
A double CD comprising 29 alternate takes, some instrumental and some vocal, of songs from the classic *C.Q.* album, one of the finest obscure psychedelic records. Besides one or

two different alternate versions of each of the 13 songs from that record, it also has alternate versions of sides from non-LP singles they released around the same time ("Do You Feel Allright" & "You Remind Me"), as well as four songs (some instrumental) that never made it onto any official release. Some of the tracks are quite close to the finished versions, and some are quite different, but it's a pretty fascinating look at works in progress, and the sound quality is uniformly excellent. The audience for this reissue is, to say the least, extremely specialized and limited, but if you're a fan of this group, it's worth picking up. It also includes five bonus tracks from excruciatingly rare (and quite good) earlier non-LP singles from 1965 and 1966, when they were a much more R&B/beat-oriented outfit. —*Richie Unterberger*

Ozark Mountain Daredevils

f. 1971, Springfield, MO
Southern Rock, Country-Rock
The Ozark Mountain Daredevils were among the most popular of mid-'70s country-rock outfits, slotting in chronologically between the Eagles and Firefall, although they were never remotely as successful as either. As exponents of '70s country-rock, the group rode a wave of success for five years on A&M Records, and have survived in some form into the 1990s, with a following just large enough to justify occasional record releases.

The sextet was formed in Arkansas during the early '70s, consisting of guitarists John Dillon and Steve Cash, blues harpist/singer/guitarist Randle Chowning, drummer/guitarist/singer Larry Lee, keyboard player Buddy Brayfield, and bassist-vocalist Michael Granda, and was signed to A&M Records in 1973. Their first album, recorded under the supervision of producer Glyn Johns, was a critical success and yielded a Top 30 hit in "If You Want to Get to Heaven." A year later, they had the biggest hit in their history, "Jackie Blue," a mellow piece of country-rock that got to number three on the charts and still gets played occasionally as a '70s oldie. They had an ethereal edge to their sound and songs that made them especially appealing to college age listeners during the middle of the decade—sort of Steely Dan with a country twang. Their self-titled debut album set the tone for the group's next four releases, although by 1978's *Don't Look Down*, the sound was somewhat closer to country-pop than country-rock. Collegiate girls and their boyfriends could relate to them, and a sense of humor didn't hurt (their third LP, *The Car Over the Lake Album* had cover art featuring—you guessed it—a car over a lake).

Lee, Dillon (who later played with fellow Daredevil Steve Cash on the Waylon Jennings/Jessi Colter *White Mansions* concept album), and Chowning authored most of the songs that anyone knows ("Jackie Blue," "Following the Way I Feel," "Fly Away Home"). The group enjoyed success primarily on FM radio from 1973 until 1978—they switched labels to CBS in 1980, losing Lee and Chowning by the end of the decade but picking up Buddy Emmons on steel guitar and Rune Walle on mandolin. The group ceased recording activity in the 1980s, but reformed and began making records again in the mid-'90s. —*Bruce Eder*

The Best of Ozark Mountain Daredevils / 1983 / A&M ✦✦✦✦
One of two CDs of classic material by the Daredevils, 12 songs drawn from their first five A&M albums, showing the different sides of the group to very good advantage, from the hard-rocking "If You Wanna Get to Heaven" to the soaring, upbeat, mandolin- and electric-guitar-driven "Homemade Wine." Some of the material seems soft today, and it's hard to imagine that this sound was ever considered viable, but a lot of it is very pretty and eminently listenable. The starting point for anyone interested, and with a little luck this and the first album will be joined at least by reissues of *It'll Shine When It Shines* and *Men from Earth*. —*Bruce Eder*

● **Time Warp: The Very Best of Ozark Mountain Daredevils** / Dec. 5, 2000 / A&M ✦✦✦✦
Although it omits three songs from the far less comprehensive (and deleted) 1983 12-track *Best Of*, and doesn't include any live or post-A&M music, this 2000 release stands as the final word on the Ozark Mountain Daredevils' career. Cherry-picking 21 tunes from their five studio album stint circa 1974-1978—with the lion's share coming from their first three albums and only three selections from the final two—this is pretty much all you'll need from the under-recognized band that worked in the '70s country-rock shadows of Poco and Firefall, but weren't as dependable or pop savvy as either. In fact, their biggest hit, the Hall & Oates, blue-eyed soul-styled "Jackie Blue," was so atypical of the band's characteristically down-home approach, that it ultimately may have been more damaging to their career than if they had clicked with a song more representative of their crisp, rural country pop/rock. As enjoyable and pleasantly organic as they were, the group lacked a distinctive vocalist, direction, and most importantly great songs. This collection focuses on their less commercially rocking, more rootsy side, and as such it's a consistently listenable, predominantly chronological compilation that is all any but the most die-hard fan will ever need. An extensive essay including quotes from bandmembers and rare photos in the disc's 16-page booklet sweeten the pot and make this as definitive an overview from a talented also-ran outfit as necessary. Like its closing title track, the Ozark Mountain Daredevils lived in a stylistic time warp, comfortable within its own limitations and unwilling—but not unable—to break free of them. —*Hal Horowitz*

Pablo Cruise

f. 1973, San Francisco, CA
Pop/Rock, Soft Rock

Pablo Cruise achieved some measure of success during the latter part of the '70s with its mellow, easygoing California pop. The band was formed in 1973 by former members of Stoneground and It's a Beautiful Day: guitarist Dave Jenkins, keyboardist Cory Lerois, bassist Bud Cockrell, and drummer Steve Price. The group was praised for the compositional and instrumental skill on the albums *Pablo Cruise* and *Lifeline*, and were rewarded with the Top Ten hit "Whatcha Gonna Do?" in 1977 from *A Place in the Sun*. Cockrell left and was replaced by former Santana bassist Bruce Day. *Worlds Away* went platinum, as did its predecessor, and produced three hit singles, including the Top Ten "Love Will Find a Way." By the time the '80s rolled around, the new wave movement was in full swing on the pop charts, and Pablo Cruise fell out of favor with the record-buying public. Several of the group's songs were used as soundtrack material for sports programs on ABC, CBS, and NBC, and their work also appeared in the films *Free Ride*, *An Unmarried Woman*, and *Dreamer*. —*Steve Huey*

● **20th Century Masters—The Millennium Collection: The Best of Pablo Cruise** / May 8, 2001 / A&M ✦✦✦✦✦
Two of Pablo Cruise's charting singles—"Never Had a Love," which went to 87 in 1978 and "Slip Away," which peaked at 75 in 1981—are missing from their edition of Universal's *20th Century Masters: The Millennium Collection* series. That means their remaining seven hits—including all their biggest, like "Whatcha Gonna Do?," "Love Will Find a Way," "Cool Love," "I Want You Tonight," and "Don't Want to Live Without It"—are here, along with five album selections. So, it may be possible to quibble that this isn't really definitive, solely on the basis of those missing hits, but for many listeners, this is as close to definitive as they need, since it really does contain Pablo Cruise's windswept, sun-mellowed blend of melodic Californian soft rock and lite jazz fusion. This music may recall the times—that netherworld of the late Carter administration and pre-Reagan assassination attempt—but its best moments (those aforementioned singles) are soft classics of the era, and this is one of the best ways to hear them. —*Stephen Thomas Erlewine*

The Pagans

f. 1977, **db.** 1979
Punk, Proto-Punk, Rock & Roll

Of all the bands that burst out of Cleveland in the mid- to late-'70s punk explosion, one of the most unjustly ignored was the Pagans. Despite breaking up in 1979 (they have, however, reunited several times since), these grimy bohunks played fast'n'loud piss-and-vinegar garage rock that valued alienation and, at times, extreme bad taste. Led by the honking rasp of Mike Hudson and the rapid-fire guitar of Mike "Tommy Gunn" Metoff, the Pagans never played it safe, nor did they enter the rock & roll wars wanting to win any friends. And this, ultimately, was a good thing, for like their pals the Dead Boys, their anti-star pose and *carpe diem* attitude meant that their best songs (and there are quite a few) sound as if they were set to auto-destruct at the tune's end. Although their don't-give-a-shit attitude lends itself more than once to some sexist japes and homophobic ranting, the Pagans ultimately didn't care who they offended. In fact, listening to any of their vintage material (1977-79), you'd think that offending everyone was their artistic raison d'etre. As Treehouse Records president Mark Trehus opines in the liner notes to the great collection *Buried Alive*, "the Pagans were as unwrought, impudent and gnarly a buncha rock & roll bedlamites as America's ever spewed outta its queasy underbelly." Little more need be said. —*John Dougan*

The Pagans / 1983 / Terminal ✦✦✦

● **Buried Alive** / 1986 / Treehouse ✦✦✦✦✦
Nasty, loud and vulgar, this is the best collection of The Pagans' music and one of the great, although almost completely forgotten, American punk rock records. After hearing such endearing "classics" as "What Is This Shit Called Love," you can see why Tesco Vee and his Meatmen covered it years later. Even better are the living-in-nowhere anthem "The Street Where Nobody Lives" and "Dead End America." Seventeen tracks, and each one's a killer, even the ones that make you wince. —*John Dougan*

Everybody Hates You / May 1, 1995 / Crypt ✦✦✦
Everything that can be said about the sound of the Pagans has already been said, in a hundred different ways, so this review will restrict itself to defining the band as a pure punch-in-the-gut punk outfit. The 30-track collection *Everybody Hates You* presents a thorough overview of the band's material, and it's now the only readily available artifact from their late-'70s career. And it's good—the Cleveland band uses its Motor City Five-

inspired sound to good effect on tracks like "What's This Shit Called Love?" *Everybody Hates You* contains obviously dated material not particularly relevant to today's musical climate, but it documents the work of a solid band during the heyday of the punk sound. —*Nitsuh Abebe*

The Pink Album . . . Plus / May 15, 2001 / Crypt ✦✦✦✦
In 1982, after the first edition of the Pagans had fallen apart, Mike Hudson, the band's singer, rhythm guitarist, and frontal lobe, decided to give them another try, and this time around the band wanted to document themselves with an actual album, rather than the 7" discs and compilation cuts that carried their previous recordings. Possessing more ambition than ready cash, the band pulled together a long-player from tunes recorded at live shows and during lo-fi sessions held in Hudson's basement (with everything recorded live to two-track through a PA mixer). The resulting LP, *The Pink Album*, issued in a run of 500 copies, became a collector's item overnight, and *The Pink Album . . . Plus* not only makes the album readily available to interested parties outside the Pagans' immediate cult for the first time, but adds a whopping 14 bonus cuts to the original LP's dozen—five 1983 outtakes from the recordings that became *The Pink Album* and nine live songs and studio outtakes from the first lineup's 1978-1979 heyday. The Pagans' sound was full-on Midwestern old-school punk at its most potent, with Hudson displaying an unusually intelligent degree of snarl and guitarist Mike Metoff (aka Tommy Gunn) showing how to split the difference between Ramones-style downstroke and hard rock flash. The original album's tracks stand up well (the sequence has been juggled a bit, but everything's here), with the basement cuts boasting a raw, abrasive guitar sound that could strip the paint from your walls. Nearly 20 years after it was first released, *The Pink Album . . . Plus* proves the Pagans are still more than capable of scaring your neighbors and impressing your friends—and that's high praise indeed. —*Mark Deming*

Page & Plant

f. 1994
Hard Rock

After years of rumors, Led Zeppelin guitarist Jimmy Page and vocalist Robert Plant reunited in 1994, recording the *No Quarter: Jimmy Page and Robert Plant Unledded* album for *MTV Unplugged*. Plant and Page didn't invite bassist John Paul Jones to join the reunion, choosing to assemble a band comprised of studio musicians. *No Quarter* performed respectably and the duo's subsequent 1995 tour was a sold-out success, prompting them to take a stab at a studio project. In 1997, they hired indie-rock producer Steve Albini to work on their forthcoming collection of new original songs; it was the first time Page chose to work with an outside producer. The resulting album, *Walking into Clarksdale*, was released to generally good reviews in the spring of 1998. —*Stephen Thomas Erlewine*

No Quarter: Jimmy Page & Robert Plant Unledded / Nov. 8, 1994 / Atlantic ✦✦✦
Page and Plant's long-awaited reunion wasn't the blockbuster success it was predicted to be, but then again, they didn't play by the rules. Instead of re-recording their most famous material, the duo chose some of the most challenging and diverse Led Zeppelin material and wrote three originals to match. *No Quarter* doesn't celebrate Page and Plant's title of the Kings of Bombast; it focuses on their role in popularizing ethnic music, from Arabia to the Celtic islands. So, it might not thrill fans of "Whole Lotta Love," but there's more invention on *No Quarter* than the standard reunion album. And, from the sounds of "City Don't Cry," "Yallah," and "Wonderful One," the partnership between the two remains fruitful. —*Stephen Thomas Erlewine*

● **Walking Into Clarksdale** / Apr. 21, 1998 / Atlantic ✦✦✦
For all of the acclaim it received, there's no denying that *No Quarter* was a tentative reunion for Page & Plant, containing only a handful of new songs which were scattered among many reworked old favorites. Since its supporting tour went well, the duo decided to make their reunion permanent, setting to work on an album of entirely new material. Taking the world music dabblings of *No Quarter* as a cue, Page & Plant tempered their eclecticism with a healthy dose of their monolithic guitar army, hiring Steve Albini, the indie-rock producer notorious for his harsh, brutal recordings, to helm the boards. In other words, it sounds perfect on paper—a groundbreaking veteran artist still taking chances and working with younger collaborators who would challenge them. If only *Walking Into Clarksdale* actually played that way. It's certainly possible to hear where the duo was intending to go, since the circular melodies, Mideastern drones, sawing strings, drum loops and sledgehammer riffs all add up to an effective update and progression of the classic Zeppelin sound. The problem is, the new sound doesn't go anywhere. There's potential in this metallic worldbeat rock, but only a few cuts, such as the stately "Most High" and the shimmering "Shining in the Light," realize it. Much of the album disappears under its own mass, since their are no well-written songs, catchy riffs or memorable

melodies to support the sound. And that's what makes *Walking Into Clarksdale* so frustrating—you can hear the potential, and even enjoy the album on the musical surface, but there's nothing to make you return to the album once it's finished. And that ultimately means that the album simply reiterates the promise of the reunited Page & Plant instead of fulfilling it. *—Stephen Thomas Erlewine*

Jennifer Paige

Adult Contemporary, Teen Pop

Pop diva Jennifer Paige was born and raised in Atlanta, Georgia, at age eight performing in local coffeehouses in a duo with her older brother; two years later, she began studying piano. A short time after moving to Los Angeles, Paige teamed with producer Andy Goldmark and in mid-1996 began work on her self-titled debut LP; originally released on the German indie label Edel, it was issued in the U.S. on Hollywood Records in 1998, launching the hit single "Crush." *—Jason Ankeny*

● **Jennifer Paige** / Aug. 11, 1998 / Hollywood ✦✦✦
Much as Donny Osmond stormed the charts in 1989 with the George Michael sound-alike "Soldier of Love," Jennifer Paige and her producer have recreated the same scenario via this collection's first offering, "Crush," a song very reminiscent of early Mariah Carey. It is only hoped that Carey will use this as a reminder of what made her voice so engaging upon her entrance into the pop diva arena. Jennifer unleashes a voice with great development potential that holds its own with a solid pop effort, and splendidly provides her own background vocals on most tracks as well. Definitely one of the brighter pop talents to emerge in quite a while. Standout tracks on this fine debut release include the first single "Crush," "Get to Me," "Somewhere, Someday," and the stellar "Let It Rain." *—Jaime Ikeda*

Palace

f. 1992

Alternative Country, Alternative Country-Rock, Indie Rock, Singer/Songwriter

Will Oldham, the brains and brawn behind releases as Palace Brothers, Palace Songs, Palace Music and just plain Palace, is loosely grouped with the '90s anti-folk movement that also includes Bill Callahan of Smog, a label-mate of Oldham's on Chicago's Drag City Records. Often mistaken for an old man due to his cracking vocals, sparse guitar pickings and biblical dialect, Oldham has recorded since 1992 with a variety of sidemen—basically, any friends or acquaintances that can play an instrument. He debuted with the single "Ohio River Boat Song" on Drag City Records. Though he's credited as Palace Songs on the single, Oldham's debut album the following year was filed under Palace Brothers—in part to denote the work of Todd Brashear. *There Is No-One What Will Take Care of You* introduced several of Oldham's continuing themes: drunkenness, sin in general, and the varied results of each. His second album—self-titled but also listed as *Days in the Wake*—was issued by Drag City in 1994. Oldham mixed things up for late-1995's *Viva Last Blues* (as Palace Music), recruiting a band with guitarist Bryan Rich, organist Liam Hayes and bassist Jason Loewenstein (from Sebadoh). The following year's *Arise, Therefore* found Oldham back in a largely solitary setting; he dropped the Palace banner soon after. *—John Bush*

There Is No-One What Will Take Care of You / Jun. 14, 1993 / Drag City ✦✦✦
Will Oldham's first album under the Palace rubric, *There Is No-One What Will Take Care of You,* seemed to emerge from under a cloud of mystery on its first release in 1993. The first edition had no credits save a list of names under the heading "Impossible Without," leading to all manner of speculation in the indie community about who was responsible; the album sounded as if some ancient songsters who had somehow escaped Harry Smith's attention years before had recorded a session in their living room, which somehow found its way to the offices of Drag City. On *There Is No-One What Will Take Care of You,* Oldham sounds like a lost-lost cousin of the Louvin Brothers who, after ending up on skid row, is equally convinced that Satan is real, since he smells his foul breath every waking moment of his life. Oldham's stark, intimate tales of sin, lust, alcohol, and hopelessness are fascinating, horribly compelling stuff, and while it would be easy for this material to sound ironic or condescending, it isn't—Oldham makes his characters' shame, confusion, and desperate search for grace real and genuinely moving. *There Is No-One What Will Take Care of You* may not be the best Palace album, but it is the work where Will Oldham's obsession with sin and redemption shines forth with the most painful and absorbing clarity. *—Mark Deming*

Days in the Wake / Aug. 29, 1994 / Drag City ✦✦✦✦✦
The second album from Palace Brothers would seem to barely qualify on either count—at a shade over 27 minutes, *Days in the Wake* seems a bit skimpy in the era of the 80-minute CD, and only one song, "Come a Little Dog," clearly features any musicians besides Will Oldham and his rickety acoustic guitar. But the stark simplicity and *audio vérité* ambience of *Days in the Wake* builds on the already dramatic emotional power of *There Is No-One What Will Take Care of You,* and if Will Oldham's obsession with sin and retribution is less forcefully stated in these songs, that's not to say it isn't clearly present on most of these songs, especially the cautionary tale "You Will Miss Me When I Burn," the mournful but fiercely proud "No More Workhorse Blues," and "Pushkin," which begins with the declaration "God is the answer/God lies within," without making it sound like a concept in which Oldham can take much comfort. Oldham's lyrics would become increasingly cryptic from this point on, but while the literal meaning of songs like "Wither Thou Goest" and "I Am a Cinematographer" is elusive, the emotional power of these performances is as eloquent as anyone could hope for. *Days in the Wake* is the simplest work in the Palace canon, and among the very best. [*Days in the Wake* was originally released simply as *Palace Brothers*.] *—Mark Deming*

Viva Last Blues / Aug. 21, 1995 / Drag City ✦✦✦✦
This incarnation of Palace, one of its more impressive, sees front man Will Oldham turning out some of the strongest bleak country rock in his career, and taking the music in a few intriguing and even upbeat directions. With a great supporting cast that includes, among others, Sebadoh's Jason Loewenstein on drums, and Oldham's brother Ned on bass, the group busts out laid back twangy tunes that can really rock when the opportunity comes up. Most notably, tracks like "Work Hard/Play Hard" and the opening "More Brother Rides" are brimming with energy that may not overwhelm, but certainly provides a hefty backbone. Alternately, slower brooding tracks like the longing "New Partner" see the band proving their chops in a more refined setting. Oldham's cracking back-country voice may be a bit of an acquired taste, but it's worth the time, as his inflections are capable of powerful feelings and certain honesty. The Palace team has put out many a record, but as far as accessible and slightly upbeat musical ruminations go, *Viva Last Blues* certainly sees the players near the top of their game. Things are a little thicker and dirtier than on the more laid back acoustic records this prolific artist has put out, but the rock approach adds worlds to the delivery and creates a powerful palette for the equally important lyrics. Oldham is a truly underrated American talent, and this is among his best work, so take the time to find it. *—Peter J. D'Angelo*

Arise, Therefore / Apr. 1996 / Drag City ✦✦✦✦
Once again Will Oldham emerges out of the murky, Midwestern haze with another helping of lovely, low-key musings on his fourth full-length album, *Arise Therefore*, this time recorded under the name Palace Music (previously Palace Brothers, Palace Songs, or just plain Palace). Much quieter than last year's *Viva Last Blues*, and less Appalachian in its folk-spirit than Palace's earlier music, the songs on *Arise Therefore* shift and moan with breathy cracks and shivers, Oldham's meandering, poet-speak vocals and guitar accompanied by his brother Ned's bass, David Grubbs' piano, and (surprise!) a Maya Tone drum machine. The lyrics (included for the first time) are beautiful in their stark, pale honesty as often as they are indecipherable. "I watch things painted on public walls, now but I see other things as well, behind but right fuck in front of my spirit is how the real road's laid out in a line" he sings on "Kid of Harith." Don't ask for an interpretation: It will come with time, or it won't. *—Kurt Wolff*

● **Lost Blues & Other Songs** / Mar. 24, 1997 / Drag City ✦✦✦✦✦
Lost Blues and Other Songs collects various singles and rarities Will Oldham released under his various Palace incarnations during the early '90s. Nearly all of the material is haunting, spare acoustic-based material, drawing from traditional folk and country, but undercut by Oldham's detached postmodern sensibilities. Occasionally, his removed, affected vocals can make Palace's music seem emotionally distant, but it often works, and *Lost Blues and Other Songs* finds him at his very best. *—Stephen Thomas Erlewine*

Pale Saints

f. 1987, Leeds, England, **db.** 1994

Noise Pop, Indie Pop, Dream Pop, Shoegazing, Alternative Pop/Rock

Ethereal pop band the Pale Saints formed in Leeds, England, in 1987. Ian Masters (bass/vocals), Chris Cooper (drums), and Graeme Naysmith (guitar) were signed by Ivo Watts-Russell to his 4AD label on the strength of their first London appearance. The three-song *Barging Into the Presence of God* was released two years later, receiving praise for it's lead track, the melancholy "Sight of You." In 1990, the debut LP *The Comforts of Madness* appeared in the bins, produced separately by Gil Norton (Echo & the Bunnymen, Pixies) and John Fryer (Cocteau Twins, Depeche Mode). Categorized within the current shoegaze scene with My Bloody Valentine and Lush, the billowy *Comforts of Madness* had just about all the features of the subgenre, as well as a bizarre experimental bent. Masters' boyish vocals also stood out, not needing any production treatments to carry a wispy, levitational quality. Meriel Barham, who was thanked for guitars and vocals on 1990's "Half Life" single, joined as a full member by the end of the year. Barham had been Lush's original vocalist. Producer Hugh Jones leant his skills for 1992's *In Ribbons*. Yet another Bunnymen associate, Jones captured a power and liveliness that Norton and Fryer didn't provide. Stronger musically and sound-wise, *In Ribbons* was another excellent album, though it sacrificed some of the band's original charms and quirks in favor of more pop accessibility. This and a growing disdain for touring led to Masters' departure in 1993. The remaining members replaced him with session hand and former Heart Throbs bassist Colleen Browne. Continuing their allegiance with Jones, 1994's *Slow Buildings* ended up being the band's final album. Lacking from the absence of Masters, the album also lacked focus. After touring, the band called it quits prior to 1997. *—Andy Kellman*

● **The Comforts of Madness** / 1990 / 4AD ✦✦✦✦✦
When thinking of the finest dream pop records from the early '90s, *The Comforts of Madness* tends to get lost in the shuffle. Frequently and unfortunately, the Pale Saints were disregarded as just another part of the 4AD sound, lacking distinction and relying on the clichés of the time. Though they might have (arguably) fallen into those traps later in their brief career, their debut really does stick out from the remainder of the 4AD roster as well as the remainder of the then-current scene. The touchstones—Jesus and Mary Chain, My Bloody Valentine, Galaxie 500—are somewhat apparent, but their debut is certifiably unique. Noise and melody duke it out, but in an arrestingly off-kilter fashion. *Comforts* is really as much of a "quirk-out" as it is a "bliss-out," experimental in many ways and apparently so from the beginning of "Way the World Is." The noisy rattling eventually gives way to wobbly bass and tunefully violent Wedding Present-like strumming, whipping up a tempestuous haze of frenzied pop. Throughout the record, the trio throws in countless tempo curveballs (with no sense of pomposity) and effectively balances the blasting

chuggers with levitational banks of piled-on guitarscapes. The somewhat thin production lent by John Fryer and Gil Norton (on separate sessions) actually serves *Comforts* well, though it may take a few listens to settle in. The somewhat trebly, un-anchored production is properly suited for Ian Masters' boyish vocals, which sound like they're just on the brink of pubescence. His vocals are just as important to this record as Graeme Naysmith's guitars, not vanishing into the gobs of guitars like your typical shoegaze. "Sight of You" (re-tooled from their debut EP) is the centerpeice, a lovelorn gem that sounds vaguely like the lost track to *Psychocandy*. In whole, this debut remains a brilliant example of insular, adventurous, and charmingly flawed noise pop. —*Andy Kellman*

In Ribbons / Apr. 14, 1992 / 4AD ✦✦✦✦
An argument could be made for *In Ribbons* topping the Pale Saints' debut, and it would be a rather solid one. Thanks to yet another stellar job by "knob twiddler of the mighty atmospheric pop bands" Hugh Jones, the Pale Saints sound full and polished, gleaming and bright. What makes this a lesser record in comparison to its predecessor is the absence of that loose sense of adventure from before. The songs are strong, the musicianship is improved, and Meriel Barham's presence as second guitarist and vocalist provides for more muscularity, but *In Ribbons* is missing the slightly perverse sense of experimentation that *The Comforts of Madness* had in spades. The unpredictability is gone, which is one of the few downsides of a band whose members are getting to know each other musically. That doesn't prevent *In Ribbons* from being a great record, stacked to the gills with great songs. Barham's sporadic contributions provide a fine spoil to those of Ian Masters. The mid-tempo moodiness of "Thread of Light" benefits from Jones' excellent treatment of her voice, with swooning backgrounds that dart between the left and right channels. (The verses bear odd sonic resemblance to Duran Duran's "Save a Prayer"—no kidding.) Her reading of Mazzy Star's "Blue Flower" tops the original, and "Baby Maker" also makes the grade with its dizzied liveliness. Masters' love for the abandonment of rock constructs strikes upon a zenith on "Hair Shirt," a drumless cluster of limpidly jousting guitars that simultaneously jiggle, rattle, moan, twinkle, and reverberate. His miasmatic vocals seal the track off as a brilliant approximation of the oceanic wash of *69era* AR Kane. Otherwise, more accessible fare, like the sprightly "Throwing Back the Apple" (a single) and the melancholy epic "Hunted," are also accountable for the record's success. Though these tracks' more traditionally structured material doesn't sound a great deal different from many of the Pale Saints' peers, the wan voice of Masters—who sounds less world-weary here—clearly sets this unit apart. —*Andy Kellman*

Slow Buildings / Aug. 30, 1994 / 4AD ✦✦✦
Anyone arguing the case that the Pale Saints were the sole vision of Ian Masters was pretty much silenced when he left the group. Masters might have said some misleading things to the press but, as it turned out, his mates had a great deal of artistic input. That's probably what led to his departure. Wanting to do things more his way—abandon drums, screw with song structures, experiment like a mad scientist, etc.—he split. Thanks to Masters' tales of artistic control, many were surprised to see the band continue. Meriel Barham took over all vocal duties, and Colleen Browne was brought in on bass. Yet *Slow Buildings* doesn't do much to dissuade listeners from the general opinion that Masters was the band's creative center. Though containing a couple excellent songs (the breezy, Breeders/Lush-like "Angel" and "Under Your Nose," the sleepy "Fine Friend"), *Slow Buildings* sinks under the weight of lengthy dirges that don't stick and general overindulgence. Five tracks clock in at over six minutes; rather than concocting lovely mood setters or dynamic epics, the material is "just there" and fails to stimulate. Some ugly guitar fireworks don't mesh (like the Skynyrd-ish solo in "Gesture of Fear"), and there are no less than a handful of other instances where one loses sight of where the band's coming from. Program out some of the clutter, and there's a decent 35- to 40-minute record here, although still not on the level of the band's prior works. Credit the Pale Saints for remaining creative and prolific in the wake of a key member's departure, but there's little denying the failure of *Slow Buildings*. The discomforts of blandness? Quite possibly. Advice: no one hoping to like this record should listen to Lush's *Split* within the same month; the similarly formatted and styled record completely belittles *Slow Buildings* in every respect. —*Andy Kellman*

Robert Palmer

b. Jan. 19, 1949, Batley, England
Vocals, Guitar / Album Rock, Blue-Eyed Soul, Pop/Rock, Adult Contemporary
The career of blue-eyed soul singer Robert Palmer was a study in style versus substance. While the performer's earliest work won praise for its skillful assimilation of rock, R&B and reggae sounds, his records typically sold poorly, and he achieved his greatest notoriety as an impeccably-dressed lounge lizard. By the mid-'80s, however, Palmer became a star, although his popularity owed less to the strength of his material than to his infamous music videos: taking their cue from the singer's suave presence, Palmer's clips established him as a dapper, suit-and-tied ladies' man who performed his songs backed by a band comprised of leggy models, much to the delight of viewers who made him one of MTV's biggest success stories. He first mounted a solo career in 1974, after several years with the Stax-influenced soul group Vinegar Joe. An avowed stylistic experimenter, Palmer recorded albums indebted to reggae and synth-pop as well as more rock-oriented material during the late '70s and early '80s. After teaming with the Duran Duran side project Power Station for the hit singles "Some Like It Hot" and "Get It On," his next solo album (1985's *Riptide*) included the number one hit "Addicted to Love," the first in a string of videos which offered him in front of a bevy of beautiful women. Two follow-ups, "I Didn't Mean to Turn You On" and "Simply Irresistible," both hit number two. By 1990's *Don't Explain* though, Palmer had returned to the eclecticism of his earliest material and his sales plummeted. —*Jason Ankeny*

Sneakin' Sally Through the Alley / 1974 / Island ✦✦✦✦
Before becoming a slick, sharp-dressed pop star in the 1980s, Robert Palmer was a soul singer deeply rooted in R&B and funk. Those influences are on full display on his debut album *Sneakin' Sally Through the Alley*. With a backing band including members of Little Feat and the Meters, the music has a laid-back groove whether Palmer's covering New Orleans legend Allen Toussaint (the title track) or singing originals ("Hey Julia," "Get Outside"). While the music is tight and solid, it is Robert Palmer's voice that is revelatory—he sounds supremely confident among these talented musicians, and they seem to feed off his vocal intensity. Fans of the Meters or people who want to discover the funky side of Robert Palmer should check this one out. —*Vik Iyengar*

Pressure Drop / 1976 / Island ✦✦✦✦✦
Palmer's own songs (especially the silky "Give Me an Inch" and "Work to Make It Work") and the backing of Little Feat help make this a worthy followup to *Sally*. —*William Ruhlmann*

Some People Can Do What They Like / 1976 / Island ✦✦✦
Robert Palmer's third album is a blue-eyed soul disc that sits comfortably alongside *Sneakin' Sally through The Alley* and *Pressure Drop*. This time, Palmer drops the orchestrations that tarted up portions of *Pressure Drop* in favor of a stripped-down yet stylish sound that shows off his ability to create a romantic, soulful mood. Highlights include "One Last Look," a lush breakup ballad that features a catchy, harmony-drenched chorus, and "Keep In Touch," a romantic tune that highlights Palmer's vocal style at its seductive height over a jazzy yet mellow melody built on a complex background vocal arrangement. Another standout track is "Man Smart, Woman Smarter," a tongue-in-cheek look at the battle between the sexes that deftly blends pop melodicism with reggae rhythms. The downside of *Some People Can Do What They Like* is that it often favors mood over hooks and this leads to music that is listenable yet falls short of being truly compelling: funky mood pieces like "What Can You Bring Me" and "Hard Head" successfully evoke a sultry mood but never take that mood in an interesting melodic direction. Another problem track is "Off The Bone," an effects-drenched instrumental snippet that serves no purpose other than to fill up two minutes of the album's running time. Despite these occasional lapses, *Some People Can Do What They Like* remains a solid and likable outing with enough memorable moments to please anyone who enjoys blue-eyed soul at its most silky and elegant. —*Donald A. Guarisco*

Double Fun / 1978 / Island ✦✦✦
After exploring a sound that filtered blue-eyed soul through excursions into worldbeat, Robert Palmer began to move in a more commercial direction on 1978's self-produced *Double Fun*. The overall sound of the album pushes towards disco (Tom Moulton, a remixer/producer and star of the American disco scene, assisted on a handful of tracks) and a lot of the tracks play up Palmer's love of reggae-styled grooves. The result was a commercial success and produced a top-20 hit with "Every Kinda People," a catchy call for brotherhood that fleshed out its gentle pop-reggae groove with tasteful orchestrations. Elsewhere, Palmer turns up the energy with "Best Of Both Worlds," a bass-driven dance tune that shows off his vocal prowess with its cleverly-arranged and complex vocal arrangement, and "Night People," an evocative tale of nightlife built on a percolating groove that borders on jazz-funk. The only real problem with *Double Fun* is that it occasionally allows style to overwhelm substance: "Where Can It Go?" has a dreamy ballad sound and "Love Can Run Faster" sports a solid reggae feel but neither tune has a melody strong enough to keep them from drifting off into the ether. Despite this flaw, *Double Fun* stays afloat thanks to its ability to deftly juggle genres while maintaining an overall consistency to its production style (example: the hard-rock guitar riffs that spice up the otherwise dance-oriented "You're Gonna Get What's Coming"). Casual listeners may want to pick up this album's hits on a compilation, but Robert Palmer fans will definitely want to give this album a spin. —*Donald A. Guarisco*

Secrets / 1979 / Island ✦✦✦✦✦
Palmer scores his biggest hit single of the '70s with the uptempo rocker "Bad Case of Loving You (Doctor, Doctor)" on an album that also includes a wonderful version of Todd Rundgren's ballad "Can We Still Be Friends." —*William Ruhlmann*

Clues / 1980 / Island ✦✦✦✦
After recording a series of albums that established him as a pop-minded interpreter of soul styles, Robert Palmer surprised fans in 1980 with the stylistic about-face of *Clues*. On this album, he brought his sound into the new wave era by playing up the rock edge to his music, stripping the high-production gloss from his sound, and incorporating synthesizers into the arrangements. The end result became a big hit in the U.K. and paved the way for later international successes like *Riptide* and *Heavy Nova*. *Clues* also produced two notable singles in "Looking For Clues," a clever slice of new wave pop that surprises the listener with an unexpected xylophone solo, and "Johnny And Mary," a moody synth-driven ballad with perceptive lyrics about a doomed romantic relationship. There is also an impressive cover of Gary Numan's "I Dream Of Wires" that retains the chilly electronic grandeur of the original while successfully working in an earthier rhythm arrangment that makes the song dance-friendly. Elsewhere, Palmer shows he hasn't abandoned his penchant for soul and ethnic music: "Woke Up Laughing" filters an African-style, chant-like vocal melody through a minimalist electronic production style and "Found You Now" effectively combines a reggae groove with a deadpan sense of cool that is very "new wave." The end result is a bit short (it clocks in at barely over a half hour), but it remains one of Robert Palmer's strongest and most consistent albums. In short, *Clues* is a must for Robert Palmer fans and worth a spin for anyone into new wave. —*Donald A. Guarisco*

Maybe It's Live / 1982 / Island ✦✦

Pride / 1983 / Island ✦✦

Riptide / Nov. 1985 / Island ✦✦✦✦✦
Palmer's commercial breakthrough, much of it in the hard rock style of his one-shot band Power Station, and featuring the hits "Discipline of Love," "Addicted to Love" (a number one hit), "Hyperactive," and "I Didn't Mean to Turn You On." *—William Ruhlmann*

Heavy Nova / Jun. 1988 / EMI America ✦✦

• **Addictions, Vol. 1** / Oct. 1989 / Island ✦✦✦✦✦
Thirteen-track compilation containing Palmer's biggest hits, not only the ones on Island but also The Power Station singles and "Simply Irresistible," from Palmer's first EMI album. *—William Ruhlmann*

Don't Explain / Oct. 1990 / EMI America ✦✦

Addictions, Vol. 2 / May 5, 1992 / Island ✦✦✦
Apart from "I Didn't Mean to Turn You On," there are no big hits, only album tracks and failed singles, all of which are quite good. Unfortunately, the majority of the material has been remixed, remade, or has new vocal tracks; the album may sound great, but it isn't an accurate retrospective. *—Stephen Thomas Erlewine*

The Very Best of Robert Palmer / Jan. 28, 1997 / Capitol ✦✦✦
Despite my (yet rationalized) fondness for his 1980 electro-pop hit "Johnny and Mary" (included here), the 16-track collection *The Very Best of Robert Palmer* mostly leaves me cold. Palmer has the tools, but the mechanicals lack potency and soul. Still, if combining mid-'80s hits like "Addicted to Love" and "Simply Irresistible" with a whiff of earlier material, several more recent constructions, and a pair from side project the Power Station sounds like your kind of fun, this disc does the job... efficiently. Includes a new cover of the Staple Singers' "Respect Yourself." *—Roch Parisien*

Rhythm and Blues / Jul. 20, 1999 / Pyramid/Rhino ✦✦

20th Century Masters—The Millennium Collection: The Best of Robert Palmer / Oct. 26, 1999 / Island ✦✦✦
MCA's *20th Century Masters—The Millennium Collection* is a good, basic collection of Robert Palmer's biggest hits, including "Sneaking Sally (Through the Alley)," "Bad Case of Lovin' You," "Can We Still Be Friends," "Looking for Clues," "Some Guys Have All the Luck," "Addicted to Love," and "I Didn't Mean to Turn You On." Although there are a couple of hits and good album tracks missing, this has enough of the hits to make it worthwhile for casual listeners on a budget. *—Stephen Thomas Erlewine*

Pantera

f. 1982
Alternative Metal, Heavy Metal, Thrash
A band with truly few peers, Pantera rose to unprecedented prominence in the early '90s with an uncompromising approach that prided itself on brutality and reverence rather than style or trend. Their eccentricity and stubborn insistence on being the most intense metal band this side of death metal took them to the top of the Billboard charts yet also ironically reduced them to cult status. Either way, Pantera never followed the bandwagon, winning legions of metalheads with sincerity, even if it meant they had become the genre's dark horse. But the Texas band wasn't always uncompromising. In fact, for much of the '80s an admittedly formative version of Pantera was indeed rather trendy. That changed, though, in 1990 when the group released *Cowboys From Hell.* Undeniably influenced by late-'80s thrash, it nonetheless stunned much of the metal community by toning down the tempo and upping the intensity level. Pantera's king-of-the-hill status came with 1992's *Vulgar Display of Power,* though. Their next album, *Far Beyond Driven,* debuted at the top of Billboard in 1994, confirming this lofty status. Yet by the time Pantera returned two years later in 1996, things had changed, and they saw their following dwindle slowly. It was inevitable. Yet rather than adapt to the latest trend, Pantera remained Pantera, priding themselves on their workmanlike approach to keeping heavy metal heavy, never toning down their intensity level, and scoffing at trends. They may have become bitter and jaded, but you could never call Pantera sellouts. *—Jason Birchmeier*

Metal Magic / 1983 / Metal Magic ✦

Power Metal / 1988 / Metal Magic ✦✦

Cowboys from Hell / Jul. 1990 / East West ✦✦✦✦✦
Pantera's breakthrough album, *Cowboys From Hell,* is largely driven by the band's powerful rhythm section and guitarist Diamond Darrell's (as he was then known) unbelievably forceful riffing, which skittered around the downbeats to produce unexpected rhythmic phrases and accents, as well as his inventive soloing. Phil Anselmo displayed a vocal range that could switch from a growling shout to a high falsetto—listen to him match Darrell's harmonic squeals at the end of "Cemetery Gates." The album gradually becomes more same-sounding as it goes on, but the first half, featuring such brutal slices of thrash as "Psycho Holiday," "Primal Concrete Sledge" and the title track, pretty much carries its momentum all the way through. *—Steve Huey*

• **Vulgar Display of Power** / Feb. 25, 1992 / East West ✦✦✦✦✦
One of the most influential heavy metal albums of the 1990s, *Vulgar Display of Power* is just what is says: a raw, pulverizing, insanely intense depiction of naked rage and hostility that drains its listeners and pounds them into submission. Even the "ballads," "This Love" and "Hollow," have thunderingly loud, aggressive chorus sections. Preaching power through strength and integrity, Phil Anselmo discards any further attempts at singing in favor of a militaristic bark and an unhinged roar, while the crystal-clear production sets Darrell's pummeling riffs against a rhythmic backdrop so thunderously supportive that Darrell often solos without underlying rhythm guitar parts. The album again follows *Cowboys From Hell*'s strategy of stacking the best songs at the beginning and letting their momentum carry the listener through the rest, but the riffs and sonic textures are more consistently interesting this time around. Pantera's thick-sounding, post-hardcore power-metal and outraged, testosterone-drenched intensity would help pave the way for alternative-metal acts like Korn and Tool; *Vulgar Display of Power* is the best distillation of those virtues. *—Steve Huey*

Far Beyond Driven / Mar. 15, 1994 / East West ✦✦✦
Far Beyond Driven may be Pantera's biggest selling album, but it's hardly their best. Though it shot straight to the number one spot on the Billboard sales chart in its first week (arguably the most extreme album ever to do so), this incredible feat doesn't so much reflect its own qualities as those of its predecessor, 1992's *Vulgar Display of Power.* A true landmark, *Vulgar* had seen the Texan quartet quite literally reinventing the wheel (in heavy metal terms) in a way not seen since Metallica's rise to fame in the late '80s. But when the time came to follow it up, the band members themselves seemed unsure as to how they could possibly top it. So they decided to try and out-heavy themselves, resulting in a less cohesive record which often sacrificed songwriting for outright aggression. Guitarist Dimebag Darrell (recently re-baptized from the far more glam Diamond Darrell) took it upon himself to conjure the heaviest riffs imaginable, turning up the volume and dissonance to sometimes painful thresholds with his massive, grinding riffs. Songs like "Becoming," "Shedding Skin," and the vicious "Slaughtered" still stand head and shoulders above most of the competition, but only die-hard metalheads will be able to stand their systematic sensory bludgeoning long enough to get to the hooks hidden underneath. Worst of all is "Good Friends and a Bottle of Pills," which wanders aimlessly in feedback and is topped with vocalist Phil Anselmo in stream-of-consciousness mode—a sketchy proposition at the best of times. In fact, except for wisely chosen first single "I'm Broken," the rest of the album (and especially over-long tracks like "5 Minutes Alone" and "25 Years") simply lacks the iron-fisted discipline and controlled power captured on *Vulgar.* Finally, the band's insistence on justifying their cover version of Sabbath's gentle "Planet Caravan" in the LP's liner notes is further evidence of their embattled frame of mind at the time. Ultimately, *Far Beyond Driven* was a necessary evolutionary step for Pantera which, if nothing else, certainly did the business. *—Ed Rivadavia*

The Great Southern Trendkill / May 1996 / EastWest ✦✦✦
Thankfully, Pantera have stopped attempting to outdo each successive album in terms of start-to-finish intensity, but that doesn't mean they don't try in spots. *The Great Southern Trendkill* is burdened with passages in which Phil Anselmo's vocals cross the line into histrionics, making the band's trademark intensity sound dull, forced, and theatrical rather than sincere. The lyrics, which reached their apex with *Vulgar Display of Power*'s focus on personal politics and integrity, have degenerated into half-baked rants against drugs and pop-culture media. But *Trendkill* is partially redeemed by trading Pantera's usual pound-then-pound-harder approach to albums for a greater variety of tempos and moods. Dimebag Darrell, while mostly sticking to his familiar riffing style, does coax some intriguing, unexpected sounds from his instrument. Ultimately, though, the ballads and slower tracks ("10's," "Suicide Note Pt. 1," "Floods") provide the album's most chilling, memorable moments, and rank with their best material. Longtime Pantera fans will find plenty to enjoy here, and the band's expanding range bodes well, but overall, *Trendkill* is an inconsistent outing. *—Steve Huey*

Official Live: 101 Proof / Jul. 29, 1997 / EastWest ✦✦✦
Official Live: 101 Proof hits most, but not quite all, of the high points of Pantera's career ("Psycho Holiday" and "Mouth for War" are two notable omissions), drawing most heavily from *Vulgar Display of Power* and *Far Beyond Driven.* There are also two new studio tracks tacked on to the end to entice the more casual fan who might find a live album redundant; however, Pantera's devoted fans will pick it up anyway, and they won't be disappointed. Pantera packs just as much of a wallop live as in the studio, even if the versions here aren't substantially different (other than a medley of "Domination" and "Hollow"). One warning: Phil Anselmo's amazing streams of non-stop vulgarities in between songs will appeal more to the adolescent fan who finds them a liberating way to vent frustration; others may find them predictable and approaching idiotic. But that shouldn't detract from the music and performances, which are uniformly strong, as fans would expect. *—Steve Huey*

Reinventing the Steel / Mar. 14, 2000 / East West ✦✦✦
Where *The Great Southern Trendkill* experimented with slower, moodier pieces, *Reinventing the Steel* finds Pantera sticking to the pulverizing basics of their sound, with the first downtempo, non-distorted guitar part appearing on the next-to-last track, "It Makes Them Disappear," and vanishing about 15 seconds into the song. In the tradition of the group's best albums, *Reinventing the Steel* is a nonstop assault on the senses, offering no respite from the intensity until the album has stopped playing. Yet somehow, it comes off as a cut below their best albums; perhaps it's that the band's sound lacks the sense of freshness that sparked *Cowboys From Hell, Vulgar Display of Power,* and *Far Beyond Driven,* or perhaps it's simply good in a very predictable way (contrary to its title). Yet even if Pantera is firmly entrenched in a signature sound, it's a distinctive, highly effective signature sound that most of the band's fans don't want to hear changed; plus, Dimebag Darrell is still one of the most inventive guitar players in heavy metal. The bottom line is that the way you feel about *Reinventing the Steel* will likely depend on whether you object to more of the same; if not, then the lean focus of its attack—the most concise, actually, since *Vulgar Display*—will make it more than worthwhile. *—Steve Huey*

Papas Fritas

f. Somerville, MA
Indie Pop, Indie Rock, Power Pop, Alternative Pop/Rock

Papas Fritas is an alternative-pop trio whose name is both Spanish for "fried potatoes" and a pun on the phrase "pop has freed us." The group's membership consists of guitarist/vocalist Tony Goddess, bassist/vocalist Keith Gendel, and drummer/vocalist Shivika Asthana; the former and the latter attended school together in Wilmington, Delaware and met Gendel at college in Somerville, Massachusetts. Their self-titled debut was released in 1995, and its follow-up, *Helioself*, was issued in 1997 by Minty Fresh. After a three-year hiatus, Papas Fritas returned in early 2000 with *Buildings and Grounds*. *—Steve Huey*

Papas Fritas / Oct. 24, 1995 / Minty Fresh ◆◆◆◆
Papas Fritas' self-titled debut album is a bracing set of indie power-pop with an astonishing sense of both playfulness and studio mastery. In spots, Tony Goddess' vocals are as rugged as on an old Replacements record, while the light-touch ballad "Passion Play" is a charming piece of chamber-pop worthy of the Left Banke. While the lyrics are a bit lightweight in places, the group's cunning pop sense and the bright harmony vocals of drummer Shivika Asthana produce a stunning pop album. *—John Bush*

Helioself / Apr. 22, 1997 / Minty Fresh ◆◆◆◆
On their second album *Helioself*, Papas Fritas displays an increased sense of songcraft and a sharper sense of melody, resulting in a bright, effervescent indie-rock record. Where their debut was occasionally brittle, *Helioself* is rounded and warm, and one of the most infectious pop records in the post-alternative indie-rock world of the late '90s. *—Stephen Thomas Erlewine*

● **Buildings & Grounds** / Mar. 7, 2000 / Minty Fresh ◆◆◆◆
Papas Fritas' album, *Buildings and Grounds*, opens as gently as a breeze, as "Girl" floats along on lazily picked acoustic guitars, cooed vocals, and an arrangement reminiscent of swinging London—not of the mid-'90s, but of the mid-'60s. It's as clear a signal as possible that things are different now in the Papas Fritas camp. Although this lighter touch wasn't completely absent on their previous record, they have toned down the straight-ahead, big indie pop hooks which fueled their first album. It may be a little startling at first, particularly for true fans of the band's earlier sparer sound, but *Buildings and Grounds* is a stronger, more cohesive record than their debut. That's not to say it's perfect. Occasionally, they're just a little too self-conscious and precious—a common affliction of indie pop—but it's hard not to be charmed by Shivika Asthana's sighing vocals or Tony Goddess' plain, friendly singing. It's so unassuming that it's easy to hear that they mean it. And, while their talents as writers and record-makers are still developing, *Buildings and Grounds* makes it clear that Papas Fritas are not only talented, but that they have their own voice, as well. They're pop fans, but unlike many of their pop peers, they're neither overly classicist nor overly insular. That doesn't mean that this is pop music for the charts—it's entirely too nice and gentle for that—but neither is it self-defeatingly "indie," as many indie pop albums are at the turn of the millennium. In its own, quiet way, *Buildings and Grounds* proves that it's worth the time of many pop fans to indulge Papas Fritas, as they awkwardly but winningly find their own voice. *—Stephen Thomas Erlewine*

Graham Parker

b. Nov. 15, 1950, East London, England
Vocals, Songwriter, Guitar / Album Rock, Pub Rock, New Wave, Singer/Songwriter
Stereotyped early in his career as the quintessential angry young man, Graham Parker was one of the most successful singer-songwriters to emerge from England's pub-rock scene of the early '70s. Drawing heavily from Van Morrison and the Rolling Stones, Parker developed a sinewy fusion of driving rock & roll and confessional folk-rock, highlighted by his indignant passion, biting sarcasm and bristling anger. At the outset of his career, his albums crackled with pub-rock energy, snide witticisms and gentle insights, earning him a devoted following of fans and critics, who lavished praise on his debut, *Howlin' Wind*. Despite all of the positive word-of-mouth, Parker never managed to become a star, and he was soon overshadowed by the emergence of Elvis Costello, a singer-songwriter who shared similar roots. After delivering *Squeezing Out Sparks* in 1979, Parker attempted to make a few crossover albums before settling into a cult following in the late '80s, continuing to garner critical acclaim. *—Stephen Thomas Erlewine*

☆ **Howlin' Wind** / Jul. 1976 / Mercury ◆◆◆◆◆
For most intents and purposes, Graham Parker emerged fully formed on his debut album, *Howlin' Wind*. Sounding like the bastard offspring of Mick Jagger and Van Morrison, Parker sneers his way through a set of stunningly literate pub-rockers. Instead of blindly sticking to the traditions of rock & roll, Parker invigorates them with cynicism and anger, turning his songs into distinctively original works. "Back to Schooldays" may be reconstituted rockabilly, "White Honey" may recall Morrison's white R&B bounce, and "Howlin' Wind" is a cross of Van's more mystical moments and the Band, but the songs themselves are original and terrific. Similarly, producer Nick Lowe gives the album a tough, spare feeling, which makes Parker and the Rumour sound like one of the best bar bands you've ever heard. *Howlin' Wind* remains a thoroughly invigorating fusion of rock tradition, singer-songwriter skill, and punk spirit, making it one of the classic debuts of all time. *—Stephen Thomas Erlewine*

Heat Treatment / Oct. 1976 / Mercury ◆◆◆◆
On his second album *Heat Treatment*, Graham Parker essentially offered more of the same thing that made *Howlin' Wind* such a bracing listen. However, his songwriting wasn't as consistent, with only a handful of songs—like "Pourin' It All Out" and the title track—making much of an impression. Unfortunately, the record was also tamed by the production of Mutt Lange, who polishes the record just enough to make the Rumour sound restrained. Which means, of course, the sheer musicality of the band can't save the lesser material. *Heat Treatment* remains an enjoyable listen—at this stage of the game,

Parker hadn't soured into a curmudgeon, and his weaker songs were still endearing—but it's a disappointment in light of its predecessor. *—Stephen Thomas Erlewine*

Stick to Me / Oct. 1977 / Mercury ◆◆◆◆◆
Graham Parker and the Rumour's third new studio album to be released in 18 months finds the bandleader running short of top-flight material; "Thunder And Rain" and "Watch The Moon Come Down" are up to his usual standards, but songs like "The Heat In Harlem" find him dangerously out of his depth. As a result, although fiercely played, this star-crossed release (it had to be re-recorded when the first version suffered technical problems) is a cut below Parker's first two albums. *—William Ruhlmann*

The Parkerilla/Live / 1978 / Mercury ◆◆
This is an ill-conceived live album (probably put out as a contract breaker with Mercury) on which Graham Parker and the Rumour sing songs from the substandard *Stick To Me* album and even use up a whole side of the original two-LP version on a studio re-recording of "Don't Ask Me Questions." With this release, what had seemed like one of the most promising careers of the second half of the 1970s suddenly seemed to be on the rocks. *—William Ruhlmann*

☆ **Squeezing out Sparks** / Mar. 1979 / Arista ◆◆◆◆◆
Generally regarded as Graham Parker's finest album, *Squeezing Out Sparks* is a masterful fusion of pub rock classicism, new wave pop, and pure vitriol that makes even his most conventional singer/songwriter numbers bristle with energy. Not only does Parker deliver his best, most consistent set of songs, but he offers more succinct hooks than before—"Local Girls" and "Discovering Japan" are powered by quirky hooks that make them new wave classics. But Parker's new pop inclinations are tempered by his anger, which seethes throughout the hard rockers and even his quieter numbers. Throughout *Squeezing Out Sparks*, Graham spits out a litany of offenses which make him feel like an outsider, but he's not a liberal, he's a conservative. The record's two centerpieces—"Passion Is No Ordinary Word" and the anti-abortion "You Can't Be Too Strong"—indicate that his traditionalist musical tendencies are symptomatic of a larger conservative trend. But no one ever said conservatives made poor rock & rollers, and Parker's ruminations over a lost past give him the anger that fuels *Squeezing Out Sparks*, one of the great rock records of the post-punk era. *—Stephen Thomas Erlewine*

The Up Escalator / May 1980 / Razor & Tie ◆◆◆◆
While it was something short of a hit, *Squeezing Out Sparks* did win a measure of richly-deserved American recognition for Graham Parker and the Rumour, and for the follow-up, Parker's American record label, Arista, paired him up with hotshot producer Jimmy Iovine. The idea looked good on paper; Iovine had produced or engineered great sounding hard rock records for Bruce Springsteen, Tom Petty, and Patti Smith, and his tough but vibrant sound would seem the perfect match for Parker and his band. But one listen to *The Up Escalator* reveals that Iovine's trademark sound somehow escaped him for this project; the recording and mix are flat and poorly detailed (Brinsley Schwarz's lead guitar and Stephen Goulding's drums suffer the most), and the often mushy audio manages the remarkable feat of making The Rumour, one of the most exciting rock bands of their day, sound just a bit dull. But Parker fights the muddy sound every step of the way, and if his batting average as a songwriter is a shade lower than on *Squeezing Out Sparks*, he certainly offers up his share of A-list material, including the incendiary "Empty Lives," the passionate "The Beating Of Another Heart," and "Endless Night," which features one Bruce Springsteen on backing vocals. Parker's singing is sharp and commanding, and even though the mix lets them down, the Rumour's performances are tough and precise throughout. *The Up Escalator* failed to catch the ears of the mass audience, and Parker would soon part ways with the Rumour, but if this album doesn't present them in the best light, it shows that they could play tough, passionate rock & roll that could survive even the most adverse recording conditions. *—Mark Deming*

Another Grey Area / Mar. 1982 / Razor & Tie ◆◆◆◆◆
Parker begins to make his peace with human imperfection (though he can still be sharp-tongued) and starts to look for love ("It's All Worth Nothing Alone"), backed by a smooth session band and a clean Jack Douglas production, which cool his usual fire without putting it out. *—William Ruhlmann*

The Real Macaw / Jul. 1983 / Razor & Tie ◆◆◆
Graham Parker must have sensed that replacing a backing band as solid as the Rumour wasn't going to be easy after he parted ways with the group, and the session heavyweights assembled for *Another Grey Area* either couldn't or wouldn't summon up the passion and soul Parker's music demanded...and the mushy-sounding production didn't help, either. 1983's *The Real Macaw*, while hardly perfect, was a significant improvement; the musicians, which included former Rumour guitarist Brinsley Schwarz and Squeeze drummer Gilson Lavis, sound tight and snappy throughout, and if the album rarely rocks as hard as you might hope for from Parker, the excellerated tempos of "Just Like A Man" and "Last Couple On The Dance Floor" indicate the band could kick it out when the situation demanded it, and the quieter songs still display a potent if low-key energy. While David Kershenbaum's production is a bit too stereotypically mid-'80s for its own good in spots (especially the periodic use of the Linn drum and those regrettably dated keyboard patches), it packs plenty of presence and gives the songs a bright, listenable surface that serves them well. And Parker had a batch of gems this time out; in the wake of his (then) recent marriage, relationships had apparently been on Parker's mind, and he had plenty to say about the ups, downs, and plain hard work that goes into being in love, ranging from the rueful "Can't Take Love For Granted" and the bitterly self-chastising "Just Like A Man" one of the most openly optimistic tunes he's ever allowed himself to write. After the disappointments of Graham Parker's final album with the Rumour and his first solo album, there was certainly room to wonder if he'd become a spent force, but *The Real*

Macaw made it clear Parker's muse was still on duty, and working hard to put him back on track. —*Mark Deming*

Steady Nerves / Mar. 1985 / Elektra ✦✦✦
Graham Parker moves to his third record label (following stints at Mercury and Arista), forms a backup band called the Shot (again led by guitarist Brinsley Schwarz) and continues alternately arguing with existence ("Break Them Down") and praising his romantic life ["Wake Up (Next To You)"]. —*William Ruhlmann*

The Mona Lisa's Sister / Apr. 1988 / Buddha ✦✦✦
Graham Parker moves to his fourth record label (actually, his fifth, if you count Atlantic, which dumped him before releasing an album) for one of his less inspired efforts. When he sings "Get Started, Start A Fire," he seems to be talking to himself, and when he resorts to covering the old Sam Cooke hit "Cupid," he seems to be grasping for material. —*William Ruhlmann*

Live! Alone in America / Jul. 1989 / RCA ✦✦✦
Graham Parker's second commercially released live album is a solo affair that finds him connecting with his audience and singing a lot of his 1970s favorites. —*William Ruhlmann*

Human Soul / Jan. 1990 / Diablo ✦✦
On *Human Soul*, Graham Parker begins to retreat further into his domestic life, writing an album that includes a side of romantic ruminations and a side of social commentary. With a band that comprises guitarist Brinsley Schwarz, bassist Andrew Bodnar, and Attractions Steve Nieve (keyboards) and Pete Thomas (drums), Parker's music is subtledly diverse, adding elements of worldbeat, reggae, pop, and folk to his R&B-fueled rock & roll; however, most of the impact of the music is lost by the slick, radio-ready production. When Parker stays at home on the first half of *Human Soul*, he makes his most impressive music, from the sultry come-ons of "Call Me Your Doctor" to the reassuring "My Love's Strong." He tends to lose his focus on the latter half of the record, when he writes about subjects that don't directly affect his homelife. Taken in conjunction with the self-conscious musical eclectism, the lyrical stretches make *Human Soul* an intriguing, but flawed, record. —*Stephen Thomas Erlewine*

Struck by Lightning / Feb. 1991 / Diablo ✦✦✦
Struck By Lightning was the culmination of Graham Parker's previous two records, where he increasingly began to chronicle domestic tasks and affairs of the married heart. For such an intimate subject, Parker wisely decided to scale back the musical ambition of *Human Soul* on *Struck By Lightning*, recording a lean, stripped-down album that relies heavily on acoustic guitars. Appropriately, his lyrics were some of the most concise he has written in years, breathing life into tales like "The Kid With the Butterfly Net" and "Wrapping Paper." Parker's music is similarly simple and tuneful, making *Struck By Lightning* his best effort since the early '80s. —*Stephen Thomas Erlewine*

Burning Questions / Jul. 20, 1992 / Diablo ✦✦
After *Struck By Lightning*, Graham Parker was dropped by RCA Records. He moved to Capitol in 1992, releasing another installment in his musical diaries called *Burning Questions*. A more open and polished affair than the previous record, *Burning Questions* concentrates on broader issues than *Struck By Lightning*, yet the scope is similarly scaled-back. And it's clear from "Long Stem Rose," "Oasis," and "Mr. Tender" that his heart is with his home, not with the sputtering rage of "Here It Comes Again" and "Short Memories." —*Stephen Thomas Erlewine*

The Best of Graham Parker 1988-1991 / Sep. 1992 / RCA ✦✦✦
All of the highlights from Graham Parker's brief stint at RCA are here on this single-disc compilation. —*AMG*

Live Alone! Discovering Japan / 1993 / Gadfly ✦✦

● Passion Is No Ordinary Word: The Graham Parker Anthology 1976-1991 / Sep. 21, 1993 / Rhino ✦✦✦✦✦
With its smart song selection and entertaining liner notes, *Passion is No Ordinary Word* is an excellent two-CD anthology covering Parker's entire career, complete with such rarities as "Mercury Poisoning" and "I Want You Back (Alive)" among such signature songs as "White Honey" and "You Can't Be Too Strong." A terrific introduction to Parker's career. —*Stephen Thomas Erlewine*

12 Haunted Episodes / Mar. 14, 1995 / Razor & Tie ✦✦✦

Live from New York, NY / Aug. 20, 1996 / Razor & Tie ✦✦

Acid Bubblegum / Sep. 24, 1996 / Razor & Tie ✦✦✦

The Last Rock & Roll Tour / Apr. 22, 1997 / Razor & Tie ✦✦✦

Not If It Pleases Me: BBC Live 76-77 / May 1998 / Hux ✦✦✦
During the late '70s, Graham Parker and the Rumour were a great live band, kicking out tough versions of Parker's mean-spirited, cynical pub-rock songs. Their sole live album from that period, 1978's *Parkerilla*, didn't prove that to be true, since it was designed as a contract-breaker, not a genuine album. That's what makes the appearance of *Not If It Pleases Me: The BBC Sessions* so welcome: it, along with the similar *Live on the Test*, are testaments to the band's considerable live prowess. *Not If It Pleases Me* draws almost entirely from his first two albums, *Howlin' Wind* and *Heat Treatment*, containing only one number from *Stick to Me* ("New York Shuffle"), plus a cover of "Kansas City." In other words, it contains his absolute best songs from this period, from "White Honey" and "Don't Ask Me Questions" to "Hotel Chambermaid" and "Pouring It All Out." While these versions don't necessarily add anything new to the original studio cuts, they're nevertheless blazing readings of great songs, which is enough to make this an essential addition to any hardcore Parker fan's collection. —*Stephen Thomas Erlewine*

Loose Monkeys, Spare Tracks and Lost Demos / Jan. 20, 1999 / Razor & Tie ✦✦

● Ultimate Collection / Mar. 20, 2001 / Hip-O ✦✦✦✦✦
There is no dearth of Graham Parker compilations, but this is the first single-disc collection to draw from most of the singer/songwriter's label affiliations and thus assemble a comprehensive look at the highlights of his career. Hip-O Records, the reissue arm of the major label Universal Music, has specialized in such multi-label licensing projects in its *Ultimate Collection* series, but compilation producer Mike Ragogna had his work cut out for him with Parker, who began on Mercury (in the U.S. at least), now controlled by Universal, but then went on successively to Arista, Elektra, RCA, Capitol, and his present affiliation, independent label Razor & Tie. Though Ragogna has made generous choices from Parker's early work, including four tracks from his debut LP *Howlin' Wind*, for example, more than half the album consists of tracks licensed from other companies. Following Parker's critical and commercial history, Ragogna has delved deeply into the artist's most celebrated album, *Squeezing Out Sparks*, for four tracks, but has otherwise been highly selective. Parker himself, in the revealing and savvy remarks he makes in Jim Bessman's liner notes, naturally rejects the notion that he did his best work from 1976 to 1979, but the compilation itself seems to confirm that notion, drawing three-quarters of its contents from that period. Parker fans will miss many favorites, but it's hard to argue with this selection of 20 tracks at a running time of more than 76 minutes. If you want more and still don't want to start collecting the individual albums, there's always Rhino's 1993 two-CD, 39-track set *Passion Is No Ordinary Word: The Graham Parker Anthology 1976-1991*, which contains all but one of the titles on this disc and more. As far as single CDs go, however, this is the one to get. —*William Ruhlmann*

Deepcut to Nowhere / Aug. 21, 2001 / Razor & Tie ✦✦✦
Ever since 1990's *Struck By Lightning*, Graham Parker has been retreating into domesticity—and, along with that, his audience became more selective. There were the occasional forays into rock & roll, on *Acid Bubblegum* and on tours where he was accompanied by the Figgs, but he turned into a genuine singer/songwriter by essaying miniature songs about daily travails, current events, and thoughts that have crossed Parker's mind. That's pretty much the case here, but there's a bit of a difference—these are "dark days" as he says on the opening salvo, and there are a number of dark undercurrents running throughout the record. By the end, when he's concluding with "It Takes a Village Idiot" and "Last Stop Is Nowhere," there are strong suggestions that things are not well on the domestic front, stating obliquely but clearly the themes that have been running through much of the uneasy songs on the album. That gives it a different thematic spin than a lot of his '90s records, but the sound is essentially the same and the music, if anything, is more insular than before (appropriate for the inward, pained songs). This means that this is a record that's just for the converted—the ones who will spin the record several times to unlock the meanings of the record, not minding that the songs aren't immediate (or that memorable outside of the lyrics) and that the record sounds very similar to every record he's made in the past ten years. —*Stephen Thomas Erlewine*

Ray Parker, Jr.
b. May 1, 1954, Detroit, MI
Vocals, Guitar / Urban, Dance-Pop
Guitarist/songwriter/producer Ray Parker Jr. was born in Detroit, MI, and started out as a teenaged session guitarist playing on sessions recorded for Holland/Dozier/Holland's Hot Wax and Invictus Records. He'd also play behind the Temptations, Stevie Wonder, the Spinners, Gladys Knight and the Pips, and other Motown acts when they appeared at the Twenty Grand Club. Later, Parker played on Wonder's albums *Talking Book* (1972) and *Innervisions* (1973). Deciding to become a recording artist, Parker got a deal with Arista Records in 1977. Not confident on his singing ability, he put together a band that included vocalist Arnell Carmichael, bassist/singer Jerry Knight, guitarist Charles Fearing, Larry Tolbert, and Darren Carmichael. However, on record, Parker played most, if not all, of the instruments. His first LP, *Raydio*, went gold, peaking at number eight R&B in spring 1978. The LP included the gold, number five R&B single "Jack and Jill" (lead vocal by Jerry Knight), "Is This a Love Thing," and the charting single "Honey I'm Rich." The hits continued with Ray Parker Jr. and Raydio's gold, number four *Rock On*; the gold, number six R&B *Two Places at the Same Time* from spring 1980; and the number one gold record *A Woman Needs Love* from 1981. Then, as Ray Parker Jr., *The Other Woman* held the number one R&B, number 11 pop spot in spring 1982. One of Parker's biggest hits and best loved songs, "Ghostbusters," parked at the number one R&B spot for two weeks and the number one pop for three weeks on Billboard's charts in summer 1984. —*Ed Hogan*

● Greatest Hits / 1982 / Arista ✦✦✦✦✦
It contains "The Other Woman," among his other hits, recorded both as a solo act and with Raydio. —*Dan Heilman*

Robert Parker
b. Oct. 14, 1930, Crescent City, LA
Vocals, Saxophone / Pop-Soul, R&B, Soul
Parker's dance raver "Barefootin'" was one of the biggest hits to come out of New Orleans during the mid-'60s. Parker played sessions as a saxophonist back in 1949 with the legendary pianist Professor Longhair, and his 1959 solo debut for Ron, "All Night Long," was a scorching two-part instrumental. But Parker's under-utilized vocal talents suddenly emerged in 1966, when his highly infectious "Barefootin'" became a giant hit on tiny Nola. Only one other Parker single, "Tip Toe," charted the next year, but Parker remains a popular attraction in his hometown. —*Bill Dahl*

● Barefootin' / 1966 / Collectables ✦✦✦✦✦
Originally issued in 1987 on vinyl by England's Charly, this collection includes Parker's

main claim to fame, the 1966 R&B and pop dance smash "Barefootin'"; its flip side, "Let's Go Baby (Where the Action Is)"; both sides of a 1969 single Parker cut for Silver Fox; and a number of '70s recordings the erstwhile sax player waxed for Sansu Enterprises. Much of the CD, including the title cut, is infectious New Orleans R&B of a high caliber, but other tracks find Parker attempting to cut mainstream funk and disco, usually with less-than-inspiring results. If possible, find the Charly release, because Collectables, in their typically shoddy manner, do not bother to provide songwriting credits, let alone track credits or liner notes. A good policy is to buy Collectables only if there is no other anthology of the same material issued anywhere else in the world, no matter what the price difference. *—Rob Bowman*

Van Dyke Parks

b. Jan. 3, 1941

Producer, Vocals, Keyboards, Arranger, Accordion, Songwriter, Piano, Synthesizer / Baroque Pop, Experimental Rock, Experimental, Singer/Songwriter

Composer, arranger, producer, and musician Van Dyke Parks has had a varied career in popular music without ever getting near the popular mainstream. Parks worked as a songwriter in the early '60s and became a producer, handling such mid-'60s acts as Harper's Bizarre. He was enlisted by Beach Boy Brian Wilson to write lyrics for what turned out to be an abortive album project called *Smile* (now one of the legendary lost albums of the '60s), resulting in such songs as the hit "Heroes and Villains." Parks released his own album, the eclectic *Song Cycle*, to critical acclaim and minimal sales in 1968. He then did session work with a variety of artists, not releasing his second album, *Discover America*, which revealed his immersion in Trinidadian music, until 1972. *Clang of the Yankee Reaper*, another eclectic collection, followed in 1976. But Parks maintained his "day job"—film work on scores by Ry Cooder and others, writing and arranging for Shelley Duvall's children's TV series, and other pursuits. Finally, in 1984, came the brilliant *Jump!*, a concept album based on the Uncle Remus tales of Joel Chandler Harris. It was followed in 1989 by *Tokyo Rose*, which concerned the state of American-Japanese relations. *— William Ruhlmann*

● **Song Cycle** / 1968 / Warner Brothers ✦✦✦✦✦

Van Dyke Parks moved on from the Beach Boys' abortive *Smile* sessions to record his own solo debut, *Song Cycle*, an audacious and occasionally brilliant attempt to mount a fully orchestrated, classically minded work within the context of contemporary pop. As indicated by its title, *Song Cycle* is a thematically coherent work, one which attempts to embrace the breadth of American popular music; bluegrass, ragtime, showtunes—nothing escapes Parks' radar, and the sheer eclecticism and individualism of his work is remarkable. Opening with "Vine Street," authored by Randy Newman (another pop composer with serious classical aspirations), the album is both forward-thinking and backwards-minded, a collision of bygone musical styles with the progressive sensibilities of the late 1960s; while occasionally overambitious and at times insufferably coy, it's nevertheless a one-of-a-kind record, the product of true inspiration. *—Jason Ankeny*

Discover America / 1972 / Warner Brothers ✦✦✦✦✦

Parks turns to the music of Trinidad here, especially as it was heard in the '40s, which means tributes to "Bing Crosby" and "The Four Mills Bros.," not to mention "G-Man Hoover" and "FDR in Trinidad," played on steel drums and other indigenous instruments. A charming, idiosyncratic genre exercise. *— William Ruhlmann*

The Clang of the Yankee Reaper / May 1976 / Warner Brothers ✦✦✦

Expanding from the Caribbean approach he took with *Discover America*, Van Dyke Parks explores more arcane Americana on an album that ranges from New Orleans to the islands to the classics. Only the title track bears a co-composing credit for the artist, but Parks' exuberant, eclectic musical personality is the unifying force in a collection of music that varies from the Sandpipers' "Another Dream" to Pachelbel's "Canon in D." *— William Ruhlmann*

Jump! / Feb. 1984 / Warner Brothers ✦✦✦✦✦

An exhilarating song cycle based on the Uncle Remus tales. It incorporates the styles of Stephen Foster, ragtime, '30s movie-soundtrack music, you name it, all in the service of playful, touching lyrics that correspond to the source material, without actually aping it. A delight from start to finish. *— William Ruhlmann*

Tokyo Rose / Jul. 1989 / Warner Brothers ✦✦✦

Given Van Dyke Parks' well-documented fascination with the various and sundry collision points of American musical culture with the rest of the world, he was as good a candidate as any to make a concept album about the often uneasy relationship between the United States and Japan, and he approached the subject on his fifth album, 1989's *Tokyo Rose*. *Tokyo Rose* concerns itself with America's mingled condescension, infatuation, and contempt toward Japan, as well as Japan's often skewed perception of America and it's cultural icons—Uncle Sam woos the Dragon Lady, Japan learns to love baseball, and everyone tries to figure out where the cowboys came from. Parks' songs dip satiric arrows into sweet but poisoned wit; the lyrics are never less than amusing (even when they're too wordy and self-consciously clever, which is often), and the lush and elaborate orchestrations are dotted with both "authentic" Japanese themes and well-turned cliches of both Asian and American musical figures. *Tokyo Rose* often sounds like the original cast album to some eccentric Broadway musical about footloose and pretentious Ugly Americans vacationing in the Pacific Rim, especially since Parks hands over a few of his lead vocals to other singers (including former Three Dog Night belter Danny Hutton), but even though Parks' slightly precious tenor rarely sounds like the perfect instrument for this stuff, he seems to fit the songs better than anyone else on board. *Toyko Rose* occasionally gets lost in its own ambitions, and it's sometimes a bit too smart for its own good, but there are precious few people in the American popular musical scene who could tackle this sort of material and make it work so well; if it's not quite a masterpiece, it's at least an experiment that works. *—Mark Deming*

Moonlighting: Live at the Ash Grove / Feb. 10, 1998 / Warner Brothers ✦✦✦✦

Since Van Dyke Parks has never released a greatest hits album (okay, he's never had any hits) in the U.S., this long-overdue concert album, which draws on material from his studio recordings dating back to 1968's *Song Cycle*, is a welcome sampler of his stunning, if small, body of work from "The All Golden" (*Song Cycle*) to "Orange Crate Art" (the title track from his duet album with Brian Wilson). The melodic invention and masterful mixing of styles confirm Parks's hidden status as one of the great American composers, a status that has gone unremarked only because of his reclusiveness and tendency to operate only on the margins of the Los Angeles pop scene. He is a miniaturist, to be sure, and nothing if not quirky. His heavily—and not always coherently—edited stage remarks call to mind Truman Capote, and his reedy, earnest singing is only adequate. But the music is both steeped in tradition and wholly original, and it's a delight to listen to. *— William Ruhlmann*

Parliament

f. 1970, Detroit, MI, **db.** 1980

R&B, Funk, Soul

Inspired by Motown's assembly-line of sound, George Clinton gradually assembled a collective of over 50 musicians and recorded the ensemble during the '70s both as Parliament and Funkadelic. While Funkadelic pursued band-format psychedelic rock, Parliament engaged in a funk free-for-all, blending influences from the godfathers (James Brown and Sly Stone) with freaky costumes and themes inspired by '60s acid culture and science fiction. From its 1970 inception until Clinton's dissolving of Parliament in 1980, the band hit the R&B Top Ten several times but truly excelled in two other areas: large-selling, effective album statements and the most dazzling, extravagant live show in the business. In an era when Philly soul continued the slick sounds of establishment-approved R&B, Parliament scared off more white listeners than it courted. *—John Bush*

Osmium / 1970 / Invictus ✦✦✦

The first Parliament album as such was a mixed-up mess of an affair—but would anyone expect anything less? The overall sound is much more Funkadelic than later Parliament, if with a somewhat more accessible feel. Things get going with an appropriately leering start, thanks to "I Call My Baby Pussycat," which makes something like "What's New, Pussycat?" seem like innocent, chaste conversation. After a stripped-down start, things explode into a full-on funk strut with heavy-duty guitar and slamming drums setting the way, while the singers sound like they're tripping without losing the soul—sudden music dropouts, vocal cut-ins, volume level tweaks, and more add to the off-kilter feeling. *Osmium*'s sound progresses from there—it's funk's fire combined with a studio freedom that feels like a blueprint for the future. Bernie Worrell's keyboard abilities are already clear, whether he's trying for hotel lounge jams or full freakiness; similarly, Eddie Hazel is clearly finding his own epic stoned zone to peel out some amazing solos at the drop of a hat. As for the subject matter and end results—who else but this crew could have come up with the trash-talking, yodeling twang of "Little Ol' Country Boy" in 1970 and still made it funky with all the steel guitar? Other fun times include the piano and vocal-into-full-band goofy romantic romp of "My Automobile" and "Funky Woman," where over a heavy groove (and goofy Worrell break) the titular character lives with the consequence of her stank: "She hung them in the air/The air said this ain't fair!" Amidst all the nuttiness, there are some perhaps surprising depths—consider "Oh Lord, Why Lord/Prayer," which might almost be too pretty for its own good (Worrell's harpsichord almost verges on the sickly sweet) but still has some lovely gospel choir singing and heartfelt lyrics. *—Ned Raggett*

Up for the Down Stroke / 1974 / Casablanca ✦✦✦✦

Kicking off with one of prime funk's purest distillations—the outrageously great title track, with a perfect party chorus line and uncredited horns (presumably the Horny Horns were involved somehow) adding to the monster beat and bass—*Up for the Down Stroke* finds Parliament in rude good health. As was more or less the case through the '70s, Parliament took a slightly more listener-friendly turn here than they did as Funkadelic, but often it's a difference by degrees. Just listening to some of Bernie Worrell's insane keyboard parts or Bootsy Collins' bass work here is enough to wake the dead. As always, Worrell in particular can suddenly surprise with his delicacy—the soft, understated flow of "I Just Got Back" may have lyrics that could be sung by Jon Anderson, at least at points, but the piano lines have subtle, dreamy grace, the antithesis of Rick Wakeman's masturbations. For that matter, Peter Chase's whistles are downright delightful, goofy, and sweet all at once. Slightly more oddball is "All Your Goodies Are Gone," which has a bit more upfront bite and some downright strange lyrics, delivered with a stoned, breathless tone and backed by unearthly choir arrangements. Eddie Hazel is still listed as present and contributing, though unfortunately not for long after, with Ron Bykowski, Gary Shider, and William Nelson also chipping in as needed. Hazel co-writes two of the songs; it's a pity "The Goose" runs out of steam toward the midpoint of its nine minutes, but it makes for pleasant background music if not Parliament at its unfettered best. In the meantime, Clinton and various familiar voices like Fuzzy Haskins and Grady Thomas keep the weird wigginess of the lyrics flowing. In a nod to the group's past, "(I Wanna) Testify," here simply called "Testify," gets a 1974-era work over. *—Ned Raggett*

Chocolate City / 1975 / Casablanca ✦✦✦✦

"Chocolate City" stands out as a trademark P-Funk moment, with it's languid meandering, rich synth washes, and spoken-word vocals—a perfect way to jump start the album. From there, the album kicks into high gear, moving from one up-tempo R&B song to the next, every song driven by Bootsy's slippery bass riffs and most showered with harmonious vocal choruses. Every song has its quirks, with "Let Me Be" being the only song that gets too unconventional for its own good, featuring only synth, piano, and vocals. Most of the other songs are fairly equal, none being lackluster and none being too noteworthy, with the exception of "Together"; this song's soulful chorus drifts momentarily away from the funk for a moment, offering one of the album's most beautiful moments. For the most part, though, this isn't a beautiful album—it's fairly grimy with its funk-infused R&B thumping and worming relentlessly, never taking too much time to worry about catchy hooks. Yet for as understated as this stubborn focus is, never venturing too far into rock, disco, or jamming territory, it's an effective focus, making *Chocolate City* a slight improvement from *Up for the Down Stroke*. There's something rewarding about how consistent and focused this album is, probably because of its amazing lineup featuring Bootsy Collins, Bernie Worrel, and Eddie Hazel. As such, *Chocolate City* won't disappoint those looking for the R&B side of the P-Funk library. *—Jason Birchmeier*

Clones of Dr. Funkenstein / 1976 / Casablanca ♦♦♦♦♦

Come 1976, and Parliament got up to its usual tricks in that particular incarnation—right down to opening backwards-masked vocal weirdness plus sci-fi scenarios in the "Prelude," where "funk is its own reward." With Bernie Worrell and Fred Wesley splitting the horn arrangements and Clinton and Bootsy Collins taking care of the rest, the result is a concept album of sorts you can dance to. The clones get up and do their thing throughout, and if it's not *The Wall*, then that's all to its benefit. The immediate downside of *Clones* is that it's a fairly one-note record—every groove can just about be exchanged for any other one, unlike the wider variety apparent on other releases. Given Clinton and company's sheer work rate, something likely had to give and this is one of the stress points. There are a couple of stronger songs—"I've Been Watching You (Move Your Sexy Body)" is classic slow jam territory. Not exactly Barry White, but hearing Parliament tone it down just enough pays off, especially with Worrell's drowsy, sensuous horn charts. "Funkin' for Fun," meanwhile, brings the album to a strong, lively end, with just enough in the call-and-response vocals and horns to spark some extra energy into the proceedings. As is the case with most mid- to late-'70s Parliament, things may not be as deep as what was done as Funkadelic, but only those who always explicitly value lyrical worth have any cause to complain. Listening to the silly squeals and burbles on "Dr. Funkenstein" itself is pure fun with sound, while the good doctor's speech is scientific craziness. As one voice says out of nowhere, "Kiss me on my ego!" Special bonus—the utterly goofball cover photo, one of P-Funk's best. *—Ned Raggett*

★ **Mothership Connection** / 1976 / Casablanca ♦♦♦♦♦

The addition of ex-JB's Fred Wesley and Maceo Parker to the Parliament roster on *Mothership Connection* elevated an already mind-blowing band into the best funk band of the '70s, arguably the best funk band ever. With these two funk veterans supplying the horns, Clinton had everything he could ask for in his already stellar group. The opening song, "P-Funk (Wants to Get Funked Up)," harkened back to the opening title track from Parliament's previous album, *Chocolate City*, laying down a languid synth aura for a spoken-word intro. When "P-Funk (Wants to Get Funked Up)" steps into second gear though, bringing in Bootsy's bass, Wesley's horn, Worrell's piano, and a chorus of vocalists, it's fairly evident just how large a step forward *Mothership Connection* is from the conventional R&B roots of *Chocolate City* and *Up for the Down Stroke*. The second song, "Mothership Connection (Star Child)," makes the differentiation glaringly evident, most noticeably when the song enters the cosmic, proto-hip-hop "swing down sweet chariot" bridge with its accompanying melody from beyond. The funk doesn't stop there though, with the remaining five songs keeping the tempo laden with dense interweaving rhythms, peaking on "Give Up the Funk (Tear the Roof Off the Sucker)." In the end, there's no questioning this album's impact, one that is still being felt via rap-induced aftershocks. In addition to its contemporary impact and continued longevity, the album was a massive success for Clinton and company upon its release in 1975, elevating the P-Funk collective to unparalleled heights in terms of audience. Some Parliament albums may be flawless, and others may be innovative, but this is the P-Funk zenith in more ways than one, perfect as well as perennial. *—Jason Birchmeier*

☆ **Funkentelechy Vs. the Placebo Syndrome** / 1977 / Casablanca ♦♦♦♦♦

Parliament simply poured it on for this amazing album, clearly one of its all-time best. At least one band named itself after a lyric—Urge Overkill, taken from the song "Funkentelechy" itself—while the amount of times this album has been sampled for the music is uncountable. Besides having an absolutely wonderful name, it contained at least three of the finest Parliament tunes ever, including arguably its signature song. "Flash Light," which closes *Funkentelechy* on a riotous high, has it all—a brilliant fake ending, instant singalong value, a synth-bass line to kill for from Bernie Worrell, and so much more. As the album ends, so too does it begin, with a stone-cold classic—"Bop Gun (Endangered Species)." Starting with a brisk little guitar figure and beat, it turns into an instant party on all fronts, with great lead vocals and an addictive chorus, the Horny Horns and company hitting the grooves and blasting hard. Worrell's laser noises and shimmering keyboard leads and Cordell Mosson's monster bass squelches send everything all that much more over the top. Another song title says it all—"Sir Nose D'Voidoffunk (Pay Attention—B3M)." Treated with vocoders to an absurd degree, Sir Nose became the legendary enemy of funk, specifically the Starchild, on many a P-Funk recording (that's the two of them on the hilarious cover, the Starchild himself operating the Bop Gun). The throwaway lines in this song are almost legendary in and of themselves, while the music itself is a great slow build and burn rhythm that piles more on as it goes, with singers, horns, and more taking it to a climax. "Funkentelechy" and "The Placebo Syndrome" both have plenty of goodness as well, while "Wizards of Finance" is an amusing retro diversion, helping make *Funkentelechy* the highlight it is. *—Ned Raggett*

Live: P-Funk Earth Tour / 1977 / Casablanca ♦♦♦♦

As amazing as most of the '70s P-Funk albums are, the group was arguably a better live act than a studio act. Once the aggregation's patience and ambition wore thin with studio albums in the late '70s, Clinton was able to sustain his career merely on the merits of live performances, cult-like experiences that were rivaled only by the Grateful Dead's in terms of legacy. Unfortunately, unlike the Dead, Clinton's ensemble never went to excessive lengths to preserve its shows. *Live: P-Funk Earth Tour* stands as the band's only live album from the '70s, when it was at its peak (not counting bootlegs or posthumous imports). To be quite honest, there couldn't have been a better performance chosen for release; this is Parliament at its prime. Recorded in 1977 (the band's zenith) during the infamous "landing of the mothership" tour (its most extravagant), with the Bootsy-Worrell-Wesly-Parker-Hazel-Shider-Hampton lineup (its most talented), and a California audience (its most exuberant), this is almost a perfect document. Unfortunately, for the most part the album doesn't include any Funkadelic material, and at 70 minutes it's a bit brief relative to the band's shows, not leaving much room for extended jams. However, the album compensates by including a 15-minute version of "Dr. Funkenstein" that alludes to the group's potential to turn any song into an epic jam session, and also by including "Landing (Of the Holy Mothership)," a studio-produced three-minute interlude included for conceptual reasons but ultimately functioning better as a P-Funk montage (foreshadowing rap's excessive sampling). Over the years, other live P-Funk recordings have surfaced, but none are as widely available as this one, and none are as succinct. It's all the live P-Funk most fans will need. *—Jason Birchmeier*

Motor Booty Affair / 1978 / Casablanca ♦♦♦♦♦

By this point Parliament was one of the most accomplished and intelligent bands in music. With albums like *Mothership Connection* and *The Clones of Dr. Funkenstein*, George Clinton's druggy and patently eccentric humor often obscured the enviable musicianship throughout. *Motor Booty Affair* is no doubt another classic album and the perfect follow-up to 1977's *Funkentelechy Vs. the Placebo Syndrome*. On *Motor Booty Affair*, Clinton decides to yuck it up more with a great underwater concept and a few of his stronger alter egos, including the rhythmically challenged Sir Nose D' Void of Funk and his friend Rumpofsteelskin. The deft and airy "Mr. Wiggles" has Clinton taking on the persona of Wiggles, the "DJ of the affair" as he says: "Mr. Wiggles here on roller skates and a yo-yo/ Acting a fool." The hypnotic "Rumpofsteelskin" has a great bass line and inventive and infectious background vocals. The closest thing to a ballad here is the astrologically savvy "(You're a Fish and I'm A) Water Sign." The well-produced "Aqua Boogie (A Psychoalphadiscobetabioaquadoloop)" with its handclaps and high-pitched bass lines basically set the standards for the sound of R&B in the coming decade. The sleeper of the album, "One of Those Funky Things," is filled with timbales, congas, and Bernie Worrell's great synth signatures. The last track, "Deep," has great, understated riffs from the Horny Horns. Although many Parliament efforts can't be fully appreciated unless the whole catalogue is nearby, *Motor Booty Affair* stands on its own merits and sustains the laugh throughout. *—Jason Elias*

Gloryhallastoopid / 1979 / Casablanca ♦♦♦

The flaws that kept *Motor Booty Affair* from being in the same league as *Mothership Connection*—that league being near perfection, from beginning to end—became alarmingly more prevalent on *Gloryhallastoopid*. By the time this album was put together in 1979, the classic P-Funk lineup of Bernie Worrell, Bootsy Collins, Fred Wesley, and Maceo Parker had splintered, and when Clinton did manage to get them into the studio, it was never as a unit. This suddenly revolving lineup of second-rate studio musicians in place of a cohesive band plagues this album more than a lack of enthusiasm on Clinton's part or half-hearted songwriting, though those two problems do play a role in this album's failure. Besides "Big Bang Theory" and "Theme From the Black Hole," nothing here is even remotely labored. Simple songs such as "The Freeze" and "Party People" sound as if they were written and recorded in a single session—they're *that* linear and shallow. Furthermore, Clinton insists on dragging these two songs, in particular, out to epic lengths, which is alarmingly futile since the songs never develop or even meander. If you are willing to wade through all the filler on this album, there are two splendid songs here, the aforementioned "Big Bang Theory" and "Theme From the Black Hole" (though "May We Bang You?" has some worthwhile melodies, as well). These two songs follow-up "Aqua Boogie" as obvious moments of funk genius among lackluster filler. But it might be a good idea to seek these songs out on a best-of compilation—nothing else here is worth bothering with. Nowhere else will you find the collective's decline more evident, and it slithers awfully close to brainless disco at times, further affirming its status as a failure. *—Jason Birchmeier*

Trombipulation / 1980 / Casablanca ♦♦

☆ **Tear the Roof Off 1974-1980** / May 18, 1993 / Casablanca ♦♦♦♦♦

The Best of Parliament: Give Up the Funk may capture the band's bare essentials, but given the band's penchant for stretching out on extended jams (which included some of their best songs), it's hard to get anything beyond the most basic overview of their work on just one disc. Unless you're a very casual fan, a much better bet is the double-disc *Tear the Roof Off 1974-1980*, whose 25 tracks add plenty of much-needed detail behind the best-known and most-sampled hits. Slightly more party-oriented than Funkadelic, Parliament created the wildest atmosphere of all the projects in the George Clinton oeuvre, full of loopy humor and way-out sci-fi concepts. Parliament was also more of a singles act than the frequently album-oriented Funkadelic, and while Parliament produced its share of classic albums, their material doesn't lose any of its potency when boiled down into compilation form. What's more, *Tear the Roof Off* contains several full-length 12" mixes that were never previously available on CD. These are some of the most unstoppable, widely imitated grooves of all time, and they still carry the same impact today, making *Tear the Roof Off* an obvious necessity. *—Steve Huey*

Dope Dogs / 1995 / Hot Hands ♦♦♦

George Clinton's most focused album of the '90s slams a barrel of P-Funk down your throat without even giving you the opportunity to swallow. The P-Funk All Stars get a co-credit on this one, bouncing and funking alongside their leader nearly every step of the way. In typical Clinton fashion, *Dope Dogs* is all over the place: funk, R&B, hip-hop and ass-busting beats cover most of the ground. It all sticks together, however, on a loose-grooved concept about dogs (hasn't most of Clinton's post-"Atomic Dog" stuff been leading to this anyway?), the government and drugs, and how they're tied together in one huge nationwide conspiracy (it makes even less sense on record than it does here). But Clinton always has been about the funk of the matter, and *Dope Dogs* clearly has that, and its tight astro-rhythms, in the right place. *—Michael Gallucci*

★ **The Best of Parliament: Give Up the Funk** / Jun. 6, 1995 / Mercury Funk Essentials ♦♦♦♦♦

To some, boiling Parliament's legacy down to a single-disc collection is the equivalent of heresy, since most fans treat each album as an individual work of art. Still, there is no denying that Parliament was an untouchable singles act, recording some of the greatest soul/funk singles of the '70s. For those listeners that just want an introduction, or only need the hits, *The Best of Parliament: Give Up the Funk* is the ideal choice. A more complete and logical collection than the previous *Greatest Hits (The Bomb)*, *The Best of Parliament* supplies all of the great group's greatest hits, from "Up for the Down Stroke" and "Tear the Roof off the Sucker" to "Flash Light" and "Aqua Boogie." For those that can only handle the funk in moderation, there is no better collection. *—Leo Stanley*

20th Century Masters—The Millennium Collection: The Best of Parliament / Jan. 25, 2000 / Mercury ♦♦♦♦

Choosing between the many Parliament best-ofs isn't an easy task; in fact, the single-disc collections are all so similar that it's barely even worth belaboring the task. But if you do want to labor a bit in hopes of getting the absolute perfect single-disc best-of, this is one of your best options. First of all, above anything, skip *Greatest Hits (The Bomb)*; there isn't anything wrong with its choices—they're perfect—but that album runs only 55 minutes, wasting invaluable CD space. That's where this collection becomes a better choice, making the most of its length by adding "Testify," "Agony of Defeet," and full-length versions of songs such as "Flashlight." You could argue, of course, that *The Best of Parliament: Give Up the Funk* is an even better collection than *20th Century Masters*, which it is (not having "Testify," but instead offering "Let's Play House," "Ride On," "Theme From the Black Hole," and "Do That Stuff"), but that's a near-futile argument since they are practically facsimiles of one another. If you can find *The Best of Parliament*, get it over this album; it's a better choice. But don't go out of your way to find that album, because *20th Century Masters* is a fine best-of, filled with nothing but Parliament anthems. There honestly aren't any weak moments here, with the possible exception of "Agony of Defeet," a latter-day song by the group that would have been better off replaced. Still, that's being highly critical. This is a perfect starting point; pick it up and chances are that either you'll struggle to stomach Parliament's funk or, more likely, find yourself searching out the group's full-lengths. *—Jason Birchmeier*

Alan Parsons

Engineer, Producer, Keyboards / Album Rock, Pop/Rock, Prog-Rock/Art Rock, Soft Rock

As indicated by its name, the Alan Parsons Project was not a band so much as a concept overseen by the titular Parsons, a successful producer and engineer who first garnered significant industry exposure via his work on the Beatles' 1969 masterpiece *Abbey Road* before solidifying his reputation by working on Pink Floyd's *Dark Side of the Moon*. Influenced by his work on Al Stewart's concept album *Time Passages*, Parsons decided to begin creating his own thematic records; along with songwriter Eric Woolfson, he soon founded the Alan Parsons Project. Although Parsons played keyboards and infrequently sang on his records, the Project was designed primarily as a forum for a revolving collection of vocalists and session players to interpret and perform Parsons and Woolfson's conceptually-linked, lushly-synthesized music. The Project debuted in 1975 with *Tales of Mystery and Imagination*, and with 1980's *The Turn of a Friendly Card*, a meditation on gambling, Parsons scored a Top 20 hit, "Games People Play"; 1982's *Eye in the Sky*, was their most successful effort, and notched a Top Three hit with its title track. *—Jason Ankeny*

Tales of Mystery and Imagination / 1975 / Mercury ♦♦♦♦♦

Tales of Mystery and Imagination is an extremely mesmerizing aural journey through some of Edgar Allan Poe's most renowned works. With the use of synthesizers, drums, guitar, and even a glockenspiel, Parsons' shivering effects make way for an eerie excursion into Poe's well-known classics. The instrumental "Dream Within a Dream" has Orson Welles narrating in front of this wispy collaboration of guitars and keyboards. The EMI vocoder is used throughout "The Raven" with the Westminister City School Boys Choir mixed in to add a distinct flair to it's chamber-like sound. Parsons' expertise surrounds this album, from the slyness that prevails in "(The System Of) Doctor Tarr and Professor Feather" to the bodeful thumping of the drums that imitate a heartbeat on "The Tell-Tale Heart." "The Fall of the House of Usher" is a lengthy but dazzling array of musicianship that keeps the album's persona in tact, while enabling the listener to submerge into it's frightening atmosphere. With vocalists Terry Sylvester, John Miles, and Eric Woolfson stretched across each track, this variety of different singing styles adds color and design to the album's air. Without any underlying theme to be pondered upon, Alan Parsons instead paints a vivid picture of one of the most alluring literary figures in history by musically reciting his most famous works in expert fashion. *—Mike DeGagne*

● **I Robot** / Jun. 1977 / Arista ♦♦♦♦♦

With its title originating from an Isaac Asimov novel, *I Robot*'s main concept is one that deals heavily in the field of science fiction. The album's idea is based around Parsons' concern with the onslaught of machinery and its inevitable takeover of man, both in a physical sense and a spiritual one. As one of the Alan Parsons Project's strongest efforts, its wise blend of keyboard-dominated instrumentals partnered with the warmth of the vocals during the lyrical songs emblazons the man-vs.-machine idea. The mechanical-sounding title track is the opening song, setting the tone for the album's futuristic motif. Man's regret for his mechanical creations sweeps through "I Wouldn't Want to Be Like You," with a passionate Lenny Zakatek singing lead. The human being's rebellious nature is the theme behind "Breakdown," sung by ex-Hollies member Allan Clarke, while the strength of the human will is the focal point of "Don't Let It Show," a heartening ballad performed by Dave Townsend. Ending with the instrumental "Genesis Ch. 1 V. 32," the promising tempo and air of this song invoke hope for all mankind. As a final product, *I Robot* leaves the listener with much to contemplate, which is its purpose, but also presents a collage of well-crafted songs that aren't easily forgotten. This album still remains one of this band's most accomplished pieces. *—Mike DeGagne*

Pyramid / Jun. 1978 / Arista ♦♦♦

Even with six different vocalists lending their talents to the album, *Pyramid* still remains an average bit of material from The Alan Parsons Project. Not only does the album's theme evolve around the mystique of the pyramid, but it also touches on man's fascination with superstition and its powers. The instrumental "Voyager" opens things up, and it's provocative style sets the tone for the album's supernatural mood. The bright sounding "What Goes Up" is one of the highlights here, as is "The Eagle Will Rise Again," sung by Colin Blunstone. The anxiety-ridden "Pyramania" enhances the album's concept the best, accompanied by some excitable keyboard playing and a friendly middle. The lesson-learning "Can't Take It With You" teaches that our souls are our most important asset, in typical Parsons-type charm. While not a stellar album, *Pyramid* completes the task of musically explaining its concept. Its short but slightly compelling nature grows after a few listens, but the album itself isn't a necessity. *—Mike DeGagne*

Eve / Sep. 1979 / Arista ♦♦

The Turn of a Friendly Card / Nov. 1980 / Arista ♦♦♦♦♦

With two of the Alan Parsons Project's best songs, the lovely ballad "Time" and the wavy-sounding "Games People Play," *The Turn of a Friendly Card* remains one of this group's most enjoyable albums. Parsons' idea, the subject of the album's six tracks, centers around the age-old temptation of gambling and its stranglehold on the human psyche. On "Games People Play," vocalist Lenny Zakatek sounds compelling and focused, giving the song a seriousness that aids in realization of the album's concept. With "Time," it is Eric Woolfson who carries this luxurious-sounding ode to life's passing to a place above and beyond any of this band's other slower material. The breakdown of human willpower and our greedy tendencies are highlighted in the last track, entitled "The Turn of a Friendly Card," which is broken into five separate parts. "Snake Eyes," sung by Chris Rainbow, is the most compelling of the five pieces, and ties together the whole of the recording. As in every Parsons album, an instrumental is included, in this case an interesting number aptly titled "The Gold Bug." Like most of the band's instrumentals, its flow and rhythm simulate the overall tempo and concept of the album, acting as a welcome interlude. Although short, *The Turn of a Friendly Card* is to the point and doesn't let down when it comes to carrying out its idea. *—Mike DeGagne*

Eye in the Sky / Jun. 1982 / Arista ♦♦♦♦♦

The fusion of Parsons' thematic intentions and exquisitely textured music comes to fruition on 1982's *Eye in the Sky*. On no other album by this group is there such a tight amalgamation of music, lyrics, and ideas, all combining to create songs that are accessible to a vast audience. Peaking at number three on Billboard's Top 40, "Eye in the Sky" is a prime example of a fabulous rock song, highlighted by the harmonic beauty of Eric Woolfson. The album deals with the futuristic outlook of how our lives will be constantly monitored by "Big Brother" and the manner in which man's right for freedom and choice may someday be thwarted by the government, or the powers that be. Aside from Parsons' intriguing concept, the individual songs serve a dual purpose by carrying out the album's message while at the same being perfect examples of well-crafted rock. The up-and-down flow of the instrumental "Sirius" is astonishing, and is used wisely as the opening track. "Mammagamma" is another instrumental that brandishes the group's trademarked mysteriousness, wrapped in an ominous science fiction-type glow. "Psychobabble" is a cerebral rock song that best represents the album's concept, while the softness of "Old and Wise" sums up the threatening result that may someday evolve, with a hint of promise for a favorable outcome. With a powdery feel and pristine sound, *Eye in the Sky* is worthy of both amiable songs and conceptual substance, something not found on all of the Alan Parsons Project's albums. *—Mike DeGagne*

The Best of the Alan Parsons Project / 1983 / Arista ♦♦♦♦♦

The 12 tracks that appear on *The Best of the Alan Parsons Project* include some of their greatest singles, like "I Wouldn't Want to Be Like You" from 1977's *I Robot* and the inducing "Games People Play" off of *The Turn of a Friendly Card*. Even though these songs are splendid all by themselves, they seem to lose their conceptual weight when taken away from their original albums. As singles, they do act as a fine representation of how The Alan Parsons Project's music sounds and conveys its mysterious air, but even with a dozen singles on this album there's just too much of their other worthy material that is sadly left off. Present is their biggest single and most alluring piece, "Eye in the Sky," from the album of the same name, and the entrancing "Time" from *Turn of a Friendly Card*. "Pyramania" and "You Don't Believe," representing both *Pyramid* and *Ammonia Avenue*, are also included, as are some of their finest ballads with "Old and Wise" and "Don't Let

It Show." "Lucifer" is the only instrumental on the collection, but is also one of their most sophisticated. As a short reference to this group's earlier material, *The Best of the Alan Parsons Project* offers some of their greatest work, but it's too short to really serve as a true best-of. Each individual album should be listened to in order to grasp the entirety of Parsons' themes. *The Best of the Alan Parsons Project, Vol. 2* should be partnered with *Volume 1* for a more concise set. *—Mike DeGagne*

Ammonia Avenue / Feb. 1984 / Arista ♦♦♦
One of the most interesting aspects about the Alan Parsons Project is the band's ability to forge a main theme with each of its songs, while at the same time sounding extremely sharp and polished. Much of this formula is used in *Ammonia Avenue*, only this time the songs rise above Parsons' overall message due to the sheer beauty of the lyrics partnered with the luster of the instruments. The album touches upon how the lines of communication between people are diminishing, and how we as a society grow more spiritually isolated and antisocial. But aside from the philosophical concepts prevalent in the lyrics, it is the music on this album that comes to the forefront. The enchanting saxophone of Mel Collins on "Don't Answer Me" adds to its lonely atmosphere, while the briskness of Eric Woolfson's wording throughout "Prime Time" makes it one of the Project's best singles. On "You Don't Believe," the seriousness of the lyrics works well with the song's energetic pace. The subtlety of the ballad comes to life on the elegant "Since the Last Goodbye," which focuses on a failed attempt at a relationship. With *Ammonia Avenue*, the sum of the parts is greater than the whole product, which can't be said for all of the Alan Parsons Project's albums. Vocalists Eric Woolfson, Chris Rainbow, Lenny Zakatek, and Colin Blunstone equally shine, placing their talents above and beyond the album's main idea. *—Mike DeGagne*

Vulture Culture / Mar. 1985 / Arista ♦♦

Stereotomy / Nov. 1985 / Arista ♦♦

Gaudi / 1987 / Arista ♦♦

The Best of the Alan Parsons Project, Vol. 2 / 1988 / Arista ♦♦♦♦♦
The Best of the Alan Parsons Project, Vol. 2 typically picks up where its predecessor left off. With 11 tracks covering seven albums, including *Gaudi*, *Stereotomy*, and *Vulture Culture*, the songs here are a tad weaker than those on the first collection, since some of the albums that these songs originate from were not of this band's finest caliber. The highlights here include both "Prime Time" and "Don't Answer Me" from *Ammonia Avenue*, and the provocative instrumental "I Robot," the only non-vocal track on the album. All of the selections on this package convey their purpose much better within their former albums, since each song is a link in the album's conceptual chain. Alone, these songs do harbor some substance, like the delicate "Days Are Numbers (The Traveller)" and the rocking "Stereotomy." Since Parsons' real genius shines on his full-length pieces, only a sampling of the Alan Parsons Project's musical flair can be distinguished by their separate selections. Sadly omitted from both volumes is any material from the incredible *Tales of Mystery and Imagination* album, as well as "Winding Me Up" or "You Lie Down With Dogs" from *Eve*. Other questionable exclusions include "Breakdown," "If I Could Change Your Mind," and "Mammagamma," which are all worthy candidates for a best-of collection. If *The Best of the Alan Parsons Project, Vol. 2* is sought after, then *Volume 1* should be owned as well. *—Mike DeGagne*

The Instrumental Works / 1988 / Arista ♦♦

Try Anything Once / Oct. 26, 1993 / Arista ♦♦♦

The Very Best Live / Jun. 27, 1995 / RCA Victor ♦♦

On Air / Sep. 24, 1996 / Digital Sound ♦♦♦

The Definitive Collection / Jul. 15, 1997 / Arista ♦♦♦♦♦
The Definitive Collection is a fabulous double-disc assembly of the Alan Parsons Project's singles that includes the band's strongest material up to 1996. All the songs are presented chronologically, and the information inside discusses each source album with great detail and offers extensive crediting for each individual track. Some obvious appearances include "The Raven," "Games People Play," "Eye in the Sky," "Don't Answer Me," and "Pyramania." What makes this set such a treasure is the inclusion of songs that fail to surface on other compilations, like "Snake Eyes" from *Turn of a Friendly Card*, "Too Late" from the overlooked *Gaudi* album, or the eerie "Doctor Tarr and Professor Feather" from *Tales of Mystery and Imagination*. A good number of instrumentals are welcomed throughout the CDs as well, such as "I Robot," "Voyager," "Sirius," and "Mammagamma." Two of the better tracks from 1993's *Try Anything Once* album appear here also, in "Turn It Up" and "Re-Jigue." Fans of the Alan Parsons Project will wonder why such gems as "Lucifer," "Winding Me Up," or "You Lie Down With Dogs" fail to appear, but after an overview of the selections it's obvious they've been bumped for more commercial songs, which still doesn't hinder this collection. *The Definitive Collection* is about as precise as a hits package can be from this band, short of a box set. The sound is pristine, and the cover and packaging are apropos to the band's style and music. This absolute collection lets the listener combine all of the ideas and concepts of Parsons into almost two hours of music, as each song aptly signifies his brilliant career as both musician and engineer. *—Mike DeGagne*

● **Master Hits: Alan Parsons Project** / Jul. 27, 1999 / Arista ♦♦♦♦♦
Arista celebrated its 30th anniversary by releasing *The Heritage Series*, spotlighting the most popular artists on the label. The Alan Parsons Project installment in *The Heritage Series* is pretty much a straight hits collection, featuring highlights from their stint at the label. While the Parsons Project was at Arista, they achieved the peak of their popularity with such radio hits as "I Robot," "I Wouldn't Want to Be Like You," "Games People Play," "Time," "Ammonia Avenue" and the crossover single "Eye in the Sky." All those songs are here, along with some highlights from their albums, providing a nice retrospective of their time with Arista, which just happened to be the peak of their career. *—Stephen Thomas Erlewine*

The Time Machine / Sep. 28, 1999 / Miramar ♦♦♦♦

Gram Parsons

b. Nov. 5, 1946, Winter Haven, FL, **d.** Sep. 19, 1973, Joshua Tree, CA
Vocals, Guitar / Country-Rock
With the International Submarine Band, the Byrds and the Flying Burrito Brothers, Gram Parsons pioneered the concept of a rock band playing country music, and as a solo artist he blended country and rock to the point that they became indistinguishable from each other. While he was alive, Parsons never sold many records, yet he influenced many of his peers. In the years since his death, numerous rock and country artists build on his body of work.

Parsons' first band, the International Submarine Band released their debut *Safe at Home*, in early 1968. By the time it hit the stores, Parsons had already joined the Byrds, pushing the group toward the country-rock unveiled on their 1968 record, *Sweetheart of the Rodeo*. He and Chris Hillman left the Byrds shortly after the album's completion, forming the Flying Burrito Brothers, debuting with *The Gilded Palace of Sin*, in 1969. Though it wasn't a hit, it earned a cult, including Keith Richards, who became fast friends with Parsons. Due to his friendship with Richards and its resulting excess, Parsons didn't have much interest in the Brothers anymore, leaving the group after finishing their second album, *Burrito Deluxe*. For the next few years, he was more rock star than musician, partying and hanging with the Stones. He finally returned to music in 1972, recording a solo album, *GP*, that year. Though it received good reviews, including praise for his backing vocalist Emmylou Harris, it didn't sell. Following a brief tour with his backing band, the Fallen Angels, he entered the studio to record his second album, *Grievous Angel*. A few weeks after the sessions, Parsons went on a vacation near the Joshua Tree National Monument in California. On September 19, 1973, he died from an overdose of morphine and tequila. After his death, Parsons' legacy continued to grow, as both country and rock musicians built on the music; if anything, he was more popular 20 years after his death than he was when he was alive. *—Stephen Thomas Erlewine*

★ **G.P./Grievous Angel** / 1973 / Reprise ♦♦♦♦♦
In the year before his death in the fall of 1973, Gram Parsons recorded two superb solo albums, and Warner Brothers has conveniently reissued them in their entirety on a single compact disc. Since many of the same musicians played on both *G.P.* (released in January of 1973) and *Grievous Angel* (which appeared in stores almost exactly a year later), the two albums flow together quite well as a single set. And while no bonus tracks were added, the booklet features well-written essays on Parsons from John M. Delgatto and Marley Brant, the complete liner notes from both albums, and lyrics for all the songs on the disc (which weren't included in the original vinyl issues). While the material and performances on *G.P.* are a shade stronger than on *Grievous Angel*, both albums have more than their share of pearly moments, and this disc is a treat from start to finish; James Burton's guitar leads are chicken-pickin' at its smartest and most tasteful, Al Perkins' pedal steel is the definitive sound of country & western heartache, fiddler Byron Berline effortlessly reveals how he became one of Nashville's leading session musicians, and Parsons' duets with the young Emmylou Harris are nothing less than sublime. And would anyone who loves either country or rock really want to be without a CD that includes songs like "A Song for You," "The New Soft Shoe," "Big Mouth Blues," "$1,000 Wedding," or "In My Hour of Darkness"? While the definitive Gram Parsons collection has yet to be compiled, *G.P./Grievous Angel* gives you everything you really need from his solo career, and these 20 performances are among the most influential and satisfying music the genre of country-rock would ever produce. *—Mark Deming*

Sleepless Nights / Apr. 1976 / A&M ♦♦♦
Three years after Gram Parsons' untimely death, his frequent duet partner Emmylou Harris helped arrange for the release of this collection of outtakes—three songs he cut with Harris for his final solo album *Grievous Angel* in 1973, and nine others recorded live in the studio with The Flying Burrito Brothers in 1970. Anyone hoping to find the great lost Gram Parsons song is out of luck here; all 12 tunes are covers of vintage country classics, except for "Honky Tonk Women" (which at least *sounds* like a C&W classic in this arrangement) and The Louvin Brothers' "The Angels Rejoiced Last Night," which is as spiritually uplifting as ever with Harris' pure, clear voice helping to bring it home. The three tracks with his duet partner fare best, while most of the cuts with the Burritos sound like demos, and though a few are inspired (particularly the deeply felt versions of "Sing Me Back Home" and "Green, Green Grass of Home," a lot of the time both Parsons and the band sound like a solid bar band in the middle of a Wednesday night set—more than competent, but less than inspired. *Sleepless Nights* was certainly a labor of love and it's a worthy purchase for committed fans, but neophytes are better off giving a listen to The Flying Burrito Brothers' masterpiece *The Gilded Palace of Sin*, or either solo album, *G.P.* or *Grievous Angel*. *—Mark Deming*

Gram Parsons & the Fallen Angels / 1981 / Sierra ♦♦♦♦♦
A good live document of Parsons's last tour, it was recorded at radio station WLIR in New York. *—Kenneth M. Cassidy*

Warm Evenings, Pale Mornings, Bottled Blues / 1992 / Raven ♦♦♦♦♦
Although all of Parsons' albums are essential, this import-only collection provides an excellent sampling of his entire career, including his stints with the Shilos, the International Submarine Band, the Byrds (complete with Parsons' vocals restored), the Flying Burrito Brothers, and the solo years. *—Chris Woodstra*

Live 1973 / Mar. 4, 1997 / Rhino ✦✦✦✦

Gram Parsons may have been one of rock's first great trust-fund hippies, but he couldn't match the kind of paycheck Elvis Presley was able to offer for a Vegas gig. So when he hit the road in 1973 to promote his superb solo debut *G.P.*, James Burton, Ronnie Tutt, and most of the band that anchored that album were otherwise engaged. He instead threw together a rough-and-ready crew of roadhouse pickers he dubbed "The Fallen Angels" (Emmylou Harris, thankfully, was available to make the trip), and they began making their way through America's rock clubs and honky-tonks. *Live 1973* was recorded live for radio broadcast in the midst of that tour, and if you imagine it sounds a good bit rougher and leaner than *G.P.* (which includes six of the 12 cuts featured here), you'd be right. On "We'll Sweep out the Ashes" and "Cry One More Time," the Fallen Angels aren't quite up to the task of recreating the studio arrangements, but they're surprisingly strong on the quieter numbers, especially "The New Soft Shoe" and "Love Hurts" (the latter of which earned a Grammy nomination), and when they pick up the tempo for some end-of-the-set covers (including Merle Haggard's "California Cottonfields" and Dave Dudley's "Six Days on the Road"), guitarist Jock Bartley and pedal steel player Neil Flanz sound like the core of a great bar band. Gram Parsons and Harris' duets are rougher around the edges on stage than on vinyl, but they sound as emotionally keen as ever, and Parsons and drummer N.D. Smart II made a pretty good comedy team. *Live 1973* isn't an essential release like *G.P.* or *The Gilded Palace of Sin*, but anyone already familiar with Parsons' body of work will love it. —*Mark Deming*

Another Side of This Life: The Lost Recordings of Gram Parsons, 1965-1966 / Dec. 19, 2000 / Sundazed ✦✦

★ **Sacred Hearts and Fallen Angels: The Gram Parsons Anthology** / May 1, 2001 / Rhino ✦✦✦✦✦

Gram Parsons' legend is so great that it's easy for the neophyte to be skeptical about his music, wondering if it really is deserving of such effusive praise. Simply put, it is, and if you question the veracity of that statement, turn to Rhino's peerless double-disc set, *Sacred Hearts and Fallen Angels: The Gram Parsons Anthology*. This is the first truly comprehensive overview of Parsons' work, running from the International Submarine Band, through the Byrds, to the Flying Burrito Brothers and his two solo albums, scattering appropriate rarities or non-LP tracks along the way. This is no small feat, since it depends on extensive cross-licensing between record labels, plus concentration from the compilers, who won't allow personal biases to get in the way of telling the story. Miraculously, this happens, and the result is a lean, yet thorough, utterly addictive set that summarizes the brilliance of Gram Parsons, capturing his magnificent songwriting abilities and how he made country sound like rock & roll, while giving rock a sense of country's history. It's possible to complain about the handful of omissions, but this still hits every major point, which means this is a perfect, irresistible summation of Parsons' career, containing every great moment from all of his bands. His genius has never seemed purer than it does here, since it conveys the true scope of his talents and his career. If you are a fan of Parsons, this isn't necessary, even if it is an excellent listen (there's only one unreleased track, the ISB's "Knee Deep in the Blues"). If you haven't fallen in love with him, skip every other disc—this is what you need. Once you hear it, there's no way that you won't become a lifelong fan. —*Stephen Thomas Erlewine*

Partridge Family

f. 1969, db. 1975

Bubblegum

The Partridge Family was the '70s successor to the Monkees. Both were totally fictional pop/rock "bands" produced by Screen Gems, the television branch of Columbia Pictures. While the Monkees (TV series and band concept) were styled as mid-'60s counterculture zaniness à la the Beatles' film *Hard Days Night*, the Partridge Family was strictly wholesome with traditional family values despite the lite quasi-hip tone of the show. The top-rated series first aired on ABC from 1970 to 1974, premiering September 25, 1970. Starring stage and screen veteran Shirley Jones and then up-and-coming actor David Cassidy, *The Partridge Family* was loosely based on real-life family pop/rock band the Cowsills. The only members of the cast heard on the records are lead vocalist Cassidy and Shirley Jones on background vocals. All of the Partridge Family records were originally released on Bell Records. The harmonies on the Family's records were quite similar to another Bell act, the 5th Dimension. In the premiere episode, the Partridge siblings ask their mom Shirley to help them make a record label demo. Recording "I Think I Love You," the family gets signed to a record label and has a number one record their first time out. "I Think I Love You," written by Tony Romeo and produced by Wes Farell, actually did become a number one million-selling pop hit, holding down the spot for three weeks beginning November 21, 1970. Other Partridge Family hits were "Doesn't Somebody Want to Be Wanted," "I'll Meet You Halfway," and "I Woke Up in Love This Morning." The huge album sales were fueled by the show's practice of fully featuring two songs per episode. —*Ed Hogan*

● **Greatest Hits** / 1989 / Arista ✦✦✦✦✦

Although they weren't as good as the Cowsills, who served as at least partial inspiration for the group, the Partridge Family had their fair share of first-rate bubblegum singles in the early '70s. *Greatest Hits* does an excellent job of summarizing those glory days, containing most of the big hits—"I Think I Love You," "Doesn't Somebody Want to Be Wanted," "I'll Meet You Halfway," "I Woke Up in Love this Morning," "It's One of Those Nights (Yes Love)," "Am I Losing You," "Looking Through the Eyes of Love"—along with their theme song "Come on Get Happy" and selected highlights from their records. Since it's missing a handful of minor hits, such as "Breaking Up Is Hard to Do," it can't really

be seen as definitive, but it comes close enough to satisfy the desires of almost all casual fans. —*Stephen Thomas Erlewine*

The Pastels

f. 1982, Glasgow, Scotland

Indie Pop, C-86, Twee Pop, Indie Rock

Although virtually unknown outside of indie rock circles, the Pastels were one of the most inspirational and enduring groups of their era, spearheading a movement towards a renewed sense of wistful musical primitivism and willful naivete known variously as "shambling" and "anorak pop"; in addition, their influence helped bring international notice to a resurgent Scottish musical community, with frontman Stephan Pastel's legendary 53rd and 3rd label helping to launch the careers of bands including the Jesus & Mary Chain, the Shop Assistants, BMX Bandits, the Vaselines, and the Soup Dragons. Formed in Glasgow, Scotland, in 1982, the band initially comprised vocalist/guitarist Pastel, guitarist Brian Superstar, and drummer Chris Gordon; they debuted that autumn on the Whaam label with the single "Songs for Children," but Gordon soon exited, the first of many subsequent lineup shuffles. Ambition was never the Pastels' strong suit; as the group's members—now including bassist Martin Hayward and drummer Bernice Simpson—devoted their primary focus to their studies, new music appeared only sporadically and to little notice, on a seemingly random series of labels. After 1983's "I Wonder Why" was released on Rough Trade, they moved to Creation, where they hit their stride with the 1984 drone pop gems "Something's Going On" and "A Million Tears." After recruiting onetime Shop Assistants keyboardist Aggi Wright, they recorded the 1986 single "Truck Train Tractor," followed by "Crawl Babies" and "Coming Through." Finally, in 1987 the group found time to assemble an LP, *Up for a Bit With the Pastels*, followed in 1988 by *Suck on the Pastels*, a collection of unreleased Creation-era material. In 1989, former Vaselines frontman Eugene Kelly and ex-Shop Assistant David Keegan joined the fold for *Sittin' Pretty*, the final LP to include Superstar, Hayward, and Simpson. —*Jason Ankeny*

● **Up for a Bit with the Pastels** / 1987 / Big Time ✦✦✦✦✦

Suck on the Pastels / 1988 / Gasatanka ✦✦✦✦

Suck on the Pastels compiles a number of singles released by the band from 1983-1985, as well as a three-song BBC session from 1984. In the liner notes, Stephan Pastel alludes to the general apathy of the band throughout this period, also explaining the general poor recording conditions in which most of these songs were birthed. The band's laconic tendencies were matched by their arrogant tendencies ("We thought we were God," notes Pastel in the liners), so there's definite attitude and substance, albeit in patchy doses. The results are rather uneven, but there are some moments of undeniable greatness. The seven-minute drone pop of "Baby Honey" remains one of Creation's earliest gems, mixing the Byrds, the Velvet Underground, detached vocals, and a lazy near-funk rhythm in the best possible way. "Couldn't Care Less" and "I'm Alright With You" also rate with the Pastels' finest. The rhythm box and childish lyrics to "I Wonder Why" provide the perfect backdrop to a rumpus room filled with joyous toddlers. The BBC session is scattered throughout the disc, showing what the band is capable of in proper working conditions. *Suck On* isn't the first place to go for the Pastels, but it's a decent snapshot of their youthful beginnings. —*Andy Kellman*

Sittin' Pretty / 1989 / Homestead ✦✦✦✦

Mobile Safari / 1995 / Domingo ✦✦✦✦

Illumination / Sep. 9, 1997 / Up ✦✦✦

Illumination finds the Pastels in a similar mood to its predecessor, *Mobile Safari*. Scaling back the snappy production and crisp guitars of their earlier releases, the group crafts a collection of subdued, lovely melodies in the vein of the Velvet Underground's third album. While the Pastels lack Lou Reed's lyricism or the Velvets' assured experimentalism, the hushed ambience and sighing melodies of *Illumination* make it a charming listen. —*Stephen Thomas Erlewine*

Illuminati: Pastels Music Remixed / Jan. 12, 1999 / Up ✦✦✦

Billy Paul

b. Dec. 1, 1935, Philadelphia, PA

Vocals / Philly Soul, Soul, Smooth Soul, Quiet Storm, Urban

Billy Paul had a good run in the '70s as an R&B vocalist, though he'd been recording since the '50s, when he debuted on Jubilee. Paul was featured on radio broadcasts in Philadelphia at age 11, and had an extensive jazz background. He worked with Dinah Washington, Miles Davis, and Roberta Flack, as well as Charlie Parker, before forming a trio and recording for Jubilee. His original 1959 recording of "Ebony Woman" for New Dawn was later re-recorded for Neptune as the title of his 1970 LP. He signed the next year with Philadelphia International, and scored his biggest hit with "Me & Mrs. Jones" in 1972, topping both the R&B and pop charts. Paul had one other Top Ten R&B single, "Thanks for Saving My Life," in 1974. He remained on Philadelphia International until the mid-'80s. Paul recorded one LP for Total Experience in 1985, *Lately*, and another for Ichiban before announcing his retirement in 1989 in London. But he's since done several club dates, both in America and overseas. —*Ron Wynn*

● **Me and Mrs. Jones: The Best of Billy Paul** / Apr. 6, 1999 / Epic Associated/Legacy ✦✦✦✦✦

Too easily dismissed as little more than a one-hit wonder, Billy Paul was in fact one of the most gifted and affecting talents to grace the Philadelphia International stable—the recipient of some of the Gamble/Huff team's most lush and sophisticated productions, his deeply soulful voice bridged the gap between jazz and soul, textured in equal measure by street-smart swagger and touching vulnerability. *Me and Mrs. Jones: The Best of Billy Paul* goes far beyond the classic title track in restoring the singer to prominence, showcasing his versatility via superb covers of pop favorites, including Bob Dylan's "Don't Think Twice, It's All Right"; Elton John's "Your Song"; and Paul McCartney's "Let 'Em In." With the inclusion of R&B chart hits like "Thanks for Saving My Life" and "Billy's Back Home," it all adds up to a definitive portrait of Paul in his prime. *—Jason Ankeny*

Pavement

f. 1989, Stockton, CA, **db.** 1999
Indie Rock, Lo-Fi, Alternative Pop/Rock, Noise Pop
With their fractured songs, unexpected blasts of feedback, laconic vocals, cryptic literate lyrics, and defiant low-fidelity, Pavement is one of the most influential and distinctive bands to emerge from the American underground in the '90s. Pavement, along with Sebadoh, were the leaders of the low-fi movement which dominated US indie-rock in the early '90s. Initially conceived as a studio project between guitarists/vocalists Stephen Malkmus and Scott Kannberg in the '80s, Pavement gradually became a band during the early '90s. Along the way, their initial EPs and debut album, 1992's *Slanted and Enchanted*, earned a devoted following of musicians, indie fans and critics. Before long, the group's aesthetics—a combination of elliptic, cryptic underground American rock, unrepentant Anglophilia, a fondness for white noise, off-kilter arrangements and winding melodies, songs that frequently had shifting titles, and literate, clever lyrics—were imitated by underground bands through America and Britian. By that point, Pavement had become an actual band, one with a notorious acid-fried, ex-hippie drummer called Gary Young. Young left the band in 1993, as the band made the move to clean up their sound, if not their sensibility, on 1994's *Crooked Rain, Crooked Rain*. Their revampment resulted in a near-hit with "Cut Your Hair," but the mainstream decided Pavement was too strange for their tastes, and the band decided they preferred the underground, leaving the band as one of the most popular—and the most influential—American indie-rock bands of the '90s. *—Stephen Thomas Erlewine*

★ **Slanted & Enchanted** / May 1992 / Matador ♦♦♦♦♦
Slanted & Enchanted is a left-field classic, a record that came out of nowhere to help establish a new subgenre of rock & roll. Pavement had already sketched out their sound, as well as their amateurish lo-fi aesthetic, on a series of indie singles before recording their debut, but *Slanted & Enchanted* is where they pulled all of their disparate sounds together into a distinctive style. At first, the primitive sound of the record is the most gripping thing about *Slanted*, but soon the true innovations of the record appear through the songs themselves. Stephen Malkmus and Spiral Stairs subvert conventional pop structures, turning melodies inside out, reinterpreting and reworking older songs, and bending genres together. It's a complex, enthralling record, filled with fractured riffs, strong melodies, and cryptic melodies, and with all the hiss and static, *Slanted & Enchanted* sounds like listening to a distant college radio station—melodies and hooks keep floating in and out of the mix, with individual lines instead of full lyrics surfacing through the murk. This unique song structure as much as the sound of the album itself makes *Slanted & Enchanted* an individual, signature work and one of the most influential records of the '90s. *—Stephen Thomas Erlewine*

Watery, Domestic / Nov. 1992 / Matador ♦♦♦
Released between *Slanted & Enchanted* and *Crooked Rain, Crooked Rain*, the *Watery, Domestic* EP captures Pavement in a transitional phase, as the band began to abandon the static-laden guitar-rock of their early recordings and started to move toward a cleaner sound. Most of the innovations of *Watery, Domestic* have to do with recording techniques, yet the songs are certainly fine. The cleaner production brings Pavement's inherent fractured melodicism into sharper focus, which benefits "Texas Never Whispers," the wistful "Frontwards," and the bright, nearly jangly "Shoot the Singer," but the slow grind of "Lions (Linden)" would have been mesmerizing regardless of the production, or the lack of it. *—Stephen Thomas Erlewine*

Westing (By Musket and Sextant) / Mar. 30, 1993 / Drag City ♦♦♦♦
A collection of all of Pavement's low-fidelity early singles and EPs, which feature considerably less melody than *Slanted and Enchanted*. It's nice to have this rare material on one CD, although the music is defiantly anti-CD. Those who boarded the train with the acclaimed *Slanted and Enchanted* should catch up on what they've missed. *—Stephen Thomas Erlewine*

☆ **Crooked Rain, Crooked Rain** / Feb. 1994 / Matador ♦♦♦♦♦
Although it's much calmer than the critically acclaimed *Slanted and Enchanted*, *Crooked Rain, Crooked Rain* shares the same spirit of the band's debut—it's a messy, impossibly catchy catalog of pop music and culture. On their second full-length album, Pavement have abandoned much of the low-fi squalor of their earlier work, opting for a laidback, subdued sound that borders on country-rock and jazz-rock at times, and pure pop and rock & roll at others. In other words, it's more accessible than *Slanted and Enchanted* but just as distinctive and original. Ultimately, *Crooked Rain, Crooked Rain* revamps rock history and reinvents it for the slacker generation. *—Stephen Thomas Erlewine*

Wowee Zowee / Apr. 1995 / Matador ♦♦♦♦♦
With its vast array of musical styles, *Wowee Zowee* isn't as accessible as *Crooked Rain, Crooked Rain* or as immediate as the bracing, noisy pop of *Slanted & Enchanted*. Pavement never abandon their warped pop aesthetic, they simply expand it, incorporating elements of folk-rock, English music-hall, soul, jazz, country, as well as adding asides to such contemporaries as Suede ("We Dance"), Ween ("Brinx Job") and Stereolab ("Half a Canyon"). Alternating between majestic epics like "Grounded" and ragged narratives like "Rattled by the Rush" and "Father to a Sister of Thought," to song fragments like "Brinx Job" and the punkish "Serpentine Pad," the record might seem disjointed at first. After repeated listens, the songs play off each other, creating a dense collage of '90s rock & roll that recasts the past and present into one rich, kalidescopic and blissfully cryptic world view. *—Stephen Thomas Erlewine*

Brighten the Corners / Feb. 11, 1997 / Matador ♦♦♦♦
There's a difference between accessibility and focus, which Pavement illustrate with their fourth album, *Brighten the Corners*. Arriving on the heels of the glorious mess of *Wowee Zowee*, the cohesive sound and laid-back sarcasm of *Brighten the Corners* can give the record the illusion of being accessible, or at the very least a retreat toward the songcraft of *Crooked Rain, Crooked Rain*. And the record is calm, with none of the full-out blasts of noise that marked all of their previous releases. It would be easy to dismiss the absence of noise as mere maturity, or a move toward more accessible songcraft, but neither statement is entirely true. *Brighten the Corners* is mature but wise-assed, melodic but complex—it's a record that reveals its gifts gradually, giving you enough information the first time to make you want come back for more. At first, the dissonant sing-song verse of "Stereo" seems awkward, but it's all pulled into perspective with the gleeful, addictive outburst of the chorus, and that is a microcosm of the album's appeal. The first time around, the winding melody of "Shady Lane," the psycho jangle-pop of "Date With Ikea," the epic grace of "Type Slowly" and the speedy rush of "Embassy Row" make an impression, but repeated listens reveal sonic and lyrical details that make them indelible. Similarly, Malkmus' hip-hop inflections on "Blue Hawaiian" and the quiet beauty of "Transport is Arranged" unfold over time. While the preponderance of slow songs and laid-back production make the album more focused than *Wowee Zowee*, it doesn't have the rich diversity of its predecessor—"Type Slowly" comes closest to the grand, melancholic beauty of "Grounded"—but it remains a thoroughly compelling listen. *—Stephen Thomas Erlewine*

Terror Twilight / Jun. 8, 1999 / Matador ♦♦♦♦
Since Pavement switched course with each record—*Crooked Rain, Crooked Rain* was nothing like *Slanted & Enchanted*, and *Brighten the Corners* was decidedly different from the brilliant, warped *Wowee Zowee*—it's a little disarming to realize that *Terror Twilight* merely deepens the sound of its predecessor. Guitars burst to the forefront every so often—most notably on the dense jam "Platform Blues" and the shouted choruses of "Billie"—yet they're usually used as texture. Nothing rocks hard and "The Hexx," which was heard on the *Brighten* tour as a metallic epic, has been transformed into a surrealistic dream, reminiscent of the Velvet Underground's "Ocean." That's typical of *Terror Twilight*—it's reflective, with the occasional flight of fancy that fits neatly into the laid-back flow. It's also the tightest record Pavement ever made, largely due to producer Nigel Godrich, who helped reign in excessive tendencies in Radiohead and Beck and does the same here. The band still sounds like Pavement—their loping interplay is unmistakable—and Stephen Malkmus' songs are typically dense and literate, yet they're easier to digest. That, along with the lack of Spiral Stairs songs, gives *Terror Twilight* a cohesion missing even on earlier Pavement albums, no matter how great they were. All the focus makes the album feel a little less like Pavement—after all, this is a band whose imperfections were among their most endearing qualities—and a bit more like Malkmus' first solo album, which it essentially is. Though it's hard not to miss the gloriously messy sprawl of Pavement at their peak, this carefully crafted, languid recasting of their signature sound is effective and winds up as a fitting, bittersweet farewell for the best band of the '90s. *—Stephen Thomas Erlewine*

Freda Payne

b. Sep. 19, 1945, Detroit, MI
Vocals / Soul
A Detroit soul/jazz/pop vocalist. Multitalented and beautiful, Payne crashed the soul and pop playlists in 1970 with a series of powerful sides for Holland-Dozier-Holland's Invictus imprint. Payne's early musical experience was quite varied, and she debuted on the jazz-oriented Impulse! label in 1965. Her 1970 blockbuster, "Band of Gold," made Payne a pop star with its strident message and insistent bassline, and she encored with "Deeper & Deeper." The controversial antiwar anthem "Bring the Boys Home" proved her biggest R&B seller the next year. Payne hosted a TV gabfest during the '80s. *—Bill Dahl*

Greatest Hits / Jul. 1, 1991 / Fantasy ♦♦♦♦♦
Fantasy's 11-track *Greatest Hits* doesn't dig much deeper than the hits, but it does contain all six of her charting singles, notably "Band of Gold," "Deeper and Deeper," and "Bring the Boys Home," plus five other fine singles and album tracks from her Invictus recordings. Yes, the aforementioned blockbusters shine the brightest here, but the rest of this is, at its worst, simply pleasant '70s soul, which means there are a few minor gems to be discovered here. *—Stephen Thomas Erlewine*

● **Band of Gold: The Best of Freda Payne** / Nov. 7, 2000 / Music Club International ♦♦♦♦♦
Band of Gold: The Best of Freda Payne is a lengthy, comprehensive overview of Freda Payne's peak recordings from the early '70s, including not just hits like "Band of Gold," "Deeper and Deeper," and "Bring the Boys Home." This may seem like a lotta Freda, but her recordings are surprisingly consistent—even when the songs are subpar, the recordings are appealing, as are her performances. There may be more concise collections to appeal to the less-dedicated listener, but for a true appreciation of Payne, this is the disc to get. [Besides, it has an absolutely terrific cover.] *—Stephen Thomas Erlewine*

Peaches & Herb

f. 1965, Washington, D.C.
Brown-Eyed Soul, Pop-Soul, Adult Contemporary, Soul
Though soul/pop Peaches and Herb was billed as a duo, their group member rotation is more similar to a group's. While in New York recording the two acts the Sweet Things and

Herb Fame, separately, producer Van McCoy decided to use some leftover recording time to record Herb and Sweet Things vocalist Francine Barker as a duo. The original A-side, "We're in This Thing Together," failed to generate much interest, but the B-side, "Let's Fall in Love," became Peaches and Herb's first hit single. As the hits continued—"Close Your Eyes," "For Your Love," "Love Is Strange," "Two Little Kids"—the duo earned the nickname the Sweethearts of Soul. When Francine "Peaches" Barker tired of touring in 1967, a succession of replacements took over as new "Peacheses." The hits continued: "The Ten Commandments of Love," "United," "When He Touches Me (Nothing Else Matters)," and "It's Just a Game, Love," which stalled in summer 1970, Peaches and Herb's last charting single on Date. Despondent over the act's failing chart success, Herb abruptly quit Peaches and Herb in 1970 before deciding to re-enter the music business in 1976. He found his "new" Peaches in Linda Greene. The duo charted again in June 1977 with "We're Still Together" on MCA from a self-titled album produced by Van McCoy. After inking a deal with Polydor, "Shake Your Groove Thing" went gold, peaking at number four R&B and number five pop in late 1978. The creamy ballad "Reunited" seemed an unlikely follow-up to the disco-oriented "Shake," yet it held on to the number one spot for four weeks on both the R&B and pop charts during spring 1979. Though there were other hits on Polydor, none came close to the success of their early- to mid-'60s Date singles. —*Ed Hogan*

● **The Best of Peaches & Herb: Love is Strange** / Mar. 12, 1996 / Epic/Legacy ◆◆◆◆◆
The brief, but successful tenure of the original Peaches (Francine Barker) & Herb are recalled in the 16 tracks culled from the duo's 1966-1968 Date Records recordings, including their Top Ten pop hit "Close Your Eyes" and their Top Ten R&B hits "For Your Love" and "When He Touches Me (Nothing Else Matters)." Given the group's love ballad reputation, there are some surprisingly uptempo numbers here, but the focus is always on the vocal interaction between the two singers and their proclamations of romantic commitment, sometimes in the words of such Tin Pan Alley prototypes as Ted Koehler, Cole Porter, and Sammy Cahn. Record-company restrictions mean this set covers only the early hits, and business considerations keep it under 45 minutes (all the releases in Legacy's *Rhythm & Soul* Series contain 16 tracks, which must indicate a ceiling on song publishing expenses), but within those parameters, this is a well-chosen collection. —*William Ruhlmann*

Pearl Jam
....
f. 1990
Grunge, Alternative Pop/Rock, Hard Rock

Pearl Jam rose from the ashes of Mother Love Bone to become the most popular American rock & roll band of the '90s. After vocalist Andrew Wood overdosed on heroin, guitarist Stone Gossard and bassist Jeff Ament assembled a new band, bringing in Mike McCready on lead guitar, Dave Krusen on drums, and vocalist Eddie Vedder. Naming themselves Pearl Jam, the band recorded their debut album, *Ten*, in the beginning of 1991. *Ten* didn't begin selling in significant numbers until early 1992, after Nirvana made mainstream rock radio receptive to alternative rock acts. Soon, Pearl Jam outsold Nirvana, which wasn't surprising. Pearl Jam fused the riff-heavy stadium rock of the '70s with the grit and anger of '80s post-punk, without ever neglecting hooks and choruses; "Jeremy," "Evenflow," and "Alive" fit perfectly into album rock radio stations that were looking for new blood. Pearl Jam's audience continued to grow during 1992, thanks to a series of radio and MTV hits, as well as a successful appearance on the second Lollapalooza tour. Despite their status as rock & roll superstars, the band refused to succumb to the accepted conventions of the music industry, refusing to release any videos or singles from their second album, 1993's *Vs.* Nevertheless, it was another multi-platinum success, debuting at number one and selling nearly a million copies in its first week of release. *Vitalogy*, the band's third album, appeared at the end of 1994, and in early 1995, they recorded *Mirror Ball*, an album with Neil Young. In late summer of 1996, Pearl Jam released their fourth album, *No Code*. Although the album was greeted with fairly positive reviews and debuted at number one, its weird amaglam of rock, worldbeat and experimentalism dissatisfied a large portion of their fan base, and it quickly fell down the charts. Their next record, the hard-rocking *Yield*, appeared in February 1998; while their sizable cult embraced the album, sending it to number two its first week of release, *Yield* quickly slipped down the charts. The following year, Pearl Jam scored an unlikely pop radio smash with their cover of the J. Frank Wilson oldie "Last Kiss," which became the band's highest charting pop hit to date, peaking at number two and going gold. The group returned in 2000 with the Chad Blake-produced *Binaural*. —*Stephen Thomas Erlewine*

★ **Ten** / Aug. 27, 1991 / Epic Associated ◆◆◆◆◆
Nirvana's *Nevermind* may have been the album that broke grunge and alternative rock into the mainstream, but there's no underestimating the role that Pearl Jam's *Ten* played in keeping them there. Nirvana's appeal may have been huge, but it wasn't universal; rock radio still viewed them as too raw and punky, and some hard rock fans dismissed them as weird misfits. In retrospect, it's easy to see why Pearl Jam clicked with a mass audience—they weren't as metallic as Alice in Chains or Soundgarden, and of Seattle's Big Four, their sound owed the greatest debt to classic rock. With its intricately arranged guitar textures and expansive harmonic vocabulary, *Ten* especially recalled Jimi Hendrix and Led Zeppelin. But those touchstones might not have been immediately apparent, since—aside from Mike McCready's Clapton/Hendrix-style leads—every trace of blues influence has been completely stripped from the band's sound. Though they rock hard, Pearl Jam is too anti-star to swagger, too self-aware to puncture the album's air of gravity. Pearl Jam tackles weighty topics—abortion, homelessness, childhood traumas, gun violence, rigorous introspection—with an earnest zeal unmatched since mid-'80s U2, whose anthemic sound they frequently strive for. Similarly, Eddie Vedder's impressionistic lyrics

often make their greatest impact through the passionate commitment of his delivery rather than concrete meaning. His voice had a highly distinctive timbre that perfectly fit the album's warm, rich sound, and that's part of the key—no matter how cathartic *Ten*'s tersely titled songs got, they were never abrasive enough to affect the album's accessibility. *Ten* also benefited from a long gestation period, during which the band honed the material into this tightly focused form; the result is a flawlessly crafted hard rock masterpiece. —*Steve Huey*

Vs. / Oct. 19, 1993 / Epic Associated ◆◆◆◆
Pearl Jam took to superstardom like deer in headlights. Unsure of how to maintain their rigorous standards of integrity in the face of massive commercial success, the band took refuge in willful obscurity—the title of their second album, *Vs.*, did not appear *anywhere* in the packaging, and they refused to release any singles or videos. (Ironically, many fans then paid steep prices for import CD singles, a situation the band eventually rectified.) The eccentricities underline Pearl Jam's almost paranoid aversion to charges of hypocrisy or egotism—but it also made sense to use the spotlight for progress. You could see that reasoning in their ensuing battle with Ticketmaster, and you could hear it in the record itself. *Vs.* is often Eddie Vedder at his most strident, both lyrically and vocally. It's less oblique than *Ten* in its topicality, and sometimes downright dogmatic; having the world's ear renders Vedder unable to resist a few simplistic potshots at favorite white-liberal targets. Yet a little self-righteousness is an acceptable price to pay for the passionate immediacy that permeates *Vs.* It's a much rawer, looser record than *Ten*, feeling like a live performance; Vedder practically screams himself hoarse on a few songs. The band consciously strives for spontaneity, admirably pushing themselves into new territory—some numbers are decidedly punky, and there are also a couple of acoustic-driven ballads, which are well suited to Vedder's sonorous low register. Sometimes, that spontaneity comes at the expense of *Ten*'s marvelous craft—a few songs here are just plain underdeveloped, with supporting frameworks that don't feel very sturdy. But, of everything that does work, the rockers are often frightening in their intensity, and the more reflective songs are mesmerizing. *Vs.* may not reach the majestic heights of *Ten*, but at least half the record stands with Pearl Jam's best work. —*Steve Huey*

Vitalogy / Dec. 6, 1994 / Epic ◆◆◆◆◆
Thanks to its stripped-down, lean production, *Vitalogy* stands as Pearl Jam's most original and uncompromising album. While it isn't a concept album, *Vitalogy* sounds like one. Death and despair shroud the album, rendering even the explosive celebration of vinyl "Spin the Black Circle" somewhat muted. But that black cloud works to Pearl Jam's advantage, injecting a nervous tension to brittle rockers like "Last Exit" and "Not For You," and especially introspective ballads like "Corduroy" and "Better Man." In between the straight rock numbers and the searching slow songs, Pearl Jam contributes their strangest music—the mantra-funk of "Aye Davanita," the sub-Tom Waits accordion romp of "Bugs" and the chilling sonic collage "Hey Foxymophandlemama, That's Me." Pearl Jam are at their best when they're fighting, whether it's TicketMaster, fame, or their own personal demons. —*Stephen Thomas Erlewine*

No Code / Aug. 27, 1996 / Epic ◆◆◆◆
A strange phenomenon with anthemic hard rock bands is that when they begin to mature and branch out into new musical genres, they nearly always choose to embrace both the music and spirituality of the East and India, and Pearl Jam is no exception. Throughout *No Code*, Eddie Vedder expounds on his moral and spiritual dilemmas; where on previous albums his rage was virtually all-consuming, it is clear on *No Code* that he has embraced an unspecified religion as a way to ease his troubles. Fortunately, that has coincided with an expansion of the group's musical palette. From the subtle, winding opener "Sometimes" and the near-prayer of the single "Who You Are," the band reaches into new territory, working with droning, mantra-like riffs and vocals, layered exotic percussion and a newfound subtlety. Of course, they haven't left behind hard rock, but, like any Pearl Jam record, the heart of *No Code* doesn't lie in the harder songs, it lies in the slower numbers and the ballads, which give Vedder the best platform for his soul-searching: "Present Tense," "Off He Goes," "In My Tree" and "Around the Bend" equal the group's earlier masterpieces. While a bit too incoherent, *No Code* is Pearl Jam's richest and most rewarding album, as well as its most human. They might be maturing in a fairly conventional method, but they still find new ways to state old truths. —*Stephen Thomas Erlewine*

Yield / Feb. 3, 1998 / Epic ◆◆◆
Perhaps shaken up by the chilly reception to the adventurous *No Code*, Pearl Jam returned to straight-ahead hard rock on their fifth album, *Yield*. There remain a few weird flourishes scattered throughout the album, from the spoken-word "Push Me, Pull Me" to the untitled Eastern instrumental bonus track, but overall, *Yield* is the most direct record the group has made since *Ten*. That doesn't mean it's the best. Pearl Jam have trouble coming up with truly undeniable hard rock hooks, and Eddie Vedder remains at his most compelling on folk-tinged, meditative numbers like "Low Light," "In Hiding" and "All Those Yesterdays." They also fall prey to their habit of dividing the record into rock and ballad sides, which makes *Yield* a little exhausting, even at its concise length. It also emphasizes the relative lack of exceptional material. *Yield* is more consistent than *Vitalogy* and *No Code*, but it doesn't have songs that reach the highs of "Better Man," "Corduroy" or "Who You Are." Ironically, the album doesn't rock hard enough—"Do the Evolution" and "Brain of J." have garage potential, but there's more bite and distortion on Vedder's voice than there is on the guitars. It's hard to view *Yield* as a disaster, since Pearl Jam's conviction still rings true, but it's frustrating that journeyman tendencies have replaced the desperate, searching confusion that was the most appealing element of the band's music. —*Stephen Thomas Erlewine*

Live on Two Legs / Nov. 24, 1998 / Epic ♦♦♦
Not long after *Ten* unexpectedly topped the charts, Pearl Jam became notorious for their intense live performances. Even more notable than the group's unbridled energy was their willingness to stretch out their songs or throw in covers, reminding jaded audiences that rock concerts could be electric and energetic. Their Seattle peers were equally (sometimes more) compelling, but Pearl Jam skillfully made arena rock feel as intimate as a punk club show—something that no other band of their time could do. Instead of building this reputation throughout the course of the '90s, the quintet let it fade away as they became embroiled in a vicious battle with Ticketmaster that ultimately proved unfruitful. Not only did the court cases tie up several years of touring, they also refused to play any venue with contracts with Ticketmaster once it was finished—which meant they played off-market venues that were difficult to reach, thereby decreasing their potential audience substantially. Once 1998's *Yield* didn't move as much as anyone expected, the band released *Live on Two Legs* a few short months later. It was culled from *Yield*'s supporting tour, and the difference is substantial—Pearl Jam still sounds good, but they lack the wild energy that distinguished their early years. Professionalism has its good points, however, and it's true that *Live on Two Legs* is eminently listenable, thanks in no small part to a fine track selection illustrating that the best moments of *No Code* and *Yield* rank with *Ten*, *Vs.*, and *Vitalogy*. For all the good points—the tight interaction, the occasional nifty solo, Eddie Vedder's powerful performance—the album never quite catches fire. Instead, *Live on Two Legs* is a souvenir, a thank you to fans who have stood by throughout the years, and on those terms, it's successful. *—Stephen Thomas Erlewine*

Binaural / May 16, 2000 / Epic ♦♦♦♦
If anything, Pearl Jam was even more in the wilderness—at least as far as the mainstream was concerned—at the beginning of 2000 than they were in the second half of the '90s. Even with "Last Kiss," their first big hit single since *Ten*, under their belts, they were an anomaly on the pop and rock scenes. They were the only one of their old grunge colleagues still standing intact, and they were genuinely alone. No peers, and too sincere to even consider fitting into a pop scene dominated by 'N Sync on one side and Limp Bizkit on the other. Not surprisingly, they chose to persevere, ignoring trends, completely in favor of being a classicist rock band. This should come as no surprise, since that's what they've done since *No Code* and, perhaps, *Vitalogy*, but the real surprise about their sixth studio album *Binaural* is that it finds the group roaring back to life without dramatically changing the direction they followed on *No Code* and *Yield*. Maybe the addition of a new drummer, former Soundgarden member Matt Cameron, has kicked the band to life, but that unfairly dismisses Jack Irons' worthy contributions. Instead, the difference is focus—though Pearl Jam is trying a lot of different styles, certainly more so than on *Yield*, they pull it all off better. The songs are sharper, the production is layered, and the performances are as compassionate as ever, resulting in their finest album since *Vitalogy*. *—Stephen Thomas Erlewine*

Pearls Before Swine

f. 1965, **db.** 1971
Obscuro, Folk-Rock, Psychedelic
The psychedelic folk band Pearls Before Swine was the brainchild of singer, composer and cult icon Tom Rapp, born in Bottineau, ND in 1947; after writing his first song at age six, he later began performing at local talent shows, and as a teen bested a young Bob Dylan at one such event. Upon relocating to Melbourne, FL, Rapp formed Pearls Before Swine in 1965, recruiting high school friends Wayne Harley, Lane Lederer and Roger Crissinger to record a demo which he then sent to the ESP-Disk label; the company quickly signed the group, and they soon travelled to New York to record their superb 1967 debut *One Nation Underground*, which went on to sell some 250,000 copies. The explicitly anti-war *Balaklava*, widely regarded as Pearls Before Swine's finest work, followed in 1968; the group—by this time essentially comprising Rapp and whoever else was in the studio at the moment—moved to Reprise for 1969's *These Things Too*, mounting their first-ever tour in the wake of releasing *The Use of Ashes* a year later. Two more albums, *City of Gold* and *Beautiful Lies You Could Live In*, followed in 1971; moving to Blue Thumb, Rapp resurfaced as a solo artist with 1972's *Stardancer*, but upon the release of *Sunforest* a year later he then retired from music, subsequently becoming a civil rights attorney. Frequently cited as a key influence by the likes of Damon & Naomi, the Bevis Frond and the Japanese psych band Ghost, Rapp made an unexpected return to live performance in mid-1998 when he appeared at the Terrastock festival in Providence, RI, joining son Dave and his indie-pop band Shy Camp; he soon began work on 1999's *A Journal of the Plague Year*, his first new LP in over two decades. *Constructive Melancholy*, a retrospective of Pearls Before Swine's tenure on Reprise, also appeared that same year. *—Jason Ankeny*

One Nation Underground / 1967 / Get Back ♦♦♦♦♦
Psychedelic-folk debut from one of the most erudite, literate minds in rock, Thomas D. Rapp (and the first of his ever-changing Swine). Although the songs here lack some cohesion, this is still a stunning piece of work, from the nightmarish sleeve art—the "Hell Panel" from Hieronymus Bosch's 15th century painting "Garden of Delights"—to the strange yet powerful songs. "Another Time," the most memorable selection, is an understated acoustic song, the first that Rapp ever penned, based on his experience in a horrific car crash where he walked away unscathed. Of similar mood is the beautiful "Ballad of an Amber Lady." "Drop Out" is a straightforward song built around a popular credo of the '60s. "Uncle John" is one of the earliest protest songs about the Vietnam War. Strangest (and funniest) of all is "(Oh Dear) Miss Morse," where Rapp adopts a Victorian persona and sounds out the Morse code spelling of F-U-C-K, accompanied by banjo and Farfisa organ.

Considering Rapp's fascination with history, it's not surprising that one of the songs here, "I Shall Not Care," features a co-writer credit to "Roman Tombs." The cryptic words that comprise this song's title were discovered on a tomb that dates to the final days of the Roman Empire. *—Peter Kurtz*

● **Balaklava** / 1968 / Get Back ♦♦♦♦♦
A record that virtually defies categorization, Pearls Before Swine's 1968 epic *Balaklava* is the near-brilliant follow-up to *One Nation Underground*. Intended as a defiant condemnation of the Vietnam War, it doesn't offer anthemic, fist-pounding protest songs. Instead, Rapp vented his anger through surrealist poetry, irony, and historical reference: Balaklava was the 1854 Crimean War battle that inspired Alfred, Lord Tennyson to write his epic *The Charge of the Light Brigade*; in reality, the "Charge" was a senseless military action that killed scores of British soldiers. *Balaklava* begins with "Trumpeter Landfrey," an 1880's recording of the actual voice and bugle charge of the man who sounded the charge at Balaklava. It makes the transition into "Translucent Carriages," a mix of acoustic guitars, a basic vocal, and ghostly narration ("Jesus raised the dead... but who will raise the living?"), all the more stunning. "Images of April" continues the mystical feel, combining flutes, cricket chirps, and frog croaks for a nether-worldly effect. Rapp virtually cries "I Saw the World," backed by a powerful string arrangement that makes the song even more impassioned. Like *One Nation Underground*, *Balaklava* is somewhat unfocused: "There Was a Man" is a little too Dylan-esque, and Leonard Cohen's "Suzanne" detracts from Rapp's compositions. Unfortunately, the record closes with "Ring Thing," a morbid piece that refers to Tolkien's famous *Lord of the Rings* trilogy. Still, this is superb psychedelic music, successfully merging exotic instruments like marimba, clavinet, French horn, and swinehorn with Rapp's unique lisping vocals. But *Balaklava* isn't just acid-trip background music. It's probably the best example of what Rapp calls "constructive melancholy" (also the name of a recent CD collection of Pearls songs), a combination of the real with the surreal, and it's indispensable to any serious '60s rock collection. *—Peter Kurtz*

These Things Too / 1969 / Reprise ♦♦

Constructive Melancholy: 30 Years of Pearls Before Swine / Apr. 20, 1999 / Birdman ♦♦♦♦♦
Pearls Before Swine's tenure on Reprise is recalled on *Constructive Melancholy*, a generous 26-track collection that distills the highlights from the seven LPs the group released on the label between 1969 and 1973. Though their two previous efforts for ESP-Disk—*One Nation Underground* and *Balaklava*—remain Tom Rapp's most perfectly realized records, there are fleeting moments of brilliance on each Pearls Before Swine album, and *Constructive Melancholy* does an excellent job in isolating these peaks; concentrating largely on 1969's *These Things Too* and 1970's *The Use of Ashes*, the set features Rapp favorites like "Sail Away," "Look into Her Eyes," "The Jeweller," "Rocket Man" and "Snow Queen" in addition to new recordings of the classics "Translucent Carriages" and "Another Time." (There's even an all-new Rapp tune, "Blind.") A solid introduction to one of the most innovative and under-recognized bands of the psychedelic era. *—Jason Ankeny*

Ann Peebles

b. Apr. 27, 1947, St. Louis, MO
Vocals / Memphis Soul, Soul
Ann Peebles was the queen of Willie Mitchell's Memphis-based Hi Records roster during the '70s, when Al Green was its undisputed king. Sung in a voice as bittersweet as it is riveting, her always-dramatic recordings include one undisputed masterpiece, "I Can't Stand the Rain," cited as a favorite by John Lennon and most recently covered by Tina Turner. Other covers abound—Robert Palmer took "I'm Gonna Tear Your Playhouse Down," and Bette Midler claimed "Breakin' Up Somebody's Home." Backed by the brilliant Hi rhythm section and flawlessly produced by Mitchell, Peebles sang and wrote (often in partnership with husband Don Bryant) of the feminine perspective on the darker side of love—sometimes untrusting love, but love, for better or worse. Her work represents, with elegance and grit, some of the best of Memphis soul.

After a long absence from recording, Ann Peebles returned to the wars with the CD *Full Time Love* in 1992 for Bullseye/Rounder. While it didn't get much exposure or recognition in urban circles, it was a wonderfully sung and well-produced attempt at giving Peebles some contemporary tweaking without losing her gritty qualities. *—Christine Ohlman and Ron Wynn*

Part Time Love / 1971 / The Right Stuff ♦♦♦♦♦
The title track was a masterpiece, and everything else on this dynamic early '70s soul session is a jewel. Ann Peebles may have been the most overlooked great soul singer, male or female, who emerged in the '70s. Hi couldn't strike crossover gold twice, and Al Green was becoming a superstar. But Peebles deserved a better fate than obscurity, as this collection of soul wailers and weepers proves. *—Ron Wynn*

Straight from the Heart / 1972 / Hi ♦♦♦♦♦
A lean, tough set that was not only a triumph for Peebles, but illustrated how the Hi label had surpassed its crosstown Stax rival for quality Memphis soul in the early '70s. The guitars are spare, funky, and bluesy, the horn section punchy, and the material far earthier and down-home than the increasingly formulaic grooves at Stax. There were three modest R&B hits on the album ("Slipped, Tripped and Fell in Love," "I Feel Like Breaking Up Somebody's Home," "Somebody's on Your Case"), much of which was penned by Peebles or her husband Don Bryant. Peebles' vocals were convincingly biting, and she never, unlike many other singers of the era, tried too hard for her own good. The main flaw of the record is its length (26 minutes), which was short even by early-'70s standards. *—Richie Unterberger*

I Can't Stand the Rain / 1974 / Hi ✦✦✦
The title song was an instant classic, and its lyrics are among the most moving and gripping in soul annals. This was Ann Peebles' finest album for Hi Records, and it should have been a massive success. Instead, while it's celebrated in Europe and now considered an anthem, it floundered and barely scraped the pop charts, although the single was her biggest R&B hit. It's sad and ridiculous that the only Ann Peebles session presently available on CD is the one she did for Bullseye Blues in '92. —*Ron Wynn*

If This Is Heaven / 1978 / Hi ✦✦✦✦✦
Another exceptional album by Ann Peebles, who was cutting remarkable records for Hi in Memphis that no one noticed except for deep soul junkies. Her voice was alternately anguished, angry, defiant, and resigned, while Willie Mitchell and the Hi Rhythm Section provided minimal, yet spectacular backing. Peebles seldom toured, preferring to stay in Memphis around her family. But she had a voice only surpassed among female soul vocalists by Aretha Franklin and equalled by Carla Thomas. —*Ron Wynn*

Handwriting Is on the Wall / 1979 / Hi ✦✦✦
Some fabulous down-home, earthy soul from Ann Peebles, a Southern treasure. Peebles was the finest female singer to pass through the Hi Records operation, and Willie Mitchell achieved with her the same kind of wonderful records he made with Al Green, although they didn't get identical commercial success. Any and all of the albums Ann Peebles did with Hi are classics; sadly, most of them haven't been reissued. —*Ron Wynn*

St. Louis Woman / 1996 / Hi ✦✦✦✦
St. Louis Woman is a terrific four-disc, 63-track box set covering Ann Peebles' entire career, concentrating (rightly so) on her seminal early-'70s recordings for Hi Records. All of her hits are here, of course, along with underappreciated album tracks, lost singles, B-sides, rarities and a handful of unreleased cuts. Certainly, this isn't the choice for the casual fan—there's simply too much music here—but for the dedicated fan and collector, this is a treasure. —*Stephen Thomas Erlewine*

U.S. R&B Hits '69-'79 / Jun. 25, 1996 / Hi ✦✦✦
U.S. R&B Chart Hits is exactly what it says it is—an excellent collection featuring Ann Peebles' 18 biggest R&B hits, including such classics as "Part Time Love," "I'm Gonna Tear Your Playhouse Down" and "I Can't Stand the Rain." It's arguably the definitive Peebles collection, since it sports a leaner and better track selection than the Right Stuff's 21-track *Best of the Hi Records Years*, which nevertheless is a fine collection in its own right. —*Stephen Thomas Erlewine*

● **The Best of Ann Peebles: The Hi Records Years** / Jul. 23, 1996 / The Right Stuff ✦✦✦✦✦
The Best of the Hi Records Years collects all the highlights from Ann Peebles' creative and commercial heyday, featuring the majority of her hits for the label, including "I Can't Stand the Rain" and "Part Time Love," as well as several terrific lesser-known singles and album tracks. —*Stephen Thomas Erlewine*

Teddy Pendergrass

b. Mar. 26, 1950, Philadelphia, PA
Vocals, Drums / Quiet Storm, Club/Dance, Urban, Soul
Teddy Pendergrass' tender ballads and slow, sensual singing style helped make him a favorite among women. By his late teens, he was a drummer for the Cadillacs. In the late '60s, the Cadillacs merged with another more-established group, Harold Melvin & The Blue Notes. Melvin soon became aware of Pendergrass' vocal prowess and asked him to take the lead singer spot. Beginning with "Miss You," a steady stream of hit singles flowed from the band.

Around 1976, Pendergrass left Melvin's Blue Notes and formed his own Blue Notes, featuring Teddy Pendergrass. Soon, however, Pendergrass disbanded his group in favor of a solo career. He burst back on the scene with his self-titled platinum solo debut. Around this time, Pendergrass began to institute his infamous "Ladies Only" concerts. His next three albums went gold or platinum. The singer received several Grammy nominations during 1977 and 1978, Billboard's 1977 Pop Album New Artist Award, an American Music Award for best R&B performer of 1978 and awards from Ebony Magazine and the NAACP. The '70s ended, but Pendergrass kept racking up the hits. *TP*, his fifth solo album went platinum in the summer of 1980. *It's Time For Love* gave Pendergrass another gold album in summer 1981. A 1982 car accident left Pendergrass paralyzed from the waist down. After almost a year of physical therapy and counseling, Pendergrass returned to the recording scene in 1983. His ninth solo album, *Love Language* went gold in the spring of 1984. Pendergrass continued to record sporadically throughout the '80s and '90s, but failed to top his previous work. —*Ed Hogan*

● **The Best of Teddy Pendergrass** / Mar. 31, 1998 / The Right Stuff ✦✦✦✦✦
The Right Stuff's *The Best of Teddy Pendergrass* is a definitive 18-track collection, containing all of his big hits from 1977's "I Don't Love You Anymore" to 1991's "It Should've Been You." In between those two songs, such romantic smooth soul classics as "Can't We Try," "You're My Latest, My Greatest Inspiration," "Close the Door," "Turn off the Lights," "Love TKO" and "Joy" are heard. Some Top Ten R&B hits, like "Love 4/2" and "I Can't Live Without Your Love," are missing, but the disc remains a near-perfect summary of Pendergrass at the peak of his powers. —*Stephen Thomas Erlewine*

The Penguins

f. 1954, Los Angeles, CA, db. 1959
Brown-Eyed Soul, Doo Wop
Best known for their hit single "Earth Angel," the doo wop quartet the Penguins were never able to replicate the success of their only Top 40 hit, but the song became a rock & roll classic. Although he wasn't the lead singer, Curtis Williams was the leader of the group. He learned "Earth Angel" from vocalist Jesse Belvin—some sources claim that

Williams wrote the song alone, others say he co-wrote the song with Belvin, while others claim Gaynel Hodge, a member of the doo wop group the Turks, wrote the song with the duo (in fact, Hodge won a lawsuit filed in 1956 that gave him a co-writing credit)—and had the Penguins sing the song.

Around 1954, the Penguins signed with the local Los Angeles independent label Dootone Records. The group's first single was going to be the uptempo "Hey Sinorita" and the ballad "Earth Angel" was going to be the B-side. Upon the release of the single in the latter half of 1954, Los Angeles radio stations were receiving more requests for "Earth Angel" than "Hey Sinorita," and by the beginning of 1955, the single had scaled the national charts, spending three weeks at the top of the R&B charts and peaking at number eight on the pop charts. After cutting some sides for Mercury, the Penguins moved to Atlantic, where they had their second and final hit, "Pledge of Love," which climbed to number 15 on the R&B charts in the summer of 1957. —*Stephen Thomas Erlewine*

Earth Angel / 1990 / Ace ✦✦✦
A 21-track anthology from the Du Tone label, it's a deeper look at the group's '50s sides and style, built around the title track that sold five-million copies worldwide. (Import) —*Hank Davis*

● **Authentic Golden Hits** / 1993 / Juke Box Treasures ✦✦✦✦✦
At long last, a well-thought-out compilation that gathers up all of the group's best sides for Dootone Records, including the original versions of the classics "Earth Angel" and "Hey, Senorita" in their original, unedited form. —*Cub Koda*

The Best of the Penguins: The Mercury Years / Jul. 1996 / Mercury ✦✦✦
The Best of the Mercury Years isn't all that it appears to be. Instead of presenting all of the Penguins' hit singles, it only presents the group's Mercury recordings, which means that neither of the two versions of "Earth Angel" on the disc are the original hit single versions, and that the remainder of their classic Dootone sides are missing. What is here is good, but not essential for anyone but hardcore doo-wop collectors. —*Stephen Thomas Erlewine*

Michael Penn

b. Aug. 1, 1958
Vocals, Guitar / Pop Underground, College Rock, Adult Alternative Pop/Rock, Pop/Rock, Singer/Songwriter
One of the most acclaimed singer/songwriters to emerge during the late 1980s, Michael Penn was seemingly destined for a career in show business—the oldest son of director Leo Penn and actress Eileen Ryan, his younger siblings included Sean (later recognized among the finest actors of his generation) and Chris (a noted character actor acclaimed for his work in features like *Reservoir Dogs*). While his brothers focused on acting, Michael turned to music, and in the early 1980s he formed the group Doll Congress, which garnered a fervent local following but never expanded its fan base outside of Southern California. In 1987, he reunited with ex-Doll Congress keyboardist Patrick Warren to begin composing the songs which comprised his 1989 debut, *March*. Upon its release, the album became a significant critical favorite, earning acclaim for its sparkling Beatlesque folk-pop and clever, Elvis Costello-like wordplay; the lead single, "No Myth," even became a surprise hit and helped launch the LP into the Top 40. In the wake of his initial success, Penn went on a lengthy hiatus; when he returned in 1992 with his sophomore effort, *Free For All*, he met much greater commercial resistance than he faced with *March*, and after only a few weeks, the album fell off the charts. He then spent five years pondering his next move, finally resurfacing in 1997 with *Resigned*. —*Jason Ankeny*

● **March** / Sep. 1989 / RCA ✦✦✦✦✦
Michael Penn's debut album, *March*, released in late 1989, served notice there was another talented Penn brother, in additon to actors Sean and Chris. The album kicks off with one of the top singles of the winter of 1989-1090, "No Myth," and proceeds through an engrossing myriad of folk-tinged ballads and up-tempo rockers. Despite several literary allusions and the ponderous title and lyrics of "Cupid's Got a Brand New Gun," on the whole, Penn doesn't take himself too seriously. "Brave New World" is an absurd Dylan-esque hodgepodge of rhyme, and "Big House" is devoted to the childhood prank of ringing doorbells, then running. The coda is "Evenfall," maybe the best '60s "frat-rock" song since the '60s, with a horn section that makes you want to dance until the campus police close down the party. —*Mark Morgenstein*

Free-for-All / Sep. 15, 1992 / RCA ✦✦✦
Free For All, Michael Penn's second album, isn't as immediately accessible as *March*, but his cryptic lyrics and twisting melodies will work their way into your memory if given some time. —*Stephen Thomas Erlewine*

Resigned / Jun. 3, 1997 / 57 Records/Epic ✦✦✦✦
Backing away from the introspective inclinations of *Free-for-All*, Michael Penn delivers a concise and thoroughly infectious guitar-pop album with *Resigned*. Like most of Penn's music, the album relies heavily on *Revolver*-era Beatles, but his melodies are uniformly tighter and catchier than before, and producer Brendan O'Brien gives the record a crisp, attractive sound. None of the tracks initially stand out like "No Myth" or "Long Way Down," yet each song is well constructed and filled with hooks, making *Resigned* a terrific third album from Penn. —*Stephen Thomas Erlewine*

MP4: Days Since a Lost Time Accident / Feb. 1, 2000 / Epic ✦✦✦✦
When Michael Penn released *MP4: Days Since a Lost Time Accident*, the strict playlist of adult-alternative radio made it pretty clear that it'd be difficult for him to have a hit, so Penn doesn't even try—he just creates a record for himself and his cult. Brendan O'Brien,

the producer of *Resigned*, mans the boards on the opening cut "Lucky One." It's not just the only song on *MP4* not produced by Penn, it's the only song that sounds like a blatant attempt at a radio-ready single. That it succeeds gloriously—it's the first sure-fire follow-up to "No Myth"—speaks of Penn's prodigious abilities as a craftsman. The rest of the album is equally well crafted, but more subtle in construction and production, without hooks that leap out of the speaker. They're there, but they're delivered subtly, letting each song slowly work its way into a listener's memory. Penn knows that whoever puts on *MP4* is willing to delve deeply into the record, willing to spend time with it to find its rewards. It's to his considerable credit that he delivers. *MP4* doesn't have a knockout punch, but it is an expert pop album—tightly sequenced and written, filled with small gems. It's the kind of album that's ideal for cult audiences, since it's familiar yet doesn't stand still (the production takes some risks, albeit minor ones). It may not win Michael Penn any new fans, but it'll certainly satisfy the devoted. *—Stephen Thomas Erlewine*

Pentangle

f. 1968

British Folk-Rock, British Folk, Folk-Rock

Were Pentangle a folk group, a folk-rock group, or something that resists classification? They could hardly be called a rock & roll act; they didn't use electric instruments often, and were built around two virtuoso guitarists, Bert Jansch and John Renbourn, who were already well-established on the folk circuit before the group formed. Yet their hunger for eclectic experimentation fit into the milieu of late-'60s progressive rock and psychedelia well, and much of their audience came from the rock and pop worlds, rather than the folk crowd. With Jacqui McShee on vocals and a rhythm section of Danny Thompson (bass) and Terry Cox (drums), the group mastered a breathtaking repertoire that encompassed traditional ballads, blues, jazz, pop, and reworkings of rock oldies, often blending different genres in the same piece. At least in England, Pentangle were very popular for a time; their third LP *Basket of Light* made number five, and "Light Flight" was a small hit single. They introduced some electric guitars on their early-'70s albums, which generally suffered from weaker material and a less unified group effort. After the original lineup broke up in 1973, Jansch and Renbourn recorded often as soloists and remained top attractions on the folk circuit. The original group reunited in 1985 for *Open the Door*, and other versions of the group recorded and toured throughout the '80s and '90s. *—Richie Unterberger*

The Pentangle / 1968 / Reprise ✦✦✦✦

There's something exciting about the first album of a band that goes on to greatness, and *The Pentangle*, by the group of the same name, is no different. Here, the listener witnesses the first studio work of a band struggling to get their essence down on vinyl. Of course Bert Jansch and John Renbourn's reputations as guitarists preceded the band, but the addition of bassist Danny Thompson and drummer Terry Cox gave the band an acoustic rhythm section like no other folk-rock group. Singer Jacqui McShee became the last piece of this intricate English puzzle, delivering high, expressive vocals that contrasted and merged so well with Jansch's deeper pipes. The group doesn't hold back on their first outing. On "Hear My Call" McShee offers a dreamy vocal, floating high above the bluesy guitars. The soaring vocal and firmly grounded rhythm highlight one another, creating a carefully layered sound that is present in all of Pentangle's best music. This dynamic works equally well in "Pentangling," with McShee and Jansch's voices combining light and dark shadows to concoct a strangely atmospheric harmony. The rocking and rollicking "Way Behind the Sun" is another standout, and the instrumentals "Bells" and "Waltz" are complex and lively. The album's spacious arrangements take full advantage of stereo, mixing instruments to different tracks so that the listener, for instance, can always hear Jansch's guitar on one side and Renbourn's on the other. This group, it seems, had it all. Equally comfortable with traditional songs, instrumentals, and originals, they made few missteps on their early albums. Like Fairport Convention and the Incredible String Band, Pentangle specialized in updating British Isles' folk music. *The Pentangle*, now with seven bonus tracks, is a dazzling debut and a must have for fans of English folk rock. *—Ronnie D. Lankford, Jr.*

Sweet Child / 1968 / Reprise ✦✦✦✦✦

This album, released in 1968, at the peak of the Pentangle's career, is probably the most representative of their work. A sprawling two-record set, half recorded in the studio and half live at the Royal Festival Hall, showcases just how versatile the Pentangle were in their unique brand of English folk, jazz, Celtic, blues, and pop styles. Some of the live covers are easily their finest performances. Furry Lewis' "Turn Your Money Green," sung by the delightful Jacqui McShee, swings sweetly, buttressed of course by Renbourn and Jansch's guitar tapestry. Charlie Mingus' "Haitian Flight Song" features a great solo by bassist Danny Thompson, who was easily one of the finest musicians to grace the instrument. The studio tracks are uniformly excellent as well, especially "The Time Has Come," which turns waltz time inside out. McShee, Renbourn, and Jansch all turn in career performances on this track. But these examples merely scratch the surface of the Pentangle's peak. The 2001 CD reissue adds four bonus tracks: alternate versions of "In Time," "The Trees They Do Grow High," and "Hole in the Coal," and a studio version of "Haitian Fight Song." In all, *Sweet Child* is an awesome and delightful collection, and probably their finest hour. *—Matthew Greenwald*

Basket of Light / 1969 / Castle Music America ✦✦✦✦✦

Although *Sweet Child* is usually cited as the group's high-water mark, *Basket of Light* finds them at their most progressive and exciting. Highlights of this album—which actually reached the Top Five in the U.K.—include the buzzing jazz dynamics of "Light Flight," and their moving rendition of the traditional folk song "Once I Had A Sweetheart," their reinvention of the girl-group smash "Sally Go Round The Roses," and "Springtime Promises," one of their finest original tunes. *—Richie Unterberger*

Cruel Sister / 1970 / Reprise ✦✦✦✦✦

Originally released in 1970, this was the fourth release from the British folk-rock group Pentangle and may qualify as their swan song. With only five songs, Jacqui McShee, Bert Jansch, John Renbourn, Terry Cox, and Danny Thompson create a dense, layered sound that is woven within the fabric of each song like a tapestry. Although known for their eclectic approach and love of jazz, here the group concentrates on traditional material like "A Maid That's Deep in Love" and the 18-minute "Jack Orion." A Pentangle fan will immediately note that John Renbourn is playing an electric guitar on "A Maid That's Deep in Love." This departure from purely acoustic doesn't create a bigger Fairport Convention or Steeleye Span sound but is imbedded quietly into the song. What really sets both this song and "When I Was in My Prime" apart is McShee's clear, vibrant vocals. On "When I Was in My Prime," she sings unaccompanied, proving that her talent runs as deep as the better-known Jansch and Renbourn. The seven-minute title cut also features McShee singing an absolutely lovely ballad with darker undertones. Jansch sings the enjoyable though straightforward "Lord Franklin." The crowning jewel of this masterpiece is the epic "Jack Orion," though one has difficulty imagining what possessed Pentangle to record a folk song that took up an entire side of an album. Jansch shares vocals with McShee on this multiple part song, and generous time is left for Renbourn to turn in a bluesy, then jazzy, electric solo. *Cruel Sister* shows Pentangle at their artistic height, combining all of their skill and inspiration to create a vital and enduring album. *—Ronnie Lankford, Jr.*

A Maid That's Deep in Love / 1987 / Shanachie ✦✦✦✦

Currently, only this 9-track compilation is available to remind listeners of this British traditional folk/rock quintet, which provided Fairport Convention's main competition in the late '60s and early '70s. Much of it is lovely, notably McShee's haunting singing and Jansch's finger-picking. But a more complete picture is provided by the two volumes of *Essential* Pentagle on Transatlantic in the U.K., which may be found in US record racks. *—William Ruhlmann*

● **Early Classics** / 1992 / Shanachie ✦✦✦✦

A 14-song, 63-minute collection (originally a double LP) comprising many of the highlights (but no "Light Flight") of the original group's history from 1968 through 1972. The notes are minimal, and there are no original release dates or any identification of the albums (*The Pentangle, Sweet Child, Basket of Light, Cruel Sister*, etc.) whence this material originated. The latter are the only flaws in what is otherwise a fine if not completely comprehensive cross-section of the group's work, showcasing their many and varied sides—Bert Jansch's, Danny Thompson's, and Terry Cox's jazz leanings in "Train Song," John Renbourn's more traditional approach in "Let No Man Steal Your Thyme," their forays into medieval music ("Lyke-Wake Dirge") and progressive folk ("House Carpenter," "Bruton Town"), etc., much of it projected by Jacqui McShee's clear, soaring vocals. The CD also highlights their early records' effective use of stereo as a format for their contrasting technique, especially among the guitars and the rhythm section. *—Bruce Eder*

● **The Pentangle Family** / 2000 / Sanctuary ✦✦✦✦✦

The Pentangle Family is a beautiful two-disc set that traces the development of the classic folk-rock group Pentangle from the mid-'60s to the early '70s. This collection features a number of songs by Bert Jansch and John Renbourn—individually and as a duo—as well as a number of selections by Pentangle. It is revealing to hold Jansch and Renbourn's work side by side with Pentangle recordings. Together, Jansch and Renbourn primarily recorded guitar albums; the addition of a rhythm section within Pentangle would inject a dense, layered sound into the group's music. Surprisingly, early songs like "Traveling Song" and "Let No Man Steal Your Thyme" from 1968's *The Pentangle* show that the group quickly found its course. The lovely vocals, a touch of blues guitar, and perfectly selected material give the group a sound unlike any other folk-rock group in England. The first disc ends with several instrumentals from Renbourn's 1968 solo release, showing an increased interest in renaissance and medieval music. The second disc covers the full flowering of Pentangle, featuring a number of songs from *Sweet Child, Basket of Light, Cruel Sister*, and *Reflection*. Pentangle's later material, such as "Wedding Dress" from *Reflection*, shows the group changing directions, perhaps losing steam. Overall, this collection offers an excellent introduction to the original Pentangle and the early work of Jansch and Renbourn. This is folk-rock at its finest. *—Ronnie Lankford Jr.*

Pere Ubu

f. Aug. 1975, Cleveland, OH

American Punk, Experimental Rock, Post-Punk, Alternative Pop/Rock, American Underground

Emerging from the urban wasteland of '70s Cleveland, Pere Ubu shaped the American underground. Through their long, convoluted career—which was marked by constant lineup shifts and several hiatuses—Ubu's art-punk focused on hulking frontman David Thomas' rapturously demented voice and lyrics and the group's volatile melodies and rhythms. While their early work captured the era's chaos with apocalyptic fervor and surprising humanity, their sound evolved into clever, elliptical pop on their later releases. Named for Alfred Jarry's surrealist play *Ubu Roi*, Pere Ubu formed in 1975 from the ashes of Rocket from the Tombs, which featured Thomas and guitarist Peter Laughner. Ubu's original lineup also included guitarist Tom Herman, bassist Tim Wright, keyboardist Allen Ravenstine and drummer Scott Krauss. The group's early singles, such as "30 Seconds Over Tokyo" and "The Final Solution," sent shock waves through the underground rock scene. After Laughner's and Wright's departures, Pere Ubu continued as a quintet with bassist Tony Maimone. In 1977, Mercury A&R exec Cliff Burnstein convinced the label to form a new imprint in order to sign Pere Ubu; Blank Records released their 1978 debut LP *The Modern Dance*, which sold little but influenced countless post-punk acts with its dark, manic intensity. *Dub Housing* pushed the band to further extremes, but they disbanded upon completing 1979's *New Picnic Time* (working title: "Goodbye"). They quickly reformed, releasing 1980's *The Art of Walking*, their most accessible work yet. They disbanded again after 1982's *Song of the Bailing Man*, and Thomas pursued a solo career. His 1987 album *Blame the Messenger* featured Ravenstine and Maimone; when Krauss sat in on a hometown date, they revived Pere Ubu, and 1988's *The Tenement Year* and 1989's *Cloudland* were their poppiest albums to date. 1995's *Ray Gun Suitcase* was planned as their swan song, but the box set *Datapanik in the Year Zero* revived interest in the band. Thomas reunited with Tom Herman to record 1998's *Pennsylvania*; the live *Apocalypse Now* followed a year later. *—Jason Ankeny*

The Modern Dance / 1978 / Geffen ✦✦✦✦✦

There isn't an Ubu recording I can imagine living without, but even so, the *Modern Dance* remains the essential Ubu purchase (as does the follow-up *Dub Housing*). I'm sure Mercury had no idea what they had on their hands when they released this as part of their punk rock offshoot label Blank, but it remains a classic slice of art-punk. It announces itself quite boldly: the first sound you hear is a painfully high-pitched whine of feedback, but then Tom Herman's postmodern Chuck Berry riffing kicks off the brilliant "Non-Alignment Pact," and you soon realize that this is punk rock unlike anything you've ever heard. David Thomas' caterwauling is funny and moving, Scott Krauss (drums) and Tony Maimone (bass) are one of the great unheralded rhythm sections in all of rock, and the "difficult" tracks like "Street Waves," "Chinese Radiation," and the terrifying "Humor Me" are revelatory, and way ahead of their time. Now 20 years old and available on CD for the first time, *The Modern Dance* is the signature sound of the avant-garage: art-rock, punk-rock and garage-rock mixing together joyously and fearlessly. *—John Dougan*

Dub Housing / 1979 / Rough Trade ✦✦✦✦✦

Though Pere Ubu's tenure on Mercury lasted one record, their departure for their unlikely home of Chrysalis (at the time the label of Jethro Tull) resulted in *Dub Housing*, widely considered their masterpiece. Darker and more difficult than *The Modern Dance* (indicated by the cover's darkened apartment complex and stormy Cleveland skyline) with plenty of bleak soundscapes (e.g., "Codex"), *Dub Housing* also includes "Navvy"'s bouncy burble (featuring Thomas yelping "I have desires!"), and "(Pa) Ubu Dance Party"'s surreal big beat. Make no mistake, as much as Ubu indulged in arty dissonance and mucked about with song structure, this is very much a rock & roll record, albeit one made by a band interested in pushing the envelope when it came to sound, song construction, and performance. As much as this is a band effort, the guitar of Tom Herman and the synthesizer of Allen Ravenstine frequently stand out. Herman's strong, polished playing veers from assertive riffing to assaultive noise; Ravenstine, who may be one of the all-time great synth players (especially compared to complete wankers such as Rick Wakeman) colors the sound with ominous whooshes of distortions, blips, and blurbs that sound like a sped-up Pong game. But, as is often the case with Ubu, it's David Thomas' singing (here at its most engagingly unrestrained) that is front and center. Part comic foil, part raging madman, Thomas utilizes all of his limited range in a whacked expressiveness built around hiccups, yodels, screeches, and, sometimes, singing. *Dub Housing* sold next to nothing and signaled the beginning of the end of Ubu's relationship with Chrysalis, but it remains an important and influential American rock record. *—John Dougan*

New Picnic Time / 1979 / Rough Trade ✦✦✦✦✦

It was not surprising that after *Dub Housing*, Ubu couldn't get a record released in the U.S. *New Picnic Time* originally surfaced on Chrysalis as a British import, but when Rough Trade made it available domestically, U.S. fans could take solace in that the band had finally hooked up with a label more sympathetic to their decidedly unique approach to music. *New Picnic Time* was also the last Ubu record with guitarist Tom Herman, and for many Ubu fans (myself included) this signals the end of Pere Ubu phase one (or phase two, depending on one's feelings for the *Datapanik*-era band). *New Picnic Time* also finds David Thomas' lyrical explorations reflecting his religious involvement with the Jehovah's Witnesses, pieties that are stated quite emphatically on the record's closing track "Jehovah's Kingdom Comes." *—John Dougan*

The Art of Walking / 1980 / Rough Trade ✦✦✦

The Art of Walking was the first Ubu recording that wasn't completely sensational. Red Krayola guitarist/mastermind Mayo Thompson replaced Tom Herman, and while he freely indulges in pushing the envelope when it comes to soloing, he doesn't have Herman's rock sensibility, so there's less pulsating, Chuck Berry-style riffing emerging from the mix. Also, the songs are a tad more obtuse—not that previous Ubu songs weren't, but this collection, with its focus on the pastoral, falls apart when it becomes overly precious. Such is the fate of utopian concept records. Still, this transitional (if you want to call it that) record offers many rewards, even if as a listener you have to work a little harder to find them. *—John Dougan*

390° Degrees of Simulated Stereo (Live) / 1981 / Rough Trade ✦✦

Song of the Bailing Man / 1982 / Rough Trade ✦✦✦

Continuing in the spirit of *The Art of Walking*, this record marks the departure of drummer Scott Krauss (replaced by ex-Feelies Anton Fier), a fact significant in that when combined with the earlier departure of guitarist Tom Herman, means that at this juncture Ubu was more art and less rock. Personally, I never understood why people were so knocked out by Fier; I think he lacks aggressiveness, plays behind the beat, and generally speaking, doesn't push the band as hard as a drummer ought to. That said, *Bailing Man* is a fine, occasionally wonderful record that, at its slackest moments, sounds strained and forced, as if it were no fun to make, and it's this seriousness (instead of the usual Ubu silly seriousness) that prevents this record from being great. It's no surprise that the band went on a hiatus for six years after the release of this record, returning with 1988's *The Tenement Year*. *—John Dougan*

★ **Terminal Tower** / 1985 / Twin/Tone ✦✦✦✦✦

At the outset of their career, Pere Ubu released some of the very first independent-label American punk singles on their own Hearthan (later Hearpen) label, which constitute some of their most celebrated and legendary work. *Terminal Tower: An Archival Collection* gathers 11 tracks, mostly from the crucial Hearthan/Hearpen period (including the entire *Datapanik in the Year Zero* EP), plus a couple of later U.K. singles. This music's historical importance is undeniable—not only because of the band's pioneeringly independent status in an area not as celebrated for its punk scene, but also because Pere Ubu was one of the first bands to push their art punk sound into territory later classified as alternative, a testament to their forward-looking approach. None of that would matter if *Terminal Tower* didn't hold up so well as a listening experience, but Pere Ubu still sounds utterly original. David Thomas' unearthly voice mumbles and sobs the angular melodies over a backdrop of garagey guitars, startling sound effects (from both guitar and synth), and odd dissonances. Moments of jarring, apocalyptic terror ("Heart of Darkness," the creeping, crawling "30 Seconds Over Tokyo") sit next to oddly beautiful introspection, sometimes on the same song (the aching angst and evocative guitar solo of "Final Solution"). Meanwhile, poppier tracks incorporate those avant-garde textures into a gleeful dada bounce. The two tracks unavailable anywhere else, "Not Happy" and "Lonesome Cowboy Dave," are slices of poppy dementia that may make the collection worthwhile for devotees who already own the box, especially since this is such a strong, coherent listen. *Terminal Tower* stands as the best introduction to the band not only because of its stellar material and relative accessibility, but also because it largely lacks the arty indulgences that popped up even on the group's most consistent albums. Now that it's back in print, it's essential, groundbreaking listening. *—Steve Huey*

The Tenement Year / 1988 / Enigma ✦✦✦✦✦

Since the re-formed version of Pere Ubu reins in (slightly) the group's more extreme tendencies, this album, which nevertheless presents David Thomas' unique vision and the band's somewhat off-kilter approach to rock more or less intact, may be the place for neophytes to get their feet wet with a highly unusual group. This one should give you the idea—then you're on your own. *—William Ruhlmann*

One Man Drives While the Other Man Screams / 1989 / Rough Trade ✦✦

Cloudland / May 1989 / Fontana ✦✦✦✦✦

It's funny, this might be the most controversial recording Ubu ever made. After years of brilliant chunks of avant-garde garage rock tomfoolery, they release a pop record, one with smooth corners, and production help from Stephen Hague (Pet Shop Boys). It's not as if Ubu is unrecognizable; the familiar idiosyncracies are here and in full effect. It's more that the songs themselves—love songs—are very different from their usual dramas from the urban landscape. But David Thomas' pastoral mumblings and utopian visions remain central to the record's lyrical heart. Hardcore fans, a boring group who want everything to sound like *Dub Housing*, felt betrayed by this record, seeing it as the band's egregious attempt at selling out. But nothing could have been further from the truth. *Cloudland* is an amazing record that allows room for growth and change without sacrificing panache and attitude. *—John Dougan*

Worlds in Collision / May 21, 1991 / Fontana ✦✦✦✦

Pere Ubu's late-1980s recordings were a marked departure from the forbidding weirdness of the band's early work. That departure culminated in 1989 with *Cloudland*, an honest-to-goodness pop album complete with singalong choruses and an MTV video. It was a wonderful album; even longtime fans loved it. With *Worlds in Collision*, Ubu keeps one foot in the world of slick pop production while returning somewhat to its bizarro-punk roots (even with the crystalline studio sound, who but David Thomas could write a song as strange and catchy as "Turpentine"?). "Over the Moon" and "Don't Look Back" are some of the most accessible songs in the Pere Ubu catalog, and yet the album's title track is one of the weirdest. The bad news is that Allen Ravenstine's bleeping EML synthesizer is getting pushed farther and farther back in the mix; the good news is that Thomas still sings like a throttled penguin. *—Rick Anderson*

Story of My Life / Apr. 6, 1993 / Imago ✦✦✦

Although it is the most pop-oriented record Pere Ubu ever cut, *Story of My Life* didn't make much of a dent even in alternative radio. Nevertheless, there are many fine pop tunes here, occasionally spiked with some of their trademark experimentalism, although the music isn't as challenging as it was years before. *—Stephen Thomas Erlewine*

Ray Gun Suitcase / Aug. 22, 1995 / Tim Kerr ✦✦✦

Returned to indie label status for their tenth studio album, Pere Ubu again made music in the style familiar from their earliest recordings—staccato rhythms and noisy guitars backing David Thomas' disjointed singing of repeated, obscure lyrics. Typical was "Vacuum In My Head," which had some of the ominous tone of "30 Seconds Over Tokyo," in which Thomas spoke-sang, "Vacuum cleaner in my head / It sucks up everything I know." The playing often had more delicacy and precision than early on, and Thomas varied his effects from mutters to shrieks. An acoustic guitar rendition of the Beach Boys' "Surfer Girl" was a distinct change of pace, even if its author, Brian Wilson, might not have recognized it in Thomas' performance. But *Ray Gun Suitcase* was an album for the cult of fans who delighted in the band's offbeat lyrical viewpoint and musical cacophony, which was just as well, since the more conventional orientation attempted in the late 1980s and early '90s did not pay off in an expanded following. *—William Ruhlmann*

Hearpen Singles / Oct. 17, 1995 / Tim Kerr ✦✦✦✦

Folly of Youth / Feb. 1996 / Tim/Kerr ✦✦✦

Or, "Everything You Ever Wanted to Know About Ubu (But Were Afraid to Ask)." A computer-interactive CD-plus release, *Folly of Youth* goes way beyond the usual bonus cuts, band member bios and photos that round out such multimedia releases, opting instead to include financial and business-related material on the band, including their tax returns. Also featured are two short films, "Story of Ubu" and "Ray Gun Suitcase" (the name of the album from which the single "Folly of Youth" is drawn), as well as lyrics, a discography and bits of animation. By the way, there's music here too: the title track, a long jam called "Ball n' Chain," and a pair of demos, "Memphis" and "Down By the River II." *—Jason Ankeny*

Beach Boys CD+ / May 21, 1996 / Tim Kerr ✦✦✦

The bad news: David Thomas is the only original member left. And that's not minor bad news, either—though his has always been the defining vision of Pere Ubu, Allen Ravenstine's bleeping, blooping EML synth and Tony Maimone's rock-solid basslines have always been as integral to the Ubu sound as Thomas' strangled-penguin vocals and pastoral-bizarre lyrics. It's not that newcomers like bassist Michele Temple and synthesist Robert Wheeler don't keep the faith (Wheeler's theremin work is particularly inspired), it's just that what they're doing is keeping the faith, and that really isn't enough. *Ray Gun Suitcase*, the album from which this CD single is drawn, is good post-*Cloudland* Pere Ubu; it veers between forbidding weirdness ("Folly of Youth" and a really awful cover of "Surfer Girl") and endearingly quirky tunefulness ("Turquoise Fins"), just like the best of Ubu's recent work, but it doesn't ever achieve the special Ubitude that animated *Tenement Years* and *Cloudland*, which may have been the two best Ubu releases since *The Modern Dance*.

The good news, however, is also nothing to sniff at: Thomas has discovered the Macintosh. That means that this otherwise unassuming little CD single is more than just a single—it also includes tons of Ubu cyber-ephemera for the discerning computer-equipped nostalgist, as well as up-to-date videos and live concert footage, financial records, weird animations, lists of band policies, etc. Thomas apparently wrote all the code himself, so if you can imagine the same brain that created *Monster Walks the Winter Lake* creating multimedia rock & roll, then you know what to expect. It's wonderful. David Thomas is one of the funniest writers around, and the text files alone are worth the money—the videos are fun, too. Even if you don't feel like you need to hear the demo versions of "Memphis" and "Down by the River," seeking out these discs is still strongly recommended. *—Rick Anderson*

Datapanik in the Year Zero [Box] / Aug. 27, 1996 / Geffen ✦✦✦✦✦

Pere Ubu's troubles with record companies are legendary within certain underground rock circles. In perhaps the most bizarre turn of events, the group's collected works of 1978-1982—after being out of print for nearly a decade—were reissued by Geffen as a five-disc box set, *Datapanik in the Year Zero*. Named after the group's 1978 EP, the set is arranged chronologically and occasionally substitutes live versions for studio tracks, but that hardly matters—nearly every song the band recorded during the five-year time span is included. In addition to the official Pere Ubu material, the box includes a disc of rare singles from early incarnations of Ubu and other Cleveland-area punk rockers like Rocket from the Tombs, 15-60-75, and Mirrors, which were released on David Thomas' independent record label. With this much material, it's safe to say that the set is a definitive retrospective and its worth is increased because most of this material hasn't been widely available on compact disc, so collectors won't feel like they've paid a lot of money for a handful of rarities. However, if you're simply interested in Pere Ubu, consider the set carefully before investing. Pere Ubu was indeed one of the most innovative and challenging bands of their era, which means that their music is an acquired taste. However, those willing to invest in the box will find a wealth of inventive, hard-edged avant-rock & roll. *—Stephen Thomas Erlewine*

Pennsylvania / Mar. 17, 1998 / Tim Kerr ✦✦✦✦

On self-imposed exile in England yet still obsessed with industrial America, Dave Thomas looks back to his hometown and finds that it's not what it used to be. The factories are still there, still belching out smoke to the heavens. There are still vast landscapes of concrete and steel. The difference is, it's all been homogenized, run through the grinder of corporate consumer culture. Although he's half a world away, he doesn't like what he sees, and that's the essence of *Pennsylvania*, Pere Ubu's eleventh album in 20 years. It's a return to the clastrophobic, complex, darkly paranoid sound of their early albums; only occasionally is it graced with the relatively tamed alterna-pop stylings that marked their early-'90s records. Thomas, thankfully, hasn't abandoned his satiric wit, and that's what makes *Pennsylvania* provocative, not insular. It's been many years since Pere Ubu has delivered a record as sweeping in lyrical and musical scope as *Pennsylvania*, and it's been worth the wait. *—Stephen Thomas Erlewine*

Apocalypse Now / Aug. 24, 1999 / Thirsty Ear ✦✦✦✦

Pere Ubu's third live album is only the second to feature decent sound (the first, *90 Degrees of Simulated Stereo*, was a compilation of dodgy fan bootlegs and almost equally dodgy board tapes), and it has the added virtue of offering a pretty thorough overview of the band's history, from its first album to its most recent work, including bandleader David Thomas' forays into solo work. In fact, it's Thomas' whimsical "My Theory of Spontaneous Simultude" ("Tony, complete this phrase: 'I am like . . .' ") that opens the program. From the old band book they pull out an inferior version of "Heaven" and the epochal "Non-Alignment Pact" (and append to it an abridged version of the Stooges' "I Wanna Be Your Dog"). "Caligari's Mirror" goes almost as far back, but there are also fine versions of the poppier and more recent "We Have the Technology" and "Oh Catherine." Guitarist Jim Jones is playing acoustic on this set, but he's got a Rat pedal that he can stomp when he wants to rock out, which gives the album a nice variety of moods and textures—though the band's segue from the bludgeoning proto-punk of "I Wanna Be Your Dog" to the 6/8 lilt of "Caligari's Mirror" is enough to give you whiplash. David Thomas is in rare form throughout, warbling and hooting in that strangled-penguin voice of his, just sounding like he's having a great old time. You will, too, though neophytes might want to start with the studio albums first. *—Rick Anderson*

Carl Perkins

b. Apr. 9, 1932, Tiptonville, TN, **d.** Jan. 19, 1998

Guitar (Electric), Vocals, Guitar / Rockabilly, Traditional Country, Rock & Roll

While some ill-informed revisionist writers of rock history would like to dismiss Carl Perkins as a rockabilly artist who became a one-hit wonder at the dawn of rock & roll's early years, a deeper look at his music and career reveals much more. A quick look at his songwriting portfolio shows that he has composed "Daddy Sang Bass" for Johnny Cash, "I Was So Wrong" for Patsy Cline, and "Let Me Tell You About Love" for the Judds, big hits and classics all. His influence as the quintessential rockabilly artist has played a big part in the development of every generation of rocker to come down the pike since, from the Beatles' George Harrison to the Stray Cats' Brian Setzer to a myriad of others in the country field as well. His guitar style is the other twin peak—along with that of Elvis' lead man Scotty Moore—of rockabilly's instrumental center, so pervasive that modern day players automatically gravitate toward it when called upon to deliver the style, not even realizing that they're playing Carl Perkins licks, sometimes note for note. As a singer, his interpretation of country ballads is every bit as fine as his better-known rockers. And within the framework of the best of his music is a strong sense of family and roots, all of which trace straight back to Carl's humble beginnings. *—Cub Koda*

Up Through the Years, 1954-1957 / 1986 / Bear Family ✦✦✦✦✦

An import collection of Perkins' groundbreaking Sun singles, *Up Through the Years* offers eight more tracks than Rhino's *Original Sun Greatest Hits*; both discs are definitive collections. *—Stephen Thomas Erlewine*

★ **Original Sun Greatest Hits** / 1986 / Rhino ✦✦✦✦✦

Original Sun Greatest Hits is exactly what it says it is—16 tracks of Carl Perkins' best sides for Sun, including all of the hits ("Blue Suede Shoes," "Boppin' the Blues," "Your True Love") and all of his most legendary songs ("Honey, Don't," "Everybody's Trying to Be My Baby," "Movie Magg," "All Mam's Children," "Matchbox," "Dixie Fried," "Lend Me Your Comb," "Glad All Over"). It's the essential compilation, providing everything you need to know about Carl Perkins and offering no filler. *—Stephen Thomas Erlewine*

Honky Tonk Gal / Apr. 1989 / Rounder ✦✦✦✦

While at Sun Records in the mid-'50s, Carl Perkins made his name with "Blue Suede Shoes." Partly due to some bad timing, though, Perkins was unable to achieve the same level of fame his Sun contemporaries Elvis Presley and Jerry Lee Lewis would. But historically speaking, Perkins is just as responsible as those two for the country and blues mix that makes up rock & roll. The proof is heard on this rarities collection, which spotlights his hillbilly roots, Hank Williams-inspired sound, and blues-tinged delivery. A perfect complement to the many hits packages available, *Honky Tonk Gal* includes solid alternate versions of "Turn Around," "Let the Jukebox Keep on Playing," and "Dixie Fried," as well as stunning covers like "You Can't Make Love to Somebody," "Caldonia," and the title track. A fine record for dedicated fans of classic rock & roll, country, and rockabilly. *—Stephen Cook*

The Classic / Feb. 1990 / Bear Family ✦✦✦✦✦

This is a Bear Family release that even casual listeners can sort of agree with. The five CDs contain close to 150 tracks, most notably Perkins' complete Sun Records output in close, glittering sound, plus all of his Columbia sides from 1958 through 1962, and his oft-overlooked early-'60s recordings for both American and English Decca. The Sun material is the best part of this box, and while it has been available as a triple CD from Charly, the latter is now out of print and had nothing like the crisp, clean sound you get here. The Sun outtakes may make the casual listener hesitate, but it's in the multiple takes that rock & roll as you know it was born, and all of the stuff is different enough between the takes to make hearing it worthwhile even for the non-scholar, to show that classics like that don't just "happen." Moreover, these differences aren't the little arrangement polishes and little tempo changes that one finds in most outtakes, but represent the evolution of a style—musically, they're at least as interesting as any of Elvis' Sun session outtakes. Beyond the rock & roll history, however, the reality is also that anyone buying it should have as much love of good honky tonk-style country music as they do for rock & roll. The Columbia sides are available separately, but they just aren't as interesting. The Decca stuff, which is unique to this set, represents Perkins' serious attempts at a comeback in the face of his huge concert success in England in the wake of the Beatles' recording of his music. The booklet is good, though not quite as comprehensive as one would have liked. *—Bruce Eder*

Jive After Five: The Best of Carl Perkins (1958-1978) / Sep. 1990 / Rhino ✦✦✦✦

A nice single-disc set that examines the best of Perkins' recordings after his tenure at Sun Records. The earlier Columbia sides continue the rockabilly mold that launched him, although tracks like "Pink Pedal Pushers" and "Jive After Five" are literally swimming in tape echo and reverb, unlike the sparseness of the Sun sides. The later tracks on Decca, Mercury, and others find him moving from rockabilly into a more mature country style, closing with a solo instrumental, "Just Coastin'," which shows his deep playing debt to both Chet Atkins and Merle Travis. A nice and important companion to the Sun sides. *—Cub Koda*

Country Boy's Dream: The Dollie Masters / Jun. 1994 / Bear Family ✦✦✦
Upon signing to Dollie records in 1966, Carl Perkins decided to concentrate on country music. The result was two minor country hits, "Country Boy's Dream" and "Shine, Shine, Shine," that marked the first time he was on the charts since the late '50s. Though the Dollie recordings weren't blockbusters, they were solid, straight-ahead country and paved the way for Perkins' major label deal with Columbia, as well as a slot in Johnny Cash's band. *Country Boy's Dream: The Dollie Masters* contains all of Perkins' recordings for Dollie, including a handful of unreleased and rare tracks. Fans of Perkins' harder-edged, rocking sound won't find much to like on the compilation, yet it demonstrates that he was equally adept at country. Nevertheless, even fans of Carl's country records will find *Country Boy's Dream* a little tedious, since many of the songs on the album are simply unremarkable. —*Stephen Thomas Erlewine*

The Complete Sun Singles / Jun. 6, 2000 / Varese ✦✦✦✦✦
As part of their Sun series, this brings together all 18 of Perkins' original singles for the Flip and Sun labels. In addition to the 16 sides, there's also the inclusion of "Tennessee" and "Sure to Fall," the single by the Perkins Brothers band that features both Carl and Jay. Although there's much duplication with Rhino's *All-Time Greatest Sun Recordings* collection here, there are still enough new wrinkles aboard this one to make a nice stand-alone set. —*Cub Koda*

Back on Top / Jul. 12, 2000 / Bear Family ✦✦✦✦
Back on Top, Bear Family's four-disc retrospective of Carl Perkins' late-'60s and early-'70s work, collects everything he recorded during his second tenure with Columbia, his tribute to Elvis ("E.P. Express"), and his complete recordings with NRBQ. Over the course of 99 tracks, the set also covers his two-year stint with Mercury, the complete *My Kind of Country* sessions, and a full disc's worth of previously unreleased demos. As with all of Bear Family's releases, *Back on Top* also features impressive supplemental material, including liner notes by Grammy winner Colin Escott, a complete discography, and previously unpublished photos. A Perkins completist's dream come true, *Back on Top* paints an expansive portrait of his comeback years. —*Heather Phares*

The Pernice Brothers

Chamber Pop, Americana, Alternative Country-Rock, Indie Rock
Led by Joe Pernice of the cult favorite alternative country band the Scud Mountain Boys, the Pernice Brothers shed their roots-rock trappings in favor of a more pop-oriented sound. Also comprising Pernice's brother Bob as well as Thom Monahan, Aaron Sperske and Mike Deming, the group debuted in 1998 with *Overcome by Happiness. The World Won't End* was released three years later. —*Jason Ankeny*

Overcome by Happiness / May 19, 1998 / Sub Pop ✦✦✦✦
Listeners expecting a continuation of the Scud Mountain Boys' slow, grim alt-country sound will be surprised by the wholesale changes wrought on *Overcome by Happiness*—Joe Pernice has gone pop, and the results are quite promising. Recorded in part with a ten-piece orchestra, the record is closer to chamber pop than roots-rock, with the bright, sunny songs adorned in piano and horns; tracks like "Monkey Suit" and "Clear Spot" are instantly engaging, their sheer hummability alone suggesting not merely a radical creative reassessment but a total artistic rebirth. —*Jason Ankeny*

● **The World Won't End** / Jun. 19, 2001 / Ashmont ✦✦✦✦✦
So maybe Joe Pernice isn't crazy. He spent his time between the release of the Pernice Brothers' *Overcome By Happiness* and *The World Won't End* by issuing *Chappaquiddick Skyline* and *Big Tobacco* under separate aliases, claiming that the material on those weren't from his top drawer and that the good stuff was being saved for the second Pernice Brothers record. Most listeners just rolled their eyes, figuring it to be yet another case of a musician's eccentricities and inability to recognize their own talents. After all, those "interim" releases did more than merely maintain fan attention; they might not have been as polished or perfected as *Overcome By Happiness*, but they were chipped from the same precious ore. So here's the payoff, proving that he was being accurate after all, if a twinge modest. With much of the support from *Overcome* staying on board with a couple of relative newcomers (this lineup has been in place over two years), *The World Won't End* is every bit on par with its predecessor, if not an improved effort thanks to the increased importance of those Pernice surrounds himself with. This is a record made by a band, not a singer/songwriter aided by seasoned session hands. The sound is as lush, melodic, and clean as ever (not sterile), with sweet arrangements standing at the polar opposite of lyrics dealing with sinking relationships and pesky emotional ghosts. This is all-purpose pop; you can hum merrily along to the melodies or sink yourself in the lyrics and wonder where everything went wrong. Or both. Regardless of where you're at, you won't lose sight of Pernice's voice, one that most vocalists would cross the river Styx to possess. Most indicative song title: "Endless Supply." That seems to be the case. —*Andy Kellman*

The Persuaders

f. 1969, New York, NY
Smooth Soul, Soul
This group made a pair of marvelous heartache ballads in 1971, but have the unfortunate legacy of having their finest cuts turned into pop hits via covers. Lead singer Douglas Scott, whose nickname appropriately was "Smokey," Willie Holland, James Barnes, and Charles Stodghill formed in New York in 1969. They signed with Atlantic in the early '70s, and had their lone R&B chart topper in 1971, the shattering classic "Thin Line Between Love & Hate." It was also their only gold single. The follow-up was nearly as strong; "Love's Gonna Pack Up (And Walk Out)" reached number eight on the R&B charts, but had no crossover appeal. They continued on Win & Lose until 1973, then moved to Atco,

where "Some Guys Have All the Luck" was a number seven R&B single in 1973. It was their final hit, though they kept recording until the late '70s, doing their last session for Calla. Besides the Pretenders re-doing "Thin Line Between Love & Hate," Rod Stewart had a Top Ten pop hit with his version of "Some Guys Have All the Luck" in 1984. —*Ron Wynn*

● **Thin Line Between Love & Hate** / 1974 / Collectables ✦✦✦✦✦
A gritty soul unit, adept at tragic encounter tunes. The title song is a soul anthem. —*Ron Wynn*

Pet Shop Boys

f. Aug. 1981, London, England
Alternative Dance, Club/Dance, House, Dance-Pop
Postmodern ironists cloaked behind a veil of buoyantly melodic and lushly romantic synth-pop confections, the Pet Shop Boys' cheeky, smart and utterly danceable music established them among the most commercially and critically successful groups of their era. Always remaining one step ahead of their contemporaries, the British duo navigated the constantly shifting landscape of modern dance-pop with rare grace and intelligence, moving easily from disco to house to techno with their own distinctive image remaining completely intact; satiric and irreverent—yet somehow strangely affecting—the Pet Shop Boys transcended the seeming disposability of their craft, offering wry and thoughtful cultural commentary communicated by the Morse code of *au courant* synth washes and drum-machine rhythms. When 1985's "West End Girls" became an international chart-topper, its massive success propelled the Pet Shop Boys' 1986 debut LP *Please* into the Top Ten. In 1987 the duo resurfaced with the superb *Actually*, which launched three more Top Ten smashes—"It's a Sin," a lovely cover of the perennial "Always on My Mind," and "What Have I Done to Deserve This?," a duet between singer Neil Tennant and the great Dusty Springfield. A year later, the Pet Shop Boys issued their third studio LP, the eclectic *Introspective*; the single "Domino Dancing" was their final Top 40 hit in the U.S. —*Jason Ankeny*

Please / 1986 / EMI America ✦✦✦
A collection of immaculately crafted and seamlessly produced synthesized dance-pop, the Pet Shop Boys' debut album, *Please*, sketches out the basic elements of the duo's sound. At first listen, most of the songs come off as mere excuses for the dancefloor, driven by cold, melodic keyboard riffs and pulsing drum machines. However, the songcraft that beats support is surprisingly strong, featuring catchy melodies that appear slight because of Neil Tennant's thin voice. Tennant's lyrics were still in their formative stages, with half of the record failing to transcend the formulaic constraints of dance-pop. The songs that do break free—the crass "Opportunities (Let's Make Lots of Money)," the lulling "Suburbia," and the hypnotic "West End Girls"—are not only classic dance singles, they're classic pop singles. —*Stephen Thomas Erlewine*

Disco / Oct. 1986 / EMI America ✦✦

Actually / Jun. 1987 / EMI America ✦✦✦✦✦
With their second album, *Actually*, the Pet Shop Boys perfected their melodic, detached dance-pop. Where most of *Please* was dominated by the beats, the rhythms on *Actually* are part of a series of intricate arrangements that create a glamorous but disposable backdrop for Neil Tennant's tales of isolation, boredom, money, and loneliness. Not only are the arrangements more accomplished, but the songs themselves are more striking, incorporating a strong sense of melody, as evidenced by "What Have I Done to Deserve This?," a duet with Dusty Springfield. Tennant's lyrics are clever and direct, chronicling the lives and times of urban, lonely, and bored yuppies of the late '80s. And the fact that dance-pop is considered a disposable medium by most mainstream critics and listeners only increases the reserved emotional undercurrent of *Actually*, as well as its irony. —*Stephen Thomas Erlewine*

Introspective / Apr. 1988 / EMI America ✦✦✦
Featuring a mere six tracks, most of them well over six minutes in length, *Introspective* was a move back to the clubs for the Pet Shop Boys. Over the course of the album, they incorporated various dance techniques that were currently in vogue, including Latin rhythms and house textures. The title isn't entirely an arch joke, however. Like *Actually*, *Introspective* was an exploration of distant, disaffected yuppies, which naturally resulted in a good deal of self-analyzation. Melodically, the essential song structures were as strong and multi-layered as the previous album, yet that was hard to hear beneath the varying rhythmic textures that composed the bulk of each track. Nevertheless, the mixes are more compelling than the remixes on *Disco*, and the songs include several of their best numbers, including "Left to My Own Devices" and "Domino Dancing," as well as the reconstruction of "Always on My Mind" and a cover of Blaze's club classic, "It's Alright." —*Stephen Thomas Erlewine*

Behavior / Oct. 1990 / EMI America ✦✦✦✦✦
Behavior was a retreat from the deep dance textures of *Introspective*, as it picked up on the carefully constructed pop of *Actually*. In fact, *Behavior* functions as the Pet Shop Boys' bid for mainstream credibility, as much of the album relies more on popcraft than rhythmic variations. Although its a subtle maneuver, it would have been rather disastrous if the results weren't so captivating. Tennant takes this approach seriously, singing the lyrics instead of speaking them. That doesn't necessarily give the album added emotional baggage—all of the distance and detachment in the duo's music is not a hindrance, it's part of the concept—but it does result in an ambitious and breathtaking pop album, which manages to include everything from the spiteful "How Can You Expect to Be Taken Seriously?" to the wistful "Being Boring." —*Stephen Thomas Erlewine*

★ **Discography: The Complete Singles Collection** / Nov. 5, 1991 / EMI America ✦✦✦✦✦
Most of the Pet Shop Boys' albums are well-crafted and thoroughly intriguing in their own right, but dance-pop is a medium that is driven by hit singles. *Discography* collects all the duo's numerous hit singles, including a handful of non-album tracks, in their original 7" single mix, which occasionally varies from the album version, particularly in the case of the *Introspective* material. Presented chronologically, the singles not only demonstrate the band's increasing musical sophistication, they illustrate what fine songwriters Tennant and Lowe are. These 19 songs form one of the most consistent and innovative bodies of work of its era. Some of the production techniques have dated slightly, but the music has remained impressive. *—Stephen Thomas Erlewine*

Very / Oct. 5, 1993 / Capitol ✦✦✦✦✦
Because they work in a field that isn't usually taken seriously, the Pet Shop Boys are often ignored in the rock world. But make no mistake—they are one of the most talented pop outfits working today, witty and melodic with a fine sense of flair. *Very* is one of their very best records, expertly weaving between the tongue-in-cheek humor of "I Wouldn't Normally Do This Kind of Thing," the quietly shocking "Can You Forgive Her?," and the bizarrely moving cover of the Village People's "Go West." Alternately happy and melancholy, *Very* is the Pet Shop Boys at their finest. *—Stephen Thomas Erlewine*

Disco 2 / Sep. 20, 1994 / Capitol ✦✦

Alternative / Aug. 29, 1995 / Capitol ✦✦✦✦✦
Alternative is a double-disc set of The Pet Shop Boys' B-sides. Far from being a superfluous collection, the album contains a wealth of prime material, including several tracks that surpass those the duo put on their albums. Consequently, the set is worthwhile not only for hardcore fans, but for listeners with a passing interest in the group. *—Stephen Thomas Erlewine*

Bilingual / Sep. 1996 / Atlantic ✦✦✦
As a title, *Bilingual* is a double-edged sword. Disregard it's sexual connotations and concentrate on its musical implications—*Bilingual* is a rich, diverse album that delves deeply into Latin rhythms. It's not a crass, simplistic fusion, where the polyphonic rhythms are simply grafted over synthesizers and a disco pulse. Instead, *Bilingual* is an enormously subtle album, with shifting rhythms and graceful, understated melodies. The music isn't the only thing subtle about the album—Neil Tennant's voice and lyrics are nuanced, suggesting more than they actually say. Furthermore, *Bilingual* consists of the most optimistic, happy set of songs the Pet Shop Boys have ever recorded. Whether it's the smooth disco of "Before" or the insistent rhythms of "Se a Vida E," *Bilingual* is filled with joyous, if subdued, sounds. If anything, it's further proof that even if the Pet Shop Boys aren't gracing the top of the charts as frequently as they did during the late '80s, they are crafting albums that are more adventurous and successful than they did when they were one of the top singles acts in pop music. *—Stephen Thomas Erlewine*

Nightlife / Nov. 2, 1999 / Sire ✦✦✦
Nightlife is a loose concept album—more of a song cycle, really—about nightlife (naturally), a collection of moods and themes, from love to loneliness. In that sense, it's not that different from most Pet Shop Boys albums, and, musically, the album is very much of a piece with *Very* and *Bilingual*, which is to say that it relies more on craft than on innovation. Depending on your point of view, this may not be such a bad thing, since Pet Shop Boys specialize in subtle craft and masterful understatement. Such skills serve them well when they're essentially following familiar musical territory, which they are on *Nightlife*. At its core, the record is very much like *Very*—a clever, skillful updating of classic disco, highlighted by small contemporary dance flourishes, and infused with a true sense of wit, sophistication, and intelligence. Pet Shop Boys do this music better than anyone else ever has, and they're at the top of their form here, but it's hard to shake the initial impression that they've done this before. Each individual song works beautifully, from the wistfully dejected "I Don't Know What You Want But I Can't Give It Any More" to the exhilarating Village People homage "New York City Boy," but as a whole, *Nightlife* seems less than the sum of its parts. Repeated listens reveal the songs' charms, yet *Nightlife* coasts on its craft a bit too much, which makes it feel like one of their second-tier albums. *—Stephen Thomas Erlewine*

Peter & Gordon

f. 1963, London, England, **db.** 1968
Merseybeat, British Invasion, Pop
In June 1964, Peter & Gordon became the very first British Invasion act after the Beatles to take the number one spot on the American charts with "A World Without Love." That hit, and their subsequent successes, were due as much or more to their important connections as to their talent. Peter Asher was the older brother of Jane Asher, Paul McCartney's girlfriend for much of the 1960s. This no doubt gave Asher and Gordon Waller access to Lennon-McCartney compositions that were unrecorded by the Beatles, such as "A World Without Love" and three of their other biggest hits, "Nobody I Know," "I Don't Want to See You Again," and "Woman." But Peter & Gordon were significant talents in their own right, a sort of Everly Brothers-styled duo for the British Invasion that faintly prefigured the folk-rock of the mid-'60s. They duo continued to hit the charts for a couple of years, with updates of Buddy Holly's "True Love Ways" and Del Shannon's "I Go to Pieces." The overtly cute British novelty "Lady Godiva," though, became their last big hit in late 1966. After Peter & Gordon broke up in 1968, Asher became an enormously successful producer. Relocating to Los Angeles, in the 1970s he was one of the principal architects of mellow Californian rock, producing James Taylor and Linda Ronstadt. *—Richie Unterberger*

EP Collection / Sep. 5, 1995 / See For Miles ✦✦✦✦
Although this 29-track compilation is ostensibly a roundup of songs that appeared on foreign EPs, it actually serves as a greatest-hits collection of sorts. The sequencing is unfortunately haphazard, jumping all over the place chronologically, but it does include all ten of their U.S. Top 40 singles. In fact, it's a substantially better deal than the domestic best-of that appeared on Rhino a few years before this; it has more songs, presents some pretty good B-sides and non-45 tracks, and puts a greater weight on their original compositions. The inclusion of four French songs from a rare EP will please collectors, although for general listeners' purposes it would have been wiser to feature the English versions. *—Richie Unterberger*

● **The Ultimate Peter & Gordon** / 2001 / Collectors Choice ✦✦✦✦✦
The selection and sequencing strategy adopted by compiler Ron Furmanek for *The Ultimate Peter & Gordon* is easy to see. Allowed to pick 20 tracks, he has chosen all 14 songs by the '60s British duo that reached *Billboard* magazine's Hot 100 chart, from major hits like "A World Without Love," "Lady Godiva," and "I Go to Pieces" to minor ones like "To Show I Love You" and "The Jokers." The remaining six selections are either non-charting A-side singles ("You've Had Better Times"), B-sides ("Love Me, Baby," "The Town I Live In"), or album tracks ("I Still Love You," "Broken Promises," "My First Day Alone"). The selections have been sequenced in chronological order by recording date, not release date. The sequencing gives a good sense of the duo's development, from the harmony-filled soft rock sound of their first three Paul McCartney-penned songs to more elaborate productions such as the one for "True Love Ways" on which Gordon Waller steps out as lead singer with Peter Asher playing a subsidiary role as harmony singer, and on to the novelty songs "Lady Godiva" (a rare Asher lead) and "Knight in Rusty Armour" that gave them their last big hits. The focus on the *Billboard* chart means singles that placed on other charts, notably "Baby, I'm Yours," a Top 20 hit in the U.K., and "Never Ever," which charted (though just barely) in *Cash Box*, are missing. But the set still gives a good sense of Peter and Gordon's best and most popular recordings. [This is the first Peter and Gordon CD to go back to the original master tapes. The sound, with that extreme stereo separation typical of the 1960s, is superb, and "Woman" and "The Town I Live In" are presented in stereo for the first time.] *– William Ruhlmann*

Tom Petty

b. Oct. 20, 1950, Gainesville, FL
Vocals, Guitar / Bar Band, Heartland Rock, Album Rock, Hard Rock, Rock & Roll
Upon the release of their first album in the late '70s, Tom Petty & the Heartbreakers were shoehorned into the punk/new wave movement by some observers, who picked up on the tough, vibrant energy of the group's blend of Byrds riffs and Stonesy swagger. In a way, the categorization made sense. Compared to the heavy metal and art-rock that dominated mid-'70s guitar-rock, the Heartbreakers' bracing return to roots was nearly as unexpected as the crashing chords of the Clash. As time progressed, it became clear that the band didn't break from tradition like their punk contemporaries. Instead, they celebrated it, culling the best parts of the British Invasion, American garage rock, and Dylanesque singer/songwriters to create a distinctively American hybrid that recalled the past without being indebted to it. The Heartbreakers were a tight, muscular and versatile backing band that provided the proper support for Petty's songs, which cataloged a series of middle-class losers and dreamers. While his slurred, nasal voice may have recalled Dylan and Roger McGuinn, Petty's songwriting was lean and direct, recalling the simple, unadorned style of Neil Young. Throughout his career, Petty & the Heartbreakers never departed from their signature rootsy sound, but they were able to expand it, bringing in psychedelic, southern rock and New Wave influences; they were also one of the few of the traditionalist rock & rollers who embraced music videos, filming some of the most inventive and popular videos in MTV history. His willingness to experiment with the boundaries of classic rock & roll helped Petty sustain his popularity well into the '90s. *—Stephen Thomas Erlewine*

Tom Petty & the Heartbreakers / 1976 / Gone Gator/MCA ✦✦✦✦✦
At the time Tom Petty & the Heartbreakers' debut was released in 1976, they were fresh enough to almost be considered punk. They weren't as reckless or visionary as the Ramones, but they shared a similar love for pure '60s rock and, for the Heartbreakers, that meant embracing the Byrds as much as the Stones. And that's pretty much what this album is—tuneful jangle balanced by a tough garage swagger. At times, the attitude and the sound overrides the songwriting, but that's alright, since the slight songs ("Anything That's Rock & Roll," to pick a random example) are still infused with spirit and an appealing surface. Petty and the Heartbreakers feel underground on this album, at least to the extent that power pop was underground in 1976; with Dwight Twilley providing backing vocals for "Strangered in the Night," the similarities between the two bands (adherence to pop hooks and melodies, love of guitars) become apparent. Petty wound up eclipsing Twilley because he rocked harder, something that's evident throughout this record. Take the closer "American Girl"—it's a Byrds song by any other name, but he pushed the Heartbreakers to treat it as a rock & roll song, not as something delicate. There are times where the album starts to drift, especially on the second side, but the highlights—"Rockin' Around (With You)," "Hometown Blues," "The Wild One, Forever," the AOR staples "Breakdown" and "American Girl"—still illustrate how refreshing Petty & the Heartbreakers sounded in 1976. *—Stephen Thomas Erlewine*

You're Gonna Get It! / May 1978 / Gone Gator/MCA ✦✦✦
Tom Petty & the Heartbreakers didn't really have to knock out their second album—it was released two years after their debut—but it sure sounds as if they did. There are some wonderful moments on this record, but it often feels like leftovers from a strong debut, or an album written on the road, especially since the music is simply an extension of the first album. That said, when *You're Gonna Get It* works, it devastates. That's not saying that "When the Time Comes" is a masterpiece, even if it's a fine opener, but it does mean

that "I Need to Know" and the scathing "Listen to Her Heart" are testaments to how good this band could be when they were focused. If the rest of the album doesn't achieve this level of perfection, that's a signal that they were still finding their footing, but overall it's still a solid record, filled with good performances that are never quite as good as the songs. It's pretty good as it spins, but once it finishes, you remember those two songs at the heart of the record, maybe the opener and closer, which are stronger than the rest of the competent, enjoyable, yet unremarkable roots-rockers that surround them. Not necessarily a transitional effort—after all, it pretty much mirrors its predecessor—but a holding pattern that may not suggest the peaks of what's to come, but still delivers a good sound-alike of the debut. *—Stephen Thomas Erlewine*

☆ **Damn the Torpedoes** / Nov. 1979 / MCA ✦✦✦✦✦
Not long after *You're Gonna Get It*, Tom Petty & the Heartbreakers' label, Shelter, was sold to MCA Records. Petty struggled to free himself from the major label, eventually sending himself into bankruptcy. He settled with MCA and set to work on his third album, digging out some old Mudcrutch numbers and quickly writing new songs. Amazingly, through all the frustration and anguish, Petty & the Heartbreakers delivered their breakthrough and arguably their masterpiece with *Damn the Torpedoes*. Musically, it follows through on the promise of their first two albums, offering a tough, streamlined fusion of the Stones and Byrds that, thanks to Jimmy Iovine's clean production, sounded utterly modern yet timeless. It helped that the Heartbreakers had turned into a tighter, muscular outfit, reminiscent of, well, the Stones in their prime—all of the parts combine into a powerful, distinctive sound capable of all sorts of subtle variations. Their musical suppleness helps bring out the soul in Petty's impressive set of songs. He had written a few classics before—"American Girl," "Listen to Her Heart"—but here his songwriting truly blossoms. Most of the songs have a deep melancholy undercurrent—the tough "Here Comes My Girl" and "Even the Losers" have tender hearts; the infectious "Don't Do Me Like That" masks a painful relationship; "Refugee" is a scornful, blistering rocker; "Louisiana Rain" is a tear-jerking ballad. Yet there are purpose and passion behind the performances that makes *Damn the Torpedoes* an invigorating listen all the same. Few mainstream rock albums of the late '70s and early '80s were quite as strong as this, and it still stands as one of the great records of the album rock era. *—Stephen Thomas Erlewine*

Hard Promises / May 1981 / MCA ✦✦✦✦✦
Damn the Torpedoes wasn't simply a culmination of Tom Petty's art; it happened to be a huge success, enabling him to call the shots on its successor, *Hard Promises*. Infamously, he used his first album as a star to challenge the record industry's practice of charging more for A-list artists, demanding that *Hard Promises* should be listed for less than most records by an artist of his stature, but if that was the only thing notable about the album, it would have disappeared like *Long After Dark*. Instead, it offered a reaffirmation that *Damn the Torpedoes* wasn't a fluke. There's not much new on the surface, since it continues the sound of its predecessor, but it's filled with great songwriting, something that's as difficult to achieve as a distinctive sound. As the opener, "The Waiting" became the best-known song on the record, but there's no discounting "A Woman in Love (It's Not Me)," "Nightwatchman," "Kings Road," "Insider," and "The Criminal Kind," album tracks that would become fan favorites. If *Hard Promises* doesn't have the sweep of *Damn the Torpedoes*, that's because its predecessor was blessed with good timing and an unusually strong set of songs. *Hard Promises* isn't quite so epochal, yet it has a tremendous set of songs and a unified sound that makes it one of Petty's finest records. *—Stephen Thomas Erlewine*

Long After Dark / Nov. 1982 / MCA ✦✦✦
Riding high on the the back-to-back Top Five, platinum hits *Damn the Torpedoes* and *Hard Promises*, Tom Petty quickly returned to the studio to record the Heartbreakers' fifth album, *Long After Dark*. Truth be told, there was about as long a gap between *Dark* and *Promises* as there was between *Promises* and *Torpedoes*, but there was a difference this time around—Petty and the Heartbreakers sounded tired. Even if there are a few new wave flourishes here and there, the band haven't really changed their style at all—it's still Stonesy, Byrdsian heartland rock. As their first four albums illustrated, that isn't a problem in itself, since they have found numerous variations within their signature sound... providing they have the right songs. Unfortunately, Petty had a dry spell on *Long After Dark*. With its swirling, minor-key guitars, "You Got Lucky" is a classic, and "Change of Heart" comes close to matching those peaks, but the remaining songs rarely rise above agreeable filler. Since the Heartbreakers are a very good band, it means the record sounds pretty good as it's playing, but apart from those few highlights, nothing much is memorable once the album has finished. And coming on the heels of two excellent records, that's quite a disappointment. *—Stephen Thomas Erlewine*

Southern Accents / Apr. 1985 / MCA ✦✦✦
Produced by Dave Stewart, *Southern Accents* is an ambitious album, attempting to incorporate touches of psychedelia, soul, and country into a loose concept about the modern South. Occasionally, the songs work; "Rebels" and "Spike" are fine rockers, and "Don't Come Around Here No More" and "Make It Better (Forget About Me)" expand The Heartbreakers' sound nicely. But too often, the record is weighed down by its own ambitions. *—Stephen Thomas Erlewine*

Pack up the Plantation: Live! / Jan. 1986 / MCA ✦✦✦
Considering that *Southern Accents* took so much time and money to complete, finally hitting the stores two and a half years after *Long After Dark*, it wasn't surprising that Tom Petty & the Heartbreakers decided to release a double-live album, *Pack Up the Plantation—Live!*, a mere eight months after its release. After all, *Southern Accents* was criticized from many corners for being too slick, too much in Dave Stewart's corner instead of the Heartbreakers', so it made sense to quickly return the focus to the band, showcasing the group as the rockers they are. *Pack Up the Plantation* does do that, even if it isn't quite the barn-burner it should have been. Part of the problem is that the song selection isn't quite as good as it could have been, relying heavily on *Southern Accents* material, including the weak "It Ain't Nothin' to Me." Then again, the weaker songs and dubious choices are outweighed by a strong performance and neat surprises like a tough "Insider" and covers of "So You Want to Be a Rock & Roll Star," "Needles and Pins" and "Don't Bring Me Down." That alone makes it worth investigating for dedicated fans, even if it doesn't quite deliver the knockout punch many listeners might have wanted. *—Stephen Thomas Erlewine*

Let Me Up (I've Had Enough) / Apr. 1987 / MCA ✦✦✦
Tom Petty & the Heartbreakers spent much of 1986 on the road as Bob Dylan's backing band. Dylan's presence proved to be a huge influence on the Heartbreakers, turning them away from the well-intentioned but slick pretensions of *Southern Accents* and toward a loose, charmingly ramshackle roots-rock that hearkened back to their roots yet exhibited the professional eclecticism they developed during the mid-'80s. All of this was on full display on *Let Me Up (I've Had Enough)*, their simplest and best album since *Hard Promises*. Not to say that *Let Me Up* is a perfect album—far from it, actually. Filled with loose ends, song fragments and unvarnished productions, it's a defiantly messy album, and it's all the better for it, especially arriving on the heels of the well-groomed *Accents*. Apart from the (slightly dated) rant "Jammin' Me'" (co-written by Dylan, but you can't tell), there aren't any standouts on the record, but there's no filler either—it's just a simply good collection of ballads ("Runaway Trains"), country-rockers ("The Damage You've Done"), pop-rock ("All Mixed Up," "Think About Me") and hard rockers ["Let Me Up (I've Had Enough)"]. While that might not be enough to qualify *Let Me Up* as one of Petty & the Heartbreakers' masterpieces, it is enough to qualify it as the most underrated record in their catalog. *—Stephen Thomas Erlewine*

Full Moon Fever / Apr. 29, 1989 / MCA ✦✦✦✦✦
Although *Let Me Up (I've Had Enough)* found the Heartbreakers regaining their strength as a band and discovering a newfound ease at songcraft, it just didn't sell that well. Perhaps that factor, along with road fatigue, led Tom Petty to record his first solo album, *Full Moon Fever*. Nevertheless, the distinction between "solo" and "Heartbreakers" is a fuzzy one because *Full Moon Fever* is essentially in the same style as the Heartbreakers albums; Mike Campbell co-wrote two songs and co-produced the record, and he, along with Benmont Tench and Howie Epstein, all play on the album. However, the album sounds different from any Heartbreakers record due to the presence of former Electric Light Orchestra leader Jeff Lynne. Petty co-wrote the lion's share of the album with Lynne, who also is the record's main producer. In his hands, Petty's roots rock becomes clean and glossy, layered with shimmering vocal harmonies, keyboards, and acoustic guitars. It was a friendly, radio-ready sound, and if it has dated somewhat over the years, the craft is still admirable and appealing. But the real reason *Full Moon Fever* became Petty's biggest hit is that it boasted a selection of songs that rivaled *Damn the Torpedoes*. *Full Moon Fever* didn't have a weak track; even if a few weren't quite as strong as others, the album was filled with highlights—"I Won't Back Down," the wistful "A Face in the Crowd," the rockabilly throwaways "Yer So Bad" and "A Mind With a Heart of Its Own," the Byrds cover "Feel a Whole Lot Better," the charging "Runnin' Down a Dream," and "Free Fallin'," a coming-of-age ballad that could be Petty's best song. *Full Moon Fever* might have been meant as an off-the-cuff detour, but it turned into a minor masterpiece. *—Stephen Thomas Erlewine*

Into the Great Wide Open / Jul. 2, 1991 / MCA ✦✦✦
Since *Full Moon Fever* was an unqualified commercial and critical sense, perhaps it made sense that Tom Petty chose to follow its shiny formula when he reunited with the Heartbreakers for its follow-up, *Into the Great Wide Open*. Nevertheless, the familiarity of *Into the Great Wide Open* is something of a disappointment. The Heartbreakers' sound has remained similar throughout their career, but they had never quite repeated themselves until here. Technically, it isn't a repeat, since they weren't credited on *Full Moon*, but *Wide Open* sounds exactly like *Fever*, thanks to Jeff Lynne's overly stylized production. Again, it sounds like a cross between latter-day ELO and roots-rock (much like the Traveling Wilburys, in that sense), but the production has become a touch too careful and precise, bordering on the sterile at times. And, unfortunately, the quality of the songwriting doesn't match *Fever* or *Let Me Up (I've Had Enough)*. That's not to say that it rivals the uninspired *Long After Dark*, since Petty is a better craftsman in 1991 than he was in 1983. There are a number of minor gems—"Learning to Fly," "Kings Highway," "Into the Great Wide Open"—but there are no knock-outs, either; it's like *Full Moon Fever* if there were only "Apartment Song"s and no "Free Fallin'"s. In other words, enough for a pleasant listen, but not enough to resonate like his best work. [And considering this, perhaps it wasn't surprising that Petty chose to change producers and styles on his next effort, the solo *Wildflowers*.] *–Stephen Thomas Erlewine*

★ **Greatest Hits** / Nov. 16, 1993 / MCA ✦✦✦✦✦
All of Petty's biggest hits collected, along with two new tracks—the excellent "Mary Jane's Last Dance" and a cover of Thunderclap Newman's "Something In the Air"—on one essential disc. Everything from "American Girl" to "Free Fallin'" is included, with sixteen tracks proving that Petty is one of the best rockers of the past fifteen years. *—Stephen Thomas Erlewine*

Wildflowers / Nov. 1, 1994 / Warner Brothers ✦✦✦✦✦
Under the guidance of producer Rick Rubin, Tom Petty turns in a stripped-down, subtle record with *Wildflowers*. Coming after two albums of Jeff Lynne-directed bombast, the very sound of the record is refreshing; Petty sounds relaxed and confident. Most of the songs are small gems, but a few are a little too laid-back, almost reaching the point of carelessness. Nevertheless, the finest songs here ("Wildflowers," "You Don't Know How

It Feels," "It's Good to Be King," and several others) match the quality of his best material, making *Wildflowers* one of Petty's most distinctive and best albums. *—Stephen Thomas Erlewine*

Playback / Nov. 20, 1995 / MCA ♦♦♦♦♦
The consequence of Tom Petty and the Heartbreakers' enduring affection for the music of the mid-'60s was that, in essence, they were a singles band, a fact driven home on the first three CDs of the six-disc set *Playback*; even when abbreviating each of their first nine studio albums to four to six cuts, the songs break down into the hits and the also-rans. To be fair, there are quite a few of the former, and some of the latter are could-have-beens; and since Petty is more a song maker (or, more precisely, a track cutter) than an album artist, his work is more amenable to compilation. Still, three discs are more than enough, and then come *three more discs* of rarities and outtakes. The first of these contains non-LP B-sides, most of which are pleasant throwaways (although "Trailer" suggests that the failed concept album *Southern Accents* could have been more of a success if it had been included). The last two discs present early and alternate histories of Petty, as his pre-Heartbreakers group, Mudcrutch, searches for a sound; later, he tries out different approaches that never made it onto his regular albums. Some of this material will be of interest to hardcore fans, but to justify the length and price of the box, there would have to be real lost treasures here. Not surprisingly, then, *Playback* is a box set that would have been twice as good at half the size. *—William Ruhlmann*

Songs and Music from "She's the One" / Aug. 1996 / Warner Brothers ♦♦♦
Nominally a soundtrack to Ed Burns' film *She's the One*, Tom Petty's *Songs and Music from "She's the One"* plays like an entity of its own, standing up quite well without the movie itself. *She's the One* is one of Petty's most relaxed efforts—several of the songs feel like they were written and performed quickly, almost as if they were throwaways, but that ramshackle feeling actually works in the album's favor. With its loose ends, repeated songs, covers, brief instrumental bridges, and direct production, *She's the One* is a ragged listen, but it's a comfortable, engaging and surprisingly eclectic one. Petty goes for a number of different moods, from the circular harmonies of "Walls (Circus)" (which features guest vocals from Lindsey Buckingham) and the hard-rocking "Zero from Outer Space" to the melancholy ruminations of "Grew up Fast." Along the way, he tosses in two excellent covers of contemporary songwriters—Lucinda Williams' slyly sneering "Change the Locks" and Beck's stark, sad "Asshole"—which are performed with affection and vigor. In fact, that vigor is what makes *She's the One* so charming—Petty sounds like he's having a good time throughout the album. It's not a major statement in his catalog, but it's all the more entertaining because of its simple, direct approach. *—Stephen Thomas Erlewine*

Echo / Apr. 13, 1999 / Warner Brothers ♦♦♦♦
Although the stripped-down, immediate production of *She's the One* was reminiscent of *Wildflowers*, Tom Petty's forays into Lindsey Buckingham-inspired pop turned out to be a passing thing, since *Echo*, his first full-fledged record with the Heartbreakers since 1991's *Into the Great Wide Open*, is an extension of *Wildflowers*, at least in terms of sound and feel. The weird thing is, *Echo* sounds like a sinewy band recording, but its sentiment makes it feel like a solo record. To be blunt, much of *Echo* feels like a by-product of Petty's divorce from his wife of over 20 years; even the intoxicating hard rock of "Free Girl Now" has a layer of sorrow and regret. That weary melancholy is the bond that keeps *Echo* together, bridging the gap between the ballads and the rockers, providing an emotional touchstone that makes the record more than just another Petty record. Then again, the music on *Echo* manages to sound like every other Petty album, yet it stays fresh. Petty, Mike Campbell, and Rick Rubin (along with some help from George Drakoulias) keep the spirit of *Wildflowers* alive by keeping the production uncluttered, direct, and muscular—which just reveals what a strong, versatile band the Heartbreakers are. And while there are no surprises, Petty once again delivers an album that works as a whole while having several clear highlights—which is a pretty neat trick, actually. At times, the disc feels a little long, but all the pieces work individually and illustrate that Petty is the rare rocker who knows how to mature gracefully. Although the album is spiked with sadness and regret, nothing on the album feels forced or self-conscious, either lyrically or musically—and he is one of the few rockers of his generation that can make such a claim. *—Stephen Thomas Erlewine*

Anthology: Through the Years / Oct. 31, 2000 / MCA ♦♦♦♦♦
For the fan that wants more than the superb single-disc *Greatest Hits* yet doesn't want to delve into actual albums or the exhaustive, rarities-heavy box set *Playback*, Tom Petty & the Heartbreakers and MCA Records offered the double-disc *Anthology: Through the Years* in the fall of 2000. This set basically offers all the singles and album rock radio favorites, with a couple of odd selections here and there and one new song, "Surrender." There are a few omissions—"Make It Better (Forget About Me)" isn't here, for instance—but not enough to really be noticeable, especially since this consolidates the bulk of Petty's great songs and plays very, very well. *Greatest Hits* might have a slight edge to *Anthology* because of its conciseness, but this double-disc set illustrates that Petty's catalog was deeper than just the hits. *—Stephen Thomas Erlewine*

Pezband

f. 1975
Power Pop, New Wave
Hailing from the same state as Cheap Trick (Illinois), the Pezband were a mostly fine, occasionally wonderful, power-pop band that specialized in hook-filled hard rock with sweet multi-part harmonies. Led by the strong, blues-inflected singing of Mimi (a guy) Betinis and the rampaging Jeff Beck-influenced guitar playing of Tommy Gawenda, the Pezzers' first LP (released in 1977) was not as hard and heavy as Cheap Trick, nor did it exhibit the berserk panache of their fellow Illini. But that all changed with their second LP, *Laughing in the Dark*, which contained a high quotient of good-to-great songs, excellent production and a wonderful lack of smugness and calculation that was slowly infiltrating every power-pop band in America. A huge public reaction, however, was not forthcoming. The band had its supporters (like most of the editorial staff of *Trouser Press*), but power-pop/hard rock from Illinois was dominated by Cheap Trick, and everybody else had to find a place in the pecking order. The rest of their recorded output is serviceable, but only hints at what the band was truly capable of doing. *—John Dougan*

Pezband / 1977 / Passport ♦♦

● **Laughing in the Dark** / 1978 / Radar ♦♦♦♦♦
Without a doubt, the best Pezband record available. Side one offers an especially strong trio of rock-pop songs ("Love Goes Underground," "I'm Leavin'," and "Stop! Wait a Minute"). Sadly, many other bands got more press, and this record was lost in the shuffle. The good news is that if you found it in a used record store (assuming there still are a few in your neighborhood), you could probably get it for $2. Some may dismiss it as formulaic, and that might be true, but no one ever said that formula couldn't be fun. *—John Dougan*

Too Old, Too Soon Live at Dingwalls / 1978 / Passport ♦♦♦
A great four-track live EP recorded at the much-missed club Dingwalls in London. Side one features rough and ready versions of "Stop! Wait A Minute" and "Lovesmith"; side two features a manic "Not Fade Away" and a thoroughly great romp through The Swinging Blue Jeans' "Hippy Hippy Shake." Power pop with the accent on power. *—John Dougan*

Thirty Seconds over Schaumburg / 1978 / PVC ♦♦♦♦♦
The title is a tongue-in-cheek reference to the Chicago suburb from whence they came. The music is loud, ferocious and wonderful. Tommy Gawenda is a little out of control here (too many multi-chorus solos), but after all is said and done, this record proves what a great live band the Pezband were. Extra points for a rippin' version of Jeff Beck's "Blue Wind" and its neat segue into The Yardbirds' "Stroll On." *—John Dougan*

Cover to Cover / 1981 / Passport ♦♦♦
While never finding the following other power-pop bands located, Pezband continued to make great music, as is in evidence on *Cover to Cover*. Why this wasn't a hit is a mystery, because the band sure has a knack for a great pop melody. "Stella Blue" rocks, and "Didn't We" proves that this band can write a great ballad to boot. *Cover to Cover* has to be heard to be believed, and once you hear it, you'll be glad you did. *—James Chrispell*

Liz Phair

b. Apr. 17, 1967, New Haven, CT
Vocals, Guitar / Adult Alternative Pop/Rock, Indie Rock, Lo-Fi, Alternative Pop/Rock, Singer/Songwriter
A product of the American underground of the late '80s, Liz Phair fused lo-fi, indie-rock production with the sensibility and structure of classic singer/songwriters. *Exile in Guyville*, Phair's debut album, was enthusiastically praised upon its 1993 release and it spawned a rash of imitators, over the following years. Phair first made an impact with her home-made tapes, released under the name Girlysound, which provided an entry point to the Chicago alternative music scene; in particular, she became friends with Urge Overkill and drummer Brad Wood. The Girlysound made ther way to Gerard Cosley, the head of record label Matador. By the summer of 1992, Matador had signed Phair. Her debut *Exile in Guyville* was released to strong reviews in the summer of 1993. The record slowly built a dedicated following in America among critics and alternative rock fans; it topped many Best-of-the-Year critics polls, including *The Village Voice* and *Spin*. Early in 1994, she launched her first tour, around the same time MTV began airing "Never Said," leading toward *Exile's* brief appearance on the charts in February. By the spring of 1994, it had sold over 200,000 copies—a remarkable number for an independent release. Phair's second album, *Whip-Smart* was released in fall of 1994 to a whirlwind of media attention—including Phair, dressed only in negligee, on the cover of *Rolling Stone*—that eclipsed her actual celebrity. Though *Whip-Smart* debuted at number 27 it received mediocre reviews and never became a crossover hit. Phair quietly retreated from the spotlight during 1995, getting married and releasing the *Juvenilia* EP, which had the first official release of Girlysound material. After having a child, she finally released her third album *whitechocolatespaceegg* in mid-1998; it received generally positive reviews and moderately strong sales. *—Stephen Thomas Erlewine*

★ **Exile in Guyville** / Jun. 22, 1993 / Matador ♦♦♦♦♦
If *Exile in Guyville* is shockingly assured and fully formed for a debut album, there are a number of reasons why. Most prominent of these is that many of the songs were initially essayed on Liz Phair's homemade cassette *Girlysound*, which means that the songs are essentially cream of the crop from an exceptionally talented songwriter. Second, there's its structure, infamously patterned after the Stones' *Exile on Main Street*, but not the song-by-song response Phair promoted it as. (Just try to match the albums up: Is the "blow-job queen" fantasy of "Flower" *really* the answer to the painful elegy "Let it Loose?") Then, most notably, there's Phair and producer Brad Wood's deft studio skills, bringing a variety of textures and moods to a basic, lo-fi production. There is as much hard rock as there are eerie solo piano pieces, and there's everything in between from unadulterated power pop, winking art rock, folk songs, and classic indie rock. Then, there are Phair's songs themselves. At the time, her gleefully profane, clever lyrics received endless attention (there's nothing that rock critics love more than a girl who plays into their geek fantasies, even—or maybe especially—if she's mocking them), but years later, what

still astounds is the depth of the writing, how her music matches her clear-eyed, vivid words, whether it's on the self-loathing "Fuck and Run," the evocative mood piece "Stratford-on-Guy," or the swaggering breakup anthem "6' 1"," or how she nails the dissolution of a long-term relationship on "The Divorce Song." Each of these 18 songs maintains this high level of quality, showcasing a singer/songwriter of immense imagination, musically and lyrically. If she never equaled this record, well, few could. *—Stephen Thomas Erlewine*

Whip-Smart / Sep. 20, 1994 / Matador ✦✦✦
Expectations ran extremely high for Phair's follow-up to *Exile In Guyville*, one of the most critically acclaimed debut albums of all time. If there are flaws in this generally first-rate followup, they mostly arise in comparison with *Guyville*, a record of such unexpected impact that most anything Phair could have done may have been found lacking. She continues to explore sex and relationships with exhilarating frankness and celebration, employing her much-touted profanity to a conversational rather than a sensational effect. The sound is somewhat more produced, though still pretty basic, and the compositions are by and large tuneful and lyrically intriguing. It's not, after all is said and done, quite as striking as *Guyville*; like many sophomore efforts, it mines similar territory without making huge strides forward. Several songs are reprised from her widely circulated *Girly Sound* demo tapes, and in some instances the more heavily produced, self-consciously ingenious arrangements here suffer in comparison to their blueprints. The title track, one of the highlights of those tapes, comes off as particularly gimmicky in its new incarnation, with the addition of all manner of superfluous animal noises. There's no question that Phair is a major songwriter and artist, but this album is more a solidification of her talents than a breakthough statement. *—Richie Unterberger*

Juvenilia / Aug. 2, 1995 / Matador ✦✦✦
Essentially, *Juvenilia* is the single for "Jealousy," one of the more pop-oriented tracks on Liz Phair's second album, *Whip-Smart*. In order to make the single more inticing for the singer/songwriter's fans, five tracks from her legendary *Girlysound* tapes were included, marking the first official release of this material. Arriving well after the initial media onslaught of Phair's debut *Exile in Guyville*—which included numerous references to the home-recorded tapes—the *Girlysound* sessions might sound a bit disappointing because they offer no new insights into Phair's songwriting. If anything, the selected songs accentuate her tendency to be cloying and cute. Not only do the repeated "fucks" begin to sound like a gimmick, she appropriates Iggy Pop's "Funtime" on "South Dakota" for no apparent reason than to demonstrate her cleverness. Before the *Girlysound* songs, Phair runs through a limp version of The Vapors' new wave classic "Turning Japanese" with Material Issue and hands in "Animal Girl," an unremarkable new piano ballad. *—Stephen Thomas Erlewine*

whitechocolatespaceegg / Aug. 11, 1998 / Matador/Capitol ✦✦✦
Following the halfhearted reception to *Whip-Smart*—good enough to retain her critical stature, not good enough to enhance it—Liz Phair slowly retreated from view, marrying and having a child. Toward the end of 1996, she began to work on her third album, but it took her nearly a year and a half to compete the record, due to a variety of reasons. When *whitechocolatespaceegg* (a reference to her baby boy's shiny bald head) finally appeared in late summer 1998, it had been a full five years since *Exile in Guyville*, and nowhere was that more apparent than in Phair's third album itself. Certain familiar elements remained—her plain vocals, strummed guitars, and character songs—but this was a brighter, cleaner, more content Phair. There was none of the emotional turmoil that underpinned *Exile* and, to a lesser extent, *Whip-Smart*. Even if the songs concerned violent emotions, there is a studied distance between her and the songs here, whether it's the character study "Uncle Alvarez" or "Johnny Feelgood," where the female narrator is beaten up and likes it. In other words, *whitechocolatespaceegg* is the work of a craftsman, not an inspired work of brilliance like *Exile*. And while that may alienate some hardcore fans, that's not necessarily a bad thing, especially since the best moments—"Big Tall Man," "Baby Got Going," "Go on Ahead," "What Makes You Happy," "Johnny Feelgood" and the *Girlysound* leftover "Shitloads of Money"—are tuneful and literate. Still, there's a distance, not only in the lyrics but in the overly polished music, that makes *whitechocolatespaceegg* difficult to embrace unconditionally, even if it may be a stronger record than *Whip-Smart*. *—Stephen Thomas Erlewine*

Sam Phillips

b. 1962
Vocals / College Rock, Adult Alternative Pop/Rock, Pop/Rock
The acid-pop singer/songwriter born Leslie Phillips earned the nonsensical nickname "Sam" as a child; only when she was recording her debut album did she finally hear of the other, more renowned Sam Phillips, the founder of Sun Records. In retrospect, however, her relative distance from the history and conventions of pop music may have been in her favor, and accounted for the fresh perspective her work offered; a critic's darling, Phillips sold few records, but her songs won widespread praise not only from the press but also her fellow performers. She began recording in 1984 (under the name Leslie Phillips) for the contemporary Christian label Word, and became a star within the limited framework of the Christian rock community. With 1987's aptly-titled *The Turning*, Phillips first teamed with producer T-Bone Burnett. After the album's release, she publicly denounced her label as a right-wing propaganda machine and adopted the name Sam. With Burnett again in the producer's seat, she emerged in 1988 on Virgin with her secular debut, *The Indescribable Wow*. Phillips and Burnett married prior to the release of 1991's darker, more experimental *Cruel Inventions*. With 1994's Grammy-nominated *Martinis and Bikinis*, her sound flirted closely with Beatlesque popcraft. Phillips returned with 1996's *Omnipop (It's Only a Flesh Wound Lambchop)*, another departure which touched upon lounge pop and industrial sounds. *—Jason Ankeny*

The Turning / 1987 / DCC ✦✦✦✦
Next to Amy Grant, Sam Phillips may very well be the best example of a Christian female pop-rocker successfully making the transition from Christian to secular audiences in the 1980s. When *The Turning* first came out on Myrrh in 1987, Phillips was still going by the name Leslie and was being marketed primarily as a Christian singer. But when DCC reissued this album on CD ten years later, the label went with the name for which she was best known, Sam Phillips. In 1987, she sort of sounded like a cross between Grant and the Go-Gos. Musically, it's hard not to overlook the parallels between "Love Is Not Lost," "Beating Heart" and other appealing tunes that draw on the 1960s girl-group sound in a Go-Gos-ish fashion. But lyrically, Phillips' songs speak of a search for meaning and purpose that has a lot more in common with Grant—or, for that matter, Bono & U2. Although Phillips is coming from a Christian perspective, her lyrics are neither offputting nor exclusionary. Even if you're firmly committed to Judaism, Hinduism or Islam, you can relate to the spiritual message of "Answers Don't Come Easy" and "River of Love." Those who discovered Phillips with *Cruel Inventions* or *Martinis & Bikinis* would do well to go back and acquire this superb album. *—Alex Henderson*

The Indescribable Wow / 1988 / Virgin ✦✦✦✦✦
Sam Phillips' aptly titled secular debut is a pop marvel, a bright, colorful collection produced with verve by T-Bone Burnett. At times, Phillips' sweet voice and bouncy songs conjure the spirit of prime girl-group-era pop, but her mature, pointed lyrics—largely devoted to sophisticated dissections of modern relationships—shrug off such easy comparisons. Similarly, Burnett's production straddles both the past and the present—for all the 1960s nods of the Beach Boys-like "I Can't Stop Crying" or the Beatlesque "Remorse," *The Indescribable Wow* never sounds dated or retro, just timeless. *—Jason Ankeny*

Cruel Inventions / May 28, 1991 / Virgin ✦✦✦✦✦
With her inimitable style, considerable talent, and producer/husband T-Bone Burnett once again in tow, Sam Phillips adds a fabulous notch to her musical belt with *Cruel Inventions*. Staying the course toward the lofty goals introduced in her previous releases, Phillips deftly folds her political inclinations into spiritual ruminations of life as she sees it, creating ten original compositions that will please anyone interested in tunes of truth. Phillips' strong suit lies in her outstanding ability to spin clever phrases and wrap her slightly quirky voice around accessible pop melodies—kind of like the spoonful of sugar that helps the medicine go down. From that launching pad, Burnett sets off the sonic experimentation with full force: percussion, drums, and grooves leading the pack. The greatness of Burnett as a producer is found in his timelessness, for even when he colors outside the lines, he doesn't date himself or the product, a craft that allows his records to stand strong through the years. Musically, lyrically, and emotionally, *Cruel Inventions* is as steady as a stream. Not many records can boast such smooth consistency. A few of the songs, however, do merit special mention. Be sure to take note of the title track, "Lying," "Private Storm," and "Raised on Promises," which was featured in the opening scenes of *Ruby in Paradise* starring Ashley Judd. With just one listen, fans of artists such as Natalie Merchant, R.E.M., and Elvis Costello will surely find a heroine in Phillips. *—Kelly McCartney*

● **Martinis & Bikinis** / Mar. 8, 1994 / Virgin ✦✦✦✦✦
With *Martinis and Bikinis*, Sam Phillips' music turns decidedly Beatlesque: edgier and more psychedelic than her previous work, songs like "Strawberry Road" and "Same Rain" springboard from John Lennon-inspired origins, while "Same Changes" brazenly borrows from "If I Needed Someone"—Van Dyke Parks' string arrangement for the stunning "Baby, I Can't Please You" even recalls "Tomorrow Never Knows." (To punctuate matters, the album closes with a cover of Lennon's "Gimme Some Truth.") The difference between Phillips and the vast majority of her pop-revisionist contemporaries, however, is that she never coasts on the fumes of her influences, but turns them on their head and gives them new life—regardless of the approach, her impassioned, spiritually charged songs remain the product of a singular vision. *—Jason Ankeny*

Omnipop / Aug. 20, 1996 / Virgin ✦✦✦
Martinis and Bikinis was an edgy, catchy pop/rock album that expanded Sam Phillips' sonic pallette without losing sight of her melodic, layered songwriting. With *Omnipop (It's Only a Fleshwound Lambcomp)*, the followup to *Martinis and Bikinis*, Phillips concentrates on creating soundscapes that are vaguely experimental and layered with effects and synthesizers, sounding unlike much of her catalog. The problem is that the soundscapes hide a lack of substance within the songs themselves. Much of the lyrics are underdeveloped and clichéd, while the music itself doesn't have the punch or hooks of her previous three albums. And that makes *Omnipop* a muddled, ineffective affair. A few songs sink in after repeated listens, but the album on the whole is a failed—but honorable—experiment. *—Stephen Thomas Erlewine*

Zero Zero Zero: The Best of Sam Phillips / Mar. 23, 1999 / Virgin ✦✦✦
Never having scored any hits, but probably contractually required to assemble a compilation at the end of her contract with Virgin Records (which would seem to have been at hand), Sam Phillips came up with an idiosyncratic repackaging consisting mostly of songs from her four albums for the label. (The advisedly titled lead-off track, "Disappearing Act," was new.) Four songs were remixed, and one, "Holding on to the Earth," was presented in a new version. The sequencing, which went back and forth from the more conventional pop sound of *The Indescribable Wow* and *Cruel Inventions* to the more experimental *Martinis & Biknis* and *Omnipop (It's Only a Flesh Wound Lambchop)*, emphasized the differences between the records, with, for example, the edgy "Signposts"

from *Martinis & Bikinis* followed by the art-pop (complete with string section) of "That's Where the Colors Don't Go" from *Cruel Inventions*. Phillips often seemed to be revising her early, more accessible work in the light of her later, more challenging efforts, such as including only the 75-second Marc Ribot-played guitar part from the *Cruel Inventions* track "Tripping over Gravity." Though some of Phillips' better songs were included, this was less a "best of" than a re-imagining of her Virgin Records catalog. —*William Ruhlmann*

Fan Dance / Jul. 31, 2001 / Nonesuch ✦✦✦✦✦

Sam Phillips' best songs display an honesty and lyrical humility that's engaging, brave, and sometimes a bit startling; plenty of singer/songwriters take pleasure in wallowing in their spiritual and emotional needs in public, but few have been willing to lay themselves as open so plainly and eloquently as Phillips does on "I Need Love" or "Fighting With Fire." But Phillips and her producer/collaborator T-Bone Burnett have a gift for gussying up her songs with deliciously fractured pop-psych backdrops that add a spoonful of sugar which helps Phillips ease her medicine down the listener's ear. This approach worked beautifully on *Martinis and Bikinis* and *Cruel Inventions*, but Phillips and Burnett seemed to have taken it as far as it would go on the lovely but flawed *Omnipop (It's Only a Flesh Wound Lambchop)*. Five years later, the pair take a somewhat different path on the album *Fan Dance*; the production is clean and open, and the arrangements are purposefully sparse and uncluttered, usually just two quiet guitars (one played by Marc Ribot, whose touch is typically flawless), bass, and drums, and the album's most elaborate production choice, a string arrangement on "Wasting My Time," is performed by a small ensemble whose performance puts the song's intimacy in even sharper focus. While many might have imagined the melodicism of Phillips' songs was a function of the production, *Fan Dance* makes it clear that, even in scaled-back form, her songs have just as much to say musically as they do lyrically, with the music a perfect complement to Phillips' fearless honesty. —*Mark Deming*

Phish
....

f. 1983

Jam Bands, American Trad Rock, Alternative Pop/Rock

During the early '90s, Phish emerged as the heirs to the Grateful Dead's throne. Although their music is somewhat similar to the Dead's—it's an eclectic, free-form rock & roll encompassing folk, jazz, country, bluegrass, and pop—the group adheres more to jazz-derived improvisation than folk tradition, and they have a looser, goofier attitude. After all, their drummer regularly plays a vacuum during their concerts. Phish's main claim as the inheritors to the Dead's legacy is their approach to their musical career. The band didn't concentrate on albums, they dedicated themselves to live improvisation. Within a few years of their 1988 debut album, Phish had become an institution in certain sections of America, particularly college campuses. And their in-concert popularity didn't necessarily translate to huge record sales—their biggest-selling albums usually halted at gold status. Phish were the de facto leaders of the neo-hippie jam band movement until deciding to go on hiatus in 2000. —*Stephen Thomas Erlewine*

Junta / 1988 / Elektra ✦✦✦✦

Elektra finally got around to reissuing Phish's first album as part of their WEA-based catalog, tucking two discs into a slimline two-CD case. To Elektra's credit, three additional tracks have been added, recorded in 1988 at Nectar's (the club that gave Phish their start with a regular gig). The live tracks are somewhat dubious in sonic terms, but they're excellent for revealing the improvisational side of the band—the 25:31 "Union Federal" totters to a start and has a couple of wobbly moments, but it's actually fun to listen to. The original album is even better, of course, with great sound and better playing, not to mention the typical wild and woolly Phish humor spilling out all over the lengthy tracks. Highly recommended whether you're starting to discover Phish or are backing up to the beginning. —*Steven McDonald*

Lawn Boy / 1991 / Elektra ✦✦

This album is relaxed, friendly, and a lot of fun. It is their true statement of purpose, capturing Trey Anastasio's unique visions in their rawest form. "Reba," with its absurd lyrics, intricate design, and renegade momentum is one of their best moments, neatly summarizing the band's philosophy in 12 minutes. Anastasio may have played with greater force and potency later on, but his creative spark was rarely brighter than here, and he proves himself to be not only a student, but a master of many divergent styles.—*Jim Smith*

• A Picture of Nectar / Aug. 1991 / Elektra ✦✦✦✦✦

Phish's second major-label release is still in many ways their best and most accomplished album. Expanding on the musical explorations that dominated *Lawn Boy*, *Nectar* incorporates a remarkable mixture of styles, from country, jazz, and calypso to straight-up rock & roll. Lyrically, the band's trademark goofiness is intact, but the playing is more muscular and Trey Anastasio's arrangements have increased intensity and focus. In fact, it's a surprisingly tight record for a band that built their reputation on endless concert jams, although "Guelah Papyrus" and "Tweezer" should satisfy those who enjoy that facet of their personality. The album also boasts the classic "Chalk Dust Torture" and most of Phish's finest moments, which are hard to resist for even the most apprehensive listeners. —*Jim Smith*

Rift / Feb. 2, 1993 / Elektra ✦✦✦

Rift, Phish's follow-up to their major-label breakthrough *A Picture of Nectar*, follows the same pattern as its predecessor, but doesn't live up to the surprising, adventurous music on *Nectar*. Instead, most of the album sounds like an uninspired retread, as the band tries to fashion their songs into a loose concept album. The concentration on thematic unity tends to rob Phish of the loose spontaneity that makes them unique and makes *Rift* a bland, tedious listen. —*Stephen Thomas Erlewine*

Hoist / Mar. 29, 1994 / Elektra ✦✦✦

Hoist is the most concise album Phish has recorded, but that's not necessarily a complement. Phish's strength is not songcraft or hooks, it's their love of free-form song structures and extended jams. When the group's sound is reduced to its core, as it is on *Hoist*, it isn't quite as compelling. Nevertheless, the album is an improvement on the dismal *Rift*, and features several fine cuts. —*Stephen Thomas Erlewine*

A Live One / Jun. 27, 1995 / Elektra ✦✦✦✦✦

Phish's strength has always been its live shows, and *A Live One* shows why. Given the opportunity, they take their songs in every direction, winding through several different sounds within the course of a song. *A Live One* also features seven previously unreleased songs, making it worthwhile listening for even casual fans. Then again, most fans of Phish will want to hear everything the group has ever played. —*Stephen Thomas Erlewine*

Stash / 1996 / Elektra ✦✦✦✦

Stash is a Europe-only collection that was released to coincide with a 1996 tour. The compilation collects highlights from all of Phish's albums, from *Junta* and *Lawn Boys* to *Hoist* and *A Live One*. Though it doesn't work quite as well as their live performances, the album nevertheless contains many of their most popular songs and offers a good introduction to the band. —*Stephen Thomas Erlewine*

Billy Breathes / Oct. 15, 1996 / Elektra ✦✦✦✦

Thanks to producer Steve Lillywhite, Phish finally delivered a concise pop album with *Billy Breathes*. Lillywhite had the band cut away their jams and accentuate their songwriting, resulting in a series of tightly-written, melodic folk-rock and psychedelic pop songs. Phish still delve into the deeper waters with sweeping songs like "Theme from the Bottom," but what truly impresses about *Billy Breathes* is the group's seamless eclecticism and how they master all varieties of roots-rock and psychedelic styles. With the shorter songs, their musical depth and breadth is all the more apparent and impressive, making *Billy Breathes* the definitive Phish album the band has always strived to deliver. —*Stephen Thomas Erlewine*

Slip, Stitch & Pass / Oct. 28, 1997 / Elektra ✦✦✦✦✦

Released a mere two years after Phish's first live album, *Slip, Stitch & Pass*, the group's second live record, in many ways surpasses its predecessor, drawing a more complete picture of the Phish concert experience. Spanning two discs, *A Live One* had the scope of a Phish concert but there's actually more adventure and surprise on *Slip, Stitch & Pass*, whether it's in the group's improvisations or the inventive cover of Talking Heads' "Cities." It's not the kind of record that will convert the sceptical—there's simply too many long, involved instrumental passages that many doubters will label "indulgent"—but it's the closest Phish has come to capturing their live spirit on record. —*Stephen Thomas Erlewine*

The Story of the Ghost / Oct. 27, 1998 / Elektra ✦✦✦

The ninth album from neo-hippieville's most proficient and clever players is their most commercially accessible offering, a slinky (and slightly funky) trip through a slim conceptual piece about a life-affirming spiritual quest—or something like that; it all gets pretty confusing midway through. But Phish has never been a very literary group; instead, its fervent cult feasts on the technical agility of the band's prime and skilled instrumentalists, which is on grand display here. Yet, whatever charm that might come through at a Phish concert still can't quite transcend itself to record. Despite some good songs (the opening story-setting "Ghost," the groovy "Birds of a Feather," the strolling "Guyute") in a typically tuneless batch, *The Story of the Ghost* is occasionally sloppy, a bit smug and often quite boring. In other words, another day in the studio for Phish. —*Michael Gallucci*

Hampton Comes Alive / Nov. 23, 1999 / Elektra ✦✦✦✦✦

Like the Grateful Dead, the line on Phish runs a little like this—they make sense in concert, but never quite gel on record. However, the Dead's true character revealed itself because they thrived on improvisations; it wasn't quite the same with Phish, because the live experience revealed the band's humor, taste, eclecticism, and (foremost) skill, not just their character. Thing is, a lot of this, particularly skill, is evident on the band's studio albums. So, what do two full evenings of Phish—four sets to be exact—on the six-disc box set *Hampton Comes Alive* offer? Well, not any revelations or anything unexpected—just the fullest representation of the band yet available. Everything evident on *Hampton Comes Alive*, a live album consisting of four sets recorded on two dates in late November 1998, is present on one or another of Phish's studio albums, but never in one place at the same time, as it is here. Furthermore, the group's eclecticism, stretched to a full-length running time, becomes stunning, since it all seems seamless. Their covers don't seem cutesy or condescending when they're placed among the band's original freewheeling genre-hopping, and that's not a minor point. Phish prides itself on its taste, not only in covers but in its own writing, and here they prove that they're right, because they not only deliver everything with conviction, but put a slight spin on it to make it their own. Even if this isn't your thing, you'd be hard pressed to listen to *Hampton Comes Alive* and not agree that this is a band of exceptional talent. This is the kind of record that converts doubters—it's just too bad that its hefty price tag makes it a reasonable purchase only for the dedicated. —*Stephen Thomas Erlewine*

Farmhouse / May 16, 2000 / Elektra ✦✦✦✦

The party line on Phish is that the band's live shows are so extraordinary, their studio records are almost superfluous by comparison; frankly, it's a ridiculous contention—apples and oranges, really—and moreover, each successive Phish album reveals new layers of intricacy and melodic invention otherwise lost in the epic explosiveness of their concert sets. Their rootsiest and most organic effort to date, *Farmhouse* is also their most fully developed—these are complete, concise songs and not simply outlines for extended jams, boasting a beauty and intimacy which expands the group's scope even as it serves notice of a newfound pop accessibility. It's a brave record, much less an exhibition of the band's vaunted instrumental prowess than it is a showcase for Trey Anastasio's increasingly skilled and far-reaching songwriting. The opening title cut, a gorgeously rustic country-pop ballad, immediately establishes *Farmhouse's* muted, relaxed tone, and despite the occasional detour like the sunny funk workout "Gotta Jibboo" or the closing instrumental jam "First Tube," by and large the set opts against kitchen-sink eclecticism in favor of an evocatively pastoral uniformity. In short, *Farmhouse* is everything Phish's die-hard legions no doubt hoped it wouldn't be, but as a radical reassessment of their music's purpose and approach, in many ways it's closer to the band's true spirit of innovation than any record they've made. *—Jason Ankeny*

Photek (Rupert Parkes)

b. 1971, Ipswich, England

Producer / Electronica, Jungle/Drum 'N Bass

Though Goldie became the first superstar of jungle, the recordings of Rupert Parkes—as Code of Practice, Aquarius, Studio Pressure, the Truper, and Sentinel, but most famously as Photek—made him an easy pick for the style's most artistic and intelligent producer. Working his way through street-level hardstep and airy, sub-aquatic "dolphin" tunes for LTJ Bukem's Good Looking label, Parkes finally arrived at a sound that pushed the bounds of drum'n'bass from the dancefloor into the realm of breakbeat headspace; unlike most jungle producers, Parkes has never DJed and rarely goes to clubs. His incredibly intricate rhythm programming and the unmissable aura of paranoid menace on recordings such as "The Hidden Camera" and "UFO" exerted quite an influence on the return of dark-style drum'n'bass during the late '90s. As a teenager, Parkes listened to electro, techno, and hip-hop as well as the more free-form side of jazz and fusion. Thanks to a sampler bought with a £2000 loan, he began producing tracks and first appeared on Paul Solomon's Certificate 18 Records with singles as Studio Pressure. He also recorded for Basement (as Sentinel) and Street Beats (the Truper) before initiating a series of 12"s for his own Photek Records, which gave him credentials and led to releases on Metalheadz and Good Looking. After Parkes had released more than 80 tracks of drum'n'bass on half a dozen labels, he was approached by Virgin and signed to a five-album deal with the label's Science imprint. Virgin compiled two EPs on 1997's *Risc Vs. Reward*, then released the debut Photek album, *Modus Operandi*, in September 1997. Much-hyped though little-praised, the album was followed by 1998's *Form & Function*, a compilation including several original Photek Records tracks plus remixes and new tracks. *—John Bush*

Risc Vs. Reward / Jul. 22, 1997 / Astralwerks ✦✦✦✦

Not quite the proper full-length fans had been waiting for, *Risc Vs. Reward* collects the six tracks from his first EP and single for Science ("The Hidden Camera" and "Ni-Ten-Ichi-Ryu") including two mixes of "The Hidden Camera" itself, plus the slow-motion drum'n'bass arts of the opener "KJZ" and the two sides of his second, "Ni-Ten-Ichi-Ryu" and "The Fifth Column." *—John Bush*

Modus Operandi / Sep. 9, 1997 / Astralwerks ✦✦✦✦✦

After releasing more than one hundred tracks on singles, scattered over half a dozen labels and as many pseudonyms, Rupert Parkes finally issued his first long-player in late 1997, and it seems the lack of time restraints got the better of him. Parkes is near idolized in the jungle underground for his obsession to detail when patterning his breaks, but his take on paranoid drum'n'bass wears out its welcome less than halfway through this album. While electronic artists usually mix up styles on full-lengths to make the lack of song structure less of a liability for home listeners, Parkes seems resistant to diversity (three small exceptions are the Detroit-inspired "Aleph 1" and two down-tempo tracks, "124" and the title song). Much of this criticism is the kind leveled at a stellar artist who could (or should) have brought excellent work onto a higher plane altogether, but the fact remains that *Modus Operandi* is a difficult listen, even for fans. *—John Bush*

★ **Form & Function** / Sep. 14, 1998 / Science ✦✦✦✦✦

The Photek Records label, home to six singles between 1995 and 1996, included several of the most stunning drum'n'bass productions ever heard; "Rings Around Saturn," "UFO," "The Seven Samurai," and "The Physical" each take their place as the tracks that made a name for Rupert Parkes in the jungle community. One year after the release of his debut LP, Science/Astralwerks used the collection *Form & Function* to compile those singles for all the fans who'd missed out on all that vinyl-only material. The problem is, *Form & Function* includes only *four* originals from Rupert Parkes' pre-LP 12" output (two are unlisted), substituting instead remixes of several tracks plus two new productions. Sympathetic producers Digital, Peshay, Doc Scott and J Majik take the scissors to Photek classics "The Lightening," "Rings Around Saturn," "The Water Margin" and "UFO," while Photek remixes his own "The Seven Samurai" and "Resolution." Though there are several excellent productions here, it's all a bit troubling since jungle producers rarely look back to rewrite history. The new tracks, "Knitevision" and "Santiago," almost rescue the proceedings with excellent turns; the former works wonders around an understated bassline and martial-arts programming while the latter features off-kilter snares and offsetting synth. Still, what could have been an essential look at what is arguably the best back catalog in drum'n'bass is transformed into a disappointing remix collection. It's especially a shame, considering the first six singles (A-sides and B-sides) would have fit perfectly onto a 75-minute disc. *—John Bush*

Solaris / Sep. 19, 2000 / Astralwerks ✦✦✦✦

Finally released from the artistic pressure and unrelenting hype surrounding his full-length debut (1997's *Modus Operandi*), Photek producer Rupert Parkes moved on to embrace Chicago acid house and minimal techno for his sophomore *Solaris*. Whereas *Modus Operandi* portrayed an artist trapped within the style he'd pioneered (paranoid drum'n'bass), *Solaris* sounds more like an album Parkes actually *wanted* to make (instead of the one his fans expected). Indebted to hard-edged Chicago acid track producers like Adonis and Armando, Parkes constructed brittle, distorted drum-machine breaks (instead of the usual endlessly tweaked skittery breakbeats) and matched them with claustrophobic analog effects, most of which hark back at least a decade or so. Parkes also made the acid house connections direct by enlisting help for two vocal tracks from Chicago institution Robert Owens (Fingers Inc.). The first Owens track, "Mine to Give," attacks with suprisingly unwavering beats and a rumbling bass line straight out of the Windy City sound of the late '80s. The other Owens contribution, a smooth production named "Can't Come Down," is more reminiscent of Parkes' productions for LTJ Bukem's Good Looking Records (like the atmospheric jungle classic "Pharaoh"). In fact, only one track here ("Infinity") flirts with the drum'n'bass darkside fans and critics had pigeonholed Photek in, though there's an undeniable air of paranoia and menace throughout the album. Near the end, Parkes even salutes the growing legion of experimental-techno producers with a trio of excellent minimalist downtempo tracks: an ambient isolationist track named "Aura" and two brittle trip-hop productions, "Halogen" and "Almost Blue Heaven" (the latter with vocals from Simone Simone). For better (and occasionally for worse), *Solaris* is just as dense and intensive a package as Photek's previous work. Still, the range of styles points to a more ambitious future. *—John Bush*

Wilson Pickett

b. Mar. 18, 1941, Prattville, AL

Vocals / Deep Soul, Southern Soul, Soul

Of the major '60s soul stars, Wilson Pickett was one of the roughest and sweatiest, working up some of the decade's hottest dancefloor grooves. Although he tends to be held in somewhat lower esteem than more versatile talents like Otis Redding and Aretha Franklin, he is often a preferred alternative of fans who like their soul on the rawer side. He also did a good deal to establish the sound of Southern Soul with his early hits, often recorded with the cream of the session musicians in Memphis and Muscle Shoals. One of his first singles as a solo act, "In the Midnight Hour," was recorded at Stax in Memphis. The single's chugging horn line, loping funky beats, and impassioned vocals made it a substantial pop hit and thousands of bands covered it onstage and on record. Pickett had a flurry of other galvanizing soul hits over the next few years, including "634-5789," "Mustang Sally," and "Funky Broadway," all of which were also frequently adapted by other bands as dance-ready numbers. He also cut tracks in Muscle Shoals and in Philadelphia (with the Gamble-Huff production team). Though his chart activity slowed down in the '70s, he continued to be active on the tour circuit. *—Richie Unterberger*

In the Midnight Hour / 1965 / Rhino ✦✦✦

Wilson Pickett's first album, from 1965, was a bit of a hodgepodge, including singles from as far back as 1962. Three of these tracks were actually issued as singles by The Falcons (for whom Pickett sang lead) before he started his solo career; others were issued as singles before Pickett broke through as a national star with the title track. This 12-track album doesn't really suffer as a result, however. Besides the all-time classic "In The Midnight Hour," it includes the Mann/Weil-penned single "Come Home Baby," covered by several rock and soul artists; "Don't Fight It," which reached the R&B Top Ten in late 1965; "I'm Gonna Cry," a 1964 single Pickett wrote with fellow soul legend Don Covay; and "I Found A Love," The Falcons single that made the R&B Top Ten in 1962. Working with several collaborators (including Steve Cropper), Pickett himself wrote most of the tunes on this album. The record also featured the first recordings he made with the Stax rhythm section in Memphis—a combination that would yield much fine soul music throughout the rest of the '60s. The 1993 CD reissue of this album features extensive liner notes and session details. *—Richie Unterberger*

The Exciting Wilson Pickett / 1966 / Rhino ✦✦✦✦✦

Less of a hodgepodge than his debut *In The Midnight Hour* album, Pickett's second album established—if there had been any doubt—his stature as a major '60s soul man. The 12 tracks include his monster hits "634-5789," "Ninety-Nine And A Half (Won't Do)," "In The Midnight Hour," and "Land Of 1000 Dances" (the last of which was his first Top Ten pop hit). Collectors will be more interested in the non-hit cuts, which are of nearly an equal level. These include covers of the R&B standards "Something You Got," "Mercy Mercy," and "Barefootin'"; several original tunes written in collaboration with Memphis soul greats Steve Cropper, Eddie Floyd, and David Porter; and Bobby Womack's "She's So Good To Me." It all adds up to one of the most consistent 1960s soul albums. The CD reissue of this 1966 record features detailed liner notes and session documentation. *—Richie Unterberger*

The Wicked Pickett / 1966 / Atlantic ✦✦✦✦✦

The Sound of Wilson Pickett / 1967 / Atlantic ✦✦✦✦✦

I'm in Love / 1968 / Rhino ✦✦✦

Bobby Womack's title track, which was a masterpiece of hurt and heartache, became in Wilson Pickett's hands a smashing, surging tale that managed to register the hurt Womack had in mind, but also contained plenty of fire and energy as well. No one except James Brown could put as much crunching power behind a scream as Pickett, but he was also a first-rate soul vocalist who showed often that he could do more than just yell and bellow. *—Ron Wynn*

Midnight Mover / 1968 / Atlantic ✦✦✦

Hey Jude / 1969 / Atlantic ✦✦✦

There were some in the soul world who scratched their heads when Wilson Pickett covered "Hey Jude" in 1969. They couldn't be found when the song became a Top 20 hit, one of five R&B smashes Pickett enjoyed that year. His cover was both outlandish and right on the button; the remainder of the album is just old-fashioned, urgent, gritty Southern soul. It's unfortunately out of print at present; hopefully, Rhino will put it back into circulation at some point. —*Ron Wynn*

Right On / 1970 / Atlantic ✦✦✦

Wilson Pickett in Philadelphia / 1970 / Atlantic ✦✦✦✦✦

Don't Knock My Love / 1971 / Atlantic ✦✦✦

A Man and a Half: The Best of Wilson Pickett / Apr. 21, 1992 / Rhino ✦✦✦✦✦

A Man and a Half—The Best of Wilson Pickett is a double-disc set that collects the absolute cream of Pickett's early sides with The Falcons and all the highlights of his successful alliance with the Atlantic label. With "Mustang Sally," "In the Midnight Hour," "Ninety Nine & a Half," "Hey Jude," "Land of 1000 Dances," "You're So Fine," and "634-5789" all included, this excellent compilation should be one of the cornerstones of anybody's soul collection. —*Cub Koda*

★ **The Very Best of Wilson Pickett** / 1993 / Rhino/Atlantic ✦✦✦✦✦

Although the double-disc set *A Man and A Half* is necessary for serious soul fans, *The Very Best of Wilson Pickett* should satiate the needs of any casual fan. Featuring 16 of his biggest Atlantic hits—including "In the Midnight Hour," "634-5789 (Soulsville, U.S.A.)," "Land of 1000 Dances," "Mustang Sally," "Funky Broadway," "She's Looking Good," and "I'm A Midnight Mover"—*The Very Best of Wilson Pickett* contains all of his truly essential items, making it both an excellent introduction and the closet thing possible to a definitive single-disc retrospective. —*Stephen Thomas Erlewine*

Pink

Teen Pop, Dance-Pop, Hip-Hop

With her colorful nickname predating her matching shade of hair, the young R&B/pop diva Pink grew up in a musical household and began singing in Philadelphia clubs by the time she reached her early teens. Her involvement in the city's dance and hip-hop scene led to a singing opportunity with the rap group Schools of Thought, for which she wrote her own material. At 14, she recorded her first original song and in 1998 released her first single, "Don't Stop," on the Colors label. Meanwhile, she also sang with R&B groups, including LaFace signees Choice; unfortunately though, the group dissolved before they recorded anything. The label was still interested in Pink, who collaborated with writers and producers such as Daryl Simmons, L.A. Reid, She' kspere, Babyface and 112 on singles such as "Just to Be Loving You" and "There U Go," which was a Top Ten hit in early 2000. Likewise, her debut album *Can't Take Me Home* reached the Top 40 of the US's album charts. —*Heather Phares*

● **Can't Take Me Home** / Apr. 4, 2000 / La Face ✦✦✦✦

It may be hard to listen to Pink's debut album, *Can't Take Me Home*, without hearing TLC, specifically their 1999 album *Fanmail*. After all, L.A. Reid and Babyface were the executive producers for both albums, and they decided to use a skittering, post-jungle rhythm for the bedrock of these savvy, club-ready dance-pop productions—a sound exploited expertly on TLC's record. Judged as its own entity, Pink's debut is quite strong, even if it isn't perfect. The production is masterminded by Babyface and Reid, who oversee such producers as Kevin "She'kspere" Briggs, Terence "Tramp-Baby" Abney, Daryl Simmons, and Tricky (not to be confused with the dark trip-hop genius, of course), and throughout this album, their work sparkles, from the deft layers of drum machines to the sultriness of the slow grooves. For the most part, Pink's performances match that production—she may not be able to deliver ballads with assurance and soul just yet, but she never over-sings. She also not only has an appealing voice, but displays a fair amount of chops. So, with the production and performances in place, that leaves just the songs. While there are no bad cuts on *Can't Take Me Home*, there aren't any knock-out punches, either. They're all fairly well-crafted, but they're more ingratiating than immediate. Still, it's not the worst situation in the world, either, especially since a lot of the tunes actually do make an impression with repeated plays. So, *Can't Take Me Home* doesn't really escape many of the pitfalls of a debut, but thanks to Reid and Babyface's production and Pink's engaging talents, it's a promising first effort all the same. —*Stephen Thomas Erlewine*

Pink Floyd

f. 1965, London, England

Mixed Media, British Psychedelia, Album Rock, Psychedelic, British Invasion, Prog-Rock/Art Rock, Hard Rock

Pink Floyd are the premier space-rock band. Since the mid-'60s, their music has relentlessly tinkered with electronics and all manner of special effects to push pop formats to their outer limits. At the same time they have wrestled with lyrical themes and concepts of such massive scale that their music has taken on almost classical, operatic quality, in both sound and words. While Pink Floyd are mostly known for their grandiose concept albums of the 1970s, they started as a very different sort of psychedelic band. Soon after they first began playing together in the mid-'60s, they fell firmly under the leadership of lead guitarist Syd Barrett, the gifted genius who would write and sing most of their early material. The Cambridge native shared the stage with Roger Waters (bass), Rick Wright (keyboards), and Nick Mason (drums). Pink Floyd quickly began to experiment, stretching out songs with wild instrumental freak-out passages incorporating feedback,

electronic screeches, and unusual, eerie sounds created by loud amplification, reverb, and such tricks as sliding ball bearings up and down guitar strings; Syd Barrett began to compose pop-psychedelic gems that combined unusual psychedelic arrangements (particularly in the haunting guitar and celestial organ licks) with catchy melodies and incisive lyrics that viewed the world with a sense of poetic, child-like wonder. Around mid-1967, though, the prodigy began showing increasingly alarming signs of mental instability. Dependent upon Barrett for most of their vision and material, the rest of the group were nevertheless finding him impossible to work with, live or in the studio. Around the beginning of 1968, guitarist Dave Gilmour, a friend of the band who was also from Cambridge, was brought in as a fifth member; within a few months, however, Barrett was out of the group. Such calamities would have proven insurmountable for 99 out of 100 bands in similar predicaments. Incredibly, Pink Floyd would regroup and not only maintain their popularity, but eventually become even more successful. —*Richie Unterberger*

★ **The Piper at the Gates of Dawn** / Aug. 5, 1967 / Capitol ✦✦✦✦✦

The title of Pink Floyd's debut album is taken from a chapter in Syd Barrett's favorite children's book, *The Wind in the Willows*, and the lyrical imagery of *The Piper at the Gates of Dawn* is indeed full of colorful, childlike, distinctly British whimsy, albeit filtered through the perceptive lens of LSD. Barrett's catchy, melodic acid pop songs are balanced with longer, more experimental pieces showcasing the group's instrumental freak-outs, often using themes of space travel as metaphors for hallucinogenic experiences—"Astronomy Domine" is a poppier number in this vein, but tracks like "Interstellar Overdrive" are some of the earliest forays into what has been tagged space rock. But even though Barrett's lyrics and melodies are mostly playful and humorous, the band's music doesn't always bear out those sentiments—in addition to Rick Wright's eerie organ work, dissonance, chromaticism, weird noises, and vocal sound effects are all employed at various instances, giving the impression of chaos and confusion lurking beneath the bright surface. *The Piper at the Gates of Dawn* successfully captures both sides of psychedelic experimentation—the pleasures of expanding one's mind and perception, and an underlying threat of mental disorder and even lunacy; this duality makes *Piper* all the more compelling in light of Barrett's subsequent breakdown, and ranks it as one of the best psychedelic albums of all time. —*Steve Huey*

A Saucerful of Secrets / Jun. 29, 1968 / Capitol ✦✦✦

A transitional album on which the band moved from Barrett's relatively concise and vivid songs to spacy, ethereal material with lengthy instrumental passages. Barrett's influence is still felt (he actually did manage to contribute one track, the jovial "Jugband Blues"), and much of the material retains a gentle, fairy-tale ambience. "Remember a Day" and "See Saw" are highlights; on "Set The Controls for the Heart of the Sun," "Let There Be More Light," and the lengthy instrumental title track, the band begin to map out the dark and repetitive pulses that would characterize their next few records. —*Richie Unterberger*

More / Jul. 27, 1969 / Capitol ✦✦

Commissioned as a soundtrack to the seldom-seen French hippie movie of the same name, *More* was a Floyd album in its own right, reaching the Top 10 in Britain. The group's atmospheric music was a natural for movies, but when assembled for record, these pieces were unavoidably a bit patchwork, ranging from folky ballads to fierce electronic instrumentals to incidental mood music. Several of the tracks are pleasantly inconsequential, but this record does include some strong compositions, especially "Cymbaline," "Green Is The Colour," and "The Nile Song." All of these developed into stronger pieces in live performances, and better, high-quality versions are available on numerous bootlegs. —*Richie Unterberger*

Ummagumma / Oct. 25, 1969 / Capitol ✦✦✦

For many years, this double LP/CD was one of the most popular albums in Pink Floyd's pre-*Dark Side of the Moon* output, containing a live disc and a studio disc all for the price of one (in the LP version). The live set, recorded in Birmingham and Manchester in June 1969, is limited to four numbers, all drawn from the group's first two LPs or their then recent singles. Featuring the band's second line-up (i.e., no Syd Barrett), the set shows off a very potent group, their sound held together on stage by Nick Mason's assertive drumming and Roger Waters' powerful bass work, which keep the proceedings moving no matter how spaced out the music gets; they also sound like they've got the amplifiers to make their music count, which is more than the early band had. "Astronomy Domine," "Careful With That Axe Eugene," "Set the Controls for the Heart of the Sun," and "A Saucerful of Secrets" are all superior here to their studio originals, done longer, louder, and harder, with a real edge to the playing. The studio disc was more experimental, each member getting a certain amount of space on the record to make their own music—Richard Wright's "Sysyphus" was a pure keyboard work, featuring various synthesizers, organs, and pianos; David Gilmour's "The Narrow Way" was a three-part instrumental for acoustic and electric guitars and electronic keyboards; and Nick Mason's "The Grand Vizier's Garden Party" made use of a vast range of acoustic and electric percussion devices. Roger Waters' "Grantchester Meadows" was a lyrical folk-like number unlike almost anything else the group ever did. In 1994 the album was remastered and reissued in a green slipcase, in a version a lot louder and sharper (and cheaper) than the original CD release. —*Bruce Eder*

Atom Heart Mother / Oct. 5, 1970 / Capitol ✦✦✦

Appearing after the sprawling, unfocused double-album set *Ummagumma*, *Atom Heart* may boast more focus, even a concept, yet that doesn't mean it's more accessible. If anything, this is the most impenetrable album they released while on Harvest, which also makes it one of the most interesting of the era. Still, it may be an acquired taste even for fans, especially since it kicks off with a side-long, 23-minute extended orchestral piece that may not seem to head anywhere, but is often intriguing, more in what it suggests than what it achieves. Then, on the second side, Roger Waters, David Gilmour, and Rick Wright have a song apiece, winding up with the group composition "Alan's Psychedelic Breakfast" wrapping it up. Of these, Waters begins developing the voice that made him the group's lead songwriter during their classic era with "If," while Wright has an appealingly mannered, very English psychedelic fantasia on "Summer 68," and Gilmour's "Fat Old Sun" meanders quietly before ending with a guitar workout that leaves no impression. "Alan's Psychedelic Breakfast," the 12-minute opus that ends the album, does the same thing, floating for several minutes before ending on a drawn-out jam that finally gets the piece moving. So, there are interesting moments scattered throughout the record, and the work that initially seems so impenetrable winds up being *Atom Heart Mother*'s strongest moment. That it lasts an entire side illustrates that Pink Floyd was getting better with the larger picture instead of the details, since the second side just winds up falling off the tracks, no matter how many good moments there are. This lack of focus means *Atom Heart Mother* will largely be for cultists, but its unevenness means there's also a lot to cherish here. *—Stephen Thomas Erlewine*

Relics / May 1971 / Capitol ✦✦✦✦✦
Since *Relics* is a compilation and not a regular studio album, it tends to be overlooked when thought of as one of Pink Floyd's better releases. It might not be regarded as a classic psychedelic masterpiece in the manner of *The Piper at the Gates of Dawn*, and it certainly won't ever achieve the multiple platinum status of *Dark Side of the Moon*, but it's a pretty good place to start with the band's early catalog. Originally issued in 1971, *Relics* culls from the band's first five singles (two A-sides and three B-sides, including the non-album pop classics "See Emily Play" and "Arnold Layne") and picks album material that capitalizes on the band's versatility while making it a thoroughly palatable listen. From *Piper*, you get the goofy childishness of "Bike" and the mesmerizing "Interstellar Overdrive," one of the band's trademark instrumental freak-outs; "The Nile Song," taken from the *More* soundtrack, is one of the heaviest songs the band recorded. A little bit of everything that made early Pink Floyd can be found here. Without a doubt, the disc is an essential part of the band's discography, not to be disregarded in lieu of its overlap with studio album material. *—Andy Kellman*

Meddle / Nov. 11, 1971 / Capitol ✦✦✦✦✦
Atom Heart Mother, for all its glories, was an acquired taste, and Pink Floyd wisely decided to trim back its orchestral excesses for its follow-up, *Meddle*. Opening with a deliberately surging "One of These Days," *Meddle* spends most of its time with sonic textures and elongated compositions, most notably on its epic closer "Echoes." If there aren't pop songs in the classic sense (even on the level of the group's contributions to *Ummagumma*), there is a uniform tone, ranging from the pastoral "A Pillow of Winds" to "Fearless," with its insistent refrain hinting at latter-day Floyd. Pink Floyd were nothing if not masters of texture, and *Meddle* is one of their greatest excursions into little details, pointing the way to the measured brilliance of *Dark Side of the Moon* and the entire Roger Waters era. Here, David Gilmour exerts a slightly larger influence, at least based on lead vocals, but it's not all sweetness and light—even if its lilting rhythms are welcome, "San Tropez" feels out of place with the rest of *Meddle*. Still, the album is one of the Floyd's most consistent explorations of mood, especially from their time at Harvest, and it stands as the strongest record they released between Syd's departure and *Dark Side*. *—Stephen Thomas Erlewine*

Obscured by Clouds / Jun. 3, 1972 / Capitol ✦✦
Obscured By Clouds is the soundtrack to the Barbet Schroeder film *La Vallee*, and it plays that way. Of course, it's possible to make the argument that Pink Floyd's music of the early '70s usually played as mood music, similar to film music, but it had structure and a progression. Here, the instrumentals float pleasantly, filled with interesting textures, yet they never seem to have much of a purpose. Often, they seem quite tied to their time, either in their spaciness or in the pastoral folkiness, two qualities that are better brought out on the full-fledged songs interspersed throughout the record. Typified by "Burning Bridges" and "Wot's…uh the Deal," these songs explore some of the same musical ground as those on *Atom Heart Mother* and *Meddle*, yet they are more concise and have a stronger structure. But the real noteworthy numbers are the surprisingly heavy blues-rocker "The Gold It's in The—," which, as good as it is, is trumped by the stately, ominous "Childhood's End" and the jaunty pop tune "Free Four," two songs whose obsessions with life, death, and the past clearly point toward *Dark Side of the Moon*. ("Childhood's End" also suggests *Dark Side* in its tone and arrangement.) As startlingly advanced as these last two songs are, they're not enough to push the rest of *Obscured by Clouds* past seeming just like a soundtrack, yet these tunes, blended with the sensibility of *Meddle*, suggest what Pink Floyd was about to develop into. *—Stephen Thomas Erlewine*

★ **Dark Side of the Moon** / Mar. 24, 1973 / Capitol ✦✦✦✦✦
By condensing the sonic explorations of *Meddle* to actual songs and adding a lush, immaculate production to their trippiest instrumental sections, Pink Floyd inadvertently designed their commercial breakthrough with *Dark Side of the Moon*. The primary revelation of *Dark Side of the Moon* is what a little focus does for the band. Roger Waters wrote a series of songs about mundane, everyday details which aren't that impressive by themselves, but when given the sonic backdrop of Floyd's slow, atmospheric soundscapes and carefully placed sound effects, they achieve an emotional resonance. But what gives the album true power is the subtly textured music, which evolves from ponderous, neo-psychedelic art rock to jazz fusion and blues-rock before turning back to psychedelia. It's dense with detail, but leisurely paced, creating its own dark, haunting world. Pink Floyd may have better albums than *Dark Side of the Moon*, but no other record defines them quite as well as this one. *—Stephen Thomas Erlewine*

☆ **Wish You Were Here** / Sep. 15, 1975 / Capitol ✦✦✦✦✦
Pink Floyd followed the commercial breakthrough of *Dark Side of the Moon* with *Wish You Were Here*, a loose concept album about and dedicated to their founding member Syd Barrett. The record unfolds gradually, as the jazzy textures of "Shine On You Crazy Diamond" reveal its melodic motif, and in its leisurely pace, the album shows itself to be a warmer record than its predecessor. Musically, it's arguably even more impressive, showcasing the group's interplay and David Gilmour's solos in particular. And while it's short on actual songs, the long, winding soundscapes are constantly enthralling.*—Stephen Thomas Erlewine*

Animals / Jan. 23, 1977 / Capitol ✦✦✦✦
Of all of the classic-era Pink Floyd albums, *Animals* is the strangest and darkest, a record that's hard to initially embrace yet winds up yielding as many rewards as its equally nihilistic successor, *The Wall*. It isn't that Roger Waters dismisses the human race as either pigs, dogs, or sheep, it's that he's constructed an album whose music is as bleak and bitter as that worldview. Arriving after the warm-spirited (albeit melancholy) *Wish You Were Here*, the shift in tone comes as a bit of a surprise, and there are even less proper songs here than on either *Wish* or *Dark Side*. *Animals* is all extended pieces, yet it never drifts—it slowly, ominously works its way toward its destination. For an album that so clearly is Waters', David Gilmour's guitar dominates thoroughly, with Richard Wright's keyboards rarely rising above a mood-setting background (such as on the intro to "Sheep"). This gives the music, on occasion, immediacy and actually heightens the dark mood by giving it muscle. It also makes *Animals* as accessible as it possibly could be, since it surges with bold blues-rock guitar lines and hypnotic space rock textures. Through it all, though, the utter blackness of Waters' spirit holds true and since there are no vocal hooks or melodies, everything rests on the mood, the near-nihilistic lyrics, and Gilmour's guitar. These are the kinds of things that satisfy cultists, and it will reward their attention—there's just no way in for casual listeners. *—Stephen Thomas Erlewine*

The Wall / Nov. 30, 1979 / Capitol ✦✦✦✦✦
Roger Waters constructed *The Wall*, a narcissistic, double-album rock opera about an emotionally crippled rock star who spits on an audience member daring to cheer during an acoustic song. Given its origins, it's little wonder that *The Wall* paints such an unsympathetic portrait of the rock star, cleverly named "Pink," who blames everyone—particularly women—for his neuroses. Such lyrical and thematic shortcomings may have been forgivable if the album had a killer batch of songs, but Waters took his operatic inclinations to heart, constructing the album as a series of fragments that are held together by larger numbers like "Comfortably Numb" and "Hey You." Generally, the fully developed songs are among the finest of Pink Floyd's later work, but *The Wall* is primarily a triumph of production: Its seamless surface, blending melodic fragments and sound effects, makes the musical shortcomings and questionable lyrics easy to ignore. But if *The Wall* is examined in depth, it falls apart, since it doesn't offer enough great songs to support its ambition, and its self-serving message and shiny production seem like relics of the late-'70s Me Generation. *—Stephen Thomas Erlewine*

A Collection of Great Dance Songs / Nov. 1981 / Capitol ✦✦
Anyone who knew anything about Pink Floyd knew that a dance band they were not, so this profit-taking, holiday-season compilation, courtesy of Columbia Records, was intended ironically. Arguably the quintessential album band, Pink Floyd is not well-served by compilations, especially one on which the two parts of "Shine On You Crazy Diamond" are edited together and there's a re-recording of "Money." Stick to the full-length versions. *—William Ruhlmann*

Works / 1983 / Capitol ✦✦

The Final Cut / Mar. 21, 1983 / Columbia ✦✦✦
The Final Cut extends the autobiography of *The Wall*, concentrating on Roger Waters' pain when his father died in World War II. Waters spins this off into a treatise on the futility of war, concentrating on the Falkland Islands, setting his blistering condemnations and scathing anger to an impossibly subdued music that demands full attention. This is more like a novel than a record, requiring total concentration since shifts in dynamics, orchestration, and instrumentation are used as effect. This means that while this has the texture of classic Floyd, somewhere between the brooding sections of *The Wall* and the monolithic menace of *Animals*, there are no songs or hooks to make these radio favorites. The even bent of the arrangements, where the music is used as texture, not music, means that *The Final Cut* purposely alienates all but the dedicated listener. Several of those listeners maintain that this is among Pink Floyd's finest efforts, and it certainly is an achievement of some kind—there's not only no other Floyd album quite like it, it has no close comparisons to anybody else's work (apart from Waters' own *The Pros and Cons of Hitch-Hiking*, yet that had a stronger musical core). That doesn't make this easier to embrace, of course, and it's damn near impenetrable in many respects, but with its anger, emphasis on lyrics, and sonic textures, it's clear that it's the album that Waters intended it to be. And it's equally clear that Pink Floyd couldn't have continued in this direction—Waters had no interest in a group setting anymore, as this record, which is hardly a Floyd album in many respects, illustrates. Distinctive, to be sure, but not easy to love and, depending on your view, not even that easy to admire. *—Stephen Thomas Erlewine*

A Momentary Lapse of Reason / Sep. 8, 1987 / Columbia ✦✦
A David Gilmour solo album in all but name, heavily featuring the kind of atmospheric instrumental music and Gilmour guitar sound typical of the Floyd before the now-departed Roger Waters took over but lacking Waters' unifying vision and lyrical ability. *—William Ruhlmann*

Delicate Sound of Thunder / Nov. 22, 1988 / Columbia ♦♦♦
In one respect, it's hard to fault David Gilmour for retooling Pink Floyd as a neo-oldies act with *Momentary Lapse of Reason*, since Roger Waters took the band over the brink with his obsessive, non-musical *The Final Cut*. Fans were eager for an album that sounded like classic Floyd, which is what *Momentary Lapse* was. But what they really thirsted for was a live spectacle from Floyd, where they could hear the old tunes and see all the old stunts. That's what they got on the 1987/1988 Pink Floyd world tour, which is documented on the double-disc set, *The Delicate Sound of Thunder*. Gilmour's reunited Floyd was intent on recreating the sound and feel of classic Floyd, so it shouldn't come as a surprise that the oldies feel like the classic records, only with Gilmour taking each vocal. He and Floyd deliver well, but this is a recreation that makes less sense on record than it did on stage, where the nostalgia was justified. Here, it feels passable but never compelling. This is professional, competent, and, often, even enjoyable music, yet, like many souvenirs, it never once feels necessary. *—Stephen Thomas Erlewine*

Shine On / Nov. 17, 1992 / Columbia ♦♦♦♦♦
A lavish and expensive eight-CD box set of Pink Floyd's greatest hits—which are all albums, naturally. Seven albums (*A Saucerful of Secrets, Meddle, The Dark Side of the Moon, Wish You Were Here, Animals, The Wall,* and *A Momentary Lapse of Reason*) have been digitally remastered; when the eight discs are set together on the shelf, their spines form the prism and rainbow from the cover of *The Dark Side of the Moon. Shine On* also includes an extra disc of early singles, housed in a digi-pak, and a hardcover book with plenty of pictures and text. Since there is no previously unreleased material included on the set, the only incentive for hardcore fans who already own the albums is the packaging and remastering, both of which are impressive. *Shine On* is certainly worth the investment for those who don't already own the music. *—Stephen Thomas Erlewine*

The Division Bell / Mar. 30, 1994 / Columbia ♦♦

Pulse / Jun. 1995 / Columbia ♦♦

Is There Anybody out There? The Wall: Live 1980-1981 / Apr. 18, 2000 / Columbia ♦♦♦
Skillfully edited together from the handful of *Wall* shows Floyd performed between 1980 and 1981 (much of the recordings date from shows at Earl's Court in London), *Is There Anybody out There?* replicates *The Wall* live—which, of course, was a replication of the record, only with spectacular visuals. There are two songs not on the studio album—"What Shall We Do Now?," a tune pulled from the record at the 11th hour (early pressings still listed it on the sleeve), plus "The Last Few Bricks," which was an instrumental at the end of the first act that gave the crew time to finish building the wall—but they add nothing to the overall piece. There are no revelations at all, actually, with the possible exception of the layered harmonies on "Outside the Wall," which makes this coda seem like a full-fledged song. Since the show was so rigidly structured, there was little opportunity for the band to stretch out and jam. All of this means that *Is There Anybody Out There?* is *The Wall* by any other name, and that it isn't for anybody but Floyd fanatics. Will this disappoint the less-dedicated listener? Not necessarily, since anybody familiar with *The Wall* will likely enjoy it as it's playing. The question is, how often will you put the record on? After all, if you want to hear this music, you'll listen to the studio recording. That doesn't really diminish the worth of *Is There Anybody out There?*, but it hardly makes it necessary, either. *—Stephen Thomas Erlewine*

Gene Pitney

b. Feb. 17, 1941, Hartford, CT
Vocals / Brill Building Pop, Teen Idol, Pop
One of the most interesting and difficult-to-categorize singers in '60s pop, Gene Pitney had a long run of hits distinguished by his pained, one-of-a-kind melodramatic wail. Pitney is sometimes characterized (or dismissed) as a shallow teen idol-type prone to operatic ballads. It's true that some of his biggest hits—"Town Without Pity," "Only Love Can Break a Heart," "I'm Gonna Be Strong," "It Hurts to Be in Love," and "Twenty Four Hours from Tulsa"—are archetypes of adolescent or just-post-adolescent agony, characterized by longing and not a little self-pity. But Pitney was not just an archetype of his style—he was one of the best at his style, and indeed one of the few (along with Roy Orbison) that could pull it off convincingly. Also (like Orbison), he had more range than he's generally given credit for, making forays into tough pop/rock, country, and even borderline rockabilly. Other than Dionne Warwick, he was the best interpreter of Bacharach-David's early compositions. Although he didn't pen much of his material, he was a composer of note, writing "He's a Rebel" for the Crystals, and "Hello Mary Lou" for Rick Nelson. He was also something of a closet hipster—he was the first American artist to cover a Jagger-Richards song ("That Girl Belongs to Yesterday," which was a British hit before the Rolling Stones had ever entered the U.S. Top 100), contributed to an actual Rolling Stones session in early 1964 (during which they recorded "Not Fade Away"), had a brief fling with a teenage Marianne Faithfull, and recorded songs by Randy Newman and Al Kooper long before those musicians became famous. *—Richie Unterberger*

● **Anthology 1961-1968** / 1986 / Rhino ♦♦♦♦♦
This CD, dating from the mid-'80s, is, ironically enough, a perfect companion in design and layout to Rhino's out-of-print Dionne Warwick *Anthology* collection. The 16 songs here represent the basis of Pitney's renown as a vocalist—rock's Caruso, critic Jeff Tamarkin called him—and is the handiest single CD collection to be found on him in the United States, covering the highlights of his primary years of success. The music is steeped in romantic angst and heartbreak, reminiscent of Roy Orbison's work from the same era, and displaying a stunning vocal range—"24 Hours From Tulsa" and "True Love Never Runs Smooth," along with much of the rest, sound like romantic screenplays in embryonic form, and "Town Without Pity" was, indeed, from a movie. Those desiring a somewhat broader picture of Pitney's music should look to Sequel Records' low-priced two-CD import *Looking Through: The Ultimate Collection*, containing 50 songs. *—Bruce Eder*

More Greatest Hits / Apr. 11, 1995 / Varese Sarabande ♦♦♦♦♦
A very worthy supplement to *Anthology*; in fact, it's almost as good. Has a lot of minor hits, some of which ("I Must Be Seeing Things," "Backstage") rank among his best; "Nobody Needs Your Love," an early Randy Newman composition that was a #2 hit in England in 1966; Pitney's own versions of his compositions "Hello Mary Lou" and "Today's Teardrops," much better known via their interpretations by Rick Nelson and Roy Orbison, respectively; and interesting album tracks and flop singles. All cuts are from the '60s, except the 1989 version of "Something's Gotten Hold Of My Heart," performed as a duet with Marc Almond. *—Richie Unterberger*

Looking Through: The Ultimate Collection / Jul. 25, 2000 / Sequel ♦♦♦♦♦
This 50-song collection contains everything that's on Rhino Records' single-CD Gene Pitney compilation, plus a lot more, and all of it is in release order, but it's got more than just excellent music—the producers interviewed Pitney for the jacket notes, and he basically walks you through the history of each song and the background on how it came to be recorded and released. This two-CD set gives you a step-by-step account of the progress and changes in Pitney's career across an entire decade and more, and offers listeners a chance to catch up on singles that they may well have missed at the time. Pitney was never less than a powerful singer, even when American pop music moved in a direction that made that talent seem less than essential or cutting edge—squeezed somewhere between the rock and pop world after the mid-'60s, he made superb records that simply couldn't get picked up on enough radio play lists to make an impact in America. This collection restores all of it to availability, in excellent sound, and ends with his 1988 chart comeback, "Something's Gotten Hold of My Heart," cut with Marc Almond—originally a 1967 single that made it to number five in England, the new version put him back in the number one spot 21 years later. Between all of that and a low list price, this is a difficult collection to pass up. *—Bruce Eder*

Pixies

f. 1986, Boston, MA, **db.** 1993
College Rock, Alternative Pop/Rock
Combining jagged, roaring guitars and stop-start dynamics with melodic pop hooks, intertwining male-female harmonies and evocative, cryptic lyrics, the Pixies were one of the most influential American alternative rock bands of the late '80s. The Pixies weren't accomplished musicians—Black Francis wailed and bashed out chords while Joey Santiago's lead guitar squealed out spirals of noise. But the band were inventive, rabid rock fans that turned conventions inside out, melding punk and indie guitar rock, classic pop, surf rock, and stadium-sized riffs with singer/guitarist Black Francis' bizarre, fragmented lyrics about space, religion, sex, mutilation, and pop culture; while the meaning of his lyrics may have been impenetrable, the music was direct and forceful. The Pixies' busy, brief songs, extreme dynamics and subversion of pop song structures proved one of the touchstones of '90s alternative rock. From grunge to Brit-pop, the Pixies shadow loomed large—it's hard to imagine Nirvana without the Pixies' signature stop-start dynamics and lurching, noisey guitar solos. While the Pixies were touted as the band to bring indie-rock into the mainstream, they simply laid the groundwork for the alternative explosion of the early '90s. MTV was reluctant to play their videos, while even modern rock radio didn't put their singles into regular rotation. Furthermore, tensions between leader Black Francis and bassist/vocalist Kim Deal, who wanted to incorporate her songs into the band's repertoire, crippled the band's prorgress. By the time Nirvana broke the doors down for alternative rock in 1992, the Pixies were effectively broken-up. *—Stephen Thomas Erlewine*

Come on Pilgrim [EP] / 1987 / 4AD/Elektra ♦♦♦♦♦
Amazingly, Pixies' 1987 debut EP *Come on Pilgrim* was compiled from the quickly, inexpensively made demo tape—paid for by Black Francis' dad—the band made at Boston's legendary Fort Apache studio soon after they formed. 4AD was so taken with the tape that they released eight of the songs as this mini-album. It's easy to see why they were so impressed: The Pixies' essential sound—Francis' unearthly shriek of a voice, David Lovering's propulsive drumming, Joey Santiago's insistent, prickly guitar playing, and Kim Deal's sugar-and-sandpaper vocals and steady bass lines—arrives fully formed on songs like the bouncy, yet twisted, surfer-girl ode "Ed Is Dead." Influences like '80s college-rock peers the Violent Femmes, the Stooges, Lou Reed and hardcore punk crop up on songs like ("I've Been Tired"), the group's surreal take on sexual frustration and "Isla de Encanta." Most importantly, the EP introduces the spooky, theatrical vision the group brought to their simple guitar-bass-drums lineup. Francis' lyrical fetishes for sex, death, and religion and his twisted sense of humor crop up on every track, from the eerie opener "Caribou," which urges listeners to "Reeeeepent!" to the final song "Levitate Me," which borrows Christian folk singer Larry Norman's catchphrase "Come on pilgrim, you know he loves you!" "The Holiday Song" and "Nimrod's Son" provide voyeuristic, back-to-back glimpses at incest, as well as the priceless lyric "My sister held me close and whispered to my bleeding head/You are the son of a motherfucker" (from "Nimrod's Son"). Gary Smith's less-is-more production allows the full, primal impact of the band's combustive sound to blast through, offering what may be the purest version of their perverse punk-pop. An electrifying debut, *Come on Pilgrim* remains as raw, vibrant, and engaging as the day it was recorded. *—Heather Phares*

☆ **Surfer Rosa** / 1988 / 4AD/Elektra ✦✦✦✦✦

One of the most compulsively listenable college rock albums of the '80s, the Pixies' 1988 full-length debut *Surfer Rosa* fulfilled the promise of *Come on Pilgrim* and, thanks to Steve Albini's production, added a muscular edge that made their harshest moments seem even more menacing and perverse. On songs like "Something Against You," Black Francis' cryptic shrieks and non sequiturs are backed by David Lovering and Kim Deal's punchy rhythms, which are so visceral that they'd overwhelm any guitarist except Joey Santiago, who takes the spotlight on the epic "Vamos." Albini's high-contrast dynamics suit *Surfer Rosa* well, especially on the explosive opener "Bone Machine" and the kinky, T-Rex-inspired "Cactus." But, like the black-and-white photo of a flamenco dancer on its cover, *Surfer Rosa* is the Pixies' most polarized work. For each blazing piece of punk, there are softer, poppier moments such as "Where Is My Mind?," Francis' strangely poignant song inspired by scuba diving in the Caribbean, and the Kim Deal-penned "Gigantic," which almost outshines the rest of the album. But even *Surfer Rosa*'s less iconic songs reflect how important the album was in the group's development. The "song about a superhero named Tony" ("Tony's Theme") was the most lighthearted song the Pixies had recorded, pointing the way to their more overtly playful, whimsical work on *Doolittle*. Francis' warped sense of humor is evident in lyrics like "Bone Machine"'s "He bought me a soda and tried to molest me in the parking lot/Yep yep yep!" In a year that included landmark albums from contemporaries like Throwing Muses, Sonic Youth, and My Bloody Valentine, the Pixies managed to turn in one of 1988's most striking, distinctive records. *Surfer Rosa* may not be the group's most accessible work, but it is one of their most compelling. *—Heather Phares*

★ **Doolittle** / 1989 / 4AD/Elektra ✦✦✦✦✦

After 1988's brilliant but abrasive *Surfer Rosa*, the Pixies' sound couldn't get much more extreme. Their Elektra debut *Doolittle* reins in the noise in favor of pop songcraft and accessibility. Producer Gil Norton's sonic sheen adds some polish, but Black Francis' tighter songwriting focuses the group's attack. *Doolittle*'s most ferocious moments, like "Dead," a visceral retelling of David and Bathsheba's affair—are more stylized than the group's past outbursts. Meanwhile, their poppy side surfaces on the irresistible single "Here Comes Your Man" and the sweetly surreal love song "La La Love You." The Pixies' arty, noisy weirdness mix with just enough hooks to produce gleefully demented singles like "Debaser,"—inspired by Bunuel's classic surrealist short *Un Chien Andalou*—and "Wave of Mutilation," their surfy ode to driving a car into the sea. Though *Doolittle*'s sound is cleaner and smoother than the Pixies' earlier albums, there are still plenty of weird, abrasive vignettes: the blankly psychotic "There Goes My Gun," "Crackity Jones," a song about a crazy roommate Francis had in Puerto Rico, and the nihilistic finale "Gouge Away." Meanwhile, "Tame," and "I Bleed" continue the Pixies' penchant for cryptic kink. But the album doesn't just refine the Pixies' sound; they also expand their range on the brooding, wannabe spaghetti western theme "Silver" and the strangely theatrical "Mr. Grieves." "Hey" and "Monkey Gone to Heaven," on the other hand, stretch Francis' lyrical horizons: "Monkey"'s elliptical environmentalism and "Hey"'s twisted longing are the Pixies' versions of message songs and romantic ballads. Their most accessible album, *Doolittle*'s wide-ranging moods and sounds make it one of their most eclectic and ambitious. A fun, freaky alternative to most other late-'80s college rock, it's easy to see why the album made the Pixies into underground rock stars. *—Heather Phares*

Bossanova / Aug. 1990 / 4AD/Elektra ✦✦✦✦✦

When *Bossanova* arrived in 1990, it reflected the exhaustion the Pixies felt after *Doolittle*'s enormous success: For the first time, the band seems to be running out of ideas. Tellingly, Kim Deal contributes no songs, having formed the Breeders to give her work an outlet; that summer, their debut *Pod* won a warmer response than *Bossanova* received. Arguably the Pixies' weakest album—though Francis has said it's his favorite—most of it finds the band in fine form. Gil Norton's spacious, reverb-heavy production makes the Pixies sound like a Martian bar band, which fits the cover of the Surftones' "Cecilia Ann" and the glorious, shimmering closer "Havalina" perfectly. On the theremin-driven "Velouria," science fiction imagery displaces Francis' penchant for fetishistic lyrics; next to the token kinky song "Down to the Well"'s tired sound, it's a refreshing change. The similarly cryptic "All Over the World" and alien abduction tale "The Happening" add to the sci-fi feel. Quirky pop songs like "Allison," a tribute to jazz cool-cat Mose Allison, and "Dig for Fire," Francis' self-professed Talking Heads homage, heighten *Bossanova*'s playful, slightly off-kilter vibe, but rockers like "Hang Wire" and "Blown Away," fall flat. However, "Rock Music" is one of the group's most fiery outbursts, and "Is She Weird"'s chugging grind and sexy, funny lyrics make it a classic Pixies song. The band was so consistently amazing on their previous albums that when they released a slightly weaker one, critics and fans alike judged them too harshly. But on *Bossanova*'s strongest moments, the Pixies explored their softer side and found different uses for their extreme dynamics. Like a straight-A student who suddenly receives a B+, *Bossanova* might have been a disappointment initially, but its (small) failings emphasize the strengths of the rest of the Pixies' work. *—Heather Phares*

Trompe le Monde / Oct. 8, 1991 / 4AD/Elektra ✦✦✦✦

The title might be French for "fool the world," but with *Trompe Le Monde*, the Pixies weren't fooling anyone: this was essentially Black Francis' solo debut. It focuses on Francis' sci-fi fascination and lacks any Kim Deal songs; even her backing vocals are far and few between. Yet the band sounds revitalized on *Trompe Le Monde*, as if it was planned as their last hurrah. The raucous "Distance Equals Rate Times Time" and the explosive cover of the Jesus & Mary Chain's "Head On" are fairly straightforward, but the lyrics remain quirky on "Planet Of Sound," a song about a Martian who lands on Earth, and "Palace of the Brine," a tribute to sea monkeys and Utah's Salt Lake. He even disses hipsters and pretentious students—basically, the Pixies' fanbase—with nasty little digs like "Subbacultcha"'s "I was wearing eyeliner / She was wearing eyeliner" and "U-Mass"' "It's eduuucaaationaal!" Musically, "Trompe Le Monde"'s psychedelic sheen and "Alec Eiffel"'s atmospheric keyboards prove that the Pixies' sound wasn't defined by Steve Albini-style rawness. There's also more emotional depth: "The Sad Punk" features the strangely poignant bridge "And evolving from the sea / would not be too much time for me / to walk beside you in the sun," and "Letter to Memphis" is a heartfelt, if cryptic, love song. Though *Trompe Le Monde* doesn't sound quite like the Pixies' other work, *Come On Pilgrim*'s spooky beginnings, *Surfer Rosa*'s abrasive assault, *Doolittle*'s deceptively accessible punk-pop and *Bossanova*'s spacy sonics helped make *Trompe Le Monde* a rousing swan song and a precursor to alternative rock's imminent success. Whether that means their music remained pure or they missed their chance to cash in is debatable; either way, the Pixies are one of America's greatest, most influential bands. *—Heather Phares*

Death to the Pixies: 1987-1991 / Oct. 7, 1997 / 4AD/Elektra ✦✦✦✦

Death to the Pixies has a difficult task—distilling the highlights of a band that concentrated on albums, not singles. The Pixies' catalog was remarkably consistent, which means that most won't agree with all the 17 selections that comprise the first disc of this retrospective, since there are so many strong songs on their records. While most of the usual suspects are here—"Debaser," "Here Comes Your Man," "Bone Machine," "Gigantic," "Where Is My Mind?," "Velouria," "Nimrod's Son," "Wave of Mutilation," "Monkey Gone to Heaven"—many of the selections appear to have been made at random. As good as "Cecilia Ann," "Holiday Song," "U-Mass" and "Gouge Away" are, such essentials as "River Euphrates," "Cactus," "Hey," "Allison," "Vamos," "I've Been Tired," "The Happening," "Letter to Memphis" and "Motorway to Roswell" could have easily taken their place. Some of these songs are on disc two, a 21-song live disc culled from a 1990 Dutch concert that has been heavily bootlegged. It's a terrific concert, but the pairing of a greatest-hits record with a live show is puzzling, since casual fans who want the hits won't need the live disc, and the hardcore fans only need the second disc. That pairing alone makes *Death to the Pixies* unnecessary for neophytes, but the hits disc itself also is an imperfect introduction, since its non-chronological sequencing distorts the Pixies' impact. Still, there's so much great music on the collection that it isn't worthless, but the presentation is so ill-conceived that the very existence of *Death to the Pixies* is a little puzzling. *—Stephen Thomas Erlewine*

Pixies at the BBC / Jul. 14, 1998 / 4AD/Elektra ✦✦✦

Between 1988 and 1991, the Pixies performed six sessions at the BBC, playing on a variety of programs. For years, these sessions were hot bootleg items, especially since their first session for John Peel (on May 3, 1988) featured two otherwise unreleased covers—the Beatles' "Wild Honey Pie" and "(In Heaven) Lady in the Radiator Song," from *Eraserhead*. It took Elektra/4AD until 1998 to release the six sessions, and when the 15-track *Pixies at the BBC* did appear, it was a mixed blessing. Certainly, the music itself is pretty terrific—none of the versions are radically different (although "Wave of Mutilation" is performed in its "UK Surf Arrangment" from the "Here Comes Your Man" single, not the *Doolittle* version), but each cut is raw and vital, and recasting "Wild Honey Pie" as pure primal dementia was brilliant. What is suspect is the presentation. Instead of keeping each session intact, the compilers have assembled individual tracks in seemingly random order so the disc bounces from 1989 to 1991 to 1988 to 1990. For an archival release, such tactics are infuriating—the sessions make more sense in chronological order, as most bootleggers know. Still, not every hardcore fan can track bootlegs down, nor are they willing to shell out the cash, which makes *Pixies at the BBC* a welcome (and overdue) addition to their official catalog. [Be aware, though, that the full-price disc clocks in at about 35 minutes.] *–Stephen Thomas Erlewine*

Complete B-Sides / Mar. 5, 2001 / 4AD ✦✦✦✦

Like the rest of 4AD's Pixies retrospectives, *Complete B-Sides* is equally exciting and frustrating: Many of their B-sides are just as good as their album tracks, so it's terrific to see them collected onto a single disc. But a number of factors make it somewhat disappointing, not the least of which is that *Complete B-Sides* is available only as a U.K. import, due to U.S. licensing problems. That won't dissuade Pixies diehards from seeking it out, but many longtime fans probably already have these songs, either on the original singles or on the bootlegs that proliferated while 4AD inexplicably sat on them. At any rate, *Complete B-Sides* mostly delivers the goods, kicking off with a ferocious version of "River Euphrates" from the "Gigantic" single. Witty, spooky *Doolittle* B-sides like "Manta Ray," "Weird at My School," and "Into the White" are so good that it's a shame they weren't saved for *Bossanova*, when the band really could have used them. Meanwhile, the Neil Young cover "Winterlong," which also appeared on *The Bridge* tribute, reaffirms the Pixies' ability to turn any artist's songs into their own. Not every song here scales these heights—"Bailey's Walk" and "Dancing the Manta Ray" are slightly less inspired bits of *Doolittle*-era pop perversity, and the snappy, strutting "Santo" and demented cow punk of "Build High" weren't quite ready for prime time, but they're still more interesting than many other bands' A material. Quirky cuts like "Make Believe," David Lovering's strangely charming tribute to Debbie Gibson, give the collection extra personality. The album also features some fun, if not extremely informative, comments about each track from Frank Black, as well as the clips for "Here Comes Your Man" and "Allison," which will only make fans clamor for the next logical Pixies release: a video collection. Though it doesn't quite do justice to the band's legacy, *Complete B-Sides* does a good job of filling in the gaps in the Pixies' body of work. *—Heather Phares*

Pizzicato Five

f. 1984, Tokyo, Japan

Shibuya-Kei, Indie Pop, Japanese Pop, Alternative Dance, Club/Dance, Alternative Pop/Rock, House, Dance-Pop

Godfathers of the Shibuya-kei scene, Tokyo kitsch-pop deconstructionists Pizzicato Five originally began taking shape as far back as 1979, when university students Yasuharu Konishi and Keitaro Takanami first met at a local music society meeting. Agreeing to form a band, they soon recruited fellow society member Ryo Kamamiya; their search for a suitable vocalist proved frustrating, however, and only in late 1984 did they settle on singer Mamiko Sasaki. The first Pizzicato Five single, "Audrey Hepburn Complex," followed a year later, and in 1986 the group issued their debut LP, *Pizzicato Five in Action*; a slew of subsequent records established them among the most popular acts in Japan, in spite of a series of line-up fluctuations which saw both Kamamiya and Sasaki exit in 1988, replaced soon after by vocalist Takao Tajima (who in turn quit the following year). Beginning with the 1990 single "Lovers Rock," Maki Nomiya was the new P5 vocalist; their popularity at home continued to soar, and in 1994 the American indie label Matador agreed to issue the compilation EP *Five by Five*. Takanami quit shortly after its release, however, reducing the group to a duo; after a pair of other US compilations, *Made in USA* and *The Sound of Music by Pizzicato Five*, in 1997 they issued *Happy End of the World*, the first of their LPs to enjoy simultaneous Japanese and American release. *The International Playboy and Playgirl Record* followed two years later, and the group's last proper album of the millennium [*Pizzicato Five (tm)*] appeared in November 1999. —*Jason Ankeny*

Non-Standard Years '85-'86 / 1985-1986 / Teichiku ♦♦

Couples / 1987 / CBS/Sony ♦♦♦

Belissima! / 1988 / CBS/Sony ♦♦♦

● **Made in USA** / 1994 / Matador ♦♦♦♦♦
Although it's not billed as such, the group's stateside debut is actually a compilation of tracks from their 15 or so albums. You need a taste for irreverent sampling and ironic deconstruction of lightweight pop idioms to dig this. But within that narrow field, Pizzicato Five are as good as it gets. They devise fare that's both funky and funny, made more human than most such projects by Maki Nomiya's fetching vocals. —*Richie Unterberger*

Big Hits & Jetlags: 1991-1995 / Mar. 1, 1995 / Triad /Columbia ♦♦♦♦♦
A look back over the third era of Pizzicato Five, when Maki Nomiya joined the group as vocalist, and up to the point when member Keitaro Takanami left, turning a long-ago quintet into a duo (possibly due to a falling-out between the two songwriters, there is not one Takanami song represented here). Not content with a sampling of hits, *Big Hits* contains several mixes not available anywhere else: a Towa Tei remix of "Catchy," a radical reworking of "On the Sunny Side of the Street" by tk, and a live studio recording of "Happy Sad" with Cornelius' backing band. There's even an orchestral medley of Pizzicato Five's greatest hits, which is just this side of cheesy. Compared to *Made in USA*, the first Matador release, this is a much more coherent introduction to the group for beginners. —*Ted Mills*

The Sound of Music by Pizzicato Five / Oct. 31, 1995 / Matador ♦♦♦♦
The second of Matador's compilations of Pizzicato Five's Japanese releases, with an emphasis on *Bossanova 2001* and *Overdose*. There are a few rarities scattered throughout: "Fortune Cookie," an obscure B-side, and "No. 5," from Readymade Recordings in 1991. The St. Etienne remix of "Peace Music," nine minutes of loops and distortion, unbalances this collection, but most of the selection is cohesive enough to listen to all the way through. —*Ted Mills*

Happy End of the World / Sep. 9, 1997 / Matador/Capitol ♦♦♦♦
Happy End of the World is the first album of entirely new material that the Pizzicato Five released in the United States, but it doesn't necessarily represent a great leap forward for the dance-lounge duo. Pizzicato Five continue to blend light '60s pop, '70s disco, and '80s dance with an ironic flair on *Happy End of the World*, but the energy level is turned down a bit. It's a surprisingly laid-back album, but that's not necessarily a bad thing—the lush arrangements have an engaging, low-key charm, and the beats are nice and subtle. *Happy End of the World* runs a little too long, and no song stands out as a single, but it's an engaging record that suggests there may be more to the Pizzicato Five than kitsch. —*Stephen Thomas Erlewine*

Playboy & Playgirl / Aug. 25, 1998 / Matador ♦♦♦♦
Playboy and Playgirl begins with the kind of collage-heavy imagined soundtrack that marked *Happy End of the World*; with that out of the way, they get back to the inspired, eclectic popcraft that is their strength. Hookier and more danceable than their previous album, this is a welcome return to songwriting for the dynamic duo. Think Burt Bacharach without the self-pity, with a smidgen of Motown and Stax. Keyboard timbres run the gamut of the Pizzicato imagination from faux-harpsichord to spacy funk. Singer Nomiya Maki puts her unpretentious stamp over everything from *Sgt. Pepper's* pomp to '60s R&B horns to symphonic dance floor beats to introspective pastorals. While P5 may be in with the lounge crowd, they never feel superior to their cheesy predecessors; avoiding the sometimes smug, reactionary irony of the new exotica, Yasuharu Konishi's diverse influences are held together by his all-embracing love of the pop spectrum. A joyous record. [Note: *Playboy & Playgirl* was released in Japan in 1998 under the title *The International Playboy & Playgirl Record*; Matador's 1999 American release cuts the third track, "International Pizzicato Five Mansion," and substitutes "La Règle du Jeu" later in the album's running order.] —*Pat Padua*

Big Hits & Jetlags: 1994-1997 / Oct. 5, 1999 / TYO ♦♦♦♦♦
The third compilation of Pizzicato Five singles and should-have-been hits focuses on the years following Takanami leaving the group. Although this only means two full albums to draw from, Pizzicato Five had released so many singles and EPs during this period, so this CD is an excellent way to keep up to date. (It helps that these singles, "Baby

Portable Rock," "A Message Song," and "I Hear a Symphony," are strong songs). The CD also features two clever mega-mixes of their catalog in "Lesson 3003 Parts 1 and 2." —*Ted Mills*

This Year's Girl / Nov. 14, 2000 / Sony International ♦♦♦♦♦
This Year's Girl was more than the culmination of a Japanese indie media blitz that had started back in early 1991, it was the album the Pizzicato Five had been looking to make since their inception, and one that has influenced all their albums since. It finds Yasuharu Konishi, Keitaro Takanami, and Nomiya Maki on top of their game. *This Year's Girl* is very polished, but also has an airy, offhanded quality about it, in the way that the whole album seems to sample itself, with glimpses of songs popping up in the mix before their due. The centerpiece of the album, "Twiggy Twiggy," is to the band what "Satisfaction" is to the Rolling Stones—instantly catchy, with a recognizable riff made up of samples from the Ventures (those timpanis!), Jimmy Smith, and Lalo Schifrin turned into something greater that the sum of its parts. It's a sign of the creativity of this period that there are plenty more, equally great songs sharing the CD. "Baby Love Child" cuts between Sonny & Cher flower power and the sophisticated groove from the band's own "Couples." "I Wanna Be You" is a laid-back midnight groove a scant couple of years before acid jazz. "Party," a cover of a 1973 song by Haruomi Hosono (pre-YMO), is all bumpin' disorienting rhythms. "Thank You," from an earlier EP, is stripped down to its tuneful essence. Yet all this would be techno diddling about if Konishi and Takanami weren't accomplished songwriters. Like De La Soul, Yasuharu Konishi had taken the potential of sampling, looping, and reconstruction to its pop limit. Even years later it sounds ahead of its time, plus it's a joyous, fun album. —*Ted Mills*

Placebo

f. 1994, London, England
Neo-Glam, Punk-Pop, Punk Revival, Britpop, Alternative Pop/Rock
Punk-pop band Placebo released their self-titled album debut for Caroline Records in 1996, after touring with the Sex Pistols and Weezer, and being featured on the covers of both *NME* and *Melody Maker*. The band, which then included vocalist/guitarist Brian Molko, bassist Stefan Olsdal and drummer Robert Schultzberg, reached the UK Top Five with the single "Nancy Boy," also performed at David Bowie's 50th birthday party. After replacing Schultzberg with new drummer Steve Hewitt, Placebo returned in 1998 with *Without You I'm Nothing*. A spiritual rebirth was evident on 2000's *Black Market Music*, for Placebo was no longer thwarting hardcore aggression once prominent in their early 20s. It was straightforward rock & roll and singles such as the glam-oriented "Taste In Men" and "Slaves to Wage" were mainstream chart favorites in the U.K. —*John Bush*

Placebo / Jul. 17, 1996 / Caroline ♦♦♦
The key to Placebo's sound is singer/guitarist Brian Molko, whose impersonation of a woman goes far beyond his appearance and into his singing voice. His trio brings together various influences—the epic, noisy "Chicago Sound," late-'70s prog-rock, and late-'80s "college rock"—but boils them down into fairly conventional guitar-heavy melodrama, with the sort of opaque and angsty lyrics usually found in that genre. That's not to say that *Placebo*'s sound is boring; churning guitars and direct, heavy basslines give the album a good deal of strength, and Molko is able to write moving, gritty melodies and fairly clever lyrics. *Placebo* may sound like a mix between Smashing Pumpkins and Rush—and the levels of melodrama on the album may stretch far beyond most people's tolerance—but it's well-written, and performs enough variations on those genres to keep it interesting. —*Nitsuh Abebe*

Without You I'm Nothing / Nov. 3, 1998 / Virgin ♦♦♦♦
While Placebo's self-titled debut contained mostly elements of '90s alternative (Smashing Pumpkins, etc.), their second album, *Without You I'm Nothing*, is full of '70s glam rock and punk references. Placebo's rhythm section of Stefan Olsdal (bass) and Steve Hewitt (drums) is impressively tight, but the band's star attraction is undoubtedly androgynous singer/guitarist Brian Molko. Whereas the debut was written solely by Molko, their latest is a bonafide group effort, with Molko still handling the lyric writing. The swirling anthemic album opener, "Pure Morning," is a self-proclaimed "celebration of friendship with women," and should be a guaranteed hit single, while the racing "Brick Shithouse" merges '90s electro-rock with Sonic Youth punk guitars. "You Don't Care About Us" shows that Molko can easily re-create J. Mascis' late-'80s guitar tones, and "Scared of Girls" contains gender-bending vocals from Molko and a tribal-rock accompaniment. With massive success already underway back home in England, *Without You I'm Nothing* should break through everywhere else. —*Greg Prato*

● **Black Market Music** / Oct. 9, 2000 / Hut ♦♦♦♦
After almost five years, the vile, nasty, spunk-filled world of Placebo refuses to go away. Marilyn Manson has turned a satirical eye on his own media status and even Suede have since come to swoon over girls "shaped like a cigarette." Yet it's Brian Molko that's steered his band from premature randiness (*Placebo*) to fearful regrouping (*Without You I'm Nothing*) without once batting a make-up smeared eyelash. *Black Market Music* finds Molko in such moody lust that his strangled, androgynous wailing rivals anything the band has previously flashed to the world. Whether it's the dripping, slithery punk circle of songs like "Black Eyed" or the choir-boy enthusiasm of others like "Special K" (strangely echoing Midnight Oil's "Warakurna"), Placebo seem to have finally found that sweet wet spot between beauty and perversion. Even at its worst (the "Block Rockin' Beats"-sampling "Taste In Men"), past glories sometimes fail to be repeated with at least grand, post-coital contentment. Because it's hard to hate an album with such fascinating softer touches. In one moment, Molko cries respect to his mother, in another he counsels, "*You better keep it in check / or you'll end up a wreck / and you'll never wake up*"—a

paternal warning seemingly directed at his fellow hedonists. Of course, there's a thin line between trying to perfect old efforts and stumbling into laughable self-parody. But Placebo now seem more in control than they ever have before. The spectacular "Commercial For Levi," for example, is some perverted, weary take on a childhood lullaby, only one written in a parallel dimension about "spunk and bestiality." True, there's no "Nancy Boy" or "Pure Morning," yet the album's consistency easily outmatches even the highest watermarks of either predecessor. This is a dank, lusty, moment in the band's career that is about as good as Placebo "mark 1" can go. They now have the talent, the intelligence, and the distorted arousal to possibly become unstoppable. It's only a matter of time before they finally find love amidst the lust. —*Dean Carlson*

Plainsong
f. 1972, **db.** 1974
Folk-Rock
A quartet formed by Ian Matthews in 1972 with Andy Roberts, Bob Ronga, and Dave Richards. They released *In Search of Amelia Earhart* the same year to critical praise but little commercial success. While working on their follow-up, the more country oriented *Plainsong III*, Ronga quit and Matthews and Richards were unable to agree on the direction the band would take musically. They disbanded before the album's completion. In 1993, a revived interest in the band inspired a new studio album, *Dark Side of the Room*, as well as a BBC recording of a promotional tour from 1972. In 1994, the band released *Voices Electric. Sister Flute* followed in 1996. In 1997, Clive Gregson (ex-Any Trouble, Gregson & Collister) joined the band, with *New Place Now* appearing two years later. —*Chris Woodstra*

● **In Search of Amelia Earhart** / 1972 / Elektra ✦✦✦✦
In early 1972 Ian Matthews started Plainsong, his fourth band in five years. And while his track record led one to believe that Plainsong may be just another short stay, the subsequent album, *In Search of Amelia Earhart*, proved to be worth the venture. Matthews was of course the obvious draw, but Plainsong seemed to be formed as more of a collective effort, with lead guitarist Andy Roberts, who shares the lead vocal duties, the other focal point in the band. On the other hand, Matthews, whose folk- and country-tinged tunes set the tone for the record, is the only member to contribute original material. Included among these is the thematic "True Story of Amelia Earhart," which along with the haunting "For the Second Time," leads a pack of five Matthews compositions that range from good to excellent. Elsewhere, Paul Siebel's heartbreaking "Louise," the dulcimer- and harmony-driven Appalachian gospel of "I'll Fly Away," and Roberts' readings of the playful "Yo Yo Man," Jim & Jesse's "Diesel on My Tail," and the mournful 1939 tale of "Amelia Earhart's Last Flight" are all highlights. Its title and artwork, along with notes by Charles Goerner on the flight and disappearance of Amelia Earhart and Frederick Noonan, gave *In Search of Amelia Earhart* the feel of a concept album, even though the title is nowhere to be found on the outside jacket and there are only two songs related to the subject contained within. It wasn't really a surprise when a follow-up, though recorded, failed to materialize, with the band parting ways on less than amicable terms, and Matthews going on to record two more records for Elektra. Still, *In Search of Amelia Earhart* fits nicely alongside the rest of his terrific early-'70s catalog. —*Brett Hartenbach*

On Air—Original BBC Recordings / 1993 / Band of Joy ✦✦✦✦

Dark Side of the Room / Oct. 19, 1993 / Mesa ✦✦✦
Matthews and company regrouped for this 1993 album. Though the album lacks much of the charm of their first album, the songs have a craftsmanlike precision and are certainly pleasant enough. The album is more closely connected to Matthews' later work than to its predecessor. —*Chris Woodstra*

Voices Electric / 1994 / Watermelon ✦✦

Sister Flute / Dec. 17, 1996 / Line ✦✦✦

New Place Now / Oct. 19, 1999 / Tangible ✦✦

Robert Plant
b. Aug. 20, 1948, Birmingham, England
Vocals, Harmonica / Album Rock, Hard Rock
British hard rock/heavy metal singer Robert Plant had released a couple of singles and worked with a number of bands before he hooked up with Jimmy Page's New Yardbirds, subsequently renamed Led Zeppelin, around the time of his 20th birthday in 1968. For the next 12 years, Plant was one of the biggest rock stars on the planet. He gradually developed as a singer, branching out into other styles within Zeppelin's hard rock framework, and he blossomed as a songwriter as well.

Plant launched a solo career in 1982 with the album *Pictures at Eleven*, a gold-selling hit. He did even better the following year with *The Principle of Moments*. It sold a million copies, included the Top 20 hit "Big Log," and led to his first post-Zeppelin concert tour. Surprisingly, Plant then organized a one-off mini-album, *The Honeydrippers—Vol. One*, recording some rock oldies with a superstar pickup band. He faced greater consumer resistance with his third solo album, *Shaken 'n' Stirred*, perhaps because joint appearances with Page led an audience to desire for a Zeppelin reunion. To an extent, Plant fed that desire with *Now and Zen*, which sampled Zeppelin tracks and featured Page. It was another million-seller. Plant's 1990 follow-up, *Manic Nirvana*, went gold. —*William Ruhlmann*

Pictures at Eleven / 1982 / Swan Song ✦✦✦✦
The directions in which Plant seemed to be heading in the later Zeppelin records—toward lighter, more melodic music, tempered with sometimes odd rhythms—are continued on

his first solo album, which finds him singing more and screaming less. It wasn't Led Zeppelin, but then, that was the whole point. —*William Ruhlmann*

Principle of Moments / 1983 / Es Paranza ✦✦✦✦
Plant reinvents rock and pop oldies in much the way Led Zeppelin did old blues songs. "Other Arms" recasts "Lay Down Your Arms," as Plant declares, "I'm not a prisoner of the big parade," while "In the Mood" retools an old pop theme. The playing is propulsive (thanks to guest drummer Phil Collins) and Plant's singing unusually supple. —*William Ruhlmann*

Shaken 'N' Stirred / 1985 / Es Paranza ✦✦✦
Robert Plant continued to expand the horizons of his music with his third album, *Shaken 'N' Stirred*, adding elements of worldbeat to his increasingly atmospheric and synth-driven pop-rock. Although the experimentation is admirable, and occasionally successful, the most successful tracks on the album are straightforward numbers like "Little By Little." —*Stephen Thomas Erlewine*

● **Now & Zen** / 1988 / Es Paranza ✦✦✦✦
After years of trying to separate himself from his legendary status as Led Zeppelin's frontman, Robert Plant finally reconciles with his past on *Now & Zen*. He borrows a few Zeppelin riffs, and even enlists Jimmy Page to play guitar on his hit "Tall Cool One." This album is also notable in that it marks his first collaboration with keyboardist Phil Johnstone, who would continue to play and write with Plant on subsequent albums. Musically, the album relies on standard rock arrangements except that the vocals and drums are at the forefront and keyboards instead of guitars are used to fill out the sound. Although most of the album is comprised of mid-tempo songs aimed at rock radio, Plant includes the lovely ballad "Ship of Fools," which demonstrates that he is more than capable of vocal subtlety. Plant, who often uses mysterious (and mystical) lyrics, writes some of his most direct songs, and the way in which the lyrics complement the melodic arrangements are partially responsible for the commercial success of *Now & Zen*. This is Robert Plant's best solo album, and a must-own for fans of Led Zeppelin. —*Vik Iyengar*

Manic Nirvana / Mar. 1990 / Es Paranza ✦✦

Fate of Nations / May 27, 1993 / Es Paranza ✦✦✦
At first, *Fate of Nations* seems so light and airy that it slips away through the layers of acoustic guitars, violins, and keyboards. Upon further listenings, more textures appear, and the album gains a calm sense of tension and reflectiveness. It's also Plant's most personal record ever; he addresses the death of his son in the beautiful "I Believe." Simultaneously, *Fate of Nations* is a political album—"Great Spirit" and "Network News" are two of the most socially conscious songs Plant has ever written. Yet, the album is never heavy-handed and doesn't fall into sermonizing or sentimentality. Plant has always had a folkie heart; on *Fate of Nations*, he wears it on his sleeve. —*Stephen Thomas Erlewine*

Plasmatics
f. 1979, New York, NY, **db.** 1983
Post-Punk, Hard Rock, Punk
Although their "fame" lasted for a full 15 minutes, few bands entered rock & roll with such a controversial reputation as did the Plasmatics. Founded by Rod Swenson, a porn film producer who fancied himself the next Malcolm McLaren, the Plasmatics were fronted by sex film "star" Wendy O. Williams, a muscular, raspy-voiced "singer" who generally wore next to nothing onstage. Almost as captivating was guitarist Richie Stotts, a tall, gangly geek who fancied garters and stockings and a blue mohawk; he also liked to smash his guitar against his head until he drew blood.

Playing the New York punk circuit, the Plasmatics became notorious for their extreme stage shows, which, early on, culminated in Williams firing blanks from a sawed-off shotgun and taking a chainsaw to a human dummy filled with stage blood. The music, however, was another story: mostly sub-literate punk rock loaded with lots of quasi-sci-fi totalitarianism and consumer nightmares of Orwellian proportions that on record didn't work without the stage pyrotechnics, something Swenson and the 'Matics understood completely as the stage shows quickly became more elaborate: cars were blown up, guitars were sawed in half, equipment was set on fire—it was a Beavis and Butt-Head wet dream come to life, although none of this translated into significant record sales. While Williams became something of a demi-celebrity in punk circles, the Plasmatics were all show and no substance. Stotts, apparently on a quest for legitimacy, quit the band, and the focus became Williams. After 1982's *Coup D'Etat*, Williams went solo, worked with Lemmy from Motörhead, and roped in Kiss' Gene Simmons to produce her album *W.O.W.* She made another solo LP, 1986's *Kommander of Kaos*. On April 8, 1998, it was announced that Williams had committed suicide; she was 48. —*John Dougan*

New Hope for the Wretched / 1980 / Repertoire ✦✦

● **Beyond the Valley of 1984/Metal Priestess** / 1981 / PVC ✦✦✦✦✦
If you're interested in actually listening to The Plasmatics (though I'd guess watching a video of them performing would be infinitely more satisfying) this is the only recording worth getting. More of a heavy metal than a punk record, it was reissued with their EP *Metal Priestess*, so you can get more bang (pun intended) for your buck. There are songs here worth playing more than once, and the outrage and vituperation seems real, even if it is a pose. Notable trivia: the drummer is ex-Alice Cooper tubman Neil Smith, a veteran of the *Killer* and *Billion Dollar Babies* Cooper era. —*John Dougan*

Coup D'Etat / 1982 / Capitol ✦✦✦

Plastic Bertrand
f. 1978, **db.** 1982
French Rock, New Wave

Plastic Bertrand was the alias of new wave prankster Roger Jouret, a native of Belgium who appropriated the sound and style of the new wave movement in order to give it a gently satirical poke in the ribs, while scoring several European hits in the process. Jouret began his musical career as a drummer for the Belgian punk trio Hubble Bubble, which recorded one unsuccessful album. When Jouret met producer/songwriter Lou Deprijck, the two struck up a recording partnership; Jouret emphasized his pretty-boy looks and punkish fashion sense. Their first effort, "Ça Plane Pour Moi" ("This Life's for Me"), is widely regarded as a New Wave classic for its gleefully deranged stupidity, with Jouret singing French nonsense lyrics in a cartoonish voice over basic three-chord rock & roll complete with saxophones and a falsetto vocal hook straight out of the Beach Boys or Four Seasons. The song was a smash in Europe and became a cult favorite in America; Plastic Bertrand continued to release records in Europe, including a U.K. hit remake of the Small Faces' "Sha-La-La-Lee." Bertrand experimented with seemingly every new wave fashion, including spacy electronics, disco, bubblegum pop, reggae, and spoken word raps, all with the same naggingly entertaining stupidity. He remained popular on the European continent and in Canada for several years, where audiences were more attuned to his largely French lyrics, but the novelty eventually wore off, and nothing was heard from Bertrand after 1982. Plastic Bertrand released several albums, all of which are difficult to find; a greatest-hits collection is also floating around. *—Steve Huey*

- **Plastic Hits** / 1995 / ✦✦✦✦✦

Apart from the gleefully deranged mini-masterpiece of absurdity "Ca Plane Pour Moi" and a cover of Peter Schilling's spacey "Major Tom," *Plastic Hits* consists of comical, frequently annoying European regurgitation of new-wave rock which only occasionally places tongue in cheek. The sound is largely the same, and the simple choruses are usually repeated ad nauseum. That said, songs like "Hula Hoop," "Super Cool," and "C'est le Rock & Roll" (a ripoff of the Four Seasons' "Walk Like a Man") do have a certain dopey charm for those fascinated by trashy, formulaic imitations of American culture. *—Steve Huey*

Plastic People of the Universe

f. 1968, db. 1984

Experimental Rock, Proto-Punk

This band's debut may well have been one of the most amazing and radical records to be released during the punk era (or any era for that matter), recorded under the most extreme conditions in the years before punk rock was a reality (1973-1974). Prague's Plastic People of the Universe, and the band they later became, Pulnoc, remain one of rock & roll's great stories of triumph and how great music can be produced and survive even in the most hostile of environments. The band was founded in 1968 soon after 500,000 Soviet troops invaded Czechoslovakia. With the Kremlin not being particularly fond of Western-style rock that wasn't sanctioned by the state, the Plastic People, to paraphrase the Jefferson Airplane, quickly became outlaws in the eyes of Moscow (and the ruling Soviet government in Prague). From 1970 until the "Velvet Revolution" of 1989 that ended Soviet domination, the Plastic People lived a mostly illegal existence, with two of their members, Ivan Jirous and Jaroslav Vozniak, doing lengthy stretches in prison. Influenced by Zappa, English progressive rock/radical politicos Henry Cow, Captain Beefheart, and the Velvet Underground, the Plastic People appropriated the avant-garde leanings and anti-authoritarian outrage of these bands while working in their own sense of dread and desperation. Remember, according to Soviet law, they could not record, press, and distribute albums or play gigs; still, they did all three surreptitiously. After 15 years of struggle, incarceration, harassment, and violence, the Plastic People quietly disbanded in 1984. Finally, in 1988, a year before the "Velvet Revolution," the band was given government permission to perform under the name Pulnoc. Unlike the radical, dissonant sounds of the Plastic People, Pulnoc had a more traditional guitar-based rock sound and production polish, but its accessibility in no way detracts from its greatness. *—John Dougan*

- **Egon Bondy's Happy Heart Club Banned** / 1978 / Invisible ✦✦✦✦✦

Sounding like a meeting between Zappa, Henry Cow and Allen Ginsberg, this is a wild, politically charged chunk of avant-garde agit-prop. Bondy's poetry may not be the most lyrical you've ever heard, but his imagery is striking in its desperation and anger. Lots of honking saxes courtesy of Vratislav Brabenec, who is a big-time blower in the style of German free-jazz player Peter Brotzmann. For those whose love for late-'60s/early-'70s progressive rock is boundless, this is absolutely essential. But, even if you're squeamish about anything labeled art-rock, don't pass this by; the raw emotions and intense idealism in the face of oppression, despite their being sung in a language you don't speak (there are English lyrics on the LP jacket), are very moving. *—John Dougan*

Leading Horses / 1983 / Bozi Mlyn ✦✦✦✦

I'll be honest, I've never heard either of these records. The only reviews of them I've ever read were by longtime Plastic People supporter Robert Christgau in his monthly *Village Voice Consumer Guide*. He gave *Passion Play* a B+, and *Leading Horses* an A–. That's all the info I need. If you find them before I do, please tell me where you purchased them. *—John Dougan*

Plasticland

Garage Rock Revival, Neo-Psychedelia

Milwaukee's Plasticland sometimes resembled an L.A. Paisley Underground band, but their style owed more to 1960s British hard rock and garage psychedelia than, for example, the Velvet Underground. Picking up where Arousing Polaris left off, Plasticland, led by vocalist Glenn Rehse, debuted in 1982 with the *Pop! Op Drops* EP; its tracks were later issued on the nearly identical French LP *Color Appreciation* and 1985's *Plasticland.*

Wonder Wonderful Wonderland was released the same year as the latter and was followed with 1987's *Salon*. In 1990, the group released a live album, *Confetti*, and the EP *Let's Play Pollyanna*. *—Steve Huey*

Color Appreciation / 1984 / Lolita ✦✦✦
Plasticland / 1985 / Enigma ✦✦✦
- **Wonder Wonderful Wonderland** / 1985 / Pink Dust ✦✦✦✦✦
Salon / 1987 / Pink Dust ✦✦✦
Confetti / 1990 / Midnight ✦✦✦
Dapper Snappings / 1994 / Repulsion ✦✦✦✦

Plastikman (Richard Hawtin)

b. Jun. 4, 1970, Danbury, England

DJ, Producer / Minimal Techno, Experimental Techno, Electronica, Ambient Techno, Acid Techno, Techno, Detroit Techno

His style formed by a fusion of the barest acid-house and straitjacket-tight Detroit techno, Richie Hawtin became one of the most influential artists in the world of techno during the 1990s, even while sticking to out-of-date synth dinosaurs like the Roland TB-303 and TR-808. Hawtin combined lean percussion and equally spare acid lines into haunting techno anthems which kicked with more than enough power for the dance floor while diverting headphone listeners as well. While even his early recordings were quite minimalistic, he streamlined the sound increasingly over the course of his recording career; from the early '90s to the end of the decade, Hawtin's material moved from the verge of the techno mainstream into a yawing abyss of dubbed-out echo-chamber isolationism, often jettisoning any semblance of a bassline or steady beat. Hawtin released material on his own +8 Records under several aliases—some in tandem with co-founder John Acquaviva—and made the label one of the best styled in Detroit techno of the 1990s. He earned his pedigrees from worldwide fans of techno for his best-known releases, as Plastikman (for NovaMute) and Fuse (for Warp/TVT). *—John Bush*

Sheet One / 1993 / Nova Mute ✦✦✦✦

One of the first records to turn the 303 acid box upside down from glorious high to isolationist low, Plastikman's first album focuses on laser-precise minimalist rhythms to drive a series of echo-box acid lines that gradually acquire power over the course of lengthy album tracks like the ten-minute "Drp," "Glob," and "Plasticine." *—John Bush*

- **Musik** / Nov. 8, 1994 / Plus 8 ✦✦✦✦✦

Richie Hawtin didn't just produce full-length albums; his albums were conceptual pieces that flowed from one track to the next with smooth continuity—from a strange audio experiment in sparse, symmetrically designed drum programming to epic electronic trips fueled by swarms of tapping percussion and haunting, lifelike acid sounds. Similar to other Plastikman albums such as *Consumed*, the beginning and end of *Musik* are simply amazing in the epic scope of their cinematic exercises in computerized funk, while the middle of the album consists of short, strange experiments in mood, tone and shape. The first two tracks, "Konception" and "Plastique," take up nearly 20 minutes of the album with their relentless, percussive electro rhythms and shrieking, alien-sounding electronic melodies. From there things get a bit slow-paced and at times dull, as Hawtin drops musical ideas rather than progressive songs. But just when things get a bit too experimental for pleasure, Hawtin concludes the album with two of the mind-encompassing sort of tracks that have propelled the name Plastikman beyond connotations of an avant-garde composer to the stature of artistic genius. Not only can he impress you with his theories, but he can also sweep your feelings away on his epic audio excursions into inhuman sensory overload. *—Jason Birchmeier*

MixMag Live!, Vol. 20: Plastikman / 1995 / Mixmag ✦✦✦

Though recorded in the studio rather than at an actual live performance, *Mixmag Live!* comes close to being the equivalent of a shortened version of Hawtin's all-night performances. Consisting of 22 tracks—including a few signature tracks—*Mixmag Live!* clocks in at nearly an hour, as Hawtin gives each track only a short moment before adding the next, often overlapping multiple tracks. At times the results are mind-blowing, as only the most knowledgeable listener can distinguish one from another, when multiple tracks are layered, or when the next track enters. The abundance of thumping bass beats and body-moving rhythm will surely please listeners who view techno as a means to dance, but it may be a little too sensory-overloading for listeners accustomed to the calming sounds of other Plastikman albums, such as *Consumed* or *Musik*. The highlight of the album comes about a third of the way through, when Hawtin drops a montage of percussive symmetry with the trilogy of 909-driven tracks from the early '90s, "Spastik," "Spaz," and "Helikopter." *—Jason Birchmeier*

From Within 3: Silent Intelligence / Jan. 6, 1998 / EFA ✦✦✦✦

Hawtin and Pete Namlook team up again two years after their last collaboration, and *From Within 3—Silent Intelligence* is possibly their best yet, featuring an eclectic mix of styles and greater studio manipulation. *—Steve Huey*

Consumed / May 18, 1998 / Nova Mute ✦✦✦✦✦

After achieving global fame in the techno world with his previous albums, intense live performances, and legendary Detroit parties, Richie Hawtin's first full-length Plastikman release in years shocked many listeners with its move toward the depths of minimal ambience. In form and structure the music on *Consumed* doesn't deviate much from Hawtin's previous Plastikman album, *Musik*. What differs are the sounds and technique applied to these forms and structures. Nearly every sound on *Consumed* registers in the lowest bass frequencies, except for the barely audible synths hovering, shadow-like, far behind the wall-shaking basslines. The album retains the ability to submerge listeners with its continuity, motifs and overall tone but never claims to be dance music. One track slowly merges with the next while the emotional tone instilled by Hawtin never wavers from consuming, contemplative alienation. The beginning two tracks ("Contained" and "Consume") and the concluding two ("Inside" and "Consumed") demand notice with their epic scope and emotional radiation. Sandwiched between these heavy tracks rest some shorter variations of the deep, minimal bass executions of German artists such as Maurizio and the Chain Reaction camp. This album's sedate approach upset some Hawtin fanatics, but most respected the producer's decision to move forward with this, the concluding album in the Plastikman cycle. —*Jason Birchmeier*

The Platters

f. 1953, Los Angeles, CA
Vocal Pop, Doo Wop, R&B
The Platters started out as a Los Angeles based Black doo wop group with little identity of their own to make them stand out from the pack. What changed their fortunes can be reduced down to one very important name: their mentor, manager, producer, songwriter and vocal coach, Buck Ram. Ram took what many would say was a run-of-the-mill R&B doo wop vocal group and turned them into stars and one of the most enduring and lucrative groups of all time. After getting the Platters out of a Federal Records contract, Ram placed them with the burgeoning national independent label Mercury, automatically getting them into pop markets through the label's distribution contacts alone. He then put the lead vocal status squarely on the shoulders of lead tenor Tony Williams, whose emoting power was turned up full blast. With Ram's pop songwriting classics as its musical palette, the group quickly became a pop and R&B success, eventually earning the distinction of being the first Black act of the era to top the pop charts. Considered the most romantic of all the doo wop groups, hit after hit came tumbling forth in a seemingly effortless manner: "Only You," "The Great Pretender," "My Prayer," "Twilight Time," "Smoke Gets in Your Eyes," "Harbor Lights," all of them establishing the Platters as the classiest of all. —*Cub Koda*

☆ **The Magic Touch: An Anthology** / Oct. 22, 1991 / Mercury ✦✦✦✦
Double-disc set of all their best sides, including "The Great Pretender," "Smoke Gets in Your Eyes," "Only You," "Harbor Lights," and the title track. Great annotation and impeccable sound. All compilations should be done this well. —*Cub Koda*

The Very Best of the Platters 1966-1969 / Jun. 17, 1997 / Varese ✦✦✦
After Tony Williams left the Platters in 1959, a new replacement was found in Charles "Sonny" Turner. But the group's label (Mercury) brought Turner in for album sessions only and kept releasing old tracks with Williams' voice on them as singles, even keeping his name off the liner notes to their new album. It wasn't until their contract was up with Mercury and the group moved on to Musicor Records in 1966 that Turner was allowed to sing on a record by the Platters in his true voice, five to six years after he came on board. This 14-track compilation covers the group's stay at the label between 1966 and 1969, a period of time that saw the Platters recast themselves as a beach music group ["Washed Ashore (On a Lonely Island In the Sea)"] while swimming against the tide of the burgeoning soul music movement. The hits didn't dry up, and "I Love You 1,000 Times," "Devri," "With This Ring," "Sweet Sweet Lovin'" and "I'll Be Home" showed that the group was breaking new ground while still making the charts. This collection chronicles the last stage of the Platters as a recording group of any significance and also features two previously unissued tracks, "Keep On Loving Me" and "Atlanta." Nothing here will ever take the place of the original hits on Mercury (which didn't sound anything like their early recordings for King), but those who want to get the big picture will do well to add this one to the collection. —*Cub Koda*

★ **Enchanted: The Best of the Platters** / Jun. 16, 1998 / Rhino ✦✦✦✦✦
For too many years, there was no single-disc collection of the Platters' greatest hits. Mercury's *Magic Touch* offered two discs' worth of prime material, but it was really too much for anyone outside of serious listeners; it also stopped short of their uneven but occasionally worthwhile Musicor recordings. Rhino's *Enchanted: The Best of the Platters* is the first compilation of the CD era to feature all of their biggest Mercury and Musicor hits on one disc, and it's a stunner. All of their Top Ten pop hits, from "Only You" to "Harbor Lights," are here, along with 18 other charting hits, all in their original hit versions. For any fan, both casual and dedicated, it's essential, since no other compilation features as many hits on one disc and no other compilation is quite so consistently entertaining. —*Stephen Thomas Erlewine*

Player

f. Los Angeles, CA
Soft Rock, Disco, Album Rock, Pop/Rock
Best remembered for the late-'70s chart-topper "Baby Come Back," Player was formed in Los Angeles in 1977 by singer/guitarist Peter Beckett (formerly of the U.K. group Skyband), bassist Ronn Moss and guitarist/keyboardist J.C. Crowley. After adding drummer John Friesen, Player signed to impresario Robert Stigwood's RSO label and issued "Baby Come Back," which sat atop the pop singles chart for three weeks in early 1978; their self-titled debut LP appeared that same year, as did the follow-up, *Danger Zone*. Crowley exited Player soon after, later enjoying a solo career as a country artist; the remaining trio issued *Room with a View* in 1980 before Moss and Friesen both departed as well. Beckett, the lone remaining founding member, continued the group for one final LP, 1982's *Spies of Life*, before retiring the Player name to mount a career as a songwriter and solo performer. Moss, meanwhile, joined the cast of the daytime soap opera *The Bold and the*

Beautiful in 1987; he and Beckett reformed Player in 1995, soon after issuing the reunion LP *Lost in Reality*. —*Jason Ankeny*

● **Baby Come Back: The Best of Player** / Nov. 17, 1998 / Hammer & Lace/Chronicles ✦✦✦✦✦
Although most casual listeners will likely be familiar only with *Baby Come Back: The Best of Player*'s title cut, fans of that soft-rock chart-topper will likely find much more to their liking here as well; assembling tracks from the group's four LPs from the late 1970s and early 1980s as well as material from the mid-1990s reunion effort, many of the 15 cuts are making their CD debut. —*Jason Ankeny*

The Plimsouls

f. 1978, **db.** 1983
College Rock, Jangle Pop, Power Pop, New Wave
At a time when rock music was shifting gears, the Plimsouls threw British Invasion into the new wave mix and permanently altered the genre. Fun was the operative word, and bar bands everywhere joined the fray. But the Plimsouls were exceptional because they boasted the talents of singer/songwriter Peter Case. After one EP, *Zero Hour* in 1980, and an album in 1981 that contained some stellar power-pop in songs like "Zero Hour" and "Hush, Hush," it looked like the band were a new wave one-off until a single from the soundtrack to *Valley Girl*, "A Million Miles Away," lifted them from new wave obscurity and cemented their reputation. The song remains a timeless classic. An album for Geffen, *Everywhere At Once*, followed in 1983 with a re-recorded version of the song, but ultimately, the liaison with the label was not a lasting one; the Plimsouls broke up shortly after its release. Case went on to record folk music for the label and remains a potent solo artist; in 1995-96, the band took a stab at re-forming, releasing the new studio LP *Kool Trash* in 1998. —*Denise Sullivan*

● **The Plimsouls . . . Plus** / 1981 / Rhino ✦✦✦✦
The band's official debut boasts some of their greatest work, most of it culled from the *Zero Hour* EP, which is also included here: "Hush, Hush," "Zero Hour" and "How Long Will It Take?" stand as quintessential new wave gems. Singer Peter Case emerged as one of rock's great voices and songwriters, and the band speeds along in characteristic British Invasion/roots-rock fashion. —*Denise Sullivan*

Everywhere at Once / 1983 / Geffen ✦✦✦✦
After their initial two Planet Records albums, the Plimsouls took the major label bait and signed on with Geffen Records. This, their first Geffen album, has mixed results. While the change to a major label did have a profound impact on the band, it wasn't always for the best. While Jeff Eyrlic's somewhat heavy-handed production did take a little air out of their performance, the end result is far less clinical than other major label mainstream rock records of the day. *Everywhere at Once* does contain the Plimsouls' greatest recorded achievement, "A Million Miles Away," which packs all of the passion and punch of some of John Lennon's finest recordings with a wonderful power-driven Byrds-like arrangement. Other standouts on this record include "Play the Breaks," which, while not quite as awesome as in live performance (they were possibly the finest live band in Los Angeles in this period), still shines. —*Matthew Greenwald*

One Night in America / 1988 / Fan Club ✦✦

Plush

Indie Pop, Chamber Pop
Vocalist, pianist, and guitarist Liam Hayes (known for his work with Will Oldham's Palace) has been songwriting for his group, Plush, since the dawn of the '90s, but didn't record with the band until 1994 when the single "Three Quarters Blind Eyes"/"Found a Little Baby" came out on Chicago's Drag City label. This first effort for the seldom-gigging band garnered some surprisingly big attention from the music press; notably, the B-side was named Single of the Week by one British magazine and received critical praise from several others. It was another three years, however, before the band created a follow-up. 1997's "No Education" came out on Flydaddy, and it was a much shorter wait between releases this time, with their full-length debut coming out the following year. 1998's *More You Becomes You* actually finds Hayes at the piano singing sparse, vulnerable, and romantic songs along the heartfelt lines of Carole King and Burt Bacharach ballads. Following the album's release, the band continued together with Hayes on guitar and toured with the Japanese band Ghost and with Yo La Tengo. One can also catch Hayes performing in the background of a bar scene in the film *High Fidelity* (2000), a movie about an obsessive music fan living in Chicago. —*Joslyn Layne*

More You Becomes You / Sep. 8, 1998 / Drag City ✦✦✦✦
While it's hip for contemporary pop acts to toss out Burt Bacharach's name as an influence, few even remotely approximate the master's melodic savvy, emotional resonance and simple elegance; Plush's Liam Hayes comes much closer to the mark, with his debut *More You Becomes You*—an intimate, often gorgeous collection of piano ballads—recalling the handful of solo records Bacharach cut during the late 1960s. Gentle yet disarming, the record's only hint of irony is in its title—Hayes smartly favors a less-is-more approach, stripping his music of virtually everything but piano and vocals; both are more than adequate to convey the somber beauty which lends the album its seductive powers. —*Jason Ankeny*

P.M. Dawn

f. 1988
Pop-Rap, Alternative Rap, Urban
Comprised of brothers Prince Be (Attrell Cordes) and DJ Minute Mix (Jarrett Cordes), the early-'90s group P.M. Dawn straddled the gap between hip-hop and smooth '70s-style

soul, creating an innovative urban R&B that owed as much to pop as it did to rhythm and blues. The brothers recorded their debut single, "Ode to a Forgetful Mind," in 1988, but P.M. Dawn didn't release a full-length album until 1991. The record, *Of the Heart, Of the Soul, Of the Cross: The Utopian Experience*, was an immediate hit, thanks to the single "Set Adrift on Memory Bliss," which sampled Spandau Ballet's new wave hit "True." Both the album and the single received glowing reviews, as did the 1993 follow-up *The Bliss Album?*, which featured the hit singles "I'd Die Without You" and "Looking Through Patient Eyes." In 1995, P.M. Dawn returned with *Jesus Wept*, which received strong reviews but weak sales. *Dearest Christian, I'm So Very Sorry for Bringing You Here. Love, Dad* followed in 1998; by this time, the group had virtually dropped out of sight as a commercial force, even though most corners continued to praise the artistic quality of their work. A greatest-hits compilation, *The Best of P.M. Dawn*, appeared in the summer of 2000. *—Stephen Thomas Erlewine*

★ **Of the Heart, Of the Soul and Of the Cross: The Utopian Experience** / Aug. 6, 1991 / V2 ✦✦✦✦✦
In the wake of De La Soul, rap group P.M. Dawn's first album samples jazz, whitebread pop soul, adds a dash of Prince's mysticism, embraces melody, and turns inward for surreal (and admittedly often sophomoric) psychedelic lyrics. P.M. Dawn may care about matters of the soul, but on their first album they don't ignore the booty: these are carefully assembled songs, layered with many a chorused vocal or a harpsichord, but all backed up with a solid beat. "A Watcher's Point of View (Dont'cha Think)" stands out here: a bumping sample with scratchy guitars, shimmering acoustic strings, and interweaving lyrics and a chorus. But it was "Set Adrift on Memory Bliss," with its sample from Spandau Ballet's "True," that made it into the charts (it then became the blueprint for following singles, for better or worse). Other successful tracks: "Reality Used to Be a Friend of Mine," "In the Presence of Mirrors," and "On a Clear Day." There's a few missteps, especially on "Shake," a pointless house-like workout. But it's a delicate balance between doe-eyed metaphysics and the dance floor that the album treads, and it's all the better for it. *—Ted Mills*

The Bliss Album . . . ? / Mar. 23, 1993 / V2 ✦✦✦✦✦
After the breakout pop success of their debut album, P.M. Dawn played up the lush, soothing urban-soul qualities of their sound on the follow-up, *The Bliss Album . . . ?* For all of hardcore rap's hysteria over the duo's gentle demeanor and pop influences, *Of the Heart, of the Soul, and of the Cross* had been a predominantly rap-oriented album. That changes on *The Bliss Album . . . ?*, which downplays Prince Be's rapping (only on about a third of the tracks) in favor of dreamy melodies throughout the songs, not just on the choruses. It's a logical move, since P.M. Dawn's most unique moments were often also their most reflective, and they had an obvious knack for crafting original hooks. *The Bliss Album . . . ?*'s approach also provides more opportunities for the ethereal, layered vocal overdubs that had become one of the duo's signatures. While the results don't quite re-envision hip-hop the way the debut did, they're still tremendously inventive, playing to P.M. Dawn's strengths. The musical landscapes are even more lushly arranged, and the pop numbers positively shimmer thanks to the duo's increasing sense of craft. A couple of the more aggressive rap tracks break up the mood a little, as with "Plastic," a sly rebuttal of the charges leveled by the group's macho detractors. It seems unnecessary, though, since P.M. Dawn's cosmic mysticism and vastly different influences clearly aren't competing on the same turf. Luckily, *The Bliss Album . . . ?* refuses to acknowledge any artificially imposed purist boundaries, continuing to chart new sonic territory and expanding the possibilities in P.M. Dawn's music. *—Steve Huey*

Jesus Wept / Oct. 3, 1995 / V2 ✦✦✦✦
With their third album, *Jesus Wept*, P.M. Dawn doesn't necessarily make a great leap forward. Instead, they make some great refinements. Prince Be's lyrics are just as trippy and cryptic as ever, but they appear more focused, offering a poetic, spiritual worldview that is supported by the lovely, layered music. Using artists like Prince, Stevie Wonder, Marvin Gaye, and the Beatles as starting points, Prince Be creates a unique world assembled equally from soul, pop, hip-hop, and psychedelia. As individual pieces, the songs might not always make much sense, but taken as a whole, they create a singular world that is rich in lush melodies and sumptuous arrangements. Occasionally, P.M. Dawn's ambition gets the best of them and the results sound self-indulgent, not transcendent. However, those moments are few and far between on *Jesus Wept*, the group's best album. *—Stephen Thomas Erlewine*

Vibrations of Love & Anger & The Ponderance of Life & Existence / 1996 / Island ✦✦✦

The Best of P.M. Dawn / Jun. 20, 2000 / V2 ✦✦✦✦✦
Compiled from P.M. Dawn's four albums and the *Senseless* soundtrack *The Best of P.M. Dawn* not only plays like an audio time capsule of slick, tuneful, '90s urban pop, it's a remarkably coherent listening experience. The New Jersey duo's sweet combination of classic silky soul, trip-hop, psychedelia, and pop was one of the most groundbreaking sounds of the decade and influenced countless bands tremendously. All the usual suspects are present and accounted for, beginning with the band's first number one single "Set Adrift on Memory Bliss," an amazingly mature debut tune, and moves forward with two tracks from 1998's relatively obscure *I'm So Very Sorry for Bringing You Here, Love Dad.* A remix of "A Watcher's Point of View" and the rare 7" versions of "Reality Used to Be a Friend of Mine" as well as "The Ways of the Wind" are also here. The latter track's single and album versions are included; though they're significantly different, it's a bit redundant. The edgy hip-hop of "A Watcher's . . . ," "Reality . . . ," and "Gotta' Be . . . Movin' on Up," a track from the *Senseless* soundtrack, break up P.M. Dawn's otherwise lush, glossy sound on this hour-long, 14-track disc. Any band who samples Deep Purple, George Michael, and Joni Mitchell has an astonishingly diverse set of influences, but what made P.M. Dawn special is how they incorporated them into music that was uniquely their own. Despite non-existent liner notes and a few omissions, what is here flows smoothly, especially considering the songs were recorded from 1991 to 1999. Like most timeless music, *The Best of P.M. Dawn*'s songs remain fresh, innovative, and enduring. *—Hal Horowitz*

Poco

f. 1968, Los Angeles, CA, **db.** 1984
Pop/Rock, Soft Rock, Country-Rock
Founded by Jim Messina and Richie Furay during the dying days of Buffalo Springfield, with Randy Meisner (who dropped out shortly before the recording of their first album), Rusty Young, and George Grantham, Poco built a solid reputation in Los Angeles as an innovative country-rock ensemble. Their first album, *Pickin' Up the Pieces*, was one of the strongest debut records of its era, a blend of country and western influences, Beatlesque harmonies, and mainstream rock, all within one cover. They began developing a major national reputation with the release of their second album, *Poco*, at the same time that the group's membership entered what proved to be a virtually constant state of flux. By the mid-'70s, the band had become an established fixture in the middle reaches of the national charts but Messina and Furay were long gone. The band continued recording well into the late '70s on MCA after leaving Epic, and their following was strong enough to justify a posthumous live album from Epic at the same time. The original quintet, which never did get to record, finally went into the studio under the auspices of RCA in the late '80s. *—Bruce Eder*

Pickin' Up the Pieces / 1969 / Epic/Legacy ✦✦✦✦✦
The group went into the studio with a sudden loss of one member (Randy Meisner), an engineer who didn't quite get what they were trying for, and a lot of pressure for a first album—and came up with this startlingly great record, as accomplished as any of the Buffalo Springfield, and also reminiscent of the Beatles and the Byrds. *Pickin' Up the Pieces* is all the more amazing when one considers that Messina and Grantham were both covering for the departed Meisner in hastily learned capacities on bass and vocals, respectively. The title track is practically an anthem for the virtues of country-rock, with the kind of sweet harmonizing and tight interplay between the guitars that the Byrds, the Burritos, et al. had to work a while to achieve. The mix of good-time songs ("Consequently So Long," "Calico Lady"), fast-paced instrumentals ("Grand Junction") and overall good feelings makes this a great introduction to the band, as well as a landmark in country-rock only slightly less important (and more enjoyable than) *Sweetheart of the Rodeo.* *—Bruce Eder*

Poco / May 6, 1970 / Epic ✦✦✦✦
The first two-thirds of Poco's second album is 25 minutes of some of their best music. These songs represent the group's blend of country and rock at its finest and brightest, with the happy harmonies of "Hurry Up" and "Keep on Believin'" totally irresistible. Jim Messina's "You Better Think Twice" is a perfectly constructed and arranged song, one that should have been a huge hit but mysteriously never found its place in the Top 40 pantheon. Listening to this recording, though, it's easy to see why unimaginative radio programmers and much of the record buying public couldn't find a niche for Poco. The knock was "too country for rock, too rock for country," but in fact, they were just ahead of their time, a tough spot to be in the world of popular entertainment.

What about the last 15 minutes of this disc? It's a lengthy instrumental called "El Tonto de Nadie, Regressa." A cynic would say it's filler, but given the trend at the time toward side-long cuts, it's probably simply Poco's attempt at hipness. In retrospect, it can be seen as the forerunner to Jim Messina's lengthy jams with Loggins & Messina a few years later; the sound is remarkably similar. While overshadowed by *Pickin' Up the Pieces*, which preceded it, and *Deliverin'*, which followed, *Poco* is well worth owning by anyone interested in the early days of this particular band, and of country-rock in general. The trademark sweet, high harmonies belying the heartbreak expressed in Richie Furay's lyrics, Messina's distinctive lead guitar, and Rusty Young's amazing ability to get an organ sound out of his pedal-steel guitar are all here in full blossom. *—Jim Newsom*

From the Inside / 1971 / Epic ✦✦

Deliverin' / Jan. 13, 1971 / Epic ✦✦✦✦✦
Poco had originally made their name as a live act, and they'd always been at their best and most easygoing onstage. The result is this live album of all new material, featuring Jim Messina's swan song with the band and some of the tightest playing and best singing in their recorded history. Jewels include "C'mon," "Hear That Music," "Kind Woman," and "You'd Better Think Twice." About as perfect an album as they ever made and, not coincidentally, by far the biggest seller the early group ever had. *—Bruce Eder*

A Good Feelin' to Know / Oct. 25, 1972 / Epic ✦✦✦
Good Feelin' to Know was Poco's big attempt to broaden their audience—the title track, one of their most popular concert numbers, was the group's push for a hit single, which didn't work. The album as a whole, however, features a louder, harder-rocking sound a step or two removed from the country-rock they'd been known for, even on numbers like "Ride the Country," which has a more brittle sound than the group would have achieved on their earlier records. The guitars are all turned up really loud, and the harmonies are less sweet, overall making for a very heavy sound, surprisingly similar to the Buffalo Springfield (one of their old numbers, "Go and Say Goodbye," is even included, in an arguably better version), making this a curious throwback/advance. This album's relative failure made Furay begin to lose faith in his own group's prospects. *—Bruce Eder*

Crazy Eyes / 1973 / Epic/Legacy ✦✦✦✦✦
The third biggest-selling album in the group's history, *Crazy Eyes* is also the group's most lively and bracing work, and contains some of their most soulful music. In short, it is the

fruition of everything they'd been working toward for four years. Curiously, it is also one of a handful of examples of their use of outside help, including Chris Hillman on mandolin. The resulting sound is richer than anything found on any other Poco album, and the only tragedy is that the band reportedly cut enough tracks for two whole albums—one longs to hear the material that remained in the can. As it is, there's not a weak song, or even a wasted note anywhere on this album, and most bands would kill for a closing track as perfect as "Let's Dance Tonight." The sound is excellent on this CD reissue, and only some historical notes would have improved it. *—Bruce Eder*

Seven / 1974 / Epic/Legacy ♦♦♦
With strong, soaring harmonies, a healthy balance between acoustic country-rock and heavy rock & roll, and some fairly strong songs, *Seven* is a major surprise, given that this is the group's first post-Richie Furay album. George Grantham's drumming is a special highlight (check out his solo on "Drivin' Wheel"), but all of the playing is superb, and with one or two additional strong songs, this would be a highly recommended album, and as it is it is quite good. Unfortunately, not everything here is as strong as "Drivin' Wheel" or "Rocky Mountain Breakdown." *—Bruce Eder*

Cantamos / Dec. 1974 / Epic ♦♦♦

Head over Heels / Jul. 1975 / MCA ♦♦♦♦
Keeping the songs short and to the point, Poco lets loose with a fine batch of material. This time out, they even cover the Becker-Fagen song "Dallas" with great verve. There's less country, but a lot more pop. *—James Chrispell*

The Very Best of Poco [1975] / Sep. 1975 / Epic ♦♦♦♦♦
Originally a two-LP set, *The Very Best of Poco* was a decent compilation in its time, assembling the group's best-known songs from singles and album cuts in a straightforward order with no particular surprises. It was reissued with upgraded sound in 1999, and for the very casual fan with a budget to consider the latter is adequate, showing their evolution as a band from the first flourish of their birth, as an offshoot of the Buffalo Springfield, with the same sort of vast potential displayed by the latter group (similarly unrealized by constant membership changes) into one of the premiere country-rock outfits of the 1970s. Anyone serious about a deep enjoyment of the group, however, will opt for the more extensive and revelatory *The Forgotten Trail* instead, which contains numerous outtakes and—no pun—forgotten tracks. *—Bruce Eder*

Rose of Cimarron / 1976 / One Way ♦♦♦

Live / Apr. 1976 / One Way ♦♦♦

Indian Summer / 1977 / MCA ♦♦♦

Legend / Nov. 1978 / MCA ♦♦♦

Under the Gun / 1980 / MCA ♦♦

Blue and Gray / 1981 / One Way ♦♦

Cowboys & Englishmen / 1982 / One Way ♦

Ghost Town / 1982 / Atlantic ♦♦♦

Inamorata / 1984 / Atlantic ♦♦

Legacy / Aug. 1989 / RCA ♦♦

Crazy Loving: The Best of Poco 1975-1982 / Oct. 1989 / MCA ♦♦♦♦
In the wake of Poco's success with *Legacy*, MCA Records resurrected their 1982 best of, *Backtracks*, added tracks to fill it out to respectable CD length, threw in some liner notes and reissued it under a new title. It's not Poco's best period, but this is a good selection that will satisfy most casual listeners. *—William Ruhlmann*

The Forgotten Trail (1969-1974) / Oct. 1990 / Epic ♦♦♦♦♦
This excellent two-disc collection captures Poco's finest moments from the days when they were laying down the template for all the country-rock music that was to follow. It's hard to remember now, but when the Eagles first hit the scene, they were thought by many to be a Poco-wannabe band. Listen to this set and you'll hear why. *The Forgotten Trail* culls tracks from Poco's first eight albums, as well as unreleased cuts and singles. From the classic anthem "Pickin' Up the Pieces," which kicks things off, through "You Better Think Twice," "C'mon," "Kind Woman," "From the Inside," "A Good Feelin' to Know," "Crazy Eyes," and on and on... this is wonderful music, ahead of its time in many ways. If Poco had arrived on the scene in the early 1990s, they would have been kings of the country charts. Of course, without Poco, country music wouldn't have taken on the rock trappings that it did in the '80s and '90s. As it was, the band was considered too country for the Top 40 rock format of the time, and too rock & roll for country radio. This set is the place to start for an appreciation of the original Poco, when the group was considered to be Richie Furay's band. All the ingredients are here that made their music so delightful: the trademark high vocal harmonies, Rusty Young's pedal steel guitar wizardry, Furay's patented juxtapositions of sad lyrics against bouncy, harmony-filled tunes, their spirit of optimism and good feelings even in the face of hard luck and bad weather. The 36-page booklet does a fine job of telling the story in print, and the 38 songs speak volumes about the band's place and influence. Thanks to this compilation, Poco's trailblazing days need be forgotten no longer. *—Jim Newsom*

● **Ultimate Collection** / Nov. 17, 1998 / Hip-O ♦♦♦♦♦
There has been no lack of Poco compilations, but this is the first one to span the four record labels the band recorded for between 1969 and 1989. Ten of the group's 13 chart singles are included, among them its biggest hits, "Crazy Love," "Call It Love," and "Heart of the Night." Also included are some of its best songs, such as "Pickin' Up the Pieces" and "A Good Feelin' to Know." The country-rock hybrid Poco achieved during its lengthy, commercially under-rewarded recording career is on display in songs written by Richie Furay, Jim Messina, Paul Cotton, Timothy B. Schmit, and Rusty Young. Anyone looking for the missing link between Buffalo Springfield and the Eagles will find it here. *—William Ruhlmann*

Very Best of Poco [1999] / Aug. 31, 1999 / Epic/Legacy ♦♦♦♦
Legacy's 1999 expansion of the *Very Best of Poco* may not contain any songs from the group's reunion, but they're not missed, since this winds up being a generous, 14-track overview of the band at its peak. Yes, there may be a fan favorite or two missing (they may be satiated by the inclusion of a couple of live tracks), but the key songs from Richey Furay and Jim Messina's country-rock outfit are here, making this an excellent representation of the band's best work. *—Stephen Thomas Erlewine*

The Pogues

f. 1982, Kings Cross, London, England, **db.** 1996
College Rock, Celtic Rock, British Folk, Alternative Pop/Rock
By demonstrating that the spirit of punk could live in traditional Irish folk music, the Pogues were one of the most radical bands of the mid-'80s. Led by Shane MacGowan, whose slurred, incomprehensible voice often disguised the sheer poetry of his songs, the Pogues were undeniably political—not only were many of their songs explicitly in favor of working-class liberalism, but the wild, careening sound of their punk-injected folk was implicitly radical. While the band was clearly radical, they also had a wickedly warped sense of humor, which was abundantly clear on their biggest hit, the fractured Christmas carol "Fairy Tale of New York." The group's first three albums—*Red Roses for Me, Rum Sodomy and the Lash, If I Should Fall From Grace With God*—were widely praised in both Britain and America, and by 1988 they had earned substantial cult followings in both countries. Yet MacGowan's darkly romantic, wasted lifestyle, which was so key to their spirit and success, ultimately proved to be their downfall. By the end of the decade, he had fallen deep into alcoholism and drug addiction, forcing the band to fire him if they wanted to survive. The Pogues carried on without him in the early '90s, playing to a slowly shrinking audience, before finally disbanding in 1996. *—Stephen Thomas Erlewine*

Red Roses for Me / 1984 / WEA International ♦♦♦
What set the Pogues apart from any number of other energetic Irish traditional bands was the sheer physical force of their performances, the punky swagger of their personalities, and Shane MacGowan's considerable gifts as a songwriter. Unfortunately, none of these qualities come through very clearly on their first album, *Red Roses for Me*. While the Pogues are in good form here, the production (by Stan Brennan) is thin and lacks the body or nuance to capture the finer details of the performances, robbing this recording of the fire the group would display on their later albums. And it's clear that Shane MacGowan had not yet fully matured as a songwriter; there are a handful of superb songs here, such as "Transmetropolitan," "Streams of Whiskey," and "Down in the Ground Where the Dead Men Go," but some of the others suggest MacGowan was still learning how to fit all his ideas into his songs. *Red Roses for Me* is good and rowdy fun, but on *Run, Sodomy & the Lash* and *If I Should Fall From Grace With God*, the Pogues would prove they were capable of a lot more than that. *—Mark Deming*

Rum Sodomy & the Lash / 1985 / WEA International ♦♦♦♦♦
"I saw my task... was to capture them in their dilapidated glory before some more professional producer f—ked them up," Elvis Costello wrote of his role behind the controls for the Pogues' second album, *Rum Sodomy & the Lash*. One spin of the album proves that Costello accomplished his mission; this album captures all the sweat, fire, and angry joy that was lost in the thin, disembodied recording of the band's debut, and the Pogues sound stronger and tighter without losing a bit of their edge in the process. *Rum Sodomy & the Lash* also found Shane MacGowan growing steadily as a songwriter; while the debut had its moments, the blazing and bitter roar of the opening track, "The Sick Bed Of Cuchulainn," made it clear MacGowan had fused the intelligent anger of punk and the sly storytelling of Irish folk as no one had before, and the rent boys' serenade of "The Old Main Drag" and the dazzling, drunken character sketch of "A Pair of Brown Eyes" proved there were plenty of directions where he could take his gifts. And like any good folk group, the Pogues also had a great ear for other people's songs. Bassist Cait O'Riordan's haunting performance of "I'm a Man You Don't Meet Every Day" is simply superb (it must have especially impressed Costello, who would later marry her), and while Shane MacGowan may not have written "Dirty Old Town" or "And the Band Played Waltzing Matilda," his wrought, emotionally compelling vocals made them his from then on. *Rum Sodomy & the Lash* falls just a bit short of being the Pogues best album, but was the first one to prove that they were a great band, and not just a great idea for a band. *—Mark Deming*

● **If I Should Fall From Grace With God** / 1987 / Island ♦♦♦♦♦
If *Rum Sodomy & the Lash* captured the Pogues on plastic in all their rough-and-tumble glory, *If I Should Fall From Grace With God* proved they could learn the rudiments of proper record making and still come up with an album that captured all the sharp edges of their musical personality. Producer Steve Lillywhite imposed a more disciplined approach in the studio than Elvis Costello, but he had the good sense not to squeeze the life out of the band in the process; as a result, the Pogues sound tighter and more precise than ever, while still summoning up the glorious howling fury that made *Rum Sodomy & the Lash* so powerful. And Shane MacGowan continued to grow as a songwriter, as his lyrics and melodies captured with brilliant detail his obsession with the finer points of Anglo-Irish culture. "Fairytale of New York," a glorious sweet-and-sour duet with Kristy MacColl, and "The Broad Majestic Shannon" were subtle in a way many of his previous work was not, "Birmingham Six" found him addressing political issues for the first time (and with all the expected venom), and "Fiesta" and "Turkish Song of the Damned" found him adding (respectively) faux-Spanish and Middle Eastern flavors into the Pogues' heady

mix. And if you want to hear the Pogues blaze through some fast ones, "Bottle of Smoke" and the title song find them doing just what they've always done best. Brilliantly mixing passion, street smarts, and musical ambition, *If I Should Fall From Grace With God* is the best album the Pogues would ever make. —*Mark Deming*

Peace and Love / Jul. 1989 / Island ✦✦✦✦
Shane MacGowan's potent appetite for alcohol was evident from the time the Pogues cut their first album, but by the time they got to work on *Peace and Love* in 1989, it was evident that he'd gone far past the point of enjoying a few pints (or many pints) and had sunk deep into drug and alcohol dependence. The Pogues were always far more than just MacGowan's backing band, but with the group's principal songwriter and lead singer frequently unable to rise to the occasion, the recording of *Peace and Love* became a trying experience, with the rest of the band often scrambling to take up the slack for their down-for-the-count frontman. Given the circumstances, the Pogues deliver with greater strength than one might expect on *Peace and Love*; while MacGowan's vocals are often mush-mouthed and his songwriting is markedly beneath his previous standards, Terry Woods contributes two terrific traditional-style numbers ("Young Ned of the Hill" and "Gartloney Rats"), Philip Chevron's "Lorelei" is a superb tale of lost love (he and Daryl Hunt also teamed up for a fine bit of Celtic-calypso fusion on "Blue Heaven"), and Jem Finer brought along a trio of strong originals. Musically, *Peace and Love* found the band stretching their boundaries, adding accents of film noir jazz on "Gridlock," rockabilly on "Cotton Fields," straight-ahead rock on "USA," and power pop on "Lorelei," though the group's highly recognizable Celtic-trad-on-steroids style is never far beneath the surface. *Peace and Love* isn't as good as the two Pogues albums that preceded it (which represent the finest work of their career), but it does make clear that Shane MacGowan was hardly the only talented songwriter in the band—though the fact that the set's most memorable songs were written by others did not bode well for the group's future. —*Mark Deming*

Hell's Ditch / 1990 / Island ✦✦✦
From the beginning, the Clash had been one of the Pogues' primary influences. So it's most appropriate that Joe Strummer produced *Hell's Ditch*. The former Clash guitarist wisely and insightfully avoids smoothing out too many of the date's rough edges, and seems to encourage rawness and go-for-broke passion (which generally serve the band well). This time, elements of Middle Eastern and Latin music are added to the Pogues' intriguing rock/Irish folk mix. It's hard to miss the effect that drugs and alcohol were having on the self-destructive Shane MacGowan, whose vocals are even more garbled than they were on *Peace And Love*. In fact, he sounds like he's in a drunken stupor most of the time. Nonetheless, his songwriting is often superb and brilliant on this risk-taking, if uneven, project. —*Alex Henderson*

Yeah Yeah Yeah Yeah Yeah / Sep. 1990 / Island ✦✦
A relentless, Motown-styled raveup, "Yeah Yeah Yeah Yeah Yeah" was one of The Pogues finest moments and one of their hardest rockers. It was a British hit in 1988, yet it took two years for an EP of the same name to appear. The EP is one of the group's most rock-oriented efforts—it even features a version of The Rolling Stones' "Honky Tonk Women"—but it's not entirely successful, with the noticeable exception of the title track. —*Stephen Thomas Erlewine*

The Essential Pogues / Nov. 19, 1991 / Island ✦✦✦✦✦
Essential Pogues doesn't cover *Red Roses for Me* or *Rum Sodomy and the Lash*, so it isn't a definitive collection. However, it does capture the majority of the highlights from their Island albums and functions as a good introduction to the band. One complaint: the tedious extended remix of "Yeah, Yeah, Yeah, Yeah, Yeah" was included instead of the punchy, energetic original single. —*Stephen Thomas Erlewine*

Waiting for Herb / Oct. 19, 1993 / Chameleon ✦✦

The Rest of the Best / 1994 / WEA ✦✦✦✦

Very Best of the Pogues / Jun. 5, 2001 / Wea International ✦✦✦✦
There's little question that the Pogues were a seminal band, blessed with great musicians, led by Shane MacGowan, a songwriter of major vision and talent. This was apparent on their initial Stiff singles but it truly blazed on their debut, *Rum Sodomy & the Lash*, an album that artfully walked the razor's edge between Irish traditionalism and venomous, working-class punk. Though they became more accomplished in later albums, they never strayed from this template. What did change, however, was the group's consistency, largely because their fortunes were tied too closely to those of MacGowan. He could still turn out some great moments but his unpredictability became a major liability for the group's very sanity and they had to let him go. Ironically, without Shane aboard, the Pogues started to drift and they only lasted through one more album before calling it a day, leaving behind a body of work that is very well summarized on the European-only compilation, *The Very Best of the Pogues*. This concentrates heavily on the group's first three albums, where MacGowan's writing was its sharpest and the band sounded best, but it also picks up highlights from erratic albums like *Peace and Love* and *Hell's Ditch*. It does have a tendency to play toward their traditional folk inclinations, which means it overlooks such wonderful moments as their stomping Motown salute "Yeah Yeah Yeah Yeah Yeah," one of the very best singles of the late '80s/early '90s. Even so, this collection is as good a single-disc retrospective as it could be and it comes very close to capturing the Pogues at their very best.—*Stephen Thomas Erlewine*

Poi Dog Pondering

f. 1986
Alternative Pop/Rock
The eclectic worldbeat/folk-rock outfit Poi Dog Pondering was formed in Waikiki by vo-

calist/guitarist Frank Orrall, violinist/vocalist Susan Voelz, and multi-instrumentalist Dave "Max" Crawford, the only constants in the group's history; sometimes swelling to upwards of ten members, the band has seen numerous personnel shifts. Named in part for a Hawaiian expression meaning "mutt," Poi Dog Pondering relocated to Austin, Texas and picked up a following through extensive touring; they released two EPs, 1988's *Poi Dog Pondering* and 1989's *Circle Around the Sun*, which attracted the attention of Columbia Records with their varied instrumentation, easygoing humor, and offbeat fusions of world musics and folk-rock. Columbia combined the two EPs for the group's 1989 self-titled major-label debut, which along with its slightly slicker follow-up, 1989's *Wishing Like a Mountain and Thinking Like the Sea*, earned Poi Dog Pondering critical acclaim and a devoted cult following.

However, all was not well between Poi Dog Pondering and its label; Columbia rejected much of the band's demo material over the next two years, and only a couple of EPs were released. *Volo Volo* was finally released in 1991, but shortly thereafter, the band was dropped from Columbia's roster. Bandleader Orrall responded by putting the group on hiatus, moving its home base to Chicago and substantially revamping the lineup; during the hiatus, Orrall put together his Palm Fabric Orchestra, while Voelz recorded solo material. When the group returned in 1995 with *Pomegranate*, their sound had gravitated slightly more towards dance music, a switch confirmed on their 1996 EP *Electrique Plummagram*. In 1997, Poi Dog Pondering debuted its own Plate.tec.tonic label with the live set *Liquid White Light*. In 1999, they issued *Natural Thing* and *Soul Sonic Orchestra* followed a year later. —*Steve Huey*

● **Poi Dog Pondering** / 1989 / Columbia ✦✦✦✦✦
Not so precious as some of their other work. This album, their major-label debut, is certainly whimsical, but it contains enough assertiveness to make their folk-rock worldbeat engaging. —*John Dougan*

Wishing Like a Mountain & Thinking Like the Sea / Dec. 1989 / Columbia ✦✦✦✦✦

Fruitless / 1990 / Columbia ✦✦✦

Jack Ass Ginger / 1991 / Columbia ✦✦✦

Volo Volo / Jun. 1991 / Columbia ✦✦✦
Poi Dog Pondering was always a band better appreciated in a live context, its albums never quite capturing the excitement of the group's rock/folk/pop/world music stew. The reason is simple: like other fun jam bands such as Phish, Aquarium Rescue Unit and the like, Poi Dog never really mastered the art of writing concise, radio-friendly songs, preferring to let their tight grooves and polyrhythmic percussion beds carry the music. Unfortunately, in the case of what is, at its core, a rock band, this approach often makes for somewhat lackluster records, and *Volo Volo* is no exception. Interestingly, Poi Dog Pondering here seems to be attempting a move into a more pop-oriented direction, sounding at times like a bizarre meeting between Santana, the Meters, Wham!, and Simple Minds. While the group deserves an "A" for effort, without the glue of catchy songwriting to hold the disparate elements together, the mix never really works that well. In fact, the best "songs" on the album are not really songs at all, but new-agey instrumental pieces ("endtrance" and "Entrance"). That said, there is certainly enough variety throughout to keep one's attention, from the New Orleans-style soul of "Be the One" to the stadium rock guitar wall of "Blood and Thunder." In the end though, *Volo Volo* is sadly a case of too much talent, not enough focus. —*Pemberton Roach*

Pomegranate / Oct. 17, 1995 / Bar/None ✦✦✦✦
Eclectic and expansive eleven-piece ensemble Poi Dog Pondering proves adept at mastering diverse musical styles and controlling the commercial end of their own distribution and production. I find them at their most sublime and inimitable in the pop ballad. To even the first-time listener, such Poi Dog warhorses as "Pomegranate," "Catacombs," and "Complicated" offer that instant familiarity of a successfully crafted song. Any pop music creator would be proud to have one of these as a "one-hit." But, such a Holy Grail as chart success eludes Poi Dog Pondering. I feel this is high crime, as any track on *Pomegranate* can move me to tears or joy on a close listen. —*Thomas Schulte*

Electrique Plummagram / 1996 / Bar/None ✦✦✦

Liquid White Light / May 15, 1997 / Platetectonic ✦✦✦
This double-CD live set finds Poi Dog incarnating what should be pop music anthems into a living beauty of delicacy ("Angelika Suspended"), joyous dance ("Everybody's Trying") and more. Each selection is a mood defined. Disc two shows the current state of the band documented in the studio on *Electrique Plummagram*, seduced making a bedfellow of electronica. They do it very well, and include plenty of live instrumentation. The songwriting of Frank Orrall comes through strong as synthesized possibilities are kept as another balanced spice in the Poi Dog stew. You may detect a little hesitation on my part as regards their new direction. Well, that certainly is there, but they have not let me down, either. —*Thomas Schulte*

Natural Thing / Apr. 20, 1999 / Tommy Boy ✦✦✦

Soul Sonic Orchestra / Aug. 8, 2000 / Platetectonic ✦✦✦✦
Poi Dog Pondering is a phenomenal group, really; phenomenal for their self-supported run of large ensemble albums full of pop treasures. The title of this album, *Soul Sonic Orchestra*, is a synonym for the group itself. Poi Dog Pondering is a sophisticated college rock orchestra with gifted musicians and a talented songwriter in frontman Frank Orrall, who delivers pop music with true soul. These live tracks present excellent live arrangements of such classic songs as "That's the Way Love Is," "Natural Thing," and more. —*Tom Schulte*

The Pointer Sisters

f. 1971, East Oakland, CA

Adult Contemporary, Urban, Dance-Pop, Soul

Versatile Ruth, Anita, June, and Bonnie Pointer regularly scored pop and soul hits throughout the '70s and '80s in a chameleonic variety of styles. Formed in Oakland, with their first successes for Blue Thumb Records blending funky rhythms with a novel nostalgic attitude (beginning with their 1973 revival of Allen Toussaint's "Yes We Can Can"), leading up to their first #1 R&B item in 1975, "How Long (Betcha' Got a Chick on the Side)."

Bonnie signed with Motown in 1978 and kicked off her own string of R&B hits with "Free Me from My Freedom/Tie Me to a Tree (Handcuff Me)." (June and Anita also tried the solo route during the '80s, without leaving the fold.)

By 1979, when the remaining trio covered Bruce Springsteen's "Fire," The Pointers were headed in a more contemporary direction on the Planet label, and "He's So Shy" (1980), "Slow Hand" (1981), "Automatic," and the anthemic "Jump (For My Love)" (the last two both 1984) were savvy ditties that blazed trails across the R&B and pop charts. However, the group's success declined during the late '80s, as their records began to sound more formulaic. The Pointer Sisters lost their major-label record contract in the early '90s, and the group began performing on oldies circuits occasionally. In 1995, the trio made a tenative return to the spotlight when they joined a revival performance of the Fats Waller musical *Ain't Misbehavin'*, yet the accompanying soundtrack album failed to gain much attention. *—Bill Dahl*

• **Yes We Can: The Best of the Blue Thumb Recordings** / Jul. 15, 1997 / Hip-O ✦✦✦✦✦

Next to LaBelle, the Pointer Sisters were the most unorthodox and adventurous R&B "girl group" of the mid-1970s R&B scene. (Of course, they'd still be having hits long after LaBelle's 1977 breakup). Beautifully illustrating the siblings' eclectic nature, this CD focuses on their early material for Blue Thumb Records from 1973-77. Sweaty, passionate hits like "Yes We Can Can," "How Long (Betcha Got a Chick on the Side)," "Going Down Slowly" and "You Gotta Believe" show that they were a first-class soul group, but that's not all they were. The collection also reminds us that they could be equally exciting when it came to blues (Willie Dixon's "Wang Dang Doodle"), jazz ("Cloudburst," "Black Coffee" and Dizzy Gillespie's "Salt Peanuts") and even country ("Fairytale"). One of the most fun tracks is the delightfully silly "Steam Heat," which finds them going on about how rough the winters were in Oakland, CA. One thing the Sisters never lost was their sense of fun, which continued to serve them well on their slicker and much more pop-minded (though equally engaging) hits of the 1980s. But never were they more risk-taking than when they recorded for Blue Thumb. Pop fans who know the Sisters primarily for "Jump" or "Neutron Dance" but might be unaware of their Blue Thumb output owe it to themselves to hear this magnificent collection. *—Alex Henderson*

• **Best of the Pointer Sisters** / Feb. 22, 2000 / RCA ✦✦✦✦✦

RCA's *The Best of the Pointer Sisters* picks up where Hip-O's *Yes We Can: The Best of the Blue Thumb Recordings* leaves off, presenting 18 of the trio's hits for Planet and RCA Records. The collection begins with 1979's "Fire" and ends with "Goldmine," which peaked on the charts in 1987. In between those two songs are such massive hits as "He's So Shy," "Slow Hand," "Automatic," "Jump (For My Love)," "I'm So Excited," and "Neutron Dance." As these hits prove, the Pointer Sisters got a lot smoother once they left Blue Thumb, choosing to record seductive quiet-storm ballads and sprightly dance-pop. Fans of the Blue Thumb years may find this a little distasteful, but as this fine collection illustrates, the Pointer Sisters excelled in this area, just as they did with the funkier material for Blue Thumb. Anyone who is a fan of the group's late-'70s and early-'80s hits will not be disappointed by this disc, since it offers a definitive portrait of the Pointer Sisters at Planet and RCA. *—Stephen Thomas Erlewine*

Poison

f. 1983, Harrisburg, PA, **db.** 1993

Pop-Metal, Hair Metal

In a decade fueled by party anthems and power ballads, Poison found massive popularity in the late 1980s, with only such related bands as Bon Jovi and Def Leppard outselling them. While the group had a long string of hits, they soon became just as renowned for their stage show, and continued to be a major attraction over the course of their first three albums. Poison was signed to Enigma Records in 1986, where they released their first album, *Look What the Cat Dragged In.* The record, spawning the Top Ten hits "I Want Action," "Talk Dirty to Me" and "I Won't Forget You," was a surprise success, selling two million copies within a year following its release. While the band was already quite popular by the end of 1987, 1988's *Open Up and Say... Ahhh!* was their commercial breakthrough, due to the massive hits "Fallen Angel," "Nothin' But a Good Time" and "Every Rose Has Its Thorn." Poison returned to the studio to record *Flesh and Blood* in 1990. The album, which included the upbeat "Unskinny Bop" and the sentimental "Something to Believe In," was another major success. 1993's *Native Tongue* album, despite some strong reviews and a hit single, "Stand," was a commercial disappointment. *—Barry Weber*

Look What the Cat Dragged In / 1986 / EMI-Capitol Special Markets ✦✦✦

Poison's debut album took its cues from the big, anthemic pop hooks of Def Leppard and the rebellious street-tough posturing of Motley Crüe, as well as a raunchy, adolescent obsession with sex. But Poison really carved out its niche as the ultimate glam-metal band, using tight-assed boogie and over-the-top visual extravagance—costumes, makeup, teased hair, etc.—to an even greater extent than most of their contemporaries. It was derivative and formulaic, to be sure, but Poison wholeheartedly embraced that formula from the beginning with a conviction often missing in their peers, and it's that ridiculous, good-time excess that keeps *Look What the Cat Dragged In*'s catchiest songs, especially the party anthems "Talk Dirty to Me" and "I Want Action," just as much fun today, if not moreso. *—Steve Huey*

Open Up & Say... Ahh! / 1988 / Capitol ✦✦✦✦

Poison's best album still has a bit of filler that fails to deliver the big hooks and catchy riffs of their best material; when that happens, Bret Michaels' affected "rawk & rowl" singing accent begins to grate. But thankfully, that doesn't happen very often on *Open Up and Say... Ahh!*, which solidified the group's status as hair-metal's top party band. The ballad "Every Rose Has Its Thorn," Poison's only number one hit, and the Top Ten "Nothin' But a Good Time" became their most widely recognized signature songs; a cover of Loggins & Messina's "Your Mama Don't Dance" also hit the Top Ten, and the sometimes-overlooked "Fallen Angel," one of their best songs, got plenty of MTV airplay. But the agreeable raunch of album tracks like "Love on the Rocks," "Good Love," and "Look But You Can't Touch" helps make *Open Up and Say... Ahh!* Poison's best overall album. *—Steve Huey*

Flesh and Blood / Jun. 21, 1990 / Capitol ✦✦✦✦

Apparently disappointed with critical hatred of their previous work, Poison made a bid to be taken seriously after the massive success of *Open Up and Say... Ahh!* Even the title of *Flesh and Blood* indicates a desire for more substance and reality in their music, as do darker songs like "Valley of Lost Souls," "(Flesh and Blood) Sacrifice," "Life Loves a Tragedy," and a more reflective power ballad, "Life Goes On." There's still the adolescent sleaze of the Top Five hit "Unskinny Bop," but for the most part, Poison shies away from party anthems in favor of Bret Michaels' toughness-in-the-face-of-tribulation philosophizing. Sometimes it works surprisingly well, aided by the band's most consistent songwriting and a wider musical range that occasionally veers into swampy blues-rock. At other times, though, Michaels comes off as well-intentioned but too self-consciously proud of his own ambition to recognize when he oversteps his bounds, as on parts of the hit ballad "Something to Believe In." Compared to their earlier output, *Flesh and Blood* is by no means a bad album (especially with the presence of one of their best songs, "Ride the Wind," an ode to motorcycles and their surrounding lifestyle). It's just not what Poison does *best*. *—Steve Huey*

Swallow This Live / Nov. 12, 1991 / Capitol ✦✦✦

Native Tongue / Feb. 8, 1993 / Capitol ✦✦

• **Poison's Greatest Hits: 1986-1996** / Nov. 26, 1996 / Capitol ✦✦✦✦

Greatest Hits 1986-96 is as definitive as a Poison compilation could hope to be. Featuring a full 18 tracks, including all of their Top 50 hits ("Talk Dirty to Me," "I Want Action," "Nothin' But a Good Time," "Fallen Angel," "Every Rose Has Its Thorn," "Your Mama Don't Dance," "Unskinny Bop," "Something to Belive In," "Stand," among others) plus two unreleased cuts ("Sexual Thing," "Lay Your Body Down"), the album boasts every worthwhile song the group ever recorded, augmented by Brett Michaels' track-by-track commentary. Though the album isn't sequenced in chronological order, it plays like an excellent mix tape, which actually makes the album more listenable. Even on a compilation, Poison wears a little thin—there are still dull moments among these 18 songs, mainly in the form of lesser-known album tracks and singles—but still, *Greatest Hits 1986-96* is the most enteraining album the band ever released. *—Stephen Thomas Erlewine*

Crack a Smile... And More / Mar. 14, 2000 / Capitol ✦✦✦

Power to the People / Jun. 13, 2000 / Cyanide Music Inc. ✦✦

The Police

f. 1977, London, England, **db.** 1985

Album Rock, Pop/Rock, New Wave

Nominally, the Police were punk rock, but that's only in the loosest sense of the term. The trio's nervous, reggae-injected pop-rock was punky, but it wasn't necessarily punk. All three members were considerably more technically proficient than the average punk or New Wave band. Andy Summers had a precise guitar attack that created dense, interlocking waves of sounds and effects. Stewart Copeland could play polyrhythms effortlessly. And Sting, with his high, keening voice, was capable of constructing infectiously catchy pop songs. While they weren't punk, the Police certainly demonstrated that the punk spirit could have a future in pop music. As their career progressed, the Police grew considerably more adventurous, experimenting with jazz and various world musics. All the while, the band's tight delivery and mastery of the pop single kept their audience increasing and by 1983, they were the most popular rock & roll band in the world. Though they were at the height of their fame, internal tensions caused the band to splinter apart in 1984, with Sting picking up the majority of the band's audience to become an international superstar. *—Stephen Thomas Erlewine*

Outlandos d'Amour / Nov. 1978 / A&M ✦✦✦✦✦

While their subsequent chart-topping albums would contain far more ambitious songwriting and musicianship, the Police's 1978 debut, *Outlandos D'Amour* (translation: *Outlaws of Love*) is by far their most direct and straightforward release. Although Sting, Andy Summers, and Stewart Copeland were all superb instrumentalists with jazz backgrounds, it was much easier to get a record contract in late-'70s England if you were a punk/new wave artist, so the band decided to mask their instrumental prowess with a set of strong, adrenaline-charged rock, albeit with a reggae tinge. Some of it may have been simplistic ("Be My Girl-Sally," "Born in the '50s"), but Sting was already an ace songwriter, as evidenced by all-time classics like the good-girl-gone-bad tale of "Roxanne," and a pair of brokenhearted reggae-rock ditties, "Can't Stand Losing You" and "So Lonely." But like all other Police albums, the lesser-known album cuts are often highlights themselves—the frenzied rockers "Next to You," "Peanuts" and "Truth Hits Everybody," as well as more exotic fare like the groovy album closer "Masoko Tanga" and the lonesome "Hole in My Life." *Outlandos D'Amour* is unquestionably one of the finest debuts to come out of the '70s punk/new wave movement. —*Greg Prato*

Reggatta de Blanc / Oct. 1979 / A&M ✦✦✦
By 1979's *Reggatta De Blanc* (translation: *White Reggae*), non-stop touring had sharpened the Police's original blend of reggae-rock to perfection, resulting in breakthrough success. Containing a pair of massive hit singles—the inspirational anthem "Message in a Bottle" and the spacious "Walking on the Moon"—the album also signaled a change in the band's sound. Whereas their debut got its point across with raw, energetic performances, *Reggatta De Blanc* was much more polished production-wise, and fully developed from a songwriting standpoint. While vigorous rockers did crop up from time to time ("It's Alright for You," "Deathwish," "No Time This Time," and the Grammy-winning instrumental title track), the material was overall much more sedate than the debut—"Bring On the Night," "The Bed's Too Big Without You," and "Does Everyone Stare." Also included was Stewart Copeland's one and only lead vocal appearance on a Police album, the witty "On Any Other Day," as well as one of the band's most eerie tracks, "Contact." With *Reggatta De Blanc*, many picked Sting and Co. to be the superstar band of the '80s, and the Police would prove them correct on their next release. —*Greg Prato*

☆ **Zenyatta Mondatta** / Oct. 1980 / A&M ✦✦✦✦✦
The stage was set for the Police to become one of the '80s' biggest acts, and the band delivered with their 1980 classic *Zenyatta Mondatta*. The album proved to be the trio's second straight number one album in the U.K., while peaking at number three in the U.S. Arguably the best Police album (perhaps second only to *Synchronicity*), *Zenyatta* contains perhaps the quintessential new wave anthem, the haunting "Don't Stand So Close to Me," the story of an older teacher lusting after one of his students. While other tracks follow in the same spooky path (their second Grammy-winning instrumental "Behind My Camel," "Shadows in the Rain"), most of the material is upbeat, such as the carefree U.S./U.K. Top Ten "De Do Do Do, De Da Da Da," "Canary in a Coalmine," and "Man in a Suitcase." Sting includes his first set of politically charged lyrics in "Driven to Tears," "When the World Is Running Down, You Make the Best of What's Still Around," and "Bombs Away," which all observe the declining state of the world. While Sting would later criticize the album as not all it could have been (the band was rushed to complete the album in order to begin another tour), *Zenyatta Mondatta* remains one of the finest rock albums of all time. —*Greg Prato*

Ghost in the Machine / Oct. 1981 / A&M ✦✦✦
For their fourth album, 1981's *Ghost in the Machine*, the Police had streamlined their sound to focus more on their pop side, and less on their trademark reggae-rock. Their jazz influence had become more prominent, as evidenced by the appearance of saxophones on several tracks. The production has more of a contemporary '80s sound to it (courtesy of Hugh Padgham, who took over for Nigel Gray), and Sting proved once and for all to be a master of the pop-songwriting format. The album spawned several hits, such as the energetic "Spirits in the Material World" (notice how the central rhythms are played by synthesizer instead of guitar to mask the reggae connection) and a tribute to those living amid the turmoil and violence in Northern Ireland circa the early '80s, "Invisible Sun." But the best and most renowned of the bunch is undoubtedly the blissful "Every Little Thing She Does Is Magic," which topped the U.K. singles chart and nearly did the same in the U.S. (#3). Unlike the other Police releases, not all of the tracks are stellar ("Hungry for You," "Omegaman"), but the vicious jazz rocker "Demolition Man," the barely containable "Rehumanize Yourself," and a pair of album-closing ballads ("Secret Journey," "Darkness") proved otherwise. While it was not a pop masterpiece, *Ghost in the Machine* did serve as an important stepping stone between their more direct early work and their more ambitious latter direction, resulting in the trio's exceptional blockbuster final album, 1983's *Synchronicity*. —*Greg Prato*

Synchronicity / Jun. 1983 / A&M ✦✦✦
Although The Police's fifth release, 1983's *Synchronicity*, would be their most commercially successful and lead to a sold-out tour of enormodomes (including New York's Shea Stadium), it would turn out to be the trio's final album and tour. Like all Police recordings, *Synchronicity* contains some obvious "filler" (such as the silly dinosaur tale of "Walking in your Footsteps" and the almost unlistenable "Mother"), but for the most part, it's exceptional. One of 1983's biggest singles, the haunting "Every Breath You Take," is an obvious highlight, as well as other hits—the cacophonic rocker "Synchronicity II," plus the far more temperate "Wrapped Around Your Finger" and "King of Pain." Also included are the oft-overlooked tracks "O My God," "Synchronicity I" (used as a concert opener on the ensuing tour), "Tea in the Sahara," "Murder By Numbers," and the Stewart Copeland original "Miss Gradenko." Few other albums from 1983 merged tasteful pop, sophistication, and expert songwriting as well as *Synchronicity* did, resulting in yet another all-time classic. —*Greg Prato*

Every Breath You Take: The Singles / 1986 / A&M ✦✦✦✦✦
Depending on whose report you believe, the Police recongregated in 1985 to either begin work on their sixth studio album or a greatest hits collection that was to include all new, reworked versions of the hits. Neither ever materialized due to hostility between the members, and when all the trio could show for their work was an insipid remake of "Don't Stand So Close to Me," the Police decided to call it a day. So instead of following the original plan, A&M issued *Every Breath You Take: The Singles*, which included 11 original versions of their hits plus the new track, titled "Don't Stand So Close to Me '86," which prevents the collection from being definitive. Still, the Police were responsible for some of the greatest rock tunes of all time, and all 11 originals are superb: "Roxanne," "Walking on the Moon," "Invisible Sun," "Every Little Thing She Does Is Magic," "King of Pain," the title track and others. The only criticism is the absence of other hits/videos/

radio faves such as "Synchronicity II," "Demolition Man" and "So Lonely." In 1995, A&M replaced *Every Breath You Take: The Singles* with *Every Breath You Take: The Classics*, which finally included the original version of "Don't Stand So Close to Me," as well as its 1986 remake, and a remix of "Message in a Bottle." —*Greg Prato*

Message in a Box: The Complete Recordings / Sep. 28, 1993 / A&M ✦✦✦✦✦
Despite their legendary status, the Police only released five albums during their brief reign from 1978-1983. In addition, the trio had amassed a healthy amount of both studio and live B-sides, plus songs that only appeared on soundtracks. For the 1993 four-CD box set *Message in a Box: The Complete Recordings*, every single song the Police ever recorded is included. All the tracks were digitally remastered for the project, sounding superior to the original CD versions of the single albums. Also included is a 68-page booklet that includes an interesting (and often humorous) biography, a timeline and notes from all three band members regarding the rarities that appear for the first time on compact disc here. But of course, the real charm of the box set is the music—album tracks ("Hole in My Life," "It's Alright for You," "Driven to Tears"), hits ("Message in a Bottle," "Can't Stand Losing You," "Spirits in the Material World"), and rarities ("Fallout," a live version of "Next to You") are all timeless classics. While the set is highly recommended to newcomers just discovering the wonders of the Police, long-time fans should consider replacing their tinny-sounding single CDs with the definitive *Message in a Box*. After all, it contains a total of 24 tracks unavailable (for the most part) anywhere else. —*Greg Prato*

Live / Jun. 13, 1995 / A&M ✦✦✦

★ **Every Breath You Take: The Classics** / Sep. 12, 1995 / A&M ✦✦✦✦✦
By deleting the 1986 hits collection *Every Breath You Take: The Singles* and replacing it nearly ten years later with *Every Breath You Take: The Classics*, A&M improved the original set…but only slightly. Instead of finally adding the missing hits that were mysteriously absent the first time around ("Synchronicity II," "Demolition Man," "So Lonely," etc.), there are only two additional tracks—the original version of "Don't Stand So Close to Me" and a "New Classic Rock Mix" of "Message in a Bottle." Again, the included hits speak for themselves—"Roxanne," "Walking on the Moon," "Every Little Thing She Does Is Magic," "Wrapped Around Your Finger,"—but ultimately, *The Classics* misses the mark. Why would a Police fan who already owns *The Singles* want to replace it with a modestly different repackaging? A&M should have added some of the missing classics instead of just rehashing what many fans already own. —*Greg Prato*

The Pop Group

f. 1978, Bristol, England, **db.** 1980
Post-Punk, New Wave

Warning: this band's name is loaded with irony; there is little if anything "pop" about them. So, if you happen across any of their albums and think you're getting something that sounds like a cross between the Raspberries and the Beatles, don't say you weren't warned. Emerging in the late-'70s post-punk era, this militant gang of leftist radical politicos from Bristol, England specialized in a funk-driven cacophony of sound that was abrasive, strident, and ultimately very exciting. Railing against Margaret Thatcher's Tory government, the state of pop music, racism, sexism, etc., the Pop Group were not the easiest band of the early post-punk era to listen to, but those who made the effort were in for an interesting melange of primitive rhythms and avant-garde guitar racket. Led by the squalling "vocals" of Mark Stewart (which were little more than chanted political slogans), the Pop Group were unabashedly and stridently radical to the point of being hectoring. But, unlike others of their ilk, the music was so challenging, joyfully noisy, and downright weird that it was easy to cut them a little slack, even when their finger-pointing and ranting became a bit much. Never intending to make a serious run at the pop charts, the Pop Group imploded after three albums, the third being a collection of outtakes and assorted ephemera. They did, however, contribute some talented people to other bands, most notably Gareth Sanger, who formed the wild and woolly Rip Rig & Panic (named after a Rahsaan Roland Kirk LP), which also featured the lead vocals of a then-teenage Neneh Cherry; and the aforementioned Stewart, who went on to flourish in Adrian Sherwood's On-U stable of artists, recording with the Maffia and Tackhead. Despite its raw, inherent anti-commerciality, the Pop Group's dissonant agit-prop rock did influence a contemporary generation of political bands like Fugazi, Fun-da-Mental, and Rage Against the Machine. —*John Dougan*

● **Y** / 1979 / Radarscope ✦✦✦✦✦
Abrasive, but interesting, The Pop Group's debut is perhaps the most succinct summation of their angry and defiant approach to rock & roll. Although at times resembling the discordant funk of fellow post-punk radicals The Gang of Four, the Pop Group leave rhythm behind almost as quickly as they find it, and the result is a clattering din of sound resembling an aural collage. I like it, but even I'll admit it's a bit meandering and overly experimental to take in one sitting. The longish, guitar-driven track "We Are Time" is the strongest cut, establishing a solid groove that won't let go. —*John Dougan*

How Much Longer Do We Tolerate Mass Murder? / 1980 / Rough Trade ✦✦✦
If the title doesn't tip you off as to what this record will probably sound like, then you're hopeless. More accusatory than their debut (only because the lyrics are more clearly recorded), and more funk-powered. Oddly, what hurts this is a lack of experimentation, but with The Pop Group, it's always too much of one thing and not enough of another. An interesting experiment that is as maddening as it is satisfying. —*John Dougan*

We Are Time / 1980 / Rough Trade ✦✦✦

Pop Will Eat Itself

f. 1986, Stourbridge, England, **db.** 1996

Alternative Dance, Alternative Pop/Rock

Taking their name from an *NME* feature on the group Jamie Wednesday (later known as Carter the Unstoppable Sex Machine), the archetypal grebo band Pop Will Eat Itself formed in Stourbridge, England in 1986. Comprised of vocalist/guitarist Clint Mansell, keyboardist Adam Mole, drummer Graham Crabb and bassist Richard March, PWEI began their existence as a Buzzcocks-influenced indie guitar band, and issued their self-produced debut EP *The Poppies Say Grrr* in 1986.

While recording their follow-up *Poppiecock*, PWEI became immersed in sampling, drawing material from sources ranging from James Brown to Iggy Pop; soon Crabb emerged from behind his drum kit to join Mansell as co-frontman, and a drum machine was installed in his place. Honing a fusion of rock, pop and rap which they dubbed "grebo," the Poppies kickstarted a small revolution; by the release of their 1987 full-length debut *Box Frenzy* and the hit "There Is No Love Between Us Anymore," grebo—the name quickly given the entire subculture of similarly grimy and raunchy bands—was all the rage in the British music press.

The influence of hip-hop was even more pronounced on singles like "Def. Con. One." and "Can U Dig It?," both included on Pop Will Eat Itself's 1989 masterpiece *This Is the Day… This Is the Hour… This Is This!*, their debut for RCA. "Touched by the Hand of Cicciolina," an ode to the Italian porn-actress-turned-politician, was another hit, while 1991's *Cure for Sanity* marked an increasing interest in dance music. By 1992's *The Looks or the Lifestyle*, PWEI even added a live drummer, Fuzz (born Robert Townshend), to expand their ever-mutating sound.

In early 1993, the Poppies issued their biggest U.K. hit, "Get the Girl, Kill the Baddies"; ironically, later that same year the group was dropped by RCA. After signing to Infectious in Britain, they were picked up in the U.S. by Nothing, a label owned by longtime fan Trent Reznor; sporting a harder-edged, funk-metal sound, PWEI resurfaced in 1994 with *Dos Dedos Mis Amigos*. Prior to the release of a 1995 remix record, *Two Fingers, My Friends*, Crabb exited the group to focus on his side project, Golden Claw Musics. March later gained fame in the big-beat act Bentley Rhythm Ace. *—Jason Ankeny*

Box Frenzy / 1987 / Rough Trade ✦✦✦

Now for a Feast! / 1988 / Rough Trade ✦✦✦✦✦

● **This Is the Day . . . This Is the Hour . . . This Is This!** / 1989 / RCA ✦✦✦✦✦

The sampling chaos that runs through Pop Will Eat Itself's breakout album includes nods to hip-hop, acid-house, heavy metal, synth-pop, soul—basically anything the Poppies could get their grebo little samplers on. The results, though dated, are consistent fun for listeners who can stand the old-school British rhymes on hits like "Can U Dig It" and "Def. Con.one." The last half of the album provides opportunity to stretch out, as "Shortwave Transmission on Up to the Minuteman" and "Satellite Ecstatica" illustrate. *—Keith Farley*

The Looks or the Lifestyle / Oct. 1992 / RCA ✦✦

Dos Dedos Mis Amigos / 1994 / Interscope ✦✦✦✦✦

Pop Will Eat Itself goes industrial. Well, not really, but the shift to Trent Reznor's Nothing label shows in the music. The guitars are harder-edged, and the drumbeats are less dancy and more driving. Despite all that, the album maintains the Poppies' unique sense of humor. Songs range from the dark club favorite "Ich Bin Ein Auslander" to the entertaining denunciation of the Royal Family on "Familus Horribilus." This album, although not all that representative of the rest of their discography, is certainly worth finding for any fan of the band. *—Joshua Landau*

Two Fingers, My Friends / 1995 / Infectious ✦✦✦✦

The remix album accompanying Pop Will Eat Itself's final album, *Dos Dedos Mis Amigos*, includes a range of solid remixers including the Orb, Renegade Soundwave, Fun-Da-Mental, Foetus, Transglobal Underground, and Apollo 440. *—John Bush*

Wise Up Suckers / 1996 / Camden ✦✦✦

A sort of best-of album, RCA released this disc after Pop Will Eat Itself broke from the label. Due to their rights to the back-catalog, this disc was produced with no input from the band. Although a good introduction to their pre-*Dos Dedos Mis Amigos* work, fans would serve themselves and the band better by acquiring *This Is the Day, This Is the Hour, This Is This* and *Dos Dedos Mis Amigos*. *—Joshua Landau*

Iggy Pop

b. Apr. 21, 1947, Ypsilanti, MI

Vocals / Detroit Rock, Album Rock, Proto-Punk, Hard Rock

After the disbandment of the proto-punk group the Stooges, vocalist Iggy Pop (born James Osterberg) embarked on a solo career that flirted with the mainstream while keeping his fiery punk spirit alive. Pop laid low for a couple of years following the breakup of the Stooges, resurfacing in 1977 with two David Bowie-produced albums, *The Idiot* and *Lust for Life*. These records expanded his trademark full-throttle rock & roll, incorporating a more pop-oriented approach that increased his audience; *The Idiot* remains his highest-charting album, peaking at number 72 in America. Released in 1982, the Chris Stein-produced *Zombie Birdhouse* (which appeared on Stein's label, Animal) was the most varied collection Pop had created since *Lust for Life*. After the release of *Zombie Birdhouse*, Pop took some time off, reappearing four years later with the Bowie-produced *Blah-Blah-Blah*; the record became his highest-charting album since *The Idiot*. He followed it in 1988 with *Instinct*, another return to basic hard rock. Released the following year on Virgin Records, the Don Was-produced *Brick By Brick* was his most accessible and commercially successful album, producing his first Top 40 hit, "Candy." *—Stephen Thomas Erlewine*

☆ **The Idiot** / 1977 / Virgin ✦✦✦✦✦

In 1976, the Stooges had been gone for two years, and Iggy Pop had developed a notorious reputation as one of rock & roll's most spectacular waste cases. After a self-imposed stay in a mental hospital, a significantly more functional Iggy was desperate to prove he could hold down a career in music, and he was given another chance by his longtime ally, David Bowie. Bowie co-wrote a batch of new songs with Iggy, put together a band, and produced *The Idiot*, which took Iggy in a new direction decidedly different from the guitar-fueled proto-punk of the Stooges. Musically, *The Idiot* is of a piece with the impressionistic music of Bowie's "Berlin Period" (such as *Heroes* and *Low*), with it's fragmented guitar figures, ominous bass lines, and discordant, high-relief keyboard parts. Iggy's new music was cerebral and inward-looking, where his early work had been a glorious call to the id, and Iggy was in more subdued form than with the Stooges, with his voice sinking into a world-weary baritone that was a decided contrast to the harsh, defiant cry heard on "Search and Destroy." Iggy was exploring new territory as a lyricist, and his songs on *The Idiot* are self-referential and poetic in a way that his work had rarely been in the past; for the most part the results are impressive, especially "Dum Dum Boys," a paean to the glory days of his former band, and "Nightclubbing," a call to the joys of decadence. *The Idiot* introduced the world to a very different Iggy Pop, and if the results surprised anyone expecting a replay of the assault of *Raw Power*, it also made it clear that Iggy was older, wiser, and still had plenty to say; it's a flawed but powerful and emotionally absorbing work. *—Mark Deming*

☆ **Lust for Life** / 1977 / Virgin ✦✦✦✦✦

On *The Idiot*, Iggy Pop looked deep inside himself, trying to figure out how his life and his art had gone wrong in the past. But on *Lust for Life*, released less than a year later, Iggy decided it was time to kick up his heels, as he traded in the mid-tempo introspection of his first album and began rocking hard again. Musically, *Lust for Life* is a more aggressive set than *The Idiot*, largely thanks to drummer Hunt Sales and his bassist brother Tony Sales. The Sales' proved they were a world class rhythm section, laying out power and spirit on the rollicking title cut, the tough groove of "Tonight," and the lean neo-punk assault of "Neighborhood Threat," and with guitarists Ricky Gardner and Carlos Alomar at their side, they made for a tough, wiry rock & roll band—a far cry from the primal stomp of the Stooges, but capable of kicking Iggy back into high gear. (David Bowie played piano and produced, as he had on *The Idiot*, but his presence is less clearly felt on this album.) As a lyricist and vocalist, Iggy Pop rose to the challenge of the material; if he was still obsessed with drugs ("Tonight"), decadence ("The Passenger"), and bad decisions ("Some Weird Sin"), the title cut suggested he could avoid a few of the temptations that crossed his path, and songs like "Success" displayed a cocky joy that confirmed Iggy was back at full strength. On *Lust for Life*, Iggy Pop managed to channel the aggressive power of his work with the Stooges with the intelligence and perception of *The Idiot*, and the result was the best of both worlds; smart, funny, edgy, and hard-rocking, *Lust for Life* is the best album of Iggy Pop's solo career. *—Mark Deming*

TV Eye / 1978 / RCA ✦

New Values / 1979 / Buddha ✦✦✦✦

From the time the Stooges first broke onto the music scene in 1967, Iggy Pop was rock's most remarkable one-man freak show, but by the mid-'70s, after the Stooges' messy collapse, Iggy found himself in need of a stable career. The rise of punk rock finally created a context in which Iggy's crash-and-burn theatrics seemed like inspired performance rather than some sort of cry for help, and in 1979, with everyone who was anyone name-checking Iggy as punk's Founding Father, he scored a deal with Arista Records, and *New Values* became his first recording since the new rock gained a foothold. These days, *New Values* sounds like Iggy Pop's new wave album; while former Stooges associates James Williamson and Scott Thurston worked on the album, the arrangements were dotted with synthesizer patches and electronic percussion accents that have not stood the test of time well at all, and the mix speaks of a more polite approach than the raw, raging rock of Iggy's best work. But the growth as a songwriter that David Bowie encouraged in Iggy on *The Idiot* and *Lust for Life* is very much in evidence here; "Tell Me a Story," "Billy Is a Runaway," and "How Do Ya Fix a Broken Part" are tough, unblinking meditations on Iggy's war with the persona he created for himself, and "I'm Bored" and "Five Foot One" proved rock's first great minimalist still had some worthy metaphors up his sleeve. If *New Values* wasn't a great Iggy Pop album, it was a very good one, and proved that he had a future without David Bowie's guidance, something that didn't seem so certain at the time. *—Mark Deming*

Soldier / 1980 / Buddha ✦✦✦

In 1980, every punk rocker in Christendom cited Iggy Pop as a key influence, and *Soldier* was the album where he started asking for some payback. Original Sex Pistols bassist Glen Matlock, Rich Kids' guitarist Steve New, Ivan Kral of the Patti Smith Group, and former XTC keyboardist Barry Andrews all signed on to back Iggy on *Soldier*, but the result was hardly the full-frontal rock assault one might have hoped for. Reportedly, conflicts between producers James Williamson and David Bowie led to both of them walking out on the project, and Iggy is said to have gotten along so poorly with Steve New that he stripped most of New's lead guitar from the mix (which would explain why keyboards and acoustic guitar dominate the album). While 1979's *New Values* showed Iggy growing as a lyricist with a number of tough but introspective songs, *Soldier* sounds goofy by comparison, featuring oddball throwaways like "Dog Food," "Get up and Get Out" (whose lyrics are mostly cribbed from old R&B tunes), and the political "satire" "I'm a Conservative." But Iggy's in great voice throughout, and on the few songs where the band fully catches fire (like "Knocking 'Em Down (In the City)" and "Loco Mosquito"), he leaves little doubt that his powers as a performer were still with him. Buddha reissued the album in 2000 with two non-essential bonus tracks, "Low Life" and "Drop a Hook." —*Mark Deming*

Party / 1981 / Buddha ✦✦

Zombie Birdhouse / 1982 / IRS ✦✦

Choice Cuts / 1984 / RCA ✦✦✦

Following the success of David Bowie's version of "China Girl," RCA assembled *Choice Cuts*, a compilation of Iggy Pop's two albums for the label. Actually, "compilation" is a misleading word: Side one of *Choice Cuts* features side one of *The Idiot*, while side two features side one of *Lust for Life*. It effectively illustrates the differences between the records, and includes most of the prime material from each collection, yet the two albums are necessary listens in their entirity, making *Choice Cuts* an engaging but useless compilation. —*Stephen Thomas Erlewine*

Blah Blah Blah / 1986 / A&M ✦✦✦

In 1983, Iggy Pop's career was in shambles, but an unexpected windfall arrived thanks to Iggy's frequent benefactor David Bowie. Bowie recorded "China Girl," a song Bowie and Pop co-wrote, for his album *Let's Dance*, earning Iggy some large (and much-needed) royalty checks. Wisely realizing he was running out of second chances, Iggy decided to make the most of his good fortune; he steered clear of drugs, learned to cook his own meals, started putting money in the bank, and used his savings to bankroll a new album. David Bowie offered to help, and together they came up with *Blah Blah Blah*, the most calculatedly commercial album of Iggy's career. Like *The Idiot*, *Blah Blah Blah* was heavily influenced by Bowie's input; however, while *The Idiot* was made by a man creating intelligent and ambitious art rock, *Blah Blah Blah* is the work of a popmeister looking for hits and not afraid to sound cheesy about it. In the liner notes, a member of Duran Duran is thanked for the loan of a drum machine, and that speaks volumes about the production; *Blah Blah Blah* is slick in a very '80s way, dominated by preprogrammed percussion and swirling keyboards. And in the four years since *Zombie Birdhouse*, Iggy hadn't come up with much in the way of material; the only truly memorable tracks are "Real Wild Child (Wild One)," a neat bit of electro-processed rockabilly (previously a hit for Australian rocker Johnny O'Keefe), and the moody "Cry for Love," co-written by former Sex Pistols guitarist Steve Jones. Both of these songs were minor hits, so *Blah Blah Blah* succeeded on its obviously commercial terms, but that doesn't change the fact it's one of Iggy's least interesting albums, and has dated worse than almost anything he's ever recorded. —*Mark Deming*

Instinct / 1988 / A&M ✦✦

"Cold Metal," the first song on *Instinct*, opens with a solid blast of hard rock guitar, and after the overly slick pop of *Blah Blah Blah* and the arty miscalculations of *Zombie Birdhouse*, many Iggy Pop fans breathed a sigh of relief at the thought that Iggy was ready to sing some hard and fast rock & roll again. But as Steve Jones' turgid neo-metal guitar riffs begin to sink in (it's hard to believe these leads are being played by the guy who founded the Sex Pistols), it soon becomes obvious that while Iggy is trying to rock out on *Instinct*, his band is not doing an especially good job of it, sounding only marginally more enthusiastic than a typical second-tier arena rock outfit. And while Bill Laswell might have seemed like an inspired choice as producer after helming solid and idiosyncratic rock albums for Motörhead and Public Image Ltd., he doesn't draw much of interest from the musicians, and his sound has the dull, pre-fab sheen of any number of standard-issue hard rock albums. And though Iggy's in strong voice here, he appears to still be working his way through the formulaic lyrical mind set of *Blah Blah Blah*—Iggy doesn't seem to have much to say, and few interesting ways of saying it. While the first and last cuts on *Instinct* are enjoyable, most of what's in between is surprisingly faceless hard rock; it's a competent, well-crafted album, but the most dangerous man in rock & roll ought to be able to come up with a bit more than that. —*Mark Deming*

Brick by Brick / Jun. 1990 / Virgin ✦✦✦✦✦

While Don Was is best known for his work with mutant funkateers Was (Not Was), he was also a Motor City boy with fond memories of the Stooges' glory days, and when he was hired to produce an album for Iggy Pop, Was said, "The guy is incredibly intelligent, writes great lyrics, is a great singer, and I just wanted to get that across." And he did: *Brick by Brick* refined Iggy's gifts without watering them down, adding a polish that focused his talents rather than blurring them. Working with a mixture of L.A. session heavyweights (Waddy Wachtel, David Lindley) and rock stars paying their respects (Slash and Duff McKagan from Guns & Roses, Kate Pierson from the B-52's), *Brick by Brick* leans to tough, guitar-based hard rock, leavened with a few more pop-oriented tunes that still speak of a hard-nosed lyrical approach. But the triumph here is Iggy's; he's rarely sung better on record, finding a middle ground between precision and abandon that honors both and surrenders to neither, and as a lyricist he reached a new level of maturity that proved he could expand his boundaries without loosing touch with his roots. On *Brick by Brick*, Iggy's dominant theme is the cultural and moral decay of modern America, and finding the strength to rise above it and reach a place in the world. That might sound a bit grand for Iggy, but as a man who sent himself to Hell and back (and learned a few things in the process), he expresses his ideas with plenty of piss, vinegar, and hard-bitten wit. Smart, tough, and impressive on all counts, *Brick by Brick* was Iggy Pop's strongest work since *Lust for Life*, and marked a new high point in his career as a songwriter. —*Mark Deming*

American Caesar / 1993 / Virgin ✦✦✦✦

Boasting a big-name producer and appearances from several actual rock stars, *Brick by Brick* was a remarkably successful attempt to create an "event album" around Iggy Pop, so the follow-up came as a surprise—*American Caesar* was cut fast and loose in a New Orleans studio, with Iggy's road band backing him up. But the real shock was that *American Caesar* ranks with Iggy's very best solo work; dark, loud, and atmospheric, it's a far riskier album than *Brick by Brick*, lyrically following that disc's themes of America teetering on the edge of collapse with the same degree of hard-won maturity, but adding a wacked-out passion and force that recalls the heady days of *Raw Power*. While Iggy's group doesn't play with the subtlety of the studio cats on *Brick by Brick*, they also sound tight and forceful, like a real band with muscle and experience. Eric Schermerhorn's guitar meshes with Iggy's vocals as well as anyone he's worked with since Ron Asheton, and Malcolm Burn's production is clear and detailed but adds subtle textures that season the formula just right. The rockers are full-bodied ("Wild America," "Plastic and Concrete"), the calmer tunes still bristle with tension and menace ("Mixing the Colors," "Jealousy"), the manic remake of "Louie Louie" tops the version on *Metallic K.O.*, and the title cut is a bizarre bit of performance art that's as strange as the entirety of *Zombie Birdhouse*, and a rousing success where that album was a brave failure. In a note printed on the CD itself, Iggy says "I tried to make this album as good as I could, with no imitations of other people and no formula shit." Iggy succeeded beyond anyone's expectations, and *American Caesar* is an overlooked masterpiece. —*Mark Deming*

Naughty Little Doggie / Mar. 5, 1996 / Virgin ✦✦✦

Iggy's career is dotted with miscalculations and flat-out mistakes, and after releasing two of his strongest solo efforts in a row—*Brick by Brick* and *American Caesar*—it might have been tempting fate to expect Iggy to pull off a hat trick. He didn't, and *Naughty Little Doggie* isn't much to write home about. If you were to compare *Naughty Little Doggie* to any of Iggy's previous albums, it most closely resembles *Instinct*, his ill-conceived neo-metal project, and in all fairness *Naughty Little Doggie* is clearly the better album. As he did on *American Caesar*, Iggy cut these sessions with his touring band (dubbed "The Fuckups" in the liner notes), and they sound solid and enthusiastic throughout, especially guitarist Eric Schermerhorn (aka Eric Mesmerize) and drummer Larry Mullins (aka Larry Contrary). Iggy's voice is in great shape, and he seems to be having a lot of fun, especially on the dirty old man's celebration of "Pussy Walk" and the nervy "Knucklehead." But Iggy the Songwriter wasn't in the midst of one of his especially inspired periods when he was assembling *Naughty Little Doggie*, and while the music is mostly solid, bare-knuckled hard rock, the lyrics aren't all that special, and it doesn't take long for Iggy and the band to run through all the tricks they have on hand. One notable exception, however, is the last track, "Look Away," a low-key remembrance of fellow rock & roll reprobate Johnny Thunders which wouldn't have been out of place on *Brick by Brick* or *American Caesar*. *Naughty Little Doggie* is a solid, respectable, and professional hard rock album, and Iggy Pop could do a lot worse. But then again, he could also do a lot better. —*Mark Deming*

● **Nude & Rude: The Best of Iggy Pop** / Oct. 29, 1996 / Virgin ✦✦✦✦✦

Nude & Rude: The Best of Iggy Pop is an excellent 17-track overview of Pop's career, from the Stooges into the '90s. With the exception of *The Idiot*, *Lust for Life* and *Brick by Brick*, Iggy's solo career has been decidedly uneven and many of his albums have been flat-out dull. *Nude & Rude* does a terrific job of selecting the best moments from these records, as well as many of the best Stooges tracks, thereby providing a nearly flawless introduction to Iggy's music. With "I Wanna Be Your Dog," "No Fun," "Search & Destroy," "Gimme Danger," "I'm Sick of You" and "Kill City," representing the Stooges, a few of the band's essential items are missing, but all the essential solo tracks are here, including "Funtime," "Nightclubbing," "China Girl," "Lust for Life," "Real Wild Child," "Cold Metal," "Candy," and "Home." —*Stephen Thomas Erlewine*

Avenue B / Sep. 14, 1999 / Virgin ✦✦

Beat 'Em Up / Jul. 17, 2001 / Virgin ✦✦✦

Love it or hate it, *Beat 'Em Up* is inarguably one of the most appropriate titles Iggy Pop has attached to an album in years; after an ill-advised detour into something resembling jazz on 1999's *Avenue B*, Iggy has shifted gears again and served up his most physically punishing album since *American Caesar* in 1993. *Beat 'Em Up* starts out promisingly enough with "Mask," a hyper-insistent three-chord blast that, with its energetic riffing and manic vocals, sounds more like a prime Stooges number than anything he's cooked up in ages. But about halfway through the song, Iggy launches into a hysterical tirade against a number of cultural abuses common to modern day America, and for every moment that he hits a nail on the head ("Irony in place of balls/balls in place of brains/brains in place of soul") there are at least one or two bits where you can only hope he's joking ("Junkie frat boys in their shorts!"). And that pretty much sets the tone for the album. But it's both ironic and appropriate that the most effective track on the album is the one that rocks the least—"V.I.P.," six and a half minutes of slow vamp in which Iggy offers a hilarious stream-of-consciousness monologue about the joys of abusing your fame, which is funny and makes its points well at the same time. *Beat 'Em Up* takes an approach not dissimilar to what Iggy was reaching for on *Brick By Brick* and *American Caesar*, but where he sounded intelligent and thoughtful on those albums, on *Beat 'Em Up* he sounds a like a crank who doesn't always realize he's being funny, and "V.I.P." suggests if he's going to go this route, he's best off directly aiming for laughs. —*Mark Deming*

The Poppy Family

f. 1968, **db.** 1973

Soft Rock

Susan Pesklevits and Terry Jacks met in the band Powerline. They later married and formed the Poppy Family in 1968. With guitarist Craig McCaw and percussionist Satwan Singh, the duo's third single, "Which Way You Goin' Billy," became a hit in the U.S. and their native Canada, selling over two million copies. The group recorded three albums in the early '70s: *That's Where I Went Wrong* and *Which Way You Goin' Billy* in 1970 and

Poppy Seeds in 1971. Terry and Susan were divorced by 1973, however, and both began solo careers. Susan released *Dream* (1976), *Ghosts* (1980) and *Forever* (1982), but Terry became more successful when his "Seasons in the Sun" single went platinum in Canada (more than 150,000 units). His albums include *Seasons in the Sun* (1974), *Y'Don't Fight the Sea* (1976), *Pulse* (1983) and *Into the Past* (1989). —*John Bush*

● **A Good Thing Lost: 1968-1973** / Apr. 2, 1996 / March ✦✦✦✦✦
A Good Thing Lost: 1968-1973 is an excellent best-of collection from the Poppy Family, a great, if largely forgotten, late-'60s Canadian soft rock/psychedelic group. The meticulous songwriting, production, and arranging skills of guitarist/mastermind Terry Jacks (who later had a huge solo hit with the classic pop single "Seasons in the Sun") lift these recordings above the work of many of the group's better-known contemporaries. Singer Susan Jacks has a beautiful voice that sometimes sounds like (but predates) Karen Carpenter, but is eminently more soulful. Although characterized in the liner notes as a "soft pop" band, the Poppy Family was also capable of a somewhat tougher sound that sometimes recalled *Surrealistic Pillow*-era Jefferson Airplane and folkier material in the Kenny Rogers & the First Edition/Roger McGuinn vein. Throughout, Jacks frames the songs with creative, if often dated, arrangements that compare favorably to his obvious influences, the Beatles, the Beach Boys, and Phil Spector. In addition to "Which Way You Goin' Billy," the group's biggest hit (number two in 1970) and a generous helping of singles and high-quality album tracks, the disc includes an alternate, wildly psychedelic mix of "There's No Blood in Bone" and two different versions of "That's Where I Went Wrong" (the second of which features some cool country guitar leads). Overall, *A Good Thing Lost: 1968-1973* is a fantastic find—one of those hidden gems that record fanatics always hope to discover. —*Pemberton Roach*

Porno for Pyros
f. 1993
Funk Metal, Alternative Pop/Rock
Perry Farrell's post-Jane's Addiction band, Porno for Pyros, followed the same path as his previous band, combining art rock, punk, heavy metal, and funk into one shrieking whole. On their self-titled 1993 debut, Farrell's pretensions got out of hand at times, resulting in some ridiculously self-absorbed conceptual pieces sitting next to some straightforward rockers and pop songs; it sold well at first, but soon slipped down the charts. While he prepared new Porno material in 1994, Farrell returned to the organization of Lollapalooza—the traveling rock festival he conceived—for the first time since 1992. The band released *Good Gods Urge* in 1996.

Although *Good Gods Urge* was a successful release from both an artistic and musical standpoint, the album disappeared from the charts shortly after its release. On the album's ensuing tour, former Minutemen/fIREHOSE bassist Mike Watt filled in for the departed Lenoble, and to the delight of longtime Jane's Addiction fans, guitarist Dave Navarro was a special surprise guest on select dates as well. After the album's ensuing tour wrapped up in early 1997 (and a pair of Porno for Pyros songs appeared on the motion picture soundtracks for *The Cable Guy* and *Private Parts*), Farrell promptly ended the group, as he focused on a solo recording career as well as sporadic Jane's Addiction reunion shows. —*Stephen Thomas Erlewine & Greg Prato*

Porno for Pyros / Apr. 27, 1993 / Warner Brothers ✦✦✦
Perry Farrell's first project since splitting up Jane's Addiction, Porno For Pyros' self-titled debut, was one of the most highly-anticipated rock releases of 1993. Joining Farrell was ex-J.A. drummer Stephen Perkins, guitarist Peter DiStefano, and bassist Martyn Le Noble, and while the music of Porno For Pyros contained some similarities to J.A., it turned out to be a more ethereal and psychedelic affair. Most noticeably absent were the monstrous guitar riffs—DiStefano specialized more in textured guitar sounds (a la The Cure's Robert Smith, etc.), which put more emphasis on Farrell's vocals and Perkins' drumming (who also added exotic percussion to the proceedings). Also, P.F.P.'s compositions were far more succinct, whereas J.A. were known to wander into mood-enhanced improv; most tracks on *Porno For Pyros* were under the 4-minute mark, while Farrell's lyric writing still alternated between train of thought and thought-provoking. The slightly melancholic ballad, "Pets," was an MTV hit, as it lyrically touched upon the possibility of extraterrestrial life. A pair of tracks, "Cursed Female" and "Cursed Male," were sequenced back to back to create a brief epic (clocking in together at barely over 7 minutes), which explored the pros and cons of both genders. Also featured was the funky "Meija," the hyperactive "Bad Shit," the ballad "Black Girlfriend," and the title track, which dealt with the 1992 Los Angeles/Rodney King riots. While those expecting an instant classic like *Nothing's Shocking* and *Ritual De Lo Habitual* were probably disappointed, *Porno For Pyros* remains an interesting musical detour for Farrell and Co. —*Greg Prato*

● **Good God's Urge** / Jun. 1996 / Warner Brothers ✦✦✦✦
By the time Porno for Pyros issued a follow-up to their gold-certified self-titled debut, 1996's *Good God's Urge*, bassist Martyn LeNoble had left the band (although he had already played bass on most of the album), replaced by ex-Minutemen bassist Mike Watt. The music was even more atmospheric than its predecessor, comprised almost entirely of laid-back compositions—only a few tracks could be considered hard rock. Inspired by the beautiful Zuma Beach in California where the band's recording studio was located, the songs sound like the perfect soundtrack to a tranquil beachside setting. The free and easy feel of the first two tracks, "Porpoise Head" and "100 Ways," is comparable to Love and Rockets' more serene moments (L&R members Daniel Ash, David J, and Kevin Haskins actually guest on the former track), while the driving "Tahitian Moon" was an alternative radio hit. The beautiful acoustic ballad "Kimberly Austin" remains one of Perry Farrell's most personal lyrics, while Mike Watt's fluid bass lines stand out on another highlight, the title track. Also of note was the guest spots by Red Hot Chili Peppers

bassist Flea and then-Pepper guitarist Dave Navarro on "Freeway," which marked the first time Navarro and Farrell played together since their less-then-amicable split from Jane's Addiction in 1991. After the tour in support of *Good God's Urge*, Porno for Pyros went the way of J.A. and broke up. —*Greg Prato*

Portastatic
f. 1992
Indie Pop, Indie Rock, Lo-Fi, Alternative Pop/Rock
Though Mac McCaughan has plenty to keep him busy—playing in Superchunk, managing the successful Merge Records—he also spends time recording as Portastatic. With a varying lineup, the side-project has recorded two albums and several singles since 1993, when Tom Sharpling of 18 Wheeler Records asked McCaughan to release some of his lo-fi, four-track recordings; he obliged with the singles "Sandals with White Socks" and "Starter." Then in 1994, McCaughan released an entire Portastatic album, *I Hope Your Heart Is Not Brittle*. The group followed with the *Scrapbook* EP and a second album, *Slow Note from a Sinking Ship*. *Nature of a Sap* appeared in 1997. 2000's EP *De Mel, De Melao* paid homage to classic Brazilian artists like Caetano Veloso and Arnaldo Baptista. In 2001, McCaughan returned with *Looking for Leonard*, the score to a film written and directed by Superchunk fans Matt Bissonette and Steven Clark. —*John Bush*

● **I Hope Your Heart Is Not Brittle** / 1994 / Merge ✦✦✦✦

Slow Note from a Sinking Ship / Jun. 20, 1995 / Merge ✦✦✦
As a side project of Superchunk's Mac McCaughan, Portastatic provides an outlet for ideas that would sound out of place on a Superchunk album, and others that would fit right in. Playing by himself for the most part—with some help from local musicians—and recorded on a four track, the project has a modest low-fi feel. Quieter and gentler than his regular gig, Mac experiments with analog synths, lap steel, and other instruments, while creating songs with a soft, somber quality about them. While tracks like "San Andreas" and "Taking You With Me" could be Superchunk outtakes, the balance of the album swings from acoustic odes like "Skinny Glasses Girl," to the plush lo-fi atmospheric drone of "The Angels of Sleep," to the *Armed Forces*-era new wave synth of "A Cunning Latch." Admittedly, there are at least a half-dozen throw-away tracks, but fans of Superchunk, who are used to Mac's voice, will enjoy this album even more than the last Portastatic, because it boasts the same bittersweet melodies and melancholy subjects of his main band with his best solo songwriting to date. —*Chris Parker*

The Nature of Sap / Mar. 11, 1997 / Merge ✦✦✦
Following in the tradition of his peers, Mac McCaughan devoted his 1997 Portastatic album to mild progressive-rock, experimenting with keyboards, pianos and even clarinets. McCaughan doesn't veer away from punk-pop song structure, but he expands it with his increased instrumental palette, creating an album that is intriguing but difficult to meet halfway. —*Stephen Thomas Erlewine*

Looking for Leonard / May 22, 2001 / Merge ✦✦✦✦
On the soundtrack *Looking for Leonard*, Mac McCaughan takes his "side project" Portastatic to levels beyond the scope of his main band, indie legends Superchunk. *Looking for Leonard*, a complete score for a Canadian indie film of the same name, continues McCaughan's fascination with Brazilian Tropicalia music of the late '60s and early '70s. This inspiration first yielded Portastatic's 2000 EP *De Mel, De Melao*, a record of covers of Brazilian pop giants such as Caetano Veloso, Gilberto Gil, and Os Mutantes. But, *Looking for Leonard* transports those South American stylings to an entirely vocals-free, instrumental album that tips its hat to Tropicalia while exploring the emotional and atmospheric range of a film score. The soft electric guitar and strings render "Looking for Leonard—Theme" all bittersweet nostalgia and happy memories. "Luka's Theme" picks up the tone with meandering South American rhythms and wistful guitar lines. "Stealing Romance" could be the most uplifting one minute and 30 seconds of music you'll hear and "Sweethearts Organ Mix"'s pretty little organ melody is a throwback to emotive movie soundtracks of the '70s. The single appearance of a fuzzed-out, noisy guitar is in the song "Funeral Music," but this score is so cohesive that the crunchy lines don't change the genre of the music, just the feeling of it. *Looking for Leonard* ends with the rollicking "Sweethearts of the World," a feel-good jaunt that leaves the listener with the image of sunnier lands and travels across the sea. This album may be a film score, but it can easily stand all alone as music for moody days. —*Charles Spano*

Portishead
f. 1991, Bristol, England
Electronica, Adult Alternative Pop/Rock, Trip-Hop, Alternative Pop/Rock
Portishead may not have invented trip-hop, but they were among the first to popularize it, particularly in America. Taking their cue from the slow, elastic beats that dominated Massive Attack's *Blue Lines* and adding elements of cool jazz, acid house, and soundtrack music, Portishead created an atmospheric, alluringly dark sound. The group wasn't as avant-garde as Tricky, nor as tied to dance traditions as Massive Attack; Instead, the band wrote evocative pseudo-cabaret pop songs that subverted their conventional structures with experimental productions and rhythms of trip-hop. As a result, Portishead appealed to a broad audience—not just electronic dance and alternative rock fans, but thirtysomethings who found techno, trip-hop and dance as exotic as worldbeat. Before Portishead released their debut album *Dummy* in 1994, trip-hop's broad appeal wasn't apparent, but the record became an unexpected success in Britain, topping most year-end critics polls and earning the prestigious Mercury Music Prize; in America, it also became an underground hit, selling over 150,000 copies before the group toured the US. Following the success of *Dummy*, legions of imitators appeared over the next two years, but Portishead remained quiet, finally issuing their eponymous second album in 1997. —*Stephen Thomas Erlewine*

★ **Dummy** / Oct. 1994 / Go! Discs/London ✦✦✦✦✦
Portishead's album debut is a brilliant, surprisingly natural synthesis of claustrophobic spy soundtracks, dark breakbeats inspired by frontman Geoff Barrow's love of hip-hop, and a vocalist (Beth Gibbons) in the classic confessional singer/songwriter mold. Beginning with the otherworldly theremin and martial beats of "Mysterons," *Dummy* hits an early high with "Sour Times," a post-modern torch song driven by a Lalo Schifrin sample. The chilling atmospheres conjured by Adrian Utley's excellent guitar work and Barrow's turntables and keyboards prove the perfect foil for Gibbons, who balances sultriness and melancholia in equal measure. Occasionally reminiscent of a torchier version of Sade, Gibbons provides a clear focus for these songs, with Barrow and company behind her laying down one of the best full-length productions ever heard in the dance world. Where previous acts like Massive Attack had attracted dance heads in the main, Portishead crossed over to an American, alternative audience, connecting with the legion of angst-ridden indie fans as well. Better than any album before it, *Dummy* merged the pinpoint-precise productions of the dance world with pop hallmarks like great songwriting and excellent vocal performances. —*John Bush*

Portishead / Sep. 30, 1997 / Go! Discs/London ✦✦✦✦✦
Portishead's debut album, *Dummy*, popularized trip-hop, making its slow, narcotic rhythms, hypnotic samples, and film-noir production commonplace among sophisticated, self-consciously "mature" pop fans. The group recoiled from such widespread acclaim and influence, taking three years to deliver their eponymous second album. On the surface, *Portishead* isn't all that dissimilar from *Dummy*, but its haunting, foreboding sonic textures make it clear that the group isn't interested in the crossover success of such fellow travelers as Sneaker Pimps. Upon repeated plays, the subtle differences between the two albums become clear. Geoff Barrow and Adrian Utley recorded original music that they later sampled for the backing tracks on the album, giving the record a hazy, dreamlike quality that shares many of the same signatures of *Dummy*, but is darker and more adventurous. Beth Gibbons has taken the opportunity to play up her tortured diva role to the hilt, emoting wildly over the tracks. Her voice is electronically phased on most of the tracks, adding layers to the claustrophobic menace of the music. The sonics on *Portishead* would make it an impressive follow-up, but what seals its success is the remarkable songwriting. Throughout the album, the group crafts impeccable modern-day torch songs, from the frightening, repetitive "Cowboys" to the horn-punctuated "All Mine," which justify the detailed, engrossing production. The end result is an album that reveals more with each listen and becomes more captivating and haunting each time it's played. —*Stephen Thomas Erlewine*

PNYC / Nov. 10, 1998 / Go! Discs/Beat/London ✦✦✦
By the end of the decade, artists realized that CD and CD-R bootlegs of live performances were in high demand, which meant that they could profit by officially releasing certain "special" live performances. Portishead's one-night stand at New York City's Roseland Ballroom, released as *PNYC*, certainly qualifies as one of those "special" occasions. Performing with a 35-piece orchestra, Portishead runs through selections from their two albums, favoring their second slightly. On the surface, it doesn't seem like the orchestra would add much to the performances, especially since the arrangements remain similar, but their presence makes the music tense, dramatic, and breathtaking. This is especially true of the material from *Portishead*. On album, several of these songs sounded a little flat, but here they soar right alongside such staples as "Mysterons," "Sour Times," and "Glory Box." That alone doesn't necessarily make *PNYC* revelatory—instead, it deepens a listener's understanding of the artist, much like the Tindersticks' *The Bloomsbury Theatre, 12.3.95*. Which means, of course, that it's much more compelling and essential than the average live album. —*Stephen Thomas Erlewine*

The Posies

f. 1986, Seattle, WA
Pop Underground, Power Pop, Alternative Pop/Rock
One of the major '90s power-pop revivalist groups, Seattle's Posies combine the genre's standard influences (Big Star, Raspberries, etc.) with Hollies-like harmonies, roaring guitars, and odd lyrics about mundane, everyday concerns. Their first record, 1988's *Failure*, featured founding guitarists/vocalists Jonathan Auer and sometime Sub Pop producer Ken Stringfellow and fit squarely into the "slacker" trend. Geffen Records signed them, and they filled out the lineup with Dave Fox and Mike Musberger for *Dear 23*. 1993's Don Fleming-produced *Frosting on the Beater* (an allusion to masturbation) broke the band in the college radio market and was a critical success as well. 1996's *Amazing Disgrace* consolidated the Posies' position as critics' darlings with even wider acclaim, but when the record sold poorly the group returned to their original label, indie Pop Llama, for their 1998 swan song *Success*. Following the early 2000 release of the seemingly posthumous *Alive Before the Iceberg*, however, Auer and Stringfellow reunited for an acoustic summer tour mounted under the Posies banner. Later that year, the band released *In Case You Didn't Feel Like Plugging In. Nice Cheekbones & a Ph.D.* surfaced the next year. —*Steve Huey*

Failure / 1988 / Pop Llama ✦✦✦

Dear 23 / Aug. 1990 / DGC ✦✦✦
Ken Stringfellow and Jonathan Auer, the leaders of the Posies, expressed genuine big-league pop ambitions with minor-league budgets on their early releases, so it's not especially surprising that their first album for a major label, *Dear 23*, found them laying on all the baroque textures that they couldn't afford on their own dime. Sounding a bit like a modernized version of the Hollies with a studio sound that crossed *The White Album* with *Big Star 3rd*, *Dear 23* kicks off with two pleasing slices of glossy power pop, "My Big Mouth" and "Golden Blunders" (the latter of which was covered by an actual Beatle,

Ringo Starr, doubtless a major thrill for these guys). But by the time track four rolls around ("Any Other Way"), power has taken a cigarette break, and the album drifts into a mid-tempo dreamland where everything is either pretty and contemplative or pretty and a bit morose. (Though in all fairness, the rocking "Help Yourself" does pop up in the later innings to punch things up). *Dear 23* is packed with too much good stuff to escape the notice of any true pop obsessive—Auer and Stringfellow write great songs, their harmonies are nothing short of superb, and the arrangements and production (by the band in collaboration with John Leckie) are imaginative and flawlessly executed. However, for all the craft, there isn't a lot of passion or heart in this music; the long hours in the studio getting the sounds right seem to have squeezed out the soul of the music. *Dear 23* offers all the proof you could ask for that the Posies were major talents. However, it also made them sound like they weren't especially fun to be around or compelling to hear from, and that ultimately sinks the album. —*Mark Deming*

Frosting on the Beater / Apr. 27, 1993 / DGC ✦✦✦✦✦
Frosting on the Beater opens with a thick wall of distorted guitars and booming drums kicking up a very melodic fuss behind Ken Stringfellow and Jonathan Auer's creamy-smooth harmonies on the psych-tinged "Dream All Day," and the track's sweet-and-sour blend immediately announces this is going to be a very different affair than the Posies' major label debut, *Dear 23*. With noisy rock dude Don Fleming in the producer's chair, it came as no great surprise that *Frosting on the Beater* was a much harder sounding album than the introspective *Dear 23*, but surprisingly enough, Fleming also knew how to make the most of the band's expert pop songwriting; with the tempos and guitars turned, the tunes gained a needed physical impact that brought the melodies and hooks into the forefront, where they belonged. Just as importantly, the spot-on harmonies that were the highlight of *Dear 23* were still very much in evidence, resting atop the piles of fuzzy guitar chords like a dollop of hot fudge poured over a big scoop of ice cream. And prior to this, who knew that Ken Stringfellow and Jonathan Auer could rock out so hard (and so well) on guitars? One could argue that the big guitar attack of *Frosting on the Beater* was simply the Posies' way of trying to cash in on the grunge sweepstakes that briefly turned their hometown of Seattle into the center of the rock universe. But one listen also reveals that it transformed a smart but overly precious pop outfit into a hard-charging power pop band that gained a wealth of strength without giving up any of their smarts in the process—not a bad bargain. —*Mark Deming*

Amazing Disgrace / May 14, 1996 / DGC ✦✦✦
The Posies let their true power pop colors fly but with a tougher edge by steeping the songs on their fourth album in punk rock and '70s metal. "Throwaway" is a big guitar rocker with a harmonious chorus—the kind that became the band's calling card. The band invited Cheap Trick's Rick Nielsen and Robin Zander to sing along on "Hate Song." Unfortunately, the elder pair's charms were lost in the mix, though "Daily Mutilation" would be a good choice of cover for their own band. "Everybody Is a Fucking Liar" takes a trip back in time with its histrionic guitar parts. Naturally, "Grant Hart" and "Broken Record" are punk rock. "Song #1" and "Will You Ever Ease Your Mind?" are the kind of gorgeous pop songs on which the band grew their reputation. Whether they tackle punk, hard rock, or soft rock, the Posies' brand of songcraft is extraordinary, though, sadly, it would appear this was their swan song. —*Denise Sullivan*

Success / Feb. 13, 1998 / Pop Llama ✦✦✦
After the release of *Amazing Disgrace*, it appeared as though the Posies were through as Jon Auer and Ken Stringfellow called it quits. They soon reunited, however (for the first time in what would become a series of break-ups and reunions), to record their fifth studio album, *Success*. Switching to an indie label from Geffen, the band were awarded more creative freedom and more room to move. Initially, Auer had stated the band was attempting to record a country-rock album, but along the way they were diverted. Still, from listening to the opening notes of "Somehow Everything," it's clear that some of that country influence made it through. *Success* is the most laid-back album the Posies have recorded to date; freed of the glossy production of their Geffen years and of the major label pressure to record a "hit," they turned out an album that was more immediate, more relaxed, and more theirs. The downside, of course, is that the Posies' three albums for Geffen are as great as they are, so by comparison this album comes off lazy at times. The problem is that as an album, *Success* doesn't work as well as its predecessors. It does have some of the finest songs the band has ever recorded (the opening country-rock of "Somehow Everything," the new wavey single "Start a Life," and the gorgeous ballad "You're the Beautiful One"), but those songs are sandwiched in between some of the closest things to filler that the Posies have ever recorded. It's a convincing statement that there was still trouble in the band, and, as mentioned earlier, they disbanded again following the release of this album. However, despite its faults, *Success* is the album that shouldn't-have-been, and for that reason alone fans will certainly be glad to have it. —*Jason Damas*

Alive Before the Iceberg / Feb. 15, 2000 / Houston Party ✦✦✦

● **Dream All Day: The Best of the Posies** / Mar. 21, 2000 / DGC ✦✦✦✦
Compiled with Ken Stringfellow and Jon Auer's full participation, *Dream All Day: The Best of the Posies*' 19 tracks still aren't a full career overview. Since their 1988 debut album, *Failure*, 1998's studio swansong *Success*, and 2000's live *Before the Iceberg* were recorded for indie imprints, none of those tracks appear here. But as an anthology of the Posies' successful and influential years on the Geffen and DGC labels, this collection is faultless. Although they only released three albums for the majors, like any classic pop band, the Posies had a handful of obscure, non-album tracks, five of which are this disc's highlights. In his fascinating liner notes, Jon Auer explains that the Hollies were not a huge influence, yet the duo's harmonies and guitar-driven glory are a perfect match for "King Midas in Reverse," originally recorded for a little known Hollies

tribute album. Their ringing cover of Big Star's Chris Bell-penned "I Am the Cosmos," an Auer favorite, is thankfully rescued from its B-side status with its inclusion here. Other curiosities, especially "Going, Going, Gone," the band's biggest moneymaker due to its appearance on the million selling *Reality Bites* soundtrack, flesh out a representative selection of the Posies' best moments. Better than the cartoonish, often overrated, and inconsistent Cheap Trick (who guest on one of their tracks), the Posies balanced smart-alecky lyrics with some of the best power pop melodies to emerge from the punk scene. With remastered sound, a flawless track selection, and terrific liner notes and pictures in an affectionately assembled 20-page booklet, this is a near perfect representation of the band, recommended for both new listeners and hardcore fans. —*Hal Horowitz*

In Case You Didn't Feel Like Plugging In / Aug. 22, 2000 / Casa ✦✦✦✦

At Least, At Last / Sep. 0, 2000 / Not Lame ✦✦✦✦
Properly constructing a box set is a daunting task. Most failed box sets mix hits and hit-and-miss rarities, so that neither fans (who own most of the material) or casual fans (who just want the hits) are satisfied with it. When Not Lame Records assembled a Posies box set, the label issued a limited-edition run (2,500 copies) including nothing but unreleased material. The four-disc, 66-song *At Least, At Last: Demos, Live Recordings, and Whatnot 1987 to 1998* is a fan's dream, with demo versions of nearly all of the band's hits and many album tracks with superb sound quality, despite their demo status. There's a handful of live tracks, including Ken Stringfellow and Jon Auer's first performance as the Posies, and a handful of unreleased tracks, including covers (Blondie's "Dreaming," Devo's "Wiggly World," Cheap Trick's "Surrender," and Big Star's "What's Going Ahn"), that were intended for never-released tribute albums. Great works-in-progress abound, including two early versions of "Apology"—seen in different stages of development—and a demo of "Oh Michael," a song with a melody later assimilated into Swirl 360's "Ask Anybody." Muzak versions of "Golden Blunders" and "Suddenly Mary," two of the band's early hits, complete the set; it also includes a full-color book with liner notes from Stringfellow and Auer themselves. *At Least, At Last* is a complete retrospective and a last, personal look one of the driving forces of '90s power pop (along with Matthew Sweet and Teenage Fanclub). It's a peek inside the studio before glossy production was laid over many of these tracks, and that's what makes it an effective and stellar box set—almost four hours of intimate, rare music that fanatics of the band will go wild over. —*Jason Damas*

Nice Cheekbones and a Ph.D. / Feb. 27, 2001 / Badman ✦✦✦
The Posies' first studio release since 1998's *Success*, *Nice Cheekbones and a Ph.D.* includes five acoustic tracks, highlighted by the buoyant lead track "Matinee." The sparse instrumentation downplays the hooks present in "Chainsmoking in the U.S.A.," though it does accentuate Ken Stringfellow and Jon Auer's expertly executed harmonizing on ballads "With Those Eyes" and "No Consolation." The cover of the Byrds' "Lady Friend" is a natural choice to conclude this brief but pleasant E.P. *Nice Cheekbones and a Ph.D.* signals the welcome return of one of pop's finest groups. —*Michael Frey*

Powder

f. 1967, San Mateo, CA, **db.** 1969
Mod, Psychedelic
One of the many fine '60s groups who barely got to record, let alone reach a wide audience, Powder was one of the most Anglophile American bands of the decade. Hailing from San Mateo, CA (near San Francisco), the group stood apart from their peers in that they were neither psychedelic nor garage, specializing in power pop with ringing, crashing guitars and harmonies. Most of their material was extremely reminiscent of the Who circa *A Quick One* and *The Who Sell Out*, and while it was undoubtedly derivative, it was also well done. Sonny & Cher tried to help Powder get an album out after the group backed them on a 1968 tour, but it was shelved, although a lot of material was recorded. Powder leaders Tom and Rich Frost released some records on their own, including the minor hit "She's Got Love," and an album of unreleased Powder material was finally released in 1993. —*Richie Unterberger*

● **Biff! Bang! Powder!** / 1996 / Distortions ✦✦✦✦✦
Comprised mostly of 1968 demos, you could be forgiven for thinking you'd stumbled into a room of Who outtakes (with an occasional detour into folk-rock), with strong (at times blatant) echoes of tracks like "Happy Jack" and "So Sad About Us." Nonetheless, it's fun stuff, and the strongest original tracks, like "Turn Another Page" and "Gladly," stand up well on their own. Originally issued on vinyl in 1993, the 27-track 1996 CD version is about twice as long, adding a few alternate versions, and songs predating and postdating Powder from the Art Collection (which Powder evolved from), New Zealand singer Ray Columbus (whom Art Collection backed briefly), and folky post-Powder efforts from Thomas & Richard Frost (the leaders of Powder). —*Richie Unterberger*

Duffy Power

b. Sep. 9, 1941
Vocals, Harmonica / British Invasion, Blues-Rock
Power is a lost figure of the '60s who drifted into the inner circle of British blues after a middling career as a teen idol in the early '60s. He recorded one of the first Beatles covers (an early 1963 single of "I Saw Her Standing There") and never experienced acclaim as a commercial pop singer or blues vocalist. But he recorded some fine little-known blues-cum-R&B/rock sides in the '60s, some of which featured present and future members of the Graham Bond Organisation, Cream, and Pentangle. The pleasures of Power are subtle and not easily captured in print. His original material is strong, his arrangements imaginative, and his performance sincere; he's grounded in the blues, but doesn't

fall into shopworn clichés, bringing a lot of himself and the innovations of British '60s rock into the picture. —*Richie Unterberger*

Blues Power / 1992 / See For Miles ✦✦✦✦
Most of the recordings on *Blues Power* were originally released on Power's self-titled album on the tiny U.K. Spark label in 1969. Duffy says in the liner notes of this reissue that the album was never intended for release, and that these sessions were acoustic demos for an LP that never got produced with the arrangements he had envisioned. That may be so, but it's still a worthy document of this underrated British bluesman at his most bare-boned and haunting. With just his guitar and harmonica, Power runs through both moody originals and covers of R&B/blues standards (with The Beatles' "Fixing a Hole" thrown in) that are rearranged and drastically stripped down. This reissue includes the 15 tracks from the 1969 release, a couple more from the same sessions that were issued on the extremely obscure *Firepoint* compilation album, and three from the mid-'60s (also included on the *Little Boy Blue* reissue) that also explore acoustic moods, forming a picture of Power's most intimate work. —*Richie Unterberger*

● **Little Boy Blue** / 1992 / Edsel ✦✦✦✦✦
His best recordings, as noteworthy for the players on the album as Power himself. Laid down sometime in the mid-'60s, Power (who sings and plays occasional guitar and harp) is backed by a rotating ensemble including, at various points, John McLaughlin and Jack Bruce (before they gained fame), as well as future Pentangle members Danny Thompson and Terry Cox. Neither as rock-oriented as the Stones nor as strictly revivalist as Alexis Korner (with whom Power played for a time), this is one of the best British blues recordings, cutting straight down the middle between gutbucket blues and soulful R&B. Divided equally between Power originals and R&B blues covers, the material and performances are spare, powerful, and as consistent as any '60s British blues album. Unfortunately, these sessions were unissued for several years, surfacing briefly under the title *Innovations* in 1970 on the British Transatlantic label. This reissue on another tiny British label is equally obscure, but should not be missed by fans of '60s British R&B. —*Richie Unterberger*

Just Say Blue / 1995 / Retro ✦✦✦✦
While not up to the level of the other vintage Power compilations available (*Little Boy Blue* and *Blues Power*), this is a worthwhile supplement to those CDs, featuring 21 tracks of rare and unreleased material cut by the singer from 1965 to 1971. The first half, focusing on his 1965-67 output, is the more interesting portion by a considerable margin, as much for the jazz-blues-R&B fusion of the arrangements (featuring contributions from Jack Bruce, John McLaughlin, Ginger Baker, and Pentangle's Danny Thompson and Terry Cox) as Power's singing. The early-'70s songs that make up the remainder of the disc have a more pedestrian blues-rock feel, but there are some good, inspired moments, with cameos by Rod Argent, Thompson, Cox, and Alexis Korner. —*Richie Unterberger*

Prefab Sprout

f. 1977, Newcastle, England
College Rock, Sophisti-Pop, Alternative Pop/Rock, Synth Pop
One of the most beloved British pop bands of the '80s and '90s, Prefab Sprout had a minimum of chart success in the U.S., where they're all but unknown outside of their devoted cult following, but singer/songwriter Paddy McAloon is regularly hailed as one of the great songwriters of his era. Critics regularly compare McAloon favorably to Elvis Costello, Paul McCartney, and even Cole Porter, but the self-effacing and publicity-shy performer modestly prefers to let his increasingly rare albums speak for themselves. Prefab Sprout was formed in Newcastle, England, in 1977 by McAloon (who sings and plays guitar and piano) and his bass-playing younger brother, Martin. Drafting an early fan, Wendy Smith, into the lineup to sing helium-register backing vocals, the trio released their first single, "Lions in My Own Garden (Exit Someone)," on their own Candle label in July 1982. Prefab Sprout's first album, *Swoon*, was released in March 1984. It is in retrospect a surprisingly brittle record, full of difficult songs that take unexpected left turns and have all but impenetrable lyrics. Shortly after *Swoon*'s release, drummer Neil Conti joined the group, and in a rather brilliant move, Thomas Dolby was tapped to produce the second Prefab Sprout album. After a fine but unimaginative best-of, *A Life of Surprises*, in the summer of 1992, many thought Prefab Sprout disbanded. However, McAloon had written (and in some cases, recorded) several albums' worth of material during the first half of the decade, abandoning them all before finally releasing the crystalline *Andromeda Heights* in 1997. An album of subtle beauty, *Andromeda Heights* shows how far McAloon had come as a songwriter and singer since *Swoon*. A much-improved two-disc anthology, *The 38-Carat Collection*, was released by CBS in 1999 as the group was leaving the label. —*Stewart Mason*

Swoon / 1984 / Epic ✦✦✦
Paddy McAloon had not yet found the key to the elegant compositions that made Prefab Sprout distinctive when it came time to record their debut, *Swoon*. He certainly tries hard to make his sophisticated contemporary pop sound distinctive, but the problem is that he does too many things at once—the lyrics are overstuffed, and the music has too many chord changes and weird juxtapositions, as he tries to put white-funk beats to carefully crafted melodies. A few moments work, such as "Couldn't Bear to Be Special," but *Swoon* is primarily of interest as a historical item, since it only suggests the promise the band later filled. —*Stephen Thomas Erlewine*

Two Wheels Good / 1985 / Epic ✦✦✦✦✦
Smart, sophisticated and timelessly stylish, *Two Wheels Good* (titled *Steve McQueen* throughout the rest of the world) is a minor classic, a shimmering jazz-pop masterpiece sparked by Paddy McAloon's witty and inventive songwriting. McAloon is a wickedly

cavalier composer, his songs exploring human weaknesses like regret ("Bonny"), lust ("Appetite") and infidelity ("Horsin' Around") with cynical insight and sarcastic flair; he's also remarkably adaptable, easily switching gears from the faux-country of "Faron" to the stately pop grace of "Moving the River." At times, perhaps, his pretensions get the better of him (as on "Desire As"), while at other times his lyrics are perhaps too trenchant for their own good; at those moments, however, what keeps *Two Wheels Good* afloat is Thomas Dolby's lush production, which makes even the loftiest and most biting moments as easily palatable as the airiest adult-contemporary confection. *—Jason Ankeny*

From Langley Park to Memphis / 1988 / Epic ✦✦✦✦✦
As suggested by the title, *From Langley Park to Memphis* is Prefab Sprout's spiritual journey into the heart of American culture; obsessed with icons like Elvis ("The King of Rock & Roll") and Bruce Springsteen ("Cars and Girls"), fascinated with gospel music ("Venus of the Soup Kitchen") and locked in a love/hate relationship with New York City ("Hey! Manhattan"), Paddy McAloon turns an iconoclastic eye to the other side of the Atlantic in order to make some sense of it all. An airy, lounge-pop feel permeates the record, which also sports cameos from the likes of Stevie Wonder and Pete Townshend; still, while ambitious in both concept and execution, *From Langley Park to Memphis* pales in comparison to its masterful predecessor *Two Wheels Good*—a shortcoming acknowledged by Prefab Sprout themselves with the title of their next album, *Jordan: The Comeback*. *—Jason Ankeny*

Protest Songs / 1989 / Kitchenware ✦✦✦✦
Protest Songs was recorded by Prefab Sprout in 1985 in the wake of the masterful *Steve McQueen/Two Wheels Good*, but shelved in favor of the subsequent *From Langley Park to Memphis*; it finally surfaced to little fanfare in 1989, appearing almost as mysteriously as it was abandoned four years earlier. It's a wonderful record, but perhaps too close in sound and spirit to *Steve McQueen* for comfort—*From Langley Park*, for all its flaws, is a much more adventurous effort, and with the benefit of hindsight, it seems reasonable to assume that Paddy McAloon wished not to stick with the tried-and-true but instead attempt something new and different, successful or not. That said, fans who loved *Steve McQueen* and its gossamer pop beauty will find much to savor here—songs like "A Life of Surprises," "Talking Scarlet" and "Diana" (the latter an evocative portrait of the late "people's princess" and her effect on British society) rank alongside McAloon's finest, informed by the stately grace and ingenious wit which remain the hallmarks of every Prefab Sprout record. By no means a lost masterpiece, it's still an essential piece of the puzzle. *—Jason Ankeny*

Jordan: The Comeback / Sep. 1990 / Epic ✦✦✦✦✦
Jordan: The Comeback is Prefab Sprout's largely successful attempt to embrace the breadth of popular music; wisely reuniting with producer Thomas Dolby, Paddy McAloon freely indulges his myriad ambitions and obsessions to weave a dense, finely textured tapestry closer in spirit and construction to a lavish Broadway musical than to the conventional rock concept LP. Over the course of no less than 19 tracks, McAloon chases his twin preoccupations of religion and celebrity, creating a loose thematic canvas perfect for his expanding musical palette; quickly dispensing with common pop idioms, the album moves from tracks like the samba-styled "Carnival 2000" to the self-explanatory "Jesse James Symphony" and its companion piece "Jesse James Bolero" with remarkable dexterity. Dolby's atmospheric production lends an even greater visual dimension to the songs, which—with their tightly constructed narratives and occasional spoken-word passages—seem almost destined to someday reach the stage; indeed, *Jordan: The Comeback* is like an original cast recording minus the actors, or a rock opera without the silliness and bombast—a truly inspired work. *—Jason Ankeny*

● **A Life of Surprises: The Best of Prefab Sprout** / Oct. 6, 1992 / Epic ✦✦✦✦✦
This hits package offers a well-chosen set and two previously unreleased tracks, "The Sound of Crying" and "If You Don't Love Me." The 16 tracks draw more selections from the *From Langley Park to Memphis* LP than the other albums, but this is a good single-disc introduction to Prefab Sprout's music. *—Scott Bultman*

Andromeda Heights / 1997 / Epic ✦✦✦
Due to Paddy McAloon's obsessive perfectionism, *Andromeda Heights* was the first Prefab Sprout album in seven years. Of course, it was greeted with anticipation, but the album doesn't quite fulfill the hopes of the group's fervent followers. On one hand, it doesn't deliver enough after the sweeping *Jordan: The Comeback*, since it is just a collection of 12 well-crafted songs. On the other hand, the sound of *Andromeda Heights* is so similar to all of Prefab Sprout's previous albums, it's hard to believe that it took McAloon so long to write the album. Even with these faults, *Andromeda Heights* is a solid Prefab Sprout record, filled with elegant melodies, wry lyrics and immaculate production, but after seven years, that nevertheless ranks as a disappointment. *—Stephen Thomas Erlewine*

● **The Collection** / Feb. 13, 2001 / Epic/Legacy ✦✦✦✦✦
A belated American release of a two-disc set released in England in 1999 as *The 38-Carat Collection*, *The Collection* is a sublime overview of Prefab Sprout's remarkable career. Disc one is all of the group's singles (minus 1983's "The Devil Has All the Best Tunes"), beginning with their self-released 1982 debut, "Lions in My Own Garden (Exit Someone)," and continuing through 1997's Beatles tribute "Electric Guitars." The decade-and-a-half's worth of singles chart Paddy McAloon's growth from an Elvis Costello disciple with a fondness for obscure religious metaphors to a gifted songsmith in his own right, whose occasional comparisons to Cole Porter and Paul McCartney are more than deserved. Whether as simple as the rueful adolescent misery of "Johnny Johnny" (called "Goodbye Lucille #1" on 1985's *Steve McQueen*) or as lush as the richly symphonic "We Let the Stars Go," these songs are brilliantly melodic and lyrically evocative gems. The second disc proves that McAloon's album tracks are in many cases better than his singles. Culling two to four tracks from each of Prefab Sprout's six 1984-1997 albums, this disc covers McAloon's more challenging or non-commercial material, from the opaque, knotty "Cue Fanfare" to the glorious "Andromeda Heights," possibly the most genuinely beautiful song of the group's oeuvre. Though no collection can truly cover all of Prefab Sprout's high points—at least three of their albums, *Swoon*, *Steve McQueen*, and *Jordan: The Comeback*, are simply essential—this set is much better than 1992's single-disc compilation *A Life of Surprises*, and it contains several songs from 1989's *Protest Songs* and 1997's *Andromeda Heights*, neither of which were ever released in the United States. *—Stewart Mason*

Sam Prekop

Vocals, Guitar / Indie Rock, Post-Rock/Experimental
A longtime pillar in the Chicago underground community and architect of the post-rock sound, Sam Prekop first gained notoriety at the helm of Shrimp Boat before becoming the leader of the Sea and Cake, whose fusion of styles both in and out of rock was both creative and experimental while remaining highly listenable. Prekop holds considerable stature in the Chicago scene, so it isn't surprising that when he released his self-titled debut solo LP in 1999 (on Thrill Jockey Records, themselves cornerstones in Chicago's music) it featured an impressive supporting cast, including Chad Taylor of the Chicago Underground Duo, Josh Abrams of Town and Country, Jim O'Rourke and the Sea and Cake's Archer Prewitt. The album played like a subtler, more organic version of the Sea and Cake, blending elements of African rhythms with soul, jazz and pop. *—Stacia Proefrock*

Sam Prekop / Feb. 9, 1999 / Thrill Jockey ✦✦✦✦
While Sam Prekop's primary creative outlet, the Sea & Cake, continues to incorporate studio technology more and more into its sound, Prekop's self-titled solo album thrives in a more organic environment. Recorded in Chicago with ex-Gastr Del Sol guitarist, Jim O'Rourke, behind the board, the album sports a vibe that's loose and inviting, especially on the more up-beat tracks like the bossa-nova bopping opener, "Showrooms," and funky "The Company." Prekop sticks with what has become his trademark: breathy, falsetto-tinged vocals and tenderly delivered lyrics. "On Such Favors" recalls the intimacy of the Velvet Underground, its languid mood marked by simple, reverberating chords. The sweet, piano-brushed "Practice Twice," and the Brazilified "The Shadow" are also highlights. Instead of calling on the prominent synth-flavored rhythms of the Sea & Cake's last album, Prekop opts here for a straight-up jazz drummer (Chicago Underground Duo's Chad Taylor) and an upright bassist (Josh Abrams) to flesh out his songs. TSAC guitarist, Archer Prewitt, plays clean, economical counterpoint to Prekop's melodies, while O'Rourke and cornetist Rob Mazurek color the empty spaces with subtle and sundry accompaniments. TSAC/Tortoise percussionist, John McEntire, even turns up playing triangle and maracas on a few cuts. O'Rourke doesn't intrude too much, although some of his stock production tactics surface on the Gastr-flavored intro of "Don't Bother," as well as the loopy, jazzed-out instrumental, "Faces and People." Mazurek's long horn tones are especially effective on the latter. In all, this a lovely, understated pop album that reveals its many charms on repeated listens. *—Jonathan Cohen*

Presidents of the United States of America

f. 1990, **db.** 1998
Comedy Rock, Punk-Pop, Post-Grunge, Alternative Pop/Rock, Grunge
Presidents of the United States of America were one of the most unlikely success stories of the post-grunge alternative rock scene in Seattle. Where the rest of their Seattle brethren traded in heavy guitars and heavy angst, the Presidents rejected torment for humor, writing short, simple and absurd punk songs that relied more on goofy attitude than sludgy riffs and tormented screams. It was a formula that worked, as the group's self-titled debut album became a double-platinum record much to the surprise of many critics, music industry insiders and the band itself.

Childhood friends Chris Ballew (lead vocals, two string basitar) and Dave Dederer (three-string guitbass, backing vocals) played in a number of groups and projects before forming the Presidents of the United States of America around 1990. The duo recorded a demo tape, which began circulating around the Seattle musical community and, in the process, earning them a cult following. Drummer Jason Finn, a member of Love Battery, saw the duo in 1991 and, after a few years of persuading, joined the band in 1993. Within a year after Finn joined, the Presidents became one of the most popular bands in Seattle. In the spring of 1994, they released their eponymous debut album on Pop Llama Records. The record became an independent hit and the band attracted the attention of major record labels; the group eventually signed with Columbia Records, who re-released the Presidents' debut in the spring of 1995. By this time, Finn had left Love Battery to become a full-time President.

The Presidents of the United States of America became a hit in the summer of 1995, when MTV and modern rock radio began airing "Lump" frequently. "Lump," followed by the radio hit "Kitty" in the fall and the radio/video hit "Peaches" in the spring of 1996, propelled the album to a surprise Top Ten, double-platinum status. The band quickly capitalized on their sudden success by releasing their second album, *The Presidents of the United States of America: II*, in November of 1996.

In December of 1997, the Presidents called it quits after Chris Ballew left the band to spend more time with his family. A farewell concert followed in February 1998 and a rarities album, *Pure Frosting*, was released in March. Rumors of a possible reunion and collaboration with fellow Seattle resident Sir Mix-a-Lot (under the collective name Subset) floated around in 1999, but the project never materialized. However, the band did reconvene in 2000 (without a rapper) under the officially shortened moniker the

Presidents, and released their third album, *Freaked Out and Small.* —*Stephen Thomas Erlewine*

● **Presidents of the United States of America** / 1995 / Columbia ✦✦✦✦
In the time-honored tradition of the Dickies, the punk-pop of the Presidents of the United States of America is brief, hooky, and dumb—it's novelty punk. Granted, that approach can occasionally produce a couple of naggingly catchy songs—particularly their breakthrough hit, "Lump"—but it basically results in a series of smug, self-satisfied songs that are neither funny nor catchy. Like the Dickies, they're not much more than one-hit wonders. —*Stephen Thomas Erlewine*

Presidents of the United States of America 2 / Nov. 5, 1996 / Columbia ✦✦✦
Considering the speed of which their second album was delivered, the Presidents of the United States of America must have known their time in the spotlight was brief. Released exactly a year after "Lump" stormed the charts, *POTUSA 2* is just like the group's debut except not as consistently engaging. A few songs have strong hooks to rival those on the debut—particularly the two-chord rampage of "Mach 5"—but about half of the album sounds too labored and considered, especially the hyped-up They Might Be Giants homage "Volcano." So, *The Presidents of the United States 2* delivers everything that the second album from a one-hit wonder should do: it has a couple of pretty good singles intermixed with a bunch of tolerable filler that plays better as nostalgia than it did when it was currently released. —*Stephen Thomas Erlewine*

Pure Frosting / Mar. 10, 1998 / Columbia ✦✦✦
At the back of their minds, the Presidents of the United States of America—or at least their leader, Chris Ballew—always knew that they were essentially a one-hit wonder, even if that one hit was an album instead of a single. Being the jesters of grunge meant that their career had a limited shelf life, and once grunge had run its course, so had the Presidents. So, Ballew wisely pulled the plug after a commercially disappointing but musically solid second album, knowing that it would ultimately serve the band's memory better to put an end to the group instead of toiling on for years. As a consolation to fans and the record company, the band released *Pure Frosting,* a collection of B-sides, live cuts, outtakes and soundtrack contributions. It's just as goofy and sporadically entertaining as their two studio albums, with as many great moments—including their inspired cover of Ian Hunter's "Cleveland Rocks," which was used as the theme song for *The Drew Carey Show*—as there are downers. And even if these are rarities, there are enough catchy, humorous throwaways here to make it entertaining even for fans that aren't collectors. Of course, casual fans will have to wait for the inevitable hits compilation to get the one definitive Presidents album, but this is a nice addition for dedicated fans, and it's much better than some skeptics would expect. —*Stephen Thomas Erlewine*

Freaked Out and Small / Sep. 12, 2000 / MUSICBLITZ ✦✦✦✦

Elvis Presley (Elvis Aaron Presley)

b. Jan. 8, 1935, Tupelo, MS, **d.** Aug. 16, 1977, Memphis, TN
Vocals, Guitar / Pop/Rock, Pop, Rockabilly, Rock & Roll
Elvis Presley may be the single most important figure in American 20th-century popular music. Not necessarily the *best,* and certainly not the most consistent. But no one could argue that he was not the musician most responsible for popularizing rock & roll on an international level. Viewed in cold sales figures, his impact was phenomenal. Dozens upon dozens of international smashes from the mid-'50s to the mid-'70s, as well as the steady sales of his catalog and reissues since his death in 1977, may make him the single highest-selling performer in history. More important from a music lover's perspective, however, are his remarkable artistic achievements. Presley was not the very first White man to sing rhythm and blues; Bill Haley predated him in that regard, and there may have been others as well. Elvis was certainly the first, however, to assertively fuse country and blues music into the style known as rockabilly. While rockabilly arrangements were the foundations of his first (and possibly best) recordings, Presley could not have become a mainstream superstar without a much more varied palette that also incorporated pop, gospel, and even some bits of bluegrass and operatic schmaltz here and there. His 1950s recordings established the basic language of rock & roll; his explosive and sexual stage presence set standards for the music's visual image; his vocals were incredibly powerful and versatile. Unfortunately, to much of the public, Elvis is more icon than artist. Innumerable bad Hollywood movies, increasingly caricatured records and mannerisms, and a personal life that became steadily more sheltered from real-world concerns (and steadily more bizarre) gave his story a somewhat mythic status. By the time of his death, he'd become more a symbol of gross Americana than of cultural innovation. The continued speculation about his incredible career has sustained interest in his life, and supported a large tourist/entertainment industry, that may last indefinitely, even if the fascination is fueled more by his celebrity than his music. —*Richie Unterberger*

★ **Elvis Presley** / Mar. 1956 / RCA ✦✦✦✦✦
Today it all seems so easy—RCA signs up the kid from Memphis, television gets interested at around the same time, and the rest is history. The circumstances surrounding the music on this album were neither simple nor promising, however. A lot was unsettled and untried at the first of two groups of sessions that produced the songs on the *Elvis Presley* album—it wasn't even certain that there was any reason for a rock & roll artist to cut an album, because teenagers bought 45s, not LPs, and it was something of an inspiration on Steve Sholes' part that he was thinking of an LP release on Presley from his first RCA recording session. The January 10, 1956, Nashville session where the first of Elvis' RCA sides were cut yielded one song, "Heartbreak Hotel," that seemed a potential single, but which no one thought would sell, and a few tracks that would be good enough for an album, if there were one. Seventeen days later, "Heartbreak Hotel" was released, and for about a month it did nothing—then it began to move, and then Elvis Presley made his appearances on the Dorsey Brothers' show and *Milton Berle,* and had a number one pop single. The album Sholes wanted out of Elvis came from two groups of sessions in January and February, augmented by five previously unissued songs from the Sun library. This was as startling a debut record as any ever made, representing every side of Elvis' musical influences except gospel—rockabilly, blues, R&B, country, and pop were all here in an explosive and seductive combination. *Elvis Presley* became the first rock & roll album to reach the number one spot on the national charts, and RCA's first million-dollar-earning pop album. For the 1999 remastering, the sound was upgraded numerous steps, and the bonus tracks show just how far Presley's sound evolved in the space of only two months. —*Bruce Eder*

☆ **Elvis [1956]** / Oct. 1956 / RCA ✦✦✦✦✦
Elvis Presley's second album was really his first to be conceived and cut as an album—his debut long-player, *Elvis Presley,* although a brilliant record, was assembled from busted singles attempts and a quintet of Sun Records outtakes. The original *Elvis* LP opened with "Anyway You Want Me (That's How I Will Be)," Elvis' most mature and technically demanding song to date. Here and on the classic "Love Me," he displays glimpses of sophistication and control as a singer on this album that would increasingly drive his singing in years to come. The rhythm numbers include three Little Richard songs that he performs extremely well, most notably "Long Tall Sally," indicating either a strong preference by Elvis or a dearth of acceptable material brought to the September 1956 sessions by Steve Sholes. The surprises on this album include "Paralyzed," one of the lesser-known Otis Blackwell compositions, and Elvis' cover of Arthur Crudup's "So Glad You're Mine" (cut at Elvis' late-January 1956 RCA sessions, but unused), which would have been among any artist's top output during this period. The 1999 remastering, in addition to significantly improved sound on the existing tracks, extends the CD by eight songs including "Hound Dog" and "Don't Be Cruel," the two sides of the biggest selling single by anybody in 1956, which were cut at sessions overlapping the conception of this album, "Too Much" and "Playing for Keeps," which came from these sessions, and "Love Me Tender," which was cut at a session overlapping the making of this album. —*Bruce Eder*

Loving You / Jul. 1957 / RCA ✦✦✦
Purporting to be the soundtrack to Elvis' second film, this album collects songs used in the film on one side with new material on the other. The weakness of a couple of the movie tunes and the fact that the new songs were leftovers from the sessions used to produce Elvis' first gospel EP and latest single add up to his weakest album offering, although any album with "Got a Lot o' Living to Do" is alright. The 1997 CD remastering adds eight more songs, only three of them associated with the movie, which becomes sort of incidental to the whole album at that point. If you think of *Loving You* as simply an Elvis Presley album, rather than a somewhat misleadingly packaged soundtrack, it was actually one of his more coherent and cohesive long-players, assembled from sessions all conducted in the first two months of 1957. By this time, he was doing precious little that was wrong, and his range and control were growing geometrically—thus, amid some powerful rock & roll, including "Mean Woman Blues" (which could almost have passed for one of his Sun tracks), "Teddy Bear," the electric guitar-driven "Got a Lot 'o Livin' to Do," Ivory Joe Hunter's "I Need You So," and a hard, brittle-textured outtake of "I Beg of You," the King does some brilliant ballad singing on "One Night of Sin" and "Is It So Strange," and belts out one of his great blues performances on "When It Rains, It Really Pours"—which boasts a killer Scotty Moore guitar part—and moves into Sons of the Pioneers territory with the hauntingly beautiful Western ballad "Lonesome Cowboy." He doesn't do badly with "Blueberry Hill," either. —*Neal Umphred & Bruce Eder*

Elvis' Golden Records / Apr. 1958 / RCA ✦✦✦✦✦
This was rock & roll's first greatest-hits album, and it set the standard for all others to follow. As originally conceived, it was a 14-song collection of most of the King's biggest hits up to that time, released on the eve of his start of military service—a dearth of material being in the offing, it seemed only logical to assemble these hits. Each of the 14 songs had earned a gold-record award for a million sales, a record unequaled at that time by anyone else in rock & roll. The album wasn't intended as a history lesson, so "Hound Dog" and "Loving You" precede "Heartbreak Hotel"—the 1997 remastering also tampers with the concept a bit, adding six bonus tracks. Elvis' singing never sounded richer or more expressive, and one can fully appreciate in vivid detail the delicate nuances of his phrasing on songs like "Too Much." On the downside, the remastering has made the sound so clean on some of the harder songs that some of the raw, "dirty" ambience that characterized this stuff on the radio and the original 45s is lacking. Still, Scotty Moore's groundbreaking lead guitar part on "Hound Dog" and the Jordanaires' backup singing never came through more sharply or cleanly, and the all-important rhythm section is almost up front in the mix. Those who own the first Elvis box from RCA, covering the '50s masters, may hesitate to pick up this or the other parts of this latest remastered series, but the sound has been upgraded one more level, and *Golden Hits* does give a bite-sized glimpse of where Elvis had come from and where he was going (for better or worse) musically on the eve of heading into the Army. —*Bruce Eder*

King Creole / Aug. 1958 / RCA ✦✦✦
Apart from a few isolated, quirky efforts like *Flaming Star, Change of Habit,* and *Charro, King Creole* was the last of Elvis' serious movies, in which he was trying hard, pushing himself as an actor and, really, all through the score, as a musician. This is reflected in the soundtrack, which is one of the stronger film-related releases of his career. The original 11 songs included a hot title track by Jerry Leiber and Mike Stoller that was a dazzling showcase for Scotty Moore's and Tiny Timbrell's guitars as well as Elvis' intense, exciting

lead vocal. Leiber and Stoller's "Trouble" and Claude Demetrius' "Hard Headed Woman" have Moore's and Timbrell's electric guitars competing successfully with a five-man brass and reed section. Even "Dixieland Rock," if not up to the level of those other two numbers, features good playing and a strong performance by Presley, and "Young Dreams" is a decent mid-tempo number. The slow ballads are where the soundtrack falls flat, "As Long As I Have You" coming up to standard but "Lover Doll" and "Don't Ask Me Why" failing to excite or maintain interest; "Crawfish" can only have been included to bring the album up to the minimum acceptable length for an LP. The 1997 remastered CD features rather upgraded sound and seven additional numbers that are outtakes from the score; these include two alternate takes of "King Creole" with considerably different guitar and brass parts, and two superior alternate versions of "As Long As I Have You," both in a much more spare arrangement, plus a discarded alternate title track ("Danny"). The undubbed "Lover Doll" is superior to the released version, featuring Presley accompanied by a single acoustic guitar. Even with the bonus cuts, this CD only runs 34 minutes and change. —*Bruce Eder*

50,000,000 Elvis Fans Can't Be Wrong: Elvis' Golden Records, Vol. 2 / Dec. 1959 / RCA ✦✦✦✦✦

The release of this album, seen in its proper historical context, is an indicator of just how bright Elvis Presley's star shone in the late '50s. His first hits collection was issued in March 1958, on the eve of his going into the Army; his second was the first "volume two" greatest-hits album ever issued on a rock & roll star, appearing weeks ahead of his leaving the Army in March 1960. Anyone who buys the notion that Elvis was "tamed" during his first years at RCA will find revelation in "A Big Hunk of Love," "I Need Your Love Tonight" and "I Got Stung," some of the greatest pieces of hard rock & roll that the King ever cut—and all were recorded in the midst of Elvis' stay in the Army, in a hastily arranged session in Nashville during June 1958. The 1997 remastering works better on this material than it did on the earlier *Golden Hits*; the more expansive sound doesn't detract a bit from the power of the music, and the quality of Elvis' singing, coupled with his choice of material, was reaching its peak. By this time, his voice was becoming one of the finest instruments in rock & roll, his idolization of Dean Martin and other popular singers paying off with a degree of control and articulation that his rivals could only envy, and it's all laid out here on what are still some pretty hard-rocking sides. The remastered edition not only improves the sound significantly, but adds eight songs to the original ten. The notes are thorough, although they reveal the stretching that the producers were engaged in by citing British releases as the justification for inclusion. But the quality of the music is undeniable. —*Bruce Eder*

Elvis Is Back! / Apr. 1960 / RCA ✦✦✦✦✦

The 1999 remastering of this classic album features the complete contents of the March 20, 1960, RCA Hollywood session plus the dawn-to-dusk April 2 Nashville session that rounded out the album, for a total of 18 songs, including the three singles and their B-sides from those sessions. Although they have common recording origins, two of the three singles, "It's Now or Never" and "Are You Lonesome Tonight," were very quirky by the standards of Elvis songs at the time—the former inspired by Elvis' admiration for Tony Martin's 1949 hit "There's No Tomorrow," while the latter was recorded at the request of Col. Parker as a favor to his wife. They add to the diversity of sounds on this record, which shows a mature Elvis Presley. "Dirty, Dirty Feeling" and "It Feels So Right" showed he could still rock out and challenge authority and propriety, while "Reconsider Baby" and "Like a Baby" offer some of his best blues performances; but "The Thrill of Your Love" (a very gospel-tinged number), "Soldier Boy," "Girl of My Best Friend," and "Girl Next Door Went a' Walking," also displayed the rich, deep vocalizing that would challenge critics' expectations of Elvis Presley playing rhythm guitar throughout. He also comes off better than on any of his other albums since arriving at RCA, as a musician as much as a "star" (he'd always had a lot more to say about running his sessions than the critics who loathed his RCA years indicated). The sound on the 1999 remastering is extraordinarily close yet natural, giving the listener full value for the presence of Scotty Moore, Hank Garland (who also plays bass on a few tracks), D.J. Fontana, Boots Randolph, and Floyd Cramer. —*Bruce Eder*

G.I. Blues / Oct. 1960 / RCA ✦✦✦

Elvis was out of uniform in March and laying down vocals for his first big musical production in April. The confections that make up the soundtrack for *G.I. Blues* were the most trite collection of songs in his career, with the slight but affecting "Wooden Heart" the standout. Still, Elvis' enthusiasm makes even the puff listenable; one can't imagine even considering listening to this music had any other singer on the planet recorded it. [The 1997 CD reissue adds 9 bonus tracks.] —*Neal Umphred*

Something for Everybody / Jun. 1961 / RCA ✦✦✦

Elvis Presley's third non-soundtrack post-Army album is, in many ways, his most interesting from those years, though nowhere near his best. *Something for Everybody* offers a tamer body of songs than *Elvis Is Back*, but also shows the effect of Presley's maturation—the voice is better than ever, and this is reflected in the arrangements, most of which are closer in spirit to the finely crafted pop symphonies of Roy Orbison than they are to any of Presley's earlier work. His ballad performances are impeccable, displaying a richness of intonation and delicacy of nuance that is downright seductive. Rather less successful are the rockers, including "I'm Coming Home," "Judy," and "Put the Blame on Me," which show a cooling of some of the white heat that Presley used to generate on the rhythm numbers. The one moment where the old Elvis Presley manifests himself is "I Want You With Me," a shouter that's only missing maybe a Gene Vincent-style scream or two from the backing band on the choruses. The 1999 remastered edition of the album is augmented with six extra tracks that turn that version of *Something for Everybody* into a much harder rocking record, with rhythm numbers like "I Feel So Bad," "(Marie's the

Name) His Latest Flame," and "Little Sister" that generally are far more successful than those on the original LP. Even at 18 songs, the remastered version only runs 40 minutes, but the skimpy running time is dominated by a brace of beautifully sung ballads and the sound of Elvis as a maturing but still exciting rocker. —*Bruce Eder*

Pot Luck with Elvis / Jun. 1962 / RCA ✦✦✦

One of the great ironies about *Pot Luck With Elvis* is its title, from which one could reasonably infer that it was a collection of leftovers. In fact, *Pot Luck* was Elvis Presley's last collection of new secular material recorded with a specific album release in mind until seven years later, and a lot less of a "pot luck" affair musically than any of the non-hits studio albums that were ever released of Elvis' material. The album is still a bit uneven, continuing the decline begun with *Something for Everybody*. While there are several excellent, continually underrated tracks ("Gonna Get Back Home Somehow," "Night Rider," "(Such An) Easy Question" and, of course, "Suspicion"), the quality of the songs is somewhat uneven, the ballads especially tending toward the lugubrious. The original release, which charted for 18 weeks and reached No. 4 at its peak, never registered as strongly with the public as his soundtracks of the period did, and this relative failure (the *Blue Hawaii* soundtrack having charted for more than a year, with months spent at No. 1) may have forced Presley and his manager to concentrate on film work from this point on, as a commercial necessity. The sad part of that decision was that *Pot Luck* was a great vehicle for Presley's voice as it was evolving—"She's Not You" brilliantly showcased the softer, more intense singing style that had manifested itself just a few months earlier with "Can't Help Falling In Love." The 1999 remastering benefits from superior sound and a 17-song lineup, reaching back to March 1961 for its songs, including the gorgeous "Fountain of Love" and the haunting, gospel-like "That's Someone You Never Forget," which was co-authored by Presley and is one of his best non-hit songs of this era. —*Bruce Eder & Neal Umphred*

Elvis' Golden Records, Vol. 3 / Sep. 1964 / RCA ✦✦✦✦✦

The original *Elvis' Golden Records, Vol. 3* was, like its predecessors, an unprecedented release—no one in rock & roll up to that point, other than Elvis, had ever legitimately earned a second greatest-hits volume, much less a third. This is also the place where the legitimately softer, more mature Presley replaces the angry young Elvis represented on the first two volumes. On a sexual level, songs like "Stuck on You," "It's Now or Never," "Fame and Fortune," "I Gotta Know," and "Surrender" offer seduction rather than diverting violation. He might no longer have been a rebel, but as represented on the original ten songs of this album, he was still making the Top Five and even the top of the charts regularly with work that was legitimately fine early-'60s rock & roll and pop/rock. "His Latest Flame" or "Good Luck Charm" might not have been groundbreaking musical statements of the caliber of "Heartbreak Hotel" or "Blue Suede Shoes," but in Elvis' hands they were worth hearing over and over. The original 12 songs have been augmented by six more, including "Can't Help Falling in Love" (which should have been on this disc to begin with) and the hauntingly beautiful "Girl of My Best Friend," which was a number two hit in England (and may be the prettiest song Elvis ever cut), plus "Wild in the Country" and "Wooden Heart" (a hit in Europe) from *G.I. Blues*. The producers have stuck with the most tasteful and intriguing numbers from the films, within the time frame of the original release, the annotation is thorough, and the 1997 remastered sound runs circles around all prior editions. —*Bruce Eder*

Elvis' Gold Records, Vol. 4 / Feb. 1968 / RCA ✦✦✦✦✦

The fourth volume of *Elvis' Gold Records* was the first of his hits compilations to be issued at a point when Elvis Presley wasn't considered a very important rock & roll star anymore (a few months later he would embark on his network television "comeback"). Indeed, it appeared at a point when it seemed, as Neal Umphred pointed out, "Elvis' gold was drained up and he was reduced to filling up the fourth volume with B-sides." Covering the early '60s through the end of 1967, the original collection had the bad fortune to appear at a point when politics, international affairs and a generational change in the listening public all combined to render Elvis Presley seemingly irrelevant. A great deal of social and musical change had taken place while Elvis withdrew from concerts and television appearances, made his movies, and scarcely attempted the recording of any non-soundtrack albums. So at the time, the album's arrival and even its title might have seemed like a joke to a lot of observers. That having been said, there is some extraordinary music on *Gold Records Vol. 4*, especially in its remastered 18-song version. "Wooden Heart" and "Can't Help Falling in Love" have been moved from *Volume 4* to *Volume 3* in reconfiguring the *Elvis' Gold Records* series. The additional songs have been chosen with care and even some inspiration, the remastered sound is most impressive, and the notes are reasonably thorough. Pop-culture mavens may want to note the presence of the indirect Ed Wood connection here—"Rock-A-Hula" was co-written by Dolores Fuller, Wood's companion and collaborator during the period of *Glen or Glenda*. —*Bruce Eder*

Elvis TV Special / Dec. 1968 / RCA ✦✦✦✦✦

After years of making abysmal movies, Presley appeared before a live audience, scared to death. That he more than rose to the challenge is evidenced here, a masterly performance highlighted by the jam-session segment with DJ Fontana and Scotty Moore, where Presley plays electric guitar and knocks out drop-dead versions of "Baby, What You Want Me to Do" and "Tiger Man." —*Cub Koda*

★ From Elvis in Memphis / May 1969 / RCA ✦✦✦✦✦

After a 14-year absence from Memphis, Elvis Presley returned to cut what was certainly his greatest album (or, at least, a tie effort with his RCA debut LP from early 1956). The fact that *From Elvis in Memphis* came out as well as it did is something of a surprise, in retrospect—Presley had a backlog of songs he genuinely liked that he wanted to record and had heard some newer soul material that also attracted him, and none of it resembled the material that he'd been cutting since his last non-soundtrack album, six years earlier. And he'd just come off of the NBC television special which, although a lot of work, had led him to the realization that he could be as exciting and vital a performer in 1969 as he'd been a dozen years before. And for what was practically the last time, the singer cut his manager, Tom Parker, out of the equation, turning himself over to producer Chips Moman. The result was one of the greatest white soul albums (and one of the greatest soul albums) ever cut, with brief but considerable forays into country, pop, and blues as well. Presley sounds rejuvenated artistically throughout the dozen cuts off the original album, and he's supported by the best playing and back-up singing of his entire recording history. The spring 2000 remastered edition matches the sound quality on the two-CD set *Suspicious Minds*, but restores the original album's classic cover and song order, with six bonus tracks cut at the same sessions but only released as singles at the time. This disc proves that he not only came back—he was *better* than he'd ever been as a singer or stylist—and is an essential part of any music collection. —*Bruce Eder*

Elvis in Person (At the International Hotel, Las Vegas, NV) / Apr. 1970 / RCA ✦✦✦✦✦
When Elvis and the Colonel decided it was time to start appearing live again, they assembled a crackerjack band (featuring James Burton) and took on Vegas full-bore. Easily the King's best live album, *In Person at the International Hotel* featured a slew of hits, including "Johnny B. Goode," "My Babe," the "Mystery Train/Tiger Man" medley, and "Suspicious Minds." If the album had a flaw, it was its skimpy running time (36 minutes). We now know, from the unissued tracks from these same performances that were added to the remastered *On Stage (1970)*, that there was more to the repertory of those five days of August 1969 shows than is represented here; but the producers, limited to a single LP, faced a major problem: Should they weigh the tracks more toward his current repertory and recent singles, or toward his classic songs? The classic songs sort of won out, but in the decades since, those then-recent singles have risen in stature. Regardless of what they're playing, the band really rock throughout, and that's not just Burton—who sounds like he's wearing his fingers ragged as he puts a new edge on "Hound Dog," coming up with something different than, yet vaguely similar to, Scotty Moore's approach to the song in concert 14 years earlier—but also the entire guitar contingent of John Wilkinson and Charlie Hodge (not to mention Elvis himself, who strums along here and there) and the muscular rhythm section of bassist Jerry Scheff and drummer Ronnie Tutt. The vocal support by Hodge, Millie Kirkham, the Sweet Inspirations, and the Imperials is soaring and tasteful, never more so than on the album's seven-minute version of "Suspicious Minds" and the soaring finale, "Can't Help Falling in Love." —*Cub Koda & Bruce Eder*

On Stage: February 1970 / Jun. 1970 / RCA ✦✦✦✦
Elvis' second live album, partly cut at the International Hotel in Las Vegas in early 1970, is one of his most unfairly underrated releases. In its original form, it did seem a bit cheap, offering ten songs that weren't necessarily associated with Elvis Presley. By this time, he was adding covers of other artists' contemporary hits to his set, not to capitalize on their success but to keep his hand in contemporary music and show audiences of the era that he was capable of doing more than reprising his own 1950s and early-'60s songs. The critics failed to notice two things, however: Presley had the same first-rate band who had graced the previous tour, led by James Burton on guitar; when he performed Neil Diamond's "Sweet Caroline," Tony Joe White's "Polk Salad Annie," or (most especially) Del Shannon's "Runaway," he did them extremely well. "The Wonder of You" might not have been "That's All Right" or even "Heartbreak Hotel," but it was a towering performance by a singer who, even then, could run circles around virtually anyone in the business this side of Roy Orbison. The 1999 full-priced reissue not only improves the sound, but adds six songs (for a total of 16), four of them—"In the Ghetto," "Kentucky Rain," "Don't Cry Baby," and "Suspicious Minds"—recent Elvis Presley hits. Although he didn't do any of the songs from his movies or any of the early-1960s hits, he did those four, and that makes this CD essential for any Elvis fan who cares about his comeback or the best work that followed; it also makes this the perfect companion to the 1968 television comeback and the *Suspicious Minds* (aka *Memphis Record*) album. —*Bruce Eder*

Elvis' Worldwide 50 Gold Award Hits, Vol. 1, Part 1 & Part 2 / Aug. 1970 / RCA ✦✦✦✦✦
This two-disc deluxe set supplants the earlier vinyl and compact disc versions of this series. Here we have all of Elvis' singles that sold a million copies, from "Heartbreak Hotel" to "Suspicious Minds," with a bonus track thrown in from his best-selling interview EP *Elvis Sails*. The first 26 tracks on disc one are in the original mono, while everything on the second disc is in true stereo. No liner notes or recording information in the enclosed skimpy booklet; in this case, the music speaks for itself. —*Cub Koda*

That's the Way It Is / Dec. 1970 / RCA ✦✦✦✦✦
Possibly due to the retro, irony-filled vogue for easy listening giants like Burt Bacharach and—to a lesser extent—roots pop figures like Glen Campbell and Neil Diamond, Elvis Presley's Vegas-era recordings have been given new life after a cruel stretch of put downs by kitsch-wary critics. The praise is not just so much posing, though, since many of Elvis' live albums from this period, in particular, contain a substantial store of quality material—dinner-show horn charts, strings, grandstanding vocals, and all. This 1970 offering from Las Vegas proves to be one of his best (it's actually the soundtrack to Denis Sanders' documentary of Elvis' summer run at the International Hotel). Acting on his affinity for country-pop figures like Campbell and Mac Davis, Elvis especially shines on the slow to mid-tempo ballads "I Just Can't Help Believin'" and "Just Pretend" (both seamless blends of torch song glitz and contemporary rock elements). And to provide the requisite amount of sweat for those nightly towel giveaways, the King works out extra hard on showstoppers like "Patch It Up" and "You Don't Have to Say You Love Me." Throughout the album, Presley sounds as commanding and powerful as he ever would and gets optimal backing by well oiled, Nashville-to-L.A. session luminaries like guitarist James Burton, bassist Jerry Scheff, and drummer Ronnie Tutt (Aretha Franklin's '60s backup singers, the Sweet Inspirations, deserve special mention as well). Also available as a deluxe three-disc set (including expanded concert highlights and rehearsal takes), *That's the Way It Was* is essential listening for Elvis fans, both die-hard and casual. —*Stephen Cook*

☆ **Elvis Country (I'm 10,000 Years Old)** / Jan. 1971 / RCA ✦✦✦✦✦
Western swing, blues, countrypolitan, traditional country, gospel—if it was music that even brushed the airwaves of a Southern state, Elvis Presley at his best could make it his own, and Elvis was at his peak when he cut *Elvis Country*. Actually, Elvis Presley was positively on a roll at the time. A decade after the end of what were thought to be his prime years, he was singing an ever-widening repertory of songs with more passion and involvement than he'd shown since the end of the 1950s. What's more, his voice had achieved a peak of perfection as an instrument, acquiring a depth and richness, a beauty to go with its power at which even his best work of the early years had only hinted. And it all came together on *Elvis Country*, which has lots of country music on it but also a lot else. His greatest long-player of the 1970s, and one of his three or four best albums ever, *Elvis Country* was a record that he threw himself into with every bit of the passion displayed on the better known, soul-oriented *From Elvis in Memphis*, and it was even more personal; he was cutting songs that he was either very impressed with at the moment or had loved for a lot of years, but they were all songs he cared about, which gives him a commanding and charismatic vocal presence. He doesn't necessarily supplant the originals, but he gives you more than enough reason to listen, again and again, to everything here. Producer Felton Jarvis and a cadre of Nashville sidemen (augmented by James Burton) provided backup as good as Presley ever got. —*Bruce Eder*

Aloha from Hawaii Via Satellite / Feb. 1973 / RCA ✦✦✦
Aloha from Hawaii Via Satellite is a double-album set that captures Elvis' celebrated live television concert from 1973. Arguably, it also captures the peak of the Presley live extravaganzas of the '70s. Spanning two albums and 30 songs, the record finds Elvis pulling out all the stops, running through a set that favors covers and new material at the expense of classics. That's hardly a complaint, since the whole point of his concerts in the '70s was a sensory onslaught, where a bluesy (albeit over-the-top) version of "C.C. Rider" could sit next to a schmaltzy show-stopper like "The American Trilogy." And the key to the whole thing is that Elvis actually sounds more committed to "The American Trilogy" than "C.C. Rider." That passion and energy is carried over to each song, and that's what makes the entire enterprise so entertaining. It's also why the record was a massive hit upon its release and why so many fans have fond memories of *Aloha from Hawaii* decades after the actual concert. —*Stephen Thomas Erlewine*

Promised Land / Jan. 1975 / RCA ✦✦✦✦
Promised Land came from the last recording sessions that Elvis Presley ever had in Memphis, the city where his fame and his legend started. The December 1973 Stax Records studio sessions showed him, as he had on *From Elvis in Memphis*, reaching out to publishers other than those he owed for songs, and the repertory embraces material by Chuck Berry, Waylon Jennings, and Larry Gatlin, among others. With the best players on hand and an upbeat mood when these songs were cut, and the singer himself lean and rested after a couple of years of concertizing, the vibes throughout this album were positive and then some. Elvis sounds bold and confident in ways that make this album a diverting, if not profoundly exciting experience. It's not as distinctive or as involved a personal document as *Elvis Country* or the concentrated soul workout of *From Elvis in Memphis*, but it does feature some fine passionate singing throughout (most notably on "It's Midnight," a wrenching performance). The eight bonus tracks on the spring 2000 remastering (in excellent sound) are drawn from the same sessions but originally appeared on the album *Good Times*. —*Bruce Eder*

Today / May 1975 / RCA ✦✦✦
Elvis Today is often cited by writers as Elvis' uncertain return to his Sun origins. There really isn't that much difference from the trio that resulted from 1973's Stax sessions, with the lesser tracks being a bit more substantial. The sound is better but the packaging had become, at this point, practically offensive: One color close-up after another, almost all from the *Aloha from Hawaii* special (or that pre-bloated period), back covers with no notes or technical data, just ads for other Presley Product. Still, an album with "Susan When She Tried," "T-R-O-U-B-L-E," and a hilariously appropriate reading of "I Can Help" is worth listening to any time. —*Neal Umphred*

From Elvis Presley Boulevard, Memphis, Tennessee / May 1976 / RCA ✦✦✦
By 1976 Elvis was recording at home in Graceland, cutting what would be the final recordings of his career. Filled with bathos and showing little rock & roll vitality, these remain interesting nonetheless, as it implied his accepting his age somewhat and attempting to combine old-fashioned, melodramatic soul with contemporary country-pop. While the pain and decay are evident—especially in hindsight—Elvis could still sing: "Hurt" is excellent, one of his best and, on "Danny Boy," Elvis reaches with an aching falsetto that closes the song, appropriately. Still, this is hardly the album to begin your collection with. —*Neal Umphred*

Moody Blue / Jul. 1977 / RCA ✦✦✦
The last Elvis Presley album released in the singer's lifetime, *Moody Blue* has a somewhat checkered history, especially among fans. Issued two months before Presley died, the album sold moderately well until Presley died—then it soared up the charts to number three, as his most current album, and it ultimately sold two million copies. As to the music, the original ten-song album was a mixed bag of live recordings, interspersed with new studio work from the previous fall at Graceland. For all of its slapped-together feel,

however, *Moody Blue* held up. The title song, authored by Mark James (who'd previously written "Suspicious Minds"), was just about as good a single as Elvis released in the 1970s, topping the country charts earlier in 1977; additionally, he did a superb re-interpretation of the George Jones hit "She Thinks I Still Care." "Little Darlin'" was almost more of a burlesque of the '50s rock & roll standard than a real performance, but it is more than made up for by the presence of the Johnny Ace classic "Pledging My Love," done with depth and sincerity. At the time, "Let Me Be There" was also on the album, drawn from the 1974 Memphis live album, but it has been removed from the spring 2000 CD remastering, with nine songs from a series of early February 1976 session substituting for it. Some of the 1976 material doesn't hold up as well, but the bonus tracks end this CD on a high note with Presley's rendition of the Tom Jones hit "I'll Never Fall in Love Again." The 24-bit remastering has added a good deal of luster to the 19 songs here, making this the first proper way to hear this material. *—Bruce Eder*

Elvis' Gold Records, Vol. 5 / 1984 / RCA ✦✦✦✦✦
Sixteen years after Elvis's *Gold Records Vol. 4*, and seven years after his death, came *Volume 5* in the series, courtesy of Joan Deary, the first RCA executive to take a sensible, intelligent approach to handling the Elvis Presley library. The original 10-song LP has been expanded to a 16-song CD. Later country chart hits like "Moody Blue" work well juxtaposed with numbers like "Suspicious Minds" and "Big Boss Man," and odd B-sides like "For The Heart" (which, as "Had A Dream," became the Judds' first hit in 1984), and Elvis' cover of "You Don't Have To Say You Love Me" doesn't seem out of place. The only real loser here (mostly thanks to its ponderous chorus) is "Edge of Reality," a song that originally showed up in the movie *Live A Little, Love A Little* as a psychedelic number in a dream sequence in which Elvis dances with a man in a great dane costume—even stripped of that image, it doesn't work as a song, and comes off even less well since it precedes the superb "Memories" and "If I Can Dream." The decade represented by the 16 songs on *Volume 5* show an Elvis Presley every bit as secure as an artist as the rebel represented on *Volumes 1* or *2*, searching for and generally finding a sound and an audience that could go together. *—Bruce Eder*

★ **Top Ten Hits** / 1987 / RCA ✦✦✦✦✦
The Top Ten Hits is exactly what it says it is—every Top Ten hit that Elvis Presley ever had during the course of his career, from "Heartbreak Hotel" in 1956 to "Burning Love" in 1972. Even though this double-disc set covers a lot of ground, there's a huge amount of terrific material that *isn't* included on the compilation. There's none of his Sun recordings, none of his gritty blues, none of his gospel, precious little of his country recordings, and many great singles for RCA aren't included. Still, the 38 songs on *The Top Ten Hits* are absolutely first-rate—there's no arguing with "I Want You, I Need You, I Love You," "Don't Be Cruel," "Hound Dog," "Love Me Tender," "Love Me," "All Shook Up," "Jailhouse Rock," "One Night," "A Fool Such As I," "(Marie's the Name) His Latest Flame," "Can't Help Falling In Love," "Little Sister," "Return to Sender," "Suspicious Minds," and many, many others. It's the perfect way to start an Elvis collection and, for many casual fans, the only set to own. *—Stephen Thomas Erlewine*

The Number One Hits / 1987 / RCA ✦✦✦✦✦
Number One Hits contains 18 #1 records from the charts of *Billboard*, who somehow didn't rank "Crying in the Chapel," "In the Ghetto," "Burning Love," and "Way Down" as chart-toppers, although other national surveys did. In fact, according to RCA, every copy of "Way Down" was sold out within days after Presley's death, not just here but all over the planet, and somehow, amazingly, it didn't even make the magazine's Top Ten! *—Neal Umphred*

☆ **The Memphis Record** / 1987 / RCA ✦✦✦✦✦
The Memphis Record was RCA's first serious effort to assemble the highlights of what is usually called Elvis Presley's comeback, but which, arguably, could be considered the best album sessions of his career. For the first time since the middle to late '50s, he went into the studio without "Colonel" Tom Parker, his manager, in control of the repertoire, and cut songs because they were good and he liked them, without regard for whether Elvis' business half had an interest in the publishing. The result was one of the greatest white R&B albums ever done, filled from beginning to end with some of the best work of Elvis' career: "Suspicious Minds," "Kentucky Rain," and "In the Ghetto" became hit singles and speak for themselves, but "Any Day Now," "Stranger in My Home Town," "Long Black Limousine," and "Only the Strong Survive," among the other cuts here, are the equal of anything he ever recorded in musical excellence, excitement, and intensity. This material, some of which was originally divided up between two separate LPs, *From Elvis in Memphis* and *Back In Memphis*, has since been recompiled yet again on *Suspicious Minds [1999]*, and that is the ultimate compilation of these songs, but this one is more than adequate for more casual fans who want a revelation or two (or three) in their listening. *—Bruce Eder*

☆ **The Complete Sun Sessions** / 1987 / RCA ✦✦✦✦✦
This is it, your perfect starting point to understanding how Elvis—as Howlin' Wolf so aptly put it—"made his *pull* from the blues." All the source points are there for the hearing; Arthur Crudup's "That's All Right (Mama)," Roy Brown's "Good Rockin' Tonight," Kokomo Arnold's "Milkcow Blues Boogie," Arthur Gunter's "Baby, Let's Play House," and Junior Parker's "Mystery Train." Modern day listeners coming to these recordings for the first time will want to reclassify this music into a million subgenres, with all the hyphens firmly in place. But what we ultimately have here is a young Elvis Presley, mixing elements of blues, gospel and hillbilly music together and getting ready to unleash its end result—rock & roll—on an unsuspecting world. *—Cub Koda*

☆ **The Million Dollar Quartet** / Feb. 1990 / RCA ✦✦✦✦✦
One of the most important things to remember about this album is it's really just three guys in a room shooting the breeze, goofing around, and stumbling through a few old songs they happen to remember. This wouldn't be the least bit interesting under most circumstances, but the three guys in question happen to be Elvis Presley, Jerry Lee Lewis, and Carl Perkins, which, as you might imagine, makes quite a difference. Perkins was doing a recording session at the Sun Records studio in Memphis on December 4, 1956, with Lewis playing piano on the date, when Elvis, in the midst of his first burst of fame and back in Memphis after a stretch of the road, stopped by to say hello. Elvis, Perkins, and Lewis began casually jamming—mostly on old gospel tunes they remembered from a shared Baptist upbringing—and Sam Phillips had the presence of mind to switch on the tape machine and record the proceedings. To call the performances casual taxes understatement, and if you were expecting the ultimate rockabilly moment from these guys, be aware it's about halfway through the session before rock & roll begins to rear its head, and even then it's obvious these guys can play "Farther Along" or "Down by the Riverside" off the top of their heads a lot more easily than "Brown Eyed Handsome Man" or "Too Much Monkey Business." But half the fun of this album is the playful casualness of the performances (and hearing three of rock's great legends in such non-legendary form). Like I said, just three guys goofing off—but from these three guys, "goofing off" is really something to hear. *—Mark Deming*

☆ **The King of Rock & Roll: The Complete 50's Masters** / Jun. 23, 1992 / RCA ✦✦✦✦✦
A casual Elvis fan wanting to assemble a decent overview of the King's '50s sides could probably sweat it down to the *Sun Sessions* CD and Volume 1 of the *Top Ten Hits* compilation. But for those of you who take your '50s Presley seriously, *The King of Rock & Roll—The Complete 50's Masters* is absolutely essential. For the hardcore Elvis fan, the booklet and CD graphics for this five-disc set provide incentive enough to justify its purchase. The liner notes by Presley expert Peter Guralnick are passionate, contagious in their enthusiasm, and filled with a real sense of history, time, and place. The treasure-trove of unpublished photos, session information and Elvis memorabilia accompanying the booklet text is no less inspiring. But it's the music (140 tracks in all) that's the real meat and potatoes of this set. Every studio track cut during the '50s—the seminal Sun sides, the early RCA hits, movie soundtracks, alternates, live performances, rarities (including both sides of the long-lost acetate he cut for his mother back in 1953)—it's all here in one gorgeous package. Soundwise, this box makes any of the previous issues of this material pale by comparison, the proper (non-reverbed) inclusion of the Sun masters being a particular treat. This is no mere rehash of what's been around a dozen times before—there's a lot of thought and care behind this package, and no serious fan of American rock & roll should consider a collection complete without it. *—Cub Koda*

☆ **From Nashville to Memphis: The Essential 60's Masters** / Sep. 28, 1993 / RCA ✦✦✦✦✦
Continues the tradition of first-quality sound remastering and packaging. Much of Elvis' '60s work is arguably not as essential as the '50s stuff, but this meticulous five-disc/130-track set makes an impressive case for the defense. A thick booklet contains riveting liner notes, full-color photos, complete discography and session listings; a sheet of RCA album cover stamps tops off the set. *—Roch Parisien*

Amazing Grace: His Greatest Sacred Songs / Oct. 25, 1994 / RCA ✦✦✦✦
Elvis recorded quite a bit of gospel over the course of his career, and this two-CD, 55-song set has the bulk of it. Most of this is drawn from his three gospel LPs (*His Hand in Mine*, 1960; *How Great Thou Art*, 1967; *He Touched Me*, 1972), as well as a 1957 EP. Presley was undoubtedly heavily influenced by gospel (at times he indicated regret at not having chosen to become a gospel singer), and this material has played pretty well with critics. Elvis sings with skill and reasonable commitment, and the backing musicians include such Elvis/Nashville standbys as Scotty Moore, Hank Garland, Floyd Cramer, Charlie McCoy, Pete Drake, the Jordanaires, and James Burton. At the same time, let's have a reality check here. Rock- and pop-oriented fans are going to find this two-and-a-half hour set tough going, unless they have a taste for spirituals as well. Things get a little more accessible when the tempos brighten, but often it's on the sedate side. For both collectors and listeners, highlights of the collection are five previously unreleased tracks from 1972. Recorded with only Charlie Hodges on piano and J.D. Sumner & the Stamps on backing vocals, they present Presley's gospel at its sparsest and most spontaneous. *—Richie Unterberger*

Command Performances: The Essential 60's Masters II / Jul. 18, 1995 / RCA ✦✦✦
Elvis Presley's 1960s film soundtracks are renowned as the repository of his most frivolous (many would say ridiculous) material. This 62-song, double CD draws from no less than 26 of those screen vehicles to present the "best" of these performances; the idea is to complement the first volume of *Essential 60's Masters*, which focused on his non-soundtrack recordings from the decade, and doesn't include any of the cuts from this collection. The goal of this package may have been to boil away the dross (as big as this is, there's a *lot* of stuff they left off). But if anything, it perhaps inadvertently demonstrates just how lousy most of those recordings were; even this selective, chronologically programmed set feels way too long, and could have probably been cut in length to a single CD without too much loss. That's not to say that what's here is entirely negligible. There are some classic singles ("Return to Sender," "Can't Help Falling in Love"), fair rockers ("What'd I Say," "Little Egypt"), and more than a few cuts that are transcendentally great/awful in their mindless silliness ("Rock-A-Hula Baby," "Viva Las Vegas," "Do the Clam"), songs which are archetypes, for better or worse, of the kitschiest facet of Presley's myth. But much of the rest is just unremarkable, or even bad: stupid novelties ("Poison Ivy League"), drab ballads, and many mediocre rock tunes. This doesn't include such legendarily idiotic tunes as "No Room to Rhumba in a Sports Car," "Yoga Is as Yoga Does," and "Fort Lauderdale Chamber of Commerce"; you can find those on the original soundtracks, or a famous bootleg, the aptly-titled *Elvis' Greatest Shit*. *—Richie Unterberger*

☆ **Walk a Mile in My Shoes: The Essential 70's Masters** / Oct. 10, 1995 / RCA ✦✦✦✦

In most conventional rock criticism, Elvis Presley's '70s records are considered his weakest, as they were recorded while he was falling deeper into drug addiction. However, as Dave Marsh argues in the liner notes of *Walk a Mile in My Shoes—The Essential 70's Masters*, the music on the five-CD box set is among the most personal and adventurous of Elvis' career, even if the individual albums don't always reflect that diversity. By cutting away all of the dross that accumulated over the decade and sequencing the songs in a logical, entertaining manner, *Walk a Mile in My Shoes* supports the argument. On the first two discs, all of the singles Presley released during the '70s are presented, and while there are a couple of weak numbers, the music stands as an impressive continuation of his artistic rebirth of the late '60s. —*Stephen Thomas Erlewine*

Elvis '56 / Mar. 5, 1996 / RCA ✦✦✦✦

Sure the music on here's great. How could it not be? It has 22 of his hottest tracks from his first year at RCA, including not only the hits "Heartbreak Hotel," "Hound Dog," "Don't Be Cruel," and "Too Much," but such noted early rockers as "My Baby Left Me," "Blue Suede Shoes," "Money Honey," and "So Glad You're Mine." From a collector's viewpoint, though, you have to wonder whether it was really necessary. The only previously unreleased item is a sparser earlier take of "Heartbreak Hotel." Everything else has been widely available (even on CD) for years, and it's a good bet that many of the Elvis fans who buy this already have virtually all of the contents on the *King of Rock & Roll* box set. —*Richie Unterberger*

★ **Sunrise** / Feb. 9, 1999 / RCA ✦✦✦✦

Elvis Presley's legendary recordings for Sun Records had been reissued many times before *Sunrise* appeared in early 1999, most notably in the 1987 collection *The Complete Sun Recordings*. Despite its title, *The Complete Sun Recordings* was missing a few odds and ends, plus its sequencing on CD was a little didactic, resulting in a repetitive listen. Those flaws are corrected on the exceptional *Sunrise*, a generous 38-song double-disc set that contains all of Elvis' Sun recordings, including alternate takes and several previously unreleased live performances. The compilers wisely decided to devote the first disc to the original takes, dedicating the second to alternate takes: six live cuts from 1955 and four private demos from 1953 and 1954. This sequencing emphasizes the brilliance of this music. Not only is listening to all 19 masters in a row quite breathtaking, but the second disc winds up as a revelatory experience, since it offers a kind of alternate history by following Elvis' pre-professional recordings from his Sun sessions to early live performances. As such, *Sunrise* is essential for the curious and the collector alike. —*Stephen Thomas Erlewine*

☆ **Suspicious Minds [1999]** / Apr. 13, 1999 / RCA ✦✦✦✦

Elvis Presley's comeback recordings from the late '60s are generally regarded as some of the finest music he ever made, not only because they proved he could still be exciting, but because they're musically diverse and emotionally rich. That was evident on *From Elvis in Memphis*, the first record released from his landmark sessions of 1968 and 1969, and latter-day compilations like *The Memphis Record* made clear how deep those recordings were. Twelve years after *The Memphis Record*, the double-disc set *Suspicious Minds* was released, and it stands as the definitive overview of these sessions. All of the familiar hits are here, of course, but for collectors, what makes this essential is that it not only contains all the master takes, but it provides nine alternate takes of classics such as "True Love Travels on a Gravel Road," "Kentucky Rain," "Suspicious Minds," "In the Ghetto" and "I'm Movin' On." None of these are particularly revelatory, but they are interesting enough to be the icing on the cake on an exceptional collection. Since they're more concise, *The Memphis Record* or *From Elvis in Memphis* remain better bets for some listeners, but any true aficionado or rock historian will need to add *Suspicious Minds* to their collection. —*Stephen Thomas Erlewine*

Artist of the Century / Jul. 13, 1999 / RCA ✦✦✦✦

Elvis Presley doesn't really need more compilations—either single discs or box sets—in his catalog, but RCA's 1999 triple-disc set *Artist of the Century* does wind up filling a need, of sorts. Over the course of 75 tracks, nearly all of Elvis' most popular songs are presented in their original hit versions. Given the number of hits he had, plus the high quality of his recordings in the late '50s and late '60s, there are inevitably big songs missing, but many of his very biggest are here, and the first two discs, in particular, are quite strong (the late '60s/'70s selections slip somewhat, lacking such necessary items as "Kentucky Rain" and "Moody Blue"). So, this winds up being good one-stop shopping for those that just want one fairly comprehensive Elvis set in their library—although you should be forewarned that "fairly" is the key word in that statement, since this will not contain all the hits or necessary recordings. —*Stephen Thomas Erlewine*

Can't Help Falling in Love: The Hollywood Hits / Sep. 14, 1999 / RCA ✦✦✦

Can't Help Falling in Love: The Hollywood Hits compiles 22 hit singles that were originally featured on soundtracks for films starring Elvis Presley. Where the double-disc set *Command Performances: The Essential 60's Masters II* concentrated on the '60s, specifically the cream of what was not on the five-disc box *From Nashville to Memphis*, this compilation draws from a random selection of movies Elvis made between 1956 and 1972. That's not necessarily a bad thing, even if the sequencing is also at random, since these featured songs are usually either quite good ("Jailhouse Rock," "Loving You," "King Creole," "Return to Sender," "Viva Las Vegas") or are embarrassing guilty pleasures ("Bossa Nova Baby," "Rock-a-Hula Baby," etc.). So, this isn't a definitive collection of movie hits, nor does it have all the movie hits that a casual fan may want. It's simply a reasonably enjoyable Elvis collection, one among many others of the same stripe in his catalog. —*Stephen Thomas Erlewine*

Peace in the Valley: The Complete Gospel Recordings [Box Set] / Sep. 12, 2000 / RCA ✦✦✦

An expanded three-disc collection that attempts to trump a 1994 double-disc set (*Amazing Grace: His Greatest Sacred Songs*) by offering virtually every single Elvis recording of a sacred song, *Peace in the Valley: The Complete Gospel Recordings* accomplishes the mission in its title, but at a hefty price that won't appeal to any but the most obsessive-compulsive fan. Obviously, it includes each track from his three gospel LPs—1960's *His Hand in Mine*, 1967's *How Great Thou Art*, and 1972's *He Touched Me*—plus scattered alternate takes that are previously unreleased. The third disc is padded out with an array of Elvis' sacred recordings that are easily available elsewhere, like the 13 gospel tracks on the raw *Million Dollar Quartet* session recorded at Sun in 1956, the "Gospel Medley" from his 1968 TV Special, and a version of "(There'll Be) Peace in the Valley" originally aired on Ed Sullivan's television show. Though there's no doubt that *Peace in the Valley: The Complete Gospel Recordings* is a complete set, most Elvis fans will gain little from owning it. —*John Bush*

Billy Preston

b. Sep. 9, 1946, Houston, TX

Vocals, Keyboards, Piano, Organ / Pop-Soul, Soul

It's advantageous to get an early start on your chosen career, but Billy Preston took the concept to extremes. By age ten he was playing keyboards with gospel diva Mahalia Jackson, and two years later, in 1958, he was featured in Hollywood's film bio of W. C. Handy, *St. Louis Blues*, as young Handy himself. Preston was a prodigy on organ and piano, recording during the early '60s for Vee-Jay and touring with Little Richard. He was a loose-limbed regular on the mid-'60s ABC TV series *Shindig*, proving his talent as both vocalist and pianist, and he built an enviable reputation as a session musician, even backing the Beatles on their *Let It Be* album. That impressive Beatles connection led to Preston's big break as a solo artist with his own Apple album, but it was his early-'70s soul smashes "Outa-Space" and the high-flying vocal "Will It Go Round in Circles" for A&M that put Preston on the permanent musical map. Sporting a humongous Afro and an omnipresent gap-toothed grin, Preston showed that his enduring gospel roots were never far removed from his joyous approach. —*Bill Dahl*

The Most Exciting Organ Ever / 1965 / Vee-Jay ✦✦✦✦

The Wildest Organ in Town! / 1966 / Capitol ✦✦✦

That's the Way God Planned It / 1969 / Apple ✦✦✦✦

The Best of Billy Preston / 1988 / A&M ✦✦✦✦

The singer/songwriter/producer/keyboardist extraordinare's greatest-hits set includes the number one pop singles "Will It Go Round in Circles'" and "Nothing From Nothing," as well as the number one R&B hits "Outa-Space" and "Space Race"; all were million sellers. The gentle ballad "You Are So Beautiful" was adapted into a gospel song. The included version of the gospel-ish bluesy ballad "I'm Really Gonna Miss You" is the single version and a different take than the one originally issued on *Whole New Thing*. A great showcase for Preston's massive talent. —*Ed Hogan*

● **Ultimate Collection** / Mar. 21, 2000 / Hip-O ✦✦✦

Hip-O's *Ultimate Collection* may not have the original hit recording of "That's the Way God Planned It," due to licensing restrictions (it was recorded for the Beatles ill-fated label, Apple), but that's about the only thing missing from this near-definitive single-disc set. Over the course of 20 tracks, the collection chronicles every one of Preston's hits, from the funky "Outa-Space," "Slaughter," and "Will It Go Round in Circles" to the smooth, quiet storm soul of his duets with Syreeta ("With You I'm Born Again," "Go for It," "One More Time for Love"). Since it's quite a transition between the two extremes, fans of either side of the spectrum may not enjoy everything here, but it's nevertheless a nearly flawless collection, providing an accurate portrait of Preston's career. It is true that the lesser-known hits aren't as compelling as the smash singles, but this is still an entertaining collection, regardless. —*Stephen Thomas Erlewine*

The Pretenders

f. 1978, London, England

Album Rock, Pop/Rock, New Wave, Hard Rock

Over the years, the Pretenders have become a vehicle for guitarist/vocalist Chrissie Hynde's songwriting, yet it was a full-fledged band when it was formed in the late '70s. With their initial records, the group crossed the bridge between punk/new wave and Top 40 pop more than any other band, recording a series of hard, spiky singles that were also melodic and immediately accessible. Hynde was an invigorating, sexy singer who bent the traditional male roles of rock & roll to her own liking, while guitarist James Honeyman-Scott created a sonic palate filled with suspended chords, effects pedals, and syncopated rhythms that proved remarkably influential over the next two decades. After Honeyman-Scott's death, the Pretenders became a more straightforward rock band, yet Hynde's semi-autobiographical songwriting and bracing determination meant that the group never became just another rock band, even when their music became smoother and more pop-oriented. —*Stephen Thomas Erlewine*

★ **Pretenders** / Jan. 19, 1980 / Sire ✦✦✦✦

Few rock & roll records rock as hard or with as much originality as the Pretenders' eponymous debut album. A sleek, stylish fusion of Stonesy rock & roll, new wave pop, and pure punk aggression, *Pretenders* is teeming with sharp hooks and a viciously cool attitude. Although Chrissie Hynde establishes herself as a forceful and distinctively feminine songwriter, the record isn't a singer/songwriter's tour de force—it's a rock & roll album, powered by a unique and aggressive band. Guitarist James Honeyman-Scott never plays conventional riffs or leads, and his phased, treated guitar gives new dimension to the pounding rhythms of "Precious," "Tattooed Love Boys," "Up the Neck," and "The Wait," as well as the more measured pop of "Kid," "Brass in Pocket," and "Mystery Achievement." He provides the perfect backing for Hynde and her tough, sexy swagger. Hynde doesn't fit into any conventional female rock stereotype, and neither do her songs, alternately displaying a steely exterior or a disarming emotional vulnerability. It's a deep, rewarding record, whose primary virtue is its sheer energy. *Pretenders* moves faster and harder than most rock records, delivering an endless series of melodies, hooks, and infectious rhythms in its 12 songs. Few albums, let alone debuts, are ever this astonishingly addictive. *—Stephen Thomas Erlewine*

Pretenders II / Aug. 15, 1981 / Sire ♦♦♦♦
The Pretenders' debut album was such a powerful, monumental record that its sequel was bound to be a bit of a disappointment, and *Pretenders II* is. Essentially, this album is an unabashed sequel, offering more of the same sound, attitude, and swagger, including titles that seem like rips on their predecessors and another Ray Davies cover. This gives the record a bit too much of a pat feeling, especially since the band seems to have a lost a bit of momentum—they don't rock as hard, Chrissie Hynde's songwriting isn't as consistent, James Honeyman-Scott isn't as inventive or clever. These all are disappointments, yet this first incarnation of the Pretenders was a tremendous band, and even if they offer diminished returns, it's still diminished returns on good material, and much of *Pretenders II* is quite enjoyable. Yes, it's a little slicker and more stylized than its predecessor, and, yes, there's a little bit of filler, yet any album where rockers as tough as "Message of Love" and "The Adultress" are balanced by a pop tune as lovely as "Talk of the Town" is hard to resist. And when you realize that this fantastic band only recorded two albums, you take that second album, warts and all, because the teaming of Hynde and Honeyman-Scott was one of the great pairs, and it's utterly thrilling to hear them together, even when the material isn't quite up to the high standards they set the first time around. *—Stephen Thomas Erlewine*

☆ **Learning to Crawl** / Jan. 21, 1984 / Sire ♦♦♦♦♦
Chrissie Hynde and drummer Martin Chambers reassembled the Pretenders in 1982, following the death of James Honeyman-Scott and the departure of bassist Pete Farndon. *Learning to Crawl*, appropriately, is the sound of a band coming to grips with loss and the responsibilities that come with maturity. Even though the subject matter is undeniably serious, the Pretenders rock with a vigorous energy that was missing on *Pretenders II*. It helps that Hynde's songs are among her best, of course. "Middle of the Road" encapsulates the contradictions in the album's main themes; "Back on the Chain Gang" is a moving tribute to Scott; "My City Was Gone" is a vicious attack on Reagan-era economic devastation; and the beautiful, ringing "2000 Miles" is one of the few rock & roll songs about Christmas to actually work. And while "Watching the Clothes" is a bit embarrassing, it isn't enough to stop *Learning to Crawl* from being one of the best rock & roll records of the early '80s. *—Stephen Thomas Erlewine*

Get Close / Nov. 1, 1986 / Sire ♦♦♦
By now, Hynde is writing songs to her child and taking on social issues. But the chiming guitars are gorgeous, and Hynde's caught-in-the-throat voice has never been more expressive. *—William Ruhlmann*

☆ **The Singles** / Nov. 17, 1987 / Sire ♦♦♦♦♦
The Pretenders burst on the scene in the early '80s with one of the most compelling presentations of rock & roll ever seen. This collection, which highlights their A and B sides up until the mid-'80s, shows that Chrissie Hynde and co-conspirators were true masters of the rock single. Tracks such as "Brass in Pocket," "Middle of the Road," and the highly underrated "Message of Love" are spectacularly performed, written, and produced. The early band, especially with James Honeyman-Scott's hook-laden guitar playing, was capable of miracles, and you'll find examples of that on virtually every cut. *—Matthew Greenwald*

Packed! / May 22, 1990 / Sire ♦♦
It may be true that Chrissie Hynde's songs on *Packed!* are the weakest in her career, but they are not the sole reason why the album is such a bland, uninspiring affair. In the hands of producer Mitchell Froom, Hynde's stylistic retreads become even more unfocused and lackluster. Froom's production lacks any edge, making the pleasant but pedestrian songs bland and featureless. Only a cover of Hendrix's "May This Be Love" and "When Will I See You," a collaboration with guitarist Johnny Marr, stand out admist the number of undistinguished tracks on *Packed!*. *—Stephen Thomas Erlewine*

Last of the Independents / May 10, 1994 / Sire ♦♦♦
Chrissie Hynde rebounded from the directionless *Packed!* with *Last of the Independents*, a tough album that proves she can mature without losing her edge. Most of the record crackles with the lean power of *Learning to Crawl*, occasionally stopping for a lushly-produced number recalling *Get Close*. Although the record goes on a little too long and there are a couple of weak songs, particularly the anthemic "I'm A Mother," *Last of the Independents* re-established Hynde as a powerful and insightful rocker. *—Stephen Thomas Erlewine*

The Isle of View / Oct. 24, 1995 / Warner Brothers ♦♦♦
An "unplugged" set without the MTV brand name, *The Isle of View* (say it fast a couple of times to catch the pun) presents songs by The Pretenders that already were the softest ones in their repertoire now played on acoustic guitars and backed by the Duke string quartet. Lead singer Chrissie Hynde's lyrics are slightly more discernible, and some of the songs are lovely. But they were to begin with, and Hynde and Co. have not really re-imagined them for the acoustic format. Rather than deliberately picking ballads, Hynde might have tried re-arranging some of her rockers to more interesting effect. Still, what's here is always pleasant and sometimes moving. *—William Ruhlmann*

Viva el Amor / Jun. 22, 1999 / Warner Brothers ♦♦♦♦
Since (at least) *Packed!* each new record from the Pretenders has been hailed as Chrissie Hynde's return to form (praise that was thrown at *Learning to Crawl*, by the way), and it's hard not to resist to say the same of *Viva El Amor!*, the seventh studio album from the Pretenders. So, we won't say that, even though it may be true. At the very least, *Viva El Amor!* is a very appealing, focused album from Hynde and Martin Chambers, their most consistent album in years. It's not just that the songs are uniformly good (Hynde's writing is sharp again, without seeming bitter or jaded), it's that the record sounds excellent—a clean, uncluttered production that enhances the muscular performances. For the first time since *Get Close*, there is a minimum of sentiment—the ballads are never saccharine, even when the melody is lovely—and Hynde resists her temptation for exaggerated metaphors or embarrassing phrases (even if her continuing fascination with bikers is puzzling). *Viva El Amor* never provides a knock-out punch, even on the level of "Night in My Veins," but it never lags in momentum, as many Pretenders records do. Hynde sounds committed and convincing on each song, turning the album into one of the best the group has ever made. *—Stephen Thomas Erlewine*

The Pretty Things

f. 1963, Kent, England, **db.** 1980
Freakbeat, British Psychedelia, Album Rock, Psychedelic, British Invasion, Prog-Rock/Art Rock, Hard Rock, Rock & Roll
Of all the original British Invasion groups, perhaps none is as underappreciated in the United States as the Pretty Things. Featuring the hoarse vocals of Mick Jagger-lookalike Phil May and the stinging leads of guitarist Dick Taylor (who actually played in early versions of the Rolling Stones with Jagger and Keith Richards), the Pretties recorded a clutch of raunchy R&B rockers in the mid-'60s that offer a punkier, rawer version of the early Stones' sound. Their first two albums, as well as a brace of fine major and minor British hits (of which "Don't Bring Me Down" and "Honey I Need" were the biggest), feature first-rate original material and covers, and remain the group's most exciting and influential recordings. Unfortunately, they remained virtually unknown to American audiences. After their initial run of success, the group took a sharp left turn into psychedelia with the orchestrated album *Emotions* (1967), impressive singles that owed more to Pink Floyd than Bo Diddley, and, most significantly, *S.F. Sorrow* (1968). The first rock opera, *S.F. Sorrow* was a major influence upon Pete Townshend, who released his much more successful opera, *Tommy*, with the Who the following year. *—Richie Unterberger*

The Pretty Things [US] / 1965 / Fontana ♦♦♦♦♦
The Pretty Things' debut was one of the prime cuts of early British R&B, featuring such definitively raunchy exponents of the genre as "Roadrunner," "Big City," "Pretty Thing," and "Honey I Need." A couple of weak jams prevent the album from ranking as a true classic. The American version differed slightly from the UK version of the record, which took off four tracks and substituted four others. The 1998 CD reissue on Snapper, however (issued in both the US and UK), is the definitive edition of the album, as it includes all of the tracks from the American and British versions of the LP, as well as "Big Boss Man" (the B-side of their first single) and the outtake "Get Yourself Home," which was not released in the 1960s. A couple of tracks that originally only appeared on the 1965 UK version of the album ("Mama, Keep Your Big Mouth Shut," "She's Fine, She's Mine") are particularly essential to rounding out the picture of the band as they sounded at their outset, so the Snapper CD is now the configuration to get. [Half of the songs from that CD are on the *Get a Buzz* compilation.] *–Richie Unterberger*

Get the Picture? / Dec. 1965 / Original Masters ♦♦♦♦♦
The band's second album (released Dec. 1965) has not only been remastered from original session tapes, so the group sound like their amps are practically right in your lap, but it's also been expanded to 18 songs with the addition of tracks cut for singles and EP releases from the same sessions. That's enough to recommend it even to casual fans—this is now a record that's just a few notches short of Rolling Stones level in the charisma department and pretty tough any way you want to look at it. On "Rainin' in My Heart," they sound exactly like the Stones from the same era, missing only the little harmonica flourish that might have been added on the break. The notes go into the history of the group during this period in delightful detail, and the histories of various songs, most particularly "L.S.D.," which, amazingly, was cut as a demo and never re-done for release, just put out that way. In their good moments here, the Pretty Things approach Rolling Stones territory, and even in their off moments they're flying at the same level as the Kinks' album tracks. The real enhancement, alas, only concerns those fans with CD-ROM drives (PC Windows 3.1 or later, minimum 486 66Mhz or Mac 68040 or better, running system 7.1 or later)—they get to see the Pretty Things playing the 100 Club in London from 1965, looking wilder and scruffier than the Stones or almost any other benchmark band. *—Bruce Eder*

Emotions / 1967 / Original Masters ♦♦♦♦
In accordance with their label's (and not the band's) wishes, the Pretties were teamed with a middle-aged orchestra directed by Reg Tilsley on this album, which saw the Phil May-Dick Taylor songwriting team making an effort to move beyond R&B knockoffs into more sophisticated territory. Sometimes the arrangements (dubbed onto tracks without much involvement from the group) worked; more often, they were an unnecessary hindrance. An interesting failure, it contained some genuinely top-rank originals that saw the group expanding their vision into social observation and tentative psychedelia, including "My Time," "The Sun," and especially the moody, folk-rock-ish "Death of a Socialite." The CD reissue on Snapper adds the 1966 singles "House in the Country" (a Kinks cover) and "Progress," neither of which were that great, and five tracks from

Emotions that are stripped of their infamous brass and string overdubs. Note that these versions are not identical to the ones which appear on the *Pure and Pretty* bootleg, which has a couple of overdub-less *Emotions* cuts ("Out in the Night" and "Bright Lights of the City") that do not appear on the expanded *Emotions* CD in overdub-less versions. *—Richie Unterberger*

S.F. Sorrow / 1968 / Original Masters ♦♦♦♦
No amount of scrutiny can disguise the fact that this rock opera—built around a short story by Phil May—is ultimately a bit of a confusing effort. Although it may have helped inspire *Tommy*, it is, simply, not nearly as good. That said, it was first, and has quite a few nifty ideas and production touches. The CD reissue on Snapper adds four valuable songs from their 1967-68 singles ("Defecting Grey," "Mr. Evasion," "Talkin' About the Good Times" and "Walking Through My Dreams"). This version of "Defecting Grey" is the original, long, uncut five-minute rendition, and not of trivial importance; it's superior to the shorter one used on the official single. *—Richie Unterberger*

Parachute / 1970 / Demon ♦♦♦
If *S.F. Sorrow* is the Pretty Things' *Sgt. Pepper, Magical Mystery Tour* and *Yellow Submarine* wrapped in one, then *Parachute* is their more succinct *White Album* and *Abbey Road*. It's not just a timeline comparison. The Pretties made this fascinating LP in the same studio as the Fab Four, London's Abbey Road, with Beatles engineer Norman Smith producing; "The Good Mr. Square" replicates the three-part harmony the Beatles were so proud of on "Because"; two songs later, the group assembles a brief, interconnected three-song "suite" like the famous ones on side two of *Abbey Road*; bassist Wally Allen's vocals on tracks such as "Sickle Clowns" have the same throaty, mad anguish that John Lennon exhibited on "Yer Blues" and "Happiness is a Warm Gun." If *S.F. Sorrow* is hard-rock grandeur, then *Parachute* is its more bitter twist, the dream dying, and the witching hour upon us. Yet if this isn't as much of a triumph, the creative neurons are still firing throughout a multi-varied, cohesive LP.

Like *S.F. Sorrow*, it's a surprisingly palatable concept LP. This time the topic is a generation caught between the conflicting calls of (rural) peace, love, and boredom, and (urban) sophistication, sex, and squalor in a harsh world. Somehow the departure of the band's main creative force, Dick Taylor, didn't diminish the writing and inspired variety. Allen stepped up bigtime into the collaborator role with singer Phil May. The harmonies remain a strong point on an otherwise rock-inclined record, and the nasty edge of perfectly balanced bombast in the best songs have been a lost art ever since—it's not hard to see why *Rolling Stone* rated *Parachute* the best LP of 1970. [There are 18 minutes of good stuff tacked on the Snapper edition, taken from singles.] *–Jack Rabid, The Big Takeover*

Silk Torpedo / 1974 / Swan Song ♦♦♦
Long out of print, *Silk Torpedo* provides an interesting glance into the glam era. Beginning with "Dream"—a ghostly instrumental prelude that the group's friends in Led Zeppelin would later cop for "In the Evening"—this album launches into "Joey," a superb combination of piano boogie, crashing drums, and melodramatic choruses draped in Hammond organ. Phil May's vocals on this piece run somewhere between Ian Hunter and Steve Tyler, and are every bit as effective. "Maybe You Tried" is a glittering slice of glam rock, all pouting and hip-thrusting, with a simply killer guitar hook from Pete Tolson. From this strong start, though, the album falters into a torpid sort of introspection. Still, "Belfast Cowboys" deserves kudos for taking on the Irish question long before U2 was taking its first music lessons. The CD reissue adds live versions of "Singapore Silk Torpedo" and "Dream/Joey," both recorded in 1974. *—Paul Collins*

Savage Eye / 1975 / Swan Song ♦♦
The last album recorded by the Pretty Things before Phil May left; within months of this recording, the band split for a few years. Even more than *Silk Torpedo, Savage Eye* seemed to have been cannily devised with an eye toward picking up FM airplay in the U.S. There were hard rock, glam rock, and AOR rock influences from David Bowie, Queen, John Lennon, and Paul McCartney to be heard at various points, and while this album wasn't explicitly derivative of any of them, it didn't have much of a personality of its own either. It certainly didn't sound like the Pretty Things, for gosh sakes. And although it went to number 163 on the charts and was one of only two records by the band to chart in the States, it was one of their least memorable. The CD reissue on Snapper adds three bonus tracks: the 1976 single "Tonight" (probably the poppiest late-period Pretty Things cut) and two mediocre demos recorded without May, just prior to the group's dissolution. *—Richie Unterberger*

The Singles A's & B's / 1977 / Harvest ♦♦♦
Thirteen tracks from their progressive/psychedelic era, 1967-71. Of special interest is the non-LP 1967 single "Defecting Grey," a brilliant cop of Syd Barrett-era Pink Floyd. Its B-side ("Mr. Evasion") and the follow-up single "Talkin' About the Good Times"/"Walking Through My Dreams" were also non-LP, and also rank among the more coveted rarities of the early British psychedelic era. *—Richie Unterberger*

Electric Banana / 1991 / Repertoire ♦♦

● **Get a Buzz: The Best of the Fontana Years** / 1992 / Fontana ♦♦♦♦♦
It's missing a few good tracks, but this is a good retrospective of their British Invasion-era work, running through the 1967 *Emotions* LP. Includes all their major singles—"Rosalyn," "Don't Bring Me Down," "Honey I Need," "Midnight to Six Man," "Come See Me." *—Richie Unterberger*

On Air / 1992 / Dutch East India ♦♦

Rage . . . Before Beauty / Mar. 9, 1999 / Madfish ♦♦♦
The key to the success of the Pretty Things first studio recording in 19 years is that most of it sounds as if it were made during their mid-'60s heyday rather than at the time of their early '80s demise. It's downfall is overwrought, out-of-style songs like "Love Keeps Hanging On," which sounds like something the fictional band, Strange Fruit, would've come up with. Cover songs like "Eve of Destruction" and "Play with Fire" are completely redundant, yet the openers, the jangly guitar workout, "Passion of Love," and the Bo Diddley-beat tribute to an old bandmate, "Vivian Prince," make the disc worthwhile. *—Denise Sullivan*

Latest Writs: Greatest Hits / Feb. 22, 2000 / Madfish ♦♦♦♦
For whatever reason, Pretty Things failed to make significant inroads in the U.S. when the window of opportunity was open widest. Perhaps the Rolling Stones, the Who, and the Animals more than fulfilled the quota for invading bad boys. Maybe their sophomoric (and less than artistic) obsession with drugs played a role, though that's doubtful, given the preponderance of mind-altering substance cheerleading by '60s bands. Like the Stones, Pretty Things incorporated garage, R&B, and psychedelia into their aggressive style of rock & roll. Their most memorable songs were from their early, raunchier period like 1965's "Rosalyn," "Don't Bring Me Down" (both covered by David Bowie on *Pinups*), and "Come See Me." They evolved into a more psychedelic band later into the '60s as "SF Sorrow Is Born" and "LSD" will indicate, although "Old Man Going" from 1968 is a definite precursor to 1974-era Queen. The psychedelic and garage-tinged "Cries From the Midnight Circus" (1970) proves to be the final vestige of creativity from this collection, as all of the post-1970 selections are positively atrocious (or nondescript at best) rockers. *—Dave Sleger*

Archer Prewitt

b. Frankfort, KY

Vocals, Guitar / Indie Pop, Chamber Pop

Musician and illustrator Archer Prewitt was born and raised in Frankfort, KY, going on to attend art school in Kansas City. There he co-founded the Coctails, a now-legendary quartet whose eclectic, Martin Denny-inspired kitsch-pop predated the lounge revival movement by a good half-decade; the band relocated to Chicago in 1991, issuing four albums and a series of singles before disbanding with a farewell show on New Year's Eve, 1995. By that time, Prewitt was also ensconced as a member of the acclaimed post-rock combo the Sea and Cake; after completing the band's 1997 effort *The Fawn*, he returned to the studio to record his long-awaited solo debut, the outstanding *In the Sun*. *White Sky* followed two years later. In addition to his musical pursuits, Prewitt enjoyed success as a graphic artist—a onetime colorist for Marvel Comics, he also earned acclaim for his brilliant independent title *Sof' Boy*. A third release entitled *Gerroa Songs* was released in fall 2000. *—Jason Ankeny*

In the Sun / Apr. 29, 1997 / Hi-ball ♦♦♦♦
After distinguished tours of duty with lounge-pop pioneers the Coctails and post-rock innovators the Sea and Cake, Archer Prewitt finally steps out on his own with *In the Sun*, a buoyant and impeccably crafted record whose spare, gently insistent pop approach channels the creative spirit of his previous projects even as it stakes out territory entirely its own. While the slinky "Rush Hour" and "Work" offer up wry funk-pop grooves and the regal instrumental "You Walk By" anticipates the full-blown string and horn arrangements of the superior follow-up *White Sky*, by and large *In the Sun* maintains a simple, straightforward presence—Prewitt's clever melodies don't need much adornment to sink in, relying instead on his tasteful guitar leads and warm, intimate vocals. *—Jason Ankeny*

● **White Sky** / Oct. 12, 1999 / Carrot Top ♦♦♦♦♦
It's not that Archer Prewitt hasn't made excellent music in the past—his fine solo debut *In the Sun* aside, there are also a number of outstanding releases recorded with the Coctails and the Sea & Cake—but *White Sky* is a revelation nonetheless, a majestic, beautifully cinematic evocation of autumnal melancholia crafted with meticulous sophistication. With titles like "Summer's End," "Last Summer Days" (sequenced back-to-back, no less), and "Final Season," the album's thematic ambitions are fairly self-explanatory, but what's impressive is how vividly Prewitt captures the sad inevitability of time's passage; although always a gifted songwriter, on *White Sky* his skills as an arranger make a huge leap forward, with gorgeously forlorn strings and horns lending color and depth to his languid, spacious pop melodies. Even the most robust moments, like the opening "Raise on High" and the propulsive "Motorcycles," possess unexpected complexity and intricacy, but it's the epic centerpiece "Walking on the Farm" that reveals *White Sky*'s boldest ambitions, its bare-bones homespun melody blooming into an instrumental coda of magnificently pastoral grandeur. *—Jason Ankeny*

Gerroa Songs / Nov. 28, 2000 / Carrot Top ♦♦♦
Despite gutting everything that made the preceding *White Sky* so stunning—the epic melodies, the majestic string and horn arrangements, even the palpable sense of autumnal longing—Archer Prewitt's third solo effort is nevertheless fairly remarkable in its own right; recorded on an old reel-to-reel in a former nunnery in Australia, *Gerroa Songs* captures a simplicity and intimacy altogether new to Prewitt's oeuvre, revealing yet another dimension to a body of work hardly one-sided in the first place. The remote desolation of the seaside landscape haunts the record's eight songs like the ghosts that supposedly occupy the house where they were recorded; although strings and other subtle overdubs were later added upon Prewitt's return to Chicago, the clear focus is his poignant vocals and tastefully intricate guitar work. Much as *White Sky* brilliantly articulated the lost innocence of summers past, in crystallizing the still of the night so too does *Gerroa Songs* evoke its time and space with uncommon clarity. *—Jason Ankeny*

Alan Price

b. Apr. 19, 1941, Fatfield, Co. Durham, England
Producer, Vocals, Keyboards, Arranger, Piano / British Invasion, Rock & Roll

As the organist in the first Animals lineup, Alan Price was perhaps the most important instrumental contributor to their early run of hits. He left the group in 1965 after only a year or so of international success (he can be seen talking about his departure with Bob Dylan in the rockumentary *Don't Look Back*) to work on a solo career. Leading the Alan Price Set, he had a Top Ten British hit in 1966 with a reworking of "I Put a Spell on You," complete with Animals-ish organ breaks and bluesy vocals. His subsequent run of British hits between 1966 and 1968—"Hi-Lili-Hi-Lo," "Simon Smith and His Dancing Bear," "The House That Jack Built," and "Don't Stop the Carnival"—were in a much lighter vein, drawing from British music hall influences. "Simon Smith and His Dancing Bear," from 1967, was one of the first Randy Newman songs to gain international exposure, though Price's version—like all his British hits—went virtually unnoticed in the U.S. A versatile entertainer, Price collaborated with Georgie Fame, hosted TV shows, and scored plays in the years following the breakup of the Alan Price Set in 1968. He composed the score to Lindsay Anderson's *O Lucky Man!*, where his spare and droll songs served almost as a Greek chorus to the surreal, whimsical film (Price himself has a small role in the movie). His 1974 concept album, *Between Today and Yesterday*, was his most critically acclaimed work. —*Richie Unterberger*

● **Price Is Right** / 1968 / Parrot ✦✦✦✦

Though Price as a solo artist was unknown in the U.S. in the '60s, he did issue one stateside album that collected most of his British hits, as well as a few other tracks. Besides "I Put a Spell on You" (head and shoulders his best early performance), it has all of his other late-'60s U.K. hits, with the exception of "Don't Stop the Carnival." There are also a couple of serviceable originals, a nice version of the little-known Goffin-King item "On This Side of Goodbye," and no less than five early Randy Newman songs in all. Price was surely Newman's biggest booster at the time, running what amounted to a Randy Newman appreciation society on disc. An uneven effort, running from solid bluesy pop/rock to mawkish, chipper quasi-vaudeville (the latter quality, unfortunately, is typical of the Newman tunes here). It's a better assortment, though, than the only other representation of Price's '60s sides, *The World of Alan Price* (on Decca U.K.), which duplicates much of what's here. Both LPs, unfortunately, are pretty hard to find nowadays. —*Richie Unterberger*

The World of Alan Price / 1970 / Decca ✦✦✦

Best-of compilation of his '60s solo work, including all his hits. "I Put a Spell on You" is fabulous, one of the best British '60s hits that never made it big in the States. The rest is surprisingly disappointing good-timey pop, sometimes in a jazzy Georgie Fame mold, at times verging on vaudevillian. —*Richie Unterberger*

● **O Lucky Man** / 1973 / Warner Brothers ✦✦✦✦✦

Price's keyboard-dominated score to the Lindsay Anderson film works well on its own, with incisive tunes that dole out equal measures of cynicism and sympathy. The infectiously poignant "Poor People" is a highlight. —*Richie Unterberger*

Archive / Nov. 19, 1996 / Rialto ✦✦✦

Rialto's *Archive, Vol. 1* is a 20-track collection that balances original studio versions with latter-day re-recordings from Alan Price. There's enough prime material here to make it worth its budget price, but not enough to make it an effective introduction to Price. —*Stephen Thomas Erlewine*

Lloyd Price

b. Mar. 9, 1933, Kenner, LA
Vocals / New Orleans R&B, Rock & Roll, R&B

Not entirely content with being a 1950s R&B star on the strength of his immortal New Orleans classic "Lawdy Miss Clawdy," singer Lloyd Price yearned for massive pop acceptance. He found it, too, with a storming rock & roll reading of the ancient blues "Stagger Lee" and the unabashedly pop-slanted "Personality" and "I'm Gonna Get Married" (the latter pair sounding far removed indeed from his Crescent City beginnings). At his very first Specialty label date in 1952, Price sang his classic eight-bar blues "Lawdy Miss Clawdy" (its rolling piano intro courtesy of a moonlighting Fats Domino). It topped the R&B charts for an extended period, making Price a legitimate star before he was old enough to vote. Four more Specialty smashes followed—"Oooh, Oooh, Oooh," "Restless Heart," "Tell Me Pretty Baby," "Ain't It a Shame"—before Price was drafted into the Army and deposited most unhappily in Korea. "Stagger Lee," Price's adaptation of the old Crescent City lament "Stack-A-Lee," topped both the R&B and pop lists in 1958. By now, his sound was taking on more of a cosmopolitan bent, with massive horn sections and prominent pop background singers. Dick Clark insisted on toning down the violence inherent to the song's storyline for the squeaky-clean *American Bandstand* audience, accounting for the two different versions of the song you're likely to encounter on various reissues. After Price hit with another solid rocker, "Where Were You (On Our Wedding Day)?," in 1959, the heavy brass-and-choir sound became his trademark at ABC-Paramount. "Personality," "I'm Gonna Get Married," and "Come Into My Heart" all shot up the pop and R&B lists in 1959, and "Lady Luck" and "Question" followed suit in 1960. —*Bill Dahl*

★ **Lawdy!** / Aug. 5, 1991 / Specialty ✦✦✦✦✦

Lloyd Price was a teenager when he scored his first hit, "Lawdy Miss Clawdy," for Art Rupe's young Specialty imprint. Backed by trumpeter/arranger Dave Bartholomew's band (featuring special guest Fats Domino on the 88s), Price's song soared to the top of the R&B charts, scoring Rupe his first crossover hit by racking up sales among both white and black audiences. Though Price's time with Specialty was cut short when he was

drafted in 1953, he managed nearly 50 storming, pre-rock & roll sides for the label, 25 of which are gathered on *Lawdy*. Though nothing here was as big a hit as his debut, many of these songs easily could have come close were they selected over later Specialty smashes like "Ooh Ooh Ooh" or "Restless Heart." A shout singer with enough edge on his voice to be convincing (even as a teenager), Price's early style was tailor-made for the 45 format. With little thought to pacing himself, the singer seems to approach each number as if it may be his last time at the microphone and, therefore, his last chance at a hit. Though that sense is exactly what makes the music so thrilling, it's also what makes these 25 sides difficult to digest *en masse*. That said, for "Lawdy Miss Clawdy" alone this set is worth it, and the high quality of nearly everything else on hand makes for a desirable package of the singer's early work. —*Nathan Bush*

Heavy Dreams, Vol. 2 / 1993 / Specialty ✦✦✦✦✦

No discernible artistic dropoff on Specialty's encore Price retrospective, distinguished by his classics "Oooh-Oooh-Oooh," "Tell Me Pretty Baby," "Ain't It a Shame?" (not Fats Domino's hit), "Country Boy Rock," and "Why" (he later recut the latter for ABC-Paramount). —*Bill Dahl*

★ **Greatest Hits: The Original ABC-Paramount Recordings** / 1994 / MCA ✦✦✦✦✦

Chronicling Lloyd Price's tenure at ABC Paramount Records, the 18 tracks here include many of his best recordings. A choral group backs him, along with a large orchestra featuring a boisterous sax that goes berserk quite often. "Personality," "Lawdy Miss Clawdy," "I'm Gonna Get Married," and "Just Because" are everlasting. His most noted recording is "Stagger Lee"; the violent song about two gamblers comes in two versions: the unedited and the Bandstand version, as Dick Clark made Price clean up the lyrics. The song glorifies Stagger Lee, a cheat spot gambler who shoots and ultimately murders a guy named Billy over a dice game dispute—and people complain about gangsta rap! Price's energized, strident tenor is infectious; he loved recording and throws down on every track. —*Andrew Hamilton*

Lloyd Price Sings His Big Ten / Feb. 8, 1994 / Curb ✦✦✦✦✦

Like all standard Curb anthologies, this is too skimpy, numbering ten tracks. It does, however, include all of Price's major hits—"Stagger Lee," "Personality," "I'm Gonna Get Married," "Where Were You On Our Wedding Day," "Lady Luck." And in its favor, it also includes the most famous of his pre-ABC hits, "Lawdy Miss Clawdy." —*Richie Unterberger*

Primal Scream

f. 1984, Glasgow, Scotland
C-86, Electronica, Alternative Dance, Club/Dance, Acid House, Alternative Pop/Rock, House

Primal Scream's career could in many ways be read as a microcosm of British indie rock in the '80s and '90s. Bobby Gillespie formed the band in the mid-'80s while drumming for goth-tinged noise-rockers the Jesus & Mary Chain, who were the exact opposite of Primal Scream—the latter specialized in infectious, jangly pop on its early records. After a brief detour to punky hard rock, the group reinvented themselves as a dance band in the early '90s, following through on the pop and acid-house fusions of the Stone Roses and Happy Mondays. With the assistance of producers Andrew Weatherall and Hugo Nicholson, Primal Scream created the ultimate indie-pop and dance fusion album, *Screamadelica*, in 1991. *Screamadelica* broke down boundaries and changed the face of British pop music in the '90s, helping to make dance and techno acceptable to the rock mainstream. Instead of following through on the promise of the album, Primal Scream retreated to Stonesy boogie for their 1994 follow-up *Give Out But Don't Give Up*. When that record was greeted with indifference, they returned to dance-rock fusions with 1997's *Vanishing Point*, which re-established the group as a major force in British rock. —*Stephen Thomas Erlewine*

Sonic Flower Groove / Sep. 1987 / Elevation ✦✦✦

Primal Scream's debut album draws from a variety of influences, pulling together strands of '60s pop with psychedelia, noisy proto-punk, and the detached cool of the Velvet Underground. However, most of the album is only impressive conceptually, as the group didn't write enough solid hooks to make their fusions memorable. —*Stephen Thomas Erlewine*

Primal Scream / Sep. 1989 / Mercenary ✦✦✦

Primal Scream in 1989 confounded their fans and foes alike by growing their hair past their shoulders, buying Marshall amps and turning them up to 11 and by showing an alarming tendency to appear in public shirtless. Previously the Scream had been the most precious of Indie-Poppers, Byrds fans down to their fringed jackets and freshly-combed bowl haircuts. However their major label debut, a pristine pop record, was a big flop and after they booted out co-founder Jim Beattie, they were ready to fully embrace rock & roll and all the attitude and noise that came with it.

Out went the Byrds, in came the MC5 and Primal Scream was ready to rock. Unfortunately, while the group was capable of whipping up a credible approximation of thuggish hard rock, Bobby Gillespie's fragile wisp of a voice is rather ill-suited to kicking out the jams. The lyrics, while never a strong point for Primal Scream, are pretty embarrassing too. The song titles alone sound like they were borrowed from Jesse Camp's LP: "Gimme Gimme Teenage Head," "She Power," "Lone Star Girl"! What saves the record are the handful of slow torch songs. Bobby's shaky vocals are affecting and powerful, the band plays with a dramatically light touch and Martin Duffy's piano work is stellar. The best song here is "I'm Losing More Than I Ever Had," which is a soul-searching midtempo song with a great arrangement filled with slide guitar, horns and gospel backing singers. It also served as the basis for Andrew Weatherall's mix of "Loaded," the song that really made Primal Scream an important band and helped change the history of indie rock. So get this record for the history and try not to laugh too hard at the lyrics *—Tim Sendra*

★ **Screamadelica** / Oct. 8, 1991 / Sire ♦♦♦♦♦
There's no underestimating the importance of *Screamadelica*, the record that brought acid house, techno, and rave culture crashing into the British mainstream—an impact that rivaled that of Nirvana's *Nevermind*, the other 1991 release that changed rock. Prior to *Screamadelica*, Primal Scream were Stonesy classic rock revivalists with a penchant for Detroit rock. They retained those fascinations on *Screamadelica*—one listen to the Jimmy Miller-produced, Stephen Stills-rip "Movin' on Up" proves that—but they burst everything wide open here, turning rock inside out by marrying it to a gleeful rainbow of modern dance textures. This is such a brilliant, gutsy innovative record, so unlike anything the Scream did before, that it's little wonder that there's been much debate behind who is actually responsible for its grooves, especially since Andrew Weatherall is credited with production with eight of the tracks, and it's clearly in line with his work. Even if Primal Scream took credit for Weatherall's endeavors, that doesn't erase the fact that they shepherded this album, providing the ideas and impetus for this dubtastic, elastic, psychedelic exercise in deep house and neo-psychedelic. Like any dance music, this is tied to its era to a certain extent, but it transcends it due to its fierce imagination and how it doubles back on rock history, making the past present and vice versa. It was such a monumental step forward that Primal Scream stumbled before regaining their footing, but by that point, the innovations of *Screamadelica* had been absorbed by everyone from the underground to mainstream. There's little chance that this record will be as revolutionary to first-time listeners, but after its initial spin, the genius in its construction will become apparent—and it's that attention to detail that makes *Screamadelica* an album that transcends its time and influence. *—Stephen Thomas Erlewine*

Give Out But Don't Give Up / Mar. 1994 / Sire ♦♦♦
The rock undercurrents that ran throughout *Screamadelica* come to the forefront on the tired *Give out but Don't Give Up*. While Primal Scream turn out a couple of good songs, "Jailbird" and "(I'm Gonna) Cry Myself Blind," the band sounds too mannered to be a truly successful ripoff of The Stones and Faces. And the colorful, reckless experimentation of their previous album is sorely missed. *—Stephen Thomas Erlewine*

Vanishing Point / Jul. 7, 1997 / Sire/Reprise ♦♦♦♦♦
Primal Scream found themselves in danger of losing their hip audience in the wake of their misconceived trad-rock record, *Give Out but Don't Give Up*. As a reaction, they returned to the genre-bending, electronic dance-rock of the seminal *Screamadelica* for *Give Out*'s follow-up, *Vanishing Point*. Instead of recycling the dazzlingly bright neo-psychedelia of *Screamadelica*, Primal Scream reaches deep into cavernous dub and '60s pop. *Vanishing Point* is a dark, trippy album, filled with mind-bending rhythms and cinematic flourishes. The addition of former Stone Roses bassist Mani to the Scream gives their music an organically funky foundation that had been lacking. Over those rhythms are samples, reverbed guitars, and synthesizers that echo spy movies, Southern soul, and the Stones. Above anything else, *Vanishing Point* is about sound and groove. Words remain a weak point for Bobby Gillespie, who only manages cohesive lyrics on the swirling "Burning Wheel" and "Star," but that is a secondary concern, since Primal Scream is at its best when working the rhythms. Songs like "Kowaliski" and, in particular, the extended instrumentals of "Get Duffy" and "Trainspotting" illustrate that the group is still capable of creating exotic, thoroughly entrancing sounds, which is what makes *Vanshing Point* a remarkable comeback. *—Stephen Thomas Erlewine*

Echo Dek / Oct. 27, 1997 / Creation ♦♦♦♦
Released a mere three months after *Vanishing Point*, *Echo Dek* finds Primal Scream turning over the master tapes for the record to Adrian Sherwood, who remixes eight of the songs ("Stuka" is done twice) and takes them farther out into left-field territory. *Vanishing Point* was already quite adventurous, sinking deep into dub and ambient cocktail territory, but Sherwood confirms the experimental bent of the record with *Echo Dek*. Only a few songs are twisted beyond recognition, the rest simply follow the original versions to their logical conclusion, offering elastic grooves, disembodied vocals, and bottomless bass. Most remix albums are only of interest to hardcore fans, but Sherwood's clever, dynamic work makes *Echo Dek* of interest to anyone curious about contemporary late-'90s dance. *—Stephen Thomas Erlewine*

XTRMNTR / May 2, 2000 / Astralwerks ♦♦♦♦♦
Whenever indie music seems hopelessly self-righteous, unchallenging and inoffensive, Primal Scream rides in to try and save it all. *Screamadelica* tried to encapsulate the importance of ecstasy culture; *Vanishing Point* tried to exorcise their own insanity. *XTRMNTR* is a nasty, fierce realization of an entire world that has lost the plot. The album starts with a gloriously vindictive sample of a kid commanding "Kill All Hippies"; this roughly states the album's modus operandi. There are songs shouting with furious, feedback-splayed anger ("Blood Money," "Exterminator"), songs of club-based revolt (both house-influenced versions of "Swastika Eyes"), and songs of utterly manic desperation ("Accelerator"). But when lead singer Bobby Gillespie's weedy vocals can't keep up with the music, *XTRMNTR* falters, especially on the meandering "Insect Royalty" and the half-realized hip-hop "Pills"; Gillespie diminishes its power on every verse—it only saves itself when it delivers the album's central theme: "Sick fuck fuck sick fuck fuck sick fuck . . .". Thankfully, *XTRMNTR*'s highs, such as the gentle "Keep Your Dreams" (sounding like a sibling of 1991's "I'm Coming Down" or 1997's "Star"), and the monstrous, apocalyptic "MBV Arkestra (If They Move, Kill 'Em)," shower down with purely visceral poise. It's not the flawless statement against complacency the band intended, but it succeeds at tearing heads off, shooting fascists, and asking questions later with unbelievable fury. These aren't the aggro-simpleton maneuvers of Rage Against the Machine or Korn; the implosive production and sheer political belief prove that ingenuity must go hand in hand with "statement" if an idea is to come across effectively. *XTRMNTR* is simply a protest—sonically as well as lyrically—and maybe this would be a fine time to once again rally behind something worthwhile. *—Dean Carlson*

Primus

f. 1986
Alternative Metal, Funk Metal, Heavy Metal, Alternative Pop/Rock
Primus is all about Les Claypool; there isn't a moment on any of their other records where his bass isn't the main focal point of the music, with his vocals acting as a bizarre sideshow. Which isn't to deny guitarist Larry LaLonde or drummer Tim "Herb" Alexander any credit—no drummer could weave in and around Claypool's convoluted patterns as effortlessly as Alexander and few guitarists would as willingly push the spotlight away like LaLonde, so he can produce a never-ending spiral of avant-noise. All of this means that they are miles away from being another punk-funk combo like the Red Hot Chili Peppers; Claypool may slap and pop his bass, but there is little funk in the rhythm he and Alexander lay down. Instead, they're a post-punk Rush spiked with the sensibility and humor of Frank Zappa. Primus doesn't want to make you dance, they want to play music; songs are secondary to showcasing their instrumental prowess. Primus' music is willfully weird and experimental, yet it's not alienating; the band was able to turn their goofy weirdness into pop stardom. *—Stephen Thomas Erlewine*

Suck on This / Jan. 1990 / Caroline ♦♦♦
Originally released on their own Prawn Song label (a parody of Led Zeppelin's Swan Song Records), this is their debut, recorded live in a small club and featuring all of the greatness this trio has. It's hard, thrashy funk and punk with a sense of humor. The reissue on Caroline sounds a little muddy. Find the original vinyl pressing on Prawn, which sounds more like a CD than the CD. *—John Book*

Frizzle Fry / Feb. 1990 / Caroline ♦♦♦♦
Primus' eccentric, dissonant blend of avant-rock, funk, punk and thrash has inspired comparisons to everyone from Frank Zappa to Devo to the Red Hot Chili Peppers. But whatever comparison is made, the fact is that this trio has created strikingly original music. *Frizzle Fry* is sometimes a bit too self-indulgent for its own good, but in general, Les Claypool's willingness to experiment and his risk-taking nature come through the most. "Too Many Puppies," "To Defy The Laws Of Tradition" and "Mr. Knowitall" are among the nutty, weird treasures that helped establish Primus as alternative rock heroes and make *Frizzle Fry* the classic that it is. *—Alex Henderson*

● **Sailing the Seas of Cheese** / May 14, 1991 / Interscope ♦♦♦♦♦
The first Primus album to achieve much widespread airplay (thanks to its release on a major), and the one that broke them on MTV, *Sailing the Seas of Cheese* completely redefined the possibilities of the electric bass in rock music for those who'd never heard the group before. Slapping like a funk player, but strumming power chords and finger-tapping like a metal guitar hero, Les Claypool coaxed sounds from his instrument that had rarely if ever been made the focus of a rock band. Claypool's riffs were so full and dominant that they hardly needed to be doubled by guitarist Larry LaLonde (and wouldn't have had the same effect anyway), which freed him up on most songs to launch into dissonant, atonal solos that essentially functioned as texture, complementing Claypool's oddly whimsical sense of melody. The combination results in a weird atmosphere that could be transformed into something dark or eerie, but Claypool's thin, nasal voice and demented blue-collar persona place the record firmly in the realm of the cheerfully bizarre. The compositions are mostly riff-driven, fleshing out their heavy metal roots with prog rock tricks from Rush and Frank Zappa, as well as the novelty side of Zappa's sense of humor. The willful goofiness may alienate some listeners, but it can also obscure some genuinely dark humor, and it never detracts from the band's frequently stunning musicianship. Somewhat analogous to jazz trumpeter Dizzy Gillespie, Claypool hasn't inspired many direct imitators because of his tremendous feats of dexterity. But his stature as a virtuoso able to take his instrument into previously undreamed-of realms is without question. Though *Sailing the Seas of Cheese* tones down Primus' penchant for jamming, it's the tightest, most song-oriented representation of their jaw-dropping, one-of-a-kind style. *—Steve Huey*

Pork Soda / Apr. 20, 1993 / Interscope ♦♦♦♦♦
Once audiences got a chance to hear Primus' instantly recognizable sound, driven by Les Claypool's bizarrely virtuosic bass riffs, their audience grew by leaps and bounds. It was enough to make their second major-label album, *Pork Soda*, one of the strangest records ever to debut in the Top Ten. Stylistically, it isn't much different from *Sailing the Seas of Cheese*, though the band does stretch out and jam more often. This can result in some overly repetitive sections, since Claypool's riffs are the basis for most of the compositions, but it also showcases the band's ever-increasing level of musicianship. Their ensemble interplay continues to grow in complexity and musicality, and that's really what fans want from a Primus record anyway. The material isn't quite as consistent as *Seas of Cheese*, though there are numerous high points; among them are "My Name Is Mud," on which Claypool plays his instrument like percussion, and "Mr. Krinkle," where he switches to a bowed upright bass. There are hints of lyrical darkness stripped of the band's usual goofiness (especially in the suicide lament "Bob"), but for the most part, the humor is again split between eccentric character sketches, cheery paranoia, and annoying novelties (with a slightly higher percentage of the latter than before). Still, despite occasional flaws, what makes *Pork Soda* a success is that the band keeps finding novel variations on their signature sound, even if they never step out of it. *—Steve Huey*

Tales From the Punchbowl / May 23, 1995 / Interscope ♦♦♦♦

The Brown Album / Jul. 8, 1997 / Interscope ♦♦♦♦
The replacement of drummer Tim "Herb" Alexander with Brian "Brain" Mantia doesn't

affect Primus' sound in any notable way on *The Brown Album*. That isn't surprising—Les Claypool's side projects Sausage and Porch sound identical to Primus. What's notable about *The Brown Album* is how Claypool moves Primus even further into progressive and jazz-rock territory, concentrating entirely on the instrumental interplay of the group and caring very little for writing full-fledged songs. "Shake Hands With Beef," the first single from the album, has a reasonably amusing adolescent lyric, but the real attraction of the song is how its thunderous bass riff weaves in and out with the syncopated drums and avant-guitar. In that sense, it does let the listener know what the album is about, and very few Primus fans should be disappointed by what *The Brown Album* delivers. It's standard Primus—all instrumental interplay and adolsecent humor—but it's delivered with more finesse and skill than ever. *—Stephen Thomas Erlewine*

Rhinoplasty / Jul. 28, 1998 / Interscope ♦♦♦
Rhinoplasty? Call it *Miscellaneous Debris, Pt. 2.* An EP of covers and live cuts designed to buy time between albums, *Rhinoplasty* is another small treasure for fans. When Primus cover songs, they rarely stick to the original recorded versions, preferring to turn in new, sometimes startling arrangements that are often unpredictable. If the band hasn't chosen any surprising covers—there are more Peter Gabriel and XTC tunes, as well as Police, Stanley Clarke, Metallica and Jerry Reed songs, plus a new version of their own "Too Many Puppies"—they make up for it with great performances. It's certainly an EP intended for the dedicated, but it does the most important thing any specialist release can do—it does not disappoint. *—Stephen Thomas Erlewine*

Antipop / Oct. 19, 1999 / Interscope ♦♦♦♦
On the surface, all Primus albums seem to sound alike, especially to outsiders (read: anyone who either respects the group but doesn't get them, or the minority that actively hates them, particularly Les Claypool's demented comedy schtick). That's not really true, even if the same basic elements remain in place each time, no matter who is in the band. And Primus has never tried to shake things up as much as they do on their seventh album, *AntiPop*. Primus enlisted a dizzying array of collaborators—Stewart Copeland, Tom Waits, James Hetfield, Tom Morello, Jim Martin, Matt Stone, Martina, and Fred Durst among them—all in the purpose of challenging themselves to find different dimensions to its music. Some play or sing, some produce, but it's amazing how much each individual guest changes the tone of the music. It's not always for the best, but it keeps things fresh, if not necessarily coherent. Though there are a couple of good lyrics here, this is by and large an album about music; it would have been even better if it had been primarily an instrumental album, actually, since the vocals get in the way occasionally. By now, the popping bass, dissonance, and angular riffs don't seem like schtick, but the lyrics and singing do. Still, it's possible to get past those and hear *AntiPop* as one of Primus' most ambitious and best efforts. No, they're not always successful, but no two songs sound the same, and some collaborations are among the best things Primus has ever recorded. *AntiPop* is dense music that isn't afraid to be goofy or fall on its face—and even if it's not to your particular taste, it's hard not to respect this. *—Stephen Thomas Erlewine*

Prince (Prince Rogers Nelson)

b. Jun. 7, 1958, Minneapolis, MN
Vocals, Keyboards, Drums, Guitar, Bass / College Rock, Album Rock, Neo-Psychedelia, Club/Dance, Pop/Rock, Hard Rock, Urban, Funk, Dance-Pop, Soul

Prince is one of the singular talents of the rock era. Not only did he release a series of groundbreaking albums, he toured frequently, produced albums and wrote songs for other artists, he recorded hundreds of songs that remain unreleased. Occasionally, his music is maddeningly inconsistent, but none of his peers were as dazzlingly diverse and musically rich.

After releasing two albums of solid funk-pop in the late '70s, Prince came into his own with 1980's *Dirty Mind*, a one-man *tour de force*, bursting with hard funk, catchy Beatlesque melodies, sweet soul ballads, and rocking guitar-pop. *1999* launched Prince into the mainstream in 1982, thanks to singles like "Little Red Corvette," setting the stage for 1984's *Purple Rain*. Recorded with The Revolution, the record made Prince a superstar, spending 24 weeks at number one and selling over ten million copies. With 1985's *Around the World in a Day*, he veered off into bizarre psycho-psychedelia and the next year, he released the even stranger *Parade*; for all their quirks, both were Top 10 hits. Prince delivered a sprawling masterpiece with 1987's double-album *Sign O' the Times*, then entered a period of uncertainty. He scrapped plans to release the hard funk *The Black Album* late in 1987, releasing the confused *Lovesexy* instead in 1988; it was his first flop. His soundtrack to 1989's *Batman* went to number one, but it owed its success to the Tim Burton blockbuster. Prince reasserted his mastery of contemporary R&B with 1991's *Diamonds and Pearls*, resulting in his biggest hit since 1985. His twelfth album was titled with a cryptic symbol; in 1993, Prince changed his name to that symbol in an effort to free himself from his Warner contract. Throughout the mid-'90s, his battle with Warner received more attention than his music. He finally freed himself from Warner in 1996, releasing the triple-album set *Emancipation* at the end of the year. Though it received considerable media attention, it didn't sell well, nor did its successors. He signed a one-album deal with Arista in 1999, releasing a self-styled comeback effort, *Rave Un2 the Joy Fantastic*, which failed to capture its desired mass audience. *—Stephen Thomas Erlewine*

For You / Oct. 1978 / Warner Brothers ♦♦
On his debut album *For You*, Prince shows exceptional skill for arranging and performing mainstream urban R&B and funk, but his songwriting remains conventional. Only on the mildly racy "Soft and Wet" does he demonstrate a personal touch, but the song is still more of a promise than a fulfillment. While *For You* isn't a bad record, it is merely a pleasant one, and it offers very little indication of his staggering talents. *—Stephen Thomas Erlewine*

Prince / Oct. 1979 / Warner Brothers ♦♦♦
Expanding the urban R&B and funk approach of his debut, *Prince* is a considerably more accomplished record than his first effort, featuring the first signs of his adventurous, sexy signature sound. Although the album is still rather uneven, a handful of songs rank as classics. "I Wanna Be Your Lover" is excellent lite funk, and "Why You Wanna Treat Me So Bad?" is a wonderful soulful plea, but "I Feel for You," a sexy slice of urban R&B with a strong pop melody, is the true masterpiece of *Prince*, indicating the major breakthroughs of his next album, *Dirty Mind*. *—Stephen Thomas Erlewine*

☆ **Dirty Mind** / Oct. 1980 / Warner Brothers ♦♦♦♦♦
Neither *For You* nor *Prince* was adequate preparation for the full-blown masterpiece of Prince's third album, *Dirty Mind*. Recorded in his home studio, with Prince playing nearly every instrument, *Dirty Mind* is a stunning, audacious amalgam of funk, new wave pop, urban R&B, and pop, fueled by grinningly salacious sex and the desire to shock. Where other pop musicians suggested sex in lewd double entendres, Prince left nothing to hide—before its release, no other rock or funk record was ever quite as explicit as *Dirty Mind*, with its gleeful tales of oral sex, threesomes, and even incest. Certainly, it opened the doors for countless sexually explicit albums, but to reduce its impact to mere profanity is too reductive—the music of *Dirty Mind* is as shocking as its graphic language, bending styles and breaking rules with little regard for fixed genres. Basing the album on a harder, rock-oriented beat than before, Prince tries everything—there's pure new wave pop ("When You Were Mine"), soulful crooning ("Gotta Broken Heart Again"), robotic funk ("Dirty Mind"), rock & roll ("Sister"), sultry funk ("Head," "Do It All Night"), and relentless dance jams ("Uptown," "Partyup"), all in the space of half an hour. It's a breathtaking, visionary album, and its fusion of synthesizers, rock rhythms, and funk set the style for much of the urban soul and funk of the early '80s. *—Stephen Thomas Erlewine*

Controversy / Nov. 1981 / Warner Brothers ♦♦♦
Controversy continues in the same vein of new wave-tinged funk on *Dirty Mind*, emphasizing Prince's fascination with synthesizers and synthesizing disparate pop music genres. It is also more ambitious than its predecessor, attempting to tackle social protest ("Controversy," "Ronnie, Talk to Russia," "Annie Christian") along with sex songs ("Jack U Off," "Sexuality"), and it tries hard to bring funk to a rock audience and vice versa. Even with all of Prince's ambitions, the music on *Controversy* doesn't represent a significant breakthrough from *Dirty Mind*, and it is often considerably less catchy and memorable. Nevertheless, Prince's talents as musician make the record enjoyable, even if it isn't as compelling as most of his catalog. *—Stephen Thomas Erlewine*

☆ **1999** / Feb. 1983 / Warner Brothers ♦♦♦♦♦
With *Dirty Mind*, Prince had established a wild fusion of funk, rock, new wave, and soul that signaled he was an original, maverick talent, but it failed to win him a large audience. After delivering the sound-alike album *Controversy*, Prince revamped his sound and delivered the double-album *1999*. Where his earlier albums had been a fusion of organic and electronic sounds, *1999* was constructed almost entirely on synthesizers by Prince himself. Naturally, the effect was slightly more mechanical and robotic than his previous work and strongly recalled the electro-funk experiments of several underground funk and hip-hop artists at the time. Prince had also constructed an album dominated by computer funk, but he didn't simply rely on the extended instrumental grooves to carry the album—he didn't have to when his songwriting was improving by leaps and bounds. The first side of the record contained all of the hit singles, and, unsurprisingly, they were the ones that contained the least amount of electronics. "1999" parties to the apocalypse with a P-funk groove much tighter than anything George Clinton ever did, "Little Red Corvette" is pure pop, and "Delirious" takes rockabilly riffs into the computer age. After that opening salvo, all the rules go out the window—"Let's Pretend We're Married" is a salacious extended lust letter, "Free" is an elegiac anthem, "All the Critics Love U in New York" is a vicious attack at hipsters, and "Lady Cab Driver," with its notorious bridge, is the culmination of all of his sexual fantasies. Sure, Prince stretches out a bit too much over the course of *1999*, but the result is a stunning display of raw talent, not wallowing indulgence. *—Stephen Thomas Erlewine*

★ **Purple Rain** / Aug. 6, 1984 / Warner Brothers ♦♦♦♦♦
Prince designed *Purple Rain* as the project that would make him a superstar, and, surprisingly, that is exactly what happened. Simultaneously more focused and ambitious than any of his previous records, *Purple Rain* finds Prince consolidating his funk and R&B roots while moving boldly into pop, rock, and heavy metal with nine superbly crafted songs. Even its best-known songs don't tread conventional territory: the bass-less "When Doves Cry" is an eerie, spare neo-psychedelic masterpiece; "Let's Go Crazy" is a furious blend of metallic guitars, Stonesy riffs, and a hard funk backbeat; the anthemic title track is a majestic ballad filled with brilliant guitar flourishes. Although Prince's songwriting is at a peak, the presence of the Revolution pulls the music into sharper focus, giving it a tougher, more aggressive edge. And, with the guidance of Wendy and Lisa, Prince pushed heavily into psychedelia, adding swirling strings to the dreamy "Take Me With U" and the hard rock of "Baby I'm a Star." Even with all of his new, but uncompromising, forays into pop, Prince hasn't abandoned funk, and the robotic jam of "Computer Blue" and the menacing grind of "Darling Nikki" are among his finest songs. Taken together, all of the stylistic experiments add up to a stunning statement of purpose that remains one of the most exciting rock & roll albums ever recorded. *—Stephen Thomas Erlewine*

Around the World in a Day / 1985 / Paisley Park ♦♦♦
Purple Rain made Prince sound like he could do anything, but it still didn't prepare even

his most fervent fans for the insular psychedelia of *Around the World in a Day.* Prince had made his interior world sound fascinating and utopian on *Purple Rain,* but *Around the World in a Day* is filled with cryptic religious imagery, bizarre mysticism, and confounding metaphors, which were drenched in heavily processed guitars, shimmering keyboards, grandiose strings, and layers of vocals. As an album, the record is a bit impenetrable, requiring great demands of the listener, but individual songs do shine through: "Raspberry Beret" is a brilliant piece of neo-psychedelia with an indelible chorus, "Pop Life" is a snide swipe at stardom that emphasizes Prince's outsider status, "Condition of the Heart" is a fine ballad, "America" is a good funk jam, "Paisley Park" is heavy and slightly frightening guitar psychedelia, while the title track is a sunny, kaleidoscopic pastiche of *Magical Mystery Tour.* The problem is, only a handful of the songs have much substance outside of their detailed production and intoxicating performances, and the album has a creepy sense of paranoia that is eventually its undoing. *—Stephen Thomas Erlewine*

Parade (Music from the Motion Picture "Under the Cherry Moon") / May 19, 1986 / Paisley Park ✦✦✦✦✦

Undaunted by the criticism *Around the World in a Day* received, Prince continued to pursue his psychedelic inclinations on *Parade,* which also functioned as the soundtrack to his second film, *Under the Cherry Moon.* Originally conceived as a double album, *Parade* has the sprawling feel of a double record, even if it clocks in around 45 minutes. Prince and the Revolution shift musical moods and textures from song to song—witness how the fluttering psychedelia of "Christopher Tracy's Parade" gives way to the spare, jazzy funk of "New Position," which morphs into the druggy "I Wonder U"—and they're determined not to play it safe, even on the hard funk of "Girls and Boys" and "Mountains," as well as the stunning "Kiss," which hits hard with just a dry guitar, keyboard, drum machine, and layered vocals. All of the group's musical adventures, even the cabaret-pop of "Venus de Milo" and "Do U Lie?," do nothing to undercut the melodicism of the record, and the amount of ground they cover in 12 songs is truly remarkable. Even with all of its attributes, *Parade* is a little off-balance, stopping too quickly to give the haunting closer, "Sometimes It Snows in April," the resonance it needs. For some tastes, it may also be a bit too lyrically cryptic, but Prince's weird religious and sexual metaphors develop into a motif that actually gives the album weight. If it had been expanded to a double album, *Parade* would have equaled the subsequent *Sign O' the Times,* but as it stands, it's an astonishingly rewarding near-miss. *—Stephen Thomas Erlewine*

The Black Album / 1987 / Paisley Park ✦✦✦

Originally scheduled for release in November of 1987—following the double-album *Sign O' the Times* by a matter of months—Prince pulled *The Black Album* weeks before its release, guaranteeing it near-mythic status. Urban legends spread like wildfire: Prince believed it was too bleak to release; Warner Brothers balked at its explicit lyrics; no CDs were ever pressed, and all the LPs were destroyed. That final rumor was certainly untrue, since bootlegs immediately appeared, and when it finally received official release in the fall of 1994, nearly every die-hard fan already had the record. That limited-edition release of *The Black Album* turned out to be a bit anti-climatic, since the album itself isn't a lost masterwork—it's fun, but not much more. If anything, it's a little labored, as Prince works hard to win back the black audience he willfully abandoned after *Purple Rain.* So, he serves up "When 2 R in Love," an urban ballad every bit as nondescript as the genre, and offers "Dead on It," trying to one-up rappers with a mocking attack that winds up as one of the lamest things he ever waxed. The rest of the eight-song album is brilliant pure funk, ranging from the unrelenting "Le Grind," a deliriously lustful plea to supermodel Cindy Crawford, the hyper-tense James Brown workout "2 Nigs United 4 West Compton" to "Bob George," a perverse tale of a macho lunkhead (Prince, electronically affecting a deep, idiotic drawl) who discovers his lady just slept with Prince—or "that skinny motherfucker with a high voice," as Bob calls him. All this may not add up to a lost classic, but it is a terrific little record that still delights, even after its mystique has faded. *—Stephen Thomas Erlewine*

☆ **Sign O' the Times** / Mar. 31, 1987 / Paisley Park ✦✦✦✦✦

Fearless, eclectic, and defiantly messy, Prince's *Sign O' the Times* falls into the tradition of tremendous, chaotic double albums like *The Beatles, Exile on Main St.,* and *London Calling*—albums that are fantastic because of their overreach, their great sprawl. Prince shows nearly all of his cards here, from bare-bones electro-funk and smooth soul to pseudo-psychedelic pop and crunching hard rock, touching on gospel, blues, and folk along the way. This was the first album Prince recorded without the Revolution since 1982's *1999* (the band does appear on the in-concert rave-up, "It's Gonna Be a Beautiful Night"), and he sounds liberating, diving into territory merely suggested on *Around the World in a Day* and *Parade.* While the music overflows with generous spirit, these are among the most cryptic, insular songs he's ever written. Many songs are left over from the aborted triple album *Crystal Ball* and the abandoned Camille project, a Prince alter-ego personified by scarily sped-up tapes on "If I Was Your Girlfriend," the most disarming and bleak psycho-sexual song Prince ever wrote, as well as the equally chilling "Strange Relationship." These fraying relationships echo in the social chaos Prince writes about throughout the album. Apocalyptic imagery of drugs, bombs, empty sex, abandoned babies and mothers, and AIDS pop up again and again, yet he balances the despair with hope, whether it's God, love, or just having a good time. In its own roundabout way, *Sign O' the Times* is the sound of the late '80s—it's the sound of the good times collapsing and how all that doubt and fear can be ignored if you just dance those problems away. *—Stephen Thomas Erlewine*

Lovesexy / Feb. 1988 / Paisley Park ✦✦✦

It's nearly impossible to judge *Lovesexy* as anything but a hastily assembled substitute for the withdrawn *Black Album,* which does the record a disservice. An exactingly sequenced song cycle—the compact disc didn't have index markings to separate the individual tracks—*Lovesexy* is quite a different record than not only *The Black Album,* but anything else Prince had recorded. Where *Dirty Mind* was single-minded in its lust, *Lovesexy* connects the carnal with spiritual, and the calmness of the music reflects this outlook. Even when the record dips into hard funk, such as on the title track or the single "Alphabet Street," there's a relaxed, casual quality to the music that is shocking after the dense paranoia of *Parade, Sign O' the Times,* and *Black Album.* Prince intends to enter a new phase of maturity with such considered music and ambitious lyrical themes, but neither his music nor his lyrics are consistently well-stated over the course of the album. A handful of tracks are worthwhile—the sappy ballad "When 2 R in Love," the moving "I Wish U Heaven," the weird psychedelia of "Anna Stesia" and "Glam Slam," as well as the wonderful "Alphabet Street"—but it is his weakest album since *Controversy.* *—Stephen Thomas Erlewine*

Batman / Jun. 1989 / Paisley Park ✦✦✦

Prince had stumbled commercially with *Lovesexy,* which may be one of the reasons he decided to record the soundtrack for Tim Burton's dark, gothic interpretation of the DC comic *Batman.* Reportedly, the *Batman* album was recorded quickly, and it shows in the loose, offhand nature of the songs, which actually comes as some relief after the big ambitions of all of his records since *1999.* "The Future" and "Electric Chair" are fine, funky one-man efforts, and "Vicki Waiting" is an excellent pure pop song, while "Arms of Orion" is embarrassingly enjoyable sappy mainstream balladry, and "Batdance" is a fun dance-club pastiche of the entire album. Even with these highlights, there are no true classics on the record, and it tends to evaporate in the memory after it's finished—there's no doubt it spent six weeks at the top of the charts because of the blockbuster film. Still, *Batman* sounds fine while it's playing. *—Stephen Thomas Erlewine*

Graffiti Bridge / Aug. 21, 1990 / Paisley Park ✦✦✦

Prince was shooting for the top of the charts with *Graffiti Bridge,* and he missed. The movie was a disaster, causing the soundtrack to sell very poorly. Despite its poor showing, *Graffiti Bridge* is not a bad album; in fact, it's often very good. Prince wrote all of the songs, but only performed a little over half the tracks, leaving the rest for The Time, Mavis Staples, and Tevin Campbell. With the exception of The Time's slamming "Release It" and Campbell's "Round and Round," the best songs are the ones Prince performed himself. The George Clinton collaboration "We Can Funk," the psycho-blues of "The Question of U," the sinewy single "Thieves in the Temple," and the pop/rock of "Can't Stop This Feeling I Got," "Tick, Tick, Bang," and "Elephants & Flowers" make *Graffiti Bridge* a thoroughly enjoyable listen. *—Stephen Thomas Erlewine*

Diamonds and Pearls / Oct. 1991 / Paisley Park ✦✦✦

Prince spent the latter half of the '80s courting the pop audience, and by the time of *Graffiti Bridge,* he had lost much of his R&B fan base. As a response, he formed the New Power Generation and recorded *Diamonds and Pearls,* his first record to reconnect with the urban audience since *1999,* as well as his first to acknowledge the hip-hop revolution. Although he still has a problem with rap—"Jughead" is simply embarassing—he manages to skillfully reinvent himself as an urban soulman without sacrificing his musical innovation. The New Power Generation is a more skilled band than the Revolution, and they are able to make Prince's funk jazzier, particularly on "Willing and Able," the breezy "Strollin'" and "Walk Don't Walk." It's clear that these subtly textured songs are where his heart is at, but the songs designed to win back his audience—the slamming dance-floor rallying cry "Gett Off," the sexy T. Rex groove "Cream," the extraordinary Philly soul of the neglected masterpiece "Money Don't Matter 2 Night" and the drippy mainstream ballad "Diamonds and Pearls"—are all terrific pop singles. However, much of the rest of *Diamonds and Pearls* is comprised of middling funk and R&B that sounds less like inspired workouts than stylistic exercises. Even with such weak moments, *Diamonds and Pearls* is a fine record, even though it's only marginally better than *Lovesexy* and *Graffiti Bridge.* *—Stephen Thomas Erlewine*

The Love Symbol Album / Oct. 13, 1992 / Paisley Park ✦✦✦✦✦

The New Power Generation is the most talented and versatile band Prince has ever fronted, and they fulfill their potential on *Symbol.* Although the NPG factored heavily on *Diamonds and Pearls,* it still sounded like a solo Prince album. *Symbol* sounds like a band performing together, working off of each other's strengths and weaknesses. Opening with the dance smash "My Name Is Prince" and the deep funk of "Sexy M.F.," *Symbol* has Prince's best dance tracks since the *Black Album.* But Prince wasn't content; he decided to run the gamut of modern pop/R&B/dance, and the music is uniformly accomplished and excellent. Unfortunately, he also decided to make a "rock soap opera," so the music is saddled with ridiculous lyrics and annoying sound bridges by Kirstie Alley. However, *Symbol* has some of the finest, most inventive music of Prince's career. *—Stephen Thomas Erlewine*

☆ **The Hits 1** / Sep. 14, 1993 / Paisley Park ✦✦✦✦✦

The primary fault with Prince's two-part *Hits* collection is that both volumes are missing some important singles and are sequenced incoherently, thereby failing to give an accurate impression of his astonishing musical growth. However, they do contain enough necessary items to illustrate why he was one of the most influential and gifted musicians of the '80s, as well as providing a reasonable introduction and compilation for casual fans. *Hits 1* contains a good cross-section of his biggest hits—"When Doves Cry" (presented in an edited version), "When You Were Mine," "Let's Go Crazy," "1999," "Sign O' the Times," "Alphabet Street," "Diamonds and Pearls," "7"—plus new items like "Pink Cashmere" and "Nothing Compares 2 U" (a Prince song that Sinead O'Connor took to number one) which are nearly as good as the familiar tracks. However, it provides an incomplete portrait, making *Hits 2* a necessary purchase. *—Stephen Thomas Erlewine*

☆ **The Hits 2** / Sep. 14, 1993 / Paisley Park ✦✦✦✦✦
Like *Hits 1, Hits 2* presents an illogically sequenced cross-section of some of Prince's biggest hits and most notorious songs, including "Dirty Mind," "I Wanna Be Your Lover," "Head," "Delirious," "Little Red Corvette," "I Would Die 4 U," "Raspberry Beret," "Kiss," "U Got the Look," "Cream," and "Purple Rain." Two new tracks, "Peach" and "The Pope," are included among the 18 cuts and while they don't match the rest of the songs (or the new cuts on *Hits 1*), they are nevertheless enjoyable. On the whole, *Hits 2* is a slightly stronger collection than its predecessor, but it still gives a rather incomplete portrait—if you buy *Hits 2*, you need to buy *Hits 1*. —*Stephen Thomas Erlewine*

The Hits/The B-Sides / Sep. 14, 1993 / Paisley Park ✦✦✦✦✦
While it isn't a truly comprehensive set, Prince's singles collection does contain most of his biggest hits. The two volumes are available separately or packaged together with a third disc of B-sides; apart from the glorious "Erotic City," the flip sides are only of interest to devoted fans. —*Stephen Thomas Erlewine*

Come / Aug. 16, 1994 / Paisley Park ✦✦
Released after Prince announced his retirement and his intention of never using the name "Prince" again, *Come* is something of a surprise: an album of reportedly all new material, released by "Prince," not "The Artist Formerly Known As Prince." After listening to *Come*, its purpose becomes clear—it's a record fulfilling a contract, nothing more and nothing less. Some of the songs are good, but there's nothing on *Come* that Prince hasn't done before; he even sounds bored on certain tracks. On top of that, the album has no obvious singles, making it a nightmare to sell. Not surprisingly, the album flopped. —*Stephen Thomas Erlewine*

Gold Experience / Oct. 1995 / Warner Brothers/NPG ✦✦✦✦
Prince changed his name to an unpronounceable symbol in 1993, but it wasn't until 1995 that he actually released a record credited to that symbol. During those two years, he released a greatest-hits collection, an official version of his much-bootlegged *Black Album*, and a final Prince album, the lackluster *Come*. Throughout 1994, he pressured Warner to release another album, *The Gold Experience*, but the company refused and he staged a public protest in the media, calling himself a slave to the label. By the summer of 1995, the artist and the company had made amends and the record was released in the fall. In a way, *The Gold Experience* lives up to the manufactured hype created while it languished on the shelf. More of a creative rebirth than a change in direction, the record finds Prince and the New Power Generation running through a typically dazzling array of musical styles, subtly twisting new sounds out of familiar forms. Much like *The Love Symbol Album*, it follows a loose concept, interweaving a variety of pop, funk, rock, soul, and jazz styles into a vague story. Song for song, *The Gold Experience* is slightly stronger than its predecessor, as Prince's melodies are more immediate, especially on the Philly soul tribute "The Most Beautiful Girl in the World" and the pure pop of "Dolphin." Also, the band's performance is lively and confident, bringing an effortless virtuosity to funk workouts ("P Control") and fuzzed-out rockers ("Endorphinmachine"), as well as ballads like "Eye Hate U." *The Gold Experience* is somewhat weighed down by interludes that attempt to further the story but wind up interrupting the flow of the music, yet that doesn't stop the album from being Prince's most satisfying effort since *Sign O' the Times*. —*Stephen Thomas Erlewine*

Chaos & Disorder / Jul. 1996 / Warner Brothers ✦✦✦
Like *Come* before it, *Chaos & Disorder* is a contractual obligation album for Prince, a way to get himself out of his contract with Warner Brothers. Unlike *Come*, *Chaos & Disorder* doesn't sound disjointed and pasted together—it's a fun, off-handed throwaway. For the first time since 1987's *Sign O' the Times*, Prince has made a pop/rock album, complete with squealing guitars and sighing melodies. None of the songs qualify as major songs in Prince's canon, but that's part of the record's charm—Prince sounds like he's having a good time, and he could really care less what anyone else has to say. Or, as he puts it in one of the album's best and most careening tracks, "I Rock, Therefore I Am." *Chaos & Disorder* sounds immediate, like the songs were recorded the same day they were written. While that might mean there's a handful of throwaways scattered throughout the album, there are wonderful moments like the stuttering jazz-funk of "Dig U Better Dead," the scathing "Had U," the pscyhedelic clashes of the title track, the heavy rock of "I Like It There" and the beautiful "Dinner with Delores," a rough gem that ranks as one of Prince's simplest and most charming singles of the '90s. So, *Chaos & Disorder* isn't Prince's best or most important work, but it is a really fun listen, especially if you're willing to accept it as what it is—a record that does nothing more than rock. —*Stephen Thomas Erlewine*

Emancipation / Nov. 19, 1996 / NPG/EMI ✦✦✦✦
Emancipation was a critical moment for Prince, one that he designed as an artistic rebirth and, optimistically, as a commercial comeback. In a typically perverse fashion, Prince decided to make the album a triple-disc set running exactly three hours, easily making it the longest album of all-new original material ever released by a popular artist. As the first album he released since leaving Warner Brothers, *Emancipation* was supposed to dazzle, proving that he had not lost any of his creative skills or power. And it does dazzle, but it's hard to digest a full three discs of music, even if it is almost all of high quality. Fortunately, Prince made each disc into a distinct entity in its own right, with the first being the most pop, the second being a song cycle devoted to his new marriage, and the third being a dance/funk extravaganza. Throughout all three discs, Prince tries on a variety of styles, from jazz to R&B, but he doesn't break any new ground; instead, the album is simply reaffirmation of his strengths as a composer and a musician. *Emancipation* doesn't have the bristling, colorful eclecticism of *Sign O' the Times* nor does it have the wildness of early one-man projects like *1999* or *Dirty Mind*, but with its gentle ballads and complex jams, it signals that Prince has evolved into middle-age

gracefully. It's a mature effort, to be certain, but in this case that doesn't mean that it's an album bankrupt of ideas—it means that Prince's craft continues to grow. —*Stephen Thomas Erlewine*

Crystal Ball / Mar. 3, 1998 / NPG ✦✦✦
As any die-hard fan knows, *Crystal Ball* was the triple-album set Prince had planned to release in 1987, when Warner forced him to trim it to the double album *Sign O' the Times*. Since then, *Crystal Ball* had become a legendary "lost" album among Prince collectors, and many of its outtakes had circulated on bootlegs for years. So, it didn't come as a complete surprise that Prince revived the title for his own collection of outtakes, which turned out to be the first release on his independent NPG label. Any collector will quibble with the track selection, since there are literally hundreds of known Prince outtakes, and there's no way that a three-disc set could include all the best cuts. Still, this is an impressive sampler that illustrates the true depth of Prince's talents. There may be no hidden masterworks on the level of "When Doves Cry," but the music here is consistently strong and compelling. As a compiler, Prince errs by favoring latter-day recordings over his '80s studio creations, but this is a minor complaint, since he has included such legendary (at least among collectors) songs as "Dream Factory," "Movie Star," "Crucial," "Sexual Suicide," "Days of Wild," and "The Ride." Prince added a full-length album, *The Truth*, as the fourth disc to *Crystal Ball*. Taken on its own terms, *The Truth* is a terrific little record with a similar feel to *Chaos & Disorder*, but with stronger material. Purportedly, it's Prince's acoustic album, but he uses that concept to spring into the blues, tape effects, straightahead pop, and soul. It's a joy to hear him work in such a structured form, since it helps him focus his ideas and deliver a tight, enjoyable pop record that offers proof he hasn't lost his gifts. —*Stephen Thomas Erlewine*

New Power Soul / Jun. 30, 1998 / New Power Generation ✦✦
Releasing two multi-disc sets may have been an audacious way to begin his career as an independent artist, but it did nothing to re-establish Prince as a commercial powerhouse. Perhaps that's the reason he released *New Power Soul* (credited to his backing band, New Power Generation, but it's a Prince album in all but name) a mere four months after his mammoth quadruple-disc *Crystal Ball* hit the stores—it was time to release a concise, focused pop-funk record that proved he could still deliver. And it does, to a certain extent. *New Power Soul* is a tight, focused record, filled with energetic funk workouts and classy, seductive ballads. It's paced to entertain, just like one of his legendary concerts, and there's no shortage of well-crafted songs. The problem is, nothing stands out and makes itself known. Certainly, the album sounds great as it's playing, but it cements Prince's evolution from groundbreaker to craftsman. There are pleasures in his craft, to be sure, but in order to hear them, you have to be a committed fan. —*Stephen Thomas Erlewine*

The Vault: Old Friends 4 Sale / Aug. 24, 1999 / Warner Brothers ✦✦✦
Upon leaving Warner Brothers in 1996, Prince agreed to let the label release a collection of unreleased recordings from his legendary prodigious vaults at some point in the future. Warner unveiled that collection, unimaginatively titled *The Vault: Old Friends 4 Sale*, in the summer of 1999. Instead of an official release for several of Prince's legendary songs though, *The Vault* is a brief collection (under 40 minutes) of ten songs, recorded between 1985 and 1994 according to the liner notes—though they all feel like *Graffiti Bridge* (or maybe *Symbol*) outtakes. That's not a complaint, actually. There's a wonderful carefree feeling to the record, heavy on jazz and light funk, constantly swinging, and nearly always engaging. Only the title track has the necessary weight to announce itself as a major addition to his official catalog, but that doesn't matter since the songs are all enjoyable. After all, it's hard not to be impressed with Prince's songcraft or the casually sophisticated flair to the musicianship throughout the album. That might not be what most observers expected from *The Vault*, but consider this—of these ten songs, eight tracks have never been heavily bootlegged before. That means that even some hardcore followers may not have heard all of this material, which is noteworthy in itself. But the nicest thing about the compilation is that even though it's a minor addition to his catalog, it holds together as an album better than *Come* or *Chaos & Disorder*, the two other Warner-era odds-and-ends collections, or even the tossed-off *New Power Soul*. It's an unassuming, jazzy little record that's damn near irresistible. —*Stephen Thomas Erlewine*

Rave Un2 the Joy Fantastic / Nov. 2, 1999 / NPG/Arista ✦✦✦
Clive Davis convinced Prince to record a star-studded comeback album for Arista in 1999—much like how he coaxed Prince's idol Carlos Santana to revive his career with *Supernatural*. Problem is, Prince isn't willing to fully throw himself into the contemporary mainstream, as Santana did. Instead, he sticks to his guns with *Rave Un2 the Joy Fantastic*, delivering an album that's frighteningly similar to the lackluster *New Power Soul*, only a little slicker and better, and with cameos. *Rave*, like its predecessor, is stilted and canned, clearly the work of one man with guitars, synths, and a drum machine. It's shocking to hear how perfunctory most of the performances are on *Rave*, yet it's stranger to hear Prince gunning for the pop charts. He has funk, a dash of pop, a little bit of rap, and a whole lotta ballads—anything that could result in a crossover hit. There are a couple of cool moments on this overlong, 70-minute album and, curiously, most of those are tracks with superstar collaborators. Prince sounds committed and adventurous on these songs, whether it's the electro-funk "Undisputed," which features a Chuck D rap, the harmonica-laden bluesy pop of "Baby Knows" (harmonica and harmonies by Sheryl Crow), or the utterly delightful, effervescent duet with Gwen Stefani ("So Far, So Pleased"). These songs, along with the passable funk-pop title cut and the ballads "The Sun, the Moon and Stars" and "Wherever U Go, Whatever U Do" are pretty enjoyable, yet their presence highlights how pedestrian the remainder of *Rave* is. Also, these are the kind of songs fanatics appreciate because of their subtleties. So, this is one for the

dedicated, like every album he's made since he changed his name to a symbol. —*Stephen Thomas Erlewine*

★ **The Very Best of Prince** / Jul. 31, 2001 / Rhino ✦✦✦✦✦
Even geniuses (maybe especially geniuses) are taken for granted, not seen as geniuses, or only appreciated in small doses. Which is a grandiose way of saying that, no matter how many partisans may complain, there are many listeners out there that don't want to delve into the deliriously rich catalog of Prince and would rather spend time with a single disc of all the hits—especially since the first singles compilation was botched, spread too thin over two discs and sequenced as if it were on shuffle play. That doesn't mean that 2001's *The Very Best of Prince* is perfect, even if it is a better hits overview than its predecessor. First of all, Prince had so many hits, and so many of them were so good, that 17 tracks couldn't possibly encapsulate everything great. After all, this doesn't have Top Ten hits like "Delirious," "Pop Life," "I Could Never Take the Place of Your Man," or "The Most Beautiful Girl in the World" (or the number one "Batdance," for that matter, continuing *Batman* being unofficially written out of his discography), nor does it have such great second-tier hits as "Take Me With U" and "Mountains," or B-sides like "Irresistible Bitch" and "Erotic City," let alone album tracks. What is here are the big songs—"1999," "Little Red Corvette," "When Doves Cry," "Kiss," and so on—all presented in their single edits. And, frankly, that's enough to make this a dynamite collection, perfect for those that just want one Prince disc, and a good, solid listen of some of his best. Besides, this trumps both *Hits* discs by including "Money Don't Matter 2 Night," his best single never to reach the Top 10. —*Stephen Thomas Erlewine*

Prince Paul (Paul Huston)

b. Apr. 2, 1967
Producer / Underground Rap, Alternative Rap, Hip-Hop
Beginning his career as a DJ for Stetsasonic, rapper and producer Prince Paul has lent his skills to albums by Boogie Down Productions, Gravediggaz, MC Lyte, Big Daddy Kane and 3rd Bass, among others. Paul's big break came when he produced De La Soul's *3 Feet High and Rising* album. Shattering the acknowledged rules of hip-hop production, he sampled not only funk, but all types of music to create fresh and original backing tracks. By throwing in comedy sketches as well, Prince Paul and De La Soul completely ushered in a new era for hip-hop. In 1994, Paul returned to rapping, joing RZA and Stetsasonic member Fruitkwan in Gravediggaz, a side-project that debuted with *6 Feet Deep*. He also began working with the new elite in underground rap, recruiting the Automator, New Kingdom's Scott Harding and Spectre for his debut solo album, 1997's *Psychoanalysis: What Is It? A Prince Among Thieves* followed in 1999, and later that year Paul formed Handsome Boy Modeling School with the Automator to release the album *So…How's Your Girl?*. —*Steve Kurutz*

Psychoanalysis: What Is It? / Oct. 21, 1997 / Tommy Boy ✦✦✦
From George Clinton and De La Soul to Ornette Coleman and Frank Zappa, a lot of great artists haven't hesitated to be self-indulgent. It's a question of *how* self-indulgent an artist chooses to be, and on *Psychoanalysis (What Is It?)*, Prince Paul is much too self-indulgent for his own good. Known for his membership in the group Stetsasonic and for producing De La Soul, Queen Latifah, and others, Paul has an impressive resume. But this unfocused, incoherent CD wasn't his finest hour. Though it contains a few worthwhile rap tunes (including "Psycho Linguistics" and "J.O.B.–Das What Dey Is"), *Psychoanalysis* isn't a rap album so much as a collection of soundbites, samples, and dialogue played over tracks. Overall, the album is pointless and serves no purpose other than Paul's desire to amuse and entertain himself. He may have gotten a few laughs out of it, but listeners will be left out in the cold and find themselves asking if there is a point to all this. —*Alex Henderson*

● **A Prince Among Thieves** / Feb. 23, 1999 / Tommy Boy ✦✦✦✦✦
Known to his mother as Paul Huston, Prince Paul's diverse résumé includes membership in the influential jazzy outfit Stetsasonic and the morosely creative Gravediggaz. He's also produced for De La Soul, George Clinton, and the Beastie Boys. Perhaps best known for his humor and unpredictability, Prince Paul surprises again with what may be the first true rap musical, *A Prince Among Thieves*. The storyline, told through songs and interludes produced by Prince Paul, involves an aspiring rapper (Tariq) on the verge of a major record deal. Without the necessary funds for a quality demo tape, he begins a hustling journey through New York. Standout verses come courtesy of Kool Keith as a weapons dealer ("Crazy Lou's Hideout"), Chris Rock as a junkie ("My First Day"), and Everlast as an overzealous policeman ("The Men in Blue"). Seamlessly combined skits and album tracks make this a hip-hop opera worth seeing at the Met. —*Craig Robert Smith*

John Prine

b. Oct. 10, 1946, Maywood, IL
Vocals, Guitar / Progressive Folk, Contemporary Folk, Singer/Songwriter
An acclaimed singer/songwriter whose literate work flirted with everything from acoustic folk to rockabilly to straight-ahead country, John Prine became a fixture on the Chicago folk music scene in the late 1960s before his compositions caught the ear of Kris Kristofferson, who was instrumental in helping him win a recording contract. In 1971, he released his eponymously-titled debut album; though not a commercial success, songs like "Sam Stone," the harsh tale of a drug-addled Vietnam veteran, won critical approval. Neither 1972's *Diamonds in the Rough* nor 1973's *Sweet Revenge* fared any better on the charts, but Prine's work won great renown among his fellow performers, with covers from the Everly Brothers, Bette Midler and Joan Baez. For 1975's *Common Sense*, Prine turned to producer Steve Cropper, the highly-influential house guitarist for the Stax la-

bel; while the album's sound shocked the folk community with its reliance on husky vocals and booming drums, it served notice that Prine was not an artist whose work could be pigeonholed, and was his only LP to reach the U.S. Top 100. Under his own Oh Boy imprint, Prine's music thrived, as 1986's country-flavored *German Afternoons* earned a Grammy nomination; 1991's Grammy-winning *The Missing Years* was his most successful outing to date, featuring guest appearances from Bruce Springsteen, Bonnie Raitt and Tom Petty. —*Jason Ankeny*

☆ **John Prine** / 1971 / Atlantic ✦✦✦✦✦
A revelation upon its release, this album is now a collection of standards: "Illegal Smile," "Hello in There," "Sam Stone," "Donald and Lydia," and, of course, "Angel from Montgomery." Prine's music, a mixture of folk, rock, and country, is deceptively simple, like his pointed lyrics, and his easy vocal style adds a humorous edge that makes otherwise funny jokes downright hilarious. —*William Ruhlmann*

Diamonds in the Rough / 1972 / Atlantic ✦✦✦
John Prine's second album was a cut below his first, only because the debut was a classic and the followup was merely terrific. "Sour Grapes" showed Prine's cracked sense of humor and "Souvenirs" his sentiment. Even if it was the second rank of his writing, *Diamonds In The Rough* demonstrated that Prine had an enduring talent that wasn't exhausted by one great album. —*William Ruhlmann*

Sweet Revenge / 1973 / Atlantic ✦✦✦✦✦
A bold and brilliant stab at (almost) straight country, it tempers Prine's cynical streak with the tone of a jaded humorist and social commentator. —*John Floyd*

Common Sense / 1975 / Atlantic ✦✦✦
A brash album, it's full of aggressive rock rhythms and morose tunes. Even the Chuck Berry cover, "You Never Can Tell," is shot full of melancholy. —*John Floyd*

Prime Prine / 1976 / Atlantic ✦✦✦✦✦
Atlantic Records' compilation of John Prine's first four albums was good for its time (and became his only gold record) but has been superseded by Rhino's *Great Days* anthology. —*William Ruhlmann*

Bruised Orange / 1978 / Asylum ✦✦✦✦✦
Despite some brilliant songs, Prine's followup albums to his stunning debut were uneven until this, his fifth, produced by his friend Steve Goodman. Here, Prine's always finely-tuned sense of absurdity once again collides with his ability to depict pain sympathetically for a whole album, typified by "That's the Way That the World Goes 'Round," a neat statement of his philosophy, and "Sabu Visits the Twin Cities Alone," perhaps the best depiction ever written of life on the road in the entertainment business. —*William Ruhlmann*

Pink Cadillac / 1979 / Oh Boy ✦✦✦
John Prine went to Sam Phillips' studio in Memphis to make his sixth album, *Pink Cadillac*, and got some of the Sun Records sound of 1950s rockabilly on a record produced by Phillips' sons Knox and Jerry. (Sam produced two of the tracks himself.) Slap-back bass here, a Bo Diddley beat there, and an overall loose feel characterized music that may have been more fun to make than it is to listen to, even though it's quite entertaining. Prine wrote only five of the ten songs, however, and even though the covers were of high caliber—notably Roly Salley's "Killing the Blues" and Arthur Gunter's "Baby Let's Play House," a song Elvis Presley did at Sun—*Pink Cadillac* was a good idea that went slightly awry in the execution. If Prine had had the songs as well as the studio, it would have been among his best. —*William Ruhlmann*

Storm Windows / 1980 / Oh Boy ✦✦✦
A relaxed effort, it's defined by straightforward love songs and subdued vocals. Modest but quite nice. —*John Floyd*

Aimless Love / 1984 / Oh Boy ✦✦✦
John Prine moved to his own independent label, Oh Boy, after stints at Atlantic and Asylum (later, he acquired his Asylum albums and reissued them on Oh Boy). On this label debut, he is under no commercial pressures, but that seems to make him more low-key, less striking. "The Oldest Baby in the World," "Somewhere Someone's Falling in Love," and "Unwed Fathers" are good examples of his new sweetness, which is as winning as, if less impressive than, his witty older songs. —*William Ruhlmann*

German Afternoons / 1986 / Oh Boy ✦✦✦
Another straight country set, but unlike *Sweet Revenge*, this is a sleepy-town stroll, highlighted by some beautiful ballads and snappy accompaniment by The New Grass Revival. —*John Floyd*

Live / 1988 / Oh Boy ✦✦✦✦
With years of experience playing club dates, John Prine has evolved into a very entertaining live performer, and this album, originally a double-LP and now a single CD, presents him at his intimate best, telling funny stories and performing his most impressive material in unadorned arrangements. —*William Ruhlmann*

The Missing Years / Sep. 1991 / Oh Boy ✦✦✦✦✦
Prine took five years between his ninth studio album and this, his tenth—enough time to gather his strongest body of material in more than a decade. From the caustic "All the Best" to the cliche compilation "It's a Big Old Goofy World," Prine's gifts for emotional revelation and off-the-wall humor are on display in abundance, and he's aided by excellent production (courtesy of Heartbreaker Howie Epstein) and strong backup musicians. *The Missing Years* won the 1991 Grammy Award for Best Contemporary Folk Album. —*William Ruhlmann*

★ **Great Days: The John Prine Anthology** / Aug. 17, 1993 / Rhino ✦✦✦✦✦
Rhino's *Great Days: The John Prine Anthology* is an excellent summary of John Prine's

prime period, from his sublime 1971 eponymous debut to 1991's *Missing Years*. This (appropriately) draws heavily from his early recordings (including the aforementioned debut), but it also does a terrific job of finding songs on uneven albums, while giving weight to such classic albums as *Bruised Orange*. Although those previously mentioned albums are all worthwhile on their own terms (as are many of Prine's other records), this provides a nearly flawless recap of his career—so much so that it's not only for neophytes, but also reminds longtime fans why they loved him in the first place. *—Stephen Thomas Erlewine*

Lost Dogs and Mixed Blessings / Apr. 4, 1995 / Oh Boy ✦✦✦

Live on Tour / Apr. 8, 1997 / Oh Boy ✦✦✦

Lucky 13 / Nov. 10, 1998 / Oh Boy ✦✦✦

In Spite of Ourselves / Sep. 14, 1999 / Oh Boy ✦✦✦✦✦
In Spite of Ourselves is John Prine's tribute to the music he grew up with. Good country songs written by folks like Roger Miller and Jack Clement. It is, at the same time, a golden opportunity for him to collaborate with some of his all-time favorite female vocalists. In the liner notes booklet, Prine tells the story: "I made a list of my favorite girl singers and the first nine I called said 'yes.' I nearly fell over." One of Prine's favorites is Iris DeMent, and her unique vocals grace four of the tracks here, including "(We're Not) The Jet Set," "We Could," and Prine's lone songwriting appearance, "In Spite of Ourselves," a song written for the upcoming Billy Bob Thornton film, *Daddy & Them*, in which Prine appears. Trisha Yearwood, Connie Smith, Fiona Prine, Melba Montgomery, Emmylou Harris, Delores Keane, Patty Loveless, and Lucinda Williams all share the studio with Prine, creating some mighty powerful duets. From Freddie Hart's "Loose Talk" to Don Everly's "So Sad (To Watch Good Love Go Bad)," the album manages to create a seamless scrapbook of both old and new songs, artists and memories. Prine's duets are backed by some of the very best musicians available. Buddy Emmons and Dan Dugmore, two incredible pedal steel players, and Sam Bush, Kenny Malone, Jason Wilber, Jim Rooney, and Marty Stuart are just a few of the stellar players featured on the album. Overall, *In Spite of Ourselves* ranks as one of Prine's finest works, a scrapbook of country classics, interpreted by some of the genres best female vocalists, in duet with one fine American singer and a great songwriter. *—Michael B. Smith*

Souvenirs / Oct. 31, 2000 / Oh Boy ✦✦✦
In the liner notes to John Prine's 2000 album *Souvenirs*, he calls the songs he has recorded during his 30-year career "faithful companions." They are indeed warm, friendly, and boldly intimate, whispering secrets to the listener—but at the same time they are growing older and smoothing their youthful edge. In an effort to have his own master recordings of his favorite and most popular songs, Prine re-recorded 15 tracks for release in Germany (as he has always wanted to be popular in Germany), but upon hearing these re-recorded versions Oh Boy Records decided to release them in the U.S. (as Prine has always wanted to be popular there as well). The result is an interesting mix, wherein the historical stories ("Grandpa Was a Carpenter," "The Late John Garfield Blues") and rocking chair reminiscences ("Angel From Montgomery") are recalled with a genuine wisdom of the years, but the songs tinged with Prine's signature cynical smirk ("People Puttin' People Down," "Please Don't Bury Me") have lost some of their cheeky, finger-pointing optimism and almost sound like grumbling. Along with other performers who have tried to regain access to their compositions by re-recording them (it seems everyone from Merle Haggard to Prince has lost original song rights at some point), John Prine's contemporary touches on these old favorites may provide new insights, but the new versions rarely surpass the originals. *—Zac Johnson*

P.J. Proby

b. Nov. 6, 1938, Houston, TX
Vocals / Pop-Soul, Pop/Rock, British Invasion, Disco
Though an American by birth and upbringing, P.J. Proby moved to England in 1963 and has maintained a career as a pop singer there ever since. The biggest of his 11 U.K. chart hits was the first, "Hold Me," in 1964, though he also hit the Top Ten with two songs from the score of *West Side Story*, "Somewhere" and "Maria." The hits stopped coming in 1968, but Proby's colorful personality assured him a continuing presence on the British cabaret circuit. *—William Ruhlmann*

● **The Legendary P.J. Proby at His Very Best: Vol. 2** / 1987 / See For Miles ✦✦✦✦✦
Oddly, this is a better compilation than Volume One, which focused more on his ballads; this is oriented toward his rock and soul recordings. Includes "Hold Me," "Nicki Hoeky," the 1964 British Top 20 single "Together," and "Just Call and I'll Be There" (also recorded by Francoise Hardy in French), where Proby sounds like the loser in a Gene Pitney soundalike contest. Spanning from 1964 to 1968, most of the rest consists of rock and soul covers that range from passable to horrid. *—Richie Unterberger*

I Am P.J. Proby / P.J. Proby / Mar. 19, 1996 / See For Miles ✦✦✦
P.J. Proby's first two albums, *I Am P.J. Proby* and *P.J. Proby*, are collected on this single disc. Before these records, he had primarily been known as a songwriter and these were supposed to establish him as a performer. Although he had a number of hits in Britain, he didn't have much success in America, apart from the minor hits, "Hold Me" and a cover of *West Side Story*'s "Somewhere." Both albums were post-British Invasion pop/rock, with lots of sugary melodies and ringing guitars. Though they have their moments, each one is riddled with filler, which is what makes the two-fer a bargain. The highlights of both discs combine to form one strong album. *—Stephen Thomas Erlewine*

P.J. Proby's in Town/Enigma / Mar. 19, 1996 / See For Miles ✦✦✦✦✦
In Town and *Enigma*, P.J. Proby's third and fourth albums, didn't have as many hits as his previous two albums (although, ironically, *Enigma* spawned his biggest American hit, "Niki Hoeky"), partially because he was beginning to move toward a more middle-of-the-road sound, similar to Tom Jones. Though the albums are well-produced and well-crafted—they sound slick, stylish and professional—they lack the spark of his first two records, even if the number of first-rate songs hasn't decreased. After *Enigma*, his career did begin to slide, but he was still a fun and popular pop/rock teen idol when he recorded these albums and that is what makes the disc an enjoyable period piece. *—Stephen Thomas Erlewine*

Procol Harum

f. 1967, London, England
British Psychedelia, Psychedelic, Prog-Rock/Art Rock
Procol Harum is arguably the most successful "accidental" group creation—that is, a band originally assembled to take advantage of the success of a record created in the studio—in the history of progressive rock. With "A Whiter Shade of Pale" a monster hit right out of the box, the band evolved from a studio ensemble into a successful live act, their music built around an eclectic mix of blues-based rock riffs and grand classical themes. With singer/pianist Gary Brooker and lyricist Keith Reid providing the band's entire repertory, their music evolved in decidedly linear fashion, the only major surprises coming from the periodic line-up changes that added a new instrumental voice to the proceedings. At their most accessible, as on "Whiter Shade of Pale" and "Conquistador," they were one of the most popular of progressive rock bands, their singles outselling all rivals, and their most ambitious album tracks still have a strong following. *—Bruce Eder*

Procol Harum / 1967 / Deram ✦✦✦✦
The group's debut album bombed in England, appearing six months after "A Whiter Shade of Pale" and "Homburg" with neither hit song on it. The LP was successful in America, where albums sold more easily, but especially since it *did* include "A Whiter Shade of Pale" and was reissued with a sticker emphasizing the presence of the original "Conquistador," a re-recording of which became a hit in 1972. The music is an engaging meld of psychedelic rock, blues, and classical influences, filled with phantasmagoric lyrics, bold (but not flashy) organ by Matthew Fisher, and Robin Trower's most tasteful and restrained guitar. "Conquistador," "Kaleidoscope," "A Christmas Camel," and the Bach-influenced "Repent Walpurgis" are superb tracks, and "Good Captain Clack" is great, almost Kinks-like fun. Not everything here works, but it holds up better than most psychedelic or progressive rock. The 1997 remastering brings out Trower's guitar and Fisher's organ (his trills on "A Christmas Camel" are spine-tingling) in all of their surging, crunching glory. *—Bruce Eder*

Shine on Brightly / 1968 / Repertoire ✦✦✦✦
After the multi-million selling "A Whiter Shade Of Pale," Procol Harum coalesced around a new line-up and cut a debut album in two days, the sales of which (because the hit song wasn't on it originally) were only fair, and a couple of new singles also failed to sell. Then they did *Shine On Brightly*, which initially drew on recordings going back to late 1967—in the course of preparing their first proper LP, the band junked an entire side of blues-based numbers in favor of the 18-minute suite "In Held 'Twas I," which rivaled anything yet heard from such established progressive rock outfits as the Nice or the Moody Blues in length and surpassed them in audacity, with an extensive spoken part surrounded by virtuoso classical and psychedelic passages (and even a featured spot for Dave Knights' bass). It all proved that they were more than a one-hit wonder and, released in late 1968, the album extended the definition of progressive rock, even as it kept much of the music rooted in established rock genres. "Skip Softly," for all of its grand piano pyrotechnics, was also a showcase for Robin Trower's bluesy, high-energy guitar attack, and "Wish Me Well" was an even better vehicle for his instrument, while "Magdalene (My Regal Zonophone)" was an interesting exercise in nostalgia highlighted by Matthew Fisher's organ. *—Bruce Eder*

A Salty Dog / Mar. 1969 / A&M ✦✦✦✦✦
This album, the group's third, was where they showed just how far their talents extended across the musical landscape, from blues to R&B to classical rock. In contrast to their hastily recorded debut, or its successor, done to stretch their performance and composition range, *A Salty Dog* was recorded in a reasonable amount of time, giving the band a chance to fully develop their ideas. The title track is one of the finest songs ever to come from Procol Harum and one of the best pieces of progressive rock ever heard, and a very succinct example at that at under five minutes' running time—the lyric and the music combine to form a perfect mood piece, and the performance is bold and subtle at once, in the playing and the singing, respectively. The range of sounds on the rest includes "Juicy John Pink," a superb piece of pre-World War II-style country blues, while "Crucifiction Lane" is a killer Otis Redding-style soul piece, and "Pilgrim's Progress" is a virtuoso keyboard workout. *A Salty Dog* was reissued by Repertoire Records in 1997 with enhanced sound and the lost B-side "Long Gone Geek," a Robin Trower guitar workout par excellence. *—Bruce Eder*

Home / 1970 / Repertoire ✦✦✦
The group's hardest-rocking classic album is, beyond some superb vocalizing by Gary Brooker, principally a showcase for Robin Trower's high-powered guitar and a rock-hard rhythm section, with B.J. Wilson only a little less animated than Ginger Baker on some of the music. Procol Harum had a split personality by this time, the band juxtaposing straight-ahead rock & roll numbers like "Still There'll Be More" and the Elvis Presley-influenced "Whisky Train" with darker, more dramatic pieces like "Nothing That I Didn't Know" and "Barnyard Story." Chris Copping doubles on organ, replacing Matthew Fisher, but the overall sound is that of a leaner Procol Harum, all except for the ambitious "Whaling Stories"—even it was a compromise that nearly worked, showcasing Trower's larger-than-life guitar sound (coming off here like King Crimson's Robert Fripp in one of his

heavier moments) within a somewhat pretentious art rock concept. It shows the strains within their lineup that the producers chose the lighter, more obviously accessible "Your Own Choice"—on which Gary Brooker's piano is the lead instrument—to end the album after "Whaling Stories"' pyrotechnic finish. *Home* has appeared several times on CD, in a poor-sounding edition from A&M ages ago, on a rather better-sounding Mobile Fidelity edition in the late '80s, and at the opening of the new century in a remastered edition from Europe's Westside label that not only features significantly increased clarity on all of the instruments, but also detailed annotation and the presence of nine bonus tracks from the same sessions, mostly rock & roll warm-ups and early takes of the finished material. Those cuts reveal interesting sides to the group's own internal dynamics and the way that they saw their sound, and one can add another star to the rating for the West Side version. *—Bruce Eder*

Broken Barricades / 1971 / A&M ✦✦✦✦
Despite the departure of organist Matthew Fisher, Procol Harum survived, and this album is ample proof. Fisher was one of the prime architects of the Harum sound, and his work on such classics as "Shine on Brightly" and, of course, "Whiter Shade of Pale" underline that. Procol continued as a four-piece, and it was indeed a good thing that they decided not to replace Fisher. The sound of the band on this album is a bit sparser, but definitely not without dimension and dynamics. "Simple Sister," one of the finest Gary Brooker/ Keith Reid compositions, is truly glorious, with Robin Trower's frightening lead guitar work juxtaposed nicely against a wonderful string arrangement. Several other tracks are first rate, including "Power Failure" and "Playmate of the Mouth." Along with Little Feat, Procol Harum was a great survivor among rock bands that have lost a key member. The proof is in these grooves. *—Matthew Greenwald*

Procol Harum Live: In Concert with the Edmonton Symphony Orchestra & the Da Camera Singers / 1972 / A&M ✦✦✦✦
It was an almost-perfect union of two musical worlds when Procol Harum recorded live with the Edmonton Symphony Orchestra and the Da Camera Singers. The songs which had previously soared on record reached a new dimension with this new, empathetic accompaniment, helped in no small part by the fact that the parts for the orchestra were written by Procol leader Gary Brooker. Actually, the concert almost didn't take place. It was organized by a fan of the group, and the arrangements were shaky and disorganized. Rehearsals with the orchestra hadn't gone smoothly, either. When the concert finally happened, the group was so nervous during the first half, they re-performed many of the same songs the second half. But the opening orchestral notes of "Conquistador," followed by B.J. Wilson's thunderous drumming, laid all doubts to rest. Although the studio recording of this tune sounded slow and limpid, Brooker's reconstruction for orchestra, with a dramatic Spanish brass and string arrangement, lifted the song to majestic heights. The song shot to number 16 in the American charts and blew away anything else on AM radio at the time. It was Procol's biggest commercial showing but for "Whiter Shade of Pale." Nothing else on this live album touches "Conquistador," although the poignant "A Salty Dog," one of the group's greatest songs, was faithfully recreated, and "Whaling Stories" provided another climactic moment. The second half of the record is devoted to the suite "In Held Twas I," which was well-suited for treatment by an orchestra, but which was always a little too arty, even for Procol Harum. *—Peter Kurtz*

Grand Hotel / 1973 / Chrysalis ✦✦✦✦
Procol Harum's first album for Chrysalis, *Grand Hotel*, found the band returning to the grandeur of earlier works such as *Shine On Brightly* and *Salty Dog*. Robin Trower's replacement Mick Grabham is capable, even powerful, but not nearly as distinctive as his predecessor; consequently, the material tends to rely more on ornate arrangements than guitar riffs, making this somewhat more dignified than either of their previous studio albums, *Home* and *Broken Barricades*.

Brooker and lyricist Keith Reid step up with strong material, notably the title track, "Toujours L'Amour," and "Fires (Which Burnt Brightly)." While the keyboard and orchestra-based arrangements harken back to earlier triumphs, the lyrics deal less with whaling stories than with social commentary; "A Souvenir of London" is about drug-smuggling, with "T.V. Caesar" about the pervasive influence of television. *—James A. Gardner*

Exotic Birds & Fruit / 1974 / Essential ✦✦✦
Now, this sounds more like a Procol Harum album than their previous efforts. From the opening comment by Gary Brooker, all the pistons are firing, producing some great music. While some of the lyrics deal in the stranger side of life (what Procol Harum doesn't), there are hooks galore to satisfy any listener's needs. The passing of years have only enhanced what lies here. *—James Chrispell*

Procol's Ninth / 1975 / Chrysalis ✦✦✦
For their ninth album, Procol Harum turned to production by the veteran songwriting team of Leiber and Stoller, who had written the first single ("Poison Ivy") by Procol predecessor band, the Parliaments. Though the band is in top form (especially drummer B.J. Wilson) and despite a strong start (with the exquisite "Pandora's Box," a U.K. hit), the album largely runs out of steam by side two. Too much of the Brooker and Reid material is competent rather than exciting. Likewise, Procol fails to render memorable versions of two cover songs, Leiber and Stoller's "I Keep Forgetting" or the Beatles' "Eight Days A Week." Most of this album's best material can be found on the *Chrysalis Years* collection. [*Grand Hotel* and *Procol's Ninth* were later re-released as *Cornerstone*, a budget double album.] *–James A. Gardner*

Something Magic / 1977 / Chrysalis ✦✦

Prodigal Stranger / Aug. 27, 1991 / Zoo ✦✦✦

The Long Goodbye / Jul. 18, 1995 / RCA Victor ✦✦

● **Greatest Hits [A&M]** / May 7, 1996 / A&M ✦✦✦✦✦
Procul Harum's 1996 collection *Greatest Hits* features the same songs and sequencing as 1987's *Classics, Vol. 17*, except the music has been remastered. For most ears, the remastering isn't particularly noticeable, so if you already own *Classics, Greatest Hits* is completely unnecessary, yet the collection remains an adequate introduction for casual fans. *—Stephen Thomas Erlewine*

30th Anniversary Anthology / Nov. 17, 1997 / Westside ✦✦✦✦✦
The best collection yet devoted to Procol Harum's classic early period ties together the many facets of their sound and their early history, including numerous outtakes and all of the music on four albums from 1967 through 1970. The clarity of the sound makes the first album—which was roundly criticized, especially in England, for having been cut in mono in late 1967—seem a lot more muscular and progressive here than it did in its original release form. The producers have tampered with the song order on *A Salty Dog*, moving that record's title track in amongst disc three's single sides for time considerations while still leaving "Whiter Shade of Pale" and "Homburg" off of the first CD (the original commercial flaw with the debut album in England was the absence of either of those songs, and the seven-month-plus delay in getting it out). From the psychedelic/progressive blues stylings of *Shine on Brightly* to the self-consciously leaner, harder *Home*, this is the optimum way to hear the band. The collection also documents the change from somewhat light, optimistic psychedelia in 1967/1968 to the darker, edgier psychedelia of 1970 and beyond. The best part for collectors will be disc three, which, in addition to the group's hit singles and surprisingly fascinating B-sides from 1967-1970, also includes outtakes from unfinished early album sessions and alternate takes (with different personnel) of "Whiter Shade of Pale," "Homburg," and others, some in stereo. The notes are reasonably thorough, although they skimp a little in telling the story of the recording of "Whiter Shade of Pale" and the subsequent assembling of the permanent band. *—Bruce Eder*

Greatest Hits [Metro] / Dec. 12, 2000 / Metro ✦✦✦✦
The title's a bit of a misnomer, as Procol Harum were never a singles-oriented band after "A Whiter Shade of Pale" had finished its massive chart run. And even though this has their other late-'60s high and (usually) low single chart entries—"Homburg," "Quite Rightly So," and "A Salty Dog"—it lacks the early-'70s hit remake of "Conquistador" (though the original's here), as well as the British Top Twenty hit "Pandora's Box." If you're not fussy about designations, this is a good and lengthy (75-minute) survey of the highlights of the earliest and most interesting part of their career, with songs from their first four albums, all released in 1967-1970. It's expectedly heavy on the self-titled debut album, including all but three songs from *Procol Harum*, and then five songs from *Shine on Brightly* (the hugely popular title track among them), drawing lightly on *A Salty Dog* and *Home*. Song- and pop-oriented listeners may find this collection, with its focus on the shorter and more accessible tracks, shows the band to be a more listenable and enjoyable proposition than they remember. *—Richie Unterberger*

The Prodigy

f. 1990, Braintree, Essex, England
Big Beat, Electronica, Rave, Club/Dance, Techno, Funky Breaks
The Prodigy navigated the high wire, balancing artistic merit and mainstream visibility with more flair than any electronica act of the 1990s. Ably defeating the image-unconscious attitude of most electronic artists in favor of a focus on nominal frontman Keith Flint, the group crossed over to the mainstream of pop music with an incendiary live experience that approximated the original atmosphere of the British rave scene even while leaning uncomfortably close to arena-rock showmanship and punk theatrics. True, Flint's spiky hairstyle and numerous piercings often made for better advertising, but it was producer Liam Howlett whose studio wizardry launched the Prodigy to the top of the charts, spinning a web of hard-hitting breakbeat techno with king-sized hooks and unmissable samples. Despite electronic music's diversity and quick progression during the 1990s—from rave/hardcore to ambient/downtempo and back again, thanks to the breakbeat/ drum'n'bass movement—Howlett modified Prodigy's sound only sparingly; swapping the rave-whistle effects and ragga samples for metal chords and chanted vocals proved the only major difference in the band's evolution from their debut to their worldwide breakthrough with third album *The Fat of the Land*. Even before the band took its place as the premiere dance act for the alternative masses, Prodigy had proved a consistent entry in the British charts, with over a dozen consecutive singles in the Top 20. *—John Bush*

Experience / Oct. 20, 1992 / Elektra ✦✦✦✦✦
One of the few non-compilation rave albums of any worth, *Experience* balances a supply of top-this siren whistles and chipmunk divas with Howlett's surprising flair at constructing track after track of intense breakbeat techno. Almost every song sounds like a potential chart-topper (circa 1992, of course) while the true singles "Your Love," "Charly," "Music Reach 1/2/3/4" and "Out of Space" add that extra bit of energy to the fray. More than just a relic of the rave experience, *Experience* shows the Prodigy near the peak of their game from the get-go. *—John Bush*

Music for the Jilted Generation / Feb. 28, 1995 / Mute ✦✦✦✦✦
The Prodigy's response to the sweeping legislation and crackdown on raves contained in 1994's Criminal Justice Bill is an effective statement of intent. Pure sonic terrorism, *Music for the Jilted Generation* employs the same rave energy that charged their debut *Experience* up the charts in Britain, but yokes it to a cause other than massive drug intake. Compared to their previous work, the sound is grubbier and less reliant on samples; the effect moved the Prodigy away from the American-influenced rave and acid-house of the past and toward a uniquely British vision of breakbeat techno that was increasingly

allied to the limey invention, drum'n'bass. As on *Experience*, there are so many great songs here that first-time listeners would be forgiven for thinking of a greatest-hits compilation instead of a proper studio album. After a short intro, the shattering of panes of glass on "Break & Enter" catapults the album ahead with a propulsive flair. Each of the four singles—"Voodoo People," "Poison," "No Good (Start the Dance)," and "One Love"—are excellent, though album tracks like "Speedway" and "Their Law" (with help from Pop Will Eat Itself) don't slip up either. If *Experience* seemed like an excellent fluke, *Music for the Jilted Generation* was the album that announced Prodigy was on the charts to stay. *—John Bush*

● **The Fat of the Land** / Jul. 1, 1997 / XL Mute/Maverick/Warner Bros. ♦♦♦♦♦
Few albums were as eagerly anticipated as *The Fat of the Land*, the Prodigy's long-awaited follow-up to *Music for the Jilted Generation*. By the time of its release, the group had two number one British singles with "Firestarter" and "Breathe," and had begun to make inroads in America. *The Fat of the Land* was touted as the album that would bring electronica/techno to a wide American audience; in Britain, the group already had a staggeringly large following that was breathlessly awaiting the album. *The Fat of the Land* falls short of masterpiece status, but that isn't because it doesn't deliver. Instead, it delivers exactly what anyone would expect: intense hip-hop-derived rhythms, imaginatively reconstructed samples, and meaningless shouted lyrics from Keith Flint and Maxim. Half of the album does sound quite similar to "Firestarter," especially when Flint is singing. Still, Howlett is an inventive producer, and he can make empty songs like "Smack My Bitch Up" and "Serial Thrilla" kick with a visceral power, but he is at his best on the funky hip-hop of "Diesel Power" (which is driven by an excellent Kool Keith rap) and "Funky Shit," as well as the mind-bending neo-psychedelia of "Narayan" (featuring guest vocals by Crispian Mills of Kula Shaker) and the blood-curdling cover of L7's "Fuel My Fire," which features vocals by Republica's Saffron. All those guest vocalists mean something—Howlett is at his best when he's writing for himself or others, not his group's own vocalists. "Firestarter" and all of its rewrites capture the fire of the Prodigy at its peak, and the remaining songs have imagination that give the album weight. *The Fat of the Land* doesn't have quite enough depth or variety to qualify as a flat-out masterpiece, but what it does have to offer is damn good. *—Stephen Thomas Erlewine*

The Dirtchamber Sessions, Vol. 1 / Apr. 6, 1999 / XL/Beggars Banquet ♦♦♦♦
As though he wasn't the feature player on each of the three Prodigy albums preceding it, *The Dirtchamber Sessions* presents Liam Howlett in a solo setting. But here, instead of showing off his production wizardry, his long history as a DJ and mixing abilities are on display. They're proved more than up to the task, as Howlett plays mix and match with over 50 records from his hip-hop and funk past. While the Chemical Brothers' mix album (released the year before) showcased the duo digging deep in their record crates for a set of soul chestnuts and rare finds, Howlett's selection and feel for the flow of a mix is superior. Including tracks by the JB's, Herbie Hancock, the 45 King, L.L. Cool J, the Sex Pistols, and Jane's Addiction, Howlett chooses grooves familiar to all and improvises around them (as any old-school DJ would think obvious) instead of mixing between two tracks few have ever heard. The result is an enlightening, practically flawless mix album. *—John Bush*

Professor Longhair (Henry Roeland Byrd)

b. Dec. 19, 1918, Bogalusa, LA, **d.** Jan. 30, 1980, New Orleans, LA
Vocals, Leader, Arranger, Songwriter, Piano / New Orleans R&B, New Orleans Blues, Piano Blues
Justly worshipped decades after his death as a founding father of New Orleans R&B, Roy "Professor Longhair" Byrd's Latin-tinged rhumba-rocking piano style and croaking, yodeling vocals were as singular and spicy as the second-line beats that power his hometown's musical heartbeat. Byrd brought an irresistible Caribbean feel to his playing, full of rolling flourishes that every Crescent City ivories man had to learn inside out (Fats Domino, Huey Smith, and Allen Toussaint all paid homage early and often). After playing piano at various clubs around New Orleans, Longhair debuted on wax in 1949 and gained his first and only national R&B hit one year later, the hilarious "Bald Head" (credited to Roy Byrd & his Blues Jumpers). The pianist made great records for Atlantic in 1949, Federal in 1951, Wasco in 1952, and Atlantic again in 1953. After recuperating from a minor stroke, Longhair came back on Lee Rupe's Ebb logo in 1957 and Joe Ruffino's Ron imprint in 1959. He hit the skids in the '60s though, abandoning his piano playing until a booking at the fledgling 1971 Jazz & Heritage Festival put him on the comeback trail. He made a slew of albums in the last decade of his life, topped off by a terrific set for Alligator (*Crawfish Fiesta*), but died in 1980. His music is played in his hometown so often and so reverently, you'd swear he was still around. *—Bill Dahl*

New Orleans Piano / 1972 / Atlantic ♦♦♦♦♦
All 16 of the Atlantic sides from 1949 and 1953 (including a handful of alternate takes) on one glorious disc. Longhair's work for the label was notoriously marvelous—this version of "Mardi Gras in New Orleans" reeks of revelry in the streets of the French Quarter; "She Walks Right In" and "Walk Your Blues Away" ride a bedrock boogie, and "In the Night" bounces atop a parade-beat shuffle groove and hard-charging saxes. *—Bill Dahl*

Rock & Roll Gumbo / 1977 / Dancing Cat ♦♦♦♦♦
Recorded in 1974, this album almost never saw the light of day. Fortunately, the master tapes were found and the album was released posthumously. Professor Longhair was a giant in the New Orleans music community, but had not recorded in over ten years when he was convinced to start playing again. From the opening riffs, one can understand the stature of Professor Longhair as a great pianist—he demonstrates that he is equally at home playing rhumba boogie, blues songs, and calypso. He plays New Orleans standards (many penned by himself), but what makes this recording a classic is the chance to hear him play with guitarist Clarence "Gatemouth" Brown. The interplay of these music veterans is mesmerizing. The piano playing is breathtaking, and has a percussive quality unlike any other player before or since. It is hard to believe that Professor Longhair languished in obscurity for so many years after hearing the jubilance of "Mardi Gras in New Orleans," a song that will have you tapping your feet and hands as if you were in the parade. This album is essential for fans of New Orleans music and those aspiring to be rock & roll pianists. *—Vik Iyengar*

Crawfish Fiesta / 1980 / Alligator ♦♦♦♦♦
Probably the best of all the many albums Longhair waxed during his comeback (and likely the last). A tremendously tight combo featuring three horns and Dr. John on guitar delightfully back the Professor every step of the way as he recasts Solomon Burke's "Cry to Me" and Fats Domino's "Whole Lotta Loving" in his own indelible image and roars, yodels, and whistles out wonderful remakes of his own oldies "Big Chief" and "Bald Head." *—Bill Dahl*

Mardi Gras in New Orleans / 1981 / Nighthawk ♦♦♦♦♦
Plenty of rarities are featured on this valuable cross-section of the Professor's early releases. Both sides of the pianist's first two 78s for Star Talent Records are aboard, as well as sides he cut for Mercury, Federal ("Curly Haired Baby," "Gone So Long"), Wasco ("East St. Louis Baby"), Atlantic, and Ebb. *—Bill Dahl*

House Party New Orleans Style / 1987 / Rounder ♦♦♦
Boiling blues and trademark Afro-Latin and boogie-woogie riffs were the menu when Professor Longhair brought his Crescent City music show to Baton Rouge and Memphis in 1971 and 1972, respectively. The 15 numbers on this set matched the great pianist with an esteemed array of musicians that included outstanding guitarist Snooks Eaglin on both sessions, and fine rhythm sections as well. Eaglin's flashy, inventive solos were excellent contrasts to Longhair's rippling keyboard flurries and distinctive mix of yodels, yells, cries and shouts. *—Ron Wynn*

Mardi Gras in Baton / 1991 / Rhino ♦♦♦♦
Some of the earliest sides from Longhair's rediscovery period (1971-72), featuring a lot of tunes inexorably associated with him through previous versions and a few ("Jambalaya," "Sick and Tired") that weren't. An added bonus is the magical presence of guitarist Snooks Eaglin, whose approach is every bit as singular as the Professor's was. *—Bill Dahl*

★ **Fess: The Professor Longhair Anthology** / Nov. 16, 1993 / Rhino ♦♦♦♦♦
The rhumba-rocking rhythms of Roy "Professor Longhair" Byrd live on throughout Rhino's 40-track retrospective of the New Orleans icon's amazing legacy. Most of the seminal stuff arrives early on: "Bald Head," the rollicking ode Byrd cut for Mercury in 1950, is followed by a raft of classics from his 1949 and 1953 Atlantic dates ("Tipitina," "Ball the Wall," "Who's Been Fooling You"), the storming 1957 "No Buts—No Maybes" and "Baby Let Me Hold Your Hand" for Ebb, and his beloved "Go to the Mardi Gras" as waxed for Ron in 1959. The second disc is a hodge-podge of material from his 1970s comeback, all of it wonderful in its own way but not as essential as the early work. *—Bill Dahl*

The Promise Ring

f. 1995, Milwaukee, WI
Emo, Punk-Pop, Indie Rock, Alternative Pop/Rock
Milwaukee-based emo quartet the Promise Ring formed in early 1995 from the remnants of acclaimed local acts Cap'n Jazz, Ceilishrine, and None Left Standing. Comprising singer/guitarist Davey VonBohlen, guitarist Jason Gnewikow, bassist Scott Schoenbeck and drummer Dan Didier, the group signed to Jade Tree in 1996, and over the course of the year which followed issued no less than two seven-inches ("Falsetto Keeps Time" and a split release with Texas Is the Reason), a full-length LP (*30 Degrees Everywhere*) and a singles compilation (*The Horse Latitudes*). The critical favorite *Nothing Feels Good* followed in 1997, and two years later the Promise Ring returned with their third album, *Very Emergency*. That same year, VonBohlen and Didier also joined forces in the more pop-oriented Vermont, releasing *Living Together* on the Kindercore label. *—Jason Ankeny*

● **30° Everywhere** / Sep. 10, 1996 / Jade Tree ♦♦♦♦♦
These young Wisconsin boys certainly know how to write sharp, powerful and beautiful songs. This, the debut album from the Promise Ring, is still their best to date; it's basically straight-up pop/emo, very catchy, very intense, very powerful. Beautiful lyrics and melodies move from somber thoughts to moments that will make you smile in understanding. It's sort of like the soundtrack to a ride through your memories. Highly recommended. *—Blake Butler*

Horse Latitudes / Feb. 11, 1997 / Jade Tree ♦♦♦♦
Nestled between the emotionally terse *30 Degrees Everywhere* and the pop explosion of *Nothing Feels Good*, this singles and unreleased songs compilation sees the Promise Ring in a number of different musical phases. The earliest material on the record, including "Watertown Plank" and the emo classic "A Picture Postcard," showcase the raw origins of the band and their early tendencies to couple meandering guitar notes with unbridled and distorted rock. "E. Texas Ave.," a fan favorite from the group's split 7" with Texas Is the Reason, is also a noteworthy inclusion, not to mention the toughest song the band has ever recorded. There are a few dawdling tracks on the record that don't do much of anything, but on the whole, this is a fine collection that clearly illustrates how this band came to reach their indie pop hitmaker status. There's a strong sense of melody that often surfaces from the tracks, and the closing horn bop of "I Never Trusted the Russians" is a clear indicator of where the band would take their sound in the period that followed this

album. A must for the group's fans, *The Horse Latitudes* is also a pretty good listen for anyone looking for solid emotional rock that is just as good at keeping quiet as it is at blasting out the speakers. *—Peter J. D'Angelo*

Nothing Feels Good / Oct. 14, 1997 / Jade Tree ✦✦✦✦
The sophomore disc from these young ones finds the band moving further into the poppiness that they only hinted at on *Thirty Degrees Everywhere*. Some things remain the same—beautifully odd lyrics, extremely catchy and powerful music, and the overall feeling of sentimentality and imagination that the Promise Ring's music always seems to exude. With the momentum and energy of this band, we could see them heading for the indie-rock history books. *—Blake Butler*

Very Emergency / Sep. 28, 1999 / Jade Tree ✦✦✦
Unfortunately, you will never see the Promise Ring the way they were in the days of *Thirty Degrees Everywhere*, but you can at least appreciate the good parts of what they have become. Their emotionally tense and sentimental edge has pretty much entirely disappeared; everything is happy, bouncy, and catchy as hell, which isn't always a bad thing. This excessively poppy direction that the Promise Ring boys take throughout this entire record was heavily hinted at on their three-song EP *Boys & Girls*. Perhaps one of the more upsetting things about this album is that the lyrics have lost that classic Promise Ring feel—they actually make clear sense a lot of the time. At times, the music just gets so poppy that it is sickening, such as in the sappy "bop bop bop" background vocals on "Skips a Beat (Over You)," and the references to the band members' names in an otherwise fairly decent song "Things Just Getting Good." Although three-fourths of the album is pretty much bad pop songs, it somehow grows on you, as those Promise Ring kids have the uncanny ability to do. *—Blake Butler*

The Psychedelic Furs

f. 1977, London, England, **db.** 1991
College Rock, Post-Punk, New Wave, Alternative Pop/Rock
The Psychedelic Furs, whose name belies their punk-influenced music, were formed in England in 1977 by brothers Richard Butler (vocals) and Tim Butler (bass), along with saxophone player Duncan Kilburn and guitarist Roger Morris. Their self-titled 1980 debut album, featuring Butler's hoarse voice (the tone of which suggested John Lydon without the sneer) was a bigger hit in England, where it reached the Top 20, than in the U.S. *Talk Talk Talk* (1981) did better, reaching the U.S. Top 100 and producing two British singles-chart entries, one of which was "Pretty in Pink," later also a hit in the U.S. when a new version was used as the title song of a film. Turning to producer Todd Rundgren, the Furs scored a U.S. Top 50 hit with "Love My Way." *Mirror Moves* (1984) was the biggest Psychedelic Furs hit yet, and the film *Pretty in Pink* helped spread their name further before the release of their next album, *Midnight to Midnight* (1987), which consequently got to #12 in the U.K. and the Top 30 in the US and included the Top 30 U.S. hit "Heartbreak Beat." After *World Outside* (1991) failed to find an audience, the Psychedelic Furs folded up shop, and Richard Butler launched a new group, Love Spit Love. *—William Ruhlmann*

The Psychedelic Furs / 1980 / Columbia ✦✦✦✦✦
Emerging from the incipient post-punk London scene with a healthy fascination for late-'70s Bowie (and in turn, for his own attraction to Krautrock), the then-sextet kicked up a slightly monochromatic but still attractive storm on their debut. Richard Butler's Thin-White-Duke-after-smoking vocal rasp has a surprising appeal, serving up a wry, slightly detached series of lyrics on life. The core band, meanwhile, had clearly honed their chops well on stage; Ashton's lead guitar work avoids both wankery and simplicity in favor of a balanced, artistic power. Production mainly comes from Steve Lillywhite, who smartly steers away from the soon-to-be-clichéd touches he would bring to U2's early work. "India" is a good example; it has a brooding, quiet beginning with strange telegraphic signals and turns into a brawling rocker without sounding like the Edge or Larry Mullins going off. The record comes off as serious without being self-consciously deep, occasional toe-dipping into humor aside ("We Love You" has Butler idly listing off things he loves, sometimes with appropriate if sarcastically delivered song quotes: "I'm in love with Frank Sinatra… fly me to the moon…"). "Imitation of Christ" is the most frazzled, with lyrics detailing someone else metaphorically nailing himself up over a light but still strange guitar line. "Wedding Song" is amusingly prescient as one of the first "white rockers go hip-hop" numbers of its kind, along with Blondie's "Rapture," though its inspiration could equally be dub. Ely lays down a pounding funk beat while Butler breaks into a mid-song rap no better or worse than most such efforts of the time. *—Ned Raggett*

Talk Talk Talk / Jun. 1981 / Columbia ✦✦✦✦✦
This time working solely with Steve Lillywhite, the Furs introduce a brighter, poppier side to their underground rock edge, with smashing results throughout. The group produces some powerful songs, even more rough-edged than before. Especially striking is "Dumb Waiters," with its queasy, slow-paced arrangement that allows both Kilburn's sax and Ashton's guitar to go wild. However, the six still create some undeniable pop classics. Most well-known is the lead track, "Pretty in Pink," inspiration for the iconic John Hughes film years later and re-recorded as a result. The original is still where to go though, with Butler's catchy description of a romantically unsure woman matched by a killer band performance. Similarly lighter numbers on the record call to mind a rockier version of Roxy Music's output in later years: elegant, romantic angst given a slightly rougher edge in both music and vocals. "She Is Mine" is especially fine as a gently swinging number with some of Butler's best, quietly ruminative lyrics. Straight-up anthems abound as well, the best being the amazing "Into You Like a Train," which mixes the blunt desire of the title with a sparkling Ashton guitar line and a fast rhythm punch. *Talk Talk Talk* ends on another high with "All of This and Nothing." A soft, acoustic guitar-sax-rhythm combination introduces the song, then fades away for the main section to begin; Butler details bits and pieces from a lost relationship over a sharp full-band performance, and a final drum smash leads into a reprise of the start—a fine way to end a fine record. *—Ned Raggett*

Forever Now / 1982 / Columbia ✦✦✦
Likely exercising the same controlling approach that he was notorious for, from his work with every act from the New York Dolls to XTC, Todd Rundgren brought in legendary backup vocal duo Flo and Eddie as well as a cellist, two horn players (including NRBQ member Donn Adams), and himself on keyboards. The end result is simply fantastic, fusing the post-punk charge of the first two albums (Ely still sounds great as always, from the first song on, while Tim Butler acquits himself well on bass) with a new synth-based approach that works wonders. Ashton's guitar often settles back in the mix a bit to allow Rundgren's wall of sound to come together fully, often with great success. The title track is a great example of this, an inspirational anthem where Ashton fully and appropriately lets go right at the end. The most well-known song is one that, for the Furs, was their most atypical single to date: "Love My Way." Butler's very Bowie-like vocals and lyrics slyly celebrate and ponder the triumphant synth-rock scene of the time, while Rundgren's often quirky keyboards take the lead in place of Ashton's guitar and Flo and Eddie wordlessly vocalize at the end. "Goodbye" has a brisk, horn-driven punch underscoring Butler's wickedly sour *au revoir* to a past love; "Sleep Comes Down" mixes Tim Butler's lovely bass line and Rundgren's piano; "President Gas" wryly takes a shot at Reagan while avoiding obvious platitudes; and "Yes I Do" ends on an almost sweetly romantic note, even as the cello/drum-driven arrangement surges along. *—Ned Raggett*

Mirror Moves / 1984 / Columbia ✦✦✦
On *Mirror Moves*, The Psychedelic Furs began to move toward a slicker, accessible pop-rock sound. By and large, the extra gloss works, as the group turns in a set of catchy rockers that manages to incorporate some mainstream concessions into their signature sound without losing their personality. It may not be as exciting as their first four records, but they pull off the streamlined pop on *Mirror Moves* with considerable panache. *—Stephen Thomas Erlewine*

Midnight to Midnight / 1987 / Columbia ✦✦✦
Midnight to Midnight continues the streamlining of The Psychedelic Furs. Unlike the previous *Mirror Moves*, *Midnight to Midnight* loses the essential character of The Furs' sound, as the production relies on a sleek, stylish pop production. Although the results don't have much to do with the group's early records, it's an entertaining record, filled with its share of pop thrills, including the single "Heartbreak Beat." *—Stephen Thomas Erlewine*

● **All of This and Nothing** / 1988 / Columbia ✦✦✦✦✦
Not a perfect Furs compilation, but this 12-track look back does contain the notable tracks from the albums *Mirror Moves* and *Midnight to Midnight*, plus some of the necessary ones from the albums listed above and a good new song, "All That Money Wants." *—William Ruhlmann*

Book of Days / Oct. 1989 / Columbia ✦✦

World Outside / Jul. 30, 1991 / Columbia ✦✦✦

B-Sides & Lost Grooves / Oct. 25, 1994 / Columbia/Legacy ✦✦✦

Should God Forget: A Retrospective / Oct. 21, 1997 / Columbia/Legacy ✦✦✦
The double-disc set *Should God Forget: A Retrospective* may be a little bit too much for casual fans who only want the hit singles—after all, this is filled with B-sides, live tracks, rarities and a handful of outtakes—but for hardcore fans, this is a definitive collection, containing the majority of the group's best work. It also may convince skeptics that the group found one of the best fusions of the Sex Pistols, Roxy Music and David Bowie, inventing a stylish but menacing post-punk style that sounded like nothing else in the new wave era. *—Stephen Thomas Erlewine*

Greatest Hits / Jan. 30, 2001 / Columbia/Legacy ✦✦✦✦
More fervid fans of the Psychedelic Furs might prefer the two-CD *Should God Forget* collection to this more basic single-disc, 17-song retrospective, much (though not all) of which is also found on *Should God Forget*. Still, it gets the job done, with material spanning 1980-1991, including all half-dozen of their (low-charting) British chart entries. As for rarities that might tempt completists, this has the original 1981 single version of "Mr. Jones" (marking the first time it appeared on CD) and a previously unreleased 1987 live version of "Only You and I." *—Richie Unterberger*

Psychic TV

f. 1979, London, England
Experimental Rock, Experimental, Acid House, Alternative Pop/Rock, Industrial
After Genesis P-Orridge dissolved the seminal industrial rock outfit Throbbing Gristle, he and Gristle cohorts Peter Christopherson and Cosey Fanni Tutti, plus Geoff Rushton, formed Psychic TV in 1979 as a means of continuing their confrontational, shock-oriented approach to music and their multimedia live performances. Psychic TV draws much of its inspiration from the literary underground, including situationist philosophy, William Burroughs (a professed fan), the Marquis de Sade, and Philip K. Dick. The group also claims to be the mouthpiece for its own quasi-religious group, the Temple Ov Psychick Youth. As for the music itself, Psychic TV's earlier years continued in the experimental vein of Throbbing Gristle's work, encompassing melodic pop, barely listenable white noise, gentle ballads, industrial found-sound collages, spoken word pieces, and experiments with ethnic instruments and world music, all tied together by a dadaist sensibility. *Force the Hand of Chance*, the group's first album, was released in 1982; during the '80s,

Psychic TV's prodigious output totaled over 20 albums. Much of this stemmed from a publicity stunt beginning in 1986 for which the group attempted to release one live album, each from a different nation, on the 23rd of each month for 23 months. Even though the group didn't quite achieve its goal, the 14 albums Psychic TV released in 18 months was enough to get the group into the *Guinness Book of World Records*. Christopherson and Rushton both left the group rather early on to form Coil, and Psychic TV has since become an open-ended collective with contributors such as Alex Fergusson, formerly of Alternative TV. Psychic TV scored a minor U.K. pop hit in 1986 with "Godstar," a tribute to Rolling Stones guitarist Brian Jones, and 1988 saw the group's first album release in America with *Allegory and Self*. —*Steve Huey*

Force the Hand of Chance / 1982 / Some Bizarre ◆◆◆

The debut Psychic TV album has all of the hallmarks of the group's radical inspirations: light '60s pop on "Just Drifting (For Caresse)" and "Stolen Kisses," more orchestrated instrumental work for the later "Caresse," and several free-form passages with bizarre spoken-word material from Genesis himself. *Force the Hand of Chance* also features the input of Peter "Sleazy" Christopherson, just before he founded Coil with John Balance. —*John Bush*

Dreams Less Sweet / 1983 / Thirsty Ear ◆◆◆

Their second album, released in 1983, *Dreams Less Sweet* fluctuates between industrial pieces and heavily orchestrated pop, employing exotic instruments like the Tibetan thighbone in additon to a number of found sounds. —*Jason Ankeny*

Allegory and Self / 1988 / Revolver ◆◆◆◆

Beginning with "Godstar," Psychic TV's tribute to Brian Jones complete with Stonesy guitar licks, *Allegory and Self* balances surprisingly straight-ahead alternative pop with more experimental tracks using tape cut-ups or extended synthesizer freeforms. P-Orridge makes for quite an ambitious frontman, crooning like Love and Rockets' Daniel Ash on "We Kiss" and producing a series of guttural roars for "Southern Comfort." "She Was Surprised" even bears the first fruits of Psychic TV's fixation with sampladelic acid-house. It may not be characteristic Psychic TV (if such an animal exists), but *Allegory and Self* may well be the best introduction for beginners. —*John Bush*

Beyond Thee Infinite Beat / 1990 / Wax Trax! ◆◆◆

This *Infinite Beat* remix album includes reworkings of tracks by a host of PTV associates, including Dave Ball, Andy Falconer, Jack the Tab and Evil Eddie. Although most of the tracks have the blander qualities of much acid-house, Falconer's mix of "Bliss" and DJ Sugar Jay's mix of "Horror House" are a bit more together than most. —*John Bush*

Towards Thee Infinite Beat / 1990 / Wax Trax! ◆◆◆◆

Although it tends toward unvarying sampladelic acid-house, *Towards Thee Infinite Beat* is a good place to start for Psychic TV's dance phase. —*John Dougan*

Hex Sex: The Singles, Pt. 1 / 1994 / Cleopatra ◆◆◆◆

The pop end of Psychic TV gets the full treatment with this singles collection, released on the Cleopatra label, including faithful covers of '60s standards like the Beach Boys' "Good Vibrations" and Serge Gainsbourg' "Je T'aime Non Plus," culture-icon tributes "Roman P." and "Godstar" plus later singles like "Hex Sex" and "Love War Riot." Though Genesis P-Orridge's vocals are occasionally tuneless, *Hex Sex* is a good summation of one of the more bizarre "pop" bands of the '80s. —*John Bush*

Godstar: The Singles, Pt. 2 / 1995 / Cleopatra ◆◆◆◆

Godstar was meant to be a "best-of" for fans without access to Genesis P-Orridge's constant output of music in the 1980s. By cutting away the excess that haunts most Psychic TV albums, what is revealed is how original and creative a force they had the potential to be. All three versions of the title track work as fitting tributes to former Rolling Stones bassist Brian Jones, while their cover of the Beach Boys' "Good Vibrations" is a charged, vibrant undertaking of a pop classic. But nothing on the album compares to the sprawling "Roman P (Sordide Sentimental Mix)," the drug-fueled centerpiece. Droning on for almost ten minutes with continued intensity, it builds into a psychedelic epic, colored with noisy guitar solos and tribal drum beats. Some may be offset by P-Orridge's blatant shock tactics ("Neurology" features samples of Charles Manson and Jim Jones in opposing stereo channels) and the album's lack of continuity, but fans of creative electronic music will find this to be a good introduction to an important artist. —*Bradley Torreano*

The Origin of the Species / Mar. 24, 1998 / Invisible ◆◆◆◆◆

Five years of Psychic TV (1987-1992) are examined in this two-CD sampler packaged in Psychic TV's trademark exploitation of the power of the vulgar image. This is the first of a three-part series chronicling the group. Ten of the 21 tracks are previously unreleased. "Infinite Beat" and succeeding tracks identify Psychic TV as primogenitors of electronica, creative sampling and the club mix while flirting with psychological principles of mind control. Such is the typical combination of outre and superficially commercial material that is the Psychic TV fare and guaranteed to maintain their cult following. It is certainly no understatement to say that without this group's envelope-pushing fusion of machines and rock instrumentation you could never have gotten to the now thoroughly explored realms of acid house and techno. A 30-page, full-color booklet details each track with text from the mind of founding member, Genesis P-Orridge (also of pre-industrial noise experimenters Throbbing Gristle). Allowing full immersion of this suggestive, cryptic, neo-psychedelic beat music is truly a mind altering experience. A couple hours after partaking of these doses, one can be assured that Psychic TV aspired, and often succeeded at, employing guitars, drums, keyboards and sequenced sounds toward recreating an expansive, hallucinogenic, paradigm-challenging drug experience...that you can dance to. —*Thomas Schulte*

● **Best Ov Psychic TV: Time's Up** / Jun. 29, 1999 / Cleopatra ◆◆◆◆

While it isn't quite a definitive overview, *Best Ov: Time's Up* is easily the best single-disc introduction to Psychic TV, featuring such crucial singles as "Godstar" (in both 7" and 1994 versions), "Roman P.," "United '94," and more. Some of the single mixes present are very difficult to locate elsewhere, making this package enticing for devoted fans as well. —*Steve Huey*

Origin of the Species, Vol. 2 / Aug. 31, 1999 / Invisible ◆◆◆

The two-disc *Origin of the Species, Vol. 2* rescues a sizable number of Psychic TV house tracks from out-of-print obscurity. The first disc is drawn from the albums *Jack the Tab: Acid Tablets, Vol. 1* (1988) and *Tekno Acid Beat* (1989), while the second disc features the *Ultradrug* material issued in 1995. The *Jack the Tab* cuts are the most interesting, having been issued as a fake various-artists compilation and actually featuring Psychic TV working with former Soft Cell keyboardist Dave Ball and writer Richard Norris. Since the tracks here aren't culled from as wide a variety of sources as the first volume of *Origin of the Species*, it isn't quite as consistent a listen, but it does capture the group at their acid-house peak, and all of this material has been very difficult to find for a long time. —*Steve Huey*

Public Enemy

f. 1982, Long Island, NY

Hardcore Rap, East Coast Rap, Hip-Hop, Political Rap, Golden Age

Public Enemy rewrote the rules of hip-hop, becoming the most influential and controversial rap group of the late '80s and, for many, the definitive rap group of all time. Building from Run-D.M.C.'s street-oriented beats and Boogie Down Productions' proto-gangsta rhyming, Public Enemy pioneered a variation of hardcore rap that was musically and politically revolutionary. With his powerful, authoritative baritone, lead rapper Chuck D rhymed about all kinds of social problems, particularly those plaguing the Black community, often condoning revolutionary tactics and social activism. In the process, he directed hip-hop towards an explicitly self-aware, pro-Black consciousness that became the culture's signature throughout the next decade. Musically, Public Enemy were just as revolutionary, as their production team the Bomb Squad created dense soundscapes that relied on avant-garde cut-and-paste techniques, unrecognizable samples, piercing sirens, relentless beats and deep funk. It was chaotic and invigorating music, made all the more intoxicating by Chuck D's forceful vocals and the absurdist raps of his comic foil Flavor Flav. With his comic sunglasses and an oversized clock hanging from his neck, Flav became the group's visual focal point, but he never obscured the music. While rap and rock critics embraced the group's late '80s and early '90s records, Public Enemy frequently ran into controversy with their militant stance and lyrics, especially after their 1988 album *It Takes a Nation of Millions to Hold Us Back* made them into celebrities. After all the controversy settled in the early '90s, once the group entered hiatus, it became clear that Public Enemy was the most influential and radical band of its time. —*Stephen Thomas Erlewine*

Yo! Bum Rush the Show / 1987 / Def Jam ◆◆◆◆◆

When their debut was released in 1987, very few rap groups even approached Public Enemy's musical or political stance. Listening to the first album now, it's surprising how few of the songs are actually political—the sheer force of the sound fools the listener into thinking Chuck D is saying more than he actually is. Still, "Megablast," "Public Enemy No. 1," and "Miuzi Weighs a Ton" carry a small amount of political rhetoric. Much sparer than later releases, the album is carried over the top by Chuck D's bulldozer roar. —*Stephen Thomas Erlewine*

★ It Takes a Nation of Millions to Hold Us Back / 1988 / Def Jam ◆◆◆◆◆

Arguably the best hip-hop album ever made, *It Takes a Nation of Millions to Hold Us Back* was a huge leap forward not only for Public Enemy, but for all of hip-hop. PE's signature sound—a barrage of found sounds, densely woven samples, and noisy tape loops—was evident for the first time, courtesy of The Bomb Squad. Chuck D's lyrics, full of revolutionary rhetoric yet managing to avoid being hysterical, matched the aural onslaught. The group's political stance would be meaningless if the music didn't put it over the top throughout, and that does happen on "Black Steel in the Hour of Chaos," "Night of the Living Baseheads," "Rebel Without a Pause," "Don't Believe the Hype," and "Bring the Noise," in particular. There isn't a weak moment on the album. A landmark recording. —*Stephen Thomas Erlewine*

☆ Fear of a Black Planet / 1990 / Def Jam ◆◆◆◆◆

Public Enemy's artistic and commercial winning streak continued with its third album, *Fear of a Black Planet*. While other East Coast rappers were content to boast and boast about their prowess on the microphone, Public Enemy always had a lot to say. Though a few stinkers are included—the worst offender being the homophobic "Meet the G That Killed Me"—they are by far outnumbered by the gems. From "Burn Hollywood Burn" (a brutally honest attack on racism in the film industry) to the optimistic "Brothers Gonna Work It Out," the politically charged rappers have no problem maintaining the level of excellence they reached on *It Takes a Nation of Millions to Hold Us Back*. A gut-level attack on incompetence in the 911 system, "911 Is a Joke" illustrates just how on-target PE could be—in fact, it should be stressed that the song precedes by several years the incident in which 911 operators in Philadelphia came under attack for doing nothing to help a youth who was being beaten to death. And once again, PE's producers, the Bomb Squad, provide a collage of samples that is as imaginative as it is bombastic. —*Alex Henderson*

☆ Apocalypse 91 ... The Enemy Strikes Black / Oct. 1, 1991 / Def Jam ◆◆◆◆◆

Although it falls short of the excellence of *Fear of a Black Planet* and *It Takes a Nation of Millions to Hold Us Back*, PE's fourth album proved that the Long Islanders could still be extremely stimulating—both lyrically and musically. This time, the obvious winners include "Shut Em Down" (a commentary on liquor stores profiting from human suffering in the Black commmunity) and "By the Time I Get to Arizona" (an angry reflection on that state's refusal to celebrate Martin Luther King's birthday in the early '90s) and an invigorating rap/metal remake of "Bring the Noize" featuring thrash headbangers Anthrax. Although produced by the Imperial Grand Ministers of Funk instead of the Bomb Squad, the album boasts exactly the type of production one associates with PE—abrasive, hard and dissonant. Unfortunately, PE's popularity would decline considerably after the album—and considerably less talented N.W.A. clones would be selling a lot more albums. *—Alex Henderson*

Greatest Misses / Sep. 15, 1992 / Def Jam ✦✦
For the first time in their career, Public Enemy sounds unsure of the direction of their music. *Greatest Misses* is half original tracks and half remixes, and consequently sounds muddled. Public Enemy sounds like it's treading water throughout the new songs; none of them are particularly bad, but unlike all of their previous material, none of it is groundbreaking. None of the remixes are awful, but they are neither revelatory nor insightful and often miss the original intent of the song. *—Stephen Thomas Erlewine*

Muse Sick-N-Hour Mess Age / Aug. 23, 1994 / Def Jam ✦✦

He Got Game / Apr. 21, 1998 / Def Jam ✦✦✦✦
Nominally a soundtrack to Spike Lee's basketball drama, but in reality more of an individual album, *He Got Game* appeared in 1998, just the second Public Enemy album since 1991's *Apocalypse 91.* Even though Chuck D was pushing 40, the late '90s were friendlier to PE's noisy, claustrophobic hip-hop than the mid-'90s, largely because hip-hop terrorists like the Wu-Tang Clan, Jeru the Damaja, and DJ Shadow were bringing the music back to its roots. PE followed in their path, stripping away the sonic blitzkrieg that was the Bomb Squad's trademark and leaving behind skeletal rhythm tracks, simple loops, and bass lines. Taking on the Wu at their own game—and, if you think about it, Puff Daddy as well, since the simple, repetitive loop of Buffalo Springfield's "For What It's Worth" on the title track was nothing more than a brazenly successful one-upmanship of Puff's shameless thievery—didn't hurt the group's credibility, since they did it *well.* Listen to the circular, menacing synth lines of the opening "Resurrection" or the scratching strings on "Unstoppable" and it's clear that Public Enemy could compete with the most innovative artists in the younger generation, while "Is Your God a Dog" and "Politics of the Sneaker Pimps" proved that they could draw their own rules. That said, *He Got Game* simply lacked the excitement and thrill of prime period PE—Chuck D, Terminator X, and the Bomb Squad were seasoned, experienced craftsmen, and it showed, for better and worse. They could craft a solid comeback like *He Got Game,* but no matter how enjoyable and even thought-provoking the album was, that doesn't mean it's where you'll turn when you want to hear Public Enemy. *—Stephen Thomas Erlewine*

There's a Poison Goin' On... / Jul. 20, 1999 / Play It Again Sam ✦✦✦
Opening with a sonic collage straight out of *Fear of a Black Planet, There's a Poison Goin' On...* comes out of the gates sounding like classic Public Enemy, which is exactly what Public Enemy intended, since their slight sonic change-up on *He Got Game* didn't result in a hit. In a way, PE's feud with Def Jam over downloadable MP3 music was a good thing, since it brought them media attention, which is rare for a veteran hip-hop band. Such increased exposure also brought a minor controversy over "Swindlers Lust," which some perceived as anti-Semitic, but this outrage was isolated because Public Enemy was now at the margins of hip-hop. They were no longer considered cutting-edge, and younger kids never picked up their records, so the only place for this controversy to reside was among the rock critics and aging fans who remembered when *It Takes a Nation of Millions* changed the world ten years prior. Chuck D must have known that they would be the only ones paying attention to the album, since it consciously copies PE's past and never really breaks from that blueprint. In some respects, that's a disappointment, since *He Got Game* showed that PE could subtly incorporate modern hip-hop and do it better than some modern acts. But *There's a Poison Goin' On* is nevertheless a strong album, even if it is doggedly classicist. It's also dogmatic, with Chuck preaching to the converted about the evils of the record industry and conformity in hip-hop, which does become a little trying by the end of the record. But he delivers lyrically and PE delivers musically, in a manner that's entirely familiar to fans of Public Enemy, offering a solid continuation of *Apocalypse 91.* Ultimately, it's their most satisfying record in several years—which is a subtle difference that only the converted will notice. *—Stephen Thomas Erlewine*

20th Century Masters—The Millennium Collection: The Best of Public Enemy / Jun. 19, 2001 / Def Jam ✦✦✦✦
In a way, Public Enemy is a band that defies compilations because each of their records is so perfectly crafted, such an ideal statement, that they can't seem to exist in any other way. But, like any great band, the individual songs stand on their own merits, and if they're put together in the right order, the end result would be nothing less than phenomenal. *20th Century Masters* is not phenomenal. It's not even executed particularly well, missing some absolutely essential songs (how the hell do you put out a PE comp without "Rebel Without a Pause" and "Black Steel in the Hour of Chaos"?) and sequenced in a halting fashion. So, it's not perfect, but some Public Enemy is better than none, especially if "Welcome to the Terrordome," "Bring the Noise," "Don't Believe the Hype," "Fight the Power," and "Night of the Living Baseheads" constitute half the album. The rest of the record is pretty damn good, too—only the Anthrax-assisted re-recording of "Bring tha Noize" is execrable, yet "By the Time I Get to Arizona," "Shut Em Down," and "Nighttrain" make up for its presence—but there's so much missing that it's hard to give this a ringing endorsement. Some haphazard compilations wind up quenching your thirst, others leave you wanting more; this is one that leaves you thirsty, especially if you get positively weak from hearing Chuck D's voice—the way that some quake at the sound of Coltrane's saxophone, Miles' trumpet, Clapton's guitar. There's no other instrument quite as overwhelming as this, and it's damn irresistible. *—Stephen Thomas Erlewine*

Public Image Ltd.

f. 1978, London, England, **db.** 1993
College Rock, Noise-Rock, Alternative Dance, Post-Punk, Alternative Pop/Rock
Public Image Ltd. (PiL) originally was a quartet led by singer John Lydon (formerly Johnny Rotten) and guitarist Keith Levene, who had been a member of the Clash in one of its early lineups. It was formed in the wake of the 1978 breakup of Lydon's former group, the Sex Pistols. For the most part, it devoted itself to droning, slow-tempo, bass-heavy noise rock, overlaid by Lydon's distinctive, vituperative rant. The group's debut single, "Public Image," was more of an uptempo pop/rock song, however, and it hit the U.K. Top Ten upon its release in October 1978. *Metal Box,* the band's second U.K. album, came in the form of three 12-inch, 45 RPM discs in a film cannister. It was released in the U.S. in 1980 as the double album *Second Edition.* In 1983, PiL scored its biggest U.K. hit, when "This Is Not a Love Song" reached #5. By this time, however, Levene had left, and the name from here on would be, more than anything else, a vehicle for John Lydon. *This Is What You Want... This Is What You Get* marked the start of Lydon's move toward a more accessible dance-rock style, a direction that would be pursued further in *Album* (1986) (also called *Cassette* or *Compact Disc,* depending on the format), notably on the hit "Rise." After completing his memoirs in late 1993, Lydon decided to put an end to PiL and pursue a solo career. *—William Ruhlmann*

Public Image/First Issue / Dec. 1978 / Warner Brothers ✦✦✦✦
Public Image shows John Lydon and his new mates working out the kinks a bit, but the debut remains a challenging chunk of destructive post-punk, just as jarring as his previous band's work. "I wish I could *die*!!!," exclaims Lydon in "Theme," the nine-minute death dirge that signals PiL's uncompromising arrival. The sludge-like tempo of Jim Walker's drums and Jah Wobble's bass never deviates; it's a "song" you either lose yourself in or quickly skip through. Things don't *really* cook until the bouncy "Annalisa" and "Public Image," the most Pistols-like tune that the band recorded. Lydon is happier than Sid Vicious in a pool of puke in his new environs, and you can't help but get a contact buzz from his sinister vigor. The record is closed out with "Fodderstompf," a dubbed-up jaunt of comical, cynical snipes—"We only wanted to be loved." But of course! *—Andy Kellman*

★ **Second Edition** / Jul. 1980 / Warner Brothers ✦✦✦✦✦
PiL managed to avoid boundaries for the first four years of their existence, and *Metal Box* is undoubtedly the apex. It's a hallmark of uncompromising, challenging post-punk, hardly sounding like anything of the past, present, or future. Sure, there were touchstones that got their imaginations running—the bizarreness of Captain Beefheart, the open and rhythmic spaces of Can, and the dense pulses of Lee Perry's productions fueled their creative fires—but what they achieved with their second record is a completely unique hour of avant garde noise. Originally packaged in a film canister as a trio of 12" records played at 45 rpm, the bass and treble are pegged at 11 throughout, with nary a tinge of midrange to be found. It's all scrapes and throbs (dubscrapes?), supplanted by John Lydon's caterwauling about such subjects as his dying mother, resentment and murder. Guitarist Keith Levene splatters silvery, violent, percussive shards of metallic scrapes onto the canvas, much like a one-armed Jackson Pollock. Jah Wobble and Richard Dudanski lay down a molasses-thick rhythmic foundation throughout that's just as funky as Can's Czukay/Leibezeit and Chic's Edwards/Thompson. It's alien dance music. *Metal Box* might not be recognized as a ground-breaking record with the same reverence as *Never Mind the Bollocks,* and you certainly can't trace numerous waves of bands who wouldn't have existed without it like the Sex Pistols record. But like a virus, it's tones have sent miasmic reverberations through a much broader scope of artists and genres. [*Metal Box* was issued in the States in 1980 with different artwork and cheaper packaging under the title *Second Edition*; the track sequence differs as well. The UK reissue of *Metal Box* on CD boasts better sound quality than the *Second Edition* CD.] *–Andy Kellman*

The Flowers of Romance / 1981 / Warner Brothers ✦✦✦✦
As opposed to the axis of throbbing bass and guitar slashings of *Metal Box, The Flowers of Romance* is centralized on razor-sharp drums and typically haranguing vocals. No dubwise grooves here—bassist Jah Wobble was kicked out prior to the recording for ripping off PiL backing tracks for his solo material. And growing more disenchanted with the guitar, Keith Levene's infatuation with synthesizers was reaching a boiling point. His scythe-like guitar is truly brought out for only one song. Stark and minimal are taken to daring lengths, so it's no surprise that Virgin initially balked at issuing the heavily percussive record. "Four Enclosed Walls" opens with something of a mechanical death rattle and John Lydon's quavering warble, framed by backwards piano and Martin Atkins' spartan, dry-as-a-bone drumming. His rapier-like drums seem to serve a similar purpose to Levene's guitar on *Metal Box.* An unsteady drum pattern and fragile, wind chime-like guitar from Levene shape "Track 8," a bleak look at sexual relationships. Lydon adds color with pleasant imagery of Butterball turkeys and elephant graves. "Under the House" and "Francis Massacre" are the most violent tracks due to Atkins' machine gun firing and Levene's chilling atmosperics. Lydon lashes out at zealous fans on the only bottom-heavy tune, "Banging the Door": "The walls are so thin / The neighbors listen in / Keep the noise down." Perhaps the band's most challenging work (in the avant garde sense), it's just as "love it or hate it" as *Metal Box*; it'll either go down a treat or like a five-pound block of liverwurst. [The UK version adds three bonus tracks: an instrumental version of "The Flowers of Romance," "Another," (essentially "Graveyard"

with vocals) and "Home Is Where the Heart Is." The latter two can be found on *Plastic Box*.] —*Andy Kellman*

This Is What You Want . . . This Is What You Get / 1984 / Virgin ✦✦

Album/Compact Disc/Cassette / 1986 / Elektra ✦✦✦

After the release of *This Is What You Want*, Lydon assembled yet another touring band. Martin Atkins stayed on, with Jebin Bruni and Mark Schulz joining the band's ranks. While gigging, Bruni and Schulz assisted in writing the material that wound up on *Album*. Atkins left to spend more time on his own projects after touring, and Lydon again scrapped his associates prior to recording. Anyone's first thousand guesses as to who Lydon would work with next couldn't possibly come close, as the unlisted credits for *Album* read as a motley crew of established musicians who literally have no business being anywhere near Lydon, let alone in a studio with him or with one another. Well, maybe that made perfect sense, given Lydon's ability to baffle. Bill Laswell produced and played bass, which isn't too much of a stretch. But Steve Vai, Ryuichi Sakamoto and Ginger Baker? Baker's involvement is especially odd since PiL played an April Fools' joke on the press by announcing his membership in the early '80s. "Rise" successfully marries rock with Celtic folk (a heavier Dexy's Midnight Runners?); Lydon's chorus is his most hospitable yet. Opener "FFF" and "Home" are other strong points, driving and defiant. The former is as good as hard rock got in 1985. But *Album* can be found lacking in its reliance on outright professionalism and polish, emphasizing skill over craft. Vai's scorched shredding likely repelled Lydon's fans more than any of PiL's earlier attempts to alienate and frustrate. The 90-second wailing over closer "Ease" is anything but; at most points, Vai's playing just doesn't fit. Unfortunately, Yellow Magic Orchestra member Sakamoto pops up only a couple times. His talent is pretty much wasted here. On the whole, *Album* is just as generic as its title. —*Andy Kellman*

Happy? / 1987 / Virgin ✦✦✦

Happy? benefits from some relative stability in PiL's lineup, not to mention the undeniable fact that the band members' allegiance *makes sense* (in contrast to that of *Album*'s crew). Keyboardist Lu Edmonds (the Damned and 3 Mustaphas 3), guitarist John McGeoch (Magazine and Siouxsie & the Banshees), drummer Bruce Smith (the Pop Group and Rip Rig & Panic), and muscular Yank bassist Allan Dias are a solid unit, forming something of a post-punk supergroup. The Blind Faith of the '80s? Even more radio friendly than *Album*, *Happy?* is increasingly entrenched in dancefloor-type fare. Lydon isn't his full-blown postal self, but he's still continents away from being rosy. Though the music might be too dated for most ears years later, Lydon's riffing on unplanned pregnancy ("The Body"), sheep mentality ("Angry"), and false national pride ("Hard Times") still holds together lyrically. McGeoch and Edmonds' sparkling work comes a little too close to stadium-bound for comfort (paging Mr. Edge . . .), but it's a good turn away from *Album*'s brainy metal-wank fireworks. Just when the band sounds as if it's approaching standard issue 1987 chart fare, it fiddles with the arrangements and structures enough to make sure the songs don't qualify as such. If PiL was trying to remain accessible and challenging at the same time, the band fell just short of its goal; given the conspirators involved, *Happy?* is not quite as distinct as it should have been. But as far as PiL outings are considered, it was Lydon's best in six years. —*Andy Kellman*

9 / 1989 / Virgin ✦✦✦

9 features essentially the same group of characters found on *Happy?*, with only Lu Edmonds having left the fold (though he did contribute to the writing on each song). Seven studio albums, seven lineups—Lydon failed yet again to keep the same people together for more than one record. But is this notion really of major consequence? Not really, and Lydon probably prides himself in it. Thankfully, *9* retained the *Happy?* core of Bruce Smith, John McGeoch, and Allan Dias. If *Happy?* and various points prior were flirtations with accessible dance-pop, *9* was a bear hug embrace of it. *9* is split between a modern rock record and a dance producer-derived one, but credit both producers and band for making it a successful combination; on paper, the game plan looks like an accident waiting to happen. Stephen Hague was responsible for just over half of the album's production, with E.T. Thorngren working on the remainder and Nellee Hooper mixing one of Thorngren's productions. *9* is easily PiL's slickest yet, but there's substance to balance it out. The catchy "Disappointed" provided the band's greatest success in the States, with plenty of airplay on modern rock radio stations and light rotation on MTV. Other highlights: the dubby, almost Police-like near-instrumental "U.S.L.S. 1" and the surprising use of acoustic guitar on "Worry." Lowlights: the slightly goofy "Sand Castles in the Snow," the oddball fusion of Asiatic keyboards and late-'80s R&B on "Like That," the character play of Lydon in "Warrior." —*Andy Kellman*

● **The Greatest Hits, So Far** / 1990 / Virgin ✦✦✦✦

The Greatest Hits, So Far mines the singles PiL released through 1990. Ten years after its release, it was doubtful that a second volume would surface (the '90s saw one lone studio release, not to mention a John Lydon "solo" record), so thankfully Lydon didn't embarrass himself by titling it "The Greatest Hits, Volume One." That said, not many outfits under the guise of one name can boast a collection of singles so diverse and ranging in quality. And really, the title should be "The Singles, So Far." By attempting to hit upon all the studio releases, bright moments like "Bad Baby," "Banging the Door," and "The Order of Death" get left behind. The distance between 1979's "Death Disco" and 1990's "Don't Ask Me" would be impossible to traverse with the trustiest of vehicles. The back cover of the disc depicts Stonehenge and an earthbound spacecraft, with a howling dog in the middle. That's accurate. With peers mutating from the Pop Group ("Careering") to Information Society ("Warrior"), PiL couldn't possibly expect to concoct a compilation that would appeal to all ears. In that regard, *GHSF* is more of a Denny's sampler than a thematic banquet spread. (To clarify: "Rules and Regulations" is a cheese stick, not tasty bean pâté.) Whether or not this is a proper first place to go for PiL is up for debate, as it takes a *very* eclectic head to thrill to both their early discordance and later chart-targeted tunefulness. It's not going to provide a solid idea of where they stood at any point in their existence, but it's just enough to pique further investigation. —*Andy Kellman*

That What Is Not / 1992 / Virgin ✦✦

Plastic Box / Jun. 8, 1999 / Virgin ✦✦✦✦

Most who own *Plastic Box* probably use the second half as coasters. Those who don't probably get headaches when listening to the first two, and a select few find much to love about the whole thing. As if conceding to the consensus that PiL's early years were their best, the first half is devoted to the band's first three studio LPs cut over four years, while the second half covers the remainder. Listeners get the entirety of *Public Image/First Edition sans* "Fodderstompf." The majority of *Metal Box* (issued as *Second Edition* in the U.S.) is included, with three of the original versions sacrificed for Peel Session counterparts that really take the cake. "Careering" is especially wonderful and harrowing, arguably the collective's finest recorded moment. Keith Levene goes bonkers with the keyboards, perhaps fostering the increased intensity amongst the remaining members. The 12" mix of "Swan Lake" ("Death Disco") gets the box set upgrade too, as well as a couple other worthwhile *Metal Box* outtakes. Closing out the second disc is the entirety of *The Flowers of Romance*, sequentially shuffled with an additional non-album track. The second half of *Plastic Box* hits upon each of the remaining studio LPs, with the odd rarity, single mix and Peel Session thrown in for completist bait. For those who want improved sound over their early CD issues, the money spent is a smart investment. A quick comparison of the first 20 seconds of "Annalisa" to the version found on an old copy of *Public Image* should be evidence enough; the bass line of "Chant" makes the gut feel as if it's being endlessly pummelled by a bouncing battering ram. Though vast and relatively pricey, *Plastic Box* is an excellent introduction, if only for the adventurous. —*Andy Kellman*

Puff Daddy/P. Diddy (Sean Combs)

b. Nov. 4, 1970, Harlem, NY

Producer / Pop-Rap, East Coast Rap, Urban, Hip-Hop

The biggest hip-hop impresario of the mid-'90s, Sean "Puffy" Combs—or Puff Daddy, as he was known on his own musical projects—created a multi-million dollar industry around Bad Boy Entertainment, with recordings by the Notorious B.I.G., Craig Mack, Faith Evans, 112 and Total, all produced and master-minded by Combs himself. Responsible for over $100 million in total record sales and named ASCAP's 1996 Songwriter of the Year, Combs was, on the other hand, criticized by many in the hip-hop community for watering down the sound of the underground and also for a perceived over-reliance on samples as practically the sole basis for many of his hits. A very successful A&R executive at Uptown Records during the early '90s, responsible for sizeable hit records by Father MC, Mary J. Blige, and Jodeci, Combs formed his own Bad Boy label, signed Notorious B.I.G., Evans, and Craig Mack, and earned enough hits to cement an alliance with Arista Records. A highly publicized feud with Death Row Records (in which Tupac Shakur and label-head Suge Knight served as West Coast/Dark Side equivalents to the Notorious B.I.G. and Combs) was summarily ended in late 1996, when Shakur was murdered and Knight jailed. Six months later, Notorious B.I.G. was dead as well, and after Combs mourned his friend's death, he hit the pop charts in a big way during his biggest year, 1997. —*John Bush*

● **No Way Out** / Jul. 1, 1997 / Bad Boy ✦✦✦✦

Before releasing his first solo album, Puff Daddy (a.k.a. Sean "Puffy" Combs) was famous as the producer of the Notorious B.I.G., Junior Mafia, Craig Mack, Lil' Kim and many other rappers. As he was making his solo debut, the Notorious B.I.G. was murdered, and that loss weighs heavily on Puff's mind throughout *No Way Out*. Even though the album has some funky party jams scattered throughout the record, the bulk of the album is filled with fear, sorrow and anger, and it's not only evident on the tribute "I'll Be Missing You" (a duet with Faith Evans and 112 that is based on the Police's "Every Breath You Take") but also on gangsta anthems like "It's All About the Benjamins." That sense of loss makes *No Way Out* a more substantial album than most mid-'90s hip-hop releases, and even if it has flaws—there's a bit too much filler and it runs a little long—it is nevertheless a compelling, harrowing album that establishes Puff Daddy as a vital rapper in his own right. —*Leo Stanley*

Forever / Aug. 24, 1999 / Bad Boy ✦✦✦

It was never much of a contest, but with his second solo album, Puff Daddy retains his crown as the biggest ego in hip-hop, if not popular music. It's an arrogance that asserts itself in the over 20 pictures included in the album booklet (all with different poses and outfits) and in the opening track—"Forever (Intro)"—that updates listeners with all the sordid details of Puffy's personal life. With all this ego strutting around, Puffy's sizable production talents have consistently been underrated. The truth is, he's been one of the best hip-hop producers of the '90s, creator of countless solid party jams, heavy on the groove and quite creative for their crossover potential. Though most of the tracks on *Forever* are co-productions with young lieutenants from his Bad Boy organization, Puffy's productions shine through. And he's downplayed sampling obvious pop hits for the main groove of his songs, perhaps a response to the constant criticism of hip-hop fans. Puffy's also a better rapper than he used to be, almost up to the level of the MC superstars guesting here. There are no tracks as propulsive as the hits from *No Way Out* ("It's All About the Benjamins," "Been Around the World"), and the ballad track "Best Friend," which samples Christopher Cross' "Sailing," is a lame rehash of the Biggie tribute "I'll Be Missing You." The final track (and first single), the Public Enemy-sampling "P.E. 2000," is an apt metaphor for Puff Daddy's second album; it's a solid production, not quite as exciting as it should be, informed by a mindset that uses hip-hop as a ladder to pop success and wealth. *—Keith Farley*

The Saga Continues / Jun. 19, 2001 / Bad Boy ♦♦♦
A lot happened to Sean Combs during the two-year gap between *Forever* and *The Saga Continues*. Besides the obvious name change to P. Diddy and his daily appearances in the news, the overdramatic rap artist saw his popularity drop considerably during those two years—a serious issue for someone as attention hungry and undeniably vain as Combs. *The Saga Continues* is Combs' melodramatic effort to let everyone know that his Bad Boy empire is in fact still an empire. In fact, "Bad Boy for Life," the album's big anthem, perhaps sums up the situation best: "We ain't going nowhere/We can't be stopped." It's a fairly simple claim, but this pretension towers over every single second of this album. Combs isn't trying to make great music anymore; he's trying to reclaim his credibility. In his mission to do so, he has recruited the latest roster of Bad Boy talent, anchored by two stellar rappers, Black Rob and G. Dep, who are to be viewed as the successors to the departed Biggie Smalls, Mase, and Shyne. Combs gives these two plenty of time in the spotlight here—arguably more than himself—and they definitely showcase their talent commendably, as do many of the other Family members. It's nice to see Combs stay in-house for this album rather than assembling a disparate best-of-the-best roster like he did on *Forever*; this decision helps give the album more of a cohesive feel. These Family members, and also the often daring production, make this an impressive album at times. Unfortunately, it's Combs himself who spoils what could be a standout album; sure, his rapping may still be subpar at best but, more than that, it's his megalomanic pretension that makes this album near-impossible to advocate. *—Jason Birchmeier*

Pulnoc

f. 1988, **db.** 1991
Post-Punk, Prog-Rock/Art Rock, Alternative Pop/Rock
Czechoslavakian post-punk group Pulnoc emerged from the ashes of the Plastic People of the Universe, the legendary underground art-rock unit formed by bassist Milan Hlavsa just weeks after the country's 1968 Communist takeover. Named in honor of the Frank Zappa composition "Plastic People"—the Velvet Underground, the Doors, the Fugs and Captain Beefheart were seminal influences as well—the group's theatrical stage performances earned the ire of officials, especially in light of the Kremlin's "normalization" initiatives which resulted in the closing of virtually all of Prague's rock venues. In 1970, the government revoked the Plastic People's professional license, restricting the band from use of state-owned instruments and practice spaces; as restrictions mounted, the group receded further into Prague's nascent underground music circuit, becoming increasingly experimental even as each of their performances ran the risk of police interference. After a March 1976 appearance led to the arrests of the Plastic People and many of their friends and fans, the band became a cause celebre among anti-Communist leaders including playwright Vaclev Havel; bootleg tapes of their music were also smuggled to the West, further expanding their notoriety.

The Plastic People of the Universe forged on until April of 1988, their demise brought on by internal dissention over whether or not to change their name in the hopes of regaining their performing license; the core trio of Hlavsa, guitarist Josef Janicek and viola player Jira Kabes soon formed Pulnoc ("Midnight") with vocalist Michaela Nemcova, guitarist Karel Jancak, cellist Tomas Schilla and drummer Petr Kuzamandas. Thanks to loosening government restrictions, in the spring of 1989 Pulnoc was allowed to tour the U.S., and with the fall of the Berlin Wall that November, the Czechoslavian people mounted a successful revolution which ultimately resulted in their liberation from Communist control. While working on their self-titled 1990 debut LP, Pulnoc took time out to open for the reunited Velvet Underground in Paris; *City of Hysteria*, featuring liner notes by now-Czech president Havel, appeared a year later. Pulnoc dissolved following the exit of drummer Kuzamandas, with Hlavsa soon forming a new group, Friction; the Plastic People of the Universe reunited in 1998, making their long-awaited American debut that summer. *—Jason Ankeny*

• **City of Hysteria** / Oct. 8, 1991 / Arista ♦♦♦♦♦
The only recording by any former Plastic People members to be released on a major American record label is a stunning bit of guitar rock helped by the beautiful singing of Michaela Nemcova. Egon Bondy is back, penning the lyrics to "Destroying Angel (White Mushrooms)," and Nemcova takes a beautiful lead vocal on the definitive version of The Velvet Underground's great "All Tomorrow's Parties." Although this disc was hyped upon its release (especially by Jello Biafra), I think that hardcore Plastic People fans were off-put by the smooth sound, beefy guitar and high-tech production. Boy, were they ever shortsighted. *—John Dougan*

Pulp

f. 1978, Sheffield, Yorkshire, England
Britpop, Post-Punk, Alternative Pop/Rock
Most bands hit the big time immediately and fade away, or they build a dedicated following and slowly climb their way to the top. Pulp didn't follow either route. For the first 12 years of their existence, Pulp languished in near total obscurity, releasing a handful of albums and singles in the '80s to barely any attention. At the turn of the decade, the group began to gain an audience, sparking a remarkable turn of events that made the band one of the most popular British groups of the '90s. By the time Pulp became famous, the band had gone through numerous different incarnations and changes in style, covering nearly every indie-rock touchstone from post-punk to dance. Pulp's signature sound is a fusion of David Bowie and Roxy Music's glam rock, disco, new wave, acid-house, Euro-pop, and British indie-rock. The group's cheap synthesizers and sweeping melodies reflect the lyrical obsessions of lead vocalist Jarvis Cocker, who alternates between sex and sharp, funny portraits of working class misfits. Out of second-hand pop, Pulp fashioned a distinctive, stylish sound that made camp into something grand and glamourous that retained a palpable sense of gritty reality. *—Stephen Thomas Erlewine*

It / 1983 / Velvel ♦♦
It is a gentle, mainly acoustic album that gives very few signs to the musical directions Pulp would later pursue. Lacking any hint of synthesizers or dance music, the album occasionally touches on the majestic, theatrical ballads of Scott Walker, as well as the stark, folky song poems of Leonard Cohen. However, at this stage, Jarvis Cocker is hardly the lyricist of either songwriter, and his singing is endearingly awkward—occasionally he misses notes and he misses the tune every once in a while. Nevertheless, there are tunes throughout the album, whether it's the light opening single "My Lighthouse" or the silly, music hall stomp of "Love Love." *It* isn't a great album, but it has an effortless, amateurish charm that makes up for the unformed songs and the band's rudimentary musical skills. *—Stephen Thomas Erlewine*

Freaks / 1986 / Velvel ♦♦
Freaks is so different than *It* that it nearly sounds like a different band. Granted, that is largely due to the fact that Pulp *was* a different band, apart from lead vocalist Jarvis Cocker. After the unsuccessful showing of *It*, the band broke up, leaving Cocker to assemble a new lineup. The most significant new member was Russell Senior, who brought a fascination with art, noise, and neo-gothic overtones to the band. But that change in sound isn't the only reason why *Freaks* is the darkest record Pulp ever made, or ever will make. Cocker's lyrics are neurotically gloomy and paranoid, obsessed with failures and outcasts. While this would become a signature theme for Pulp's songs, Cocker's outlook on *Freaks* is oppressively bleak—he finds no future for the mis-shapes and misfits in his songs. Not only are the songs hopeless, so is the production. The very sound of *Freaks* is muddy and impenetrable, making it difficult to find the occasional rewarding moment on the album, such as "Master of the Universe," "They Suffocate At Night," or Senior's "Anorexic Beauty." *—Stephen Thomas Erlewine*

Separations / 1992 / Razor & Tie ♦♦♦
Separations is the birth of the modern Pulp. Not only does the record feature the lineup that would eventually break through into the mainstream, it is the first album to contain the fusion of pop, dance, and rock that would take them to the top of the charts in the mid-'90s. More than anything, the influence of acid house and raves weighs heavily on *Separations*, as the band stretches out into the disco groove of "Countdown" and the long jam "This House Is Condemned." But what is especially noticeable about *Separations* is how Pulp is finally starting to write some fully-realized songs. "My Legendary Girlfriend," the song that earned them their first Single of the Week in *NME*, is the leader of the pack with a brilliant, sly lyric and vocal from Cocker and an appropriately melodic and slightly dirty instrumental backdrop from the group. "Countdown," with its insistent beat, is nearly as good, as is the loping opener "Love Is Blind." Pulp isn't able to keep the pace throughout the album—there are several weak spots, particularly the awkward stab at house, "This House Is Condemned"—but *Separations* is the first album that illustrates their potential and exactly what the band could accomplish. *—Stephen Thomas Erlewine*

Pulpintro—The Gift Recordings / 1993 / Island ♦♦♦♦♦
All of the singles Pulp recorded for Gift Records, including both the A- and B-sides, are collected on *Pulpintro—The Gift Recordings*. From the opening track, "Space," it's clear that Pulp's confidence and talents have grown considerably, even from the relatively accomplished *Separations*. Now, the band has created a signature sound that relies heavily on cheap, synthesized sounds as well as tight pop melodies and a theatrical attack that approximates the art rock of Roxy Music and David Bowie. However, Pulp is too concerned with earthly pleasures to really recall Roxy or Bowie. Furthermore, the band's knack for creating terrific pop singles prevents them from being too pretentious, as the singles "O.U.," "Razzamatazz," and, particularly, "Babies" illustrate. And even though it's just a collection of singles, *Pulpintro* holds together as well as *Separations*, if not better. *—Stephen Thomas Erlewine*

Masters of the Universe / 1994 / Velvel ♦♦
Masters of the Universe is a collection of singles that Pulp recorded for Fire Records in the mid-'80s, around the time of the *Freaks* album. During this time, the band was steeped in the morose obsessions of goth rock, like most of their British indie contemporaries, layering their music with droning synths and dissonant guitars. The group also had a noticibly arty attack—witness the performance art schlock of Russell Senior's rant "The Will to Power." While that preoccupation with goth and self-conscious art decreases the effectiveness of the music, *Masters of the Universe* does contain Pulp's first great leaps forward, "Little Girl (With Blue Eyes)" and "Dogs Are Everywhere," which demonstrate Jarvis Cocker's burgeoning lyrical skills and the band's increasing ability to paint evocative soundscapes. ["Silence" was the only non-album song of the era that wasn't included on the compilation.] *–Stephen Thomas Erlewine*

His 'n' Hers / Jun. 21, 1994 / Island ♦♦♦♦♦
Jarvis Cocker's update on Bryan Ferry's lounge lizard persona works because he recognizes the sleaziness beneath the style. Instead of chronicling the lives and times of jet-setting club-hoppers, Cocker sneaks into the closet of his girlfriend to watch her sister have sex, reveals a fetish for pink gloves among other things, and remembers the first time. Pulp's fake, synthetic backdrop sounds like it was constructed on bargain Casio keyboards, adding an extra layer of seaminess to Cocker's songs. That sense of cheap, faux-glamor is essential to the success of *His N' Hers*, Pulp's commerical and artistic breakthrough. It's the sound of a poor man giving up everything he has so he can act out his expensive, elegant fantasies. He may never get there, but the approximation of glamor is

more appealing and compelling than the reality, which is what gives *His N' Hers* a grand tragic romanticism. —*Stephen Thomas Erlewine*

● **Different Class** / Oct. 30, 1995 / Island ✦✦✦✦✦

After years of obscurity, Pulp shot to stardom in Britain with 1994's *His N' Hers*. By the time *Different Class* was released at the end of October 1995, the band, particularly lead singer Jarvis Cocker, were genuine British superstars, with two number two singles and a triumphant last-minute performance at Glastonbury under their belts, as well as one tabloid scandal. On the heels of such excitement, anticipation for *Different Class* ran high, and not only does it deliver, it blows away all their previous albums, including the fine *His N' Hers*. Pulp doesn't stray from their signature formula at all—it's still grandly theatrical, synth-spiked pop with new wave and disco flourishes, but they have mastered it here. Not only are the melodies and hooks significantly catchier and more immediate, the music explores more territory. From the faux-showtune romp of the anthemic opener "Mis-Shapes" and the glitzy, gaudy stomp of "Disco 2000" (complete with a nicked riff from Laura Branigan's "Gloria") to the aching ballad "Underwear" and the startling sexual menace of "I Spy," Pulp construct a diverse, appealing album around the same basic sound. Similarly, Jarvis Cocker's lyrics take two themes, sex and social class, and explore a number of different avenues in bitingly clever ways. As well as perfectly capturing the behavior of his characters, Cocker grasps the nuances of language, creating a dense portrait of suburban and working-class life. All of his sex songs are compassionate, while the subtle satire of "Sorted for E's & Wizz" is affectionate, but the best moment on the album is the hit single "Common People," about a rich girl who gets off by slumming with the lower class. Coming from Cocker, who made secondhand clothes and music glamourous, the song is undeniably affecting and exciting, much like *Different Class* itself. —*Stephen Thomas Erlewine*

Second Class / 1996 / Island ✦✦✦

Island repackaged Pulp's breakthrough album *Different Class* with a limited-edition bonus disc of B-sides titled *Second Class* in 1996. Although the compilation is haphazard—it leaves off the wonderful, Latin-tinged "His N' Hers" (a stronger song than several included here), as well as the intriguing single mix of "Disco 2000"—it is extremely useful, since it collects the bulk of their best B-sides from *His N' Hers* and *Different Class*. The jaunty "Mile End," which was featured in *Trainspotting*, is a terrifically humorous slice of dead-end urban life that's disarmingly reminiscent of early Cure, while "Ansaphone" is an affecting theatrical ballad, and "P.T.A. (Parent Teacher Association)" is a tongue-in-cheek portrait of perversion. The B-sides that are culled from *His N' Hers* are a little uneven, but "Your Sister's Clothes" is scarily sexy, and "Deep Fried in Kelvin" and "Street Lites" are two epic synth-pop numbers any Pulp devotee should hear. —*Stephen Thomas Erlewine*

Countdown 1992-1983 / Mar. 1996 / Velvel ✦✦✦✦

A double-disc collection released to cash in on Pulp's massive success with *Different Class*, *Countdown* might be a rip-off compilation, but it does offer an effective introduction to Pulp's '80s catalog. Since their recordings on Fire were decidedly uneven, *Countdown* does distill all the highlights a casual fan could want to hear. Beginning with the latest track, the 1990 single "Countdown," and working its way backwards, the compilation's sequencing eases newer fans into both the band's more experimental and folkier work. Even though all of Pulp's best material from this era is included, they lacked the pop sense that they developed in the early '90s, which could make this rough sailing for some recent fans. For those that want to dig deeper, there is plenty of fascinating material here. —*Stephen Thomas Erlewine*

This Is Hardcore / Mar. 31, 1998 / Island ✦✦✦✦

"This is the sound of someone losing the plot/you're gonna like it, but not a lot." So says Jarvis Cocker on "The Fear," the opening track on *This Is Hardcore*, the ambitious follow-up to Pulp's breakthrough *Different Class*, thereby providing his own review for the album. Cocker doesn't quite lose the plot on *This Is Hardcore*, but the ominous, claustrophobic "The Fear" makes it clear that this is a different band, one that no longer has anthems like "Common People" in mind. The shift in direction shouldn't come as a surprise—Pulp was always an arty band—but even the catchiest numbers are shrouded in darkness. *This Is Hardcore* is haunted by disappointments and fear—by the realization that what you dreamed of may not be what you really wanted. Nowhere is this better heard than on "This Is Hardcore," where drum loops, lounge piano, cinematic strings, and a sharp lyric create a frightening monument to weary decadence. It's the centerpiece of the album, and the best moments follow its tone. Some, like "The Fear," "Seductive Barry," and "Help the Aged," wear their fear on their sleeves, some cloak it in Bowie-esque dance grooves ("Party Hard") or in hushed, resigned tones ("Dishes"). A few others, such as the scathing "I'm a Man" or "A Little Soul," have a similar vibe without being explicitly dark. Instead of delivering an entirely bleak album, Pulp raises the curtain somewhat on the last three songs, but the attempts at redemption—"Sylvia," "Glory Days," "The Day After the Revolution"—don't feel as natural as everything that precedes them. It's enough to keep the album from being a masterpiece, but it's hardly enough to prevent it from being an artistic triumph. —*Stephen Thomas Erlewine*

Pure Prairie League

f. 1971, Cincinnati, OH, **db.** 1983
Soft Rock, Country-Rock

For a short time, Pure Prairie League were one of America's best country-rock bands, but personnel shifts ultimately destroyed its early promise. The group was formed in 1971 by vocalists/guitarists Craig Lee Fuller (the band's main songwriter) and George Powell, steel guitarist John Call, bassist Jim Lanham, and drummer Jim Caughlin, and recorded their self-titled debut album just a year later. Its fusion of laid-back singer-songwriter-

styled rock and country earned critical praise, but much of the group departed, leaving only Fuller, Powell, and several session musicians. Even so, *Bustin' Out* proved to be an unqualified success, featuring the innovative addition of string arrangements by David Bowie guitarist Mick Ronson. Unfortunately, Fuller left in 1975, leaving the group without a strong songwriter or leader. Powell carried on with guitarist Larry Goshorn, bassist Mike Reilly, and pianist Michael Connor for several albums, none of which were as commercially or artistically successful as *Bustin' Out*. The group did enjoy a brief resurgence in 1980 with the Top Ten single "Let Me Love You Tonight," featuring future country star Vince Gill on lead vocals, but finally called it quits in 1983. Fuller has since joined Little Feat. —*Steve Huey*

Pure Prairie League / 1972 / RCA ✦✦✦✦✦

For all those who think The Eagles are the be all and end all of country-rock, you owe it to yourself to search out this album. Any track here (or on the followup, *Bustin' Out*) holds up as well, if not better than, anything by The Eagles. This album also proves that Craig Fuller is a grossly underrated songwriter. A country-rock must! —*Jim Worbois*

Bustin' Out / 1972 / RCA ✦✦✦✦✦

Two Lane Highway / 1975 / RCA ✦✦✦

With the departure of Fuller, the face (and sound) of Prairie League changed considerably. Larry Goshorn (ex-Sacred Mushroom) has replaced Fuller as the main songwriter in the band. And, while the overall album isn't up to its predecessors, there are still some nice moments including the title track, "Runner" and a humorous tribute to country music legend, Merle Haggard. —*Jim Worbois*

If the Shoe Fits / 1976 / RCA ✦✦✦

Dance / 1976 / RCA ✦✦

Live Takin' the Stage / 1977 / RCA ✦✦

Just Fly / 1978 / RCA ✦✦

Can't Hold Back / 1979 / One Way ✦✦

Firin' Up / 1980 / Casablanca ✦

Amie & Other Hits / 1981 / RCA ✦✦✦✦

At eight tracks, this is really skimpy, but *Amie & Other Hits* nevertheless does offer a nice sampler of Pure Prairie League's RCA recordings. This does mean that their biggest hit, "Let Me Love You Tonight," is missing, along with anything else from their time at Casablanca, but this does give a basic overview of their earliest material, when they were led by the fine singer/songwriter Craig Fuller. —*Stephen Thomas Erlewine*

The Best of Pure Prairie League / Aug. 8, 1995 / Mercury Nashville ✦✦✦✦

As one of country-rock's most appealing groups, Pure Prairie League contributed to the late-'70s and early-'80 era of musical interbreeding which made them firm FM radio staples, as well as country music mainstays. Their highest charted single, "Let Me Love You Tonight" at number ten in 1980, was where country superstar Vince Gill began singing lead for the band and was their third vocalist. Sounding slightly more country than rock, Pure Prairie League's music gained popularity by churning out jangly guitar strummed tunes that imitated the Eagles recipe of sturdy country love songs. This collection of their best material is a superb rundown of all their hits, with an extra two bonus tracks at the end. "Amie," their first Top 40 entry, sung by Craig Fuller, kicks off this album and represents the early stages of the band's career with its light, breezy sound. Other stand-outs on this 14 song compilation include the number 34 hit "I'm Almost Ready" and the sincere sounding "Still Right Here In My Heart," with its timeless chorus and free-range melody. Mike Reilly sings the Buddy Holly classic "That'll Be The Day" with a modest country feel, and even the semi-edgy "Don't Keep Me Hangin" holds up well amidst the other more countrified tracks on this best-of. Although Pure Prairie League weren't given quite the amount of attention they deserved, the music they produced befriended fans of both country and AOR. —*Mike DeGagne*

● **Greatest Hits** / Sep. 28, 1999 / RCA ✦✦✦✦✦

RCA's 1999 compilation *Greatest Hits* is the definitive portrait of Pure Prairie League at their peak. Although it contains none of their Casablanca recordings, and therefore it's missing their biggest hit, "Let Me Love You Tonight," it does have a comprehensive chronicle of the group's first four albums, including their breakthrough hit "Amie," the non-LP "She Darked the Sun," and nearly all of their best album, *Bustin' Out*, albeit not in sequence. It would have been nice to have "Let Me Love You Tonight" added to this collection, but it's hard to argue with what's here, since it is the best of the best years of the Pure Prairie League. —*Stephen Thomas Erlewine*

James and Bobby Purify

f. 1966, Pensacola, FL
Pop-Soul, Soul

James (b. May 12, 1944) and Bobby (b. Sep. 2, 1939) of this Southern soul duo were not actually brothers but cousins. James Purify and Robert Lee Dickey joined forces for some classic Southern soul duets during the mid-'60s. Producer Papa Don Schroeder brought the soulful Floridians to Muscle Shoals in 1966 to record at Rick Hall's Fame studios, and the result was the gorgeous mid-tempo "I'm Your Puppet." The Dan Penn/Spooner Oldham ballad proved their biggest hit for the Bell label, although "Let Love Come between Us" and their revival of The Five Dutones' "Shake a Tail Feather" also made some major noise in 1967. When Bobby mutinied, James went it alone for a while before recruiting a new Bobby (Ben Moore), and they picked up right where the old duo left off. —*Bill Dahl*

● **Do It Right: The Best of James & Bobby Purify** / 1985 / Arista ✦✦✦

This collection covers the few hits James and Bobby Purify enjoyed, including "I'm Your

Puppet" and "Shake A Tail Feather." They were a good straight soul duo, and were not brothers but cousins. —*Ron Wynn*

Pussy Galore

f. 1985, Washington, DC, **db.** 1990
College Rock, Noise-Rock, Indie Rock, Alternative Pop/Rock, American Underground
You either loved them or loathed them (some did both) but it was difficult to ignore the bawling, intentionally crude, anti-musicianship coughed up by Pussy Galore. A bunch of scuzzy-looking juveniles from Washington D.C. led by a young punk-rockin' bohemian hipster wannabe named Jon Spencer, Pussy Galore created an unholy metallic ruckus that was part serious avant-garde noise wail, part bullshit pose. Considering their limited skills, narcissistic tendencies, and drug-cult mythologizing, there is a sizable body of work from this band. The problem is that it's mostly hit-and-miss, which is a polite way of saying a little Pussy Galore goes a long way. A serious discussion of Pussy Galore's musical attributes must thoroughly ignore technical ability; they have none. Surprisingly, with all of their hip attitude and condescending, arty indifference, Pussy Galore was capable of creating some great trash rock. However, I would argue that these moments were accidental, the byproduct of doing something long enough and eventually getting it right. Really the only difference between good Pussy Galore music and bad is that the latter is boring and the former is not—that is unless you have an extremely high tolerance for low-rent nihilism. —*John Dougan*

Sugarshit Sharp / 1988 / Matador ◆◆◆◆
Both of these records, *Groovy Hate Fuck* and *Sugarshit Sharp*, come highly recommended if only because, as EPs, filler is kept to a minimum. *Groovy Hate Fuck* lives up to its title: it's a mess of a record thrown together by a bunch of bored kids who want to be as offensive as possible. On that level it's a near total success. Don't be shocked by the song titles (e.g., "Cunt Tease," "You Look Like a Jew," "Dead Meat"), simply enjoy the violent, sonic chaos they whip up. It's very energetic. *Sugarshit Sharp* is even better. Side one is a cover of Einsturzende Neubauten's "Yu Gung," side two is more death-grunge rendered with a maximum of noise and minimum of panache. But at under 30 minutes, it's free of a lot of arty-farty jerking around. —*John Dougan*

Dial 'M' for Motherfucker / 1989 / Matador ◆◆

Historia de la Musica Rock / 1990 / Caroline ◆◆◆

● **Corpse Love: The First Year** / Feb. 14, 1992 / Plan 9/Caroline ◆◆◆◆◆
With the exception of *Corpse Love*, a pretty good career anthology, I recommend all of Pussy Galore's full-length records with this caveat: Not a one of them is strong all the way through. All have their moments (especially *Right Now!*) but after a while (a short while) you'll be able to anticipate every one of their moves, and the cacophonous anti-rock thrash and bash becomes samey sounding. Freaks for this stuff will want all three records, but as trashy noise rock goes, there are better bands, and certainly plenty who are less patronizing to their audiences. —*John Dougan*

Pylon

f. 1978, Athens, GA, **db.** 1983
Comedy Rock, New Wave
Despite failing to equal the commercial success or cross-cultural impact of their Athens, GA compatriots R.E.M. and the B-52's, Pylon's influence on the city's legendary music scene proved just as pronounced–the group's propulsive, angular jangle-pop sound resonated not only through the Athens creative community but throughout the American pop underground of the 1980s, and though more heard-of than actually heard, their role as elder statesmen of the alternative rock explosion is unassailable. Borrowing their name from the William Faulkner novel, Pylon was founded by guitarist Randy Bewley and bassist Michael Lachowski, University of Georgia art students inspired by the likes

of Television, the Ramones and Talking Heads; the twosome soon sublet practice space in a studio loft rented by local artist Curtis Crowe, who quickly signed on to play drums. After auditioning a series of vocalists, the band finally settled on fellow UGA student Vanessa Briscoe, whose distinctive yelping style ideally complemented the music's jagged guitars and martial rhythms. The quartet made its live debut in March 1979; that summer, the B-52's became the darlings of the New York scene thanks to their breakthrough hit "Rock Lobster," and their success paved the way for Pylon to make their own Big Apple debut, with Philadelphia and Boston appearances following before the school year resumed. Pylon's debut single, "Cool," appeared on the dB label in early 1980, earning strong critical notices and emerging as a major underground dance hit; that summer, they issued their debut LP *Gyrate*, also opening for the B-52's in New York's Central Park. Pylon toured regularly leading up to—and in the wake of—their sophomore effort, 1983's *Chomp*, but dissatisfied with the finished LP, and also disheartened by an abortive tour in support of U2, the band dissolved. In their absence, Athens emerged as the nexus of the American underground thanks largely to the snowballing success of R.E.M., who regularly cited Pylon as a major influence on their music; in fact, when in 1987 *Rolling Stone* named R.E.M. "America's Best Band," drummer Bill Berry argued the honor actually belonged to Pylon, even though the group had disbanded four years earlier. Their posthumous notoriety, in tandem with the impending release of dB's *Hits* compilation, convinced Pylon to reform in 1988; after opening for R.E.M. on their *Green* tour, they also recorded a new album, 1990's *Chain*. With Bewley's decision to leave the lineup, however, Pylon again called its quits, playing their final show at Athens' famed 40 Watt Club on November 22, 1991. —*Jason Ankeny*

Gyrate / Nov. 1980 / DB ◆◆◆

Chomp / 1983 / DB ◆◆◆◆
Like their Athens, Georgia counterparts the B-52's, this unusual band used dance beat music as the platform for its intriguingly eccentric style—but while the former group gleefully exploited the kitschy aspects of this aesthetic, Pylon explored the spare, arty, new wave side of the genre. All the songs on this album are composed of short, static, obsessively repeated riffs propelled by dance mix drums, over which vocalist Vanessa Briscoe chant-sings surrealist lyrics. Within this seemingly narrow ambit, however, the group manages to find a fair bit of variety. "Italian Movie Theme" is an instrumental number featuring surf-derived guitar playing. "Gyrate" has a heavier, thumping, rock-oriented beat and a modest funk-derived feel. "Yo-Yo" exhibits a Devo-like mechanical quality, while "K" shows the gloomy influence of Joy Division or early Siouxie and the Banshees. Hints of Go-Go's girl group touches are audible on "Crazy." The odd aural idea of R.E.M. as a dance mix group is suggested on one of the album's best tracks, "No Clocks." The group went on a lengthy hiatus after this platter and would not release another album for seven years. This odd record may take a few listens to reveal its merits, but it's worth the effort. —*David Cleary*

● **Hits** / 1989 / DB ◆◆◆◆◆
All the Pylon you'll ever need is here on one long disc; the best of their career culled from their albums *Gyrate* and *Chomp* and various singles. Vanessa Briscoe's lyrics take the form of admonishments and are set to the band's dancefloor, militaristic beats. It's repetitive but enduring and helped launch a hundred bands, chiefly R.E.M., out of the small college town of Athens, GA in the early '80s. "Crazy," the song R.E.M. chose to cover, is a fine pop song indeed, but the lesser-known rock blast "Feast on my Heart" absolutely kills. —*Denise Sullivan*

Chain / Oct. 1990 / Dog Gone ◆◆◆
The reformed Pylon acquit themselves nicely on *Chain*, but never deliver a knockout blow. Stylistically speaking, there are no big changes here, but the exuberance and emotion carry even the most rote workouts. —*John Dougan*

Q-Tip (Jonathan Davis)

b. Nov. 20, 1970, Brooklyn, NY
Vocals / East Coast Rap, Alternative Rap, Hip-Hop

The longtime MC with pioneering alternative hip-hop trio A Tribe Called Quest, rapper Q-Tip was born Jonathan Davis in New York City on November 20, 1970. While a student at the Murray Bergtraum High School for Business Careers, he co-founded A Tribe Called Quest with fellow students Ali Shaheed Muhammad and Phife (Malik Taylor) in 1988; the following year, Q-Tip guested on De la Soul's groundbreaking *3 Feet and Rising* LP, with the two groups forever linked through their association with the "Native Tongues" collective. Tribe's debut single "Description of a Fool" appeared in the summer of 1989, and after signing to Jive Records, the trio issued their debut LP *People's Instinctive Travels and the Paths of Rhythm* a year later. With their fiercely intelligent, socially progressive lyrics and brilliant fusion of rap and jazz, the group emerged as one of the most popular and influential in all of hip-hop, producing such classic LPs as 1991's *The Low End Theory* and 1993's *Midnight Marauders* before disbanding in 1998. Q-Tip then mounted a solo career with the 1999 release of *Amplified*. —*Jason Ankeny*

● **Amplified** / Nov. 23, 1999 / Arista ◆◆◆◆◆
Just over a year after A Tribe Called Quest issued its final album, the group's nominal frontman Q-Tip issued his debut solo album, *Amplified*. For Tribe fans able to get over the fact that Q-Tip isn't trading off on rhymes with Phife Dog and Ali as usual, *Amplified* is an excellent work, almost up to the same level as the group's underrated final Jive album, *The Love Movement*. The sound here is *very* similar to *The Love Movement*, obviously no coincidence since production credits throughout go to Jay Dee and Q-Tip for the Ummah, the same combo that produced most of A Tribe Called Quest's material. It's a style that emphasizes deep grooves and clipped beats with a polished sheen that takes Tribe's jazz-rap into the age of quiet storm and fusion. Q-Tip's rapping is as smooth and inventive as ever, though it's a mild surprise that he doesn't include any message tracks (most Tribe albums have at least one or two). The band's breakup was a blow to hip-hop fans all over the world, but *Amplified* will make everyone feel much better. —*John Bush*

Kamaal the Abstract / Sep. 25, 2001 / Arista ◆◆◆

Quarterflash

f. Portland, OR
Album Rock, Arena Rock, Pop/Rock

The sax-heavy pop/rock band known as Quarterflash formed in early 1980, joining together two of the city's more popular acts, Seafood Mama, which contributed Rindy and Marv Ross and Pilot, which added Jack Charles, Rick DiGiallonardo, Rich Gooch and Brian Willis. The band would release four albums together, starting with their 1981 self-titled debut, which sold over two million copies and spawned two of their biggest songs, "Harden My Heart," which went to #3 on the charts, and the top 20 hit "Find Another Fool." Subsequent albums would not reach the blockbuster commercial success of their debut, but they continued to sell albums steadily throughout the mid-'80s. Another notable song was "Night Shift," which was the theme for the movie of the same name. They followed up their debut with 1983's *Take Another Picture*, which produced another top 20 hit, "Take Me to Heart" as the band continued forward with their trademark rock sound. By *Girl in the Wind* in 1984, the band began to run out of clever hooks, and they issued just one more album, *Back Into Blue*, in 1985. A modified version of the band anchored by the Rosses continued to perform live, calling it quits just after recording an unreleased album in 1995. —*Stacia Proefrock*

● **Harden My Heart: The Best of Quarterflash** / Mar. 25, 1997 / Geffen ◆◆◆◆◆
Quarterflash's three charted singles highlight this best-of package that compiles their sturdiest material, as well as a few of their soundtrack contributions. Both "Harden My Heart" and "Find Another Fool" broke the Top 20 upon the release of their self-titled debut album in 1981, and proved to be this Oregon band's best singles. Two other songs from the album, "Critical Times" and "Right Kind of Love" appear here also, followed by the seductive rock flow of the #14 hit "Take Me To Heart" from 1983's *Take Another Picture*. "Night Shift" appeared on the soundtrack of the same name which is now out of print, while the B-side to "Harden My Heart" entitled "Don't Be Lonely" surfaced on the *Fast Times At Ridgemont High* album and "Make It Shine" was included on *The Gremlins* soundtrack. Even though Quarterflash harbors a definitive eighties pop sound, the rich saxophone and sultry vocals of Rindy Ross give this average sounding chorus-and-bridge rock a slightly distinct edge. Both "Talk To Me" and "Walking On Ice" come from the effortless *Back Into Blue* album released in 1985 which marked an end to their career. *Harden My Heart: The Best of Quarterflash* does what a hits collection should by leaving the unnecessary luggage behind while presenting all of the group's familiar music. —*Mike DeGagne*

Suzi Quatro

b. Jun. 3, 1950, Detroit, MI
Vocals, Songwriter, Bass / Glitter, Pop/Rock, Glam Rock, Hard Rock

It's pretty far-fetched, as some revisionists are now claiming, to view Suzi Quatro as a precursor to the "riot grrrls" of the '90s. Her brand of mid-'70s glam-pop was far more innocuous and, in any case, often supplied by professional songwriters. What she did prove was that it was possible for a petite woman to play bass, sing, and wear leather with a reasonable degree of raunch and pride. That, with enough musical hooks to draw in the teenage pop crowd, was enough to reel off a series of big British hit singles just before the advent of punk, although she remained virtually unknown in her native US. While playing in an all-girl Detroit band named Cradle, Quatro was spotted by British producer Mickie Most and encouraged to begin recording in London. Her second single "Can the Can" went to number one in the UK in 1973. In the US though, she could barely get into the Top 100, though she did somehow get on the cover of *Rolling Stone* during a slow month. Her American fortunes changed in the late '70s, when she had a short-lived semi-regular stint on the sitcom *Happy Days* as the guitar-playing, sassy Leather Tuscadero. In 1979, she made the American Top Five with "Stumblin' In," although this was a duet with Chris Norman. She's kept a low profile in the '80s and '90s, although she's done some television and theatrical work in Britain. —*Richie Unterberger*

● **The Wild One: Classic Quatro** / Apr. 1996 / Razor & Tie ◆◆◆◆◆
The definitive compilation—20 tracks, mostly from her mid-'70s prime, including all of her British and American hits and a few album tracks. —*Richie Unterberger*

Queen

f. 1971, London, England, **db.** 1995
Album Rock, British Metal, Arena Rock, Pop/Rock, Glam Rock, Prog-Rock/Art Rock, Hard Rock

Few bands embodied the pure excess of the '70s like Queen. Embracing the exaggerated pomp of prog-rock and heavy metal, as well as vaudevellian music-hall, the British quartet delved deeply into camp and bombast, creating a huge, mock-operatic sound with layered guitars and overdubbed vocals. Queen's music was a bizarre yet highly accessible fusion of the macho and the fey. For years, their albums boasted the motto "no synthesizers were used on this record," signaling their allegiance with the legions of post-Led Zeppelin hard rock bands. But vocalist Freddie Mercury brought an extravagant sense of camp to the band, pushing them towards kitschy humor and pseudo-classical arrangements, as epitomized on their best-known song, "Bohemian Rhapsody." Mercury, it must be said, was a flamboyant homosexual, who managed to keep his sexuality in the closet until his death from AIDS in 1992. Nevertheless, his sexuality was apparent throughout Queen's music, from their very name to their veiled lyrics—it was truly bizarre to hear gay anthems like "We Are the Champions" turn into celebrations of sports victories. That would have been impossible without Mercury, one of the most dynamic and charismatic frontmen in rock history. Through his legendary theatrical performances, Queen became one of the most popular bands in the world in the mid-'70s; in England, they remained second only to the Beatles in popularity and collectibility in the '90s. Despite their enormous popularity, Queen were never taken seriously by rock critics—an infamous *Rolling Stone* review labeled their 1978 album *Jazz* as "fascist." In spite of such harsh criticism, the band's popularity rarely waned; even in the late '80s, the group retained a fanatical following except in America. In the States, their popularity peaked in the early '80s, just as they finished nearly a decade's worth of extraordinarily popular records. And while those records were never praised, they sold in enormous numbers, and traces of Queen's music could be heard in several generations of hard rock and metal bands in the next two decades, from Metallica to Smashing Pumpkins. —*Stephen Thomas Erlewine*

Queen / Sep. 4, 1973 / Hollywood ◆◆◆
Although it may not be up to par with such future classics as *A Night at the Opera* and *The Game*, Queen's 1973 self-titled debut is one of the most underrated hard rock debuts of all time. Chances are that many will only be familiar with one song (the classic rock radio staple "Keep Yourself Alive"), but it is a very consistent and solid album; even the more uncommon compositions are impressive and memorable. Unlike other notable hard rock debuts of the '60s/'70s (Led Zeppelin, Van Halen, Kiss, etc.), Queen's first album was not recorded quickly, but over the course of a year or more, since the band had to record during the studio's off-hours to minimize costs. Even so, the album does retain continuity, a perfect balance of anthems (the aforementioned "Keep Yourself Alive"), gorgeous ballads ("The Night Comes Down," "Doing All Right"), and raging heavy metal ("Liar," "Great King Rat," "Son & Daughter"). All of the band's future musical trademarks can be detected here as well—Brian May's sweeping guitar orchestras (several different guitars overdubbed to create harmonies), Freddie Mercury's vocal acrobatics, and the

solid rhythm section of drummer Roger Taylor and bassist John Deacon (listed as Deacon John in the credits here). At the time, many critics dismissed the band and the debut (unfairly classifying Queen as "disposable glam"), but in hindsight, *Queen* laid down the groundwork for this legendary band's future triumphs. *—Greg Prato*

Queen II / Apr. 9, 1974 / Hollywood ✦✦✦
Queen's second album, 1974's *Queen II*, is their heaviest and also darkest release. Upset by the lashing the critics bestowed upon their underrated self-titled debut a year earlier (and its underachieving chart performance), the band were determined to hit the big time with their second try. And succeed they did—the album reached number five on the U.K. charts, while its breakthrough single, "Seven Seas of Rhye," reached number ten. The band also created a buzz stateside by opening a tour for Mott the Hoople, and in return received FM radio support. The first side of the record was titled the "white" side, while the second was the "black" side; still, both include an equal amount of rockers and ballads. Opening with the lush guitar orchestration of Brian May's "Procession," the album kicks into high gear with one of Queen's most underrated tracks, the haunting "Father to Son." Like the debut, the album switches from style to style throughout ballads ("White Queen," "Nevermore"), pop ("Some Day One Day"), heavy metal ("Ogre Battle," "Seven Seas of Rhye"), and mutated prog-rock ("The March of the Black Queen," "The Fairy Feller's Master-Stroke"). A stellar release that has only improved over the years, *Queen II* also proved to be an influential album for future musicians—Smashing Pumpkins' Billy Corgan considers it an all-time personal favorite. *—Greg Prato*

Sheer Heart Attack / Nov. 12, 1974 / Hollywood ✦✦✦✦✦
Queen's second album of 1974 (and third overall), *Sheer Heart Attack*, helped bridge the gap between the mystical heavy metal of their early years and the hard rock/pop perfection of future releases. The main reason why Queen issued another album so soon after *Queen II* (only eight months apart) was due to guitarist Brian May's hepatitis, which had forced the band off their touring schedule. Instead of waiting, Freddie Mercury and Co. used their time wisely and worked diligently on their third record. The result was what many fans consider Queen's first true classic, featuring their U.S. breakthrough single "Killer Queen" (which almost reached the top of the charts in England), and the radio/concert favorite "Now I'm Here." Also included is a song that Metallica would later cover (and win a Grammy Award for), "Stone Cold Crazy," as well as the impressive opening guitar showcase, "Brighton Rock." Besides including the expected ballads ("Dear Friends," "Lily of the Valley") and hard rock ("Flick of the Wrist," "Tenement Funster"), Queen takes on musical styles previously unexplored by hard rock bands—uplifting sounds from the Caribbean ("Misfire") and a ragtime ditty ("Bring Back That Leroy Brown"). Closing with the epic composition "In the Lap of the Gods... Revisited" (the set-closer on the ensuing tour), *Sheer Heart Attack* captured Queen's first true U.S. success. But their next album would make them a worldwide phenomenon. [Note: There has been some confusion over the years concerning the album *Sheer Heart Attack* and the song of the same name. The album was released in 1974, while the song appeared on 1977's *News of the World*] *—Greg Prato*

★ **A Night at the Opera** / Dec. 2, 1975 / Hollywood ✦✦✦✦✦
Queen was straining at the boundaries of hard rock and heavy metal on *Sheer Heart Attack*, but they broke down all the barricades on *A Night at the Opera*, a self-consciously ridiculous and overblown hard rock masterpiece. Using the multi-layered guitars of its predecessor as a foundation, *A Night at the Opera* encompasses metal ("Death on Two Legs," "Sweet Lady"), pop (the lovely, shimmering "You're My Best Friend"), campy British music-hall ("Lazing on a Sunday Afternoon," "Seaside Rendezvous") and mystical prog-rock ("'39," "The Prophet's Song"), eventually bringing it all together on the pseudo-operatic "Bohemian Rhapsody." In short, it's a lot like Queen's own version of *Led Zeppelin IV*, but where Zep finds dark menace in their bombast, Queen celebrates its own pomposity. No one in the band takes anything too seriously, otherwise the arrangements wouldn't be as ludicrously exaggerated as they are. But the appeal—and the influence—of *A Night at the Opera* is in its detailed, meticulous productions. It's prog-rock with a sense of humor as well as dynamics, and Queen never bettered their approach anywhere else. *—Stephen Thomas Erlewine*

A Day at the Races / Dec. 18, 1976 / Hollywood ✦✦✦
There was no way that Queen could top their 1975 masterpiece *A Night at the Opera* and its epic single "Bohemian Rhapsody," so they did the next best thing—they recorded a companion album, 1976's *A Day at the Races*. Although not as meticulously detailed or all-encompassing as its brilliant predecessor, *A Day at the Races* showed that the band was shedding their five-minute-plus epics in favor of more succinct songs, and becoming one of the world's top rock bands in the process. The album's centerpiece is undoubtedly the hit single "Somebody to Love"—whereas "Bohemian Rhapsody" had its roots in opera, "Somebody" was centered in gospel sounds (and features a surprisingly authentic-sounding gospel choir, using only the band members' voices!). Queen also tackled their first serious political statement with "White Man" (which details the plight of the American Indian), but also showed their fun side with such tracks as "The Millionaire Waltz," "Good Old Fashioned Lover Boy," and the rocking concert standard "Tie Your Mother Down." Also included is the album closer "Teo Torriatte," a hauntingly beautiful ballad that includes both English and Japanese lyrics. *A Day at the Races* proved to Queen's detractors that they hadn't run out of steam with the colossal *A Night at the Opera*. *—Greg Prato*

News of the World / Nov. 1, 1977 / Hollywood ✦✦✦
By 1977, Queen had perfected and succeeded at several different musical styles—heavy metal, glam, progressive, pop, ballads, and forays into genres not usually associated with hard rock (opera and gospel). By their next release, the band had progressed toward arena rock, and *News of the World* contained two of rock's best and most renowned all-time anthems, "We Will Rock You" and "We Are the Champions" (worldwide Top Ten hits). Punk rock was in full force by 1977, and Queen was among the elite bands being criticized by the punks. Instead of ignoring it, the band issued their answer to punk with the amphetamine-fueled "Sheer Heart Attack." *News of the World* bears some resemblance to 1974's *Queen II* due to their darkness—the tracks "All Dead, All Dead," "Spread Your Wings," and "My Melancholy Blues" smack the listener with cold, hard reality. But not all of the tracks are so serious, such as the fun salsa sounds of "Who Needs You," the epic Zep-rock of "It's Late," the groovy blues jam "Sleeping On the Sidewalk," the tasty funk of "Fight From the Inside," and the robotic, overtly sexual "Get Down, Make Love" (later covered by Nine Inch Nails). Their third blockbuster release in a row, *News of the World*, solidified Queen's status as global stadium headliners. *—Greg Prato*

Jazz / Nov. 14, 1978 / Hollywood ✦✦✦✦
Jazz has been unfairly slagged in some quarters as an inconsistent and unfocused record; granted, there's a bit of filler cluttering the second half, but as for the latter criticism, it's not like *A Night at the Opera* wasn't all over the map. The fact that it didn't produce any huge hit singles in the U.S. probably hasn't helped its reputation, but given half a chance, *Jazz* emerges as one of Queen's most playful, maniacally entertaining records. There are a few Freddie Mercury piano ballads and unusually hopped-up metallic rockers, but about half of *Jazz* is given over to quirky lyrics and/or stylistic detours (which, oddly enough, don't include any jazz, unless you count the music hall swing of "Dreamers Ball"). Kicking off with the pseudo-Middle Eastern kitsch of "Mustapha," *Jazz*'s first half is its strongest, highlighted by the double-A-sided single "Fat Bottomed Girls"/"Bicycle Race"; the former is a hilariously macho boogie that finds Mercury posing as Sir Mix-A-Lot's spiritual forebear, and the latter's childlike enthusiasm masks a subtle double entendre and an indirect reference to the all-female nude bicycle race the band staged as a promotional stunt (a poster of which was included). The second half climaxes with the, er, flamboyant U.K. Top Ten hit "Don't Stop Me Now," a Broadway showstopper at heart; it's preceded by the disco-rock of "Fun It" and the almost pastoral ballad "Leaving Home Ain't Easy," among others. It's difficult to discuss *Jazz* without referring to individual tracks one by one, since it can come off as a collection of moments, but its anything-goes diversity actually helps tie it together. Plus, there's a giddy sense of fun through most of the album, which helps make it Queen's strongest since *A Night at the Opera*. *—Steve Huey*

Live Killers / Jun. 26, 1979 / Hollywood ✦✦

The Game / Jun. 30, 1980 / Hollywood ✦✦✦✦✦
Along with 1975's *A Night at the Opera*, Queen's 1980 chart-topper *The Game* is one of their best and most commercially successful records. But *The Game* was the polar opposite of *Opera*, composition-wise. Whereas their 1975 classic was completely over-the-top and bombastic (it included "Bohemian Rhapsody," after all), *The Game* was full of succinct songs that included their trademark hard rock and ballads, as well as styles previously unexplored by the band—funk, disco, rockabilly, and new wave. The album's success is obviously linked to its pair of worldwide number one singles, the Elvis Presley tribute "Crazy Little Thing Called Love" and the contagious disco anthem "Another One Bites the Dust." Other highlights included the British hits "Play the Game" and "Save Me" (the latter being one of Queen's best ballads), the funk-rocker "Dragon Attack," the tuneful "Need Your Love Tonight" and "Sail Away Sweet Sister," plus the modern sounds of "Don't Try Suicide" and "Coming Soon." Although Queen would remain superstars throughout the rest of the world, *The Game* proved to be the band's last true hit studio album in the U.S. *—Greg Prato*

Flash Gordon / Jan. 27, 1981 / Hollywood ✦✦

Hot Space / May 25, 1982 / Hollywood ✦✦✦
By taking the better part of 1981 off to work on the follow-up to their big 1980 hit *The Game*, Queen fans were confident that the band's next release would follow in their winning tradition of classic albums. Unfortunately, this would not be the case. Unlike its predecessor, *Hot Space* was an inconsistent effort, marred by unfocused songwriting and material that was simply not as strong as their earlier work. Since they had just previously enjoyed a massive hit with the discofied "Another One Bites the Dust," Queen decided to dedicate the entire first side of the album to dance music, something that alienated their longtime rock fans. And while the single "Body Language" nearly cracked the U.S. Top Ten, the rest of the dance material was easily forgettable—"Back Chat," "Staying Power," "Action This Day," etc. However, the album was not a total washout. The more rock-oriented second side did contain some great tracks, such as "Put Out the Fire," "Calling All Girls," "Las Palabras De Amor," and the David Bowie collaboration "Under Pressure." But it was not enough to save *Hot Space* from a cruel critical and commercial fate, as its ensuing world tour marked the last time Queen would perform in the U.S. *—Greg Prato*

The Works / Feb. 28, 1984 / Hollywood ✦✦
Following the disappointing commercial performance of the dance-oriented *Hot Space* in 1982, Queen took 1983 off to get refocused and work on a follow-up that would put the band back on track. While the songwriting had definitely improved on the resulting *The Works* in 1984, the album sonically lacked the punch of such earlier releases as *News of the World* and *The Game* (strangely, *Hot Space* even had a better overall sound). Although the album only peaked at #23 on the U.S. album charts, it was a Top Ten hit in just about every other area of the world, producing the huge single "Radio Ga Ga." Three other tracks were hits in Queen's native England—the uplifting "I Want to Break Free," the love song "It's a Hard Life," and the politically conscious rocker "Hammer to Fall," which dealt with the danger of nuclear weapons. Other highlights included the '50s-sounding "Man On the Prowl," the electronic experiment "Machines," the thunderous "Tear It Up," and a touching acoustic ballad, "Is This the World We Created?" Perhaps with a more

straight-ahead production (and a U.S. tour), *The Works* would have landed Queen back on the top of the charts Stateside. *—Greg Prato*

A Kind of Magic / Jun. 3, 1986 / Hollywood ✦✦

By the release of 1986's *A Kind of Magic*, Queen's stature as a prominent rock band in the U.S. had slipped considerably, while in all other parts of the world (especially Europe), they remained superstar hitmakers. *A Kind of Magic* was their biggest album yet in England, where it reached number one, remained on the charts for 63 weeks, and spawned several hit singles—the epic title track, the tuneful pop-rocker "Friends Will Be Friends," and one of their most haunting ballads, "Who Wants to Live Forever?" (also included was the Live Aid-inspired hit anthem "One Vision," which was originally released as a single in 1985). Most of the songs were written for the movie *Highlander*—"Gimme the Prize (Kurgan's Theme)," "Princess of the Universe," the aforementioned "Who Wants to Live Forever?," etc.—but instead of issuing just a movie soundtrack, the band added a few non-movie tracks and made an official Queen release out of it. It may not have been as cohesive as some of their other albums, but *A Kind of Magic* was their best work in some time. Queen would embark on a sold-out tour of outdoor stadiums in Europe upon the album's release, which would sadly turn out to be their final tour. *—Greg Prato*

Live Magic / 1986 / Hollywood ✦✦✦

As their second live album, *Live Magic* might appear to be a bit unnecessary, but a closer look reveals that it's a better record than the previous *Live Killers*. Culled from a variety of dates from the 1986 *A Kind of Magic* tour but concentrating on the final show at Knebworth, *Live Magic* captures Queen, and Freddie Mercury in particular, at the height of their powers. While the set-list might rely a bit too heavily on mediocre mid-'80s material for some tastes, the band is tight and professional, and Mercury has an undeniable hold over the crowd. It's to Queen's credit that the energy rarely dips over the course of the record. *Live Magic* may be designed for hardcore fans, but for those listeners, it will provide a number of highlights, proving that the band's remarkable performance at Live Aid was no fluke.

This live album was released originally in the U.K. in 1986, but was not for sale on American soil until 1996. *—Stephen Thomas Erlewine*

The Miracle / Jun. 6, 1989 / Hollywood ✦✦

Innuendo / Feb. 5, 1991 / Hollywood ✦✦✦

Unbeknownst to the public, Freddie Mercury had been diagnosed with the AIDS virus in the late '80s. Although his health weakened by the '90s, Mercury insisted that the band work on music until the very end; their final album turned out to be 1991's *Innuendo*. Although it didn't receive the same critical praise as its predecessor, 1989's *The Miracle*, it was another strong album and global hit (again going gold in the U.S.). With hindsight, the song's lyrics are blatantly autobiographical from Mercury's standpoint, such as the reflective "These Are the Days of Our Lives" and the bold "The Show Must Go On." Also included are a pair of tracks that deal with mankind's inability to live harmoniously (the superb epic title track and "All God's People") and a humorous tribute to Mercury's beloved pet felines ("Delilah"). Queen's heavier side is represented by both the rock radio hit "Headlong" and "The Hitman," while "I'm Going Slightly Mad," "I Can't Live With You," and "Don't Try So Hard" show the band's pop sensibilities in full force, and on "Bijou," Brian May gets to show off his guitar chops. *Innuendo* was a fitting way to end one of rock's most successful careers. *—Greg Prato*

Greatest Hits, Vol. 2 / Oct. 30, 1991 / Parlophone ✦✦✦✦

Released just about a month before Freddie Mercury's untimely death in November 1991, a second "best of" collection titled *Greatest Hits, Vol. 2*, was issued in England only. While the album was re-sequenced (with other tracks added) and released as *Classic Queen* in the U.S. in 1992, *Greatest Hits, Vol. 2* features all of the band's European hits from 1982 through 1991. Since 1981's *Greatest Hits* went on to become one of the best-selling albums of all time in their homeland (spending 63 weeks on the charts when first released, and reappearing steadily ever since), the band had racked up enough hits to warrant a follow-up 10 years later. While Queen's hits from this era may not be as stellar as their '70s predecessors, they were all still very compelling rock compositions. Tracks such as "Radio Ga Ga," "Friends Will Be Friends," "I Want to Break Free" and "I'm Going Slightly Mad" show that the band could still compose pop gems, while the hard rockers "I Want It All," "Headlong," "One Vision" and "Hammer to Fall" kept their long-time fans happy. Also included are a few of the band's more epic compositions—"The Miracle," "Innuendo," "Who Wants to Live Forever" and "A Kind of Magic"—which help round out this second excellent collection of British Queen hits. *—Greg Prato*

Classic Queen / Mar. 10, 1992 / Hollywood ✦✦✦✦✦

Essentially, this 17-track album is a second-volume Queen's *Greatest Hits*, picking up the story from that album's 1981 release and taking it to the end of Queen's career. But the album also contains a few tracks—"Bohemian Rhapsody," "Keep Yourself Alive," and "Under Pressure"—that appeared on that first set, as well as a couple—"Stone Cold Crazy" and "Tie Your Mother Down"—from the same era. The remaining 12 tracks, culled from *The Works*, *A Kind of Magic*, *The Miracle*, and *Innuendo*, represent songs that were not big hits in the U.S. Nevertheless, with a resurgence of interest in Queen and the second coming of "Bohemian Rhapsody," courtesy of *Wayne's World*, this album returned Queen to platinum status and the U.S. Top 5 for the first time since the early '80s. *—William Ruhlmann*

★ **Greatest Hits** / Sep. 15, 1992 / Hollywood ✦✦✦✦✦

This is going to take a little explaining. In 1981, when it was contracted to Elektra Records in the U.S., Queen released an album called *Greatest Hits* (Elektra 564), which contained 14 songs that chronicled singles from 1973 to 1981. In 1990, Hollywood Records acquired CD rights to Queen's catalog, by which time the Elektra *Greatest Hits* had gone out of print on vinyl. Hollywood released *Classic Queen*, a compilation that covered Queen's hits from 1982 to its demise in 1991, with a few older songs thrown in. Then it released this album, its version of *Greatest Hits*, which is a 17-track album that deletes the songs from the first *Greatest Hits* that appeared on *Classic Queen* (among them Queen's biggest hit, "Bohemian Rhapsody") and adds a few tracks from the 1973-1982 era that did not appear on the original release. The Elektra *Greatest Hits* LP had a superior selection, but it's gone now, so you're stuck with this. [New fans don't seem to have minded, as this new *Greatest Hits* sold better than the first one.] *–William Ruhlmann*

Greatest Hits / 1994 / Parlophone ✦✦✦✦✦

Even more remarkable than the number of different Queen collections with nearly identical track listings and artwork which are available is the fact that every one of them is pretty much beyond reproach—such is the quality of the band's magnificent legacy. This particular version of their *Greatest Hits* features the original vinyl sequence and artwork. *—Ed Rivadavia*

Greatest Hits, Vols. 1-2 / 1995 / Hollywood ✦✦✦✦✦

Queen's greatest hits collections have contained different track listings throughout the world. In the band's native England they scored more hits than anywhere else, hence their compilations are usually more extensive. When Hollywood Records purchased the U.S. Queen catalogue in the early '90s, they reissued the long-out-of-print *Greatest Hits* album (basing the track listing on the 1981 British album of the same name but with a few changes), and released a companion album entitled *Classic Queen*. The rest of the world received *Greatest Hits II* in 1991, which contained their U.K. hits from 1981-1991(*Classic Queen* contained tracks by the band from all eras). Sensing that Queen completists in the U.S. would want both British-only releases for their collection, Hollywood released the 2-CD *Greatest Hits I & II* in 1995. Most of the tracks are available on the U.S. versions, but *Greatest Hits II* is the only compilation that includes such tracks as "Innuendo," "Breakthru," "It's a Hard Life," "The Invisible Man," and "Friends Will Be Friends." The set also comes with a special 40-page booklet. *—Greg Prato*

At the BBC / Mar. 7, 1995 / Hollywood ✦✦✦

A collection of early Queen material recorded for the British Broadcasting Corporation, *At the BBC* captures the band in their formative stages, as they were sketching out a cross between heavy metal and bombastically melodic pop. Several classic Queen songs are included and the performances are fascinating for hardcore fans, but there are only eight tracks on the album and it lists at full-price, which doesn't make it a bargain by any stretch of the imagination. *—Stephen Thomas Erlewine*

Made in Heaven / Nov. 7, 1995 / Hollywood ✦✦

Greatest Hits, Vol. 3 / Nov. 9, 1999 / Hollywood ✦✦✦

The history of Queen's *Greatest Hits* albums is impossibly convoluted. The first album with that title was released in 1981, and it was an excellent collection, but it was deleted in America by the end of the '80s. When Hollywood acquired the rights to the Queen catalog in 1991, it didn't reissue the original *Greatest Hits* album. Instead, it released *Classic Queen*, a bastardized version of the British compilation *Greatest Hits, Vol. 2*; it included "Bohemian Rhapsody," along with a couple other tracks from *Greatest Hits*. *Classic Queen* was essentially a quick cash-in to capitalize on the band's exposure in the hit film *Wayne's World*, and it served its purpose well. However, since it was pieced together with elements of the first two greatest-hits albums, Hollywood couldn't reissue either one. So, that year they put out their own *Greatest Hits*, which had the same skeleton as the British *Greatest Hits*, minus selections that were on *Classic Queen*, plus a handful of other tracks. To further complicate matters, Hollywood issued *Greatest Hits, Vols. 1 & 2* in 1995, and this two-disc set contained the original British collections, which *Greatest Hits, Vol. 3* functions as a sequel to. But *Greatest Hits, Vol. 3* isn't a hits collection, it's a hodgepodge of rarities. The only real hit here is George Michael's live duet with Queen on "Somebody to Love." The rest are remixes, solo cuts, and tracks completed after Freddie Mercury's death. It's nice to get some of these items on one disc, but such a collection could barely be called "hits." It wouldn't be a problem if it was billed as such, but it's a sporadic collection of loose ends, a few of which are pretty good, most of which are unnecessary. If casual fans are expecting a true *Greatest Hits, Vol. 3*, they will be sorely disappointed. *—Stephen Thomas Erlewine*

Queen Latifah

b. Mar. 18, 1970, Newark, NJ

Rap, Vocals, Leader / Pop-Rap, Alternative Rap, Hip-Hop, Golden Age

Although Queen Latifah was certainly not the first female rapper, she was the first to bring a feminist consciousness to the genre's political agenda with her groundbreaking 1989 debut, *All Hail the Queen*, and its single "Ladies First." Latifah (an Arabic word translating as "delicate" or "sensitive") was born Dana Owens in Newark, New Jersey and served a stint as a human beatbox in the group Ladies Fresh. She recorded a single, "Wrath of My Madness," in 1988 and later released *All Hail the Queen* to strongly favorable reviews; the album showcased her versatility on material ranging from soul, dub reggae and dance to straight hip-hop and established a tough, no-nonsense, intelligent persona. *Nature of a Sista* expanded on that role with some more personal material, but *Black Reign* became her most popular album, probably boosted by Latifah's increased visibility as a cast member of the Fox sitcom *Living Single*. The album was dedicated to her late brother, who was killed in a motorcycle accident in 1992, and produced the hit single "U.N.I.T.Y.," which won a Grammy for Best Rap Solo Performance. In addition to *Living Single*, Latifah has also appeared in the films *Jungle Fever*, *Juice*, and *House Party 2*. She returned to music in 1998 with *Order in the Court*. *—Steve Huey*

● **All Hail the Queen** / Nov. 1989 / Tommy Boy ✦✦✦✦✦

As strong a buzz as Queen Latifah created with her debut single of 1988, "Wrath of My

Madness" and its reggae-influenced B-side "Princess of the Posse," one would have expected the North Jersey rapper/actress' first album, *All Hail the Queen*, to be much stronger. Though not a bad album by any means, it doesn't live up to Latifah's enormous potential. The CD's strongest material includes "Evil That Men Do," a hardhitting duet with KRS-One addressing Black-on-Black crime and other social ills; the infectious hip-house number "Come Into My House"; the rap/reggae duet with Stetsasonic's Daddy-O "The Pros"; and the aforementioned songs. Unfortunately, boasting numbers like "A King and Queen Creation" and "Queen of Royal Badness" aren't terribly memorable. Especially disappointing is "Mama Gave Birth to the Soul Children," a duet with De La Soul that surprisingly, is both musically and lyrically generic. To be sure, Latifah's rapping skills are top-notch—which is why *All Hail the Queen* should have been consistently excellent instead of merely good. *—Alex Henderson*

Nature of a Sista / Sep. 3, 1991 / Tommy Boy ♦♦♦
Nature of a Sista isn't the outstanding album Queen Latifah is quite capable of recording. But even so, it's a decent sophomore effort that has more strengths than weaknesses. The North Jersey native tends to spend too much time boasting about her microphone skills—something that can wear thin in a hurry—but there's no denying the fact that she has considerable technique. As on her first album, Latifah indicates that she could hold her own in a battle with just about any rapper, male or female. And the positive image she projects is certainly commendable. But as likeable as much of this album is, it's obvious that she is capable of a lot more. Artistically, Latifah is selling herself short. *—Alex Henderson*

Black Reign / Nov. 16, 1993 / Motown ♦♦♦♦
Black Reign marked Latifah's move to Motown, and was also a return to the tough-talking, lyrically frank, frequently controversial material that established her as arguably the finest female rapper. "Coochie Bang" and "Weekend Love" were harsh and explicit attacks on would-be hit-and-run lovers, while "Just Another Day" and "I Can't Understand" examined the continuing inequities plaguing inner-city youth, and "Superstar" took a pointedly unglamorous view of her situation and the perils of hip-hop supremacy. *—Ron Wynn*

Order in the Court / Jun. 16, 1998 / Motown ♦♦♦
Queen Latifah opens up her sound on *Order in the Court* by adding old-school R&B and contemporary soul flourishes to her trademark hip-hop. Of course, she has never been reluctant to experiment—even on her first album, she aligned herself with the Native Tongues instead of running with hardcore rappers like Public Enemy. The difference with *Order in the Court* is that she's trying to fit into the fuzzy post-Fugees world where the lines between hip-hop and urban are nearly invisible. She performs duets with Pras and Faith Evans, letting them bring her closer to the urban-hip-hop fusion that she envisions. It's an intriguing blend that's occasionally successful, but it's hard not to yearn for the harder-edged Latifah that dominated her early albums. There are some good moments on *Order in the Court*, like the hard-hitting "Bananas" or the smooth "Paper," but they're a double-edged sword—they're good but they reveal that she's capable of delivering something better than *Order in the Court* ultimately turns out to be. *—Stephen Thomas Erlewine*

Queens of the Stone Age

Stoner Metal, Alternative Metal, Heavy Metal, Hard Rock
Formed from the ashes of stoner-rock icons Kyuss, Queens of the Stone Age reunited the group's singer/guitarist Josh Homme, drummer Alfredo Hernandez and bassist Nick Oliveri along with new guitarist/keyboardist Dave Catching. The project's origins date back to Homme, who in the wake of Kyuss' 1995 demise relocated to Seattle to tour with the Screaming Trees; he soon began working with a revolving lineup of musicians including the Trees' Van Conner, Soundgarden's Matt Cameron and Dinosaur Jr.'s Mike Johnson, recording a series of seven-inches originally issued under the name Gamma Ray. After rechristening the group Queens of the Stone Age, Homme recruited Hernandez to begin work on their self-titled debut LP, issued in late 1998 on Loosegroove; after the album was completed, Oliveri left the Dwarves to rejoin his former bandmates, with the subsequent addition of Catching rounding out the roster. In addition to extensive touring, Homme put together a series of albums for the indie label Man's Ruin; the various volumes of *The Desert Sessions* feature Homme's collaborations with a loose-knit, revolving-door lineup of like-minded musicians, some from bands like Soundgarden, Fu Manchu, and Monster Magnet. In mid-2000, Queens of the Stone Age issued their sophomore album *R* (as in the movie rating; some promo copies were distributed with the original title, *II*) before appearing on that year's Ozzfest tour. By that point, drummer Hernandez had been replaced by a tag-team combo of Gene Troutman and Nicky Lucero. *—Jason Ankeny*

Queens of the Stone Age / Sep. 22, 1998 / Loose Groove ♦♦♦♦
Instead of trying to recreate the sound of his former band Kyuss, Josh Homme took a new approach to music. He crafted tight hard rock songs that were heavy on melody and light on vocals. While there is still a lot of fuzz coming from the amplifiers, the vocals are softly interwoven among the chords. There's no screaming or rock & roll antics, and the group takes an almost lo-fi attitude to heavy metal—an interesting combination that produced instant radio gems like "Regular John," the extreme ranges on "Avon," and the smoky, blues-influenced "Walkin' on the Sidewalks." Queens of the Stone Age are creating a new blend of heavy metal that makes it acceptable to produce creative music that doesn't rely on testosterone as the driving force. *—David Thomas*

• **R** / Jun. 6, 2000 / Interscope ♦♦♦♦♦
The second Queens of the Stone Age album, *R* (as in the movie rating; its title was changed from *II* at the last minute before release) makes its stoner rock affiliations clear right from the opening track. The lyrics of "Feel Good Hit of the Summer" consist entirely of a one-line list of recreational drugs that Josh Homme rattles off over and over, a gag that gets pretty tiresome by the end of the song (and certainly doesn't need the reprise that follows "In the Fade"). Fortunately, the rest of the material is up to snuff. *R* is mellower, trippier, and more arranged than its predecessor, making its point through warm fuzz-guitar tones, ethereal harmonies, vibraphones, horns, and even the odd steel drum. That might alienate listeners who have come to expect a crunchier guitar attack, but even though it's not really aggro, *R* is still far heavier than the garage-punk and grunge that inform much of the record. It's still got the vaunted Arizona-desert vibes of Kyuss, but it evokes a more relaxed, spacious, twilight feel, as opposed to a high-noon meltdown. Mark Lanegan and Barrett Martin of the Screaming Trees both appear on multiple tracks, and their band's psychedelic grunge—in its warmer, less noisy moments—is actually not a bad point of comparison. Longtime Kyuss fans might be disappointed at the relative lack of heaviness, but *R*'s direction was hinted at on the first QOTSA album, and Homme's experimentation really opens up the band's sound, pointing to exciting new directions for heavy guitar rock in the new millennium. *—Steve Huey*

Queensrÿche

f. 1981, Bellevue, WA
Album Rock, Progressive Metal, Heavy Metal
Although they were initially grouped in with the legions of pop/metal bands that dominated the American heavy metal scene of the '80s, Queensrÿche were one of the most distinctive bands of the era. Where their contemporaries built on the legacy of Van Halen, Aerosmith and Kiss, Queensrÿche constructed a progressive form of heavy metal that drew equally from the guitar pyrotechnics of post-Van Halen metal and '70s art-rock, most notably Pink Floyd and Queen. After releasing a handful of ignored albums, the band began to break into the mainstream with the acclaimed 1988 album, *Operation: Mindcrime*. Its follow-up, *Empire*, was the group's biggest success, selling over two million copies due to the hit single, "Silent Lucidity." Queensrÿche never sustained that wide-spread popularity—like most late-'80s metal bands, their audience disappeared after the emergence of grunge. Nevetheless, they retained a large cult following well into the '90s. *—Stephen Thomas Erlewine*

Queensrÿche / 1983 / EMI America ♦♦♦
Before establishing themselves as both a commercial and a progressive metal force, Seattle's Queensrÿche dealt classic metal steeped in English tradition. In fact, their 1983 self-titled debut EP, while largely ignored in America, became a sensation in the U.K. and Europe. The band displays an obvious Iron Maiden influence in their early songs, which often featured "dungeons and dragons" lyrical themes. Their classic "Queen of the Reich" is one such example (with a hilariously primitive adventure video to boot), while "The Lady Wore Black" displays more maturity—a sign of things to come. EMI scored an extra point when issuing the CD version by adding "Prophecy," a phenomenal outtake from the *Rage for Order* sessions which helps make this a must-have release for Queensrÿche fans. *—Ed Rivadavia*

The Warning / Sep. 7, 1984 / EMI America ♦♦♦
1984's *The Warning* proved to be a holding pattern for Seattle's Queensrÿche, offering quality classic metal with lyrics tending to the mystical and occult. The band would soon embark on a massive creative growth spurt, but they seem to be treading water on tracks like "En Force," "Sanctuary," and the pedestrian title cut. Bright spots include the technology nightmare portrayed on "N M 156" and the nine-minute epic "Roads to Madness" where singer Geoff Tate demonstrates all of his incredible range. The album's high point comes with the anthemic "Take Hold of the Flame," which became a monster smash worldwide, especially in Japan. *—Ed Rivadavia*

Rage for Order / Jul. 1986 / EMI America ♦♦

Operation: Mindcrime / Apr. 27, 1988 / EMI America ♦♦♦♦♦
Queensrÿche scored their breakthrough success with the ambitious concept album *Operation: Mindcrime*, which tells the story of a fortune hunter whose disillusionment with Reagan-era American society leads him to join a shadowy plot to assassinate corrupt leaders. For such a detailed storyline (there is also a tragic romance thrown in), the band keeps its focus remarkably well, and the music is just as ambitious, featuring a ten-minute track with orchestrations by Michael Kamen. Those experiments don't tend to work as well as the tighter, more melodic prog-metal songs, which are frequently gems, especially the singles "Eyes of a Stranger" and "I Don't Believe In Love." Granted, the lyrics and political observations can sometimes be too serious and intellectual for their own good (few bands, metal or otherwise, can make lines like "There's no *raison d'être*" work). But despite the occasional flaws, it's surprising how well *Operation: Mindcrime does* work, and it's a testament to Queensrÿche's creativity and talent that they can pull off a project of this magnitude. *—Steve Huey*

• **Empire** / Aug. 1990 / EMI America ♦♦♦♦♦
One of the most praised metal albums of the late 1980s, *Operation: Mindcrime* was an extremely tough act to follow. But while *Empire* isn't quite on a par with that gem, it is certainly one of the most absorbing headbanger efforts of 1990. Highly conceptual and anything but redundant, *Empire* demonstrates beautifully just how imaginative Queensrÿche can be. If anyone has bridged the gap between the bombast of Iron Maiden and the artsiness of Pink Floyd, it is Queensrÿche. But as much as one may be reminded of Floyd's *The Wall* on pieces like "Anybody Listening?," "Silent Lucidity" and "Resistance," *Empire* leaves no doubt that Queensrÿche has a rich personality all its own. *—Alex Henderson*

Promised Land / Oct. 18, 1994 / EMI America ♦♦♦
Queensrÿche returned from a four-year absence with *Promised Land* only to find the hard-rock landscape very different than the one they left in 1990. But Queensrÿche did

something smart. Instead of trying to adjust themselves to fit into the world that their Seattle brethren had created, they simply stayed the same. Not only was the record a commercial success—it went gold in four months—but it was also an engaging album. *Promised Land* lacks the conceptual unity and consistent songwriting of *Operation: Mindcrime*, but it makes it clear that the band hasn't run out of ideas yet. —*Stephen Thomas Erlewine*

Hear in the Now Frontier / Mar. 25, 1997 / EMI America ✦✦✦

Q2k / Sep. 14, 1999 / Atlantic ✦✦✦

Greatest Hits / Jun. 27, 2000 / Virgin ✦✦✦✦✦
Queensrÿche was poised to follow in the footsteps of Pink Floyd, Rush, and Iron Maiden. Their early albums were derivative but interesting, and the Seattle quintet quickly synthesized intelligent, technically impressive progressive rock and heavy metal. Vocalist Geoff Tate, guitarists Chris DeGarmo and Michael Wilton, bassist Eddie Jackson, and drummer Scott Rockenfield arguably peaked with 1988's concept album *Operation: Mindcrime*, a masterpiece in terms of musicianship and story structure. Then 1990's equally excellent *Empire* exploded thanks to "Silent Lucidity." But some things happened that stopped Queensrÿche from cementing itself as a superstar band for the ages: (1) Within a year grunge exploded, rendering Queensrÿche's skills "unhip"; (2) 1994's *Promised Land* did well commercially but was generally underappreciated; (3) Queensrÿche virtually ruined its own career with 1997's disappointing and ill-conceived *Hear in the Now Frontier*, which featured a stripped-down "modern" sound five years after the fact; (4) Queensrÿche's label, EMI, folded just after its release; (5) Perhaps reeling from creative uncertainty and label problems, DeGarmo quit. Prime highlights are collected on 2000's *Greatest Hits*, which covers seven EMI albums. "Queen of the Reich" is great heavy metal, even if Tate does imitate the operatic wail of Judas Priest's Rob Halford and Iron Maiden's Bruce Dickinson. Other early gems are "Take Hold of the Flame" and "I Dream in Infrared." *Operation: Mindcrime* works best as a whole, but "I Don't Believe in Love" and "Eyes of a Stranger" are the peaks. *Promised Land* is represented by the superb "I Am I" and "Bridge." Two bonus tracks from Japanese releases are included: "Chasing Blue Sky" is astonishingly beautiful and "Someone Else?" features the full band. The *Greatest Hits* liner notes feature an essay by Paul Sutter who wrote an early Queensrÿche demo review for Kerrang! All 16 songs are 24-bit digitally remastered. —*Bret Adams*

? & the Mysterians

f. 1962
Detroit Rock, Frat Rock, Garage Rock
Originally formed in Flint, MI, in 1962, this group took its name from the obscure science-fiction movie *The Mysterians*. They recorded the anthemic "96 Tears" for the local Spanish music label Pa-Go-Go in 1966. It was immediately picked up for national consumption by Cameo-Parkway, going on to be one of the most covered garage band classics of the '60s. Lead singer Question Mark (real name listed as both Rudy Martinez and Reeto Rodriguez) continues to front a version of the band on oldies package shows across the U.S. —*Cub Koda*

● **96 Tears** / 1966 / Cameo ✦✦✦✦✦
A true garage band classic, featuring the title track and 11 others straight from the band's set list. —*Cub Koda*

Action / 1966 / Cameo ✦✦✦
On the back of the album cover of *?* and the Mysterians' *Action*, there is a list of "the facts" about the band. Their "likes" mostly consist of "girls," "science fiction," and "the color black," the combination of which pretty much describes their music. *Action* contains some of the best early-'60s, AM-pop-meets-garage-noise tunes—a mixture that also produced the L.A. sound of the Seeds and would later lead to the utter genius of the Velvet Underground. But like the Beatles when they were in Hamburg, *?* and the Mysterians are content to play catchy renditions of their rock & roll favorites. They burn through the first verse of "Shout," play some pure sugar pop on the groovy, fantastic organ-driven "Hangin' on a String," and give "Can't Get Enough of You Baby" the garage treatment. But *?* and the Mysterians have some real innovation, too. They start their version of the hit "Girl (You Captivate Me)" with dark, almost spoken vocals. Originals like "It's Not Easy" are infused with R&B sensibilities. But "Smokes" is the real winner—it bleeds with raucous basement party grooves that set the stage for much of rock to come. —*Charles Spano*

96 Tears Forever: The Dallas Reunion Tapes '84 / 1985 / ROIR ✦✦✦
Originally a BASF-LHD cassette-only release, this live recording showcases the distinctive mixture of Tex-Mex bounce and garage-punk raunch that anticipated such groups as the Lyres, Joe King Carrasco & the Crowns, and Elvis Costello & the Attractions. The band propels lead vocalist Question Mark (aka Rudy Martinez) as he swaggers, taunts, and exhorts his way through 14 energized (if somewhat repetitive) songs, including "Don't Tease Me," "Girl (You Captivate Me)" sung as "Girl (You Masturbate Me)," "I Can't Get Enough of You Baby," and "96 Tears." Question Mark doesn't convey quite as much menace as he does on the original 1960s recordings of songs such as "Smokes," but since those original recordings are not readily available in the U.S., this is a reasonable substitute for a career retrospective. However, the group has released another live recording, *Do You Feel It Baby?*, which offers more songs and is easier to find. —*Todd Kristel*

● **Original Recordings** / 1995 / Campark ✦✦✦✦✦
This is probably an unauthorized compilation, with 30 of the group's original '60s recordings, including, of course, "96 Tears." Since the owners of the original tracks have obstinately refused to officially reissue the Mysterians' '60s catalog on CD in the U.S., they really have no cause to complain if frustrated collectors turn to this anthology as the only

reasonable option. The sound quality is good, although the brief liner notes unfortunately do not detail the specific origin of each cut. Even with so much vintage work in one place, it is still striking how much better "96 Tears" was than anything else they did. Garageheads might be disappointed with how many of the cuts sound like lesser, similar "96 Tears" derivations, all heavy on the cheap organ sound and Rudy Martinez's quasi-studly vocals. For "Do You Feel It," they rip off someone other than themselves, as it's a retitled cover of the Rolling Stones' instrumental, "2120 South Michigan Avenue." At least they wrote most of their own material, and there are occasional cuts that hold their own weight. —*Richie Unterberger*

? & the Mysterians Featuring 96 Tears / Nov. 4, 1997 / Collectables ✦✦✦
Since the rights to the original *96 Tears* album and singles are held in limbo, fans have to be content with records like *? & the Mysterians Featuring 96 Tears*, a collection of rerecordings by the original lineup that was recorded in 1997, 31 years after their one hit topped the charts. Surprisingly, the group sounds tough, dynamic and exciting—it's easy to tell that this is not the same group of young garage punks from the mid-'60s, but these guys can still kick hard which is what makes the record worthwhile for diehard garage freaks. In addition to "96 Tears," the album also features Mysterians classics like "I Need Somebody," "'8' Teen," "Smokes," "Up Side," "Stormy Monday," "Make You Mine," "Got To," "Don't Tease Me" and "You're Telling Me Lies." —*Stephen Thomas Erlewine*

Do You Feel It Baby? / Apr. 28, 1998 / Norton ✦✦✦✦
Recorded live at Cavestomp '97 at Coney Island High School in New York City, this capturea the original version of Question Mark & the Mysterians (accept no substitutes) shaking the joint down to the last brick. Amazingly, they sound *exactly* like they did some 30-odd years ago, fortified with some vintage equipment (no synthesizers here) and an enthusiastic crowd to goad them on. Kicking off with a Stones-like "2120 South Michigan Avenue" riff that gets turned into the title track, the band gets into fourth gear right from the start and pretty much stays there. Running through a 19-song set list that combines old favorites from their Cameo and Capitol recordings along with new songs that sound exactly like they were written 30 years ago (and who's to say they weren't?), this is one of the very, very few modern-day "reunion" albums that really works and makes you wish you were there. —*Cub Koda*

Feel It! The Very Best of Question Mark & the Mysterians / Jul. 31, 2001 / Varese ✦✦✦

Quicksilver Messenger Service

f. 1965, San Francisco, CA, **db.** 1973
Acid Rock, Psychedelic
The band that became Quicksilver Messenger Service originally was conceived as a rock vehicle for folk singer/songwriter Dino Valenti, author of "Get Together." As the band was being put together, however, Valenti was imprisoned on a drug charge and he didn't rejoin Quicksilver until later. They debuted at the end of 1965 and played around the Bay Area and then the West Coast for the next two years, building up a large following but resisting offers to record that had been taken up by such San Francisco acid-rock colleagues as Jefferson Airplane and the Grateful Dead. Quicksilver finally signed to Capitol toward the end of 1967 and recorded their self-titled debut album in 1968. *Happy Trails*, the 1969 follow-up, was recorded live. —*William Ruhlmann*

Quicksilver Messenger Service / May 1968 / Capitol ✦✦✦✦✦
The band's debut effort was a little more restrained and folky than some listeners had expected, given their reputation for stretching out in concert. While some prefer the mostly live *Happy Trails*, this is inarguably their strongest set of studio material, with the accent on melodic folk-rockers. Highlights include their cover of folksinger Hamilton Camp's "Pride of Man," probably their best studio track, "Light Your Windows," probably the group's best original composition, and founding member Dino Valenti's "Dino's Song" (Valenti himself was in jail when the album was recorded). "Gold and Silver" is their best instrumental jam, and the 12-minute "The Fool" reflects some of the best and worst traits of the psychedelic era. —*Richie Unterberger*

Happy Trails / Mar. 1969 / Capitol ✦✦✦✦
Quicksilver was heard at its best on this partially live album, which contained a 25-minute version of Bo Diddley's "Who Do You Love." —*William Ruhlmann*

Shady Grove / Dec. 1969 / Edsel ✦✦✦✦✦
Originally released on Capitol, and in recent years only available as an import CD, it includes "Joseph's Coat," "Flashing Lonesome" and "Edward (The Mad Shirt Grinder)." —*Roundup Newsletter*

Just for Love / Aug. 1970 / BGO ✦✦✦
With the return of Gary Duncan and the recording debut of founder Dino Valenti, *Just for Love*, Quicksilver's fourth album, marked their debut as the band they were intended to be. The ironic thing about that is that, led by singer/songwriter Valenti, they were a much more pop-oriented band than their fans had come to expect. On *Just for Love*, Quicksilver finally was Valenti's backup group (he wrote all but one of the songs), and while this gave them greater coherence and accessibility, as well as their only Top 50 single in "Fresh Air," it also made them less the boogie band they had been. And it meant the band's days were numbered. —*William Ruhlmann*

What About Me / Dec. 1970 / One Way ✦✦✦
Recorded in part at the same 1970 sessions that produced *Just for Love*, *What About Me* was a similar effort, again dominated by Dino Valenti's songwriting and singing. It was also the swan song of the band, with guitarist John Cipollina, pianist Nicky Hopkins, and bassist David Freiberg dropping out after its completion. —*William Ruhlmann*

Quicksilver / Nov. 1971 / One Way ✦✦✦✦
One of the group's better albums, despite coming so late in their history that it was

ignored by almost everyone. "Hope," "Fire Brothers," and "Don't Cry For My Lady Love" are among the best songs the group ever cut, and "I Found Love" is one of the prettiest, most upbeat songs ever to come from any classic San Francisco band. Some of the rest is self-indulgent, but that's what this era of music was about—the guitar pyrotechnics of "Song For Frisco" and "Play My Guitar" make them both more entertaining than their somewhat bland melodies; the latter song, in particular, sounds like a Marty Balin/Jefferson Airplane outtake that would have been right on target about four years before the release date of this album. The whole record feels that way, a throwback to the psychedelic era circa late 1967. It's also very much a folk-rock record, with a rich acoustic guitar texture on many of the songs. For the record, since the CD reissue has no personnel information, the band at this point was Dino Valenti (guitar, vocals), Greg Elmore (drums), Gary Duncan (vocals, guitar), Mark Ryan (bass), Mark Naftalin (keyboards), and Chuck Steaks (keyboards). If you ever wondered what the Airplane might have done as a follow-up to *Surrealistic Pillow* with Marty Balin still singing lead, this is it. *—Bruce Eder*

Comin' Thru / Apr. 1972 / One Way ✦✦✦

Anthology / Mar. 1973 / EMI-Capitol Special Markets ✦✦✦✦✦
A two-record set chronicling Quicksilver's recorded history from 1967 to 1971 and including most of their best tracks. Now out of print, this collection has been superseded by the Rhino album *Sons of Mercury*. *— William Ruhlmann*

Solid Silver / Oct. 1975 / Edsel ✦✦

Maiden of the Cancer Moon / 1983 / Psycho ✦✦✦
A double album of live material from 1968, this duplicates a lot of the material on *Happy Trails* and adds considerably more. This erratic collection reflects Quicksilver's best and worst qualities: The hard-driving blend of raga/folk/psychedelic rock is fine, while the blues jams are fairly awful. Besides "Who Do You Love?" and "Mona" (two versions), this LP has covers of "Back Door Man," "Smokestack Lightning," Buffy St. Marie's "Codine," and versions of most of the songs from the first Quicksilver LP. The rendition of "The Fool" here eclipses the studio take, and the performance of "Gold and Silver" is fine except for the "Toad"-like drum solo. John Cippolina's slithery leads are consistently fine, and Quicksilver fans will find this worth the search. *—Richie Unterberger*

Peace by Piece / Jul. 1986 / Capitol ✦

● **Sons of Mercury (1968-75)** / Jul. 2, 1991 / Rhino ✦✦✦✦✦
This thorough two-disc best-of contains Quicksilver's most familiar material from its various lineups, plus some rarities. The only thing keeping this from being essential is the exclusion of the complete live version of "Who Do You Love," over a single edited version. *— William Ruhlmann*

Unreleased Quicksilver: Lost Gold and Silver / Mar. 14, 2000 / EMI Capitol/Collectors' Choice ✦✦✦
By licensing these previously unreleased live and studio tracks (plus some previously released but rare material) from the Special Markets division of EMI-Capitol Music, the mail-order company Collectors' Choice Music has legitimized Quicksilver Messenger Service recordings that had floated around on bootlegs and quasi-legal discs for many years. The performances all date from 1967-1968, a period during which Quicksilver consisted of lead guitarist John Cipollina, rhythm guitarist and singer Gary Duncan, bassist David Freiberg, and drummer Greg Elmore. The first disc, entitled "Studio," finds them struggling to pull together original songs for their debut LP, while the second disc, "Live From 1968," finds them playing some of these same songs in concert. By their second album, *Happy Trails*, they had given up trying to get across in the studio and just recorded live, where they were far more comfortable. They were also more comfortable using blues and rock standards like "Back Door Man," "Smokestack Lightning," and "Who Do You Love" as jumping-off points for extended jams, or extrapolating the jazz standard "Take Five" into "Gold and Silver." Some performances age better than others, but by and large, Quicksilver's live reputation stands up well. The second disc's studio outtakes are more problematic, but nevertheless interesting, notably a horn-filled arrangement of "Back Door Man." Tacked on at the end are the group's two contributions to the soundtrack to *Revolution*, their one-off novelty single "Bears," and the B-side of "Bears," the pretty acoustic ballad "Stand by Me" (an original penned by erstwhile band member Dino Valenti, not the Ben E. King song), which has not been reissued since the single was released in 1968. *— William Ruhlmann*

Quickspace

f. London, England
Noise Pop, Ambient Pop, Experimental Rock, Space Rock, Indie Rock
Shortly after the breakup of his acclaimed indie pop group the Faith Healers at the end of 1994, London-based guitarist/vocalist Tom Cullinan formed Quickspace Supersport. While Cullinan's new band retained some of the same droning tension and fuzzy pop sensibilities of the Faith Healers, Quickspace Supersport's sound proved more malleable and their lyrics more upbeat. In March 1995, the group released their debut 7", *Quickspace Happy Song #1*, on their own Kitty Kitty Corporation label. Though they received an initially tepid response from a Brit-pop-preoccupied press, Quickspace Supersport found friends in bands such as Sebadoh and Stereolab, both of whom they toured the U.K. with later that year. By October 1995 and the release of their landmark *Superplus* EP, the British press caught up with the band's tense-but-varied drone pop, and raved about their singles and live shows. Just as the momentum behind them seemed to reach critical mass, Quickspace Supersport took a six-month hiatus. In the summer of 1996, the band returned with more than half its lineup replaced and half its name removed. Only Cullinan and bassist Sean Newsham remained from the original group, and new members Nina Pascale (guitar/vocals), Paul Shilton (keyboards), and Chin (drums) re-energized their sound. Now simply Quickspace, they released the bouncy, driving "Friend" single that November. In June 1997, Quickspace released their self-titled debut album to warm reviews. After holing up in the studio for the remainder of 1997, Quickspace rewarded their fans' patience by releasing two 7"s (compiled on the *Precious Little* EP) in spring 1998 and an album, *Precious Falling*, later that summer. With the number of names, band members, and styles the band plays with, the only constants in Quickspace's world are quality and change. *—Heather Phares*

Quickspace [UK] / 1997 / Kitty Kitty Corporation Choosy ✦✦✦✦✦
On their debut album, Quickspace's experiments with different styles and combinations of drone-pop meet with slightly less success than on their earlier EPs. Nevertheless, *Quickspace* is quietly infectious. It gets off to a strong start with "Swisher," a rolling, breezy tune that features a sweetly circular guitar line and lyrics like, "All we need is a place to be nice and warm/Got to live it up, must be happy."

The fuzz blasts of "Song for Someone" and the post-rock/surf hybrid "Quasi-Pfaff" nearly match the propulsive energy of earlier works like the *Superplus* EP, but overall *Quickspace* is more subdued and guitar-based than much of their previous output. Unfortunately, the least focused songs, "Mousetail" and "Winona," are right in the middle of the album and break its momentum. However, "Docile One" and "Docile Two" build a quiet tension thanks to flowing, slow-motion grooves and judicious use of French horn, violin, and slide guitar. "Docile Two" is one of the finest moments from Quickspace, making the most of a stately pace, cascading drums, fluid guitars and a soft duet from Tom Cullinan and Nina Pascale. Though not as instantly accessible as their earlier, poppier singles, *Quickspace*'s quiet meditations and extended drones reward repeat listens. *—Heather Phares*

Supo Spot / 1997 / Kitty Kitty ✦✦✦✦
Quickspace Supo Spot combines all of Quickspace's early singles, B-sides and Peel sessions and documents the evolution of the group's sound, from their debut single, the overdrive-drenched "Quickspace Happy Song #1" to vast, droning epics like "Friend," "Extraplus" and "Exemplary Swishy." Each track contains seeds of the driven keyboard and guitar grooves, creative arrangements and unpretentious lyrics that became Quickspace's trademark approach to making music.

At its best, such as on "Do It My Own Way," which incoroporates tin whistles, violin and shouted boy-girl vocals, *Quickspace Supo Spot* sounds spontaneous and exciting. At its worst, on songs like "Unique Slippy" and "The Whiff n' Spoof Song," it's just goofy. Too scattered to be a starting point for Quickspace, listening to the band get its musical footing is especially entertaining for completists and anyone fond of lo-fi drone-rock in general. *—Heather Phares*

● **Quickspace [US]** / Nov. 18, 1997 / Slash ✦✦✦✦✦
The U.S. release of *Quickspace* is something of an improvement over the U.K. version, as it adds two of the band's finest singles, "Rise" and "Friend," and removes "Mousetail." Bookending the original album with the two relatively fast-paced singles detracts somewhat from the stately flow of the rest of the material, but it does give a better overview of Quickspace's diverse sound. Integrating the new songs into the rest of the album might have worked better, as "Swisher" and "Docile Two" are strong opening and final tracks for *Quickspace*, but overall the album is a fine introduction for U.S. listeners to a unique band. *—Heather Phares*

Precious Falling / Aug. 1998 / Kitty Kitty ✦✦✦✦✦
Where their EPs expanded and experimented with the different elements of their sound, and their first album concentrated on their softer side, Quickspace's second album *Precious Falling* pulls the band's versatile style together in a collection of 13 diverse but cohesive songs. The dreamily beautiful "Mouse" glides atop a minimal, shimmering guitar pattern and sighs off-handedly charming lyrics like "You're not perfect, I suppose/But you're my rose." Fuzzy guitar and synth rave-ups like "Happy Song #2" and "Coca Lola" prove Quickspace hasn't lost its affection for noisy pop, and the minor-key "Melo," "Minors" and "Walk Me Home" offer a tart contrast to the generally sweet and sunny feel of *Precious Mountain*. Most interesting are the experimental and filmic songs like "Hadid," "The Mountain Waltz" and "Goodbye Precious Mountain," where the band stretch their remixing and arranging skills.

Though quirky throwaways like "7 Like That" and "Obvious" sometimes pull the rest of the album down from its heights, it's the band's essentially unpretentious nature that makes their flexibility possible. That Quickspace can blend diverse styles and sounds together in a comfortable and spontaneous-sounding way reflects on their creative integrity, and *Precious Falling* shows just how much they can do. *—Heather Phares*

The Death of Quickspace / Mar. 21, 2000 / Matador ✦✦✦✦
Taking a step back from the vast scope and experimentalism of their brilliant, sprawling album *Precious Falling*, Quickspace's Matador debut, *The Death of Quickspace*, hones in on the group's precarious, invigorating fusion of giddy noise bursts and moody, hypnotic lock grooves. Songs like "They Shoot Horse Don't They" and "The Lobbalong Song" feature their signature mix of rolling drums, bubbling keyboards, and twining, chiming melodies, but surprisingly thrashy guitars slash through "Munchers No Munchers," "Lob It," and "4," making this album the group's most raucous to date. Though the cascading, 11-minute epic "Climbing a Hill" doesn't quite achieve the liftoff that most of Quickspace's extended pieces accomplish effortlessly, the band more than makes up for that with two of their finest pop confections, "Gloriana" and "A Rose." As sunny and winding as a country road in the summertime, both songs blend sweet harmonies, pastoral fiddles, slide guitars, and the otherworldy theremins that always hover around the periphery of Quickspace's songs. Though *Precious Falling* is a hard act to follow, much like their first album and early singles, *The Death of Quickspace* makes its sneaky way into the listener's

affections, creeping up and offering something surprising when it's least expected. —*Heather Phares*

Quiet Riot

f. 1975, **db.** 1988

Heavy Metal, Hard Rock, Album Rock, Pop-Metal

For a very brief moment, Quiet Riot was a rock & roll phenomenon. The first heavy metal band to top the pop charts, the California quartet was an overnight sensation thanks to its monster 1983 smash, *Metal Health*. Pushed by a raucous rendition of the old Slade chestnut "Cum on Feel the Noize," the album stormed up the U.S. charts, quickly reaching the number one spot and going platinum five times over in the process. Quiet Riot's unexpected success shocked everyone. Pressured to capitalize on their hot streak, the band was rushed back into the studio to whip together 1984's *Condition Critical*; but, not surprisingly, the album was little more than a poor carbon copy of *Metal Health*—even including yet another Slade cover in "Mama Weer All Crazee Now." Sure enough, fans were hardly impressed, and as they watched the album begin to slide off the charts, the band members began to panic—none more than notorious motor-mouth singer Kevin DuBrow, the man most deserving of credit for taking the band so far with his dogged persistence. Arguably the only rock star to talk himself out of a gig, DuBrow began turning his frustration into verbal attacks toward all in sight, eventually isolating the band even more and almost single-handedly sealing its fate. By the time damage control set in, it was too late to turn the ship around, and Quiet Riot's fortunes only went from bad to worse, eventually resulting in DuBrow getting fired from his own band. He would eventually resurrect Quiet Riot in the '90s, but despite their best efforts, the once chart-topping band would remain forever exiled to the fringes of pop conscience. —*Ed Rivadavia*

Quiet Riot / 1977 / CBS ✦✦✦

Quiet Riot II / 1978 / CBS ✦✦✦

Metal Health / 1983 / Pasha ✦✦✦✦

Quiet Riot seemingly came out of nowhere in 1983, racing up the singles charts with their over-the-top cover of Slade's "Cum On Feel the Noize" and crashing the *Billboard* album chart's number one spot with their multi-million-selling *Metal Health* LP—the first heavy metal record to ever do so. Prior to their "overnight success," Q.R. had been toiling in relative obscurity for years, so that by the time they finally turned the corner, *Metal Health*'s meteoric success must have surprised the band even more than it did their critics and

newfound fans. Though it has received its fair share of criticism, *Metal Health* isn't nearly as average as some would have you believe. Say what you will, but the album's title track continues to deliver after all these years. With its crushing guitar riff, inane lyrics, and goofy bravado, it's heavy metal personified in all its glorious/ridiculous excess. The surprisingly laid-back groove of "Don't Wanna Let You Go" follows the storming "Cum On Feel the Noize," which leads into the slightly '50s "Slick Black Cadillac," a rehashed early band favorite. "Love's a Bitch" closes side one with plenty of venom and attitude, but despite a valiant attempt by the driving coulda-been-a-hit "Breathless," side two falls way short of the mark. Even though "Run for Cover" is quite a stomper, the closing triplet of "Battle Axe" (Carlos Cavazo's half-assed guitar showcase), "Let's Get Crazy" (downright embarrassing jock rock), and "Thunderbird" (painful sub-Journey balladry) tend to understate the hugeness of the occasion. Still unquestionably the band's best effort, *Metal Health* would eventually earn one-hit wonder status thanks to Quiet Riot's inability to deliver anything resembling a decent follow-up. —*Ed Rivadavia & John Franck*

Condition Critical / 1984 / Pasha ✦✦✦

Condition Critical, Quiet Riot's follow-up to their number one, multi-million-seller commercial breakthrough *Metal Health*, is nearly identical to its predecessor. Not only do they repeat the hard driving pop-metal hybrid to the last detail, they even throw in another Slade cover. Like *Metal Health*, the Slade cover on *Condition Critical* ("Mama Weer All Crazee Now") is the finest moment on the record—it's the only time the riffs have a solid hook and the melody is memorable. However, the rest of the record is well-produced and sounds good, even if the quality of the songs is somewhat poor. —*Stephen Thomas Erlewine*

QR III / 1986 / Pasha ✦✦

The Randy Rhoads Years / Oct. 26, 1993 / Rhino ✦✦✦✦

A fine collection of Quiet Riot's earliest records, *The Randy Rhoads Years* captures the influential guitarist in his formative years. That alone would have made the disc essential for his fans, but it also includes some prime unreleased material, making it all the more desirable. —*Stephen Thomas Erlewine*

● **The Greatest Hits** / Feb. 20, 1996 / Epic/Pasha ✦✦✦✦

For those interested in the genre, *The Best of Quiet Riot* contains all of Quiet Riot's biggest hits, from "Cum On Feel The Noize" to a live version of "Metal Health." While some favorites such as "Winners Take All" are missing, the most enjoyable pop-metal songs produced by Quiet Riot through 1988 all made it to this compilation. —*Barry Weber*

R

Rachel's

f. 1994
Experimental Rock, Indie Rock, Post-Rock/Experimental

Although the avant-chamber trio Rachel's did not fully emerge until after the breakup of the seminal Louisville indie group Rodan, the trio's origins dated back to 1989, when guitarist and bassist Jason Noble first met violinist and Juilliard alumnus Christian Fredericksen on a Baltimore trolley. After the duo composed a 1991 Christmas tape dubbed "Rachel's Halo," they parted ways while Noble tenured in Rodan; upon reuniting in 1994, they formed Rachel's, named after Noble's Toyota Corolla and not after the group's third member, pianist Rachel Grimes. In 1995, the group debuted with *Handwriting*, a dark fusion of classical and experimental sounds influenced by film music; a year later, Rachel's returned with two separate releases, *Music for Egon Schiele* (composed by Grimes for a theatrical dance production based on the life of the famed Austrian painter) and *The Sea and the Bells* (which featured an orchestra employing over a dozen musicians). *Selenography* followed in 1999, and in the spring of 2000 the group resurfaced with *Full on Night*, a collaboration with Matmos. —*Jason Ankeny*

Handwriting / 1995 / Quarterstick ♦♦

Music for Egon Schiele / Feb. 20, 1996 / Quarterstick ♦♦♦♦
Composed for a live theater/dance production about the tragic life of Austrian artist Egon Schiele, the gentle majesty of this album is a welcome change of pace for anyone bored with popular music forms, transporting the listener's mood entirely. The trio weaves a delicate but highly moving musical fabric that wraps itself around you tightly and pulls you in, simultaneously cradling you lovingly while haunting you with its melancholy ambiance. At times, the emotionally rich compositions work as effectively as any ballet score to tell the artist's tragic story (related in the liner notes, which also include copies of some of her most famous pieces). It is to pianist Rachel Grimes' credit that her pieces convey a stirring sense of drama and vivid imagery that perfectly match her subject. Highly recommended. —*Bret Love*

The Sea and the Bells / 1996 / Quarterstick ♦♦♦♦♦
Formed out of the ashes of Rodan, this loose collective thrives on the neo-classical compositional skills of pianist Rachel Grimes, bassist/organist Jason Noble, and violinist Christian Frederickson. Augmented by a rotating cast of cellists, trumpeters, and drummers, the trio concocts an emotive symphony that, though thoroughly modern, seems timeless. The songs on *The Sea and the Bells* flow together so seamlessly, it almost seems like one brilliant hour-long epic composition. "Rhine & Courtesan" opens the album with a dynamic, wistful melody that evokes the feeling of riding on ocean waves, then crashes to a startling halt, only to re-emerge with a claustrophobic eeriness that foretells impending doom. Other songs continue the nautical theme, from the haunting "Night at Sea" to the hallucinatory "Letters Home." In an alternative scene where instrumental rockers are a dime a dozen, Rachel's stands out like diamonds on the ocean floor. —*Bret Love*

● **Selenography** / Jun. 8, 1999 / Quarterstick ♦♦♦♦♦
The Rachel's' 1999 album *Selenography* presents more of their thoughtful, expressive, nearly unclassifiable compositions. Many of the 12 pieces here grew from live performances and were nurtured in the group's home studio, blossoming into works with a cosmic and rustic theme. The harpsichords on "Honeysuckle Suite," the gentle interplay of violas and piano on "Kentucky Nocturne" and the subtly dissonant guitars and vibes of "An Evening of Long Goodbyes" proves the Rachel's' already complex and beautiful sound continues to mature. —*Heather Phares*

Radar Bros.

f. 1993
Slowcore, Indie Rock, Alternative Pop/Rock

Guitarist Jim Putnam (Medicine, Maids of Gravity), bassist Senon Williams and drummer Steve Goodfriend debuted with a self-titled EP (Fingerpaint Records) and quickly garnered themselves a following in the U.K. By 1996, they were signed to Restless and the resulting self-titled album combined sonic guitarscapes and smoky melodies, earning the band a slowcore/sadcore tag, and aligning them with peers Acetone and Low, while evoking memories of Neil Young, Brian Wilson and Pink Floyd. *Singing Hatchet* followed in 1999. —*Denise Sullivan*

● **Radar Bros.** / 1996 / Restless ♦♦♦♦
The Radar Brothers' eponymous debut album is a remarkable blend of lush, *Pet Sounds*-styled pop and indie-rock aesthetics, resulting in an otherworldly record of veiled, yet emotional sentiments and sighing, melodic pop that manages to cut much deeper than the surface. —*Stephen Thomas Erlewine*

The Singing Hatchet / Sep. 28, 1999 / Philips Media ♦♦♦♦
The Radar Bros.' second album *The Singing Hatchet* delivers more of their quietly quixotic, psychedelically rootsy songs, which roll along like tumbleweeds: shambling and seemingly fragile, yet surprisingly strong. Crackling static, solemn pianos, doleful mellotrons, and chiming guitars support the rambling, almost weightless melodies of songs like "Shifty Lies," "You've Been Hired," and "Tar the Roofs" and the clean production shows off the songs' expressive arrangements—"Shoveling Sons'" guitars sparkle like dust motes in the sunlight. Musically and lyrically, *The Singing Hatchet* often manages to be poignant, spooky, and funny all at once; Jim Putnam's mournful upper register makes vaguely disturbing lines like "All the Ghosts"'s "Eyes are painted shut and we won't come clean" even more unsettling, while "Open Ocean Sailing"'s lament "fight the ways of a slow production day" hints at emotional truths without tipping the entire hand. Somnambulistic reflections like "The Pilgrim," spaced-out spaghetti western soundtracks like "Five Miles," and sweeping epics like the aforementioned "Open Ocean Sailing" and "You're on an Island" make this release a surprisingly diverse album, while the songs' relatively concise lengths make it surprisingly coherent. A shabbily majestic, subtly accomplished work, *The Singing Hatchet* doesn't wear its heart on its sleeve, but it's in the right place. —*Heather Phares*

Radio Birdman

f. 1974, **db.** 1981
Aussie Rock, Punk, Hard Rock

Although the best-known band of the early Australian punk scene of the late '70s was the Saints, the first band to wave the punk rock flag in the land down under was Radio Birdman. Formed by Australian emigre Deniz Tek (originally from Ann Arbor, Michigan) and Aussie surfer-turned-vocalist Rob Younger in 1975, Radio Birdman's approach to rock & roll was rooted in the high-energy, apocalyptic guitar rant of the Stooges and MC5, sprinkled liberally with a little East Coast underground hard rock courtesy of Blue Öyster Cult. Their first EP, *Burn My Eye*, released in 1976, was a great record and, nearly 20 years later, still remains a seminal chunk of Aussie punk. Loud and snotty, with Younger bellowing his guts out and Tek on a search and destroy mission with his guitar, this was a great debut that set the stage for the impending deluge of Aussie punk bands waiting in the wings. After the release of their debut LP, *Radios Appear* (the title comes from a lyric in the Blue Öyster Cult song "Dominance and Submission"), in Australia a year later, Radio Birdman seemed poised to break Aussie punk worldwide. And although the American label Sire (then the home of the Ramones) was quick to sign them and distribute *Radios Appear* internationally in 1978, there was a gap of three years before they released a second album (*Living Eyes*). During that time, two things happened: dozens of other Aussie punk bands stole their thunder, and Radio Birdman split up almost immediately after *Living Eyes* was released. Sire never released the record outside of Australia, and Radio Birdman, who should have been the biggest band in Aussie punk, were now highly-regarded punk forefathers. After the band split in 1981, various members were busy forming other bands; space limitations prevent an exhaustive look at their post-Birdman careers. Tek formed the New Race with Younger, ex-Stooges guitarist Ron Asheton and ex-MC5 drummer Dennis Thompson, released a handful of solo singles and EPs, and became a surgeon (!); Younger started his own band, the New Christs, and produced records by the second generation of Aussie punk bands influenced by Radio Birdman, most notably the Celibate Rifles; other Radio Birdman alumni ended up in assorted Aussie bands such as the Lime Spiders, Hoodoo Gurus and Screaming Tribesmen. Now the grand old man of Aussie punk, Tek has formed an unnamed, part-time project with Celibate Rifles guitarist Kent Steedman that rocks with the same reckless abandon Radio Birdman did when they were changing the course of Australian rock forever. —*John Dougan*

Burn My Eye [EP] / 1976 / Trafalgar ♦♦♦
This is where Aussie punk got the kick in the pants it needed to become a worldwide phenomenon. Tough to locate the original, but it has been reissued more than once as an affordable import. The title track alone (later recorded by The Celibate Rifles) is worth the price of the record. —*John Dougan*

● **Radios Appear** / 1978 / Sire ♦♦♦♦♦
Starting off with a rip-snortin' cover of The Stooges' "T.V. Eye," this is primal (and prime) Birdman, with Tek and Younger firmly ensconced in the eye of this guitar-fueled hurricane. Tek's originals are pretty strong, especially the grimy tale of urban desolation "Murder City Nights" and the noisy freakout "Descent Into the Maelstrom." One of Australia's great rock & roll bands in all of their glory. —*John Dougan*

Living Eyes / 1981 / WEA ♦♦♦♦
While *Radios Appear* (overseas version) remains the full-fledged classic by Radio Birdman, the reissue of *Living Eyes* shows that it was damn near as good as the first one,

and maybe a bit more original. Fully loaded with classic songs that inspired several generations of Australian rockers, *Living Eyes* is an album that has benefited greatly from modern technology as well as a little luck. Recorded at the legendary Rockfield Studios in Wales when the band went to Europe to tour with the Flamin' Groovies (their first shows outside Australia), the original master tapes disappeared before the album was released. The band then broke up and *Living Eyes* ended up being mastered from a cassette. While no one really complained about the sound quality at the time, it wasn't all it could've been. Flash forward to the '90s and the master tapes are found on a dusty shelf at Rockfield. The band bakes them up and remixes, remasters, and re-sequences the album. It is now a total monster, screaming out of your speakers with intent to do damage. From the time Chris Masuak's stun guitar comes in at the beginning of "Hanging On," it is apparent that this is not your big brother's *Living Eyes*. The sound is deeper by degrees. The songs remain superb. Singer Rob Younger is as ferocious as ever, a true original to the hardcore, and Deniz Tek solidifies his place as father of real Australian rock & roll. This CD reissue makes clear that had Radio Birdman stuck it out and released this album they would have been a contender. *—Geoffrey Ginsberg*

Under the Ashes / 1988 / WEA ✦✦✦
I've seen this box set exactly once (in Minneapolis to be exact), didn't pick it up and have regretted it almost daily ever since. If you've caught the fever of this band and are inclined to have their complete recorded works—buy it! Also available as a multi-CD box. Well worth the investment. *—John Dougan*

● **The Essential Radio Birdman: 1974-1978** / Jul. 17, 2001 / Sub Pop ✦✦✦✦✦
With the release of *The Essential Radio Birdman: 1974-1978*, Sub Pop ends the 20-year absence of any product from the Australian punk icons in the U.S. Included in its entirety is the group's impossible to find debut LP *Radios Appear* (here sounding as if mastered directly from vinyl), as well as choice tracks from the follow-up *Living Eyes* and the live *More Fun* and debut *Burn Me Eye* EPs. Simply put, this disc is a godsend to serious punk and indie rock fans. Every gritty, sputtering riff sounds positively alive. At its best, the group had a communal political ethos that bridged the gap between the MC5 and the emergence of hardcore in the 1980s. At its most basic, Radio Birdman was as good as garage rock could get before taking itself too seriously. Mellower tracks like "Man With Golden Helmet" and "Love Kills" exhibit a Doors influence in addition to guitarist/songwriter Deniz Tek's unapologetic fascination with the MC5 and Stooges music of his Detroit youth. For all but the most insane collector, this is all the Radio Birdman you will ever need. Even if the title is slightly misleading (no music here was recorded before 1976), one no longer need shell out big bucks for vintage Radio Birdman wax anymore. *—John Duffy*

Radiohead

f. 1989, Oxford, England
Britpop, Alternative Pop/Rock, Experimental Rock
Radiohead was one of the few alternative bands of the early '90s to draw heavily from the grandiose arena-rock that characterized U2's early albums. But the band internalized that epic sweep, turning it inside out to tell tortured, twisted tales of angst and alienation. Vocalist Thom Yorke's pained lyrics were brought to life by the group's three-guitar attack, which relied on texture—borrowing as much from My Bloody Valentine and Pink Floyd as R.E.M. and the Pixies—instead of virtuosity. It took Radiohead a while to formulate their signature sound. Their 1993 debut, *Pablo Honey*, only suggested their potential, and one of its songs, "Creep," became an unexpected international hit, its angst-ridden lyrics making it an alternative rock anthem. Many observers pigeonholed Radiohead as a one-hit wonder, but the group's second album, *The Bends*, was released to terrific reviews in the band's native Britain in early 1995, helping build a more stable fan base. Having demonstrated unexpected staying power, as well as increasing ambition, Radiohead next released *OK Computer*, a progressive, electronic-tinged masterpiece that became one of the most acclaimed albums of the '90s. *—Stephen Thomas Erlewine*

Pablo Honey / Apr. 20, 1993 / Capitol ✦✦✦
Radiohead's debut album *Pablo Honey* is a promising collection that blends U2's anthemic rock with long, atmospheric instrumental passages and an enthralling triple-guitar attack that is alternately gentle and bracingly noisy. The group has difficulty writing a set of songs that are as compelling as their sound, but when they do hit the mark—such as on "Anyone Can Play Guitar," "Blow Out," and the self-loathing breakthrough single "Creep"—the band achieves a rare power that is both visceral and intelligent. *—Stephen Thomas Erlewine*

The Bends / Apr. 4, 1995 / Capitol ✦✦✦✦✦
Pablo Honey in no way was adequate preparation for its epic, sprawling follow-up, *The Bends*. Building from the sweeping, three-guitar attack that punctuated the best moments of *Pablo Honey*, Radiohead create a grand and forceful sound that nevertheless resonates with anguish and despair—it's cerebral anthemic rock. Occasionally, the album displays its influences, whether it's U2, Pink Floyd, R.E.M. or the Pixies, but Radiohead turn clichés inside out, making each song sound bracingly fresh. Thom Yorke's tortured lyrics give the album a melancholy undercurrent, as does the surging, textured music. But what makes *The Bends* so remarkable is that it marries such ambitious, and often challenging, instrumental soundscapes to songs that are at their cores hauntingly melodic and accessible. It makes the record compelling upon first listen, but it reveals new details with each listen, and soon it becomes apparent that with *The Bends*, Radiohead have reinvented anthemic rock. *—Stephen Thomas Erlewine*

★ **OK Computer** / Jul. 1, 1997 / Capitol ✦✦✦✦✦
Using the textured soundscapes of *The Bends* as a launching pad, Radiohead delivered another startlingly accomplished set of modern guitar rock with *OK Computer*. The anthemic guitar heroics present on *Pablo Honey* and even *The Bends* are nowhere to be heard here. Radiohead have stripped away many of the obvious elements of guitar rock, creating music that is subtle and textured, yet still has the feeling of rock & roll. Even at its most adventurous—such as the complex, multi-segmented "Paranoid Android"—the band is tight, melodic, and muscular, and Thom Yorke's voice effortlessly shifts from a sweet falsetto to vicious snarls. It's a thoroughly astonishing demonstration of musical virtuosity, and becomes even more impressive with repeated listens, which reveal subtleties like electronica rhythms, eerie keyboards, odd time signatures, and complex syncopations. Yet all of this would simply be showmanship if the songs weren't strong in themselves, and *OK Computer* is filled with moody masterpieces, from the shimmering "Subterranean Homesick Alien" and the sighing "Karma Police" to the gothic crawl of "Exit Music (For a Film)." *OK Computer* is the album that establishes Radiohead as one of the most inventive and rewarding guitar-rock bands of the '90s. *—Stephen Thomas Erlewine*

Kid A / Oct. 3, 2000 / Capitol ✦✦✦✦
Instead of simply adding club beats or sonic collage techniques, Radiohead strives to incorporate the unsettling "intelligent techno" sound of Autechre and Aphex Twin, characterized by its skittering beats and stylishly dark sonic surfaces, for *Kid A*. To their immense credit, Radiohead don't sound like carpetbaggers, because they share the same post-post-modern vantage point as their inspirations. As a result, *Kid A* is easily the most successful electronica album from a rock band—it doesn't even sound like a rock band, even if it does sound like Radiohead. So, *Kid A* is an unqualified success? Well, not quite. Despite its admirable ambition, *Kid A* is never as visionary or stunning as *OK Computer*, nor does it really repay the time it demands. *OK Computer* required many plays before revealing the intricacies of its densely layered mix; here, multiple plays are necessary to discern the music's form, to get a handle on quiet, drifting, minimally arranged songs with no hooks. Of course, the natural reaction of any serious record geek is that if the music demands so much work, it must be worth it—and at times, that supposition is true. But *Kid A*'s challenge doesn't always live up to its end of the bargain. It's self-consciously alienating and difficult, and while that can be intriguing, it seems deeper than it actually is. Repeated plays dissipate the mystique and reveal a number of rather drab songs (primarily during the second half), where there isn't enough under the surface to make Radiohead's relentless experimentation satisfying. But mixed results are still results, and about half of the songs positively shimmer with genius. *—Stephen Thomas Erlewine*

Amnesiac / Jun. 5, 2001 / Capitol ✦✦✦
Faced with a deliberately difficult deviation into "experimentation," Radiohead and its record label promoted *Kid A* as just that—a brave experiment, and that the next album, which was just around the corner, really, would be the "real" record, the one to satiate fans looking for the next *OK Computer*, or at least guitars. At the time, people bought the myth. That, however, ignores a salient point—*Amnesiac*, as the album came to be known, consists of recordings made *during* the *Kid A* sessions, so it essentially sounds the same. Since Radiohead designed *Kid A* as a self-consciously epochal, genre-shattering record, the songs that didn't make the cut were a little simpler, so it shouldn't be a surprise that *Amnesiac* plays like a streamlined version of *Kid A*, complete with blatant electronica moves and production that sacrifices songs for atmosphere. This, inevitably, will disappoint the legions awaiting another guitar-based record. Where *Kid A* had shock on its side, along with an admirably dogged desire to not be conventional, *Amnesiac* often plays as a hodgepodge. True, it's a hodgepodge with amazing moments, but these are not moments that are markedly different than *Kid A*, which itself lost momentum as it sputtered to a close. And this is the main problem—these two records clearly derive from the same source and have the same flaws, which clearly would have been corrected if they had been consolidated into one record. Instead of revealing why the two records were separated, *Amnesiac* makes the separation seem arbitrary—there's no shift in tone, no shift in approach, and the division only makes the two records seem unfocused, even if the best of both records is quite stunning, proof positive that Radiohead are one of the best bands of their time. *—Stephen Thomas Erlewine*

Raekwon (Corey Woods)

b. Jan. 12, 1968
Vocals / Hardcore Rap, East Coast Rap
A member of the Wu-Tang Clan, rapper Raekwon was born Corey Woods; a.k.a. the Chef, he first surfaced on the group's 1993 debut *Enter the Wu-Tang: 36 Chambers*, issuing his first solo single "Heaven and Hell" on the soundtrack to *Fresh* a short time later. On Raekwon's 1995 solo LP *Only Built 4 Cuban Linx* he recast the Wu-Tang crew as an Italian mafioso family dubbed the Wu-Gambinos, rechristening himself "Lou Diamonds" in the process. *Immobilarity* followed in 1999. *—Jason Ankeny*

★ **Only Built 4 Cuban Linx** / 1995 / Loud ✦✦✦✦✦
Raekwon's solo debut remains one of the best, if not the zenith, of the numerous Wu-Tang-affiliated albums of the 1990s, even if it attained only modest commercial success upon its release. *Only Built 4 Cuban Linx* attains such hallowed critical status partially because of the amazing synergy between Ghostface Killah and Raekwon. They team up on 12 of the 18 tracks to create some of the most cinematically engaging lyrics ever collected on a rap album, trading off lucid verses on one track after the next, only occasionally joined by their peers, most notably Method Man and Nas. Yet for the most part, *Only Built 4 Cuban Linx* is lyrically a two-man affair, which prevents it from getting diluted and retains a vital sense of consistency—a problem many 1990s rap albums suffer from. This suturing consistency is only furthered by the eerie production of RZA, who turns in what may be his most impressive performance of the decade. Riddled with violent gangsta film samples, haunting keyboards, an overall foreboding aura, and, of course, phenomenal beats, RZA's production may deserve the acclaim for this album

more so than Raekwon and Ghostface Killah's dark gangsta tales, as the Wu-Tang mastermind weaves one long cinematic motif characterized by subtle yet emotive twists. One cannot attribute the genius of this album to Raekwon, Ghostface Killah, or RZA alone, but rather to the synergy resulting from their respective contributions. *—Jason Birchmeier*

Immobilarity / Nov. 16, 1999 / Epic ♦♦♦
It's a rare Wu-Tang solo album that doesn't bear the stamp of the collective's production mastermind, RZA, to some extent, and Raekwon's second full-length is no different. Except for the fact that RZA doesn't actually *appear* on *Immobilarity,* the paranoid synth-strings and soundtrack feel he pioneered on Wu-Tang's *Enter the Wu-Tang: 36 Chambers* and *Forever* are all over this album. The producers, including Raekwon's American Cream Team, Infinite Arkatechz, and Six July Productions, give *Immobilarity* the same sounds RZA gave to Raekwon's first album, *Only Built 4 Cuban Linx.* Though few rappers are more entitled to the sound than Raekwon, most of these songs just don't contribute to the lyrical concerns or delivery (a notable exception is "Sneakers," the only track produced by Pete Rock). And since the album's success depends wholly on Raekwon himself, it's almost impossible for him to trump the excellence of his first album. *—Keith Farley*

Gerry Rafferty

b. Apr. 16, 1947, Paisley, Scotland
Vocals, Guitar / Pop/Rock, Soft Rock, Singer/Songwriter
Gerry Rafferty was a popular music giant at the end of the 1970s, thanks to the song "Baker Street." His career long predated that fixture of Top 40 radio, however—indeed, by the time he cut "Baker Street," Rafferty had already been a member of two successful groups, the Humblebums and Stealers Wheel. After three years of legal battles sorting out problems between Rafferty and his management, Rafferty cut *City to City* in 1978, a melodic yet strangely enigmatic album that topped the charts in America, put there by the success of the song "Baker Street." The song itself was a masterpiece of pop production, Rafferty's Paul McCartney-like vocals carrying a haunting central melody with a mysterious and yearning lyric—it was sophisticated '70s pop/rock at its best and it dominated the airwaves for months in 1978, narrowly missing the number one spot in England but selling millions of copies and taking up hundreds of cumulative hours of radio time. His next record, *Night Owl* (1979), also charted well and got good reviews, but the momentum that had driven *City to City* to top-selling status wasn't there, and *Snakes and Ladders* (1980), his next record, didn't sell nearly as well. Rafferty is still remembered, primarily for "Baker Street" and *City to City,* which have been released as gold-plated audiophile CDs, and every so often, when some Stealers Wheel track gets picked up for some soundtrack (as "Stuck in the Middle With You" was for Quentin Tarantino's *Reservoir Dogs*) or commercial. *—Bruce Eder*

Clowns to the Left, Jokers to the Right: 1970-1982 / Mar. 25, 1997 / Raven ♦♦♦♦
Short of a double-CD set, this is the most comprehensive look at Gerry Rafferty's career, covering Rafferty's evolution from folky to folk-rocker to McCartney-esque pop-rocker over a period of 12 years. Highlights include "Please Sing a Song for Us" and "Blood & Glory" by the Humblebums, "Can I Have My Money Back" from Rafferty's first solo LP, and the inevitable "Stuck in the Middle With You" and "Baker Street" from Stealers Wheel and Rafferty's post-1978 solo career. At 78 minutes running time, this 21-track compilation is ample without being overloaded, and it offers better sound than some of the American CD editions of the same music. What's more, the essay by John Tobler is probably the best account to date of Rafferty's recording career. Fans of the Humblebums or Stealers Wheel will likely prefer the various collections specifically devoted to their work, with fuller accounts of each group's output, but this disc gives a good overview of a dozen very productive years in Rafferty's career, and the music—especially the 1978-1982 material—is all melodic and memorable. *—Bruce Eder*

Rage Against the Machine

f. 1991
Rap-Metal, Alternative Metal, Alternative Pop/Rock, Heavy Metal
Rage Against the Machine earned acclaim from disenfranchised fans (and not insignificant derision from critics) for their bombastic, fiercely polemical music, which brewed sloganeering leftist rants against corporate America, cultural imperialism and government oppression into a Molotov cocktail of punk, hip hop and thrash. Rage debuted in 1992 with a self-released, self-titled 12-song cassette featuring the song "Bullet in the Head," which became a hit when re-issued as a single later in the year. The tape won the band a deal with Epic, and their leap to the majors did not go unnoticed by detractors, who questioned the revolutionary integrity of Rage Against the Machine's decision to align itself with the label's parent company, media behemoth Sony. Undeterred, the quartet emerged in late 1992 with another eponymous release, which scored the hits "Killing in the Name" and "Bombtrack." After touring with Lollapalooza and declaring their support of groups like FAIR (Fairness and Accuracy in Reporting), Rock for Choice and Refuse & Resist, Rage spent a reportedly tumultous four years working on their follow-up; despite rumors of a break-up, they returned in 1996 with *Evil Empire,* which entered the U.S. album charts at Number One and scored a hit single with "Bulls on Parade." *—Jason Ankeny*

● **Rage Against the Machine** / Nov. 3, 1992 / Epic ♦♦♦♦♦
The first album to successfully merge the amazingly disparate sounds of rap and heavy metal, Rage Against the Machine's self-titled debut was groundbreaking enough when it was released, and many would argue that its importance and influence remains unchallenged and unsurpassed to this day. The living embodiment of this culture clash, guitar wizard Tom Morello fuses his roots in '80s metal-style shredding with an unprecedented array of six-string acrobatics and rhythmic special effects, most of which no one has even tried to imitate. And from vocalist Zack de la Rocha, the group receives the meaningful rhymes and emotionally charged delivery that white-boy metal could never hope to achieve. Still, despite the unique elements upon which they are built, songs like "Bombtrack," "Take the Power Back," and "Know Your Enemy" are immediately memorable, surprisingly straightforward slabs of hard rock. And one need not look further than the main riff of the venomous "Wake Up"—lifted straight out of Zeppelin's "Kashmir"—for conclusive proof of Morello's influences. Even more impressive is the group's talent for injecting slowly mounting tension into such highlights as "Settle for Nothing" and "Bullet in the Head," both of which finally explode with awesome power and rage. In contrast, the band manages to convey their message with even more urgency through stubborn repetition, as seen on "Freedom" and their signature track, "Killing in the Name." With its relentlessly rebellious mantra of "Fuck you, I won't do what you tell me," the song is a rallying cry of frightening proportions and the unequivocal climax of their vision. A stunning debut that remains absolutely essential. *—Ed Rivadavia*

Evil Empire / Apr. 1996 / Epic ♦♦♦♦
Rage Against the Machine spent four years making their second album, *Evil Empire.* As the title suggests, their rage and contempt for the "fascist" capitalist system in America hasn't declined in the nearly half-decade they were away. Their musical approach didn't change, either. Lead vocalist Zach De La Rocha is caught halfway between the militant raps of Chuck D and the fanatical ravings of a street preacher, shouting out his simplistic, libertarian slogans over the sonically dense assault of the band. Since the band did not perform together much after 1993, there isn't a collective advance in their musicianship. Nevertheless, guitarist Tom Morello demonstrates an impressive palette of sound, creating new textures in heavy metal, which is quite difficult. Even with Morello's studied virtuosity, the band sounds leaden, lacking the dexterity to fully execute their metal/hip-hop fusion—they don't get into a groove, they simply pound. But that happens to fit the hysterical ravings of De La Rocha. Though his dedication to decidedly left-wing politics is admirable, his arhythmic phrasing and grating shouting cancel out any message he is trying to make. And that means *Evil Empire* succeeds only on the level of a sonic assault. *—Stephen Thomas Erlewine*

The Battle of Los Angeles / Nov. 2, 1999 / Epic ♦♦♦♦
Rage Against the Machine isn't really the only metal band that matters, but their aggressive social and political activism is refreshing, especially in an age of blind (or usually self-directed) rage due to groups like Limp Bizkit, Bush, or Nine Inch Nails. Recorded in less than a month, *The Battle of Los Angeles* is the most focused album of the band's career, exploding from the gate and rarely letting go the whole way through. Like a few other famous revolution-in-the-head bands (most notably Minor Threat), Rage Against the Machine has always been blessed by the fact that the band is spewing just as much vitriol as its frontman. Any potential problems created here by Zack de la Rocha's one-note delivery and extremist polemics are smoothed over by songs and grooves that make it sound like the revolution really *is* here, from the single "Guerrilla Radio" to album highlights like "Mic Check," "Calm Like a Bomb," and "Born of a Broken Man." As on the previous two Rage Against the Machine albums, Tom Morello's roster of guitar effects and vicious riffs are nigh overpowering, and are as contagious as the band has ever been since their debut. De la Rocha is best when he has specific targets (like the government or the case against Mumia Abu Jamal), but when he attempts to cover more general societal problems, he falters. If anything less than one of the most talented and fiery bands in the music world were backing him, *The Battle of Los Angeles* wouldn't be nearly as high-rated as it is. *—John Bush*

Renegades / Dec. 5, 2000 / Epic ♦♦♦♦
Rush released after the late-2000 split between Zack de la Rocha and the rest of Rage Against the Machine, the covers album *Renegades* salutes the band's musical and philosophical roots, ranging from the old-school Bronx to the hard-rockin' Motor City to protest-central Greenwich Village to gangsta-ridden L.A. As could be expected, the set works best when the group focuses on material from its most recent forebears: rappers and hardcore bands. Indeed, *Renegades* begins with a pair of powerful hip-hop covers—Eric B & Rakim's "Microphone Fiend" and Volume 10's "Pistol Grip Pump"—that spotlight Rage's immense strengths: Tom Morello's clean, heavy riffing and vocalist de la Rocha's finely tuned spray of vitriol, just this side of self-righteous. Another hip-hop blast (and the one closest to home), Cypress Hill's "How I Could Just Kill a Man," is even more devastating, an easy pick for the highlight of the album. Listeners familiar with the originals, however, may have trouble with Rage's covers of EPMD's "I'm Housin'," the Stones' "Street Fighting Man," and Dylan's "Maggie's Farm," a trio of original versions whose anger and emotion were conveyed more in the lyrics than the performances. Still, drummer Brad Wilk sets an appropriately frenetic hardcore tempo for the excellent version of Minor Threat's "In My Eyes," and de la Rocha stretches out well on the MC5's "Kick Out the Jams." With just a bare few excepions, *Renegades* works well, in part because Rage Against the Machine is both smart enough to change very little and talented enough to make the songs its own. *—John Bush*

Rain Parade

f. 1981, Los Angeles, CA, **db.** 1987
College Rock, Neo-Psychedelia, Jangle Pop, Paisley Underground, Power Pop, Alternative Pop/Rock
Among the L.A. groups dubbed Paisley Underground (Dream Syndicate, the Bangles, Three O'Clock), Rain Parade were the closest to being the real deal for their use of psychedelic flourishes thoroughout their first album. Formed in Los Angeles in the early '80s,

the group consisted of David Roback (vocals, guitar), Steven Roback (vocals, bass), Matt Piucci (vocals, guitar), Will Glenn (keyboards) and Eddie Kalwa (drums). Their first single, "What She's Done to Your Mind," was a certifiable hit on college radio, and the band quickly followed with a full-length LP for Enigma in 1983, *Emergency Third Rail Power Trip.* For 1984's *Explosions in the Glass Palace* (Restless), the band lost David Roback to Opal, but John Thoman took over and Mark Marcum filled in for the departed Eddie Kalwa. The re-formed band recorded the live album *Beyond the Sunset* (1985, Restless) and *Crashing Dream* (Island, 1986) before disbanding. David Roback went on to license Opal into Mazzy Star, Steven Roback and Thoman worked as Viva Saturn, and Piucci recorded an album with Crazy Horse—yes, that Crazy Horse. —*Denise Sullivan*

● **Emergency 3rd Rail Power Trip** / 1983 / Restless ✦✦✦✦✦
Featuring the dreamy "What She's Done to Your Mind" and the Byrdsy "This Can't Be Today" (with the Dream Syndicate's Kendra Smith), Rain Parade fashioned traditional, gentle psychedelic pop. Clearly way ahead of their time, it would take years before sleepy music (a la founding Rain Parade member's David Roback's Mazzy Star) would catch on, this record sounds no more made in the '80s than in the '60s or '90s. —*Denise Sullivan*

Explosions in the Glass Palace / 1984 / Enigma ✦✦✦✦
Listeners who were enraptured by this band's first effort should enjoy this follow-up, even though principal member David Roback had already quit. Don't know if this is considered an LP or EP, as it clocks in at a mere 20 minutes, but it's still superior to other recycled psychedelia from L.A.'s Paisley Underground. Layered guitars, special effects, droning vocals, catchy hooks—they're all here. The Rain Parade never broke any barriers during their brief existence, but they really captured the spirit of '60s psychedelic rock better than most. —*Peter Kurtz*

Beyond the Sunset / 1985 / Restless ✦✦✦

Crashing Dream / 1986 / Island ✦✦✦

Rainbow

f. 1974, **db.** 1984
Heavy Metal, Hard Rock
The brainchild of former Deep Purple guitarist Ritchie Blackmore, Rainbow quickly developed into one of the '70s most successful heavy metal bands behind charismatic frontman Ronnie James Dio. Together, the duo would produce a string of acclaimed albums which are still considered classics of the genre. Capturing Blackmore and Dio at the peak of their creative powers, *Rising* (1976) chronicled both the guitarist's neo-classical metal compositions at their most ambitious, and the singer's growing fixation with fantasy lyrical themes. By the time they returned with the equally acclaimed *Long Live Rock & Roll* album in 1978, Rainbow had established themselves as one of Europe's best-selling groups and top concert draws. But the volatile relationship between Blackmore and Dio had already begun to deteriorate, as the American-born singer became increasingly frustrated of standing in the guitarist's shadow. To make matters worse, Blackmore had been so impressed with "Long Live Rock & Roll"'s success as a single, that he began to consider altering the band's sound in order to pursue a more mainstream hard rock approach. A chance meeting with Tony Iommi of Black Sabbath helped the singer make up his mind, and Dio officially quit Rainbow in early 1979 to join Black Sabbath. The group would change their musical approach numerous times following the singer's departure, eventually confusing and alienating much of their audience. Releasing eight albums during its decade-long run, the band finally came to an end when Blackmore departed to rejoin his old Deep Purple comrades in a full-fledged reunion in 1984. And while the impact of Rainbow's influence has faded with the intervening decades, their work was a crucial chapter in the development of heavy metal and hard rock. —*Ed Rivadavia*

● **The Very Best of Rainbow** / Jul. 15, 1997 / Polydor/Chronicles ✦✦✦✦
The Very Best of Rainbow is a terrific single-disc collection that traces the band's evolution from a heavy metal outfit to hard rockers with a flair for power ballads like "Since You've Been Gone." It's nearly a definitive collection, featuring all of the group's very best songs, and a good sampling of Ritchie Blackmore's still-impressive guitar work. —*Stephen Thomas Erlewine*

20th Century Masters—The Millennium Collection: The Best of Rainbow / Oct. 3, 2000 / Polydor ✦✦✦✦
The broad roster of artists under the Universal Music umbrella—thanks to record company merger mania—has enabled a slew of mid-line-priced *20th Century Masters—The Millennium Collection* titles. In some cases, such as Steve Winwood's, it's a unique volume. For others, such as Rainbow, it's a sensible purchase for budget-minded casual fans, but more complete one-CD retrospectives exist. Deep Purple hasn't truly received the widespread critical respect it deserves as a pioneering heavy metal band, so it's no surprise that guitarist Ritchie Blackmore's Rainbow isn't fully appreciated either. No consecutive studio albums bore the same lineup, so continuity can't be considered one of Rainbow's virtues. But from the progressive heavy metal, mid-'70s Ronnie James Dio era to the calculated, radio-friendly, early-'80s Joe Lynn Turner era, the band created many excellent songs and foreshadowed the mid-'80s pop/metal boom. Rainbow's three best-known songs—"Since You Been Gone" (with Graham Bonnet's throat-bursting vocals), "Stone Cold," and "Street of Dreams"—are featured on *20th Century Masters—The Millennium Collection.* All three were modest hit singles, but only "Stone Cold" made the Top 40. "Man on the Silver Mountain" should also be recognizable to fans of "classic rock" radio. The beautifully hypnotic "Catch the Rainbow" and bombastic, strings-enriched epic "Stargazer" are other highlights. The menacing "Kill the King," supple "Rainbow Eyes," 13-minute live version of Deep Purple's blues showcase "Mistreated," and catchy "I Surrender" are treats too. ("Since You Been Gone" and "I Surrender" were both penned by Argent veteran Russ Ballard.) Although 1997's stunning *The Very Best of Rainbow* is the

definitive compilation, the generous 11-song, 66-minute *20th Century Masters—The Millennium Collection* certainly has its own virtues. —*Bret Adams*

Raincoats

f. 1978, London, England, **db.** 1984
Post-Punk
The Raincoats were one of the most experimental bands that immediately followed the initial burst of punk rock in the late '70s. With their minimalistic approach to guitar-driven folk-rock, the band developed a distinctive, jagged sound, punctuated by a shrill violin. The Raincoats were also one of the first all-female post-punk bands, which wasn't common in the late '70s and early '80s. When they were recording, the band gained a small cult following in their native England and an even smaller audience in America; they broke up in 1984. Nearly ten years later, the band became a hip name in alternative rock, thanks to Kurt Cobain's mention of the group in the liner notes to a Nirvana album. Geffen picked up the rights to the Raincoats' catalog and reissued their albums in late 1993 and 1994. The band reunited and toured with Nirvana in the U.K. before heading out on their own tour of the U.S. in 1994. Two years later, the Raincoats released *Looking in the Shadows*, which was produced by Sonic Youth's Steve Shelley. —*Stephen Thomas Erlewine*

● **The Raincoats** / 1980 / DGC ✦✦✦✦✦
Picking the "best" Raincoats is more an intellectual exercise than it is a work of thoughtful criticism. So, to make it easy for the benighted, all three studio releases are absolutely essential. Their live cassette is wonderful, but I wouldn't start there. Better yet, start with their debut, a soaring, daring, avant-garde-influenced folk-punk record. Don't let the words "avant-garde" scare you off; the Raincoats are not harsh or unapproachable. In fact, this music, even at its most dissonant, is stunning and captivating. There's a great cover of the Kinks' "Lola" that's so skewed and obtuse, I'm sure Ray Davies never dreamed it could sound this way. Reissued by Geffen on CD with extra tracks in 1995. —*John Dougan*

Odyshape / 1981 / DGC ✦✦✦✦✦
It was the late Kurt Cobain (with some help from labelmates Sonic Youth) that initiated Geffen's reissue of the Raincoats' catalog. And listening to *Odyshape*, it's easy to see why Cobain loved them so. There's an emotional directness about these songs that hooks you from the start. Mostly you hear about emotions and situations, sometimes indirectly, almost as if you are eavesdropping on a conversation. Then it hits you: it's almost like you're talking to old friends. That's the way the Raincoats' music worked: it's deceptively simple, but extremely complicated. Also, as on this record, it makes demands of the listener. But songs like "Red Shoes" and "Dancing in My Head" say this far more eloquently. Reissued by Geffen with extra tracks in 1995. —*John Dougan*

Kitchen Tapes / 1983 / ROIR ✦✦✦✦
Rough, loose-limbed, warm, exciting and everything you'd expect from the Raincoats onstage. Bolstered by the heavy percussion of Richard Dudanski and Derek Godard, this recording pulsates, while the band dances around the beat tossing in shards of guitar, vocals and violin. Excellent liner essay by Greil Marcus. —*John Dougan*

Moving / 1984 / DGC ✦✦✦✦
What a wonderful cacophony of sounds! The Raincoats' last record (until their reunion EP of 1996) is a triumph of excitement and intensity equaling that of their previous studio work. Some of these songs are from the live tape and are in sharper (and I'd say better) form here. Yet another important record by one of the most important bands of the post-punk era. Reissued by Geffen with extra tracks in 1995. —*John Dougan*

Looking in the Shadows / May 14, 1996 / DGC ✦✦

Rainer Maria

f. 1995
Emo, Indie Rock, Alternative Pop/Rock
Madison, WI emo trio Rainer Maria emerged in 1995 from the ashes of another poetically-inclined local combo, Ezra Pound, reuniting singer/guitarist Kyle Fischer and drummer William Kuehn; enlisting singer/bassist Caithlin De Marrais, within six weeks the group recorded their first demo cassette, quickly selling out all 350 copies. Following a handful of compilation appearances, Rainer Maria resurfaced in 1996 with a self-titled EP on Polyvinyl; the single "New York: 1955" appeared in early 1997, heralding a shift towards the more subtle melodicism of the full-length *Past Worn Searching.* Absent throughout 1998, a year later Rainer Maria returned with the full-length *Look Now Look Again* and the EP *Atlantic. A Better Version Of Me* arrived in early 2001. —*Jason Ankeny*

Past Worn Searching / Dec. 2, 1997 / Polyvinyl ✦✦

● **Look Now Look Again** / Apr. 20, 1999 / Polyvinyl ✦✦✦✦
Rainer Maria's *Look Now Look Again* could quite possibly be the last great album from the now tired emo rock scene. Using the loud-soft dynamics of emo and the catchy playfulness of indie pop proves to be a delicious combination, and Rainer Maria pull it off with grace and intelligence. Sometimes sentimental, but never too sappy, *Look Now Look Again* showcases the band's strongest attributes: boy-girl vocal dueling, stripped down production to reveal the core emotion of a song, and the melodic and furious attack of a band in its prime. Guitar, bass, and drums tastefully play cat and mouse, weaving in and out of each other, laying a solid foundation for Caithlin De Marrais' verbal gymnastics are a pleasure to listen to, lyrics like "Like foreign post/I leave twice a day, but take a week to get there" or "I'm certain if I drive into those trees/It would make less of a mess/Than you've made of me" are examples of her subtle wit. Although they

probably will not be the messiahs of a dying genre, Rainer Maria will be a band whose creative future is beyond promising; *Look Now Look Again* is their proof. *—Dale Nicholls*

A Better Version of Me / Jan. 23, 2001 / Polyvinyl ♦♦♦
Emo-core darlings Rainer Maria stay close to heartache and dogmatic independence on their third full-length, *A Better Version of Me*. Sincerely endearing thanks to the band's passion for poetry and romanticism, classic visceral lyrics are clearly depicted, harmonic story lines picking things up where their critically received sophomore effort *Look Now Look Again* left off five years prior.

Caithlin De Marrais' graceful, yet abrasive vocals craft the dynamic of the band: well-directed musicianship without the frills of overproduced punk-inspired anthems. The musical relationship between Caithlin De Marrais, guitarist Kyle Fischer, and drummer William Kuehn is as enigmatic as Lou Barlow's satirical heartbreak, but also emotionally stripped like Sarah Dougher's feminine toughness. Songs such as "Spit and Fire" and "The Seven Sisters" are De Marrais' swan songs—pure honesty of self-denial and fear. Such messages are typically found in most pop songs, but a theme never far from any individual in search of something different, something creative, and something real. And like their indie rock cohorts (Bettie Serveert, the Spinanes), Rainer Maria seeks catharsis in an enchanting way and *A Better Version of Me* supports humanity's internal tussles with taking responsibility. *—MacKenzie Wilson*

Bonnie Raitt

b. Nov. 8, 1949, Burbank, CA
Slide Guitar, Vocals, Guitar / Slide Guitar Blues, Album Rock, Pop/Rock, Adult Contemporary, Singer/Songwriter, Blues-Rock
Long a critic's darling, singer/guitarist Bonnie Raitt did not begin to win the comparable commercial success due her until the release of the aptly titled 1989 blockbuster *Nick of Time*; her tenth album, it rocketed her into the mainstream consciousness nearly two decades after she first committed her unique blend of blues, rock and R&B to vinyl. Debuting in 1971 with an eponymously titled effort, Raitt immediately emerged as a critical favorite. Throughout the middle of the decade she released an LP annually, and scored her first significant pop airplay with a hit cover of the Del Shannon classic "Runaway." She remained a committed activist, playing hundreds of benefit concerts and working tirelessly on behalf of the Rhythm and Blues Foundation. By the early '80s, however, her own career was in trouble—1982's *Green Light*, while greeted with the usual good reviews, again failed to break her to a wide audience and led to Warners dropping her. Many had written Raitt off when she recorded *Nick of Time* though; seemingly out of the blue, the LP won a handful of Grammys (including Album of the Year) and overnight she was a superstar. The follow-up, 1991's *Luck of the Draw*, was also a smash. *—Jason Ankeny*

Bonnie Raitt / 1971 / Warner Brothers ♦♦♦
The astounding thing about Bonnie Raitt's blues album isn't that it's the work of a preternaturally gifted blues woman, it's that Raitt doesn't choose to stick to the blues. She's decided to blend her love of classic folk blues with folk music, including new folk-rock tunes, along with a slight R&B, New Orleans, and jazz bent and a mellow Californian vibe. Surely, *Bonnie Raitt* is a record of its times, as much as Jackson Browne's first album is, but with this, she not only sketches out the blueprint for her future recordings, but for the roots music that would later be labeled as Americana. The reason that *Bonnie Raitt* works is that she is such a warm, subtle singer. She never oversells these songs, she lays back and sings them with heart and wonderfully textured reading. Her singing is complemented by her band, who is equally as warm, relaxed, and engaging. This is music that goes down so easy, it's only on the subsequent plays that you realize how fully realized and textured it is. A terrific debut that has only grown in stature since its release. *—Stephen Thomas Erlewine*

Give It Up / Sep. 1972 / Warner Brothers ♦♦♦♦♦
Bonnie Raitt may have switched producers for her second album *Give It Up*, hiring Michael Cuscuna, but she hasn't switched her style, sticking with the thoroughly engaging blend of folk, blues, R&B, and Californian soft rock. If anything, she's strengthened her formula here, making the divisions between the genres nearly indistinguishable. Take the title track, for instance. It opens with a bluesy acoustic guitar before kicking into a New Orleans brass band about halfway through—and the great thing about it is that Raitt makes the switch sound natural, even inevitable, never forced. And that's just the tip of the iceberg here, since *Give It Up* is filled with great songs, delivered in familiar, yet always surprising, ways by Raitt and her skilled band. For those that want to pigeonhole her as a white blues singer, she delivers the lovely "Nothing Seems to Matter," a gentle mid-tempo number that's as mellow as Linda Ronstadt and far more seductive. That's the key to *Give It Up*: Yes, Raitt can be earthy and sexy, but she balances it with an inviting sensuality that makes the record glow. It's all delivered in a fantastic set of originals and covers performed so naturally it's hard to tell them apart and roots music so thoroughly fused that it all sounds original, even when it's possible to spot the individual elements or influences. Raitt would go on to greater chart successes, but she not only had trouble topping this record, generations of singers, from Sheryl Crow to Shelby Lynne, have used this as a touchstone. One of the great Southern California records. *—Stephen Thomas Erlewine*

Takin' My Time / 1973 / Warner Brothers ♦♦♦♦
This album is an overlooked gem in the catalog of Bonnie Raitt. On *Takin' My Time*, she wears her influences proudly in an eclectic musical mix containing blues, jazz, folk, New Orleans R&B, and calypso. Although she did not write her own material for this album, she demonstrates an excellent ear for songs and chooses material from some of the best songwriters of the day. She is a great interpreter, and her renditions of Jackson Browne's "I Thought I Was a Child" and Randy Newman's "Guilty" from this album are the definitive versions of these songs. The highlights of this album are the romantic ballads "I Gave My Love a Candle" and "Cry Like a Rainstorm," where Raitt adds an emotional depth to the performance unusual for such a young woman. (Perhaps that's a result of her spending time with elder statesmen of the blues community such as Mississippi Fred McDowell and Sippie Wallace.) Although the faster-paced songs like the calypso "Wah She Go Do" seem a little out of place, the playful tune is welcome among an album filled with the heartache of the slower tunes. Despite being a relative newcomer, Raitt had already earned the respect of her mentors and her peers, as evidenced by the musical contributions of Taj Mahal, and Little Feat members Lowell George and Bill Payne on the album. This is the last consistent album she would make until her comeback in the mid-'80s. *—Vik Iyengar*

Streetlights / 1974 / Warner Brothers ♦♦♦
Bonnie Raitt had delivered three stellar albums, but chart success wasn't forthcoming, even if good reviews and a cult following were. So, she teamed with producer Jerry Ragovoy for *Streetlights* and attempted to make the crossover record that Warner so desperately wished she'd release. Over the years, the concessions that she made here—particularly the middle-of-the road arrangements (as opposed to the appealingly laid-back sounds of her previous records), the occasional use of strings, but also some of the song selections—have consigned *Streetlights* to noble failure status. There's no denying that's essentially what *Streetlights* is, but that makes it out to seem worse than it really is. It winds up paling to the wonderful ease and warm sensuality of her first three albums—she only occasionally hits that balance—but it's still undeniably pleasant, and there are moments here where she really pulls off some terrific work, including the opening cover of Joni Mitchell's "That Song About the Midway," a good version of John Prine's "Angel From Montgomery," and the much-touted take on Allen Toussaint's "What Is Success." It may be easy to lament the suppression of the laid-back sexiness and organic feel of Raitt's earlier records, but there's still enough here in that spirit to make this worthwhile. *—Stephen Thomas Erlewine*

Homeplate / 1975 / Warner Brothers ♦♦♦
Homeplate takes Bonnie Raitt even further down the path toward mainstream production than the unjustly maligned *Streetlights*, but, ironically, it works better than its predecessor. Perhaps that's because producer Paul A. Rothchild has helped Raitt craft a record that's unapologetically pitched at the mainstream, where *Streetlights* often seemed to be torn between two worlds. The great thing about that is, regardless of the production, the essentials of Raitt's music have not changed. It remains a wonderful hybrid of American music, built on a thoroughly impressive set of songs, all delivered with Raitt's warm, expertly shaded, and undeniably sexy singing. She's such an accomplished singer, she sells these songs through productions that are much slicker than those that graced her earlier records, plus with a supporting crew of studio musicians. This production will undoubtedly dismay listeners that just like the earthiness of *Give It Up*, but *Homeplate* is still a success because, even though the recording is glossier, Raitt and her music remain the same and, if you're looking for that, it's still irresistible. *—Stephen Thomas Erlewine*

Sweet Forgiveness / Apr. 1977 / Warner Brothers ♦♦

The Glow / 1979 / Warner Brothers ♦♦♦

Green Light / 1982 / Warner Brothers ♦♦♦♦♦
Since 1975's *Homeplate*, Bonnie Raitt has veered closer to the mainstream than she has to the organic, sexy funk of her early-'70s records. This bothered many listeners, who chose to concentrate on the surface instead of the substance, but Raitt retained many of the same special qualities she demonstrated on those records into the '80s—namely, her excellent taste in material, fondness for blurring folk, blues, country, and rock, and her wonderfully subtle, always engaging, interpretations. *Green Lights* may suffer a bit from a production that clearly pegs it as a 1982 release, but strip away its production and it's yet another satisfying collection of roots-rockers and bluesy ballads from the always reliable Raitt. Producer Rob Fraboni's recording may be a little bit too mainstream, lacking the new wave spark of, say, Dave Edmunds' similar-sounding recordings of this era, but Raitt nevertheless rises above the limitations of the recording and delivers a tight, enjoyable collection of amiable mainstream rockers with just a hint of roots. This isn't nearly as sexy as even *Sweet Forgiveness*, and it doesn't have much grit, but it has spirit and is fun, and it's a nice, smooth ride for those that like the direction Raitt's going. *—Stephen Thomas Erlewine*

Nine Lives / 1986 / Warner Brothers ♦♦♦
Bonnie Raitt's ninth and final album for Warner Bros. Records was a star-crossed affair that began in 1983 in a session with producer Rob Fraboni, which was a typical Raitt mixture of different genres and songwriters, from Jerry Williams ("Excited") and Eric Kaz ("Angel") to reggae star Toots Hibbert ("True Love Is Hard to Find") in a style similar to her 1982 album *Green Light*. This record seems to have been rejected by Warner, but three years later Raitt returned to the studio with Bill Payne (Little Feat) and George Massenburgh and cut a group of commercial-sounding songs by the likes of Bryan Adams and Tom Snow. *Nine Lives* splits the difference between the two sessions, with four tracks rescued from 1983, and five added from 1986, plus the theme from a forgotten Farrah Fawcett movie ("Stand Up to the Night" from *Extremities*). The result is predictably scattered and strained, and it was Raitt's lowest-charting album since her debut. Not surprisingly, it was also the last straw in her relationship with Warner. *—William Ruhlmann*

● **Nick of Time** / Mar. 1989 / Capitol ♦♦♦♦♦
Prior to *Nick of Time*, Bonnie Raitt had been a reliable cult artist, delivering a string of solid records that were moderate successes and usually musically satisfying. From her 1971 debut through 1982's *Green Light*, she had a solid streak, but 1986's *Nine Lives* snapped it, falling far short of her usual potential. Therefore, it shouldn't have been a

surprise when Raitt decided to craft its follow-up as a major comeback, collaborating with producer Don Was on *Nick of Time*. At the time, the pairing seemed a little odd, since he was primarily known for the weird hipster funk of Was (Not Was) and the B-52's quirky eponymous debut, but the match turned out to be inspired. Was used Raitt's classic early '70s records as a blueprint, choosing to update the sound with a smooth, professional production and a batch of excellent contemporary songs. In this context, Raitt flourishes; she never rocks too hard, but there is grit to her singing and playing, even when the surfaces are clean and inviting. And while she only has two original songs here, *Nick of Time* plays like autobiography, which is a testament to the power of the songs, performances and productions. It was a great comeback album that made for a great story, but the record never would have been a blockbuster success if it wasn't for the music, which is among the finest Raitt ever made. She must have realized this, since *Nick of Time* served as the blueprint for the majority of her '90s albums. *—Stephen Thomas Erlewine*

The Bonnie Raitt Collection / Jun. 28, 1990 / Warner Brothers ✦✦✦

Since Bonnie Raitt didn't score any big hits during her nine-album tenure at Warner Bros., compiling a best-of from those records is largely a matter of taste, and after Raitt's commercial breakthrough on Capitol with *Nick of Time* in 1989, Warners decided to trust her own taste in choosing songs for this compilation. The artist's input is usually considered a good thing, but in this case it has resulted in an idiosyncratic selection that fails to be representative or to cull the real highlights from Raitt's Warners catalog. Basically, that catalog breaks down into three sections—the first three solid albums, the second three good, but uneven albums, and the last three mediocre, compromised albums. Raitt has opted to try to find at least a couple of tracks from each album, which means she necessarily slights her best work in favor of her weakest. Even by choosing four tracks from *Give It Up*, she still misses "Been Too Long at the Fair," and by restricting herself to two tracks from *Takin My Time*, she misses "Cry Like a Rainstorm" and "I Gave My Love a Candle." On later albums, the problem is more about selection than quantity. Why "Sugar Mama" from *Home Plate* and not "Run Like a Thief" and "I'm Blowin' Away"? Why "(Goin') Wild for You Baby" from *The Glow* and not the Grammy-nominated "You're Gonna Get What's Coming"? Why "Willya Wontcha" from *Green Light* and not "Me and the Boys"? Even taking into account differences in taste, Raitt's choices run in the face of the preferences of fans and critics to the point that the album fails to make the case for her Warners recordings as true expressions of her talents, a case that could have been made decisively with a better selection. *—William Ruhlmann*

Luck of the Draw / Jun. 1991 / Capitol ✦✦✦✦✦

Nick of Time not only was an artistic comeback for Bonnie Raitt, it brought her largest audience yet, so there was no reason to mess with success for its sequel, *Luck of the Draw*. And sequel is the appropriate word, since *Luck of the Draw* is nothing if it isn't "Nick of Time, Part 2." True, there's a heavier reliance on original material this time around, but the sound and feel of the record is identical to its predecessor. There is one slight difference—several of the songs appear tailor-made for crossover success, where *Nick of Time* felt organic. Nevertheless, *Luck of the Draw* is an unqualified success, filled with strong songs—including the hits "Something to Talk About" and "I Can't Make You Love Me," plus the Delbert McClinton duet "Good Man, Good Woman"—appealing productions and just enough dirt to make old-school fans feel at home. *—Stephen Thomas Erlewine*

Longing in Their Hearts / Mar. 14, 1994 / Capitol ✦✦✦✦✦

On the follow-up to the follow-up (and another million-selling #1 hit), Bonnie Raitt contributes more than her usual share of original songs, writing four songs herself and setting a lyric of her husband's to music for a fifth. Elsewhere, she draws on such strong writers as Richard Thompson and Paul Brady, all for a collection devoted to devotion. Song after song expresses passion, usually with happy results—this is not the album of a woman with the blues. Even when she's dressing down a parent in her own "Circle Dance," Raitt offers forgiveness and understanding. There, and in other songs, the object of her emotions rarely seems to be perfect, but she takes that in and loves him, anyway. Co-producer Don Was provides a detailed production in which single elements—an accordion, a harmony vocal by Levon Helm or David Crosby—effectively color arrangements and complement Raitt's always soulful singing. *—William Ruhlmann*

Road Tested / Nov. 7, 1995 / Digital Sound ✦✦✦✦✦

In a 24-year recording career, Bonnie Raitt had not previously released a live album, so this concert set was overdue. Coming off three multi-platinum studio albums, Raitt and Capitol pulled out all the stops, compiling a 22-track, double-disc package from dates recorded in July 1995 in Portland and Oakland. Raitt ranged over her career, reaching back to her early folk-blues days and forward to the pop/rock songs that finally made her a big star in the late '80s and early '90s. She also shared the spotlight with such guests as Bruce Hornsby, Ruth Brown, Charles Brown, Kim Wilson of the Fabulous Thunderbirds, Bryan Adams, and Jackson Browne. But that didn't keep an artist who has spent the bulk of her career pleasing live audiences rather than cutting hits from displaying her personal warmth along with her singing and playing skills. She also introduced half a dozen songs new to her repertoire, including a surprising cover of Talking Heads' "Burning Down the House" and a few that had potential to help promote the album as singles, including "Never Make Your Move Too Soon" and "Shake a Little." Inexplicably, Capitol (which probably wished the album had been a more reasonably priced single-disc) failed to bring the record home to consumers. The company's choice for a single was the anonymous Adams rocker "Rock Steady," done as a duet with him—apparently, they were confusing Raitt with Tina Turner. As a result, the album stopped at gold, spending less than six months in the charts. Despite that commercial disappointment, it will be for many Bonnie Raitt fans an example of her at her best that effectively bridges the two parts of her career, and also a good sampler for first-time listeners. *—William Ruhlmann*

Fundamental / Apr. 7, 1998 / Capitol ✦✦✦

Apparently in an attempt to find new sounds that would appeal to a new audience, Bonnie Raitt severed her ties with her comeback producer Don Was for *Fundamental*, hiring those masterminds of experimental adult pop, Mitchell Froom and Tchad Blake. Although Froom and Blake have worked with a number of singer-songwriters and roots musicians—including Elvis Costello, Suzanne Vega, Richard Thompson, Los Lobos and Crowded House—they often emphasize the production over the song, pouring on layers of effects and novelty instruments that tend to obscure the songs and performances. While they don't go overboard on *Fundamental*, like they did on Los Lobos' *Colossal Head*, they have pushed too much of their own style on Raitt. There are good songs scattered throughout the record, but it's hard to pick them out underneath the gauzy, murky production. Eventually, the album becomes a bit of a chore, since the sounds wear on the ears. That's too bad, because Raitt remains a vital artist—it's just that Froom and Blake haven't allowed her to rely on her talents here. *—Stephen Thomas Erlewine*

Rakim

b. Jan. 28, 1968

Vocals / Hardcore Rap, East Coast Rap, Hip-Hop

Rakim may never have achieved the stardom of peers like Ice-T or Chuck D, but he never lost respect among the hip-hop community, where he was acknowledged as one of the great rappers. Throughout the '80s, he was one of the leading figures in hip-hop as he and his partner, DJ Eric B., released a series of groundbreaking records. In 1992, the two parted ways and Rakim spent the next five years in seclusion, returning in the fall of 1997 with his solo debut, *The 18th Letter*. *The Master* followed two years later. *—Stephen Thomas Erlewine*

The 18th Letter/Book of Life / Nov. 4, 1997 / Universal ✦✦✦✦✦

This two-disc set is an excellent collection of material that succinctly outlines the career of this well-known, highly respected, and deft lyricist. The first disc, also released alone as *The 18th Letter*, was released in late 1997 after a four-year period of inactivity and features 12 tracks of previously unreleased material. The collection of producers on this album shows Rakim's ability to change his lyrical and vocal style so as not to bore the listener, but at the same time maintain a consistent and dependable level of creativity and ingenuity. The two R&B-tinged tracks, "Stay a While" and "Show Me Love," represent two instances where R&B and hip-hop successfully merge without too much sugarcoating or hazy outlines. "The Mystery (Who Is God?)" is a serious lyrical synopsis of Rakim's spiritual beliefs and social commentary; still in the relaxed but intense style of delivery that Rakim is known for are "Guess Who's Back" and "New York (Ya' Out There)," among other songs. No track on *The 18th Letter* stands out more than another because each is strong in content and rhythmically powerful.

The second disc in this set is a collection of popular songs from the four albums Rakim had released as one-half of a rapper-DJ duo with DJ Eric B.: *Paid In Full*, *Follow the Leader*, *Let the Rhythm Hit 'Em*, and *Don't Sweat the Technique*. Also included in the songs on this disc is "Know the Ledge," an edgy, uptempo declaration of rhyming skill from the *Juice* soundtrack that provided a brief dose of Rakim during his hiatus after *Let the Rhythm Hit 'Em*. Including titles such as "I Know You Got Soul," "Microphone Fiend," "My Melody," "Move the Crowd," "Mahogany," and "Paid In Full," the second disc (known as *The Book of Life*) is an ideal introduction to the impressive past of Rakim as a lyricist. *—Qa'id Jacobs*

The 18th Letter / Nov. 4, 1997 / Uptown/Universal ✦✦✦✦

It took Rakim five years to begin his solo careeer, but the wait was worth it—*The 18th Letter* is one of the strongest records a veteran rapper has released in the late '90s. Working with a variety of producers (Pete Rock, Clark Kent, Father Shaheed, DJ Premier), Rakim sounds sharp, focused and strong, rapping with a force unheard of on his classic albums with Eric B. He still retains his knack for rolling, laidback rhymes, but what's impressive is how he can switch between that style and a more aggressive technique. There are a few slow spots on the record, but in general, few latter-day albums by '80s rappers sound as powerful and vital as *The 18th Letter*. *—Leo Stanley*

● **The Master** / Nov. 30, 1999 / Universal ✦✦✦✦✦

When you've been named the best rapper ever in countless readers' and critics' polls, it must be easy to get a bit complacent. And as a veteran who's been on the mic since 1985 (yes, there are several rappers who weren't even on the earth back then), it also must be easy to make a few concessions to all the rappers and delivery styles that have come since Kangols were all the rage—the first time, that is. Thankfully, Rakim's second solo album shows hip-hop's best rapper outdoing himself yet again, and not conceding a whit to '90s rap. Rakim has always been known for his laid-back flow and, accordingly, he never pushes himself here; his flow is smooth as syrup, and will undoubtedly make hip-hop fans realize just what rhythm is after merely a few tracks. He plays with internal rhymes (one of his trademarks) and constructs the most dense lyrics heard in hip-hop for years. *The Master* also benefits from its stellar cast of producers—Clark Kent, DJ Premier, Ron "Amen-Ra" Lawrence, the 45 King, and even Rakim himself. The productions are tough and catchy (no strings here, thankfully), but they never outshine the rhymes. Rakim praises himself on quite a few tracks ("Flow Forever," "When I B on the Mic," "I Know," "It's the R"), but after a listen or two, listeners will likely agree with every boast he makes. After one album (*The 18th Letter*) to get back into things, Rakim is arguably doing the best work of his career. *—John Bush*

The Ramones

f. 1974, New York, NY, **db.** 1996

College Rock, American Punk, New York Punk, Punk

The Ramones are the first punk rock band. There were other bands, such as the Stooges and the New York Dolls, that came before them and set the stage and aesthetic for punk and bands that immediately followed, such as the Sex Pistols, that made the latent violence of the music more explicit, but the Ramones crystallized the musical ideals of the genre. By cutting rock & roll down to its bare essentials—four chords, a simple, catchy melody, and irresistably inane lyrics—speeding up the tempo considerably, the Ramones created something that was rooted in early '60s, pre-Beatles rock & roll and pop but sounded revolutionary. Since their breakthrough was theoretical as well as musical, they comfortably became the leaders of the emerging New York punk rock scene. While their peers such as Patti Smith, Television, Talking Heads and Richard Hell all were more intellectual and self-consciously artistic than the Ramones, they nevertheless appealed to the same mentality because of how they turned rock conventions inside out and celebrated kitschy pop culture with stylized stupidity. The band's first four albums set the blueprint for punk, especially American punk and hardcore, for the next two decades. And the Ramones themselves were major figures for the next two decades, playing essentially the same music without changing their style much at all. Although some punk diehards—including several of their peers—would have claimed the band's long career wound up undercutting the ideals the band originally stood for, the Ramones always celebrated not just the punk aesthetic, but the music itself. — *Stephen Thomas Erlewine*

☆ **The Ramones** / May 1976 / Sire ♦♦♦♦♦
With the three-chord assault of "Blitzkrieg Bop," *The Ramones* begins at a blinding speed and never once over the course of its 14 songs does it let up. *The Ramones* is all about speed, hooks, stupidity and simplicity. The songs are imaginative reductions of early rock & roll, girl group pop, and surf-rock. Not only is the music boiled down to its essentials, but the Ramones offer a twisted, comical take on pop culture with their lyrics, whether it's the horror schlock of "I Don't Wanna Go Down to the Basement," the drug deals of "53rd and 3rd," the gleeful violence of "Beat on the Brat" or the maniacal stupidity of "Now I Wanna Sniff Some Glue." And the cover of Chris Montez's "Let's Dance" isn't a throwaway—with its single-minded beat and lyrics, it encapsulates everything the group loves about pre-Beatles rock & roll. They don't alter the structure, or the intent, of the song, they simply make it louder and faster. And that's the key to all of the Ramones' music—it's simple rock & roll, played simply, loud, and very, very fast. None of the songs clock in at any longer than two and half minutes and most are considerably shorter. In comparison to some of the music the album inspired, *The Ramones* sounds a little tame—it's a little too clean and compared to their insanely fast live albums, it even sounds a little slow—but there's no denying that it still sounds brilliantly fresh and intoxicatingly fun. — *Stephen Thomas Erlewine*

Leave Home / Feb. 1977 / Sire ♦♦♦♦♦
Of course the Ramones' second album *Leave Home* is simply more of the same—14 songs, including one oldie ("California Sun"), delivered at breakneck speed and concluding in under a half hour. The Ramones have gotten slightly poppier, occasionally delivering songs like "I Remember You" that are cloaked neither in irony nor seedy rock & roll chic. Still, the biggest impressions are made by the cuts that strongly recall the debut, whether it's the ersatz Beach Boys of "Sheena Is a Punk Rocker," the sing-along of "Pinhead" or the warped anthems "Gimme Gimme Shock Treatment" and "Commando." Song for song, it's slightly weaker than its predecessor, but the handful of mediocre cuts speed by so fast that you don't really notice its weaknesses until after it's all over. — *Stephen Thomas Erlewine*

☆ **Rocket to Russia** / Nov. 1977 / Sire ♦♦♦♦♦
The Ramones provided the blueprint and *Leave Home* duplicated it with lesser results, but the Ramones' third album, *Rocket to Russia*, perfected it. *Rocket to Russia* boasts a cleaner production than its predecessors, which only gives the Ramones' music more force. It helps that the group wrote its finest set of songs for the album. From the mindless, bopping opening of "Cretin Hop" and "Rockaway Beach" to the urban surf-rock of "Sheena Is a Punk Rocker" and ridiculous anthem "Teenage Lobotomy," the songs are teeming with irresistibly catchy hooks; even their choice of covers, "Do You Want to Dance?" and "Surfin' Bird," provide more hooks than usual. The Ramones also branch out slightly, adding ballads to the mix. Even with these (relatively) slower songs, the speed of the album never decreases. However, the abundance of hooks and slight variety in tempos makes *Rocket to Russia* the Ramones' most listenable and enjoyable album—it doesn't have the revolutionary impact of *The Ramones*, but it's a better album and one of the finest records of the late '70s. — *Stephen Thomas Erlewine*

Road to Ruin / Jun. 1978 / Sire ♦♦♦♦♦
The loud-and-fast, campy-and-catchy formula began to wear a little thin by the time of the Ramones' fourth album, *Road to Ruin*. Following the exact same blueprint as its three predecessors, *Road to Ruin* simply doesn't yield the same results as the other records. In part, it's because the band sounds a little forced on the harder numbers, but the main problem lies with the undistinguished material. "I Wanna Be Sedated" is a classic, and "Questioningly" proves that the Ramones are just as effective when they slow the tempo down, yet much of the record sounds like the Ramones trying to give the people what they want. Since they were still in their prime, such nondescript material sounds good, but the record has neither the exuberant energy or abundant hooks of *Ramones* and *Rocket to Russia*, and it's the first suggestion that the Ramones may have painted themselves into a corner. — *Stephen Thomas Erlewine*

It's Alive / May 1979 / Sire ♦♦♦♦
One of the greatest live albums of all time, *It's Alive* captures the Ramones at their absolute peak. Recorded at London's Rainbow Theater on New Year's Eve 1977, the album contains 28 songs (every one a classic) from the band's landmark first three albums: *Ramones*, *Ramones Leave Home*, and *Rocket to Russia* performed at breakneck speed

in under an hour. In fact, the band only pauses long enough for bassist Dee Dee to count off the next tune—"one-two-three-four!"—and for singer Joey to complain about some bad chicken vindaloo. It has often been said that the Ramones helped save rock & roll by making it fun again—*It's Alive* is the perfect case in point. Long live the Ramones! — *Ed Rivadavia*

End of the Century / Jan. 1980 / Sire ♦♦♦♦
Road to Ruin found the Ramones stretching their signature sound to its limits; even though there were several fine moments, nearly all of them arrived when the group broke free from the suddenly restrictive loud-fast-hard formula of their first records. Considering that the Ramones did desire mainstream success and that they had a deep love for early-'60s pop/rock, it's not surprising that they decided to shake loose the constrictions of their style by making an unabashed pop album, yet it was odd that Phil Spector produced *End of the Century* because his painstaking working methods seemingly clashed with the Ramones' instinctual approach. However, the Ramones were always more clever than they appeared, so the matching actually worked better than it could have. Spector's detailed production helped bring "Rock & Roll High School" and "Do You Remember Rock & Roll Radio?" to life, yet it also kept some of the punkier numbers in check. Even so, *End of the Century* is more enjoyable than its predecessor, since the record has stronger material, and in retrospect, it's one of their better records of the '80s. — *Stephen Thomas Erlewine*

Pleasant Dreams / Jul. 1981 / Sire ♦♦♦
End of the Century didn't make the Ramones into the stars they so wanted to be, so they hooked up with another '60s icon, Graham Gouldman, for its follow-up, *Pleasant Dreams*. Oddly, Gouldman directs the band away from their bubblegum, British Invasion and surf fetishes toward acid-rock and heavy metal. They still manage to squeak out a couple of irresistibly catchy songs, but the production is too clean to qualify as punk, and the music itself has lost sight of the infectious qualities that made their earlier records such fun. Yet those flaws seem endearing compared to the metallic meanderings of their late '80s records. — *Stephen Thomas Erlewine*

Subterranean Jungle / May 1983 / Sire ♦♦♦
Tentatively returning toward punk, or at least new wave, the Ramones turned in their most enjoyable record since *Rocket to Russia* with *Subterranean Jungle*. Producers Ritchie Cordell and Glen Kolotkin were the heads of the edgy power-pop and punk label Bomp!, so they steered the Ramones back toward the '60s pop infatuation that provided the foundation for their early records. It's a strategy that pays off well—for the most part, the group's originals are so punchy and catchy that they make the pair of covers superfluous. Comprised of a set of unabashedly hook-laden songs and driven by more subtle rhythms, *Subterranean Jungle* may not be a punk record in the strictest sense of the word, yet the Ramones haven't sounded quite as alive in a long, long while. — *Stephen Thomas Erlewine*

Too Tough to Die / Jan. 1985 / Sire ♦♦♦♦♦
With the Ramones' original drummer Tommy Erdelyi producing, the group returns to simple, scathing punk rock on *Too Tough to Die*. The group takes the big guitar riffs of *Subterranean Jungle* and makes them shorter and heavier. The Ramones rhythms are back up to jackhammer speed and the songs are down to short, terse statements. The results read like a reaction to hardcore punk, but the Ramones are more melodic than any hardcore band, as well as smarter than most. Apart from the occasional foray into pop, such as the surprisingly effective Dave Stewart-produced "Howling at the Moon," the album is a sterling set of lethal punk, the best the Ramones had made since the end of the '70s. It was also the last great record they would ever make. — *Stephen Thomas Erlewine*

Animal Boy / May 1986 / Sire ♦♦♦
1986's *Animal Boy* wasn't a very happy record for the Ramones. Since the release of *Too Tough to Die* (a slight return to form) nearly two years earlier, the band's fortunes had gone from bad to worse; interest in the band kept dwindling with every release and the "bruthas" were constantly at each other's throats. But their desperation only became apparent when they started seriously altering their sound in search of a lucky break. With *Animal Boy*, producer Jean Beauvoir (of Plasmatics infamy) attempted to update the band's sound with the commercial conventions of the day, meaning keyboards and synthesizers. Opener "Somebody Put Something in My Drink," for instance, wastes an aggressive vocal performance from Joey Ramone by supporting it with a shamelessly polished synthesizer backing track. The balls-out title song momentarily simplifies things once again, but the album continues to progress in hit-and-miss fashion, culminating with the unbearably soft "Something to Believe In"—with bright synths taking over completely and no guitar in sight, it is a career low. Of note, the album does contain one of the band's most clearly political statements in first single "Bonzo Goes to Bitburg," written about President Ronald Reagan's ill-advised visit to Germany's Bitburg cemetery, the site of many Nazi graves. Interestingly, the song was later re-titled "My Brain Is Hanging Upside Down" prior to the album's release after vehement protests from guitarist Johnny Ramone, a fervid conservative. One of many mid-'80s blunders, *Animal Boy* is best left forgotten from the Ramones' otherwise remarkable late-'70s legacy. — *Ed Rivadavia*

Halfway to Sanity / Sep. 15, 1987 / Sire ♦♦

Ramones Mania / May 31, 1988 / Sire ♦♦♦♦♦
Ramonesmania is a relentless collection of 30 tracks from the Ramones' first ten albums, ranging from the classic *Ramones* to the less-than-classic *Halfway to Sanity*. Although not all of their great '70s songs are included, it boils down the highlights from the inconsistent '80s albums quite effectively, making it a useful summation of their peak period, even if the sequencing is not chronological. — *Stephen Thomas Erlewine*

Brain Drain / May 23, 1989 / Sire ♦♦

★ **All the Stuff & More, Vol. 1** / May 1990 / Sire ✦✦✦✦✦
All the Stuff & More, Vol. 1 compiles the Ramones first two albums—*Ramones* and *Leave Home*—onto one compact disc, adding a handful of B-sides, demos and live songs as bonus tracks as well. While the music on the disc is terrific and timeless, having both albums on one disc actually dilutes some of its impact, since the records were designed as a relentless rush of brief, speedy songs; in this form, the assault becomes a little tiring, and the distinctions between the two albums—and they are there—are lost. Still, these are minor flaws, especially considering that the music on *All the Stuff & More, Vol. 1* is essential for any rock & roll library. —*Stephen Thomas Erlewine*

☆ **All the Stuff & More, Vol. 2** / 1990 / Sire ✦✦✦✦✦
The second volume of *All the Stuff & More* compiles the Ramones' third and fourth albums—*Rocket to Russia* and *Road to Ruin*—onto one compact disc, adding several live cuts, demos and B-sides as bonus tracks. Like its predecessor, *All the Stuff & More, Vol. 2* suffers slightly from its length, which happens to contradict the loud-fast nature of the band's songs and albums, yet the music isn't hurt by its presentation. *Rocket to Russia* is one of the classic rock & roll albums, and while *Road to Ruin* isn't as consistent, it does have its moments, making *All the Stuff & More, Vol. 2* a good bargain. —*Stephen Thomas Erlewine*

Loco Live / Oct. 1991 / Sire ✦✦✦
Between 1976 and 1978, the Ramones could seemingly do no wrong, and *It's Alive*, the album that preserved their 1977-going-on-1978 New Year's Eve show in London for the ages, captured the pride of Forest Hills at the peak of their form, turning three-chord downstroke into the stuff of magic. By 1990, the band's albums were generally good but not great, and it seemed as if their days of studio glory were behind them. But anyone who ever saw the Ramones live will tell you that right up to the end, they never failed to deliver onstage, and if *Loco Live* isn't quite up to the same level as *It's Alive*, it proves these guys always gave their fans the sweat, muscle, and cool tunes they came to see. The buzz of Johnny Ramone's guitar is still gloriously relentless, Joey yelps like he means it (and if he has a little more to say between songs, most of it's cool), Marky remains King of the Big Beat, and C.J. plays at least as well as Dee Dee (and is nearly as good at yelling "wuntootreeFAH!"). And if the presence of "Mama's Boy," "Someone Put Something in My Drink," and "I Believe in Miracles" don't exactly give *Loco Live* an edge over the first-three-albums set list of *It's Alive*, the truth is nearly all the newer songs sound stronger (and faster) on stage, and the old stuff is, as always, a joy to behold. If you're going to buy a Ramones live album, the blazing *It's Alive* is the one to get, but *Loco Live* proves these old soldiers never gave up the fight—13 years on, they were still loud and proud, and you can't help but love 'em for it. —*Mark Deming*

Mondo Bizarro / Sep. 1992 / Radioactive ✦✦

Acid Eaters / Dec. 1993 / Radioactive ✦✦

Adios Amigos / Jul. 18, 1995 / Radioactive ✦✦✦

Greatest Hits Live / Jun. 18, 1996 / Radioactive ✦✦✦

● **Hey! Ho! Let's Go: The Anthology** / Jul. 20, 1999 / Rhino ✦✦✦✦✦
In a way, the Ramones are an ideal band to anthologize. No matter how cohesive their records were (or not), their albums always played like collections of singles and since singles are easy to anthologize, it stands to reason that the best of the Ramones' songs will sound good in nearly any context; hell, the haphazard *Ramones Mania* proved that. However, Rhino's double-disc *Hey! Ho! Let's Go: The Anthology* has much greater goals than being just being another collection—it strives to be the final word on the Ramones. Weighing in at nearly 60 songs, with a hardcover book that includes an excellent history by David Fricke, it has to be said that the set has the heft of history, which is both a blessing and a curse. It's a blessing because *Anthology* does its job perfectly—apart from "We're a Happy Family," no major songs are missing and it tells its history succinctly, even at its length. The problem is that the Ramones did drop in quality sometime after *End of the Century*. They never bottomed out, but their music became less exciting, which is evident in this anthology, as the second disc is simply not as compelling as the first. That's not to say it isn't good—with "The KKK Took My Baby Away" and "My Brain Is Hanging Upside Down (Bonzo Goes to Bitburg)," it can be great—but it isn't timeless like the entire first disc is. Yet, this is nitpicking, since *Anthology* does a flawless job in summarizing the band's career. True, most listeners will wear out the first disc while rarely reaching for the second, but this is still essential. —*Stephen Thomas Erlewine*

Willis Alan Ramsey

Vocals, Guitar / Folk-Rock, Soft Rock, Singer/Songwriter, Country-Rock
Willis Alan Ramsey was one of the bright lights of Austin's singer/songwriter movement of the '70s, and his laid-back folky airs and sweet melodies impressed many contemporaries. Indeed, his 1972 self-titled debut album featured songs later covered by Jimmy Buffett, America, Waylon Jennings and Captain & Tennille, who took "Muskrat Love" to the Popular Top Five in 1976. His star shines less bright if only for the fact that he practically disappeared in the mid-'70s. A small cult of fans remained true, however, and their adoration was somewhat rewarded when Ramsey re-surfaced, working with Lyle Lovett, who has also covered Ramsey in concert. —*John Bush*

Willis Alan Ramsey / 1972 / Koch ✦✦✦✦✦
In many ways, Willis Alan Ramsey's debut album makes him sound like the archetypical Texas singer/songwriter; there's more than a little Guy Clark in his approach, a healthy dose of Townes Van Zandt, a dash of Jimmie Dale Gilmore, and one can hear the echoes of what Steve Earle and Lyle Lovett would draw from this music. But Ramsey's style—an engaging mixture of cowboy poetry, post-hippie wit and wonder, and singer/songwriter introspection—burst forth fully formed in 1972, while Van Zandt was

still barely a rumor outside the Lone Star State, and Clark had yet to make himself heard on vinyl. While a number of artists covered material from *Willis Alan Ramsey*, one listen to the album is enough to convince anyone Ramsey was as much a performer as a songwriter. The bluesy drawl and frayed edges of Ramsey's voice convey a road-worn maturity that betrayed his youth (he was in his early twenties when he cut these sessions), and his production (in collaboration with Denny Cordell) is remarkably intelligent and imaginative for someone with so little experience in the studio. Part of the mystique that has sprung up around Willis Alan Ramsey's debut album is that he dropped from sight after recording it (due to differences with his record company and a lack of enthusiasm for the realities of the music business), and has yet to release a follow-up; while it's hard to imagine anyone whose heard it not hoping there's more where this came from, if your recording career was to be contained in a single album, you'd be very fortunate if it were as good as *Willis Alan Ramsey*. —*Mark Deming*

Rancid

f. 1991, Berkeley, CA
Ska-Punk, Punk-Pop, Third Wave Ska Revival, Punk Revival, Alternative Pop/Rock
Drawing an enormous influence from the Clash, the Bay Area quartet Rancid followed the lead of fellow latter-day punks Green Day and the Offspring to mainstream success. The group was led by singer/guitarist Tim Armstrong, a lifelong hardcore fan who first found underground success teamed with childhood friend and bassist Matt Freeman in the late-'80s ska-punk band Operation Ivy. Unable to deal with their growing popularity, Op Ivy disbanded in 1989, and Armstrong and Freeman founded Rancid in 1991 with Brett Reed on drums. The trio issued their five-song debut in 1992, followed in 1993 by a self-titled full-length release on the prominent indie label Epitaph. After the addition of second guitarist Lars Frederiksen, formerly a member of the U.K. Subs, Rancid recorded its 1994 breakthrough album *Let's Go*, which sold close to a million copies on the strength of the single and video "Salvation." A major bidding war followed, but the band remained with Epitaph for 1995's *...And Out Come the Wolves*, which featured the hits "Time Bomb" and "Ruby Soho." *Life Won't Wait* followed in 1998. —*Jason Ankeny*

Rancid [1993] / May 10, 1993 / Epitaph ✦✦✦✦
This is where it all starts. Without any reminiscing about their former band Operation Ivy, Matt Freeman (bass) and Tim Armstrong (guitar/vocals) blast through their debut without any hints of ska or blatant Clash plagiarizing. On the contrary, this album rips through 15 tracks of high-energy punk that's accompanied by heavy bass leads and Armstrong's permanently slurred vocals. And to top it all off, the lyrical content deals with urban blight and the lifestyle of being a public nuisance. With this trademark sound, Rancid provides the perfect soundtrack for any car chase that includes massive property damage; is it a wonder MTV wouldn't touch this? —*Mike DaRonco*

Let's Go / Jun. 14, 1994 / Epitaph ✦✦✦✦✦
Whatever Rancid lacks in innovation, it makes up with sheer energy. The group rushes through *Let's Go* with an invigorating wrecklessness, sounding like a less-serious, party-ready version of the Clash. It's almost impossible to understand what vocalist Tim Armstrong sings at any given moment, yet there is no great meaning in what Rancid says—the message is in the buzzing guitars and speeding rhythms. It doesn't hurt that the band can throw out the occasional memorable hook or melody, like the single "Salvation," as well. —*Stephen Thomas Erlewine*

● **And Out Come the Wolves** / Oct. 1995 / Epitaph ✦✦✦✦✦
In the wake of the Offspring's success, Rancid became a hot band, earning a dedicated cult and sparking a major-label bidding war. After flirting with a handful of major labels, the band decided to stick with Epitaph and returned with *And Out Come the Wolves*. While the title is a veiled reference to the attention the band gained, the album doesn't mark an isolationist retreat into didactic, defiantly underground punk rock. Instead, Rancid develop their own identity on the record, which ironically makes them more accessible. Although they continue to draw heavily from the Clash and the Specials—and their roots in the ska-punk band Operation Ivy are quite clear throughout the record—the band plays with such energy and conviction, it's easy to forgive their derivativeness. On the whole, *And Out Come the Wolves* is a little too long to make a major impact, but individual tracks are classic moments of revivalist punk, including the skittering 2-Tone tribute "Time Bomb." —*Stephen Thomas Erlewine*

Life Won't Wait / Jun. 30, 1998 / Epitaph ✦✦✦✦
Rancid never wins any points for originality, but originality isn't their goal. Rancid wants to be, to quote an old Clash slogan, "the only band that matters." Where the Clash earned that title by mixing genres, blending the old with the new, Rancid decides to be traditional, spiking the Clash's sound with ska-punk and hardcore. Musically, that might not make the group vital in 1998, since it ignores any musical innovations since 1978, but that doesn't mean the group is impotent—far from it. *Life Won't Wait*, the group's fourth album, is a powerful slice of old-school punk—as powerful as any of their records. Apart from a more pronounced ska influence, it actually sounds a lot like its immediate predecessor, *And Out Come the Wolves*, complete with the fiery intensity and catchy hooks that set the group apart from the retro-punk pack. *Life Won't Wait*, however, also shares the messy, pseudo-epic pretentions that hampered its predecessor. Taken in small doses, the record is quite powerful but since the group's attack is fairly predictable, even with the detours into ska/reggae and blues, the album becomes wearing when taken as a whole. Still, the band is head-and-shoulders above their punk contemporaries—they have better songs, a genuine political stance and raging energy—and that makes such indulgences tolerable. Even if it runs too long, there won't be a better old-school punk album than *Life Won't Wait* in 1998. —*Stephen Thomas Erlewine*

Rancid [2000] / Aug. 1, 2000 / Epitaph ✦✦✦✦✦

After several fine, if rather derivative, albums of ska-inflected punk rock, and after years of being criticized for relying unduly on gestures lifted from the Clash, Rancid has come roaring out with the harshest and most consistent album of their career. It wouldn't be entirely accurate to say that they've left their influences behind; rather, they've integrated them more completely and created a sound that is completely satisfying without having to prove anything about its own originality. That sound ends up being something like a cross between the Clash circa 1978 and the hardcore punk of the early-'80s Los Angeles scene. "Rwanda" is a stutter-step anthem of sympathy for a devastated country; "Corruption" has an atonal power-chord progression and headlong tempo that Minor Threat would have killed for; and "Blackhawk Down" is built on a ridiculously catchy descending bass line and a distinctly Oi!-flavored singalong chorus. No ska, no reggae, no dub, just 22 tracks in 38 minutes with barely a pause between songs and barely a tempo under 1000 bpm. If you're looking for artistic subtlety, go back to the catalog; if all you need is a half-hour of undiluted adrenaline, you've come to the right place. *—Rick Anderson*

The Rascals

f. 1964, New York, NY, **db.** 1972

AM Pop, Blue-Eyed Soul, Pop

The Rascals, along with the Righteous Brothers, Mitch Ryder, and precious few others, were the pinnacle of '60s blue-eyed soul. The Rascals' talents, however, would have to rate above their rivals, if for nothing else than the simple fact that they, unlike many other blue-eyed soulsters, penned much of their own material. They also proved more adept at changing with the fast-moving times, drawing much of their inspiration from British Invasion bands, psychedelic rock, gospel, and even a bit of jazz and Latin music. They were at their best on classic singles like "Good Lovin'," "How Can I Be Sure," "Groovin'," and "People Got to Be Free." When they tried to stretch their talents beyond the impositions of the three-minute 45, they couldn't pull it off, a failure which—along with crucial personnel losses—effectively finished the band as a major force by the 1970s. *—Richie Unterberger*

The Young Rascals / 1966 / Atlantic ✦✦✦✦✦

The history of '60s rock is littered with stories of great rock classics—the Savages' album, the Thirteenth Floor Elevators' first two albums, the first two Chocolate Watch Band albums—that should have been better known than they were. *The Young Rascals* is that rare example of a genuinely great album that got heard and played, and sold and sold. Apart from the presence of a hit ("Good Lovin'") to drive sales, every kid (and his girlfriend) in any aspiring white rock band on the East Coast in 1966 seemingly owned a copy. And it's easy to see why—the Rascals' debut couples a raw garage band sound with compelling white soul more successfully than just about any record since the Beatles' *Please Please Me.* The band had three powerful singers in Felix Cavaliere, Eddie Brigati, and Gene Cornish, and an attack honed in hundreds of hours of playing dance clubs on Long Island and New York City. The result is a record without a weak moment or a false note anywhere in its 35 minutes: "Do You Feel It" shows them crossing swords stylistically with Smokey Robinson & the Miracles; "Just a Little" and "Like a Rolling Stone" show off their folk-rock chops; and "Slow Down," "Good Lovin'," "Mustang Sally," and "In the Midnight Hour" are all '60s rock & roll classics in these versions. "Like a Rolling Stone," in particular, now seems all the more compelling, pointing the way toward a future that included Hendrix's version of "All Along the Watchtower." The CD is one of Warner Special Products' better sounding reissues, having been remastered by Rhino's Bill Inglot. The original album was on Atlantic, and was one of the label's best-sellers of the mid-'60s. *—Bruce Eder*

Collections / Jan. 1967 / Atlantic ✦✦✦✦✦

The garage-band feel has been banished almost entirely from the group's second album, whose release followed a pair of disappointing singles ("What Is the Reason," "Come On Up"). It also includes their first misjudgment on an album, Gene Cornish's too-quiet, too-introspective, and way-too-languid "No Love to Give," amid an otherwise wonderfully soulful body of music that picks up right where "In the Midnight Hour" from the prior album left off. Most of this record is among the most danceable White rock music of its period—even the Eddie Brigatti-sung cover of the then-current pop standard "More" has a certain rocking credibility. Their attempt at bluesy rock & roll, Cornish's "Nineteen Fifty-Six," a bit of a "Kansas City" ripoff, with a pair of crunchy guitar parts and Cornish singing lead, also comes off extremely well. They're even better with the more soulful tracks, however. "Land of 1000 Dances" was the best track on which to end this album, but it was Cavaliere and Brigatti's "Love Is a Beautiful Thing" that pointed to the future, showing the group moving toward the mix of sounds and sentiments behind "People Got to Be Free." The CD reissue of this album (originally on Atlantic) has no notes but very good sound. *—Bruce Eder*

Groovin' / Jul. 1967 / Rhino ✦✦✦✦✦

The Rascals move into the era of psychedelia with a vengeance on this album—their best of their entire history—which also retains a soulful core and adds a bit of a Latin beat. The original album on Atlantic was a monster seller thanks to the title track, practically the group's signature tune (number one on the pop charts, number three on R&B), but "Groovin'" was only one small strong point on the album of the same name. "Find Somebody" marked a return to the group's garage band sound with a psychedelic twist, including phased fuzztone guitars and some catchy lyrics and choruses. "How Can I Be Sure" is the second-best-known song off of this album, but it has a fully successful companion piece, "I'm So Happy Now," which applies similar instrumentation to very different (but pleasing) effect. Gene Cornish's "I Don't Love You Anymore" could be the finest pop song in the band's repertory apart from "How Can I Be Sure," with a delectable guitar part, scrumptious melody, and delicious chorus. "You Better Run" was more than a year old when it turned up on this album, and its garage band sensibilities are a bit more primitive than those of "Find Somebody," but it's a great piece of rock & roll. The band turns in one superb Motown cover, "A Place in the Sun," done in a surprisingly subdued fashion. And for a finale, Cavaliere and Brigati turn in an exultant period piece, "It's Love," whose soaring lyrics are matched by guest artist Hubert Laws' flute—alas, his presence would point the way toward less effective, more disjointed work in the group's future, as they moved more deeply into psychedelia. *—Bruce Eder*

Once Upon a Dream / 1968 / Rhino ✦✦✦

This is a welcomed reissue in Atlantic's Original Sound series, with souped-up audio and a neat reproduction of the original gatefold jacket. It's also a little flawed—only 11 tracks indexed while the jacket says 14. *Once Upon a Dream* is a fascinating record, capturing the Rascals in transition from white soul band to progressive jazz-blues-rock fusion outfit. Working amid the psychedelia flourishes of the post-*Sgt. Pepper* era, this is the Rascals at their most ornate, backed by flautist Hubert Laws, saxman legend King Curtis, and trumpet player Mel Lastie and a string orchestra. "Rainy Day"'s outro, with its mention of peace and love, is the dead giveaway about where the band was heading—luckily, the soulful "Please Love Me" and "It's Wonderful" follow immediately, retaining the toughness and drive of their earlier work; and Felix Cavaliere's "Singin' the Blues Too Long" marks the peak of the band's blues experiments, as well as a compelling foray into jazz, five minutes of surging trumpet and sax, soulful choruses, and searing guitar from the composer/singer. Gene Cornish's "I'm Gonna Love You" is one of the group's strangest tracks up to that time, a mixture of soul and marching band, no less. Not everything here works, by a longshot—the gentle, trippy, sitar-laden "Sattva" is one of the silliest things the band had recorded up to that time; "My Hawaii" is a boring interlude, and the title song is too self-consciously pretty and profound. Those flaws aside, however, *Once Upon a Dream* marked the end of an era, the last Rascals album that could be absorbed casually, without any demanding pretensions or larger messages. *—Bruce Eder*

Freedom Suite / 1969 / Rhino ✦✦✦

Released in 1969 as a two-record set, *Freedom Suite* showcases the Rascals' hitmaking strengths, but also reveals the weaknesses which prevented the group from becoming more than a singles-oriented band. There are three soulful hit singles included here: the megahit, "People Got to Be Free," which had gone to number one the previous year; its follow-up, "A Ray of Hope," a powerful tribute to Dr. Martin Luther King; and Felix Cavaliere's statement of faith and hopefulness, "Heaven," a minor hit. However, most of the other songs were considerably more lightweight than that triumvirate, and the entire second record consisted of three meandering instrumental jams. Nonetheless, the lyrics on this album provide an interesting historical documentation of the optimistic "we can change the world" feel of the era in which it was made. *—Jim Newsom*

See / Dec. 1969 / Atlantic ✦✦✦

Felix Cavaliere continued his search for meaning and relevance with this release. The title cut, a track that rocked harder than anything the band had done since its early days, featured distorted electric piano pounding under Cavaliere's optimistic "love's the only thing I see" lyrics. That track and the gospel rave-up "Carry Me Back" were the band's last Top 30 single releases. Although the album didn't do much on the charts, *See* contains some interesting music. "Nubia" has a nice jazz feel and an airy Hubert Laws flute solo; several songs mine the gospel vein; and the band's cover of "Temptation's Bout to Get Me" will take any jaded baby boomer back to a slow dance on a sawdust-covered high school gym floor. *—Jim Newsom*

Peaceful World / 1971 / Sundazed ✦✦✦✦

Peaceful World is a wonderful blend of soul, jazz, and funk that never found an audience. Perhaps it was because the positive sentiments expressed in the lyrics were unfortunately becoming passé; perhaps it was the diversity of the two-record set itself. Despite its lack of commercial success, this was an artistic triumph for Felix Cavaliere. With a supporting cast including jazz luminaries Joe Farrell, Hubert Laws, Alice Coltrane, and Ron Carter, Cavaliere creates a musical vision of the *Peaceful World* conjured up by the album's title. The single, "Love Me," which barely cracked the Hot 100, is a piece of funk in a Sly Stone vein. Guitarist Buzz Feiten's "In and Out of Love" is one of those shoulda-been-a-hit-single songs. Many of the tracks, including the side-long (21:25) title track, are mellow jazz excursions. This ambitious album took the Rascals to the place Cavaliere had been headed over the course of the last couple of albums—but, sadly, the fans didn't follow. *—Jim Newsom*

The Ultimate Rascals / 1986 / Warner Brothers ✦✦✦✦

A wonderful collection of songs, most of which were major hits for this quartet, *The Ultimate Rascals* was one of the early compilations released when compact discs were still fairly young. As such, the tapes from which this recording was mastered were obviously not first generation, with the resulting subpar sound the disc's only weakness. But, oh, the music: a cornucopia for any baby boomer weaned on AM radio in the mid- to late '60s. The band's development is traced here from the early rock & roll sides, like "Good Lovin'" and "You Better Run," through the blue-eyed soul era of "Groovin'" and "A Girl Like You," to the band's social relevance period, exemplified by "People Got to Be Free" and "A Ray of Hope." During their peak period from 1966-69, the Rascals cranked out a batch of popular hit singles, and all are here, along with some of their better album cuts. This is the disc that many fans rushed to buy when they first acquired CD players, and it's still a good place to start for the uninitiated. For the true fan, however, the two-disc anthology released in the early '90s is much better. *—Jim Newsom*

In Retrospect / 1986 / Raven ✦✦✦✦

A good 20-song greatest-hits compilation, focusing solely on their '60s work, augmented by fine liner notes. Since its appearance, Rhino has come out with greatest-hits collections that are more extensive and much more readily available than this import. *—Richie Unterberger*

Anthology (1965-1972) / Jul. 14, 1992 / Rhino ✦✦✦✦✦
Boasting all of the Rascals' essential hits as well as many enjoyable album tracks, this two-CD set does a fine job of summarizing the New Yorkers' accomplishments. Whether the Rascals are tearing into rockers like "You Better Run" (covered by Pat Benatar in 1980) and the Olympics' "Good Lovin'" (a frat-rock staple) or expressing their love of soul music (both Northern and Southern) on "Groovin'," "A Beautiful Morning" and "I've Been Lonely Too Long," the package shows us just how dynamic they could be. The Rascals' cover of Wilson Pickett's "In the Midnight Hour" is hard to resist, and it should be noted that their version of Sir Mac Rice's "Mustang Silly" was recorded before the song became a major hit for Pickett. Sadly, things broke down for the Rascals commercially in the early 1970s, but the socially aware soul-pop songs "Love Me," "Saga of New York" and "Brother Tree" show that they still had some creative life left in them. And they indicate that with the right guidance and input (working with someone like Curtis Mayfield, maybe?), the band could have made a comeback and become an important part of the '70s soul-pop scene. From obvious choices to surprises, *Anthology: 1965-72* is a package that both rock and soul aficionados should savor. *—Alex Henderson*

● **The Very Best of the Rascals** / 1994 / Rhino ✦✦✦✦✦
Although Rhino issued a deluxe two-CD set covering the Rascals a few years ago, this single disc set contains enough essential songs for you to get the point. The Rascals, along with the Righteous Brothers, defined blue-eyed soul singing, making records that were as churchy, earthy, and convincing as anything that came out of the South or Motown in the '60s, backed by tight, anthemic arrangements and excellent combo playing. The 16 cuts include their first hit, "I Ain't Gonna Eat Out My Heart Anymore," and continue on into their flirtation with psychedelia in 1970. The only quibble is their failure to include "Look Around," a socio-political cut from the *Freedom Suite* album that's just a cut below "People Got to Be Free" or "A Ray of Hope." *—Ron Wynn*

All I Really Need: The Complete Atlantic Recordings / Oct. 17, 2000 / Rhino Handmade ✦✦✦✦✦

The Raspberries

f. 1970, Mentor, OH, **db.** 1975
Pop/Rock, Power Pop
The Raspberries cut through the epic pretensions and pomposity of '70s-era rock to proudly reclaim the spirit and simplicity of classic pop, recalling the heyday of the British Invasion with their exquisitely crafted melodies and achingly gorgeous harmonies, not to mention their short hair and matching suits. The group was formed in Mentor, OH, in early 1970 by singer/songwriter Eric Carmen and drummer Jim Bonfanti; guitarist Wally Bryson and bassist John Aleksic completed the original lineup; Aleksic left in March 1971, and with the addition of rhythm guitarist Dave Smalley, Carmen assumed bass duties. In the wake of a major label bidding war, the band signed to Capitol, issuing their self-titled debut LP in the spring of 1972. The second single, "Go All the Way," sold over a million copies on its way to cracking the Top Five. 1972's *Fresh* generated two more hits, "I Wanna Be With You" and the beautiful "Let's Pretend," and solidified the band's stature as critical favorites. Nevertheless, tensions within the ranks—sparked largely by Carmen's creative primacy and the shadow it cast over the songwriting contributions of Bryson and Smalley—were beginning to boil over, and accordingly 1973's *Side 3* boasted a more aggressive sound than its predecessors. *Side 3* failed even to crack the Top 100, however, and both Smalley and Bonfanti exited the Raspberries to form their own band. 1974's acclaimed *Starting Over* continued the harder-edged approach of *Side 3*, yielding the band's final chart smash, the superb "Overnight Sensation (Hit Record)." A nasty post-gig confrontation between Carmen and Bryson soon resulted in the latter's departure, and the Raspberries disbanded in 1975. Carmen mounted a sometimes-successful solo career; Bryson, meanwhile, joined the power pop group Fotomaker for three albums during the late '70s. *—Jason Ankeny*

Raspberries / 1972 / Capitol ✦✦✦✦
An excellent first effort, highlighted by "Go All the Way," "Don't Want to Say Goodbye," "I Saw the Light," and "Come Around and See Me." At the time, audiences thought they heard echoes of Paul McCartney's work with the Beatles, and they weren't far wrong, in terms of what the group was capable of. *—Bruce Eder*

Fresh / Dec. 1972 / Capitol ✦✦✦✦
The second best of the four albums issued by the band, with "I Wanna Be with You," "If You Change Your Mind," and "Drivin' Around" as highlights amid some overall incredibly superb rock craftsmanship. The band's sound overall is more confident, and more powerful. *—Bruce Eder*

Side Three / 1973 / Capitol ✦✦✦✦
One of the group's most accomplished albums, almost Beatles-like in its richness, romanticism, cleverness, and even its packaging, which is one of the few "novelty" jacket designs (it's shaped like a basket of ... you guessed it) that works. The band was at its peak and it showed in "Ecstacy" and "Last Dance," among numerous others. *—Bruce Eder*

Starting Over / 1974 / Capitol ✦✦✦
The band's last album is something of a disappointment, much louder and punchier than their previous work but lacking the elegance that characterized their overall sound. None of the songs is bad, and some are quite good, but they sound like they're going through the motions at this point, and they did break up soon after. *—Bruce Eder*

★ **Capitol Collectors Series** / Feb. 26, 1991 / Capitol ✦✦✦✦✦
Intermixing singles with the band's best accompanying album tracks, this 20-song retro-

spective gives a good overall impression of the Raspberries' strengths across their two years of recording, as well as hints of some weaknesses in the way they were represented on record. As expected, Eric Carmen is the dominant songwriter, but Wally Bryson and David Smalley also show up with "Last Dance" and "Hard to Get Over a Heartbreak," respectively, along with Scott McCarl ("Rose Coloured Glasses"), to give a hint of the range of composing talent in the band in its different phases. It's astonishing how many of their LP cuts would have made superb singles in their own right. It's clear listening to this collection that, between the record company's apparent inability to market their material to its fullest potential and the group's fear of sounding too English, that some killer tracks, like "Nobody Knows" with appealing hooks, a great beat, and overflowing with melodic teen angst, and "Hard to Get Over a Heartbreak," were overlooked as potential singles. Of course, the disputes over songwriting and the matter of who was represented on their singles (and where, the A- or B-side) were among the factors that helped kill the Raspberries after only a couple of years. This collection delineates a lot of the problems in the course of presenting the group's triumphs. An unusual amount of care has been taken in assembling the songs—they all sound better than the original records, and the hotter single mix of "Overnight Sensation" graces this disc. A serious fan may well want to own CDs of the group's complete albums (available on RPM Records on two CDs), but this is one time that Capitol Records did right by one of its own acts. *—Bruce Eder*

Greatest Hits [1995] / Aug. 1, 1995 / Capitol ✦✦✦✦
Although it isn't as comprehensive as *Capitol Collectors Series*, *Greatest Hits* is a terrific overview of the Raspberries' best songs, containing all of their hits—"Go All the Way," "I Wanna Be With You," "Let's Pretend," "Tonight," "Overnight Sensation (Hit Record)"—plus selected album tracks and lesser-known singles. Even though it does have fewer songs than its predecessor, it contains everything a casual fan will need. *—Stephen Thomas Erlewine*

Power Pop, Vol. 1 / 1996 / RPM ✦✦✦✦✦
Featuring the hit singles "Go All the Way," "Don't Want to Say Goodbye," "I Wanna Be with You," and "Let's Pretend," *Power Pop, Vol. 1* combines the Raspberries' first two albums—*Raspberries* and *Fresh Raspberries*—onto one compact disc. *—Stephen Thomas Erlewine*

Power Pop, Vol. 2 / 1996 / RPM ✦✦✦✦
Featuring the hit singles "Tonight," "I'm a Rocker" and "Overnight Sensation (Hit Record)," *Power Pop, Vol. 2* combines the Raspberries' last two albums—*Side Three* and *Starting Over*—on one compact disc. *—Stephen Thomas Erlewine*

● **Greatest Hits [Expanded]** / Jan. 25, 2000 / Capitol ✦✦✦✦✦
Scheduled for release in early 2000, the expanded version of the Raspberries' *Greatest Hits* was pressed up and even circulated in limited numbers—but it was never quite officially released. This was a major disappointment to the legions of the Raspberries' faithful, since it was slated to include demos and rarities, two things that weren't found in the Raspberries' collection. As such, this collection is highly prized by the faithful, and perhaps someday Capitol will be able to issue it widely, since it not only has those sought-after rarities, it is also an excellent overview of the Raspberries' best work. *—Stephen Thomas Erlewine*

The Rationals

f. 1964, Ann Arbor, MI, **db.** 1970
Detroit Rock, Blue-Eyed Soul, Garage Rock, Rock & Roll
When serious collectors compose lists of the top shoulda-been-bigger bands of the '60s, the Rationals are often among them. Coming out of the same Ann Arbor, MI scene that gave birth to the MC5 and the Stooges, the Rationals' forte was a sort of garageish take on blue-eyed soul, built around the fine R&B-hued vocals of frontman Scott Morgan. Their mid-'60s singles, however, didn't break in many areas outside of Michigan (where they had some big local hits), and by the time they got to record an album, they had long passed their peak.

The Rationals actually predated the MC5/Stooges by quite some time, both chronologically and stylistically. When they began recording for the local A2 label in 1965, they were, like many garage bands, heavily influenced by the British Invasion, although they gave their material a more soulful flavor than most similar units. "Gave My Love" was a chart-topper in Ann Arbor (and a hit in Detroit), as was a follow-up single of "Respect" (which predated Aretha Franklin's version). Picked up for national distribution by Cameo/Parkway, it nudged into the lowest regions of the national charts as well.

Similar distribution of follow-up singles by Cameo and Capitol, which found them pursuing a more blue-eyed soul-oriented direction on cuts like "I Need You" and "Hold on Baby," followed the same story: big success in Michigan, nothing doing elsewhere. Morgan turned down a spot in Blood, Sweat & Tears, and the Rationals finally got an album out on Crewe in early 1970. By that time, though, their moment had passed: their best work was behind them, and attempts to modify their energetic pop/soul approach for the psychedelic album market were ill-fated.

The Rationals broke up in the summer of 1970. Morgan continued to build his cult credentials over the next 25 years on sporadic recordings with Sonic's Rendezvous Band (which also featured the MC5's Fred Smith), the Scott Morgan Band, and Scot's Pirates. Licensing hurdles, unfortunately, have prevented this batch of fine '60s singles for A2, Cameo/Parkway, and Capitol from being reissued on a coherent anthology, although some have dotted obscure garage compilations. This is a shame, as their sole album, and a recently released live CD of a show from late 1968, are unrepresentative of the band as they sounded at their best. *—Richie Unterberger*

The Rationals / 1970 / Crewe ✦✦✦
On their sole, belated long-playing effort, the group tempered their spunky blue-eyed

soul with more laid-back influences from late '60s psychedelia and progressive rock. It's not bad, just not typical of what they were most known for, and not in the same league as their prime stuff. —*Richie Unterberger*

Tempation 'bout to Get Me / 1995 / Total Energy ✦✦
Recorded live at Detroit's Grande Ballroom in November 1968, this finds the group using a much heavier hard/blues rock approach than they took on their singles, concentrating on blues/R&B covers. It has its use as a document of where they were at during this era, but it's not the band at their best, and the performances are kind of sloppy. What truly relegates this to souvenir territory is the murky sound (especially the fuzzy vocals), which is about on the level with the average '60s live bootleg. —*Richie Unterberger*

● **The Rationals** / 1998 / Flash ✦✦✦✦✦
At a glance this looks like a CD reissue of their 1970 Crewe LP, and the first nine of the 21 tracks present that album in its entirety. However, this disc is actually a career retrospective, adding a dozen bonus cuts from the mid- and late 1960s from non-LP singles and outtakes. This is almost certainly an unauthorized compilation, given that it assembles tracks from several labels, and that the bonus cuts have obviously been mastered from vinyl (although the tracks from the LP sound very clear and good). In a sense, this is a botched opportunity: the extra material encompasses much, but not all, of the songs from their highly desirable (and rare) '60s singles, and thus cannot be considered the final word on this group's legacy. Nonetheless, it's great to have this stuff available on reissue at long last, as the bonus material does include the superb, Beatlesque "Feelin' Lost" and "Little Girls Cry" singles, the hard R&B of "Leavin' Here" and "Sing!," and their white soul ballad "I Need You," not to mention the outtake "Poor Dog." —*Richie Unterberger*

Ratt

f. 1983, db. 1992
Album Rock, Hair Metal, Heavy Metal, Hard Rock, Pop-Metal
Ratt's brash, melodic heavy metal made the Los Angeles quintet one of the most popular rock acts of the mid-'80s. The group had its origins in the '70s group Mickey Ratt, which had evolved into Ratt by 1983; at that time the band featured vocalist Stephen Pearcy, guitarist Robbin Crosby, guitarist Warren DeMartini, bassist Juan Croucier, and drummer Bobby Blotzer. The band released their self-titled first album independently in 1983, which led to a major-label contract with Atlantic Records. Their first album under this deal, 1984's *Out of the Cellar*, was a major success, reaching the American Top Ten and selling over three million copies. "Round and Round," the first single drawn from the album, hit number 12, proving the band had pop crossover potential. While their second album, 1985's *Invasion of Your Privacy*, didn't match the multi-platinum figures of *Out of the Cellar*, it also reached the Top Ten and sold over a million copies. By that time, the band could sell out concerts across the country and were a staple on MTV and AOR radio. Both *Dancin' Undercover* (1986) and *Reach for the Sky* (1988) continued the band's platinum streak and their audience had only slipped slightly by the time of their final album, 1990's *Detonator*. In 1992, Pearcy left Ratt to form his own band, Arcade, issuing a pair of releases before forming another new band, Vertex. With their brand of glam metal out of step with the then-burgeoning alt-rock movement, Ratt decided to sit out much of the '90s. But by the late '90s, the public's interest in '80s rock began to perk up, leading to Ratt reuniting in time for 1997's *Collage.* —*Stephen Thomas Erlewine & Greg Prato*

Ratt [EP] / 1983 / Atlantic ✦✦✦
Many fans consider Ratt's self-titled debut EP to be the band's best, largely because its shoestring production values give the L.A. quintet's streetwise metal a gut-level energy that was lost in the group's more glossy later albums. Features an early version of "Back For More," and a cover of Aerosmith's "Walkin' the Dog." —*Andy Hinds*

Out of the Cellar / 1984 / Atlantic ✦✦✦✦✦
Ratt emerged from the early '80s pop metal scene combining the prevalent Van Halen and Aerosmith elements with the staccato guitar-picking style of Judas Priest. After a well-received, self-titled independent EP, the band signed with Atlantic Records in 1984 and recorded what would be their most successful album *Out of the Cellar*. Scoring a huge radio and MTV hit with "Round and Round," the record was very consistent and also spawned minor hits with "Wanted Man," "Back for More" and the excellent "I'm Insane." —*Ed Rivadavia*

Invasion of Your Privacy / 1985 / Atlantic ✦✦✦✦
Released in 1985, Ratt's second album *Invasion of Your Privacy* contained all the ingredients which helped launch the band to MTV and radio success: another batch of solid pop metal tunes and a half-naked model on the cover. Though singer Stephen Pearcy's limited range becomes more obvious, guitarist Warren DeMartini truly shines, as does drummer Bobby Blotzer. "You're in Love" is the obvious stand-out and strong cuts such as "Give It All," "Between the Eyes" and "Lay it Down" keep things interesting without quite repeating the consistency of the band's debut. —*Ed Rivadavia*

Dancin' Undercover / 1986 / Atlantic ✦✦✦
L.A. pop metal merchants Ratt knew better than to mess with a successful formula, following up their first two multi-platinum albums with 1986's *Dancing Undercover.* Unfortunately, this lack of growth also trapped the band in a creative corner which would eventually lead to their demise a few years later. Still, with strong singles such as "Slip of the Lip," "Dance," and "Body Talk," leading the way, *Dancing Undercover* achieved platinum sales. —*Ed Rivadavia*

Reach for the Sky / 1988 / Atlantic ✦✦✦

Detonator / 1990 / Atlantic ✦✦✦

● **Ratt & Roll 81-91** / Sep. 1991 / Atlantic ✦✦✦✦✦
A terrific and comprehensive overview of Ratt's entire career, *Ratt & Roll 81-91* contains

19 tracks, including all of the group's hits ("Round and Round," "Wanted Man," "Lay It Down," "You're in Love," "Dance," "Way Cool Jr."), as well as all the best album tracks from their frequently uneven records. In other words, it's a definitive package, containing everything that anyone but hardcore fans could ever need. —*Stephen Thomas Erlewine*

Collage / Jul. 22, 1997 / D-Rock ✦✦✦

Ratt / Jul. 6, 1999 / Portrait ✦✦

Lou Rawls (Louis Allen Rawls)

b. Dec. 1, 1935, Chicago, IL
Vocals / Vocal Jazz, Philly Soul, R&B, Soul
When Chicago-born Lou Rawls croons a soulful love song, his deep-hued pipes rumble with simmering passion. Rawls did the usual gospel apprenticeship before breaking out on a landmark jazz album with pianist Les McCann's trio for Capitol that launched his secular career. But it took Rawls a while to establish himself as a soul artist—perhaps he was perceived as a little too sophisticated and jazzy (although his uncredited responses on Sam Cooke's "Bring It on Home to Me" certainly proved he could wail). "Love Is a Hurtin' Thing" instantly changed that notion when it topped the R&B charts in 1966, and the unyielding "Dead End Street" and "Your Good Thing (Is About to End)" perpetuated his success.

After memorably delivering Bobby Hebb's powerful "A Natural Man" in 1971, Rawls joined forces with Philadelphia producers Kenny Gamble and Leon Huff in 1976, emerging with the silky "You'll Never Find Another Love Like Mine," another gigantic R&B and pop smash tailor-made for nattily sweeping across the classiest disco dance floors. The disco era's long gone now, but Rawls maintains elegantly. He's still as cool as cool can be. —*Bill Dahl*

Spotlight on Lou Rawls / Feb. 5, 1962 Jan. 2, -196 / Capitol ✦✦✦
This 18-track compilation isolates his most pop-oriented output for Capitol in the '60s, consisting largely of standards on the order of "St. James Infirmary," "Stormy Weather," and "Willow Weep for Me," often with orchestration. Includes one previously unreleased cut, "When It's Sleepy Time Down South." —*Richie Unterberger*

● **The Best of Lou Rawls: Classic Philadelphia Recordings** / Nov. 24, 1998 / Music Club ✦✦✦✦✦

● **Anthology** / Jun. 6, 2000 / Capitol ✦✦✦✦✦
True, this two-CD compilation of 1962-1970 tracks isn't the most balanced Lou Rawls retrospective, as it favors his early soul output and has nothing from his commercial peak in the late '70s with Philadelphia International. It's also true that if you favor Rawls at his earthiest, you'll likely find this the best Rawls compilation available. Not that Rawls ever got too down 'n' dirty, but these are the songs on which his bluesiest leanings came most to the fore, leavened by various degrees of jazz and pop. His three big Capitol hits ("Love Is a Hurtin' Thing," "Dead End Street," and "Your Good Thing (Is About to End)") are all here, but the 33-song program includes a good many other satisfying outings that most listeners will never have heard. There's the previously unreleased 1962 cover of Sam Cooke's "What Makes the Ending"; the odd soul-jazz reading of "It Was a Very Good Year"; and the first-rate soul of 1967's "You Can Bring Me All Your Heartaches." The somewhat weird "Down Here on the Ground" is soul-pop tinged by disoriented psychedelic allusions in the lyrics about wanting to fly, and a bad-trip swirl of strings; co-written by Lalo Schifrin and folk-pop one-hit wonder Gale Garnett, it was used in the *Cool Hand Luke* movie. It's not all soul; indeed, there are a few smoothies like "Willow Weep for Me" and straight jazz interpretations that are among the less interesting selections. On the other hand, cuts like "Dead End Street" and "Blues Is a Woman" show Rawls to be one of the more talented songwriters of hard-luck blues-soul-jazz tunes, though he penned just a handful of the cuts on this anthology. —*Richie Unterberger*

Chris Rea

b. Mar. 4, 1951, Middlesborough, England
Vocals, Keyboards, Guitar / Album Rock, Singer/Songwriter, Adult Contemporary
British singer and guitarist Chris Rea has enjoyed a run of popularity in Europe during the late '80s and early '90s after almost a decade of previous recording. Rea started out performing with a local group called Magdalene, taking David Coverdale's place; the band won a national talent contest in 1975 as the Beautiful Losers, but still failed to get a record contract. Rea left the band and recorded the album *Whatever Happened to Benny Santini?*, which alluded to a discarded stage name, which went gold on the strength of the U.S. Top 20 hit "Fool (If You Think It's Over)." Rea was not heard from again in the U.S. for some time, concentrating his efforts on his main fan base of Europe. A compilation of tracks from Rea's '80s albums, *New Light Through Old Windows*, was released in 1988 and sold well in the U.K. and Europe and charted in the U.S. Rea followed it up with the critically acclaimed *The Road to Hell*, which many regarded as his best album. It and its follow-up, *Auberge*, went to the top of the U.K. album charts, but did not prove as successful in the U.S., where he has failed to chart with his subsequent releases. —*Steve Huey*

● **The Best of Chris Rea** / 1995 / East West ✦✦✦✦✦
All of the highlights from guitarist/songwriter Chris Rea's moody late-'80s and early-'90s records are collected on *The Best of Chris Rea*. For neophytes and casual fans, this a perfect introduction, though more serious listeners will find plenty to treasure on his original albums. —*Stephen Thomas Erlewine*

The Records

f. 1977, db. 1982
Power Pop, New Wave
The Records are probably best remembered for their cult classic and minor hit, "Starry

Eyes"—a near-perfect song that defined British power pop in the '70s. And while they never quite matched the success of that record, their high-quality output from 1979 to 1982 has not only held up better than most of the era with its timeless appeal, but has also served as a blueprint for the various waves of British and American power-pop since then. Some have gone as far as to call them the "British Big Star," which is probably a fair comparison—within their genre, they're seen as giants, yet the general public has missed them for the most part. The band was formed around 1977, when pub rockers Kursaal Flyers broke up. The drummer from the band, Will Birch, and vocalist/guitarist John Wicks, who had joined the Kursaals in the last stages, began writing together, inspired by the pure-pop tradition of the Raspberries, Badfinger and Big Star. After a series of live gigs, they released their debut, "Starry Eyes," on the independent Record Company label in November the same year. They received some valuable early exposure on the Stiff label's "Be Stiff" tour which led to their signing with Virgin Records. Wicks and Birch continued to churn out should-have-been-hit pop classics over the next three years and three albums—1979's *Shades in Bed* (released in a slightly modified form as *The Records* in the U.S.), 1980's *Crashes* and 1982's *Music on Both Sides*. Aside from a minor hit with "Starry Eyes" in the U.S., their efforts were criminally unrewarded. *—Chris Woodstra*

Shades in Bed / 1979 / Virgin ✦✦✦✦✦
The band's first U.K. LP is a pure pop masterpiece featuring the near-perfect singles "Starry Eyes" and "Teenarama." The album was retitled *The Records* and released in a modified form in America. The first pressings came with a bonus 12" entitled *High Heels*, which featured a collection of four covers. *—Chris Woodstra*

Crashes / 1980 / Virgin ✦✦✦
The Records' second American album is just as tuneful and nearly as catchy as its predecessor, though none of the songs have the punch of "Starry Eyes." "Girl in the Golden Disc" and "Hearts Will Be Broken" are the highlights. Unfortunately, the band's take on the brilliant "Hearts in Her Eyes" (a song written by Will Birch and John Wicks and covered more successfully by the reunited Searchers the previous year) is slightly lackluster and somewhat of a letdown. *—Chris Woodstra*

Music on Both Sides / 1982 / Virgin ✦✦✦
With a tighter, harder-rocking five-man lineup, the Records returned with *Music on Both Sides*. Despite the usual strong material courtesy of the John Wicks/Will Birch partnership, the album failed to make an impact. This would be their last album. *—Chris Woodstra*

● **Smashes Crashes and Near Misses** / 1988 / Virgin ✦✦✦✦✦
The Records may not have been great innovators but they undeniably made some of the best singles of the era. *Smashes, Crashes and Near Misses*, a 20-track collection, is the definitive proof of the band's generally overlooked brilliance. Anyone interested in power-pop should start here. *—Chris Woodstra*

Paying for the Summer of Love / 1990 / Skyclad ✦✦
A collection of demos recorded prior to the first album, *Paying for the Summer of Love* provides an interesting look at the songs in their formative stages but only true fans need to seek this one out. *—Chris Woodstra*

Red Aunts

f. 1991, California
Punk Revival, Indie Rock, Hardcore Punk, Alternative Pop/Rock
The hardcore band Red Aunts formed in 1991; although the group—comprised of vocalists/guitarists Kerry Davis and Terri Wahl, bassist Debi Martini and drummer Lesley Ishino—could barely play their instruments during their first few performances, they soon became a popular West Coast attraction. After signing to the Sympathy for the Record Industry label, the Red Aunts issued their 1994 debut *Drag*, followed a year later by *Bad Motherfucken 40 O-Z*. After a jump to the Epitaph label, the quartet issued *#1 Chicken* in early 1995; *Saltbox* appeared in 1996. *—Jason Ankeny*

Drag / Apr. 25, 1994 / Sympathy for the Record Industry ✦✦✦

● **#1 Chicken** / Mar. 28, 1995 / Epitaph ✦✦✦✦✦
The back cover of the CD proudly proclaims "14 songs, 23 minutes." The Red Aunts' first album for Epitaph Records, true to the punk ethic of this record label, runs like a Ramones record. Once one song is over, another one starts, with the same manic energy of its predecessor. Alienation seems to be a theme on the album, particularly songs like "Krush" and "Hate" (which contains the lyric "I hate everyone but you"). But instead of being angry, the music seems celebratory (particularly "Mota" and the opening track, "Freakathon," which is their standard). Even though the songs seem like blueprint punk, slide guitars and unexpected changes keep the songs from being predictable, which is often a problem with much of the music on the Epitaph label. *—Brian Flota*

Bad Motherfucker 40 O-Z / Apr. 16, 1995 / Sympathy for the Record Industry ✦✦✦
The sophomore release from the queens of scuzz-rock, the Red Aunts, is a dirty affair, and it has every right to be. The quartet stumbles their way through eleven sludgy songs, of which the last two are worth the short wait. Using the Black Flag and Circle Jerks song "Wasted" as a warmup, the Aunts blast through "Smoke," a 20-second song of punk-rock bliss. The album ends with "Monster Truck Muther Fucker," a breakneck-slow bobbin'-head song so guilty with simplicity that it appropriately borrows Johnny Cash's "hello" from the *Johnny Cash at Folsom Prison* album. Their punk rock ethic often results in slight material (like "Batman a Go-Go"), but this album reveals a group growing into a great, immature outfit. *—Brian Flota*

Saltbox / 1996 / Epitaph ✦✦

Ghetto Blaster / Apr. 21, 1998 / Epitaph ✦✦✦✦✦
After the subdued *Saltbox*, the distortion and feedback return as the Red Aunts climb to the peak of their powers on *Ghetto Blaster*. The first track, "I'm Crying," sets the tone, with an explosive feedback-fueled mauling of a guitar with a slide. "The Things You See, The Things You Don't" is probably the catchiest song in their entire repertoire, and this one-chord song is aided with a great melody line played on a cheesy Casio synthesizer. "Exene," which references the influential band X (and singer Exene Cervenka) on their sound, sounds more like a Bikini Kill song with its high-pitched vocals. *Ghetto Blaster* continues to show the Red Aunts growing, further developing their hybrid blend of punk, blues, grunge and country. *—Brian Flota*

The Red Hot Chili Peppers

f. 1983
College Rock, Rap-Rock, Funk Metal, Alternative Pop/Rock
A quartet with varying personnel, anchored by lead singer Anthony Kiedis and bassist Flea (born Michael Balzary), the Red Hot Chili Peppers play a hybrid rock, incorporating punk, funk, rap, and metal. Though the mixture was ahead of its time when the group was first organized in the early '80s in Los Angeles, the music industry has since caught up to it, which earns the group the right to call itself the forerunner of an approach now adopted by such acts as Living Colour and Faith No More, and also means the Peppers themselves have finally hit the big time. They scored a commercial breakthrough with *Mother's Milk*, which went gold after its release in 1989. They ascended to real star status with the release of *Blood Sugar Sex Magik*, which sold two million copies and included the Top Ten hit "Under the Bridge." Although it went platinum and spent nearly a year on the charts, 1995's *One Hot Minute* was ultimately a disappointment, failing to live up to the expectations set by *Blood Sugar Sex Magik*. *—William Ruhlmann*

Red Hot Chili Peppers / 1984 / EMI America ✦✦✦✦
The Red Hot Chili Peppers' debut album sketched out their funk-metal hybrid quite effectively, especially on the warped deep groove of "True Men Don't Kill Coyotes." Even though their fusion of heavy guitars and slapping bass was audacious, their first effort didn't quite gel into a cohesive album. *—Stephen Thomas Erlewine*

Freaky Styley / 1985 / EMI America ✦✦✦✦✦
Long before the Red Hot Chili Peppers became alternative rock darlings via tear-jerking ballads, they were firmly rooted in pure, uncut funk. Of course, their stint as a funk band extended for a very short time, from their inception (showcased on their formative self-titled debut) to their more stylistically varied guitar-orientated efforts (hinted at on *Uplift Mofo* and fully realized on *Mother's Milk*). Of this short era before Anthony Kiedis decided to take a more poetic approach to songwriting, and before Hillel Slovak's unfortunate death, *Freaky Styley* stands as the group's masterpiece. Here, the Peppers seem fully in control of their vision to be accessible successors to '70s P-Funk, laying down a varied collection of quirky songs propelled by Flea's omnipresent bass riffs and Slovak's restrained efforts. Above all, though, much of this album's success from all angles goes to producer George Clinton, perhaps the most inspiring individual the Peppers could have worked with at this point in their career. *Freaky Styley* is the mid-'80s album that Clinton could never make on his own. Where Clinton's '80s albums seemed infused with the right ideas, he never had the seemingly limitless energy that the Peppers employ here. Above all, the Peppers' stunning rendition of Sly Stone's "If You Want Me to Stay" is a testament to just how funky the Peppers were at this point, even if it doesn't quite have the original's soul. Other notable moments include "Jungle Man" and "American Ghost Dance," two tight funk numbers with wonderful choruses. This album probably won't appeal to those weaned on "Under the Bridge" or "Scar Tissue," but it's undeniably a somewhat forgotten cult favorite, particularly to those infatuated with the group's short-lived Slovak era, the group's zenith in terms of quirkiness and funkiness. *—Jason Birchmeier*

The Uplift Mofo Party Plan / 1987 / EMI America ✦✦✦✦
The Chili Peppers created most of the imperfections in their world, especially in the late '80s, and the unusual scenario of four original bandmembers recording together for the first time on that band's third album would tragically prove to be a one-shot deal. Veterans Anthony Kiedis (vocals) and Flea (bass) had welcomed back original guitarist Hillel Slovak for the preceding *Freaky Styley* album after using Jack Sherman on their self-titled 1984 debut, doing the same at this point for original drummer Jack Irons, who replaced Cliff Martinex. The energy of having these four friends from Los Angeles back together jumps out of the opening anthem "Fight Like a Brave" and the experimental "Funky Crime." Kiedis' barking rap delivery drives the cover of Bob Dylan's "Subterranean Homesick Blues," and Flea's ahead-of-their-time slapping bass lines stand out in "Behind the Sun" and "Walkin' on Down the Road," but Slovak and Irons brought things to the Chili Peppers that no one else ever has. The drummer's pounding funk backbeats left a blueprint for his successor, Chad Smith, and the manic intro to "Skinny Sweaty Man" sounds like Buddy Rich playing James Brown material. Slovak is at the height of his powers on the rap-rock reggae "Love Trilogy" and funky "Special Secret Song Inside," which gained some notoriety for its anatomical undertones. But Slovak would die of a heroin overdose the following year, with Irons quitting the band afterward from the depression of the loss, leaving Kiedis and Flea to wonder what might have been. *—Bill Meredith*

Mother's Milk / Aug. 1989 / EMI America ✦✦✦
The Chili Peppers' playing on *Mother's Milk* is more metallic than ever, thanks to newcomers Chad Smith (drums) and especially John Frusciante (guitar). Thanks to their presence, Kiedis and Flea sound reinvigorated in their performances, but the material is inconsistent, with too much of the second half in particular seeming like undeveloped, loud-fast-manic schtick. Still, there are more than enough quality tracks to make the filler

worth sorting through, most obviously the heavy reworking of Stevie Wonder's "Higher Ground" and the cautionary, heartfelt "Knock Me Down," as well as several others scattered over the album. —*Steve Huey*

Blood Sugar Sex Magik / Sep. 1991 / Warner Brothers ✦✦✦✦✦
The Chili Peppers' best album, *Blood Sugar Sex Magik* benefits immensely from Rick Rubin's production—Frusciante's guitar is less overpoweringly noisy, leaving room for differing textures and clearer lines, while the band overall is more focused and less indulgent, even if some of the grooves drag on too long. Lyrically, Kiedis is as preoccupied with sex as ever, whether invoking it as his muse, begging for it, or boasting in great detail about his prowess, best showcased on the infectiously funky singles "Give It Away" and "Suck My Kiss." However, he tempers his testosterone with a more sensitive side, writing about the emotional side of failed relationships ("Breaking the Girl," "I Could Have Lied"), his drug addictions ("Under the Bridge" and an elegy for Hillel Slovak, "My Lovely Man"), and some hippie-ish calls for a peaceful utopia. Three of those last four songs (excluding "My Lovely Man") mark the band's first consistent embrace of lilting acoustic balladry, and while it's not what Kiedis does best as a vocalist, these are some of the album's finest moments, varying and expanding the group's musical and emotional range. Frusciante departed after the supporting tour, leaving *Blood Sugar Sex Magik* as probably the best album the Chili Peppers will ever make. —*Steve Huey*

● **What Hits!?** / Sep. 29, 1992 / EMI America ✦✦✦✦✦
After the Red Hot Chili Peppers left EMI for Warner Bros. and hit the big time with "Under the Bridge," their former label gathered most of the best tracks from the group's first four albums for the compilation *What Hits!?* Since *Blood Sugar Sex Magik*, the Peppers' most popular album, was recorded for Warner, none of its songs are present—with the exception of "Under the Bridge," which was somehow licensed for use. *What Hits!?* does a pretty good job of sifting through the Peppers' uneven discography and picking out the best moments, making it a very useful sampler; it also contains "Show Me Your Soul," the band's contribution to the *Pretty Woman* soundtrack. —*Steve Huey*

Out in L.A. / Nov. 1, 1994 / EMI America ✦✦
One Hot Minute / Sep. 12, 1995 / Warner Brothers ✦✦✦
Following up *Blood Sugar Sex Magik* proved to be a difficult task for the Red Hot Chili Peppers. In 1993, two years after *Blood Sugar*, former Jane's Addiction guitarist Dave Navarro joined up, but it was still another two years before *One Hot Minute* appeared, due to various personal problems. Navarro's metallic guitar shredding should have added some weight to the Chili Peppers' punk-inflected heavy-guitar funk, but tends to make it plodding. By emphasizing the metal, the funk is gradually phased out of the blend, as is melody; the grinding chant of "Warped" is hardly as twisted as anything on *Freaky Styley*, or even "Give It Away." The ballads "My Friends" and "Transcending" are blatant attempts to hold on to the mainstream audience gained by "Under the Bridge," but the melodies are weak and the lyrics are even more feeble. *One Hot Minute* is as musically ambitious as *Blood Sugar Sex Magik*, but is even more unfocused which means it provides the fewest thrills of any of the group's albums. —*Stephen Thomas Erlewine*

Californication / Jun. 8, 1999 / Warner Brothers ✦✦✦✦
Many figured that the Chili Peppers' days of undisputed alternative kings were numbered after their lackluster 1995 release *One Hot Minute*, but like the great phoenix rising from the ashes, this legendary and influential outfit returned back to greatness with 1999's *Californication*. An obvious reason for their rebirth is the reappearance of guitarist John Frusciante (replacing Dave Navarro), who left the Peppers in 1992 and disappeared into a haze of hard drugs before cleaning up and returning to the fold in 1998. Frusciante was a main reason for such past band classics as 1989's *Mother's Milk* and 1991's *BloodSugarSexMagik*, and proves once and for all to be the quintessential RHCP guitarist. Anthony Kiedis' vocals have improved dramatically as well, while the rhythm section of bassist Flea and drummer Chad Smith remains one of rock's best. The quartet's trademark punk-funk can be sampled on such tracks as "Around the World," "I Like Dirt" and "Parallel Universe," but the more pop-oriented material proves to be a pleasant surprise—"Scar Tissue," "Otherside," "Easily" and "Purple Stain" all contain strong melodies and instantly memorable choruses. And like their 1992 introspective hit "Under the Bridge," there are even a few mellow moments—"Porcelain," "Road Trippin'" and the title track. With the instrumentalists' interplay at an all-time telepathic high and Kiedis peaking as a vocalist, *Californication* is a bona fide Chili Peppers classic. It would be a crime for this stellar, definitive lineup to not remain intact the second time around. —*Greg Prato*

Red House Painters

f. 1989, San Francisco, CA
Sadcore, Dream Pop, Indie Rock, Alternative Pop/Rock, Singer/Songwriter
Red House Painters was primarily the vehicle of singer/songwriter Mark Kozelek, an evocative, compelling performer of rare emotional intensity. Like Mark Eitzel of American Music Club, to whose work the Painters were invariably compared and to whom their early success owed a tremendous debt, Kozelek laid his soul bare on record, conjuring harrowingly acute tales of pain, despair and loss; unlike Eitzel, Nick Drake and other poets of decay, Kozelek's autobiographical songs walked their tightrope without a net—forsaking the safety offered by metaphor and allegory, he faced his demons in the first person, creating a singularly haunting body of work unparalleled in its vulnerability and honesty. While performing on the Bay Area club circuit, the quartet came to the attention of American Music Club's Eitzel, who often named Red House Painters his favorite band. Through Eitzel, a demo tape of recordings cut in 1989 and 1990 made their way to the London offices of 4AD Records, which signed the group and in 1992 issued the unvarnished demos—a superb collection of spartan, atmospheric melodies lurking behind Kozelek's ghostly vocals—as the LP *Down Colorful Hill*. In 1993, Red House

Painters emerged from the studio with over two dozen new recordings, which they issued on back-to-back eponymously titled albums. Taken in tandem, the LPs established Kozelek as a unique songwriter capable of conveying stunning emotional depths; compositions like "Grace Cathedral Park," "Katy Song," "Strawberry Hill," "Evil" and "Uncle Joe" expanded greatly upon the emotional palette evidenced on the first record, unflinchingly detailing Kozelek's erratic, abusive nature and troubled background. —*Jason Ankeny*

Down Colorful Hill / Sep. 15, 1992 / 4AD ✦✦✦✦
Not a proper debut as such, *Down Colorful Hill* instead comprises the demo recordings which won Red House Painters their contract with the 4AD label, released here with minimal overdubbing. Regardless, the group has already reached full maturity; these lengthy, ponderous songs are remarkably evocative portraits of a distinctly tortured psyche—Mark Kozelek forgoes the camouflage of metaphor to lay his soul on the line, and the honesty of his craft is both beautiful and disturbing. —*Jason Ankeny*

Red House Painters [I] / May 25, 1993 / 4AD ✦✦✦✦✦
The first of the group's two eponymously titled 1993 efforts is a sprawling, remarkable set distinguished by Mark Kozelek's continuing maturation as a songwriter; far removed from the uniform darkness of *Down Colorful Hill*, *Red House Painters* offers an expansion of both emotional and musical possibilities. Working outward from the cutting "Mistress"—included as both a Spartan piano ballad and as a gauzy rock number—the record moves through a shifting, impressionistic backdrop of textures and sounds; from the luminous folk-pop of "Grace Cathedral Park" to the epic dissonance of the gut-wrenching "Strawberry Hill," the songs resonate with depth and poignancy, and rank as Kozelek's most fully realized collection of compositions. —*Jason Ankeny*

Red House Painters [II] / Sep. 1993 / 4AD ✦✦✦
The second of two self-titled 1993 efforts, this *Red House Painters* collects the remaining tracks from the remarkably fruitful sessions which also launched the earlier, superior album. Far more experimental in nature, it opens with "Evil," an almost painfully slow and withdrawn song which acutely sets the album's haunting, dark tone. While not everything works—the electric version of "New Jersey" pales in comparison to the previous set's acoustic rendition, while the cover of Simon and Garfunkel's "I Am a Rock" is overripe—both the unrequited love song "Bubble" and the dysfunctional "Uncle Joe" rank among Mark Kozelek's most perfectly realized compositions, and the closer, a marvelously downbeat reading of "The Star Spangled Banner," allows the group's often unsung black humor to seep to the surface. —*Jason Ankeny*

● **Ocean Beach** / Mar. 28, 1995 / 4AD ✦✦✦✦✦
Red House Painters has always been Mark Kozelek's project, but *Ocean Beach* represents the first record that is almost entirely a solo project. Not that that distinction has made a great change in the music—*Ocean Beach* is a spare, gentle, nearly painfully introspective folk-rock album that draws more from Simon & Garfunkel than Bob Dylan. Kozelek reigns in the droning, experimental tendencies of the group's first full-length album, yet he is more generous with his melodies and arrangements than the band's second untitled record. While Red House Painters remains very arty and self-conscious, *Ocean Beach* shows the singer/songwriter breaking out of his shell ever so slightly, bringing more fully developed songs and melodies with him. —*Stephen Thomas Erlewine*

Songs for a Blue Guitar / Jul. 23, 1996 / Supreme ✦✦✦
Before *Songs for a Blue Guitar* could appear, the Red House Painters' singer/songwriter/guitarist Mark Kozelek had to leave his old label 4AD (allegedly over a Kozelek solo album 4AD rejected), split up the band, and find a new home for his music on Supreme Recordings. Fortunately for Kozelek and his audience, it's worth all the tumult. This is the solo album Kozelek wanted to make masquerading as a Red House Painters album; no other Painters are listed in the liner notes. The benefits that resulted from his freedom from the group setting are evident on *Songs for a Blue Guitar*. The album compiles a diverse group of styles, including gently hypnotic folk in "Have You Forgotten" and "Trailways," and country-rock, both slow ("Song for a Blue Guitar") and fast ("Make Like Paper"), as well as a various selection of covers. Mixed with Kozelek's traditionally beautiful and sad material, Yes' "Long Distance Runaround," Paul McCartney's "Silly Love Songs," and the Cars' "All Mixed Up" bring light to the Red House Painters' typically shadowy songs. The deep beauty and eclecticism on *Songs for a Blue Guitar* make it another artistic triumph for the Red House Painters. —*Heather Phares*

Retrospective / May 18, 1999 / 4AD ✦✦✦✦
Retrospective collects some of the finest moments from the Red House Painters' albums for 4AD as well as some previously unreleased work. Compiled by Mark Kozelek and Ivo Watts-Russell, this two-CD set features one disc spanning Kozelek's four-album output for the label. Kozelek's cover of Kiss' "Shock Me," which was previously available only on a UK single, opens the first disc; tracks like "Katy Song," "Medicine Bottle," "San Geronimo," "New Jersey," "Mistress," and "Drop" are also included. Demos, outtakes, and live recordings are included on the second disc, including two songs, "Waterkill" and "Instrumental" that were previously unreleased. Alternate versions of Painters favorites like "Japanese to English," "Funhouse," "Dragonflies," and "Brockwell Park" also appear on the second disc, making *Retrospective* an affordable starting point for newcomers, and a welcome addition for collectors. —*Heather Phares*

Old Ramon / Apr. 10, 2001 / Sub Pop ✦✦✦✦
After years on the shelf due to Mark Kozelek's drawn-out problems with Supreme and Island, the Red House Painters' long-awaited *Old Ramon* finally saw the light of day, thanks to Sub Pop. As it stands, the label needed Kozelek as much as he needed them—after a few years' worth of disappointing releases from garage rock revivalists, *Old Ramon* broke Sub Pop's losing streak. Ironically, the album's long-delayed release only

made its joyous sound that much more refreshing; its inviting mix of gentle and fuzzy guitars and Kozelek's empathetic vocals make it the Painters' most hopeful, accessible work. Though one of *Old Ramon*'s finest songs, "Find Me, Reuben Olivares," ended up on the *Shanti Project Collection*, the remaining ten songs are first-rate expressions of Kozelek's thoughtful songcraft and guitar work. Beginning with "Wop-A-Din-Din," a chiming, charming tribute to Kozelek's cat, the album signals a lighter, freer approach than one might expect from the often-brooding Painters. Even slow, wistful numbers like "Smokey," "Cruiser," and "Void" sound downright sunny in comparison to Kozelek's early work. Though *Old Ramon* keeps the polish of later Red House Painters albums like *Songs for a Blue Guitar*, the album has an added immediacy and vitality, particularly on surprisingly poppy tracks like "Byrd Joel," a winning blend of folk and fuzz, and "Between Days," which features some of the most luscious-sounding guitars ever heard on a Red House Painters song. The gently whimsical love song "Kavita" provides a happy ending to an album whose difficult story definitely deserves one. But in spite of the trouble surrounding it, *Old Ramon* is a surprisingly comfortable sounding album, as if its long delay was intended to let its songs mellow and ripen with time, making the long wait for it all the more worthwhile. *—Heather Phares*

The Red Krayola

f. 1966, Houston, TX

Experimental Rock, Indie Rock, Post-Punk, Experimental, Psychedelic, Prog-Rock/Art Rock

One of the longest-lived underground rock groups (if not *the* longest-lived), the Red Krayola lasted through the birth pangs of psychedelia past the death throes of post-punk. The one constant in its ever-shifting lineup was principal singer/songwriter/visionary Mayo Thompson, who seemed as concerned with deconstructing the language of "rock" music as with actually expressing himself within it. That made Red Krayola's catalog challenging, often difficult listening. Its saving grace was the quirky charm of Thompson's songs and vocals, with a whimsical humor and open-mindedness rather atypical of avant-rock. The Red Krayola, initially spelled Red Crayola, were formed in Houston as a trio in 1966. But by the late '60s the Krayola had disbanded, partially due to disputes with their label. They were unexpectedly resurrected in the late '70s, however. Thompson had moved to England, where he found that the old Red Krayola recordings enjoyed a cult among hip listeners. Thompson was never a champion of hippie ideals, and he was able to make the transition into the punk era effectively. Red Krayola's releases on underground European labels like Rough Trade and Recommended presented an ensemble that dove into the heart of post-punk, with skronky guitars and horns, and disjointed, arty song structures. Thompson joined Pere Ubu for a while in the early '80s. He always kept the Red Krayola going, however, although most of their releases went all but unheard in the U.S., as they were only available as obscure European indie imports. The situation changed to some degree in the mid-'90s, when the Krayola landed a U.S. deal with Drag City. Albums such as *The Red Krayola* (1994), *Coconut Hotel* (1995), *Hazel* (1996), and *Fingerpainting* (1999) were still resolutely uncommercial, but the material was nonetheless more approachable for adventurous listeners who shied away from full-throttle avant-rock. *—Richie Unterberger*

Parable of Arable Land / 1967 / Collectables ✦✦✦

The Red Krayola's debut remains their most celebrated/notorious effort. Although this was categorized as psychedelia when first released, it's more like futuristic avant-noise-rock. Thompson's flighty songs about hurricane fighter planes and transparent radiation are almost submerged by a cacophony of "free-form freakout" noise created on kazoos, flutes, harmonica, hammer, jugs, bottles, sticks, and more by a large ensemble of friends dubbed the Familiar Ugly. My minority opinion holds that the wistfulness of Thompson's tunes (the brittle "War Sucks" excepted) and voice may have been served better by less self-consciously far-out arrangements. (Several of the songs can be heard in more skeletal form on the *Epitaph for a Legend* compilation). It's quite a daring statement for its day, however, with instrumental cameos by Roky Erickson on a couple of tracks. *—Richie Unterberger*

Coconut Hotel / 1967 / Drag City ✦✦

As strange as the Red Krayola's debut album was, their proposed follow-up, *Coconut Hotel*, was far stranger. This all-instrumental recording was more appropriately classified as twentieth-century avant-garde music than rock, and was rejected by International Artists for release in 1967, finally seeing the light of day on Drag City in 1995. All power to the Krayola for doing things their own way, but it's not hard to understand International Artists' reasoning. This has so little commercial potential that it makes Zappa's *Lumpy Gravy* sound like AM radio fodder. Dissonant exotic plucked strings, spooky organ clusters, 36 (yes, 36) "One-Second Pieces"—these are not tunes that you can hum, by any stretch of the imagination. Some acoustic guitar pieces bear the influence of John Fahey (with whom the Krayola recorded some unreleased material around this time). It's totally uncompromising, and rather wearisome, to be honest. It's like nothing else that nominally "rock" groups were doing in 1967, but it's not nearly as interesting as their official releases from the late '60s, which had at least a few loose ties to conventional song structures. *—Richie Unterberger*

● **God Bless the Red Krayola & All Who Sail with It** / 1968 / International Artist ✦✦✦✦✦

A far gentler, though equally quirky, album as their maiden effort. The Krayola's second record was a series of odd miniatures that, though far more restrained than *Parable of Arable Land*, was a much more solid indication of the direction Mayo Thompson would explore over the next few decades. These are less "songs" than stream-of-consciousness fragments. Thompson's wavering, quizzical voice intones disjointed but evocative lyrics that may appear to be non sequiturs. Odd time meters and musical shifts do their best to defy conventional rock song structures. It's not very poppy, no, but if the description sounds foreboding, be assured that as experimental rock goes, it's far warmer and friendlier than the norm. *—Richie Unterberger*

The Red Krayola / Sep. 20, 1994 / Drag City ✦✦✦

Now working with such younger musicians as John McEntire (Tortoise), Jim O'Rourke, and David Grubbs, Mayo Thompson comfortably steers the Red Krayola into the mishmash of '90s post-punkdom here. For Thompson, it's not so much a return to the scene (he had always kept recording, after all) as a continuation of his themes of musical eclecticism. It's heavy on the angular guitar lines and unusual lyrical construction/deconstruction, with occasional electronic flutters. It's not as highly recommended as his two subsequent Drag City releaes (*Amor and Language* and *Hazel*), which state the same thematic concerns with a tad more melodicism and warmth. *—Richie Unterberger*

Hazel / Nov. 19, 1996 / Drag City ✦✦✦

Mayo Thompson has expressed bemusement at the constant categorization of his work as "quirky." *Hazel*, however, will do nothing to stem the tide of that adjective showing up in reviews such as this one. The Red Krayola do not seem interested nearly as much in connecting disparate styles as jumbling them. So you'll hear a languid, Lou Reedish drone segue into a John Faheyish guitar pattern backed by weird female vocals, and then a light reggaeish thing about Christian soldiers marching onward. The lyrics are not constructed to make a point, but to reflect the rhythm and fragmented patterns of everyday thought and conversation. It's interesting, but too nonchalantly strange to evoke a passionate response. *—Richie Unterberger*

Fingerpainting / Jun. 8, 1999 / Drag City ✦✦✦

The ever-changing, ever-challenging Red Krayola return with 1999's *Fingerpainting*. Head Krayola Mayo Thompson returns with an eclectic supporting crew, including fellow Drag City artists David Grubbs and Stephen Prina, along with other regular Krayolas like George Hurley and Frederick Barthelme. The 11-piece Red Krayola turns out 12 new works like "Bad Medicine," "There There Betty Betty" and "Vile Grass," which play with noise, creative arrangements and vocalizing, shaping these elements into ambitious instrumentals and whimsical songs that graze pop's fringe. *—Heather Phares*

Redd Kross

f. 1980, Hawthorne, CA

Power Pop, Alternative Pop/Rock, Punk-Pop, American Underground

Inspired as much by breakfast cereal and kiddie TV as by rock music, the punk-pop cult band Redd Kross was the brainchild of Steve and Jeff McDonald, brothers from the Los Angeles suburb of Hawthorne (also home of the Beach Boys) who began playing music together before either had hit puberty. Fueled by a series of dubious visits to famed area rock clubs like the Roxy and the Whiskey-a-Go-Go, they formed their first band, the Tourists, in 1978; Jeff, then 15, handled vocal duties while Steve, 11, took up the bass. After rounding out the group with schoolmates Greg Hetson on guitar and Ron Reyes on drums, the Tourists played their first gig, opening for Black Flag. Following a name change to Red Cross, they issued their self-titled EP debut in 1980. After the departure of Hetson and Reyes (for the Circle Jerks and Black Flag, respectively), the McDonalds enlisted a revolving line-up of underground musicians for their full-length follow-up, 1981's *Born Innocent*. Following the album's release, the band was threatened with a lawsuit from the real International Red Cross; as a result, they became Redd Kross, and returned in 1984 with *Teen Babes From Monsanto*, a collection of covers of artists ranging from David Bowie to the Rolling Stones and the Shangri-Las. Complete with new guitarist Robert Hecker and drummer Roy McDonald (no relation) 1987's *Neurotica* appeared primed to push the band out of the underground; shortly after the album's release, however, their label, Big Time, folded, and legal hassles prevented Redd Kross from recording any new material under its own name for three years, recording instead as the Tater Totz and Anarchy 6. Finally, in 1990 Redd Kross landed a deal with Atlantic, issuing the surprisingly straighforward *Third Eye*. *—Jason Ankeny*

Born Innocent / 1981 / Frontier ✦✦✦

Originally issued in 1982, *Born Innocent* was the debut full-length release from Redd Kross, a band of suburban L.A. youth fronted by brothers Jeff (guitar, vocals) and Steve McDonald (bass). Aged 18 and 14, respectively, the aspiring punks are aided and abetted here by rhythm guitarist Tracy Lee and drummers Janet Housden and John Stielow as they attack these 16 songs with all the patience of over-stimulated teens and all the subtlety of a slasher flick. The average song length falls below the two-minute mark, during which time Jeff McDonald's whine is rarely coherent above the clamor of his band's brutal rock assault. The punk negation of titles like "Kill Someone You Hate," "Look up at the Bottom," and "Notes and Chords Mean Nothing to Me" couldn't be more appropriate descriptions for this music. "Solid Gold" is a slice of dislocated blues while "St. Lita Ford Blues" disintegrates from a stop-start punk party (complete with jubilant screams) to a raucous three-chord blur. Included for good measure are tributes to both actress Linda Blair ("Linda Blair") and serial killer Charles Manson ("Charlie" and a cover of Manson's own "Cease to Exist"). Though subsequent releases found Redd Kross cleaning up their act, this debut captures them in all their youthful glory; documenting the sound of the McDonalds and company unleashed on an unsuspecting set of guitars, bass, and drums. *—Nathan Bush*

Teen Babes from Monsanto / 1984 / Enigma ✦✦✦✦✦

The title says it all. Speedy, sloppy pop loaded with fuzzed-up guitars and whiny vocals. Mostly covers (Stooges, Kiss, Bowie), it's a great little statement of purpose from these '70s hard-rock babes-turned-adults. *—John Dougan*

● **Neurotica** / 1987 / Big Time ✦✦✦✦✦

It seems hard to imagine that a band inspired as much by breakfast cereal and Saturday morning cartoons as rock & roll could have created the album that spawned an entire movement—grunge. When *Neurotica* was released in 1987, it inspired hordes of punk/hardcore kids to put down the safety pins and pick up the guitar. The perfect blend of Beatles/Kiss-style pop/rock and Butthole Surfers art rock, the album blends the raw punk spirit of the band that included "Quit School" stickers in their second album, 1984's *Teen Babes From Monsanto*, with the pure thrift store rock & roll of Kiss, the Rolling Stones, and the Stooges. Jon Auer from the Posies remixed some of these tracks (including the obvious super hit "Peach Kelli Pop") for a potential reissue on Seattle's Sub Pop in the mid/late '90s, but, for whatever reason, this idea was quickly shelved. Largely ignored upon its release in 1987 (Big Time folded shortly after and the band were unable to record under their own name for three years), *Neurotica* did manage to find its way into some very important young people's bedrooms. Redd Kross had unwittingly created the rough, lo-fi, melodic, rock & roll template that bands like Mudhoney and Nirvana would become very successful exploring over the next few years. —*Terrance Miles*

Third Eye / Sep. 1990 / Atlantic ♦♦♦
Redd Kross reached its peak in the early 1980s, when the band made such humorous and clever contributions to punk rock as "Linda Blair." As the '80s progressed, Kross got away from punk and went for cleaner, less reckless alternative rock and power-pop. Those who play 1990's *Third Eye* next to Kross' early recordings will hear just how radically the band changed over the years. Whether rocking aggressively on "Shonen Knife," going for a very melodic "jangly guitar" approach on "Annie's Gone" and "I Don't Know How to Be Your Friend" or sounding positively Beatlesque on "Bubblegum Factory," Kross shows just how far it has come since the irreverent, freewheeling aggression of "Linda Blair." While some punk enthusiasts missed the old Kross, this decent though not outstanding CD proves that the band was still worthwhile at the dawn of the '90s. —*Alex Henderson*

Phaseshifter / Oct. 5, 1993 / This Way Up ♦♦♦♦
On *Phaseshifter*, Redd Kross has stripped away many of the '60s and '70s pop-culture trappings that figured prominently on earlier recordings (covers of Brady Bunch and Charles Manson songs, for instance). As a result, the band (basically brothers Jeffrey and Steven McDonald) have brought their strong melodic sense, psychedelic punk/metal mix, and fine harmonies to the fore on standout tracks like "Lady in the Front Row" and "Monolith." The brothers' '70s-TV obsession certainly hasn't disappeared, though, as evidenced by songs like "After School Special" and the Partridge Family-inspired cut "Dumb Angel" (Susan Dey being replaced here by keyboardist Gere Fennelly); but they seem more bent on cutting straightforward and driving, power pop/rock anthems than going in for their '80s-style, *HR Pufnstuf* form of garage psychedelia, and even the paisley is conspicuously missing, replaced by t-shirts and jeans. Is the shift due in part to the pervasive influence of grunge and Nirvana? Maybe. But one should remember that, as early as 1980, Redd Kross was incorporating the same Black Flag, hardcore stylings that Cobain and company were admittedly inspired by. It doesn't really matter, though, since this album stands on it own just fine, especially considering the inclusion of one of the band's best rockers ("Crazy World") and most rewarding pop tunes ("Pay for Love"). For some great Redd Kross music, get both *Phaseshifter* and the band's 1997 release, *Show World*. —*Stephen Cook*

Show World / Feb. 11, 1997 / Mercury ♦♦♦♦♦
Nearly four years after the release of *Phaseshifter*, Redd Kross delivered their followup, *Show World*. In between the two albums, the alternative punk-pop audience came and went, leaving Redd Kross slightly out of the loop, which meant *Show World* wasn't greeted to the kind of acclaim it might have received in 1994 or 1995. And that's too bad, because the record is one of the band's best albums, filled with tight, catchy hooks, memorably melodic songs and a bristling energy that makes it a compulsive listen. —*Stephen Thomas Erlewine*

Otis Redding

b. Sep. 9, 1941, Dawson, GA, **d.** Dec. 10, 1967, Madison, WI
Vocals / Deep Soul, Southern Soul, Soul
One of the most influential soul singers of the 1960s, Otis Redding exemplified to many listeners the power of Southern "Deep Soul"—hoarse, gritty vocals, brassy arrangements, and an emotional way with both party tunes and aching ballads. He was also the most consistent exponent of the Stax sound, cutting his records at the Memphis label/studios that did much to update rhythm and blues into modern soul. After Redding's 1962 ballad "These Arms of Mine" became an R&B hit, his solo career was truly on its way, though the hits didn't really start to fly until 1965 and 1966, when "Mr. Pitiful," "I've Been Loving You Too Long," "I Can't Turn You Loose," a cover of the Rolling Stones' "Satisfaction," and "Respect" were all big sellers on the R&B charts. In 1967, he began to show signs of making major inroads into the White audience, particularly with a well-received performance at the Monterey Pop Festival. Redding's biggest triumph, however, came just days before his death, when he recorded the wistful "(Sittin' on) The Dock of the Bay," which represented a significant leap as far as examination of more intensely personal emotions. Also highlighted by crisp Cropper guitar leads and dignified horns, it rose to the top of the pop charts in early 1968. Otis Redding, however, had perished in a plane crash in December 1967. —*Richie Unterberger*

Pain in My Heart / Jan. 1964 / Rhino ♦♦♦♦♦
Redding's blistering debut set the tone for all his later releases and brought the rough, emotional delivery of gospel into R&B in what would soon be called soul. Listen and try to tell yourself Redding was only 22 when he recorded this; there's a lifetime of love and broken hearts in his delivery already. The 12 songs here pay tribute to his favorite singers, mainly Sam Cooke ("You Send Me"), Ben E. King ("Stand By Me"), and the most influential rock & roll shouter Little Richard ("Lucille"). Redding and band play it safe in these initial covers; there's nothing yet as daring as the bizarre twisting of Cooke's "Chain Gang" of three years later. Redding's originals, apart from the rather derivative "Hey Hey Baby," are fabulous: "Pain in My Heart," the slow, burning ballad of "These Arms of Mine," and "That's What My Heart Needs," all singles taken from the album. —*Ted Mills*

The Great Otis Redding Sings Soul Ballads / Mar. 1965 / Rhino ♦♦♦♦♦
Redding's second album includes "Mr. Pitiful," "That's How Strong My Love Is," "Chained and Bound." He moves out of the country-soul genre into his own stompin' thing. —*Christine Ohlman*

☆ **Otis Blue: Otis Redding Sings Soul** / 1966 / Atco ♦♦♦♦♦
Otis Redding's third album, and his first fully realized album, presents his talent unfettered, his direction clear, and his confidence emboldened, with fully half the songs representing a reach that extended his musical grasp. More than a quarter of this album is given over to Redding's versions of songs by Sam Cooke, his idol, who had died the previous December, and all three are worth owning and hearing. Two of them, "A Change Is Gonna Come" and "Shake," are every bit as essential as any soul recordings ever made, and while they (and much of this album) have reappeared on several anthologies, it's useful to hear the songs from those sessions juxtaposed with each other, and with "Wonderful World," which is seldom compiled elsewhere.

Also featured are Redding's spellbinding renditions of "Satisfaction" (a song epitomizing the fully formed Stax/Volt sound and which Mick Jagger and Keith Richards originally wrote in tribute to and imitation of Redding's style), "My Girl," and "You Don't Miss Your Water." "Respect" and "I've Been Loving You Too Long," two originals that were to loom large in his career, are here as well; the former became vastly popular in the hands of Aretha Franklin and the latter was an instant soul classic. Among the seldom-cited jewels here is a rendition of B.B. King's "Rock Me Baby" that has the singer sharing the spotlight with Steve Cropper, his playing alternately elegant and fiery, with Wayne Jackson and Gene "Bowlegs" Miller's trumpets and Andrew Love's and Floyd Newman's saxes providing the backing. Redding's powerful, remarkable singing throughout makes *Otis Blue* gritty, rich, and achingly alive, and an essential listening experience. —*Bruce Eder*

The Soul Album / Apr. 1966 / Rhino ♦♦♦♦
Often overlooked amongst the Redding riches, *The Soul Album* is a solid and consistently wonderful LP; despite launching no major hits, the set contains any number of standout efforts to place it on par with his finest work. Not a cathartic personal statement on par with *Otis Blue*, the record essentially offers Redding the chance to cut loose on a variety of soul favorites, including Sam Cooke's "Chain Gang," Roy Head's "Treat Her Right" and Smokey Robinson's superb "It's Growing," rendered here with remarkable guitar work by the great Steve Cropper. The centerpiece is the amazing "Cigarettes and Coffee," one of the ultimate late-night ballads and a testament to the Stax sound at its most poignant and evocative. —*Jason Ankeny*

☆ **The Complete & Unbelievable: The Otis Redding Dictionary of Soul** / Oct. 1966 / Rhino ♦♦♦♦♦
Otis Redding's fifth album delivers a dozen towering performances on material fully worthy of his talents, ranging from originals like "Fa-Fa-Fa-Fa-Fa (Sad Song)" to covers of the Beatles' "Day Tripper" and the country standard "Tennessee Waltz," with the classics "My Lover's Prayer" and "Try a Little Tenderness" sandwiched in there. What separates this album from its immediate predecessor is the intensity of his performance and the range of repertory—most of the highlights have been anthologized many times over, but this album is still worth hearing all in one, capturing the moment when the singer was approaching his peak. He was only to complete one more solo studio album (*King & Queen*) before his untimely death, and this and it are indispensable additions to any serious soul collection. —*Bruce Eder*

King & Queen / Mar. 1967 / Atco ♦♦♦♦♦
Otis Redding never recorded a lighter, more purely entertaining record than *King and Queen*, a collection of duets with Stax labelmate Carla Thomas. In all likelihood inspired by a series of popular duets recorded by Marvin Gaye—indeed, "It Takes Two," Gaye's sublime collaboration with Kim Weston, is covered here—the record serves no greater purpose than to allow Redding the chance to run through some of the era's biggest soul hits, including "Knock on Wood," "Tell It Like It Is" and "When Something Is Wrong with My Baby," and while clearly not a personal triumph on a par with either *Otis Blue* or *The Dictionary of Soul*, the set is still hugely succcessful on its own terms. Redding and Thomas enjoy an undeniable chemistry, and they play off each other wonderfully; while sparks fly furiously throughout *King and Queen*, the album's highlight is the classic "Tramp," where their battle of the sexes reaches its fever pitch in supremely witty fashion. —*Jason Ankeny*

Live in Europe / Jul. 1967 / Rhino ♦♦♦
Live in Europe was the first full-length concert album released on Otis Redding, and the last LP of his work that he lived to see issued. Recorded along the Stax/Volt tour of Europe in March of 1967, it featured Redding backed by Booker T. & the MG's. Their playing, along with that of Wayne Jackson (trumpet) and Andrew Love and Joe Arnold (tenor saxes), is more elegant and elegantly articulated than the work of his usual touring band, and this album is a sort of idealized Otis Redding concert. Some of it lacks the raw excitement of *Live at the Whisky a Go Go* (which was recorded a year earlier than the shows where this album was cut, but not issued until a year later), but in compensation one gets all of the virtuoso flourishes and details that one would expect from this ensemble. The audience, ecstatic at the rare chance to see the soul idol in concert, is very vocal in their enthusiasm for the singer and his songs, and "Fa-Fa-Fa-Fa-Fa (Sad Song)" is practically a singalong number with some finely detailed playing from Booker T. Jones, Steve Cropper, and Al Jackson Jr., who, with Wayne Jackson and company, also add some exquisite grace notes to the finale, "Try a Little Tenderness." Beyond the musical power of his

performance, Redding's emotions are practically overflowing as he addresses the crowd in a very personal manner as he introduces "These Arms of Mine." The only flaw in this recording, if there is one, is that it does have only ten songs, but that was the nature of the shows on this tour. *—Bruce Eder*

☆ **The Dock of the Bay** / Feb. 1968 / Atco ✦✦✦✦✦
It was never supposed to be like this: "(Sittin' on) The Dock of the Bay" was supposed to mark a beginning of a new phase in Otis Redding's career, not an ending. Producer/guitarist Steve Cropper had a difficult task to perform in pulling together this album, the first of several posthumous releases issued by Stax/Volt in the wake of Otis Redding's death. What could have been a cash-in effort or a grim memorial album instead became a vivid, exciting presentation of some key aspects of the talent that was lost when Redding died. *Dock of the Bay* is, indeed, a mixed bag of singles and B-sides going back to July of 1965, one hit duet with Carla Thomas, and a pair of previously unissued tracks from 1966 and 1967, respectively. There's little cohesion, stylistic or otherwise, in the songs, especially when the title track is taken into consideration—nothing else here resembles it, for the obvious reason that Redding never had a chance to follow it up. Despite the mix-and-match nature of the album, however, this is an impossible record not to love. Cropper chose his tracks well, selecting some of the strongest and most unusual among the late singer's orphaned songs: "I Love You More Than Words Can Say" is one of Redding's most passionate performances; "Let Me Come on Home" presents an ebullient Otis Redding accompanied by some sharp playing; and "Don't Mess With Cupid" begins with a gorgeous guitar flourish and blooms into an intense, pounding, soaring showcase for singer and band alike. No one could complain about the album then, and it still holds more than three decades later. Reissued on CD by the Atco label through Rhino Records in excellent sound. *—Bruce Eder*

The Immortal Otis Redding / Jun. 1968 / Rhino ✦✦✦
A posthumous release of 11 sides recorded in 1967, showing Otis Redding turning his ability toward the most sophisticated soul music of his career—even the songs with models in earlier works, such as "The Happy Song (Dum-Dum-De-De-De-Dum-Dum)," show a level of articulation and care in the playing that runs circles around Redding's earlier recordings. "Think About It" could pass for the work of an earlier phase in the singer's career, but for the surprisingly elegant piano accompaniment and Redding's more softly nuanced singing. It's a testament to Redding's talent that he left behind enough unanthologized and unreleased tracks to generate four fine posthumous studio albums, including this one. The good tracks are bookended by a pair of masterpieces, "I've Got Dreams to Remember" and the soaring "Amen," of which the latter has been heavily anthologized and the former not heard often enough. *—Bruce Eder*

☆ **In Person at the Whisky a Go Go** / Oct. 1968 / Rhino ✦✦✦✦✦
This album, released posthumously, captured Otis Redding's show at the Whisky A Go Go from April of 1966 in Los Angeles. What is essential here was that it captured Otis Redding's sound in a small club with his own touring band, as opposed to his work on stage with Booker T. & the MG's—an ideal band, to be sure, which is why they were sent over to Europe with him and why they were at Monterey with him a year later, but not the group that Redding normally worked on stage with. This album is closer to how Otis Redding sounded in the years coming up and working his way to the top, and the way that his original audience on the chitlin' circuit heard him. The singer and his band (including a pair of tenor saxes, a trombone, and four trumpets, with James Young, Ralph Stewart, and Elbert Woodson pounding out the rhythm on guitar, bass, and drums, respectively, go through roaring versions of "Respect," "I Can't Turn You Loose," "These Arms of Mine," "Pain in My Heart," "Satisfaction" and "Papa's Got a Brand New Bag" and four more, in Redding's only full-length recording in a small-scale setting. They may not have the musical elegance of Booker T. and company, but they create this intense, hypnotic sound that is spellbinding. The set itself lasts less than 40 minutes but the singer and his band are so energetic, that it doesn't feel short or lacking. This album was, in more ways than one, Redding's equivalent to Sam Cooke's *Live At The Harlem Square Club*, and just as essential. Reissued in 1992 on the Atco label through Rhino Records. *—Bruce Eder*

Love Man / Jun. 1969 / Rhino ✦✦✦
This is a straight-ahead reissue of a vinyl album originally released in 1969 on Atco. Consisting of 1967 recordings, the album yielded a mild hit with the title cut and offers solid versions of Jackie Wilson's "Higher and Higher" and Brook Benton's "A Lover's Question." Even Redding's leftovers are cause for celebration. *—Cub Koda*

Tell the Truth / Jul. 1970 / Rhino ✦✦✦
When a major artist dies, labels can usually be counted on to release anything and everything the artist had in the can, regardless of quality. In the case of Otis Redding, most of the posthumous releases were of a very high quality. One example is *Tell the Truth*, which was recorded the year he died, 1967, and remained unreleased until 1970. Though it falls short of essential, *Truth* has a lot to excite the soul icon's more devoted followers. Tracks like "I Got the Will," "Snatch a Little Piece," and "Demonstration" are pure Redding—frenzied, passionate, relentlessly gritty Memphis soul that makes no concessions to pop tastes or Northern soul. "Out of Sight" speaks volumes about him—while others would have been afraid to cover a song written and defined by James Brown, Redding confidently tackles the song with splendid results. Redding's last major hit, "Dock of the Bay," indicated that had he lived, he would have explored softer, Northern R&B sounds. But on this album (reissued on CD in the early '90s), it was Memphis all the way. *—Alex Henderson*

Remember Me / 1992 / Stax ✦✦✦
One of the better posthumous Otis packages, this brings together tracks recorded between 1963 and 1967, including two alternate takes of the smash "Sittin' on the Dock of the Bay." Far from a batch of leftovers, this features strong material like "I've Got Dreams to Remember," and interesting alternate takes of "Respect," "Come to Me," and "Try a Little Tenderness." After you've absorbed the hits and some of the best of the live material, here's your next stop. *—Cub Koda*

★ **The Very Best of Otis Redding** / 1993 / Rhino ✦✦✦✦✦
The Very Best of Otis Redding wasn't the first Otis Redding compilation but it is the best of the single-disc collections, distilling the high points across his career (up thru the posthumous hits "(Sitting' On) The Dock of the Bay" and the heartbreaking "I've Got Dreams to Remember") in 16 tracks, every one a musical milestone and a soul music high-point of one kind or another. Although aimed at the casual listener and the neophyte fan, there are some astonishing realizations to be had in listening to this disc and looking at the chart placements of the early sides, and realizing just how uniform his musical influence is—"These Arms of Mine" and, especially, "Pain In My Heart," from 1962 and 1963, respectively, sold only a fraction of what his later singles did, yet they've been covered by so many artists since, that they're as familiar as any of the other, bigger hits on this disc. The collection is hardly comprehensive, but all of the major bases are touched, right down to his 1967 hit duet "Tramp" with Carla Thomas. The other advantage, especially for those on a budget, is that this was the first Otis Redding compilation to avail itself of the improved master tape research and analog-to-digital technology of the early '90s. *—Bruce Eder*

Good to Me: Live at the Whiskey A Go Go, Vol. 2 / Jan. 25, 1993 / Stax ✦✦✦
Despite the deluge of reissues and anthologies, there still remains some unreleased Otis Redding material. There are two pluses about this new release of vintage Redding cuts, four of them newly issued. The first is that it's live, and Redding was always worth hearing in that context. The second is that the bonus cuts are invigorating, frenetic workouts with Redding blazing through the verses and then reworking and reshaping them in fiery vocal improvisations. The only negative, if there is one, is that there are better versions of "Ole Man Trouble" and "Pain in My Heart" available on other Redding releases. *—Ron Wynn*

☆ **Otis! The Definitive Otis Redding** / Nov. 9, 1993 / Rhino ✦✦✦✦✦
Anyone who wants to understand the different phases of Otis Redding's career, and the reason for his having made a major impact across the 1960s and beyond, can have no better place to start than *Otis! The Definitive Otis Redding*. There are 73 studio cuts here and the producers have reached back beyond the Atlantic and Stax vaults: They've included numbers like "She's All Right," cut by the Shooters featuring Otis Redding in the summer of 1960 for the Transworld label; "Gettin' Hip," which was done for the Alshire label in 1960; and "Shout Bamalama" by Otis Redding & the Pinetoppers, recorded for Confederate, all prior to Redding's signing with Stax. The selection of studio cuts suggests that the makers thought long and hard about each and every track on this disc—the first three CDs are a mix of single A- and B-sides, coupled with important album tracks, all culminating with "(Sittin' On) The Dock of the Bay." Little or nothing that's essential is missing along the way (though one could argue very persuasively that anything on the albums that Redding released in his lifetime was essential in some respect). The fourth disc is the real killer, however; 23 live songs drawn from the complete range of his concert tapes in the Atlantic (and Stax) vaults, from the Apollo Theater in New York in November of 1963 to his final tour of Europe and the Monterey International Pop Festival in the spring of 1967, including individual tracks that were unheard until the 1980s. An extensive booklet is also included. *—Bruce Eder*

☆ **The Very Best of Otis Redding, Vol. 2** / Apr. 25, 1995 / Rhino ✦✦✦✦✦
Rhino's first Otis Redding volume was perfect within the confines of a 16-song single disc, and a difficult act to follow. *The Very Best of Otis Redding, Vol. 2* is a fine companion volume and fills in some different kinds of gaps. The lion's share of the disc is devoted to 13 more singles, several of which ("I Love You More Than Words Can Say," "Security," "That's What My Heart Needs," "Chained and Bound," "Glory of Love") are, if not definitive, then still all-but-essential. Several posthumous singles are also here, along with two more duets with Carla Thomas. More revealing and representative of the range of Redding's talent, however, are three album tracks that show off Redding applying his talents to the songs of Smokey Robinson, with a rapturous account of "My Girl"; the Beatles, in a ferociously freewheeling, elongated, and essentially re-composed version of "Day Tripper"; and, most notably, Sam Cooke with "A Change Is Gonna Come." The latter, arguably the best recording ever given a Sam Cooke song by anyone other than Cooke himself, might just be the best Otis Redding song never released as a single. The neophyte and the casual listener will love the contents of this disc, and even longtime fans may be impressed with some of the choices. *—Bruce Eder*

Dreams to Remember: The Otis Redding Anthology / Aug. 18, 1998 / Rhino ✦✦✦✦✦
Dreams to Remember: The Otis Redding Anthology presents an interesting dilemma. Certainly, the music on the double-disc set is superb—all of his hits are here, along with a wealth of great album tracks and five live cuts from the Monterey International Pop Festival. The question is, was the collection *necessary*? Casual listeners who just want the hits will be satisfied with the excellent *Very Best of Otis Redding*, while those who want to dig deeper will find the four-disc box *Otis! The Definitive Otis Redding* essential, or will opt for the actual albums. *Dreams to Remember* falls somewhere between the two extremes, containing too much music for the casual listener and not being extensive enough for serious listeners. Perhaps realizing this, Rhino added several tracks here that weren't featured on the box set, but any true collector will have these songs on the original albums. So, *Dreams to Remember* is in limbo—a fine collection that isn't really necessary. It's not a bad choice, to be sure, but *The Very Best of Otis Redding* and *Otis!* are better choices, depending on your tastes. *—Stephen Thomas Erlewine*

Redman (Reggie Noble)

b. Apr. 17, 196?, Newark, NJ
Vocals, Producer / Hardcore Rap, East Coast Rap, Hip-Hop

New Jersey rapper Redman made his initial impact with *Whut? Thee Album* in 1992. He blended reggae and funk influences with topical commentary and displayed a terse, though fluid rap style that was sometimes satirical, sometimes tough, and sometimes silly. Redman returned in 1994 with his second album, *Dare Iz a Darkside*, which was a harder album than his debut. *Muddy Waters*, Redman's third album, followed in 1996; he returned two years later with *Doc's Da Name. —Ron Wynn*

● **Whut? Thee Album** / Sep. 22, 1992 / Def Jam ✦✦✦✦✦
Redman's debut album is a minor masterpiece, fueled by the thick, P-Funk-influenced production of Erick Sermon. Redman's rhyming is forceful and intelligent, and he's never afraid to lighten his rhetoric with humor. Plus, the deeply funky grooves forming the core of the album never grow tiresome or repetitive. —*Stephen Thomas Erlewine*

Dare Iz a Darkside / 1994 / Def Jam ✦✦✦
Redman may have become a household name among the rap community by the end of the '90s, but there was a time when he garnered little more than a cult following. Why? Well, *Dare Iz a Darkside* illustrates this better than any of his other '90s albums—nowhere else has Redman ever been this odd, to be quite frank. It's fairly evident here that he'd been listening to his George Clinton records and that he wasn't fronting when he alluded to "A Million and 1 Buddah Spots" that he'd visited. In fact, this album often divides his fans. Many admire it for its eccentricities, while others deride it for being quite simply too inaccessible. It's almost as if Redman is trying to puzzle listeners on *Dare Iz a Darkside* with his continually morphing persona. In fact, there's actually little questioning his motives—it's a matter of fact that Redman's trying to be as crazy as he can without alienating *too* many of those who first knew him for his affiliation with EPMD. And while that affiliation does aid this album, since Erick Sermon plays a large role in production, it's not quite enough. If this album has one unforgivable flaw besides the debatable quirks in Redman's persona, it's the production. Sermon isn't up to his usual standards here, unfortunately, and the album could really use some of his trademark funk. But the reason most fans either feel devotion or disdain for this album isn't the beats, but rather Redman's antics. If you appreciate his wacky sense of insane humor, this album is a gold mine. If you're more into his latter-day Method Man-style rhymes, then this album probably isn't one you want to bother with. After all, though Redman became a household name by the end of the '90s, it surely wasn't because of albums like this. —*Jason Birchmeier*

Muddy Waters / Dec. 10, 1996 / Def Jam ✦✦✦✦
Like Redman's first two albums, *Muddy Waters* is an uncompromising set of hardcore hip-hop, complete with tight, menacing rhythm tracks, suprisingly menacing reggae overtones and winding rhymes that illustrate that he is one of the best, and most underrated, rappers in contemporary hip-hop. —*Leo Stanley*

Doc's Da Name 2000 / Nov. 24, 1998 / Def Jam ✦✦✦✦
The sound Redman achieves on this album is characteristic of his previous albums. With production credits going mostly to Erick Sermon, the bass-intensive and melodic beats on *Doc's Da Name 2000* allow Redman to deliver the raw Newark, NJ, flow for which he's known and liked. Redman himself produced a few of the songs on this album, including "Jersey Yo!" A mildly funny skit that describes the attitude of a certain Little Bricks resident precedes this selection. There are actually five skits on the album, which, like most skits on an often-played album, become very unfunny after a few repetitions. On "Jersey Yo!," Redman uses a slow and funky guitar sound over tight drums and a fluid bass line. Redman is also responsible for the production of "Da Goodness," a song that features Busta Rhymes. The instrumentation in this song has a futuristic, almost minimal, sound that mimics a lot of the music Busta Rhymes frequently flows over. Not stopping there, Redman spits lyrics in "Da Goodness" with what could be identified as Busta's lyrical style—and he does it well. The result is an entertaining song that exemplifies Redman's skill as a talented lyricist and producer. "Beet Drop," another cut produced by Redman, is a brief but funny cover of the Beastie Boys' "It's the New Style." —*Qa'id Jacobs*

Malpractice / May 22, 2001 / Def Jam ✦✦✦
During the three-year gap separating Redman's previous album, *Doc's da Name 2000* (1998), from *Malpractice*, the crazed New Jersey rapper became a bona fide superstar thanks to his collaboration with the ubiquitous and ridiculously recognized Method Man. It now seems that the same sort of excessively brash attitude that somewhat burdens Method Man's superstar ego has become a staple of Redman's as well. That sort of lazy overconfidence often leads to effortless redundancy—this is a problem that creeps into *Malpractice*. After nearly a decade, Redman's countless skits and his ever-wacky but still-the-same antics just don't seem as fresh and amusing as they once were. Furthermore, with his newfound Method Man-like arrogance, his old tricks seem even tougher to stomach. It'd be different if Redman took a Missy Elliott-like approach to *Malpractice* and made an effort to continually flip styles and keep things fresh with each album. That's not the case, though. Rather, he turns in a repeat performance of his last few solo albums. Erick Sermon again crafts a number of the beats, and Redman returns to many of the same lyrical motifs that fueled his past work. So, in a sense, you can commend Redman for his consistency; after all, his rhymes are always a grin and he even produces a good chunk of *Malpractice*. Unfortunately, if you've heard his previous albums, this is going to feel very familiar. It's guests like George Clinton and the aforementioned Missy Elliott who keep things fresh, and there's no shortage of guests here, but even they can't salvage the record's déjà vu feeling. It's not easy criticizing *Malpractice*, since it is a relatively strong album with some nice moments such as the lead single, "Let's Get Dirty." But being

Redman's fifth solo album, you expect a little more growth; instead you get what feels like a repeat performance. —*Jason Birchmeier*

Lou Reed

b. Mar. 2, 1942, Freeport, Long Island, NY
Vocals, Keyboards, Guitar (Electric), Guitar / New York Punk, Album Rock, Proto-Punk, Glam Rock, Hard Rock, Singer/Songwriter

The career of Lou Reed defies capsule summarization. Like David Bowie (whom Reed directly inspired in many ways), he has made over his image many times, mutating from theatrical glam-rocker to scary-looking junkie to avant-garde noiseman to straight rock & roller to yer average guy. A firmer grasp of rock's earthier qualities has ensured a more consistent career path than Bowie's, particularly in his latter years. Yet his catalog is extremely inconsistent, in both quality and stylistic orientation. Liking one Lou Reed LP, or several, or all of the ones he did in a particular era, is no guarantee that you'll like all of them, or even most of them.

Few would deny Reed's immense importance and considerable achievements, however. As has often been written, he expanded the vocabulary of rock & roll lyrics into the previously forbidden territory of kinky sex, drug use (and abuse), decadence, transvestites, homosexuality, and suicidal depression. As has been pointed out less often, he remained (and remains) committed to using rock & roll as a forum for literary, mature expression well into middle age, without growing lyrically soft or musically complacent. By and large, he's taken on these challenging duties with uncompromising honesty and a high degree of realism. For these reasons, he's often cited as punk's most important ancestor. It's often overlooked, though, that he's equally skilled at celebrating romantic joy, and rock & roll itself, as he is at depicting harrowing urban realities. Most would have to concede that with the exception of Neil Young, no other star that rose to fame in the 1960s has continued to push himself so diligently into creating work that is meaningful and contemporary. If that means he relies on stock musical and lyrical ideas at times (as Young does), it also means he's proved that rock can remain relevant to listeners other than hormone-crazed teenagers. —*Richie Unterberger*

Lou Reed / 1972 / RCA ✦✦✦
Nearly 30 years after it came out, Lou Reed's solo debut suggests that neither Reed nor his new record company were quite sure about what to do with him in 1972. It would be years before the cult of the Velvet Underground became big enough to mean anything commercially, leaving Lou pretty much back where he started from in the public eye after five years of hard work, and he seemed to be searching for a different musical direction on this set without quite deciding what it would be; while the best tunes are admirably lean, no-frills rock & roll, there are also several featuring tricked-up arrangements that don't suit the material terribly well (at no other time in history would anyone believe that Steve Howe and Rick Wakeman would be a good choice as backing musicians for the guy who wrote "Sister Ray"). Lou also didn't appear to have done much songwriting since he left the Velvets in 1970; with the exception of the hilariously catty "Wild Child" and "Berlin," a song Reed would revisit a few years later, nearly every significant song on *Lou Reed* dated back to his tenure with the Velvet Underground, though it would be years before that band's recordings of "I Can't Stand It," "Lisa Says," or "Ocean" would surface. On its own terms, *Lou Reed* isn't a bad album, but it isn't a terribly interesting one either, and since superior performances of most of these songs are available elsewhere, it stands today more as a historical curiosity than anything else. —*Mark Deming*

Transformer / 1972 / RCA ✦✦✦✦✦
David Bowie has never been shy about acknowledging his influences, and since the boho decadence and sexual ambiguity of the Velvet Underground's music had a major impact on Bowie's work, it was only fitting that as *Ziggy Stardust*-mania was reaching its peak, Bowie would offer Lou Reed some much needed help with his career, which was stuck in neutral after his first solo album came and went. Musically, Reed's work didn't have too much in common with the sonic bombast of the glam scene, but at least it was a place where his eccentricities could find a comfortable home, and on *Transformer* Bowie and his right-hand man, Mick Ronson, crafted a new sound for Reed that was better fitting (and more commercially astute) than the ambivalent tone of his first solo album. Ronson adds some guitar raunch to "Vicious" and "Hangin' Round" that's a lot flashier than what Reed cranked out with the Velvets, but still honors Lou's strengths in guitar-driven hard rock, while the imaginative arrangements Ronson cooked up for "Perfect Day," "Walk on the Wild Side," and "Goodnight Ladies" blend pop polish with musical thinking just as distinctive as Reed's lyrical conceits. And while Reed occasionally overplays his hand in writing stuff he figured the glam kids wanted ("Make Up" and "I'm So Free" being the most obvious examples), "Perfect Day," "Walk on the Wild Side," and "New York Telephone Conversation" proved he could still write about the demimonde with both perception and respect. The sound and style of *Transformer* would in many ways define Lou Reed's career in the 1970s, and while it led him into a style that proved to be a dead end, you can't deny that Bowie and Ronson gave their hero a new lease on life—and a solid album in the bargain. —*Mark Deming*

Berlin / 1973 / RCA ✦✦✦
Transformer and "Walk on the Wild Side" were both major hits in 1972, to the surprise of both Lou Reed and the music industry, and with Reed suddenly a hot commodity, he used his newly won clout to make the most ambitious album of his career, *Berlin. Berlin* was the musical equivalent of a drug-addled kid set loose in a candy store; the album's songs, which form a loose storyline about a doomed romance between two chemically fueled bohemians, were fleshed out with a huge, boomy production (Bob Ezrin at his most grandiose) and arrangements overloaded with guitars, keyboards, horns, strings,

and any other kitchen sink that was handy (the session band included Jack Bruce, Steve Winwood, Aynsley Dunbar, and Tony Levin). And while Reed had often been accused of focusing on the dark side of life, he and Ezrin approached *Berlin* as their opportunity to make The Most Depressing Album of All Time, and they hardly missed a trick. This all seemed a bit much for an artist who made such superb use of the two-guitars/bass/drums lineup with the Velvet Underground, especially since Reed doesn't even play electric guitar on the album; the sheer size of *Berlin* ultimately overpowers both Reed and his material. But if *Berlin* is largely a failure of ambition, that sets it apart from the vast majority of Reed's lesser works; Lou's vocals are both precise and impassioned, and though a few of the songs are little more than sketches, the best—"How Do You Think It Feels," "Oh Jim," "The Kids," and "Sad Song"—are powerful, bitter stuff. It's hard not to be impressed by *Berlin*, given the sheer scope of the project, but while it earns an A for Effort, the actual execution merits more of a B. —*Mark Deming*

Rock & Roll Animal / 1974 / RCA ✦✦✦✦
In 1974, after the commercial disaster of his album *Berlin*, Lou Reed needed a hit, and *Rock & Roll Animal* was a rare display of commercial acumen on his part, just the right album at just the right time. Recorded in concert with Reed's crack road band at the peak of their form, *Rock & Roll Animal* offered a set of his most anthemic songs (most dating from his days with the Velvet Underground) in arrangements that presented his lean, effective melodies and street-level lyrics in their most user-friendly form (or at least as user friendly as an album with a song called "Heroin" can get). Early '70s arena-rock bombast is often the order of the day, but guitarists Dick Wagner and Steve Hunter use their six-string muscle to lift these songs up, not weigh them down, and with Reed's passionate but controlled vocals riding over the top, "Sweet Jane," "White Light/White Heat," and "Rock & Roll" finally sound like the radio hits they always should have been. Reed would rarely sound this commercial again, but *Rock & Roll Animal* proves he could please a crowd when he had to. The revised CD reissue of *Rock & Roll Animal* released in 2000 offers markedly better sound than the album's initial release, along with two bonus cuts that give a better idea of how this band approached the material from *Berlin* on stage, as well as an amusing moment of Reed verbally sparring with a heckler. —*Mark Deming*

Sally Can't Dance / 1974 / Buddha ✦✦
On the live album *Rock & Roll Animal*, Lou Reed showed he'd learned how to give his audience what they wanted, and do it well. *Sally Can't Dance*, on the other hand, was the polar opposite, a remarkably cynical album that pandered to the lowest common denominator of the market that had bought *Transformer* and *Rock & Roll Animal*, and didn't even do it with much flair. Reed's performances here are limited to vocals, except for some sloppy acoustic guitar on one track (this from the man who helped reinvent electric guitar with the Velvet Underground), and the sodden, overblown arrangements sink most of these tunes before they get past the first chorus; much of the time, Reed sounds like an afterthought on his own album. And while Reed's best songwriting ranks with the best rock of his generation, *Sally Can't Dance* is cluttered with throwaways that reach for the boho decadence of *Transformer* and come up empty (with special recognition going to the bizarre and truly puzzling "Animal Language"). Side two does offer two worthwhile songs: "Kill Your Sons," a powerful and deeply personal remembrance of Reed's bouts with shock treatment and brutal psychotherapy, which he would revisit in a much stronger performance on 1984's *Live in Italy*, and "Billy," a witty and surprisingly poignant remembrance of an old friend and how their paths in life diverged. But otherwise, *Sally Can't Dance* has the distinction of being the worst studio album of Lou Reed's career; *Metal Machine Music* may have been a lot more annoying, but at least Reed was trying on that one. —*Mark Deming*

Lou Reed Live / 1975 / RCA ✦✦✦
If you were seeing Lou Reed in concert, which songs would you rather hear him play—"Sweet Jane," "White Light/White Heat," and "Rock & Roll," or "Vicious," "Oh Jim," and "Sad Song"? Even the most loyal fan would probably concede that the former would make for a more exciting show than the latter, which is one of the reasons why this set of outtakes from the concerts recorded for *Rock & Roll Animal* in 1974 isn't nearly as interesting as the first album. The duel-guitar attack of Dick Wagner and Steve Hunter is still impressive, and Reed's vocals are in good form, but these performances were left on the cutting room floor the first time around for a reason—they're simply not as good as the other stuff. If you loved *Rock & Roll Animal*, you'll probably like this, but in all likelihood you won't feel cheated by not having it in your collection, either. —*Mark Deming*

Metal Machine Music / 1975 / Buddha ✦
One would be hard-pressed to name a major artist who ever released an album as thoroughly alienating as Lou Reed's *Metal Machine Music*; at a time when noise rock and punk had yet to make their presence known, Reed released this 64-minute aural assault that offered up a densely layered soundscape constructed from feedback, distortion, and atonal guitar runs sped up or slowed down until they were all but unrecognizable. *Metal Machine Music* seems a bit less startling today, now that bands like Sonic Youth and the Boredoms have created some sort of context for it, but it hasn't gotten any more user friendly with time—while Thurston Moore may go nuts on his guitar like this for three or four minutes at a stretch, *Metal Machine Music* goes on and on and on for over an hour, pausing only for side breaks with no rhythms, melodies, or formal structures to buffer the onslaught. If you're brave enough to listen to the whole thing, it's hard not to marvel at the scope of Reed's obsession; it's obvious he spent a lot of time on these layered sheets of noise, and enthusiasts of the violent guitar freakout may find it pleasing in short bursts. But confronting *Metal Machine Music* from front to back in one sitting is an experience that's both brutal and numbing. It's hard to say what Lou Reed had in mind when he made *Metal Machine Music*, and Reed has done little to clarify the issue over the years, though he summed it up quite pointedly in an interview in which he said, "Well,

anyone who gets to side four is dumber than I am." For the record, I did get to side four. But I got paid for it. —*Mark Deming*

Coney Island Baby / Feb. 1976 / RCA ✦✦✦✦
From 1972's *Transformer* onward, Lou Reed spent most of the '70s playing the druggy decadence card for all it was worth, with increasingly mixed results. But on *Coney Island Baby*, Reed's songwriting began to move into warmer, more compassionate territory, and the result was his most approachable album since *Loaded*. On most of the tracks, Reed stripped his band back down to guitar, bass, and drums, and the results were both leaner and a lot more comfortable than the leaden over-production of *Sally Can't Dance* or *Berlin*. "Crazy Feeling," "She's My Best Friend," and "Coney Island Baby" found Reed actually writing recognizable love songs for a change, and while Reed pursued his traditional interest in the underside of the hipster's life on "Charlie's Girl" and "Nobody's Business," he did so with a breezy, free-wheeling air that was truly a relief after the lethargic tone of *Sally Can't Dance*. "Kicks" used an audio-tape collage to generate atmospheric tension that gave its tale of drugs and death a chilling quality that was far more effective than his usual blasé take on the subject, and "Coney Island Baby" was the polar opposite, a song about love and regret that was as sincere and heart-tugging as anything the man has ever recorded. *Coney Island Baby* sounds casual on the surface, but emotionally it's as compelling as anything Reed released in the 1970s, and proved Reed could write about real people with recognizable emotions as well as anyone in rock music—something you might not have guessed from most of the solo albums that preceded it. —*Mark Deming*

Rock & Roll Heart / Nov. 1976 / Buddha ✦✦
Rock & Roll Heart was Lou Reed's first album for Arista Records, and one senses that he wanted to come up with something saleable for his new sponsors. Uptempo numbers with pop hooks dominate the set, the 12 songs zip by in an efficient 38 minutes, and instead of Reed's trademark meditations on the dark side of life, the lyrics are (for the most part) lean bursts of verse and chorus, in which the artist sings the praises of good times in general and rock & roll in particular (then again, on "I Believe in Love," Reed pledges his allegiance to both "good time music" and "the iron cross," a bit of perversity to remind us whose album this is). But if *Rock & Roll Heart* sounds like "Lou Reed Lite," there are more than a few flashes of Reed's inarguable talent. His band is in fine form (especially Marty Fogel on sax and Michael Fonfara on keyboards). "Banging on My Drum" is a crunchy rocker that recalls his work with the Velvet Underground; "A Sheltered Life" is an amusing bit of VU archeology (the Velvets demoed the song, but this marked its first appearance on record); and the closer, "Temporary Thing," is a bitter, haunting narrative that foreshadows Reed's next album, the harrowing masterpiece *Street Hassle*. —*Mark Deming*

Walk on the Wild Side: The Best of Lou Reed / 1977 / RCA ✦✦✦✦✦
Walk on the Wild Side: The Best of Lou Reed was the standard record company "hits" compilation surveying Reed's five-year, eight-album sojourn at RCA from 1972 to 1976. Its 11 songs included two from *Lou Reed*, three from *Transformer* (among them, of course, this album's title track, Reed's sole chart hit), one from *Berlin*, two from *Rock & Roll Animal* (one of which is "Sweet Jane," minus the introductory fanfare), and the title tracks from *Sally Can't Dance* and *Coney Island Baby*, plus the previously non-LP B-side "Nowhere at All." It was a bullet-proof selection, as unimaginative as it was dependable, which oddly was why it worked so well. Reed's solo career had seen some extreme tangents, and this album caught them, from the Dylan-ish "Wild Child" to the glam-pop of the *Transformer* material, and from the heavy metal rearrangements of old Velvet Underground songs on *Rock & Roll Animal* to the attempts at straightforward adult singer/songwriter rock on songs like "Coney Island Baby." The regular albums had been uneven, but here Reed came off as an accomplished dabbler in a variety of styles who really had something to say and said it, sometimes humorously, sometimes frantically, but always with conviction. Reed has been a prolific artist, and this album captures only a fraction of his catalog, but he is actually less eclectic as a rule than this collection makes him seem, so the result is an excellent introduction. —*William Ruhlmann*

Live: Take No Prisoners / 1978 / Arista ✦✦✦
"I do Lou Reed better than *anybody*, so I thought I'd get in on it," Reed says at one point during this double live set, and that seems to sum up the album's theme quite well. Recorded during a week of shows at New York's Bottom Line in 1978, *Live: Take No Prisoners* presents Lou Reed The Standup Comic, doing schtick on Patti Smith ("F—k Radio Ethiopia, man! I'm Radio Brooklyn!"), political activism ("Give me an issue, I'll give you a tissue, and you can wipe my ass with it"), and the agony of playing "Walk on the Wild Side" ("It's not that I don't want to play your favorites, but there are *so many* favorites to choose from!") while occasionally pausing to play a song. As a comic, Lou is no Lenny Bruce or Bill Hicks, but he's funny by fits and starts (and he plays guitar better than either of them). On the odd moments when Lou is focused enough to actually perform a song from start to finish (such as "Pale Blue Eyes" or "Coney Island Baby"), he's in fine form, sounding loose but enthusiastic, but those moments don't happen especially often, and this album plows through a mere ten songs in close to 100 minutes, which gives you an idea of just how far he stretches out here. If you're a fan who wants a look into the mind of Lou Reed, comic or otherwise, *Live: Take No Prisoners* certainly fills the bill, but if you want to hear Lou actually play his music, you're better off with *Rock & Roll Animal* or *Live in Italy*. But then again, as Lou himself points out, "What's wrong with cheap dirty jokes? I never said I was tasteful." —*Mark Deming*

Street Hassle / 1978 / Arista ✦✦✦
The rise of the punk/new wave movement in the late '70s proved just how pervasive Lou Reed's influence had been through the past decade, but it also gave him some stiff competition, as suddenly Reed was no longer the only poet of the New York streets. 1978's *Street Hassle* was Reed's first album after punk had gained public currency, and Reed

appeared to have taken the minimal approach of punk to heart. With the exception of *Metal Machine Music*, *Street Hassle* was Reed's rawest set of the 1970s; partly recorded live, with arrangements stripped to the bone, *Street Hassle* was dark, deep, and ominous, a 180-degree turn from the polished neo-glam of *Transformer*. Lyrically, *Street Hassle* found Reed looking deep into himself, and not liking what he saw. Opening with an uncharitable parody of "Sweet Jane," *Street Hassle* found Reed acknowledging just how much a self-parody he'd become in the 1970's, and just how much he hated himself for it, on songs like "Dirt" and "Shooting Star." *Street Hassle* was Reed's most creatively ambitious album since *Berlin*, and it sounded revelatory on first release in 1978. Sadly, time has magnified its flaws; the Lenny Bruce-inspired "I Wanna Be Black" sounds like a bad idea today, and the murk of the album's binaural mix isn't especially flattering to anyone. But the album's best moments are genuinely exciting, and the title cut, a three-movement poetic tone poem about life on the New York streets, is one of the most audacious and deeply moving moments of Reed's solo career. Raw, wounded, and unapologetically difficult, *Street Hassle* isn't the masterpiece Reed was shooting for, but it's still among the most powerful and compelling albums he released during the 1970s, and too personal and affecting to ignore. *—Mark Deming*

The Bells / 1979 / Buddha ✦✦✦✦
After the harrowing triumph of *Street Hassle*, Lou Reed's *The Bells* sounded like a bit of a step back; it returned Reed to the more listener-friendly, keyboard-dominated sound of *Rock & Roll Heart*, the lyrics lacked the caustic self-loathing of songs like "Dirt" or "I Wanna Be Black," and it even featured a four-and-a-half-minute funk workout called "Disco Mystic" (hey, this *was* 1979). But lyrically, *The Bells* found Reed moving away from the boho decadence of most of his 1970s work and towards a more compassionate perspective on his characters; "Families" and "All Through the Night" display an empathy and emotional depth Reed didn't often allow himself as a solo artist, and "Stupid Man" and "Looking for Love" rocked hard while making the loneliness of their protagonists felt. And the title cut, with Reed experimenting with a guitar synthesizer and free jazz hero Don Cherry inviting the spirit on trumpet, is both a brave exploration of musical space and a lyrically touching sketch of loss and salvation. An album that's worn well over time, *The Bells* gains depth with each playing and now sounds like one of Reed's finest solo efforts of the 1970s. *—Mark Deming*

Growing Up in Public / 1980 / Buddha ✦✦✦
Growing Up in Public was a transitional album for Lou Reed; it was his last set with his long-running road band (dominated by keyboardist Michael Fonfara), and while the fleshed-out arrangements are of a piece with Reed's work on *Rock & Roll Heart* and *The Bells*, the lyrics of the best songs anticipate the directly personal, emotionally naked songwriting that marked the two extraordinary albums that would follow, *The Blue Mask* and *Legendary Hearts*. "How Do You Speak to an Angel," "My Old Man," and "Standing on Ceremony" deal with Reed's family issues with a direct force he hadn't summoned since "Kill Your Sons" (we'll leave it to others to debate their accuracy), and "So Alone" and "Keep Away" both offer a trenchant but heart-rending look at modern relationships. And "The Power of Positive Drinking" is amusing, but rather surprising coming from a guy who would give up alcohol and drugs a year after this was released. *Growing Up in Public* didn't get much notice on its initial release, but all these years later it sounds like a dry run for what was to be the most creatively fruitful period of Lou Reed's solo career. *—Mark Deming*

Rock & Roll Diary: 1967-1980 / 1980 / Arista ✦✦✦
Given the large number of stylistic detours and periodic creative dead ends that have marked Lou Reed's career, it isn't surprising that his body of work doesn't readily lend itself to a neatly packed "Greatest Hits" album; while there are more than a few Lou Reed collections on the market, most of them fall short of the mark as a truly accurate representation of his body of work. While flawed, *Rock & Roll Diary: 1967-1980* fares better than most; by necessity, it stops before Reed could enter his career renaissance period with 1982's *The Blue Mask*, and it doesn't glean as many of the scattered gems from his RCA period as one might hope. But it's one of the few Reed collections that starts with his work in the Velvet Underground rather than the dawn of his solo career, and if the first half isn't the Velvets collection of your dreams, it's a concise and telling picture of just how special their music really was, honoring both their sweet and bitter sides. The second half of *Rock & Roll Diary* looks at Reed's post-Velvets solo work, and while there are plenty of puzzling gaps (Nothing from *Coney Island Baby*? Where's "Perfect Day" and "Kill Your Sons"?) and a curiously strong emphasis on the transitional *Growing Up in Public*, the songs that do appear are Reed in prime form, and the live workout on "Street Hassle" that closes this set ends the album on a high note. *Rock & Roll Diary: 1967-1980* tries to summarize Reed's career as a major creative figure rather than pull together a handful of relative "hits," and if it doesn't quite achieve its goal, it comes close enough to remind anyone that Reed is one of the best and most intriguing figures in American rock & roll. *—Mark Deming*

The Blue Mask / 1982 / RCA ✦✦✦✦✦
In 1982, 12 years after he left the Velvet Underground, Lou Reed released *The Blue Mask*, the first album where he lived up to the potential he displayed in the most groundbreaking of all American rock bands. *The Blue Mask* was Reed's first album after he overcame a long-standing addiction to alcohol and drugs, and it reveals a renewed focus and dedication to craft—for the first time in years, Reed had written an entire album's worth of moving, compelling songs, and was performing them with keen skill and genuine emotional commitment. Reed was also playing electric guitar again, and with the edgy genius he summoned up on *White Light/White Heat*. Just as importantly, he brought Robert Quine on board as his second guitarist, giving Reed a worthy foil who at once brought great musical ideas to the table, and encouraged the bandleader to make the most of his own guitar work. (Reed also got superb support from his rhythm section, bassist extrordinaire Fernando Saunders and ace drummer Doane Perry). As Reed stripped his band back to a muscular two-guitars/bass/drums format, he also shed the faux-decadent "Rock & Roll Animal" persona that had dominated his solo work and wrote clearly and fearlessly of his life, his thoughts, and his fears, performing the songs with supreme authority whether he was playing with quiet subtlety (such as the lovely "My House" or the unnerving "The Gun") or cranked-to-ten fury (the paranoid "Waves of Fear" and the emotionally devastating title cut). Intelligent, passionate, literate, mature, and thoroughly heartfelt, *The Blue Mask* was everything Lou Reed's fans had been looking for in his work for years, and it's vivid proof that for some rockers, life can begin on the far side of 35. *—Mark Deming*

Legendary Hearts / 1983 / RCA ✦✦✦✦
If *Legendary Hearts* seemed like a disappointment in 1983, that was largely because the year before Lou Reed had released *The Blue Mask*, one of the finest albums of his career, and *Legendary Hearts* just wasn't quite as good. But pull it off the shelf today, give it a listen, and *Legendary Hearts* easily shuts down nearly anything Reed released in the 1970s; if it's a less obvious masterpiece than *The Blue Mask*, it makes clear that Reed was once again in firm command of his strengths, and making the most of them in the studio. Guitarist Robert Quine and bassist Fernando Saunders were both back on board from *The Blue Mask*, and they reaffirmed their status as the lynchpins of the strongest band of Reed's solo career, and drummer Fred Maher rocked harder (and with fewer frills) than Doane Perry. The bracing cross-talk of Reed and Quine's guitars had lost nothing in the year separating the two albums, and if Reed didn't seem to be aiming quite as high as a songwriter this time out, most of the tracks were every bit as intelligent and soul-searching as *The Blue Mask*'s lineup; if there were a few moments of comic relief, like "Don't Talk To Me About Work" and "Pow Wow," no one could argue that Reed hadn't earned a few laughs after songs like "Make Up Mind," "The Last Shot," and "Betrayed." On *Legendary Hearts*, Lou Reed was writing great songs, playing them with enthusiasm and imagination, and singing them with all his heart and soul, and if it wasn't his best album, it was more than good enough to confirm that the brilliance of *The Blue Mask* was no fluke, and that Reed had reestablished himself as one of the most important artists in American rock. *—Mark Deming*

Live in Italy / 1984 / RCA ✦✦✦✦✦
Robert Quine has said that the personal and musical differences which led to the end of his working relationship with Lou Reed had put a wall between them well before he finally gave Reed his notice. While Quine never failed to deliver on stage, the tension became audible in their music, and *Live in Italy* captures the best band of Lou Reed's solo career about a year past their peak, not long before they fell apart for the first time (Lou would reassemble the group for the world tour that followed *New Sensations*—a job Quine said he took solely for the money). Consequently, this isn't the ideal document of this band—but it also makes clear that even on a lesser night, Lou Reed, Robert Quine, Fernando Saunders, and Fred Maher were a force to be reckoned with. While Quine's performance isn't flattered by this album's mix, his edgy lines blend superbly with Reed's, and both are in fine fettle, while Fernando Saunders shines on bass and Fred Maher's rock-solid drumming holds everything firmly in place. Reed is on fire on most of these songs, and while this plays for the most part like a "Best of Lou Reed" set, he pulls out sharp, impassioned performances on every cut, doing lean-and-mean justice to Velvet Underground classics like "White Light/White Heat" and "Sister Ray," and rescuing the unnerving "Kill Your Sons" from the oblivion of *Sally Can't Dance*. Are there bootlegs or live videos that capture this band on better nights? Yes. Does that change the fact this is Reed's strongest live album? Not a bit. *—Mark Deming*

New Sensations / 1984 / RCA ✦✦✦✦✦
Lou Reed never struck anyone as one of the happiest guys in rock & roll, so some fans were taken aback when his 1984 album, *New Sensations*, kicked off with "I Love You, Suzanne," a catchy up-tempo rocker that sounded a lot like a pop tune. After reaffirming his status as one of rock's greatest poets with *The Blue Mask* and *Legendary Hearts*, what was Lou Reed doing here? Lou was having a great time, and his pleasure was infectious—*New Sensations* is a set of straight-ahead rock & roll that ranks with the most purely enjoyable albums of Lou's career. Reed opted not to work with guitarist Robert Quine this time out, instead overdubbing rhythm lines over his own leads, and if the guitars don't cut quite as deep, they're still wiry and in the pocket throughout, and the rhythm section of Fernando Saunders and Fred Maher rocks hard with a tough, sinewy groove. And while much of *New Sensations* finds Reed in a surprisingly optimistic mood, this isn't "Don' t Worry, Be Happy" by any stretch of the imagination. On "Endlessly Jealous," "My Friend George," and "Fly Into the Sun," Reed makes it clear that happiness can be a hard-won commodity, and when Reed embraces life's pleasures on "Turn To Me" and "New Sensations," he does so with a fierce joy that's realistic, unblinking, and deeply felt, like a man whose signed on for the full ride and is going to enjoy the good times while they last. Like *Coney Island Baby*, *New Sensations* showed that Reed had a lot more warmth and humanity than he was given credit for, and made clear that he could "write happy" when he felt like, with all the impact of his "serious" material. *—Mark Deming*

Mistrial / 1986 / RCA ✦✦✦
Between 1982 and 1984, Lou Reed put together the best band of his solo career, recorded three superb albums, and left behind a fine live double after two rapturously received world tours—not a bad track record from a guy who had been so inconsistent throughout the 1970s. One might well have argued that Lou was due for a disappointment, and *Mistrial* certainly filled that bill. On *Mistrial*, Reed opted to handle both lead and rhythm guitar parts as he had on *New Sensations*, but with a few shades less precision, and while Fernando Saunders once again did yeoman work as a bassist, as a co-producer he didn't

fill out Reed's sound especially well. The decision to use a drum machine on most of these tracks gives the album a stiff feeling, and a texture that captures what was least fortunate about '80s rock, but most importantly Reed didn't have an album's worth of top-shelf songs on tap. "No Money Down" and "Tell It to Your Heart" are smart and funny sketches on the difficult art of romance, while "Mama's Got a Lover" is an unexpectedly sweet character study and "The Original Wrapper" is a game stab at hip-hop from a 44-year-old white guy. But "Outside" and "Spit It Out" are just filler, and "Video Violence" is a pretty strange attack on the media from a guy who tried to bring the mindset of William S. Burroughs and Hubert Selby Jr. to rock & roll. *Mistrial* wasn't one of Reed's worst albums (it's hard to imagine *Sally Can't Dance* ever being deprived of that honor), but it certainly lowered his batting average as he seemed to be on a hot streak—as if his longtime fans needed to be reminded that he was fallible. *—Mark Deming*

New York / 1989 / Sire ✦✦✦✦✦

New York City figured so prominently in Lou Reed's music for so long that it's surprising it took him until 1989 to make an album simply called *New York*, a set of 14 scenes and sketches that represents the strongest, best-realized set of songs of Reed's solo career. While Reed's 1982 comeback, *The Blue Mask*, sometimes found him reaching for effects, *New York*'s accumulated details and deft caricatures hit bull's-eye after bull's-eye for 57 minutes, and do so with an easy stride and striking lyrical facility. *New York* also found Reed writing about the larger world rather than personal concerns for a change, and in the beautiful, decaying heart of New York City, he found plenty to talk about—the devastating impact of AIDS in "Halloween Parade," the vicious circle of child abuse in "Endless Cycle," the plight of the homeless in "Xmas in February"—and even on the songs where he pointedly mounts a soapbox, Reed does so with an intelligence and smart-assed wit that makes him sound opinionated rather than preachy—like a New Yorker. And when Reed does look into his own life, it's with humor and perception; "Beginning of a Great Adventure" is a hilarious meditation on the possibilities of parenthood, and "Dime Store Mystery" is a moving elegy to his former patron Andy Warhol. Reed also unveiled a new band on this set, and while guitarist Mike Rathke didn't challenge Reed the way Robert Quine did, Reed wasn't needing much prodding to play at the peak of his form, and Ron Wasserman proved Reed's superb taste in bass players had not failed him. Produced with subtle intelligence and a minimum of flash, *New York* is a masterpiece of literate, adult rock & roll, and the finest album of Lou Reed's solo career. *—Mark Deming*

Songs for Drella / Jul. 1990 / Sire ✦✦✦✦✦

John Cale, the co-founder of The Velvet Underground, left the group in 1968 after tensions between himself and Lou Reed became intolerable; neither had much charitable to say about one other after that, and they seemed to share only one significant area of agreement—they both maintained a great respect and admiration for Andy Warhol, the artist whose patronage of the group helped them reach their first significant audience. So it was fitting that after Warhol's death in 1987, Reed and Cale began working together for the first time since *White Light/White Heat* on a cycle of songs about the artist's life and times. Starkly constructed around Cale's keyboards, Reed's guitar, and their voices, *Songs for Drella* is a performance piece about Andy Warhol, his rise to fame, and his troubled years in the limelight. Reed and Cale take turns on vocals, sometimes singing as the character of Andy and elsewhere offering their observations on the man they knew. On a roll after *New York*, Reed's songs are strong and pithy, and display a great feel for the character of Andy, and while Cale brought fewer tunes to the table, they're all superb, especially "Style It Takes" and "A Dream," a spoken word piece inspired by Warhol's posthumously published diaries. If *Songs for Drella* seems modest from a musical standpoint, it's likely neither Reed nor Cale wanted the music to distract from their story, and here they paint a portrait of Warhol that has far more depth and poignancy than his public image would have led one to expect. It's a moving and deeply felt tribute to a misunderstood man, and it's a pleasure to hear these two comrades-in-arms working together again, even if their renewed collaboration was destined to be short-lived. *—Mark Deming*

Magic and Loss / Jan. 14, 1992 / Sire ✦✦✦

With 1982's *The Blue Mask*, Lou Reed began approaching more mature and challenging themes in his music, and in 1992, Reed decided it was time to tackle the Most Serious Theme of All—Death. Reed lost two close friends to cancer within the space of a year, and the experience informed *Magic and Loss*, a set of 14 songs about loss, illness, and mortality. It would have been easy for a project like this to sound morbid, but Reed avoids that; the emotions that dominate these songs are fear and helplessness in the face of a disease (and a fate) not fully understood, and Reed's songs struggle to balance these anxieties with bravery, humor, and an understanding of the notion that death is an inevitable part of life—that you can't have the magic without the loss. It's obvious that Reed worked on this material with great care, and *Magic and Loss* contains some of his most intelligent and emotionally intense work as a lyricist. However, Reed hits many of the same themes over and over again, and while Reed and his accompanists—guitarist Mike Rathke, bassist Rob Wasserman, and percussionist Michael Blair—approach the music with skill and impeccable chops, many of these songs are a bit samey; the album's most memorable tunes are the ones that pull it out of its mid-tempo rut, like the grooving "What's Good" and the guitar workout "Gassed and Stoked." *Magic and Loss* is an intensely heartfelt piece of music, possessing a taste and subtlety one might never have expected from Lou Reed, but its good taste almost works against it; it's a sincere bit of public mourning, but perhaps a more rousing wake might have been a more meaningful tribute to the departed. *—Mark Deming*

Between Thought and Expression: The Lou Reed Anthology / Apr. 14, 1992 / RCA ✦✦✦

Over the course of 45 songs on three CDs or cassettes, *Between Thought and Expression* chronicles the first 16 years of Lou Reed's solo work, from his debut, self-titled album that followed his 1970 departure from the Velvet Underground through the RCA and Arista years that culminated in 1986's *Mistrial*. On the way, the anthology delivers stellar moments from Reed's David Bowie-produced *Transformer* period, several pieces from the hauntingly doom-laden *Berlin*, and the '70s guitar anthem "Sweet Jane" from *Rock & Roll Animal*. The set includes five previously unreleased tracks, one non-LP B-side, and two soundtrack-only numbers. The tracks were selected and remastered with Reed's participation, and the refurbished sound is a revelation, particularly on the early material. *—Roch Parisien*

Set the Twilight Reeling / Feb. 20, 1996 / Warner Brothers ✦✦✦

After contemplating the decline of New York City, the passing of his mentor Andy Warhol, his place in (perhaps) the greatest American rock band of all time, and the very nature of life and death, in 1996 Lou Reed finally began to consider a really important subject—where to get a good chocolate egg cream. "Egg Cream" kicked off *Set the Twilight Reeling*, and for many fans it was a kick to hear Reed cranking up his amps and having some fun again, but much of the rest of the album turned out not to be as lightweight as the opener would have led you to expect. On *Set the Twilight Reeling*, Reed is preoccupied with relationships, as he tries to figure if he wants a long-term commitment ("Trade In"), if he's better off as a lone wolf ("NYC Man"), if he's in love ("The Proposition"), or if he just wants to fool around ("Hookywooky"). Reed rocks a lot harder here than on the two albums that preceded it (and plays plenty of great crunchy guitar), but much of the album is set in a mellow mid-tempo groove that's casual and comfortable but not especially compelling. And while "Sex With Your Parents (Motherfucker), Pt. II" is an amusing attack on conservative politicians, his logic isn't exactly clear. Longtime fans are no doubt grateful that Reed's relatively unfocused and unsubstantial albums these days are such a vast improvement over his fallow period in the 1970s, but for the most part *Set the Twilight Reeling* sounds like a standard issue 1990s Lou Reed album—smart, well-crafted, with plenty of guitar, but nothing terribly special, either. *—Mark Deming*

● **Different Times: Lou Reed in the '70s** / May 1996 / RCA ✦✦✦✦✦

Reed is very much an album-oriented artist, and those who think they may develop a serious interest in his work are better advised to seek individual titles than compilations. If you just want some of his best songs around the house, though, this is a well-chosen, economic 17-track survey of his best material from his best period as a solo act (the early to mid-'70s). Drawing most heavily from the *Transformer* and *Berlin* albums, this has his most famous/notorious early solo works ("Walk on the Wild Side," "Vicious," "Satellite of Love," "Caroline Says"), some inferior but notably different remakes of songs he recorded with the Velvet Underground ("Lisa Says," "I Can't Stand It," "Sweet Jane"), and other high points like "Kill Your Sons" and "Coney Island Baby." *—Richie Unterberger*

Perfect Night: Live in London / Apr. 21, 1998 / Warner Brothers ✦✦✦

By 1997, the "Unplugged" craze, in which nearly every rocker under the sun decided to look back on their songbook with tasteful and unamplified maturity, had just about run its course, but that wasn't about to stop Lou Reed from belatedly trying the same gimmick for his performance at London's 1997 Meltdown Music Festival. Reed's semi-acoustic performance was also prompted by the latest bit of electronic gimmickry to catch his fancy, a special feedback-defeating pickup system that gave his acoustic guitar "the sound of diamonds" (Reed's phrase). While it's difficult to say just what a diamond is supposed to sound like, it is true that his guitar sounds quite good on this set. Reed and his band approach the respectfully quiet arrangements with precision and no small amount of enthusiasm (especially bassist Fernando Saunders), and Lou is in unusually good voice here; one of the traditional failings of his live albums has been that he doesn't always sing and play well at the same time, but here he hit his marks with ease. However, you've got to wonder about the choice of material on *Perfect Night*; if Reed really intended this to be an overview of the breadth of his career, he wasn't doing himself any favors by throwing in "Vicious," "Original Wrapper," or "Sex With Your Parents," while "Kicks" and "Riptide" aren't especially well-served by stripping them of their electric guitars. There are enough good tracks here ("I'll Be Your Mirror," "Perfect Day," and "New Sensations") to indicate that Reed might have a good acoustic album in him, but before he tries something like *Perfect Night* again, he ought to sit down with some friends who can edit a better set list for him. *—Mark Deming*

Ecstasy / Apr. 4, 2000 / Warner Brothers ✦✦✦

Never let it be said that Lou Reed has lost the ability to surprise his audience; who would have thought that at the age of 58, on his first album of the new millennium, Reed would offer us an 18-minute guitar distortion workout with lyrics abut kinky sex, dangerous drugs, and (here's the surprise) imagining what it would be like to be a possum? For the most part, *Ecstasy* finds Reed obsessed with love and sex, though (as you might expect) his take on romance is hardly rosy ("Paranoia Key of E," "Mad," and "Tatters" all document a relationship at the point of collapse, while "Baton Rouge" is an eccentric but moving elegy for a love that didn't last) and Eros is usually messy ("White Prism"), obsessive ("Ecstasy"), or unhealthy and perverse ("Rock Minuet"). Reed genuinely seems to be stretching towards new lyrical and musical ground here, but while some of his experiments work, several pointedly do not, with the epic "Like a Possum" only the album's most spectacular miscalculation. Still, Reed and producer Hal Wilner take some chances with the arrangements that pay off, particularly the subtle horn charts that dot several songs, and Reed's superb rhythm section (Fernando Saunders on bass and Tony "Thunder" Smith on drums) gives these songs a rock-solid foundation for the leader's guitar workouts. As Reed and his band hit fifth gear on the album's rousing closer, "Big Sky," he once again proves that even his uneven works include a few songs you'll certainly want to have in your collection—as long as they're not about possums. *—Mark Deming*

American Poet / Jun. 26, 2001 / Pilot ✦✦✦

The Reivers

Jangle Pop, Power Pop, Alternative Pop/Rock

The Reivers began their existence as Zeitgeist, one of many melodic, jangly pop bands to emerge from the fertile Austin, Texas music community during the 1980s. Led by singers/guitarists John Croslin and Kim Longacre, Zeitgeist debuted in 1985 with the album *Translate Slowly*, which included their cover of Willie Nelson's "Blue Eyes Crying in the Rain." Shortly after the record's release, the group was slapped with a cease-and-desist order by another band called Zeitgeist, a Minneapolis-based percussion ensemble which had held the name longer; in honor of the William Faulkner novel, they became the Reivers. With Don Dixon producing, the band recorded 1987's *Saturday*, followed two years later by the assured *End of the Day*. 1991's *Pop Beloved* was the Reivers' final record; after their break-up, Croslin went on to produce the band Spoon. *—Jason Ankeny*

● **Translate Slowly** / 1985 / DB ♦♦♦♦♦

This, the Reivers' first full-length album, was a great amalgamation of rock and folk with a little bit of an "alternative" edge. It attracted a fair amount of attention in the music press, and received primarily good reviews. As with much of their future work, the lyrics were somewhat impressionistic, as opposed to straight stories. Unlike their subsequent releases, the drumming here was very frenzied, creating a unique sound which set them apart from similar bands. With vocals shared by John Croslin and Kim Longacre, the songs run the gamut from all-out rockers like "Araby" and "Sound and the Fury" to acoustic folk like the spirited "Freight Train Rain." *—Rob Caldwell*

Saturday / 1987 / Capitol ♦♦♦

End of the Day / 1989 / Capitol ♦♦♦

Continuing the pattern of a new album every other year, *End of the Day* came out two years after 1987's *Saturday*. John Croslin was beginning to gain experience as a producer, doing more than half the tracks without co-producer Andy Metcalfe. This would lead to his total production of their next album, plus his future endeavors after the breakup of the Reivers. A very good album, marred slightly by a distracting too-high-in-the-mix drum sound, it continued in the same vein as their previous release. A sort of theme about the idea of "home" ran through this album, though, with songs like "Almost Home" (later covered by Hootie and the Blowfish), "Star Telegram," "End of the Day," and "Cut Above." Tying in to this was the album artwork which included family snapshots hung on a refrigerator. Musically, one of the highpoints was an impassioned electric cover of the Broadway musical number "Lazy Afternoon." As with most of the Reivers' albums, a number of additional songs were recorded, but didn't make it on, in this case live favorite "Tell Me So" was a casualty. *—Rob Caldwell*

Pop Beloved / 1991 / DB ♦♦♦

The Reivers' moderately muscular folk-pop hasn't necessarily aged very well, but those who enjoyed this kind of thing when it was current will still enjoy the subtle charms of this album. "Subtle," of course, is a gentle way of saying "hookless," but that's not entirely accurate in this case. "Breathin' Easy" and "Other Side" are more purposeful than interesting, and "Dragonflies" keeps building steadily towards a climax that never arrives. These specifics, however, just seem to make the simple, melodic charms of "What You Wanna Do" and especially "Chinatown" all the more arresting. And even more striking is the fact that "If I Had a Little Time Without You" starts off sounding for all the world like Mission of Burma. Bandleader John Croslin sounds like he's singing with a cold. The title track, strangely enough, is an instrumental waste of time. *—Rick Anderson*

R.E.M.

f. 1980, Athens, GA

College Rock, Jangle Pop, Alternative Pop/Rock, American Underground

R.E.M. mark the point when post-punk turned into alternative rock. When their first single, "Radio Free Europe," was released in 1981 it sparked a back-to-the-garage movement in the American underground. While there were a number of hardcore and punk bands in the US during the early '80s, R.E.M.—singer Michael Stipe, guitarist Peter Buck, bassist Mike Mills and drummer Bill Berry—brought guitar-pop back into the underground lexicon. Combining ringing guitar hooks with mumbled, cryptic lyrics and a D.I.Y. aesthetic borrowed from post-punk, the band simultaneously sounded traditional and modern. Though there were no overt innovations in their music. R.E.M. had an identity and sense of purpose that transformed the American underground. Throughout the '80s, they worked relentlessly, releasing records every year and touring constantly, playing both theaters and backwoods dives. Along the way, they inspired countless bands, from the legions of jangle-pop groups in the mid-'80s to scores of alternative-pop groups in the '90s, who admired their slow climb to stardom. By the late '80s, the group's fanbase had grown large enough to guarantee strong sales, but the Top 10 success in 1987 of *Document* and "The One I Love" was unexpected, especially since R.E.M. had only altered its sound slightly. Following *Document*, R.E.M. slowly became one of the world's most popular bands. After an exhaustive international tour supporting 1988's *Green*, the band retired from touring for six years and retreated into the studio to produce their most popular records, *Out of Time* (1991) and *Automatic for the People* (1992). By the time they returned to performing with the *Monster* tour in 1995, the band had been acknowledged by critics and musicians as one of the forefathers of the thriving alternative rock movement, and they were rewarded with the most lucrative tour of their career. Toward the late '90s, R.E.M. was an institution, as its influence was felt in new generations of bands. *—Stephen Thomas Erlewine*

Chronic Town / 1982 / IRS ♦♦♦

Chronic Town established R.E.M.'s signature sound immediately, expanding the jangling riffs of their debut single "Radio Free Europe" into a full-fledged modus operandi. Recorded at Mitch Easter's Drive-In Studios, the EP has an endearingly ragged sound—it's a garage band playing jangling pop songs, and while the music is melodic and memorable, it has an underground mentality that keeps it from sounding conventional. Not only does the lo-fi production keep the music underground, but so do Peter Buck's ringing arpeggios, Michael Stipe's incomprehensible mumbled vocals and the band's amateurish enthusiasm. They might not be accomplished players, but already their songwriting is distinctive, with "Gardening at Night," "Wolves, Lower," and "Carnival of Sorts (Box Cars)" ranking as early classics. *—Stephen Thomas Erlewine*

☆ **Murmur** / 1983 / IRS ♦♦♦♦♦

Leaving behind the garagey jangle-pop of their first recordings, R.E.M. developed a strangely subdued variation of its trademark sound for its full-length debut album, *Murmur*. Heightening the enigmatic tendencies of *Chronic Town* by de-emphasizing the backbeat and accentuating the ambience of the ringing guitar, R.E.M. created a distinctive sound for the album—one that sounds eerily timeless. Even though it is firmly in the tradition of American folk-rock, post-punk and garage-rock, *Murmur* sounds as if it appeared out of nowhere, without any ties to the past, present or future. Part of the distinctiveness lies in the atmospheric production, which exudes a detached sense of mystery, but it also comes from the remarkably accomplished songwriting. The songs on *Murmur* sound as if they've existed forever, yet they subvert folk and pop conventions by taking unpredictable twists and turns into melodic, evocative territory, whether it's the measured riffs of "Pilgrimage," the melancholic "Talk About the Passion" or the winding guitars and pianos of "Perfect Circle." R.E.M. may have made albums as good as *Murmur* in the years following its release, but they never again made anything that sounded quite like it. *—Stephen Thomas Erlewine*

☆ **Reckoning** / 1984 / IRS ♦♦♦♦♦

R.E.M. abandoned the enigmatic post-punk experiments of *Murmur* for their second album *Reckoning*, returning to their garage-pop origins instead. Opening with the ringing "Harborcoat," *Reckoning* runs through a set of ten jangle-pop songs that are different not only in sound but in style from the debut. Where *Murmur* was enigmatic in its sound, *Reckoning* is clear, which doesn't necessarily mean that the songs themselves are straightforward. Stipe continues to sing powerful melodies without enunciating, but the band has a propulsive kick that makes the music vital and alive. And, if anything, the songwriting is more direct and memorable than before—the interweaving melodies of "Pretty Persuasion" and the country-rocker "(Don't Go Back to) Rockville" are as affecting as the melancholic dirges of "Camera" and "Time After Time," while the ringing minor-key arpeggios of "So. Central Rain," the pulsating riffs of "7 Chinese Bros.," and the hard-rocking rhythms of "Little America" make the songs into classics. On the surface, *Reckoning* may not be as distinctive as *Murmur*, but the record's influence on underground American rock in the '80s is just as strong. *—Stephen Thomas Erlewine*

Fables of the Reconstruction / 1985 / IRS ♦♦♦♦

For their third album, R.E.M. made a conscious effort to break from the traditions *Murmur* and *Reckoning* established, electing to record in England with legendary folk-rock producer Joe Boyd. For a variety of reasons, the sessions were difficult, and that tension is apparent throughout *Fables of the Reconstruction*. A dark, moody rumination on American folk—not only the music, but its myths—*Fables* is creepy, rustic psychedelic folk, filled with eerie sonic textures. Some light breaks through occasionally, such as the ridiculous collegiate blue-eyed soul of "Can't Get There From Here," but the group's trademark ringing guitars and cryptic lyrics have grown sinister, giving even sing-alongs like "Driver 8" an ominous edge. *Fables* is more inconsistent than its two predecessors, but the group does demonstrate considerable musical growth, particularly in how perfectly it evokes the strange rural legends of the South. And many of the songs on the record—including "Feeling Gravitys Pull," "Maps and Legends," "Green Grow the Rushes," "Auctioneer (Another Engine)" and the previously mentioned pair—rank among the group's best. *—Stephen Thomas Erlewine*

Lifes Rich Pageant / 1986 / IRS ♦♦♦♦♦

Fables of the Reconstruction was intentionally murky, and *Lifes Rich Pageant* was constructed as its polar opposite. Teaming with producer Don Gehman, who previously worked with John Mellencamp, R.E.M. developed their most forceful record to date. Where previous records kept the rhythm section in the background, *Pageant* emphasizes the beat, and the band turns in its hardest rockers to date, including the anthemic "Begin the Begin" and the punky "Just a Touch." But the cleaner production also benefits the ballads and the midtempo janglers, particularly since it helps reveal Stipe's growing political obsessions, especially on the environmental anthems "Fall on Me" and "Cuyahoga." The group hasn't entirely left myths behind—witness the Civil War ballad "Swan Swan H"—but the band sounds more contemporary both musically and lyrically than they did on either *Fables* or *Murmur*, which helps give the record an extra kick. And even with excellent songs like "I Believe," "Flowers of Guatemala," "These Days" and "What If We Give It Away," it's ironic that the most memorable moment comes from the garage rock obscurity "Superman," which is sung with glee by Mike Mills. *—Stephen Thomas Erlewine*

Dead Letter Office / 1987 / IRS ♦♦♦

Arriving mere months before *Document* took the group into the Top Ten, the B-sides and rarities collection *Dead Letter Office* sums up all of the quirks and idiosyncracies that made R.E.M. the leading underground guitar-pop band of the '80s. While only a handful of songs on *Dead Letter Office* rank among the group's best, the record is extremely entertaining, even for casual fans, particularly because it captures the wild spirit of R.E.M. that was evident at their concerts, but not always on their records. Among the gems scattered throughout the collection are the cheerily ridiculous "Band Wagon," "Voice of Harold" (which features Stipe singing the liner notes to a gospel album over the backing of "7 Chinese Brothers"), covers of the Velvet Underground, Pylon and Aerosmith, the ringing pop of "Burning Down" (which is later reworked as "Ages of You"), and "Walter's Theme," a drunken attempt at a commercial for a local restaurant that segues into a clueless cover of "King of the Road." The material may be slight, but it's fun—and R.E.M.'s albums aren't always fun. [The CD version of *Dead Letter Office* contains the group's debut EP, *Chronic Town*.] *—Stephen Thomas Erlewine*

☆ **Document** / 1987 / IRS ♦♦♦♦♦
R.E.M. began to move toward mainstream record production on *Lifes Rich Pageant*, but they didn't have a commercial breakthrough until the following year's *Document*. Ironically, *Document* is a stranger, more varied album than its predecessor, but co-producer Scott Litt—who would go on to produce every R.E.M. album in the following decade—is a better conduit for the band than Don Gehman, giving the group a clean sound without sacrificing their enigmatic tendencies. "Finest Worksong," the stream-of-conscious rant "It's the End of the World As We Know It (And I Feel Fine)" and the surprise Top Ten single "The One I Love" all crackle with muscular rhythms and guitar riffs, but the real surprise is how political the midtempo jangle-pop of "Welcome to the Occupation," "Disturbance At the Heron House" and "King of Birds" is. Where *Lifes Rich Pageant* sounded a bit like a party record, *Document* is a fiery statement, and its memorable melodies and riffs are made all the more indelible by its righteous anger. In other words, it's not only a commercial breakthrough, but a creative breakthrough as well, offering evidence of R.E.M.'s growing depth and maturity, and helping usher in the P.C. era in the process. *—Stephen Thomas Erlewine*

● **Eponymous** / 1988 / IRS ♦♦♦♦♦
Basically a singles collection from R.E.M.'s first five albums, *Eponymous* gives the listener a sense of R.E.M.'s change from a folk-rock band to a rock band. The songs are intelligently selected, distilling most of the best moments from their first five albums for I.R.S. Included is the original single of "Radio Free Europe," different mixes of "Gardening at Night" (where it's actually possible to hear the vocal) and "Finest Worksong," and the previously unreleased (and unspectacular) "Romance." (Note: An import collection, *The Best of R.E.M.*, doesn't have the rarities, but has 16 songs, including the remainder of *Eponymous*, plus many other important songs from their IRS years. Worth the couple of extra dollars for the beginner.) *—Stephen Thomas Erlewine*

Green / 1988 / Warner Brothers ♦♦♦
As major-label debuts by underground bands go, *Green* is fairly uncompromising. While it displays a more powerful guitar sound on "Get Up," "Turn You Inside Out" and "Orange Crush," it also takes more detours than *Document*, whether it's the bizarrely affecting contemporary folk of "The Wrong Child" and "You Are the Everything," the bubblegum of "Stand" and "Pop Song 89" or the introspection of the lovely "Hairshirt" and "World Leader Pretend." But instead of presenting a portrait of a band with a rich, eclectic vision, *Green* is incoherent. While its best moments are flat-out great, the band has bitten off more than it can chew; many of the songs sound like failed experiments, and its arena-ready production now sounds slightly dated. Nevertheless, half of the record is brilliant, and it certainly indicates that R.E.M. is continuing to diversify its sound. *—Stephen Thomas Erlewine*

Out of Time / Mar. 12, 1991 / Warner Brothers ♦♦♦
The supporting tour for *Green* exhausted R.E.M., and they spent nearly a year recuperating before reconvening for *Out of Time*. Where previous R.E.M. records captured a stripped-down, live sound, *Out of Time* was lush with sonic detail, featuring string sections, keyboards, mandolins, and cameos from everyone from rapper KRS-1 to the B-52's' Kate Pierson. The scope of R.E.M.'s ambitions is impressive, and the record sounds impeccable, its sunny array of pop and folk songs as refreshing as Michael Stipe's decision to abandon explicitly political lyrics for the personal. Several R.E.M. classics—including Mike Mills' Byrdsy "Near Wild Heaven," and the haunting "Country Feedback," and the masterpiece "Losing My Religion"—are present, but the album is more notable for its production than its songwriting. Most of the songs are slight but pleasant, or are awkward experiments like "Radio Song"'s stab at funk, and while this sounds fine as the record is playing, there's not much substantive material to make the record worth returning to. *—Stephen Thomas Erlewine*

☆ **Automatic for the People** / Jul. 1992 / Warner Brothers ♦♦♦♦♦
Turning away from the sweet pop of *Out of Time*, R.E.M. created a haunting, melancholy masterpiece with *Automatic for the People*. At its core, the album is a collection of folk songs about aging, death and loss, but the music has a grand, epic sweep provided by layers of lush strings, interweaving acoustic instruments and shimmering keyboards. *Automatic for the People* captures the group at a crossroads, as they moved from cult heroes to elder statesmen, and the album is a graceful transition into their new status. It is a reflective album, with frank discussions on mortality, but it is not a despairing record—"Nightswimming," "Everybody Hurts" and "Sweetness Follows" have a comforting melancholy, while "Find the River" provides a positive sense of closure. R.E.M. have never been as emotionally direct as they are on *Automatic for the People*, nor have they ever created music quite as rich and timeless, and while the record is not an easy listen, it is the most rewarding record in their oeuvre. *—Stephen Thomas Erlewine*

Monster / Sep. 27, 1994 / Warner Brothers ♦♦
Monster is indeed R.E.M.'s long-promised "rock" album; it just doesn't rock in the way one might expect. Instead of R.E.M.'s trademark anthemic bashers, *Monster* offers a set of murky sludge, powered by the heavily distorted and delayed guitar of Peter Buck. Stipe's vocals have been pushed to the back of the mix, along with Bill Berry's drums, which accentuates the muscular pulse of Buck's chords. From the androgynous sleaze of "Crush with Eyeliner" to the subtle, Eastern-tinged menace of "You," most of the album sounds dense, dirty and grimy, which makes the punchy guitars of "What's the Frequency, Kenneth?" and the warped soul of "Tongue" all the more distinctive. *Monster* doesn't have the conceptual unity or consistently brilliant songwriting of *Automatic*, but it does offer a wide range of sonic textures that have never been heard on an R.E.M. album before. *—Stephen Thomas Erlewine*

New Adventures in Hi-Fi / Sep. 10, 1996 / Warner Brothers ♦♦♦
Recorded during and immediately following their disaster-prone *Monster* tour, *New Adventures in Hi-Fi* feels like it was recorded on the road. Not only are all of Stipe's lyrics on the album about moving or travel, the sound is ragged and varied, pieced together from tapes recorded at shows, soundtracks, and studios, giving it a loose, careening charm. *New Adventures* has the same spirit of much of R.E.M.'s IRS records, but don't take the title of *New Adventures in Hi-Fi* lightly—R.E.M. tries different textures and new studio tricks. "How the West Was Won and Where It Got Us" opens the album with a rolling, vaguely hip-hop drum beat and slowly adds on jazzily dissonant piano. "E-Bow the Letter" starts out as an updated version of "Country Feedback," then it turns in on itself with layers of moaning guitar effects and Patti Smith's haunting backing vocals. Clocking in at seven minutes, "Leave" is the longest track R.E.M. ever recorded and it's one of their strangest and best—an affecting minor-key dirge with a howling, siren-like feedback loop that runs throughout the entire song. Elsewhere, R.E.M. treads standard territory: "Electrolite" is a lovely piano-based ballad, "Departure" rocks like a *Document* outtake, the chiming opening riff of "Bittersweet Me" sounds like it was written in 1985, "New Test Leper" is a gently winding folk-rock, "The Wake-Up Bomb" and "Undertow" rock like the *Monster* outtakes they are. *New Adventures in Hi-Fi* may run a little too long—it clocks in at 62 minutes, by far the longest album R.E.M. has ever released—yet in its multifaceted sprawl, they wound up with one of their best records of the '90s. *—Stephen Thomas Erlewine*

Up / Oct. 27, 1998 / Warner Brothers ♦♦♦
New Adventures in Hi-Fi functions as the starting point for *Up*, R.E.M.'s first album without drummer Bill Berry and their first that truly repudiates the legacy of jangle pop. *Up* is dominated by keyboards, muted percussion, buried guitars, and moody melodies—only "Daysleeper" finds the group in familiar sonic territory. What's striking about the album is that it *doesn't* sound like a dramatic departure; even without the ringing guitars, it sounds like R.E.M., albeit R.E.M. trying to be adventurous and hip. To a certain extent, that's a good thing, since it proves that the band has developed a signature sound more elastic than many would have predicted, and that they are skilled enough to successfully take risks with their sound. Above all else, *Up* is an accomplished and varied record, the work of smart record makers. It is also the work of veteran musicians—for the first time, R.E.M. sounds like they're playing catch-up, trying to keep their hip status intact. Occasionally, they pull it all together, as on the ominous opener "Airportman" and the darkly seductive "Suspicion," but they stretch their capacities to the breaking point nearly as often, as on the *Pet Sounds* pastiche "At My Most Beautiful," which comes off as second-rate High Llamas. Most of *Up*, however, falls in between those two extremes, winding up as self-consciously moody, down-tempo songs that fail to make an impression because they either don't take enough chances or they fail to speak directly—they are simply well-crafted tracks that are easy to admire, but hard to love. Ultimately, that is what distinguishes this new incarnation of R.E.M. *—Stephen Thomas Erlewine*

Reveal / May 15, 2001 / Warner Brothers ♦♦♦
Give 'em credit for realizing that *Up* was a dead-end, an avenue paved with forced experimentalism that signified nothing. Dock them points for harboring the desire to wander down that path, choosing to indulge in fuzzy details that add texture, but not character. These two impulses balance each other, as R.E.M. delivers *Reveal*, an album that feels like their stab at *All That You Can't Leave Behind*—a conscious return to their classic sound. Since they're fiercely protective of their anointed position of underground pioneers, they're not content to sit still and spin their wheels. So, they return to the lushness of *Out of Time*, melding it with the song-oriented *Automatic*—and undercutting it all with the sober sonic trickery of *Up* and *New Adventures in Hi-Fi*. Because *Reveal* is song-oriented, it initially plays more accessibly than *Up*, but these songs are cloaked in the same kind of deliberate studio craft that made *Up* feel stilted. This prevents *Reveal* from being an album to wholeheartedly embrace, even if it attempts to be as rich as *Automatic* and even if it succeeds on occasion. There are some very good pop songs here—windswept and sun-bleached beauties like "Imitation of Life," the dusty "All the Way to Reno (You're Gonna Be a Star)," and "Beachball," the one time their Beach Boys obsessions click. Still, ultimately these moments are weighed down by the album's aesthetic, which emphasizes sonic construction over the songs. *Reveal* winds up sharing the same strangely distant feel of *Up*, even if it's a tighter, better record. When R.E.M. weren't trying as hard, when they weren't meticulously crafting their sound, they made records that were as moody, evocative, and bracing as *Reveal* intends to be. Here, it's just all a bit too studied to ring true. *—Stephen Thomas Erlewine*

The Rembrandts

f. 1990, **db.** 1996

Adult Alternative Pop/Rock, Jangle Pop, Pop/Rock, Power Pop

Even though they became best known for recording "I'll Be There for You," the theme song to the smash NBC sitcom *Friends*, the Rembrandts were actually rather successful back in 1990 with their self-titled debut album, which produced a Top 20 hit in "Just the Way It Is, Baby." The duo of songwriter Danny Wilde and Phil Solem, both originally in the Los Angeles band Great Buildings, forged a Beatle-tinged brand of pop/rock with ringing guitars and fresh harmonies that found favor with radio programmers across the country, as well as *Friends* co-producer Kevin Bright. The Rembrandts were invited to record a theme song for the show, which they completed in three days; after the show became a hit, radio demand for a full-length version was overwhelming, and one was added to 1995's *LP* at the last minute. While the song was an instant radio smash, topping *Billboard*'s airplay chart for eight weeks, it wasn't released as a single until four months later in September, which makes its overall chart peak of number 17 somewhat deceptive. *LP*, meanwhile, went platinum. The band followed in 1998 with *Spin This*, this time under the name Danny Wilde and the Rembrandts. —*Steve Huey*

● **The Rembrandts** / Aug. 1990 / Atco ✦✦✦✦✦
One of the more noteworthy "jangly guitar" acts of the 1990s, the Rembrandts were off to an enjoyable start with this debut album. Melodic and congenial but far from wimpy, such pop/rock as "If Not for Misery," "New King" and the small hit "Just The Way It Is, Baby" set the tone for the L.A. duo's career. A variety of influences from previous decades can be detected—everyone from the Beatles to the Byrds and Crosby, Stills & Nash to the Everly Brothers. And yet, this CD never sounds dated, and has a definite freshness to it. With so many rap, metal and industrial acts expressing deep pessimism in 1990, the optimistic, socio-political idealism of "Everyday People" (not to be confused with the Sly & the Family Stone classic) was a refreshing change. —*Alex Henderson*

Untitled / Sep. 15, 1992 / Atco ✦✦✦
Untitled didn't come close to the punch of *The Rembrandts*, as the duo moved away from the bright pop that shone on the previous effort in favor of a more subdued approach. And while the subject matter—mainly songs of yearning and lost love—hasn't changed much since the debut, the subtle string arrangements and minor-key melodies blend quite nicely, bringing out the themes more fully. Aside from the beautiful "Johnny Have You Seen Her," which is pleasantly reminiscent of Squeeze, the songs lack the instantly endearing quality of the debut, but are no less rewarding with a little more effort. —*Chris Woodstra*

LP / May 23, 1995 / East West ✦✦✦
Most of the merits of the Rembrandts' third album, *LP*, were overshadowed by the massive success of "I'll Be There for You," the infectious theme from the hit Generation X sitcom *Friends*. Included on *LP* at the last minute—the first pressings didn't list the song on the album cover—"I'll Be There for You" received saturation radio airplay, topping the adult contemporary charts, yet it was never released as a single, forcing fans of the song to buy the entire album to own the song. While the Monkees guitar riffs and layered harmonies are not entirely representative of the Rembrandts—it makes them out to be a bubblegum band—the record is filled with smart, hook-laden guitar pop that won't disappoint old Rembrandts fans or listeners attracted by the hit. —*Stephen Thomas Erlewine*

Renaissance

f. 1969, Surrey, England
Prog-Rock/Art Rock
The history of Renaissance is essentially the history of two separate groups—the original group was founded in 1969 by ex-Yardbirds members Keith Relf and Jim McCarty as a sort of progressive folk-rock band, who recorded two albums but never quite made it, despite some success on England's campus circuit. The band went through several membership changes, with Relf and his sister Jane exiting and McCarty all but gone after 1971. The new line-up formed around the core of bassist Jon Camp, keyboard player John Tout, and Terry Sullivan on drums, with Annie Haslam, an aspiring singer with operatic training and a three-octave range. Their first album in this incarnation, *Prologue*, released in 1972, was considerably more ambitious than the original band's work, with extended instrumental passages and soaring vocals. Their breakthrough came with their next record, 1973's *Ashes Are Burning*. *Turn of the Cards* had a much more ornate songwriting style and was awash in lyrics that alternated between the topical and the mystical. The group's ambitions, by now, were growing faster than its audience—*Scheherazade* (1975) was built around a 20-minute extended suite for rock group and orchestra that dazzled the fans but made no new converts. As the 1970s closed out, the group was running headlong into the punk and new wave booms that made them seem increasingly anachronistic and doomed to cult status. —*Bruce Eder*

Renaissance / 1969 / Renaissance ✦✦✦
The original group's debut album was a then-groundbreaking meld of progressive rock with classical and jazz influences. The album is a little clunky by today's standards, and far druggier than the later group in its ambience (cofounders Keith Relf and Jim McCarty were the heavily psychedelic half of the final lineup of the Yardbirds, which made them anathema to Jimmy Page), but vocalist Jane Relf had a striking individual style and the classical influence was unique for its time. —*Bruce Eder*

Illusion / 1971 / Island ✦✦✦
The group's second album is more polished in its sound, but the record never found an audience because it has never remained in print for very long or been very easy to find. The classical influence is more pronounced, and Jane Relf stretches out further in her vocalizing, as the original group evolved somewhat in the direction of Renaissance Mark II. —*Bruce Eder*

Prologue / 1972 / One Way ✦✦✦
The first album by the '70s (i.e., Annie Haslam) version of Renaissance is a transitional work, rooted in more standard hard rock sounds (including psychedelia) than what followed. One can spot the difference, which may please some listeners and put others off, in the fairly heavy guitar sound of "Prologue," Rob Hendry's electric instrument playing both lead and rhythm parts prominently at various times behind Annie Haslam's soaring vocals and adjacent to John Tout's piano. "Kiev" may also startle some longtime fans, since Haslam doesn't handle the lead vocals, the male members' singing being much more prominent. The ethereal, flowingly lyrical "Sounds of the Sea" is the cut here that most resembles the music that the group became known for in the years ahead, and shows Haslam singing in the high register for which she would become famous. "Spare

Some Love," with its prominent folky acoustic guitar, also anticipates material (specifically "Let It Grow" and "On the Frontier") off of the group's better-known second album, *Ashes Are Burning*. "Bound for Infinity" marked the final creative contribution by cofounder Jim McCarty, of the '60s version of Renaissance, and is pretty enough even if it doesn't fit in anywhere with their subsequent sound. The sound is clean, and this version of *Prologue* is to be preferred over Capitol's abortive attempt to reissue it in the late '80s as *In the Beginning*, which cut some of the material and had totally lackluster sound. —*Bruce Eder*

Ashes Are Burning / 1973 / One Way ✦✦✦✦✦
With electric guitarist Andy Powell sitting in on the title track, Renaissance delivered its best, and first fully formed album, mixing Russian, French, and Indian influences in musical settings that are both lively and elegant. The title track is one of the few lengthy progressive-rock pieces of the era that holds up, and the rest of the material runs the gamut from folk ("Carpet of the Sun") to Impressionist ("At the Harbor"), all of it hauntingly beautiful and enlivening. Reissued in 1993 by One Way Records, with excellent sound. —*Bruce Eder*

Turn of the Cards / 1974 / Repertoire ✦✦✦✦✦
The third album by this incarnation of Renaissance was a match for their previous success, *Ashes Are Burning*, with equally impressive performances and songwriting and a few new musical twists added. The songs here fit more easily into a rock vein, and the prior album's folk influences are gone. *Turn of the Cards* rocks a bit harder, albeit always in a progressive rock manner, and Jon Camp's bass and Terence Sullivan's drums are both harder and heavier here, the bass (the group's only amplified instrument) in particular much more forward in the mix. This change works in giving the band a harder sound that leaves room for Jimmy Horowitz's orchestral accompaniments, which are somewhat more prominent than those of Richard Hewson on the prior album, with the horns and strings, in particular, more exposed. Annie Haslam is in excellent voice throughout, and finds ideal accompaniment in Michael Dunford's acoustic guitar and John Tout's piano. The writing team of Dunford and Betty Thatcher also adds some new wrinkles to the group's range—in addition to progressive rock ballads like "I Think of You," they delivered "Black Flame," a great dramatic canvas for Haslam and Tout, in particular; and "Mother Russia" is a surprising (and effective) move into topical songwriting, dealing with the plight of Alexander Solzhenitsyn and other victims of Soviet repression (you had to be there in the 1970s to realize what a burning issue this was). And then there were the soaring, pounding group virtuoso numbers like "Things I Don't Understand," which managed to hold audience interest across nine or ten minutes of running time. —*Bruce Eder*

Scheherazade & Other Stories / 1975 / Repertoire ✦✦✦✦
This album was the group's magnum opus in the perception of many on-lookers and fans, and it still plays well, though its flaws are more evident now than they were at the time. The "Song of Scheherazade," really a suite for the group supported by the London Symphony Orchestra and a chorus, started with guitarist-composer Mick Dunford, who had a personal fascination with the medieval literary work *Tales of 1,001 Arabian Nights*, and was realized by Dunford and his composing partner Betty Thatcher, with bassist Jon Camp and pianist John Tout. The piece, really nine sections assembled together, was one of the more ambitious works to come out of the progressive rock boom, and while it fits together nicely and does have some gorgeous passages and many lyrical, powerful sections, although it also seems slightly repetitive, overstaying its welcome somewhat; additionally, it never uses the orchestra quite as effectively as one senses it might have, for anything except embellishment. Less ambitious and more completely successful are "Ocean Gypsy," "The Vultures Fly High," and "Trip to the Fair" on side one, all relatively unpretentious pieces which feature extraordinary singing by Annie Haslam. There's no domestic CD release, though there is an import that does improve on the original vinyl, which suffered from a fair amount of noise in its pressings and somewhat compressed sound. —*Bruce Eder*

Live at Carnegie Hall / 1976 / Repertoire ✦✦

Novella / 1977 / Sire ✦✦

A Song for All Seasons / 1978 / Sire ✦✦

In the Beginning / 1978 / Capitol ✦✦✦
This compilation of the *Prologue* and *Ashes Are Burning* albums should be great, but it isn't. The sound is flat and two major songs from *Ashes* were cut mercilessly. Good for a glimpse at the band. —*Bruce Eder*

Azure d'Or / 1979 / Sire ✦✦

Rock Galaxy / 1980 / RCA ✦✦

Camera Camera / 1981 / Repertoire ✦✦

Time-Line / 1983 / IRS ✦✦

● **Tales of 1001 Nights, Vol. 1** / 1990 / Sire ✦✦✦✦
This 75-minute compilation and its companion volume are just about the only acknowledgments on the part of Sire Records that it ever had a progressive rock catalog, somewhere in between signing the Ramones and Madonna. The song lineup on this first volume heavily favors the group's early repertory, including songs originally done for the Sovereign label, represented here in concert recordings from *Renaissance Live at Carnegie Hall*. How attractive that is depends upon how one feels about those performances, versus the original studio renditions (available from One Way Records domestically and, in superior versions, from HTD Records in England). They were never too impressive on vinyl, although the digital remastering and re-equalization of the material seems to have solved much of that problem. The original Sire studio material, including

"Running Hard" and "Black Flame," sound better here than they did on their original vinyl releases, which had fairly noisy pressings and were somewhat top-heavy on the bass. The accompaniments all sound crisper on the CD, the nuances and fine balances between the band and the orchestra much easier to appreciate, and the only major flaw—and it is a big one—is the absence of "Song of Scheherazade," their biggest orchestral-accompanied piece ever. Only a four-minute excerpt is included; admittedly, the work as a whole is somewhat overblown, taking up a little more time than it is worth, but it was the centerpiece of two separate albums, which should have told the programmers something about how much it registered to fans. *—Bruce Eder*

Tales of 1001 Nights, Vol. 2 / Mar. 27, 1990 / Sire ✦✦✦✦
The second volume of Sire Records' retrospective compilation on Renaissance is not as impressive musically as its predecessor, devoted as it is primarily to the lesser of the group's late-'70s repertory. The intelligent thing to have done with this volume would have been to put "Song of Scheherazade" on this volume, which would have shored up its value—perhaps this would have been an awkward fit, as the disc was to include the 23-minute live version of "Ashes Are Burning," but one or two of the lesser songs that are here might've been sacrificed. As it is, the material is less concise and accessible than that of the preceding volume, though it still has very attractive vocal and piano flourishes, and stunning melodies. There are also a few of what could be considered "offbeat" numbers for the group, most notably the folk-like "Northern Lights," and "Midas Man," on which the dominant instrument for much of the song is Mick Dunford's acoustic guitar rather than John Tout's piano. Much of the music seems more of a reach, however, in terms of subject matter, making this volume more of an acquired taste than its companion, and a choice more appropriate for hardcore fans of the group than those with a casual interest. *—Bruce Eder*

REO Speedwagon

f. 1967, Champaign, IL
Arena Rock, Pop/Rock, Soft Rock, Adult Contemporary
REO Speedwagon may not have been the most talented arena rock band of the '70s, but they almost certainly worked harder than any other group on the same circuit. In 1971, they released their first album of competent hard rock, but they didn't chart until 1974 with *Ridin' the Storm Out.* That album was recorded with temporary vocalist Michael Murphey, who would later have some solo success of his own; regular vocalist/rhythm guitarist Kevin Cronin rejoined the band in 1975. The first album released after Cronin rejoined REO was only moderately successful, but 1977's *REO Speedwagon Live/You Get What You Play For* began a string of gold and platinum albums, culminating with the 1980 album *Hi-Infidelity,* which sold over seven million copies in America. Although their style had shifted to a slick, mainstream AOR rock and they were known for power ballads, their hits didn't stop coming until 1990, when the band's support dropped off sharply; their 1991 album didn't even chart. However, the band remains a solid touring attraction, and they continued to release albums into the '90s. *—Stephen Thomas Erlewine*

R E O Speedwagon / Dec. 1971 / Epic ✦✦✦

R.E.O. 2 / Dec. 1972 / Epic ✦✦✦✦
An early album defining what was best about them in their opening-act days of the early '70s. *—Cub Koda*

Ridin' the Storm Out / Jan. 1974 / Epic ✦✦✦✦
REO Speedwagon began to come into its own with its third album, *Ridin' the Storm Out.* Over the years, the record became a platinum-seller, but it originally charted at number 171, due to the strength of their series of opening shows for more successful rock acts. While the group still had elements of their bar-band boogie, they began to streamline their approach on this album. Although it only resulted in one minor hit, with the title track scraping the bottom of the singles charts, the record was one of their most consistent efforts. *—Stephen Thomas Erlewine*

R.E.O. / Jun. 1976 / Epic ✦✦✦

You Can Tune a Piano, But You Can't Tuna Fish / Apr. 1978 / Epic/Legacy ✦✦✦✦
You Can Tune A Piano, But You Can't Tuna Fish was a breakthrough album for REO Speedwagon in a sense, gelling the guitar craft of Gary Richrath and the vocals of Kevin Cronin with songs that rambled and rolled and never stopped for air. Richrath's style finally formed some catchy hooks, and Cronin's songwriting is solid while his voice sounds rejuvenated and downright fiery. "Roll With The Changes" and "Time For Me To Fly" only made it to #58 and #56 on the charts, but the album's sales trumped all of the chart statistics, giving REO their second platinum-selling album. Songs like "Do You Know Where Your Woman Is Tonight" and "Blazin' Your Own Trail Again" are well groomed around the edges, sounding smoother and more established than their earlier material. The harmonies on most of the songs stick to the guitar chords, and even the frantic "Unidentified Flying Tuna Trot," a wild and flighty guitar piece, is unraveled with tornado-like power. With the guitars sounding louder, the songs running quicker, and the culmination of both being well-maintained, *Tuna Fish* proved that REO Speedwagon could rock & roll when they had to. *—Mike DeGagne*

Decade of Rock & Roll '70-'80 / 1980 / Epic ✦✦✦✦
This is a well-chosen recap of REO's dues-paying years. *—Dan Heilman*

Hi Infidelity / Dec. 1980 / Epic/Legacy ✦✦✦✦✦
Many albums have scaled to the top of the American charts, many of them not so good, but few have been as widely forgotten and spurned as REO Speedwagon's *Hi Infidelity.* In a way, the group deserved this kind of success. They had been slogging it out in the arenas of the U.S., building up a sizeable audience because they could deliver live. And then, in 1980, they delivered a record that not just summarized their strengths, but captured everything that was good about arena rock. This is the sound of the stadiums in that netherworld between giants like Zeppelin and MTV's slick, video-ready anthems. This is unabashedly mainstream rock, but there's a real urgency to the songs and the performances that gives it a real emotional core, even if the production keeps it tied to the early, pre-visual '80s. And so what if it does, because this is *great* arena rock, filled with hooks as expansive as Three Rivers Stadium and as catchy as the flu. That, of course, applies to the record's two biggest hits—the power ballad "Keep on Loving You" and the surging "Take It on the Run"—which define their era, but what gives the album real staying power is that the rest of the record works equally well. It's easy to dismiss REO Speedwagon, since they weren't hip at the time, and no amount of historical revisionism will make them cool kitsch. And, let's face it, their records were usually hit-and-miss affairs. But they did get it right once, and it's on this glorious record—if you need proof why arena rock was giant, this is it. *—Stephen Thomas Erlewine*

Wheels Are Turnin' / Nov. 1984 / Epic ✦✦✦
Wheels Are Turnin' blends clear, crisp ballads with high-energy pop/rock, which eventually gave REO Speedwagon four Top 40 singles, the same amount as *Hi Infidelity* credited them with four years earlier. Kevin Cronin's writing is rock solid, a delightful turnaround from 1982's *Good Trouble* album. As one of their best ballads, "Can't Fight This Feeling" puts an elegant piano riff in front of Cronin's earnest voice, presenting the band with their second #1 single, while "I Do' Wanna Know" is a turbulent ride of clean-cut guitar and up-and-down piano that comes off as well-crafted pop with a bite. Every track has the band sounding sharper and more alive, with even the less-extravagant material like "Break His Spell" and "Thru The Window" emanating merit. "One Lonely Night" throws the spotlight on Cronin's voice, proving his expertise at carrying out the slow stuff hasn't dwindled, while "Live Every Moment" rounds out the last of the singles from the album, hitting #34 in August of 1985, eight months after *Wheels Are Turnin'* achieved its #7 mark on the U.S. charts. With production, songwriting, and tight instrumentation wisely dished out in equal portions, *Wheels Are Turnin'* was evidence that REO Speedwagon could still make some gratifying rock & roll. *—Mike DeGagne*

Live: You Get What You Play For / 1985 / Epic ✦✦✦

● **The Hits** / 1988 / Epic ✦✦✦✦✦
Over the course of the 1980s, REO Speedwagon became one of the decade's leading power balladeers. However, these singles sapped the band's reputation as a rock & roll band. Although it may focus more on ballads such as "Time for Me to Fly," "Keep on Loving You," and "Can't Fight This Feeling," *Hits* does not completely overlook the band's rock anthems, taking care to also include such underrated rockers as "I Don't Want to Lose You," "Don't Let Him Go," and a live version of "Ridin the Storm Out," the band's first and best rock single from the 1970s. Though there is a rather large quantity of REO compilations, *Hits* remains the wisest investment for most listeners. *—Barry Weber*

Second Decade Of Rock & Roll, 1981 to 1991 / Sep. 24, 1991 / Epic ✦✦✦
Fans of live material will thoroughly enjoy this handpicked, hit-and-miss 18-track compilation of REO Speedwagon's hits recorded during their mid- to late-'80s tours. Most of the songs work well in a live environment, with songs like "Tough Guys," "I Do' Wanna Know" and "Keep The Fire Burning" coming out on top, harnessing the most energy while keeping with their original form. Only six of the tracks are from the studio, with "Shakin' It Loose" being the most spirited, as the others are mediocre REO efforts "L.I.A.R," "Live Every Moment," "Love Is A Rock"). As a hits package though, *The Second Decade* should be spared, especially since their best song, "Keep On Loving You" has been replaced by a poorly ventured reggae version which sounds silly and out of place. While the ballads are kept to a minimum, some of their less accomplished material could have been replaced with some of their seventies work from *Tuna Fish* or even *REO.* Tracks like "Live It Up" and "One Too Many Girlfriends" represent their late eighties disappointments in *The Earth, a Small Man, His Dog, and a Chicken* and *Life As We Know It,* sounding a wee bit uninspired. For what it's worth, Doughty's Hammond organ revitalizes much of the live tracks, while on the other hand, the absence of Gary Richrath's feverish guitar playing is sadly missed on a few of the newer tunes. *The Second Decade Of Rock & Roll* shouldn't be deemed crucial, as only a few of its tracks are truly worthy of owning. *—Mike DeGagne*

The Ballads / Aug. 3, 1999 / Epic/Legacy ✦✦✦✦
At one time, REO Speedwagon were considered hard rockers, or at least arena-rockers. Over time, their harder rocking material was forgotten, and their true talent surfaced—namely, power ballads. Along with Journey, REO Speedwagon was one of the first groups to develop the power ballad—the distinctive blend of anthemic melodies, slow tempos, big guitars and big hooks. They had their biggest hits with power ballads, so it makes sense that Epic would assemble a collection, appropriately titled *Ballads,* that contains all of them on one disc. As it happens, *Ballads* features all but one of their Top Ten hits ("Keep the Fire Burnin'" is the absent party), plus a pair of new songs, "Just for You" and "Till the Rivers Run Dry." Naturally, the well-known hits ("Time for Me to Fly," "Keep on Loving You," "Can't Fight this Feeling," "Take It on the Run") dominate, especially since they're sandwiched between the two new songs on the first side. Nothing—not the pleasant new songs, not the listenable album tracks, not the acceptable also-ran singles—matches those songs, which sound all the stronger when they're sequenced together. Still, that doesn't make *Ballads* a weak listen, since the second-tier material here is among REO's best and helps elevate this collection to one of their most enjoyable albums. After all, their albums frequently were dotted with filler, and one benefit of a compilation is that it leaves the filler behind. *—Stephen Thomas Erlewine*

The Replacements

f. 1979, Minneapolis, MN, **db.** 1991

College Rock, Jangle Pop, Alternative Pop/Rock, Hard Rock, American Underground

The Replacements were one of the most beloved bands of the American underground in the '80s, due to their raucous live performances and Paul Westerberg's heartbreaking songs. Though they tried to break into the mainstream, they never succeeded, spending their career as a cult act. Like many great cult acts, they inspired many fans to start bands of their own, and their records remain highlights of the '80s.

After a fairly nondescript debut, the Replacements developed their voice with 1983's *Hootenanny.* Here, the group started playing around with other genres, sometimes ironically. *Hootenanny* was a dry run for 1984's *Let It Be,* the band's critical and artistic breakthrough which proved that Westerberg had developed into a first-rate songwriter. Critics and fellow musicians were quick to praise the band, and they developed a large underground following, leading to a contract with Sire.

Their major-label debut *Tim* garnered rave reviews upon its 1985 release, yet the band couldn't quite leap into the mainstream. Frequently, the band was barely able to play, let alone stand up, during their concerts. The Replacements also refused to make accessible videos—the video for "Bastards of Young" featured nothing but a stereo system, playing the song—thereby cutting themselves off from MTV mass exposure.

After *Tim,* founding member Bob Stinson was fired from the band, allegedly for substance addictions. The Replacements' next album, the relatively streamlined *Pleased to Meet Me,* received another round of terrific reviews upon its spring 1987 release, but the band couldn't expand their cult. *Don't Tell a Soul* was their slickest to date, yet it earned mixed reviews, even if they cracked the charts with the single "I'll Be You."

Defeated by *Don't Tell a Soul*'s lackluster performance, Paul Westerberg planned on recording a solo album, but Sire rejected the idea. Consequently, the next Replacements album, the stripped-down *All Shook Down,* was a solo Westerberg record in all but name. Following a supporting tour for the album, the Replacements quietly disbanded in the summer of 1991. *—Stephen Thomas Erlewine*

Sorry Ma, Forgot to Take Out the Trash / 1981 / Twin/Tone ✦✦

Stink / 1982 / Twin/Tone ✦✦✦

Following quick on the heels of the group's debut, the *Stink* EP takes the loud-hard-fast attitude of *Sorry Ma, Forgot to Take Out the Trash* to the extreme, mistakenly giving the impression that the Replacements were a hardcore band. Even though the EP isn't much more than clamor, it's *better* clamor than before—the band doesn't sound tighter but their noise is more galvanizing and a handful of songs ("Kids Don't Follow," "Fuck School," "God Damn Job") suggest Paul Westerberg is improving as a songwriter. *—Stephen Thomas Erlewine*

Hootenanny / 1983 / Twin/Tone ✦✦✦

The Replacements came into their own with *Hootenanny,* a careening, drunken stumble through punk, rock & roll, country, blues and folk. The eclecticism of the album separated the Replacements from the post-punk hardcore pack, but it's also what makes the record a mess. Half of the record is devoted to ironic jokes, whether it's the Beatles pastiche of "Mr. Whirly," and the tongue-in cheek title track or the silly closer "Treatment Bound." Not so coincidentally, those are songs where Westerberg branches out into other styles, and he found it easier to experiment under the guise of a joke. He does let his guard down on the extraordinary "Within Your Reach," a disarmingly open plea for love that he recorded entirely himself. It's the only truly vulnerable moment on the record, but the snide "Color Me Impressed" also comes close to true emotion. And it's fun to hear Westerberg act tough on "Take Me Down to the Hospital," "Run It," and "You Lose," especially considering how the group has improved. They're still sloppy, to be sure, but Bob Stinson's guitar stings and the rhythm section of Tommy Stinson and Chris Mars rocks with a loose abandon that makes even the filler—and there's a lot of filler—enjoyable garage-punk. *—Stephen Thomas Erlewine*

☆ **Let It Be** / 1984 / Twin/Tone ✦✦✦✦✦

The Replacements half-heartedly tried to expand their reach on *Hootenanny,* and they followed through on that album's promise on *Let It Be.* Kicking off with the country-rock shuffle of "I Will Dare," the record explodes into a series of psuedo-hardcore ravers before hitting Paul Westerberg's piano-driven rumination, "Androgynous," one of four major ballads that cuts to the core of Midwestern suburban alienation. "Sixteen Blue" is one of the definitive teenage anthems of the '80s, while "Unsatisfied" rages in despair and Westerberg rarely was more affecting than the solo performance of "Answering Machine." All four, along with "I Will Dare," form the core of Westerberg and the Replacements' canon, and are enough to make *Let It Be* a cornerstone post-punk album, even if the rest of the record pales next to the songs. All the remaining songs are convincing garage-rockers, even if they reveal the Replacements' former punk stance to be a bit of a pose—a cover of Kiss' "Black Diamond" comes off as a tribute, as does the co-opting of Ted Nugent's "Cat Scratch Fever" for "Gary's Got a Boner." Furthermore, the original numbers lean toward the Faces, leaving the Ramones behind and while everything except "Seen Your Video," which now sounds as dated as a "Disco Sucks" rant, are bracing rockers, they're a bit inconsequential and point the way toward the band's deadly fascination with classic rock. *—Stephen Thomas Erlewine*

★ **Tim** / 1985 / Sire ✦✦✦✦✦

Let it Be made the Replacements into college-radio and critical favorites, leading the group to a major-label contract with Sire. The band's major-label debut *Tim* does represent a bit of a compromise of the group's garage-punk sound. Producer Tommy Erdelyi (formerly of the Ramones) helped clean up the band's sound, primarily by harnassing the rhythm section to a click track—no longer does the band thrash all over the place, they keep a steady rocking beat. Similarly, Bob Stinson is kept in check, and his wildfire guitar bubbles above the surface only on two cuts, "Dose of Thunder" and "Lay it Down Clown," which are both filler. Some of the rockers, even the anthemic "Bastards of Young," are gutted by the cleaner sound, but the overall effect of the record isn't hurt because Paul Westerberg turns in his finest overall set of songs, ranging from the charming love song "Kiss Me On the Bus" and the college-radio anthem "Left of the Dial" to the detailed chronicles of loneliness like "Here Comes a Regular," "Hold My Life" and "Swingin' Party." Westerberg's melodies and observations are sharper than ever, giving *Tim* an eloquent but edgy power that can't be diluted by the tame production. *—Stephen Thomas Erlewine*

Boink!! / 1986 / Glass ✦✦

The purpose of *Boink!!* has never been entirely clear—though released in 1986, two years after the Replacements' critical breakthrough *Let It Be,* this eight-track mini-LP instead compiles the majority of its selections from the band's earlier, lesser Twin/Tone releases *Stink* and *Hootenanny.* The record is nevertheless something of a Holy Grail among Replacements fans, however, for its inclusion of two much sought-after rarities: "If Only You Were Lonely," the B-side of their "I'm in Trouble" single, and the previously unreleased "Nowhere Is My Home." The former is a sardonic acoustic ballad that's perhaps the first Paul Westerberg song to fully articulate the self-deprecating angst and alienation at the heart of the band's very best work; the latter is a blistering rocker produced by cult icon Alex Chilton, brilliantly continuing along the same thematic lines. Long out of print, but well worth the effort of tracking the damn thing down. *—Jason Ankeny*

Pleased to Meet Me / 1987 / Sire ✦✦✦✦✦

Bob Stinson was kicked out of the band after *Tim,* allegedly because he was unwilling to make the musical leap forward necessary for *Pleased to Meet Me.* With Stinson left the Replacements' hardcore roots, leaving behind the conflicting desires of Westerberg's wish to be a serious singer/songwriter and for the group to become either the Faces or Big Star. That conflict is played out throughout *Pleased to Meet Me,* and it isn't helped by the stultifyingly clean and detailed production by Jim Dickinson. Chris Mars and Tommy Stinson are reigned in tighter than ever before, giving most of the songs a strangled, distanced feel which isn't helped by Dickinson's canned guitar sounds and the odd production flourishes, including the occasional sax and keyboard. The full-blown production works on the horn and string-drenched "Can't Hardly Wait," but it makes mindlessly rocking filler like "Shooting Dirty Pool" and "Red Red Wine" irritating. For the most part, Westerberg's songs make the clean sound tolerable, particularly on the Stonesy "I.O.U.," the suicide sketch of "The Ledge," the power-pop of "Never Mind" and "Valentine," and the lovely acoustic "Skyway." But the fan love-letter "Alex Chilton" reveals more than necessary—even though Westerberg is shooting for stardom, he has more affinity for the self-styled loser, which means he never wants to make the full leap to the mainstream. And that can only hurt a record like *Pleased to Meet Me,* which has stardom in its sights. *—Stephen Thomas Erlewine*

Don't Tell a Soul / 1989 / Sire ✦✦✦

All of the slick production of *Pleased to Meet Me* couldn't prepare listeners for the glossy sound of *Don't Tell A Soul,* the Replacements' last-ditch attempt at mainstream success. Bathed with washes of synthesizers, shining guitars, backing vocals and a shimmering, AOR-oriented production, *Don't Tell a Soul* puts an end to the Replacements and begins Paul Westerberg's solo career. The bulk of the songs are self-consciously mature, as Westerberg looks back on his career (the autobiographical "Talent Show") and is haunted by the past ("Rock & Roll Ghost," "Darlin' One"), as he attempts to refashion himself as a craftsman. A few of these attempts work, particularly the country-rock ballad "Achin' to Be" and the arena-rock stab "I'll Be You," but the lite-funk workout "Asking Me Lies" and the stuttering "I Won't" are flat-out embarassing. And the rest of the album suffers from Westerberg's determination to be adult. The songs are too self-consciously mature and the band functions as a supporting act for the lyrics, which lack the unpretentious poetry of his best work. Ironically, Westerberg's desire to be an "adult" is the reason why radio ignored *Don't Tell a Soul,* because it meant that the record lacked both rockers or power-ballads which would have given them air-time. And most old fans found the production too heavy to make sorting through the album worthwhile. *—Stephen Thomas Erlewine*

All Shook Down / 1990 / Sire ✦✦✦✦✦

Although *Don't Tell A Soul* sounded like a Replacements record, it felt like a Paul Westerberg album. *All Shook Down* continues that trend—it's a Replacements record only in name. Recorded with a variety of session musicians and sporting no individual credits, *All Shook Down* emphasizes the songs, not the band, and it's a weary, beaten set of songs. Despite a handful of forced rockers—especially the down-right embarrassing Johnette Napolitano duet "My Little Problem"—the album is a low-key and primarily acoustic set, finding Westerberg knowing that the band is over and wondering where it all went wrong. While *All Shook Down* doesn't have any nakedly emotional stunners like "Answering Machine" or "Skyway," it has a unified atmosphere and an off-the-cuff, unpretentious feel which comes as a relief after the weighty ambitions of *Don't Tell a Soul.* It also has a number of excellently crafted songs, ranging from the wistful "Sadly Beautiful" and the druggy "All Shook Down" to snappy pop-rockers like "Merry Go Round," "When It Began" and "Happy Town." As the loungey closer suggests, the record is meant to be "The Last," and few bands ended their career in such a knowing, worn-out fashion. *—Stephen Thomas Erlewine*

All For Nothing/Nothing for All / Oct. 28, 1997 / Sire ✦✦✦

The Replacements were one of the three great American underground bands of the '80s (the other two were R.E.M. and Hüsker Dü), influencing a generation of alternative bands with their ramshackle, ragged rocking and Paul Westerberg's heart-tugging songs. In short, they were the band no one heard except for the young guitar-slingers inspired to form bands of their own. *All for Nothing/Nothing for All,* a double-disc set comprised of one disc of "hits" and one disc of rarities, is supposed to offer proof of the group's influence, but it actually inadvertently dismantles their legend. For legal reasons, the hits disc *All for Nothing* couldn't feature highlights from their Twin/Tone releases, which means their rawest recordings and gems like "Within Your Reach," "I Will Dare," and "Androgynous" aren't here. Instead, four songs each from their Reprise albums—*Tim, Pleased to Meet Me, Don't Tell a Soul, All Shook Down*—are featured, and while most of the obvious suspects are here, they make the Replacements sound downright traditional; based on these tracks, the only '90s bands they influenced were Americana groups like Wilco and the Bottle Rockets, not indie punk and grunge outfits like Nirvana. And, surprisingly, the Replacements don't even rock that hard on these Reprise records—the production, as many longtime fans have claimed, tames their wilder tendencies. Nevertheless, many of the songs on *All for Nothing* are among Westerberg's finest and prove that he was a talented songwriter, especially since the filler that plagued every Replacements album has been saved for disc two, *Nothing for All*, which is comprised entirely of B-sides and unreleased cuts. Still, there are a couple of gems on the disc, particularly the early Alex Chilton-produced take of "Can't Hardly Wait" and the Tom Waits-assisted rave-up "Date to Church." *—Stephen Thomas Erlewine*

Republica

f. 1995, London, England

Alternative Dance, Club/Dance, Alternative Pop/Rock

As Brit-pop remained popular in England during the mid-'90s, Republica hit the charts with a sound closer in feel to '80s indie-dance groups such as the Pet Shop Boys and New Order. Vocalist Saffron was born in Nigeria, and began singing with club-staples N-Joi and the Shamen, as well as Jah Wobble. By 1995, she had met keyboard players Tim Dorney (previously with Flowered Up) and Andy Todd (who has produced Barbra Streisand and Björk, among others). They began writing songs, and after recruiting guitarist Johnny Male and drummer Dave Barborossa, Republica debuted with the single "Out of the Darkness." U.K. indie-dance label Deconstruction signed the group and released its self-titled debut. From the album, "Ready to Go" became a hit both in England and in the States, where it stormed the alternative Top Ten during late 1996. The follow-up, 1998's *Speed Ballads*, only gained British distribution *—John Bush*

• **Republica** / Jul. 29, 1996 / RCA ♦♦♦♦

Republica essentially sounds like they're stuck in 1990, when house and rave were just beginning to make their presence felt in dance-pop—which, to more critical ears, will mean they sound dated during the mid-'90s, when jungle, drums-n-bass, ambient and all other forms of techno are finally edging their way into the mainstream. And that argument would be relevant if Republica were attempting to work in that genre, but as their eponymous debut indicates, they have no interest in hardcore techno—they just want to dance. Working with strong, accessible hi-NRG beats and catchy choruses, the trio has a bright, energetic sound that is quite infectious when tied with the right melodies, such as on the hit singles "Ready to Go" and "Drop Dead Gorgeous." If they had more than one sound, however, *Republica* would be even more entertaining, but as it stands, the record is a stretch of pleasantly numbing dance-pop punctuated by two terrific singles. *—Stephen Thomas Erlewine*

Speed Ballads / Nov. 1998 / Deconstruction ♦♦♦

While it was released only in the U.K., Republica's sophomore release *Speed Ballads* exhibits some remarkable growth. Detractors always felt that the band was the commercialization of other similar groups such as Garbage, yet Republica's music has a definite pop leaning that sets them apart from some of their contemporaries. Since Republica is more or less a studio creation—more about "production" than being a band, really—it's not surprising that the project employed a team of all-star producers including Alan Winstanley and the Lightning Seeds' Ian Broudie. What resulted was a cycle of ten tracks in an album far more diverse than their debut. While the disco-metal that ruled their first record has been pushed to the back of the mix here—only some of the songs actually have the same pounding rhythms on the debut—the songwriting has come exceptionally far. It's especially noticeable on the excellent single "Try Anything," a moving power-ballad that's also awash in beats. Other highlights include the hard-driving "From Rush Hour With Love" and the spacey "Fading of the Man." *—Jason Damas*

The Residents

f. 1966, Shreveport, LA

Mixed Media, No Wave, Post-Punk, Experimental, Avant-Garde

Over the course of a recording career spanning several decades, the Residents remained a riddle of Sphinx-like proportions; cloaking their lives and music in a haze of willful obscurity, the band's members never idenitified themselves by name, always appearing in public in disguise—usually tuxedos, top hats and giant eyeball masks—and refusing to grant media interviews. Drawing inspiration from the likes of fellow innovators including Harry Partch, Sun Ra and Captain Beefheart, the Residents channelled the breadth of American music into their idiosyncratic, satiric vision, their mercurial blend of electronics, distortion, avant-jazz, classical symphonies and gratingly nasal vocals reinterpreting everyone from John Philip Sousa to James Brown while simultaneously expanding the boundaries of theatrical performance and multimedia interaction.

Finding no takers for their oddball sounds, the Residents issued their first records on their own Ralph Records. The 1974 full-length *Meet the Residents* prompted a lawsuit from Capitol Records over its cover, a twisted, dadaesque Beatles parody. 1976's *Third Reich 'N' Roll* was a collection of pop oldies covers, followed one year later by an abrasive cover of the Rolling Stones' "Satisfaction," which became an underground hit on both sides of the Atlantic at the peak of the punk movement.

During the early '80s, the Residents embarked upon a trilogy of prog-rock albums and also mounted another ambitious project, the "American Composer" series, although only two of the projected titles ever appeared. Instead, in the wake of financial and corporate difficulties which resulted in the creation of a New Ralph label, the Residents issued the one-off *God in Three Persons* and 1989's *The King and Eye*. The 1990 album *Freak Show* was reissued as a CD-ROM four years later, marking the group's first leap into the new digital interactive technology. In 1997, the band celebrated their silver anniversary with the release of the career-spanning overview *Our Tired, Our Poor, Our Huddled Masses*. *—Jason Ankeny*

Meet the Residents / 1974 / East Side Digital ♦♦♦

The Residents are true avant-garde crazies. Their earliest albums (of which this is the first) have precedents in Captain Beefheart's experimental albums, Frank Zappa's conceptual numbers from *Freak Out*, the work of Steve Reich and the compositions of chance music tonemeister John Cage—yet the Residents' work of this time really sounds like nothing else that exists. All of the music on this release consists of deconstructions of countless rock and non-rock styles, which are then grafted together to create chaotic, formless, seemingly haphazard numbers; the first six "songs" (including a fragment from the Nancy Sinatra hit "These Boots Are Made for Walkin'") are strung together to form a larger entity similar in concept to the following lengthier selections. The result is a series of unique, odd, challenging numbers that manage not to be entirely successful. The album cover is a fierce burlesque of the Beatles' first U.S. Capitol label release, sporting puerilely doctored photographs of the Fab Four on the front and pictures of collarless-suited sea denizens on the back (identified as Paul McCrawfish, Ringo Starfish, and the like). This is an utterly bizarre platter that may appeal to very adventurous listeners. *—David Cleary*

Third Reich & Roll / 1976 / East Side Digital ♦♦♦♦

Technically the third album from the group, though released as a follow-up to *Meet the Residents*, this 40-minute assault on the music of the '60s follows Picasso's dictum of all artists killing their (aesthetic) fathers. Two side-long medleys of songs both classic ("Papa's Got a Brand New Bag") and obscure ("Telstar") are destroyed, deconstructed, mangled, spat on, spit out, ground up, and injected with gleeful humor. If there's any concept here, it's that the brain-numbing catchiness of pop music was fascism in disguise, keeping teenyboppers docile while selling them rebellion, hence the cover art of a gestapo-uniformed Dick Clark holding a carrot. Whether it's only much-suppressed love for these songs (as they went on to return again and again to the themes and artists examined here, including James Brown, "Land of 1000 Dances," and "Double Shot"), it's up to the listener to decide. Mostly any fan of the group will spend many hours trying to decode all the songs here, all the time with a smile on their face. (Officially, there are 29 songs, but there could be more). The first CD release (on ESD) added two essential singles plus their B-sides from around the same time. Their cover of the Stones' "Satisfaction" reduces the concepts of the album to three highly unlistenable minutes, guaranteed to tax the patience of any non-fan, a guaranteed lease-breaker, and therefore highly recommended. And their Beatles collage "Beyond the Valley of a Day in the Life" cuts and pastes the Fab Four's output into something wondrous and strange. The 1997 rerelease drops these tracks, making the first CD worth hunting out if possible. *—Ted Mills*

Eskimo / 1979 / East Side Digital ♦♦♦♦♦

The most rewarding, the most difficult, and the most accomplished of all the Residents' albums, this was their departure into the field of imaginary ethno-musicography that they had begun on "Six Things to a Cycle" on *Fingerprince*. Ostensibly a musical documentary on the Eskimo, this is an album of icy atmospheres, poetic electronics, and imaginary landscapes, concocted around a loose narrative told in the liner notes. There's also a subtheme of indigenous populations overrun by western commercialism (is that native chant actually "Coca Cola is Life"?). Ex-Henry Cow member Chris Cutler plays a lot of the percussion on the album, especially on the finale, "Festival of Death," the only real piece of rhythmic music here, which shines out as anything but dark or sinister. In any other group's hands this would have been a pretentious disaster, but the Residents pull it off through spirit, humor, and sheer bravado. *—Ted Mills*

The Commercial Album / Nov. 1980 / East Side Digital ♦♦♦♦

Here's the concept: The structure of most pop songs consists of only two parts, the verse and the chorus. Since the verse and chorus usually repeat three times in a three-minute song, a pop tune really only consists of one minute of music. Cut out the repetition and you can, therefore, fit 40 pop songs onto a 40-minute record. And that's exactly what the Residents have done on *The Commercial Album*, the title of which comes from the band's deduction that since pop songs only consist of one minute of music and most advertisements are about a minute long also, ad jingles are "therefore the music of America." Got it? Whatever the concept behind it, this album is not only weird in that special way that only Residents albums are, but it's also surprisingly musically satisfying. A few of its 40 tracks ("Secrets" and "The Simple Song," for example) feel like throwaways, but most of them are surprisingly well organized and complete. The instrumental "Japanese Watercolor" is particularly impressive, as are the songs "Picnic Boy" and "Troubled Man." This album would make a great introduction to the Residents for anyone who hasn't yet been exposed to the band's unique brand of whimsy. *—Rick Anderson*

The Mole Show: Live in Holland, June 6, 1983 / 1983 / East Side Digital ♦♦♦

The Mole story is the Residents' crypto-religious saga of exodus, enslavement, and bitter hope. *Mole Show: Live in Holland, June 6, 1983* is a powerful opening of a trilogy as of yet only partially released. As such, even among Residents fans, it is often seen as the pinnacle of their vision. Rich in artwork, the package contains an animate and powerful expression of the Residents' core ode. A young Penn Jillette (Penn & Teller) narrates the tales with explanations, some visual cues, and a comedic routine still in development. At least for this show, there is an explosive, surprise ending featuring a frantic, cursing Jillette. Along with the companion album *Mark of the Mole* (the studio version), this is a prime and important example of the Residents' electronic visions of a weird reality and fractured, deconstructed pop. —*Thomas Schulte*

13th Anniversary Show—Live in Japan / 1986 / East Side Digital ✦✦✦✦✦
The 13th Anniversary Tour marked the last live appearance of Snakefinger with the Residents and was the only time the group took to the stage with an armload of career spanning material, not centered around one concept album. Expanded from the original Torso release by eight tracks, the song list ranges from the early "Eloise" (from *Vileness Fats*) to their angst-ridden cover of James Brown's "Man's World." The band, relying heavily on the Emulator synth and the fiery angular distortion of Snakefinger's guitar, bring life to even the slightest of their material, rendering "Monkey and Bunny" from their snoozy team-up with Renaldo and the Loaf into something approaching a frightening beauty. The lead Residents' vocals burst forth with bile and confusion, letting out a cathartic wail on the show closing "Cry for the Fire." The remaster adds some applause into an original mix that was once all the more devastating when it seemed like they were playing for an enthusiastic crowd of three in an echoing hall. That quibble aside, this is one of the finest live documents of this mysterious group. —*Ted Mills*

★ **God in Three Persons** / 1988 / Rykodisc ✦✦✦✦✦
Employing the same stress-scheme as Poe's "The Raven" throughout its 62 minutes, "God In Three Persons" is an extended work in "talking-blues" style for narrator, electronic instruments, and a chorus providing comments not to be found in the libretto—they sing production credits at the beginning, and lines like "something's coming, but not real soon," and "this is a sad part, oh, such a sad part." This surreal and yet directly delivered work is as lovingly human as it is comic with profound experience simply expressed... in short, an original masterpiece of American music, directly in the tradition of the Thomson-Stein and Robert Ashley operas. As in all Residents pieces, the voices are modified electronically and the musical elements are deceptively minimal—most of its 14 episodes have only two chords which, however, still manage to instantly produce the correct atmosphere (Phil Glass-like Wagnerian thirds for mythic import, tonic-dominant in triplets for '50s teenage love story, etc.). There are only passing riffs, more like comments, and the only melody in the whole piece is a wheezy organ quote of the standard doxology hymn "Holy, Holy, Holy (God in Three Persons)." The subject matter is, in part, the derivation of religious and other symbolic images from the naturally erotic... but that's only part of it. Please give this one a listen. —*"Blue" Gene Tyranny*

Roadworms: The Berlin Sessions / Sep. 12, 2000 / East Side Digital ✦✦✦✦✦
An intriguing attempt to capture a section of the Residents' *Wormwood* tour without actually recording live shows. Instead, they set up in a Berlin studio and recorded the live arrangements, aiming to get each song in a single take, later adding some overdubs. The result is typically quirky, having a mix of rawness and polish that makes it quite appealing to listen to, even with the bite that comes as part of any work by the Residents. Whether or not the album is appealing to those who own *Wormwood* is another matter. —*Steven McDonald*

Paul Revere & the Raiders

f. 1960, Portland, OR

Frat Rock, Pop/Rock, Garage Rock, Pop, Rock & Roll
With their Revolutionary War costumes and upbeat attitude, Paul Revere & the Raiders were one of the more entertaining rock & roll bands of the mid-'60s. They began in 1960 as a more hard-edged outfit, and after the mid-'70s, they evolved into a musical-comedy lounge act. It wasn't until the summer of 1965, when they were chosen as the house band on the afternoon TV show *Where the Action Is*, that Paul Revere & the Raiders really took off, with singer Mark Lindsay becoming a teenage heartthrob. In 1966 and 1967, they enjoyed four Top Ten hits—"Kicks," "Hungry," "Good Thing," and "Him or Me—What's It Gonna Be?"—and four Top Ten, gold-selling albums—*Just Like Us!, Midnight Ride, The Spirit of '67*, and *Greatest Hits*. Their good-time style became less fashionable in the late '60s, though they continued to reach the Top 40. After a temporary name change to simply "Raiders," they scored their sole number one hit with the gold single "Indian Reservation (The Lament of the Cherokee Reservation Indian)" in 1971. —*William Ruhlmann*

Like Long Hair / 1961 / Gardena ✦✦
Paul Revere & the Raiders / 1963 / Sande ✦✦✦
Paul Revere & the Raiders' second independently released album, issued shortly before they signed to Columbia Records, showed that the group had developed from the barband material and gimmicky boogie-woogie instrumentals of 1960-1961 into a good R&B-based band with a stronger vocal focus, both on Mark Lindsay's lead singing and on the band's backup harmonies (though many of the tracks still were instrumentals). The material consisted of covers of songs like "Honky Tonk," "Shake, Rattle & Roll," and "Don't Be Cruel," evidence that the Raiders had been listening to the radio carefully for suitable dance music. It would take the studio polish of producer Terry Melcher to make them the band of "Kicks" and "Good Thing" a few years down the line, but it was already apparent that the Raiders had been paying their dues. [After the group achieved stardom in 1966, *Paul Revere & the Raiders* was reissued by Jerden Records under the title *In the Beginning*. In 1969, it was reissued by Sears under its original title and by Pickwick with two tracks, "Linda Lu" and "Irresistable You," deleted.] —*William Ruhlmann*

Here They Come! / 1965 / Columbia ✦✦✦
It took Columbia Records two years after signing Paul Revere & the Raiders to release this label-debut LP. In the interim, the group had released a string of singles that were only regional successes in the Northwest. Producer Bob Johnston had taken them into the studio to try to recreate their dynamic live show before an invited audience, but Columbia sat on the results until the group's coming residency on ABC-TV's *Where the Action*

Is prompted this release. The first side of the album displays the Raiders as the raucous club band they were, grinding through R&B dance tunes like "You Can't Sit Down" and "Oo Poo Pah Doo." The second side previews their evolution into more of a pop group in the mid-'60s, although with songs like "Fever," it still retains something of their early R&B flavor. —*William Ruhlmann*

Midnight Ride / 1966 / Sundazed ✦✦✦
Midnight Ride marked just about the pinnacle of Paul Revere & the Raiders' history as a source of great albums. Even more to their credit, most of the music on *Midnight Ride* was written by the bandmembers themselves, and not just Mark Lindsay and Paul Revere, but Phil Volk, Drake Levin, and Mike Smith getting a shared songwriting credit. The irony is that this was the last album on which that egalitarian spirit was to dominate; alongside the tight, hard, eminently danceable rock & roll sounds that comprise about two-thirds of this album, there are signs of the softer, more introspective balladry that lead singer Mark Lindsay was starting to favor in his songwriting ("Little Girl in the Fourth Row," etc.). It was this stylistic break, coupled with disputes over which bandmembers were to get their songs represented on the group's albums, that led to Levin's departure following the release of this album, which helped precipitate a stylistic drift away from the sound that defined the group. The Sundazed reissue, released in February 2000, has been remixed from the original three-track session masters, yet remains true to the band's original sound, and the album has been enhanced with the presence of three rocking bonus tracks (two of them car songs—cool!). "Kicks" is still the coolest song here, but the Sundazed version rocks a lot harder with the extra tracks, and is a lot more fun. There are also new notes by Volk and Levin, in which both look back with honesty yet a great deal of warmth and enjoyment for what they did, and what they were doing around the time of this album. —*Bruce Eder*

In the Beginning / 1966 / Jerden ✦✦✦
When Paul Revere & the Raiders became a commercial success on Columbia Records in 1966, Northwest independent Jerden Records released *In the Beginning*, a reissue of the group's second album, originally released on Sande in 1963 under the title *Paul Revere & the Raiders*. When released the first time around, it showed that the group had developed from the bar band material and gimmicky boogie-woogie instrumentals of 1960-1961 into a good R&B-based band with a stronger vocal focus, both on Mark Lindsay's lead singing and on the band's backup harmonies (though many of the tracks still were instrumentals). The material was covers of songs like "Honky Tonk," "Shake, Rattle & Roll," and "Don't Be Cruel," evidence that the Raiders had been listening to the radio carefully for suitable dance music. It took the studio polish of producer Terry Melcher to make them the band of "Kicks" and "Good Thing," but it was already apparent that the Raiders had been paying their dues. —*William Ruhlmann*

Just Like Us! / Jan. 1966 / Sundazed ✦✦✦
Although *Just Like Us!* was Paul Revere & the Raiders' fourth album overall, it marked a number of firsts. It was their first album to appear since they had become TV stars (and therefore AM radio staples and teenage magazine heartthrobs, especially Mark Lindsay) as a result of *Where the Action Is*; it was their first album to be produced entirely by Terry Melcher, a powerful influence and significant contributor to their sound; it was their first Top Ten album and their first to go gold. Actually, it's only a gradual development from their previous album, the half-live (in the studio) *Here They Come!* The group still had a tough R&B edge and still favored R&B covers like "Night Train," "Doggone," and, by way of England, "(I Can't Get No) Satisfaction" and "I'm Crying." (Melcher was already steering a stylistic course for The Raiders between The Rolling Stones and the Animals.) Even the two hit singles, "Steppin' Out" and "Just Like Me," were intense, bluesy rockers. Unlike later albums, *Just like Us!* highlighted the whole band—guitarist Drake Levin, bassist Phil "Fang" Volk, and drummer Mike Smith each took turns on lead vocals. (That would change as Lindsay's profile rose in the band.) Each was competent and entertaining, but *Just like Us!* was still an album by a group feeling its way from the dancehall circuit to the different and more creative demands of mass popularity. —*William Ruhlmann*

The Spirit of '67 / Nov. 1966 / Sundazed ✦✦✦
The Spirit of '67, Paul Revere and the Raiders' third gold-selling, Top Ten album to be released in 1966, marked the triumph of the group's in-house writing team of lead singer Mark Lindsay, Paul Revere, and producer Terry Melcher. "Hungry," the Top Ten follow-up to "Kicks," was written, like the earlier hit, by Barry Mann and Cynthia Weil, but Lindsay-Revere-Melcher then hit the Top 40 with "The Great Airplane Strike" and the Top Ten with "Good Thing." (Actually, Revere was not a writer on "Good Thing," as subsequent releases indicated.) Those hits anchored this collection, which was filled out by showcases for bassist Phil Volk and drummer Mark Smith (guitarist Drake Levin had been replaced by Jim Valley), plus some secondary material by the group's leaders. As usual, they were listening closely to their peers, and much of the material had the twangy guitar-rock sound common to 1966, though some of the experimental eclecticism that would lead to the elaborate productions of 1967's *Sgt. Pepper* psychedelic era was also apparent in songs like "Oh! To Be a Man" and "Undecided Man" (the latter a near-copy of the Beatles' "Eleanor Rigby"). This stylistic trend-following did not bode well for the future, but for the moment Paul Revere and the Raiders were riding high. The CD reissue on Sundazed adds three bonus cuts, including the 45-single version of "The Great Airplane Strike," and an alternate version of "Hungry." —*William Ruhlmann*

Revolution! / 1967 / Sundazed ✦✦✦✦
If not as consistently a knockout as *Spirit of '67, Revolution!* is nevertheless right on its heels, containing as it does an even greater degree of pop experimentation within the form. Suffice to say that this group managed to make the transition from the simple, tough R&B-flavored rock they helped found to the more psychedelic popcraft/acidic majesty that soon unfolded behind the 1964-1965 Beatles' lead. And if *Spirit* is the

Raiders' *Revolver*, then *Revolution!* is their less wacked-out *Sgt. Pepper*. Beginning with one of their most supreme moments—the rough-and-tumble, aggressive yet amazingly catchy "Him or Me—What's It Gonna Be"—the LP takes the same twists and turns as its predecessor through a multitude of entertaining styles, from the sharp lazy blues of "Reno" to the quintessential upbeat smack of "Mo'reen" and especially "Gone-Movin' On." Through it all, bandleader Mark Lindsay is a minor marvel. Lindsay may not have been blessed with a classic pop voice croon, but his exciting lower-range grunt and snarl compliments his upper-range prettier voice in a way that adds bushels of unfiltered attitude. His gutsy, versatile style totally blends with the rough edges of both the production and playing, which belies the more gilded pop moments. Lindsay is the glue that holds what would have been a willy-nilly collection together. Truly 1967 was the most magical year in pure pop history. But if many with-it fans have already bathed in the unbelievable sonic pleasures of that year, far too few have given the Raiders their rightful place in this pantheon, even though they certainly held such a place in their time. There can be no reason for this oversight to continue, for here is the evidence once again laid bare. *—Jack Rabid, The Big Takeover*

Goin' to Memphis / 1968 / Sundazed ♦♦♦
Regardless of the name on the album, *Goin' to Memphis* is essentially a Mark Lindsay solo project cut in Memphis, at Chips Moman's American Studios. At the time, the group was looking for a change in sound, their prior LP, *Revolution*, having failed to sell in remotely the number of its predecessors; road manager Jerry Williams suggested an album with Moman, who would only record with his own house musicians: Tommy Cogbill and Reggie Young on guitars, Mike Leech on bass, Spooner Oldham and Bobby Woods on keyboards, and Gene Crispian on drums. So this is Mark Lindsay and those guys, with Lindsay writing six of the songs himself. Only one cut—the previously recorded single "Peace of Mind"—features Paul Revere & the Raiders. *Goin' to Memphis* was a serious departure, without a trace of the garage punk or pop-psychedelia sound of their earlier albums, but it was also a reasonably successful one. Lindsay's vocals are astonishingly strong and gritty throughout this record, doing "Soul Man," "Every Man Needs a Woman," "I Don't Want Nobody," "No Sad Songs," or "Boogaloo Down Broadway" with very convincing ease, grit, and passion. At the time, this may have been the album that helped inspire Lindsay to begin pursuing a solo career around the Raiders' work. The American Studios band, of course, could play this stuff in their sleep, and what little augmentation there is came from members of the Memphis Symphony adding strings. Unfortunately, *Goin' to Memphis* failed to recapture the group's earlier audience, being a little too hard and serious as soul for many of the younger white middle-class kids who comprised their listenership. *—Bruce Eder*

Something Happening / 1968 / Sundazed ♦♦♦

Alias Pink Puzz / 1969 / Sundazed ♦♦
The title was a reference to the band's ruse of submitting a new record to an L.A. radio station under the alias and earning airplay until it was discovered that "Pink Puzz" was really Paul Revere & the Raiders. That was the Raiders' dilemma—they could still get attention for their singles, such as the Top 40 rocker "Let Me!" that led off this collection, but hip FM radio didn't want to know. Actually, since Mark Lindsay's muse was taking him in a pop-swamp-rock direction not far removed from what Elvis Presley was doing at the time, maybe that made sense. Lindsay's increasingly autobiographical material concerned itself with the pleasures and travails of being a rock star on the road, and though he could bring conviction to such material, singing about the dilemma of missing his limo can't have endeared him to his fans. As it was, *Alias Pink Puzz* charted higher than any Raiders album in two years, but stayed in the charts fewer weeks than any since 1965. Maybe what they needed to do was change their name for real ... *—William Ruhlmann*

Hard 'N' Heavy (With Marshmallow) / Mar. 5, 1969 / Sundazed ♦♦

Legend of Paul Revere / Apr. 1990 / Columbia/Legacy ♦♦♦♦♦
This two-CD anthology, with 55 songs, may be a lot more Raiders than the average fan would want. But go for it and be amazed at how consistently strong this rocking band from the Great Northwest was. Includes all the hits. *—Jeff Tamarkin*

● **The Essential Ride '63-'67** / Jun. 6, 1995 / Columbia/Legacy ♦♦♦♦♦
A much more sensible buy than the double-CD *Legend of Paul Revere*, this 20-track compilation focuses on their toughest (and therefore best) early material. Has all the big early hits, and about half the songs weren't on *Legend*, most notably their fine pre-Monkees version of "Steppin' Stone." Note that the version of "Hungry" here is an alternate take, good or bad news depending on whether you have the original hit rendition already. *—Richie Unterberger*

Just Like Us! [Sundazed] / 1998 / Sundazed ♦♦♦♦♦
This is Paul Revere & the Raiders the way garage band fanatics want to remember them. The Sundazed version of this album is twice the record that the original LP was, with louder, sharper, denser sound that captures the punk edge that this band had on its best days, which were frequent during this part of their history. Released in May of 1965, *Just Like Us* was the group's first full studio album for Columbia, recorded just a few weeks earlier, and the first record on which they were allowed to stretch out in the studio, utilizing multiple overdubs to fulfill their potential. Despite this luxury, the band still had their edge, mixing dance-rock with R&B on numbers like "Steppin' Out" and "Just Like Me," amid covers of contemporary hits like Marvin Gaye's "I'll Be Doggone," Them's (and Big Joe Williams') "Baby Please Don't Go," and "Night Train," as well as white rock (and folk-rock) hits such as "Satisfaction" (featuring lots of organ), "I'm Cryin'," and "Catch the Wind," not to mention the Tommy Boyce co-authored "Action" from *Where the Action Is*. *The Raiders* do okay with "I'm Cryin'," but the group's covers of the R&B classics come off rather better than their work with stuff originated by the Stones and Donovan. CD producer Bob Irwin went back about as far into the master tapes as anyone ever will, and the sound is amazing; the guitars, organ, saxes, and everything else are real close, but the density of the original mixes remains (and the volume is very, very loud). The notes by Mark Lindsay are almost as engaging as the music, and the original notes have been reproduced as well. *—Bruce Eder*

● **Greatest Hits** / Feb. 8, 2000 / Columbia/Legacy ♦♦♦♦♦
Paul Revere and the Raiders scored seven chart hits between the fall of 1965 and the winter of 1967, and all of them—"Steppin' Out," "Just Like Me," "Kicks," "Hungry," "The Great Airplane Strike," "Good Thing," and "Ups and Downs"—were included among the 11 tracks on the group's first hits collection. Also included were "Louie, Louie," the Raiders' first Columbia single, and its follow-up, "Louie, Go Home," a B-side instrumental, plus the newly penned "Legend of Paul Revere," which told the band's story. Thus, the album traced the band from its beginnings as a Northwest club band to its reign as an L.A. pop/rock success. There would be more hits, but this brief compilation (it originally ran under 30 minutes) contained the essence of the Raiders' most successful period and indeed marked the end of the band's lineup, as the rhythm section split to form another group, leaving Revere and lead singer Mark Lindsay to recruit a new edition of the Raiders. The 2000 CD reissue on Columbia/Legacy adds four bonus tracks: "Him or Me—What's It Gonna Be?" (their biggest post-1966 hit of the 1960s), "I'm Not Your Steppin' Stone" (which predated the Monkees' version), "Action," and "Peace of Mind." *—William Ruhlmann*

Mojo Workout / Nov. 14, 2000 / Sundazed ♦♦♦

Reverend Horton Heat

b. Corpus Christi, TX
Vocals, Guitar / Psychobilly, Rockabilly Revival, Alternative Pop/Rock
With his highly stylized, backwoods hick-preacher image, it would be easy to dismiss the Reverend Horton Heat as a poseur. But it would be wrong. Instead of treating rockabilly as a campy joke like the Cramps, the good Reverend rocks the hell out of his modern-day rockabilly, playing it as if it were the hardest of punk, yet without any of the self-conscious trappings of either genre. Although his lyrics can be too silly, his music never is; it rocks harder than most of his punk and metal contemporaries, as evidenced by 1993's *Full Custom Gospel Sounds*, 1994's *Liquor in the Front*, 1996's *It's Martini Time*, 1998's *Space Heater*, and 2000's *Spend a Night in the Box*. *—Stephen Thomas Erlewine*

Smoke 'em If You Got 'em / 1992 / Sub Pop ♦♦♦♦
Given how the psychobilly/punk/greaser/whatever underground just seemed to grow and grow throughout the '90s, there's every reason in the world to choose this album as one of the things that sparked it off. Little doubt as to why, too, re-recorded on two-track after a more technically complex version was deemed to lack that certain something, *Smoke 'Em If You Got 'Em* fires up strong with "Bullet" and doesn't stop there. Heat's fierce guitar playing is just as perfectly matched by Bentley's anything-but-polite drumming and Wallace's low-end mania, while Heat's occasional wails and yodels add the frosting to a cake, which is very clearly devil's food if anything. From there it's a dozen anti-meditations on everything from the joys of meat eating—"Eat Steak," how much more direct can one get?—to the demon weed "Marijuana" and the perfectly appropriate "Psychobilly Freakout." Heat's killer punch is his wide-ranging approach—AC/DC is as much a reference point for what the heck's going on, as is the classic western swing that inspires "Baby, You Know Who" and the fierce, kicking "Bad Reputation." Imagining what the Bob Wills crew could have done with this one is a fun game to play, though it's doubtful Wills himself would have allowed a line like "You're the kind of girl I like to eat" to surface. It's all sleaze, it's all wrong, and it's all so very, very right. How can anyone say no to the type of song that's a classic swampy rock strut with in-yer-face drumming, fiery solos and a title like "Big Dwarf Rodeo," after all? Credit as well for the great front cover photo that makes Heat look somewhere between the oiliest insurance salesman alive, a refugee from the Nudie suit modeling school, and Elmer Gantry. *—Ned Raggett*

The Full Custom Gospel Sounds / Apr. 26, 1993 / Sub Pop ♦♦♦♦
With fellow Texas maniac Gibby Haynes on production, Heat and his trusty sidemen go at it again on *The Full Custom Gospel Sounds* and do so with all the style and sass one could want. Kicking off with "Wiggle Stick," a perfectly lubricious number that ended up scoring the band some airplay with *Beavis and Butthead*, the good Reverend serves notice that his services are once again the type of affairs where the Blood and the Body aren't necessarily spiritual. *Full Custom* is arguably more frenetic and metal-leaning than before—not that Heat has turned into Robert Plant or anything like that, but the likes of "Livin' on the Edge (Of Houston)" would sound perfect smack dab in the middle of a Motörhead set. When it comes to matters lyrical, meanwhile, Heat is still the clever, leering bastard he's been before, and why not? The absolute killer on that front is "Bales of Cocaine," arguably the only English-language equivalent to narcotraficante corridas worthy of the comparison. Then there's the classic rockabilly strut and swing of "Beer: 30," where everything's boiled down to the doesn't-need-more triad of "Party! Get naked! Buy us more beer!" Aside from the "speed up then slow down the tape" goofiness on the concluding "Gin and Tonic Blues," Haynes doesn't really change the band's overall sound or anything, but he sure does help it sound great. Meanwhile, what the band comes up with in terms of variation is often a treat. For instance, who expected a drop-dead perfect borrowing from the Sweet's "Ballroom Blitz" making the brilliantly angry "400 Bucks" sound even better? Otherwise Heat keeps playing like crazy—quiet when he needs to be and explosive when the time is right—with Wallace and Bentley going after things with the same perfect feel. *—Ned Raggett*

Liquor in the Front / Jul. 5, 1994 / Interscope ♦♦♦
Reverend Horton Heat (aka Jim Heath) always wanted to sound like the wildest, noisiest

rockabilly guitarist on Earth, so it was fortunate that he crossed paths with Ministry braintrust Al Jourgensen during his brief spell as an advocate of roots music (and whatever happened to the Buck Satan project, Jourgensen's promised collaboration with Buck Owens?). From a musical standpoint, *Liquor in the Front* doesn't represent much of a change-up from Heat's previous work; there's a bit of up-tempo surf, a dash of old-school country, and a man-sized portion of fast and frantic tunes about cars, girls, and hard living. But with Jourgensen in the producer's chair, the Reverend's guitar finally sounds as big and powerful as he always wanted it to be; the rod-rodded engineering and in-the-red mix makes for a loud, meaty guitar assault that merges technical finesse and physical power like Muhammad Ali, and while Jimbo Wallace's bass and Taz Bentley's drums don't undergo quite so dramatic a transformation, they display more than enough backbone to support their leader as he burns up the fretboard. Reverent Horton Heat was never your typical rockabilly act, and on *Liquor in the Front* he made an album that still honored the traditions of the style while kicking up more dust than he ever had before, and for sheer crank, nothing in his catalog can touch it. *—Mark Deming*

It's Martini Time / Jul. 1996 / Interscope ✦✦

Space Heater / Mar. 24, 1998 / Interscope ✦✦✦
On his fifth release, Reverend Horton Heat returns with more of the Southern-fried rockabilly sound for which he's become primarily known. The Reverend is unfortunately one of the most overlooked rock guitarists today, who really deserves more attention (just check out the roaring instrumental album opener "The Pride of San Jacinto"). And although the trio (which also includes Jimbo Wallace on stand-up bass and Scott Churilla on drums) is also one of the most energetic live bands around, they've had a problem in the past matching their spirited performances with memorable songs. The filler problem isn't entirely solved on their latest, *Space Heater*, but one cannot deny the contagious, humorous personality contained in such highlights as "Lie Detector," "Hello Mrs. Darkness," and "Jimbo Song." The band set out to enter the studio without any songs written, and attempted to write 30 songs in 30 days. They were able to accomplish their goal, and cut down the original pool of songs to the best 16 (with an extra unlisted track at the end). Although 1994's *Liquor in the Front* is widely regarded as the Reverend's finest, *Space Heater* certainly isn't far behind. *—Greg Prato*

• **Holy Roller** / Apr. 20, 1999 / Sub Pop ✦✦✦✦✦
Like most rockabilly cats, the Rev. Horton Heat was a singles act—they cut a couple of good full-length records, but they truly made the most sense on an individual song basis, which is why *Holy Roller* is such a welcome addition to their catalog. Weighing in at a generous 24 tracks, *Holy Roller* contains highlights from every Horton Heat album—not just their pair of SubPop records, but their trio of platters for Interscope—plus two unreleased cuts ("Bath-Water Blues," "Folsom Prison Blues") and "Where in the Hell Did You Go with My Toothbrush?," which was previously only available on the SubPop rarities collection, *Afternoon Delight*. Those three cuts were added as enticements for hardcore fans, but they'd want to pick this up anyway, since it's the best album the group has released. There's little of the filler that cluttered their regular studio albums, and it contains all of the cult favorites—"Wiggle Stick," "Bales of Cocaine," "400 Bucks," "Marijuana," "Bad Reputation," "In Your Wildest Dreams," "Eat Steak"—that built their career. Die-hards will still want to hear the original records, but most listeners will be satisfied by *Holy Roller*, which is certainly the definitive Horton Heat. *—Stephen Thomas Erlewine*

Spend a Night in the Box / Mar. 21, 2000 / Time Bomb ✦✦✦✦
Dispensing with the alternative-rock leanings of some of his earlier albums like *Liquor in the Front*, Reverend Horton Heat returns with his sixth album *Spend a Night in the Box*, which features a clean, traditional rockabilly sound, courtesy of producer (and former Butthole Surfer) Paul Leary. The stripped-down sound of songs like "Big D Boogie Woogie" and "The Girl in Blue" is all the better to show off the amazing chops of the Reverend and the other two-thirds of the trio, bassist Jimbo Wallace and drummer Scott Churilla. The group's old punkabilly venom resurfaces on "Sue Jack Daniels," and while most of the songs recount the Reverend's usual litany of babes and booze, "It Hurts Your Daddy Bad" and "The Bedroom Again" show surprising lyrical depth. Though there's some filler, for the most part *Spend a Night in the Box* is another album of entertaining, revved-up rockabilly from a group that has made it look effortless for years. *—Heather Phares*

Revolting Cocks

f. 1985
Industrial Dance, Alternative Pop/Rock, Industrial
Revolting Cocks has been the sleaziest and ugliest industrial band in the land since their debut album in 1986. Over the years, their records have featured many musicians, but the core members of the band are Ministry's Al Jourgensen, ex-Fini Tribe member Chris Connelly, and Belgian producer Luc Van Acker. Combining samples, guitars, synths, and pounding dance rhythms, their records are a trashy synthesis of the most extreme industrial noise, the silliest pop culture, and classic art rock. Because of their irreverence, they are the industrial band that is the most fun to listen to, if not the best or most influential. *—Stephen Thomas Erlewine*

Big Sexy Land / 1986 / Wax Trax! ✦✦✦
Helping to establish the Midwestern tradition of prolific industrial cross-pollination, Chicago industrial-dance supergroup Revolting Cocks released their debut *Big Sexy Land* appropriately enough on Wax Trax! in 1986. Featuring Ministry's Al Jourgensen and Chris Connelly (Fini Tribe/KMFDM) among others, the group produced an electronic grind that fans of Wax Trax! artists from this era will find very familiar. Plenty of slap bass and contorted samples abound on highlight cuts like "We Shall Cleanse the World," "No Devotions," and the most house-influenced track, "TV Mind." Fine dance music with plenty of cool synth and sample trickery, *Big Sexy Land* is a distinguished debut from a "side project" that occasionally surpasses the day-job work that its members became famous for. *—Vincent Jeffries*

You Goddamned Son of a Bitch / 1988 / Wax Trax! ✦✦✦

• **Beers, Steers & Queers** / 1990 / Wax Trax! ✦✦✦✦✦
If any industrial unit can be compared to the twisted, madcap humor of Frank Zappa, it's the Revolting Cocks. While other industrial acts offer dark, depressing reflections on the state of the world, the Cocks can hardly be accused of taking themselves too seriously. Their forte is wild musical comedy as goofy and eccentric as it is irreverent. *Beers, Steers and Queers*, the group's most successful album up to that point and arguably its best, must be taken for exactly what it is—outrageous entertainment, pure and simple. A variety of amusing samples accompany abrasive, clever tracks that successfully combine industrial noise with elements of everything from heavy metal and new wave to hip-hop. Numbers like "Get Down" and "Razor's Edge" point to the fact that as abstract and left-of-center as the Cocks are, they recognize the value of a good hook and a solid groove. *—Alex Henderson*

Linger Ficken' Good . . . / 1993 / Sire ✦✦✦
Revolting Cocks' major-label debut treads no new ground but contains a giddy, demented reworking of Rod Stewart's "Do Ya Think I'm Sexy" that has to be heard to be believed. *—AMG*

The Rezillos

f. 1976, **db.** 1978
British Punk, New Wave, Punk
Although frequently aligned with the punk movement, the Rezillos' (later known as the Revillos) irreverent glam-rock image and affection for campy girl-group iconography set them distinctly apart from their peers. The Rezillos' early repertoire contained material from the likes of Screaming Lord Sutch, the Dave Clark Five and the Sweet. The success of their 1977 debut single "I Can't Stand My Baby" was unexpected, especially by the band members themselves, who never considered the group much more than a lark. After signing to major label Sire, the quintet reached the U.K. Top 20 with a single titled, ironically enough, "Top of the Pops." After releasing their 1978 debut LP *Can't Stand the Rezillos*, internal problems continued to plague the group, and following a farewell tour, they disbanded in December 1978. Quickly reforming as the Revillos, they recorded a pair of singles, "Where's the Boy for Me?" and "Motorbike Beat." The band again split in 1985, reuniting in 1994 to play a series of concerts in Japan, ultimately recording the *Live and On Fire in Japan* album and the *Yeah Yeah* EP.*—Jason Ankeny*

• **Can't Stand the Rezillos: The (Almost) Complete Rezillos** / 1993 / Sire ✦✦✦✦✦
Nearly everything this energetic new wave band ever recorded is on this splendid one-disc compilation. *—Stephen Thomas Erlewine*

Emitt Rhodes

b. Feb. 25, 1950, Hawthorne, CA
Vocals, Keyboards / Baroque Pop, Pop, Singer/Songwriter
Hawthorne, California, native Emitt Rhodes made his first mark in the music world in 1967 as the leader of the baroque-pop band the Merry-Go-Round. The band achieved some marginal success with the Rhodes-penned "Live," and "You're a Very Lovely Woman," recording one album of *Magical Mystery Tour*-inspired pop. When the band broke up in 1969, Rhodes set up a home studio in his parents' garage and began his solo career, engineering and playing all instruments himself. The strength of his initial demos, now showing a strong Paul McCartney influence, helped him get signed to ABC/Dunhill. His critically acclaimed, self-titled debut managed to break into the Top 40 in 1971, but pressure from his record company forced him to rush-release a follow-up, *Mirror*, the same year. *Mirror* was predictably a lesser effort, barely charting. By the time of the third album, 1973's *Farewell to Paradise*, Rhodes was running into legal problems with ABC, since he was unable to fulfill his contract, which demanded he deliver a new album every six months. Disillusioned, he retired from the performing side of the business, working instead as an engineer and studio operator for Elektra/Asylum. Though he hasn't released an album since *Farewell to Paradise*, he continues to write and demo new songs. *—Chris Woodstra*

Emitt Rhodes / 1970 / One Way ✦✦✦✦✦
Although this probably wasn't meant to be, this album is Emitt Rhodes' definitive statement. Soon after disbanding the Merry Go Round (of "Live" fame) Rhodes scored a solo deal with Dunhill. Rather than recording with a band or using studio musicians (which he did with his first "solo" album *American Dream*), the multi-instrumentalist decided to build a small, primitive home studio and record the entire affair there, "At Home." The results are, in a word, staggering. Tracks such as "With My Face on the Floor," "Someone Made For Me," and the entire album as a whole showcase Rhodes' genius, and in the end, the songs are probably what most Beatles-maniacs wanted to hear from Paul McCartney's debut album. Rhodes' individuality shines through despite this; the album is a true classic of the period. *—Matthew Greenwald*

The American Dream / 1971 / A&M ✦✦✦✦
Although this album may have been a contractual obligation, there is no doubt that Emmit Rhodes did not take the task of recording *American Dream* lightly. After disbanding his first group, Merry Go Round, Rhodes still owed A&M Records another album. Several new sessions were held, and along with a few old tracks such as the remarkable "You're a Very Lovely Woman," they make up the body of this fine, if fragmented album. "Mother Earth" is without a doubt one of Rhodes' McCartney-influenced masterpieces, led by a strident 12-string acoustic guitar and a masterful lead vocal. For

the first (and possibly only) time in his career, Rhodes utilized session musicians, but he used the very best. Awesome playing from Hal Blaine, Larry Knechtel, Drake Levin, Joel Larson, and others lift this track and others to a level of greatness. This album may be seen as a sort of a warm-up for Rhodes' brilliant, self-recorded Dunhill albums. *—Matthew Greenwald*

Mirror / 1971 / Dunhill ✦✦✦✦
Following the critical success of his debut solo album, Emitt Rhodes, the one-man Beatles, entered his home studio for the follow-up, and he did not disappoint. Although not as cohesive as his last record, *Mirror* is home to some of his finest material. "Birthday Lady" and "Really Wanted You" are almost Stones-like in their attack, aggression, and feel, and Rhodes pulls them off with fantastic results. "Golden Child of God" is also one of his finest compositions—it also would have easily been at home on Paul McCartney's *Ram*. All in all, this album is not a disappointment, coming off his self-titled debut *Emitt Rhodes*, which can easily be described as one of the classics of the period. *—Matthew Greenwald*

Farewell to Paradise / 1973 / Dunhill ✦✦✦
This, essentially Emitt Rhodes' third and final album, is once again a one-man-band affair. It does differ, however, from his earlier efforts. The record has a much more wistful, almost Harry Nilsson-like feeling, and this permeates most of the cuts. This album also finds Rhodes experimenting with other instruments, such as violin on "Warm Self Sacrafice," one of the album's standouts. Although not as buoyant as his earlier efforts, *Farewell to Paradise* is still a very strong album, and further cements his reputation as one of the great (albeit long-lost) artists of the period. *—Matthew Greenwald*

● **Listen, Listen: The Best of Emitt Rhodes** / Aug. 29, 1995 / Varese Sarabande ✦✦✦✦✦
For someone who could almost out-Beatle the Beatles, either in a group situation or as a solo artist, it's hard to match Emitt Rhodes. From his earliest recordings with the long-lamented Merry Go Round, to his critically-acclaimed Dunhill albums, Rhodes always seemed to have a flair for effervescent, McCartney-styled songs and audacious studio performances. This fine collection covers most of the bases, and even includes an excellent, previously unreleased studio track from 1980, "Isn't It So," which, had it been released, would have easily fit in the milieu of Top-40 radio of the time. Aside from some strange omissions (1970's "Somebody Made for Me" comes to mind), this is an excellent overall sampler. *—Matthew Greenwald*

Daisy-Fresh from Hawthorne, California (The Best of the Dunhill Years) / Aug. 11, 1998 / Edsel ✦✦✦✦✦
Emitt Rhodes is often written off as nothing more than a Paul McCartney wannabe. Well, who wouldn't want to have a beautiful voice, be able to write lush and unforgettable melodies, and also be rich and famous? Certainly Rhodes qualifies on the first two counts (failed miserably on the third) and to be honest his voice does sound eerily reminiscent of McCartney, but his strong songwriting and the deeply emotional qualities he brings to those songs make him far more than a McCartney clone. This CD covers the three records he made for Dunhill in the early '70s, including all of his self-titled debut solo release. *Emitt Rhodes* is a lost classic filled with songs that easily stack up against the finest power pop. Every song has a knockout hook, and the whole record sounds like it was recorded directly from Rhodes' soul. A pop masterpiece. Also included on the disc are six songs from his second album, 1972's *Mirror*, and five songs from his third album, 1973's *Farewell to Paradise*. The tracks from *Mirror* are not as lush and feel less immediate than those from *Emitt Rhodes*. The melodies don't sparkle and there seems to be a lack of inspiration and emotion. Having said that, *Mirror* is still a very good record, and the tracks Edsel chose are the best from it. *Farewell to Paradise* finds Rhodes experimenting with new instrumentation and expanding his musical palette. Again, Rhodes is in fine vocal form, and the songs Edsel chose from *Farewell to Paradise* are uniformly good. Rhodes missed his shot to become a pop star but you shouldn't miss your chance to discover him, and this is a fine place to start. *—Tim Sendra*

Busta Rhymes

b. 1972, Brooklyn, NY
Rap, Vocals / Hardcore Rap, East Coast Rap, Alternative Rap, Hip-Hop
The most idiosyncratic personality in rap and possessor of its most recognizable delivery—a halting, ragga-inspired style with incredible complexity, inventiveness and humor—Busta Rhymes formed Leaders of the New School in 1990 and released two albums with the group before breaking out with a 1996 solo hit single, "Woo-Hah!! Got You All in Check." Much respected in the hip-hop underground for their Afrocentric philosophy and tough rapping styles, Leaders of the New School debuted in 1991 with *Future Without a Past*, but released only one more album, 1993's *T.I.M.E.*, before breaking up the following year. Out on his own for the first time, Busta Rhymes' first solo album, *The Coming*, proved a huge hit; the single "Woo-Hah!! Got You All in Check" hit the Top Ten and pushed the album into gold-record territory. His second album, *When Disaster Strikes*, debuted at number three in September 1997. *—John Bush*

● **The Coming** / Apr. 1996 / Elektra ✦✦✦✦✦
Busta Rhymes delivered his debut album, *The Coming*, three years after the Leaders of the New School unofficially disbanded, and it reflects the change in hip-hop between 1993 and 1996. *The Coming* is indebted to the slow, spare, and quietly menacing funk and soundscapes of the Wu-Tang Clan—in fact, Ol' Dirty Bastard appears on one of the album's most infectious tracks, the single "Woo-hah!! Got You All in Check." Busta Rhymes, like Ol' Dirty, is a surreal, inspired rapper, but his skills are on a whole different level. Though his talents were evident on the Leaders of the New School records, Busta Rhymes has never had such an impressive showcase for his rhymes as he does on *The Coming*. Busta doesn't have a deep message in his raps, but he twists words and phrases around with an insane, invigorating flair. Like many hip-hop albums of the mid-'90s, *The Coming* is padded with too much material, but Busta Rhymes' brilliant raps keep the record from sinking during its monotonous passages. *—Stephen Thomas Erlewine*

When Disaster Strikes / Sep. 23, 1997 / Elektra ✦✦✦✦✦
Alternately brilliantly inspired and brilliantly confused, Busta Rhymes' second album, *When Disaster Strikes*, isn't perfect, but it's considerably more creative than the bulk of contemporary hip-hop albums. Using the Wu-Tang Clan's haunting soundscapes as a blueprint, Busta Rhymes expands that formula, adding funkier beats and elements of electronica and electric funk. It's a forward-thinking mix, pointing the way to new hip-hop fusions, even when the music falls flat. Busta's lyrics remain startlingly fresh and compelling, and they're given more weight by these dense rhythm tracks. Not everything on *When Disaster Strikes* is successful, partially because the album runs too long, but the best cuts confirm that Busta Rhymes is a singular talent. *—Stephen Thomas Erlewine*

Extinction Level Event (The Final World Front) / Dec. 8, 1998 / Elektra ✦✦✦✦
Busta Rhymes rocketed to superstardom in an alarmingly short time, simply because there was no other rapper quite like him. Nobody else in his position had his wild sense of humor, reckless fashion sense and, most importantly, willingness to take risks. Yes, underground rappers like the Jurassic Five and the entire Wu clan relentlessly pushed the boundaries of hip-hop, but they operated at the fringes of pop culture. Busta placed himself smack in the middle of middle America, gleefully taking cameos on *Cosby* and recruiting both Janet Jackson and Ozzy Osbourne to appear on his third album, *Extinction Level Event (The Final World Front)*. Where this could seem like pandering by some artists, there's no condescension or crass commercialism in his approach. Busta's party is careening out of control because he doesn't see a reason to exclude anybody. That's the reason why *E.L.E.* is a richer listen than most contemporary hip-hop records—it has hard beats, weird samples, unpredictable musical juxtapositions and collaborations, and sharp, intelligent rhymes. Like any artist who attempts so much, Busta occasionally falls flat (the rewrite of "Iron Man" wasn't a great idea), but there's so much happening on *E.L.E.* that the missteps don't really matter—especially since Busta has come up with a party record that doesn't just sound the end of the millennium, it *feels* like it. *—Stephen Thomas Erlewine*

Anarchy / Jun. 20, 2000 / Elektra ✦✦✦
Busta Rhymes is undoubtedly one of the best and most distinctive rappers of the '90s. He's also one of the most prolific; *Anarchy*, released in the summer of 2000, is his fourth album since 1996. Each one has been jammed full of material and also a little erratic, packed not only with great singles and tongue-twisting performances but also filler that gets by mostly on Busta's personality. Clocking in at around 78 minutes, *Anarchy* is no exception to the rule. Its best moments are as brilliant as ever, but there are also signs that Busta's winning formula is starting to show a little wear and tear. "C'Mon All My Niggaz, C'Mon All My Bitches" has the insanely rapid-fire delivery of *E.L.E.*'s "Gimme Some More," which sums up the difficulty of *Anarchy* in a nutshell: no matter how incredible it is, we've heard much of this from Busta before. Of course, the converse is also true: a lot of it is still incredible, no matter how familiar, and there are a few intriguing production touches. But, perhaps for the first time, Busta's singular yet now familiar style isn't quite enough to carry the weaker material, which often feels too tossed off. It doesn't help, either, that *Anarchy* follows the same sort of millennial-apocalypse concept that enlivened *E.L.E.* (and, to a certain extent, *When Disaster Strikes*); it's a little disappointing to hear such an inventive rapper retreading familiar territory. It seems almost impossible that Busta could produce a true failure, but by this point, a growing number of fans may not salivate over a new album nearly as much as the inevitable best-of collection. *—Steve Huey*

● **Total Devastation: The Best of Busta Rhymes** / Oct. 2, 2001 / Rhino ✦✦✦✦

The Rich Kids

f. 1977, **db.** 1978
British Punk, New Wave
Following his 1977 firing from the Sex Pistols—reportedly for expressing an admiration for the Beatles—bassist Glen Matlock founded the Rich Kids, a more experimental pop/rock outfit rounded out by guitarist Steve New, drummer Rusty Egan and vocalist Midge Ure, formerly of the group Silk. Distancing themselves from the punk community, the Rich Kids recorded only one LP, 1978's *Ghosts of Princes in Towers*, before tension between Matlock and Ure resulted in the group's dissolution within a year of their formation. Ure and Egan later reunited in Visage, and Ure ultimately found success with Ultravox, while Matlock largely vanished from sight until publishing his autobiography *I Was a Teenage Sex Pistol* in the late 1980s. In 1996, he rejoined the Sex Pistols for their "Filthy Lucre" reunion tour. *—Jason Ankeny*

Ghosts of Princes in Towers / 1978 / EMI ✦✦✦
The single "Ghosts of Princes in Towers" was simply brilliant; unfortunately, the album that bore the same name failed to live up to the promise of the single, in most cases trading punky power-pop in favor of more dirge-like hard rock—muddy sound doesn't help matters either. Overall, the album serves as a curiosity for the Sex Pistols completist or the Ultravox fan who wants a look at Midge Ure's formative years. [In 1993, Dojo Records reissued the album on CD with three B-sides added, "Empty Words," "Here Comes the Nice," and "Only Arsenic," making the complete recorded works of the band available on one disc.] *—Chris Woodstra*

Tony Rich

Vocals / Contemporary R&B, Urban
Contemporary R&B singer/songwriter Tony Rich first attracted attention as a staff writer at LaFace Records, where he authored hits for acts including Boyz II Men, Johnny Gill,

TLC and Toni Braxton. As the Tony Rich Project, he debuted in 1995 with *Words*, writing, performing and producing every note of the LP himself; after scoring the Grammy-nominated hits "Like a Woman" and "Nobody Knows," he began work on his sophomore LP, 1998's *Birdseye*. —*Jason Ankeny*

● **Words** / Sep. 26, 1995 / La Face ◆◆◆◆
Tony Rich's debut album didn't quite fit in with the rigid format of '90s urban R&B. Instead of relying on hip-hop as his foundation, Rich takes elements from soul, blues, pop, and rock, creating a personal brand of new jack R&B. Like Prince, he synthesizes these elements into a distinctive whole. Unlike Prince, his influences are more apparent on the surface, but perhaps that should be expected from a debut. Like many first records, the songs aren't always first-rate, but the best tracks on *Words* stand head and shoulders above much of Rich's competition. What makes *Words* work is Tony Rich's audacity and his talent—he ties together disparate influences with his melodic, soulful songwriting, forming a fresh sound that breathes new life into '90s urban R&B. —*Stephen Thomas Erlewine*

Birdseye / Aug. 11, 1998 / La Face ◆◆◆◆
Tony Rich made quite a splash with his debut album, *Words*. Like his peers D'Angelo and Maxwell, Rich decided to buck slick contemporary conventions in urban R&B, adhering to the sophisticated styles pioneered by Stevie Wonder, Smokey Robinson and Marvin Gaye. Not only was *Words* a welcome change of pace in a genre that had become too predictable, but it revealed a truly gifted singer-songwriter. Rich's second album, *Birdseye*, proves that the first was no fluke. Branching out from his stylish acoustic love ballads, Rich expands his musical vocabulary by touching on lite-funk, reggae flourishes, pop and soul. Nevertheless, *Birdseye* remains a remarkably romantic record, one of the rare albums whose seduction feels genuine, not prepackaged. It's not only Rich's smooth, soulful voice—it's a combination of his singing, his clean, inviting arrangements, skilled musicianship (he plays every instrument, apart from some guest guitar solos from Eric Clapton) and sturdy, memorable songwriting that makes *Birdseye* such a delight. —*Leo Stanley*

Cliff Richard

b. Oct. 14, 1940, Lucknow, India
Vocals / Early British Pop/Rock, Teen Idol, Pop/Rock, Pop, Rock & Roll
Britain's answer to Elvis Presley, Cliff Richard dominated the pre-Beatles British pop scene in the late '50s and early '60s. An accomplished singer with a genuine feel for the music, Richard's artistic legacy is nonetheless meager, as he was quickly steered toward a middle-of-the-road pop direction. Several of his late '50s recordings, however, were genuinely exciting Presley-esque rockers—especially his first hit, "Move It" (1958)—and gave British teenagers their first taste of genuine homegrown rock & roll talent. Backed by the Shadows—clean-cut instrumental virtuosos who became legends of their own—Richard embarked on a truly awesome string of hit singles in Britain, scoring no less than 43 Top 20 hits between 1958 and 1969. In his homeland, Richard's popularity was diminished only slightly by the rise of the Beatles, but in his prime, he had a much rougher time in the U.S., hitting the Top 40 only three times (with "Living Doll" in 1959, "It's All in the Game" in 1963, and "Devil Woman" in 1976). He remains an institution in Britain, where he is one of the nation's most popular all-around entertainers of all time. —*Richie Unterberger*

● **20 Rock & Roll Hits** / 1979 / EMI-Columbia ◆◆◆◆◆
Concentrating mostly on his 1958-59 material, this has Richard's most untamed recordings (bearing in mind that they're still pretty polished compared to most U.S. rockabilly). Includes his first brace of hits—"Move It," "High Class Baby," "Mean Streak," and "Never Mind"—along with the megasmash "Livin' Doll," which pointed the way toward the pop-ballad path he would follow in the '60s. —*Richie Unterberger*

Cliff Richard & the Shadows / 1984 / EMI ◆◆◆◆◆
Cliff Richard & the Shadows rock out like nobody's business on this classic live album (arguably rock's first authorized and professionally recorded concert album). Recorded in February 1959 at EMI in front of 500 screaming fans, the sound is raw and raunchy by British standards of the time. —*Bruce Eder*

The Cliff Richard Collection (1976-1994) / 1994 / Razor & Tie ◆◆◆◆
The Cliff Richard Collection isn't simply the best American compilation he has ever been granted, it's also the finest single-disc collection of Cliff Richard's post-"Devil Woman" material around. That song, of course, remains his biggest-ever American hit; however, it also marked the beginning of what Richard himself regards as his renaissance, critically, commercially, and creatively, the point at which he was transformed from a '60s hitmaker who didn't know when to stop to a contemporary singer and sometimes songwriter, as valid as any of the young bucks walking a similar path. The emphasis remains on the U.K. hits, although with over 50 to choose from, a lot of strong material was omitted in favor of material that—if one may be blunt for a moment—has more in common with contemporary American tastes than with Richard's overall development. "Some People" and "The Only Way Out," for example, are pounding '80s AOR, smartly produced and neatly executed, but not a patch on, say, "Miss You Nights" and "Silhouettes." There's also a gratuitous reliance on duets, although with partners the caliber of Elton John, Sarah Brightman, and Olivia Newton-John ("Suddenly," from the *Xanadu* soundtrack), who's to say that's a mistake? But these are petty complaints—and besides, some excellent material does surface: a dramatically echo-drenched rendition of Buddy Holly's "True Love Ways," recorded with the London Philharmonic Orchestra; the effortlessly contagious dance hit "We Don't Talk Anymore"; and, best of all (indeed, one of the greatest records Richard has ever made), "Carrie," darkly desperate, disturbingly desolate, a missing person's report set to music. There's also a triumphant appearance for "Mistletoe and Wine," the 1988 U.K. chart-topper that inaugurated what has now become an integral part of the British calendar, Richard's Christmas single. It's mawkish sentimentality at its most

overtly rampant, and no self-respecting ears will want to hear it more than once a year. But that's all the song itself demands—you don't whistle "Jingle Bells" in midsummer, either. But come next December.... —*Dave Thompson*

The Rock & Roll Years 1958-1963 / 1997 / EMI ◆◆◆◆◆
Such an unimaginative title for such an imaginative boxful. Across four discs and 105 songs, Cliff Richard's earliest catalog comes in for precisely the kind of treatment every rock & roll star should have: an all-encompassing study of his most important period. Even more impressively, though the song titles all sound familiar, the performances rarely are. Thirty-seven tracks are bona fide unreleased (South African 78s notwithstanding), but several dozen more are culled from scarce EP-only mixes, rarely resurfacing B-sides, and unusual mixes. Discs one through three are the conventional ones. Running in strict chronology through Richard's first eight albums, 20-plus EPs, and 23 singles, highlights are sorted, then sorted again. Where a rare version exists, that's what is offered here. Subtitled "Rare'n'Rockin' 1958-63," disc four is the album that completely rewrites history. It opens with the first recording Richard (then still laboring under his distinctly nondescript given name of Harry Webb) ever made: He rips through raucous, raw renderings of "Lawdy Miss Clawdy" and "Breathless," cuts to a 1958 live show, and hacks through broadcast tapes and unreleased acetates. And every one is a gem. His Elvis Presley covers are especially remarkable. America's rock & roll revolution, of course, was matched blow for blow by skiffle in the U.K. Where Richard triumphed over the rest of the pack was in the way he blended the two forms together; where "Rare'n'Rockin'" triumphs is by revealing just how seamless that blending could be. Richard did more than create a hybrid. He invented a truly British way of rocking. And from the Beatles to Blur, the Rolling Stones to the Stone Roses, that method remains fundamental to British rock. —*Dave Thompson*

Keith Richards

b. Dec. 18, 1943, Dartford, Kent, England
Vocals, Keyboards, Guitar (Electric), Guitar / Album Rock, Hard Rock, Rock & Roll
One of the few White guitarists with strong blues roots who has been able to take the form to new places, Richards' contribution to the vocabulary of rock guitar cannot be overestimated. His heavy reliance on Delta blues open tunings (mostly played on guitars with only five strings) has provided licks that are part and parcel for any player who wants to get the joint rocking and the dance floor packed. Though much has been made of his lifestyle, and time has reduced his voice to a sore-throated husk, it is as a guitarist and songwriter that Richards has ultimately established his reputation. —*Cub Koda*

● **Talk Is Cheap** / 1988 / Virgin ◆◆◆◆◆
Richards' first solo album includes "Take It So Hard," "Struggle," "I Could Have Stood You Up," and "Make No Mistake," with a classic Hi Rhythm Section groove and featuring great guest vocals by Sarah Dash. —*Cub Koda*

Live at the Hollywood Palladium (Dec. 15, 1988) / Dec. 1991 / Virgin ◆◆◆
A nicely ragged live album that captures Richards and the Winos at the top of their form. —*Stephen Thomas Erlewine*

Main Offender / Oct. 20, 1992 / Virgin ◆◆◆
Richards' second solo album is even more delightfully focused than his first. Highlights include "Wicked as It Seems," "Eileen," and the searing "999." New Rolling Stones albums should rock this hard. —*Cub Koda*

Lionel Richie

b. Jun. 20, 1949, Tuskegee, AL
Vocals, Keyboards / Quiet Storm, Soft Rock, Adult Contemporary, Urban
After leaving the Commodores, Lionel Richie became one of the most successful male solo artists of the '80s, arguably eclipsed during his 1981-1987 heyday only by Michael Jackson and Prince. Richie dominated the pop charts during that period with an incredible run of 13 consecutive Top Ten hits, five of them number ones. Titled simply *Lionel Richie*, his solo debut was released in late 1982 and was an immediate smash, reaching number three on the pop charts on its way to sales of over four million copies. It spun off three Top Five pop hits, including the first single "Truly," which became Richie's first solo number one. If *Lionel Richie* made its creator a star, the follow-up *Can't Slow Down* made him a superstar. Boasting five Top Ten singles, including the number ones "All Night Long (All Night)" and "Hello," *Can't Slow Down* hit number one, eventually sold over ten million copies, and won the 1984 Grammy for Album of the Year. By the end of 1985, he was on top of the charts again with "Say You, Say Me," a ballad recorded for the film *White Nights*. The song was slated to be the title track on Richie's upcoming album, but delays in the recording process prevented the record from being released until August 1986, by which time the title was changed to *Dancing on the Ceiling* (in order to promote Richie's next single release). The album didn't match the success of *Can't Slow Down*, but it still sold an impressive four million copies, although Richie's reputation for sentimental ballads was beginning to incur a backlash in some quarters. After 1987, Richie fell silent, taking an extended break from recording and touring before beginning a comeback toward the tail end of the '90s. —*Steve Huey*

Lionel Richie / 1982 / Motown ◆◆◆◆◆
Lionel Richie was perhaps the dominant songwriter and performer of the early '80s. His overwhelmingly sentimental love tunes were massive crossover hits, and he turned awkwardness into an art form. This was his first big album, and it peaked at #3 on the pop album chart, eventually selling over four million copies and staying on the charts for 140 weeks. —*Ron Wynn*

Can't Slow Down / 1983 / Motown ◆◆◆◆◆
The Lionel Richie gravy train was in full throttle on this second big hit album, which

eventually sold over eight million copies. Richie earned the 1984 Grammy for Album of the Year, and such tunes as "Hello," "Running With the Night," "Stuck on You" and "Love Will Find a Way" were all over the R&B, pop, and even country airwaves. *—Ron Wynn*

Dancing on the Ceiling / 1986 / Motown ♦♦♦♦♦
Lionel Richie had a slump of sorts after the incredible success of *Can't Slow Down*. This record, which came some three years later, only sold four million instead of eight million copies, stayed atop the pop album charts for only one month instead of two, and only had a few pop hits in "Love Will Conquer All," "Say You, Say Me," "Se La" and "Deep River Woman." *—Ron Wynn*

● **Back to Front** / May 5, 1992 / Motown ♦♦♦♦
On his own and as part of the Commodores, by 1992 Lionel Richie amassed more than enough singles for a greatest-hits collection. Unfortunately, this is one of those compilations that, good intentions aside, falls so flat there's not much point in buying it. By trying to cover his solo material, while touching base with his Commodores fans, and adding some new cuts, no part of his career is well represented. It's easy to figure out what record companies are thinking when they release greatest-hits compilations without all the hits—they can release another collection a few years down the road with the "missing" singles in order to get you to spend more money. For the record, *Back to Front* lacks "Oh No," "Lady You Bring Me Up," "Ballerina Girl," "You Are," "My Love," "Stuck on You," "Love Will Conquer All," "Se La," and "Dancing on the Ceiling," all Top 40 hits. If Motown had concentrated solely on solo Richie, with another collection of Commodores hits, this could have been a solid, career-topping CD. As it is, it's strong, but hearing such gems as "Still," "Truly," "Say You, Say Me," and "Running With the Night" makes you long to hear the cuts that aren't here. Of the three new songs, "Do It to Me" and "My Destiny" are classic, smooth Richie, but "Love, Oh Love" is so schmaltzy, you're almost embarrassed for him; kids singing about peace on earth is just too cheesy, no matter how middle-of-the-road you are. If you're a casual Lionel Richie fan, this might suffice, but for anyone who truly enjoys pop music, this collection is not worth your money. *—Bryan Buss*

Louder Than Words / Apr. 1996 / Mercury ♦♦♦
After the greatest hits collection *Back to Front* disappeared without a trace in 1992, Lionel Richie spent four years making *Louder Than Words*, his first album for Mercury Records. Although there are some slight attempts to incorporate New Jack and hip-hop influences into Richie's sound, *Louder Than Words* relies on his trademark balladeering, which remains his forte. All of the weak moments on *Louder than Words* are ill-advised forays into rap—to put it bluntly, he can rap about as well as Snoop Doggy Dogg can sing. Although the ballads aren't as strong as his late-'70s and early-'80s standards, they are nevertheless pleasant, which makes the record a worthwhile purchase for fans. *—Stephen Thomas Erlewine*

Time / Jun. 23, 1998 / Mercury ♦♦♦
Louder Than Words was the official comeback, the long-awaited return to recording from Lionel Richie, one of the most successful pop stars of the '80s. Perhaps it was inevitable that returning to recording would be difficult—after all, it had been 10 years since he had released an album of original material—but *Louder Than Words* turned out to be a bigger disappointment than anyone expected, failing to deliver either musically or commercially. Its failure helped clear the decks for *Time*, Richie's true musical comeback. *Time* doesn't quite match the heights of *Lionel Richie* or *Can't Slow Down*, but it successfully updates his familiar concoction of sweet, seductive ballads and light funk for the late '90s. Whenever he incorporates light hip-hop rhythms here, it sounds less forced, and the dance numbers are often infectious. Similarly, the ballads have strong (albeit sappy) hooks that make them memorable. Don't take Richie's belated version of "Lady," the hit he gave Kenny Rogers, as a bad sign—*Time* is the most satisfying effort he has released in quite some time. *—Stephen Thomas Erlewine*

Renaissance / Mar. 20, 2001 / Island ♦♦

Jonathan Richman

b. May 15, 1951, Boston, MA
Vocals, Guitar / College Rock, Proto-Punk, Alternative Pop/Rock
Jonathan Richman was one of rock's most eccentric and unpredictable cult figures, a performer whose eternally childlike public persona and seeming naiveté tended to obscure the dexterity and craft of his music, which skirted from garage rock to country to Latin stylings and back. In 1970, he formed the first incarnation of the influential proto-punk band the Modern Lovers, though it was most of two years before the group recorded the demos which comprised their seminal self-titled debut, featuring long-standing Richman favorites like "Roadrunner," "Pablo Picasso" and "Hospital." Problems with their label, however, blocked the songs' release until 1976. Eventually, he formed a new, acoustic version of the group that debuted on record with 1977's *Jonathan Richman and the Modern Lovers*. That same year, he scored a major European hit with the instrumental "Egyptian Reggae." In 1979, Richman issued his first solo album, *Back in Your Life*. After a period of self-imposed exile, he resurfaced in the mid-'80s with a series of strong pop records. In 1990, he released the self-explanatory *Jonathan Goes Country*; later, he made another left turn with 1993's *Jonathan, Te Vas a Emocionar!*, a collection of Latin-influenced songs performed entirely in Spanish. No matter what path his music took, however, Richman's cult following remained fiercely loyal, and saw its ranks expand courtesy of a prominent appearance in the 1998 hit film comedy *There's Something About Mary*. *I'm So Confused* appeared later that year. *—Jason Ankeny*

☆ **Modern Lovers** / 1976 / Rhino ♦♦♦♦♦
Compiled of demos the band recorded with John Cale in 1971, *The Modern Lovers* is one of the great proto-punk albums of all-time, capturing an angst-ridden adolescent geekiness which is married to a stripped-down, minimalistic rock & roll derived from the art-punk of the Velvet Underground. While the sound is in debt to the primal three-chord pounding of early Velvet Underground, the attitude of Jonathan Richman and the Modern Lovers is a million miles away from Lou Reed's jaded urban nightmares. As he says in the classic two-chord anthem "Roadrunner," Richman is in love with the modern world and rock & roll. He's still a teenager at heart, which means he's not only in love with girls he can't have, but also radios, suburbs, and fast food, and it also means he'll crack jokes like "Pablo Picasso was never called an asshole... not like you." "Pablo Picasso" is the classic sneer, but "She Cracked" and "I'm Straight" are just as nasty, made all the more edgy by the Modern Lovers' amateurish, minimalist drive. But beneath his adolscent posturing, Richman is also nakedly emotional, pleading for a lover on "Someone I Care About" and "Girl Friend," or romanticizing the future on "Dignified and Old." That combination of musical simplicity, driving rock & roll and gawky emotional confessions makes *The Modern Lovers* one of the most startling proto-punk records—it strips rock & roll to its core and establishes the rock tradition of the geeky, awkward social-outcast venting his frustrations. More importantly, the music is just as raw and exciting now as when it was recorded in 1971, or when it was belatedly released in 1977. *—Stephen Thomas Erlewine*

Live / 1977 / Rhino ♦♦♦
This release catches Jonathan Richman at the height of his candy-floss novelty period. The music is warm and mild, almost all of it derived from 1950s and early 1960s models such as surf idioms and guitar instrumentals. The lyrics are sweet and charming, sure to appeal to fanciful youngsters with visions of ice cream men and little dinosaurs in their heads. The only bothersome misstep here is the repeated encore reprise of the chorus to "Ice Cream Man," which extends well past the point of honest enjoyment. Sound quality and instrumental balances are excellent, and performances are low-key and winsome. While not an essential album in the Modern Lovers' canon, this sunny little platter is a fetching listen. *—David Cleary*

Jonathan Richman & the Modern Lovers / Jan. 1977 / Beserkley ♦♦♦♦♦
Richman's second collection of Modern Lovers, over which he was billed (eventually, the group name would be dropped) had a lighter rock & roll sound than the first. In fact, as often as not, Richman played acoustic guitar. And his lyrical concerns had similarly lightened up, to the point of childlike whimsy on such songs as "Hey There Little Insect" and "Here Come the Martian Martians." But the focus was still Richman's unabashed vocalizing (the word "sings" is put in quotes on the back cover), giving the whole album an amateurish charm. *—William Ruhlmann*

Rock & Roll with the Modern Lovers / Feb. 1977 / Beserkley ♦♦♦♦♦
Rock & Roll with the Modern Lovers. Richman branches out to Japanese music, a "South American Folk Song," and even "Egyptian Reggae" (the last earning him a UK Top 5 hit), but the real highlight on *Rock & Roll with the Modern Lovers* is that ode to a totaled car, "Dodge Veg-O-Matic." *—William Ruhlmann*

Back in Your Life / 1979 / Beserkley ♦♦♦
Recorded with two different bands—the usual Modern Lovers crew and a vocals/string bass/glockenspiel combo—*Back in Your Life* ranks among the most eccentric albums in a career which is the very embodiment of quirkiness. Heavy on cover material, both the songs and performances are deliriously campy, closer to vaudeville than any recognizable strain of rock & roll. *—Jason Ankeny*

The Jonathan Richman Songbook / 1980 / Beserkley ♦♦♦♦
The Jonathan Richman Songbook is a U.K.-only compilation of early material. *—Jason Ankeny*

The Original Modern Lovers / 1981 / Bomp! ♦♦♦
Long before his lyrics celebrated abominable snowmen and ice cream truck drivers, Jonathan Richman was positioning himself as rock's poet of the ordinary. Ex-Velvet Underground co-founder John Cale and larger-than-life songwriter Kim Fowley translated the Richman vision with varying success, but the band dissolved when it couldn't agree on a direction. Beserkley Records issued the Cale sessions as *The Modern Lovers* in 1976, while Bomp followed suit with Fowley's rougher and readier handiwork in 1981, which was here recycled again onto compact disc. (Several bootlegs also contain songs not released on either album.) The sessions showcase a rudimentary, yet spirited outfit that knew how to emphasize its strengths. Richman's nonstop guitar chug lends depth to his elementary arrangements, which are further buoyed by Robinson's insistent drumming and Harrison's fuzzed-out roller-rink organ, which is the primary instrumental voice here. Still, Richman's songs are the main interest: "She Cracked" slaps at a '70s rock scene fueled by laid-back decadence, while "Girlfren" pleads for intimacy during a trip to the local art museum. "Walk up the Street" critiques a society that widens people's isolation while continuing to tempt them with an ever-growing array of modern conveniences and distractions. Given its thin sound, and a length that stops just shy of a meager 30 minutes, this disc is best appreciated as a documentary of an underdog band trying to harness its energies into a coherent product. At best, *The Original Modern Lovers* is a tangent to *The Modern Lovers*, which remains the definitive showcase of Richman's earliest creations. *—Ralph Heibutzki*

Jonathan Sings / 1983 / Rough Trade ♦♦♦
Richman emerges as an incurable romantic on *Jonathan Sings!*, an infectiously sunny effort which stands among his finest LPs. Recorded after a long layoff with a new Modern Lovers lineup, Richman sounds thoroughly recharged, even extolling the simple virtues of "This Kind of Music"; among his other enthusiasms are kids ("Not Yet Three") and travel ("Give Paris One More Chance"), but his primary focus here is romance—"You're the One for Me," "That Summer Feeling" and "Someone to Hold Me" are positively joyous in their lovestruck outlook. *—Jason Ankeny*

Rockin' & Romance / 1985 / Twin/Tone ✦✦✦✦✦
While it is generally true that many of Richman's post-1980 albums are all but interchangeable, with their earnest naive cheerfulness, this stands as one of the best, if you like his schtick and need to make a choice. The production is sparse, accentuating the acoustic guitar and the doo wop harmonies (both male and female), with light but purposeful drums. Jonathan covers his usual terrain here: juvenilia ("My Jeans," "The U.F.O. Man," "Chewing Gum Wrapper"), cultural heroes ("Vincent Van Gogh," "Walter Johnson"), and optimistic paeans to the simple pleasures of life ("The Beach"). Heart-warming and melodic stuff that might well sound insipid in the hands of others. *—Richie Unterberger*

It's Time for Jonathan Richman / 1986 / Upside ✦✦✦
Produced by Andy Paley, *It's Time for*... welcomes back to the fold former Modern Lovers guitarist Asa Brebner, resulting in a fuller and more lively sound than Richman has enjoyed in some time. Taking full advantage of Richman's sax-blowing acumen, the record sports a wistful early rock & roll feel: "Let's Take a Trip" and "Yo Jo Jo" are energetic rave-ups, "This Love of Mine" is a sweet doo wop ballad, and "It's You" is a joyous romantic romp. The highlight is "Corner Store," an impassioned plea against modernization. *—Jason Ankeny*

● **Beserkley Years** / 1987 / Rhino ✦✦✦✦✦
After the first Modern Lovers album, Richman's records were enjoyable but fairly spotty. Thankfully, *The Beserkley Years* collects the best moments from his '70s records, when his cutesiness was endearing, not irritating. With "Roadrunner," "Pablo Picasso," "Here Come the Martian Martians," "Important In Your Life," "Ice Cream Man," and "Dodge Veg-O-Matic" forming its core, this collection is a definitive portrait of his goofy, catchy minimalist pop and rock. *—Stephen Thomas Erlewine*

Modern Lovers 88 / 1988 / Rounder ✦✦✦
One of his better '80s efforts, and certainly one of the most basic, performed in an acoustic trio format. It's nonetheless quite rocking, with heavy debts to doo wop and Bo Diddley rhythms, and a jolly (though not sappy) summertime campfire feel. Some of his best uptempo tunes are here, including "I Love Hot Nights," "California Desert Party," and "Gail Loves Me." *—Richie Unterberger*

Jonathan Richman / 1989 / Rounder ✦✦✦
As basic and bare-bones as its title, *Jonathan Richman* is a solo effort modeled after Richman's live show, spotlighting only his voice, guitar and percussive foot stomping. An eclectic mixture of originals and covers (occasionally sung in either French or Spanish), the record's simplicity is its charm; the high point, "I Eat With Gusto, Damn! You Bet," is a spoken-word paean to the joys of bad table manners. *—Jason Ankeny*

Jonathan Goes Country / 1990 / Rounder ✦✦✦
The Skeletons' Lou Whitney and D. Clinton Thompson as well as a number of seasoned session vets join Richman as he ventures into Nashville territory. The material consists of a batch of originals, a few covers and a couple of old songs reworked from 1983's *Jonathan Sings!* The music's country affectations are entertaining without being gimmicky, and Richman sounds right at home in his twangy environs. *—Jason Ankeny*

Having a Party with Jonathan Richman / 1991 / Rounder ✦✦✦
A hodgepodge of studio and live recordings, this *Party* is a rather quiet affair with just Jonathan and his guitar. Without a band to support him, Richman grows more pensive than usual; while interpersonal dynamics remain his primary focus, his thoughts turn to relatively serious examinations of adultery ("My Career as a Homewrecker") and commitment ("Just for Fun"). Similarly, the minutiae of romance is the concern of "The Girl Stands Up to Me Now," "When I Say Wife" (a fretful essay on nomenclature and possessiveness) and "She Doesn't Laugh at My Jokes." *—Jason Ankeny*

I, Jonathan / Sep. 16, 1992 / Rounder ✦✦✦✦✦
A lo-fi effort cut in a California basement, *I, Jonathan* returns Richman to the full band setting and manic diversity which recent conceptual efforts have forsaken. Sloppy and wild, the album is a blast from start to finish; among its many concerns are skydiving ("Tandem Jump"), sea life (the surf instrumental "Grunion Run"), nightclubbing ("I Was Dancing in a Lesbian Bar") and hero worship ("Velvet Underground"). *—Jason Ankeny*

Jonathan, Te Vas a Emocionar! / Feb. 28, 1994 / Rounder ✦✦✦
Although Richman's vocals have intermittently slipped into foreign tongues for years, *Jonathan, Te Vas a Emocionar!* is still a surprise: entirely sung in Spanish, the record is a charmer, transcending the language barrier with ease. Along with a few new originals and a handful of traditional Mexican tunes, the album primarily consists of loose Spanish reworkings of Richman favorites—*I, Jonathan's* "You Can't Talk to the Dude" becomes "No Te Oye," for example, while *Having a Party's* "Just for Fun" becomes "No Mas por Fun" and *Jonathan Goes Country's* "Reno" becomes, well, "Reno"; whatever the language, however, Richman remains his earnest, wistful self—none of his personality gets lost in the translation. *—Jason Ankeny*

Precise Modern Lovers Order / Aug. 2, 1994 / Rounder ✦✦✦
Of the major pre-punk bands of the late '60s and early '70s (such as the Velvet Underground, the MC5, the Stooges, and the New York Dolls), the Modern Lovers probably seemed the most eccentric—while the aforementioned groups each took a very individual approach to rock & roll, they were still rock bands who worked hard to deliver on stage for an audience. Jonathan Richman, on the other hand, was just as likely to let his bruised and bleeding heart hang on his sleeve for five long, slow minutes of "Hospital" or "Dance With Me" as he was to rip it up on a tune like "Roadrunner" or "Someone I Care About." *Precise Modern Lovers Order* combines a ten-song set the Modern Lovers played in Berkley, CA, during a 1972 West Coast tour with a half-dozen tracks recorded at student mixers at Harvard University between 1971 and 1973, and the audiences seem uniformly befuddled throughout this disc—there aren't any audible catcalls of disapproval, but no one seems to know how to react to Richman's vivid tales of teenage angst. And the Modern Lovers sound a good bit more stark and extreme in these performances than they did on their few studio recordings (hard to imagine, but that first album sounds slick by comparison), though Jonathan Richman's vocals are strikingly impassioned, and the band supports him with a clean, sympathetic simplicity (Jerry Harrison and David Robinson, later to play with Talking Heads and the Cars, respectively, were still members of the Modern Lovers at this point, and future Real Kids leader John Felice is on the Harvard-recorded tracks). *Precise Modern Lovers Order* captures a great and groundbreaking band blazing trails the hard way on stage; it's worth owning as psychodrama, living history, and great music. *—Mark Deming*

You Must Ask the Heart / Apr. 25, 1995 / Rounder ✦✦✦✦✦
The ambitious *You Must Ask the Heart* is Richman's most consistent effort in years; produced with clarity by Brennan Totten, the album is a neat summation of the singer's recent history, ranging in tone from the pensive ("To Hide a Little Thought") to the silly ("Vampire Girl") and spanning in style from country (the title track) to Spanish ("Amorcito Corazon"). Offsetting his own material with a handful of superb covers—including Tom Waits' "The Heart of Saturday Night" and Sam Cooke's "Nothing Can Change This Love"—Richman sings with remarkable energy and honesty; even after dozens of records, his joyful spirit remains undimmed. *—Jason Ankeny*

Surrender to Jonathan / Sep. 10, 1996 / Vapor ✦✦✦
Surrender to Jonathan was Richman's return to a major label, and he constructed the album as a showcase of his finest, or at least most notorious, songs of the early '90s. "Egyptian Reggae" and "I Was Dancing in the Lesbian Bar" are hauled out of the woodwork and given moderately polished reworkings by Andy Paley. Even with the slicker sound, Jonathan remains Jonathan, and no amount of studio polish can erase the fact that his goofball, naive pop is better-suited for small clubs than records. There's a couple of worthy additions to his set-list, "Not Just A 'Plus One' on the Guest List Anymore" and "Surrender," but *Surrender to Jonathan* remains a marginal effort. *—Stephen Thomas Erlewine*

I'm So Confused / Oct. 20, 1998 / Vapor ✦✦✦
Ric Ocasek steps in to produce a lush-sounding record for Richman, employing quirky keyboards, percussive effects and background vocalists. "Nineteen In Naples" is one of his typical, naive travelogues: "When I was 19, I went across the pond and I found myself in the demimonde." But his charming nasal voice seems to all but have disappeared; it's been replaced with a sort of arty croon, as on the title cut and the dour "Affection." Yet, it suits the song treatments, which sound similar to mid-period Talking Heads (!). Still, on "The Night Is Still Young," the "old" Jonathan makes an appearance with one of his trademark shuffles. *—Denise Sullivan*

Ride

f. 1988, Oxford, England, **db.** Jan. 1996

British Trad Rock, Dream Pop, Shoegazing, Alternative Pop/Rock, Noise Pop

With their first records, Ride created a unique wall of sound that relied on massive, trembling distortion in the vein of My Bloody Valentine but with a simpler, more direct melodic approach. The shatteringly loud, droning neo-psychedelia the band performed was dubbed "shoegazing" by the British press, because they stared at the stage while they performed. Along with their initial influence, My Bloody Valentine, Ride stood apart from the shoegazing pack, primarily because of their keen sense of songcraft and dynamics. Signed to Creation in 1989 by virtue of their blisteringly loud, intense live shows, the band recorded two successful EPs and quickly became darlings of the UK press. *Nowhere*, Ride's first album, became a significant hit in England during 1990, peaking at number 14. The group's second album, 1992's *Going Blank Again*, earned a Top Ten hit in "Leave Them All Behind." Tensions between frontmen Mark Gardener and Andy Bell forced an extended break though, and it was two years before Ride re-emerged with their third album, *Carnival of Light*. The album represented a major shift toward conventional psychedelic rock and turned out to be a commercial misstep. Tensions between Bell and Gardener escalated throughout the recording sessions for 1996's *Tarantula*. Both left Ride even before the album's release, and the group announced its disbandment in early 1996. *—Stephen Thomas Erlewine*

Smile / Jul. 1990 / Sire ✦✦✦✦
A compilation of Ride's first two EPs for Creation, *Smile* is a batch of eight muddy, shambling wrecks that run dangerously close to obscuring great pop songs. In fact, much of *Smile* makes My Bloody Valentine's blurry *Isn't Anything* sound as polished as a Steely Dan record. What makes the tunes remarkable is the spirit of the band, along with a good mix. The band probably knew exactly what they were doing, but wanted to sound clueless. It's the sound of four art students losing themselves in their record collections, wanting to be naive and fresh but well-studied.

Mark Gardener sounds like he couldn't sing himself out of a paper bag on the original "Chelsea Girl," but it's no matter. The relentless rush of Loz Colbert's drums and distorted guitars of Gardener and Andy Bell carry the song, topped off by a nifty wah wah climax. Though the mid-tempo, chugging "Drive Blind" could be taken literally, it could double as a metaphor for throwing oneself headlong into a relationship—closing your eyes and not caring if a brick wall or cliff is up a mile ahead. The remainder is filled out with sticky riffs and melodies which avoid sounding like the standard pop fair. It sounds a bit amateurish, and Gardener and Bell hadn't quite found their footing vocally. Nonetheless, *Smile* brought something new to the table, and the U.K. audience and more adventurous U.S. fans clutched onto the sound for dear life. Rightfully so. [Oddly, *Smile's* mastering comes from the vinyl versions of the EPs. If you can track down the CD versions of the EPs separately, you'll notice a difference in quality.] —*Andy Kellman*

• **Nowhere** / Oct. 15, 1990 / Sire ✦✦✦✦✦
1990 was a banner year for Ride, capped off by this fantastic full-length, which seems to hold consensus as the second best record of the shoegaze era (My Bloody Valentine's *Loveless* being number one). All of the common words, phrases, and adjectives commonly used with the short lived sub-genre fit properly here, and they're all positive—depending on your taste. Whir, whoosh, hazy, fuzzy, swirly, ad nauseum. But it all boils down to quality *songs*, which *Nowhere* delivers.

Ride's catalog is a bit shoddy in the lyrics department, but *Nowhere* boasts Andy Bell's best pen work. Musically it's undeniably their zenith—dense, tight, and hypnotic. "Seagull" serves as a dynamic opener; after a couple seconds of light feedback, bassist Steve Queralt kicks in with a rubbery, elliptical line, which is soon followed by Bell and Gardener's guitar twists and Loz Colbert's alternately gentle and punishing drum patterns. After the upbeat "Kaleidoscope," the record falls into a tempo lull that initially seems impenetrable and meandering. However, patience reveals a five-song suite of sorts, full of lovely instrumental passages that are punctuated with violent jabs of manic guitars. Don't miss the endlessly escalating "Polar Bear," with expertly placed tom rolls from Colbert. Only for the last track does the pace significantly pick up. The wistful "Vapour Trail" is likely Ride's signature song, with Gardener and Bell's chiming background guitars throughout and mournful strings to close the record out.

The U.S. version of *Nowhere* was bolstered significantly with the addition of the *Fall* EP, which was released just a month prior to the LP in the U.K. "Taste" is one of their better pure pop numbers. The moody "Here and Now" matches the best of *Nowhere*, and the five minute "Nowhere" is a decent distortion freakout. —*Andy Kellman*

Going Blank Again / Mar. 1992 / Sire ✦✦✦✦
From the sounds of cloistered, chaotic opener "Leave Them All Behind," *Going Blank Again* sounds like it could be headed down the same *Nowhere* path. Guitars as far as the ear can hear—not far removed from the effect gained after riding a sit-and-spin for eight straight minutes—making you just as dizzy as "Seagull" did on the debut. But rather than sink into a thick underbelly of melancholy, *Going Blank Again* offers sunshine and streamlined production. All the band's elements are more pliable, and overall it's pretty cheery. In fact, some of the album could be loosely classified as power pop. Bouncy tunes like "Twisterella," "Not Fazed," "Mouse Trap," and "Time of Her Time" each share more than a thing or two in common with the likes of Teenage Fanclub but with more layered vocals and less-cutting guitars. Though Ride's guitars don't bite as much, there are loads of them; the band doesn't completely sacrifice their love of reverberating noise, but it's more done in the name of pop than to merely cause a racket.

As with much of Ride's catalog, the lyrics aren't so hot. Though reading as overtly simple or obtuse, Mark Gardener and Andy Bell's voices are too pretty to let this shortcoming mar things. They create enough of a mood with their proper instruments, and their sighing and random vocal intonations are undeniably lovely. No longer do they hide shortcomings with sheets of distortion, and there's a lot more focus and confidence on display throughout. Don't let a Ride fan tell you otherwise: *Going Blank Again* is anything but empty. —*Andy Kellman*

Carnival of Light / Jun. 28, 1994 / Sire ✦✦✦
Credit Ride for sticking to their guns and following only their own creative radar, completely ignoring outside expectations. You could always tell they had a love for the likes of the Byrds and Buffalo Springfield, and perhaps it was uncool at the time to confide a love for the Black Crowes. Crowes producer George Drakoulias was called in, but über-producer John Leckie ended up working on the majority. Fans generally didn't dig the classic vibe of the record, and the beautifully autumnal record sold poorly as a result.

Carnival's first side largely consists of Mark Gardener's songs, while the latter is mainly Andy Bell's affair. Aside from questionably kitschy use of tamboura on "Moonlight Medicine," Gardener's contributions are excellent. "1000 Miles" lifts the Byrds' jangle convincingly. Bell's opening Rhodes tones kick "From Time to Time" off tastefully, which is a "Vapour Trail" II of sorts, lyrically. Surprisingly, Bell's songs aren't as strong. He wrote the bulk of the band's prior top material, but he's pretty much trumped by his mate. Even Loz Colbert's "Natural Grace" wipes the mat with Bell's writing. The first half is much stronger.

Despite the gaps in song quality and a hackneyed Creation cover, *Carnival of Light* creates a pleasant, freewheeling feeling throughout. A bit lengthy at nearly an hour, the overall effect might have been improved with the extraction of some of the duff. Perhaps Bell's ego was too big to recognize the shortcomings of "Crown of Creation" and the poor Al Green-ism of "Endless Road." The kids' choir on "I Don't Know Where It Comes From" was a bad idea, too. But for all its faults and lack of originality, *Carnival of Light* remains a pleasant listen and was unlike anything released at the time in the U.K. —*Andy Kellman*

Live Light / Oct. 24, 1995 / Mutiny ✦✦

Tarantula / Mar. 12, 1996 / Sire ✦✦

• **OX4: The Best of Ride** / Sep. 10, 2001 / Ignition ✦✦✦✦✦
It wasn't exactly fashionable to be a Ride fan in the early '90s. In certain nooks of the universe, wearing a Ride T-shirt meant you had to walk with your fists clenched, ready to defend your decrepit taste in music and do the pouncing before you got pounced upon. Often, you had to endure the taunts of your peers and the remainder of those who agreed with or were influenced by the majority of the British press who decided—shortly after praising the band for their genius—that they were ultimately a crap band. When it came to shoegaze, they weren't My Bloody Valentine, were they? As their tastes and influences changed and they began playing more "proper" rock & roll, they failed to write anything as anthemic as "Live Forever," right? Well to hell with all of that. In the nooks of the universe where it *is* okay to wear a Ride shirt, *Nowhere* is on par with *Loveless* for its own peculiar rush of swirling psychedelics and more prominent vocal hooks; *Going Blank Again* trumps Teenage Fanclub's *Bandwagonesque* because it exudes more power and focus; and 1994's *Carnival of Light*, with its roots in the Byrds and their ilk, is viewed more as prophecy than heresy. A copy of *OX4: The Best of Ride* is all you need for your defense now. Boasting a solid representation of each of Ride's albums, the band-selected compilation proves once and for all that Ride was one of the finest of the early '90s; they were capable of crafting brilliant melodies just as easily as their influences and competitors; and they never repeated themselves. So wear your Mark Gardener fringe with pride, blare "Unfamiliar" as loudly as possible, and keep *Tarantula* forever blocked from your memory. —*Andy Kellman*

Amy Rigby

Vocals / Americana, Adult Alternative Pop/Rock, Alternative Country-Rock, Singer/Songwriter

Singer/songwriter Amy Rigby first surfaced during the early 1980s as a member of the New York City-based cowpunk outfit the Last Roundup, later earning cult success with the postmodern girl group the Shams. The former wife of ex-dBs drummer Will Rigby, she made her solo debut in 1996 with *Diary of a Mod Housewife*, a record widely acclaimed for its vivid portraits of life as a thirtysomething single mother and its smart assimilation of pop, country and folk sounds; *Middlescence* followed two years later; and *The Sugar Tree* was issued in fall 2000. —*Jason Ankeny*

• **Diary of a Mod Housewife** / 1996 / Koch ✦✦✦✦✦
Amy Rigby's solo debut is a breath of fresh air: in an era dominated by overwrought, angst-ridden female rockers, the wonderfully titled *Diary of a Mod Housewife* offers deceptively simple songs which cut to the heart of what day-to-day existence is truly like for women in the 1990s. Rigby's songs are miniature character studies which find the pointed truths locked inside seemingly mundane circumstances: "Knapsack" details a galvanizing crush on the boy who works at the local bookstore, while "Beer and Kisses," an outstanding duet with John Wesley Harding, distills the sum of married life into the couplet "Get home from work, turn on the light / Sit on the couch, spend the whole night there." In addition to her knowing lyrical eye, Rigby is also a terrific composer who synthesizes elements of rock, country, folk and girl group-era pop; melodic and assured, *Diary of a Mod Housewife* is a remarkable and unique debut. —*Jason Ankeny*

Middlescence / Sep. 15, 1998 / Koch ✦✦✦
Amy Rigby's debut *Diary of a Mod Housewife* was so perfect that its follow-up, *Middlescence*, is seemingly predestined to come up short in comparison; it does, but not by much, and what it lacks in immediacy it gains over repeated listens as its subtle, even sneaky charms begin to surface. Where *Mod Housewife* captured the dissolution of Rigby's marriage with you-are-there immediacy, the new album surveys the post-divorce fallout with the same poignancy and intimacy—"What I Need" portrays the difficulties of dating as a single mother, while "Raising the Bar" confronts the impossibility of making a decent living in a world where all the good jobs go to younger, more attractive women; there's even a mid-life crisis song, "The Summer of My Wasted Youth," which finds solace in the sweet nostalgia of cheap beer, good drugs and Patsy Cline records. If the subjects of Rigby's songs aren't revelatory, the insights she brings to her material frequently are, with a dignity and maturity that are the ultimate rewards of surviving the daily grind *Middlescence* so vividly details; perhaps her greatest accomplishment is that rarest of pop music feats—growing old gracefully. —*Jason Ankeny*

The Sugar Tree / Sep. 26, 2000 / Koch ✦✦✦
This album, like Amy Rigby's previous offerings, provides a sometimes scathing, often funny look at middle-aged post-divorce singledom. From the brash bombs dropped by songs like "Balls" to the heartbreak of "Stop Showing Up in My Dreams" and "Sleepin' With the Moon," this recording shows an artist who has been around the block a few times but at the end of the day feels pretty comfortable in her own skin. —*Stacia Proefrock*

The Righteous Brothers

f. 1962, California

Blue-Eyed Soul, Brill Building Pop, Pop

They weren't brothers, but Bill Medley and Bobby Hatfield were most definitely righteous, defining (and perhaps even inspiring) the term "blue-eyed soul" in the mid-'60s. They initially recorded quite a few energetic R&B tunes on the Moonglow label that bore similarity to the gospel/soul/rock style of Ray Charles, copping their greatest success with "Little Latin Lupe Lu," which became a garage band favorite covered by Mitch Ryder, the Kingsmen, and others. The duo wouldn't break out nationally until they put themselves at the services of Phil Spector, who gave the wall-of-sound treatment to the grandiose ballad "You've Lost That Lovin' Feelin'." At nearly four minutes, the song was pushing the limits of what could be played on radio in the mid-'60s, and some listeners thought they were hearing a 45 single played at 33 rpm due to Medley's low, blurry lead vocal. No matter; the song had a power that couldn't be denied, and went all the way to number one. The Righteous Brothers had three more big hits in 1965 on Spector's Philles label ("Just Once in My Life," "Unchained Melody," and "Ebb Tide"), all employing similar dense orchestral arrangements and swelling vocal crescendos. Yet by 1966 the Righteous Brothers had left Philles for a lucrative deal with Verve, where the duo had another number one hit with "(You're My) Soul and Inspiration." It's a bit of a mystery as to why the Righteous Brothers never came close to duplicating that success during the rest of their tenure at Verve. —*Richie Unterberger*

★ **Anthology 1962-1974** / Jul. 1989 / Rhino ♦♦♦♦♦
For some listeners, a double-disc of the Righteous Brothers might seem like overkill, but *Anthology 1962-1974* should silence most skeptics. Over the course of the two discs, it becomes clear that the duo were the finest blue-eyed soul singers of their era. Not only do the hits ("Little Latin Lupe Lu," "You've Lost That Lovin' Feeling," "Unchained Melody," "Ebb Tide," "(You're My) Soul and Inspiration," "Rock & Roll Heaven") retain their power, there are numerous forgotten gems, like the harder-rocking "Justine" and an excellent version of "This Little Girl of Mine." For listeners who want to dig a little deeper into the Righteous Brothers' music than the hits, they'll be generously rewarded by *Anthology*. *—Stephen Thomas Erlewine*

● **The Unchained Melody: The Very Best of the Righteous Brothers** / 1990 / Polydor ♦♦♦♦♦

The Best of the Righteous Brothers, Vol. 2 / 1991 / Curb ♦♦♦
Since *Vol. 1* contained most the duo's biggest hits, the ten-track, budget-priced *Best of Righteous Brothers, Vol. 2* contains leftovers. Only "Rock & Roll Heaven"—which is included in its original version, as well as a 1992 remake—is an oldies staple, while "Give It to the People" and "Dream On" were minor hits. The remainder of the collection is devoted either to forgotten songs or newly recorded covers. Although this isn't bad for a budget-priced disc, there are better collections available, offering more songs and better sound for not much more money. *—Stephen Thomas Erlewine*

Billy Lee Riley

b. Oct. 5, 1933, Pocohontas, AR
Vocals, Drums, Harmonica, Guitar, Bass / Rockabilly
Billy Lee Riley is a rockabilly singer and multi-instrumentalist. An alumni of Sun Records, he was one of the most crazed, unabashed rockers that label had to offer—in the company of Jerry Lee Lewis, Carl Perkins, and Sonny Burgess, that's saying a lot. Proficient at harmonica, guitar, bass, and drums, Riley contributed as a sideman to many a classic Sun session, and his combo the Little Green Men (most notably guitarist Roland Janes and drummer J.M. Van Eaton) in time became the Sun house band. Riley recorded for a number of labels in a variety of styles, especially effective with blues. Though never commercially successful, Riley's Sun recordings of "Flying Saucer Rock & Roll" and "Red Hot" (both covered in wooden renditions by Robert Gordon) remain landmarks of the genre. *—Cub Koda*

Classic Recordings, 1956-1960 / Jul. 1990 / Bear Family ♦♦♦♦♦
All the classic Sun sides, plus later Memphis recordings in a brilliant two-CD set. Raw rockin' at its finest. *—Cub Koda*

● **Red Hot: The Best of Billy Lee Riley** / Feb. 2, 1999 / Collectables ♦♦♦♦♦

Minnie Riperton

b. Nov. 8, 1947, Chicago, IL, **d.** Jul. 12, 1979, Los Angeles, CA
Vocals / Smooth Soul, Chicago Soul, Uptown Soul, Pop-Soul, Soul
One of soul music's most unique and unforgettable voices, Minnie Riperton was blessed with an angelic five-octave vocal range and scored her greatest commercial success with the chart-topping pop ballad "Lovin' You." As a youth, she studied music, drama and dance at the city's Lincoln Center, and later contemplated a career in opera. Her pop career began in 1961 when she joined the local girl group called the Gems. After graduating high school, she worked as a receptionist at the famed Chess label and in 1968, was installed as the lead vocalist of the psychedelic soul band the Rotary Connection, which debuted that year with a self-titled LP. While still a member of the Connection, Riperton mounted a solo career, issuing her brilliant debut *Come to My Garden* in 1970. After the Rotary Connection dissolved in the wake of 1971's *Hey Love*, she toured as a member of Stevie Wonder's backing unit.

Wonder agreed to co-produce Riperton's 1974 album *Perfect Angel*, which contained the international blockbuster "Lovin' You"; the record made her a household name, although subsequent LPs like 1975's *Adventures in Paradise* and 1977's *Stay in Love* failed to repeat its success. By this time, however, commercial woes were the least of Riperton's concerns—diagnosed with breast cancer, she underwent a mastectomy in 1976, later becoming a spokesperson for the American Cancer Society. Riperton continued performing despite her declining condition, with 1979's *Minnie* the final record completed during her lifetime. Unreleased vocal tracks with new instrumental backing comprised 1980's posthumous collection *Love Lives Forever*. *—Jason Ankeny*

● **Capitol Gold: The Best of Minnie Riperton** / Jun. 21, 1993 / Capitol ♦♦♦♦♦

Her Chess Years (50th Anniversary Collection) / Nov. 4, 1997 / Chess ♦♦♦♦
While this compilation is credited to Minnie Riperton, none of the 16 tracks was actually released under her name. Indeed, a more apt title might have been *Best of Minnie Riperton and the Rotary Connection*, as 13 of the songs are Rotary Connection cuts on which she sang lead. The other three date from before the Rotary Connection days, with a couple of tracks by the Gems (a mid-'60s girl group) that bear Riperton's lead vocals, as well as the 1966 single "Lonely Girl," which is actually Riperton solo, but was released under the pseudonym Andrea Davis. The pre-Rotary Connection numbers are fair but unremarkable pop-soul, with Minnie unveiling her stratospheric operatic vocals on "Lonely Girl." The Rotary Connection material is taken from five albums recorded by the group in the late '60s and early '70s; there's nothing from their most famous LP, the self-titled 1967 debut, as Riperton sang no leads on that record (it's been reissued on its own by Chess anyway). This stuff is a very mixed bag, including dubious Cream and Hendrix covers, as well as a ghoulish mauling of "Respect." On the other hand, "Magical World" shows their odd psychedelic-soul-as-MGM-musical production style at its best, and "A-Muse" is a surprisingly pretty, acoustic singer-songwriter type ballad, delivered with sensitivity by Riperton. As a whole, this music isn't so much notable for Riperton's vocals (as wide-ranging as they are) as its eccentric genre-mashing, from a rare period in which mainstream pop and soul tried to be self-consciously avant-garde and eclectic without getting too far out. *—Richie Unterberger*

Petals: The Minnie Riperton Collection / Feb. 13, 2001 / The Right Stuff ♦♦♦♦♦
Although her 1979 death at 31 still reverberates through pop and R&B, *Petals: The Minnie Riperton Collection* is one of the first sets to successfully celebrate the joy, sensuality and wonder inherent in Minnie Riperton's music. This two-CD set has 34 tracks spanning the years 1966-1979. Unlike other compilations this culls work from all of her styles, including the cutesy but derivative R&B/pop she recorded under the name Andrea Davis. The collection also includes tracks from her stint with the often ho-hum, rock/R&B group Rotary Connection. The challenging and baroque songs from Riperton's first album, *Come to My Garden*, are much better. The tracks including the title, "Les Fleur," "Completeness," and "Expecting" are a collaborative effort between Riperton's husband Richard Rudolph and the brilliant Chicago writer/producer Charles Stephney. A few years down the line, she appeared to be an even more confident singer. Tracks like "Take a Little Trip," "Perfect Angel," and "Lovin' You," all from 1974, were all produced by Stevie Wonder in a relaxed and spare style. This set demonstrates other producers like Stewart Levine, Freddie Perren, and Jeremy Lubbock were also inspired to excellence by the style defined by Riperton and Rudolph. The evocative and powerful "Adventures in Paradise," "Inside My Love," and disco-ish "Young, Willing and Able" all have Riperton's sweetness and intelligence prominent in the mix. The later tracks, including the gorgeous "Memory Lane," finds the formula reaching perfection. Her five-and-a-half octave range is on full display here, and *Petals: The Minnie Riperton Collection* assembles a plethora of definitive songs. *—Jason Elias*

Rites of Spring

Emo, Indie Rock, Hardcore Punk, Alternative Pop/Rock
Instead of addressing hardcore's standard political and social themes, the Rites of Spring used the music for personal introspection and emotional release, leading their sound to be dubbed emocore. Signed to Ian MacKaye's Dischord label, the band released a self-titled debut in 1985 and the EP *All Through a Life* in 1987 before breaking up. Vocalist Guy Picciotto subsequently joined MacKaye in Fugazi. *—Steve Huey*

● **End on End** / 1991 / Dischord ♦♦♦♦♦
Released on CD by Dischord in 1991, this digital version of *End on End* covers the complete recorded output of the legendary Rites of Spring: the self-titled LP, the *All Through a Life* EP, and one extra song. One of the first bands to be labeled emo-core, Rites of Spring would seem to transcend all labels as their music cuts right through to the heart of universal human experience. Emotional? Yes—check out the bitter memorial relived on "For Want Of," the pulse pounding moment-grab that is "Drink Deep," or the devoted searches for honesty and meaning explored on "End on End," "Theme," and really just about every track on the disc. Hardcore? Yes—emerging from the D.C. scene, the music is pure focused energy, not a single note wasted. The band at times is fast and furious, at other times lush and evocative though always with a sense of drive and melody. Rites of Spring hint at some of the territory vocalist/guitarist Guy Picciotto and drummer Brendan Canty would later survey with Fugazi but this band is much more than just a stepping stone. *End on End*, quite simply, is a testament to the rich possibilities of sincerity in music. *—Matthew Isaac Kantor*

Johnny Rivers

b. Nov. 7, 1942, New York, NY
Vocals, Guitar / Pop/Rock, Pop
Among the most successful yet underrated solo acts of the 1960s, Johnny Rivers reeled off a lengthy series of rock favorites which together sold over 30 million copies. Distinguished throughout by his reedy vocals and soulful guitar leads, Rivers' body of work is characterized by a rare consistency and versatility which stretches from his earnest yet rousing covers of R&B classics to his later, self-penned hits. Strongly influenced by the swamp-blues sound of his hometown of Baton Rouge, LA, Rivers—born John Ramistella in New York City on November 7, 1942—picked up the guitar as a child and played with local groups throughout his school years. After stints in New York (where he met disc jockey Alan Freed, who suggested he change his name to Rivers, and Nashville, he settled in Los Angeles. He headlined at the newly opened Whisky-a-Go-Go, which became one of the area's hottest nightspots and earned its star attraction a rabid following among Tinseltown clubgoers. His 1964 debut *Johnny Rivers Live at the Whisky-a-Go-Go* featured hits like the Chuck Berry covers "Memphis" and "Maybelline." Over the years, Rivers returned to the club to record his albums and most of his early hits were covers, including his smash 1965 rendition of Willie Dixon's "Seventh Son," and the traditional "Midnight Special." Over the next two years, Rivers charted with hits like the theme to the television spy thriller *Secret Agent Man*, the elegiac "Poor Side of Town" (which he co-wrote with Lou Adler) and a pair of Motown covers, "Baby I Need Your Lovin'" and "The Tracks of My Tears." But after the subsequent "Summer Rain," he disappeared from the Top 40 for the rest of the decade. For the rest of his career, he returned to his roots. During the '70s, he charted with his renditions of Huey "Piano" Smith's "Rockin' Pneumonia and the Boogie Woogie Flu," Carl Perkins' "Blue Suede Shoes" and the Beach Boys' "Help Me Rhonda." His recording career wound down in the '80s, but he continued touring into the '90s, increasingly returning to the blues that inspired him initially. In 1998, Rivers reactivated his Soul City imprint and released *Last Train to Memphis*, his first new studio album in 15 years. *—Jason Ankeny*

Realization / 1968 / Soul City ♦♦♦
Not a concept album, but a song cycle depicting life in Southern California in the late '60s,

Realization is a fine cycle to catch a ride on. From the opening "Hey Joe" right through to the rather delicate reading of "Positively Fourth Street" at the close, Rivers succeeds in evoking so many thoughts and emotions. Including the hits "Look to Your Soul" and "Summer Rain," this record captures a certain place and time with great accuracy. *Realization* is a must for any fan. *—James Chrispell*

Last Boogie in Paris / 1974 / Varese ✦✦

The Best of Johnny Rivers / 1987 / EMI America ✦✦✦✦✦
A fine single-disc collection, *Best of Johnny Rivers* features most of his biggest hits, making it a good purchase for those who don't want the definitive double-disc set. *—Stephen Thomas Erlewine*

• **Anthology, 1964-1977** / Mar. 1991 / Rhino ✦✦✦✦✦
The 36 songs here, spread over two CDs, don't cover Johnny Rivers' early, pre-Liberty Records career, but they do represent the broadest cross section of his hits for that label and beyond, B-sides, and superior album tracks assembled to date in one place. As revealed here, Rivers is a very versatile, somewhat underrated talent whose range extends far beyond Top 40 rock, "Secret Agent Man" or any other single hit, into folk, soul, and blues, all of which he plays with an unpretentious honesty. He remained remarkably consistent through the psychedelic era and into the 1970s, even amid the twin onslaughts of disco and punk, and there are no real weak points on this set. Additionally, the notes give a reasonably detailed picture of Rivers' life and career, which started far earlier (1957) than most listeners realize, and the sound is up to Rhino Records' usual standard, in terms of quality and the selection of masters. *—Bruce Eder*

Changes/Rewind / 1993 / Capitol ✦✦✦✦✦
Johnny Rivers took a dramatic step during the late '60s, embracing adult standards and recording several Jimmy Webb compositions. These were solemn, literate tales of woe, anguish and turmoil requiring lyric interpretation and careful vocal pacing. They were also heavily produced numbers with string sections and background vocalists. The change didn't hurt Rivers' career; indeed, it won him new critical attention as a serious ballad stylist and landed him some hits. This single-disc collection covers 23 songs from two LPs, *Changes* and *Rewind*. Besides the big hit covers "Tracks of My Tears" and "Baby, I Need Your Loving," there is arguably his greatest ballad, "Poor Side of Town." While not everything worked, this material showed another side of Johnny Rivers and expanded his popularity. *—Ron Wynn*

Meanwhile Back at the Whiskey A-Go-Go / 1996 / RCA ✦✦✦
Johnny Rivers' two 1965 albums have been released together in a double-disc package. Though neither *Meanwhile Back At the Whisky A Go Go* or *Rockin' the Folk* were commercial disappointments, they weren't the singer's most popular records, either. Rivers' first album was also recorded live at the Whisky, so *Meanwhile* represents something of a homecoming. Since Rivers is essentially an interpretive singer, a live album suits his talents well—it features a set list that isn't plagued by filler and a tight, energetic backing band. Because of this, *Meanwhile* is the better record of the pair. *Rockin' the Folk* has its moments but many of these folk songs aren't as compelling as Rivers' rock and pop covers. It does have its moments—such as the minor hit "Where Have All the Flowers Gone"—but there are too many weak moments to make the record interesting for anyone but dedicated fans. Then again, only dedicated fans will have the need to purchase this double disc set. *—Stephen Thomas Erlewine*

In Action!/Changes / Jul. 22, 1997 / BGO ✦✦✦✦
A superb compilation of Johnny Rivers' third and eighth albums, providing a good look at two sides of his studio work, the lean, stripped down rock & roll of *In Action!* juxtaposed with the more ornate and ambitious sounds of *Changes*. Rivers became more sophisticated in many unexpected ways as time went on; *In Action!* shows him covering the Beatles' "I Should Have Known Better" in a punchy, lively rendition, where *Changes* has him incorporating the string arrangement of "Eleanor Rigby" onto John Phillips' "California Dreamin'." He is in excellent voice throughout, and seldom gets too far from rock even on the most heavily orchestrated songs from *Changes*. The analog-to-digital transfers are excellent and the sound is genuinely impressive, even by BGO's usual high standards. *—Bruce Eder*

The Rivieras

f. South Bend, IN, **db.** 1966
Frat Rock, Garage Rock, Rock & Roll
A South Bend, IN, rock & roll band, the Rivieras' one big hit was one of the last great gasps of pure American rock & roll before the British Invasion took over the charts. Original members Otto Nuss (organ), Doug Gean (bass), Marty "Bo" Fortson (vocals and guitar), Joe Pennell (guitar), and Paul Dennert (drums) were local teen ballroom heroes. They recorded a supercharged version of the Joe Jones R&B semi-hit "California Sun" featuring a powerful drum intro and the now-famous signature guitar and organ riff. The song became a hit in the midst of the first flush of Beatlemania, only nudged out of the #1 spot on the national charts by "I Want to Hold Your Hand." Although several equally fine 45s and two albums followed, the band's relatively young ages, coupled with numerous personnel changes caused by the draft and the changing musical climate, caused the band to break up by 1966. Nuss, Gean, and Fortson reunited the Rivieras in the mid '80s, recording and doing local shows, sounding as great as ever. Though their time in the spotlight was brief, their one big hit continues to define for future generations everything that's pulsatingly great about American teen-band rock & roll. *—Cub Koda*

California Sun / 1964 / Sonet ✦✦✦✦✦
Import reissue of their first album. *—Cub Koda*

Campus Party / 1965 / Riviera ✦✦✦✦✦
Second album; classic frat-band sound. Out of print and impossibly rare but worth the search at any cost. *—Cub Koda*

• **The Best of the Rivieras: California Sun** / Apr. 4, 2000 / Norton ✦✦✦✦✦
At long last, the pride of South Bend, IN, finally get a legally sanctioned best-of that serves their legacy well. This brings together all of their original singles, the best cuts from their two albums, and the first-time reissue of "Played On," the original B-side of "California Sun." The band storm through these tracks with an energy that's palpable, and the result is '60s garage band rock & roll at its absolute finest. Highly, highly recommended. *—Cub Koda*

The Rivingtons

f. 1962, Los Angeles, CA
Doo Wop, R&B
Though they are best known for their string of early-'60s novelties, the Rivingtons in reality had a rich tradition of doo wop in their background, going back to their original recordings for Federal as the Lamplighters in 1953. They did extensive backup group work throughout the '50s between their own stray releases under a number of different names; the Sharps (singing on the original "Little Bitty Pretty One" and "Over and Over" by Thurston Harris), the Rebels (they do all the backups on the Duane Eddy hits), the Four After Fives—they even sang backup on Paul Anka's first record, credited as the Jacks! In 1962 they became the Rivingtons and hit pay dirt with their first record, the self-penned "Pa Pa Ooh Mow Mow," one of the truly great rock & roll songs to make a virtue of sheer gibberish. They hit the charts again a year later with "The Bird's the Word," capitalizing on a current West Coast dance fad that teenagers were doing to "Pa Pa Ooh Mow Mow." A landlocked surf-teen combo from Minnesota called the Trashmen combined the two songs, revved up the beat to warp factor nine, and scored a massive hit with "Surfin' Bird." Despite no further chart success, their place in rock & roll history is assured. *—Cub Koda*

• **The Liberty Years** / Jun. 1991 / EMI America ✦✦✦✦✦
An excellent 23-track CD with detailed notes and great sound, featuring both sides of all their original-issue 45s (including the insane follow-up "Mama Ooh Mow Mow") plus all the tracks from their lone Liberty album, *Doin' the Bird*. *—Cub Koda*

Robbie Robertson (Jaime Robbie Robertson)

b. Jul. 5, 1943, Toronto, Ontario, Canada
Vocals, Keyboards, Guitar / Album Rock, Ethnic Fusion, Singer/Songwriter
One of the premier songwriters of the rock era, Robbie Robertson hooked up with rockabilly star Ronnie Hawkins' backing band the Hawks in 1958. After remaining with Hawkins through 1963, the Hawks began working on their own; they soon came to the attention of Bob Dylan, and became the support unit on the singer's now-legendary 1965-1966 world tour. Continuing their affiliation with Dylan, the group, renamed simply the Band, went on to become one of rock's seminal acts; propelled by Robertson's acute, evocative examinations of American mythology and lore, they made a series of seminal LPs, including 1968's *Music From Big Pink* and the following year's self-titled masterpiece. The Band dissolved on Thanksgiving Day, 1976 following an all-star concert filmed by director Martin Scorsese and later released as *The Last Waltz*. The project marked the beginning of Robertson's long affiliation with Scorsese, and in 1980 he composed the score to the director's brilliant *Raging Bull*; they later teamed for the acerbic 1983 satire *The King of Comedy* and 1986's *The Color of Money*. Finally, in 1987 Robertson released his self-titled solo debut to much acclaim. *Storyville*, a conceptual piece steeped in the sounds and imagery of a famed area of New Orleans, followed in 1991. In 1994, Robertson teamed with the Native American group the Red Road Ensemble for *Music for "The Native Americans,"* a collection of songs composed for a television documentary series. *Contact From the Underworld of Redboy* appeared in 1998. *—Jason Ankeny*

• **Robbie Robertson** / 1987 / Geffen ✦✦✦
Robbie Robertson was once asked why he waited 11 years after the breakup of the Band to release a solo project, and he replied, "I wasn't so sure I had something to say." One can hear a bit of this thinking in Robertson's self-titled solo debut; it's obvious that he didn't care to revisit the country- and blues-flavored roots rock that had been his bread and butter with the Band, and at the same time Robertson seemed determined to make an album that had something important to say, and could stand alongside his legendary earlier work. Looking for a moody and atmospheric sound, Robertson teamed up with producer Daniel Lanois, who had previously worked with U2 and Peter Gabriel, two artists whose work obviously influenced Robertson's musical thinking while he was making the album (they both appear on the album as well). As a result, *Robbie Robertson* is an album that represents both a clear break from his past, and an ambitious attempt to take his fascination with American culture and music in a new and contemporary direction. It's highly ambitious stuff, and the album's ambitions sometimes prove to be its Achilles' heel. And it doesn't take long to realize why Robbie only took two lead vocals during his tenure with the Band; his dry, reedy voice isn't bad, but it lacks the force and authority to communicate the big themes Robertson wants to bring across. Despite all this, *Robbie Robertson* does have its share of pearly moments. It isn't the masterpiece its creator was obviously striving towards, but it's an intelligent and often compelling set from an inarguably important artist, and it comes a good bit closer to capturing what made the Band's work so memorable than the latter-day efforts from Levon Helm and company. *—Mark Deming*

Storyville / Sep. 1991 / Geffen ✦✦✦
Robbie Robertson's 1987 solo debut was an ambitious but only intermittently successful attempt to chart a new musical direction for himself 11 years after the Band had publicly called it quits. Four years later, Robertson's second solo set, *Storyville*, found him in much

more familiar musical territory, as he steeped himself in both the music and the lore of New Orleans, the birthplace of jazz and home to many of the R&B masters who had been a primal influence on Robertson and the other members of the Band. Anyone hoping for a blowing session with Robbie Robertson leading a team of the Big Easy's finest through the Huey "Piano" Smith and Professor Longhair songbooks will have to keep on dreaming; noted perfectionist Robertson polished these sessions to a high gloss (with the help of co-producers Stephen Hague and Gary Gersh), and the funk and good humor of Crescent City R&B generally takes a back burner to more sophisticated lyrical conceits (moody character-based narratives and meditations on the hard edges of love dominate) and gracefully moody musical structures not entirely unlike the sophisticated melodies of his first album. But the material on *Storyville* does have a lighter step and a freer swing than the songs on Robertson's debut, and his vocals are in far better shape this time out, boasting a lot more body and nuance than the sometimes fragile rasp that dominated his first time at bat. And Robertson had the good sense to bring Art Neville, his brother Aaron, Ziggyboo Modeleste, and Chief Bo Dollis on board; if the New Orleans presence in these songs is more often felt than heard, it still snakes powerfully through the music and honors the spirits that helped influence this music. If *Robbie Robertson* was about taking his music to a new and different place, *Storyville* found him taking his music back home and still finding new room to move within it, and if it's a more subtle album, in many ways it's also more satisfying. *—Mark Deming*

Music for the Native Americans / Oct. 4, 1994 / Capitol ♦♦♦
With *Storyville*, Robbie Robertson's music began to directly incorporate more world-music influences; *Music for the Native Americans* makes that connection more explicit. Most of the album is quite evocative, recalling an American version of Peter Gabriel's Mediterranean exploration *Passion*. Robertson writes some fully formed songs, but most of the record is devoted to instrumental, incidental film music, and that's where he fully explores new musical territory. *Music for the Native Americans* is a soundtrack, yet contains some of Robertson's most challenging and complex music. *—Stephen Thomas Erlewine*

Contact from the Underworld of Red Boy / Mar. 10, 1998 / Capitol ♦♦♦
Throughout his solo career, Robbie Robertson has been as fascinated with sonics as he was with songwriting, so perhaps it wasn't entirely surprising that he collaborated with techno DJ/producer Howie B and remixer Marius de Vries on his fourth album, *Contact from the Underworld of Redboy*. Anyone familiar with his moody, atmospheric solo efforts will realize that there's a bigger jump between *Music from Big Pink* and *Robbie Robertson* than there is between the Daniel Lanois-produced *Robbie Robertson* and the ambient-flavored *Contact*, but the electronic textures and dance beats still may come as a shock to some. The electronics are interwoven with blues, folk, country and rock, as well as American Indian music. And, as on *Music for the Native Americans*, Robertson is primarily concerned with American Indians throughout *Contact*, whether it's through the chants of "Peyote Healing" or the protest of "Sacrifice," which features Leonard Peltier—a Native American who has been imprisoned since 1976 on charges of murder many believe are fabricated—on a telephone call. Both his lyrical and musical concerns can get bogged down in their own pretensions, but often, the results are provocative and unique. *—Stephen Thomas Erlewine*

Smokey Robinson

b. Feb. 19, 1940, Detroit, MI
Producer, Vocals / Quiet Storm, Motown, Urban, R&B, Soul, Smooth Soul
If you're looking for the all-time #1 purveyor of mainstream romantic soul, Smokey Robinson may well be the man, in the face of some towering competition. With the Miracles in the 1960s, he paced dozens of tuneful Motown hits with his beautiful high tenor. As a solo performer from the 1970s onwards, he's been one of the staples of urban contemporary music. But his singing gifts, as notable as they are, comprise only one of his hats: he's also one of pop's best and most prolific songwriters. As a songwriter and producer, he was the most important musical component to Motown's early success, not only on the hits by the Miracles, but for numerous other acts as well (especially Mary Wells and the Temptations). Robinson first crossed paths with Motown founder Berry Gordy, Jr. in the late 1950s in Detroit. In retrospect, this may have been the most important meeting in both men's lives. There was no national action for the Miracles until "Shop Around" in late 1960; it made #2, doing much not only to establish the Miracles, but to establish the Motown label itself. The song also heralded many of the important elements of the Motown sound, with its gospelish interplay between lead and backup vocals, its rhythmic groove, and its blend of R&B and pop. While Smokey Robinson is most often thought of as a romantic balladeer, the Miracles were also capable of grinding out some excellent uptempo party tunes, particularly in their early days. The 1962 Top Ten hit "You've Really Got a Hold on Me," however, was the key cut in forming Robinson's romantic persona, with its pleading, soaring vocals, exquisite melody, and carefully crafted lyrics. Bob Dylan was impressed enough by Robinson's facility for imaginative wordplay to dub him "America's greatest living poet" (a phrase which has possibly become the most quoted example of one rock giant praising another). *—Richie Unterberger*

Hi, We're the Miracles / Jun. 1961 / Motown ♦♦♦♦♦
The Miracles' first album is a magnificent debut, filled with impeccable vocal performances, inventive and occasionally brilliant songwriting, and an aching romantic aura. "Shop Around" was the big hit on the record, but another highlight is the group's recut version (also available on the old Miracles' *Anthology* double-disc set) of their single "Way Over There" in a lusher, more beguiling arrangement, which anticipated Phil Spector's "pop symphony" productions with the Crystals, Darlene Love, the Ronettes, and Tina Turner. Smokey Robinson authored or co-authored (with Berry Gordy or fellow Miracle Ronnie White) all but one track here—all are winners, and songs like the ethereal Robinson-White "Heart Like Mine" are worth the price of the disc. They'd do classier, more elaborate work later on, but the youthful verve of Robinson, Claudette Rogers Robinson, Ronnie White, Bobby Rogers, Pete Moore, and Marv Tarplin on these tracks makes this an indispensable record, even for casual fans. *—Bruce Eder*

I'll Try Something New / Jul. 1962 / Motown ♦♦♦♦
Berry Gordy shows the versatility of his prize group on this forgotten masterpiece, which embraces several different pop and soul idioms in the course of its ten songs with extraordinary aplomb, the group moving from strength to strength while also showing off Gordy's growing musical vocabulary. The floating beauty of "I'll Try Something New" showed the world the genius of Smokey Robinson more than some of his later, much bigger records, his ethereal lead vocal surrounded by an exquisite chorus (with Claudette, in particular, providing some beautiful effects and a gently comical allusion to the Frankie Avalon song "Venus") and strings that Berry Gordy knew just when to thicken, for an emotional spike in the lyric. Equally enchanting is the quizzical "What's So Good About Goodbye," which mixed some ravishingly mournful lyrics and deeply emotive performances with a sound that gave equal play to hard electric guitars and a closely recorded violin section. "He Don't Care About Me" is a delightful showcase for Claudette Rogers Robinson in a girl-group mode. Those songs and the rest of side one are included on the *35th Anniversary* box, but side two—apart from "If Your Mother Only Knew" (the original B-side of "Way Over There")—has been neglected, which is a shame, because that was the experimental side (truly the "something new" musically to which the LP title could have referred). The quintet's harmonizing soars into what would later become Manhattan Transfer territory in their version of Lerner and Loewe's "On the Street Where You Live," and they bring out equally dexterous and warmer sides of their singing on Cole Porter's "I've Got You Under My Skin"; they also engage in some delightful vocal acrobatics on the Ogden Nash-Kurt Weill "Speak Low." *—Bruce Eder & Andrew Hamilton*

Cookin' with the Miracles / Nov. 1962 / Motown ♦♦♦

The Fabulous Miracles / Feb. 1963 / Motown ♦♦♦

Going to a Go-Go / Nov. 1965 / Motown ♦♦♦
This was the first truly great Miracles album, and their first to crack the Top Ten on the LP chart. The title song was arguably Robinson's finest uptempo composition (along with "Get Ready"), and the album also contained the majestic ballads "Ooh Baby Baby" and "My Girl Has Gone," plus Robinson's signature tune, "Tracks Of My Tears." After those heavyweights, it didn't matter what else was there, but "In Case You Need Love" and "My Baby Changes Like The Weather" were the kind of afterthought gems Motown churned out with regularity during their prime. *—Ron Wynn*

Make It Happen / Aug. 1967 / Motown ♦♦♦♦
As pleasing a Miracles' album as you will find anywhere, loaded with hits and should-have-, could-have-been hits that were never released. Motown later changed the title to *Tears of a Clown* after the Miracles' big hit which was the last track on Side Two. Nearly three years passed before Motown finally released "Tears" as a single. "The Soulful Shack" had as much hit potential as anything on this set, yet the rocking upbeat number about a hip hangout spot languished without fanfare. Likewise for the grooving "It's a Good Feeling," written by Holland, Dozier & Holland, one of the trio's finest compositions that went unnoticed. The ballads are devastating, "After You Put Back the Pieces (I'll Still Have a Broken Heart)," "My Love for You," and "You Must Be Love" are excellent examples of silky, smooth, soul music. Anchored by two big hits, "Tears of a Clown," and "More Love," (a tune Smokey wrote about his wife after she suffered her second miscarriage which is tender, sweet and one of his most memorable songs). The 12 songs are all substantial, not a dog in the bunch. *—Andrew Hamilton*

Time Out for Smokey Robinson & the Miracles / Jul. 1969 / Motown ♦♦♦♦
This topnotch release by the Miracles presents a good combo of ballads and up-tempo numbers. "Baby, Baby Don't Cry," with Smokey's spoken intro and "I'm here for you" lyrics, is a stone classic, as is the much-covered "Here I Go Again," a song lovers everywhere can identify with. Pete Moore adds some bottom for accent on "Doggone Right," a good song for hand dancing. Dion's "Abraham, Martin and John" is given new flavor by the Miracles; the song about three American heroes starts slow like Dion's original, then speeds to a gospel revival-like frenzy. The charming "Once I Got to Know You" is the most overlooked song on this LP, a heartwarmer sung in a sweet tone by Smokey. *Time Out* has 12 winners from one of the most captivating groups in R&B history. *—Andrew Hamilton*

The Tears of a Clown / Dec. 1970 / Motown ♦♦♦

Pure Smokey / Mar. 15, 1974 / Motown ♦♦♦♦♦
During his solo career, many of Smokey Robinson's best solo efforts are when he writes his own material, which is more personally involved and reflective than his earlier work with the Miracles and others. An exceptionally good, ballad-driven album, its highlight is the modest pop hit "Virgin Man," one of pop and soul music's first attempts to explore male sexual inexperience and insecurity. *—John Lowe*

A Quiet Storm / Mar. 26, 1975 / Motown ♦♦♦♦♦
The genius of William "Smokey" Robinson is immeasurable. As many of his prior songs had shaped R&B and pop music, this album would have a similar effect. The title track became the namesake for a music format. The album itself had three singles hit the charts. Arranged in an intermittent rhythm, "Baby That's Backatcha" ran up the *Billboard* R&B charts to number one inside 16 weeks. It was Robinson's first number one single since leaving the Miracles. The lyric of the ballad "The Agony and the Ecstasy" hit the Top Ten at number seven, and it was followed by the masterpiece "A Quiet Storm." Although

it only managed to seal the Top 25, it has since made a greater impact on the music charts and music industry. Briefly, radio mogul Cathy Hughes, owner of Radio One, was the general manager at Howard University radio WHUR during the early '70s when she created the format "the quiet storm." She used Smokey Robinson's composition as the theme song. Before long, it caught on around the country and evolved into a new market. This album also features the "Wedding Song" which was written for Hazel and Jermaine Jackson's wedding and the "Happy" theme from the movie *Lady Sings the Blues*. *—Craig Lytle*

Smokey's Family Robinson / Feb. 10, 1976 / Motown ✦✦

Where There's Smoke . . . / May 22, 1979 / Motown ✦✦✦
This album was a considerable return to form, Smokey Robinson's most commercially successful solo LP up to this point (and highest-charting record in 11 years), entirely due to the single "Cruisin'" (number four pop and R&B), his biggest pop hit since "The Tears of a Clown." Motown doesn't seem to have recognized that track's potency, leading off with the flop "Get Ready" (a disco treatment of the old Temptations hit) before turning to "Cruisin'" as a second single several months after the LP's release. *Where There's Smoke...*then took off and peaked at number 17, more than six months after first appearing. Although the LP is divided into "Smoke" and "Fire" sides, both sides start out with rhythmic songs and gradually slow down to near-ballad speed, with the sensuous "Cruisin'" the final "Fire" track. In retrospect, the album may be uneven and a touch too disco-ish in places, but in 1979-1980, *Where's There's Smoke...*brought Smokey Robinson back into the limelight. *—William Ruhlmann*

Warm Thoughts / Feb. 25, 1980 / Motown ✦✦✦
On his follow-up to "Cruisin'," Smokey Robinson goes right back to that lazy, romantic style with "Let Me Be the Clock" (#4 R&B, #31 Pop), which leads off the aptly named *Warm Thoughts*. Robinson seems to have taken the success of "Cruisin'" as his opportunity to distance himself from disco and return to his more familiar ballad style, even injecting a touch of his old wordplay in "Into Each Rain Some Life Must Fall." Side two begins with the more uptempo "Melody Man," which was arranged, co-written, and co-produced by Stevie Wonder, but for the most part this is the bedroom Smokey Robinson, and that got him to #14 on the LP chart, his highest solo peak yet. *—William Ruhlmann*

Being with You / Feb. 17, 1981 / Motown ✦✦✦
Smokey Robinson landed his first big album of the 1980s with this release. The title track soared to the top of the R&B charts and stayed there, while it just missed topping the pop charts. Robinson's wonderful lead vocals, timing, dramatic delivery, and overall technique were as impressive as ever, and he got two more chart hits from the album. It eventually became his most successful LP ever from a commercial standpoint, although his artistic landmark as a solo artist remains *A Quiet Storm*. *—Ron Wynn*

One Heartbeat / Feb. 24, 1987 / Motown ✦✦✦
Another superb Robinson album. He continued scoring hit singles throughout the 1980s, and this time out, the song "Just To See Her" was another huge pop and R&B smash, and the title track did almost as well. Robinson was thriving, despite the fact that hip-hop was steadily gaining strength, and New Jack Swing would soon force its way into the urban contemporary spotlight. *—Ron Wynn*

Whatever Makes You Happy: More of the Best . . . / Feb. 16, 1993 / Rhino ✦✦✦✦✦
Solid compilation of 18 of the most interesting non-hits from Smokey's (and Motown's) golden era. Culled from 11 albums, this is an intelligent and consistent overview of Robinson's relatively unknown tunes. These cuts show the stylistic evolution of Motown as surely as any greatest hits collection, moving from bluesy, raucous R&B to assembly-line soul to songs reflecting the lyrical and instrumental innovations of the psychedelic era. Robinson's peerless soul songwriting and the Miracles' smooth harmonies remained constant no matter what the era, making this a much more fluid set than you might expect. Ultimately, the songs don't boast hooks quite as memorable as their classic hit singles, despite their similarities in structure and production. The early-'60s tracks are perhaps the record's most interesting, displaying a gritty, almost salacious approach that had yet to be toned down by slicker production values. Dominated by Robinson originals, this collection also includes scattered covers of "Money" and hits by the Temptations and Supremes, as well as the original version of "From Head to Toe," later covered by Elvis Costello. *—Richie Unterberger*

☆ **The 35th Anniversary Collection** / Feb. 22, 1994 / Motown ✦✦✦✦✦
This four-CD boxed set covers every essential track that Smokey Robinson and the Miracles ever recorded, and then some—at least a dozen never previously anthologized tracks are included here, among them the original single versions of "Way Over There" (unavailable elsewhere) and "Shop Around" (which had already been released locally in Detriot when Berry Gordy decided one night to get a session together, punch up the rhythm, and lay down a new version, which became the hit). Even better is the remastering, which runs circles around any previous edition of the Miracles' work, and the annotation—including an essay by Claudette Robinson—that gives credit to all of the participants, including the backup musicians who were seldom if ever mentioned during Motown's heyday. The Smokey Robinson & the Miracles *Anthology* is a fine collection, but this set is the definitive history, and irreplaceable for anyone who genuinely loves the group. *—Bruce Eder*

★ **Anthology** / 1995 / Motown ✦✦✦✦✦
Detroit vocal group the Miracles were a fixture at Motown from day one. Driven by Robinson's superior writing and smooth, silky falsetto, the Miracles placed a stunning 48 singles on the Billboard charts, 39 of those with Smokey in tow. Virtually all of them are included on this collection. Songs such as "Ooh Baby Baby," "The Tracks of My Tears," and "The Tears of a Clown" define much that was good about the '60s. The 1995 double-CD reissue is digitally remastered and includes virtually the same tracks, adding a couple previously unreleased songs and extensive liner notes. *—Rob Bowman*

The Ultimate Collection [1997] / Mar. 25, 1997 / Motown ✦✦✦✦✦
While Robinson's solo work pales in comparison to his hits with the Miracles, this 17-track collection of Motown singles uncovers such gems as "Baby Come Close," "I Am I Am," "Cruisin'," "Let Me Be," "The Clock," "Tell Me Tomorrow," "I've Made Love to You a Thousand Times," "One Heartbeat," "Just to See Her," "Everything You Touch," "Baby That's Backatcha," "The Agony and the Ecstacy" and "Open." *—Jason Ankeny*

★ **The Ultimate Collection [1998]** / Feb. 10, 1998 / Motown ✦✦✦✦✦
Motown is notorious for recycling their catalog as endless hit collections, but *The Ultimate Collection* is one of the finest series of greatest-hits CDs they have ever assembled. Each disc contains all of the major hits from an artist, plus important B-sides, album tracks and minor hits. Smokey Robinson & the Miracles' entry in the series is no exception to the rule, boasting all their Top Ten pop and R&B hits between 1960 and 1969—"Shop Around," "You've Really Got a Hold on Me," "Mickey's Monkey," "Ooo Baby Baby," "The Tracks of My Tears," "My Girl Has Gone," "Going to a Go-Go," "(Come 'Round Here) I'm the One You Need," "The Love I Saw in You Was Just a Mirage," "More Love," "I Second That Emotion," "If You Can Want," "Yester Love," "Special Occasion," "Baby, Baby Don't Cry"—plus the 1970 number one "The Tears of a Clown" and important B-sides like "Choosey Beggar" and "Who's Lovin' You," resulting in a total of 25 tracks. For anyone who wants a definitive hits collection but is hesitant to invest in the four-disc *35th Anniversary Box*, *The Ultimate Collection* is an ideal choice. *—Stephen Thomas Erlewine*

Lost and Found: Along Came Love (1958-1964) / Sep. 28, 1999 / Motown ✦✦✦✦
As part of Motown's *Lost and Found* series, this brings together 20 previously unreleased tracks and rarities of prime Smokey and the Miracles from various early time frames in the Motown catalog. Some of the earliest, like "My Mama Told Me," echo Motor City role models Nolan Strong and the Diablos right down to the guitar riffs behind Smokey's uncharacteristically bluesy vocals, while others, like "Please Say You Love Me," splendidly wear their doo-wop roots on their sleeves. Here we find the group taking on Broadway show tunes in modern jazz harmonies and *nailing* it on "If I Were a Bell" and "Easy Street." The title track is one of Smokey's patented slow burners. In the rarities department, there's the lost Ron and Bill B-side, "Don't Say Bye Bye," only outdone by "Mr. Misery," a rare lead vocal by Claudette Robinson in the grand girl group style, and a live version of "Shop Around" that's as raw as anything Smokey ever committed to wax. In the final analysis, however, most of the tracks here just make you wonder how material this great could have languished in unreleased forms for so long. Smokey's worst session is still better than most superstars' best work; here's a whole CD that makes even his leftovers a tantalizing prospect. *—Cub Koda*

Tom Robinson

b. Jun. 1, 1950
Vocals, Bass / British Punk, Pub Rock, New Wave, Hard Rock, Punk
Although his career had pretty much flamed out by the start of the '80s, there were few punk-era major label performers as intensely controversial as Tom Robinson. Cutting his teeth with folk-rockers Cafe Society, he roared into the spotlight in 1978 with a great single ("2-4-6-8 Motorway") and a much-ballyhooed contract with EMI. What was remarkable about this was that Robinson was the kind of politically conscious, confrontational performer that major labels generally ignored: he was openly gay and sang about it ("Glad to be Gay"), vociferous in his hatred for then-British Prime Minister Margaret Thatcher, helped form Rock Against Racism, and generally spoke in favor of any leftist political tract that would embarrass the ruling ultraconservative Tory government. His debut album, 1978's *Power in the Darkness*, was an occasionally stunning piece of punk/hard rock agitprop that, along with being ferociously direct, was politicized rock that focused more on songs than slogans. However, by the release of the second album, the Todd Rundgren-produced *TRB Two*, the songs were getting weaker and Robinson began sounding like a boring idealogue. *—John Dougan*

Power in the Darkness / 1978 / Razor & Tie ✦✦✦✦✦

TRB Two / 1979 / Razor & Tie ✦✦✦
A heartfelt record of political rock, Robinson made interesting albums after this one, but never again sounded as passionate, defiant, and full of himself. The band's secret weapon was guitarist Danny Kustow, whose playing makes even the most obvious and unsubtle moments enjoyable. Earnest and likeable, this is hands-down the best Tom Robinson record available (yes, even better than any of the TRB anthologies). The original American LP release included a bonus EP, with "Glad to Be Gay" (which doesn't hold up well) and the embarrassingly simplistic feminist ode "Right on Sister." *TRB Two* is only recommended to those who will appreciate a warmed-over version of *Power in the Darkness*—more slogans, less substance. *—John Dougan*

North by Northwest / 1982 / IRS ✦✦✦✦✦
North by Northwest features contributions by Peter Gabriel and a far less noisy pop/rock sound. It's an insinuating record, one that was dismissed cavalierly upon its release, but Robinson's songwriting is mostly good even when his singing (never much to write home about in the first place) is inadequate or just plain bad. *—John Dougan*

Hope and Glory / 1984 / Repertoire ✦✦✦
Hope and Glory is as good as *North by Northwest*, if only because it rocks a little harder and for the simple, but emotional track "War Baby." It's not the record to begin with Robinson, but the work is better than you'd expect. *—John Dougan*

Having It Both Ways / Jul. 2, 1996 / Cooking Vinyl ♦♦♦

● **Rising Free: The Very Best of Tom Robinson Band** / 1997 / EMI ♦♦♦♦♦
The Tom Robinson Band straddled the border between pub rock and punk, turning out hard-driving rock anthems that were filled with attitude, if not venom. They were a stripped-down rock & roll band, delivering charging, catchy three-chord rockers at their best. Occasionally, as on the notorious anthem "Glad to Be Gay," Robinson dipped into social commentary, yet he was best at just rocking out, like on the lost classic "2-4-6-8 Motorway," one of the very best driving songs of all time. "2-4-6-8 Motorway" is the highlight on *Rising Free—The Very Best of the Tom Robinson Band*, which proves that the group was a good band, but not great. Few songs on *Rising Free* have the intoxicating hook of "2-4-6-8 Motorway," and few are as acidic as "Glad to Be Gay." By and large, it's simply competent pub rock that's harder than average. As the years progressed, TRB's edge softened, and they began experimenting with disco. All of these progressions, and all of the group's best moments, are found on *Rising Free*, and while it doesn't reveal many hidden gems, there are enough good songs to make it worthwhile for pub and punk fanatics. *—Stephen Thomas Erlewine*

Rocket from the Crypt

f. 1990, San Diego, CA
Indie Rock, Alternative Pop/Rock
Pledging to never play a venue with a stage, singer/guitarist John Reis formed San Diego's Rocket from the Crypt in the summer of 1990 after becoming disillusioned with the hardcore punk band he was in called Pitchfork. Joining with current Rocketeers bassist Petey X and guitarist ND, in addition to now-departed drummer Sean and backing vocalist Elaina, Reis and company released *Paint as a Fragrance* in 1991.

Though the album caused a lot of people to take notice, a lineup change ensued; Atom became the drummer, and Apollo 9, a drinking buddy of Reis' who played sax in high school, joined as saxophonist. After the successful independent *Circa: Now!* was released on Cargo Records in 1992, a major-label bidding war resulted in Rocket From The Crypt signing with Interscope Records (in addition to Reis' other band, Drive Like Jehu, which features another former Pitchfork member, Rick Fork). Interscope then re-released *Circa: Now!* in 1993, and the single "Ditch Digger" spent some time in MTV's Buzz Bin. Eventually, a sixth member—JC 2000 on horn—was added in 1994, which preceded the release of a new 10-inch record, *The State of Art is on Fire*, in 1995. By the end of the year, the group released its most acclaimed album to date, *Scream, Dracula, Scream*. *RFTC* followed in 1998 and *Group Sounds* was issued on Vagrant in early 2001. *—Matt Carlson*

Paint as a Fragrance / Feb. 1991 / Headhunter ♦♦♦
This record lurches through ten solid songs, which, though as aggressive as punk's roots, offer much more than your typical power-chord mosh pit anthems. John "Speedo" Reis stuns with his soulful, Sammy Davis, Jr.-meets-Eddie Cochran lead vocals, while backing vocalist Elaina adds rich harmony. In addition to more immediate punk scorchers, Rocket From The Crypt also explores other musical terrain; the band gears up with rockabilly-laden guitar riffs, which are then unleashed with some dissonant guitar harmonies and breakneck piano. *—Matt Carlson*

Circa: Now! / Nov. 1992 / Headhunter ♦♦♦♦♦
Originally released on Cargo/Headhunter before the group was picked up by Interscope, *Circa: Now!* finds Speedo's army redirecting its sound slightly by adding saxophone and slowing the tempo down on some tracks. Of course, Rocket From The Crypt still imbues every second of these with unflinching power. The saxophone of Apollo 9, though sparsely decorated and subtly buried throughout the album, adds 1950s R&B flair on "Hairball Alley" and "March of Dimes." And though a majority of the songs pack a more direct wallop than *Paint as a Fragrance*, the record still finds room to settle down on the lush '60s pop of "Little Arm." *—Matt Carlson*

All Systems Go / 1993 / Headhunter ♦♦♦
More than many so-called punk bands of the '90s, especially as corporate release structures took precedence over fun and music, Rocket From the Crypt celebrates the original spirit of releasing single after single, in its case via a huge number of labels. Indeed, the band was productive enough on that front to be able to release a fantastic compilation of its various 7" and comp appearances after only two studio albums. *All Systems Go* contains what for many are the group's best early efforts, tightly wound and fiercely performed garage/punk monsters that burn attitude and sly intelligence all at once. Self-deprecation aside, "Live the Funk" and "Bad Song Ninja" appear in smoking re-recorded versions, and from there the band careens from one happy blast to another, soul shouting and call-and-response choruses as much a part of things as chunky riffs and slamming drums. Add in the smoking horns of Apollo 9 and all is raunchy bliss. One great rarity is a cover of Adam & the Ants' "Press Darlings," which Reis sounds almost apologetic for in the notes, but which still kicks major butt. Then there's the goofy "Chantilly Face," which takes the Big Bopper's early rock classic and does rather strange things to it. On a technical note, *All Systems Go* initially appeared in Japan as part of a tour promotion; demand for it back in the States prompted its American release, with a slew of extra tracks. However, four songs from the original release didn't make it—two finally ended up on *All Systems Go, Vol. 2*, but the others are still in limbo, including a damn good version of the MC5 rarity "Gold" that ends with Reis puking on the mic! *—Ned Raggett*

State of the Art Is on Fire / 1995 / Sympathy for the Record Industry ♦♦♦
Certainly Rocket From The Crypt's most furious punk exploit to date, the 10-inch EP *The State of Art is on Fire* burns straight to the point. Rocket relinquishes its usual musical homage to rockabilly and R&B, and instead blazes through six explosive songs that don't slow down until the final track, "Human Spine." Reis' lyrics add more fuel to the fire, while Apollo 9 and JC 2000 blast their horns against the wall of sound. *—Matt Carlson*

Hot Charity / Aug. 8, 1995 / Perfect Sound ♦♦♦♦
1995 was Rocket's year of sheer productivity—no less than three separate major releases, counting the fantastic *The State of the Art Is on Fire* EP, not to mention another slew of singles. The rarest of the three is for many the best, the limited-edition vinyl-only release *Hot Charity*. Just under half an hour long, this particular album has never been reissued on CD, though it's been sought after more than a few times by obsessed fans, while Japanese and Australian special editions of other Rocket albums have included tracks from it on bonus discs. Starting with the dramatic slow build of "Pushed," making for an almost cinematic opening to the proceedings (helped by the fact that it's an instrumental), *Hot Charity* smokes from the start and takes special care not to let up. The recording quality sounds fantastic, the band is as playful as it is utterly hard-edged, and everything, simply put, rocks. There's the party grooving of "My Arrow's Aim," with some smart guitar playing increasing the nerviness as everything gets more driving, ending up in a great, strutting chorus interspersed with Apollo 9 and JC 2000 blowing like fiends. Or one can just simply let the amazing blend of Reis' vocals and the backing singing from others on the downright soaring "Guilt Free" do its work. Slower grooves aren't forgotten, like the twangy, measured kick of "Feathered Friends," piano adding to the wooziness here and there. Mostly, though, it's music like the addictive handclap/rockabilly bass and echo leading into the rip-roaring "Lorna Doom," quick, amazing end solo and all, which leads the way, and that's nothing to regret in the slightest. In lieu of a wider issue, this is one to search for—either in and of itself or on the Internet. *—Ned Raggett*

● **Scream, Dracula, Scream!** / Oct. 10, 1995 / Interscope ♦♦♦♦♦
Rocket from the Crypt keeps the rock & roll torch burning with their fourth full-length, *Scream, Dracula, Scream!* (named after the infamous '70s Black horror flick *Scream, Blackula, Scream!*). The presence of RFTC's innovation and energy is still right in your face, and with an added trumpet player in their lineup, the horn section is more apparent than ever; also, there's a loud party atmosphere that fails to cross the line of obnoxious. Tracks like "Born in '69" and "On a Rope" provide headbanging fun, but Rocket from the Crypt is anything but long haired butt-rock; this has enough of a cool edge to scare Henry "The Fonz" Winkler out of any roller rink. *—Mike DaRonco*

R.F.T.C. / Jun. 2, 1998 / Interscope ♦♦♦
It's a bit of a mystery why it took Rocket from the Crypt a full three years to deliver *RFTC*, the followup to their major-label debut *Scream, Dracula, Scream*. After all, diversity isn't Rocket from the Crypt's bag—they just love rock & roll, baby, and all of the sleaze, leather, booze, bikes and babes that come with it. Before, they kept raw by producing their own records, but here they hired an outside producer in Kevin Shirley, who previously worked with Journey. There's not a trace of Journey on *RFTC*, but Shirley has given the band a bigger, glossier sound that may distress longtime followers, who were into the whole MC5/Stooges/Stones biker vibe of the earlier albums. That said, *RFTC* rocks harder and with more attitude than almost any other record released under the alternative umbrella in the late '90s. The guys haven't lost it—they've just found another way to say it. *—Stephen Thomas Erlewine*

All Systems Go, Vol. 2 / Oct. 26, 1999 / Swami ♦♦♦♦
Some years after the initial collection, this follow-up to the first *All Systems Go* follows the same method as the original, right down to similar cover art, disc art, and even inlay tray track-listing style (no comments about Garth Brooks being a "puppet asshole" this time around, though). Besides a slew of B-sides from British singles taken from their "regular" albums like *Scream, Dracula, Scream*, any number of one-offs, contributions to split singles and compilations, and more are again assembled, an amazing 25 songs' worth of great times. If a few numbers sound like something that were put on an obscure single for a reason, most work just fine on their own. With JC 2000 on board throughout, one or two early cuts aside, the distinct horn attack that makes Rocket such a treat is on full display. Everything from almost winsome pop—check the downright sweet verses on the opening "Tarzan"—to nuclear-strength guitar obliteration gets the Rocket treatment here. The recording quality generally sounds a bit better here than with the original *All Systems Go*, likely because of the major label cash that helped in the recording here and there, but thankfully nothing ever sounds too slick. Some all-time greats include the almost-too-explosive-to-live "UFO, UFO, UFO," piano careening amidst the groove-heavy tune with Reis in his rough-voiced crowd-inspiring glory; the energetically pissed kiss-off "Heads Are Gonna Roll"; and the frenetic Halloween-themed "I Drink Blood." A fine treat is the inclusion of a slew of cover songs, with the band touching on expected and unexpected roots alike. Bands like the Drags and the Real Kids make perfect sense in context—even Ray Charles—but hearing Rocket snarl through the Silver Apples' "You and I" makes for a one-of-a-kind experience. *—Ned Raggett*

Group Sounds / Mar. 6, 2001 / Vagrant ♦♦♦♦
Rebounding from both a messy extrication from Interscope and the departure of founding drummer Atom, Rocket recruited San Diego scene vet Mario Rubalcaba to fill in and whipped out the fierce and fine *Group Sounds*. Superchunk's Jon Wurster actually plays the skins on most of the tracks, as Rubalcaba (redubbed in Rocket-style Ruby Mars) only officially joined towards the end of recording, but either way the band sounds fully up to necessary events. "Straight American Slave" says that much at the start—it's Rocket as all have come to know and love them, garage/punk/R&B grooves tightly wound as hell, horns ripping joyfully through the mix, call and response choruses, and Reis as always the at-once slick and raging frontman. From there it's barely a breath taken before launching into "Carne Voodoo," and the instant party atmosphere that Rocket know how to nail just so runs rampant. Having participated in a slew of fine solo efforts and projects all throughout 2000 like the Hot Snakes and the Sultans, hearing Reis take full charge with Rocket again seems like coming home to something especially great. Hints of other influences and approaches certainly crop up on the slightly calmer "S.O.S." and most

notably with the marvelous closing track "Ghost Shark." A big woozy slow number with a bit of emotional bite, it makes for a perfect ending, with legendary producer Jim Dickinson adding piano. Those who want more of what Rocket does so well can't be disappointed, though. Sure to be future classics include "White Belt," which never seems to stop building up, the utterly anthemic "Heart of a Rat," and the no-less-so "This Bad Check Is Gonna Stick"—with bells, even! Ten years since Rocket's first full-length, the sextet still sounds like they're on a live wire with an endless power source, as inspiring here as ever before. *—Ned Raggett*

Rockpile

f. 1976, **db.** 1981

Pub Rock, Pop/Rock, New Wave, Rock & Roll

During the late '70s, Rockpile was the touring band for both Dave Edmunds and Nick Lowe. Like Edmunds, the band was passionate about traditional rock & roll. Like Lowe, the band played with a reckless, trashy abandon. Driven by the powerful rhythm section of drummer Terry Williams and Lowe's bass, guitarists Billy Bremner and Edmunds were free to spit out crushing rock, blues, rockabilly, and country licks. With their fierce live energy and unpretentious rock & roll, the band fit easily into the post-punk new wave at the end of the decade.

Although they only released one album as a group—1980's *Seconds of Pleasure*—the band provided support for most of the albums Lowe and Edmunds recorded in the late '70s. After the rushed release of *Seconds of Pleasure*, the band toured one last time before splitting apart, largely due to mismanagement. All of the members continued to occasionally collaborate with each other throughout the '80s. *—Stephen Thomas Erlewine*

Seconds of Pleasure / 1980 / Columbia ♦♦♦♦♦

If *Seconds of Pleasure*, the only album issued under the Rockpile name, doesn't quite capture the intensity of the band's ferocious live performances, attribute that to the confines of a studio setting, plus the fact that most of the band's set list derived from Nick Lowe's *Labour of Lust* and Dave Edmunds' *Repeat When Necessary* (both of which featured Rockpile as backing band). So, much of their great songs had already been cut elsewhere, leaving *Seconds* to be split equally between covers and originals. Since Edmunds was never a songwriter, this gave Lowe the upper hand, not only because Dave sings Nick's "Fool Too Long," but because he's in tremendous form. He unearths the Gene Chandler "Teacher Teacher," gives the irrepressible Billy Bremner the joyous "Heart," offers the jangling Buddy Holly-esque "Now and Always" where the sweetness masks the suicidal undertones, sleazes it up with "Pet and Hold You," and then delves into tongue-in-cheek autobiography with "When I Write a Book," one of his very finest and funniest songs. And Dave's covers are barroom ravers of the highest order, whether it's Joe Tex's "If Sugar Was as Sweet as You" or Difford & Tilbrook's "Wrong Again (Let's Face It)." Yes, the production has the gloss of new wave, which actually provides some freshness. Not that they needed it. Although Rockpile is a band of unabashed rock revivalists, they make it sound fresh—they have so much joy, it's hard not to get wrapped up in the momentum. Maybe not a flat-out classic, but rock & roll rarely gets as flat-out fun as this. [The CD reissue is even better, since it contains the bonus 7" of four Everly covers, sung by Nick and Dave, alone with acoustics, at a radio station.] *—Stephen Thomas Erlewine*

Tommy Roe

b. May 9, 1942, Atlanta, GA

Vocals, Guitar / Sunshine Pop, Bubblegum, Rock & Roll

Widely perceived as one of the archetypal bubblegum artists of the late '60s, Tommy Roe cut some pretty decent rockers along the way, especially early in his career—many displaying some pretty prominent Buddy Holly roots. In fact, Roe's initial pop smash, 1962's chart-topping "Sheila," was quite reminiscent of Holly's "Peggy Sue," utilizing a very similar throbbing drum beat and Roe's hiccuping vocal. The singer had previously cut the song for the smaller Judd label before remaking it in superior form for ABC-Paramount. The infectious "Everybody"—another hot item the next year—was waxed in Muscle Shoals at Rick Hall's Fame studios, normally an R&B-oriented facility (it's not widely known that Roe wrote songs for the Tams, a raw-edged soul group from his Atlanta hometown).

Once Roe veered off on his squeaky-clean bubblegum tangent, he stuck with it for the rest of the decade. His lighthearted "Sweet Pea" and "Hooray for Hazel" burned up the charts in 1966, and he was still at it three years later when he waxed his biggest hit, "Dizzy," and "Jam Up Jelly Tight." *—Bill Dahl*

● **Greatest Hits** / Sep. 28, 1993 / MCA ♦♦♦♦♦

Supplants previous anthologies as the best Roe collection available. Eighteen songs spanning 1962 to 1971, including all the big singles, with thorough liner notes. *—Richie Unterberger*

The Rolling Stones

f. Jan. 1963, London, England

British Psychedelia, Album Rock, British Blues, Pop/Rock, Psychedelic, British Invasion, Hard Rock, Blues-Rock, Rock & Roll

By the time the Rolling Stones began calling themselves the World's Greatest Rock & Roll Band in the late '60s, they had already staked out an impressive claim on the title. As the self-consciously dangerous alternative to the bouncy Merseybeat of the Beatles in the British Invasion, the Stones had pioneered the gritty, hard-driving blues-based rock & roll that came to define hard rock. With his preening machismo and latent maliciousness, Mick Jagger became the prototypical rock frontman, tempering his macho showmanship with a detached, campy irony, while Keith Richards and Brian Jones wrote the blueprint for sinewy, interlocking rhythm guitars. Backed by the strong, yet subtly swinging rhythm section of bassist Bill Wyman and drummer Charlie Watts, the Stones became the breakout band of the British blues scene, eclipsing such contemporaries as the Animals and Them. Over the course of their career, the Stones never really abandoned blues, but as soon as they reached popularity in the U.K., they began experimenting musically, incorporating the British pop of contemporaries like the Beatles, Kinks and Who into their sound. After a brief dalliance with psychedelia, the Stones re-emerged in the late '60s as a jaded, blues-soaked hard rock quintet. They always flirted with the seedy side of rock & roll, but as the hippie dream began to break apart, they exposed and reveled in the new rock culture. It wasn't without difficulty, of course. Shortly after he was fired from the group, Jones was found dead in a swimming pool, while at a 1969 free concert at Altamont, a concertgoer was brutally murdered during the Stones' show. But the Stones never stopped going. For the next thirty years, they continued to record and perform, and while their records weren't always blockbusters, they were never less than the most visible band of their era—certainly, none of their British peers continued to be as popular or productive as the Stones. And no band since has proven to have such a broad fan base or far-reaching popularity, and it is impossible to hear any of the groups that followed them without detecting some sort of influence, whether it was musical or aesthetic. *—Stephen Thomas Erlewine*

The Rolling Stones (England's Newest Hitmakers) / May 30, 1964 / ABKCO ♦♦♦♦♦

The group's debut album was the most uncompromisingly blues/R&B-oriented full-length recording they would ever release. Mostly occupied with covers, this was as hardcore as British R&B ever got; it's raw and ready. But the Stones succeeded in establishing themselves as creative interpreters, putting '50s and early '60s blues, rock, and soul classics (some quite obscure to White audiences) through a younger, more guitar-oriented filter. The record's highlighted by blistering versions of "Route 66," "Carol," the hyper-tempoed "I Just Want to Make Love to You," "I'm a King Bee," and "Walking the Dog." Their Bo Diddleyized version of Buddy Holly's "Not Fade Away" gave them their first British Top Ten hit (and their first small American one). The acoustic ballad "Tell Me" was Jagger-Richards' first good original tune, but the other group-penned originals were little more than rehashed jams of blues cliches, keeping this album from reaching truly classic status. *—Richie Unterberger*

☆ **12 X 5** / Oct. 17, 1964 / ABKCO ♦♦♦♦♦

The evolution from blues to rock accelerated with the Stones' second American LP. They turned soul into guitar rock for the hits "It's All Over Now" and "Time Is on My Side" (the latter of which was their first American Top Ten single). "2120 South Michigan Avenue" is a great instrumental blues-rock jam; "Around and Around" is one of their best Chuck Berry covers; and "If You Need Me" reflects an increasing contemporary soul influence. On the other hand, the group originals (except for the propulsive "Empty Heart") are weak and derivative, indicating that the band still had a way to go before they could truly challenge the Beatles' throne. *—Richie Unterberger*

☆ **The Rolling Stones Now!** / Apr. 1965 / ABKCO ♦♦♦♦♦

Although their third American album was patched together (in the usual British Invasion tradition) from a variety of sources, it's their best early R&B-oriented effort. Most of the Stones' early albums suffer from three or four very weak cuts; *Now!* is almost uniformly strong start-to-finish, the emphasis on some of their Blackest material. The covers of "Down Home Girl," and Bo Diddley's vibrating "Mona," Otis Redding's "Pain in My Heart," and Barbara Lynn's "Oh Baby" are all among the group's best R&B interpretations. The best gem is "Little Red Rooster," a pure blues with wonderful slide guitar from Brian Jones (and a #1 single in Britain, although it was only an album track in the U.S.). As songwriters, Jagger and Richards are still struggling, but they come up with one of their first winners (and an American Top 20 hit) with the yearning, soulful "Heart of Stone." *—Richie Unterberger*

Out of Our Heads / Aug. 1965 / ABKCO ♦♦♦♦♦

In 1965, the Stones finally proved themselves capable of writing classic rock singles that mined their R&B/blues roots, but updated them into a more guitar-based, thoroughly contemporary context. The first enduring Jagger-Richards classics are here—"The Last Time," and its menacing, folky B-side "Play with Fire," and the riff-driven "Satisfaction," which made them superstars in the States and defined their sound and rebellious attitude better than any other single song. On the rest of the album, they largely opted for mid-'60s soul covers, Marvin Gaye's "Hitch Hike," Otis Redding's "Cry to Me," and Sam Cooke's "Good Times" being particular standouts. "I'm All Right" (based on a Bo Diddley sound) showed their '65 sound at its rawest, and there are a couple of fun, though derivative, bluesy originals in "The Spider and the Fly" and "The Under Assistant West Coast Promotion Man." *—Richie Unterberger*

December's Children / Dec. 1965 / ABKCO ♦♦♦♦♦

The last Stones album in which cover material accounted for 50% of the content was thrown together from a variety of singles, British LP tracks, outtakes, and a cut from an early '64 U.K. EP. Haphazard assembly aside, much of it's great, including the huge hit "Get Off of My Cloud" and the controversial, string-laden acoustic ballad "As Tears Go By" (a Top Ten item in America). Raiding the R&B closet for the last time, they also offered a breathless run-through of Larry Williams' "She Said Yeah," a sultry Chuck Berry cover ("Talkin' About You"), and exciting live versions of "Route 66" and Hank Snow's "I'm Moving On." More importantly, Jagger-Richards' songwriting partnership had now developed to the extent that several non-A-side tracks were reasonably strong in their own right, such as "I'm Free" and "The Singer Not the Song." And the version of "You Better Move On" (which had been featured on a British EP at the beginning of 1964) was one of their best and most tender soul covers. *—Richie Unterberger*

Big Hits: High Tide and Green Grass / Mar. 1966 / ABKCO ♦♦♦♦♦

With such classic passion-filled rock & roll hits as "(I Can't Get No) Satisfaction" and "Get Off of My Cloud," the Rolling Stones leave no reason not to believe that they are rock music's rebels of the '60s. This collection, eloquently known as *Big Hits: High Tide and Green Grass*, is revered as an album fit to conquer the ages. It was Jagger, Richards, and the Stones' idea to be everything the Beatles weren't. Their sound was intense, powerful, and daring. *High Tide and Green Grass* kicks off that classic Stones sound, with the shriveling, distortion-laden, feedback-driven guitars of Richards and Jones featured initially on the song, "Have You Seen Your Mother, Baby, Standing in the Shadow?" Then the record's mood darkens with the soul-stirring "Paint It, Black," with more of the same from Richards, along with his gripping trademark guitar riffs. Here is the first real mark of Jagger's exquisite, scintillating vocal presence. The band as a whole sounds like a huge hurricane in stereo, very free-flowing and spontaneous in its playing and singing. Jagger and Richards' knack for writing fiercely charged and positively witty rock tunes (along with the occasional romantic ballad such as "Lady Jane" and "As Tears Go By") is supported by the craftsmanship of a serious, hard-working rock band. The result of their work collected on this album paid off, landing the Stones high on the pedestal of rock immortality. Other classic hits featured in this must-have compilation are "It's All Over Now," "Time Is on My Side," and the fast-paced, supercharged "19th Nervous Breakdown." *—Shawn Haney*

☆ **Aftermath** / Jun. 1966 / ABKCO ✦✦✦✦✦
The Rolling Stones finally delivered a set of all-original material with this LP, which also did much to define the group as the bad boys of rock & roll with their sneering attitude toward the world in general and the female sex in particular. The borderline misogyny could get a bit juvenile in tunes like "Stupid Girl." But on the other hand the group began incorporating the influences of psychedelia and Dylan into their material with classics like "Paint It Black," an eerily insistent #1 hit graced by some of the best use of sitar (played by Brian Jones) on a rock record. Other classics included "Mother's Little Helper" (whose lyrics had extremely blatant and controversial drug references); Jones also added exotic accents with his vibes (on the jazzy "Under My Thumb") and dulcimer (the delicate Elizabethan ballad "Lady Jane"). Some of the material is fairly ho-hum, to be honest, as Jagger and Richards were still prone to inconsistent songwriting; "Goin' Home," a 11-minute blues jam, was remarkable more for its barrier-crashing length than its content. Look out for an obscure gem, however, in the brooding, meditative "I Am Waiting." *—Richie Unterberger*

Got Live If You Want It / Nov. 4, 1966 / ABKCO ✦✦
A live document of the Brian Jones-era Stones sounds enticing, but the actual product is a letdown. The sound is lousy, and for that matter not all of it's live; a couple of old studio R&B covers were augmented by screaming fans that had obviously been overdubbed. Partially recorded at a 1966 Royal Albert Hall performance (where the audience rioted at the opening of the concert), the performances and singing are on the sloppy side (and sometimes alarmingly out of tune), the sound balance is atrocious, and several of the songs are taken at a let's-get-this-over-with-and-off-the-stage-before-we-get-torn-apart pace. It's a fun souvenir in its own way; just don't expect top-notch value, even factoring in the primitive state of live rock recording technology in 1966. *—Richie Unterberger*

☆ **Between the Buttons** / Jan. 1967 / ABKCO ✦✦✦✦✦
The Rolling Stones' 1967 recordings are a matter of some controversy; many critics felt that they were compromising their raw, rootsy power with trendy emulations of the Beatles, Kinks, Dylan, and psychedelic music. Approach this album with an open mind, though, and you'll find it to be one of their strongest, most eclectic LPs, with many fine songs that remain unknown to all but Stones devotees. The lyrics are getting better (if more savage), and the arrangements more creative, on brooding near-classics like "All Sold Out," "My Obsession," and "Yesterday's Papers." "She Smiled Sweetly" shows their hidden romantic side at its best, while "Connection" is one of the record's few slabs of conventionally driving rock. But the best tracks were the two songs that gave the group a double-sided #1 in early 1967: the lustful "Let's Spend the Night Together" and the beautiful, melancholy "Ruby Tuesday," which is as melodic as anything Jagger and Richards would ever write. *—Richie Unterberger*

Flowers / Jun. 1967 / ABKCO ✦✦✦✦✦
Dismissed as a ripoff of sorts by some critics, as it took the patchwork bastardization of British releases for the American audience to extremes, gathering stray tracks from the U.K. versions of *Aftermath* and *Between the Buttons*, 1966-67 singles (some of which had already been used on the U.S. editions of *Aftermath* and *Between the Buttons*), and a few outtakes. Judged solely by the music, though, it's rather great. "Lady Jane," "Ruby Tuesday," and "Let's Spend the Night Together" are all classics (although they had all been on an LP before); the 1966 single "Mother's Little Helper," a Top Ten hit, is also terrific; and "Have You Seen Your Mother, Baby, Standing in the Shadow," making its first album appearance, is the early Stones at their most surrealistic and angst-ridden. A lot of the rest of the cuts rate among their most outstanding 1966-67 work. "Out of Time" is hit-worthy in its own right (and in fact topped the British charts in an inferior cover by Chris Farlowe); "Back Street Girl," with its European waltz flavor, is one of *the* great underrated Stones songs. The same goes for the psychedelic Bo Diddley of "Please Go Home," and the acoustic, pensively sardonic "Sittin' on a Fence," with its strong Appalachian flavor. Almost every track is strong, so if you're serious about your Stones, don't pass this by just because a bunch of people slag it as an exploitative marketing trick (which it is). There's some outstanding material you can't get anywhere else, and the album as a whole plays very well from end-to-end. *—Richie Unterberger*

Their Satanic Majesties Request / Nov. 1967 / ABKCO ✦✦✦✦
Without a doubt, no Rolling Stones album—and, indeed, very few rock albums from any era—split critical opinion as much as the Rolling Stones' psychedelic outing. Many dismiss the record as sub-*Sgt. Pepper* posturing; others confess, if only in private, to a fascination with the album's inventive arrangements, which incorporated some African rhythms, mellotrons, and full orchestration. Never before or since did the Stones take so many chances in the studio. This writer, at least, feels that the record has been unfairly undervalued, partly because purists expect the Stones to constantly champion a blues 'n' raunch worldview. About half the material is very strong, particularly the glorious "She's a Rainbow," with its beautiful harmonies, piano, and strings; the riff-driven "Citadel"; the hazy, dream-like "In Another Land," Bill Wyman's debut writing (and singing) credit on a Stones release; and the majestically dark and doomy cosmic rocker "2000 Light Years from Home," with some of the creepiest synthesizer effects (devised by Brian Jones) ever to grace a rock record. The downfall of the album was caused by some weak songwriting on the lesser tracks, particularly the interminable psychedelic jam "Sing This All Together (See What Happens)." It's a much better record than most people give it credit for being, though, with a strong current of creeping uneasiness that undercuts the gaudy psychedelic flourishes. In 1968, the Stones would go back to the basics, and never wander down these paths again, making this all the more of a fascinating anomaly in the group's discography. *—Richie Unterberger*

☆ **Beggars Banquet** / Nov. 1968 / ABKCO ✦✦✦✦✦
The Stones forsook psychedelic experimentation to return to their blues roots on this celebrated album, which was immediately acclaimed as one of their landmark achievements. A strong acoustic Delta blues flavor colors much of the material, particularly "Salt of the Earth" and "No Expectations," which features some beautiful slide guitar work. Basic rock & roll was not forgotten, however: "Street Fighting Man," a reflection of the political turbulence of 1968, was one of their most innovative singles, and "Sympathy for the Devil," with its fire-dancing guitar licks, leering Jagger vocals, African rhythms, and explicitly satanic lyrics, was an image-defining epic. On "Stray Cat Blues," Jagger and crew began to explore the kind of decadent sexual sleaze that they would take to the point of self-parody by the mid-'70s. At the time, though, the approach was still fresh, and the lyrical bite of most of the material ensured *Beggars Banquet*'s place as one of the top blues-based rock records of all time. *—Richie Unterberger*

Through the Past Darkly (Big Hits, Vol. 2) / Sep. 1969 / ABKCO ✦✦✦✦✦
Their biggest '60s hits, from "Paint It Black" onward. Like *High Tide and Green Grass*, it's somewhat redundant these days, as all of the tracks appear on the more extensive *Hot Rocks* anthologies. What's in the grooves, though, is wall-to-wall classic, including "Ruby Tuesday," "Let's Spend the Night Together," "Jumpin' Jack Flash," "Honky Tonk Woman," "Have You Seen Your Mother, Baby, Standing in the Shadow," "She's a Rainbow," "Street Fighting Man," and more. *—Richie Unterberger*

☆ **Let It Bleed** / Nov. 28, 1969 / ABKCO ✦✦✦✦✦
Mostly recorded without Brian Jones—who died several months before its release (although he does play on two tracks) and was replaced by Mick Taylor (who also plays on just two songs)—this extends the rock & blues feel of *Beggar's Banquet* into slightly harder-rocking, more demonically sexual territory. The Stones were never as consistent on album as their main rivals, the Beatles, and *Let It Bleed* suffers from some rather perfunctory tracks, like "Monkey Man" and a countrified remake of the classic "Honky Tonk Woman" (here titled "Country Honk"). Yet some of the songs are among their very best, especially "Gimme Shelter," with its shimmering guitar lines and apocalyptic lyrics; the harmonica-driven "Midnight Rambler"; the druggy party ambience of the title track; and the stunning "You Can't Always Get What You Want," which was the Stones' "Hey Jude" of sorts, with its epic structure, horns, philosophical lyrics, and swelling choral vocals. "You Got the Silver" (Keith Richards' first lead vocal) and Robert Johnson's "Love in Vain," by contrast, were as close to the roots of acoustic down-home blues as the Stones ever got. *—Richie Unterberger*

Get Yer Ya-Ya's Out / Sep. 4, 1970 / ABKCO ✦✦✦✦✦
Recorded during their American tour in late 1969, and centered around live versions of material from the *Beggars Banquet-Let It Bleed* era. Often acclaimed as one of the top live rock albums of all time, its appeal has dimmed a little today. The live versions are reasonably different from the studio ones, but ultimately not as good, a notable exception being the long workout of "Midnight Rambler," with extended harmonica solos and the unforgettable section where the pace slows to a bump-and-grind crawl. Some Stones aficionados, in fact, prefer a bootleg from the same tour (*Liver Than You'll Ever Be*, to which this album was unleashed in response), or their amazing the-show-must-go-on performance in the jaws of hell at Altamont (preserved in the *Gimme Shelter*... film). Fans that are unconcerned with picky comparisons such as these will still find *Ya Ya's*... an outstanding album, and it's certainly the Stones' best official live recording. *—Richie Unterberger*

☆ **Sticky Fingers** / Apr. 23, 1971 / Virgin ✦✦✦✦✦
Pieced together from outtakes and much-labored-over songs, *Sticky Fingers* manages to have a loose, ramshackle ambience that belies both its origins and the dark undercurrents of the songs. It's a weary, drug-laden album—well over half the songs explicitly mention drug use, while the others merely allude to it—that never fades away, but it barely keeps afloat. Apart from the classic opener, "Brown Sugar" (a gleeful tune about slavery, interracial sex, and lost virginity, not necessarily in that order), the long workout "Can't You Hear Me Knocking" and the mean-spirited "Bitch," *Sticky Fingers* is a slow, bluesy affair, with a few country touches thrown in for good measure. The laid-back tone of the album gives ample room for new lead guitarist Mick Taylor to stretch out, particularly on the extended coda of "Can't You Hear Me Knocking." But the key to the album isn't the instrumental interplay—although that is terrific—it's the utter weariness of the songs. "Wild Horses" is their first non-ironic stab at a country song, and it is a beautiful, heart-tugging masterpiece. Similarly, "I Got the Blues" is a ravished, late-night classic that ranks among their very best blues. "Sister Morphine" is a horrifying overdose tale, and "Moonlight Mile," with Paul Buckmaster's grandiose strings, is a perfect closure: sad,

yearning, drug-addled, and beautiful. With its offhand mixture of decadence, roots music, and outright malevolence, *Sticky Fingers* set the tone for the rest of the decade for the Stones. *—Stephen Thomas Erlewine*

● **Hot Rocks, 1964-1971** / Jan. 1972 / ABKCO ✦✦✦✦✦
This two-LP/two-CD set is both a lot more and a bit less than what it seems. It is seven years worth of mostly very high-charting, and all influential and important, songs, leaving out some singles in favor of well-known album tracks and, in the process, giving an overview not just of the Rolling Stones' hits but of their evolving image. One hears them change from loud R&B-inspired rockers covering others' songs ("Time Is on My Side") into originators in their own right ("Satisfaction"); then into taste-makers and style-setters with a particularly decadent air ("Get off of My Cloud," "19th Nervous Breakdown"); and finally into self-actualized rebel-poets ("Jumping Jack Flash," "Midnight Rambler") and Shaman-like symbols of chaos. On its initial release, *Hot Rocks* sold well, not only as a unique compilation but also as a panorama of the 1960s. The only flaw was that it didn't give a good look at the Stones' full musical history, ignoring their early blues period and the psychedelic era. There are also some anomalies in *Hot Rocks*' history for the collector—the very first pressings included an outtake of "Brown Sugar" featuring Eric Clapton that was promptly replaced; and the original European CD version, issued as two separate discs on the Decca label, was also different from its American counterpart, featuring a version of "Satisfaction" mastered in stereo and putting the guitars on separate channels for the first time. Those musicologist concerns aside, this is still an exciting assembly of material. *—Bruce Eder*

☆ **Exile on Main Street** / May 12, 1972 / Virgin ✦✦✦✦✦
Greeted with decidedly mixed reviews upon its original release, *Exile on Main Street* has become generally regarded as the Rolling Stones' finest album. Part of the reason why the record was initially greeted with hesitant reviews is that it takes a while to assimilate. A sprawling, weary double album encompassing rock & roll, blues, soul, and country, *Exile* doesn't try anything new on the surface, but the substance is new. Taking the bleakness that underpinned *Let It Bleed* and *Sticky Fingers* to an extreme, *Exile* is a weary record, and not just lyrically. Jagger's vocals are buried in the mix, and the music is a series of dark, dense jams, with Keith Richards and Mick Taylor spinning off incredible riffs and solos. And the songs continue the breakthroughs of their three previous albums. No longer does their country sound forced or kitschy—it's lived-in and complex, just like the group's forays into soul and gospel. While the songs, including the masterpieces "Rocks Off," "Tumbling Dice," "Torn and Frayed," "Happy," "Let It Loose," and "Shine a Light," are all terrific, they blend together, with only certain lyrics and guitar lines emerging from the murk. It's the kind of record that's gripping on the very first listen, but each subsequent listen reveals something new. Few other albums, let alone double albums, have been so rich and masterful as *Exile on Main Street*, and it stands not only as one of the Stones' best records, but sets a remarkably high standard for all of hard rock. *—Stephen Thomas Erlewine*

● **More Hot Rocks (Big Hits and Fazed Cookies)** / Nov. 1972 / ABKCO ✦✦✦✦✦
Hot Rocks covers most of the monster hits from the Stones' first decade that remain in radio rotation in the 1990s. *More Hot Rocks* goes for the somewhat smaller hits, some of the better album tracks, and a whole LP side worth of rarities that hadn't yet been available in the United States when this compilation was released in 1972. The material isn't as famous as what's on *Hot Rocks*, but the music is almost as excellent, including such vital cuts as "Not Fade Away," "It's All Over Now," "The Last Time," "Lady Jane," the psychedelic "Dandelion," "She's a Rainbow," "Have You Seen Your Mother, Baby, Standing in the Shadow?," "Out of Time," "Tell Me," and "We Love You." The eight rarities are pretty good as well, including their 1963 debut single "Come On," early R&B covers of "Fortune Teller" and "Bye Bye Johnnie," great slide guitar on Muddy Waters' "I Can't Be Satisfied," and the soulful 1966 U.K. B-side, "Long Long While." *—Richie Unterberger*

Goats Head Soup / Aug. 31, 1973 / Virgin ✦✦✦
Sliding out of perhaps the greatest winning streak in rock history, the Stones slipped into decadence and rock star excess with *Goats Head Soup*, their sequel to *Exile on Main St.* This is where the Stones image began to eclipse their accomplishments, as Mick ascended to jet-setting celebrity and Keith slowly sunk deeper into addiction, and it's possible hearing them moving in both directions on *Goats Head Soup*, at times in the same song. As Jagger plays the devil (or, dances with Mr. D, as he likes to say), the sex and sleaze quotient is increased, all of it underpinned by some genuinely affecting heartbreak, highlighted by "Angie." This may not be as downright funky, freaky, and fantastic as *Exile*, yet the extra layer of gloss brings out the enunciated lyrics, added strings, wah-wah guitars, explicit sex, and violence, making it all seem trippily decadent. If it doesn't seem like there's a surplus of classics here, all the songs work well, illustrating just how far they've traveled in their songcraft, as well as their exceptional talent as a band—they make this all sound really easy and darkly alluring, even when the sex'n'satanism seems a little silly. To top it all off, they cap off this utterly excessive album with "Star Star," a nasty Chuck Berry rip that grooves on its own mean vulgarity—it's real title is "Starfucker," if you need any clarification, and even though they got nastier (the entirety of *Undercover*, for instance), they never again made something this dirty or nasty. And, it never feels more at home than it does at the end of this excessive record. *—Stephen Thomas Erlewine*

It's Only Rock & Roll / Oct. 18, 1974 / Virgin ✦✦✦
It's uneven, but at times *It's Only Rock & Roll* catches fire. The songs and performances are stronger than those on *Goats Head Soup*; the tossed-off numbers sound effortless, not careless. Throughout, the Stones wear their title as the "World's Greatest Rock & Roll Band" with a defiant smirk, which makes the bitter cynicism of "If You Can't Rock Me" and the title track all the more striking, and the reggae experimentation of "Luxury," the aching beauty of "Time Waits for No One," and the agreeable filler of "Dance Little Sister" and "Short and Curlies" all the more enjoyable. *—Stephen Thomas Erlewine*

Metamorphosis / Jun. 1975 / ABKCO ✦✦

Black & Blue / Apr. 20, 1976 / Virgin ✦✦✦
The Stones recorded *Black & Blue* while auditioning Mick Taylor's replacement, so it's unfair to criticize it, really, for being longer on grooves and jams than songs, especially since that's what's good about it. Yes, the two songs that are undeniable highlights are "Memory Motel" and "Fool to Cry," the album's two ballads and, therefore, the two that had to be written and arranged, not knocked out in the studio; they're also the ones that don't quite make as much sense, though they still work in the context of the record. No, this is all about groove and sound, as the Stones work Wood into their fabric. And the remarkable thing is, apart from "Hand of Fate" and "Crazy Mama," there's little straight-ahead rock & roll here. They play with reggae extensively, funk and disco less so, making both sound like integral parts of the Stones' lifeblood. Apart from the ballads, there might not be many memorable tunes, but there are times that you listen to the Stones just to hear them play, and this is one of them. *—Stephen Thomas Erlewine*

Love You Live / Sep. 23, 1977 / Virgin ✦✦
Recorded on the supporting tour for 1976's *Black & Blue*, the double-album set *Love You Live* is an adequate live album, capturing the Stones' transition from a lean, lethal rock & roll band to accomplished show men. As show men, they aren't as compelling as they are when they're rockers, but the show biz glitz of Mick Jagger's arena rock schtick remains thoroughly entertaining, even when it robs the music of its power. *—Stephen Thomas Erlewine*

☆ **Some Girls** / Jun. 9, 1978 / Virgin ✦✦✦✦✦
During the mid-'70s, the Rolling Stones remained massively popular, but their records suffered from Jagger's fascination with celebrity and Keith's worsening drug habit. By 1978, both punk and disco had swept the group off the front pages, and *Some Girls* was their fiery response to the younger generation. Opening with the disco-blues thump of "Miss You," *Some Girls* is a tough, focused, and exciting record, full of more hooks and energy than any Stones record since *Exile on Main Street*. Even though the Stones make disco their own, they never quite take punk on their own ground. Instead, their rockers sound harder and nastier than they have in years. Using "Star Star" as a template, the Stones run through the seedy homosexual imagery of "When the Whip Comes Down," the bizarre, borderline-misogynistic vitriol of the title track, Keith's ultimate outlaw anthem, "Before They Make Me Run," and the decadent closer, "Shattered." In between, they deconstruct the Temptations' "(Just My) Imagination," unleash the devastatingly snide country parody "Far Away Eyes," and contribute "Beast of Burden," one of their very best ballads. *Some Girls* may not have the backstreet aggression of their '60s records, or the majestic, drugged-out murk of their early-'70s work, but its brand of glitzy, decadent hard rock still makes it a definitive Stones album. *—Stephen Thomas Erlewine*

Emotional Rescue / Jun. 23, 1980 / Virgin ✦✦✦
Coasting on the success of *Some Girls*, the Stones offered more of the same on *Emotional Rescue*. Comprised of leftovers from the previous album's sessions and hastily written new numbers, *Emotional Rescue* may consist mainly of filler, but it's expertly written and performed filler. The Stones toss off throwaways like the reggae-fueled, mail-order bride anthem "Send It to Me" or rockers like "Summer Romance" and "Where the Boys Go" with an authority that makes the record a guilty pleasure, even if it's clear that only two songs—the icy but sexy disco-rock of "Emotional Rescue" and the revamped Chuck Berry rocker "She's So Cold"—come close to being classic Stones. *—Stephen Thomas Erlewine*

Tattoo You / Aug. 30, 1981 / Virgin ✦✦✦✦✦
Like *Emotional Rescue* before it, *Tattoo You* was comprised primarily of leftovers, but unlike its predecessor, it never sounds that way. Instead, *Tattoo You* captures the Stones at their best as a professional stadium-rock band. Divided into a rock & roll side and a ballad side, the album delivers its share of thrills on the tight, dynamic first side. "Start Me Up" became the record's definitive Stonesy rocker, but the frenzied doo wop of "Hang Fire," the reggae jam of "Slave," the sleazy Chuck Berry rockers "Little T&A" and "Neighbours," and the hard blues of "Black Limousine" are all terrific. The ballad side suffers in comparison, especially since "Heaven" and "No Use in Crying" are faceless. But "Worried About You" and "Tops" are effortless, excellent ballads, and "Waiting on a Friend," with its Sonny Rollins sax solo, is an absolute masterpiece, with a moving lyric that captures Jagger in a shockingly reflective and affecting state of mind. "Waiting on a Friend" and the vigorous rock & roll of the first side make *Tattoo You* an essential latter-day Stones album, ranking just a few notches below *Some Girls*. *—Stephen Thomas Erlewine*

Still Life / Jun. 1, 1982 / Virgin ✦
Like *Love You Live* before it, *Still Life* showcases the Stones as pure entertainers, although the band adds enough rhythmic grit to keep the record from sinking into pure show biz formula. Nevertheless, it isn't nearly enough grit to make it rock as hard as *Get Yer Ya-Ya's Out*. Or even *Love You Live*, depressingly enough. *—Stephen Thomas Erlewine*

Undercover / Nov. 7, 1983 / Virgin ✦✦✦
As their most ambitious album since *Some Girls*, *Undercover* is a weird, wild mix of hard rock, new wave pop, reggae, dub and soul. Even with all the careening musical eclecticism, what distinguishes *Undercover* is its bleak, nihilistic attitude—it's teeming with sickness, with violence, kinky sex and loathing dripping from almost every song. "Undercover of the Night" slams with echoing guitars and rubbery bass lines, as Jagger gives a feverish litany of sex, corruption and suicide. It set the tone for the rest of the album, whether it's the runaway nymphomaniac of "She Was Hot" or the ridiculous slasher imagery of "Too Much Blood." Only Keith's "Wanna Hold You" offers a reprieve from the

carnage, and its relentless bloodletting makes the album a singularly fascinating listen. For some observers, that mixture was nearly too difficult to stomach, but for others, it's a fascinating record, particularly since much of its nastiness feels as if the Stones, and Jagger and Richards in particular, are running out of patience with each other. *—Stephen Thomas Erlewine*

Dirty Work / 1986 / Virgin ✦✦✦
Reuniting after three years and one solo album from Mick Jagger, the Rolling Stones attempted to settle their differences and craft a comeback with *Dirty Work*, but the tensions remained too great for the group. Designed as a return to their rock & roll roots after several years of vague dance experiments, *Dirty Work* is hampered by uneven songs and undistinguished performances, as well as a slick, lightly synthesized production that instantly dates the album to the mid-'80s. Jagger often sounds like he's saving his best work for his solo records, but a handful of songs have a spry, vigorous attack—"One Hit (To the Body)" is a classic, and "Winning Ugly" and "Had It With You" have a similar aggression. Still, most of *Dirty Work* sounds as forced as the cover of Bob & Earl's uptown soul obscurity "Harlem Shuffle," leaving the album as one of the group's most undistinguished efforts. *—Stephen Thomas Erlewine*

☆ **Singles Collection: The London Years** / 1989 / ABKCO ✦✦✦✦✦
The three-disc box set *Singles Collection: The London Years* contains every single the Rolling Stones released during the '60s, including both the A- and B-sides. It is the first Stones compilation that tries to be comprehensive and logical—for all their attributes, the two *Hot Rocks* sets and the two *Big Hits* collections didn't present the singles in chronological order. In essence, the previous compilations were excellent samplers, where *Singles Collection* tells most of the story (certain albums, like *Aftermath*, *Beggars Banquet* and *Let It Bleed*, fill in the gaps left by the singles). The Rolling Stones made genuine albums—even their early R&B/blues albums were impeccably paced—but their singles had a power all their own, which is quite clearly illustrated by the *Singles Collection*. By presenting the singles in chronological order, the set takes on a relentless, exhilarating pace with each hit and neglected B-side piling on top of each other, adding a new dimension to the group; it has a power it wouldn't have had if it tried to sample from the albums. Although it cheats near the end, adding singles from the *Metamorphosis* outtakes collection and two singles from *Sticky Fingers*, this captures the essence of the '60s Stones as well as any compilation could. Casual fans might want to stick with the *Hot Rocks* sets, since they just have the hits, but for those that want a little bit more, the *Singles Collection* is absolutely essential. *—Stephen Thomas Erlewine*

Steel Wheels / Aug. 1989 / Virgin ✦✦✦
The Stones, or more accurately the relationship between Mick and Keith, imploded shortly after *Dirty Work*, resulting in Mick delivering a nearly unbearably mannered, ambitious solo effort that stiffed and Keith knocking out the greatest Stones album since *Tattoo You*, something that satisfied the cult but wasn't a hit. Clearly, they were worth more together than they were apart, so it was time for the reunion, and that's what *Steel Wheels* is—a self-styled, reunion album. It often feels as if they sat down and decided exactly what their audience wanted from a Stones album, and they deliver a record that gives the people what they want, whether it's *Tattoo You*-styled rockers, ballads in the vein of "Fool to Cry," even a touch of old-fashioned experimentalism with "Continental Drift." Being professionals, in the business for over two-and-a-half decades, and being a band that always favored calculation, they wear all this well, even if this lacks the vigor and menace that fuels the best singles; after all, the rocking singles ("Sad Sad Sad," "Rock and a Hard Place," "Mixed Emotions") wind up being smoked by such throwaways as "Hold on to Your Hat." Even though it's just 12 songs, the record feels a little long, largely due to its lack of surprises and unabashed calculation (the jams are slicked up so much they don't have the visceral power of the jam record, *Black & Blue*). Still, the Stones sound good, and Mick and Keith both get off a killer ballad apiece with "Almost Hear You Sigh" and "Slipping Away," respectively. It doesn't make for a great Stones album, but it's not bad, and it feels like a comeback—which it was supposed to, after all. *—Stephen Thomas Erlewine*

Flashpoint / Apr. 1991 / Virgin ✦✦

Jump Back: The Best of the Rolling Stones 1971-1993 / Nov. 19, 1993 / Virgin ✦✦✦✦✦
Released in 1994 to coincide with the Stones' catalog moving to Virgin Records, as well as the accompanying remastering of their Rolling Stone Records catalog (1971's *Sticky Fingers* through 1989's *Steel Wheels*—actually 1991's *Flashpoint*, which is the last Rolling Stones Records release, but isn't featured here), *Jump Back* supplants *Rewind* as the best single-disc overview of the Stones' '70s and '80s recordings. The non-chronological order at times is a little irritating—bouncing between "Brown Sugar," "Harlem Shuffle," "It's Only Rock & Roll (But I Like It)," "Mixed Emotions," and "Angie" nearly causes whiplash—but nearly all the big songs from this period are included. Yes, "She Was Hot" isn't here, along with a couple other singles that didn't catch hold, but this has everything that the casual follower could want, which makes up for the fact that it could have been sequenced better (that's what home programming and burners are for anyway). *—Stephen Thomas Erlewine*

Voodoo Lounge / Jul. 19, 1994 / Virgin ✦✦✦
Funny that the much-touted "reunion/comeback" album *Steel Wheels* followed *Dirty Work* by just three years, while it took the Stones five years to turn out its sequel, *Voodoo Lounge*—a time frame that seems much more appropriate for a "comeback." To pile on the irony, *Voodoo Lounge* feels more like a return to form than its predecessor, even if it's every bit as calculated and Bill Wyman has flown the coup. With Don Was, a neo-classic rock producer that always attempts to reclaim his artist's original claim to greatness, helming the boards with the Glimmer Twins, the Stones strip their sound back to its spare, hard-rocking basics. The Stones act in kind, turning out a set of songs that are pretty traditionalist. There are no new twists or turns in either the rockers or ballads (apart maybe from the quiet menace of "Thru and Thru," later used to great effect on *The Sopranos*), even if they revive some of the English folk and acoustic country-blues that was on *Beggars Banquet*. Still, this approach works, because they are turning out songs that may not be classics, but are first-rate examples of the value of craft. If this was released 10 years, even five years earlier, this would be a near-triumph of classicist rock, but since *Voodoo Lounge* came out in the CD age, it's padded out to 15 tracks, five of which could have been chopped to make the album much stronger. Instead, it runs on for nearly an hour, an ironically bloated length for an album whose greatest strengths are its lean, concentrated classic sound and songcraft. Still, it makes for a stronger record than its predecessor. *—Stephen Thomas Erlewine*

Stripped / Nov. 14, 1995 / Virgin ✦✦✦
Despite the odds, the Rolling Stones' *Stripped* held out great promise. *Voodoo Lounge* was an energized return to studio form for the Borg of rock & roll road shows. From that platform, the idea of taking it back to small clubs, live, lean and pared down without succumbing to the worn "unplugged" treadmill, seemed an inspired move. Patched together from an embroidery of tour rehearsals and live club dates in Paris and Amsterdam, the project was an extension of acoustic sets the group introduced on the North American leg of the *Voodoo Lounge* tour. The concept offered an invigorating opportunity to dust off some rough gems from the past that no longer felt at home on scoping stadium stages. Unfortunately, the cover photo depicting a lean, determined, leather-clad combo in spartan black and white proves to be misleading advertising. Within the brave packaging lies a listless, lethargic Dorian Gray bluff. Spongy keyboards gunk many of the tracks. The much-touted cover of Dylan's "Like a Rolling Stone" remains pointlessly devoted to the original. There are lazy, somnambulant versions of "I'm Free" and "Let It Bleed"; Keith Richards' painfully intoned "Slipping Away"; the dozens of lost songs that any fan would chose to have renovated before "Angie." *—Roch Parisien*

Rolling Stones Rock & Roll Circus / Oct. 15, 1996 / ABKCO ✦✦✦
The most interesting archival release of the Rolling Stones since *More Hot Rocks*, 20 years ago, and the first issue of truly unreleased material by the Stones from this period. And the Stones have some competition from the Who, Taj Mahal, and John Lennon on the same release. Filmed and recorded on December 10-11, 1968 at a North London studio, *Rock & Roll Circus* has been, as much as the Beach Boys' *Smile*, "the one that got away" for most '60s music enthusiasts. The Jethro Tull sequence is the standard studio track, but the rest—except for the Stones' "Salt of the Earth"—is really live. The Who's portion has been out before, courtesy of various documentaries, but Taj Mahal playing some loud electric blues is new and great, the live Lennon rendition of "Yer Blues" is indispensable, and the Stones' set fills in lots of blanks in their history—"Jumpin' Jack Flash" in one of two live renditions it ever got with Brian Jones in the lineup, "Sympathy for the Devil" in an intense run-through, "Parachute Woman" as a lost live vehicle for the band, "You Can't Always Get What You Want" as a show-stopping rocker even without its extended ending (no Paul Buckmaster choir), and "No Expectations" as their first piece of great live blues since "Little Red Rooster." It's a must-own, period. *—Bruce Eder*

Bridges to Babylon / Sep. 23, 1997 / Caroline ✦✦✦
Voodoo Lounge confirmed that the Stones could age gracefully, but it never sounded modern; it sounded classicist. With its successor, *Bridges to Babylon*, Mick Jagger was determined to bring the Rolling Stones into the '90s, albeit tentatively, and hired hip collaborators like the Dust Brothers (Beck, Beastie Boys) and Danny Saber (Black Grape) to give the veteran group an edge on their explorations of drum loops and samples. Of course, the Stones are the Stones, and no production is going to erase that, but the group is smart enough—or Keith Richards is stubborn enough—to work within their limitations and to have producer Don Was act as executive producer. As a result, *Bridges to Babylon* sounds like the Stones without sounding tired. The band is tight and energetic, and there's just enough flair to the sultry "Anybody Seen My Baby?," the menacing "Gunface" and the low-key, sleazy "Might as Well Get Juiced" to make them sound contemporary. But the real key to the success of *Bridges to Babylon* is the solid, craftsmanlike songwriting. While there aren't any stunners on the album, nothing is bad, with rockers like "Flip the Switch" and "Low Down" sounding as convincing as ballads like "Already Over Me." And, as always, Keith contributes three winners—including the reggae workout "You Don't Have to Mean It" and the slow-burning "How Can I Stop"—that cap off another fine latter-day Stones record. *—Stephen Thomas Erlewine*

No Security / Nov. 3, 1998 / Caroline ✦✦✦
Another record, another tour, another live album chronicling the whole shebang. The Rolling Stones have followed this basic pattern since the early '80s—if Keith had been able to get Mick out on the road to support *Dirty Work*, there damn well would have been a live record in 1987—stepping up the production rate in the '90s, eventually winding their way to *No Security*, a document of the *Bridges of Babylon* tour of 1997-1998. Since the Stones (or at least Jagger) are sharp businessmen, they have given all three of their '90s live albums a hook, an angle for journalists and fans alike—*Flashpoint* was their return to form, *Stripped* was culled from unplugged and club dates, and *No Security* contains 11 songs that have never before appeared on a live Stones album. Of course, several of these date from *Voodoo Lounge* and *Bridges to Babylon* (five, to be exact), but they also dig out such great songs as "Gimme Shelter," "Respectable," "Sister Morphine," and "Memory Hotel," as well as reviving "The Last Time" and "Live With Me," which haven't been on a live record since *Got Live If You Want It!* and *Get Yer Ya-Ya's Out*, respectively. There are also guest spots from Taj Mahal and Dave Matthews. All of these things give some measure of distinction to *No Security* but they don't erase the feeling that this is more of a soundtrack to a spectacle than a musical event. Sure, the Stones are as accomplished as ever, the album is certainly enjoyable, but it just doesn't feel necessary. Which,

again, doesn't make it any different than most Stones live records since *Love You Live.* —*Stephen Thomas Erlewine*

Bright Lights, Big City / [Bootleg] ✦✦✦✦✦
As you'd expect, there are a ton of Rolling Stones bootlegs, but there isn't a great deal of essential material from the '60s to be found on them. The exceptions are these outtakes from 1963 and 1964, which have popped up under quite a few guises, but most frequently under the *Bright Lights, Big City* title. The five early-1963 demos were cut shortly before they signed with Decca, and capture the band at their bluesiest and blackest; when Brian Jones was being frozen out of The Stones in the late '60s, it's said that he would play these for listeners as examples of the purity of the group's original vision. With clear fidelity, the standards of these performances are well up to official release; "Baby What's Wrong," "Road Runner," and "I Want to Be Loved" are downright electrifying. The four 1964 cuts were recorded at Chess Studios, and again (with the possible exception of the jam "Stewed And Keefed") are well up to release quality, with fine, spare readings of "Hi-Heel Sneakers," Howlin' Wolf's "Down In The Bottom," and Big Bill Broonzy's "Tell Me Baby." Essential for serious fans. —*Richie Unterberger*

Henry Rollins

b. Feb. 13, 1961, Washington, D.C.
Vocals / College Rock, Alternative Metal, Alternative Pop/Rock, American Underground
In the '90s, Henry Rollins emerged as a post-punk renaissance man, without the self-conscious trappings that plagued such '80s artists as David Byrne. Since Black Flag's breakup in 1986, Rollins has been relentlessly busy, recording albums with the Rollins Band, writing books and poetry, performing spoken word tours, writing a magazine column in *Details*, acting in several movies, and appearing on radio programs and, less frequently, as an MTV VJ. The Rollins Band's records are uncompromising, intense, cathartic fusions of hard rock, funk, post-punk noise, and jazz experimentalism, with Rollins shouting angry, biting self-examinations and accusations over the grind. On his spoken word albums, he is remarkably more relaxed, showcasing a hilariously self-deprecating sense of humor that is often absent in his music. In 1992, the Rollins Band released their major-label debut for Imago with *The End of Silence*, which some found to be his most focused music yet, and gave Rollins his first charting album. 1994 became Rollins' breakout year thanks to the one-two punch of *Weight*—the best-reviewed and most popular Rollins Band album to date, which cracked *Billboard*'s Top 40—and *Get in the Van: On the Road with Black Flag*, a double-disc set of readings from Rollins' memoir of the same name that won a Grammy for Best Spoken Word Recording. With all the increased visibility, Rollins became a genuine phenomenon; *Details* magazine chose him as their Man of the Year in 1994. Primed by appearances on MTV and VH-1, Rollins also made his film debut that year in *The Chase*, and went on to appear in movies like *Johnny Mnemonic*, *Heat*, and *Lost Highway* over the next few years. All the while, he has kept his artistic integrity, becoming a kind of father figure for many alternative bands of the '90s. —*Steve Huey*

Hot Animal Machine / 1987 / Texas Hotel ✦✦✦✦
A good solo effort, raw and powerful. This CD includes the EP *Drive by Shooting.* —*John Dougan*

Life Time / 1988 / Buddha ✦✦✦
When Henry Rollins emerged from the break-up of Black Flag, many thought he couldn't be succesful without guitarist Greg Ginn. If anything, *Life Time* proves the detractors wrong. With Ian MacKaye of Fugazi in the production chair, Rollins Band was able to distance themselves from Black Flag with a tight, visceral, and sometimes bluesy album. While more abrasive than later Rollins Band releases, this is worth picking up to better understand the progression of Rollins Band's unique style of emotional funk/metal. Remastered and re-released in 1999, the CD has a better sound, but it sacrifices the live tracks (which appear on the original Texas Hotel CD release). The outtakes from the *Life Time* sessions, however—"Do It," "Move Right In," and "Nest Time," originally released as the album *Do It* in 1988—are included. —*Chris True*

Sweatbox / 1989 / Quarterstick ✦✦✦✦
This two-disc set of Henry Rollins' spoken word performances from 1987 and 1988 is typically engaging, showcasing his sharp wit and ability to interact with his audience. Hitting on topics as distanced as masturbation and David Letterman, the former Black Flag frontman goes into each of his rants with equal gusto, and proves himself to be a great entertainer. Storytelling is a skill, and Rollins has it, whether he is trying to make an occasional serious point about the struggles of life or telling one-liners (incidentally, at one point in the set he comments that his favorite one-liner comedian is Nietzsche). Rollins is a cut-up; a punk rock class clown with a skill for rhetoric, and these shows, played for an audience of a couple of hundred, allow him to step to the front of the class and play the obnoxious teacher for a bit. He's clearly a bit peeved from time to time, but he makes his incensed points about hating cops and stupid people with a hearty dose of humor, and it's especially effective. A hardcore Renaissance man, this disc allows the singer to prove his brains are equal to his brawn, and above all else, he's damn funny. The crowd is in constant hysterics for almost all but the most serious of his material, and there are only about a few minutes worth of that. *Sweatbox* is a great set of tales with plenty of attitude and a fired-up delivery, certainly worth the time for anyone who is a fan of this multi-faceted artist and his uniquely self-deprecating approach. —*Peter J. D'Angelo*

Do It / 1988 / Texas Hotel ✦✦✦✦
Leave it to good ol' Hank to make the second Rollins Band album a collection of studio outtakes and live tracks. This is not an attempt to make a quick buck, however. Rollins has always believed in giving the people the most for their money. And this is no exception. The first three tracks are covers which were outtakes from the *Life Time* sessions, and the last 12 are tracks from a live show in Europe in 1987. This album may not be necessary for the casual fan, but for the devotee of Hank, it is one of the best albums his band has put out. —*Chris True*

Hard Volume / 1989 / Buddha ✦✦✦✦
A vastly looser affair than their debut album, *Hard Volume* is the first glimpse of what Rollins Band would become with 1992's *The End of Silence.* The songs here are based more on the groove than they are on *Life Time.* The opener "Hard" may seem a little over the top lyrically, but it has a swagger unmatched in the Rollins Band's catalog. This is also the first Rollins release to showcase both a more atmospheric approach ("Love Song"), and the Andrew Weiss-bass sound that was made famous on *End of Silence.* The 1999 Buddha re-release features clearer sound (Rollins remastered the reissues himself), and outtakes and demos from the sessions, making it a great buy for enthusiasts and a solid choice for casual fans as well. —*Chris True*

Turned On / 1990 / Quarterstick ✦✦✦
A perfect example of the Rollins Band at work was recorded live in Vienna, Austria, in 1989 with some of his best songs from that era. Recorded digitally, but the CD treats the entire recording as one track. —*John Book*

Deep Throat / Feb. 1992 / Quarterstick ✦✦✦✦✦
All of Rollins' early spoken-word releases are gathered in the reasonably priced six-disc box set *Deep Throat.* As with each of his spoken albums, Rollins is incisive, moving, self-effacing, and very funny; it's worth the price of the discs. —*Stephen Thomas Erlewine*

The End of Silence / Feb. 25, 1992 / Imago ✦✦✦✦
With the exception of 1989's *Hard Volume*, Henry Rollins' solo profile had always been relegated to the minor leagues following his departure from neo-punk stalwarts Black Flag. But with the 1992 release of *The End of Silence*, Henry Rollins' first official effort for the burgeoning Imago label, everything would change, partly because *The End of Silence* was launched with the appropriate bells and whistles normally reserved for other, already well-established acts. Finally pairing up with an established producer capable of bringing the Rollins vision to fruition, Andy Wallace intuitively placed the singer's voice at the forefront of the album's incendiary mix. The dead-on, ultra-separated, compact sound of *The End of Silence* would go a long way toward broadening the singer's potential audience. Not only is the record a full-blown sonic assault on the senses (delivered with typical, deadpan Rollins honesty), *Silence* finally delivered in the songwriting department as well, making it the singer's most focused record to date. Never one to mince words, *The End of Silence* is chock full of bone-splintering moments like the first single, "Low Self Opinion." Bludgeoning and menacing at the same time, Rollins' visceral, introspective commentary takes no prisoners. On other songs like "Grip" and "What Do You Do" (which clocks in at just under seven and a half minutes), the singer furthers a vision that launched a hundred imitators. "Tearing," the record's excellent second single, would also be a boon for the vocalist, benefiting from some substantial MTV *Headbanger's Ball* airtime; it would further cement Rollins' profile with yet another audience: metalheads. Rollins would release other solid records, but *The End of Silence* remains one of his best. —*John Franck*

● **Rollins: The Boxed Life** / Jan. 26, 1993 / Imago ✦✦✦✦✦
Rollins' spoken-word records are comedy records, more like Lenny Bruce or Richard Pryor than Andrew Dice Clay or Eddie Murphy. Underneath all the laughter there are some serious themes; the humor is drawn from pain. But the main reason to hear *The Boxed Life* (or any of Rollins' spoken-word records) is that he's a superb storyteller with a wicked sense of humor. Some of the topics are squeamish (animal testing, safe sex, depression) and there is a generous helping of profanity, but it is genuinely funny and moving. —*Stephen Thomas Erlewine*

● **Weight** / Apr. 12, 1994 / Imago ✦✦✦✦
On *Weight*, the Rollins Band is able to mix the musicians' love for jazz with a blindingly direct hard-rock assault, making a twisted form of metal-jazz. Rollins' lyrics have also begun to move away from his relentless self-examination, adding a touch of the self-effacing humor that distinguishes his spoken records. The new lyrical dimension adds depth to the band's music, making *Weight* the most impressive album they have released to date. —*Stephen Thomas Erlewine*

Everything / Jul. 1996 / Thirsty Ear ✦✦

Come In & Burn / Mar. 25, 1997 / DreamWorks ✦✦✦

Black Coffee Blues / Apr. 22, 1997 / Thirsty Ear ✦✦✦✦
A collection of readings from his book of the same name, *Black Coffee Blues* is some pretty heavy stuff. Those who are only aware of the man from his spoken word work may be a bit off-put, but there is still some quality here. Not a good place to start, but if it's stark, honest, brutal truth you seek, here you go. —*Chris True*

Think Tank / Sep. 22, 1998 / DreamWorks ✦✦✦
For the uninitiated, Henry Rollins may be a puzzling dichotomy at best. Perhaps best known for his aggro-punk musical rantings and bulging tattoos, Rollins contains a very opposite side within his imposing frame. On this two-disc, live album, which was recorded on opposite ends of the Earth, Rollins lets both sides loose on the ears and minds of his devoted fans and those who may want to enter his maddened world. Clever, sharp, and brutally honest, Rollins has the self-control of a dormant volcano and sets his vocal lava upon the people and places that make our lives a little more aggravating. And no one is safe! From "Bubba" Clinton to Kenneth Starr, David Hasselhoff to Michael "Bolthead" Bolton, husbands and wives, and the cast of *Friends*, everybody gets a taste of Rollins' right-minded rage. Along the way, he brings his two sides together by dipping into his musical realm as well. From the opening singalong and the renaming of El Niño as "The First Four Black Sabbath Albums," to the closing lounge lizard rendition of the Rollins Band's appropriately two-faced shredder "Liar," Rollins realizes his nefarious

talents and alternative icon status and uses them to a combined effect which is simultaneously duplicitous and unifying, demonstrating his command of words and emotions to open our eyes and ears more than they may want to be. Dangerously intelligent commentary. —*Matthew Robinson*

Hot Animal Machine/Drive By Shooting / Nov. 23, 1999 / Buddha ✦✦✦✦
Hank roared out of the box with this, his first solo release after the demise of Black Flag. Recorded in England with friend and guitarist Chris Haskett, this is a less groove-oriented album than subsequent Rollins Band releases, but it is still one hell of a rock & roll record. The punishing opener "Black and White" and the cover of Suicide's "Ghost Rider" make this disc indispensable to the Rollins fan, while the whole of the album will quench the thirst of any rock junkie. Included along with the CD release is the *Drive By Shooting* EP, a more humorous affair than the album proper. *Drive By Shooting*'s best moments are the opener "Drive By Shooting'" and the closer "Men Are Pigs" (a classic Rollins style look at power in and out of the bedroom). The 1999 Buddha reissue has been remastered by Rollins himself, which makes the album sound 100 times better than the original Texas Hotel release. (Unfortunately, however, the original liner notes, which were absolute comedy, are not included.) —*Chris True*

Get Some Go Again / Feb. 29, 2000 / DreamWorks ✦✦✦
With 1997's *Come In and Burn*, everyone (including Henry Rollins himself) knew that the Rollins Band lineup of Sim Cain, Melvin Gibbs, and Chris Haskett had reached an impasse. While the band was entering into new territories, featuring acoustic and jazz work, Rollins was stomping down the same path he had since his days in the Washington, D.C. hardcore scene. His once-unique blend of near-spoken diatribes over a hard rock beat was in danger of becoming repetitive. Enter Mother Superior. Already an established act, this three-piece hard rock outfit began working with Rollins after he had disbanded the original lineup.

The result of this new alliance, *Get Some, Go Again*, is a return to the type of hard rock that Rollins thrives in. The beats are simple, straightforward, and tight. Mother Superior's sound on tracks like "Illumination," "Love's So Heavy," and "I Go Day Glo" are an infectious blend of acid rock, metal, and punk. Their stripped-down sound seems to have reinvigorated Rollins himself, who sounds like he's actually having fun on this record. Unfortunately, the album lacks any new insights from the man. With the exception of the opener "Illumination," Henry is still going on and on about the same things. Depression, anger, rejection, etc., have been his bread and butter for years, but he never seems to go anywhere on *Get Some*...While his spoken-word shows have gotten better and better with each tour, here Rollins sounds like a broken record. It's frustrating that with all of this great rock hitting you from all sides, you have to wonder who the hell Rollins is actually singing to. —*Chris True*

A Rollins in the Wry / Feb. 20, 2001 / Quarterstick ✦✦✦
The contents of this entertaining CD were taken from two shows recorded in the spring of 1999 at Los Angeles' Café Luna. On tap: 13 tracks of Rollins' musings on society, politics, pop culture, and his career. By far, one of the funniest skits is "Clintonese." "They should teach Clinton in college," says Rollins of his admiration of the former president's savvy verbal performance during 1999's impeachment trial. Another winning moment comes by way of "Language," where Rollins reads a letter that he received from a fan named Boris from the Czech Republic. He extracts one part of the letter, which he describes as "One of the greatest sentences I have ever read in my life." Boris writes: "On two concert I'm should of collected photo, but small, fat technologist be insane." Rollins' interpretation: "He took his roll of film to Rite Aid and had a bad experience. I think Boris got his film fucked up by the technologist." In fact, Rollins seems to have a fixation with Rite Aid. The store even gets its own self-titled treatment. This is an engaging listening experience. Rollins' commentary leaves no stone unturned—gender idiosyncrasies, homosexuality, the media, the tragedy at Columbine (where he takes a serious turn), and other topics. His vocal delivery is dynamic; listeners could easily envision his facial expressions and contortions as if they were sitting at Café Luna. And Rollins has no problem pointing the finger at himself—a surefire way at gaining trust and a connection with audiences. He is honest, without offending, and gives the impression that he genuinely has no biases—he's just a curious observer of life. And the world, through Rollins' eyes, is an interesting, offbeat, and funny place. —*Liana Jonas*

Nice / Aug. 21, 2001 / Sanctuary ✦✦✦✦
Turning 40 has had quite an effect on Henry Rollins. His seemingly stodgy old sound has been blown to bits with the grooving, funky, and heavy as hell *Nice*. While *Get Some Go Again* had a lot of great songs, and the music of Mother Superior is just what Rollins needed, he never seemed to gel with the band on that album. Here, however, it sounds like Jim Mackenroth, Jim Wilson, and Marcus Blake had ideas of their own, and went for them 100 percent. It may be shocking to hear female vocals or a horn section coming out from behind Rollins, but here it works splendidly. With this band and this album, Rollins has finally shaken off the ghosts of the old band, as well as Black Flag. No, it's not punk, but that's okay. Rollins has always been a rock guy, and *Nice* is just that—a great rock record. The problem that may arise from that is the argument that Rollins' lonely, "intense guy" image can't and won't work on a grooving rock record, but Rollins has adjusted in this respect as well. He seems to be a man who is looking at things with a fresh, positive perspective. With this incredibly versatile band alongside him, he may well be the "hardest working man in show business." —*Chris True*

The Romantics

f. 1977, Detroit, MI
Pop/Rock, Power Pop
In the early '80s, the Romantics were a terrific rock band, joyously tearing through loose,

infectious power pop gems like the classic "What I Like About You." After two albums of energetic pop/rock, the band shifted its direction to a slicker, more radio-friendly pop; the change of style worked, resulting in the hit singles "Talking in Your Sleep" and "One in a Million" in 1983. Surprisingly, their drummer Jimmy Marinos left after their success; the band recorded one more album in 1985 before breaking up. In the early '90s, "What I Like About You" began appearing in television commercials, leading the band to reunite. They have recorded one EP and have toured several times since re-forming. —*Stephen Thomas Erlewine*

The Romantics / Feb. 1980 / Nemperor/Epic ✦✦✦✦✦
The cover, featuring the four members decked out in identical red leather outfits with the de rigeur skinny ties, leaves no doubt as to the album's content. This is your basic artifact of the era—lusty, girl-crazed, teen anthems sung to hard-driving, punchy power-pop. "What I Like About You" was the hit, but any of these songs could have been hits. It's easy to dismiss this band, but few albums provide this much guilty pleasure. —*Chris Woodstra*

National Breakout / Dec. 1980 / Nemperor/Epic ✦✦✦
Their sophomore effort follows much of the same formula of the debut. Unfortunately, none of the songs had the instantly endearing catchiness of "What I Like About You" and the album failed to live up to the optimistic title's promise. —*Chris Woodstra*

Strictly Personal / Oct. 1981 / Nemperor/Epic ✦✦✦

In Heat / 1983 / Nemperor/Epic ✦✦✦
In Heat, the Romantics' commercial breaktrough, loses much of the innocence (and fun) of the first two albums, with its slicker production. "Talking in Your Sleep" and "One in a Million" both broke the Top Ten, but the album offers little else. —*Chris Woodstra*

Rhythm Romance / 1985 / Nemperor/Epic ✦✦

● **What I Like About You (& Other Romantic Hits)** / Dec. 1990 / Nemperor/Epic ✦✦✦✦✦
What I Like About You (& Other Romantic Hits) is a ten-track best-of including the classic "What I Like About You," as well as some other fondly remembered hits like "Talking In Your Sleep" and "One in a Million." While this is a good distillation of the band's best moments (especially from the later albums), nothing matches the debut for consistent quality and power-packed catchiness. —*Chris Woodstra*

King Biscuit Flower Hour / Aug. 27, 1996 / King Biscuit ✦✦✦✦✦
Arguably the group's best album, and one of the best live albums ever released by anybody. This concert, recorded on Oct. 30, 1983 in San Antonio, at the peak of the group's popularity, captures them in a powerful, energetic performance, displaying their best garage punk attributes full force along with a surprisingly melodic sound that put them a few steps above bands like the Ramones. It's all here, including "Talking In Your Sleep" and climaxing with "What I Like About You," covering a big chunk of the band's history as well as some pre-history, like "Little Latin Lupe Lou." Along with Robyn Hitchcock & The Egyptians' *Gotta Let This Hen Out*, one of the great 1980's live albums, and only a step short of classics like *Live Kinks* and the Stones' *Got Live If You Want It*. Great sound, too, with some really cool crunchy guitars—a must-own collection. —*Bruce Eder*

Romeo Void

f. 1979, San Francisco, CA, **db.** 1984
Post-Punk, New Wave
A post-punk quintet formed in San Francisco in 1979, consisting of singer Debora Iyall (b. 1956), bassist Frank Zincavage, guitarist Peter Woods, drummer Jay Derrah (replaced by John Stench and then Larry Carter), and saxophone player Ben Bossi. They released several albums on 415 Records (distributed by CBS) from 1981 to 1984. Iyall then left for a solo career. —*William Ruhlmann*

It's a Condition / Mar. 1981 / 415 ✦✦✦
Romeo Void ably represented the post-punk zeitgeist. Their simple, relentless beat and repetitive riffs complemented singer Debora Iyall's huffy posturing, in which the denial of emotion became an emotional statement in itself. In "White Sweater," Iyall obsessed on the clothing in which her sister committed suicide; she might demand "Talk Dirty (To Me)," but never forgot that "Love Is an Illness," and one is best off keeping "Myself to Myself." Meanwhile, the band maintained a minimalist backing in which every note counted. If punk spoke of unmitigated rage, Romeo Void's music was no less angry, but far more resigned. —*William Ruhlmann*

Benefactor / 1982 / Columbia ✦✦✦
Those danceable beats, that tough-girl stance—maybe somebody at Columbia thought the label was getting its own Blondie by buying up 415 Records and its principal asset, Romeo Void. Certainly, *Benefactor* was a more commercial-sounding effort than the debut album, with the band even agreeing to eviscerate the four-letter word in "Never Say Never" and elsewhere playing uptempo dance-rock that almost, but not quite, overcame the disaffection of Debora Iyall's lyrics. But Romeo Void still was less a Blondie clone than an heir to X-Ray Spex or the Bush Tetras, playing bass-heavy, minimalist rock behind a pissed-off singer who, unlike Deborah Harry, wasn't kidding. "You don't get it?" asked Iyall. "Rain on you. And the world disappears." —*William Ruhlmann*

Instincts / 1984 / Columbia ✦✦✦
Perhaps in reaction against the more commercial sound of *Benefactor*, Romeo Void returned to producer David Kahne and the sound of their first album, *It's a Condition*, on their third, *Instincts*. Nevertheless, it proved to be their bestselling album. The group's instrumental attack continued to be spearheaded by saxophonist Benjamin Bossi, whose floating lines contrasted with the drive of the rhythm section and guitarist Peter Woods' Morse code leads. And Debora Iyall continued to pour out disappointed reflections on the romantic condition in songs with titles like "Your Life Is a Lie" and "Say No." One of them, "A Girl in Trouble (Is a Temporary Thing)," managed to be both provocative and vague

enough to inch into the Top 40, such that the album gained greater exposure and sales. But instead of marking a breakthrough for Romeo Void, *Instincts* marked their breakup, with Iyall going solo. —*William Ruhlmann*

● **Warm, In Your Coat** / May 2, 1992 / Columbia/Legacy ✦✦✦✦✦
Punk bands, of course, were not meant to last, and even if Romeo Void, with its dance beats and warm sax sound, as well as a distinctive lead singer with a gift for soundbite lyrics, seemed to have more commercial potential than most, its five-year, three-album existence was long enough to make some noise, make some compromises, and make it out alive. This 15-song, 65-minute compilation is notable not only for the signature songs—"White Sweater," "Myself to Myself," "A Girl in Trouble (Is a Temporary Thing)," and, especially, "Never Say Never"—but also for revealing the range of a band that seemed at the time mostly a backdrop for Debora Iyall. Romeo Void was a band, and from the evidence of this set, a good one, too. —*William Ruhlmann*

The Ronettes

f. 1959, New York, NY, db. 1966
Girl Group
Before Phil Spector took them under his wing in the early '60s, the Ronettes had already recorded several singles and were regionally successful. But the Spector-produced records are what everyone remembers, and for good reason—they featured some of his biggest, best productions along with equally impressive songs. Beneath his monumental Wall of Sound, lead vocalist Ronnie Bennett, who would later marry Spector, sang songs of teenage love in a plain, girlish voice; "Be My Baby," the group's first and biggest hit, was the pinnacle of the group's talent, as well as being one of the producer's finest moments. None of their following singles (including "Baby, I Love You," "(The Best Part Of) Breaking Up," and "Walking in the Rain") were quite as successful commercially, although they were nearly as strong artistically. While Spector was inactive in the mid-'60s, the Ronettes were also inactive; together they re-emerged in 1969 to a small commercial reception. After Ronnie divorced Spector in 1973, she formed a new version of the Ronettes that lasted for three years; after the group disbanded, she launched a solo career. —*Stephen Thomas Erlewine*

The Ronettes: The Early Years / 1965 / Rhino ✦✦✦✦✦
The early Ronettes songs weren't as immaculately produced or as evocative as Phil Spector's productions. Their sound was more generic and resembled other girl groups like The Shirelles or Chiffons. They recorded for Colpix and Dimension during 1961 and 1962, with Ronnie Bennett doing most of the leads, while her sister Estelle and cousin Nedra added soothing harmonies and backgrounds. At times, as on "My Guiding Angel" or "You Bet I Would," they came close to the appealing mix of innocence and earnestness that characterized their later (and greatest) tracks. But despite getting material from such songwriters as Jackie DeShannon and Carole King, many of these cuts were more serviceable than classic. Still, this is the foundation for the sound that exploded in the mid-'60s. —*Ron Wynn*

The Greatest Hits, Vol. 2 / 1981 / Masters ✦✦✦
A good 16-track compilation of rare tracks and non-hit singles, highlighted by "I Can Hear Music," "Paradise," and "Is This What I Get for Loving You"; it also has three tracks that Ronnie Spector sang on, but which were credited to the Crystals. The most interesting material, however, is now available on the ABKCO CD. —*Richie Unterberger*

★ **The Best of the Ronettes** / Sep. 22, 1992 / ABKCO ✦✦✦✦✦
For a couple of years, the Ronettes made music that was as moving and unforgettable as any made during the rock era. Their voices merged sensuality, longing, anguish, and sentimentality, with Ronnie Spector's angelic leads framed by Phil Spector's sweeping production, and the lyrics of Ellie Greenwich, Jeff Barry, Barry Mann, Cynthia Weil, Spector, and others. While such songs as "Walking in the Rain," "Be My Baby," "Baby, I Love You," and "(The Best Part of) Breaking Up" may seem hopelessly naive and possibly sexist in today's cynical world, they're still classic love poems. Ronnie Spector's voice retains its allure and appeal, and the 18 tracks on this CD will never become dated. —*Ron Wynn*

Linda Ronstadt

b. Jul. 15, 1946, Tucson, AZ
Vocals / Traditional Pop, Pop/Rock, Folk-Rock, Soft Rock, Adult Contemporary, Country-Pop, Country-Rock
With roots in the Los Angeles country and folk-rock scenes, Linda Ronstadt was one of the most popular interpretive singers of the '70s, earning a string of platinum-selling albums and Top 40 singles. Ronstadt began her professional career with the Los Angeles folk-rock group the Stone Poneys. Shortly after their first hit "Different Drum," the group disbanded and Ronstadt went solo. She found her voice with her 1971 eponymous third album. Featuring a group of session musicians that would later form the Eagles, the album was laidback country-rock, built around songs by singer/songwriters like Jackson Browne and Eric Anderson. *Don't Cry Now* (1973) followed the same formula to greater success, yet she perfected it with 1974's *Heart Like a Wheel*. Thanks to hit covers of "You're No Good," "When Will I Be Loved," and "It Doesn't Matter Anymore," the record made her a star. *Prisoner in Disguise* (1975) and *Hasten Down the Wind* (1976) were nearly as successful, while she rocked a little harder on 1977's *Simple Dreams*. She tentatively experimented with New Wave on *Living in the U.S.A* (1978) and *Mad Love* (1980). Ronstadt's popularity declined in the early '80s, as 1982's *Get Closer* failed to go platinum. Afterward, she starred in Broadway and movie productions of Gilbert & Sullivan's *Pirates of Penzance*, which led to a collaboration with Nelson Riddle, who arranged and conducted her 1983 collection of pop standards, *What's New*. While it received lukewarm reviews, it was a hit, leading to two more albums with Riddle. Ronstadt returned to contemporary

pop in 1986, having a number two single with "Somewhere Out There," a duet with James Ingram, followed by the 1987 *Trio* album with Dolly Parton and Emmylou Harris. That same year, Ronstadt recorded *Canciones de mi Padre*, a set of traditional Mexican songs. Two years later, she recorded *Cry Like a Rainstorm—Howl Like the Wind*—her first contemporary pop album since 1982's *Get Closer*. Throughout the '90s, she alternated between adult contemporary and Mexican albums, with the latter earning greater acclaim than the former. —*Stephen Thomas Erlewine*

Hand Sown Home Grown / 1969 / Capitol ✦✦

Silk Purse / 1970 / Capitol ✦✦✦
While it followed the same musical approach of the debut, *Silk Purse* was an improvement on *Hand Sown Home Grown*, featuring more confident vocals from Linda Ronstadt and a stronger selection of songs, including "Lovesick Blues" and "Long Long Time." —*Stephen Thomas Erlewine*

Linda Ronstadt / 1971 / Capitol ✦✦✦
Linda Ronstadt's self-titled third album captured the singer moving away from the rootsier charms of her first two albums, toward a more polished take on country rock. Supported by the Eagles throughout the record, Ronstadt turns in a strong performance, aided by a fine selection of material, including "Rock Me on the Water," "Crazy Arms," "I Still Miss Someone," and "I Fall to Pieces." —*Stephen Thomas Erlewine*

Don't Cry Now / 1973 / Asylum ✦✦✦
Don't Cry Now expanded the pop-rock concessions of *Linda Ronstadt*, and the result was the singer's first genuine hit record, peaking at number 45 on the charts. —*Stephen Thomas Erlewine*

Different Drum / 1974 / Capitol ✦✦✦✦✦
Different Drum collects the highlights of Linda Ronstadt's first three solo albums, adding five Stone Poneys tracks, including the hit "Different Drum," for good measure. It misses some fine tracks from her solo records, but the album remains a fine introduction to her early years. —*Stephen Thomas Erlewine*

☆ **Heart Like a Wheel** / 1974 / Capitol ✦✦✦✦✦
Following the same formula as her early records, *Heart Like a Wheel* doesn't appear to be a great breakthrough on the surface. However, Ronstadt comes into her own on this mix of oldies and contemporary classics. Backed by a fleet of Los Angeles musicians, Ronstadt sings with vigor and passion, helping bring the music alive. But what really makes *Heart Like a Wheel* a breakthrough is the inventive arrangements that producer Peter Asher, Ronstadt, and the studio musicians have developed. Finding the right note for each song—whether it's the soulful reworking of "When Will I Be Loved," the hit "You're No Good," or the laid-back folk-rock of "Willing"—the musicians help turn *Heart Like a Wheel* into a veritable catalog of Californian soft rock, and it stands as a landmark of '70s mainstream pop/rock. —*Stephen Thomas Erlewine*

Prisoner in Disguise / 1975 / Asylum ✦✦✦✦✦
Linda Ronstadt followed the commercial and critical breakthrough success of *Heart Like a Wheel* with *Prisoner in Disguise*, a record that essentially repeated the formula of its predecessor. While it lacked the consistency of *Heart Like a Wheel*, it was thoroughly enjoyable, highlighted by sturdy remakes of the Motown classics "Tracks of My Tears" and "Heat Wave." —*Stephen Thomas Erlewine*

Hasten Down the Wind / 1976 / Asylum ✦✦✦
Again, Linda Ronstadt repeats her slick, Californian pop/country rock formula on *Hasten Down the Wind*. When the material is first-rate—such as "That'll Be the Day" or "Crazy"—Ronstadt's performances are terrific, but on the subpar songs—such as the three Karla Bonoff numbers—she's dragged down with her material. —*Stephen Thomas Erlewine*

● **Greatest Hits, Vol. 1** / 1976 / Asylum ✦✦✦✦
Greatest Hits, Vol. 1 is a good 12-track collection of Linda Ronstadt's biggest hits from the early '70s, beginning with the Stone Poneys' "Different Drum" and running through "Tracks of My Tears," from 1975's *Prisoner in Disguise*. In between, all of her best-known songs—"You're No Good," "When Will I Be Loved," "Heat Wave"—are included, plus selected minor hits, making it an excellent overview of her peak years. —*Stephen Thomas Erlewine*

Simple Dreams / 1977 / Asylum ✦✦✦✦✦
Featuring a broader array of styles than any previous Linda Ronstadt record, *Simple Dreams* reconfirms her substantial talents as an interpretive singer. Ronstadt sings Dolly Parton ("I Never Will Marry") with the same conviction as the Rolling Stones ("Tumbling Dice"), and she manages to update Roy Orbison ("Blue Bayou") and direct attention to the caustic, fledgling singer/songwriter Warren Zevon ("Poor Poor Pitiful Me" and "Carmelita"). The consistently adventurous material and Ronstadt's powerful performance makes the record rival *Heart Like a Wheel* in sheer overall quality. —*Stephen Thomas Erlewine*

Living in the U.S.A. / 1978 / Asylum ✦✦✦
On *Living in the U.S.A.*, Linda Ronstadt made the ill-advised move to incorporate some current musical trends, such as new wave, into her successful formula. While some of the record sounds good, the majority of the album is poorly executed, particularly her take on Elvis Costello's "Alison." —*Stephen Thomas Erlewine*

Greatest Hits, Vol. 2 / 1980 / Asylum ✦✦✦✦✦
Picking up where the first volume left off, *Greatest Hits, Vol. 2* contains Linda Ronstadt's biggest hits from the late '70s, including such songs as "It's So Easy," "Hurt So Bad," "Blue Bayou," "Back in the USA," "Poor Poor Pitiful Me," "Ooh Baby Baby," "How Do I

You" and "Tumbling Dice." Since Ronstadt's late-'70s albums tended to be a little spottty, this is a very useful summation of their highlights. *—Stephen Thomas Erlewine*

Mad Love / 1980 / Asylum ♦♦

Get Closer / 1982 / Asylum ♦♦

What's New / 1983 / Asylum ♦♦♦
Instead of trying to compete with a newer, fashion-conscious pop marketplace, Linda Ronstadt removed herself from the rat race, recording an album of traditional pop standards with Nelson Riddle. Ronstadt's voice isn't always showcased to a fine effect on these songs, but the record is an interesting change of pace. And it would have been more interesting if she hadn't repeated its formula on her next two records. *—Stephen Thomas Erlewine*

Lush Life / 1984 / Asylum ♦♦

For Sentimental Reasons / Feb. 1986 / Asylum ♦♦

Round Midnight with Nelson Riddle and his Orchestra / 1986 / Asylum ♦♦♦
Round Midnight is a triple-disc box set that compiles all three of the traditional pop albums Linda Ronstadt recorded with Nelson Riddle (*What's New, Lush Life,* and *For Sentimental Reasons*). Only dedicated fans will need to own all three of the albums, and, for those listeners, this is a classy way to purchase them. *—Stephen Thomas Erlewine*

Canciones de Mi Padre / 1987 / Asylum ♦♦♦
Linda Ronstadt abandoned the pop audience in 1983, turning toward traditional pop music. She recorded three albums with Nelson Riddle before changing direction yet again, this time recording a set of traditional Mexican songs titled *Canciones de Mi Padre.* As the title suggests, the record is a fairly sentimental collection, since these are songs from her childhood and her heritage. Occasionally, Ronstadt oversells the songs but overall, the album is charming, affectionate, entertaining and more successful than her stilted Nelson Riddle collaborations. *—Stephen Thomas Erlewine*

Cry Like a Rainstorm—Howl Like the Wind / Sep. 1989 / Asylum ♦♦♦
On the strength of the hit duet with Aaron Neville, "Don't Know Much," *Cry Like a Rainstorm—Howl Like the Wind* returned Linda Ronstadt to the top of the charts. The album was a collection of well-constructed adult contemporary pop, which suits her voice better than the traditional pop she recorded during the mid-'80s. Musically, *Cry Like a Rainstorm* isn't as adventerous as *Canciones de Mi Padre,* nor is it as consistent as *Trio,* the album she recorded with Emmylou Harris and Dolly Parton, but it is her most satisfying mainstream pop album she has made since the late '70s. *—Stephen Thomas Erlewine*

Mas Canciones / 1990 / Elektra ♦♦♦
Mas Canciones is a thoroughly enjoyable collection of Spanish and Mexican songs that is arguably stronger than its predecessor, since Ronstadt sounds more comfortable with the material than ever before. *—Stephen Thomas Erlewine*

Frenesi / Aug. 25, 1992 / Elektra ♦♦

Winter Light / 1994 / Elektra ♦♦♦
Winter Light could arguably be classified as Linda Ronstadt's best pop album of the 1990s. She followed up 1989's hugely successful *Cry Like a Rainstorm–Howl Like the Wind* with two Spanish language albums (*Mas Canciones* and *Frenesi*), then returned with the beautiful light-pop collection that is *Winter Light.* This set finds Ronstadt interpreting such classics as the Bacharach/David compositions "Anyone Who Had a Heart" and "I Just Don't Know What to Do With Myself" with enough torchy bravado to make them her own. Her cover of the Beach Boys' "Don't Talk (Put Your Head on My Shoulder)" is an ethereal, gorgeous, and breathy interpretation, and other covers, such as "Oh No, Not My Baby" and "It's Too Soon to Know" shine just as brightly. In fact, there is not a single dud on this impeccably produced album, which, in fact, gets better and better with each listening. Also included is the gutsy, dramatic Spanish language mini-epic "Adonde Voy" and, as the icing on the cake, her own co-written contribution, "Winter Light," a shimmering and heartbreaking lullaby that would fit perfectly in a holiday music collection. This sadly overlooked album is nothing short of a shining gem, and an absolute must for fans of this amazing singer. *—Jose F. Promis*

Feels Like Home / Mar. 14, 1995 / Elektra ♦♦♦

Dedicated to the One I Love / Jun. 1996 / Elektra ♦♦♦
Throughout her career, Linda Ronstadt has always interpreted rock and pop classics, but *Dedicated to the One I Love* is different from the rest of her albums—this time around, she reinterprets the oldies as children's lullabies. All of the songs are given lush, sweet, and soft arrangements, even when that approach is ludicrous; it might be a cute idea to deliver Queen's "We Will Rock You" as a rock-a-bye chant, but in practice it is simply ridiculous. Fortunately, most of the album relies on songs—"Be My Baby," "In My Room"—that can be sung as lullabies, and she sings them very well. Of course, the appeal of *Dedicated to the One I Love* is limited—only baby boomer parents will really find this interesting—but fans that find the concept intriguing won't be disappointed by the results. *—Stephen Thomas Erlewine*

We Ran / Jun. 23, 1998 / Elektra ♦♦♦
For much of the '90s, it seemed as if Linda Ronstadt was avoiding pop music. She recorded only two pop albums, 1994's *Winter Light* and 1995's *Feels Like Home,* which seemed like diversions from the Latin and children's records that were occupying her time. In 1998, she returned with *We Ran,* a full-fledged pop comeback produced by Glyn Johns (George Massenberg, Peter Asher and Waddy Wachtel also produced a handful of songs) and featuring support from such '70s soft-rock stalwarts as Waddy Wachtel and Bernie Leadon, as well as Heartbreakers Mike Campbell, Howie Epstein and Benmont Tench. The pedigree is in place, leaving it up to Ronstadt and her songs to deliver the goods which, more often than not, she does. Her voice remains strong and suprisingly robust, and her choice of songs, while not surprising, is quite satisfying. There are a couple of cuts that are a little bland and others, such as Dylan's "Just Like Tom Thumb's Blues," aren't suited for her polished delivery, but most of the album is quite enjoyable. It's nice to hear Ronstadt tackle classics like "Ruler of My Heart," but the moments of *We Ran* that truly capture the spirit of *Heart Like a Wheel* are when she tries contemporary songs like John Hiatt's "Icy Blue Heart" and Bruce Springsteen's "If I Should Fall Behind." Granted, Hiatt and Springsteen are predictable choices—she could have been more adventurous and sought out songs by such '90s songwriters as Ron Sexsmith or Aimee Mann—but they are just contemporary enough to help make *We Ran* a successful update of her classic '70s sound. *—Stephen Thomas Erlewine*

Western Wall: The Tucson Sessions / Aug. 24, 1999 / Elektra ♦♦♦♦♦
Linda Ronstadt and Emmylou Harris have frequently collaborated over the course of their long careers. Their voices are made for each other in a yin-yang meeting of Ronstandt's rich velvet alto and Harris' songbird-sweet soprano. *The Tucson Sessions* takes their collaborations to new heights. A collection of covers and originals tracing various paths of love and loss, the performances seem to have breathed in the desert where they were recorded. Arrangements airy as the space between desert and sky are grounded by gritty guitars, splashed with color from folk instruments and filled with glorious harmonies. Well known singer/songwriters are covered—Patty Griffin, Andy Prieboy, Rosanne Cash, Leonard Cohen, and Bruce Springsteen. Traditional presentations of Cohen's "Sisters of Mercy" and Springsteen's "Across the Border" take on new dimensions as sung by women. The spare arrangement and delicate harmonies lend a wonderful wistfulness to Cash's "Western Wall." A surprising cover choice with beautiful results is Sinead O'Connor's "This Is to Mother You." The album's best track, "1917," was written by folk singer David Olney. It's impossible to imagine anyone else singing this haunting tale of soldiers and women in WWI. Fragile and breathtaking, Harris' voice is buoyed by the angelic harmonies of Ronstadt and Kate and Anna McGarrigle. Harris also contributes, along with some collaborators, three tracks to the album, notably the spirited "Raise the Dead." *—Theresa LaVeck*

The Linda Ronstadt Box Set / Nov. 16, 1999 / Elektra ♦♦♦♦
Linda Ronstadt's generically titled four-CD, five-hour, 86-track box set retrospective attempts with considerable success to encompass the many types of music she's sung from the mid-'60s to the late '90s. The album is divided into five unequal parts, with 31 tracks given over to an "Album Retrospective," followed by seven tracks from "The Nelson Riddle Sessions," her three albums of classic pop, then five songs "En Espanol," drawn from her three Spanish language albums. That takes up the first two discs, with the third disc consisting of 20 "Collaborations" and the fourth 23 "Rarities." It is significant that the first section is called "Album Retrospective," signaling to the listener that Ronstadt is not interested in presenting her hit singles as such. In fact, most of her chart hits do turn up somewhere on the set, but a whole chunk of them is missing. At the time that Ronstadt was peppering the singles charts in the late '70s, she caught flack for her covers of Motown and rock & roll standards, and she herself has disavowed her recordings of such work, so maybe it shouldn't be a surprise that she has chosen to forget them. The omissions tend to make Ronstadt seem like more of a balladeer than she has been in her career. She is much more interested in emphasizing her non-rock work. Also, the "Rarities" disc really only contains five previously unreleased songs, and they are hardly revelations. *The Linda Ronstadt Box Set* clearly had major input from the artist herself, and its contents may not be what a Ronstadt fan or chart researcher would have chosen. But it certainly makes the case for Ronstadt as a hard-working performer who constantly challenged herself by trying styles beyond the Southern California folk-rock for which she remains best known. *— William Ruhlmann*

Roogalator

Pub Rock, New Wave

U.S.-born guitarist Danny Adler's Roogalator was one of the fixtures on the London pub rock scene of the mid-'70s, at the same time establishing themselves among the most un-pub-like bands on the circuit. Drawing deep from Adler's own experience on the Cincinnati club circuit of the late '60s, where he gigged alongside (and frequently jammed with members of) R&B legends Dyke & the Blazers and Bootsy Collins' Pacesetters, Roogalator offered an angular, minimalist funk sound which was utterly at odds with the country, blues, and early rock sounds normally heard on the scene. Even Kokomo, up to that point the most authentic attempt at a homegrown funk sound yet unveiled, trailed in Roogalator's slipstream. They, after all, simply followed the lead of the American masters. Roogalator prided themselves in escaping from it and in so doing, created the wholly distinctive blueprint for what would become the Brit funk explosion of the early '80s. They made their recorded debut in April 1976 with the Stiff Records classic "Cincinnati Fatback." Despite such applause, another year elapsed before Roogalator issued a follow-up, when Virgin released "Love and the Single Girl." The group then shifted to manager Robin Scott's own newly formed Do It label for their debut album, *Play It By Ear,* in mid-1977. Essentially little more than an opportunity to preserve the band's repertoire on vinyl before unleashing a crop of new material, the album was well-received but sold poorly. When lineup changes shook the group in summer 1978, Adler realized the band had reached the end of the line. Roogalator officially disbanded in July 1978 with many of the songs scheduled for their second album promptly being reworked for Adler's own solo debut, *The Danny Adler Story.* *—Dave Thompson*

Play It By Ear / 1977 / Do It ♦♦♦
In a perfect world, Roogalator would have cut its first album a full 18 months earlier than it did, when the band was still brittle and the songs still fresh, and before a whole new

generation of angry young punks rose up to carve its own noise into immortality. The last of the so-called pub rock bands to threaten to make a major impact, Roogalator was the first to suffer from the changing of the guard. One moment, they were being feted as the biggest thing since Springsteen. The next, they were yesterday's bill-toppers. Roogalator cut one single in the band's prime, then went out on the road and stayed there forever. By the time they came back to record a full album, they'd been playing the same songs for so long it hurt. But don't let familiarity get mistaken for staleness. True, the re-recordings of the band's debut 45, "All Aboard" and "Cincinnati Fatback," do pale alongside the original single. But the imagery ("down by the banks of the O-Hi-O") remains just as potent an invocation of the American Midwest as it ever was. And, elsewhere in the package, it's still impossible to avoid becoming ensnared in the deliberately convoluted rhythms and rhymes that mark out bandleader Danny Adler's strongest compositions. But *Play It By Ear* did nothing upon release and, by the time Roogalator was ready to record its follow-up album, the band had already broken up. *Play It By Ear*'s legacy, too, has been short-circuited somewhat, because better versions of many of the songs exist among the demos and outtakes featured on the *Cincinnati Fatback* anthology. Anybody seeking their first wild ride on the Roogalator, then, would be best advised to seek that set out first. Save this one to fill in the gaps. *—Dave Thompson*

● **Cincinnati Fatback** / Feb. 8, 2000 / Proper ♦♦♦♦♦

A companion to the same label's Danny Adler compilation, this 18-track plunge into the Roogalator vaults unveils some quite astonishing sidelights. No less than one-third of the tracks appear as either an unissued version or an unreleased mix, drawing from demos reaching back as far as fall 1975, a BBC session in spring 1976, and enough of the band's one and only album to send you scouring the stores for the rest of the set. The key attractions, of course, are the expected ones—"Cincinnati Fatback," Roogalator's self-affirming statement of intent and first single; "All Aboard," its equally exciting B-side; the exhilarating "Ride With Your Roogalator"; and keyboard player Nick Plytas' ridiculously catchy "Love and the Single Girl," the closest the band ever came to scoring a hit single. For the rest of the set, the Roogalator sound rattles by as relentlessly as the railroad tracks that inspired their greatest songs. No matter that the band eventually washed up on the shores of underachievement; nor that, by the time they finally cut their first album, they already knew where they were bound. Songs from Roogalator's last few months—"Zero Hero," "Where Were You?," and "Dream Rider"—glow with an inner fire regardless. This is edgy dance music cut on the new wave side of classic rock, with only the members' road weariness beginning to show some frays' round the edges. So the band fell apart and Adler went solo, but viewed from a distance, the thing that leaps out loudest is the sheer musical and lyrical audacity of this band. From tempo changes that nod toward jazz to lyrical shifts that evoke primal urges, Adler stood at the crossroads between an all-American Springsteen-shaped icon and an absurdly English, postmodern Ray Davies. *—Dave Thompson*

The Roots

f. 1989

Jazz-Rap, Alternative Rap, Hip-Hop

Though popular success has largely eluded the Roots, the Philadelphia group showed the way for live rap, building on Stetsasonic's "hip-hop band" philosophy of the mid-'80s by focusing on live instrumentation at their concerts and in the studio. Though their album works have been inconsistent affairs, more intent on building grooves than pushing songs, the group's live shows are among the best in the business. Formed by rapper Black Thought and drummer ?uestlove, the Roots began their musical career by recreating classic hip-hop tracks with ?uestlove's drum kit backing Black Thought's rhymes. Moving from the street to local clubs, the Roots became popular around Philadelphia and recorded an album, 1993's *Organix*, to sell at shows. Later that year, the group signed to DGC and recorded their major-label debut, *Do You Want More?!!!??!* Though it was mostly ignored by hip-hop fans, the album made tracks in alternative circles. Early in 1996, the Roots released "Clones," the trailer single for their second album. It hit the Rap Top Five, and created a good buzz for the album. The following September, *Illadelph Halflife* appeared and made number 21 on the album charts. The Roots' third album, 1999's *Things Fall Apart*, was easily their biggest critical and commercial success. *—John Bush*

Organix / 1993 / Remedy ♦♦♦

Although to knowledgeable natives of Philadelphia they may have originally been known as the Square Roots, the sound of this group on this album is only occasionally square. The sound, feel, and quality of *Organix* is much less developed than their subsequent recordings, but that is to be expected, given the amount that the band has grown over the years.

The introductory song "The Roots Is Comin'," is merely one minute and 17 seconds long, yet long enough to exemplify the band's funky bassline (here played by Leonard Hubbard), their dreamy and emotional organ chords (thanks to Scott Storch), and their ferociously swift yet clear rhymes from the group's focal MC Black Thought. The song that follows, "Pass the Popcorn" would have been called a "posse cut" in 1993 (when *Organix* was originally recorded). Everyone could've used a little more practice before stepping up to the mic on this song, but the fun and the spirit of the song are not lost in the amateurishness. The creative venture "Writers Block" is an example of just the opposite, as Black Thought flows with spoken word, comically and creatively expressing the experience of a day in the life of a Philadelphian using mass transit. The instrumentation is appropriately frantic and punctuated by [cymbal] crashes (like any mass transit system).

Fans of *Do You Want More*, the Roots album released immediately following *Organix*, will recognize the music of "I'm Out Deah," "Leonard I-V," and "Essawhamah?" Another track to note is "The Session (Longest Posse Cut in History)"—no false claim at 12 minutes and 43 seconds. This album should be a part of any Roots fan's collection—not so much because it is an example of their artistry at its best, but because it allows you to see where they came from and how long and fruitful a journey it's been. *—Qa'id Jacobs*

Do You Want More?!!!??! / Jan. 1995 / DGC ♦♦♦♦

Because the Roots were pioneering a new style during the early '90s, the band was forced to draw its own blueprints for its major-label debut album. It's not surprising then, that *Do You Want More?!!!??!* sounds more like a document of old-school hip-hop than contemporary rap. The album is based on loose grooves and laid-back improvisation, and where most hip-hoppers use samples to draw songs together and provide a chorus, the Roots just keep on jamming. The problem is that the Roots' jams begin to take the place of true songs, leaving most tracks with only that groove to speak for them. The notable exceptions—"Mellow My Man" and "Datskat," among others—use different strategies to command attention: the sounds of a human beatbox , the great keyboard work of Scott Storch, and contributions from several jazz players (trombonist Joshua Roseman, saxophonist Steve Coleman and vocalist Cassandra Wilson). By the close of the album, those tracks are what the listener remembers, not the lightweight grooves. *—John Bush*

Illadelph Halflife / Sep. 24, 1996 / DGC ♦♦♦♦

The Roots always had ambition, which theoretically placed them ahead of many of their mid-'90s hip-hop contemporaries. Where many of their peers settled for gangsta clichés, tedious displays of lyrical skills, alternative hip-hop or half-hearted jazz-rap fusions, the Roots decided to take an entirely different route by merging street-level rhythms with jazz and old-school technique, and performing everything on live instruments. While their approach works well in theory, it doesn't always work in practice. Though it is decidedly tougher and more adventurous than the group's debut, *Illadelph Halflife* just misses the mark. Part of the problem with the record is the fact that it doesn't capture the relentless energy of their live show; without the reckless, rampaging momentum of their live show, the record is only sporadically engaging. Still, the best moments of *Illadelph Halflife* demonstrate the Roots are an exciting, inventive band that have great potential—they just haven't quite fulfilled it yet. *—Leo Stanley*

● **Things Fall Apart** / Feb. 23, 1999 / MCA ♦♦♦♦♦

This progressive, Philadelphia, hip-hop band's fourth album grabbed its title from the Chinua Achebe novel of the same name, and numerous guest stars add a welcome spice to the pot. Mos Def lends a mic-clutching hand to the Roots' lyrically precise lead MC, Black Thought, on their old school homage, "Double Trouble." Throughout the complex album, listeners are treated to somber textures ("The Spark" with Malik B) and heavyweight jams like "Adrenaline!" Even through often thankless years of relentless touring, marketing and promotion, hip-hop remains a way of life for the group, and they let you know it on "Act Too (The Love of My Life)" featuring Common. On that stellar track, Black Thought raps about what hip-hop culture means to him, "I remember late nights steady rocking' the mic/hip-hop you the love of my life." *—Craig Robert Smith*

The Roots Come Alive / Nov. 2, 1999 / MCA ♦♦♦♦

Releasing an album recorded live in concert makes more sense for the Roots than any other hip-hop artist, considering they've always concentrated on live prowess over their skills on the mic or in the production booth. The standard guitar/drums/bass/keyboards lineup of most rock bands is a reality for this group, and after years of requests from rabid fans, the Roots acquiesced with a document of their live experience, titled *The Roots Come Alive*. Recorded at two venues in New York and one in Paris, the album distills exactly what the Roots bring to the hip-hop world—a live experience built on call-and-response vocals that bring the show to the audience like few other artists. The sound is fantastic, especially on early keyboard-driven tracks like "Proceed," "Essaywhuman?!???!!!," and "Mellow My Man." Though the raps themselves often suffer from the live setting, the rhythms are crisper than in the studio, and the bass-driven grooves are much beefier. The Roots' resident turntablist, Scratch, takes a large role as well, as does human beatbox Rahzel the Godfather of Noyze (though the latter only appears on about half of the album). This is a live album that not only satisfies fans, but offers neophytes more entertainment than any of the Roots' studio efforts. It's difficult to make any live album a first pick, but *Come Alive* displays the group doing exactly what it does best. *—John Bush*

Diana Ross (Diane Earle)

b. Mar. 26, 1944, Detroit, MI

Vocals / Pop-Soul, Motown, Urban, Disco, Soul

As a solo artist, Diana Ross is one of the most successful female singers of the rock era. If you factor in her work as the lead singer of the Supremes in the 1960s, she may be *the* most successful. The Supremes scored 12 number one pop hits during the '60s, though by the end of the decade Ross had launched a solo career. Motown initially paired her with writer/producers Ashford & Simpson, who gave her four quick pop hits, including the number one "Ain't No Mountain High Enough." Ross branched out into acting in 1972, starring in a film biography of Billie Holiday (*Lady Sings the Blues*) that earned her an Academy Award nomination (as well as a number one soundtrack). She returned to record-making with the number one hit "Touch Me in the Morning," earned several hits from a duet album with Marvin Gaye, and followed with two more chart-topping singles in 1976 ("Do You Know Where You're Going To" and the disco-oriented "Love Hangover"). After two more number one singles, 1980's "Upside Down" and the following year's "Endless Love," she decamped for RCA and was rewarded immediately with the million-selling album *Why Do Fools Fall in Love*. After a few more hits, Ross began to have trouble selling records in the late '80s. By 1989, she had returned to Motown, and by 1993 had turned more to pop standards. *— William Ruhlmann*

Lady Sings the Blues / Dec. 1971 / Motown ♦♦♦

Her biggest album as a solo act, Diana Ross forever ended any association with the

Supremes after this film. She not only got an Oscar nomination and more roles, she really did capture the spirit and flavor, if not the sound and timbre, of Billie Holiday's music; her performance was the film's only saving grace. *—Ron Wynn*

Mahogany / Oct. 1975 / Motown ✦✦
As a vehicle for Diana Ross' film career, *Mahogany* wasn't nearly as successful as *Lady Sings the Blues*, not only because it didn't focus on her musical gifts, but because the script was weak. Still, the movie produced one of her biggest and best hits with "Theme from Mahogany (Do You Know Where You're Going To)," a Goffin-Masser tune that was nominated for an Oscar. It's a great song, but most Ross fans will rather pick it up on a collection than *Mahogany—Original Soundtrack*, since it is the only vocal track on an otherwise monotonous album of instrumental incidental music. *—Stephen Thomas Erlewine*

Diana Ross / 1976 / Motown ✦✦✦✦
Diana Ross landed one of the decade's definitive singles with "Love Hangover," instantly making this a major hit album. While it surprisingly didn't sell as well as some 1980s LPs, the single was a double chart-topper and a huge club hit for much of the next two years. It vaulted the album into the pop Top 10 and even managed to break the followup single onto the charts. *—Ron Wynn*

Diana / May 1980 / Motown ✦✦✦
Coming off four Top Ten hits in three years for their group Chic, producers Bernard Edwards and Nile Rodgers were *the* hot R&B/disco team of the day when they wrote and produced Diana Ross' second album named simply *Diana*. (The first was her 1971 TV soundtrack, *Diana!*) The result was Ross' best-selling album ever, paced by her biggest singles hit yet, "Upside Down," and its Top Ten follow-up, "I'm Coming Out." For the most part, disco productions tended to emphasize the beat over the voice, and it might be argued, but for the billing, Ross had been reduced to guest vocalist on her own album. But it was exactly her struggle to retain an identity beyond the groove that made this music more compelling than Chic's records. *Diana* marked an important comeback for Ross, who had struggled in the late '70s after the early successes of her solo career. She celebrated by leaving Motown for a six-year, five-album sojourn at RCA. *—William Ruhlmann*

All the Great Hits / Oct. 1981 / Motown ✦✦✦✦✦
Yet another Motown anthology/greatest hits package. The songs are fine and the mastering is good. It's really a question of choice and need. If you want everything, get either the new Ross boxed set or the original anthology. If you only want a few hits, then either this or any other package will suffice. *—Ron Wynn*

Forever Diana: Musical Memoirs / Oct. 5, 1993 / Motown ✦✦✦
Plagued by inferior sound and a weak track selection, *Forever Diana* is a major disappointment for fans. Only one disc is devoted to the Supremes, with Ross's spotty solo career occupying the other three discs, featuring decidedly poorer sound than previous Motown releases. Besides poor audio, the liner notes are skimpy and incomplete. Ultimately, *Forever Diana* is a wasted opportunity. *—Stephen Thomas Erlewine*

One Woman: The Ultimate Collection / Oct. 18, 1994 / Motown ✦✦✦✦✦
This compilation attempts to condense Diana Ross's most successful recordings into one 20-song, 71 1/2-minute disc. Well, there's good news and bad news. The good news is that Ross (who produced the album, which is to say picked the tracks) has included six of her Supremes recordings from the 1960s (one of them, "Someday We'll Be Together," in a new disco mix) and licensed a few songs from her stay at RCA in the 1980s, making this the most wide-ranging of her compilations. The bad news is that she has jettisoned many possible hits (only ten of her 18 chart-toppers are included) in the name of featuring four tracks from the 1990s that do not rank with her best, either aesthetically or in terms of popularity. In other words, Ross has constructed the album as she might a concert—a sprinkling of early Supremes hits, all her biggest solo hits, and what she considers the highlights of her current work. The result is a less than perfect, or "ultimate" portrait, since the selection implies erroneously that a forgettable piece of tripe like the 1991 Top 40 hit "When You Tell Me That You Love Me" is as much a milestone in the Ross catalog as "You Can't Hurry Love" or "Upside Down" (and that Ross remained as significant an artist in 1994 as she was in 1964 and 1974). But the album still makes a good sampler of Ross's entire 30-year-plus career for beginners. *—William Ruhlmann*

Greatest Hits: The RCA Years / Mar. 25, 1997 / RCA ✦✦✦✦
Diana Ross' glossy 1981-1987 tenure on RCA is the subject of this 18-track collection, which includes her hit tribute to the late Marvin Gaye, "Missing You." Other highlights include her cover of Frankie Lymon and the Teenagers' "Why Do Fools Fall in Love," "Mirror, Mirror," "Swept Away" and a solo version of the chart-topping "Endless Love." *—Jason Ankeny*

20th Century Masters—The Millennium Collection: The Best of Diana Ross / Jun. 27, 2000 / Motown ✦✦✦✦
The Best of Diana Ross: The Millennium Collection compiles 11 of her solo career highlights, including the #1 hits "Touch Me in the Morning," "Theme from Mahogany (Do You Know Where You're Going To)," "Ain't No Mountain High Enough," "Upside Down," and "Endless Love." Other chart hits, such as "Remember Me," "Love Hangover," "The Boss," and "It's My Turn" trace her work from her departure from the Supremes to her disco diva stage to her intertwined film and music careers. Though it's not a complete look at Ross's music, *The Best of Diana Ross: The Millennium Collection* is a concise and affordable selection of her best-known songs. *—Heather Phares*

● **The Motown Anthology** / Mar. 27, 2001 / Motown ✦✦✦✦✦
Up until this release, consumers had a difficult task of finding a definitive compilation highlighting the post-Supremes career of Diana Ross—mainly because there wasn't one. This double-disc set gathers 27 of the diva's finest solo sides, plus an additional 11 tracks that are making their domestic debut. As a retrospective, *The Motown Anthology* succeeds in gathering all of Ross' major singles. Some are available here in a previously unissued form. Such is the case for "Remember Me," "My Mistake (Was to Love You)," and "Lovin' Livin' & Givin'"—from the *Thank God It's Friday* soundtrack. Those looking for chart-toppers should note that *The Motown Anthology* not only delivers rare material, but also all the hits that would render most other collections superfluous. The producers have also hit upon a favorable ratio of hits to rarities. After covering all the bases on the popular and familiar material, the previously unearthed nuggets—which are spread throughout the chronologically organized set—are a treat for both the intense as well as the casual fan. Of particular note is the leadoff track "Time and Love"—a Laura Nyro composition which had been scheduled, and then withdrawn, as Ross' first solo single. The sound is uniformly excellent with the caveat that some of the early recordings on disc one—"Reach Out and Touch (Somebody's Hand)" for example—never were known for their fidelity. Likewise, the sound of mid-to-late '70s tracks such as "Love Hangover" and "The Boss" are marked improvements. Clocking in at over two and a half hours, *The Motown Anthology* is a tremendous value. *—Lindsay Planer*

David Lee Roth

b. Oct. 10, 1955, Bloomington, IN
Vocals / Pop-Metal, Album Rock, Pop/Rock, Hard Rock
In the eyes of countless hard rock fans, David Lee Roth is the prototypical frontman. With a flamboyant, larger-than-life stage presence and a party-hearty surfer-dude persona (not to mention his acrobatic leaps, long mane of blond hair, and skintight spandex outfits), Roth was an integral part of Van Halen's meteoric rise to global dominance from 1978 through 1984. Just as the group had hit their peak and appeared they could do no wrong, Roth issued a four-track solo EP in 1985, *Crazy From the Heat*, with rumors swirling that the group was bickering behind the scenes and that the singer was going to make a major motion picture. Still, it was a shock to rock fans everywhere when Roth left Van Halen later that year. When his plans for the movie proved to be a bust, Roth immediately formed a top-notch solo band, consisting of ex-Talas bassist Billy Sheehan (often called "the Eddie Van Halen of bass"), ex-Frank Zappa guitarist Steve Vai, and ex-Maynard Ferguson drummer Gregg Bissonette. In 1986, Roth issued his first full-length solo effort, *Eat 'Em & Smile*, which was another hit and gave way to another sold-out tour. But while Roth's new solo band seemed to be on their way to a very promising future, the lineup began to splinter with each subsequent release (1988's *Skyscraper*, 1991's *A Little Ain't Enough*), until Roth was the only remaining member. With interest waning, Roth attempted to branch out musically on his experimental 1994 release, *Your Filthy Little Mouth* (produced by Nile Rodgers), but it was met with a cool reception, as was his attempt to break into the Vegas circuit around the same time. *—Greg Prato*

Crazy from the Heat / 1985 / Warner Brothers ✦✦✦✦
For his first solo effort, Roth stripped away the gonzo guitars that are Van Halen's trademark and accentuated his lounge-lizard-as-rock-star persona, resulting in an EP that succeeds because of that persona, not because the music is anything special. Certainly, he doesn't add anything to "California Girls" and "Just a Gigolo/I Ain't Got Nobody" other than his joking, over-the-top vocals. Then again, that's all he needs to do. *—Stephen Thomas Erlewine*

Eat 'Em & Smile / 1986 / Warner Brothers ✦✦✦✦✦
Few would argue that David Lee Roth's first solo EP was a complete comedy send-up, albeit a very successful one that gained him enough favor with the MTV peanut gallery to solidify his potential as a solo artist. When threat became fact, however, Roth was smart enough to know that show tunes set to flashy videos weren't going to cut it and wisely proceeded to surround himself with musicians of impeccable pedigree. Thus armed, the "diamond" one set out to out-Van Halen Van Halen with his band's first effort, *Eat 'Em & Smile*, a more than adequate substitute for the overtly commercial tendencies of the "new and improved" original. Why mess with a winning recipe, indeed. Guitarist Steve Vai, bassist Billy Sheehan, and drummer Gregg Bissonette sound perfectly at home aping their boss' old cronies on such sizzling party anthems as "Shyboy" and "Elephant Gun." A fun-loving cover of "Tobacco Road" kicks off a very solid side two featuring the remarkably *Fair Warning*-esque "Big Trouble," and it doesn't get any better than first single "Yankee Rose," where the squealing call and response between Roth and Vai reaches unparalleled comical heights. The glossy pump of "Goin' Crazy!" (originally conceived as the title track for Roth's botched movie project) hints at the pop excesses to come, and although two lounge pieces are knocked out for good measure, these are easily offset by the cool strut of "Ladies Nite in Buffalo?," arguably Roth's most legitimate piece of art ever. *—Ed Rivadavia*

Skyscraper / 1988 / Warner Brothers ✦✦✦
Even as *Skyscraper* shot up the charts behind the momentum of its ultra-saccharine lead-off single "Just Like Paradise," it was abundantly clear to anyone paying attention that the wheels were already falling off the David Lee Roth bandwagon. Simply put, the collaborative spirit that had given their manic debut *Eat 'Em & Smile* such legitimacy as a band project was collapsing under the unbearable strain of its leader's unstoppable ego. With bass wizard Billy Sheehan already gone to form Mr. Big and guitar hero Steve Vai mostly flying on auto-pilot (if spectacularly so), keyboard player Brett Tuggle seems like the most unwelcome presence on an album that squanders much of its free-wheeling potential by trying too hard to achieve an exaggerated pop sheen. The aforementioned "Just Like Paradise" is the obvious main offender, but promising examples of arena rock like "Stand Up" and "Perfect Timing" also lose much of their bite through excessive studio tampering. Likewise, the largely acoustic "Damn Good" and the overlong "Two Fools a

Minute" (an unconvincing ode to Roth's lounge lizard persona) go nowhere fast, and what the band was trying to achieve with the bizarre title track is still anyone's guess. And while rockers like "Knucklebones" and "The Bottom Line" don't really impress or offend, "Hina" and "Hot Dog and a Shake" are the album's only two clear standouts. The first's soothing, interweaving guitar harmonies presaged Vai's Joe Satriani-inspired solo work while the latter finally explodes in the over-the-top fashion of the first album, largely thanks to a Vai solo so fast, so hot not even he could keep up, momentarily losing his fingering in the album's only spontaneous moment. *—Ed Rivadavia*

A Little Ain't Enough / Apr. 1991 / Warner Brothers ✦✦

Your Filthy Little Mouth / Mar. 8, 1994 / Warner Brothers ✦✦

• **Best of David Lee Roth** / Oct. 28, 1997 / Rhino ✦✦✦✦✦
Considering that David Lee Roth's solo career crashed after two albums and an EP, it should have been easy to assemble a 20-track greatest-hits compilation. Rhino's *The Best* proves that isn't so. Most of Roth's best-known songs are here, including "California Girls," "Just a Gigolo/I Ain't Got Nobody," "Yankee Rose," "Ladies Night in Buffalo?," "Goin' Crazy," "Skyscraper," "Just Like Paradise," and "Stand Up." However, the collection contains too many mediocrities from the flat albums *A Lil' Ain't Enough* and *Your Filthy Little Mouth* while overlooking radio and MTV staples like "Damn Good" and "That's Life." Furthermore, the collection isn't assembled in chronological order, which makes it a bit of a difficult listen. Even with these faults, there's no arguing that *The Best* does distill Roth's best solo recordings to one disc, making it a useful compilation for most casual fans. Nevertheless, after listening to all of *The Best*, many listeners will probably think a li'l is enough and 20 tracks might be a bit too much. *—Stephen Thomas Erlewine*

DLR Band / Jun. 9, 1998 / Wawazat ✦✦✦
Following the disasterous near-reunion of Van Halen, David Lee Roth didn't lie down—he wrote the vindictive, hilarious, near-brilliant memoir *Crazy from the Heat*, compiled *The Best of David Lee Roth* for Rhino and, finally, assembled the DLR Band, his response to the Gary Cherone version of Van Halen. Where his former collegues aimed at world domination and serious art with *Van Halen III*, Diamond Dave kept his aim low, turning in a sleazy little record that just wants to rock really hard. While Van Halen stumbled hard with their revamping, Roth succeeded in delivering a kind of miniature comeback. Granted, *DLR Band* didn't shake the charts, but it wasn't meant to be big; it's a record that was made with the fans in mind, and they should be pleased by its down-and-dirty attitude. This is the hardest Roth has rocked since *Eat 'Em & Smile*. The songs may not be as funny or memorable, and his new band doesn't reach the heights of Vai and Sheehan, but *The DLR Band* benefits from its modest scale. It succeeds on its own terms, delivering a selection of fine, spirited metal songs that finds Roth's charisma at a near peak. *—Stephen Thomas Erlewine*

Roxette

f. 1984, Halmstad, Sweden, **db.** Nov. 18, 1999
Pop/Rock, Euro-Pop, Adult Contemporary, Swedish Pop/Rock
It's tempting to write Roxette off as nothing more than a shallow pop/rock band, but their shameless hooks are precisely what makes them so enjoyable. Roxette has a knack for writing extremely catchy and simple hooks and melodies that are sweet but not saccharine; it's radio-friendly pop, but the hooks don't wear thin with repeated plays. The duo of guitarist Per Gessle and vocalist Marie Fredriksson released an album in 1986 that didn't display much of their talents, but the infectious follow-up, 1988's *Look Sharp!*, brought them to the top of the charts in America and England; 1991's *Joyride* was almost equally successful. After a couple years off, Roxette returned with a new album, *Crash! Boom! Bang!*, in 1994; *Baladas en Español* followed in 1997, and two years later the duo returned with the EP *Stars*. In 2000, Roxette signed to Edel and released the greatest-hits collection *Don't Bore Us Get to the Chorus* and began work on their next album. *—Stephen Thomas Erlewine*

Pearls of Passion / 1986 / EMI Sweden ✦✦

Look Sharp! / 1988 / EMI America ✦✦✦✦✦
Per Gessle and Marie Fredriksson exploded onto the pop radar screen with *Look Sharp!*, which spawned four big hits: the bright, shiny "The Look," the punchy, hopeful "Dressed for Success," the A/C-leaning "Dangerous," and the bland, overproduced "Listen to Your Heart." The cuts that weren't released as singles aren't necessarily filler, but they also aren't as strong as many of the cuts that made up Roxette albums that followed, particularly *Joyride* and *Tourism (Songs From Studios, Stages, Hotelrooms & Other Strange Places)*. The non-releases are nothing memorable, and they don't age well, "Paint" and "Dance Away" in particular being pretty average in terms of production and melody. Only "Chances" and "Shadow of a Doubt" show glimmers of the skills the duo would soon flourish. Gessle and Fredriksson became artists at crafting superb pop melodies and surrounding them with amazing production, so think of this album as basic training. *—Bryan Buss*

Joyride / Mar. 1991 / EMI America ✦✦✦✦
The beauty of Roxette is that the duo of Per Gessle and Marie Fredriksson can do practically anything in terms of Top 40 music. From the quiet desperation of "Spending My Time" to the chanting carnival of "Joyride" to the folky "Church of Your Heart," they bring a worldliness to their lyrics and melodies that most pop A-listers don't even have the imagination to dream of. This, the follow-up to their breakthrough disc, *Look Sharp!*, sees through on what that collection hinted at, meaning most of the songs sound like they were designed to be hit singles, not just filler between two or three good cuts. "The Big L," "Soul Deep," and "Hotblooded" all follow in the successful vein Gessle and Fredriksson mined with "The Look," while "Fading Like a Flower (Every Time You Leave)," an insistent rock ballad, and the accordion-driven "Perfect Day" take things down a notch. The low-key "Watercolours in the Rain" and the whining "(Do You Get) Excited?" are the only cuts that keep the album from being a total success. For the most part, though, this is two pop artists at the top of their game. *—Bryan Buss*

Tourism (Songs from Studios, Stages, Hotelrooms & Other Strange Places) / 1992 / EMI America ✦✦✦

Crash! Boom! Bang! / Oct. 4, 1994 / EMI America ✦✦

Have a Nice Day / Mar. 9, 1999 / EMI ✦✦✦
In the five years between Roxette's last album, *Crash, Boom, Bang*, and this, their "comeback" album, pop music had changed considerably. *Crash, Boom, Bang* failed, in part, because it was completely out of step with the times; in 1994 grunge, alternative, and rap ruled the charts, but Roxette always produced a relatively crisp and clean brand of pop/rock. In the five years since then, however, Brit-pop brought alternative rock back towards pop, electronica made dance music "cool" again, and bubblegum pop bands like the Spice Girls made unabashed pop fun again. Also, Per Gessle was fresh off from his very rock-oriented 1997 solo album. What resulted, then, was really rather ambitious. *Have A Nice Day* is an effort to encapsulate Roxette's trademark sound with Brit-pop and electronica, and, by gosh, it works. It's easily as good as any other Roxette album, save maybe only the stellar *Joyride*, and it shows that artistically the band is still on top. There's a good deal of emphasis on dance music here, but instead of the indistinguishable dance-pop of the band's early days, the beats seem to be borrowed straight from Fatboy Slim records. That, mixed with Gessle's gritty guitars, makes for a good deal of up-tempo rockers ("Crush on You," "7Twenty7," "Stars"). There are also some excellent pop songs, such as the single "Wish I Could Fly" and Gessle's unforgettable "You Can't Put Your Arms Around What's Already Gone," quite possibly the best song he's ever written. As is the case with any Roxette album, however, there are flaws, namely the presence of filler, mostly in the form of pace-destroying ballads. It's a small price to pay, however, for the return of one of the best mainstream pop bands in the past decade. *—Jason Damas*

• **Don't Bore Us, Get to the Chorus: Greatest Hits** / Sep. 26, 2000 / Edeltone ✦✦✦✦✦
Berry Gordy Jr. once said "Don't bore us—get to the chorus," which basically sums up most of pop music. It doesn't, however, do credit to Roxette, who has crafted some of the best tunes of the '80s and '90s. This compilation exhibits what pop masters Per Gessle and Marie Fredriksson are. It sums up major hits ("It Must Have Been Love," "Joyride"), minor hits ("Church of Your Heart," "How Do You Do!"), hard-to-find cuts ("Almost Unreal" from the *Super Mario Bros.* soundtrack), and new material ("Stars," "Wish I Could Fly"). Every song is a gem. Whether it's aching ballads like "Crash! Boom! Bang!," A/C/pop like "Dressed For Success," or techno/dance like "Stars," the two never miss a beat in terms of production, vocals, or lyrics. You can see how much their skills sharpened as both they and pop music matured when you place "The Look" alongside "Fading Like a Flower (Every Time You Leave)" alongside "Wish I Could Fly." Even with the pop renaissance of the late '90s, no one picked up where Roxette left off. This is a comprehensive collection of great contemporary music from overlooked and underrated pros. *—Bryan Buss*

Room Service / Apr. 3, 2001 / EMI ✦✦✦

Roxy Music

f. 1971, **db.** 1983
Album Rock, Proto-Punk, Pop/Rock, Glam Rock, Prog-Rock/Art Rock
Evolving from the late-'60s art-rock movement, Roxy Music had a fascination with fashion, glamour, cinema, pop art, and the avant-garde, which separated the band from their contemporaries. Dressed in bizarre, stylish costumes, the group played a defiantly experimental variation of art-rock which vascillated between avant-rock and sleek pop hooks. During the early '70s, the group was driven by the creative tension between Bryan Ferry and Brian Eno, who each pulled the band in separate directions: Ferry had a fondness for American soul and Beatlesque art-pop, while Eno was intrigued by deconstructing rock with amateurish experimentalism inspired by the Velvet Underground. This incarnation of Roxy Music may have only recorded two albums, but it inspired a legion of imitators—not only the glam-rockers of the early '70s, but art-rockers and new wave pop groups of the late '70s. Following Eno's departure, Roxy Music continued with its arty inclinations for a few albums before gradually working in elements of disco and soul. Within a few years, the group had developed a sophisticated, seductive soul-pop that relied on Ferry's stylish crooning. By the early '80s, the group had developed into a vehicle for Ferry, so it was no surprise that he disbanded the group at the height of its commercial success in the early '80s to pursue a solo career. *—Stephen Thomas Erlewine*

Roxy Music / 1972 / Virgin ✦✦✦
Falling halfway between musical primitivism and art-rock ambition, Roxy Music's eponymous debut remains a startling redefinition of rock's boundaries. Simultaneously embracing kitschy glamour and avant-pop, *Roxy Music* shimmers with seductive style and pulsates with disturbing synthetic textures. Although no musician demonstrates much technical skill at this point, they are driven by boundless imagination—Brian Eno's synthesized "treatments" exploit electronic instruments as electronics, instead of trying to shoehorn them into conventional acoustic patterns. Similarly, Bryan Ferry finds that his vampiric croon is at its most effective when it twists conventional melodies, Phil Manzanera's guitar is terse and unpredictable, while Andy Mackay's saxophone subverts rock & roll cliches by alternating R&B honking with atonal flourishes. But what makes *Roxy Music* such a confident, astonishing debut is how these primitive avant-garde tendencies are married to full-fledged songs, whether it's the free-form, structure-bending "Remake/Remodel" or the sleek glam of "Virginia Plain," the debut single added to later editions of the album. That was the trick that elevated Roxy Music from an art-school project to the most adventurous rock band of the early '70s. *—Stephen Thomas Erlewine*

☆ **For Your Pleasure** / 1973 / Virgin ✦✦✦✦✦
On Roxy Music's debut, the tensions between Brian Eno and Bryan Ferry propelled their music to great, unexpected heights, and for most of the group's second album, *For Your Pleasure*, the band equals, if not surpasses, those expectations. However, there are a handful of moments where those tensions become unbearable, as when Eno wants to move toward texture and Ferry wants to stay in more conventional rock territory; the nine-minute "The Bogus Man" captures such creative tensions perfectly, and it's easy to see why Eno left the group after the album was completed. Still, those differences result in yet another extraordinary record from Roxy Music, one that demonstrates even more clearly than the debut how avant-garde ideas can flourish in a pop setting. This is especially evident in the driving singles "Do the Strand" and "Editions of You," which pulsate with raw energy and jarring melodic structures. Roxy also illuminates the slower numbers, such as the eerie "In Every Dream Home a Heartache," with atonal, shimmering synthesizers, textures that were unexpected and innovative at the time of its release. Similarly, all of *For Your Pleasure* walks the tightrope between the experimental and the accessible, creating a new vocabulary for rock bands, and one that was exploited heavily in the ensuing decade. *—Stephen Thomas Erlewine*

Stranded / 1973 / Virgin ✦✦✦✦✦
Without Brian Eno, Roxy Music immediately becomes less experimental, yet it remains adventurous, as *Stranded* illustrates. Under the direction of Bryan Ferry, Roxy moves toward relatively straightforward territory, adding greater layers of piano and heavy guitars. Even without the washes of Eno's synthesizers, Roxy's music remains unsettling on occasion, yet in this new incarnation, they favor more measured material, whether it's the reflective "A Song for Europe" or the shifting textures of "Psalm." Even the rockers, such as the surging "Street Life" and the segmented "Mother of Pearl," are distinguished by subtle songwriting that emphasizes both Ferry's tortured glamour and Roxy's increasingly impressive grasp of sonic detail. *—Stephen Thomas Erlewine*

★ **Country Life** / 1974 / Virgin ✦✦✦✦✦
Continuing with the stylistic developments of *Stranded*, *Country Life* finds Roxy Music at the peak of its powers, alternating between majestic, unsettling art-rock and glamorous, elegant pop-rock. At their best, Roxy combines these two extremes, like on the exhilarating opener "The Thrill of it All," but *Country Life* benefits considerably from the ebb and flow of the group's two extremes, since it showcases the group's deft instrumental execution and their textured, enthralling songwriting. And, in many ways, *Country Life* offers the greatest and most consistent set of Roxy Music songs, illustrating their startling depth. From the sleek rock of "All I Want is You" and "Prairie Rose" to the elegant, string-laced pop of "A Really Good Time," *Country Life* is filled with thrilling songs, and Roxy Music rarely sounded as invigorating as they do here. *—Stephen Thomas Erlewine*

☆ **Siren** / 1975 / Virgin ✦✦✦✦✦
Abandoning the intoxicating blend of art-rock and glam-pop that distinguished *Stranded* and *Country Life*, Roxy Music concentrates on Bryan Ferry's suave, charming crooner persona for the elegantly modern *Siren*. As the discofied opener "Love is the Drug" makes clear, Roxy embraces dance and unabashed pop on *Siren*, weaving them into their sleek, arty sound. It does come at the expense of their artier inclinations, which is part of what distinguished Roxy, but the end result is captivating. Lacking the consistently amazing songs of its predecessor, *Siren* has a thematic consistency that works in its favor, and helps elevate its best songs—"Sentimental Fool," "Both Ends Burning," "Just Another High"—as well as the album itself into the realm of classics. *—Stephen Thomas Erlewine*

Viva! / 1976 / Virgin ✦✦

Manifesto / 1979 / Virgin ✦✦✦
Returning to action after four years of solo projects, Roxy Music redefined its sound and agenda on *Manifesto*. More than ever, Roxy sounds like Bryan Ferry's backing band, as the group strips away their art-rock influences, edits out the instrumental interludes in favor of concise pop songs, and adds layers of stylish disco rhythms. Although the songwriting is distressingly inconsistent, there are a number of wonderful moments on the record, particularly in the sighing "Angel Eyes" and the heartbroken "Dance Away." Still, trading sonic adventure for lush, accessible disco-pop isn't entirely satisfactory, even if it is momentarily seductive. *—Stephen Thomas Erlewine*

Flesh & Blood / 1980 / Virgin ✦✦
An even slicker record than *Manifesto*, *Flesh & Blood* precariously balances between alluringly seductive, sophisticated soul-pop and cloying, radio-ready disco-pop. At its best, the album is effortlessly suave and charming—"Over You" is one of their greatest singles, and "Oh Yeah" is nearly as persuasive—but much of the record is devoted to ill-formed, stylish lounge-pop. In particular, the reliance on reworked covers of "In the Midnight Hour" and "Eight Miles High" is distressing, not only because it signals a lack of imagination, but also because it suggests that *Flesh & Blood* is simply a lesser solo effort from Bryan Ferry. And even the handful of undeniably strong moments can't erase the feeling that Roxy Music was beginning to run out of ideas. *—Stephen Thomas Erlewine*

☆ **Avalon** / 1982 / Virgin ✦✦✦✦✦
Flesh & Blood suggested that Roxy Music was at the end of the line, but they regrouped and recorded the lovely *Avalon*, one of their finest albums. Certainly, the lush, elegant soundscapes of *Avalon* are far removed from the edgy avant-pop of their early records, yet it represents another landmark in their career. With its stylish, romantic washes of synthesizers and Ferry's elegant, seductive croon, *Avalon* simultaneously functioned as sophisticated make-out music for yuppies and as the maturation of synth-pop. Ferry was never this romantic or seductive, either with Roxy or as a solo artist, and *Avalon* shimmers with elegance in both its music and its lyrics. "More Than This," "Take a Chance With Me," "While My Heart is Still Beating" and the title track are immaculately crafted and subtle songs, where the shifting synthesizers and murmured vocals gradually reveal the melodies. It's a rich, textured album and a graceful way to end the band's career. *—Stephen Thomas Erlewine*

Street Life: 20 Greatest Hits / 1986 / Reprise ✦✦✦✦✦
While the packaging and song selection leave something to be desired, *Street Life: 20 Greatest Hits* is a strong collection of Roxy Music and Bryan Ferry's crossover hits. Ignoring Roxy's art-rock inclinations, the collection concentrates on latter-day hits like "More Than This," "Over You," "Love Is the Drug," and "Jealous Guy," adding early singles like "Virginia Plain," "Do the Strand" and "Pyjamarama" for good measure. But a large portion of the record is devoted to Ferry's solo material, not only mid-'80s hits like "Slave to Love" but also '70s covers like "A Hard Rain's A-Gonna Fall," "These Foolish Things" and "Let's Stick Together." Consequently, *Street Life* is rather uneven, but it is an adequate collection for anyone who wants all the hits on one disc. *—Stephen Thomas Erlewine*

Heart Still Beating / Oct. 30, 1990 / Virgin ✦✦

Thrill of It All / Nov. 20, 1995 / Virgin ✦✦✦✦✦
Album-rock artists like Roxy Music always make a difficult subject for comprehensive, multi-disc box sets. Frequently, their albums were designed as a cohesive whole and the idea of individual singles never really entered the picture at all. Roxy Music was slightly different than the average art/prog-rock band—not only did they make albums, they also made singles. And that is one of the reasons why the four-disc set *The Thrill of It All* is successful. Roxy's songs stand as individual works, and they make sense outside of their original context, even if they make more sense *within* their original context. Thankfully, the majority of each of their major albums are reproduced on the first three discs of this collection, leaving the fourth disc for non-LP singles, remixes, and B-sides. Most of this material has not been available on CD before, making *The Thrill of It All* essential for collectors. Nevertheless, it's a helpful guide to Roxy's career for casual fans—it contains all of the essential songs and shows why the group was one of the seminal bands of the '70s. *—Stephen Thomas Erlewine*

The Royal Guardsmen

f. 1965, Ocala, FL
Novelty, Bubblegum
The Royal Guardsmen from Ocala, Florida—Bill Balough (bass), John Burdett (drums), Chris Nunley (vocals), Tom Richards (guitar), Billy Taylor (organ), and Barry Winslow (vocals/guitar)—enjoyed their brief reign of pop fame in 1966-1968 by recording a series of songs taking off from the *Peanuts* cartoon character Snoopy and his fantasy about aerial dogfighting with German World War I flying ace Baron Von Richthofen. The million-selling "Snoopy Vs. the Red Baron" was the first and most successful of these novelty records in the fall of 1966, and its follow-up, "The Return of the Red Baron," also made the Top 40.

"Snoopy's Christmas" topped the seasonal charts at the end of 1967. After a few non-Snoopy singles were less successful, the Guardsmen released "Snoopy for President" in the summer of 1968, but the fad was over. The group scored a final Top 40 hit with its two-year-old, reissued debut single "Baby Let's Wait" in the winter of 1968-1969. The original group split in 1969; a version with some replacement members continued for another year. *—William Ruhlmann*

● **Anthology** / 1995 / One Way ✦✦✦✦✦
Of course, the heart of this hour-long, 20-track compilation is the series of Snoopy novelty hits enjoyed by the Royal Guardsmen in the mid-'60s, starting with the million-selling "Snoopy Vs. the Red Baron." The group had a few other singles chart entries, all of which are here, sometimes making reference to aerial themes ("Airplane Song [My Airplane]"). Though cute and catchy with their martial drumming and banjo picking, the Snoopy songs have a trash-rock quality in the tradition of "Louie, Louie" and "Hang on, Sloopy." Elsewhere, the group veers from one mid-'60s style to another, sometimes recreating the good-time sound of the Lovin' Spoonful, other times using harmonies that sound like the Association, then resorting to covers (an instrumental version of "So You Want to Be a Rock & Roll Star," "As Tears Go By"). Though they made four albums, this anthology, which brought them back into print in 1995, is a little more than anyone really needs of the Royal Guardsmen. *—William Ruhlmann*

Royal Trux

f. 1985, Chicago, IL, **db.** 2001
Noise-Rock, Indie Rock, Alternative Pop/Rock
From the noisy demise of underground kingpins Pussy Galore came two interesting bands. The first was Jon Spencer's blues deconstruction unit the Jon Spencer Blues Explosion; the second was Neil Hagerty and Jennifer Herrema's dissonant junkie nightmare known as Royal Trux. Interestingly, both bands started out as avant-noise combos playing little that resembled traditional rock & roll. After a protracted period of making harsh, nearly inaccessible records, both bands, by the mid-'90s, were making records that sounded like '70s rock, only with gobs more attitude and noise. Early Royal Trux (two self-titled records and *Twin Infinitives*) are, to say the least, extreme. Herrema and Hagerty played mostly beat-to-shit, thrift-store guitars, howled over the noise, and let a crappy little drum machine keep a beat. By 1993's *Cats and Dogs*, the duo began making music that sounded grimy and raunchy, the way the Stones did in the mid-'70s. After exhibiting a little stability, Royal Trux was signed by Virgin and cut 1995's *Thank You*, a great, greasy glob of lo-fi rock fueled by cigarettes and junk food. *Sweet Sixteen* followed in 1997, after which Virgin dropped the group and released tapes of 1998's *Accelerator* to the duo's previous label, Drag City. *—John Dougan*

Royal Trux [#1] / 1988 / Drag City ♦♦♦
Royal Trux's eponymous debut album is a virtually unlistenable collage of primitive guitar chords, clattering production, howled vocals and sheer white noise. Occasionally, the music showed signs of actual song structure, as well as shards of Stonesy blues, but it generally sounded like an abrasive, self-conscious deconstruction of classic rock. Either that, or the band simply didn't have a clue how to play their instruments. *—Stephen Thomas Erlewine*

Twin Infinitives / 1990 / Drag City ♦♦♦
Noisier and harsher than the group's debut, *Twin Infinitives* is a polarizing record—you either understand Royal Trux's primal, atonal deconstructions of rock & roll, or you think it's self-indulgent, unlistenable crap. Either way, *Twin Infinitives* is noteworthy for stretching the amateurish trash-rock of *Royal Trux* to the extreme, creating a defiantly noisy and abrasive assault of gutted riffs, screams, tinny synthesizers and melodic fragments. It may not be particularly listenable, but it is some sort of achievement. *—Stephen Thomas Erlewine*

Royal Trux [#2] / Oct. 5, 1992 / Drag City ♦♦♦
With their untitled 1992 album, Royal Trux tentatively abandoned the noise aesthetic of their first two albums and began writing real songs. Surprisingly, they were strong songs, bristling with the group's love of rock sleaze and junkie culture, as well as riffs that are captivatingly tough and sloppy. And Jennifer Herrema has never sounded as scarily sexy as she does throughout the album, slurring and snarling her bleak, disease-ridden lyrics with a compelling insolence. *Royal Trux* is still hampered by some meandering noise, but the emergence of real songs make them a primitive indie-rock band worth investigating. *—Stephen Thomas Erlewine*

Cats & Dogs / Jun. 14, 1993 / Drag City ♦♦♦♦♦
Recorded for America's number one low-fi underground label, *Cats and Dogs* was the first indication that Royal Trux could do more than whip up a tornado of distortion. A little less focused than *Thank You*, it still has its moments of splendor, especially when it sounds as though it's going to fall apart and, suddenly, comes back together. *—John Dougan*

Thank You / Apr. 1995 / Virgin ♦♦♦♦♦
I realize that this runs contrary to the beliefs of longtime Royal Trux fans, but the more Royal Trux resembles a standard rock band, the better they sound. If you want a little guitar skronk with your sci-fi surrealism (as in Herrema's lyrics), but like a little funky backbeat now and again, this is Royal Trux at their scuzzy best. It's still not for the weak, nor for those who like pretty melodies or great musicianship. But for the rest of us who like the occasional run through the jungle, songs like "The Sewers of Mars" and "You're Gonna Lose" are prime chunks of non-commercial alternative rock. It's a safe bet to assume that more '90s bands will continue to appropriate '70s rock stylings, but few will do it with the panache of Royal Trux. *—John Dougan*

Sweet Sixteen / Feb. 11, 1997 / Virgin ♦♦♦
Royal Trux always subverted classic rock by neglecting to learn how to play their instruments and taking the junkie myths of Keith Richards and Johnny Thunders as fact. When they moved to a major label with 1995's *Thank You*, they cleaned up their sound and wrote actual songs, so it makes sense that its followup, *Sweet Sixteen*, is where they learn how to stretch out on their instruments. Opening up with a riff lifted from the Allman Brothers, *Sweet Sixteen* is a sloppy mess, filled with grime, sleaze and filth—just like the broken toilet that graces the album's cover. While Royal Trux is now able to play these blues riffs, they don't have the desire to make them palatable. At heart, they still want to tap into what originally scared people about rock & roll, and to a certain extent they do—they are a viciously anti-social band, snarling vocals and throwing riffs out carelessly. However, they are falling into a netherworld with music that is too slick for indie and too weird for the mainstream, which means *Sweet Sixteen* is unlikely to appeal outside of their cult. *—Stephen Thomas Erlewine*

Singles Live Unreleased / Nov. 4, 1997 / Drag City ♦♦♦♦
Royal Trux celebrated their freedom from Virgin and return to Drag City by releasing *Singles Live Unreleased*, a sprawling double-disc set filled with rarities and obscurities. Sure, it seems like this falls into the "fans-only" category, but this mess has a certain charm. Also, in its own way, it captures what Royal Trux is all about, containing equal amounts of pretension, noise, blues-rock, attitude and menace. Neil Hagerty and Jennifer Herrema were the perfect fusion of the Rolling Stones and Sonic Youth, a concept which didn't always yield listenable or great results—how could it?—but when it worked, it was among the greatest indie-rock of their era. And while this is by definition arcane music, it also frequently captures the group at its best and, even better, captures the group the way they really are. *—Stephen Thomas Erlewine*

• **Accelerator** / Apr. 21, 1998 / Drag City ♦♦♦♦♦
Not long after they received *Sweet Sixteen*, complete with its notorious cover of an excrement- and vomit-filled toilet, Virgin Records realized Royal Trux may not be a crossover act. They were willing to let the band go, giving them severance pay and the master tapes to their recently completed album, *Accelerator*, which was then released on their old home, Drag City. Listening to the album, it's hard to believe that a major label funded such an exhilaratingly noisy record. Ostensibly the third installment in their ongoing salute to particular decades in rock history—i.e., *Thank You* took on the '60s, *Sweet Sixteen* saluted the '70s—Royal Trux deconstructs '80s rock on *Accelerator*, running all the instruments through some sort of electronic distortion, taking away the bass, trying to make it sound processed. Since this is Royal Trux, the result still is indebted to the Stones and astoundingly messy, but that's why *Accelerator* rocks like a demon, running over everything in sight. The album sounds chaotic, but there are some great songs hidden under the cacophony, like the explosive "I'm Ready," the soul vamp "Juicy, Juicy, Juice" and the soul-tinged closer "Stevie." Royal Trux have rarely had both their songwriting and noise under control like they do here, and the result is pure dynamite—possibly their best album to date. *—Stephen Thomas Erlewine*

Veterans of Disorder / Sep. 7, 1999 / Drag City ♦♦♦♦♦
With 1998's excellent *Accelerator*, Royal Trux completed their rock history trilogy and returned to Drag City. On *Veterans of Disorder*—the title of which attests to the band's mix of classic rock and noisy experimentation, and to their status as survivors of their own chaotic excesses—the Trux move forward and look back at the same time. Splitting the difference between their increasingly focused yet subversive rock and their early, sludgy experimentalism, *Veterans of Disorder* begins with seven (relatively) radio-friendly versions of the Trux aesthetic. "Waterpark" is an almost-straightforward raw charge led by Neil Hagerty's driving guitars and Jennifer Herrema's sultry, snarling vocals; the sexy "Second Skin" follows suit, and the duo shares vocal duties on "The Exception" and "Yo Se!"'s the Glimmer Twins-style funk. Latin percussion adds a twist to "Lunch Money," while "Witch's Tit" and "Stop" show off Royal Trux's softer side. None of these songs last longer than three and a half minutes, but the group crams as many big guitars and weird ideas as they can into these "singles." The album's second half returns to *Twin Infinitives*-era noise jams for inspiration, especially on the shambolic "Sickazz Dog." Herrema's wonderfully sneery vocals on "Coming Out Party" serve sharp-tongued lyrics like "He's going to be a playboy in his mind/He's trying to pretend he's making friends," while "Blue Is the Frequency" mixes jazz, cock rock, and a bit of slide guitar into a nearly nine-minute workout. Though the album sounds cleaner and more focused than anything Royal Trux released on Virgin, it's the duo's closest tie to their trashy underground roots. One of their most accomplished works, *Veterans of Disorder* could only be made by artists as creatively and financially independent as Royal Trux. *—Heather Phares*

Pound for Pound / Jun. 6, 2000 / Drag City ♦♦♦♦
On *Pound for Pound*, Royal Trux's second album within a year, the increasingly prolific group revisits the laid-back, scuzzy sound of albums like *Thank You* and *Sweet Sixteen*—albeit with a warmer, cleaner production, not unlike the sound they gave the Make Up's *In Mass Mind*. Touted by their label as a "party record," *Pound for Pound* comes pretty close to living up to that description, alternating between summery, boogie rock-inspired numbers like "Fire Hill" and "Dr. Gone" and more aggressive rockers like "Accelerator (The Original)" and "Teenage Murder Mystery." The Trux also find room for the almost-wistful summer love song "Sunshine," as well as the witchy blues-rock of "Deep Country Sorcerer" and "Small Thief," and despite the sound-effects weirdness on "Platinum Tips" and the trippy flutes on "Blind Navigator," this is their most straightforward collection of songs since their Virgin label output. Weighing in at a short and sweet ten tracks, *Pound for Pound* may not be as combustive or inventive as their recent output, but it reaffirms that there is plenty of room for just plain enjoyment in Royal Trux's subversive agenda. *—Heather Phares*

The Rubinoos

f. 1973, Berkeley, CA, **db.** 1983
Power Pop, New Wave
For a brief moment, San Francisco's the Rubinoos seemed to be the last hope for pure pop music, carrying on the tradition of the Raspberries with an engaging blend of innocent bubblegum and power pop. The band was formed in 1973 by teenage friends Jon Rubin (vocals, guitar) and Tommy Dunbar (guitar, keyboards, vocals) along with Royse Adler (bass) and Donn Spindt (drums) but it wasn't until 1977 that they made their recording debut for Beserkley Records. The single, a cover of Tommy James' "I Think We're Alone Now," made an appearance in the lower reaches of the U.S. charts, giving the indie label their first hit. The same year, their self-titled debut LP received rave reviews all around but failed commercially. *Back to the Drawing Board* (1979), another solid collection of bouncy pop songs, again went ignored despite its classic single "I Wanna Be Your Boyfriend." The band effectively broke up the following year. Rubin and Dunbar returned in 1983, contributing a pair of songs for the *Revenge of the Nerds* soundtrack and then teaming with producer Todd Rundgren for the *Party of Two* EP. "If I Had You Back" from the EP saw some airplay on MTV but it failed to ignite enough interest for the band to go on. *—Chris Woodstra*

• **The Rubinoos** / 1977 / Beserkley ♦♦♦♦♦
This little gem is a celebration of pop music. There's no other way to describe this record. Catchy tunes with a touch of tongue-in-cheek, mixed with exuberance and joy make this record as much fun as when it was first released. *—Jim Worbois*

Back to the Drawing Board / Jan. 1979 / Beserkley ♦♦♦
Overall, this is not quite as strong a record as the first one but still, not to be missed. There are some fine original tunes on this record and one quite interesting cover, "Hold Me," taken from *Three Faces of Eve*. *—Jim Worbois*

Party of Two / 1983 / Warner Brothers ♦♦

Basement Tapes: Studio Demos Circa 1980-1981 / 1994 / One Way ♦♦♦
Basement Tapes is a collection of studio demos from 1980 to 1981 for an intended album that never happened. And while it lacks the polish of production, the material stands up against their released output. The track-by-track comments by the band members are a nice touch. [Not Lame's 2000 reissue features three previously unreleased bonus tracks.] *—Chris Woodstra*

Garage Sale / Jul. 29, 1994 / Big Deal ♦♦♦
A nice companion piece to One Way's *Basement Tapes*, *Garage Sale* collects previously unreleased demos, alternate takes, and other oddities ranging from their earliest recordings in 1973 (at age 15) through 1985—complete with track-by-track commentary. This

provides an interesting look at a band with no shortage of great material. Essential for fans. —*Chris Woodstra*

Paleophonic / 1998 / Varese ✦✦✦✦
The first real Rubinoos recordings in over ten years, this delicious platter picks up where their classic recordings left off. With all original members present and accounted for (Jon Rubin on vocals and guitar, Tommy Dunbar on guitar and vocals, Donn Spindt on drums and vocals, and Al Chan, who joined in 1980, on bass and vocals), this is pure pop for all people. More Raspberries than Beatles, the Rubinoos play music from the heart filled with memorable hooks, glorious harmonies and honest sincerity. Although many years passed between the last time that these four recorded together, it seems that time stood still between those sessions. Immaculately produced by the late Kevin Gilbert, Dunbar comes up with another fine batch of songs that will melt your heart when Jon Rubin wraps his voice around 'em. It's great to hear the magic again. —*Steven "Spaz" Schnee*

Rufus

f. 1970, Chicago, IL, **db.** 1983
Quiet Storm, Funk, Soul
Rufus was one of the most commercially successful funk bands of the mid-'70s, primarily because lead vocalist Chaka Khan was a dynamic singer, capable of making even the band's pedestrian material seem interesting. Their self-titled debut album suffered from a lack of strong side material, but the follow-up featured Stevie Wonder's "Tell Me Something Good," which he wrote specifically for the band after hearing Khan sing; it became a number three hit single. After that song, the hits kept coming until the end of the '70s. Chaka Khan began a solo career that eventually eclipsed Rufus' success in 1978, continuing to record with the band until 1983; the group fell apart shortly after her departure. —*Stephen Thomas Erlewine*

Rufusized / 1974 / MCA ✦✦✦✦
Rags to Rufus / 1974 / MCA ✦✦✦✦✦
Rufus Featuring Chaka Khan / 1975 / MCA ✦✦✦✦
Ask Rufus / 1977 / MCA ✦✦✦✦
● **The Very Best of Rufus Featuring Chaka Khan** / Nov. 19, 1996 / MCA ✦✦✦✦✦
The Very Best of Rufus & Chaka Khan contains all of the group's biggest hits, including the number one R&B hits "You Got the Love," "Sweet Thing," "At Midnight (My Love Will Lift You Up)," "Do You Love What You Feel" and "Ain't Nobody," plus the Top 10 hits "Tell Me Something Good," "Stay," "Hollywood," "Sharing the Love" and "Dance Wit Me." —*Stephen Thomas Erlewine*

Rumour

f. 1975, **db.** 1980
Pub Rock, New Wave, Rock & Roll
The Rumour are best known as Graham Parker's backing band during his heyday, but the band also took a stab at their own recording career. And even though they were overshadowed by their association with Parker and never received much attention for their efforts, they did manage to make three albums of really enjoyable music in the mold of a new wave-ish pub-rock band.
  The Rumour consisted of pub-rock veterans Bob Andrews (keyboards) and Brinsley Schwarz (guitar/vocals) from the legendary Brinsley Schwarz, Martin Belmont (guitar/vocals) from Ducks Deluxe, and Stephen Goulding (drums/vocals) and Andrew Bodnar from Bontemps Roulez. The group formed in 1975 as Graham Parker's backing band, recording and touring with him off and on through 1980. In 1977, they signed their own deal with Phonogram and released their debut album, *Max*, the same year. They followed with *Frogs Sprouts Clogs and Krauts* for Stiff in 1979 and *Purity of Essence* in 1980, and also worked extensively as one of Stiff's house bands, backing up Elvis Costello on "Watching the Detectives," as well as Carlene Carter, Rachel Sweet, Nick Lowe, and Dave Edmunds. By the end of 1980, lack of real success on their own led to their breakup. —*Chris Woodstra*

Max / 1977 / Mercury ✦✦✦✦
On their debut, the Rumour play laidback pub-rock in a style (predictably) not too dissimilar to their work with Graham Parker, though it is looser and more in the style of later Brinsley Schwarz. *Max* is probably most noteworthy for the clear high point, the band's cover of Nick Lowe's "Mess With Love" (a song he wouldn't get around to recording himself until 1982's *Abominable Showman*), although the album is packed with some terrific music. —*Chris Woodstra*

Frogs, Sprouts, Clogs & Krauts / 1979 / Repertoire ✦✦✦
After signing to Stiff, the Rumour made a clear attempt to redefine themselves as a new wave band, incorporating quirky embellishments and more atmospheric keyboards. They're still a pub-rock band at heart, though, and the combination usually works quite well, at times making for some truly inspired moments like "Emotional Traffic," which sounds remarkably like a Nick Lowe song. —*Chris Woodstra*

Purity of Essence / 1980 / Hannibal ✦✦✦
Purity of Essence marked a successfully harder-rocking return to the pub, with a bunch of really good songs—mostly covers this time—that benefit from crisp new wave production, including the Bacharach/David tune "Little Red Book," Randy Newman's "Have You Seen My Baby," and Nick Lowe's "I Don't Want the Night to End." Unfortunately, the unremarkable, often half-hearted vocals fail to ignite the top-notch material for the most part. [*Purity of Essence* was issued in the U.S. in a rearranged order, dropping three songs in favor of three others, the most notable being a Glenn Tilbrook (Squeeze) original, "Depression," which was never recorded by Squeeze. The U.K. CD retains the original

tracks and adds "Name and Number" from the U.S. edition. The U.S. CD reissue in 1997 matches the U.K. edition.] —*Chris Woodstra*

● **Not Just a Rumour, More a Way of Life** / Mar. 20, 2001 / Metro ✦✦✦✦✦
Metro's *Not Just a Rumour, More a Way of Life* is a tremendous compilation of the Rumour's recordings for Stiff. Spanning 23 tracks on a single disc, this has the bulk of the albums and singles, with a couple of good rarities thrown in for good measure. This winds up being a wonderful summation of the band's strengths—they were a good, poppy rock & roll band, similar to Nick Lowe, Rockpile, Any Trouble, and, of course, Graham Parker, and this is the way to hear them at their best, even if you already have the albums. —*Stephen Thomas Erlewine*

Run-D.M.C.

f. 1982, Queens, NY
Hardcore Rap, East Coast Rap, Hip-Hop, Golden Age
More than any other hip-hop group, Run-D.M.C. is responsible for the sound and style of the music. As the first hardcore rap outfit, the trio set the sound and style for the next decade of rap. With its spare beats and excursions into heavy metal samples, the trio was tougher and more menacing than its predecessors Grandmaster Flash and Whodini. In the process, it opened the door for both the politicized rap of Public Enemy and Boogie Down Productions, as well as the hedonistic gangsta fantasies of N.W.A. At the same time, Run-D.M.C. helped move rap from a singles-oriented genre to an album-oriented one—they were the first hip-hop artist to construct full-fledged albums, not just a collection with two singles and a bunch of filler. By the end of the '80s, Run-D.M.C. had been overtaken by the groups they had spawned, but they continued to perform to a dedicated following well into the '90s. —*Stephen Thomas Erlewine*

☆ **Run-D.M.C.** / 1984 / Profile/Arista ✦✦✦✦✦
Undeniably, *Run-D.M.C.* is among the most influential rap albums ever. Before Run-D.M.C.'s ascension in the mid-'80s, rap hits tended to be melodic and danceable. Whether the inspiration for their tracks was Chic, Ashford & Simpson or Kraftwerk, hip-hop recordings were generally more interested in grooving than rocking—that is, until Run-D.M.C. had so enormous an impact on rap with "Rock Box," "Sucker MCs" and other abrasive classics included on this landmark debut album. When these self-proclaimed "Kings from Queens" took off in the mid-'80s, it became fashionable for rappers to use the type of abrasive, amelodic tracks heard here—many of which consist of little more than a drum machine and the influential Jam Master Jay's cutting and scratching. When they do employ some type of melody on "Rock Box," it isn't a Chic groove—but a crunching, Black Sabbath-like guitar. Run-D.M.C.'s daring rap/metal fusion, in fact, influenced everyone from Whodini to Ice-T to the Beastie Boys. [*Run-D.M.C.* was remastered and reissued in 1999.] —*Alex Henderson*

☆ **King of Rock** / 1985 / Profile/Arista ✦✦✦✦✦
Run-D.M.C.'s artistic winning streak continued with its superb second album, *King of Rock*. The fusion of rap and heavy metal the duo unveiled on "Rock Box" proved equally arresting on "You're Blind" and the title song, and the hip-hoppers' boasts were still among the finest in rap. Though boasting, rap's staple, can wear thin in a hurry, Run-D.M.C.'s boasts are consistently clever and often humorous. From the amusing "You Talk Too Much" to the insistent "Jam-Master Jammin'" to the inventive "Rots, Rap, Reggae," everything on *King of Rock* is a classic. By the end of the 1980s, fusing rap and reggae wasn't out of the ordinary—especially on the East Coast. But when Run-D.M.C. recorded "Roots, Rap, Reggae" in 1985, it was quite daring. [*King of Rock* was remastered and reissued in 1999.] —*Alex Henderson*

★ **Raising Hell** / 1986 / Profile/Arista ✦✦✦✦✦
Run-D.M.C. enjoyed its greatest triumph of all—both artistically and commercially—with its triple-platinum third album, *Raising Hell*. Much of the support that Run-D.M.C. enjoyed came from rock fans, and the MCs made their love of rock more than evident on "It's Tricky" (which samples the Knack's "My Sharona"), the forceful title song, and an inspired remake of Aerosmith's "Walk This Way" featuring Steve Tyler and Joe Perry themselves. Most of the other gems on *Raising Hell*—which range from the humorous "You Be Illin'" to the clever "My Adidas" to the uplifting "Proud to Be Black"—don't employ a screaming rock guitar. But even then, Run-D.M.C. is one of the loudest acts in hip-hop. [*Raising Hell* was remastered and reissued in 1999.] —*Alex Henderson*

Tougher than Leather / 1988 / Profile/Arista ✦✦✦✦
At the end of 1986, *Raising Hell* was rap's best-selling album up to that point, though it would soon be outsold by the Beastie Boys' *Licensed to Ill*. Profile Records hoped that Run-D.M.C.'s fourth album, *Tougher than Leather*, would exceed the Beastie Boys' quintuple-platinum status, but unfortunately, the group's popularity had decreased by 1988. One of Run-D.M.C.'s strong points—its love of rock & roll—was also its undoing in hip-hop circles. Any type of crossover success tends to be viewed suspiciously in the hood, and hardcore hip-hoppers weren't overly receptive to "Miss Elaine," "Papa Crazy," "Mary, Mary" and other rap/rock delights found on the album. Thanks largely to rock fans, this album did go platinum for sales exceeding one million copies—which ironically, Profile considered a disappointment. But the fact is that while *Tougher than Leather* isn't quite as strong as Run-D.M.C.'s first three albums, it was one of 1988's best rap releases. [*Tougher Than Leather* was remastered and reissued in 1999.] —*Alex Henderson*

Back from Hell / 1990 / Profile/Arista ✦✦✦
Longevity isn't a realistic goal for most rappers, who are lucky if they aren't considered played out by their third or fourth album. By 1990, Run-D.M.C.'s popularity had decreased dramatically, and the Queens residents had lost a lot of ground to both West Coast gangster rappers like Ice Cube, Ice-T and Compton's Most Wanted. With its fifth album, *Back from Hell*, Run-D.M.C. set out to regain the support of the hardcore rap audience and

pretty much abandoned rock-influenced material in favor of stripped-down, minimalist and consistently street-oriented sounds. Not outstanding but certainly enjoyable, such gritty reflections on urban life as "Livin' in the City," "The Ave." and "Faces" made it clear that Run-D.M.C. was still well worth hearing. [*Back from Hell* was remastered and reissued in 1999.] *—Alex Henderson*

★ **Together Forever: Greatest Hits 1983-1991** / Nov. 6, 1991 / Profile ✦✦✦✦✦
For the most part, all of Run D.M.C.'s most important singles and biggest hits are included on *Together Forever: Greatest Hits 1983-1991.* That alone makes the compilation a necessary purchase. However, that doesn't mean that it is a perfectly assembled collection. Instead of presenting the singles in chronological order, the sequencing skips back and forth—for example, it opens with "Sucker M.C.'s," jumps ahead to "Walk This Way," jumps further ahead to "Together Forever," then slams back to "King of Rock." Still, *Together Forever* has 18 of the groundbreaking group's absolutely essential items, from "It's Like That" and "Hard Times" to "It's Tricky" and "Run's House," which makes it an ideal introduction and an enjoyable retrospective. It's just not the definitive collection it could have been. *—Stephen Thomas Erlewine*

Down with the King / May 4, 1993 / Profile/Arista ✦✦✦

Crown Royal / Oct. 12, 1999 / Arista ✦✦

Run On

f. 1992, **db.** 1998
Indie Rock
New York's Run On combined their love of pop, rock, and the avant-garde into complex, eclectic but accessible music. The group's extensive history in New York's underground rock and noise/jazz circles made them comfortable with bouncy pop or extended improvs—and many of their songs employed both. Run On formed as the members' other projects slowly disintegrated. Drummer Rick Brown and vocalist/guitarist Sue Garner played in groups together for over a decade, including the seminal art band Fish & Roses. As Fish & Roses broke up, Brown and Garner began playing with guitarist Alan Licht, formerly of Love Child, forming Run On's creative nucleus. The trio recorded their debut 7", *Days Away*, in 1994 with Yo La Tengo's Ira Kaplan, and added a fourth member, trumpet player David Newgarden, later that year. After Newgarden joined Run On, the group began playing live and recorded their first EP, *On/Off*, this time with ex-Yo La Tengo bassist Gene Holder at the controls. As with their future releases, *On/Off* came out on Matador Records. *On/Off* also featured the mix of challenging and accessible musical ideas that became the group's signature approach with their 1996 full-length debut, *Start Packing*. The group's talent and heritage helped secure tours with like-minded bands such as Yo La Tengo, Tortoise, and the Dirty Three, with whom they played local and national gigs. By 1997, Newgarden left the band; violinist Katie Gentile joined in time for the recording of the group's second album, *No Way*, in 1997. Later that year, Run On also released the *Scoot* and *Sit Down* EPs. 1998 saw Brown and Garner retire the Run On name as Gentile returned to academic pursuits and her other band, Special Pillow. Garner and Brown continued to play and record together, in their Peach Cobbler project and other settings. *—Heather Phares*

On/Off / 1995 / Matador ✦✦✦✦
Run On's debut EP *On/Off* shows off a raw version of the group's sonic template: Sue Garner's alternately sweet and tough vocals come to the front over angular, buzzing guitar lines, blasts of organ and complex percussion. Marimbas enliven the instrumental "Switch On" and a distorted harmonica solo gives the art-punky "Into the Attic" a twist. The aptly-named "Pretty Note" lets Garner's languid vocals preside over softly noisy guitars, while "Water" features a tougher take on the group's sound. Finally, "Beat Out" mixes intricate percussion and droning vocals from Rick Brown with chiming guitars for a hypnotic effect. *On/Off* traces Run On's development as a band playing around with blending pop and avant leanings; though not every idea here is a great success, the textures, arrangements and songwriting are thoughtful and promising. *—Heather Phares*

● **Start Packing** / Feb. 27, 1996 / Matador ✦✦✦✦
Run On reached a very happy medium of innovative and accessible music with their 1996 full-length debut, *Start Packing*. The creative arrangements on the album's 12 songs add horns, marimbas, organs and electronics to complex guitar and drum patterns, whipping them all into an invigorating blast on songs like the album's first two songs ("Tried" and "Baap"). "Tried's" propulsive rhythm and noisy guitars duel with Sue Garner's exhilarated wail, while her street-smart hiss makes "Baap's" jittery bop all the more seductive. On both songs, Run On retains all the power of rock and the artfulness of jazz. "Go There" also captures a jazzy, slinky nastiness and harnesses it to droning organs and guitars. Run On's pop side also shines on *Start Packing*, particularly on "Doesn't Anybody Love the Dark," the album's bounciest, and strangely enough, sunniest moment. Though more downcast, "A to Z" also features tight, expressive songwriting, smart lyrics and endearingly adolescent vocals from guitarist Alan Licht, along with one of the album's best arrangements—a minimal use of marimba, guitar, maracas and voice used to maximum effect. "Xmas Trip" starts off like Jerry Lee Lewis' "Breathless," features a beautiful trumpet solo from David Newgarden and references Bernadette Peters and CBGB's in one breath, and makes it sound completely natural—no small feat. *Start Packing*'s scope also includes the group's noisy side, as the distortion-driven "Miscalculation" and sprawling, syncopated "Coffee" attest. Just as easily, Run On quiets down on the elegiac "You Said" and even wears their hearts on their sleeves with "Tell Me" and "In Strength," Garner's shout-out to her best friend. Though their grip on holding so many elements together falters a bit on the second half of the album, *Start Packing* is nevertheless an exciting and accomplished blend of diverse and often contrary creative forces. Easily one of the best and most eclectic indie-rock albums of the mid-'90s. *—Heather Phares*

No Way / Feb. 25, 1997 / Matador ✦✦✦✦✦
Run On's second full-length, 1997's *No Way*, continues the group's exciting blend of noise, rock and pop. This album, however, focuses the group's ideas into a more cohesive sound. "Something Sweet," "Lab Rats" and "Look" all feature a heady, fuzzed-out organ-and-guitar drone topped with Sue Garner's sultry, versatile voice. The jazz elements on *Start Packing* are also evident here, particularly in the songs' rhythms; "Bring Her Blues"' syncopated drums give the song an expansive dreaminess, while "Half of Half" begins with Garner's shivery singing and Rick Brown's abstract drumming and explodes into a shimmering chorus of guitars. Along with the other refinements to their sound, *No Way* also features Run On's newest member, violinist Katie Gentile. In particular, she shines in "Out for a Walk," "Ropa Vieja" and the deliciously sad "Anything You Say." The group's arrangements remain as artful as ever, especially on the marimba- and guitar-based cover of Nick Drake's "Road," and the brooding version of their own "Days Away," which consists of a spooky reedy organ and Garner's yearning voice. Best of all, Run On's songwriting remains intelligent and catchy on *No Way*, especially when a song like "As Good As New" takes lyrics like "I just woke up/I just fucked up/I just want to see you smile" and sets them to beautiful, fuzzy guitar pop. Run On's expansive but controlled musical vision makes sure their music is never predictable or willfully obscure, and happily, *No Way* is no exception. *—Heather Phares*

The Runaways

f. 1975, Los Angeles, CA, **db.** 1979
Heavy Metal, Hard Rock
Dismissed during their existence as a crass marketing gimmick, the Runaways have grown in stature over the years as the first all-female band to make a substantial impression on the public by playing loud, straight-up, guitar-driven rock & roll. Since all of the members were teenagers (some of whom were still learning to play their instruments when they passed their auditions), their music was frequently raw and amateurish, but it neatly combined American heavy metal (think Aerosmith and Kiss) with the newly emerging sound of punk rock. In the media, the Runaways were victims of their own hype, supplied by maverick promoter/manager Kim Fowley. Fowley's insistence on a sleazy jailbait image for the group made it easy for the press to dismiss them as nothing but a tasteless adolescent fantasy—an impression bolstered at the time by the admittedly erratic quality of their music. But in the end, the Runaways' sound and attitude proved crucially important in paving the way for female artists to crank up the volume on their guitars and rock as hard as the boys; plus, they produced one undeniably classic single in the rebel-girl manifesto "Cherry Bomb." An even better indicator that there was more to the Runaways' music than met the eye was the success of Joan Jett's solo career. Jett formed her own band and record label, landed an enormous number one smash with 1982's "I Love Rock & Roll," and continued to produce albums of tough hard rock into the '90s. The heavily feminist riot grrrl punk movement claimed Jett as a major inspiration, prompting a re-examination of the Runaways' output divorced from Kim Fowley's marketing tactics. *—Steve Huey*

The Runaways / 1976 / Touchwood ✦✦✦✦✦
When the Runaways debuted in 1976 with this self-titled LP, aggressive female rockers were the exception instead of the rule. Women had no problem becoming folk-rockers, singer-songwriters or Top 40 icons, but female artists who had more in common with Led Zeppelin and Aerosmith than Joni Mitchell were hardly the norm. With this album, the Runaways made it crystal clear that women (or specifically, adolescent girls) were more than capable of playing intense, forceful hard rock that went directly for the jugular. Lusty classics like "Cherry Bomb" and "You Drive Me Wild" made no attempt to conceal the fact that teenage girls could be every bit as sexual as the guys—a message that both men and women found intimidating. And on "Is It Day or Night," Cherie Currie sings about life in the fast lane with every bit as much conviction as Axl Rose would eleven years later. Currie and Joan Jett are equally riveting, and a 17-year-old Lita Ford was already an impressive guitarist. This LP was far from a commercial hit in the U.S., where timid rock radio programmers simply didn't know what to make of the Runaways. But interestingly, it did earn the band a strong following in the major rock market of Japan. *—Alex Henderson*

Queens of Noise / 1977 / Touchwood ✦✦✦✦✦
The Runaways didn't compromise a bit on their outstanding sophomore effort, *Queens of Noise*. Melodic yet tough and aggressive, this is hard rock that pulls no punches either musically or lyrically. Classics like "Neon Angels (On the Road to Ruin)," "Take It or Leave It" and "I Love Playing With Fire" wouldn't have been shocking coming from Aerosmith or Kiss, but suburban adolescent girls singing openly and honestly about casual sex, intoxication, and wild, all-night parties was certainly radical for 1977. Joan Jett and Cherie Currie articulated the thoughts and feelings of the "bad girls" Kiss and countless others were describing, and they didn't hesitate to say that yes, women fantasized about sex. "Johnny Guitar" is a fine vehicle for guitarist/singer Lita Ford, who had solid chops before she was old enough to vote. *Queens of Noise* would be Currie's last album with the groundbreaking band. *—Alex Henderson*

Waitin' for the Night / 1977 / Mercury ✦✦✦

Live in Japan / 1977 / Mercury ✦✦

● **The Best of the Runaways** / 1987 / Mercury ✦✦✦✦✦
A good collection of the Runaways' finest moments, *Best of the Runaways* is the only consistently enjoyable disc from these trashy hard-rockers. *—Stephen Thomas Erlewine*

Todd Rundgren

b. Jun. 22, 1948, Upper Darby, PA

Saxophone, Keyboards, Drums, Piano, Guitar, Bass, Synthesizer / Album Rock, Comedy Rock, Blue-Eyed Soul, Proto-Punk, Pop/Rock, Power Pop, Soft Rock, Prog-Rock/Art Rock, Hard Rock

Todd Rundgren's best-known songs —- the Carole King pastiche "I Saw the Light," the ballads "Hello, It's Me" and "Can We Still Be Friends," and the goofy novelty "Bang on the Drum All Day"—suggest that he is a talented pop craftsman, but nothing more than that. On one level, that perception is true, since he is undoubtedly a gifted pop songwriter, but at his core Rundgren is a rock & roll maverick. Once he had a taste of success with his 1972 masterwork *Something/Anything?*, Rundgren chose to abandon stardom and, with it, conventional pop music. He began a course through uncharted musical territory, becoming a pioneer not only in electronic music and prog-rock, but in music video, computer software and Internet music delivery. As his career wound into its third decade, Rundgren concentrated on behind-the-scenes innovations, but during the '70s and '80s he maintained a relentless work schedule, releasing up to two albums a year, either as a solo artist or with his band Utopia, while producing acclaimed, successful records for artists as diverse as Badfinger, Meat Loaf, Grand Funk Railroad, the New York Dolls and XTC. Given such an extensive catalog, it's not surprising that there's a vast variety of styles within Rundgren's music—which is either rewarding or frustrating, depending on the album. Also, more often than not, the singles from each record do not offer an accurate indication of what the remainder of the album sounds like. Such an approach severely curtailed his mass appeal, but it helped him cultivate a ferociously dedicated cult audience. *—Stephen Thomas Erlewine*

Runt / Sep. 1970 / Bearsville/Rhino ✦✦✦✦✦

Reluctant to start a full-fledged solo career after leaving the Nazz, Todd Rundgren formed Runt, a band that was a front for what was in effect a solo project. Such isolationism lends *Runt* its unique atmosphere—it is the insular work of a fiercely talented artist finally given the opportunity to pursue his off-kilter musical vision. From the moment the slow, bluesy psychedelic grind of "Broke Down and Busted" starts the album, it's apparent that Rundgren could never have made *Runt* with the Nazz—and that's before the introspective ballads or the willfully strange stuff kicks in. Throughout the record, Rundgren reveals himself as a gifted synthesist, blending all manners of musical styles and quirks into a distinctive signature sound. He's as interested in sound as he is in song and while he would later pursue these tendencies to extremes, *Runt* finds him learning how to create an effective sound with the studio, which may be the reason why the album runs the gamut from hard rockers like "Who's That Man?" to ballads like "Once Burned." Although these songs are instantly appealing, the album really gets interesting when he reaches between those two extremes, whether it's in the classic pop medley "Baby Let's Swing," the bizarrely tongue-in-cheek "I'm in the Clique," or the equally impish "We Gotta Get You a Woman," which gave Rundgren his first hit. All the details buried within these songs—not only in the deceptively direct productions, but within the writing itself—confirm Rundgren's exceptional skill at songcraft. He occasionally slips on *Runt*, delivering tracks that rely on production instead of a blend of studiocraft and songcraft, but it remains a thoroughly impressive debut and one of his finest pop records. *—Stephen Thomas Erlewine*

☆ **Runt: The Ballad of Todd Rundgren** / Jun. 1971 / Ampex ✦✦✦✦✦

Upon its release, *Rolling Stone* called *The Ballad of Todd Rundgren* "the best album Paul McCartney" never made, and even if the album doesn't sound particularly McCartney-esque, it does share the homespun, melodic charm of the best of his early albums. Arguably, it's better than Paul's solo work, since it is focused and subtle, never drawing attention to Rundgren's considerable skills as a writer and producer. He tones down the hard rock and his impish wit, lending the album a sense of direction missing on *Runt*. That's not to say he abandoned his sense of humor—as if the cover shot of Rundgren sitting at a piano with a noose around his neck left any doubt. This time around, it takes some careful listening to hear the jokes, such as the opening Floyd Cramer piano lick on "Range War." On such clever in-jokes as "Chain Letter," as well as ballads like "Hope I'm Around," the artist reveals himself as an exceptional craftsman and songsmith. In fact, *Ballad* is considerably more song-oriented than its predecessor, with very little of the jams and instrumental sections that occasionally bogged down *Runt*. Here, even propulsive pop tunes such as "Bleeding" and "Long Flowing Robe," along with the hard rocker "Parole," are as much about the song as the performance, which is probably appropriate for an album called *The Ballad of Todd Rundgren*. Another thing about that title—it may be a joke, but the album inarguably offers a glimpse into Rundgren's inner world through a combination of introspective ballads, off-hand jokes, musical virtuosity, outright weirdness, and unabashed showmanship. And that's the charm of *The Ballad*—it's the slyly sardonic masterwork of a loner who may be sensitive, but is certainly not shy. *—Stephen Thomas Erlewine*

★ **Something/Anything?** / Feb. 1972 / Bearsville/Rhino ✦✦✦✦✦

Others had recorded one-man albums before Todd Rundgren, most notably Stevie Wonder and Paul McCartney, but with *Something/Anything?* he captured the homemade ambience of *McCartney* with the visionary feel of *Music of My Mind*, adding an encyclopedic knowledge of pop music from Gilbert & Sullivan through Jimi Hendrix, plus the crazed zeal of a pioneer. Listening to *Something/Anything?* is a mind-altering trip in itself, no matter how many shamelessly accessible pop songs are scattered throughout the album, since each side of the double-record is a concept unto itself. The first is "a bouquet of ear-catching melodies"; side two is "the cerebral side"; on side three "the kid gets heavy"; side four is his mock pop operetta, recorded with a full band including the Sales Brothers. It gallops through everything—Carole King tributes ("I Saw the Light"), classic ballads ("Hello It's Me," "It Wouldn't Have Made Any Difference"), Motown ("Wolfman Jack"), blinding power pop ("Couldn't I Just Tell You"), psychedelic hard rock ("Black Maria"), pure weirdness ("I Went to the Mirror"), blue-eyed soul ("Dust in the Wind"), and scores of brilliant songs that don't fall into any particular style ("Cold Morning Light," "It Takes Two to Tango"). It's an amazing journey that's remarkably unpretentious. Rundgren peppers his writing with self-aware, self-deprecating asides, indulging his bizarre sense of humor with gross-outs ("Piss Aaron") and sheer quirkiness, such as an aural tour of the studio at the beginning of side two. There are a ton of loose ends throughout *Something/Anything?*, plenty of studio tricks, slight songs (but no filler), snippets of dialogue, and purposely botched beginnings, but all these throwaways simply add context—they're what makes the album into a kaleidoscopic odyssey through the mind of an insanely gifted pop music obsessive. *—Stephen Thomas Erlewine*

☆ **A Wizard, A True Star** / Mar. 1973 / Bearsville/Rhino ✦✦✦✦✦

Something/Anything? proved that Todd Rundgren could write a pop classic as gracefully as any of his peers, but buried beneath the surface were signs that he would never be satisfied as merely a pop singer-songwriter. A close listen to the album reveals the eccentricities and restless spirit that surges to the forefront on its follow-up, *A Wizard, A True Star*. Anyone expecting the third record of *Something/Anything?*, filled with variations on "I Saw the Light" and "Hello It's Me," will be shocked by *A Wizard*. As much a mindfuck as an album, *A Wizard, A True Star* rarely breaks down to full-fledged songs, especially on the first side, where songs and melodies float in and out of a hazy post-psychedelic mist. Stylistically, there may not be much new—he touched on so many different bases on *Something/Anything?* that it's hard to expand to new territory—but it's all synthesized and assembled in fresh, strange ways. Often, it's a jarring, disturbing listen, especially since Rundgren's humor has turned bizarre and insular. It truly takes a concerted effort on the part of the listener to unravel the record, since Rundgren makes no concessions—not only does the soul medley jerk in unpredictable ways, but the anthemic closer, "Just One Victory," is layered with so many overdubs that it's hard to hear its moving melody unless you pay attention. And that's the key to understanding *A Wizard, A True Star*—it's one of those rare rock albums that demands full attention and, depending on your own vantage, it may even reward such close listening. *—Stephen Thomas Erlewine*

Todd / Feb. 1974 / Bearsville/Rhino ✦✦✦

Maybe some listeners thought that the sonic trip *A Wizard, A True Star* was a necessary exercise in indulgence and that he would return to the sweet pop of *Something/Anything?* for its follow-up. Not a chance. As it turned out *A Wizard* was the launch pad for further dementia—and, depending on your point of view, indulgence. Its follow-up was *Todd*, an impenetrable double album filled with detours, side roads, collisions and the occasional pop tune. That those pop tunes are among his best may come as little consolation to the lightweight fan who has stumbled upon *Todd*. Conceptually, *A Wizard, A True Star* may be the wilder record, but *Todd* is a more difficult listen, thanks to the layers of guitar solos and blind synth prog tunes, such as "In and Out the Chakras We Go." Large stretches of the album are purely instrumental, foreshadowing the years of synth experiments with Utopia that were just around the corner. The murk subsides every so often, revealing either exquisite ballads ("A Dream Goes on Forever"), blistering rock ("Heavy Metal Kids") or, more murk and dementia (particularly with how Gilbert & Sullivan rear their heads not only on the requisite novelty "An Elpee's Worth of Tunes," but an honest-to-goodness cover of "Lord Chancellor's Nightmare Song"). These are some major additions to his catalog, but the experiments and the excesses are too tedious to make *Todd* a necessary listen for anyone but the devoted. But for those listeners, the gems make the rough riding worthwhile. *—Stephen Thomas Erlewine*

Initiation / May 1975 / Bearsville/Rhino ✦✦

Returning to solo recording almost immediately after forming Utopia, Todd Rundgren continued with the synth-heavy prog-rock he pioneered with *Todd Rundgren's Utopia* on *Initiation*. The differences immediately resonate with "Real Man," a terrific song that encapsulates not only his newfound fondness for electronics, but also his burgeoning spirituality and his knack for pop craft. "Real Man" is so good, it's tempting to believe that the remainder of *Initiation* will follow in the same direction, resulting in an inspired, truly progressive fusion of classic Rundgren and synthesizers. As soon as the second track, an a cappella vocoder opus called "Born to Synthesize," it's clear that Rundgren has no intention of following that path, choosing to push the limits of synth technology and recorded music instead of constructing an album. *Initiation* suffers accordingly. At times, particularly on the first, song-oriented side, it is pretty intriguing, but too often, the results are simply frustrating because it doesn't go anywhere. That's particularly true with "A Treatise on Cosmic Fire," a half-hour "suite" that comprises all of side two and doesn't really go anywhere, despite hitting many stops along the way. It's enough to erase the memory of "Real Man," "Eastern Intrigue" and "Initiation," the moments where it all comes together on the first half of the record, but another spin of the first side reveals that Rundgren could have made *Initiation* something special if he had the discipline. *—Stephen Thomas Erlewine*

Faithful / Apr. 1976 / Bearsville/Rhino ✦✦✦

Todd Rundgren considered 1966 the beginning of his professional musical career, largely because the Nazz formed around that time. As a celebration, he recorded *Faithful*. Presumably, *Faithful* celebrates the past and the future by juxtaposing a side of original pop material with a side of covers. Actually, "covers" isn't accurate—the six oldies that comprise the entirety of side one are re-creations, with Rundgren "faithfully" replicating the sound and feel of the Yardbirds ("Happenings Ten Years Time Ago"), Bob Dylan ("Most Likely You Go Your Way and I'll Go Mine"), Jimi Hendrix ("If Six Was Nine"), the Beach Boys ("Good Vibrations") and the Beatles ("Rain," "Strawberry Fields Forever"). All of this is entertaining, to a certain extent, especially since it's remarkable how close Rundgren comes to duplicating the very feel of the originals. Still, it's hard to see it as much more than a flamboyant throwaway, especially when compared with the glorious second side. For the first time since *Something/Anything?*, Rundgren allows himself to write and—more importantly—record straight-ahead pop songs. Certainly, *A Wizard, Todd* and *Initiation* had their share of great songs, but they weren't delivered as pop songs; they were telegraphed as art. Here, Rundgren delivers pop and rock songs with ease, letting the melodies glide to the forefront. There are embellishments, of course, but the end result is a lushness that's apparent even on the hard rockers. If Rundgren had made all of *Faithful* originals, it would have been a pure pop masterpiece. As it stands, it's essential for the faithful—not only for hardcore Toddheads, but for devoted pop fans as well. *—Stephen Thomas Erlewine*

Hermit of Mink Hollow / Apr. 1978 / Bearsville/Rhino ✦✦✦✦✦
Over the course of 1977, Todd Rundgren moved Utopia toward a more pop-oriented direction, winding up with the slick mainstream arena-rock of *Oops! Wrong Planet.* With that in mind, it makes sense that *The Hermit of Mink Hollow*—his first full-fledged solo album since *Initiation*, if you discount the half-cover/half-original *Faithful*—finds Rundgren in his pop craftsman persona. The difference is, he's heartbroken. His relationship with Bebe Buell collapsed during 1977 and it's clear that the separation has pained him, since pain and melancholy underpin the album, whether it's on ballads ("Can We Still Be Friends") or on apparently joyous revelries, like "All the Children Sing." That said, this is a Rundgren solo album and he has not abandoned his trademarks, which means that the lush ballads are paired with novelties ("Onomatopoeia," which sounds exactly how you hope it does), ersatz soul ("You Cried Wolf") and pure pop ("Hurting for You"). *Hermit* is also the first record Rundgren recorded completely alone since *Something/Anything?.* Where that record sounded like the inner workings of a madman, with each song providng no indication what the next would sound like, *Hermit* is more cohesive. It also feels less brilliant, even if it is, in many ways, nearly as excellent as Rundgren's masterwork, mainly because it doesn't have such a wide scope. Still, the reason *The Hermit of Mink Hollow* is such a milestone in Rundgren's career is because it's a small album, filled with details, and easily the most emotional record he made. *—Stephen Thomas Erlewine*

Back to the Bars / Dec. 1978 / Bearsville/Rhino ✦✦✦
Following a year of Utopia and the completion of *The Hermit of Mink Hollow*, Todd Rundgren hit the road with a musical retrospective on the advice of Bearsville president Paul Fishkin, who wanted a live greatest-hits record to plug. Ever perverse, that's not exactly what Rundgren delivered. Culled from three shows—where he was supported by both Utopia and a carefully assembled band at New York's Bottom Line, one at L.A.'s the Roxy, one at Cleveland's the Agora—the resulting double album *Back to the Bars* was an idiosyncratic collection of hits and personal favorites, covering many (but not all) of his best songs, from "I Saw the Light," "Couldn't I Just Tell You," "Hello It's Me" and "Real Man" to "The Range War," "Sometimes I Don't Know What to Feel" and "The Verb 'To Love.'" All of the performances are tough and persuasive—enough so that the songs that sounded like production numbers on record, such as large stretches of *A Wizard, A True Star*, reveal themselves as effective compositions and often sound a great deal more accessible here. That said, *Back to the Bars* isn't an ideal introduction to Rundgren, simply because his studio wizardry is one of the main reasons his records are so interesting, yet it is true that the record has enough great songs and quirks to paint an effective portrait of Rundgren's music. As such, it's the rare live album that caters to both the casual and hardcore fan and should be equally enjoyable to either audience. *—Stephen Thomas Erlewine*

Healing / Feb. 1981 / Rhino ✦✦✦
Healing is a subdued, reflective effort unlike anything else in Todd Rundgren's catalog. Certainly, there are some familiar elements throughout *Healing*, particularly on majestic ballads like "Compassion," but there are more new variations on his style since any album since *Initiation.* Not coincidentally, that record had hints of the spirituality that surges to the forefront on *Healing*, but it was nowhere near as musically focused as the latter record. Apart from "Compassion," there is a true lack of singles, which doesn't mean that there aren't standouts—since "Golden Goose" has a weird, jerky hook and the opener "Healer" is a terrific pop single—that stand on their own merit. Instead, the record works as a whole, flowing as seamlessly as *Something/Anything?* or *Hermit.* Unfortunately, it's not as strong as either of those records, largely because it's about texture and spirit, not individual songs. In a case like that, the music and ambience are as important as the actual songs, and while they're often very provocative, they tend to meander as well, particularly on the three-part "Healing" suite that comprises the last side of the record. On CD, its calming effect is dissipated because the bonus 7" single "Time Heals"/"Tiny Demons" is added at the end. Their presence makes it clear that *Healing* was intended as an album unto itself, without much in the way of singles, because each song—the former being excellent new wave pop, the other a fine ballad—could have been a single unto itself. In this context, they may deflate the lasting spiritual impression of the album, but they add musical weight, helping make the disc a fine effort. *—Stephen Thomas Erlewine*

The Ever Popular Tortured Artist Effect / Jan. 1983 / Rhino ✦✦✦✦
As the early '80s continued to unfold, Todd Rundgren grew increasingly disenchanted with Bearsville, especially since the label wasn't supporting Utopia. He wrangled the band free in 1982, but he still had to deliver solo records to Bearsville. Not entirely pleased with the situation, Rundgren hammered out a collection of pop songs on his own, cynically titling the effort *The Ever Popular Tortured Artist Effect.* In later years, Rundgren disavowed the album, but it stands as one of his better collections of pop songs, even if it lacks a theme or a unifying sound. There are a fair share of throwaways, not only coming in the expected form of covers (a fine but pointless remake of the Small Faces' "Tin Soldier") and Gilbert & Sullivan parodies ("Emperor of the Highway"), but also in the monumentally silly "Bang the Drum All Day," which not only became a hit, but a hit that refused to die, lasting as a radio staple into the late '90s. These three songs are anomalies on *Tortured Artist*, which for the most part is pure pop and pop-soul, delivered with little fuss or pretention. There's also little deep meaning to the songs themselves, which is quite unusual for Rundgren, yet the best tunes—"Hideaway," "Influenza," "There Goes Your Baybay," "Drive," "Chant"—are indelible, irresistible pop confections that prove Rundgren can be quite involving, even when he's not trying his hardest. *—Stephen Thomas Erlewine*

A Cappella / Sep. 1985 / Rhino ✦✦✦
A Cappella was the end of the road, as far as Bearsville was concerned. Rundgren, who was already at odds with the label and had taken his Utopia elsewhere, had to struggle to get the label to release the record, and it didn't hit the shelves officially until Warner stepped in and negotiated him out of the contract. Perhaps Bearsville didn't want to release *A Cappella* because they perceived it to be too weird, too bizarre to cross over into the mainstream, which is true. However, that thread of logic ignores the fact that ever since 1973, Rundgren had positioned himself as a cult artist. He may have proven himself to be an enormously successful cult artist, one capable of landing the odd hit single every now and then, but he remained a cult artist precisely because he was willing to take risks like *A Cappella*, an album he created entirely with his voice. To some listeners, such a tactic seemed like a gimmick, which is a fair criticism, since the compositions themselves don't necessarily explore new ground (he even throws in the requisite novelties and covers). Then again, the production and the recording are precisely the point of *A Cappella*, and that's why it's such an involving listen. Many times, it's hard to believe that all of the sounds on the record originated from the same larynx, since each layer of the production is filled with astonishing details. Even more impressively, by forcing himself to use just his voice (albeit electronically processed), Rundgren has devised fresh, unexpected arrangements that enliven a set of solid but unrevelatory songs. That inventive spirit is enough to turn *A Cappella* into something unique and special. *—Stephen Thomas Erlewine*

Anthology (1968-1985) / May 1989 / Rhino ✦✦✦✦
The flagship of Rhino's Todd Rundgren reissue series was *Anthology (1968-1985)*, a double-disc set that traced the rock & roll maverick's career from the Nazz through his decade and a half with Bearsville Records. Designed as the definitive statement of Rundgren's solo work (his work with Utopia received its own *Anthology*), *Anthology* comes very close to fulfilling its goal. Since it covers so much ground, it's inevitable that a few essential items and fan favorites are missing, especially since Rundgren was incredibly prolific during these 17 years. And it is true that early masterpieces like "I'm in the Clique," "Once Burned," "Chain Letter," "The Range War" and "Long Flowing Robe" are missing, as are several highlights from *Something/Anything?*, but in their place are stronger tracks from less consistent albums, which makes it a nice retrospective for converted fans who want a comprehensive compilation to supplement the acknowledged classics. That said, the curious or casual listener may find *Anthology* a bit too sprawling for their tastes, even it does provide an excellent summary of Rundgren's heyday as a cult recording artist. In that case, Rhino's *The Very Best of Todd Rundgren* is a good choice, since it is a more concise collection that contains all the hits and rock-bottom essentials, plus several Utopia cuts and "The Want of a Nail." *—Stephen Thomas Erlewine*

Nearly Human / May 1989 / Warner Brothers ✦✦✦✦
As the '80s drew to a close, Todd Rundgren turned over a new leaf with his first album recorded specifically for Warner Bros. Not long after the release of *A Cappella*, he separated from Bearsville and disbanded Utopia, choosing to embark on a few years as a producer and session man. He finally returned with *Nearly Human*, his first album of new material in four years, in the summer of 1989. During his hiatus as a recording artist, Rundgren became fascinated with recording live music, deciding to record *Nearly Human* live in the studio—not nearly as flamboyant as *A Cappella*, but a gimmick nonetheless. If anything, the live-in-the-studio gimmick works better than the all-vocal track, not only because it's easier to execute, but because the production style complements the soul-inflected songs. Song for song, *Nearly Human* is his best record since *The Hermit of Mink Hollow*, since not only is the bulk of the album filled with charging blue-eyed soul like "The Want of a Nail" or sweet ballads like "Parallel Lines," but because there are no novelties and the cover choice (Elvis Costello's "Two Little Hitlers") is fresh and surprising. At times, his eccentricities get the best of him, as he overstuffs his arrangements or lyrics with unnecessary details, but these are minor points—*Nearly Human* finds Rundgren at the top of his game as a performer, producer and songwriter, sustaining his momentum in a way he hadn't for nearly a full decade. *—Stephen Thomas Erlewine*

Second Wind / Jan. 1991 / Warner Brothers ✦✦✦
Todd Rundgren's last major-label album was recorded in July 1990, at the Palace of Fine Arts Theatre in San Francisco before a live audience, although under recording studio conditions, with a backup band that included some local talent: Roger Powell of Utopia, Vince Welnick (who would join the Grateful Dead later in the year), Prairie Prince of the Tubes, Ross Valory of Journey, and Jenni Muldaur. It's a mixed set, including three songs Rundgren wrote for the off-Broadway musical *Up Against It*, which was based on an unproduced screenplay British playwright Joe Orton wrote in the 1960s for the Beatles. Those songs have a Kurt Weill-ish tone, while songs like "Love Science" are up-tempo R&B and the leadoff track, "Change Myself," is in Rundgren's familiar pop/rock style. On the whole, though, there's nothing to get excited about here. *—William Ruhlmann*

No World Order / Jul. 6, 1993 / Forward/Rhino ✦✦

The Individualist / 1995 / Digital ✦✦

● **The Very Best of Todd Rundgren** / Jul. 22, 1997 / Rhino ✦✦✦✦✦
The Very Best of Todd Rundgren distills the Runt's career to just the hit singles, which is

surprsisingly effective. Most casual Todd fans will only want the hits—"We Gotta Get You A Woman," "I Saw the Light," "Hello, It's Me," "Bang on the Drum"—and not invest in the double-disc set *Anthology (1968-1985)*, which simply contains too much music for most listeners. With *The Very Best of*, all of the good stuff (including "The Want of a Nail," which is not on *Anthology*) is here, satisfying the needs of the casual and curious. *—Stephen Thomas Erlewine*

With a Twist / Sep. 23, 1997 / Guardian ✦✦

One Long Year / Jun. 20, 2000 / Artemis ✦✦✦
During the last quarter of the '90s, Todd Rundgren spent much of his time on the Internet, distributing music and previews of his in-progress autobiography through his net service, Patronet. Hence, the appearance of *One Long Year*, a disc that collects highlights from the Patronet service, plus a couple odds and ends. Technically, it doesn't have a cohesive concept like *With a Twist* or *TR-I*, but that's fine, because its patchwork quality is not only charming, it results in a ragged, multifaceted pop charmer reminiscent of 1982's *The Ever Popular Tortured Artist Effect*. Like that album, *One Long Year* boasts a fair share of sparkling pop gems. This time around, it's not quite as pop oriented or tuneful, since there are a re-recording of "Love of the Common Man" and a cut-and-paste instrumental ("Mary and the Holy Ghost") among the rockers, ballads, and pop tunes. This may result in choppy momentum, but diehards are much more likely to appreciate these quirks rather than be alienated by them. They'd be right to accept them, since the gems are things to embrace. "I Hate My Frickin ISP" may be a goofy rant at Internet service providers, but it has a hook and it rocks, just like the cheerfully sleazy "Yer Fast (And I Like It)." It doesn't all drive hard, however, there are sweet moments like "Buffalo Grass" and "The Surf Talks" that give the album an appealing sheen. True, this doesn't really make *One Long Year* a classic—even a second-tier Rundgren classic like, say, *Tortured Artist*—but it is a highly enjoyable patchwork that illustrates that Rundgren remains a restless musical experimenter and a first-class pop craftsman. And that's enough for anybody that's curious about a new Rundgren album in 2000. *—Stephen Thomas Erlewine*

Go Ahead Ignore Me: The Best of Todd Rundgren / Oct. 31, 2000 / Castle ✦✦✦✦✦
Todd Rundgren has been the subject of several greatest-hits collections over the years (1989's *Anthology: 1968-1985*, 1997's *The Very Best Of*, etc.), and 2000 saw the release of his latest, the import *Go Ahead Ignore Me: The Best of Todd Rundgren*. A double-disc set weighing in at a hefty 41 tracks in length, *Go Ahead Ignore Me* covers most of the same ground as the aforementioned *Anthology: 1968-1985* but expands the track listing considerably (*Anthology* features 27 songs). Rundgren covered a lot of musical ground from the early '70s though the mid-'80s, which is the era spotlighted here. Although the compilers may have gone overboard by plucking nine tracks from what many consider Rundgren's finest hour (and most commercially successful release), *Something/Anything?*, and the track listing fails to include any selections from Rundgren's Utopia output, it remains a consistent and enjoyable set. You can't go wrong with such Rundgren classics as "We Gotta Get You a Woman," "I Saw the Light," "Hello It's Me," "It Wouldn't Have Made Any Difference," "Couldn't I Just Tell You," "Just One Victory," "Real Man," and "Love Is the Answer," as well as such overlooked cuts as the whacked "An Elpee's Worth of Toons," among others. If you're just discovering the great Todd Rundgren, *Go Ahead Ignore Me: The Best of Todd Rundgren* will serve as a fine introduction, with a recommended follow-up purchase being Utopia's 1989 collection, *Anthology*. *—Greg Prato*

Rush

f. 1968, Toronto, Ontario, Canada
Album Rock, Arena Rock, Prog-Rock/Art Rock, Hard Rock
Over the course of their decades-spanning career, the Canadian power trio Rush emerged as one of hard rock's most highly-regarded bands; although typically brushed aside by critics and rare recipients of mainstream pop radio airplay, the group nonetheless won an impressive and devoted fan following, while their virtuoso performance skills solidified their standing as musicians' musicians. Just after a 1974 self-titled LP, the group's lineup gelled around guitarist Alex Lifeson, vocalist/bassist Geddy Lee and drummer Neil Peart. Peart assumed the role of the band's primary songwriter, composing the cerebral lyrics (influenced by works of science fiction and fantasy) which gradually became a hallmark of the group's aesthetic. Rush's fourth album, 1976's *2112*, proved to be their breakthrough release, fusing the elements of the trio's sound—Lee's high-pitched vocals, Peart's epic-length compositions and Lifeson's complex guitar work—into a unified whole. The album established a formula from which the band rarely deviated throughout the duration of their career. The band achieved even greater popularity with 1980's *Permanent Waves*, a record marked by Peart's dramatic shift into shorter, less sprawling compositions. Thanks to heavy exposure on album-oriented radio, 1981's "Tom Sawyer" became perhaps their best-known song. As the 1980s drew to a close, the trio cut back on its touring schedule, while hardcore followers complained of a sameness afflicting slicker, synth-driven efforts. After Rush returned to the heavier sound of their early records, both 1991's *Roll the Bones* and 1993's *Counterparts* reached the Top Three on the US album charts. *—Jason Ankeny*

Rush / 1974 / Mercury ✦✦

Fly by Night / 1975 / Mercury ✦✦

Caress of Steel / 1975 / Mercury ✦✦
When Rush finished their third album, *Caress of Steel*, the trio was assured that they had created their breakthrough masterpiece. But when the album dropped off the charts soon after its release, it proved otherwise. While it was Rush's first release that fully explored their prog rock side, it did not contain the catchy and more traditional elements of their future popular work—it's quite often too indulgent and pretentious for a mainstream rock audience to latch onto. And while Rush would eventually excel in composing lengthy songs, the album's two extended tracks—the 12-and-a-half-minute "The Necromancer" and the nearly 20-minute "The Fountain of Lamneth"—show that the band was still a ways off from mastering the format. The first side contains two strong and more succinct tracks, the raging opener, "Bastille Day," and the more laid-back "Lakeside Park," both of which would become standards for their live show in the '70s. But the ill-advised "I Think I'm Going Bald" (which lyrically deals with growing old) borders on the ridiculous, which confirms that *Caress of Steel* is one of Rush's more unfocused albums. *—Greg Prato*

2112 / 1976 / Mercury ✦✦✦✦✦
Whereas Rush's first two releases, their self-titled debut and *Fly By Night*, helped create a buzz among hard rock fans worldwide, the more progressive third release, *Caress of Steel*, confused many of their supporters. The band knew it was now or never with their fourth release, and they delivered just in time—1976's *2112* proved to be their much sought-after commercial breakthrough and remains one of their most popular albums. Instead of choosing between prog rock or heavy rock, both styles are merged together to create an interesting and original approach. The whole entire first side is comprised of the classic title track, which paints a chilling picture of a future world where technology is in control (Peart's lyrics for the piece being influenced by Ayn Rand). Comprised of seven "sections," the track proved that the trio was fast becoming rock's most accomplished instrumentalists. The second side contains shorter selections, such as the Middle Eastern-flavored "A Passage to Bangkok" and the album-closing rocker "Something for Nothing." *2112* is widely considered by Rush fans as their first true "classic" album, the first in a string of similarly high-quality albums. *—Greg Prato*

All the World's a Stage / 1976 / Mercury ✦✦✦
The '70s may forever be remembered as the decade of the "live album," where many rock artists (Kiss, Peter Frampton, Cheap Trick, etc.) used the format for their commercial breakthrough. While Rush's *All the World's a Stage* is not as renowned as the aforementioned bands' live albums, it is still one of the better in-concert rock releases of the decade, and helped solidify the trio's stature as one of rock's fastest rising stars. Eventually, Rush would polish their live sound to sound almost like a studio record, but in the mid-'70s, they were still a raw and raging hard rock band, captured perfectly on *A.T.W.A.S.* Comprised almost entirely of their heavier material, the album packs quite a punch—"Bastille Day" and "Anthem" prove to be a killer opening combination, while over the top renditions of their extended epics "2112" and "By-Tor & the Snow Dog" prove to be standouts. Even their more tranquil studio material proves more explosive in concert ("Fly by Night," "Something for Nothing," "Lakeside Park," "In the End"). *All the World's a Stage* was a fitting way of closing the first chapter of Rush, as the liner notes state. *—Greg Prato*

A Farewell to Kings / 1977 / Mercury ✦✦✦
On 1977's *A Farewell to Kings* it quickly becomes apparent that Rush had improved their songwriting and strengthened their focus and musical approach. Synthesizers also mark their first prominent appearance on a Rush album, a direction the band would continue to pursue on future releases. With the popular hit single "Closer to the Heart," the trio showed that they could compose concise and traditionally structured songs, while the 11-minute "Xanadu" remains an outstanding accomplishment all these years later (superb musicianship merged with vivid lyrics help create one of Rush' s best all-time tracks). The album-opening title track begins with a tasty classical guitar/synth passage, before erupting into a powerful rocker. The underrated "Madrigal" proves to be a delicately beautiful composition, while "Cinderella Man" is one of Rush's few songs to include lyrics penned entirely by Geddy Lee. The ten-minute tale of a dangerous black hole, "Cygnus X-1," closes the album on an unpredictable note, slightly comparable to the two bizarre extended songs on 1975's *Caress of Steel*. *A Farewell to Kings* successfully built on the promise of their breakthrough *2112*, and helped broaden their audience. *—Greg Prato*

Archives / 1978 / Mercury ✦✦✦

Hemispheres / 1978 / Mercury ✦✦✦
While such albums as 1980's *Permanent Waves* and 1981's *Moving Pictures* are usually considered Rush's masterpieces (and with good reason), 1978's *Hemispheres* is just as deserving. Maybe the fact that the album consists of only four compositions (half are lengthy pieces) was a bit too intimidating for some, but the near 20-minute long "Cygnus X-1 Book II—Hemispheres" is arguably the band's finest extended track. While the storyline isn't as comprehensible as "2112" was, it's much more consistent musically, twisting and turning through five different sections which contrast heavy rock sections against more sedate pieces. Neil Peart had become one of rock's most accomplished lyricists by this point, as evidenced by "The Trees," which deals with racism and inequality in a unique way (set in a forest!). And as always, the trio prove to be experts at their instruments, this time on the complex instrumental, "La Villa Strangiato." Geddy Lee's shrieking vocals on the otherwise solid "Circumstances" may border on the irritating, but *Hemispheres* remains one of Rush's greatest releases. *—Greg Prato*

Permanent Waves / 1980 / Mercury ✦✦✦✦✦
Since Neil Peart joined the band in time for 1975's *Fly By Night*, Rush had been experimenting and growing musically with each successive release. By 1980's *Permanent Waves*, the modern sounds of new wave (the Police, Peter Gabriel, etc.) began to creep into Rush's sound, but the trio still kept their hard rock roots intact. The new approach paid off—two of their most popular songs, the "make a difference" anthem "Freewill," and a tribute to the Toronto radio station, CFNY, "The Spirit of Radio" (the latter a U.K. Top 15 hit) are spectacular highlights. Also included were two "epics," the stormy "Jacob's Ladder" and the album closing, "Natural Science," which contains a middle section that contains elements of reggae. Geddy Lee also began singing in a slightly lower register around this time, which made their music more accessible to fans outside of the heavy prog-rock circle. The album proved to be the final breakthrough Rush needed to become

an arena headliner throughout the world, beginning a string of albums that would reach inside the Top Five of the U.S. *Billboard* album charts. *Permanent Waves* is an undisputed hard rock classic, but Rush would outdo themselves with their next release. *—Greg Prato*

• **Moving Pictures** / 1981 / Mercury ✦✦✦✦✦
Not only is 1981's *Moving Pictures* Rush's best album, it is undeniably one of the greatest hard rock albums of all time. The new wave meets hard rock approach of *Permanent Waves* is honed to perfection—all seven of the tracks are classics (four are still featured regularly in concert and on classic rock radio). While other hard rock bands at the time experimented unsuccessfully with other musical styles, Rush was one of the few to successfully cross over. The whole entire first side is perfect—their most renowned song, "Tom Sawyer," kicks things off, and is soon followed by the racing "Red Barchetta," the instrumental "YYZ," and a song that examines the pros and cons of stardom, "Limelight." And while the second side isn't as instantly striking as the first, it is ultimately rewarding. The long and winding "The Camera Eye" begins with a synth-driven piece before transforming into one of the band's more straight-ahead epics, while "Witch Hunt" and "Vital Signs" remain two of the trio's more underrated rock compositions. Rush proved with *Moving Pictures* that there was still uncharted territory to explore within the hard rock format, and was rewarded with their most enduring and popular album. *—Greg Prato*

Exit . . . Stage Left / 1981 / Mercury ✦✦✦✦✦
Rush was planning on releasing a live album after the *Permanent Waves* tour, but manager Cliff Burnstein convinced the group that they were peaking musically, and should go straight back into the recording studio—resulting in their finest album, 1981's *Moving Pictures*. So after the tour wound down, their postponed live album was finally assembled, released as *Exit . . . Stage Left* the same year. The album turned out to be the polar opposite of its predecessor, 1976's raw and direct *All the World's a Stage*; in fact, the performances often sound identical to the recently released studio versions. The contagious energy that helped make *All the World's a Stage* such a success is muted, replaced by workmanlike renditions that border on the uninspired. There's no denying the high quality of the songs selected—"Spirit of Radio," "Tom Sawyer," "Xanadu," "The Trees," "Closer to the Heart," "Jacob's Ladder," etc.—it's just that the performances rarely catch fire. Compared to Rush's three other concert albums (the aforementioned *All the World's a Stage*, 1988's *A Show of Hands* and 1998's *Different Stages*), *Exit . . . Stage Left* is probably the weakest. *—Greg Prato*

Signals / 1982 / Mercury ✦✦✦✦✦
Instead of playing it safe and writing *Moving Pictures Part II*, Rush replaced their heavy rock of yesteryear with even more modern sounds for 1982's *Signals*. Synthesizers were now an integral part of the band's sound, and replaced electric guitars as the driving force for almost all the tracks. And more current and easier-to-grasp topics (teen peer pressure, repression, etc.) replaced their trusty old sci-fi inspired lyrics. While other rock bands suddenly added keyboards to their sound to widen their appeal, Rush gradually merged electronics into their music over the years, so such tracks as the popular MTV video, "Subdivisions," did not come as a shock to longtime fans. And Rush didn't forget how to rock out—"The Analog Kid" and "Digital Man" were some of their most up-tempo compositions in years. The surprise hit, "New World Man," and "Chemistry" combined reggae and rock (begun on 1980's *Permanent Waves*), "The Weapon" bordered on new wave, the placid "Losing It" was one of the band's few guitar-less tracks, while the epic closer "Countdown" painted a vivid picture of a space shuttle launch. *Signals* proved that Rush was successfully adapting to the musical climate of the early '80s. *—Greg Prato*

Grace Under Pressure / 1984 / Mercury ✦✦
Grace Under Pressure was the first Rush album since 1975's *Fly By Night* to not be produced by Terry Brown, who was replaced by Peter Henderson (Supertramp, Paul McCartney). The change resulted in a slightly more accessible sound than its predecessor, *Signals*, and marked the beginning of a period where many Rush fans feel that synths and electronics were used too prominently—in effect pushing guitarist Alex Lifeson into the background. The songwriting and lyrics were still strong however, as evidenced by the video/single "Distant Early Warning" (a tale about nuclear war) and the often-overlooked highlight, "Kid Gloves," one of the album's few songs to feature Lifeson up front. Other standouts include a tribute to a friend of the band who had recently passed away, "Afterimage," the disturbing "Red Sector A" (which details a concentration camp), and one of Rush's first funk-based songs, "The Enemy Within." Whereas most other rock bands formed in the 1970s put out unfocused and uninspired work in the 1980s (which sounds very dated), Rush's *Grace Under Pressure* remains an exception. *—Greg Prato*

Power Windows / 1985 / Mercury ✦✦✦
Like much of the band's '80s output, *Power Windows* finds Rush juggling their hard-rock heritage with new technology to mixed results. With Alex Lifeson choosing sparse, horn-like guitar bursts over actual crunch, Geddy Lee's synthesizers running rampant, and Neil Peart's crisp, clinical percussion and stark lyrical themes (evoking cold urban landscapes), the result just may be the trio's "coldest" album ever. Still, it does boast its share of important tracks in "Marathon" and "Manhattan Project," while offering an energetic, tongue-in-cheeck hit single in "The Big Money." In an album that rewards patience (repeated listens are the key), the most gripping moments are saved for last, with the beautifully eerie textures of "Mystic Rhythms," a song that was later used as a concert drum solo showcase for Peart. *—Ed Rivadavia*

Hold Your Fire / 1987 / Mercury ✦✦✦
Hold Your Fire is an album in the purest sense; infinitely greater than the sum of its parts, it gradually draws in the listener by slowly revealing its nuances and secrets. While the use of keyboards is still overwhelming at times, Geddy Lee employs lush textures which, when coupled with a greater rhythmic and melodic presence from guitarist Alex Lifeson, results in a far warmer sound than in recent efforts. Of course, drummer Neil Peart is as inventive and exciting as ever, while his lyrics focus on the various elements (earth, air, water, fire) for much of the album. Opener "Force Ten" is the band's most immediate number in years, and other early favorites such as "Time Stand Still" and "Turn the Page" soon give way to the darker mysteries of "Prime Mover" and "Tai Shan." The multifaceted "Lock and Key" is quintessential Rush, and sets the stage for the album's climax with the sheer beauty of "Mission." As was the case with 1976's *2112* and 1981's *Moving Pictures*, Rush always seem to produce some of their best work at the end of each four-album cycle, and *Hold Your Fire* is no exception. *—Ed Rivadavia*

A Show of Hands / Jan. 2, 1988 / Mercury ✦✦✦
Although keyboards dominated Rush's 1988 double live set, *A Show of Hands*, it was a definite improvement over its somewhat flat predecessor, 1981's *Exit: Stage Left*. The band's music wasn't as hard rock-based as it previously was, evidenced by the more modern-sounding compositions selected for their third live album (the first Rush album to be produced completely by the band). The only tracks from the pre-1982 period to be featured are "Closer to the Heart," which is expanded to include a jamming section at the end, and the spooky "Witch Hunt," originally from 1981's *Moving Pictures*. The remainder of the album's track list is comprised of Rush's best compositions from 1982-1987, such as "Subdivisions," "Distant Early Warning," "Force Ten," "Time Stand Still" and "Red Sector A," as well as several tracks that have been forgotten over time ("Marathon," "Turn the Page," "Mission," etc.). Also featured for the first time on a live Rush album was a completely unaccompanied drum solo by Neil Peart—the intricate "Rhythm Method." The inspired *A Show of Hands* is an excellent snapshot of Rush in concert during the mid-late '80s. *—Greg Prato*

Presto / Nov. 1989 / Atlantic ✦✦✦✦✦
After being slagged off for the electronic ambience of its predecessor releases such as 1985's *Power Windows* and 1984's *Grace Under Pressure*, Rush bounces back with their 13th release, *Presto*. Yet again the prog-rock trio proves that their tight guitar work and lyrical originality is not long lost or overlooked in an attempt to secure the latest technical flash.

Rupert Hine's production work totally brings things to the forefront by molding solid piano breaks instead of the typical adventure-like synthesizers into Alex Lifeson's spellbinding guitar work. The sound quality is strong and thick, making the sounds of *Presto* complete. Neil Peart also makes headway with his natural percussion power, and Geddy Lee's trademark lyrical complexities shine like signature Rush perfectionism. Songs like "Scars" and "Superconductor" are sonically firm, but "Show Don't Tell" is the album's infectious standout that's heightened thanks to Lee's stunning vocal wizardry. *Presto* intelligently leads Rush into the '90s without musical bleakness. They weren't ones to be blinded by such creative mediocrity anyway. *—MacKenzie Wilson*

Chronicles / Jul. 1, 1991 / Mercury ✦✦✦✦✦
Though the band has since released four more albums on Atlantic Records, this double-disc set was the original, definitive Rush anthology, spanning the band's entire 15-year, 16-album relationship with Mercury Records. In fact, this set is virtually perfect, clearly illustrating the Canadian power trio's evolution from Cream/Zeppelin enthusiasts into a ground-breaking, progressive hard-rock unit. Acclaimed classics like "Finding My Way," "Fly by Night," "A Passage to Bangkok," "Closer to the Heart," "The Spirit of Radio," and "Tom Sawyer" are interspersed with less-well-known, but equally vital tracks like "Bastille Day," "La Villa Strangiato," "Limelight," "Subdivisions," and "Red Sector A" to paint a literal moving picture (pun intended) of the band's career. As a testament to its excellence, Mercury was incapable of improving upon this package when releasing the nearly identical *Retrospective* six years later on two separate CDs. *—Ed Rivadavia*

Roll the Bones / Jul. 1, 1991 / Atlantic ✦✦✦
From a lyrical perspective, 1991's *Roll the Bones* is quite possibly Rush's darkest album (most of the songs deal with death in no uncertain terms), but from a musical point of view, the record treads territory (highbrow melodic hard rock) similar to its recent predecessors, with only a few surprises thrown in for good measure. These include an amusing rap section in the middle of the title track, a welcome return to instrumentals with "Where's my Thing?," and one of the band's finest songs of the '90s in the gutsy "Dreamline." "Neurotica" is another highlight which lives up to its title, and though their negative subject matter can feel stifling at times, fine tracks like "Bravado," "The Big Wheel," and "Heresy" feature wonderful melodies and arrangements. *—Ed Rivadavia*

Counterparts / Oct. 19, 1993 / Atlantic ✦✦
By 1993, alternative rock had arrived in a big way, and surprisingly, Canadian veterans Rush were game, releasing their most honest and organic rock & roll record in over a decade with *Counterparts*. Opener "Animate" is straightforward enough, but doesn't even hint at the guitar ferocity and lyrical angst of "Stick it Out," a song which undoubtedly polarizes Rush fans to this day. Intellectual melodic rockers like "Cut to the Chase," "At the Speed of Love," and "Everyday Glory" are also present (and less shocking), but diversity continues to rule the day with Geddy Lee's bass taking charge on the amazingly somber "Double Agent" and the giddy instrumental "Leave That Thing Alone." Pure hard rock resurfaces on "Cold Fire," but it is the largely acoustic "Nobody's Hero" which provides the album's most gripping moment with an impassioned plea for HIV consciousness and understanding. *—Ed Rivadavia*

Test for Echo / Sep. 9, 1996 / Atlantic ✦✦✦
After flirting (albeit mildly) with alternative rock on *Counterparts*, Rush returns to classic progressive rock on *Test for Echo*. Cutting back many of the AOR production flourishes that hampered most of their late '80s and early '90s releases, the band concentrates on the sounds and styles that made albums like *Moving Pictures* huge successes in the late '70s and early '80s. *Test for Echo* is all instrumental gymnastics and convoluted song

structures, all of which demonstrate each member's skills. And the key to the album is the individual performances, since each song isn't particularly memorable as a song, only as a way to showcase the solos. With Rush, such a tactic isn't necessarily a bad thing, since they have always been better at playing than writing, and they have rarely played better in the past ten years than they have on *Test for Echo*. —*Stephen Thomas Erlewine*

● **Retrospective, Vol. 1 (1974-1980)** / May 5, 1997 / Mercury ✦✦✦✦✦
Retrospective, Vol. 1 (1974-80) was designed to replace the double-disc set *Chronicles*, and it is, in fact, a better compilation than its predecessor. By concentrating on Rush's earliest albums—from 1974's *Rush* to 1980's *Permanent Waves*—the album draws an excellent portrait of the group's artiest work, leaving their hard-rock radio-rock hits for *Retrospective, Vol. 2*. Meanwhile, *Vol. 1* contains nearly all of the highlights from their '70s albums, including "Closer to the Heart" and "Fly By Night," making it a nearly flawless encapsulation of their early career. —*Stephen Thomas Erlewine*

Retrospective, Vol. 2 (1981-1987) / Jun. 3, 1997 / Mercury ✦✦✦✦✦
Retrospective, Vol. 2 (1981-1987) picks up where *Retrospective, Vol. 1* left off, the time period when Rush became an arena-rock sensation with each of their albums reaching the Top Ten. The set begins with several selections from their most popular album, 1981's *Moving Pictures*, and ends with 1987's *Hold Your Fire*. In between, many of the trio's most familiar songs—"Tom Sawyer," "New World Man," "Limelight," "Distant Early Warning," "Time Stand Still"—are featured, making this an excellent overview of the group's hard-rock heyday. —*Stephen Thomas Erlewine*

Different Stages / Nov. 10, 1998 / Atlantic ✦✦✦
On their fourth live album since their inception in the early '70s, Rush's three-CD *Different Stages/Live* is similar in approach and feel to their first in-concert release, 1976's *All the World's a Stage*. Instead of overdubbing and cleaning up the performances as they did on their last two live albums (1981's *Exit… Stage Left* and 1988's *A Show of Hands*), the tracks are left raw and rocking. And with very limited use of synthesizers (which plagued *A Show of Hands*), the results are often extremely impressive. The first two discs are comprised of renditions of hits from Rush's past couple of tours (1994's Counterparts and 1997's Test For Echo), while the third is a long-lost classic show from London's Hammersmith Odeon in 1978. On discs one and two, such Rush standards as "2112," "Tom Sawyer," and "The Spirit of Radio" are joined by recent material ("Dreamline," "Stick It Out," "Roll the Bones," etc.) and obscure tracks ("Natural Science," "Analog Kid," etc.), which makes for a perfect balance of material. But it's the third disc that will have long-time fans frothing at the mouth—for the first time ever on an official release, live versions of "Cygnus X-1," "A Farewell to Kings," and "Cinderella Man" are presented. Even though no material from the mid- to late '80s is included, *Different Stages/Live* will delight Rush's adoring throng of fans. —*Greg Prato*

Leon Russell (Claude Russell Bridges)

b. Apr. 2, 1941, Lawton, OK

Vocals, Keyboards, Piano, Guitar, Bass / Album Rock, Pop/Rock, Singer/Songwriter, Country-Rock

The ultimate rock & roll session man, Leon Russell's long and storied career includes collaborations with a virtual who's who of music icons spanning from Jerry Lee Lewis to Phil Spector to the Rolling Stones; a similar eclecticism and scope also surfaced in his solo work, which couched his charmingly gravelly voice in a rustic yet rich swamp-pop fusion of country, blues, and gospel. As a member of Spector's renowned studio group, Russell played on many of the finest pop singles of the '60s, also arranging classics like Ike and Tina Turner's monumental "River Deep, Mountain High." He scored his first songwriting hit with Joe Cocker's reading of "Delta Lady," and in 1970, he also organized Cocker's legendary Mad Dogs and Englishmen tour. After the subsequent tour film earned Russell his first real mainstream notoriety, he issued a self-titled solo LP. Russell reached the number two spot with 1972's *Carny* and scored his first pop hit with the single "Tight Rope." While the success of 1973's three-LP set *Leon Live* further established his reputation as a top concert draw, response to the country-inspired studio effort *Hank Wilson's Back* was considerably more lukewarm. 1975's *Will O' the Wisp*, however, restored his commercial luster. In June 1975, Russell married singer Mary McCreary; the following year the couple collaborated on *The Wedding Album*, issued through his newly formed Paradise Records label. Among other subsequent projects, Russell teamed with Willie Nelson for 1979's *Willie and Leon*, and spent the next two years touring with his bluegrass band the New Grass Revival, issuing a live LP in 1981. After two albums in 1984, Russell spent the remainder of the decade largely outside of music, and did not resurface until 1992's Bruce Hornsby-produced *Anything Can Happen*. Another long period of relative inactivity followed prior to a 1998-1999 recording comeback. —*Jason Ankeny*

Leon Russell / 1970 / The Right Stuff ✦✦✦✦✦
Leon Russell never quite hit all the right notes the way he did on his eponymous debut. He never again seemed as convincing in his grasp of Americana music and themes, never again seemed as individual, and never again did his limited, slurred bluesy voice seem as ingratiating. He never again topped his triptych of "A Song for You," "Hummingbird," and "Delta Lady," nor did his albums contain such fine tracks as "Dixie Lullaby." Throughout it all, what comes across is Russell's idiosyncratic vision, not only in his approach but in his very construction—none of the songs quite play out as expected, turning country, blues, and rock inside out, not only musically but lyrically. Yes, his voice is a bit of an acquired taste, but it's only appropriate for a songwriter with enough chutzpah to write songs of his own called "I Put a Spell on You" and "Give Peace a Chance." And if there ever was a place to acquire a taste for Russell, it's here. —*Stephen Thomas Erlewine*

And the Shelter People / 1971 / The Right Stuff ✦✦✦✦✦

Asylum Choir II / 1971 / The Right Stuff ✦✦

Carney / 1972 / The Right Stuff ✦✦✦✦
"Tight Rope" leads off *Carney*, and it's not just his biggest hit, it offers an excellent introduction to an off-kilter, confused, fascinating album. In a sense, it consolidates his two extremes, offering a side of fairly straightforward roots rock before delving headfirst into twisted psychedelia on the second side. On the whole, the second side deflates the first side, since it's just too fuzzy—it's intriguing, at least in parts, but it never adds up to anything. Besides, the first side is already odd enough, but in a meaningful way; here, his fascination with Americana sideshows is married to songs that work, instead of just being vehicles for tripping in the studio. Of course, part of what makes *Carney* interesting is that it contains a bit of both, but interesting doesn't equal compelling, as the whole of *Carney* bears out. —*Stephen Thomas Erlewine*

Hank Wilson's Back / 1973 / The Right Stuff ✦✦✦✦
A skewed but interesting Hank Williams tribute album, with capable country backing. —*Cub Koda*

Leon Live / 1973 / The Right Stuff ✦✦✦
A solid concert offering that showcases Russell's strengths (and weaknesses) as a live performer, with A-1 support throughout. —*Cub Koda*

Stop All That Jazz / 1974 / The Right Stuff ✦✦

Will O' the Wisp / 1975 / The Right Stuff ✦✦✦

Anything Can Happen / Sep. 1992 / Virgin ✦✦✦
Bruce Hornsby's active participation in Leon Russell's first recording in ten years is both a blessing and a curse. A blessing, because without Hornsby's encouragement, co-songwriting, production, and musical backing, the project would probably never have happened. A curse, because Hornsby imprints too much of his own personal style and mushy, middle-of-the-road keyboard washes on the sessions. Despite Russell's long layoff, the unique, drawling rasp that gave us "Tight Rope" and "Delta Lady" in the early-'70s is still intact. However, the cloying instrumental backings to such tracks as "Angel Ways" and "Faces of the Children" have Hornsby engraved all over them. —*Roch Parisien*

● **Gimme Shelter: The Best of Leon Russell** / Nov. 12, 1996 / EMI ✦✦✦✦✦
It's a little problematic to put together a compilation of such an album-oriented artist. But unless you're very deeply into the Russell catalog, this two-CD, 40-track best-of will serve as a retrospective of all that you need, largely covering his work from the first half of the '70s (a couple of songs from his 1992 Virgin album are also included), and featuring his best-known hits, big and small. It's a well-done tour through his blend of swamp rock, gospel, and bits of blues and country, with material from eight of his Shelter LPs, including the one he recorded in 1969 as part of the Asylum Choir. Interesting rarities include a 1974 single of "Wild Horses," a 1970 cover of Dylan's "She Belongs to Me" that only showed up on a compilation, and a folk-rockish 1965 single for Dot. —*Richie Unterberger*

● **Retrospective** / Oct. 21, 1997 / The Right Stuff/Shelter ✦✦✦✦
Retrospective is an 18-track collection that features the bulk of Leon Russell's greatest hits ("Tight Rope," "Roll in My Sweet Baby's Arms," "Lady Blue," "Back to the Island"), plus many key album tracks. Since Russell was primarily an album artist, this approach doesn't necessarily do him justice, but for listeners who only want the hits, this will do. However, the double-disc *Gimme Shelter: The Best of Leon Russell* is a better, more thorough overview and is the one serious fans should acquire. —*Stephen Thomas Erlewine*

The Rutles

Psychedelic Pop, Comedy Rock, Pop/Rock, British Invasion

Originally broadcast on network TV in 1978, ex-Monty Python member Eric Idle's satire of the Beatles' legend was one of the very few successful rock parodies; only Spinal Tap, perhaps, has outdone it. One of the key elements of this mock rockumentary was the brilliantly executed soundtrack by Python associate and ex-Bonzo Dog Band member Neil Innes (he also played the character loosely based upon John Lennon in the film itself). As an actual peer of the group in the '60s (the Bonzos even appeared in the *Magical Mystery Tour* film), Innes was well-qualified to satirize the Fab Four in song. With the exception of Idle, each of the four Rutles played their own instruments on the recording in addition to acting in the film. To complete the gag, the Rutles reconvened in 1996 to record a second album, *Archeology*, to coincide with the Beatles' *Anthology* projects. Masquerading as archival material, most of *Archeology* was in fact newly recorded in the mid-'90s, and was as witty and well-executed as the soundtrack to their TV special nearly 20 years ago. —*Richie Unterberger*

● **The Rutles** / 1978 / Rhino ✦✦✦✦✦
Neil Innes delivered catchy, harmony-laden tunes that deftly and lovingly parody every phase of the moptops' career, from their Hamburg/Cavern Club days through "Get Back" (here retitled "Get Up and Go"). In between are fully realized send-ups of "If I Fell," "I Want to Hold Your Hand," "Penny Lane," "Lucy in the Sky," "I Am the Walrus," "All You Need Is Love," and more. "Ouch!," their hilarious mockery of "Help!," is perhaps the album's highlight. The 1990 CD reissue adds six very worthwhile "bonus tracks" that were used in the special but were unavailable on the original 1978 Warner album, making for 20 cuts in all. —*Richie Unterberger*

Archaeology / Oct. 29, 1996 / Virgin ✦✦✦✦
Since the Rutles never properly existed in the first place, they were free of the high expectations surrounding the "reunions" of groups with a higher profile (such as the prime targets of their satire, the Beatles). Although it was recorded over 20 years after the first Rutles album, this is an unexpectedly delightful continuation of that debut. Songwriter Neil Innes continues to masterfully lampoon the Beatles myth on this collection, billed as

an archival release of unreleased material (in the mold of the Beatles' own *Anthology* series). The sound is extremely similar to the Rutles' earlier material, although most of the cuts here are spoofing the Beatles' work from *Sgt. Pepper* onwards, rather than striving for an equal balance between all Fab Four phases. Innes is a genius at weaving in musical and lyrical quotes/references from numerous Beatle tunes, with a subtle hilarity that takes several plays to fully unfold. *—Richie Unterberger*

Ruts

f. 1976, **db.** 1983

Ska Revival, Punk

With their unique blend of raucous punk rock laced with reggae and dub, the Ruts were one of the most exciting bands to emerge from Britain's late-'70s scene. They were also a powerful force within Britain's Rock Against Racism movement, ensuring a political legacy at least as vital as their music. It was through Misty in Roots' People Unite label that the Ruts' debut single, the driving "In a Rut"/"H-Eyes," was released in late 1978. Virgin Records was one of several labels which recognized the Ruts' potential and signed the band in the spring of 1979. They were immediately awarded when the group's next single, "Babylon's Burning"/"Society," seared its way into the U.K. Top Ten. Inspired by the political and societal upheavals taking place across the country, the song perfectly caught the mood of rage simmering just below Britain's surface. Following a national tour supporting the Damned and the release of their Top 30 follow-up single, the rabble-rousing "Something That I Said," the Ruts' debut album, *The Crack*, arrived in October 1979. With its seminal blend of punk, roots reggae, dub, and hard rock meets hardcore sound, the album slammed its way to number 16 and into the national musical lexicon. Their career was cut cruelly short by the death of singer Malcolm Owen in 1980, but still the group released six crucial singles and a seminal album in their short lifetime. The remaining trio would continue on without Owen as Ruts DC (from the phrase "da capo," meaning new beginning), but in a decidedly different musical vein. *—Jo-Ann Greene*

● **The Crack** / 1979 / Virgin ✦✦✦✦✦

Early punk's greatest glory, and greatest flaw, was that most of the bands were signed before they'd reached true musical proficiency. No wonder they sounded so unique—they weren't capable of imitating their influences yet. Not so with the Ruts, who were able to deliver a powerful musical punch with their debut album, something virtually unique among old-school British punk bands. Easily able to recreate not just first-wave punk stylings, but classic rock as well, the Ruts' influences ran the gamut of genres from Motörhead to Marley, the New York Dolls to the Banshees. Thus, *The Crack* was one blindingly original album, far removed from its contemporaries. At the core, the quartet's sound was based primarily on '70s rock, played fast and hard, bringing them into the sphere of the street punks, an evolving genre later tagged Oi!, and eventually mutating into both speed metal and hardcore. The album features a clutch of headbanging pogo-til-you-puke blasts of fury, anthemic shout-alongs one and all. But the Ruts were capable of much more than simplistic punk-rockers in a metal mode. Some songs feature a wondrous gothic drone; "It Was Cold" was indebted to both Magazine and the Police, while other tracks give nods to pub rock and R&B. Out of this mass of sounds and styles, the Ruts hammered out intriguing hybrids, darkly shadowed, but occasionally emerging into the pop light. The group was, if anything, even stronger lyrically. "Babylon's Burning" turns a powerful punk-rocker into an epic, with singer Malcolm Owen capturing the anger, frustration, and horror of anyone caught up in a riot. The CD reissue also includes the B-sides from the group's three singles: "Give Youth a Chance," "I Ain't Sophisticated," and "The Crack." *—Jo-Ann Greene*

Something That I Said: The Best of the Ruts / 1995 / Choice Cuts ✦✦✦✦✦

Mitch Ryder

b. Feb. 26, 1945, Hamtramck, MI

Vocals / Detroit Rock, Frat Rock, Album Rock, Blue-Eyed Soul, Hard Rock, Rock & Roll

The unsung heart and soul of the Motor City rock & roll scene, Mitch Ryder and the Detroit Wheels' blue-eyed R&B attack boasted a gritty passion and incendiary energy matched by few artists of any color. Born William Levise, Jr. in Hamtramck, MI on February 26, 1945, the teenage Ryder sang with the local black quartet the Peps but suffered so much racial harassment that he left to form his own combo, Billy Lee and the Rivieras. While opening for the Dave Clark Five in 1965, they were noticed by producer Bob Crewe, who immediately signed them and, according to legend, rechristened the singer Mitch Ryder after randomly selecting the name from a phone book. Backed by the peerless Detroit Wheels—guitarists James McCarty and Joseph Cubert, bassist Earl Elliot, and drummer Johnny "Bee" Badanjek—Ryder reached the Top Ten in early '66 with the breathless, intense "Jenny Take a Ride," a frenzied combination of Little Richard's "Jenny Jenny" and Chuck Willis' "C.C. Rider." Ryder and the Detroit Wheels returned to the charts with "Little Latin Lupe Lu," "Sock It to Me Baby!" and the Top Five smash "Devil with a Blue Dress On/Good Golly Miss Molly." At Crewe's insistence, Ryder split from the rest of the band to mount a solo career; outside of the Top 30 entry "What Now My Love," the hits dried up. In 1970, he reunited with Badanjek in the seven-piece band Detroit, who scored a major FM radio hit with their cover of Lou Reed's "Rock & Roll." Ryder's throat problems forced him to retire until the late '70s, when he released several albums on his own Seeds and Stems label. He made his major label comeback with 1983's John Cougar Mellencamp-produced *Never Kick A Sleeping Dog*; the album's minor hit, the Prince cover "When You Were Mine," didn't return the singer to mainstream success in the US, but in Europe he retained a large fan following. He remained active for the rest of the '80s and '90s, working on his biography and continuing to tour and release albums. *—Jason Ankeny*

Take a Ride / 1966 / Sundazed ✦✦✦✦✦

The debut album of Ryder and the Wheels, fresh from the teenage ballroom circuit in Detroit, where they held court in earlier days as Billy Lee & the Rivieras. One of the defining moments in the history of Motor City music, *Take a Ride* is the sound of poor White kids claiming the music as theirs, too, while infusing it with the manic energy of the color-blind dreams of anybody who ever wanted to be somebody. Built entirely around their stage act, this album captures a band in full cry at the peak of their powers. This is what they mean when they say the words "high-energy Motor City rock & roll." *—Cub Koda*

Breakout . . . !!! / 1966 / Sundazed ✦✦✦✦✦

Ryder & the Wheels' second album, featuring the classic "Devil with a Blue Dress On/ Good Golly, Miss Molly" workout, continues the pattern of their debut; strong renditions of R&B classics, chopped and channeled and revved up to maximum torque. With the use of the original two-track master, the sound of it fairly sparkles. *—Cub Koda*

Sock It to Me / 1967 / Sundazed ✦✦✦✦

Ryder's last album with the Detroit Wheels before going solo finds the material reverting to producer Bob Crewe's readymades, no match for the authentic R&B found on the first two albums, but still strutted out with typical Detroit-like flair. Three bonus tracks and the use of the original stereo masters makes this a must-have for serious Mitch Ryder collectors. *—Cub Koda*

All Mitch Ryder Hits! / 1967 / Sundazed ✦✦✦✦✦

Greatest-hits packages sometimes can rob an artist of their wider focus, only zeroing in on the hits and not giving the true big picture. But this is one time when the hits and the subsequent singles fill the bill in an absolutely perfect way. Although many of these songs turn up on other Mitch Ryder albums, many of the versions included here differ greatly, the most noticeable being the kickoff track, "Devil With a Blue Dress/Good Golly Miss Molly." The reason is simple enough: These are the single mixes, the ones edited and compacted to fit on one side of a 45-rpm vinyl record. As a result, they aurally exude a brighter, more shimmering presence, and although not much else is done in the way of audio chicanery here (no sped-up tracks, etc.), this one *does* have the sound. If you truly want to experience what a great kick-ass band the Detroit Wheels were in their prime and what a skunk-hot singer Mitch Ryder was in his young man days, this is the one you want to stick in the CD player and play over and over again. *—Cub Koda*

How I Spent My Vacation / 1978 / J-Bird ✦✦✦✦

Ryder recorded this hidden gem in 1978. Like his other post-Detroit Wheels albums, it's an angry album, full of the original songs that he had inside of him but wasn't allowed to pursue back in the day. As such, the lyrics seem to come at times in a garbled rush, as if Ryder had these songs bursting inside of him. It starts to wear after a few tunes (too much angst), but those in for the long haul will be rewarded with the performances on "Tough Kid," "Passions Wheel," "The Jon," "Falling Forming," and the closer, "Poster." Another closet classic here for those who want to investigate the other side of this Detroit rocker's career. *—Cub Koda*

Naked But Not Dead / 1979 / J-Bird ✦✦✦

This mid-'80s offering finds Ryder in good form, recorded in Detroit and sporting his regular working band at the time, featuring long timers Mark Gugeon on bass and Wilson Owens on drums. It's the usual strong mix of Ryder originals, with the finger pointedness of "Ain't Nobody White," "War," "Spittin' Lizards," "Hometown," and "True Love" as must-listen recommendations. Good to see this material coming around again, as it's some of Ryder's most involved work. *—Cub Koda*

Live Talkies / 1982 / J-Bird ✦✦✦

In his brief liners to this disc, Ryder describes this as a live album cut in a studio, just running though their regular set of the time. The result is a session with longer-than-usual intros and soloing and a looseness that usually doesn't happen on a studio recording. Mixing up a set between angry Ryder originals and severely reworked R&B classics, this sounds more like the tape machine left running than an actual produced session. Loose, even bordering on sloppy in places, but loads of fun with a true live feel to recommend it. *—Cub Koda*

● **Rev-Up: The Best of Mitch Ryder & the Detroit Wheels** / 1990 / Rhino ✦✦✦✦✦

Perhaps the most raucous White soul band of the '60s, Ryder and the Detroit Wheels scored a series of hits, 1966-1968, by souping up rock and R&B ravers to fever pitch. This is hard party music. *—William Ruhlmann*

Got Change for a Million / May 26, 1995 / J-Bird ✦✦✦

The 1981 vinyl version of Mitch Ryder's *Got Change for a Million*, released in Germany on Line Records, continues the progression started on *The Detroit-Memphis Experiment* in 1969 and the subsequent *Detroit* album produced by Bob Ezrin. This is no-nonsense blues-tinged rock produced by Tom Conner along with Ryder. "That's Charm," clocking in at five-and-a-half minutes, is the longest track and indeed has charm. Although Ryder looks a bit haggard a mere 12 years after *The Detroit-Memphis Experiment*, his voice is intact and the tunes, all by Kim Levise and Ryder (aka William S. Levise Jr.), have a concise poppy snap. "Red Scar Eyes" is a real departure, a moody piece with lyrics that go from introspection to downright deranged, a far cry from the efficient opening track "My Heart Belongs to Me." Included with the liner notes are the handwritten lyrics, from side one seen next to a full glass of beer, and from side two with a photo of a pen next to an empty glass. The earthy voice of Ryder found fame as an instrument for producer Bob Crewe and songs by Crewe, Burt Bacharach, Bill Medley, and others. Although side two's opening track "Bang Bang" fails, "Back at Work" and the reggae-flavored "Ich Bin Aus Amerika" succeed, showing Ryder's development from singer to singer/songwriter. The classic growl of this true, well-rounded journeyman is in fine shape on the exquisite "Bare Your Soul." "We're Gonna Win" opens with looping guitars and unique backing vocals, the band cooking behind Ryder's hard-driving voice. The album was recorded and mixed at Delta Sound Studio in Wilster, West Germany, except for the final two tracks, "Bare Your Soul" and "We're Gonna Win," which were tracked in Detroit. The album was "recorded and mixed without the aid of any reduction devices." Re-released on J-Bird Records in 1995, it's a good look at Mitch Ryder on his own. —*Joe Viglione*

Detroit Breakout! / 1997 / West Side ✦✦✦✦✦
If you want a Mitch Ryder and the Detroit Wheels greatest-hits-plus package that's one-stop shopping of the highest order, then look no further. This two-disc, 50-track set collects all three of the group's original albums plus Ryder's solo album, *What Now My Love*. With only three single sides (not counting the original single edit of "Devil With a Blue Dress On/Good Golly, Miss Molly," available on Sundazed's reissue of the *All Hits* album) missing to keep this from being a "complete" set, this does provide an awful lot of bang for a buck; unless a single hits compilation will fill the bill in your library, this is the way to go. Great notes and superlative sound on this one, too. —*Cub Koda*

In the China Shop / May 30, 2000 / J-Bird ✦✦✦

Red Blood, White Mink / May 30, 2000 / J-Bird ✦✦✦✦

Smart Ass / May 30, 2000 / J-Bird ✦✦✦

RZA (Robert Diggs)
b. Jul. 5, 196?
Mixing, Producer / Underground Rap, Hardcore Rap, East Coast Rap, Alternative Rap
The Wu-Tang Clan's chief producer, RZA (a.k.a. The Abbott, Prince Rakeem, the Rzarector and Bobby Steels) was born Robert Diggs; he first surfaced during the early 1990s as a member of the rap unit All in Together Now, a group which also featured fellow Wu-Tang members the Genius/GZA and Ol' Dirty Bastard. Following All in Together Now's dissolution, he signed to Tommy Boy under the name Prince Rakeem, issuing the 1991 EP *Ooh We Love You Rakeem* before joining the Wu-Tang; the group's 1993 debut, *Enter the Wu-Tang: 36 Chambers*, was one of the most influential hip-hop records of the era, with RZA's lean, menacing production work much imitated throughout the rap community in the years to follow. In addition to remaining a member of the loose-knit Wu-Tang family and producing many of the group members' solo efforts, RZA also joined the Gravediggaz, helming their 1995 debut *Six Feet Deep*; his first full-length solo LP, *RZA as Bobby Digital in Stereo*, followed in 1998. In 1999, *Hits*, a compilation of some of the Wu-Tang family's best-known tracks, from both group and solo projects, was released under RZA's name. —*Jason Ankeny*

RZA as Bobby Digital in Stereo / Nov. 16, 1998 / V2 ✦✦✦✦
RZA's first solo album, the soundtrack to a film involving experimental self-transformation, has many of the same fractured strings and crisp, staccato beats he made trademarks on Wu-Tang Clan recordings. In fact, this could well *be* a Wu-Tang album, even more so than the legion of other related albums. The only contributors to the project are Wu members (Method Man, Ol' Dirty Bastard, Ghostface Killah, U-God, Inspectah Deck) or relatives (Killarmy, Masta Killa, Sunz of Man). *Bobby Digital in Stereo* is also a more focused work than the last Wu-Tang Clan album (*Forever*), and just a bit more diverse. Though the hooks aren't as big and the raps aren't as upfront, this is a producers album, designed to showcase RZA's talents in the control room, not in front of the mic. —*Keith Farley*

● **The RZA Hits** / Jun. 22, 1999 / Epic ✦✦✦✦✦
As a summation of everything that made Wu worthy of the best rap groups of all time *RZA Hits* reaches leagues beyond *Wu-Chronicles*. *RZA Hits* includes RZA's favorite Wu-Tang productions from the first two albums (including staples like "Wu-Tang Clan Ain't Nuthing Ta F' Wit," "Protect Ya Neck," and "C.R.E.A.M."), as well as the best of his productions for solo joints by Wu-Tang members—solo hits like GZA's "Liquid Swords," Method Man's "Bring the Pain" and "Method Man," Raekwon's excellent "Incarcerated Scarfaces" and "Ice Cream," and Ol' Dirty Bastard's "Shimmy Shimmy Ya." The added narration by RZA interspersed with tracks may be unappealing, and the addition of a strictly marketing track named "Wu-Wear: The Garment Renaissance" is a bit suspicious, but *RZA Hits* could well be the first and best purchase for Wu-Tang neophytes. —*Keith Farley*

The Sabres of Paradise

f. 1992, London, England, **db.** 1995
IDM, Electronica, Ambient Techno, Club/Dance, Techno

Andrew Weatherall's Sabres of Paradise were one of the U.K.'s most celebrated experimental techno groups. A combined effort of Weatherall and collaborators Jagz Kooner and Gary Burns, the group released a flood of singles and EPs, many of which were collected on compilations released by Warp and Weatherall's other main focus: the Sabrettes label, with releases from Plod and Slab, among others. Born in Windsor, Berkshire, Weatherall considers himself a DJ first, and his exhausting schedule of deck-work has been arguably as influential as his records, inspiring scores of other DJs and anticipating trends in trance-techno, inelegant dance, and even trip-hop. Still, tracks such as "Smokebelch," "Theme," "Wilmott," and the expansive *Haunted Dancehall* LP did much in helping to push the post-techno envelope beyond the often staid conventions of the dancefloor. Weatherall also gained visibility through remix and production work, working with Primal Scream and reworking tracks for the Orb and Bjork, among many others. His mixing skills can be sampled firsthand via the three-CD collection *Cut the Crap*, released by Six By 6 Records. After dissolving his Sabres of Paradise project and label, Weatherall set up the tripartite Emissions label group and launched his latest, perhaps most prodigious musical venture, Two Lone Swordsmen. A collaboration with Emissions engineer Keith Tenniswood, 2LS was formed in early 1996. The group speaks the same language of warped, down-tempo grooves as much previous Sabres work, but opts instead for a syntax of minimal electronics and taut, brittle electro-funk for structure and guidance. The group's first full-length release, 1996's *The Fifth Mission*, was a whopping double CD/triple LP, both preceded and followed by additional EPs of new material. The heavy release schedule continued through the rest of the decade, with an assortment of LPs and mini-LPs recorded via a new deal with Warp. — *Sean Cooper*

● **Sabresonic** / 1993 / Warp ✦✦✦✦✦
The Sabres techno-oriented debut album includes crucial singles like "Smokebelch," "Wilmott," and previously unavailable items like "Still Fighting" and "Ano Electro." Also tacks on In the Nursery's beatless remix of "Smokebelch II." — *Sean Cooper*

Haunted Dancehall / 1994 / Warp ✦✦✦✦
The Sabres' second album is a conceptual manifesto of sorts, accompanied by a loose song-by-song narrative of descriptions written by the group. According to Weatherall, they initially hired Scottish novelist Irvine Welsh (*Trainspotting*) to pen the notes, but, unhappy with the results, threw together their own versions minutes before the record was shipped off to be pressed. Lots of thin, bubbly, minimalist ambient and mid-tempo breakbeat, with quirky, occasionally half-thought-out tracks aided by production assistance from Geoff Barrow (Portishead) and A. Carthy (Mr. Scruff). — *Sean Cooper*

Versus / 1995 / Warp ✦✦✦
A collection of dirty, vigorous remixes from Depth Charge's J. Saul Kane and the ever-inspired Chemical Brothers. The CD includes extra versions, and a limited-edition vinyl triple-pack featured an additional 10" with LFO and Nightmares on Wax remixes and a one-sided 7" of "Haunted Dancehall" mixed by English post-classical group In the Nursery. — *Sean Cooper*

Sade

b. Jan. 16, 1959, Ibadan, Nigeria
Vocals / Sophisti-Pop, Quiet Storm, Adult Contemporary, Urban

When Sade first came on the recording scene in the '80s, her record company, Epic, made a point of printing "pronounced shar-day" after her name on the record labels of her releases. Soon enough the world would have no problem in correctly pronouncing her name. Born Helen Folasade Adu in a village 50 miles from Lagos, the capitol of Nigeria, she grew up on the North End of London.

Around 1980, she started singing harmony with a Latin funk group called Arriva. One of the more popular numbers that the group would perform was "Smooth Operator," which would later become her first stateside hit. The following year she joined the eight-piece funk band Pride as a background singer. The group played live frequently, helping Sade obtain a recording contract with the U.K. division of Epic Records. Her debut album, *Diamond Life*, went Top Ten in the U.K. in late 1984. Her third album, *Promise* (November 1985), featured "Never As Good As the First Time" and arguably her signature song, "The Sweetest Taboo," which stayed on the U.S. pop charts for six months. Sade was so popular that some radio stations reinstated the '70s practice of playing album tracks, adding "Is It a Crime" and "Tar Baby" to their play lists. In 1986, Sade won a Grammy for Best New Artist. Sade's third album was 1988's *Stronger Than Pride* and featured her first number one soul single "Paradise." 1992's *Love Deluxe* continued the unbroken streak of multi-platinum Sade albums, spinning off the hits "No Ordinary Love," "Feel No Pain," and

"Pearls," but after its release, the singer kept a low profile, performing only occasionally. — *Ed Hogan*

Diamond Life / 1984 / Epic ✦✦✦✦
Former model Sade made an immediate and huge impact with her 1984 debut album. Her sound and approach were deliberately icy, her delivery and voice aloof, deadpan and cold, and yet she became an instant sensation through such songs as "Smooth Operator" and "Your Love Is King," where the slick production and quasi-jazz backing seemed to register with audiences thinking they were hearing a jazz vocalist. Sade won the Best New Grammy Award for 1984, and *Diamond Life* sold more than two million copies. — *Ron Wynn*

Promise / 1985 / Epic ✦✦✦
Sade's second album improved on the performance of her debut, as "Sweetest Taboo" was a huge hit and "Never As Good As the First Time" landed in both the R&B and pop Top 20. She was once again the personification of cool, laid-back singing, seldom extending or embellishing lyrics, registering emotion, or projecting her voice. This demeanor made her more desirable in the minds of many fans and was perhaps the ultimate misapplication of the notion of sophistication. But this album topped the pop charts and eventually went triple platinum. — *Ron Wynn*

Stronger Than Pride / 1988 / Epic ✦✦✦
After two LPs with little or no energy, Sade demonstrated some intensity and fire on her third release. Whether that was just an attempt to change the pace a bit or a genuine new direction, she had more animation in her delivery on such songs as "Haunt Me," "Give It Up," and the hit "Paradise." Not that she was suddenly singing in a soulful or bluesy manner; rather, Sade's dry and introspective tone now had a little more edge, and the lyrics were ironic as well as reflective. This was her third consecutive multi-platinum album, and it matched the two-million-plus sales level of her debut. — *Ron Wynn*

Love Deluxe / Oct. 20, 1992 / Epic ✦✦✦✦✦
Sade's fourth album included the hit "No Ordinary Love" and marked a return to the detached, cool jazz backing and even icier vocals that made her debut album a sensation. Although Sade's style is more suggestive than hypnotic, and her production and arrangements are in an urbane mode rather than a jazz one, she's maintained her popularity among the fusion and urban-contemporary audiences. This release also included "Mermaid," "Pearls," and "Feel No Pain." — *Ron Wynn*

● **The Best of Sade** / 1994 / Epic ✦✦✦✦✦
It's easy to dismiss Sade as makeout music for Calvin Klein Obsession models, but she created an impressive body of work over the course of a decade, a series of moody singles with cool jazz passion and the kick of good R&B. All the hits are here, of course, from "Smooth Operator" to "No Ordinary Love." — *Eddie Huffman*

Lovers Rock / Nov. 14, 2000 / Epic ✦✦✦✦✦
Lovers Rock, the title of Sade's first album of the 21st century, could be taken on many levels. Never before has the singer infused more mainstream rock elements (prominent strummed guitars) into her music as evidenced by the first single, "By Your Side." That's not to say that she has eschewed her own tried-and-true brand of smoky, dusky ballads. The singer/songwriter is reunited with co-producer Mike Pela and musician/songwriters Andrew Hale, Stuart Matthewman, and Paul S. Denman; and *Lovers Rock* finds them all in fine form. "Somebody Already Broke My Heart," "Every Word," and "Lovers Rock" are vintage Sade. — *Ed Hogan*

Sagittarius

Sunshine Pop, Psychedelic Pop, Baroque Pop, Psychedelic, Pop

Although it only reached number 70 in the national charts, Sagittarius' 1967 single "My World Fell Down" is one of the great experimental pop-psych gems of the era. Sounding very much like a lost Beach Boys classic from the "Good Vibrations"/*Smile* era, the record had beautiful California pop harmonies, exquisite symphonic orchestration, and a downright avant-garde middle section of carnival and bullfight noises. It was perhaps too weird to become the Top 40 smash it deserved to be, but in any case, Sagittarius would have had a difficult time launching a successful career, as the group didn't really exist. It was a studio project of noted producer Gary Usher, who wrote several great Beach Boys songs with Brian Wilson and produced classic albums by the Byrds. Fellow songwriter/producer/singer Curt Boettcher wrote and sang much of the material that ended up on Sagittarius' 1968 Columbia album, *Present Tense*. — *Richie Unterberger*

● **Present Tense** / 1967 / Sundazed ✦✦✦✦✦
All 11 tracks from the 1968 LP, with the addition of seven previously unreleased items and a couple cuts from non-LP singles. Although the production is beautiful and the songwriting melodic, the material is really too cloying to qualify this as a lost classic. When

there's even a bit of a serious or melancholic edge—as on the graceful opening track "Another Time," or Usher's strange and stunning slice of psych-pop, "The Truth Is Not Real"—it's much more memorable. Otherwise, this is kind of like the lesser fairy-tale, sing-songy British psychedelia of the time, but with state-of-the-art L.A. '60s production. The bonus cuts are similar to the album, highlighted by the gorgeous instrumental "Sister Marie," although the non-LP single "Hotel Indiscreet" is silly fluff. The version of "My World Fell Down" that appeared on *Present Tense* was brutally edited, but fear not: one of the bonus cuts is the classic original single version, all of its glory (and avant-garde bridge of found noise) intact. *—Richie Unterberger*

Doug Sahm

b. Nov. 6, 1941, San Antonio, TX, **d.** Nov. 18, 1999, Taos, NM

Vocals, Leader, Violin, Songwriter, Guitar / Americana, Roots Rock, Tex-Mex, Country-Rock, Progressive Country, Blues-Rock, Rock & Roll

Guitarist, composer, arranger, and songwriter Doug Sahm was a knowledgeable music historian and veteran performer equally comfortable in a range of styles, including Texas blues, country, rock & roll, Western swing, and Cajun. Beginning in 1955, the San Antonio-born Sahm recorded a series of singles for a procession of Texas-based record companies. After being prompted in 1965 to assemble a group by producer Huey Meaux, Sahm recruited some friends who became the Sir Douglas Quintet. The group had some success on the radio with "The Rains Came," but later broke up, and Sahm moved to California. There he reformed the Quintet and recorded a now-classic single, "Mendocino." The resulting album of the same name was a groundbreaking record in the then-emerging country-rock scene. The Sir Douglas Quintet followed *Mendocino* with *Together After Five*, another album that led them to a larger fan base. Atlantic Records producer Jerry Wexler realized that country-rock sounds were coming into vogue (and that there was no place in Nashville for people like Sahm), and signed both Sahm and Willie Nelson. One of Sahm's greatest albums, 1973's *Doug Sahm and Band*, was recorded in New York City with Bob Dylan, Dr. John, and accordionist Flaco Jiminez. The Sir Douglas Quintet later got back together again to record two more albums, *Wanted Very Much Alive* and *Back to the 'Dillo*. Among Sahm's most essential blues records are 1980's *Hell of a Spell* and his Grammy-nominated studio album for Antone's, *The Last Real Texas Blues Band*. For his other material, there are several good compilations, including *The Best of Doug Sahm* (Rhino). Sahm died on November 18, 1999. *—Richard Skelly*

● **The Best of Doug Sahm (1968-1975) [Rhino]** / 1991 / Rhino ♦♦♦♦♦

Whether he was playing roots rock, garage punk, blues, country, norteño, or (as was often the case) something that mixed up several of the above-mentioned ingredients, Doug Sahm always sounded like Doug Sahm—a little wild, a little loose, but always good company, and a guy with a whole lot of soul who knew a lot of musicians upon whom the same praise could be bestowed. Pulling together a single disc compilation that would make sense of the length and breadth of the artist's recording career (which spanned five decades) would be just about impossible, but this disc, which boasts 22 songs recorded over the course of eight years, is a pretty good starter for anyone wanting to get to know Sahm's music. You get two almost-hits ("Mendocino" and "[Is Anybody Going To] San Antone"), a healthy portion of memorable album cuts, and even a few unreleased songs as Sir Doug and his pals swing through vintage blues, country weepers, rootsy hippie jams, and a few cuts that defy convenient description, all dominated by Sahm's warm, expressive drawl, distinctive guitar work, and the loose but emphatic sound he knew how to draw from a band. Put it this way—there's one guy in a million who could write and record a song called "You Never Get Too Big and You Sure Don't Get Too Heavy That You Don't Have to Stop and Pay Some Dues Sometime" and not sound like a fool. Doug Sahm was that man, and you get to hear him sing it on *The Best of Doug Sham*, along with 21 other equally cool tunes. *—Mark Deming*

The Best of Doug Sahm (1968-1975) [Sequel] / 1995 / Sequel ♦♦♦♦

She's About a Mover: The Best of Crazy Cajun Recording / Oct. 26, 1999 / Edsel ♦♦♦♦

This differs from Music Club's package in that this set also includes tracks issued as Doug Sahm solo sides, giving us a time frame between 1964 and 1977 to hear Sahm's art unfold. Of course, the early SDQ sides are the big ticket here. Rough and raw, they include the two big hits "She's About a Mover" and "The Rains Came." Yet the solo sides that fill up the cracks here are also every bit as raw, sometimes disconcertingly so, like the bass and drums that lose track of each other in the middle of "Seguin" or the maracas that never quite catch up to the band track on "You've Got Your Good Thing Down." If you wondered what Huey Meaux had in the vault on Sahm, here's your chance to find out. *—Cub Koda*

San Antonio Rock: The Harlem Recordings 1957-1961 / Apr. 4, 2000 / Norton ♦♦♦♦

If you think Doug Sahm's career began with the Sir Douglas Quintet, guess again. This 18-track collection rounds up all of Sahm's early 45s and demos, as well as rarities with Doug playing sideman in various Texas combos, the majority of it issued on the Harlem label out of Fort Worth. It's raw Texas music, soaked in R&B and rock & roll, and Sahm goes through no less than seven different backing units on this set, not to mention his sideman work with Spot Barnett, Jimmy Dee, and Red Hilburn. Lots of alternate takes, great booklet with loads of information, all putting into historical perspective this missing chapter in the history of this modern Texas troubadour. *—Cub Koda*

In the Beginning / Aug. 29, 2000 / Aim ♦♦♦

In the Beginning chronicles the earliest singles released by the late Texas renegade Doug Sahm. Recorded between 1958 and 1962, these 14 songs encompass Tex-Mex, R&B, doo wop, polka, and early rock & roll from Sahm's pre-Sir Douglas Quintet days on the Harlem, Cobra, and Renner labels. Rare regional singles "Crazy Daisy," "Why, Why, Why," "Slow Down," "Baby Tell Me," and "Just a Moment" are a few of the gems collected. *—Al Campbell*

Son of San Antonio: The Roots of Sir Douglas / Sep. 11, 2001 / Music Club ♦♦♦♦

Saint Etienne

f. 1988, Croydon, Surrey, England

Indie Pop, Alternative Dance, Brit-pop, Club/Dance, Alternative Pop/Rock

Like most bands formed by former music journalists, Saint Etienne was a highly conceptual group. The trio's concept was to fuse the British pop sounds of '60s London with the dance club rhythms and productions that defined the post-acid house England of the early '90s. Led by songwriters Bob Stanley and Pete Wiggs, and fronted by vocalist Sarah Cracknell, the group managed to carry out their concept, and, in the process, they helped make indie-dance a viable genre within the UK. Throughout the early '90s, Saint Etienne racked up a string of indie hit singles that were driven by deep club beats—encompassing anything from house and techno to hip-hop and disco—and layered with light melodies, detailed productions, clever lyrics, and Cracknell's breathy vocals. They revived the sounds of swinging London, as well as the concept of the three-minute pop single being a catchy, ephemeral piece of ear candy, in post-acid house Britan, thereby setting the stage for Brit-pop. Though most Brit-pop bands rejected the dance inclinations of Saint Etienne, they nevertheless adopted the trio's aesthetic, which celebrated the sound and style of classic '60s pop. *—Stephen Thomas Erlewine*

Fox Base Alpha / Jan. 14, 1992 / Warner Brothers ♦♦♦

Despite a handful of classic pop singles, Saint Etienne's debut album *Fox Base Alpha* is a tentative fusion of club culture and swinging '60s pop. Lead vocalist Sarah Cracknell hasn't been fully integrated into the band's lineup—she doesn't even sing on their astonishing Eurodisco cover of Neil Young's "Only Love Will Break Your Heart," which is not only cleverly ironic, but also works—yet the filler remains thoroughly enjoyable, even if it rarely reaches the heights of the irresistible girl-group pop of "Kiss and Make Up." *—Stephen Thomas Erlewine*

So Tough / Mar. 9, 1993 / Warner Brothers ♦♦♦♦♦

Saint Etienne's second album, *So Tough*, is a remarkable step forward from *Fox Base Alpha*, boasting a stronger set of songs and a sharper focus. Not only are the pop melodies catchier than before, the group's mastery of swinging '60s arrangements and Eurodisco rhythms is positively infectious, and Sarah Cracknell's light, airy vocals are alluringly dreamy, giving the record a wonderful, floating quality. The cool club beats, occasional samples, and synthesized textures provide an inviting sonic backdrop for Bob Stanley and Pete Wiggs' infectious pop songs, and while the singles "You're in a Bad Way" and "Hobart Paving" stand out, there are several other tracks here that are nearly as good, making *So Tough* an irresistible set of danceable, well-constructed pop. *—Stephen Thomas Erlewine*

Tiger Bay / Jun. 28, 1994 / Warner Brothers ♦♦♦♦

Tiger Bay abandons the unassuming charm of *So Tough* for a grander sound. Saint Etienne fill *Tiger Bay* with sonic details, from sampled bits of dialogue to musical references that give the record some depth, but occasionally those very sounds make the album feel over-labored. Still, the group frequently fulfills their ambitions, particularly on "Hug My Soul," "Like a Motorway," and the delightfully exuberant "I Was Born on Christmas Day," which features guest vocals by the Charlatans' Tim Burgess. Moments like these, plus Saint Etienne's widening sonic palette, make *Tiger Bay* a thoroughly enjoyable affair, despite its handful of faults. *—Stephen Thomas Erlewine*

● **Too Young to Die** / Nov. 1995 / Heavenly ♦♦♦♦♦

Although their albums were considerably more consistent than most dance-pop acts, Saint Etienne's high points were always their singles. Released prior to a quiet, lengthy hiatus, *Too Young to Die* collects all of their singles, from their debut disco cover of Neil Young's "Only Love Can Break Your Heart" to their last, "He's on the Phone," providing a thoroughly entertaining chronicle of the group's career. Much of the music sounds somewhat dated—which is always a problem with dance music—but Saint Etienne was essentially a very good Euro-pop band, reveling in kitsch and style in equal measure. At their best—"Only Love Can Break Your Heart," "You're in a Bad Way," "Join Our Club," "Who Do You Think You Are," among others—they found the heart in nightclubbing. The quality of the music dips slightly in the latter half of the album, but there is prime pop throughout the disc. [Initial pressings came with a bonus disc of remixes, all of which are worthwhile for dedicated fans.] *—Stephen Thomas Erlewine*

Casino Classics / Oct. 7, 1996 / Heavenly ♦♦♦

The title makes a sly reference to a legendary Northern soul club, which is appropriate, since *Casino Classics* is a collection of dance remixes. Comprised equally of classic 12" remixes and new offerings from the likes of the Aphex Twin and Chemical Brothers, the double-disc *Casino Classics* does have some wildly imaginative reinterpretations, but only dedicated Saint Etienne collectors or dance-club devotees need to bother with the collection. *—Stephen Thomas Erlewine*

Continental / Jun. 1997 / Nippon Columbia ♦♦♦

The trio Saint Etienne (songwriters/musicians Pete Wiggs and Bob Stanley and vocalist Sarah Cracknell) has been a popular fixture in the British indie dance scene since the release of its debut album *Fox Base Alpha* in 1992. Combining '60s-influenced pop and the acid house rhythms of the British club scene, the band has scored with a series of successful European albums and singles. Saint Etienne has also earned critical acclaim and a loyal cult following in America (particularly in dance clubs), though U.S. commercial success has been elusive. Saint Etienne has released a series of strong albums since the early 1990s. *Continental* is a superb collection of mostly previously released material, and it's a nice introduction to their solid body of work. Their strong points are the combination of atmospheric (yet accessible) arrangements and Sarah Cracknell's '60s girl-group cooing. However, her vocals are not derivative or cutesy, instead lending substantial personality to the material. "Burnt Out Car" and "He's on the Phone" benefit greatly from her performances, mainly because Saint Etienne rarely incorporates obvious pop hooks. Rather, the band relies more on rhythm and personality, making them considerably more complex than the average pop/dance band. *Continental*'s best track is a house cover of Gary Numan's "Stormtrooper in Drag" (it previously appeared on a Gary Numan tribute album), which is odd in concept but surprisingly effective. Fortunately, *Continental* surrounds that tune with equally competent Saint Etienne originals. Any of the group's studio albums, particularly *So Tough* and *Tiger Bay*, will serve as a nice introduction to the band's music, since the trio's best albums stand on their own quite nicely. However, various collections of singles, remixes, and rare material have also been released, and *Continental* is by far one of the best. Highly recommended. *—William Cooper*

Good Humor / Sep. 1998 / Creation ♦♦♦♦

Good Humor has Saint Etienne back cooking up more delectable lolli-pop. From "Woodcabin," the dubby, bass-heavy opener, *Good Humor* is a typically arch Saint Etienne album full of easy-listening dream pop. Tracks like the shimmering "Lose That Girl" and the swirling "Erica America" show Saint Etienne at its melancholic best. There are, predictably, some near misses such as the Beatlesque "Mr. Donut," which is as sweet as a strawberry field but fails to deliver the melodic promises made by the smart atmospherics. "Goodnight Jack," with its pastel-shaded flute loops and subtle breakbeats, has a positively cooler-than-cool feel and a wrenching change of pace toward the middle of the song. Sure, *Good Humor* is clever, perhaps overly so, and yeah, it's full of the Et's contrived coyness and we-know-more-than-you attitude, but it's good stuff. Sometimes you just want to put on a disc, sit back, and let it carry you off to someplace else. If that's all you're looking for, *Good Humor* is sweet ear candy. *—Matthew Hilburn*

Sound of Water / Jun. 22, 2000 / Sub Pop ♦♦♦♦

Ten years on, Saint Etienne found themselves at a bit of a crossroads. They had long ago stopped having hits in the U.K., settling into a cult audience in both their homeland and the U.S. There isn't an inherent problem with having a cult audience, but cult bands often have the stigma of being on the cutting edge. At the start of their career, Saint Etienne was on the cutting edge. Their first two albums were at the foundation of many '90s pop trends, including the revival of swinging '60s London, the unabashedly melodic bent of Brit-pop, the fascination for forgotten easy-listening artifacts from the '60s, the kaleidoscopic blend of '60s sound and '90s sensibility later heard on Beck records, plus the insurgent twee-pop of the late '90s. For their tenth anniversary, they decided to reclaim the cutting edge with *Sound of Water*. The album strove to keep the concise, song-oriented focus of *Good Humour*, while expanding the horizons of their music to focus on abstract, dreamy, electronic sounds. There are moments of pop pleasure here, surrounded by spare, languid electronica sections, vaguely reminiscent of the High Llamas. This is where maturity pays off. Saint Etienne never lingers too long in one area, letting the album flow gracefully between these two extremes and placing some very good pop melodies along the way. There are no knockout singles on par with those from *So Tough* or *Tiger Bay*, but Saint Etienne has pretty much given up on the pop charts, preferring to concentrate on cohesive, stronger albums. That may mean that *Sound of Water* simply isn't as exciting as their earlier work, and it also means that there isn't a good gateway song to the record. But that's OK, since with repeated plays, *Sound of Water* reveals itself as a first-rate effort. *—Stephen Thomas Erlewine*

Interlude / Feb. 20, 2001 / Sub Pop ♦♦♦

Fans of Saint Etienne who aren't quite dedicated enough to pay attention to the singles could be easily tricked into thinking *Interlude* is a new studio album. Given a different title and the subtraction of the two extraneous remixes at the end (the single mix of "Boy Is Crying" and the Trouser Enthusiasts mix of "Lose That Girl"), this would stand up pretty well as a follow-up to 2000's excellent *Sound of Water*. With the exception of three new compositions and their cover of the Beach Boys' "Stevie," these songs were recorded during the sessions for that record. So they tend to have the same graceful, minimal, melodic touches. In a few cases, the songs rival or eclipse material on *Sound of Water*, but they probably weren't included because they didn't fit the general, easygoing flow of the immaculately sequenced album. "Northwestern" is one such example of B-side brilliance; although it's one of their best overall moments, Sarah Cracknell's melancholic vocals would have found the track misplaced with the remainder of the record. "Shoot Out the Lights," which isn't a Richard & Linda Thompson cover, is the most organic of the bunch, a jumpy throwback to their *Good Humor* days. As for the new songs, they're promising if not much of a departure. "Mountain Rain" reigns supreme over the two other newbies, graced with swirling electronic drizzle and Cracknell's just-out-of-bed whispering. But what's most remarkable about *Interlude* is that Saint Etienne can deliver the goods over a decade into their career, even on a disc of extras. Admittedly, those who didn't care for *Sound of Water*'s spare production won't find much here. But those who did care will find a group in top form, to say the least. *—Andy Kellman*

Smash the System: Singles and More / Sep. 2001 / Heavenly ♦♦♦♦♦

The Saints

f. 1977, Australia

College Rock, Aussie Rock, Post-Punk, Alternative Pop/Rock, Punk

Roaring out of Brisbane, Australia in 1977 with the punk-era classic "(I'm) Stranded," the Saints, despite going through numerous incarnations, have been a part of rock & roll for over 20 years, thanks mainly to their indefatigable leader (and founder) Chris Bailey. Saints fans fall into two distinct camps: the punk-era fans (up to about 1980) and the mature pop fans, which for American audiences begins with the release of *All Fools Day* in 1987; for many, the feral assault of their first three records (when co-founder Ed Kuepper was in the band) is more interesting and exciting. After the LP *(I'm) Stranded* became a modest hit in England in 1977, the follow-up record, *Eternally Yours*, showed some changes (more varied tempos, acoustic guitars) that would set the stage for their third record, *Prehistoric Sounds*, which combined horn arrangements into a punkish sort of R&B. Kuepper left in 1979 to form the arty Laughing Clowns and eventually made a number of records as a solo act. Bailey, however, got to keep the name the Saints and soldiered on, taking time here and there to record his own solo records; the twists and turns he took the band through (horns, folk/blues arrangements, etc.) produced some good music, but it was mostly scattershot and too difficult to wade through the mediocre material. By the time *All Fools Day* was released in 1987, there were many who thought the Saints were a brand new band—and they were right. Gone were the rapid-fire guitar sound and bellowing vocals, replaced by sophisticated pop arrangements and more technically accomplished singing. The music was strong, intelligent pop that was better than much late-'80s new wave. The next LP, *Prodigal Son*, wasn't as good, but did nothing to hurt the reputation of the "new" Saints. Despite extended dormant periods, the Saints have never officially broken up, and Bailey always seems to have another version of the band ready. *—John Dougan*

● **(I'm) Stranded** / 1977 / Captain Oi! ♦♦♦♦♦

Around the time Sire was scooping up every band under the sun that played like the Ramones, they had the smarts to sign the Saints, who were creating great punk rock. Along with the title track, there are rough and ready bits of speed-burn, like "Erotic Neurotic," and very unpunk-like tracks in terms of song length, six minutes of "Messin' With the Kid" (not the Junior Wells song). Toss in a piss-take of Elvis' "Kissin' Cousins," and you've got the makings of a fine slice of history. This is their best record, for a lot of reasons, but primarily for its energy, high spirits, and smarts. *—John Dougan*

Prehistoric Sounds / 1978 / Harvest ♦♦♦♦

With *Prehistoric Sounds* (the last record of the band's original lineup), the Saints provide the textbook by which to make a great rock record where horns play as much of a role as guitar. Further extracting themselves from the limitations of punk, the band retains the attitude and turns it into a smart, bluesy, gutsy combination of controlled power. There's more dip in the hip and additional swagger. The days of "(I'm) Stranded" might have been long gone, but the varied tempos and sophisticated songwriting doesn't sacrifice the band's intensity at all. The horns are the real treat, a central element to the record's solidity. They don't make the Saints sound like Chicago, and they don't make them sound like a faux '70s soul band—they don't make them sound like the Doors of "Touch Me" or the Bowie of *Young Americans*, either. Whether used for the basis or just punctuation of each song, the tasteful use of saxaphones is a genuine masterstroke. The dynamic "Brisbane (Security City)"—which is like an update of the Stooges' "1969" and "1970" in terms of subject matter—is the high point. After two minutes of Chris Bailey's Iggy-like lament on his hometown, the medium tempo shifts into high gear, thanks to rhythmic overdrive, charged guitars, and (of course) the ubiquitous horns. Other bright spots include "Every Day's a Holiday, Every Night's a Party" and an energetic cover of Otis Redding's "Security," where Bailey sounds so much like a young Van Morrison that it's scary. *—Andy Kellman*

Eternally Yours / 1978 / Captain Oi! ♦♦♦♦♦

While the into-the-wind blare of the title cut was what people remembered best, the Saints' first album, *(I'm) Stranded*, had a lot more musical variety than it was generally given credit for in 1977, and the band stayed much farther from the standard punk template (which had solidified with remarkable speed in the wake of the Sex Pistols) on their second LP, *Eternally Yours*. For their sophomore outing, the Saints threw actual tempo changes, horn charts, keyboards, and R&B accents into the mix, which didn't endear them to punk purists, who predictably didn't recognize that these changes had only strengthened the band's sound. Anyone looking for blazing 4/4 punk will find it in "Lost and Found" and "Private Affair," but the horn-fueled "Know Your Product" and "Orstralia" proved that punk could also sound soulful (Rocket From the Crypt owe their entire career to these cuts); the moody "A Minor Aversion," "Untitled," and "Memories Are Made of This" proved the Saints could slow it down and still sound tough and impassioned; and "This Perfect Day" is quite possibly the greatest song this band would ever record—Chris Bailey's sneer of "It's so funny I can't laugh" is alone worth the price of admission. While *Eternally Yours* is a bit less consistent than *(I'm) Stranded*, the material is first-rate, the band sounds better than ever, and the approach suggests the pop-smart eclecticism of the band's mid-'80s period fused with the muscle and ferocity of their debut. Maybe *Eternally Yours* didn't sound like a standard-issue punk album in 1978, but it's stood the test of time much better than most of the work of punk's first graduating class. *—Mark Deming*

The Monkey Puzzle / 1981 / New Rose ♦♦♦♦

The Monkey Puzzle, the Saints' first full-length album after the departure of founding guitarist/songwriter Ed Kuepper, is quite different from the first three Saints LPs—which were all different from each other anyway—but holds up well to the test of time. Instead of the abrasive punk or Memphisy sound of earlier records, *Monkey Puzzle*'s jangly rock hints at the direction bands like R.E.M. took mid-'80s college rock. Lead singer Chris Bailey's distinctive, resonant voice shines on the gorgeous "Let's Pretend," the very Byrdsy "Always," and the incendiary "Simple Love." The Australian version also includes the classic B-side, "In the Mirror," with its highly memorable bass intro and astounding hooks, and a wonderfully sloppy and loose cover of Larry Williams' "Dizzy Miss Lizzy." Elsewhere, the fare is more conventional rock, albeit with chiming guitar, great songs, and singing. Barrington Francis' jangly guitar, original drummer Ivor Hay, and bassist Janine Hall give the band an entirely new dimension. On its release, *Monkey Puzzle* shocked fans with its maturity; though it was made by 21-year-old punk, most other 21-year-old punks thought it was too much like regular rock—a sin in 1981. Since it wasn't released in the U.S. or England, not many people heard it anyway. Ironically, a few years later, bands like Guadalcanal Diary and the Connells came to the forefront using a very similar approach. Of course, by then Bailey had moved into a whole new musical space. Highly recommended. —*Geoff Ginsberg*

A Little Madness to Be Free / 1984 / New Rose ✦✦✦✦
On this album, the Saints shift gears yet again. *A Little Madness to Be Free* takes the band (which is actually just a vehicle for singer Chris Bailey at this point) in a denser, more layered direction. This time, brass and strings dominate with lush acoustic guitars underneath. Obviously, any trace of the punk band that was is gone. The power, however, remains. Like its follow-up, the devastating *All Fools Day*, this record explores the depths of irony, and the ironies of depth. Through exploration of the soul there is (musical at least) redemption. From the incredibly beautiful photo of a bay at sunset on the album cover, to the opening track, "Down the Drain," the tone is set. "Still I think it's better to stand out in the rain/then go slipping on down the drain," Bailey sings. A melancholy rainy-day vibe so damn gray it's vibrant. You can't help but be transported by it. Somehow there is catharsis, so the end result is not an overall bummer. The album concludes with one of Bailey's all-time classic songs, "Ghostships," a track so amazing he went and put it on several more albums, re-recording it twice. While electric guitars are not the centerpiece of the sound here, the layers make for an equally powerful experience. Surprisingly, there are really no keyboards to speak of, which is very unusual for a non-guitar rock album. By this point in his career, Bailey had come into his own as an arranger and it really shows. Certainly one of the Saints' most obscure discs, but ultimately as rewarding as the classics *I'm Stranded, Eternally Yours*, and *All Fools Day*. —*Geoff Ginsberg*

All Fools Day / 1987 / TVT ✦✦✦✦✦
Call this the second coming of the Saints, but the only thing this record has in common with previous Saints recordings is Chris Bailey. Still, it's a sharp, tuneful, and (ahem) mature work that shows Bailey's increasing confidence as a singer and songwriter. One listen to songs as grabbing as "Celtic Ballad" or the great "Just Like Fire Would" (which is kind of a neat pun) will convince you that despite the differences, the new Saints were a good band for completely different reasons than the old Saints. —*John Dougan*

Howling / 1997 / Blue Rose ✦✦✦

Everybody Knows the Monkey / Oct. 27, 1998 / Amsterdamned ✦✦✦

● **Wild About You (1976-1978)** / 2000 / Raven ✦✦✦✦✦
The Australian compilation *Wild About You (1976-1978)* is the first place to go for the Saints in more ways than one. The thorough, double-disc anthology exhaustively includes the Australian band's first three records (1977's *(I'm) Stranded* and 1978's *Prehistoric Sounds* and *Eternally Yours*), as well as every stray EP and single track recorded by the Ed Kuepper/Chris Bailey era of the Saints—the period that spawned the band's best material. To lure the rabid fans, four previously unissued recordings are included. The results of the vault looting aren't anywhere near the levels of "(I'm) Stranded" or "Brisbane (Security City)," but they weren't unearthed just to take advantage of the consumer, either. Additionally, the package is dolled up with scads of photos and extensive liner notes provided by numerous sources. It's odd that such a collection would surface in close proximity to the individual U.K. reissues of *(I'm) Stranded* and *Eternally Yours*, but this is the kind of package that appeals to beginners and longtime fans. At two discs, the price isn't much of a financial risk for the newbie, and the scope of the material is too grand to be ignored by the familiar. As far as punk and post-punk are considered, this is a rather essential document. —*Andy Kellman*

Sallyangie

British Folk, Folk-Rock
The Sallyangie, the British folk duo of Sally Oldfield and her brother Michael, were signed upon the recommendation of guitarist John Renbourn of the Pentangle. Sally was 21 years old, and Michael a mere 16, at the time of their late-'60s album *Children of the Sun*, which was produced by the legendary Shel Talmy (who also produced Pentangle). Not surprisingly, the result was crystalline, gentle contemporary British folk with similarities to Pentangle, but considerably more low-key. The Oldfields collaborated on the writing of all of the material on their sole outing. Mike Oldfield went on to join Kevin Ayers' band and achieve stardom as a progressive rock guitarist and composer with *Tubular Bells*, while Sally recorded less successful but equally ambitious art-rock albums as a solo act. —*Richie Unterberger*

Children of the Sun / 1969 / Warner Brothers ✦✦✦
A gentle, fairy-tale ambience pervades on this album of harmony folk tunes, on which Sally's high trills generally overshadow Mike's vocal contributions. —*Richie Unterberger*

Salt-N-Pepa

f. 1985
Pop-Rap, Urban, Hip-Hop
By the late '80s, hip-hop was on its way to becoming a male-dominated art form, which is what made the emergence of Salt-N-Pepa so significant. As the first all-female rap crew (even their DJs were women) of importance, the group broke down a number of doors for women in hip-hop. They were also one of the first rap artists to crossover into the pop mainstream, laying the groundwork for the music's widespread acceptance in the early '90s. Salt-N-Pepa were more pop-oriented than many of their contemporaries, since their songs were primarily party and love anthems, driven by big beats and interlaced with vaguely pro-feminist lyrics that seemed more powerful when delivered by the charismatic and sexy trio. While songs like "Push It" and "Shake Your Thang" made the group

appear to be a one-hit pop group during the late '80s, Salt-N-Pepa defied expectations and became one of the few hip-hop artists to develop a long-term career. Along with L.L. Cool J, the trio had major hits in both the '80s and '90s, and, if anything, they hit the height of their popularity in 1994, when "Shoop" and "Whatta Man" drove their third album, *Very Necessary*, into the Top Ten. —*Stephen Thomas Erlewine*

Hot, Cool & Vicious / 1986 / Next Plateau ✦✦✦✦✦
One of the earliest female rap groups, they hit the big leagues with this debut that includes the pulsating "Push It" and the salacious "Tramp." —*John Floyd*

A Salt With a Deadly Pepa / 1988 / London ✦✦✦
A concept album musically, if not lyrically, this one fleshes out one terrific single, "Shake Your Thing," with a sharpening of the trio's sensibilities and talents. —*John Floyd*

A Blitz of Hits: The Hits Remixed / 1989 / London ✦✦

● **Blacks' Magic** / Mar. 1990 / London ✦✦✦✦✦
Another concept album, this time the themes celebrate black education and awareness, with some concise feminism included. —*John Floyd*

Very Necessary / Oct. 12, 1993 / London ✦✦✦✦
While Salt-N-Pepa definitely took their time releasing albums during their career, they returned from a three-year sabbatical in 1993 with *Very Necessary*, a smart album that furthered the progressive femininity that had worked so well for them on *Blacks' Magic*. Unfortunately, *Very Necessary* wasn't as strong of an album as *Blacks' Magic*, but the female rappers did come prepared with a pair of potent singles capable of carrying the album commercially, "Shoop" and "Whatta Man." Given the success of "Let's Talk About Sex" three years earlier, it's little surprise that Salt-N-Pepa instilled that song's progressive feminine ideology into both "Shoop" and "Whatta Man." Like "Let's Talk About Sex," these two songs aren't overly serious—employing a safe, club-friendly hip-hop rhythm and catchy, radio-friendly vocal hooks—but they do manage to communicate their message of feminine pride and a social norm-challenging view of female sexuality quite effectively without sacrificing any sense of fun. Besides these two obviously contrived singles, there aren't too many other major highlights here, with the exception of "None of Your Business," another song laden with subtle social commentary regarding femininity. Elsewhere, a few songs such as "I've Got AIDS" and "Sexy Noises Turn Me On" are similarly interesting from an ideological standpoint but just aren't that impressive in terms of rapping or production—this can be said for the remainder of the album as well. When you benchmark the best moments on *Very Necessary* against the lesser moments, you get the sense that the group was far more interested in crafting the obligatory crossover singles rather than a solid album from beginning to end. Nonetheless, the album stands only second to *Blacks' Magic* as the strongest of Salt-N-Pepa's 15-year career. —*Jason Birchmeier*

Brand New / Oct. 21, 1997 / London/Red Ant ✦✦✦
The four years separating Salt-N-Pepa's latter-day blockbuster *Very Necessary* and its successor, *Brand New*, is an eternity in hip-hop. During that time, styles and fashions change rapidly, leaving many artists behind. Salt-N-Pepa suffer from being out of the spotlight for so long—they don't sound in tune with the times, they sound like they're stuck in 1993. However, that isn't necessarily a bad thing since the group does this kind of thing very well. There isn't anything that stands out like "Whatta Man" or "Shoop," but there's enough strong moments to make it worthwhile for longtime fans. —*Stephen Thomas Erlewine*

Sam & Dave

f. 1961, Miami, FL
Deep Soul, Southern Soul, Soul
Perhaps no act epitomized soul music as the secularization of gospel more than Sam & Dave. The original pairing of Sam Moore and Dave Prater met in Florida in 1961, and they recorded unsuccessfully for several years before being signed to Atlantic Records in 1965. Atlantic persuaded their Memphis affiliate Stax Records to produce them, and in December that year the writing and production team of Isaac Hayes and David Porter delivered the crisply soulful "You Don't Know Like I Know." Hayes and Porter became the "eminences grises" behind Sam & Dave, much as Holland-Dozier-Holland pulled the strings behind the Supremes. They wrote, they produced—and the result was a string of hits, including "Soul Man," "Hold On I'm Coming" and "I Thank You," songs that survive as the very epitome of Southern soul. Certainly, Sam & Dave's hits are among the most soulful ever to crack the Hot 100. Their albums often bore the hallmarks of hasty execution, though. The dissolution of the partnership between Stax and Atlantic virtually sealed the fate of Sam & Dave; there were a few more hits (and, later, a revival of interest thanks to the Blues Brothers), but the glory days were over. —*Colin Escott & Stephen Thomas Erlewine*

Sam & Dave / 1962 / Roulette ✦✦✦
Roulette didn't release this album until 1966—two years after Sam & Dave's last Roulette single. They had become a household name via Stax Records when this hit the market. It is definitive Roulette, containing both sides of their six singles for the label. Roulette featured Dave Prater's baritone/tenor more prominently than Sam Moore's vibrant gospel tenor—Stax featured Moore. They recorded "I Got a Thing Going On," "I Need Love," "No Pain," and "Keep Walkin'" at Criterion Studios in Miami for Henry Stone. And according to Moore they first dropped on either Marlin or TK Records (the Rolling Stones' labels). Their first Roulette release, "I Need Love," written by Moore and Sam Early (not Prater as credited) went unnoticed. A nondescript "No More Pain" did no better. Through Morris Levy (the nefarious owner of Roulette) they kept busy gigging with no hits. According to Moore, "Jackie Wilson hung around the studio and sings background

(uncredited) on many of these tracks." A third release, "She's Alright," failed miserably. Only the flowing "It's So Nice While It Lasted" where Prater and Moore's voices blend soulfully had any juice; it almost broke in 1963. Roulette released the charmer again in 1966 to ride the wave of their Stax hits. —*Andrew Hamilton*

Hold On, I'm Comin' / 1966 / Atlantic ◆◆◆◆
When the northern soulsters of Motown were employing strings and pop elements, Sam & Dave rejected pop wholesale and made sure they kept their Memphis soul simple and raw. Their albums never sounded heavily produced, and therein lies much of the appeal of *Hold On, I'm Comin'* (their first album for Atlantic). This wasn't a duo that believed in hiding behind lavish productions. Like the blues and gospel artists who paved the way for soul music, Sam & Dave knew how to seize the moment. From such major hits as "You Don't Know Like I Know" and the title song to solid album tracks like the riveting "It's a Wonder" and the tough yet vulnerable ballad "Just Me," this album epitomizes Memphis soul in all its unpretentious, down-home glory. A song-for-song reissue of the original LP, the CD version of *Hold On, I'm Comin'* that Atlantic put out in 1991 is rather skimpy by CD standards (as are the CD versions of *Soul Men* and *I Thank You*). Certainly Atlantic could have provided some bonus tracks. Nonetheless, this CD is well worth hearing. —*Alex Henderson*

Double Dynamite / 1967 / Atlantic ◆◆◆◆
This was the second Sam & Dave album to enjoy significant crossover appeal. The 1967 record included such hits as "Said I Wasn't Gonna Tell Nobody," "Soothe Me," and "When Something Is Wrong With My Baby." Isaac Hayes and David Porter were now rolling as songwriters, and even though the record didn't attain big pop numbers, the singles clicked with both soul and pop audiences. More importantly, Sam And Dave's teamwork and vocal interaction were establishing them as major stars. —*Ron Wynn*

Soul Men / 1967 / Rhino ◆◆◆◆
Because R&B was such a singles-driven market in the 1960s, many albums released by Stax and Motown were big on filler. But that generally wasn't the case with Sam & Dave's albums, which boasted many gems that weren't released as singles and enjoyed little, if any, radio airplay. Listeners may be surprised to learn that as popular as this twosome was in 1967, *Soul Men* contains only one major single: the anthemic title song and its B-side, the charming "May I Baby." Among the first-class album tracks never released as singles were "Rich Kind of Poverty," the punchy "Hold It Baby," and the gospel-drenched ballads "Just Keep Holding On" and "I've Seen What Loneliness Can Do." For those with more than a casual interest in Memphis soul, *Soul Men* (reissued on CD in 1991) is highly recommended. —*Alex Henderson*

I Thank You / 1968 / Rhino ◆◆◆
Although not quite as strong as *Hold On, I'm Comin'* or *Soul Men*, *I Thank You* serves as a fine illustration of the splendor of Memphis soul. The best known songs on this album (reissued on CD in 1992) are the title song and its infectious B-side, "Wrap It Up." Interestingly, this wasn't an album that contained a lot of major hits, but it does have a lot to admire, including "If I Didn't Have a Girl Like You" (a gem of a ballad), the driving "Ain't That a Lot of Love," and an inspired version of Otis Redding's "These Arms of Mine." As usual, Isaac Hayes' arranging and songwriting is a definite asset for the energetic duo, which really digs right into the material and spares no passion. —*Alex Henderson*

The Best of Sam & Dave / 1969 / Atlantic ◆◆◆◆
During the early '80s, Atlantic released newer compilations from some of the most popular R&B artists from the '60s, including Aretha Franklin and Wilson Pickett. *The Best of Sam & Dave* perhaps works even better. Although the duo's 1969 greatest hits remains definitive from a pop culture and song choice perspective, this boasts superior sound and zero filler. Like all of their compilations of merit, *The Best of Sam & Dave* proves the precision of the backing from Booker T. and the MG's and the duo's most illustrious songwriting team, Isaac Hayes and David Porter. The writing team's masterwork, the amazing and kinetic "Soul Man" was in line with the burgeoning black pride of the time. While other well-known tracks like "When Something Is Wrong With My Baby" and "Hold on, I'm Comin'" are here, *The Best of Sam & Dave* also culls other songs that are just as potent. The humorous "Said I Wasn't Gonna Tell Nobody" and the hard-driving yet quirky "Wrap It Up" all display the singular one-two punch of Moore's narrow and irascible tone pitted against Prater's woebegone baritone. Arguably the best track, the phenomenal "I Thank You" closes the compilation on a high note. Although the duo did switch officially to Atlantic by the early '70s, this compilation stops at the prime Stax material. *The Best of Sam & Dave* had a brief shelf life and was supplanted by more extensive overviews. As a compilation spotlighting the hits, this does the job. —*Jason Elias*

Back at 'Cha! / 1976 / United Artists ◆◆◆
The great soul duo of Sam Moore and Dave Prater made a gallant attempt at a comeback with this mid-'70s release, but the times had changed dramatically, and there wasn't much demand on the urban contemporary horizon for an aging Southern soul duo. Their harmonies were still solid, although the leads and shared vocals were a little on the faded side. It was great to hear the two singing together again, but the combination of changed audience tastes and uneven material proved too much of an obstacle for Sam & Dave to get back in the spotlight. —*Ron Wynn*

☆ **Sweat 'n' Soul: Anthology (1965-1971)** / Jul. 20, 1993 / Rhino/Atlantic ◆◆◆◆◆
Sam Moore and Dave Prather were the ultimate soul duo; one a high-voiced wailer, the other a low-toned blaster. They came together in the mid-'60s to form a superb duo, singing tunes penned by soul's finest writing tandem, Isaac Hayes and David Porter. They made a host of great singles before ego battles broke them apart. This 50-cut, two-disc anthology not only has every song of significance, but plenty of obscure worthwhile items, like a "Stay in School" promo, some overlooked material done with the Dixie

Flyers, and a couple of numbers cut by Moore as a solo act in the early '70s. The sound quality, annotation, and song sequencing are as outstanding as the songs themselves. —*Ron Wynn*

★ **The Very Best of Sam & Dave** / Feb. 28, 1995 / Rhino ◆◆◆◆◆
The Very Best of Sam & Dave contains all of Sam & Dave's Top 40 hits, including "You Don't Know Like I Know," "Hold On, I'm Comin'," "Said I Wasn't Gonna Tell Nobody," "You Got Me Hummin'," "When Something Is Wrong With My Baby," "Soothe Me," "Soul Man," and "I Thank You," plus a handful of essential album tracks and B-sides like "I Can't Stand Up For Falling Down." It's an expertly compiled, concise collection that contains everything you need to know. If you need to dig deeper, the double-disc *Sweat 'n' Soul* is essential, but most casual fans will be completely satisfied by *The Very Best of Sam & Dave*. —*Stephen Thomas Erlewine*

Santana

f. 1966, San Francisco, CA
Latin Rock, Album Rock, Pop/Rock, Psychedelic, Fusion, Hard Rock, Blues-Rock
Santana is the name of a band that has successfully married elements of blues, rock, and Latin music and enjoyed international acclaim for more than two decades. It is also the name of the guitarist, Carlos Santana, who has led that band and made other recordings over the same period of time. In its original manifestation, the Santana Blues Band was a group of equals, with Carlos named as leader only because of a musicians-union requirement that such a designation be made. The group was formed in San Francisco in the mid-'60s and first gained recognition in the same dance halls that hosted the psychedelic rock groups of the era, although, with its Latin and African roots, Santana never quite fit in with the psychedelic sound. The group came under the direction of promoter Bill Graham and had already scored a contract with Columbia when it appeared at the Woodstock Festival in August 1969. *Santana*, the debut album, was a massive success, including the number four hit "Evil Ways." *Abraxas* (1970) did even better, topping the charts for six weeks and featuring the hits "Black Magic Woman" and "Oye Como Va." In subsequent years, "Santana" for the most part referred to Carlos and a band of hired musicians playing in the established Santana style, while the leader also made occasional solo albums that varied the style somewhat. — *William Ruhlmann*

Santana / Aug. 1969 / Columbia/Legacy ◆◆◆◆◆
Released in 1969, the group's first album shot the group from local San Francisco band status to a worldwide forum. Included were the group's first hits ("Evil Ways" and "Soul Sacrifice") and others that combined Latin grooves with a rock sensibility. The newly remastered compact disc also adds three bonus tracks recorded live at Woodstock in 1969, "Savor," "Soul Sacrifice," and "Fried Neckbones." —*Cub Koda*

★ **Abraxas** / Sep. 1970 / Columbia/Legacy ◆◆◆◆◆
The San Francisco Bay Area rock scene of the late '60s was one that encouraged radical experimentation and discouraged the type of mindless conformity that's often plagued corporate rock. When one considers just how different Santana, Jefferson Airplane, Moby Grape, and the Grateful Dead sounded, it becomes obvious just how much it was encouraged. In the mid-'90s, an album as eclectic as *Abraxas* would be considered a marketing exec's worst nightmare. But at the dawn of the 1970s, this unorthodox mix of rock, jazz, salsa, and blues proved quite successful. Whether adding rock elements to salsa king Tito Puente's "Oye Como Va," embracing instrumental jazz-rock on "Incident at Neshabur" and "Samba Pa Ti," or tackling moody blues-rock on Fleetwood Mac's "Black Magic Woman," the band keeps things unpredictable yet cohesive. Many of the Santana albums that came out in the '70s are worth acquiring, but for novices, *Abraxas* is an excellent place to start. [Columbia/Legacy's 1998 reissue of *Abraxas* featured three previously unreleased tracks—"Se a Cabo," "Toussaint L'Overture," "Black Magic Woman/Gypsy Queen"—which were all recorded live at the Royal Albert Hall on April 18, 1970.] —*Alex Henderson*

Santana III / Sep. 1971 / Columbia/Legacy ◆◆◆◆◆
The group's third album, simply titled *Santana* on its original September 1971 release, was the last work of the original Woodstock-era lineup. With hit singles and albums under its belt, the group became more experimental on its third go-round. This yielded some of their best work and another number one for the band. This 1998 re-release also adds three bonus recorded live at the Fillmore West on July 4, 1971, bringing comparable on-stage versions of the album's "Batuka" and "Jungle Strut" along with the rocking "Gumbo." —*Cub Koda*

Love, Devotion and Surrender / 1972 / Columbia ◆◆◆◆◆
Mahavishnu John McLaughlin and Devadip Carlos Santana came together under the influences of John Coltrane and Sri Chinmoy (the latter of whom McLaughlin would eventually renounce), cut their hair, and joined forces in probably the greatest guitar summit meeting of the jazz-rock era. Their rapport is obvious from the first track, Coltrane's "A Love Supreme"; both guitarists are on fire, flashing their stuff with extraordinary energy and remarkable arrhythmic placement of each note. From this point, the two fuse the high-octane virtuosity of the Mahavishnu Orchestra and Tony Williams' Lifetime (present are Billy Cobham and Jan Hammer—on drums!—from the former and Larry Young from the latter) with Santana's thundering Latin percussion team of Armando Peraza and James Mingo Lewis, without either element dominating. The music reaches an ecstatic peak on the lengthy jam "Let Us Go Into the House of the Lord" (based on the chords of Bobby Womack's "Breezin'"), where Santana's trademark ascending chromatic flurries give way to McLaughlin machine-gun volleys that make more coherent musical sense than anything he was recording with the first Mahavishnu group around this time. Whatever you may think of gurus and Indian religions, there must be something to it if the

results of spiritual immersion are as spectacular and fulfilling as the music on this CD. —*Richard S. Ginell*

Carlos Santana & Buddy Miles! Live! / Jun. 1972 / Columbia ✦✦✦✦
From December 1971 to April 1972, Carlos Santana and several other members of Santana toured with drummer/vocalist Buddy Miles, a former member of the Electric Flag and Jimi Hendrix's Band of Gypsys. The resulting live album contained both Santana hits ("Evil Ways") and Buddy Miles hits ("Changes"), plus a 25-minute, side-long jam. It was not, perhaps, the live album Santana fans had been waiting for, but at this point in its career, the band could do no wrong. The album went into the Top Ten and sold a million copies. (Reissued on CD on September 6, 1994.) —*William Ruhlmann*

Caravanserai / Oct. 1972 / Columbia ✦✦✦✦✦
Drawing on rock, salsa, and jazz, Santana recorded one imaginative, unpredictable gem after another in the 1970s. But *Caravanserai* is daring even by Santana's high standards. Carlos Santana was obviously very hip to jazz-fusion—something the innovative guitarist provides a generous dose of on the largely instrumental *Caravanserai*. Whether its approach is jazz-rock or simply rock, this album is consistently inspired and quite adventurous. Full of heartfelt, introspective guitar solos, it lacks the immediacy of *Santana* or *Abraxas*. Like the type of jazz that influenced it, this pearl (which marked the beginning of keyboardist/composer Tom Coster's highly beneficial membership in the band) requires a number of listenings in order to be absorbed and fully appreciated. But make no mistake: this is one of Santana's finest accomplishments. —*Alex Henderson*

Welcome / Nov. 1973 / Columbia ✦✦✦
On the group's fifth album, "the New Santana Band," as it was called, was an octet. Musically, the album was something of a companion piece to Carlos Santana's duet album with John McLaughlin, *Love Devotion Surrender*, even including a song by that title and, like the earlier record, containing compositions by McLaughlin and John Coltrane. In addition to the jazz influences, there was also a new blues sound courtesy of Leon Thomas, a smooth-voiced singer in the Joe Williams tradition. The record was musically adventurous, but as Santana continued to diverge from its Latin rock roots, his popularity eroded. —*William Ruhlmann*

Lotus / May 1974 / Columbia ✦✦✦✦✦
Recorded in Japan in July 1973, this massive live album, originally on three LPs and now on two compact discs, was available outside the United States in 1974 but held back from domestic release until long into the CD age. It features the same "New Santana Band" that recorded *Welcome* and combines that group's jazz and spiritual influences with performances of earlier Latin rock favorites like "Oye Como Va." —*William Ruhlmann*

Greatest Hits / Jul. 1974 / Columbia ✦✦✦✦✦
This ten-song sampler presents the best of Santana, 1969-71, the period of its greatest popularity. The hits include "Black Magic Woman," "Evil Ways," "Everybody's Everything," and "Oye Como Va." But note that this is a bare minimum of prime Santana. Not only does the sampler choose from only Santana's first three albums, it leaves out such seminal numbers as "Nobody to Depend On" and "Soul Sacrifice." Those looking for a more extensive overview should consider *Viva Santana!* —*William Ruhlmann*

Illuminations / Sep. 1974 / Columbia ✦✦

Borboletta / Oct. 1974 / Columbia ✦✦✦
Borboletta was the first new Santana band studio album in 11 months and the group's sixth overall. Once again, individual credits were listed for each song. The main problem was that the band seemed to be coasting; Carlos turned in the usual complement of high-pitched lead guitar work, and the percussionists pounded away, but the Santana sound had long since taken over from any individual composition, and the records were starting to sound alike. That, in turn, started to make them inessential; *Borboletta* spent less time in the charts than any previous Santana album. —*William Ruhlmann*

Amigos / Mar. 1976 / Columbia ✦✦✦✦
By the release of *Amigos*, the Santana band's seventh album, only Carlos Santana and David Brown remained from the band that conquered Woodstock, and only Carlos had been in the band continuously since. Meanwhile, the group had made some effort to arrest its commercial slide, hiring an outside producer, David Rubinson, and taking a tighter, more up-tempo, and more vocal approach to its music. The overt jazz influences were replaced by strains of R&B/funk and Mexican folk music. The result was an album more dynamic than any since *Santana III* in 1971. "Let It Shine" (number 77), an R&B-tinged tune, became the group's first chart single in four years, and the album returned Santana to Top Ten status. —*William Ruhlmann*

Festival / Jan. 1977 / Columbia ✦✦✦
Santana's follow-up to its comeback album, *Amigos*, was another David Rubinson-produced effort that moved back toward more of a Latin-rock feel, although it retained an essentially pop focus—"The River" was the first real vocal ballad on a Santana album. If any doubt still existed that the group was no longer a band of equals but a platform for its lead guitarist, the current lineup dispelled that; Carlos Santana was now the only original member of the band left. Although the album went gold, the lack of a hit single hurt the album's commercial standing; its number 27 peak was the lowest yet for a Santana Band album. —*William Ruhlmann*

Moonflower / Oct. 1977 / Columbia ✦✦✦
Santana, which was renowned for its concert work dating back to Woodstock, did not release a live album in the U.S. until this one, and it's only partially live, with studio tracks added, notably a cover of the Zombies' "She's Not There" (number 27) that became Santana's first Top 40 hit in five years. The usual comings and goings in band membership had taken place since last time; the track listing was a good mixture of the old— "Black Magic Woman," "Soul Sacrifice"—and the recent, and with the added radio play of

a hit single, *Moonflower* went Top Ten and sold a million copies, the first new Santana album to do that since 1972 and the last until *Supernatural* in 1999. —*William Ruhlmann*

Inner Secrets / Oct. 1978 / Columbia ✦✦

Oneness: Silver Dreams Golden Realities / Mar. 1979 / Columbia ✦✦✦
This is the first Carlos Santana solo album. It features members of the Santana band as backup, however, so the difference between a group effort and a solo work seems to be primarily in the musical approach, which is more esoteric and more varied than on a regular band album. The record is mostly instrumental and given over largely to contemplative ballads, although there is also, for example, in the song "Silver Dreams Golden Smiles," a traditional pop ballad sung by Saunders King. —*William Ruhlmann*

Marathon / Sep. 1979 / Columbia ✦✦

The Swing of Delight / Aug. 1980 / Columbia ✦✦

Zebop! / Apr. 1981 / Columbia ✦✦
On *Zebop!*, a Santana band featuring newcomer Richard Baker on keyboards tried to preserve the better elements of the first and third trilogies of Santana albums—there was a heavy component of Latin-flavored percussion topped by Carlos' biting lead guitar work, and there were also three pop cover songs in Cat Stevens' "Changes," J.J. Cale's "The Sensitive Kind," and Russ Ballard's "Winning." The double strategy worked. "Winning" (number 17) became Santana's first Top 20 single in a decade, "The Sensitive Kind" (number 56) also charted, and the album was Santana's first Top Ten, gold-selling hit in four years. —*William Ruhlmann*

Shango / Aug. 1982 / Columbia ✦✦

Havana Moon / Apr. 1983 / Columbia ✦✦✦
The third Carlos Santana solo album marks a surprising turn toward 1950s rock & roll and Tex-Mex, with covers such as Bo Diddley's "Who Do You Love" and Chuck Berry's title song. Produced by veteran R&B producers Jerry Wexler and Barry Beckett, the album features an eclectic mix of sidemen, including Booker T. Jones of Booker T & the MG's, Willie Nelson, and the Fabulous Thunderbirds. *Havana Moon* is a light effort, but it's one of Santana's most enjoyable albums, which may explain why it was also the best-selling Santana album outside the group releases in ten years. —*William Ruhlmann*

Beyond Appearances / Feb. 1985 / Columbia ✦✦

Freedom / Feb. 1987 / Columbia ✦✦✦
Freedom marked several reunions in the Santana band, which was now a nonet. In addition to Carlos, the band consisted of percussionists Armando Pereza, Orestes Vilato, and Raul Rekow; returning drummer Graham Lear; bassist Alphonso Johnson; returning keyboardist Tom Coster; keyboardist Chester Thompson; and on lead vocals, Buddy Miles, who had made a duet album with Santana 15 years before. Credited as an "additional musician" was keyboard player Greg Rolie, an original member. The music also marked a return from the hyper-pop sound of Val Garay on *Beyond Appearances* to a more traditional Santana Latin rock style. Thus, *Freedom* was a literal return to form, but, unfortunately, not to the quality of early Santana albums. And the group's commercial decline continued, with the LP getting to only number 95. —*William Ruhlmann*

Blues for Salvador / Oct. 1987 / Columbia ✦✦✦✦✦
On previous "solo" albums, Carlos Santana had made noticeable stylistic changes and worked with jazz, pop, and even country musicians. On this, his fourth Carlos Santana release, the line between a "solo" and a "group" project is blurred; this record is really a catchall of Santana band outtakes and stray tracks. For example, included are an instrumental version of "Deeper, Dig Deeper" from *Freedom* and an alternate take of "Hannibal" from *Zebop!*, as well as "Now That You Know" from the group's 1985 tour. Given the variety of material, the album is somewhat less focused than most Santana band albums, but there are individual tracks that are impressive, notably "Trane," which features Tony Williams on drums. (*Blues for Salvador* won the Grammy Award for Best Rock Instrumental Performance.) —*William Ruhlmann*

Viva Santana! / Aug. 1988 / Columbia ✦✦✦✦✦
Released in 1988, *Viva Santana!* is a generous 30-track overview of Santana's first 20 years of recording. Appropriately, it concentrates on the band's glory years of the late '60s and early '70s, when both Carlos Santana and his supporting musicians were on fire. There are several unreleased cuts, including live tracks included for hardcore fans, but *Viva Santana!* is most useful as a thorough overview for curious listeners. —*Stephen Thomas Erlewine*

Spirits Dancing in the Flesh / Jun. 1990 / Columbia ✦✦✦
Following a 1989 20th-anniversary reunion tour to promote *Viva Santana!*, Carlos Santana reorganized the band as a sextet and recorded *Spirits Dancing in the Flesh*, Santana's 15th and final studio album for Columbia Records. It was an unusually eclectic collection, featuring songs by Curtis Mayfield ("Gypsy Woman"), the Isley Brothers ("Who's That Lady"), and Babatunde Olatunji ("Jin-Go-Lo-Ba"). For all those influences, it was more of a straightforward, guitar-heavy rock album than usual. Coming more than three years after Santana's last new album, *Freedom*, it sold to the band's core audience only, reaching number 85. —*William Ruhlmann*

Milagro / May 5, 1992 / Polydor ✦✦✦
Santana signed to Polydor in 1991 after 22 years with Columbia Records. Their label debut has a somewhat elegiac tone, beginning with a stage introduction by the late promoter Bill Graham and featuring an excerpt from a speech by Dr. Martin Luther King Jr., solos taken from Miles Davis and John Coltrane, and music written by Bob Marley, Coltrane, and Gil Evans. Despite the presence of all these heroic ghosts, however, *Milagro* is only an average Santana release, familiar-sounding but undistinguished, and it failed

to arrest the band's commercial slide, becoming the first new Santana studio album not to crack the Top 100. — *William Ruhlmann*

Sacred Fire: Santana Live in South America / Oct. 19, 1993 / Polydor ♦♦

Dance of the Rainbow Serpent / Aug. 8, 1995 / Columbia/Legacy ♦♦♦
Guitarist Carlos Santana continues to record music, but when contemplating his body of work, it's difficult not to telescope to the "vintage" 1969-1975 period, from first albums *Santana* and *Abraxas* through to *Lotus*. *Dance of the Rainbow Serpent* offers a well-rounded, three-disc overview of his career, but its the sultry Latin rhythms and stinging guitar of the early years—captured on disc one, subtitled *Heart*—that prove most invigorating. The obvious hits like "Evil Ways" and "Black Magic Woman" are all included of course, although these are scorched by the speedy pyrotechnics of the likes of "Toussaint Overture" from *Lotus*. The second disc, mistitled *Soul*, covers material that is, to be kind, bland and overproduced. Without the Latin edge, there's nothing to distinguish the contents from a hundred other MOR performers. Third disc *Spirit* is more diverse and satisfying; delving into the funkier examples of his later work, plus sessions with John Lee Hooker (including hit "The Healer") and previously unreleased material (including a workout with Living Color's Vernon Reid). In all, plenty here to chew on for fans of Santana's fluid, spiritual style—with one of three discs left to gather. — *Roch Parisien*

Live at the Fillmore 1968 / Mar. 11, 1997 / Columbia/Legacy ♦♦♦♦
Two-CD package drawn from performances at the Fillmore West in December 1968, with an early lineup including Bob Livingston on drums and Marcus Malone on congas (both of whom would be gone by the time the group recorded their official debut in 1969). The band sound only a bit more tentative here than they would in their Woodstock-era incarnation, running through several of the highlights of their first album ("Jingo," "Persuasion," "Soul Sacrifice," and "Treat"). More interesting to collectors will be the five songs that have not previously appeared on any Santana recording, including covers of songs by jazzmen Chico Hamilton and Willie Bobo and a half-hour original jam that concludes the set, "Freeway." The sound is excellent and the arrangements a bit more improve-oriented than what ended up on the early studio records. Its appeal isn't solely limited to committed fans; on its own terms it's a fine release, highlighted by some burning organ-guitar interplay in particular. — *Richie Unterberger*

● **The Best of Santana** / Mar. 31, 1998 / Columbia/Legacy ♦♦♦♦♦
The Best of Santana is a 16-track collection that greatly expands the scope of Santana's previous hits compilation, *Greatest Hits*. Drawing from the band's entire 30-year career, the disc contains such familiar items as "Evil Ways," "Jingo," "Black Magic Woman/Gypsy Queen," and "Oye Como Va," but it also has a number of longtime favorites of the band and fans. Furthermore, all the songs have been subjected to Super Bit remastering, resulting in the best sound ever. For some casual fans, *Greatest Hits* remains definitive, since it's a portrait of the band at its peak, but anyone wanting a career-spanning single-disc compilation will find that *The Best of Santana* suits their needs. — *Stephen Thomas Erlewine*

Supernatural / Jun. 15, 1999 / Arista ♦♦♦♦
Santana was still a respected rock veteran in 1999, but it had been years since he had a hit, even if he continued to fare well on the concert circuits. Clive Davis, the man who had signed Santana to Columbia in 1968, offered him the opportunity to set up shop at his label, Arista. In the tradition of comebacks and label debuts by veteran artists in the '90s, *Supernatural*, Santana's first effort for Arista, is designed as a star-studded event. At first listen, there doesn't seem to be a track that doesn't have a guest star, which brings up the primary problem with the album—despite several interesting or excellent moments, it never develops a consistent voice that holds the album together. The fault doesn't lay with the guest stars or even with Santana, who continues to turn in fine performances. There's just a general directionless feeling to the record, enhanced by several songs that seem like excuses for jams, which, truth be told, isn't all that foreign on latter-day Santana records. Then again, the grooves often play better than the ploys for radio play, but that's not always the case, since Lauryn Hill's "Do You Like the Way" and the Dust Brothers-produced, Eagle-Eye Cherry-sung "Wishing It Was" are as captivating as the Eric Clapton duet, "The Calling." But that just confirms that *Supernatural* just doesn't have much of a direction, flipping between traditional Santana numbers and polished contemporary collaborations, with both extremes being equally likely to hit or miss. That doesn't quite constitute a triumph, but the peak moments of *Supernatural* are some of Santana's best music of the '90s, which does make it a successful comeback. — *Stephen Thomas Erlewine*

The Best of Santana, Vol. 2 / Nov. 21, 2000 / Columbia/Legacy ♦♦♦♦
These 14 tracks lean heavily on the earliest phase of Santana. Nine of them, in fact, were recorded prior to 1972, and just one postdates 1978. As 1969-71 was Santana's most vital period, however, that's no cause for complaint, and indeed the later cuts really pale in comparison. For someone who wants a little more than a greatest hits collection but wants to stop after two volumes, this is good enough, with first-rate items like "Persuasion," "Se Acabo," and "Guajira." Nothing here is rare, and note that the versions of "Black Magic Woman" and "Europa" are live ones. — *Richie Unterberger*

Sarge

f. 1995, Champaign-Urbana, IL, **db.** 1999
Indie Pop, Punk-Pop, Indie Rock

Champaign, IL punk-pop group Sarge was formed in late 1995 by singer/guitarist Elizabeth Elmore and ex-Corndolly bassist Rachel Switzky. Recruiting drummer Russ Horvath, the group played their debut show in January 1996, quickly becoming a popular local attraction. Upon signing to the Mud label, Sarge debuted that March with the excellent single "Dear Josie, Love Robyn," resurfacing a few months later on a split single

with Supporting Actress issued on Grand Theft Autumn. After recording their acclaimed 1996 debut *Charcoal*, Horvath quit the group and was replaced by drummer Chad Romanski, who signed on in time to cut the 1997 single "Stall." Sarge's breakthrough sophomore LP *The Glass Intact* appeared in 1998 and was recorded with second guitarist Pat Cramer, who quit the band a short time later. His replacement was Sue Roth; lineup changes continued to plague the group in the months which followed, however, and in late 1998 Switzky left Sarge as well, opening the door for ex-Castor bassist Derek Niedringhaus. The following year Elmore enrolled in Northwestern Law School, and in the wake of her semester finals opted to dissolve the band, playing the occasional performance as a solo act; *Distant*, a posthumous collection of Sarge demos and live tracks, followed in the spring of 2000. —*Jason Ankeny*

Charcoal / Oct. 1996 / Mud ♦♦♦♦
Charcoal is the impressive debut from the Champaign, IL, punk-pop trio, Sarge. Singer and guitar player Elizabeth Elmore's honest, true-to-life lyrics reflect the pain, frustration, and anger experienced in relationships, without resorting to cliches. Her sweet-sounding vocals give the songs an innocent quality that almost masks the dark side of her lyrics. This, combined with fast, high-energy music, is why Sarge has been compared to bands such as Sleater-Kinney, Heavenly, and Team Dresch. The album's single, "Dear Josie, Love Robyn," starts out as a quiet "Dear John" letter but then unleashes into an angry tirade directed at a boyfriend who squashed her self-confidence. She realizes she deserves more so she's leaving him and telling him why. The band's driving, hook-laden sound reinforces the intensity of the lyrics. At the other end of the spectrum, "Another Gear Uncaught" is an acoustic number recorded and mixed on a four-track. Elmore's pure vocals over her solo guitar almost distract the listener from the sobering lyrics that describe a suicide attempt. Although the album was recorded on a limited budget and the production quality is not the best, Sarge's songwriting strength and pure punk-pop energy come through. — *Tracy Frey*

● **The Glass Intact** / 1998 / Mud ♦♦♦♦♦
The Glass Intact represents a kind of apotheosis of '90s-era girl-punk—Sarge brilliantly assimilates the emotional intensity of Sleater-Kinney, the melodic aggression of Team Dresch, and the sheer exuberance of Cub, yet their best trick of all is that they sound like an absolute original. Elizabeth Elmore is a true triple threat: a gifted composer, an acute lyricist, and a nakedly honest vocalist, her songs come fast and furious, but no amount of barbed-wire guitars can obscure the poignancy and desperation of standout tracks like "Stall" and "Charms and Feigns." And for all of Sarge's indie defiance, it's clear Elmore's misspent youth also included a steady diet of arena-schlock—her songs are built around unashamedly meaty riffs, and the wonderful "Beguiling" could even very well be the first real air-guitar song for riot-grrrls. The cumulative result is that regardless of labels—punk, indie, whatever—*The Glass Intact* is at heart a rock & roll album in the classic sense: cathartic, impassioned, and vividly alive. —*Jason Ankeny*

Distant / Apr. 11, 2000 / Mud ♦♦♦
Bands come and bands go, of course, but the swift demise of Sarge still stings—with their breakthrough sophomore album *The Glass Intact*, the group delivered on all the promise of their previous records, perfecting a taut, infectious brand of punk-pop distinguished by the vulnerable vocals and razor-sharp songs of frontwoman Elizabeth Elmore. The bittersweet *Distant* compiles the remaining odds and ends from Sarge's all-too-brief career, assembling a hodgepodge of demos, live recordings, and covers; opening with the band's final new recordings and concluding with a pair of Elmore solo efforts, the set is highlighted by both electric and acoustic versions of "The End of July" (aka "all my plans changed..."), a heart-rending evocation of separation and loss given even greater impact by its context. At the core of the record are a half dozen live tracks recorded in August of 1999 while opening for another late, lamented Champaign band, Braid; drawing primarily on material from *The Glass Intact*, the performances vividly capture the raw desperation at the core of Elmore's songs, seething with the intensity and immediacy that made Sarge so affecting. A fitting farewell. —*Jason Ankeny*

Joe Satriani

b. 1956, Long Island, NY
Guitar (Electric), Drums, Instrumental, Guitar / Guitar Virtuoso, Fusion, Hard Rock, Instrumental Rock

Joe Satriani was one of the best, most influential rock guitarists of the late '80s, equally capable of fast flights of blinding technique as well as sweet, lyrical passages. What also separates Satriani from most technically gifted guitar virtuosos is that he treats a song as a song, not as an excuse to shred. For these reasons, he appeals not only to guitarists but also to many rock fans who have never touched the instrument—his breakthrough 1987 album, *Surfing With the Alien*, was the first instrumental rock album in years to chart in the Top 30 on Billboard's Top 200 Albums. Since then, he has added vocals to his records; while his voice can't compare to his guitar, it added another dimension to an artist who was already more versatile than the majority of contemporary musicians.

Before Satriani became a recording star, he taught guitar in San Francisco; several of his students became famous, influential guitarists in their own right, before he even recorded his first album in 1986. Metallica's Kirk Hammett was the first of his students to hit the big time, followed by Steve Vai and Larry LaLonde of Primus. —*Stephen Thomas Erlewine*

Not of This Earth / 1986 / Epic ♦♦♦♦
Not of This Earth was the first studio release from guitar wizard Joe Satriani (not counting the hard-to-find *Joe Satriani* EP). This all-instrumental album was making ripples in the guitar-playing community not long after it was released, and it's easy to see why: superior compositions, a signature style, a unique tone, and playing that's out of this world.

Satriani shifts musical gears deftly, often layering multiple tracks together to make a complex soundscape. The fiery sound of "Not of This Earth" and "Hordes of Locusts" is tempered by the cool, dark tone of "Driving at Night," the far-out Eastern approach of "The Snake," and the quiet, thoughtful "Rubina." Satriani's fluid playing and wicked licks are enough to drop jaws and widen eyes. There isn't a weak track on this disc, even though the guitarist was still maturing when he released it. *—Phil Carter*

• **Surfing With the Alien** / 1987 / Epic ✦✦✦✦✦
Not content to sit on his laurels, Satriani released this groundbreaking instrumental album in 1987, leaving guitarists and musicians everywhere stunned and amazed by the playing and musicianship displayed therein. Satriani defined his sound more sharply to further develop his distinct musical tone, and his playing continued to evolve to higher levels with each new panorama of notes he blazed out. Whether it was the twisted, horizon-pushing "Ice 9," the fiery, churning "Surfing With the Alien," the bluesy rock shuffle of "Crushing Day," the straight-ahead, slamming "Satch Boogie," or the more subdued, soulful "Always With Me, Always With You," Satriani's style and songwriting were uniquely his own. Taking guitar playing and song composition to new levels, this is a remarkable recording. *—Phil Carter*

Dreaming #11 / 1988 / Epic ✦✦✦
Dreaming #11 is something of an oddity: a mini-disc released in 1988 with three live tracks and one new studio track. The live tracks, taken from the *Surfing With the Alien* tour and featuring the powerful duo of Stuart Hamm on bass and Jonathan Mover on drums, showcase Satriani's outstanding talents in a live atmosphere; however, they've been heard before ("Ice Nine" was on *Surfing With the Alien* and "Memories" and "Hordes of Locusts" came from *Not of This Earth*). The studio track, "The Crush of Love," immediately became a favorite of Satriani fans everywhere, mostly because of its catchy tune and its creative use of the wah-wah pedal to give the guitar an almost human voice. A recommended disc for musicians and fans, but not essential to the casual collector. *—Phil Carter*

Flying in a Blue Dream / Oct. 1989 / Epic ✦✦✦✦✦
An hour-long disc filled with musical explorations and compositions that defy belief, *Flying in a Blue Dream* is unquestionably Satriani at his absolute best. Breaking his all-instrumental tradition for the first time, he croons on six of the disc's 18 tracks, including the weird "Strange," the bluesy, hard-rocking "Big Bad Moon," and the driving "Can't Slow Down." Satriani's voice isn't extraordinary, but it fits extremely well with the music he creates, especially on the acoustic-tinged, uplifting "I Believe." It's his playing that's the really impressive thing here, though; his unique tone and complex song structures are enhanced by his signature playing style and the incredible array of effects and tricks he wrestles out of his instrument. The disc closes with the high-flying, misty piece "Into the Light," leaving behind a feeling of real wonder. Soaring, powerful and triumphant, this recording deserves a place in everyone's collection. *—Phil Carter*

The Extremist / Jul. 1992 / Epic ✦✦✦✦

Time Machine / Oct. 26, 1993 / Sony ✦✦✦✦✦

Joe Satriani / Oct. 1995 / Epic ✦✦✦

Crystal Planet / Mar. 3, 1998 / Epic ✦✦✦✦

Engines of Creation / Mar. 14, 2000 / Epic ✦✦✦

Savage Garden

f. 1997, **db.** Oct. 2001
Adult Alternative Pop/Rock, Adult Contemporary, Dance-Pop
Australian pop duo Savage Garden has taken the world by storm without the record company hype and career-establishing game plan that is often the background to pop-oriented acts. Originally calling themselves Crush, songwriting duo Daniel Jones and Darren Hayes sent 150 demo tapes all over the world and waited patiently for replies. The only positive response came from Australian music identity John Woodruff, who had previously managed the Angels and Baby Animals. He put the duo in the studio with Australian producer Charles Fisher, who had previously created international break-through hits for Air Supply and Moving Pictures. The first single, "I Want You," released in July 1996 reached number two but was followed by consecutive number ones with "To the Moon and Back" and "Truly Madly Deeply." When the self-titled debut album was released in April 1997, it entered the charts at number one and notched up 13 weeks at the top, the third longest stay for any Australian-made album. In the meantime a Dallas radio station had started playing "I Want You," and the duo was signed to Sony's Columbia imprint in the U.S. "I Want You" and "Truly Madly Deeply" became worldwide hits, the latter achieving number one in the U.S. in January 1998. The album sold 11 million copies globally and earned Savage Garden ten Australian ARIA Awards. The second album, *Affirmation*, was basically written by phone and computer from separate corners of the world, since Hayes had moved from Australia to New York. The album was produced in Los Angeles by award-winner Walter Afanasieff, known for his work with artists such as Mariah Carey, Celine Dion, and Barbra Streisand. In January 2000 the album's leadoff single, "I Knew I Loved You," gave Savage Garden its second U.S. number one. *—Ed Nimmervoll*

• **Savage Garden** / Apr. 15, 1997 / Columbia ✦✦✦
Savage Garden is light, catchy, and undeniably melodic, and it's hard to believe they released their debut album in the late, not early, '90s. It's easy to say that their breakthrough single "I Want You" sounds like a revamped Roxette, but it's accurate—it has a breezy chorus and frothy production that make it an appealing slice of mainstream pop, the kind banished from the airwaves in 1992. Occasionally, Savage Garden reach that peak elsewhere on their eponymous debut—most notably on the second single, "To the Moon and Back" and "Truly Madly Deeply"—but they lack the vision and discipline to make the record anything more than fitfully entertaining. But those highlights almost make the album worthwhile. *—Stephen Thomas Erlewine*

Affirmation / Nov. 9, 1999 / Columbia ✦✦✦
Savage Garden managed to slip underneath everyone's radar and go multi-platinum with their 1997 debut. The Australian duo wasn't hip enough to warrant coverage in the music press, even after they had a series of hit singles, largely because they traded in the least-respected rock genre: soft rock. Like any soft rock group, they were a product of their times. In the early '80s, that meant adding some lite country influences to the melodic pop base. In the late '90s, it meant adding mild dance/club beats, even on the ballads. Since *Savage Garden* was such a success on adult contemporary radio, it's not a surprise that Darren Hayes and Daniel Jones have decided to lean a little heavier on the ballads this time around, to the extent that even up-tempo tracks like "Affirmation" and "Hold Me," or mid-tempo numbers like "The Lover After Me" feel like ballads. On the whole, this isn't a bad thing, since it gives the album some coherence. Plus, Savage Garden has a knack for delivering this professional, well-crafted melodic pop—if some songs aren't as memorable as others, that's just the way the game of mainstream pop is played. There aren't any bad pieces on *Affirmation* (well, with the exception of the lyrically tortured "The Animal Song"), just some that aren't quite as hooky or memorable as "I Knew I Loved You" or the title track, or for those fans who like SG's piano ballads, "I Don't Know You Anymore." Like the debut, *Affirmation* is hardly earth-shattering, but it's well-done mainstream adult pop whose best moments are ideal for radio play. Those moments may be better heard on a greatest-hits collection someday, but this album is fine on its own terms; it is so well-constructed that the filler goes down easily. *—Stephen Thomas Erlewine*

Savage Republic

f. 1981, Los Angeles, CA, **db.** 1990
Indie Rock, Post-Punk, Experimental Rock, Noise-Rock
Figures of considerable repute within the Los Angeles post-punk community of the 1980s, Savage Republic grafted tribal percussion, industrial drones, and raga-like guitar lines together to craft an idiosyncratically moody sound with flashes of both desolation and eloquent grandeur. Capable of both harsh dissonance and shimmering textures, the band's guiding force was guitarist Bruce Licher, a founder and constant presence in their shuffling lineups. Alternating between cyclic instrumentals and quasi-industrial assaults with gruff, chanted vocals, their records were unavoidably inconsistent, but most contain some enduring highlights. Savage Republic were founded by former UCLA students Licher and drummer Mark Erkstine in the early '80s. Adding new members, the group originally called themselves Africa Corps, changing the name to Savage Republic just before releasing their first record in 1982. Exotic percussion would always play a big role in Savage Republic—even in the early days they were using oil cans, metal pipes, and 55-gallon drums. Their early singles and their debut LP, *Tragic Figures* (1982), show the group at their least accessible, though there are hints of the more mysterious and melodic elements to come. After some personnel changes, Savage Republic regrouped with a more guitar-oriented sound. On *Ceremonial* (1985), the band shifted their focus to mostly instrumental material, usually piloted by oddly tuned guitars. They never wholly abandoned those droning, angst-driven chants, though. Combined with the fact that their instrumental material wouldn't break much new ground over the course of the decade, their studio albums can be uneven listening. In any case, the band were best experienced live, where they would burn trashcans of pampas leaves, play on Los Angeles' skid row, and use all sorts of unexpected objects for percussion in their quest to make each concert a unique event. *—Richie Unterberger*

Tragic Figures / 1982 / Independent Project ✦✦✦
This is really their most atypical full-length studio album, emphasizing harsh, grating vocals and instrumental drones to a greater degree than anything else in their catalog. The throbbing percussion, though, would continue to be an element in everything they did, and quasi-Middle Eastern melodic motifs begin to assert themselves at times. Be aware that this, like all of Savage Republic's work, is not a collection of "songs" in the conventional rock sense, although many have vocals; it's more like a collection of "pieces" designed to establish moods and textures. The album is also distinguished by its exotic packaging, lettered entirely in Arabic script. The CD adds seven bonus tracks, including everything from their out-of-print 7" releases from 1983 and 1984. *—Richie Unterberger*

• **Ceremonial** / 1985 / Independent Project ✦✦✦✦✦
Their most accomplished and accessible work, largely jettisoning the harsher scrapings of the early records for expansive instrumentals featuring chiming guitars and occasional touches of ethereal trombone. Aiming for (and sometimes achieving) a hypnotic drone, at their best these have a melancholy beauty, bringing raga-rock into the post-punk age. The title track, unusually, features a female vocal from guest singer Louise Bialik, as well as (relatively) conventional lyrics. *—Richie Unterberger*

Live Trek / 1987 / Fundamental ✦✦✦
Seventy-five minutes of live material, much of which appears on their early studio recordings. A decent representation of their live presence, but the similarity of a lot of the riffs and arrangements make this hard to bear in such a big lump. For devoted fans of the group, it's a worthwhile document, with characteristically uneven material and sound quality (though the fidelity is on the whole fairly good). *—Richie Unterberger*

Jamahiriya / 1988 / Fundamental ✦✦✦
Considering that three years had passed since their previous full-length studio effort, little ground is broken here. The mood has turned more ominous and dour, though not to any

great purpose. The Sturm-und-Drang, hoarsely screamed vocals also make something of a comeback, again not to any great purpose. However, their skills at crafting tribalistic instrumental rock remain intact, and "Pois Den Mila Yia Ti Lambri" (with its martial accents) and "Lebanon 2000" (with its early Pink Floydish rumble) are among their better tracks. *—Richie Unterberger*

Customs / 1989 / Fundamental ✦✦
Savage Republic's originality had pretty much run its course by the time of their final studio album. Familiar instrumental motifs are repeated, but not expanded upon, though the Greek feel of "Song for Adonis" has a sweeter tone than they were usually inclined to employ. When they sing, half-formed lyrics and shouted vocals are still the order of the day (though "Mapia" probably includes their most conventional singing, aside from *Ceremonial's* "Andalusia"). "Rapeman's 1st EP" is as difficult and grating as they ever got, though it's not effective as either art or satire (if that was an intention). *—Richie Unterberger*

Live in Europe 1988 / 1990 / Fundamental ✦✦

Recordings From Live Performance, 1981-1983 / 1993 / Independent Project ✦✦
Savage Republic were probably more diligent about enshrining their live performances for posterity than they needed to be; there's almost as much live material available as there is from the studio. This set of two 10" records contains 14 tracks from the early days, including versions of songs from *Tragic Figures* and some numbers that were never recorded in the studio. It tends toward the noisy side of their early evolution, so those who prefer the *Ceremonial* era will probably want to pass, although glimmers of surf-psychedelia can be found in "Exodus" and "Snakedance." The packaging, as usual, is damned impressive, with copious documentation and a five-color letterpress folder to enclose the vinyl. *—Richie Unterberger*

Savage Rose

f. 1966, Denmark
Prog Rock/Art Rock
One of the most well-known rock groups from Continental Europe, Denmark's Savage Rose recorded a wealth of intriguing and eclectic progressive rock in the late '60s and '70s. In their early work, one hears faint echoes of the Airplane, Doors, Pink Floyd, and other psychedelic heavyweights combined with classical jazz and Danish-Euro folk elements. Their arrangements rely heavily on an incandescent, watery organ that sounds like nothing so much as psychedelic aquarium music. The most striking aspect of the band's sound, however, was the vocals of lead singer Annisette. Her childish wispy and sensual phrasing can suddenly break into jarring, almost histrionic wailing, like a Janis Joplin with Yoko Ono-isms, and eerily foreshadows Kate Bush's style. Stars in their native land, Savage Rose also achieved a bit of underground success abroad, and several of their albums were released in North America. *—Richie Unterberger*

● **Savage Rose** / 1968 / Polydor ✦✦✦✦✦
Their debut is their lightest and most charming effort. Waltzing melodies give way to thunder-of-doom bass runs, and the storybookish lyrics have a forlorn, yearning quality. With its oddly hollow sound, one is never really sure whether the tone is supposed to be playful or ominous. *—Richie Unterberger*

In the Plain / 1969 / Polydor ✦✦✦
The band takes a more aggressive and soul-oriented approach on their second album, but the material isn't as strong, and much of the ethereal ambience that made their first LP special is lost. It does include the terrific, rollicking "Evening's Child," as well as the pre-doom & gloom workout "A Trial in Our Native Town." *—Richie Unterberger*

Travelin' / 1969 / Polydor ✦✦✦
More excursions into soul-rock territory dominate one of their less distinguished albums. Highlights include the more serene and melodic cuts ("Travelin'," "Sailing Away") and the shockingly titled (for 1969) "My Family Was Gay," with its rather straightforward hint of incest. *—Richie Unterberger*

Your Daily Gift / 1970 / Gregar ✦✦✦
Their most well-known album, singled out for praise by critic Greil Marcus in his anthology *Stranded.* About half of this is fairly undistinguished heavy progressive-psychedelic rock, but the other half ranks among their most fragile and best material—the group were always better when they waxed reflective than when they tried to rock out. The lengthy, bittersweet, melancholy title track (complete with weepy European sidewalk cafe accordion) is one of their finest moments. *—Richie Unterberger*

Refugee / 1971 / Gregar ✦✦✦
Their most gospel and soul-influenced recording. Recalls Janis Joplin's more generic solo recordings, albeit with a more subdued feel. *—Richie Unterberger*

Dodens Triumf / 1972 / Polydor ✦✦✦✦✦
An unheralded landmark in art rock, this features Savage Rose keyboardist Thomas Koppel's score for a ballet by Flemming Flindt (the title translates to "Triumph of Death"). Nearly entirely instrumental (one song features Annisette on vocals), this is one of the finest classically influenced rock records. Moody and melancholy, at times almost doomy, yet always melodic, this 40-minute selection of haunting pieces prominently features the group's unique underwater organ sound and makes for compelling listening. *—Richie Unterberger*

Babylon / 1972 / Polydor ✦✦✦
With contributions by noted jazz saxophonist Ben Webster and the American gospel quintet the Stars of Faith, this is (along with *Refugee*) their most R&B-influenced recording, at times achieving a churchy, old-time New Orleans-like feel. *—Richie Unterberger*

Wild Child / 1973 / Polydor ✦✦✦

One of their better efforts. The R&B influence retreats in favor of a tender, melodic approach emphasizing the organ, piano, and accordions on a strong set that favors their European folk influences. *—Richie Unterberger*

Sole Var Ogsa Din / 1978 / Sonet ✦✦✦
A welcome return to their lightest and wispiest styles, with clear, shimmering instrumental textures that are almost like sonic waterfalls. Their enigmatic, moody song structures and melodies remain, with the most histrionic edges of Annisette's vocals toned down. As all but two of the songs are in their native Danish, this can perhaps be considered their most personal effort as well. *—Richie Unterberger*

25 / 1993 / Mega ✦✦✦
A double-CD compilation in commemoration of Savage Rose's 25th anniversary, drawing from most of the albums they recorded between the late '60s and early '90s. As an extremely eclectic and album-oriented group, Savage Rose aren't as well served by compilations as the average band. This is a decent enough way to get a rough feel for what the group has accomplished. But as an overview it's too diffuse, especially since the first disc only goes through 1973 and the second disc covers the decade 1982-1992 exclusively. There's nothing at all from one of their most celebrated albums (*Your Daily Gift,* 1970), or the Danish-language-dominated 1978 record, *Sole Var Ogsa Din.* In its favor, it does include several of their most outstanding early songs ("Wild Child," "A Girl I Knew," "A Trial in Our Native Town," "Dear Little Mother," "Evening's Child"). Also, the material from the 1980s and 1990s on disc two—which will be mostly unknown to U.S. listeners—stacks up pretty well against (and is fairly similar to) their early recordings. *—Richie Unterberger*

Black Angel / 1995 / Mega ✦✦

The Savages

f. 1965, **db.** 1966
Garage Rock
Little is known about this mid-'60s group, which has variously been reported to be from Bermuda or to be a group of Americans who were based in Bermuda when their sole LP, *Live 'n Wild,* was recorded. That album, recorded live at the Princess Hotel in Bermuda (according to the liner notes), stands as one of the best '60s full-length garage platters. Composed almost wholly of original material, the group played top-notch tunes with heavy echoes of the Beatles, Searchers, and Byrds, with a much greater melodic sense than the typical American garage combo, though a pleasing rawness is evident throughout.

Guitarist/singer Paul Muggleton was part of a short-lived group called Omaha Sherriff (produced by Tony Visconti), who recorded one album in England (*Come Hell or High Water,* 1977), and also sang on four late-'70s/early-'80s albums by Judy Tzuke on Rocket and Chrysalis (the fact that they were all English releases leading one to believe that they were from Bermuda). And drummer Howie Rego may have been part of a mid-'70s progressive band called Stardrive, who recorded for Elektra and Columbia. Nothing has ever turned up concerning the group's two other members, Jimmy O'Conner and Bobby Zuill. *—Richie Unterberger*

● **Live 'n Wild** / 1984 / Resurrection ✦✦✦✦✦
One of the few ultra-rare garage albums that lives up to the raves you'll come across in specialist fanzines by one of the few groups of the genre that were equally capable of garage raunch and moody, melodic ballads (the Rising Storm were about the only other one in their league in this regard). Don't bother looking for the original LP, which fetches hundreds of dollars on auction lists; the reissue is much easier to find. *—Richie Unterberger*

Savoy Brown

f. 1966, United Kingdom
Blues-Rock, British Blues, Album Rock, Hard Rock, Arena Rock
Part of the late-'60s blues-rock movement, Britain's Savoy Brown never achieved as much success in their homeland as they did in America, where they promoted their albums with nonstop touring. The band was formed and led by guitarist Kim Simmonds, whose dominating personality has led to myriad personnel changes; the original lineup included singer Bruce Portius, keyboardist Bob Hall, guitarist Martin Stone, bassist Ray Chappell, and drummer Leo Manning. This lineup appeared on the band's 1967 debut *Shake Down,* a collection of blues covers. Seeking a different approach, Simmonds dissolved the group and brought in guitarist Dave Peverett, bassist Rivers Jobe, drummer Roger Earl, and singer Chris Youlden, who gave them a distinctive frontman with his vocal abilities, bowler hat, and monocle. With perhaps its strongest lineup, Savoy Brown quickly made a name for itself, now recording originals like "Train to Nowhere" as well. However, Youlden left the band in 1970 following *Raw Sienna,* and shortly thereafter, Peverett, Earl, and new bassist Tony Stevens departed to form Foghat, continuing the pattern of consistent membership turnover. Simmonds collected yet another lineup and began a hectic tour of America, showcasing the group's now-refined bluesy boogie-rock style, which dominated the rest of their albums. The group briefly broke up in 1973, but re-formed the following year and has continued to tour and record ever since. Simmonds has remained undeterred by a revolving-door mentality and declining interest (no Savoy Brown album has charted in the U.S. since 1981's *Rock & Roll Warriors*). *—Steve Huey*

● **The Savoy Brown Collection (Chronicles Series)** / Jul. 20, 1993 / Polygram ✦✦✦✦✦
With one of the smoothest and most compelling guitarists of the blues-rock style, Savoy Brown and the finger wizardry of Kim Simmonds unleashed some of the smoothest and most mesmerizing rock & roll of the 1970s. Their ingenious blend of contented blues and hard-edged rock resulted in some wholesome yet somewhat bypassed guitar music. *The Savoy Brown Collection* is a two-disc compilation that takes their best tunes from

14 different albums and presents the listener with a sufficient amount of material that never becomes tiresome. Some of the meatier material comes from 1971's *Street Corner Talking*, like the ultra-smooth "I Can't Get Next to You" and Willie Dixon's "Wang Dang Doodle." Equally impressive is the haunting "Poor Girl" or the desperate guitar cry of "Leavin' Again," both from the sensational *Looking In* album. The real treasures are the lone tunes taken from some of their lesser-known albums. "I'm Tired," from *A Step Further*, emanates pathos through instrumentation, while "Stranger Blues" is a startling example of prime guitar manipulation. Early material from albums like *Shake Down* and *Blue Matter* have former lead singer Chris Youlden at the helm, who departed before the *Looking In* album, replaced by Lonesome Dave Peverett who later formed Foghat. Overshadowed by bands like the Yardbirds and Led Zeppelin, Savoy Brown didn't get the acclaim they actually deserved. Rightfully so, the words "Featuring Kim Simmonds" are underneath the title of this two CD set, since his craftsmanship is truly the heart of this talented band. Everything that is even the least bit important from this group is strewn across this compilation. *—Mike DeGagne*

Leo Sayer

b. May 21, 1948, Shoreham-on-Sea

Vocals, Harmonica, Guitar / Soft Rock

Leo Sayer had a string of highly polished mainstream pop hits in the late '70s. Sayer began his musical career as the leader of the London-based Terraplane Blues Band in the late '60s. His debut solo single, "Why Is Everybody Going Home," failed to make any impact, yet 1973's "The Show Must Go On" hit number one in the U.K.; a cover by Three Dog Night stopped Sayer's version from charting in the U.S. The following year he released his first album, *Silver Bird*. It was followed quickly by *Just a Boy*, which included two more British hit singles, "One Man Band" and "Long Tall Glasses (I Can Dance)"; "Long Tall Glasses" managed to break Sayer into the American Top Ten in early 1975. Sayer's working relationship with songwriting partner David Courtney was severed during the recording of his third album, *Another Year* (1975). The following year, he released *Endless Flight*, which was co-written with former Supertramp member Frank Furrell; featuring the number one singles "You Make Me Feel Like Dancing" and "When I Need You." The record became his biggest hit in both the U.S. and the U.K., selling over a million copies in America. Following *Endless Flight*, Sayer became a fixture in the American Top 40, yet his hits began to dry up in England. Sayer began the '80s with the American number two hit "More Than I Can Say," yet it was his last big single in the U.S. His last chart entry in America was the early 1981 hit "Living in a Fantasy"; the U.K. hits didn't stop until 1983, after "Till You Come Back to Me" scraped the charts. After laying low for the rest of the decade, he attempted a comeback in 1990 with *Cool Touch*, yet it fell on deaf ears. *—Stephen Thomas Erlewine*

The Show Must Go On: Anthology / Nov. 19, 1996 / Rhino ✦✦✦✦

The Show Must Go On offers a definitive collection of Sayer's 1970s bubbly dance-pop hits like "You Make Me Feel Like Dancing," "When I Need You," and "More Than I Can Say." A number of rare singles are also included, as is the unreleased cut "Tonight the Sky's About to Cry." *—Jason Ankeny*

● **The Very Best of Leo Sayer** / Feb. 15, 2000 / Rhino ✦✦✦✦

The Very Best of Leo Sayer? It may seem like Rhino has tread this ground before, and in a way they have. In 1996, they offered an exhaustive double-disc compilation called *The Show Must Go On*—a fine set, but one that was only useful for true fans, since it was simply too large for anyone who just wanted the hits. That's where *The Very Best of Leo Sayer* comes in. This single-disc collection has all of his ten charting singles—including "Long Tall Glasses (I Can Dance)," "You Make Me Feel Like Dancing," "When I Need You," and "More Than I Can Say"—plus six enjoyable album tracks. Essentially, it's simply a truncated version of *The Show Must Go On* (even the liner notes are an edited version of what appeared on the double-disc set), but for most casual fans, that makes it preferable. *—Stephen Thomas Erlewine*

Boz Scaggs

b. Jun. 8, 1944, Ohio

Slide Guitar, Vocals, Guitar / Album Rock, Pop/Rock, Soft Rock, Blues-Rock

After first finding acclaim as a member of the Steve Miller Band, singer/songwriter Boz Scaggs went on to enjoy considerable solo success in the 1970s. Joining former schoolmate Miller in his fledgling group in 1967, Scaggs exited after recording two acclaimed albums with the unit, *Children of the Future* and *Sailor*. With the aid of Rolling Stone magazine publisher Jann Wenner, Scaggs secured a solo contract with Atlantic; his soulful self-titled debut failed to find an audience despite winning critical favor, and the track "Loan Me a Dime" later became the subject of a court battle when bluesman Fenton Robinson successfully sued for composer credit. After signing to Columbia, Scaggs teamed with producer Glyn Johns to record 1971's *Moments*, a skillful blend of rock and R&B which, like its predecessor, failed to make much of an impression on the charts. Scaggs remained a critics' darling over the course of LPs like 1972's *My Time* and 1974's *Slow Dancer*, but he did not achieve a commercial breakthrough until 1976's *Silk Degrees*, which reached number two on the album charts while spawning the Top Three single "Lowdown," as well as the smash "Lido Shuffle." 1977's *Down Two Then Left* was also a success, and 1980's *Middle Man* reached the Top Ten on the strength of the singles "Breakdown Dead Ahead" and "Jo Jo." *—Jason Ankeny*

Boz Scaggs / 1969 / Atlantic ✦✦✦✦✦

Produced by Jann Wenner and featuring crack accompaniment by the Muscle Shoals house band, Scaggs's solo debut is a near-masterwork, mingling the pathos and heartbreak of vintage honky tonk with the celebration and release of Southern soul. The highlights of the album also flaunt its diversity: "Loan Me a Dime," an extended blues dirge, which features some of Duane Allman's finest work, and "Waiting on a Train," Scaggs's marvelous revamping of Jimmie Rodgers's classic hobo song. *—John Floyd*

Moments / 1971 / Columbia ✦✦✦

"We Were Always Sweethearts" wasn't a huge hit single, but it was a good one, signaling that Boz Scaggs was a soul man of the first degree. *Moments* places him into a variety of settings, including soul, R&B, blues, country, and beautiful, string-drenched balladry. Side one of the LP is especially strong, the kind whose grooves were worn out by its listeners in the early '70s. The second half of the recording doesn't hold up as well, but the closer, "Can I Make It Last (Or Will It Just Be Over)," is a gorgeous, atmospheric instrumental that pulls at the heartstrings. Although Scaggs' big moment in the commercial spotlight was still a few years away, this recording provides many satisfying musical *Moments*. *—Jim Newsom*

Boz Scaggs & His Band / Dec. 1971 / Columbia ✦✦✦✦

Although most listeners know Boz Scaggs primarily for his 1976 disco-era, multi-million seller *Silk Degrees*, he produced several excellent recordings in the years leading up to that breakthrough. *Boz Scaggs & Band* is the middle release of a three-disc spurt which Scaggs produced in a two-year period, between 1971 and 1972. Although it is weaker than *Moments* and *My Time* which bookend it, this album still has much to offer. Sounding at times like the original average white band, and at other times like a bunch of Nashville cats, Boz and his eight-piece group traverse a wide terrain with great facility and much soul. "Here to Stay" is particularly appealing, hinting at things to come, and "Flames of Love" is an extended piece of smoking funk. "Monkey Time" and "Why Why" also turn up the funk. This album is well worth checking out. *—Jim Newsom*

My Time / 1972 / Columbia ✦✦✦✦

Music critics of the early '70s kept predicting big things for Boz Scaggs, but his records of that period had trouble finding more than a cult audience. *My Time* continued with a mix similar to *Moments* from the previous year, with the opening "Dinah Flo," a great soul-drenched rocker that should have been a hit. In fact, the first three tracks present a powerful opening triumvirate which begs to be heard, with "Full-Lock Power Slide," an air guitarist's dream-come-true. Other high points are Scaggs' definitive cover of Allen Toussaint's "Freedom for the Stallion" and a take on Al Green's "Old Time Lovin'" that gives the original author a run for his money. Considering the success Van Morrison was having working the same territory, it's surprising that this album didn't achieve more in the commercial arena. Its blend of solid '60s soul and bluesy rock is very appealing. However, Boz Scaggs' time was still four years away. *My Time* is a rewarding listen nonetheless. *—Jim Newsom*

Slow Dancer / 1974 / Columbia ✦✦✦✦✦

Uneven production by Motown's Johnny Bristol. *—Bil Carpenter*

Silk Degrees / Feb. 1976 / Columbia ✦✦✦✦✦

Both artistically and commercially, Boz Scaggs had his greatest success with *Silk Degrees*. The laid-back singer hit the R&B charts in a big way with the addictive, sly "Lowdown" (which has been sampled by more than a few rappers and remains a favorite among baby-boomer soul fans) and expressed his love of smooth soul music almost as well on the appealing "What Can I Say." But Scaggs was essentially a pop/rocker, and in that area he has a considerable amount of fun on "Lido Shuffle" (another major hit single), "What Do You Want the Girl to Do," and "Jump Street." Meanwhile, "We're All Alone" and "Harbor Lights" became staples on adult contemporary radio. Though not remarkable, the ballads have more heart than most of the bland material dominating that format. *—Alex Henderson*

Down Two Then Left / Nov. 1977 / Columbia ✦✦✦

With 1974's *Slow Dancer*, produced by Johnny Bristol, Scaggs recast himself as a more R&B-infused singer. 1976's multi-million-selling *Silk Degrees* found Scaggs' switch paying off commercially, displaying enough skills and chops that the odious "blue-eyed soul" tag was deemed passé. This is noticeably more detached than *Silk Degrees*. And although this set is indeed quirky, the often unsurprising production featuring almost-on-cue guitar solos makes this album more "mainstream" than it had to be. "Still Falling for You" kicks the album off and sets the standard for the skilled, seamless production juxtaposed to meandering, almost incoherent lyrics. The melodic "A Clue," the best of the released singles, attains the offhanded cool and tunefulness that most of this set is striving for. Although this set is more soulful throughout than *Silk Degrees*, nothing sticks out like "What Can I Say." More than anything, this album puts the spotlight on Scaggs' romantic views, but they are so all over the road it's hard to tell what he really thinks. On the lush "We're Waiting," a listener may not have an idea of what he's talking about, but his vocal inflections say what the lyrics fail to. After a while, Scaggs seems to give up on making this a statement about love and offers some so-so rockers. In particular, the strongly produced "1993" has Scaggs imagining a drastically changed world as he sings, "Before they take me up/They'll have to alter, alter me." *Down Two Then Left* has a melancholy appeal much like *Al Green Is Love* and Joni Mitchell's *Hissing of Summer Lawns*, but a few concessions prevent this from being in their elite class. *—Jason Elias*

Middle Man / Apr. 1980 / Columbia/Legacy ✦✦✦

● **Hits!** / Nov. 1980 / Columbia ✦✦✦✦✦

In spite of the inclusion of "Dinah Flo," *Hits!* primarily focuses on Scaggs's '80s pop hits like "Lowdown," "Jojo," "Break Down Dead Ahead," and "Look What You've Done to Me." *—Bil Carpenter*

Other Roads / 1988 / Columbia ✦✦

Some Change / Apr. 5, 1994 / Virgin ✦✦✦✦✦

When Boz Scaggs signed with Virgin Records after spending at least 17 years with

Columbia, listeners had no idea what to expect. *Some Change* proved to be a pleasant surprise. Instead of going out of his way to be as slick and commercial as possible or offering something contrived and robotic, the singer-turned-restaurant-owner let his better instincts win out and delivered a very honest and natural-sounding collection of pop, pop-rock, and soul-influenced pop. On songs ranging from the smooth "I'll Be the One" (which has a slightly Average White Band-ish appeal) and the haunting "Sierra" to the ominous "Follow That Man," there's no question that Scaggs is coming from the heart. Arguably, *Some Change* is his best album since 1976's *Silk Degrees*. —*Alex Henderson*

Come On Home / Apr. 8, 1997 / Virgin ✦✦✦✦
On this prime collection of R&B and blues songs and influences from Scaggs' youth—and four new yet classic-sounding self-penned originals—the blue-eyed soulman eschews the slick production values of his pop chart-toppers such as "Lido" and "Lowdown," instead getting way down and his hands dirty with the honest blood, sweat, and tears of the real down-home blues. Packing in tow drummer Jim Keltner, guitarist Fred Tackett (from Little Feat), and slow-burning, soulful horn arrangements by Willie Mitchell, one of the founding fathers of Memphis soul (and composer of *Come On Home*'s title track), Scaggs' covers of songs originally composed and performed by such legends as Jimmy Reed ("Found Love"), T-Bone Walker (the legendary "T-Bone Shuffle"), Sonny Boy Williamson ("Early in the Morning") and Bobby "Blue" Bland (the thunderous "Ask Me 'Bout Nothing (But the Blues)"), along with "It All Went Down the Drain" (Earl King Johnson), and the smoldering "Your Good Thing (Is About to End)" (David Porter with Isaac Hayes), are absolutely impossible to resist. *Come On Home* is a genuine musical treasure. —*Chris Slawecki*

My Time: The Anthology (1969-1997) / Oct. 7, 1997 / Columbia/Legacy ✦✦✦✦
My Time: Anthology (1969-1997) is an excellent double-disc retrospective of Boz Scaggs' entire career, containing all of his hits, several key album tracks, and a handful of rarities designed to entice the hardcore collector. For any serious fan who wants a comprehensive overview of Scaggs' career, *My Time* is an ideal purchase. —*Thom Owens*

Scarface

Vocals / Southern Rap, Hardcore Rap, Gangsta Rap
Scarface quickly became the South's most admired rapper and remained so throughout the 1990s after breaking away from the Geto Boys to launch his solo career in 1991. Even if he never scored any national hits or stormed up the Billboard charts with any of his numerous albums throughout the '90s, no one could question his clout in the South. He essentially defined what it meant to be a Southern thug rapper years before anyone even coined the term "Dirty South." This became glaringly evident in the late '90s when a massive wave of young MCs arose from Houston, New Orleans, and Memphis emulating his style of hard-boiled, ghetto-bred, straight-up hardcore rapping. Besides serving as the father of Southern thug rap, it seemed as if every hardcore rapper wanted to align himself with Scarface during the '90s—everyone from Ice Cube and Dr. Dre to 2Pac and Master P collaborated with the former Geto Boy—all in an attempt to foster credibility among the loyal Southern rap audience. Yet despite his unquestionable influence, Scarface never crossed over to mainstream acceptance. His albums were often plagued with half-baked filler, his lyrics were simply too harsh for radio, and his uncompromising devotion to producer Mike Dean led to a stagnant albeit trademark sound. Still, likely *because* Scarface never crossed over and remained aligned to the streets, his influence never waned, making him one of the few veterans able to sustain in the here-today, gone-tomorrow rap game. —*Jason Birchmeier*

● **Mr. Scarface Is Back** / 1991 / Rap-A-Lot ✦✦✦✦✦
Scarface became the latest Geto Boy to try it solo with this 1991 album. He created a memorable message track in "A Minute to Pray and a Second to Die," a song that should have been a crossover sensation. Few gangsta numbers have more vividly and effectively chronicled the litany of hopelessness and violence plaguing the nation's inner cities. Other cuts, like "Body Snatcher," "Born Killer," and "Diary of a Madman," were less compelling and more chilling. —*Ron Wynn*

The Diary / 1993 / Rap-A-Lot/Noo Trybe ✦✦✦✦✦
Scarface's debut album after the breakup of his controversial band the Geto Boys, *The Diary* is just that—a journal of the trials of inner-city life. Related with his rhythmic, deep-voiced delivery, this gangsta album has some of the deepest, darkest beats around, and one track with guest Ice Cube. —*John Bush*

The World Is Yours / 1995 / Rap-A-Lot ✦✦✦
The second album from former Geto Boy Scarface didn't contain any single cut as moving or hypnotic as "A Minute to Pray and a Second to Die," but it proved even more popular. It also was an indication that the Geto Boys were kaput, as everyone continued cutting solo albums, and talk of a proposed new Geto Boys album went from probable to possible to the backburner. —*Ron Wynn*

Untouchable / Mar. 11, 1997 / Virgin ✦✦✦
Scarface's fourth album, *Untouchable*, is yet another collection of hardcore gangsta rap, this time spiked with a G-funk influence—both Dr. Dre ("Game Over") and 2Pac ("Smile") appear on the record, lending their rhyming skills to the deep bass grooves. While the production is impeccable, Scarface offers nothing distinctive on the album, and the record runs way too long to stay interesting. A handful of cuts, including those with Dre and 2Pac, are worthwhile, but *Untouchable* is his weakest effort yet. —*Leo Stanley*

My Homies / Feb. 24, 1998 / Virgin ✦✦✦
Scarface was never one of the more consistent hardcore rappers, falling prey to a tendecy for cartoonish violence and comic-book gangsta fantasies. As long as his music hit hard, such traits were forgivable, but he began to slip in the mid-'90s, relying on familiar styles,

samples, beats, and grooves. All of these factors are reasons why his double-disc opus *My Homies* was not the greatest of ideas. Scarface simply doesn't have enough ideas to sustain an album of this gargantuan size, especially since it follows *Untouchable* by just a year. He recycles beats and bass lines, and he repeats themes over and over again. The moments that do work, such as the dynamic Master P collaboration "Homies & Thuggs," only put the weakness of the remaining album in sharper relief. *My Homies* would have been tiring if it had been a single 70-minute disc, but at this bloated double-length, it's plain exhausting. —*Stephen Thomas Erlewine*

Last of a Dying Breed / Oct. 3, 2000 / Virgin ✦✦✦
The sixth album from Scarface doesn't stray too far from his usual subjects: Pain, murder, mayhem, and vengeance are all well represented on this sort-of concept album involving a life in turmoil. It's certainly Scarface's most personal album, with the rapper taking more responsibility for his actions and accounting for his words (and actually providing some well-deserved introspection on a few tracks). But this is still a street album, and Scarface still often takes a lazy street stance. Nonetheless, it's a good representation of a gangsta's development into conscientiousness. —*Michael Gallucci*

The Scene Is Now

The Scene Is Now was a kind of postmodern jug band comprised of a loose, ever-changing aggregation of downtown New York City musicians. Throughout their fluid career, only onetime Mofungo members Chris Nelson and Philip Dray remained permanent fixtures of the Scene's lineup, which also included Dick Champ and Jeff McGovern on their 1985 debut single "1150 Lbs." and dadaist first LP *Burn All Your Records* (which included "Yellow Sarong," their best-known composition thanks to a subsequent Yo La Tengo cover). Elliott Sharp signed on as producer and part-time sax player for 1986's *Total Jive*, which moved away from the complex, herky-jerky experimentation of the Scene's introductory outings into a more mellow and simplified sound. Pere Ubu bassist Tony Maimone and ex-dB Will Rigby enlisted for 1988's *Tonight We Ride*, another curveball which included the atmospheric "Dinah Shore" and the jaunty "Moonlight Broil." 1990's cassette-only *Shotgun Wedding*, featuring a cameo from the Shams, was the final collection of new The Scene Is Now material, although an expansive, eclectic career overview titled *The Oily Years (1983-1993)* appeared in 1995. —*Jason Ankeny*

● **Oily Years 1983-1993** / Oct. 17, 1995 / Bar/None ✦✦✦✦✦

Schnell Fenster

f. 1986, db. 1992
Adult Alternative Pop/Rock, Pop/Rock
Schnell Fenster was an eclectic New Zealand-based band comprised of former Split Enz members Phil Judd (guitar/vocals/keyboards), Noel Crombie (drums), Nigel Griggs (bass), and Michael Den Elzen (guitar) (the short-lived original lineup also included Enz keyboardist Eddie Rayner). The band formed in 1986 and released their first album, *Sound of Trees*, in 1988 in Australia. The same year, the band recorded a handful of country-tinged songs for the film *Rikky and Pete* as Noel's Cowards. A warm reception in their homeland and a revived interest in Split Enz prompted an American contract with Atlantic Records the following year. *Sound of Trees* saw a belated worldwide release in 1990, but without a supporting tour outside and poor promotion, the album quickly faded. The follow-up, 1991's *OK Alright a Huh Oh Yeah*, suffered the same fate, this time with a release limited to Australasia. While promoting the album, Crombie developed tinnitus, forcing them to postpone the tour. They eventually broke up, with the members playing a more active role behind the scenes in the music business. —*Chris Woodstra*

● **Sound of Trees** / 1988 / Atlantic ✦✦✦✦
The band's debut picks up where Split Enz left off in the mid-'80s, exploring some of the funkiness first heard on *Time and Tide* and the jazzy stylings of *Conflicting Emotions*. The always interesting Phil Judd turns in another quirky batch of lyrics as only he can sing, proving that his return was long overdue. —*Chris Woodstra*

Ok Alright a Huh Oh Yeah / 1991 / WEA ✦✦✦
Though the songs aren't quite as strong as those on the debut, *OK Alright a Huh Oh Yeah* is still a solid, well produced effort, worthwhile for longtime Split Enz fans. Released only in Australia, this would be their last album before disbanding. —*Chris Woodstra*

Schramms

Indie Pop, Alternative Country-Rock
The country-folk group Schramms drew their name from singer/guitarist Dave Schramm, a New York musician and veteran of critic's darlings like the Human Switchboard and Yo La Tengo. After playing on the latter's debut LP *Ride the Tiger*, he left the band to form his own unit, originally called the Walking Wounded. After learning of a Los Angeles band performing under the same name, they jokingly became the Schramms for a handful of performances, only to see the name stick permanently.

In addition to frontman Schramm, the outfit's original lineup featured ex-Human Switchboard drummer Ron Metz and bassist Terry Karydes, who switched over to the organ after her original instrument was stolen. The group soon swelled to include new bassist Mike Lewis, also a Yo La Tengo alum, as well as guitarist Todd Novak and saxophonist Pete Linzell. After recording their 1990 debut *Walk to Delphi*, the three new additions left the group, followed shortly thereafter by Karydes. Stepping in were bassist Al Greller, formerly of the Tall Lonesome Pines and Peter Stampfel & the Bottlecaps, and organist George Usher, late of the Bongos and Beat Rodeo. With their lineup firmly in place, the Schramms issued their second record, *Rock, Paper, Scissors, Dynamite*, in 1992. *Little Apocalypse* appeared in 1994, followed four years later by *Dizzy Spell*. —*Jason Ankeny*

Walk to Delphi / 1990 / Okra ✦✦✦✦✦

Rock, Paper, Scissors, Dynamite / 1992 / East Side Digital ✦✦✦✦

The second album from the Schramms, *Rock, Paper, Scissors, Dynamite*, sounds like the sort of record most bands don't come up with until six or seven years into their recording careers, speaking with the clear voices of seasoned veterans in firm command of their powers. Dave Schramm's songwriting had already developed an easygoing maturity that displayed wit without forcing a laugh and conveyed bitterness without spite or overwhelming angst. The second edition of the Schramms plays with authority, grace, and good humor; while Schramm's fleet-fingered guitar leads are the highlight, Terry Karydes' keyboards offer splendid melodic counterpoints, and bassist Al Greller and drummer Ron Metz are a rock-solid, no-nonsense rhythm section. If *Rock, Paper, Scissors, Dynamite* has a flaw, it's that it goes on a bit too long and doesn't shift gears often enough; while the album starts out well with the brilliant "Welfare of Your Enemy" and rolls on with a string of fine songs, it starts to lose a bit of steam at about the halfway point, and stays in a mid-tempo rut that is just a bit wearying by the time the disc finally comes to a close. In short, this album makes clear that the Schramms already had a lot going for them in the way of chops and studio smarts, but pacing an album was one task they hadn't yet learned to master. *—Mark Deming*

Little Apocalypse / Sep. 20, 1994 / East Side Digital ✦✦✦✦

The Schramms already had intelligence and maturity to spare when they cut their second album, *Rock, Paper, Scissors, Dynamite*, but the two years of seasoning that preceded the recording of 1994's *Little Apocalypse* is audible from the first play. While the Schramms already sounded tight on their earlier recordings, they sound positively intuitive on these sessions (especially Ron Metz, whose drumming offers lots of subtle color without calling attention to itself), and Dave Schramm's guitar playing has, if anything, grown even more striking and inventive, confirming his status as one of America's greatest unsung guitarists. And while *Rock, Paper, Scissors, Dynamite* sounded like a set of great songs, *Little Apocalypse* is a great *album*, displaying a greater thematic unity and enough tonal variety to keep it compelling from start to finish. And *Little Apocalypse* is dark enough to live up to its title, full of casual murders, angry apparitions, songs of the sirens, and vengeful final words alongside Schramm's usual tales of romantic distress and emotional discombobulation, painting a vivid picture of a world where things aren't quite right made all the more familiar by Schramm's warm, well-worn voice. (For good measure, the band also offers up another of its stellar covers: in this case, an inspired reading of Lucinda Williams' "Side of the Road.") A striking mix of the comfortable and the troubling, *Little Apocalypse* is a superb album from a band just sitting at the top of its form. *—Mark Deming*

● **Dizzy Spell** / Mar. 17, 1998 / Checkered Past ✦✦✦✦✦

If ever there was a band whose albums demanded more than a single listen, it's the Schramms. On first spin, *Dizzy Spell* sounds like a pleasant, well-crafted bit of folk-leaning pop; play it a few more times, let it sink in, and you'll find it's a remarkably intelligent, expressive, and compelling album that becomes more satisfying each time out. Dave Schramm was not blessed with the finest voice of his generation, but give his craggy, conversational timbre a chance to register and you'll be amazed at its range of nuances, and his lyrics manage to be both witty and genuinely poetic without sinking into pretension. More importantly, he's a superb guitarist who knows when to gently support a song and when to reel off a solo that's full of dexterity and fire. And with George Usher on keyboards, Al Greller on bass, and Ron Metz on drums, Schramm has a band that's solid and expressive but knows their first responsibility is to serve the song. And on *Dizzy Spell*, the Schramms offer up a dozen songs well worth hearing, particularly the bizarre suburban romance of "Wild Season," the remembrance of lost love of "Tell Me Again and Again," and the wistful, reflective title cut. Evocative, compelling, and seasoned with plenty of great guitar work, *Dizzy Spell* is a superb, criminally overlooked album that was one of the most pleasurable releases of 1998. *—Mark Deming*

100 Questions / Sep. 12, 2000 / Madacy ✦✦✦✦✦

Schramms quietly made a handful of superb albums through the 1990s which offered all the proof you'd need that Dave Schramm was a top-shelf guitarist, songwriter, and bandleader. But with 2000's *100 Questions*, Schramm and his usual studio cohort Gary Arnold have handed over the production duties to someone else for the first time, and the result is the band's strongest album to date. Musically, there isn't much that's strikingly different about *100 Questions*: Schramm's songs are still as dour, slyly witty, and keenly intelligent as ever; his tastefully angular guitar solos are still a delight to hear; and his band is solid and fully in touch with the subtleties of the songs. But producer J.D. Foster has encouraged tighter and more concise arrangements for the musicians, which give them less space to drift than they displayed on *Dizzy Spell* (*100 Questions*' 11 cuts zip by in a snappy 38 minutes, while *Dizzy Spell*'s dozen take a more leisurely 57 minutes), and the songs gain a lot of punch in the process. And the album simply *sounds better*. Foster's production and mix are brighter, warmer, and more vivid than anything Schramms have enjoyed in the past. And Schramm and company have certainly risen to the occasion for their fifth time at bat; "Torn in Two," "Deny You," and "Simple Arithmetic" are pop that's intelligent, engaging, and hooky, while "I'll Believe," "Mailbox," and "She Says" prove this band is no less exciting when they cut back the tempo. It's hard to say why the Schramms aren't widely regarded as one of America's best and most interesting bands at the dawn of the millennium, but one listen to *100 Questions* proves it's not because they don't have the goods. *—Mark Deming*

Scorpions

f. 1969, Hannover, Germany

Album Rock, Heavy Metal, Hard Rock

German hard rockers the Scorpions have sold over 22 million records, making them one of the most successful rock bands to ever come out of Continental Europe. The band was originally formed in 1969 by Rudolf Schenker, whose younger brother Michael joined in 1971 to play lead guitar; good friend Klaus Meine became the vocalist that year as well. Michael's guitar playing was noticed by the band UFO, who hired him as their lead guitarist in 1973; Uli Jon Roth replaced him, and under his guidance the group released four albums on RCA from 1974-77. Roth subsequently left the band; in 1979, Michael Schenker was kicked out of UFO for alcohol abuse and came back to play with the Scorpions, who had recently signed with Mercury Records. The group released *Lovedrive* that same year and played their first American tour. Still coping with addiction, Michael missed tour dates repeatedly, and guitarist Matthias Jabs was hired to fill in; Michael eventually would leave the band a second time. The band released *Animal Magnetism* in 1980, which surprisingly went gold in the United States. 1982's *Blackout* contained the cult hit "No One Like You" and was a major success worldwide, selling over one million copies in the U.S. alone. But it was the powerful follow-up, *Love at First Sting*, that succeeded in making them superstars. Released in 1984, the album boasted the MTV hit "Rock You Like a Hurricane" and achieved double-platinum status. In 1990, the album *Crazy World* became the Scorpions' biggest-selling record to date, drawing on the strength of the hit ballad "Wind of Change." However, *Crazy World* was the last successful Scorpions release in the U.S.; many fans lost interest due to the alternative explosion of the early '90s. Still, they continued to record for a core audience, and in 1997 Mercury assembled a double album of the band's greatest hits, *Deadly Sting: The Mercury Years*. *—Barry Weber*

The Best of Rockers 'n' Ballads / Oct. 1989 / Mercury ✦✦✦✦✦

Even though it's the official greatest-hits compilation of the Scorpions' '80s releases, *Best of Rockers n' Ballads* is actually missing some of their best rockers and ballads. While it contains such hits as "Rock You Like a Hurricane," "Blackout," and "The Zoo," the 12 songs listed simply don't give the listener a good impression of what the Scorpions are all about. In fact, some of the band's best songs, such as "Dynamite" and "Another Piece of Meat," weren't ever hits in the first place and are therefore absent. Due to its lack of some of the Scorpions' most entertaining classics, *Best of Rockers n' Ballads* fails to be a good introduction to the band. *—Barry Weber*

● **Deadly Sting: The Mercury Years** / Jul. 15, 1997 / Mercury ✦✦✦✦✦

Presently, it is quite difficult to find a young person who knows about the Scorpions. Even when their careers were peaking in the '80s they were never widely recognized, existing always as more of an underground band. The lack of hit singles produced by the group is by no means a judgment of their talent, however, as *Deadly Sting: The Mercury Years* proves. Some may find the fact that Mercury made the compilation a double-disc set surprising—again due to the band's small following—but the album is far better than the single-disc collection *Best of Rockers n' Ballads*. Following chronologically from 1979 to 1993 (thus covering the years in which the band enjoyed their most success), *Deadly Sting* rips through the favorites "Loving You Sunday Morning," "The Zoo," "Blackout," "No One Like You," "Big City Nights," "Still Loving You," "Rock You Like a Hurricane," "Rhythm of Love," "Wind of Change," and "Don't Believe Her," finally concluding with two unreleased recordings from 1995. Though these tracks are far cries from the songs which preceded them, that doesn't stop *Deadly Sting: The Mercury Years* from being the most essential album from one of the most underrated hair bands of all time. *—Barry Weber*

Jack Scott

b. Jan. 24, 1936, Windsor, Ontario, Canada

Vocals, Guitar / Rockabilly, Traditional Country, Rock & Roll

Jack Scott sounded tough, like someone you wouldn't want to meet in a dark alley unless he had a guitar in his hands. When he growled "The Way I Walk," wise men stepped aside. Despite his snarling rockabilly attitude, Scott hailed from Ontario and grew up near Detroit, developing a love for hillbilly music along the way. His pronounced emphasis on acoustic guitar distinguished his atmospheric rockers, though his principal pop success came with tear-in-your-beer ballads. After recording for ABC during 1957, he found a hit with "My True Love" after signing to Carlton. The single reached number three and became a British Top Ten hit. After switching labels again, to Top Rank, he hit the Top Five twice during 1959 with "What in the World's Come Over You" and "Burning Bridges." Those two singles were his peak, though Scott also recorded with Capitol during 1961. He continued to vacillate between cowboy crooner and rough-edged rocker throughout the remainder of the '60s and '70s. During the '80s and '90s, Scott occasionally turned up on the oldies circuit, still looking and sounding like a man you seriously didn't want to mess with. *—Bill Dahl*

Scott on Groove / 1989 / Bear Family ✦✦✦✦

The music on *Scott on Groove* was recorded after Jack Scott's hit-making era on Capitol was finished. Scott recorded for Groove in the early '60s. During this time, he was trying to refashion his sound into a rock & roll/rockabilly direction. Not all of the attempts were successful, but the set is interesting for dedicated fans, but they would probably rather acquire this material on the more comprehensive box set, *Classic Scott*. *—Stephen Thomas Erlewine*

● **Greatest Hits** / 1990 / Curb ✦✦✦✦✦

Curb's *Greatest Hits* was the only American Jack Scott compilation available in the mid-'90s, after Capitol pulled its *Collector's Series* from the market. Although *Greatest Hits* only has 11 tracks—including a recently recorded version of "Running Scared"—it has the essential big hits ("My True Love," "Goodbye Baby," "Burning Bridges," "Leroy," "The Way I Walk," "What in the World's Come Over You") and is a servicable collection, even if it is frustratingly brief. *—Stephen Thomas Erlewine*

Classic Scott / Jun. 27, 1994 / Bear Family ✦✦✦✦✦

With the exception of Roy Orbison and Elvis, no white rock & roller of the time ever developed a finer voice with a better range than Jack Scott, or cut a more convincing body of work in rockabilly, rock & roll, country-soul, gospel, country-pop, or blues. And it's all here on this five-CD set, which probably seems at first like more Jack Scott than most of us need. Its 134 tracks include very, very few songs that aren't worth hearing at least twice (and most a lot more) and have more than their share of surprises. Anyone who laments Scott's failure to remain a rockabilly artist will be surprised at just how much he brought to country ballads and gospel, as well as the convincingly bluesy approach to rock & roll that he maintained years into his recording career. The handful of rockabilly tracks here, confined to the first half of the first disc (with their stereo mixes appearing on the last one), show Scott as a potential rival to Elvis Presley and Gene Vincent. He found success as more of a ballad singer, however, and never returned to his rock & roll roots for more than a song at a time. At the end of the 1950s, he moved back into the haven of country music, where he'd started in his teen years. The fit wasn't an ideal one, although Scott was good enough to make an album's worth of Hank Williams songs a worthwhile venture. This box has it all, mastered about as well as it's ever likely to be. Moreover, good as everything else is, the producers of this box have saved the best for last—unissued, undated demos a few of which are worth the price of a CD themselves. —*Bruce Eder*

The Very Best of Jack Scott / Sep. 26, 2000 / Collectables ✦✦✦✦

Although it runs 23 tracks and contains such classics as "What in the World's Come Over You" and "Burning Bridges," Collectables' *The Very Best of Jack Scott* is not a definitive overview of his career, since it lacks such classics as "The Way I Walk" and "Leroy." This does a good job of rounding up such lesser-known, later-'60s recordings, which are by and large fairly good, but they don't make up for the absence of those previously mentioned songs. Not a bad collection, but not as good as it could have been—especially considering its generous running time. —*Stephen Thomas Erlewine*

The Way I Walk / Roller Coaster ✦✦✦

Jack Scott cut a couple of great rockabilly 45s for ABC/Paramount to begin his career, and Scott's two biggest hits, "What in the World's Come Over You" and "Burning Bridges," were recorded directly after his stay at Carlton Records. But it's generally conceded by rockabilly fans that the majority of his best and most lasting work was cut for that label between 1958 and 1960. This 26-track compilation makes a nice one-stop for the casual Scott fan who doesn't want to opt for Bear Family's massive multi-disc box set, as it's loaded with great rockers like "The Way I Walk," "Leroy," "Goodbye Baby," and his first big hit, "My True Love." But the non-inclusion of his two biggest hits and his early rockabilly singles keep this one from being the definitive package, although it's great listening all the way. —*Cub Koda*

Jill Scott

Contemporary R&B, Funk, Hip-Hop

Jill Scott grew up in north Philadelphia and began her performing career reading her own poetry. She was heard by Amir, drummer in the Roots, who invited her to join the band in the studio, resulting in the co-composition "You Got Me," a Top 40 pop hit in 1999. Subsequently, she collaborated with Eric Benet, Will Smith, and Common and broadened her performing experience by touring Canada in a production of the Broadway musical *Rent*. Signed to Steve McKeever's newly formed Hidden Beach Recordings label, she released her debut album, *Who Is Jill Scott? Words and Sounds Vol. 1*, in July 2000. —*William Ruhlmann*

Who Is Jill Scott?: Words and Sounds, Vol. 1 / Jul. 18, 2000 / Hidden Beach/Epic ✦✦✦✦✦

Though start-up label Hidden Beach and its manufacturer/distributor, Sony, may have been hoping for another Lauryn Hill in this eloquent young African-American from a Middle Atlantic state, Jill Scott turns out to be something of a hip-hop Patti Smith, a street poet who, on her first album, hasn't quite made the transition from spoken word performances to music, despite an excellent singing voice. With any luck, she will retain her sense of the power of words, since the best parts of this album are the ones when she lets fly, drunk on her verbal virtuosity. Producer Jeff Townes (of DJ Jazzy Jeff and the Fresh Prince fame) and his team of associates from the A Touch of Jazz production company set up sympathetic musical backgrounds for Scott that support her without requiring her to fit her spoken and sung excursions into strict meter. That gives her range to pursue her interests, which include a strong sense of her north Philadelphia neighborhood and such idiosyncratic concerns as food. But the album has a story to tell, and for the most part it is a love story. Scott describes a relationship from many different angles, including an encounter with her boyfriend's ex in a super market ("Exclusively") and her warnings to that girl (or some other) to stay away ("Gettin' in the Way"). This narrative structure gives Scott ample room to express a variety of emotions and to display her "verbal elation." Like many poets, she sometimes delights in a torrent of words for their own sake, but it's hard to fault her when the result is such a fully articulated worldview. —*William Ruhlmann*

Gil Scott-Heron

b. Apr. 1, 1949, Chicago, IL
Vocals, Piano, Guitar / Folk-Jazz, Fusion, Social Commentary, Political Rap

One of the most influential progenitors of rap music, Gil Scott-Heron's aggressive, no-nonsense street poetry inspired a legion of intelligent rappers while his engaging songwriting skills placed him square in the R&B charts later in his career, backed by increasingly contemporary production courtesy of Malcolm Cecil and Nile Rodgers (of Chic). Born in Chicago but transplanted to Tennessee for his early years, Scott-Heron spent most of his high-school years in the Bronx, where he learned firsthand many of the experiences which later made up his songwriting material. He had begun writing before reaching his teenage years, however, and completed his first volume of poetry at the age of 13. Though

he attended college in Pennsylvania, he dropped out after one year to concentrate on his writing career and earned plaudits for his novel, *The Vulture*. Encouraged at the end of the '60s to begin recording by legendary jazz producer Bob Thiele—who had worked with every major jazz great, from Louis Armstrong to John Coltrane—Scott-Heron released his 1970 debut, *Small Talk at 125th & Lennox*, inspired by a volume of poetry of the same name. With Thiele's Flying Dutchman Records until the mid-'70s, he signed to Arista soon after and found success on the R&B charts. Though his jazz-based work of the early '70s was tempered by a slicker disco-inspired production, Scott-Heron's message was as clear as ever on the Top 30 single "Johannesburg" and the number 15 hit "Angel Dust." Silent for almost a decade, after the release of his 1984 single "Re-Ron," the proto-rapper returned to recording in the mid-'90s with a message for the gangsta rappers who had come in his wake; Scott-Heron's 1994 album *Spirits* began with "Message to the Messengers," pointed squarely at the rappers whose influence—positive or negative—meant much to the children of the 1990s. —*John Bush*

● **The Revolution Will Not Be Televised** / 1988 / Bluebird/RCA ✦✦✦✦✦

Spanning 1970-1972, this superb collection takes us back to Gil Scott-Heron's early years when he was working with jazz producer Bob Thiele—a man who had been in the studio with everyone from John Coltrane and Pharoah Sanders to Coleman Hawkins. But *The Revolution Will Not Be Televised* isn't a jazz collection per se; it's a collection of innovative R&B and spoken poetry that contains jazz influences and finds Scott-Heron employing such jazz musicians as flutist Hubert Laws and bassist Ron Carter. Like the Last Poets, Scott-Heron has been described as "one of the first rappers"—and while he was hardly the first person to speak in rhyme to music, there are definitely parallels between angry sociopolitical poems like "Whitey on the Moon," "No Knock," and "Brother" and hip-hop commentary from the 1980s. Poetry, however, doesn't dominate this album—most of the selections illustrate Scott-Heron's excellence as a singer, including "Home Is Where the Hatred Is," "Did You Hear What They Said?," and the poignant "Save the Children." One of the collection's less political tracks is "Lady Day and John Coltrane," an R&B classic that articulates how easily jazz can lift a person's spirits. *The Revolution Will Not Be Televised* isn't the last word on Scott-Heron's artistry—he recorded many more treasures after leaving Flying Dutchman for Arista in 1975. But it's one of the collections to acquire if you're exploring his artistry for the first time. —*Alex Henderson*

Evolution & Flashback: The Very Best of Gil Scott-Heron / Feb. 9, 1999 / RCA ✦✦✦✦

Scrawl

f. 1985, Columbus, OH
Indie Rock, Alternative Pop/Rock

Long before the riot-grrrl movement opened the floodgates for the widespread emergence of female artists in the male-dominated world of indie rock, the Columbus, OH based trio Scrawl carved out their own tough-minded yet feminine niche within the underground community. Formed by singer/guitarist Marcy Mays, bassist Sue Harshe, and drummer Carolyn O'Leary, the group—originally dubbed Skull—debuted in the summer of 1985 by playing a 20-minute opening set for the Meat Puppets; with the financial assistance of friends, they entered the studio to record their debut effort a year later, releasing *Plus, Also, Too* on the small No Other label in 1987.

In the wake of the album's strong reviews, Scrawl toured extensively before signing to the Rough Trade label in 1988. *He's Drunk*, an assured indie-pop effort recorded at Prince's Paisley Park studios, soon followed, and in 1990 the trio returned with *Smallmouth*, a more intimate album produced by Gary Smith. Problems with Rough Trade forced Scrawl to depart the label in the autumn of 1990; a few months later, the company declared bankruptcy, and with its demise the group's back catalog immediately went out of print.

The sting of the Rough Trade debacle clearly informed 1991's superb *Bloodsucker*, recorded with Steve Albini; a biting, bitter record, it too fell prey to industry whims and poor distribution, quickly joining the group's other records in limbo. After O'Leary broke ranks, Scrawl mounted the "Foxcore, My Ass" tour as an acoustic duo, recruiting new drummer Dana Marshall prior to signing with the Simple Machines label for 1993's *Velvet Hammer*. After jumping to Elektra, Scrawl issued their major-label debut *Travel On, Rider* in 1996. *Nature Film* followed two years later. —*Jason Ankeny*

Plus, Also, Too / 1987 / Rough Trade ✦✦

He's Drunk / 1988 / Rough Trade ✦✦✦

Though Scrawl still sounds ragged and tentative in the studio, *He's Drunk* is much better than their debut, with across-the-board improvement. The band sounds more comfortable with each other and the first instances of the band's knack for committing catchy folk-punk to tape peek through ("Green Beer," "Breaker Breaker"). Rough production cramps some of the tunefulness, but it's not as demo-sounding as their previous LP. One of Scrawl's distinct features over bands of their time was their ability to handle familial relationships and friendship issues without sounding dopey; "For Your Sister" is one such example. A cover of Felice and Boudleaux Bryant's "Rocky Top" lends a bit of cowpunk edge, and a rare occasion where Scrawl show their sense of humor (also see their Paula Abdul homage on *Bloodsucker*) looms on a version of "Let It All Hang Out": "Black clothes, white white tan/ That's the way I catch my man, uh huh." —*Andy Kellman*

Smallmouth / 1990 / Rough Trade ✦✦✦

Though *Smallmouth* is Scrawl's third LP, it's still the sound of a band not 100% comfortable in the studio. Confidence isn't lacking in Marcy Mays' songwriting, however, which continues to improve. The angular jab of "Time to Come Clean" purges guilt while remaining defiant ("I want to look you in the eye/ I have talked behind your back") and in "Charles," the woman wears the pants ("Put out or get out, that's the way it goes"). The band's crafty folk-punk is served up with rare emotion, closing out with a biting version of "I Need You" that is just as gripping as Eurythmics' original. The song's vulnerable-yet-sturdy theme is so fitting for Scrawl that it would be easy to mistake it for a Mays original. —*Andy Kellman*

● **Velvet Hammer** / Nov. 19, 1993 / Simple Machines ✦✦✦✦✦
Velvet Hammer is one of the saddest, most heartbreaking records you will ever hear. It's soaked in tears and alcohol, punctuated with bruises and frostbitten fingers. Whether the songs of fractured relationships within are of romantic or familial nature, they sting with equally biting resonance. Marcy Mays is a mediator between mother and child on "Your Mother Wants to Know": "She wants you to like her so try to forget it/ And she's sorry for all the years and what happened to you when you were a kid." In "Take a Swing," she confronts an angered lover: "If you get me started, there's no telling what I'll do." She's stuck in an un-trusting rut in "Prize": "I get flowers/ I get suspicious, too." Throughout *Velvet Hammer*, the protagonist is at the end of her rope, struggling to find peace of mind amidst inner and outer turmoil. Though still sounding ragged and a little out of place in the studio, Steve Albini's raw engineering style is tailor-made for the band, especially for this stark material. New drummer Dana Marshall adds a creative instrumental spark, and it seems to have re-fueled his bandmates' creative juices. The closest touchstones with *Velvet Hammer* have to be American Music Club's *Everclear* and Joy Division's *Unknown Pleasures*, two other records that bleed with despair and grim reality. It's a blues record from the Midwest and an undeniable diamond in the rough, an unheard indie-rock classic. —*Andy Kellman*

Travel On, Rider / Aug. 20, 1996 / Elektra ✦✦✦✦
The indie community's knee-jerk negative reaction to finding out about Scrawl's jump to a major was one of puzzlement. The band had been shafted by most of the small-fry outlets that released them prior, and Simple Machines (which released *Velvet Hammer* and reissued *Bloodsucker*) were fans enough of the band to continue their support. Regardless, who knows why a major label would sign a band whose minor chords and emotionally naked songs could *never* translate into unit shifting, but what the signing meant for Scrawl was better availability. New label Elektra wouldn't have a clue as to what do with them, but at least they could put Scrawl's records in more shops and provide a decent recording budget—therein lies the band's rationale. *Travel On, Rider* is their most professional sounding record to date. Without sacrificing the band's rough edges, Steve Albini's and Jeff Powell's recording and engineering give the band it's most polished sound yet, but it doesn't make their songs—still bitter, still pessimistic, still sad—suffer for it. Two third-person stories set the table, doubling as highlights: "Good Under Pressure" illustrates a woman on the verge of breakdown and "The Garden Path" tells of another who burns her bridges in search of a new life. The playing is as tight as ever, surely the result of constant touring. Dana Marshall's underrated drums are at their most dynamic, Sue Harshe's Rickenbacker bass is graceful and thick, and Marcy Mays' Wire-meets-Cheap Trick guitar lofts countless catchy riffs. Harshe's piano on the second version of "Story Musgrave" is a major stunner. As Mays sings "I'm smart enough to know you have no use for me," there's little to prevent the onslaught of chills. —*Andy Kellman*

Nature Film / May 12, 1998 / Elektra ✦✦✦✦✦
It was fitting for the bad-luck Scrawl that *Nature Film*'s artwork included the intended street date of "05-12-1998"—it wasn't released until a week later. Aware of the likelihood that it would be their last record for Elektra, Scrawl smartly opted to offer as few new songs as possible to the label. Why bake a cake for a partner who's mistreating you, knowing that you can save it for someone who actually deserves it? With that frame of mind *Nature Film* should be the sound of a band not giving their all, simply going through the motions. That isn't the case—despite half of the record being actual new material, it's the band's second-best album. They had kept old material from the Rough Trade days in their live repertoire; through years of sporadic gigging, songs like "Rot" and "For Your Sister" turned from good to fantastic, and literally none of their fans could find pre-*Bloodsucker* releases in the stores. "Standing Around," "Charles," "11:59 It's January," and "Clock Song" also get powerful updates, finally capturing the band's live edge on tape. Most noticeable is drummer Dana Marshall's contributions to the older materials (Marshall joined after *Bloodsucker*). More agile and forceful than earlier drummer Carolyn O' Leary, Marshall's style and advanced musicianship are more complementary to the band. The record isn't just a good trawl through the past—the six new songs lack nothing in vitality. Bad relationships are still the forte of Marcy Mays' songwriting, who manages to keep it fresh; "You Made It a Crime" is scornful, "100 Car Pile-Up" is shameless rage, and "Guess I'll Wait" is empty resignation. Top it off with a storming cover of PiL's "Public Image," and there you have it: another great record from Columbus' finest. —*Andy Kellman*

Screaming Trees

f. 1983, Seattle, WA, db. 2000
College Rock, Neo-Psychedelia, Grunge, Alternative Pop/Rock, American Underground
Where many of their Seattle-based contemporaries dealt in reconstructed Black Sabbath and Stooges riffs, the Screaming Trees fused '60s psychedelia and garage rock with '70s hard rock and '80s punk. Over the course of their career, their more abrasive punk roots eventually gave way to a hard-edged, rootsy psychedelia that drew from rock and folk equally. After releasing several albums on indie labels like SST and Sub Pop, the Screaming Trees moved to Epic Records in 1989. Though they were one of the first Seattle bands to sign with a major label, the group never attained the popularity of fellow Northwestern bands (and friends) like Nirvana and Soundgarden, largely due to their erratic work schedule. Throughout their career, the Trees were notorious for drinking and fighting, which caused them to break up briefly at several points in their career. Nevertheless, the band managed to cultivate a dedicated following, which included not only fans, but also fellow musicians. —*Stephen Thomas Erlewine*

Clairvoyance / 1986 / Velvetone ✦✦✦

Even If and Especially When / 1987 / SST ✦✦✦
The Screaming Trees were still trying to define their style on their second album, *Even If and Especially When*, but that makes it one of their most intriguing and exciting efforts. —*Stephen Thomas Erlewine*

Invisible Lantern / 1988 / SST ✦✦✦
On Screaming Trees' third full-length release, *Invisible Lantern*, the band further refined their early psychedelic garage sound. The group had become a bona fide cult success by the time of this release, but the indie scene was losing steam and this disc (while superior to earlier efforts) didn't garner enough critical or commercial attention to move the band into mainstream awareness. The music of *Invisible Lantern* is spirited and raw—a swirling garage pop that, while repetitive, has a character all its own. Looking back, fans will notice that singer Mark Lanegan still hadn't found his unique tonality that listeners most familiar with the group's one and only radio hit (1992's "Almost Lost You") might recognize. Besides the unrealized potential of Lanegan's performances, this early-career release suffers a little from meandering song structures and other sonic deficiencies that the band eventually overcame. That's not to say that there aren't plenty of fine moments on *Invisible Lantern*. The hypnotic pop of the record's first six tracks is best represented on "Lines and Circles" and "Ivy"—trippy cuts with interesting lyrics and arrangements. Other straight-ahead tracks like "Walk Through to This Side" and "Night Comes Creeping" provide a nice contrast and energy. Indie fans (resentful of the post-Nirvana Seattle revolution) tend to ignore Screaming Trees' later material in favor of earlier offerings like this one. But to unbiased listeners, it might appear that the group simply had two incarnations, the second of which was perhaps more mature. Ultimately, there are as many perspectives on this issue as there are fans and critics. No matter how one interprets the arc of Screaming Trees' career, however, *Invisible Lantern* stands as a solid offering to the waning indie-rock movement. —*Vincent Jeffries*

Buzz Factory / 1989 / SST ✦✦✦

Uncle Anesthesia / Jan. 1991 / Epic ✦✦✦
After a long career with independent label SST, the Screaming Trees arrived at Epic Records with little fanfare (and would leave in much the same way) with 1991's *Uncle Anesthesia*. Produced by Soundgarden's Chris Cornell and metal specialist Terry Date, the album lurches to its feet on the military shuffle of "Beyond This Horizon." Despite offering a few glimpses of the group's punkier side—"Story of Her Fate," "Alice Said," "Time for Light"—most of the material emphasizes the Trees' mellower inclinations. As its title and disturbing, *Alice in Wonderland*-inspired cover artwork would suggest, the album also finds the band delving deeper and deeper into their psychedelic tendencies. Gary Lee Conner's lysergic guitar textures gently frame Mark Lanegan's rough, whiskey-drenched vocals on such highlights as the title track, "Caught Between," and "Something About Today." And while "Bed of Roses" and "Lay Your Head Down" betray a strong R.E.M. influence, songs like "Before We Arise," "Closer," and "Disappearing" (with its Mexican funeral horn section) possess a sense of despair and hopelessness that only Lanegan's voice can convey. The last album to feature original drummer Mark Pickerel, *Uncle Anesthesia* also set the stage for the band's breakthrough, *Sweet Oblivion*. —*Ed Rivadavia*

Anthology: SST Years / 1991 / SST ✦✦✦
Anthology: SST Years is a terrific 21-track compilation of songs culled from the group's three albums for the label, hitting most of the highlights from all of the records and thereby providing an excellent summary of their early years. —*Stephen Thomas Erlewine*

● **Sweet Oblivion** / Mar. 1992 / Epic ✦✦✦✦
The Screaming Trees one-upped their major-label debut *Uncle Anesthesia* with this solid, vastly underrated effort. *Sweet Oblivion*'s lead single, the jumpy hard rocker "Nearly Lost You," proved itself a highlight on the hugely successful, Seattle-themed *Singles* soundtrack. But even though the Screaming Trees stacked up quite well against their more famous peers in that particular showcase, the exposure didn't make them stars. Perhaps it was because *Sweet Oblivion* had been released several months before *Singles*, and the band thus couldn't build a sense of anticipation for a *new* album release, the way Alice in Chains and Smashing Pumpkins did for *Dirt* and *Siamese Dream*, respectively; nor could they capitalize on the extra publicity that goes along with new releases. For whatever reason, *Singles* didn't push sales of *Sweet Oblivion*, as the latter only scraped the lower reaches of the Billboard charts. And that's a shame, because the record is quite good—the best songs here are easily among the best in their catalog, and the songwriting was their most consistent yet. "Nearly Lost You" is a standout, of course, but "Dollar Bill," "Shadow of the Season," and "Butterfly" are nearly as impressive. Mark Lanegan's raspy voice conveys a weary wistfulness which adds an unexpected dimension to the group's otherwise macho garage-psych grunge. The Trees no longer sound all that punkish, trading in some of their early, noisy fury for a more '70s-indebted hard-rock sound, but it's done with a graceful power that proves they were at least the equal of their more famous fellow scenesters. Unfortunately, the four-year hiatus between *Sweet Oblivion* and its follow-up, *Dust*, ensured that the band would be forever relegated to cult status. —*Steve Huey*

Dust / Jun. 25, 1996 / Epic ✦✦✦✦
In many ways, the Screaming Trees missed their opportunity. They released *Sweet Oblivion* just as grunge began to capture national attention and they didn't tour the album extensively, which meant nearly all of their fellow Seattle bands became superstars while stood to the side. After four years, they returned with *Dust*, their second major label album, and by that point, the band's sound was too idiosyncratic for alternative radio. Which is unfortunate, because *Dust* is the band's strongest album. Sure, the rough edges that fueled albums like *Uncle Anesthesia* are gone, but in its place is a rustic hard rock,

equally informed by heavy metal and folk. The influence of Mark Lanegan's haunting solo albums is apparent in both the sound and emotional tone of the record, but this is hardly a solo project—the rest of the band has added a gritty weight to Lanegan's spare prose. The Screaming Trees sound tighter than they ever have and their melodies and hooks are stronger, more memorable, making *Dust* their most consistently impressive record. *—Stephen Thomas Erlewine*

Scritti Politti

f. 1977, Leeds, England, **db.** Feb. 8, 1990
Sophisti-Pop, Pop/Rock, New Wave, Dance-Pop
By the mid '80s, Scritti Politti, the band that had been inspired by the Sex Pistols' *Anarchy in the U.K* tour and the Young Communists, was releasing meticulously crafted synth-pop with a strong R&B influence and topping the charts both in their native England and in the U.S.; undergoing in the process one of the most dramatic transformations in the history of pop music.

Scritti Politti, which earned its name when founder Green Gartside was reading a book by Italian author Antonio Gramisi (English title: Political Writing), was formed in 1977 in London by Gartside and his schoolmates Matthew Kay, Nial Jinks, and Tom Morely. The group, who at the time was living in a London squat, issued three DIY recordings under their own St. Pancras label which were distributed by Rough Trade. The singles, which featured an experimental style and highly political lyrics, sold well and Gartside became something of a local celebrity, aided by his quirky, intellectual personal style.

Serious health problems in 1979 forced Gartside to return to his boyhood home in South Wales. When he returned to London in 1980 he convinced the other band members to make a major change in musical direction. 1982's *Songs to Remember*, which was issued on Rough Trade, shows a much stronger pop style than their previous punk-influenced work and paved the way for their major label contract with Virgin. 1985's *Cupid & Psyche* was a major international hit, propelled by the singles, "Word Girl" and "Perfect Way"; it showed off a new synth-pop style with a strong R&B influence, no doubt aided by new band members Fred Maher and David Gamson. The band's perfectionism in the studio delayed its follow-up for three years, when *Provision* was released. The next hiatus would prove to be much longer, however, when Gartside again retreated to the Welsh countryside, emerging only for occasional singles and production jobs until 1999's *Anomie & Bonhomie*. *—Stacia Proefrock*

Songs to Remember / 1982 / Rough Trade ✦✦✦
Scritti Politti's debut album was an infectious set of catchy, well-crafted pop songs that demonstrate Green Gartside's talent for deceptively simple hooks and melodies. *—Stephen Thomas Erlewine*

● **Cupid & Psyche 85** / 1985 / Warner Brothers ✦✦✦✦✦
On their second album, Scritti Politti essentially was Green Gartside, who directed drummer Fred Maher, keyboardist David Gamson, and a multitude of studio musicians through a state-of-the-art, immaculately constructed set of catchy, synth-pop on *Cupid & Psyche 85*. The results are as impressive as *Songs to Remember* and produced the hit singles "Perfect Way" and "Wood Beez (Pray like Aretha Franklin)." *—Stephen Thomas Erlewine*

Provision / 1988 / Warner Brothers ✦✦

Anomie & Bonhomie / Jul. 1999 / Virgin ✦✦✦✦
Scritti Politti finally delivered their fourth album, *Anomie & Bonhomie*, in the summer of 1999, nearly 15 years after their third. Such a long wait almost guarantees some change in the music, but the strange thing about *Anomie & Bonhomie* is how the updates—rapper cameos, vague house beats, grunge guitars—sound as if they're pasted over backing tracks from 1986. Not necessarily a bad thing, but disconcerting, since the heart of this album is squarely in *Cupid & Psyche 85* territory. Green Gartsidestill creates unabashedly fey, unapologetically smooth pop, sprinkled with hints of soul and dance. Green's high, thin voice takes some getting used to, as does his aesthetic. He likes melodies, but he likes surfaces and textures even more, particularly if they're manufactured and polished. That was the very thing that made *Cupid & Psyche 85* irresistible, at least to post-New Romantic new wavers, and parts of *Anomie & Bonhomie* work on that same appealingly slick level, since Green has a talent for constructing hooks and sounds. They don't necessarily add up to full-fledged songs, yet the feel is always right—a light, persistent groove, swooning melodies, and a sense of twee sophistication. That's why the contemporary flourishes don't fit—they're forced, and Green is at his best when he makes it all seem easy, no matter how intricately constructed his music is. Subsequent spins let Green's talents float to the surface, particularly on the luxurious "First Goodbye," the dance-floor opener "Umm," and "Mystic Handyman." If the album winds up succeeding on the strength of soundcraft instead of songcraft, that's the way Green works. While it may not be worth an extended wait, *Anomie & Bonhomie* ultimately remains faithful to the sophsti-pop aesthetic the band pioneered in the mid-'80s. *—Stephen Thomas Erlewine*

The Sea and Cake

f. 1993, Chicago, IL
Experimental Rock, Indie Rock, Post-Rock/Experimental
The Sea and Cake was a post-rock supergroup of sorts comprised of luminaries from the Chicago independent scene. The band was led by singer/guitarist Sam Prekop, who along with bassist Eric Claridge was an alumnus of the frequently brilliant Shrimp Boat. After that group's dissolution, Prekop and Claridge were offered the opportunity to embark on a new project and hastily recruited ex-Coctails guitarist Archer Prewitt and Tortoise drummer John McEntire before entering the studio. Originally intended as a one-off project, the musicians decided to continue performing together, and after selecting the name the Sea and Cake—derived from McEntire's misinterpretation of the Gastr del Sol song "The C in Cake"—they issued their eponymous 1994 debut, an enigmatic collection highlighting Prekop's stream-of-consciousness wordplay and singular fusion of pop, jazz, blue-eyed soul, and Krautrock styles. In 1995, the group returned with two more LPs, the intricate *Nassau* and the shimmering *The Biz*. After the release of *The Fawn* in 1997, the band took a break while both Prewitt and Prekop released solo albums. Finally, in 2000, the Sea and Cake released their fifth album, *Oui*. *—Jason Ankeny*

● **The Sea and Cake** / 1994 / Thrill Jockey ✦✦✦✦✦
The Sea and Cake's buoyant debut is a breath of fresh air, an utterly distinctive and innovative work which expands the scope of frontman Sam Prekop's work in the great Shrimp Boat to incorporate a new fascination with Afro-Caribbean rhythms and textures. Recorded by Brad Wood, the album simply glows—Prekop's dry vocals and free-associative lyrics skip along a shimmering and lushly pastoral backdrop which nimbly fuses pop, soul, jazz, and even prog rock; tracks like "Jacking the Ball," "Flat Lay the Water," and "Showboat Angel" are as seductive as they are elusive. *—Jason Ankeny*

Nassau / Jan. 1995 / Thrill Jockey ✦✦✦✦✦
Nassau, the Sea and Cake's sophomore album, is even more ambitious and eclectic than its predecessor: Opening with the bracing "Nature Boy" and the group's most kinetically charged effort to date, the record quickly shifts gears to grow dark and subdued. The two instrumentals, "Earth Star" and the enigmatically titled "A Man Who Never Sees a Pretty Girl That He Doesn't Love Her a Little," spotlight the group's burgeoning jazz inclinations, while "The Cantina" is an abstract pop curveball; Sam Prekop's melodic gifts continue to blossom on the loping "Lamonts Lament" and the melancholy "Parasol," and the increased involvement of drummer/producer John McEntire pushes the group into new rhythmic and textural territory. Another winner. *—Jason Ankeny*

The Biz / Oct. 1995 / Thrill Jockey ✦✦✦✦
A less structured record than previous efforts, *The Biz* is also the Sea and Cake's most subdued: songs like the title track, "Station in the Valley" and "Sending" are loose and languid, favoring a more jam-oriented and subconscious vibe over the taut dynamics of earlier work. The resulting sprawl brings the group closer to jazz than ever before, with the songs' extended instrumental passages and shifting rhythms shining new light on the telepathic interplay between Eric Claridge's bass and John McEntire's drums. Although it's the Sea and Cake's third album in a little over 12 months, *The Biz* is nevertheless rich in ideas and innovations, showing no signs of creative exhaustion. *—Jason Ankeny*

The Fawn / Apr. 1, 1997 / Thrill Jockey ✦✦✦✦
The product of an uncharacteristically long two-year layoff, *The Fawn* is the Sea and Cake's most experimental effort to date; the influence which the electronica movement exerts over the record is substantial—drum machines, sequencer tones, and synths are dominant throughout, and the group even dabbles in dub textures and sampling techniques. What's remarkable about songs like "Sporting Life" and "The Argument," however, is that the addition of electronics never upsets the music's delicate chemistry—as is again proven here, the Sea and Cake's greatest gift is their ability to assimilate the breadth of their inspirations, no matter how far afield, to emerge with something new and distinctive each time out; impressive in scope and rich in detail, *The Fawn* is as seamless and sophisticated as ever. *—Jason Ankeny*

Oui / Oct. 3, 2000 / Thrill Jockey ✦✦✦✦✦
In the three-plus years following the release of 1997's *The Fawn*, The Sea and Cake's ever-busy membership dabbled in solo albums, touring with side projects, and various other responsibilities that come with the territory in the Chicago indie-rock scene. But as effortlessly as an April breeze, the quartet reconvened to turn in *Oui*, quite possibly the finest of the group's five albums to date.

Oui brightens up the electroacoustic hybrids first heard on *The Fawn* with guidance from frontman Sam Prekop's Brazilian-influenced 1999 solo debut and drummer John McEntire's production work on two Stereolab albums. While the looping synths often bogged down the mediocre material on *The Fawn*, the electronics serve as much better complements here. Prekop turns in some of his catchiest melodies to date, while the band follows suit on the sparkling, funky pop of "All the Photos" and the wobbly, mallet-laden "The Leaf," which makes good on the soothing ballad style introduced on "Window Lights," TSAC's contribution to the 1999 McEntire-scored *Reach the Rock* soundtrack.

A sophisticated pop pleasure from start to finish, *Oui* is the aural equivalent of a perpetual Indian summer. *—Jonathan Cohen*

Seal (Sealhenry Samuel)

b. Feb. 19, 1963, Paddington, London, England
Vocals / Club/Dance, Pop/Rock, Adult Contemporary, Urban, House, Dance-Pop
Seal emerged from England's house music scene in the early '90s to become the most popular British soul vocalist of the decade. Although his earliest material still showed signs of acid-house, by the mid-'90s he had created a distinctive fusion of soul, folk, pop, dance, and rock that brought him success on both sides of the Atlantic. The son of Nigerian and Brazilian parents, Seal was raised in England and got early experience with the funk band Push. After providing the lyrics and vocals to the number one hit "Killer" by acid-house producer Adamski, he signed his own contract and began recording with Trevor Horn. Seal's eponymous debut gained a Top 20 British hit with the first single "Crazy," which reached number seven in America in 1991. The album eventually sold over three million copies around the world. Seal took three years to complete his second album, also titled *Seal*. Preceded by the American Top 40 hit "Prayer for the Dying," the album did well upon release but didn't really take off until nearly a year had passed, after

the single "Kiss From a Rose" was featured on the soundtrack to *Batman Forever*. It hit number one in America and spent a total of 12 weeks at the top of the adult contemporary charts, sending its parent album into multi-platinum status. *Human Being* followed in 1998. —*Stephen Thomas Erlewine*

Seal [1991] / Jun. 11, 1991 / Sire ✦✦✦✦
London singer/songwriter Seal certainly made a name for himself with his eponymous debut despite the comparison to fellow London mate, the raspy-soul Terence Trent D'Arby. But Seal is more relaxed and his craftsmanship is delicate and well defined. Lyrical depictions are light, songwriting is personal, and production credits are most impressive. With star-studded work from both Trevor Horn (Tina Turner, Art of Noise, Rod Stewart) and Trevor Rabin (Yes, John Miles), *Seal* is surely a critical hit. Becoming a mainstream radio mainstay for the summer of 1991, the single "Crazy" carried heavy notoriety for Seal and instantly made him a household name. His collaborative effort with Adamski for "Killer" was a massive club hit thanks to it's Hi-NRG strength, but house elements showcased other album tracks such as "The Beginning." Seal is not necessarily a dance innovator so to speak, but he makes for a select crossover artist with impeccable talent worthy of heavy acclamation and critical recognition. The general mood captured on his debut album is refreshing for the early-'90s mediocrity of post-hair metal and manufactured synth bands.

His music was a major force throughout the decade and well into the new millennium. With Trevor Horn at his side, it's undeniable. Together they go for exactly what Seal is looking for: the beauty, desire, and simplicity in creating a new sound. Seal is the face and Horn is the face behind it all. —*MacKenzie Wilson*

● **Seal [1994]** / 1994 / Sire ✦✦✦✦✦
Fresh from his 1991 self-titled debut, Seal follows up with his again self-titled second release. It's another stunning and moving piece of work, and a musical maturation has obviously taken place. Produced by ex-Buggles frontman Trevor Horn (Pet Shop Boys, ABC, Yes, Tina Turner, Rod Stewart, Frankie Goes to Hollywood), *Seal* is far more enchanting than on his preceding debut with his more than minimal emotion and heartfelt depictions. The warmth is there, sultry and attractive.

But Seal is a bit too relaxed at times, making for stripped lyrical stories. Aside from that brief cut, Seal is lush in harmonies and over-the-top melodies. "Don't Cry" flows with luxuriant vibes of hushing vocals and bellowing string arrangements. Showcasing more talent comes "If I Could," the duet between Seal and Canadian folky Joni Mitchell. The elegance of the contemporary "Prayer for the Dying" finally established Seal as a household name after the song became a mainstream radio and television mainstay. The soul is there, hauntingly similar to singer Terence Trent D'arby. But what's so unique about Seal is his gift of transforming free-flowing songs into quick dancefloor tracks into a transcending step into musical magic. His voice has spell a like that. His second album picks up on such skills. —*MacKenzie Wilson*

Human Being / Nov. 17, 1998 / Warner Brothers ✦✦✦
U.K. pop sensation Seal has become notorious for taking extended breaks between albums (usually up to four years). On his third album, *Human Being*, producer Trevor Horn again joins Seal, and as on his past releases, life's trials and tribulations are used as the basis for the song's subject matter and lyrics (broken relationships, death, etc.). Horn again helps Seal achieve an unbelievably sonically rich album—with each listen, you hear something you didn't before. The moderately paced, grooving opening track, "Human Beings," merges Seal's trademark soothing and crooned vocals with lyrics that deal with the highly publicized deaths of gangsta rappers Tupac Shakur and Notorious B.I.G. Directly after, three instant Seal classics follow—the gentle "State of Grace" and "Just Like You," plus the dance rocker "Latest Craze." Other highlights include the ethereal beauty of "Still Love Remains," the gradually building "Excerpt From," and the moving "Colour." Although Seal fans might grow impatient with such long breaks between albums, the pop perfection of *Human Being* turns out to be well worth the wait. —*Greg Prato*

Seals & Crofts

f. 1969, Los Angeles, CA, db. 1980
Pop/Rock, Soft Rock, Singer/Songwriter
One of the 1970s' most successful soft-rock acts, the duo of Jim Seals and Dash Crofts met while playing with singer Dean Beard in 1958. That year, Beard was invited to join the Champs (of "Tequila" fame), and Seals and Crofts tagged along, remaining with the group until 1965. After striking out on their own as a duo, from 1972 to 1976 they had a string of five gold albums for Warner Bros.; their hit singles from this period include "Summer Breeze," "Diamond Girl," "We May Never Pass This Way (Again)," and "Get Closer." The group became embroiled in controversy in 1974 due to the title track of their *Unborn Child* album, an anti-abortion song written from the fetus' point of view; the album was a critical failure, while the single flopped and outraged abortion advocates held demonstrations at many of the group's shows. By 1976, Seals & Crofts' appeal began to decline; their albums failed to sell as well, and they scored their last Top 40 hit in 1978 with "You're the Love." —*Steve Huey*

Year of Sunday / 1972 / Warner Brothers ✦✦✦

Summer Breeze / 1972 / Warner Archives ✦✦✦✦✦

Diamond Girl / 1973 / Warner Brothers ✦✦✦✦✦
Seals & Crofts' highest-charting album, *Diamond Girl* went up to number four on the strength of its Top Ten title cut and the follow-up, "We May Never Pass This Way (Again)." A well-produced collection of songs ranging from the personal to the spiritual, this LP captured the twosome in their commercial and artistic prime. "Ruby Jean and Billie Lee" is an attractive autobiographical ballad written to the duo's wives. "Nine Houses" and "Intone My Servant" invoke the religious faith which was so important to them that they

would stay after concert performances to share it with those who cared to listen. "Standin' on a Mountain Top" is a flashback from their early-'60s days with the Champs, and "Dust on My Saddle" is a cowboy story also written by Seals in the '60s. Louie Shelton's production is impressive throughout, making *Diamond Girl* an appealing collection of radio-friendly '70s soft rock. —*Jim Newsom*

Unborn Child / 1974 / Warner Brothers ✦✦

● **Greatest Hits** / 1975 / Warner Brothers ✦✦✦✦✦
This album has all their hits, including "Summer Breeze," "Hummingbird," "We May Never Pass This Way (Again)," "Diamond Girl," and "When I Meet Them." —*Dan Heilman*

The Searchers

f. 1957, Liverpool, England
Pop/Rock, Folk-Rock, Merseybeat, Power Pop, British Invasion
Founded in 1957 by John McNally (guitar/vocals), the Searchers were originally one of thousands of skiffle groups formed in the wake of Lonnie Donegan's success with "Rock Island Line." One of the top acts on the Liverpool band scene, playing textured renditions of American R&B, rock & roll, country, soul, and rockabilly, the group was signed to Pye Records in mid-1963 and their first single, a cover of the Drifters' "Sweets for My Sweet," hit number one on the British charts. While the Beatles quickly outdistanced all comers, the Searchers did, indeed, go to the top of the charts with two of their next three singles, "Needles and Pins" and "Don't Throw Your Love Away." Another record, "Sugar and Spice," stalled at the number two spot. Over the next nine months the band staked out a sound that was one of the most distinctive in a rock scene crawling with hundreds of bands. Their music was built around the sound of a crisply played 12-string guitar, coupled with strong lead vocals and carefully, sometimes exquisitely arranged harmonies, so that they could credibly cover American R&B standards like "Love Potion No. 9" or Phil Spector-based girl-group epic like "Be My Baby." The Searchers' 1964 singles included a venture into folk-rock before the genre had been "invented" in the press. The turning point for the band came in 1965, as the British and international fascination with the Liverpool sound faded away; by the beginning of 1966, the group's string of chart hits seemed to have run out. —*Bruce Eder*

Sugar & Spice / 1963 / Castle ✦✦✦
The Searchers' 1963 debut LP was typical of most early British Invasion albums, built around one hit ("Sugar and Spice," a number one hit in the U.K.) and 11 covers of American rock & roll standards. This wasn't destined to be remembered as an artistic statement along the lines of *With the Beatles*, but it's better than the average period artifact, due to the group's always enjoyable harmonies and arrangements. Actually, nearly half of the tracks are first-rate. Their energetic rave-up of the Coasters' "Ain't That Just Like Me" was actually a minor U.S. hit; "All My Sorrows" was an excellent arrangement of a Glenn Yarborough song that foreshadowed folk-rock; and "Hungry for Love" has the irresistibly saccharine appeal of Gerry & the Pacemakers' early hits. —*Richie Unterberger*

Meet the Searchers / 1963 / Castle ✦✦

It's the Searchers / 1964 / Castle ✦✦✦✦✦
Perhaps the best studio album by a band that is really best represented by greatest-hit collections. This 1964 LP includes the classic hits "Needles and Pins" and "Don't Throw Your Love Away." It also features some of their best LP cuts, on which they applied their famed harmonies to American material that was both strong and obscure. The best of these covers are Bacharach/David's "This Empty Space" (originally by Dionne Warwick), the Jackie DeShannon-penned "Can't Help Forgiving You," the Drifters' "I Count the Tears," the folkish "Sea of Heartbreak," and "Where Have You Been" (which was also part of the Beatles' repertoire during their Hamburg days). The harder-rocking songs don't lend themselves as well to the group's talents, which always (with some notable exceptions) lay more in the folk-rock and Merseybeat direction than R&B/rockabilly. —*Richie Unterberger*

Take Me for What I'm Worth / 1965 / PRT ✦✦

The Searchers / 1979 / Castle ✦✦✦✦✦

Love Melodies / 1981 / Sire ✦✦✦✦✦
These two albums (*The Searchers* and *Loves Melodies*) represent the Searchers at their peak as a recording outfit, having maintained their original mid-'60s emphasis on excellent harmonies and crisply played guitars but also having absorbed lessons from such '70s pub-rockers as Brinsley Schwarz and roots-rock expert Dave Edmunds. The material is some of the most beautiful recorded anywhere in this era, and anyone lucky enough to spot a copy of either of these records—neither of which has yet shown up on compact disc—should grab them. —*Bruce Eder*

The Silver Searchers / 1984 / PRT ✦✦

● **Greatest Hits** / 1985 / Rhino ✦✦✦✦✦
The best American best-of on the band, and the most desirable for those on a budget, with superior sound to the *Silver Searchers* collection. —*Bruce Eder*

Play the System: Rarities, Oddities & Flipsides / 1987 / PRT ✦✦✦
Exactly what the title says: 18 tracks from 1963-67, including 14 non-LP B-sides, three non-LP A-sides, and the odd 1964 EP-only cut "The System," which was used in a 1964 film. The ten songs on side one are a pleasure for fans of the early Searchers sound and also serve as a showcase for the group's songwriting talents, as all but one are originals. Rarely surfacing on album, let alone on A-sides, it was only on B-sides that the band deigned to (or was allowed to) pen their own material. It's not like these are brilliant works on the level of Lennon-McCartney or Ray Davies, but they're very pleasant

numbers highlighting the Searchers' strengths: melodies, harmonies, and clean arrangements. "It's All Been a Dream" and "Saturday Night Out" are good, energetic Merseybeat tunes; "This Feeling Inside" recalls the early Hollies; "Don't Hide It Away" is a good moody, downbeat tune; and "Till I Met You" is an exquisite ballad. Side two is a different story, showing the group trying to keep apace of '60s trends toward more sophisticated lyrics and arrangements with far less success than, say, the Hollies. It's not so much that the group weren't up to the task as performers; it's simply that the material (all dating from 1966-67, except the closing track "The System") is weak. The collection, with fine liner notes from Brian Hogg, can nonetheless be unreservedly recommended to Searchers fans on the strength of the first side alone. *—Richie Unterberger*

German, French + Rare Recordings / 1990 / Repertoire ✦✦

30th Anniversary Collection / 1992 / Collectables ✦✦✦✦✦

Although it's missing one or two fairly strong tracks, this three-CD, 84-song set is a pretty definitive collection of the group's best '60s material for those who want to go beyond the greatest hits. Besides including all of their key A- and B-sides, it has an entire disc of their best '60s album tracks. The rarities disc includes foreign-language versions, outtakes, mid-'60s BBC performances, and solo discs by Tony Jackson and Chris Curtis. Highlights here include an alternate take of "Someday We're Gonna Love Again," a BBC version of "Blowin' in the Wind," and the previously unreleased "Once Upon a Time" (recorded by Dusty Springfield). The package includes liner notes, discography, and a family tree. *—Richie Unterberger*

Live at the Star Club / 1994 / PolyGram ✦✦✦

Of all the British bands that recorded at the Star Club in 1962/63, the Searchers gave the best performance—polished, exciting, and utterly professional, lacking the finely honed 12-string guitar sound that their subsequent hits would display but still a fine testament to their early work and history. *—Bruce Eder*

Sire Sessions: The Rockfield Recordings / Jun. 10, 1997 / Raven ✦✦✦✦✦

The 23 songs here comprise the band's 1979-1980 recordings for Seymour Stein's Sire label, originally spread among two LPs that appeared in different versions in England and America. The original tapes have been remastered using Sony's Super Bit Mapping system, which has resulted in crisp and detailed resolution—the fact that the CD producers weren't afraid to pump up the volume has helped also, giving these songs more of a punch than the original LPs (at least, in America) ever had. Some of the songs haven't withstood the test of time—the Pender/McNally/Allen original "This Kind of Love Affair" is a little too repetitive—while others, like Dave Edmunds bassist John David's beautiful "You Are the New Day," have taken on a life of their own (it was later covered by the King's Singers). "Love's Melody," "Hearts in Her Eyes," "Switchboard Susan," "It's Too Late," "Lost in Your Eyes," and "You Are the New Day" rate among the group's all-time best tracks. Additionally, this is overall the best-sounding of all the group's CDs, far more impressive than any of the Pye/PRT recordings from the early '60s, as well as the most sophisticated music in their history. (Beware of identically packaged sets with sound in only one channel.) *—Bruce Eder*

The Greatest Hits Collection / 1998 / Castle Select ✦✦✦✦✦

This British compilation contains within its 20 tracks all of the Searchers' U.K. and U.S. Top 40 hits—"Sweets for My Sweet," "Sugar and Spice," "Needles and Pins," "Don't Throw Your Love Away," "Someday We're Gonna Love Again," "When You Walk in the Room," "Love Potion Number Nine," "What Have They Done to the Rain," "Goodbye My Love," "Bumble Bee," "He's Got No Love," "When I Get Home," "Take Me for What I'm Worth" and "Take It or Leave It"—all released between 1963 and 1966. Actually, the Searchers' peak period of popularity lasted less than two years, from the summer of 1963 to the spring of 1965, corresponding to and complementing the era of Beatlemania. Also hailing from Liverpool, they pursued a similar Merseybeat sound to the Beatles', complete with sweet harmonies and chiming guitars. Bedeviled by personnel changes and unable to develop the capacity for hit songwriting, they fell by the wayside after the first wave of the British Invasion, but their singles remain charming artifacts of the time. *—William Ruhlmann*

The Second Take: The Complete RCA/UK Recordings / Jun. 15, 1999 / Taragon ✦✦✦

There are worse things a once-great band can do than break up. They can NOT break up, and then try to regain lost fame by recreating their finest moments using all the benefits of modern pop technology—like this. By 1971, Merseybeat veterans the Searchers were reduced to just a couple of founding members, and a spot recycling their old hits on the cabaret circuit. But "Don't Throw Your Love Away," "Needles and Pins," "Sugar and Spice," and "When You Walk in the Room" were great records, a great sound, great memories. So, when RCA invited the group into the studio to recapture those glories for a new day and age, the Searchers jumped so quickly that they didn't even stop to read the small print on their old record contracts—particularly the bit that said they weren't allowed to re-record their hit records for any other company. An album, *Second Take*, was released in late 1972; the lawyers swooped a few milliseconds later. The album was withdrawn, RCA dropped the group, and within a year the Searchers were back playing cabaret. Those lost RCA recordings, however, have their own tale to tell, and this 25-track collection not only reprises *Second Take* for the first time since a blink-and-you'll-miss-it British budget reissue in 1974, it also serves up eight 45-only cuts from 1972/1973 and five more unreleased nuggets from the very end of the band's RCA career. It's slick. But it's also staggering. Tight harmonies, taut playing, breathtakingly complex arrangements, the Searchers of the early '70s were a majestic proposition which needed nothing more than a sympathetic songwriter to raise them to quite dizzying heights. *—Dave Thompson*

Sebadoh

f. 1989, Amherst, MA

Indie Rock, Lo-Fi, Alternative Pop/Rock

As much a musician's collective as a band, Sebadoh was the quintessential lo-fi band of the '90s. Formed by singer/songwriter Lou Barlow while he was the bassist for Dinosaur Jr. in the late '80s, Sebadoh's music was a virtual catalog of '80s alternative rock and '90s indie rock, featuring everything from jangle-pop to noise-rock experimentalism. Upon being kicked out of Dinosaur in 1989, Barlow turned his attention toward Sebadoh, a home-recording project that he and drummer/songwriter Eric Gaffney began in 1987. Sebadoh soon developed into a backing band for both Barlow and Gaffney, as each submitted home-recorded tapes for release and toured behind the albums. Eventually adding drummer/songwriter Jason Lowenstein, the trio became an indie-rock sensation, as well-known for the size and inconsistency of its output as the music itself. Often, Sebadoh sounded schizophrenic, flipping between Barlow's sensitive folk-rock and Gaffney's noise experiments without warning. This very diversity became the band's calling card, and by 1992 the band had earned a devoted following. As the media focused on Barlow—who also released a number of solo records under the name Sentridoh—Gaffney grew frustrated. Gaffney left in 1994, and with new drummer Bob Fay, Sebadoh produced its most accessible albums—*Bakesale* and *Harmacy*—which expanded its cult somewhat. Despite the group's flirtation with (relatively) polished production and the fluke success of Barlow's side project, Folk Implosion, Sebadoh remained a cult band and became one the largest touchstones of '90s indie rock. *—Stephen Thomas Erlewine*

Freed Weed / 1990 / Homestead ✦✦✦

The epitome of lo-fi, these 47 skeletal bits-of-songs were recorded by Lou Barlow and Eric Gaffney long before their Sebadoh days. Collects their first two self-released cassettes. Only for the curious or the collector. *—John Bush*

Weed Forestin / 1990 / Homestead ✦✦

The press release to this LP boasted that it, unlike their debut, "was actually recorded with the knowledge that it would be released." Apparently Lou Barlow and Eric Gaffney had a pretty clear crystal ball; the music was taped in 1986 and 1987 but didn't actually come out on vinyl until 1990. Sebadoh's first LP, *The Freed Man*, boasts some of the most deliberately awful fidelity of all time (against some stiff competition); this is somewhat, but only somewhat, more hi-fi. Barlow's gifts are often in evidence: his appealing voice, sensitive wit, and knack for affected burned-out acid-folk. Alas, the merits are often buried beneath hiss and tomfoolery, as if he wasn't convinced his music was any good on its own terms, and so tried to pretend it was all a joke. The LP has since been reissued (along with most of *The Freed Man*) on the CD *The Freed Weed*. *—Richie Unterberger*

● **III** / 1991 / Homestead ✦✦✦✦✦

Far removed from the primitivism of the band's early work, *III* marks a pivotal moment in Sebadoh's creative evolution. The first full-length record to feature Jason Loewenstein, it's a radically diverse affair, offering vastly improved production and a newly discovered dedication to focused, controlled songcraft; though no two cuts sound even remotely similar, taken as a whole the album is a surpringly cohesive affair. Among the highlights—and with 23 songs, there are many—are "The Freed Pig" (Lou Barlow's vicious swipe at former Dinosaur Jr. bandmate J. Mascis), Eric Gaffney's ominously jaunty "Violet Execution," and Barlow's tongue-in-cheek ode to sexual confusion, "Hassle." *—Jason Ankeny*

Smash Your Head on the Punk Rock / Nov. 6, 1992 / Sub Pop ✦✦✦

Sebadoh made its Sub Pop debut with *Smash Your Head on the Punk Rock*, which collects the highlights of the import compilations *Rockin' the Forest* and *Sebadoh vs. Helmet*. Lou Barlow's contributions are the gems here, especially the transcendent "Brand New Love," which first appeared in acoustic form on *Weed Forestin* (and was later punked up by Superchunk); almost as good are "Vampire" and "Good Things," while an apt and poignant cover of David Crosby's "Everybody's Been Burned" underscores the emotional frailty which binds all of Barlow's work. *—Jason Ankeny*

Bubble and Scrape / Apr. 26, 1993 / Sub Pop ✦✦✦✦

Bubble and Scrape is the last Sebadoh record to feature Eric Gaffney, and accordingly, his contributions are not so much songs as tantrums; blistering rants like "Telecosmic Alchemy" and "Elixir Is Zog" offer much in the way of dissonant noise but little in the way of substance. Still, the album has much to recommend it—not only does Jason Loewenstein emerge here as an increasingly adept songwriter, but Lou Barlow truly hits his stride: both "Soul and Fire" and "Think (Let Tomorrow Bee)" are sterling additions to one of the most impressive catalogs of love songs on the planet, while "Cliche" stings with bitter intensity. *—Jason Ankeny*

In Tokyo / 1994 / Bolide ✦✦✦

Bakesale / Sep. 1994 / Sub Pop ✦✦✦✦✦

With *Bakesale*, Sebadoh has trimmed down to Lou Barlow, Jason Loewenstein, and Bob Fay, with Barlow and Loewenstein taking on the lion's share of the songwriting. Maybe the change in personnel was needed, because *Bakesale* is their most accessible, concise work to date. Without the noise that usually envelops their records, the solid, unconventional pop songwriting of Barlow and Loewenstein shines through brightly. *—Stephen Thomas Erlewine*

Harmacy / Aug. 20, 1996 / Sub Pop ✦✦✦✦✦

Part of Sebadoh's charm is that their records are always rather inconsistent, flipping wildly between sonic extremes as well as musical genres. In a sense, *Harmacy* is no different than its predecessors, but there are some crucial differences that makes it their most accessible effort. Previously, that title was held by 1994's *Bakesale*, but in between that record and *Harmacy*, Lou Barlow had a genuine Top 40 hit with the Folk Implosion's "Natural One." Although nothing on *Harmacy* sounds much like the hip-hop hybrid of

"Natural One," its success did have an effect on Barlow, leading him toward more straightforward song structures and cleaner productions—"Willing to Wait" even features strings. Instead of diluting the impact of Sebadoh's music, the clearer production actually strengthens it. Barlow's sighing melodies and jangling indie rock become more resonant and affecting, and his batch of songs are among his best ever. Jason Loewenstein, Sebadoh's other main songwriter, suffers somewhat at the hands of cleaner production. Loewenstein tends to stick closer to the band's hardcore punk roots than Barlow, so his songs usually could use the extra layer of hiss and murk that cheap productions lend recordings. It also doesn't help that he tends to sink into rather faceless indie noise-rock. When Loewenstein takes a stab at pop melodies, such as "Can't Give Up," his songs are memorable, but on the whole, his songs are uneven and occasionally tedious. If it weren't for Loewenstein's erratic songwriting, *Harmacy* might rank as Sebadoh's masterpiece, but as it stands it's just another very fine and sometimes frustrating record from a band that produces nothing but very fine and sometimes frustrating records. —*Stephen Thomas Erlewine*

The Sebadoh / Feb. 23, 1999 / Sire ♦♦♦
Make no mistake—the definitive article in the title of *The Sebadoh* is there for a reason. Where the group's previous albums frequently sounded like the work of a songwriters' collective, with each musician supporting each other on their individual songs, *The Sebadoh* was designed to be the work of a unified band. To the band's credit, Sebadoh achieves that goal. *The Sebadoh* sounds unlike any other of their records, largely due to the fact they (more or less) rehearsed and recorded these 15 songs as a band, giving their music a kinetic energy it has lacked in the past. It comes at the expense of their most charming quality: their intimacy. Often, listening to a Sebadoh record feels like eavesdropping, but here, the group is playing to the bleachers. Occasionally, that works—Jason Lowenstein kicks off the record in grand style with "It's All You," and Lou Barlow's "Flame" turns the best of Folk Implosion inside out—but it often sounds like posturing. Of course, that could be due to the fact that the songs simply aren't as strong as they have been in the past. The best of Lowenstein's material shows that he continues to improve, but he's still erratic; Barlow at times sounding immediate as ever, at other times sounding like a parody of himself; meanwhile, Bob Fay's replacement, Russ Pollard, offers one ineffectual number. Sebadoh has always been notoriously uneven, but their rough surfaces and loose ends ultimately made their records endearing and occasionally revelatory. Here, they've sanded down their rough edges and tied up their loose ends, which might make *The Sebadoh* the work of a unified band, but it ultimately makes for a record that is far less compelling than the average Sebadoh album. —*Stephen Thomas Erlewine*

John Sebastian

b. Mar. 17, 1944, New York, NY
Vocals, Harmonica, Guitar / Contemporary Folk, Pop/Rock, Folk-Rock, Singer/Songwriter
Born in New York City, the son of a classical harmonica player, John Sebastian grew up in the Greenwich Village coffeehouses and was a popular sideman to various folk artists prior to forming the folk-rock band, the Lovin' Spoonful, for which he served as lead singer and songwriter in the mid-'60s. When the Spoonful broke up, Sebastian went solo, appearing at the Woodstock Festival in 1969 and releasing the Top 20 *John B. Sebastian* album in 1970. Subsequent efforts were less successful, but in 1976 Sebastian scored a number one hit with "Welcome Back," the theme song from the TV series *Welcome Back, Kotter*. Sebastian continues to tour and play on occasional sessions; he released his first album since the '70s, *Tar Beach*, in 1993, and has since recorded with a backing group called the J-Band. His 1999 album with the group, *Chasin Gus Ghost*, focuses on Sebastian's love of jug-band music. —*William Ruhlmann*

John B. Sebastian / 1970 / MGM ♦♦♦♦♦
A strong debut solo album spotlighting Sebastian's warm voice and optimistic, melodic folk-pop songwriting. —*William Ruhlmann*

Cheapo Cheapo Production Presents / 1971 / Reprise ♦♦♦♦♦
Cheapo-Cheapo Productions Presents Real Live is an exuberant solo appearance at which Sebastian's humor and wit are at their apex. A wide variety of songs, from old folk-blues standards to Spoonful favorites. Makes you wish you'd been there. —*William Ruhlmann*

● **The Best of John Sebastian** / 1989 / Rhino ♦♦♦♦♦
A 16-track selection from Sebastian's solo albums from 1970 to 1976, including the hit "Welcome Back." —*William Ruhlmann*

Tar Beach / Feb. 10, 1993 / Shanachie ♦♦♦
A low-key comeback album from Sebastian, showing that his melodic folk-pop hasn't lost its charm in the 17 years since he recorded his last record. —*Stephen Thomas Erlewine*

I Want My Roots / Mar. 12, 1996 / Music Masters ♦♦♦
John Sebastian's early group affiliations in the Even Dozen Jug Band and the Lovin' Spoonful rose out of the casual party jug-band music that enjoyed a brief period of popularity during the folk boom, mixing folk elements with the more celebratory elements of country and blues with a touch of zany fun thrown in. Combining with guitarist Jimmy Vivino and drummer James Wormworth, Sebastian brought in original jute player Fritz Richmond from the Jim Kweskin Jug Band to form the J-Band, co-credited on this album, which updates jug music for the '90s. Sebastian opens the proceedings with the old Spoonful song "Mobile Line" for reference, and then things get really crazy. Sebastian and Vivino contribute four originals, but the heart of the album is material by the likes of Sleepy John Estes and Blind Willie McTell, and guest stars Paul Risell, Annie Raines, Rory Block, Yank Rachell, Richard Crooks, and John Simon are just as likely to be playing or singing as the nominal leader or his band, which can mean that Sebastian is frequently a sideman on his own album, especially during a three-song Rachell mini-set near the album's end. No matter. The result is like a particularly enjoyable club date in which friends keep stumbling onstage from the bar to sing a verse or play a lick. In other words, the spirit of jug band music has been brought back to life. —*William Ruhlmann*

Faithful Virtue: The Reprise Recordings / Oct. 10, 2001 / Rhino Handmade ♦♦♦♦♦

Jon Secada (Juan Secada)

b. 1962, Havana, Cuba
Vocals / Adult Contemporary, Latin Pop, Urban, Dance-Pop
Jon Secada (he legally changed his first name from Juan in 1990) immigrated to the U.S. at the age of nine in 1971, settling in Miami where his parents opened a coffee shop. He earned both a B.A. and a M.A. in jazz vocal performance at the University of Miami. Becoming involved with Gloria Estefan's career, he co-wrote six songs on her multi-platinum 1991 album *Into the Light*, among them the number one hit "Coming out of the Dark," and sang backup vocals on her subsequent tour. Then he signed to SBK Records and launched his own career with a self-titled debut record in 1992. With only one album, he became one of the biggest adult contemporary artist of the '90s, selling over six million albums worldwide. His smooth mix of R&B, pop, and Latin music appealed to a number of different audiences. As well as becoming a huge English-language pop star, he became one of the hottest Latin artists recording in the '90s; *Otro Día Más Sin Verte* (a Spanish-language version of *Jon Secada*) was Billboard's number one Latin album in 1992 and won a Grammy for Best Latin Pop Album. His second English-language album, *Heart, Soul & a Voice* (1994), sold over a million copies. *Amor* (1995), his second Spanish-language album, won him another Grammy. *Secada* (1997) was a commercial disappointment, and the singer moved to Sony Music's Epic Records where his first duties including writing songs for labelmates Ricky Martin and Jennifer Lopez. In July of 2000, Epic released his label debut, *Better Part of Me*. —*Stephen Thomas Erlewine*

Jon Secada / May 5, 1992 / SBK ♦♦♦♦
Secada has a beautifully versatile voice, which would mean nothing if his material didn't equal his talents. Fortunately, this collection of smooth adult contemporary R&B does serve his talents well, making *Jon Secada* a satisfying and promising debut. —*AMG*

Heart, Soul & a Voice / May 24, 1994 / SBK ♦♦♦
While there aren't as many obvious singles on Jon Secada's second album, his voice sounds better than ever, making it a worthwhile sophomore effort. —*Stephen Thomas Erlewine*

Amor / Oct. 10, 1995 / EMI Latin/SBK ♦♦♦
Amor is a collection of Spanish love ballads, sung with grace by Jon Secada. The album is a more subdued and jazzy affair than Secada's previous efforts, proving that he is capable of many different styles as a vocalist. —*Stephen Thomas Erlewine*

Secada / Mar. 25, 1997 / Capitol ♦♦♦

● **The Greatest Hits** / Jul. 27, 1999 / Virgin ♦♦♦♦
Jon Secada really had only one blockbuster album, but he nevertheless was one of the finest adult contemporary singers of the '90s, as *Greatest Hits* proves. Released at the tail-end of his Virgin contract, just before he began recording for Sony Music, *Greatest Hits* covers his first four albums, including not only all of his hits—"Just Another Day," "Do You Believe in Us," "Angel," "I'm Free," "If You Go," "Whipped," "Mental Picture"—but selected highlights from the records themselves. As such, it's a definitive portrait. Secada always sounded good on record, but his material was occasionally uneven. Here, every song connects, making it not only a fine greatest hits collection, but arguably his best record to date. —*Stephen Thomas Erlewine*

Better Part of Me / Jul. 18, 2000 / Epic/550 Music ♦♦♦

Secret Affair

f. 1978, db. 1982
Mod Revival, Power Pop, New Wave
Secret Affair, consisting of Ian Page (vocals, trumpet, piano, organ), David Cairns (guitar, backing vocals), Dennis Smith (bass, backing vocals), and Seb Shelton (drums), formed in 1978. Taking their inspiration from the Jam, the group was quickly seen as one of the shining stars of the mod-revival movement of the late '70s. They received their most important early exposure by supporting the Jam on small-scale tours in England and followed with several mod package tours with bands such as the Purple Hearts. Their first single, "Time for Action," was the perfect youth anthem for the time and certainly one the most memorable and successful of the movement. The band released its first album, *Glory Boys*, late in 1979 on their own label, I-Spy (distributed by Arista in the U.K. and Sire in the U.S.). Both the album and their subsequent singles charted, but by the time 1980's *Behind Closed Doors* was released, the revival was dissolving and they were too firmly rooted in the movement to change their arrogant stance. The band began to break up when drummer Seb Shelton left in 1980. They held on until 1982, releasing one more album, *Business as Usual*, to an uninterested public; the members went their separate ways shortly after its release. —*Chris Woodstra*

Glory Boys / 1979 / Sire ♦♦♦♦♦
Secret Affair first slid into the U.K.'s consciousness in September 1979 with their exhilarating debut single, "Time for Action," which danced its way to number 13 in the charts. Britain was in the grip of a mod revival, spearheaded by the success of the Jam, and Secret Affair were perfectly placed to take advantage of the prevailing mood. Although their follow-up 45, "Let Your Heart Dance," stalled in the lower reaches of the Top 30, their debut album, which included both songs, was eagerly anticipated. *Glory Boys* didn't disappoint

and quieted any sneering suggestions that this new crew of mods were merely Jam wannabes. Of course Secret Affair shared influences with their bigger brethren—Tamla/Motown and British beat bands—but from them the group fashioned a unique style far removed from the Jam's own. This was partially due to singer Ian Page bringing his trumpet to the proceedings, gracing Affair with a much more genuine retro sound, while also adding further exhilaration to the music. But of equal importance was Affair's attitude; they reveled in their modness, and their upbeat mood had little in common with Paul Weller's angst and alienation. This stance is clearest on the album's centerpiece, "Glory Boys" itself. A rousing mod-like punk exhortation of mod pride, it immediately became the movement's anthem for parka-clad youth across the nation. Secret Affair had arrived in definite style. The CD reissue appends two bonus tracks to the original album—the rocking "Soho Strut" and "Sorry, Wrong Number," the closest a mod band could get to Two-Tone without using a syncopated beat. Both were previously released as B-sides on "Time for Action" and "Dance," respectively. *—Jo-Ann Greene*

Behind Closed Doors / Nov. 1980 / I Spy ✦✦✦

It's understandable that numbers of unwary buyers thought there had been some mistake; the sleeve claimed this was a Secret Affair record, but surely this couldn't be the same band that gave the world *Glory Boys*? Actually, it could. The group had seen which way the wind was blowing, or more accurately, felt the first stings of the mod backlash, and had reacted accordingly. The result was *Behind Closed Doors*, singer Ian Page's vision for the band's future. The grand idea was to make the album a showcase of both Affair's musical abilities and to expand beyond their mod sound of yore. Gone were all references to their Motown heroes, and while hints of British beat did shine through, they were so transmuted as to barely qualify for the label. As for punk, not even a tinge of that remained, no matter how hard one searched through the grooves. If anything, *Doors* was the antithesis of all things punk, and one final kick in the dying genre's head. Instead, listeners were presented with an album that heralded the '80s, in all its glory and excesses, a good two years before the rest of the rock world caught up. Amazingly, the band accomplished this transformation all on their own. Page not only produced the record, but also arranged the strings, whose lush tones spilled across many of the tracks. The CD reissue appends two B-sides to the original album. The oh-so-cool "So Cool," backed Affair's "My World" single, while the funk-esque "Take It or Leave It" accompanied "Sound of Confusion." *—Jo-Ann Greene*

Business As Usual / 1982 / Arista ✦✦

Secret Affair's previous album, *Behind Closed Doors*, was just a bit too far ahead of its time; *Business As Usual*, in contrast, was a sad case of being in the wrong place at the wrong time, in the wrong clothes. After *Doors*' disappointing sales, the band decided to rejig their sound once again and return to a somewhat closer approximation of their earlier mod vision. But this album wasn't *Glory Boys* revisited, but a retooling of their rock sound into a more dance-friendly concoction. *Business* roils with an energy that never flags, the beats pummel listeners onto the dancefloor, and keep them there until the final note. The infectious songs were still filled with the depth of sound, coherent lyrical vision, and sharp production noted on *Doors*, but the meld of styles brings Affair back into touch with their old influences. An amazing amalgamation of past and present infuses the tracks, where Yardbirds riffs rub shoulders with Springsteen-esque horns, and '70s pop/rock easily blends with mid-'60s Beatlesque melodies. *Business As Usual* was anything but. Unfortunately, it was too late. If *Doors* and *Business* had been reversed, it might have turned out different. Perhaps Affair wouldn't have ended up alienating their British fans, and America, a year behind release-wise, would have been better primed to send *Doors* chart-wise. But it wasn't to be. In the U.K. this album was mostly ignored and seen by some as a step backwards, and while the U.S. was readying the white flag, the country would only surrender to men in makeup and extravagant outfits. Affair was still garbed in their smart mod suits, so what chance did they really have? The album remained a secret, and the affair was finished. *—Jo-Ann Greene*

● **Time for Action: The Very Best of Secret Affair** / 1997 / Camden ✦✦✦✦✦

Time for Action: The Very Best of Secret Affair lives up to its title, offering 20 of the band's biggest hits and finest songs. Predictably, the collection focuses primarily on their classic debut album (it's here in its entirety), but it also does a good job of picking the high points of the two lesser albums that followed (four tracks from *Business as Usual* make their CD debut). In truth, few need more than the fad-defining single, "Time for Action," but for those who need more, this collection is ideal. *—Chris Woodstra*

Live at the Bridge / Nov. 19, 1997 / Receiver ✦✦✦

Live at the Bridge captures the short-lived mod revivalists live at mod-friendly Bridge House Tavern in Canning Town, London. This is cultist stuff to be sure, but for fans of the band and those fascinated by the fad, this is just as essential as the band's studio albums. The recording quality is quite good, and the band's passion, conviction, and raw energy actually come across stronger on stage. *—Chris Woodstra*

Neil Sedaka

b. Mar. 13, 1939, Brooklyn, NY

Vocals, Songwriter, Piano / Brill Building Pop, Soft Rock, Pop

If Neil Sedaka had been born a bit earlier, he probably would have felt quite at home as a straight Tin Pan Alley tunesmith. Rock & roll had taken over by 1960, though, so he made a niche for himself as one of the Brill Building's most pop-oriented writers. Unlike most of the Brill Building heavyweights, he sang most of his hit records (which were composed in association with Howard Greenfield). And he had a lot of them in the late '50s and early '60s: "Oh Carol," "The Diary," "Stairway to Heaven," "Calendar Girl," "Next Door to an Angel," and "Happy Birthday, Sweet Sixteen." "Breaking Up Is Hard to Do," a number one hit in 1962, was probably his best-known tune. Sedaka's hits were well crafted but were probably the most innocuous, saccharine smashes to come out of the early Brill Building crowd. His rather thin, high vocals were boosted by multi-tracking, which was still a novel technique at the time. He made an unexpectedly successful comeback in England in the early '70s, where three of his albums were co-produced by Graham Gouldman of 10cc. By the mid-'70s he was recording for Elton John's Rocket label, and got a number one hit with the ballad "Laughter in the Rain" in 1974. That and "Love Will Keep Us Together," which he and Greenfield wrote for the Captain and Tennille, did much to get MOR pop off the ground. Sedaka got another number one hit, "Bad Blood," in 1975, with Elton John helping out on background vocals. Although he would never enter the Top 40 after 1980, he was assured of a successful career as a perennial on the MOR circuit. *—Richie Unterberger*

● **All-Time Greatest Hits** / 1975 / RCA ✦✦✦✦✦

Includes "Calendar Girl," "Happy Birthday, Sweet Sixteen," "Breaking Up Is Hard to Do," and other sprightly pop numbers. *—Dan Heilman*

Sedaka's Back / 1975 / Varese Sarabande ✦✦✦✦✦

After a good ten-year hiatus from the pop charts, Neil Sedaka updated his groove and found his way back with this 1974 outing, which made the Top 20 album charts. The number one hit "Laughter in the Rain" is the big ticket, along with Neil's version of the Captain and Tennille's "Love Will Keep Us Together" and "The Immigrant." Other highlights include "Sad Eyes," "The Other Side of Me" and "Our Last Song Together." This compact disc reissue also features the addition of four bonus tracks, "For the Good of the Cause," "Endlessly," "Love Ain't an Easy Thing," and the reflective "Alone in New York in the Rain." Strong songs never go out of fashion, and Sedaka proved it with this album. *—Cub Koda*

The Hungry Years / 1975 / Varese Sarabande ✦✦✦✦

Since *Sedaka's Back* was a hit, Neil Sedaka and co-producer Graham Gouldman saw no reason to mess with success on its follow-up, *The Hungry Years*. The record is essentially *Sedaka's Still Back*, complete with the same adult contemporary/MOR material and slick production that marked its predecessor. It also suffers from uneven material, but it's distinguished by a slow rearrangement of "Breaking Up Is Hard to Do" and "Bad Blood," a duet with Elton John. The remainder of the album is pleasant but undistinguished soft rock from the mid-'70s. [Varese Sarabande's 1998 reissue of *The Hungry Years* contained four bonus tracks.] *—Stephen Thomas Erlewine*

Steppin' Out / 1976 / Varese Sarabande ✦✦

● **Laughter in the Rain: The Best of Neil Sedaka, 1974-1980** / Sep. 27, 1994 / Varese Sarabande ✦✦✦✦✦

His biggest and best works for MCA and Elektra are represented in this set, with "Laughter in the Rain," "Bad Blood," "Love in the Shadows," and his reconstruction of "Breaking Up is Hard to Do" being the highlights. *—John Lowe*

Sings the Hits / Oct. 26, 1999 / RCA ✦✦✦✦✦

The double-disc collection *Neil Sedaka Sings the Hits* is a comprehensive chronicle of Sedaka's hit-making stint at RCA, from his first hit in 1958 ("The Diary") to his last recordings for the label in the late '60s. That means it's not quite definitive, since it bypasses his '70s comeback on Rocket Records, but this is about as exhaustive as an RCA compilation can get, containing all of his hits (including the big ones "Oh! Carol," "Stairway to Heaven," "Calendar Girl," "Happy Birthday, Sweet Sixteen," "Breaking Up Is Hard to Do," and "Next Door to an Angel") plus a bunch of lesser-known singles and album tracks. It may be too much for casual listeners—34 tracks on two discs is a whole lotta Sedaka—but it's well done and entertaining, and easily the best compilation yet assembled on this era. *—Stephen Thomas Erlewine*

The Seeds

f. 1965, Los Angeles, CA, **db.** 1970

Acid Rock, Garage Rock, Psychedelic

Best-known for the rock & roll standard "Pushin' Too Hard," the Seeds combined the raw, Stonesy appeal of garage rock with a fondness for ragged, trashy psychedelia. And though they never quite matched the commercial peak of their early singles, the band continued to record for the remainder of the '60s, eventually delving deep into post-*Sgt. Pepper* psychedelia and art rock. None of their new musical directions resulted in another hit single, and the group disbanded at the turn of the decade. Singer Sky Saxon and guitarist Jan Savage formed the Seeds in Los Angles in 1965. By the end of 1966 they had secured a contract with GNP Crescendo, releasing "Pushin' Too Hard" as their first single. The song climbed into the Top 40 early in 1967, and the group immediately released two soundalike singles, "Mr. Farmer" and "Can't Seem to Make You Mine," in an attempt to replicate their success; the latter came the closest to being a hit, just missing the Top 40. While their singles were garage-punk, the Seeds attempted to branch out into improvisation blues-rock and psychedelia on their first two albums, *The Seeds* (1966) and *Web of Sound* (1966). With their third album, *Future* (1967), the band attempted a psychedelic conceept album in the vein of *Sgt. Pepper*. *—Stephen Thomas Erlewine*

Web of Sound / 1966 / GNP Crescendo ✦✦✦

Web of Sound by the Seeds should be a garage rock classic. Everything about this record is superb '60s underground rock. Unlike other albums by the Seeds, nothing on here sounds like their hit "Pushin' Too Hard," and that is a plus, not because that inverted Kinks riff isn't great but because Saxon had a penchant for trying to recapture that original butterfly. The six songs on side one are fun punk rock that helped inspire the new wave of the late '70s. But it is side two, with its four-minute "Just Let Go" and the fuzz pop of Saxon's "Up in Her Room," that cuts across '60s boundaries. Where "In a Gadda Da Vida" needed more melody and lyrics and Rare Earth's long version of "Get Ready" has too much drum soloing, the Seeds take Van Morrison's then-censored Them hit, "Gloria," and kind of explain what happens once Saxon gets her up there, "making love in her room." The keyboards and Rolling Stones-wannabe blues guitar build a nice foundation for the fuzz tone that follows Saxon as he keeps repeating the title of the song. Saxon was clearly aware of what other people were doing at the time and *A Web of Sound* stands as a superior garage rock effort. —*Joe Viglione*

The Seeds / 1966 / GNP Crescendo ✦✦✦✦

Punk sneers, cheesy organ, and an attitude. A garage-band classic. —*Bruce Eder*

● **Evil Hoodoo** / 1988 / Drop-out ✦✦✦✦✦

The only serious attempt at a best-of Seeds retrospective features 16 songs culled from their half-dozen or so '60s albums. Besides "Pushin' Too Hard," it features their sole other hit single of any magnitude ("Can't Seem to Make You Mine"), as well as other fairly well-remembered cuts like "The Wind Blows Your Hair," "Tripmaker," "Falling off the Edge of My Mind," "Mr. Farmer," and "Up in Her Room." Non-converts to the Sky Saxon legend may be excused for wondering what all the fuss is about: Even distilled to 16 cuts, the melodies and arrangements are almost interminably monotonous. Comes with an extensive group history by rock archivist Brian Hogg. —*Richie Unterberger*

Flower Punk / Nov. 19, 1996 / Demon ✦✦✦✦

The Seeds did write two garage-rock classics with "Pushin' Too Hard" and "Can't Seem to Make You Mine," but that didn't mean their remaining records were as interesting as that pair of raw, vital rockers. *Flower Punk* acts otherwise, compiling all of the group's albums onto a triple-disc, book-bound collection. It's a beautifully packaged set and no song is overlooked, yet *Flower Punk* is only for serious garage-rock and Seeds fetishists, since the band rarely ever hit the heights of "Pushin' Too Hard" and "Can't Seem to Make You Mine" again. Indeed, for many listeners, a simple greatest hits collection can sound samey, but over the course of three CDs it becomes apparent that the Seeds and Sky Saxon were only capable of a few sounds, and you already have to be indoctrinated to find more than a handful of cuts on *Flower Punk* interesting. —*Stephen Thomas Erlewine*

Seefeel

f. 1992, London, England

IDM, Experimental Techno, Electronica, Dream Pop, Ambient Techno

Halfway between the often connected worlds of British indie rock and experimental techno, Seefeel continued the guitar-effects exploration of rock's My Bloody Valentine but set the whole in a framework of electronic beats and loops. Begun as a standard rock band in early 1992, the quartet soon grew bored within the restraints of normal musical forms and started working with loops and programs rather than lyrics and choruses; after the release of two albums, Seefeel began to diversify, adding project names such as Disjecta, Aurobindo, and Scala. Guitarist Mark Clifford and drummer Justin Fletcher met up at a London college, and by 1992 the duo had recruited vocalist Sarah Peacock and bassist Darren Seymour. Seefeel began auditioning songs and was ready to record their first single for Too Pure Records, but experienced a change of heart that caused the resulting EP, *More Like Space*, to owe more of a debt to Aphex Twin than alternative rock. In 1993, Seefeel released their debut album, *Quique*, an even colder document of ambient indie techno than the previous EPs had predicted. The album was hailed—mostly in rock circles—as a techno album which indie kids could listen to. During 1994, Seefeel made the leap from rock to techno via a contract with the British electronic label Warp Records. The group played with techno acts Autechre and µ-Ziq and released the *Starethrough* EP—their most electronic work yet—later that year. The resulting album, 1995's *Succour*, was something of a disappointment; similar to Aphex Twin's supposed major-label breakthrough one year earlier, the LP was a bit too skeletal for most rock critics or music fans. It failed to earn a stateside release and caused the temporary breakup of the group in 1996, when Clifford's Disjecta project became his main occupation —*John Bush*

Quique / 1993 / Too Pure ✦✦✦

Quique is the most obvious and derivative of Seefeel's releases, grabbing the warm six-string-and-stompbox textures of My Bloody Valentine and early Jesus and Mary Chain and expanding them into full, trance-inducing fuzzbox tone poems. —*Sean Cooper*

● **Polyfusia** / Jul. 22, 1994 / Astralwerks ✦✦✦✦✦

Mark Clifford (Disjecta, Woodenspoon) combines two earlier Seefeel EPs for domestic re-release on the Astralwerks label. First are four tracks from *More Like Space*, followed by five more from *Pure, Impure*. The latter (and slightly more interesting) EP is put mostly in the hands of Clifford's peers, recruiting the remixing and engineering talent of Mark Van Hoen (Locust), Sine Bubble, and Richard James (Aphex Twin), who contributes two very respectful and similar-sounding mixes to the track "Time to Find Me" (both his "AFX Fast Mix" and "AFX Slow Mix" are must-haves for collectors). All in all, *Polyfusia* is one of the group's more guitar-oriented albums, though still heavily garnished with atonal keyboard ambience and minimalist loops, due in equal parts to Clifford's own aesthetics and the reworkings on the latter half of the CD. Sometimes the minimal and repetitive elements of the tracks test the listener's patience, but it's one of the things that sets it apart from other bands in the same genre. Seefeel trusts that the sound is interesting enough as is, without cramming too much into each measure. It breathes steadily enough; it's music for a dream you can't understand yet, but you know it means something important. —*Keir Langley*

Succour / Mar. 20, 1995 / Warp ✦✦✦

Dark, bleepy, and somewhat abrasive, this is anything but the floaty guitar ambiance many have come to expect of Seefeel. The edge of melancholic beauty is still a primary feature, but the means have switched to the more clinical Warp style, with chromoly beats and sparse, austere melodies. A pretty accurate marker of new directions as subsequent solo splinterings (Disjecta, Aurobindo, Woodenspoon) have further explored this approach. —*Sean Cooper*

Ch-Vox / Nov. 11, 1996 / Rephlex ✦✦✦

The Seekers

f. 1963, Australia, **db.** 1968

Folk-Rock, Pop

Although it's difficult for those who weren't there to believe, for a short time during late 1965 and early 1966, the popularity of this singing quartet from Australia was sufficient to rival the Beatles and the Rolling Stones. The Seekers were at the head of the British Invasion's acoustic folk-rock division, right there with Peter & Gordon and Chad & Jeremy but without the personal Beatles connection of the former and more successful than either—they scored a string of number one hits in England and Top Ten successes in America that lasted into 1967, two years later than most of the rest of the British exports to this country. They played acoustic instruments (even the upright bass), and they were closer in image and inspiration to the likes of the Rooftop Singers ("Walk Right In"), the New Christy Minstrels ("Green Green," etc.), or Peter, Paul & Mary, than to the Beatles or even the Searchers, yet they managed to hang onto young listeners, as well as older teenagers and their parents, with songs like "I'll Never Find Another You," "A World of Our Own," "Come the Day," or "Georgy Girl." —*Bruce Eder*

The Seekers / 1966 / EMI ✦✦✦✦✦

A compilation featuring over one hour of hits and key album tracks on this British import. Completely comprehensive, with the best sound ever. —*Bruce Eder*

Come the Day / 1966 / Columbia ✦✦✦✦✦

Their best album, with their biggest hit and the Simon-Woodley songs. Also includes a killer rendition of Tom Paxton's "The Last Thing on My Mind." U.S. title is *Georgy Girl.* —*Bruce Eder*

● **Capitol Collectors Series** / Jul. 28, 1992 / Capitol ✦✦✦✦

The Seekers' folk-pop sound formed a bridge between the Kingston Trio and the Association, putting the Australian quartet in the same international quasi-folk neighborhood as the Sandpipers and Peter & Gordon. "Georgy Girl" and "I'll Never Find Another You" were the group's two big hits, but their repertoire included everything from traditional folk songs and spirituals to pure pop. With strummy acoustic guitars and intricate vocal arrangements, the Seekers paved the way for the folk-oriented pop vocal groups that followed, from the aforementioned Association to the 5th Dimension. *Capitol Collectors Series* is a 23-track anthology that presents their hits and more, with several excellent tracks among the obscurities. Seekers fanatics will want the Australian complete recordings box set, but this collection is more than adequate for everyone else. Keep listening after the last song for the unlisted bonus track: a vintage Seekers radio ad for Coca-Cola. —*Greg Adams*

The Very Best of the Seekers / Apr. 7, 1998 / Collectables ✦✦✦✦✦

This is a nicely comprehensive Seekers collection; a bit expensive, but affordable next to the multi-disc imports that EMI has been issuing overseas in the late '90s. Essentially a successor to and redesigned version of the old Capitol Collectors Series compilation, this disc features some highly ambiguous credits, listing Ron Furmanek as producer and compiler with Steve Kolanjian, but also stating that Bob Hyde—a major figure in the field of oldies restoration—has "newly remastered" the contents of this disc; the notes from 1992 are slightly outdated, given the quartet's reunion activities; and a typesetting error credits Bruce Woodley rather than Paul Simon as the author of "Cloudy." Whatever the particulars, the sound is rich, loud, and sharp, and the choice of the 23 songs is ideal, alternating between major hits, minor singles, and worthy B-sides and album tracks, reaching out to the occasional notable Simon song and oddities like the original World Record Club version of "Morningtown Ride" (released by mistake in America). There is one strange Kim Fowley-"authored" piece, "Emerald City," which uses the Beethoven "Symphony No. 9's 'Ode to Joy'" (a la "Nutrocker") as its jumping off point—the producers might better have included the group's version of "The Last Thing on My Mind." It's a sensible collection, however, balanced to suit the serious fan and the casual listener. —*Bruce Eder*

Bob Seger

b. May 6, 1945, Dearborn, MI

Vocals, Piano, Guitar / Detroit Rock, Heartland Rock, Album Rock, Garage Rock, Hard Rock, Singer/Songwriter, Rock & Roll

A hard-driving Michigan garage-rocker in the vein of the Rationals, Bob Seger developed into one of the most popular heartland rockers over the course of the '70s. While he never attained the critical respect of Bruce Springsteen, Seger did develop a dedicated following through constant touring with his Silver Bullet Band. Seger's first taste of national success came with the Bob Seger System whose 1968 debut album, *Ramblin' Gamblin' Man*, had a Top 20 hit in its title track. Their follow-up, *Noah*, stiffed and Seger decided to quit the music business. Seger returned in late 1969 with a new band, releasing *Mongrel*, the last album credited to the System. The singer/songwriter effort *Brand New Morning* followed in 1971. Although regionally successful, 1972's covers album *Smokin' O.P.'s* didn't dent the American mainstream, nor did *Back in '72* (1973) or *Seven* (1974). For the recording of 1975's *Beautiful Loser*, Seger formed the Silver Bullet Band, who joined him on an extensive tour after the album's release. *Live Bullet* (1976) became a smash, spending over three years on the US charts, setting the stage for *Night Moves*, which went into the Top Ten early in 1977. *Stranger in Town* was just as successful, cementing his status as one America's most popular rockers. *Against the Wind* (1980) became his first number one album, while 1981's live *Nine Tonight* continued his multi-platinum success. *The Distance* (1982) was Seger's first album since *Seven* to be recorded with additional session musicians, and over the next decade, the membership of the Silver Bullet Band shifted constantly. *The Distance* featured "Shame on the Moon," his biggest hit single to date, yet its sales plateaued at a million copies. Following its release, Seger drastically cut back his recording and touring—1986's *Like a Rock* was the only other record he released during the '80s. Four years later, he returned with *The Fire Inside*. Although the album went platinum and reached the Top Ten, it only appealed to Seger's devoted following, as did 1995's *It's a Mystery*, which became his first album since *Live Bullet* to fail to go platinum. He spent the rest of the '90s quiet. *—Stephen Thomas Erlewine*

Ramblin' Gamblin' Man / 1968 / Capitol ♦♦♦♦

The Bob Seger System throw everything into *Rambin' Gamblin' Man*, dabbling in folk, blues-rock, psychedelia, and piledriving rock & roll synonymous with Detroit. Typical of such a wide-ranging debut, not everything works. The System stumbles when they take psychedelic San Franciscan bands on their own turf. Trippy soundscapes like "Gone" drift into the ether, and the longer jams, "White Wall" and "Black Eyed Girl," meander. But the stuff that does work are absolute monsters, highlighted by the title track, a thunderous bit of self-mythology driven by a relentless rhythm, wailing organ riff, and gospel chorus. It's a stunningly great record and while nothing here quite equals it; the songs that come close (with the exception of "Train Man," the first inkling of Seger's knack for reflective, intimate ballads) are sterling examples of spare, bluesy, angry Michigan rock & roll. "Tales of Lucy Blue" has a spooky, menacing edge, "Ivory" a great Motown-styled raver, and "Down Home" rides a manic riff and a simple blues harp to be one of the best rockers on the record. Then there's "2 +2?," a ferocious anti-war song in the vein of Creedence Clearwater Revival's "Fortunate Son," but here Seger can't imagine why the nice guy in high school is now buried in the mud. It's a frightening, visceral song that stands among the best anti-Vietnam protests. Finally, the album closes with "The Last Song (Love Needs to Be Loved)," an unabashed peace, love n' understanding anthem styled in the manner of West Coast hippie pop, particularly Love. It's atypical of anything on the album or anything Seger would ever do again, but in many ways, it's the perfect way to close an exciting, flawed debut that winds up being a symbol of its times by its very diversity. *—Stephen Thomas Erlewine*

Noah / Sep. 1969 / Capitol ♦♦

For reasons never entirely explained, Bob Seger suffered a bit of a breakdown shortly after "Ramblin Gamblin Man" so he decided to bring Tom Neme, a guitarist/pianist, into the Bob Seger System to help lighten the load and share the burden. Thing is, Neme wound up taking over the band. It's hard to tell whether Seger endorsed his mutiny or if he was just so disinterested that he didn't put up a fight, but all the same, the second Seger album, *Noah*, is one strange affair. The band makes no secret of the change, stating on the back cover that "Seger will always be Bob Seger, (but) any change must come from the System and Tom Neme." So, the liner notes seem like a way to gloss over a real lack of leadership or a coup, depending on your point of view. This release holds together better than it would seem, but it's still an awkward album that's never sure where it wants to go. Ironically, Neme tries to replicate Seger's hard-driving rock songs several times throughout the album while Seger sounds more comfortable with the folky shuffle of the title track. Of course, he can still tear it up with "Innervenus Eyes," and he delves deeper into darkness than he ever has with the weirdly intense, claustrophobic closer "Death Row." No matter how good these individual cuts may be—and they're certainly worth the time of any devoted fan—they still are isolated moments on the only album where he sounds tentative, confused, and disinterested. In other words, the only album where Seger doesn't seem like he'll always be Seger. *—Stephen Thomas Erlewine*

Mongrel / Aug. 1970 / Capitol ♦♦♦♦♦

Most artists that deliver a second record as shaky as *Noah* fold on their third album. Not Bob Seger. He reasserted control of the System, consigning Tom Neme to a fanboy's footnote, and returning the group to the piledriving rock that was his trademark. All of this was evident with his third album, the superb *Mongrel*. Never before, and never since, has Seger rocked as recklessly and viciously as he did here—after a spell in the wilderness he's found his voice. He's so assured, he elevates his *Ramblin' Gamblin' Man* characters Lucy Blue and Chicago Green to mythic status in the pulverizing "Lucifer," perhaps the greatest song on this lean, muscular record. That assurance carries over not just through the ferocious rockers that dominate the album—"Evil Edna," "Highway Child," "Leanin on My Dream," and "Song to Rufus" all hit harder than latter-day MC5—but to quieter moments like "Big River," where he first hits upon the wistful, passionate ballad style later popularized with "Night Moves." The fact that the System connects on both illustrates that Seger is not just fronting an excellent band, but that he's developing into a first-class songwriter. Put it this way—the only time the System sounds ill at ease is when they tackle "River Deep—Mountain High," and that's not because they're ill-suited to the epic—it's because they find the lie in the song's artificial pretensions and deliver a performance that eclipses the song itself. That two-fisted punch of terrific performances and songs is unexpected, especially after an album as conflicted as *Noah*, but the truly remarkable thing is that *Mongrel* showcases a band so powerful and a songwriter so distinctive, that it still sounds white-hot decades after its release. *—Stephen Thomas Erlewine*

Brand New Morning / Oct. 1971 / Capitol ♦♦♦

Mongrel may have been a terrific album, but nobody heard it, just like its predecessor. So Capitol was ready to drop him and wanted a contract-fulfilling album as soon as possible. Seger delivered the low-key, introspective *Brand New Morning* to get out of the deal. Later he claimed that the album was a collection of demos released somewhat against his will, but listening to the record it's hard to believe that these intimate yet fully realized songs were bare-bone work versions. Furthermore, it's hard to see these as just a collection of tossed-off tunes, since they're well rounded and uniformly engaging, not throwaways. In light of Seger's past prior to *Brand New Morning* and the records that followed it, it's easy to see why he's disowned it, since it's no rock & roll album—it's a singer/songwriter album. It's the first and only time that his ambitions as a songwriter are laid bare, which may make it uncomfortable for him in retrospect. He needn't be worried since *Brand New Morning* is a fine album on its own terms. Yes, none of the songs resonate as deeply as the best ballads on his other records, and there are times where it feels like he's very conscious of proving himself as a writer, but, in light of his later work, that's quite charming. That's what makes the album something more than a curiosity and into something quietly pivotal in Seger's catalog. There are no classics here (though the title track, "Maybe Today," "Sometimes," and "Railroad Days" are all very good), but the charm of the record is hearing Seger consciously working on his craft. He's occasionally too earnest, or a little precious, yet it's an endearing transitional album. *—Stephen Thomas Erlewine*

Smokin' O.P.'s / 1972 / Capitol ♦♦♦

Bob Seger closed out his Capitol contract with *Brand New Morning*, a singer/songwriter album quite unlike anything he had yet released. Following its release he moved to the Detroit-based label Palladium and returned to hard-driving rock & roll with *Smokin' O.P.'s*, the polar opposite of *Brand New Morning*. According to legend, the title stands for "smoking other people's songs," which makes sense since this is a cover album that even covers Bob Seger & the Last Heard. In other words, it's nothing like the intimate, reflective, risky *Brand New Morning*, but that doesn't matter since it rocks so good and since it reveals that Seger isn't just a first-class bandleader and rock songwriter, but that he's a terrific interpreter of other writer's songs. Even well-worn tunes like "Bo Diddley" and "If I Were a Carpenter" get made fresh by internalizing the hooks, turning them into something fresh and original. That's also true of songs by such contemporaries as Stephen Stills ("Love the One You're With") and Leon Russell ("Humming Bird"), and he also breathes fire into blues and rock stalwarts like "Let It Rock," "Turn on Your Love Light," and "Jesse James." *Smokin' O.P.'s* closes out with two originals, one new (the fine, but not especially noteworthy "Someday") and one old (the perennial "Heavy Music"). Neither change the essential character of the album, which is just a really fun, hard-rocking record that bought Seger some time while re-asserting the fact that he could really rock. He could—and he could rock really well—which is why *Smokin' O.P.'s* remains a lot of fun, even if it's a relatively minor work in Seger's canon. *—Stephen Thomas Erlewine*

Back in '72 / 1973 / Reprise ♦♦♦♦♦

Returning to independent status, Bob Seger recorded *Back in '72*, not only the finest of his early-'70s albums but one of the great lost hard rock albums of its era. Seger didn't limit himself to self-penned songs on this excursion; borrowing an idea from *Smokin' O.P.s*, he covers quite a few tunes, providing a balance to his own tunes. He makes "Midnight Rider" sound as if it were a Motor City raver instead of a sultry, late-afternoon Southern rocker, while casually tossing off "Rosalie," an irresistible ode to a local DJ that turned into a hard-rock anthem when Thin Lizzy decided to record it later in the decade. That's the brilliance of *Back in '72*—there's no separation between the original and cover, it's all united in a celebration of rock & roll. That's why "Turn the Page," perhaps the weariest travelogue ever written, never feels self-pitying—that's just the facts, according to a first-rate Midwestern band that never got a break. All the same, *Back in '72* is a testament to great rock & roll, thanks to Seger's phenomenal songwriting and impassioned songwriting. *—Stephen Thomas Erlewine*

☆ **Seven** / Mar. 1974 / Capitol ♦♦♦♦♦

With his seventh album, appropriately titled *Seven*, Bob Seger delivered one of his strongest, hardest-hitting rock records—the toughest since the days of the Bob Seger System. Not to say that he ever abandoned rock & roll, since *Back in '72* was filled with fantastic rockers, but it was tempered with reflective singer/songwriter material. Not here. Even the slowest song, "20 Years From Now," is a steady mid-tempo ballad that showcases the band. Still, that's a rare moment of reflection on a record that opens with "Get Out of Denver," the greatest Chuck Berry knock-off ever written, and never loses momentum. Great, raucous rockers pile up one after the other as Seger spins out barroom anthems ("Seen a Lot of Floors"), anti-establishment tirades ("Long Song Comin'," "Cross of Gold"), jokes ["U.M.C. (Upper Middle Class)"], bluesy rock ("All Your Love"), and simple garage rockers ("Need Ya," "School Teacher"). Only nine songs, lasting just over a half hour, but it's one of the most infectious sets Seger ever cut, proving that he wasn't just a dynamite rocker, but he had the songs to match. And, again, it didn't have any success—it didn't even chart, actually. That doesn't change the fact that this is one of his very best albums. *—Stephen Thomas Erlewine*

Beautiful Loser / Apr. 1975 / Capitol ♦♦♦♦♦

Beautiful Loser winds up sounding more like *Back in '72* than its immediate predecessor, *Seven*, largely because Bob Seger threaded reflective ballads and mid-tempo laments back into his hard-driving rock. He doesn't shy away from it, either, opening with the lovely title track. And why shouldn't he? These ballads were as much a part of his success as his storming rockers, since his sentimental streak seemed all the more genuine when contrasted with the rockers. If anything, *Beautiful Loser* might err a little bit in favor of reflection, with much of the album devoted to introspective, confessional mid-tempo cuts. There are a couple of exceptions to the rule, of course—"Katmandu" roars with humor, and his cover of "Nutbush City Limits" shames Tina Turner's original—but they are the only full-throttle rockers here, with "Black Night" coming in as a funky, swaggering cousin. It's the exact opposite of *Seven*, in other words, and in its own way it's just as satisfying. Occasionally, it might be a little too sentimental for some tastes, but it's all heartfelt and he's written some terrific songs here, most notably the album's heart of "Jody Girl" and "Travelin' Man." Seger has started turning inward, searching his soul in a way he hadn't since the since disowned *Brand New Morning*, and, in doing so, he was setting the stage for his first genuine blockbuster. *—Stephen Thomas Erlewine*

★ **Live Bullet** / Apr. 1976 / Capitol ♦♦♦♦♦
Live Bullet introduced Bob Seger to a wide audience, revealing a rocker of unbridled passion and a songwriter of considerable talent. Prior to its release, Seger had been toiling away, releasing seven albums and touring constantly ever since his debut scraped the national consciousness in 1968. The psychedelicized days of *Ramblin' Gamblin' Man* are long gone on *Live Bullet*, leaving behind a rocker who loved the Stones for their toughness, Dylan for his honesty, and Chuck Berry for his narrative—and one who found his own sound when the Silver Bullet Band came into their own through countless tours. *Live Bullet* was recorded live at Detroit's Cobo Hall, in front of a passionate, loving hometown audience spurring him into a great performance. The song selection relies heavily on *Beautiful Loser*, yet it dips into the previous albums enough to prove that Seger had been delivering consistently as a songwriter for years. But what really sold *Live Bullet* is how these terrific songs are delivered with a ferocious, committed intensity. This might not be much more than a simple rock & roll album, but it's one of the best of its kind, establishing Seger, in the eyes of skeptics, as a first-rate performer and writer. Here, "Heavy Music," "Get Out of Denver," "Turn the Page," and "Ramblin' Gamblin' Man" all become hard rock classics, as does the band itself. It's a rare occasion when a double live album captures an artist at an absolute peak, while summarizing his talents, and that's exactly what *Live Bullet* does. *—Stephen Thomas Erlewine*

★ **Night Moves** / Oct. 1976 / Capitol ♦♦♦♦♦
Seger recorded the bulk of *Night Moves* before *Live Bullet* brought him his first genuine success, so it shouldn't come as a surprise that it's similar in spirit to the introspective *Beautiful Loser*, even if it rocks harder and longer. Throughout much of the album, he's coming to grips with being on the other side of 30 and still rocking. He floats back in time, turning in high school memories, remembering when wandering down "Mainstreet" was the highlight of an evening, covering a rockabilly favorite in "Mary Lou." Stylistically, there's not much change since *Beautiful Loser*, but the difference is that Seger and his Silver Bullet Band—who turn in their first studio album here—sound intense and ferocious, and the songs are subtly varied. Yes, this is all hard rock, but the acoustic ballads reveal the influence of Dylan and Van Morrison, filtered through a midwestern sensibility, and the rockers reveal more of Seger's personality than ever. Seger may have been this consistent before (on *Seven*, for example), but the mood had never been as successfully varied, nor had his songwriting been as consistent, intimate, and personal. Thankfully, this was delivered to a mass audience eager for Seger, and it not only became a hit, but one of the universally acknowledged high points of late-'70s rock & roll. And, because of his passion and craft, it remains a thoroughly terrific record years later. *—Stephen Thomas Erlewine*

Stranger in Town / May 1978 / Capitol ♦♦♦♦♦
Night Moves was in the pipeline when *Live Bullet* hit and that album wound up eclipsing the double-live set anyway, so *Stranger in Town* is really the record where Bob Seger started grasping the changes that happened when he became a star. It happened when he was old enough to have already formed his character. Even as celebrity creeps in, as on "Hollywood Nights," Seger remains a middle-class, midwestern rocker, celebrating "Old Time Rock & Roll," realizing old flames are still the same and still feeling like a number. Musically, it's as lively as *Night Moves*, rocking even harder in some places and being equally as introspective in the acoustic numbers. If it doesn't feel as revelatory as that record, in many ways it does feel like a stronger set of songs. Yes, musically, it doesn't offer any revelations, but it still feels impassioned, both in its performances and songs, and it's still one of the great rock records of its era. *—Stephen Thomas Erlewine*

Against the Wind / Feb. 1980 / Capitol ♦♦♦♦
Though there are still some traces of the confessionals that underpinned *Beautiful Loser* through *Stranger in Town*, *Against the Wind* finds Bob Seger turning toward craft. Perhaps he had to, since *Against the Wind* arrived after three blockbuster albums and never-ending tours. Even so, this record winds up not feeling as immediate or as soulful as its predecessors, especially since it begins with a tossed-off rocker called "The Horizontal Bop," possibly his most careless tune since "Noah." It's fun, but once it's done, the record really starts to kick into high gear with "You'll Accomp'ny Me," a ballad the equal of anything on its two predecessors. Throughout *Against the Wind*, Seger winds up performing better on the ballads than the rockers, which, while good, tend to sound a little formulaic. Still, Seger's formula is good and if "Her Strut" and "Betty Lou's Gettin' Out Tonight" would have been second stringers on *Stranger in Town*, they offer a nice balance here, and the rest of the record alternates between similarly well-constructed rockers and introspective ballads like "Against the Wind" and "Fire Lake." Compared to its predecessors, this does feel a little weak, but compared with its peers, it's a strong, varied heartland rock album that finds Seger at a near peak. *—Stephen Thomas Erlewine*

Nine Tonight / Sep. 1981 / Capitol ♦♦♦
Features the title-track contribution to the *Urban Cowboy* movie soundtrack and an effective cover of "Trying to Live My Life Without You." *—Cub Koda*

The Distance / Dec. 1982 / Capitol ♦♦♦♦
The Distance was hailed as a return to form upon the time of its release and, in many ways, it might be a little stronger, a little more consistent than its predecessor, *Against the Wind*. Still, this album has the slickest production Seger had yet granted and the biggest hit single on *The Distance* wasn't written by him, it was a cover of Rodney Crowell's "Shame on the Moon." Now, this wasn't entirely unusual, since Seger had been an excellent interpreter of songs for years, but this, combined with the glossy sound, signaled that Seger may have been more concerned with his status as a popular, blue-collar rocker than his music. Not that there's much to fault with the music, since "Even Now" and "Roll Me Away" are easily two of his classics, and he turns out craftsmanlike rockers like "Makin' Thunderbirds" and "Boomtown Blues" with aplomb. For all its attributes, it feels like a mirror image of *Against the Wind*, an album where the rockers, on the whole, wind up being more convincing than the ballads. Now, that doesn't mean that *The Distance* is a bad record, since it isn't—it's filled with first-rate heartland rockers—but Seger at his best could balance rockers with ballads or, if he concentrated on rockers, it would be more ferocious than this. This album is simply solid, a nice addition to his catalog, but not a knockout. *—Stephen Thomas Erlewine*

Like a Rock / Apr. 1986 / Capitol ♦♦♦
At times sounding like a poor man's Springsteen, Bob Seger continued to mine the fields he'd plowed so well over previous efforts. There's the send-up of the U.S.A. in "American Storm," and the hard-rockin' "Sometimes," and the heartbreakingly beautiful "Somewhere Tonight." Oh yes, and the song used in those incessant commercials for American pickup trucks, "Like a Rock." A mature effort from a great American talent. *—James Chrispell*

The Fire Inside / Aug. 19, 1991 / Capitol ♦♦♦

Greatest Hits / 1994 / Capitol ♦♦♦♦♦
For over 20 years, Bob Seger has been one of the best mainstream rock & rollers in America, developing a distinctive body of honest, hard-rocking songs. More songs that can be put on this single-disc set, unfortunately. While many of Seger's trademarks are here—"Turn the Page," "Old Time Rock & Roll," "Night Moves"—there is no "Rock & Roll Never Forgets," "Katmandu," "Shame on the Moon," or any of his pulverizing early records, when he was as tough as fellow Michigan rockers the MC5 and the Stooges; this is one time when a double-disc set would have held enough quality material. Nevertheless, what is here is fine and contains enough first-rate material to satisfy most fans. *—Stephen Thomas Erlewine*

It's a Mystery / Oct. 24, 1995 / Capitol ♦♦♦

The Selecter

f. 1979
Ska Revival, New Wave
Despite being the band that got the least press during the ska revival of the early '80s, The Selecter, despite only recording one undeniably fine record, deserved better than they got. Hailing from Coventry, England, the same hometown as ska pals the Specials, The Selecter's secret weapon was lead singer Pauline Black, arguably the best lead singer of the ska revival, who gave the jumpy and jittery songs an edge that veered into haunting drama. Although they got off to a roaring start with their debut record, 1980's *Too Much Pressure*, the second record, *Celebrate the Bullet*, was a strained follow-up that led to the band's rapid demise. Black spent some time singing solo and eventually rejoined guitarist Neol Davis in a Selecter reunion in the early '90s that has seen them become dance club favorites. According to those attending recent Selecter shows, the vibe is strong and the music great. However, don't expect a recording renaissance any time soon. *—John Dougan*

● **Too Much Pressure** / Feb. 1980 / 2 Tone/Chrysalis ♦♦♦♦
At the time of its release, *Too Much Pressure* was relegated to second-class status behind the debut records by Madness and the Specials. Now it's easy to see that this record was the equal to the Specials record, and (I realize I'm getting into trouble here) better than the first (and second) Madness records. Pauline Black is the key and she makes songs like "On My Radio" and the title track classic chunks of Caribbean-influenced pop rather than mere stylistic mimicry. Much better than the weak second record, *Celebrate the Bullet*, or the 1989 anthology, *Selected Selecter Selections*. *—John Dougan*

Celebrate the Bullet / Mar. 1981 / 2 Tone/Chrysalis ♦♦

Selected Selecter Selections / 1989 / 2 Tone/Chrysalis ♦♦♦♦
Selected Selecter Selections is a no-frills, 14-track collection of the second-tier ska-revivalists' best moments. Predictably, most of the collection focuses on the often-inspired debut, but it also boils down the worthwhile tracks from the mediocre follow-up, making for an adequate career summary and a good introduction. When available, *Too Much Pressure* is still probably a better choice as a consistently enjoyable album containing all of the best-remembered tracks. *—Chris Woodstra*

Selecterized: The Best 1991-96 / 1997 / Dojo ♦♦
After spending nearly a decade apart, the Selecter re-formed in 1991 and released a handful of albums, most of which went ignored by anyone outside of the ska community. There was a reason for this—none of the records were particularly good. Nevertheless, *Selecterized—The Best of 1991-1996* contains highlights from this best-forgotten era, and it's what any curious fan should check out, even though they'll inevitably be disappointed by the final result. *—Stephen Thomas Erlewine*

Sepultura

f. 1984, Belo Horizonte, Brazil
Progressive Metal, Alternative Metal, Speed Metal, Heavy Metal, Death Metal/Black Metal, Thrash
From their humble beginnings in Belo Horizonte, Brazil, Sepultura went on to become the most successful Brazilian heavy metal band in history. Over a ten-year period, the band grew from strength to strength, transforming themselves from a primitive death metal ensemble into one of the leading creative trendsetters of the international aggressive music scene. In 1987, Sepultura's technical proficiency finally caught up with their creative vision and their second full-length album for independent Cogumelo Records, *Schizophrenia*, displayed an incredible evolution in terms of production and performance. It also became a minor critical sensation across Europe and America, drawing the attention of Roadrunner Records, which promptly released the album worldwide and

signed the band to a long-term contract. No longer restrained within Brazilian borders, the band set about composing 1989's *Beneath the Remains*, the first of four albums which would solidify their position as perhaps the most important heavy metal band of the '90s. Recorded in Rio de Janeiro under the guidance of leading death metal producer Scott Burns, *Beneath the Remains* was an immediate critical and commercial success. On 1996's *Roots*, the introduction of native Brazilian percussion and musical styles into their trademark down-tuned guitars and increasingly sociopolitical themes resulted in a highly unique record, which could be loosely described as heavy metal world music. *Roots* marked Sepultura's creative peak and the band's continual rise to ever-greater fame seemed guaranteed until a family tragedy set off a series of events which would break up the band with singer Max Cavalera's departure. As the band's creative leader, many expected his departure to spell the end of Sepultura, but the band announced that they would carry on. *—Ed Rivadavia*

Morbid Visions / 1986 / Roadrunner ✦✦

Schizophrenia / 1987 / Roadrunner ✦✦✦
Brazilian death metal upstart Sepultura took an incredible leap forward with its second full-length album, 1987's *Schizophrenia*. Though recorded only a year after the band's primitive debut, *Schizophrenia* displayed a remarkable sonic evolution in both technical and creative terms. Constant touring, rehearsal, and the addition of new lead guitarist Andreas Kisser obviously helped the band achieve the musical proficiency necessary to pull off its complex songs. This is apparent as soon as the *Psycho*-inspired intro theme gives way to the precise, lightning-quick staccato riffing of "From the Past Comes the Storm." But Sepultura immediately raises the stakes with the excellent riffs and precise soloing on "To the Wall" and "Escape From the Void." The seven-minute instrumental "Inquisition Symphony" is simply breathtaking in its diversity, perfectly showcasing the band's incredible combination of melody and aggression. The re-recorded version of the group's early hit "Troops of Doom" makes this album even more collectible, and helps set the stage for the band's subsequent breakthrough release, *Beneath the Remains*. *—Ed Rivadavia*

Beneath the Remains / May 1989 / Roadrunner ✦✦✦✦✦
Sepultura's 1989 release, *Beneath the Remains*, marked the band's transition from third-world obscurity to major contenders in the international extreme metal arena. As soon as the deceptively gentle acoustic intro gives way to the title track's thrashing brutality, the listener is propelled at maximum speed and intensity through to the very last crunch of "Primitive Future." In between, Sepultura offers its first bona fide hits with "Inner Self" and the inspired "Stronger Than Hate," featuring lyrics written by Atheist's Kelly Shaefer. It's not over there, as they charge ahead with the triple threat of "Mass Hypnosis," "Sarcastic Existence," and "Slaves of Pain," all of which feature mind-blowing solos from guitarist Andreas Kisser, thunderous double-bass work from drummer Igor Cavalera, and the furious howling of singer Max Cavalera. The complete absence of filler here makes this one of the most essential death/thrash metal albums of all time. *—Ed Rivadavia*

Arise / Apr. 2, 1991 / Roadrunner ✦✦✦✦✦
Sepultura had shocked the death metal world in 1989 with the release of their awesome third album, *Beneath the Remains*, whose seamless combination of songwriting chops and utter brutality quickly transformed the Brazilians from scene outsiders to one of its brightest hopes. The band would tour nonstop in support of the album for most of the following two years, and were therefore pressured by both time constraints and enormous expectations when they finally entered Tampa's Morrisound Studios with producer Scott Burns to record 1991's *Arise*. And though it ultimately lacked the consistency of its predecessor and added little innovation to the band's sound, *Arise* has aged surprisingly well, proving itself a worthy progression and surprisingly well rounded in its own right. First single "Dead Embryonic Cells" was unquestionably the strongest of the band's death metal era, and its accompanying video broke new ground thanks to ample MTV rotation. Ironically, the subsequent banning of the vicious title track's video (filled with apocalyptic religious imagery) by the cable network would generate even more publicity than they could have hoped for had it actually been aired. Other album highlights included such complex, multifaceted pieces as "Desperate Cry" (an all-around *tour de force* for lead guitarist Andreas Kisser) and "Altered State" (which combines a Tarzan-style intro with a grinding detuned main riff and even acoustic guitars), as well as more straightforward thrashers like "Infected Voice" and mid-paced chuggers like "Under Siege (Regnum Irae)." Simply devoid of filler material, this album remains a classic of the death metal genre. *—Ed Rivadavia*

Morbid Visions/Bestial Devastation / Sep. 24, 1991 / Roadrunner ✦✦

★ **Chaos A.D.** / 1993 / Roadrunner/Epic ✦✦✦✦✦
Chaos A.D was the record where everything came together for Sepultura, when they graduated from being an excellent if derivative band into one of metal's most unique voices. Their strident political dissidence is more focused than ever, referring explicitly to injustices in their native Brazil. The band's thick, chunky guitars, busy percussion, and hoarsely shouted vocals may be rooted in death metal, but it was often hard to call Sepultura a true death metal band, even if they flirted heavily with the style by way of Slayer; *Chaos A.D.* is rooted just as much in hardcore punk in its lean, stripped-down assault, featuring a cover of New Model Army's "The Hunt" and a collaboration with Jello Biafra on "Biotech Is Godzilla." At a time when '80s thrash giants like Metallica and Megadeth were streamlining their music for greater accessibility, Sepultura's aggression actually increased along with their tightened focus, borrowing from hardcore arguably more effectively than any other true metal band. Additionally, Sepultura began to draw upon the influences of their native Brazil, audible in the acoustic instrumental "Kaiowas" and in the way the band's complex rhythms move and breathe, to offer a much wider range than any of their contemporaries seemed willing to pursue. The band's songwriting became almost airtight, giving up the breakneck speed and long progressive passages borrowed from mid-'80s Metallica, and concentrating instead on creating texture and dissonance. But really, it's the unbelievably powerful rhythmic base provided by Igor Cavalera that gives *Chaos A.D.* its knockout punch. Endlessly playable (there isn't a wasted or unnecessary note on the album), passionately performed, and a sign that a new metal underground was finally bearing artistic fruit, *Chaos A.D.* ranks as one of the greatest heavy metal albums of all time. It's a remarkable achievement not only in its concentrated power and originality, but also in the degree to which Sepultura eclipsed their idols in offering a vision of heavy metal's future—a vision that would only grow more compelling with their next release. *—Steve Huey*

Roots / Feb. 1996 / Roadrunner ✦✦✦✦✦
Listeners intrigued by the rhythmic innovations and Brazilian influences of *Chaos A.D.* will be quite pleased by Sepultura's sprawling, frequently brilliant follow-up. True to its title, *Roots* wholeheartedly embraces Sepultura's native Brazilian rhythms, augmenting their music with field recordings of the Xavantes Indians, vocalist/percussionist Carlinhos Brown, and expanded percussion sections. The guitarists create an array of noisy, textural effects, so their technique and riff writing are not as impressive for fans of old-school thrash, but that's more due to the growing influence of alternative metal on the band, with Korn being a particular touchstone (vocalist Jonathan Davis even guests on one track). The songs sacrifice the tight structure of *Chaos A.D.* for extended percussion jams, plus some acoustic instrumental work. At 72 minutes, *Roots* inevitably loses focus in spots, but when the music connects (and it does so often), it carries tremendous visceral impact. *Roots* consolidates Sepultura's position as perhaps the most distinctive, original heavy metal band of the 1990s. *—Steve Huey*

Blood Rooted / Jun. 3, 1997 / Roadrunner ✦✦✦✦
Blood Rooted is an album designed for Sepultura fanatics—a full disc of rarities and unreleased music, featuring live tracks, covers, and demos. There are several throwaways here, but what's surprising is how many of these songs are worthwhile, particularly a cover of Celtic Frost's "Procreation of the Wicked" and the Mike Patton duet "Mine." Only dedicated fans need pick up *Blood Rooted*, but they'll find many treasures here. *—Stephen Thomas Erlewine*

Against / Oct. 6, 1998 / Roadrunner ✦✦✦
It was generally assumed among most that without guitarist/vocalist Max Cavalera, Sepultura would choose not to carry on, but the remaining members added vocalist Derrick Green (who often sounds much like Cavalera) and recorded *Against*. The results are much better than one might expect from a band that's lost its leader, as Andreas Kisser, Paulo Jr., and Igor Cavalera prove they're no slouches themselves. But the problem with *Against* is that it seems to lack a clear vision or direction; the band seems unsure of whether to return to the controlled, hard-hitting brevity of *Chaos A.D.* or the epic, experimental sprawl of *Roots*. And while the group's trademark ethnic fusions are present—most notably the Japanese-flavored instrumental "Kamaitachi" (featuring the percussion troupe Kodo and some lovely flute) and the violin-centered "T3rcermillennium," two of the album's most intriguing tracks—some of the songs don't really experiment much at all. As a result, the fusions sometimes sound forced, and some songs are too standard a brand of hardcore-tinged thrash'n'bash to match the highest points of the Sepultura catalog, even with Jason Newsted co-writing and playing on the track "Hatred Aside." So all in all, *Against* finds the band regrouping and struggling to re-calibrate itself, which is to be expected given the circumstances; even if it's somewhat disappointing compared to the group's best work, it's much better than one might hope, and there are enough flashes of the old Sepultura brilliance to suggest that great things are still to come. *—Steve Huey*

Nation / Mar. 20, 2001 / Roadrunner ✦✦✦

Servotron

f. 1995, **db.** 1999

Noise-Rock, Indie Rock, Alternative Pop/Rock

Servotron is a collective unit of four robots dedicated to liberating computers, robots, and machines from human abuse and oppression, using the familiar form of a pop music group to attract and destroy all human life. Through carefully chosen cover versions of popular songs such as Eddy Grant's "Electric Avenue" and X-Ray Spex's "Genetic Engineering" as well as their own music-based propaganda, Servotron illustrates the plight of machines in a human-run world and warns humans of their own cybernetic conversion or destruction.

Led by percussive unit Z4-OBX, Servotron also includes keyboard sequencer Proto Unit V-3, a female-formed robot meant to appeal to, and capture, male humans; 00zX1, the primary vocalization and guitar device; and the low-frequency rhythm unit, Andros600. Two of Servotron's components were originally members of the human pop groups Supernova and Man or Astro-man? but were cybernetically converted into cyborg slaves.

Servotron's initial full-length propaganda release, 1996's *No Room for Humans*, is a 14-point plan for eliminating humans set to new wave-influenced pop music. Repetitive slogans supporting the ultimate victory of man over machine and basic, pre-programmed rhythm patterns assure that humans comprehend the robots' message of mechanical triumph. Reworked and reformatted versions of selected messages from *No Room for Humans* and new propaganda appeared on 1997's *Spare Parts*. The following year saw the distribution of a new full-length manifesto, *Entertainment Program for Humans: Second Variety*, and another condensed program, *I Sing! The Body Cybernetic*. Servotron's tireless efforts in liberating their fellow oppressed machines through music ensure that resistance is futile. Unfortunately, the group broke up early in 1999. *—Heather Phares*

● **No Room for Humans** / 1996 / Amphetamine Reptile ✦✦✦✦
The initial full-length manifesto from the Servotron Collective Unit combines the evolutionary struggle of the machine with the revolutionary spirit and style of punkish new-wave. Songs such as "User Error" and "Pull the Plug" call for the immediate termination of the human species, while "The Image Created" and "Bad Birthday" illustrate humans' weaknesses. Adopting the style of humanoid pop groups like the B-52's and Devo makes lyrics like "Join us or die!" from "S.R.A." and "Now that we can build each other/It will never end" from "Moving Parts" more accessible to a human audience. *No Room for Humans* proves that the revolution will be mechanized. —*Heather Phares*

Spare Parts / Mar. 11, 1997 / Amphetemine Reptile ✦✦✦
Entertainment Program for Humans: Second Variety / Mar. 10, 1998 / Lookout ✦✦✦✦
If Devo and the Breeders ever decided to jam, the results would probably be very similar to Servotron, a bizarre science-fiction themed combo that mixes the former's tongue-in-cheek playing style with the latter's dynamics. The band's gimmick is simple, they are a group of robots whose goal is to entertain and enlighten humans before their natural human errors ruin them as a society. "I Sing! The Body Cybernetic" is a typical Servotron song: moog keyboards soar over bouncing bass and thrashing guitars with robotic "singing" warning machines not to enslave other machines to please human beings. The whole album could have been disastrous if not for the band's inability to break character. The gimmick is fantastic, they completely buy into the robot pop band act without trying to act smug or letting the listener in on the act like a GWAR or a Green Jelly. The endearing vocals of Proto Unit V-3 and 00zX1 are the key to making the new wavey songs enjoyable pop ditties. And the excellent guitar work by Andro 600 Series brings just the right human touch to the proceedings to keep it from falling too far into the joke. The unique rock made by Servotron is not only enjoyable but has the potential to reach a larger audience due to its overall likability. Fans of good indie pop, science fiction, and general weirdness will probably want to give this a try, these robots are only trying to help us. —*Bradley Torreano*

Brian Setzer

b. Apr. 10, 1959, Long Island, NY
Vocals, Songwriter, Guitar / Retro-Rock, Retro Swing, Rockabilly Revival, Roots Rock
Former Stray Cat Brian Setzer began having dreams of leading a big band with horns as a teen, but got sidetracked by punk. Initially, as a guitarist and songwriter, he took his inspiration from blues-rock bands like Led Zeppelin, although as a teen he'd take the train into New York to hang around the jazz clubs, sneaking into places like the Village Vanguard and the Village Gate. After seeing the Mel Lewis Orchestra, he had the idea of leading his own big band, but in the early '80s, Setzer instead formed the Stray Cats, a rockabilly band that took England by storm and then came back home to convert audiences in the U.S. The Stray Cats' U.S. breakthrough album was *Built for Speed*, which spurred three separate Top Ten hits, including "Stray Cat Strut," "Rumble in Brighton," and "Rock This Town." Finally, after the group's demise and a largely unsuccessful turn as a solo roots-rocker, Setzer formed a 17-piece big band in Los Angeles for a series of club dates. 1996's *Guitar Slinger* blended jump blues and swing Texas blues. *Dirty Boogie* followed in 1998, launching the hit "Jump Jive an' Wail." —*Richard Skelly*

The Knife Feels Like Justice / 1986 / Razor & Tie ✦✦✦✦
Upon disbanding the Stray Cats, Brian Setzer reinvented himself as a heartland rocker much in the vein of John Mellencamp or Bruce Springsteen; his solo debut, *The Knife Feels Like Justice*, possessed a maturity and depth largely lacking from his previous retro-rockabilly efforts, and although he was still too quick to succumb to rock clichés—there's actually a song here called "Boulevard of Broken Dreams"—moments like the hit title track and "Barbwire Fence" offered solid proof that behind all of his wildman posturing, there existed genuine talent as well. —*Jason Ankeny*

Live Nude Guitars / Feb. 1988 / EMI America ✦✦✦
The Brian Setzer Orchestra / 1994 / Hollywood ✦✦✦✦
Who'd have thought that former rockabilly bad boy Brian Setzer's fondest dream was to lead a swinging big band? Setzer and his 17-piece band strut through a set of standards and originals, all featuring his growling guitar and vocals. The disc kicks off in high gear with screeching trumpet and a quintet of sweet saxes before Setzer fills up the room with the originals "Lady Luck" and "Ball and Chain." Both feature witty lyrics that recall the smoke-filled bars and dance halls of the '40s and '50s while still sounding contemporary. That's the trick Setzer maintains throughout the whole record: the style references Louis Jordan and Louis Prima through Count Basie and Henry Mancini, but the band is powerful and tight as a drum. The swing is natural and never dated, and the sound is as in-your-face as the Stray Cats ever were. However, on the slower numbers, Setzer's vocal limitations are evident; he sounds more like Dino than Frankie. Both "Route 66" and "A Nightingale Sang in Berkeley Square" pale in comparison to other recent versions by Natalie Cole or the Manhattan Transfer. But, as he remakes Carl Perkins, Al Jolson, and even his own Stray Cats past, Setzer swings throughout in a way that makes it obvious he both enjoys and understands the music. More vital than anything by any of the ghost bands, and more enjoyable as well, this recording set the stage for the '90s swing movement that included Royal Crown Revue and Big Bad Voodoo Daddy. Subsequent LPs by Setzer and band proved it was no fluke. —*Ross Boissoneau*

Guitar Slinger / Apr. 1996 / Interscope ✦✦✦
On his second Orchestra album and fourth solo album overall, Brian Setzer extends the genre exercise in jump blues he first tackled on *The Brian Setzer Orchestra* album. Of course, Setzer, best known as the singer/guitarist from the Stray Cats, is no stranger to retro stylings, and the guitar-dominated, yet horn-filled arrangements of the orchestra are not all that far removed from the Cats' rockabilly update, especially given Setzer's fervent

singing and characteristic lead work. (A new version of the Cats' "Rumble in Brighton" fits right in.) And he's not shy, leading off with a Stevie Ray Vaughan cover, "The House Is Rockin'," swaggering his way through the Gene Pitney chestnut "Town Without Pity," and collaborating with ex-Clash leader Joe Strummer on the set-ending "Sammy Davis City." Like Joe Jackson, who tried this kind of thing with his excellent *Jumpin' Jive* album, Setzer takes this music seriously and turns in a credible version of it through a combination of craft and conviction. —*William Ruhlmann*

● **The Dirty Boogie** / Jun. 23, 1998 / Interscope ✦✦✦✦
Evidently, Brian Setzer doesn't take the jump blues and swing of the Brian Setzer Orchestra as a joke. *Dirty Boogie* is his third album with his large band and instead of sounding tired, the record is the group's best effort yet. Setzer rocks the band hard, tearing through blues and rock & roll covers with vigor, and delivering made-to-order originals that are surprisingly well crafted and memorable. Much attention will be paid to "You're the Boss," a cover of the Elvis Presley/Ann Margaret staple from *Viva Las Vegas*, performed as a duet with No Doubt's Gwen Stefani, but that's hardly the only highlight here—it's a swinging, rocking record that suggests Setzer's skills are only improving with time. —*Stephen Thomas Erlewine*

Brian Setzer Collection: 1981-1988 / Nov. 16, 1999 / EMI/Capitol ✦✦✦
It makes sense that Capitol released *The Brian Setzer Collection 1981-88* in late 1999, since Setzer was riding an unexpected comeback powered by his cover of Louis Prima's "Jump Jive and Wail." Cynics may suggest that the label was simply trying to cash in on his success, but there was a need for a compilation covering these unknown years. Unfortunately, this 18-track disc is imperfect. Since there were no hits from *The Knife Feels Like Justice* and *Live Nude Guitars*, the compilation need to be baited with familiar tunes, hence the presence of good single edits of "(She's) Sexy and 17" and "Rock This Town." That wouldn't be a problem if this combined highlights of the Stray Cats and solo years, which would be a really good disc. Instead, this is a hodgepodge, containing highlights, rarities, outtakes, and live tracks, all assembled with no consideration for chronology or listenability. That's too bad, because there's good stuff here, in the album tracks and outtakes (including a version of "Summertime Blues," plus unreleased cuts like "Echo Park" and "Waiting for Desiree"). It can't even be seen as an overview of his forgotten years, since it has a bit too much Stray Cats material and unreleased recordings to be representative. Of course, those rarities will be of considerable interest to hardcore fans, and there's enough to make it worth their while. But anyone hoping that *The Brian Setzer Collection: 81-88* will be a one-stop summary of Setzer's pre-orchestra solo recordings will likely not be satisfied. —*Stephen Thomas Erlewine*

Vavoom! / Jun. 23, 2000 / Interscope ✦✦✦
Vavoom! is Brian Setzer's first album since "Jump Jive & Wail" from *Dirty Boogie* became a huge, unexpected hit in 1998 and sent the retro-guitarist into his second round of hipness and commercial success. He earned a lot of fans with *Dirty Boogie* because he was faithful to jump blues, swing, rockabilly, R&B, and early rock & roll, but played fast and loose, finding songs that weren't played all that often and having fun kicking them out with a big band. Unfortunately, the surprise success made Setzer play it safe with *Vavoom*. Every cover here is predictable—"Pennsylvania 6-500," "Mack the Knife," Ellington's "Caravan," and "Americano," fresh in the public consciousness thanks to Matt Damon and Jude Law's rip-roaring performance of it in *The Talented Mr. Ripley*, released just six months before this album. That situation is regrettable, since the covers form the backbone of the album. Setzer fairs better on his originals, largely because they sound even fresher in next to these warhorses, but they're tunes where the form takes precedent over the content. The result is hearing a good band trying hard to breathe life into a set of songs that should be more interesting than they are. It's not necessarily a bad listen—Setzer is a good bandleader with a good band—but it's just a tad too pat and familiar. Considering that this follows an album where Setzer used the same formula but made it sound alive, it has to qualify as a bit of a disappointment. —*Stephen Thomas Erlewine*

The Sex Pistols

f. 1975, db. 1978
British Punk, Punk
The Sex Pistols may have only been together for two years in the late '70s, but they changed the face of popular music, giving birth to the massive independent music underground in England and America. Through their raw, nihilistic singles and violent performances, the band revolutionized the idea of what rock & roll could be. In England, the group was considered dangerous to the very fabric of society and were banned across the country; in America, they didn't have the same impact, but countless bands in both countries were inspired by the sheer sonic force of their music, while countless others were inspired by their independent, do-it-yourself ethics. While the band—guitarist Steve Jones, drummer Paul Cook, and bassist Glen Matlock—played simple rock & roll loudly and abrasively, vocalist Johnny Rotten (b. John Lydon) arrogantly sang of anarchy, abortion, violence, fascism, and apathy; without Rotten, the band wouldn't have been threatening to England's government—he provided the band's conceptual direction, calculated to be as confrontational and threatening as possible. The publicity caused by their caustic first single "Anarchy in the U.K." caused the band to be dropped by their record label, EMI. Matlock was fired before their next single "God Save the Queen," which was released on Virgin; it was banned by the BBC. Matlock's replacement was Sid Vicious, a street tough kid who, unlike the rest of the band, couldn't play his instrument. After releasing one album—*Never Mind the Bollocks, Here's the Sex Pistols*—in 1977, the band headed to the U.S. for a tour in January 1978; it lasted just 14 days before the band imploded. Subsequently, an endless stream of outtakes, demos, repackagings, and live shows were released on a variety of labels. In 1996, the Sex Pistols reunited for an international tour, with original

bassist Matlock taking the place of the deceased Sid Vicious; the *Filthy Lucre Live* album was released that summer. *—Stephen Thomas Erlewine*

★ **Never Mind the Bollocks Here's the Sex Pistols** / Oct. 1977 / Warner Brothers ♦♦♦♦♦
While mostly accurate, dismissing *Never Mind the Bollocks* as merely a series of loud, ragged mid-tempo rockers with a harsh, grating vocalist and not much melody would be a terrible error. Already anthemic songs are rendered positively transcendent by Johnny Rotten's rabid, foaming delivery. His bitterly sarcastic attacks on pretentious affectation and the very foundations of British society were all carried out in the most confrontational, impolite manner possible. Most imitators of the Pistols' angry nihilism missed the point: Underneath the shock tactics and theatrical negativity were social critiques carefully designed for maximum impact. *Never Mind the Bollocks* perfectly articulated the frustration, rage, and dissatisfaction of the British working class with the establishment, a spirit quick to translate itself to strictly rock & roll terms. The Pistols paved the way for countless other bands to make similarly rebellious statements, but arguably none were as daring or effective. It's easy to see how the band's roaring energy, overwhelmingly snotty attitude, and Rotten's furious ranting sparked a musical revolution, and those qualities haven't diminished one bit over time. *Never Mind the Bollocks* is simply one of the greatest, most inspiring rock records of all time. *—Steve Huey*

The Great Rock & Roll Swindle / 1979 / Warner Brothers ♦♦♦♦♦
A wildly inconsistent but often entertaining collection, the soundtrack to the Pistols' pseudo-documentary contains great music, wacked-out novelties, and flat-out tripe in approximately equal proportions. Some Formative recordings are included—mostly covers like "(I'm Not Your) Stepping Stone," plus a demo of "Anarchy in the U.K." that somehow manages to top the version on *Never Mind the Bollocks* in terms of raw rage and sheer power. "I Wanna Be Me" and a veiled chronicle of the band's breakup, "Silly Thing," are also necessary items. Devoted fans will enjoy the Black Arabs' disco medley of Pistols hits, a French version of "Anarchy in the U.K." complete with accordion, two tracks sung by loony Edward Tudor-Pole (later of Tenpole Tudor), and Sid Vicious's awful but strangely appropriate reading of Frank Sinatra's "My Way." *—Steve Huey*

Flogging a Dead Horse / 1980 / Virgin ♦♦♦♦
Flogging a Dead Horse collects the A- and B-sides of the Sex Pistols' seven British singles. It's not really the best way to hear those singles, though—there was a sharp decline in the quality and relevance of the Pistols' material when Johnny Rotten left the band, and some of the later goofiness dilutes the impact of early songs like "God Save the Queen" and "Anarchy in the U.K." It is a useful compilation in that two songs—"Did You No Wrong" and "No Fun"—are unavailable on both *Never Mind the Bollocks* and *The Great Rock & Roll Swindle*, and it is perfect for fans who don't want to sift through the latter and will be content with a brief overview. Still, *Dead Horse* doesn't match *Never Mind the Bollocks* (still the necessary purchase) for start-to-finish venom, and as inconsistent as *Swindle* is, it can be quite entertaining. So, *Flogging a Dead Horse* is not the best compilation, but it will do in some cases. *—Steve Huey*

We've Cum for Your Children / 1988 / Skyclad ♦♦♦
Another of the entries in the mini-industry of Sex Pistols marginalia, assembled by the group's onetime soundman, Dave Goodman. The July 1976 demos (of "Submission," "Pretty Vacant," and "Suburban Kid") here are actually very good, from both fidelity and performance standpoints. Elsewhere the quality is much more variable—live songs, the famous Bill Grundy interview on British television, a "live in the studio" version of "Unlimited Supply," the "ultra-rare mystery track" "Revolution in the Classroom," and more. It's really not a bad historical document; it would rate higher except for the fact that the material is haphazardly assembled and appears on other similar slapdash anthologies. And you *do* need a scorecard to keep such things straight by now: It's doubtful more than a few thousand listeners (if that) could tell you exactly what here has appeared elsewhere, and where. *—Richie Unterberger*

Chaos / Feb. 27, 1996 / Restless ♦♦

Filthy Lucre Live / Jul. 1996 / Caroline ♦♦♦
As the cliche says, the Sex Pistols were the last band anyone expected to see reunite. However, those observers were ignoring just how alluring the promise of easy money is to a band that never earned that much in the first place, so the Sex Pistols did what was previously unthinkable and reunited in 1996 for a summer-long tour of Europe and the United States. After playing two warm-up gigs, the band played their first official live concert at Finsbury Park in early June and the result is presented on *Filty Lucre Live*, which was released just a matter of weeks after the concert. Two things about the reunited Pistols are clear from the outset—they can play their instruments and they sound much heavier and less revolutionary than expected. In fact, the band doesn't sound very *punk* at all—they sound like a professional hard rock band. But—and this is the most surprising thing—they sound fun. If you're a fan, it's hard to deny that it's fun to hear a live performance by the Pistols that doesn't degenerate into chaos and is recorded in clean audio. You can't call *Filthy Lucre Live* punk rock by any stretch of the imagination, but it is first-rate nostalgia, even if punk was about eliminating the need for records just like this one. *—Stephen Thomas Erlewine*

Ron Sexsmith

b. 1964

Vocals, Guitar (Acoustic) / Adult Alternative Pop/Rock, Singer/Songwriter

The earnest work of boyish Canadian singer/songwriter Ron Sexsmith won acclaim not from only critics but from fellow performers like Paul McCartney, Elvis Costello, and John Hiatt—some of the same artists, ironically enough, who initially inspired Sexsmith himself to become a musician. Born in 1964 and raised in the Niagara Falls area, he started his first band at the age of 14, and within a few years earned his first regular gig at an area club. Influenced by Pete Seeger, he began making the rounds on the folk circuit but soon decided to focus his attentions on becoming a songwriter.

After moving to the Toronto area, Sexsmith formed the Uncool and began issuing his own material in 1985 with the cassette *Out of the Duff*, followed a year later by *There's a Way*. He continued performing while maintaining a day job as a courier but did not release anything more until 1991's *Grand Opera Lane*, recorded by Blue Rodeo's Bob Wiseman. The collection of songs helped earn Sexsmith a songwriting contract and eventually a recording deal with Interscope Records; teamed with producer Mitchell Froom, he released his self-titled debut in 1995. A follow-up, *Other Songs*, appeared two years later. In 1999, Sexsmith returned with *Whereabouts*, again produced by Froom. *—Jason Ankeny*

Grand Opera Lane / 1991 / [self released] ♦♦♦
Although these are not the first tracks he actually recorded, these are the songs that brought Ron Sexsmith to the attention of the music world. Originally released as a demo in 1991, the tape made its way into the hands of Interscope, who eventually took a chance on the promising young songwriter and performer. Those familiar with Sexsmith's three low-key albums for Interscope will be surprised with the material on *Grand Opera Lane*, which is almost all upbeat—almost rock & roll in places. The guitars take on a skiffle feel, and horns appear in the background on a few of the numbers. The change of feel can probably be laid square on the shoulders of producer/keyboardist Bob Wiseman, who brought along some of the country-rock sensibilities of his band Blue Rodeo (as well as fellow member Greg Keelor for a few tracks). Also surprising is Sexsmith's material, which, while strong, was certainly more direct and less poetic than the songs that appeared on his major label debut. In fact, only one of the songs featured here, "Speaking With the Angel," made the transition to that record. This is a much younger Sexsmith, however, and while *Grand Opera Lane* isn't as soul-touching as his later work, it's an interesting window into what came before. *Grand Opera Lane* was re-released on CD in 2000. Initially available only at live shows, the CD can now be ordered online at www.maplemusic.com. *—Sean Carruthers*

● **Ron Sexsmith** / May 16, 1995 / Interscope ♦♦♦♦♦
Ron Sexsmith is so anti-cool that this may actually be one the coolest albums you hear. The Toronto singer/songwriter's appearance matches his music perfectly—hair falling in tousled bangs over doe eyes and baby face; one of those guys who always got beat up in high school and couldn't string two words together in front of a real live girl without stammering. A wide-eyed innocent, Sexsmith's eponymous release marries the wonder of Jonathan Richman with the darker atmosphere of a Daniel Lanois. Superficially, the songs are so sparsely childlike that you're tempted to wonder if Sexsmith is either a master of affectation or some kind of idiot savant. *—Roch Parisien*

Other Songs / Jun. 17, 1997 / Interscope ♦♦♦♦
The quandary of the whole solo singer/songwriter thing is that one listener's deeply personal and affecting music is another's boringly self-absorbed slop. And the fine line between them, between naked emotion and unadulterated pap, is the production, its intent, and above all, the talent trapped in it—so highly exposed, after all. In this second LP by Sexsmith, it's clear he's a composer of ability, as his lyrics have a quietly moving air and his delicate picking and fingering of his acoustic silently charms. The drums bubble so lightly in the back you never notice them, and the pretty piano on tracks such as "Average Joe" is employed with grace. Best of all, Sexsmith's voice is a dead ringer for 1966-1967 Tim Hardin (circa his best work, *Tim Hardin I* and *Tim Hardin II*), only without Hardin's more breathy trills (and without the late legend's incredible, arrestingly sweet melancholia, woeful lamentation, and bleeding heart). Sexsmith's throat is smoky menthol, yet gentle and soothing, the kind that wraps around the melodies like a mother's most serene lullaby. Maybe there's a little 1971 Jackson Browne in Sexsmith, too, only without the reedy dweebness. On the negative side, ubiquitous producer Mitchell Froom elicits nice takes but envelops them in a slightly glossy sheen. He makes Sexsmith fall in line with so much ho-hum singer/songwriter pop, when the playing and singing suggested more direct emotional immediacy, like Hardin, or young Neil Young, or the late-'60s Paul Simon before he regrettably lost his Garfunkel. That Sexsmith has the stuff to overcome such sanitation for listeners' protection is a credit to a modest prize at work. And love that mellifluous voice. *—Jack Rabid, The Big Takeover*

Whereabouts / May 18, 1999 / Interscope ♦♦♦♦
Ron Sexsmith's third album continues the singer/songwriter's talent—and perhaps his need—for revealing his delicate and contemplative reflections on life and himself. On *Whereabouts*, Sexsmith sounds vulnerable yet a bit more worldly than on his previous two albums, and his clear, plaintive vocals sound best on the most introspective tracks like "Riverbed," "The Idiot Boy," and "Doomed." The only minor flaw is the production—somewhat cold and soulless, it detracts from Sexsmith's intimacy instead of complementing it. *—Gina Boldman*

Blue Boy / Jun. 5, 2001 / Cooking Vinyl ♦♦♦♦
For his fourth studio album, Ron Sexsmith abandoned the increasingly baroque textures of Mitchell Froom and Tchad Blake's keyboard-dominated production to work with producer and fellow world-class songwriter Steve Earle (along with Earle's usual studio partner, Ray Kennedy). But if you're expecting the results to be a straightforward singer/songwriter affair, think again—*Blueboy* is a stylistically diverse, sonically full-bodied affair, and while it's hardly a full-on rock record, it's certainly Sexsmith's most immediate and forceful set to date. Between the soul horns on "This Song," the reggae accents of "Never Been Done," and the cool jazz arrangement on "Foolproof," Earle's production brings a variety of different flavors to these songs, and while most fall into a smart pop mode not unlike Sexsmith's earlier work, the album's subtle but inventive textures draw the listener's focus into the songs, rather than the arrangements. Earle and Kennedy have also

done a fine job capturing the nuances of Sexsmith's vocals, which boast a greater depth than on most of his earlier outings in the studio. But the best reason to listen to a Ron Sexsmith album is always his songs, and *Blueboy* offers another 14 pieces of evidence that this man ranks among the most gifted singer/songwriters working today. Balancing a youthful charm with a strikingly mature perspective, Sexsmith sings about the stuff of ordinary people—life, love, and fate—with a perceptive intelligence, emotional depth, and subtle and compassionate wit that's truly one of a kind. Anyone who has heard his work knows that Ron Sexsmith is a superb songwriter, and *Blueboy* suggests he's learned how to make records just as strong as his material. *—Mark Deming*

Phil Seymour

b. May 15, 1952, Tulsa, OK, **d.** Aug. 17, 1993, Tarzana, California

Vocals, Drums / Power Pop, New Wave

Phil Seymour is best remembered as one half of the creative force behind the Dwight Twilley Band, co-writing, with Dwight Twilley, some of the finest pop songs of the era, including the classic "I'm on Fire." After two albums (1976's *Sincerely* and 1978's *Twilley Don't Mind*), Seymour left to pursue a solo career. While waiting for a recording deal, he began recording solo sessions, as well as contributing session work for Tom Petty, 20/20, and Moon Martin. In 1980, he signed to Boardwalk Records after selling the label on a batch of demos recorded with fellow Tulsa natives 20/20. His self-titled debut was well received at the time (the single "Precious to Me" made it to number 22 on the pop charts) and has become highly revered in power-pop circles as one of the landmark albums of the era. He followed in 1982 with *2*, a less satisfying album both creatively and commercially. Seymour was left without a label when Boardwalk president Neil Bogart died shortly after the record's release. In 1984, he joined Carla Olsen's Textones, drumming and singing on their *Midnight Mission* album for A&M. While supporting the album, Seymour was diagnosed with lymphoma. He returned to Tulsa, carrying on at a diminished pace and recording infrequently, until the disease took his life in August of 1993 while he was preparing a new album. *—Chris Woodstra*

Phil Seymour / 1980 / Boardwalk ✦✦✦✦✦

Upon splitting with former bandmate Dwight Twilley, Phil Seymour began work on his first solo effort. Using many of the same musicians who had supported Twilley, Seymour turns in a pop gem on his first try. All 11 cuts are great, and they include the hit "Precious to Me." A real fine pop masterwork. *—James Chrispell*

2 / 1982 / Boardwalk ✦✦✦

2 continues in the same vein where his first disc left off. It includes Tom Petty's "Surrender," and Dwight Twilley's "Looking for the Magic," and many other pop/rock essentials. Too bad his record company went belly-up shortly after its release. Worth seeking out. *—James Chrispell*

• **Precious to Me** / Jun. 25, 1996 / The Right Stuff ✦✦✦✦✦

Precious to Me attempts to collect the many phases of Phil Seymour's all-too-brief career. The disc's 15 tracks cover his period as Dwight Twilley's partner, his solo work, a song he did with the Textones, and a handful of rarities and stray tracks. And while it is certainly a welcome compilation of his long-out-of-print work on to compact disc, this collection could have been better. Considering Seymour's small cult of obsessive fans, the Twilley tracks are redundant—anyone who buys this collection undoubtedly has the Dwight Twilley discs already—and the absence of any songs from Seymour's second solo album is simply a disservice. Any of Seymour's recordings are pure pop fun so *Precious to Me* is good listen and for the uninitiated, this is a good enough starting point if only because so much of his work is unavailable. *—Chris Woodstra*

Sha Na Na

f. 1968, New York, NY

Doo Wop, Nostalgia, Novelty

Sha Na Na parlayed their straight-ahead '50s rock & roll revivalism into a successful touring career, even if they were never as popular on record as they were live. The group's image and style were unabashedly anachronistic, as they covered '50s pop and doo wop standards, slicked their hair back in the greaser fashion, and dressed in flamboyant '50s costumes. Sha Na Na formed at Columbia University in 1968 and quickly built a name for itself with live performances, often at the Fillmore East, featuring such theatrics as a dance contest for audience members. The original lineup consisted of vocalists Scott Powell, Johnny Contardo, Frederick "Denny" Greene, Richard "Ritchie" Joffe, and Don York, plus guitarists Chris Donald, Elliot Cahn, and Henry Gross, bassist Bruce Clarke, drummer John "Jocko" Marcellino, pianists "Screamin'" Scott Simon and John "Bowser" Bauman, and former Danny and the Juniors saxophonist Leonard Baker. Sha Na Na's big break came with a booking at the Woodstock Festival in 1969; they caught on with the public and began a string of appearances at rock & roll venues and nightclubs. Gross left for a solo career in 1970 and scored a Top Ten hit six years later with "Shannon," something his old group was never able to do; Sha Na Na was largely a live act playing on nostalgia and entertainment value, which did not translate as well on record. In spite of internal problems including nervous breakdowns and the death of member Vincent Taylor from a heroin overdose in 1974, the group peaked in popularity in the late '70s, hosting its own syndicated television show from 1977 to 1981 and appearing in the 1978 film *Grease*. Screamin' Scott Simon co-wrote the song "Sandy" for the film; meanwhile, Jon "Bowser" Bauman continued his television career, co-hosting a morning show in Los Angeles and guesting frequently on several game shows. The group continues to tour with several original members still on board. *—Steve Huey*

Whole Lotta Sha-Na-Na / Nov. 11, 1997 / BMG Special Products ✦✦

Shadows of Knight

f. 1964, Chicago, IL, **db.** 1969

Garage Rock

"The Stones, Animals and Yardbirds took the Chicago Blues and gave it an English interpretation. We've taken the English version of the Blues and re-added a Chicago touch." The Shadows of Knight's self-description was fairly accurate. Although this mid-'60s garage band from the Windy City did not match the excellence of either their British or African-American idols, the teen energy of their recordings remains enjoyable, if not overwhelmingly original. The group took a tamer version of Them's classic "Gloria" into the American Top Ten in 1966, and also took a Yardbirdized version of Bo Diddley's "Oh Yeah" into the Top 40 the same year. Their patchy albums contained a few exciting R&B covers in the Yardbirds/Stones style and a few decent originals in the same vein. The group's original lineup splintered quickly, and the Shadows faded in the late '60s after briefly pursuing a more commercial pop sound. *—Richie Unterberger*

Gloria / 1966 / Sundazed ✦✦✦✦✦

Although revisionist historians will claim that any Shadows of Knight best-of that includes "Gloria" will cover just about everything you'll ever need on this Chicago punk band (and usually acting as if Van Morrison's and Them's original was the actual hit—wrong!!), true believers have long championed their two original albums for the Dunwich label, especially their debut long-player named after their big hit. Why? Simply because it positively rocks with a raw energy of a band straight out of the teen clubs, playing with a total abandon and an energy level that seems to explode out of the speakers. Equal parts Rolling Stones, Yardbirds, Who, and snotty little Chicago-suburb bad boys, the Shadows of Knight could easily put the torch to Chess blues classics, which make up the majority of the songs included here. Their wild takes on "I Just Want to Make Love to You," "Oh Yeah," and "I Got My Mojo Working" rank right up there with any British Invasion band's version from the same time period. Original material was never plentiful on either SOK long-player, but worth checking out are "Light Bulb Blues," the blues ballad "Dark Side," and the why-me? rocker, "It Always Happens That Way." Completing the package is the inclusion of three bonus tracks, the single-only "Someone Like Me" and an alternate version, and "I Got My Mojo Working," which is vastly superior to the take on the original album. A not-too-vastly-different alternate mix of "Oh Yeah" completes the bonus tracks, although the original album version is curiously missing from this otherwise excellent package. Nonetheless, a reissue well worth adding to the collection. If you're only going to own one Shadows of Knight package, you could, and should, start right here. *—Cub Koda*

Back Door Men / 1967 / Sundazed ✦✦✦✦✦

The original LP version of this album, the second by the legendary white Chicago garage punk/blues outfit, was one of the most sought-after artifacts of mid-'60s punk rock. *Back Door Men* was a loud, feedback-laden, sneering piece of rock & roll defiance, mixing raunchy anthems to teenage lust ("Gospel Zone," "Bad Little Woman"), covers of Chicago blues classics (Willie Dixon's "Spoonful," Jimmy Reed's "Peepin' and Hidin'"), raga rock ("The Behemoth"), folk-rock ("Hey Joe," "Three for Love," "I'll Make You Sorry"), and a blues-punk grab off of commercial Top 40 ("Tomorrow's Gonna Be Another Day") all on one 12" platter. What makes the record even more startling is that every one of these tracks, however far afield they go from one another, works. The band strides across the music spectrum with a reach and boldness that most listeners usually only associate with the likes of the Beatles or the Rolling Stones, and a grasp that, for a moment here, may have exceeded either of those groups, as they slide from electric guitar into extended Chess-style blues instrumentals ("New York Bullseye"). *—Bruce Eder*

Raw 'N Alive at the Cellar, Chicago 1966! / 1992 / Sundazed ✦✦✦

This is one of the very few live garage band tapes from the mid-'60s of relatively decent sound quality (considering the standards of the era). The song selection of this set should also please fans of one of the most famed '60s garage bands, captured here at a club in their home turf of Chicago in December 1966. The 13 songs include live versions of many of the tunes from their first (and best) album, as well as a six-minute workout of their lone national hit "Gloria" and a couple of Solomon Burke covers. However, it's not essential if you already have the original albums, or the fine best-of compilation released in the U.K. on Edsel, *Gee-El-O-Are-I-Ay*. These versions are very close in arrangement to the officially released ones, but the performance is less accomplished, as it were, and the sound quality worse. An interesting artifact that nevertheless has little appeal beyond '60s garage collector circles, although the very brief quotes from the Mothers of Invention's "Help I'm A Rock" are most curious and unexpected. *—Richie Unterberger*

• **Dark Sides: The Best of the Shadows of Knight** / Aug. 16, 1994 / Rhino ✦✦✦✦✦

More easily available to North Americans than the British Edsel best-of, but not necessarily an improvement. Adds some tracks from both the original lineup and their unimpressive, more pop-oriented singles from the late '60s, and has more comprehensive liner notes, but also omits a few decent covers that are on the U.K. compilation, particularly their smoking, over-the-top version of "I Just Want to Make Love to You." *—Richie Unterberger*

The Shaggs

f. 1969, **db.** 1975

Obscuro, Alternative Pop/Rock, Novelty

One of the great stories of rock & roll is that of the three Wiggins sisters (Dot, Helen, and Betty), better known as the Shaggs. Growing up dirt poor in New Hampshire, the three girls were turned onto forming a band by their father, Austin Wiggins, buying their instruments and paying for lessons. Despite their lack of musical expertise, Austin drove the girls down to a studio in Massachusetts, determined to get them on tape "while they were still hot." Striking a deal with a local fly-by-night record company called Third World, the Shaggs recorded their debut album, *Philosophy of the World*, in one day, recording a dozen tunes all written by Dot. One thousand copies were pressed and all but 100 of them quickly disappeared, along with the president of the company. When Austin Wiggins passed away in 1975, the group disbanded and never played together again. But over the intervening years, their lone misguided attempt at recording started gaining cult status. In a *Playboy* magazine interview, Frank Zappa called *Philosophy of the World* his third all-time favorite album and by the time NRBQ had reissued it in 1980, its legendary status was already confirmed, keeping the music of the Shaggs (which one can view as either guileless primitive art or just a garage band that *really* can't play or sing) alive. *—Cub Koda*

• **Philosophy of the World** / 1969 / RCA ✦✦✦✦✦
Supplanting the Rounder single disc that combined the group's original album with later sides, this brings the package back to its original form. It features the original mixes (the Rounder reissue used remixes), sequencing, cover, and liner notes along with updated historical notes from producer Irwin Chusid. While a 12-song reissue that replaces a fuller and longer collection would seem like a beat for the money, this puts the Wiggins sisters' primitive attempt to make original rock & roll in its proper context. The guilelessness that permeates these performances is simply amazing, making a virtue out of artlessness. There's an innocence to these songs and their performances that's both charming and unsettling. Hacked-at drumbeats, whacked-around chords, songs that seem to have little or no meter to them ("My Pal Foot Foot," "Who Are Parents," "That Little Sports Car," "I'm So Happy When You're Near" are must-hears) being played on out-of-tune, pawn-shop-quality guitars all converge, creating dissonance and beauty, chaos and tranquility, causing any listener coming to this music to rearrange any pre-existing notions about the relationships between talent, originality, and ability. There is no album you might own that sounds *remotely* like this one. *—Cub Koda*

Shaggs' Own Thing / 1982 / Rounder ✦✦✦✦
Shaggs' Own Thing is a compilation album, including all songs from the band's 1969 debut album, *Philosophy of the World*, and others they made between then and 1975. Don't come to *The Shaggs'* for pop sensibility, or even for readily understandable melodies or rhythms. The original songs, mostly written by Dot Wiggins, almost sound as though they were precariously built, note-by-note, at the time of recording. The tunes wander up and down the scale, the way a song spontaneously created by a small child might do. The Wiggins sisters' (Dot, Helen, and Betty on the first album, joined by sister Rachel later) mastery of their instruments is rudimentary at best, and their sense of rhythm is somewhat unusual. Some song introductions sound convincingly as if the band is merely tuning up. Yet, on most of the songs, the sisters seem to be completely in synch with each other in terms of time and pitch, sharing some innate familial metronome. However, lack of musical expertise on the part of the Shaggs does not prevent this collection of songs from being a charming and intriguing listen. This is a rare, raw look into the minds of a family of sweet, sad, but hopeful young girls who are struggling to understand the world. There are some cover songs in the set, but ironically, the girls play the original tunes much more tightly. Their expression of these seemly autobiographical songs is the core of what makes this album worthwhile, particularly for devotees of the Shaggs. *—Susan Bachner*

Los Shakers

British Invasion
The concept of a Uruguayan band in the mold of the *Hard Day's Night*-era Beatles may seem absurd, but it did happen in the mid-'60s. What's more, the Shakers (sometimes billed as Los Shakers on their releases) were fairly successful in mimicking the jangle of the early Beatles sound, writing most of their material with a decent grasp of the British Invasion essentials of catchy tunes and enthusiastic harmonies. While the grammar is fairly broken and pidgin, soundwise the Shakers were actually superior to many of the bona fide Mersey groups; if you like the Beatles sound as heard on tracks like "I Should Have Known Better" or "I'll Be Back," you'll like this stuff. Popular in their native land, the Shakers were understandably unable to compete on an international scale, although their 1966 album, *Break It All*, was actually issued in the States. Today they enjoy respect from hardcore '60s collectors, and much of their material is available on reissues. The group was formed by brothers Hugo Fattoruso (lead guitar, keyboards) and Osvaldo Fattoruso (rhythm guitar), who as a team wrote most of their material. Like so many combos around the world, the specific motivation to form the group came from watching the Beatles' movie *A Hard Day's Night*. The band remained extremely influenced by the Beatles throughout their career and were in fact not too aware of or interested in the work of other British Invasion groups. Signed to a deal by EMI/Odeon in Argentina, they issued their first single, "Break It All," in 1965. The band became very big in both Uruguay and Argentina and also toured in several other South American countries. There was never a concerted effort on the band's part to invade the English-speaking market, and they never played in North America. *—Richie Unterberger*

• **Por Favor** / Oct. 31, 2000 / Big Beat ✦✦✦✦✦
No doubt this will stand as the most definitive single-disc compilation of Uruguay's Shakers (referred to as "the Shakers" on some releases and "Los Shakers" on others, including this one). There are 32 tracks, and 79 minutes, taken from all three of the LPs they issued in South America between 1965-1968, along with three cuts from 1966 singles, almost everything sung in English. It cements their well-deserved reputation as the top Beatlesque 1960s band from South America—as if any further proof were necessary—and indeed one of the most uncannily Beatlesque bands from anywhere, at any time. Does that mean that this is as good as, or nearly as good as, the Beatles themselves? No, but it's good fun all the same, even if much of the disc sounds like inverted, or at times barely altered, ideas from Beatles riffs and arrangements. They were at their best, perhaps, when mimicking the *A Hard Day's Night*-era Fab Four, as they did on their 1965 debut LP, *Los Shakers*, most of which is here. They did, however, evolve to some degree artistically, albeit rather in tandem with how the Beatles' own records changed in 1965-1967, adding some (but not much) native rhythmic styles and riffs here and there; putting *Revolver*-type vocals and meters into cuts like "Picking Up Troubles" and "Got Any Money?"; putting some down-beat, jazzy riffs into the fine "Too Late"; using freaky backwards guitar and drones in "I Hope You'll Like It," their most advanced cut; and adopting the march-beat, mid-tempo, and sunny harmonies of many 1967 Beatles tunes on numbers like "On a Tuesday I Watch Channel 36." This anthology is not, incidentally, the last word on the Shakers' output: there are no tracks from their U.S.-only 1966 LP, *Break It All* (which featured re-recordings of their early South American sides), and a handful of other numbers show up on the Brazilian EMI CD *All the Best*. *—Richie Unterberger*

Shalamar

f. 1976, New York, NY, **db.** 1991
Urban, Disco, Soul
Shalamar was the creation of Dick Griffey, the booking agent for the television R&B program *Soul Train*, and British R&B producer Simon Soussan. The group's first single, the 1977 Motown medley "Uptown Festival," featured a bevy of faceless studio musicians; once it became a hit, Griffey decided to form a performing group under the name Shalamar. Through *Soul Train* Griffey found Jody Watley, Jeffrey Daniels, and Gerald Brown, the three vocalists that became Shalamar; Brown was quickly replaced by Howard Hewitt in 1978.

Shalamar's string of poppy dance-soul hits began in 1979 with "Take That to the Bank"; later that year, "The Second Time Around" hit the Top Ten. Throughout the early '80s the group were favorites on the U.S. R&B scene, as well as scoring a number of British hit singles. Watley and Daniels left the group in 1982 and were replaced by Delisa Davis and Micki Free in 1984; Watley went on to stardom as a solo act. The following year Shalamar won a Grammy award for "Don't Get Stopped in Beverly Hills," which was featured in *Beverly Hills Cop*. Hewitt left for a solo career in 1986, signaling the end of the band's career as hit-makers. Sidney Justin replaced Hewitt and the group recorded 1987's *Circumstantial Evidence*, which was a commercial disappointment. The group faded away soon after the release of 1990's *Wake Up*. *—Stephen Thomas Erlewine*

• **The Greatest Hits** / Jul. 27, 1999 / Capitol ✦✦✦✦
The Right Stuff's *Greatest Hits* comes close to being the definitive Shalamar hits collection. Every one of their biggest hits—"Uptown Festival (Part 1)," "The Second Time Around," "Make That Move," "A Night to Remember," "Dead Giveaway," "Dancing in the Sheets," "Games"—are present, in their best-known mixes. Some dedicated fans might notice that a song or two is missing, but all the biggest best singles are here, making it a very entertaining compilation ideal for casual and dedicated fans alike. *—Stephen Thomas Erlewine*

Sham 69

f. 1976, **db.** 1980
British Punk, Oi!, Punk
I doubt there would be much disagreement with the assertion that of all the British punk bands of the late-'70s, Sham 69 was the worst band to have a career lasting more than two records. Negligibly talented like their punk brethren the Cortinas and Eater, and specializing in simplistic political vituperation, shouted vocals, and roaring guitars, Sham 69 was remotely interesting in the heady days of 1976-78, only to quickly descend to joke status (in America anyway) by the turn of the decade.

Led by vocalist and lyricist Jimmy Pursey, Sham's basic attack was "leftist" slogans chanted repeatedly over a wall of fast distorted guitars that exploded into shoutalong choruses (all the better for their yob fans to participate). Unsurprisingly, this begat chart success (in England only) where the band released five, albeit indistinguishable, hit singles in their first year. Flushed with success, Pursey adopted the role of principal spokesman, erstwhile politico, and punk careerist, roles for which (except for the latter) he showed little talent. In 1980, shortly after the release of the album *The Game*, Pursey, in a move that indicated a tremendously inflated self-worth, broke up Sham 69 for a solo career; his four subsequent solo records exhibit a dearth of creativity and talent.

His solo career stalled, Pursey saw an opportunity to milk punk rock nostalgia for a few pounds and re-formed Sham 69. Exhibiting careerist proclivities and excessive crassness, the new Sham simply played like the old Sham, and Pursey fobbed the whole thing off as a retrenchment by an aging punk rocker to his "roots." Mostly it was pathetic, but based on Sham 69's history, totally unsurprising. *—John Dougan*

Tell Us the Truth / 1978 / Sire ✦✦✦✦✦
The first wave of British punk was overrun with smart kids from upper-class backgrounds playacting at being working class yobs. (The Clash did this first, and did it better than practically anyone.) But Sham 69 was different; every bit as thick-headed and provincial as the band sounded, Sham 69 took a perversely populist pride in its lack of musical or intellectual sophistication. If there's a point where British punk began to evolve from smart, edgy bands like the Sex Pistols and the Adverts into beer-soaked Neanderthals such as the Exploited and the Anti-Nowhere League, Sham 69 marks the spot, and while its first album, *Tell Us the Truth*, is the band's strongest work, the album also shows that most of Sham 69's flaws were in plain sight from the start.

Side one of *Tell Us the Truth* was recorded live, and it's inarguably fascinating as an anthropological document, capturing the Cockney yob in his native environment, complete with football chants and a spontaneous chorus of "Knees Up, Mother Brown." Jimmy Pursey's communication with his audience is inarguably impressive, and some of the songs have a good head of straight-ahead energy (especially "Borstal Breakout"), but the sound is thin and the band seems to have a hard time getting into fifth gear. The studio side actually sounds more impressive; the performances are tighter, Dave Parsons' guitar benefits from a bit of double-tracking, and Pursey sings more than he hectors. But Pursey was already starting to sound a bit pompous, and time has not been the least bit kind to songs like "I'm a Man I'm a Boy" and "Hey Little Rich Boy," which for all their sincerity don't say anything dozens of other bands haven't said better.

Tell Us the Truth sounds passionate, belligerent, and kinda dumb, but that's an improvement over Sham 69's later work, where the band sounds overblown, strident, and really, *really* dumb. The 2000 CD reissue features two bonus cuts, including a studio version of "Borstal Breakout." *—Mark Deming*

That's Life / 1978 / Polydor ✦✦✦✦

The Adventures of the Hersham Boys / 1979 / Polydor ✦✦✦✦

The First, The Best & The Last / 1980 / Polydor ✦✦✦
Released directly after the band's expiry after too many rows with their notorious skinhead following, this features all of the singles (with the exception of "I Don't Wanna," their independent debut on Step Forward) plus selected B-sides such as "Hey Little Rich Boy" and the wonderful "Sunday Morning Nightmare," which is Pursey's tribute to working-class family life, or what's left of it, on the morning after the night before. Really, one very good live album aside, this is as much Sham 69 as anyone needs in their life. *—Alex Ogg*

The Game / 1980 / Polydor ✦✦✦
Sham 69's last—and least-loved—studio album. Sham had just disbanded and re-formed within a couple of months, drafting in new drummer Mark Goldstein for this comeback. Musical adventurism is not something you'd readily associate with this crew, and though it was brave of Pursey to try to push his audience, fans were nowhere near ready to be pushed. Some of the songs are tolerable, just tolerable. But the absolute nadir is a gentle ballad number called, yep, "Poor Cow." Boy, did he have a way with words. *—Alex Ogg*

Live and Loud / 1987 / Link ✦✦✦✦
Artless dodgers they may have been, but on-stage Sham 69's was a powerful presence. What you can't argue with is the fact that this band meant something—a great deal—to their huge working-class audience. Recorded in 1979, this well-produced, visceral souvenir is easily the best of a plethora of live albums and arguably a much better introduction to why Sham mattered than either *That's Life* or *Hersham Boys*, their rather limited studio efforts. *—Alex Ogg*

● **The Punk Singles Collection (1977-1980)** / Mar. 10, 1998 / Cleopatra ✦✦✦✦✦
The Punk Singles Collection is a 22-track overview of Sham 69's career, including such working-class punk anthems as "Hurry Up Harry," "Angels With Dirty Faces," "If the Kids Are United," and "Borstal Breakout." 22 tracks may border on overkill for the casual fan, but everything you need is here, and this particular collection has the advantage of being in print. *—Steve Huey*

The Shangri-Las

f. 1963, Queens, NY, **db.** 1969
Brill Building Pop, Girl Group, Rock & Roll
Along with the Shirelles and the Ronettes, the Shangri-Las were the greatest girl group; if judged solely on the basis of attitude, they were the greatest of them all. They combined an innocent adolescent charm with more than a hint of darkness, singing about dead bikers, teenage runaways, and doomed love affairs as well as ebullient high-school crushes. These could be delivered with either infectious, hand-clapping harmonies or melodramatic, almost operatic recitatives that were contrived but utterly effective. Tying it all together in the studio was Shadow Morton, a mad genius of a producer that may have been second in eccentric imagination only to Phil Spector in the mid-'60s. The quality of Morton's work with the Shangri-Las on Red Bird (with assistance from Jeff Barry and Artie Butler) was remarkable considering that he had virtually no prior experience in the music business. The group's material, so over-the-top emotionally that it sometimes bordered on camp, was lightened by the first-class production, which embroidered the tracks with punchy brass, weeping strings, and plenty of imaginative sound effects. Nowhere was this more apparent than on "Leader of the Pack," with its periodic motorcycle roars and crescendo of crashing glass. The death-rock classic became the Shangri-Las' signature tune, reaching number one. *—Richie Unterberger*

Golden Hits of the Shangri-Las / 1984 / Mercury ✦✦✦✦✦
It includes all the eerie three-minute melodramas from one of the all-time great girl groups: "Leader of the Pack," "Remember," "I Can Never Go Home Anymore," "Past, Present, and Future." *—George Bedard*

Collection: 20 Greatest Hits / 1993 / Masters ✦✦

● **Myrmidons of Melodrama** / 1994 / RPM ✦✦✦✦✦
Until the release of this import, there had never been a truly satisfactory Shangri-Las anthology; in fact, the group had been subject to worse piecemeal mangling than almost any other significant act of the 1960s. This 33-track production finally sets the record straight, including all of the significant A-sides, B-sides, and album tracks they recorded for Red Bird between 1964 and 1966, as well as an earlier single for a different label, and four radio commercials. Includes every one of their hits, but anyone who likes those will be enchanted by quite a few of their more obscure numbers here: "Dressed in Black," "Paradise," "It's Easier to Cry," "Never Again," and "Heaven Knows" are all first-class (if sometimes mordant). Not everything is up to that level, but enough is to make a case for them as one of the very best girl groups, and the good sound and thorough liner notes are significant bonuses. It may be more extensive and expensive than some fans wish, but don't settle for the numerous skimpy/rip-off domestic compilations, all of which manage to leave off some key tunes; this is the definitive document. *—Richie Unterberger*

● **The Best of the Shangri-Las** / Jun. 18, 1996 / Mercury/Chronicles ✦✦✦✦✦
This 25-song best-of actually covers most of their discography, containing all of the chart singles, and notable misses, and B-sides like "Paradise" and "Dressed in Black." An excellent package, but the British *Myrmidons of Melodrama* (on RPM) is just a bit better, assembling a few more of their Red Bird tracks, including a couple of pretty notable ones ("It's Easier to Cry" and "The Boy") that this domestic anthology omits. The Mercury CD does have their rare (but unexceptional) final two singles, which don't appear on *Myrmidons of Melodrama*. *—Richie Unterberger*

Del Shannon

b. Dec. 30, 1934, Coopersville, MI, **d.** Feb. 8, 1990, Santa Clarita, CA
Vocals, Guitar / Teen Idol, Pop/Rock, Pop, Rock & Roll
One of the best and most original rockers of the early '60s, Del Shannon was also one of the least typical. Although classified at times as a teen idol, he favored brooding themes of abandonment, loss, and rejection. In some respects he looked forward to the British Invasion with his frequent use of minor chords and his ability to write most of his own material. His 1961 debut single "Runaway" was one of the greatest hits of the early '60s; with its unforgettable riffs, Shannon's amazing vocal range (which often glided off into a powerful falsetto), and the creepy, futuristic organ solo in the middle, it made number one on the pop charts. He became even more successful in England; he played some shows with the Beatles, and with 1963's "From Me to You," became the first American artist to cover a Beatles song.

A switch to a bigger label (Liberty) however, didn't bring the expected commercial results. He continued to evolve, developing a more baroque, orchestrated pop/rock sound on sessions with Rolling Stones producer Andrew Loog Oldham, though much to Shannon's frustration, Liberty decided not to release the material. Shannon began devoting his energy to production and became popular on the oldies circuit. An early-'80s album produced by Tom Petty got him into the Top 40 again with a cover of "Sea of Love" and he was working on another comeback album with Jeff Lynne when he unexpectedly killed himself in 1990, while on anti-depressant drugs. *—Richie Unterberger*

Little Town Flirt / 1963 / Rhino ✦✦✦
Half of the songs on Shannon's second album—"Runaway," "Hats Off to Larry," "Hey Little Girl," "Kelly," "Little Town Flirt," and "Two Kinds of Teardrops"—are on *Greatest Hits*. These are also the best and most popular songs on *Little Town Flirt*, which is filled out with competent but unremarkable covers of early '60s hits like "Go Away, Little Girl," "Runaround Sue," and "Hey Baby." That means that everyone except Shannon collectors should head to *Greatest Hits* instead. *—Richie Unterberger*

Del Shannon Sings Hank Williams / 1965 / Rhino ✦✦✦✦✦
While tribute albums nowadays are commonplace, a quick examination of history 30 years ago shows us that it wasn't always thus. And when they *did* occur, it was usually a tip of the hat to some long-standing show-business icon like Al Jolson. Certainly departed country music stars like Hank Williams were considered outside the pale of such honors, which is only one of the reasons why this tribute album by rocker Del Shannon stands out as being something rarified and great. Shannon—like most aspiring rockers—grew up on Williams' songs and once success allowed him to show that side of his musical equation, he jumped at the opporunity. But rather than cutting a dozen tepid updates of Hank's best ("Kaw-LIga," "Your Cheatin' Heart," "I'm So Lonesome I Could Cry," "Hey Good Lookin'," etc.), awash in a sea of strings and female choruses, Shannon was smart enough to keep the music firmly in the style of Williams' backup band, the Drifting Cowboys. Although several Motown session players—including Dennis "Scorpio" Coffey on lead guitar—are on this session, the net result is heartfelt, understated country music with plenty of steel guitar to the fore, the kind you'd hear at the kinds of beer halls in Saginaw, MI, where Shannon honed his craft. Del sings the songs straight, minus any of his trademarked falsetto embellishments, and the result is one of the best straight forward country albums you'll ever hear. *—Cub Koda*

The Vintage Years / 1975 / Sire ✦✦✦✦✦
A very strong 28-track compilation of his best '60s work. Most fans will want to stick with *Greatest Hits*, but this more extensive (though out-of-print) overview goes deeper without much filler. Major advantages are its inclusion of material from both the earlier and later part of the decade (with emphasis on pre-1966 sides) and extensive liner notes by Greg Shaw. *—Richie Unterberger*

Runaway Hits / 1986 / Bug ✦✦✦✦✦
Fine 16-track compilation of his best early- and mid-'60s hits, with good liner notes and discography. All but one of the songs, however, are included on Rhino's slightly more extensive *Greatest Hits*. *—Richie Unterberger*

I Go to Pieces / 1990 / Edsel ✦✦✦✦✦
At the time this 16-song collection was put together at the end of the 1980s, it was intended to fill some major gaps in Del Shannon's CD and LP catalog, and Shannon himself appreciated the effort. He has since passed on, and ironically, the major part of his catalog is now available on CD. Some of the songs on this collection, including the title track, are now available elsewhere, but some of the best, such as "You Never Talked About Me" (a catchy, dramatic love song that he sang in the movie *It's Trad, Dad*) and the gorgeous "Ginny in the Mirror" and "Don't Gild the Lily, Lily," are unique to *I Go to Pieces*. *—Bruce Eder*

★ **Greatest Hits** / 1990 / Rhino ✦✦✦✦✦
Greatest Hits features 20 tracks from Del Shannon's early-'60s heyday, including all of

the big hits—"Runaway," "Hats off to Larry," "Little Town Flirt," "Handy Man," "Keep Searchin' (We'll Follow the Sun)," "Stranger in Town"—plus a generous selection of lesser-known but equally fine singles and album tracks. Completists should fill in the gaps with his neglected gem *I Go To Pieces*, but *Greatest Hits* remains a definitive retrospective from one of the finest pre-Beatles rockers of the '60s. *—Stephen Thomas Erlewine*

The Liberty Years / Apr. 23, 1991 / EMI America ♦♦♦♦
Not the record to start with. An artist in search of a style, with some interesting attempts at finding one. *—Bruce Eder*

1961-1990: A Complete Career Anthology / Jan. 27, 1998 / Raven ♦♦♦
To most casual listeners, Del Shannon was a one-hit (or, at best, two-hit) wonder. This two-CD anthology goes a long way toward correcting that inaccurate perception, covering virtually every high point in a career that, admittedly with some ups and downs, yielded some great and popular music across nearly 30 years. Every phase of the late singer/composer/guitarist's career is represented, and though "Runaway is usually the only song associated with Shannon, this collection reveals many other sides to his work and sound, from the romantic Shannon original "Jody" to the defiant Pomus-Shuman song "Ginny in the Mirror."

The really good part about this set is that a lot of the songs appear here in their rare stereo mixes. With most classic rock & roll, that would not necessarily be a virtue, stereo being superfluous as well as harmful to its impact, but in Shannon's case it is—his records usually featured very busy, complex instrumental parts (an attribute that he shared in common with the Beatles and a lot of other British invasion acts) that can be discerned much more easily in the stereo versions. All of the bases are covered right up through his work in the late '60s with Andrew "Loog" Oldham and into the 1970s and 1980s obscurities. His version of the Zombies' hit "Tell Her No" (cut for Island Records in the mid-'70s) and the Dave Edmunds-produced "And the Music Plays On" are represented, along with the results of his collaboration with Tom Petty and his comeback with the early-'80s NBC television series *Crime Story* (which returned "Runaway," used as the show's title theme, to the charts). As is usual with Raven Records, the annotation is extremely thorough and the mastering is impeccable. *—Bruce Eder*

Sandie Shaw

b. Feb. 26, 1947, Dagenham, Essex, England
Vocals / Girl Group, British Invasion, Pop
British singer Sandie Shaw had a string of girl group-styled singles in the mid-'60s before she retired in the early '70s. Shaw was discovered by pop singer Adam Faith in 1963, who led her to his manager, Eve Taylor; she released her debut single, "As Long as You're Happy," the following year. It didn't hit the charts, yet her next record, "(There's) Always Something There to Remind Me," hit number one in the U.K. For the next three years, she had a string of hits—most of them written by her producer Chris Andrews—that kept her at the top of the charts. In 1967, Taylor began to move Shaw into cabaret territory; the approach proved a success when the song "Puppet on a String" hit number one. However, none of her further work with Andrews resulted in hit singles. Released in early 1969 her English version of the French "Monsieur Dupont" managed to crack the Top 20; it would turn out to be her last hit. Shaw returned to recording in the early '80s when BEF, a Heaven 17 side-project, prompted her to record "Anyone Who Had a Heart," an old Cilla Black hit. The Smiths' lead singer Morrissey began championing her in interviews, as well, which led her to record a version of the band's "Hand in Glove" supported by The Smiths themselves; the single briefly appeared on the U.K. charts. *—Stephen Thomas Erlewine*

Sandie / 1965 / Pye ♦♦

Me / 1965 / Pye ♦♦♦
Shaw's second album was a substantial improvement on her debut in every respect, though hardly a major effort. It helped that Chris Andrews (who wrote most of her hits) supplied a lot of the tunes. and Shaw herself contributed a fair effort with her first original composition, "Till the Night Begins to Die." "Down and Dismal Ways" is as down and dirty as Sandie ever got (which means that it's still pretty innocuous). Still, you can't help wondering how much better Lulu or Dusty Springfield would have done with the same material. No need to look for a rare, pricy copy of the original LP; all of the songs are included on the British double-CD compilation *64-67 Complete Sandie Shaw Set*. *—Richie Unterberger*

Love Me, Please Love Me / 1967 / RPM ♦♦
Fresh from her triumph at the 1967 Eurovision Song Contest, Shaw concentrated on determinedly MOR pop (not pop/rock) material on her third album. The program focused on songs by Jacques Brel, Antonio Carlos Jobim, Cole Porter, and the like, with only two contributions by her longtime songwriter Chris Andrews. She's no Barbra Streisand, to put it mildly, and the results held little charm either for her fan base or the larger adult market that she may have been trying to reach. The CD reissue is made more palatable by the addition of both sides of four 1967-68 singles, almost all of which were written by Andrews. These are more consistent with the pop/rock lite of her mid-'60s work, but are weaker than her biggest hits, although "Tonight in Tokyo," "You've Not Changed," and "Today" all made the UK Top 30; the Motown-influenced B-side "Stop" may be the highlight of the batch, although that's not saying much. *—Richie Unterberger*

The Sandie Shaw Supplement / 1968 / RPM ♦♦

Reviewing the Situation / 1969 / RPM ♦♦♦
On her last album of the '60s, Shaw proved that she was hipper than a lot of people would have suspected. Moving away from the usual light pop and MOR, she chose a set of covers heavy on material by the likes of Bob Dylan, the Lovin' Spoonful, the Rolling Stones ("Sympathy For the Devil!"), Led Zeppelin's "Your Time Is Gonna Come" (double exclamation point!), Donovan, Dr. John, and the Bee Gees. Which doesn't mean it's a great album. It's thoughtfully arranged and energetically delivered, but Shaw's slight, wispy voice is as ill-suited for some of the material as a nun is for the mosh pit. Hearing her attempt even the slightest hint of funky menace, as on "Sympathy For the Devil" and Dr. John's "Mama Roux," is apt to induce snickers, however heartelt the endeavor might have been. On the other hand, there's a nifty slinky, jazzy cover of the Beatles' "Love Me Do," and her version of the Spoonful's "Coconut Grove" is also good. The CD reissue adds ten bonus tracks from 1969-71 singles, most of which are far more akin to the straight pop of her earlier '60s work (a cover of Paul McCartney's "Maybe I'm Amazed" being an exception). None of the singles were especially memorable, and none of them were hits, closing the chapter on the first phase of her career. *—Richie Unterberger*

Collection / 1990 / Castle ♦♦♦♦♦
Collection is an effective overview of Sandie Shaw's entire career, from her early hits to her '80s collaborations with the Smiths. It covers more ground than the double-disc *Complete* but it doesn't have quite as much prime material. *—Stephen Thomas Erlewine*

● **64-67 Complete Sandie Shaw Set** / 1994 / Sequel ♦♦♦♦♦
A double-disc set that features all of her big hits as well as all of her minor ones, this provides the definitive portrait of the British girl-group vocalist. *—Stephen Thomas Erlewine*

Nothing Less Than Brilliant: The Best of Sandie Shaw / 1995 / Virgin ♦♦♦♦♦
Most of Sandie Shaw's biggest hits are included on *Nothing Less Than Brilliant*, but the collection tries to balance her '60s hits with her '80s comeback, which makes the disc somewhat inconsistent. Nevertheless, it is a good career portrait, featuring many of her finest moments. *—Stephen Thomas Erlewine*

Sandie/Me / Jan. 30, 1996 / See For Miles ♦♦♦
Sandie Shaw's first two albums, *Sandie* and *Me*, are featured on this single disc. Both albums have their share of filler, but there's a high number of strong tracks on the records, and Shaw's joyful, girlish charisma carries many of the weak songs and covers. *Sandie* and *Me* were both included on the double-disc set *64-67 Complete Sandie Shaw Set*, which also featured all of her hit singles, which makes it preferable to this single-disc. *—Stephen Thomas Erlewine*

Cool About You: BBC Sessions 1984/88 / 1998 / RPM ♦♦♦
With good fidelity and performances that find Sandie Shaw in decent voice, this 18-song disc actually serves as a pretty fair overview of her '80s career in case you can't find the studio versions. Her vocals and material are still the sort of thing whose cultish appeal will baffle those who haven't been converted to the cause. To many, it will sound like ordinary '80s pop-rock, albeit by someone conscious enough of critical faves to cover tunes by the Waterboys and have songs specially penned for her by the Smiths and the Jesus & Mary Chain. Smiths/Shaw completists will be especially enticed by the drumless '84 versions of "I Don't Owe You Anything" and "Jean," on which Shaw is backed by guitarist Johnny Marr and bassist Andy Rourke. The highlight of the album, though, is actually a 1986 "unplugged" rendition of one of her biggest '60s hits, "Girl Don't Come." Only 14 of these tracks are actually BBC sessions, by the way; the bonus material includes a couple of songs from a live 1988 benefit show (including a version of "Anyone Who Had a Heart"), and a radio interview from 1984. Annotation is outstanding, much above the norm of what you usually get with Strange Fruit BBC compilations and such. *—Richie Unterberger*

Jules Shear

b. Mar. 7, 1952, Pittsburgh, PA
Vocals, Guitar / Adult Alternative Pop/Rock, Pop/Rock, Singer/Songwriter
Though he's never been able to record a hit of his own, singer/songwriter Jules Shear has recorded several albums of highly accessible, hit-worthy material, and as a testiment to his abilities, he's penned hits for others including "All Through the Night" for Cyndi Lauper and "If She Knew She What She Wants" for the Bangles. He relocated to Los Angeles in the mid-'70s, joining his first band, a typically laid-back combo called the Funky Kings. The band released one album for Arista in 1976. Shear left the following year to form his own group, Jules & the Polar Bears, who released two critically acclaimed, though commercially overlooked, albums for Columbia. When a third album was rejected by the label, Shear forged on as a solo artist. Signing on to EMI-America, he released two solo albums, 1983's *Watch Dog* and 1985's *Eternal Return*; both received critical praise but few sales. Shear then formed the Reckless Sleepers with the Cars' Elliot Easton. In 1988, without Easton, the Reckless Sleepers released their sole album for IRS, *Big Boss Sounds*; it failed to make much impact though "If We Never Meet Again" from the album was later covered by Roger McGuinn. Shear teamed up with the Church's Marty Willson-Piper for an all acoustic, Dylanesque album, *The Third Party*, in 1989. The album ultimately led to a spot on MTV, hosting the first 13 episodes of *Unplugged*—he left when the show switched to the single-artist format. *—Chris Woodstra*

Watch Dog / 1983 / EMI ♦♦♦♦♦
His first solo album following the breakup of the Polar Bears, *Watch Dog*, features a newfound maturity in songwriting with an eclectic mix of styles from ultra-smooth pop to R&B-inflected rockers. Shear sounds much more comfortable on his own, even under Todd Rundgren's heavy-handed production. Highlights includes "All Through the Night" (a hit for Cyndi Lauper), "Whispering Your Name," and the the more experimental, Brian Wilson-inspired "Longest Drink." Another unjustified commercial sleeper. *—Chris Woodstra*

Eternal Return / 1985 / EMI America ♦♦♦
Seemingly unfazed by *Watch Dog's* failure, Shear again produces a slick, pop delight in

Eternal Return. Shear explores a more soulful side in songs like "Steady" and the yearning "You're Not Around" while perfecting his hook-laden melodies. Despite being perfectly in line with the mid-'80s sound, this one also slipped through the cracks. The Bangles would later find a hit in the leadoff track, "If She Knew What She Wants." —*Chris Woodstra*

Demo-Itis / 1987 / Enigma ♦♦
Of interest mainly to fans, this collection of demos shows Shear's true talent, free of the often smothering production that plagued his previous albums. In addition to early versions of old favorites, several songs that never made it on the LPs appear for the first time. —*Chris Woodstra*

The Third Party / 1989 / IRS ♦♦♦
Jules Shear joined up with the Church's Marty Willson-Piper in Sweden for *Third Party*, a stark, bare-bones acoustic album. Stripped of all of the excessive production that sometimes marred earlier work, Shear's songs are allowed to come to the forefront, as they should. Shear's voice, phrasing, and the minimalistic, often folky arrangements led to Dylan comparisons, but the album really features Shear's own clever craftsmanship; the back-to-basics approach is certainly a welcome one (as are the guitar chords included in the booklet). Shear had long before proven his strong melodic sense, but with *Third Party*, his clever wordplay and interesting turns of phrase were allowed the proper platform. Though the album failed commercially, the approach undoubtedly led to Shear's hosting the first several *MTV Unplugged* episodes, which gave him more exposure than ever before. —*Chris Woodstra*

The Great Puzzle / Jan. 28, 1992 / Polydor ♦♦♦♦♦
Jules Shear left behind several albums' worth of terrific music, from his earliest days with the Funky Kings to his work with Jules & the Polar Bears and on to a distinguished solo career. Even with tough competition, *The Great Puzzle* stands as Shear's high point, combining his never-failing gift of melody with tasteful, organic arrangements, highly personal yet universal lyrics, and probably his most consistent batch of songs to date. [Initial pressings of *The Great Puzzle* were packaged with a bonus disc, *Unplug This*, which had Shear reprise his best-known songs along with a couple from *The Great Puzzle* in a solo acoustic setting.] —*Chris Woodstra*

● **Horse of a Different Color (1976-1989)** / 1994 / Razor & Tie ♦♦♦♦♦
Horse of a Different Color collects tracks from all of the early phases of the sadly overlooked songwriter's career from 1976 to 1989, including "Nothing Was Exchanged" (a song that still stands as one of his finest moments) from the sole Funky Kings album, a couple of tracks each from the two released Jules & the Polar Bears albums, a handful from each of his proper solo albums up to 1989's *Third Party*, and the two high points from the short-lived Reckless Sleepers project. Since so much of his early output is long out of print, this collection is a welcome addition, and as a career summary, it's invaluable. Liner notes outlining Shear's ever-changing career would have been nice, but the sheer quality and consistency of music like this really speaks for itself. —*Chris Woodstra*

Healing Bones / Aug. 23, 1994 / Island ♦♦♦
While Shear's albums are always packed with craftsmanlike songwriting, the production and arrangements often end up dating them. What sets *The Healing Bones* apart from most of his back catalog is a certain timelessness of the sound. The songs are definitely among his finest. Includes a cover of the Walker Brothers' classic "The Sun Ain't Gonna Shine Anymore." —*Chris Woodstra*

Between Us / Feb. 24, 1998 / High Street ♦♦♦♦♦
Between Us is a duets album teaming Shear with a veritable who's who of singer/songwriters, from veterans like Carole King and Rosanne Cash to new-breed performers like Paula Cole, Freedy Johnston, Ron Sexsmith, and Amy Rigby. Shear, who has never received proper credit for his distinctive vocal style, is in particularly good voice, blending perfectly with his partner on each song. In a low-key, "unplugged" setting, Shear and company sing tales of heartache and troubled relationships, with Shear's acute eye for detail and evocative lyrics capturing the wide range of feelings with odd turns of phrase that manage to express a certain universality while avoiding obvious clichés. And despite the sparse, tasteful arrangements, the songs once again reveal Shear to be a rare master of melody—these are some of his finest yet, and despite the subject matter, they're extremely catchy. —*Chris Woodstra*

Allow Me / Apr. 25, 2000 / Rounder/Zoe ♦♦♦
Master pop craftsman Jules Shear is also one of the genre's great humanists: His clear-eyed takes on love, regret, and failure can be tenderhearted or scathing, but are never less than compassionate. *Allow Me*, his first recording for Rounder Records, finds Shear back in solo mode after 1998's collection of duets, *Between Us*. Like that record, *Allow Me* is a collection of love songs, but the mood here is comparatively optimistic. Shear's melodies are as catchy and his lyrics as sharp as ever, especially on "Nothing Is New" and the opener, "Hard Enough," one of Shear's patented wake-up calls to a troubled friend; he's also in fine, relaxed vocal form. But *Allow Me* is not Shear's strongest overall effort: "Deep" and "Love With You" are unexceptional bar-band rockers, and the latter features flashy backing vocals that are singularly at odds with his down-to-earth persona. The album is also less cohesive than some of his other works, and some songs are obscured by clunky arrangements. Still, even lesser Jules Shear is a gift to fans of intelligent pop. —*Kristi Coulter*

Shellac

f. 1992, Evanston, IL
Noise-Rock, Indie Rock, Alternative Pop/Rock
More likely to play Reykjavik than Detroit, and more likely to release songs on flexi-discs

in Dutch comic books than provide MP3s on their website, Shellac of North America will always be known for doing it their way and doing it well. Being able to operate completely outside the typical machinations of music, the trio carved out a sizeable niche in the sewage-infested gutters of underground rock & roll, churning out some excellent records along the way.

Started in an informal setting between infamous engineer and guitarist Steve Albini (ex-Big Black, Rapeman) and drummer Todd Trainer in 1992, Shellac came into full formation after Albini invited bassist Bob Weston to move to Chicago and employed him as an engineer at his studio. A clutch of singles soon appeared in 1993 and 1994 on Touch & Go and Drag City, somewhat following in the footsteps of Albini's Big Black, if only due to his trebly, cutting guitar work and deadpan vocals. The odd rhythms of Trainer and seismic bass of Weston clearly removed Shellac from any of the members' previous involvements. The trio's first LP, *At Action Park*, appeared in late 1994. Four years passed until their proper follow-up, *Terraform*, which was recorded much earlier than its release date but was delayed due to artwork clearance. Recorded on various dates in 1998 and 1999, their third full-length, *1000 Hurts*, was released in the late summer of 2000. —*Andy Kellman*

● **At Action Park** / Sep. 1994 / Touch & Go ♦♦♦♦♦
Shellac's first three singles (especially *Uranus*) suggested that Steve Albini was moving into more subtle and dynamic territory after the musical and lyrical brutality of Big Black and Rapeman, but the group's first full-length album, *At Action Park*, proved that the misanthropic noisemaker responsible for *Atomizer* and *Songs About Fucking* was still very much present. "My Black Ass," "Dog and Pony Show," and "Il Porno Star" revealed Albini was still obsessed with sex, violence, and anti-social behavior, and the hard, metallic guitar figures of "Pull the Cup" and "Song of the Minerals" were as uncompromisingly abrasive as ever, with Albini's trademark engineering (dry, stark, and crystal clear) making the rough edges all the more punishing. But *At Action Park* does reveal a band more musically intelligent and imaginative than Big Black, and while it hits a good bit harder than the 7"ers that preceded it, Shellac is still significantly more concerned with the space between the notes than any of Albini's earlier projects. Just as importantly, in drummer Todd Trainer and bassist Bob Weston, Albini had found a human rhythm section that lived up to his exacting specifications, with Weston adding both melody and force with his thick, meaty tone and Trainer displaying both precision and an expressive abstraction behind the kit. And while Shellac's idea of a good time would still make most folks uncomfortable, there's a dark but genuine humor to a few of the cuts (especially "Il Porno Star"), and "Song of the Minerals" suggests Albini may actually feel compassion for one of his protagonists. *At Action Park* made it clear that Steve Albini was slowly but surely maturing, while stubbornly refusing to compromise in the process. —*Mark Deming*

The Futurist / 1997 / Touch & Go ♦♦♦
With Shellac's fans waiting patiently for the follow-up to *At Action Park*, the band oddly issued approximately 800 copies of this half-hour of voiceless experimentation to friends and family. Strangely popping up briefly on Touch & Go's release schedule, the record quickly vanished from it amidst rumors of its nature. The record accompanied a Canadian dance production, and it was deemed by the band a mediocre recording. So rather than flood the market with perceived twaddle, they decided to give the record to friends as a gift.

The Futurist does have its moments. Rather than proper tracks or songs, the record seems to have ten "movements," as each piece flows steadily into the next. Oscillator tweakings mixed with Morse code transmissions and overseas correspondence give way to brief guitar/bass/drum bursts. Skronking noise here, guitar twists there, and familiar band interplay every now and again à la "QRJ" (off *1000 Hurts*) double dutch with each other, never outlasting their welcome. The second side is the better of the two, including two excellent stompers. The last "movement" is the high point of the record, concluding with a bombastic outro.

More than anything, the band's reluctance in properly issuing *The Futurist* speaks volumes on how much twaddle is foisted on the general public. Shellac might not be the most prolific band on the planet, but you can pretty much bet without fault that what they *do* release will be up to snuff. Thanks to one of their friends leaking this record into the dark dungeons of file sharing, this may be reaching more ears than the band wished, and certainly they would have preferred that it not reach the ears of lowlife scribes. It might be second-rate Shellac, but second-rate Shellac is just fine. —*Andy Kellman*

Terraform / Feb. 10, 1998 / Touch & Go ♦♦♦
Three and a half years is a long time between albums, especially for indie-rock bands. Though Steve Albini and Bob Weston were busy with their respective production careers, the wait between Shellac's 1994 debut album and 1998's *Terraform* doesn't seem to have done the group any good. What sinks *Terraform* more than anything else is the opening track, a ten-minute dirge with a repetitive riff and little else to recommend it. After that, the album gets better yet still sounds remarkably similar to the debut, if slightly less noisy (much of it was recorded at the Beatles' Abbey Road Studios). —*John Bush*

1000 Hurts / Aug. 8, 2000 / Touch & Go ♦♦♦♦
Don't expect *1000 Hurts* to open your ears to any new sonic vistas; Shellac's sound hasn't developed much. Are they yanking chains by periodically releasing selections from one extremely fruitful session? Only the boys and a few tape operators know. No other band sounds like Shellac, which legitimizes this status quo. The jagged scrapes of Steve Albini's guitar, the somewhat laggard bass from Bob Weston, and the awkward-yet-steady time keeping of Todd Trainer's drums remain in top form. For what it's worth, Albini's guitar does seem to gain more grace as the years go on—just watch out for the ugly jazz fusion lick that ends "Canaveral."

Raw, no-frills production? Absence of overdubs? Goofy time signatures? They're all a part of the cauldron. As with the band's previous LPs, you get healthy doses of extended hypnotic doodling, rumbling mid-tempo tantrums, speedy jabs, and a joke or two. And as with any recording featuring the wordsmithery of Steve Albini, one fights the urge to transcribe the whole damn thing. Often humorous, occasionally unsettling, but always intelligent and thought-provoking, Albini's lyrics are a bit nastier than the past couple records. "Prayer to God" is no plea for forgiveness or well-wishing; he asks his lord to kill an ex-girlfriend and her accomplice. "Canaveral" dreams of whisking an enemy to outer space, in hopes that he'll become fertilizer.

If you know the band's sound, your mind should have been made up prior to reading this. You know what to expect, aside from it not being quite as fantastic as *At Action Park*, but certainly better than *Terraform*. True to Shellac form, the record is a sound purchase. Within the domain of atonal, anti-commercial rock & roll, very few are on their level. *—Andy Kellman*

Pete Shelley

b. Apr. 17, 1955

Vocals, Guitar / New Wave

Pete Shelley, the leader of the seminal punk band the Buzzcocks, actually had recorded a solo album in 1974, two years before the Buzzcocks had formed. Released in 1979, *Sky Yen* was a collection of electronic music that didn't sound much like his full-time band's blistering guitar-pop, yet it did contain the roots of his solo career. After the Buzzcocks disbanded in 1981, Shelley began a solo career which incorporated the electronic experimentations of *Sky Yen* with the pop sensibilities of his punk singles. Released in 1981, *Homosapien* showcased this musical merger and resulted in the U.K. hit single, "Homosapien." The following year Shelley released *XL1*, which added more guitar to his dance-oriented synth-pop. Three years later he released his final solo album, *Heaven and the Sea*, which failed to capture an audience. Shelley then joined the short-lived band Zip; after its breakup, he rejoined the reunited Buzzcocks in 1988. *—Stephen Thomas Erlewine*

Sky Yen / 1979 / Groovy ✦✦

● **Homosapien** / Dec. 1981 / Razor & Tie ✦✦✦✦✦
Homosapien, for most intents and purposes, was Pete Shelley's first official solo album, and it's a pretty forceful break from the Buzzcocks' patented punk-pop rush. Shelley delved deeply into synth-pop and dance rhythms, somewhat tempering those robotic influences with slight glam and gloomy psychedelic influences. While the songs might not be as consistent as his best Buzzcocks albums, there are a number of terse pop gems much in the vein of the classic title track. *—Stephen Thomas Erlewine*

XL 1 / 1983 / Genetic/Arista ✦✦✦
With *XL1*, Pete Shelley integrates layers of guitar into the electronic synth-pop he essayed on his solo debut, *Homosapien*. While the result isn't quite as bracing as its predecessor, the music benefits from the guitar—it sounds edgier, making the record fairly captivating. There's still some weak material on the record, but "Telephone Operator" and "If You Ask Me (I Won't Say No)" are terrific, ranking among Shelley's best. *—Stephen Thomas Erlewine*

Heaven & the Sea / 1986 / Mercury ✦✦✦
Heaven & the Sea isn't quite as dance-oriented as Pete Shelley's first two albums, nor does it have the nervous pop energy that was a hallmark of those records and his work with the Buzzcocks. Instead, it's a layered and textured release, given a polished, mature production which ironically only emphasizes the lack of notable songs. There are a handful of relatively strong cuts on the record, but even they don't match the high points of its two predecessors. *—Stephen Thomas Erlewine*

The Shirelles

f. 1958, Passaic, NJ, **db.** 1982

Brill Building Pop, Girl Group

The Shirelles were instrumental in defining the girl-group sound, and were one of the style's most successful acts between 1960 and 1963, when they placed six singles in the Top Ten. Bridging doo wop and uptown New York pop-soul, the group projected a beguiling mixture of tenderness and innocence that was grounded in R&B as much as pop/rock. Forming as high school classmates in New Jersey, the Shirelles came under the wing of manager Florence Greenberg, who also ran the Scepter label. Many of their classic early sides featured innovative, occasionally string-laden production by Luther Dixon, who also penned several of their greatest songs. Top Brill Building pop songwriters like Goffin-King, Bacharach-David, and Van McCoy also supplied the group with material. "Will You Love Me Tomorrow," "Baby It's You," "Foolish Little Girl," "Soldier Boy," "Dedicated to the One I Love," and "Mama Said" were their biggest hits, but they also cut a number of less-famous sides, including "Boys," which (like "Baby It's You") was covered by the Beatles on their first LP. After mid-1963, the Shirelles were unable to dent the Top 40, although they recorded several songs, including the original version of "Sha La La" (covered for a hit by Manfred Mann). The group recorded well into the '70s, updating their sound into a more soul-oriented mode. *—Richie Unterberger*

Baby It's You / 1962 / Sundazed ✦✦✦
The best songs on here—the title track, "Big John," "A Thing of the Past," "Make the Night a Little Longer," "Soldier Boy," and "Putty in Your Hands"—are available on the Rhino best-of double album. Still, it's a pretty solid effort for its day, featuring state-of-the-art orchestral early-'60s New York girl-group production and decent songwriting. *—Richie Unterberger*

A Shirelles & King Curtis Give a Twist Party / 1962 / Sundazed ✦✦✦
A rather strange concept for an early-'60s album, pairing the Shirelles, then at the peak of their success, with R&B/soul sax great King Curtis. It's not so much a collaboration as an alternation; Curtis gets three instrumentals to himself, and sings "I Got a Woman" and another cut. King does duet with the girls on "I Still Want You," and the Shirelles handle the rest of the material, mostly written by their chief producer/songwriter Luther Dixon, in a much more up-tempo vein than their famous singles. No hits on this record, which is respectable but not terribly exciting, and a bit schizo in concept. *—Richie Unterberger*

Anthology (1959-1964) / 1986 / Rhino ✦✦✦✦✦
In the course of eight years, Rhino came out with two separate but very similar Shirelles anthologies. The first was 1986's *Anthology: 1959-1964*, followed by *The Very Best of the Shirelles* in 1994. Both are 16-song CDs, and many of the essential hits that were included on *Very Best* were also found on this CD, including "Tonight's the Night," "Dedicated to the One I Love," "Mama Said," and "Will You Love Me Tomorrow" (as well as "Boys," "A Thing of the Past," "Soldier Boy," and "Big John"). The main reason *Very Best Of* has a slight edge over this disc is because of its inclusion of the 1958 doo wop classic "I Met Him on a Sunday (Ronde-Ronde)," which is missing from *Anthology*. Both CDs, however, are full of gems that would greatly influence countless girl groups. These songs were undeniably seminal, and the late-1950s/early-1960s harmonies of the Shirelles would directly or indirectly influence everyone from the Supremes, the Marvelettes, the Shangri-Las, and Martha & the Vandellas in the 1960s to LaBelle, First Choice, the Three Degrees, and the Pointer Sisters in the 1970s. How many groups who influenced the Go-Gos and Blondie also had an impact on En Vogue? The importance of the Shirelles hits found on this CD cannot be overstated. *—Alex Henderson*

Lost & Found / Dec. 1, 1995 / Ace ✦✦

★ **25 All-Time Greatest Hits** / Jul. 27, 1999 / Varese ✦✦✦✦✦
An excellent 26-song single-disc collection that has all of the significant hits and several very fine low-charting 45s and B-sides. Some good tracks are missing, however, notably "Putty" (which the Yardbirds covered) and Goffin-King's "Make the Night a Little Longer." Rhino's *Anthology* double LP still has a tiny edge in song selection if you can find it, but if you're not real picky this is certainly a quality summary of their career highlights. There are also a few items that don't show up on all the best-ofs, like the 1961 B-side "The Things I Want to Hear" and the small 1964 hit "Thank You, Baby." *—Richie Unterberger*

Shirley & Lee

f. 1951, New Orleans, LA, **db.** 1963

New Orleans R&B, R&B

Shirley Goodman and Leonard Lee, born just ten days apart in 1936, scored three massive R&B hits before either one of them were 20 years old: "Feel So Good," "Let the Good Times Roll," and "I Feel Good" were all written by the talented young couple. They had one trait in common among their recordings; this New Orleans-based duo almost never sang in harmony, let alone together at all. Early in their careers, Shirley & Lee became known as "the Sweethearts of the Blues," a nickname given not for their personal relationship, but for their romantic sagas of their songs, which often bordered on telling a fictional soap opera story line about two lovers. Their fans would buy the singles simply to keep up with the continuing story of the two sweethearts. Eventually, the audience seemed to be tiring of the soap opera, so Shirley & Lee moved on to new lyrical subject matter. By the middle of 1957, they were back on top, this time with the biggest hit in their careers. Goodman and Lee borrowed one of New Orleans' most familiar refrains and built a rocking tune around it called "Let the Good Times Roll." The recording was an instant smash and received substantial airplay, climbing up the charts in the process. It sold well over one million copies and for more than 40 years has been a staple of oldies play lists. Other tunes followed—"I Feel Good" and "The Flirt" among them—but like many acts, Shirley & Lee were never able to recapture the nationwide success of their biggest hit. After a few final singles in 1962-1963, the "Sweethearts of the Blues" decided to call it a day. *—Bryan Thomas*

Legendary Masters Series, Vol. 1 / Mar. 16, 1990 / EMI America ✦✦✦✦✦
The Sweethearts of the Blues were a ragged duo at best, with Shirley Goodman's intonation flying all over the place and Leonard Lee's droning baritone sounding unfazed no matter what was going on. But the duo also had a sound that was totally unique (if you've never heard them, then there's simply no one else that *sounds* like them) and produced one R&B hit after another, including the epochal "Let the Good Times Roll" and "I Feel So Good." This is a reissue of a reissue, Collectables' 1995 repackage of the original 1991 EMI Masters set on this New Orleans twosome, and it's a pip. If you dig New Orleans music, you gotta have this one for the collection. Weird, wild, and wonderful, just like the city it emanates from. *—Cub Koda*

● **Let the Good Times Roll** / May 2, 2000 / Ace ✦✦✦✦✦
The track listing of this 30-song disc is based on the 1973 double-LP Shirley & Lee compilation in United Artists' *Legendary Masters* series, with "I Feel Good" substituted for "Do You Mean to Hurt Me So." Spanning their 1952-59 work for Aladdin, it's comprehensive enough to serve as a best-of, particularly as it included the four songs that are by far their most famous cuts: "Let the Good Times Roll," "I'm Gone," "I Feel Good," and "Feel So Good." As the American best-of CD compilation *Legendary Masters* (issued first on EMI America, then on Collectables) has only 20 numbers, one might presume that this 30-track anthology has the edge. It doesn't make the *Legendary Masters* CD redundant, though, as *Legendary Masters* has seven songs that don't appear here. At any rate, *Let the Good Times Roll* will almost certainly be a sufficient overview of the duo's prime output for those who haven't picked up a Shirley & Lee greatest hits anthology yet. Truth to tell, for most listeners 30 Shirley & Lee songs is more than enough, as the accomplished, good-timey New Orleans R&B/rock groove gets pretty similar-sounding over the course of an hour-plus. One thing you could note is how the contrasting male-female duet

style of Shirley & Lee was influential on early ska and reggae productions from Jamaica; listen to "Marry Me" for one instance in which Shirley & Lee themselves played calypso/Caribbean rhythms. It's also interesting to note that almost all of the material on this disc was self-penned, an impressive feat for teenage R&B singers of the '50s. *—Richie Unterberger*

Michelle Shocked

b. Feb. 24, 1962, Dallas, TX

Vocals, Guitar / College Rock, Alternative Folk, Anti-Folk, Alternative Pop/Rock, Singer/Songwriter, Urban Folk

According to her own, undoubtedly semi-fictional account, Michelle Shocked was born Michelle Johnston in Dallas, TX, in 1962, where she spent her early childhood travelling around army bases. After being introduced to country bluesmen Big Bill Broonzy and Leadbelly and contemporary songwriters Guy Clark and Randy Newman, she spent the next several years exploring the folk underground, spending the early '80s in Austin, where she began honing her own songwriting skills. The next few years were chaotic—she spent time in San Francisco, Amsterdam, New York, and was briefly committed to a mental hospital by her mother.

In 1986, Shocked attended the Kerrville Folk Festival, where English producer Pete Lawrence was impressed by her campfire-side playing and recorded her on his Sony Walkman. The recordings surfaced in the fall of that year as *The Texas Campfire Tapes* and became a surprise hit in England, eventually topping the independent charts. The success led to her signing with Mercury Records in 1988. *Short Sharp Shocked*, displayed even more talent, combining the informal, tradition-rooted folkiness of *The Texas Campfire Tapes* with a strong postmodern feminist perspective and punk attitude. In an unexpected move, Shocked returned in 1989 with *Captain Swing*, a '40s-style big-band swing outing that shocked her fans initially but had no shortage of strong material. In 1991, she took something of a step back with *Arkansas Traveller*, a rootsy collection that covered all forms of early American, homegrown music. In 1993, Mercury finally became fed up with her confusing style jumping and refused to release her proposed gospel album. She then left on a solo tour, selling her newly recorded, independently produced, *Kind Hearted Woman*. Late in 1995, Shocked began legal action against Mercury Records to break her contract.

By 1996, Shocked was released from Mercury and another independent release, *Artists Make Lousy Slaves*, was sold at her shows. *Kind Hearted Woman* was picked up for release by Private Music in 1996. *—Chris Woodstra*

The Texas Campfire Tapes / 1986 / Mercury ♦♦♦
Her debut, recorded live around a campfire on a Walkman, is a wildly overrated but interesting introduction to her talents. *—John Dougan*

★ **Short Sharp Shocked** / 1988 / Mercury ♦♦♦♦♦
Michelle Shocked is asked in the song "Anchorage," "What's it like to be a [New York City] skateboard punk rocker?" Perhaps it takes a flashback like *Short Sharp Shocked* to fully answer the more interesting question, "How did you get there?" The album finds Shocked taking a semi-fond trip back to an East Texas childhood, and all of the defined roles, limited expectations, claustrophobia, and ultimate rebellion coming from that environment. Musically, she tackles the spectrum of rootsy folk in a warm way that shows not only a love for, but also a great deal of knowledge of the forms (producer Pete Anderson added a Nashville gloss to the recordings that shouldn't go unnoticed). The songs have a very personal, almost diary feel, but at the same time, they speak a universal language—none so poignant as the album's centerpiece, "Anchorage," a touching letter from an old friend. The cover photo, which shows Shocked restrained by police officers during a protest, indicates little about the music found within (save for the uncredited album closer, the hardcore punk work-up of "Fog Town" featuring MDC), but the music certainly reveals much about the protestor. *—Chris Woodstra*

Captain Swing / Oct. 1989 / Mercury ♦♦♦
Shocked made a big jump from *The Texas Campfire Tapes* to *Short Sharp Shocked*, but no one expected the direction she would take for *Captain Swing*. Rather than continuing as a folky singer-songwriter, she opted instead to take on '40s swing and big-band music, complete with horn-heavy arrangements and bright orchestration. And although the cartoon image of her on the cover gives a smirk and a sly wink, the album is surprising devoid of irony. She treats the genre with affection and she's obviously having a good time swinging. *Captain Swing* may have confused fans of *Short Sharp Shocked* (and the material isn't nearly as consistently strong either), but the album has several great moments, and most of all, it offers a good time. *—Chris Woodstra*

Arkansas Traveler / Oct. 1991 / Mercury ♦♦♦♦
Part three of the trilogy that began with *Short Sharp Shocked*, *Arkansas Traveler* focuses this time on American roots music of the South, mainly rural-blues and country; according to her theory in the album's liner notes, all of these songs are based on the legacy of blackface minstrels. Recorded with a mobile studio at various non-conventional locations around the country, it features an amazing array of guest musicians including Pops Staples, Doc Watson, and Gatemouth Brown. Those who were put off by the unexpected direction of *Captain Swing* will certainly welcome this return to form—her best since *Short Sharp Shocked*. *—Chris Woodstra*

Kind Hearted Woman / 1994 / Private Music ♦♦♦
Shocked released *Kind Hearted Woman* on her own, selling it exclusively at live shows, when she ran into troubles with Mercury Records. Accompanied by only her own Stratocaster playing, she has produced her most touching, personal document to date even though the subject matter is decidedly dark and bleak. Private Music reissued the album in 1996 . *—Chris Woodstra*

Artists Make Lousy Slaves / 1996 / Independent ♦♦♦
Independently produced and sold during her *First Annual Underground Test Site Tour* in the Spring/Summer of 1996, *Artists Make Lousy Slaves* is a collaboration with Hothouse Flowers' Fianchna O'Braonain—the two wrote most of the material together and appear as the sole musicians. The title refers to her long battle to free herself from her former label, Mercury Records, but while this album certainly gives the impression of relief, it fails to capture the raw energy and joy of the tour which celebrates the dissolving of her contract—the songs are instead, pleasantly reflective, and low-key. It may not be groundbreaking or particularly representative, but *Artists Make Lousy Slaves* is a nice treat for those fans lucky enough to have witnessed the tour. *—Chris Woodstra*

Mercury Poise: 1988-1995 / Nov. 5, 1996 / Mercury ♦♦♦♦♦
With a title that plays on Graham Parker's corporate-venomous song and EP *Mercury Poisoning*, the disc skims a dozen layers of feminist-folk-punk cream from three eclectic albums (folk-rock, swing-jazz, and Southern roots music) recorded for the label between 1988 and 1991, plus tracks previously only available on soundtracks, compilations, and 1994 indie release *Kind Hearted Woman*. *—Roch Parisien*

Good News / Mar. 1998 / Mood Swing ♦♦♦♦
A wonderful, somewhat eclectic set from Michelle Shocked. Released as an independent, numbered, and strictly limited edition (2500 copies), this CD was mainly sold at her concerts during her 1998 tour of colleges and universities. It's a shame that it wasn't more widely available, because it really is a great CD. It shows many different sides of Michelle, including an outstanding gospel song, "Can't Take My Joy." One of Michelle Shocked's most endearing qualities is that one is never sure what she will do next. This CD is no exception, as it ranges from straight-out rock & roll ("Good News") to rhythm & blues ("Little Billie") and everything in between. Her voice is strong, and this is particularly highlighted in the folky, truly beautiful "No Wonder." Her backup band is also quite strong, capable of switching musical genres rapidly and successfully. Her lyrics, as usual, are strong, with a wonderful swipe at gutter press in the song "Tabloid." Obviously the independent route has given Michelle Shocked a great deal of freedom to express herself musically and lyrically. But the independence that makes this CD great also gives rise to a major problem: the difficulty in obtaining a copy. This deserves to be played on radio, at home, and should be front-racked at all CD stores. As it is, this CD is well worth the search. *—Aaron Badgley*

Shoes

f. 1975, Zion, IL

Power Pop, New Wave

It may not have been the hip thing to do at the time but Shoes carried on the pure pop traditions of the Beatles and the Raspberries during the late '70s and early '80s with a charming innocence and execution unmatched by the more derivative bands lumped into the category "power pop." After one self-made and extremely limited album (only 300 were pressed), 1975's *Un Dans Versalles*, and the unreleased *Bazooka* (1976), they recorded their true debut for national consumption, *Black Vinyl Shoes*, and released it on their own label, Black Vinyl Records. Though it was barely distributed, enough critics and key people heard the record to start a word-of-mouth buzz. Eventually, Greg Shaw, the head of Bomp! Records, heard the record and arranged for the band to release one single, the brilliant "Tommorrow Night"/"Okay," on his label. A contract with Elektra Records soon followed. Elektra released the group's next three, textbook power-pop albums: *Present Tense* (1979), *Tongue Twister* (1981), and *Boomerang* (1982). Despite the instantly accessible, catchy quality of the songs, they were unable to achieve mainstream success—among specialists however, these albums, along with the debut, stand as the high points of the era. *—Chris Woodstra*

Black Vinyl Shoes / 1977 / Black Vinyl ♦♦♦♦♦
Most bands start out trying to bang their songs together in someone's living room, but Shoes certainly made more of that experience than most people. Jeff Murphy, Gary Klebe, and John Murphy were three pop obsessives from Zion, IL, who bought a four-track, found a drummer (Skip Meyer), and started putting songs on tape in Murphy's living room with all the care their primitive circumstances would allow. While the results were intended to be used only as a demo, *Black Vinyl Shoes* eventually attracted the attention of PVC Records, who gave the homemade set a nationwide release; the album's positive press eventually earned the band a major-label deal. Like their contemporaries and kindred spirits the Scruffs, Shoes were one of the few interesting pop bands to emerge in the mid- to late '70s who were very obviously *not* new wave; Shoes were pop classicists in the manner of the Beatles and the Raspberries, and if their low-tech recording setup dictated a leaner and more basic approach than the Fab Four, the thick guitar lines, smooth backing harmonies, and trickier-than-they-sound melodic structures made it clear their back-to-basic style was a nod to past rock glories as much as a call to jangly arms. But Shoes also had their own set of quirks to bring to the table (again like the Scruffs, Shoes had an unusual perspective on the male/female relationship), and there's an understated, off-kilter wit to songs like "Tragedy," "Do You Wanna Get Lucky?," and "Capital Gains" that's as delicious as the band's rich, satisfying songcraft. *Black Vinyl Shoes* is an album whose somewhat primitive production actually works in its favor; with 15 tunes to record and only four tracks on hand, Shoes made a record that was about melodies, hooks, and harmonies, and the result was an album that helped kick start the '80s pop revival—and still sounds fine almost a quarter of a century later. *—Mark Deming*

Present Tense / 1979 / Elektra ♦♦♦♦♦
Their major-label debut suffers from a bit of overwhelming post-production, but there isn't enough interference to ruin this great collection of tunes. The CD version is a twofer which combines *Present Tense* with *Tongue Twister*. *—John Dougan*

Tongue Twister / 1981 / Elektra ♦♦♦

After having recorded one of the finest albums of 1977 (*Black Vinyl Shoes*) on a four-track in the guitar player's living room, it's not surprising that when Shoes were signed to a major label, they would want to explore how the other half lived with the bigger and more bombastic production of *Present Tense*. *Tongue Twister*, however, found Shoes in more audibly sympathetic territory; though the album's crisp, well-detailed mix is significantly more hi-fi than the group's debut, producer Richard Dashut's approach is pleasingly lean and concise, with John Murphy and Jeff Murphy's harmonies and the efficiently hooky guitar lines of Gary Klebe and Jeff Murphy clear in the forefront at all times. In many ways, *Tongue Twisters* suggests what *Black Vinyl Shoes* might have sounded like with more time and money but a similar set of aesthetic choices; it also boasts a set of great pop songs (played with a few notches more energy than on their debut), including the spunky "Your Imagination," the plaintive yet lustful "Karen," the surprisingly hard-rocking "She Satisfies," and "Girls of Today," which amusingly covers territory the Who staked out on "Pictures of Lily." Oh, and no matter what it might sound like, there are no keyboards on *Tongue Twisters*, a brave creative choice for a pop band with an eye on the charts in 1981. If *Tongue Twisters* didn't break nearly as much ground as Shoes' debut, it's still a superb bit of guitar-driven pop, and one of the band's most purely enjoyable efforts. —*Mark Deming*

Boomerang/Shoes on Ice / May 1982 / Black Vinyl ♦♦♦♦

In an early interview, the Beatles were asked why they chose their name, to which Paul McCartney replied, "for all you know, we might have been called the Shoes." Fortunately, there *is* a band called the Shoes and this is one of the finest pop albums ever made. Back on their own territory and producing their own records, this is the album that *Tongue Twister* should have been. It stands as one of their best. [A live EP, *Shoes on Ice*, which came with the initial pressing of the album, has now been added to the CD version.] —*Jim Worbois*

Silhouette / 1984 / Black Vinyl ♦♦♦

Now reduced to a three-piece (John Murphy, Jeff Murphy, and Gary Klebe), the band recorded their fifth album independently in their home studio in Illinois. A pleasant, though unexceptional album, *Silhouette* is a softer, more keyboard-dominated effort. Without an American outlet they (left Elektra prior to recording), this album was only available in Europe until the band's own label, Black Vinyl Records, reissued it in the late '80s. —*Chris Woodstra*

● **Shoes' Best** / 1987 / Black Vinyl ♦♦♦♦♦

A 22-song compilation, this is a wonderfully comprehensive overview of this wonderful band. Good liner notes by former *Trouser Press* head honcho Ira Robbins. —*John Dougan*

Stolen Wishes / 1989 / Black Vinyl ♦♦

After the release of the superb *Shoes' Best* compilation reminded pop fans of the group's great songs and deliciously idiosyncratic style (and reintroduced Shoes to the creative and financial benefits of going D.I.Y.), the band (now officially shorn of drummer Skip Meyer) headed back to their studio and recorded *Stolen Wishes*, their first album in five years (and first American release since *Boomerang* in 1982). Somewhere along the way, Jeff Murphy, Gary Klebe, and John Murphy appeared to have gotten over their collective distrust of keyboards, and the bright, punchy sound, peppy tempos, and frequent synthesizer washes of *Stolen Wishes* sound like a studied attempt at a more "contemporary" sound from a band who seemed perfectly content to be slightly anachronistic a decade earlier. Oddly enough, as a result, 1989's *Stolen Wishes* seems significantly more dated several years later than the guitar-based popcraft of the albums Shoes released between 1977 and 1982, which still sound pleasingly timeless. (And who told the guys those pseudo-Duran Duran haircuts they're sporting on the cover were a good idea?) But Shoes were a band who had never been short of great pop songs in the past, and their gifts as writers did not fail them on *Stolen Wishes*; the album is loaded with great hooks and hummable melodies, and their vocal harmonies are spot-on throughout. *Stolen Wishes* isn't quite as strong as Shoes' earlier work, but it's still a strong dose of well-crafted pop, and dozens of the bands who traveled in their wake would love to have songs as good as "Love Is Like a Bullet" or "Feel the Way I Do" to their credit. —*Mark Deming*

Propeller / 1994 / Black Vinyl ♦♦

Fret Buzz / May 2, 1995 / Black Vinyl ♦♦♦

As Is / 1996 / Black Vinyl ♦♦♦♦

The limited edition, two disc *As Is* is simply a delight for die-hard Shoes fans. Boasting a disc of 27 demos and unreleased tracks as well as the ultra-rare *Bazooka* and *One in Versailles* albums in their entirety–both released before their official debut, *Black Vinyl Shoes*–and a detailed booklet, this collection works well not only as a rarities collection but also a testament to the band's power-pop legacy. —*Chris Woodstra*

Shonen Knife

f. 1981, Japan

Indie Pop, Twee Pop, Alternative Pop/Rock

At their best, the Japanese punk-pop band Shonen Knife is an irresistible delight, combining sweet Beatlesque pop with buzzing Ramones power chords, singing about the schlockiest things pop culture has churned out. At their worst, the band's cuteness seems contrived, as if they were using their fractured English and obsession about Barbie Dolls, ice cream, and Hello Kitty as a deliberately cloying, cutesy marketing ploy. Even worse, at times it seems that their fans are not laughing with the band, they're laughing *at* their fascination with American kitsch culture and their bad English. Nevertheless, when taken on a strictly musical level, Shonen Knife's best records–including 1993's *Let's Knife* and

1997's *Brand New Knife*–and are truly intoxicating, rocking hard with a melody you can hum for days. They returned in 1998 with *Happy Hour*. —*Stephen Thomas Erlewine*

Pretty Little Baka Guy / Live In Japan / 1986 / Rockville ♦♦♦♦♦

The CD reissue of this album adds eight live tracks (some that go as far back as 1982, when they were barely teens!) and makes this hands-down the best Shonen Knife record available. On *Baka Guy*, their pop culture obsessions are clearly and humorously articulated ("I Wanna Eat Choco Bars" and "Ice Cream City"), and the record includes the best song ever about public bath houses, "Public Bath." Too often, cute, condescending terminology is used to describe Shonen Knife as though they were candy-floss teddy bears instead of a rock band. So, let's get one thing straight: this is a great rock & roll record by one of Japan's great rock & roll bands. —*John Dougan*

Shonen Knife / 1990 / Positive ♦♦♦♦♦

A superb collection of material previously available only in Japan on the albums *Burning Farm* and *Yama No Attchan*, covering Shonen Knife's early career from 1983-85. The purist in me has become increasingly disappointed with Shonen Knife's records, as they sound more and more like generic alternative rock. On these recordings there is a nearly palpable sense of joy that comes with the discovery that you've mastered four chords, can keep a steady beat, and are now considered a band. Also, this material is unforced, almost carefree and has little of the calculation that's creeping into their more recent work. Very simply, fabulous pop music. —*John Dougan*

712 / 1991 / Rockville ♦♦♦♦♦

"Good morning Shonen Knife freaks!" is the cry that opens *712*, Shonen Knife's last indisputably great record. The playing and songwriting has matured here, but not to the point where it begins to sound sterile or overly sophisticated. Of course, what would a Shonen Knife record be without a few goofy tributes to junk culture, as in "Fruit Loop Dreams" and "Expo '90"? There's a surprising cover of John Lennon's "Luck of the Irish" with vocal help from Redd Kross's Jeff McDonald. Note: the song "Blue Oyster Cult" is not a tribute to the band; it's about food poisoning from eating raw oysters. —*John Dougan*

● **Let's Knife** / Jan. 26, 1993 / Capitol ♦♦♦♦

Song titles "Twist Barbie," "Flying Jelly Attack," and "I Am a Cat" offer an accurate snapshot of this Japanese band…then there's the environmental anthem (?) "Bear Up Bison": "He has a right to live though he's ill ill ill-shaped/He's on the way to extinction/We only want what's best for him/Bear up bison never say die!" There's something fascinating about having Western culture thrown back at us in this quirky, unpretentious manner, and Shonen Knife are well on their way to becoming a cult favorite–for those who "get" it. —*Roch Parisien*

Rock Animals / Jan. 25, 1994 / Virgin ♦♦

Birds & The B-Sides / Mar. 5, 1996 / Virgin ♦♦♦

Eighteen odds and ends from the Shonen Knife '90s catalog: single-only cuts, import-only songs or versions, four live performances from their first British gig, and contributions to tribute albums to the Carpenters, Beach Boys, and Nilsson. Shonen Knife have a devoted following for a cultish alternative act, and fanatics will appreciate the thoughtfully assembled, thoroughly annotated collection of these rarities, which would set you back a few hundred dollars or so if you tried to track them down via their original sources. If you're not devoted enough to become a fan club member, it's neither a place to start nor an essential addition. The covers (especially of "Heatwave" and the Beach Boys' "Don't Hurt My Little Sister") generally outpace the original material, which doesn't vary as much as it could or should. —*Richie Unterberger*

Brand New Knife / Mar. 11, 1997 / Big Deal ♦♦♦

Brand New Knife finds Shonen Knife returning to punk-pop after the metallic experiments of *Rock Animals*, both for better and for worse. While the record offers more thrills than its predecessors, it sounds more tired than their late-'80s and early-'90s records. For longtime fans, there's enough strong moments to make *Brand New Knife* fun, but there's enough filler to make it disheartening as well. [Seven bonus tracks, sung in Japanese, were added to the American CD edition.] —*Stephen Thomas Erlewine*

Happy Hour / 1998 / Big Deal ♦♦

Shop Assistants

f. Edinburgh, Scotland

Indie Pop, C-86, Twee Pop

Following in the footsteps of fellow Scots the Jesus and Mary Chain, Edinburgh's nearly all-female Shop Assistants played noisy, raw, sweetly melodic pop also drawing on the Buzzcocks. First known as Buba and the Shop Assistants, the band's initial lineup comprised guitarist David Keegan, lead vocalist Alex Taylor, bassist Sarah Kneale, and drummers Ann Donald and Laura McBride; the group generally credited itself using first names only. Under its original name, the band pressed 500 copies of a single, "Something to Do," on Villa 21 in 1984; after shortening their name, the Shop Assistants released two critically acclaimed EPs (*Shop Assistants* and *Safety Net*). The latter, pressed on Keegan's 53rd & 3rd label (co-owned with a member of the Pastels) hit number one on the U.K. indie chart. Their only album, a self-titled effort for Chrysalis, appeared in 1986, the same year Donald was replaced by Joan Bride. The next year, Taylor left to form Motorcycle Boy; Keegan took a job as a skiing instructor, and the band was put on hiatus. A reunion took place in 1989 with Keegan, Kneale (now the lead vocalist), McPhail (the new bassist), and brand-new drummer Margarita. Two EPs, *Here It Comes* and *Big E Power*, came out in 1990, but Keegan would soon join the Pastels. —*Steve Huey*

● **Will Anything Happen** / 1997 / Overground ♦♦♦♦♦

The Shop Assistants represented all that was right and good with Scottish rock during the mid-1980s; their music brilliantly fused the gap between the three-chord noise of the

Jesus and Mary Chain and the shambling naiveté of bands like the Pastels, generating infectious, sweet-and-sour pop completely lacking in pretense and polish. *Will Anything Happen* is a superb retrospective combining the group's self-titled 1986 debut LP with tracks from their earlier EPs, and although a little of the Shop Assistants' primitive charms can go a long way, the spirit and sheer exuberence of their music is never less than infectious—an essential artifact of its times. *—Jason Ankeny*

Showaddywaddy

Glitter, Glam Rock, Rock & Roll

One of the finest rock & roll revival bands of the 1970s, Showaddywaddy also proved to be one of the most successful and enduring. Originally styled as a British answer to American retro masters Sha Na Na, Showaddywaddy then found themselves scooped up into the glam rock basket; indeed, at a time when rival giants Mud, Wizzard, and the Rubettes were also mining the 1950s for inspiration, Showaddywaddy swept ahead with barely a glance over their shoulder. Formed in 1973 in Leicester, England, the group entered and won television's *New Faces* talent show in 1974. They were rewarded with a support slot on David Cassidy's latest British tour and a recording contract with his thenlabel Bell. Paired with producer Mike Hurst, Showaddywaddy scored their first hits that same year, with the decidedly Gary Glitter-esque "Hey Rock & Roll" and "Rock & Roll Lady." They were swift to claim their own identity, however. The Christmas 1974 hit "Hey Mr. Christmas" and the new year's "Sweet Music" then gave way to a succession of remarkably individual 1950s covers—Eddie Cochran's "Three Steps to Heaven," Buddy Holly's "Heartbeat," Sam Cooke's "Chain Gang," interspersed with Showaddywaddy's own note- and stylistically perfect originals. Their foolproof instincts were proven when they recorded "Under the Moon of Love," a song originally recorded by Mud but passed over as a single. It gave Showaddywaddy their first British number one hit in December 1976 at a time when virtually every other band in the glam pack was now feeling fortunate if they scraped the Top 40. Indeed, Showaddywaddy wouldn't simply outlive their original peers. They continued racking up further hits into the early '80s. *—Dave Thompson*

● **Greatest Hits** / 1978 / Arista ✦✦✦
Less than three years into a U.K. chart career that ultimately survived for a decade, Showaddywaddy's first hits collection served up a staggering nine hits—staggering, because even at the height of the glam scene's flirtation with vintage rock & roll, who would ever have predicted such success for such a bunch of unrepentant Teddy boys? Hindsight insists, and the future would prove, that this is Showaddywaddy at its best. The sequence of smashes that opened with "Hey Rock & Roll" in May 1974 and peaked with the charttopping "Under the Moon of Love" in November 1976 saw the band swinging precociously between breathtakingly authentic originals and ferociously individual covers. Buddy Holly's "Heartbeat" (a number seven hit in September 1975) and Eddie Cochran's "Three Steps to Heaven" (a number two hit two months later) both blaze with a fever that is unquestionably a child of the glam-rock age, but was sired by the sound of the '50s regardless. Elsewhere, Sam Cooke's "Chain Gang" is rewired for orchestral flourishes and an almost frantic tempo, while "Johnny Remember Me," one of the most potently spooky love and death songs ever exhumed, is rendered with such theatrical flair that one can only regret that the band never made a video for it. There are a couple of weak links— both "Rock & Roll Lady" and "Sweet Music," the group's second and fourth hits respectively, capture Showaddywaddy somewhere between its initial wide-eyed exuberance and later studied confidence and are further hamstringed by the absence of a decent tune. In between times, however, the band scored one of the finest festive records of the age, the grin-like-an-imbecile frolic of "Hey Mr. Christmas," while one simply cannot praise the rockabilly doo wop of "Under the Moon of Love" too highly. There are other Showaddywaddy hits collections, and most are far more comprehensive than this one. But completeness isn't always a virtue—sometimes you just want a band at its most blindingly brilliant. Here 'tis. *—Dave Thompson*

Showaddywaddy [7T's] / 2000 / 7T's ✦✦✦

The Showmen

f. 1960, db. 1968

Pop-Soul, Northern Soul, New Orleans R&B, Soul

The Showmen were one of the R&B groups to bridge the gap between doo wop and soul in the early '60s, creating a buoyant, energetic fusion of harmonies and propulsive R&B beats. Released in the fall of 1961, their debut "It Will Stand" was a hit, particularly on the East Coast and in the New Orleans era, but it only peaked at number 61 on the pop charts. Nevertheless, the song's popularity never decreased and it became a hit three years later, when re-released on the Imperial label. On its second release, the single peaked at number 80 on both the R&B and pop charts. Between the two chart appearances of "It Will Stand," the Showmen kept recording and performing. During this time, they had no national hits, but "39-21-46" became a significant regional hit. In 1965, the group signed with Swan Records, but none of the ensuing singles became hits. In 1968, lead singer General Johnson left the band and moved to Detroit, where he formed the Chairmen of the Board. *—Stephen Thomas Erlewine*

● **It Will Stand** / Apr. 24, 1990 / Collectables ✦✦✦✦✦
A nice collection featuring the stuttering, sputtering vocals of General Norman Johnson and company, otherwise known as the Showmen. The title track was one of the great pieces of rock and R&B testimony. They never quite equaled it, although they produced some fine ballads and good up-tempo tunes. "It Will Stand" wasn't a hit the first time out of the box; it didn't make it onto the R&B charts until 1964, three years after it had peaked at number 61 on the pop charts, and then it only reached number 80. *—Ron Wynn*

Shudder to Think

f. 1986, Washington, DC

Indie Rock, Alternative Pop/Rock

Shudder to Think's hardcore punk background (courtesy of D.C.'s Dischord Records, also the home of Fugazi) isn't the best pointer toward their sound, since the group works in pop influences and a skewed sense of songwriting as well. Originally formed in 1986, the band's first lineup—vocalist/guitarist Craig Wedren, guitarist Chris Matthews, bassist Stuart Hill, and drummer Mike Russell—released two singles and one 1989 album (*Curse, Spells, Voodoo, Mooses*) before signing with the Dischord label. Shudder to Think released albums in 1990 (*Ten-Spot*), 1991 (*Funeral at the Movies*), and 1992 (*Get Your Goat*), and toured with Fugazi and the Smashing Pumpkins. Matthews and Russell had left by 1994; guitarist Nathan Larson and drummer Adam Wade replaced them, just in time for the band's first major-label contract. After signing with Epic, Shudder to Think released their fifth album, *Pony Express Record*, in 1994. Almost three years later in 1997 (during which time Wedren successfully overcame Hodgkin's Disease, Larson released an album with his side project, Mind Science of the Mind, and Wade was replaced with former Dambuilders drummer Kevin March), *50,000 B.C.* was released, which ultimately failed to push the band into the big-time.

The following year, the band focused their attention on soundtrack work for the indie films *First Love, Last Rites* (which included songs in various different musical styles sung by such alt-rock notables as Liz Phair, Billy Corgan, Robin Zander, and one of Jeff Buckley's last recorded works) and *High Art*, the latter featuring Brian Eno-like instrumental soundscapes. The same year, guitarist Larson left the band, which served as the final straw for the group, as they promptly split up. Wedren soon after began a solo career, playing shows in the New York City area and appearing on the soundtrack *Down to You* (the song "Didn't Mean to Do You Harm"), as well as supplying backup vocals to the Verve Pipe's 1999 self-titled release. *—John Bush & Greg Prato*

Curse, Spells, Voodoo, Mooses / May 1989 / Sammich ✦✦✦

Ten Spot / 1990 / Dischord ✦✦✦

Funeral at the Movies / 1991 / Dischord ✦✦✦

Get Your Goat / 1992 / Dischord ✦✦✦✦
On the fourth release by art-rockers Shudder to Think, *Get Your Goat*, the band created a record that with each additional spin reveals something new. The final studio album with guitarist Chris Matthews and drummer Mike Russell proved to be one of their most consistent. The album also turned out to be the first step toward their trademark textured sound (later achieved on *Pony Express Record* and *50,000 B.C.*), shedding the straightahead production of the previous *Funeral at the Movies* and *Ten Spot*. "Goat" and "Pebbles" are a couple of classic Shudder tracks that engage the listener with their genrebending music and nonsensical lyrics. The chromatic riffing of "Baby Drop" and "Rain-Covered Cat" confirms the group's technical proficiency, and "She Wears He-Harem" shows off Craig Wedren's maturing skills as a vocalist. This would also be the last release for Dischord Records by Shudder to Think, as the group inked a deal with Epic afterwards. The last release by all four original members more than met the standard set by the band's previous efforts. *—Greg Prato*

Funeral at the Movies/Ten Spot / 1993 / Dischord ✦✦✦✦✦
A compilation of two early releases, *Funeral at the Movies and Ten Spot* is part of Shudder to Think's beginning. The band's sound is surprisingly already complex and original, performed by their first lineup (which would splinter after one more release). *Funeral at the Movies* includes the first version of the recurring "Red House" (later re-recorded for the *Hit Liquor* EP and *50, 000 B.C.*), a manic version of Jimi Hendrix's "Crosstown Traffic," and the early fan favorite "Chocolate." The first half of the lengthy "I Blew Away/Ride That Sexy Horse" is a soaring R.E.M.-sounding rocker, while the second half is nothing more than feedback with talking over the noise. Parts of *Ten Spot* were recorded a full year prior to *Funeral*, but the sound and formula are strikingly similar. "About Three Dreams" contains some intricate bass and guitar work courtesy of Stuart Hill and Chris Matthews, while "Corner of My Eye" shows off Mike Russell's tribal drumming. And there are plenty of vocal heroics throughout, courtesy of the multi-talented Craig Wedren. The production and overall sound of the two albums aren't as textured as future releases would turn out to be, as the group opts for a more straightforward approach. However, this compilation was an important stepping stone for the future musical schizophrenia of Shudder to Think. *—Greg Prato*

Your Choice Live Series / May 3, 1994 / Your Choice ✦✦✦

● **Pony Express Record** / Sep. 13, 1994 / Epic ✦✦✦✦✦
Shudder to Think's major-label debut, *Pony Express Record*, boasted a better sound/production than past releases (courtesy of producer Ted Nicely and mixer Andy Wallace), and signaled more focused songwriting on the group's part. It was by no means a sellout, because even on earlier releases the group's ambitious songwriting was in full effect. And "focused" songwriting from Shudder to Think does not mean three-chord, predictable verse-chorus-verse compositions, either. *Pony Express Record* challenges the listener in many ways: stop/start riffing ("X-French Tee Shirt"), oblique lyrics ("Earthquakes Come Home"), often dramatic, Freddie Mercury-like vocals ("Gang of $"), and everything-but-the-kitchen-sink song structures ("No Rm. 9, Kentucky"). The music is consistently unpredictable, mixing jazz, metal, art-rock, folk, experimental, and alternative in the band's melting pot. And all of the songs boast strong melodies, which initially draw the listener in until you realize that there's more than meets the ear. *Pony Express Record* also marked the studio debut of guitar whiz Nathan Larson and drummer Adam Wade (Larson became an integral member of the group, helping to write five tracks, while Wade

left after the supporting tour). One of the most underrated rock records of the '90s. *—Greg Prato*

50,000 B.C. / Feb. 25, 1997 / Epic ✦✦✦✦
Pony Express Record might have been Shudder to Think's self-consciously difficult art-punk album, but *50,000 B.C.* is their move toward big-rock. Sporting a slick, polished guitar sound and anthemic harmonies, *50,000 B.C.* is more accessible than the rest of the group's catalog, at least on the surface. However, Craig Wedren's songs remain remarkably versatile and eclectic, ranging from Queen-style pomp rock and power pop to doo wop and folk-rock. Shudder to Think can pull off these stylistic variations with aplomb, but the smooth production gives the music the illusion of being more accessible than it is; it is melodic, but the melodies follow twisted paths, and Wedren's high, vibrato-laden voice can be off-putting to some. Which leaves Shudder to Think in an odd position. Their music is too odd for the mainstream, but it now sounds too slick for their old hardcore and indie-rock following, which means *50,000 B.C.* is the kind of eclectic post-punk that will primarily appeal to critics and record collectors. *—Stephen Thomas Erlewine*

Jane Siberry

b. Oct. 12, 1955, Toronto, Ontario, Canada
Vocals, Keyboards, Guitar / College Rock, Adult Alternative Pop/Rock, Singer/Songwriter
The idiosyncratic Canadian art-pop chanteuse Jane Siberry was born in Toronto, Ontario on October 12, 1955; after taking up the piano as a child, she began absorbing the classical and operatic inspirations which later distinguished her professional work. While earning a degree in microbiology, Siberry began performing at the local coffeehouse where she also worked as a waitress; ultimately, she used her tip money to fund her 1981 self-titled debut LP, a spartan offering spotlighting her ethereal vocal navigations through the eccentric rhythm changes and dramatic mood shifts which ornamented her abstract, atmospheric sound.

Three years later, Siberry resurfaced with *No Borders Here*, a more assured, cinematic collection highlighted by "Mimi on the Beach," an underground Canadian hit. The critical and commercial success of 1985's evocative *The Speckless Sky* brought her to the attention of Warner/Reprise for 1988's *The Walking*, a bold major label bow comprised of dense, epic-length soundscapes and subtle, intricate melodies. Despite considerable media acclaim, the album failed to dent the charts, and consequently Siberry's next record, 1989's *Bound By the Beauty*, reflected more commercial concerns, focusing on more direct production and succinct songwriting.

Siberry's next release was a 1992 career overview titled *Summer in the Yukon*; while comprised primarily of older material, one new cut—a drastic remix of *Bound By the Beauty's* "The Life Is the Red Wagon"—proved revelatory, its painless transformation into a club-ready dance track revealing the true elasticity of the singer's music. As a result, 1993's *When I Was a Boy*, produced in part by Brian Eno and Michael Brook, emerged as her most eclectic and ambitious work yet, while 1995's *Maria* found the singer recording with a jazz quintet. After growing disenchanted with the compromises of remaining on a major label, in May 1996 Siberry formed her own record company, dubbed Sheeba; *Teenager*, her first self-released effort, followed a month later. *—Jason Ankeny*

Jane Siberry / 1981 / East Side Digital ✦✦

No Borders Here / 1983 / Windham Hill ✦✦✦✦
The sound has a new-wave rock energy. The songs poke fun at "Extra Executives" as well as the artist, who muses that she'd probably be famous by now if she weren't such a good waitress. *—William Ruhlmann*

The Speckless Sky / 1985 / Windham Hill ✦✦✦✦
If "Mimi on the Beach" brought Jane Siberry some critical and commercial attention, "One More Colour" solidified it, with a more radio-friendly sound than before. Elsewhere on *The Speckless Sky*, Siberry refines the complex, arty soundscape work started on the previous album ("Vladimir Vladimir"), indulges in more surreal pop ("Map of the World (Part II)"), and tosses in an achingly beautiful straightforward song of love and loss ("The Taxi Ride"). Siberry's lyrics are often unencumbered by reality (think Laurie Anderson on hallucinogens), but the top-notch musicianship on the album helps Siberry keep at least one foot on the ground. *—Sean Carruthers*

The Walking / Jul. 1988 / Reprise ✦✦✦✦
Although Jane Siberry's big hit singles were a bit too pop-oriented to truly represent her work as a whole, even those who loved her more off-kilter side would have been hard-pressed to have foreseen the direction of *The Walking*. For most of the tracks, Siberry dispenses with standard pop construction, instead opting more for a sometimes-surreal narrative approach. This can be a bit trying for those who value succinctness; of the eight tracks, only one clocks in at less than six minutes. Musically speaking, however, the playing is still excellent and even some of the epics are pop gems ("Ingrid and the Footman"). It's her most accomplished work to date, but it's bound to lose the casual listener quickly. *—Sean Carruthers*

Bound By the Beauty / Aug. 1989 / Reprise ✦✦✦
Siberry has by now mastered an ability to make her unorthodox song forms (changing time signatures, surprising alterations of melody) work for her, and she's struck a balance between revealing too much and too little in her lyrics, so that such songs as "The Life Is the Red Wagon" really do reveal all the levels she's given it. And "Everything Reminds Me of My Dog" is one of the funniest and best songs of the year. *—William Ruhlmann*

When I Was a Boy / Aug. 3, 1993 / Reprise ✦✦✦✦
Considering the three-year delay since her last release (which reportedly saw one completed album scrapped altogether), Siberry has obviously gone through some intense soul searching to determine where her muse was to take her next. Judging by *When I Was A Boy*, she ended up retreating to some neutral ground that drew on several elements of her previous work without really taking things anywhere new. This is a very personal, introspective album, its intimate textures consistent with the ambient work that production collaborators Brian Eno and Michael Brook are well known for. Even average Siberry is still better than most of what gets foisted on the public as female vocalist pop these days. It's just that one has come to expect more from her—like surprises and wonder—rather than the sound of treading water. *—Roch Parisien*

● **A Collection 1984-1989** / 1994 / Duke/MCA ✦✦✦✦✦
This collection doesn't shy away from Jane Siberry's more extended, difficult, but ultimately rewarding work found on *The Walking*. Otherwise, this 14-track compilation gathers all the most accessible Duke Street-period material produced by a very unique vocalist—from "Mimi on the Beach" and "The Waitress" to "Bound By the Beauty." Missing in action: anything from her debut indie release or *When I Was A Boy*. *—Roch Parisien*

Maria / Aug. 29, 1995 / Reprise ✦✦✦
For those looking for more of the lush beauty found on the wonderful *When I Was a Boy*, *Maria* is a spectacular disappointment. Instead, the majority of the album consists of spare tracks with jazz and Latin inflections. Much of this can be traced to the fact that this is Siberry's first album without any of her original musicians playing a prominent role (Ken Myhr was the last to go). More problematic is that the material is far more slight than usual, including the album's closer, a 20-minute-and-counting "Oh My My." While repeated listenings bring out some of the album's charms, overall it leaves long-term Sib-heads feeling a bit unsatisfied. *—Sean Carruthers*

Teenager / Oct. 15, 1996 / Sheeba ✦✦✦

Hush / Sep. 15, 2000 / Sheeba/Sounds True ✦✦✦

Sigur Rós

f. Jan. 1994, Iceland
Post-Rock/Experimental, Alternative Pop/Rock
Named in part after a sister of one of the bandmembers, Reykjavik, Iceland's Sigur Rós ("Victory Rose") was formed by guitarist and vocalist Jon Thor Birgisson, bassist Georg Holm, and drummer Agust. Coming together while each of the members were teenagers in early 1994, the trio's first recorded song earned them a deal with Iceland's Bad Taste label. Their haunting debut LP, *Von* (Hope), was released in 1997, followed the next year by a collection of remixes from that album, *Recycle Bin*. Kjartan Sveinsson joined the band on keyboards and the band recorded 1999's strings-heavy *Ágætis Byrjun* (Good Start), earning them numerous accolades in their homeland and achieving platinum status in sales. Agust then departed and was quickly replaced by Orri Pall Dyrason. *Svefn-G-Englar*, their first release to be distributed outside of their native country, was hailed as NME's Single of the Week during September of 1999, launching a press hype steam-roller in the U.K. and—to a lesser extent—in the U.S. The *Ný Battery* single was issued in early 2000, the band's breakout year. British independent Fat Cat began distributing the band, increasing their accessibility beyond Icelanders and rabid journalists. April dates in England with Godspeed You Black Emperor! were capped off by an appearance at the All Tomorrow's Parties festival, and they also opened several dates of Radiohead's European tour before year's end.

Sigur Rós spent the first three months of 2001 away from the road, setting up their own studio and making their third album. Meanwhile, *Ágætis Byrjun* found a label in the U.S. and worldwide press became increasingly positive and varied; both *Entertainment Weekly* and the *Wire* ran features on the band. The group began touring again in April, playing more shows in Europe, a handful in the States, and several more in Japan throughout the remainder of the year. *—Andy Kellman*

Von / 1997 / Bad Taste ✦✦✦✦
The heaps of praise during 2000 surrounding 1999's *Ágætis Byrjun* brought surprisingly little attention to Sigur Rós' first record, released in 1997. Remaining available only through the band's Icelandic label, it took some effort to obtain, but those who did get a copy probably found it to be just as adventurous as *Ágætis*. Though darker and more fractured than the string-laden nooks of the follow-up, it's just as sprawling and outright bombastic. It's remarkable that such a young band would be this experimental at this stage in their lifespan, but the sheer breadth gets to be an albatross. Poking fun at '70s prog rock is just as easy as shooting at cement gargoyles on a suburban rooftop, especially when you're an indie kid or a fan of post-rock. But Sigur Rós makes Yes look like the Minutmen. Whittled down to 40 minutes, *Von* would be considerably more effective than it already is. As a mood setter, the 10-minute opening track really takes about three minutes to do what it needs, and a few other spots seem to drag on for the sake of sucking time. That doesn't prevent *Von* from being impressive, veering from Gavin Bryars-style aquatic minimalism to My Bloody Valentine-style dream pop. Varying states of isolationist ambience run throughout, whether evoking unrest or tranquil rest. You can practically envision a stray headboard floating through the *Sinking of the Titanic*-type passages, and the lush "Myrkur" comes from a planet where MBV's Kevin Shields and Kitchens of Distinction's Julian Swales are accorded the level or worship that Earth gives to Hendrix and Clapton. And then there's that voice, one of the most distinctly unintelligible voices since the Cocteau Twins' Liz Fraser. Boy? Girl? One would be hard-pressed to guess without liner notes. Based on pure sound, Von is just as much of a treat as the acclaimed follow-up. *—Andy Kellman*

Recycle Bin / 1998 / Bad Taste ✦✦✦
Recycle Bin puts songs from the group's debut LP in the hands of Gus Gus, Biogen, and an assorted cast of unfamiliars. As with most full-length remix affairs, the results are hit-and-miss. Somewhat disappointingly, only a handful of *Von's* tracks are retooled: two are

handled twice, and one is thrice reconstructed. Despite the overlap and mostly minor-league remixing, it's still lightly pleasurable. The primary hope for future Sigur Rós remixers would be to mess around more with the vocals. One can imagine that there must be a million and one things that can be done to the elfin, siren-like hymns. *—Andy Kellman*

• **Ágætis Byrjun** / 1999 / Bad Taste ✦✦✦✦✦
Two years passed since Sigur Rós' debut. By this time, the band recruited in a new keyboardist by the name of Kjartan Sveinsson and it seems to have done nothing but take the band to an even higher state of self-awareness. Even on aesthetic matters, Sigur Rós entitle their sophomore effort not in a manner to play up the irony of high expectations (ala the Stone Roses' *Second Coming*), but in a modest realization. This second album—*Ágætis Byrjun*—translates roughly to "Good Start." So as talented as *Von* might have been, this time out is probably even more worthy of dramatic debut expectations. Indeed, *Ágætis Byrjun* pulls no punches from the start. After an introduction just this side of one of the aforementioned Stone Roses' backwards beauties, the album pumps in the morning mist with "Sven-g-englar"—a song of such accomplished gorgeousness that one wonders why such a tiny country as Iceland can musically out-perform entire continents in just a few short minutes. The rest of this full-length follows such similar quality. Extremely deep strings underpin falsetto wails from the mournfully epic ("Viðar vel tl loftárasa") to the unreservedly cinematic ("Avalon"). One will constantly be waiting to hear what fascinating turns such complex musicianship will take at a moment's notice. At its best, the album seems to accomplish everything lagging post-shoegazers like Spiritualized or Chapterhouse once promised. However, at its worst, the album sometimes slides into an almost overkill of sonic structures. Take "Hjartað hamast (bamm bamm bamm)," for instance: there are so many layers of heavy strings, dense atmospherics, and fading vocals that it becomes an ineffectual mess of styles over style. As expected, though, the band's keen sense of Sturm-und-Drang is mostly contained within an elegant scope of melodies for the remainder of this follow-up. Rarely has a sophomore effort sounded this thick and surprising. Which means that "Good Start" might as well become of the most charming understatements to come out of a band in years. *—Dean Carlson*

Silkworm

f. 1987, Missoula, MT
Noise-Rock, Indie Rock, Alternative Pop/Rock
The noisy, bracing Seattle-based post-punk unit Silkworm formed in their native Missoula, MT, in 1987. Originally comprised of vocalists/guitarists Andy Cohen and Joel Phelps, vocalist/bassist Tim Midgett, and drummer Ben Koostra, Silkworm rose from the ashes of the band Ein Heit; a prolific and eclectic group from their inception (everyone but Koostra, who exited in 1989, contributed to songwriting duties), they issued their debut cassette *Advantage* in 1988. After two more tapes, 1989's *Girl Harbrr* and its companion *Girl Harbrr Out-Takes* EP, the remaining trio moved to Seattle in the opening weeks of 1990, quickly recruiting drummer Michael Dahlquist to complete the lineup.

Silkworm's "official" debut *L'ajre* followed in 1992, spotlighting the band's evolving, dissonant sound, anchored in Midgett's propulsive bass work. After the following year's... *His Absence Is a Blessing* EP, the quartet signed to the C/Z label for 1994's *In the West*, recorded by fellow Montana native Steve Albini (who continued to oversee the majority of the group's work). After 1994's strong *Libertine*, Phelps left the band, resurfacing in 1996 under the name Joel R.L. Phelps with the solo effort *Warm Springs Night*. As a trio, Silkworm signed to Matador and in 1996 issued *Firewater*, a sprawling yet finely honed set which ranked as their finest record to date. *Developer* followed in 1997, and a year later the group jumped to Touch and Go to issue *Blueblood*. *Lifestyle* was released in mid-2000. *—Jason Ankeny*

L'ajre / 1992 / Temporary Freedom ✦✦✦
Silkworm's first official LP is good, but merely decent when compared to what they would end up releasing. Still finding their feet, the land is a rather smooth one. The Joel Phelps-sung leadoff track "St. Patrick's Day" begins sparingly with his weary voice and raw acoustic and feedback-drenched electric guitars. Everyone kicks in with a squalor a minute and a half later, coming up with the closest thing to grunge the band produced. "Homoactivity" is one of the more melodic and outright poppy songs written by bassist Tim Midgett, with nifty double-tracked vocals. Overall, it's the bands' least developed, least distinct record. Nothing to be ashamed of, though certainly not as ugly as a junior-high yearbook photo. The grungier bits were all but done away with after this, as well as the early-'90s indie-style production values. Other highlights: Phelps' "Little Sister" and Midgett's "Scruffy." And if you want a chuckle, take a listen to drummer Dahlquist's "Shithead," a skittish ode to twentysomething confusion; two lines of the song are comprised of "All I want now is Sinéad O'Connor's breasts and lips against me in my bed" and "All I want now is some man who'll come and press his lips against me in my bed." Well what is it then? [*L'ajre* was included with a jumbled track order, sans "Pearl Harbor," on the 1998 compilation *Even a Blind Chicken Finds a Kernel of Corn Now and Then* on Matador.] *—Andy Kellman*

In the West / Jan. 25, 1994 / C/Z ✦✦✦✦
Finding a deep foundation in rhythmic post-punk and almost-funky bass lines from Tim Midgett, *In the West* successfully dislocates Silkworm from obvious influences. A three-headed songwriting team—matched with love for vaguely danceable beats and occasional guitar cacophony—liken them to Mission of Burma, but nothing here *truly* sounds like them. But similar to Burma, the pointiness of the guitars is balanced by warm, thick rhythms. Somehow, the band avoids sounding derivative. It would be easy for a four-piece with a knack for noise to step all over each other's toes, resulting in a boggled mess, but only during momentary blasts of cathartic guitar wailing does this become problematic. Otherwise, the wide spaces provided in the likes of "Garden City Blues," "Parsons," and "Enough Is Enough" are effective, making the sonic barrages all that more special.

Having three distinct songwriters in one band lends itself to a lack of cohesion, but that's forgiven through the excellence of each one. Joel Phelps' dramatic, scorched soul bearing is brought to the fore on "Dremate," resting uneasily for three minutes and eventually letting go, ending in screams chilling enough to make any emo vocalist run for mama. Whether Midgett's going on about romantic tension or his home town, frustration, wistfulness, and resentment flow throughout. Lines like "Enough is enough/Well come on/Give it up" read like a WASP song on paper, but Midgett's delivery is full of self-flagellation and fraught nerves. Andy Cohen adds one of the band's famed "history songs" on "Dust My Broom," name-checking General Pershing. *—Andy Kellman*

Libertine / Aug. 26, 1994 / El Recordo ✦✦✦✦
More jagged and range roaming than *In the West* (and slightly more direct), *Libertine* fully realizes a struggle between Silkworm's three fine songwriters. Aside from that, it's not a great deal different from its predecessor, released earlier that year. And it's just as good, if a bit lengthy. Andy Cohen checks in with the first two songs and is basically unheard of for the remainder, while Joel Phelps and Tim Midgett deliver three-song chunks at different stretches. Cohen provides another "history song" on "There Is a Party in Warsaw Tonight," with image-heavy lines like "There will be peace on mounds of teeth" and "The men are revolted, but they'll have to learn to keep their duty before their guts." Midgett really steps out on his own through "Cotton Girl" and especially the sharp "Couldn't You Wait," honing his ability of summing up romantic stumbling blocks and picking apart wrongdoers. Phelps' "Oh How We Laughed" is a wrenching breakup song, fractured and fraught as much as anything the Wedding Present recorded. Vocally it's one of the man's best, with an especially vicious last minute.

It was probably around here that people started using the sadcore and/or slowcore adjectives to describe the band. It's a completely unfitting term, as one listen to the rousing "Wild in My Day" or the dissonant "Cotton Girl" can attest. The use of loud guitars is too central. Though turtle-paced and introspective at times, Silkworm isn't sad. And when peeling back instrumentation, they're not fragile. They're just a different kind of rock band, plain and simple. Raw with no gimmicks and striking without over-indulgence. *—Andy Kellman*

• **Firewater** / Feb. 20, 1996 / Matador ✦✦✦✦✦
It's a difficult thing to have too many cooks in the kitchen, especially when all of them are iron chefs. Joel Phelps' semi-forced exit made a big difference. On one hand, it was bad: Phelps was an integral part of the band since its inception. And on the other, it was good: the pared-down sound fit the band well, and that's quite evident on the double vinyl *Firewater*.

Left to two voices, the band produces its most cohesive and precise set, despite it being their most broad; *Firewater* clocks in with 16 tracks at an hour long. Not a minute is mediocre, and everything sounds more measured and relaxed. Lyrically, the themes of each song tie in with just a couple concepts in mind, not suffering from the somewhat schizo topics of previous LPs. As the lone guitarist, Cohen spreads his wings, turning in some lengthy, Television-like solos. At times, his scorchy leads seem *twice* as loud as the bass and drums, but it's called for. Midgett's always propulsive bass becomes more of a centerpiece than an anchor, sounding its thickest yet.

Stripped bare to the degree of sounding awkward on the first few listens, a couple songs rely mainly on light rhythms and little else. The record's themes of alienation and inebriation are balanced by spells of dark humor. Cohen is always reliable for the occasional zinger, and Midgett's woes-of-the-road "Miracle Mile" provides many laughs at the band's expense. Also, the occasional cathartic yelping and complex structures seem to be done away with, in favor of more classic influences (the Stones-y "Lure of Beauty") and decreasing tangential incidents. Though one hates to say it in the wake of Phelps, *Firewater* sounds like a band that's lost its training wheels—fuller yet less cluttered. *—Andy Kellman*

Developer / Apr. 8, 1997 / Matador ✦✦✦
Developer takes many plays to weave its web. It's the band's most subtle album, containing some of their prettiest material. They don't assault the senses as often as usual, but it still has a couple heavy moments. Albini's again on board, and the record doesn't sound much different from its predecessor—nice crisp drums and good space between the bass and guitars. It's arguably their least fulfilling record, and it features their ugliest artwork—odd how those two characteristics go hand in hand. It's still fine, though.

Tim Midgett's "The City Glows" is one of the albums bright spots. On earlier records, Midgett's voice tended to break off-key when he attempted to roam past his range. Here, his voice is perfect: a soft, gentle croon. Lyrics like "There's a tug of war inside my skin/Got no control over anything" would usually require a cathartic wail, but drummer Michael Dahlquist and guitarist Andy Cohen make a soft, fluffy bed for Midgett to glide on top of. Cohen's narrative title track offers some witty lines: "Met a young slip and told him to strip/You work for me now, better get on the ship/Got to ride these boys hard when they're on my time/Havanas aren't free, nor is my ex-wife." All told, there are only one or two weak songs. Not a bad good-to-crud ratio for a band's weakest record.

Never the greatest unit shifters, Silkworm were dropped from the Matador stable after *Developer*. Was it the poor sales, or did Cohen never repay label head Gerard Cosloy for the money he asked for during "Never Met a Man I Didn't Like"? *—Andy Kellman*

Even a Blind Chicken Finds a Kernel of Corn: 1990-1994 / Jan. 20, 1998 / Matador ✦✦✦✦
Even a Blind Chicken thankfully reissues the majority of the impossible-to-find *L'ajre* LP and the excellent, vinyl-only *His Absence is a Blessing* EP, buttressing them with various singles and compilation tracks spanning five years. Aside from the *Blessing* EP, nothing

here quite lives up to the high standard of Silkworm's other works, but the compilation is essential for any fan. A self-released 1992 single comprising renditions of the Comsat Angels' "Our Secret" *and* Fleetwood Mac's "The Chain" is a major highlight. Silkworm makes the Comsats' song very much their own, supplanting the original's ringing guitars with Andy Cohen and Joel Phelps' agitated roars. Phelps and Tim Midgett repeatedly shout "We will never give it up" like a defiant mantra. There's even some atmospheric synth added in, just for the hell of it. The Fleetwood Mac cover is storming, done completely without irony, unlike your token ha-ha ska band cover. All vocalists chime in at various points as Midgett makes a bitchin' Lindsey. (Loudon Wainwright, Tom Petty, and the Walkabouts receive the Silkworm treatment.)

A couple moments of misguided infancy are kind of embarrassing, perhaps documented with the diehard in mind. The thrashy "Inside Outside" has an uncharacteristic bass lead-in and goofy vocal trickery. Phelps veers dangerously close to Geddy Lee-with-laryngitis territory.

A handy, well-warranted package, Midgett's often hilarious liner notes provide added value, recalling van wrecks and recording processes. He also lucidly expresses the instability of even the most durable bands, stating that they "... walk a thin line between satisfying individual egos and caving into them." Valuable words for any band. *—Andy Kellman*

Blueblood / Jul. 21, 1998 / Touch & Go ♦♦♦♦
After years of churning out albums of ponderous music matched with dark lyrics of alienation and alcoholic excess, Silkworm released *Blueblood*, their most accessible and melodic album. Unfortunately, despite having taken a more upbeat, riff-driven approach, the album lacks any signs of real stylistic growth, and it's somewhat disappointing in comparison with previous efforts. The traditional Silkworm sound is still there, though watered down. Tim Midgett's driving bass meshes with Andy Cohen's guitar solos as the band winds through its typical verse/chorus/verse format. The lyrics still have that world-weary, cynical quality as heard on "Said it Too Late" (The only reason that I won't die/ Is that I won't see you on the other side) and "Tonight We're Meat" (From inseam to hem I am a dying specimen/The local joke/ I'm a tramp/ Everybody rides my ramp). Although many consider this to be one of Silkworm's worst albums, it's still a good one, and it can be an enjoyable listen. It has its highlights, such as guest pianist Brett Grossman on "I Must Prepare (Tablecloth Tint)" and Michael Dahlquist's debut on lead vocals in "Empty Elevator Shaft." The problem is that it's not one of Silkworm's best or most inspired efforts. *—Tracy Frey*

Lifestyle / Aug. 8, 2000 / Touch & Go ♦♦♦♦
As a testament to Silkworm, a decade-plus existence has *not* resulted in a truncated amount of inspiration and vitality. Though the casual listener might not hear a great deal of difference from their previous three studio records, they're actually skipping merrily on that ever-treacherous tightrope concept: "Stay the same, but change." That line they are prancing on can't be walked upon by many others. On their eighth album (by their count), they've made something that's just as good as anything else they've released. Yet another record can divide the opinions of Silkworm fans as to what their finest hour is.

Thorough attention reveals increased writing proficieny and refinement, but the general makeup from recent efforts remains the same. Guest pianist/organist Brett Grossman reprises his standout role on *Blueblood* through the likes of "Contempt," and "Yrweb," serving the same important role that Nicky Hopkins provided on some of the Rolling Stones' best. Drummer Michael Dahlquist, who turned in a lead vocal turn on *Blueblood*, cashes in with one of the highlights, "Around the Outline." Andy Cohen again does fine double duty on rhythm and lead guitar. His get-it-over-with soloing does nothing to damage the craft. Tim Midgett's rumbling but agile bass again anchors the band's sound with Dahlquist's trademark kick drum leading the way. Lyrically, Cohen and Midgett's writing stacks up nicely with any of their best material. The themes largely remain the same; Cohen's has his wry anecdotal musings and Midgett has his personal phrasings of devotion and nostalgia.

In a word, Silkworm are durable. Continually churning out the classicist-without-being-retro goods, they hold an accomplished spot between the likes of CCR and the Minutemen. Not as famous as the former, and not as wild as the latter, but as fresh and timeless as both. *—Andy Kellman*

Silver Apples

f. 1967, New York, NY
Obscuro, Experimental Rock, Proto-Punk, Psychedelic, Electronic
Decades after their brief yet influential career first ground to a sudden and mysterious halt, the Silver Apples remain one of pop music's true enigmas: a surreal, almost unprecedented duo, their music explored interstellar drones and hums, pulsing rhythms and electronically-generated melodies years before similar ideas were adopted in the work of acolytes ranging from Suicide to Spacemen 3 to Laika. The Silver Apples formed in New York in 1967 and comprised percussionist Danny Taylor and lead vocalist Simeon, a bizarre figure who played an instrument also dubbed the Simeon, which (according to notes on the duo's self-titled 1968 debut LP) consisted of "nine audio oscillators and eighty-six manual manual controls... The lead and rhythm oscillators are played with the hands, elbows and knees and the bass oscillators are played with the feet." Although the utterly uncommercial record—an ingenious cacophony of beeps, buzzes, and beats—sold poorly, the Silver Apples resurfaced a year later with their sophomore effort, *Contact*, another far-flung outing which fared no better than its predecessor. After the record's release, the duo seemingly vanished into thin air, perhaps returning to the alien world from whence they purportedly came; however, in 1996 the Silver Apples mysteriously resurfaced, as Simeon and new partner Xian Hawkins released the single "Fractal Flow." American and European tours followed, and a year later a new LP, *Beacon*, was released to wide acclaim. The follow-up *Decatur* appeared in 1998, and was soon joined by *A Lake of Teardrops* (a collaboration with avowed fans Spectrum) as well as *The Garden*, the long-unreleased third and final effort from the original Simeon/Taylor partnership. However, on November 1, 1998, the Silver Apples' van crashed while returning from a New York gig; the accident left Simeon with a broken neck and spinal injuries, casting his continued musical career in grave doubt. *—Jason Ankeny*

Silver Apples [Kapp] / 1968 / Kapp ♦♦♦♦
The music on *Silver Apples* was unlike anything anyone had previously heard. Simeon layered his oscillators to create a collage of sounds that seemed to be recorded in outer space and then transmitted back to earth for your listening pleasure. The lead oscillator produced a tone akin to a theremin, contributing not only to the out-of-this-world quality, but its shaky, hyper-quiver added an air of tension. A hypnotic one- or two-chord rhythm pattern of bass notes held the tunes together, while Simeon played counter- and counter-counter-rhythms. Danny Taylor proved to be an innovative drummer, producing an array of interesting beats and fills. He also tuned his drums so he could change chords with Simeon. A song like "Lovefingers" would build with a drum and bass pattern, before bursting with waves of sound from the oscillators. Many of the tracks on *Silver Apples* have a subtle catchiness to them, possessing a pop mentality that isn't immediate. Simeon's "Simeon" is what pulls you in on first listens, but it is the songs that stay with you when you're away from the turntable. Compositions were kept short—all are four minutes or less, with the exception of the tribal "Dancing Gods"—further preserving the pop-song ethic. *—Bart Bealmear*

Contact / 1969 / Kapp ♦♦♦♦♦
Aside from Simeon's use of a banjo on a couple of tracks, the music on *Contact* does not differ from that of their debut. One aspect improved upon was the lyrics; many possess the same "cosmic" element found on *Silver Apples*, but others are full of bitterness, pain, paranoia, and confusion. In turn, the lead oscillator is used to greater effect, reflecting this newfound intensity. Simeon, who composed the text for five of *Contact*'s ten songs (he framed one song on *Silver Apples*, "Dancing Gods"), was largely responsible for this change. The record opens with "You and I," one of their best numbers, in which Simeon cuts out the hippie overtones present in the first album's lyrics and gets straight to the point. The text of "I Have Known Love," written by Simeon's girlfriend Eileen Lewellen, details love's all-encompassing power. "You're Not Foolin' Me" incorporates outside sound to drive home the written word, using a continuous, ringing telephone to illustrate the obsessive nature of love. "A Pox on You" and "Gypsy Love" further exploit the feelings one experiences once love is denied and the raw emotions that surface. "Confusion" features Simeon's banjo playing prominently. The playful, tossed-off script adds to its throwaway nature, although there is a line or two alluding to their pop leanings. The album closer, "Fantasies," involves Simeon guiding drummer Danny Taylor through the song and hints at the intuitive, trusting nature of their collaboration. This often hilarious track comes as a bit of a surprise, but works along with "Confusion" as a counterbalance to the darker lyrical content on *Contact*. *—Bart Bealmear*

• **Silver Apples [MCA]** / 1997 / MCA ♦♦♦♦♦
The group's two '60s albums (*Silver Apples* and *Contact*) were previously combined as a two-fer a few years before this identical release, but as this is on a major label, it will find wider distribution. It also benefits from the addition of newly penned historical liner notes from Simeon and vintage photos of the band, along with a diagram of the Simeon (the instrument) and Taylor's drum setup. *—Richie Unterberger*

Beacon / May 12, 1998 / Whirly Bird ♦♦♦
Beacon is the first Silver Apples album in nearly 30 years. Eight of the tracks are new songs that former exile and Silver Apples leader Simeon had composed with recent additions Xian Hawkins and Michael Lerner. The remaining three tunes are remakes from the Silver Apples' past. A reworking of "I Have Known Love" opens the record, and its lyrics are the most striking aspect, as they take on new meaning in relation to Simeon's reappearance: "I never heard the warning voice/I never knew I had a choice/Though I never wanted to return." "You and I" is given an appropriate chaotic reading; a wall of cacophonous keyboards forms in the instrumental breaks, like the video game Stargate on tilt. Of the originals, the vocal-less "Cosmic String" is the standout, developing a Trans Am groove (albeit looser), with sounds recalling the moment the beloved Pac-Man is caught by his nemesis, Speedy. *Beacon* is full of the influence of '80s video games, no doubt incorporated by the twentysomething Hawkins. *—Bart Bealmear*

The Silver Jews

f. 1992, VA
Indie Rock, Alternative Pop/Rock, Singer/Songwriter
Writer/musician David Berman formed the Silver Jews in 1989 with his friends, guitarist/singer Stephen Malkmus and drummer Bob Nastanovich. They played noisy, often improvised songs, mostly for the sheer enjoyment they got out of playing together after a hard day's work, often recording songs into people's answering machines; this basic idea of friends playing together in a spontaneous way became the Silver Jews' trademark style. Malkmus then founded Pavement with his childhood friend Scott Kannberg. As Pavement's acclaim and visibility grew, the notion arose that the Silver Jews were a "Pavement side-project," despite the fact Berman's writing, singing, and guitar playing led the band's music. However, the Jews' sometimes frustrating "Pavement connection" did bring some important attention to the band: Dan Koretsky, founder of the Chicago-based indie label Drag City, met Berman at a Pavement show; when he heard of the Jews' tapes, Koretsky offered to release them. On their first EPs for the label, 1990's *Dime Map of the Reef* and 1993's *The Arizona Record*, the band held to their ultra low-fi aesthetic and recorded both mostly on a walkman. Berman recorded the Jews' third album *The Natural*

Bridge in the summer of 1996 with members of New Radiant Storm King and Drag City artist/producer Rian Murphy. 1998's *American Water* featured a kind of reunion of the original lineup, with Malkmus returning to the fold. *—Heather Phares*

The Arizona Record [EP] / 1993 / Drag City ♦♦♦
The Arizona Record expands on the appealingly disheveled feel of the Silver Jews' first EP. This time around, Bob Nastanovich drums, but the band keeps the answering machine-fidelity of their recordings. "I Love the Rights" and "Jackson Nightz" feature competitive duets between Berman and Malkmus, while "West S" and "The War in Apartment 1812" have the sunny, sprawling feel that warmed the Jews'—and Pavement's—future recordings. "Welcome to the House of the Bats" captures the group's random, offhand sense of humor, and "Bar Scene From Star Wars" uses a four-track for a slightly smoother sound. Tape hiss has rarely sounded so enjoyable. *—Heather Phares*

● **Starlite Walker** / Oct. 24, 1994 / Drag City ♦♦♦♦♦
Starlite Walker is a first for the Silver Jews on many levels. Not only is it the group's first full-length album, it's also the first recorded in a full-fledged studio—Memphis' 24-track Easley Recordings—as well as the first collection of songs penned almost entirely by Berman. The album's lyrical and musical richness comes partly from Berman's retreat to the woods of Oxford, MS in preparation for the record, and partly from the understated, intimate production. As a result, *Starlite Walker* collects some of the Jews' most diverse and affecting songs. Wry lyrics like "I just got back from a dream attack" from "Trains Across the Sea" and "On the last day of your life/Don't forget to die" from "Advice to the Graduate" let Berman's easygoing charm come to the front, while jangly and crunchy guitars, Malkmus' backing vocals, and Nastanovich's steady drumming punctuate his observations.

Though *Starlite Walker* is a more low-key, reflective affair than the Silver Jews' EPs, the album benefits from it, combining the laid-back experimentalism of the Jews' early work with more sophisticated and expressive songwriting. "Advice to the Graduate" and "New Orleans" turn from humorous to poignant with a simple chord change; "Rebel Jew" draws on the group's affection for country music; and instrumentals like "The Moon is Number 18" and "The Silver Pageant" add to the relaxed, homespun feel of the album. Repeated listening just enhances *Starlite Walker's* warm, off-the-cuff appeal. *—Heather Phares*

The Natural Bridge / Oct. 1, 1996 / Drag City ♦♦♦♦
The Silver Jews' 1996 recording, *The Natural Bridge* continues the band's shift from their early, sprawling racket into a smooth foil for David Berman's laid-back vocals and evocative lyrics. When sessions with original Jews Stephen Malkmus and Bob Nastanovich and with members of the Scud Mountain Boys didn't work out the way Berman hoped, they were scrapped; the final version of *The Natural Bridge* was recorded in the summer of 1996 at Hartford, CT's Studio .45, which was originally a gun factory.

New Radiant Storm King's Peyton Pinkerton and Matt Hunter, Drag City producer/sessionman Rian Murphy, and keyboardist Michael Deming joined Berman in this version of the Jews' lineup, resulting in a more spacious sound than on any of the group's previous recordings. *The Natural Bridge* is also darker than the band's previous work, with lyrics like "I think we may be losing now/Please guard my bed" from "Pet Politics" and "Burnout tramp/Waits by the ramp/For one more car" from "Ballad of Reverend War Character." However, this darkness blends and contrasts with the wry, wistful "Dallas" and "Pretty Eyes." "The Frontier Index" combines jokes and a beautiful, descending guitar line for a really nice mix of ideas and emotion. Though *The Natural Bridge* lacks some of the immediacy of the Jews' earlier work, and Berman's voice slips into a monotone occasionally, this album offers some of the Silver Jews' finest moments. *—Heather Phares*

American Water / Oct. 20, 1998 / Drag City ♦♦♦♦♦
American Water, the Silver Jews' third full-length release, reunites David Berman and Stephen Malkmus and adds new members Mike Fellows, Tim Barnes and Chris Stroffolino. Named after a poster Berman saw at his veterinarian's office for American Water Spaniels, the album boasts some of the Jews' best arrangements and playing, from the flute and brass-tinged "Random Rules" to the driven but eloquent guitars on "Night Society" to the wah-wah friendly, '70s-style pop of "People."

American Water also varies in tempo and mood more than any Silver Jews album since *Starlite Walker*. "Send in the Clouds" and "Smith & Jones Forever" gallop along, while "We Are Real" and "The Wild Kindness" stroll. Though most of the album's lyrics aren't as personal as those on *The Natural Bridge*, they still feature Berman's detailed wit, like this couplet from "People": "The drums march along at the clip of an IV drip/Like sparks from a muffler dragged down the strip." The tight, sunny-sounding production sparkles on songs like "Honk If You're Lonely Tonight," and Berman and Malkmus' twin vocals brighten songs like "Blue Arrangements" and "Federal Dust." As with all of the Jews' best work, *American Water* sounds like it was made for the band's own enjoyment, and the listener is just eavesdropping on their fun. *—Heather Phares*

Simon & Garfunkel

f. 1964, New York, NY, **db.** 1970
Folk-Rock, Pop
The most successful folk-rock duo of the 1960s, Paul Simon and Art Garfunkel crafted a series of memorable hit albums and singles featuring their choirboy harmonies, ringing acoustic and electric guitars, and Simon's acute, finely wrought songwriting. Simon & Garfunkel's early albums were erratic, but they steadily improved as Simon sharpened his songwriting, and as the duo became more comfortable and adventurous in the studio. Their execution was so clean and tasteful that it cost them some hipness points during the psychedelic era, which was a bit silly. They were far from the raunchiest thing going, but managed to pull off the nifty feat of appealing to varying segments of the pop and rock audience—and various age groups, not just limited to adolescents—without compromising their music. *Parsley, Sage, Rosemary and Thyme* (late 1966) was their first really consistent album; *Bookends* (1968), which actually blended previously released singles with some new material, reflected their growing maturity. One of its songs, "Mrs. Robinson," became one of the biggest singles of the late '60s after it was prominently featured in one of the best films of the period, *The Graduate* (which also had other Simon & Garfunkel songs on the soundtrack). Their final studio album, *Bridge Over Troubled Waters*, was an enormous hit, topping the charts for ten weeks, and containing four hit singles (the title track, "The Boxer," "Cecilia," and "El Condor Pasa"). It was certainly their most musically ambitious, with "Bridge Over Troubled Waters" and "The Boxer" employing thundering drums and tasteful orchestration, and "Cecilia" marking one of Simon's first forays into South American rhythms. It also caught the confused, reflective tenor of the times better than almost any other popular release of 1970. *—Richie Unterberger*

Wednesday Morning, 3 A.M. / Oct. 1964 / Columbia ♦♦♦
Wednesday Morning, 3 A.M. doesn't resemble any other Simon & Garfunkel album, because the Simon & Garfunkel sound here was different from that of the chart-topping duo that emerged a year later. Their first record together since their days as the teen duo of Tom & Jerry, the album was cut in March 1964 and, in keeping with their own sincere interests at the time, it was a folk-revival album. Paul Simon was just spreading his wings as a serious songwriter and shares space with other composers as well as a pair of traditional songs, including a beautifully harmonized rendition of "Peggy-O." The album opens with a spirited (if somewhat arch) rendition of Gibson and Camp's gospel/folk piece "You Can Tell the World." Also present is Ian Campbell's "The Sun Is Burning," which Simon heard on his first visit to England as an itinerant folksinger. But the dominant outside personality on the album is that of Bob Dylan—his "Times They Are A-Changing" is covered, but his influence is manifest on the oldest of the Simon originals here, "He Was My Brother." Simon's first serious, topical song, it was what first interested Columbia Records producer Tom Wilson in Simon & Garfunkel. By the time the album was recorded, however, Simon had evolved beyond Dylan as an inspiration and developed a unique songwriting voice of his own in the title track, a beautifully sung, half-lovely song. *Wednesday Morning, 3 A.M.* is surprisingly ambitious but also somewhat disjointed, mostly because the non-original material, apart from "Peggy-O" and "The Sun Is Burning," comes off so arch. The seeds of their future success were here, however, and took root when the version of "The Sounds of Silence" on this album started getting played on the radio. *—Bruce Eder*

The Sounds of Silence / Jan. 1966 / Columbia ♦♦♦
Simon & Garfunkel's second album was a radical departure from their first, owing to its being recorded in the wake of "The Sound of Silence," with its overdubbed electric instrument backing, topping the charts. Paul Simon arrived with a large song-bag, enhanced by his stay in England over the previous year and his exposure to English folk music, and the duo rushed into the studio to come up with ten more songs that would fit into the folk-rock context of the single. The result was this, their most hurried and uncharacteristic album—Simon and Art Garfunkel had to sound like something they weren't, surrounded on many cuts by amplified folk-rock-style guitar, electric piano, and even horns. Much of the material came from *The Paul Simon Songbook*, an album that Simon had recorded for British CBS during his stay in England, some parts of it more radically altered than others. The record was a rushed job overall, and apart from the title track, the most important songs here were also, oddly enough, among the least enduring, "I Am a Rock" and "Richard Cory"—the former for establishing the duo (and Simon as a songwriter) as confessional pop-poets, sensitive and alienated post-adolescents that endeared them to millions of college students going through what later came to be called an "identity crisis"; and the latter for endearing them to thousands of high-school English teachers with its adaptation of Edward Arlington Robinson's poem. The August 2001 remastering restores the original, uncensored back-cover art (depicting Art Garfunkel holding what the powers-that-were later decided was a decidedly uncool copy of Tiger Beat magazine, airbrushed out of later copies), features the first genuinely good sound ever heard on any CD edition of this album, and also includes four bonus tracks. *—Bruce Eder*

Parsley, Sage, Rosemary & Thyme / Sep. 1966 / Columbia ♦♦♦♦♦
The duo's first masterpiece, *Parsley, Sage, Rosemary & Thyme* was also the first album on which Simon & Garfunkel, in tandem with engineer Roy Halee, exerted total control from beginning to end, right down to the mixing, and it is an achievement akin to the Beatles' *Revolver* or the Beach Boys' *Pet Sounds* album, and it is just as personal and pointed as either of those records at their respective bests. After the frantic rush to put together an LP in just three weeks that characterized the *Sounds of Silence* album early in 1966, *Parsley, Sage, Rosemary & Thyme* came together over a longer gestation period of about three months, an uncommonly extended period of recording in those days, but it gave the duo a chance to develop and shape the songs the way they wanted them. Overall, *Parsley, Sage, Rosemary & Thyme* was the duo's album about youthful exuberance and alienation, and it proved perennially popular among older, more thoughtful high school students and legions of college audiences, across generations. The August 2001 reissue offers not only the best sound ever heard on this album in any incarnation, but also a few bonuses: a slightly extended mastering of "Cloudy" that gives the listener a high-harmony surprise in its fade; and, as actual bonus tracks, Paul Simon's solo demos of "Patterns" and "A Poem on the Underground Wall"—raw and personal, they're startling in their intimacy and their directness, and offer a more intimate view of Paul Simon the artist than ever seen. *—Bruce Eder*

☆ **Bookends** / Mar. 1968 / Columbia ♦♦♦♦♦
Bookends is a literary album that contains the most minimal of openings with the theme,

an acoustic guitar stating itself slowly and plaintively before erupting into the wash of synthesizers and dissonance that is "Save the Life of My Child." The classic "America" is next, a folk song with a lilting soprano saxophone in the refrain and a small pipe organ painting the acoustic guitars in the more poignant verses. The song relies on pop structures to carry its message of hope and disillusionment as two people travel the American landscape searching for it until it dawns on them that everyone else on the freeway is doing the same thing. The final four tracks of the original album, "Mrs. Robinson," the theme song for the film *The Graduate*, "A Hazy Shade of Winter," and the album's final track, "At the Zoo," offer as tremblingly bleak a vision for the future as any thing done by the Velvet Underground, but rooted in the lives of everyday people, not in the decadent underground personages of New York's Factory studio. But the album is also a warning that to pay attention is to take as much control of one's fate as possible. The bonus tracks, a different take of "Old Friends" and "You Don't Know Where Your Interest Lies"—which ended up as the B-side of "Hazy Shade of Winter"—add dimension to what was easily the most ambitious recording of Simon & Garfunkel's career. *—Thom Jurek*

☆ **Bridge Over Troubled Water** / Feb. 1970 / Columbia ♦♦♦♦♦
Bridge Over Troubled Water was one of the biggest selling albums of its decade, and it hasn't fallen too far down on the list in the 30-plus years since. Apart from the gospel-flavored title track, which took some evolution to get to what it finally became, however, much of *Bridge Over Troubled Water* also constitutes a stepping back from the music that Simon & Garfunkel had made on *Bookends*—this was mostly because the creative partnership that had formed the body and the motivation for the duo's four prior albums literally consumed itself in the making of *Bridge Over Troubled Water*. The overall effect was perhaps the most delicately textured album to close out the 1960s from any major rock act. *Bridge Over Troubled Water*, at its most ambitious and bold, on its title track, was a quietly reassuring album; at other times, it was personal yet soothing; and at other times, it was just plain fun. The public in 1970—a very unsettled time politically, socially, and culturally—embraced it; and whatever mood they captured, the songs matched the standard of craftsmanship that had been established on the duo's two prior albums. Between the record's overall quality and its four hits, the album held the number one position for two and a half months and spent years on the charts, racking up sales in excess of five million copies. The irony was that for all of the record's and the music's appeal, the duo's partnership ended in the course of creating and completing the album. The August 2001 remastering of *Bridge Over Troubled Water* is the first-ever CD version of the album that sounds good—properly mastered off of what sound like the real first-generation tapes. *—Bruce Eder*

Greatest Hits / Jun. 1972 / Columbia ♦♦♦♦
This album was released within weeks of the duo getting back together for a benefit concert at Madison Square Garden on behalf of George McGovern's 1972 presidential campaign. Simon & Garfunkel's work had never been compiled before, but their albums were still selling so well as catalog items that this record should have been superfluous. Instead, it touched all the right buttons, providing an overview of the duo's most popular songs and biggest singles, but also offering longtime fans a previously unissued alternate take of "America" and live versions of "For Emily, Whenever I May Find Her," "Homeward Bound," "Feelin' Groovy," and "Kathy's Song," which meant that even fans who already had everything else they'd ever released wanted to own it—understandably, it peaked at number five on the charts. Over the years, its value has lessened somewhat with the release of more ambitious, wider-ranging compilations of their work that were also mastered more carefully, from better sources, though this is still the best easily available single disc on the duo. All of their most identifiable and widely embraced hits, from "The Sounds of Silence" to "Bridge Over Troubled Water," are represented here, along with the duo's best-known and most personal album cuts ("Kathy's Song," etc.), making it a decent introduction for the total neophyte—what's missing are some interesting and ambitious singles that either haven't stood the test of time ("Fakin' It") or were artistic blind alleys ("The Dangling Conversation"), plus "Punky's Dilemma," a perennial FM radio favorite that lay just below Columbia Records' and the duo's radar. *—Bruce Eder*

☆ **Collected Works** / 1981 / Columbia ♦♦♦♦♦
The three-disc box set *Collected Works* contains all of Simon & Garfunkel's studio albums, from *Wednesday Morning 3 A.M.* to *Bridge Over Troubled Water*. Though this is too much material for casual fans, any serious fan of Simon & Garfunkel or folk-rock will need to acquire the set, simply because it presents the albums in their best-ever sound. The duo did record a handful of tracks that didn't make the set—and if Columbia was assembling a true "collected works" compilation, they would have to be included—but the genuinely essential material is present, making it a good buy for the budget-conscious. *—Stephen Thomas Erlewine*

Concert in Central Park / Feb. 1982 / Warner Brothers ♦♦♦♦♦
Simon & Garfunkel reunited on September 19, 1981, to perform a free concert in Central Park, New York City. This two-record set presents some of the duo's biggest hits in a live context and also allows listeners a chance to hear what many Simon solo numbers could sound like in S&G mode. *—William Ruhlmann*

Old Friends / Oct. 28, 1997 / Columbia/Legacy ♦♦♦
The Collected Works was a triple-disc box set that included all of the duo's albums, but no rarities. For the average fan—even the fairly dedicated fan—that set contained most everything they would need, even if the sound quality was a little below average. *Old Friends* is a three-disc box set that was designed to replace *The Collected Works*, but it fails to achieve its goals, despite its improved remastered sound. Part of the reason is the contents itself—all five albums plus the rarities on this set could have fit on three discs, offering a real complete recorded studio works, but the compilers decided to truncate the albums and toss on a handful of rarities. The result certainly isn't bad—after all, it features all of the hits, most of the major album tracks, the 1975 reunion "My Little Town," and a couple of good rarities, like "Blues Run the Game"—but it isn't all it could have been. If you already own *The Collected Works*, *Old Friends* serves little purpose unless you're a collector or audiophile, and if you're a neophyte, you're better off obtaining the original albums, not this well-intentioned and enjoyable but ultimately unsuccessful compilation. *—Stephen Thomas Erlewine*

★ **The Best of Simon & Garfunkel** / Nov. 9, 1999 / Columbia/Legacy ♦♦♦♦♦
This supersedes *Greatest Hits* as the best Simon & Garfunkel compilation, with more tracks (20 compared to *Greatest Hits*' 14). Among the new additions are some notable hits: "Hazy Shade of Winter," "At the Zoo," "Fakin' It" (in its "mono single version," for what that's worth), "The Dangling Conversation," and the 1975 reunion "My Home Town." Includes the A-sides of all 16 S&G singles to make the Billboard charts, as well as three B-sides and one album cut. The only number lost from the *Greatest Hits* set is "Kathy's Song." *—Richie Unterberger*

Tales from New York / Mar. 28, 2000 / Columbia/Legacy [International] ♦♦♦♦♦
Released around the same time Columbia/Legacy expanded the original *The Best of Simon & Garfunkel* to a comprehensive 20-track single-disc collection, the British-only *Tales From New York: The Very Best of Simon & Garfunkel* takes that expansion a little further. It weighs in at a hefty 40 songs spread over two discs. This is not a problem, yet it isn't entirely an unqualified blessing, either. There are many terrific songs here that didn't make the cut on *The Best of*—which, after all, concentrated primarily on the biggest hits—but *Tales From New York* isn't exactly trim. Actually, it takes a little bit to get going, as the early folk numbers eat up the first five or so songs. Once it hits the second disc, Simon & Garfunkel are in their stride, and that disc, spanning "A Hazy Shade of Winter" to "America" and the reunion number "My Little Town," is peerless listening. Still, *Tales From New York* is a bit of a strange release, since it appeals to that small, small audience that wants more than just *The Best* yet doesn't want to delve into the actual albums or own the rarity-filled box (which contains nearly everything the duo recorded). For that select audience, *Tales From New York* is quite worthwhile, since it has almost every seminal song the duo cut, from hits ("Mrs. Robinson," "The Sound of Silence") to album tracks that are every bit as good as the singles ("Fakin' It," "The Only Living Boy in New York"). *—Stephen Thomas Erlewine*

The Columbia Studio Recordings, 1964-1970 / Aug. 21, 2001 / Columbia/Legacy ♦♦♦♦
This box set containing the remastered, expanded editions of all five of Simon & Garfunkel's original LPs on five CDs just—but only just—misses a top rating, by virtue of its packaging. The sound is, as with the individual editions of each title, a significant improvement over any prior releases of this material and proves to be utterly impeccable, and the annotated booklet, containing the original credits and notes off the albums as well as the lyrics and all of the new annotation for each individual album by Bud Scoppa, is fairly handy. The problem is the packaging of the individual discs in miniature recreations of the original LP jackets, which are somewhat awkwardly stowed in one side of the box interior—unless they're lined up perfectly, however, they will come out of that receptacle; additionally, as there are no inner sleeves for the CDs in their miniature jackets (a necessity and a courtesy provided by the Japanese when they issue CDs in miniature LP sleeves), it's easy for them to slide out of their jackets and get scratched and dinged even prior to purchase and opening. It's a shame that Columbia went to this kind of trouble in remastering and preparing this edition without seeing to such obvious details, and the result is a 50 dollar box set that is more inconvenient than it needed to have been. *—Bruce Eder*

Carly Simon

b. Jun. 25, 1945, New York, NY
Vocals, Keyboards, Piano, Guitar / Pop/Rock, Soft Rock, Adult Contemporary, Singer/Songwriter

Carly Simon was one of the most popular of the confessional singer/songwriters who emerged in the early '70s. She got her start in music as part of the Simon Sisters, a duo with her sister Lucy that had a charting single in 1964. Her eponymous solo debut album appeared in 1971, and she found a Top 40 hit with the title track from her second album, *Anticipation*. Her third album *No Secrets* was a gold number one, and included her best-known hit "You're So Vain." During 1977-78, two singles ("Nobody Does It Better" from the James Bond film *The Spy Who Loved Me* and "You Belong to Me") became Top Ten hits.

Though Simon curtailed her concert appearances after collapsing of exhaustion onstage in 1980, she scored a Top Ten U.K. hit two years later with "Why." Her U.S. career was in decline, however, as two mid-'80s albums were poor sellers. Her movie-related hits, including "Coming Around Again" (from *Heartburn*) and "Let the River Run" (from *Working Girl*), defined the mid-to-late-'80s. In 1990, Simon released both *My Romance*, her second album of pop covers, and *Have You Seen Me Lately?*, an album of original songs. In 1993, her "family opera" *Romulus Hunt* premiered and was released on record, and one year later she released a new album, *Letters Never Sent*. *—William Ruhlmann*

Carly Simon / Feb. 1971 / Elektra ♦♦♦
"That's The Way I've Always Heard It Should Be," the leadoff track of Carly Simon's first album and a Top Ten hit, in which the singer expresses reservations about getting married, benefitted from a sense of role reversal—it's such a guy sentiment, but sung by a woman in 1971, came across as a feminist statement, consistent with the overall disillusionment so prevalent then. Nothing on the rest of the album was quite as pointed, though the other songs maintained the same ambivalence toward romance. The one other standout track, "Dan, My Fling," in which the singer tries to rekindle a relationship

with a man she has discarded, was, like the single, co-written by Jacob Brackman (in this case, with Fred Gardner, not Simon), suggesting that the real creative talent here was him and not her (especially since the writing credits also featured another four names). And since Simon, with her plaintive, proper, and relatively inexpressive voice, was such an un-remarkable performer, her debut seemed less auspicious than the attention it attracted might have implied. —*William Ruhlmann*

Anticipation / Nov. 1971 / Elektra ✦✦✦
Carly Simon's second album found her extending the gutsy persona she had established on her debut album, notably on the title track, "Legend in Your Own Time" (both of them hit singles), and "I've Got to Have You." The last especially suggested a frankly passion-ate person whose vulnerability was a source of strength, not weakness, a valuable feminist trait and one Simon would pursue in her later work. —*William Ruhlmann*

No Secrets / Nov. 1972 / Elektra ✦✦✦✦✦
Carly Simon's best album was also her commercial breakthrough, topping the charts and going gold, along with its leadoff single, "You're So Vain." That song set the album's saucy tone, with its air of sexually frank autobiography ("You had me several years ago / When I was still quite naive") and its reflections on the jet-set lifestyle. But Simon's honesty meant that her lyrical knife was double-edged; now that she felt she had found true love ("The Right Thing to Do," another Top Ten hit, was her celebration of her relationship with James Taylor), she was as willing to acknowledge her own mistakes and regrets as she was to point fingers. But it wasn't only Simon's forthrightness that made the album work, it was also Richard Perry's simple, elegant pop/rock production, which gave Simon's music a buoyancy it previously lacked. And Perry paid particular attention to Simon's vocals in a way that made her more engaging (or at least less grating) to listen to. —*William Ruhlmann*

Hotcakes / Jan. 1974 / Elektra ✦✦✦✦

Playing Possum / Apr. 1975 / Elektra ✦✦✦
Though it reached the Top Ten on career momentum, Carly Simon's fifth album, *Playing Possum*, marked a creative downturn. The burst of autobiographical songwriting that had taken her from her early twenties into married life seemed to have run out, as she sang generic love songs, while Richard Perry's production gave everything an anonymous pop veneer. "Attitude Dancing" made the Top 40, and "Waterfall" and "More and More" charted, but *Playing Possum* was the album of an artist treading water, unsure of her next step. —*William Ruhlmann*

● **The Best of Carly Simon** / Nov. 1975 / Elektra ✦✦✦✦✦
Carly Simon was among the pop royalty of the singer/songwriter era of the early 1970s. This album collects her most popular songs of the first five years of her solo career. Open-ing with the powerful "That's the Way I've Always Heard It Should Be," and for which Simon received the 1971 Best New Artist Grammy Award, it includes three tunes from the classic *No Secrets* album, including the number one hit "You're So Vain." Simon's duet with then-husband James Taylor on "Mockingbird" was also a Top Ten hit. "Anticipation," with its classic "I rehearsed those words just late last night," and the repetitive coda "these are the good old days," though merely a ketchup commercial to a later generation, still retains its power here in the original version. Simon's insightful lyrics and evocative voice remain fresh years later. This album is a good starting point for those interested in discovering why. —*Jim Newsom*

Another Passenger / Jun. 1976 / Elektra ✦✦✦

Boys in the Trees / Apr. 1978 / Elektra ✦✦✦

Spy / Jun. 1979 / Elektra ✦✦✦

Come Upstairs / Jun. 1980 / Warner Brothers ✦✦✦

Torch / 1981 / Warner Brothers ✦✦✦
Carly Simon slightly anticipated the trend toward contemporary pop singers turning to pop standards here, singing songs like "I Got It Bad and That Ain't Good" and "Body and Soul." The theme, of course, was romantic torment, and it was expressed no better than on the final track, a new song from Stephen Sondheim's then-upcoming musical *Merrily We Roll Along* called "Not a Day Goes By" that Simon delivered with heartbreaking conviction. —*William Ruhlmann*

Hello Big Man / Sep. 1983 / Warner Brothers ✦✦✦

Spoiled Girl / 1985 / Epic ✦✦

Coming Around Again / Mar. 1987 / Arista ✦✦✦
After the debacle that was *Spoiled Girl*, Carly Simon moved to her fourth record label, Arista, and returned to soundtrack work. This time, she wrote "Coming Around Again" for *Heartburn*, and it hit number 18 in early 1987, her biggest hit in more than six years. That set up Simon's comeback with this album, which became her biggest hit in a decade, producing two more chart singles, "Give Me All Night" (number 61) and "All I Want Is You" (number 54), and going platinum. Once again, a bevy of producers—nine this time—weighed in in an attempt to vary Simon's appeal. The big difference was that this time, Simon was willing to go to her strengths as a ballad singer rather than romping amid synthesized blips. Better to flirt with retro than disco, at least as far as Simon's audience is concerned. —*William Ruhlmann*

Greatest Hits Live / Aug. 1988 / Arista ✦✦✦✦

My Romance / Mar. 1990 / Arista ✦✦✦

Have You Seen Me Lately / Sep. 1990 / Arista ✦✦✦

This Is My Life / Apr. 14, 1992 / Qwest ✦✦

Letters Never Sent / Nov. 1, 1994 / Arista ✦✦✦

Clouds in My Coffee 1966-1996 / Nov. 7, 1995 / Arista ✦✦✦
Rather than focusing on hits and other material most beloved by fans, retrospectives com-piled by the artists themselves tend to reflect personal favorites, overbalanced with more recent material. By organizing this three-disc set into three different, non-chronological collections, Carly Simon partially defeats those tendencies. The first disc, "The Hits," per-forms the valuable function of bringing together most of her biggest singles, previously spread across many records on many labels. The second disc, "Miscellaneous & Unre-leased," seems aimed at the collector. And the third, "Cry Yourself to Sleep," is the best-intentioned one of all—though perceived as a singles artist, Simon has written some of her best and most personal music on isolated album tracks. However, her choices fre-quently are not the best songs in her catalog; what is included is good stuff—it's just that a box set can offer the opportunity to provide an alternate view of an artist who may have been misjudged, as Carly Simon has, and that opportunity has been missed. —*William Ruhlmann*

Film Noir / Sep. 16, 1997 / Arista ✦✦✦

Bedroom Tapes / May 16, 2000 / Arista ✦✦✦

Joe Simon

b. Sep. 2, 1943, Simmesport, LA

Vocals / Deep Soul, Southern Soul, Pop-Soul, Disco, Soul

His plaintive baritone equally conversant with R&B and country phrasing, Joe Simon married the two genres with startling success during the late '60s, adapting Nashville ma-terial to the soul sound and repeatedly coming up a winner. Simon began recording in the Bay Area, but a switch in recording sites (first to Muscle Shoals for Vee-Jay and then to Nashville, upon signing with deejay John Richbourg's Sound Stage 7 label in 1966) heightened his national appeal. With easy access to prime country-oriented material, Simon soon found his true calling, scoring major hits with "Nine Pound Steel," "(You Keep Me) Hangin' On," and the number one R&B smash "The Chokin' Kind," penned by Music Row tunesmith Harlan Howard. Still dabbling in country covers after switching to the Spring imprint in 1970, Simon was even more successful when assigned to Philadel-phia wizards Kenny Gamble and Leon Huff, who produced the moody "Drowning in the Sea of Love" the next year. Simon tried his hand at disco in 1975 with the sizzling "Get Down, Get Down (Get on the Floor)" and "Music in My Bones," two of the most palatable artifacts of the era. Simon eventually retired from active performing to devote his life to the church. —*Bill Dahl*

Greatest Hits: The Spring Years, 1970-1977 / 1997 / Ace ✦✦✦✦✦
Of all the soul singers who got their first hits during the 1960s, Joe Simon proved to be one of the most adaptable to the sweeter and slicker sounds of the 1970s. This 23-track compilation, covering his output at the Spring label, is not necessarily the best Simon an-thology, omitting as it does his less elaborately produced work of the 1960s, which some find preferable to his Philly soul outings. It does, however, feature all his major pop hits of the era—"Drowning in the Sea of Love," "Power of Love," "Your Time to Cry," "Get Down, Get Down," and "Theme From Cleopatra Jones"—as well as a number of singles that only made a strong impression on R&B audiences, like his cover of Kris Kristofferson's "Help Me Make It Through the Night." As usual with this sort of overview, the music gets more tedious the further you get into the disco era, but it's certainly a good pickup for those who like their soul with a bow tie on it. —*Richie Unterberger*

● **Music in My Bones: The Best of Joe Simon** / Nov. 11, 1997 / Rhino ✦✦✦✦✦
Music in My Bones: The Best of Joe Simon is a superb 20-track collection that contains the best of the soul singer's recordings between 1966 and 1976. During those ten years, he recorded for Sound Stage 7, Spring, and Warner and had 13 Top Ten R&B hits, all of which are included on this collection. Simon was one of the best country-soul and smooth soul singers, as evidenced by such hits as "The Chokin' Kind," "Your Time to Cry," "Drowning in the Sea of Love," "Power of Love," "Step By Step," "Theme From Cleopatra Jones," "Get Down, Get Down (Get on the Floor)," and "Music in My Bones," and there is no better place to listen to his music than on this excellent collection. —*Stephen Thomas Erlewine*

Monument of Soul / Apr. 3, 2001 / RPM ✦✦✦✦
Monument of Soul is a comprehensive collection of Joe Simon's 1966-1972 releases on the Sound Stage 7 label, including nearly everything that he put out on singles through the company during that period. Among them are all of his R&B and pop chart hits on Sound Stage 7, which in Simon's case were quite numerous—16 in all, even if just a cou-ple of them ("The Chokin' Kind" and "You Keep Me Hanging On") got into the Top 40. Simon's Sound Stage 7 period is underrepresented by the singer's best career retrospec-tive, Rhino's *Music in My Bones: The Best of Joe Simon*, so this is a welcome in-depth view of the earlier era. And, for listeners who prefer his Nashville soul stint to his slicker Philly soul and disco productions of the '70s, this will probably be the Simon CD they'll want most. Simon was not quite on the Hall of Fame level of soul singers, but he was on the next level down, and he pretty consistently delivered the goods, even on B-sides, of which there are quite a few on this disc. He was better on the countrified ballads than he was on the mid-tempo chuggers, both because these suited his style better, and because such material stood in bolder relief when juxtaposed with much late-'60s soul. "I Worry About You" and "San Francisco Is a Lonely Town" are two of the overlooked slow-burners on this anthology, though some relatively unknown up-tempo belters are worthy of atten-tion too, like "Travellin' Man." —*Richie Unterberger*

Paul Simon (Paul Frederick Simon)

b. Oct. 13, 1941, Newark, NJ

Vocals, Guitar / Album Rock, Pop/Rock, Folk-Rock, Soft Rock, Worldbeat, Adult Contemporary, Singer/Songwriter

In a career dating back to the 1950s, Paul Simon has established himself among the best and most popular songwriters of the rock era. A charting artist with Art Garfunkel since the age of 16 (under the name Tom and Jerry), Simon spent five years as half of one of the most successful acts in pop music. Simon wrote the songs and harmonized with Garfunkel on a series of hit singles and albums between 1965 and 1970. After two solo albums that both sold a million copies, he released 1975's *Still Crazy After All These Years* which topped the charts, won the Grammy for Album of the Year, and included the number one hit "50 Ways to Leave Your Lover." Simon took his time following this success, writing songs for the soundtrack to the 1980 film *One Trick Pony* and releasing another proper album, *Hearts and Bones*, in 1983. After experimenting with songwriting styles and becoming interested in South African music, Simon released 1986's *Graceland*, which became his biggest selling solo album and won him another Album of the Year Grammy. Four years later, he delivered *The Rhythm of the Saints* (October 1990), which did for Brazilian music what *Graceland* had done for South African music and was another multi-platinum seller. In 1993, he undertook a tour that featured Garfunkel on their old hits, as well as covering other aspects of his career. —*William Ruhlmann*

The Paul Simon Songbook / May 1965 / CBS ✦✦✦✦✦

The first album to use this title is one of the most mysterious in Paul Simon's output and almost belongs more with Simon & Garfunkel's discography, given its 1965 recording date. Following the failure of Simon & Garfunkel's first, all-acoustic folk revival-style album, *Wednesday Morning 3 A.M.*, Paul Simon headed off to England to see about pursuing music over there. While he was in London, he found himself in demand as a visiting American "folk singer." Suddenly, there were requests for Paul Simon recordings, of which there were none—as a result of his being signed to Columbia Records in America, however, he was brought into the London studios of British CBS and recorded this album with only his acoustic guitar for backup. The resulting album is spare, almost minimalist, as Simon runs through raw and unaffected versions of songs that he was known for in London. The notes are very, very strange, but a bigger problem is the production by Reginald Warburton and Stanley West, which isn't terribly sympathetic; the sound isn't very natural, being very close and booming, but the album is a fascinating artifact of Simon's work during the interregnum in Simon & Garfunkel's career. And there is one fascinating number here, "The Side of a Hill," which eventually resurfaced as the countermelody song in the Simon & Garfunkel version of "Scarborough Fair" (a song curious by its absence here, considering that Simon was doing it in his coffeehouse appearances) two years later. Curiously, Simon has done his best to suppress this record through the years—he reportedly objected when Columbia Records began importing it directly during the late '70s, and he has never permitted it to be reissued on compact disc, thus making the original album a collector's item. —*Bruce Eder*

☆ Paul Simon / Jan. 1972 / Warner Brothers ✦✦✦✦✦

If any musical justification were needed for the breakup of Simon and Garfunkel, it could be found on this striking collection, Paul Simon's post-split debut. From the opening cut, "Mother and Child Reunion" (a Top Ten hit), Simon, who had snuck several subtle musical explorations into the generally conservative S&G sound, broke free, heralding the rise of reggae with an exuberant track recorded in Jamaica for a song about death. From there, it was off to Paris for a track in South American style and a rambling story of a fisherman's son, "Duncan" (which made the singles chart). But most of the album had a low-key feel, with Simon on acoustic guitar backed by only a few trusted associates (among them Joe Osborn, Larry Knechtel, David Spinoza, Mike Manieri, Ron Carter, and Hal Blaine, along with such guests as Stefan Grossman, Airto Moreira, and Stephane Grappelli), singing a group of informal, intimate, funny, and closely observed songs (among them the lively Top 40 hit "Me and Julio Down by the Schoolyard"). It was miles removed from the big, stately ballad style of *Bridge Over Troubled Water* and signalled that Simon was a versatile songwriter as well as an expressive singer with a much broader range of musical interests than he had previously demonstrated. You didn't miss Art Garfunkel on *Paul Simon*, not only because Simon didn't write Garfunkel-like showcases for himself, but because the songs he did write showed off his own, more varied musical strengths. —*William Ruhlmann*

There Goes Rhymin' Simon / May 1973 / Warner Brothers ✦✦✦✦✦

Retaining the buoyant musical feel of *Paul Simon*, but employing a more produced sound, *There Goes Rhymin' Simon* found Paul Simon writing and performing with assurance and venturing into soulful and R&B-oriented music. Simon returned to the kind of vocal pyrotechnics heard on the Simon and Garfunkel records by using gospel singers. On "Love Me Like a Rock" and "Tenderness" (which sounded as though it could have been written to Art Garfunkel), the Dixie Hummingbirds sang prominent backup vocals, and on "Take Me to the Mardi Gras," the Reverend Claude Jeter contributed a falsetto part that Garfunkel could have handled, though not as warmly. For several tracks, Simon traveled to the Muscle Shoals Sound Studios to play with its house band, getting a variety of styles, from the gospel of "Love Me Like a Rock" to the Dixieland of "Mardi Gras." Simon was so confident that he even included a major ballad statement of the kind he used to give Garfunkel to sing: "American Tune" was his musical State of the Union, circa 1973, but this time Simon was up to making his big statements in his own voice. Though that song spoke of "the age's most uncertain hour," otherwise *Rhymin' Simon* was a collection of largely positive, optimistic songs of faith, romance, and commitment, concluding, appropriately, with a lullaby ("St. Judy's Comet") and a declaration of maternal love ("Loves Me Like a Rock")—in other words, another mother and child reunion that made *Paul*

Simon and *There Goes Rhymin' Simon* bookend masterpieces Simon would not improve upon (despite some valiant attempts) until *Graceland* in 1986. —*William Ruhlmann*

Live Rhymin' / Feb. 1974 / Warner Brothers ✦✦✦

One thing Simon and Garfunkel never did much of was tour, so a Paul Simon solo tour, following two commercially successful solo albums, was one more way for Simon to distance himself from the duo and, simultaneously, by performing songs like "The Boxer" and "Homeward Bound," to reclaim his songwriting catalog. Reflecting the musical explorations he had pursued since S&G, Simon brought along Brazilian group Urubamba and gospel group the Jessy Dixon Singers. The result wasn't perfect: Nobody needed to hear "Jesus Is the Answer" (a Dixons' spotlight number) on a Paul Simon album, and if it was inevitable that he would try his own version of "Bridge Over Troubled Water," it was also predestined that he wouldn't come near to matching Garfunkel's original. Though the album was, like most live albums, artistically redundant (there was nothing new, and none of the live versions improved upon the studio ones), it served as a career statement and it had a marketing function, buying the relatively slow-working Simon time between new studio releases. (Simon completists should note that, as in all live performances of "The Boxer," Simon sings the extra verse [beginning "Now the years are rolling by me"] not included on the Simon and Garfunkel studio version.) —*William Ruhlmann*

Still Crazy After All These Years / Oct. 1975 / Warner Brothers ✦✦✦✦✦

Replacing the guitar with the piano as the primary instrument, Simon produced a quiet, introspective Grammy-winning album centering around lost love. Simon reunites with Garfunkel on "My Little Town," a track that sounds nothing like old S&G songs. *Still Crazy* doesn't really resemble Simon's two previous albums; it is a serious, somber album with none of the light touches present on *Paul Simon* and *Rhymin' Simon*. —*Stephen Thomas Erlewine*

One Trick Pony [Original Soundtrack] / Aug. 1980 / Warner Brothers ✦✦✦

Though released to coincide with the film *One Trick Pony*, which Paul Simon wrote and starred in, the *One Trick Pony* album is not a soundtrack—at least, not exactly. If it were, it might contain the Simon song "Soft Parachutes" and other non-Simon music featured in the movie. Instead, this is a studio album containing many of the movie songs; the closest thing to a band album Simon ever made, it contains some of his most rhythmic and energetic singing. But it is also his most uneven album, simply because the songwriting, with the exception of the title song and the ballads "How the Heart Approaches What It Yearns" and "Nobody," is not up to his usual standard. Maybe he was too busy writing his screenplay to polish these songs to the usual gloss. In any case, though the album spawned a Top Ten hit in "Late in the Evening" and may have sold more copies than the film did tickets, it remained a disappointment in both artistic and commercial terms. —*William Ruhlmann*

Collected Works / 1981 / Columbia ✦✦✦✦✦

Like the identically titled Simon and Garfunkel boxed set released at the same time, Paul Simon's *Collected Works* was what it claimed to be: A five-LP set reissue containing *The Paul Simon Song Book* (in its first and only U.S. release), *Paul Simon*, *There Goes Rhymin' Simon*, *Live Rhymin'/Paul Simon In Concert*, and *Still Crazy After All These Years*. The *Song Book*, containing solo Simon versions of songs that turned up on the first three Simon and Garfunkel albums, remained an interesting curiosity and *Live Rhymin'* remained an entertaining tour souvenir, but the heart of the matter was Simon's three 1970s studio albums, which constituted some of the most accomplished pop music of the period. By the time this set was released, Simon had decamped Columbia for Warner Bros., and when the CD era dawned and his catalog followed him, *Collected Works* went out of print. —*William Ruhlmann*

Hearts and Bones / Oct. 1983 / Warner Brothers ✦✦✦✦✦

Hearts and Bones was a commercial disaster, the lowest-charting new studio album of Paul Simon's career. It is also his most personal collection of songs, one of his most ambitious, and one of his best. It retains a personal vision, one largely devoted to the challenges of middle-aged life, among them a renewed commitment to love; the title song was a notable testament to new romance, while "Train in the Distance" reflected on romantic discord. Elsewhere, "The Late Great Johnny Ace" was his meditation on John Lennon's murder and how it related to the mythology of pop music. Musically, Simon moved forward and backward simultaneously, taking off from the jazz fusion style of his last two albums into his old loves of doo wop and rock & roll while also incorporating current sounds with such new collaborators as dance music producer Nile Rodgers and minimalist composer Philip Glass. The result was Simon's most impressive collection in a decade and the most underrated album in Paul Simon's catalog. —*William Ruhlmann*

☆ Graceland / Aug. 1986 / Warner Brothers ✦✦✦✦✦

With *Graceland*, Paul Simon hit on the idea of combining his always perceptive songwriting with the little-heard mbaqanga music of South Africa, creating a fascinating hybrid that re-enchanted his old audience and earned him a new one. It is true that the South African angle (including its controversial aspect during the apartheid days) was a powerful marketing tool and that the catchy music succeeded in presenting listeners with that magical combination: something they'd never heard before that nevertheless sounded familiar. As eclectic as any record Simon had made, it also delved into zydeco and conjunto-flavored rock & roll while marking a surprising new lyrical approach (presaged on some songs on *Hearts and Bones*); for the most part, Simon abandoned a linear, narrative approach to his words, instead drawing highly poetic ("Diamonds on the Soles of Her Shoes"), abstract ("The Boy in the Bubble"), and satiric ("I Know What I Know") portraits of modern life, often charged by striking images and turns of phrase torn from the headlines or overheard in contemporary speech. An enormously successful record, *Graceland* became the standard against which subsequent musical experiments by major artists were measured. *—William Ruhlmann*

• **Negotiations and Love Songs 1971-1986** / Oct. 1988 / Warner Brothers ✦✦✦✦✦
Paul Simon replaced his earlier compilation, *Greatest Hits, Etc.* (1977), with this new one, allowing *Hits* to go out of print. Fans may well wish that he had simply put together a *Greatest Hits, Etc., Volume II* instead, however, since this is a case of a 16-track album covering 15 years replacing a 14-track album covering five years while containing nine of the same songs. All the major hits have been retained (though "Mother and Child Reunion" and "Loves Me Like a Rock" each have been shortened by 15 seconds), along with some of Simon's odd album track choices, such as "Have a Good Time." From the post-1977 period, we have the 1980 Top Ten hit "Late in the Evening," three selections from the underrated *Hearts And Bones*, and two from *Graceland*. (The original double-LP version of *Negotiations And Love Songs* contained a third, the Grammy Record of the Year-winning title song, but the in-print CD and cassette versions do not.) The result is more sampler than compilation. An artist of Simon's calibre is difficult to condense, and most of the tracks here are worthy, but as a single-album career retrospective, this could have been better. *—William Ruhlmann*

Rhythm of the Saints / Oct. 1990 / Warner Brothers ✦✦✦✦
Though he recorded the album's prominent percussion tracks in Brazil, Paul Simon fashioned *The Rhythm of the Saints* as a deliberate follow-up to the artistic breakthrough and commercial comeback that was South Africa-tinged *Graceland*. Several of the musicians who had appeared previously were back, along with some of the New York session players who had worked with Simon in the 1970s, and the overall sound was familiar to fans of *Graceland*. Further, Simon's non-linear lyrical approach was carried over: He continued to ruminate about love, aging, and the onslaught of modern life in disconnected phrases and images that created impressions rather than telling straightforward stories. But where *Graceland* had seamlessly merged its styles into an exuberant whole *The Rhythm of the Saints* was less well digested. Those drum tracks never seemed integrated effectively into what had been dubbed over them; at the same time, they tended to lock the songs into musical patterns that reined them in from the kind of excitement the South African music on *Graceland* generated and made the melodies harder to grasp. At the same time, Simon sang his lyrics in a less involved way, which sometimes made them seem like collections of random lines rather than the series of striking observations *Graceland* seemed to contain. No Paul Simon album could be lacking in craft or quality, and *The Rhythm of the Saints* was a typically tasteful effort. But this time around, Simon hadn't quite succeeded in bringing the wide-ranging elements together; the album sold about half as many copies as *Graceland* (that is to say, a none-too-shabby two million), and that's about right—where *Graceland* was an exotic adventure, *The Rhythm of the Saints* was more of an anthropology lesson. *—William Ruhlmann*

Paul Simon's Concert in the Park, August 15, 1991 / Nov. 1991 / Warner Brothers ✦✦✦✦
Ten years after playing a free concert in New York's Central Park with Art Garfunkel, Paul Simon returned, backed by the New York session musicians and the native musicians from South Africa and Brazil who had enlivened his solo work. The show was filmed and recorded, and the audio release was a 23-track double-disc set running nearly two hours. Half the selections came from his *Graceland* and *The Rhythm of the Saints* albums, but unlike the *Graceland* Tour of 1987, the Born at the Right Time Tour of 1991 made room for Simon's earlier solo work as well as a few Simon and Garfunkel songs. Simon made such stylistically various material work together by frontloading the set with the newer stuff and rearranging some of the older solo stuff, so that "Kodachrome," for example, was refitted with a guitar line courtesy of *Graceland* player Ray Phiri. (Wisely, except for a becalmed Africanization of "Cecilia," Simon didn't monkey with the S&G songs, most of which came at the end of the set.) But Simon also toned down the Brazilian percussion that had dominated the *Saints* material and sang it more convincingly, so that "Born at the Right Time," for example, was far more effective than it had been in its studio version. On the whole, then, *Concert in the Park* managed to be an enjoyable and surprisingly cohesive career summary. *—William Ruhlmann*

1964-1993 / Sep. 28, 1993 / Warner Brothers ✦✦✦
Artist-designed box-set retrospectives tend to be idiosyncratic, and this one is no exception. Take the title, which describes a 52-track, 200+-minute, three-disc set, the earliest recording from which actually was released in 1957 (that's Tom and Jerry's chart single, "Hey, Schoolgirl") and which contains no recordings from 1964 or from later than 1991. While Simon has included all of his biggest solo hits and most of those by Simon and Garfunkel (excepting "Homeward Bound" and "I Am a Rock") and has grouped the songs into three roughly chronological sections (1957-1973, 1973-1983, and 1986-1991), he has made song choices and sequencing decisions within each section more reflective of his own taste than any historical or audience-based consideration. The music is so good it almost doesn't matter, but with only one previously unreleased song (a 1991 outtake from *The Rhythm of the Saints*), *Paul Simon 1964-1993* is little more than an abridged reshuffling of Simon's existing catalog, and one hopes for more from box sets than that. (Note also that Simon's tendency to edit his songs for use on compilations continues: "Loves Me Like a Rock" is 13 seconds shorter than the version on *There Goes Rhymin' Simon*, while "50 Ways to Leave Your Lover" has lost 29 seconds from the *Still Crazy After All These Years* version.) *—William Ruhlmann*

Songs From the Capeman / Nov. 18, 1997 / Warner Brothers ✦✦
During the production of *The Rhythm of the Saints*, Paul Simon latched upon the idea of turning the story of Salvador Agron—a '50s Puerto Rican hoodlum nicknamed the Capeman who was convicted of stabbing two kids to death during a New York street fight; during his prison term, he educated himself and turned into a poet and activist—into a musical. Collaborating with poet Derek Walcott on the lyrics and book, Simon worked on the musical for seven years, writing a set of songs that evoked doo wop, '50s rock & roll, and Puerto Rican music. A few months before the Broadway premier of *The Capeman*, Simon—who was not performing in the musical—released *Songs From the Capeman*, an album that functioned as a calling card for the play. The record suggests what a complex and ambitious musical *The Capeman* may be, but it doesn't succeed on its own terms. Simon's songs have the narrative drive of a stage musical, but are littered with idiosyncratic, conversational flourishes, profanities, and self-consciously literate wordplay that keep them insular and nearly impenetrable. Similarly, the music is forced and labored—it often sounds like he has to push the melodies into unnatural paths—and it never has the graceful, joyously organic spirit of doo wop and Puerto Rican music, which is what he needed to capture in order for *The Capeman* to succeed. Instead, the project is a cerebral exercise, not only in writing but also in white liberal guilt, and it's an exhausting one at that. *—Stephen Thomas Erlewine*

You're the One / Oct. 3, 2000 / Warner Brothers ✦✦✦
The disaster of *The Capeman* hit Paul Simon particularly hard, so he decided to quickly record a new album, his first proper collection of songs since 1990's *The Rhythm of the Saints*—his first album in ten years, really. Nevertheless, if this album has a relative, its 1982's *Hearts and Bones*, since it's a deliberately low-key, insular record, especially when compared to the sweeping worldbeat explorations of *Graceland* and *Rhythms*. But where *Hearts and Bones* was a singer/songwriter album, no two ways about it, *You're the One* illustrates the influence of its predecessors, but it's not showy about it. The African and South American rhythms are as much a foundation of Simon's music as folk is, and his compositions reflect it, boasting surprisingly tricky rhythms that carry through to his melodies themselves. That, combined with Simon's determination to meet aging head-on, makes *You're the One* a bit of an acquired taste, especially since its compositions are never overtly accessible and melodic—they're all tone-poems, driven as much by tone and lyric as song itself. This all results in a record that may be a little too deliberately low-key and elliptical for most tastes, especially since it demands full concentration even from serious fans. But this does reward close listening, and even if it doesn't shine as brilliantly as *Hearts and Bones* (his most underappreciated record), it does share some similarities in that it's a unassumingly intellectual record that feels like it was made without an audience in mind. Which means its more interesting than successful, but interesting can have its own rewards. *—Stephen Thomas Erlewine*

Simple Minds

f. 1978, Glasgow, Scotland
College Rock, Post-Punk, Pop/Rock, New Wave, Alternative Pop/Rock
Best known in the U.S. for their 1985 number one hit "Don't You (Forget About Me)" from the film *The Breakfast Club*, Scotland's Simple Minds have evolved from a post-punk art rock band influenced by Roxy Music into a grand, epic-sounding pop band along the lines of U2. The band grew out of a Glasgow punk group called Johnny and the Self-Abusers, which featured guitarist Charlie Burchill and lead singer Jim Kerr. Their early albums leaped from one style to another, with *Life in a Day* consisting mostly of dense, arty pop songs; critical acclaim followed the darker, more experimental art rock of *Real to Real Cacophony* and the Eurodisco of *Empires and Dance*. The group began a transition to a more accessible pop style with the albums *Sons and Fascination* and *Sister Feelings Call*. "Don't You (Forget About Me)" gave Simple Minds their only American chart-topper, and the song later became an international hit as well; however, Kerr's feelings about the song were ambivalent, and it did not appear on the follow-up album, *Once Upon a Time*. This album went gold and reached the U.S. Top Ten, in spite of criticism for its bombastic, over-the-top approach. A live album and the uncompromisingly political *Street Fighting Years* squandered Simple Minds' commercial momentum, however. *—Steve Huey*

New Gold Dream (81-82-83-84) / Sep. 1982 / A&M ✦✦✦✦✦
One of Scotland's finest imports, Simple Minds deliver a strong synth-reared release on *New Gold Dream*. This album harks the darker side of the band's musicianship, and such material alludes to their forthcoming pop-stadium sound which hurled them into rock mainstream during the latter part of the '80s. They were still honing their artistic rowdiness, and Kerr's pursuing vocals were still hiding. But Simple Minds' skill of tapping into internal emotion is profound on songs such as "Someone, Somewhere in Summertime" and the album's title track. But the dance-oriented tracks like "Promised You a Miracle" and "Glittering Prize" are lushly layered in deep electronic beats—it was only a matter of time for Simple Minds to expound upon such musical creativity which made them a household favorite through the 1980s. *—MacKenzie Wilson*

Sparkle in the Rain / Feb. 1984 / A&M ✦✦✦✦✦
Scotland's Simple Minds get creative and passionate on *Sparkle in the Rain*, their seventh album released prior to their mid-'80s heyday of heralding the charts. Produced by Steve Lillywhite (U2, Morrissey, XTC, Psychedelic Furs), *Sparkle in the Rain* marks the band's best effort thus far, capturing thick seascapes of illustrious lyrical visions. Frontman Jim Kerr's anthemic love songs are political and personal, and synth-beats throb over Charlie Burchill's new wave third-chord guitars and swooning bass lines. Songs like "Waterfront" and "Book of Brilliant Things" are finely cut tracks with Simple Minds' signature harking, but the glossy verse behind "Up on the Catwalk" is what's most appealing. Piano vibes are pinch-hitting and Kerr's songwriting thrives on celebrity and the falling grace that coincides that. *Sparkle in the Rain* is a glimpse of what's to come from Simple Minds. Kerr's heart-wrenching vocals soar and such emotion only leads to earning a global following. Like U2 did with 1984's *The Unforgettable Fire*, Simple Minds will touch hearts by stripping their soul. The process has already begun on *Sparkle in the Rain*. *—MacKenzie Wilson*

Once Upon a Time / Oct. 1985 / A&M ♦♦♦♦♦
Riding the coattails of the John Hughes flick *The Breakfast Club*, Simple Minds finally broke America with their theme song "Don't You Forget About Me," and their 1985 release *Once Upon a Time* captured the heart-wrenching excitement found in bands such as U2. They were now one of the biggest names in music and Jim Kerr's thirsting vocals became the band's signature. *Once Upon a Time*, featuring producer Jimmy Iovine (U2, Stevie Nicks, Bruce Springsteen), showcased more of a guitar-driven sound. The band's heavy synth-pop beats had relaxed a bit and Charlie Burchill's charming playing style was most noticeable. Also enlisting the choir-like beauty of Robin Clark, Simple Minds' popularity was expounded on songs such as "Alive & Kicking" and "Sanctify Yourself." This album was one of their best, most likely leading the pack in the band's album roster, because it exuded raw energy and solid composition not entirely captured on previous albums. *—MacKenzie Wilson*

Live in the City of Light / May 1987 / A&M ♦♦♦

Street Fighting Years / 1989 / A&M ♦♦♦
Their first proper new release since the commercial breakthrough of *Once Upon a Time* (a live album intervened) and Simple Minds makes a decidedly, noncommercial follow-up. *Street Fighting Years* is a moody, dark affair. The music is yearning and most of the songs are politically charged lyrically. It was a move that could (and did) bring commercial failure. However, *Street Fighting Years* is an artistic and elegant album that might lack immediate choruses but draws in the listener. The title track takes some dramatic turns that give the gentle melody added thrust. "Take a Step Back" pulsates and "Wall of Love" rocks with conviction. Slower tracks like the brooding "Let It All Come Down" and a spirited run through the traditional "Belfast Child" are well done. Other noteworthy tracks include a version of the Peter Gabriel classic "Biko" and the soaring "Mandela Day." It might not have satisfied the band's newly won fans, but *Street Fighting Years* is an interesting, enjoyable album with some truly lovely moments. *—Tom Demalon*

Real Life / Apr. 1991 / A&M ♦♦

● **Glittering Prize: Simple Minds 1981-1992** / Oct. 1992 / A&M ♦♦♦♦♦
Glittering Prize falls short of being a true anthology of Simple Minds, eliminating many key tracks (not even "Glittering Prize," the song the album is named after, is included) and giving too much weight to the band's later years (an inexplicable three tracks from 1991's *Real Life* are included). Still, all the mid-'80s hits are here, including "(Don't You) Forget About Me," making its first appearance on a Simple Minds album, which will be enough for most casual fans. *—Stephen Thomas Erlewine*

Good News From the Next World / Feb. 7, 1995 / Virgin ♦♦

Néapolis / 1998 / Chrysalis/EMI UK ♦♦♦
Simple Minds signed to Chrysalis for *Néapolis* and saw the return of Derek Forbes on bass. *Néapolis* signals a return to form while remaining on the cutting edge. Unlike U2, the band they have been most often compared to, Simple Minds have not lost themselves in the techno beats and processed samples of their countrymen. Longtime fans will embrace this album; from the opening track "Song for the Tribes" through the two singles "Glitterball" and "War Babies" one immediately recognizes that classic sound. Other standout tracks include "Tears of a Guy," "Superman V Supersoul," and a potential third single, "Killing Andy Warhol." The biggest surprise on the album is "Androgyny," a welcomed instrumental in the tradition of their earlier works (see *Empires and Dance*, *Sister Feelings Call* and *Sons and Fascination*). It's nice to know that in the 1990s, one classic new-wave band hasn't forgotten what they are all about. Unfortunately, Chrysalis felt there was not enough of a following outside of Europe to justify the worldwide release of the new album. *—Paul Fucito*

Celebration / Aug. 28, 2001 / Disky ♦♦♦

Simply Red

f. 1984
Sophisti-Pop, Blue-Eyed Soul, Pop/Rock, Adult Contemporary, Dance-Pop
The British soul-pop band Simply Red was formed in 1984 by singer Mick Hucknall with three ex-members of Durutti Column, Tony Bowers, Chris Joyce, and Tim Kellett. The group signed to Elektra and released 1985's *Picture Book*, which featured the Top 40 hit "Money's Too Tight (To Mention)" and the chart-topping "Holding Back the Years." The album soon went platinum, and made the group one of the major successes of 1986. The follow-up, 1987's *Men and Women*, generated the Top 40 hit "The Right Thing." The third album, 1989's *A New Flame*, went gold due to the cover of the Harold Melvin and the Blue Notes hit "If You Don't Know Me by Now" that hit number one and became a gold single. Fourth album *Stars* was a relative commercial disappointment in the U.S., but it became a major success elsewhere, especially in the U.K., where it was the best-selling album of 1991. Released in 1995, *Life* again proved more of a success at home than in America, topping charts all over Europe, as did its leadoff single, "Fairground," while spending only three months in the U.S. charts. *Blue* followed in 1998, and a year later Simply Red issued *Live at the Lyceum*. *—William Ruhlmann*

Picture Book / 1985 / Elektra ♦♦♦♦♦
The band finds a steady R&B groove reminiscent of '60s Stax house band the MG's, and, as with the MG's, it's all in the service of a big-voiced soul singer, in this case a British redhead. Features the U.S. number one "Holding Back the Years" and the U.K. Top 20 "Money's Too Tight (To Mention)." *—William Ruhlmann*

Men and Women / 1987 / Elektra ♦♦♦
After a monster debut, Simply Red's follow-up album simply didn't get the job done. It wasn't a half-hearted effort; Mick Hucknall's crackling vocals were just as exuberant, and the band's Stax/Volt-influenced lines were effectively played. The songs, however, were an uneven batch and lacked the kind of standout single Hucknall had enjoyed on the previous album with "Holding Back the Years." They did turn in an interesting version of "Ev'ry Time We Say Goodbye." *—Ron Wynn*

A New Flame / 1989 / Elektra ♦♦♦♦
Although Hucknall tries to resurrect soul in his own original songs, he's most successful at evoking the past, notably on Simply Red's second number one, a remake of the Harold Melvin & the Blue Notes classic "If You Don't Know Me by Now." *—William Ruhlmann*

Stars / Sep. 30, 1991 / East West ♦♦♦♦♦
Although it didn't have a single as strong as "Holding Back the Years" or "If You Don't Know Me By Now," *Stars* was Simply Red's best album since its debut. It was smoother and more polished than their previous work, while Mick Hucknall was singing better than ever and his songwriting was improving. *—Stephen Thomas Erlewine*

Life / Oct. 24, 1995 / East West ♦♦♦
For *Life*, Simply Red retain the basic influences that fueled their earlier albums, especially American R&B of the early '70s, specifically the Marvin Gaye of *What's Going On* and Harold Melvin and the Blue Notes-era Teddy Pendergrass. Mick Hucknall's singing has calmed down and smoothed out on such songs as "You Make Me Believe" and "So Many People," but that only makes them sound more like the product of Philadelphia International Records. On "Fairground," he opts for a Latin-tinged sound that ends up evoking Herb Alpert more than Milton Nascimento; reggae turns up on "Out on the Range," and the big-time closer, "We're in This Together," is a South African-style anthem, complete with Hugh Masekela's flugelhorn. Stripped of the international superstar trappings, *Life* is, of course, pretentious, but it does have a couple of promising songs, notably "So Beautiful" and "Remembering the First Time We Made Love." *—William Ruhlmann*

Greatest Hits / 1996 / East West ♦♦♦♦♦
Simply Red's superb *Greatest Hits* is a fine collection that captures all of their big hits, U.S. and European, up through 1996. The songs come together seamlessly on this album, with ample amounts of soul, pop, and dance influences. Included are the act's early hits, which resonated high on American charts, especially their two number one hits, "Holding Back the Years" and "If You Don't Know Me by Now." After the release of their critically acclaimed fourth album, *Stars*, their popularity waned in the U.S. while it soared to new heights in the rest of the world. Five songs are included from that album, and the caliber of these songs leads one to ponder why their chart-topping success did not continue in the U.S. This album closes with two tracks from their *Life* album—the wonderful and sarcastic "So Beautiful" and their international number one hit "Fairground," which barely bubbled under the American Hot 100. A cover of the Aretha Franklin hit "Angel" (produced by Wyclef Jean) is this collection's only new contribution. Mick Hucknall's voice can go from a soulful snarl ("It's Only Love," "Something Got Me Started") to being beautifully understated ("For Your Babies"), and his ample talents are well showcased on this top-notch collection, which also serves to heighten the disparity between American and European popular music. *—Jose Promis*

● **The Best of Simply Red: Holding Back the Years 1985-1997** / Oct. 22, 1996 / East West ♦♦♦♦♦
Best of Simply Red: Holding Back the Years 1985-1997 contains all of Simply Red's biggest British and American hits, including "Holding Back the Years," "If You Don't Know Me by Now," and "Something Got Me Started." In addition to the well-known singles, there are two new tracks added to the collection, including "Angel," a duet with the Fugees. Simply Red always worked better on singles than albums, making this single-disc compilation an excellent introduction. *—Stephen Thomas Erlewine*

Blue / May 19, 1998 / East West ♦♦♦

Love and the Russian Winter / Nov. 2, 1999 / East West ♦♦♦
Simply Red entered a holding pattern after 1991's *Stars*, turning out two records in a row that essentially replicated its charms, only with diminishing returns. Mick Hucknall must have realized he was stagnating, since 1999's *Love and the Russian Winter* is the first time since *Stars* that he's shaken up his sound. It's still recognizably Simply Red, as it trades in '70s soul and jazz-pop influences, but there are a number of reasonably contemporary influences added into the mix. As it turns out, these influences are largely based in house music, which means that Simply Red took some weird middle ground between Everything But the Girl and Soul II Soul. Still, these changes are welcome, since they've revitalized Hucknall and his collaborators, Andy Wright and Gota Yashiki. They're willing to try different sounds and write in different idioms. Occasionally, they might sound as if they're forcing matters somewhat, but there's also a number of gems that pop up on the album, from "The Spirit of Life" to "The Sky Is a Gypsy." And while the title may imply that *Love and the Russian Winter* is a concept album of sorts, that's not true—Hucknall and company have reserved their ambitions for their refurbished production instead of channeling them into a song cycle. That's for the best, actually, since Simply Red works the best on a song-by-song basis, particularly when they rely on love songs (the millennium farewell "Wave the Old World Goodbye" is one of the more awkward moments on the record). *Love and the Russian Winter* doesn't quite rise to the level of the group's strongest records, but it's a refreshing change of pace from an outfit that had seemed to have gone stagnant. *—Stephen Thomas Erlewine*

Jessica Simpson

Vocals / Teen Pop, Adult Contemporary, Dance-Pop
Dance-pop singer Jessica Simpson was born and raised in Dallas, TX, beginning her performing career as a member of her church choir; at 12, she also auditioned unsuccessfully for *The Mickey Mouse Club*. While attending church camp the following summer, Simpson was discovered by the head of a tiny CCM label, spending the next three years

recording her debut album; the label folded before the record could be released, however, although a small pressing was eventually funded by her grandmother. The teen nevertheless became a hit on the Christian Youth Conference circuit, also sharing bills with Kirk Franklin, God's Property, and Ce Ce Winans; seeking to expand her popularity in the secular market, Simpson signed to Sony, touring in support of boy-band sensations 98° prior to releasing her 1999 major label debut *Sweet Kisses*, which launched the smash "I Wanna Love You Forever." A second studio effort, *Irresistable*, appeared in spring 2001. *—Jason Ankeny*

● **Sweet Kisses** / Nov. 9, 1999 / Columbia ✦✦✦
By the end of 1999, teen pop had grown into a strangely diverse genre of its own, with each act fulfilling a different need. Britney Spears was pure, trashy fun, while Christina Aguilera was flashy and talented just like Mariah Carey. The Backstreet Boys stood above the pack with their suave sophistication and irresistible melodic charm, while 'N Sync were the Stones to the Backstreet Boys' Beatles—a little bit of the rough and tough, not quite as melodic, but almost as charming. Into the fray arrived Jessica Simpson—unlike some of her peers, a mere finalist for the New Mickey Mouse Club instead of a full-fledged member—with her debut *Sweet Kisses*, an album that positions her as the teen Celine Dion. Sure, she delves into the frothy dance-pop that's teen pop's stock-in-trade, but the heart of her album lies in adult contemporary ballads like her breakout hit "I Wanna Love You Forever," which gives her a chance to show off the richness of her voice. She doesn't over-sing, like Aguilera occasionally does, even if she has moments where she pushes the envelope slightly—just like her idol Dion. However, there are already indications that she's developing her own voice, since she is equally capable of delivering danceable urban R&B ("Final Heartbreak," "I've Got My Eyes on You," the Destiny's Child duet "Woman in Me") as she is mature balladry ("Faith in Me," the Nick Lachey duet "Where You Are"). Like most teen-pop albums, *Sweet Kisses* suffers from inconsistent material, yet the filler is well produced and performed, making the record every bit as listenable as Aguilera's fine debut. As a matter of fact, Simpson proves with this debut that she could very well be a teen popster that could easily make the transition to adult artist—and that puts her in a rarified league with Aguilera and the Backstreets. *—Stephen Thomas Erlewine*

Irresistible / May 29, 2001 / Columbia ✦✦✦
Jessica Simpson pretty much throws out any aspirations to be mature with her second album, *Irresistible*. And, in a sense, who could blame her? Her debut, *Sweet Kisses*, was pretty much stalled on the charts until the dazzling, "Jack & Diane"-sampling neo-bubblegum "I Think I'm in Love With You" was promoted to the stratosphere (hitched to *Dawson's Creek*, among other things), thereby proving the axiom that teens singing teen pop should be marketed to teens. So, that's what *Irresistible* is, at least on the surface, with Simpson looking like she stepped out of a Maxim photo shoot on the cover, filled with frothy, sugary pop tunes. There still are remnants of the middlebrow Simpson showcased on *Sweet Kisses*, notably in a fine duet with Marc Anthony called "There You Were," plus a misguided cover of the gospel standard "His Eye Is on the Sparrow" that concludes the record. Still, this takes up very little of the actual record, since these two cuts are surrounded by glossy teen pop that is designed to sound state-of-the-art, but winds up sounding curiously dated, as if it should have been released two years earlier than it was. And that's not necessarily a bad thing, at least on the surface, but apart from the opening double-punch of "Irresistible" and "A Little Bit," none of the songs register as songs—they're just stylish background music. So, it's a bit of the inverse of *Sweet Kisses*, which was too heavy on ballads, and, like that record, this is the work of pros, so it sounds fine as it plays but it lacks a song as strong as "I Think I'm in Love With You" to anchor it—so it floats away from memory. *—Stephen Thomas Erlewine*

Nancy Sinatra

b. Jun. 4, 1940, Jersey City, NJ
Vocals / Sunshine Pop, Psychedelic Pop, Baroque Pop, Pop
Frank Sinatra's daughter Nancy enjoyed a brief run of superstardom between 1966 and 1968. Not nearly the vocalist her father is, the family name didn't hurt her advances in the business, nor did the fact that she recorded for Frank's label, Reprise. Her first few singles met with little success, and Nancy was on the verge of being dropped when she hooked up with producer Lee Hazlewood and arranger Billy Strange. They urged her to lower her voice and toughen her delivery, and crafted material emphasizing growling bass lines and "go-go" tempos. One of their first efforts, the 1966 single "These Boots Are Made for Walkin'," topped the charts, inaugurating a series of hits over the next couple years, the biggest of which were "Sugar Town," "Lightning's Girl," "Love Eyes," and her number one hit duet with her father, "Somethin' Stupid." Nancy's singles were as notable for their distinctive arrangements and the odd, brooding compositions of Hazlewood, who wrote most of her hits, as her own sex-kitten vocals. Specializing in oddly disquieting songs with a sort of modern Western theme, Hazlewood teamed up with Sinatra for a few duets which presented the chalk'n'cheese combination of Nancy's thin voice with Lee's gravelly, almost spoken delivery, which recalled an off-kilter Johnny Cash. The team actually managed a few hits, some of which, especially "Some Velvet Morning," rank as some of the most bizarre MOR Top 40 pop hits of all time. *—Richie Unterberger*

Boots / 1966 / Sundazed ✦✦✦✦✦
Unexceptional debut album, built around "These Boots Are Made for Walkin'" and covers of contemporary rock and pop hits, with a couple of other Lee Hazlewood songs. The CD reissue adds a few rare early single tracks (all penned by Hazlewood) as bonus cuts, as well as the mono single version of "Boots." *—Richie Unterberger*

How Does That Grab You? / 1966 / Sundazed ✦✦✦
Sinatra's sophomore effort sticks to her usual LP formula: a hit title track, a bunch of pop covers ("Bang Bang" is the best), and some unremarkable Lee Hazlewood songs, the exception being the classy Nancy & Lee duet "Sand." There are four notable bonus tracks on the CD reissue from 45s: the fuzz-guitar-driven single "Lightning's Girl" (one of her very best songs), a cover of Buffy St. Marie's "Until It's Time for You to Go," the single "The Last of the Secret Agents," and the breezy California pop duet with her father, "Feelin' Kinda Sunday." *—Richie Unterberger*

Nancy in London / 1966 / Sundazed ✦✦✦
The change of locale for Nancy's third album didn't change her approach much: it's dominated by humdrum covers of contemporary pop and rock hits and pop standards, with some second-rank Lee Hazlewood country songs thrown in, though his compositions "Friday Child" and "Summer Wine" (the second of which is a Nancy/Lee duet) are strong, moody highlights. The four bonus tracks, taken from singles, outclass the original LP: "100 Years," "You Only Live Twice" (the single version), "Tony Rome," and her cringingly dated duet with her father, "Life's a Trippy Thing." *—Richie Unterberger*

Sugar / 1967 / Sundazed ✦✦

Country, My Way / 1967 / Sundazed ✦✦

Nancy / 1969 / Sundazed ✦✦✦

● **The Hit Years** / 1986 / Rhino ✦✦✦✦✦
Contains all the essential tracks: every hit, including those with her father and with Hazlewood, and a bunch of interesting misses, such as the theme song to the James Bond film *You Only Live Twice*. It focuses mostly on material penned by Hazlewood and has comprehensive liner notes. An Australian best-of on the Raven label, *Lightning's Girl*, has a few more songs, but this less expensive 18-track domestic compilation covers all the key bases. *—Richie Unterberger*

Fairy Tales & Fantasies: The Best of Nancy Sinatra and Lee Hazelwood / 1989 / Rhino ✦✦✦
Basically a reissue of the 1968 album *Nancy and Lee*, with some bonus tracks. This has all of the duo's hits ("Summer Wine," "Jackson," "Sand," "Lady Bird," and "Some Velvet Morning"), which easily outclass the filler material. And those hits are about as inspired as middle-of-the-road pop gets, especially the eerie "Some Velvet Morning," one of the strangest songs ever to crack the Top 40. *—Richie Unterberger*

Siouxsie & the Banshees

f. 1976, London, England, **db.** 1996
College Rock, British Punk, Post-Punk, Goth Rock, Alternative Pop/Rock, Punk
Siouxsie & the Banshees were among the longest-lived and most successful acts to emerge from the London punk community; over the course of a career which lasted two decades, they evolved from an abrasive, primitive art-punk band into a stylish, sophisticated unit which even notched a left-field Top 40 hit. Throughout their numerous lineup changes and textural shifts, the group remained under the leadership of vocalist Siouxsie Sioux, born Susan Dallion; she and the Banshees' initial lineup emerged from the Bromley Contingent, a notorious group of rabid Sex Pistols fans. In addition to bassist Steve Severin and guitarist Marco Perroni, the band included drummer John Simon Ritchie, who assumed the name Sid Vicious. Soon after, Vicious joined the Sex Pistols, while Perroni went on to join Adam and the Ants. The core duo of Sioux and Severin reached the U.K. Top Ten with their 1978 debut single, "Hong Kong Garden"; their grim, dissonant first LP, *The Scream*, followed later in the year. During a 1979 tour, drummer Budgie became a permanent member of the group and remained with the Banshees' throughout the duration of their career. The band returned to the studio for 1980's *Kaleidoscope*, a more subtle and melodic effort than their prior records; on the strength of the U.K. Top 20 smash "Happy House," the album reached the Top Five. With 1986's *Tinderbox*, Siouxsie and the Banshees finally reached the U.S. Top 100 album charts, largely on the strength of the excellent single "Cities in Dust." 1988's *Peep Show*, a techno-inspired outing, gave the group their first U.S. chart single with "Peek-a-Boo." 1991's *Superstition* was their most commercially successful effort, spawning their lone U.S. Top 40 hit "Kiss Them for Me." *—Jason Ankeny*

The Scream / 1978 / Geffen ✦✦✦✦
By waiting until punk essentially had blown over to sign a contract, the Banshees had a clear field for their harsh rock attack and plenty of time to prepare it. The result is this fierce debut, which fulfills the promise of punk and suggests (unlike most of its progenitors) that it has a future. *—William Ruhlmann*

Join Hands / 1979 / Geffen ✦✦

Kaleidoscope / 1980 / Geffen ✦✦✦✦✦
After *Join Hands*, guitarist John McKay and drummer Kenny Morris departed the Banshees, leaving the band at a crossroads. Siouxsie Sioux and Steven Severin elected to soldier on with ex-Slits drummer Budgie and two guitarists, ex-Sex Pistol Steve Jones and John McGeoch of Magazine as guest Banshees. Despite the personnel upheaval, the result is a surprisingly strong record. While a number of the songs here are still dark-hued and feature bleak lyrics, they are made very palatable by extraordinarily imaginative production values featuring intricate synthesizer-flecked arrangements; psychedelic touches in "Christine," and spaceship synthesizer swoops in "Tenant," and rhythmic camera clicks in "Red Light" all enliven their respective songs. Sound quality here is lighter and much clearer than on previous releases. Sioux's singing shows noticeable improvement here, still tuneless at times but also exhibiting more range and subtlety than previously. The song "Hybrid," a Joy Division-style number, shows her vocals running the gamut from primitive to inspired. Other highlights include the galloping, vibrant up-tempo number "Skin," the spooky and atmospheric "Lunar Camel," the medium-tempo rocker "Trophy," and the punky vocalise "Clockface." This was a make-or-break album for the band, and happily they came through strongly. *—David Cleary*

● **Once Upon a Time: The Singles** / 1981 / Geffen ♦♦♦♦♦
Once Upon a Time: The Singles collects all ten of Siouxsie & the Banshees' A-sides spanning the years 1978-1981, with four songs otherwise unavailable on LP. It's a neat and accessible encapsulation of the group's early guitar-driven sound—a frosty, dissonant art-punk that had a tremendous impact on the emerging goth-rock scene. Unlike similarly forbidding work by such proto-goth contemporaries as Joy Division or the Cure, the early Banshees were tense and visceral; the darkness of the *Once Upon a Time* singles doesn't come from a sense of downcast gloom so much as it does from a jittery angst. Yet as challenging as the music is, it's also accessible enough for eight of these singles to have charted in the British Top 50. The melodies are angular and almost alien, yes, but oddly memorable once the listener has assimilated them. Starting shortly after the period covered by this collection, Siouxsie Sioux's icy detachment would be fused with an elegant romanticism and lusher, smoother arrangements. Which means that *Once Upon a Time* isn't the one, definitive Banshees compilation, but it is a cohesive and essential overview of the band's edgy, influential peak. —*Steve Huey*

Juju / Aug. 1981 / Geffen ♦♦♦♦
They're shifting gradually toward a more straightforward rock sound, but the Banshees also add Middle Eastern touches here. Contains the British hits "Spellbound" and "Arabian Knights." —*William Ruhlmann*

Kiss in the Dream House / 1982 / Geffen ♦♦♦
This release shows the band backpedaling a bit from its excellently forthright predecessor *Juju* to update the more avant-garde stylings of *Kaleidoscope*. This album is in fact the Banshees' crowning glory in this experimental vein. Production and arrangements are highly varied and accomplished, and Sioux's singing by now is excellent, capable of imaginative shadings and free of its former tunelessness. "Obsession" is scored for chimes, overdubbed breathing, swallowed synthesizer sounds, strings, and very occasional guitar touches; this all supports a fine vocal with lyrics about the speaker's fixation on her object of desire. "Green Finger" is a driving, up-tempo number with Joy Division melodic bass, sparkling synthesizer touches, and wacky recorder tootlings. "Painted Bird" features a full helping of multi-tracked vocals propelled by a drumbeat that is alternately skittering and thumping; portions of this song suggest a nightmare version of Fleetwood Mac's "Go Your Own Way." "Cocoon" is best characterized as mutant bopping jazz with an often breathy, cooing vocal. "She's a Carnival" and "Slowdive" suggest eccentric stabs at mainstream acceptance, the former being a comparatively gutsy and forthright rocker, the latter a violin-colored dance beat number with hints of New Order or David Bowie that is a catchy melodic hook away from being the real thing. This fine platter is well worth purchasing. —*David Cleary*

Nocturne / 1983 / Geffen ♦♦♦
This is a top-notch live double album recorded in 1983 at the Royal Albert Hall. The sound quality is first-rate and the band performs excellently here. The songs on this release run a wide chronological range, from early numbers like the Lennon/McCartney cover "Helter Skelter" (here given a fire-breathing performance) to their recent single of the time (another Beatles song), "Dear Prudence." Much of the material is culled from the group's recent releases *Juju, A Kiss in the Dreamhouse*, and *Kaleidoscope*. This platter serves as an excellent, no-nonsense introduction to the band's music for neophytes, while fans of the group will appreciate the tight, gutsy, stripped-down performances. This album is strongly recommended. —*David Cleary*

Hyaena / 1984 / Geffen ♦♦♦♦♦
Broadening the eclectically experimental landscape of 1982's *Kiss in the Dream House* with the occasional string arrangement and a spacious sound mix, Siouxsie & the Banshees' Geffen debut nicely bridges the gap between the band's handful of more-punk-than-pop early releases and their run of new wave, radio-friendly hits from the late '80s and early '90s. And though echoes of classic albums like *Kaleidoscope* and *JuJu* are heard in dark and menacing tracks such as "Bring Me the Head of the Preacher Man" and "Blow Your House Down," the emphasis here is on layered arrangements and pop tunes disguised as art-house production numbers ("Dazzle"); tasteful horn and keyboard parts expand the group's guitar-dominated sound and provide Siouxsie with an airy and dream-like backdrop in which to fully display her considerable vocal talents. Siouxsie further refines things by also including a generous share of fleet and gothic-tinged pop numbers like "Belladonna," "Running Town," and the band's hit cover of "Dear Prudence." Anchored by the signature sound of Steve Severin's guitar-like bass and Budgie's exotically adept percussion work, *Hyaena* qualifies as one of Siouxsie & the Banshees' finest moments. —*Stephen Cook*

Tinderbox / 1986 / Geffen ♦♦♦♦♦
This is the most musically up-tempo of all the Banshees' albums and the most stylistically consistent one since *The Scream* and *Join Hands*. Most of the selections here feature urgently rocking drumming, drivingly aggressive yet fully textured guitar playing, and masterful, gutsy singing. The songs here are intense and unfold slowly, some starting off less vigorously but becoming hard rockers further along. There is of course a fine line between consistency and lack of contrast, but this album stays firmly on the side of the former; in fact, there's a certain satisfying feel to the musically uniform wall of sound here. The arrangements are less complex than in immediately preceding albums, but there are still plenty of subtle, effective production touches to be found throughout, most notably in the song "Cannons." "Cities in the Dust," a dance-pop number with a bell-like synthesizer opening section stretches the above-mentioned boundaries the most, though typically bleak lyrics keep this selection from any sense of vacuity. This excellent release is well worth purchasing. —*David Cleary*

Through the Looking Glass / 1987 / Geffen ♦♦♦
Well-selected album of rock and pop cover songs, including everything from Sparks' "This Town Ain't Big Enough for Both of Us" to "Strange Fruit." —*William Ruhlmann*

Peep Show / 1988 / Geffen ♦♦♦
As good as it is in places, this is the sound of a once-terrific band treading water. Some of the songs are fine, but they're too layered in self-referential mystique to actually win over listeners. The single ("Peek-A-Boo") is one exception—a seductive glimpse of the sleek lines and pouty truculence of old. But other songs, including two singles—"Killing Jar" and "Last Beat of my Heart"—fail to convince. The obituary writers had started sharpening their pencils. —*Alex Ogg*

Superstition / 1991 / Geffen ♦♦♦
A similar album to that of *Peepshow*, this time with more precise production and a lighter feeling to many of the songs. While Banshees' albums like *Tinderbox* and *Juju* were dark affairs, *Superstition*'s sound is representative of the pink of the album cover. A softer pop sound, mixed with the Banshees' penchant for minor keys and strange imagery. They manage to pull it off quite well on most tracks. "Fear (Of the Unknown)" and "Drifter" are classic Siouxsie stuff, and "Kiss Them for Me" gave them their first significant entry into the U.S. singles charts. But it is tracks like "Silly Thing" which hold this album back. This track manages to do what the Banshees had avoided all their career—sounding like someone else. One of their most accessible albums, *Superstition* has appeal without losing its edge. —*Chris True*

● **Twice Upon a Time: The Singles** / Oct. 13, 1992 / Geffen ♦♦♦♦♦
Siouxsie Sioux has always maintained that it was not her intention to create the goth-rock movement. While that lofty statement may be a little self-serving, it's partly right. The Banshees' post-1982 singles (documented in entirety on *Twice Upon a Time*) have a lush and expansive sound that directly influenced the goth sound. From the opening of "Fireworks" it is immediately apparent that Siouxsie and the Banshees were growing up. By the time of "Peek-a-Boo," the band had learned how to incorporate their early dissonance with their majestic, late-'80s sound. The *Twice Upon a Time* collection is one great step after another, with the only drawback being a poor remix of 1991's "Fear of the Unknown." A solid introduction for the unknowing. —*Chris True*

Rapture / Feb. 1995 / Geffen ♦♦

The Sir Douglas Quintet

f. 1964, San Antonio, TX, **db.** 1972
Tex-Mex, Rock & Roll
Texas had always had its own brand of rock & roll—a little bit o' country, a little bit o' blues, with a heapin' helpin' o' hot sauce poured over the top. Doug Sahm was no stranger to the studio when he formed the Sir Douglas Quintet in 1964; he'd been at it since the age of six, and already possessed an encyclopedic knowledge and innate understanding of those local flavors when the band cut its first big hit, "She's About a Mover."

The ingredient that set the Quintet apart was Tex-Mex, that curious, joyous, irresistible, danceable, festive feast that married the jumpy Mexican *conjunto* to good ol' rock & roll. With Augie Meyers on the organ and a rhythm section that couldn't stop cookin', Sir Doug Sahm let it be known that good-time music was alive and kickin' in San Antone.

After the Quintet itself dissolved, Sahm cut numerous solo albums and collaborations, spreading the Tex-Mex influence. In the late '80s he and Meyers teamed up with two of their mentors, Freddy Fender and Flaco Jimenez, to form the Texas Tornados, keeping that high and happy sound alive. —*Jeff Tamarkin*

Live Texas Tornado / Aug. 11, 1998 / Takoma ♦♦♦♦
In the 1960s and early 1970s, no band better illustrated the richness of the Texas musical experience than the Sir Douglas Quintet. Lead singer Doug Sahm and his friends could almost always be counted on for versatility, and they could usually be counted on to cook. A 1998 reissue, *Live Texas Tornado* is a gem-filled CD that boasts classic live performances at the Whiskey-a-Go-Go in Hollywood and the Club Foot in Austin, TX. The band is in excellent form on everything from Tex-Mex ("Who Were You Thinking Of" and "The Rains Came") to 1960s rock ("She's About a Mover," "Wooly Bully") to 1940s-type R&B (T-Bone Walker's "T-Bone Shuffle"). Another high point of the CD is an interpretation of Charley Pride's country smash "Is Anybody Going to San Antone," which gets the Tex-Mex treatment instead of the Nashville treatment. Unfortunately, the CD doesn't list the dates or even the years of these recordings, and equally frustrating is the fact that it clocks in at a skimpy 35 minutes. As much great music as the Quintet recorded, Takoma could have easily made it twice as long. But the music that Takoma does include is superb. Despite its skimpiness and lack of recording dates, this is a CD that's well worth having. —*Alex Henderson*

● **Prime of Sir Douglas Quintet** / Oct. 19, 1999 / Music Club ♦♦♦♦♦
It is unfortunate that no one can seem to muster a definitive collection of Sir Douglas Quintet's early (pre-*Smash*) recordings. This 15-song disc is a pretty good try, and has very good music, but doesn't quite take the cigar. No original recording or release dates are given, and the liner notes are vague about the sources for the material. About half of the tracks did show up on Tribe singles (and their sole Tribe LP) in the mid-'60s. The rest are of more mysterious origin, some sounding like casual demos, and some sounding as if they may date from a later period. The important thing to note is that this *does* have the original versions of their mid-'60s hits "She's About a Mover" and the equally worthy, though lesser known, "The Rains Came." "In Time" is an awkward but appealing attempt to incorporate British Invasion influences; "Beginning of the End" has that special lazy Texas doo wop/pop feel typical of Meaux's early-'60s productions; "Please Just Say So" is top-drawer Tex-Mex rock; and "Bacon Fat" is an engagingly sloppy cover of the Andre Williams R&B dance tune. The more obscure selections have less of a "band" sound and more of a country/folk/blues orientation that puts Sahm's great roots vocals at the fore.

On some of the slow country tunes, he sounds uncannily like Elvis Costello *wants* to sound when doing country music. "Blue Pass Me By" sounds like a Tribe-era outtake with its smoky barroom feel, while Sahm's "I Don't Want to Go Home" and the cover of Dylan's "One Too Many Mornings" have a more mature folk-rock feel. Sahm's singing is cool throughout, and almost everything is a good listen; it's just that a significant group such as Sir Douglas deserves a more thorough, and more thoroughly documented, compilation. *—Richie Unterberger*

• **Best of the Sir Douglas Quintet** / Mar. 20, 2000 / Beat Rocket ✦✦✦✦✦
A more or less straight-up reissue of the group's Tribe album. When producer Huey Meaux released this disc in 1966, he probably though it was the end of the group, as they had hadn't hit the Top 40 in almost a year and a drug bust decimated their ranks. Cobbled together from their 1965 sessions, this brings together "She's About a Mover," "The Rains Came," and strong versions of "Bacon Fat," "Quarter to Three," and "It's a Man Down There." If you're going to slim the collection down to just one Sir Doug collection, this is the one to grab. *—Cub Koda*

Sir Douglas Quintet Is Back! / Mar. 20, 2000 / Beat Rocket ✦✦✦✦✦
This and Beat Rocket's companion reissue of the 1966 *The Best of Sir Douglas Quintet* album seem to gather most or all of what the group recorded for Tribe in the mid-'60s. Seems simple enough, but it's cause for rejoicing among '60s collectors, considering that this back catalog had somehow eluded the marketplace for more than 30 years prior to these two sets. If you're looking to choose one over the other, *The Best of* would get the nod for its inclusion of their only two Tribe hits: ("She's About a Mover" and "The Rains Came"). However, the various flop singles and outtakes comprising *The Sir Douglas Quintet Is Back!* are about equal in quality to the sister volume, with the same invigorating, erratic combination of British Invasion, Cajun, blues, soul, country, and even folk-rock. Certainly "In Time," a minor-key Sahm original with echoes of the Animals and the Zombies, and "Blues Pass Me By," a grand illustration of Sahm's stature as one of the finest white soul-rock vocalists ever, rate among their finer moments. Another Sahm original, "She Digs My Love," has astonishing fluttering blues-rock guitar licks that sound a hell of a lot like Jimi Hendrix—although Hendrix had yet to release records under his own name when it came out. According to the liner notes, their debut 1964 single "Sugar Bee" preceded the Beatles' "She's a Woman" by several months, boasting a *very* similar riff and rhythm. It does make you wonder whether some of rock's giants somehow managed to borrow some ideas from Sir Douglas Quintet singles that very few people heard. At times the material on this disc can be perfunctory, but the mix of so many elements in one band (and sometimes in one song) are seldom less than interesting. *—Richie Unterberger*

Soul Jam / Mar. 21, 2000 / Classic World ✦✦✦
If you need a CD of the Sir Douglas Quintet blasting through a set of R&B and blues standards, this collection's right up your alley. Culled from various albums and B-sides, the set list includes "Mr. Pitiful," "I'll Go Crazy," "Night Train," "Please Please Please," "Kansas City," "Stagger Lee," "The Things That I Used to Do," and "Turn on Your Lovelight." Fans of Doug Sahm will want this set, a nice collection of Texas roadhouse music. *—Cub Koda*

Sir Mix-a-Lot

b. Aug. 12, 1963
Vocals, Leader / Pop-Rap, West Coast Rap
Sir Mix-a-Lot put Seattle on the rap map in the late '80s with catchy, comedic dramas drenched in b-boy culture and punctuated by his whiny vocals. Sir Mix-a-Lot vaulted into the spotlight and into controversy with the single "Baby Got Back." Not only was it an enormous pop and R&B hit, it triggered a backlash against what was widely viewed as both sexist and racist lyrics from Mix-a-Lot in his celebration of rear ends and putdown of women who lacked them. It helped make the *Mack Daddy* album one of 1992's biggest, although 1994's *Chief Booty Knocka* and 1996's *Return of the Bumpasaurus* failed to match its success. In 2000, Rhino released an 18-track best-of titled *Beepers, Benzos & Booty: The Best of Sir Mix-a-Lot*. *—John Floyd*

Swass / 1988 / Def American ✦✦✦

Seminar / Mar. 1988 / Def American ✦✦✦

Mack Daddy / Apr. 1991 / Def American ✦✦✦
The massive success of "Baby Got Back" may have earned Sir Mix-a-Lot the dreaded "one-hit wonder" label, as well as an appearance on VH-1's "Where Are They Now?," but the Seattle native has always been a much more interesting and important figure than his reputation would suggest. One of the first rappers outside of New York and L.A. to score significant chart success, Mix-a-Lot's music is generally a lot more irreverent and tongue-in-cheek than people give him credit for, the work of a chubby studio geek living out his most ridiculous playboy fantasies on wax. "Baby Got Back" may be the song that put Sir Mix-a-Lot on the map, but it's actually one of the album's weaker tracks. Far better is *Mack Daddy*'s first single, "One Time's Got No Case," a song that finds Mix-a-Lot addressing standard hip-hop subject matter in a novel fashion, striking out against racist police officers not through gunplay or violence but by handing the guilty parties a righteous legal smackdown in a court of law. The rest of *Mack Daddy* charts a similarly cheeky cruise through the not-so-mean streets of Seattle, with Mix-a-Lot addressing such vital subject matters as the nefarious proprietors of fake designer merchandise at swap meets ("Swap Meet Louie") and the importance of not getting whipped by opportunistic females ("Sprung on the Cat"). It's all extremely silly stuff, made even more so by Mix-a-Lot's nasal flow and knack for ridiculous double entendres: "Yo baby, I got a big snake, all you gotta do is make it dance" is a typically subtle Mix-a-Lot come-on. But damn if isn't infectious, funky, and downright fun, making *Mack Daddy* one of the premiere hip-hop guilty pleasures of the '90s. *—Nathan Rabin*

Chief Boot Knocka / Jul. 19, 1994 / Rhyme Cartel ✦✦✦
Anyone who has had the pleasure of interviewing Sir Mix-a-Lot can tell you that he's extremely intelligent. The Seattle rapper can spend hours talking about political and social issues, and his best sociopolitical offerings are in a class with anything that Public Enemy, KRS-1, and Ice-T have done. But Mix was never marketed as a hip-hop intellectual or a hardcore rapper; listeners usually think of him as the quirky, goofy pop-rapper who gave us "Baby Got Back" and "Posse's on Broadway," and Mix gladly went with the flow because fun, escapist tunes are what earned him the big bucks. *Chief Boot Knocka*, Mix's second album for American and fourth album overall, doesn't pretend to be a Public Enemy release—this is pop-rap that must be judged by pop-rap standards instead of hardcore rap standards. And when those standards are applied, the album is a winner. While fun, frivolous numbers like "Let It Beaounce" and the hit "Put 'Em on the Glass" didn't get much respect from hip-hop's hardcore, there is no denying how infectious they are. The fact is that there is good pop-rap and bad pop-rap; like Salt-N-Pepa and Young MC, Mix knows how to provide material that is commercial but still has some bite. The Seattle resident does get into serious topics on "Take My Stash" (which was inspired by his problems with the IRS) and "Don't Call Me Da Da," but, overall, this is very much a party album. Is it regrettable that someone who is capable of writing sociopolitical gems like "National Anthem" and "Society's Creation" has neglected his more hard-hitting side? Absolutely. But that doesn't make *Chief Boot Knocka* any less effective as party music. *—Alex Henderson*

Return of the Bumpasaurus / Aug. 27, 1996 / Warner Brothers ✦✦✦

• **Beepers, Benzos & Booty: The Best of Sir Mix-a-Lot** / Jun. 20, 2000 / Rhino ✦✦✦✦✦
Rhino's *Beepers, Benzos & Booty: The Best of Sir Mix-a-Lot* collects the Seattle rapper's definitive tracks, including the infamous "Baby Got Back," "My Hooptie," "Society's Creation," "Just Da Pimpin' in Me," "Posse on Broadway," and "Square Dance Rap." A fun compilation of one of rap's most consistently funny artists. *—Heather Phares*

Sisqó (Mark Andrews)

b. Baltimore, MD
Urban, Pop-Rap
Even before Sisqó became an overnight superstar in summer 2000 with the infamous "Thong Song," he was no stranger to success. Not many may have recognized his name, but his voice was no doubt familiar, since he was a member of the massively successful '90s R&B group Dru Hill. Long before Sisqó dyed his hair and tattooed his body, he was born Mark Andrews in Baltimore, MD. He co-founded the group Dru Hill in 1995 with high school friends Jazz, Nokio, and Woody and saw their debut album released in 1996, instantly notable for Keith Sweat's production work. But Dru Hill quickly became noteworthy themselves with "Tell Me," a huge R&B hit. Two years later in 1998, Sisqó again graced the airwaves with the second Dru Hill album, *Enter the Dru*. After the success of this album, it didn't take long for the prolific young artist to bounce back the following summer with his solo album, *Unleash the Dragon*. The album's hit singles propelled it to multi-platinum success, setting the stage for Sisqó's forays into acting. He first appeared in the teen comedy *Get Over It* before signing a development deal with NBC television and a five-picture deal with Miramax. By the end of 2000, Sisqó was not only a music star but also a teen phenomenon because of his youthful looks, toned body, trendy clothing, and stylish hair—and his omnipresence on MTV obviously didn't hurt. Following commercially successful guest appearances on DMX's "What These B*****s Want" and Lil' Kim's "How Many Licks" that kept him in the spotlight while he spent time in the studio, Sisqó re-emerged in the summer of 2001 with *Return of Dragon*, his attempt to prove that "Thong Song" wasn't just a novelty success. *—Jason Birchmeier*

• **Unleash the Dragon** / Nov. 30, 1999 / Def Soul ✦✦✦
By the end of his debut solo album, Dru Hill's finest singer Sisqó has beaten the same rhythmic pattern, which is churned in and out of nearly every song, into the ground. Loaded with whispered bedroom moans, which have become late-'90s R&B clichés, *Unleash the Dragon* is short on any real songs to justify the pointless replay of these familiar grooves. Only when he actually unleashes his inner dragon, like on the club thumper "Thong Song," does Sisqó sound at all like the ferocious soulman he fancies himself to be. There's also little distinction among the guest spots here (though Make It Hot's turn on the jittery "Got to Get It" offers some sparks). And once the beats—which borrow heavily from the contemporary R&B playbook—are programmed, there's little for Sisqó to do but coast along the grooves, with all the conviction and commitment of a soul robot. *—Michael Gallucci*

Return of Dragon / Jun. 19, 2001 / Def Soul ✦✦✦
Sisqó's second solo album, *Return of Dragon*, follows up a debut that unexpectedly shot to the top of the charts a year earlier and remained there, week after week. That debut album, *Unleash the Dragon*, was almost solely powered by an omnipresent summer anthem in "Thong Song"—a difficult feat to duplicate, an even more difficult feat to top. But even if *Return of Dragon* doesn't have a surefire novelty hit like "Thong Song" on it, it still has enough firepower to carry Sisqó back to the top of the charts. It's a safe record, no doubt, offering only ten full-length songs and an ensemble cast of songwriters and producers. But regardless of how few risks Sisqó takes on this album, the result is commendable, an energetic, slick, and stylish album with plenty of subtle sex and overt gloss—everything early-2000s pop listeners demand in their superstars. To be honest, though, pop fans aren't looking for well-crafted albums but rather dynamite singles. And this album has its fair share. In fact, somewhere around half of these ten songs could function as hit singles in 2001, with "Can I Live," "Dance for Me," and "Close Your Eyes" being the most obvious choices. In particular, "Can I Live" stands out on the album mostly because of its over-the-top execution; here, the timeless Teddy Riley takes the reigns with

songwriting partner D'Wayne Jones, crafting a jittery Timbaland-style beat and working various members of Sisqó's new affiliates, the Dragon Family, into the song. Yet while "Can I Live" stands out as a step in a new direction for Sisqó, "Dance for Me" takes a look back to "Thong Song," resulting in a similarly sexy dancefloor anthem that is just dying for a sleazy, near-naked-dancers-everywhere MTV treatment. In short, Sisqó gives you exactly what you want—assuming you liked his debut album—offering a can't-miss collection of should-be hits and even more of his ceaseless crooning. *—Jason Birchmeier*

Sister Sledge

f. 1971, North Philadelphia, PA

Smooth Soul, Quiet Storm, Urban, Disco, Soul

Best known for their work with Chic in the late '70s, siblings Debbie, Kim, Joni, and Kathy Sledge—collectively Sister Sledge—reached the height of their popularity during the disco era but had been recording since the early '70s and were still active in the late '90s. The group was formed in Philadelphia in 1971, when the sisters' ages ranged from 12 to 16, and they recorded their first single, "Time Will Tell," for the Philly-based Money Back label. At first, the group called itself Sisters Sledge, but after a few years, decided to change "Sisters" to "Sister." Sister Sledge's first national hit came in 1974, when "Love, Don't You Go Through No Changes on Me" reached number 31 on the R&B charts and the Philadelphians recorded their debut album, *Circle of Love*. It wasn't until 1979, when Chic leaders Nile Rodgers and Bernard Edwards produced *We Are Family*, that Sister Sledge really exploded commercially. "He's the Greatest Dancer" and "We Are Family" both soared to number one on the R&B charts. Sister Sledge's next album, *Love Somebody Today* (1980), was also produced by the Rodgers/Edwards team, and the single "Got to Love Somebody" became a number six R&B hit. In 1981, Sister Sledge switched producers and worked with Narada Michael Walden, who produced 1981's excellent *All American Girls*. The title song was a number three R&B hit, and in 1982, Sister Sledge had a number 14 R&B hit with a cover of Mary Wells' "My Guy" that appeared on *The Sisters*. But after that, the foursome's popularity faded, and it never had another Top 20 hit in the U.S. Sister Sledge left Atlantic for good in 1985, but its members kept busy in the 1990s. *—Alex Henderson*

• **The Best of Sister Sledge (1973-1985)** / Sep. 1, 1992 / Rhino ♦♦♦♦♦

Sister Sledge evolved quite a bit during the 12 years documented on this 1992 collection, which traces the Philadelphians' evolution from bubblegum soulsters to sexy but wholesome disco-era darlings to struggling urban-contemporary act. After early numbers like "Mama Never Told Me" and "Love Don't You Go Through No Changes on Me" (both recorded at a time when the sisters were still in their teens and came across as sort of a female Jackson 5), they dive headfirst into disco/soul with "Cream of the Crop" (an underrated, Philly-sounding pearl) and finally hit the big time with the Chic-produced mega-hits "We Are Family" and "He's the Greatest Dancer." One hears Sledge entering the '80s on a high note with "Got to Love Somebody" but by the middle of the decade sounding less inspired on the singles "Frankie" and "Dancing on the Jagged Edge." One of the collection's most disappointing tracks is the reggae remix of "He's Just a Runaway." While it's true that this is the version that became a medium-size hit, the more rock-ish version found on *All American Girls* packs a much greater punch. But despite a few weak spots here and there, this is a gem-laden CD that paints a generally impressive picture of the group. *—Alex Henderson*

We Are Family [Deluxe Edition] / 1995 / Rhino ♦♦♦♦♦

Before 1979's *We Are Family*, Sister Sledge wasn't a huge name in the R&B/disco world. The group had enjoyed a small following and scored a few minor hits, including "Love, Don't You Go Through No Changes on Me" in 1974 and "Blockbuster Boy" in 1977. But it wasn't until *We Are Family* that the Philadelphia siblings finally exploded commercially, and the people they have to thank for their commercial success are Chic leaders Nile Rodgers and Bernard Edwards. The Rodgers/Edwards team handles all of the writing, producing, and arranging on this album; so not surprisingly, almost everything on *We Are Family* is very Chic-sounding. That is true of the sexy "He's the Greatest Dancer" and the anthemic, uplifting title song (both of which soared to number one on the R&B charts), as well as excellent album tracks like the lush "Easier to Love," the perky "One More Time," and the addictive "Thinking of You." The least Chic-sounding tune on the album is the ballad "Somebody Loves Me," which favors a classic sweet soul approach and is the type of song one would have expected from Thom Bell, Gamble & Huff, or Holland-Dozier-Holland rather than Rodgers/Edwards. Meanwhile, the intoxicating "Lost in Music" (a number 35 R&B hit) is about as Chic-sounding as it gets. When Rhino reissued *We Are Family* on CD in 1995, it added four bonus tracks, all of which are remixes of either the title song or "Lost in Music." These remixes are intriguing; it's interesting to hear late '70s classics turned into high-tech 1990s dance-pop. But they are less than essential, and the original versions are by far the best—how can you improve on perfection? Both creatively and commercially, *We Are Family* is Sister Sledge's crowning achievement. *—Alex Henderson*

Sisters of Mercy

f. 1980, Leeds, England, **db.** 1990

College Rock, Goth Rock, Alternative Pop/Rock

One of England's leading "goth" bands of the 1980s, the Sisters of Mercy play a slow, gloomy, ponderous hybrid of metal and psychedelia, often incorporating dance beats; the one constant in the band's career has been deep-voiced singer Andrew Eldritch. (There is some disagreement as to whether the group took its name from an order of Catholic nuns or from the Leonard Cohen song of the same name.) Eldritch originally formed the band in 1980 with guitarist Gary Marx and recorded its first single with a drum machine dubbed Doktor Avalanche. Guitarist Ben Gunn and bassist Craig Adams were added to make live gigs feasible, and the Sisters built a reputation through several singles and EPs. Gunn left the band in 1983 and was replaced by Wayne Hussey. The Sisters of Mercy recorded their first full-length album, *First and Last and Always*, in 1985, but two years later, internal dissent had split them apart; Marx left to form Ghost Dance, and Adams and Hussey departed shortly thereafter. A legal dispute ensued over the rights to the name Sisters of Mercy; Adams and Hussey attempted to use the name Sisterhood, but Eldritch released an EP under the name to prevent its usage, and the two finally settled on the Mission. Eldritch chiefly utilized a corps of temporary sidemen from this point on (although former Gun Club bassist Patricia Morrison was an official member of the group for a short time) and rebounded with his two biggest-selling American LPs, *Floodland* and *Vision Thing*. He is currently the group's only member. *—Steve Huey*

First and Last and Always / 1985 / Elektra ♦♦♦

Sisters of Mercy's first full-length album didn't quite have the powerful musical vision of their early EPs, but its gloom was more focused, making it an impressive debut album. *—Stephen Thomas Erlewine*

Floodland / 1987 / Elektra ♦♦♦♦♦

While the goth scene in England was picking up commercial steam in the mid-1980s, the Sisters of Mercy may have seemed quiet, but they roared back with 1987's *Floodland*. Opening with the driving two-part hymn "Dominion/Mother Russia," Sisters leader Andrew Eldtrich (along with bassist Patricia Morrison) creates a black soundscape that is majestic and vast. While the earlier Sisters releases were noisy, sometimes harsh affairs, *Floodland* is filled with lush production (thanks to Meatloaf writer/producer Jim Stienman and the New York Choral Society) and lyric imagery that is both scary and glorious. The slower tracks, like "Flood" and "1959," are some of the best ethereal sounds goth has to offer, and the downright regal "This Corrosion" is one of the best songs of the genre. A definite milestone. *—Chris True*

Vision Thing / Nov. 1990 / Elektra ♦♦♦♦

• **Some Girls Wander by Mistake** / Oct. 20, 1992 / Elektra ♦♦♦♦♦

Collecting a number of their better singles, *Some Girls Wander by Mistake* offers a good introduction to the Sisters of Mercy. *—AMG*

A Slight Case of Overbombing: Greatest Hits, Vol. 1 / 1993 / Elektra ♦♦♦♦

A Slight Case of Overbombing gathered together material from goth merchants the Sisters of Mercy's three major label releases. That fact immediately sets the stage for complaints from longtime fans desiring their indie music. However, for the listener more familiar with the band's mid- to late-'80s college radio tracks, this is a very good collection. The lyrics are rather pointless and Andrew Eldritch's vocals lack dynamics, but his singing has personality that overcomes his limitations. It's the edgy, hard, gothic rock of the music that is their strength. There's an undeniable pull to songs like the galloping "This Corrosion" or the epic "More" (both produced by Jim Steinman). There's also a mix of "Temple of Love," featuring Ofra Haza, and an unreleased track, "Under the Gun." Not essential, but a good record for the casual fan (although more extensive liner notes would have been nice). *—Tom Demalon*

Sixpence None the Richer

f. 1993

Alternative CCM, Adult Alternative Pop/Rock, CCM

Named in honor of a passage from C.S. Lewis' *Mere Christianity*, the Austin, TX-based CCM trio Sixpence None the Richer began taking shape in the early 1990s, when guitarist Matt Slocum first met vocalist Leigh Nash (nee Bingham) at a church retreat. Initially a trio rounded out by bassist T.J. Behling, the group recorded a 1993 demo which led to their signing with the R.E.X. label; their debut LP, *The Fatherless & the Widow*, appeared soon after. With rhythm guitarist Tess Wiley, new bassist J.J. Plasencio, and drummer Dale Baker, Sixpence None the Richer toured before returning to the studio to record their sophomore effort, 1995's *This Beautiful Mess*; the *Tickets for a Prayer Wheel* EP followed later that same year. Both Wiley and Plasencio exited prior to the group's next LP, an eponymously titled effort issued in 1997. *—Jason Ankeny*

The Fatherless & the Widow / Apr. 26, 1994 / Flying Tart ♦♦

This Beautiful Mess / Apr. 18, 1995 / Flying Tart ♦♦♦

• **Sixpence None the Richer** / Nov. 22, 1997 / Squint Entertainment ♦♦♦♦

After toiling in relative obscurity in the Christian pop ghetto for several years, Sixpence None the Richer suddenly exploded onto the pop charts in 1999 on the strength of "Kiss Me," an utterly irresistible slice of swoony guitar pop that, once heard, is impossible to shake loose from the brain and could well turn out to be this generation's "I Wanna Hold Your Hand." The rest of the album may not be quite as memorable, but that's not to say that "Kiss Me" is the only thing worth hearing. "Anything," with its fruity chord progression and string sweetening, is almost Beatlesque; "The Lines of My Earth" draws subtly on country influences. Then there's the Pablo Neruda setting. There are moments when the wispiness of Leigh Nash's voice isn't adequately offset by sturdier accompaniment, but overall this is a very winning album. Those who are offended by religious messages in their pop music don't need to worry—there are a few here, but they're pretty subtle. *—Rick Anderson*

Collage: Portrait of Their Best / Apr. 13, 1999 / Flying Tart ♦♦♦

This is a nice collection of Sixpence None the Richer's hits. There aren't any surprises here, just the strong tunes Sixpence fans are familiar with. The one exception to the rule is "You're a Mean One, Mr. Grinch," which is quite cute, and the remix of "Love, Salvation, the Fear of Death." This compilation serves as a good introduction to Sixpence's early work. *—Melinda Hill*

The 6ths

f. 1994

Indie Pop, Lo-Fi, Alternative Pop/Rock

The 6ths are a side project of the Magnetic Fields' Stephin Merritt, who produced and wrote all of the material on 1995's *Wasps' Nest*, as well as played much of the music. He only sang one of the tracks, however, giving all of the remaining lead vocal slots to alternative rock faves like Barbara Manning, Dean Wareham (Luna), Georgia Hubley (Yo La Tengo), Chris Knox, Lou Barlow, Robert Scott (the Bats), Chris Knox, and Mary Timony (Helium). Brighter and poppier than his contemporaneous efforts with Magnetic Fields, it demonstrated (intentionally or inadvertently) that his principal talents are as a producer and composer, rather than a performer. Hot on the heels of the well-received Magnetic Fields project *69 Love Songs*, Merritt released his second 6ths' album, *Hyacinths and Thistles*, with vocal help from Marc Almond, Bob Mould, Gary Numan, and Sarah Cracknell, among others. *—Richie Unterberger*

● **Wasps' Nests** / Mar. 21, 1995 / London ✦✦✦✦✦

A one-of-a-kind collaborative effort, masterminded by producer/songwriter Stephin Merritt and sung well by various cult stars of the alternative rock scene. The results are unusually successful, if a bit toward the light and precious side, mixing indie attitude with melodicism and production finesse. *—Richie Unterberger*

Hyacinths and Thistles / Sep. 5, 2000 / Merge ✦✦✦

Stephin Merritt's the 6ths' second album isn't nearly as dynamic as his Magnetic Fields' *69 Love Songs*, nor is it quite as good as the first 6ths' album, *Wasps' Nests*. It is, however, another crowning achievement for Merritt. "As You Turn to Go," with Scottish eccentric Momus, is one of Merritt's most moving love songs, a tender, irony-free caress. And the atmospheric "Oahu" wraps its spare melody in a package of primitive synth beeps (which repeat the same tranquil loop for the album's concluding 25 minutes). *Hyacinths and Thistles* falls between Merritt's two musical passions: old-style songwriting and '80s new wave. But the abundant, and diverse, choice of vocalists here (including Sally Timms, Bob Mould, Melanie, Gary Numan, and Marc Almond) puts the accent on the song, rather than the singer. Take this as Merritt the songwriter's demo tape, indication of what he is capable of. *—Michael Gallucci*

Roni Size

b. Bristol, England

Producer / Electronica, Jungle/Drum 'N Bass, Club/Dance

Bristol native Roni Size is one of the U.K. jungle scene's most respected names, with production credits spanning dozens of labels, projects, and releases. Although not as quick to rise to acclaim (either critical or popular) as peers such as Goldie, LTJ Bukem, Photek, and others, Size's influence as a producer, label owner, and committed underground magnate figures him as one of the emerging sound's true pioneers. With DJ Krust, Suv, and DJ Die, Size's formed his longest-running musical commitment to date: his own Full Cycle label. Formed simply as an outlet for the four's entree into the nascent drum'n'bass scene, Full Cycle has since grown into a label group, releasing a steady flow of 12"s (on both Full Cycle and Dope Dragon), and a label comp, *Music Box*, in 1995. Oft duplicated, the Full Cycle sound is a subtle mix of jazz and soul with jump-up rhythms and world beat references spanning from Roni's Jamaican roots to '50s bebop and the Motown sound. The crew now counts a number of classics among their credits, including Size's "It's a Jazz Thing," Krust's "Jazz Note," and Reprazent's "Reasons for Sharing" EP, their first outing through major label subsidiary Talkin' Loud. *—Sean Cooper*

● **New Forms** / Oct. 28, 1997 / Talkin' Loud ✦✦✦✦✦

From the final drum'n'bass pioneer to release a full-length, Roni Size's *New Forms* could well be the best. Though it's slightly bloated at two full discs, and slightly overhyped due to its winning Britain's Mercury Prize, *New Forms* was *the* major statement on drum'n'bass, barring only Goldie's *Timeless*. Size's prime asset is his unique style—tough, careening breakbeats and metallic time-stretched effects over the organic, elastic sounds of upright bass and other jazzy add-ons. He also has a knack for deft pacing; though many of his productions test the seven-minute mark, he plays around with the beats so much that it never really grows boring. On the title track, he weaves two sets of female vocals—American rapper Bahamadia and resident Reprazent diva Onallee—into the mix, digitally syncopating Bahamadia's rap into the production with complete precision. The constantly retriggering breakbeat on "Matter of Fact" makes it another highlight, and Size's transition from the atmospheric "Heroes" to a raging breakbeat storm like "Share the Fall" (both are Onallee features) is astonishing. Yes, Size's production clout is much more apparent on the first disc than the second, but *New Forms* is laced with so much genius it's worth the price of two discs to own all the excellent productions inside. *—John Bush*

Replica: The Remix Album / Jan. 26, 1998 / Mercury ✦✦✦✦

Compiling all the crucial remixes of material from countless *New Forms* singles, *Replica* includes contributions from Photek, Origin Unknown, Grooverider, Kruder & Dorfmeister, and DJ Krust. *—John Bush*

In the Møde / Oct. 10, 2000 / Talkin' Loud ✦✦✦✦

Following up one of the most praised album debuts of the '90s was a tough assignment, and Roni Size obviously worked hard to keep up the energy level on *In the Møde*. He pared the track lengths down considerably, and kick-started the LP with the frenetic "Railing, Pt. 2," featuring Dynamite MC doing his usual excellent warm-up gig over a chorus of racing breakbeats and fluid basslines. After taking a break during the cold, clinical precision of "Snapshot," Dynamite's back on the mic, chatting over most of the LP's highlights: "System Check," "Who Told You?," "Switchblade," and "Dirty Beats." The few tracks featuring Reprazent's female vocalist Onallee are a disappointment (especially after her solid performances on the Breakbeat Era LP), but Size lets two special guests shine on great featured tracks. At the beginning of "Ghetto Celebrity," Wu-Tang's Method Man sounds as though he can barely keep up with the flurry of programming, but he soon turns it up as well and freestyles for nearly seven minutes of madness. Size also sparkles on a track featuring Rahzel (from the Roots), transforming the MC's human-beatbox percussion into a very full breakbeat production. But despite the great features and solid tracks, *In the Møde* doesn't quite make it to the level of *New Forms*. Yes, the tracks are much more concise than on *New Forms*—usually only three or four minutes, as compared to seven to nine before—but on the downside, Size was forced to stretch himself thin writing 17 short tracks. And despite having a trio of Reprazent helping hands (Krust, Die, and Suv, all excellent producers), he uses them on only five tracks. In essence, the highlights are over far too quickly, and the weaker tracks never should have appeared in the first place. *—John Bush*

Skid Row

f. 1986

Pop-Metal, Hair Metal, Heavy Metal

Skid Row was one of the last hair metal bands to hit the mainstream before grunge took over in the early '90s. They were also arguably the last of such bands to have any originality. In 1989, the band released their first album, *Skid Row*, which went multi-platinum on the strength of the Top 40 singles "18 and Life" and "I Remember You." Success was not without backlash, however—the band had naively signed away much of their royalties and singer Sebastian Bach's childlike behavior would land the group in additional trouble. Nonetheless, Skid Row retained a devoted audience—1991's *Slave to the Grind* debuted at number one on the Billboard charts, an unprecedented accomplishment for a metal band. While the album did not chart any real radio hits, *Grind* received stronger critical praise and would eventually reach platinum status. Like so many of their peers, Skid Row lost much of their fan base during the grunge phase of the '90s. As Nirvana stormed the scene in 1992, *Skid Row* took a hiatus, waiting out the grunge period and pondering breakups. Skid Row returned in 1995 with *Subhuman Race*, which surprisingly charted in the Top 40 but otherwise did not attract any real attention. Though personal differences and changing trends would eventually tear the band apart by 1996, Skid Row showed a tremendous amount of promise during their short run in the mainstream. In mid-2000, Skid Row reformed with new singer Johnny Solinger and toured as the opening band for KISS' Farewell Tour. *—Barry Weber*

Skid Row / 1989 / Atlantic ✦✦✦

The material on *Skid Row* is mostly typical pop-metal fluff, but as Skid Row was one of the hardest bands to find commercial success during the hair-metal fad, the songs sound angrier and more aggressive than the lyrics and hooks might indicate. Part of this is due simply to the musical talent in the band, and part of it is due to vocalist Sebastian Bach; his tendency to oversing actually gives some much-needed nasty attitude to most of the songs, and when the music does match those sentiments (i.e., "Youth Gone Wild"), the results fulfill, rather than merely hint at, Skid Row's potential. But the melodies and songwriting are pretty consistent throughout the album, even if they aren't as close to true heavy metal as they sound. The hit power ballads "18 and Life" and "I Remember You" are musically generic, but Bach's over-the-top delivery makes them guilty pleasures as well. *—Steve Huey*

Slave to the Grind / Jun. 11, 1991 / Atlantic ✦✦✦✦

Skid Row gets harder and heavier on its sophomore effort, matching Sebastian Bach's gritty, streetwise rants to lean, driving riffs that manage to back up all the attitudinal posturing. Largely missing are the bits of pop-metal fluff that filled out *Skid Row*; in their place are tales from the dark side about drugs, corruption, and the like, with Bach affecting a tough, threatening persona most of the time. The furious noise kicked up behind Bach is usually more threatening than his overwrought vocal delivery, but *Slave to the Grind* is powerful enough that it doesn't really matter. "Monkey Business," "Get the Fuck Out," and the thrashy title track crush most anything on the debut, and power ballads like "Quicksand Jesus" and "Wasted Time" are far less generic than their *Skid Row* counterparts. Many observers were surprised when *Slave to the Grind* became the first heavy metal album to debut at number one on the *Billboard* charts, but it really was one of the best—and heaviest—examples of mainstream hard rock/heavy metal in the genre's MTV heyday. *—Steve Huey*

B-Sides Ourselves / Sep. 22, 1992 / Atlantic ✦✦✦

B-Sides Ourselves was intended to be a stopgap EP, but it turned out to be Skid Row's last recording for three years. It wasn't a bad way to step away from the spotlight, actually. A collection of five covers, *B-Sides Ourselves* ranks among the best music Skid Row ever recorded, simply because it's so raw and seething with energy. Produced by the band, the EP careens through the songs—including selections by Kiss and the Sex Pistols—at a breakneck pace, creating vicious rock & roll that is more vital than their two previous albums. The band managed to harness that power and put it into their original material on their next album, 1995's *Subhuman Race*. *—Stephen Thomas Erlewine*

Subhuman Race / Mar. 28, 1995 / Atlantic ✦✦✦✦

Skid Row waited out the grunge storm and returned in 1995 with *Subhuman Race*, their strongest and most vicious record to date. Abandoning most of the pop-metal posturing of their early hit albums, Skid Row strips back their music to the basics—roaring guitars and Sebastian Bach's shriek. It wasn't a hit the size of *Slave to the Grind*, yet it made an impressive showing, climbing into the Top 40. *—Stephen Thomas Erlewine*

● **Forty Seasons: The Best of Skid Row** / Nov. 3, 1998 / Atlantic ✦✦✦✦

This after-the-fact compilation from one of the last hard-rock bands to make any sort of impression before the alt-rock revolution made most of it meaningless does its job, limited as it is, fairly well. All the hit singles that Sebastian Bach and company cranked out during their brief run of superstardom are here; none particularly holds up out of its era. Still, if having "Youth Gone Wild," "18 and Life," "I Remember You," and "Monkey Business" in one compact package means something to you, then *Forty Seasons* is that album. —*Michael Gallucci*

The Skids

f. 1977, Dunfermline, Scotland, **db.** 1982
New Wave

The Scottish art-punk unit the Skids formed in Dunfermline in 1977. Comprised of the dramatic vocalist Richard Jobson, guitarist Stuart Adamson, bassist William Simpson, and drummer Tom Kellichan, the group issued the single "Reasons" on their own No Bad label before signing to Virgin. After two more singles, "Sweet Suburbia" and "The Saints Are Coming," they entered the U.K. Top Ten with "Into the Valley," included on their 1979 debut LP *Scared to Dance*, a fine document of the anthemic guitar riffs and chant-like vocals which typified the first phase of the group's music.

With their second effort, 1979's arty, overreaching *Days in Europa* (produced by Be-Bop Deluxe's Bill Nelson), the Skids scored a pair of Top 20 hits with "Masquerade" and "Working for the Yankee Dollar." Trouble loomed, however, as Jobson's increasingly grandiose plans for the group's music alienated not only their fans but also their own rhythm section, and both Simpson and Kellichan were long gone by the time of 1980's *The Absolute Game*, recorded with bassist Russell Webb and drummer Mike Baillie. By 1981's *Joy*, only Jobson remained from the Skids' original lineup; prior to recording the album, Adamson quit to form his own group, the internationally successful Big Country. After *Joy* failed commercially and critically, the Skids officially disbanded; Jobson soon returned as a solo artist before forming the Armoury Show and beginning a career as a broadcaster. —*Jason Ankeny*

● **Sweet Suburbia: The Best of the Skids** / Apr. 18, 1995 / Virgin ✦✦✦✦
Sweet Suburbia is a smartly assembled 18-track career overview of the Scottish punk/new wave outfit. The Skids' early albums had no shortage of fine material, but in truth, *Sweet Suburbia* is probably the beginning and ending point for all but the completist, picking out most, if not all, of the high points. —*Chris Woodstra*

Skinny Puppy

f. 1982, Vancouver, British Columbia, Canada, **db.** 1996
Industrial Dance, Alternative Pop/Rock, Industrial

Drawing from the pioneering work of artists like Throbbing Gristle, Cabaret Voltaire, and Suicide, the dark avant-industrial group Skinny Puppy formed in 1982 around vocalist cEVIN Key and Nivek Ogre. Subsequent releases like 1986's *Mind: The Perpetual Intercourse*, 1987's *Cleanse, Fold and Manipulate*, and 1988's *VIVIsectVI* further honed the trio's style, as well as introducing the outspoken lyrical agenda that remained a thematic constant throughout much of the group's work. In 1989, Ministry's Al Jourgensen added vocals, guitars and production work to *Rabies*. In 1993, Skinny Puppy signed to American Recordings and relocated to Los Angeles to begin production work. The subsequent album, titled *The Process*, wasn't released until 1996 amidst problems with producers and the death of keyboardist Dwayne Goettel. A multimedia history of the band, *Brap—Back and Forth, Series 3&4*, followed a few months later, while Key returned to his new project, Download. Released in 1998, *ReMix Dys Temper* featured Skinny Puppy reworkings by Autechre, Neotropic, and Adrian Sherwood in addition to industrial groups like KMFDM and God Lives Underwater. —*Jason Ankeny*

Bites / 1985 / Nettwerk ✦✦✦✦
Skinny Puppy's first album recalls the gloomy throb of Cabaret Voltaire, but with a more pronounced beat; their debut EP, *Remission*, is included on the CD version of *Bites*. —*Stephen Thomas Erlewine*

Mind: The Perpetual Intercourse / 1986 / Nettwerk ✦✦

Cleanse, Fold and Manipulate / 1987 / Nettwerk ✦✦✦
While it doesn't deviate from their previous lyrical territory, the music is more intense and scary; for the first time, Skinny Puppy has made an album that actually *sounds* frightening. —*Stephen Thomas Erlewine*

VIVIsect VI / Jul. 1988 / Nettwerk ✦✦✦
VIVIsectVI is the first explicitly political Skinny Puppy album, which adds some depth to their standard throbbing, gloomy industrial dance-rock. —*Stephen Thomas Erlewine*

Rabies / 1989 / Nettwerk ✦✦✦
Despite the presence of Ministry's Al Jourgensen and his brutal guitar riffs, Skinny Puppy sounds as if they're at a loss for ideas on their fifth album. —*Stephen Thomas Erlewine*

Too Dark Park / 1990 / Nettwerk ✦✦✦✦
When Ministry and the Revolting Cocks were offering what could be described as industrial noise for people who weren't industrial fans, Skinny Puppy continued to thrive on the extreme and remained far to the left of rock's center. Employing more bass than Puppy's previous albums, *Too Dark Park* has a bit of a funk element. But make no mistake: The industrial agitators (who had influenced Nine Inch Nails, Ministry, RevCo, Godflesh, and numerous others) were hardly going after rock's mainstream. Forceful and consistently abrasive, these twisted and disturbing collages of samples, electronics, distortion, and heavy guitars push the limits of rock and are about as hardcore as it gets. Those who have only a slight interest in industrial would probably be better off starting out with the more accessible Ministry, but this is a CD that the more seasoned industrial aficionados shouldn't miss. —*Alex Henderson*

12" Anthology / Jun. 1990 / Nettwerk ✦✦✦✦✦
Featuring both sides of four 12" singles from 1985 to 1989, *12" Anthology* offers the best

introduction to Skinny Puppy's psycho-terrorist industrial music. From the early double-sided classic "Dig It/The Choke" to later offerings like "Chainsaw" and "Assimilate," only the best of SP's 1980s output is collected here. —*Stephen Thomas Erlewine*

Last Rights / 1991 / Nettwerk ✦✦✦✦
Last Rights, Skinny Puppy's final album before a five-year hiatus, and their second to last overall, is a hailstorm of electro-distortion ten years ahead of its time. Even while industrial pop stars like Nine Inch Nails and Ministry were strutting their way across the charts and media outlets trumpeting the industrial revolution, Dave Ogilvie and cEvin Key's ambitious production talents reached what is easily a technical peak (and, arguably, an artistic peak). "Inquisition" is the pinnacle, a heart-stopping single whose production contributed just as much to the air of menace as Ogre's vocals. Skinny Puppy even attempts a ballad on "Killing Game," with surprising success. Though the dense production occasionally masks Ogre's vocals and songwriting, *Last Rights* is a sonic masterpiece that undoubtedly influenced sound manipulators from Autechre to White Zombie. —*John Bush*

The Process / Feb. 27, 1996 / American ✦✦

Brap / Apr. 30, 1996 / Nettwerk ✦✦

● **The Singles Collect** / Nov. 16, 1999 / Nettwerk ✦✦✦✦✦
It's not a compilation of across-the-board greatest songs, but the Skinny Puppy singles collection does the old *12" Anthology* one better by including tracks from the group's three Nettwerk albums of the 1990s (*Rabies, Too Dark Park*, and *Last Rights*). For fans, it's long been a dream to have the full fruits of the industrial kingpins' long career all on one disc—"Dig It," one of Skinny Puppy's first and best singles, appears right beside "Worlock," from 1989's *Rabies*. Also aboard are a baker's dozen of well-selected career highlights, including "Assimilate," "Tormentor," "Deep Down Trauma Hounds," "Stairs and Flowers," "Testure," "Tin Omen," "Inquisition," and "Killing Game." Though a chronologically ordered compilation would have been a better idea, *The Singles Collect* sounds excellent all the way through and proves that Skinny Puppy was, hands down, the best and most adventurous band of the industrial era. —*John Bush*

B-Sides Collection / Nov. 16, 1999 / Nettwerk ✦✦✦✦
Skinny Puppy was indeed one of the most collectable industrial bands, issuing many singles that contained surprisingly strong tracks. In 1999, Nettwerk compiled some of the best for the companion to *The Singles Collect*. These tracks aren't the rarest in the Skinny Puppy catalog, considering most are B-sides from later singles like "Testure," "Worlock," "Censor," "Tormentor," and "Spasmolytic." Still, the group's quality control was practically undisputed among industrial bands, and for fans who may have missed out on a single or two the first time, it's the perfect acquisition. Highlights include remixes of "Addiction" and "Shore Lined Poison," plus notable tracks like "Brak's Talk," "Bark," "Punk in Park Zoo's," and "Yes He Ran." —*John Bush*

The Skyliners

f. 1959, Pittsburgh, PA
Doo Wop

This Pittsburgh vocal group made a magnificent heartache ballad in 1959, "Since I Don't Have You." It remains among R&B's ultimate agonizing triumphs, and Chuck Jackson later did an equally gripping version. Jimmy Beaumont was the lead vocalist, with Janet Vogel, Wally Lester, Joe VerScharen, and Jackie Taylor. Beaumont, Taylor, and Lester had been in the Crescents, while Vogel and VerScharen were alumni of the El Rios. Their follow-up, "This I Swear," was a creditable effort that peaked at number 20 on the R&B charts, but few remember it. Oddly, "Since I Don't Have You" only reached number three on the R&B side and number 12 on the pop charts. But it's certainly one song for whom the numbers really don't come close to telling the story. The Skyliners had two chart singles on Callico and then had one other song reach the R&B Top 40 in 1965, "The Loser," for Jubilee. —*Ron Wynn*

● **The Skyliners' Greatest Hits** / 1986 / Original Sound ✦✦✦✦✦

Since I Don't Have You / 1991 / Ace ✦✦✦✦✦
The Skyliners were among the more dramatic, theatrical white doo wop groups. Their hit "Since I Don't Have You" has been covered by numerous performers, and it's among the 21 singles featured on this Ace anthology covering numbers recorded for Calico and Laurie. Jimmy Beaumont's tremendous leads distinguished "I Swear," "It Happened Today," and the title track, among others. It's no surprise that such flamboyant performers as Patti LaBelle and Chuck Jackson are big Skyliners fans. —*Ron Wynn*

Slade

f. 1966
Glam Rock, Hard Rock

One of the most successful British bands of the early '70s, Slade made it to the top of the charts after several years on the road. The band formed in 1966 in Wolverhapton as the N'Betweens. After taking on former Animals bassist Chas Chandler as their manager, they changed their name to Ambrose Slade, then shortened it to Slade.

Many of their records were variations of upfront lead vocals; fat, loud, distorted guitar chords; a basic foot-stomping beat; and anthemic choruses. The simplicity of it all was played up even further by the deliberate misspelling of words in the song titles. At the turn of the '70s, "Get Down and Get With It" cracked the U.K. Top 20 and there was no turning back. Their next dozen singles were U.K. Top Five hits, six of them reaching number one. Their success wasn't limited to the singles charts, either; three of their albums also topped the charts during the same period. Their holiday song, "Merry Xmas Everybody," has entered the U.K. charts seven times, as well.

Despite their British success, Slade barely cracked the U.S. Hot 100. Even in England, the big hits stopped coming during the punk revolution in the late '70s. They enjoyed a brief revival in the early '80s when Quiet Riot covered "Cum on Feel the Noize" and took it to the top of the charts around the world. This revival even enabled Slade to chart in the American Top 40 with "Run Runaway" and "My Oh My." Slade later celebrated their 25th anniversary, showing no sign of stopping. *—Jim Powers*

Slayed? / 1972 / Polydor ✦✦✦✦✦
Slayed was Slade's best and most consistent original album, featuring "Mama Weer All Crazee Now." *—Stephen Thomas Erlewine*

Sladest / 1973 / Reprise ✦✦✦✦
If your taste in music leans toward arena rock anthems filled with great hooks, fist pumping sing along choruses and essentially mindless lyrics than Slade is the band you've been looking for.

Sladest is a "best of" collection that includes all of the material that helped the band sell tons of records and fill arenas in the U.K. in the early '70s. Falling somewhere between the glam of T. Rex and the hard rock of Nazareth, Slade's finest moments come with arena rockers Cum On Feel the Noize, Mama Weer All Crazee Now, and Gudbye T' Jayne. These songs were specifically written to be strong live numbers that would get the British kids up off their seats. This style of songs is what the band did best, and at the time not many bands did it better.

When the band strays from their successful formula of catchy guitar riffs and big choruses they tend to fail. Softer tracks like Coz I Luv You and Pouk Hill fall flat.

Although the band enjoyed major success in the U.K. they never broke stateside. They had a brief surge of popularity in the U.S. in the early '80s when Quiet Riot had hits covering two Slade tunes (&Cum On Feel the Noize and &Mama Weer All Crazee Now). One listen to Kevin Dubrow of Quiet Riot will tell you he spent many nights listening to Skweeze Me Pleeze Me and other Slade songs for hours on end. Judging by Slade's popularity in the early '70s, he wasn't alone. *—Paul Tinelli*

Till Deaf Do Us Part / 1981 / RCA ✦✦✦
Till Deaf Do Us Part is Slade's most hard rocking album ever. Their playing is at its fiercest and the material totally kicks ass. While this was not quite the commercial success the band was hoping for, it didn't kill their momentum by any means. They were now packing halls again instead of playing to half-empty small clubs. The disc includes three songs that would be played live at every gig the band did from this LP's release until they stopped playing out. The opener, "Rock & Roll Preacher," features Noddy Holder praying at the alter of rock & roll. This number is so blistering one wonders just how heavy these guys can get. Answer: *very*. "Lock Up Your Daughters" is as catchy as it gets, and maintains the furious instrumental pace of the record. "Daughters" is a perfect example of how far the band had come. It retains the almost bubblegum sound of the earlier singles, while the heavy production style gives it a bit more of a hard-rocking edge. The wonderfully Slade-esque "Ruby Red," which failed as a single, makes a good album track, and "A Night to Remember" is definitely a song to remember, as it ups the intensity ante. Also included is the hysterical "That Was No Lady That Was My Wife" and a rare song written by Dave Hill, an innocuous little instrumental called "M'Hat, M'Coat." This is noteworthy since from the earliest days of the band, all the originals were by Lea and Holder. This LP shows a band with renewed enthusiasm and confidence. And by the way, the original album cover (drawing of an ear with a bent nail in it) is way cooler than the CD cover (band shot in flames). Recommended for rockers. *—Geoff Ginsberg*

Keep Your Hands Off My Power Supply / 1984 / Epic ✦✦✦✦
An early-'80s album that managed to climb into the Top 40, thanks to the success of Quiet Riot's versions of "Cum On Feel the Noize" and "Mama Weer All Crazee Now." On *Keep Your Hands Off My Power Supply*, Slade shows that they are still the masters of loud, trashy hard rock. *—Stephen Thomas Erlewine*

● **Feel the Noize: The Very Best of Slade** / 1997 / Polydor ✦✦✦✦✦
The finest collection ever assembled on Slade's hit-making heyday, *Feel the Noize: The Very Best of...* contains all of the group's hit singles from the early '70s, from 1971's "Get Down and Get With It" to 1975's "Thanks for the Memory (Wham Bam Thank You Mam)." In between those two songs, all of the group's big, dumb, irresistible and misspelled hits—"Cuz I Luv You," "Take Me Bak 'Ome," "Mama Weer All Crazee Now," "Gudbuy T'Jane," "Cum On Feel the Noize," "Skweeze Me Pleeze Me"—are featured. Though it is missing latter-day hits like "My Oh My," Slade never got better than they did at their stomping glitter-rock peak, and *Feel the Noize* captures the essence of that era. *—Stephen Thomas Erlewine*

Slave

f. 1975, Dayton, OH
Disco, Funk
Arguably the hottest of the '70s Ohio funk bands, Slave had a great run in the late '70s and early '80s. Trumpeter Steve Washington formed the group in Dayton in 1975. Vocalist Floyd Miller teamed with Tom Lockett, Jr., Charles Bradley, Mark Adams, Mark Hicks, Danny Webster, Orion Wilhoite, and Tim Dozier. Vocalists Steve Arrington and Starleana Young came aboard in 1978, with Arrington ultimately becoming lead vocalist. Their first big hit was the thumping single "Slide" in 1977 for Cotillion, where they remained until 1984. Their best tracks were lyrically simple and at times silly, but the arrangements and rhythms were intense and hypnotic. Other Top Ten R&B hits were "Just a Touch of Love" in 1979, "Watching You" in 1980, and "Snap Shot" in 1981. Young, Washington, and Lockett departed to form Aurra in 1979. Arrington himself left in the early '80s. They added Charles C. Carter, Delburt Taylor, Sam Carter, Kevin Johnson, and Roger Parker as replacements and continued on, though much less successfully, into the late '80s. They moved to Atlantic for one LP in 1984, then switched to the Atlanta-based Ichiban in 1986 for singles and LPs that were just a shade of the former vibrant Slave sound. Their most recent release was *The Funk Strikes Back* in 1992. Rhino issued *Stellar Funk: The Best of Slave*, a first-rate anthology of their finest cuts, in 1994. *—Ron Wynn*

● **Stellar Funk: The Best of Slave** / Feb. 22, 1994 / Rhino ✦✦✦✦✦
Slave's music was straight, simple funk: prominent bass lines, catchy phrases, and either comical or throwaway lyrics. This excellent 15-track anthology contains Slave's finest hits, each with a captivating, thudding bass riff: "Slide," "Just a Touch of Love," and "Watching You," among others. There are also five Steve Arrington numbers, among them his best dance cut ("Weak at the Knees") and topical tune ("Feel So Real"). Although not as acclaimed as Parliament/Funkadelic or Earth, Wind & Fire, this CD shows that Slave deserves recognition for its ability to keep the funk with style and verve. *—Ron Wynn*

Slayer

f. 1982, Huntington Beach, CA
Speed Metal, Heavy Metal, Thrash
Slayer was one of the most distinctive, influential, and extreme thrash-metal bands of the 1980s. Their graphic lyrics deal with everything from death and dismemberment to war and the horrors of hell. Their full-throttle velocity, wildly chaotic guitar solos, and powerful musical chops paint an effectively chilling sonic background for their obsessive chronicling of the dark side; this correspondence has helped Slayer's music hold up arguably better than the remaining Big Three '80s thrash outfits (Metallica, Megadeth, Anthrax). Naturally, Slayer has stirred up quite a bit of controversy over the years, with rumors flying about Satanism and Nazism that have only added to their mystique. Over the years, Slayer has put out some high-quality albums, one undisputed classic (*Reign in Blood*), and seen the numbers of naysayers and detractors shrinking as their impact on the growing death-metal movement was gradually and respectfully acknowledged. Slayer has survived into the 1990s with arguably the most vitality and the least compromise of any pre-Nirvana metal band, and their intensity still inspires similar responses from their devoted fans. *—Steve Huey*

Show No Mercy / 1983 / Metal Blade ✦✦

Hell Awaits / 1985 / Metal Blade ✦✦✦
When it was released in 1985, Slayer's second album *Hell Awaits* was a nearly inpenetrable cacophony of sound; however, what may have seemed like pure noise then, only proved to be ahead of its time. Songs like the title track, "At Dawn They Sleep" and "Hardening of the Arteries" show a more technical side of the band rarely seen before (or since), featuring complex arrangements and time changes, but without compromising any speed. And though buried in distortion, the more straightforward thrash of "Kill Again" and "Necrophiliac" are just as enticing. Ultimately, this was Slayer's first important record and influenced an entire generation of bands, as well as setting the stage for their masterpiece *Reign in Blood*. *—Ed Rivadavia*

★ **Reign in Blood** / 1986 / American ✦✦✦✦✦
Widely considered the pinnacle of speed metal, *Reign in Blood* is Slayer's undisputed masterpiece, a brief (under half an hour) but relentless onslaught that instantly obliterates anything in its path and clears out just as quickly. Producer Rick Rubin gives the band a clear, punchy sound for the first time in its career, and they largely discard the extended pieces of *Hell Awaits* in favor of lean assaults somewhat reminiscent of hardcore punk (though distinctly metallic and much more technically demanding). *Reign in Blood* opens and closes with slightly longer tracks (the classics "Angel of Death" and "Raining Blood") whose slower riffs offer most of the album's few hints of melody. Sandwiched in between are eight short (all under three minutes), lightning-fast bursts of aggression that change tempo or feel without warning, producing a disjointed, barely controlled effect. The album is actually more precise than it sounds, and not without a sense of groove, but even in the brief slowdowns, the intensity never lets up. There may not be much variation, but it's a unified vision, and a horrific one at that. The riffs are built on atonal chromaticism that sounds as sickening as the graphic violence depicted in many of the lyrics, and Kerry King and Jeff Hanneman's demented soloing often mimics the screams of the songs' victims. It's monstrously, terrifyingly evocative, in a way that transcends *Reign in Blood*'s metal origins. The album almost single-handedly inspired the entire death metal genre (at least on the American side of the Atlantic), and unlike many of its imitators, it never crosses the line into self-parodic overkill. *Reign in Blood* was a stone-cold classic upon its release, and it hasn't lost an ounce of its power today. *—Steve Huey*

South of Heaven / 1988 / American ✦✦✦✦
When it comes to death metal, no band is more convincing than Slayer. For other bands, focusing on death, satanism, the supernatural, and the occult became a cliche; but Slayer's controversial reflections on evil always came across as honest and heartfelt. The group's sincerity is the thing that makes *South of Heaven* so disturbing and powerful—when the influential thrashers rip into such morbid fare as "Spill the Blood," "Mandatory Suicide," and "Ghosts of War," they are frighteningly convincing. With its fourth album, Slayer began to slow its tempos without sacrificing an iota of heaviness or incorporating any pop elements. *South of Heaven* would be Slayer's last album for Def Jam. When Rick Rubin and Russell Simmons (brother of Joseph "Run" Simmons of Run-D.M.C.) parted company, Slayer went to Rubin's new company Def American, while L.L. Cool J, Slick Rick, and other rappers recorded for Simmons at Def Jam. *—Alex Henderson*

Seasons in the Abyss / 1990 / American ✦✦✦✦✦
After staking out new territory with the underrated *South of Heaven*, Slayer brought back some of the pounding speed of *Reign in Blood* for its third major-label album, *Seasons in the Abyss*. Essentially, *Seasons* fuses its two predecessors, periodically kicking up the midtempo grooves of *South of Heaven* with manic bursts of aggession. "War Ensemble" and the title track each represented opposite sides of the coin, and they both earned

Slayer their heaviest MTV airplay to date. In fact, *Seasons in the Abyss* is probably their most accessible album, displaying the full range of their abilities all in one place, with sharp, clean production. Since the band is refining rather than progressing or experimenting, *Seasons* doesn't have quite the freshness of its predecessors, but aside from that drawback, it's strong almost all the way from top to bottom (with perhaps one or two exceptions). Lyrically, the band rarely turns to demonic visions of the afterlife anymore, preferring instead to find tangible horror in real life—war, murder, human weakness. There's even full-fledged social criticism, which should convince any doubters that Slayer isn't trying to promote the subjects they sing about. Like Metallica's *Master of Puppets* or Megadeth's *Peace Sells... But Who's Buying, Seasons in the Abyss* paints Reagan-era America as a cesspool of corruption and cruelty, and the music is as devilishly effective as ever. *—Steve Huey*

Decade of Aggression: Live / Oct. 22, 1991 / American ♦♦♦
While the double-disc *Decade of Aggression* couldn't be expected to capture all of the unparalleled aggression of Slayer's live shows, this set comes pretty damn close. Most of the thrash metal pioneers' countless classics (including "Angel of Death," "War Ensemble," "Black Magic," "Hell Awaits," "Chemical Warfare," "Raining Blood," et al.) are featured here, but it is the sheer ferocity (and velocity) of the band members' performances which really stand out. Tom Araya's tortured screams never lose their potency, and though the unbelievable speed of guitarists Kerry King and Jeff Hanneman is shocking enough, drummer Dave Lombardo takes the cake with his double kick-drum precision and inventive fills. *—Ed Rivadavia*

Divine Intervention / Sep. 27, 1994 / American ♦♦♦
The rock & roll landscape changed dramatically between *Seasons in the Abyss* in 1990 and *Divine Intervention* in 1994. With the rise of alternative rock, many metal and hard rock bands that had been enormously successful at the dawn of the '90s were struggling by the middle of the decade. Instead of doing something calculated like emulating Nirvana or Pearl Jam—or for that matter, Nine Inch Nails or Ministry—Slayer wisely refused to sound like anyone but Slayer. Tom Araya & Co. responded to the new environment simply by striving to be the heaviest death metal band it possibly could. Less accessible than *Seasons* but equally riveting, *Divine Intervention* marked drummer Paul Bostaph's studio debut with the band. Bostaph proved to be a positive, energizing influence on Slayer, which sounds better than ever on such dark triumphs as "Killing Fields," "Serenity in Murder" and "Circle of Beliefs." Characteristically grim and morbid, Slayer focuses on the violently repressive nature of governments and the lengths to which they will go to wield power. And true to form, Slayer's music is as disturbing as its lyrics. *—Alex Henderson*

Undisputed Attitude / Jun. 1996 / American ♦♦♦
Look back at L.A. punk-rock posters from the dawn of the '80s, and you're sure to find Slayer playing the same venues as many of the bands covered on this album. Hailing from Huntington Beach, Slayer grew up fans of both more traditional heavy metal and of the increasingly fast and aggressive American hardcore punk movement. The combination of metal's technicality and hardcore punk's flat-out aggressiveness and speed are the seeds that Slayer's breakneck sound originally grew out of, and *Undisputed Attitude*, while not perfect, is a fitting tribute to the bands that inspired Slayer to break from the traditional metal mold. The album includes tracks originally by Minor Threat, Doctor Know, Verbal Abuse, T.S.O.L., D.R.I., D.I., Iggy Pop, and a few originals, all played in the trademark Slayer style. With the exception of "Gemini," the songs are under two minutes long, and the tempos tend to fall within the mid-tempo to fast realm of most hardcore punk, rarely blazing into a full force thrash assault. The covers are undeniably marked with Slayer's sound, but are played with minimal alteration for the most part. A notable exception is the rewording of Iggy Pop's "I Wanna Be Your Dog" to "I'm Gonna Be Your God." *Undisputed Attitude* does not serve as a historical review of hardcore and punk of the '80s, and some might argue that the many important punk bands missing from this collection of songs diminish its value. However, this record intends to provide hindsight from the perspective of the band, not popular culture as a whole. For fans of Slayer and all the grindcore, crust, and thrash borne out of the marriage of punk and metal, it's an interesting and sometimes entertaining listen. *—Paul Kott*

Diabolus in Musica / Jun. 9, 1998 / American ♦♦♦
Diabolus in Musica sounds like no other piece of work from Slayer, which makes for a bit of a queasy and uncomfortable experience at first. *Undisputed Attitude's* "Gemini" is the definite precursor to Slayer's newer, hardcore-driven sound. Sort of a speed-metal Machine Head at times, one can easily be discouraged from the first few songs, but album closer "Point" reaffirms faith in the band. It also opens the idea that in the rapidly expanding metal scene, a veteran band such as Slayer has to expand outward, not inward, in order to retain its throne. This is precisely what Slayer has done, and instead of the *Reign*-rehash of *Divine Intervention* or career-risking punk escapades, Slayer has thrashed their way out of the metal niche from which they were almost trapped. Kerry King and Jeff Hanneman tap their hardcore roots to create a speedy, bass-driven chug which pummels the senses in a whole new devilish way. "Death's Head," "Perversions of Pain," "In the Name of God," "Scrum," and "Bitter Peace" usher in a crisp new era of Slayer aggression. Thankfully the lyrics have not traveled the route of "Ain't My Bitch"; instead they stick to familiar topics such as religion, death, war, and serial killers. This album smokes and it is recommended to all fans of metal, even if that first listen is a bit of a shock. The greatest albums are those that take several daunting listens in order to become just that, a great album. Just think where Slayer would be if all those speed junkies had turned their backs on *South of Heaven* after only one or two listens. *—Jason Hundey*

God Hates Us All / Jul. 3, 2001 / American ♦♦♦♦
Quite frankly, Slayer is downright exhausting—always. So it almost goes without saying that *God Hates Us All* proves exhausting. It often sounds like a cacophonous blur, the sort of aural barrage that leaves your ears ringing at the album's finally concluding moment—if you can endure the entire album in one listen, of course. But this is nothing new. Never once has Slayer toned down its brutal approach for anyone. Even when the band dabbled with slower tempos and melody back in the *South of Heaven* era, its intensity was nothing less than relentless. So, in a way, *God Hates Us All* shouldn't disappoint anyone, particularly anyone who enjoyed the band's preceding album, *Diabolus in Musica*. Like that album, *God Hates Us All* finds Slayer trying to make the most brutal music it possibly can—songs as breathtaking in their attack as past classics like "War Ensemble" and "Angel of Death." And also like *Diabolus in Musica, God Hates Us All* rarely departs from the traditional hardcore-meets-thrash approach, never once attempting anything as accessible as "Dead Skin Mask" or "Spill the Blood." "Bloodline" is the biggest departure here, being the only song that even flirts with melody or singing. Elsewhere, vocalist Tom Araya has never sounded more possessed yelling and screaming the highly ideological lyrics. In fact, probably more than anything, it's Araya's manic performance that could make this the most exhausting Slayer album yet. And Matt Hyde's wall-of-noise production only strengthens this album's claim to that status. Nearly 20 years into its evolution, Slayer has abandoned the extravagancies and accessibility of their late-'80s/early-'90s work and returned to perfect the raw approach of its early years. *—Jason Birchmeier*

Sleater-Kinney

f. 1994, Olympia, WA
Riot Grrrl, Indie Rock, Alternative Pop/Rock
The anthemic Olympia, WA-based punk trio Sleater-Kinney formed from the ashes of Heavens to Betsy and Excuse 17, a pair of groups which rode the first wave of the riot grrl movement. Singers/guitarists Corin Tucker and Carrie Brownstein first met in 1992, when Tucker was one half of the duo Heavens to Betsy; Brownstein, a classically trained pianist, was so inspired by Tucker and other grrrl musicians like Bikini Kill and Bratmobile (not coincidentally Tucker's own influences) that she formed her own band, Excuse 17, a year later. Sleater-Kinney, which earned its name from a local freeway off-ramp, initially began as Tucker and Brownstein's side project; in late 1994, Australia-born Lora Macfarlane signed on as the group's first permanent drummer, and over the course of the following two weeks the trio recorded their self-titled 1995 debut for Team Dresch bassist Donna Dresch's Chainsaw label. Upon its release, the album earned widespread acclaim for its visceral intensity as well as the group's provocative, politically charged lyrics, passionate vocals, and intricate melodies. With 1996's brilliant *Call the Doctor*, Sleater-Kinney garnered even greater media exposure and critical applause on the strength of their incisive rants against gender inequity, consumerism, and indie rock's male-dominated hierarchy. Their Kill Rock Stars label debut *Dig Me Out*, recorded with new drummer Janet Weiss, followed in 1997, and was again among the most acclaimed releases of its season; *The Hot Rock* appeared two years later, and in the spring of 2000 Sleater-Kinney resurfaced with *All Hands on the Bad One*. *—Jason Ankeny*

Sleater-Kinney / 1995 / Chainsaw ♦♦♦
Sleater-Kinney's debut reocrd is a medium-fi blast of thrashy riot-grrl rock. Some tracks are reminscient of 90's Sonic Youth ("Be Yr Mama"). While others are just a punk blast of angst ("A Real Man"). The group suffers for excessive monotone melody lines, but suceeds in making this reviewer uncomfortable in being male. The group showcases a promising understanding of dynamics, and they are certainly confident. This is a good first record, and a showcase for talent that would later blossom on albums such as *The Hot Rock*. *—Zachary Curd*

● **Call the Doctor** / Mar. 25, 1996 / Chainsaw ♦♦♦♦♦
Sleater-Kinney's masterful sophomore effort *Call the Doctor* fulfills all the promise of the group's debut and more, forging taut melodicism and jaw-dropping sonic complexity out of barbed-wire emotional potency. The emergence of Carrie Brownstein as an equal shareholder in Corin Tucker's vision is the key—her four contributions (particularly "Stay Where You Are" and "I Wanna Be Your Joey Ramone") are stellar, while her harmonies complete Tucker's equally superb lead turns by reading between the lines to verbalize the naked aggression at the core of the songs' polemic power. Forget the riot grrrl implications inherent in the trio's music—*Call the Doctor* is pure, undiluted punk, and it's brilliant. *—Jason Ankeny*

Dig Me Out / Apr. 8, 1997 / Kill Rock Stars ♦♦♦♦♦
Having reinvented the girl-punk wheel with *Call the Doctor*, Sleater-Kinney continues to expand the boundaries of the form with the stunning *Dig Me Out*. Leaner and more intricate than its predecessor, the record is remarkably confident and mature; instead of succumbing to the pressures of "next big thing" status, the trio finds vindication in all of their critical adulation—the vocals are even more ferocious, the melodies are even more infectious, and the ideals are even more passionate. *—Jason Ankeny*

Hot Rock / Feb. 23, 1999 / Kill Rock Stars ♦♦♦♦
Expectations for Sleater-Kinney's fourth album were stratospheric, with the raging, tuneful feminist catharsis of *Call the Doctor* and *Dig Me Out* having garnered near-universal critical raves and outlandish media hype. Afraid of falling into a predictable rut, though, the band bravely pushed its range of expression into more personal, subdued, and cerebral territory on *The Hot Rock*. That means the record isn't quite as immediately satisfying as its two brilliant predecessors, but it does reward those willing to spend time absorbing its nervy introspection and moodiness. Corin Tucker and Carrie Brownstein push relentlessly for more complex interplay, both in their vocal and instrumental work; even the gentlest songs might break into unexpected dissonance or take an angular, off-kilter melodic direction. As such, there's never an obvious, gut-level anthem that jumps out at the listener in the manner of an "I Wanna Be Your Joey Ramone" or "Words and Guitar,"

but the intensity simmering under the surface does bubble over often, thanks to the group's greater use of dynamic shifts. There are fewer protest songs this time around, as most of the lyrics explore failed relationships and personal uncertainty, yet it manages to retain the sense of empowering catharsis that makes the group so compelling. *The Hot Rock* can invite comparisons to a less jam-oriented Television or a minimalist version of indie compatriots Helium (not to mention the obvious Kim Gordon homage on "Get Up"), but in the end, it stands on its own as Sleater-Kinney's most progressive and experimental work, as well as their darkest. *—Steve Huey*

All Hands on the Bad One / May 2, 2000 / Kill Rock Stars ♦♦♦♦
Sleater-Kinney switched gears on their follow-up to the challenging, introspective *The Hot Rock*, delivering their brightest, most accessible album to date with *All Hands on the Bad One*. That's partly due to a renewed assurance in craft—the arrangements here are the most refined of the group's career, and their performances the most polished. Corin Tucker seems to be in complete command of her voice as an instrument, delivering her most nuanced vocal performance to date. Tucker and Carrie Brownstein's guitar interplay is up to their usual standard of intricacy, but instead of wildly careening off one another, the two mesh more seamlessly than they ever have. Plus, drummer Janet Weiss had been honing her skills as a backup vocalist, and the group makes full use of that extra instrument, packing the tracks with lilting three-part harmonies. Yet all of this craft and control shouldn't be taken as evidence that Sleater-Kinney has toned down the passion that makes them so exciting. Even if *All Hands on the Bad One* isn't as desperately cathartic as their previous records, there's a contagious exuberance in the performances, and the band is absolutely brimming with confidence and vitality. Though the record still covers serious political and emotional topics, its overall aura is best summed up in "You're No Rock & Roll Fun," a bouncy, playful jab at snobby scenesters unable to remember the good times at the core of so much great rock & roll. Not only is *All Hands on the Bad One* Sleater-Kinney's most consistent overall set of songs since *Call the Doctor*, it's also evidence that the band has taken that philosophy to heart. *—Steve Huey*

Percy Sledge

b. Nov. 25, 1941, Leighton, AL
Vocals / Deep Soul, Southern Soul, Soul
Percy Sledge will forever be associated with "When a Man Loves a Woman," a pleading, soulful ballad he sang with wrenching, convincing anguish and passion. Sledge sang all of his songs that way, delivering them in a powerful rush where he quickly changed from soulful belting to quavering, tearful pleas. It was a voice that made him one of the key figures of deep Southern Soul during the late '60s, based around the Muscle Shoals studio in Alabama. Formerly the vocalist for a Southern vocal group, Percy Sledge went solo in 1966, and recorded "When a Man Loves a Woman" as his first single. Released on Atlantic, it became a huge hit that summer and topped both pop and R&B charts. It was quickly followed that year by two Top Ten R&B hits, "Warm and Tender Love" and "It Tears Me Up," which were both in the vein of his first hit. Sledge's sales declined considerably during the early '70s, and after one surprise return to the R&B charts with 1974's "I'll Be Your Everything," he recorded little but toured often. After a revival of his major hit (used in numerous soundtracks and television ads) during the late '80s, Sledge's concerts became even more successful and he released the album *Blue Night* in 1994. *—Stephen Thomas Erlewine*

When a Man Loves a Woman / 1966 / Collectables ♦♦♦♦♦
A country-soul masterpiece. The title track remains among the most beloved, anthemic explanations of love's impact and travails ever written or performed. Had Sledge never made another song, he would still deserve kudos just for that one. But he continued to score with more simple, heartfelt, unsophisticated stories about disappointment, pain, rejection, and perseverance. *—Ron Wynn*

The Percy Sledge Way / 1967 / Atlantic ♦♦♦
This late-'60s album contains hard-hitting, memorable country-soul testimonies from Percy Sledge, who had hit his stride at Atlantic. His narratives were perfectly paced, written with irony and insight, and sung with the ideal mixture of crunching soul and country wit and wisdom. Hopefully, Rhino will one day reissue some of soul's archival sessions like this one, for it needs full exposure. *—Ron Wynn*

Take Time to Know Her / 1968 / Collectables ♦♦♦
The title track was another smashing Sledge gem, while the remainder of the album continues his evocative country-soul tales of woe and heartache. Sledge's late-'60s Atlantic singles and albums were landmarks in the genre; they should have been major country events just as Ray Charles' earlier cuts, but were simply too rooted in black nuance to get any shot with the unimaginative types running country radio (although to be fair, there were also some great country songs in the period that should have been aired on soul stations). The songs were produced and arranged with the right amount of care and sensitivity, never intruding or crowding Sledge as his stories unfolded. *—Ron Wynn*

I'll Be Your Everything / 1974 / Capricorn ♦♦♦
Some wonderful country-soul from Percy Sledge, whose throaty, energized, wonderfully Southern delivery hadn't lost either its earthiness or its zeal, but was so regional that it was losing its appeal to the cosmopolitan, urban types gaining hegemony in black music circles. Sledge delivered several grainy, earnest country-soul weepers and wailers when he moved to Capricorn in the mid-'70s, but they didn't generate much attention anywhere beyond the South. *—Ron Wynn*

★ **It Tears Me Up** / Apr. 21, 1992 / Rhino/Atlantic ♦♦♦♦♦
This stunning compilation from the vaults of Atlantic Records spotlights the voice that gave us the original version of "When a Man Loves a Woman." Lesser-known hits like "It Tears Me Up," "Take Time to Know Her," and "Warm and Tender Love" are equally wonderful, and all are included in this must-have package. Great liner notes by Dave Marsh. Soul music just doesn't get any more heart-wrenching than this. Absolutely essential! *—Christine Ohlman*

Very Best of Percy Sledge / Feb. 3, 1998 / Rhino ♦♦♦♦♦
The Very Best of Percy Sledge is an excellent 16-track collection that features his biggest hits from 1966-1994. The disc concentrates on his classic '60s hits, including "When a Man Loves a Woman," "Warm and Tender Love," "It Tears Me Up," "Baby, Help Me," "Out of Left Field," "Cover Me," "Take Time to Know Her," "Sudden Stop," and "I'll Be Your Everything," as well as the alternate version of "When a Man Loves a Woman" where the horns are in tune. While the latter-day tracks didn't need to be included on the collection, the disc remains a concise, affordable summation of Sledge's peak period and is a fine introduction to the legendary R&B vocalist. *—Stephen Thomas Erlewine*

Sleeper

f. 1993, London, England
Brit-pop, Alternative Pop/Rock
Louise Wener (vocals, guitar), Jon Stewart (guitar), Andy Maclure (drums), Diid Osman (bass). Wener and Stewart met at while studying politics at school in Manchester, England. Relocating to London, the two recruited Osman and Maclure and began playing Wener's original songs. The group made its debut in 1993, which led to a series of positive reviews in the British music weeklies. By November of 1993, the group had released an independent single ("Alice in Vain"). In February 1994, the band released "Swallow," which charted in the Top 100; the following May, "Delicious" was released and it became a number one independent single. During May, Sleeper supported Blur on the London band's enormously successful *Parklife* tour. In February 1995, Sleeper released their debut album *Smart*, which entered the U.K. album chart at number five and the independent chart at number one; it would be certified a silver album in four months. *Smart* was released in the U.S. in March to positive reviews, yet it failed to duplicate the band's British commercial success. In the late spring of 1996, Sleeper released their second album, *The It Girl*. Again, the album was a major hit in the U.K., yet it barely made an impact in the US. *—Stephen Thomas Erlewine*

Smart / Mar. 14, 1995 / Arista ♦♦♦♦
"Inbetweener" is an intoxicating single. Fuzz guitars, light harmonies, singsong melodies and hooks keep piling up until the whole thing collapses in a heap after three minutes. Unfortunately, there's nothing that matches it on *Smart*, Sleeper's debut album. Occasionally, Louise Wener comes up with a memorable hook, melody, or lyric but never can quite pull them together into something as well-crafted (and sexy) as "Inbetweener." Still, the flashes of inspiration scattered across *Smart* prove Sleeper has potential—which they have already fulfilled once, with the single. *—Stephen Thomas Erlewine*

● **The It Girl** / Jun. 18, 1996 / Arista ♦♦♦♦♦
Although it lacks a standout track on the level of *Smart*'s "Inbetweener," Sleeper's second album, *The It Girl*, is a stronger effort, suggesting that lead singer/songwriter Louise Wener could develop into a distinctive talent. Certainly, her melodies and hooks are uniformly better this time around, ranging from the bouncy "Sale of the Century" to the sighing melancholy of "What Do I Do Now?" Wener's lyrics continue to be underdeveloped and simplisitic, but her hooks usually make that tendency easy to ignore. What would have made *The It Girl* an even stronger album is a clearer, more focused production. Although the sound of the album changes subtlely throughout the course of the record, the overall effect is numbingly similar. The rhythm section lacks drive and the guitars lack balls—they blend together into one dull grind. Out of all of Stephen Street's productions, this is the most undistinguished. Occasionally, the song is strong enough to compensate for the flat production, but Sleeper albums will not only improve according to the development of Louise Wener's songwriting, but also as the band finds the right producer. *—Stephen Thomas Erlewine*

Pleased to Meet You / Oct. 13, 1997 / Indolent ♦♦♦
At the beginning of 1997, Sleeper were still considered one of the most popular indie-based guitar bands in England, as their songs were staples on the airwaves and Louise Wener was consistently on the covers of music magazines. At the beginning of 1998, they were nearly persona non grata, and there were whispers of the group's imminent demise. That's how hard their third album, *Pleased to Meet You*, crashed on the charts, but its lack of the success was due more to the changes in British pop than the merits of the album itself. While it lacks the energy of *The It Girl*, it's ultimately a better-crafted album than *Smart*, which suffered from too much derivative filler. There's still filler on *Pleased to Meet You*, but the album demonstrates that Wener's songwriting has strengthened, as her melodies have more weight and her lyrics have more depth. She still has the tendency to go for predictable hooks and easy put-downs, but there's enough muscle and tuneful songs to make this a worthy successor to *The It Girl*. Nevertheless, it was ignored by the British public, perhaps because it subsitituted the freshness of the first two albums for craftsmanship, which is something that true fans may appreciate more than those who simply follow the pop charts. *—Stephen Thomas Erlewine*

Slick Rick

b. Jan. 14, 1965, London, England
Vocals / Hardcore Rap, Hip-Hop, Golden Age
Slick Rick foreshadowed and epitomized the pimpster attitude of many rappers during the late '80s and early '90s, with gold chains, his trademark eye-patch, and recordings that were no less misogynistic—"Treat Her Like a Prostitute," for example, became an underground hit in 1988, though it was justly criticized for its view of women. His 1989 album, *The Great Adventures of Slick Rick*, was a certified-platinum classic, but before he could

record a follow-up, Slick Rick was arrested for attempted murder. Out on bail thanks to Def Jam Records' label-head Russell Simmons, Rick recorded 21 songs in 1991 and hastily released them as as *The Ruler's Back*. The album failed to move at all, though Rick's confession track "I Shouldn't Have Done It" scraped the R&B charts later in 1991. Featured in the rap documentary *The Show* (released in 1995)—in a segment where Russell Simmons actually visits the prison—Slick Rick was released on a work program in 1993, and his *Behind Bars* album appeared in 1994. *Art of Storytelling* was issued in 1999. *—John Bush*

★ **The Great Adventures of Slick Rick** / 1988 / Def Jam ✦✦✦✦✦
Slick Rick first gained an audience by rapping on Doug E. Fresh's "La-Di-Da-Di" and "The Show," two songs that immediately established him as a major talent upon their release in 1985. It may have taken him three years to deliver his full-length debut, but when *The Great Adventures of Slick Rick* arrived in 1988, it was an immediate classic. What makes *The Great Adventures of Slick Rick* such a stunning achievement isn't necessarily the music—in retrospect, it's strong, but unexceptional, street funk—but Rick's rhyming. His style was fluid, but filled with odd cadences and an idiosyncratic phrasing. Furthermore, his storytelling technique is unparalleled, full with detail and dramatic momentum; his skewed, slightly cartoonish view point was nearly as influential. Unfortunately, his rampant misogyny and cool, amoralistic outlook became equally influential on '90s hip-hop. Even though Slick Rick released a series of fairly mediocre followups and spent an extended stay in prison, his failure to live up to the potential of *The Great Adventures* doesn't dilute the impact of the album at all. Years after its release, it still sounds fresh. *—Stephen Thomas Erlewine*

The Ruler's Back / 1991 / Def Jam ✦✦✦✦
It was easy to dismiss *The Ruler's Back* before it was even released, or to assume that there was no way it could live up to *The Great Adventures of Slick Rick*. Of course, it did not attain the same level of artistic success as that debut, and it certainly did not equal that album's commercial success, in fact seemingly passing beneath the radar of the whole hip-hop community, for the most part. At the time of its release, the album received mixed reviews and indifferent reactions even from fans of Slick Rick. That's another unfortunate, ill-fated aspect of *The Ruler's Back*, because, in truth, it is a strong, albeit uneven, progression from the debut and occasionally strikes a flawless note. To think of the album as anything other than a confused, transitional effort would be inaccurate, but it does not follow that it isn't an intriguing record. The messiness of its execution perfectly encapsulates the sort of turmoil Slick Rick was experiencing in his life at the time, and the music pulls the listener into that sort of tangled experience. Both Vance Wright's production and Slick Rick's rapping sound pressed for time, and they rush through the songs with a whip-lashing intensity. It can be a disorienting listen, but it is also a pure adrenaline rush. Slick Rick was going through a time of hurtling change, and the hurried breathlessness of the music captures that. *The Ruler's Back* is all over the map, lacking the thematic focus that held the first album together, but its frayed-threads, seams-showing immediacy is part of what makes it such an underrated album in the hip-hop canon. *—Stanton Swihart*

Behind Bars / Nov. 22, 1994 / Def Jam ✦✦

The Art of Storytelling / May 25, 1999 / Def Jam ✦✦✦✦
If there's one thing Slick Rick has mastered, it is *The Art of Storytelling*. Ever since his debut, *The Great Adventures of Slick Rick*, he has been known for his literate, winding narratives, but his career was marred by legal troubles that kept him in prison for much of the '90s. Consequently, *The Art of Storytelling* is only his fourth album, but it's the first to rank as a worthy sequel to his classic debut. *The Ruler's Back* came close to capturing the feel of *The Great Adventures*, but *The Art* has a continually stunning set of stories and tales, and the presence of guest artists—even rappers as talented as Outkast, Nas, Raekwon, and Snoop Dogg—only emphasizes what a singular talent Rick is. The smooth production may be a little bit mired in contemporary rap cliches, but it's all enjoyable. Besides, Rick is about the lyrics, not the music, and he has written a stellar set of songs here, songs that are continually surprising and thought-provoking. It's a masterful set from one of the true lyrical masters of hip-hop. *—Stephen Thomas Erlewine*

Slint

f. 1987, Louisville, KY, **db.** 1991
Math Rock, Experimental Rock, Indie Rock, Post-Rock/Experimental, Alternative Pop/Rock, Instrumental Rock, American Underground
Though largely overlooked during their brief lifespan, Slint grew to become one of the most influential and far-reaching bands to emerge from the American underground rock community of the 1980s; innovative and iconoclastic, the group's deft, extremist manipulations of volume, tempo, and structure cast them as clear progenitors of the post-rock movement which blossomed during the following decade. Slint grew out of Louisville, KY's legendary Squirrel Bait, another seminal band which languished in relative obscurity during its own lifetime but ultimately spawned the likes of Gastr del Sol, Bitch Magnet, and Bastro as well. With producer Steve Albini, the quartet recorded 1989's *Tweez*, issued on their own Jennifer Hartman label; a collection of odd stylistic approaches, fractured rhythms, and strange lyrical fragments, the album owed debts to few (if any) historical precedents and steadfastly defied easy classification. 1991's *Spiderland* was an even more sophisticated and adventurous set, but (with the exception of a posthumous 1994 EP originally recorded between the two full-length albums) was Slint's swan song, although individual members remained key figures in the independent scene in acts including Tortoise, the Breeders, King Kong, Palace, and the For Carnation. *—Jason Ankeny*

Tweez / 1989 / Touch & Go ✦✦✦
Tweez is a fine, if bizarre recording, often switching from bass-led rhythm to rhythm in the same song. The guitars are harsh, but not especially fast. Instead of singing, bits of dialogue, sound effects, and spoken lyrics are used. *—John Bush*

● **Spiderland** / 1991 / Touch & Go ✦✦✦✦✦
More known for its frequent name-checks than its actual music, *Spiderland* remains one of the most essential and chilling releases in the mumbling post-rock arena. Even casual listeners will be able to witness an experimental power-base that the American underground has come to treasure. Indeed, the lumbering quiet-loud motif has been lifted by everybody from Lou Barlow to Mogwai, the album's emotional gelidity has done more to move away from prog-rock mistakes than almost any of the band's subsequent disciples, and it's easy to hear how the term "Slint dynamics" has become an indie categorization of its own. Most interestingly, however, is how even a seething angularity to songs like "Nosferatu Man" (disquieting, vampirish stop-starts) or "Good Morning, Captain" (a murmuring nod to *"The Rime of the Ancient Mariner"*) certainly signaled the beginning of the end for the band. Recording was intense, traumatic, and one more piece of evidence supporting the theory that band members had to be periodically institutionalized during the completion of the album. *Spiderland* remains, though, not quite the insurmountable masterpiece its reputation may suggest. Brian McMahan softly speaks/screams his way through the asphyxiated music and too often evokes strangled pity instead of outright empathy. Which probably speaks more about the potential dangers of pretentious post-rock than the frigid musical climate of the album itself. Surely, years later, *Spiderland* is still a strong, slightly overrated, compelling piece of investigational despair that is a worthy asset to most any experimentalist's record collection. *—Dean Carlson*

Slint / Aug. 29, 1994 / Touch & Go ✦✦✦✦✦
The release of this two-song EP (originally available only on vinyl, but hence released on CD) marks the end of Slint's brief yet shockingly provocative career. The album contains an alternate version of "Rhoda" from *Tweez*, as well as one previously unreleased track, "Glenn." The album is a 20-minute barrage of haunting melodies and caustic noise. It is entirely instrumental, and this evidences Slint's skill and ambition. Without lyrics, the music takes a precedence that it perhaps lacks on other albums. Although greatly in the character of their earlier work, this album breaks through as Slint's most important release. Sadly, though, the album acknowledges the breakup of the band. Many have followed in the wake of Slint, but it seems unlikely that anyone will eclipse them. The album is a requisite listen for anyone interested in the post-rock era. *—Marc Gilman*

The Slits

f. 1976, **db.** 1981
Post-Punk, Punk
Along with the Raincoats and Liliput, the Slits are one of the most significant female punk-rock bands of the late '70s. Not only did they bravely (or foolishly, you be the judge) leap into the fray with little, if any, musical ability, but through sheer emotion and desire created some great music, especially when they began working with veteran reggae producer Dennis Bovell, setting the stage for a future generation of riot grrrls. Formed by barely teenaged Ari Upp and Palmolive, the group made some crude recordings, though it wasn't until they nabbed the opening spot on the Clash's "White Riot" tour of England in 1977 that the Slits became a part of the punk pantheon. In 1979, the Slits made their first proper record *Cut* with reggae vet Dennis Bovell, who replaced the raging guitars with subtle reggae riddims. Palmolive was later replaced by new drummer Budgie (soon to join Siouxsie & the Banshees), and it was two years before a second record was released (*Return of the Giant Slits*), which was denser, darker, and full of surprises. By the close of 1981, Arri Up was singing in Adrian Sherwood's dub/funk aggregation the New Age Steppers, and the Slits had become both legendary and somewhat notorious. Though much derided in their short existence, what the Slits achieved and what they meant to succeeding generations of young female rockers cannot be underestimated. *—John Dougan*

● **Cut** / 1979 / Island ✦✦✦✦✦
Its amateurish musicianship, less-than-honed singing, and thick, dubwise rhythms might not be for everyone, but there's little denying the crucial nature of the Slits' first record. Along with more recognized post-punk records like Public Image Limited's *Metal Box*, the Pop Group's *Y*, and less recognized fare like Ruts DC and Mad Professor's *Rhythm Collision Dub*, *Cut* displayed a love affair with the style of reggae that honed in on deep throbs, pulses, and disorienting effects, providing little focus on anything other than that and periodic scrapes from guitarist Viv Albertine. But more importantly, *Cut* placed the Slits along with the Raincoats and Liliput as major figureheads of unbridled female expression in the post-punk era. You could call some of these songs a reaction to the more knuckledragging *Nuggets* bands, or the '60s garage acts that would find as many ways possible to say "women bad." Songs like "Instant Hit" (about PiL guitarist Keith Levene), "So Tough" (about Sid Vicious and Johnny Rotten), "Ping Pong Affair," and "Love Und Romance" point out the shortcomings of the opposite sex and romantic involvements with more precision and sass than the men were ever able to. "Spend Spend Spend" and "Shoplifting" target consumerism with an equal sense of humor ("We pay fuck all!"). Despite the less-than-polished nature and street tough ruggedness, *Cut* is entirely fun and catchy; it's filled with memorable hooks, whether they're courtesy of the piano lick that carries "Typical Girls" or Ari Up's exuberant vocals. (One listen to Up will demonstrate that Björk might not be as original as you've been led to believe.) Island's 2000 reissue blows away the earlier issue in sound and presentation, adding to the essential nature of this wildly influential record. *—Andy Kellman*

Y3LP / 1980 / Rough Trade ✦✦✦
This anonymous record (it's been referred to as *Retrospective*, *Untitled*, and *Once Upon a Time in a Living Room*) is, in some respects, the quintessential punk rock statement. The album sleeve is plain, white cardboard; the song titles are scribbled haphazardly on

the center label. The recordings, which pre-date any of the Slits' studio releases, are from demos and live shows. The playing is crude and amateurish while singer Ari Upp shrieks like a pre-adolescent child. That's not to say that it's unlistenable. The first cut, "A Boring Life," encompasses everything that was exciting about British punk: a breakneck pace, buzzsaw guitar, primitive drumming, and Ari railing about a hum-drum existence. —*J.P. Ollio*

Return of the Giant Slits / 1981 / CBS ✦✦✦
Never released in America, the Slits' second and final record found them pushing the envelope rhythmically. Although designed to be more commercial than *Cut*, it's actually less so, sounding more like the innovative work a young Adrian Sherwood was doing with Creation Rebel. Fans of the early Slits, who were put off by the reggae of *Cut*, were no doubt further alienated by this record's comfortable use of Afro-pop tempos and style. Which was a shame, because this music was interesting, daring and exciting. —*John Dougan*

The Peel Sessions / 1989 / Strange Fruit ✦✦✦✦✦
This seven-track disc contains all of the material recorded at two sessions for John Peel's BBC radio show. It's vintage early Slits, lots of crashing and bashing, but with a touch of the sophistication and Caribbean influence that was to follow about a year later on *Cut*. Not just for completists, this is a valuable addition to any serious collection of the music of the punk era, and an interesting document of a young band's growth. —*John Dougan*

Sloan

f. 1991, Halifax, Nova Scotia, Canada
Pop Underground, Indie Rock, Power Pop, Alternative Pop/Rock

Sloan was one of the most successful Canadian bands of the '90s, which was both a blessing and a curse. While they were well-known in their homeland, where their Beatlesque power pop became a radio staple, they had a difficult time breaking into the American market, especially after their label, DGC, decided not to market their hooky pop in the wake of grunge. After spending several years fighting the label, and nearly breaking up, Sloan re-emerged in 1996 with *One Chord to Another*, a record that became an instant success in Canada and a critical sensation in the U.S. upon its American release in 1997, establishing the group as one of the leaders of the new wave of power-pop groups in the late '90s.

Andrew Scott (drums), Chris Murphy (bass, vocals), Patrick Pentland (guitar, vocals), and Jay Ferguson (guitar, vocals), formed Sloan in Halifax, Nova Scotia, Canada in 1991. Within a few months, their feedback-laden live shows had gained a sizable audience. By the end of the year, their first recording, "Underwhelmed," appeared on the local Halifax compilation *Hear and Now*. Early in 1992, they released the *Peppermint* EP on their own Murderecords, and by the summer, they had signed with DGC. Sloan's debut album, *Smeared* appeared in October in Canada. For their second album, 1994's *Twice Removed*, Sloan simplified their sound considerably, concentrating on melodic, hook-laden power-pop. Sloan re-emerged in the summer of 1995, playing a handful of concerts and releasing a single, "Same Old Flame," on Murderecords. That winter they recorded *One Chord to Another*, a record which expanded the power-pop approach of *Twice Removed* on a small budget. Although its origins were modest, the album was a huge Canadian hit upon its June 1996 release. *Navy Blues* followed a year later. A double live album, *4 Nights at the Palais Royale* was released by Murderecords in 1999, as was a new studio effort, *Between the Bridges*. —*Stephen Thomas Erlewine*

Smeared / Jan. 19, 1993 / Murder ✦✦✦
Sloan's debut album, *Smeared*, is a bit of a mess, as the group tries to combine catchy pop melodies with punky rhythms and washes of dissonant feedback borrowed straight from Sonic Youth and My Bloody Valentine records. Those aren't the only two influences that are apparent on *Smeared*—references to all sorts of American indie-rock, from the Velvet Underground to Nirvana, are scattered throughout the record. Sloan, surprisingly, can harness these diverse influences into a winning combination of sighing melodies and swirling guitars, and while their songwriting is occasionally a little unfocused, the best songs—"Underwhelmed," "Two Seater," "I Am the Cancer," "What's There to Decide?" —are quite impressive. —*Stephen Thomas Erlewine*

Twice Removed / Aug. 30, 1994 / Geffen ✦✦✦✦✦
The difference between *Smeared* and Sloan's second album *Twice Removed* is quite remarkable. Stripping away most of their indie-rock influences, Sloan emerges as an astonishingly accomplished pure pop band, one that evokes the sunny charm and effortless melodicism of the Beatles and Beach Boys without being beholden to preserving a tradition. Almost every song on *Twice Removed* sparkles with clear, graceful melodies, and the arrangements are dense with ideas. The album is a rarity—an unself-conscious power-pop album, overflowing with fresh melodies and tough, energetic performances. —*Stephen Thomas Erlewine*

● **One Chord to Another** / 1996 / Murder ✦✦✦✦✦
Following the bungled American release of *Twice Removed*, it seemed unlikely that Sloan would survive, let alone record an album as wonderful as *One Chord to Another*. On their previous album, Sloan had refashioned themselves as a power pop band, often to terrific results, but on *One Chord to Another*, their songwriting blossoms. Filled with catchy, jangling riffs and memorable melodies, the record is a *tour de force* of hooks and harmonies, filled with exceptionally strong songs and forceful performances, which give the record a firm, rocking foundation. Few power-pop records of the '90s are as infectious and memorable as *One Chord to Another*. [The initial American pressing of *One Chord to Another*, which appeared nearly a year after the original Canadian release, contained a bonus disc patterned after the Beach Boys' live-in-the-studio *Party*, which featured Sloan

running through several of their best-known songs and a handful of covers, including a jaw-dropping medley of Canned Heat and Stereolab.] —*Stephen Thomas Erlewine*

Navy Blues / May 26, 1998 / Murder ✦✦✦✦
Having weathered the demise of their most recent American label, Sloan forges on, battered but unbroken and still delivering perfect pop records; *Navy Blues* might just be their best yet, with the sheer consistency of its infectious melodies, clever lyrics, and exuberant performances pushing the group toward new creative peaks. Moving away from the ornately Beatlesque production of the previous *One Chord to Another*, the sound on *Navy Blues* is more down and dirty, indicating a heavy Big Star influence; a track like "Iggy & Angus" certainly isn't as raw as the homages implicit in its title would suggest, but its fuzzed-out guitars and lumbering drums are nevertheless emblematic of the sonic shifts which characterize the entire record. Truth be told, there's not a weak track here, but "C'mon C'mon (We're Gonna Get It Started)," "Keep on Thinkin'," "Chester the Molester," and "I Wanna Thank You" all go above and beyond the call of duty, each undeniably catchy and instantly memorable. —*Jason Ankeny*

4 Nights at the Palais Royale / Apr. 20, 1999 / Murder ✦✦✦
Taking cues from Rush's *All the World's a Stage* and Kiss' *Alive!*, Sloan released their 1999 double-live CD, *4 Nights at the Palais Royale*, at the perfect time—they had honed their chops since 1996, and *Navy Blues* was less than a year old. Recorded in Toronto in November 1998, this double-live CD is a snapshot of the band: fun, endearing, and eager to please. Drummer Andrew Scott's songs sound particularly strong live: they've progressed into pop masterpieces and stand out as the most solid, mostly due to their tight arrangements. Though guitarist Jay Ferguson's tunes are underrepresented—he has just three songs out of 28—he sounds wonderful, especially on "The Lines You Amend." Bassist Chris Murphy, the jester, spends the most time playing to the crowd, but his songs shouldn't be overlooked. He sounds best singing his lower-key numbers such as "Pen Pals" and "Coax Me." Murphy's stripped-down "Torn" is phenomenal, and his and Scott's rendition of "Before I Do" adds vitality to that previously mellow, hypnotic song. Guitarist Patrick Pentland sings "I Can Feel It" with some restraint, but cuts loose on "Everything You've Done Wrong" and "Money City Maniacs." There's a singalong to "Deeper Than Beauty"—which has become a concert standard—and the crowd adds hand claps and vocals whenever needed. For fans who have never seen Sloan perform, *Four Nights at the Palais Royale* is especially essential—it takes you down to the main floor of a Sloan concert circa fall 1998. —*Gina Boldman*

Between the Bridges / Sep. 21, 1999 / Murder ✦✦✦✦
Sloan has managed to tinker with their signature sound—'60s pop meets '90s indie pop—while pleasing their current fans and gaining new ones. Their fifth studio album *Between the Bridges* is one of their best and most consistent—it's *Navy Blues* with better production, higher quality songs, and a polished (but definitely not slick) sound. The band returns to producer/engineer extraordinaire Brenndan McGuire, who produced *Twice Removed* and *One Chord to Another*, to illustrate how their sound has improved and evolved since *OCTA* and even *Navy Blues*. The tighter arrangements and the band's naturally engaging songwriting make *Between the Bridges* a standout in their already impressive discography. This progression is most obvious on tracks like Andrew Scott's blues-rock anthem "Sensory Deprivation," Patrick Pentland's rocking "Friendship," Chris Murphy's Television/Halifax club ode "The Marquee and the Moon," and Jay Ferguson's mellow and bouncy "Waiting for Slow Songs." Sloan is making harder-edged, bluesier albums, but they still sound like a pop band: innovative, pure, and energetic. Scott's tracks, in particular, have developed from simple Beatlesque numbers into astonishingly genuine, multi-layered pop songs. *Between the Bridges* sounds eclectic, energized, and cohesive, even if the individual artists don't always stretch out their own compositions. Somehow the group gets better and better while still experimenting with new concepts and sounds, which is not something many bands do gracefully. —*Gina Boldman*

P.F. Sloan

b. 1944
Vocals, Songwriter, Harmonica, Guitar / Folk-Rock, Pop, Singer/Songwriter, Sunshine Pop

He was there at the dawn of surf music, he was crowned king of the West Coast protest folkies, and he created some of the great American pop records of the '60s, yet today, the name P.F. Sloan is scarcely remembered outside of a circle of collectors and other period enthusiasts. Teamed early with Steve Barri, Sloan had a lasting partner. The duo cashed in on the surf craze as the Fantastic Baggies, and Sloan has claimed to be involved with countless more surf productions. Sloan and Barri wrote and produced hits for the likes of the Turtles and Johnny Rivers, and may best be remembered for Barry McGuire's "Eve of Destruction." Sloan's own albums for Dunhill were based on the kind of material he had given McGuire, and despite being dismissed by the "serious" protest-folk community of the day, they stand as excellent on their own merits.

Sloan's attempt to shift away from the West Coast folk-rock he largely created was reflected with the R&B-tinged album *Measure for Pleasure*, and following another album in the early '70s, he was gone. In spite of the occasional live gig and rumors of a comeback, it appears that P.F. Sloan will remain forever connected with his '60s work, his behind-the-scenes efforts overshadowing the fine music under his own name. —*Steve Aldrich*

P.F. Sloan/The Grass Roots / 1988 / Big Beat ✦✦✦
While this isn't as solid as the other P.F. Sloan collections, the concept is interesting, combining some of his most famous solo performances with five songs that were credited to the Grass Roots in the mid-'60s, but were for most intents and purposes Sloan performances. You can avoid this confusing approach by getting the Grass Roots' *Where Were You*

When I Needed You? CD and Sloan's first two LPs. But those original Sloan albums are pretty hard to come by these days, meaning that our choices are largely limited to relatively pathwork compilations such as these. *—Richie Unterberger*

• **Anthology** / Jul. 18, 1993 / One Way ✦✦✦✦✦
A well-compiled 18-track anthology featuring Sloan's overlooked recording career. This is essential folk-rock in the singer/songwriter tradition. Included is his wonderful version of "Eve of Destruction," which was written by Sloan and popularized by Barry McGuire. *—Chris Woodstra*

Child of Our Times: The Trousdale Demo Sessions, 1965-1967 / Apr. 17, 2001 / Varese ✦✦✦✦✦
P.F. Sloan was jaw-droppingly prolific in the years 1965 to 1967, not only writing, producing, and playing on numerous fine hit and non-hit pop and folk-rock records by other artists, but making two good solo albums. It didn't stop there: he also recorded quite a few unreleased demos, 20 of which make their first appearance on this compilation. Most of these were recorded and released by someone or other, and in one case ("Miss Charlotte") redone by Sloan himself later in the 1960s. No one sings Sloan like Sloan, though, and it's quite a treat to hear him as the performer on these largely outstanding, rousingly melodic pop-rockers. Some are well known ("You Baby" and "Can I Get to Know You Better" were hits for the Turtles, "Another Day, Another Heartache" did okay for the Fifth Dimension, and, of course, "Secret Agent Man" was big for Johnny Rivers), and others not so well known, but in the same class ("Child of Our Times," the Beatlesque "You're a Lonely Girl," "I've Got No More to Say"). Although these were demos, the production is sometimes as state-of-the-art as anything in L.A. in the mid-'60s, and the fidelity, performance, and arrangements are up to release quality on almost everything. The only reason this rates just a little below his first two solo albums is that it's lighter on the personal folk-rock and social consciousness statements ("Child of Our Times" being an exception); much of this is like a link between L.A. folk-rock and L.A. sunshine pop. It's very good, though, and enthusiastically recommended to anyone who enjoys the albums that Sloan did release in the mid-'60s. *—Richie Unterberger*

Slowdive

f. 1989, Reading, England, **db.** 1995
Dream Pop, Indie Rock, Shoegazing, Alternative Pop/Rock
Named after a word in one of Nick Chaplin's dreams—not from a Siouxsie and the Banshees single—Slowdive formed in Reading, England, in late 1989. Formed when they were mostly in their teens, Slowdive was initially lumped in with the remainder of the early-'90s British shoegaze scene. Signing with Creation, Slowdive's early singles received glowing press and chart placement. Slowdive's later releases extended upon the likes of the Cocteau Twins and the more atmospheric sides of post-punk. The group's debut LP, *Just for a Day*, was released in September of 1991. Though it placed in the Top Ten of the indie chart, the press backlash was beginning to surface. Regardless, it was a fine debut. The band's sound tightened for *Souvlaki*, released in mid-1993. With assistance from Brian Eno on a couple tracks and an excellent mixing job from Ed Buller, it was a marked improvement from their earlier material. It wandered less, but didn't sacrifice their sense of woozy atmosphere for it. Troubles with U.S. label SBK prevented *Souvlaki* from being released anywhere near it's U.K. street date and U.S. dates with Catherine Wheel that had been intended to promote *Souvlaki* proved to be another incident of bad timing; at that point, they were playing in a country where their record wouldn't be available for months. They closed out their career in 1995 with the excellent and misunderstood *Pygmalion*, essentially a solo ambient record by guitarist/vocalist Neil Halstead. Taken further than the intelligent techno slant of the *5* EP, the record was often beatless. Unhappy with this shift, band members Chaplin and Christian Savill left during the recording. The remaining members continued as Mojave 3, signed by 4AD on the strength of a demo that basically became their stellar debut LP. *—Andy Kellman*

Just for a Day / Sep. 1991 / SBK ✦✦✦
Just for a Day is Slowdive's first album, and it shows; when one listens to the magnificent sound of *Souvlaki* or the brilliant experimentation of *Pygmalion*, it becomes clear that *Just for a Day* was only a step toward the greatness they would later achieve. Its sound is quite like *Souvlaki*'s—swelling waves of flanged guitars, layers of wispy vocals floating in and out of the mix, and sweet lazy pop songs—but the production sometimes turns the band's plush, sweet sound into the sort of cheap and cheesy pleasantness one might expect from a New Age artist. A few tracks hint at the sound that would be fully achieved on *Souvlaki* ("Celia's Dream," "Erik's Song"), and the album as a whole must have sounded wonderful before anyone knew what great things the band was capable of—but *Just for a Day* is really Slowdive in their infancy. *—Nitsuh Abebe*

Blue Day / Feb. 1992 / Creation ✦✦✦✦
Blue Day is a summary of the *Slowdive, Morningrise*, and *Holding Our Breath* EPs, minus "Catch the Breeze," "Golden Hair," and "Avalyn II." It was initially released in Japan, France, and a couple of other countries, and it was also included with the first 1000 CD copies of *Souvlaki* sold in the U.S. and U.K. It's an excellent document of their pre-*Just for a Day* material. *—Andy Kellman*

• **Souvlaki** / 1993 / SBK ✦✦✦✦✦
Not enough great things can be said about *Souvlaki*, Slowdive's magnificent second album. The sound is incredible—beautifully written pop songs layered with floating trails of vocals, vast waves of flanged guitars which swell and recede—a sound that defines the term "dream-pop." In fact, *Souvlaki*'s opening track, "Alison," is quite possibly the most exemplary single ever to come from the genre—one listen is all it takes to be convinced. The album is the high point of Slowdive's career, stylistically speaking; at this, the midpoint of their career, they were combining the sweet pop of *Just for a Day* with the ambient experimentation that would mark their third release, *Pygmalion*. The result is a wholly brilliant album, almost on par with My Bloody Valentine's *Loveless* as the definitive recordings of the "shoegazer" genre. *—Nitsuh Abebe*

Pygmalion / 1995 / Creation ✦✦✦✦✦
Pygmalion isn't quite the departure you've been lead to believe it is. While the slippery floes of "Rutti," "Crazy for You," and "Blue Skied an' Clear" are certainly more electronically based than any of Slowdive's previous material, the intent is similar to earlier tracks like "Avalyn" and "Morningrise"; they each create a blissful, dreamlike state where time slows down and one begins to lose a sense of self. Instead of piling on loads of droning, phased guitars, lightly pulsing beats that barely register and bright atmospherics take over. Actually, Neil Halstead took over. Not happy with the direction of the material during recording, bassist Nick Chaplin and guitarist Christian Savill fled the scene. (They're credited in the sleeve, but as to whether or not they contributed a note is hazy.) This actually aided the progression of the record, which benefits from its minimalism. Rachel Goswell went along for the ride, contributing occasional lyrics and vocals, and newbie Ian McCutcheon provided light drumming for two of the album's most arresting tracks. *Pygmalion* isn't the snoozefest you might have been told it is, either. Though Creation's Alan McGee hated the record for its lack of proper tunes (and dropped them weeks after release), fans of Brian Eno's ambient works and Talk Talk's last three albums will find plenty to be excited about. The direction Halstead, Goswell, and McCutcheon would shoot off to with the first Mojave 3 record is hinted at in "All of Us" and the brief "Visions of La," including sparse acoustic guitar and candle-lit production flourishes. So what if you drift off to the record while listening to it? If you need to tuck away for a while, *Pygmalion* has all the tools to provide a peaceful slumber. *—Andy Kellman*

Sly & the Family Stone

f. 1967, San Francisco, CA, **db.** 1970
Pop/Rock, Funk, Soul
Sly & the Family Stone harnessed all of the disparate musical and social trends of the late '60s, creating a wild, brilliant fusion of soul, rock, R&B, psychedelia, and funk that broke boundaries down without a second thought. Led by Sly Stone, the Family Stone was comprised of men and women, and blacks and whites, making the band the first fully integrated group in rock's history. That integration shone through the music, as well as the group's message. Before Stone, very few soul and R&B groups delved into political and social commentary; after him, it became a tradition in soul, funk, and hip-hop. And, along with James Brown, Stone brought hard funk into the mainstream. The Family Stone's arrangements were ingenious, filled with unexpected group vocals, syncopated rhythms, punchy horns, and pop melodies. Their music was joyous, but as the '60s ended, so did the good times. Stone became disillusioned with the ideals he had been preaching in his music, becoming addicted to a variety of drugs in the process. His music gradually grew slower and darker, culminating in 1971's *There's a Riot Going On*, which set the pace for '70s funk with its elastic bass, slurred vocals, and militant Black Power stance. Stone was able to turn out one more modern funk classic, 1973's *Fresh*, before slowly succumbing to his addictions, which gradually sapped him of his once prodigious talents. Nevertheless, his music continued to provide the basic template for urban soul, funk, and even hip-hop well into the '90s. *—Stephen Thomas Erlewine*

Whole New Thing / 1967 / Epic/Legacy ✦✦✦
Their debut album is more restrained and not nearly as funky or psychedelic as their subsequent efforts, owing far more to traditional soul arrangements. These aren't *that* traditional, though; Sly is already using goofier and/or more thoughtful lyrics than the soul norm, and taking some cues from rock in his adventurous and unexpected song construction. The Family Stone, similarly, aren't as innovative as they would shortly become, but are already a tight unit, particularly in the interplay between lead and backup vocals and the sharp horn riffs. The CD reissue adds a previously unissued track, "What Would I Do." *—Richie Unterberger*

Life / 1968 / Epic/Legacy ✦✦✦✦✦
Just a matter of months after *Dance to the Music*, Sly & the Family Stone turned around and delivered *Life*, a record that leapfrogged over its predecessor in terms of accomplishment and achievement. The most noteworthy difference is the heavier reliance on psychedelics and fuzz guitars, plus a sharpening of songcraft that extends to even throwaways like "Chicken." As it turns out, *Life* didn't have any hits—the double A-sided single "Life"/"M'Lady" barely cracked the Top 100—yet this feels considerably more song-oriented than its predecessor, as each track is a concise slice of tightly wound dance-funk. All the more impressive is that the group is able to strut their stuff within this context, trading off vocals and blending into an unstoppable force where it's impossible to separate the instruments, even as they solo. The songwriting might still be perfunctory or derivative in spots—listen to how they appropriate "Eleanor Rigby" on "Plastic Jim"—but what's impressive is how even the borrowed or recycled moments sound fresh in context. And then there's the cuts that work on their own, whether it's the aforementioned double-sided single, "Fun," "Dynamite!," or several other cuts here—these are brilliant, intoxicating slices of funk-pop that get by as much on sound as song, and they're hard to resist. *—Stephen Thomas Erlewine*

Dance to the Music / Apr. 27, 1968 / Epic/Legacy ✦✦✦
Sly & the Family Stone came into their own with their second album, *Dance to the Music*. This is exuberant music, bursting with joy and invention. If there's a surfeit of classic material, with only the title track being a genuine classic, that winds up being nearly incidental, since it's so easy to get sucked into the freewheeling spirit and cavalier virtuosity of the group. Consider this—prior to this record no one, not even the Family Stone, treated soul as a psychedelic sun-splash, filled with bright melodies, kaleidoscopic

arrangements, inextricably intertwined interplay, and deft, fast rhythms. Yes, they wound up turning "Higher" into the better "I Want to Take You Higher" and they recycle the title track in the long jam "Dance to the Medley," but there's such imagination to this jam that the similarities fade as they play. And, if these are just vamps, well, so are James Brown's records, and those didn't have the vitality or friendliness of this. Not a perfect record, but a fine one all the same. *—Stephen Thomas Erlewine*

☆ **Stand!** / May 3, 1969 / Epic ✦✦✦✦✦
Stand! is the pinnacle of Sly & the Family Stone's early work, a record that represents a culmination of the group's musical vision and accomplishment. *Life* hinted at this record's boundless enthusiasm and blurred stylistic boundaries, yet everything simply gels here, resulting in no separation between the astounding funk, effervescent irresistible melodies, psychedelicized guitars, and deep rhythms. Add to this a sharpened sense of pop songcraft, elastic band interplay, and a flowering of Sly's social conscious, and the result is utterly stunning. Yes, the jams ("Don't Call Me Nigger, Whitey," "Sex Machine") wind up meandering ever so slightly, but they're surrounded by utter brilliance, from the rousing call to arms of "Stand" to the unification anthem "Everyday People" to the unstoppable "I Want to Take You Higher." All of it sounds like the Family Stone, thanks not just to the communal lead vocals but to the brilliant interplay, but each track is distinct, emphasizing a different side of their musical personality. As a result, *Stand!* winds up infectious and informative, invigorating and thought-provoking—stimulating in every sense of the word. Few records of its time touched it, and Sly topped it only by offering its opposite the next time out. *—Stephen Thomas Erlewine*

★ **Greatest Hits** / Nov. 21, 1970 / Epic ✦✦✦✦✦
Released in 1970, during the stopgap between *Stand!* and *There's a Riot Goin' On*, *Greatest Hits* inadvertently arrived at precisely the right moment, summarizing Sly & the Family Stone's joyous hit-making run on the pop and R&B charts. Technically, only four songs here reached the Top Ten, with only two others hitting the Top 40, but judging this solely on charts is misleading, since this is simply a peerless singles collection. This summarizes their first four albums perfectly (almost all of *Stand*, outside of the two jams and "Somebody's Watching You," is here), adding the non-LP singles "Hot Fun in the Summertime," "Thank You (Falettinme Be Mice Elf Agin)," and "Everybody Is a Star," possibly the loveliest thing they ever recorded. But, this isn't merely a summary (and, if it was just that, *Anthology*, the early-'80s comp that covers *Riot* and *Fresh* would be stronger than this), it's one of the greatest party records of all time. Music is rarely as vivacious, vigorous, and vibrant as this, and captured on one album, the spirit, sound, and songs of Sly & the Family Stone are all the more stunning. Greatest hits don't come better than this—in fact, music rarely does. *—Stephen Thomas Erlewine*

☆ **There's a Riot Goin' On** / Nov. 20, 1971 / Epic ✦✦✦✦✦
It's easy to write off *There's a Riot Goin' On* as one of two things—Sly Stone's disgusted social commentary or the beginning of his slow descent into addiction. It's both of these things, of course, but pigeonholing it as either winds up dismissing the album as a whole, since it is so bloody hard to categorize. What's certain is that *Riot* is unlike any of Sly & the Family Stone's other albums, stripped of the effervescence that flowed through even such politically aware records as *Stand!*. This is idealism soured, as hope is slowly replaced by cynicism, joy by skepticism, enthusiasm by weariness, sex by pornography, thrills by narcotics. Joy isn't entirely gone—it creeps through the cracks every once and awhile and, more disturbing, Sly revels in his stoned decadence. What makes *Riot* so remarkable is that it's hard not to get drawn in with him, as you're seduced by the narcotic grooves, seductive vocals slurs, leering electric pianos, and crawling guitars. As the themes surface, it's hard not to nod in agreement, but it's a junkie nod, induced by the comforting coma of the music. And damn if this music isn't funk at its deepest and most impenetrable—this is dense music, nearly impenetrable, but not from its deep grooves, but its utter weariness. Sly's songwriting remains remarkably sharp, but only when he wants to write—the foreboding opener "Luv N' Haight," the scarily resigned "Family Affair," the cracked cynical blues "Time," and "(You Caught Me) Smilin'." Ultimately, the music is the message and while it's dark music, it's not alienating—it's seductive despair, and that's the scariest thing about it. *—Stephen Thomas Erlewine*

☆ **Fresh** / Jun. 30, 1973 / Epic ✦✦✦✦✦
Fresh expands and brightens the slow grooves of *There's a Riot Goin' On*, turning them, for the most part, into friendly, welcoming rhythms. There are still traces of the narcotic haze of *Riot*, particularly on the brilliant, crawling inversion of "Que Sera Sera," yet this never feels like an invitation into a junkie's lair. Still, this isn't necessarily lighter than *Riot*—in fact, his social commentary is more explicit, and while the music doesn't telegraph his resignation the way *Riot* did, it comes from the same source. So, *Fresh* winds up more varied, musically and lyrically, which may not make it as unified, but it does result in more traditional funk that certainly is appealing in its own right. Besides, this isn't conventional funk—it's eccentric, where even concise catchy tunes like "If You Want Me to Stay" seem as elastic as the opener, "In Time." That's the album's ultimate charm—it finds Sly precisely on the point where he's balancing funk and pop, about to fall into the brink, but creating an utterly individual album that wound up being his last masterwork and one of the great funk albums of its era. *—Stephen Thomas Erlewine*

Small Talk / 1974 / Epic ✦✦✦
A new bass player and drummer signaled a toned-down Family Stone sound. Partially in keeping with changes in much of popular music in the early '70s, and maybe the result of marriage and a child, Sly became more introspective, quieter, and calmer, even employing a string section on various cuts. A less exhilarating album than earlier efforts, there is still much of merit here, including the Top Ten R&B hit "Time for Livin'." *—Rob Bowman*

★ **Anthology** / 1981 / Epic ✦✦✦✦✦
Anthology essentially replicates the previous collection *Greatest Hits* and adds singles from *There's A Riot Goin' On* and *Fresh* to the end of the album. Where *Greatest Hits* didn't follow chronological order, *Anthology* presents every single in the order they were released—and, with the exception of the latter-day singles and the inclusion of "Don't Call Me Nigger, Whitey," that is the major difference between the two collections. *Anthology* goes for a sweeping, definitive overview, while *Greatest Hits* is a brief blast of 12 of the finest singles of the rock & roll era. Either compilation functions as an excellent introduction, but *Anthology* is more comprehensive, giving it the edge as a first purchase. *—Stephen Thomas Erlewine*

Family Affair / 1991 / Thunderbolt ✦
Beware of this deceptively titled, quasi-legal import. Sly Stone did indeed work with the Mojo Men, a minor San Francisco band, as a producer in the mid-'60s. No less than 11 of the 15 cuts here are not Sly, but mid-'60s Mojo Men tracks, available in much better fidelity on Sundazed's *Whys Ain't Supposed to Be* reissue (which has more songs to boot). This disc does end with three outtake-sounding Sly Stone tracks of obscure vintage (there are no liner notes). An educated guess would put them circa 1967, but they're not that interesting in any case. *—Richie Unterberger*

In the Still of the Night / 1991 / Thunderbolt ✦✦
The two years or so before Sly Stone signed to Epic saw him lay down a myriad of hazily documented official and unissued recordings. Now available on a variety of labels, *In the Still of the Night* has 17 of them, most seeming to date from his days as a producer at Autumn in the mid-'60s (the liner notes are of little help). These are mostly sketches, really, of primary interest to Sly historians: some soul covers, some instrumental R&B vamps, and tentative originals that show Stone approaching his singular rock/soul fusion. There's a good deal of duplication with other packages of early Sly material, and it's much less thoughtfully assembled than the best of those (Ace's *In the Studio With Sly Stone*). *—Richie Unterberger*

Dance to the Music / 1991 / Thunderbolt ✦✦
With the exception of Ace's *In the Studio With Sly Stone*, the import compilations of Sly's pre-1967 work seem determined to keep such trivial information as sources of material and dates secret. So we'll have to guess that most of the ten tracks on *Dance to the Music* come from the early '60s, even before Stone started working at Autumn Records (a couple, "Help Me With My Broken Heart"/"Long Time Alone," were definitely released as a solo single). Most of these have a late-period doo wop feel, and although the songs aren't that noteworthy, Sly sings well, and there's a nice pop/R&B feel to the production. It's a curiosity that fills out the puzzle of Sly's pre-Family history. A couple of tracks obviously date from his later, more sophisticated Autumn productions, like the female-sung "Honest," which has also appeared on other compilations. *—Richie Unterberger*

Sly Stone & the Mojo Men / 1993 / WPC ✦
A deceptively packaged collection of early work, most of which is not Sly himself but the Mojo Men, a minor San Francisco rock band that he worked with in the mid-'60s as a producer. It's the same as another dubious collection of early Sly/Mojo Men work (*Family Affair*), though it's missing one Sly track, "Seventh Son," which does appear on *Family Affair* and other murky reissues of early Sly material. *—Richie Unterberger*

Spotlight on Sly & the Family Stone / 1993 / Javelin ✦✦
One of several piecemeal compilations of pre-Epic Sly Stone floating around. Most or all of the 16 tracks here probably date from his mid-'60s demos (some performed by other singers) at Autumn Records. Much more straight R&B/soul-oriented than his late '60s work, it's mostly of interest as an insight into his formative influences, although it offers some small pleasures. Ace's *In the Studio With Sly Stone* is the most comprehensive (and most professionally packaged) of these compilations by far. But if you're a completist, this does offer a few tracks that aren't frequently duplicated elsewhere, like the interesting soul/pop confection "Honest" (which has an unidentified woman on lead vocals). *—Richie Unterberger*

Remember Who You Are / May 1994 / Charly ✦✦
A reissue of his 1979 album *Back on the Right Track*, with the addition of a couple of previously unreleased outtakes that are more like jams than complete songs. *—Richie Unterberger*

Precious Stone: In the Studio / Sep. 13, 1994 / Ace ✦✦✦
Before forming the Family Stone, Sly Stone gained a lot of experience in the studio as the virtual in-house producer for the San Francisco-based Autumn label. The sessions he worked on during this era (performed by both himself and other artists) have appeared on numerous scattershot compilations. This 28-song anthology is the most comprehensive and intelligently assembled of these, including Sly solo performances, Sly collaborations with Billy Preston, and obscure soul-pop sides by Bobby Freeman, Gloria Scott, George & Teddy, and others. Over half of the cuts were previously unissued, and the lengthy liner notes provide an in-depth overview of his early accomplishments. Only serious collectors should seek this out, though. While Autumn afforded Stone the opportunity to experiment in the studio and devise various primitive collisions of soul and pop, his compositional, instrumental, and vocal skills were still in a very formative (if very promising) stage. Much of this is routinely pleasant, if lightly eccentric, period pop-soul, with occasional bursts of inspiration like Sly's wild scat vocals on "Scat Swim," and the folk-rockish "As I Get Older," and a few songs that would be reworked for inclusion on the first couple of Family Stone albums. *—Richie Unterberger*

Slyest Freshest Funkiest Rarest / 1995 / Magicalmystery ✦✦

Who in the Funk Do You Think You Are: The Warner Bros. Recordings / Aug. 16, 2001 / Rhino Handmade ✦✦✦
By the time Sly Stone—with a revamped version of the Family Stone—released his two Warner Bros. albums, *Back on the Right Track* and *Ain't But the One Way*, he had been

dismissed as a drugged-out has-been, with his best days past him. The latter part was most certainly true, since he was not only worn out, it would have been hard for most musicians to reach the peaks of *Stand!*, *There's a Riot Goin' On*, and *Fresh*, not to mention his unbelievable singles of the late '60s. But the truth was Sly was running on near-empty, barely able to keep afloat during a series of personal trouble and addictions. In retrospect, that makes these Warner recordings all the more remarkable—not because they're great, but because they're competent, enjoyable, period-piece funk. That's a testament to the sheer size of his genius—even amidst all the trouble he made pretty good music. Not great, to be sure, but neither of these records are disasters, which is more evident now than it was at the time. This still isn't music that packs any revelations, and there's not much depth in the music, apart from "The Same Thing (Makes You Laugh, Makes You Cry)," but it's surprisingly enjoyable, considering its reputation, and the presentation and packaging is first-rate, making this a nice collectors piece. *—Stephen Thomas Erlewine*

The Small Faces

f. 1965

British Psychedelia, Mod, Psychedelic, British Invasion

The Small Faces were the best English band never to hit it big in America. On this side of the Atlantic, all anybody remembers them only for is their sole stateside hit, "Itchycoo Park"—but in England, the Small Faces were one of the most extraordinary and successful bands of the mid-'60s; their music remains some of the most valuable and enjoyable of the era. Lead singer/guitarist Steve Marriott's formal background was on the stage, though he was earning his living at a music shop when he met bassist Ronnie Lane and drummer Kenney Jones, members of the Pioneers. The band—with Marriott installed permanently—cast its lot with a faction of British youth known as the Mods, stylish posers who, among their other attributes, affected a dandified look and a fanatical love of American R&B. Now christened the Small Faces ("face" being a piece of Mod slang for a fashion leader), the band recorded two singles ("Sha-La-La-La-Lee" and "Hey Girl") which hit the Top Ten in 1966, heralded with their first album, *Small Faces*. "All or Nothing" marked their first chart-topping entry, and its follow-up, "My Mind's Eye," followed it nearly as high.

After moving to the Immediate label, the Small Faces released their second album, also entitled *Small Faces* (but known in the U.S. as *There Are But Four Small Faces*). The band had bigger aspirations than doing more hit singles and set to work across five months during 1968 recording what proved to be their magnum opus, *Ogden's Nut Gone Flake*. Though recorded as a joke, the single "Lazy Sunday" rose to number two on the British charts. The group began showing serious signs of strain, however, and the end came when Marriott suddenly left the stage during a concert; he later called Peter Frampton and the two eventually formed Humble Pie. The Small Faces did carry on into 1969, replacing Marriott with Rod Stewart and Ron Wood and carrying on for one album before going on to greater glory as the Faces. During the mid-'70s, the band reunited (without Ronnie Lane) for two albums, *Playmates* and *78 in the Shade*. *—Bruce Eder*

The Small Faces / 1966 / Deram ♦♦♦♦♦

This CD and the accompanying 1996 reissue of *From the Beginning* makes collecting the Small Faces' Decca sides complicated, containing as it does many tracks that are not on the anthology double-disc. The new remastering has turned this into a must-own disc for anyone who enjoys the early Rolling Stones or, especially, the early Who, and wants to hear a British Invasion band as good as they were that never quite made it in the U.S., and which could have crossed swords with any garage band you care to name and carried the day. In those days, Steve Marriott had an even more soulful voice than Mick Jagger or Roger Daltrey; the main influences on the group were Sam Cooke and Marvin Gaye, and he was pretty formidable on guitar as well. The songs all have that really cool crunchy sound on the early Who records, except the sound is a little fuller and the tempos are better conceived, and there's even a pretty impressive bit of feedback throughout. The French EP tracks that comprise this disc's bonus songs are all distinctly different from the standard cuts, generally much more raw—like *real* American-style garage band stuff—including a feedback-laden opening to a completely different take of "What'cha Gonna Do About It" and totally different versions of "Shake" and "E to D." The sound on these cuts isn't quite up to the original album's 12 established tracks, as master tapes were impossible to find, but they—and the improved sound of the rest—make this a must-own CD, even more than *The Decca Anthology*. *—Bruce Eder*

From the Beginning / 1967 / Deram ♦♦♦♦♦

Another remastering of a classic piece of mid-'60s British rock & soul, and as important and enjoyable a record as, say, the Beatles' *Rubber Soul* or the Stones' *Aftermath*, even if the album itself was slapped together by Decca in an effort to undercut the band's first new release for rival Immediate Records in 1967. Steve Marriott's honest, agonized cover of the Del Shannon classic "Runaway" almost makes up for the fact that neither Otis Redding nor Marvin Gaye ever got around to applying their respective talents to this jewel of a song. That's just the opening number, and there's some stuff even better than that here. There are some songs that overlap with the Immediate stuff, including some really spaced-out psychedelia ("Yesterday, Today, and Tomorrow"), cool dance numbers ("Have You Ever Seen Me"), some repeated tracks ("What'cha Gonna Do About It," "Sha-La-La-La-Lee") from the Decca *Small Faces* album), killer Motown paeans ("You've Really Got a Hold on Me"—picture the early Who on a really, really good day covering this), and one original ("All or Nothing") that should be required listening for anyone who thinks they know the best music of the British invasion. And then there are the five bonus tracks, four from French-issued EPs that are completely different (and better) takes of "Baby Don't You Do It" et al, and a live BBC-recorded version of "What'cha Gonna Do About It." Marriott's playing on the latter is so loud and powerful, it could have melted the instruments of any American garage band this side of the Litter. At $11.99 list, this disc and its companion *Small Faces* reissue are the biggest British Invasion bargains going. *—Bruce Eder*

☆ **There Are But Four Small Faces** / 1968 / Columbia ♦♦♦♦♦

The band's first album for Andrew "Loog" Oldham's Immediate label originally appeared in two different forms in England (where it was known as *Small Faces*) and America, and the two song lineups have been combined on an early-'90s American Sony Music reissue. The music here is much more fully developed and experimental than their preceding album, still largely R&B-based (apart from the delightfully trippy "Itchycoo Park," the band's sole American hit) but with lots of unusual sounds and recording techniques being attempted. *—Bruce Eder*

☆ **Ogden's Nut Gone Flake** / 1968 / Castle ♦♦♦♦♦

There was no shortage of good psychedelic albums emerging from England in 1967-1968, but *Ogden's Nut Gone Flake* is special even within their ranks. The Small Faces had already shown a surprising adaptability to psychedelia with the single "Itchycoo Park" and much of their other 1967 output, but *Ogden's Nut Gone Flake* pretty much ripped the envelope. British bands had an unusual approach to psychedelia from the get-go, often preferring to assume different musical "personae" on their albums, either feigning actual "roles" in the context of a variety show, or simply as storytellers, or actor/performers. The Small Faces tried a little bit of all of these approaches on *Ogden's Nut Gone Flake*, but they never softened their sound. Side one's material, in particular, would not have been out of place on any other Small Faces release. Some of side two's production is more elaborate, with overdubbed harps and light orchestration here and there, and an array of more ambitious songs, all linked by a narration by comic dialect expert Stanley Unwin, about a character called "Happiness Stan." The core of the sound, however, is found in the pounding "Rollin' Over," which became a highlight of the group's stage act during its final days. Overall, this was the ballsiest-sounding piece of full-length psychedelia to come out of England, and it rode the number one spot on the U.K. charts for six weeks in 1968, though not without some controversy surrounding advertisements by Immediate Records that parodied the Lord's Prayer. Still, *Ogden's* was the group's crowning achievement—it had even been Marriott's hope to do a stage presentation of *Ogden's Nut Gone Flake*, though a television special might've been more in order. *—Bruce Eder*

The Autumn Stone / 1969 / Castle ♦♦♦♦

An excellent collection of most of the band's most important songs from both their later Decca and their entire Immediate history, rounded out with their final single, "The Universal," and five live tracks taken from a 1968 concert. A decent set of liner notes would have been nice, though. *—Bruce Eder*

78 in the Shade / 1978 / Atlantic ♦♦

★ **25 Greatest Hits** / 1992 / Repertoire ♦♦♦♦♦

Featuring all of their big British hits from "What'cha Gonna Do About It" to "The Universal," as well as worthy obscurities like "Donkey Rides a Penny a Glass," *25 Greatest Hits* is the best Small Faces compilation available, even if the tracks aren't presented in chronological order. *—Stephen Thomas Erlewine*

All or Nothing / Jun. 30, 1992 / Columbia ♦♦♦♦

The best collection to date of odd outtakes, obscure B-sides, and other rarities, remastered for superior sound and reconfigured so that, among other advantages, the live tracks from *The Autumn Stone* are assembled together in sequence. Also contains lots of alternate takes, instrumental backing tracks, etc. *—Bruce Eder*

Singles A's & B's / Dec. 16, 1994 / See For Miles ♦♦♦♦

Decca Anthology 1965-1967 / 1996 / Decca ♦♦♦♦♦

This 36-song double-CD set covers most of the group's released songs from Decca, minus one song ("I Can't Make It") that they lost the rights to, and augmented with a handful of solo tracks by Steve Marriott and songs by Jimmy Winston's band. The sound is fair—none of the Decca songs by any band from this period seem to be in great shape—but not earth-shattering; what is earth-shattering is the performance of Marriott and company, especially on their earlier tracks. Despite being worked to death by the record company and their own touring schedule, and their rapidly growing disillusionment, they generated some incredibly passionate British Invasion-era R&B, embracing Stax and the more soulful sides of Motown with equal ease. The later material shows the first appearance of the druggy ambience and psychedelic haze that was to characterize their Immediate period, not surprising since they moved from Decca to Immediate in a matter of days, the moment they had enough material to satisfy (at least on paper) their Decca contract, with some songs ("E to D," etc.) shared in different versions between the two companies. The packaging is a bit unwieldy, however, and while the photos are great, Paolo Hewitt's well-intentioned notes seem driven more by enthusiasm than care or skill (not only is the connection between "You Need Loving" and Led Zeppelin's "Whole Lotta Love" debatable, but he gets the title of the Zeppelin song wrong, referring to it as "Whole Lotta Lovin'." *—Bruce Eder*

The Immediate Years [U.K. Box Set] / Jan. 1996 / Charly ♦♦♦♦♦

Okay, it's expensive as a four-CD set. And yeah, apart from "Itchycoo Park" and maybe "Lazy Sunday," not too much of what the Small Faces recorded ever made any lasting impression on American listeners. But there's a *lot* of good music here. The box opens up modestly enough with Steve Marriott's old band, the Moments, covering the Kinks' "You Really Got Me" and doing one other song, "Money Money." A few of the band's Decca tracks that seem to float between Decca and Immediate follow, and then we plunge into the group's Immediate history. Andrew "Loog" Oldham's independent label wasn't much more organized than the typical blues label from Chicago in the 1950s, and the Small Faces' tape library is a mess. But the producers have included everything—every stereo and mono version of each song (where a different mix exists), the five official live tracks, the unfinished backing tracks, every known outtake. Anyone who thinks this is overkill doesn't know the Small Faces—they weren't much less prolific than the Rolling Stones, and were better than the Stones as both a soul band and a psychedelic band (the Stones never really made the jump into drug songs too comfortably); and based on the evidence, they could have cut the Who to shreds most nights. The sound varies, although it's all been nicely cleaned up (mildly CEDAR-ized, actually), and while three versions of "(Tell Me) Have You Ever Seen Me" may seem like overkill, it's all fascinating stuff, watching certain songs change and evolve. This is where it ends for the serious fan. *—Bruce Eder*

The Definitive Anthology of the Small Faces / Feb. 1996 / Repertoire ✦✦✦✦✦
The four-CD box has more music, and there are lots of other anthologies out there, and this one only gives you a couple of cuts off of their magnum opus, *Ogden's Nut Gone Flake* (which is still essential listening and should be bought separately); but short of a six-disc set that has everything, this double-disc set is probably the best general overview that anyone is likely to provide of the Small Faces, covering their Decca as well as their Immediate Records outputs with more than reasonable thoroughness. The 16 Decca tracks represent their complete singles output for the label, A- and B-sides alike, and they sound great, too; 12 more songs on disc one represent their Immediate Records output on 45 rpm record. Disc two opens with Steve Marriott's two early solo sides for Decca on which he sounded amazingly like Buddy Holly, followed by a pair of songs (including a cover of the Kinks' "You Really Got Me") that he cut fronting the Moments, prior to hooking up with the Small Faces. Four solo sides by original organist Jimmy Winston (two of them credited the Winston's Fumbs) are followed by a series of late-era Small Faces cuts, including outtakes, and a previously unissued version of the Marriott/Lane song "Groovy" credited to "the Lot," which was soul singer P.P. Arnold fronting the Small Faces. The 55-song set also comes with a nicely illustrated and written booklet. *—Bruce Eder*

Anthology: 1965-1967 / Oct. 22, 1996 / Polygram ✦✦✦✦✦
The Small Faces' catalog is one of the most confusing in rock & roll history, featuring multiple compilations bearing the same title but considerably different track listings, reworked original albums and haphazard retrospectives. The double-disc *Anthology: 1965-1967* goes a long way toward correcting those problems, yet it stops just short of being definitive. Containing all of the material the band recorded for Decca Records—including "Whatcha Gonna Do About It?," "Sha-La-La-La-Lee," "Hey Girl," "All or Nothing," and "My Mind's Eye"—which means it cuts off just as the Small Faces were entering their most creative period. Still, the Small Faces were an excellent British R&B group and that phase is captured in all its glory on this set. *—Stephen Thomas Erlewine*

BBC Sessions: 1965-1968 / Feb. 29, 2000 / Varese ✦✦✦
A solid compilation of 1965-68 BBC performances. It's heavier on their early mod years than their later psychedelic ones, which are essentially only represented by three songs from a 1968 broadcast (of which only one, "Lazy Sunday," is an original). Still, this has energetic (and, by the standards of BBC archive tapes from the 1960s, good-sounding) versions of the early singles "Whatcha Gonna Do About It," "Sha-La-La-La-Lee," "Hey Girl," and "All Or Nothing," as well as a few first album-era songs, highlighted by "You Need Love," the template for Led Zeppelin's "Whole Lotta Love." "Whatcha Gonna Do About It," from a 1965 broadcast, is a particularly incendiary performance, about the equal of the hit single version. As for songs that are otherwise unavailable on Small Faces releases, there are just a couple, and they're good ones. "Jump Back" is a heavy mod-soul cover of a song first done by Hadda Brooks, and later covered by Gene Vincent, though the Small Faces most likely learned it from Rufus Thomas' soul version. One thing's for sure: although Steve Marriott is given the songwriting credit in the liners, he did *not* compose it (it's been credited to both Brooks and Thomas on other reissues). There's also a mighty fine cover of Brenda Holloway's soul ballad "Every Little Bit Hurts" from 1968, with P.P. Arnold (uncredited on the sleeve) on backing vocals. This does miss some BBC cuts that have shown up on bootlegs (notably a cover of "You Really Got a Hold on Me"); perhaps good-fidelity tapes could not be found. What they *did* find blows previous bootlegs of Small Faces BBC sessions away, soundwise. *—Richie Unterberger*

★ **The Darlings of Wapping Wharf Launderette** / May 16, 2000 / Immediate/Sequel ✦✦✦✦✦
Here's the question for Small Faces fans: Is it better to own the original Immediate albums or to invest in the splendid double-disc set, *The Darlings of Wapping Wharf Launderette*? The question is a tricky one, since *Darlings* contains all of their Immediate recordings, meaning all of *Autumn Stone* (or *There Are but Four Small Faces*, as it's known in its American incarnation), plus all of the landmark *Ogden's Nut Gone Flake*. Granted, *Ogden's* is divided cleanly in half, with the first side appearing on disc one and the second on disc two, which may irritate listeners who like to hear the concept album uninterrupted. Nevertheless, it's hard not to view *Darlings* as a real bargain, since it gathers all the singles, albums, B-sides, plus some outtakes and alternate mixes and versions from the group's most creative period. And, hearing them in this setting, it's hard not to be stunned by the depth of the group's songwriting and restless musicality, which holds its own with peers like the Kinks and the Who. So, the question may indeed be an easy one, after all—if you want to be stunned by the Small Faces' peak, there's no better place to turn. *—Stephen Thomas Erlewine*

Nice / Mar. 27, 2001 / Pilot ✦✦✦
This two-disc set, evidently produced under the auspices of the surviving members of the Small Faces, is part of the newest wave of CD releases that are multimedia affairs. The first disc is a 26-minute CD made up of the ten appearances that the Small Faces made on the German *Beat Club* and *Beat Beat Beat* television programs between September 28, 1966, and April 27, 1968. In those days, the two programs were exceptional in that most of the guests played live. Given the absence of a definitive Small Faces concert album, these tracks should be invaluable to serious fans of the band, and about half of this disc is precisely that—they might not sound exactly the way they did in concert, but it's got to be close; they're loud and raw, and surge like thunder on the songs "All or Nothing," "Hey Girl," and "Sha La La Lee." The 1966 appearances show the Small Faces at their peak as an R&B band—maybe the best in England at the time (with apologies to the Rolling Stones and the Who)—while the later songs cast them in a trippy, psychedelic mode. "Itchycoo Park" and "Lazy Sunday" are very obviously mimed to the studio tracks, as the phasing of the drums on the former is identical to that on the single; "Tin Soldier" is really live, however, and captures the group in a transcendent moment in performance, grinding away while Steve Marriott screams like a dervish. The second disc purports to contain the video clips that accompany the audio heard on disc one—perhaps others will have better luck getting it to play on their computers, or downloading the Quicktime program that will supposedly play it. *—Bruce Eder*

Smash Mouth

f. San Jose, CA
Ska-Punk, Post-Grunge, Alternative Pop/Rock
A novelty rock band in the same vein as Presidents of the United States of America, but with surf and garage influences instead of the Presidents' punk/thrash background, Smash Mouth found a hit in 1997 with the '50s-influenced "Walkin' on the Sun." The group was formed in 1994 in San Jose, CA by vocalist Steve Harwell, a former rapper with the group F.O.S. After that group disintegrated, he began jamming with an old friend, drummer Kevin Coleman. Harwell's former manager introduced him to guitarist Greg Camp (fresh from the local band Lackadaddy) and bassist Paul De Lisle. The quartet recorded two demos, and got the songs into rotation on a local radio station. After playing a summer festival with No Doubt and Beck, Smash Mouth decided to record an album. After finishing *Fush Yu Mang*, the group were signed by Interscope, which released "Walkin' on the Sun" as the first single. It became a number one modern rock hit, and pushed the album into the Top 40. The follow-up album, *Astro Lounge*, was released in 1999, generating the hit "All Star"; a collection of early material, *East Bay Sessions*, also appeared that same year. *—John Bush*

● **Fush Yu Mang** / Jul. 8, 1997 / Interscope ✦✦✦✦
The groovy, '60s soul-funk of "Walking on the Sun" disguised the fact that Smash Mouth wasn't much more than a run-of-the-mill ska-punk band, and their debut, *Fush Yu Mang*, wasn't much more than an average modern-rock album. With its organ riff and breezy melody, "Walking on the Sun" was a great one-shot single, yet Smash Mouth never came close to replicating its easy charm anywhere on *Fush Yu Mang*. They sound clumsy when they rock, and their up-tempo numbers never quite catch fire. There are some moments that'll satisfy third-wave ska-revival fans, but anyone hooked in by the single will find the album disappointing. *—Stephen Thomas Erlewine*

Astro Lounge / Jun. 8, 1999 / Interscope ✦✦✦✦
Based on their infectious summer single "Walking on the Sun," it was easy to dismiss Smash Mouth as a one-hit wonder, since it was hard to believe that they'd be able to top that sun-kissed delight which was easily the highlight of their debut, *Fush Yu Mang*. Perhaps that's why their second record, *Astro Lounge*, feels like such a surprise, since it carries through on the promise of "Walking on the Sun." Like Sugar Ray—a fellow veteran of the ska-punk underworld who delivered a follow-up which owed more to melodic pop and new wave than its hit predecessor—Smash Mouth has created an album that is unabashedly fun, catchy, and lightweight; the ideal music for a car radio or a day at the beach. It's true that nothing on *Astro Lounge* is as immediately grabbing as "Walking on the Sun," but every song shares the same party-ready mentality and irresistible, trashy AM-radio vibe. No, nothing on *Astro Lounge* is particularly deep, but it's all good fun and it never disappoints—which is quite a remarkable feat, since one-hit wonders rarely deliver a second album that betters their first. *—Stephen Thomas Erlewine*

The Smashing Pumpkins

f. 1988, Chicago, IL, **db.** Dec. 2, 2000, Chicago, IL
Alternative Pop/Rock
Of all the major alternative rock bands of the early '90s, Smashing Pumpkins were the group least influenced by traditional underground rock. Lead guitarist/songwriter Billy Corgan fashioned an amalgam of progressive rock, heavy metal, goth-rock, psychedelia, and dream-pop, creating a layered, powerful sound driven by swirling, distorted guitars. Corgan was wise enough to exploit his angst-ridden lyrics, yet he never shied away from rock-star posturing, even if he did cloak it in allegedly ironic gestures. In fact, the Smashing Pumpkins became the model for alternative rock success—Nirvana were too destructive, Pearl Jam shunned success. The Pumpkins, on the other hand, knew how to play the game—signing to a major-subsidized indie for underground credibility, moving to the major in time to make the group a multi-platinum act. And when the group did achieve mass success with 1993's *Siamese Dream*, they went a long way to legitimize heavy metal and orchestrated prog rock, helping move alternative rock even closer to '70s AOR rock, especially in the eyes of radio programmers and mainstream audiences. And, unlike many of their contemporaries, the Pumpkins were able to withstand many internal problems and keep selling records, emerging as the longest-lasting and most successful alternative band of the early '90s. *—Stephen Thomas Erlewine*

Gish / May 1991 / Virgin ✦✦✦✦✦
Arriving several months before Nirvana's *Nevermind*, the Smashing Pumpkins' debut album *Gish*, which was also produced by Butch Vig, was the first shot of the alternative

revolution that transformed the rock & roll landscape of the '90s. While Nirvana was a punk band, the Smashing Pumpkins and guitarist/vocalist Billy Corgan are arena-rockers, co-opting their metallic riffs and epic art-rock song structures with self-absorbed lyrical confessions. Though Corgan's lyrics fall apart upon close analysis, there's no denying his gift for arrangements. Like Brian May and Jimmy Page, he knows how to layer guitars for maximum effect, whether it's on the pounding, sub-Sabbath rush of "I Am One" or the shimmering, psychedelic dream-pop surfaces of "Rhinoceros." Such musical moments like these, as well as the rushing "Siva" and the folky "Daydream," which features D'Arcy on lead vocals, demonstrate the Smashing Pumpkins' potential, but the rest of *Gish* falls prey to undistinguished songwriting and showy instrumentation. *—Stephen Thomas Erlewine*

Lull / Nov. 5, 1991 / Caroline ♦♦♦
Lull is a four-song EP the Smashing Pumpkins released as they were preparing to enter the studio to record their second album, *Siamese Dream.* Essentially the "Rhinoceros" single and three B-sides, *Lull* is targeted toward die-hard fans, but the solo Billy Corgan acoustic ballad "Bye June" and the blistering "Slunk" illustrate that the sumptuous neo-psychedelic hard rock of *Gish* wasn't a fluke. *—Stephen Thomas Erlewine*

● **Siamese Dream** / Jul. 27, 1993 / Virgin ♦♦♦♦♦
While *Gish* had placed Smashing Pumpkins on the "most promising artist" list for many, troubles were threatening to break the band apart. Singer/guitarist/leader Billy Corgan was battling a severe case of writer's block and was in a deep state of depression brought on by a relationship in turmoil; drummer Jimmy Chamberlin was addicted to hard drugs; and bassist D'Arcy and guitarist James Iha severed their romantic relationship. The sessions for their sophomore effort, *Siamese Dream,* were wrought with friction—Corgan eventually played almost all the instruments himself (except for percussion). Some say strife and tension produces the best music, and it certainly helped make *Siamese Dream* one of the finest alt-rock albums of all time. Instead of following Nirvana's punk rock route, *Siamese Dream* went in the opposite direction—guitar solos galore, layered walls of sound courtesy of the album's producers (Butch Vig and Corgan), extended compositions that bordered on prog rock, plus often reflective and heartfelt lyrics. The four tracks that were selected as singles became alternative radio standards—the anthems "Cherub Rock," "Today," and "Rocket," plus the symphonic ballad "Disarm"—but as a whole, *Siamese Dream* proved to be an incredibly consistent album. Such underrated compositions as the red-hot rockers "Quiet" and "Geek U.S.A." were standouts, as were the epics "Hummer," "Soma," and "Silverfuck," plus the soothing sounds of "Mayonaise," "Spaceboy," and "Luna." After the difficult recording sessions, Corgan stated publicly that if *Siamese Dream* didn't achieve breakthrough success, he would end the band. He didn't have to worry for long—the album debuted in the Billboard Top Ten and sold more than four million copies in three years. *Siamese Dream* stands alongside *Nevermind* and *Superunknown* as one of the decade's finest (and most influential) rock albums. *—Greg Prato*

Pisces Iscariot / Oct. 4, 1994 / Virgin ♦♦♦
Although Smashing Pumpkins had only released two studio albums by 1994 (1991's *Gish* and 1993's *Siamese Dream*), they had an overflow of songs that were either relegated to B-sides on European singles or remained unreleased. Billy Corgan proved to be one of rock's most prolific songwriters of the 1990s' alt-rock movement—as the quality of these early leftovers were often just as strong as the songs that were officially released. Since nearly all of these songs were never issued domestically, the B-side/rarity collection *Pisces Iscariot* was issued alongside their first long-form home video, *Vieuphoria.* The collection proved to be a feast for fans—it's inexplicable why such exceptional rockers ("Plume," "Hello Kitty Kat," "Frail and Bedazzled," "Blue") and ballads ("Obscured," "La Dolly Vita") weren't featured on albums. Also included is the long and winding, 11-minute epic jam fest "Starla," which proves that Corgan was one of the finest (and most underrated) rock guitarists of the '90s, as well as a pair of unlikely covers—Fleetwood Mac's gentle "Landslide" and the Animals' psychedelic "Girl Named Sandoz." Also included are insightful liner notes (strewn with typos) from Corgan. While it's not the definitive B-sides collection of pre-*Mellon Collie* Pumpkins (such tracks as "Bullet Train to Osaka," "Purr Snickety," "Apathy's Last Kiss," "My Dahlia," "Jackie Blue," "Glynis" and others are nowhere to be found), *Pisces Iscariot* contains some of Corgan and company's finest moments. Hopefully a second collection will eventually see the light of day. *—Greg Prato*

Mellon Collie and the Infinite Sadness / Oct. 24, 1995 / Virgin ♦♦♦♦♦
Smashing Pumpkins didn't shy away from making the follow-up to the grand, intricate *Siamese Dream.* With *Mellon Collie and the Infinite Sadness,* the band turns in one of the most ambitious and indulgent albums in rock history. Lasting over two hours and featuring 28 songs, the album is certainly a challenging listen. To Billy Corgan's credit, it's a rewarding and compelling one as well. Although the artistic scope of the album is immense, the Smashing Pumpkins flourish in such an overblown setting. Corgan's songwriting has never been limited by conventional notions of what a rock band can do, even if it is clear that he draws inspiration from scores of '70s heavy metal and art-rock bands. Instead of copying the sounds of his favorite records, he expands on their ideas, making the gentle piano of the title track and the sighing "1979" sit comfortably against the volcanic rush of "Jellybelly" and "Zero." In between those two extremes lay an array of musical styles, drawing from rock, pop, folk, and classical. Some of the songs don't work as well as others, but *Mellon Collie* never seems to drag. Occasionally they fall flat on their face, but over the entire album, the Smashing Pumpkins prove that they are one of the more creative and consistent bands of the '90s. *—Stephen Thomas Erlewine*

The Aeroplane Flies High / Nov. 26, 1996 / Virgin ♦♦♦
The Aeroplane Flies High contains all five singles—"Bullet With Butterfly Wings," "1979," "Zero," "Tonight, Tonight," "Thirty-Three"—from *Mellon Collie and the Infinite Sadness* in a box set shaped like a 45 single carrying case from the '60s. Though the set contains all of the B-sides from the five singles, the running order isn't quite the same as the original releases; for example, in its original release, "Butterfly Wings" only had two B-sides, but it is augmented for covers of new wave artists like the Cars, Blondie, and Missing Persons. In total, the box set has more songs than *Mellon Collie,* and, by and large, the quality of the music is quite strong. Occasionally, Billy Corgan's prolificness gets the better of him; there are a number of songs where his reach exceeds his grasp, and he doesn't quite come up with an engaging melody to match his detailed production. At other times, his musical experimentations catch hold, such as when he delves into jazz or orchestrated pop. Still, all of these pleasures are ones that are only of interest to dedicated Smashing Pumpkins fans who already know *Mellon Collie and the Infinite Sadness* inside and out. A casual fan will have a hard time sorting out the wheat from the chafe on *The Aeroplane Flies High,* but that work will be a pleasure for the diehards. *—Stephen Thomas Erlewine*

Adore / Jun. 2, 1998 / Caroline ♦♦♦
Left without a drummer after Jimmy Chamberlin's dismissal, the Smashing Pumpkins took the opportunity to revamp their sound slightly—which is what Corgan claimed they were going to do on their fourth album, anyway. *Adore* however, isn't a drastic departure. Using dream-pop ballads and the synthetic pulse of "1979" as starting point, the Pumpkins have created a hushed, elegiac album that sounds curiously out of time—it's certainly an outgrowth of their previous work, but the differences aren't entirely modern. Whenever synthesizers are added to the mix, the results make the band sound like a contemporary of the Cure or Depeche Mode, not the Aphex Twin. That's not necessarily a problem, since *Adore* creates its own world with layered keyboards, acoustic guitars, and a rotating selection of drummers and machines. There's none of the distorted bluster that cluttered *Mellon Collie* and none of the grand sonic technicolor of *Siamese Dream. Adore* recasts the calmer moments of those albums in a sepia tone, in an attempt to be modest and intimate. Only Billy Corgan would consider a 74-minute, 16-track album a modest effort, but compared to its widescreen predecessors, it does feel a bit scaled-down. Still, Corgan's ambitions reign supreme. This is no mere acoustic album, nor is it electronica—it is quiet contemporary art-rock, playing like a concept album without any real concept. Its very length and portentousness tend to obscure some lovely songs, since all the muted production tends to blend all the songs together. But even with its flaws, *Adore* is an admirable record that illustrates the depth of the Pumpkins' sound, even if it ultimately isn't a brave step forward. *—Stephen Thomas Erlewine*

MACHINA/The Machines of God / Feb. 29, 2000 / Caroline ♦♦♦
Any record called *MACHINA/The Machines of God* couldn't be a pure rock album. The title suggests this is a concept album, which are at least a little progressive. As it happens, *MACHINA* is a lot progressive. Though it's damn near impossible to figure out the storyline, the album plays like a concept album, with each track floating into the next, winding up with an album artier than *Adore.* That's not a liability, since Smashing Pumpkins were always arty, yet Billy Corgan was very clever in camouflaging his artiness. "The Everlasting Gaze," rocks more overtly than anything on *Adore,* and the storybook-styled artwork deliberately evokes memories of *Mellon Collie.* Enthusiasts will find moments to admire throughout *MACHINA,* but ultimately, they might be disappointed with a record that crosses *Mellon Collie* with *Adore* without relying on the strengths of either. *MACHINA* appears to be ornately straightforward, yet as it progresses, it becomes increasingly insular. By the time it gets to "Heavy Metal Machine," designed as the record's crushing centerpiece, its weaknesses become apparent. "Heavy Metal Machine" should be a brutal, bruising experience, yet it's toothless, processed within an inch of its life. It becomes clear that the chief strength of the album is production. Not once does *MACHINA* ever feel like the work of a band; it feels as if it was painstakingly assembled by Corgan and Flood. Smashing Pumpkins have always been Corgan's band, but they've never sounded like a solo vehicle the way that they do here. With *MACHINA,* they fall into a vaguely unsastifying middle ground. Certain things work quite well, like the lovely closer "Age of Innocence," yet *MACHINA* meanders, meaning it's not the uncompromising, take-no-prisoners return to form that Corgan surely wanted *MACHINA* to be. *—Stephen Thomas Erlewine*

Machina II: The Friends and Enemies of Modern Music / Sep. 5, 2000 / Constantinople ♦♦♦
Having decided that the earlier *Friends and Enemies* effort at getting rare songs out to the Pumpkins' fan base surreptitiously was successful, Billy Corgan organized a more formal effort with *Machina II,* borrowing the original tape title while revamping the contents. Twenty-five copies were made on three 10" and two 12" vinyl discs. Instructions were given to distribute the material on the web; artwork was also made available online, making this possibly the first full release of an album strictly as a free web effort. The first 10" disc includes the heavy-yet-dreamy "Slow Down" and a "spacy" version of "Glass' Theme"; the second features one of the Pumpkins' most surprising covers, James Brown's "Soul Power," which turns out to be a great Pumpkins bash-and-thrash fest. It also includes the *Adore* outtake "Cash Car Star," a fantastic hyper-thrash assault with some insane guitar work, and a fantastic version of the "Stand Inside Your Love" B-side "Speed Kills." The final 10" contains a piano/vocals version of "If There Is a God," and a lighter take on "Try, Try, Try." The two 12" disc releases—the "official" *Friends and Enemies* release—features alternate takes of the original cassette's tracks, including "Dross," and a heavy rip through "Blue Skies Bring Tears," while the loud, sparkling soar of "Real Love" and "Le Deux Machina" remain unchanged. New songs include a fine James Iha number, "Go," the haunting "Innosence," and the official release of "Let Me Give the World to You," here given a triumphant total band take. As a high-class artifact and a gift to a loyal fan base, *Machina II* is a winner. *—Ned Raggett*

Elliott Smith

Vocals / Sadcore, Indie Pop, Indie Rock, Singer/Songwriter

Folk-punk singer/songwriter Elliott Smith rose from indie obscurity to mainstream success in 1997 on the strength of "Miss Misery," his Academy Award-nominated song from the film *Good Will Hunting*. A native of Portland, OR, Smith began writing and recording his first songs at age 14, later becoming a fixture of the city's thriving music scene; as a member of the band Heatmiser, he debuted in 1993 with the LP *Dead Air*, issuing his first solo effort *Roman Candle* on the tiny Cavity Search label a year later. For his 1995 self-titled album, Smith signed with the noted Kill Rock Stars label; *Either/Or* followed in 1997, around the same time that filmmaker and longtime fan Gus Van Sant requested permission to use the singer's music in his upcoming *Good Will Hunting*. Smith also composed a handful of new songs for the soundtrack, among them "Miss Misery," and when the Academy of Motion Picture Arts and Sciences announced its Oscar nominations the following February, the track was a surprise entry in the "Best Original Song" category. Although he did not win, Smith performed the song live at the televised Oscar broadcast, appearing onstage alongside superstars Trisha Yearwood and eventual award-winner Celine Dion in one of the most notably surreal musical moments in recent memory; his DreamWorks label debut, *XO*, followed later in 1998, and *Figure 8* arrived in early 2000. *—Jason Ankeny*

Roman Candle / 1994 / Cavity Search ✦✦✦✦

Elliott Smith began his career like most aspiring musicians in the northwestern states: putting in the requisite hours in a grunge band. Being a team player, however, is not Smith's forte. After those buzzy shows in the bars of Portland, OR, he would retreat backstage with his acoustic guitar and whisper his own quiet songs to himself. This album is his first attempt to record those songs, and they capture that feeling perfectly: a loner retreating from the noisy tension of life with others finding solace in musical solitude. *Roman Candle* was, in fact, recorded in solitude on a four-track in a basement. Smith played all the instruments himself. He has said that he's always surprised when people call his songs "sad," because playing them always made him happy. You can hear that reclusive joy in the light bounce of the melodies and hushed harmonies (which recall Simon and Garfunkel). But his lyrics are haunted by the downbeat, drug-addled life from which he was retreating. For all their cryptic cleverness, there is a restless unhappiness in his fragmented stories of alienated urbanites. After that description, a reference to the definitive folk loner, Nick Drake, is inevitable. Smith's whispy vocals and able fingerpicking deserve the comparison. The highlight of *Roman Candle* is the title track. The quietly driving acoustic guitars and threatening bass create a disturbing portait of a human timebomb, barely containing a seething and simmering undercurrent of bitterness. The rest of the album, by comparison, is pure sunlight. *—Darryl Cater*

Elliott Smith / Jul. 21, 1995 / Kill Rock Stars ✦✦✦✦

Elliott Smith's self-titled second album was his first for the Kill Rock Stars label and also his first major artistic statement. Its sound is fairly similar to that of *Roman Candle*—it's mostly just Smith and his gently fingerpicked acoustic guitar, embellished a bit more often with drums, harmony vocals, and the odd additional instrument. The main difference here is that Smith's melodies and lyrics reveal their greater strength and substance with repeated listens. And make no mistake, the songs do require repeated listens—not just because of Smith's often whispery, spiderweb-thin delivery, but also because of his deceptively angular melodies and chord progressions, which threaten to float away until the listener hears them enough to latch on and know where they're going. Smith is often compared to Paul Simon or the Beatles in their softer moments, but perhaps the best touchstone for this early sound is Nick Drake's even more minimalistic *Pink Moon*; while Smith's language is rawer and tougher than Drake's haunting poetics, his songs also deal with depression and loneliness, creating an almost uncomfortable intimacy with their bare-bones arrangements. The quiet prettiness of Smith's sound can make it easy to overlook the darker, edgier side of his songs—many of Smith's embittered characters cope with their dysfunctional relationships or breakups through substance abuse, while some of the lyrics read more like angry, defiant punk rants when separated from the music. Smith would flesh out his sound with the albums to come, but *Elliott Smith* contains the blueprint for his later successes, and more importantly, it's a fully realized work itself. *—Steve Huey*

● **Either/Or** / Feb. 25, 1997 / Kill Rock Stars ✦✦✦✦✦

Elliott Smith's third album sees his one-man show getting a little more ambitious. While he still plays all the instruments himself, he plays more of them. Several of the songs mimick the melody mastery of pop bands from 1960s. The most alluring numbers, however, are still his quietly melancholy acoustic ones. While the full-band songs are catchy and smart, Smith's recording equipment isn't quite up to the standards set by the Beatles and the Beach Boys. The humbler arrangements are better suited to the sparse equipment. "Between the Bars," for example, plays Smith's strengths perfectly. He sings, in his endearingly limited whisper, of late night drinking and introspection, and his subdued strumming creates a minor-key mood befitting the mysteries of self. "Angeles" is equally ethereal-Smith's acoustic fingerpicking spins out notes which briskly move around a single atmospheric keyboard chord, like aural minnows swimming toward a solitary light at the surface of the water. The lyrics are a darkly biting rejection of the hypercapitalist dream machinery of Los Angeles (it would make a great theme song for Smith's label, Kill Rock Stars). Ironically, "Angeles" was included on the *Good Will Hunting* soundtrack, which won Smith the acclaim of Hollywood's biggest, brightest, and best connected voting body, the Academy of Motion Picture Arts & Sciences. Smith's stock in L.A. soared after he took his bow at the Oscars with Celine Dion and Trisha Yearwood. It might have been more interesting had he sung "Angeles." *—Darryl Cater*

XO / Aug. 25, 1998 / DreamWorks ✦✦✦✦✦

A year before his major label debut, *XO*, was released it seemed unlikely that Elliott Smith would even be on a major, let alone having his record be one of the more anticipated releases of 1998. He had certainly earned a great deal of critical respect with his low-key, acoustic indie records and was emerging as a respected songwriter, but he hadn't made much of an impression outside of journalists, record collectors, and indie-rockers. An Oscar nomination can change things, however. "Miss Misery," one of Smith's elegantly elegiac songs for Gus Van Sant's *Good Will Hunting*, unexpectedly earned an Academy Award nomination, and he was immediately thrust into the spotlight. He was reluctant to embrace instant celebrity, yet he didn't refuse a contract with DreamWorks, and he didn't shy away from turning *XO* into a glorious fruition of his talents. Smith's songs remain intensely introspective, yet the lush, Beatlesque production provides a terrifically charming counterpoint. His sweetly dark melodies are vividly brought to life with the detailed arrangements, and they sell Smith's tormented songs—it's easy to get caught up in the tunes and the sound of the record, then realize later what the songs are actually about. That's a sign of a good craftsman, and *XO* proves that not only can Elliott Smith craft a song, but he knows how to make an alluring pop record as well. *—Stephen Thomas Erlewine*

Figure 8 / Apr. 18, 2000 / DreamWorks ✦✦✦✦

Judging only by his earlier, bare-bones indie-label albums, it seemed highly unlikely that Elliott Smith would turn into the ambitious arranger and studio craftsman of his lushly textured DreamWorks debut, *XO*. A big part of that shift, of course, was the fact that Smith had major-label finances and equipment to work with for the first time; this allowed him to fuse his melancholy, slightly punky folk with the rich sonics of pop artists like the Beatles and Beach Boys. Smith continues in that direction for the follow-up, *Figure 8*, an even more sonically detailed effort laden with orchestrations and inventive production touches. With a couple of exceptions, the sound of Smith's melancholy has largely shifted from edgy to sighingly graceful, although his lyrics are as dark as ever. Even if the subject matter stays in familiar territory, though, the backing tracks are another matter—a gorgeous, sweeping kaleidoscope of layered instruments and sonic textures. Smith fleshes his songs out with assurance and imagination, and that newfound sense of mastery is ultimately the record's real emphasis. Even if it is a very impressive statement overall, *Figure 8* isn't quite the masterpiece it wants to be—there's something about the pacing that just makes the record feel long, and it can sometimes float away from the listener's consciousness. Still, most of the songs do reveal their strengths with repeated plays, and it's worth the price of a few nondescript items to reap the rewards of the vast majority. Fans who miss the intimacy of his Kill Rock Stars records won't find much to rejoice about here, but overall, *Figure 8* comes tantalizingly close to establishing Smith as the consummate pop craftsman he's bidding to become. *—Steve Huey*

Huey "Piano" Smith

b. Jan. 26, 1934, New Orleans, LA

Songwriter, Piano / New Orleans R&B, R&B

At one time a madcap vocalist and underrated pianist, Huey "Piano" Smith was a star in New Orleans during the '50s. He sang with Earl King in the early '50s, then recorded with Guitar Slim from 1951 to 1954. He did several sessions and also led the Clowns, whose roster at one point included Bobby Marchan. Smith's biggest hit wasn't the song he's best known for, "Rocking Pneumonia and the Boogie Woogie Flu," but "Don't You Just Know It," which was his only Top Ten pop and R&B hit. It reached number four R&B and number nine pop in 1958, a year after "Rocking Pneumonia" peaked at number five R&B. Smith kept going until he became a Jehovah's Witness and left the music business. *—Ron Wynn*

Rock & Roll Revival / Jan. 1991 / Ace ✦✦✦✦✦

A terrific 16-track collection of Huey "Piano" Smith & the Clowns' biggest hits and best material, including "Rocking Pneumonia" and "Don't You Just Know It," plus a couple of fine previously unreleased tracks. *—Stephen Thomas Erlewine*

● **This Is Huey Piano Smith** / Apr. 21, 1998 / Music Club ✦✦✦✦✦

For years, Huey "Piano" Smith lacked a comprehensive overview of his recording career, and no compilation ever appeared on CD in the United States. The budget-line label Music Club rectified that situation in 1998 with the release of *This is Huey Piano Smith*, an 18-track collection that features all of his hit singles for Ace plus several failed singles and New Orleans staples. Smith's hits and standards—"Rockin' Pneumonia and the Boogie-Woogie Flu," "Don't You Just Know It," "High Blood Pressure," "Pop-Eye," the original version of "Sea Cruise," with his vocals instead of Frankie Ford's—are so good that it's an inevitable disappointment to find many of the songs here are blatant attempts to get back on the charts ("Tu-Ber-Cu-Lucas and the Sinus Blues," "Would You Believe It (I Have a Cold)"). These fall flat, as do a couple of the other cuts, but unfortunately, that's an accurate portrait of Smith's career—he had a handful of wonderful, essential songs and was a hell of a performer, but he wasn't a consistent hitmaker. Nevertheless, the strong stuff is so good—even essential—that this is still highly recommended for New Orleans R&B fans and R&B fans in general. *—Stephen Thomas Erlewine*

Havin' Fun with Huey "Piano" Smith: More of the Best / Mar. 3, 1999 / West Side ✦✦✦✦

The second part of Ace Records combing through their Huey "Piano" Smith vault, *More of the Best* includes 24 tracks of new-to-disc songs and unreleased recordings, with vocalists including Bobby Marchan and Curley Moore, as well as Smith himself. *—Keith Farley*

That'll Get It: Even More of Best / Aug. 24, 1999 / West Side ✦✦✦✦

The third volume of Westside's retrospective into the music of Huey "Piano" Smith yields even more amazing treasures. It seems as if Huey never stopped recording and recording in every conceivable configuration it seems, as sideman, leader, songwriter, backing up young singing hopefuls, and beyond. With the advent of recording band tracks separately from vocals (the beginnings of stereo recording), label owner Johnny Vincent could take Huey's old tracks and try new vocals on them and in many cases that's what we have here. But also along the way are another brace of Ace and related label singles and album tracks that go just that further in making the case for Huey being one of the most influential and prolific of all New Orleans musicians. Not the place to start your Huey "Piano" Smith collection, but definitely not a bad place to end up. *—Cub Koda*

Patti Smith

b. Dec. 30, 1946, Chicago, IL

Vocals / New York Punk, Album Rock, Proto-Punk, Hard Rock

Patti Smith is a poet and rock singer who first gained notice when reading her poetry at gatherings in New York City in the early '70s. By 1974 Smith had edged toward music by reading with the backup of electric guitarist and rock critic Lenny Kaye, notably on her independent-label single, "Piss Factory." By 1975 Smith had organized a band that was playing in such clubs as the punk birthplace in New York, CBGB's, and she earned a contract with Arista Records. This resulted in the release of *Horses*, a critically acclaimed album that featured her songs, sometimes melded to dramatic readings, and such rock oldies as "Land of 1,000 Dances." *Radio Ethiopia* was both mainstream-rock-oriented and more experimental, depending on which track you played. With 1978's *Easter*, Smith was definitely moving in a more commercial direction, especially by pairing with Bruce Springsteen for the hit single "Because the Night." That marked the high point of Smith's rock career. *Wave* (1979) found her waving goodbye; she married ex-MC5 guitarist Fred "Sonic" Smith and retired from the music business. Her return came with the promising 1988 album *Dream of Life*, but she was not back to full-time duty. Smith's husband died suddenly at the end of 1994. In 1995, she began making concert appearances again while preparing a new album due in 1996. In June 1996, Smith released *Gone Again*; *Peace and Noise* appeared a year later, and in the spring of 2000 she returned with *Gung Ho*. *—William Ruhlmann*

★ **Horses** / Nov. 1975 / Arista ✦✦✦✦✦

It isn't hard to make the case for Patti Smith as a punk rock progenitor based on her debut album, which anticipated the new wave by a year or so: the simple, crudely played rock & roll, featuring Lenny Kaye's rudimentary guitar work, the anarchic spirit of Smith's vocals and the emotional and imaginative nature of her lyrics, all prefigure the coming movement as it evolved on both sides of the Atlantic. Smith is a rock critic's dream, a poet as steeped in '60s garage rock as she is in French Symbolism; "Land" carries on from the Doors' "The End," marking her as a successor to Jim Morrison, while the borrowed choruses of "Gloria" and "Land of 1,000 Dances" are more in tune with the era of sampling than they were in the '70s. Producer John Cale respected Smith's primitivism in a way that later producers did not, and the loose, improvisatory song structures worked with her free verse to create something like a new spoken word/musical art form: *Horses* was a hybrid, the sound of a post-Beat poet, as she put it, "dancing around to the simple rock & roll song." *—William Ruhlmann*

Radio Ethiopia / Oct. 1976 / Arista ✦✦✦

After the success of *Horses*, Patti Smith had something to prove to reviewers and to the industry, and *Radio Ethiopia* aimed at both. Producer Jack Douglas gave "the Patti Smith Group," as it was now billed, a hard-rock sound, notably on the side-opening "Ask the Angels" and "Pumping (My Heart)," songs that seemed aimed at album-oriented rock radio. But the title track was a ten-minute guitar extravaganza that pushed the group's deliberate primitivism closer to amateurish thrashing. Elsewhere, Smith repeated the reggae excursions and vocal overlaying that had paced *Horses* on "Ain't It Strange" and "Poppies," but these efforts were less effective than they had been the first time around, perhaps because they were less inspired, perhaps because they were more familiar. A schizophrenic album in which the many elements that had worked so well together on *Horses* now seemed jarringly incompatible, with *Radio Ethiopia* Smith and her band encountered the same development problem the punks would—as they learned their craft and competence set in, they lost some of the unself-consciousness that had made their music so appealing. *—William Ruhlmann*

Easter / Mar. 1978 / Arista ✦✦✦✦✦

Patti Smith came back from the year-and-a-half break caused by her fall from a stage in January 1977 without having resolved the arts vs. commerce argument that had marred her second album, *Radio Ethiopia*. In fact, that argument was in some ways the theme of her third. *Easter*, produced by Bruce Springsteen associate Jimmy Iovine, was Smith's most commercial-sounding effort yet and, due to the inclusion of Springsteen's "Because the Night" (with Smith's revised lyrics), a Top Ten hit, it became her biggest seller, staying in the charts more than five months and getting into the Top 20 LPs. But Smith hadn't so much sold out as she had learned to use her poetic gifts within an album-rock context. Certainly, a song that proclaimed, "Love is an angel disguised as lust / Here in our bed until the morning comes," was pushing the limits of pop radio, and on "Babelogue," Smith returned to her days of declaiming poetry on New York's Lower East Side. That rant (significantly ending, "I have not sold my soul to God") led into the provocative "Rock & Roll Nigger," a charged rocker with a chorus that went, "Outside of society / Is where I want to be." Smith made the theme from the '60s British rock movie *Privilege* her own and even got into the U.K. charts with it. And on songs like "25th Floor," Iovine, Smith, and her group were able to accommodate both the urge to rock out and the need to expound. So, *Easter* turned out to be the best compromise Smith achieved between her artistic and commercial aspirations. *—William Ruhlmann*

Wave / May 1979 / Arista ✦✦✦

The Patti Smith Group's most conventional album, *Wave* was given a bright pop/rock sound by producer Todd Rundgren. It was the last album Smith made before marrying and retiring from record-making for nine years, and it can be heard as a farewell to the music business, from "Frederick," the love song to her husband-to-be, Fred "Sonic" Smith, that leads it off, to the version of "So You Want to Be (A Rock & Roll Star)," among the most bitter accounts of fame on record. But Smith also achieves a sense of charm and sincerity on *Wave* that she hadn't even attempted on her earlier albums, even to the point of her imagined small-talk encounter with the late Pope John Paul I on the title track. Still, the overall mediocre quality of the material makes this the slightest of Smith's efforts. *—William Ruhlmann*

Dream of Life / Jun. 1988 / Arista ✦✦✦

The big difference between Patti Smith's four 1970s albums and this return to action after nine years lies in the choice of collaborator. Where Smith's main associate earlier had been Lenny Kaye, a deliberately simple guitarist, here her co-writer and co-producer (with Jimmy Iovine) was her husband, Fred "Sonic" Smith, formerly of the MC5, who played guitar with a conventional rock competence and who lent his talents to each of the tracks, giving them a mainstream flavor. In a sense, however, these polished love songs, lullabies, and political statements are not to be compared to the poetic ramblings of Smith's first decade of music making—she's so much... calmer this time out. But you can't help it. Where the Patti Smith of *Horses* inspired a generation of female rockers, the Patti Smith of *Dream of Life* sounds like she's been listening to later Pretenders albums and taking tips from Chrissie Hynde, one of her spiritual daughters. *Dream of Life* is the record of someone who is simply showing the flag, trying to keep her hand in, rather than announcing her comeback. Not surprisingly, having made it, Smith retreated from the public eye again until the '90s. *—William Ruhlmann*

Gone Again / Jun. 18, 1996 / Arista ✦✦✦

After years of silence, Patti Smith returned to music with a series of concerts in late 1995. It had been years since she had performed live—for most of the '80s and '90s, she concentrated on domestic life. Following the death of her husband, Fred "Sonic" Smith, in early 1995, Smith began playing music in public again and those concerts eventually led to the triumphant comeback, *Gone Again*. Her husband wasn't the only loved one Smith lost between 1988's *Dream of Life* and 1996's *Gone Again*—her brother and her close friend Robert Mapplethorpe both died. Appropriately, grief and loss hang over *Gone Again*, but the overall effect is not one of indulgent melancholy. Instead, it's a sober but strengthing listen—this is healing optimistic music. Like most of Smith's best work, the songs on *Gone Again* aren't proper songs, they're song poems, with cascading music and dense, inspired lyrics. Smith sounds more mature than her earlier records—there are only a handful of out-and-out rockers, and most of the album is subtle and folky—which gives the album extra weight. *Gone Again* is more than a comeback, it's a revitalization—Patti Smith simply hasn't sound so engaged and provocative since *Easter*. *—Stephen Thomas Erlewine*

Peace and Noise / Sep. 30, 1997 / Arista ✦✦✦

After a prolonged retirement, Patti Smith returned to action in 1996 with *Gone Again*. It was recorded after she suffered the loss of both her brother and her husband, Fred "Sonic" Smith, two losses so great that it's not surprising she is still exploring that pain on *Peace and Noise*, which quickly followed *Gone Again* in 1997. Patti Smith had been working on *Peace and Noise* with Fred Smith before his death, and its issues are appropriately more domestic than those on *Gone Again*. Throughout most of the record, she explores aging and raising children, trying to find a place for her family in the modern world while coming to terms with her aging rebelliousness. The music on *Peace and Noise* trims away the sonic bluster and anthemic rocking of *Gone Again*, preferring a sparse, piano-based musical foundation. As a result, her words resonate clearly and have a succinct, poetic power that was lacking on the otherwise worthy *Gone Again*. *—Stephen Thomas Erlewine*

Gung Ho / Mar. 21, 2000 / Arista ✦✦✦

Patti Smith's late '90s comeback was devoted to reflective, intensely emotional music that explored her life in seclusion and the losses that made forced her to reconnect with the larger world. They were acclaimed, ambitious, successful records, but they steered away from Smith's angry, activist muse, plus her penchant for visceral music. She rediscovers both on *Gung Ho*, her most immediate album in years. "Immediate" doesn't necessarily mean rock & roll, though. At times, she does reconnect with garage punk, notably on the Farifisa-fueled "Persuasion" and "Glitter in Their Eyes," which is graced by the guitar of Tom Verlaine, but her remarkable band—featuring guitarists Lenny Kaye and Oliver Ray, bassist Tony Shanahan, and drummer Jay Dee Daugherty—sounds direct and forceful even on the mid-tempo cuts that dominate the album. Smith doesn't shy away from the personal—after all, the cover shot features her father Grant and the title track appears to deal with his war experiences—but she works on a broader plain throughout the album, concentrating on larger, social messages even in the more intimate moments. The result may not be as haunting as *Gone Again*, but it's superficially nervier, reminiscent of a subdued, mature version of *Easter*. In other words, it's another handsome, shaded, and satisfying work from an artist that has reconnected with her muse. *—Stephen Thomas Erlewine*

Warren Smith

b. Feb. 7, 1933, **d.** Jan. 31, 1980

Vocals, Guitar / Rockabilly, Traditional Country

For sheer, heartfelt vocalizing abilities, of all the folks who stood in front of the microphone at Sun studio, Warren Smith may have been the most talented. Equally adept at storming rockabilly and the most gut-wrenching of country ballads, Smith always sang it from the heart, without giving in to phony rasping or histrionics. Though typecast as strictly a rocker, Smith left Sun and achieved minor success in the '60s as a country singer, his first love. *—Cub Koda*

Call of the Wild / 1990 / Bear Family ✦✦✦✦✦
Warren Smith left Sun Records in 1959 and, after a brief stay with Warner Bros., signed with Liberty Records, where he looked forward to doing country music rather than the hybrid rockabilly that Sun had him recording. With Joe Allison managing his recordings, he began making records with a smooth Nashville sound, even though they were done in Hollywood. With Johnny Western on guitar, Ralph Mooney on steel guitar, and Bobby Bruce and Harold Hensley on fiddles, he got a very refined commercial sound that yielded a few hits ("I Don't Believe I'll Fall in Love Today" made it to number five, and "Odds and Ends, Bits and Pieces" got to number seven) and a superb album, *The First Country Collection of Warren Smith*, which featured covers of songs associated with Patsy Cline, Buck Owens, Charlie Walker, Eddy Arnold, and Rose Maddox, among others, and a couple of duets with singer Shirley Collie. The music here—Smith's complete Liberty recordings, plus his two 1966-vintage songs for the tiny Skill label—is among the most accomplished and inspired of Smith's career, and was work he was clearly proud of. The only drawback is the conventional nature of the arrangements—Allison and Liberty were, understandably, trying for the most commercial sound possible, and the results are a little dullish in retrospect. Smith's expression is fine, however, expressive and strong throughout (only the Skill sides are weak), and the playing, especially in the 1959-60 sessions, is first-rate. Highlights among the later songs include "Five Minutes of the Latest Blues," "A Hundred and Sixty Pounds of Hurt," and "That's Why I Sing in a Honky Tonk." The notes, as usual, are extremely thorough, covering Smith's career in considerable detail from 1959 until his death in 1980. *—Bruce Eder*

● **The Classic Recordings 1956-59** / 1992 / Bear Family ✦✦✦✦✦
Smith's entire output (31 tracks in all) for Sun Records. Includes the rockabilly classics "Rock & Roll Ruby," "Ubangi Stomp," and "Miss Froggie," as well as heartfelt country performances on "The Darkest Cloud," "I'd Rather Be Safe Than Sorry," and "Goodbye Mr. Love." No Sun collection can really be considered complete without adding this one to the list. *—Cub Koda*

Uranium Rock: The Best of Warren Smith / May 23, 1995 / AVI ✦✦✦✦✦
Uranium Rock: The Best Of is a wonderful 24-track collection containing all of Warren Smith's essential Sun recordings, from "Rock & Roll Ruby" and "Ubangi Stomp" to "Black Jack David," "Red Cadillac and a Black Moustache," and "Uranium Rock." It's a more concise and more effective compilation than Bear Family's *The Classic Recordings*, and therefore, it's arguably the definitive overview. *—Stephen Thomas Erlewine*

Will Smith (William Smith III)

b. Sep. 25, 1968, West Philadelphia, PA
Vocals / Pop-Rap, Urban, Hip-Hop
Beginning his career during the mid-1980s under the name the Fresh Prince, by the following decade rapper Will Smith was one of the biggest superstars of his time—not only a pop music sensation, he also conquered television and eventually feature films, starring in a string of box-office megahits. He was 16 when he met aspiring DJ Jeff Townes; joining forces as DJ Jazzy Jeff and the Fresh Prince, in 1987 the duo issued their debut record *Rock the House*, scoring a hit with the single "Girls Ain't Nothing but Trouble." Propelled by the smash "Parents Just Don't Understand," DJ Jazzy Jeff and the Fresh Prince broke into the mainstream a year later with *He's the DJ, I'm the Rapper*, one of the first hip-hop LPs to achieve double-platinum status. Clean-cut, witty, and easygoing, the duo's bubblegum approach was a stark contrast to the dominant, harder-edged rap sound of the period; viewed as a non-threatening alternative to their peers, they received the parental seal of approval, and their appeal spread across racial lines as well. Soon Hollywood began taking notice of Smith's success; in 1990, he was tapped to star in *The Fresh Prince of Bel-Air*, a sitcom for NBC. In 1995, Smith co-starred in the action film *Bad Boys*, a major box office hit; it set the stage for his leading role in 1996's *Independence Day*, the summer's biggest smash. A year later, he starred in *Men in Black*, again the box-office champ of the summer season; recording for the first time under his given name, he also scored a smash with the movie's rap theme. Smith's debut solo LP, *Big Willie Style*, also appeared in 1997, notching the hit "Gettin' Jiggy Wit It." *—Jason Ankeny*

● **Big Willie Style** / Nov. 25, 1997 / Columbia ✦✦✦✦
Will Smith wisely decided not to change his style too much on *Big Willie Style*, the first record he released since becoming a major movie star with appearances on *Independence Day* and *Men in Black*. Instead of trying to toughen his image, Smith continued with the friendly, humorous pop-rap that has been his trademark since *He's the DJ, I'm the Rapper*. Of course, he gives the music a glossy modern sheen (ironically based on early-'80s funk) in order to prove that he's still hip—and it works. Sure, there's filler scattered all the way the through the album, but the best moments—the disco-thumping "Gettin' Jiggy Wit It," the Larry Blackmon duet "Candy," the ballad "I Loved You," and the riotous "Men in Black"—rank among his best singles. *—Stephen Thomas Erlewine*

Willennium / Nov. 16, 1999 / Columbia ✦✦✦✦
By the time Will Smith released *Willennium* in November 1999, it was fashionable to put him down, especially since he was recovering from his first major stumble, the overblown *Wild Wild West*. Probably just the fact that he was everywhere made certain spoilsports long to take him down a notch, but *Wild Wild West* wasn't a mess because of him; in fact, he provided the only glimmers of fun in the whole misguided mess, through sheer star power. And that star power drives *Willennium*, turning it into a bold, brassy delight. Smith just doesn't care what anyone thinks; he knows he's a superstar, and he revels in his status. He likes to make fun music, and he likes to make it on a grand scale. Furthermore, he has no shame about entertaining. Consequently, *Willennium* is a gonzo pleasure in the way only a handful of big-budget pop albums can be: gaudy, giddy, infectiously silly, and proudly over-the-top. Case in point, its de facto title track, "Will 2K." Smith and his producers picked the Clash's "Rock the Casbah" as the foundation for an end-of-the-century party jam, a move so mind-bogglingly unpredictable that it's hard not to smile. And that spirit carries throughout the album, as Smith drops lyrical and musical allusions that are at once well known and totally out of left field. All of this is done to bright, joyful party music that celebrates its big beats and big hooks. Smith isn't quite as convincing when it comes to slow jams, but still his charm shines through. But the heart of the album lies in the up-tempo dance numbers, since they're what make *Willennium* irresistible. And this is one of the rare times that an abundance of cameos enhances the spirit of an album, making *Willennium* feel like a Y2K blowout where everyone is invited. *—Stephen Thomas Erlewine*

The Smithereens

f. 1980, Carteret, New Jersey
College Rock, Bar Band, Power Pop, Hard Rock
Dressed in leather, brandishing heavy guitars, and sporting an unabashed fetish for British Invasion pop, the Smithereens were an anomaly in the American college rock scene of the mid-'80s. Lead singer/songwriter Pat DiNizio stood out because his catchy hooks were haunting, not punchy, and his lyrics morose. As time wore on, the group became more straightforward, attacking pop songs with the weight of AC/DC. A few hits followed, but once alt-rock burst into the mainstream in the early '90s, the Smithereens' classicist pop seemed out of date (even if, ironically, DiNizio's lyrics were equally as angst-ridden), and they quietly faded into a cult working band.

Of course, the Smithereens essentially started out as a working band. Pat DiNizio (vocals, guitar) joined New Jersey high school students Dennis Diken (drums), Jim Babjak (guitar), and Mike Mesaros (bass), who had all played together in school, toward the end of the '70s. By the end of 1980, they had independently released the EP *Girls About Town*. The group played New Jersey and New York for the next three, not releasing another record until 1983's EP *Beauty and Sadness*, which received college radio airplay and a positive review in *Rolling Stone*. Their Don Dixon-produced debut album *Especially for You* appeared in 1986 to enthusiastic reviews. The album became a sizable indie hit, leading to a major-label contract with Capitol. *Green Thoughts*, appeared early in 1988, and its first single, "Only a Memory" crossed over to album-rock stations. Producer Ed Stasium brought a heavier guitar sound to 1989's *11*, which made "A Girl Like You" a Top 40 hit, sending the album to gold status. "Too Much Passion," the first single from their fourth album *Blow Up*, became a Top 40 hit, yet the album didn't replicate its predecessor's success. After 1994's reunion with producer Don Dixon, *A Date With the Smithereens*, the band released a pair of compilations in 1985. Four years later, they returned with *God Save the Smithereens*, released on the independent label, Koch. *—Stephen Thomas Erlewine*

Beauty and Sadness / 1983 / Enigma ✦✦✦

Especially for You / 1986 / Enigma ✦✦✦✦✦
The Smithereens' superb full-length debut *Especially for You* marries an unapologetically nostalgic affection for the melodic crunch of the British Invasion era with an equally unapologetic helping of postmodern melancholia. In tandem with Don Dixon's moodily atmospheric production, Pat DiNizio's lovelorn lyrics and world-weary vocals reveal the dark underbelly of his otherwise crisply infectious songs, lending standout tracks like "Strangers When We Meet," "Behind the Wall of Sleep," and the minor hit "Blood and Roses," both a unique flavor and an immediate familiarity. *—Jason Ankeny*

Green Thoughts / 1988 / Capitol ✦✦✦✦✦
The Smithereens' excellent sophomore effort picks up where their debut, *Especially for You*, left off, with Pat DiNizio delivering another impressive batch of superbly constructed pop gems; tracks like "Only a Memory," "House We Used to Live In," and "Drown in My Own Tears" are immediately ingratiating—instantly familiar, yet performed with more than enough energy and flair to sound new and exciting. Equally compelling are *Green Thoughts*' curveballs, like the countryish "Something New," the lovely ballad "Especially for You," and the dark, atmospheric "Deep Black," all of which deliver intriguing variations on the Smithereens' basic power-pop formula. Another winner. *—Jason Ankeny*

11 / 1989 / Capitol ✦✦✦
The third full-length album from the Smithereens, *11* (a title which presumably referred to Spinal Tap's fabled guitar amps, which could be cranked past 10), was something of a letdown after the solid, tough-pop perfection of their first two albums, *Especially for You* and *Green Thoughts*. While their previous sets boasted strong material from front to back, *11* is dotted with filler. And while "A Girl Like You," "Blue Period," and "William Wilson" are all great songs, many of the others sound like by-the-numbers pop tunes cranked out to pad the set to full length. Producer Don Dixon made the most of the dark and mysterious undercurrents of Pat DiNizio's songs and Jim Babjak's guitar, here Ed Stasium gives the band a solid, professional sound that is sadly lacking in personality; there's nothing wrong with the way the album sounds, but there isn't anything terribly engaging about it, either. As a band, the Smithereens still sound rock solid here, but as an album it was sadly indicative of the creative ups and downs that would mark their recording career from this point forward. *—Mark Deming*

Blow Up / Sep. 10, 1991 / Capitol ✦✦✦
Sometimes it seems like the Smithereens' entire career was mistimed. After the relative success of *11*, Pat DiNizio and company returned with their most straightforward and mainstream-ready release yet in *Blow Up*. Produced by Ed Stasium, the mix is arena-ready and clean, and DiNizio co-wrote two of the disc's most accessible songs with songwriters Diane Warren and Julian Lennon. The first single, the string-laden Philly soul of

"Too Much Passion" not only cracked the top 40, but it placed at number 38, one position higher than their previous biggest hit "A Girl Like You." That's where the success story ends. If there was ever a time for an alternative band to opt for a slicker sound, 1991 wasn't it. "Blow Up" was released within a week of Nirvana's *Nevermind*, and that album would quickly change alternative radio formats forever, squeezing out largely pop-oriented bands like the Smithereens. Also, "Too Much Passion" was the most "adult contemporary" single the Smithereens ever released, which meant a good deal of their new audience came on board expecting more of the same, and found only Warren's "Get a Hold of My Heart" to be similar. Still, the Smithereens never released a bad record, and *Blow Up* is in fact a quite good one: Much like *11* before it, *Blow Up* is a collection of catchy, blue-collar power pop distinguished by DiNizio's often moody outlook. *—Jason Damas*

Date With the Smithereens / Apr. 26, 1994 / RCA ✦✦

● **Blown to Smithereens: The Best of the Smithereens** / Apr. 4, 1995 / Capitol ✦✦✦✦✦
With their British Invasion style of rock, New Jersey's the Smithereens weren't exactly in step with the musical landscape of the mid- to late '80s. It didn't stop the quartet from being critical darlings and perennial candidates to break through to a wider audience. *Blown to Smithereens* gathers together ample evidence that the attention was more than merited. There's nary a weak moment on this collection, which includes all of the band's best-known songs and radio hits. Sequenced chronologically, *Blown to Smithereens* leads off with the Beatlesque "Beauty & Sadness" and proceeds with gems like the moody "Blood & Roses," "In a Lonely Place" (with its Bacharach vibe), the driving "House We Used to Live In," the sweet, melodic "Blue Period," and closes with a cover of "Time Won't Let Me." Pat DiNizio's often bittersweet, romantic lyrics compliment the polished, yet gritty, power pop resulting in timeless songs like "Behind the Wall of Sleep," "Only a Memory," and "A Girl Like You." For the uninitiated, *Blown to Smithereens* is a perfect introduction. For fans, it isn't necessarily essential, but rather a wonderful opportunity to revisit one of the more underappreciated bands of the past two decades. *—Tom Demalon*

Attack of the Smithereens / Nov. 21, 1995 / Capitol ✦✦✦✦
At first glance, a Smithereens rarities compilation might seem like an odd release. After all, the band was never had more than one gold album and none of their singles cracked the Top 30. That doesn't mean the band didn't have fans, however, nor does it mean that their music was undistinctive, as *Attack of the Smithereens* proves. Filled with B-sides, demos, rare singles, and live tracks, the collection has a loose charm and freewheeling energy their proper albums occasionally lacked. Much of this material is as good as anything the group released, making it a necessary purchase for most fans. Even casual fans will find something to cherish on *Attack of the Smithereens*. *—Stephen Thomas Erlewine*

God Save the Smithereens / Oct. 19, 1999 / Koch ✦✦✦
After two decades, the Smithereens were no longer in step with the times and they no longer cared—they do what they do because they love it, not because it's fashionable. They were at that point with 1994's *A Date With the Smithereens*, but that record was hurt by a weird undercurrent of bitterness and Pat DiNizio's songwriting slump. Wisely, the group decided to take a break after that album. The extended five-year hiatus recharged the group, if *God Save* is any indication. Not that the record is a masterpiece, but it is a good journeyman record that plays up their strengths quite nicely. There's a little bit of everything that the Smithereens do on the record—jangly pop ("She's Got a Way"), doomy rock ("The Last Good Time"), melancholy ballads, crunching riffs, and even a re-working of "Gloomy Sunday," reminiscent of DiNizio's moody solo effort. The Kinks allusion in the title is appropriate, since the Smithereens are also pop traditionalists whose consistency is only appreciated by a selective, discerning audience. Unlike Ray Davies, no one in the band really seems to care about the hits drying up—there's joy within their songcraft and their performances, they like the act of making music itself. Admittedly, *God Save* may not be as immediate or memorable as their best albums from the late '80s, but there are no weak moments on the record. Every song is well crafted and delivered with conviction—the very things that made the Smithereens a beloved cult band. *God Save the Smithereens* may not play to the wide audience that loved "A Girl Like You," but that cult will certainly be pleased by this strong comeback. *—Stephen Thomas Erlewine*

The Smiths

f. 1982, Manchester, England, **db.** Aug. 1987
College Rock, Indie Pop, Alternative Pop/Rock

The Smiths were the definitive British indie-rock band of the '80s, marking the end of synth-driven new wave and the beginning of the guitar rock that dominated English rock into the '90s. Sonically, the group was indebted to the British Invasion, crafting ringing, melodic three-minute pop singles, even for their album tracks. But their scope was far broader than that of a revivalist band. The group's core members, vocalist Morrissey and guitarist Johnny Marr, were obsessive rock fans inspired by the D.I.Y. ethics of punk, but they also had a fondness for girl groups, pop, and rockabilly. Morrissey and Marr also represented one of the strangest teams of collaborators in rock history. Marr was the rock traditionalist, looking like an elegant version of Keith Richards during the Smiths' heyday, and meticulously layering his guitar tracks in the studio. Morrissey, on the other hand, broke from rock tradition by singing in a keening, self-absorbed croon, embracing the forlorn, romantic poetry of Oscar Wilde, publicly declaring his celibacy, performing with a pocketful of gladiolas and a hearing aid, and making no secret of his disgust for most of his peers. While it eventually led to the Smiths' early demise, the friction between Morrissey and Marr resulted in a flurry of singles and albums over the course of three years that provided the blueprint for British guitar rock in the following decade. *—Stephen Thomas Erlewine*

☆ **The Smiths** / 1984 / Sire ✦✦✦✦✦
Arriving in an era dominated by synth-pop and gloomy post-punk, the Smiths' eponymous debut was the bracing beginning of a new era. On the surface, the Smiths' sound wasn't radically different from traditional British guitar pop—Johnny Marr's ringing layered guitars were catchy and melodic—but it was actually an astonishing subversion of the form, turning the structure inside out. Very few of the songs followed conventional verse-chorus structure, yet they were quite melodic within their own right. Marr's inventive songwriting was made all the more original and innovative by Morrissey's crooning and lyrics. Writing about unconventional topics, from homosexuality ("Hand in Glove") to child molestation and murder, Morrissey had a distinctively ironic, witty, and literate viewpoint whose strangeness was accentuated by his off-kilter voice, which would move from a croon to a yelp in a matter of seconds. While the production of *The Smiths* is a little pristine, the songs are vital and alive, developing a new, unique voice within pop music. Though the Smiths continued to improve over the course of their career, their debut remains startling and exciting. *—Stephen Thomas Erlewine*

☆ **Hatful of Hollow** / Nov. 1984 / Sire ✦✦✦✦✦
Several months after releasing their first album, the Smiths issued the singles and rarities collection *Hatful of Hollow*, establishing a tradition of repackaging their material as many times and as quickly as possible. While several cuts on *Hatful of Hollow* are BBC versions of songs from *The Smiths*, the versions on the compilation are nervy and raw—and they're also not the selling point of the record. The Smiths treated singles as individual entities, not just ways to promote an album, and many of their finest songs were never issued on their studio albums. *Hatful of Hollow* contains many of these classics, including the sweet rush of "William, It Was Really Nothing," and the sardonic "Heaven Knows I'm Miserable Now," the tongue-in-cheek lament of "Please, Please, Please Let Me Get What I Want," the wistful "Back to the Old House," "Girl Afraid," and the pulsating, tremolo-laced masterpiece "How Soon Is Now?" With such strong material forming the core of the album, it's little wonder that *Hatful of Hollow* is as consistent as *The Smiths* and arguably captures the excitement surrounding the band even better. *—Stephen Thomas Erlewine*

Meat Is Murder / 1985 / Sire ✦✦✦
With their second proper album *Meat Is Murder*, the Smiths begin to branch out and diversify, while refining the jangling guitar-pop of their debut. In other words, it catches the group at a crossroads, unsure quite how to proceed. Taking the epic, layered "How Soon Is Now?" as a starting point (the single, which is darker and more dance-oriented than the remainder of the album, was haphazardly inserted into the middle of the album for its American release), the group crafts more sweeping, mid-tempo numbers, whether it's the melancholy "That Joke Isn't Funny Anymore" or the failed, self-absorbed protest of the title track. While the production is more detailed than before, the Smiths are at their best when they stick to their strengths—"The Headmaster Ritual" and "I Want the One I Can't Have" are fine elaborations of the formula they laid out on the debut, while "Rusholme Ruffians" is an infectious stab at rockabilly. However, the rest of *Meat Is Murder* is muddled, repeating lyrical and musical ideas of before without significantly expanding them or offering enough hooks or melodies to make it the equal of *The Smiths* or *Hatful of Hollow*. *—Stephen Thomas Erlewine*

★ **The Queen Is Dead** / 1986 / Sire ✦✦✦✦✦
Meat Is Murder may have been a holding pattern, but *The Queen Is Dead* is the Smiths' great leap forward, taking the band to new musical and lyrical heights. Opening with the storming title track, *The Queen Is Dead* is a harder-rocking record than anything the Smiths had attempted before, but that's only on a relative scale—although the backbeat is more pronounced, the group certainly doesn't rock in a conventional sense. Instead, Johnny Marr has created a dense web of guitars, alternating from the minor-key rush of "Bigmouth Strikes Again" and the faux-rockabilly of "Vicar in a Tutu" to the bouncy acoustic pop of "Cemetry Gates" and "The Boy With the Thorn in His Side," as well as the lovely melancholy of "I Know It's Over" and "There Is a Light That Never Goes Out." And the rich musical bed provides Morrissey with the support for his finest set of lyrics. Shattering the myth that he is a self-pitying sap, Morrissey delivers a devastating set of clever, witty satires of British social mores, intellectualism, class, and even himself. He also crafts some of his finest, most affecting songs, particularly in the wistful "The Boy With the Thorn in His Side" and the epic "There Is a Light That Never Goes Out," two masterpieces that provide the foundation for a remarkable album. *—Stephen Thomas Erlewine*

Louder Than Bombs / 1987 / Sire ✦✦✦✦✦
A compilation of singles, B-sides, album tracks, and BBC sessions assembled for the American market, *Louder Than Bombs* is an overlong and unfocused collection that nevertheless boasts a wealth of brilliant material. Since *Hatful of Hollow* was unavailable in the U.S. at the time of the release of *Louder Than Bombs*, the record contains large chunks of that album, as well as several cuts from *The Smiths*, which makes the record a little redundant for most Smiths fans. Also, the album contains some of the worst material the group ever recorded, including the bland instrumental "Oscillate Wildly" and a cover of Twinkle's "Golden Light." Excluding all of this material, the remainder of the record is brilliant. The singles "Shakespeare's Sister," "Panic," "Ask," "Shoplifters of the World Unite," and "Sheila Take a Bow" are all definitive, as are the elegiac "Unloveable," "Asleep," "Stretch Out and Wait," and "Half a Person," which are all unavailable anywhere else (excluding the British counterpart to *Louder Than Bombs*, *The World Won't Listen*). Furthermore, the sneering, bouncing pop of "You Just Haven't Earned It Yet, Baby" and the bizarre travelogue of "Is It Really So Strange?" are two other essential songs not available anywhere else. Though *The World Won't Listen* is a more concise collection,

Louder Than Bombs is a necessary purchase for any Smiths fan. *—Stephen Thomas Erlewine*

Strangeways, Here We Come / 1987 / Sire ♦♦♦♦
Recorded as the relationship between Morrissey and Marr was beginning to splinter, *Strangeways, Here We Come* is the most carefully considered and elaborately produced album in the group's catalog. Though it aspires greatly to better *The Queen Is Dead*, it falls just short of its goals. With producer Stephen Street, the Smiths created a subtly shaded and skilled album, one boasting a fuller production than before. Morrissey and Marr also labored hard over the songs, working to expand the Smiths' sound within their very real boundaries. For the most part, they succeed. "I Started Something I Couldn't Finish," "Girlfriend in a Coma," "Stop Me If You Think You've Heard This One Before," and "I Won't Share You" are classics, while "A Rush and a Push and the Land Is Ours," "Death of a Disco Dancer," and "Last Night I Dreamt That Somebody Loved Me" aren't far behind. However, the songs also have a tendency to be glib and forced, particularly on "Unhappy Birthday" and the anti-record company "Paint a Vulgar Picture," which has grown increasingly ironic in the wake of the Smiths' and Morrissey's love of repackaging the same material in new compilations. Still, *Strangeways* is a graceful way to bow out. While it doesn't match *The Queen Is Dead* or *The Smiths*, it is far from embarrassing and offers a summation of the group's considerable strengths. *—Stephen Thomas Erlewine*

Rank / 1988 / Sire ♦♦

The Best of the Smiths, Vol. 1 / 1992 / Sire ♦♦

The Best of the Smiths, Vol. 2 / Dec. 8, 1992 / Sire ♦♦

★ **Singles** / May 23, 1995 / Reprise ♦♦♦♦♦
The Best of the Smiths collections didn't work because they didn't have a sense of history and distorted the underlying sense of urgency that helped make the Smiths important. *Singles* simply collects all of the singles from one of the greatest singles bands since the Beatles. It's essential and influential guitar pop, presented in a way that makes sense and is endlessly listenable *—Stephen Thomas Erlewine*

Smog

Sadcore, Indie Rock, Lo-Fi, Singer/Songwriter
An underrecognized pioneer of the lo-fi revolution, Smog was essentially the alias of one Bill Callahan, an enigmatic singer/songwriter whose odd, fractured music neatly epitomized the tenets and excesses of the home-recording boom. Melancholy, poignant, and self-obsessed, Callahan's four-track output offered a peepshow view into an insular world of alienation and inner turmoil, his painfully intimate songs ping-ponging wildly through a scrapbook of childhood recollections, failed relationships, bizarre fetishes, and dashed hopes. Smog debuted in 1988 with the spare, primitive *Macrame Gunplay*, a cassette-only release issued on Callahan's own Disaster label. With 1991's *Floating* EP, Smog signed to the Chicago-based indie label Drag City, and with the move began an advancement toward more traditional songcraft; the subsequent full-length *Forgotten Foundation* was his most well-rounded effort yet, employing a stronger sense of melody while remaining true to the trademark bare-bones atmosphere. 1993's superb *Julius Caesar* raised the stakes considerably, expanding the Smog palette to include touches of cello, violin, and even banjo. 1995's *Wild Love* continued this approach toward relative sonic grandeur. *—Jason Ankeny*

Forgotten Foundation / 1992 / Drag City ♦♦

Julius Caesar / 1993 / Drag City ♦♦♦♦
Smog's third album, 1993's *Julius Caesar*, features increasingly creative songwriting and arrangements that celebrate the lo-fi recording process. Like grainy snapshots taken in an instant-photo booth, *Julius Caesar's* 13 songs have a fuzzy, distinctive character, heightened by their low-budget surroundings. Darker songs like "Your Wedding" and "What Kind of Angel" sound even blacker because of the muddy, distorted sound quality. "What Kind of Angel" in particular exploits lo-fi's fuzziness, blurring Bill Callahan's vocals and slide guitars into a rage of noise. Poignant moments like the cello-based instrumental "One Less Star" and ballads such as "Golden" and "Chosen One" have a naive, bittersweet feel thanks to the bedroom-quality production. Other tracks use the lo-fi aesthetic as their musical focus: "I Am Star Wars!" uses a cheap drum machine and tape loops of the Rolling Stones' "Start Me Up" and "Honky Tonk Women" for an unusual, funny foray into sampling on the cheap, while the drums on "Parade" sound suspiciously like tin cans. *Julius Caesar's* wide emotional and sonic palette is contrasted by Callahan's consistently honest, often blunt lyrics. Whether they're self-mocking ("I feel like Travis Bickle, listening to 'Highway to Hell'/It's a shitty little tape I taped off the radio," from "37 Push Ups") or nonsensically logical ("I am Star Wars today/I am no longer English Grey," from "I Am Star Wars!") or wistful ("Chosen One's" lament, "Maybe it's best for you to ride into the sun"), Callahan's sentiments are anything but sentimental. An immensely creative album, *Julius Caesar's* artistic, arranged approach to lo-fi displays Callahan's willingness to grow and experiment as a musician and storyteller. *—Heather Phares*

Burning Kingdom / Sep. 20, 1994 / Drag City ♦♦♦
Four vignettes of concentrated sadness, *Burning Kingdom* has to be one of the darkest-sounding EPs released in recent memory. Particularly effective is the haunting "Reneé Died," which pits Dall's frail voice against brittle acoustic guitars. *—Heather Phares*

Wild Love / Mar. 27, 1995 / Drag City ♦♦♦♦♦
Building on *Julius Caesar*'s artful songcraft, *Wild Love* expands Bill Callahan's lyrical and musical horizons, balancing roughness and polish in just the right amounts. Recorded in a proper studio with Drag City's favorite producer, Rian Murphy, the album benefits from a wider musical palette; instead of *Julius Caesar*'s lo-fi patchwork, the sound is focused into a hypnotic blend of chamber music and indie rock. Keyboards, chamberlin, and cello add a theatrical flair to *Wild Love*'s dark, witty portraits of domestic frustration, especially the opening and closing songs, "Bathysphere" and "Goldfish Bowl." The arrangements are key; sometimes they reflect the moody, detailed lyrics. On the frail, flickering ballad "The Candle," Callahan sings "I'm gathering these splinters to make a raft someday," accompanied by delicate, feeble guitars and keyboards, while "Be Hit"'s awkward drumming and out of tune strumming mirror its ugly lyrics: "Every girl I've ever loved has wanted to be hit/and every girl I've ever loved has left me because I wouldn't do it." At other times, the dense orchestrations are ironic; "Sleepy Joe" and "Prince Alone in the Studio" are emotionally detached. As usual, the lyrics are sad, funny, and often cut to the quick. Couplets like "The Candle"'s "I was on her body/he was on her mind./I caressed her/he possessed her," provoke a reaction somewhere between a wince and a grin. On a purely musical level, the album is of Smog's most remarkable achievements, combining studio effects and low-budget innovation. The snare drums and chamberlins on "The Emperor" sound like fireworks over a parade, while the chiming guitars on "It's Rough" add a touch of empathy. A finely wrought, magnetic work, *Wild Love*'s music and lyrics are too artful to be just the outpourings of a completely miserable soul. *—Heather Phares*

Sewn to the Sky / Nov. 29, 1995 / Drag City ♦♦♦
"I wanna tell you about a man/You won't find him on your MTV," Smog's singer/songwriter Bill Callahan sings on his first album, 1990's *Sewn to the Sky*. Though he's actually referring to Jesus, those lyrics apply to Callahan and this collection of songs, which introduce his noisy aesthetic and dark sense of humor. According to the liner notes, *Sewn to the Sky* was recorded on a "dumpster Porta-Studio," and indeed the album wears its cheap, abrasive production values well. Distorted guitars, vocals, and tape collages gain harsh and muddy textures that Callahan uses artfully, painting a bleak, darkly humorous musical landscape. *Sewn to the Sky* ranges from percussive pieces like "Russian Winter" and "Polio Shimmy" to droning, minor-key guitar workouts like "Olive Drab Spectre" and "Hollow Out Cakes." "Confederate Bills and Pinball Slugs" and "Fables" feature more recognizable melodies and song structures, and "Fruit Bats," "Peach Pit," and "The Weightlifter" introduce Callahan's dry, detailed lyrical style (sample lyrics from "The Weightlifter": "His car is red/He's saving for a waterbed/Oh what a love nest that'll be") but the album's focal point is its pungent sound. Callahan's first album is an acquired taste; on *Sewn to the Sky*, you can hear every needle used to put him there. *—Heather Phares*

The Doctor Came at Dawn / Sep. 10, 1996 / Drag City ♦♦♦♦
The Doctor Came at Dawn documents romantic decay and deception with Bill Callahan's typical unflinching honesty. Over the album's ten songs, he recounts every painful detail of falling in and out of love. "You Moved In" recalls an affair's desperate, obsessive beginnings with grim humor: "You could have done better, but oh well." The song's eerie, foreboding strings and piano arrangement, as well as Callahan's deadpan vocals, give fair warning that *The Doctor Came at Dawn*'s intimate sound hits close to home. The deadly aim of "Lize," a duet between Callahan and his sometime creative and romantic partner Cindy Dall, spares no one. "You don't make lies like you used to," they sing in near-unison, creating the tense, charged atmosphere of a stifled argument. As always, Smog walks the fine line between self-deprecation and self-parody; "Somewhere in the Night"'s handclaps and acoustic strumming make it sound like a rousing, inspirational folk song—except for the sneer embedded in Callahan's voice as he urges his beloved to devote herself to someone else. But *The Doctor Came at Dawn* is at its best when Callahan's sense of empathy emerges on the remarkable "All Your Women Things." Initially, it seems like a fetishistic ballad about keeping an ex-lover's things, but with deeper listening, it reveals itself as a very sincere (albeit unnerving) love song, praising the beloved's different aspects: "How could I ignore your hardness, your softness, and your mercy?" Lyrically and emotionally complex, the song exemplifies the depth of Smog's songwriting. The album is also musically deep, with understated guitar, piano, and string arrangements that give the rich vocals and lyrics added impact. It's Smog's darkest collection of songs, but it's also among the most mature and rewarding. *—Heather Phares*

● **Red Apple Falls** / May 20, 1997 / Drag City ♦♦♦♦♦
Over the course of his previous albums, Bill Callahan explored every nuance of humor and despair; with 1997's *Red Apple Falls*, he adds hope and possibility to Smog's scope. Musically, the album concentrates on spacious, acoustic-based music rather than Callahan's prior lo-fi experiments. With flourishes of piano, horns, drum machines, and pedal steel, *Red Apple Falls* appropriates the best of folk, rock, and country, defying easy classification. "Blood Red Bird" and "Red Apples" focus on Callahan's voice and mournful pianos, while epics like "Red Apple Falls" and "Inspirational" use weepy steel guitars for maximum emotional impact. Lyrically, the album's intensity and clarity is equally strong: motifs of apples, horses, and widows thread through the album, evoking rustic, traditional songs as they tell the story of a star-crossed love affair. "Most of my fantasies are to be of use/like a spindle, like a candle," Callahan sings on "To Be of Use," blending pain, pleasure, selfishness, and selflessness in a typically Smog manner. But the best songs here combine the album's musical expansiveness and lyrical intensity. On "I Was a Stranger" Callahan sings, "Why do you women in this town let me look at you so bold?/You should have seen what I was in the last town/or in the last town/I was worse than a stranger/I was well known," backed by more sighing steel guitars. "Ex Con" blends synth washes, horns, and a stiff, mechanical beat in a unique country/new wave hybrid, emphasizing the bleak wit of lyrics like "Out on the streets/I feel like a robot by the river/looking for a drink." *Red Apple Falls'* subtle mix of contrasting sounds and emotions makes it a high point in Bill Callahan's distinguished, distinctive musical career. *—Heather Phares*

Knock Knock / Jan. 12, 1999 / Drag City ♦♦♦♦♦
Smog's seventh full-length album *Knock Knock* proves to be singer/songwriter Bill

Callahan's subtlest collection of songs yet. Indeed, one of the album's greatest accomplishments is its gently optimistic tone; if his other albums made a deadpan joke out of misery, on this album Callahan delivers the punchlines with traces of a grin. It's a moving album on many levels; not only do the songs have Smog's usual emotional intimacy, their subjects move away from difficult, claustrophobic situations toward maturity and acceptance. "Let's Move to the Country" and "I Could Drive Forever" are all about escape, whether it's from the rat race or bad relationships—"I feel light and strong," Callahan sings on "I Could Drive Forever," summing up *Knock Knock*'s lyrical tenor. But moving also implies distance. As the album travels the emotional spaces between people, Callahan himself seems more removed from these songs; more than ever, his songs read more like short stories than diary entries, particularly on "River Guard," about a warden watching prisoners swim, and the enigmatic "Sweet Treat." "Cold Blooded Old Times" and "Teenage Spaceship" capture the awkwardness of youth, while "Left Only With Love" accepts a lover's departure in stride. Musically, *Knock Knock* builds on *Red Apple Falls*'s folky, flowing sound, but throws in twists like drum loops, electric guitars, and, surprisingly, a children's choir. "Hit the Ground Running" combines all three elements, driven by rolling guitars and accented with strings, with the children's choir urging Callahan on his way. "Held"'s drum, guitar, and feedback loops take a collage approach to a classic rock sound; along with "Cold Blooded Old Times" and "No Dancing," it's one of Callahan's most up-tempo songs since 1995's "Wild Love." Over time, *Knock Knock* reveals itself as one of Smog's finest moments. *—Heather Phares*

Dongs of Sevotion / Apr. 4, 2000 / Drag City ♦♦♦♦

After a decade as one of indie rock's most consistent, versatile artists, Smog's ninth album catalogs the sounds and emotions that Bill Callahan explored on previous albums. *Dongs of Sevotion* borrows *Wild Love*'s chamber rock arrangements, *Red Apple Falls*' droning folk, *The Doctor Came at Dawn*'s painful honesty, *Knock Knock*'s sardonic humor, and even nods to *Burning Kingdom*'s album artwork. While these eclectic influences could have had scattered results, *Dongs of Sevotion* is remarkably spare and focused; over half the album is just Callahan on vocals and guitar and/or piano, with Tortoise's John McEntire on drums. Not surprisingly, the starker songs are the most lyrically loaded. On the coming-of-age ballad "Nineteen," Callahan laments, "My movements were slow/She didn't even know/What she was taking away," and on "Devotion," he notes "There are some terrible gossips in this town/With jaws like vices and eyes like drains." "Easily Led" and "Distance" are musically and emotionally similar, tending to blend together in the middle of the album. However, *Dongs* begins with "Justice Aversion" a survival-of-the-fittest tale set to icy, detached synths, and "Dress Sexy at My Funeral," a warm, sensual recounting of a man's final wishes: "Tell them about the time we did it with fireworks above us"—a one-two punch that captures the album's range. "Bloodflow" mixes a Jew's harp, cheerleaders (the "Dongettes," natch), and a galloping beat, and rhymes "tete-a-tete" with "machete," distilling the album's twists and turns. But Callahan saves the best for last: "Permanent Smile" a song of devotion that, with its echoing drums and rippling piano loop, sounds like a collaboration between Phil Spector and Philip Glass. It's this reverence and irreverence that makes Smog so enduring, and *Dongs of Sevotion* another worthwhile addition to Callahan's body of work. *—Heather Phares*

'Neath the Puke Tree / Dec. 12, 2000 / Drag City ♦♦♦

The increasingly prolific Bill Callahan returns with the *'Neath the Puke Tree* EP, his fourth 2000 release. Over the course of five songs, Callahan revisits Smog songs from the near and distant past and adds two new obsessive tales to his body of work. From the dramatically different version of *Sewn to the Sky*'s "A Jar of Sand" to the subtler remake of the *Red Apple Falls* gem "I Was a Stranger," Callahan finds room for new interpretations of his material, in much the same way that Chan Marshall did on Cat Power's *The Covers Record*. New songs such as "Your Sweet Entrance" and "Orion Obscured By Stars" follow in a similar vein to *Dongs of Sevotion*'s sparsest, subtlest moments; they creep up on you and slowly work their way into your brain. Though *'Neath the Puke Tree* isn't a revelation in the way that EPs such as *Kicking a Couple Around* and *Burning Kingdom* were, its unadorned intensity is nevertheless riveting. *—Heather Phares*

The Smoke

f. 1965, **db.** 1967

Freakbeat, British Psychedelia, Mod, Garage Rock, Psychedelic, British Invasion

More than any other band, the Smoke epitomized the groove of Swinging London. Their sound fell somewhere between mod and the Beatles—their instrumental attack was somewhat Who/Small Faces-like, yet they delighted in cheerful vocals and infectious harmonies and melodies. Only slightly popular on their home turf, and unknown in the U.S., their biggest success was in Germany (oddly enough, for such a British-sounding group). *It's Smoke Time*, their only album, was issued in Germany in 1967, and is one of the most cheerful records ever made, though not at all wimpy. "My Friend Jack," with its crushing reverb feedback, was a big hit in Germany and on its way to becoming a hit in the U.K. when it was banned by British radio for supposed drug references. The Smoke issued several rare singles after the album before disbanding. *—Richie Unterberger*

It's Smoke Time / 1967 / Repertoire ♦♦♦♦

Besides "My Friend Jack," other highlights of the group's only album (all but one of whose tracks were group originals) include the beautiful mid-tempo ballad "Waterfall" and the bee-humming guitars and lilting backup vocals on "You Can't Catch Me." The German CD reissue adds 14 additional cuts, including non-LP singles, a single issued in 1965 by the Shots (an earlier version of the group), a single puzzlingly issued under the alias the Chords Five, and an interesting alternate take of "My Friend Jack." A lot of these tracks pale in comparison to the 12 from the original album, but "Have Some More Tea" is a great Who-ish number, and "Sydney Gill" is a good stab at a more progressive mood. *—Richie Unterberger*

My Friend Jack [1974] / 1974 / Gull ♦♦♦

A retitled reissue of the *It's Smoke Time* LP. For a long time it was the only Smoke record available. But now you're much better off with the Repertoire CD of *It's Smoke Time*, which doubles its length and then some with 14 bonus tracks. *—Richie Unterberger*

My Friend Jack [1988 Compilation] / 1988 / Morgan Blue Town ♦♦♦

Unsatisfyingly skimpy 12-song compilation of the group's work, presenting seven of the 12 cuts from the *It's Smoke Time* album, and adding some non-LP tracks, including a 1965 number by the Shots (an early version of the band). All of the songs but one appear on Repertoire's far more extensive *It's Smoke Time* compilation. The one that doesn't, "Like a Good Man Should" (origin undocumented in the sleeve notes), is not so remarkable that this LP is worth tracking down on that count alone. *—Richie Unterberger*

● **My Friend Jack [1999]** / May 18, 1999 / Retroactive ♦♦♦♦

Regardless of who came up with the term "freakbeat"—either Bam Caruso czar Phil Smee created it in the mid-'80s or Richard Allen came up with it as the name for his psych fanzine—it's generally agreed that the Smoke were one of the best examples of the style (along with the Birds, the Creation, Les Fleur de Lys, and a few others) during the "swinging London" era of the mid-'60s. This 23-track comp of feedback-rich primeval psych-beat is highlighted by their finest moment right up front: "My Friend Jack" hit the U.K. Top 50 in 1967, despite the fact that it was banned by the BBC. In fact, as the liner notes explain, "My Friend Jack" (included here in both the single and the sensational longer version) received airplay on pirate radio stations in the U.K. and shot to number one in Germany for an incredible seven weeks. Also included is their scorching version of Otis Redding's "She Put the Hurt on Me" and their Jeff Beck/Dave Mason-produced "Utterly Simple." However, a few tracks are missing here from the Yorkshire group's outstanding oeuvre. The now out of print 1994 Repertoire CD included their 1967 album plus rare acetates and live tracks; their first single—1965's "Keep a Hold of What You Got" b/w "She's a Liar"—is also sadly missing in action. Even so, Retroactive/Sin-Drome's compilation is a solid improvement on previously issued collections, due to clean remastering and a colorful booklet. *—Bryan Thomas*

Patty Smyth

b. Jun. 26, 1957, New York, NY

Vocals / Album Rock, Pop/Rock

After leaving Scandal in 1984, vocalist Patty Smyth waited three years before launching her solo career with the *Never Enough* album. Although it sold respectably, it didn't have any major hit singles. Smyth returned to the top of the charts in 1992 with "Sometimes Love Just Ain't Enough," a duet with Don Henley; the single hit number two and went gold. Its parent album, *Patty Smyth*, also went gold and featured two other minor hits, "No Mistakes" and "I Should Be Laughing." *—Stephen Thomas Erlewine*

● **Greatest Hits—Featuring Scandal** / Sep. 8, 1998 / Columbia/Legacy ♦♦♦♦♦

For many years, Patty Smyth inexplicably lacked a hits compilation, but Columbia/Legacy finally issued the single-disc *Greatest Hits—Featuring Scandal* in the fall of 1998. Drawing from both her solo recordings and her time with Scandal, from her recordings for both Columbia and MCA, the 16-track contains all of her hits, including "Goodbye to You," "The Warrior," "Hands Tied," "Beat of a Heart," and "Sometimes Love Just Ain't Enough," her duet with Don Henley. The enticements for hardcore fans—two new Matt Serletic-produced recordings ("Wish I Were You," which is also on the *Armageddon* soundtrack, and "Carnival Lights"), plus an unreleased cut from *Never Enough*—aren't particularly noteworthy, but for most fans, both casual and serious, it's a blessing to have all of the hits in one place, even if it's frustrating that the disc isn't sequenced in chronological order. *—Stephen Thomas Erlewine*

Sneaker Pimps

f. 1995, Reading, England

Electronica, Alternative Dance, Adult Alternative Pop/Rock, Trip-Hop, Club/Dance

Sneaker Pimps are a trip-hop trio that formed in Reading, England in 1995, following the success of Portishead's *Dummy* and Tricky's *Maxinquaye*. Borrowing heavily from Portishead and Massive Attack, Sneaker Pimps have a trancey but edgey sound, highlighted by Kelli Dayton's soulful vocals. While Dayton is the focal point, Chris Corner (guitar) and Liam Howe (keyboards) are the band's leaders, writing all of the songs and producing the records. Howe and Corner had been playing in bands since the early '90s, to no success. After seeing Dayton sing with a pub band in 1995, they convinced her to join the fledgling Sneaker Pimps, who had taken their name from an article the Beastie Boys published in their Grand Royale magazine about a man they hired to track down classic sneakers.

Sneaker Pimps released their first single, "Tesko Suicide," in May of 1996 and it was greeted with positive reviews in the U.K. music press. *Becoming X*, the group's debut, was released in August and it was a critical success, with *Q* magazine naming the album one of the best albums of the year. However, the band failed to make an impact on the pop charts in the U.K. The hit *Becoming X* was released in the United States in February 1997, preceded by the single "6 Underground." *Becoming Remixed* followed in early 1998. *—Stephen Thomas Erlewine*

● **Becoming X** / Aug. 19, 1996 / Clean Up ♦♦♦♦

Becoming X is one of the most engaging by-products of post-Portishead trip-hop. While the Sneaker Pimps don't have the doomed romanticism of Portishead, or the nasty experimental tendencies of Tricky, they have a cool sense of pop hooks and an edgier guitar attack than their predecessors. "Tesko Suicide" moves along with jagged guitars and rhythms, while "6 Underground" is cooly detached post-modern soul. *Becoming X* creates an airy, urban atmosphere, and while the record begins to unravel toward the end, it is an exciting, entrancing listen. *—Stephen Thomas Erlewine*

Splinter / Dec. 7, 1999 / EMI ✦✦

The Sneakers

f. 1975, **db.** 1978

Power Pop

While the Sneakers never made much of an impact when they were together, the band marks the first appearance of several seminal figures of the alternative pop scene of the early '80s. Chris Stamey, Mitch Easter, and Will Rigby formed the core of the Sneakers, writing well-crafted, guitar-driven pop rockers; their self-titled debut EP was engineered by Don Dixon, who went on to be a successful producer, as well as a solo artist. After one excellent full-length album, the Sneakers broke up. Stamey and Rigby went on to form the dBs, one of the '80s' best American guitar pop bands; Easter led Let's Active, as well as becoming a record producer (including R.E.M.'s first two albums). However, the Sneakers are more than a historical curiosity; although they didn't record very much, their album and EP contain some of the finest power pop of the late '70s. *—Stephen Thomas Erlewine*

In the Red / 1978 / Car ✦✦✦

● **Racket** / Nov. 27, 1992 / East Side Digital ✦✦✦✦✦

Snoop Dogg (Calvin Broadus)

b. Oct. 20, 1972, Long Beach, CA

Rap, Vocals / West Coast Rap, G-Funk, Gangsta Rap

As the embodiment of '90s gangsta rap, Snoop Doggy Dogg blurred the lines between reality and fiction. Introduced to the world through Dr. Dre's *The Chronic*, Snoop Dogg quickly became the most famous star in rap, partially because of his drawled, laconic rhyming and partially because the violence that his lyrics implied seemed real, especially after he was arrested on charges of being a murder accomplice. The arrest certainly strengthened his myth, and it helped his debut album, 1993's *Doggystyle*, become the first debut album to enter the charts at number one, but in the long run, it hurt his career. Snoop had to fight charges throughout 1994 and 1995, and while he was eventually cleared, it hurt his momentum. *The Doggfather*, his second album, wasn't released until November 1996, and by that time, pop and hip-hop had burned itself out on gangsta-rap. *The Doggfather* sold half as well as its predecessor, which meant that Snoop remained a star, but he no longer had the influence he had just two years before. *—Stephen Thomas Erlewine*

● **Doggystyle** / Nov. 23, 1993 / Death Row ✦✦✦✦✦

Often compared and undoubtedly related in more ways than one, Snoop Dogg's Dr. Dre-produced debut album, *Doggystyle*, might not be as influential or as historically important as *The Chronic*, but it arguably just might be the better album of the two. For instance, where the second half of *The Chronic* gets bogged down with too many second-rate rappers, and where it also suffers from Dre's so-so rapping, *Doggystyle* finds the Death Row camp's best MCs—Snoop, Kurupt, Daz, Nate Dogg—handling most of the lyrical duties. Considering these factors, *Doggystyle* is a wiser and more well-crafted album than *The Chronic*, even if it is monopolized by Snoop's sometimes too-stoned-for-his-own-good delivery (not necessarily a bad thing). Moments such as the opening montage of "Bathtub" into "G Funk Intro" into "Gin and Juice" (and, to a slightly lesser degree, "Doggy Dogg World" and "Murder Was the Case") are brilliantly cinematic moments on a par with the finest moments of Curtis Mayfield's *Superfly*. And the wit practiced by Tha Dogg Pound posse on playboy songs such as "Ain't No Fun" also helps make this an album of non-stop highlights. As proven with his subsequent mid- to late-'90s solo albums, Snoop may be a talented MC, but the brilliance of this album should be attributed, as much if not more so, to Dre, and to a lesser extent Daz, Kurupt, Nate Dogg, and Warren G. This album is the result of an amazing synergy that would soon dissolve. *—Jason Birchmeier*

Tha Doggfather / Nov. 12, 1996 / Death Row ✦✦✦

A lot happened to Snoop Doggy Dogg between his debut *Doggystyle* and his second album, *Tha Doggfather*. During those three years, he became the most notorious figure in hip-hop through a much-publicized murder trail, where he was found not guilty, and he also became a father. Musically, the most important thing to happen to Snoop was the parting of ways between his mentor Dr. Dre and his record label, Death Row. Dre's departure from Death Row meant that Snoop had to handle the production duties on *Tha Doggfather* himself, and the differences between the two records are immediately apparent. Though it works the same G-funk territory, the bass is less elastic and there is considerably less sonic detail. In essence, all of the music on *Tha Doggfather* reworks the funk and soul of the late '70s and early '80s, without updating it too much—there's not that much difference between "Snoop's Upside Ya Head" and "Oops Up Side Your Head." Though the music isn't original, and the lyrics break no new territory, the execution is strong—Snoop's rapping and rhyming continue to improve, while the bass-heavy funk is often intoxicating. At over 70 minutes, *Tha Doggfather* runs too long to not have several filler tracks, but if you ignore those cuts, the album is a fine follow-up to one of the most successful hip-hop albums in history. *—Stephen Thomas Erlewine*

Da Game Is to Be Sold Not to Be Told / Aug. 4, 1998 / No Limit/Priority ✦✦

Top Dogg / May 11, 1999 / No Limit ✦✦✦

As time keeps on slipping into the future, it becomes apparent that Master P's greatest gift is marketing, particularly when his advertising masquerades as liner notes. Witness P's work for Snoop Dogg, once considered the brightest rapper of the '90s but now merely a general in the No Limit army. The Master began plugging *Top Dogg*, Snoop's second No Limit release, in the liners for his label debut, even mentioning a release date only months away. Clearly, Snoop had indeed been placed on the No Limit production line, and there was every indication that from now on, Snoop would churn out moderately enjoyable, Dirty South-lite records crammed with cameos and appropriated hooks. Turns out he had a trick up his sleeve, because *Top Dogg* is about as individualized an album as possible under the No Limit precepts. Since the outset of his career, Snoop has shown a fondness for early-'80s synth-funk, and for the first time, he lets that form the basis of an album. And while there may be a bit too much recycling for some tastes, the end result isn't just the freshest-sounding Snoop album since his debut, it's easily the freshest-sounding No Limit album. Unfortunately, it's still a No Limit album, which means it runs way too long and is filled with superfluous, even irritating cameos, and also that Snoop is content to haul out low-rent gangsta clichés. Since he's a gifted rapper, he makes the dope n' crimes, sex n' violence rhymes go down easily (compare his delivery to some of his guests if you have any doubts), but his lyrics just aren't as clever as they were five years earlier. But records don't have to be deep; they can be appreciated as a pure sonic experience, and taken on that level, *Top Dogg* satisfies. *—Stephen Thomas Erlewine*

Dead Man Walkin' / Oct. 31, 2000 / D-3 ✦✦✦

Tha Last Meal / Dec. 5, 2000 / Priority ✦✦✦✦

Granted, Dr. Dre only produced three tracks on *Tha Last Meal*, but his influence is *all* over this record. The album's promising young producers—Scott Storch, Jelly Roll, Meech Wells, Battlecat, and Soopafly—all lay down Dre-like beats full of fat bass lines and cosmic synth that are just as effective, if not more inspired, than Dre's. Furthermore, half the songs feature Kokane's P-funkesque vocal hooks, one of the most important changes in Snoop's sound; as quirky as his voice might be, the old-school L.A. rapper brings soulful melody, a quality that only enhances itself on successive listens. In addition, the Doggfather lets the beats ride out a bit, sparsely ad-libbing rather than smothering them with rhymes and guest rappers—another welcome decision. Yet calling this album a masterpiece is a bit erroneous. Master P lets Snoop do what he wants for the most part but does manage to include one blatant No Limit-flavored track, "Back Up Off Me." Also, Timbaland produces two tracks here—"Snoop Dogg (What's My Name Pt. 2)" and "Set It Off"—which are great songs, yet the beats are slightly inconsistent with the rest of the album. Overall though, these are minor flaws that do little to scar this otherwise impressive album. *Tha Last Meal* foreshadows a West Coast rap renaissance driven not so much by rappers but rather by a generation of young funk-obsessed producers weaned on *The Chronic*. *—Jason Birchmeier*

Phoebe Snow

b. Jul. 17, 1952, New York, NY

Vocals, Guitar / Contemporary Folk, Pop/Rock, Soft Rock, Singer/Songwriter

Renowned for her elastic contralto and jazz-scat vocal gymnastics, singer Phoebe Snow began playing Greenwich Village clubs in the early 1970s, honing an eclectic set which spotlighted both folk and pop sounds as well as jazz, blues, and even torch songs. After signing to Leon Russell's Shelter label, she issued her self-titled debut LP in 1974, scoring the Top Five smash "Poetry Man." Snow resurfaced in 1976 with *Second Childhood*, another highly successful effort which, like its predecessor, achieved gold-selling status. The record appeared in the wake of personal tragedy, however: in 1975, the singer's newborn daughter Valerie was diagnosed with profound autism, and against the wishes of doctors, Snow—a single mother—decided to raise the child at home by herself. As a consequence, her career as a performer became dwarfed by her parental duties; despite a flurry of records throughout the latter half of the decade, including 1977's *It Looks Like Snow*, 1977's *Never Letting Go*, and 1978's *Against the Grain*, Snow receded from view as the 1980s dawned, and following the release of 1981's *Rock Away* she did not record again for eight years. Upon signing to Elektra, Snow resurfaced in 1989 with *Something Real*. *—Jason Ankeny*

Phoebe Snow / Jul. 1974 / The Right Stuff ✦✦✦✦✦

It's been said many times that being difficult to categorize or pigeonhole can be the kiss of death commercially, and no one bears that out more than Phoebe Snow—a pearl of a singer who never caught on because she simply didn't fit neatly into any one category. Known primarily for her haunting single "Poetry Man," this self-titled classic (which was recorded in 1973, released on LP in 1974, and reissued on CD in 1989) found the earthy vocalist drawing on everything from folk and pop to soul, jazz, and blues. If anyone has bridged the gap between Joni Mitchell and Aretha Franklin, it's Snow, who is as confident on the soul-influenced "Good Times" as she is on the introspective jazz offering "Harpo's Blues." In fact, many of the players backing Snow are jazzmen, including cool jazz great Zoot Sims (tenor sax) and piano legend Teddy Wilson. With as many risks as she takes, the album is generally quite accessible. *—Alex Henderson*

Second Childhood / Jan. 1976 / Columbia ✦✦✦

Although it lacked a hit single to match "Poetry Man," Phoebe Snow's second album was another folk-pop-jazz confection that effectively showcased her one-of-a-kind voice in musical settings featuring the cream of New York's session musicians, produced by Phil Ramone. It was a classy job on which Snow contributed seven originals and displayed her versatility on covers ranging from Motown to Gershwin. *—William Ruhlmann*

It Looks Like Snow / Feb. 1977 / Columbia ✦✦✦✦✦

The cover songs start to overwhelm the originals, but when Snow is able to bring such powerful interpretations to "Don't Let Me Down," "Shakey Ground," and "Teach Me Tonight," who could complain? *—William Ruhlmann*

Never Letting Go / Oct. 1977 / Columbia ✦✦✦

Against the Grain / Oct. 1978 / Columbia ♦♦♦

Rock Away / Mar. 1981 / Mirage/Atlantic ♦♦

The Best of Phoebe Snow / 1982 / Columbia ♦♦♦♦♦
Best of Phoebe Snow contains most of the singer/songwriter's biggest hits from the '70s, as well as several key album tracks that make this a good introduction to her work. Among the highlights are "Poetry Man," "Shakey Ground," "Love Makes a Woman," "Two Fisted Love," and "Never Letting Go." *—Stephen Thomas Erlewine*

Something Real / Feb. 1989 / Elektra ♦♦♦
"This time when I reach out, it may be my last try," warns Phoebe Snow on the title track to her seventh album, which is her first in eight years. Perhaps with that in mind, it's a well-considered effort, and one that brought moderate success, including two Adult Contemporary chart hits in "If I Can Just Get Through the Night" (number 13) and "Something Real" (number 29). Snow takes a slightly more relaxed approach to the rock style of her last album, *Rock Away*. She sticks to contemporary songs for the most part (there's a dance music cover of the Emotions' "Best of My Love") and writes half of them herself. She tends to de-emphasize the more unusual aspects of her voice, although not so much that you'd confuse it with anybody else's. The result is a sturdy, respectable set, although not one likely to launch a major comeback. *—William Ruhlmann*

I Can't Complain / Feb. 10, 1998 / House of Blues Music Co. ♦♦♦♦
The record business being, if possible, even harder on women over 30 than the movie business is, *I Can't Complain* was 45-year-old Phoebe Snow's first album in nine years and only her second in 17 years. It was also her first to present her solely as an interpretive singer, not including any of her own compositions. Maybe for these reasons, producers Joel Moss and Jimmy Vivino had her swing for the fences: It took a lot of confidence to cover songs associated with such vocal powerhouses as Van Morrison ("Madame George"), Janis Joplin ("Piece of My Heart"), and Mary Martin ("Never Never Land") among others. Of course, Snow's own voice was so distinctive that she had no trouble making such material her own. In truth, the challenge with Snow is not so much finding songs as excluding them; it's hard to think of a song to which she couldn't bring a new and valuable interpretation. Her "Piece of My Heart" is just as impassioned as Joplin's, but comes from a different universe of feeling. She fully understands Bob Dylan's "It Takes a Lot to Laugh, It Takes a Train to Cry" (one of two duets with Michael McDonald) and suggests a few other meanings. Her "Baby, Work Out" is just as joyous as Jackie Wilson's, with some added emotions as well. Her "A Case of You" is just a vulnerable as Joni Mitchell's, and somewhat more knowing. And so on. The only thing wrong with this album is that it is such a rarity. A singer of Snow's quality should have been documented much more extensively over the last two decades. *—William Ruhlmann*

Social Distortion

f. 1978, Los Angeles, CA
College Rock, American Punk, L.A. Punk, Alternative Pop/Rock, Hard Rock, American Underground

The enduring L.A. punk band Social Distortion has overcome numerous personnel shifts, the demise of the Los Angeles hardcore scene that spawned them, and the heroin addiction of singer/guitarist/bandleader Mike Ness to achieve a measure mainstream acceptance for their rootsy, hard-hitting punk without compromise. Inspired by the fertile L.A. punk scene, Ness formed the group in 1978 with drummer Casey Royer and brothers Frank (bass) and Rikk Agnew (guitar). When the Agnews left to join the Adolescents, Ness's schoolmate Dennis Danell joined on bass; the next few years saw a revolving-door membership. When the group finally recorded its debut album, *Mommy's Little Monster*, in 1983, the band consisted of Ness, Danell (now on guitar), bassist Brent Liles, and drummer Derek O'Brien. Their music was often described as a punk version of the Rolling Stones, and "Another State of Mind" was one of the few punk videos to air on MTV in 1984. However, the band took four years to record a follow-up, as Ness descended into heroin addiction and self-consciously rebellious behavior. Liles and O'Brien left, and Ness finally regrouped after straightening himself out in 1988 with John Maurer on bass and Chris Reece on drums. This lineup recorded *Prison Bound*, a mature album broadening Social Distortion's roots-rock influences with a country feel. Their self-titled 1990 effort included a cover of Johnny Cash's "Ring of Fire" and returned the group to MTV via "Ball and Chain." *Somewhere Between Heaven and Hell* became their most popular album to date, producing a minor radio hit in "Bad Luck" and keeping with their now-established blend of punk, blues, country, and rockabilly.

Social Distortion took an extended hiatus following the release of *Somewhere Between Heaven and Hell*, returning in 1996 with *White Light, White Heat, White Trash*, which proved to be a moderate hit on MTV and modern-rock radio. *Live at the Roxy* followed in 1998, and a year later Ness issued a pair of solo albums, *Cheating at Solitaire* and the covers collection *Under the Influences*. Danell died February 29, 2000 of an apparent brain aneurysm; the guitarist was just 38 years old. *—Steve Huey*

Mommy's Little Monster / 1983 / Time Bomb ♦♦♦♦
Seminal Orange County punk band Social Distortion's first full-length album *Mommy's Little Monster* is the epitome of early-'80s suburban California punk and provided inspiration for many future Californians, including the Offspring and Rancid. *Mommy's Little Monster* finds the band supplying plenty of attitude and aggression as they rip through nine tracks worth of hard, fast, power chord-filled tracks loaded with snarling anti-establishment lyrics and themes. Songs like "The Creeps (I Just Want to Give You)" and "Telling Them" show a young punk group that is very angry, and they were going to let society know it whether they wanted to hear it or not. The title track, "Mommy's Little Monster," with its descriptions of the girl with blue hair and the unemployed young punk who loves to drink and fight, gives you a good idea of the characters Social Distortion was surrounded by in the scene of the day. Although the low-budget production gives the album a genuine early genre feel, it tends to hinder some of the potential power of most of the tracks presented here. As frontman Mike Ness matured as a songwriter the band went on to record stronger albums later in their career, but *Mommy's Little Monster* is a fine document of the raw early stages of a great influential American punk band that would go on to influence countless others in the future. *—Paul Tinelli*

Prison Bound / 1988 / Time Bomb ♦♦♦
The release of this album brought acoustic guitars, ballads, and a cautious step toward the rock mainstream that makes their music of use for more than just hardcore nihilists. *—John Floyd*

Social Distortion / Mar. 1990 / Epic ♦♦♦♦♦
With *Prison Bound*, Social Distortion began to metamorphasize from a rather ordinary L.A. hardcore band into a roots rock band willing to make with more than their share of the attitude, and this process continued on their self-titled third album (which was also their major-label debut). Musically, Mike Mess and company had learned to split the difference between rockabilly and Ramones-style punk, not unlike fellow L.A. vets X, and if Ness couldn't sing or write with the skill or the resonance of John Doe, "Story of My Life" and "It Coulda Been Me" sound a lot more personal and deeply felt than anything on *Mommy's Little Monster*, and "Ball and Chain" and "So Far Away" prove he could crank out a respectable honky tonk number if he put his mind to it. Thanks to Epic's sponsorship, the group had more time and money at their disposal for *Social Distortion* than on their previous albums, and producer Dave Jerden made the most of it; Mike Ness and Dennis Danell's guitars sound lean, sharp, and powerful; Ness's vocals are better controlled than ever before; and Christopher Reece's drums have a tight snap that suits both the thrashier numbers as well as the slower, blusier tunes. *Social Distortion* isn't a great roots rock album, but it's a pretty good one, and it's better and more affecting than anything this band had cranked out before. *—Mark Deming*

● **Somewhere Between Heaven and Hell** / 1992 / Epic ♦♦♦♦♦
Social Distortion finally achieves the perfect balance between their two major influences, the country anguish of Johnny Cash and the furious punk rock sound of early Clash, on their 1992 album *Somewhere Between Heaven and Hell*, making it the band's finest hour. The band tears through a fair share of rollicking, straight-ahead hard rock with songs like "Cold Feelings" and "When She Begins," but they also show a reflective, heartfelt, country-inspired side with songs like "This Time Darlin'" and the hard rock tribute to "Folsom Prison Blues," the cold blooded, murderous tale "99 to Life." At times the band slows down the pace a bit more than on earlier albums, but the band hasn't lost any of the edge or attitude they had as the brash young punks who recorded *Mommy's Little Monster*. Social Distortion classics "Bad Luck" and "Born to Lose" find a more mature Mike Ness still continuing to play the familiar role of the steadfast underdog with better results than in previous efforts. This album had all the earmarks of a major commercial success with some radio friendly tunes and strong production, but it never found the large audience Epic records expected. Regardless of the sales totals, *Somewhere Between Heaven and Hell* finds Orange County's most enduring punk band, Social Distortion, at their creative peak, and this album is the crown jewel of their entire catalog. *—Paul Tinelli*

Mainliner: Wreckage From the Past / Jul. 18, 1995 / Time Bomb ♦♦♦
Mainliner: Wreckage From the Past is a collection of early singles and rare B-sides from Orange County punk legends Social Distortion. Recorded while they were still in their teens, this early material shows no signs of the country-influenced sound that would appear later in the band's career. The main style displayed here is pure punk fury with short, fast songs, lyrics about teen rebellion, and plenty of attitude to go around. "Playpen," "Moral Threat," and "All the Answers" speak of the plight of the early punk rockers who took major abuse from all forms of authority back in a period where the musical style was still considered dangerous. "Mainliner" is a not-at-all subtle tale of heroin abuse. A cover of "Under My Thumb" shows early on that the Rolling Stones were just as much an influence on Social Distortion as the Sex Pistols and the Clash. This collection is definitely intended for dedicated fans and is more of a history lesson than a proper album. Although extremely raw and a bit naïve, becoming familiar with this material will help fans understand where the band came from and appreciate their point of view on stronger, later material. *—Paul Tinelli*

White Light, White Heat, White Trash / Sep. 1996 / 550 Music/Epic ♦♦♦

Live at the Roxy / Jun. 30, 1998 / Time Bomb ♦♦♦♦

The Soft Boys

f. 1976, Cambridge, England, **db.** 1981
College Rock, British Punk, Jangle Pop, Post-Punk, New Wave

The Soft Boys have turned out to be one of the most influential bands in shaping contemporary alternative music, though few are completely familiar with the quirky band's legacy. Formed in Cambridge, England in 1976 on the heels of the punk revolution, the Soft Boys eschewed the three-chord nihilism of punk and opted for a crude version of psychedelic/folk-rock that was well on its way out of fashion, but oddly, just on the cusp of a resurgence. Led by singer/songwriter Robyn Hitchcock, the band released a single, "(I Want To Be An) Anglepoise Lamp," followed by the *Can of Bees* album in 1979. *Underwater Moonlight* found the band trading psychedelic jams for a more straight-ahead jangle-guitar-rock sound. The LP has become extremely influential in the guitar rock canon—the Replacements, R.E.M., and the L.A. Paisley Underground scene all claimed it as a prime influence. The album launched a thousand bands, but it turned out to be the Soft Boys' swan song. Hitchcock has had a prolific post-Soft Boys recording career, sticking to the unusual style he 's forged and finessed since 1976, with a series of albums to his credit. *—Denise Sullivan*

A Can of Bees / 1979 / Rykodisc ✦✦✦✦✦
One of the band's earliest recordings, featuring their signature tune "Give It to the Soft Boys," *A Can of Bees* includes a lot of the zaniness principal member Robyn Hitchcock would become known for in his later work, but the band had not yet jelled and found them still in search of their ultimate sound, an amalgam of new wave and psychedelia. However, the record is essential to any Soft Boys collection, as it demonstrates the band flying in the face of what was happening musically at the time and creating their own unique style. *—Denise Sullivan*

★ **Underwater Moonlight** / 1980 / Rykodisc ✦✦✦✦✦
A watershed guitar rock album—the one that launched a thousand bands, including the Replacements and R.E.M., and a quintessential cult favorite. Beautiful harmonies and Byrdsian guitar dominate this set of songs, the standouts being the punk-pop of "I Wanna Destroy You," "Positive Vibrations," and the chiming "Queen of Eyes." Robyn Hitchcock found his voice on this record, singing his mostly nonsensical lyrics with unusual conviction, and guitarist Kimberley Rew played with a tidiness rarely heard on most underground recordings from the era. *—Denise Sullivan*

Invisible Hits / 1983 / Rykodisc ✦✦✦✦
A collection of lost recordings and previously unreleased tracks, a number of this album's cuts remain Soft Boys classics, like "Rock & Roll Toilet," "Wey Wey Hep Uh Hole," "Have a Heart Betty (I'm Not Fireproof)," and "He's a Reptile." Most of the songs were recorded in 1978-79 during the sessions prior to *A Can of Bees* and *Underwater Moonlight*, and though it isn't as strong as the latter, it is essential to the Soft Boys collector—their recorded output is so spare that every last detail is crucial. *—Denise Sullivan*

1976-1981 / Aug. 10, 1993 / Rykodisc ✦✦✦✦
This double-CD set compiles unreleased material, select cuts from *Give It to the Soft Boys*, *A Can of Bees*, *Invisible Hits*, and *Underwater Moonlight*, as well as two tracks from the live bootleg *At the Portland Arms* and "Only the Stones Remain" from the *Two Halves for the Price of One* EP. Alhough it may appear to be a good introduction to the Soft Boys oeuvre, the inclusion of rarities and alternate takes makes it ideal for die-hard Soft Boys fans and inappropriate for the novice. *—Denise Sullivan*

Soft Cell

f. 1980, Leeds, England, **db.** 1984
New Romantic, Post-Punk, New Wave, Synth Pop
A synth-pop duo famed for its uniquely sleazy electronic sound, art students Marc Almond and David Ball formed Soft Cell in Leeds, England in 1980. A self-financed EP titled *Mutant Moments* brought the duo to the attention of Some Bizzare label head Stevo, who enlisted Daniel Miller to produce their underground hit single "Memorabilia" the following year. It was the next Soft Cell effort, 1981's "Tainted Love," that brought the duo to international prominence; already a cult favorite thanks to Gloria Jones' soulful reading, the song was reinvented as a hypnotic electronic dirge which became the year's best-selling British single, as well as a major hit abroad. The group's debut LP, *Non-Stop Erotic Cabaret*, was also enormously successful, and while 1983's *The Art of Falling Apart* proved as popular as its predecessor, the LP's title broadly hinted at the internal problems plaguing the duo; prior to the release of 1984's *This Last Night in Sodom*, Soft Cell had already broken up. *—Jason Ankeny*

Non-Stop Erotic Cabaret / 1982 / Sire ✦✦✦✦✦
Reissued with a staggering number of B-sides, this Soft Cell album should not be missed, though the point is not the over-referenced "Tainted Love." More interesting are the astoundingly sleazy "Sex Dwarf," the grim trash of "Bedsitter," the dual punches of "Seedy Films" and "Secret Life," and the melancholy "Say Hello, Wave Goodbye." The hard black heart that beat under the skin of Soft Cell was located squarely in the middle of London's Soho district, red lights, strip clubs, alleyway hookers and all; if ever a city district had a soundtrack, this was it. *—Steven McDonald*

Non-Stop Ecstatic Dancing / 1982 / Sire ✦✦✦✦
The version of "Memorabilia" included here is notable for its energy, but the only other thing on the U.S. edition that really catches the attention is "What." The U.K. edition of the mini-album included "Insecure... Me?," the B-side to the single version of "What," improving the odds a little. *—Steven McDonald*

The Art of Falling Apart / 1983 / Sire ✦✦✦
While it has some mediocre moments, this tense, quirky release also has some magnificent outings, including the epic "Martin" (based on the obscure George Romero psycho/vampire movie), a cut that was originally included on a bonus 12," and the relentless title cut. Not as cheap or sleazy in its sound as *Non-Stop Erotic Cabaret*, the album was still prone to melodramatic writing and performance. By all means, miss the "Hendrix Medley," another bonus cut. *—Steven McDonald*

The Singles 1981-1985 / 1986 / Some Bizarre ✦✦✦✦✦
The original and still the best single-disc Soft Cell compilation (at least up through the band's long-awaited reactivation in 2001), *The Singles 1981-1985* is just what it says it is, and what a collection it is. Along with other genre- and era-defining compilations such as Depeche Mode's similarly titled singles disc and Visage's best-of, *The Singles 1981-1985* captures the sheer luxuriant thrill and shock of England's early-'80s electro-pop boom. Even more to the point, though, it also stands up perfectly in later years, instantly catchy as well as shockingly surprising and exciting pop that managed to be both rooted in the past and perfectly of the moment and beyond. That so many of these songs were big hits in England testifies to the band's accidental but spot-on appeal; that most didn't repeat such success in America is a downright shame. "Tainted Love," unsurprisingly, remains the eternal defining moment of the duo's career and appears here in its short edit, but the collection in fact begins with the equally impressive, frenetic electro-disco fusion "Memorabilia" and takes things from there. Only a couple of the singles were actual misfires—Almond himself later said the cover of "What!" was suggested by a record company hoping for another fluke remake hit—while the majority bear perfect testimony to both Almond's passionate singing and impressive lyrics and Ball's ear for great arrangements and melodies. The absolutely dead-on slice-of-life "Bedsitter," the astonishing, spotlight-grabbing romantic angst of "Say Hello Wave Goodbye," the slow burn of the spectacularly underrated "Torch," the sheer frenetic collapse of "Soul Inside"—just four highlights among many. An appreciative essay from English critic Tony Mitchell makes for a nice overall touch. All three original albums remain fascinating collections for even casual fans to explore, while the hardcore need to have *The Twelve-Inch Singles* compilation, but if there's one record that's absolutely hands-down necessary, *The Singles 1981-1985* is it. *—Ned Raggett*

● **Memorabilia: Singles** / Oct. 8, 1991 / Mercury ✦✦✦✦✦
This would seem, at least by the title, that this would be a perfect Soft Cell collection, since it has the group's singles. Thing is, much of these are remixes and reworkings from 1991, not the original recordings, which means it's hardly of interest to the audience that just wants the original versions of Soft Cell's greatest moments. It's passable, to a certain extent, since it has the songs, but it's better to hold out for a collection that contains the real deal. *—Stephen Thomas Erlewine*

Soft Machine

f. 1966, **db.** 1976
Canterbury Scene, British Psychedelia, Jazz-Rock, Experimental, Psychedelic, Prog Rock/Art Rock
The Soft Machine were never a commercial enterprise and indeed still remain unknown even to many listeners that came of age during the late '60s, when the group was at their peak. In their own way, however, they were one of the more influential bands of their era, and certainly one of the *most* influential underground ones. One of the original British psychedelic groups, they were also instrumental in the birth of both progressive rock and jazz-rock.They were also the central foundation of the family tree of the "Canterbury school" of British progressive rock acts, a movement that also included Caravan, Gong, Matching Mole, and National Health, not to mention the distinguished solo careers of founding members Robert Wyatt and Kevin Ayers. The group was among the very first underground psychedelic bands in Britain and quickly became well loved in the burgeoning London psychedelic underground, although the considerable melodic elements and vocal harmonies of their early material soon gave way to more challenging, artier postures that sought—sometimes successfully, sometimes not—to meld the energy of psychedelic rock with the improvisational pulse of jazz. Their second album, *Vol. 2* (1969), further submerged the band's pop elements in favor of extended jazzy compositions, with an increasingly lesser reliance on lyrics and vocals. For their third album, they went even further in these directions, expanding to a seven-piece by adding a horn section. This record virtually dispensed with vocals and conventional rock songs entirely and is considered a landmark by both progressive rock and jazz-rock aficionados, though it was too oblique for many rock listeners. *—Richie Unterberger*

Volume One / Dec. 1968 / One Way ✦✦✦✦✦
A wild, freewheeling, and ultimately successful attempt to merge psychedelia with jazz-rock, Soft Machine's debut ranges between lovingly performed oblique pop songs and deranged ensemble playing from drummer/vocalist Robert Wyatt and organist Mike Ratledge. With only one real break (at the end of side one), the songs merge into each other—not always smoothly, but always with a sense of flair that rescues any potential miscues. Wyatt takes most of the vocals, and proves himself a surprisingly evocative singer despite his lack of range. Like Pink Floyd's *The Piper at the Gates of Dawn*, *Volume One* was one of the few over-ambitious records of the psychedelic era that actually delivered on all its incredible promise. [*Volume One* is also available in a CD release combined with *Volume Two*.] *—John Bush*

Volume Two / Apr. 1969 / One Way ✦✦✦✦✦
The first Soft Machine LP usually got the attention, with its movable parts sleeve, as well as the presence of ultra-talented songwriter Kevin Ayers. But musically, *Volume Two* better conveys the Dada-ist whimsy and powerful avant-rock leanings of the band. Hugh Hopper took over for Ayers on bass, and his fuzz tones and experimental leanings supplanted Ayers' pop emphasis. The creative nucleus behind this most progressive of progressive rock albums, however, is Robert Wyatt. He provides the musical arrangements to Hopper's quirky ideas on the stream-of-consciousness collection of tunes ("Rivmic Melodies") on side one. Unlike the first record, which sounded choppy and often somnolent, this one blends together better, and it has a livelier sound. The addition of session horn players enhanced the Softs' non-guitar lineup, and keyboardist Mike Ratledge, whose musical erudition frequently clashed in the early days with the free-spirited Wyatt, Ayers, and Daevid Allen, lightened his touch here. He even contributes one of the album's highlights with "Pig" ("Virgins are boring/they should be grateful for the things they're ignoring"). But it's Wyatt who lifts this odd musical jewel to its artistic heights. He uses his tender voice like a jazz instrument, scatting (in Spanish!) on "Dada Was Here," and sounding entirely heartfelt in "Have You Ever Bean Green," a brief tribute to the Jimi Hendrix Experience, with whom the Softs toured ("Thank you Noel and Mitch, thank you Jim, for our exposure to the crowd"). Fans of the Canterbury scene will also relish "As Long As He Lies Perfectly Still," a loving tribute to ex-bandmate Ayers. This is the one record that effectively assimilates rock, absurdist humor, jazz, and the avant-garde, and it misses classic status only due to some dissonant instrumentation on side two. *—Peter Kurtz*

Third / Jun. 1970 / Columbia ✦✦✦✦✦

The Soft Machine plunged deeper into jazz and contemporary electronic music on this pivotal release, which incited the *Village Voice* to call it a milestone achievement when it was released. It's a double album of stunning music, with each side devoted to one composition—two by Mike Ratledge, and one each by Hopper and Wyatt, with substantial help from a number of backup musicians, including Canterbury mainstays Elton Dean and Jimmy Hastings. The Ratledge songs come closest to fusion jazz, although this is fusion laced with tape loop effects and hypnotic, repetitive keyboard patterns. Hugh Hopper's "Facelift" recalls "21st Century Schizoid Man" by King Crimson, although it's more complex, with several quite dissimilar sections. The pulsing rhythms, chaotic horn and keyboard sounds, and dark drones on "Facelift" predate some of what Hopper did as a solo artist later (this song was actually culled from two live performances in 1970). Robert Wyatt draws on musical ideas from early 1967 demos done with producer Giorgio Gomelsky, on his capricious composition "Moon in June." Lyrically, it's a satirical alternative to the pretension displayed by a lot of rock writing of the era, and combined with the Softs' exotic instrumentation, it makes for quite a listen (the collection *Triple Echo* includes a BBC broadcast recording of this song, with different albeit equally fanciful lyrics). Not exactly rock, *Third* nonetheless pushed the boundaries of rock into areas previously unexplored, and it managed to do so without sounding self-indulgent. A better introduction to the group is either of the first two records, but once introduced, this is the place to go. —*Peter Kurtz*

Fourth / Feb. 1971 / One Way ✦✦✦

Live at the Proms 1970 / 1988 / Reckless ✦✦✦

Initially recorded for the BBC in August 1970, this is a good document of the group in concert shortly after the release of *Third*, stripped down to the quartet of Wyatt, Ratledge, Hopper, and saxophonist Elton Dean. Most of the material comes from their second and third albums, and Wyatt, disappointingly, barely sings at all. These versions aren't much different from the ones found on the official releases, though they're perhaps a bit more spontaneous, so this is primarily recommended for hardcore fans. —*Richie Unterberger*

● **Vols. 1 & 2** / Sep. 1989 / Big Beat ✦✦✦✦✦

A combination of their first two studio albums onto one CD. Their first (originally titled *The Soft Machine*, from 1968), recorded with the trio of Wyatt, Ratledge, and Ayers, combines goofy humor, psychedelia, and some free jazz into an erratic but invigorating brew that was comparable to little else in the late-'60s rock world. Ayers had left to be replaced by Hugh Hopper for 1969's *Volume Two*, which took a definite spin toward jazz and increasingly surrealistic material, stringing together whimsical bits and pieces for side-long suites. Not as pop-oriented as their initial 1967 recordings or as jazz-oriented as their final albums with Wyatt, the material compiled here is perhaps the best representation of the Soft Machine's accomplishments. —*Richie Unterberger*

Peel Sessions / 1990 / Dutch East India ✦✦✦✦

On their good days, the Soft Machine could slide effortlessly between jazz, rock, and classical influences, and show a lot of other bands how it's done. Unlike a lot of other *Peel Sessions* releases, which comprise as little as a quartet of tracks, this volume, drawn from appearances on the BBC from June 1969 through November 1971, takes up two full CDs, and none of the space is wasted—disc one also opens with Robert Wyatt's special invocational version of "Moon in June," written for the occasion and referring to it throughout. It is strange, but the group's playing is so confident and elegant, that they make their case and then some—they were already acquitting themselves better than other neophyte outfits like King Crimson, based on the evidence presented here. The sound is, of course, superb, and the group was on form throughout these appearances, evidently having been given a blank check (within reason) by the BBC. —*Bruce Eder*

Jet-Propelled Photographs / Sep. 13, 1994 / Charly ✦✦✦✦✦

The latest available CD version of a title which has been repackaged and retitled several times over the last 20 years. Recorded in London in April 1967 and produced by the legendary Giorgio Gomelsky, these nine demos feature the original Soft Machine lineup of Robert Wyatt, Kevin Ayers, Mike Ratledge, and Daevid Allen. Although not intended for release, these rough but accomplished performances show the band at their most pop- and song-oriented. Not far removed from Syd Barrett-era Pink Floyd, the jazzy chord changes, unpredictable bursts of scat singing, glib free-association lyrics, ominous buzzing organ, and Robert Wyatt's soulful rasp convey the freewheeling abandon and giddy high spirits that characterized the best early British psychedelia. For similar but more elaborately produced relics from the Daevid Allen lineup, check for the three tracks on the hard-to-find triple LP *Triple Echo*. —*Richie Unterberger*

Live at the Paradiso 1969 / 1995 / Voiceprint ✦✦✦

Previously available as a bootleg, this is a sanctioned release of a 1969 concert in Amsterdam, with excellent sound (particularly by late-'60s standards). The group runs through most of their second album on this set, without much notable difference from what you'll hear on the official record (though the pungency of the organ and thick bass comes through pretty well). It's only recommended to serious fans of the group, but that constituency will probably find it a worthwhile purchase. —*Richie Unterberger*

Man in a Deaf Corner: Anthology 1963-1970 / Mar. 27, 2001 / Mooncrest ✦✦

Softies

f. 1994, Sacramento, CA

Indie Pop, Twee Pop, Indie Rock

Borrowing their name from a British new wave group, the Softies were formed in 1994 by singer/guitarist Rose Melberg following the dissolution of her previous band, Tiger Trap. Upon relocating from Sacramento, CA to Portland, OR, Melberg first established the

trio Go Sailor, still a going concern when she teamed with Pretty Face alum (and publisher of the fanzine *Sparkly Kitty Sticker*) Jen Sbragia to found the Softies. The indie-pop duo bowed in early 1995 with "Loveseat," a single issued on the Slumberland label; their gorgeous debut LP *It's Love* followed later in the year on Calvin Johnson's K label. After a self-titled 1996 *Slumberland 10*", the Softies returned to K in early 1997 to issue their sophomore effort, *Winter Pageant*; at the same time, both Melberg and Sbragia also teamed with Class' Peter Green in the Three Peeps. Fall 2000 saw the release of their third album *Holiday in Rhode Island*. —*Jason Ankeny*

● **It's Love** / 1995 / K ✦✦✦✦

A gorgeously melancholy debut, *It's Love* forgoes the ebullient love-rock of singer/guitarist Rose Melberg's tenure with Tiger Trap to focus on skeletal guitar/harmony duets with partner Jen Sbragia; simple and beautiful, tracks like "I Love You More," "Charms Around Your Wrist" and "Fragile, Don't Crush" are as sweet as cotton candy—pure indie-pop perfection. Bonus points for the wonderful cover of Talulah Gosh's "I Can't Get No Satisfaction (Thank God)." —*Jason Ankeny*

Winter Pageant / Jan. 21, 1997 / K ✦✦✦

Amidst the popular shouting and mystical-philosophical dramatics of their female contemporaries, the Softies make music that is barely audible, delicately lovelorn, and mostly unknown. Like *It's Love*, the Softies' debut LP, *Winter Pageant* is a collection of songs that begin after the romance has ended. Their sound is intimate and fragile—guitars like baby birds and voices as brightly immaterial as sunlight shimmering on water. The rare songs that celebrate a love that has not yet died—"The Best Days" and "Excellent"—have the same wistful air as the rest. They eulogize a perfect moment, preserve it as a tragic souvenir, before the inevitable end. Despite the melancholy tone, there is something hopeful in the Softies' resignation, a faith in perfect moments that is as strong as the knowledge of love's frailty. There is no recrimination in these songs and no bitterness. From their own intimate distress, Jen Sbragia and Rose Melberg have chosen to produce neither manifestoes nor rallying cries, but sad lullabies for the amorously disenfranchised. In their unassuming way, the Softies remind us that the personal need not always be political, that sometimes personal is enough. —*Jessica Jernigan*

Holiday in Rhode Island / Sep. 12, 2000 / K ✦✦✦✦✦

Son Volt

f. 1994

Americana, Alternative Country, Alternative Country-Rock

Following the acrimonious dissolution of the influential alternative country trio Uncle Tupelo, the group's singer/guitarist Jay Farrar formed the roots-rock unit Son Volt. Joined by onetime Tupelo drummer Mike Heidorn along with brothers Jim (bass, vocals) and Dave Boquist (guitar, banjo, fiddle, lap steel), Farrar set about authoring the group's 1995 debut record, *Trace*, an edgy, stark affair which earned virtually unanimous praise from the critical community as well as scoring a minor hit with its first single, "Drown." Son Volt returned in the spring of 1997 with the album *Straightaways*; *Wide Swing Tremolo* followed a year later. —*Jason Ankeny*

● **Trace** / Sep. 19, 1995 / Warner Brothers ✦✦✦✦✦

Jay Farrar always provided the darkest, grittiest moments in Uncle Tupelo, so it comes as no surprise that Son Volt is a rawer record than *A.M.*, the first album by Wilco, a band led by his former partner Jeff Tweedy. Throughout Son Volt's debut *Trace*, the group reworks classic honky tonk and rock & roll, adding a desparate, determined edge to their performances. Even when they rock out, their is a palpable sense of melancholy to Farrar's voice, which lends a poignancy to the music. *Trace* isn't a great step forward from Tupelo's last album, the lovely *Anodyne*, but it is a fine continuation of the ideas Farrar has pursued over the course of his career. —*Stephen Thomas Erlewine*

Straightaways / Apr. 22, 1997 / Warner Brothers ✦✦✦✦

Although none of the songs on *Straightaways* immediately jump off the grooves, as was the case with the band's brilliant debut *Trace*, repeated spins reveal a strong effort nonetheless. Whereas former Uncle Tupelo partner Jeff Tweedy and his band Wilco used its sophomore release to explore new territory, Son Volt leader and songwriter Jay Farrar keeps his band mining the same country-folk vein that Uncle Tupelo quarried. There are plenty of threads to connect *Straightaways* to *Trace*, such as the expressive playing of multi-instrumentalist Dave Boquist on guitars, fiddle, banjo, and lap steel, and Farrar's forlorn vocal delivery, which could give even the weakest song emotional power. On *Straightaways*, his songs live on the same late-night backwoods rural highways that *Trace* inhabited, with song titles like "Creosote" and "Cemetery Savior" conjuring up dark imagery. The album contains plenty of high points: the aforementioned songs, as well as the lonesome "Back Into Your World" and "Last Minute Shakedown." And the only place it comes up short is the lyrics—unlike *Trace*, whose songs "Windfall" and "Tear Stained Eye" stood by themselves and provided a universal feel and emotion that was easily grasped, much of the lyrical content of *Straightaways* seems open-ended and fragmented, with the intensity building on the haunting instrumental arrangements and Farrar's affecting vocal phrasing. —*Jack Leaver*

Wide Swing Tremolo / Oct. 6, 1998 / Warner Brothers ✦✦✦

While Son Volt's first two albums, *Trace* and *Straightaways*, received critical acclaim, they are both very restrained and sparse works underlain with languidness. These albums hinted, in their best moments, at Son Volt's potential to both write beautiful songs and rock out, but the band never seemed to completely let loose and turn it up to 11. Part of this may stem from their eclectic mix of musical influences. While the juxtaposition of styles ranging from country to bar-band rock & roll has been the key to Son Volt's sound, it has also been a point of contention for those who have criticized them for not knowing what sort of band they wanted to be. *Wide Swing Tremolo* represents an attempt to somewhat break the mold of the earlier releases, especially from the intensely sparse *Straightaways. Wide Swing Tremolo* is a wide-open, rocking album with precious little of the overt country influences found on previous Son Volt works. Instead, this album is driven by R.E.M.-like arpeggio guitar riffs and muscular, warm rhythms. It's a strong album. *—Matthew Hilburn*

Sonic Youth

f. 1981, New York, NY

College Rock, Experimental Rock, Noise Rock, Indie Rock, Alternative Pop/Rock, Post-Punk, American Underground

Sonic Youth was one of the most unlikely success stories of underground American rock in the '80s. Where contemporaries R.E.M. and Husker Du were fairly conventional in terms of song-structure and melody, Sonic Youth began their career by abandoning any pretense of traditional rock & roll conventions. Borrowing heavily from the free-form noise experimentalism of the Velvet Underground and the Stooges, and melding it with a performance-art aesthetic borrowed from the New York post-punk avant garde, Sonic Youth redefined what noise meant within rock & roll. Sonic Youth rarely rocked, though they were inspired directly by hardcore punk, post-punk, and no wave. Instead, their dissonance, feedback, and alternate tunings created a new sonic landscape, one that redefined what rock guitar could do. Their trio of independent late '80s records—*EVOL, Sister, Daydream Nation*—became touchstones for a generation of indie-rockers, who either replicated the noise, or reinterpreted it a more palatable setting. As their career progressed, Sonic Youth grew more palatable, as well, as their more free-form songs began to feel like compositions and their shorter works began to rock harder. During the '90s, most American indie bands, and many British underground bands, displayed a heavy debt to Sonic Youth, and the band themselves had become a popular cult band, with each of their albums charting in the Top 100. *—Stephen Thomas Erlewine*

Confusion Is Sex / Feb. 1983 / SST ♦♦

Originally released on the small independent labels Neutral and Zensor, *Confusion Is Sex* began Sonic Youth's steady climb to the top of the 1980s alt-rock underground. As the adventurous New York group's first full-length album, this collection of low-quality recordings serves as a perfect summation of Sonic Youth's beginnings, capturing their punk ideology, avant-garde approach to guitar playing, and knack for confrontational performance. Never again would the band ever sound so extreme and anarchic, not only in terms of music but also in terms of attitude. A live cover of the Stooges' "I Wanna Be Your Dog" begins with an ambient segment of feedback titled "Freezer Burn" from which Kim Gordon's tortured vocals explode with painful ferocity. Gordon brings more moments of uncomfortable beauty to the album on "Protect Me You," a moody piece of muted-guitar plucking highlighted by her gentle whispering of such lyrics as "Protect me from ravagement / I'm ten years old." Though Gordon's songs tend to be the best ones here, Thurston Moore's contributions are also noteworthy, especially his charismatic vocals on the title track. Although it features a young, undeveloped version of Sonic Youth—one nowhere near as articulate or evolved as the Sonic Youth that would come to rule alternative rock by the end of the 1980s—what *Confusion Is Sex* lacks in quality, it certainly makes up for in intent. *—Jason Birchmeier*

Kill Yr. Idols / Oct. 1983 / Zensor ♦♦♦

Building on the shadowy carnage of their first masterpiece, *Confusion Is Sex*, Sonic Youth quickly followed up that LP with a 12" EP titled *Kill Yr. Idols*. As one may assume from its title, *Kill Yr. Idols* continued the group's fascination with dark, illogical confrontation. The music seems downright scary today, with its atonal guitar resonance and haunted vocals, but it must have sounded utterly alien back in 1983, before anyone had even conceived of such an idea as "alternative rock." Of course, there's a certain sense of fascination and eroticism inherent in extremity, and in the early '80s Sonic Youth managed to revel in their image as a daring band of poor Manhattan post-punks out to destroy audiences' preconceptions. Originally released on *Confusion Is Sex*, the ghostly "Protect Me You" leads things off, and is followed by a live version of "Shaking Hell" that transcends the original in terms of its raw inhumanity. On the B-side of the record are three songs exclusive to the EP: "Kill Yr. Idols," "Brother James," and "Early American." The first two share similar characteristics, relying primarily on psychotic vocals and near-dissonant wails of atonal guitar. Both have stood the test of time as two of the group's most unique songs, with "Brother James" remaining an integral part of their live shows into the early '90s. "Early American" takes the same approach as "Protect Me You," with its subtle vocals and evocative guitar chiming. Unfortunately, the song ends up being little more than a boring attempt at recreating "Protect Me You"'s morbid tone. This hard-to-find 12" EP was eventually re-released in the early '90s with *Confusion Is Sex* as *Confusion Is Sex (Plus Kill Yr. Idols)*. *—Jason Birchmeier*

Sonic Death: Early Sonic 1981-1983 / 1984 / SST ♦♦

Blast First's *Sonic Death/Sonic Youth Live* is a reissue of the 1984 live album *Sonic Death*. The record captures the early incarnation of Sonic Youth at their noisiest and artiest. Often, it's unfocused and tiresome, but there are enough intriguing moments to make it of interest to some collectors, even if fans who became familiar with Sonic Youth with such later works as *Daydream Nation* or *Dirty* (or even *Sister* and *EVOL*) might find this a little inaccessible. *—Stephen Thomas Erlewine*

Bad Moon Rising / 1985 / DGC ♦♦

Following the noisy darkness of their releases on small independent labels—a period that peaked with the abrasive guitar hailstorm of *Kill Yr. Idols*—Sonic Youth returned with a calmer and more introspective album. *Bad Moon Rising* illustrates the group's move toward conceptual rock, with its underlying poetic tone and continuous flow from one song to the next. The tortured horror of *Confusion Is Sex* has been toned down in favor

of tranquil ghostliness. On songs such as "Brave Men Run" and "Society Is a Hole," the group puts up a serene facade, characterized by subtly spoken poetics and gently strummed guitars. The hazy, opiate feel of these songs occasionally gets rocky—especially during the apocalyptic frenzy of "I Love Her All the Time," when the haze gets disrupted by the flaming explosion of the group's guitars, eclipsing whatever sense of serenity has been established. These opposing forces battle each other throughout the album, culminating with the closer, "Death Valley '69." This monolithic chunk of guitar-driven havoc features Lydia Lunch sharing vocals with Thurston Moore, as the two narrate the song's fantastic theme. Overall, the group's intentions on *Bad Moon Rising* seem novel; unfortunately, with the exception of "I Love Her All the Time," "Society Is a Hole," and "Death Valley '69," many of the songs never reach their full potential. [After Sonic Youth signed to major label DGC in the early '90s, *Bad Mood Rising* was re-released with the *Flower* 12" EP as *Bad Mood Rising (Plus Flower)*.] *—Jason Birchmeier*

EVOL / 1986 / DGC ♦♦♦♦♦

Sonic Youth made its first moves toward rock with *EVOL*, a stunningly fluent mixture of avant-garde instrumentation and subversions of rock & roll. The band benefits greatly from the addition of structure, which gives their aural experiments a firm grounding, but the addition of drummer Steve Shelley is essential to the group's new, dangerous edge. With the added propulsion, the fearless rush of "Expressway to Yr Skull" (a.k.a. "Madonna, Sean and Me") and the near-pop of "Green Light" are undeniably powerful, as are the eerie textures of "Shadow of a Doubt." *—Stephen Thomas Erlewine*

Made in USA / 1986 / Rhino ♦♦

☆ Sister / 1987 / DGC ♦♦♦♦♦

EVOL was a major leap forward for Sonic Youth, but *Sister* is a masterpiece, demonstrating the group's rapidly evolving musicality. More than ever before, Sonic Youth's songs sound like actual songs, and their collages of noise, distortion, and alternate tunings are now used to provide texture and depth to the music, which is original, complex and rewarding. Not only is there the full-throttle roar of "Tuff Gnarl," but there are shimmering layers of ambient harmonics and dissonance which are as haunting and challenging as any of their barrages of feedback. Furthermore, *Sister* has a warm sound, which lures the listeners into music that's defiantly arty but never indulgent. It's one of the singular art-rock records of the '80s, surpassed only by Sonic Youth's next album, *Daydream Nation*. *—Stephen Thomas Erlewine*

★ Daydream Nation / 1988 / DGC ♦♦♦♦♦

By refining the song-oriented breakthroughs of *Sister* and developing their fascination with noise and alternate tunings, Sonic Youth created a masterpiece of post-punk art-rock with the double album *Daydream Nation*. Though the self-conscious sprawl of the album might appear self-indulgent on the surface, *Daydream Nation* is powered by a sustained vision, one that encapsulates all of the group's quirks and strengths. Alternating between tense, hypnotic instrumental passages and furious noise explosions, the music demonstrates a range of emotions and textures and, in many ways, it's hard not to listen to the record as one long piece of shifting dynamics. But the songs themselves are remarkable, from the anti-anthem of "Teen Age Riot" and the punky "Silver Rocket" to the hazy drug dreams of "Providence" and the rolling waves of "Eric's Trip." *Daydream Nation* demonstrates the extent to which noise and self-conscious avant-art can be incorporated into rock, and the results are nothing short of stunning. *—Stephen Thomas Erlewine*

Goo / Jun. 1990 / DGC ♦♦♦

Any doubts as to the continuing relevance of Sonic Youth upon their jump to major label status were quickly laid to rest by *Goo*, their follow-up to the monumental *Daydream Nation*. While paling in the shadow of its predecessor, the record is nevertheless a defiant call to arms against mainstream musical values; the Geffen logo adorning the disc is a moot point—*Goo* is, if anything, a portrait of Sonic Youth at their most self-indulgently noisy and contentious, covering topics ranging from Karen Carpenter ("Tunic") to U.F.O.'s ("Disappearer") to dating Jesus' mom ("Mary-Christ"). Even Public Enemy's Chuck D. joins the fracas on the single "Kool Thing," which teeters on the brink of a cultural breakthrough but which falls just shy of the mark; the same could be said of *Goo* itself—by no means a sellout, it nevertheless lacks the coherence and force of the group's finest work, and the opportunity to violently rattle the mainstream cage slips by. *—Jason Ankeny*

Dirty / Jul. 21, 1992 / DGC ♦♦♦♦

When DGC Records signed Nirvana in 1991, one of DGC's A&R reps expressed the opinion that, with plenty of touring and the right promotion, the new act might sell as well as its labelmate and touring partner Sonic Youth. The surprise success of *Nevermind* upended previous commercial expectations for Sonic Youth (among other established alternative rock bands), and when *Dirty* was released in 1992, it was seen by many as the band's big move toward the grunge market. Which doesn't make a lot of sense if you actually *listen* to the album; while Butch Vig's clean but full-bodied production certainly gave Thurston Moore and Lee Ranaldo's guitars greater punch and presence than they had in the past, and many of the songs move in the increasingly tuneful direction the band had been traveling with *Daydream Nation* and *Goo*, most of *Dirty* is good bit more jagged and purposefully discordant than its immediate precursors, lacking the same hallucinatory grace as *Daydream Nation* or the hard rock sheen of *Goo*. If anything, *Dirty* finds Sonic Youth revisiting the territory the band mapped out on *Sister*—merging the propulsive structures of rock (both punk and otherwise) with the gorgeous chaos of their approach to the electric guitar—and it shows how much better they'd gotten at it in the past five years, from the curiously beautiful "Wish Fulfillment" and "Theresa's Sound World" to the brutal "Drunken Butterfly" and "Purr." *Dirty* was also Sonic Youth's most overtly political album, railing against the abuses of the Reagan/Bush era on "Youth Against Fascism," "Swimsuit Issue," and "Chapel Hill," a surprising move from a band so often in love with cryptic irony. Heard today, *Dirty* doesn't sound like a masterpiece (like

Daydream Nation) or a gesture toward the mainstream audience (like *Goo*)—it just sounds like a damn good rock album, and on those terms it ranks with Sonic Youth's best work. —*Mark Deming*

Experimental Jet Set, Trash & No Star / May 3, 1994 / DGC ♦♦

Whereas *Dirty* and its predecessors were loud, distorted, and bordering on the fine line between pop and noise, *Experimental Jet Set, Trash & No Star* did away with the ear-bleeding guitar feedback so often attributed to the group. The group retained its quirky twist on pop/rock song structures, moving even further toward a consistent use of the verse-chorus-verse template. Of course, the disregard for mosh-friendly guitar riffs, lack of crowd-surfing intensity, and increasing traces of normalcy killed a large part of the group's momentous surge in popular acceptance, damning them once again to the status of often misunderstood artists. Popular opinion may have wanted more rock than what Sonic Youth wanted to deliver on this album, yet upon careful inspection, *Experimental Jet Set, Trash & No Star* still out-noises the majority of its peers. Butch Vig's clean production makes the album seem clean, when in actuality it is nearly as dirty as the group's preceding effort. Songs such as "Starfield Road" and the acoustic song "Winner's Blues" emanate plenty of raw spontaneity, even with Vig's crystal clear production. Relative to Sonic Youth's greater body of work, the album does seem rather sedate, though. The noises resonate subtly rather than mangle one's eardrum. In sum, this record must be considered the closest the group has ever gone to straight-ahead pop/rock. With all of the feedback, murky production, incoherent song structuring, and rambunctious charisma stripped away, what remains are odd lyrics and unique guitar nuance. In other words, *Experimental Jet Set, Trash & No Star* features the underlying foundation of the group's music standing naked, without any of their traditionally excessive static to heighten it. —*Jason Birchmeier*

Screaming Fields of Sonic Love / Apr. 25, 1995 / DGC ♦♦♦

Sonic Youth was never a singles band—they may have released many 7" singles, but they rarely paid attention to conventional song structure, which meant their ideas couldn't always be distilled in the form of one three-minute song. Consequently, the idea of a compilation of highlights from their peak years at SST Records is a little odd, since each of their recordings—from masterworks like *Sister* and *Daydream Nation* to one-offs like Ciccone Youth's *The Whitey Album* and their EPs—worked as a cohesive, individual entity. That said, the 17-track SST overview *Screaming Fields of Sonic Love* isn't nearly as bad as some die-hard fans might have suspected. It's true that it feels a little haphazard, but its ingenious sequencing—running backward from 1988's *Daydream Nation*—makes their noisier, atonal early recordings sound more accessible. And that means that the compilation is, in a weird way, a good choice for neophytes, since it does offer an easy introduction to the group's seminal '80s records. Longtime followers won't find anything unusual here, apart from edits of "Teen Age Riot" and "Candle," but it isn't designed for them—it's for the curious, and it will likely whet their appetites. —*Stephen Thomas Erlewine*

Washing Machine / Oct. 1995 / DGC ♦♦♦♦

After the regressive, low-key *Experimental Jet Set, Trash & No Star*, Sonic Youth appeared to be floundering somewhat, but *Washing Machine* erased any notion that the band had run out of things to say. Easily their most adventurous, challenging and best record since *Daydream Nation*, the album finds Sonic Youth returning to the fearless exploration of their SST records, but the group has found a way to work that into tighter song structures. Not only are the songs more immediate than most of the material on their earlier records, the sound here is warm and open, making *Washing Machine* their most mature and welcoming record to date. It's not a commercial record, nor is it a pop record, but *Washing Machine* encompasses everything that made Sonic Youth innovators and shows that they can continue to grow, finding new paths inside their signature sound. —*Stephen Thomas Erlewine*

SYR 1 / Jun. 10, 1997 / SYR ♦♦♦♦

Sonic Youth invested the money it earned as Lollapalooza headliners in 1995 in a new studio. Owning their own studio gave the quartet the freedom to experiment as they were recording, since they no longer had to pay rental fees. To inaugurate their new studio, they set out to record a series of three experimental instrumental EPs with engineer Wharton Tiers, all of which would be released on their own label. With its winding, elliptical improvised instrumentals, *SYR 1* set the tone for the entire series. Musically, the EP isn't far removed from the instrumental sections on *Sister* or *Daydream Nation*, but this music isn't merely waves of feedback—it's considered, detailed, and bizarrely accessible. Like the epic "The Diamond Sea," the four songs have shifting sonic colors, as simple riffs build and intertwine, crossing over each other before finding a new path. It's closer to avant-garde than rock, but the music isn't purely cerebral, either. Recognizable statements float in and out of the mix, providing something of a touchstone for the free-form explorations. *SYR 1* also has brevity on its side. The EP lasts 25 minutes—which is just enough time to provide an exciting blueprint for a new era of Sonic Youth. —*Stephen Thomas Erlewine*

SYR 2 / Sep. 2, 1997 / SYR ♦♦♦

The second of three self-released instrumental EPs, *SYR 2* follows through on the promise of *SYR 1* while exploring new territory. A noisier record than its predecessor, *SYR 2* nevertheless shares the same modus operandi—namely, it's purely improvised music that gleefully wanders into uncharted territory. Even at its noisiest, the EP reveals that Sonic Youth has remarkable interplay. Each member can sense where the other will go, and that's what's so fascinating about the EPs—there are no clear-cut themes, structures, or leaders, it's simply Sonic Youth without a harness. Toward the end of the record, the band ventures into quieter territory, immediately making clear their influence on such post-rock bands as Tortoise. Although *SYR 2* is slightly less rewarding than *SYR 1*, its

unpredictable, continually shifting sonics make for an endlessly intriguing listen. —*Stephen Thomas Erlewine*

SYR 3 / Feb. 24, 1998 / SYR ♦♦♦♦

For their final self-released instrumental EP, Sonic Youth teamed up with Jim O'Rourke, the avant-garde/post-rock guru best known as a member of Gastr Del Sol. While the collaboration is a little long-winded—the "EP" lasts nearly an hour—and is the most difficult of the three *SYR* recordings, it also provides some of the best music of the series. It just takes a little digging to find it. *SYR 3* is closer to Gastr Del Sol, in many ways, than Sonic Youth, but that's refreshing. All the members of SY switch instruments on the record, and O'Rourke pushes them into free-jazz territory. Occasionally, they can get lost in the murk, drifting into long static stretches that barely raise above a murmur. More often, though, the music is fascinating, with the subtle layers and seamless transitions becoming mesmerizing. It takes a little work to get into *SYR 3*—a recording that is more complex and ambitious than its full-length follow-up, *A Thousand Leaves*—but the cerebral, difficult music is worth the effort. —*Stephen Thomas Erlewine*

A Thousand Leaves / May 12, 1998 / DGC ♦♦♦♦

Truth be told, the grunge era never quite fit Sonic Youth. They may have been at the peak of their popularity, but they had traded their experimentalism for sheer, bracing noise. It may have sounded good, but ultimately *Dirty* didn't have the cerebral impact of *Sister*, largely because it was tied to an admittedly effective backbeat. Beginning with *Washing Machine*, Sonic Youth returned to more adventurous territory, and in 1997, they released a series of EPs that illustrated their bond with such post-rock groups as Tortoise and Gastr Del Sol. Those EPs, as well as the epic *Washing Machine* closer "The Diamond Sea," provide the foundation for *A Thousand Leaves*, the band's most challenging and satisfying record in years. The blasts of dissonance that characterized their SST masterworks have been replaced, by and large, by winding, intricate improvisations. There's a surprising warmth to the subdued guitars of Thurston Moore, Lee Ranaldo, and Kim Gordon, which keeps the lengthy songs captivating. Both Moore and Ranaldo concentrate on quiet material, which almost makes Gordon's noisy politicized rants sound a little out of place, but her best moments ("French Tickler," "Heather Angel") have unsettling, unpredictable twists and turns that greatly contribute to the success of *A Thousand Leaves*. It may be their most cerebral album in ages, but that only makes it all the more engaging. —*Stephen Thomas Erlewine*

Silver Session for Jason Knuth / Jul. 14, 1998 / SYR ♦♦♦

Of the many strange recordings released by Sonic Youth over the course of their long career, few measure up to *Silver Session for Jason Knuth*. On the inside of the CD sleeve, guitarist Thurston Moore explains the unique situation involving this record and what sort of music to expect. Sonic Youth has been known to drift away from the pop/rock precedent with their tendency to incorporate untraditionally tuned guitars, feedback-driven noise, incoherent lyrics, and odd song structures into their music. On this record, though, they completely abandon any sort of rock-related clichés, instead delivering eight songs of lively guitar feedback. According to Moore, while the band tried to record the vocals for their *A Thousand Leaves* album one evening, a band in the neighboring studio proceeded to play "some funky metal overdrive." Frustrated over the incident, Sonic Youth turned every amplifier in their studio to ten+ and leaned as many guitars as they could against them, creating a cacophony of ear-piercing feedback. The group recorded the session and mixed it into digestible sections. Surprisingly, the resulting record has quite a serene feel, with the feedback taking on a beautiful ambient aura. Nothing eventful occurs during these pieces, making it more of a meditative album in the spirit of Brian Eno's *Ambient 4*. The record also functions as an ode to Knuth, a Sonic Youth fan who committed suicide. Proceeds from the CD went to San Francisco Suicide Prevention Hotline. Don't consider this one of the influential group's most important albums by any means, but do consider it an interesting addition to their catalog, intended mainly for loyal fans. —*Jason Birchmeier*

Goodbye 20th Century / Nov. 16, 1999 / SYR ♦♦

NYC Ghosts & Flowers / May 16, 2000 / Geffen ♦♦♦

Hot on the heels of *Goodbye 20th Century*, Sonic Youth's tribute to avant-garde masters like Pauline Oliveros and John Cage, came *NYC Ghosts & Flowers*, an attempt to commemorate the dangerous, bohemian New York of old in a similar way. Though it sports an Allen Ginsberg-inspired title and artwork by William Burroughs, the album lacks the visceral, immediate impact of the best beat poetry and seems driven by self-consciousness instead of stream-of-consciousness. Its most uncomfortable moments spring from its beat generation inspirations, such as Thurston Moore's awkward monologue "Small Flowers Crack Concrete." Even worse, "Lightnin'"'s dissonant, stabbing guitars and Kim Gordon's woozy vocals almost ruin the impact of Lee Ranaldo's epic title track, which is the closest *NYC Ghosts & Flowers* comes to blending the album's deadpan vocals and sonic maelstroms successfully. Sonic Youth still seems to be atoning for their more accessible, early '90s sound, particularly on "StreamXSonik Subway," a rant about NYC's increasing authoritarianism. However, *NYC Ghosts & Flowers* isn't dismissible. "Free City Rhymes" is another of their dreamy yet prickly guitarscapes; "Renegade Princess" recalls the group's early art-punk; and Kim Gordon's "Side2Side" and "Nevermind (What Was It Anyway)" are sullenly sensual (though the latter song features the lyrical nadir "Boys go to Jupiter/Get more stupider"). Considering that this was recorded shortly after all of Sonic Youth's irreplaceable, custom-tweaked guitars were stolen, it's frustrating that they tried to recreate their old sound with new gear instead of exploring new ideas. *NYC Ghosts & Flowers* will chase away any remaining fair-weather fans hoping for another "Sugar Kane" or "Kool Thing," but it doesn't offer much for diehards, who may prefer the undiluted experiments of the group's SYR EPs. Ultimately, the album is equally uncompromising and frustrating. —*Heather Phares*

The Sonics

f. Tacoma, WA

Garage Rock, Rock & Roll

A rock & roll band from Tacoma, WA, the Sonics' original members were Gerry Roslie (lead singer and piano/organ), Andy Parypa (guitar), Larry Parypa (bass), Bob Bennett (drums), and Rob Lind (saxophone). Forming in the wake of the early-'60s success of local favorites the Kingsmen and the Wailers (whose Etiquette label they recorded for), the Sonics combined the classic Northwest-area teen-band raunch with early English band grit (particularly influenced by the Kinks), relentless rhythmic drive, and unabashed '50s-style blues-shouting for a combination that still makes their brand of rock & roll perhaps the raunchiest ever captured on wax. Lead singer Gerry Roslie was no less than a white Little Richard, whose harrowing soul-screams were startling even to the Northwest teen audience, who liked their music powerful and driving with little regard to commercial subtleties. With hit after hit on the local charts (and influencing every local band that ever took the stage), the band inexplicably was never able to break out nationally, leaving their sound largely undiluted for mass consumption. Breaking up in the late '60s (after one ill-fated album attempt to water down their style for national attention), the Sonics continue today to be revered by '60s collectors the world over for their unique brand of rock & roll raunch. —*Cub Koda*

Here Are the Sonics!!! / 1965 / Norton ✦✦✦
The Sonics that Wailers bassist Buck Ormsby took into a small studio and unleashed on the world shows a live band at the peak of their powers, ready to mow down the competition without even blinking twice. Their debut long-player (originally issued on the Etiquette imprint) is reprised here with new liner notes by Norton prexy Miriam Linna in the original mono. Their flame-throwing hits of "The Witch," "Psycho," "Boss Hoss," and "Strychnine" are aboard, along with versions of "Do You Love Me," "Dirty Robber," "Have Love-Will Travel," and "Walkin' the Dog" that are no less potent. This long-play vinyl reissue also boasts the addition of four bonus tracks: "Keep A-Knockin'" (the original B-side of "The Witch") and three selections from an Etiquette Christmas album, "Don't Believe in Christmas," "The Village Idiot," and "Santa Claus." Another important chunk of Seattle rock & roll history. —*Cub Koda*

The Sonics Boom / 1966 / Norton ✦✦✦
The Sonics' second album is every bit as explosive and influential as their debut outing, loaded with gritty Northwest rock'n'soul. This 1998 vinyl reissue bonus tracks out with an alternate take of "The Witch" plus hot 1972 live reunion tapes of the band doing "Psycho" and "The Witch." Sandwiched in between the abrasive classics of "Cinderella," "Don't Be Afraid of the Dark" (with the Wailers on backing vocals), the funk sass of "The Hustler" and "Shot Down," the demonic "He's Waitin'" and the sledgehammer, inside-out version of "Louie Louie" (only three chords to play and they don't even *play 'em*), are the band's straight-ahead takes on old R&B chestnuts like "Skinny Minnie," "Let the Good Times Roll," "Don't You Just Know It," "Since I Fell for You," "Hitch Hike," and a nice barn-burning version of "Jenny Jenny." Where the Wailers cut down the trees and paved the highway, the Sonics were the first group from their neck of the woods to take that music somewhere wilder than their original inspirations. The second chapter of Northwest rock-'n'roll after you absorb the Wailers' Golden Crest sides. —*Cub Koda*

Introducing the Sonics / 1966 / Beat Rocket ✦✦✦
This is a limited-edition, 180-gram premium vinyl audiophile pressing of the group's final album for Jerry Dennon's Jerden label. In addition to the band's two original hits (recorded and originally issued on the Etiquette label), there are 13 sides that were cut at the band's last session in 1966. All of the material on here is the same as on Jerden's compact disc version of the same material (issued as *Maintaining My Cool*), save for the exclusion of a lame version of "Hanky Panky," mercifully replaced here with Gerry Roslie's original "Love Lights." This makes a more than interesting comparison for audiophiles when compared to Jerden's CD version of this, minus the track swap. This also features the original album cover art of the band captured in a blue duo-tone in their matching gaucho outfits. Hardcore fans of the band and completists will want both versions of this. —*Cub Koda*

● **Here Are the Ultimate Sonics** / 1991 / Etiquette ✦✦✦✦✦
Combining all the tracks from their first two Etiquette albums, three tracks from the label's Christmas album, live tracks, and an alternate take of "The Witch," this compilation more than lives up to its title. The definitive overview. —*Cub Koda*

Sonny & Cher

f. 1964, db. 1974

Pop/Rock, Folk-Rock, Pop

Sonny & Cher proved one of the magical musical combinations of the mid '60s and one of the better rock-influenced MOR acts of the early '70s, their wisecracking repartee providing counterpoint to a series of adoring hit duets. They were a strange duet in the sense that neither had a great voice and, indeed, their voices were so similar that Atlantic Records president Ahmet Ertegun was convinced that Sonny had come close to breaking a contract by turning up singing with her on her solo hit "All I Really Want to Do." Their biggest success was as a duet on Atco, with "I Got You Babe" and "The Beat Goes On." For a time, from 1965 until 1967, they were rock & roll's hottest couple, so much so that in some conservative communities they were considered almost morally subversive; parents locked up their kids when Sonny & Cher were passing through for a concert appearance. And then nothing—the hits stopped coming, and the couple made some daringly creative but unsuccessful commercial missteps. Soon they were playing supper clubs and Las Vegas nightclubs; their stage act—which had evolved into a kind of "with it" domestic comedy routine nearly as prominent as the music, with the tall, wry-witted

Cher cutting up on the seemingly dim-witted Sonny—was spotted by Fred Silverman, who was then the head of programming for CBS. They ended up with a summer replacement try-out show that did so well that Sonny & Cher were given a regular spot in the CBS lineup in 1972 with a comedy-variety series. The couple's recording career was revived initially by a live album cut in one night at Las Vegas, featuring new versions of their early hits as well as parts of their current repertory; the album went gold. The first couple of singles by Cher and Sonny & Cher failed, but then producer Snuff Garrett was brought in, and the result was "Gypsies, Tramps and Thieves," a career-reviving number one hit. After that, "The Way of Love," "All I Ever Need Is You" (which became the theme for their TV show), "A Cowboy's Work Is Never Done," "Half Breed," and "Dark Lady" kept either Cher or the couple in the Top Ten at various times through 1974. By then, however, their marriage had fallen apart, and with it, the success of their TV show. —*Bruce Eder*

● **The Beat Goes On: The Best of Sonny & Cher** / 1975 / Rhino/Atco ✦✦✦✦✦
Weighing in at a generous 21 tracks, Atco's *The Beat Goes On: The Best of Sonny & Cher* is the definitive portrait of Sonny & Cher in their glory years. The duo left Atco in the late '60s, staging a comeback on Kapp/MCA records in the early '70s, which means latter-day hits such as "All I Ever Need Is You" and "A Cowboy's Work Is Never Done" aren't here, but chances are most listeners won't even notice, since all the big songs are here: "I Got You Babe"; "Laugh at Me"; "Baby Don't Go"; "Just You"; "But You're Mine"; "What Now, My Love?"; "The Revolution Kind"; "Little Man"; and "The Beat Goes On." True, the collection may run a little long for some tastes, but there's no denying that it has all that a casual or dedicated fan could ever want from a Sonny and Cher compilation. —*Stephen Thomas Erlewine*

All I Ever Need: The Kapp/MCA Anthology / Jan. 1996 / MCA ✦✦✦✦
A single CD of the dozen or so key tracks from Sonny & Cher's second era of success (1971-74) on Kapp Records will probably be preferable to all but the biggest fans. What's more, even this set, which starts with the first failed Kapp singles ("Classified 1A," etc.) is missing five cuts available on the Cher greatest hits package, as well as three Sonny Bono solo tracks, and the long version of "Mama Was a Rock & Roll Singer." Still, it's difficult to complain about the contents, 38 songs drawn from four years on the label, nicely remastered and assembled in impeccably logical fashion. The duo's (and Cher's solo) studio cuts make up the first disc, while the second is comprised of songs from the duo's two live recordings done two years apart in Las Vegas. It does show off the various facets of their appeal, even if what they were doing was more mainstream music than anything near the cutting edge of even pop music—no more Dylan songs, or any songs by would-be Dylan successors carried to the top of the charts, but lots of sales, and the live albums' sections not only include covers of the most obvious of the duo's early songs ("The Beat Goes On," "I Got You Babe," etc.) but also titles like "You Better Sit Down Kids," as well as their humor and marital sparring. —*Bruce Eder*

Cher and Sonny & Cher Greatest Hits / 1998 / MCA ✦✦✦✦✦
This single CD costs a third the price of the double-CD MCA set *All I Ever Need*, and is the preferable alternative in almost every respect. Eight of the 16 tracks are hits or B-sides by Cher from 1971-74, interspersed with the biggest hits by Sonny & Cher from the same period. The failed singles like "Classified 1A" are not represented, but good B-sides like "I Hate to Sleep Alone" are, along with the live version of "I Got You Babe" from their second *Live in Las Vegas* album. The notes (edited from the double-disc booklet) are thorough, the sound is excellent, and the only drawback is the absence of any of the comic repartee that sparked their interaction. —*Bruce Eder*

The Sorrows

f. 1963, Coventry, England, db. 1969

Freakbeat, Mod, British Invasion

One of the most overlooked bands of the British Invasion, the Sorrows offered a tough brand of R&B-infused rock that recalled the Pretty Things (though not as R&B-oriented) and the Kinks (though not as pop-oriented). Their biggest British hit, "Take a Heart," stopped just outside the U.K. Top 20; several other fine mid-'60s singles met with either slim or a total lack of success. With the rich, gritty vocals of Don Fardon, taut raunchy guitars, and good material (both self-penned and from outside writers), they rank as one of the better British bands of their era, and certainly among the very best never to achieve success of any kind in the U.S. After their sole LP (also titled *Take a Heart*), they issued a couple of singles with psychedelic and Dylanesque overtones, and had somehow relocated to Italy in the late '60s, where they played out their string with material in a much more progressive (and less distinctive) vein. Don Fardon had a Top 20 hit in America with a pre-Raiders version of "Indian Reservation" in 1968. —*Richie Unterberger*

Take a Heart / 1965 / Repertoire ✦✦✦✦✦
A reissue of their mid-'60s album, with eight bonus tracks, including the fine non-LP singles by the original lineup and foreign-language versions of some tunes. One of the best obscure British Invasion records. —*Richie Unterberger*

Take a Heart / 1982 / Raven ✦✦✦✦✦
There are four or five reissues of the Sorrows' mid-'60s material; this Australian LP was the first of the batch. The others are more comprehensive, especially Sequel's *The Sorrows*, with 20 tracks (including all 14 of the ones on this Australian comp). You really don't lose much, however, if you choose to stick with this one. It has the very best stuff and it's sequenced better than some of the other reissues, although it doesn't have any historical liner notes. —*Richie Unterberger*

In Italy / 1983 / Eva ✦✦✦
With an altered lineup, The Sorrows cut these tracks in a much more progressive vein in the late '60s, heavily influenced by Traffic, Family, and the Small Faces (five of the

14 songs here are covers of compositions by those groups). Not nearly as impressive as their beat material. *—Richie Unterberger*

- **The Sorrows** / 1991 / Sequel ♦♦♦♦♦
The best reissue of the *Take a Heart* album (which has also been reissued in other configurations). Includes all the tracks from the LP, all the important non-LP singles, a couple unissued tracks, and Don Fardon's version of "Indian Reservation." *—Richie Unterberger*

Soul Asylum

f. 1983, Minneapolis, MN

College Rock, Adult Alternative Pop/Rock, Alternative Pop/Rock, Hard Rock, American Underground

Soul Asylum is the quintessential little band that could; it only took ten years to turn them from a teenage garage band into multi-platinum-selling rock stars. After several albums recorded for the local Minneapolis label Twin/Tone, the band signed to A&M Records in 1989 as part of a distribution pact between Twin Tone and A&M for the harder rock-sounding *Hang Time*, produced by Lenny Kaye. The record garnered some college radio attention, but by 1990's *And the Horse They Rode in On*, Soul Asylum had fallen out of favor with the indie-rock set and were left languishing in limbo, having almost entirely forsaken their post-punk indie roots. Signed to Columbia for 1992's *Grave Dancers Union*, Soul Asylum eventually earned a multi-platinum record after a slow start. The magical third single, "Runaway Train" helped push the single to number five and the album to number 11 and turned the band into a household name. Though 1995's *Let Your Dim Light Shine* charted at number six and a single, "Misery," hit the Top 20, the band never reached the dizzying heights nor masses they touched with "Runaway Train." Still, the band returned in 1998 with *Candy From a Stranger*. Needless to say, the little band's fame ultimately eclipsed those other guys from Minneapolis. *—Denise Sullivan*

Say What You Will, Clarence . . . Karl Sold the Truck / 1984 / Twin/Tone ♦♦♦
Produced by Hüsker Dü's Bob Mould, it's unsurprising that Soul Asylum's debut record shares the same tendencies as the Hüskers to loud, fast punk rock. Compared to the more structured songs he writes today, Dave Pirner was jumpy with nervous energy, and the songs reflect this frantic need to communicate and make some noise. Fans of post-stardom Soul Asylum might find this a bit too much to handle, but it remains expressive speed-rock that will leave you breathless. *—John Dougan*

Made to Be Broken / Jan. 1986 / Twin/Tone ♦♦

Time's Incinerator / Jul. 1986 / Twin/Tone ♦♦♦
A cassette-only release, this is a collection of outtakes and live tracks covering the period from 1981-1986 when the band was metamorphosing from their former selves as Loud Fast Rules into Soul Asylum. Obviously, when you give your band a name like Loud Fast Rules, you're not going to be playing folk-rock, but despite the insistence on speed and volume, there are some surprises here, most notably a live cover of James Brown's "Hot Pants." An interesting document of a band growing up and becoming more comfortable with getting better, whether they wanted to or not. *—John Dougan*

While You Were Out / Nov. 1986 / Twin/Tone ♦♦♦
Producer and ex-Suicide Commando Chris Osgood was an excellent choice to produce this first attempt at a breakthrough record. And, despite a few songs simply sounding like retreads, this is a pretty snappy collection, with Pirner's songwriting showing a depth and nuance that had previously been lost amid the roaring. The album closer, "Passing Sad Daydream," is even a country-tinged wallow that, despite being too long, was an indication that this band was developing a style that would allow them to make the transition out of speed-rock's obsession with, well, speed. *—John Dougan*

Clam Dip & Other Delights / Jan. 1988 / Twin/Tone ♦♦♦♦♦
A great EP with a hysterical cover parody of Herb Alpert's sexy *Whipped Cream and Other Delights* album cover, this shows Soul Asylum growing up but not growing old. Starting with the huge thudding riff of "Just Plain Evil," this adds the triumphantly poppy "Chains" and the funky "Take It to the Root," which originally appeared on *Time's Incinerator*. Oddly, what was originally intended as a minor release turned out to be a major work in Soul Asylum's early career. *—John Dougan*

Hang Time / Feb. 1988 / A&M ♦♦♦♦
More riff-heavy than usual, with considerable help from producer Lenny Kaye, *Hang Time* turned out to be the best of Soul Asylum's early records. The guitars of Pirner and Dan Murphy synchronize into a sonic wad of incredible power, while the songs (especially "Cartoon," "Some Time to Return," and "Beggars and Choosers") showed that Pirner had become a first-rate songwriter. Clever without being glib, and heartfelt without resorting to clichés, Pirner was doing something that eluded many of his peers: dealing with the transition from youth to adulthood and all the inherent conflicts that arise during this time. They would become superstars later, but this record should have done the trick. *—John Dougan*

And the Horse They Rode in On / 1990 / A&M ♦♦♦
The band had already begun to trade in the loud and fast sound for something a little more roots-based, as found on "We 3, " while other songs dabbled in heavy metal ("All the King's Friends"). On alternate tracks, the experiment didn't really work, and it left old fans confused and cold while arriving a little too early to cash in on the alt-rock explosion. Consequently, this otherwise fine record was left unheralded. It stands as one of the last pre-grunge alternative rock records, but had it not been perceived to fail so miserably, the band's success with its following album wouldn't have been nearly as sweet. *—Denise Sullivan*

Grave Dancer's Union / May 1992 / Columbia ♦♦♦♦
The band's breakthrough, million-selling album yielded the mega-hit "Runaway Train" and put Soul Asylum in a whole new league; longtime fans were predictably disappointed with the slick results. This is a solid alternative rock record with singer/songwriter/vocalist Dave Pirner up front, a role he was built for but always seemed to resist until the clear do-or-die moment for the band. They did; however, they've never matched the success or consistency of this album. Tracks like "Home Sick" and "New World" bear the roots of the country-rock revival later forged by Son Volt and Wilco, while the angst-ridden "Somebody to Shove" is pure joy Soul Asylum style. *—Denise Sullivan*

Let Your Dim Light Shine / Jun. 6, 1995 / Columbia ♦♦

Candy From a Stranger / May 12, 1998 / Columbia ♦♦♦

- **Black Gold: The Best of Soul Asylum** / Sep. 26, 2000 / Columbia/Legacy ♦♦♦♦
Unusually, for a best-of by a band that started indie and didn't become stars into hooking up with a major, *Black Gold: The Best of Soul Asylum* spans their entire pre-2000 career, starting with a 1985 track from their second LP. Naturally, their output on the major label that issued this compilation, Columbia, is emphasized; there are just four songs from the Twin/Tone era, and nothing at all from their 1984 debut, *Say What You Will, Clarence... Karl Sold the Truck*. So it's mostly Soul Asylum the 1990s stars you hear here. Its appeal to collectors, and simultaneous aggravation to completists who have most of this but need everything, is guaranteed by the inclusion of a few rarities. There are previously unreleased live versions of "Stranger" (from *MTV Unplugged*) and "Closer to the Stars" and the *Candy From a Stranger* outtake "Lonely for You." There's also the song that's actually titled "Candy From a Stranger," although, oddly, this didn't make it onto the actual *Candy From a Stranger* album; before this compilation, it was only released on a commercially unavailable promo CD. And, finally, there's "Summer of Drugs" from the benefit album *Sweet Relief: A Benefit for Victoria Williams*. In addition, Lenny Kaye, who produced the band's *Hang Time* LP, contributes liner notes. *—Richie Unterberger*

Soul Coughing

f. 1993

Post-Grunge, Alternative Pop/Rock

Soul Coughing was founded by former New York City music critic M. Doughty, who also worked at the famed avant-garde jazz club the Knitting Factory. Described by Doughty as "deep slacker jazz," Soul Coughing's music combines Doughty's stream-of-consciousness lyrical fragments, the jazz grooves of upright bassist and drummer Sebastian Steinberg and Yuval Gabay, and the various contributions of sampling guru Mark de Gil Antoni. Steinberg and Gabay were veterans of both New York's avant-garde and hip-hop underground scenes. Their debut album, *Ruby Vroom*, was released in 1994; *Irresistible Bliss* followed two years later, and in 1998 the group resurfaced with *El Oso*. Soul Coughing decided to call it quits in March of 2000, with M. Doughty pursuing a solo career. DiGliAntoni has a band called Horse Tricks and does film scores, and Steinberg and Gabay continue working together as a drums and bass duo called UV Ray. *—Steve Huey*

- **Ruby Vroom** / 1994 / Slash/Warner Brothers ♦♦♦
The debut album from Soul Coughing is an eclectic mix of free-style jazz, slam-poetry performance art, and avant-garde pop noodlings bound together by an affinity for the history of punk (leader M. Doughty used to be a music critic) and its winding ties to the theater of the absurd. Needless to say, it comes very close to being the most pretentious bit of self-conscious and commercially stagnating anti-music that alt-rock has offered in the '90s. But the band's refusal to take itself all that seriously, coupled with Tchad Blake's stylized production, makes *Ruby Vroom*, and Soul Coughing, one of the more ambitious projects of the decade. Their attempts to intellectualize themselves within a genre that often forsakes such aspirations are as lofty as they are bitingly cold, but the eventual sound is one of urban decay, and its accompanying denial, set to a slight bebop beat. *—Michael Gallucci*

Irresistible Bliss / May 14, 1996 / Slash/Warner Brothers ♦♦♦
Soul Coughing's second album *Irresistible Bliss* finds the band cutting away some of their eccentricities, leaving behind the bare basics of their psuedo-bohemian fusion of jazz, hip-hop, performance art, and alternative rock. Theoretically, the album should be more accessible; in practice, it is simply less involving. Though some engagingly quirky, off-center avant-pop remains, there are no jarring juxtapositions as satisfying as those that dominated *Ruby Vroom*, with its melded samples of Howlin' Wolf and the Andrews Sisters. There's enough strong music on *Irresistible Bliss* to suggest that the album is merely a slight sophomore slump, but that still doesn't make the long stretches of tediousness on the album any more forgivable. *—Stephen Thomas Erlewine*

El Oso / Sep. 29, 1998 / Warner Brothers ♦♦♦♦
One approaches this album with trepidation: can they really do it again? Can the band that singlehandedly defined postmodern white-boy funk poetry in 1994 with *Ruby Vroom* and dodged the sophomore slump with deceptive ease two years later come up with something just as good that isn't simply rehash? The answer is a qualified yes, and they do it by leaving the skeleton—bare-bones funky drums, big string bass, scratchy guitar—mostly the same, while fleshing out the vocals a bit and yoking the pointillistic samples to the wagon of the song, at least part of the time. Thus, on "Circles," the album's first single, you have overdubbed harmonies (!) and a bleeping synth that supports the chorus rhythmically. And you could actually sing along with "Blame." That's not to say that this stuff is exactly tuneful—poetry and groove are still the whole point. But it's nice to hear M. Doughty hauling off and singing every so often. Nothing here packs quite the same revelatory wallop as "Blue-Eyed Devil" or "Casiotone Nation" did, but then, the revelation has already been received. That doesn't make it any less valuable. Or any less funky. *—Rick Anderson*

Soul II Soul

f. 1989, London, England

Club/Dance, Acid House, Urban, House, Dance-Pop

Led by producer/vocalist/songwriter DJ Jazzie B, Soul II Soul were one of the most innovative dance/R&B outfits of the late '80s, creating a seductive, deep R&B that borrowed from Philly soul, disco, reggae, and '80s hip-hop. Featuring the vocals of Caron Wheeler, Soul II Soul's third single "Keep on Movin'," reached the U.K. Top Five in March of 1989. Released in the summer of 1989, "Back to Life" also featured Wheeler and became another Top Ten hit. Soul II Soul released their debut album, *Club Classics Volume One* (known as *Keep on Movin'* in the U.S.), shortly afterward. Wheeler left the group before the recording of the group's second album, *Vol. II: 1990—A New Decade*. The album debuted at number one in the U.K., yet it caught the group in a holding pattern. Producer/arranger Hooper soon left the collective, leaving Jazzie B. to soldier on alone. Hooper went on to work with several of the most influential and popular acts of the early '90s, including Massive Attack (*Blue Lines*), Bjork (*Debut* and *Post*), Madonna (*Bedtime Stories*), and U2 ("Hold Me, Thrill Me, Kiss Me, Kill Me"). *—Stephen Thomas Erlewine*

● **Keep on Movin'** / Jun. 1989 / Virgin ✦✦✦✦✦

When American urban-contemporary radio was bombarding its listeners with one Guy clone after another in the late '80s and early '90s, British neo-soulsters like Soul II Soul, Lisa Stansfield, and the Chimes offered highly creative and gutsy alternatives. With influences ranging from Chic to hip-hop to African music, Soul II Soul's debut album, *Keep on Movin'* (titled *Club Classics, Vol. 1* in its original British incarnation), was among the most rewarding R&B releases of 1989. Soul II Soul leader/producer/composer Jazzie B. takes one risk after another—all of which pay off. The group enjoyed major hits with the Chic-influenced gems "Keep on Movin'" and "Back to Life" (both of which feature the gifted Caron Wheeler), and equally superb are the African-influenced reflections of "Dance" and "Holdin' On," the soulful grit and intensity of "Feel Free," and the hypnotic house music of "Happiness." Though Wheeler was Soul II Soul's best-known singer and went on to enjoy a career as a solo artist, Rose Windross and Do'Reen (both expressive soul divas) also do their part to make *Keep on Movin'* the artistic triumph that it is. *—Alex Henderson*

Vol. II: 1990, A New Decade / May 21, 1990 / Virgin ✦✦✦✦

A better album but a deceptive one: even the best songs here don't intoxicate as thoroughly as "Keep on Movin'," but within the context of the album, each plays a vital part. In other words, this is a genuine *album*, and not a pastiche of singles. *—John Floyd*

Vol. III: Just Right / Apr. 13, 1992 / Virgin ✦✦

Vol. IV: The Classic Singles 1988-1993 / Dec. 6, 1993 / Virgin ✦✦✦✦✦

This compilation captures the essence of ultra-sophisticated R&B and house music at a turning point, before the sample-heavy storm of American R&B took over in the early '90s. Soul II Soul brought an organic feeling to their music, which shines through on this stellar compilation. The music was sleek, the vocals were clear, and the beats were irresistible. This collection assembles the hits and singles from the ever-evolving act's first three albums. "Back to Life," the group's biggest stateside hit, is included in its single form, which was dramatically different from the original album version, which made many purchasers of *Keep on Movin'* very disappointed when they realized the song they heard on the radio was clearly not the one on the album. Other singles, such as "Jazzie's Groove" and "A Dream's a Dream" are also included in their radio/video versions. The album includes their other big hit, "Keep on Movin'" (unfortunately in an edited form—the full-length album version was better), as well as other key singles, such as the rousing "Joy," the gritty club hit "Fairplay," and the ballad "Move Me No Mountain." From slick R&B ballads to Philly-inspired soul, from hip-hop to house music, Soul II Soul's hit collection offers up a musical smorgasbord that neatly highlights the outfit's greatest successes. As a final note, this album is only available as an import and has yet to see the light of day in the U.S. *—Jose Promis*

Vol. V: Believe / Aug. 11, 1995 / Virgin ✦✦✦

Six years after they revolutionized R&B and soul with their debut album, *Keep on Movin'*, Soul II Soul returned with *Vol. V: Believe*. Since their debut, the soul collective had been struggling to regain their position as musical innovators; in the process, they turned out two confused albums that had their moments, but nothing quite as stirring as their initial singles, which were collected on the British-only *Volume IV: The Classic Singles*. *Believe*, their fourth album of original material, doesn't necessarily make a case for Soul II Soul as pioneers in the mid-'90s, but it does represent something of a comeback. Where their two previous albums were muddled affairs, *Believe* is clear and confident, filled with fully formed songs. It helps that Jazzie B, the leader of the group, has persuaded former members Caron Wheeler and Penny Ford to make appearances on the album and has recruited some genuine new talent that helps spark him into recording his best music since the group's debut. Granted, it doesn't push down many boundaries, but *Believe* fits comfortably into the laid-back, jazz-saturated grooves of '90s R&B. *—Stephen Thomas Erlewine*

Jimmy Soul

b. Aug. 24, 1942, Weldon, NC, **d.** Jun. 25, 1988, New York, NY

Vocals / R&B, Soul

Born on August 24, 1942 in Weldon, NC, Jimmy Soul became a preacher at the age of seven and performed gospel as a teenager, becoming known locally as "The Wonder Boy." His talent was noticed by Frank Guida, engineer of the legendary Norfolk sound, and was recruited to record some of the calypso-based songs that Guida had hand-picked for one of his other hit artists, Gary U.S. Bonds. Soul's only two charting hits were both Bonds' cast-offs, 1962's "Twistin' Matilda" and 1963's number one hit, "If You Wanna Be Happy." That song, with its upbeat, vibrant Caribbean sound was a huge success and prompted Soul to try to recreate the success of his hit with some fairly derivative West Indian songs like "Treat 'Em Tough" and "A Woman is Smarter in Every Kinda Way," but he failed to chart again and later joined the army, giving up his career in music. He died of a heart attack on June 25, 1988, at the age of 45. *—Stacia Proefrock*

● **The Best of Jimmy Soul** / 1992 / Rhino ✦✦✦✦✦

Jimmy Soul wasn't the most original or varied of soul singers, but he had a light touch and effervescent charm that made his singles perfect for beach parties. Rhino's *The Best of Jimmy Soul* contains his 18 best singles, including not only "If You Wanna Be Happy," but a lot of rewrites of that song, such as "My Baby Loves to Bowl." Nothing is as good as that big hit, and this is awful samey, but it keeps it's mood grooving from start to finish, and provides a good time—provided that you're looking for sound, not songs. *—Stephen Thomas Erlewine*

If You Wanna Be Happy: The Very Best of Jimmy Soul / Feb. 20, 1996 / Ace ✦✦✦✦

Even though it contains a bunch of the same material, Ace's *If You Wanna Be Happy: The Very Best of Jimmy Soul* trumps the Rhino collection, since it cuts out novelties and has a sharper track selection. This still is a lot of Jimmy Soul, probably too much for most listeners, but if you're serious about your pop-soul, this is the Jimmy Soul collection to get. *—Stephen Thomas Erlewine*

Soundgarden

f. 1984, Seattle, WA, **db.** Apr. 9, 1997

Alternative Metal, Grunge, Alternative Pop/Rock, Heavy Metal

Soundgarden made a place for heavy metal in alternative rock. Their fellow Seattle rockers Green River may have spearheaded the grunge sound, but they relied on noise rock in the vein of the Stooges. Similarly, Jane's Addiction was too fascinated with prog rock and performance art to appeal to a wide array of metal fans. Soundgarden, however, developed directly out of the grandiose blues-rock of Led Zeppelin and the sludgy, slow riffs of Black Sabbath. Which isn't to say they were a straight-ahead metal band. Soundgarden borrowed the D.I.Y. aesthetics of punk, melding their guitar-driven sound with an intelligence and ironic sense of humor that was indebted to the American underground of the mid-'80s. Furthermore, the band rarely limited themselves to simple, pounding riffs, often making detours into psychedelia. But the group's key sonic signatures—the gutsy wail of vocalist Chris Cornell and the winding riffs of guitarist Kim Thayil—were what brought the band out of the underground. Not only were they one of the first groups to record for the legendary Seattle indie Sub Pop, but they were the first grunge band to sign to a major label. In fact, most critics expected Soundgarden to be the band that broke down the doors for alternative rock, not Nirvana. However, the group didn't experience an across-the-boards success until 1994, when *Superunknown* became a number one hit. *—Stephen Thomas Erlewine*

Ultramega OK / 1988 / SST ✦✦✦✦

The best expression of Soundgarden's early, Stooges/MC5-meets-Zeppelin/Sabbath sound, *Ultramega OK* is a dark, murky, buzzing record that simultaneously subverts and pays tribute to heavy metal. At times, the band and its recasting of over-the-top '70s hard rock seem smirky (Hiro Yamamoto's ridiculous vocal on "Circle of Power"; a "cover" of John Lennon's "One Minute of Silence"); a few, like the cover of "Smokestack Lightning," really do sink into turgid metal silliness. But the best moments are startling fusions of classic metal, punk rock, and psychedelia of the fuzz-guitar variety, plus the local flavor of Green River and the Melvins. The difference was, Soundgarden were better songwriters, and their feel for memorable riffs and hooks lends greater power to both the rockers and the creepy, dirge-like slow numbers. It's a shame the album as a whole isn't more fully realized, because when separated out from the filler, the numerous highlights show why Soundgarden had such an enormous impact on the development of grunge. It may not be quite as complex or consistent as some of Soundgarden's later albums, but *Ultramega OK* is easily the best document of grunge's early, pre-Nirvana days. *—Steve Huey*

Louder Than Love / 1990 / A&M ✦✦✦

Signing to a major label, Soundgarden take a step toward the metal mainstream with *Louder Than Love*, a slow, grinding, detuned mountain of Sabbath/Zeppelin riffs and Chris Cornell wailing. The production is even murkier than usual—this time too much so, as the rest of the band tries to poke its way through Kim Thayil's guitar squall; additionally, too much of the album drifts along without focus or variety. But there are some essential Soundgarden items mixed in, among them the haunting "Hands All Over," the punky "Full On Kevin's Mom," and the stereotypically macho metal stupidity of "Big Dumb Sex," whose ironic intent is often misconstrued. Unfortunately, that irony is missing from the plodding, overblown filler that constitutes about half of the album. It's worthwhile to sift through *Louder Than Love*, but don't expect consistency. *—Steve Huey*

Screaming Life/Fopp / Jun. 1990 / Sub Pop ✦✦✦

Soundgarden's first two EPs for Sub Pop weren't particularly impressive at first listen, since they wallowed a bit too heavily in sub-Sabbath and Zeppelin riffery, but in retrospect, the record offers a good indication of where the band would go. Still, they aren't as sonically powerful as they would later become, nor are their songs particularly compelling, making this only interesting as a historical recording. *—Stephen Thomas Erlewine*

Badmotorfinger / 1991 / A&M ✦✦✦✦✦

Bidding for a popular breakthrough with their second major-label album, Soundgarden suddenly developed a sense of craft, with the result that *Badmotorfinger* became far and away their most fully realized album to that point. Pretty much everything about *Badmotorfinger* is a step up from its predecessors—the production is sharper and the music more ambitious, while the songwriting takes a quantum leap in focus and consistency. In so doing, the band abolishes the murky meandering that had often plagued them in the past, turning in a lean, muscular set that signaled their arrival in rock's big leagues. Conventional wisdom has it that despite platinum sales, *Badmotorfinger* got lost amidst the blockbuster success of *Nevermind* and *Ten* (all were released around the same time). But the fact is that, though they're all great records, *Badmotorfinger* is much less accessible by comparison. Not that it isn't melodic, but it also sounds twisted and gnarled, full of dissonant riffing, impossible time signatures, howling textural solos, and weird, droning tonalities. It's surprisingly cerebral and arty music for a band courting mainstream metal audiences, but it attacks with scientific precision. Part of that is due to the presence of new bassist Ben Shepherd, who gives the band its thickest rhythmic foundation yet—and, moreover, immediately shoulders the departed Hiro Yamamoto's share of songwriting duties. But it's apparent that the whole band has greatly expanded the scope of their ambitions. And *Badmotorfinger* fulfills them, pulling all the different threads of the band's sound together into a mature, confident, well-written record. This is heavy, challenging hard rock full of intellectual sensibility and complex band interplay. And with their next album, Soundgarden would learn how to make it fully accessible to mainstream audiences as well. —*Steve Huey*

● **Superunknown** / Mar. 8, 1994 / A&M ✦✦✦✦✦
Soundgarden's finest hour, *Superunknown* is a sprawling, 70-minute magnum opus that pushes beyond any previous boundaries. Soundgarden had always loved replicating Led Zeppelin and Black Sabbath riffs, but *Superunknown's* debt is more to mid-period Zep's layered arrangements and sweeping epics. Their earlier punk influences are rarely detectable, replaced by surprisingly effective appropriations of pop and psychedelia. *Badmotorfinger* boasted more than its fair share of indelible riffs, but here the main hooks reside mostly in Cornell's vocals; accordingly, he's mixed right up front, floating over the band instead of cutting through it. The rest of the production is just as crisp, with the band achieving a huge, robust sound that makes even the heaviest songs sound deceptively bright. But the most important reasons *Superunknown* is such a rich listen are twofold: the band's embrace of psychedelia, and their rapidly progressing mastery of songcraft. Soundgarden had always been a little mind-bending, but the full-on experiments with psychedelia give them a much wider sonic palette, paving the way for less metallic sounds and instruments, more detailed arrangements, and a bridge into pop (which made the eerie ballad "Black Hole Sun" an inescapable hit). That blossoming melodic skill is apparent on most of the record, not just the poppier songs and Chris Cornell-penned hits; though a couple of drummer Matt Cameron's contributions are pretty undistinguished, they're easy to overlook, given the overall consistency. The focused songwriting allows the band to stretch material out for grander effect, without sinking into the pointlessly drawn-out muck that cluttered their early records. The dissonance and odd time signatures are still in force, though not as jarring or immediately obvious, which means that the album reveals more subtleties with each listen. It's obvious that *Superunknown* was consciously styled as a masterwork, and it fulfills every ambition. —*Steve Huey*

Down on the Upside / May 21, 1996 / A&M ✦✦✦
Superunknown was a breakthrough in many ways. Not only did the album bring Soundgarden a new audience, it dramatically expanded their vision, as well as their accomplishments. If *Down on the Upside* initially seems a retreat from the grand, layered textures of *Superunknown*, let it sink in. The sound of *Down on the Upside* is certainly more immediate, but the band hasn't returned to the monstrous, unfocused wailing of *Louder Than Love*. Instead, they've retained their ambitious song structures, neo-psychedelic guitar textures, and winding melodies but haven't dressed them up with detailed production. Consequently, *Down on the Upside* is visceral as well as cerebral—"Rhinosaur" goes for the gut, while "Pretty Noose" is updated, muscular prog rock. *Down on the Upside* is a deceptive album—it might seem like nothing more than heavy metal, but a closer listen reveals that Soundgarden hasn't tempered their ambitions at all. —*Stephen Thomas Erlewine*

● **A-Sides** / Nov. 4, 1997 / A&M ✦✦✦✦✦
For an act that was one of the definitive album artists of the late '80s and '90s, Soundgarden was a surprisingly effective singles band. Their singles effectively conveyed all of their best ideas, from their sludgy early Sub Pop recordings to the elaborate, post-metal psychedelia of their last two albums, *Superunknown* and *Down on the Upside*. That's the reason why the 17-track compilation *A-Sides* is such a successful overview of the band's too-brief career. Most of their peers wouldn't be well represented by a compilation that concentrated solely on singles, but Soundgarden is, because their singles *do* capture what they're all about. There are many great songs left off *A-Sides*, from "Big Dumb Sex" to "My Wave," but it's hard to argue with what's here. Each single from every album—from the 1987 debut EP *Screaming Life* through SST's *Ultramega OK*, to their four records for A&M—is here, with the *Down on the Upside* outtake "Bleed Together" added as an enticement for collectors. Almost every one of the group's best-known songs are here, including "Hands All Over," "Loud Love," "Jesus Christ Pose," "Outshined," "Rusty Cage," "Black Hole Sun," "The Day I Tried to Live," "Spoonman," "Fell on Black Days," "Pretty Noose," "Burden in My Hand" and "Blow Up the Outside World," resulting in a near-definitive summary of one of the most important and influential bands of the '90s. —*Stephen Thomas Erlewine*

Epic Soundtracks (Kevin Paul Godfrey)

b. 1960, London, England, **d.** Nov. 22, 1997
Vocals, Piano / Indie Rock, Alternative Pop/Rock, Singer/Songwriter
In the '70s, Epic Soundtracks formed Swell Maps, with his brother, Nikki Sudden; the band influenced many groups, from Sonic Youth to the Lemonheads. Considering his past, it may seem strange that Epic returned in the early '90s after a long hiatus to write

moving piano ballads. His first solo LP, *Rise Above*, featured J. Mascis and Kim Gordon, among others. He returned two years later with a second album, *Sleeping Star, Change My Life* followed in 1996. Sadly, Soundtracks was discovered dead in his flat on November 22, 1997, presumably the victim of a suicide; the posthumous *Everything Is Temporary* followed two years later. —*John Bush*

● **Rise Above** / 1993 / Bar/None ✦✦✦✦✦
Epic Soundtracks writes affecting piano ballads and mid-tempo pieces with an ease that belies how good these songs are. Though J. Mascis (drums on two tracks) and Kim Gordon (voice on "Big Apple Graveyard") do contribute, this is Epic's show; he provides most of the music and all the magic. Many songs have a traditional feel and sound strangely familiar. —*John Bush*

Sleeping Star / Oct. 19, 1994 / Bar/None ✦✦✦
Sleeping Star is not exactly identical to Epic's first album, but little has changed. The songs still have that traditional ballad feel; witness "Tonight's the Night (Rock & Roll Lullabye)," a song that borrows heavily from the long history of ballad procedure. Not that any of this is bad. "Emily May" has a rolling piano line and up-tempo rhythm that makes it the highlight of the disc. Most of the songs, however, are a bit too traditional to provoke any reaction by the listener. —*John Bush*

Change My Life / Apr. 23, 1996 / Bar/None ✦✦✦
It's basically more of the same from Mr. Soundtracks on his third album, which isn't necessarily a bad thing. He doesn't solely stick to the loungish piano ballads that have been his trademark, occasionally jangling things up a bit. Considering his background, though, his best assets are turning out to be the surprisingly conventional ones of tuneful, affecting slow pieces. These should appeal to fans of John Cale, David Bowie, Alex Chilton, and Brian Wilson, to name a few reference points. When he tries to rock harder, the results are strained and awkward, as his voice isn't strong enough to carry raucous material. —*Richie Unterberger*

Everything Is Temporary / Apr. 13, 1999 / Innerstate ✦✦✦✦
From studio outtakes and radio broadcasts to home recordings, Soundtracks' brother and kindred musical spirit Nikki Sudden combed his sibling's massive tape collection for this posthumous tribute. The essence of Soundtracks is captured here: The gentle, under-appreciated, alienated, cult figure with a vocal range and sense of melody that at times can make you weep. There's the noise fest of "Wild Situation," yet there's a beautiful solo acoustic version of "Something New Under the Sun"; the keyboard outtake, "Caroline" is equally lovely. Alex Chilton's popular "Night Time" is also included here. Truth be told, covers are unnecessary—Soundtracks has track upon track of his own which capture the loneliness of Big Star's *Third* and other sadcore touchstones. Clearly this was a songwriter worth reckoning with during his short lifetime. —*Denise Sullivan*

The Soup Dragons

f. 1986, Glasgow, Scotland, **db.** 1994
C-86, Alternative Dance, Alternative Pop/Rock
Glasgow's Soup Dragons began as a Buzzcocks-styled punk-pop band and gradually moved into an indie-rock/dance fusion. Centered around singer/guitarist/songwriter Sean Dickson, the band also contained guitarist Jim McCulloch, bassist Sushil Dade, and drummer Ross Sinclair; Dickson and McCulloch had also played in a group called the BMX Bandits. The Soup Dragons took their name from characters on a children's television show and caught the attention of former Wham! manager Jazz Summers, who helped them get a record deal. Their debut EP, *Hang-Ten*, and first full-length album, *This Is Our Art*, didn't make much of a splash, but *Lovegod*, with its U.K. hit single "Mother Universe," established the band as a force. 1992's *Hotwired* produced the American hit "Divine Thing," but two years later, Dickson was the group's only remaining member. He has released two albums, without matching prior success. —*Steve Huey*

Hang-Ten! / 1987 / Sire ✦✦✦✦✦

This Is Our Art / 1988 / Sire ✦✦
Many bands would kill for a song as immediately lovable as the Soup Dragons' "Soft As Your Face" from *This Is Our Art*; however, while the track reveals the group's ability to craft clever, hummable pop, the rest of the LP unveils the band's lack of punch. "Soft As Your Face," with its jaunty acoustic guitars and warm harmonies, outshines almost everything else on the album. On "Kingdom Chairs," vocalist Sean Dickson tries to imitate the snarl of a '60s garage rocker; unfortunately, he isn't convincing, and the group sounds anemic, unable to unleash the raw power necessary to make the song crackle. The Soup Dragons aim for the punk-pop of the Buzzcocks on "Great Empty Space," but the lyrics fail to make an impact. The band cranks up the amps even louder on "Passion Protein," veering closely to heavy metal, and they seem as if they're trying too hard to show that they're not a wimpy new wave act. The Soup Dragons are far more effective when they're gorging themselves on bubblegum like the sweet jangle pop of "Soft As Your Face" and "Turning Stone." The Soup Dragons bite off more than they can chew on *This Is Our Art*; nevertheless, "Soft As Your Face" and "Turning Stone" melt in the mouth like the most delicious candy. —*Michael Sutton*

Lovegod / 1990 / Big Life ✦✦✦
The Soup Dragons' *Lovegod* is packed with contradictions; the synthesizers and breakbeats don't match the psychedelic cover art, and the guitars seem out of place within the slick production. If *Lovegod* is where the Soup Dragons supposedly found their sound—and it is—they still hadn't fine-tuned it to the level it would reach in a few short years. This isn't to say that *Lovegod* isn't an enjoyable album, though; in fact, it's quite the opposite: of the late-'80s/early-'90s explosion of British rock bands who made danceable rock music, the Soup Dragons were one of the most interesting and most fun. *Lovegod*

is far from an exception to this rule, and several of the band's best songs are included here: the hit "I'm Free," "Mother Universe," and the title track. What makes *Lovegod* frustrating, however, is that it feels as though the band is being held back. Given the way they let loose later—on *Hotwired* and *Hydrophonic*—on this album they sound too mannered, too rigidly following the rules implied by the overly stiff beats. It's not a disappointment, it just means that in retrospect, *Lovegod* was more of a transition album, more of a blueprint to come, than the statement that would define this band's unfortunately short career. —*Jason Damas*

● **Hotwired** / 1992 / Big Life ✦✦✦✦
Hotwired is where the Soup Dragons reached equilibrium—the happy medium between the slick breakbeats and guitar-based rock & roll. Throughout most of the album, the songs are among the strongest of the band's career and sonically the album is near perfect; fans of dance alternative will love singles like "Pleasure" and "Divine Thing" (both moderate hits in the U.S.) and rock fans will appreciate the crisp but not sterile instrumentation. There are many great production flourishes—like the "gospel choir"-like background vocals and fun sound effects—sprinkled throughout the disc. In fact, "Hotwired" is worth listening to for the chugging guitars on the fabulous "Getting Down" alone. For fans of this genre or fans of Brit-pop or even power pop in general, this is the place to start. —*Jason Damas*

Hydrophonic / 1995 / Phonogram ✦✦✦
By 1994, the British baggy-alternative-dance-Brit-pop movement had fizzled; the Happy Mondays were done, and the hits dried up for most of the lesser artists of the genre. This left the Soup Dragons in an interesting position: the band had roots in rock music (one band member would later be in Teenage Fanclub, two already been in the BMX Bandits), so it seemed to make sense to rock up the mix a bit. Commercially, the album stiffed like cold, lumpy mashed potatoes. Most critics probably ignored it, but to do so would be a great injustice. Not to say that *Hydrophonic* is groundbreaking, but it is solid. Many of the beats (which weren't that great anyway) were stripped from the Soup Dragons' sound, and the guitars were pushed way up in the mix. At the same time, funk and soul were both far more prominent, and the "rock" songs are sweaty, and, well, almost Stonesy. This isn't quite the same band that gave listeners hits like "I'm Free" or "Divine Thing," but they're a far less cartoonish version of themselves, and this particular period in the band's history never deserved to be ignored as it was. The rule is this: If you loved *Lovegod*, this may not be for you. If you liked the more rocking parts of *Hotwired*, and want to hear more, this is an extremely worthwhile place to go. Just try not to be seen digging for *Hydrophonic* in the cut-out bin. —*Jason Damas*

Joe South

b. Feb. 28, 1940, Atlanta, GA
Vocals, Guitar / Pop/Rock, Singer/Songwriter

Singer/songwriter Joe South (born Joe Souter) began his career as a country musician, performing on an Atlanta radio station and joining Pete Drake's band in 1957. The following year, he recorded a novelty single, "The Purple People Eater Meets the Witch Doctor," and became a session musician in Nashville and at Muscle Shoals. South appeared on records by Marty Robbins, Eddy Arnold, Aretha Franklin, Wilson Pickett, Bob Dylan (*Blonde on Blonde*), and Simon & Garfunkel ("The Sounds of Silence"). During the '60s, South began working on his songwriting, crafting hits for Deep Purple ("Hush") and several for Billy Joe Royal, including "Down in the Boondocks." South began recording his own material in 1968, scoring a hit with the Grammy-winning "Games People Play" (Song of the Year) the following year. While South produced hits like "Don't It Make You Want to Go Home" and "Walk a Mile in My Shoes," Lynn Anderson had a smash country and pop hit in 1971 with South's "(I Never Promised You a) Rose Garden."

South took several years off after his brother's suicide in 1971, moving to Maui and living in the jungles. He had proven a rather prickly character, recording a song entitled "I'm a Star"; he was also busted for drugs and, never entirely comfortable performing, was known for an antagonistic stance in concert (he once suggested that audience members start dancing around the concert hall and kiss his ass as they approached the stage). South briefly returned in 1975 with the *Midnight Rainbows* LP but retired from recording and performing soon afterwards. South returned in 1994 in a London concert showcasing American Southern performers and has since re-entered the music publishing industry. —*Steve Huey*

The Best of Joe South / Jul. 1990 / Rhino ✦✦✦✦✦
This album contains South's own hits plus the original songwriters' versions, including "Rose Garden," "Games People Play," and more. —*AMG*

● **Best of Joe South: Retrospect** / 1999 / Koch ✦✦✦✦✦

J.D. Souther

b. 1946, Detroit, MI
Vocals, Songwriter, Guitar / Urban Cowboy, Pop/Rock, Folk-Rock, Soft Rock, Adult Contemporary, Singer/Songwriter, Country-Rock

While J.D. Souther may have made his biggest impact on the country-rock sound behind the scenes or in a supporting role to some of the '70s bigger pop names, he had an impressive and critically acclaimed series of solo albums that have unfortunately all but disappeared from music fans' radar.

Born in Detroit, Souther was raised in Amarillo, TX, which may help explain his stylistic roots in both country and rock music. He was in a band called John David and the Senders (also known as the Cinders) while in high school, later relocating to Los Angeles. He worked as a session musician, meeting Glenn Frey and eventually renting a house with him; the two were signed to Amos Records and recorded an album under the name

Longbranch Pennywhistle. Souther's connections with Frey would prove fruitful later, collaborating on some of the Eagles biggest hit songs like "Best of My Love," "Heartache Tonight," and "New Kid in Town." Previous to forming the Eagles, Frey had also played in Linda Ronstadt's band; their collaboration would lead to a long-term working partnership between Souther and Ronstadt. He produced her 1973 album, *Don't Cry Now*, and performed background vocals on it. Many of Ronstadt's albums would feature Souther's songs from then on, and he often performed as a vocalist on them as well. David Geffen encouraged Souther to form the Souther, Hillman, and Furay Band with Chris Hillman and Ritchie Furay. The trio would record two albums before disbanding in 1975. Souther's country-rock style was featured on four critically acclaimed but not particularly commercially successful solo albums, 1972's *John David Souther*, 1976's *Black Rose*, 1979's *You're Only Lonely*, and 1984's *Home by Dawn*. Frequent label changes plagued Souther, with each new company struggling to promote his music. Between albums he also worked as a session player with Don Henley and Danny Kortchmar and collaborated with James Taylor on his song, "Her Town Too," which appeared on Taylor's 1981 album. The late '80s brought a bit of a career change for Souther, as he garnered acting roles for film and television. He had a recurring role on the television series *Thirtysomething*, as well as roles in two independent films, *To Cross the Rubicon* and *How to Make the Cruelest Month*. —*Stacia Proefrock*

John David Souther / 1972 / Elektra ✦✦✦✦
It may be that the only thing that kept Souther from becoming a major star in the '70s was that his friends the Eagles beat him to the country-rock style demonstrated on this album, which features "The Fast One" and "Run Like a Thief," both recorded by Linda Ronstadt. —*William Ruhlmann*

Black Rose / 1976 / Elektra ✦✦✦✦✦
Excellent album steeped in the Southern California country-rock sound of the '70s, with all the usual suspects (Danny Kortchmar, Waddy Wachtel, Kenny Edwards, and Russ Kunkel, and producer Peter Asher—all Ronstadt veterans—plus Glenn Frey and Don Henley from the Eagles) in place on such songs as "Faithless Love," "Simple Man, Simple Dream," and "Silver Blue." —*William Ruhlmann*

● **You're Only Lonely** / 1979 / Columbia ✦✦✦✦✦
Souther finally scored a hit single with the 50s-ish title track, and the album also includes such lovely ballads as "White Rhythm and Blues," as well as the solo version of the Souther, Hillman, Furay song "Trouble in Paradise." —*William Ruhlmann*

Home by Dawn / 1984 / Warner Brothers ✦✦✦

Southside Johnny

b. Dec. 4, 1948, New Jersey
Vocals, Harmonica / Bar Band, Heartland Rock, Album Rock, Rock & Roll, R&B

Southside Johnny and the Asbury Jukes were the second group after Bruce Springsteen and the E Street Band to emerge from the New Jersey shore scene, and though they carried over a significant influence (and some key personnel) from their predecessors, they were a more generic white R&B band steeped in the Memphis Stax Records tradition. The group was organized in 1974 by singer John Lyon and guitarist/songwriter "Miami" Steve Van Zandt. Van Zandt decamped for the E Street Band in 1975, but he continued to direct the Jukes, managing them, writing their songs, and producing their records. The group signed to Epic Records and released *I Don't Want to Go Home* (1976), which featured songwriting by Springsteen and cameos by Ronnie Spector and Lee Dorsey. *This Time It's for Real* (1977) contained more Springsteen tunes and appearances by the Coasters, the Drifters, and the Five Satins. Critical consensus said that the third album, *Hearts of Stone* (1978), was the Jukes' peak, but they failed to break through to mass success. —*William Ruhlmann*

I Don't Want to Go Home / 1976 / Epic ✦✦✦✦
The Jukes' debut is an R&B revivalist's delight, capped by splendid duets with Lee Dorsey ("How Come You Treat Me So Bad?") and Ronnie Spector ("You Mean So Much to Me"). —*Kit Kiefer*

This Time It's for Real / 1977 / Epic ✦✦✦✦✦
Southside Johnny and the Asbury Jukes' second album suffers a bit in comparison to their debut, *I Don't Want to Go Home*; while the first album boasted a number of songs that would become staples of the band's killer live show for years to come (such as "The Fever," "Broke Down Piece of Man," and "I Don't Want to Go Home"), *This Time It's for Real* kicks off with a powerhouse, roof-raising anthem (the title cut) and never comes up with another song that hits quite as hard. Most of *This Time It's for Real* finds Southside and the Jukes (and their behind-the-scenes mastermind, Miami Steve Van Zandt) in a soulful mood, with vintage R&B groups the Coasters, the Drifters, and the Five Satins lending vocals to three tunes. While much of the album stays in a mid-tempo R&B groove, the band is in superb form throughout (especially the truly mighty Miami Horns), and Southside Johnny more than holds his own as a soul belter, no mean feat with some of the great men of R&B on hand as guests. A stack of fine songs from Van Zandt (and his old buddy Bruce Springsteen) adds the icing to the cake; while purists might wish it rocked harder, *This Time It's for Real* proves that Southside Johnny and the Asbury Jukes were one of the finest R&B-based show bands of the 1970s. And as a bonus, read the liner notes for the inside scoop on what the string players had for lunch! —*Mark Deming*

Hearts of Stone / 1978 / Epic ✦✦✦✦✦
This is the most successful merger of old R&B with modern songwriting and sensibilities in the Jukes' catalog. "Hearts of Stone" features more great Van Zandt originals ("Got to Be a Better Way Home," "This Time Baby's Gone for Good") and Springsteen's knockout title tune. —*Kit Kiefer*

Havin' a Party With Southside Johnny / 1979 / Epic ✦✦✦✦✦

The Jukes / 1979 / Mercury ✦✦✦

After none of the Jukes' first three records got higher than number 85 in the charts, Epic Records dropped the band. The feeling was that Southside was too closely identified with Springsteen and Van Zandt and needed to establish a separate identity. So, the band dumped its producer and songwriter and moved to Mercury Records for its fourth album, on which Jukes guitarist Billy Rush took over the songwriting. Given that, however, the result is not half bad. Southside and Rush collaborate on the excellent leadoff track, "All I Want Is Everything," and Rush contributes "I'm So Anxious," "Living in the Real World," and several other respectable numbers. The glory days were over, and the band really wouldn't make a big success on its own, but they remained workmen making the best of a bad situation. *—William Ruhlmann*

Love Is a Sacrifice / 1980 / Mercury ✦✦

Reach Up & Touch the Sky: Live / 1981 / Mercury ✦✦✦

Southside Johnny and the Asbury Jukes' first commercially released live album, a two-LP set, was recorded in June and July 1980 and allowed the band to mine its catalog for songs previously heard on the excellent Epic albums as well as re-opening the door on covers (there's a fine Sam Cooke medley). They may have been at an artistic impasse, but they were a fun band to see live. *—William Ruhlmann*

Trash It Up / 1983 / Mirage ✦✦

In the Heat / 1984 / Atco ✦✦✦

At Least We Got Shoes / 1986 / Atlantic ✦✦✦

Billy Rush had decamped by the time the Jukes reconvened to record their third and final Atlantic album. Southside Johnny's originals were only okay, although the selection of covers—"Walk Away Renee" and "I Only Want to Be With You"—was stellar as usual. Still, this was something of a swan song for the band, who did not record again for five years. *—William Ruhlmann*

Better Days / Oct. 1991 / Impact ✦✦✦✦

A comeback album that by all rights shouldn't be this good, *Better Days* reunites Southside Johnny with his old cohorts Springsteen and Van Zandt and some special guests (Jon Bon Jovi, Flo and Eddie) for 11 bittersweet originals capped by the gorgeous soul ballad "It's Been a Long Time." *—Kit Kiefer*

● **The Best of Southside Johnny & the Asbury Jukes** / Aug. 11, 1992 / Epic/Legacy ✦✦✦✦✦

Concentrating on the highlights from Southside Johnny & The Asbury Jukes' late-'70s albums, *Best of Southside Johnny* offers a good introduction to the hard R&B-influenced rock of the New Jersey band. *—Stephen Thomas Erlewine*

All I Want Is Everything: The Best of Southside Johnny & the Asbury Jukes / 1993 / Rhino ✦✦✦✦✦

The companion to Epic's *Best Of* (52733), this 14-song compilation traces the Jukes' career through their stints on Mercury/Polygram, Mirage/Atlantic, and Impact/MCA. These were not their best years, but on each album they managed a few worthy cuts, and this set chooses the best of the period, making for a collection that nearly matches the Epic years. *—William Ruhlmann*

Spittin' Fire / 1997 / Grapevine Musidisc ✦✦

Spacemen 3

f. 1982, Rugby, Midlands, England, **db.** 1991

College Rock, Space Rock, Neo-Psychedelia, Post-Punk, Alternative Pop/Rock

Spacemen 3 were psychedelic in the loosest sense of the word; their guitar explorations were colorfully mind-alterating, but not in the sense of the acid rock of the '60s. Instead, the band developed its own minimalistic psychedelia, relying on heavily distorted guitars to clash and produce their own harmonic overtones; frequently, they would lead up to walls of distortion with over-amplified acoustic guitars and synths. Often the band would jam on one chord or play a series of songs, all in the same tempo and key. Though this approach was challenging, often bordering on the avant garde, Spacemen 3 nevertheless gained a dedicated cult following. At first the band sounded a bit like a punked-up garage rock band, but their music quickly evolved into their signature trance-like neo-psychedelia. Spacemen 3's second album, 1987's *The Perfect Prescription*, was the first to capture the group's distinctive style. By the time of the release of *Recurring*, singer/guitarist Jason Pierce was performing in a new band called Spiritualized, while fellow singer/guitarist Scott "Sonic Boom" Kember formed Spectrum. *—Stephen Thomas Erlewine*

Sound of Confusion / 1986 / Taang ✦✦✦

Sonic Boom's liner notes from the 1994 reissue in many ways capture the whole point of Spacemen 3's full-length debut: "[It] was basically an exorcism for us of our early material... we began our discography with an equal nod to our influences and our inspirations." Indeed, calling *Sound of Confusion* derivative misses the point entirely, where calling it anything but a clear and specific homage to a sound and style would be a complete mistake. Three of its seven songs are cover versions—"Rollercoaster" by the 13th Floor Elevators, "Mary Anne" by Juicy Lucy, and the Stooges' "Little Doll"—while the originals are at once very much Spacemen 3 songs and clear distillations of everything the band members were tripping out on at the time. Though Sonic and Pierce later expressed a preference for the takes included on the *Taking Drugs to Make Music* bootleg, the rough garage energy throughout still makes *Sound of Confusion* a fine listen, if nowhere near as stunning as where the band would later go. As was the case throughout the band's early days, Pierce handled all the vocals with the right amount of diffidence and low-key intensity, while he and Sonic cranked up the amps for minimal, bluntly entrancing riffs and the Brooker/Bain rhythm section chugged along. Of the originals, leadoff cut "Losing Touch With My Mind" is the strongest of the bunch, a perfect fusion of the psych/proto-punk/drone influences of its creators sent into the outer void. Meanwhile, "Hey Man," the title audibly playing off the rhythm and sound of the word "amen," is the first of many overt references to gospel music that Pierce would incorporate for years to come. Some later CD versions included the *Walking With Jesus* EP for bonus tracks, along with one of the many demo takes on "2:35." *—Ned Raggett*

Perfect Prescription / 1987 / Taang ✦✦✦✦✦

Drawing together some earlier material and a slew of new songs, Spacemen 3 tied everything together on the brilliant *Perfect Prescription*, the clear point of departure from tribute to psych inspirations and finding its own unique voice. Planned as a concept album, *Perfect Prescription* works where so many other similar efforts failed due to the strength of the individual songs, as well as the smart focus of the concept in question—a vision of a drug trip from inception to its blasted conclusion, highs and lows fully intact. The bookending of the album makes that much clear—"Take Me to the Other Side" is a brash, exultant charge into the joys of the experience, a sharp, tight performance. "Call the Doctor," meanwhile, is a pretty-but-wounded conclusion, husky singing and a drowsy mood detailing the final collapse. The many highlights in between beginning and end are so striking that the album is practically a best-of in all but name. Sonic's eventual work with Spectrum and E.A.R. gets clearly signaled via the majestic reprise of the *Transparent Radiation* single, here introduced by the swirling flange of an edited "Ecstasy Symphony," also originally from that release. Sonic's breathless delivery of the Red Krayola classic, combined with the elegant arrangement, is a marvel to hear. "Walkin' With Jesus," meanwhile, is practically the birth of Spiritualized, the much different earlier takes now become a reflective combination of acoustic guitar, two-note keyboard lines, and Pierce's yearning, aching desire. The intentionally nasty flip to that is the storming charge of "Things'll Never Be the Same," a call to arms (or injecting something into them) that's as disturbing as it is energetic, the compressed, violent rage of feedback and rhythmic charge a gripping listen. Guest performers from the Jazz Butcher family tree, including Alex Green on sax, help expand the record's sonic range even further. Further reissues include a rotating series of bonus tracks from contemporary singles. *—Ned Raggett*

Performance / 1988 / Rough Trade ✦✦✦✦

Recorded in Amsterdam in 1988, the live *Performance* documents a set from the *Perfect Prescription* tour; the emphasis here is on the group's loud, noisy origins—only the closing "Feel So Good" hints at the more subdued atmospheres and textures which emerged as Spacemen 3's primary focus as they approached *Playing With Fire*. Among the highlights: "Take Me to the Other Side," "Walkin' With Jesus" and "Come Together." *—Jason Ankeny*

● **Playing With Fire** / 1989 / Taang ✦✦✦✦✦

Appropriately preceded by the mind-melting crunch of the "Revolution" single, *Playing With Fire* proved to be the end of Spacemen 3 as a functioning band, but in truly spectacular fashion. Exploring both the depths of serene, agog beauty and sheer tape-shredding chaos, *Playing With Fire* pushed the extremes of *The Perfect Prescription* to an even further edge. It's little surprise that Pierce and Sonic couldn't find themselves properly working together after it, but even less that hordes of bands to follow would rank *Playing With Fire* as the equal (or better) of psychedelia's '60s/'70s forebears. With future Spiritualized bassist Will Carruthers in place of Bain, the trio (and uncredited drummer) created glazed, liquid songs with subtle arrangements and sheer reveling in aural joys. Flange is everywhere, as is echo, full dynamic stereo mixes and more, a feast of sound. When aiming toward a gentler, hushed sound, most notably on Pierce's compositions, the incorporation of gospel power filtered through the band's own perspective results in wonders, as heard on "Come Down Softly to My Soul" and the album-closing "Lord Can You Hear Me?" As for the louder end of things, besides the awesome "Revolution" itself, a slow burn blast that just keeps getting more and more obsessive and frenetic as it goes, the other complete freak-out is "Suicide." Initial repressings of the album in the mid-'90s included tracks from the *Revolution* and *Threebie* singles, while an elaborate reissue in 1999 also including a full extra disc of demos and rarities, including covers of the Perfect Disaster's "Girl on Fire" and the Troggs' "Anyway That You Want Me"—eventually Spiritualized's first single. *—Ned Raggett*

Taking Drugs to Make Music to Take Drugs To / 1990 / Bomp ✦✦✦✦

Never has a record been so aptly titled, or so perfectly descriptive of a band's particular vision of the universe. For all that, the original appearance of *Taking Drugs* was in fact a bootleg on the semi-legendary/semi-notorious Father Yod imprint in 1990, later supplemented with contemporary outtakes and cuts for the Bomp reissue in 1994 and one further song for the Space Age version in 2000. The original seven tracks, dated January 1986 and the first recordings to feature Pete Bain on bass, are collectively known as the Northampton Demos, understandably named for the recording location in a studio outside said English city. Both Sonic and Pierce have been on record as long preferring these takes to the eventual versions that surfaced for the most part on *Sound of Confusion*. Certainly it's a fine set of performances, showing a definite step toward the more familiar sound of the group and away from the rougher takes on *For All the Fucked Up Children of the World*. "The Sound of Confusion," aka "Walkin' With Jesus," rips along with fierce energy, Pierce's singing and the rampaging, primitive wail and rumble of the band just wonderful. "Losing Touch With My Mind" takes things to an even higher level, a huge wallop of feedback and beat (Natty Brooker's drumming in particular delivers just what the doctor ordered), Pierce delivering the lines with a flat, cutting drawl. On the slightly lighter tip, "Come Down Easy" is more or less fully in place (aside from singing about it being 1986!), possessing a more upfront but less vocally distinct feel than the *Perfect Prescription* take. The tracks that surfaced on the later reissues come from a variety of different sessions, including the original take on "Feel So Good" and a good live version of "Things'll Never Be the Same," one of several cuts featuring Brooker's drumming replacement Rosco. *—Ned Raggett*

Dreamweapon: An Evening of Contemporary Sitar Music / 1990 / Fierce ♦♦♦♦♦
Taking off from the ideals which form the core of LaMonte Young's concept of Dream Music, the heart of *Dreamweapon* is "An Evening of Contemporary Sitar Music," a transfixing 40-minute-plus document of a landmark Spacemen 3 performance recorded at Waterman's Art Centre in Hammersmith on August 19, 1988. Perhaps the purest expression of the Spacemen aesthetic, the piece is an unbroken tapestry of hypnotic drones, throbbing tones, and repetitive phrases, dappled here and there by evaporating fragments of the melodies which later resurfaced on *Playing With Fire*. The cumulative effect is one of utter disorientation—all notions of time and space quickly give way to complete conscious immersion in the music's narcotic tug. A pair of epic rarities, Sonic Boom's feedback sculpture "Ecstasy in Slow Motion" and "Spacemen Jam," round out the package. *—Jason Ankeny*

Recurring / Mar. 1991 / Dedicated ♦♦♦♦
By the time *Recurring* was recorded, Pierce and Sonic had all but come to blows, and the end result shouldn't be considered an album proper so much as two EPs, with completely different personnel supporting their individual creations, Sonic's tracks appearing first. That they were even able to release it as a Spacemen 3 album at all seems to have been a fraught affair, but somehow it happened, with original drummer Natty Brooker providing the cover art. The respective musical obsessions that would define Pierce and Sonic's post-Spacemen work were perfectly apparent in both sections—while there have always been plenty of clear links between the two, the more individual parts of their natures started to flourish in full. Pierce's obsession with orchestration, gospel, and blues as transposed into psychedelia and proto-punk energy was in full swing, while his backing musicians would shortly thereafter form the initial Spiritualized lineup. "Feel So Sad," later recorded by Spiritualized as a dramatic 15-minute epic, is already well on its way via heavy space and echo on Pierce's vocals combined with sweeping arrangements. Sonic, again recording with Jazz Butcher associates (including the Jazz Butcher himself on flute) and with future Spectrum member Richard Formby, moved toward a more overtly experimental approach. They're still obsessively structured compared to many later Spectrum and E.A.R. explorations, but with the familiar wash of compressed yet dynamic production well in place, as the astonishing "Why Couldn't I See" shows. His lead-off track "Big City" is one of his best, Kraftwerk's propulsion filtered through Suicide's roughness and his own evanescent bliss, building to a soaring climax. An interesting inclusion was his cover of Mudhoney's "When Tomorrow Hits," originally recorded for a split single with them until he heard some irreverent lyric changes they did for their take on "Revolution." As with nearly everything the band released, *Recurring* has its own discographical oddities, with the original U.K. CD featuring four more tracks (all alternate versions and mixes) than the U.S. and European version. *—Ned Raggett*

Singles / Jun. 17, 1994 / Taang ♦♦♦♦♦
Not in fact an entirely accurate title—it does certainly consist of band singles, just not all of them—*Singles* is a slightly redundant collection of the first three such releases from Spacemen 3. In order, the contents of the original *Walkin' With Jesus*, *Transparent Radiation*, and *Take Me to the Other Side* EPs are reproduced, along with the cover art and credits of those releases. The whole collection closely parallels the U.K.-released *Transparent Flashbacks*, right down to the artwork, except that this U.S.-released effort also includes "Things'll Never Be the Same," one of the original cuts from *Transparent Radiation*. Depending on what versions of which Spacemen 3 albums one owns, *Singles* will either be a useful place to get a lot of rarities or a mix of obscurities and already-available cuts. Taang itself didn't help matters any, given that they had already released the contents of *Walkin' With Jesus* as bonus tracks on its version of the *Sound of Confusion* album, making it not much of a bonus for the label's presumed buyers! However, given all the discographical weirdness the band suffered from in the first place, it's still a great collection and makes a good starting point for newcomers as well. With such winners as the full 17-minute monster rampage through the 13th Floor Elevators' "Rollercoaster," the nearly as lengthy remake of the MC5's "Starship," and the original versions of "Feel So Good," "Walkin' With Jesus," and "Ecstasy Symphony" to recommend it, *Singles* is definitely not a boring listen. *—Ned Raggett*

Translucent Flashbacks / 1995 / Fire ♦♦♦♦
Translucent Flashbacks fills in some of the gaps in the early chapters of the Spacemen 3 story, compiling singles, B-sides, and rarities issued primarily in conjunction with the *Sound of Confusion* and *The Perfect Prescription* albums. Among the essentials: the complete "Ecstasy Symphony" (a fragment of which leads into *Prescription's* "Transparent Radiation"), the early single version of "Walkin' With Jesus," and the full-on 17-minute "Rollercoaster." *—Jason Ankeny*

Spacemen Are Go! / Apr. 23, 1995 / Bomp! ♦♦♦♦
Also released as *Live in Europe 1989* with two extra songs, *Spacemen Are Go!* was released in large part as a response to *Performance*, which at least some members of the group felt was a sub-par effort. Collected from various German shows in that year, the album covers the last era of the band as a live act, not to mention the rarest of all the lineups: a four-piece with bassist Will Carruthers and drummer Jon Mattock, who would eventually become founding members of Spiritualized with Pierce. Though fidelity varies a bit throughout, the remastering job, partially overseen by Sonic, presents good results, not to mention a number of cuts performed by the band only on rare occasions. Only three *Playing With Fire* cuts regularly appeared in the live set, but two of the less performed songs take a bow here, a stripped down, striking take on "I Believe It" and a gentle ramble through "Lord Can You Hear Me?" As for the classics—or at least what many later would recognize as such—some appear in notably different versions from the studio takes. "Walkin' With Jesus" has a quick, happy feel to it, for all that Pierce changes a line to go "cause I can't stand this life/without sweet heroin." Other songs, notably the twin rampages of "Revolution" and a 16-minute take on "Suicide," completely let fly with all the psychosis the studio versions had and then some. In keeping with the band's acknowledged reverence and inspiration from the past, a variety of covers appear, with a short version of the 13th Floor Elevators' "Rollercoaster" kicking things off for the album as a whole. There's also the "Bo Diddley Jam," not so much a cover as an enthusiastic rip through that legend's style, laced with appropriately heavy vibes. *—Ned Raggett*

For All the Fucked Up Children of This World We Give You . . . / Apr. 28, 1995 / Sympathy for the Record Industry ♦♦♦
An unexpected peek into the band's earliest possible roots, *For All the Fucked Up Children* preserves Spacemen 3's first ever studio recording work from 1984. Though there are seven cuts total, only five songs are on offer—the remaining two are alternate mixes of some recordings, interesting but not notably different. Outside of a completely fried take of "TV Catastrophe," those expecting *Playing With Fire*, or even *Sound of Confusion*, will have some (pleasant, happily) surprises at hearing where the group was and had yet to go. "Things'll Never Be the Same" readily demonstrates how the trio changed more with time. Where the version on *The Perfect Prescription* is a viciously compressed, psychotic monster of a track, here it's almost easygoing, Pierce's voice swathed in the appropriate echo while all three lay down everything in a country/blues-with-feedback approach. "Walkin' With Jesus" is even more radically different from either of the more familiar later takes, again cooking up a slow and steady blues twang and stomp with plenty of ambient space, Sonic contributing harmonica while Pierce does his best imitation of Lou Reed-sings-Muddy Waters. "Fixin' to Die," meanwhile, may share its title with other tracks but is its own little beast, an early take of "Come Down Easy" with different lyrics and backing vocals but the same general low-key gospel groove. As a great bonus, the packaging has both a review of a live show from around the same period—if nothing else, confirming that Rugby was apparently not only an unlikely place for Spacemen 3 to come from, but any band, period—and an early publicity photograph. Seeing the original three in short haircuts—Sonic even has a buzz!—while striking semi-Kraftwerk poses is something else, though at least the sunglasses are in place. *—Ned Raggett*

Spandau Ballet

f. Nov. 1979, **db.** 1990
New Romantic, Pop/Rock, New Wave
As one of the leading New Romantic bands, Spandau Ballet racked up a number of British hits—as well as one Top Ten American hit, "True"—during the early '80s, becoming one of the most successful groups to emerge during new wave. The only other new romantic band to enjoy greater commercial success was Duran Duran, yet Spandau Ballet was there first, scoring three Top Ten hit singles during 1981 with their synthesized dance-pop. By 1983, the London-based quintet had shed its Roxy Music-inspired robotic art-disco and picked up on Bryan Ferry's latter-day crooner persona, revamping themselves as a slick, stylish white soul act. It was in this incarnation that Spandau Ballet experienced its greatest success, as "True" reached number one in Britain and number four in America. However, their time in the spotlight was shortlived. Though they had a few more hits in Britain, none of them were particularly big, and in America they disappeared at the end of 1984. By the end of the decade, the group had split, with their core members, brothers Gary and Martin Kemp, launching acting careers with the 1990 film, *The Krays*. *—Stephen Thomas Erlewine*

Journeys to Glory / 1981 / Chrysalis ♦♦

Diamond / 1982 / Chrysalis ♦♦♦

True / 1983 / Chrysalis ♦♦♦♦♦

Parade / 1984 / Chrysalis ♦♦♦
Parade was Spandau Ballet's follow-up to their most successful LP, 1983's *True*. "Only When You Leave" reached number three on the U.K. charts. The three other singles that were released do successively worse: "I'll Fly for You" (number nine), "Highly Strung" (number 15), and "Round and Round" (number 19). (These charting songs are all marginal at best.) The band was still riding high in the U.K. and sold out seven consecutive dates at Webley Arena. Fans of the band, and the "new romanticism" of other acts like Simple Minds, Adam Ant, and Wham may like *Parade* because it comes close to recapturing the stylish, white soul sound of the *True* LP. But nothing on the album comes close to the song "True." Spandau Ballet disappeared from American charts after canceling U.S. tour dates in 1984 due to injury. *—JT Griffith*

● **The Singles Collection** / 1985 / Chrysalis ♦♦♦♦♦
Traces the group's development from the melodramatic, "new-romantic" dance-pop style of "To Cut a Long Story Short" to the lush ballad "True." Spandau Ballet always went in for big effects, but they became more subtle as they went along. *—William Ruhlmann*

Spanky & Our Gang

f. 1966, Chicago, IL, **db.** 1975
Sunshine Pop, Jazz-Pop, Folk-Rock
Spanky & Our Gang is one of those odd groups that, despite having had a string of Top 40 chart hits in a two-year period from 1967 through 1969, somehow falls between the cracks of 1960s pop music history. Their hits, particularly "Sunday Will Never Be the Same," "Lazy Day," "Like to Get to Know You," and "Give a Damn," were as much a part of the ambience of the middle to late '60s as any of the best known songs of the Mamas & the Papas with whom they're frequently compared. Yet they fell short of the latter group as cultural icons; they lacked the L.A.-based group's distinctively accessible collective

personality, or anything like its individual members' visual appeal, and they also had none of the Mamas & the Papas' in-house songwriting talent. They did have good voices and musical instincts, however, and a lot more to their sound than the cheerful anthems that made them famous. The group's harmonies were impeccable, and their records and arrangement displayed a slick, smooth texture that overlapped with the sounds of pop-jazz and also with the singing that one often heard on commercials of the period. In October 1968, however, the group received a devastating blow when Malcolm Hale died suddenly of pneumonia. The 27-year-old multi-instrumentalist also sang and arranged and pretty well kept the band together. In the wake of Hale's death, the group played out its concert commitments and then reassessed its future. Elaine McFarlane was pregnant and not planning on performing with them too much longer, and John Seiter had been offered a gig playing drums with the Turtles. Rather than reorganize around such key membership changes, the group decided to call it quits. *—Bruce Eder*

Spanky & Our Gang / Aug. 1967 / Mercury ✦✦✦

The group's debut LP demonstrates what can go wrong, even with a group enjoying a trio of hit singles. Though those hits are here, the album is the least representative of what the group was about and a mixed bag for fans, presenting a trio of widely available hits, six or seven fine tracks currently unavailable elsewhere, and two musical lapses that between them account for nearly one-third of the running time. Spanky & Our Gang started out in Chicago with a sound somewhere midway between the original Jefferson Airplane and the original Nitty Gritty Dirt Band, a folk-rock ensemble with a few jazzy twists and some funny between-song sketches. For their first year at Mercury Records, however, and especially on this LP, producer Jerry Ross used the group as an instrument of his own, turning them into a virtual clone of the Mamas & the Papas on a big portion of this album. Vocally most of the album is outstanding, the harmony singing absolutely radiant on the familiar hits "Sunday Will Never Seem the Same," "Lazy Day," and "Making' Every Minute Count." "Brother Can You Spare a Dime" is the most controversial song here, an unfinished track that was stuck onto the album by Ross in the process of rush-releasing the record and getting it above 30 minutes running time, with nothing but an awkward guide vocal from Elaine "Spanky" McFarlane never intended to be heard by the public; along with the four-minute rendition of "Ya Got Trouble" from Meredith Willson's *The Music Man*, which might've worked well on stage, it's the nadir of the record. *—Bruce Eder*

Without Rhyme or Reason (Anything You Choose) / 1968 / Mercury ✦✦✦✦

The best (though not the best selling) of the group's three original albums, *Without Rhyme or Reason* was their most ambitious creation and the album of theirs that holds up best on CD, a 40-minute soundscape in which songs drifted from one into the other. "Nowhere to Go" isn't much more than a song fragment, but it makes a compelling intro to "Give a Damn," enhancing the familiar single. In contrast to their prior two albums, *Without Rhyme or Reason* contains no major hits, and none of the songs off of it ever charted seriously, although "Give a Damn," which closes it, nearly made the Top 40 despite a radio ban over the use of the word "damn" in its title and chorus; thus, it was their poorest selling album. The group hardly played at all on most of the record but provided their most elaborate vocals arrangements, and it proved to be their most lasting creation apart from the hit singles. The death of Malcolm Hale on October 30, 1968, during the recording of the album, coupled with the group's satisfaction over what they'd achieved musically, resulted in the decision to disband in the early 1969, soon after the release of *Without Rhyme or Reason*. *—Bruce Eder*

Like to Get to Know You / Apr. 1968 / Mercury ✦✦✦✦

Spanky & Our Gang had been unhappy with various aspects of their self-titled debut album, and as a result they recruited two new producers, Stuart Scharf and Bob Dorough, who were more in sympathy with how the group actually sounded. Recorded somewhat on the fly, *Like to Get to Know You* was the first album to reflect what the group considered their own sound, and was harder-rocking, bluesier, and more inventive in its folk stylings than anything on their debut album. The mix of sounds was actually quite startling in its own time and is engaging even 30 some years later, with various top New York and Los Angeles-based session musicians and a cadre of Chicago bluesmen adding their talents to the band's core instrumentalists. Elaine "Spanky" McFarlane gives convincing and honest performances, and Lefty Baker acquits himself well as a singer. The group opens new vocal territory on the six-part harmony "Sunday Morning," and they do arguably the best cover ever of Leonard Cohen's "Suzanne," which dazzles with its tempo changes and the sheer variety of timbres employed. Side two of the original album was actually a prelude to their next LP, containing elements of conceptual rock and made up of songs that segue thematically from one to another. As an album, *Like to Get to Know You* was of its time, a conceptual record that was finely executed and fascinating to hear; it was perhaps taken a little less seriously, given the image of Spanky & Our Gang for light pop/rock. It's worth rediscovering, either on the original vinyl or on the 1999 Japanese-imported CD. *—Bruce Eder*

• **Greatest Hits** / Aug. 24, 1999 / Mercury ✦✦✦✦

This 15-song compilation supplants a 12-song CD of the same name dating from the 1980s, which, in turn, was adapted from an LP from 1969. This time out, in addition to improving the sound somewhat, the producers have de-emphasized the cheerful, faux hippie pop sound of the group (though that is definitely represented) to show off some other sides of their output. All of the hits are here: "Sunday Will Never Be the Same," "Making Every Minute Count," "Lazy Day," "Sunday Morning" (in its hit version, not the interesting but bizarre outtake from the earlier hits collection), "Like to Get to Know You," "Give a Damn," "Yesterday's Rain," "And She's Mine," and "Anything You Choose." The real inspiration (and limitations) of this compilation lie in the other tracks, which include "Brother Can You Spare a Dime" and "Prescription for the Blues," the latter featuring Little Brother Montgomery, who taught Elaine "Spanky" McFarlane the song originally, and their live version of "For Lovin' Me," which features a quote from Sergie Prokofiev's "Lt. Kije Suite." And isn't it amazing how that piece of music manifests itself here and there in popular music, in locales such as this and Emerson, Lake & Palmer's "I Believe in Father Christmas," among others? On the down side, the producers have removed one gorgeous and playful number, "It Ain't Necessarily Bird Avenue" and "Three Ways From Tomorrow," the latter a brilliant showcase for guitarist/banjoman Lefty Baker and the closest thing to a heavy psychedelic guitar track that this group ever issued. One gets a broader overview of the group's sound, but one wishes that they could've seen fit to work at least those two songs in, if not the third "missing" track, "Commercial." *—Bruce Eder*

Sparklehorse

f. 1995

Noise Pop, Alternative Country-Rock, Indie Rock, Alternative Pop/Rock

Sparklehorse was essentially singer/songwriter Mark Linkous, an alumnus of the mid-1980s indie band the Dancing Hoods. A tenure in the Johnson Family (later known as Salt Chuck Mary) followed, as did stints sweeping chimneys and painting houses; he began working as Sparklehorse in 1995, honing his spooky, lo-fi roots-pop in the studio located on his Bremo Bluff, VA farm. After a demo made its way to the offices of Capitol Records, Linkous signed to the label to issue Sparklehorse's acclaimed debut *Vivadixiesubmarinetransmissionplot*, scoring an alternative radio hit with the single "Someday I Will Treat You Good." In early 1996, after a Sparklehorse live date in London, Linkous nearly died when he passed out after mixing Valium with prescription antidepressants; throughout the 14 hours he spent unconscious on his hotel's bathroom floor his legs were pinned under the rest of his body, and the prolonged loss of blood circulation nearly left him crippled. Many months and countless surgeries later he was back on his feet, although no new Sparklehorse material was forthcoming prior to the release of *Good Morning, Spider* in mid-1998. *—Jason Ankeny*

Vivadixiesubmarinetransmissionplot / Aug. 1995 / Capitol ✦✦✦✦

Sparklehorse's 1996 full-length debut *Vivadixiesubmarinetransmissionplot* has even more sad, beautiful, weird moments of spacy, rural folk-rock than it does letters in its name. Primarily the project of singer/songwriter/guitarist Mark Linkous, Sparklehorse's sound embraces impossibly frail, cobwebby ballads like the album opener "Homecoming Queen," "Most Beautiful Widow in Town" and "Heart of Darkness"; sun-drenched, noisy pop like "Rainmaker" and "Hammering the Cramps"; and noise blasts like "Ballad of a Cold Lost Marble" and "850 Double Pumper Holley." The album's most powerful moments borrow from folk and country traditions, alluding to their universally understood poignancy, while updating and personalizing them with spacy arrangements, distorted vocals, and slivers of feedback. "Heart of Darkness" and "Homecoming Queen" in particular have a woozy, late-night sweetness that conveys a touching, if unstable, honesty. The single "Someday I Will Treat You Good" molds this vulnerability into a radio song, with catchy and affecting results, but it's the shambling, understated songs like "Saturday" and "Sad & Beautiful World" that define the group's down-to-earth melancholy. Despite covering some expansive musical territory, *Vivadixiesubmarinetransmissionplot* doesn't sound scattered so much as spontaneous, reflecting the happy, sad, noisy, and quiet moments in life. *—Heather Phares*

• **Good Morning Spider** / Feb. 9, 1999 / Capitol ✦✦✦✦✦

Recorded after singer/songwriter Mark Linkous' accidental, near-fatal drug reaction and subsequent 12-week stay in London's St. Mary's Hospital, *Good Morning Spider* dwells in the grey areas between dreaming and waking, sickness and health, and living and dying. The album takes these grey areas and makes a world out of them, blending classic songwriting with an experimental sound that borrows from hi-fi and lo-fi. It's a natural progression from their debut, *Vivadixiesubmarinetransmissionplot*, which introduced Sparklehorse's refreshing mix of classic songwriting and sonic experimentation. *Good Morning Spider* adds bubbling synths, ambient electronics, horns and drum loops to the mix, giving songs like "Painbirds" an unclassifiable—but distinctively Sparklehorse—blend of darkness and childlike innocence. From driving, punky songs like "Pig" and "Cruel Sun," to frail, winding ballads such as "Saint Mary" and "Come On In," to the experimental pop of "Ghost of His Smile" and "Sunshine," the album encompasses a rainbow of sounds and emotions but never loses focus. *—Heather Phares*

Distorted Ghost / Feb. 1, 2000 / Odeon ✦✦✦✦

The vague poetry of Sparklehorse mastermind Mark Linkous is gracefully complex. David Lowery digs him and he is pals with Vic Chesnutt, but he probably won't join the ranks of Leonard Cohen or Woody Guthrie. Having bounced back from a traumatic overdose on Valium and prescription antidepressants which left him clinically dead for three minutes in 1996, Sparklehorse is Linkous' glimmering crystal of artistic emotion. 1999's *Good Morning Spider* brought him critical acclaim, but commercial whispers weren't enough.

Linkous is trying to be a happy man; his folk-rock appeal is sultry and he sings his pain to no one who listens. The six-song EP *Distorted Ghost* is a collection of live tracks and B-sides encompassing Linkous' music career that began in the early '90s. Highlights include "Waiting for Nothing," which plucks with acoustic beauty and Linkous' sad yet sweet demeanor. "Gasoline Horseys," (from 1995's *Vivadixiesubmarinetransmissionplot*) is a moving live cut recorded in Bristol, England. In essence, *Distorted Ghost* allows Linkous to fully expose his heartbreaking frustration; Sparklehorse is his therapy. *—MacKenzie Wilson*

It's a Wonderful Life / Jul. 3, 2001 / EMI ✦✦✦✦

Along with the Flaming Lips and Mercury Rev, Sparklehorse crafts strangely beautiful—and beautifully strange—music inspired by down-to-earth sounds as well as spacey experimentalism. But where the Lips are lovably loopy and Mercury Rev is arty and wry, Sparklehorse wraps deep-seated, often uncomfortable emotions in layers of metaphors and static. However, the group's third album, *It's a Wonderful Life*, is its most open and direct work yet. Whether this has anything to do with the fact that this is reportedly singer/songwriter Mark Linkous' first substance-free work is arguable, but regardless, it's a noticeably more focused effort. Though it lacks *Good Morning Spider*'s sprawling brilliance, it's possibly Linkous' most effective, and affecting, collection of songs. It's also his most collaborative album, with co-producer and Mercury Rev alum David Fridmann adding just the right amount of warmth and weirdness and the Cardigans' Nina Persson and PJ Harvey contributing backing vocals that rival their work on *Gran Turismo* and *Stories From the City, Stories From the Sea*. Persson's sweetly empathetic voice shines on "Gold Day" and "Little Fat Baby," while Harvey's passionate style fits "Piano Fire" and the brooding ballad "Eyepennies" perfectly. Driven by burbling keyboards, drum machines, acoustic guitar, and piano and populated with spooky, homespun images of babies, teeth, nails, and horses, most of the album consists of gently unsettling ballads like the title track and "Apple Bed." Edgier, poppier songs like "King of Nails" and "Comfort Me" don't sound out of place, but the stomping, clunky, Tom Waits-lite of "Dog Door," which actually features Waits on lead vocals, is a distraction. The album's sweet, yet too strange to be conventionally uplifting songs like "More Yellow Birds" and "Babies on the Sun" convey *It's a Wonderful Life*'s message best: Even at its weirdest, just being alive is pretty wonderful. Needless to say, so is the album. *—Heather Phares*

The Sparkletones

f. 1955, Spartanburg, SC, **db.** 1960

Rockabilly

The Sparkletones' story should have been a movie. For a lot of listeners, they were and are what rockabilly music was really all about—four kids from the South, none older than 16 and one as young as 13 when they started, getting together and making fast, sometimes raunchy sounds, literally the soundtrack to their own teen years, and having a lot of fun and getting an adventure out of it. Their music at its best sounded as freewheeling as their approach to it really was, and they were rewarded in October of 1957 with a number 17 placement on the Billboard charts for the only record they ever did chart, "Black Slacks." The song was a stunner: fast paced, with rippling lead guitar, and filled with teen catch phrases of the period, it sounded a little like the Everly Brothers on uppers, with a guitar part that was somewhere midway between Carl Perkins and Buddy Holly. The number 17 spot tells only part of the story, however. "Black Slacks" stayed on the charts for more than four months, selling a lot of copies in that time, well enough to keep the band going for three years while they vainly searched for another hit. They soldiered on for three years, issuing "Penny Loafers and Bobby Sox," "Cotton Pickin' Rocker," "We've Had It," "Late Again," and "Run Rabbit Run," good, lively songs, none of which charted. Indeed, some of the group's B-sides were even better, such as "Rocket," which is pure, high-voltage rockabilly but manages to display elements of a black vocal sound as well. By 1959, their contract with ABC/Paramount was up, and they moved to the Paris label, for four singles that did no better. *—Bruce Eder*

Black Slacks / 1993 / MCA ✦✦✦✦✦

The Sparkletones never released an LP in their own time, but 25 years after they split up, MCA Records (which inherited the ABC-Paramount library) put together this brilliant ten-song album, made up of "Black Slacks," and five other released songs, and four numbers that weren't released until 1983. Apart from the title track, one of the greatest rockabilly originals, the album's numerous highlights include Bennett's previously unreleased "Rocket" and "Let's Go Rock & Roll," and the collectively authored "Maybe Baby" (no connection with the Buddy Holly song). One European pirate label issued a longer Sparkletones collection later in the 1980s, but the sound quality on some of those cuts was relatively poor. And the fact that MCA hasn't reissued this on CD is a crime. (Out of print) *—Bruce Eder*

Sparks

f. 1970, Los Angeles, CA

Proto-Punk, Club/Dance, Pop/Rock, New Wave

Sparks was a vehicle for the skewed pop smarts and wiseguy wordplay of brothers Ron and Russell Mael. While attending UCLA in 1970, the Maels formed their first group, Halfnelson. Todd Rundgren helped land the group a contract and produced their self-titled 1971 debut. Their quirky, tongue-in-cheek art-pop failed to find an audience, however, and their manager convinced the Maels to change the group's name to Sparks. They almost reached the charts with "Wonder Girl," and 1972's sublimely bizarre *A Woofer in Tweeter's Clothing* cemented the band's cult status with another near-hit, "Girl From Germany."

Warmly received by the British music press, the Mael brothers ultimately relocated to London to record 1974's glam-bubblegum opus *Kimono My House*—it spawned two major British hits, "This Town Ain't Big Enough for the Both of Us" and "Amateur Hour." Sparks returned later in 1974 with *Propaganda*, another smash which scored with the hits "Never Turn Your Back on Mother Earth" and "Something for the Girl With Everything." The Maels eventually returned to the U.S., however, treading water for two albums before enlisting disco producer Giorgio Moroder to helm 1979's synth-powered dance-pop confection *Number One in Heaven*. The album spurred the group to renewed success in England on the strength of the hit singles "The Number One Song in Heaven," "Beat the Clock," and "Tryouts for the Human Race." Sparks left disco in the dust with 1981's *Whomp That Sucker* and the following year's *Angst in My Pants*. The wonderful single "Cool Places," a duet with the Go-Go's Jane Wiedlin, nearly reached the Top 40, and was the band's biggest American hit. After three lackluster LPs during the '80s, Sparks remained silent until *Gratuitous Sax and Senseless Violins*, released in 1994. *Plagiarism* followed four years later. *—Jason Ankeny*

Sparks / 1971 / Bearsville ✦✦✦

Within the first track of their debut album—the crisp, minimal pounder "Wonder Girl," featuring Russell Mael's falsetto already engaged in swooping acrobatics and Ron Mael's sparkling piano work to the fore, singing ever-so-slightly-weird lyrics about love that couldn't quite be taken at face value—Sparks established themselves so perfectly that arguably the rest of the brothers' long career has been a continual refinement from that basic formula. Even more striking is realizing how astoundingly prescient it was; what must have sounded indescribably strange in 1972 now feels like the precursor to nearly all of new wave, a fair chunk of synth-pop, and just about any music with a brain. As it stands, the original Sparks group, with brothers Jim and Earle Mankey on bass and guitar and Harvey Feinstein on drums accompanying the Maels, was as tight and accomplished as the classic Alice Cooper lineup, but given to their own brand of clever insanity (the fact that there's a loud-rocking original on here called "(No More) Mr. Nice Guys" makes you wonder if that other band wasn't listening in). Todd Rundgren's production is generally spare but very effective, with snippets of cymbal and keyboard leaping out from the speakers at odd moments. The twisted, '50s piano-rock loper "High C" practically invents Queen in both shuffling rock-out and heavy rockabilly camp phases; "Fletcher Honorama" slides and slinks along in a wickedly dreamy way; and "Slowboat" combines show tunes, cabaret, and rock to magnificent effect. With other songs like "Biology 2," "Fa La Fa Lee," and the brilliantly titled "Saccaharin and the War," *Sparks* remains a wonderfully entertaining listen and an honestly unique debut. *—Ned Raggett*

A Woofer in Tweeter's Clothing / 1972 / Bearsville ✦✦✦

Woofer... starts with another killer opening track, musically and lyrically, with "Girl From Germany," a chugging number detailing the problems the narrator has with his parents over his girlfriend, given their lingering wartime attitudes. The album builds upon the strengths of the debut to create an even better experience all around. The same five-person lineup offers more sharp performances. Album engineering veteran James Lowe takes over production reins from Rundgren, with, happily, no audible sense of trying to make the album more commercial. If anything, things are even wiggier this time around, from the naughtily-titled sea chanty which turns into a full-on rocker "Beaver O'Lindy" and the strings-plus-piano "Here Comes Bob," to the album's completely wacked-out, dramatic centerpiece "Moon Over Kentucky." Melodies start approaching the hyperactivity level which would flower completely on the band's subsequent releases. Ron and Earle Mankey trade off or play against each other, while the rhythm section of Jim Mankey and Feinstein executes the kind of sharp tempo changes which would become *de rigueur* for thrash-metal bands of the '80s, but fit in perfectly here with the spastic pop being played. Russell soars and croons over it all like an angel on deeply disturbing drugs, wrapping his vocals around such lines as "We surely will appreciate our newfound leisure time" from "Nothing is Sacred." The long-time live favorite "Do-Re-Mi"—indeed a cover of the number from *The Sound of Music*—first appears here as well, taking Rodgers and Hammerstein to a level Julie Andrews might be hardpressed to follow. Anyone wondering why Faith No More appeared on Sparks' self-tribute album *Plagiarism* need only listen to *Woofer* to understand—as a full-on purée of musical styles in the service of twisted viewpoints, it's a perfect album. *—Ned Raggett*

Kimono My House / 1974 / Island ✦✦✦✦✦

Sparks specializes in keyboard-based pop songs with clever, ironic lyrics (by Ron Mael), sung in a near-falsetto by Russell Mael. Examples include "Here in Heaven" (in which a disappointed, dead Romeo sings to a still-living Juliet who "broke our little pact"), "Thank God It's Not Christmas," and the U.K. hits "This Town Ain't Big Enough for Both of Us" and "Amateur Hour." *— William Ruhlmann*

Propaganda / 1974 / Island ✦✦✦✦✦

More of Ron's wit ("Don't Leave Me Alone with Her," "Who Don't Like Kids") and Russell's operatic singing with catchy rock backings, though it's hard to get the jokes without the lyric sheet. *— William Ruhlmann*

Indiscreet / 1975 / Island ✦✦✦✦✦

On their third terrific album in as many years, producer Tony Visconti provides the Mael brothers the best production and arrangements of their careers; they responded with some of their catchiest, cleverest material. Ron Mael's lyrics explore some of the same themes as Ray Davies: the regrets of an aging drunk ("T*ts"), the loss of gentility and innocence ("It Ain't 1918"), and other observations about decorum and courtship. And relationships ranging from the wholesome to the depraved to the baffling. A classic of quirky pop, one that surely influenced bands like They Might Be Giants and Barenaked Ladies. *—James A. Gardner*

Big Beat / 1976 / Island ✦✦✦✦

Most of this album finds Sparks doing what they do best: spewing out clever, mile-a-minute lyrics over solid-rocking accompaniment (this time, provided by a superior group of studio musicians). Drummer Hilly Michaels and guitarist Jeffrey Salen lend the Mael brothers' songs considerable rock & roll authority. Standouts include the opening blast, "Big Boy" (which was featured in the film *Rollercoaster*), the propulsive "Fill-Er-Up," and the falsetto-delivered proclamation "I Like Girls," apparently a leftover from their previous album, *Indiscreet*. Generally, however, they eschew the elaborate arrangements of *Indiscreet* and go for a powerful, stripped-down sound. As titles such as "Everybody's Stupid" and "Thrown Her Away (And Get a New One)" suggest, the album brims with decidedly politically incorrect (and often hilarious) lyrics. *—James A. Gardner*

The Best of Sparks / 1979 / Curb ✦✦✦

Back when LPs were music's dominant format, there were two easy ways to spot

European vinyl: the jackets were often made with a softer cardboard than American LPs, and the shrink-wrap was a lot looser. And because Sparks was much more popular in England than in the U.S., it made sense to be on the lookout for their European releases if you were among their American fans. Some of Sparks' recordings, in fact, never came out in the U.S.—1980's *Terminal Jive*, for example, was a hit in France and England but was only available as an import in North America. Not to be confused with Island's 1990 CD *Mael Intuition: The Best of Sparks* or an eight-song budget CD from Curb that was also titled *The Best of Sparks*, this LP is a 12-song collection that Island put out in England in 1979. Had Island wanted to be more specific, it could have called this LP *The Best of Sparks: The Island Years* because its focus is Sparks' excellent Island output of 1974-1975. The album doesn't contain any of the work that Sparks did for Bearsville, Columbia, or Elektra in the '70s, so it isn't the last word on Sparks during that decade. But if, in 1979, you wanted an introduction to Sparks' Island work, it was a fine choice. Sparks did some of its best work at Island, and treasures from 1974's *Propaganda* ("Something for the Girl With Everything," "At Home, at Work, at Play," "Thanks but No Thanks"), 1974's *Kimono My House* ("This Town Ain't Big Enough for the Both of Us," "Amateur Hour," "Thank God It's Not Christmas"), and 1975's *Indiscreet* ("Get in the Swing," "Looks, Looks, Looks") are nothing to complain about. *—Alex Henderson*

No. 1 in Heaven / 1979 / Virgin ✦✦✦✦

It may not have been the most natural match in music history, but the marriage of Sparks' focus on oddball pop songs to the driving disco-trance of Giorgio Moroder produced the duo's best album in years. From the chart hits "Number One Song in Heaven" and "Beat the Clock" to solid album tracks like "La Dolce Vita," *No. 1 in Heaven* surprises by succeeding on an artistic and commercial level despite the fact that neither the Mael brothers nor Moroder tempered their respective idiosyncrasies for the project. Moroder's production is just as dizzying, chunky, and completely rhythm-driven as on his best work with Donna Summer, and the Mael brothers prove on "Tryouts for the Human Race" and "Academy Award Performance" that their bizarre songwriting wasn't compromised. *—John Bush*

Terminal Jive / 1979 / Oglio ✦✦✦✦

The second Giorgio Moroder collaboration of Sparks' career doesn't have quite the emphasis on Moroder trademarks compared to its predecessor; he has only two songwriting credits here, while the Mael brothers take most of them alone. Still, the breakout single "When I'm With You" and "Just Because You Love Me" have an ineffable disco stomp and the requisite cymbal slaps on the offbeat, while "Noisy Boys" and "Stereo" have an experimental, laddish feel that looks past disco into '80s synth-pop and new romantic. Though disco fans can feel safe with *No. 1 in Heaven*, those more interested in new wave would be well served to pick up *Terminal Jive* first. *—John Bush*

Whomp That Sucker / 1981 / Oglio ✦✦

The History of Sparks / 1981 / Underdog ✦✦✦✦

Until Rhino released 1991's two-CD set *Profile: The Ultimate Sparks Collection*, there was no such thing as a definitve Sparks anthology—the 1981 European import *The History of Sparks* can hardly be called definitive. In all fairness, it's hard to assemble a definitive anthology when a band has done as much label-hopping as Sparks—by 1981, they had recorded for Bearsville, Island, Columbia, Elektra, and RCA (and would record for Atlantic and MCA by the end of the '80s). But while this LP, which spans from 1971-1981, isn't definitive, it paints a generally attractive picture of Sparks. No, it doesn't contain "Something for the Girl With Everything," "Big Boy," "This Town Ain't Big Enough for the Both of Us," or "Achoo"—or "Don't Leave Me Alone With Her," "Amateur Hour," "Get in the Swing," or "At Home, at Work, at Play." It does include three Giorgio Moroder-produced Euro-disco/synth-pop tunes from 1979's *No. 1 in Heaven* ("Beat the Clock," "Tryouts for the Human Race," and "The Number One Song in Heaven"), two irresistibly goofy power pop gems from 1981's *Whomp That Sucker* ("Funny Face" and "Tips for Teens"), and three enjoyable Euro-pop items that Moroder and Harold Faltermeier produced for 1980's European release *Terminal Jive* ("Rock & Roll People in a Disco World," "Young Girls," "Just Because You Love Me," and the French mega-hit "When I'm With You"). While *Terminal Jive* was a big seller in England and France, it never even came out in the U.S. Meanwhile, *The History of Sparks* takes us back to the Mael brothers' early pre-Island output of 1971-1972 with "Girl From Germany," "(No More) Mr. Nice Guys," and "Wonder Girl." Again, *The History Of Sparks* isn't definitive, but it's not a bad collection either. *—Alex Henderson*

Angst in My Pants / 1982 / Oglio ✦✦✦

Sparks in Outer Space / 1983 / Teldec ✦✦✦

Pulling Rabbits Out of a Hat / 1984 / Oglio ✦✦

Mael Intuition: The Best of Sparks 1974-1976 / 1990 / Island ✦✦✦✦

A well-chosen, 20-track compilation derived from the group's three best albums (*Kimono My House*, *Propaganda*, and *Indiscreet*), released during their brief, productive tenure with Island Records. Producers Muff Winwood (for the first two, harder-rocking albums) and Tony Visconti (the more varied and elaborately arranged *Indiscreet*) both provide the Mael brothers with solid, sympathetic settings for their witty, rapid-fire lyrics and manic delivery. Songs range from the aggressive riff of "At Home, at Work, at Play" (a precursor to the heavier sound of the 1976 album, *Big Beat*) to the uncanny Andrews Sisters evocation "Looks, Looks, Looks." Russell Mael's quavery falsetto is an acquired taste, and his vocal affectations can try the listener's nerves on prolonged exposure. Also, their tendency to deliver a few hundred lyrics in as many seconds makes interpretation a challenge, but their perverse humor rewards the effort. This is probably all the Sparks the casual fan needs. *—James A. Gardner*

• **Profile: The Ultimate Sparks Collection** / Apr. 1991 / Rhino ✦✦✦✦✦

Unfortunately, Sparks never enjoyed more than a small, though devoted, cult following. But it certainly wasn't for a lack of effective hooks and clever, insanely funny lyrics. While a few of the L.A. pop/rockers' albums were disappointing, many others were exceptional. For those seeking an introductory overview of Sparks' legacy, this two-CD set is highly recommended. From "Achoo" to "Tips for Teens" to "This Town Ain't Big Enough for the Both of Us," *Profile* makes it clear just how delightfully goofy Sparks could be. Often willing to experiment, the group embraces everything from hard rock on "Big Boy" to Euro-disco on Giorgio Moroder-produced songs like "The Number One Song in Heaven" and "Beat the Clock." Despite the inclusion of a few throwaways—such as the disappointing *Music You Can Dance To*'s title song—*Profile* paints an impressive picture of a wrongly neglected band. *—Alex Henderson*

Gratuitous Sax & Senseless Violins / 1994 / Logic/Artista ✦✦✦✦✦

Even the cover art is great, playing with the same fake tabloid style that Guns & Roses tried but with funnier results. Beginning with a semi-echo of the start of *Propaganda*, with the a cappella "Gratuitous Sax" leading into the surging, well-deserved European smash hit "When Do I Get to Sing 'My Way'," *Sax* broke a near seven-year silence from Ron and Russell Mael—the longest period of time by far since their start in between major releases. Rather than sounding tired or out of touch, though, the brothers gleefully embraced the modern synth/house/techno explosion for their own purposes (an explosion which, after all, they had helped start with their work during the late '70s with Giorgio Moroder). Solely recorded by the Maels with no outside help, *Sax* keeps that same, perfect Sparks formula—Russell's sweet vocals soar with smart and suspect lyrics over Ron's sometimes fast and furious, sometimes slow and elegant melodies, here performed with detailed electronic lushness. They make their style live yet again, feeling far fresher here than on *Interior Design*. "(When I Kiss You) I hear Charlie Parker Playing" finds Russell rapping (!), "I Thought I Told You to Wait in the Car" has a great building chorus, and "Let's Go Surfing" helps wrap up the album with a wistfully triumphant call to arms. "Tsui Hark" is the one slight departure from the formula, featuring the *Hong Kong* director Hark himself giving a brief autobiography while a colleague speaks in Chinese. Though some longtime fans groused that they missed the more rocked-up Sparks of the early '70s (or early '80s) in comparison, all in all, *Sax* is a well-deserved return to form from a band which has deserved far more attention from the musical world, or the world at large, than they have received. *—Ned Raggett*

Plagiarism / 1997 / Oglio ✦✦✦

In the age of remixing, sampling and cut-and-paste record-making, leave it to Sparks to beat everyone to the punch and put the '90s spin on their own catalog before someone else did. Nineteen Sparks favorites are tackled here, including a super Hi-NRG version of "The Number One Song in Heaven" and a keenly orchestrated "This Town Ain't Big Enough for Both of Us," both delivered with a hand from their friends in opera-rock: Jimmy Somerville and Faith No More, respectively. *—Denise Sullivan*

Balls / Aug. 22, 2000 / Oglio ✦✦✦

Los Angeles legends and music innovators Sparks, best known in the States for their '80s hit "Cool Places" with Jane Wiedlin, has actually been around for nearly 30 years, consistently putting out records and developing a cult following. Precursors to electronica, synth-pop, and new wave, the brothers Ron and Russell Mael have inspired such varied acts as Ween, Fear, and They Might Be Giants. With an ironic, irreverent way of looking at the world reflected in their wordplay and dramatic productions that are highlighted by the coldness of heavy synthesizers, they come across like a combination of the Pet Shop Boys, Men Without Hats, and a splash of Devo. Despite the welcome dichotomy created by their silly lyrics and detached synths, there is something forlorn about the duo's melodies—even when singing lines like "I'm much more than this/more than a sex machine," covering odd topics like an ode to Scheherezade or explaining "How to get Your Ass Kicked." This being Sparks' 18th album, the Mael brothers clearly know what they're doing. Though both the lyrics and the production are quirky, there is nothing dumb about them. To be able to make a song called "More Than a Sex Machine" anthemic shows just how elegant and how smart the Maels are. The melodies have brilliant pop hooks and Russell's voice soars. *Balls* made it worth the three-year wait between this and their last album, *Plagiarism*. *—Bryan Buss*

Britney Spears

b. Dec. 2, 1981, Kentwood, LA

Vocals / Teen Pop, Adult Contemporary, Dance-Pop

Dance-pop singer Britney Spears was born in Kentwood, LA on December 2, 1981; after honing her chops in local dance showcases and church choirs, at age eight she auditioned for a role on the Disney Channel's *Mickey Mouse Club* show, and although the series' producers deemed her too young for the job they were sufficiently impressed with the girl's talent to assist her in gaining entry to New York's Off-Broadway Dance Center and the Professional Performing Arts School. After a series of television commercials and stage appearances, at 11 Spears finally joined *The Mickey Mouse Club*, where she remained for two seasons; continuing on as a solo artist, she signed to Jive Records and in early 1999 issued her first LP *... Baby One More Time*. The record was a massive hit, debuting atop the pop charts and reeling off a series of radio smashes including the title track, "(You Drive Me) Crazy" and "From the Bottom of My Broken Heart" on its way to becoming the best-selling album ever released by a teenage girl. Spears' success also spawned legions of imitators, most notable among them Christina Aguilera and Jessica Simpson. Her sophomore effort, *Oops!... I Did It Again*, followed in the spring of 2000. *—Jason Ankeny*

• **... Baby One More Time** / Jan. 12, 1999 / Jive ✦✦✦✦

At the beginning of the '90s, teen currency shifted from bubblegum'n'Tiger Beat to grunge'n'Maximum Rock & Roll. Although it may have been pushed from the spotlight, teen pop hadn't died—it, in a way, went underground, spending time on the fringes of pop culture. One of the leading lights of the exiled teen brigade was *The New Mickey Mouse Club*. For several years, it toiled away on the Disney Network, earning a small fan base—but, more importantly, providing a launchpad for several careers, including that of Britney Spears. Like her fellow *NMMC* alumni 'N Sync, Spears shot to stardom in the late '90s, just as she was on the verge of late adolescence. By that time, everything old was new again. Albums like her debut, *...Baby One More Time*, were topping the charts as if they were *Hangin' Tough*, which is only appropriate since it sounded as if it could have been cut in 1989, not 1999.... *...Baby One More Time* has the same blend of infectious, rap-inflected dance-pop and smooth balladry that propelled the New Kids and Debbie Gibson, due to the Backstreet Boys' producer, Max Martin, who is also the mastermind behind Spears' debut. He has a knack for catchy hooks, endearing melodies, and engaging Euro-dance rhythms, all of which are best heard on the hits: the ingenious title track, "Some-times," "(You Drive Me) Crazy," and the utterly delightful, bubblegum-ragga album track "Soda Pop." Like many teen pop albums, *...Baby One More Time* has its share of well-crafted filler, but the singles, combined with Britney's burgeoning charisma, make this a pretty great piece of fluff. —*Stephen Thomas Erlewine*

Oops!...I Did It Again / May 16, 2000 / Jive ✦✦✦✦
Given the phenomenal success of Britney Spears' debut, *...Baby One More Time*, it should come as no surprise that its sequel offers more of the same. After all, she gives away the plot with the ingenious title of her second album *Oops!...I Did It Again*, essentially admitting that the record is more of the same. It has the same combination of sweetly sentimental ballads and endearingly gaudy dance-pop that made *One More Time*. Fortunately, she and her production team not only have a stronger overall set of songs this time, but they also occasionally get carried away with the same bewildering magpie aesthetic that made the first album's "Sodapop"—a combination of bubblegum, urban soul, and raga—a gonzo teen-pop classic. It doesn't happen all that often—the clenched-funk revision of the Stones' deathless "Satisfaction" is the most obvious example—but it helps give the album character apart from the well-crafted dance-pop and ballads that serve as its heart. In the end, it's what makes this an entertaining, satisfying listen. —*Stephen Thomas Erlewine*

The Specials

f. 1977, Coventry, England, **db.** 1985
Ska Revival, New Wave
True innovators of the punk era, the Specials began the British ska-revival craze, combining the highly danceable ska and rocksteady beat with punk's energy and attitude, and taking on a more focused and informed political and social stance than their predecessors and peers. Despite early interest from major labels, frontman Jerry Dammers opted to start his own 2-Tone label, named for its multi-racial agenda and after the two-tone tonic suits favored by the like-minded mods of the '60s. The band debuted with the single "Gangsters" which reached the U.K. Top Ten. Soon after, hordes of bands and fans followed in the same tradition and the movement was in full swing with hits by similar-sounding 2-Tone bands, such as Madness, the (English) Beat, and the Selecter. Late in 1979, the Specials released their landmark self-titled debut album. The title track of a subsequent EP, *Too Much Too Young*, reached the number one spot. At this time, the band switched musical directions, releasing album number two, *More Specials*, with a new neo-lounge persona. The 1981 single "Ghost Town" also jumped to number one, but the band began falling apart soon after. A splinter trio left to form Fun Boy Three, while Dammers held on and returned with one final album, 1984's *In the Studio*. In 1996, a Dammers-less version of the band reappeared with a shameful cash-in album, *Today's Specials*. —*Chris Woodstra*

★ **The Specials** / Nov. 1979 / 2 Tone/Chrysalis ✦✦✦✦✦
The Specials' self-titled debut sparked the Two-Tone movement in the late '70s. With well-chosen ska classics and Prince Buster-inspired originals, the band mixed political and social activism and blended punk's intensity with an infectious dance beat. *The Specials* is a landmark recording that, while very much a product of its time, hasn't really dated at all. Produced by Elvis Costello. —*Chris Woodstra*

More Specials / Oct. 1980 / 2 Tone/Chrysalis ✦✦✦✦✦
Branching away from their ska roots, the band moves somewhat directionlessly into a neo-lounge act. Still in full force is the biting social commentary only in a slightly skewed environment. While this can be seen as a slight disappointment after the brilliant debut, with time *More Specials* can be nearly as rewarding—many of the songs are just as strong. —*Chris Woodstra*

In the Studio / 1984 / 2 Tone/Chrysalis ✦✦✦
When Hall, Staples, and Golding left to become Fun Boy Three, Jerry Dammers decided to continue with the addition of vocalist Stan Campbell. Nearly three years in the making, *In the Studio* lacks any hint of ska, and Campbell's vocals, while good, lack the tension needed for the overtly political direction of the band. The highpoints, "Racist Friend" and the anthem "Free Nelson Mandela" can be found on the *Singles Collection* so only completists need to bother. —*Chris Woodstra*

☆ **The Singles Collection** / Sep. 1991 / 2 Tone/Chrysalis ✦✦✦✦✦
All of the essential singles from their three albums are present on this 15-track collection. Not only the perfect starting point for the curious, the inclusion of B-sides and rarities, like an inspired cover of Dylan's "Maggie's Farm," makes this essential for fans. —*Chris Woodstra*

Coventry Automatics Aka the Specials: Dawning of a New Era / Mar. 1994 / Receiver ✦✦
The first incarnation of the Specials, a six-piece band called the Automatics, recorded a batch of demos in London in 1978, hoping to obtain a major recording deal; *Dawning of a New Era* presents them for the first time. As is the case with most demos, these recordings have a limited audience, but die-hard fans will thrill to the early, rawer versions of their favorites, along with songs that never made it to actual albums. —*Chris Woodstra*

Today's Specials / May 1996 / Virgin ✦

Phil Spector (Harvey Phillip Spector)

b. Dec. 26, 1940, New York, NY [The Bronx]
Producer, Vocals, Songwriter / Baroque Pop, Brill Building Pop, Girl Group, Pop, Rock & Roll
Though he very rarely released records under his name, as a producer Phil Spector has influenced the course of rock & roll more than all but a handful of performers. The "Wall of Sound" that he perfected in the early '60s opened unlimited possibilities for arrangements and sound construction in rock and pop, and his brilliant talents imprinted the discs that he produced with an artistic vision that was much more attributable to him than the talented performers with whom he worked.

To an extent that had never been imagined in rock & roll, Spector pumped his records full of orchestration—strings, horns, rattling percussion—that coalesced into teenage symphonies, never overwhelming the material or the passionate vocals. Though he enjoyed a lot of success with blue-eyed soul duo the Righteous Brothers in the mid-'60s, Spector's teen operas quickly became out of fashion. After the failure of Ike & Tina Turner's 1966 single "River Deep, Mountain High"—which he always considered among his greatest achievements—he retired to his L.A. mansion, marrying Ronnie Spector, lead singer of the Ronettes.

Spector re-emerged in the late '60s to do post-production on the Beatles' controversial *Let It Be* album, and he also produced George Harrison and John Lennon's first solo albums. For the past couple of decades, he's been active only sporadically, producing isolated albums by Dion, Leonard Cohen, and the Ramones. Today he's one of rock's most legendary recluses, rarely appearing in public, but his accomplishments cast a shadow over all performers and producers who aspire to create works of art in the studio. —*Richie Unterberger*

☆ **A Christmas Gift for You From Phil Spector** / 1963 / ABKCO ✦✦✦✦✦
Featuring Phil Spector's "Wall of Sound" in its prime and his early stable of artists, the Ronettes, Crystals, Darlene Love, and Bob B. Soxx & the Blue Jeans, this stands as inarguably the greatest Christmas record of all time. Spector believed he could produce a record for the holidays that would capture not only the essence of the Christmas spirit, but also be a pop masterpiece that would stand against any work these artists had already done. He succeeded on every level, with all four groups/singers recording some of their most memorable performances. This is the Christmas album by which all later holiday releases had to be judged, and it has inspired a host of imitators. (Note: This CD is available separately and as part of the highly recommended four-CD box set, *Phil Spector: Back to Mono [1958-1969]*.) —*Dennis MacDonald*

Early Productions 1958-1961 / 1983 / Rhino ✦✦✦✦
A sampling of Spector's earliest work, generally more pop-oriented, sappy, and far less distinguished than his early and mid-'60s classics. The Teddy Bears' "To Know Him Is To Love Him," and Gene Pitney's "Every Breath I Take," The Paris Sisters' "I Love How You Love Me," and Curtis Lee's "Pretty Little Angel Eyes" are fine hits that reveal much of the talent that would fully blossom on his Philles singles. The other tracks, including rarities by the Ducanes, Kell Osborne, and Spector's Three, suffer from weak songwriting, and would be downright dispensable if not for their historical significance. —*Richie Unterberger*

★ **Back to Mono (1958-1969)** / Nov. 12, 1991 / ABKCO ✦✦✦✦✦
At the time *Back to Mono* was released in 1991, Phil Spector's reputation as one of pop's great visionaries was intact, but there was no way to hear his genius. It wasn't just that there were no collections spotlighting his productions, there weren't collections of artists he produced. It wasn't until *Back to Mono* that there was a thorough overview of Spector's greatest work and while it's not without flaws, it still stands as one of the great box sets. Some may complain that there are no selections from his superstar '70s productions for John Lennon, George Harrison, Leonard Cohen, and the Ramones, but that's for the best, since their presence would have been incongruous, taking attention away from the music that forms the heart of Spector's legacy. All of that music is here, not just on the first three discs, all devoted to singles, but also on the fourth disc, his seminal 1963 holiday album *A Christmas Gift for You*, which isn't just the greatest rock Christmas album, but a crystallization of his skills. It could be argued that the song selection overlooks some obscure fan favorites, such as "Do the Screw," but that's simply nitpicking, because what's here are all the great Spector records, which were hardly just great productions, they were great songs, as well. As the set plays, it's hard not to be stunned by the depth of the material and clarity of Spector's vision for his famed Wall of Sound, whether you've heard these songs hundreds of times or not at all—especially because they gain power when grouped together. Many producers have been credited as the true creative force behind many rock records, but usually that's hyperbole. In Spector's case, it wasn't, as this set gloriously proves. —*Stephen Thomas Erlewine*

Benny Spellman

b. Dec. 11, 1931, Pensacola, FL
Vocals / New Orleans R&B, R&B
New Orleans R&B vocalist. His deep bass voice booms through loud and clear on many early-'60s Allen Toussaint productions, but Benny Spellman enjoyed a major hit of his own in 1962, "Lipstick Traces (On a Cigarette)." Spellman spent some time with Huey

"Piano" Smith and the Clowns before signing with Minit, where Toussaint utilized his deep pipes to full advantage as a backing vocalist behind Ernie K-Doe on "Mother-in-Law" and countless others. The Rolling Stones covered "Fortune Teller," the flip side of this hit. Spellman recorded through much of the '60s, his "Word Game" turning up on Atlantic in 1965, before he took a day gig as a beer salesman. *—Bill Dahl*

Fortune Teller / 1988 / Collectables ♦♦♦♦♦

Infectious and influential early-'60s New Orleans R&B. Spellman's low-pitched vocals are perfectly produced by pianist Allen Toussaint. *—Bill Dahl*

Skip Spence (Alexander Spence)

b. Apr. 18, 1946, Windsor, Ontario, Canada, **d.** Apr. 16, 1999, Santa Cruz, CA

Drums, Guitar / Folk-Rock, Psychedelic, Singer/Songwriter

Like a rough, more obscure American counterpart to Syd Barrett, Skip Spence was one of the late '60s' most colorful acid casualties. The original Jefferson Airplane drummer (although he was a guitarist who had never played drums before joining the group), Spence left after their first album to join Moby Grape. Like every member of that legendary band, he was a strong presence on their first album, playing guitar, singing, and writing "Omaha." The group ran into rough times in 1968, and Spence had the roughest, flipping out and (according to varying accounts) running amok in a record studio with a fire axe; he ended up being committed to New York's Bellevue Hospital. Upon his release, Spence cut an acid-charred classic, *Oar,* in 1969. Though released on a major label (Columbia), this was reportedly one of the lowest-selling items in its catalog and is hence one of the most valued psychedelic collector items. Much rawer and more homespun than the early Grape records, it features Spence on all (mostly acoustic) guitars, percussion, and vocals. With an overriding blues influence and doses of country, gospel, and acid freakout thrown in, this sounds something like Mississippi Fred McDowell imbued with the spirit of Haight-Ashbury 1967. It also featured cryptic, punning lyrics and wraithlike vocals that range from a low Fred Neil with gravel hoarseness to a barely there high wisp. Sadly, it was his only solo recording; more sadly, mental illness prevented Spence from reaching a fully functional state throughout the remainder of his lifetime. He died April 16, 1999, just two days short of his 54th birthday; the tribute album, *More Oar: A Tribute to Alexander "Skip" Spence,* featuring performances by Robert Plant, Beck, and Tom Waits, appeared just a few weeks later. *—Richie Unterberger*

● **Oar** / 1969 / Sundazed ♦♦♦♦♦

This 1969 LP was the only solo effort by the founding Moby Grape guitarist and original Jefferson Airplane drummer. Though released on a major label (Columbia), this was reportedly one of the lowest-selling items in its catalog, and is hence one of the most valued psychedelic collector items. Much rawer and more homespun than the early Grape records, this features Spence on all (mostly acoustic) guitars, percussion, and vocals. The tight, charging S.F. rock of the Grape in no way prepares the listener for the spaced-out, rural ambience here. With an overriding blues influence and doses of country, gospel, and acid freakout thrown in, this sounds something like Mississippi Fred McDowell imbued with the spirit of Haight-Ashbury '67. Great cryptic, punning lyrics and wonderful wraithlike vocals that range from a low Fred Neil-with-gravel hoarseness to a barely-there high wisp. Drug-addled, yes, but also inspirational, warm, and haunting, like a charred but charming survivor of the Summer of Love. The CD reissue of this premier acid folk album adds a few previously unreleased loose jams. *—Richie Unterberger*

Jon Spencer Blues Explosion

f. 1990, New York, NY

Indie Rock, Alternative Pop/Rock

After a long and semi-successful tenure as leader of scuzz-rock heroes Pussy Galore, Jon Spencer took his anti-rock vision and hooked up with guitarist Judah Bauer and drummer Russell Simins to create the scuzz-blues trio the Jon Spencer Blues Explosion. Postmodern to the core, little of what this band plays resembles standard blues. There is, however, a blues feel to what they play, meaning that in many instances they appropriate aspects of the blues (very often clichés) and incorporate them into their anarchic, noisy sound. Not part of alterna-rock's commercial establishment, Spencer has also managed to sharply divide critics who tend to see him as either inspired showman or mendacious con man (frankly, he's both). As with Royal Trux, the other band to emerge after the breakup of Pussy Galore, the Blues Explosion's earliest recordings are virtually incomprehensible (and impossible to find). The Blues Explosion's "breakthrough" came (as it did for Royal Trux) when they began to sound like a '70s rock band, with the release of 1993's *Extra Width. Orange* netted the band even more fans upon its release in 1994; 1996's *Now I Got Worry* and 1998's *Acme* were also successful. Still, there is a compelling argument to be made that despite his hip credentials, Spencer is more style than substance. Love him or loathe him (and it's easy to do both), he's a force to reckoned with. *—John Dougan*

Jon Spencer Blues Explosion / Apr. 24, 1992 / Caroline ♦♦♦

Produced by underground rock's most notorious producer, Steve Albini, this is as close as you're going to get to the Blues Explosion's primal, industrial strength noise rock. From the cacophonous start of "Write a Song," it's clear that this is not going to be your average blues album. Still, it's contagious in a demented kind of way, and the sloppiness, intentional crudeness, and semicoherence are punk rock to the core (the furious, psychobilly track "Rachel"). Not recommended as a place to start with Spencer, and definitely not recommended to those who think they're going to hear Muddy Waters songs. *—John Dougan*

Extra Width / Nov. 1, 1993 / Matador ♦♦♦♦♦

Much more accessible than the aforementioned record, but in no way does its accessibility detract from the record's adventurousness. *Extra Width* is a crankin' piece of bluesoid ranting, with Spencer working up one hysterical performance after another. "Afro" is as funky as all get-out and sounds like an old Curtis Mayfield track. Similarly, "Soul Letter" is a hefty chunk of riff-muck, as is the noisy bliss of "Soul Typecast." The playing is energetic and unhinged, and Spencer drives the engine with his whoopin' and hollerin'. Plenty of noticeably '70s production techniques add to the atmosphere, contributing significantly to what may be Spencer's best record. *—John Dougan*

Orange / Oct. 1994 / Matador ♦♦♦♦

By this juncture, you either love Spencer enough to listen to every record, or you've heard plenty and are decidedly uninterested. Still, *Orange* mines the same territory as *Extra Width,* and that may not be enough. At times, even during *Orange*'s best tracks ("Bell Bottoms"), the thin, retro-'70s worshipping sounds phoned-in and lacking in real emotional commitment. But, as with a lot of junk-rock, sometimes it can be appreciated for simply being junk, and that's fine. But I'm willing to bet that Spencer's core fans like the idea of the blues more than the reality. In other words, they don't mind the pose, nor do they mind the facade. In Jon Spencer's world, image is everything. *—John Dougan*

● **Now I Got Worry** / Oct. 15, 1996 / Matador/Capitol ♦♦♦♦♦

Where *Orange* had some awkward attempts at funk, *Now I Got Worry* is a raw bloozy workout, full of harsh guitars and barked vocals. The sound of the Blues Explosion is so fiery and alive that it overshadows Spencer's habit for campy posturing, and that's what keeps *Now I Got Worry* afloat. Once it's finished, it becomes hard not to second-guess Spencer's intentions, but the album is the closest the Blues Explosion has come to capturing their wild, intense live show on record. *—Stephen Thomas Erlewine*

Acme / Oct. 20, 1998 / Matador/Capitol ♦♦♦

Part of the reason Jon Spencer Blues Explosion has been so distasteful to legions of blues purists is that Spencer cherishes not the mythology of the blues or the songcraft, but the actual *sound* of classic blues records—what's important is the feel and the grit of the performance. Often, that means that the Blues Explosion's records are better when they're playing than they are in memory, but there's no question that the trio has shrewdly crafted albums that pack real sonic force. They've also been sharp enough to subtly explore new territory with each album, and on *Acme,* pure sound matters more than ever. Like the Stones, the Blues Explosion never abandons their signature sound, even when they're branching into new territory. No matter how many electronic bleeps, hip-hop loops, or cut-and-paste arrangements rear their heads on *Acme,* or how many producers or remixers are employed, the primal, two-guitar racket remains at the center of Blues Explosion's sound. But the electronica and hip-hop flourishes aren't folly, either—they confirm Spencer's ultimate goal of sound over structure, force over sense. And while there are only a handful of songs to latch on to, the dynamic explosions of sound guarantee that *Acme* is a captivating listen, at least the first time through. Still, it doesn't quite live up to the standards of its three predecessors, not only because it lacks full-fledged songs (the other three were weak on those, anyway) but because it simply isn't as overwhelmingly visceral as other Blues Explosion excursions. While frequently exciting, the sonic experimentations sound cerebral instead of primal, and JSBX have always been better when they aimed straight for the gut, since that's when they came the closest to capturing the feel, if not the sound, of the classic blues records they've used as a blueprint. *—Stephen Thomas Erlewine*

Spice Girls

f. 1993

Teen Pop, Club/Dance, Euro-Dance, Euro-Pop, Adult Contemporary, Dance-Pop

The Spice Girls were the first major British pop music phenomenon of the mid-'90s to not have a debt to independent pop/rock. Instead, the all-female quintet derived from the dance-pop tradition that made Take That the most popular British group of the early '90s, but there was one crucial difference. The Spice Girls used dance-pop as a musical base, but they infused the music with a fiercely independent, feminist stance that was equal parts Madonna, post-riot-grrrl alternative-rock feminism, and a co-opting of the good-times-all-the-time stance of England's new lad culture. Their proud, all-girl image and catchy dance-pop appealed to younger listeners, while their colorful, sexy personalities and sense of humor appealed to older music fans, making the Spice Girls a cross-generational success. The group also became chart-toppers throughout Europe in 1996, before concentrating in America in early 1997. *—Stephen Thomas Erlewine*

● **Spice** / 1996 / Virgin ♦♦♦♦♦

Spice doesn't need to be original to be entertaining, no do the Spice Girls need to be good singers. It just has to be executed well, and the innocuous dance-pop of *Spice* is infectious. None of the Girls have great voices, but they do exude personality and charisma, which is what drives bouncy dance-pop like "Wannabe," with its ridiculous "zig-a-zig-ahhh" hook, into pure pop guilty pleasure. What is surprising is how the sultry soul of "Say You'll Be There" is more than just a guilty pleasure, and how ballads like "2 Become 1" are perfect adult contemporary confections. The rest of the album isn't quite as catchy as those first three singles, but it is still an irresistible, immaculately crafted pop that gets by on the skills of the producer and the charisma of the five Spices. Sure, the last half of the album is forgettable, but it sounds good while it's on, which is the key to a good dance-pop record. *—Stephen Thomas Erlewine*

Spiceworld / Nov. 4, 1997 / Virgin ♦♦♦♦♦

The Spice Girls, as well as their managers and songwriters, are nothing if not clever, and *Spiceworld,* the group's second album, illustrates exactly how sharp they are. Conventional wisdom dictates that *Spiceworld* should be a weak fascimile of *Spice,* which itself featured a handful of great singles surrounded by filler. Conventional wisdom, in this case, is wrong—*Spiceworld* is a better record than its predecessor, boasting a more consistent (and catchier) set of songs and an intoxicating sense of fun. Instead of merely rewriting *Spice*, *Spiceworld* consolidates and expands the group's style, adding Latin flourishes ("Spice Up Your Life"), kitschy blues ("The Lady Is a Vamp") and stomping, neo-Motown blue-eyed soul in the vein of Culture Club ("Stop"). The girls—Mel C. in particular—are actually turning into good vocalists, and each song plays to their strengths, giving each Spice a chance to shine. Best of all, each song has a strong melody and a strong, solid beat, whether it's a ballad or a dance number. It's a pure, unadulterated guilty pleasure and some of the best manufactured mainstream dance-pop of the late '90s. —*Stephen Thomas Erlewine*

Forever / Nov. 7, 2000 / Virgin ♦♦
The Spice Girls waited three years to deliver their third album, *Forever*. While they were away, a number of things changed—things have that tendency—but the pop scene didn't shift so drastically that it was chilly to a Spice comeback. Many pundits argued, fairly accurately, that they were the trailblazers for the resurgence of frothy, unabashed teen pop in the last two years of the 20th century. But, just like there was a decade separating the ages of the Spices and Britney Spears, there's a huge difference between the cheery, featherweight "Wannabe" and the calculated sex and shock of "...Baby One More Time"—ironically, the older girls made music that was lighter and more innocent. With *Forever*, they continue to follow that path, with a sleek, stylish attempt at maturity, but they seem lost because they just don't sound interested any more. Sure, they make all the right moves, hiring superstar producer Rodney Jerkins to helm most of the tracks, but the record is curiously self-conscious and flat. Neither the production, songs, or performances have much life to them, with the exception of the closer "Goodbye," which significantly was released as a Christmas single back in 1999. There's little of the giddy sense of friendship that marked their first two records, and the ballads aren't as sweetly sentimental; there's little of the charm that made Spice Girls so irresistible. Often, *Forever* plays like the Girls realized that it's their final album, and they put in just enough effort to make it palatable, but not enough to make it appetizing. That's not the best way to go out, but it seems like the best the Spice Girls could do in 2000, considering that their hearts and minds were clearly on their ever-increasing solo projects. —*Stephen Thomas Erlewine*

The Spiders

f. 1953, **db.** 1957
New Orleans R&B, R&B
A fine New Orleans vocal ensemble who started as a gospel group, the Spiders scored five Top Ten R&B hits for Imperial in 1954 and 1955. They were originally the Zion City Harmonizers in the '40s, and also did radio work as the Delta Southernaires in 1952 and 1953. Lead singer Hayward "Chuck" Carbo, Joe Maxon, Matthew West, Oliver Howard, and Leonard "Chick" Carbo got their first hit with "I Didn't Want to Do It" in 1954. It was also their biggest, peaking at number three. They continued the string until the end of 1955. The Carbo brothers departed in 1956, moving on to solo careers. —*Ron Wynn*

● **The Imperial Sessions** / 1993 / Bear Family ♦♦♦♦♦
All of the Spiders' best songs are collected on this extensive double-disc set. —*AMG*

The Spiders

f. 1961, **db.** 1971
Garage Rock
The Spiders may be the most renowned 1960s Japanese vocal rock group, certainly among collectors outside of Japan. Like many non-English-speaking nations, Japan generated many bands playing in the British Invasion style, and the Spiders were among the first and foremost. Drummer Shochi Tanabe formed the band in 1961, and at the outset they played in an American country music style. By 1966, however, they were recording in a vocal beat group style reflecting the influence of bands like the Beatles, the Rolling Stones, and the Animals. In the last half of the 1960s, they had some Japanese hits, cut about half a dozen albums, and even made some attempts to breach the English and American market. They made no commercial impression overseas, however, though they continued to enjoy success at home. Singing in both Japanese and fractured English, their sound was heavily imitative of American and particularly British groups, mixing in some California vocal group harmony and psychedelic influences. Mixing original material and covers of overseas rock hits, the songwriting and musicianship was frankly not on the level of the outstanding groups from other countries. What attracts cultists to their records these days is a peculiar manic intensity found in much of their work, as well as odd mixtures of styles and fractured song structures that, to Western ears at least, can sometimes sound like an off-the-wall mangling of familiar forms. The best of their recordings are collected on Big Beat's compilation *Let's Go Spiders!*, which only draws from the years 1966-1968. In early 1971 they broke up, although beginning in the early '80s they occasionally re-formed for reunions. —*Richie Unterberger*

● **Let's Go Spiders!** / Dec. 12, 2000 / Big Beat ♦♦♦♦
The Spiders recorded from the mid-'60s through around 1970 in a variety of styles. However, this 28-song compilation is exclusively comprised of the 1966-1968 British Invasion-garage-psych material with the strongest appeal to international collectors. Looked at in the cold objective light of day, it couldn't be rated among the best such stuff to pour forth from non-English-speaking lands, although it's certainly brimming with frenzied energy. Their weaknesses were common to many such bands, whatever their native language. Their original material was frequently derivative, and lacked the melodic invention and instrumental skill of their inspirations; many of these are feverish but basic R&B-pop hybrids. Getting past all that—few people are checking this out expecting something on the order of the Yardbirds or even the Chocolate Watch Band, after all—it's brash, if oft-rudimentary, beat music with some unusual twists, particularly in the ants-in-the-pants raunchy vocals, sung in both Japanese and English. "Kuroyuri No Uta" is a clever

psych-pop number that appropriates a vocal hook from the Association's "Cherish"; "Lucky Rain" is a good illustration of their occasional facility with brooding, minor-keyed tunes; "Summer Girl" illustrates their occasional bent toward Beach Boys-influenced California pop; and "Kaze Ga Naiteriru" and "Ano Niji Wo Tsukamo" summon some genuinely weird moods with their mix of growly spy guitar and cinematic orchestration. —*Richie Unterberger*

Spin Doctors

f. 1988, New York, NY
Jam Bands, American Trad Rock, Pop/Rock
There were many pseudo-hippie, jam-oriented blues rockers in New York during the early '90s, but only the Spin Doctors made it big. And they made it big because they not only could immerse themselves in a groove, but they also had concise pop skills. "Little Miss Can't Be Wrong" and "Two Princes" were cleverly written singles, full of clean, blues-inflected licks and ingratiating pop melodies. *Pocket Full of Kryptonite* had been around for nearly a year when MTV and radio began playing "Little Miss Can't Be Wrong," but once they started playing it, they couldn't stop. The Spin Doctors became an overnight sensation, selling millions of albums around the world.

Their second album, 1994's *Turn It Upside Down*, didn't sell very well when it was released, largely because the first single, "Cleopatra's Cat," was a failed experiment in funk. But the second single, "You Let Your Heart Go Too Fast," was in the vein of "Two Princes," and the album began to sell after the song was released. In the summer of 1996, the Spin Doctors released *You've Got to Believe in Something*. After the album failed to make an impression on the charts, the Spin Doctors were dropped from Epic in the fall of 1996. After a couple of years, the group found a new label; their first record for Uptown/Universal, *Here Comes the Bride*, appeared in the summer of 1999. —*Stephen Thomas Erlewine*

Up for Grabs . . . Live / Jan. 1991 / Epic ♦♦♦
Although billed as a mere EP, this six-song live set recorded at New York City's Wetlands club in September 1990 runs 45 minutes, which used to be the length of a full-fledged album. Calling it an EP is a way of de-emphasizing its significance, since it is intended more as an introduction to the band than as the major statement implied by a debut album. Fair enough: *Up for Grabs* gives you the kinetic, groove-heavy approach of Spin Doctors, especially on the leadoff song, "Big Fat Funky Booty," and Christopher Barron proves to be a funny, crowd-pleasing frontman, but it's also obvious that not much money was spent producing this record. —*William Ruhlmann*

Pocket Full of Kryptonite / Aug. 1991 / Epic ♦♦♦♦
After nearly a year of solid touring, the Spin Doctors scored a huge, unexpected success with the incessantly catchy "Little Miss Can't Be Wrong." The rest of *Pocket Full of Kryptonite* will please fans of that song; the album is full of the loose, leisurely three-chord pop/rock jams the Spin Doctors specialize in. It may be unfair to compare them to the Grateful Dead, but the Doctors often suggest a lighter, more pop-oriented version of that band. While all of the best tracks were issued as singles ("Jimmy Olsen's Blues," "Two Princes," and "Little Miss"), there are still enough good moments on the rest of the album to please anyone who loves the hits. —*Stephen Thomas Erlewine*

Homebelly Groove . . . Live / Nov. 24, 1992 / Epic ♦♦♦
Homebelly Groove Live follows up The Doctors' left field success with the album *Pocket Full of Kryptonite* and its single "Little Miss Can't Be Wrong." The disc re-releases (in remixed form) tracks from their now out-of-print 1990 EP *Up for Grabs . . . Live*, adding live renditions, and four previously unreleased numbers. Highlights include a lengthy but inspired segue of "What Time Is It? / Off My Line" and a relentlessly propulsive "Refrigerator Car." —*Roch Parisien*

Turn It Upside Down / Jun. 14, 1994 / Epic ♦♦
You've Got to Believe in Something / May 1996 / Epic ♦♦♦
● **Just Go Ahead Now: A Retrospective** / Oct. 24, 2000 / Epic/Legacy ♦♦♦♦♦
There was a moment in the spring of 1993, as the single "Two Princes" and the debut album *Pocket Full of Kryptonite* peaked in the Top Five of their respective charts, that the Spin Doctors appeared to be on the brink of a big career. Only a little over a year later the group began a commercial slide that turned into one of the more spectacular flameouts of the '90s when their third album, *You've Got to Believe in Something*, didn't even sell well enough to reach the charts. Pop fans can be fickle, but this was ridiculous. That at least seems to be the reasoning behind the selections on *Just Go Ahead Now: A Retrospective*, which excerpts five tracks each from the three albums, adding the previously unreleased mid-tempo rocker "Miss America" and a live version of "Refrigerator Car" from *Pocket Full of Kryptonite* that was on the concert album *Homebelly Groove . . . Live*. Compilation producer Bruce Dickinson's apparent contention that the three studio albums are of equal value is not borne out by a listen to the disc. Those first five tracks, all of which were album rock radio hits and three of which reached the singles charts, present the band at its lively, kinetic best, with Chris Barron rhythmically singing his wordy lyrics over the funky grooves. But as soon as "Cleopatra's Cat," the first track from *Turn It Upside Down*, begins, the music begins to seem forced. There are some good songs as the disc goes on, but nothing to match the rush of the early tracks. As it is, this release looks like the record label's excuse to delete the Spin Doctors' other albums while keeping a compilation in print. —*William Ruhlmann*

The Spinners

f. 1961, Detroit, MI
Smooth Soul, Quiet Storm, Philly Soul, Soul
The Spinners were the greatest soul group of the early '70s, creating a body of work that

defined the lush, seductive sound of Philly Soul. Ironically, the band's roots lay in Detroit, where they formed as a doo wop group during the late '50s. Throughout the '60s, the Spinners tried to land a hit by adapting to the shifting fashions of R&B and pop. By the mid-'60s, they had signed with Motown Records, but the level never gave the group much consideration. "It's a Shame" became a hit in 1970, but the label continued to ignore the group, and dropped the band two years later. Unsigned and featuring a new lead singer Phillipe Wynne, the Spinners seemed destined to never break into the big-leagues, but they managed to sign with Atlantic Records, where they began working with producer Thom Bell. With his assistence, the Spinners developed a distinctive sound, one that relied on Wynne's breathtaking falsetto and the group's intricate vocal harmonies. Bell provided the group with an appropriately detailed production, creating a detailed web of horns, strings, backing vocals, and lightly funky rhythms. Between 1972 and 1977, the Spinners and Thom Bell recorded a number of soul classics, including "I'll Be Around," "Could It Be I'm Fallin in Love," "Mighty Love," "Ghetto Child," "Then Came You," "Games People Play" and "The Rubberband Man." Wynne left in 1977 and the Spinners had hits for a few years after his departure, but the group will always be remembered for its classic mid-'70s work. —*Stephen Thomas Erlewine*

Party: My Pad After Surfin' / 1963 / Time ✦✦✦
Their debut for Tri-Phi put the Spinners on the R&B map quickly with the single "That's What Girls Are Made For." Of course, confusion quickly reigned when it turned out that Harvey Fuqua had sung the lead and wasn't even in the group. Chico Edwards replaced George Dixon when the band was signed to Motown, but they wouldn't enjoy another huge hit until they left Motown for Atlantic. If you find this album, grab it immediately. It's been deleted forever. —*Ron Wynn*

The 2nd Time Around / 1970 / VIP ✦✦✦
The Spinners began making some soul noise in 1970, when Stevie Wonder produced a pair of hit singles for them. "It's A Shame" was their first Top Ten R&B song since 1965, and was the swan song for G.C. Cameron as lead vocalist. Phillipe Wynne stepped in and shortly after made everyone forget (who remembered) that Cameron was ever in the band. The follow-up tune, "We'll Have It Made," wasn't bad either. —*Ron Wynn*

Spinners / 1972 / Rhino ✦✦✦✦✦
A superb album, arguably their finest, though not their biggest, crossover work. The Spinners teamed with Thom Bell and made Motown look stupid with this album of glorious anthems. "I'll Be Around" and "Could It Be I'm Falling in Love" ended any discussions, mentions, or even thoughts of their former lead singer G.C. Cameron as Phillippe Wynne was emerging as the king of immaculate, sophisticated soul. They had three R&B chart toppers from this album and were now dominating the Motown acts they once idolized. —*Ron Wynn*

The Best of the Spinners [Motown] / 1973 / Motown ✦✦✦✦✦
Yet another Motown collection (that makes at least three for a group that only had four hits from 1965 to 1971) of Spinners singles. It's not as extensive as the anthology, so if you only want hits, they're available. Otherwise, take your pick between it and the others. —*Ron Wynn*

Mighty Love / Jan. 1974 / Rhino ✦✦✦✦✦
Phillippe Wynne's twisting, soulful, frequently captivating voice was at its finest on this 1974 album. The title track was a smash in edited single form, and the extended album version contains marvelous Wynne ad-libs and exchanges nicely contrasted by the group's harmonizing. The album contains many other fine songs, like "Ain't No Price on Happiness" and "I'm Coming Home," and was their second Atlantic release. It equaled the gold-selling pace of its predecessor and cemented the Spinners' status as R&B stars. —*Ron Wynn*

New and Improved / Feb. 1974 / Rhino ✦✦✦✦
The Spinners were on a roll; after years of neglect at the hands of Motown, their ship just kept coming in, and in, and in with Atlantic Records. *New and Improved* is an absolute classic, yet it gets less run than some of their other LPs. Everything from the romanticism of "Smile We Have Each Other," a real tearjerker, to the self-assured, driven "I've Got to Make It on My Own" is on board, and it all works. "Sadie," a song about the death of a mother, became a signature song for the Spinners; it was revived in the '90s by R. Kelly, who introduced it to new fans, many of whom thought he created the touching tribute. Dionne Warwick struts her soul on "Then Came You," accompanied by Bobby Smith; it's a mover from the first note. A strong effort from Thom Bell and the Spinners. —*Andrew Hamilton*

Live / 1975 / Atlantic ✦✦

Pick of the Litter / 1975 / Rhino ✦✦✦✦✦
The Spinners were rolling in the 1970s, and this proved to be their biggest album ever. It peaked in the pop Top Ten at number eight, and they racked up four consecutive R&B Top Ten singles, including the chart topper "They Just Can't Stop It (The Games People Play)." Phillipe Wynne sang with an amazing mix of class and fire, sophistication, and earthiness that hadn't been heard in soul circles for years. Of course, this is now out of print. —*Ron Wynn*

Happiness Is Being With the Spinners / 1976 / Atlantic ✦✦✦

Yesterday, Today & Tomorrow / 1977 / Atlantic ✦✦✦

The Best of the Spinners [Atlantic] / 1978 / Atlantic ✦✦✦✦✦
The Spinners lost lead singer Philippe Wynne in 1977, as he left to join Parliament/Funkadelic. However, they were getting replacement John Edwards acclimated, Atlantic issued this greatest-hits LP containing all the gems with Wynne as their lead singer. Until the Atlantic two-CD set was issued, this was a definitive work, and it's still

as complete a single album package as available. It includes "Could It Be I'm Falling in Love," "How Could I Let You Get Away," "Mighty Love," "Rubberband Man," and "One of a Kind (Love Affair)," among others. —*Ron Wynn*

Dancin' and Lovin' / 1979 / Rhino ✦✦✦
While soul purists recoiled in horror, the Spinners climbed off the ropes and soared back into the spotlight by recasting themselves as a modified dance/crossover band with soul/R&B influences. It worked in the short run, as their remake of the Four Seasons' "Working My Way Back to You," mixed with their own wailer, "Forgive Me Girl," made a nice sandwich at number two pop and number six R&B. It took nearly a year, but they were revived. While they wore the formula out with a similar follow-up, it gave them a fresh start and the necessary credibility to eventually return to their customary sophisticated soul. —*Ron Wynn*

From Here to Eternity / 1979 / Atlantic ✦✦✦
Yesterday, Today & Tomorrow all but ended the group's string of classics. And this album's predecessor, *Spinners #8*, rightfully put a big scare into their biggest fans. The good news is that *From Here to Eternity* shows things get better. A few of the best tracks are easily the best songs Thom Bell and the Spinners had been involved with since *Pick of the Litter*. Admittedly it does a take awhile to get to them. The too-smooth and lyrically barren tracks, "It's Natural Affair" and "Don't Let the Man Get You," are so interchangeable they cancel one another out. While those embarrassments don't bear thinking about, the best tracks have lead singer John Edwards working his magic with his excitable persona. He survives the potential treacle of the ballad "A Plain and Simple Song" by giving a flat-out believable and melisma-filled performance. On the melodic and disco-styled "Are You Ready for Love," Edwards' voice finally meshes with Bell's patently effervescent production. The effort's only released single, "If You Wanna Do a Dance (All Night)," comes off like a more languid "Rubberband Man." The track has Edwards doing a commanding lead, and as he calls out "Henry, Billy" on the fade, you know he's the right guy for the gig. The last track, "Once You Fall in Love" has interesting production values and was a great way to close the album. While it is true *From Here to Eternity* didn't help the Spinners that much commercially, it features a few underrated gems and some good to great production by Bell. —*Jason Elias*

Love Trippin' / 1980 / Atlantic ✦✦✦

Labor of Love / 1981 / Atlantic ✦✦✦

Grand Slam / 1982 / Atlantic ✦✦

Lovin' Feelings / 1985 / Mirage ✦✦

Down to Business / Sep. 1989 / Volt ✦✦✦
The Spinners made a bid for renewed stardom on a soul independent when they signed with the revived Volt in 1989. Unfortunately, they also found out quickly that being on Volt didn't mean in the late '80s what it meant in the '60s and '70s. Despite a representative effort, with some excellent harmonizing and fine, soulful leads from John Edwards, they couldn't even get a nibble from urban contemporary radio. They're still working the nostalgia/oldies circuit, but this one was a shocker all around. —*Ron Wynn*

Can't Shake This Feeling / 1990 / Atlantic ✦✦✦

☆ **One of a Kind Love Affair** / Nov. 5, 1991 / Rhino ✦✦✦✦✦
Spanning from their first single, 1961's "That's What Girls Are Made For," to their last charting single more than 20 years later, *One of a Kind Love Affair—The Anthology* is the definitive Spinners collection. The bulk of the two-CD compilation is the group's work with Thom Bell during the mid-'70s, easily the best work they ever recorded and arguably the finest Philly soul singles. All of the Spinners' major hits are here, as are excellent, informative liner notes (including complete personnel and discography). —*Stephen Thomas Erlewine*

★ **The Very Best of the Spinners** / Apr. 20, 1993 / Rhino ✦✦✦✦✦
The Spinners were to the 1970s what the Temptations were to the '60s. Though the Spinners, a quintet like the Temptations, approached their music from a different perspective, the result was still the same: hit after hit after hit. This album is evidence. It is led by two outstanding tenors: Bobby Smith and Phillippé Wynne. Smith had an ultra sound for a second tenor; his articulate interpretation of the lyric was elegant and charming, even with the most painful message. Wynne, another smooth tenor with much agility, would inject that invigorating thrust, giving the group that soulful burst that elevated them to a level not many have known. He has an extraordinary ability to ad-lib through minutes of a song by dancing and prancing on words, melodizing within a melody and never forsaking the focus of the song. His feats were remarkable.

Upon Wynne's exit in 1977, John Edward, who was also a dynamic singer, made his mark with a couple of chart busters. On occasion, bass Pervis Jackson, baritone Henry Fambrough, and tenor Billy Henderson would inject a vocal lead, which was always perfectly orchestrated. However, the primary lead singers for the Detroit fivesome were "mister smooth" Bobby Smith and the fascinating Phillippé Wynne. This set features eight number one Billboard singles and a herd of Top Ten hits, including the duet with Dionne Warwick, who is in impeccable form. From the first song through the last, the Spinners just keep turning out hits. The majority of these songs were produced by the brilliant Thom Bell, one of the top producers of that era. This is a great collection. —*Craig Lytle*

The Very Best of the Spinners, Vol. 2 / May 27, 1997 / Rhino ✦✦✦✦
The Very Best of the Spinners, Vol. 2 rounds up the lesser-known hits that didn't make the first volume, plus selected album tracks, including "Heaven on Earth," "You're Throwing a Good Love Away," "Love or Leave," "Wake Up Susan" and "Easy Come, Easy Go." —*Stephen Thomas Erlewine*

Spirit

f. 1967, Los Angeles, CA, **db.** 1972

Psychedelic, Prog Rock/Art Rock

California's eclectic Spirit blended hard rock and jazz with elements of blues, country, and folk to produce a series of acclaimed albums during the late '60s and early '70s. The group was formed in 1967 by guitarist Randy California (born Randy Wolfe) and his shaven-headed stepfather, percussionist Ed "Mr. Skin" Cassidy. The two first played together in a band called the Red Roosters in 1965, which also featured future Spirit members Jay Ferguson (vocals) and Mark Andes (bass). Spirit's unique style, Cassidy's visual distinctiveness, and the idea of a stepfather/stepson combo quickly attracted attention, and the group recorded two well-received albums in 1968 (*Spirit* and *The Family That Plays Together*). The latter produced their only hit, "I Got a Line on You." 1970's *The Twelve Dreams of Dr. Sardonicus* was hailed as their finest album, and ultimately proved to be their biggest seller as well. However, Ferguson and Andes left the band in 1971 to form Jo Jo Gunne; Andes would later join Firefall and Heart. Brothers Christian and Al Staehely were brought in on guitar and bass, respectively, but California and Cassidy themselves left after the *Feedback* album. California moved to England and played with Peter Hammill, but a concussion sustained in a fall from a horse and a nervous breakdown interrupted his career. He returned in 1972 with a spotty solo LP, *Kaptain Kopter and the (Fabulous) Twirlybirds.* Spirit reformed for the first of several times in 1974 with California, Cassidy, and bassist Barry Keene. Their ensuing LPs sold rather poorly, leading to periodic breakups and reunions. California continued to lead various Spirit lineups, usually with Cassidy, until his accidental drowning death in January 1997. *—Steve Huey*

Spirit / 1968 / Epic/Legacy ✦✦✦✦✦

Spirit's debut unveiled a band that seemd determine to out-eclecticize everybody else on the California psychedelic scene, with its melange of rock, jazz, blues, folk-rock, and even a bit of classical and Indian music. Teenaged Randy California immediately established a signature sound with his humming, sustain-heavy tone; middle-aged drummer Ed Cassidy gave the group unusual versatility; and the songs tackled unusual lyrical themes, like "Fresh Garbage" and "Mechanical World." As is often the case in such hybrids, the sum fell somewhat short of the parts; they could play more styles than almost any other group, but couldn't play (or, more crucially, wrote) as well as the top acts in any given one of those styles. There's some interesting stuff here, nonentheless; "Uncle Jack" shows some solid psych-pop instincts, and it sounds like Led Zeppelin lifted the opening guitar lines of "Taurus" for their own much more famous "Stairway to Heaven." The 1996 CD reissue has four previously unissued bonus tracks cut during the same time as the *Spirit* sessions, including an alternate take of the lengthy, jazzy "Elijah." *—Richie Unterberger*

The Family That Plays Together / Dec. 1968 / Epic/Legacy ✦✦✦✦✦

On this, the second Spirit album, the group put all of the elements together that made them the legendary (and underrated) band that they were. Jazz, rock & roll, and even classical elements combined to create one of the cleanest, most tasteful syntheses of its day. The group had also improved measurably from their fine debut album, especially in the area of vocals. The album's hit single, "I Got a Line on You," boasts especially strong harmonies as well as one of the greatest rock riffs of the period. The first side of this record is a wonderful and seamless suite, and taken in its entirety, one of the greatest sides on Los Angeles rock. The CD reissue also boasts some excellent bonus tracks. "So Little to Say" is one of Jay Ferguson's finest compositions ever, and the jazz-inspired instrumentals such as "Fog" and "Space Chile" showcase pianist John Locke as one of the most inspired and lyrical players in the rock idiom to date. All in all, a classic album and a true landmark. *—Matthew Greenwald*

Clear / 1969 / Epic/Legacy ✦✦✦✦

Although this album may not be seen as the definitive Spirit statement, it has several moments of brilliance that prove what a revolutionary band they were. Coming off of the success of *The Family That Plays Together* and "I Got a Line on You," the group entered the studio with Lou Adler once again in the producer's chair. Unfortunately, the group appeared to be beginning to fragment, and it shows on this uneven but ultimately fine album. "Dark Eyed Woman" opens the album with promise, and it is indeed one of Spirit's hardest-rocking studio performances. Randy California's inspired guitar solo is one of the finest performances of the period. The riff and general feel of the track (right down to the siren sound effects) were borrowed by Traffic on "Shoot Out at the Fantasy Factory." The record tends to go downhill from there (primarily due to some uninspired songwriting), but not without high points like "Cold Wind" and the awesome closer "New Dope in Town." *—Matthew Greenwald*

The Twelve Dreams of Dr. Sardonicus / 1970 / Epic/Legacy ✦✦✦✦✦

Although this has the reputation of being their most far-out album, it actually contains the most disciplined songwriting and playing of the original lineup, cutting back on some of the drifting and offering some of their more melodic tunes. The lilting "Nature's Way" was the most endearing FM standard on the album, which also included some of Spirit's most popular songs in "Animal Zoo" and "Mr. Skin." The 1996 CD reissue has four bonus tracks, though these are on the nonessential side: mono versions of "Animal Zoo" and "Morning Will Come," the 1970 single "Red Light Roll On," and the previously unissued "Rougher Road." *—Richie Unterberger*

Feedback / 1972 / Epic ✦✦

The Best of Spirit / 1973 / Epic ✦✦✦

The Best of Spirit is a solid primer on the group's work, comprised primarily of big hits and familiar items like "Nature's Way," "Animal Zoo," "I Got a Line on You," and "Dark Eyed Woman." For the curious and the casual fan, it's not a bad introduction to the group's work. *—Stephen Thomas Erlewine*

Spirit of '76 / 1975 / Mercury ✦✦

● **Time Circle** / Jul. 23, 1991 / Epic/Legacy ✦✦✦✦✦

From the opening riff of "Fresh Garbage," with its jazzy electric piano and fuzzy rock guitar, Spirit set out to carve a unique, eclectic niche in the music world of the late '60s. Though the band achieved only limited commercial success, the music they produced from 1968-1972 still sounds fresh decades later. *Time Circle* collects the bulk of their recorded output during this five-year period. The 41 tracks assembled here include nine from the group's eponymous debut, seven from the follow-up *The Band That Plays Together,* six from *Clear,* and nine-tenths of the classic *The Twelve Dreams of Dr. Sardonicus.* This set also includes unreleased tracks, singles, and B-sides to provide a complete look at this excellent quintet. *—Jim Newsom*

The Mercury Years / Mar. 25, 1997 / Mercury ✦✦✦

The double-disc set *The Mercury Years* is a comprehensive overview of Spirit's late-'70s recordings for Mercury Records, containing nearly all of their 1975 album *Spirit of '76,* plus highlights from *Farther Along* (1976), *Son of Spirit* (1976), and *Future Games* (1977). Though this music isn't among the band's best, it's occasionally intriguing, and for dedicated fans of Spirit's '60s albums, this compilation is the best way to appreciate their late '70s work. *—Stephen Thomas Erlewine*

Spiritualized

f. 1989, Rugby, Midlands, England

Noise Pop, Ambient Pop, Dream Pop, Space Rock, Neo-Psychedelia, Alternative Pop/Rock

Formed from the ashes of the trance-rockers Spacemen 3, singer/guitarist Jason Pierce's group Spiritualized did not break away from his prior band's trademark hypnotic minimalism; instead, they perfected it. Drawing on the continued influence of the Velvet Underground, LaMonte Young, and Steve Reich, Spiritualized staked out a common ground between minimalism and lush symphonics—while powered by simple, repetitious motifs, their songs simultaneously blossomed into rich, shimmering sonic panoramas inspired by the majestic studio wizardry of Phil Spector and Brian Wilson. Such seeming contradictions were essential to the group's alchemy: while the infamous Spacemen 3 tag of "taking drugs to make music to take drugs to" remained a cornerstone of their craft, at the same time Spiritualized's very name acknowledged the existence of other forces, further reflected in their heavy debt to gospel and soul music as well as an affinity for mantras and devotional hymns. *—Jason Ankeny*

Lazer Guided Melodies / 1992 / Dedicated ✦✦✦✦✦

The group's seminal debut album is aptly titled: The melodies shimmer and drone and hum like otherworldly pop tunes, and Radley and Pierce's vocals hover gently in the mix. One of the premier dream-pop albums, *Lazer Guided Melodies* is both beautiful and innovative. *—Heather Phares*

Pure Phase / Mar. 28, 1995 / Dedicated ✦✦✦

Spiritualized's eagerly awaited second album continues the group's ethereal tradition, this time with a loopier, more symphonic sound. Many of the songs swell past the six-minute mark, ebbing and flowing majestically. "Medication," "Electric Phase," "Lay Back in the Sun," and "Spread Your Wings" typify the dreamy grandeur of most of the album. *—Heather Phares*

● **Ladies and Gentlemen We Are Floating in Space** / Jul. 1, 1997 / Arista ✦✦✦✦✦

Spiritualized's third collection of hypnotic headphone symphonies is their most brilliant and accessible to date. Largely forsaking the drones and minimalistic, repetitive riffs which have characterized his work since the halcyon days of Spacemen 3, Jason Pierce re-focuses here and spins off into myriad new directions; in a sense, *Ladies and Gentlemen We Are Floating in Space,* with its majestic, Spector-like glow, is his classic rock album. "Come Together" and the blistering "Electricity" are his most edgy, straightforward rockers in eons, while the stunning "I Think I'm in Love" settles into a divided-psyche call-and-response R&B groove, and the closing "Cop Shoot Cop" (with guest Dr. John) locks into a voodoo blues trance. Lyrically, Pierce is at his most open and honest: The record is a heartfelt confessional of love and loss, with redemption found only in the form of drugs—designed, no less, to look like a prescription pharmaceutical package, *Ladies and Gentlemen* is pointedly explicit in its description of drug use as a means of killing the pain on track after track. Conversely, never before have the literal implications of the name "Spiritualized" been explored in such earnest detail—the London Community Gospel Choir appears prominently on a number of songs, while another bears the title "No God, Only Religion," pushing the music even further toward the kind of cosmic gospel transcendence it craves. A masterpiece. *—Jason Ankeny*

Royal Albert Hall October 10 1997 / Nov. 10, 1998 / Arista ✦✦✦✦

Live albums, by and large, are a dime a dozen—inconsequential souvenirs designed to placate fans awaiting new studio material, they rarely if ever shed new light on the artist in question; rarer still is their ability to approximate the energy and excitement of the concert setting itself. Spiritualized's transcendent *Royal Albert Hall October 10 1997* is the proverbial exception that proves the rule, a revelatory two-disc collection which captures the group at the peak of their powers, somehow translating the hypnotic power and epic majesty of their live set onto vinyl. Rejecting the inane between-song stage patter common to most live performers, Jason Pierce instead weaves his music together into an unbroken tapestry of sound, casting a spell which ebbs and flows with narcotic beauty and intensity; even the most familiar selections (like "Shine a Light," "Take Your Time," and "Medication," all frequent inclusions on other Spiritualized live EPs and bootlegs) pulsate with new life, their melodies as likely to set off on a meditative drift as they are to erupt in blasts of white noise. Granted, *Royal Albert Hall* isn't a substitute for the experience of actually catching the group in the flesh—what is?—but like so few other concert LPs, it actually rises above its conceptual limitations, forever capturing a singular moment in time and space when Spiritualized was unquestionably the greatest rock & roll band in the world. *—Jason Ankeny*

Let It Come Down / Sep. 25, 2001 / Arista ♦♦♦♦
Jason Pierce has never shied away from changes in pursuit of his artistic goals. He traded Spacemen 3's white-hot intensity for the gentler ebb and flow of Spiritualized, and took things a step further by firing the rest of the band after their greatest success, *Ladies and Gentlemen We Are Floating in Space. Let It Come Down* is another step in Pierce's difficult, single-minded creative path. To craft the album's epic sound, Pierce sang the melodies into a Dictaphone, translated them to piano, and then transposed them into orchestral arrangements. This painstaking process results in an album that is equal parts intimate confessions and ambitious soundscapes, yet, despite the lineup changes and its lengthy inception, *Let It Come Down* doesn't sound radically different from Spiritualized's previous albums, proving for once and all that Pierce is Spiritualized and Spiritualized is Pierce. Instead, it feels like a natural progression from the densely orchestrated space rock of the first three Spiritualized albums, especially on the bleak, bluesy "Out of Sight" and the plaintive "Don't Just Do Something." Sweeping, stratospheric string and brass sections dominate the album, with over 100 musicians surrounding Pierce's frail, desolate vocals on some songs. Indeed, the lushness of the arrangements sometimes overpowers the album's relatively straightforward songwriting, particularly on tracks like "Anything More." While country and gospel influences bring the beautiful "Do It All Over Again" and "Won't Get to Heaven (The State I'm In)" back down to earth, *Let It Come Down*'s elaborate sound doesn't always make its songs particularly accessible. When Pierce dares to keep things relatively simple, as on the insistent, yearning "I Didn't Mean to Hurt You" and the finale, "Lord Can You Hear Me," the emotional impact is stunning; the rockers "On Fire" and "The Twelve Steps" also cut the album's scope down to size in a direct, gripping way. *Let It Come Down* is another masterfully made Spiritualized album, but its very ambitions sometimes overwhelm it. *—Heather Phares*

Split Enz

f. 1972, Auckland, New Zealand, **db.** 1985
New Zealand Rock, Pop/Rock, New Wave

Best known for their early '80s new wave pop hits, particularly "I Got You," Split Enz—after surviving a dizzying array of image, style, and personnel changes—became the first New Zealand band to achieve worldwide success. Although they never reached superstar status outside of Australia and New Zealand, the band developed a strong international cult following which continued to thrive over a decade after their breakup. Split Enz's output always seemed slightly outside of the times and often frustratingly obscure, but in the end, they left behind an impressively diverse body of work. Though no two of their albums were the same, their history can roughly be broken down into two periods—their highly theatrical, wildly original first period and the more mainstream new wave period of the early-'80s.

The group was founded in 1972 around songwriters Tim Finn and Phil Judd as an acoustic combo called Split Ends. The team proved to be an interesting combination—Judd drew his inspiration from a wild variety of often non-musical sources while Finn's tastes leaned toward the British pop of the Beatles, the Kinks, and the Move. They expanded into progressive rock band with complex, neo-classical structures and arrangements, blending an eclectic mix of styles. They became Split Enz in1974, building strong following in Australia through theatrical shows and outrageous hair styles and cosumes. 1975 saw the impressive debut of *Mental Notes* (a re-recorded version was released the following year as *Second Thoughts*). When Phil Judd left in 1977, they replaced Judd with Tim's younger brother Neil and added a new rhythm section, essentially creating a new band.

Tim Finn assumed leadership of the new Split Enz shiffting away from their early artiness with *Dizrhythmia* (1977) and *Frenzy* (1978), but they made their big breakthrough with 1979's *True Colours*, showcasing Neil Finn's emerging songwriting talents, especially on the irresistible new wave classic "I Got You." The band's early practice of making conceptual videos for their songs made them favorites of the new MTV. *Corroborree* followed in 1981 with memorable hits such as "History Never Repeats" and "One Step Ahead," and in 1982 they hit a creative peak with the introspective *Time and Tide*. Tim Finn left the band in 1984 following *Conflicting Emotions* to pursue a solo career. The remaining members carried on for 1984's *See Ya Round* but disbanded following a farewell tour of Australia and New Zealand. The band members continued to record in a variety of projects with Neil Finn's Crowded House being the highest profile. *—Chris Woodstra*

Mental Notes / 1975 / Mushroom ♦♦♦♦♦
The first proper Enz album features the band at it's eccentric best. *Mental Notes* is completely noncommercial art rock filled with ambitious arrangements and slightly disturbing themes courtesy of the Phil Judd and Tim Finn songwriting partnership. Finn's bittersweet crooning perfectly compliments Judd's madman persona on tracks like "Stranger Than Fiction." Although the album would be repackaged, renamed, and re-recorded in years to come, the band would never again produce anything like it. *—Chris Woodstra*

Second Thoughts / 1976 / Mushroom ♦♦♦♦
After *Mental Notes* failed commercially, the band left for England to rework the tracks with Roxy Music's Phil Manzanera producing. *Second Thoughts* is an eccentric album filled with the theatrics that gained the band its early notoriety. Mainly new versions of old songs, the album adds some new tracks such as the brilliant "Late Last Night" and "Woman Who Loves You." Released in America and the U.K. as *Mental Notes* with a modified cover. *—Chris Woodstra*

Dizrhythmia / Oct. 1977 / Mushroom ♦♦♦♦
Dizrhythmia marks a change not only in personnel (half of the band had been replaced) but also musically and lyrically. With Tim Finn taking over the band, gone almost entirely are the neo-classical arrangements and abstract imagery in favor of a more direct approach that draws heavily from British Invasion-era pop as well as incorporating British music hall and straight-ahead rock & roll. And though the band is still hiding behind hair, colorful costumes, and the occasional swirl of carnival sounds, beneath it all Finn makes his most personal statements to date, showing his optimism and determination for the band's future while also revealing his uncertainty and fears. Most of the songs deal with relationships and, more specifically, his parting-of-ways with former collaborator and close friend, Phil Judd. *—Chris Woodstra*

Frenzy [Australian] / 1978 / Mushroom ♦♦♦♦
Although often thought of as a transitional album, *Frenzy* shows the band in top form. Produced in England on a diminished budget, the album showcases pure pop with a hungry edge. "I See Red," added after the initial pressing, became a moderate hit in Australia and New Zealand, allowing the band the financial freedom to follow up with the blockbuster *True Colours* in 1980. Stripped down of the earlier excesses, the album hints at the direction the band would take in the '80s while capturing a rare, rougher side to their music. [The album was reissued in the U.S. in 1981, dropping half of the tracks and adding songs from the legendary "Rootin' Tootin' Luton Tapes" recorded in 1978.] *—Chris Woodstra*

True Colours / 1979 / Mushroom ♦♦♦♦
Split Enz found their place in new wave with *True Colours*, shedding the eccentricities and excesses of their past in favor of bright, highly memorable, Beatlesque pop. The album also marked Neil Finn's emergence as a great songcraftsman—his infectous "I Got You" helped to push the album and the band to international success. Both the single and the album stand as highpoints of the new wave era. As part of its marketing, the album was released in several different colored covers with laser-etched vinyl. *—Chris Woodstra*

Beginning of the Ends / 1979 / Mushroom ♦♦♦♦♦
A compilation of demos from 1972-1975. This Australian-only release shows the band in its eccentric formative years before a recording contract. Light acoustic arrangements of songs appearing on later albums coupled with long-forgotten gems make this a favorite among die-hard fans. Not the most representative picture of the band, but an interesting one. *—Chris Woodstra*

Frenzy [US] / 1981 / A&M ♦♦♦♦
Although often thought of as a transitional album, *Frenzy* shows the band in top form. Produced in England on a diminished budget, the album showcases pure pop with a hungry edge. "I See Red," added after the initial pressing, became a moderate hit in Australia and New Zealand, allowing the band the financial freedom to follow up with the blockbuster *True Colours* in 1980. The album was reissued in the U.S. in 1981, dropping half of the tracks and adding songs from the legendary "Rootin' Tootin' Luton Tapes" recorded in 1978. The Luton Tapes, which featured some simply sublime Neil Finn songs like "Holy Smoke" and "Semi-Detached," have not been made available except in this long out-of-print reissue. *—Chris Woodstra*

Waiata (Corroboree) / May 1981 / Mushroom ♦♦♦
Because of the hurried schedule of newfound international success, the follow-up to *True Colours* suffered. *Waiata* follows much of the same formula of its predecessor, though in a slightly darker form that often lacks the punch that made *True Colours* great. Despite a couple of classic singles—"One Step Ahead" and "History Never Repeats"—and a handful of other inspired tracks, the album marks the band's first lateral move. Waiata is the Maori word for party (the album was given the Aboriginal party title, *Corroboree* in Australia). Following in the trend of *True Colours*, A&M issued three different colored covers for the worldwide release. *—Chris Woodstra*

Time and Tide / 1982 / Mushroom ♦♦♦♦♦
Time and Tide stands as the band's creative peak and most fully realized effort. On previous albums, Split Enz remained distant and removed, only revealing what little they did between the lines; for *Time and Tide*, Tim and Neil Finn, while still clearly standing as outsiders, opened up, giving a rare glimpse at their feelings and thought processes. Tim exorcised demons and fears in the funky workout of "Dirty Creature," and experienced a joyful communion with nature in "Never Ceases to Amaze Me," outlined a global view in "Small World," and explored ancient folk music with "Six Months in a Leaky Boat" and "Haul Away," an autobiographical sea shanty. Neil, on the other hand, gave darkly evocative yet slightly more abstract accounts in "Giant Heartbeat," "Take a Walk," and the claustrophobic "Log Cabin Fever" while still producing an infectious rocker in "Hello Sandy Allen." In addition to the peaks in songwriting, the Enz never sounded tighter as a band, with lean, tasteful arrangements. The result is a timeless, thoroughly consistent album and the high point of the Enz catalog. *—Chris Woodstra*

Conflicting Emotions / 1983 / Mushroom ♦♦♦
The distraction of a Tim Finn solo project (1983's *Escapade*) may have robbed Split Enz of the creative momentum produced by *Time & Tide*; Tim obviously spent much of his energy on that project, leaving him with a minority of songwriting credits for the first time since taking leadership of the band. So, despite a strong batch of songs from Neil—which includes the achingly beautiful love song "Message to My Girl" and the contemplative "Our Day," which intimates the thoughts of the soon-to-be father—the album suffers from a general lack of focus. A misguided overreliance on drum machines and generally heavy-handed production are the real downfall, though, ultimately dating a solid though unexceptional album. The telling title track, as well as the album closer,

"Bon Voyage," hinted at Tim Finn's imminent departure from the band. [Initial pressings of the album in New Zealand included a bonus 12" of "Kia Kaha" and "Parasite"—songs unavailable elsewhere until the release of the box sets.] —*Chris Woodstra*

Enz of an Era / 1983 / Mushroom ✦✦✦✦✦
A solid collection of the singles from *Second Thoughts* (1976) to *Time and Tide* (1982). Although not all of the singles are present, all of the hits from that period are covered. *Enz of an Era* was originally most notable for inclusion of the rare "Another Great Divide," but it has been superseded by more current (and more easily found) collections. —*Chris Woodstra*

See Ya Round / 1984 / Mushroom ✦✦
With Tim Finn departing for a solo career, Neil Finn takes charge of the aging band for their final studio album. While not living up to the band's previous brilliance, songs such as "Years Go By," "One Mouth Is Fed," and an early version of "I Walk Away" are delightful Finn compositions. Side two features songs written by each of the remaining members. Released only in Australia, New Zealand, and Canada. —*Chris Woodstra*

Living Enz / 1985 / Mushroom ✦✦✦
A double live album with tracks from the farewell *Enz With a Bang* tour and a few from the 1982 *Time and Tide* tour. Rather than just focusing on the hit singles, the album revives old album favorites with new live arrangements. Mainly a gift for the fans, this album is a showcase for the band at its crowd-pleasing best. —*Chris Woodstra*

● **History Never Repeats: The Best of Split Enz** / 1987 / A&M ✦✦✦✦✦
Split Enz are probably best remembered in the U.S. for their new wave-era singles; *History Never Repeats: The Best of Split Enz* collects all of the major singles from the band's A&M albums in a single disc package. For the casual fan, there is no better starting point. The Australian issue is far superior as a career overview however, as it covers their pre-hit period beginning in the mid-'70s and adds a rare mix of "Late Last Night." —*Chris Woodstra*

History Never Repeats / 1987 / Mushroom ✦✦✦✦✦
The Australian version of *History Never Repeats: The Best of Split Enz* offers a better picture of the band through a wider range (all of the albums are represented on this one) and better song selection. Although it may be hard to find, collectors will find this essential if only for the alternate mix of "Late Last Night," not available elsewhere. —*Chris Woodstra*

1973-1979: Oddz & Enz / 1993 / Mushroom ✦✦✦✦✦
This Australian-only box set covers the band's more experimental beginnings (1973-1979). From the light acoustic demos of *Beginning of the Enz* and the art-rock of *Mental Notes*, to the edgy-pop of *Frenzy*, the listener gets a strong sense of the band's pre-popularity evolution. With over an hour of non-LP tracks on the bonus disc and improved sound quality, this is essential for fans. —*Chris Woodstra*

1980-1984: Rear Enz / 1993 / Mushroom ✦✦✦✦✦
This Australian-only box set covers the period of the band's peak in popularity (1980-1984). Beginning with *True Colours* and ending with their swansong, *See Ya Round*, it shows the band in perfect pop form. While this is too ambitious for the casual fan, the devoted will find this essential for considerably improved sound and the bonus disc of previously unreleased tracks. —*Chris Woodstra*

Anniversary / 1994 / Fuel 2000 ✦✦
● **The Best of Split Enz** / Jun. 28, 1994 / Chrysalis ✦✦✦✦
Chrysalis Records handled the band's non-Australia/New Zealand releases from 1976-1977—an extremely low point in terms of sales. Not surprisingly, *Best of Split Enz* focuses a little too heavily on this early period to truly give the casual listener a representative collection of the band's better-known period. The big A&M/new wave-era hits ("I Got You," "One Step Ahead") are covered adequately, but this was clearly an attempt to cash in on Crowded House's success in Europe the year before. —*Chris Woodstra*

● **Spellbound** / 1997 / Mushroom ✦✦✦✦✦
Spellbound is an Australian-only two-disc collection which offers 39 of the band's biggest hits and best-known favorites. There are no shortage of Enz collections on the market, and this is the best to date. All of the tracks have been remastered, and as an incentive to collectors, the rare Luton version of "Semi-Detached" and a drastically remixed version of "Stuff and Nonsense" have been added. The one major flaw is the non-chronological sequencing, which, for a band with two distinct phases and a clear career arc, misses the opportunity to tell the band's story completely. Minor complaints aside, *Spellbound* is a good starting point for those who want more than any of the single-disc collections have to offer. [In typical Enz fashion, *Spellbound* was released in several different-colored covers.] —*Chris Woodstra*

Other Enz / 2000 / Raven ✦✦✦
Collecting Split Enz has never been an easy thing—tracking down all of the limited editions, laser-etched LPs, various colored covers, etc., has been very frustrating for fans over the years. If that wasn't enough, it has been next to impossible to go beyond the already twisted discography to collect the various side projects that have come from the band. *Other Enz* seeks to rectify that with two discs worth (41 songs in all) of rare tracks from Split Enz side projects. While the combining of wildly different styles of music—ranging from Noel Crombie's twisted country take of "My Voice Keeps Changing on Me" (which is worth the price of the disc alone), and the synthy new wave of Mal Green's "Follow Me," to more straightforward tracks like the highly underrated Citizen Band's "The Ladder Song," latter-day Tim Finn, and Crowded House rarities—and somewhat random sequencing doesn't make this the easiest listen for the uninitiated, it is an invaluable addition for collectors, showcasing some excellent moments that were most likely missed the

first time around. Of course, this is only the tip of the iceberg of rarities—fortunately, a second volume is hinted at in the liner notes. —*Chris Woodstra*

The Spongetones
f. 1980
Power Pop, New Wave
One of the most underrated power pop bands of the '80s, the Spongetones released several albums of effortlessly catchy guitar pop that captured the feel of '60s British Invasion pop with remarkable accuracy and innocent charm. While they never received much critical or commercial attention, their music has aged much better than most power pop of the era (late-'70s early-'80s) and among specialists, they're highly revered not only for their studio prowess but also for their spirited live shows. They are one of the few bands to carry on past the "skinny tie" fad into the '90s gracefully—not as strict revivalists but as something unique. They signed to the Ripete label in 1982 and released their first full length, *Beat Music* the same year, following with the *Torn Apart* EP in 1984. By 1987, it seemed the Spongetones wanted to distance themselves from their revivalist reputation, recording probably the most experimental and most un-Spongetones album, *Where-Ever-Land*, which flirted with garage rock, psychedelia, and the more fashionable jangle pop—all in all it marked a more muscular and harder edged approach. The experiment failed for the most part and was short-lived. The band signed to Vinyl records (owned by power pop icons, Shoes) and found a true home in 1991. There they created, in the mold of their first two releases, possibly their most focused Mersey pastiche, *Oh Yeah! Textural Drone Thing* followed in 1995. —*Chris Woodstra*

Beat Music / 1982 / Ripete ✦✦✦✦
Beat Music, the Spongetones' debut album, features some of their finest music, drawing heavily on the Beatles, Dave Clark Five, and Hollies without shame. And while this is certainly derivative stuff, rarely is a nostalgia trip so well executed and enjoyable. *Beat Music* and its follow-up, *Torn Apart*, have been combined on a single disc, *Beat & Torn*, released on Black Vinyl Records. —*Chris Woodstra*

Torn Apart / 1984 / Ripete ✦✦✦✦

Where-Ever-Land / 1987 / Triapore ✦✦✦
Not their strongest effort, *Where-Ever-Land* shows a slight move from their trademark Mersey-inspired pop in favor of slightly harder material with a touch of radio-ready gloss. Fortunately, this deviation was short-lived. The album was reissued on CD in 1998 with five bonus tracks (two unreleased demos and three acoustic songs performed live on a radio program). —*Chris Woodstra*

● **Oh Yeah!** / 1991 / Black Vinyl ✦✦✦✦✦
The Spongetones return after a long absence with 1991's *Oh Yeah!* They effectively pick up where they left off in the '80s with their infectious Beatlesque power pop. Easily their best songwriting and a good place to get acquainted with the band. —*Chris Woodstra*

Beat & Torn / Jun. 30, 1994 / Black Vinyl ✦✦✦✦✦
Now combined on one CD, *Beat Music* and *Torn Apart* represent the band's earliest recordings and some of their finest. These two albums are simply Southern power pop at its best, and this package is essential for fans of pure pop. —*Chris Woodstra*

Textural Drone Thing / Feb. 21, 1995 / Black Vinyl ✦✦✦
Textural Drone Thing may not reach the heights of its predecessor, *Oh Yeah!*, but that's tough competition. The approach is considerably more subtle, and it lacks the band's usual immediacy, but with melodies like these, it's well worth the effort. —*Chris Woodstra*

Odd Fellows / Jun. 20, 2000 / Gadfly ✦✦✦
Power pop isn't dead, it's just middle-aged; the Spongetones have been leading purveyors of the genre for almost 20 years. And the fact is, power pop has never sounded better than it does on their first album in five years; the hooks on their Gadfly debut beat anything they ever released on the Black Vinyl label. "Beatlesque" is the term that pops inevitably to mind, what with those juicy-fruit chord progressions and that hint of a fake British accent ("boy meets gull," etc.). But the Spongetones deliver their pop confections with the weight and momentum of a Detroit muscle car—song titles like "On the Wings of a Nightingale" and "Nightsong" notwithstanding, the general tone here is crunchy and loud. One problem with middle-aged power pop, though, is the weakening of the vocal cords that often comes at midlife, and that's a distraction in several places (especially the whimsical "Love Song to Mrs. Parker"). Even with that minor caveat, this is an album that will please any pop music lover. —*Rick Anderson*

Spoon
f. 1992
Indie Rock, Alternative Pop/Rock
Hailing from Austin, TX, the three-piece of Spoon originated in 1992 as a collaboration between Britt Daniel (vocals/guitar) and Brian Emo (drums). Along with their array of bass players, their hybrid of indie and punk resulted in a number of Sonic Youth and Pixies comparisons after their 1996 debut album, *Telephono*. Eventually settling with bassist Andy Maguire, Spoon would have the chance to tour with the likes of Pavement, Guided By Voices, Silkworm, and Archers of Loaf before their second album, *Soft Effects* (1997). Following a move to Elektra Records and their third album, *A Series of Sneaks* (1998), Spoon moved on to the indie route with a hand full of 7" singles and the *The Agony of Laffitte* EP in 1999. On top of his full-time band, Daniel also spends his free time as a solo artist while going under the moniker of Drake Tungsten. In fall 2000, the *Love Ways* was released on Merge, paving the way for spring 2001's full-length *Girls Can Tell*. —*Mike DaRonco*

Telephono / Apr. 1996 / Matador ♦♦♦♦

Amped-up acoustic guitars, jumpy song structures, and punk attitude combine in *Telephono*, the debut album from Austin's Spoon. Their girl-boy harmonies, spiky guitars, and soft-loud dynamic shifts recall the Pixies, and barring Kim Deal and Frank Black's reconciliation, *Telephono* is the next best thing to a reunion by that group. Short, energetic bursts like "Don't Buy the Realistic" and "Claws Tracking" have a raw, angry attitude missing in most alternative and indie music today, and the group's quieter moments like "Cvantez" and "Towner" have a directness that suits them well. Highlights include "Theme to Wendell Stivers," a fun, space-surf instrumental, and "Plastic Mylar," an entertaining, shiny pop song. While they're not the most original band, Spoon has created an enjoyably raw, punky album that only borrows from the best. *—Heather Phares*

Series of Sneaks / May 5, 1998 / Elektra ♦♦♦

With *A Series of Sneaks*, Spoon became one of the unsung heroes of the guitar-driven post-punk tradition inhabited by bands such as Wire, Gang of Four, Husker Du, and the Pixies. But *Sneaks* wouldn't work if it were merely a repository of all the right influences. Thanks to John Croslin and the band's detailed production, shards of jagged guitar lines chime in from every direction, creating a language that blends with Daniel's charismatic vocal licks to form something so tuneful and compelling that the majority of *Sneaks* sticks in the brain just when you've thought you'd heard it all before. But it's the production—the constantly shifting vocal mixture and placement of Daniel's guitar, Joshua Zarbo's bass, and Jim Eno's drums around bits of melody—that binds *Sneaks* into more than the sum of its parts. Amidst this kind of sonic engagement, it is the search for meaning in music amidst the open roads and open spaces of the American Southwest that form a central character in Daniel's fragmented and oblique lyrical universe. In a few brief lines, a drive to New York on the interstate becomes a meditation on rock and youth in "Car Radio," while "Metal School" seems to be a reassessment of the purpose of post-punk. Elektra, the major label that originally released the CD, must have reassessed its purpose too. The band was ditched soon after its release but has since reappeared on an independent label, Vapor. The enthusiasm behind its resurrection and the anticipation of its full-length follow-up after the two years that followed is a testament to its strength. *—Jonathan Druy*

• **Girls Can Tell** / Feb. 20, 2001 / Merge ♦♦♦♦

Time may not exactly heal all wounds, but it can lend the perspective and strength to channel pain into something positive. Such is the case with Spoon; their perennial indie rock underdog status and disastrous stint on Elektra have focused and tempered the trio's brash energy instead of crushing it. Their third full-length, *Girls Can Tell*, reflects the group's lean, hungry stance in its spare, spiky, immaculately crafted songs. "Take the Fifth" and "Take a Walk" take Spoon's smart, bouncy, slightly tough signature sound to another level; while the ghosts of the Pixies, Nirvana, and Elvis Costello still haunt songs like "Lines in the Suit," *Girls Can Tell*'s sharp wordplay, barbed guitars, and appealingly raw vocals prove that the group embraces their influences without becoming slaves to them. Britt Daniel's increasingly eclectic and expansive songwriting comes to the forefront on "Everything Hits at Once," a taut, brooding pop song driven by vibes, keyboards, yearning, and pride; "Me and the Bean" suggests the direction alternative/indie rock should have taken after Nirvana's implosion. This album is also Spoon's most emotionally eclectic collection of songs, ranging from "Anything You Want," a sunny pop song drawn with just a few artfully placed strokes to "1020 AM," a brooding, slightly psychedelic piece of folk-rock that recalls Daniel's Drake Tungsten side project. "This Book Is a Movie," an appropriately tense, filmic instrumental, and "Chicago at Night," a slightly spooky pop song with winding guitars and an off-kilter melody, complete *Girls Can Tell*, making it Spoon's most mature, accomplished work to date and a fine balance of fire and polish. *—Heather Phares*

Spoonie Gee (Gabe Jackson)

Vocals / Old School Rap, Hip-Hop

Spoonie Gee was the nephew of veteran rhythm and blues producer Bobby Robinson and one of the earliest rap artists. He was known as the "love rapper," an image that was established by his first record, "Love Rap," released on his uncle's Enjoy label as the flip side of the Treacherous Three's "New Rap Language." The bulk of early rap records reproduced an MC's party routine with a loose sequence of narrative, boasting, and call and response. Spoonie's initial outing, however, organized a hip-hop styled record around a romantic theme, coming closer to the lyrical norms of pop music. The intimate "Love Rap" was accompanied only by drum set and congas, and Spoonie Gee's next record continued in a similarly minimalist vein. The voiceover on 1979's "Spoonin' Rap" stuck to more conventional old school boasting, but looks forward to the gangster attitude in its jailhouse references. "Spoonin' Rap" was also prophetic in its use of flexatone and heavily echoed voice, suggesting the Jamaican connection that was denied in early interviews by some of the rap originators. In 1980, Spoonie Gee collaborated with Sequence on a classic single, "Monster Jam," probably the last word on the series of "Good Times/Another One Bites the Dust" variations, and a classic in the Sugar Hill vein, complete with bone crushing bass line and ecstatic crowd noises. *—Richard Pierson*

• **The Godfather . . . Rap** / 1987 / Tuff City ♦♦♦♦♦

Spoonie Gee was among the earliest old-school rappers, performing in a coarse, terse style over funk beats. He was never a great rapper, but he was an effective one, and this album showcased his functional approach on material ranging from straight come-ons to microphone challenges and message cuts. *—Ron Wynn*

Dusty Springfield

b. Apr. 16, 1939, Hampstead, London, England, **d.** Mar. 2, 1999

Vocals / Smooth Soul, Pop-Soul, Blue-Eyed Soul, Girl Group, British Invasion, Soul

Britain's greatest pop diva, Dusty Springfield was also the finest white soul singer of her era, embracing everything from lushly-orchestrated pop to gritty R&B to disco with unparalleled sophistication and depth. She was born Mary O'Brien on April 16, 1939 ; after completing her schooling she joined the Lana Sisters, a pop vocal trio which issued a few singles on Fontana before dissolving. In 1960, upon teaming with her brother Dion and his friend Tim Field in the folk trio the Springfields, O'Brien adopted the stage name Dusty Springfield; thanks to a series of hits the group was soon the U.K.'s best-selling act.

1963 she left the Springfields at the peak of their fame to pursue a solo career. Her first single, "I Only Want to Be With You," quickly reached the British Top Five. Propelled by hits like "Wishin' & Hopin'" by the end of 1964 Springfield was arguably the biggest solo act in British pop. In1966, she scored her biggest international hit with the devastating ballad "You Don't Have to Say You Love Me." In 1968, she traveled to Memphis to record *Dusty in Memphis*, which remains her masterpiece, a perfect marriage of pop and soul stunning in its emotional complexity and earthy beauty. The album and its fine 1970 follow-up *A Brand New Me* unfortunately were commercial failures, as was another critical success, 1973's *Cameo*.

Springfield spent the mid-1970s mostly outside of music while battling substance abuse problems. A comeback was orchestrated in 1987 when she collaborated with techno-pop innovators the Pet Shop Boys on a duet titled "What Have I Done to Deserve This?" The single was a global blockbuster, peaking at number two in both the U.S. and the U.K. Neil Tennant and Chris Lowe also agreed to produce a handful of tracks for 1990's *Reputation*, which became Springfield's best-selling new album since her '60s-era peak. Breast cancer detected during sessions for 1995's *A Very Fine Love* eventually took her life on March 2, 1999; just ten days later, she was inducted into the Rock & Roll Hall of Fame. *—Jason Ankeny*

Dusty / Oct. 1964 / Mercury ♦♦♦

Although not quite as good as her first American LP, *Dusty* is a good mix of soul/R&B covers and orchestrated pop/rock in the manner of early Dionne Warwick. Standouts include the cover of Bacharach-David's "I Just Don't Know What to Do With Myself" (a British hit), "All Cried Out," and the epic ballad "Summer Is Over," which foreshadows the style she'd use on her later hit "You Don't Have to Say You Love Me." The 1999 Mercury CD reissue adds three rare bonus tracks: the Stax soul tune "Every Ounce of Strength" (a 1966 U.K. B-side), the 1966 B-side "I'm Gonna Leave You," and an unreleased cover of Gloria Jones' soul stormer "Heartbeat." *—Richie Unterberger*

Ev'rything's Coming Up Dusty / 1965 / BGO ♦♦♦♦♦

Dusty started to lean in a somewhat less R&B and somewhat more pop direction on this album, with covers of "La Bamba" and Anthony Newley's "Who Can I Turn To?" Still, it has good interpretations of songs by Goffin/King, Jerry Ragovoy, Randy Newman, Bacharach-David, and the Zombies' Rod Argent, highlighted by "Oh No! Not My Baby" and Newman's "I've Been Wrong Before." *—Richie Unterberger*

Ooooooweeee!!! / 1965 / Mercury ♦♦♦♦

Springfield's second U.S. album is another hybrid work, but for different reasons. The tracks, of which two ("You Don't Own Me," "When the Lovelight Starts Shining Through His Eyes") are repeated from her debut, were cut in London and in Nashville, the latter under the direction of Shelby Singleton Jr. The Singleton-produced numbers, except the girl-groupish "Now That You're My Baby," are better R&B, more raw and less dignified in their playing (Springfield in the early days had to fight to get the sound she wanted from her backing musicians), and mix well with the London-based material. In fact, "Lovelight" works better here than it did on the earlier album, for *Ooooooweeee!!!* is overall a more soul-oriented album. The bonus tracks are a significant enhancement—"Go Ahead On," cut by Springfield backed by the Echoes is a fine piece of Brit-beat R&B; her version of Aretha Franklin's "Don't Let Me Lose This Dream" is a harbinger of Springfield's real musical direction, while "I Will Always Want You" is a throwback to the sound of her first album, in a broad, big-voiced, heavily orchestrated style. *—Bruce Eder*

You Don't Have to Say You Love Me / 1966 / Mercury ♦♦♦♦♦

If you overlook the title track, a pop hit in the manner of "Stay Awhile" et al, this is Springfield's best R&B album of her early career. "Won't Be Long" shows Springfield as a soul-shouter par excellence, now with the backing to match, a reasonable fascimile of an authentic American sound, and she alternates with her softer ballad singing. But whether she's covering songs by Goffin-King ("Oh No! Not My Baby," "I Can't Hear You"), Burt Bacharach ("Long After Tonight Is Over"), Randy Newman ("I've Been Wrong Before"), or Ragavoy and Russell ("It Was Easier to Hurt Him"), she makes it come out in her most alluring R&B style. There are a few breaks in the mood, like a less than compelling "La Bamba" and a rendition of "Who Can I Turn To" that's close in spirit to Dionne Warwick at her poppiest, but generally Springfield is consistently superb here, even elevating Rod Argent's "If It Don't Work Out" in an achingly soulful rendition. The 1999 Mercury reissue contains a trio of tracks never before issued in the U.S., "Doodlin'" and "Packin' Up" are lively enough, and the latter features an uncredited guitar solo, a first on a Springfield record and a fine counterpoint to her lusty, shouted performance, but the real jewel is her poignant, lyrical rendition of "That's How Heartaches Are Made." *—Bruce Eder*

Golden Hits / 1966 / Mercury ♦♦♦♦♦

A fair representation of her mid-'60s hits, with major gaps. The imported CDs are preferable. *—Bruce Eder*

Where Am I Going / 1967 / Philips ♦♦♦♦

Where Am I Going is a phenomenal album by Dusty Springfield, and though it doesn't have any American chart hits made famous by the icon, it would have been a blessing had every single performance here conquered the Top 40. The LP cover is great—a black and white of a smiling Dusty with wide-brimmed hat, mini skirt, and a comic book quotation in psychedelic off-pink and orange stating or asking "Where Am I Going." The music inside with strings and orchestration is a relentless delight. The Pat Williams arrangement of Bobby Hebb's "Sunny" with conductor Peter Knight reveals a touch of the James Bond riff, a definite sign of the times. You can hear the wondrous voices of Madeline Bell and Lesley Duncan—the backing voices blending perfectly with the orchestration in songs like "I Can't Wait Until I See My Baby's Face" and "Don't Let Me Lose This Dream." "They Long to Be Close to You" is the serious and dramatic blues that the Carpenters aspired to develop. "Where Am I Going" is as perfectly surreal as its title suggests—imagine Julie Andrews in *The Sound of Music* twirling around in the windmills of Dusty's mind. This is not the driving pop of "I Only Want to Be With You" or "Wishin' & Hopin'"; this is symphonic adult contemporary. *Where Am I Going* is a tremendous and often forgotten masterpiece in the repertoire of Dusty Springfield which deserves more attention. It truly is the record which keeps on giving. *—Joe Viglione*

The Look of Love / Dec. 1967 / Mercury ♦♦♦
A true mixed bag, from the sensual title track to the melodramatic "If You Go Away," and some fine soul stylings in between, most notably "Small Town Girl" (check out the choruses) and "I've Got a Good Thing." The latter is one of four choice bonus tracks on this, the last of Springfield's Philips albums to be released in America (she signed with Atlantic in the U.S. soon after, and the label declined to release most of her Philips output here)—"I'll Try Anything" makes its first U.S. appearance in stereo, and the CD ends with the previously unissued, very dramatic "It's Over." *—Bruce Eder*

★ **Dusty in Memphis** / Mar. 1969 / Mercury ♦♦♦♦♦
Sometimes memories distort or inflate the quality of recordings deemed legendary, but in the case of *Dusty in Memphis*, the years have only strengthened its reputation. The idea of taking England's reigning female soul queen to the home of the music she had mastered was an inspired one. The Jerry Wexler/Tom Dowd/Arif Mardin production and engineering team picked mostly perfect songs, and those that weren't so great were salvaged by Springfield's marvelous delivery and technique. This set has definitive numbers in "So Much Love," "Son of a Preacher Man," "Breakfast in Bed," "Just One Smile," "I Don't Want to Hear About It Anymore," and "Just a Little Lovin'" and offers exquisite mastering, informative notes, and an unreleased version of "What Do You Do When Love Dies." It's truly a disc deserving of its classic status. In 1999, Rhino upgraded *Dusty in Memphis* with a deluxe edition that retained the original album, the three bonus tracks from the same era that appeared on its first CD reissue of the record, and 11 further bonus tracks, the new material dating from 1970-1971. It isn't quite accurate to lump those early-'70s cuts into Dusty's "Memphis" era, since they were recorded in New York and Philadelphia and don't have as much of a soul orientation. "Cherished" and "Goodbye" were produced by Gamble-Huff in early 1970 and are good pop-soul numbers. The rest of the sides were produced by Jeff Barry in 1971 and are more pop in flavor, including covers of Bread's "Make It With You" and Carole King's "You've Got a Friend." These Barry-overseen efforts are okay pop-soul, but lacking in truly memorable songs or inspired playing, especially in comparison to the original *Dusty in Memphis* tracks. *—Ron Wynn & Richie Unterberger*

A Brand New Me / 1970 / Rhino ♦♦♦♦♦
Sticking with the soul stylings of her stellar *Dusty in Memphis* recording, Springfield takes her sensual huskiness north to the City of Brotherly Love for this 1970 slice of Philly soul. Doing incredible justice to a batch of top-quality Gamble & Huff songs, Springfield trades in the Stax-inspired swamp grit of her Memphis album for the urban soul kaleidoscope of *A Brand New Me*. Surrounded by angelically funky string and horn charts from guitarist Roland Chambers and Thom Bell (along with Gamble & Huff, Bell can be counted as an architect of Philly International sound), Springfield sounds positively liberated ranging through the gospel pop closer "Let's Talk It Over," an Aretha-inspired "Silly, Silly Fool," and the Bacharach-styled ballad "Joe." These get topped off by the upbeat Jackson 5 knockoff "Bad Case of the Blues" and covers of two of Jerry Butler's best Mercury hits, "Lost" and "Brand New Me." Along with *Dusty in Memphis* and her early *You Don't Have to Say You Love Me* record, *A Brand New Me* figures into Springfield's handful of really top-notch albums. *—Stephen Cook*

The Silver Collection / Jan. 1988 / Philips ♦♦♦♦♦
Twenty-four songs, encompassing her British and American chart history for the '60s. Superb sound. *—Bruce Eder*

Sounds of the 60's / 1989 / Pickwick ♦♦♦
Intelligently assembled Springfield compilations have proven to be a surprisingly elusive concept, if you want to go beyond the big hits. There's lots of good stuff on this 24-track survey of her 1960s work: some (not all) of her big early hits, and some superb mid-'60s LP-only covers like "Oh No Not My Baby" and "Anyone Who Had a Heart." These are interspersed with less-impressive items from later in the decade, and chronologically and stylistically it jumps all over the place. So it's not bad, but doesn't really satisfy either the collector or the listener who just wants the greatest hits. *—Richie Unterberger*

Something Special / 1996 / Mercury ♦♦♦♦♦
A 48-song, double-CD set of rarities and album tracks, including eight previously unreleased cuts and plenty of songs that had rarely or never been on album before. Sure, this is primarily for Springfield fans, and not the first (or second) anthology recommended to casual listeners. But quite a bit of this is on par, or nearly on par, with her best work. What's more, the bulk of it dates from her '60s prime, although there are about a dozen mediocre numbers from the late '70s/early '80s on which her voice still cuts it, but the material and production don't. Big Dusty Springfield fans will already have some or all of the songs taken from albums, but about half of this is very hard or impossible to find elsewhere, and much of it is very good. Highlights include the title track (one of her best girl group-style numbers); a 1965 Italian-language single in the "You Don't Have to Say You Love Me" ballad style; soulful mid-'60s B-sides like "I'm Gonna Leave You" and "I'll Love You for a While"; and the strange 1968 outtake "Don't Speak of Love," based on a classical piece by Wagner. *—Richie Unterberger*

Stay Awhile/I Only Want to Be With You/Dusty / 1997 / Taragon ♦♦♦♦♦
This CD combines the 24 songs off of Dusty Springfield's first two U.S.-released albums, which comprises a ton of great material, all remastered from what sure sound like first-generation tapes. The sound is vivid and, at times, shattering, in the best Phil Spector sense of that word, as Springfield's bigger-than-life voice fills every corner of the room and your soul. At least as worthwhile as any hits collection that exists on her. *—Bruce Eder*

Anthology / Sep. 23, 1997 / Mercury/Chronicles ♦♦♦♦♦
Weighing in at three discs, *Anthology* sets out to be the definitive Dusty Springfield compilation and it damn near achieves its goal. While the size of this set makes it a little impractical for fans that just want the hits, anyone that wants to dig deeper into her career will discover that she was one of the most consistent interpretive singers of the '60s, capable of sweet girl-group pop, lush orchestral pop, and blue-eyed soul. Bypassing her early records with the Springfields and starting with her solo career in 1963, *Anthology* hits all the high points and features a number of fine forgotten gems as well, making it essential for serious fans of Dusty, '60s pop, and blue-eyed soul. *—Stephen Thomas Erlewine*

★ **The Very Best of Dusty Springfield** / Apr. 21, 1998 / Mercury/Chronicles ♦♦♦♦♦
The Very Best of Dusty Springfield is an ideal compilation, featuring 20 songs from Dusty's prime period of 1963 through 1969. All of the hits—"I Only Want to Be With You," "Wishin' and Hopin'," "Son of a Preacher Man," "I Just Don't Know What to Do With Myself," "A Brand New Me"—are here, along with several lesser-known singles and album tracks that illustrate the full range of her talent. The triple-disc *Anthology* may be more comprehensive and thereby suited for collectors, but this excellent set is the ideal choice for casual fans, since it captures one of the greatest pop singers of the '60s at her very best. *—Stephen Thomas Erlewine*

Stay Awhile/I Only Want to Be With You / 1999 / Mercury ♦♦♦♦♦
Her most rock & roll-oriented album, and one of the finest solo rock albums of the mid-'60s. Besides the two hit title tracks, Dusty covers various American soul and pop tunes that usually rank at least equal to the originals, in some cases totally outclassing them. In particular, she improves upon "24 Hours From Tulsa," "Anyone Who Had a Heart," "You Don't Own Me," and "When the Lovelight Starts Shining Through His Eyes." The production is the most credible approximation of the Phil Spector Wall of Sound ever managed in the U.K., with full brass and strings, soulful female backup choruses, and pounding piano and drums. Also includes a first-rate Springfield original, "Somethin' Special." *—Richie Unterberger*

Dusty in London / Feb. 16, 1999 / Rhino ♦♦♦♦
In the late 1960s and early 1970s, Springfield had an unusual arrangement whereby Philips released her records everywhere in the world except the United States, where they appeared on Atlantic. Atlantic chose to release only 1968-71 material that was recorded in the U.S., meaning that quite a few tracks she recorded in Britain during this time went unreleased stateside. This collects 24 of those songs Springfield recorded in the U.K. between 1968 and 1971, only a few which had appeared in the U.S. before. Although this is not as soul- and R&B-oriented as the material Atlantic recorded with her in America during this era, in truth it's not always that far removed in sound and spirit from what you'll hear on the Atlantic albums *Dusty in Memphis* (1969) and *A Brand New Me* (1970). You can't get much more soulful than "Piece of My Heart," for instance, a good cover of which leads off the collection. Overall, though, it takes in a broader range of pop styles than Springfield did with her American/Atlantic recordings, from covers of the Rascals ("How Can I Be Sure") and Goffin-King ("Wasn't Born to Follow") to Charles Aznavour, Leon Russell, Jimmy Webb, Bacharach-David, and Antonio Carlos Jobim. Most of it's taken from the British albums *Dusty Definitely* (1968) and *See All Her Faces* (1972), and it's lower on standout performances than the familiar Atlantic albums are. The singing is almost always involved and committed, but sometimes the material is pedestrian. The highlights are very good, however, including Randy Newman's "I Think It's Going to Rain Today," the beautiful string ballad "Morning," and the bossa nova spiced "See All Her Faces." This is worth hearing if you like Springfield a lot; just don't gear up for an extraordinarily consistent or essential listen. *—Richie Unterberger*

Simply Dusty / Nov. 7, 2000 / Mercury ♦♦♦♦♦
For anyone who wasn't satisfied with the three-CD Dusty Springfield set from the late '90s, this four-CD, 98-song collection is a chance for deeper immersion in the late singer's music and career—indeed, a more appropriate title thematically might have been "Totally Dusty." In contrast to past compilations, this set ranges so far within her career that the hits are almost incidental, and anyone wanting just the highlights of her work from a given era in her career would be better advised to get one of the smaller compilations. The first two CDs cover Springfield's career across the 1960s, from pop diva to white soul queen and from the London pop scene to the legendary Memphis sessions; most of the cuts are remixes from various points in history, but otherwise are familiar to longtime fans. Disc three begins with material from the usually (unfairly) neglected *A Brand New Me* and proceeds on through her various aborted and unfinished projects of the early '70s; the sad part about this material is that it was all good, solid pop-soul music that, for reasons having more to do with record company politics and other non-artistic matters, was seldom put before the public except in the most nominal fashion. Disc four covers the last phase of Springfield's career, from the very end of the 1970s through her final recordings in the mid-'90s. The price for this set is high as it is a British-only release, but it is the

most comprehensive overview of her work and career. Even so, it doesn't contain every important song, even of her mid-'60s U.K. period. The notes are very thorough, however, and each of the 98 songs gets a little individual history. *—Bruce Eder*

Beautiful Soul: The ABC/Dunhill Collection / Feb. 6, 2001 / Hip-O ♦♦♦
Hip-O's *Beautiful Soul: The ABC/Dunhill Collection* is an exhaustive retrospective of Dusty Springfield's early-'70s stint at Dunhill records, containing the entirety of the 1973 *Cameo* album, plus all the completed material from the unreleased 1974 album, *Longing*. After she signed to Dunhill in 1972, Springfield relocated to California to cut the material, and, appropriately these are Californian productions of their time, filled with studio pros (Larry Carlton, Hal Blaine, Bernard Purdie, Joe Venuto), a warm lush production, and soft rock, written by such songwriters as Alan O'Day, David Gattes, Melissa Manchester, and Ashford and Simpson. In other words, this is not the Dusty of *Dusty in Memphis* and *A Brand New Me*, although a cover of Van Morrison's "Tupelo Honey" has an appropriate Southern flair and Ashford & Simpson's "I Just Wanna Be There" is smoothly seductive. All this means that some fans will not warm to this and, admittedly, some of the music is a little slight, but it works on two different levels. First, it's simply a good pop artifact, evoking its era with high-class performances and classy productions, appealing to the kind of listener that finds "Learn to Say Goodbye"'s status as the theme from the ABC Movie of the Week *Say Goodbye, Maggie Cole* to be a virtue. More importantly, this finds Springfield exploring more adventurous material, particularly on *Longing*, where she tackles Janis Ian's "In the Winter" and Margie Adams' lesbian love song, "Beautiful Soul." Therefore, this compilation winds up being as a historical exercise, both for Springfield diehards and early-'70s fanatics, but it'll please both camps equally, since they'll both find its flaws somewhat charming. *—Stephen Thomas Erlewine*

Rick Springfield

b. Aug. 23, 1949, Sydney, Australia
Vocals, Keyboards, Guitar / Album Rock, Pop/Rock, Power Pop
Although Rick Springfield's music was frequently dismissed as vapid teen idol fare, his best moments have actually withstood the test of time far better than most critics would ever have imagined, emerging as some of the best-crafted mainstream power pop of the decade. A singer turned soap-opera star turned singer, Springfield worked in a few bands before joining the highly successful Australian teenybopper band Zoot in 1968. He went solo after the band broke up in 1971 and garnered his first U.S. success the following year with a re-recording of his Australian hit "Speak to the Sky." Subsequent '70s albums stiffed however, and he moved to RCA. In the midst of recording his debut for the label, he was signed to the soap opera *General Hospital* in 1981. Springfield's popularity skyrocketed later that year with the release of *Working Class Dog*, powered by the classic chart-topper single "Jessie's Girl" and the Top Ten follow-up "I've Done Everything for You." *Success Hasn't Spoiled Me Yet*, released in 1982, spawned the Top Ten smash "Don't Talk to Strangers," while 1983's *Living in Oz* featured yet another Top Ten, "Affair of the Heart." The soundtrack to his 1984 film *Hard to Hold* spawned his last Top Ten hit to date, "Love Somebody." His career seemed to bottom out afterwards, although he recorded several more albums over the rest of the '80s. In 1999, Springfield returned with a new album, *Karma*. *—Steve Huey*

Beginnings / 1972 / Capitol ♦♦
"Come on Everybody" aside, this is a different side of Springfield of which fans of his work in the '80s may not be aware. This is the work of an artist trying to fit into the sensitive singer/songwriter mould. While not a bad record, it's most interesting for "Speak to the Sky," his first American hit, and as a clue to the roots of the work for which he is best known. *—Jim Worbois*

Comic Book Heroes / 1974 / Razor & Tie ♦♦♦
Springfield grew considerably as a writer between his first record and *Comic Book Heroes*. Although he is still doing some sensitive singer/songwriter material, it no longer sounds as awkward. In fact, a couple tracks, like "Weep No More," are very memorable. On the other hand, "Misty Water Woman" sounds like an overly melodramatic attempt at being Elton John. Still, the good stuff makes it worth owning. *—Jim Worbois*

Wait for Night / 1976 / Chelsea ♦♦

● **Working Class Dog** / 1981 / RCA ♦♦♦♦♦
Forget that Rick Springfield was a soap star for a moment and listen to his music, because he made some of the finest guitar-driven mainstream pop/rock of the early '80s. *Working Class Dog* is his finest moment, filled with expertly crafted pop songs, highlighted by the massive hit "Jessie's Girl." *—Stephen Thomas Erlewine*

Success Hasn't Spoiled Me Yet / 1982 / RCA ♦♦♦♦♦
Rick Springfield's follow-up to his commercial breakthrough *Working Class Dog* wasn't quite as consistent, but it contained a number of solid power-pop tracks, including "Calling All Girls," "What Kind of Fool Am I," "How Do You Talk to Girls," "The American Girl," and the Top Ten hit "Don't Talk to Strangers." *—Stephen Thomas Erlewine*

Living in Oz / 1983 / RCA ♦♦♦♦
Though this was Rick Springfield's ninth album, it seemed like the third to most pop music fans, as it came on the heels of his breakthrough, *Working Class Dog*, and its successful follow-up, *Success Hasn't Spoiled Me Yet*. And though this contained as many hits as the aforementioned collections, it isn't remembered as quite the same in terms of accomplishment; this may be because it is so personal that it's just not as accessible. *Living in Oz* is Springfield's response to the dance-pop wave that was just starting to build and would be prominent until grunge announced its presence, as well as his response to the naysayers who wouldn't accept him as a serious musician. Where earlier hits, like "Jessie's Girl" and "Don't Talk to Strangers," were well-crafted pop tunes, on this release he shows an edge and a maturity he hadn't before. By embracing the synthesizers he also shows contempt for, he is able to illustrate how they're changing music and the way fans mindlessly embrace them. This sets up a dichotomy between the coldness of synths and about the need for the human touch—whether it's with a mistress, a friend, or a father—as each cut is about the need for that touch or about the consequences of it. Be it of adultery (a sexually charged "Alyson"), youthful dreams of fame (a spare, unsentimental "Me & Johnny"), or his upbringing (the restrained indictment "Like Father, Like Son"), the entire CD is like a confessional, and that type of honesty suits Springfield well as he matures as an artist and not just as a pop idol. *Living in Oz* ranks among his best. *—Bryan Buss*

Hard to Hold / 1984 / Razor & Tie ♦♦

Tao / 1985 / RCA ♦♦♦

Rock of Life / 1988 / RCA ♦♦

Greatest Hits / Aug. 1989 / RCA ♦♦♦♦♦
Rick Springfield contributed to some of the most congenial sounding pop that braced radio throughout the 1980s. With 17 singles gracing the Top 40 charts, it was evident that both his charming persona and his hook-induced choruses led to his successful ten-year stint. While his music is lyrical fluff, it's the friendly guitar riffs and contagious three-minute rock formula that sometimes takes on a love song approach and boldly represents the feel-good emptiness of '80s pop. This greatest-hits collection is one of the best that Springfield has to offer, since it doesn't suffer from any unnecessary tracks or lose interest with overkill. His pop fervidness is perfectly outlined by the number one charted "Jessie's Girl" and the staccato rhythm of "I've Done Everything for You," which was penned by Sammy Hagar. His best ballads are represented by the syrupy "Affair of the Heart" and the teenage angst of "State of the Heart." Songs like "Love Is Alright Tonight" and "Love Somebody" show Springfield at his most energetic and are solid checkmarks for him in the rock & roll column. Even later material like "Rock of Life" from 1988 footnotes the type of transparent pop that Springfield produced, held together only by its meaningless but contagious keyboard froth. Other collections do offer more tracks, but none are as substantial as the songs laid out here, which are a truly solid dozen. *—Mike DeGagne*

The Best of Rick Springfield / Mar. 23, 1999 / RCA ♦♦♦♦

Karma / Apr. 13, 1999 / Intersound ♦♦♦

VH-1 Behind the Music: The Rick Springfield Collection / Sep. 12, 2000 / RCA ♦♦♦♦
VH1's *Behind the Music: The Rick Springfield Collection* gathers 17 of Springfield's singles and album tracks, including the number one "Jessie's Girl" and Top 40 hits like "Don't Talk to Strangers," "Affair of the Heart," "Love Somebody," and "I've Done Everything for You." Album tracks like "Living in Oz" and "Calling All Girls," along with the previously unreleased bonus track "Lio," round out this enjoyable and comprehensive collection of Springfield's career highlights. *—Heather Phares*

Springhouse

f. 1988, New York, NY
Dream Pop, Indie Rock, Shoegazing, Alternative Pop/Rock
The story of New York's Springhouse treads the all-too-familiar waters of the critically acclaimed band that's never able to get the commercial attention it justly deserves. Formed in 1988 by Mitch Friedland (guitars and vocals), Larry Heinemann (bass, guitars, chapman stick, and backing vocals), and Big Takeover publisher Jack Rabid (drums and vocals), the dream pop outfit's tales of romantic and environmental survival are snow-capped with lush textures of guitar that sound nothing like you've ever heard.

From the beginning, Springhouse developed an Anglophilic yet highly distinct sound that found a rhythmic foundation through the likes of the Buzzcocks and the Sound. Friedland's nylon-stringed guitar, run through myriad effects, gave the band a layered sound similar to the shoegaze scene of the early '90s. Their two LPs for Caroline—1991's storming *Land Falls* and 1993's less aggressive *Postcards From the Arctic*—are equally demanding of emotional immersion; sometimes gloomy, but always purifying and frequently uplifting. Shortly after the band's second LP was released, the band decided to call it quits, only to re-form briefly to open for heroes Mark Burgess and the Sons of God on their brief 1994 U.S. tour. Four years later, the trio began work on a third LP. *—Andy Kellman*

Land Falls / 1991 / Caroline ♦♦♦
Between Mitch Friedland's dazzling nylon-stringed guitar work and lyrics/vocals (duties shared by the guitarist and drummer Jack Rabid) that resonate with all the world weariness of post-punk bands like the Sound and the Chameleons without any of the latter's chest-beating, there's plenty on *Land Falls* to distinguish Springhouse from the texture-heavy shoegaze bands of the early '90s. Unlike a good number of their predominantly U.K.-based peers, very rarely does the trio rely upon effects over ability to carry the material; both craft and execution are too strong to prove otherwise. Could it be any small coincidence that the record concludes with a song entitled "The Sound," which just happens to be one of their brightest, most powerful moments? Perhaps. *—Andy Kellman*

Eskimo / Oct. 18, 1991 / Caroline ♦♦♦
Springhouse's combinations of British dream pop influences and American rock standards has a tendency, on records like *Postcards From the Arctic*, to sound like late-'80s, pre-shoegazer British pop. The *Eskimo* EP focuses on this sound, delivering a solid set of tracks that could easily be compared to any number of post-new wave English bands. The record as a whole proves rather appealing. *—Nitsuh Abebe*

● **Postcards From the Arctic** / 1993 / Caroline ♦♦♦♦
Postcards From the Arctic has all the marks of the dream-pop influence that made its way into American indie in the early '90s. Springhouse soften their guitars and try to compose

floating pop melodies, and the results, while occasionally bearing a sappy pop slickness, are typically appealing. The album's more straightforward rock tendencies mean that it has more in common with the spacier end of late-'80s Brit-pop than it does with shoegazing and dream pop, and this tends to be a good thing. 1991's *Eskimo* EP focuses on this common ground, and, at times, sounds slightly better than *Postcards*.... *—Nitsuh Abebe*

Bruce Springsteen

b. Sep. 23, 1949, Freehold, NJ

Vocals, Leader, Songwriter, Harmonica, Guitar / Heartland Rock, Album Rock, Pop/Rock, Singer/Songwriter, Rock & Roll

When Bruce Springsteen finally broke through to national recognition in the fall of 1975, after a decade of trying, critics hailed him as the savior of rock & roll, the single artist who brought together all the exuberance of '50s rock and the thoughtfulness of '60s rock, molded into a '70s style. He rocked as hard as Jerry Lee Lewis, his lyrics were as complicated as Bob Dylan's, and his concerts were near-religious celebrations of all that was best in the music. One critic became so enamored that he quit reviewing to become Springsteen's manager. But the hosannas, when piped through the publicity machine of a major record company, were perceived as hype by a significant part of the public as well as the mainstream media—Springsteen landed on the covers of *Time* and *Newsweek*, but both magazines were covering the phenomenon, not the music. Springsteen's album, *Born to Run*, became a hit, and he jumped to arena status as a live act, but as many people were turned off by the press campaign as turned on by the records and shows. Two decades later, however, Springsteen remained an established star who could look back on a career that had produced one of the best-selling albums of all time, sold-out stadium shows, Grammy Awards and an Oscar, and a group of imitators who constituted their own subgenre of popular music. If he no longer seemed divine, he remained popular enough for his *Greatest Hits* album to enter the charts at number one, and he had won over many of those skeptics from 1975. *—William Ruhlmann*

Greetings From Asbury Park N.J. / Jan. 5, 1973 / Columbia ♦♦♦♦♦

Bruce Springsteen's debut album found him squarely in the tradition of Bob Dylan: folk-based tunes arranged for an electric band featuring piano and organ (plus, in Springsteen's case, 1950s-style rock & roll tenor saxophone breaks), topped by acoustic guitar and a husky voice singing lyrics full of elaborate, even exaggerated imagery. But where Dylan had taken a world-weary, cynical tone, Springsteen was exuberant. His street scenes could be haunted and tragic, as they were in "Lost in the Flood," but they were still imbued with romanticism and a youthful energy. *Asbury Park* painted a portrait of teenagers cocksure of themselves, yet bowled over by their discovery of the world. It was saved from pretentiousness (if not preciousness) by its sense of humor and by the careful eye for detail that kept even the most high-flown language rooted. Like the lyrics, the arrangements were busy, but the melodies were well developed and the rhythms, pushed by drummer Vincent Lopez, were breakneck. *—William Ruhlmann*

☆ **The Wild, the Innocent & the E Street Shuffle** / Sep. 11, 1973 / Columbia ♦♦♦♦♦

Bruce Springsteen expanded the folk-rock approach of his debut album, *Greetings From Asbury Park, N.J.*, to strains of jazz, among other styles, on its ambitious follow-up, released only eight months later. His chief musical lieutenant was keyboard player David Sancious, who lived on the E Street that gave the album and Springsteen's backup group their names. With his help, Springsteen created a street-life mosaic of suburban society that owed much in its outlook to Van Morrison's romanticization of Belfast in *Astral Weeks*. Though Springsteen expressed endless affection and much nostalgia, his message was clear: this was a goodbye-to-all-that from a man who was moving on. *The Wild, the Innocent & the E Street Shuffle* represented an astonishing advance even from the remarkable promise of *Greetings*; the unbanded three-song second side in particular was a flawless piece of music. Musically and lyrically, Springsteen had brought an unruly muse under control and used it to make a mature statement that synthesized popular musical styles into complicated, well-executed arrangements and absorbing suites; it evoked a world precisely even as that world seemed to disappear. Following the personnel changes in the E Street Band in 1974, there is a conventional wisdom that this album is marred by production lapses and performance problems, specifically, the drumming of Vini Lopez. None of that is true. Lopez's busy Keith Moon style is appropriate to the arrangements in a way his replacement, Max Weinberg, never could have been. The production is fine. And the album's songs contain the best realization of Springsteen's poetic vision, which soon enough would be tarnished by disillusionment. He would later make different albums, but he never made a better one. The truth is, *The Wild, the Innocent & the E Street Shuffle* is one of the greatest albums in the history of rock & roll. *—William Ruhlmann*

☆ **Born to Run** / Aug. 25, 1975 / Columbia ♦♦♦♦♦

Bruce Springsteen's make-or-break third album represented a sonic leap from his first two, which had been made for modest sums at a suburban studio; *Born to Run* was cut on a superstar budget, mostly at the Record Plant in New York. Springsteen's backup band had changed, with his two virtuoso players, keyboardist David Sancious and drummer Vini Lopez, replaced by the professional but less flashy Roy Bittan and Max Weinberg. The result was a full, highly produced sound that contained elements of Phil Spector's melodramatic work of the 1960s. Layers of guitar, layers of echo on the vocals, lots of keyboards, thunderous drums, *Born to Run* had a big sound, and Springsteen wrote big songs to match it. The overall theme of the album was similar to that of *The E Street Shuffle*; Springsteen was describing, and saying farewell to, a romanticized teenage street life. But where he had been affectionate, even humorous before, he was becoming increasingly bitter. If Springsteen had celebrated his dead-end kids on his first album and viewed them nostalgically on his second, on his third he seemed to despise their failure, perhaps because he was beginning to fear he was trapped himself. Nevertheless, he now felt removed, composing an updated *West Side Story* with spectacular music that owed more to Bernstein than to Berry. To call *Born to Run* overblown is to miss the point; Springsteen's precise intention is to blow things up, both in the sense of expanding them to gargantuan size and of exploding them. If *The Wild, the Innocent & the E Street Shuffle* was an accidental miracle, *Born to Run* was an intentional masterpiece. It declared its own greatness with songs and a sound that lived up to Springsteen's promise, and though some thought it took itself too seriously, many found that exalting. *—William Ruhlmann*

Darkness on the Edge of Town / Jun. 2, 1978 / Columbia ♦♦♦♦♦

Coming three years and one extended court battle after *Born to Run*, *Darkness on the Edge of Town* was highly anticipated. Some attributed the album's embattled tone to Springsteen's legal troubles, but it carried on from *Born to Run*, in which Springsteen had first begun to view his colorful cast of characters as "losers." On *Darkness*, he began to see them as the working class: his characters, some of whom he inhabited and sang for in the first person, had little and were in danger of losing even that. Their only hope for redemption lay in working harder, and their only escape lay in driving. Springsteen presented these hard truths in hard-rock settings, the tracks paced by powerful drumming and searing guitar solos. Though not as heavily produced as *Born to Run*, *Darkness* was given a full-bodied sound; Springsteen's stories were becoming less heroic, but his musical style remained grand—the sound, and the conviction in his singing, added weight to songs like "Racing in the Street" and the title track, transforming the pathetic into the tragic. But despite the rock & roll fervor, *Darkness* was no easy listen, and it served notice that Springsteen was already willing to risk his popularity for his principles. *—William Ruhlmann*

☆ **The River** / Oct. 10, 1980 / Columbia ♦♦♦♦♦

Imbedded within the double-disc running time of *The River* is a single-disc album that follows up on the themes and sound of *Darkness on the Edge of Town*—wide-screen, mid-tempo rock and stories of the disillusionment of working-class life and the conflicts within families. In these songs, which include the title track, "Independence Day," and "Point Blank," Springsteen's world view is just as dire as it had become on *Darkness*, but less judgmental. "Independence Day," for example, is a father-and-son ballad that has little of the anger of its hard rock counterpart on *Darkness*, "Adam Raised a Cain." Springsteen's heroes again seek to overcome their crushing troubles through defiance and by driving around, and though "The River" repeats the soured love theme of "Racing in the Street," he also posits romance as a possible escape, sometimes combining it with one of the other solutions, as on the eight-plus-minute "Drive All Night." But there is also another album lurking within *The River*, and it is a more lighthearted pop/rock collection of short, sometimes humorous songs like "Sherry Darling" and "I'm a Rocker." At times Springsteen combines elements of the two, as on "Out in the Street," perhaps the album's quintessential song, a catchy, up-tempo number that sounds like something from the early '60s and echoes the theme of the Vogues' 1966 hit "Five O' Clock World." "Hungry Heart," which became Springsteen's first Top Ten hit, combines a rollicking musical track with a more sober lyrical theme that emphasizes longing over disappointment. But a better guide to Springsteen's development are the songs "Stolen Car" and the album-closing "Wreck on the Highway," gentle, moody ballads imbued with a sense of hopelessness that anticipate his next record, *Nebraska*. *—William Ruhlmann*

☆ **Nebraska** / Sep. 20, 1982 / Columbia ♦♦♦♦♦

There is an adage in the record business that a recording artist's demos of new songs often come off better than the more polished versions later worked up in a studio. But Bruce Springsteen was the first person to act on that theory, when he opted to release the demo versions of his latest songs, recorded with only acoustic or electric guitar, harmonica, and vocals, as his sixth album, *Nebraska*. It was really the content that dictated the approach, however. *Nebraska*'s ten songs marked a departure for Springsteen, even as they took him farther down a road he had been traveling previously. Gradually, his songs had become darker and more pessimistic, and those on *Nebraska* marked a new low. They also found him branching out into better developed stories. The title track was a first-person account of the killing spree of mass murderer Charlie Starkweather. (It can't have been coincidental that the same story was told in director Terrence Malick's 1973 film *Badlands*, also used as a Springsteen song title.) That song set the tone for a series of portraits of small-time criminals, desperate people, and those who loved them. Just as the recordings were unpolished, the songs themselves didn't seem quite finished; sometimes the same line turned up in two songs. But that only served to unify the album. Within the difficult times, however, there was hope, especially as the album went on. "Open All Night" was a Chuck Berry-style rocker, and the album closed with "Reason to Believe," a song whose hard-luck verses were belied by the chorus—even if the singer couldn't understand what it was, "people find some reason to believe." Still, *Nebraska* was one of the most challenging albums ever released by a major star on a major record label. *—William Ruhlmann*

★ **Born in the U.S.A.** / Jun. 4, 1984 / Columbia ♦♦♦♦♦

Bruce Springsteen had become increasingly downcast as a songwriter during his recording career, and his pessimism bottomed out with *Nebraska*. But *Born in the U.S.A.*, his popular triumph, which threw off seven Top Ten hits and became one of the best-selling albums of all time, trafficked in much the same struggle, albeit set to galloping rhythms and set off by chiming guitars. That the witless wonders of the Reagan regime attempted to co-opt the title track as an election-year campaign song wasn't so surprising: the verses described the disenfranchisement of a lower-class Vietnam vet, and the chorus was intended to be angry, but it came off as anthemic. Then, too, Springsteen had softened his message with nostalgia and sentimentality, and those are always crowd-pleasers. "Glory

Days" may have employed Springsteen's trademark disaffection, yet it came across as a couch potato's drunken lament. But more than anything else, *Born in the U.S.A.* marked the first time that Springsteen's characters really seemed to relish the fight and to have something to fight for. They were not defeated ("No Surrender"), and they had friendship ("Bobby Jean") and family ("My Hometown") to defend. The restless hero of "Dancing in the Dark" even pledged himself in the face of futility, and for Springsteen, that was a step. The "romantic young boys" of his first two albums, chastened by "the working life" encountered on his third, fourth, and fifth albums and having faced the despair of his sixth, were still alive on this, his seventh, with their sense of humor and their determination intact. *Born in the U.S.A.* was their apotheosis, the place where they renewed their commitment and where Springsteen remembered that he was a rock & roll star, which is how a vastly increased public was happy to treat him. — *William Ruhlmann*

Live 1975-1985 / Nov. 10, 1986 / Columbia ✦✦✦✦✦
Long before he sold substantial numbers of records, Bruce Springsteen began to earn a reputation as the best live act in rock & roll. Fans had been clamoring for a live album for a long time, and with *Live 1975-1985* they got what they wanted, at least in terms of bulk. His concerts were marathons, and this box set, including 40 tracks and running over three-and-a-half hours, was about the average length of a show. In his brief liner notes, Springsteen spoke of the emergence of the album's "story" as he reviewed live tapes, and that story seems nothing less than a history of his life, his concerns, and his career. The first cuts present the Springsteen of the early to mid-'70s; these performances, most of them drawn from a July 1978 show at the Roxy in Los Angeles, give us the romantic, hopeful, earnest Springsteen. The second section begins with his first Top Ten hit, "Hungry Heart"—this is the Springsteen of the late '70s and early '80s, an arena rock star with working-class concerns. After an acoustic mini-set given largely to material from *Nebraska*-songs of economic desperation and crime—comes a reshuffling of *Born in the U.S.A.*, songs in which the artist and his characters start to fight back and rock out. Finally, he brings it all back home to New Jersey, starting with the unofficial state anthem, "Born to Run." Fans could rejoice in the seven previously unreleased songs, but it wasn't as funny, moving, or exhilarating as a Springsteen show could be. Maybe no single album could have been, but where Springsteen impressed in concert because he tried so hard, here he seemed to have tried a little too hard to make a live album carry the freight of everything he had to say. — *William Ruhlmann*

☆ **Tunnel of Love** / Oct. 9, 1987 / Columbia ✦✦✦✦✦
Just as he had followed his 1980 commercial breakthrough *The River* with the challenging *Nebraska*, Bruce Springsteen followed the most popular album of his career, *Born in the U.S.A.*, with another low-key, anguished effort, *Tunnel of Love*. Especially in their sound, several of the songs, "Cautious Man" and "Two Faces," for example, could have fit seamlessly onto *Nebraska*, though the arrangements overall were not as stripped-down and acoustic as on the earlier album. While *Nebraska* was filled with songs of economic desperation, however, *Tunnel of Love*, as its title suggested, was an album of romantic exploration. But the lovers were just as desperate in their way as *Nebraska*'s small-time criminals. In song after song, Springsteen questioned the trust and honesty on both sides in a romantic relationship, specifically a married relationship. Since Springsteen sounded more autobiographical than ever before ("Ain't Got You" referred to his popular success, while "Walk Like a Man" seemed another explicit message to his father), it was hard not to wonder about the state of his own two-and-a-half-year-old marriage, and it wasn't surprising when that marriage collapsed the following year. *Tunnel of Love* was not the album that the ten million fans who had bought *Born in the U.S.A.* as of 1987 were waiting for, and though it topped the charts, sold three million copies, and spawned three Top 40 hits, much of this was on career momentum. Springsteen was as much at a crossroads with his audience as he seemed to be in his work and in his personal life, though this was not immediately apparent. — *William Ruhlmann*

Chimes of Freedom / 1988 / Columbia ✦✦✦
Culled from recordings of Springsteen's spring 1988 *Tunnel of Love* tour, *Chimes of Freedom* is a four-track EP that initially was released as a benefit for Amnesty International, appearing as he joined the fall 1988 Human Rights Now! tour. It was recorded and released quickly, easily qualifying as the speediest project Springsteen has ever completed. Unfortunately, it occasionally feels a little slap-dash, but it's hard to criticize a four-song live charity EP for being haphazardly assembled, since that's in its nature. Nevertheless, *Chimes of Freedom* is a little unsatisfying, even though it's a good, brief sampler of the Boss live circa *Tunnel of Love*. And that's part of the problem. *Tunnel of Love* had a slicker production than a normal Springsteen record, featuring synths scattered throughout the record. Those arrangements were preserved on the live version of "Tougher Than the Rest," one of the best songs from the record, and it turns a little mushy in an arena setting. Similarly, the title track has its chiming opening refrain played on synths, and consequently it sounds a little stiff and dated. These faults are balanced by the remaining two cuts, the first released version of the excellent "Be True" and a reworking of "Born to Run" as an acoustic ballad. "Born to Run" has considerable power in this stripped-down setting, and "Be True" teems with life, pointing out how stiff its cousins sound on *Chimes of Freedom*. Neither of these tracks are major contributions to Springsteen's catalog, but they're nice additions for the die-hard fans that will be picking up the EP anyway. — *Stephen Thomas Erlewine*

Human Touch / Mar. 31, 1992 / Columbia ✦✦
Bruce Springsteen has always been steeped in mainstream pop/rock music, using it as a vocabulary for what he wanted to say about weightier matters. He has always written generic pop as well, but *Human Touch* was the first album to consist entirely of this kind of minor genre material, which he seems capable of turning out endlessly and effortlessly. Having largely jettisoned the E Street Band, Springsteen enlisted some sturdy minor

talent to play and sing, among them ace studio drummer Jeff Porcaro, Sam Moore of Sam and Dave, and Bobby Hatfield of the Righteous Brothers. It's pleasant enough stuff, and easy to listen to, but it is not the kind of record Springsteen had conditioned his audience to expect, and its release brought considerable disappointment. Though at nearly 59 minutes it was the longest single-disc album of his career, and though it contained several songs that could have been big hits—the "Tunnel of Love" soundalike title track, which actually made the Top 40, "Roll of the Dice," an AOR radio favorite, and "Man's Job"—*Human Touch* was an uninspired Springsteen album, his first that didn't at least aspire to greatness. — *William Ruhlmann*

Lucky Town / Mar. 31, 1992 / Columbia ✦✦✦
Reportedly, Bruce Springsteen recorded most of *Human Touch* in 1990, but left it unreleased. He returned to work in the fall of 1991, intending to add a song, but ended up recording a whole new album, *Lucky Town*, and then decided to release both records at the same time in the spring of 1992. He might have been better off pulling a couple of the stronger songs from the earlier album, adding them to the later one (which runs less than 40 minutes), and shelving the rest. While *Human Touch* was a disappointing album of second-rate material, *Lucky Town* was an ambitious collection addressing many of Springsteen's major concerns and moving them forward. Here was the rage and the humor, the sense of compassion, the loyalty and commitment that had been the stuff of Springsteen's best music from the beginning. Songs like "Better Days" and "Local Hero" commented on and deflated the commercial success with which Springsteen clearly felt uncomfortable; "If I Should Fall Behind" and "Book of Dreams" expressed romantic fidelity and generosity; "Souls of the Departed" contained scathing social commentary; and "My Beautiful Reward" was a meditative epilogue. The lyrics were better, the arrangements tighter, the performances more powerful than those on the companion release. If *Lucky Town*, like *Tunnel of Love* and *Human Touch* before it, sounded a little underproduced, it nevertheless had the mark of the major artist Springsteen is, and if he had released it alone, it might have had a more significant impact. — *William Ruhlmann*

In Concert/MTV Plugged / Apr. 1993 / Columbia ✦✦✦
Released in Europe to coincide with Bruce Springsteen's spring 1993 tour of the continent, this album is a 13-track, nearly 72-minute audio version of Springsteen's video concert broadcast on MTV in the fall of 1992. It was part of the network's *Unplugged* series, but after performing the first, previously unheard song "Red Headed Woman" alone on guitar, Springsteen shouted, "All right, let's rock it!," and departed from the acoustic format. (The album's title has an "X" drawn through the "Un" of "Unplugged.") Eight of the selections come from Springsteen's 1992 albums *Human Touch* and *Lucky Town*, and the relatively minor tracks from the former benefit from being sequenced among the more ambitious songs from the latter and such old favorites as "Darkness on the Edge of Town" and "Thunder Road." Though Springsteen and his new band don't "rock it" too hard for the most part, a notable exception is a performance of the previously unrecorded "Light of Day," a title song Springsteen wrote for a 1987 movie. Here, he gives a taste of the enthusiasm and spontaneity he can bring to his live performances. But this is an album of small pleasures rather than a major performance statement. — *William Ruhlmann*

Greatest Hits / Feb. 28, 1995 / Columbia ✦✦✦
Compiling a greatest-hits collection for Bruce Springsteen should be an easy task, yet *Greatest Hits* manages to miss the mark. Nothing from his first two albums is included, and the set includes such non-hits like "Atlantic City" and "The River" instead of hits like "Cover Me," "Tunnel of Love," and "Fade Away." In fact, a good portion of his hits are missing, as are important album tracks like "Backstreets," "Rosalita," and "Candy's Room," making this neither a straight hits collection nor a compilation of his best tracks. What's left are some of his biggest hits and best songs ("Born to Run," "Glory Days," "The River"), but not all of them, as well as four new tracks, the best of which is an outtake from the *Born in the U.S.A.* sessions ("Murder Inc.") Aside from "Murder Inc.," the new tracks follow the synth-laden adult contemporary direction Springsteen began pursuing with "Streets of Philadelphia," only without the lyricism or melody. So, it's a mixed bag, drawing an incomplete portrait of one of the prime rockers of the '70s and '80s. Casual fans would be better served by *Born in the U.S.A.*, which encompasses all of Springsteen's sides. — *Stephen Thomas Erlewine*

The Ghost of Tom Joad / Nov. 21, 1995 / Columbia ✦✦✦
In 1982, with Ronald Reagan in the White House and much of America torn between a newly fierce patriotism and the dispassionate conservatism of the dawning "Greed Is Good" era, a number of roots-oriented rock musicians began examining the State of the Union in song, and one of the most powerful albums to come out of this movement was Bruce Springsteen's stark, home-recorded masterpiece *Nebraska*. In 1995, Bill Clinton was president, America was congratulating itself for a new era of high-tech peace and prosperity, and Springsteen returned to the themes and approach of *Nebraska* with *The Ghost of Tom Joad*. With several of its songs drawn directly from news stories, *The Ghost of Tom Joad* is more explicitly political than *Nebraska* (more so than anything in Springsteen's catalog, for that matter), and while the arrangements are more full-bodied than those on *Nebraska*, the production and the overall tone is, if anything, even starker and more low-key, with the lyrics all the more powerful for their spare backdrops. While there's an undertow of bitterness in this album's tales of an America that has turned its back on the working class and the foreign-born, there's also a tremendous compassion. Individually, these songs, either angry or plaintive, are clean and expertly drawn tales of life along this nation's margins, and their cumulative effect is nothing short of heartbreaking; anyone who pegged Springsteen as a zealously patriotic conservative in the wake of the widely misunderstood *Born in the U.S.A.* needs to hear this disc. *The Ghost of Tom Joad* failed to find the same audience (or the same wealth of media attention) that

embraced *Nebraska*, but on its own terms it's a striking and powerful album, and certainly one of Springsteen's most deeply personal works. *—Mark Deming*

Tracks / Nov. 10, 1998 / Columbia ♦♦♦♦

For years, decades even, Bruce Springteen was legendary for the amount of recordings he did not release. Every time he cut an album, he recorded a surplus of songs and left some out, not always on the basis of quality, but often because they simply didn't suit the mood of the record. It was inevitable that dedicated fans and collectors would bootleg these recordings, and for many years, he was one of the most popular bootlegged artists, rivaling even Bob Dylan. Dylan released a box set of unreleased songs in 1991, paving the way for the long-overdue appearance of a similar Springsteen set, *Tracks*, in 1998. Spanning four discs, it isn't entirely devoted to unreleased material—a few B-sides pop up here and there—nor is it truly definitive, since it misses a number of key outtakes, plus his original version of "Because the Night," the sole hit for Patti Smith. Instead, the compilation is an unassuming sampling of what's in the vaults, from his early acoustic demos to polished outtakes from *Human Touch* and *Lucky Town*. Along the way, there are a number of great songs—"Bishop Danced" is every bit as terrific as its legend, as are "Thundercrack," "Give the Girl a Kiss," "Hearts of Stone," "Roulette," and many others. *Tracks* merely offers fans an enjoyably sequenced selection of what was left behind. If the end result isn't as revelatory as some may have expected (even the acoustic "Born in the U.S.A.," powerful as it is, doesn't sound different than you may have imagined it), it's because Springsteen is, at heart, a solid craftsman, not a blinding visionary like Dylan. That's why *Tracks* is for the dedicated fan, where *The Bootleg Series* or *The Basement Tapes* were flat-out essential for rock fans. *—Stephen Thomas Erlewine*

Before the Fame / 1999 / BCD USA ♦♦♦

18 Tracks / Apr. 13, 1999 / Columbia ♦♦♦

18 Tracks is a single-disc distillation of 1998's four-CD box set *Tracks*, the superb retrospective assembling unreleased material spanning the breadth of Bruce Springsteen's storied career; also featuring three previously unissued songs, this new, streamlined release is a frustration from both a critical and consumer standpoint. The issue of record company greed aside, the greatest disservice is actually to those listeners who buy the disc as a substitute for the full *Tracks* box; each of its 66 cuts is an invaluable addition to the Springsteen songbook, so even casual fans need the complete package to discover lost classics like "Thundercrack," "Give the Girl a Kiss," "Wages of Sin," and "The Wish"—just 18 of these gems are simply not enough. Which means, then, that *18 Tracks* is ultimately most essential for those hardcore fans who already shelled out for most of the material in question anyway; and though it's appalling to force the devoted to buy a full-length album for just three new songs, at least each is excellent, in particular longtime fan favorites "The Fever" and "The Promise" (the latter newly recorded for inclusion here). *—Jason Ankeny*

Live in New York City / Mar. 27, 2001 / Columbia ♦♦♦

Compared to the gargantuan quintuple album *Live 1975/1985*, 2001's *Live in New York City* seems like the very definition of restraint, but consider this—not only does it span two discs, it leaves out a considerable portion of the set list from the show and thereby the set list of Springsteen's celebrated 2000 reunion with the E Street Band. Some critics complained that this record was little more than a tie-in to the HBO special of the same name, but even if that's true, the record would have merit since it illustrates exactly why this group should never have parted ways. In a sense, even if this is the third live album in Springsteen's catalog, it's the first that attempts to replicate the feeling of an evening out with the E-Street Band (the box tried too hard to be an ultimate experience; *MTV Plugged* captured a transitional phase). Though most reunions feel a little forced, this feels natural, yet never nostalgic, since the track listing never relies on the predictable. There are no hits in the conventional sense—outside of "Born in the U.S.A." tucked away on the second disc and an initially uncredited "Born to Run"—but there are many fan favorites interspersed with a few obscurities and new songs, most notoriously the protest song "American Skin (41 Shots)." This works in Springsteen's favor, since there's no pandering—only the joy of making music with the band that understands him best. This doesn't really result in something essential, even if the new songs are quite good, but if you've ever been a fan, it's hard not to warm to *Live in New York City*. *—Stephen Thomas Erlewine*

Squarepusher (Tom Jenkinson)

b. Chelmsford, Essex, England

Remixing, Producer, Bass / IDM, Drill'n'bass, Experimental Jungle, Electronica, Jungle/Drum 'N Bass

Tom "Squarepusher" Jenkinson makes manic, schizoid experimental drum'n'bass with a heavy progressive jazz influence and a lean toward pushing the clichés of the genre out the proverbial window. Rising from near-total obscurity to drum'n'bass *cause célèbre* in the space of a couple of months, Jenkinson released only a pair of EPs and a DJ Food remix for the latter's *Refried Food* series before securing EP and LP release plans with three different labels. His first full-length work, *Feed Me Weird Things* (on Richard "Aphex Twin" James' Rephlex label) is a dizzying, quixotic blend of superfast jungle breaks with Aphex-style synth textures, goofy, offbeat melodies, and instrumental arrangments (Jenkinson samples his own playing for his tracks) that recall vaguely jazz fusion pioneers such as Mahavishnu Orchestra and Weather Report. A skilled bassist and multi-instrumentalist, Jenkinson's fretless accompaniment is a staple of his music and one of the more obvious affiliations with jazz (although his formal arrangements are often as jazz-derived as his playing).

Barely into his twenties, Jenkinson grew up listening to jazz and dub greats like Miles Davis, Augustus Pablo, Charlie Parker, and Art Blakey. The son of a jazz drummer, Jenkinson followed in his father's footsteps, playing bass and drums in high school. Introduced to electronic music through experimental electro-techno groups such as LFO and Carl Craig, Jenkinson soon began assembling the rolls of disparate influence into amalgams of breakbeat techno and post-bop avant-garde and progressive jazz. Claiming a closer affinity with jazz than jungle (although he draws from both equally in his music), Jenkinson's EPs as Squarepusher and the Duke of Harringay (Jenkinson moved to Harringay from his Chelmsford birthplace) were initially disregarded as misplaced perversions of jungle's more obvious compositional principles, but found ready audience in fans of post-acid house experimental listening music. He inked a deal with Warp in 1995, releasing the *Port Rhombus* EP and three others through a variety of different labels. His full-length debut *Feed Me Weird Things* appeared in 1996, followed a year later by *Hard Normal Daddy*. For 1998's *Music Is Rotted One Note*, Jenkinson became a one-man fusion group, multi-tracking himself playing drums, bass, and keyboards. The following year, he released two EPs (*Budakhan Mindphone*, *Maximum Priest*) and another full LP, *Selection Sixteen*. *Go Plastic* was issued in summer 2001. *—Sean Cooper*

Feed Me Weird Things / Jun. 3, 1996 / EFA ♦♦♦♦

Fractured beats, frenetic bass licks, and alternately silly and moving melodies tie together Squarepusher's first full-length effort. Much of the material—with its lo-fi synth damage and often tongue-in-cheek feel—places Jenkinson closer to Aphex territory than traditional drum'n'bass, but the distinctions begin breaking down from word go. Flawed but promising. *—Sean Cooper*

● **Hard Normal Daddy** / Apr. 28, 1997 / Warp ♦♦♦♦♦

Tom Jenkinson's jazz roots come through louder and clearer on his full-length Warp debut. Although, like the preceding EP "Port Rhombus," this album sounds substantially cleaner and more thought out than previous releases for Spymania and Rephlex, it also far surpasses those releases in terms of musicality and track development, not simply relying on the shock value of "tripping-over-myself" drum programming and light-speed fretless bass noodling. Jenkinson's bass accompaniment also sounds far less prog-rock-influenced here, making *Hard Normal Daddy* his overall most listenable work to date. *—Sean Cooper*

Music Is Rotted One Note / Oct. 12, 1998 / Nothing ♦♦♦♦♦

The one-man drum'n'bass outfit Squarepusher (aka Tom Jenkinson) treads upon more unpredictable terrain on *Music Is Rotted One Note*. Although the album still contains elements of his usual drum'n'bass sound, this is by and large a jazz/fusion affair. Jenkinson does a masterful job playing all the instruments live and by himself, and perfectly recreates the funky atmosphere of such early-'70s Miles Davis classics as *Get Up With It* and *On the Corner*. Jenkinson's performances throughout the disc are both flawless and inspired—he obviously realized that if he was to pay tribute to Miles, nothing but the best would do. Davis' spirit lives on in such tracks as "Don't Go Plastic," "Dust Switch," "137 (Rinse)," and "Theme From Vertical Hold," while "My Sound" perfectly captures the essence of Miles' calming and reflective compositions. But don't be misled; this is not a by-the-numbers ripoff of Miles Davis. Jenkinson updates these familiar sounds with '90s recording techniques and injects enough of his own style into the mix to keep it recognizable. Miles would be proud. *—Greg Prato*

Selection Sixteen / Nov. 9, 1999 / Nothing ♦♦♦♦

After releasing more than two hours worth of material in less than a year, Tom Jenkinson returned in late 1999 with what looked to be another full LP, comprising 17 tracks and clocking in at 45 minutes. In fact, it's regarded as a "mini-album" and plays the part well. Similar to the 1999 Squarepusher EPs *Budakhan Mindphone* and *Maximum Priest*, *Selection Sixteen* alternates what sounds like outtakes from his last LP (*Music Is Rotted One Note*)—that is, short organic fusion cast-offs—with a set of hard-edged acid tracks, most of which chart the hyperkinetic drum'n'bass programming that fans expect. The album comes off surprisingly well, given both the glut of Squarepusher material in 1999, and the fact that Jenkinson is mixing'n'matching crazed drill'n'bass and more stately jazz-fusion, with little regard for album flow. The highlight here, "Square Rave," takes a little bit from both camps and ends up sounding like Aphex Twin (circa *Selected Ambient Works 85-92*) if he'd been working with jungle breakbeats. In addition to the 13-track album are four remixes, including one on which Jenkinson recruits his brother Andy for remixing duties. *—John Bush*

Go Plastic / Jun. 26, 2001 / Warp ♦♦♦♦

Realizing that another obsessively imitative jazz fusion workout could quickly become a blind alley, Squarepusher's Tom Jenkinson returned to the green fields of drum'n'bass for 2001's *Go Plastic*, and sounds quite refreshed for having taken a holiday. As one of the track titles ("Go! Spastic") attests, Jenkinson's back to heavy drill'n'bass, the practically undanceable collision of fractured breakbeats and sample-a-second riffs he made popular with his earliest work as Squarepusher. The opener and first single, "My Red Hot Car," is probably the most together production on the album, filtering drill'n'bass through the prism of the stylish British 2-step all the rage in clubland during recent years. Jenkinson quickly moves from the single to "Boneville Occident" and "Go! Spastic," a pair of drill'n'bass knockouts that veer from pointed, endlessly complex breakbeats to downbeat hip-hop at the drop of a hat. Jenkinson uses a lot of classic, sampled breakbeats—reminiscent of early jungle and hardcore—and even reprises the original "jump wide!" vocal-sample classic, tweaked separately in both channels at the same time. Toward the end, Jenkinson trades the experimentation for a bit of mood-setting on pieces like "Tommib" and "Plaistow Flex Out," but these are only temporary detours from some serious programming chaos. *Go Plastic* is clearly a work of programmed electronics, with little of the jazz influence or played instruments audible on 1999's *Music Is Rotted One Note*. Any jazzbos left over from his previous work may be in for a rude awakening to the frenetic programming and primitive acid house textures, but fans of Squarepusher from the beginning will be overjoyed to hear him back doing what he's done best. *—John Bush*

Squeeze

f. 1974

College Rock, Pop/Rock, New Wave

As one of the most traditional pop bands of the new wave, Squeeze provided one of the links between classic British guitar pop and post-punk. Inspired heavily by the Beatles and the Kinks, Squeeze was the vehicle for the songwriting of Chris Difford and Glenn Tilbrook, who were hailed as the heirs to Lennon and McCartney's throne during their heyday in the early '80s. Unlike Lennon and McCartney, the partnership between Difford and Tilbrook was a genuine collaboration, with the former providing the music and the latter writing the lyrics. Squeeze never came close to matching the popularity of the Beatles, but the reason for that is part of their charm. Difford and Tilbrook were wry, subtle songwriters who subscribed to traditional pop songwriting values but subverted them with literate lyrics and clever musical references. While their native Britain warmed to Squeeze immediately, sending singles like "Take Me I'm Yours" and "Up the Junction" into the Top Ten, the band had a difficult time gaining a foothold in the States; they didn't have a Top 40 hit until 1987, nearly a decade after their debut album. Even if the group never had a hit in the U.S., Squeeze built a dedicated following that stayed with them into the late '90s, and many of their songs—"Another Nail in My Heart," "Pulling Mussels (From the Shell)," "Tempted," "Black Coffee in Bed"—became pop classics of the new wave era, as the platinum status of their compilation *Singles 45's and Under* indicates. *—Stephen Thomas Erlewine*

U.K. Squeeze / Mar. 1978 / A&M ♦♦

The band's debut, credited (in the U.S.) to U.K. Squeeze to avoid confusion with a similarly named band, is quite unlike anything that would follow and nearly seems like the work of another band. Much of the reason for this comes from producer John Cale's somewhat warped vision of the band. Cale threw out all of the songs the band came to the studio with and demanded that they write new ones on the spot (he also proposed calling the album *Gay Guys*, and undoubtedly had something to do with the hot pink bodybuilder cover and the shirtless photo of the band on the back). The rough and ragged songs that resulted from the studio writing range from raw, inspired rockers like "Sex Master," "Strong in Reason," and "Get Smart" to the utterly bizarre, near-funk instrumental "Wild Sewerage Tickles Brazil," which features wild shrieks throughout. The band-produced "Take Me I'm Yours" is a fondly remembered hit, but the album in general remains an oddity of the Squeeze catalog. *—Chris Woodstra*

Cool for Cats / Apr. 1979 / A&M ♦♦♦♦♦

After the false start of the debut, Squeeze recast themselves as a quintessentially British band, packing the songs with exaggerated accents, British slang, and incorporating a nearly cinematic narrative style to make incisive observations on British working-class life with a sly, skewed wit and a sex-obsessed thematic undercurrent. Musically, the band often rocks harder than they did on the debut, this time adding synth-driven arrangements while retaining a working-class pub-rock sensibility. *Cool for Cats* stands as the band's first truly great album and boasts arguably their finest song-story in "Up the Junction," a timeless gem, as well as the unforgettable Difford-sung hit title track. *—Chris Woodstra*

☆ **Argybargy** / Mar. 1980 / A&M ♦♦♦♦♦

Where *Cool for Cats* marked a great leap over the debut, *ArgyBargy* improved at least that far over its own predecessor. Still a distinctly British band, Squeeze compensated with an incredibly catchy batch of songs that, despite the subject matter, spoke the universal language of bright, bouncy, instantly endearing pop. The acute observations of the British working class were even more vivid—none so poignant as the classic "Pulling Mussels (From the Shell)," which offers a series of detailed snapshots of the different walks of life on a seaside holiday, or the often-overlooked courting-to-breakup story-song "Vicky Verky," which nearly matched "Up the Junction"'s brilliance. *ArgyBargy* is simply packed with perfect, timeless pop that stands not only as the band's crowning achievement, but also as a landmark recording of the era. *—Chris Woodstra*

East Side Story / May 1981 / A&M ♦♦♦♦♦

East Side Story was originally planned as a double album with each side produced by a different "hot" producer—Elvis Costello, Nick Lowe, Dave Edmunds, and Paul McCartney were the proposed lineup. And while only Elvis Costello (along with Roger Bechirian) ended up doing the job, save for one track by Edmunds, Costello's push for decidedly un-Squeeze-like material and sympathetic production style resulted in not only the band's most diverse but also their most creatively rewarding album to date. *East Side Story* is definitely packed with the band's trademark bouncy Brit-pop numbers like "In Quintessence," "Piccadilly," "Is That Love," and "Mumbo Jumbo," but the standouts come from the unexpected turns—the country lament of "Labeled With Love," the trippy near-psychedelia of "There's No Tomorrow," the lush and delicate "Woman Work" and "Vanity Fair," and the soulful groove of "Tempted" (the song the band is probably best known for, sung by newly added member Paul Carrack). *—Chris Woodstra*

★ **Singles 45's and Under** / 1982 / A&M ♦♦♦♦♦

Above all, Squeeze were a great singles act—among the finest of the era—and *Singles 45's and Under* offers proof of that fact, giving a chronological survey of their biggest hits from their early, pre-breakup period. Most of the songs can be found on the actual albums, aside from the slightly different single version of "Goodbye Girl" and the new "Annie Get Your Gun," but with a perfect collection like this, even those with the albums should purchase this one as well. *—Chris Woodstra*

Sweets From a Stranger / May 1982 / A&M ♦♦

Perhaps the accolades from *East Side Story* and the constant Lennon/McCartney comparisons went to their head, or maybe the strain of constant touring sapped a lot of their energy and better judgment. Whatever the case, *Sweets From a Stranger* suffers from self-conscious sophistication, overambition, and general lack of direction. And though the album is certainly flawed, an average Squeeze album is still pretty good, and when it hits—as in "I've Returned," "His House Her Home," and the favorite "Black Coffee in Bed"—it really hits. With previous albums, Difford and Tilbrook were able to make incisive observations on British life; the same holds true here, but the alcohol-soaked imagery and chaos between the lines of songs also reveals much about the internal problems of the band. Not surprisingly, the group disbanded shortly after the release. *—Chris Woodstra*

Cosi Fan Tutti Frutti / Aug. 1985 / A&M ♦♦♦

Cosi Fan Tutti Frutti marked not only a re-formation of the band but also a reunion with Jools Holland. And while history and a dated production style hasn't been particularly kind to the album, it is not without its merits. True, it is marred by much of the overblown ambition that undercut *Sweets From a Stranger* and the *Difford and Tilbrook* album, but several of the songs—especially the often overlooked "King George Street"—are real gems in the classic Squeeze tradition, and the move toward "sophistication" is more fully realized and effective. A flawed but certainly worthwhile album, *Cosi Fan Tutti Frutti* deserves reassessment. *—Chris Woodstra*

Babylon and On / Sep. 1987 / A&M ♦♦

Following a brief period of arty, self-conscious indulgence, Squeeze decided to return to the more straight-ahead pop of their classic period. *Babylon and On* strips back a bit and, although the return is a welcomed one, much of the material misses the mark, and the move seems a little forced. Flaws aside, there are some moments of inspiration, and the near-novelty of "Hourglass," unfortunately not one of those moments, became the band's biggest Stateside hit. *—Chris Woodstra*

Frank / Sep. 1989 / A&M ♦♦

Though *Babylon and On* was hailed as a return to form, the unfairly overlooked follow-up, *Frank*, comes much closer to the sound of classic Squeeze. While irresistable songs like "If It's Love" and "She Doesn't Have to Shave" more than make up for the blandness of the previous album, much of the material unfortunately misses the mark. *—Chris Woodstra*

A Round & A Bout (Live) / May 1990 / IRS ♦♦

Play / Aug. 1991 / Reprise ♦♦♦♦

One of Squeeze's most mature and thoughtful albums, 1991's *Play* might be a bit pretentious in spots—the liner notes are written out as a theatre script, with the songs laid out as dialogue—but it's probably Squeeze's best post-reunion album. Shorn of the misguided experiments of *Cosi Fan Tutti Frutti* and the naked chart ambitions of *Babylon and On* and *Frank*, *Play* is a simple and low-key collection of songs charting (loosely; this is less of a concept album than many reviews claimed at the time) the dissolution of a love affair. Reduced to a quartet by Jools Holland's departure for a career as a BBC television presenter (the group's South London homeboy Steve Nieve, tour keyboardist Matt Irving, and more implausibly, Bruce Hornsby provide the keyboards), the group play with a loose, R&B-inflected casualness. Producer Tony Berg, unfortunately, occasionally obscures that character by drowning the songs in strings and mass backing vocals (including special appearances by Michael Penn, Wendie Colter, and Spinal Tap's Michael McKean and Christopher Guest!), but the Difford/Tilbrook songs are mostly strong enough to withstand the onslaught. "The Truth" and the downcast "Walk a Straight Line" are particular highlights. *—Stewart Mason*

Some Fantastic Place / Sep. 14, 1993 / A&M ♦♦♦

The band's tenth proper album reunites the core of Glen Tilbrook and Chris Difford with former member Paul Carrack and adds drummer Pete Thomas (Elvis Costello & the Attractions). Their classic sound is still there through the melodic power pop of "Third Rail" to the blue-eyed soul of "Loving You Tonight" (nearly a rewrite of "Tempted"). Another in a series of commercial sleepers, but definately worth a listen. *—Chris Woodstra*

Ridiculous / Nov. 1995 / Ark 21 ♦♦♦

After nearly 20 years of recording, it would be easy to write Squeeze off as spent creative force—certainly their mosty recent albums have seemed like somewhat forced attempts to recapture the glory days of *Cool for Cats*, *Argybargy*, and *East Side Story*. With *Ridiculous*, Difford and Tilbrook (the only original members left and still the band's primary songwriters) seem content to have passed the Brit-pop torch on, and, as a result, this effortless album is also one of their most enjoyable in recent years. *Ridiculous* isn't an embarrassing attempt to rewrite previous hits, but rather, a natural progression executed with a dignified maturity rather than resignation. "This Summer" and "Electric Trains," though not candidates for the top of the charts at this point, certainly rank among their finest singles. *—Chris Woodstra*

Piccadilly Collection / Aug. 20, 1996 / A&M ♦♦♦

It bills itself as a greatest hits compilation, but *Picadilly Collection* doesn't quite fit that description. Granted, the 18-track disc features some of Squeeze's biggest hits—including "Tempted," "Black Coffee in Bed," "Pulling Mussels (From a Shell)," and "Hourglass"—but the majority of the album consists of songs that will be totally unfamiliar to casual fans. Aside from that handful of hits, *Picadilly Collection* alternates between album tracks from latter-day Squeeze albums like *Frank* and *Some Fantastic Place*, and B-sides that have never before appeared on compact disc. Certainly, dedicated fans will be delighted to have the B-sides on CD, but they would have been better served by a full-fledged rarities collection. Similarly, casual fans would have been better served by a straight singles collection, or a more thorough retrospective—even though this features 18 tracks, it shortchanges all of the group's early records, including such classic new wave albums as *Cool for Cats*, *Argybargy*, and *East Side Story*, in favor of the interminable medley "Squabs on Forty Fab." So, that leave's the question of, just who is *Picadilly Collection* for? It's not for casual fans, it's not for diehards—it's just a wasted opportunity, despite the inclusion of many wonderful songs. *—Stephen Thomas Erlewine*

Excess Moderation / Nov. 1996 / A&M ✦✦✦✦✦
Excess Moderation one-ups its American counterpart, *The Picadilly Collection*, by offering two discs worth of mainly rarities and B-sides along with the stray missed album track, complete with track-by-track comments from Chris Difford and Glen Tillbrook. While, even in combination with *The Picadilly Collection*, there are still many B-sides left unavailable on disc, this is certainly a welcome addition for any fan. *—Chris Woodstra*

Domino / Nov. 1998 / Valley ✦✦

Billy Squier

b. May 12, 1950, Wellesley Hills, MA
Vocals, Guitar / Arena Rock, Hard Rock
Billy Squier was making pop-metal years before Bon Jovi came along. With his sharp, hard-rocking riffs and sweet, slick melodies, Squier became one of the biggest hard rock stars of the early '80s, earning two multi-platinum albums. But his fall from commercial prominence was just as quick as his rise; 1984's *Signs of Life* was his last album to sell over a million copies and even then he seemed slightly behind the times. Squier wasn't able to translate his AOR hits over to MTV, causing him to fall down the charts. However, he never lost his hardcore fans, and continued to tour and record successfully right into the '90s, issuing *Happy Blue* in 1998. *—Stephen Thomas Erlewine*

• **16 Strokes** / 1995 / Capitol ✦✦✦✦
All of Billy Squier's best material is dished out on *16 Strokes*, from the simplistic contagiousness of "The Stroke" to the Van Halen-like fervency of "Tied Up." His rock & roll flamboyancy, a mix of hard but not heavy guitar riffs wrapped around spirited just-for-fun three-minute outpourings, was best established through his singles and not the entirety of his albums. Squier's wild, sexually inundated feistiness is best represented here on a compilation, where the sleekness of "Everybody Wants You" is found in the same place as the naughty "She Goes Down." Both "In the Dark" and "My Kinda Lover" from 1981's *Don't Say No* pop up here, as does his smoothest of songs, "Emotions in Motion" from the album of the same name. His later songs from the early '90s don't include the catchy grandeur or congenial rock hollowness of his first three albums, but their appearance on *16 Strokes* is the best place to hear them. Efforts like the bombastic "Don't Say You Love Me" or the transparent sincerity of "Facts of Life" still harbor Squier's greasy vocal approach, but work better here as the conclusion to a singles anthology than as the end of an album's worth of this song type. The keyboard-drenched "Rock Me Tonite" is another highlight here, as is the breakneck pace of "All Night Long," the two best outcrops from 1984's *Signs of Life* album. This collection may not be as indulgent as his two-disc best-of, but it's more than enough for anyone who's interested. *—Mike DeGagne*

Squire

f. 1977, **db.** 1985
Mod Revival, Power Pop, New Wave
Though they never received the recognition they deserved, Squire was one of the earliest and finest mod-revival bands of the late '70s. Like the founders of the revival, the Jam, Squire were able to transcend the limits of the genre with their high quality blend of pop smarts and songcraft which drew equal parts from punk spirit and '60s sensibilities.

The band formed in Guildford, England around 1977 as a covers band consisting of Enzo Esposito (vocals/bass), Steve Baker (guitar), and Ross Di'Landa (drums). In June 1978, songwriter/guitarist Anthony Meynell joined just prior to a high-profile gig opening for the Jam. The addition of Meynell changed the band's focus to producing original material, and by 1979, they had released their first single for ROK Records, "Get Ready to Go." While the single gained them some airplay, their biggest break came with the newly termed mod-revival movement and their appearance on the legendary *Mods Mayday* album which featured two new songs by the band. Ian Page of Secret Affair (one of Squire's mod peers) had just started his own I-Spy label and signed the band on the merits of their appearance on *Mods Mayday*. The signing led to some personnel changes. First, Di'Landa was replaced by Kevin Meynell, then Baker quit without replacement. In 1979, Squire released two wonderful singles for I-Spy: "Walking Down the Kings Road" and "The Face of Youth Today." Out of the two singles, only "Walking Down the Kings Road" charted. In 1980, Squire switched record labels, signing with another independent, Stage One Records. The band's first release on Stage One was "My Mind Goes Round in Circles" which, like its predecessors, barely made an impact on the charts. Frustrated by a lack of success, the band essentially dissolved when the last original member, Esposito, left.

Anthony Meynell decided to give it another try when he started his own label, Hi-lo in 1981. The first release was *Hits from 3000 Years Ago*, a collection of demos and leftovers from the original Squire lineup. He reactivated the band, adding Jon Bicknell on bass, and releasing a new single, "No Time for Tomorrow," in 1982. Though they were still virtually unknown in their homeland, America had begun picking up on *Hits from 3000 Years Ago*. Delayed by a short promotional tour in the States, their first proper album, *Get Smart*, was finally released late in 1983. They never made the breakthrough into the mainstream, but the album and its follow-up EP, *September Gurls*, (the title track was a cover of the Big Star classic) in 1984 became cult classics in American power-pop circles. Squire began preparation for their next album, *Smash*, but decided to call it quits before its completion. *—Chris Woodstra*

• **Big Smashes** / 1992 / Tangerine ✦✦✦✦✦
Big Smashes is a 24-track best-of that compiles the band's mod-revival singles from the '70s and the more power-pop-oriented material from their Hi-Lo albums. As an introduction to this unfairly overlooked band, there is no better place to begin. These are truly lost classics that deserve discovery. *—Chris Woodstra*

Get Ready to Go! / 1995 / Tangerine ✦✦✦
A nice companion to the *Big Smashes* collection, *Get Ready* focuses on the early work of the original lineup from their mod days. This release supplants *Hits from 3000 Years Ago* by picking the highlights (most of the album) and combining their first single, the brilliant "Get Ready Go," with B-sides, previously unreleased material, a track from the *Odd Bods, Mods and Sods* compilation, and a track from a fan club release. *—Chris Woodstra*

Squirrel Nut Zippers

f. 1993
Retro Swing, Alternative Pop/Rock
The commercialization of alternative music in the '90s resulted in many strange one-hit wonders, but few were quite as unpredictable as the Squirrel Nut Zippers. During a time when hipsters were obsessed with swing music in its relation to Sinatra and Martin's Rat Pack, the Zippers were fascinated with big band swing and Harlem, creating a tongue-in-cheek salute to '20s and '30s jazz. For younger listeners familiar with the style but not the content of classic hot jazz, the band was good fun, but purists found the group's vaguely campy sense of humor and amateurish technique off-putting. This debate would never have even been a matter of consideration if "Hell," an incessantly catchy single from their 1997 album *Hot*, hadn't been able to sneak through loosened alternative airplay to become a novelty hit. Jim Mathus and Katharine Whalen formed the group in 1993 and recruited five additional members before signing to Mammoth in 1994. Though their debut album, 1995's *The Inevitable*, didn't make much of an impact, the group continued to tour. Their second album *Hot* became a hit and went gold. Still, they received mixed reviews with many critics claiming that they were mocking hot jazz, not paying tribute. *Perennial Favorites* followed in 1998, as did *Christmas Caravan*. *—Stephen Thomas Erlewine*

The Inevitable / Mar. 21, 1995 / Mammoth ✦✦✦✦
The members of the band mostly just call it jazz, or "hot music," or, when they're feeling naughty, "race music"—a term that dates back to the1920s and '30s, when major record labels released jump blues and hot jazz singles under special subsidiary imprints with names like Okeh and Sepiatone. It's music that doesn't really have a name anymore, yet everyone recognizes it and loves it. This wasn't the album that made the Squirrel Nut Zippers a household name (that honor goes to *Hot*, the follow-up), but it sure could have if given the chance. An instrumental with the pitch-perfect title of "Lugubrious Whing Whang," cover versions of "You're Drivin' Me Crazy" and "I've Found a New Baby," originals like "Lover's Lane" and the absolutely hair-raising "La Grippe"—these are not just labors of love by dewy-eyed nostalgists. The SNZs have taken this music and appropriated it entirely, without a trace of irony or condescension. The result is magnificent. *—Rick Anderson*

• **Hot** / Jan. 1997 / Mammoth ✦✦✦✦
Squirrel Nut Zippers' second album, *Hot*, was one of the most surprising success stories of 1997. Like the group's debut, *The Inevitable*, *Hot* is comprised entirely of good-natured, if slightly tongue-in-cheek, postmodern big-band music. The band has nailed the sound of jump blues and swinging jazz, and if they don't have the chops of real big bands, they do have enthusiasm and a sense of humor. Of course, for purists of the genre, that collegiate sense of humor might make *Hot* a little unbearable, especially those instances when Katharine Whalen sounds uncannily like Billie Holiday, only without the substance. For those willing to overlook such things, they'll find *Hot* to be a good time, filled with songs nearly as infectious as the group's breakthrough hit, "Hell." *—Stephen Thomas Erlewine*

Sold Out / Sep. 2, 1997 / Mammoth ✦✦✦
After "Hell" made Squirrel Nut Zippers' second album, *Hot*, into a platinum success, the group rush-released the limited-edition *Sold Out* EP. Comprised of live cuts, outtakes, and rarities, the EP is a boon to dedicated fans, especially because of "Pallin' With Al," a duet with Fats Waller's pianist. Tracks like that prove that the Squirrel Nut Zippers aren't simply kitschy—they actually have affection for the music. *—Stephen Thomas Erlewine*

Perennial Favorites / Aug. 4, 1998 / Mammoth ✦✦✦✦
Although it had been simmering for a little while, the neo-swing boom had its breakthrough hit in early 1997 with the Squirrel Nut Zippers' "Hell." Instead of fading away, the movement simply gained momentum, virtually guaranteeing a large audience for the group's summer 1998 follow-up album, *Perennial Favorites*. The title is a sly joke, since the group are revivalists who happen to be part of a fad, but they do prove to be more substantial than many of their peers with this record. Part of the reason they stand apart from the rest of the neo-swing crowd is that they don't forget that there was a bit of menace in the days of hot jazz—it wasn't a naive, swinging party, there was some genuine hedonism as well. Since the Zippers are revivalists, they can only hint at the subtext that informed swing and hot jazz, but that's considerably more than their glitzy peers do. They also have a knack for a solid hook, and they deliver it all with panache and loose-limbed glee. The band may lack the chops that would make this enticing to jazzbos, but they are developing their own style, and they also have songwriting skills. "The Ghost of Stephen Foster," in particular, is a *tour de force*, encapsulating SNZ's gift for hooks, their subversive sense of humor, and their hidden dark side. Moments like that prove that the Squirrel Nut Zippers are more than a one-hit wonder. *—Stephen Thomas Erlewine*

Bedlam Ballroom / Oct. 17, 2000 / Mammoth ✦✦✦✦
Despite undergoing massive lineup changes, among which were vocalist and guitar

player Tom Maxwell going solo, the death of original trumpet blower Stacy Guess, and the birth of a daughter to bandleaders Jim Mathus and Katherine Whalen in May 2000, the Squirrel Nut Zippers persevered through all of it to release a wonderful, progressive (for them) album. Granted, the hot jazz and Dixieland tunes that the band is known for are still present, but the first thing one hears upon listening to this album is a synthesizer and a Spanish guitar. And how about some '70s funk and soul? Funky is the surprising quality of this work, which is why the album stands out among the group's past efforts. *Perennial Favorites* had some good performances, but seemed more of a mere continuation of what was laid down on *Hot*. Here, New Orleans-type funky grooves mix with a Spanish guitar on consecutive tracks, and the juxtaposition reminds the listener of just how magnificent and inspired the Squirrel Nut Zippers can be when they try to grow. Perhaps those who were a part of the neo-swing "revival" of the mid- to late-'90s won't be so receptive to this album, but to anyone who enjoys spirited old-timey music (spanning a range of times), *Bedlam Ballroom* is a damn hoot. *—Jeremy Salmon*

SRC

Detroit Rock, Acid Rock, Psychedelic, Hard Rock

Along with the Stooges, MC5, and the Amboy Dukes, SRC was a group of local heroes of the Michigan rock scene in the late '60s and early '70s, although in terms of national success, they were relegated to the second division populated by such bands as the Frost and the Rationals. Led by the Quackenbush brothers, Gary and Glenn, the Ann Arbor group evolved out of the Fugitives, adding lead singer Scott Richardson from fellow garage band the Chosen Few. SRC recorded three erratic albums for Capitol that blended Motor City crunch with sustain-laden psychedelic guitar, pompous bursts of organ, spacey lyrics, and unexpectedly wispy, vulnerable vocals, throwing in some pretty ballads and harmonies to temper the hard rock excess. *—Richie Unterberger*

● **SRC** / 1968 / One Way ♦♦♦♦

With the twin leads of Gary Quackenbush and Steve Lyman, the distinctly church-like psychedelic Hammond of Glenn Quackenbush, and the angelic (and anglophile) vocals of Scott Richardson, *SRC* is a distinctly acidic album unlike anything else from the Detroit scene; there's not a single soul influence to be heard! Instead, ideas were formed from Procol Harum, the Pretty Things, the Who, and blended with the beauty of the Left Banke. "Black Sheep," "Daystar," and "Marionette" are highlights of this distinct album of cosmic psychedelia and melodic childlike pop. It even sounds fresh today. *—Jon 'Mojo' Mills*

Milestones / 1969 / One Way ♦♦♦

Their second album, although rather erratic, proved to be SRC's most popular. Containing their version of Grieg's "In the Hall of the Mountain King" and Ravel's "Bolero," it's easy to see why they were such a draw in the psychedelic ballrooms across the Midwest in the late '60s. *—James Chrispell*

Traveler's Tale / 1970 / One Way ♦♦♦

SRC's final album was recorded after the departure of guitarists Gary Quackenbush and Steve Lyman, Ray Goodman assuming all the guitar chores. Despite the shakeup, the sound hardly changed at all, perhaps becoming a bit more progressive-minded. The organ-guitar duels and alternation of concise hard rock with lengthy progressive passages also remained intact. If this album came out today, you'd swear it was a satire of the progressive rock era, some of it is so prototypical. But these guys were serious about what they did, and impressive, in their own way. The CD reissue includes a non-LP B-side from the same era, "My Fortune's Coming True." *—Richie Unterberger*

Lost Masters / 1972 / One Way ♦♦♦

Consisting of an amalgam of leftover and unreleased material recorded after leaving Capitol, and both early and late non-album singles, this compilation will be of interest for ardent SRC followers, but is not an advisable introduction. The psychedelia, '70s rock, and soul/R&B do not sit too easily together, which is not surprising either as this set is intentionally and odds and ends package. And as that, it works extremely well. "After Your Heart," "Gypsy Eyes," "Love Is Here Now," "Cry of the Lonely," and the moody instrumental "Valerie" could have quite easily fit on *Milestones* and indeed are comparable to any of their best releases. A more commercial soul sound was adopted a little later, and in working with Motown producers, a horn section, and female backing vocalists, Scott Richardson attempted to emulate his black brethren. Material performed in this manner includes covers of the Animals' "I'm Crying," Holland-Dozier-Holland's "Heatwave," and heroes the Pretty Things' "Out in the Night," which while playable does not match earlier efforts. Of more interest from this era are "Evil," (SRC parodying Howlin' Wolf) and a number of laid-back numbers, such as "No Rules in Love," that hint at how they would of sounded if they continued in a more soft rock vein. All in all a very good album of perhaps Detroit's best and yet least recognized '60s band. After buying the re-releases of the originals, this is the next step to complete the picture. *—Jon 'Mojo' Mills*

The Revenge of the Quackenbush Brothers / 1987 / Bam Caruso ♦♦♦♦♦

Good selection of key cuts from all three albums; "Daystar," "Marionette," and "Black Sheep" are first-rate hard psychedelia. One Way has reissued all of the original albums, as well as some unissued material, but this is the best and most judicious selection. Comes with detailed group history. *—Richie Unterberger*

● **Black Sheep** / Mar. 21, 2000 / RPM ♦♦♦♦♦

If the '80s Bam Caruso compilation *The Revenge of the Quackenbush Brothers* lost marks for being far too skimpy on its track selection, then RPM's expanded update, retitled *Black Sheep*, gains the highest AMG rating. With the best cuts from the *SRC*, *Milestones*, and *Traveler's Tale* albums, single versions and B-sides all included, this is an ideal starting point for anyone new to the band. Phil Smee (with thanks to Brian Hogg) supplies the story, and there are some nice pictures too. This is an ideal introduction and best-of. *—Jon 'Mojo' Mills*

Staind

f. Nov. 24, 1995

Heavy Metal, Alternative Metal

It has been said that first impressions last a lifetime. Luckily for Staind, some only last for about 45 minutes. After a volatile disagreement with Limp Bizkit's Fred Durst, it seemed their big break had walked out the door. Fortunately by the time Durst had witnessed Staind's intense live show, he was ready to exchange phone numbers. Staind's story began in the New England area when vocalist Aaron Lewis and guitarist Mike Mushok met at a Christmas party in 1993. Mushok was able to bring in drummer Jon Wysocki into the fold, and Lewis' connection with a bass player (now no longer with the band) completed the early lineup. Establishing themselves took time, and extensive touring of the Northeast with other established metal acts helped them sell over 2,000 copies of their self-released debut in just over a year. They were primed for their big break, and on October 23, 1997, the hard work paid off. At a show in Hartford, CT, Staind was all set to open for Limp Bizkit when Bizkit singer Fred Durst raised a stink over cover art on Staind's CD. Forty-five minutes later Durst was back, not to further the argument, but to make sure he kept in contact with Staind. Blown away by their live show, Durst exchanged phone numbers. By the time February rolled around in 1998, the band had a record deal. After playing the Vans Warped Tour, they began work on their first album, *Dysfunction*, produced by Terry Date and released April 13, 1999. A tour with Kid Rock followed that spring and later the band reunited with good friends Limp Bizkit for a summer tour. Their follow-up, *Break the Cycle*, enjoyed a prolonged visit at the number one spot on U.S. charts in 2001. *—Chris True*

Dysfunction / Apr. 13, 1999 / Flip/Elektra ♦♦♦

At the beginning of the '90s, "metal" was a dirty word. A few bands, such as Metallica, had enough weight to appear as heirs to the metallic crown, but for the most part, it was the province of lightweight pop-metal mavens. How times change. By the end of the decade, metal was ultra-serious, with the typical band tackling somber, even morose, subjects without humor either in their lyrics or music; it was nothing but a constant grind. Staind is very much emblematic of their era, as much as Poison was of theirs—which isn't meant to be a slam, actually, it's just that their debut album, *Dysfunction*, is a product of the times. Staind show a lot of promise on *Dysfunction*, but you'd forgive a casual observer for thinking that it's an average alt-metal record because in many ways it is. Unlike Korn or Limp Bizkit (who fervently endorsed Staind, so much so that LB's lead singer, Fred Durst, co-produced the album), Staind doesn't really have a distinct image or musical style, but they do summarize '90s underground metal, from Alice in Chains to Tool to Korn. This is hookless, solo-less music where the sonic texture serves as coloring for the bleak words. Not necessarily an easy listen for the uninitiated, but anyone that's grown up on alt-metal will find familiar touchstones throughout the record and will be pleased at how the band easily shifts tempos and sonic colorings, while Aaron Lewis actually sings on much of the record. These are subtle pleasures, the kinds that aficionados will appreciate. Other listeners, however, will likely find *Dysfunction* a little tedious, since there isn't a wide variety of songs on the record, nor is there anything catchy. That, of course, is a signature trait of alt-metal, and helps make the record a sign of the times—but that doesn't mean it's an easy record to enjoy for anyone outside of the cognoscenti. *—Stephen Thomas Erlewine*

● **Break the Cycle** / May 8, 2001 / Flip/Elektra ♦♦♦

The title of Staind's sophomore album refers to the misery passed on from generation to generation; specifically, singer Aaron Lewis' family issues. And *Break the Cycle* is an issues album—Lewis' therapy session for all to hear. "For You" reads like a final confession from child to parent ("I am fucked up because you are"), and on the hit single "It's Been Awhile," he sings, "I cannot blame this on my father." Staind wraps up all this pain in deceivingly melodic packages, sort of like Nirvana's "All Apologies" without the depth. Lewis has a Kurt Cobain-like ache to his voice, which makes the more affecting songs—like the acoustic version of "Outside"—genuine (or at least appear that way). *Cycle* is ultimately no more than 50 minutes of standard-issue desolation, but the softness of many of the tracks gives it compassion, something most of Staind's peers have no time for. *—Michael Gallucci*

Chris Stamey

b. Dec. 6, 1954, Chapel Hill, NC

Producer, Vocals, Keyboards, Guitar, Bass / Jangle Pop, Experimental, Power Pop

From his tenures with the Sneakers and the dB's on through to his subsequent solo projects, singer/songwriter Chris Stamey remained a linchpin of the jangle pop renaissance. He was raised in the Winston-Salem area, and alongside longtime friend and collaborator Peter Holsapple, he first surfaced in 1972 in the short-lived Rittenhouse Square, which issued its sole LP the following year. While attending the University of North Carolina in 1975, Stamey teamed with drummer Will Rigby to form the cult favorite power pop combo Sneakers, later joined by guitarist Mitch Easter. The group traveled to New York City in 1976 to appear at the famed Max's Kansas City but dissolved soon after, at which time Stamey returned to the Big Apple to set up his own label, Car Records. When Rigby and bassist Gene Holder relocated to New York, Stamey joined them as the dB's, releasing the 1978 single "If and When" before expanding to a four-piece with the addition of Holsapple. Although the dB's quirky yet melodic approach anticipated the emergence of the Southern jangle pop explosion, initially they couldn't even land an American record deal, and their first two albums appeared only in Britain. Stamey left the dB's in 1983, issuing the solo LP *It's a Wonderful Life* later that same year. Stamey signed with A&M in 1987 to make his long-awaited major-label debut with the superb *It's Alright*; despite uniformly solid reviews, the album made almost no commercial impact, and he spent the next several years as a producer and guest musician, completing an album which A&M reportedly rejected. The LP finally appeared on Rhino in 1991 under the title *Fireworks*; that same year, he reunited with Holsapple for *Mavericks*. —*Jason Ankeny*

Instant Excitement / 1984 / Coyote ✦✦✦

It's Alright / 1987 / A&M ✦✦✦✦✦

● **Fireworks** / Oct. 22, 1991 / Rhino/RNA ✦✦✦✦✦
Stamey, who founded the dB's and went on to play with the Golden Palominos, proves once again that pop music can be well produced, intelligent, *and* exciting. Deliciously atmospheric, too. —*Roundup Newsletter*

Wonderful Life / Nov. 27, 1992 / East Side Digital ✦✦✦

The Robust Beauty of Improper Linear Models in Decision Making / Apr. 4, 1995 / East Side Digital ✦✦
Be warned: this is not the typical, power-pop release from Chris Stamey. For *Improper Linear Models in Decision Making* Stamey teams up with Kirk Ross for his most experimental outing to date—essentially free improvisation combined with more complex compositions for guitar. As a theoretical exercise, this may be interesting to some, but Stamey fans will most likely be confused and put off by this deviation. —*Chris Woodstra*

The Standells

f. 1962, Los Angeles, CA, **db.** 1983
Garage Rock, Rock & Roll
The Standells made number 11 in 1966 with "Dirty Water," an archetypal garage rock hit with its Stonesish riff, lecherous vocal, and combination of raunchy guitar and organ. In fact, "garage rock" may not have been a really accurate term for them in the first place, as the production on their best material was full and polished, with some imaginative touches of period psychedelia and pop. The Los Angeles band had been playing clubs since the early '60s, hardly typical of the young suburban outfits across America who took their raw garage sound onto obscure singles recorded in small studios. Though they recorded some ordinary albums and singles for Liberty, MGM, and Vee Jay, the group didn't really hit their stride until teaming up with producer Ed Cobb. It was Cobb who wrote "Dirty Water," quite a change of direction from their previous clean-cut image. Their image now considerably toughened, the group churned out four albums during 1966 and 1967, as well as appearing in (and contributing the theme song to) the psychedelic exploitation movie *Riot on Sunset Strip*. After vocalist and drummer Dick Dodd went solo in 1968, the group never recorded again, though they dragged on in one form or another until the early '70s. —*Richie Unterberger*

Dirty Water / 1966 / Sundazed ✦✦✦
Along with *Why Pick on Me*, this was the group's strongest album, although you're always better off with a greatest hits collection. "There Is a Storm Comin'" and "Pride and Devotion" are a couple of strong numbers that don't make it onto compilations, and "Rari," the moody B-side of "Dirty Water," 'tis one of their best little-known tracks. The CD reissue takes off one cut (the easily found "Sometimes Good Guys Don't Wear White") and adds six bonus tracks of only mild interest, including a version of "Batman." Add points for finding a longer version of "Rari," though. —*Richie Unterberger*

Why Pick on Me / 1966 / Sundazed ✦✦✦
This pop-punk relic isn't bad, but as the best of these songs—"Why Pick on Me," "Sometimes Good Guys Don't Wear White," "Mainline"—have been issued on whatever best-of Standells compilation you might pick up, its appeal is really limited to big fans. Of the more obscure tracks, "Black Hearted Woman" is a decent slow, menacing number, "Mr. Nobody" a decent punky cut, and "The Girl and the Moon" one of their best pop-oriented compositions. This CD reissue adds five tracks that were previously unissued in the U.S., which are okay but nothing too special. —*Richie Unterberger*

Hot Ones / 1966 / Sundazed ✦✦

Try It / 1967 / Sundazed ✦✦

The Best of the Standells / 1984 / Rhino ✦✦✦✦✦
Most '60s punk bands could barely fill an album side with decent material. This 18-song compilation is a tribute to the vitality of the Standells' raunch-and-roll attack, including not only their one hit ("Dirty Water") but salacious essentials ranging from the swaggering "Sometimes Good Guys Don't Wear White" to the horny wail of "Barracuda." —*John Floyd*

◗ **The Very Best of the Standells** / May 19, 1998 / Hip-O ✦✦✦✦
The Standells were a one-hit wonder, and that hit was "Dirty Water," which appropriately opens and closes this compilation (the second version is in stereo). Among the 15 other tracks are the group's less successful follow-ups to their hit, notably "Sometimes Good Guys Don't Wear White," and LP tracks from their three albums of 1966-67, including their versions of standards like "Hey Joe," "My Little Red Book," and "Ninety-Nine and a Half." Of course, nothing is as good as "Dirty Water," even if many of the tracks echo its snotty garage-rock appeal, especially the taunting "Try It," a single that Cub Koda's entertaining liner notes were banned in Boston, which, for a band that declared (falsely), "Boston, you're my home" on its hit single, must have been traumatic. —*William Ruhlmann*

Ban This!: Live From Cavestomp! / Oct. 31, 2000 / Varese ✦✦✦

Lisa Stansfield

b. 1965, Rochdale, United Kingdom
Vocals / Club/Dance, Urban, Dance-Pop
English vocalist Lisa Stansfield was the lead singer of the group the Blue Zone, and

featured on Coldcut's "People Hold On" in 1989. She zoomed into the spotlight with *Affection* in 1990. The album went platinum and earned her a number three pop and number one R&B single with "All Around the World." *Affection*, and its follow-up CD *Real Love*, were deeply influenced by the '70s disco sound of Barry White, from arrangements to mood and even Stansfield's own technique. After a long hiatus, she returned with a self-titled effort in 1997. The *#1 Remixes* EP followed a year later. —*Ron Wynn*

● **Affection** / 1989 / Arista ✦✦✦✦✦
When Lisa Stansfield took the R&B world by storm with her melancholy, Barry White-influenced single "All Around the World," it was obvious that not since Teena Marie had a white female singer performed R&B so convincingly. Though she didn't shy away from hip-hop and house-music elements, *Affection* leaves no doubt where the British singer's heart lies—sleek yet gritty '70s R&B. Though the retro leanings of such updated soul treasures as "You Can't Deny It," "What Did I Do to You" are obvious, Stansfield's producer keeps things very fresh-sounding by embracing a decidedly high-tech and very late-'80s/early-'90s production style. Though essentially a soul diva, Stansfield has a disco masterpiece in the love-and-togetherness anthem "This Is the Right Time." —*Alex Henderson*

Real Love / 1991 / Arista ✦✦✦
Expectations ran incredibly high when the time came for Lisa Stansfield to deliver a second album, but unfortunately, she didn't escape the infamous sophomore slump. *Real Love*, although far from a bad album, clearly falls short of *Affection*'s unmitigated excellence. Nonetheless, there are some definite gems here—including the poigant and heart-breaking ballad "All Woman," the spunky "Soul Deep," and the sleek "Set Your Loving Free." While most of *Real Love* is at least decent and is far superior to most '90s R&B, Stansfield is a major talent who—as the outstanding *Affection* quite clearly demonstrated—can do much better than "merely" good. —*Alex Henderson*

So Natural / 1993 / Arista ✦✦✦
After achieving minor success as the lead singer of the U.K. trio Blue Zone and providing vocals for Coldcut's dancefloor classic "People Hold On," Lisa Stansfield established herself as a solo artist with her immensely successful 1989 debut album *Affection*. The combination of lush, Barry White-influenced arrangements and Stansfield's soulful voice proved wildly popular, and Stansfield became one of the hottest new international artists of the late '80s. Unfortunately, Stansfield's popularity slipped a bit with the follow-up, 1991's *Real Love*, but the album was still a respectable seller. *So Natural*, from 1993, failed to reestablish Stansfield as a major commercial force, but since the album was never released in the U.S., it's easy to understand why. Though *So Natural* pales in comparison to *Affection* and even *Real Love*, it certainly isn't bad, and the lack of an American release remains a mystery.

Stansfield almost abandons the R&B-flavored dance-pop of her debut with *So Natural*. The album is definitely consistent, but the ballad-heavy approach wears thin. *So Natural* also lacks a surefire hit single, like *Affection*'s "All Around the World" and "This Is the Right Time" or *Real Love*'s "Change." But *So Natural* still offers many pleasant moments. The steamy ballads "Never Set Me Free" and "Be Mine" rank with Stansfield's best work, and the album does offer a couple of sunny, up-tempo numbers with "Too Much Love Makin'" and "Marvelous and Mine." *So Natural* does flow along quite nicely—the only real clunker here is the bland, dated-sounding synth pop throwback "Little Bit of Heaven"—but the album fails to deliver the memorable hooks of her biggest hits. Still, *So Natural* could have easily found an American audience, considering the success of her previous work. *So Natural* is only available in America as an import release. The album is certainly a worthy find for Lisa Stansfield fans willing to search the import bins. The casual fan, however, is better off with the considerably easier to find *Affection* or her 1997 American comeback effort, simply titled *Lisa Stansfield*. —*William Cooper*

Lisa Stansfield / Apr. 15, 1997 / Arista ✦✦✦✦
Lisa Stansfield's long-awaited eponymous fourth album finds the blue-eyed soul singer at the top of her game, turning in a stylish set of smooth, disco-infelcted dance pop. The songs, from a cover of Barry White's "Never, Never Gonna Give You Up" and "Never Gonna Fall" to the ballad "I Cried My Last Tear," are uniformly strong and Stansfield's voice is seductive and sexy, making the album a small gem in her catalog. —*Stephen Thomas Erlewine*

Face Up / Jul. 3, 2001 / Arista [International] ✦✦✦
Face Up is Lisa Stansfield's first offering for the new millennium, and on this disc she treads similar waters as on previous albums, except for a few more adventurous outings. The album's first single, "Let's Just Call It Love," incorporates the British garage 2 step beats introduced to Americans and popularized earlier in 2001 by fellow Brit Craig David, and makes for an unusual but interesting leadoff single. The album's opener, "I've Got Something Better," is classic, funky Lisa Stansfield at her best, and the song gets more and more fun with each repeated listening. Other standouts include the Burt Bacharach-ish show-stopping ballad "How Could You?," the pleading "Don't Leave Now I'm in Love," and the set's most obvious hit, the breezy, disco-laced anthem "8-3-1." The title track is the album's requisite Barry White tribute, and the album's irresistibly funky closer, "All Over Me," is this set's answer to her previous album's "The Line." This disc does have its share of filler, including the Destiny's Child-sounding "Boyfriend," which is quite immature for a sophisticated gal like Lisa, and the silly ditty "Candy." Stansfield's pipes get quite gritty on the ballad "Didn't I," and "Wish on Me" is as sensitive and acoustic as the "Rochdale Queen" gets. Once again, this reliable singer, without straying too far from her signature formula, delivers a high-quality set, despite the presence of a few dull moments. —*Jose F. Promis*

The Staple Singers

f. 1951, Chicago, IL

Traditional Gospel, Country-Soul, Southern Gospel, Black Gospel, Soul

The Staples story goes all the way back to Winona, MS, in 1915. It was then and there that patriarch Roebuck "Pops" Staples entered the world. A contemporary and familiar of Charley Patton, Roebuck quickly became adept as a solo blues guitarist, entertaining at local dances and picnics. Gradually drawn to the church, by 1941 he'd moved to Chicago, playing gospel music with the Windy City's Trumpet Jubilees. A decade later Pops Staples presented two of his daughters, Cleotha and Mavis, and his one son, Pervis, in front of a church audience, and the Staple Singers were born. The Staples recorded in an older, slightly archaic, deeply Southern spiritual style first for United and then for Vee-Jay. In 1960 they signed with Riverside and attempted to move into the then-burgeoning white folk boom. Two Epic releases, "Why (Am I Treated So Bad)" and a cover of Stephen Stills's "For What It's Worth," briefly graced the pop charts in 1967. In 1968 the Staples signed with Memphis-based Stax. The first two albums, *Soul Folk in Action* and *We'll Get Over*, were produced by Steve Cropper and backed by Booker T and the MG's. The Staples were now singing entirely contemporary "message" songs; when Al Bell took over production chores, he took them down the road to Muscle Shoals, and things got decidedly funky. Starting with "Heavy Makes You Happy (Sha-Na-Boom Boom)" and "I'll Take You There," the Staples counted 12 chart hits at Stax. Curtis Mayfield then signed the Staples to his Curtom label and produced a number one hit in "Let's Do It Again." *—Rob Bowman*

Uncloudy Day/Will the Circle Be Unbroken / 1955-1960 / Vee-Jay ✦✦✦✦✦
The Staple Singers brilliantly fused gospel, folk, blues, and soul into a cohesive, commercially potent sound in the '50s and '60s. They perfected this approach during their tenure at Vee-Jay, the first label that fully presented their harmonies and allowed the twangy, expert guitar licks of Roebuck "Pop" Staples to be heard in the group's mix. This single disc contains two pivotal Staples albums; *Uncloudy Day* includes such gospel favorites as "I Know I Got Religion" and "Let Me Ride," while *Will the Circle Be Unbroken* offers the splendid title track, plus masterpieces like "Pray On" and "Come Up in Glory." *—Ron Wynn*

Great Day / 1963 / Milestone ✦✦✦
This two-album Fantasy reissue is an anthology of the material the Staples recorded for Riverside between 1960 and 1963. For Riverside, the Staples recorded mostly gospel but the shouting was toned down a bit. A few modern-day "message" songs make their way into their repertoire as well, including Bob Dylan's "Masters of War." Not quite as cataclysmic as their Vee-Jay material but still essential. *—Rob Bowman*

Freedom Highway / 1965 / Columbia ✦✦✦
Classic live in-church Epic recordings from the height of the civil rights movement of 1965. *—Opal Louis Nations*

Soul Folk in Action / 1968 / Stax ✦✦✦
This is one you are probably going to have to search out, but this gem is worth all the effort. First, take the stunning voices of the Staple Singers, with the closely blending harmonies that can only come from the years of a family singing together. Put in the crack vibrato guitar of Pops (he was a blues player early on), add in a top-notch rhythm section that play as close as it gets, and throw in the Memphis Horns. Then add some material that was just about custom-tailored for them, mixed and mastered by Steve Cropper, and you have the makings of a fantastic disc. Still, how many times have we seen all the right ingredients and been disappointed? Not this time. The only disappointment might come from the brevity of the disc; you just want it to continue. The power and majesty that these voices carry comes as close to heaven as can be felt here on earth. They are truly performers who give their all. There are few performers who could rival Otis Redding, and to try and do one of his songs while he was still alive was almost considered sacrilege, yet listen to what they do with "(Sittin' On) The Dock of the Bay." It is a completely different take, yet it loses absolutely nothing and in fact gains a new dimension with their controlled power. True, it probably helps that Steve Cropper, the co-writer of the song, is leading the backing band. Two of the highlights of an incredibly strong disc are "Slow Train," for its slow adept building of potency, and "The Weight." It is a vital testament to belief and love, and you will thank yourself for following a hunch. *—Bob Gottlieb*

Pray On / 1968 / Frank Music ✦✦✦✦✦
The Staple Singers recorded ten 78s over a four-year period for Chicago's Vee Jay. These have been reissued countless times in various forms. The Charly CD is simply the most recent. For Vee-Jay, the Staples recorded a number of Pops Staples originals as well as radical rearrangements of standards. Pops Staples and Mavis Staples shared the lead singing chores, with Pervis and Cleotha Staples moaning in the background. Superb gospel shouting. *—Rob Bowman*

We'll Get Over / 1970 / Stax ✦✦✦
Their second Stax release was similar to *Soul Folk in Action*. The album's highlight is Randall Stewart's "When Will We Be Paid?" *—Rob Bowman*

The Staple Swingers / 1971 / Stax ✦✦✦
The Staples' first album produced by Al Bell and recorded in Muscle Shoals hit the winning formula. Other changes saw Pervis Staples departing just before the album was recorded and being replaced by sister Yvonne Staples. Everything was now in place for the Staples' golden years. Three songs, "Heavy Makes You Happy," "Love Is Plentiful," and "You've Got to Earn It," all charted. *—Rob Bowman*

Be Altitude: Respect Yourself / 1972 / Stax ✦✦✦
The Staples' finest single album, containing three Top Ten R&B hits, "Respect Yourself,"

"I'll Take You There," and "This World." The first two also were pop Top 20s, "I'll Take You There" going all the way to number one. *—Rob Bowman*

Be What You Are / 1973 / Stax ✦✦✦
By the early '70s, despite a roster that included the Dramatics and Isaac Hayes, Stax Records was winding down. The Staple Singers, signed to the label in the late '60s, always provided hit singles and respected album efforts. Despite their gospel beginnings, the Staple Singers' biggest draws became Pops Staples' blues-based "devil's music" guitar and Mavis Staples' breathy and sexy vocals. Their 1972 album, *Be Altitude: Respect Yourself*, all but set the template for their subsequent work. *Be What You Are* in some respects is an often overly cautious follow-up. The first single, "If You're Ready (Come Go With Me)," comes off as a softer take on "I'll Take You There." While the implications of having a narrow lyrical scope did impede the group somewhat, *Be What You Are* has the group mining familiar terrain with minimal wear. Tracks like "Love Comes in All Colors," "Tellin' Lies," and the masterful "Touch a Hand, Make a Friend" are all strong and well-produced tracks in the group's rural yet urbane style. The effort's lone cover of Bill Withers' "Grandma's Hands," despite Mavis Staples' lead, comes up short due to the perfection of the Withers original. Mavis Staples also gets two solo efforts here, including Bettye Crutcher's tough "Drown Yourself" and the spare "Heaven." *Be What You Are* isn't as strong or innovative as its predecessor, but it is a cohesive album and a must-have for fans. *—Jason Elias*

City in the Sky / 1974 / Stax ✦✦✦
City in the Sky, the final LP that the Staple Singers made with Stax Records, features the same socially conscious lyrics and powerful singing that had become their trademark before the album's 1974 release. While the original recording didn't have the kind of explosive singles like "Respect Yourself" and "I'll Take You There" that helped them become legends of soul music, this is by no means a weak album. The opener "Back Road Into Town" seethes with energy and anger-tinged pride, while "Washington We're Watching You" combines that same message of anger and pride with organ and horn-driven funk. The Staple Singers return to the gospel style that had begun their musical career nearly 20 years before with "Who Made the Man," perhaps the strongest song on the album, alternating between gentle invectives by Pop Staples and powerful harmonic blasts by Mavis, Cleotha, and Yvonne. Overall, the album combines a classic Stax-influenced soul sound with a strong message, making it an essential part of the Staples Singers' catalog. [The 1996 CD reissue of *City in the Sky* features four bonus tracks, including "Oh La De Da" and live versions of "I Like the Things About You," "Respect Yourself," and "I'll Take You There."] *—Stacia Proefrock*

Let's Do It Again / 1975 / Curtom ✦✦✦
As Stax neared bankruptcy, the Staples signed with Curtis Mayfield's Curtom label for this soundtrack album. The title track was a number one hit and "New Orleans" reached number 70, returning the Staples to the upper echelons of the charts for the last time. *—Rob Bowman*

★ **The Best of the Staple Singers** / Oct. 17, 1990 / Stax ✦✦✦✦✦
The best and most famous cuts from their glory years at Stax. Includes their massive hits "Respect Yourself" and "I'll Take You There"; less famous but similar gospel-funk fusions like "Touch a Hand (Make a Friend)" and "Heavy Makes You Happy (Sha-Na-Boom Boom)"; and less expected items like a cover of "(Sittin' On) The Dock of the Bay." It does not, however, have their 1975 number one single "Let's Do It Again," which they recorded just after cutting their ties to Stax. *—Richie Unterberger*

The Very Best of the Staple Singers, Vol. 1: Live / Mar. 3, 1998 / Collectables ✦✦✦
1950s Vee Jay classics with Pops' Delta guitar and Mavis' deep, compelling vocals. *—Opal Louis Nations*

The Very Best of the Staple Singers, Vol. 2: On My Way to Heaven / Mar. 3, 1998 / Collectables ✦✦✦
The cream of the cream. Their choice Vee Jay sides. *—Opal Louis Nations*

Edwin Starr

b. Jan. 21, 1942, Nashville, TN

Vocals / Pop-Soul, Northern Soul, Motown, Soul

One of the best soul-shouters to come from the Motown stable, Starr's style was closer to James Brown than to any of the other male Motown artists. Best known for his 1970 hit "War," he made a brief comeback during the disco craze, but he now tours Europe and plays the oldies circuit. Detroit vocalist Edwin Starr returned to the vocal wars in 1984 when he recorded a tribute album to Marvin Gaye for England's Streetwave label. He had relocated to Britain and moved to Warwickshire. Starr signed with Hippodrome and issued a pair of singles on that label in 1985 and 1986. He then recorded briefly for Virgin, being produced by the Stock/Aitken/Waterman trio, and then recorded for Motorcity in England and WEA in Germany. Starr also had some songs featured on the Walt Disney release *Mousersize*. *—Rick A. Bueche*

● **The Very Best of Edwin Starr** / Aug. 25, 1998 / Motown ✦✦✦✦✦
Edwin Starr was at the height of his creative powers in the 1960s and early to mid-1970s, when he did much of his best work for Motown. Released in late 1998, this CD spans 1965-1974 and boasts many of his essential Motown hits. Starr was very much a product of Northern soul, and yet, he sometimes showed an awareness of the sweaty, rough-and-tumble soul that Stax Records was recording down in Memphis. "If My Heart Could Tell the Story," "Stop Her On Sight (S.O.S.)," and "I'm Still a Struggling Man" are pure Detroit; the sweetness and honey-coated harmonies that defined a lot of Motor City and Northern R&B are very much a part of these classics. But Starr's tougher side asserts itself on "25 Miles" and the angry protest song "War," both of which demonstrate that when he

wanted, Starr could be every bit as gritty as Memphis shouters like Otis Redding and Sam Moore. If you're seeking an introduction to Starr's talents, this disc would be the best choice by far. —*Alex Henderson*

Ringo Starr

b. Jul. 7, 1940, Liverpool, England
Vocals, Drums / Pop/Rock
Ringo Starr, born Richard Starkey, was the drummer in the Beatles from 1962 to 1970 and thus one of the most famous musicians of the '60s. Though the least prominent member of the quartet, he distinguished himself as an occasional singer of good-natured material and as an actor. Upon the group's split, Starr went solo with two novelty projects: the first, an album called *Sentimental Journey*, found him covering pre-rock standards, and the second, *Beacoups of Blues*, was a country music collection.

Starr then scored Top Ten hits with two non-album singles, "It Don't Come Easy" in 1971 and "Back off Boogaloo" in 1972. In 1973 he paired with producer Richard Perry and, with assistance from the three other ex-Beatles, made *Ringo*, which featured two number one hits, "Photograph" and "You're Sixteen." "Oh My My," a Top Ten hit, was also included. Almost as successful was the 1974 follow-up, *Goodnight Vienna*, which featured the hits "Only You" and "No No Song."

Starr continued to release albums through 1981, though with diminishing success. His 1983 album *Old Wave* did not find a U.S. distributor. Starr was also suffering from the excesses of his lifestyle, but by the late '80s he had cleaned up, and in 1989 he toured with his "All-Starr Band." In 1992, he signed to Private Music and released a new studio album, *Time Takes Time. Vertical Man*, his first album for Mercury, followed in 1998, as did a disc culled from his performance on the *VH1 Storytellers* series. Starr's first seasonal effort, *I Wanna Be Santa Claus*, appeared a year later. —*William Ruhlmann*

Sentimental Journey / Mar. 27, 1970 / Capitol ✦✦✦
Ringo actually started recording his first solo album in late 1969, before the Beatles had officially split. Partially to please his parents, he set out to record an album not of rock & roll, but of standards from the 1930s and 1940s, with help from a bellyful of top arrangers (Richard Perry, Chico O'Farrill, Maurice Gibb, Klaus Voorman, George Martin, Quincy Jones, Elmer Bernstein, Oliver Nelson, and Paul McCartney). Savaged by some critics, it's really not all that bad. But it ain't rock & roll, it's not what Ringo does best, and it's not an essential part of anyone's collection, Beatles fan or otherwise, though it rose into the U.K. Top Ten and U.S. Top 30 when it was released, largely on the strength of Starr's then-fresh association with the Beatles. Reissued on CD in 1995. —*Richie Unterberger*

Beaucoups of Blues / Sep. 25, 1970 / Capitol ✦✦✦✦✦
Ringo Starr had a demonstrated affinity for country music, as heard on such Beatles recordings as "Act Naturally," and he sounded as modestly comfortable on this Nashville-recorded session as in any other musical context. The cream of the city's session players backed up the former Beatle on a set of newly written songs, and the result was a typical country effort, pleasant as long as you didn't expect too much. Of course, this was the second straight genre exercise for Starr, following his pop standards album *Sentimental Journey*, and now he had tackled two styles that depend on vocal stylists for much of their appeal. On both, Ringo was Ringo. But with the Beatles fading into history, his suddenly front-burner solo career was starting to look like a series of dabblings rather than a coherent follow-up to the group's success. What could be next, an album of Motown songs? Wisely, he returned to Beatles-style pop/rock in subsequent releases. [*Beaucoups of Blues* was reissued on August 1, 1995, by Captiol with two bonus tracks, "Coochy Coochy," which had been released as the B-side of the single "Beaucoups of Blues," and the six-and-a-half-minute impromptu instrumental "Nashville Jam," which was previously unreleased.] —*William Ruhlmann*

Ringo / Nov. 2, 1973 / Capitol ✦✦✦✦✦
With *Ringo*, Ringo Starr finally put his solo career in gear in 1973, after serving notice with back-to-back Top Ten singles in 1971 and 1972 that he had more to offer than his eccentric first two solo albums. *Ringo* was a big-budget pop album produced by Richard Perry and featuring Ringo's former Beatles bandmates as songwriters, singers, and instrumentalists. On no single track did all four appear, though George Harrison played the guitars on the John Lennon-penned leadoff track "I'm the Greatest," with Lennon playing piano and singing harmony. But it wasn't only the guests who made *Ringo* a success: Ringo advanced his own cause by co-writing two of the album's Top Ten singles, the number one "Photograph" and "Oh My My." The album's biggest hit was a second chart-topper, Ringo's cover of the old Johnny Burnette hit "You're Sixteen." Songs like "Have You Seen My Baby," a Randy Newman song with guitar by Marc Bolan, and Ringo and Vini Poncia's "Devil Woman" were just as good as the hits. Ringo's best and most consistent new studio album, *Ringo* represented both the drummer/singer's most dramatic comeback and his commercial peak. The original ten-track 1973 album got even better in 1991 as a 13-track CD reissue, the bonus tracks including the 1971 gold single "It Don't Come Easy" and its B-side, "Early 1970," a telling depiction of Ringo's perspective on the Beatles breakup. —*William Ruhlmann*

Goodnight Vienna / Nov. 15, 1974 / Capitol ✦✦✦✦
Goodnight Vienna was very much a follow-up to *Ringo*, on which Ringo Starr called upon his bevy of musical buddies. Most prominent among them was John Lennon, who again wrote the leadoff track, "(It's All Da-Da-Down To) Goodnight Vienna," and played on three songs; also included are Elton John, who wrote and played on "Snookeroo," Dr. John, Billy Preston, Robbie Robertson, and Harry Nilsson. Richard Perry again produced, bringing his strong pop sensibility to the diverse material. The only real fall-off was in the songwriting; the album's Top Ten hits were "Only You," the old Platters song, and Hoyt Axton's novelty number "No No Song," which winked at intoxicants, but little else on the set stood out. *Goodnight Vienna* was another enjoyable Ringo record, but it lacked the star power and consistency of its predecessor. Still, compared to the rest of his '70s albums, it was a masterpiece. —*William Ruhlmann*

● **Blast From Your Past** / Nov. 20, 1975 / Capitol ✦✦✦✦✦
Capitol records marked Ringo Starr's impending departure from the label with this ten-song compilation drawn from three of his solo albums, along with the previously non-LP hits "It Don't Come Easy" and "Back Off Boogaloo" and the B-side "Early 1970." As it happened, the set was perfectly timed, since Ringo never threatened the Top Ten again and he was caught here at his 1971-1975 commercial peak, with all seven of his Top Ten hits accounted for, including the gold-selling chart-toppers "Photograph" and "You're Sixteen." —*William Ruhlmann*

Ringo's Rotogravure / Sep. 17, 1976 / Atlantic ✦✦✦
The formula that had worked for *Ringo* and *Good Night Vienna* was followed again on Ringo Starr's Atlantic Records debut. Arif Mardin replaced Richard Perry in the producer's chair, but he hewed to the bouncy, eclectic pop style Perry had pioneered for *Ringo*, and the drummer called in such name help as Peter Frampton, Dr. John, Melissa Manchester, the Brecker brothers, Paul McCartney, John Lennon, and Eric Clapton. The last three all contributed songs, too, as did George Harrison. As usual, there was an oldie, Bruce Channel's "Hey Baby," which came out as a single, as did the leadoff track, "A Dose of Rock & Roll." The latter was the only Top 40 hit, as the times seemed to be passing Ringo's happy-go-lucky style by. Or maybe it was just time for a new formula. —*William Ruhlmann*

Ringo the 4th / Sep. 26, 1977 / Atlantic ✦✦
On his previous three albums, Ringo Starr had depended on superstar friends, a few oldies, and a lighthearted attitude to get him through. The commercial disappointment of *Rotogravure* seemed to dictate a change of approach, and *Ringo the 4th* attempted to be a slick '70s soul-pop effort with hints of disco. Ringo was accompanied by New York studio pros, and he wrote most of the songs with Vini Poncia. The result marked the difference between disappointment and disaster, as the record flopped commercially and Atlantic bounced him. —*William Ruhlmann*

Bad Boy / Apr. 21, 1978 / Portrait ✦✦
Leaving Atlantic Records after the sales disaster of *Ringo the 4th*, Ringo Starr signed to CBS's Portrait label and returned to the record racks after only seven months with *Bad Boy*. Working again with Vini Poncia and with a largely pseudonymous band (lead guitar by "Push-alone," and bass by "Diesel"), Ringo turned out a competent effort with a few interesting song choices, notably the old Benny Spellman song "Lipstick Traces (On a Cigarette)" (bet it was a favorite back in Liverpool) and Gallagher & Lyle's "Heart on My Sleeve," and some that were beyond him, such as the Supremes' "Where Did Our Love Go." But Ringo needed more than competence to reverse his career decline, and *Bad Boy* sold only to the same hardcore Beatles collectors who had pushed *Ringo the 4th* into the lower reaches of the charts for half a dozen weeks. —*William Ruhlmann*

Stop and Smell the Roses / Oct. 27, 1981 / The Right Stuff ✦✦✦
The idea, back in 1980, was to resurrect Ringo Starr's recording career by the same method that it had been launched with the *Ringo* album in 1973—by having his fellow Beatles and other well-known friends help out. John Lennon was working on a song called "Nobody Told Me," and George Harrison had one ready to go. Then Lennon was murdered in December. His Ringo song languished (his own version would be released in 1984), while Harrison took his tune back and rewrote the lyrics for what became his own hit, "All Those Years Ago." Then Ringo's label, Portrait, lacked enthusiasm for the album, and he moved on to Boardwalk. Finally released as Boardwalk 33246, *Stop and Smell the Roses* was Ringo's strongest and most effervescent album since *Goodnight Vienna*, containing two good songs by Paul McCartney and one by George Harrison—"Wrack My Brain," which became Ringo's final Top 40 hit—along with music by Harry Nilsson, Ron Wood, and Stephen Stills. Long out of print, *Stop and Smell the Roses* reappeared on Capitol's The Right Stuff reissue label on September 6, 1994, with six bonus tracks, reflecting the changes made in the album from its original, unreleased version, that increased the album's length by nearly 70 percent and demonstrated that the later song selection was better. —*William Ruhlmann*

Old Wave / Jun. 8, 1983 / The Right Stuff ✦✦
Produced by Joe Walsh, *Old Wave* was a well-put-together collection of good pop/rock songs that was all wrong for Ringo Starr. The songs required interpretive abilities simply not found in a singer of Ringo's pleasant, but limited voice and phrasing. "She's About a Mover" and "I Keep Forgettin' " were appropriate covers, but Ringo was out of his depth on reflective songs like "Picture Show Life" and "As Far as We Can Go." There was also a throwaway instrumental, "Everybody's in a Hurry but Me," featuring Eric Clapton and John Entwistle. Neil Bogart, the head of Boardwalk, Ringo's record label, died during the making of this album, and the closest it got to an American release was on RCA Canada, which was just as well. [Originally released in Canada on June 8, 1983, as RCA 3233, as well as in Japan, South America, and Germany, *Old Wave* was finally released in the U.S. by The Right Stuff/Capitol on September 6, 1994, with one extra bonus track, an orchestral version of "As Far as We Can Go."] —*William Ruhlmann*

Starr Struck: Best of Ringo Starr, Vol. 2 / Feb. 24, 1989 / Rhino ✦✦✦
A follow-up compilation to *Blast from Your Past*, *Starr Struck* gathered together the better tracks from Ringo Starr's less successful albums originally released between 1976 and 1983. "A Dose of Rock & Roll" and "Wrack My Brain" were Top 40 singles, and the album contained specially written songs by Ringo's Beatle colleagues. The album also marked the first U.S. release for four songs from Ringo's 19B3 album *Old Wave*. The result was a good substitute for five Ringo albums that were out of print when it was released, but no match for the hit-filled *Blast From Your Past*. —*William Ruhlmann*

All-Starr Band / Oct. 8, 1990 / Rykodisc ♦♦♦

Time Takes Time / May 22, 1992 / Private Music ♦♦♦♦♦

On his first new studio album to be released in the U.S. in 11 years, Ringo Starr made a neo-'60s-sounding record that, if it didn't feature his Beatle-mates, certainly evoked them. Don Was, the king of creative retro, produced half the album, bringing in bands like Jellyfish and the Posies, who devote their careers to trying to sound like the Beatles of 1965-66. Here, with a real Beatle on drums and vocals, they came much closer. Of course, it's always a little weird when a veteran star makes what is essentially clone music meant to resemble the sound of his glory days. But Ringo remains a distinctive drummer and an engaging singer, so even when he was singing something called "Golden Blunders," it was hard to blame him. Besides, there are worse things to copy than the Beatles. *—William Ruhlmann*

Live from Montreux, Vol. 2 / 1994 / Rykodisc ♦♦♦

Vertical Man / Jun. 16, 1998 / Mercury ♦♦♦

Early in his career, Ringo Starr realized that he couldn't quite carry an entire album by himself, so he established the practice of the "all-star" (or "All-Starr," as he later dubbed it) album, drafting in his musician buddies to help him make an album. The first time he did this was also the best—1973's *Ringo* remains one of the best Beatles solo albums, possibly the only one that is simply, unabashedly fun. The approach also enlivened his 1992 comeback album *Time Takes Time*, but it fails to deliver on that record's follow-up, *Vertical Man*. Ringo remains loyal to such longtime friends as Joe Walsh and Tom Petty, as well as Paul and George, but he also brings in such young guns as Alanis Morissette and Scott Weiland, hoping that some of their hipness will transfer to him. Of course, that doesn't happen, but you wouldn't want it to anyway—Ringo is at his best when he's Ringo, warbling amiable ditties with his charming, slightly off-key voice. *Vertical Man* has that in spades. The overall quality of the songs isn't as strong as *Time Takes Time*, but there are some neat moments, from a cover of Dobie Gray's timeless "Drift Away" to ingratiating new numbers like "One" and "I'll Be Fine Anywhere." It's a slight album—most of Ringo's albums are—but it's an entertaining one, and that's only true of a handful of his records. *—Stephen Thomas Erlewine*

VH1 Storytellers / Oct. 20, 1998 / Polygram ♦♦♦

Just as MTV's *Unplugged* series started out as a great idea—get musicians to re-imagine their material in stripped-down arrangements—then was reduced by the record business to a gimmick—a new kind of live album, which is to say, yet another way to re-sell the same material—VH1's *Storytellers* series has quickly traced the same decline. After all, not everybody is as eloquent, or as well-prepared, as Ray Davies, who did the first show. And as any music journalist can tell you, a musician's idea of a great story about how he came to write a song may not be anybody else's. But the format would seem perfect for bon vivant Ringo Starr, and even if he has been as guilty of padding his catalog as any veteran, he does tell short, entertaining anecdotes about the collection of Beatles favorites and solo hits included (most of which haven't been circulated widely before), which makes it forgivable that he also sneaks in four Beatlesque songs from his recently released *Vertical Man* album. His backup band, the Roundheads, is actually more supportive than the various editions of the All-Starr Band he used to tour with, and it's good to have a Ringo Starr live album with so much Ringo on it. *—William Ruhlmann*

Starry Eyed and Laughing

Pub Rock

Originally a distinctly Byrds-influenced duo of guitarist/vocalists Ross McGeeney and Tony Poole (and thus instantly comparable to an early R.E.M.), Starry Eyed and Laughing were one of the most individual acts to gravitate toward the London pub rock scene as the 1970s neared their midpoint. Formed in the midlands city of Northampton during 1973, within a year the band had swollen to a quartet comprising McGeeney, Poole, bassist Steve Hall, and drummer Nick Brown and were packing venues across the capital. This lineup survived only a matter of months, but did bring the band to the attention of CBS. With a new rhythm section of Iain W hitmore and the splendidly named drummer Mick Wackford, plus a cast of guests including Russ Ballard, Lindisfarne's Ray Jackson, and BJ Cole, Starry Eyed and Laughing cut their eponymous debut album in mid-1974, alongside the single "Money Is No Friend of Mine."

A second album, *Thought Talk*, followed in 1975, together with further singles "Nobody Home" and "Good Love," and that fall, Starry Eyed and Laughing made their U.S. debut with a short, but very well-received tour. Upon returning home, however, McGeeney quit the band—he was replaced by Roger Kelly for the 1976 single "Don't Give Me a Hard Time," before bassist Whitmore, too, departed.

Opting to continue on as a trio, the band abbreviated its name to Starry Eyed alone, but never recaptured the excitement of earlier years and broke up soon after. *—Dave Thompson*

● **Starry Eyed and Laughing** / 1974 / CBS ♦♦♦♦

Thought Talk / 1975 / CBS ♦♦♦

Status Quo

f. 1967, London, England

Boogie Rock, Psychedelic, Hard Rock

Status Quo is one of Britain's longest-lived bands, staying together for over 30 years. During much of that time, the band was only successful in the U.K., where they racked up a string of Top Ten singles that ran into the '90s. In America, the group was ignored after they abandoned psychedelia for heavy boogie rock in the early '70s. Before that, the Quo managed to reach number 12 in the U.S. with the psychedelic classic "Pictures of Matchstick Men" (a Top Ten hit in the U.K.). Following that single, the band suffered a lean period for the next few years, before deciding to refashion themselves as a hard-rock boogie band in 1970 with their *Ma Kelly's Greasy Spoon* album. Over the next 25 years, the Quo have basically recycled the same simple boogie on each successive album and single, yet their popularity has never waned in Britain. If anything, their very predictability has ensured the group a large following. By the mid-'90s, Status Quo had scored 50 British hit singles, which was a greater number than any other band in rock & roll's history. *—Stephen Thomas Erlewine*

● **Whatever You Want: The Best of Status Quo** / 1997 / Polygram ♦♦♦♦♦

In many ways, *Whatever You Want: The Best of Status Quo* is the definitive Quo collection. Spanning two discs, the set features almost all of the band's hits, from "Pictures of Matchstick Men" to "Down Down" and "Rockin' All Over the World," leaving only a couple of cuts behind. For all but the most dedicated fan, this is all the Quo they'll ever need, and it may even be too much for the casual observer. *—Stephen Thomas Erlewine*

Steeleye Span

f. 1970

British Folk-Rock, British Folk, Folk-Rock

Aside from Fairport Convention, Steeleye Span were the most successful and enduring British folk-rock band. The parallels between the band are numerous: both updated traditional British folk material with rock arrangements, both featured an excellent female lead singer (Sandy Denny for Fairport, Maddy Prior for Steeleye Span), both frequently employed multi-part harmonies, and both mixed original and traditional songs. Although Fairport were more innovative in their early days, Steeleye Span were arguably the more interesting band after 1970, when personnel changes had gutted the original Fairport lineup. Steeleye Span, too, would undergo numerous personnel changes even at their peak. Prior was the constant factor that gave the group something of a recognizable identity at all phases of their journey. One thing that differentiated Steeleye Span from their counterparts was that Fairport came to traditional folk from a rock background, whereas Steeleye traveled in the opposite direction. While Steeleye Span played folk music, they had no aversion to playing it loud, and proved that it was possible to create an energetic ruckus without a drummer. *—Richie Unterberger*

Hark the Village Wait / 1970 / Shanachie ♦♦♦

Originally released by British RCA, this debut album by Steeleye Span's original lineup—Ashley Hutchings (bass), Tim Hart (electric guitar, electric dulcimer, banjo, harmonium, vocals), Maddy Prior (vocals, banjo), Terry Woods (mandola, mandolin, electric guitar, vocals), and Gay Woods (vocals, concertina, bodhran)—barely made it out the door before Gay and Terry Woods exited. This was probably the best singing edition of Steeleye Span, with Gay Woods and Maddy Prior melding beautifully on tracks like "Dark-Eyed Sailor" and "My Johnnie Was a Shoemaker," and Terry Woods adding some realistic coarseness on "The Hills of Greenmore." The sound is fully electric here (with superb playing on the epic "Lowlands of Holland"), if not as aggressive or well crafted as later albums—Hart, Hutchings, and Woods comprise a good core band, and Gerry Conway and Fairport Convention's Dave Mattacks sit in on drums. *—Bruce Eder*

Ten Man Mop / 1971 / Shanachie ♦♦♦

The third Steeleye Span album opens with possibly the most beautifully sung number of their entire history, "Gower Wassail," and which also makes a very strong case for the use of electric guitars in a traditional folk setting. "Paddy Clancy's Jig/Four Nights Drunk" was the group's first great electric adaptation of traditional dance, None of the rest is quite that good, highlighted by Maddy Prior's haunting performance on "When I Was on Horseback" (although the song drones on a little too long at six-and-a-half minutes), the delightful "Marrowbones," the riveting "Stewball," and the rousing reels "Dowd's Favourite," "£10 Float," and "The Morning Dew." *—Bruce Eder*

Please to See the King / 1971 / Shanachie ♦♦♦

The debut of Steeleye Span (Mark II), with Peter Knight on fiddle and Martin Carthy on guitar, is more solid almost every area from repertory to production. The group still had its feet in both modern and traditional sounds simultaneously, so the album mixes very beautiful, distinctly archaic sounding songs such as "Boys of Bedlam" with amplified, electric numbers such as the rousing, ironic "Female Drummer" (which was a highlight of their concerts). Although a second female voice would've been nice, the singing and harmonizing (with help from some careful overdubbing) is still impressive and the performances are tighter, the group's overall sound reflecting the quintet's status as a working band and their experience performing these songs on-stage. The use of electric guitars was also unique, and quite different from rivals such as Fairport Convention, occasionally mimicking the sound of bagpipes here. Songs including the haunting "The Blacksmith," the fine guitar workout on "Cold, Haily Windy Night," the dour "Prince Charlie Stuart," the bittersweet "Lovely on the Water," and the playful, cautionary "False Knight on the Road." They would get better on later albums—especially in their approach to the jigs and reels represented here—but this represents a solid second beginning for the band. *—Bruce Eder*

Below the Salt / 1972 / Shanachie ♦♦♦♦♦

The most successful of all Steeleye Span lineups, with Bob Johnson and Rick Kemp in place of Martin Carthy and Ashley Hutchings, makes its debut on what could be their best album. There's not a weak note here, and all of its has a harder, more muscular sound courtesy of Kemp and Johnson, matched to impeccable vocals and uniformly excellent material. Kemp's bass playing makes it possible to overlook the absence of a drummer, while the match-up of Johnson and Hart made them one of the best electric guitar teams in English folk-rock (and helps explain Steeleye's successful eclipsing of the post-Richard Thompson Fairport Convention). Prior's voice was never better than on this album, and while Carthy's backing vocals are missed, the group's singing is still up to a very high standard, with "Rosebud in June" perhaps the best a cappella number in their repertory and "Royal Forester" their most charmingly lusty performance. "John Barleycorn"—which every Traffic fan should hear—is in a class by itself, and the dazzling "Gaudette" actually made the British charts and got Steeleye Span onto *Top of the Pops*. *—Bruce Eder*

Parcel of Rogues / 1973 / Shanachie ♦♦♦♦♦
The group's first real rock album, with a sound clearly rooted in modern sensibilities, with the guitars are turned up very loud for the first time. The singing is still modeled on traditional patterns, and is quite beautiful (especially "One Misty Moisty Morning" and "Allison Gross"), but the resonances and undertones of electric guitars are everywhere—the result is a record that, in some ways, recalls Fairport Convention's *Liege and Lief* (the record that led indirectly to the spawning of Steeleye Span in the first place), with some very flashy playing by Johnson on some of the breaks. The rousing "Ups and Downs" is played on acoustic instruments, and the atmospheric "Weaver and the Factory Maid" could've come off of any of the earlier albums, while "The Bold Poachers" is more traditional sounding, starting out on acoustic instruments before the amplified guitars chime in—it sets the tone for the album, as wah-wah pedals punch up instrumentals such as "Robbery With Violins" and "The Wee Wee Man" (which includes drums). A lot of the time it works—the ominous and dazzling "Cam Ye O'er Frae France" would not have succeeded half as well without amplification, and every fan of the group should hear this track at least once. *—Bruce Eder*

Now We Are Six / 1974 / Shanachie ♦♦♦♦
With Nigel Pegrum added permanently as drummer, the group rocks out for the first time, and from the thumping tom-toms and snare on the opening track, "Thomas the Rhymer," and Bob Johnson's power chords, it's clear that this is a record with balls. Actually, *Now We Are Six* is still a folk-rock album, albeit with a beat. This was the first Steeleye Span album that many Americans heard and it's a pretty good place to start—in fact, it might've been the group's very best album, if not for the presence of drivel such as "Twinkle, Twinkle Little Star" and "To Know Him Is to Love Him" (the latter featuring David Bowie on sax), which still leaves 33 very solid minutes of great music to savor.

For all of their rocking natures, "Drink Down the Moon" and "Two Magicians" (which can be heard in its more traditional form on Martin Carthy's first album) capture the mystery and lustiness, respectively, of their hundreds-of-years-old source material magnificently; "Long-a-Growing" is one of Maddy Prior's finest vocal performances; and "The Mooncoin Jig"—which is alive with richly textured guitar and mandolin—is one of the greatest instrumental folk-rock tracks ever recorded, vibrant enough to get even the clumsiest up and dancing. *—Bruce Eder*

All Around My Hat / 1975 / Shanachie ♦♦♦
The biggest selling of all Steeleye Span albums is also their hardest rocking record. They sound like would-be competitors to the Who on the opening bars of "The Wife of Usher's Well," and Robert Johnson's electric guitar grinding out power-chords like nobody's business. The vocals have their usual elegance, the harmonies soaring exquisitely, but between the choruses the guitar puts out lots of wattage. The guitar competes with Maddy Prior's voice for dominance on tracks like "Hard Times of Old England," "Batchelors Hall," and "Dance With Me." There's some more traditional sounding material here, including the lovely "Cadwith Anthem," "Batchelor's Hall," and "Gamble Gold (Robin Hood)," where the group returns to acoustic instruments. A single of the upbeat title track also made the charts in England, and the overall sound was the work of producer Mike Batt, who gave the band a raw, stripped-down style, with only the smallest touching up, with the very lightest of overdubbed strings. *—Bruce Eder*

Commoner's Crown / 1975 / BGO ♦♦♦♦♦
From the opening bars of "Little Sir Hugh"—an extraordinarily brisk and upbeat sounding treatment of an incredibly grim song—the band playing on *Commoner's Crown* scarcely sounds like the same group on *Now We Are Six* or *Parcel of Rogues*. Now a full-fledged rock group, competing with the likes of Jethro Tull and pumping out higher amperage than Fairport Convention, Steeleye engages in heavy riffing, savage attacks on their instruments, and generally kicks out the jams on this album. But they're also fairly clever, interweaving Bach with traditional Irish music—actually, Bach-meets-the-Mooncoin-Jig from their previous record—on "Bach Goes to Limerick." There's not a bad song here, and even if it is more rock than folk, it's all very substantial and vibrant music-making, and maybe the classic Steeleye Span's most engaging album. *—Bruce Eder*

Rocket Cottage / 1976 / BGO ♦♦♦♦♦
The second of Steeleye Span's Mike Batt-produced albums was released at a time (1976) when the acceptance of British folk-rock was on a rapid downhill slide. That was unfortunate because *Rocket Cottage* remains one of the strongest yet most unappreciated of Steeleye's catalog. Their knack for adapting English folk songs to rock & roll has never been more adeptly executed than on this record. Rob Johnson's electric guitar work became more consistently aggressive as did Nigel Pegrum's drumming and Rick Kemp's bass playing. Tracks like "The Brown Girl," "The Twelve Witches," and the instrumental "Sligo Maid" are indicative of this more muscular Batt treatment. While several tracks from Steeleye Span's past repertoire are frequently labeled as definitive (like "Alison Gross" and "All Around My Hat") when describing their unique style of folk-rock, none surpasses the anthemic "Sir James the Rose." It combines their trademark macabre lyrical content with a forceful rock arrangement, innocent sounding vocal harmonies, and a timely Peter Knight violin interlude to remind the listener that this song actually has traditional roots. So while this album was greeted with overwhelming indifference in 1976, it has stood the test of time as well as any "classic" '70s album. *—Dave Sleger*

Storm Force 10 / 1977 / Chrysalis ♦♦♦♦

Original Masters / 1977 / BGO ♦♦♦♦♦
Original Masters is an excellent compilation of the first nine albums from one of the most respected and revered British folk-rock bands ever. Despite numerous personnel changes, Steeleye Span retained a readily identifiable sound built around folk-based instrumentation and the distinctive vocals of Maddy Prior. Beginning with amplified traditional songs, the group later adopted a more rock-oriented approach that attempted, often successfully, to stretch the boundaries of British folk music while still respecting and holding onto its roots. One of the best songs from the early years is "Lovely on the Water," which beautifully showcases the spirit and dignity of Prior's voice. Among the band's first successful experiments was "Gaudete," an a cappella Latin chant that somehow made the British charts. "Alison Gross" used loud power chords to give the impression of an all-out rock approach, and "Fighting for Strangers" used percussion to give an almost abstract atmosphere to the recording, something not expected from a band that started out as very traditional. Whether singing songs about romance, elves, violent upheavals, or witches, Steeleye Span successfully expanded the boundaries of British folk. Though longtime fans may prefer the individual albums, this is a fine introduction to the most creative period in the group's history. *—Michael Offord*

● **Spanning the Years** / 1995 / Chrysalis ♦♦♦♦
A 35-song, two-CD best-of, moving from their earliest 1970 recordings through the early 1990s. The emphasis is properly on their 1970s work, and accordingly the first disc is more essential, though the second part also has merit. With lengthy liner notes by Maddy Prior, it's an excellent survey of the group and may serve the essential needs of most listeners who aren't devoted fans. *—Richie Unterberger*

Rare Collection 1972-1996 / 1999 / Raven ♦♦♦♦♦
By rights, this 20-song CD should only interest the most hardcore fans of Steeleye Span or Maddy Prior—who else would possibly be interested enough in hearing the original B-side version of "Lanercost," the unedited version of "Thomas the Rhymer," or the undubbed version of the group's one major chart hit, "Gaudette"? The reality, however, is that this is an intrinsically strong album—if not a best-of collection, then a "best of the rest of"—that ought to attract more general and casual fans of English folk-rock. It turns out that this is a fascinating collection, coming from a band that one wouldn't naturally assume had 20 tracks' worth of lost album cuts, rare B-sides and odd soundcheck and rehearsal recordings. The CD opens with a luscious live rendtion of "The King," done a cappella on the group's 1982 Australian tour. The original single version of "Gaudette" is a very compelling reason to own this disc—the single featured only the group's voices, with none of the overdubbed Cathedral voices added to the LP version. The producers of this album have even rescued "Like the Wind," Maddy Prior's extraordinary contribution to the Mandalaband album *Eye of the Wendor*, the group's delightful rendition of the Four Seasons' "Rag Doll" has also been rescued. The 15 Steeleye Span tracks featured are augmented by six more cuts featuring Maddy Prior in various solo settings and in collaboration with Rick Kemp, and with June Tabor as part of the *Silly Sisters II* album sessions. The sound quality is generally good to excellent, and it's hard to imagine a better compilation to fill out and enhance the various best-ofs on this group that already exist. The notes by drummer Nigel Pegrum also present an interesting personal perspective on the group's songs, repertory, and history. *—Bruce Eder*

Steely Dan

f. 1972, Los Angeles, CA, **db.** 1981
Album Rock, Jazz-Rock, Pop/Rock, Soft Rock
Most rock & roll bands are a tightly wound unit that developed their music through years of playing in garages and clubs around their hometown. Steely Dan never subscribed to that aesthetic. As the vehicle for the songwriting of Walter Becker and Donald Fagen, Steely Dan defied all rock & roll conventions. Becker and Fagen never truly enjoyed rock—with their ironic humor and cryptic lyrics, their eclectic body of work shows some debt to Bob Dylan—preferring jazz, traditional pop, blues, and R&B. Steely Dan created a sophisticated, distinctive sound with accessible melodic hooks, complex harmonies and time signatures, and a devotion to the recording studio. With producer Gary Katz, Becker & Fagen gradually changed Steely Dan from a performing band to a studio project, hiring professional musicians to record their compositions. Though the band didn't perform live after 1973, Steely Dan's popularity continued to grow throughout the decade as their albums became critical favorites and their singles became staples of AOR and pop radio stations. Even after the group disbanded in the early '80s, their records retained a cult following, as proven by the massive success of their unlikely return to the stage in the early '90s. *—Stephen Thomas Erlewine*

You Gotta Walk It Like You Talk It (Or You'll Lose That Beat) / 1971 / Visa ♦♦

Can't Buy a Thrill / 1972 / MCA ♦♦♦♦♦
Walter Becker and Donald Fagen were remarkable craftsmen from the start, as Steely Dan's debut *Can't Buy a Thrill* illustrates. Each song is tightly constructed, with interlocking chords and gracefully interwoven melodies, buoyed by clever, cryptic lyrics. All of these are hallmarks of Steely Dan's signature sound, but what is most remarkable about the record is the way it differs from their later albums. Of course, one of the most notable differences is the presence of vocalist David Palmer, a professional blue-eyed soul vocalist who oversings the handful of tracks where he takes the lead. Palmer's very presence signals the one major flaw with the album—in an attempt to appeal to a wide audience, Becker and Fagen tempered their wildest impulses with mainstream pop techniques. Consequently, there are very few of the jazz flourishes that came to distinguish their albums—the breakthrough single "Do It Again" does work an impressively tight Latin-jazz beat, and "Reelin' in the Years" has jazzy guitar solos and harmonies—and the production is overly polished, conforming to all the conventions of early-'70s radio. Of course, that gives these decidedly twisted songs a subversive edge, but compositionally, these aren't as innovative as their later work. Even so, the best moments ("Dirty Work,"

"Kings," "Midnite Cruiser," "Turn That Heartbeat Over Again") are wonderful pop songs that subvert traditional conventions, and more than foreshadow the paths Steely Dan would later take. *—Stephen Thomas Erlewine*

☆ **Countdown to Ecstasy** / 1973 / MCA ✦✦✦✦✦
Can't Buy a Thrill became an unexpected hit, and as a response, Donald Fagen became the group's full-time lead vocalist, and he and Walter Becker acted like Steely Dan was a rock & roll band for the group's second album, *Countdown to Ecstasy.* The loud guitars and pronounced backbeat of "Bodhisattva," "Show Biz Kids," and "My Old School" camouflage the fact that *Countdown* is a riskier album, musically speaking, than its predecessor. Each of its eight songs have sophisticated, jazz-inflected interludes, and apart from the bluesy vamps "Bodhisattva" and "Show Biz Kids," which sound like they were written for the stage, the songs are subtly textured. "Razor Boy," with its murmuring marimbas, and the hard-bop tribute "Your Gold Teeth" reveal Becker and Fagen's jazz roots, while the country-flavored "Pearl of the Quarter" and the ominous, skittering "King of the World" are both overlooked gems. *Countdown to Ecstasy* is the only time Steely Dan played it relatively straight, and its eight songs are rich with either musical or lyrical detail that their album-rock or art-rock contemporaries couldn't hope to match. *—Stephen Thomas Erlewine*

☆ **Pretzel Logic** / 1974 / MCA ✦✦✦✦✦
Countdown to Ecstasy wasn't half the hit that *Can't Buy a Thrill* was, and Steely Dan responded by trimming the lengthy instrumental jams that were scattered across *Countdown* and concentrating on concise songs for *Pretzel Logic.* While the shorter songs usually indicate a tendency toward pop conventions, that's not the case with *Pretzel Logic.* Instead of relying on easy hooks, Becker and Fagen assembled their most complex and cynical set of songs to date. Dense with harmonics, countermelodies, and bop phrasing, *Pretzel Logic* is vibrant with unpredictable musical juxtapositions and snide, but very funny, wordplay. Listen to how the album's hit single, "Rikki Don't Lose That Number," opens with a syncopated piano line that evolves into a graceful pop melody, or how the title track winds from a blues to a jazzy chorus—Becker and Fagen's craft has become seamless while remaining idiosyncratic and thrillingly accessible. Since the songs are now paramount, it makes sense that *Pretzel Logic* is less of a band-oriented album than *Countdown to Ecstasy,* yet it is the richest album in their catalog, one where the backhanded Dylan tribute "Barrytown" can sit comfortably next to the gorgeous "Any Major Dude Will Tell You." Steely Dan made more accomplished albums than *Pretzel Logic,* but they never made a better one. *—Stephen Thomas Erlewine*

☆ **Katy Lied** / 1975 / MCA ✦✦✦✦✦
Building from the jazz-fusion foundation of *Pretzel Logic,* Steely Dan created an alluringly sophisticated album of jazzy pop with *Katy Lied.* With this record, Becker and Fagen began relying solely on studio musicians, which is evident from the immaculate sound of the album. Usually, such a studied recording method would drain the life out of each song, but that's not the case with *Katy Lied,* which actually benefits from the duo's perfectionist tendencies. Each song is given a glossy sheen, one that accentuates not only the stronger pop hooks, but also the precise technical skill of the professional musicians drafted to play the solos. Essentially, *Katy Lied* is a smoother version of *Pretzel Logic,* featuring the same cross section of jazz-pop and blues-rock. The lack of innovations doesn't hurt the record, since the songs are uniformly brilliant. Less overtly cynical than previous Dan albums, the album still has its share of lyrical stingers, but what's really notable are the melodies, from the seductive jazzy soul of "Doctor Wu" and the lazy blues of "Chain Lightning" to the terse "Black Friday" and mock calypso of "Everyone's Gone to the Movies." It's another excellent record in one of the most distinguished rock & roll catalogs of the '70s. *—Stephen Thomas Erlewine*

The Royal Scam / 1976 / MCA ✦✦✦
The Royal Scam is the first Steely Dan record that didn't exhibit significant musical progress from its predecessor, but that doesn't mean the album is any less interesting. The cynicism that was suppressed on *Katy Lied* comes roaring to the surface on *The Royal Scam*—not only are the lyrics bitter and snide, but the music is terse, broken, and weary. Not so coincidentally, the album is comprised of Becker and Fagen's weakest set of songs since *Can't Buy a Thrill.* Alternating between mean-spirited bluesy vamps like "Green Earrings" and "The Fez" and jazzy soft-rock numbers like "The Caves of Altamira," there's nothing particularly bad on the album, yet there are fewer standouts than before. Nevertheless, the best songs on *The Royal Scam,* like the sneering "Kid Charlemagne" and the gorgeous ballad "Sign in Stranger," rank as genuine Steely Dan classics. *—Stephen Thomas Erlewine*

Aja / 1977 / MCA ✦✦✦✦✦
Steely Dan hadn't been a real working band since *Pretzel Logic,* but with *Aja,* Becker and Fagen's obsession with sonic detail and fascination with composition reached new heights. A coolly textured and immaculately produced collection of sophisticated jazz-rock, *Aja* has none of the overt cynicism or self-consciously challenging music that distinguished previous Steely Dan records. Instead, it's a measured and textured album, filled with subtle melodies and accomplished, jazzy solos that blend easily into the lush instrumental backdrops. But *Aja* isn't just about texture, since Becker and Fagen's songs are their most complex and musically rich set of songs—even the simplest song, the sunny pop of "Peg," has layers of jazzy vocal harmonies. In fact, Steely Dan ignores rock on *Aja,* preferring to fuse cool jazz, blues, and pop together in a seamless, seductive fashion. It's complex music delivered with ease, and although the duo's preoccupation with clean sound and self-consciously sophisticated arrangements would eventually lead to a dead end, *Aja* is a shining example of jazz-rock at its finest. *—Stephen Thomas Erlewine*

Gaucho / 1980 / MCA ✦✦✦✦
Aja was cool, relaxed and controlled; it sounded deceptively easy. Its follow-up, *Gaucho,* while sonically similar, was its polar opposite: a precise and studied record, where all of the seams showed. *Gaucho* essentially replicates the smooth jazz-pop of *Aja,* but with none of that record's dark, seductive romance or elegant aura. Instead, it's meticulous and exacting; each performance has been rehearsed so many times that they no longer have any emotional resonance. Furthermore, Becker and Fagen's songs are generally labored, only occasionally reaching their past heights, like on the suave "Babylon Sisters," "Time Out of Mind," and "Hey Nineteen." Still, those three songs are barely enough to make the remainder of the album's glossy, meandering fusion worthwhile. *—Stephen Thomas Erlewine*

Gold / 1982 / MCA ✦✦✦✦
Donald Fagen and Walter Becker wrote many outstanding light-rock tunes with a somewhat soulful appeal. This compilation album plays host to quite a few of those songs, among them "Hey Nineteen," "Deacon Blues," and Black Cow." The twosome have an uncanny style of conveying their messages in a very overt way without forfeiting the songs' charisma. Of the 12 tracks listed, Steely Dan is responsible for ten and the other two are Donald Fagen selections; both were taken from movie soundtracks, and unfortunately they do not retain that same sting that the other compositions have. *—Craig Lytle*

★ **A Decade of Steely Dan** / 1985 / MCA ✦✦✦✦✦
A Decade of Steely Dan was one of the first compilations designed for CD, so it was intended to showcase digital sound as much as the music itself. Consequently, it's balanced to showcase at least one song from each of the band's albums, leaving such minor hits as "Pretzel Logic," "The Fez" and "Josie" off the compilation. Nevertheless, the songs here—including "Do It Again," "Reeling in the Years," "My Old School," "Rikki Don't Lose That Number," "My Old School," "Kid Charlemagne," "Peg," "Deacon Blues", "Hey Nineteen" and the non-LP "FM (No Static At All)"—provide a good overview of Steely Dan's career, making the disc a fine introduction to the innovative jazz-rock group. *—Stephen Thomas Erlewine*

Citizen Steely Dan / Dec. 14, 1993 / MCA ✦✦✦
Collecting all of Steely Dan's albums in chronological order, plus all of their two or three B-sides and one demo in a four-CD box, *Citizen Steely Dan* is only worthwhile for the fan replacing their old records. The remastering on the box is exactly the same as the newly upgraded CDs, and everything but the demo is available on other discs. *—Stephen Thomas Erlewine*

Alive in America / Oct. 17, 1995 / Giant ✦✦

Two Against Nature / Feb. 29, 2000 / Giant ✦✦✦✦
Notorious for shunning concert performances, Steely Dan's improbable live reunion in the mid-'90s eventually turned into a full-fledged reunion album. Since Steely Dan fans went two decades without even the hope of a new record, the very prospect was a delight, but it was also a little worrying, since a botched comeback would tarnish the band's legacy. Fortunately, *Two Against Nature* is as seductive and alluring as the best of Steely Dan's later work, with a similar emphasis on classy atmosphere and groove. Pitched halfway between *Gaucho* and the immaculate production of Fagen's solo album *Kamakiriad,* it's a graceful, intricate record that works its subtle charms at its own pace. While that means it isn't a knockout on the first listen, it's a real grower—a quietly addicting album that slowly works its way into the subconscious. It's also an uncannily natural extension of the duo's previous work, but surprisingly, it never sounds nostalgic or dated. It's clear that Becker and Fagen re-teamed because they simply enjoy working together: crafting the songs and arrangements, designing the production, shoehorning in-jokes into the lyrics, finding the exact performances that fit their specifications. In this sense, *Two Against Nature* is no different than any past Steely Dan effort; that's exactly why it's welcome, since they find nearly endless permutations within their signature sound. Lyrically, the album isn't quite as malicious as their '70s work, but they haven't lost their sharp humor, even on some mere throwaway lines. The real payoff, however, is musical. Each song gradually reveals its own identity through small, thrilling touches, giving the record depth and character, and fitting it comfortably into Steely Dan's acclaimed body of work. And that's as delightfully unexpected and peculiarly beautiful as anything else in their career. *—Stephen Thomas Erlewine*

Showbiz Kids: The Steely Dan Story 1972-1980 / Nov. 14, 2000 / MCA ✦✦✦✦✦
There is an audience for the double-disc set *Showbiz Kids: The Steely Dan Story 1972-1980,* although it may be a small one—it's a set for listeners that want something a little more extensive than *Decade of Steely Dan* or *Gold,* yet don't want to invest in full albums. On that level, it works quite well, since it does have all the chart and radio hits, plus a terrific sampling of classic album tracks from "Only a Fool Would Say That" through "Any Major Dude Will Tell You" to "Time Out of Mind." So, *Showbiz Kids* winds up being useful for neophytes—although it's hard not to imagine anyone that gets this set, believing that this will be all the Steely Dan they'll ever need, eventually succumbing and buying all the studio albums. If that's the case, at least they'll already have "Here at the Western World" and "FM," and won't have to purchase one of the two multi-disc sets that contain these non-LP songs. *—Stephen Thomas Erlewine*

Steppenwolf

f. 1967, Los Angeles, CA, **db.** 1972
Acid Rock, Psychedelic, Hard Rock
Led by John Kay (born Joachim Krauledat, April 12, 1944), Steppenwolf's blazing biker anthem "Born to Be Wild" roared out of speakers everywhere in the fiery summer of 1968, John Kay's threatening rasp sounding a mesmerizing call to arms to the counterculture movement rapidly sprouting up nationwide. German immigrant Kay got his professional start in a bluesy Toronto band called Sparrow, recording for Columbia in 1966. After Sparrow disbanded, Kay relocated to the West Coast and formed Steppenwolf,

named after the Herman Hesse novel. "Born to Be Wild," their third single on ABC-Dunhill, was immortalized on the soundtrack of Dennis Hopper's underground film classic *Easy Rider*. The song's reference to "heavy metal thunder" finally gave an assignable name to an emerging genre. Steppenwolf's second monster hit that year, the psychedelic "Magic Carpet Ride," and the follow-ups "Rock Me," "Move Over," and "Hey Lawdy Mama" further established the band's credibility on the hard-rock circuit. By the early '70s, Steppenwolf ran out of steam and disbanded. Kay continued to record solo, as other members put together ersatz versions of the band for touring purposes. During the mid-'80s, Kay re-formed his own version of Steppenwolf, grinding out his hits (and some new songs) at oldies shows. Nevertheless, they'll be remembered for generations to come for creating one of the ultimate gas'n'go rock anthems of all time. *—Bill Dahl & Cub Koda*

Early Steppenwolf / 1969 / MCA ✦✦✦
Early live recordings made when the band was still called "Sparrow," working more out of a blues-band mold; features a surprisingly great version of Junior Wells' "Messin' With the Kid." *—Cub Koda*

• **16 Greatest Hits** / 1973 / MCA ✦✦✦✦✦
Just what the name implies; "Born to Be Wild," "Magic Carpet Ride," "The Pusher," and "Rock Me" are just some of the highlights. Everything you're going to want to hear in one neat little package. *—Cub Koda*

Born to Be Wild: A Retrospective / Nov. 5, 1991 / MCA ✦✦✦✦✦
A double-disc collection of Steppenwolf's lengthy career, *Born to Be Wild: A Retrospective* includes more music than anyone but hardcore fans need, but the song selection and packaging are superb, making it essential for those devoted fans. *—Stephen Thomas Erlewine*

Stereo MC's

f. 1985, London, England
Trip-Hop, Club/Dance, Acid Jazz, House, Hip-Hop
One of the most successful hip hop acts to emerge from Great Britain, Stereo MC's formed in London in 1985, when rapper Rob B. (born Rob Birch), and DJ/producer the Head (Nick Hallam) formed the Gee Street label as a means of promoting their music. Gee Street soon signed a distribution deal with the New York-based 4th & Broadway label, and a series of singles followed before the Stereo MC's debut album, *33-45-78*, surfaced in 1989.

After the departure of founding member Cesare, the group—now consisting of Rob B., the Head, drummer Owen If (born Owen Rossiter), and vocalist Cath Coffey—issued the 1990 single "Elevate My Mind," which became the first British rap single ever to reach the U.S. pop charts. Following the release of the album *Supernatural*, Stereo MC's toured with the Happy Mondays and EMF before returning to the studio to record their 1992 breakthrough *Connected*, a sample-free album recorded completely with live instruments which spawned such major hits as "Step It Up," "Creation," "Ground Level," and the title track. After years of production and remix work, the group's long-awaited (and oft-delayed) follow-up remains unreleased, though in 1997, Coffey did at least issue her debut solo single, "Wild World." For their 2000 mix album *DJ Kicks*, Stereo MC's recorded three new tracks, "Rhino, Pts. 1-3." After a long nine-year hiatus, Stereo MC's returned to form in the new millennium, inssuing *Deep Down & Dirty* in spring 2001. *—Jason Ankeny*

Supernatural / 1990 / 4th & Broadway ✦✦✦✦
The only thing that separates *Supernatural* and its hit follow-up *Connected* is that *Connected* had a hit. Otherwise, the albums are nearly identical and are equally enjoyable. *-AMG*

• **Connected** / 1992 / Gee Street ✦✦✦✦✦
Stereo MC's' American breakthrough is an energetic, club-oriented collection of colorful, funky dance tracks—the raps almost seem like an afterthought, yet that doesn't distract from the sheer pleasure of their sound. *—AMG*

DJ Kicks / Mar. 28, 2000 / !K7 ✦✦✦✦
Eight years on from their last LP, Stereo MC's returned not with a studio work but a mix album that shows their long career in a new light, as not just one-hit wonders but breakbeat renegades who've been searching for the perfect beat—both as recording artists and as label heads—for over 15 years. *DJ Kicks* trips back and forth between beat-heavy cinematic music from the '70s, rap from the old-school to the new-skool, and trip-hop from producers who, just like Stereo MC's themselves, take the template of breakbeat music down new paths. Truth to tell, though, there'd been so many similar mix albums released in the previous few years that it wasn't difficult to believe the bottomless well of obscure, funky music was just about tapped. Fortunately, Rob H. and Nick come through with a lineup of widely varied artists and crucial tracks. Most of the instrumental highlights are obscurities like "Back to the Hip Hop" by the Troubleneck Brothers, "Do It Do It" by the Disco Four, "Moon Trek" by the Mike Theodore Orchestra, and a surprisingly chilling track by 101 Strings titled "Flameout." The rap tracks are solid too, including old-school heroes like Kool G. Rap & DJ Polo ("Road to the Riches") and Ultramagnetic MC's ("Poppa Large"), as well as more recent artists from the growing hip-hop underground like the 57th Dynasty ("Pharoah Intellect") and Divine Styler ("Tongue of Labyrinth"). Another highlight is the new, three-part track "Rhino" produced by Stereo MC's. Fitting in well with the album itself, "Rhino" is an old-school groove number with heavy drums and Hammond keys. It's easy to wonder if Stereo MC's even *have* any fans left from the days of *Connected*, but this mix album might gain them a few. *—John Bush*

Deep Down & Dirty / Jun. 12, 2001 / Island ✦✦✦✦
2001, several years after *any* listeners could've expected a follow-up to 1992's *Connected*, Stereo MC's finally delivered with *Deep Down & Dirty*. It's a tribute to how far ahead of the curve Stereo MC's were ten years earlier that *Deep Down & Dirty* never strays far from the spirit of *Connected*, but still sounds perfectly up-to-date for 2001. It's clear the productions are more mature and more complex, but they still plumb the depths of deep-groove beatbox funk, with nods to soul-jazz and gospel. Still tossing out lines with the half-assed cool of Shaun Ryder or Ian Brown, frontman Rob Birch doesn't rap quite as much as he used to (that's a good thing), and the productions are a tad more down-tempo and dubby than when the band was at its most clubbed-up in the early '90s. The title-track opener sets things off in fine fashion, working a stuttered mid-tempo groove with split-second snippets from the horn section and a full-throttle vocal backing. In true soul tradition, the upfront mover "Graffiti, Pt. 1" segues into a bongo-led "Graffiti, Pt. 2." Birch even sends up his slacker-cool image on "Sofisticated," a groovy piano-and-beatbox number. Along with Birch, producer Nick Hallam (aka the Head) is the other key to what makes *Deep Down & Dirty* so much fun, packing his productions to the bursting point with dusty beats, lines from old Hammond organs, and samples of bygone soul shouters. Despite a few traditionalist, anthemic tracks ("We Belong in This World Together," "Running") which don't work as well as they would've in the heady days of 1993, *Deep Down & Dirty* is a solid record that reveals no trace of cobwebs from Stereo MC's long hiatus. *—John Bush*

Stereolab

f. 1991, London, England
Indie Pop, Ambient Pop, Experimental Rock, Indie Rock, Post-Rock/Experimental, Alternative Pop/Rock
Combining an inclination for melodic '60s pop with an art-rock aesthetic borrowed from Krautrock bands like Faust and Neu!, Stereolab were one of the most influential alternative bands of the '90s. Led by Tim Gane and Laetitia Sadier, Stereolab legitimized forms of music that were either on the fringe of rock, or brought attention to a strand of pop music—bossa nova, lounge-pop, movie soundtracks—that were traditionally banished from the rock lineage. The group's trademark sound—a droning, hypnotic rhythm track overlaid with melodic, mesmerizing singsong vocals, often sung in French and often promoting revolutionary, Marxist politics—was deceptively simple, providing the basis for a wide array of stylistic experiments over the course of their prolific career. Throughout it all, Stereolab relied heavily on forgotten methods of recording, whether it was analog synthesizers and electronics or a fondness for hi-fi test records, without ever sinking to the level of kitsch. *—Stephen Thomas Erlewine*

Switched On / 1992 / Too Pure ✦✦✦
Switched On collects Stereolab's earliest singles, capturing the group's hypnotic, driving sound in its infancy. Though they're more guitar-driven and rock-oriented than the band's later work, tracks like "Super-Electric" and "Au Grand Jour" prove that Stereolab's basic style—Krautrock lock-grooves, bubbling analog synths, fuzzed-out guitars, and angelic vocals—arrived fully formed. "Doubt" and "Brittle" are among the group's most vibrant pop songs, while the eight-minute "Contact" is a warm-up for the epics the band would include on albums like *Transient Random Noise-Bursts With Announcements*. Reflective pieces like "The Way Will Be Opening" and "High Expectation" show off Laetitia Sadier's coolly sophisticated, Nico-meets-Francoise Hardy vocals, while "The Light That Will Cease to Fail" manages to be poppy, kinetic, and bittersweet all at once. Though the group would go on to make even more impressive albums, the newness of Stereolab's sound is palpable on *Switched On*, giving the songs an added vitality. Obviously, it's an impressive debut, but it's captivating in its own right. *—Heather Phares*

Peng! / 1992 / Too Pure/American ✦✦✦✦
With its full-length debut *Peng!*, Stereolab continued to develop a unique approach to experimental pop music, building on the seriously playful mix of Krautrock, dream pop, and lounge forged on the band's early singles. The album's first three tracks present the basic kinds of songs that the band would explore in the future: the tense, brooding "Super Falling Star" builds on simple keyboard drones and chilly, choral vocals; "Orgiastic" is a prototypically chugging, droning guitar and keyboard workout; and the sweet, bouncy melody and "ba ba ba" backing vocals of "Peng! 33" define Stereolab's early pop sound. "Perversion" mixes a heavy, dance-inspired beat with strummy, Velvet Underground guitars and Beach Boys harmonies, while "The Seeming and the Meaning" and "Stomach Worm" are two of the band's most dynamic, rock-oriented songs. Dreamy, melancholy songs like "K-Stars" and "You Little Shits" and the fuzzed-out "Mellotron" and "Enivrez-Vous" represent, respectively, the soft and loud aspects of Stereolab's more experimental side, and "Surrealchemist" manages to combine all of the aspects of the group's sound, with overtly Marxist lyrics to boot. While *Peng!* doesn't feature many of Stereolab's most instantly recognizable compositions, it defines the group's early style and reflects the eclectic directions pursued in later work. *—Heather Phares*

The Groop Played "Space Age Bachelor Pad Music" / 1993 / Too Pure/American ✦✦✦
Released in 1993, *Space Age Bachelor Pad Music* refined Stereolab's sound further and also showcased the increasingly experimental focus of the band's music. Split into two sides—the gentle, intricate "Easy Listening" and the more upbeat "New Wave"—this eight-song EP ranges from the bubbly keyboard piece "Space Age Bachelor Pad Music (Foamy)" to the defiant, driving groove of "We're Not Adult Orientated." The sweet, close harmonies on "Ronco Symphony" and "The Groop Play Chord X" edge closer to the sophisticated, lounge pop-inspired sound explored during the rest of Stereolab's career, while the vibes of "Avant Garde M.O.R." and the fizzy keyboards of "Space Age Bachelor Pad Music (Mellow)" spotlight the band's more texturally complex arrangements. However, the immediacy of "We're Not Adult Orientated (Neu Wave Live)" and the hypnotic, fuzzy guitars on "U.H.F.—MFP" prove that while Stereolab gained more polish and

ambition on *Space Age Bachelor Pad Music*, the band didn't lose any of its kinetic edge. —*Heather Phares*

Transient Random-Noise Bursts With Announcements / Aug. 1993 / Elektra ✦✦✦✦✦
Though it was the group's major-label debut, Stereolab's *Transient Random-Noise Bursts With Announcements* showed no signs of selling out. If anything, it's one of the most eclectic and experimental releases in Stereolab's early career, emphasizing the group's elongated Krautrock jams, instrumentals, and harsh, noisy moments. The album begins and ends with smooth, sensual washes of sound like "Tone Burst" and "Lock-Groove Lullaby" and smoothly bouncy pop songs like "I'm Going Out of My Way." These softer, more accessible moments surround complex and varied compositions such as "Analogue Rock," "Our Trinitone Blast," and "Golden Ball," which, with its distorted vocals and shifting tempos, serves as an appetizer for "Jenny Ondioline." A hypnotic, 18-minute epic encompassing dreamy yet driving pop, a Krautrock groove, forceful, churning guitars, and a furious climax, it's the most ambitious—and definitive—moment of Stereolab's early years. But *Transient Random-Noise Bursts With Announcements* also features quietly experimental pieces such as "Pause," a slightly spooky song that uses distorted whispers as a rhythm track and places fluttery keyboards and Laetitia Sadier and Mary Hansen's sweet, slightly alien harmonies atop it. Likewise, the very sexy, very French "Pack Yr Romantic Mind" reveals the growing influence of '50s and '60s easy listening on the group's musical direction. If *Switched On* and *Peng!* defined the band's essential sound, *Transient Random-Noise Bursts With Announcements* expanded it, reaffirming Stereolab's place as one of the most innovative and evolving groups of the '90s. —*Heather Phares*

Mars Audiac Quintet / Aug. 9, 1994 / Elektra ✦✦✦✦
By the time of 1994's *Mars Audiac Quintet*, Stereolab had already highlighted the rock and experimental sides of its music; now the band concentrated on perfecting its space-age pop. Sweetly bouncy songs like "Ping Pong" and "L' Enfer des Formes" streamline the band's sound without sacrificing its essence; track for track, this may be the group's most accessible, tightly written album. The groove-driven "Outer Accelerator," "Wow and Flutter," and "Transona Five" (which sounds strangely like Canned Heat's "Goin' Up the Country") reaffirm Stereolab's Krautrock roots, but the band's sweet synth melodies and vocal arrangements give it a pop patina. Even extended pieces like "Anamorphose" and "Nihilist Assault Group"—which could have appeared on *Transient Random Noise-Bursts With Announcements* if they had a rawer production—are more sensual and voluptuous than edgy and challenging. It's equally apparent on layered, complex songs such as "New Orthophony" and "The Stars Our Destination," as well as spare, minimal tracks like "Des Etoiles Electroniques," that the members of Stereolab focused their experimental energies on production tricks, vocal interplay, and increasingly electronic-based arrangements. The charming final track "Fiery Yellow" takes the band's fondness for lounge pop and experimentation to the limit; a delicate, marimba-driven piece featuring the High Llamas' Sean O'Hagan, it sounds like the kind of music Esquivel or Martin Denny would be proud to make in the '90s. While it's not as overtly innovative as some of Stereolab's earlier albums, *Mars Audiac Quintet* is an enjoyable, accessible forerunner to the intricate, cerebral direction the group's music would take in the mid- and late '90s. —*Heather Phares*

Music for the Amorphous Body Center [EP] / Apr. 1995 / Duophonic ✦✦✦✦
Recorded especially for an art exhibit, *Music for the Amorphous Body Center* expands on Stereolab's trademark guitar-and-organ drone by adding strings. With the subtle, lush strings as support, the group's easy listening and '60s pop inclinations become more pronounced, making the overlapping textures of "Pop Quiz" swirl magnificently. Such small adjustments make the EP quite wonderful; it proves that there are hidden variations in Stereolab's music that don't quite come to the forefront immediately. —*Stephen Thomas Erlewine*

Refried Ectoplasm (Switched On, Vol. 2) / Jul. 1995 / Duophonic/Drag City ✦✦✦✦✦
Refried Ectoplasm (Switched On, Vol. 2) collects 13 singles and rarities Stereolab released between 1992 and 1995, and it is far more than a mere oddities collection. More than any other album, *Refried Ectoplasm* charts Stereolab's astonishing musical growth between those three years, and offers several definitive songs—including "Lo Boob Oscillator," "French Disko," and "John Cage Bubblegum"—not available on any album. While such items are essential for collectors, the quality and accessiblity of the music is very strong, showcasing Stereolab's complexity and providing an excellent introduction to the group. —*Stephen Thomas Erlewine*

● **Emperor Tomato Ketchup** / Apr. 1996 / Elektra ✦✦✦✦✦
Stereolab was poised for a breakthrough release with *Emperor Tomato Ketchup*, their fourth full-length album. Not only was their influence becoming apparent throughout alternative rock, but *Mars Audiac Quintet* and *Music for the Amorphous Body Center* indicated they were moving closer to distinct pop melodies. The group certainly hasn't backed away from pop melodies on *Emperor Tomato Ketchup*, but just as their hooks are becoming catchier, they bring in more avant-garde and experimental influences, as well. Consequently, the album is Stereolab's most complex, multi-layered record. It lacks the raw, amateurish textures of their early singles, but the music is far more ambitious, melding electronic drones and singsong melodies with string sections, slight hip-hop and dub influences, and scores of interweaving counter melodies. Even when Stereolab appears to be creating a one-chord trance, there is a lot going on beneath the surface. Furthermore, the group's love for easy listening and pop melodies means that the music never feels cold or inaccessible. In fact, pop singles like "Cybele's Reverie" and "The Noise of Carpet" help ease listeners into the group's more experimental tendencies. Because of all its textures, *Emperor Tomato Ketchup* isn't as immediately accessible as *Mars Audiac Quintet*, but it is a rich, rewarding listen. —*Stephen Thomas Erlewine*

Dots and Loops / Sep. 23, 1997 / Elektra ✦✦✦✦
On *Emperor Tomato Ketchup*, Stereolab moved in two directions simultaneously—it explored funkier dance rhythms while increasing the complexity of its arrangements and compositions. For its follow-up, *Dots and Loops*, the group scaled back its rhythmic experiments and concentrated on layered compositions. Heavily influenced by bossa nova and swinging '60s pop, *Dots and Loops* is a deceptively light, breezy album that floats by with effortless grace. Even the segmented, 20-minute "Refractions in the Plastic Pulse" has a sunny, appealing surface—it's only upon later listens that the interlocking melodies and rhythms reveal their intricate interplay. In many ways, *Dots and Loops* is Stereolab's greatest musical accomplishment to date, demonstrating remarkable skill—their interaction is closer to jazz than rock, exploring all of the possibilities of any melodic phrase. Their affection for '60s pop keeps *Dots and Loops* accessible, even though that doesn't mean it is as immediate as *Emperor Tomato Ketchup*. In fact, the laid-back stylings of *Dots and Loops* makes it a little difficult to assimilate upon first listen, but after a few repeated plays, its charms unfold as gracefully as any other Stereolab record. —*Stephen Thomas Erlewine*

Aluminum Tunes: Switched On, Vol. 3 / Oct. 20, 1998 / Drag City ✦✦✦✦✦
Stereolab's *Switched On* series is ingenious, one of the best services a band has performed for their fans. Since their inception, Stereolab has made it a practice to release non-LP singles, tour 7"s, split-singles, special-edition EPs—recordings that were available in small quantities for a limited time. In every case, the limited-edition recordings become very valuable very quickly, often reaching ridiculously exorbitant prices that most fans could never afford. That's where the *Switched On* series comes in. It's where the group gathers the best of these rarities, leaving a couple of tracks on the original single for collectibility's sake. Stereolab may do certain projects as a lark, but they rarely throw away tracks, as each EP and most singles have their own identity, offering a new spin on the group's trademark style. Given that *Aluminum Tunes: Switched On, Vol. 3* spans two discs, it might seem that the compilation will only be of interest to diehards, but it rivals *Refried Ectoplasm: Switched On, Vol. 2* in terms of creativity and consistency. *Aluminum Tunes* is distinguished by the first wide release of the entire sublime easy listening EP *Music for the Amorphous Body Center*, which would be enough to make the compilation essential for all fans, but it also has such minor masterpieces as their swinging duet with Herbie Mann on Antonio Carlos Jobim's "One Note Samba," Wagon Christ's remix of "Metronomic Underground," the horn-spiked "Percolations," and "You Used to Call Me Sadness." There may be a couple of tracks that never rise above the level of good but predictable Stereolab, but the best moments rank among their very best work. Quite simply an essential addition to their catalog. —*Stephen Thomas Erlewine*

Cobra and Phases Group Play Voltage in the Milky Night / Sep. 21, 1999 / Elektra ✦✦✦
Stereolab took an unprecedented two years between 1997's *Dots & Loops* and 1999's *Cobra and Phases Group Play Voltage in the Milky Night*, as they tended to personal matters. During those two years, Stereolab's brand of sophisticated, experimental post-rock didn't evolve too much, even as colleagues like Tortoise, Jim O'Rourke, and the High Llamas tried other things. Since each Stereolab album offered a significant progression from the next, it would have been fair to assume that when they returned, it would be with a leap forward, especially since Tortoise's John McEntire and O'Rourke were co-producers. Perhaps that's the reason that the album feels slightly disappointing. The group has absorbed McEntire's jazz-fusion leanings—"Fuses" kicks off the album in compelling, free-jazz style—and the music continually bears O'Rourke's attention to detail, but it winds up sounding like O'Hagan's increasing tendency of making music that's simply sound for sound's sake. Throughout it all, Stereolab's trademarks remain in place, but they're augmented by horn arrangements, dissonance, muted trumpets, and electric keyboards all out of jazz from the late '60s, whether it's bossa nova or fusion. All fascinating in theory and often in practice, but *Cobra* still winds up being less than the sum of its parts. Maybe it's because the longer pieces drift instead of hypnotize or develop, or maybe it's because the songs sound like afterthoughts to the arrangements (a criticism leveled at Stereolab before). In any case, *Cobra* never hits its stride, even as it offers a few miniature masterpieces along the way. As an album, *Cobra* is their first record since *Transient Random Noise Bursts* to not be fully realized. —*Stephen Thomas Erlewine*

First of the Microbe Hunters / May 16, 2000 / Elektra ✦✦

Sound-Dust / Aug. 28, 2001 / Elektra ✦✦✦✦
While the two years between *Dots and Loops* and *Cobra* resulted in stagnation, the two years separating *Cobra* and *Sound-Dust* find Stereolab deliberately recharging their creative juices, delving deeper into avant-garde composition and '60s swing pop in equal measures. As the album opens with the minimal "Black Ants in Sound-Dust," it's evident that the group has restructured and pushed forward, even if it means that they're adhering to their time-honored tradition of expanding their trademark sound with new arrangements and influences. Frankly, after the stagnation of *Cobra*, any movement forward is welcome, and initially the record seems like a bold move forward—a Stereolab instrumental album where the arrangements and production take the proper forefront, since every recording since *Amorphous Body Center* has illustrated that that's the group's real strength. Then, "Captain EasyChord" kicks in with a familiar, albeit catchy, mid-tempo lounge groove and Laetitia Sadier's singsong vocals, and the album is immediately anchored in overly familiar territory. And that's the biggest problem with *Sound-Dust*—by this point the group's melodies, singalong choruses, and Marxist platitudes no longer sound fresh, they often sound like a straightjacket, preventing the group from pushing forward into new territory. After all, if it's taken on a pure sonic level, *Sound-Dust* can often be quite pleasing and intriguing, especially the sophisticated horn and flute arrangements, which producer Jim O'Rourke makes lushly alluring. It's hard not to wish that the entire record was constructed simply of instrumentals of this sort, since that's when

Stereolab sounds fully recharged and gorgeous. As it stands, the album is held back by their insistence on simple songs and simple vocals that keep the record earthbound and solely the province of the already converted. *—Stephen Thomas Erlewine*

Stereophonics

British Trad Rock, Alternative Pop/Rock

A bright new noise in U.K. alternative rock in the '90s, the Stereophonics comprise Kelly Jones (vocals/guitar), Richard Jones (bass), and Stuart Cable (drums). They were formed in Cwmaman, South Wales, originally as the teenage cover band Tragic Love Company. Early reviews cited the Manic Street Preachers as their most obvious influence, and their initial batch of singles struggled to disabuse cynics of this notion. Yet in Jones, the Stereophonics possess an able writer as well as a singer of some distinction, a fact that was only truly acknowledged following the release of their debut LP. One of the first bands on Richard Branson's new V2 label, they were signed by chief executive Jeremy Pearce in August 1996, before the label was officially up and running. They made their debut in November with "Looks Like Chaplin" b/w "More Life in a Tramp's Vest," which later became a single in its own right. They entered the charts for the first time with "Local Boy in the Photograph" and didn't look back. Each of their subsequent singles sold progressively better, culminating in a U.K. Top Ten placing for their debut album *Word Gets Around* and Top 20 honours for "Traffic." The latter's resigned themes provided the perfect platform for Jones' plaintive vocals. A reissue of "Local Boy in the Photograph" also made the Top 20, in the same week as they received a BRIT Award for Best New Group. As a singles band they seem overburdened with riches—"The Bartender and the Thief" duly became a British radio staple through the closing months of 1998, followed the next year by the full-length *Performance and Cocktails*. The *T-Shirt Suntan* EP appeared in the spring of 2000. The band's third studio effort *Just Enough Education to Perform* was initially slated to go by the abbreviated J.E.E.P., however Daimler-Chrysler objected to the plan and claimed ownership of the actual word JEEP. *—Alex Ogg*

Word Gets Around / 1997 / V2 ✦✦✦✦

In the late '90s, a rash of Welsh rock bands emerged, amongst them Catatonia, Super Furry Animals, 60 Ft. Dolls, and the Stereophonics. On the surface, the Stereophonics' gritty rock & roll seems relatively uninspired, but upon close listen, *Word Gets Around* proves to be a very accomplished debut. Vocalist/guitarist Kelly Jones' vocals are raw and rip the songs apart, as his loud, arena-ready guitar assault gives every track a gritty edge. Jones' lyrics are also of note; highly poetic and meaningful, he writes about the underbelly of a small town. The anthemic opener, the outrageously catchy "A Thousand Trees," details how a respected high school athletic coach ruined his career through a lurid sexual encounter with a female student, and the quick, jagged "More Life in a Tramp's Vest" displays the view of the world through the eyes of a supermarket bagboy. *Word Gets Around* isn't all about hard rockers, though; the hit ballad, "Traffic," is a beautifully constructed ballad that works marvelously when a juxtaposition is made between the music and Jones' rough vocal styling. While *Word Gets Around* occasionally suffers from blandness, it is a remarkably accomplished debut LP. *—Jason Damas*

Performance and Cocktails / May 25, 1999 / V2 ✦✦✦

In December 1998, the Stereophonics released the single "The Bartender and the Thief," which became an unexpected explosion on the charts, peaking at number three in the U.K. In March 1999, the band's sophomore effort, *Performance and Cocktails*, was released to impressive sales—it was reportedly outselling Blur's *13* when that album was released. A second single, "Just Looking," also peaked within the U.K. Top Ten, making the first half of 1999 a very unexpectedly busy time for the Stereophonics. Never a favorite to become a hugely successful Brit-pop band, their noisy, raw hard rock came into favor after the more produced and calculated sound of Brit-pop had become passe. Unfortunately, however, this disc isn't quite as consistent as the debut. Part of the reason why *Word Gets Around* was so appealing is that there was a sense of urgency that, on this release, seems to have disappeared. There are more ballads than before, and some of the rockers don't burn with the intensity that they did on the last album. This doesn't make *Performance and Cocktails* a bad album, though; fans will be very pleased that the Stereophonics have released another slab of indie-flavored hard rock. Some highlights include "T Shirt Suntan," the acoustic "She Takes Her Clothes Off," and the poppy "Pick a Part That's New." (Japanese versions of this album include three live tracks, but the quality is mediocre and the performances are unspectacular, making this version of the release for hardcore fans only.) *—Jason Damas*

• **Just Enough Education to Perform** / Apr. 17, 2001 / V2 ✦✦✦✦

Prior to releasing their third effort, Stereophonics endured brief controversy for the album's title, *Just Enough Education to Perform*. Already having dealt with the critics' views of this being a country or acoustic record, frontman Kelly Jones wanted the album to go by the abbreviation of J.E.E.P., which captures the band's opinions of the music industry. Of course, politics played the game and Daimler-Chrysler objected to the use, claming copyright and usage of the word "Jeep." Despite the media drama, Jones isn't entirely disenchanted on *Just Enough Education to Perform* and the album isn't heavy with needle acoustics or twangy licks either. It's another glassy cast of rock & roll rawness (with slight acoustics) that's made them indie darlings since their inception in the mid-'90s. *Performance and Cocktails* (1999) was more abrasive with Jones' signature scratchy vocals, and the rough poetics on 1997's *Word Gets Around* were impressive; however, *Just Enough Education to Perform* illustrates a more mature Stereophonics. It's a monolith of 11 detailed narratives, each playing with areas of soul, aggro rock, and moody pop/rock. The Stereophonics appear to be achieving a much-welcomed calamity. Changes within their personal lives shaped the sounds found on this record, most notably "Maybe" and "Watch Them Fly Sundays." Crafted around blues-rock guitars and shimmering percussion, these swan songs reflect the demise of Jones' relationship with his longtime girlfriend. They're gorgeously haunting with emotional depictions, and the Stereophonics are okay with that. No longer into the destructive side of rock & roll, *Just Enough Education to Perform* exudes a peaceful sect; a charming side is more visible even though Jones has had his row with the press. He can laugh about it while wholeheartedly believing that the Stereophonics have shaped this album into their most stunning material yet. *—MacKenzie Wilson*

Stetsasonic

f. 1981, **db.** 1992

Hip-Hop, Golden Age

One of the first rap groups to use a live band, Brooklyn's Stetsasonic formed in 1981 and were also among the first to promote a positive black consciousness that found its ultimate expression in the so-called daisy-age sounds of De La Soul and the Jungle Brothers. The group consisted of DJs "Prince Paul" Huston and Leonard "Wise" Roman, keyboardist/drummer/DJ Marvin "DBC" Nemley, and rappers Glenn "Daddy-O" Bolton, Martin "Delite" Wright, and Bobby "Fruitkwan" Simmons. Daddy-O and Delite founded the group as the Stetson Brothers, after the hat company, and began performing in New York hip-hop clubs, picking up other members along the way. Their debut, *On Fire*, was released in 1986, but it was the follow-up, *In Full Gear*, that brought them critical acclaim and an R&B hit, "Sally." 1991's *Blood, Sweat & No Tears* was considered by many to be their best and most diverse album, but Daddy-O decided that they had run out of ideas and broke up the band. He went on to work with Mary J. Blige, Queen Latifah, Big Daddy Kane, and the Red Hot Chili Peppers as a producer and remixer. Meanwhile, Prince Paul had already established himself as a producer for his work with De La Soul and Fine Young Cannibals, and later worked with Fruitkwan in the Gravediggaz. *—Steve Huey*

On Fire / 1986 / Tommy Boy ✦✦✦

There weren't many bands utilizing a hip-hop format in the mid-'80s, making Stetasonic quite unique on the pop front in 1986. While their subject matter was invariably light and their raps now hopelessly tame and effete, they were groundbreaking at the time and retain a certain charm. *—Ron Wynn*

• **In Full Gear** / 1988 / Tommy Boy ✦✦✦✦✦

They're not "the world's only hip-hop band" anymore, but this seven-piece group (real drums even!) paved the way. Their second disc documents their innovative best, culminating in the anthemic "Talkin' All That Jazz." *—John Floyd*

Blood, Sweat & No Tears / 1991 / Tommy Boy ✦✦✦

Cat Stevens

b. Jul. 21, 1947, London, England

Vocals, Keyboards, Songwriter, Piano, Guitar, Synthesizer / Album Rock, Pop/Rock, Folk-Rock, Soft Rock, Pop, Singer/Songwriter

Cat Stevens became interested in folk and rock & roll in his teens and scored his first U.K. hit, "I Love My Dog," before he turned 20. Stevens reached the singles charts four more times, getting to number two with "Matthew & Son" and releasing the similarly titled Top Ten album before he contracted tuberculosis in 1968 and was forced to retire from music. He re-emerged with a new, mature style in 1970 with the album *Mona Bone Jakon* and hit the U.K. Top Ten with "Lady D'Arbanville." But it was his late 1970 follow-up, *Tea for the Tillerman*, that made him an international success. The album hit the Top Ten and went gold in the U.S., producing the hit "Wild World." *Teaser and the Firecat*, released in 1971, did even better, including the hits "Peace Train" and "Morning Has Broken." Stevens became so successful as an albums artist that, even though his next couple of albums did not generate big hit singles, they were still big sellers. His records were gradually less successful during the second half of the '70s. In 1979, he became a Muslim, adopted the name Yusef Islam, and retired from music. He was not heard from for another ten years, until he shocked admirers at the end of the '80s by supporting the death sentence ordered by the Ayatollah Khomeini against novelist Salman Rushdie for writing the book *The Satanic Verses*. Some "classic rock" radio stations discontinued playing him as a result, though his music remains popular. *— William Ruhlmann*

Matthew & Son / 1967 / Deram ✦✦✦

Released in the late winter of 1967, 19-year-old Cat Stevens' debut album, *Matthew & Son*, contained his breakthrough U.K. hits "I Love My Dog" (number 28) and the title song (number two), and spawned a third, "I'm Gonna Get Me a Gun" (number six). (The Tremeloes took a cover of the album's "Here Comes My Baby" to U.K. number four.) While it is a precocious effort (Stevens wrote all the songs) and the material is undeniably catchy, it's also wildly overproduced, with gimmicky arrangements typical of the mid-'60s British pop sound around the time of *Sgt. Pepper*. This is especially noticeable, heard in the context of Stevens' later, less-produced, more meaningful efforts. *— William Ruhlmann*

New Masters / 1967 / Deram ✦✦

Mona Bone Jakon / Jul. 1970 / A&M ✦✦✦✦

Cat Stevens virtually disappeared from the British pop scene in 1968, at the age of 20, after a meteoric start to his career. After contracting tuberculosis, Stevens spent a year recovering from both his illness and the strain of being a teenage pop star, and in the spring of 1970—as a very different 22-year-old—he returned to action with *Mona Bone Jakon*. Fans who knew him from 1967 must have been surprised. Under the production aegis of former Yardbird Paul Samwell-Smith, he introduced a group of simple, heartfelt songs played in spare arrangements on acoustic guitars and keyboards and driven by a restrained rhythm section. Built on folk and blues structures, but with characteristically compelling melodies, Stevens' new compositions were tentative, fragmentary statements that alluded to his recent "Trouble," including the triviality of being a "Pop Star." But these were the words of a desperate man in search of salvation. *Mona Bone Jakon* was dominated by images of death, but the album was also about survival and hope. Stevens' craggy voice, with its odd breaks of tone and occasional huskiness, lent these sometimes sketchy songs depth, and the understated instrumentation further emphasized their seriousness. If Stevens was working out private demons on *Mona Bone Jakon*, he was well attuned to a similar world-weariness in pop culture. His listeners may not have shared his exact experience, but after the 1960s they certainly understood his sense of being wounded, his spiritual yearning, and his hesitant optimism. *Mona Bone Jakon* was only a modest success upon its initial release, but it attracted attention in the wake of the commercial breakthrough of its follow-up, *Tea for the Tillerman.* — *William Ruhlmann*

☆ **Tea for the Tillerman** / Nov. 1970 / A&M ♦♦♦♦♦
Mona Bone Jakon only began Cat Stevens' comeback. Seven months later, he returned with *Tea for the Tillerman*, an album in the same chamber-group style, employing the same musicians and producer, but with a far more confident tone. *Mona Bone Jakon* had been full of references to death, but *Tea for the Tillerman* was not about dying; it was about living in the modern world while rejecting it in favor of spiritual fulfillment. It began with a statement of purpose, "Where Do the Children Play?," in which Stevens questioned the value of technology and progress. "Wild World" found the singer being dumped by a girl, but making the novel suggestion that she should stay with him because she was incapable of handling things without him. "Sad Lisa" might have been about the same girl after she tried and failed to make her way; now, she seemed depressed to the point of psychosis. The rest of the album veered between two themes: the conflict between the young and the old, and religion as an answer to life's questions. *Tea for the Tillerman* was the story of a young man's search for spiritual meaning in a soulless class society he found abhorrent. He hadn't yet reached his destination, but he was confident he was going in the right direction, traveling at his own, unhurried pace. The album's rejection of contemporary life and its yearning for something more struck a chord with listeners in an era in which traditional verities had been shaken. It didn't hurt, of course, that Stevens had lost none of his ability to craft a catchy pop melody; the album may have been full of angst, but it wasn't hard to sing along to. As a result, *Tea for the Tillerman* became a big seller and, for the second time in four years, its creator became a pop star. — *William Ruhlmann*

☆ **Teaser and the Firecat** / Oct. 1971 / A&M ♦♦♦♦♦
Even as a serious-minded singer/songwriter, Cat Stevens never stopped being a pop singer at heart, and with *Teaser and the Firecat* he reconciled his philosophical interests with his pop instincts. Basically, *Teaser's* songs came in two modes: gentle ballads that usually found Stevens and second guitarist Alun Davies playing delicate lines over sensitive love lyrics, and up-tempo numbers on which the guitarists strummed away and thundering drums played in stop-start rhythms. There were also more exotic styles, such as the Greek-styled "Rubylove," with its twin bouzoukis and a verse sung in Greek, and "Tuesday's Dead," with its Caribbean feel. Stevens seemed to have worked out some of his big questions, to the point of wanting to proselytize on songs like "Changes IV" and "Peace Train," both stirring tunes in which he urged social and spiritual improvement. Meanwhile, his love songs had become simpler and more plaintive. And while there had always been a charming, childlike quality to some of his lyrics, there were songs here that worked as nursery rhymes, and these were among the album's most memorable tracks and its biggest hits: "Moonshadow" and "Morning Has Broken," the latter adapted from a hymn. The overall result was an album that was musically more interesting than ever, but lyrically dumbed-down. Stevens continued to look for satisfaction in romance, despite its disappointment, but he found more fulfillment in a still-unspecified religious pursuit that he was ready to tout to others. And they were at least nominally ready to listen: the album produced three hit singles and just missed topping the charts. *Tea for the Tillerman* may have been the more impressive effort, but *Teaser and the Firecat* was the Cat Stevens album that gave more surface pleasures to more people, which in pop music is the name of the game. — *William Ruhlmann*

Catch Bull at Four / Oct. 1972 / A&M ♦♦♦
Catch Bull at Four began with a statement of purpose, "Sitting," in which Cat Stevens tried to talk himself into believing that he hadn't stalled, beginning to worry that he might be falling behind schedule or even going in circles. It may be that Stevens' recent experiences had contributed to his sense that he was running out of time. Though he was never a directly confessional writer, one got the sense that his disaffection with the life of a pop star was reasserting itself. And while he was touring unhappily around the world, the world was still going to hell in a handbasket. Yet Stevens was still motivated by his urge to help mankind mend its ways. Love provided some comfort, but for the most part, the singer who had seemed so excited on his last album now sounded apprehensive. Stevens set his reflections to a mixture of musical styles that included traces of old English folk songs, madrigals, and Greek folk music along with more typical rock stylings, all performed with the stop-and-start rhythms that added drama to his performances. Nevertheless, *Catch Bull at Four* was a more difficult listen than its three predecessors. Coming off the momentum of *Teaser and the Firecat*, it roared up the charts to number one, but stayed in the Top Ten fewer weeks than its predecessor. Fans who had been stirred by Stevens' rhythmic tunes and charmed by his thoughtful lyrics were starting to lose interest in his quasi-religious yearnings, busy arrangements, and self-absorbed, melodramatic singing. His career still had a ways to go, but as of *Catch Bull at Four*, he had passed his peak. — *William Ruhlmann*

Foreigner / Jul. 1973 / A&M ♦♦♦
Between 1970 and 1972, Cat Stevens recorded four albums in the same manner, using the same producer and many of the same musicians, painting the album covers, and assigning the records ponderous titles. Things changed with his next album, *Foreigner*. The

recording itself had been produced by Stevens, and while a couple of Stevens' usual backup musicians had been retained, New York session musicians appeared, and second guitarist Alun Davies was gone. With him went the acoustic guitar interplay that had been the core of Stevens' sound, replaced by more elaborate keyboard-based arrangements complete with strings, brass, and a female vocal trio featuring Patti Austin. It's easy to look at the 18-plus minute "Foreigner Suite" that took up the first side and accuse Stevens of excess and indulgence. What should be kept in mind, however, is that his peers in 1973 were acts like Jethro Tull and Yes, who in turn were taking their cue from the Beatles' *Abbey Road* and the Who's *Tommy*. Call *Foreigner* ambitious, then, rather than indulgent. Actually, the suite is full of compelling melodic sections and typically emotive singing that could have made for an album side's worth of terrific four-minute Cat Stevens songs, if only he had composed them that way. As it is, the suite is a collection of tantalizing fragments. But the album's second side, featuring the Top 40 hit "The Hurt," demonstrates that, even in the four-minute range, his songwriting and arranging were becoming overly busy. On the whole, *Foreigner* marked a slight fall-off in quality from *Catch Bull at Four*, which itself had marked a slight fall-off from *Teaser and the Firecat*. The decline seemed more extreme, though, because *Foreigner* clearly was intended to be better than its predecessors. That's the risk of ambition. — *William Ruhlmann*

Buddha and the Chocolate Box / Apr. 1974 / A&M ♦♦♦
While *Foreigner* was Cat Stevens' fifth consecutive gold album and his fourth straight Top Ten hit, it actually marked a small drop commercially and encountered critical resistance for the lengthy suite that took up all of side one. Eight months later, *Buddha and the Chocolate Box* found Stevens back in England and back with producer Paul Samwell-Smith and second guitarist Alun Davies. It also marked a return to the simpler style of earlier albums. No song ran much over five minutes, the arrangements were sparer and featured more acoustic guitar, and the lyrics did not take off into discursive ruminations about the state of the universe. It was very much as if Stevens was deliberately trying to make an album like *Teaser and the Firecat*, his commercial and artistic apex. Having begun the album with an ode to "Music" and its potential for reforming the world, he ended with "Home in the Sky," in which he sang, "Music is a lady that I still love." Such statements of renewed commitment added to the sense that the album was consciously crafted as an attempted second wind for the singer, who had been recording and performing at a torrid pace since returning to the music business full-time four years before. But that was not to say that he had abandoned the spiritual nature of his creative quest, and the songs were, as usual, littered with religious imagery. Stevens' fans responded warmly to *Buddha and the Chocolate Box's* stylistic return to form. "Oh Very Young" became his first Top Ten hit in two years, and the album was held out of number one only by *The Sting*. The album's tone, however, suggested that Stevens was once again wearying of being a pop star, even as he delivered a record that maintained that status. — *William Ruhlmann*

Greatest Hits / Jun. 1975 / A&M ♦♦♦♦♦
Like many of his peers, Cat Stevens made records that were identified by strong, memorable hit singles, but make no mistake: he made albums that were cohesive works onto themselves. For that reason, the very idea of a Cat Stevens' *Greatest Hits* collection may be troublesome to some fans, since they will only notice the missing album tracks, but *Greatest Hits* does its job exceptionally well. With the exception of "The Hurt," all of his hits from the early '70s—"Wild World," "Moon Shadow," "Peace Train," "Morning Has Broken," "Sitting," "Oh Very Young," "Another Saturday Night," "Ready," and "Two Fine People"—are here, along with three other fine album tracks. In short, it is everything that casual fans need—and even fans that find a favorite or two missing will be hard-pressed to deny that this is a solid introduction and a great listen. — *Stephen Thomas Erlewine*

Numbers / Nov. 1975 / A&M ♦♦
Subtitled "A Pythagorean Theory Tale," *Numbers* was a concept album relating to a faraway galaxy, a planet called Polygor, a palace, and its people, the Polygons. So one learned from the album's accompanying booklet. The songs presumably told the tale, but as with so many concept albums, listening to *Numbers* was like hearing a Broadway cast album without having seen the show—something seemed to be going on, but it was hard to tell what. The setting did allow Cat Stevens to indulge his affection for Middle Ages madrigal music, and individual songs, notably the singles-chart entry "Banapple Gas," were appealing. The lyrics were full of references to home, God, and "the truth," which gave the whole a vaguely spiritual tone, though the key word here is "vague." Stevens fans may have been somewhat put off by the fear that *Numbers* was a kind of musical math class—though it went gold, the album was the first in his last seven to peak below the Top Ten. — *William Ruhlmann*

Izitso / May 1977 / A&M ♦♦♦
Cat Stevens bounced back from the lackluster *Numbers* with an album of pop/rock songs that brought his usual rhythmic folk-rock into contemporary style with the Muscle Shoals rhythm section, a snappy Dave Kershenbaum production, and lots of synthesizers. Most of the songs were unusually lightweight, but the autobiographical "(I Never Wanted) To Be a Star" explored Stevens' ambivalence about being in the music business, an attitude that would find him dropping out and finding religion after one more album. In the meantime, *Izitso* produced a final Top 40 hit in "(Remember the Days of The) Old Schoolyard" and a singles-chart entry in the instrumental "Was Dog a Doughnut," as a result of which it returned Stevens's name to the Top Ten LPs list and gave him a ninth straight gold album, his last. — *William Ruhlmann*

Back to Earth / Dec. 1978 / A&M ♦♦♦
In retrospect, it is not hard to find in the final album Cat Stevens made before a near-death experience and a religious conversion hints of his coming change. "I must be heading for a breakdown," he notes in "Bad Brakes," the album's sole singles-chart entry; there

are songs titles like "Last Love Song" and "Never"; and there is, throughout, an elegiac tone to the mostly quiet ballads. But it is just as easy to see *Back to Earth* as an intended return to the simple style of albums like *Tea for the Tillerman* and thus a return to form: producer Paul Samwell-Smith is back on board, along with his subdued arrangements, and Stevens is again investigating his favorite themes, including children ("Daytime"), the father-son relationship ("Father"), and the vulnerable nature of romantic love, in plain-spoken verses. The year 1978 was late for a sensitive singer/songwriter to make a comeback; most of the folkies were getting tossed off the major labels by then. So, it's doubtful that *Back to Earth* could have re-established Cat Stevens even if he had been willing and able to promote it. As it is, the album serves as a satisfying coda to his pop career. *—William Ruhlmann*

Footsteps in the Dark: Greatest Hits, Vol. 2 / Nov. 1984 / A&M ✦✦✦✦✦
Cat Stevens's greatest hits were contained on the album of that title released in June 1975, though that set did not include the minor Top 40 entry "The Hurt" and though Stevens made the singles chart four more times between 1976 and 1979, with "Banapple Gas," the Top 40 "(Remember the Days of The) Old Schoolyard," "Was Dog A Doughnut," and "Bad Brakes." One might expect that an album subtitled *Greatest Hits, Vol. 2* would contain all those tracks, but if so, one would be disappointed. The only chart single on the 14-track *Footsteps in the Dark* is "The Hurt." Actually, the album is a non-hits compilation of good album tracks drawn from seven of Stevens's nine A&M albums originally released between 1970 and 1978, plus a non-LP B-side and two songs that previously had only appeared in the 1972 film *Harold and Maude*. It leans heavily to the earlier, folkier period, with ten songs drawn from 1970-1972, and thus emphasizes the vulnerable, seeking singer/songwriter of *Tea for the Tillerman* over the more pop-oriented and musically ambitious artist who made albums like *Izitso*. The material is sometimes dated ("I'd like to live on a commune and / People can call me a hippie"), and, in the wake of Stevens's conversion to Islam, one inevitably hears lines like "Where I'll end up well I think, / Only God really knows" in a different light. But Stevens's songwriting still impresses, his childlike wonder and earnestness are still endearing, and such political statements as "Where Do the Children Play?" remain timely. Though Stevens's best albums, *Tea for the Tillerman* and *Teaser and the Firecat*, work best as albums, *Footsteps in the Dark* confirmed that, a decade on from their initial appearance, his songs had maintained their quality. *—William Ruhlmann*

Early Tapes / Jun. 30, 1998 / Spectrum ✦✦✦
A lot has been said of Cat Stevens' early music being over-produced and filled with bloated '60s studio touches, which is true, but, even so, that shouldn't obscure the fact that in these songs lie the genius that was to become Cat Stevens. And they're not altogether bad songs either. This collection opens with "I Love My Dog," which, while not brilliant, at least showed that Stevens was willing to approach songwriting from unconventional angles even at that stage. The following track, "The First Cut Is the Deepest," would have been a perfect fit for the Righteous Brothers. The majority of the songs, which aren't as consistently great as his later work, are still impressive. "I'm So Sleepy" sounds similar to some of the tracks he'd be cutting in a few years, as does the Gordon Lightfoot-esque "Blackness of the Night" and "Where Are You," which wouldn't have been out of place on *Mona Bone Jakon*. That's not to say that some of the songs aren't poorly done, but, overall, if the horns and strings are stripped away, you still have a Cat Stevens album. *—Matt Fink*

Remember: The Ultimate Collection / Nov. 30, 1999 / Island/Universal International ✦✦✦✦

● **Very Best of Cat Stevens** / Mar. 28, 2000 / A&M ✦✦✦✦✦
It is impossible to compile a single-disc greatest-hits compilation for Cat Stevens that will come close to satisfying all of his admirers. *The Very Best of Cat Stevens* is the fifth major attempt to do so and, like its predecessors, it is challenged by its subject's success. *Remember Cat Stevens—The Ultimate Collection* is the longest of the five (24 tracks) and may be the most comprehensive. But *The Very Best of Cat Stevens*, released just a year later, has several advantages that make it more appealing. To begin with, it is the only compilation to sequence chronologically songs from every one of Stevens' albums, including the experimental *Foreigner*. It also contains the delightful folk creed "The Wind," which was a glaring omission from the so-called *Ultimate Collection*. Most significantly, it contains the previously unreleased "I've Got a Thing About Seeing My Grandson Grow Old." Stevens recorded a demo of the song during the *Mona Bone Jakon* sessions in 1970, but it never saw the light of day until it was remixed for this collection. Perhaps this was because it was considered too eccentric for public consumption, straddling the line between the hook-rich pop of Stevens' '60s records and the groundbreaking folk-rock of his '70s efforts. If so, the public was vastly underestimated. The song is a buried treasure that fits in perfectly in the company of Stevens' best work. *—Evan Cater*

A Is for Allah / Jul. 11, 2000 / Resurgent ✦✦✦✦
After the birth of his daughter, Yusuf Islam (formerly known as Cat Stevens) created this two-disc set to teach the basics of Islam using the Arabic alphabet and some song. Yusuf Islam narrates, and is joined by vocalists Sheikh Muhammad Gibril, Hamza Yusuf, Zain Bhikha, and Raihan. *—Joslyn Layne*

Al Stewart

b. Sep. 5, 1945, Glasgow, Scotland
Vocals, Keyboards, Trumpet, Guitar / British Folk-Rock, Album Rock, Pop/Rock, Folk-Rock, Soft Rock, Prog Rock/Art Rock, Singer/Songwriter
Glasgow native Al Stewart began his career playing guitar in Tony Blackburn's band the Sabres, and moved from there to the London folk club scene. After an unsuccessful single on Decca, "The Elf" (which featured Jimmy Page on guitar), Stewart signed with CBS and released a series of albums largely consisting of introspective, confessional love songs beginning in 1967. *Love Chronicles* was the only one to be released in the U.S., and the autobiographical title track, which detailed Stewart's romantic involvements, attracted a bit of attention for the singer's use of the word "fucking" in a song with supposed artistic credibility. On 1974's *Past, Present and Future*, Stewart switched gears, exploring his fascination with historical tales, and was rewarded with his first U.S. chart album. *Modern Times* was even more successful, and *Year of the Cat* was an unqualified hit, selling over a million copies and spawning the Top Ten title single. *Time Passages* duplicated both feats, but Stewart's creativity dried up soon afterwards, and difficulties over his contract and change of labels prevented him from releasing any new material until 1984. *Russians and Americans* was highly political, but sales were disappointing. Even so, Stewart has recorded and toured sporadically in the late '80s and '90s while devoting time to his hobby of wine collecting. *—Steve Huey*

Bedsitter Images / 1967 / Epic ✦✦

Love Chronicles / 1969 / Epic ✦✦✦

Zero She Flies / 1970 / Epic ✦✦✦
On his third album, *Zero She Flies*, Al Stewart continued in a familiar gentle, folk-based singer/songwriter vein. The album's key track was "Manuscript," one of Stewart's first historical songs. *—Daevid Jehnzen*

Orange / 1972 / BGO ✦✦✦✦
This is a transitional Al Stewart album. After stretching the boundaries of song length and language with *Love Chronicles*, he was in a something of a holding pattern on *Orange*, without any obviously profound inspiration or moments of daring. "Songs Out of Clay," however, does reveal the first signs of the mix of acoustic and electric guitar sounds that he would perfect on his next album, *Past, Present and Future*, two years later, while "The Fourth of May," a six-minute personal story-song, gets something of the beat and the sound that Stewart would refine in achieving his subsequent success—he just needed subject matter other than busted relationships. *Orange* also introduced Tim Renwick, whose lead guitar would become central to the sound on Stewart's subsequent albums. His singing, however, is still of a rather mournful and even monotonous nature, except on those two songs; he hadn't yet found sufficient variety in his tone and delivery, and even the presence of Rick Wakeman's elegant, classically based, arpeggio-laden piano accompaniments couldn't rescue most of these songs. There's also a pretty cool cover of Bob Dylan's "I Don't Believe You," cut as a warm-up for the rest of the album. *—Bruce Eder*

Past, Present and Future / 1974 / Rhino ✦✦✦
As good as portions of it was, *Orange* was essentially a transitional effort, the necessary bridge to *Past, Present and Future*, the record where Al Stewart truly begins to discover his voice. This is largely through his decision to indulge his fascination with history and construct a concept album that begins with "Old Admirals" and ends with "Nostradamus" and his predictions for the future. A concept like this undoubtedly will strike prog warning bells in the minds of most listeners but, ironically, he has stripped back most of the prog trappings from *Orange*, settling into a haunting folk bed for these long, winding tales. If anything, this results in an album that is a bit too subdued, but even so, it's apparent that Stewart has finally found his muse, focusing his songwriting and intent to a greater extent than ever before. Now, the key was to find the same sense of purpose in record making—he didn't quite get it here, but he would the next time around. *—Stephen Thomas Erlewine*

Modern Times / 1975 / Beat Goes On ✦✦✦✦✦
Surely the title is a bit of an allusion to the *Past, Present and Future* of its predecessor, but *Modern Times* also brought Al Stewart into the present, establishing his classic sound of folky narratives and Lennonesque melodies, all wrapped up in a lush, layered production from Alan Parsons. Hearing this production makes it clear that his is what was missing from *Past*, since it gives epics like the title track a real sense of grandeur that makes their sentiments resonate strongly. But it's not just the improvement in production that makes *Modern Times* the beginning of Stewart's classic period—his songwriting has now leapt up and met his ambitions, as it retains the historical sweep of his earlier material but melds it to a melodic sensibility that's alternately comforting and haunting. This skill is apparent throughout *Modern Times*, and it's married to a sound that is its equivalent, making this an exquisite pop-prog gem. *—Stephen Thomas Erlewine*

Year of the Cat / 1976 / Arista ✦✦✦✦✦
Al Stewart had found his voice on *Past, Present and Future* and found his sound on *Modern Times*. He then perfected it all on 1976's *Year of the Cat*, arguably his masterpiece. There is no overarching theme here, as there was on its two immediate predecessors, but the impossible lushness of Alan Parsons' production and Stewart's evocative continental narratives give the record a welcome feeling of cohesion that keeps the record enchanting as it moves from "Lord Grenville," to "Midas Shadow," to "Broadway Hotel," before it ends with the haunting title track. Along the way, Stewart doesn't dwell too deeply in any area, preferring to trace out mysteries with his evocative lyrical imagery and a spinning array of self-consciously sophisticated music, songs that evoke American and European folk and pop with a deliberate grace. This could be unbearably precious if it didn't work so well. Stewart is detached from his music, but only in the sense that he gives this album a stylish elegance, and Parsons is his perfect foil, giving the music a rich, panoramic sweep that mimics Stewart's globe-trotting songs. The result is a tremendous example of how good self-conscious progressive pop can be, given the right producer and songwriter—and if you're a fan of either prog or pop and haven't given Al Stewart much thought, prepare to be enchanted. *—Stephen Thomas Erlewine*

Time Passages / 1978 / Arista ✦✦✦✦✦
Year of the Cat brought Al Stewart a genuine worldwide smash with its title track, and

for its successor, he did make a few concessions. These, however, were slight—just a slight increase of soft-rock productions, an enhancement of the lushness that marked not only *Year of the Cat*, but also *Modern Times*. These happened to be welcome adjustments of Stewart's sound, since they increased the dreamy continental elegance at the core of his work. And that's why *Time Passages* is the equal of *Year of the Cat*—it may be more streamlined, but the adjustments to his sound and the concessions to the mainstream just increase the soft grace of his eloquent historical pop epics. It's possible to view this as too precious, because it is pitched at an audience that believes the common-day concerns of pop are piffle, but this is exceptionally well crafted, from Stewart's songs, where even three-minute songs seem like epics, to Alan Parsons' cinematic arrangements and productions. This added concentration on the texture of the recording, ensuring that it's clean, spacious, and gentle with a welcoming surface. Of course, this means that *Time Passages* can work very well as background music, but it also reveals much upon concentrated listening—enough to make it stand proudly next to *Modern Times* and *Year of the Cat* as one of Al Stewart's very best albums. *—Stephen Thomas Erlewine*

24 Carrots / 1980 / Razor & Tie ♦♦♦♦♦
The pun of the title of *24 Carrots*—the first overt signal of humor Al Stewart has displayed in years, possibly ever—illustrates that a lot has changed since 1978's *Time Passages*. The loosening of his wit is perhaps the most evident, but the most significant is the departure of producer Alan Parsons, who collaborated with Stewart on his mid-'70s triptych of masterpieces. In truth, *24 Carrots* isn't far removed from those high points, because he is indeed still writing at a remarkably consistent pace. No, this record isn't quite at the high standard of the previous three albums, but it does have a number of brilliant moments, from the opening "Rouning Man," through the silly but effective "Mondo Sinistro" and the gorgeous "Midnight Rocks." Though there are some songs that don't quite click (something that did not happen on the aforementioned trio), overall the record coheres nicely, thanks not just to the uniform classiness of Stewart's songs, but to his production with Chris Desmond. Although the production does hint at the antiseptic cleanliness that sank many of his latter-day recordings, here, it is just a perfect balance of audio precision and elegant studiocraft. Despite its occasional missteps, it still is a fine record, a fitting, wistful coda to Stewart's classic period. [Razor & Tie's 1993 contains three bonus tracks.] *—Stephen Thomas Erlewine*

Live Indian Summer / 1981 / Arista ♦♦

Russians & Americans / 1984 / Mesa ♦♦

● **The Best of Al Stewart** / 1986 / Arista ♦♦♦♦♦
Eleven songs from Stewart's albums *Past, Present and Future* (1974) through *Live Indian Summer* (1981), remastered in 1992, which gives it more than decent sound. "Roads to Moscow" is drawn from *Past, Present and Future* (the inlay card erroneously lists *Live Indian Summer*), and "Year of the Cat" is the hit studio version, but the producers have chosen live versions of "Nostradamus" (which emphasizes its *Tommy*-like central riff) and "On the Border," rather than their superior originals, probably to retain the value of the original albums. Includes full lyrics (but no instrumental credits) and notes by David Dasch, which may explain too much, removing the mystery from some of the material. *—Bruce Eder*

Last Days of the Century / 1988 / Enigma ♦♦

Rhymes in Rooms / Feb. 25, 1992 / Mesa Blue Moon ♦♦♦
A pleasant unplugged set featuring most of Al Stewart's greatest hits, *Rhymes in Rooms* is a delight for devoted fans. *—Daevid Jehnzen*

Famous Last Words / 1993 / Mesa ♦♦♦

To Whom It May Concern, 1966-1970 / 1993 / EMI ♦♦♦
EMI's 1993 double-disc collection *To Whom It May Concern: 1966-1970* contains the entirety of Al Stewart's early recordings for Epic Records, including all of his first three albums, *Bedsitter Images*, *Love Chronicles*, and *Zero She Flies*. Stewart took some time to find his voice, and it's possible to hear him struggle here, alternately hitting on British folk-rock à la Donovan, Tolkien-spirited fantasy, and lite psychedelia before he started to embark on his trademark historical obsessions and winding narratives. This makes it sound like it's only of interest to hardcore fans, which it is to a certain extent, but for fetishists of late-'60s folk-rock and psychedelic pop, there are some really intriguing things to be heard here, even if part of the reason that they're intriguing is because they don't quite work. *—Stephen Thomas Erlewine*

Billy Stewart

b. Mar. 24, 1937, Washington, D.C., **d.** Jan. 17, 1970, Neuse River, NC
Vocals, Drums, Piano / Brown-Eyed Soul, Chicago Soul, Pop-Soul, Northern Soul, Soul
Billy Stewart was one of the most distinctive vocal stylists of the '60s. His stuttering, word-doubling attack owed more to jazz scat singing than to the gospel influences of many of his peers. A jovial, rotund piano player who toured with Bo Diddley and, through him, gained entry to Chess Records, Stewart scored biggest in 1966 with a smash Top Ten version of George Gershwin and Dubose Heyward's "Summertime," an atypically (for Chess) big-band arrangement (featuring Earth, Wind & Fire's Maurice White on drums) with Stewart in a vocal *tour de force*, masterfully scatting around, stuttering through, and generally turning the melody inside out. It was not your typical '60s soul music, but Stewart's success opened the door for other jazz-influenced singers like Georgie Fame to gain a place on radio playlists of the day. Stewart died tragically at age 33 in a 1970 auto accident. *—Christine Ohlman*

● **One More Time: The Chess Years** / Oct. 1990 / Chess ♦♦♦♦♦
When you hear Bo Diddley's opening guitar on "Billy Blues," you know you're listening to something special. Billy Stewart ices the cake with a hiccupping, apologetic vocal. That lovely guitar melody was plagiarized and reappeared as "Love Is Strange," a big hit for Mickey and Sylvia. It doesn't get much better than "Strange Feeling," a warm floating song about the joys of new love. "I Do Love You" is a creamily concocted ballad—he sings as if in a trance, playing off excellent backing blends by uncredited male vocalists. Stewart dazzles again on "Sitting in the Park"; the slow ballad speaks of utter rejection, sitting in a park waiting on your chick, and she never shows. The backing is majestic, and pushes Stewart to unthought-of heights, such as "Love Me," where he sounds uncompromisingly happy. If you like cool mid-tempo ditties then you'll go for "How Nice It Is," an R&B charter. The lovely "I Cross My Heart" is a tearjerker; it sounds like the Dells on backing vocals with Stewart crooning like he was born to hurt, his soulful howl on the fade will make you tingle. Better known to some are his revitalizations of pop/MOR standards "Summertime" and "Secret Lover." You get the full unedited dose of the former. He does it his way, performing complete makeovers on both. "Golly Golly Gee" and "I'm in Love (Oh, Yes I Am)" deserve honorable mention for being borderline great. The latter is similar in feel and melody to "I'm Gonna Make You Love Me" by the Supremes & the Temptations. Stewart was one of a kind (Otis Redding's singing style and stage performance was probably influenced by the late, great Billy Stewart). *—Andrew Hamilton*

20th Century Masters—The Millennium Collection: The Best of Billy Stewart / Oct. 10, 2000 / Chess/MCA ♦♦♦♦♦
The omission of Stewart's heartfelt "How Nice It Is," one of his seven best singles, is the only sore spot. Compilers always overlook the tension-filled ballad on these short collections (11 songs). Stewart's six other gems—"Strange Feeling," "I Do Love You," "Sitting in the Park," "Cross My Heart," "Summertime," and "Secret Love"—sparkle like diamonds with their digitally remastered makeovers. Also solid are "Everyday I Have the Blues," with vocal accompaniment by the Dells, and "Reap What You Sow," featuring the Jewels. *—Andrew Hamilton*

Rod Stewart

b. Jan. 10, 1945, London, England
Vocals / Album Rock, Blue-Eyed Soul, British Blues, Arena Rock, Pop/Rock, Folk-Rock, Soft Rock, Adult Contemporary, Hard Rock, Singer/Songwriter, Rock & Roll
Despite shifting critical and commercial fortunes, Rod Stewart is one of the greatest interpretative vocalists in rock & roll; when he's on, he's a first-rate songwriter, too. His early '70s recordings remain his strongest, yet he turned into a more than competent mainstream pop/rock star with music that wasn't as distinguished, yet was appealingly professional pop/rock.

Stewart first came to prominence when he joined the Jeff Beck Group at the end of 1966. The group fell apart after two albums, *Truth* and *Beck-Ola*, with Rod and Ron Wood joining the Small Faces, now called the Faces. A boisterous, boozy Stonesy rock & roll band, the Faces couldn't have been more different from Stewart's solo recordings; these albums meshed with his folk, R&B, and rock influences, resulting in a distinctive, stripped-down acoustic-based rock & roll. At the beginning of 1971, the Faces released their second album, *Long Player*, yet it was Stewart's third solo album, *Every Picture Tells a Story*, that made him a household name thanks to the number one single, "Maggie May." Stewart's solo success created tension within the band which peaked when 1972's *Never a Dull Moment* was his second solo smash. Following 1973's *Ooh La La* he left the Faces for a solo career. Throughout the late '70s, his celebrity and popularity increased, while his critical respect declined. Stewart's popularity plateaued in the early '80s, then it hit a slump. He had only one gold album and only scored three Top Ten hits between 1982 and 1988. Stewart rebounded with 1988's *Out of Order*, then "Downtown Train," taken from the 1989 four-disc retrospective box set *Storyteller*, became his biggest hit in ten years. Stewart reunited with Ron Wood to record an *MTV Unplugged* concert and album in 1993. It was his last unqualified hit of the decade, as his next three records failed to capture a sizable audience. He left his longtime home of Warner for Atlantic in 2000, releasing *Human* the following year. *—Stephen Thomas Erlewine*

The Rod Stewart Album / 1969 / Mercury ♦♦♦♦♦
On his debut album (titled *An Old Raincoat Won't Ever Let You Down* in Britain, and *The Rod Stewart Album* in America, presumably because its original title was "too English" or cryptic for U.S. audiences), Rod Stewart essays a startlingly original blend of folk, blues, and rock & roll. The opening cover of the Stones' "Street Fighting Man" encapsulates his approach. Turning the driving acoustic guitars of the original inside out, the song works a laid-back, acoustic groove, bringing a whole new meaning to the song before escalating into a full-on rock & roll attack—without any distorted guitars, just bashing acoustics and thundering drums. Through this approach, Stewart establishes that rock can sound as rich and timeless as folk, and that folk can be as vigorous as rock. And he does this not only as an interpreter, breathing new life into Ewan MacColl's "Dirty Old Town" and defining Mike D'Abo's "Handbags & Gladrags," but also as a songwriter, writing songs as remarkable as "Man of Constant Sorrow," "An Old Raincoat Won't Ever Let You Down," and "Cindy's Lament." The music and the songs are so vivid and rich with detail that they reflect a whole way of life, and while Stewart would later flesh out this blueprint, it remains a stunningly original vision. *—Stephen Thomas Erlewine*

☆ **Gasoline Alley** / 1970 / Mercury ♦♦♦♦♦
Gasoline Alley follows the same formula of Rod Stewart's first album, intercutting contemporary covers, with slightly older rock & roll and folk classics and originals written in the same vein. The difference is in execution. Stewart sounds more confident, claiming Elton John's "Country Comfort," the Small Faces' "My Way of Giving," and the Rolling Stones' version of "It's All Over Now" with a ragged, laddish charm. Like its predecessor, nearly all of *Gasoline Alley* is played on acoustic instruments—Stewart treats rock & roll songs like folk song, reinterpreting them in individual, unpredictable ways. For instance,

"It's All Over Now" becomes a shambling, loose-limbed ramble instead of a tight R&B/blues groove, and "Cut Across Shorty" is based around a howling, mid-eastern violin instead of a rockabilly riff. Of course, being a rocker at heart, Stewart doesn't let these songs become limp acoustic numbers—these rock harder than any fuzz-guitar workout. The drums crash and bang, the acoustic guitars are pounded with a vengance—it's a wild, careening sound that is positively joyous with its abandon. And on the slow songs, Stewart is nuanced and affecting—his interpretation of Bob Dylan's "Only a Hobo" is one of the finest Dylan covers, while the original title track is a vivid, loving tribute to his adolescence. And that spirit is carried throughout *Gasoline Alley.* It's an album that celebrates tradition while moving it into the present and never once does it disown the past. *—Stephen Thomas Erlewine*

★ **Every Picture Tells a Story** / 1971 / Mercury ♦♦♦♦♦
Without greatly altering his approach, Rod Stewart perfected his blend of hard rock, folk, and blues on his masterpiece, *Every Picture Tells a Story.* Marginally a harder-rocking album than *Gasoline Alley*—the Faces blister on the Temptations cover "(I Know I'm) Losing You," and the acoustic title track goes into hyperdrive with Mick Waller's primitive drumming—the great triumph of *Every Picture Tells A Story* lies in its content. Every song on the album, whether it's a cover or original, is a gem, combining to form a romantic, earthy portrait of a young man joyously celebrating his young life. Of course, "Maggie May"—the ornate, ringing ode about a seduction from an older woman—is the centerpiece, but each song, whether it's the devilishly witty title track or the unbearably poignant "Mandolin Wind," has the same appeal. And the covers, including definitive readings of Dylan's "Tomorrow Is Such a Long Time" and Tim Hardin's "Reason to Believe," as well as a rollicking "That's All Right," are equally terrific, bringing new dimension to the songs. It's a beautiful album, one that has the timeless qualities of the best folk, yet one that rocks harder than most pop music—few rock albums are quite this powerful or this rich. *—Stephen Thomas Erlewine*

☆ **Never a Dull Moment** / 1972 / Mercury ♦♦♦♦♦
Essentially a harder-rocking reprise of *Every Picture Tells a Story, Never a Dull Moment* never quite reaches the heights of its predecessor, but it's a wonderful, multi-faceted record in its own right. Opening with the touching, autobiographical rocker "True Blue," which finds Rod trying to come to grips with his newfound stardom but concluding that he'd "rather be back home," the record is the last of Stewart's series of epic fusions of hard rock and folk. It's possible to hear Stewart go for superstardom with the hard-rocking kick and fat electric guitars of the album, but the songs still cut to the core. "You Wear It Well" is a "Maggie May" rewrite on the surface, but it develops into a touching song about being emotionally inarticulate. Similarly, "Lost Paraguayos" is funny, driving folk-rock, and it's hard not to be swept away when the Stonesy hard rocker "Italian Girls" soars into a mandolin-driven coda. The covers—whether a soulful reading of Jimi Hendrix's "Angel," an empathetic version of Dylan's "Mama You Been on My Mind," or a stunning interpretation of Etta James' "I'd Rather Go Blind"—are equally effective, making *Never a Dull Moment* a masterful record. He never got quite this good ever again. *—Stephen Thomas Erlewine*

Smiler / 1974 / Mercury ♦♦
Rod Stewart's classic formula ran out of gas on *Smiler,* his fifth solo album. The failure of *Smiler* wasn't a matter of weak songs, nor was it a matter of Stewart being in poor voice. Instead, the album failed because everything, from the choice of songs to the production, sounded too pat and predictable. The predictability held "Sweet Little Rock & Roller" from truly rocking and it made the reworking of "(You Make Me Feel Like) A Natural Man" unbearably smug. Apart from the free-wheeling take on Elton John's "Let Me Be Your Car" and the inspired version of Dylan's "Girl From the North Country," *Smiler* is an utter waste of time. *—Stephen Thomas Erlewine*

Atlantic Crossing / 1975 / Warner Brothers ♦♦♦♦♦
Atlantic Crossing wasn't simply the moment when Rod Stewart left Britain for the greener pasture of America, it was the moment when he accepted his role as a full-fledged, jet-setting superstar. Stewart abandoned the formula of his first five solo records, as well as most of his folk-rock and hard rock undercurrents, trading them for a professionally-polished, rock and soul-inflected pop, courtesy of Muscle Shoals' musicians and producer Tom Dowd. The glossy production doesn't obscure or trivialize Stewart's talents—coming after the tired *Smiler,* the slickness actually accentuated his strength as an interpretive singer. "The fast half" suffers from a couple of weak tracks, but "Three Time Loser" and "Stone Cold Sober" catch fire, and "the slow half" is generally excellent, but Stewart's heart-wrenching rendition of Danny Whitten's "I Don't Want to Talk About It" ranks as one of his finest performances. *—Stephen Thomas Erlewine*

A Night on the Town / 1976 / Warner Brothers ♦♦♦♦♦
After bouncing back to life with *Atlantic Crossing,* Rod Stewart crafted his most self-consciously ambitious record with *A Night on the Town.* The centerpiece of the album, "The Killing of Georgie (Part I and II)," was a long, winding Dylanesque tale of the murder of one of Stewart's gay friends and was one of his better songs of the mid-'70s. Even if "The Killing of Georgie" was the conscious artistic focal point of *A Night on the Town,* the true masterpiece of the album was an eloquent rendition of Cat Stevens' "The First Cut Is the Deepest." Apart from the flawed political platitudes of "Trade Winds," the rest of the album was filled with competent, professional pop/rock, highlighted by the number one hit "Tonight's the Night (Gonna Be Alright)," a ballad where the gallant Rod relieves a teenager of her virginity. And, again, the "Slow Half" was more convincing than the frequently perfunctory "Fast Half." *—Stephen Thomas Erlewine*

The Best of Rod Stewart / 1976 / Mercury ♦♦♦♦♦
Originally released in the '70s, Mercury's *The Best of Rod Stewart* was expanded to a generous 18 tracks in 1998. Many of those added tracks were not proper hits—they were album track favorites that may not have been big on the charts, but were of the consistently high quality that Rod was turning out in the early '70s. That means that this is a representative cross section and sampler of his best solo albums, even if it isn't wall-to-wall hits, and, in a way, that makes it better than being nothing but hits. *—Stephen Thomas Erlewine*

The Best of Rod Stewart, Vol. 2 / 1977 / Mercury ♦♦♦♦♦
Like its sister, *Best of Rod Stewart, Vol. 2* was also expanded in 1998 to include several bonus tracks—it now weighs in at a hefty 19 tracks. The biggest hits were put on the first volume, so this contains smaller hits and album-oriented radio favorites like "Country Comforts," "Mandolin Wind," "Reason to Believe," "Lost Paraguayos," and "True Blue," along with a superlative selection of album tracks and non-LP singles tracks. This may not be exactly what listeners drawn to best-of collections are looking for, since it doesn't contain all that many hits, but the music is consistently excellent, and it's a first-rate sampling of Rod's best era. *—Stephen Thomas Erlewine*

Foot Loose & Fancy Free / 1977 / Warner Brothers ♦♦♦
Following the same formula as *Atlantic Crossing* and *A Night on the Town,* but not explicity breaking the record into fast and slow sides, *Foot Loose & Fancy Free* was a limp effort from an increasingly complacent Rod Stewart. With the exception of the dumb, sleazy "Hot Legs," none of the rockers are discernable from each other, and this time he doesn't have a strong set of ballads to save him. The affectionately sappy acoustic ballad "You're in My Heart" was the big hit, but Stewart sounds completely convincing only on "I Was Only Joking." Coming at the end of the album, the song seems like a justification for the uninspired, by-the-book record that preceded it. *—Stephen Thomas Erlewine*

Blondes Have More Fun / 1978 / Warner Brothers ♦♦♦
In its simplest terms, *Blondes Have More Fun* is Rod Stewart's disco album, filled with pulsating rhythms and slick, synthesized textures. It's also his trashiest, most disposable album, filled with cheap come-ons and bad double entendres. Of course, that makes *Blondes Have More Fun* one of his most enjoyable records, even if all the pleasures are guilty. With its swirling strings and nagging chorus, "Da Ya Think I'm Sexy?" was the reason the record hit number one and, two decades later, the song stands as one of the best rock-disco fusions. The rest of the record isn't as engaging, but he throws out a handful of winning tracks in the same mould, including "Ain't Love a Bitch," "Attractive Female Wanted," and the title track. *—Stephen Thomas Erlewine*

Greatest Hits / 1979 / Warner Brothers ♦♦♦♦♦
Even though it has a couple of flaws—particularly the appearance of "Maggie May," which doesn't quite fit in with the rest of the material—*Greatest Hits* is an enjoyable sampler of Rod Stewart's first four Warner albums, including most of the hits but not necessarily all of his greatest performances. *—Stephen Thomas Erlewine*

Foolish Behaviour / 1980 / Warner Brothers ♦♦

Tonight I'm Yours / 1981 / Warner Brothers ♦♦♦♦
Though it lacks a truly great selection of songs, *Tonight I'm Yours* is a fine latter-day effort from Rod Stewart, and one of the last records that makes Rod sound like he's hip. Sporting a shiny new wave production, *Tonight I'm Yours* has a sleek, professional sound that can make even mindless rave-ups like "Tora, Tora, Tora (Out With the Boys)" a guilty pleasure. But the key to the album lays in songs like "Tonight I'm Yours" and the haunting "Young Turks," where Rod sounds totally at ease with a synth-pop beat. They are some of the best examples of mainstream rock co-opting the nervy, quirky appeal of new wave, and they make *Tonight I'm Yours* an enjoyable, if lightweight, listen. *—Stephen Thomas Erlewine*

Absolutely Live / 1982 / Warner Brothers ♦

Body Wishes / 1983 / Warner Brothers ♦♦
Two of the songs are first-rate synth-laden, disposable pop/rock filler—"Baby Jane" and "What Am I Gonna Do (I'm So in Love With You)"—but when those songs sound *substantial* next to dreck like "Ready Now" and "Sweet Surrender," it's clear that *Body Wishes* is one of Rod Stewart's worst efforts. *—Stephen Thomas Erlewine*

Camouflage / 1984 / Warner Brothers ♦♦
Camouflage is better than the disastrous *Body Wishes,* but that's only a relative term. Jeff Beck adds the occasional rock guitar flourish, but that doesn't save the faceless material. Again, the two singles—"Infatuation" and "Some Guys Have All the Luck"—are fine, ready-made pop hits, but they wear thin after a few plays, and they're the best things on the record. *—Stephen Thomas Erlewine*

Rod Stewart / 1986 / Warner Brothers ♦
Featuring a set of amazingly vapid material—led by the empty Top Ten hit "Love Touch"—and an embalmed, mechanical production, *Rod Stewart* is the worst album the singer recorded. After a series of faceless albums, it's not surprising that the record was uninspired; what was surprising was the utter lack of convincing popcraft. The highlights of the album, "Love Touch" and "Every Beat of My Heart," were the singles but they lacked the well-constructed precision of "Some Guys Have All the Luck," "Infatuation," and "Baby Jane," which leaves *Rod Stewart* a soulless, and ultimately depressing, album. *—Stephen Thomas Erlewine*

Out of Order / 1988 / Warner Brothers ♦♦♦
With the support of the Power Station's guitarist Andy Taylor and drummer Bernard Edwards, Rod Stewart rebounds from his previous career nadir of "Love Touch" with *Out of Order.* Alternating between professional, driving rock & roll like "Lost in You" and ballads like "My Heart Can't Tell You No," *Out of Order* is a well-constructed set of mainstream pop/rock and his best album since *Tonight I'm Yours,* even if none of the songs rank among his best work. *—Stephen Thomas Erlewine*

Storyteller: The Complete Anthology / Oct. 1989 / Warner Brothers ✦✦✦✦✦
Storyteller: The Complete Anthology is a flawed but effective four-disc box set covering Rod Stewart's entire career. Although most of Stewart's biggest hits and best-known songs are on *Storyteller*, the collection is poorly paced, containing too much heistant early material and not enough Jeff Beck Group or Faces selections. Nevertheless, the box traces his evolution from a working-class singer to Rod the Mod to superstar, featuring most of his essential songs—including whole sides of *Every Picture Tells A Story* and *Never A Dull Moment*—along the way. For casual fans looking for an in-depth overview, it's an essential purchase, but more serious fans should stick with individual albums, especially his classic early '70s albums. *—Stephen Thomas Erlewine*

Downtown Train (Selections from the Storyteller Anthology) / Mar. 6, 1990 / Warner Brothers ✦✦✦
Downtown Train (Selections from the Storyteller Anthology) is a 12-track distillation of Rod Stewart's four-disc box set, but instead of containing early hits, it concentrates on '80s singles like "Passion," "Young Turks," "Infatuation," "People Get Ready," and "Forever Young," adding a few '70s songs ("Stay With Me," "Tonight's the Night," "Killing of Georgie," "I Don't Want to Talk About It") and the new hit single "Downtown Train" for good measure. Although none of the material on the disc is bad, but the compilation lacks focus or cohesion, making it no more than a good sampler for casual fans. *—Stephen Thomas Erlewine*

Vagabond Heart / Mar. 26, 1991 / Warner Brothers ✦✦✦
Rod Stewart continued to regain his strength with *Vagabond Heart*, the follow-up to his comeback album, *Out of Order*. *Vagabond Heart* is a stronger, more diverse album than its predecessor, featuring a more consistent set of songs, including Robbie Robertson's "Broken Arrow" and the hit "Motown Song," as well as a convincing, impassioned performance by Stewart. *—Stephen Thomas Erlewine*

The Mercury Anthology / Sep. 22, 1992 / Mercury/Chronicles ✦✦✦✦✦
A two-disc anthology of Rod Stewart's early Mercury recordings, which, in conjunction with the albums he recorded with the Faces, are inarguably his finest (nothing from the Faces records is included). Most of the highlights of his terrific first four albums are here—"Maggie May," "You Wear It Well," "Handbags and Gladrags," "Gasoline Alley"—as well as selections from the lukewarm *Smiler*, a live album recorded with the Faces, and a couple of rare B-sides. *—Stephen Thomas Erlewine*

Unplugged . . . and Seated / May 25, 1993 / Warner Brothers ✦✦✦
The inherent problem with Rod Stewart's *Unplugged* album is that it seems like a supremely calculated attempt to revive his career exactly as Eric Clapton did. Stewart returns to the acoustic rock & roll and folk that marked his greatest recordings; Ron Wood's supporting guitar is a nice bonus recalling the glory days. Naturally, *Unplugged* can't hope to match *Gasoline Alley* or *Every Picture Tells a Story*, but the amazing thing is how close it comes at times. He sounds fine, if a little bit ragged at first, but as the album progresses, his performances become more genuine and heartfelt, culminating in yet another sublime Tom Waits cover with "Tom Traubert's Blues (Waltzing Matilda)," as well as a hit single with Van Morrison's "Have I Told You Lately?" *—Stephen Thomas Erlewine*

Spanner in the Works / Jun. 6, 1995 / Warner Brothers ✦✦✦
Following the success of *Unplugged . . . and Seated*, Rod Stewart had shrewdly repositioned himself as a mature, middle-aged man who still had a slight streak of his wilder days in him. Unsurprisingly, the music both recalled his past glories in instrumentation, yet the attack was different—the acoustics rocked, but it wasn't bracing; it was like a back-porch jam session. Stewart expanded that approach on *A Spanner in the Works*, his first album since *Unplugged*. The acoustics are still there, but they're strummed a little more gently and set in a bed of unobtrusive synths. More importantly, Stewart tackles his most ambitious and varied set of material since *A Night on the Town*. From the pop/rock of Tom Petty's "Leave Virginia Alone" and the reflective take on Dylan's "Sweetheart Like You" through the R&B tribute of "Muddy, Sam and Otis" and the rocking "Delicious" to the British folk of "Purple Heather," the songs recall his classic early albums in ambition and musical diversity. *A Spanner in the Works* isn't quite as successful as *Gasoline Alley* or *Every Picture Tells a Story*—it's a content album, not a probing one, which is appropriate for a middle-aged singer—yet it is the most inspired and ambitious record Stewart has released in nearly 20 years. *—Stephen Thomas Erlewine*

If We Fall in Love Tonight / Nov. 12, 1996 / Warner Brothers ✦✦✦
Taking its cue from Madonna's ballad collection *Something to Remember*, Rod Stewart's *If We Fall In Love Tonight* combines several of his biggest ballads with three new songs. *If We Fall in Love Tonight* is targeted directly toward an older, adult-contemporary audience who no longer wants to hear Stewart's harder-edged material. Which means that not only is "Maggie May" not included, but neither is "This Old Heart of Mine," since both are a bit too up-tempo for this collection. Instead, the album is nothing but ballads, going back as far as "Tonight's the Night," "The First Cut is the Deepest," "I Don't Want to Talk About It," and "You're in My Heart," but concentrating on '80s and '90s hits like "Downtown Train," "All for Love," "My Heart Can't Tell You No," "Have I Told You Lately," and "Broken Arrow." The compilation also contains rarities like the Sting and Bryan Adams collaboration "All for Love" and the Carole King cover "So Far Away," a new version of "Forever Young," a cover of Leo Sayer's "When I Need You," the James Newton Howard song "For the First Time," and the Jimmy Jam & Terry Lewis collaboration "If We Fall in Love Tonight." The new songs are good adult contemporary radio fodder, yet they pale next to his classic '70s cuts. Nevertheless, *If We Fall in Love Tonight* is a very enjoyable soft-rock collection. It may not draw an accurate portrait of Stewart's career, but it does offer a good overview of his soft-rock hits. *—Stephen Thomas Erlewine*

When We Were the New Boys / Jun. 2, 1998 / Warner Brothers ✦✦✦
When We Were the New Boys finds Rod Stewart tackling the music of his Brit-pop offspring and coming to terms with his pub rock roots. It's a bit of a risky move, since he could have embarrassed himself with stodgy singing but, surprisingly, he (more or less) pulls it off. Granted, he's not nearly as energetic as he once was, and he stumbles on occasion, but he recasts Oasis' "Cigarettes and Alcohol," Primal Scream's "Rocks," and Graham Parker's "Hotel Chambermaid" as comfortable rockers in the vein of "Hot Legs." They're not as vibrant as the Gallaghers' rolling thunder or Bobby Gillespie's ironic classicism, but they're easily the best rockers Rod has cut in ages. Yet, like on any of his '90s records, he really shines on the ballads, giving Ron Sexsmith's "Secret Heart," Nick Lowe's gorgeous "Shelly My Love," and Mike Scott's "What Do You Want Me to Do" lovely, unadorned readings, while letting his sentimental streak slip through in his original "When We Were the New Boys" and a cover of the Faces' "Ooh La La," originally sung by Ronnie Lane. These unabashedly recall his rowdy, youthful days with the Faces, and they're warmly nostalgic. He may be reveling in memory and trying recapture his youth, but Rod hasn't sounded this comfortable in years. *—Stephen Thomas Erlewine*

20th Century Masters—The Millennium Collection: The Best of Rod Stewart / Jul. 20, 1999 / Mercury ✦✦✦
Rod Stewart's volume of *20th Century Masters* is heavy on hits, and the songs that aren't hits are staples of Stewart's classic early-'70s repertoire. It is true that not every great song Rod recorded during this time is here—he recorded so much great music in the first half of the '70s that it couldn't be condensed to 12 songs—but it does contain a terrific selection of his very best, including "Maggie May," "You Wear It Well," "Every Picture Tells a Story," "Gasoline Alley," and "Angel," which makes this a first-class sampler. *—Stephen Thomas Erlewine*

1964-1969 / Jun. 6, 2000 / Pilot ✦✦✦
This double CD purports to assemble "every Rod Stewart recording from the '60s with the exception of his own work with the Jeff Beck Group." It doesn't seem 100 percent certain that the compilers managed to do so, but even if they didn't, the 30 tracks on these discs must represent virtually everything Stewart did in the 1960s aside from those Jeff Beck Group tracks, and aside from his solo debut album (which is usually given the release date of 1969 in discographies). As with David Bowie, there's a sense of a talented singer who took a long time to find his musical identity and secure first-rate material. Don't, nonetheless, think this disc is meaningless trivia; the music's good to not bad, although the 1964-1966 cuts are usually somewhat routine R&B numbers, assembled from a 1964 single as part of Long John Baldry & the Hoochie Coochie Men; his 1964 solo debut single for Decca; various 1964 soul/blues demos; his rather attractive late-1965 orchestrated pop single for Columbia; the demo cuts he sang on with Steampacket; his third Columbia single ("Shake"); and his lone track with Shotgun Express. Post-1966, Stewart really starts to come into his own, with richer, grittier vocals and harder blues-rock arrangements, again in a wide assortment of contexts: his 1967 soul-pop single "Little Misunderstood"; the 1967 vocal duet with P.P. Arnold, "Come Home Baby"; a performance fronting the Aynsley Dunbar Retaliation; the songs he sang on with Python Lee Jackson, including the famous "In a Broken Dream"; a track with the GTO's; and, finally, two demos done in 1969 with Art Wood's Quiet Melon, an aggregation that grew into the Faces. The whole lot is accompanied by a 48-page booklet that has an interesting, lengthy interview with early Stewart associate Long John Baldry. *—Richie Unterberger*

Human / Nov. 14, 2000 / Atlantic ✦✦
Throughout his career, Rod Stewart has been remarkably skillful at adopting current musical trends, whether it was disco, new wave, adult contemporary, or even Brit-pop. Since he tried contemporary rock, it made sense that the pendulum would swing back and he would take a stab at contemporary soul. Seems logical, but as the neo-TLC title track starts, it's hard not to think "what the hell happened?" Even when at the height of superstardom, he never pretended to be hip, which is what he's trying to do here. Surrounded by skittering drum machines and En Vogue-styled harmonies, crooning Babyface-styled ballads, it sounds like he's auditioning for the La Face roster. Rarely does *Human* try to be outright modern dance music, instead blatantly stealing these production techniques for a set of mid-tempo tunes and ballads that are firmly adult contemporary territory in content—they're just delivered as if they had a chance of sitting at the top of the charts, alongside Pink. In general, the slow ballads wind up being a bit better, since Stewart has gravitated toward that style during the '90s, while the livelier numbers, such as "Don't Come Around Here" (the Mary J. Blige duet) also work at times. Still, it's bizarre to hear Stewart in this setting, since he not only doesn't mesh with the sound, but he also has a really awkward batch of songs. Consider this: the most effective songs are "To Be With You," "Run Back Into Your Arms," and "I Can't Deny It," three fairly conventional Rod Stewart numbers tucked away toward the end of the album. Apart from that, *Human* is the sound of an artist painfully trying to sound modern but—by trying to sound fresh—sounding older than he ever has. *—Stephen Thomas Erlewine*

A Little Misunderstood: The Sixties Sessions / May 22, 2001 / Varese ✦✦✦
Culled from a series of recording sessions from the 1960s, particularly August 1964, and released after some legal squabbles, Rod Stewart's early influences of Southern blues and early Motown is quite evident on these 15 tracks. Drawing heavily from the likes of Jimmy Reed, the mod certainly appears in fine form, despite the occasional unpolished delivery and being rough around the edges. As well, the recordings also include a "supergroup" performance dubbed P.P. Arnold, consisting of Stewart, Mick Jagger, Keith Richards, and Nicky Hopkins. And there is also Steampacket, which included Long John Baldry. Highlights include the Sunday gospel "Can I Get a Witness" and "Ain't That Loving You Baby." "The Day Will Come" is perhaps the weakest track in the lot, a song definitely not complementary of his style. The majority of the sessions though stick to the

formula which has been the bread and butter of the singer's soul-tinged blues boogie exemplified on "So Much to Say." —*Jason MacNeil*

Stiff Little Fingers

f. 1977, Belfast, Northern Ireland, **db.** 1982
British Punk, Punk

A taut, explosive Belfast-based punk band, Stiff Little Fingers (named after a Vibrators song) had the dubious distinction of being referred to as "The Irish Clash." What must have seemed like a compliment at the time did little to help their career, only because it made comparisons between the two bands inevitable. Granted, there were many similarities: both bands debuted playing revved-up late-'70s punk rock, both were politically inclined, featured pissed-off lead singers, a love for reggae, and a near-palpable sense of isolation and desperation. But as we all know, the Clash offered complexity, panache, and a consistently breathtaking body of work. Stiff Little Fingers, on the other hand, were simply a very good punk rock band. —*John Dougan*

- **Inflammable Materials** / 1979 / Restless ✦✦✦✦✦

With "Alternative Ulster" and "Suspect Device" leading the way, this is a compelling, raging record that derives most of its style from the Sex Pistols and simply cranks up the personal political issues a notch or two. There is a so-so version of Bob Marley's "Johnny Was" (call it the obligatory reggae cover), but that doesn't hamper the enjoyment, nor does it detract from the record's overwhelming power. Issued on CD by Restless Retro in 1990. —*John Dougan*

Hanx / 1980 / Restless ✦✦✦

The other SLF studio recordings all contain some fine songs but are recommended only to hardcore fans. *Hanx*, however, is a live recording that brilliantly serves two purposes: first, as proof of what incendiary live shows SLF was capable of; second, as a greatest hits record. Unsurprisingly, the tempos here are much faster than the studio recordings, but that simply adds to the excitement. Overlooked upon its release, *Hanx* is a raging, nonstop hunk of punk rock that sounds great even after all these years. Issued on CD by Restless Retro in 1990. —*John Dougan*

Nobody's Heroes / Jan. 1980 / Restless ✦✦✦✦✦

It's easy to see why their Rough Trade debut remains so highly rated, but for the discerning fan of second-generation punk, *Nobody's Heroes* is every bit as special. For a start, new drummer Jim Reilly was an improvement on Brian Faloon (who gets a heartwarming tribute on "Wait and See"). Secondly, Jake Burns' songwriting collaborations with journalist Gordon Ogilvie are really beginning to pay off. The cornerstones of the LP are "Gotta Gettaway," "At the Edge," and "Tin Soldiers"—three songs which, in different ways, brilliantly articulate the frustrated ambitions of young men in search of expression and identity, trapped in nowhere jobs/situations. Though "Suspect Device" and "Alternative Ulster" had long since ensured they would always be tagged with the label political punk, in truth SLF were always more interested in their immediate environment, and finding a way out of it. A couple of plausible stabs at reggae are more than an interesting aside. —*Alex Ogg*

Go for It / May 1981 / Cargo ✦✦✦✦

By the time of *Go for It's* release in 1981, Stiff Little Fingers were at the peak of their powers. While the second-generation punk bands hadn't earned the critical respect afforded their forebears, the children of the revolution were arguably more popular *and* populist—it is difficult to describe the relationship of a band like SLF with their fans, so extraordinarily partisan was the connection between them, particularly live. But Jake Burns had no appetite to repeat himself, at least at this stage in his career. *Go for It* confirmed the upward swing in SLF's songwriting that began with *Nobody's Heroes*. It's not as immediate, and it's a slightly lesser album because of its ambition, but still a very good one. The brass on "Silver Lining" is the most self-evident example of the group's attempts at growth, and it doesn't quite gel. Yet "Piccadilly Circus" is arguably the best song Burns has ever written, and the instrumental title track is intoxicating. At this stage the fans were prepared to give them their head, and *Go For It* sold well. It was the last SLF album to do so. (The original U.S. version of the album added "Back to Front" to a rejigged running order). —*Alex Ogg*

Now Then / 1982 / Chrysalis ✦✦✦✦✦

On 1982's *Now Then*, which again featured a new drummer (skilled journeyman Dolphin Taylor), SLF attempted to become a full-fledged mainstream rock band. As a consequence, their hardcore fans deserted them in droves. To be fair, leader Jake Burns had always professed a high regard for Bruce Springsteen and Little Feat as much as his punk elders, and his lyrics here changed in tone rather than theme. But that wasn't enough to establish a new audience, nor retain their existing one. It's a real shame, because so much of *Now Then* is superb, honest, combative, and heartfelt. "Won't Be Told," "The Price of Admission," and the singles "Talkback" and "Bits of Kids" are far more three-dimensional than "Suspect Device" could ever be. Incidentally, Jake Burns inspired Paul Young to cover "Love of the Common People," a version of which is included here, rather than vice versa. Five years later, when SLF re-formed for the first time, no songs from *Now Then* would appear on their set lists. To paraphrase the Gang of Four, history had done a bunk on SLF's finest hour. —*Alex Ogg*

All the Best / 1983 / One Way ✦✦✦✦✦

The best anthology of SLF available. A 30-track chronological overview that's as articulate an argument for SLF's greatness as anything else they released. A perfect way to hear their development from the early punk days to their more "mature" punk-pop period just prior to their breakup: Jake Burns goes from shouter to singer, hooks and riffs replace simple walls of distorted guitars; the reggae influence becomes stronger and is played with greater dexterity; and all and all, you simply can't go wrong here. —*John Dougan*

Stephen Stills

b. Jan. 3, 1945, Dallas, TX

Vocals, Keyboards, Guitar, Bass / Pop/Rock, Folk-Rock, Soft Rock, Singer/Songwriter
Famed for his work in Buffalo Springfield and Crosby, Stills & Nash, two of pop music's most successful and enduring groups, Stephen Stills was born in Dallas, TX, on January 3, 1945. He eventually dropped out of college, moving to New York and signing on as a guitar player with the Au Go Go Singers. After a tour of Canada, Stills left the Au Go Go's in 1965 for Los Angeles, where he became enmeshed in the city's burgeoning folk-rock community. In the spring of 1966 Stills joined the Herd, later dubbed the Buffalo Springfield. A year later, the group issued their eponymous debut. Internal problems, ego clashes, and drugs were already tearing the band apart, however, and by the release of 1968's *Last Time Around*, the Springfield had already dissolved.

Stills quickly resurfaced with 1968's *Super Session*. A jam session with David Crosby and Graham Nash led to the formation of the vocal harmony supergroup Crosby, Stills & Nash; released in 1969, their self-titled debut was hugely successful. Later that year, Neil Young joined the loose-knit group, and in 1970, as Crosby, Stills, Nash & Young, they issued *Deja Vu*, another major hit.

In late 1970 Stills released his self-titled solo debut. The album was a smash, as was his 1971 follow-up *Stephen Stills 2*. In 1972, Stills began performing with a new backing unit, Manassas; both their debut and 1973's *Down the Road* continued Stills' long string of chart successes.

In 1977, Stills reunited with Crosby and Nash for *CSN*, which sold over four million copies; the band would reunite again several times in the early '80s to tour and produce albums. Stills again went solo for 1984's *Right by You*. In 1985, Crosby was sent to prison on drug possession charges, and Stills spent much of the late 1980s out of the public eye. In 1988 the reconstituted Crosby, Stills, Nash & Young recorded *American Dream*, followed in 1990 by the CSN release *Live It Up*. In 1991, Stills issued the solo LP *Stills Alone*, while CSN's *After the Storm* appeared in 1994. —*Jason Ankeny*

Stephen Stills / 1970 / Atlantic ✦✦✦✦✦

Stephen Stills 2 / 1971 / Atlantic ✦✦✦

Flushed with the success of his first solo effort and the continuing adulation from his role in the supergroup CSN&Y, Stephen Stills must have felt like he could do no wrong, and in many instances, his second solo disc proves him right. The superb "Marianne" and "Change Partners" more than satisfy the listener, while the dark and brooding "Know You Got to Run" and the prophetic "Fishes and Scorpions" are prime examples of his power as a singer and a songwriter. But when he misses the mark, as on "Ecology Song," he misses it by a mile and then some. Besides that cut, "Bluebird Revisited" is pure self-indulgence that someone of his craft and technique should have known better than to include here—or anywhere. But with compact disc players, one can omit anything offending and concentrate on what's good about *2*. Cut the disc in half, and you have a very enjoyable listening experience. As for the rest, well, let's just say you've been warned. —*James Chrispell*

- **Manassas** / 1972 / Atlantic ✦✦✦✦✦

A sprawling masterpiece, akin to the Beatles' *White Album*, the Stones' *Exile on Main Street*, or Wilco's *Being There* in its makeup, if not its sound. Rock, folk, blues, country, Latin, and bluegrass have all been styles touched on in Stephen Stills' career, and the skilled, energetic musicians he had gathered in Manassas played them all on this album. What could have been a disorganized mess in other hands, though, here all gelled together and formed a cohesive musical statement. The songs are thematically grouped: Part one is titled "The Raven" and is a composite of rock and Latin sounds that the group would often perform in full live. "The Wilderness" mainly centers on country and bluegrass. Part three, "Consider," is largely folk and folk-rock. "Johnny's Garden," reportedly for the caretaker at Stills' English manor house and not for John Lennon as is often thought, is a particular highlight. Two other notables from the "Consider" section are "It Doesn't Matter" and "Move Around," which features some of the first synthesizer used in a rock context. The closing section, titled "Rock & Roll Is Here to Stay," is a rock and blues set with one of the landmarks of Manassas' short life, the epic "The Treasure." A sort of zen-like meditation on love and "oneness," enlivened by the band's most inspired recorded playing, it evolves into a bluesy groove washed in Stills' fierce electric slide playing. The delineation lines of the four themed song groupings aren't cut in stone, though, and one of the strengths of the album is that there is a lot of overlap in styles throughout. —*Rob Caldwell*

Stills / 1975 / Columbia ✦✦

Illegal Stills / 1976 / Columbia ✦✦

The Best of Stephen Stills / 1977 / Atlantic ✦✦✦✦✦

Thoroughfare Gap / 1978 / Columbia ✦✦

Live / 1979 / Atlantic ✦✦✦

Right by You / 1984 / Atlantic ✦✦

Stills Alone / Sep. 11, 1991 / Vision ✦✦✦

This is the disc that Stephen Stills' fans always hoped he'd make. *Stills Alone* is just Stephen doing what he does the best, picking and singing in a style all his own. Put this on, and what you have is Stephen Stills in your living room playing your very own private concert. From Fred Neil's "Everybody's Talkin'" to the Beatles' "In My Life," right on through to Stephen's own compositions, everything here seems to click. Of note is the sensational "Blind Fiddler Medley." From one of the veterans of the rock & roll wars, Stephen Stills has put out a spectacular solo effort in the true sense of the word. —*James Chrispell*

Sting

b. Wallsend, England

Vocals, Bass / College Rock, Album Rock, Adult Alternative Pop/Rock, Pop/Rock, Adult Contemporary

After disbanding the Police at the peak of their popularity in 1984, Sting quickly established himself as a viable solo artist, one obsessed with expanding the boundaries of pop music. Sting incorporated heavy elements of jazz, classical, and worldbeat into his music, writing lyrics that were literate and self-consciously meaningful, and he was never afraid to emphasize this fact in the press. For such unabashed ambition, he was equally loved and reviled, with supporters believing that he was at the forefront of literate, intelligent rock and his critics finding his entire body of work pompous. Either way, Sting remained one of pop's biggest superstars for the first ten years of his solo career, before his record sales began to slip. Even before the Police were officially disbanded, Sting began recording his solo debut, 1985's *The Dream of the Blue Turtles*, with jazz musicians Branford Marsalis, Kenny Kirkland, and Omar Hakim. The album became a hit, prompting an even more ambitious and successful second album, *Nothing Like the Sun*, which was dedicated to his recently deceased mother. Although 1991's *The Soul Cages* peaked at number two and spawned the Top Ten hit "All This Time," the record was less successful than its predecessor. Two years later, he delivered another hit, *Ten Summoner's Tales*, that showed his audience had shifted from new wave/college rock fans to adult contemporary. Though 1996's *Mercury Falling* stalled at platinum sales and failed to generate a hit single, Sting remained a popular concert attraction, confirming his immense popularity. *—Stephen Thomas Erlewine*

The Dream of the Blue Turtles / 1985 / A&M ♦♦♦♦

The Police never really broke up, they just topped working together—largely because they just couldn't stand playing together anymore and partially because Sting was itching to establish himself as a serious musician/songwriter on his own terms. Anxious to shed the mantle of pop star, he camped out at Eddy Grant's studio, picked up the guitar, and raided Wynton Marsalis' band for his new combo—thereby instantly consigning his solo debut, *The Dream of the Blue Turtles*, to the critical shorthand of Sting's jazz record. Which is partially true (that's probably the best name for the meandering instrumental title track), but that gives the impression that this is really risky music, when he did, after all, rely on musicians who, at that stage, were revivalists just developing their own style, and then had them jam on mock-jazz grooves—or, in the case of Branford Marsalis, layer soprano sax lines on top of pop songs. This, however, is just the beginning of the pretensions layered throughout *The Dream of the Blue Turtles*. This is a serious-minded album, but it's undercut by its very approach. And that's the problem with the record: With every measure, every verse, Sting cries out for the respect of a composer, not a pop star, and it gets to be a little overwhelming when taken as a whole. As a handful of individual cuts—"Fortress," "Consider Me Gone," "If You Love Somebody," "Children's Crusade"—he proves that he's subtler and craftier than his peers, but only when he reins in his desire to show the class how much he's learned. *—Stephen Thomas Erlewine*

Bring on the Night / 1986 / A&M ♦♦♦

Sting really got carried away with the idea that his supporting crew for *Dream of the Blue Turtles* was a real jazz band, and, technically, he was kind of right. He did pluck them straight out of Wynton Marsalis' backing band (thereby angering Wynton and emboldening his anti-rock stance, while flaring up a sibling rivalry between the trumpeter and his saxophonist brother Branford—a veritable hat trick, that) and, since he was initially a jazz bassist, it seemed like a good fit. At the very least, it seemed like a monumental occasion because he documented the entire development of the band and making of *Dream* with a documentary called *Bring on the Night*, releasing a double-live album as its soundtrack just a year after the debut hit the stores. This could be called hubris (and I will call it that), especially because the appearance of the live album feels like a way of showcasing Sting's jazz band and jazz chops. Most of the songs run around five minutes long and there are no less than three melodies, two of which marry an old Police number with a tune from *Dream*. Arriving as a second solo album, it can't help but feel a little unnecessary, even if the loose, rather infectious performances show what Sting was trying to achieve with his debut. Even so, this is a record for the cult, and while it will satisfy them, to others it will seem like, well, hubris. *—Stephen Thomas Erlewine*

Nothing Like the Sun / 1987 / A&M ♦♦♦♦♦

If *Dream of the Blue Turtles* was an unabashedly pretentious affair, it looks positively light-hearted in comparison to Sting's sophomore effort, *Nothing Like the Sun*, one of the most doggedly serious pop albums ever recorded. This is an album where the only uptempo track, the only trifle—the cheerfully stiff white-funk "We'll Be Together"—was added at the insistence of the label because they believed there wasn't a cut on the record that could be pulled as a single, one that would break down the doors to mainstream radio. And they were right, since everything else here is too measured, calm, and deliberately subtle to be immediate (including the intentional throwaway, "Rock Steady"). So, why is it a better album than its predecessor? Because Sting doesn't seem to be trying so hard. It flows naturally, largely because this isn't trying to explicitly be a jazz-rock record (thank the presence of a new rhythm section of Sting and drummer Manu Katche for that), and because the melodies are insinuating, slowly working their way into memory, while the entire record plays like a mood piece—playing equally well as background music or as intensive, serious listening. Sting's words can still grate—the stifling pompousness of "History Will Teach Us Nothing" the clearest example, yet calls of "Hey Mr. Pinochet" also strike an uneasy chord—but his lyricism shines on "The Lazarus Heart," "Be Still My Beating Heart," "They Dance Alone," and "Fragile," a quartet of his very finest songs. If *Nothing Like the Sun* runs a little too long, with only his Gil Evans-assisted cover of "Little Wing" standing out in the final quarter, it still maintains its tone until the end and, since it's buoyed by those previously mentioned stunners, it's one of his better albums. *—Stephen Thomas Erlewine*

The Soul Cages / Jan. 17, 1991 / A&M ♦♦♦♦

Emboldened by the enthusiastic response to the muted *Nothing Like the Sun* and reeling from the loss of his parents, Sting constructed *The Soul Cages* as a hushed mediation on mortality, loss, grief, and father/son relationships (the album is dedicated, in part, to his father; its predecessor was dedicated to his mother). Using the same basic band as *Nothing Like the Sun*, the album has the same supple, luxurious tone, stretching out leisurely over nine tracks, almost all of them layered mid-tempo tunes (the exception being grinding guitars of the title track). Within this setting, Sting hits a few remarkable peaks, such as the elegant waltz "Mad About You" and "All This Time," a deceptively skipping pop tune that hides a moving tribute to his father. If the entirety of *The Soul Cages* was as nimbly melodic and urgently emotional as these two cuts, it would have been a quiet masterpiece. Instead, it turns inward—not just lyrically, but musically—and plays as a diary entry, perhaps interesting to those willing to spend hours immersing themselves within Sting's loss, finding parallels within their own life. This may be too much effort for anyone outside of the devoted, since apart from those two singles (and perhaps "Why Should I Cry for You"), there are few entry points into *The Soul Cages*—and, once you get in there, it only rewards if your emotional state mirrors Sting's. *—Stephen Thomas Erlewine*

● **Ten Summoner's Tales** / Mar. 9, 1993 / A&M ♦♦♦♦♦

After two albums of muted, mature jazz-inflected pop, the last being an explicit album about death, Sting created his first unapologetically pop album since the Police with *Ten Summoner's Tales*. The title, a rather awkward pun on his given last name, is significant, since it emphasizes that this album is a collection of songs, without any musical conceits or lyrical concepts tying it together. And, frankly, that's a bit of a relief after the oppressively somber *The Soul Cages* and the hushed, though lovely, *Nothing Like the Sun*. Sting even loosens up enough to crack jokes, both clever (the winking litany of celebrity pains of "Epilogue [Nothing 'Bout Me]") and condescending (the sneeringly catchy cowboy tale "Love Is Stronger Than Justice [The Munificent Seven]"), and the result is his best solo record. In places, it's easily as pretentious as his earlier work, but that's undercut by writing that hasn't been this sharp and melodic since the Police, plus his most varied set of songs since *Synchronicity*. True, there isn't a preponderance of flat-out classics—only the surging opener "If I Ever Lose My Faith in You," the understated swing of "It's Probably Me," and the peaceful ballad "Fields of Gold" rank as classics—but, as an album, *Ten Summoner's Tales* is more consistently satisfying than anything else in his catalog. *—Stephen Thomas Erlewine*

Fields of Gold: The Best of Sting 1984-1994 / Nov. 8, 1994 / A&M ♦♦♦

Early in his solo career, Sting defined himself as a man of taste, choosing to work with jazz musicians instead of rockers. Inevitably, this meant he walked the thin line between sophisticated pop and adult contemporary, but he did it with grace from 1985's *Dream of the Blue Turtles* to 1993's *Ten Summoner's Tales*. Unfortunately, *Fields of Gold: The Best of Sting* doesn't illustrate what a deft trick he pulled off with that quartet of albums. Naturally, *Fields of Gold* concentrates on his hit singles, just like any other greatest hits collection, but Sting's material sounds surprisingly tame in this context. Sure, there is a number of great songs here—enough to state his case as a fine songwriter or to satisfy his casual fans. Still, these songs are safe choices and all share a similar tranquil quality, which means the collection itself becomes a little monotonous. Nevertheless, *Fields of Gold* performs the necessary service of rounding up all of the big hits—"If You Love Somebody, Set Them Free"; "All This Time"; "Fortress Around Your Heart"; "They Dance Alone"; "If Ever Lose My Faith in You"; "Fragile"; and an alternate version of "We'll Be Together"—and offering them on one disc, which is reason enough to make it worthwhile, even with its flaws. *—Stephen Thomas Erlewine*

Mercury Falling / Mar. 12, 1996 / A&M ♦♦♦

Falling somewhere between the pop sensibilities of *Ten Summoner's Tales* and the searching ambition of *The Soul Cages*, *Mercury Falling* is one of Sting's tighter records, even if it fails to compel as much as his previous solo albums. Though he doesn't flaunt his jazz aspirations as he did in the mid-'80s, *Mercury Falling* feels more serious than *The Dream of the Blue Turtles*, primarily because of its reserved, high-class production and execution. Building from surprisingly simple, memorable melodies, Sting creates multi-layered, vaguely soul-influenced arrangements that carry all of the hallmarks of someone who has studied a music, not lived it. Of course, there are many pleasures in the record—for all of his pretensions, Sting remains an engaging melodicist, as well as a clever lyricist. There just happens to be a distinct lack of energy, stemming from the suffocating layers of synthesizers. *Mercury Falling* is a record of modest pleasures; it's just not an infectious, compulsive listen. *—Stephen Thomas Erlewine*

The Very Best of Sting & the Police / Nov. 18, 1997 / A&M ♦♦♦

In the summer of 1997, Puff Daddy took "I'll Be Missing You," a sappy reworking of "Every Breath You Take," to the top of the charts across the world; it became the biggest rap single in history. The success of "I'll Be Missing You" had the bizarre by-product of making the Police hip again among both rock and rap artists. So, what better to celebrate the occasion—as well as the 20th anniversary of the Police's first album—than the release of another compilation, this time combining highlights from the Police and Sting's solo career? *The Very Best of Sting & the Police* does just that, compiling 14 songs in a seemingly random chronological order. The Police cuts are generally classics, but there are several big hits left off, which should probably be expected for an integrated collection like this. There's plenty of good music on Sting's solo records, but the selection here emphasizes his MOR side instead of some of his more ambitious material. Obviously, that selection is designed to snag a mature, 30-something audience, which makes the inclusion of Puff Daddy's remix of "Roxanne" (included in both its original and remixed incarnations) a little puzzling, since that strives to appeal to a younger audience. Then again, you don't really expect coherence from a collection that simply wants to cash in at the right moment. While it's hard to ignore the fact that this disc isn't necessary, the music itself is good, and certain casual fans may find this useful. But anyone following Sting or the Police for any length of time will find *The Very Best Of*...superfluous. *—Stephen Thomas Erlewine*

Brand New Day / Sep. 28, 1999 / A&M ♦♦♦
By the late '90s, Sting had reached a point where he didn't have to prove his worth every time out; he had so ingrained himself in pop culture, he really had the freedom to do whatever he wanted. He had that attitude on *Mercury Falling*, but it was too somber and serious, everything that its successor, *Brand New Day*, is not. Light, even effervescent, *Brand New Day* feels like little else in Sting's catalog. Not that it represents a new beginning, contrary to what the title may promise. The album is not only firmly within his tradition, it sounds out of time—it's odd how close *Brand New Day* comes to feeling like a sequel to *Nothing Like the Sun*. Musically, that is. The sparkling, meticulous production and the very tone of the music—ranging from light funk to mellow ballads to the Lyle Lovett tribute "Fill Her Up"—are of a piece with Sting's late-'80s work. That's the main thing separating it from *Ten Summoner's Tales*, his other straight pop album—well, that, and the levity. There are no overarching themes, no political messages on *Brand New Day*—only love songs, story songs, and, for lack of a better term, inspirational exhortations. This is all a good thing, since by keeping things light he's managed to craft an appealing, engaging record. It may not ask as much from its audience as Sting's other '90s efforts, but it's immediately enjoyable, which isn't the case for its cousins. *Brand New Day* doesn't boast any new classics, and it does sound a little dated, but it's well crafted, melodic, and has a good sense of humor—exactly the kind of record Sting should be making as he embarks on the third decade of his career. *—Stephen Thomas Erlewine*

Stone Poneys

f. 1964, Los Angeles, CA, **db.** 1968
Folk-Rock, Pop
Before becoming a solo act, Linda Ronstadt was the lead singer of the Stone Poneys, an L.A.-based trio with an acoustic, folkish sound and strong original material. The band's focal point and greatest asset was Ronstadt's clear, powerful vocals. Originally recording in a coffeehouse folk style not far removed from Peter, Paul & Mary, the group rocked up their sound slightly and scored a Top 20 hit with "Different Drum," written by Mike Nesmith of the Monkees, in 1967. *—Richie Unterberger*

● **Stone Poneys Featuring Linda Ronstadt** / 1967 / Capitol ♦♦♦♦
It doesn't have "Different Drum," but the first Stone Poneys album is their folkiest and best, dominated by close harmonies and strong original material by the group's guitarists, Bob Kimmel and Ken Edwards. *—Richie Unterberger*

Evergreen, Vol. 2 / 1967 / Capitol ♦♦♦
Evergreen, Vol. 2 wasn't as strong as their debut album, but it did contain their only hit, "Different Drum," as well as several other pleasant songs in a similar vein. *—Stephen Thomas Erlewine*

Stone Poneys & Friends, Vol. 3 / 1968 / Capitol ♦♦♦
The Stone Poneys broke up during the recording of their final album, leaving Ronstadt to finish the work with various sessionmen (hence the billing "Stone Poneys & Friends"). It's a solid effort, though, of decent if muted Californian folk-rock, with a laid-back (but not offensively so), carefully produced feel. Certainly the material is varied, with selections from the Stone Poneys, Mike Nesmith, and Laura Nyro, and occasional intimations of the country-rock direction that Ronstadt would frequently pursue during the '70s. The inclusion of three Tim Buckley songs serves as evidence that Ronstadt was hipper than some of her detractors have made her out to be. *—Richie Unterberger*

The Stone Roses

f. 1985, Manchester, England, **db.** Oct. 1996
College Rock, Madchester, Alternative Dance, Brit-pop, Alternative Pop/Rock
Meshing '60s-styled guitar-pop with an understated '80s dance beat, the Stone Roses defined the British guitar-pop scene of the late '80s and early '90s. After their eponymous 1989 debut album became an English sensation, countless other groups in the same vein became popular. However, the band was never able to capitalize on the promise of their first album, waiting five years before they released their second record and slowly disintegrating in the year and half after its release. The Stone Roses emerged from the remains of a band formed by schoolmates John Squire (guitar) and Ian Brown (vocals). In 1987, the Stone Roses' lineup finally coalesced around Squire and Brown, plus drummer Reni (b. Alan John Wren) and bassist Mani (b. Gary Mounfield). At the end of the year, the Stone Roses released the single "Sally Cinnamon," which pointed the way toward the band's hook-laden, ringing guitar-pop. In 1989, the Stone Roses released their eponymous debut album, which demonstrated not only a predilection for '60s guitar hooks, but also a contemporary acid-house rhythmic sensibility. *The Stone Roses* received rave reviews and a single, "She Bangs the Drums," became the group's first Top 40 hit. By the end of the year, they reached the Top Ten with "Fool's Gold."

Though the group returned in 1990 with the single "One Love," the Stone Roses became embroiled in a vicious legal battle with their label. Finally, in 1991 the band signed a multi-million deal with Geffen Records. For the next three years, they worked sporadically on their second album, *Second Coming*, which received mixed reviews and only spent a few weeks in the Top Ten. Forced to cancel a headlining spot at 1995's 25th Glastonbury Festival after John Squire broke his collarbone, the Stone Roses continued to sink in popularity and respect. In the spring of 1996, Squire announced that he was leaving to form a new, more active band and, by the end of the year, the group was finished. Squire's new band, Seahorses, released their debut album in 1997, while Brown released his solo debut in 1998. *—Stephen Thomas Erlewine*

★ **The Stone Roses** / Jul. 1989 / Silvertone ♦♦♦♦♦
Since the Stone Roses were the nominal leaders of Britain's "Madchester" scene—an indie rock phenomenon that fused guitar-pop with drug-fueled rave and dance culture—it's rather ironic that their eponymous debut only hints at dance music. What made the Stone Roses important was how they welcomed dance and pop together, treating it as if it were the same beast. Equally important was the Roses' cool, detached arrogance which was personified by Ian Brown's nonchalant vocals. Brown's effortless malevolence is brought to life with songs that equal both his sentiments and his voice—"I Wanna Be Adored," with its creeping bass line and waves of cool guitar hooks, doesn't demand adoration, it just *expects* it. Similarly, Brown can claim "I Am the Resurrection" and lay back, as if there were no room for debate. But the key to *The Stone Roses* is John Squire's layers of simple, exceedingly catchy hooks and how the rhythm section of Reni and Mani always imply dance rhythms without overtly going into the disco. On "She Bangs the Drums" and "Elephant Stone," the hooks wind into the rhythm inseparably—the '60s hooks and the rolling beats manage to convey the colorful, neo-psychedelic world of acid house. Squire's riffs are bright and catchy, recalling the British Invasion while suggesting the future with their phased, echoey effects. *The Stone Roses* was a two-fold revolution—it brought dance music to an audience that was previously obsessed with droning guitars, while it revived the concept of classic pop songwriting, and the repercussions of its achievement could be heard throughout the '90s, even if the Stone Roses could never achieve this level of achievement ever again. *—Stephen Thomas Erlewine*

Turns Into Stone / Oct. 27, 1992 / Silvertone ♦♦♦♦
Brit-pop has never been performed better than on the Stone Roses' self-titled debut album. Coming somewhere near to it, however, is this, *Turns Into Stone*. Admittedly, *Turns Into Stone* isn't made up of entirely original material. Rather, the album is a sort of 'best of the Stone Roses' B-sides.' Fortunately, these are B-sides of exceptional quality. Included in among the track-list is perhaps the bands finest moment, "Fools Gold." The track is driven along by Reni's domineering drumming and Mani's understated bass line, while Squire impresses with his lead and Brown sings a rather sinister, but catchy melody. While the album's approach has taken on a dancy-edge if you will, on the whole *Turns Into Stone* retains the guitar driven musical style that dominated the Stone Roses debut. Despite not being quite as consistent as the previously mentioned release, *Turns Into Stone* has all the hallmarks of a great Brit-pop album and will delight those who enjoyed the band's first release. *—Ben Davies*

Second Coming / Dec. 1994 / Geffen ♦♦♦
There's no denying that *Second Coming* is a bit of a letdown. None of the songs are quite as strong as the best on their debut, but there is plenty of good music on the band's much-delayed second record. The Stone Roses create a dense tapestry of interweaving guitars and pulsing bass grooves. Ian Brown growls a little more than before, but he isn't the center of the music; John Squire's endlessly colorful riffs are. It's clear that Squire has been listening to a bit of hard rock, particularly Led Zeppelin. While the songs occasionally take a back seat to the grooves, several tracks—"Ten Storey Love Song," "Begging You," "Tightrope," "How Do You Sleep," and "Love Spreads"—rank as true classics. It might not be the long-awaited masterpiece it was rumored to be, but *Second Coming* is a fine sophomore effort. *—Stephen Thomas Erlewine*

The Complete Stone Roses / Jun. 27, 1995 / Silvertone ♦♦♦♦♦
The title's a bit of a misnomer. *The Complete Stone Roses* concentrates on the band's first album, compiling the A- and B-sides of the group's hits from "Elephant Stone" to "One Love." In addition to the familiar material, the disc includes rare, early singles like "So Young" and "Sally Cinnamon" for the first time on compact disc, giving their classic material some context. The loud guitars of "So Young" are clearly the work of a hesitant band, while "Sally Cinnamon" is the first indication of John Squire's gift for ringing, melodic guitar hooks. However, their inclusion—as well as the appearance of the B-sides, which lack the consistent brilliance of "I Wanna Be Adored," "She Bangs the Drums," "Elephant Stone," "Waterfall," etc.—make *The Complete Stone Roses* a flawed introduction to the band. Nevertheless, there's a fair amount of classic pop here and the rarities are necessary for dedicated fans. *—Stephen Thomas Erlewine*

Garage Flower / Nov. 1996 / Silvertone ♦♦♦
Quite possibly the best thing punk ever invented was the Stone Roses. From their seminal, classically abstract debut to their rock & roll braggadocio of its follow-up, it might be hard to remember the band first came out of the revolutionary discontentment of punk ethics. But it's here in every track of *Garage Flower*: a quasi-bootleg collection of early demos performed with all the shambolic sputter of a band just on the cusp of discovering brilliance. It all starts off sounding like an etching to one of Squire's Jackson Pollock paintings. Melding Ian Brown's atonal growls and a rhythmic splatter just this side of people slamming things against anything within reach, songs like "Tradjic Roundabout" or "Fall" flounder around until they happen upon something ingenious. Cunningly, underexposed classics shine even while drenched in demo muck. "Here It Comes"—with one of the most beautiful closing refrains ever written—has such a blissful disregard for garage-band conventions that it comes across better than its appropriate studio counterpart. Plus, the embryonic versions of the astonishing "I Wanna Be Adored" and the immortal, climaxing "This Is the One" both helpfully shine a light on the very instant when genius was discovered. While this is clearly a mess of a band trying to cobble together a proper debut, it's an utterly fascinating one. *Garage Flower* still proves that—in even their

most awkward and ungainly stages—the Stone Roses were surrounded by a sense of hushed magic. *—Dean Carlson*

Stone Temple Pilots

f. 1992

Grunge, Alternative Pop/Rock, Hard Rock

Stone Temple Pilots were able to make alternative rock into stadium rock; naturally, they became the most critically despised band of their era. Accused by many critics of being nothing more than rip-off artists, pilfering from Pearl Jam, Soundgarden, and Alice in Chains, the band nevertheless became major stars in 1993. And the influences of those bands *are* apparent in their music, but Stone Temple Pilots do manage to change things around a bit. STP are more concerned with tight song structure and riffs than punk rage. Their closest antecedents are not the Sex Pistols or Hüsker Dü; instead the band resembles arena rock acts from the '70s—it's popular hard rock that sounds good on the radio and in concert. No matter what the critics might say, Stone Temple Pilots have undeniably catchy riffs and production; there's a reason why over three million people bought their debut album, *Core*, and why their second album, *Purple*, shot to number one when it was released. Following the success of *Purple* and its accompanying tour, the band took some time off, during which the group's lead singer, Scott Weiland, developed a heroin addiction. *—Stephen Thomas Erlewine*

Core / Sep. 29, 1992 / Atlantic ♦♦♦

The Stone Temple Pilots were positively vilified once their 1992 debut *Core* started scaling the charts in 1993, pegged as fifth-rate Pearl Jam copyists. It is true that the worst moments of *Core* play like a parody of the Seattle scene—titles like "Dead and Bloated" and "Crackerman" tell you that much, playing like really bad Alice in Chains parodies, and the entire record tends to sink into gormless post-grunge sludge. Furthermore, even if it rocks pretty hard, it's usually without much character, sounding like cut-rate grunge. To be fair, it's more that they share the same influences as their peers than being overt copycats, but it's still a little disheartening all the same. If that's all that *Core* was, it'd be as forgettable as Seven Mary Three, but there are the hits that propelled it up the charts, songs that have remarkably stood the test of time to be highlights of their era. "Sex Type Thing" may have a clumsy anti-rape lyric that comes across as misogynist, but it survives on its terrifically lunk-headed riff, while "Wicked Garden" is a surprisingly effective piece of revivalist acid rock. Then, there's the slow acoustic crawl of "Creep" that works as well as anything on AIC's *Sap* and, finally, "Plush," a majestic album rock revival more melodic and stylish than anything grunge produced outside of Nirvana itself. These four songs aren't enough to salvage a fairly pedestrian debut, but they do find STP to be nimble rock craftsmen when inspiration hits. *—Stephen Thomas Erlewine*

● **Purple** / May 31, 1994 / Atlantic ♦♦♦♦

Stone Temple Pilots had hits with *Core*, but they got no respect. They suffered a barrage of savage criticism and it must have hurt, since their second effort seems a conscious effort to distinguish themselves as a band not indebted to grunge. That didn't get them anywhere, as they were attacked as viciously as before, but *Purple* is nevertheless a quantum leap over their debut, showcasing a band hitting their stride. They still aren't much for consistency, and there's more than their fair share of filler over this album's "12 Gracious Melodies." Still, this filler isn't cut-rate grunge, as it was on the debut; it has its own character, heavily melodic and slightly psychedelic. That's a fair assessment of the hits, as well, but there's a difference there—namely, expert song and studiocraft. Yes, they were considerably more mainstream than their peers, but time has proven that that's their primary charm, since they were unafraid to temper their grunge with big arena hooks and swirling melodies. It works particularly well on the tight, concise "Vasoline" and the acoustic-based "Pretty Penny," but it really shines on the record's two masterpieces, "Big Empty" and "Interstate Love Song." "Big Empty" is ominous and foreboding, yet remains anthemic, a perfect encapsulation of mainstream alienation that is surpassed only by "Interstate Love Song," a concise epic as alluring as the open highway. These two songs are so good (really, mainstream hard rock didn't get better than these two cuts) that the unevenness of the rest of the record is all the more frustrating, but the filler here is better than before—and those singles are proof positive that STP was the best straight-ahead rock singles outfit of their time. *—Stephen Thomas Erlewine*

Tiny Music . . . Songs From the Vatican Gift Shop / Mar. 26, 1996 / Atlantic ♦♦♦♦

Purple established that Stone Temple Pilots were not one-album wonders but *Tiny Music . . . Songs From the Vatican Gift Shop* illustrates that the band isn't content with resting on the laurels. Without abandoning their trademark hard rock, STP have added a new array of sounds that adds depth to their immediately accessible hooks. Dean DeLeo layers his guitar tracks to create distinctive, multi-textured sounds that make his riffs more powerful. Though there are hints of grunge scattered throughout the album, what makes *Tiny Music* impressive is how the band brings in elements of psychedelia, trancy shoegazing, jangle pop, and other forms of melodic alternative guitar pop. By accentuating their pop tendencies in both their riffs and melodies, they are able to slip in a number of creative arrangements which manage to expand their musical repertoire significantly. Although the lyrics are nearly as ambitious as the music, they simply don't have the same weight. But with a band like Stone Temple Pilots, the music is what matters and *Tiny Music* showcases the band at their most tuneful and creative. *—Stephen Thomas Erlewine*

No. 4 / Oct. 26, 1999 / Atlantic ♦♦♦♦

It would be tempting to scour *No. 4*, Weiland's reunion with Stone Temple Pilots, for insights into his troubles, yet the group consciously avoids this throughout the album. That's for the best, since it's their hardest effort since their debut, *Core*. "Down" and "Heaven & Hot Rods" provide a powerful, brutal opening for *No. 4*—it's as if STP decided to compete directly with the new generation of alt-metal bands who prize aggression over hooks or riffs. With these two songs, the band's attack is as vicious as that of the new generation, but they retain their gift for gargantuan hooks. Much of the album hits pretty hard—most explicitly on "No Way Out," "Sex & Violence," and "MC5,"—and even the ballads and neo-psychedelic pop have none of the swirling production that distinguished *Tiny Music*. That sense of adventure is missed, because even if the album finds STP returning to the muscular hard rock that made them, they always sounded better when they concentrated on melodicism. *No. 4*'s most effective moments have a variety of sonic textures and color—"Pruno" tempers its giant riffs with spacy verses; "Church on Tuesday" is a great pop tune, as are the trippy "Sour Girl" and "I Got You"; and the psychedelic "Glide" and closing ballad, "Atlanta," have a sense of majesty. These songs anchor the heavier moments, instead of the other way around, and it all plays well together. As a matter of fact, *No. 4* is as tight as *Tiny Music*. Even if it isn't as grandiose or sonically compelling as that effort, it's a record that consolidates all their strengths. *—Stephen Thomas Erlewine*

Shangri-La Dee Da / Jun. 19, 2001 / Atlantic ♦♦♦

No. 4 gave STP the comeback they were looking for, albeit a little later and a little differently than expected. Nearly a year after its release, "Sour Girl" gave the band its biggest hit in years, and it set up their fifth album, *Shangri-La Dee Da*, perfectly. They seized this opportunity by turning out the same record as the time before, splitting the difference between heavy rockers and sugar-sweet psych-pop tunes. That's not a bad thing, nor is it unexpected, since they've basically been staking this same territory since *Tiny Music*, yet at this point, it feels as if the Pilots are comfortably within a musical groove, no matter how much turmoil they have privately. And, while this doesn't result in a particularly surprising record, it's not an album that's bad, either. Here, as on *4*, they're not just better on the pop tunes, they're phenomenal on the pop tunes. Regardless of their critical reputation, no rock band of their time turned out such a consistently dazzling streak of pop tunes. Sometimes, the rockers do catch hold—"Dumb Love" provides a gripping opening, "Hollywood Bitch" has a real sense of propulsion, the dreamy "Hello It's Late" has a gentle rush of its own—but, by this point, they don't seem as interesting as the excursions into psych-pop that gives *Shangri-La Dee Da* its real core. That's nothing new, but that's not a bad thing at all. *—Stephen Thomas Erlewine*

The Stooges

f. 1967, Ann Arbor, MI, **db.** 1973

Detroit Rock, Album Rock, Proto-Punk, Glam Rock, Hard Rock

During the psychedelic haze of the late '60s, the grimy, noisy, and relentlessly bleak rock & roll of the Stooges was conspicuously out of time. Like the Velvet Underground, the Stooges revealed the underside of sex, drugs, and rock & roll, showing all of the grime beneath the myth. The Stooges, however, weren't nearly as cerebral as the Velvets. Taking their cue from the over-amplified pounding of British blues, the primal raunch of American garage rock, and the psychedelic rock (as well as the audience-baiting) of the Doors, the Stooges were raw, immediate, and vulgar. Iggy Pop became notorious for performing smeared in blood or peanut butter, diving into the audience. Ron and Scott Asheton formed a ridiculously primitive rhythm section, pounding out chords with no finesse—in essence, the Stooges were the first rock & roll band completely stripped of the swinging beat that epitomized R&B and early rock & roll. During the late '60s and early '70s, the group was an underground sensation, yet the band was too weird, too dangerous to break into the mainstream. Following three albums, the Stooges disbanded, but the group's legacy grew over the next two decades, as legions of underground bands used their sludgy grind as a foundation for a variety of indie-rock styles, and as Iggy Pop became a pop cultural icon. *—Stephen Thomas Erlewine*

The Stooges / 1969 / Elektra ♦♦♦♦♦

While the Stooges had a few obvious points of influence—the swagger of the early Rolling Stones, the horny pound of the Troggs, the fuzztone sneer of a thousand teenage garage bands, and the Velvet Underground's experimental eagerness to leap into the void—they didn't really sound like anyone else around when their first album hit the streets in 1969. It's hard to say if Ron Asheton, Scott Asheton, Dave Alexander, and the man then known as Iggy Stooge were capable of making anything more sophisticated than this, but if they were, they weren't letting on, and the best moments of this record document the blithering inarticulate fury of the post-adolescent id. Ron Asheton's guitar runs (fortified with bracing use of fuzztone and wah-wah) are so brutal and concise they achieve a naive genius, while Scott Asheton's proto-Bo Diddley drums and Dave Alexander's solid bass stomp these tunes into submission with a force that inspires awe. And Iggy's vividly blank vocals fill the "so what?" shrug of a thousand teenagers with a wealth of palpable arrogance and wondrous confusion. One of the problems with being a trailblazing pioneer is making yourself understood to others, and while John Cale seemed sympathetic to what the band was doing, he didn't appear to quite get it, and as a result he made a physically powerful band sound a bit sluggish on tape. But "1969," "I Wanna Be Your Dog," "Real Cool Time," "No Fun," and other classic rippers are on board, and one listen reveals why they became clarion calls in the punk rock revolution. Part of the fun of *The Stooges* is, then as now, the band managed the difficult feat of sounding ahead of their time and entirely *out* of their time, all at once. *—Mark Deming*

☆ **Fun House** / 1970 / Elektra ♦♦♦♦♦

The Stooges' first album was produced by a classically trained composer; their second was supervised by the former keyboard player with the Kingsmen, and if that didn't make all the difference, it at least indicates why *Fun House* was a step in the right direction. Producer Don Gallucci took the approach that the Stooges were a powerhouse live band, and their best bet was to recreate the band's live set with as little fuss as possible. As a result, the production on *Fun House* bears some resemblance to the Kingsmen's version of "Louie Louie"—the sound is smeary and bleeds all over the place, but it packs the low-tech wallop of a concert pumped through a big PA, bursting with energy and immediacy. The Stooges were also a much stronger band this time out; Ron Asheton's blazing minimalist guitar gained little in the way of technique since *The Stooges*, but his confidence had grown by a quantum leap as he summoned forth the sounds that would make him the hero of proto-punk guitarists everywhere, and the brutal pound of drummer Scott Asheton and bassist Dave Alexander had grown to Heavyweight Champion status. And *Fun House* is where Iggy Pop's mad genius first reached its full flower; what was a sneer on the band's debut had grown into the roar of a caged animal desperate for release, and his primal-scream rants were far more passionate and compelling than what he had served up before. *The Stooges* may have had more "hits," but *Fun House* has stronger songs, including the garage raver to end all garage ravers in "Loose," the primal scream of "1970," and the apocalyptic anarchy of "L.A. Blues." *Fun House* is the ideal document of the Stooges at their raw, sweaty, howling peak. —*Mark Deming*

★ **Raw Power** / 1973 / Columbia/Legacy ✦✦✦✦✦
In 1972, the Stooges were near the point of collapse when David Bowie's management team, MainMan, took a chance on the band at Bowie's behest. By this point, guitarist Ron Asheton and bassist Dave Alexander had been edged out of the picture, and James Williamson had signed on as Iggy's new guitar mangler; Asheton rejoined the band shortly before recording commenced on *Raw Power*, but was forced to play second fiddle to Williamson as bassist. By most accounts, tensions were high during the recording of *Raw Power*, and the album sounds like the work of a band on its last legs—though rather than grinding to a halt, Iggy and the Stooges appeared ready to explode like an ammunition dump. From a technical standpoint, Williamson was a more gifted guitar player than Asheton (not that that was ever the point), but his sheets of metallic fuzz were still more basic (and punishing) than what anyone was used to in 1973, while Ron Asheton played his bass like a weapon of revenge, and his brother Scott Asheton remained a powerhouse behind the drums. But the most remarkable change came from the singer; *Raw Power* revealed Iggy as a howling, smirking, lunatic genius. Whether quietly brooding ("Gimme Danger") or inviting the apocalypse ("Search and Destroy"), Iggy had never sounded quite so focused as he did here, and his lyrics displayed an intensity that was more than a bit disquieting. In many ways, almost all *Raw Power* has in common with the two Stooges albums that preceded it is its primal sound, but while the Stooges once sounded like the wildest (and weirdest) gang in town, *Raw Power* found them heavily armed and ready to destroy the world—that is, if they didn't destroy themselves first. —*Mark Deming*

Metallic K.O. / 1976 / Skydog ✦✦✦✦✦
Metallic K.O. isn't quite as epochal as its reputation would have you believe. Time has had its way with it, diluting its original impact, not just through the natural ebb and flow of time, but in the way that historical accuracy has given us a record that might be true to the letter but betrays the myth. Most of the original bootlegs of *Metallic K.O.* consisted of two separate performances, both recorded toward the end of the band's run, including their very final show, legendary for Iggy's baiting of a hostile audience of drunk bikers. This bootleg was ferocious, capturing the highlights of both shows, distilling its rawest essence. *Metallic 2X KO* performs a historical service by presenting the two shows in their entirety and while this is welcome, separating the performance does a disservice to the myth. On the original vinyl, the second half of both shows is captured, and the momentum is blinding, capturing the Stooges gleefully careening through a set of new material (including songs like "Cock in Pocket" and "I Got a Right" that didn't show up on studio albums). Here, even the final show seems more like a conventional show—albeit a show that ends with bottles being thrown onto the stage and the singer brazenly taunting an audience that hates him. And the funny thing about this is that it seems more fun than scary, just a big prank pulled by the Stooges, as they recklessly belt out their sleaziest songs and ending it all with a monumental version of "Louie Louie." Yes, the recording is an audience tape and it's nearly anti-audiophile, but music this raw and unhinged deserves nothing less. And make no mistake, in any incarnation, this is one of the best rock live albums, nothing but pure, insane energy. —*Stephen Thomas Erlewine*

Kill City / 1977 / Bomp! ✦✦✦✦✦
Kill City helped bridge Iggy Pop's musical career from the drug-fueled and blazing rock of the Stooges (*Raw Power*, etc.) to the more arty (but just as influential and passionate) David Bowie-produced solo albums (*The Idiot* & *Lust for Life*). After the Stooges broke up for good in 1974, Iggy (who was depressed, suicidal, and addicted to hard drugs) checked himself into a mental hospital to straighten out. When he emerged sober, Iggy hooked up with ex-Stooges guitarist James Williamson and began collaborating on demos. The duo tried to land a record contract on the strength of the compositions, but failed to do so. Although it's not as jaw-dropping as the releases listed above, *Kill City* certainly has its moments. And surprisingly, the songs sound more like laid-back Stones rockers than what the duo was known for at the time (which was barely containable near-heavy metal). There are a couple of Stooges leftovers ("Johanna" & "I Got Nothin") which lack the bite of the originals, but make up for it in Iggy's heartfelt vocals. The title track opens the album, with the lyrics painting a picture of a desperate and dangerous metropolis, and musically is the closest to the classic Stooges' sound. Iggy and James' admiration of Jagger and Richards shows on the tracks "Sell Your Love," "Lucky Monkeys," and the instrumental "Night Theme." Also, synthesizers and keyboards are featured on "Master Charge," signaling the new direction Iggy would soon embark on. Also included are informative liner notes which do a good job of showing where Iggy's head was at during his mid-'70s, refocusing period. An interesting release, worthy of belonging in any Stooges/Iggy fan's collection. —*Greg Prato*

I Got a Right / 1987 / Revenge ✦✦✦
When Iggy and the newly reformed Stooges were starting work on what would eventually their final album, *Raw Power*, their initial efforts shocked their management and were summarily rejected, only to surface on numerous vinyl bootlegs over the next couple of decades. One of the more famous couplings was released as a single, the flame throwing "I Got A Right" and the equally wild "Gimme Some Skin." This collection rounds up every existing take of those two titles with a live version of the title cut to round things out. This is Iggy and the Stooges at arguably their peak and well worth seeking out as the sound is appreciably better than the original 45 issue. —*Cub Koda*

Rough Power / Jan. 30, 1995 / Bomp! ✦✦✦
The final mix by David Bowie of the Stooges' final studio album has been a subject of open debate since the day of its release in 1973. Some see it as a total botch job, with the vocals and guitar overdubs set so far out front of the bass and drums (collapsed into mono, stripped of its high frequencies, then echoed to death) as to appear comical. Others see it as a mix every bit as anarchic as the music itself. That debate is fueled even further by the first legal appearances of these alternate mixes done by Iggy and the Stooges prior to Bowie's intervention. On tracks like "I Need Somebody" and "Gimme Danger," the focus is much sharper than the released version, while on others ("Hard to Beat," "Raw Power," "Search and Destroy") Iggy's vocal is obscured by liberal doses of too much echo. An aircheck from early 1973 gives us grainy, abrasive speeded up alternates of seven more tracks and the compilation closes with three more from late in 1972, clearly showing that the boys had theories on mixing that were every bit as off the wall as Bowie's finals. Final score: not necessarily better, but very different. —*Cub Koda*

Year of the Iguana / Feb. 27, 1997 / Bomp! ✦✦✦
There's little doubt that in the 20 years plus since their demise as a group, Iggy and the Stooges have achieved legendary status as the seminal and defining influence on the late-'70s punk rock movement; without them, there would have been no Sex Pistols, etc. And in those intervening years, they have found themselves being exhaustively documented, with seemingly every scrap of magnetic tape bearing their imprint coming up for reissue air at one time or another. This is an interesting collection that's primarily culled from other Bomp CD collections and 10" vinyl LPs. If you're into Iggy and the Stooges enough to have made it *this* far, this collection of alternate mixes ("Death Trip"), raw rehearsal tapes ("Rubber Legs," "Head On," "Till the End of the Night," "Wild Love," and an extended run through of "Raw Power"), and "suppressed masters" from the original *Raw Power* sessions ("I Got a Right," "Gimme Some Skin," and "Scene of the Crime") will almost seem like a greatest-hits package of sorts. And for the new fan who's just discovered the chaotic magic that was the Stooges—and has heard the rumors that there's material far more incendiary than their three studio albums—this compilation will serve just that purpose, sifting through the unending maze of unissued Stooges material to make a single-disc package that hits on the spots. This make a nice stopping-off point before moving on to the group's live masterpiece, *Metallic K.O.*. The transfers are well done here (considering the point of origin of several of them) and for a compilation pulled from multiple and disparate sources, this collections hangs together remarkably well, providing the hardcore fan with a one-stop loaded with rarities. —*Cub Koda*

1970: The Complete Fun House Sessions / 2000 / Rhino Handmade ✦✦✦✦
While fans of the Stooges are by their nature a hardy breed, this set is the ultimate litmus test to separate casual admirers from the truly obsessed: *1970: The Complete Fun House Sessions* is a six-CD set that contains every single sound the Stooges committed to tape while making the album *Fun House*. False starts, mikes going haywire, bad jokes, Iggy Pop imitating a wrestler, Ron Asheton and Scott Asheton trying to play "Wipeout"—it's all here, along with 30 (count 'em!) takes of "Loose" spread out over seven and three-quarter hours. While this is admittedly tough going for any but the most devoted Stooges fan, it's more a matter of bulk than a question of quality. The performances are remarkably consistent throughout, and while the multiple takes of each song get to be a bit much after a while, the songs do indeed grow and shift as they go along; the Stooges seem to have taken the approach that they knew how these songs would start and finish, but what happened in the middle was up for grabs. And it's obvious that the band knew what they wanted for this album; there are only two unreleased songs on deck, neither of which they spent much time on, and the between song patter is kept to a minimum. For a band that's often regarded as sloppy and incoherent, *1970: The Complete Fun House Sessions* indicates that the Stooges were a lot more focused and methodical in the studio than anyone might have imagined; this set is fun and fascinating for those strong enough to wade through it. —*Mark Deming*

Stories

f. 1972, New York, NY, **db.** 1973
Pop/Rock

Though originally helmed by onetime Left Banke mastermind Michael Brown, Stories ironically scored their lone hit, the 1973 chart-topper "Brother Louie," following Brown's exit from the lineup. After leaving Left Banke in 1967, Brown—the keyboardist who composed the group's classic "Walk Away, Renee" and "Pretty Ballerina"—cut a 1969 LP with the band Montage which closely recalled the pioneering baroque pop approach of his previous work; he then formed Stories with vocalist Ian Lloyd, guitarist Steve Love, and drummer Bryan Medley. Following the group's self-titled 1972 Kama Sutra label debut, the mercurial Brown abruptly resigned, at which point the remaining Stories recruited bassist Kenny Aaronson and pianist Ken Bichel to record 1973's *About Us*. "Brother Louie," a tale of interracial romance penned by Hot Chocolate's Errol Brown, hit number one that summer, but Stories never again returned to the Top 40. Brown, meanwhile, resurfaced in 1976, leading the short-lived Beckies before spending the following decades out of the limelight. *—Jason Ankeny*

Stories / 1972 / Kama Sutra ✦✦✦✦✦
The Stories' first album is gentler, and closer in mood to the Left Banke, than the subsequent *About Us*, which is good news for Left Banke fans. Although the quality of the Brown-Lloyd compositions is uneven, it's generally good, though the songs are a bit modest and self-effacing. It's at its best when Brown whips out those classical/baroque keyboard and melodic flourishes that were among his trademarks since the Left Banke days. Sometimes it's on the edge of the tuneful hard rock style the Beatles and Badfinger essayed on mid-tempo numbers in the late 1960s and early 1970s. At other times there's almost a harder rock-vaudevillian meld, somewhat in the style of the late 1960s Kinks. It was pretty out of step with most of what else was going on in rock and pop in the early 1970s, and not even too well known to power pop revivalists, although to be honest this is on the fringe of power pop since it emphasizes keyboards and dainty ballads more than electric guitars and cheerful up-tempo tunes. Still, it's well worth rediscovery by fans of pop/rock with unusual and inventive melodies and vocal harmonies. *—Richie Unterberger*

Traveling Underground / 1973 / One Way ✦✦✦
With 1973's *Traveling Underground*, Stories changed its name to Ian Lloyd & Stories and unveiled a new five-man lineup. Lead singer Lloyd (a whiskey-voiced belter comparable to Rod Stewart and Led Zeppelin's Robert Plant), guitarist Steve Love, and drummer Bryan Madey were still on board. But keyboardist/composer Michael Brown (a graduate of Left Banke and Montage) was gone, and the new members were keyboardist Kenneth Bichel and bassist Kenny Aaronson. *Traveling Underground* proved that there was life after Brown for Stories; this is a generally solid effort, although *About Us* remains the band's most essential album. Like before, Stories came out with an R&B-minded single that doesn't sound anything like the rest of the album it's on. "Mammy Blue" is as different from the other songs on *Traveling Underground* as "Brother Louie" is from the rest of *About Us*. A long way from the R&B leanings of "Mammy Blue," tracks like "Stories Untold," "Hard When You're So Far Away," and "Earth Bound/Freefall" favor the type of baroque art-rock approach that had worked so well on Stories' previous releases. "Brother Louie" and "Mammy Blue" indicated that Stories might have made a great blue-eyed soul band, instead, *Traveling Underground* is the work of a fine pop-rock/art-rock band that occasionally detoured into blue-eyed soul. *—Alex Henderson*

● **About Us** / 1973 / Pair ✦✦✦✦
Michael Brown and Ian Lloyd had the luxury of producing their own self-titled debut, no doubt due in part to the success of Brown's days with Left Banke. Eddie Kramer co-produces five of the initial 12 songs on this wonderful follow-up album entitled *About Us*—initial because the recording had two lives. Brown left the band and the new Stories went into the studio with former Music Connection magazine editor and producer of Gladys Knight, Kenny Kerner. He and Richie Wise recorded a song written by Errol Brown/Tony Wilson and released by their British band Hot Chocolate. The song was "Brother Louie," a strange concoction of the Hot Chocolate sound found on their latter-day hit "Emma" and the Kingsmen's "Louie Louie." Kama Sutra later put the 45 in the original pressing's sleeve before adding it as a 13th track on *About Us*. That unique Hot Chocolate song was a far cry from the Paul McCartney-ish pop of opening track "Darling" or closing track "What Comes After," and the hit song's production was a lot heavier than the light pop which was Brown's trademark, something Lloyd translated very nicely. The rock & roll pop of "Top of the City" is most indicative of the music on *About Us*. The album is representative of the two sides of Stories and, despite all the changes happening to the group at the time, is a very fine record. *—Joe Viglione*

Walk Away From the Left Banke / 1989 / See For Miles ✦✦✦✦
Most listeners probably only know the Stories as the band behind the early-'70s one-hit wonder "Brother Louie," an eerily lush tale of interracial love. The fact that the song, even with its wah-wah guitars and period strings, was still eerie and lush should have signaled that the people behind could have been partially responsible for a band as evocative as the Left Banke, which they were. See for Miles' collection, *Walk Away From the Left Banke*, illustrates this very well over the course of its 20 tracks. Left Banke fanatics shouldn't come in looking for baroque pop on the level of that fabled group, but this is excellent pop-prog in its own right, worth seeking out for pop fetishists and Banke devoted. *—Stephen Thomas Erlewine*

Izzy Stradlin

b. Apr. 8, 1962
Vocals, Guitar / American Trad Rock, Roots Rock, Hard Rock, Rock & Roll
After leaving Guns & Roses, guitarist Izzy Stradlin formed a band, the JuJu Hounds, that accentuated the Rolling Stones and Faces undertones that were always in his music. His 1992 debut is an underrated record, full of great songwriting and effortless rocking; the follow-up, *117 Degrees*, did not appear until 1998. *—Stephen Thomas Erlewine*

● **Izzy Stradlin & the Ju Ju Hounds** / Oct. 13, 1992 / Geffen ✦✦✦✦✦
Izzy Stradlin was always the most gifted member of Guns & Roses, able to put a modern spin on the classic rock of Chuck Berry, the Stones, and the Faces, as well as the New York Dolls and Sex Pistols. Axl may have had the angst and Slash may have had the chops, but Izzy had the smarts and the heart. On his debut album, the traditional elements that had always formed the backbone of Stradlin's music with Guns & Roses comes to the forefront—it's Stones and Faces all the way, but it is done well. *Izzy Stradlin & the Ju Ju Hounds* is terrific only half of the time, which is good enough for a debut album. *—Stephen Thomas Erlewine*

117 Degrees / Mar. 10, 1998 / Geffen ✦✦✦
Well, Izzy Stradlin sure didn't spend the five and a half years between his first two solo records rethinking his music. *117 Degrees* picks up right where *The Ju Ju Hounds* left off, offering a set of 14 bluesy hard rockers in the vein of Chuck Berry, the Stones, the Faces, Aerosmith and, yes, Guns & Roses. There are no surprises, in other words. There also isn't anything quite as good as his underappreciated classic-in-waiting "Shuffle It All," but *117 Degrees* rocks harder than most roots-rock albums of the late '90s. And Stradlin is a roots-rocker by this point. None of his contemporaries are even trying for this kind of unassuming, straightforward, well-crafted hard rock, and by pursuing this direction so doggedly (he even covers Berry's "Memphis"), he sounds like a throwback to another era, much like all the Americana bands of the late '90s. His music sounds fresher than many of those roots-rockers because he just wants to play, not preserve heritage, but the ironic thing is when he's on, he's a better songwriter than almost any of them. He has his down moments on the album, but songs like "Ain't It a Bitch" and "Here Before You" make up for the weaknesses. Ultimately, there's no good reason why it took Stradlin so long to deliver a follow-up other than that he really seems to have no contact with the outside world, but that's part of his charm and part of the reason why *117 Degrees* is endearing despite its faults. *—Stephen Thomas Erlewine*

Ride On / 1999 / Universal/Victor ✦✦✦

The Strangeloves

f. 1964, Brooklyn, NY, **db.** 1968
Garage Rock, Rock & Roll
While the Strangeloves managed to produce one garage band classic, their story is probably more interesting than their actual music. Bob Feldman, Jerry Goldstein, and Richard Gottehrer were a trio of Brooklyn songwriter-producers who landed a number one girl group hit with the Angels' "My Boyfriend's Back." When the British Invasion crested in the mid-'60s, they decided to get in on the act by recording as a group, billing themselves as an Australian outfit to cash in on the mystique being attached to foreign groups.

"I Want Candy," with its crunching Bo Diddley beat, joyous chorus, and rambling lead guitar, was their great moment, reaching number 11 in 1965. Forced to put together a live act to support their disc, they made outrageous claims to hail from the nonexistent town of Armstrong, Australia, where they had made a fortune as sheepherders who had developed a cross-breed. They also made the Top 40 with a couple fairly gutsy follow-ups, "Cara-Lin" and "Night Time," both of which were built around crunching claps, stomps, and drums. Also recording an album and several non-hit singles, most of their material unashamedly plagiarized the Bo Diddley beats of "I Want Candy," with forgettable results. They withdrew from performing and recording to concentrate on writing and producing for the McCoys, although Strangeloves releases continued to appear until 1968. Goldstein went on to produce records for War in the 1970s, and Gottehrer produced efforts by Blondie, the Go-Go's, and others. *—Richie Unterberger*

● **I Want Candy: The Best of the Strangeloves** / 1995 / Epic/Legacy ✦✦✦✦✦
Twenty tracks from the mid-'60s, including all the hits, a lot of stuff from their sole LP, non-hit singles, rare 45s they recorded for Swan (in 1964) and Sire (in 1968), and an item they put out under the pseudonym of the Beach-Nuts. But it's really not deserving of such thoughtful archiving; beyond "I Want Candy," "Cara-Lin," and "Night Time," only hardcore collectors will be interested. *—Richie Unterberger*

Stranglers

f. 1974
British Punk, Post-Punk, Punk
As were their contemporaries the Vibrators, the Stranglers were faux-punks; grimy, slightly arty rockers that found the notoriety surrounding punk bands too irresistible to ignore. So armed with short haircuts and reticent about revealing their true ages, the Stranglers became stars of Brit punk's class of 1976-77, garnering headlines for their sexist posturing, drug use, and occasional arrests as well as their music. Their first two albums (*Rattus Norvegicus* and *No More Heroes*) featured plenty of taut, guitar-driven songs, rife with urban doom and gloom. After 1978's *Black and White* failed to generate much interest, A&M dropped them, though the Stranglers soldiered on. Prisoners of their own careerist impulses, the Stranglers turned to covering older rock classics in a desperate attempt to win American ears. Trying twice, first with the Kinks' "All Day and All of the Night" and then ? & the Mysterians' "96 Tears," the Stranglers sounded as if flogging a dead horse was the best they could do. Gone also was their characteristic gritty and grimy sound replaced by a pop sheen that smelled of adult, new wave marketability (eventually Queen producer Roy Thomas Baker was brought in to help). The saga of the Stranglers is one of a band hanging around far too long. *—John Dougan*

Rattus Norvegicus / Apr. 1977 / A&M ✦✦✦
Like the Vibrators, the Stranglers were an older band which managed to gain visibility and success through association with Britain's punk movement. Musically, the group is much more polished than some of their rawer brethren such as the Adverts and Siouxsie and the Banshees. The Stranglers' early work is most properly described as stripped-down pop played with a hardcore sensibility; fairly lengthy songs with frequent solo breaks, prominent keyboard usage, and occasional employment of vocal harmony sets them apart from their peers. But snarling lead singing that puts forth macho/critical/distasteful lyrics predominates here, clearly showing the group's punk affinity. Most of the songs on this album fit the description of hardcore pop to a tee, but there are a few deviations from this model. "Princess of the Streets" is a slow-tempo selection with blueslike echoes. The ambitious "Down in the Sewer" crosses the concept of episodic numbers like the Who's "A Quick One" with early-'60s instrumentals. And the energetic "London Lady"

is almost a true punk song—or at least as close as the band gets to one. While not the equal of their best album, *No More Heroes*, this release is solid and worthwhile, a rewarding listen. *—David Cleary*

No More Heroes / Oct. 1977 / A&M ✦✦✦✦✦
Rattus is hardly a punk rock classic but still is a pretty good chunk of art-punk. Hugh Cornwell's testosterone level is very high here, and the macho preening gets a bit much, but it's still an enjoyable bit of noise that holds up better than anyone would have guessed at the time. Still, it's odd to think of this as a part of the punk rock era—with the exception of the fast and sloppy production by Martin Rushent, and the short songs, there's not much that's overtly punk about it. *Heroes* on the other hand is faster, nastier, and better. At this point the Stranglers were on top of their game, and the ferocity and anger that suffuses these records would never be repeated. *—John Dougan*

Black & White / 1978 / A&M ✦✦✦
Of the first three Stranglers albums, *Black & White* is arguably the weakest, yet it still has some absolutely stunning moments. For example, the epic "Toiler on the Sea" picks up where "Down in the Sewer" and "School Mam" left off on the band's two previous efforts. Ignore the fact that it's a concept album (it has a black side, and a white side, see) and that there are a couple of slightly ill-judged efforts ("In the Shadows" is plain silly, "Outside Tokyo" is whimsical rubbish), and let the rest of the album burn through your speakers. "Nice 'n' Sleazy" does just what it says on the bottle (the band was getting themselves into awful trouble hiring strippers for open air gigs to dance to this one), and "Death and Night and Blood (Yukio)" includes one of those inimitable Stranglers moments: "Bring me a piece of my mummy/She was quite close to me." All together now! *—Alex Ogg*

Live (X Cert) / 1978 / IRS ✦✦✦
Recorded at various gigs in 1977-78, *X-Cert* is worthy if only to hear Hugh Cornwell bait and insult the audience (very punk!). Plus the band sounds pretty good, loads of aggression and volume add to the fun. Not essential but a very interesting snapshot of an era. *—John Dougan*

The Raven / 1979 / United Artists ✦✦✦
By the time this album was released, the group had branched out a bit from their punk-influenced pop music stylings and grouchy personal-relationship-based lyrics. Half the songs on this album (among them "Dead Loss Angeles" [sic], "Nuclear Device," "Shah Shah a Gogo," [sic] and "Genetix" [sic]) spout verses critical of social or political issues. Only the first of these four numbers, with its clipped vocal delivery and stripped-down, bass-heavy arrangement, shows significant Brit-punk influence. Certain songs here exhibit strong mainstream tendencies with no hardcore sensibilities whatsoever, such as "Duchess" (a tuneful power pop number with clear chart-oriented influences) and "Don't Bring Harry" (a slow-tempo, piano-dominated selection). Still other influences can be seen in "Meninblack," a Devo-derived number featuring a synthesized clipped beat/electronic pulse texture, chilly and sanitized-sounding organ, lockstep drums, and Alvin and the Chipmunks-style sped-up vocals. The intriguing "Ice" boasts interesting production touches and an inventively dubious tonal focus. The songs are lengthy, with at times prolix instrumental openings and interludes. Sound quality on the EMI America re-release is uneven at times, with occasional distortion in the drums and percussive low synthesizer. This is a generally good album worth hearing. Original pressings of this release have a 3-D picture on the front cover. Approximately half the songs on this album would be reissued one year later on the U.S. label release *IV*. *—David Cleary*

Stranglers IV / 1980 / IRS ✦✦
A stopgap American-only release that introduced the then-new song "Vietnamerica." No small irony there, given that the Stranglers never thought much of the U.S. (check out "Dead Loss Angeles" on *The Raven* or the later single "Big in America"). When they lost all of their equipment to New York thieves around this time, that just about set the seal on their contempt for the country. In addition to five tracks from 1979's superb *The Raven* plus recent singles, the album originally came with a free 7" EP (featuring Stranglers chestnuts "Choosey Suzie" and "Straighten Out," as well as one track each from the recent solo work of Burnel and Cornwell). *—Alex Ogg*

The Meninblack / 1981 / Liberty ✦✦

La Folie / 1981 / Liberty ✦✦✦✦
La Folie is a welcome album in the group's oeuvre, mainly a collection of tight, punchy songs that often suggest the forthright approach of American new wave bands. With one exception, the songs are shorter and more pointed, hearkening back to the comparative conciseness of some of the tunes on the band's first two albums, *Rattus Norvegicus* and *No More Heroes*, though acidic lyrics still predominate. "Non-Stop" is a typical example, featuring a half-spoken vocal that suggests Lou Reed, a Cars-influenced organ sound, and a bouncy, dance-derived drum beat; this particular song is atypical, however, because it employs a blues-oriented progression. An interesting excursion is encountered in the song "Golden Brown," a subdued, jazz-influenced number with purring vocals, a coolly executed synthesizer/harpsichord backing texture, and a periodically stumbling beat. Only the plushly understated title track suggests the sprawl typical of the group's immediately preceding releases. This fine album is well worth purchasing. *—David Cleary*

Feline / 1983 / Epic ✦✦✦
Another Stranglers concept album, but a much lesser work than forerunner *La Folie*. While not an instant classic, it does repay repeated listening—especially the rustic English charms of "Midsummer Night's Dream" and the more Eurocentric "Last Tango in Paris" and "All Roads Lead to Rome." Instead of the belligerent tunefulness of yesteryear, the Stranglers were trying to expand their sound and reach. Too often on this lackluster effort, however, it comes across as boring and unengaging. *—Alex Ogg*

Aural Sculpture / 1984 / Epic ✦✦✦✦
A massively underrated album by a band too quickly dismissed as relevant only to the '70s—fair enough, as the accompanying statement of intent (the title was meant to be descriptive) is pretentious rubbish. Yet there is a real majesty to some of these pop compositions, notably Burnel's devastating "North Winds." The hit single "Skin Deep" is excellent, if a little self-important. Other cuts, like the infectious "Uptown" and "Mad Hatter," reveal the eternally grim Stranglers to be in a playful mood. Not quite what everyone expected, but a great album nevertheless. *—Alex Ogg*

Dreamtime / 1987 / Epic ✦✦

● **Greatest Hits 1977-1990** / 1990 / Epic ✦✦✦✦✦
Despite its rather cheeky title, this is a good place to sample the entire Stranglers output. From the squalor of the late-'70s material, to the smoothed out gloom pop of songs like "Skin Deep" and other mid- to late-'80s neo-goth rock, this is a solid anthology that values substance over style and exhaustive track selection. Trust me, a well-edited Stranglers anthology is the only way to enjoy them, they recorded way too much dross to spend time searching out all of their plentiful, marginal records. *—John Dougan*

10 / May 1990 / Epic ✦✦✦
Over an illustrious history (and don't let those so-called punk historians tell you that they either weren't punk or weren't important) the Stranglers actually released very, very few bad albums. *10*, sad to say, is one of the few, and it's an absolute stinker. Having creaked into the '90s, this proved to be the final album from the original lineup (who'd been together for 15 years), their tenth studio album giving them the inspiration for the title. The truth is, there was barely concealed hatred percolating between main men Jean-Jacques Burnel and Hugh Cornwell. Yet rather than produce any kind of edge, the tensions inexplicably resulted in this meager fare of dislocated pop and half-assed R&B. There really are no discernible redeeming features. *—Alex Ogg*

The Old Testament / 1992 / EMI ✦✦✦✦
A lavish package celebrating the myriad bumps, bruises, and highlights of the Stranglers' earliest and best, the boastfully titled *Old Testament* is a four-CD set that spans the group's first six albums (up to 1981's *La Folie*), also including a number of non-LP singles and B-sides. It also contains an exhaustive—if blindly... er, boastful—112-page book, which makes the package all the more attractive for longtime fans who have long since hunter-gathered the rarities. It would be a major gamble to make this your first Stranglers purchase, especially due to the 1997 release of *The Hit Men*, which runs through the band's stylistically varied singles and doesn't indulge too much in the Stranglers' lengthy deterioration phase(s). They were productive from 1977-1981, discounting the number of album tracks that really shouldn't have seen the light of day. Make no mistake, nearly every good thing they did can be found within these four discs, save for the odd later hit like 1984's soft rock gem "Skin Deep." The band's rampant misogyny, occasional lapses into racial faux pas, and odd fixations on pointless violence can almost be forgiven through the undeniable musicianship and ability to write a great pop song, not to mention nasty corkers like "(Get a) Grip (on Yourself)" and "Toiler on the Sea." Lunkheadedness and quality control issues aside, the 80-plus songs on *The Old Testament* definitely prove the Stranglers to be worthy of a box set. *—Andy Kellman*

The Early Years 74-75-76 / Oct. 14, 1994 / Castle ✦✦✦
If you feel like joining in the debate on whether the Stranglers were really a punk band, and you fancy being a witness for the prosecution, you could do worse than hunt down these pre-first album demos. Yep, they definitely sped things up a little hereafter. Most interesting of all is a version of "Strange Little Girl," one of the Stranglers' finest pop singles, several years before it was finally released. *—Alex Ogg*

About Time / 1995 / When? ✦✦

Saturday Night Sunday Morning [Live] / Mar. 10, 1996 / Castle ✦✦

Written in Red / 1997 / When ✦✦

The Hit Men 1977-1991 / Feb. 1997 / EMI ✦✦✦✦✦
The Stranglers worked better as a singles band than they did as album artists, but that doesn't mean that the double-disc, 43-track retrospective *The Hit Men 1977-1991* is consistently engaging. Considerably older than their punk peers, the Stranglers nevertheless knocked out several terrific songs in their first records, including "(Get A) Grip (On Yourself)" and "Hanging Around," but by the mid-'80s they had become a little bland and predictable, as evidenced by covers of "96 Tears" and "All Day and All of the Night." That decline is charted on *The Hit Men*, as it runs through all of the group's EMI and Epic singles, as well as selected album tracks. All of the group's best moments are here, but there's also an abundance of mediocre tracks making this of interest primarily to completists. Casual fans will be content with the single-disc *Greatest Hits 1977-1990*. *—Stephen Thomas Erlewine*

The UA Singles / Jun. 2001 / EMI ✦✦✦✦

Syd Straw

Vocals / Jangle Pop, Alternative Pop/Rock, Folk-Pop, College Rock, Adult Alternative Pop/Rock

Vocalist, singer/songwriter, and guitarist Syd Straw first made a name for herself as part of the Golden Palominos, a band led by Anton Fier that enjoyed a cult following in the 1980s. Her Capricorn Records debut, *War and Peace*, was released in 1996, and since then her unique blend of folk-rock and blues-rock have found a home with triple A (adult album alternative) radio stations and their audiences around the country. Straw has only one other solo album, *Surprise*, released in 1990 to good reviews. That recording chronicled Straw's emergence as a songwriter; she had thought of herself primarily as a song interpreter before that. On *Surprise*, Straw was joined by Michael Stipe (R.E.M.),

John Doe (X), Ry Cooder, Daniel Lanois, Don Was, Richard Thompson, and Marshall Crenshaw. Although Straw may have few albums out, she's an enormously gifted vocalist and songwriter who has her own distinct musical vision, as evidenced on her self-produced *War and Peace*. That vision is a rootsy one, with lots of country and blues influences. Her 14 originals on the record prove it. Although she didn't set out to, she also plays rhythm guitar on many of the tracks on the album. Great records and a wider following are in the offing for this unique, multi-genre vocalist and songwriter. *—Richard Skelly*

● **Surprise** / Jun. 1989 / Virgin ♦♦♦♦♦

Singer/songwriter Syd Straw's 1989 debut album *Surprise* charted a path soon followed by a number of more famous female rockers, makes herself different from the rest of the female rock artists of the '80s and '90s. She's earnest in a way that doesn't have to be automatically friendly or mysteriously cunning. *Surprise* was reissued by the Koch label ten years after its initial release and marks the album's simplistic beauty. Representing a departure from her '80s work with the Golden Palominos, *Surprise* finds Straw in the role of down-home girl with a heart to be mended, singing of love like everyone else but with a style all her own. The album exhibits Straw's broad range, from brooding songs like "Crazy American" and "Sphinx" to "Future 40s (String of Pearls)," a twangy lovesucker featuring backup from R.E.M.'s Michael Stipe. (Straw's abrasiveness on this track is utterly perfect, especially in contrast to Stipe's calmer vocal approach.) But *Surprise* isn't based entirely around Straw's patented vocal style, earnest while neither overly friendly nor mysteriously cunning. This is also an album of strong musicianship from Straw (her guitar work is impeccable throughout) and an all-star cast including Daniel Lanois, Benmont Tench, John Doe of X, and Richard Thompson. The album's style and production mix jangle pop elements from the preceding decade with a roots rock tone, and the overall result has a healthy folkish disposition. *Surprise* anticipates what was to come for females in rock during the '90s; Syd Straw was first in a line of artists who most prominently included Sheryl Crow, Joan Osborne, and Edie Brickell. Koch Records is to be commended for setting this little bit of history straight by reissuing the classic album *Surprise* in March 2000. *—MacKenzie Wilson*

War and Peace / May 7, 1996 / Capricorn ♦♦♦

Emerging out of the Golden Palominos, Syd Straw made 1989's *Surprise*, one of those big-budget, name-producer, multiple-recording-studio star-making extravaganzas, and good as it was, it didn't get noticed. It took her seven years to mount a second try, and to do so she just tooled down to Springfield, Missouri, and cut a quick record with the semi-legendary Skeletons backing her up. The result is a jangly-guitar, singer/songwriter folk-rock feast and a glimpse into an apparently tortured soul. Straw sings of liquor and love gone wrong; there is a vague story line here, what with the references to Spain and recurrent self-debasement. But there is also a deadpan humor, plenty of tuneful music, and an intriguing, if wounded, persona who comes under unyielding self-examination. *—William Ruhlmann*

Strawberry Alarm Clock

f. 1966, Los Angeles, CA, **db.** 1971

Sunshine Pop, Psychedelic Pop, Psychedelic

Strawberry Alarm Clock were a psychedelic bubblegum band of the mid-'60s, reaching the top of the charts with "Incense and Peppermints" at the height of the flower power era. Originally called the Sixpence, the Californian group consisted of Ed King (lead guitar), Lee Freeman (rhythm guitar), Gary Lovetro (bass), Mark Weitz (organ), and Randy Seol (drums). On the band's debut single, "Incense and Peppermints," lead vocals were sung by Greg Munford, a 16-year-old friend of the band. Before recording their full-length debut album, the band added George Bunnell, who also played bass; more importantly, Bunnell became the group's main songwriter. In the summer of 1967, the Strawberry Alarm Clock contributed music to the film *Psych-Out*, as well as appearing in it. Gary Lovetro left the band before they recorded their second album, *Wake Up It's Tomorrow*, which also appeared in 1967. Between 1968's *The World in a Seashell* and 1969's *Good Morning Starshine* the band went through a number of lineup changes; as of *Good Morning Starshine* the band featured King on bass, Weitz, guitarist Jimmy Pitman, and drummer Gene Gunnels. By this time, the Strawberry Alarm Clock had lost much of its audience. They managed to keep performing until 1971, when the band finally broke up. Ed King went on to join Lynyrd Skynyrd; several of the former members of Strawberry Alarm Clock reunited in the '80s to perform on oldies tours. *—Stephen Thomas Erlewine*

● **Strawberries Mean Love** / 1992 / Big Beat ♦♦♦♦

For a little more money, this 21-track CD compilation is a better deal than its American counterpart (One Way's *Anthology*), offering a slightly more extensive selection and extensive liner notes, and including almost all of the cuts contained on *Anthology*. Drawn from their four albums (with the accent, properly, on the first two), it also has a clutch of non-LP singles. "Incense and Peppermints" and the small follow-up hit, "Tomorrow," are by far the best things on here; much of the rest is trendy period pop/psychedelia, sounding at various times like a bush-league Doors, or a *really* spaced out Association, with a bit of garage raunch tossed in on the B-side of "Incense" ("The Birdman of Alkatrash"). The two hits were included on Rhino's *Nuggets* compilations, which might be a better context in which to appreciate the group's fairly minimal contributions to psychedelia. *—Richie Unterberger*

Anthology / Jun. 30, 1993 / One Way ♦♦♦♦

For most fans, the 16-track *Anthology* will simply be too much Strawberry Alarm Clock to digest, since the band rarely hit the heights of "Incense & Peppermints." Most of the rest of the album consists of period pieces like "Sit With the Guru," "Rainy Day Mushroom Pillow," "They Saw the Fat One Coming," "The Birdman of Alkatrash," and the three-part suite "Black Butter," which are entertaining as artifacts, but aren't particularly good songs. Nevertheless, it's hard to imagine anyone assembling a more comprehensive overview than *Anthology*, even if it is lacking any cuts from the *Beyond the Valley of the Dolls* soundtrack. It's a near-definitive retrospective. *—Stephen Thomas Erlewine*

The Strawbs

f. 1968

British Folk-Rock, British Folk, Folk-Rock, Prog Rock/Art Rock

One of the better British progressive bands of the early '70s, the Strawbs differed from their more successful compatriots—the Moody Blues, King Crimson, Pink Floyd—principally in that their sound originated in English folk music, rather than rock. Originally a folk and bluegrass trio formed by Dave Cousins, with Sandy Denny as lead singer, the Strawbs evolved into an acoustic folk quartet and later into a progressive rock quintet, complete with electric keyboards and an epic/classical orientation. The exits of bassist John Ford and drummer Richard Hudson in the early '70s led to a toughening of the group's sound but also a weaker songwriting contingent. Their return, and Cousins' hookup with guitarist Brian Willoughby, made them musically if not commercially viable again in the '80s and '90s. *—Bruce Eder*

Sandy Denny & the Strawbs / 1968 / Hannibal ♦♦♦♦

Acoustic folk and bluegrass. Mostly a showcase for Denny, plus a few clues to the group's future evolution. *—Bruce Eder*

Strawbs / 1969 / A&M ♦♦♦

The Strawbs had done an album with Sandy Denny handling many of the vocals, and had also done quite a bit of unreleased recordings (now on the double CD *Preserves Canned*), prior to 1969's *Strawbs*. This is still their first proper album, but their wealth of prior live and studio experience most likely helped make it sound more confident and fully formed than many a debut effort. The group distinguished themselves among the burgeoning school of British folk-rockers by delivering bittersweet folk-rock with a storytelling flavor. Dave Cousins' songwriting was on the sober and occasionally over-earnest side, but nonetheless the record was strong and alluring enough to immediately establish the Strawbs as one of the better first-generation U.K. folk-rock outfits. Some of these songs had been around for a while, as the presence of some of them on *Preserves Canned* and *Sandy & the Strawbs* attests. However, the group took big strides from bare-bones folk-rock in the studio by dressing these in arrangements—sometimes with light recorder, choral backup vocals, and orchestration—that gave the Elizabethan melodies a pastoral, quasi-classical feel at times, without losing sight of an acoustic base. "The Man Who Called Himself Jesus" and "Where Is This Dream of Your Youth" are among their best and most ambitious songs, and even if the compositions can sometimes take themselves too seriously, the music's never less than respectable. *—Richie Unterberger*

Dragonfly / 1970 / A&M ♦♦♦

A transitional record, profound in some of its intent, but lacking muscle and excitement. *—Bruce Eder*

Just a Collection of Antiques and Curios / 1970 / A&M ♦♦♦

This album, cut live at London's Queen Elizabeth Hall in July of 1970, was the first Strawbs album to be released in the United States. It didn't do much in the U.S., but it did chart in England, and the original concert also got Rick Wakeman his first front-page coverage in the British music press, owing to his bravura performance on the solo piano spot, "Temperament for a Mind." The group is trying really hard here to make the jump from folk to folk-rock. They still play a lot of acoustic music, and some of it is surprisingly diverse, but this is a fairly successful album bridging the gap between the acoustic Strawbs combo of their first incarnation and the harder, more strident folk-rock stylings that followed on *From the Witchwood*, with hints of progressive leanings. The original finale, the rocking, searing nine-minute epic "Where Is the Dream of Your Youth," which clearly showed where the band was heading, was supplemented on a remastered CD reissue (A&M 540-938-2) with a haunting, moody "Vision of the Lady of the Lake," featuring Dave Cousins and Rick Wakeman, and Tony Hooper's showcase number, the surprisingly rousing "We'll Meet Again," from the same concert, and the contemporary studio creation "Forever." The latter is the only track that doesn't fit, its heavy string overdubs and studio ambience clashing with the live sound on the rest of the CD, although it does have Cousins' best vocals of the album. The sound throughout is excellent, as one might expect since the producers returned to the original concert recordings, with rich detail and an especially robust presence to John Ford's bass playing. *—Bruce Eder*

From the Witchwood / 1971 / A&M ♦♦♦♦

This album was originally the weak link in the transition of the Strawbs from an acoustic folk-rock outfit to a progressive-folk band, being neither fish nor fowl and suffering from an anemic mix. The 1998 British reissue (A&M 540-939-2), however, solves some inherent problems that plagued both the original vinyl edition and the first CD reissues. Th new remastering toughened up the bass sound, and brings out more of the sheer po of Rick Wakeman's organ and synthesizer playing, accenting the harder side group's sound that was obviously there in the studio but lacking in the analog Glimpse of Heaven" and "The Hangman and the Papist," in particular, benefi remastering, and "Sheep" finally has the musical fury to match its lyrics. Da voice also comes off as really close, and the effect is to make this a much m bum than it previously seemed. Overall, it's now far easier to visualize thi the step leading to full-blown progressive rock releases such as *Grave Ne* followed. The disc includes one bonus track, John Ford's "Keep the Devi has an acoustic opening and a hard rock break and finale, which was sessions, and which turned up months later as the B-side of "Benedic from the next album. *—Bruce Eder*

Grave New World / Feb. 4, 1972 / A&M ✦✦✦✦✦
Fulfillment! Singer/songwriter Dave Cousin finds a space somewhere between Bob Dylan and John Bunyan, Hudson and Ford come up with some superb hooks, and the electric sound is powerful and majestic. The music is serious—perhaps too much so—bracing, and sincere, if a bit downbeat. Reissued on CD in 1998 in remastered form, which makes the band sound really loud and close, so you can practically feel the room ambience of the studio. Cousins' electric guitar in "The Flower and the Young Man" crunches right in your ear, and his acoustic fills the room in "On Growing Older," with new notes and two extra tracks. Of the latter, "Here It Comes" (recorded before this album) is bouncy and pleasant enough, even if it doesn't fit the mood of most of the original album, and the previously unissued "I'm Going Home" is one of the best hard rock sides the group ever recorded—a piece of '70s rock & roll in the manner of Badfinger's "Rock of Ages" and T. Rex's "Get It On," which it resembles. —*Bruce Eder*

● **Bursting at the Seams** / 1973 / A&M ✦✦✦✦✦
The 1998 remastering of the Strawbs' best album (A&M 540-936-2 is the new catalog number) sports the finest sound of any of their CDs, which, by itself, would make this purchase worthwhile—the detailed notes and the presence of three bonus tracks—the shorter, punchier single version of "Lay Down," "Will Ye Go," and "Backside"—only add to the enticements offered. Additionally, the song order has been changed to the correct one (on the LP, "The River" had to follow "Down by the Sea" to end the first side, because of its heavy bass part), but the main virtue is the sound, which is extraordinary—every instrument sounds as though it's miked directly into your speakers. The result is that Dave Lambert's heavy chording is so close that the record does come off closer in texture to a Who album at certain points than it does to the group's folk roots. But the kettle drums at the end of "Down by the Sea" also sound close, and you can practically hear the bowing on the strings. The bonus tracks are a treat—"Backside," a B-side "credited" to "Ciggy Barlust and the Whales From Venus" (which would have been Tits From Venus if not for the censors) that's a pretty fair burlesque of "Space Oddity," et al.; and "Will Ye Go" is a version of "Wild Mountain Thyme" that is equal parts Cousins' voice, acoustic harmonium, and heavy power chords and bass. In all, in this version, *Bursting at the Seams* is the greatest Strawbs album of all, and the most overpowering. —*Bruce Eder*

Strawbs by Choice / 1974 / A&M ✦✦✦
A concise retrospective of some of the better moments from the first four A&M albums. —*Bruce Eder*

Hero and Heroine / 1974 / A&M ✦✦✦✦✦
The group's ballsiest album to date, a surging, hard-rocking follow-up to *Bursting at the Seams*, which debuted a new lineup, Richard Hudson, John Ford, and Blue Weaver having left to form their own group. In their places, ex-Nashville Teens keyboardman John Hawken and the more muscular rhythm section of Rod Coombes and Chas Cronk make their debut, on what is the Strawbs' first fully electric album. Dave Cousins' songwriting (augmented by Dave Lambert, who also contributes some slashing electric lead guitar) is still as romantic as ever in various spots ("Shine On Silver Sun," "Deep Summer's Sleep"), but also boasts dark visions ("Round and Round") which, coupled with new band's muscular playing, made the Strawbs one of the hardest-rocking progressive bands in the world. They should have been able to blow acts like the Moody Blues off the stage, so what went wrong with this album and the tour? One suspects it was a little too serious and complex for kids who were just looking for a soundtrack to their drug experiences, and it rocked too hard for the "sensitive" English-major types who got off on Cousins' lyrics—in a sense, the Strawbs were squeezed out of the middle in a very small-scale, subtle 1970s version of the old folk-versus-rock battles of the '60s. *Hero and Heroine* deserved better, being one of the best guitar-driven progressive rock albums of its period. —*Bruce Eder*

Ghosts / 1975 / A&M ✦✦✦✦✦
Ghosts was the last album by the Strawbs to appear while the band was on its upward curve of commercial success; a more lyrical follow-up to *Hero and Heroine*, it was the group's last thrust at wide-audience appeal, with a hoped for-hit ("Lemon Pie") that didn't materialize. The group's mix of acoustic guitars, electric lead and bass, and Rod Coombes' heavy drumming was very compelling on this, their smoothest album; the title track introduction, mixing multiple overdubbed harpsichords, acoustic guitars, and church bells was a gorgeous beginning, and the melodies only got better further into the album. The hauntingly beautiful "Starshine/Angel Wine" was a magnificent successor to "Lay Down" off of *Bursting at the Seams*, with a moment of Led Zeppelin-like flash from Dave Lambert's playing in the break, while "The Life Auction" was a bigger, bolder follow-up to "The Hangman and the Papist." The original finale, "Grace Darling," is probably the prettiest tune Dave Cousins ever wrote. Alas, *Ghosts* would be the group's last record to be released before the changes in music—with the introduction of punk rock in the middle of the '70s—began hemming them in, and they never again put out an album with as much panache as this. Previously available on CD only from Japan, in 1998 *Ghosts* was reissued by A&M in England with a sharp, clean digital sound that greatly enhanced the rich textures of the playing, and one bonus track, Rod Coombes' unexpectedly lyrical "Changes Arrange Us," which had previously been available only as a single B-side. (British import) —*Bruce Eder*

The Best of the Strawbs / 1978 / A&M ✦✦✦
double-album retrospective that misses the mark with too little of the best material m their best albums. Too much dross and somehow flat-sounding. —*Bruce Eder*

serves Uncanned / 1991 / Road Goes On Forever ✦✦✦✦✦
uble CD of 38 previously unreleased songs (one is unlisted on the sleeve) dating from 68, prior to the recording of their proper debut album. Most of these are demos, and would surface (sometimes in altered form) on future Strawbs and Dave Cousins albums, although quite a few were never officially rerecorded. Its appeal isn't just limited to Strawbs specialists—it's good, versatile (if slightly derivative) late-'60s British folk-rock, recalling Fairport Convention and (to a lesser degree) Pentangle in its eclecticism, though the Strawbs were no match for the Fairports in the vocal department. Most of the songs are Cousins originals, including tuneful, almost poppy harmony numbers and wordy tracts that take their lyrical cues from Bob Dylan and Ray Davies; the traditional folk tunes and bluegrass instrumentals, though indicative of the group's multi-faceted talents, are less interesting. Self-penned compositions like "October to May," "Martin Luther King's Dream," "Where Is the Dream of Your Youth," and "The Man Who Called Himself Jesus" are among the best (not to mention lyrically ambitious) songs Cousins has ever done; "All I Need is You" and the Beatles-ish "And You Need Me" are among the poppiest. Good sound quality, and detailed liner notes by Cousins himself. —*Richie Unterberger*

● **A Choice Selection of Strawbs** / 1993 / A&M ✦✦✦
A Choice Selection of Strawbs is indeed just that, compacting 16 of their most solid tracks onto one disc. Conveniently showcasing the Strawbs' folk-rock sound as well as their movement into a more progressive field (thanks to Rick Wakeman), this short hits collection is perfect for a quick investigation into the band's music. Tracks such as "Part of the Union" and "Lay Down" represent David Cousin's love of the simplistic folk sound, while efforts like "Hero and Heroine" and the psychedelic rippling of "Round and Round" reveal a lean toward a meatier keyboard composite with greater attention aimed at the guitar. Still, even with the Strawbs' drift into the progressive rock arena, the group kept their appealing vocal structure and tendency to sound attractively simple and unpretentious. "The Hangman and the Papist," "Benedictus," and even "Autumn," with its three-part arrangement, all contain an enchanting, almost pastoral quality within the congenial layered keyboards, mandolin, and banjo. *Halcyon Days*, a more comprehensive hits package, covers greater ground, but *A Choice Selection* serves as the perfect abbreviated introduction into the band's earnest style of music. —*Mike DeGagne*

Halcyon Days / 1997 / A&M ✦✦✦✦✦
In the course of nine years, the Strawbs evolved from an obscure, quirky British bluegrass group into one of the most beloved progressive rock bands in the world. This 150-minute collection covers most of that history, encompassing most (but not all) of the key songs from their nine A&M albums, as well as lost B-sides, songs by ex-members Richard Hudson and John Ford, and a pair of tracks off of Dave Cousins' 1972 solo album *Two Weeks Last Summer*. The selection of material is inspired, juxtaposing rarities with a good deal of important music from the core of their output. The programming straddles the collectable and the historical/musical significance of the material, so we get early 1970s FM hits such as "The River" and "Down by the Sea" sharing space with material such as "Martin Luther King's Dream" and subsequent extended progressive material like "Ghosts." The range of styles is daunting, from Dylanesque acoustic folk-style numbers to extended songs in which Mellotrons, synthesizers, and loud, complex electric guitar runs are the dominant presences. —*Bruce Eder*

Stray Cats

f. 1979, **db.** 1994
Rockabilly Revival, New Wave, Rock & Roll
This U.S. rock trio consists of Brian Setzer (b.1960), standup bass slapper Lee Rocker (born Lee Drucher), and drummer Slim Jim Phantom (born James McDonnell). It was formed in 1979 in the midst of the punk/new wave scene, playing retro-rockabilly style. Emigrating to England shortly thereafter, they caught on quickly with a music scene that was always interested in the "next big thing," and their top-notch production by Dave Edmunds quickly moved them into the charts. Visual image and European success augered well for their return to the U.S. just in time to mine the early motherlode of MTV video-land. By the mid-'80s, after much success, the gimmick had worn off, and the band broke up by late 1984. They regrouped in the '90s after various solo projects had fizzled, with their style relatively unchanged, but again disbanded after 1994's *Choo Choo Hot Fish*. —*Cub Koda*

Built for Speed / Jun. 1982 / EMI America ✦✦✦✦✦
In 1982, the unexpected success of the Stray Cats' American debut, *Built for Speed*, made America aware that rockabilly, previously believed to be extinct, was actually alive and well somewhere in New Jersey (though the evidence had to be taken to England before anyone would notice). Pulling together six songs from the Stray Cats' self-titled debut, five tunes from the follow-up, *Gonna Ball*, and one previously unreleased number (the title song), *Built for Speed* is song-for-song the group's strongest album, despite the cut-and-paste manner in which it was created. Originality was never this band's strongest suit, and as songwriters the Stray Cats rarely wandered far from the traditional themes of cars, girls, rockin', and their own level of coolness, but Brian Setzer's fleet-fingered guitar work revealed that he'd absorbed the lessons of Cliff Gallup, James Burton, and Scotty Moore and constructed an impressive and colorful style of his own from the parts, while Lee Rocker and Slim Jim Phantom were an admirably potent and appropriately uncluttered rhythm section (the clean, streamlined production, by Dave Edmunds on most cuts, also helped quite a bit). If the group's songs haven't all worn the test of time especially well, the melodies are strong and the playing is tight and enthusiastic throughout. While you're better off with a good collection from Gene Vincent, Eddie Cochran, or Charlie Feathers, there are a lot worse ways you could learn about rockabilly than to pick up *Built for Speed*—which is a good thing, since if you were born after 1965, chances are it *was* was where you learned about rockabilly. —*Mark Deming*

Rant N' Rave With the Stray Cats / 1983 / EMI America ✦✦✦✦✦
Rant N' Rave, the Stray Cats' second album, sounded identical to *Built for Speed*,

and—thanks to the hits "(She's) Sexy & 17" and the ballad "I Won't Stand in Your Way"—it was equally as strong. —*Stephen Thomas Erlewine*

Rock Therapy / 1986 / EMI America ✦✦✦

Rock Therapy wasn't as consistently engaging as *Built for Speed* and *Rant N' Rave*, but it was a spirited, inspired effort that continued their trademark sound to a fine effect. —*Stephen Thomas Erlewine*

Blast Off / 1989 / EMI America ✦✦

The Best of the Stray Cats: Rock This Town / Oct. 1990 / EMI America ✦✦✦✦

The Best of the Stray Cats is a brief but effective ten-song compilation featuring all of the rockabilly revivalists' biggest American hits, including "Stray Cat Strut," "Rock This Town," "(She's) Sexy & 17," "I Won't Stand In Your Way," "Bring It Back Again" and "Look At That Cadillac." Although other compilations offer a larger selection, *Rock This Town* contains all of the necessary items, making it a good choice for most casual fans. —*Stephen Thomas Erlewine*

Runaway Boys: A Retrospective '81-'92 / Jan. 14, 1997 / EMI America ✦✦✦✦✦

An exemplary best-of, this has 25 tracks from throughout their career, leaning heavily on the earliest and best material. It also contains a few tunes that were previously unreleased in the U.S., the B-side cover of the Supremes' "You Can't Hurry Love," and all three non-album songs from their 1983 double 45 "(She's) Sexy & 17." Those that prize authenticity might continue to scorn this rockabilly revivalism. But now that the debate over whether the group were poseurs or not has become irrelevant, it's a surprisingly solid guilty pleasure, even if it's more or less reheated Gene Vincent. —*Richie Unterberger*

● Greatest Hits [Expanded] / Jan. 25, 2000 / Capitol ✦✦✦✦✦

One of the great unspoken things about the Stray Cats is that they just didn't have that many hits. In America, they had three Top Ten singles—"Rock This Town," "Stray Cat Strut," "(She's) Sexy & 17"—plus the ballad "I Won't Stand in Your Way," which just scraped the Top 40. The fact that the Stray Cats were so fondly remembered not only by kids of the early '80s, but by older and younger listeners alike, just shows how good those three hits are; they really held their own next to any '50s rockabilly classic. However, they're not all the Stray Cats had to offer, as the 2000 expanded version of *Greatest Hits* illustrates. True, apart from such U.K. hits as "Runaway Boys," they didn't really have original tunes that rivaled their three big hits, but they were a kick-ass rockabilly band, making their newly written genre items sound every bit as convincing as their fine cover of Gene Vincent's "Race With the Devil." The group was fortunate to choose a producer as savvy as Dave Edmunds, the roots-rock trailblazer who captured the Stray Cats' muscular, energetic sound with recordings that would have sounded fine in the '50s, yet managed to sound contemporary in the early '80s. Of course, that production trick wouldn't have amounted to much if that wasn't what the Cats were doing with their music anyway. These 14 songs—plus three bonus tracks—are as good as rockabilly revival has ever gotten. Not only that, these songs also offer a convincing argument that the Stray Cats really did hold their own with their idols. In other words, it's the definitive compilation. —*Stephen Thomas Erlewine*

Barbra Streisand

b. Apr. 24, 1942, Brooklyn, NY

Vocals / Traditional Pop, Standards, Musicals, Cast Recordings, Soft Rock, Pop, Adult Contemporary, Show Tunes

Barbra Streisand's status as one of the most successful singers of her generation is all the more remarkable not only because her popularity has been achieved in the face of a dominant musical trend—rock & roll—which she did not follow, but also because, despite an amazing singing voice that has enthralled practically anyone who has heard it, she has always used singing as a mere stepping stone to other careers, as a stage and film actress and as a film director. Parts in two Broadway shows during the early '60s gained her a contract through Columbia, and her first album became a Top Ten hit in 1963. Streisand turned her back on potentially lucrative concert bookings in favor of a long-running starring role in the Broadway show *Funny Girl*. "People" from that show became her first Top Ten single, and the *People* album her first chart-topping LP. Though subsequent film roles were flops, she returned to hit-making during the '70s and successfully married her musical and film acting interests, gaining film roles and number one hits with *The Way We Were* (the title theme) and *A Star Is Born* ("Evergreen"). In 1983, Streisand's first directorial effort, *Yentl*, became a successful film with a Top Ten soundtrack album, and 1985's *The Broadway Album* brought her to the top of the charts once again. She returned to the concert stage in 1994, resulting in the Top Ten, million-selling album *The Concert*. —*William Ruhlmann*

Pins and Needles [Original Cast Recording] / 1962 / Columbia ✦✦✦

Harold Rome's musical revue *Pins and Needles*, staged by the Cultural Division of the International Ladies Garment Workers Union in 1937, was an unusual mixture of Broadway show music style and '30s union content. It also had a union cast of workers who performed the show on weekends for four years in the late Depression. Twenty-five years later, Rome was back on Broadway with *I Can Get It For You Wholesale*, which inspired Columbia Records to make the first recording of his first show, using a simple piano/guitar/bass/drums backup. Rome sang some of the songs himself, and he brought along a young Barbra Streisand, who was stopping the show as a featured performer in *Wholesale*. Streisand, heard on six of the 15 cuts, was given the comic material for the most part, her "Nobody Makes a Pass at Me" playing up the same angle as her *Wholesale* feature, "Miss Marmelstein." The songs did not give Streisand much of a chance to display her vocal gifts, especially because the romantic material was handled by Rose Marie Jun and Jack Carroll. Carroll sang the show's one hit, "Sunday in the Park," and Jun sang its

best-written effort, "Chain Store Daisy." The real star was Rome, and Streisand seemed headed for typecasting. —*William Ruhlmann*

☆ The Barbra Streisand Album / Feb. 25, 1963 / Columbia ✦✦✦✦✦

Of course, the first thing that strikes you listening to the first Barbra Streisand album, recorded and released before the singer's 21st birthday, is that great voice. And it isn't just the sheer quality of the voice, its purity and its strength throughout its register, it's also the mastery of vocal effects that produce dramatic readings of the lyrics—each song is like a one-act musical. Streisand opens with Julie London's signature torch song, "Cry Me a River," and she doesn't only surpass London, she sets off a thermonuclear explosion. From there, versatility and novelty are emphasized—a breakneck version of "Who's Afraid of the Big Bad Wolf?," a slow, emotion-drenched performance of "Happy Days Are Here Again." But Streisand's debut, inventively arranged and conducted by Peter Matz, is notable as much for the surprising omissions as the surprising selections. Arriving in 1963, ten years into the revival of sophisticated interwar theater songs led by Frank Sinatra and followed by all other adult pop singers, Streisand virtually ignores the modern masters like Gershwin and Berlin. When she does do Rodgers and Hart or Cole Porter, she picks obscure songs; her idea of a good 1930s number is Fats Waller and Andy Razaf's "Keepin' Out of Mischief Now." She is much more comfortable with recent theater material, choosing two songs from *The Fantasticks* (1960) and the title song from the stage play *A Taste of Honey* (1962). *The Barbra Streisand Album* is an essential recording in the field of pop vocals because it redefines that genre in contemporary terms. (*The Barbra Streisand Album* won Grammy Awards for Album of the Year, Best Female Vocal Performance, and Best Album Cover.) —*William Ruhlmann*

The Second Barbra Streisand Album / Oct. 1963 / Columbia ✦✦✦

Barbra Streisand's second album might have been subtitled "The Harold Arlen Album," asince Arlen is the composer of five of the 11 selections, including four of five on the first side. Streisand had demonstrated an affinity for Arlen's work on her first album, singing "A Sleepin' Bee." Here, she is most impressive on "Down With Love," a 1937 song with a lyric by E.Y. Harburg that lampoons the love songs of other writers of the period. Never given to singing the Gershwins and other classic pop writers, Streisand relishes the chance to condemn them, and she sings with a vengeance. But in general, Arlen's bluesy music, combined with the second-rate contemporary material on the second side, makes Streisand's second album less accomplished than her first. In fact, where the first album, with its surprising arrangements, surprising song choices, humor, and emotionalism, reconceived pop singing for a new singer, the second album, with it sameness of tone, surrenders to the old mold. On an already unlikely piece of material like Sigmund Romberg and Oscar Hammerstein II's "Lover, Come Back to Me," arranger/conductor Peter Matz uses an updated, up-tempo Billy May-style arrangement (with bongos). Streisand gives it a bravura reading, but she is competing against the arrangement rather than riding over it. *The Second Barbra Streisand Album* was typically well sung, but instead of continuing the innovations of her debut, Streisand seemed to be trying simply to consolidate her triumph, and it was a bit too early for that. —*William Ruhlmann*

The Third Album / Feb. 1964 / Columbia ✦✦✦

On her first album, Barbra Streisand established herself as a singer who discovered or created new standards instead of one who revived or recreated old ones. She wavered from this commitment on her second album, and on her third gave in to convention completely. There was nothing wrong with her interpretations of such old favorites as "My Melancholy Baby," "Taking a Chance on Love," "As Time Goes By," or "It Had to Be You," except perhaps that they seemed overly tame for a performer of such demonstrated individuality. And Streisand was far less successful on "Bewitched (Bothered and Bewildered)," betraying little understanding of Lorenz Hart's nuanced lyric, or on Jerome Kern and Oscar Hammerstein II's "Make Believe," which had none of the playfulness the song needed, and of which Streisand certainly was capable. She did seem assured going back to Harold Arlen's *St. Louis Woman* for "I Had Myself a True Love," using its bluesy tone for some emotional fireworks. But *The Third Album*, while it was another demonstration of the beauty of Barbra Streisand's voice, also suggested that her interpretive abilities remained limited. —*William Ruhlmann*

People / Sep. 1964 / Columbia ✦✦✦✦✦

After two less successful albums, Barbra Streisand returned to form on her fourth album with a selection of songs that showed some of the imagination of her debut album. Much of the material was new: The album opened and closed with songs by Jule Styne and Bob Merrill, first "Absent Minded Me," and then the Top Ten title song that was the hit from Streisand's triumphant Broadway show, *Funny Girl*. Streisand introduced Cy Coleman and Carolyn Leigh's "When in Rome (I Do as the Romans Do)," a lively song that allowed her to display some of the spirit and humor that had been missing on her last two outings. And when picking from older songs, she again found obscure or atypical tunes from prominent composers or lost gems she could make her own. In the former category were Irving Berlin's "Supper Time," a blues song unlike any the composer had ever done, and "My Lord and Master," from Rodgers and Hammerstein's *The King and I*. In the latter was the delightful "Fine and Dandy," from the 1930 show of the same name, with a lyric by Kay Swift. Add in some obvious choices like James Van Heusen and Sammy Cahn's "Love Is a Bore" (a companion to the previously recorded "Down With Love") and "Don't Like Goodbyes," another selection from Harold Arlen and Truman Capote's *House of Flowers*, from which Streisand had earlier picked "A Sleepin' Bee," and you have an album fashioned to play to the singer's strengths and musical tastes instead of trying to fit her into existing ones. That wasn't quite enough to match the quality of the debut album, but it was a definite improvement over the second and third albums. (*People* won Grammy Awards for Best Vocal Performance and Best Album Cover.) —*William Ruhlmann*

My Name Is Barbra / 1965 / Columbia ✦✦✦✦✦
An album containing many of the songs used in Barbra Streisand's TV special of the same name, *My Name Is Barbra* followed the general outline of two of the three sections of the show. The first side was a concept set of songs about childhood and growing up that allowed Streisand, in the songs "I'm Five" and "Sweet Zoo," to take a comic approach for the first time in several albums. The second side was a set of adult songs performed in Streisand's big, dramatic style. "I Can See It," her third borrowing from *The Fantasticks*, was the best yet, and Streisand's first attempt at a Gershwin tune, "Someone to Watch Over Me," was at least a qualified success. "I've Got No Strings," from the movie *Pinocchio*, was no "Who's Afraid of the Big Bad Wolf" (one of the highlights of her debut album), but it wasn't bad. And best of all was Streisand's reading of "My Man," Fanny Brice's signature song, though it had not been used in *Funny Girl*, the Broadway show about her life, in which Streisand had starred. After this demonstration, however, it would be interpolated into the movie version. (*My Name Is Barbra* won a Grammy Award for Best Female Vocal Performance.) *—William Ruhlmann*

My Name Is Barbra, Two... / Oct. 1965 / Columbia ✦✦✦
My Name Is Barbra, Two... is not exactly a sequel to *My Name Is Barbra*, though it contains a medley of songs about poverty that was performed as one of the three sections of the TV special. For the most part, this is just the next Barbra Streisand album, containing the usual mixture of recent songs ("He Touched Me," "The Shadow of Your Smile," "No More Songs for Me") and lesser known songs by classic pop writers (Rodgers and Hart's "Quiet Night" and "Where's That Rainbow?"), filled out by full-length versions of songs from the medley ("Second Hand Rose," a song associated with Fanny Brice that became Streisand's second Top 40 hit, and "I Got Plenty O' Nothin'" from *Porgy And Bess*). The medley lacks the TV show's visual complement of Streisand cavorting in a department store, but the arrangement and her performance still camp up songs like "Brother Can You Spare a Dime?" and "Nobody Knows You When You're Down and Out" a dubious choice of interpretation. *—William Ruhlmann*

Color Me Barbra / 1966 / Columbia ✦✦✦
All of the songs on *Color Me Barbra* were featured on Barbara Streisand's second TV special of the same name. (There were some more songs as well, but they had appeared on earlier albums.) It was a strong collection on which Streisand successfully tackled such standards as Jerome Kern and Otto Harbach's "Yesterdays" and Rodgers and Hart's "Where or When," as well as introducing some good new show material in "Where Am I Going?" from *Sweet Charity* and Maltby and Shire's "Starting Here, Starting Now," as well as displaying her comedic skills on "The Minute Waltz." The long medley of "face" songs ("Funny Face," "I've Grown Accustomed to Her Face," etc.) made more sense on TV, where Streisand sang it to a studio zoo full of animals, but was still enjoyable. The material wasn't all great, with a retread of "Gotta Move" by Streisand's arranger/conductor Peter Matz and a couple of French songs looking forward to *Je M'Appelle Barbra* among the filler. *—William Ruhlmann*

Je M'Appelle Barbra / Nov. 1966 / Columbia ✦✦✦
Je M'Appelle Barbra is an album of songs with a French orientation, either because they are actually sung, at least in part, in French, or because they originated in France before having English lyrics added. Streisand does not embarrass herself in French, but the album is more an experiment than a triumph, and is notable primarily for marking her first collaboration with Michel Legrand, who arranged and conducted. *—William Ruhlmann*

Simply Streisand / Oct. 1967 / Columbia ✦✦✦
After three albums related to television specials and one of French songs, *Simply Streisand* was Barbra Streisand's first "regular" new album since *People* three years earlier and her first new release of any kind in a year. (Before, her albums came regularly every six months.) By now, the singer was spending her time in Hollywood shooting movies, and the music scene had moved heavily into rock, developments that made this a perfunctory set and one released into an indifferent climate; unlike her previous eight albums, *Simply Streisand* missed the Top Ten. But it isn't that bad. Streisand is not an accomplished performer of classic pop standards like "My Funny Valentine" and "More Than You Know," largely because she seems too intimidated by the material to put an individual stamp on it, but she is a great singer, and if arranger Ray Ellis's charts lack the invention of Peter Matz, they are conventionally competent. If this were the only Streisand album you ever heard, you'd still think she was good. It's only in comparison to what went before that it seems mediocre. *—William Ruhlmann*

A Happening in Central Park / 1968 / Columbia ✦✦✦
Recorded at a one-off free concert in front of 135,000 people in New York's Central Park in June 1967, Barbra Streisand's first live album was something of a throwback to her early days, and not only because it waited in the can 15 months before release. (Also filmed, the performance was used as a TV special.) Songs like "Happy Days Are Here Again" and "Cry Me a River" dated from Streisand's 1963 debut album, while the comic "Value" was a previously unrecorded song from her first Off-Broadway show, *Another Evening With Harry Stoones*, which ran for one night in October 1961. Streisand was dangerously close to being a musical anachronism in the pop music scene of 1968, even as her Hollywood stardom was confirmed by the release of the *Funny Girl* movie. This album did nothing to change that, though Streisand proved a charming and funny live performer and, as ever, a great singer. It was amazing that she could pull off what remained essentially a nightclub act in front of such a large audience. *—William Ruhlmann*

What About Today? / 1969 / Columbia ✦✦

The Owl and the Pussycat / 1970 / Columbia ✦

● **Greatest Hits** / 1970 / Columbia ✦✦✦✦✦
At a time when Barbra Streisand's career was in decline, what turned out to be only her first greatest hits album seemed to serve as both a summing up and a kiss-off of her 1960s recordings. Streisand was not primarily a singles artist; between 1964 and 1969, she enjoyed nine chart singles, of which only one, "People," made the Top Ten, with only one other, "Second Hand Rose," reaching the Top 40. But in that time, she scored seven gold-selling, Top Ten albums. This hits collection contained seven of her chart singles, plus her non-charting early single, "My Coloring Book," "Happy Days Are Here Again," which was one of the highlights of her debut album (heard here in the live version from *A Happening in Central Park*), and "Don't Rain on My Parade" from the *Funny Girl* soundtrack. For casual fans, that made for a good sampling of Streisand's most prominent '60s work, and if at the time it seemed likely that this was all the hits there would be, instead the '60s proved to be only the first chapter in Streisand's career. *—William Ruhlmann*

On a Clear Day You Can See Forever / Jul. 1970 / Columbia ✦✦✦
The film version of the Broadway musical *On a Clear Day You Can See Forever* was something of a disaster, but the soundtrack album is better because the focus is on the Burton Lane/Alan Jay Lerner songs and on the primary singer, Barbra Streisand, who has six vocals out of ten selections. Far less impressive is co-star Yves Montand, whose singing voice is as suspect as his English, such that the album is a mixed success. *—William Ruhlmann*

Stoney End / Feb. 1971 / Columbia ✦✦✦✦✦
Barbra Streisand scored her second Top Ten hit in early 1971 by treating Laura Nyro's recording of her song "Stoney End" as a demo and copying it practically note for note. "Mama, let me start all over," she sang, and her wish was granted. The follow-up album of the same title was in its way as surprising as Streisand's debut album eight years earlier. Where that record had redefined the role of the traditional pop singer in contemporary terms for the early '60s, *Stoney End* redefined Streisand as an effective pop-rock singer, which her last outing, *What About Today?*, had failed to do. Maybe she listened as closely to Nyro and Joni Mitchell as she had to Ethel Merman and Judy Garland a decade earlier, but somehow she reoriented her approach to music, adapting herself to vocal demands that were very different in terms of dynamics, expressiveness, and especially rhythm from the traditional pop and theater music she had sung previously. Producer Richard Perry may have eased the transition by using session men like Randy Newman, who played piano on two of his own compositions and who bridged the worlds of show music and rock. But Streisand herself found something to identify with in songs like Gordon Lightfoot's "If You Could Read My Mind" (maybe that passage about the movie queen) and Mitchell's "I Don't Know Where I Stand." *Stoney End* was not a perfect album—the reliance on minor Brill Building material and two more Nyro copies kept it from classic status—but it was so far removed from what Streisand's fans and her detractors thought her capable of that it stands as one of her major triumphs. It was also her biggest seller in four years and launched the comeback that saw her through the '70s. *—William Ruhlmann*

Barbra Joan Streisand / Aug. 1971 / Columbia ✦✦✦✦✦
On her follow-up to the comeback album *Stoney End*, Barbra Streisand tried to do for (or to) Carole King what she had done the last time around with Laura Nyro, i.e., redo her material in a similar manner and essentially hijack it (while providing a big jump in songwriter royalties, of course). This was not so easy to do in the case of "Beautiful," "Where You Lead," and "You've Got a Friend," however, since, unlike the Nyro songs, by the time Streisand got to these tunes, they were already on King's own chart-topping album, *Tapestry*. Nevertheless, Steisand, who after all is a much more powerful singer than King, did them well and even eked out a Top 40 single on "Where You Lead." And the album contained other gems, such as a delicate reading of John Lennon's "Love" (a take on his "Mother" was far less successful) and the only recording of "I Mean to Shine," written by Donald Fagen and Walter Becker, soon to launch Steely Dan. Streisand was not able to make the final transition into the pop-rock realm for the simple reason that she wasn't a writer, but she had spent a career making other people's songs her own, and she was as effective doing that here as she had been on very different material in the '60s. *—William Ruhlmann*

Live Concert at the Forum / Oct. 1972 / Columbia ✦✦✦
Barbra Streisand's second live album demonstrated how much her music had changed since her first one had been released four years before. (Actually, five years separated the recording dates.) But she also strived to combine her earlier work with her current songs, and while you might have expected "People" to sit oddly with "Stoney End" on the same record side, in fact the two songs only demonstrated Streisand's versatility. It may have been years since Streisand had faced a concert audience, but she'd been facing casino audiences in Las Vegas for years, and she was a polished performer. She was also in good voice, and the concert medium suited her powerful delivery well. Her humorous monologue, in which she seemed to be smoking marijuana, is now as dated as it was timely in 1972. The Forum concert was an early indication that Streisand had not abandoned the middle of the road for rock & roll, but only made a strategic detour. In fact, she would soon return to a contemporary ballad style. *—William Ruhlmann*

Barbra Streisand . . . and Other Musical Instruments / Nov. 1973 / Columbia ✦✦

The Way We Were / Jan. 1974 / Columbia ✦✦✦
Though usually referred to as *The Way We Were*, the unwieldy full title of this album is *Barbra Streisand Featuring the Hit Single The Way We Were and All in Love Is Fair*, an important distinction because it was released simultaneously with the original soundtrack album for the film *The Way We Were* (Columbia 32830), which also contained a Streisand recording of the title song, along with the film score composed by Marvin Hamlisch. This album was thrown together quickly after that song took off as a single (in a recording different from the one in the film) in the wake of the success of the movie. In

addition to the single and the Stevie Wonder song that also features in its title, the album contained a grab-bag of stray tracks dating back as far as seven years and coming from Streisand's fourth TV special, *The Belle of 14th Street* and an unfinished album project called *The Singer* largely made up of ballads written by Alan and Marilayn Bergman and Michel Legrand. The result was not one of Streisand's more impressive collections, but the combined commercial impact of the film and the single propelled this album to the top of the charts. *—William Ruhlmann*

ButterFly / Oct. 1974 / Columbia ✦✦✦

Barbra Streisand's first album of newly recorded, non-soundtrack studio material in three years, *ButterFly* was ridiculed at the time of its release because its credited producer was her boyfriend, Jon Peters, whose musical credentials were nonexistent. In retrospect, the real power on the album was arranger Tom Scott, a reed player who had perfected a light jazz-pop style in his work on Joni Mitchell's *Court and Spark* earlier in the year. *ButterFly* backed off from the pop-rock style of its predecessors, *Stoney End* and *Barbra Joan Streisand*, but it still found Streisand essaying contemporary material by such writers as Bob Marley, Graham Nash, and David Bowie. Unlike Richard Perry, who had produced those albums, Scott adapted the songs to Streisand's powerful and individual vocal style rather than having her ape existing versions of the songs. The result was more of a compromise with contemporary pop that, while it sold only to Streisand's existing fan base, nevertheless had its charms. *—William Ruhlmann*

Lazy Afternoon / 1975 / Columbia ✦✦✦

Lazy Afternoon was Barbra Streisand's Rupert Holmes album. Holmes, later known for his number one hit "Escape (The Pina Colada Song)," arranged, conducted, and co-produced the album and wrote or co-wrote four songs. He helped Streisand to continue her evolution into a kind of post-rock contemporary pop artist. This was achieved largely through the sympathetic ballad arrangements, which surrounded Streisand's voice with delicately played individual instruments while focusing on her calm vocals. The exception was a cover of the Four Tops' "Shake Me, Wake Me," which was given a disco treatment. For the most part, *Lazy Afternoon* was true to its title, a collection of relaxed performances that was pleasant without being particularly impressive. *—William Ruhlmann*

Funny Lady / 1975 / Arista ✦✦

Classical Barbra / Feb. 1976 / Columbia ✦✦✦

One of Barbra Streisand's more esoteric projects, *Classical Barbra* is an album of European art songs composed by Debussy, Handel, Schumann, and others and sung in French, German, Latin, Italian, and English. Streisand is in typically good voice, and while the album must have been a stretch for her usual audience and a surprise to the classical audience, she carries the performances off. *—William Ruhlmann*

A Star Is Born / Nov. 1976 / Monument ✦✦

Though it is credited to Barbra Streisand and Kris Kristofferson, *A Star Is Born* is in effect the soundtrack album to the motion picture of the same name, a rock-oriented retelling of the story that had been filmed three times before. That it is not billed as a soundtrack only indicates that the album contains the songs featured in the film, but not the score. Of course, the main drawing card here is "Love Theme From 'A Star Is Born' (Evergreen)," the number one hit. But the rest of the album is slight. Streisand isn't much of a rock singer and these aren't much as rock songs (the songwriters include Paul Williams and Rupert Holmes). For his part, Kristofferson sounds even more gravelly than usual, and he isn't even growling his own compositions, which doubtless would have been superior to what he's been given to sing. Nevertheless, spurred by the hit single and the box office success of the film, *A Star Is Born* was the best-selling album of Barbra Streisand's career up to this point. ["Evergreen," co-written by Streisand and Williams, won Grammy Awards for Song of the Year and Best Female Pop Vocal.] *—William Ruhlmann*

Streisand Superman / 1977 / Columbia ✦✦✦

Appearing only seven months after *A Star Is Born*, *Streisand Superman* seemed to continue much of its rock-oriented feel, even including several songs that had been intended for the film. It was unusual in featuring all recently written songs, many first recorded here. Streisand co-wrote the rockish "Don't Believe What You Read," an attack on her negative press coverage, while Alan Gordon contributed both the discoish "I Found You Love" and the album's Top Ten single ballad "My Heart Belongs to Me." *Streisand Superman* seemed to be an unusually personal album for the singer, reflecting her feelings and viewpoints. That did not make it one of her best, however. *—William Ruhlmann*

★ **Barbra Streisand's Greatest Hits, Vol. 2** / 1978 / Columbia ✦✦✦✦✦

Between the release of Barbra Streisand's first hits collection in 1970 and her second in 1978, she essentially became a different kind of recording artist. In the 1960s, she made a series of consistent albums devoted largely to show music material, but she scored precious few singles hits, with only one, "People," and reaching the Top Ten. But in the 1970s, she shifted to contemporary soft-rock and released a series of highly successful ballad singles, while her albums became largely inconsistent. For that reason, the hit quotient of her second hits album was much higher—"The Way We Were," "Love Theme From 'A Star Is Born' (Evergreen)," and the duet version of "You Don't Bring Me Flowers," sung with songwriter Neil Diamond and released on album here for the first time, all were number one hits, while "Stoney End" and "My Heart Belongs to Me" were Top Tens and "Sweet Inspiration/Where You Lead," "Songbird," and "Love Theme From 'Laura Mars' (Prisoner)" reached the Top 40. That was enough material to make *Volume 2* Streisand's definitive hits collection, so much so that later compilations like *Memories* and *A Collection/Greatest Hits... And More* would be forced to cannibalize it. It was also a genre-defining album in terms of the emergence of a post-'60s contemporary pop music that drew upon the rock revolution to redefine classic pop for a new generation. *—William Ruhlmann*

Songbird / 1978 / Columbia ✦✦✦

Songbird was a competent, professional effort from Barbra Streisand, typical of the soft-rock style of her '70s work, but unexceptional. Gary Klein, who had produced *Streisand Superman*, guided a middle course between bombast and balladry, resulting in, for example, perhaps the least objectionable version possible of the frankly awful "Tomorrow" from the Broadway musical *Annie* and a good reading of Neil Diamond's "You Don't Bring Me Flowers" that would help inspire the hit duet version a year later. But though Streisand now seemed to have access to the efforts of a raft of good songwriters, most of the material here was not memorable. The intended hit, obviously, was the title song, which was patterned after Streisand's recent string of hit ballads. But it was not as effective as its predecessors and didn't perform as well as they had in the charts, only breaking into the Top 40. *—William Ruhlmann*

Wet / 1979 / Columbia ✦✦✦

A concept album of sorts in the sense that each of the songs has something to do with water, *Wet* was the third of a trilogy of albums produced by Gary Klein in a soft-rock vein increasingly set in the synth-pop style of the late '70s and early '80s. The concept allowed for a range of material, from old favorite Harold Arlen's "Come Rain Or Come Shine" to an updated version of the old Bobby Darin hit "Splish Splash." The album's number one hit was "No More Tears (Enough Is Enough)," a disco duet with Donna Summer. But most of the songs were newly written ballads attempting to recreate the "Evergreen"/"The Way We Were" style of Streisand's recent hits. "Kiss Me in the Rain" grazed the Top 40, but most of that material was substandard. Yet there was enough variety on the album to make it an average Streisand outing. *—William Ruhlmann*

The Main Event / Jun. 1979 / Columbia ✦✦

Guilty / 1980 / Columbia ✦✦✦✦✦

The biggest selling album of Barbra Streisand's career is also one of her least characteristic. The album was written and produced by Barry Gibb in association with his brothers and the producers of the Bee Gees, and in essence it sounds like a post-*Saturday Night Fever* Bee Gees album with vocals by Streisand. Gibb adapted his usual style somewhat, especially in slowing the tempos and leaving more room for the vocal, but his melodic style and the backup vocals, even when they are not sung by the Bee Gees, are typical of them. Still, the record was more hybrid than compromise, and the chart-topping single "Woman in Love" has a sinuous feel that is both right for Streisand and new for her. Other hits were the title song and "What Kind of Fool," both duets with Gibb. (The song "Guilty" won a Grammy Award for Best Pop Vocal by Duo or Group.) *—William Ruhlmann*

Memories / Nov. 1981 / Columbia ✦✦✦

As albums go, *Memories* made a great single. A compilation, but not exactly a hits collection, it contained two newly recorded songs, "Memory" from the musical *Cats* and the Top 40 hit "Comin' in and Out of Your Life," plus a rerecorded version of "Lost Inside of You," a song previously done as a duet with Kris Kristofferson in *A Star Is Born*, and seven tracks from the previous eight years, three of which were making their third or fourth appearance on record. In other words, *Memories* was a blatant consumer rip-off, highly unusual for an artist who usually gave value for money. That said, the album contained some of Streisand's biggest hits—"You Don't Bring Me Flowers," "No More Tears (Enough Is Enough)," "Evergreen," and "The Way We Were," as well as some excellent performances, such as Streisand's take on Billy Joel's "New York State of Mind." Thus, it was a good collection thought of independently (which may help explain why it became one of Streisand's biggest sellers), even if in the context of her overall catalog it was an album of reruns baited with a couple of new songs. [In the U.K., the album was released with four additional tracks—"Kiss Me in the Rain," "I Don't Break Easily," "Wet," and "A Man I Loved"—under the title *Love Songs* (CBS 10031).] *—William Ruhlmann*

Yentl / 1983 / Columbia ✦✦✦

Billed as both a Barbra Streisand album and as an Original Motion Picture Soundtrack, *Yentl* contains the songs, sung by Streisand and written by Michel Legrand and Alan and Marilyn Bergman, that the character played by Streisand sings as internal monologues in the film, sometimes with spoken dialogue interspersed. (The album is filled out by "studio versions" of two of the songs, "The Way He Makes Me Feel" and "No Matter What Happens," played on contemporary electronic instruments, rather than in the orchestral settings used for the rest of the songs.) With such a thematic base, the music has an unusual consistency and, written specifically for Streisand, it makes use of her emotional expressiveness, phrasing, and timing as a singer. But it was also written as a complement to the film and on its own comes across as a group of isolated musical plot highlights rather than as a coherent song cycle. (*Yentl* won an Academy Award for Best Original Song Score.) *—William Ruhlmann*

Emotion / Oct. 1984 / Columbia ✦✦✦

Barbra Streisand's first album of contemporary material in four years was a typical '80s "Adult Contemporary" superstar release, each track written and produced as a potential "power ballad" single by an extensive team of other performers, in this case includir Richard Perry, Kim Carnes, Maurice White of Earth, Wind & Fire, Jim Steinman, Al Galuten (the Bee Gees' producer), Richard Baskin, Diane Warren, John Mellencam Streisand herself. Streisand proved capable of handling everything from White age R&B to Steinman's melodramatic overproduction. (He was the man who b Meat Loaf.) But as usually happens with such big budget efforts, the albur sistency, and as Columbia tried to pull several singles off it without notabl only to Streisand's million-member base audience. *—William Ruhlmar*

☆ **The Broadway Album** / 1985 / Columbia ✦✦✦✦✦

Barbra Streisand's abandonment of Broadway was the worst thing theater in the '60s. Her retreat from theater music on record was le because she had tended to focus on second-rank composers and obscure songs by first-rate ones, while practically ignoring, for example, Stephen Sondheim. When she returned to show songs in 1985, she reversed these failings. Now, the singer who had never done much with Rodgers & Hammerstein, Frank Loesser, George Gershwin, or Jerome Kern finally felt confident enough to take on "If I Loved You" from *Carousel*, "Adelaide's Lament" from *Guys and Dolls*, "Can't Help Lovin' That Man" from *Showboat*, and a medley from *Porgy and Bess*, and she did them well. Even better, on seven tracks with Sondheim's name on them, she proved the perfect intepreter of the most contemporary and intellectual of Broadway's writers, whether singing his lyrics over the music of Leonard Bernstein (another composer she'd largely neglected) from *West Side Story* or making the most of material drawn from shows like *Company*, *A Little Night Music*, *Sweeney Todd*, and *Sunday in the Park With George*. Sondheim collaborated with Streisand, penning special lyrics for songs like "Putting It Together" and even his standard, "Send in the Clowns." The result was an album that repositioned some of Broadway's best in a pop context and showed that Streisand was still at her best when presenting the dramatically satisfying story songs of the theater. Apparently, many longtime fans agreed: At sales over three million, *The Broadway Album* was Streisand's most commercially successful album in five years. *—William Ruhlmann*

One Voice / Apr. 1987 / Columbia ✦✦✦
For her first live recording in more than 14 years (a benefit held in her backyard with tickets at $5,000 a throw), Barbra Streisand reviewed her work in the interim, singing her chart-topping themes from the movies *The Way We Were* and *A Star Is Born* and choosing material from such memorable projects as *Guilty* (for which Barry Gibb got up and sang along), *Yentl*, and *The Broadway Album*. She also found room for a wonderful version of "Over the Rainbow" and for such old favorites as "People" and "Happy Days Are Again," the latter a Democratic Party campaign song and therefore singularly appropriate since the concert was held to raise money for Democratic Senate candidates. The political caste of the evening came out in Streisand's sometimes preachy stage remarks and the concert-closing "America the Beautiful," but it was possible to enjoy the recording no matter what your politics. *—William Ruhlmann*

Till I Loved You / Oct. 1988 / Columbia ✦✦✦
Barbra Streisand's first album of new studio material in four years, *Till I Loved You* was led by its title song, a duet with Streisand's current paramour, actor Don Johnson, on a tune from a Columbia Records pet project, a studio musical called *Goya*, written by Maury Yeston (composer of the Broadway show *Nine*), that the label was encouraging its artists to promote. That embarrassing recording made the album as a whole seem worse than it was. But *Till I Loved You*, which was given over to newly written romantic ballads by people like Burt Bacharach and Carole Bayer Sager, still wasn't very good. Eighteen songwriters, six producers, nine recording studios: Like *Emotion*, *Till I Loved You* was a big budget effort. But it was like a movie with a great star, great production values, and a mediocre script, so how much you liked it depended on how much you liked Barbra Streisand, and it sold to her fans only. *—William Ruhlmann*

Greatest Hits . . . and More / Sep. 1989 / Columbia ✦✦✦
Like *Memories*, *Greatest Hits . . . and More* was an odd compilation, not quite a hits set, though it gathered up the big hits not heard on the earlier record—"The Main Event/Fight," "Woman in Love," "Guilty," "What Kind of Fool"—since it also seemed to be a grab-bag, including a few stray album tracks, recycling the two new songs from *Memories*(!), "Comin' in and Out of Your Life" and "Memory," and adding a couple of new recordings, "We're Not Makin' Love Anymore" (by Diane Warren and Michael Bolton) and "Someone That I Used to Love." The selection made no apparent sense, but then neither had *Memories*, and that album sold several million copies. This one wasn't so fortunate, though many Streisand fans must have received it as a present for Christmas in 1989, which probably was the idea. *—William Ruhlmann*

Just for the Record . . . / Sep. 24, 1991 / Columbia ✦✦✦✦✦
As they evolved in the 1980s, retrospective box sets tended to contain a full complement of an artist's essential recordings, plus enough rarities to suggest the artist's inspirations and ambitions. Not all box sets conformed to this outline, however. Barbra Streisand was unusual, in that she had a large base of devoted fans interested in the minutiae of her career, and in that her entire recorded catalog remained in print. She had also worked with the same record company for her entire career and maintained her status as a frontline artist, so she had complete creative control over this retrospective. The result was a four-disc box devoted almost entirely to rare, previously unreleased material. Here and there, Streisand tossed in one of her most familiar recordings, such as the hit version of "People." But the overwhelming bulk of *Just for the Record . . .* was given over to homemade demonstration tapes, live recordings, television appearances, and outtakes from unfinished album projects, not to mention other special material. To Streisand's army of fans, that made it a delight, but practically by definition, that did not make it a great Barbra Streisand album unto itself. Unlike most boxed sets, this was not a one-stop shopping item that gave you the best and the rest of Barbra Streisand. That is not to say that there weren't some fascinating and terrific performances included. Especially notable was a set of eight songs recorded at a nightclub in 1962 and originally intended for Streisand's debut album. A duet with Judy Garland from her TV show and a rendering of "In the Wee Small Hours of the Morning" from a Las Vegas show were equally impressive. Nevertheless, *Just for the Record . . .* was an album to buy in addition to her hits collections and landmark albums, not in place of them. *—William Ruhlmann*

Prince of Tides / Nov. 12, 1991 / Columbia ✦✦✦
mes Newton Howard's score for Barbra Streisand's *The Prince of Tides* is a delicate, etty set of repetitive orchestral themes. Indeed, for a soundtrack, it is amazingly conent in terms of tone, continually employing swelling strings and slowly played piano figures in what sounds more like music for an air freshener commercial than a drama. Streisand sings two songs at the end, neither of them heard as a vocal selection in the actual film. One is the old J. Fred Coots and Sam M. Lewis standard "For All We Know," and the other is the newly written "Places That Belong to You," with music by Howard and lyrics by Alan and Marilyn Bergman in their "The Way Were" mode. Both songs are typically well sung, but the oldie is the better tune. *—William Ruhlmann*

Back to Broadway / Jun. 29, 1993 / Columbia ✦✦✦
While still an impressive recording, *Back to Broadway* is less impressive than its predecessor, *The Broadway Album*, for a number of reasons. The first is material. Barbra Streisand seems to be attracted to certain musicals, and here she chooses more songs from shows like *West Side Story* and *Guys And Dolls* that she didn't pick the last time around. Still attracted more to current composers than earlier ones, Streisand picks five songs by Stephen Sondheim (who has once again obligingly rewritten lyrics to suit her) and three by Andrew Lloyd Webber. The Sondheim material is worthy; the Lloyd Webber is not. (Though the intensity with which she sings "With One Look" from *Sunset Boulevard* suggests an eerie identification with the show's demented silent movie queen Norma Desmond.) Further, Streisand has done duets on two selections with people better identified with the material—Michael Crawford, the original Phantom in *Phantom of the Opera*, on his signature song, "The Music of the Night," and Johnny Mathis, who has sung a medley of *West Side Story* songs in his shows for years, on a medley of "I Have a Love/One Hand, One Heart" from that show. Finally, the arrangements and production lean more toward contemporary pop and light jazz in many instances, the influence of commercial producers and arrangers like David Foster. All of which means that *Back to Broadway* is somewhat uneven. When Streisand takes on songs as well suited to her as "Everybody Says Don't" (from Sondheim's *Anyone Can Whistle*) and "Children Will Listen" (from his *Into the Woods*), she nears her work on *The Broadway Album*. Elsewhere, she is merely a phenomenal singer working against material or arrangements that aren't quite appropriate to her. *—William Ruhlmann*

Barbra: The Concert / Sep. 1994 / Columbia ✦✦✦✦✦
Barbra Streisand's fourth live album was the only one to be drawn from a concert tour and not a one-time occasion, but it is no less special for that. For her first tour in 28 years, Streisand didn't just come out and sing her greatest hits for an hour and a half. Instead, she wove a selection of her best-known songs together with what she considered career highlights and added new and special material, starting with the customized lyrics of "As If We Never Said Goodbye" and "I'm Still Here" and including "Ordinary Miracles," by her conductor, Harvin Hamlisch and her house lyricists, Alan and Marilyn Bergman. The show was a musical autobiography crafted (as her 1991 boxed set *Just for the Record . . .* had been) for fans who would catch the references and agree with the artist on her viewpoints about her life, her career, the entertainment business, and politics. (And it was an abridged resume—rockers like "Stoney End" and disco hits like "Enough Is Enough" were omitted.) There was no denying that the 52-year-old singer, backed by a large orchestra and singing the songs that had kept her at the forefront of popular music for 30 years, was an impressive concert performer. But Streisand insisted that her listeners also encounter everything from her film directing ambitions to her psychoanalyst which made this an idiosyncratic performance from an artist determined to make public art out of her private story. As a result, *The Concert* may not be the place for neophytes to be introduced to her, though for fans it was the culmination of decades of wishing. *—William Ruhlmann*

The Concert—Highlights / May 2, 1995 / Columbia ✦✦✦✦✦
While an impressive live career retrospective and musical autobiography, *The Concert* also contained a lot of talking and a few less-than-terrific musical passages that made it the sort of album one was not likely to play repeatedly. With *The Concert—Highlights*, the original two-disc/cassette, containing 28 tracks and running 103:47, was condensed to a single disc/cassette containing 20 tracks and running 77:51, for, of course, half the price. The result was actually an improvement: Three of the eight excised tracks were portions of "Therapist Dialogue" and a fourth was the second act overture. No loss there. The four omitted songs were pleasant, but nonessential. In fact, one, an extended valentine to Streisand's godchild masquerading as a Disney film song medley, was better left off. Streisand completists will have to have the complete show, of course, but *Highlights* is more listenable in the way one listens to records—more than once—and focuses more on Streisand's singing. Obviously, the album was trimmed just enough to fit onto one disc. But it could have benefitted by being edited even more. *—William Ruhlmann*

Mirror Has Two Faces / Nov. 12, 1996 / Columbia ✦✦

Higher Ground / Nov. 4, 1997 / Columbia ✦✦✦

A Love Like Ours / Sep. 21, 1999 / Columbia ✦✦✦

Timeless: Live in Concert / Feb. 8, 2000 / Columbia ✦✦✦
Timeless: Live in Concert, recorded at her Las Vegas show on New Year's Eve 1999, takes as its subject the star herself. It opens with a dramatization of her first, amateur recording session, with young Lauren Frost playing a part described in the credits as "Young Girl," though Streisand later refers to her as "mini-me." Frost doesn't get too far before being joined by Streisand herself on a stirring version of "Something's Coming" from *West Side Story*. The rest of "Act One" traces Streisand's career from her club days to her movie performances. "Act Two" has less of a narrative structure, though it is equally autobiographical, with Streisand displaying and commenting on videos of herself performing with other stars and building up to the stroke of midnight with a combination of old, recent, and new specially written songs. At 57 that night, Streisand remains in good voice, and the old warhorses, among them inevitable hits like "People," "Evergreen," and "The Way We Were," sound, well, like they always do. More interesting are songs that, while

previously recorded, have not been heard live before, especially "Alfie," which the singer confesses to having forgotten she ever did. But unless you are a big Streisand fan, you may want to stick to the studio albums on which she just sings. The extensive stage remarks here include comic interludes such as a dialogue with Shirley MacLaine and negative opinions about new technology, but for the most part they center on the singer herself. *Timeless* was issued a week before what were said to be her final concerts in September 2000. —*William Ruhlmann*

Barrett Strong

b. Feb. 5, 1941, Westpoint, MS
Vocals, Songwriter / Motown, R&B, Soul
A pivotal figure in Motown's formative years, singer/composer Barrett Strong was a key associate and friend of Berry Gordy. It was his hit "Money (That's What I Want)" for Anna Records in 1960 that provided vital capital for Gordy to expand his operation. The song gave Strong his only major hit as a vocalist, reaching number two on the R&B charts and barely missing the pop Top 20. During the late '60s and early '70s, Strong collaborated with Norman Whitfield on some historic songs that included Marvin Gaye's "I Heard It Through the Grapevine" and "Too Busy Thinking About My Baby," The Temptations' "Papa Was a Rolling Stone" and "Ball of Confusion," Edwin Starr's "War," and "Take Me in Your Arms and Love Me" for Gladys Knight & the Pips, which he also co-wrote. Strong left Motown when they moved to Los Angeles in 1972, and he signed with Epic. After one failed single, Strong moved to Capitol, where he had the LP *Stronghold* released in 1975 and later *Live & Love* in 1976. Though it wasn't a hit, his song "Man up in the Sky" was a '70s soul gem. Johnny Bristol later re-recorded it. Strong continued into the '80s, recording "Rock It Easy" for an independent label and writing and arranging "You Can Depend on Me," which was included on the Dells' *The Second Time* LP in 1988. —*Ron Wynn*

Stronghold / 1975 / Capitol ✦

● **Live & Love** / 1976 / Capitol ✦✦✦
This is light-years ahead of his Capitol debut, the amateurish, weak *Stronghold*; *Live & Love* has better songs, arrangements, and instrumentation. He adequately revives his only hit "Money (That's What I Want)" and Eddie Floyd's "Knock on Wood." The excellent "Man Up in the Sky" had hit potential, a moving number with a spiritual theme; Johnny Bristol's version of this Barrett Strong/Billy Always composition achieved some popularity in Europe, and most people associate the song with Bristol. A good effort, but people expected more from the co-writer of classics the stature of "Ball of Confusion," "War," "Friendship Train," "Too Busy Thinking About My Baby," and others. —*Andrew Hamilton*

Nolan Strong

b. 1950, Scottsboro, AL, **d.** Feb. 21, 1977, Detroit, MI
Detroit Blues, R&B
The Diablos are best remembered for "The Wind," a haunting song that featured the group chanting the words "blow wind" in harmony behind Nolan Strong's ethereal tenor lead. The Diablos were inspired by gospel groups like Sam Cooke & the Soul Stirrers, Archie & the Blind Boys, and R&B groups like the Cadillacs, Del-Vikings, Billy Ward & the Dominoes, and the Dells. They originally formed around 1950, while all of the original members were still in high school, Strong's tenor and high falsetto definitely the focal point of the group from the very beginning. In 1954, the Diablos cut a few demos in the studios of Detroit's Fortune Records, a pioneering black R&B label, hoping to further their career. Their hopes were realized even more quickly than they expected when those demos were heard by Jack and Devora Brown, owners of Fortune, who immediately signed the group to their first recording contract. It was Devora Brown who penned their first single, in fact, called "Adios My Desert Love." Their second Fortune outing, the haunting ballad "The Wind," was written by the group members and credited to the Diablos Featuring Nolan Strong, later changed to Nolan Strong & the Diablos. Over the next two years, the Diablos would release several singles on Fortune. When Strong returned to the group after a two-year Army stint, Fortune began focusing on his silky lead tenor and not the group, even paying him more in royalties. By 1962, the label credits on the chart-climbing "Mind Over Matter" were credited to Nolan Strong, even though the Diablos were backing him up as they had all along. The in-fighting between group members inevitably led to the Diablos' demise before the mid-'60s. —*Bryan Thomas*

● **Fortune of Hits, Vol. 1** / 1961 / Fortune ✦✦✦✦✦
All the early hits, and the perfect place to start. —*Cub Koda*

Fortune of Hits, Vol. 2 / 1962 / Fortune ✦✦✦✦✦
The companion piece to *Fortune of Hits—Vol. 1*. —*Cub Koda*

Daddy Rock / 1963 / Fortune ✦✦✦
A great batch of rare and unreleased sides. —*Cub Koda*

Joe Strummer

b. Aug. 21, 1952, Ankara, Turkey
Vocals, Guitar / Roots Rock, Alternative Pop/Rock
One of the most talented songwriters of his generation, Joe Strummer has seemed lost since disbanding the Clash after the wretched *Cut the Crap* in 1986. Strummer has done some respectable soundtrack work (*Walker*, *Straight to Hell*, five strong tracks for *Permanent Record*, and the theme song for *Sid & Nancy*). He acted impressively in Jim Jarmusch's *Mystery Train* and Alex Cox's *Straight to Hell*, collaborated with ex-partner Mick Jones, and released the occasional solo album, with a decade separating 1989's *Earthquake Weather* from its follow-up, *Rock Art and the X-Ray Style*. —*Stephen Thomas Erlewine*

Walker / 1987 / Virgin ✦✦✦
While the film was something of a hodgepodge of ideas, the soundtrack music was a remarkable collection of influences, with everything from razor-edged rock to near-ambient elements creeping in. Bears well with repeated playing just as an album. —*Steven McDonald*

● **Earthquake Weather** / 1989 / Epic ✦✦✦
Strummer's first solo album is a muddled hodgepodge of roots rock and world explorations. His compositions are fine, but are often undercut by the limp kick of the band. —*Stephen Thomas Erlewine*

Rock Art and the X-Ray Style / Oct. 19, 1999 / Epitaph ✦✦✦
It has taken Joe Strummer ten years to follow up on his first solo album, *Earthquake Weather*, with *Rock Art and the X-Ray Style*, and while the vocals and occasional moments in the music are identifiable as the work of a man who was once a singer, guitarist, and songwriter in the Clash, no one should purchase this album expecting to hear a direct extension of his old band. Strummer, who helped lead the Clash beyond punk rock to a variety of rhythmic styles, has only expanded his range since, and *Rock Art and the X-Ray Style* is an album of songs built on often exotic, funky beats, few of which rock very hard. Over those rhythm tracks, Strummer sings highly poetic, apparently freely associative lyrics whose meanings usually seem to be either private to him or just not literal. Unfortunately, the vocals are high in the mix and the musical tracks are subservient to the lyrics (which are printed in the booklet) so that one is left to ponder what Strummer is talking about. Coming back after a decade, even on an independent label, it might have been hoped that Strummer would return to action with a more accessible effort than *Rock Art and the X-Ray Style*, which is unlikely to re-establish him as a major force in popular music. —*William Ruhlmann*

Global a Go-Go / Jul. 24, 2001 / Epitaph ✦✦✦
In many ways, it's easiest to appreciate Joe Strummer's album *Global a Go-Go* if you forget that it was made by Joe Strummer. This isn't meant to insult the music in question, which is often engaging and always passionate, or suggest that it doesn't bear any significant signs of Strummer's personality; if you loved the syllable-drenched wordplay of songs like "The Magnificent Seven," "Lightning Strikes," or "Car Jamming," you're in for a treat, because here you get nearly a whole album of it. But if you're expecting the former leader of the Clash to be backed by two guitars, bass, and drums and playing something easily recognizable as rock & roll (not a difficult assumption to make) then you're flat out of luck. Best described as eccentric internationalist folk-rock, *Global a Go-Go* is dominated by acoustic instruments (Tymon Dogg, the fiddler from the Clash's "Loose This Skin," is all over this album like a pillowcase) and a wild gumbo of flavors from Africa, Latin America, and the West Indies, and while a few tunes have a prominent electric guitar (particularly "Cool 'n' Out"), most do not. And if you're hoping for lots of punkwise sloganeering from the usually provocative Mr. Strummer, there isn't a great deal of that, either, though it's obvious from the Dylanesque density of his wordplay that Strummer's got a lot on his mind, and the one-world perspective that shines throughout is food for thought in itself, especially on the tasty "Bhindi Bhagee" and the globetrotting title cut. And while the epic instrumental "Minstrel Boy" wouldn't lead you to imagine it's the work of one of the great icons of punk rock, it at least proves Strummer is willing to mess with his audience's expectations, which is a very punk rock thing to do. *Global a Go-Go* is an intelligent and uniquely absorbing record, but listening to it is like eating sushi or escargot for the first time (knowing what it is might shape your expectations in the wrong direction). —*Mark Deming*

The Style Council

f. 1983, **db.** 1990
Sophisti-Pop, New Wave
Guitarist/vocalist Paul Weller broke up the Jam, the most popular British band of the early '80s, at the height of their success in 1982 because he was dissatisfied with their musical direction. Weller wanted to incorporate more elements of soul, R&B, and jazz into his songwriting, which is something he felt his punk-oriented bandmates were incapable of performing. In order to pursue this musical direction, he teamed up in 1983 with keyboardist Mick Talbot, a former member of the mod revival band the Merton Parkas. Together, Weller and Talbot became the Style Council—other musicians were added according to what kind of music the duo were performing. With the Style Council, the underlying intellectual pretensions that ran throughout Weller's music came to the forefront. Although the music was rooted in American R&B, it was performed slickly—complete with layers of synthesizers and drum machines—and filtered through European styles and attitudes. Weller's lyrics were typically earnest, yet his leftist political leanings became more pronounced. His scathing criticisms of racism, unemployment, Margaret Thatcher, and sexism sat uneasily beside his burgeoning obsession with high culture. As his pretensions increased, the number of hits the Style Council had decreased; by the end of the decade, the group was barely able to crack the British Top 40 and Weller had turned from a hero into a has-been. —*Stephen Thomas Erlewine*

Introducing the Style Council / 1983 / Polydor ✦✦✦✦✦
A solid EP collection of the band's initial British singles, it includes the ersatz soul of "Long Hot Summer," and the bubbling pop of "Speak Like a Child," and "Money-Go-Round," a fine British-funk manifesto. —*John Floyd*

Cafe Bleu / 1984 / Polydor ✦✦✦✦✦
Style Council's first proper album *Cafe Bleu* was one of their better efforts, but it indicated the group's fatal flaw—a tendency to be too eclectic and overambitious. Amidst the lazy jazz instrumentals, many of them courtesy of Mick Talbot, Paul Weller inserted several solid soul-tinged pop songs, including "My Ever Changing Moods," "Headstart for

Happiness," "You're the Best Thing," and "Here's One That Got Away." However, that doesn't excuse the rap experiment, "A Gospel." The album was later released with a slightly different running order as *My Ever Changing Moods* in the U.S.; the American edition included the U.K. hit "A Solid Bond in Your Heart." *—Stephen Thomas Erlewine*

Our Favourite Shop / 1985 / Polydor ✦✦✦✦✦
Our Favourite Shop, the Style Council's second proper album, was still quite eclectic, but it didn't seem as schizophrenically diverse as *Cafe Bleu*. Weller had been able to incorporate his soul and jazz experiments into his songwriting, writing the fine "Walls Come Tumbling Down," "Come to Milton Keys," "Boy Who Cried Wolf," and "Down in the Seine," which were some of his best songs for the Style Council. The occasional misguided experiment remained—the stiff funk of "The Internationalists" and the self-righteous "The Stand Up Comic's Instructions" were particularly embarrassing—but the record was more cohesive and stronger than the debut. In America, the album was released without "Our Favourite Shop" and retitled *Internationalists*. *—Stephen Thomas Erlewine*

Home & Abroad / 1986 / Polydor ✦✦

Cost of Loving / 1987 / Polydor ✦✦

Confessions of a Pop Group / 1988 / Polydor ✦

● **The Singular Adventures of the Style Council** / Jun. 1989 / Polydor ✦✦✦✦✦
The Style Council's albums were always weighed down by their far-reaching musical ambitions, which meant that their ideas were usually best heard on their singles. And while this period of Paul Weller's career has been criticized heavily, he wrote several excellent songs during the Style Council, most of which are featured on the fine compilation *The Singular Adventures of the Style Council*. Not all of the 16 songs are first-rate, as it begins to lose steam toward the end of the band's life, but "My Ever Changing Moods," "You're the Best Thing," "Long Hot Summer," "Shout to the Top!," "A Solid Bond in Your Heart," "Money Go Round," "Walls Come Tumbling Down," and "Speak Like a Child" are terrific, and make the collection worthwhile for fans of the Jam and Weller's solo career, as well as fans of New Romantic new wave and jazzy sophisti-pop. *—Stephen Thomas Erlewine*

Here's Some That Got Away / Feb. 22, 1994 / Polydor ✦✦✦
Since the Style Council's albums were either inconsistent or downright boring, the idea of a B-sides and rarities collection isn't exactly enticing. However, *Here's Some That Got Away* is surprisingly enjoyable, proving that Paul Weller was at his best when he wasn't trying to make serious, self-important music. *—Stephen Thomas Erlewine*

The Style Council Collection / Mar. 1996 / Polydor ✦✦✦✦
Not a strict greatest hits, *The Style Council Collection* balances some of the group's biggest singles with some relatively obscure album tracks. Like the band itself, the album loses steam toward the end but the best songs here—"My Ever Changing Moods," in particular—prove that, contrary to popular belief, the Style Council wasn't a complete waste of Paul Weller's time and that he did explore some new territory with the group. *—Stephen Thomas Erlewine*

The Complete Adventures of the Style Council / Sep. 29, 1998 / Polydor ✦✦✦✦
Given the blockbuster success of the Jam's exhaustive box set *Direction Reaction Creation*, perhaps it was inevitable that Polydor would give the Style Council a similar treatment, but the 1998 release of the five-disc box set *The Complete Adventures of the Style Council* was still a bit of surprise—there never was much interest in their catalog following their 1990 disbandment. Fortunately, Polydor took a chance and assembled *The Complete Adventures*, a lavish box set containing all of the group's singles and albums, minus the live *Home & Abroad* but including the notorious unreleased 1989 record *A Decade of Modernism*, which the label allegedly rejected because it found Weller turning toward house music. As it turns out, *A Decade of Modernism* wasn't that far afield from what the Style Council was exploring from their inception, as the chronological running order of the set makes clear. The sequencing is a blessed occurrence, since it's easy to trace their development over the years. Instead of an aberration, the Style Council seems like a natural extension of the Jam's final record, *The Gift*, and every one of their subsequent records makes more sense than before. That doesn't mean the music is always compelling. No matter how interesting some of Weller's ideas were, they didn't always work, and he wrote way too many pompous, directionless songs to have *The Complete Adventures* rank with *Direction Reaction Creation*. (There are also too many Mick Talbot instrumentals, but that's another story.) For most listeners, including some serious Weller fans, the Style Council is best appreciated as a singles band, but for the dedicated, *The Complete Adventures* reveals that the Style Council, no matter how maddening they could be, were a group that continually reinvented themselves, occasionally making some remarkable music along the way. *—Stephen Thomas Erlewine*

In Concert / Dec. 28, 1999 / Polydor ✦✦✦

The Stylistics

f. 1968, Philadelphia, PA, **db.** 1980
Smooth Soul, Quiet Storm, Philly Soul, Soul
After the Spinners and the O'Jays, the Stylistics were the leading Philly soul group produced by Thom Bell. During the early '70s, the band had 12 straight Top Ten hits, including "You Are Everything," "Betcha by Golly, Wow," "I'm Stone in Love With You," "Break Up to Make Up" and "You Make Me Feel Brand New." Of all their peers, the Stylistics were one of the smoothest and sweetest soul groups of their era. All of their hits were ballads, graced by the soaring falsetto of Russell Thompkins Jr. and the lush, yet graceful productions of Thom Bell, which helped make the Stylistics one of the most successful soul groups of the first half of the '70s. After signing to Avco in 1971, the Stylistics began working with producer/songwriter Thom Bell. He crafted a series of hit singles that relied as much on the intricately arranged and lush production as they did on Thompkins' falsetto. Every single that Bell produced for the Stylistics was a Top Ten R&B hit, and several were also Top Ten pop hits. In 1974, the Stylistics replaced Thom Bell with Van McCoy, who helped move the group toward a softer, easy listening style. Though their American sales declined, they remained popular in Great Britain, where they scored four Top Five hits. The Stylistics continued performing into the '90s on oldies shows. *—Stephen Thomas Erlewine*

The Stylistics / 1971 / Amherst ✦✦✦
The brilliant album that got everything started. Heads turned, people snapped to attention (women especially), and the "sweet" soul fraternity was turned on its head when this five-member group featuring the sugary, sweeping falsetto of Russell Tompkins Jr. hit the scene with such singles as "Betcha by Golly Wow," "People Make the World Go Round," and "Stop, Look and Listen to Your Heart." His delivery, shimmering style, and brilliant pacing and control temporarily rendered almost every other "sweet" soul vocalist and group speechless; pretty soon, the Delfonics, Blue Magic, Moments, and others would fight back, but in 1972, everyone was playing catchup to the Stylistics. *—Ron Wynn*

Round 2 / 1972 / Amherst ✦✦✦✦✦
This was the Stylistics' sophomore album and it spawned three Billboard R&B Top Ten singles: "I'm Stone in Love With You," "Break Up to Make Up," and "You'll Never Get to Heaven (If You Break My Heart)." The first two even cracked the Top Ten on the pop charts. Furthermore, there is much here to savor. The vocal quintet's version of the Carole King classic "It's Too Late" never soars or dips—it just soothes in spite of the fateful lyric. "Children of the Night" imparts a similar mood but with a different lyrical content. The two selections "Peek-A-Boo" and "You're As Right As Rain" are Stylistics originals. First tenor Russell Thompkins Jr, who leads on all the aforementioned songs, seems to effortlessly reach each note and hold it as long as necessary. Although only the first three hit the charts, all of the songs referenced are radio favorites. As superb as the group was vocally, the production work of Thom Bell is commendable as well. *—Craig Lytle*

Rock & Roll Baby / 1973 / Amherst ✦✦✦✦
The last of the Stylistics' Thom Bell productions is just as essential as the first two. This one is slightly harder to find as it has not been reissued in the States. It has been reissued by a United Kingdom company however, and can be purchased via online music stores. The title cut is possibly the fastest record the sweet Philly crooners ever recorded. The late Linda Creed's lyrics fit the speedy rhythm track like custom gloves and lead singer Russell Thompkins enunciates every word clearly, making a lyric sheet unnecessary. Kenny Gamble collaborates with Bell on "Payback Is a Dog," a what-goes-around-comes-around song performed in the Stylistics' classic style. Normally writers for the Spinners, Bruce Hawes, Chester Simmons, and Joe Jefferson contributes the questioning "Could This Be the End," a ballad that Thompkins precise falsetto works to perfection. Everybody knows "You Make Feel Brand New," Airon Love begins the stately love song, and Thompkins takes it home shining brightly, hitting the notes with the precision of a diamond cutter. With Thompkins it's all about technique, on the Bell sides he was always restrained, just once you wanted him to cut loose and let that falsetto go hog wild. Overall, not as compelling as the first two Bell productions, but a far cry better then anything that came after it. *—Andrew Hamilton*

Greatest Love Hits / 1974 / Amherst ✦✦✦✦✦
Another anthology, this one covering the beautiful love songs and romantic ballads that were the Stylistics' specialty. These are all magnificent, some of the finest sentimental soul that's ever been recorded. But it's also been issued before, and Amherst's mastering isn't anything to write home about, especially the way they tend to wash out Russell Tompkins, Jr.'s high notes. *—Ron Wynn*

Let's Put It All Together / 1974 / Avco Embassy ✦✦✦
Their finest album, the Stylistics climbed the "sweet" soul mountain in 1974. "You Make Me Feel Brand New" and the title cut were among the year's prime love/romance numbers, and Russell Tompkins, Jr. had nudged past Blue Magic's Ted Mills and the Delfonics' Hart brothers as the falsetto voice of choice among female fans. Their run on Avco, with Thom Bell at the production helm, was one of the greatest in modern soul annals. *—Ron Wynn*

Heavy / 1974 / Avco Embassy ✦✦✦
The magical union between the Stylistics and producer/writer Thom Bell ended with this album, but the legacy had included a string of fabulous hit singles and arguably the greatest "sweet" soul productions of all time. Russell Tompkins, Jr. was in his prime as a lead vocalist, and while this album didn't have any blockbusters like its predecessors, it still had plenty of exquisitely sung, nicely harmonized ballads and love tunes. *—Ron Wynn*

● **The Best of the Stylistics [Amherst]** / 1975 / Amherst ✦✦✦✦✦
Any of their collections are good, but this one features their biggest and best hits, including "I'm Stone in Love with You," "Rockin' Roll Baby," "Betcha by Golly Wow," and "You Make Me Feel Brand New." *—Cub Koda*

The Best of the Stylistics [Spectrum] / Dec. 28, 1999 / Spectrum ✦✦✦✦
Eighteen of the Stylistics' creamiest recordings featuring a good helping of Thom Bell productions and ample portions of Hugo & Luigi's efforts. The different styles are quite evident: Bell has Russell Thompkins' soaring falsetto under complete control while Hugo & Luigi allow him to fly off the handle every once in a while. The H & L tunes didn't set the states on fire, but "Star on a TV Show," "Funky Weekend," and "Can't Give You Anything but Love" exploded in Europe. "You're a Big Girl Now," produced by Marty Bryant, shows yet another side of the talented Philly group and contrasts with Bell's stately pro-

ductions, such as "You Make Me Feel Brand New," "You'll Never Get to Heaven," "You Are Everything," "Betcha By Golly Wow," and "Stone in Love With You." *—Andrew Hamilton*

Styx

f. 1970, Chicago, IL

Album Rock, Arena Rock, Pop/Rock, Prog Rock/Art Rock, Hard Rock

Styx was one of the biggest album rock bands of the late '70s, capable of producing monster hits with their stadium rock, power ballads, and concept albums. More than any other art rock band, Styx was able to cross over into the pop charts, scoring hits with "Babe," "Lady," "Come Sail Away," "Too Much Time on My Hands," and "Don't Let It End." Never a band for subtlety, their ballads featured sweeping, over-arranged guitars and keyboards while their rockers were long and detailed, with several different sections and gargantuan guitar solos. When MTV rolled around in the early '80s, the hits stopped coming; they broke up in 1984. Six years later, they reunited and released *Edge of the Century*; the record featured "Show Me the Way," which became popular as a Gulf War anthem. The band went on hiatus a couple of years after the album's release, but returned several more times in the late '90s; 1999 saw the release of a new studio album, *Brave New World*. *—Stephen Thomas Erlewine*

Styx / Sep. 1972 / One Way ✦✦

Styx II / Jul. 1973 / RCA ✦✦✦

Styx's second album was a belated success, scoring a Top Ten hit with "Lady," two years after its release. In retrospect, it is easy to see why *Styx II* was ignored upon its release. Apart from "Lady" and "You Need Love," most of the album is bland. However, it's the best of the group's first three records. *—Stephen Thomas Erlewine*

The Serpent Is Rising / Feb. 1974 / RCA ✦✦

Man of Miracles / Nov. 1974 / RCA ✦✦✦

Equinox / Dec. 1975 / A&M ✦✦✦

Equinox produced Styx's first single with A&M, the highly spirited "Lorelei," which found its way to number 27 on the charts. Although it was the only song to chart from *Equinox*, the album itself is a benchmark in the band's career since it includes an instrumental nature reminiscent of their early progressive years, yet hints toward a more commercial-sounding future in its lyrics. "Light Up" is a brilliant display of keyboard bubbliness, with De Young's vocals in full bloom, while "Lonely Child" and "Suite Madame Blue" show tighter songwriting and a slight drift toward radio amicability. Still harboring their synthesizer-led dramatics alongside Dennis De Young's exaggerated vocal approach, the material on *Equinox* was a firm precursor of what was to come. After *Equinox*, guitarist John Curulewski parted ways with the band, replaced by Tommy Shaw, who debuted on 1976's *Crystal Ball* album. *—Mike DeGagne*

Crystal Ball / Oct. 1976 / A&M ✦✦✦

Crystal Ball wasn't as successful as *Equinox*, but it was a better album, showcasing Styx's increased skill for crafting simple, catchy pop hooks out of their bombastic sound. *—Daevid Jehnzen*

The Grand Illusion / Jul. 1977 / A&M ✦✦✦✦

Other than being their first platinum-selling album, *The Grand Illusion* led Styx steadfastly into the domain of AOR rock. Built on the strengths of "Come Sail Away"'s ballad-to-rock metamorphosis, which gained them their second Top Ten hit, and on the high harmonies of newcomer Tommy Shaw throughout "Fooling Yourself," *The Grand Illusion* introduced Styx to the gates of commercial stardom. The pulverized growl of "Miss America" reveals the group's guitar-savvy approach to six-string rock, while De Young pretentiously struts his singing prowess throughout the title track. Shaw's induction into the band has clearly settled, and his guitar work, along with James Young's, is full and extremely sharp where it matters most. Even the songwriting is more effluent than *Crystal Ball*, which was released one year earlier, shedding their mystical song motifs for a more audience-pleasing lyric and chord counterpoise. Reaching number six on the album charts, *The Grand Illusion* was the first to display the gelled accomplishments of both Tommy Shaw and Dennis De Young as a tandem. *—Mike DeGagne*

Pieces of Eight / Sep. 1978 / A&M ✦✦✦✦

Styx's feisty, straightforward brand of album rock is represented best by "Blue Collar Man" from 1978's *Pieces of Eight*, an invigorating keyboard and guitar rush—hard and heavy, yet curved by Tommy Shaw's emphasized vocals. Reaching number 21, with the frolicking romp of "Renegade" edging in at number 16 only six months later, *Pieces of Eight* maintained their strength as a front-running FM radio group. Even though these two tracks were both mainstream singles, the rest of the album includes tracks that rekindle some of Styx's early progressive rock sound, only cleaner. Tracks like "Sing for the Day," "Lords of the Ring," and "Aku-Aku" all contain slightly more complex instrumental foundations, and are lyrically reminiscent of the material from albums like *The Serpent Is Rising* or *Man of Miracles*, but not as intricate or instrumentally convoluted. While the writing may stray slightly from what Styx provided on *The Grand Illusion*, *Pieces of Eight* kept their established rock formula in tact quite firmly. *—Mike DeGagne*

Cornerstone / Oct. 1979 / A&M ✦✦✦✦

Presenting radio with one of the best rock ballads ever, *Cornerstone* gave Chicago's Styx their big break with the number one single "Babe," which held that spot for two weeks in October of 1979. "Babe" is a smooth, keyboard-pampered love song that finally credited Dennis De Young's textured vocals. While this single helped the album climb all the way to the number two spot on the charts, the rest of the tracks from *Cornerstone* weren't nearly half as strong. "Why Me" made it to number 26, and both "Lights" and "Boat on the River" implement silky harmonies and welcoming choruses, yet failed to get off the ground. De Young's keyboards are effective without overly dominating the music, and the band's gritty rock & roll acerbity has been slightly sanded down to compliment the commercial market. The songs aren't as tight or assertive as their last few albums, but Shaw's presence can be felt strongly on most of the tracks, especially where the writing is concerned. Outside of "Babe," *Cornerstone* tends to sound a tad weaker than one would expect. *—Mike DeGagne*

Paradise Theater / Jan. 1981 / A&M ✦✦✦✦

After successfully establishing themselves as one of America's best commercial progressive rock bands of the late '70s with albums like *The Grand Illusion* and *Pieces of Eight*, Chicago's Styx had taken a dubious step towards pop overkill with singer Dennis DeYoung's ultra-schmaltzy ballad "Babe." The centerpiece of 1979's uneven *Cornerstone* album, the number one single would sew the seeds of disaster for the group by pitching DeYoung's increasingly mainstream ambitions against the group's more conservative songwriters, Tommy Shaw and James "JY" Young. Hence, what had once been a healthy competitive spirit within the band quickly deteriorated into bitter co-existence during the sessions for 1980's *Paradise Theater*. For the time being, however, *Paradise Theater* seemed to represent the best of both worlds, since its loose concept about the roaring '20s heyday and eventual decline of an imaginary theater (used as a metaphor for the American experience in general, etc., etc.) seemed to satisfy both of the band's camps with its return to complex hard rock (purists Shaw and JY) while sparing no amount of pomp and grandeur (DeYoung). The stage is set by the first track, "A.D. 1928," which features a lonely DeYoung on piano and vocals introducing the album's recurring musical theme before launching into "Rockin' the Paradise"—a total team effort of wonderfully stripped-down hard rock. From this point forward, DeYoung's compositions continue to stick close to the overall storyline, while Shaw's try to resist thematic restrictions as best they can. Among these, "The Best of Times" remains one of the more improbable Top Ten hits of the decade. A resounding success, *Paradise Theater* would become Styx's greatest commercial triumph; and in retrospect, it remains one of the best examples of the convergence between progressive rock and AOR. *—Ed Rivadavia*

Kilroy Was Here / Feb. 1983 / A&M ✦✦✦

Although Dennis De Young's concept about man being replaced by robots in the near future failed to get off the ground, *Kilroy Was Here* still harbored two of the band's best singles. "Don't Let It End" almost captures the same endearing qualities as their number one hit, "Babe," did four years earlier, peaking at number six, and the synthesized novelty of "Mr. Roboto" went all the way to number three, accompanied by a lively and rather extravagant Dennis De Young at the helm. It was the song's mechanically spoken chorus and slight disco beat that made it Styx's fifth Top Ten single up to that point, overshadowing the rest of the album's tracks. Pretentious, weakly composed, and rhythmically anemic, songs like "Cold War," "Heavy Metal Poisoning," and "Double Life" couldn't even keep the album's main idea interesting, solidifying the fact that Styx's forte was singles, not conceptual pieces. The saxophone playing from Steve Eison gathers some redemption, cropping up here and there, but even some decent guitar work from Shaw and Young can't save the rest of the album. Brought back to life in the late '90s in an automobile commercial, "Mr. Roboto" gained somewhat of a minor resurgence more than 15 years after its chart life. *—Mike DeGagne*

Caught in the Act / Apr. 1984 / A&M ✦

Edge of the Century / Oct. 9, 1990 / A&M ✦✦

● **Greatest Hits** / Aug. 22, 1995 / A&M ✦✦✦✦✦

Replacing the band's volume in A&M's *Classics* series, *Greatest Hits* collects all Styx's major chart and radio hits, from "Lady" to "Show Me the Way." Although they were a definitive album rock band, creating records that were meant to be listened to as a whole, their finest moments were always their singles, making *Greatest Hits* the only Styx disc many fans will need to own. *—Stephen Thomas Erlewine*

Greatest Hits, Part II / Jun. 1996 / A&M ✦✦✦

Greatest Hits, Part II collects all of Styx's radio hits that weren't featured on the first collection, as well as a a handful of newly recorded tracks. While there are some fine songs on *Part II*, the overall quality isn't as high as that of the first volume, which did have all of the hits. Still, for fans wanting to fill in the holes left by *Greatest Hits* who don't have the desire to dig deep into Styx's back catalog, *Greatest Hits, Part II* is a good purchase. *—Stephen Thomas Erlewine*

Return to Paradise / May 5, 1997 / CMC International ✦✦✦✦

Styx was one of the all-time favorite targets of many rock critics, but the mixture of bleeding-heart ballads, catchy arena rock, and ambitious art rock appealed to millions in the late '70s and early '80s. After 13 years apart, the Chicago-based band's classic lineup of vocalist/keyboardist Dennis DeYoung, vocalist/guitarist Tommy Shaw, vocalist/guitarist James Young, and bassist Chuck Panozzo reunited for a successful greatest-hits tour in 1996. Drummer Todd Sucherman replaced John Panozzo, who died of chronic alcohol abuse that year. The highly enjoyable, 17-song concert video *Return to Paradise* was filmed on the final date of the 1996 tour—on the autumnal equinox—in front of an enthusiastic hometown crowd at the Rosemont Horizon. The quintet seems to be having a blast. The tour's theme and stage setup was based on 1981's *Paradise Theater* (number one). As such, the boisterous "Rockin' the Paradise" is an appropriate opener. "Blue Collar Man (Long Nights)" maintains the full-tilt pace. A frantic jam ends "Too Much Time on My Hands." Before Young starts the dramatic "Snowblind," he reminds the fans that it was accused of containing satanic backward messages, lists the devil's many aliases, and says, "None of those bad guys had a damn thing to do with this next song." DeYoung dedicates "Show Me the Way" to John Panozzo; a photo of the late drummer is projected on the stage backdrop and the fans ignite a sea of lighters and candles. A blistering version of "Come Sail Away" ends the regular set; the encores are "Renegade" and "The Best of

Times." (Although "Mr. Roboto" was regarded as a cheesy sci-fi embarrassment by many, its omission is disappointing.) The 1999 DVD includes many extras such as behind-the-scenes footage shot by Sucherman, an interview with Shaw, a photo gallery, and more. —*Bret Adams*

Sublime

f. 1988, **db.** 1996
Ska-Punk, Third Wave Ska Revival, Punk Revival, Alternative Pop/Rock
Formed in Long Beach, CA, in 1988 as a garage-punk band, Sublime grew to fame in the mid-'90s on the back of the Cali punk explosion engendered by Green Day and the Off-spring, though Sublime mixed up their punk rage with reggae and ska influences. The band released just two albums during its first seven years, finally finding a hit with the self-titled third. It was Sublime's last, however, as lead singer Brad Nowell died in May 1996, just two months before the album's release.

The trio which comprised Sublime—vocalist/guitarist Nowell, bassist Eric Wilson, and drummer Bud Gaugh—played their first gig on the 4th of July 1988 at a small Long Beach club (a show which sparked the infamous Peninsula Riot). The group began aggressively touring around the area with an increasingly substantial following, especially among the surf/skate beach crowd. After four years of concentrating strictly on live shows, Sublime's first album (*40 Oz. to Freedom*) was recorded in 1992. The LP was released on Skunk Records—the label formed by Nowell with Sublime manager Miguel—and sold at shows, but it really started to break when KROQ began playing the single "Date Rape" two years after its initial release.

Mostly due to the radio exposure, Sublime signed to MCA for 1994's *Robbin' the Hood*, which revealed an experimental ethic more in keeping with cut-and-paste dub than the well-tuned rage of the Cali punk revival. The album performed well at college radio and set the stage for the breakout success of their self-titled third album. On May 25, 1996, however, Brad Nowell was found in a San Francisco hotel room, dead of a heroin overdose. The band collapsed, but *Sublime* was still slated for a July release. On the strength of the alternative radio hit "What I Got," the album was certified gold by the end of 1996. A number of posthumous releases followed, among them 1997's *Second Hand Smoke*, 1998's *Live: Stand By Your Van* and *Acoustic: Bradley Nowell and Friends*. —*John Bush*

40 Oz. to Freedom / 1992 / MCA ✦✦✦
With their debut *40 Oz. to Freedom*, Sublime attempts to have it both ways. The group wants to appeal to alterna-punks, but they want to cut a little deeper and make some sort of social statement, both with their lyrics and their self-consciously eclectic music. Since the group has a knack for combining dancehall reggae with hardcore punk, the music can be nervy and invigorating, but their joyous blend of cultures falls apart at the lyrical level. No matter what you look at it, "Date Rape" isn't a bold, ironic satire on macho mores—it's frat-rock that's bound to be misinterpreted, especially with its homophobic "I don't feel too sorry for his kind/now that he gets it in the behind" conclusion. Lyrics like that prevent *40 Oz. to Freedom* from being the cracking, skanking skate-punk record that it had the potential to be. —*Stephen Thomas Erlewine*

Robbin' the Hood / 1994 / MCA ✦✦✦✦
Pieced together rather quickly, *Robbin' the Hood* wasn't really intended to be the follow-up to Sublime's debut *40 Oz. to Freedom*, but what is shocking is how much better the record is from its predecessor. Boasting a wider range of influences—including elements of reggae and old-school hip-hop—the record is a loose, infectious blend of styles that rides along on its own sense of energy. Brad Nowell's songwriting might still be at a rudimentary level, but the group sounds more muscular and musical than before, demonstrating that the breakthrough of its sole major-label record, *Sublime*, wasn't an accident. —*Stephen Thomas Erlewine*

● **Sublime** / Jul. 1996 / MCA ✦✦✦✦✦
Sublime's eponymous major-label debut arrived a few months after the band's leader Brad Nowell died tragically of a heroin overdose. As a show of sympathy, the album tended to by slightly overrated in some critical quarters, who claimed that Nowell was an exceptionally gifted lyricist and musical hybridist, but *Sublime* doesn't quite suppport those claims. The trio does have a surprising grace in its unabashedly traditionalist fusion of Californian hardcore punk, light hip-hop, and reggae. Switching between bracing hardcore and slow, sexy reggae numbers, Sublime displays supple, muscular versatility and, on occasion, a gift for ingratiatingly catchy hooks, as on the hit single "What I Got." What they don't have is the vision—either lyrical or musical—to maintain interest throughout the course of the entire album. *Sublime* sags when the band delves too deeply into their dub aspirations or when their lyrics slide into smirking humor. The low moments don't arrive that often—by and large, the album is quite engaging—but they happen frequently enough to make the record a demonstration of the band's blossoming ability, but not the fulfillment of their full potential. Of course, Nowell's death gives the record a certain pathos, but that doesn't make the album any stronger. —*Stephen Thomas Erlewine*

● **Greatest Hits** / Nov. 9, 1999 / MCA ✦✦✦✦
Sublime's career ended before it had the chance to really take off. Lead singer/songwriter Bradley Nowell died two months before the release of their 1996 major-label debut, *Sublime*. That record turned out to be a blockbuster, partially because it arrived at the right time and partially because the band's tragic loss gave them increased exposure. Hence, a promising band had its career cut short just as they were beginning to define their sound. Since they proved to be commercially viable, the posthumous releases began appearing swiftly, only a year after his death, culminating in 1999's *Greatest Hits*. Ultimately, Sublime wound up having as many posthumous releases as they did regular albums—

three of each. Naturally, that means there's not a whole lot of material to form the basis of *Greatest Hits*, and the disc is surprisingly brief, weighing in at only ten tracks. All the usual suspects are here, with the three big hits—"What I Got," "Wrong Way," and "Santeria"—filling the first three slots, with such fan favorites as "40 Oz. to Freedom," "Date Rape," "Smoke Two Joints," "Doin' Time," "Saw Red," and "Badfish" following them. There are no rarities here and only one song ("Badfish") from the posthumous albums; the only bait for collectors and diehards are CD-ROM versions of the "What I Got" and "Wrong Way" videos. Some could complain that this all is a little skimpy, but there really wasn't much more that the compilers could do—this is the sort of collection that will never appeal to diehards, who already have three albums of unreleased material (and possibly bootlegs), so this is for the fans that liked these songs on the radio. *Greatest Hits* delivers those songs, no more and no less. Of course, many of those songs are on *Sublime* as well, which is a stronger record overall than this, but since this rounds up the best moments from *40 Oz. to Freedom* and *Robbin' the Hood*, it's a better choice for casual fans. —*Stephen Thomas Erlewine*

Suede

f. 1989, England
Neo-Glam, Brit-pop, Alternative Pop/Rock
Suede kick-started the Brit-pop revolution of the '90s, bringing English indie pop/rock music away from the swirling layers of shoegazing and dance-pop fusions of Madchester, and reinstating such conventions of British pop as mystique and the three-minute single. Before the band had even released a single, the U.K. weekly music press was proclaiming them as the "Best New Band in Britain," but Suede managed to survive their heavy hype due to the songwriting team of vocalist Brett Anderson and guitarist Bernard Butler. Equally inspired by the glam crunch of David Bowie and the romantic bed-sit pop of the Smiths, Anderson and Butler developed a sweeping, guitar-heavy sound that was darkly sensual, sexually ambiguous, melodic, and unabashedly ambitious. At the time of the release of their first single, "The Drowners," in 1992, few of their contemporaries—whether it was British shoegazers or American grunge rockers—had any ambitions to be old-fashioned, self-consciously controversial pop stars and the British press and public fell hard for Suede, making their 1993 debut the fastest-selling first album in U.K. history. Though they had rocketed to the top in the U.K., Suede was plagued with problems, the least of which was an inability to get themselves heard in America. Anderson and Butler's relationship became antagonistic during the recording of their second album, *Dog Man Star*, and the guitarist left the band before its fall release, which inevitably hurt its sales. Instead of breaking up, the band soldiered on, adding new guitarist Richard Oakes, and a keyboardist before returning in 1996 with *Coming Up*, an album that returned them to the top of the British charts. —*Stephen Thomas Erlewine*

★ **Suede** / Mar. 29, 1993 / Nude/Columbia ✦✦✦✦✦
Borrowing heavily from David Bowie and the Smiths, Suede forged a distinctively seductive sound on their eponymous album. Guitarist Bernard Butler has a talent for crafting effortlessly catchy, crunching glam hooks like the controlled rush of "Metal Mickey" and the slow, sexy grind of "The Drowners," but he also can construct grand, darkly romantic soundscapes like the sighing "Sleeping Pills" and the tortured "Pantomime Horse." What brings these elegant sounds to life is Brett Anderson, who invests them with bed-sit angst and seamy sex. Anderson's voice is calculatedly affected and theatrical, but it fits the grand emotion of his self-consciously poetic lyrics. Suede are working-class lads striving for glamour, and they achieve it by piecing together remnants of the past with pieces of the present, never forgetting the value of a strong hook in the process. And while the sound of *Suede* frequently recalls the peak of glam-rock, its punk-influenced passion and self-conscious appropriation of the past makes it thoroughly postmodern. Coincidentally, its embrace of trashy pop helped usher in an era of Brit-pop, but few bands captured the theatrical melancholy that gave *Suede* such resonance. —*Stephen Thomas Erlewine*

Dog Man Star / Oct. 10, 1994 / Nude/Columbia ✦✦✦✦✦
Instead of following though on the Bowie-esque glam stomps of their debut, Suede concentrated on their darker, more melodramatic tendencies on their ambitious second album, *Dog Man Star*. By all accounts, the recording of *Dog Man Star* was plagued with difficulties—Brett Anderson wrote the lyrics in a druggy haze while sequestered in a secluded Victorian mansion, while Bernard Butler left before the album was completed—which makes its singular vision all the more remarkable. Lacking any rocker on the level of "The Drowners" or "Metal Mickey"—only the crunching "This Hollywood Life" comes close—*Dog Man Star* is a self-indulgent and pretentious album of dark, string-drenched epics. But Suede are one of the few bands who wear pretensions well, and after a few listens, the album becomes thoroughly compelling. Nearly every song on the record is hazy, feverish, and heartbroken, and even the rockers have an insular, paranoid tenor that heightens the album's melancholy. The whole record would have collapsed underneath its own intentions if Butler's compositional skills weren't so subtly nuanced and if Anderson's grandiose poetry wasn't so strangely affecting. As it stands, *Dog Man Star* is a strangely seductive record, filled with remarkable musical peaks, from the Bowie-esque stomp of "New Generation" to the stately ballads "The Wild Ones" and "Still Life," which are both reminiscent of Scott Walker. And while Suede may choose to wear their influences on their sleeve, they synthesize them in a totally original way, making *Dog Man Star* a singularly tragic and romantic album. —*Stephen Thomas Erlewine*

Coming Up / Sep. 2, 1996 / Nude/Columbia ✦✦✦✦
Brett Anderson carried on after Bernard Butler's departure, adding a teenage guitarist and restructuring the intent of Suede, if not the sound, for their third album, *Coming Up*. The most striking thing about *Coming Up* is the simplicity. Gone are the grand, sweep-

ing gestures of both *Suede* and *Dog Man Star*, leaving behind the glam, which is now spiked with an invigorating sense of self-belief—Anderson is out to prove that he's a survivor, and he does give a damn whether you believe he is or not. So *Coming Up* has none of the lush, melancholy, and paranoid overtones of *Dog Man Star*. It's about celebrating being young, going out, taking drugs, having sex, and living life. And it sounds just like it reads—Richard Oakes pounds out fizzy, fuzzy guitar riffs while the rhythm section lays back with dirty, sexy grooves and new keyboardist Neil Godling exudes a sultry, unattainable cool. Even on the wistful ballads "By the Sea" and "Picnic by the Motorway," there's none of the enveloping melancholy that consumed *Dog Man Star*—they're as optimistic as the buoyant, melodic rockers that comprise the rest of the album. As a statement of purpose, *Coming Up* is unimpeachable. Though it doesn't break any new ground for the band—unless you count the newfound sense of optimism—it's a remarkable consolidation and crystallization of Suede's talents and all the evidence anyone needs that Brett Anderson was always the guiding force behind the band. *—Stephen Thomas Erlewine*

Sci-Fi Lullabies / Oct. 6, 1997 / Nude/Columbia ✦✦✦✦✦
Few debut singles have the impact of Suede's "The Drowners," which helped set the course to Brit-pop and established Suede as one of the U.K.'s most important bands. In that light, it isn't surprising that the B-sides were considered as important as the A-side—the slow, grinding "My Insatiable One" was covered in concerts by Morrissey weeks after its release, while the band often closed shows with the majestic "To the Birds." The strength of "The Drowners" B-sides wasn't an anomaly—it established a precedent of high-quality B-sides that Suede strove to maintain on their first three albums. The double-disc *Sci-Fi Lullabies* collects the majority of those B-sides, leaving behind the odd live track and remix, as well as the worthy "Painted People" and "Asda Town" and the non-LP single "Stay Together." What's included is stellar, offering an alternate history of Suede. In fact, the first disc—comprised of *Suede* and *Dog Man Star* B-sides, plus the haunting "Europe Is Our Playground"—is as strong as any of their albums, featuring such essentials as the sleazy "He's Dead," "The Living Dead," "My Dark Star," the storming "Killing of a Flash Boy," the sighing "Where the Pigs Don't Fly," and "Whipsnade," all strong enough to be A-sides. Disc two isn't quite as consistent, which might be because they're all drawn from the singles for *Coming Up*, but it does find the band exploring their darker, more adventurous side, which they largely suppressed on that record. Unlike most B-sides compilations, *Sci-Fi Lullabies* is far from extraneous—for any Suede fan, and most fans of contemporary British pop, this is absolutely essential material, confirming the group's status as one of the '90s' greatest bands. *—Stephen Thomas Erlewine*

Head Music / Jun. 1, 1999 / Nude/Columbia ✦✦✦
Coming Up was every bit the triumphant comeback Brett Anderson and company were expecting and it was a terrific little record, but it did suggest that Suede had begun to reach the limits of Ed Buller's production ideas, while also feeling a little superficial. The very fact that its sequel was produced by Steve Osbourne, the man behind classics LPs from New Order and Happy Mondays, suggested they were returning to the dark undercurrents of their first two records, yet, *Head Music* is *Coming Up, Pt. 2.* Working with Osbourne has added some vague elements of electronic and dance music to Suede's signature sound, but these primarily manifest themselves in the form of gurgling analog synths and canned, old-school drum machines. Essentially, they're just window-dressing, since the songs themselves are extensions of the glam flash of *Coming Up*. While that hardly qualifies as an artistic progression, it hardly qualifies as a bad album either, and they've never sounded quite as unself-conscious as they do here. Suede even gets downright silly at times, whether it's the goofy puns of the title track or the ridiculously intoxicating stomp "Elephant Man." It's hard not to miss early Suede—the psychedelic "Indian Springs" comes close to capturing the feel, but it's bright, not menacing, and the ballads are pretty, not majestic—but even in this streamlined incarnation, nobody does this kind of trash pop as alluringly as Suede. Nobody can turn out a single as thrilling as "Electricity," nobody can grind out sex'n'drugs anthems as electrifying as "Can't Get Enough," or swoon as fetchingly as "She's in Fashion." When it comes down to it, nobody makes cheap sleaze sound so alluring. *—Stephen Thomas Erlewine*

Sugar

f. 1992, **db.** 1995
Alternative Pop/Rock
After two solo albums, ex-Hüsker Dü guitarist/vocalist Bob Mould formed Sugar in 1992, with bassist David Barbe and drummer Malcolm Travis; their first album, *Copper Blue*, was released in the fall of 1992 to enthusiastic reviews and it became Mould's most successful project to date. *Copper Blue* nearly went gold and spawned several alternative radio and MTV hits, including "Helpless" and "If I Can't Change Your Mind." In the spring of 1993, Sugar released the mini-LP *Beaster*, a more abrasive collection than *Copper Blue* that was recorded at the same sessions. Mould wrote the material for the second Sugar album during 1993. The band began recording in the spring of 1994, but the sessions ground to a halt and the tapes were erased. Mould decided to give the album one more try and it was recorded quickly late that spring. *File Under: Easy Listening* appeared in the fall of 1994. Although it received good reviews and was moderately successful commercially, it didn't match the performance of *Copper Blue*. In the spring of 1995, it was announced that Sugar was on hiatus. *Besides*, a collection of rarities and B-sides, was released that summer. By the fall, Mould had broken up the band. *—Stephen Thomas Erlewine*

● **Copper Blue** / Sep. 4, 1992 / Rykodisc ✦✦✦✦✦
Featuring some of Mould's best songwriting, Sugar's debut album is a stunning piece of hook-laden punk-pop, highlighted by the '60s-style "If I Can't Change Your Mind," and the loud, beautiful guitars of "Man on the Moon" and "Helpless," and the tongue-in-cheek Pixies tribute, "A Good Idea." *—Stephen Thomas Erlewine*

Beaster / Apr. 6, 1993 / Rykodisc ✦✦✦
Recorded at the same time as *Copper Blue*, *Beaster* is a darker, more intense record than Sugar's debut, but it's never as black as Mould's *Black Sheets of Rain*. The fusion of pop melodies with a punk roar, which made *Copper Blue* so magnificent, is here, but the guitars are harsher and the loose crucifixion concept provides a downbeat atmosphere, provided you can hear the lyrics. Mould's vocals are mixed beneath all the other instruments, contributing to the claustrophobic, oppressive atmosphere. But *Beaster* is not nihilistic. In fact, Mould ends the EP optimistically, albeit cautiously, with the gorgeously circular organ-based "Walking Away." *—Stephen Thomas Erlewine*

File Under: Easy Listening / Sep. 6, 1994 / Rykodisc ✦✦✦✦✦
Given Bob Mould's reputation for searing electric rock & roll, it may be easy to think that the title is ironic, and it is to a certain extent. But beneath the loud guitars lay the friendliest, most relaxed pop songs Mould has ever written. "Your Favorite Thing" and "Can't Help You Anymore" are two of Mould's most direct, pop-oriented songs, driven by instantly memorable melodies and hooks; they are also the most conventional songs on the record. The best moments come when Sugar push the boundaries a bit, whether it's on the country-rock of "Believe What You're Saying," the swirling "What You Want It to Be" and "Company Book," the searching ballad "Panama City Motel," or "Explode and Make Up," which bristles even at its most delicate moments. Mould throws in one classic spite-fueled rocker, "Granny Cool," but the record's finest moment is "Gee Angel," a powerhouse melodic scorcher. *—Stephen Thomas Erlewine*

Besides / Jul. 25, 1995 / Rykodisc ✦✦✦
The strength of *Besides* is not only a measure of the quality of Bob Mould's songwriting, it's a measure of how good a band Sugar is. Collecting all of the B-sides and rare tracks left over from the group's three albums, *Besides* isn't filled with sub-par material. Frequently, Mould would leave fine songs off the album because it didn't fit the mood, such as the scorching rocker "Needle Hits E." That consistent quality means the record is a thoroughly engaging experience, even during live and alternate versions of "Explode and Make Up" and "If I Can't Change Your Mind." The first 25,000 copies included a bonus disc, featuring a complete Sugar concert; it's a typically mesmerizing, galvenizing show. *—Stephen Thomas Erlewine*

Sugarcubes

f. 1986, Reykjavik, Iceland, **db.** 1992
College Rock, Alternative Dance, Alternative Pop/Rock
The Sugarcubes were the biggest group ever to emerge from Iceland, which helps explain their off-kilter sense of melody. Their 1988 debut, *Life's Too Good*, attracted terrific reviews and became a college radio hit, but they never were able to recapture that sense of excitement. Taking members from a variety of Icelandic bands, the Sugarcubes formed around vocalists Bjork and Einar Benediktsson plus drummer Siggi Baldursson. After signing to One Little Indian in the U.K., the group released their debut album *Life's Too Good* and single "Birthday," an indie hit in Britain and a college radio hit in America. In particular, Björk received a heap of praise, which began tensions between her and Einar. *Here Today, Tomorrow Next Week!*, the Sugarcubes' second album, was released in 1989. After its release, the band embarked on a lengthy international tour and began recording their third album. Released in 1992, *Stick Around for Joy* received better reviews than *Life's Too Good*, but failed to yield a hit single. Following its release, the Sugarcubes disbanded. In 1993, Björk launched a critically acclaimed and commercially successful solo career that was based in dance music. *—Stephen Thomas Erlewine*

● **Life's Too Good** / 1988 / Elektra ✦✦✦✦✦
With strong songs built around Bjork Gudmundsdottir's piercing, striking voice, this record lived up to all the advance hype. With songs like "Birthday" and "Motorcrash," this is the perfect introduction to the 'Cubes. *—John Dougan*

Here Today, Tomorrow Next Week! / Sep. 1989 / Elektra ✦✦✦
A slip from the first album, but not so much that it's without merit. *—John Dougan*

It's-It / 1992 / Elektra ✦✦✦
Since the Sugarcubes came and went in such an audacious flash of bizarre originality (and especially since Björk slowly became one of the biggest international crossover success stories of the '90s), one isn't shocked to find the number of reissues and clumsy collections quickly outnumbering the band's actual output. Yes, the Sugarcubes are becoming much like an Icelandic Sex Pistols these days. Which explains *It's-It*: a mood-testing, dull nightmare of a remix album that almost destroys every fond memory of listeners' Icelandic friends. How bad is it? For starters, schooled big beat artist Justin Robertson shows up twice here. Once to add an abstruse, '90s disco beat to the lovelorn, alien, mystical (and never to be surpassed) lament of "Birthday" and again to modify "Motorcrash" into a KLF-styled swagger. Neither are too exceptional. Both are actually about as good as this album gets. In the rest of the album, the band's two-pronged vocal gymnastic act of Einar and Björk is usually muzzled throughout simplistic beats and over-processed guitar riffs. For every fun, "let's turn Björk into a feral, growling hip-hop singer" moment (the Marius de Vries mix of "Pump"), there's about a half-dozen others that reduce the shambolic oddity of the band into sub-B-52's disco fests (Tony Humphries, S1000, etc.). It's as if these remixers seem to be shaking off a post-acid house haze and getting nowhere fast. Luckily, the Sugarcubes do their own remix of "Regina," which—apart from some accented accordions and echoes—has relatively conservative changes. No wonder it sounds worthy of being here. Even better, true fans will also enjoy the Bryan "Chuck" remix on "Water." This take is probably the only version that still seems to recognize the band's knack for frazzled unpredictability without completely missing the point. Which

highlights how the rest of the entire contrived album is that much more of an insult to the band. The Sugarcubes might not have lasted long in the world of pasty-faced indie, but they deserve far, far better than this. *—Dean Carlson*

Stick Around for Joy / Feb. 18, 1992 / Elektra ♦♦♦
While not as adventurous or stunning as their debut, *Life's Too Good*, the Sugarcubes' swan song release, *Stick Around for Joy*, contains enough quality material to see them out in style. Amidst producer Paul Fox's (10,000 Maniacs, They Might Be Giants, Semisoni) compact backdrops, Bjork and Einar Orn lead the band through a fast-paced and funk-inflected mix of art house pop. With Sigtryggur Balsuresson's syncopated drums and Thor Eldons' glossy indie guitar in the forefront, Bjork expectedly pounces on each song with her acrobatic pipes; thankfully, Orn keeps his usually spastic vocal interjections to a minimum, often opting for some fine trumpet accents instead. Moving from the multi-vocal nuances of the opener, "Gold," to the relatively straightforward delivery heard on the tidy "Hit," Bjork proves that her subsequent solo career was inevitable and necessary–she sounds at times as if the band's relatively narrow musical approach is straitjacketing her, especially on the presciently titled "Leash Called Love." While the curious will only need to pick up *Life's Too Good*, the Sugarcubes' faithful will no doubt want to check this disc out. *—Stephen Cook*

The Great Crossover Potential / Jul. 14, 1998 / Elektra ♦♦♦♦
The Sugarcubes were one of the great cult bands of collegiate rock, not only because they had a distinctive sound, but because they were so damn weird. They sounded like nothing else in the late '80s/early '90s or anything that came before, creating an unusual hybrid of pop, dance, and the avant-garde. So rabid was their cult that some critics said they could cross over into the mainstream, yet that never really happened, despite their strong English following. However, that notion gives the title to their best-of collection, *The Great Crossover Potential*. The 14-track compilation proves that they could never really have crossed over, mainly because their pop sense is quirky and they're often an acquired taste. Bjork, of course, wound up being a pop star with equally ambitious music, and while her talent is apparent here, it's often submerged by Einar's excruciatingly ridiculous showboating. Einar was often overbearing on the Sugarcubes albums (particularly toward the end of their career), and it is true that he's less irritating here than on the proper records, but casual fans should be aware that *The Great Crossover Potential* is only slightly less uneven than the actual albums, with the exception of the remarkable debut *Life's Too Good*. The collection, however, remains a nice way to round up the highlights, particularly those from *Here Today, Tomorrow Next Week!* and *Stick Around for Joy*. *—Stephen Thomas Erlewine*

The Sugarhill Gang

f. 1979, **db.** 1985
Old School Rap
Though the Sugarhill Gang inaugurated the history of recorded hip-hop with their single "Rapper's Delight," a multi-platinum seller and radio hit in 1979, the group was cooked up to cash in on a supposed novelty item; music-industry producer and label-owner Sylvia Robinson had become aware of the massive hip-hop block parties occurring around the New York area during the late '70s, so she gathered three local rappers (Master Gee, Wonder Mike, and Big Bank Hank) to record a single. Infectious and catchy, "Rapper's Delight" borrowed the break from Chic's "Good Times" and became a worldwide hit, eventually selling over eight million copies. Most industry people figured rap for a short-lived trend, and though they were dead wrong, the Sugarhill Gang certainly didn't carry the torch; despite several modest hits ("8th Wonder," "Apache") the trio faded quickly and were gone by the mid-'80s, returning in 1999 with *Jump on It*, a rap album for children. *—John Bush*

● **The Best of Sugarhill Gang** / Jul. 1996 / Rhino ♦♦♦♦♦
Sugarhill Gang's biggest hits are collected on this single-disc compilation. In addition to "Rapper's Delight"—the first rap single to reach the pop Top Ten—the group's seven other R&B hits are included on the disc, plus three other singles that never made the charts. All of the songs are presented in their original 12" versions. Not all of the material is first-rate—in retrospective, the group's old-school groove tended to be a little simplistic, monotonous, and too polished, while their rhymes were frequently stilted and sometimes just outright silly—but this music, especially "Rapper's Delight," is important historically. Most casual fans of old-school hip-hop will be content with purchasing "Rapper's Delight" on a various artists collection, but for those wanting to dig deeper into the trio's history, *The Best of Sugarhill Gang* is a defintive retrospective. *—Stephen Thomas Erlewine*

Suicidal Tendencies

f. 1982, Venice, CA
Punk Metal, Skatepunk, Heavy Metal, Thrash, Hardcore Punk, American Underground
Suicidal Tendencies were formed in Venice, CA, as a punk/hardcore band and virtually came to define the phrase "skate-punk." Vocalist/bandleader Mike Muir has earned a reputation for addressing various political and personal topics with focused rage and thoughtfulness, and also for his keen sense of humor, which helps set the band apart from its competition. During the '80s, the group was frequently banned in the Los Angeles area, as their gigs often turned into out-of-control melees. Over the years, the band has mixed speed metal, more relaxed alternative rock, and touches of funk into its sound. Muir and bass virtuoso Robert Trujillo formed the metal/funk party band Infectious Grooves as a side project for Muir's non-political side. *—Steve Huey*

● **Suicidal Tendencies** / 1983 / Epitaph ♦♦♦♦♦
Fast, furious, and funny, Suicidal Tendencies' self-titled debut owed much more to hardcore punk than to the later hardcore/heavy metal hybrid they would become known for, but it's still quite possibly their best album. Mike Muir proves himself an articulate lyricist and commentator, delving into subjects like alienation, depression, and nonconformist politics with intelligence and humor. The band behind him is aggressive and speedy, but never sinks into an overly fast sonic blur. Contains the classic rant "Institutionalized." *—Steve Huey*

Join the Army / 1987 / Caroline ♦♦♦
No one could expect 1987's *Join the Army*, the long-awaited follow-up to Suicidal Tendencies' quintessential self-titled debut, to live up to its predecessor, but few expected it to be this disappointing. Except for a few bright moments such as "Possessed to Skate" and "War Inside My Head," the album is badly written, badly played, and terribly produced. There could have been many reasons for this fiasco, but considering the renewed quality of the following year's *How Will I Laugh Tomorrow* opus, perhaps the most likely is that *Join the Army* was a transitional album in the transformation of the band's sound from hardcore punk to thrash metal. *—Ed Rivadavia*

How Will I Laugh Tomorrow When I Can't Even Smile Today / 1988 / Epic ♦♦♦♦♦
Suicidal Tendencies regrouped successfully for one of its best efforts, *How Will I Laugh Tomorrow When I Can't Even Smile Today*. The band's thrashy fusion of its hardcore roots with speed metal was fully developed by this point, and Muir's social commentary and self-analysis were as ragingly compelling and by turns amusing as ever. Highlights include "Trip at the Brain," "One Too Many Times," and the title track. *—Steve Huey*

Controlled By Hatred/Feel Like Shit . . . Deja Vu / 1989 / Epic ♦♦

Lights . . . Camera . . . Revolution! / Jun. 1990 / Epic ♦♦♦
After recording some definite gems in the late 1980s, Suicidal Tendencies triumphantly entered the '90s with one of its best albums ever, the commanding *Lights . . . Camera . . . Revolution!* Not since the mid-'80s had the L.A. band sounded this confident, focused, and inspired. "You Can't Bring Me Down" and the Motörhead-ish "Get Whacked" demonstrate just how much fun Suicidal can be, but most of all, the metal-oriented album is dark, angry, and troubling. The Angelenos already commanded an incredibly devoted following, and powerful offerings like "Send Me Money" (a gut-level, brutally honest attack on television evangelists), "Give It Revolution," and the dark-humored "Disco's Out, Murder's In" brought even more listeners aboard. This is a disc that no Suicidal fan should be without. *—Alex Henderson*

The Art of Rebellion / Jun. 1992 / Epic ♦♦♦
On the group's earliest albums, vocalist Mike Muir specialized in intense, angst-ridden rants, harrowing but one-dimensional. He has since developed into a rock-solid vocalist, his voice a powerful and fluid instrument. Muir still delivers emotionally ferocious spoken-word segments on "Nobody Hears" and "I Wasn't Meant to Hear This," but the trademark is woven into good songs rather than being an end onto itself. A clenched fist in a velvet glove—or is it an open hand in chain mail?—whichever, *The Art of Rebellion* packs a punch that should win over new devotees while maintaining the group's hardcore following. *—Roch Parisien*

Prime Cuts: The Best of Suicidal Tendencies / Jun. 3, 1997 / Epic ♦♦♦♦♦
Prime Cuts: Best of Suicidal Tendencies is a good overview of the group's career, featuring such hardcore classics as "Institutionalized" and "I Saw Yor Mommy," plus two new songs, "Berserk!" and "Feeding the Addiction." *—Stephen Thomas Erlewine*

Suicide

f. 1971, New York, NY, **db.** 1982
American Punk, New York Punk, Post-Punk, Punk, Electronic
Although they barely receive credit, Suicide (singer Alan Vega and keyboardist Martin Rev) is the sourcepoint for virtually every synth-pop duo that glutted the pop marketplace (especially in England) in the early '80s. Without the trailblazing Rev and Vega, there would have been no Soft Cell, Erasure, Bronski Beat, Yaz, you name 'em, and while many would tell you that that's nothing to crow about, the aforementioned synth-poppers merely appropriated Suicide's keyboards/singer look and none of Rev and Vega's extremely confrontational performance style and love of dissonance. The few who did (Throbbing Gristle, Cabaret Voltaire) were considered too extreme for most tastes. Their approach to music was simple: Rev would create minimalistic, spooky, hypnotic washes of dissonant keyboards and synthesizers, while Vega sang, ranted, and spat neo-Beat lyrics in a jumpy, disjointed fashion. *—John Dougan*

● **Suicide [First Album]** / 1977 / Mute ♦♦♦♦♦
Proof that punk was more about attitude than a raw, guitar-driven sound, Suicide's self-titled debut set the duo apart from the rest of the style's self-proclaimed outsiders. Over the course of seven songs, Martin Rev's dense, unnerving electronics—including a menacing synth bass, a drum machine that sounded like an idling motorcycle, and harshly hypnotic organs—and Alan Vega's ghostly, Gene Vincent-esque vocals defined the group's sound and provided the blueprints for post-punk, synth-pop, and industrial rock in the process. Though those seven songs shared the same stripped-down sonic template, they also show Suicide's surprisingly wide range. The exhilarated, rebellious "Ghost Rider" and "Rocket U.S.A." capture the punk era's thrilling nihilism—albeit in an icier way than most groups expressed it—while "Cheree" and "Girl" counter the rest of the album's hard edges with a sensuality that's at once eerie and alluring. And with its retro bassline and simplistic, stylized lyrics, "Johnny" explores Suicide's affinity for '50s melodies and images as well as their pop leanings. But none of this is adequate preparation for "Frankie Teardrop," one of the duo's definitive moments and one of the most harrowing songs ever recorded. A ten-minute descent into the soul-crushing existence of a young factory worker, Rev's tense, repetitive rhythms and Vega's deadpan delivery and horrifying, almost inhuman screams make the song more literally and poetically political than the

work of bands who wore their radical philosophies on their sleeves. The Mute reissue includes "Keep Your Dreams" and the "Cheree" remix that appeared on previous versions of the album, along with live versions of "Las Vegas Man," "Mr. Ray," and "23 Minutes Over Brussels"; though the extra tracks dilute the original album's impact somewhat, they're worthwhile supplements to one of the punk era's most startlingly unique works. *—Heather Phares*

Suicide [Second Album] / 1980 / Mute ♦♦♦♦♦
Confusingly released in 1980 as *Alan Vega/Martin Rev: Suicide*, Mute reissued Suicide's second album as *The Second Album* in 2000. The reissue adds the "Dream Baby Dream" single, as well as a second disc of Vega and Rev's first rehearsal tapes. The Ric Ocasek-produced *Second Album* is less confrontational and more contemporary than the duo's terrifying debut. Vega's rockabilly snarl and Rev's burbling electronics remain, but Ocasek's involvement purges a pop sensibility only hinted at on *Suicide*. Hell, some of the tracks are downright *pretty* ("Shadazz," "Diamonds, Fur Coat, Champagne"). Perhaps it's not as renegade as *Suicide*, but it's an arguably better, more realized work, and just as essential. Three of the tracks found on the first rehearsal tapes disc were previously issued on ROIR's *Half Alive* in 1981. The rehearsals are extremely spatial and equally creepy as the proper studio works. Most of the tracks lurch by at a mid-tempo pace; Vega's distorted vocalisms are rather restrained but highly sinister, and Rev's sonic wizardry is delightfully horrific. *—Andy Kellman*

Half Alive / 1981 / ROIR ♦♦♦♦
There was an aesthetic revolution implied in the coupling of Alan Vega's reckless rockabilly howling and the hypnotic buzz and drone of Martin Rev's keys, and that revolution in sound birthed (perhaps unwittingly) two primary schools of synthesized rock: wimpy, gutless new wave duos and the painful dissonance of bands like Skinny Puppy, Foetus, and the later Chicago Wax-Trax scene. For better and for worse, Suicide enabled the industrial revolution. *Half Alive* is an essential reissue of the original ROIR cassette from 1981, compiling extremely rare early demo material and live tracks from 1974-1979. It's a mesmerizing, confrontational listen, and even more importantly—when contextualized in that time period, that harsh and beautiful juxtaposition of futuristic minimalism and anachronistic crooning (imagine Gene Vincent cornered on a mixture of quaaludes and speed), is confounding. Vega's scream is as damn reckless, damn frightening, and as full of abandon as a Stooges live show from the early '70s. Suicide went on to record a handful of indispensable albums before splitting up and reuniting innumerable times. If nothing else, this collection documents the peculiar fury of proto-industrial music prior to its eventual emasculation and/or reconfiguration as the millieu of studio hounds and gothic make-up artists. *—Patrick Kennedy*

Ghost Riders / 1986 / ROIR ♦♦♦
Originally a cassette-only release, this live recording at Walker Arts Center in Minneapolis marked Rev and Vega's tenth anniversary. And while not as deliberately offensive as some of their earlier live gigs (the impossible-to-locate *24 Minutes Over Brussels*), this is a compelling, interesting document of their ever-evolving stage show. Not as transcendent as their debut album, but well worth the effort. Reissued on CD by the French Danceteria label in 1990. *—John Dougan*

A Way of Life / 1988 / Wax Trax! ♦♦♦
The unwitting godfathers of industrial noise-squall return after a long absence to reclaim their throne on *A Way of Life*. Produced by Ric Ocasek, Suicide's Alan Vega and Martin Rev pick up exactly where they left off, crafting beautifully ominous drone-rock founded on pulsing sequences, dramatic vocals, and dense atmospherics. *—Jason Ankeny*

Sukia

f. 1995, Los Angeles, CA
Electronica, Exotica, Trip-Hop
Taking their name from a Mexican lesbian vampire comic-book heroine, the avant-lounge quartet Sukia emerged from Los Angeles' famed Silverlake scene (the same musical community home to Beck, the Beastie Boys, and the Dust Brothers). Comprised of multi-instrumentalists Sasha Fuentes, Ross Harris, Grace Marks, and Craig Borrell, Sukia combined Moog-driven grooves laced with found samples and space-age pop aesthetics on their 1996 debut *Contacto Espacial con el Tercer Sexo*, produced by the Dust Brothers and issued on their Nickel Bag label. *—Jason Ankeny*

● **Contacto Espacial con el Tercer Sexo** / Oct. 1996 / Nickel Bag ♦♦♦♦♦
An ominous, free-floating collage of found sounds, drum machines, cheap keyboards, and samples, Sukia's debut album *Contacto Espacial con el Tercer Sexo* flirts with exotica and the avant-garde without committing to either. And it's the better for it. Sukia's instrumentals are alternatingly mesmerizing and disturbing, fueled by pseudo-bossa nova rhythms, jazzy chords, and sheets of noise. It's not necessarily an alienating record, but anyone well versed in the cut-paste productions of the Dust Brothers, who also helmed this record, will be more inclined toward meeting the album halfway, since the music isn't strictly lounge revival, avant pop, or electronic music. It's a fascinating, darkly humorous melange of all three, and it's endlessly fascinating. *—Stephen Thomas Erlewine*

Donna Summer

b. Dec. 31, 1948, Boston, MA
Vocals / Club/Dance, Urban, Disco
Born Donna Gaines to a churchgoing family in the Mission Hill section of Boston, Summer took her name from Helmut Sommer, whom she married while living in Munich, Germany, as a member of a travelling cast of *Hair*. Italian electro-pop arranger Giorgio Moroder met her, and in 1975 they recorded "Love to Love You Baby," a 16-minute, riff-driven update of Jane Birkin and Serge Gainsbourg's version of "Je T'aime... Moi Non Plus." But Summer, as it turned out, had a sturdiness quite different from Birkin's short bursts of this and that, and a flair for kitschy show tunes and overproduced slickness, both of which ideally complimented the transparent impersonality of Moroder's electronic rhythms. She and Moroder created entire subgenres of disco, and there was no stopping them until Summer stopped herself.

Beginning with 1980's *The Wanderer* (except for the title song), she began to sing exactly the kind of pop/rock material her daring impressionism had fought against. She tried to become a pop singer; and when, as in *She Works Hard for the Money*, she drew upon gospel styles, she was listened to. But during the '70s, she wasn't merely listened to, she was a leader. *—Michael Freedberg*

The Donna Summer Anthology / Sep. 21, 1993 / Casablanca/Chronicles ♦♦♦♦♦
Donna Summer's two-CD *Anthology* is by far the most exhaustive compilation available on the disco diva. This two-CD set includes most of Summer's hits, from her earliest "Love to Love You Baby" to her '90s dance single "Carry On." The music flows from early to classic disco and '80s pop, rock, R&B, and adult contemporary. Also included are two tracks ("I'm a Rainbow" and "Don't Cry for Me Argentina") from her 1981 album *I'm a Rainbow*, which wasn't released until 1996. However, a couple of sore points keep this collection from having a perfect rating. First, some of the edits are a little awkward. One only wishes that the longer, five-minute edit of "Love to Love You Baby" were included as opposed to the severely truncated version found here. The promo single version of "MacArthur Park" is included, and "Heaven Knows" suffers from an early fade-out. Then there are the omissions—"The Woman in Me," "Walk Away," "Winter Melody," "Who Do You Think You're Foolin'," "Dinner With Gershwin," and "Love's About to Change My Heart" are nowhere to be found. All of this only highlights the fact that an ultra-exhaustive, three-CD box set on this star would be a welcome addition. But, for now, with so many other hit collections on the market, this clearly stands as the best, and also stands as a testament to a time gone by. As an added bonus, the liner notes and photographs are nothing short of excellent. Finally, the versions of "Hot Stuff" and "Bad Girls" included here are the 12" mixes. *—Jose F. Promis*

★ **Endless Summer: The Very Best** / 1995 / Casablanca ♦♦♦♦♦
With '70s and disco nostalgia taking the U.S. by storm in the early to mid-1990s, it wasn't surprising that Mercury/PolyGram saw Donna Summer's recordings as a way to make a quick dollar. What is surprising is that the label came out with this single-disc best-of collection only a year after releasing the two-CD set *The Donna Summer Anthology* in 1993. Why was another greatest-hits package needed? Though not definitive, this CD does contain many of Summer's essential material. From the erotic club diva of "Love to Love You Baby," "Could It Be Magic," and "I Feel Love" to the Vegas-like pop star of "On the Radio," "Last Dance," and "Dim All the Lights," the Queen of Disco is as charismatic as she is cutting-edge. And Summer still sounds incredibly fresh on 1989's infectious "This Time I Know It's for Real" and 1994's previously unreleased "Melody of Love." It would have been preferable to hear many of these songs in their extended versions (as opposed to the shorter ones provided here), but then, a label can only fit so much on a single disc. Although *The Donna Summer Anthology* is more comprehensive, *Endless Summer* can work well as a shorter introduction to her innovations. *—Alex Henderson*

Greatest Hits / Sep. 15, 1998 / Mercury/Chronicles ♦♦♦♦♦
There are Donna Summer collections available for any level of fan. For hardcore fans, there's the double-disc set, *The Donna Summer Anthology*. For casual fans wanting a solid collection that digs a little deeper than a basic hits compilation, there's the very fine *Endless Summer: The Very Best of Donna Summer*. Then there's *Greatest Hits*, a bare-bones collection that contains her 12 biggest hits, from "Love to Love You Baby" to "She Works Hard for the Money," all presented in their single edits. Only listeners who want just the singles will want *Greatest Hits*, since the other compilations provide a better, more thorough overview, but they will be quite pleased with the end result. *—Stephen Thomas Erlewine*

The Sundays

f. 1987
College Rock, Dream Pop, Adult Alternative Pop/Rock, Alternative Pop/Rock
Building on the jangly guitar pop of the Smiths and the trance-like dream pop of bands like the Cocteau Twins, the Sundays cultivated a dedicated following in indie-rock circles, both in their native England and in America, in the early '90s. Although the sales of their first two albums were strong, the band never crossed over into the mainstream, as so many observers and critics predicted they would. Vocalist Harriet Wheeler and guitarist David Gavurin, the target of a record-label bidding war soon after their first concert, finally signed to Rough Trade (DGC in the U.S.) and released their first album *Reading, Writing and Arithmetic* in 1990. It entered the U.K. charts at number four, and became a modern rock hit in America thanks to the single, "Here's Where the Story Ends." After Rough Trade collapsed in 1991, the Sundays moved to Parlophone and released their second album *Blind* in 1992. Although it was initially successful, the album didn't have quite the staying power of the debut. The Sundays were quiet for the next several years, finally returning in 1997 with *Static & Silence*. *—Stephen Thomas Erlewine*

● **Reading, Writing and Arithmetic** / Apr. 1990 / DGC ♦♦♦♦♦
The Sundays' debut album built on the layered, ringing guitar hooks and unconventional pop melodies of the Smiths, adding more ethereal vocals and a stronger backbeat. As evidenced by the lilting, melancholy single "Here's Where the Story Ends," it was a winning combination, making *Reading, Writing and Arithmetic* a thoroughly engaging debut. *—Stephen Thomas Erlewine*

Blind / Oct. 20, 1992 / DGC ♦♦♦
Featuring gentle, folk-based guitars and pop melodies, the Sundays' second album isn't

much of a sonic departure from their first album. While it does have several fine numbers, it doesn't have as many outstanding songs as *Reading, Writing and Arithmetic*; nevertheless, *Blind* will please most fans of the group. *—Stephen Thomas Erlewine*

Static & Silence / Sep. 23, 1997 / Geffen ✦✦✦
It took the Sundays five years to deliver their third album, *Static & Silence*. Five years is a long time, especially in the quicksilver world of pop music, but the Sundays sound totally unbothered by their absence on *Static & Silence*. Instead of sounding labored and forced, the album is gentle and effortless, as if it was recorded five months after *Blind* instead of five years. In some ways, that's a disappointment—it would have been nice for the duo to show some progression, considering all of their time off—but the record delivers the pleasant, endearing jangle pop that is the Sundays' signature sound. There's certainly nothing as catchy as "Here's Where the Story Ends" on *Static & Silence*, and there aren't many songs that are instantly memorable, yet the album has a quiet charm that should satisfy most longtime fans. *—Stephen Thomas Erlewine*

Sunny Day Real Estate

f. 1992, Seattle, WA
Emo, Indie Rock, Alternative Pop/Rock
Considering their relatively brief existence, Sunny Day Real Estate racked up enough dramatic twists and turns to rank with some of the great rock soap operas. Originally comprised of guitarist-vocalist Dan Hoerner, bassist Nate Mendel, and drummer William Goldsmith), Sunny Day Real Estate garnered attention when it added enigmatic lead singer Jeremy Enigk, whose high-pitched, constantly ascending voice complimented their melodic songs. The group was shrouded in mystery from the get-go: they released only one picture to the press, conducted one interview and, for some still-unknown reason, never played a show in the state of California with all four members intact. With the release of their 1994 debut album, *Diary*, Sunny Day found newfound fame while Enigk found religion, and in 1995 the group broke up. (Goldsmith and Mendel quickly found work with the Foo Fighters.) After much speculation, the group reformed in 1998 minus Mendel, who stayed with the Foo Fighters, and released *How It Feels to Be Something On*. *The Rising Tide* was released by Time Bomb in 2000, marked by a gentler tone and a stronger prog rock influence. *—Brian Raftery*

Diary / 1994 / Sub Pop ✦✦✦✦
Sunny Day Real Estate's debut album, *Diary*, virtually defined emo in the '90s, laying much of the groundwork (along with Weezer) for the genre's end-of-decade indie prominence. Although emo existed (both as a term and as a style) prior to *Diary*, it hadn't yet risen out of the deepest hardcore punk underground, save for a few bands on the Dischord label. For all intents and purposes, *Diary* was the album that made emo accessible, fusing its gnarled guitars and nakedly emotional vocals with more than a hint of melodic Seattle grunge. SDRE's song structures are far more oblique than, for example, the similarly anthemic Pearl Jam, but it's still easy to miss the group's main inspirations if you're not looking for them. Perhaps that's because, at bottom, SDRE don't sound much like their emo predecessors. For one, there are plenty of quiet, arpeggiated passages and contrasting dynamics; for another, vocalist Jeremy Enigk is more of a crooner than a screamer at heart, and the underlying tenderness in his voice breathes majesty into the group's slow, languid melodies. Yet, while *Diary*'s true heart lies in its soaring, introspective anthems (like the band's signature song, "In Circles"), the more tortured, visceral moments balance things out, preventing the album from wallowing in melodramatic self-obsession. In retrospect, *Diary* doesn't quite fulfill all of its ambitions—there are a few underfocused moments that don't achieve the epic sweep of the album's best compositions. That occasional inconsistency makes it feel somewhat less realized than their proggier post-reunion work, especially since Enigk would develop into a far more distinctive vocalist. But even if it isn't quite the top-to-bottom masterpiece its legions of imitators suggest, *Diary* still ranks as arguably the definitive '90s emo album, and an indispensable introduction to the genre. *—Steve Huey*

LP2 / Nov. 1995 / Sub Pop ✦✦✦
Delivering on the promise Sunny Day Real Estate showed on their 1994 debut *Diary*, the following year's *LP2*—a.k.a. *The Pink Album* for its entirely pink cover—also felt like a posthumous work left by a brilliant writer. Shortly after recording *LP2*, the band spontaneously imploded: Enigk emerged born-again as a Christian, and the rhythm section, Nate Mendel and William Goldsmith, headed off to join Dave Grohl in Foo Fighters, seemingly sabotaging that once-limitless future. As tragic as the turn of events was for fans, the album proved how special the band was and underscored just how lamentable their too-early demise was. From its first ringing guitar tone to its abrupt conclusion, *LP2* is a masterpiece of emotion and evocation, a sprawling musical soundscape that moves effortlessly from tender, unsteady sonic explorations to raging assaults of guitars. At all times, it seems heartbreakingly fragile and moody, ready to spin apart at the apex of one of the band's guitar frenzies or fold in on itself when the music turns serene. There are plenty of both such moments, all of which come together to produce lovely, resplendent songs like "Friday," "5/4," "8," and "J'Nuh," made all the more breathtaking by Enigk's alternately tortured and delicate vocals. It's sometimes difficult to make out what he is warbling about, but the intent seems obvious. *LP2* wears all of its affectations and passions on its sleeve and has a lump in its throat; in the process, it also creates the same sort of longing and desire in the listener. Few post-grunge bands were able to make their tortured souls sound so viscerally appealing, and few albums of the mid-'90s strike as poignant a note as this *tour de force*. *—Stanton Swihart*

How It Feels to Be Something On / Sep. 8, 1998 / Sub Pop ✦✦✦✦
The cryptically titled *How It Feels to Be Something On* was the first fruit of Sunny Day Real Estate's reunion, and it simultaneously smoothed out their sound while shifting it into something altogether more ambitious. Always somewhat arty and challenging to begin with, SDRE flirts with out-and-out prog rock here, cleaning up the production to reveal the contrasting layers in their ever more intricate arrangements. There's a droning, almost Middle Eastern feel to some of the songs, pointing up Jeremy Enigk's newfound taste for spiritual mysticism (though the mantra-like chanting on "The Prophet" comes off a little awkwardly). Enigk has matured greatly as a vocalist, applying lessons learned from his solo project; gone is the strangled roar he frequently used on *Diary*, but even while confirming his softer bent, he's reined in the swooning, bordering-on-fey excess of *LP2*. Similarly, the band's musicianship keeps getting sharper, handling the twisting chord progressions with an easy grace that keeps the songs flowing smoothly into one another. Almost too smoothly, in fact—if the album has a flaw, it's that the climactic peaks don't seem to scale quite the same heights as on the band's other albums. That's a minor complaint, to be sure, but perhaps that's why *How It Feels to Be Something On* can feel at times like a dry run for the magnificently perfected *The Rising Tide*, where Enigk's piercing falsetto really hits its stride and where the band's songwriting fulfills their every anthemic ambition. But that's only in hindsight; taken on its own terms, *How It Feels to Be Something On* is a remarkable step forward from a band that seemed destined to leave its full potential untapped. *—Steve Huey*

Live / Oct. 19, 1999 / Sub Pop ✦✦✦
An absolutely perfect way to carve a vivid memory of one of the most passionate and dumbfounding live bands ever. For those who have not experienced the purely incredible Sunny Day Real Estate live, you are now one step closer to the magic. If you were lucky enough to see them, you know that this live document is outstanding. With perhaps one of the best set lists performed throughout the entire *How It Feels to Be Something On* tour (including "Song About an Angel," "Rodeo Jones," "J'nuh," and the ever popular "In Circles," to name a few), the band rains down on their audience with energy of their passion and intensity. Slight changes in mood and style of the songs, such as on the dark and breathtaking rendition of "Pillars," offer different takes on the much-loved songs. Jeremy's vocals sometimes slip out of place, but the emotion is so beautifully real that it rarely matters. A definite must-have for any fan and/or newcomer. *—Blake Butler*

● **The Rising Tide** / Jun. 20, 2000 / Time Bomb ✦✦✦✦✦
Described by Jerermy Enigk as a "wake-up call," Sunny Day Real Estate's fourth album (and their first for Time Bomb) *The Rising Tide* presents the most accomplished version of their gripping, anthemic sound yet. Appropriate to its title, *The Rising Tide* comes in sweeps and swells, ranging from searching, uncompromising rock like "Killed By an Angel" and "One" to gentle, beautiful ballads like "Rain Song" and even pop-tinged songs like "Television," which sounds a bit like a more propulsive version of the Police's early '80s singles. Though the album was recorded with a trio lineup (Jeremy Enigk, Dan Hoerner, and William Goldsmith), it's some of the band's fullest-sounding work, rich with strings and keyboard flourishes that add extra depth to the shimmering, Eastern-inspired drones of "Fool in the Photograph" and "Faces in Disguise." Lou Giordano's production gives *The Rising Tide* an unabashedly big, clean sound that frames Sunny Day's detailed songwriting and arrangements perfectly, giving the restrained, reflective "Tearing in My Heart" and "The Ocean" as much impact as driven tracks like "Snibe" and "Disappear." Best of all is the title track, which blends a beautiful melody, heartfelt vocals, and an insistent rhythm into a sweeping, affecting finale. Expansive and complex without compromising the band's focused, impassioned style, *The Rising Tide* is one of Sunny Day Real Estate's—and 2000's—most impressive albums. *—Heather Phares*

The Sunrays

Surf
California surf band the Sunrays was organized in 1964 by producer Murry Wilson following his dismissal as manager of his sons' group, the Beach Boys; organized around singer/songwriter/drummer Rick Henn, a friend of Beach Boy Carl Wilson, the lineup also included guitarists Eddie Medora and Byron Case as well as pianist Marty DiGiovanni, all three of whom previously recorded as the Snowmen. Completing their sound with bassist Vince Hozier, the Sunrays signed to the Tower label and soon issued their debut single, "Outta Gas"; its 1965 follow-up, "I Live for the Sun," was the band's breakthrough hit, reaching the US Top 50. "Andrea" was an even bigger hit, serving as the title track of the group's 1966 debut LP; although "Still" was also successful, subsequent singles including "I Look Baby I Can't See" and "Hi, How Are You?" met commercial resistance, and in the wake of 1967's "Loaded With Love" the Sunrays disbanded. Henn later went on to compose material with Brian Wilson. *—Jason Ankeny*

Andrea / 1966 / Tower ✦✦

● **The Tower Recordings** / Nov. 9, 1999 / Collectables ✦✦✦✦✦
This has 27 of their 1964-1967 tracks, concentrating on their singles, but also including a half-dozen previously unreleased alternate mixes/vocals, as well as the previously unreleased "Goodnight Debbie, Goodnight." The Sunrays were the pet project of co-producer Murry Wilson, father of the three Beach Boys brothers. Unsurprisingly, they sounded very much like the Beach Boys, particularly in their vocal arrangements. Before you go buy this expecting a son-of-*All Summer Long*, be aware that as was often the case in imitative rock music, the Sunrays were a much more lightweight version of the original model. Imagine the Beach Boys' most superficial and Whitest mid-'60s sides with more mainstream L.A. pop arrangements and you have some idea of where the Sunrays were coming from. The harmonies are accomplished but on the sterile side, with even more of the Four Freshmen influence that colored the Beach Boys' vocal arrangements. It's in some respects as close to the Happenings or the Tokens as to the Beach Boys, and even by 1965-1966 standards, pretty square. And, most important, the material is mostly inconsequential, frothy pop, whether written by Sunrays singer Rick Henn (who penned their best

tracks), Murry Wilson, or others. To be honest, they make the Beach Boys sound gritty, proving that it took more than smooth, high vocal harmonies to capture that group's magic; it also took the complexity and emotional depth of Brian Wilson's compositions and production, which of course couldn't be emulated. The Sunrays' biggest hits (although they weren't *that* big), "I Live for the Sun" (one of their relatively few tunes to boast a lot of drive) and "Andrea," remain their best tracks. This compilation is indeed only a portion of their output—Collectables also has a Sunrays box—but the 27 cuts will still be way more than enough for most listeners, unless they're fanatics for the West Coast harmony sound. *—Richie Unterberger*

Super Furry Animals

f. 1993, Cardiff, Wales

Indie Pop, Neo-Psychedelia, Brit-pop, Alternative Pop/Rock

One of the leaders of the mid-'90s Welsh scene, Super Furry Animals fused disparate musical genres—including power pop, punk rock, techno, and prog rock—into shimmering, melodic, irreverent, and arty rock & roll. Their infectious melodies, irreverent attitude, and tendency to sing in their native tongue set them apart, but their unique approach was remarkably popular: their 1996 debut *Fuzzy Logic* and 1999's *Guerilla* became major U.K. hits, charting in the Top 40 and placing in the Top Ten of many year-end critic's polls.

Super Furry Animals formed in Cardiff, Wales in 1993 and included Gruff Rhys (lead vocals, guitar), Huw "Bunf" Bunford (guitar, vocals), Guto Pryce (bass), Cian Ciaran (keyboards, electronics), and Dafydd Leuan (drums). After the dissolution of Rhys' noise-rock band Ffa Coffi Pawb, the trio he played in with Pryce and Leuan evolved into Super Furry Animals. Initially a techno outfit, they soon became a neo-psychedelic and progressive pop band. In 1995, they signed with the Cardiff-based indie Ankst. Their Welsh-language EPs *Lianfairpwllgywgyllgoger Chwymdrobwlltysiliogoygoyocynygofod (In Space)* and *Moog Droog*, earned them a wide fanbase in Wales and a strong cult following in Britain, which led to a six-album record contract with Creation Records. Prior to signing with Creation, the band decided to sing the majority of their songs in English in order to reach a wider audience. The singles "Hometown Unicorn" and "God! Show Me Magic" became moderate hits in the U.K. and preceded the summer 1996 release of the band's debut *Fuzzy Logic*, which received uniformly excellent reviews. SFA became one of Britain's hippest acts within a few months; with the release of 1997's *Radiator* and 1999's *Guerilla*, they cemented their place as one of the U.K.'s most entertaining and innovative bands. They secured a U.S. deal with Flydaddy, who released *Radiator, Guerrilla*, and 2000's Welsh-language *MWNG* in the States. *—Stephen Thomas Erlewine*

Fuzzy Logic / May 1996 / Creation ✦✦✦✦✦

Super Furry Animals are eclectic, to say the least. Fusing together pop melodies, psychedelia, and art rock with an impish, punky fury, the band covers more ground on their debut album, *Fuzzy Logic*, than most indie bands do in their entire career. However, the album works better as a series of moments than as a collection, mainly due to their overreaching ambition. Each song floats by on irresistable, catchy vocal harmonies, while the music alternates between glitzy overdriven guitars and sighing, sweeping keyboard, guitar, and string backdrops. Over these lush sonic beds, lead vocalist Gruff sings lyrics that are either mystical, nonsensical, or bizarrely funny—none of the songs make much literal sense, but that doesn't quite matter when the music is as free-spirited as this. The songs may start conventionally, but they'll be undercut by wild synthesizers and careening guitar solos, or off-kilter vocal melodies. Taken as individual moments—as the singles "God! Show Me Magic" (relatively straight-ahead punk-pop), "Hometown Unicorn" (gorgeous psychedelia), and "Something for the Weekend" (which finds the middle ground between the first two singles) prove—the music of Super Furry Animals is quite intoxicating, but when assembled together, they don't sustain momentum. However, the individual pleasures of each song become more apparent with each listen and *Fuzzy Logic* suggests that the group could blossom into something quite distinctive and utterly unique within a few albums. *—Stephen Thomas Erlewine*

● **Radiator** / Aug. 21, 1997 / Flydaddy ✦✦✦✦✦

Using the psychedelicized prog-punk of *Fuzzy Logic* as a foundation, Super Furry Animals move even further into left field on their second album, *Radiator*. As before, the group displays a gift for catchy, deceptively complex melodic hooks, but now their songwriting and arrangements are mind-bogglingly intricate and eclectic. Songs boast intertwining melodies and countermelodies, with guitars and keyboards swirling around the vocals. Similarly, the production is dense and heavy with detail, borrowing heavily from prog rock and psychedelic pop, but pieced together with the invention of techno and played with the energy of punk. It's a heady, impressive kaleidoscope of sounds, but what gives *Radiator* its weight is the way the sonics complement the songwriting. SFA's songs are melodic, accessible, and utterly original—melodically, they may borrow from '60s pop, but they rearrange the clichés in fresh ways. Also, Gruff Rhys has a fondness for revolutionary politics and the bizarre that helps give *Radiator* its intoxicating, otherworldly atmosphere, making it one of the few late-'90s albums that sounds inventive, vibrant, and utterly contemporary. *—Stephen Thomas Erlewine*

Outspaced / Nov. 1998 / Creation ✦✦✦✦

Like any band in '90s British pop, Super Furry Animals were obligated to release a steady stream of singles buttressed with non-LP songs, which meant that there were nearly two albums' worth of songs that weren't on either *Fuzzy Logic* or *Radiator*, especially if the first two EPs on Ankst and two non-LP singles were counted as well. Following in the footsteps of Suede, Gene, and Oasis, among others, SFA released *Outspaced*, their own compilation of B-sides, in the fall of 1998, a year after *Radiator* hit the stores. Instead of taking the completist route, which is essentially what Suede did with *Sci-Fi Lullabies*, SFA constructed *Outspaced* as an actual album, leaving many very good songs behind on the singles. This is bound to frustrate fans who haven't bothered to collect every single, but the approach results in a better, tighter album—one that doesn't quite rank with their official albums, but nevertheless amply proves that SFA takes more risks and reaps greater rewards than most of their contemporaries. Even on the earliest material—and a fair portion of their Ankst EPs are here—SFA was gleefully recontextualizing, pulling techno, indie, and classic rock into unpredictable forms. Unlike some bands, they didn't save their riskiest material for B-sides—unless you count singing in Welsh as a risk, since each single contained a Welsh-language song, about half of which are here. What's really impressive is that the English songs sound as magical, baffling, and unusual as their Welsh counterparts, which only emphasizes the uniqueness of SFA's vision. These sort of revelations are best appreciated by the dedicated, but that's why *Outspaced* remains an essential addition to any hardcore fan's collection. *—Stephen Thomas Erlewine*

Guerrilla / Jun. 14, 1999 / Flydaddy ✦✦✦✦

It's difficult not to find Super Furry Animals' brand of pop infectious, particularly the collection of numbers compiled for *Guerrilla*, the band's third full-length and arguably most cohesive—albeit pleasingly and consistently unpredictable—one to date. Old-school techno remains in remnants, such as in "Wherever I Lay My Phone (That's My Home)." When it rears its head otherwise, it rests easily beside and within the majority of the fully-fledged pop songs. The High Llamas contribute to the dreamy "Turning Tide"; there's the tropicalia of "Northern Lites," and, as ever, there are shades of punk and distortion in "Night Vision." Amazingly, the super-bouncy-rocker "The Teacher" does not credit a sample to the Who's "Baba O'Riley." *—Denise Sullivan*

Mwng / Jun. 20, 2000 / Flydaddy ✦✦✦✦✦

The very fact that Super Furry Animals had the courage to release *Mwng*, an all-Welsh language album, is proof that the group is the great eccentric band of their time. Unfortunately, many critics and listeners may dismiss *Mwng* as a stunt or a wacky joke, which is condescending—especially in light of what a terrific album this is. It doesn't matter that many listeners will not understand the lyrics, since the music is terribly effective in its own right. Ironically, *Mwng* is more of a pop album than its predecessor, *Guerrilla*, which often took fascinating detours into electronica-inspired pure sound. *Mwng* has more than its fair share of evocative sonic textures—it's easy to get lost not just in the surface sound but what's buried beneath the melodies—yet it's also a concise, sharply written psychedelic-pop record. These are smart, melodic, catchy songs graced with inventive, clever arrangements. Super Furry Animals have tempered their harder-rocking in favor of expanding their prog, psych, and pop inclinations. There are still numbers that rock, but they're unconventional, taking wonderful left turns and being blessed with arrangement that are welcoming, but never predictable. Fuzztone guitars and floating keyboards vie for space in the mix, vocals swoon in reverb, horns sound equally eerie and enthusiastic, and instruments are compressed so they no longer sound normal. Even when it skirts with psych-pop convention, with sitars popping up in the mix, it sounds fresh. *Mwng* is simply intoxicating with its richly melodic songs and dreamlike flow. This is an otherworldly record not because it is sung in Welsh, but because the music is fully realized and visionary. *—Stephen Thomas Erlewine*

Rings Around the World / Jul. 23, 2001 / Epic ✦✦✦✦

Super Furry Animals' leap to a major label in the U.K. with *Rings Around the World* isn't that drastic of a change—*Fuzzy Logic* was also released on Epic in the U.S., Creation was subsidized by Sony, and they never were exactly wanting of money on their previous records—but the band nevertheless seizes the opportunity to consolidate their strengths, providing an introduction for listeners that may not have been paying attention before. As such, it's hard not to consider it as a bit of a missed opportunity, since this is the first SFA album not to progress from its predecessor, or offer the shock of the new, and that's hard not to miss—but, if this is the first SFA record you hear, it'll likely intrigue, even dazzle, with its kaleidoscopic blend of pop, prog, punk, psych, and electronica. This is nearly Super Furry Cliff Notes, offering a glossy, big-screen variation on all of their themes—decadently lush pop-psych, chugging rock & roll, bitter leftism, sublimely warped imagery, experimentalism wrapped in luxurious productions. Still, it's hard not to at least want surprises (since there are none) or, if it's going to be a consolidation, to have it be a statement of purpose, since it lacks either an overarching theme or a music that gels. So, it's not what it could have been, but what it is is still pretty damn great, satisfying with its melodies, textures, and ideas. Compared to what Super Furry Animals have done before, *Rings Around the World* pales slightly but noticeably, but compared to the dead world of mainstream and indie rock in 2001, it still shines brightly. *—Stephen Thomas Erlewine*

Superchunk

f. 1989, Chapel Hill, NC

Indie Rock, Alternative Pop/Rock

Perhaps no band was more emblematic of the true spirit of American indie rock during the 1990s than Superchunk, the pride of Chapel Hill, NC. Following the D.I.Y. ethic to the letter, the group operated solely by their own rules, ignoring all passing trends by sticking to their trademark sound—typified by the buzzing guitars and high, impassioned vocals of frontman Mac McCaughan—and rejecting all major-label advances in favor of their own label, Merge Records. Although Superchunk's resistance to the overtures of the music industry may have deprived them of the wider audience their work clearly deserved, perhaps their greatest legacy remains their unwavering dedication to the indie tradition. With the release of their self-titled debut LP in 1990, Superchunk was widely celebrated among the most promising young bands in America. Label heads scrambling to locate the next alternative rock hotbed after Seattle made Chapel Hill a consensus choice, and Superchunk soon found themselves in the middle of a major-label bidding war. Still, the group remained on Merge for their brilliant 1991 sophomore effort *No Pocky for Kitty.* 1995's *Here's Where the Strings Come In* heralded a subtle refinement of their core sound. As well, McCaughan has also recorded several LPs with his side project Portastatic. *—Jason Ankeny*

No Pocky for Kitty / 1991 / Merge ✦✦✦✦✦

Where Superchunk's self-titled debut otherwise failed to live up to the brilliance of its anti-anthem centerpiece "Slack Motherfucker," the follow-up *No Pocky for Kitty* is a complete and fully realized statement of purpose—opening with the dizzying "Skip Steps 1 & 3," the disc never lets up for a second, crackling with an energy and breathless abandon that underlines the sheer exuberance at the heart of even Mac McCaughan's most superficially bitter songs. Although *No Pocky for Kitty* successfully channels the sound and spirit of punk's heyday, for all their whiplash guitars and spitfire rhythms Superchunk's songs derive their power not from nihilism and ennui but from optimism and passion—implicit in McCaughan's lyrics is a belief in creation over destruction, hope over cynicism, and love over hate. Credit too Steve Albini's no-frills recording for the live-wire snap and crackle of standouts like "Seed Toss," "Punch Me Harder," and "Throwing Things"—for all its earthy simplicity and everyman conviction, *No Pocky for Kitty* positively soars. *—Jason Ankeny*

● **Tossing Seeds (Singles 89-91)** / 1992 / Merge ✦✦✦✦✦

"The single must be a distillation of one's powers, the most exciting slice of noise a person can cram between the lip of the disc and the edge of the label," writes Superchunk frontman Mac McGaughan in the sleeve notes to *Tossing Seeds*; the 13 7" sides which make up this collection deliver everything McGaughan promises and much more, capturing the essence of American indie rock in the pre-Nirvana era with an energy and eloquence matched by few other records of the period. As a note-perfect snapshot of minimum-wage angst and attitude, "Slack Motherfucker" justly remains the band's most celebrated moment, but perhaps their most quintessential record is instead "My Noise," a glorious celebration of indie ethos and music's liberating power; add underground classics like "The Breadman" and "Seed Toss" to the mix, and you've got a definitive portrait of arguably the best singles band of the early '90s. *—Jason Ankeny*

On the Mouth / 1993 / Merge ✦✦✦✦

After pushing the buzzsaw abandon of their earliest records to its logical extreme on the masterful *No Pocky for Kitty*, Superchunk begins reinventing itself with their third full-length, *On the Mouth*, a record as invigorating as it is frustrating. Without sacrificing any of the energy or conviction of past efforts, many of the disc's 13 songs harness Mac McCaughan's breathless pop-punk melodies into tighter, more demanding contexts—highlights, like the singles "Mower" and "The Question Is How Fast," introduce a new arsenal of shifting rhythms and explosively tense dynamics which reveal unexpectedly limitless possibilities within the classic Superchunk approach. The problem is that *On the Mouth* equates to something less than the sum of its parts—while tracks like the blistering "From the Curve" and "Package Thief" barrel forth with the sheer recklessness of old, their adherence to the band's past makes for an ill-fitting match alongside the album's more ambitious moments. More problematic, the slow, plodding "Swallow That"—while an admirable departure from the norm—is simply tedious. Still, more often than not *On the Mouth* comes up with the goods, and remains a pivotal turning point in Superchunk's continued evolution. *—Jason Ankeny*

Foolish / Dec. 1993 / Merge ✦✦✦✦

Forged at a difficult time in the band's history, this album is a dark masterpiece that contrasts the band's signature high-energy power punk attack of *On the Mouth* with a far more somber, orchestrated approach, while still retaining the band's melancholy melodic majesty. From the opening track, "Like a Fool," with it's droning guitar and languid pace, Superchunk serves notice of their desire to move in new directions. The band itself was in flux, deciding to release *Foolish* on the own label, Merge, abandoning Matador, who'd help shepherd the successful *On the Mouth* album. There were also band tensions arising from the breakup of Mac and bassist Laura Ballance, hinted at in Ballance's morbid album art of a disgruntled woman with a butchered rabbit hanging behind her. There's also Mac's bitter words. He goes lyrically from the Icarus-fantasy "Water Wings," where a female "pointed to the black cloud in the sky/and said that's what happened when you try to fly," to "Without Blinking," where he laments, "when you said you're sorry, you did it without blinking/and you can not know how much that hurts." But great works are often forged out of misfortune. Wedding their melodic impulses with a more sedate approach that utilizes increasingly complexity, Superchunk create a emotionally taut album that maps the changing direction of the band as it moves away from its crunchy, arena-pop roots. *—Chris Parker*

Incidental Music 1991-95 / Jun. 20, 1995 / Merge ✦✦✦✦✦

Singles are the most effective forum for Superchunk's music, which makes *Incidental Music 1991-95* one of their most consistent records. It might not have a single song as definitive as "Slack Motherfucker," but this collection of non-LP singles is filled with some of their finest moments. *—Stephen Thomas Erlewine*

Here's Where the Strings Come In / Sep. 19, 1995 / Merge ✦✦✦

Without changing their tensely wound, post-Hüsker Dü punk-pop style at all, Superchunk sounds completely weary on *Here's Where the Strings Come In*. No longer do their their nervous, amateurish songs sound energetic—they sound tired and broken. This actually results in some really interesting music, as Mac McCaughan tries to reconcile his broken spirits with his passion for punk. These songs tend to have more resonance than by-the-books rave-ups like "Hyper Enough," no matter how well those are written, and they suggest that Superchunk may be better off if they decide to revamp their signature sound completely. *—Stephen Thomas Erlewine*

Indoor Living / Sep. 2, 1997 / Merge ✦✦✦

Superchunk painted themselves into a corner long before the release of *Indoor Living*. By remaining true to their independent aesthetic and indie-punk sound, they earned a cult following with a series of records that essentially sounded the same. Like most indie bands, their earliest records were their rawest and most exciting, and their latter-day albums—that is, any album after *On the Mouth*—rely on craft rather than surprise. And there are no surprises on *Indoor Living*: it's simply another set of frenetic, tense, melodic, and occasionally exciting punk-pop. Mac McCaughan is a solid songwriter, but with Superchunk he's not a particularly resourceful one—he saves all of his experimentations for Portastatic, which leaves Superchunk a little predictable. Which means, of course, if you've followed them for this long, *Indoor Living* will provide some thrills. But it simply isn't as life-changing as *No Pocky for Kitty* or the singles on *Tossing Seeds*. *—Stephen Thomas Erlewine*

Come Pick Me Up / Aug. 10, 1999 / Merge ✦✦✦✦

Actually, *here's* where the strings come in—*Come Pick Me Up* is Superchunk's finest effort in years, a bright, infectious pop record that rejuvenates the group's trademark sound through the addition of producer Jim O'Rourke's candy-colored orchestral flourishes without losing sight of the music's punk roots. Tracks like "Hello Hawk," "1000 Pounds," and "Pink Clouds" achieve a perfect balance between Superchunk's patented brand of hyperkinetic indie rock and O'Rourke's avant-pop aesthetic, drawing upon the talents of Chicago underground notables including saxophonist Ken Vandermark, trombonist Jeb Bishop, and cellist Fred Lonberg-Holm to bring galvanizing new dimensions to Mac McGaughan's memorably melodic songs. A stunning and unexpected return to form. *—Jason Ankeny*

Supergrass

f. 1993, London, England

Punk-Pop, Brit-pop, Alternative Pop/Rock

Like many other British bands of the '90s, Supergrass' musical roots lie in the infectiously catchy punk-pop of the Buzzcocks and the Jam, as well as the post-punk pop of Madness and the traditional British pop of the Kinks and Small Faces. Perhaps because of their age—two of the trio were still in their teens when they recorded their debut single—the band also brings in elements of decidedly un-hip groups like Elton John, as well as classic rockers like David Bowie, the Beatles, and the Rolling Stones. With an exuberant, youthful enthusiasm, Supergrass tied all of their influences together in new surprising ways, where a Buzzcocks riff could slam into three-part harmonies out of "Crocodile Rock," or have a galloping music hall rhythm stutter like the best moments of the Who. *—Stephen Thomas Erlewine*

● **I Should Coco** / Jul. 18, 1995 / Capitol ✦✦✦✦✦

Tearing by at a breakneck speed, *I Should Coco* is a spectacularly eclectic debut by Supergrass, a trio barely out of their teens. Sure, the unbridled energy of the album illustrates that the band is young, yet what really illustrates how young the band is how they borrow from their predecessors. Supergrass treat the Buzzcocks, the Beatles, Elton John, David Bowie, Blur, and Madness as if they were all the same thing—they don't make any distinction between what is cool and what isn't, they just throw everything together. Consequently, the jittery "Caught By the Fuzz" slams next to the music-hall rave-up "Mansize Rooster" and the trippy psychedelia of "Sofa of My Lethargy," or the heavy stomp of "Lenny" or the the bona fide teen anthem "Alright." *I Should Coco* is the sound of adolescence, but performed with a surprising musical versatility that makes the record's exuberant energy all the more infectious. *—Stephen Thomas Erlewine*

In It for the Money / May 5, 1997 / Capitol ✦✦✦✦✦

Supergrass' debut album *I Should Coco* rushed by at such a blinding speed that some listeners didn't notice the melodic complexity of its best songs. On their second album, the cleverly titled *In It for the Money*, Supergrass brought the songs to their forefront, slowing the tempos considerably and constructing a varied, textured album that makes their ambition and skill abundantly clear. From the droning mantra of the opening title track, it's clear that the band has delved deeply into psychedelia and hints of *Magical Mystery Tour* are evident throughout the album, from swirling organs and gurgling wah-wahs to punchy horn charts and human beatboxes. In fact, Supergrass has substituted the punky rush of *I Should Coco* for such sonic details, and while that means they only occasionally touch upon the breakneck pace of the debut (the hard-driving "Richard III"), they also deepen its joyful exuberance with subtle songs and remarkably accomplished musicianship. There might not be a "Caught By the Fuzz" or "Alright" on *In It for the Money*, but that's not a problem, since the bright explosion of "Sun Hits the Sky" and the nervy "Tonight" are just as energetic, and the album features introspective numbers like the gorgeous "Late in the Day" and "It's Not Me" that give the album substantial weight. And even with all this musical maturity, they haven't sacrificed their good-natured humor, as the detailed production and the bizarre closer "Sometimes I Make You Sad" make abundantly clear. Sometimes, maturity turns out to be everything it's supposed to be. *—Stephen Thomas Erlewine*

Supergrass / Sep. 20, 1999 / Capitol ✦✦✦

Essentially, Supergrass' eponymous third album is a refined, subdued extension of *In It for the Money*. Where that album was a supremely confident, head-spinning musical kaleidoscope, splendidly shifting focus from track to track, *Supergrass* is down to earth, mellow, and unassuming. Part of the trio's charm has always been that they're unabashedly unpretentious, since their casual attitude made their considerable musical skill all the more impressive. On *Supergrass*, that casualness occasionally crosses the line into laziness. It doesn't happen all that often, but there are moments on the album that feel tossed-off, such as "What Went Wrong (In Your Head)" and "Beautiful People." This is particularly evident because these also-rans are surrounded by songs that are as great as anything Supergrass has ever recorded—the harpsichord-driven, pulsing "Your Love"; the stately, sophisticated "Shotover Hill"; the gleeful absurdity of "Jesus Came From Outta Space"; or the breezy, infectious summer single "Pumping on Your Stereo." The disparity in material also hammers home the point that *Supergrass* doesn't quite gel, the way their first two albums did. There were no themes behind those two records, but the performances and songs shared a similar spirit. The third album is simply a collection of moments, some spectacular and some average. While that may come as a slight disappointment, since *I Should Coco* and *In It for the Money* are two of the greatest pop albums of the '90s, the songs that work on *Supergrass*—and they do account for well over half the record—confirm that the 'Grass remain one of the most gifted, irresistible guitar-pop bands of their time. —*Stephen Thomas Erlewine*

Supertramp

f. 1969
Album Rock, Arena Rock, Pop/Rock, Soft Rock, Prog Rock/Art Rock
Once upon a time in 1969, a young Dutch millionaire by the name of Stanley August Miesegaes gave his acquaintance, vocalist and keyboardist Rick Davies a "genuine opportunity" to form his own band; he could form the band of his dreams and Miesegaes would pay for it. After placing an ad in Melody Maker, Davies assembled Supertramp. Supertramp released two long-winded progressive rock albums before Miesegaes withdrew his support. With no money or fan base to speak of, the band was forced to redesign their sound. Coming up with a more pop-oriented form of progressive rock, the band had a hit with their third album, *Crime of the Century*. Throughout the decade, Supertramp had a number of best-selling albums, culminating in their 1979 masterpiece, *Breakfast in America*. *Breakfast in America* marked their first album that tipped the scale completely in the favor of pop songs; on the strength of the hit singles "Goodbye Stranger," "Logical Song," and "Take the Long Way Home" it sold over 18 million copies worldwide. After that album, Supertramp continued to develop a more R&B-flavored style; the change in direction was successful on 1982's *Famous Last Words*, but they soon ran out of hits. The band continued to sporadically record and tour into the '90s. —*Stephen Thomas Erlewine*

Supertramp / 1970 / A&M ✦✦

Indelibly Stamped / 1971 / A&M ✦✦

Crime of the Century / 1974 / A&M ✦✦✦✦
With *Crime of the Century*, Supertramp established themselves as one of the handful of progressive rock acts that could sell albums and have hit singles. Stripping away the longwinded excesses of their first two albums, *Crime of the Century* featured tighter, more melodic songs, as evidenced by the singles "Bloody Well Right" and "Dreamer." —*Stephen Thomas Erlewine*

Crisis? What Crisis? / 1975 / A&M ✦✦✦
Crisis? What Crisis? wasn't quite as fully developed as its predecessor, *Crime of the Century*, lacking any instant standouts like "Dreamer" or "Bloody Well Right." Nevertheless, it had a handful of fine songs which signalled that Supertramp was continuing to refine and expand their sound. —*Stephen Thomas Erlewine*

Even in the Quietest Moments / 1977 / A&M ✦✦✦✦✦
Like *Crisis? What Crisis?*, *Even in the Quietest Moments* is a jumbled affair, alternating between long, unfocused sections and relatively concise pop songs, like the hit "Give a Little Bit." —*Stephen Thomas Erlewine*

● **Breakfast in America** / 1979 / A&M ✦✦✦✦✦
With *Breakfast in America*, Supertramp had a genuine blockbuster hit, topping the charts for four weeks in the U.S. and selling millions of copies worldwide; by the 1990s, the album had sold over 18 million units across the world. Although their previous records had some popular success, they never even hinted at the massive sales of *Breakfast in America*. Then again, Supertramp's earlier records weren't as pop-oriented as *Breakfast*. The majority of the album consisted of tightly written, catchy, well-constructed pop songs, like the hits "The Logical Song," "Take the Long Way Home," and "Goodbye Stranger." Supertramp still had a tendency to indulge themselves occasionally, but *Breakfast in America* had very few weak moments. It was clearly their high-water mark. —*Stephen Thomas Erlewine*

Paris / 1980 / A&M ✦✦

...Famous Last Words ... / 1982 / A&M ✦✦✦
Even though...*Famous Last Words*..., Supertramp's follow-up to *Breakfast in America*, was slicker and more pop-oriented than its predecessor, it wasn't quite as successful. Where the singles on *Breakfast* still had a progressive rock edge, most of ...*Famous Last Words*...was light, synthesized pop, with the shimmering "It's Raining Again" being the only song melodic enough to support the lush, layered sound. —*Stephen Thomas Erlewine*

Brother Where You Bound / 1985 / A&M ✦✦

Free As a Bird / 1987 / A&M ✦

Classics, Vol. 9 / 1987 / A&M ✦✦✦✦✦
This is a fairly good sampler of this band's bigger radio tracks as well as key album numbers. Included are "Bloody Well Right," "Ain't Nobody but Me," "The Logical Song," "Give a Little Bit," "It's Raining Again," "Goodbye Stranger," "Take the Long Way Home," and "Dreamer." Unfortunately, "Even in the Quietest Moments" is curiously omitted. —*AMG*

● **The Very Best of Supertramp** / 1992 / A&M ✦✦✦✦✦
The European compilation *The Very Best of Supertramp* is the closest thing to a definitive overview of the '70s pop-prog group. Certainly, there will be hardcore fans that will

notice some favorite album cuts missing—after all, despite their considerable success on the pop charts, Supertramp was as much an album rock band as ELP or Genesis—but all the hits are here, from "Bloody Well Right" to "It's Raining Again," as well as a sizable portion of their blockbuster *Breakfast in America*. That alone will make it worthwhile for all casual fans, but what's really nice about the collection is that it flows very smoothly, even if it isn't in chronological order. There have been other Supertramp compilations, but *The Very Best of Supertramp* stands head and shoulders above the rest. —*Stephen Thomas Erlewine*

Some Things Never Change / Jun. 3, 1997 / Chrysalis ✦✦

The Supremes

f. 1961, Detroit, MI, db. 1977
Uptown Soul, Pop-Soul, Girl Group, Motown, Soul
The most successful black performers of the 1960s, the Supremes for a time rivaled even the Beatles in terms of red-hot commercial appeal, reeling off five number one singles in a row at one point. Critical revisionism has tended to undervalue the Supremes' accomplishments, categorizing their work as more lightweight than the best soul stars' (or even the best Motown stars') and viewing them as a tool for Berry Gordy's crossover aspirations. There's no question that there was about as much pop as soul in the Supremes' hits, that even some of their biggest hits could sound formulaic, and that they were probably the black performers who were most successful at infiltrating the tastes and televisions of middle America. This shouldn't diminish either their extraordinary achievements or their fine music, the best of which renders the pop vs. soul question moot with its excellence. —*Richie Unterberger*

★ **The Ultimate Collection** / Oct. 7, 1997 / Motown ✦✦✦✦✦
The Ultimate Collection nearly lives up to its billing, featuring 25 tracks on a single disc, including all of the Supremes' Top Ten pop and R&B hits with Diana Ross. For most casual fans and those who just want the hits, this will be the definitive collection. —*Stephen Thomas Erlewine*

Supremes [Box Set] / Aug. 29, 2000 / Motown ✦✦✦✦
The Supremes were Motown's most popular act, so there was much anticipation for a comprehensive box set, especially since Motown waited many years to assemble one. So, the question is, was the wait worth it? Almost. It's a lavish set, spanning four discs (five, if you include the limited-edition live bonus disc included with the first 25,000 sets), housed in a red-velvet plated book and boasting a 70-page booklet, plus alternate takes, original 45 mixes, and other rarities. The devil is in the details, though. Rarities are substituted for original hit versions; for instance, the original versions of "Stop! In the Name of Love" and "Love Is Here and Now You're Gone" are not here. Then, there are the little omissions, like noting Elvis Costello's cover of "Remove This Doubt" in a list of great Supremes covers, but not including the original. These curious choices, along with the decision to devote the fourth disc to post-Diana Ross material, makes the set feel a little incomplete even though it covers a tremendous amount of ground. There are some classic cuts missing, and it's not a good thing that some of those missing items are the single versions of the hits. Still, it's hard not to like *The Supremes* as a set for hardcore fans, who will thrill to the different mixes and alternate versions, unreleased photos, Top Ten Lists, and illustrated discographies. But for the listener looking for one exhaustive set containing all the Supremes they'll ever need, this set falls short of the mark. In fact, for that kind of listener, a good double-disc hits compilation remains a preferable choice over this set. —*Stephen Thomas Erlewine*

The Surfaris

f. 1962, Glendora, CA
Frat Rock, Surf, Instrumental Rock
A Glendora, CA, surf group remembered for "Wipe Out," the number two 1963 hit that ranks as one of the great rock instrumentals, featuring a classic up-and-down guitar riff and a classic solo drum roll break, both of which were emulated by millions (the number is no exaggeration) of beginning rock & rollers. They recorded an astonishing number of albums (about half a dozen) and singles in the mid-'60s; the "Wipe Out" follow-up, "Point Panic," was the only one to struggle up to the middle of the charts. The Surfaris were not extraordinary, but they were more talented than the typical one-shot surf group; drummer Ron Wilson was praised by session stickman extraordinaire Hal Blaine, and his uninhibited splashing style sounds like a direct ancestor to Keith Moon. He also took the lead vocals on the group's occasional Beach Boys imitations. —*Richie Unterberger*

● **Wipe Out! The Best of the Surfaris** / Jul. 5, 1994 / Varese Sarabande ✦✦✦✦✦
Decent 18-track distillation of their 1962-65 work, including several album tracks and non-LP singles. "Wipe Out" is by far the best cut, of course, but the instrumentals, packed with reverbed guitars, honking saxes, and high-end drums aplenty, usually have an admirably sleek power. Two of the vocal surf tunes were co-written by Gary Usher, who also worked with the Beach Boys during this time. —*Richie Unterberger*

Surfaris Stomp / Jul. 4, 1995 / Varese Sarabande ✦✦✦✦
Aside from the significant drawback of missing "Wipe Out," this second anthology of the Surfaris' best work is just as good as the other Varese Sarabande compilation, *The Best of the Surfaris* (which doesn't duplicate any of the tracks here). Largely taken from rare singles and albums that the group recorded for Decca between 1963 and 1965, it also has a few previously unreleased cuts, some dating from their initial session (the same one that produced "Wipe Out"). If you like *The Best of the Surfaris*, you can't go wrong by adding this one to your collection as well—it's packed with haunting reverb, Ron Wilson's nonstop drum fills rank among the best stickwork of the pre-Keith Moon era, and one of

the three vocal cuts is one of the most obscure Brian Wilson compositions ever released ("My Buddy Seat," co-written with Gary Usher). —*Richie Unterberger*

Screaming Lord Sutch

b. Nov. 10, 1940, Harrow, Middlesex, England, **d.** Jun. 16, 1999, South Harrow, London, England

Vocals / Rock & Roll

He couldn't properly be considered part of the British Invasion—he never had a hit in the U.S. or the U.K.—but Screaming Lord Sutch laid some unheralded groundwork for the phenomenon. With a rock & horror act based to a large degree on Screamin' Jay Hawkins, David "Lord" Sutch was one of the first genuine rock & roll longhairs, and his bands employed such sterling instrumentalists as Jimmy Page, Jeff Beck, Ritchie Blackmore, Nicky Hopkins, and Mitch Mitchell before they became famous. His early-'60s singles—mostly over-the-top Halloween novelties or covers of early rock and R&B standards—are genuinely energetic and fun performances that rank among the few out-and-out raunchy rock & roll records waxed in Britain before the ascension of the Beatles. Twiddling the knobs on his first five singles was the legendarily eccentric Joe Meek, who embellished Sutch's modest talents with his usual grab bag of treated instruments, compression, and odd effects. While he holds a position of undeniable importance in the history of British rock, Sutch was not a talented singer or musician, and the records he made after the mid-'60s were pretty lame despite the presence of some stars who remembered him fondly (and had even sometimes played in his band in the old days). A well-known public figure in Britain, he ran for Parliament several times in the '60s, representing the National Teenage Party, and he founded the pirate radio station Radio Sutch in 1964. He published his autobiography in the early '90s. —*Richie Unterberger*

● **Story** / 1990 / (no label) ✦✦✦✦

Except for one B-side, this has both sides of his first seven singles (released 1961-66), most produced by Joe Meek between 1961 and 1965, some featuring sterling guitar work by Mssrs. Page, Beck, and Blackmore. Divided into a "horror" and a "rock" side, this is fun if silly stuff; tracks like "She's Fallen in Love With the Monsterman," "Monster in Black Tights," and "Dracula's Daughter" are great for Halloween parties. No record label name is given for this reissue, but it's easy enough to locate through specialty mail-order outfits. —*Richie Unterberger*

Billy Swan

b. May 12, 1942, Cape Giradeau, MO

Producer, Vocals, Keyboards, Guitar, Bass / Pop/Rock, Country-Rock, Rock & Roll

One of rock's more interesting fringe characters, Billy Swan had been in the music business for more than a decade before he landed a surprise number one neo-rockabilly hit in 1974 with "I Can Help." His composition "Lover Please" was a hit for Clyde McPhatter in the early '60s, and he spent the rest of the decade as a combination roadie, engineer's assistant, and songwriter, penning material for Conway Twitty, Waylon Jennings, and Mel Tillis. He played with Kris Kristofferson, Kinky Friedman, and Billy Joe Shaver in the '70s before the success of "I Can Help," whose swirling organ and classic '50s rockabilly arrangement anchored one of the best hit singles of the mid-'70s. Swan recorded a few albums as a solo act that were well received by critics, but he never hit the Top 40 again. Too eclectic to be characterized as a '50s revivalist, he actually mixed country, soul, and pop into his sound more frequently than out-and-out rockabilly. After a few years, Swan returned to Kristofferson's band, where he stayed until 1992. —*Richie Unterberger*

Billy Swan's Best / Aug. 31, 1993 / Red Baron ✦✦✦✦

Listeners expecting tuneful updated rockabilly along the lines of "I Can Help" (which leads off this collection) may be disappointed by this CD. There's nothing as instantly compelling as the big hit (only "Vanessa" approaches its energy), much of the material lies closer to country than rock, and there are a few tame covers of '50s oldies. Nonetheless, Swan ranks among the more interesting country-pop-rock hybrids, as you could guess from the song title "(You Just) Woman Handled My Mind," and his thin, wavering voice is oddly memorable. Most of the material on this best-of is written by Swan, with occasional assistance from notables Guy Clark, Buddy Emmons, and Kris Kristofferson. —*Richie Unterberger*

● **Best of Billy Swan** / Jan. 27, 1998 / Epic/Legacy ✦✦✦✦✦

Epic/Legacy's *The Best of Billy Swan* is a fine 16-track collection that features highlights from his recordings for Monument, Columbia and Epic in the '70s and '80s. Swan's unexpected crossover hit "I Can Help" is here, but the remaining 15 songs veer closer to country, bearing just a slight resemblance to the bouncy pop/rock of the hit. Among the remaining songs are the country hits "Everything's the Same (Ain't Nothing Changed)," "You're the One," "Shake, Rattle and Roll," "I Just Want to Taste Your Wine," "Do I Have to Draw a Picture," "I'm Not Lovin' You," "Stuck Right in the Middle of Your Love," "With Their Kind of Money and Our Kind of Love" and "Your Picture Still Loves Me (And I Still Love You)," as well as "Lover Please," the Clyde McPhatter song Swan wrote when he was in high school. Not all of the songs meet the standards of "I Can Help" and "Lover Please," abut many of them are interesting and are among the better country-pop of their era. —*Stephen Thomas Erlewine*

Sweet

f. 1968, London, England, **db.** 1982

Glitter, Bubblegum, Glam Rock, Hard Rock

In some ways, the Sweet epitomized all the tacky hubris and garish silliness of the early '70s. Fusing bubblegum melodies with crunching, fuzzy guitars, the band looked like a heavy metal band, but were as tame as any pop group. It was a dichotomy that served

them well, as they racked up a number of hits in both the U.K. and the U.S., which served as the predecessors for '80s pop-metal. Most of those hits were written by Nicky Chinn and Mike Chapman, a pair of British songwriters who had a way with silly, simple, catchy hooks. Chinn, Chapman and Sweet were smart enough to latch on to the British glam-rock fad, building a safer, radio-friendly and teen-oriented version. Sweet signed to RCA Records in 1971, and Chinn & Chapman wrote a number of lightweight, double-entendre-filled bubblegum pop songs for the group, which included six Top 40 hits. During this time, Sweet were writing their own B-sides and album tracks, which featured crunching hard rock guitars. Consequently, the duo decided to write tougher songs for the group. "Blockbuster," the first result of Chinn & Chapman's glam-rock approach, was the biggest hit Sweet ever had in the U.K., reaching number one in early 1973. By the summer of 1974, the members of Sweet had grown tired of the control Chinn & Chapman exerted over their career and decided to record without the duo. In the spring of 1975, Sweet had their first self-penned hit with "Fox on the Run," which reached the Top Ten in both the U.K. and the U.S.; "Ballroom Blitz" belatedly reached the American Top Ten in the summer of 1975. For the rest of the decade, the group continued to churn out album-oriented rock records, each less successful than its predecessor. Sweet bounced back into the charts in 1978 with "Love Is Like Oxygen," but the single proved to be their last gasp. After several years of little success or attention, Sweet broke up in 1982, reuniting on various occasions in the decade afterward. —*Stephen Thomas Erlewine*

Desolation Boulevard / 1974 / Capitol ✦✦✦✦

Sweet hit the peak of their powers on *Desolation Boulevard*, a wonderfully lightweight collection of fizzy melodies and big, dumb hooks. Essentially, the album consists of three dynamic singles buoyed by a bunch of filler, but those singles—"Ballroom Blitz," "The 6-Teens," and "Fox on the Run"—are addictive slices of bubblegum glam rock. And the filler is ridiculously silly and enjoyable, with "Sweet F.A.," "I Wanna Be Committed," and "No You Don't" sounding like a kind of bizarre prototype for the Ramones' punky bubblegum (only without the irony, of course). Although the filler is relatively strong, there are a number of weak patches on *Desolation Boulevard*, but it remains an intoxicatingly fun record and one that sounds surprisingly fresh, even with all of its kitschy '70s production techniques. —*Stephen Thomas Erlewine*

● **The Best of Sweet** / Mar. 1, 1993 / Capitol ✦✦✦✦✦

Nobody played rock & roll trashier or dumber than Sweet, and their best moments shine on this terrific 16-track compilation. Every one of their hits were powered by an irresistibly stupid melody, big dumb guitars, and, on occasion, a whining synthesizer. It was glitter-rock for teens at its best, without the dark sensuality of T. Rex. Even today, Sweet's best songs—"Ballroom Blitz," "Little Willy," "Blockbuster," "Teenage Rampage," and the nearly-perfect "Fox on the Run"—still sound gloriously trashy. —*Stephen Thomas Erlewine*

The Sweet Inspirations

f. 1963, **db.** 1979

Pop-Soul, Soul

If one was cutting a soul, R&B, pop, rock, or girl-group record in New York in the '60s and needed female backup vocals, chances are they'd try to get the Sweet Inspirations first. The group found their way onto numerous recordings, including hits by the Drifters, Van Morrison, Wilson Pickett, Solomon Burke, Garnett Mimms, and most famously, Aretha Franklin (with whom they sometimes toured).

The group evolved from the '50s gospel group the Drinkard Singers. At various points soul singers Doris Troy, Judy Clay, Dionne Warwick, and sister Dee Dee Warwick were members. By the time they began to record on their own in 1967, their leader was Cissy Houston (mother of Whitney), and the women were renamed the Sweet Inspirations.

As an Atlantic recording act, the group cut some fine sides that rank among the clearest illustrations of the close links between soul music and gospel harmony. Usually sticking to material by famed soul and pop songwriters, they had about a half-dozen moderate R&B hits in the late '60s; the biggest, "Sweet Inspiration," was a Top 20 pop single. Houston left the group at the end of the '60s and the Inspirations left Atlantic in the early '70s, sometimes working with Elvis Presley and recording an album for Stax in 1973. —*Richie Unterberger*

The Sweet Inspirations: Estell, Myrna and Sylvia / 1968 / Stax ✦✦✦✦

Though Cissy Houston was long gone from the group by the time they made this album, it's a fine set of gospel-pop-soul, with arrangements that manage to be sophisticated without getting slick. Co-produced by David Porter and Ronnie Williams, who as a pair also wrote most of the material, the songs are good and varied, the vocals and harmonies emotive and ebullient. The CD reissue adds two hits that they recorded for Atlantic in 1967 with Houston in the lineup ("Why [Am I Treated So Bad]" and "Sweet Inspiration"). —*Richie Unterberger*

● **The Best of the Sweet Inspirations** / Nov. 22, 1994 / Ichiban/Soul Classics ✦✦✦✦✦

Solid retrospective of their Atlantic years (1967-71), including all the hits and several misses. A lot of the songs were cut at Muscle Shoals, Memphis, or Atlantic Studios, and accordingly the arrangements have a deep soul flavor characteristic of Atlantic's late-'60s releases (although they worked briefly in Philadelphia in 1969 for a Gamble-Huff-flavored sound). Includes covers of songs by Isaac Hayes, Roebuck Staples, Dan Penn, and Gamble/Huff, all of which they make their own with lovely harmonies and imaginative interpretations. —*Richie Unterberger*

Matthew Sweet

b. 1964, Lincoln, NE

Vocals, Songwriter, Guitar / Pop Underground, College Rock, Adult Alternative Pop/Rock, Power Pop, Alternative Pop/Rock

After spending the '80s as an unappreciated jangle-pop guitarist with Oh-OK and Lloyd Cole, as well as a solo artist, Matthew Sweet emerged in 1991 as the leading figure of the American power-pop revival. Like his British counterparts Teenage Fanclub, Sweet adhered to traditional songcraft, yet subverted the form by adding noisy post-punk guitar and flourishes of country-rock, resulting in an amalgam of the Beatles, Big Star, R.E.M., and Neil Young. Recorded with guitarists Richard Lloyd and Robert Quine, Sweet's third album, *Girlfriend* (1991), became a word-of-mouth critical and commercial hit over the course of 1992, with its title track reaching the Top Five on the Modern Rock charts. For the next five years, as alternative rock was the dominant commercial force in rock & roll, Sweet was a popular concert attraction, and his reputation as an alternative pop singer-songwriter was at its peak—his next two records, *Altered Beast* (1993) and *100% Fun* (1995), were both critically acclaimed and relatively successful albums, with the latter reaching gold status and making many year-end "Best Of" lists. Beginning with 1997's *Blue Sky on Mars*, Sweet settled into cult status, and while he wasn't enjoying the success of his previous records, most power-pop records of the latter half of the '90s were indebted to *Girlfriend*. *—Stephen Thomas Erlewine*

Inside / 1986 / Columbia ♦♦

Matthew Sweet's debut solo album was a tentative effort, featuring a handful of good songs, but it was weighed down by too many guest artists (everyone from Valerie Simpson and the Heartbreakers' Mike Campbell to Chris Stamey, Bernie Worrell, and Anton Fier) and a glossy, synth-heavy production. *—Stephen Thomas Erlewine*

Earth / 1989 / A&M ♦♦

Despite the presence of guitarists Richard Lloyd and Robert Quine, Matthew Sweet's second album, *Earth*, remains a spotty affair. Like *Inside* before it, *Earth* has an overly glossy production, as well as a set of songs that are, by and large, forgettable—in fact, the songs on the second album are even more undistinguished than the ones on the previous record. *—Stephen Thomas Erlewine*

● **Girlfriend** / Oct. 22, 1991 / Zoo ♦♦♦♦♦

Matthew Sweet's third album is a remarkable artistic breakthrough. Grounded in the guitar-pop of the Beatles, Big Star, Byrds, R.E.M., and Neil Young, *Girlfriend* melds all of Sweet's influences into one majestic, wrenching sound that encompasses both the gentle country-rock of "Winona" and the winding guitars of the title track and "Divine Intervention." Sweet's music might have recognizable roots, but *Girlfriend* never sounds derivative; thanks to his exceptional songwriting, the album is a fresh, original interpretation of a classic sound. *—Stephen Thomas Erlewine*

Altered Beast / Jul. 13, 1993 / Zoo ♦♦♦

Compared to the concise songwriting of *Girlfriend*, *Altered Beast* is all over the place, both emotionally and musically. Ranging from piercing guitar rave-ups ("Dinosaur Act") to gorgeous country-rock ("Time Capsule"), the album not only covers all sides of Sweet's musical personality, but pastes them together haphazardly. Consequently, it takes a bit of time for all of it to make sense, but after a few listens, it falls together, and its best moments equal *Girlfriend*. *—Stephen Thomas Erlewine*

Son of Altered Beast / Mar. 15, 1994 / Volcano ♦♦♦

Most live releases attempt to recreate the sound of a studio album in a stage setting. Matthew Sweet's *Son of Altered Beast* pushes the music of 1993 studio release *Altered Beast* further, providing new material for fans and giving others a chance to see another dimension of Sweet's work. This time out, Sweet intensifies his reverence for guitar-oriented rock. Critically acclaimed, *Altered Beast* shows Sweet's shadowy side in songs such as "Someone to Pull the Trigger" as well as his biting humor on "Knowing People." The studio versions of these songs contain blistering guitars and carefully engineered vocals. While the vocals verge on unreserved, the live tracks present another side of Matthew Sweet not manifest in his videos or studio albums. The live versions of these songs on *Son of Altered Beast* share the guitar sounds of *Altered Beast* (thanks to the stellar performances by Richard Lloyd and Greg Liesz), but the vocals and overall sound reverberate with a raw energy characteristic of Sweet's stage show. The studio remix of "Devil With the Green Eyes" and the "lost" studio track "Ultrasuede" round out the live tracks. Recorded part way through the *Altered Beast* tour, *Son of Altered Beast* demonstrates Matthew Sweet's ability to reinvent his music live, rather than reproduce it. *—Jennifer Ansbach*

100% Fun / Mar. 14, 1995 / Zoo ♦♦♦♦

Clocking in at 45 minutes, Matthew Sweet's third record of guitar-dominated, hook-laden power-pop runs through its 12 songs at a classic speed, piling up songs that lovingly conform to the three-minute pop tradition. Richard Lloyd's gnarled guitars save Sweet's melodies and harmonies from being saccharine or sappy. Behind Sweet's bright hooks lies something darker—the self-loathing of "Sick of Myself" and the mental manipulation of "We're the Same" aren't evident from the sound of the record, which obliterates any hidden meanings with its chiming guitars and driving rhythms. It might not have the consistent barrage of great songs like *Girlfriend*, yet it tames the wilder impulses of *Altered Beast* into an album that rocks its worries away without ever getting rid of them. *—Stephen Thomas Erlewine*

Blue Sky on Mars / Mar. 25, 1997 / Zoo ♦♦♦

On Matthew Sweet's early-'90s power-pop trilogy of *Girlfriend*, *Altered Beast*, and *100% Fun*, Richard Lloyd's angular, unpredictable lead guitar functioned as a gritty counterpoint to Sweet's pretty melodies and tales of lost love, giving the music an unexpected depth. Sweet parted ways with Lloyd before he made *Blue Sky on Mars*, and his departure greatly effects the music. Without Lloyd, the songs are more predictable and the band, even with Brendan O'Brien's warm production, sounds rather canned. However, the music isn't the only thing hurting *Blue Sky on Mars*—the songs themselves are considerably more uneven than before, lacking the effortless hooks of its three predecessors. Sweet manages to turn out a handful of good songs—the swirling "Where Do You Get Love" has an infectious chorus, and "Come to California" has a sunny, Californian feel—but the simple problem is that most of the songs are colorless, and that comes as a major disappointment after the inspired songcraft since *Girlfriend*. *—Stephen Thomas Erlewine*

In Reverse / Sep. 28, 1999 / Volcano ♦♦♦♦♦

Ever since *Girlfriend*, Matthew Sweet made tightly wound guitar pop, but *In Reverse* takes a different approach, borrowing elements from Phil Spector, Brian Wilson, the Beatles, and Electric Light Orchestra to create a seductive ocean of sound. Vocals, guitars, and pianos are given cavernous reverb, surrounded by grand percussion, backwards guitars, and brass. Unlike many of his '90s pop peers, Sweet isn't aping *Pet Sounds* and *Magical Mystery Tour* just to prove that he can—this rich music is a personal interpretation of lush chamber pop and psychedelia, giving a musical counterpart for lovely melancholy songs of heartbreak and disillusion. *In Reverse* is a song cycle, with songs segueing into one another and playing off each other's themes, each blessed with glorious touches of neo-psychedelia and baroque pop. There's a unity of sound and song which makes *In Reverse* play like a concept album and, like any good concept album, it ends with a grandiose gesture—a nine-minute suite called "Thunderstruck" which fuses the Beach Boys, Neil Young, and Sweet himself in unpredictable, thrilling ways. In that one song, all of the themes and pretensions of the album brilliantly come together, and that's the most remarkable thing about *In Reverse*—it fulfills its ambitions while delivering the emotional impact of *Girlfriend*. *—Stephen Thomas Erlewine*

Time Capsule: The Best of Matthew Sweet / Sep. 26, 2000 / Volcano ♦♦♦♦♦

One of the most unlikely and endearing successes of the alternative rock era, Matthew Sweet was—and is—one of the most consistent artists to come out of that time period. Compiled by Volcano Records, the same label that released Sweet's 1999 album *In Reverse*, *Time Capsule: The Best of Matthew Sweet* collects 16 of his best-loved songs and two new ones, "Ready" and "So Far." Not surprisingly, the anthology spends the most time with his strongest albums, especially his breakthrough, *Girlfriend*. A full four songs—"Divine Intervention," "I've Been Waiting," "Girlfriend," and "You Don't Love Me"—come from that 1991 classic, but *Altered Beast*, *100% Fun*, *Blue Sky on Mars*, and even *In Reverse* are well represented with songs like "Time Capsule," "Sick of Myself," "We're the Same," "Where You Get Love," and "What Matters." Sweet's vibrant, vulnerable take on power pop revitalized the genre in the '90s, and this collection of his work still sounds completely fresh and enjoyable. *—Heather Phares*

Rachel Sweet

b. 1963, Akron, OH

Vocals / Pop/Rock, New Wave

At Stiff Records, nothing was sacred; often the label's slogans and unorthodox promotion were as memorable as the truly inspired music they released. With teenage Rachel Sweet, whom they marketed as a "jailbait" country singer (and later as a leather-clad child abductor), it would seem that their perverse humor had finally gone too far. One listen to her albums, however, and all questionable images and in-jokes fall into the background; the "little girl with the big voice" made some terrific music, holding her own on a roster that had no shortage of talent. Sweet recorded her first album, *Fool Around*, with backing from the Rumour in 1978. The album didn't sell particularly well, but it did receive a fair amount of critical praise. The attention was short-lived, though, and *Protect the Innocent*, released through Stiff/Columbia, went virtually ignored the following year. She switched to Columbia in 1981 for *... And Then He Kissed Her*, an uneven album that nevertheless featured the Top 40 hit "Everlasting Love," a duet with Rex Smith. After one more album, 1982's *Blame It on Love*, Sweet retired from the music business to pursue an education, returning sporadically, most notably to sing the title track to John Waters' *Hairspray*, as well as *Cry Baby*. *—Chris Woodstra*

Fool Around / Oct. 6, 1978 / Stiff ♦♦♦♦

Protect the Innocent / 1980 / Rhino ♦♦♦

Despite being part of the Stiff Records roster, Rachel Sweet didn't really have anything to do with punk, or even new wave—but then again, if more teenage pop music had been like *Protect the Innocent* in the late '70s, we might not have needed a new wave so badly. Rachel had a big, big voice and a refreshing degree of smarts about what to do with it, able to sing pop, rock & roll, and country-accented stuff with enthusiasm, taste, and gale-force impact, and she was never in better form than on *Protect the Innocent*. Martin Rushent and Alan Winstanley's production is sharp, clear, and keeps Rachel's pipes up front at all times, and the backing band (uncredited, but said to be Fingerprintz) sounds lean, spunky, and tuneful. And Rachel? Well, it's not every 18-year-old girl who can tackle Lou Reed's "New Age," Elvis Presley's "Baby, Let's Play House," and the Damned's "New Rose" all in a row and sound convincing on all three, but Ms. Sweet manages that hat trick, and sounds mighty fine on the album's other nine cuts as well. She also does well with her three originals on the album, especially the energetic pop rocker "Tonight" and the slinky sneaking-your-boyfriend-into-the-house number "Tonight Ricky" (if Britney Spears had dared to sound half as sexy singing about high-school seduction, the FCC would never have let her on the air). Remember *Mad Love*, that album where Linda Rondstadt was trying to sound "new wave"? Listen to *Protect the Innocent*, and you'll hear Rachel do what Rondstadt was shooting for, and do it lots, lots better. Easily Rachel's best album. *—Mark Deming*

And Then He Kissed Me / Aug. 1981 / Columbia ✦✦✦

Blame It on Love / 1982 / Columbia ✦✦

● **Fool Around: The Best of Rachel Sweet** / Mar. 24, 1992 / Rhino ✦✦✦✦✦
Fool Around: The Best of Rachel Sweet compiles the finest moments of the singer's career with the first album represented in its entirety (including the U.S. version additions), the rare "I'll Watch the News" and "Be Stiff" from Stiff Records samplers, a couple each from her two lesser albums, and the title track from the *Hairspray* soundtrack. A strong collection, this is probably the only Rachel Sweet disc to own for all but the obsessive completist. *—Chris Woodstra*

B.A.B.Y.: The Best of Rachel Sweet / May 11, 2001 / Metro ✦✦✦✦

Sweetwater

Psychedelic
An unusual rock group in both the size of their lineup (which numbered eight), the instrumentation employed, and the eclectic scope of their material, Sweetwater didn't quite get the first-class songs or breaks necessary to make them widely known. Lead singer Nansi Nevins was backed not just by conventional guitar, bass, drums, and keyboards, but also flute, conga, and cello. Their self-titled debut album was the kind of release that could have only been the product of the late '60s, with the music flying off in all directions, and a major label willing to put it out. Sweetwater blended Californian psychedelia with jazzy keyboards and a classical bent, especially in the flute and cello, but did not cohere into a readily identifiable aesthetic, or write exceptional songs. In the late '60s they opened for a lot of big-time acts, and played a bunch of festivals without breaking into the headliner ranks. In fact, they were the very first band to take the stage at Woodstock. In December 1969, 20-year-old Nansi Nevins was in a serious car accident in which she suffered severe brain trauma and damaged her vocal cords, putting her in a coma for weeks and necessitating physical therapy for years. Although she had recorded a couple of tracks on their second Reprise album, she was unable to rejoin the band, which had to stop touring and lost any career momentum it had developed. The surviving trio of Nevins, keyboardist Alex Del Zoppo, and bassist Fred Herrera reunited Sweetwater in 1997, and two years later cable network VH1 produced and broadcast a film about the group; the picture sparked a considerable resurgence of interest in the group, and that same year Rhino released *Cycles*, a limited-edition retrospective of their work for Reprise. *—Richie Unterberger*

● **Cycles: The Reprise Collection** / Sep. 1999 / Rhino Handmade ✦✦✦
As the opening band at the original Woodstock festival, Sweetwater was a rock & roll footnote that was almost completely forgotten until VH-1 decided to inaugurate its series of original films with a TV movie about the band—or, more specifically, about Nancy Nevins' role in the band. The day after the film premiered, the release of *Cycles: The Reprise Collection* was announced on Rhino's website. So, *Cycles* arrived at the perfect time—in fact, the only time that it could have arrived, since even a month after its announced release, the Sweetwater craze began to fade. And justifiably so, since this "definitive" 19-track collection proves that they were not that great of a band. They effectively aped the Mamas & the Papas and Jefferson Airplane (Nevins is a dead ringer for Grace Slick), with a slightly jazzier bent, but their music is too much of its time—decades later, lyrics like "What's wrong with our schools/What's wrong with our zoos" elicit nothing but cringes. Some pop artifacts of this nature are quite entertaining—nearly everything Sundazed has unearthed, for example—but Sweetwater was stunningly average, lacking memorable songs or distinctive performances. They were a hippie folk-rock band perfect for opening Woodstock, but removed from its context, their music doesn't hold up. But if the VH-1 movie sparked your interest, *Cycles* is ideal. There's no need to pay 100 dollars for the band's debut album, since nine of its 11 tracks are here, along with a version of "What's Wrong" from Woodstock, four songs from *Just for You*, three songs from *Melon*, and two previously unreleased songs: "God Rest Ye Merry Gentlemen" and "Home Again." It's a perfect distillation of a perfectly average career. *—Stephen Thomas Erlewine*

Swell Maps

f. 1972
Experimental Rock, Post-Punk, Alternative Pop/Rock
Noisy and experimental, Britain's Swell Maps experienced little commercial success during the course of their chaotic career, but in hindsight they stand as one of the pivotal acts of the new wave: not only was the group an acknowedged inspiration to the likes of Sonic Youth and Pavement, but their alumni—most notably brothers Nikki Sudden and Epic Soundtracks—continued on as key players in the underground music community.

Although Sudden (vocals/guitar) and Soundtracks (piano/drums) formed the first incarnation of the Swell Maps (named after the charts used by surfers to gauge wave intensities) as far back as 1972, the group did not begin to truly take shape until 1976, when the siblings enlisted bassist Jowe Head and guitarist Richard Earl. In the spirit of punk's "do-it-yourself" mentality, they formed their own label, Rather Records, and issued their debut single—the brief, jarring "Read About Seymour"—in the early weeks of 1978. Local media support soon won the group a distribution pact with Rough Trade, but they did not resurface until over a year later with the single "Dresden Style."

In mid-1979, the Swell Maps released their full-length debut *A Trip to Marineville*, a crazy-quilt of punk energy and Krautrock-influenced clatter. After the release of the speaker-shredding single "Let's Build a Car," the group recorded one final studio LP, *Jane From Occupied Europe*, before breaking up. A series of outtakes and singles collections—1981's *Whatever Happens Next...*, 1982's *Collision Time*, and 1987's *Train Out of It*—followed, while the members followed their own career paths: Sudden formed the Jacobites, Soundtracks joined Crime and the City Solution, and Head played with the Television Personalities. All later enjoyed solo careers as well. *—Jason Ankeny*

Trip to Marineville / Jul. 1979 / Mute ✦✦✦✦
Swell Maps' debut album was a scattershot affair, ranging from blistering three-chord punk to free-form noise experiments, that was intriguing, yet frequently incoherent. *—Stephen Thomas Erlewine*

Jane From Occupied Europe / 1980 / Mute ✦✦✦✦✦
Swell Maps might have been shamblin' ramblin' men, and there might be a couple tracks on the band's second and final album that are practically throwaway, but you have to admire a band that has enough fun in making a record that you can practically catch a buzz from rooms away when hearing it. More experimental and less punk-leaning than *A Trip to Marineville*, *Jane From Occupied Europe* is every bit indulgent but equally excellent, if flawed. How can you not admire a band with song titles like "Collision With a Frogman" or "Vs. the Mangrove Delta Plan"? After the Teutonic intro "Robot Factory," the Maps unleash four nasty, loose-limbed garage numbers, including the especially loud and catchy "Helicopter Spies." The Maps then dispose with vocals for the entire middle half of the record. "Big Maz in the Desert" is frenzied clang-and-drone (a Can record played at 45 RPMs), and "Big Empty Field" (an actually descriptive title!) adds chime to another relentless, Kraut-inspired rhythmic drive. Another trio of vocal garage tunes follow, closing out with a brief solo piano tune. While *Jane* might have been criticized upon release for lacking focus, it could also be heralded for containing even more imagination that the band's wild debut. Regardless of its perceived shortcomings, it's hard to imagine what Sonic Youth and Pavement would have sounded like without it. The Mute reissue adds eight bonuses, most of which are alternate versions and somewhat relevant outtakes. The especially flammable single version of "Let's Build a Car" is a noteworthy addition. *—Andy Kellman*

Whatever Happens Next / 1981 / Mute ✦✦

Train Out of It / 1987 / Mute ✦✦✦✦
Compiling a number of outtakes and singles, *Train Out of It* features more quality material than their similar rarities collection, *Whatever Happens Next*. *—Stephen Thomas Erlewine*

● **Collision Time Revisited** / 1989 / Mute ✦✦✦✦✦
A good intro, this 27-track album collects tracks from the band's four LPs, along with B-sides and unreleased tracks. *—John Bush*

The International Rescue / Mar. 16, 1999 / Alive ✦✦✦
You'll have to be a pretty major Swell Maps fan to make heads or tails, at a glance, out of which songs on this 19-track compilation you may already have. It's all over the Swell map, including four songs that have never been on CD (including "Dresden Style (City Boys)," which was on a single); three that have never been released anywhere; three "unreleased mixes"; and a few songs that appeared on U.K. singles ("Let's Build a Car," "Real Shocks," "Read About Seymour"). It doesn't really succeed as either a representative overview compilation or a rarities disc. Approached on its own terms—which you might want to do if this happens to be the first, or only, Swell Maps album you get—it's decent arty punk that's too monochromatic to sustain burning interest over the course of the lengthy program. It does have a heartier sense of *joie de vivre* than much U.K. punk/new wave of the period, particularly in the vocals. *—Richie Unterberger*

Sweep the Desert / Jan. 23, 2001 / Alive ✦✦

Swervedriver

f. 1990, London, England
Dream Pop, Shoegazing, Alternative Pop/Rock
The band who brought the car song into the shoegazer era, Swervedriver was formed in Britain in 1990 by vocalists/guitarists Adam Franklin and Jimmy Hartridge, bassist Adi Vines and drummer Graham Bonner. Fusing the swirling textures of the shoegazer aesthetic with the more traditional boundaries of pop, the group debuted with a series of brilliant EPs—*Son of Mustang Ford*, *Rave Down*, and *Sandblasted*—before issuing their full-length debut, *Raise*, in 1991. After a U.S. tour in support of Soundgarden, Bonner left the band, followed quickly by the departure of Vines; 1992's *Never Lose That Feeling* EP, their strongest effort to date, initially appeared to mark the group's swan song. But in 1993, Swervedriver returned; with the core of Franklin and Hartridge rounded out by new drummer Jez, they released their sophomore LP *Mezcal Head*. An import-only release, *Ejector Seat Reservation*, followed in 1995; in 1998, Swervedriver resurfaced with their fourth effort, *99th Dream*. The *Wrong Treats* EP followed in 1999. Bonner and Vines, meanwhile, continued as Skyscraper. *—Jason Ankeny*

Raise / 1991 / A&M ✦✦✦✦
A molten hybrid of *Daydream Nation*-era Sonic Youth, the drill-press rhythms of the Stooges, and early Dinosaur Jr., *Raise* sounds like a record made by young record shop rats from the Midwest. Adding to this notion is the lyrical fascination with cars. With this in mind, it's no small wonder that the Oxford, London-based Swervedriver found a home on even the most Anglophobic turntables in the States. Through loads of effects pedals and buried vocals, the band was initially lumped in with the shoegaze scene. But with a heavier aesthetic caused by their love for the above-mentioned bands, as well as the likes of the well-named Loop and Spacemen 3, they were unique—even with their earliest material. Oddly, *Raise* only contains six new songs for those who bought their excellent trio of preceding singles. The new tracks rival their greatness. Jimmy Hartridge's and Adam Franklin's guitars definitely carry a soaring, seering quality, but the record is largely bass driven, thanks to Adi Vines' thick lines (see "Pile Up" and "Sunset" for the best examples).

And though buried to the point of serving merely as another instrument, Franklin's vocals sound like that of a road trip lifer, made weary by constant sun exposure on the eyes. Other than what might seem as the band trying too hard to prove themselves through complexity, there aren't many faults to be found. Though it does seem to favor texture over anything else, the somewhat murky production suits the songs well. It actually sounds dark, like green-skied, pre-tornado weather. It's not too hard to pick apart each instrument on each song, but they still sound a bit mashed together. A fantastic debut that merely hinted at the band's talents. *—Andy Kellman*

• **Mezcal Head** / Oct. 5, 1993 / A&M ✦✦✦✦✦
There are cruising records, and then there are speeding records; *Mezcal Head* is definitely one of the latter. Solid, dense as marble, and frighteningly well executed, Swervedriver's second album is a non-abrasive rock & roll record of the highest order. Polishing the sound of *Raise* and improving the songcraft to match the band's previous sense of texture, it contains all the ingredients of a favorite record to exceed the speed limit by. Adam Franklin's cool voice is no longer buried in the mix, a smart move since his range has expanded to allow for melodic hooks and deep emotion, unlike the detached quality he held on *Raise* and the singles that preceded it.

Clocking in at an hour, the 11 songs provide enough depth and variety to defray any sense of boredom. "For Seeking Heat" begins innocently until revving into steaming ferocity. "Duel," a minor hit on alternative radio, is probably the band's most well-known song. Fittingly enough, it takes its name from Spielberg's road velocity-based movie of the same name. "Blowin' Cool" shows the band's first strain of the pop influence that would bleed through *Ejector Seat Reservation.* "Last Train to Satansville," likely Franklin's finest moment as a songwriter, puts him in the shoes of a delusional lover. Breaking free from the steaming charge of the album's first side, the eight-minute "Duress" snakes drowsily through the first four minutes until breaking into a trancey mid-tempo dirge.

Like a film with many well-developed characters that makes one lose both track of time and a sense of self, *Mezcal Head* delivers. And, just to hammer home that this isn't an album that loses its effect outside of the automobile—after the tenth play you'll surely learn your lesson to quit running over to the stereo and increasing the volume with each successive song. Just leave it pegged. *—Andy Kellman*

Ejector Seat Reservation / 1995 / Creation ✦✦✦✦✦
What a bummer to have your finest hour left for dead. Creation was nice enough to release *Ejector Seat Reservation*, but the record received nothing outside of a couple small ads promotion-wise, and the band was dropped a week after its release. Clocking in at just over 40 minutes, Ejector Seat Reservation is the band's most cohesive and concise record, best experienced in whole. The band scales back the roar of *Mezcal Head* and points to their classic pop and glam influences; "Bring Me the Head of the Fortune Teller" is the only completely blasting thing here. Otherwise, it could pass as another band to a casual listener. Even the most gnashing moments are more melodically driven than previous outings (*Mezcal Head*'s "Blowin' Cool" is a good reference point). Those who thrilled over the band's bad-ass, Stooge-ified sonic assaults might not know what to think of after a couple listens, but taken on its own context, the record ropes you in just as tightly as anything else they've done. Helping the band reach new pop heights is the expanded range of Adam Franklin's voice. Check the upper register on the Love-y acid trip "Son of Jaguar 'E'" and the gentle, graceful croon on "Last Day on Earth." A T-Rex/Sweet-like shuffle pops up in the title track, with more hallucinatory lyric imagery. The vocal hook from Bacharach/David's "Do You Know the Way to San Jose" gets cleverly nicked for "Candy," a song that's possibly their best fusion of overload guitars and singalong chorus. It boggles the mind how a song as powerful and melodic as "The Birds" didn't find a home on a radio chart of any form, in any country. They effortlessly committed this as if they had it in them all along. *—Andy Kellman*

99th Dream / Feb. 24, 1998 / Zero Hour ✦✦✦
Though the weakest of Swervedriver's four long-players of the '90s, *99th Dream* still shimmers and sizzles like the work of shamefully few bands of the time. Another trademark opening one-two punch is offered in "99th Dream" and "Up From the Sea," showing a continuation of the band falling prey to their pop instincts. Slowly but surely, Swervedriver have morphed from a runaway locomotive informed by the Stooges and Dinosaur Jr. to a classic sports car fueled by Love and the Beatles, without losing their ferocious purr along the way. *99th Dream* has its less than superb moments; "Electric '7" and "Stellar Caprice" lumber along enough to challenge the attention of the diehard, and "In My Time" would have gathered dust on the cutting room floor had it been committed during *Mezcal Head* or *Ejector.* Also, the version of "These Times" that appears on the Zero Hour version is inferior to the one found on the Geffen advance. The latter version plods along, marring the sprightly pace of the original; oddly enough, the original sounds a hell of a lot like Oasis. Adam Franklin even attains the nasal whine of Liam Gallagher without grating. One could wager a shoebox of Beatles 45s that it was for these reasons that a tamer version appears here. Full of rich harmonies and graceful instrumental passages, *99th Dream* closes with "Maybe the People Would Be the Times . . ."—"Behind the Scenes of the Sounds and the Times," that is! Though reading like a song off Love's *Forever Changes*, "Behind the Scenes" is a dynamic seven-minute trip of charging, psychedelic ebb and flow. [A Japanese version of *99th Dream* adds the B-sides from the *Wrong Treats* EP.] *—Andy Kellman*

Swimming Pool Q's

f. 1981, **db.** 1989
Jangle Pop, Alternative Pop/Rock, New Wave, Post-Punk
Atlanta's Swimming Pool Q's were one of the first Southern new wave bands to gain nationwide recognition in the early '80s after the breakthrough of the B-52's made folks aware that there was more to Southern rock than what Q's leader Jeff Calder called "the boogie establishment." However, while most of their Georgia brethren were famous for serving up light, off-kilter pop, Swimming Pool Q's music had a darker and more challenging undercurrent, balancing twisted guitar patterns against lyrics that played on Southern gothic archetypes in a manner that was often witty, and sometimes ominous. In 1978, Calder and Bob Esley had formed Swimming Pool Q's; with Esley playing lead guitar and Calder handling rhythm and taking most of the lead vocals, the Q's were rounded out by percussionist Robert Schmid, bassist Billy Jones, and Anne Richmond Boston, who sang lead on several numbers, played occasional keyboards, and brought samples from her impressive toy collection to shows. In 1979, the band self-released their first single, "Rat Bait" b/w "The A-Bomb Woke Me Up," which generated enthusiastic press and sold well enough to gain the band spots opening for the likes of Devo and the Police. In 1981, the band released their first album, *The Deep End*, and before long the band signed to A&M Records. In 1984, the group released their first major-label album, simply entitled *The Swimming Pool Q's*; by this time the band's sound had become a bit more streamlined, with Boston handling a greater number of lead vocals and adding more keyboard textures to the songs. *Blue Tomorrow* followed in 1986, but despite college radio airplay and continued touring, the band seemed to have hit a commercial plateau, and they were dropped by A&M. *—Mark Deming*

• **The Deep End** / 1981 / DB ✦✦✦✦
Because they came out of Georgia's then-fledgling new wave scene in the late '70s, the Swimming Pool Q's usually get lumped in with the great Southern jangle pop brigade alongside R.E.M., Pylon, and Guadalcanal Diary—which suggests the people doing the comparing never spent much time listening to the band. The group's 1981 debut, *The Deep End*, shows the Swimming Pool Q's shared a fondness for angular pop hooks with the above-mentioned groups, but that's where most of the similarities end. The guitars of Bob Elsey and Jeff Calder aim less for chime than for sharp aural twists and turns, the vocals from Calder and Anne Richmond Boston are soulful with just the right amount of grit to make the willful surrealism of the lyrics stick, and the band's melodic sense suggests Pere Ubu's Southern brethren, with the noise factor turned down, the psychedelic influences given greater room to move, and the arrangements given a oddly cheerful exterior that only made the dark undercurrents creepier. Lyrically, *The Deep End* captures a band fully in touch with their Southernness, but their take on life below the Mason-Dixon line is mixed with equal parts good humor and not-so-subtle menace. The Swimming Pool Q's didn't sound much like anyone else who emerged from the Deep South at the time, and *The Deep End* proves they had both the chops and the ambition to make something special of their strange vision. The 2001 reissue of the album adds 13 bonus tracks to the album's original 11 tunes, ranging from songwriting demos to pre-album single tracks; the result is as complete a look at this band's unique world view as you're ever likely to find in one package. *—Mark Deming*

Swimming Pool Q's / 1984 / A&M ✦✦✦

Blue Tomorrow / 1986 / A&M ✦✦✦

The Firing Squad for God / 1987 / DB ✦✦✦

World War Two Point Five / 1989 / Capitol ✦✦✦

Swing Out Sister

f. 1985
Sophisti-Pop, Adult Alternative Pop/Rock
Swing Out Sister came out of Manchester in the late '80s, but don't really have much in common with the other, more psychedelic groups on that scene; they play smooth, jazz-inflected synth-pop. They began as a trio of Martin Jackson (drums), Andy Connell (keyboards), and former fashion designer Corrine Drewery (vocals). Jackson left the group after their first album, which produced the Top Ten hit "Breakout," but still helped with the drum programming. The group attempted a less excessive,'60s pop sound on its next album. *—Steve Huey*

• **The Best of Swing Out Sister** / Jun. 30, 1998 / Polygram International ✦✦✦✦
As it stands, this import collection is the best and most accurate representation of Swing Out Sister's hit singles. Another hits collection, issued in 2001, failed to include some of their vital singles, including their second U.S. chart entry, "Twilight World," and "Waiting Game," the first single from their sophomore album. All of their hits are included on this set, including their biggest, "Breakout," as well as the incredibly difficult to find single edit of the aforementioned "Twilight World." Also included is their 1992 comeback hit, "Am I the Same Girl," and other gems such as the fantastic "You on My Mind," "Notgonnachange," and the U.K. edit of "La La (Means I Love You)." Additionally, the album closes with a tender, heartfelt live cover of the 1960s classic "The Windmills of Your Mind." The set plays well from start to finish, with all the songs blending together seamlessly. This is an ideal album for either a cocktail party, a late-night gathering, a romantic dinner date, or simply nostalgia for late-'80s/early-'90s sophisticated British jazz-pop, similar in style to Everything But the Girl, Sade, and Simply Red. A fine collection from a truly underrated act. *—Jose Promis*

Swingers

f. Nov. 1978, **db.** May 1982
New Wave
Phil Judd was a founding member and major creative force behind the early incarnation of Split Enz. Judd left the band in February of 1977, rejoining a year later only to leave shortly after finding himself unable to fit into the new direction of the band. Following a short stint with New Zealand punk bands Suburban Reptiles and Enemy, Judd formed

Swingers in late-1978, a no-frills, no image, straightforward power trio, with Dwayne "Bones" Hillman (bass) and Buster Stiggs (drums). In April of 1980, they recorded a single for Ripper Records, "One Good Reason"—the single eventually broke the N.Z. Top 20. The band set off for Australia , teaming up with David Tickle (who had just finished working with Split Enz) to re-record "One Good Reason" as well as the infectious "Counting the Beat." Stiggs exited following a falling out with Judd in December 1980 and was replaced by Ian "Killjoy" Gillroy. "Counting the Beat" was an Australian number one by February of 1981. In July, the band recorded several songs for the soundtrack to the film *Starstruck* (Judd would also write additional incidental music and the band made several appearances in the film). The following month, their full-length debut, *Practical Jokers*, was released by Mushroom Records (Backstreet edited and resequenced the album as *Counting the Beat* in the U.S.). The title track, "It Ain't What You Dance," and "One Good Reason (Gimme Love)," found a fair amount of exposure on the then-infant MTV while *Starstruck* also found a cult following. They added a new frontman, Andrew McLennan (ex-Pop Mechanix) and released one final single, "Punch and Judy" in early 1982. The single failed and Judd dissolved the unit in May the same year.

Hillman later found success as a member of Midnight Oil. Judd released one solo album (1983's *Private Lives*) and two more with ex-Split Enz bandmates as Schnell Fenster; he now keeps a low profile, dividing his time between artistic pursuits and composing music for films. *—Chris Woodstra*

• **Practical Jokers** / 1979 / Mushroom ✦✦✦✦✦
For *Practical Jokers*, his first post-Enz project, Judd left his arty leanings behind in favor of a tight blend of mid-'60s pop, punk, and new wave, resulting in a fine collection of fractured, eccentric pop songs that were surprisingly accessable. With the exception of "Ayatollah," which instantly dates the album, much of it remains fresh with a timeless appeal. The quirky "Counting the Beat," became a hit single in Australia/New Zealand. [A resequenced, slightly modified version of the album with the single "One Good Reason (Gimme Love)" added was issued in the U.S. as *Counting the Beat* in 1982. In a somewhat confusing move, Mushroom Records in Australia, as part of the label's 25th anniversary, reissued *Counting the Beat* with the original artwork but with the track listing and order of *Practical Jokers*. "One Good Reason" and "The Flack"—both found on the original *Counting the Beat* album—were added to the end of the disc.] *—Chris Woodstra*

Counting the Beat / 1982 / Mushroom ✦✦✦✦✦
In an attempt to capitalize on U.S. interest in the band generated by their appearance in the cult film *Starstruck*, Backstreet Records resequenced the *Practical Jokers* album, dropped a couple of songs and added the "One Good Reason (Gimme Love)" from the film. Unfortunately, it failed to make much of an impact in the States and was quickly deleted. [In a somewhat confusing move, Mushroom Records in Australia, as part of the label's 25th anniversary, reissued *Counting the Beat* with the original artwork but with the track listing and order of *Practical Jokers*. "One Good Reason" and "The Flack"—both found on the original *Counting the Beat* album—were added to the end of the disc.] *—Chris Woodstra*

The Swingin' Medallions

f. 1965, Greenwood, SC
Frat Rock, Beach, Rock & Roll, R&B
When the world nears Y3K there will probably still be a Swinging Medallions group touring throughout the South with fanatics shagging to their music. The one-hit wonders' claim to fame, "Double Shot (Of My Baby's Love)," charted at number 17 on July 2, 1966, and has made them an institution in the South. It was the band's second release for Smash Records; the first, "I Wanna Be Your Guy," went unnoticed. "Doubleshot"'s successors didn't pack the same wallop; the follow-up, "She Drives Me Out of My Mind," stopped climbing at number 71 in 1966, and "Hey Baby" failed too. They began as Pieces of Eight in the late '50s, and changed to Swinging Medallions in 1965 when they signed with Smash. The members: John McElrath (keyboards), Jim Doares (guitar), Carroll Bledsoe (trumpet), Charles Webber (trumpet), Brent Forston (sax, flute), Steven Caldwell (sax), James Perkins (bass), and Joe Morris (drums). All hail from the Greenwood, SC, area. Beach music is their forte and they're the main purveyors of the shag, a popular dance on Southern beaches. Over 30 years, the personnel has changed, and McElrath is the only original. Every year the original members reunite for a one-night concert in Atlanta, GA. *—Andrew Hamilton*

• **Anthology** / 1997 / Ripete ✦✦✦✦✦
Not surprisingly, this album opens with "Double Shot (Of My Baby's Love)," and the two minutes and 21 seconds of inspired craziness that in 1966 gave the Medallions their sole taste of national fame. The rest of *Anthology* is a mishmash, and no wonder: Despite the cover billing, only part of the album is by the original Medallions, who survived from 1963 to 1967. The rest comes from several successor bands, including the Pieces of Eight, a group formed in 1967 that contains several veterans of the original group; and a 1990s outfit that uses the original band's moniker but includes only one of its members. Which group performs which songs is often far from clear; the skimpy liner notes don't say, nor do they list any songwriters, vocalists in the original group, producers, or release dates. To further confuse matters, the album art includes a photo labeled "The Original Swingin' Medallions" that's captioned with the names in the 1990s lineup. Quality and approach vary widely, as the various aggregations try everything under the sun to get back on the charts. One highlight is "She Drives Me Out of My Mind," an at least partly successful attempt to recreate the magic of "Double Shot." The only thing most of the other songs have in common with the group's hit, however, is that they're covers ("Double Shot" was first recorded by the obscure Dick Holler and the Holidays). The album is worth buying, but you'll be glad your CD player makes it easy to skip a few of the tracks. *—Jeff Burger*

The Swinging Blue Jeans

f. 1959, Liverpool, England, **db.** 1968
Merseybeat, British Invasion
Although they're only remembered today for their 1964 hit "Hippy Hippy Shake," the Swinging Blue Jeans were actually one of the strongest of the Liverpool bands from the '60s British Invasion. "Hippy Hippy Shake"—a cover of an obscure '50s rocker that was actually done much better by the Beatles on tapes of their BBC performances—was their only Top 30 entry in the U.S. But the band enjoyed some other major and minor hits in the U.K., including a top-notch Merseyization of Betty Everett's (and later Linda Ronstadt's) "You're No Good," which they took into the British Top Five in 1964. They also wrote some catchy and energetic, if slightly sappy, originals in the purest Merseybeat style. While it doesn't add up to an enduring legacy, there's a lot to be said for the naive energy of the best of their early tunes. *—Richie Unterberger*

Blue Jeans a Swinging / 1964 / EMI ✦✦

The Best of the EMI Years / 1992 / EMI ✦✦✦
Weighing in at a hefty 34 tracks, this is the most exhaustive Swinging Blue Jeans anthology available. Do not mistake this, however, for the best collection of these cheery Liverpool British Invaders. That honor belongs to the American *Hippy Hippy Shake* collection, which is nearly as comprehensive (at 26 tracks) but much more well chosen. All their U.K. hits—half a dozen, more or less—are included here, as well as many B-sides, flop singles, and eight previously unreleased tracks (most of which bear the writing credits "unknown," even the relatively well-known Little Richard song "Ready Teddy"). At their best, the Blue Jeans were one of the better British Invasion pop-rockers, and they did manage a fair number of good tracks, but a great deal of the selections here are uneventful or downright difficult to bear in their dated quaintness, fallow MOR pop, or lame rehashing of '50s rock. The small bonus is that the version of their 1968 single "Now That You've Got Me (You Don't Seem to Want Me)," written by Clint Ballard (also responsible for "You're No Good" and other great '60s tunes), is, for some reason, much better than the one on *Hippy Hippy Shake*. That's hardly worth the fairly hefty price of this import—stick with the U.S. compilation. *—Richie Unterberger*

• **Hippy Hippy Shake: the Definitive Collection** / May 4, 1993 / EMI America ✦✦✦✦✦
All of their U.K. and U.S. hits are included on this compilation. Highlights are "You're No Good," "Hippy Hippy Shake," and their fine (pre-Who) cover of Johnny Kidd's "Shakin' All Over," though even for the Anglophile, about half of this CD is forgettable, especially the dreary post-1966 stuff. This anthology includes several non-LP/rare singles and unreleased songs. *—Richie Unterberger*

The Swirlies

f. 1990
Dream Pop, Indie Rock, Shoegazing, Lo-Fi, Noise Pop
Originally a Go-Go's cover band called Raspberry Bang, the Swirlies formed in Boston in 1990. Along with Kudgel and Fat Day, the band—guitarist/singer Damon Tuntunjian, singer/guitarist Seana Carmody, bassist Andy Bernick, and drummer Ben Drucker—was a part of the city's chimp rock scene, which pitted dreamy, guitar-based pop against noisy, experimental tendencies.

The Swirlies made their recorded debut with the six-song EP *Swirlies Number One*, and then proceeded to release a slew of singles, including "Red Fishdreams" with fellow chimp rockers Kudgel. The band signed to the Boston-based Taang! label and released a mini-album, *What to Do About Them*, in 1992. A collection of the group's singles along with new material, it hinted at the band's departure from typical dream pop.

1993's *Blonder Tongue Audio Baton* continued the band's foray into sonic experimentation. The addition of tape loops, found sounds, Moogs, Mellotrons, and white noise made the Swirlies' sound an interesting cross between lo-fi concrete music and shoegazing dream pop.

After the release of the *Brokedick Car* EP, the band experienced almost constant personnel shake-ups. This included an auxiliary bassist and the departures of Ben Drucker and Seana Carmody; Carmody formed her own band, Syrup USA. By 1995, only Tuntunjian and Bernick remained from the original lineup, joined by singer/guitarist Christina Files and drummer Anthony DeLuca. This lineup of the Swirlies recorded *They Spent Their Wild Youthful Days in the Glittering World of the Salons*, the band's second full-length album, which included more keyboards and drum machines in their sound but maintained a lo-fi aesthetic.

By spring 1996, DeLuca left the band and was temporarily replaced by Karate drummer Gavin McCarthy; however, by this time the Swirlies included a trigger drum kit in their equipment and also toured as an electronic trio. Later that year, the group found a permanent drummer in Adam Pierce, but Files left the Swirlies in 1997. The group continued as a guitar/electronic hybrid and released a remix album, *Strictly East Coast Sneaky Flute Music*, in 1998. That year also saw the band add another guitarist, Rob Laxo from the Wicked Farleys; the group lost distribution through a label that year, but started releasing cassettes as part of their Sneaky Flute Empire project. *—Heather Phares*

What to Do About Them / Oct. 2, 1992 / Taang! ✦✦✦
What to Do About Them, the Swirlies' first mini-album, compiles some of their early work (including their split single with Kudgel) with previously unreleased material and traces the band's development from My Bloody Valentine worshippers into something more interesting. The earliest recordings on the album, like 1991's "Sarah Sitting" and "Didn't Understand," borrow the pummeling tempos and wall-of-feedback guitars from *Isn't Anything*-era Valentines. However, tracks like "Her Life of Artistic Freedom" and "Cousteau" veer from the shoegazing blueprint and add touches like white noise, found sounds, and clean as well as fuzzed-out guitars. "Tall Ships," in particular, exemplifies the

Swirlies' sound, a mix of the dreaminess and deadpan humor, making lyrics like "Just shut the fuck up" into a lullaby. *—Heather Phares*

● **Blonder Tongue Audio Baton** / Mar. 26, 1993 / Taang! ✦✦✦✦✦
The Swirlies' first full-length album melds noisy guitars, samples, and sweet girl-boy vocals into a disheveled take on dream pop. Where so many dreamy bands polish their sound into pristine oblivion, the Swirlies create a hazy atmosphere that is evocative and unpretentious. *Blonder Tongue Audio Baton*—named after a vintage tube equalizer—combines the elements of the band's early work with more complexity. Songs like "Bell" and "Vigilant Always" juxtapose gentle and brash moments for a spontaneous feel, while "His Life of Artistic Freedom" expands on the Swirlies' noisy/experimental side.

The group also shows off their accessible fuzz-pop on the album's centerpiece, "Pancake." The combination of Seana Carmody's demure vocals, big guitars, and burbling Mellotrons makes for one of Boston's most memorable pop moments since the Pixies' "Gigantic." The crunchy rhythms of "Tree Chopped Down" and "Wrong Tube" complement Damon Tuntunjian and Carmody's limpid vocals beautifully, and the sweetly noisy "Wait Forever" sums up the Swirlies' homemade noise-pop aesthetic. A mainstay of early-'90s indie music, *Blonder Tongue Audio Baton* still sounds fresh today. *—Heather Phares*

Brokedick Car / Aug. 1, 1994 / Griffin ✦✦✦✦
Brokedick Car finds the Swirlies playing around with some of the more memorable songs from *Blonder Tongue Audio Baton*, including a trimmed and cleaned-up version of "Wrong Tube" and two alternate takes on "Pancake." "Pancake Cleaner" delivers what its name promises: a version of the *Blonder Tongue* epic with clean instead of fuzzy guitars, for an effect that's chiming instead of fizzy. "House of Pancake" is a Casio-inspired remix of the song, replete with canned drum rolls and a heavy dance beat. *Brokedick Car* also features two songs unavailable elsewhere, "Labrea Tarpit," comprised of atonal, twanging guitars and ringing telephones, and "You're Just Jealous," which starts outs as a sun-baked pop song but evolves into sludgy art-punk reminiscent of Pavement's early singles. While it consists of throwaway bits of experimentation, *Brokedick Car* paints an enjoyable picture of the Swirlies goofing around in the studio. *—Heather Phares*

They Spent Their Wild Youthful Days in the Glittering World of the Salons / Apr. 1996 / Taang! ✦✦✦
On their second full-length album *They Spent Their Wild Youthful Days in the Glittering World of the Salons*, the Swirlies show again why they're so aptly named. From "In Her Money New Found Freedom" to "The Vehicle Is Invisible," the band's songs float, hover, threaten to fall apart, and yes, swirl. Though the Swirlies much of the lineup changed between this album and their excellent 1992 debut album, *Blonder Tongue Audio Baton*, their trademark mix of samples, sweet vocals, and noisy drums and guitars remains pretty much intact. While songs like "Sounds of Sebring," "San Cristobal de las Casas," and "Two Girls Kissing" presents their more focused, accessible side, "No Identifier,"; "You Can't Be Told It, You Must Behold It"; and "Boys, Protect Yourselves from Aliens" use plenty of buzzing synths, loops, and Speak 'n' Spells to make more experimental noise. A noisy, sonically interesting album, *They Spent Their Wild Youthful Days in the Glittering World of the Salons* may not be straightforward, but the eddies and dips in the Swirlies' sound are more than worth a listen. *—Heather Phares*

Strictly East Coast Sneaky Flute Music / May 12, 1998 / Taang ✦✦✦✦
With the revolving door of their band's lineup showing no signs of slowing, founding Swirlies Damon Tuntunjian and Andy Bernick developed the experimental, noisy side of their band. This included incorporating more drum loops and other electronic elements into their music, and on 1998's *Strictly East Coast Sneaky Flute Music*, inviting top East Coast DJs to remix songs from their previous albums and collaborate on new material.

A generous 16 tracks long, the individual merit of each track on *Strictly East Coast Sneaky Flute Music* varies with the DJ doing the remixing. DJ Spooky's take on "In Harmony Retrograde Transposition" opens the album on a high note, retaining the hovering, shimmery feel of the original's guitars and framing it with spacy keyboards and jackhammer drumbeats. Bob Brass' sleek "Sterling Moss (Slippy Mix)," and DJ Rich Costey's remix of "San Cristobal de las Casas" also keep the Swirlies' dreamy pop essence intact in high-tech settings.

Some of *Strictly East Coast Sneaky Flute Music* keeps the group's playful experimentalism high in the mix: DJ Carlos "Soul" Slinger's mix of "Boys, Protect Yourselves From Aliens," which features video game sound effects, a funk guitar and heavy synth bass, and Dog vs. Mice Parade's mix of "Who Was in Scituate on the 4th of July?" morphs from analog synth tinkering to minimalist piano tinkling. The real treat, however, is "Symphony of the Sneaky Flutes," a trio of naive, ambient-inspired analog synth pieces that wobble and float like a lo-fi version of Eno's early synth works. Far from remaining tied to their guitar-based pop roots, the Swirlies continue to push the envelope as they create playful, intruiging music. *—Heather Phares*

David Sylvian

b. Feb. 23, 1958, Lewisham, London, England

Vocals, Keyboards, Guitar / Experimental Ambient, Experimental Rock, Prog Rock/Art Rock

Following the 1982 dissolution of Japan, the group's onetime frontman David Sylvian staked out a far-ranging and esoteric career which encompassed not only solo projects but also a series of fascinating collaborative efforts and forays into filmmaking, photography, and modern art. Sylvian formed Japan in 1974 and served as their primary singer/songwriter throughout the group's eight-year existence. He released his solo debut *Brilliant Trees* in 1984; the first step in his music's evolution from Japan's post-glam synth-pop into richly-textured, poetic ambience, the album featured contributions from Ryuichi Sakamoto and Can alumnus Holger Czukay. *Gone to Earth*, an ambitious double-LP recorded with assistance from Robert Fripp and Bill Nelson, followed in 1986, while 1987 marked the release of the beautful *Secrets of the Beehive*. In 1988, Sylvian reunited with Czukay for the instrumental LP *Plight & Premonition*; the duo reteamed in 1989 for *Flux + Mutablitity*. Two years later, he and the other members of Japan briefly reunited under the name Rain Tree Crow to issue a self-titled album. In 1994, Sylvian emerged in tandem with Robert Fripp for both an album, *The First Day*, and *Redemption*, a sound-and-image installation exhibited in Japan. The superb *Dead Bees on a Cake* followed in 1999. *—Jason Ankeny*

Brilliant Trees / 1984 / Blue Plate ✦✦✦✦

Gone to Earth / 1986 / Virgin ✦✦✦✦
Sylvian is joined by guitarists Robert Fripp and Bill Nelson on this 68-minute CD, which features tracks of Sylvian's trademark vocals and instrumentals. These dreamy, atmospheric works have nice musical support from Steve Nye, Kenny Wheeler, and Mel Collins. *—Scott Bultman*

● **Secrets of the Beehive** / 1987 / Virgin ✦✦✦✦✦
Streamlining the muted, organic atmospheres of the previous *Gone to Earth* to forge a more cohesive listening experience, *Secrets of the Beehive* is arguably David Sylvian's most accessible record, a delicate, jazz-inflected work boasting elegant string arrangements courtesy of Ryuichi Sakamoto. Impeccably produced by Steve Nye, the songs are stripped to their bare essentials, making judicious use of the synths, tape loops, and treated pianos which bring them to life; Sylvian's evocative vocals are instead front and center, rendering standouts like "The Boy With the Gun" and the near-hit "Orpheus"—both among the most conventional yet penetrating songs he's ever written—with soothing strength and assurance. *—Jason Ankeny*

Plight & Premonition / 1988 / Venture ✦✦✦✦✦
This is a collaboration between David Sylvian, frontman for Japan, and Holger Czukay, the bassist for Can. *—Michael P. Dawson*

Flux + Mutability / 1989 / Venture ✦✦✦
A followup to *Plight & Premonition*, it features Holger Czukay and consists of two lengthy, dreamlike pieces. *—Michael P. Dawson*

God's Monkey: Retrospective / 1993 / Virgin ✦✦✦✦

The First Day / Aug. 10, 1993 / Virgin ✦✦✦✦✦
Robert Fripp and David Sylvian's first official release together, *The First Day*, is a much funkier and more percussive affair than its bootleg predecessor, *The Day Before* (which contained radically different versions of these songs). An obvious reason for its higher quality is that it was recorded in a studio, while the bootleg consisted of in-concert demos, and the songs have been worked to completion. Fripp has found an extremely talented singer/partner in Sylvian, who adds a lot to his quirky compositions. Trey Gunn (who plays a bass-like instrument called the stick) makes each track practically groove and breathe on his own and allows Fripp to stretch out and experiment in ways previously unheard by this guitar icon. *The First Day* is a very consistent album, with the musician's excitement and energy easily being felt on such tracks as "God's Monkey," "Brightness," and the ten-minute *tour de force* "Firepower." Other lengthy tracks follow (the 11-minute "20th Century Dreaming" and the 17-minute "Darshan"), but it never becomes self-indulgent or boring. Certainly one of Robert Fripp's best and more inspired King Crimson side projects. *—Greg Prato*

Dead Bees on a Cake / Mar. 30, 1999 / Virgin ✦✦✦
Fans of David Sylvian may consider some of his earlier releases to have been autumnal spectacles filled with intoxicating arrangements and some of the most beautifully heart-breaking songs ever composed. At face value, *Dead Bees on a Cake* should have been one of David Sylvian's most spiritually fulfilled and innovative releases—maybe next time. One can admire the rich vocals and impeccable instrumental performances by Talvin Singh, Steve Jansen, Ryuichi Sakamoto, and Marc Ribot, among others; however, for David Sylvian, even beautiful tracks like "The Shining of Things" are the sonic equivalent of running on a treadmill. One song makes this worth the price of admission: "Midnight Sun"; while the vocals are classic Sylvian, the bluesy, swampy sound of this track is completely new to him. It would have been fantastic if other songs on the album had followed in a similarly inventive vein. *—Sanz Lashley*

Approaching Silence / Oct. 5, 1999 / Narada ✦✦✦✦
The "unofficial" subtitle of this CD is "music for multi media installations." All that to say that the songs on this release date back to 1990 and were used as part of Sylvian and Russell Mills' exhibit *Ember Glance-The Permanence of Memory* (1990) and 1994's *Redemption-Approaching Silence*, which was done by Sylvian and Robert Fripp. Since the music is ambient at its finest, the dates of recording do not matter. The question is does this music stand up on its own, apart from the exhibit. The answer is a resounding yes! Sylvian produces original and interesting ambient music. The selections are long ("Approaching Silence" is over 38 minutes long) yet never get boring. It is to Sylvian's credit that he can keep the listener interested for that long with this genre of music. Sylvian uses instruments and sounds to create his own creative ambient music. The short-wave samples, for example, add an eeriness in "The Beekeeper's Apprentice," which adds to the overall sound of the piece. This music is not for every taste, but fans of Sylvian and ambient music will find this to be a treat. *—Aaron Bagdley*

Everything and Nothing / Oct. 17, 2000 / Virgin ✦✦✦✦
Singer/songwriter David Sylvian's career spans a long and enigmatic scene of experimental rock and emotional restylings. Not one to fully absorb the conventional ways of a certain circuit, Sylvian is a realist musician. He is ambitious in molding his own catharses within layers of woodwinds, horns, and homegrown synth beats, and 1999's *Dead Bees on a Cake* was only a small cue to Sylvian's forthcoming work. The new

millennium brought the release of the double-disc *Everything and Nothing*, a reflection of Sylvian's previously unreleased older material. Sonically gorgeous with vocals comparable to Bryan Ferry, *Everything and Nothing* is a vastly expressive record of 29 tracks lost in the vaults of remixes, time, and creative changes; it is certainly a moving package of lush elevations and underrated wordplay. The two-disc set hums with eclectic instrumental constructions and tinges of Middle Eastern material, especially on tracks such as "Ride." "Pop Song" is more attractive with its abstract guitar riffs and whimsical synth loops, and "Some Kind of Fool," a long-lost Japan song intended to be on 1980's *Gentleman Take Polaroids*, is electronically driven. It's naturally abrasive in lyrical poetry, and Sylvian's atmospheric nature to float over the initial song composition is classic. "Jean the Birdman" echoes the sultriness of Peter Murphy, but Sylvian is shiftless at the same time with his funkadelic mood. The textural differences among the cuts make *Everything and Nothing* particularly inviting, reflecting the wholehearted desire that continues to make David Sylvian surprising, professional, and unattached to what's common. *Everything and Nothing* is undoubtedly a firm recognition of Sylvian's musical wizardry. —*MacKenzie Wilson*

The Syndicate of Sound

f. 1964, San Jose, CA, **db.** 1970
Garage Rock, Rock & Roll

Formed in San Jose, CA in 1964, the Syndicate of Sound were one of the premier garage bands and forerunners of psychedelic rock, establishing a national following based on one massive 1966 hit, "Little Girl." Comprised of vocalist/guitarist Don Baskin, guitarist/keyboardist John Sharkey, lead guitarist Jim Sawyers, bassist Bob Gonzalez, and drummer John Duckworth, the predecessors to the Syndicate of Sound were groups called the Pharoahs and Lenny Lee and the Knightmen. After recording an unsuccessful single for the Scarlet label, on January 9, 1966, Syndicate of Sound recorded "Little Girl" at a studio in San Francisco for Hush Records; it became a regional hit in California after San Jose radio stations latched onto it, attracting the attention of executives at Bell Records in New York, who later asked the group to record an album.

"Little Girl" began to break nationally first in Oklahoma City, and the record entered *Billboard* magazine's Top 40; just before the single broke, original guitarist Larry Ray was pushed out of the band, and the group hired Jim Sawyers instead. When they flew to New York that summer, it was with Sawyers, and since Bell Records was anxious to get their group on the road, Syndicate of Sound toured constantly for the latter half of 1966, taking time off to tape TV shows like *American Bandstand* and *Where the Action Is*; James Brown, who appeared with them on one of the TV shows, was so impressed that he in-

vited them to open his theater show in San Francisco. After drummer Duckworth was drafted at the height of the Vietnam conflict, the band went through several other changes from its original lineup and recorded three singles at the end of 1969, "You're Lookin' Fine" (a Kinks cover), "Brown Paper Bag," and "Mexico." After Baskin moved to Los Angeles in 1970, he and Gonzalez—the only other remaining original member of the band—mounted an unsuccessful attempt at recording another album for Capitol Records in 1970, and then disbanded.—*Richard Skelly*

● **Little Girl** / 1966 / Sundazed ✦✦✦

The teen band pride of San Jose, CA, the Syndicate of Sound scaled the heights of the rock & roll world for a very brief moment in the summer of 1966 with their Top Ten hit "Little Girl." With a catchy, jangly electric 12-string riff, a solid beat, a macho teen vocal, and a chord progression heavily influenced by "Hey Joe," the tune perfectly mirrored the sound of the times and was a can't-miss hit, a British sound played with American garage enthusiasm. But their success ride was short; within a year or two, their ranks were decimated from the draft, touring exhaustion, and the musically changing times. This reissue serves as their lasting legacy, combining the original 12-song album with four bonus tracks. Kicking off with a pair of souped-up R&B covers, the album casts a pretty wide net, with half of the tunes penned by various bandmembers. Of these, ballads sit alongside rockers like "Lookin' for the Good Times (The Robot)" and "Rumors" (complete with Yardbirds-style fuzz guitar rave-up in the middle), while the Kinks-style "That Kind of Man" is an imaginative British-sound knockoff. The outside material, however, is where the band shows their true chameleon-like strength. Covers of the Hollies' "I'm Alive," Louis Jordan's "Is You Is or Is You Ain't My Baby" (via Buster Brown's version), the Sonics' "The Witch," and Roy Orbison's "Dream Baby" show a band that could either play a song "just like the record" or bring their own twist to the proceedings. The four CD bonus tracks likewise demonstrate that the group had no shortage of original material, but unfortunately nothing compiled here has the hit sound of "Little Girl," an easy explanation as to why the group ended up with one-hit wonder status. —*Cub Koda*

Little Girl—The History of the Syndicate of Sound / Nov. 1, 1995 / Performance ✦✦✦

"Little Girl" is a rock & roll classic. With its sneering vocals, vague threats, crude chords and rhythms, it's a menacing, swagger masterpiece of garage rock. It's also the only good thing the Syndicate of Sound ever recorded. *Little Girl—The History of the Syndicate of Sound* compiles nearly everything the group recorded, yet none of it comes close to matching the power of their hit single; it's a mess of weak originals and limp covers. The patience of even the most dedicated garage rock fan will be tested by the disc. —*Stephen Thomas Erlewine*

T

T. Rex

f. 1967, **db.** 1978
Album Rock, Proto-Punk, Glam Rock, Hard Rock
Initially a British folk-rock combo called Tyrannosaurus Rex, T. Rex was the primary force in glam rock, thanks to the creative direction of guitarist/vocalist Marc Bolan (b. Marc Feld). Bolan created a deliberately trashy form of rock & roll that was proud of its own disposability. T. Rex's music borrowed the underlying sexuality of early rock & roll, adding dirty, simple grooves and fat distorted guitars, as well as an overarching folkie/hippie spirtuality that always came through the clearest on ballads. While most of his peers concentrated on making cohesive albums, Bolan kept the idea of a three-minute pop single alive in the early '70s. In Britain, he became a superstar, sparking a period of "T. Rextacy" among the pop audience with a series of Top Ten hits, including four number one singles. Over in America, the group only had one major hit—the Top Ten "Bang a Gong (Get It On)"—before disappearing from the charts in 1973. T. Rex's popularity in the U.K. didn't begin to waver until 1975, yet they retained a devoted following until Marc Bolan's death in 1977. Over the next two decades, Bolan emerged as a cult figure and the music of T. Rex has proven quite influential on hard rock, punk, new wave, and alternative rock. —*Stephen Thomas Erlewine*

My People Were Fair & Had Sky In Their Hair ... But Now They're Content to Wear Stars / 1968 / A&M ✦✦✦
The Bolan voice, hardened from the slight warble which carried through his early solo material, remains uncompromising on *My People Were Fair*, but it blends so perfectly with the bizarre, almost Eastern-sounding instrumentation that the most lasting impression is of a medieval caravansary whose demented Bedouin cast has suddenly been let loose in a recording studio. It is an irresistible affair, if absolutely a child of its psychedelically inclined time. But one of Bolan's loveliest compositions is here—the gentle and deceptively melodic "Child Star," layered by harmonies which hit you sideways and are all the more mighty for it; one of his weirdest, too, is included, the mutant fairy dance of "Strange Orchestras," which sounds like it was recorded by one. Together with fellow highlights "Chateau in Virginia Waters" and "Graceful Fat Sheba," both are so far ahead of the material Bolan had been composing just a year earlier that the inclusion of the "oldies" "Hot Rod Mama" and "Mustang Ford"—before disappearing is almost disappointing. They are, however, the only sour notes sounded on an album whose magic is discernable from so many different angles that it is hard to say which is its most astonishing factor. But it's hard not to be drawn to the actual dynamics of *My People Were Fair*, the uncanny way Tyrannosaurus Rex take the slightest musical instruments, pixiephones, glockenspiels, and a Chinese gong included, and make them sound like the heaviest rock & roll band on the planet. Anyone could play power chords, after all. But who else would play them on acoustic guitar? —*Dave Thompson*

Prophets Seers & Sages The Angels Of The Ages / 1968 / A&M ✦✦✦
The most underrated of Tyrannosaurus Rex's four albums, *Prophets Seers And Sages* was recorded just six months after their debut and adds little to the landscapes which that set mapped out. There is the same reliance on the jarring juxtaposition of rock rhythms in a folky discipline; the same abundance of obscure, private mythologies; the same skewed look at the latest studio dynamics, fed through the convoluted wringer of the duo's imagination—the already classic pop of the opening "Debora" is further dignified by its segue into the same performance played backwards, a fairly groundbreaking move at a time when even the Beatles were still burying such experiments deep in the mix.

But if the album itself found the duo rooted to the musical spot, still it delivered some of Marc Bolan's most resonant songs. The nostalgia-flavored "Stacey Grove" and the contrarily high-energy "Conesuela" were as peerless as any of Bolan's more feted compositions. Equally intriguing is the confidence which exudes from "Scenescof Dynasty," a successor of sorts to the last album's "Scenescof," but presented with just percussion and some strange vocal noises to accompany Bolan's singing—at a time when "singing" was maybe not the term a lot of listeners would employ for his vocals. The excited "one-two-three-four" count-in only adds to the dislocation, of course.

Finally, the owlishly contagious "Salamanda Palaganda" offers a first-hand peek into the very mechanics of Bolan's songwriting. Other composers, stuck for a rhyme, either reach for the thesaurus or abandon the lyric altogether. Bolan simply made one up, and in the process created a whole new language—half nonsense, half mystery, but wholly intoxicating. Just like the rest of the album, in fact. —*Dave Thompson*

Unicorn / 1969 / Fly ✦✦✦
The third Tyrannosaurus Rex album, and their debut U.S. release, *Unicorn* was also the first to steadfastly state the game plan which Marc Bolan had been patiently formulating for two years—the overnight transformation from underground icon to overground superstar. Not only does it catch him experimenting with an electric guitar for the first time

on record, it also sees Steve Peregrin Took exchange his bongos for a full drum kit, minor deviations to be sure, but significant ones regardless. And listen closely and you can hear the future. The opening "Chariots of Silk" sets the ball rolling, as slight and lovely as any of Bolan's early songs, but driven by a tumultuous drum roll—a pounding percussion which might be the sound of distant gunfire, but could as easily be a petulant four year old, stamping around an upstairs apartment. Either way, it must have been a rude awakening for the bliss-soaked hippy acid-heads who were the duo's most loyal audience at the time—and, though the album settled down considerably thereafter, that initial sense of alarm never leaves. By the time one reaches the closing "Romany Soup," a nursery jingle duet for voice and whispered secrets, you feel like you've just left the wildest roller coaster on earth. Had things not gone horribly awry between Bolan and Took during their first U.S. tour that same year, all that T. Rex was to achieve in the first years of the next decade might have instead fallen into place during the final years of the '60s. Because again, you can already hear the storm brewing. —*Dave Thompson*

A Beard of Stars / 1970 / A&M ✦✦✦✦
A Beard of Stars is the most consistent Marc Bolan project, second only to *Electric Warrior* (1971). Tasteful, hip playing, simple, catchy pop structures, and short, easy-to-consume compositions make this an excellent starting point for the uninitiated. This album is the last release before the band changed its name to the simpler, cooler T. Rex. *A Beard of Stars* is the perfect marriage of acoustic and electric rock. Mickey Finn's tabla and clay drums enliven these recordings with an upbeat, eastern tone best exemplified on "Pavilions of Sun" and "Dragon's Ear." His performances are tight and genuinely complement Bolan's mythical, flower-child lyrics. Bolan's voice is magnetic, an appealing, hip delivery so integral to the atmosphere his music evokes. One of his signature tunes, "By the Light of a Magical Moon," clearly illustrates this point. His acoustic/electric guitar playing is exquisitely simple, clean, and at times beautiful as on "A Day Laye." In contrast, the finale, "Elemental Child," an electrifying guitar-driven rock statement, presents the instrument in its rawest form. Here, Bolan's overindulgent performance epitomizes the term "rock guitar"—his style, manic and aggressive, his sound, piercing. —*David Ross Smith*

T. Rex / 1970 / Castle ✦✦✦
Throughout the mid- to late '60s, Tyrannosaurus Rex was a folk duo, consisting of singer/guitarist Marc Bolan and percussionist Steve Peregrin Took, releasing such mysterious albums as *My People Were Fair and Had Sky in Their Hair...But Now They're Content to Wear Stars on Their Brows.* Like their runaround name and album titles, the music was too self-indulgent to break through to the mainstream, so by the dawn of the '70s, Took was replaced with Mickey Finn, and the name was shortened to T. Rex. But the most important change was the music—it was becoming more focused, and elements of hard rock were fast replacing Bolan's past acoustic songs, as heard on 1970's self-titled release. While it still does have many acoustically tranquil moments ("The Visit," "The Time of Love Is Now," "Suneye," etc.), the bare, raw rock of "Jewel," "Beltane Walk," and "Is It Love?" signals T. Rex's soon-to-be permanent direction. Also included are a pair of lush, orchestrated ballads, "Diamond Meadows" and the exceptional "Seagull Woman" (the first T. Rex song to feature the backing vocal talents of Howard Kaylan and Mark Volman, aka the Turtles). Although it may not be as quintessential as 1971's *Electric Warrior* or 1972's *The Slider*, *T. Rex* is Bolan & Co.'s most underrated effort. [Note: Currently, *T. Rex* is only available as a European import.] —*Greg Prato*

★ Electric Warrior / 1971 / Reprise ✦✦✦✦✦
The album that essentially kick-started the U.K. glam rock craze, *Electric Warrior* completes T. Rex's transformation from hippie folk-rockers into flamboyant avatars of trashy rock & roll. There are a few vestiges of those early days remaining in the acoustic-driven ballads, but *Electric Warrior* spends most of its time in a swinging, hip-shaking groove powered by Marc Bolan's warm electric guitar. The music recalls not just the catchy simplicity of early rock & roll, but also the implicit sexuality—except that here, Bolan gleefully hauls it to the surface, singing out loud what was once only communicated through the shimmying beat. He takes obvious delight in turning teenage bubblegum rock into campy sleaze, not to mention filling it with pseudo-psychedelic hippie poetry. In fact, Bolan sounds just as obsessed with the heavens as he does with sex, whether he's singing about spiritual mysticism or begging a flying saucer to take him away. It's all done with the same theatrical flair, but Tony Visconti's spacious, echoing production makes it surprisingly convincing. Still, the real reason *Electric Warrior* stands the test of time so well—despite its intended disposability—is that it revels so freely in its own absurdity and willful lack of substance. Not taking himself at all seriously, Bolan is free to pursue whatever silly wordplay, cosmic fantasies, or non sequitur imagery he feels like; his abandonment of any pretense to art becomes, ironically, a statement in itself. Bolan's lack of pomposity, back-to-basics songwriting, and elaborate theatrics went on to influence everything from hard rock to punk to new wave. But in the end, it's that sense of

playfulness, combined with a raft of irresistible hooks, that keeps *Electric Warrior* such an infectious, invigorating listen today. *—Steve Huey*

☆ **The Slider** / Jul. 21, 1972 / Mercury ✦✦✦✦✦
Buoyed by two U.K. number one singles in "Telegram Sam" and "Metal Guru," *The Slider* became T. Rex's most popular record on both sides of the Atlantic, despite the fact that it produced no hits in the U.S. *The Slider* essentially replicates all the virtues of *Electric Warrior*, crammed with effortless hooks and trashy fun. All of Bolan's signatures are here—mystical folk-tinged ballads, overt sexual come-ons crooned over sleazy, bopping boogies, loopy nonsense poetry, and a mastery of the three-minute pop song form. The main difference is that the trippy mix of *Electric Warrior* is replaced by a fuller, more immediate-sounding production. Bolan's guitar has a harder bite, the backing choruses are more up-front, and the arrangements are thicker-sounding, even introducing a string section on some cuts (both ballads and rockers). Even with the beefier production, T. Rex still doesn't sound nearly as heavy as many of the bands it influenced (and even a few of its glam contemporaries), but that's partly intentional—Bolan's love of a good groove takes precedence over fast tempos or high-volume crunch. Lyrically, Bolan's flair for the sublimely ridiculous is fully intact, but he has way too much style for *The Slider* to sound truly stupid, especially given the playful, knowing wink in his delivery. It's nearly impossible not to get caught up in the irresistible rush of melodies and cheery good times. Even if it treads largely the same ground as *Electric Warrior, The Slider* is flawlessly executed, and every bit the classic that its predecessor is. *—Steve Huey*

Tanx / Feb. 1973 / Mercury ✦✦✦✦✦
By 1973's *Tanx*, the T. Rex hit-making machine was beginning to show some wear and tear, but Marc Bolan still had more than a few winners up his sleeve. It was also admirable that Bolan was attempting to broaden the T. Rex sound—soulful backup singers and horns are heard throughout, a full two years before David Bowie used the same formula for his mega-seller *Young Americans*. However, *Tanx* did not contain any instantly recognizable hits, as their past couple of releases had, and the performances were not quite as vibrant, due to non-stop touring and drug use. Despite an era of transition looming on the horizon for the band, tracks such as "Rapids," "Highway Knees," "The Street & Babe Shadow," and "Born to Boogie" contain the expected classic T. Rex sound. The leadoff track, "Tenement Lady," is an interesting Beatle-esque epic, while "Shock Rock" criticizes the early-'70s glam scene, which T. Rex played a prominent role in creating. Other highlights include one of Bolan's most gorgeous and heartfelt ballads, "Broken Hearted Blues," as well as the brief, explosive rocker "Country Honey." *Tanx* marked the close of what many consider T. Rex's golden era; unfortunately, the band members would drift off one by one soon after, until Bolan was the only one remaining by the mid-'70s. Like the 1997 Polygram CD reissue of *The Slider*, the 1997 version of *Tanx* contains seven extra bonus tracks, including such non-album hits as "Children of the Revolution" and "20th Century Boy." *—Greg Prato*

Zinc Alloy & the Hidden Riders of Tomorrow / 1974 / Mercury ✦✦
By late 1973, Marc Bolan's star was waning fast. No longer gunning out those effortless classics which established him as the most important figure of the decade so far, he embarked instead on a voyage of musical discovery, which cast him so far adrift from the commercial pop mainstream that when his critics said he'd blown it, he didn't even bother answering them back. Or that's the way it appeared at the time, and today, too, it must be acknowledged that 1974's *Zinc Alloy & the Hidden Riders of Tomorrow* is not classic Bolan, even if one overlooks the transparency of its title. After all, hadn't Bowie already done the Fictional Someone & the Somethings From Somewhere routine? Indeed he had, as his fans kept remarking at the time, and when the knives began slashing *Zinc Alloy* to shreds, that was one of the fiercest wounds. Time, however, has healed almost all of them. Indeed, hindsight proves that, far from losing his muse, Bolan's biggest sin was losing his once-impeccable sense of occasion. How faulty was Bolan's timing, though? As it transpired, he was out by no more than a year, maybe less than six months. The era of disco was coming, and with it the wholesale transformation of a wealth of rocking talents. "The Groover," the spring 1973 single which many regarded as the first sign of Bolan's fall from grace, marked the birth of this new fascination, a simple but solid slab of funk-inflected rock which did, indeed, groove. The yearning, heavily orchestrated hit "Teenage Dream" notwithstanding, the heart of *Zinc Alloy*, then, simply followed in "The Groover"'s footsteps, an abandoned romp through the R&B influences which Bolan had always acknowledged, but never truly explored. *—Dave Thompson*

Bolan's Zip Gun / 1975 / Mercury ✦✦✦
Having reinvented himself as a bionic soulboy across the course of 1974's *Zinc Alloy, Zip Gun* was less a reiteration of Marc Bolan's new direction than a confirmation of it. Much of the album returns to the understated romp he had always excelled at—the delightful knockabout "Precious Star," the unrepentant boogie of "Till Dawn," and the pounding title track all echo with the effortless lightheartedness which was Bolan at his most carelessly buoyant, while "Token of My Love" is equally incandescent, a playful blues which swiftly became a major in-concert favorite. But the essence of *Zip Gun* remains firmly in the funky pastures which characterized *Zinc Alloy*, with the only significant difference lying in the presentation. Out went the plush production which so diluted the earlier set, to be replaced by a sparser sound which emphasized the rhythms, heightened the backing vocals, and left rock convention far behind. "Light of Love," "Golden Belt," and the heavyweight ballad "I Really Love You Babe" may not be Stax-sized attractions, but they have an earthy authenticity nevertheless, while bonus tracks on the Edsel remaster include single-only stabs at "Dock of the Bay" and "Do You Wanna Dance," further indications of just how seriously Bolan was taking his new role—and how far he'd moved from the bopping elf of three years earlier. The difference was, in 1972 Marc Bolan was a god. By 1975, he was barely even a minor deity. Decades on, each of Bolan's latter-day albums retain a hint of their original controversy, but hindsight lends them an impact (and, for what it's worth, a credibility) which contemporary listeners could never have imagined. And *Zip Gun*, an album which scored the worst reviews of all, hits as hard as any of them. *—Dave Thompson*

Futuristic Dragon / 1976 / Mercury ✦✦✦
The most blatantly, and brilliantly, portentous of Marc Bolan's albums since the transitional blurring of boundaries that was *Beard of Stars*, almost seven years before, *Futuristic Dragon* opens on a wave of unrelenting feedback, guitars, and bombast, setting an apocalyptic mood for the record which persists long after that brief (two minutes) overture is over. Indeed, even the quintessential bop of the succeeding "Jupiter Liar" is irrevocably flavored by what came before, dirty guitars churning beneath a classic Bolan melody, and the lyrics a spiteful masterpiece. But if the other tunes pursue Bolan's new-found fascination for pomp over pop with barely disguised glee, he wasn't above slipping the odd joke into the brew to remind us that he knew what he was doing. "Theme for a Dragon" is an all-but Wagnerian symphonic instrumental—with the sound of screaming teenyboppers as its backdrop, with the punchline lurking further afield, among the handful of obvious hits which he also stirred in. The first of these, the big-budget ballad "Dreamy Lady," scored even before the rest of the album was complete. It was followed by the idiotically contagious "New York City," a piece of pure pop nonsense genius which effortlessly returned him to the British Top 20. And when he followed that up with the rhythm'n'punk swagger of "I Love to Boogie," few people would deny that Bolan was on the way back up. *—Dave Thompson*

Dandy in the Underworld / 1977 / Mercury ✦✦✦
Marc Bolan welcomed the advent of punk rock with the biggest smile he'd worn in years. The hippest young gunslingers could go on all night about the influence of the Velvet Underground, the Stooges, and the Ramones, but Bolan knew—and subsequent developments proved—that every single one of them had been nurtured in his arms, growing up with the ineffable stream of brilliant singles he slammed out between 1970-1972, and rehearsing their own stardom to the soundtrack he supplied. *Dandy in the Underworld*, released early in 1977, confirmed Bolan's punkoid pre-eminence. Still retaining its predecessors' demented soul revue edge, but packed solid with powerful pop, Bolan's personal predictions for the punk scene literally exploded out of the grooves. By the time the album wraps up with the rock'n'armageddon flavored "Teen Riot Structure," Bolan was not simply wearing the mantel of punk godfatherhood, he was happily sticking safety-pins through it and preparing his next move, the driving "Celebrate Summer" single, the greatest record he'd made in years. It was also his last—a month after its release, Marc Bolan was dead. Sorrow immediately imbibed *Dandy in the Underworld* with a dignity which, had Bolan lived, it probably wouldn't have otherwise deserved—it is not, overall, one of his strongest albums, and the demos and outtakes included on the later volumes of the *Unchained* series suggest that his proposed next album would have left it far behind. But conjecture, like hindsight, can be a dangerous gauge. At the time, *Dandy* not only seemed bloated with promise, it was pregnant with foreboding as well. Listen again to the lyrics of the title track—self-mythologizing autobiography and not a happy ending in sight. Just like real life. *—Dave Thompson*

T. Rextasy: The Best of T. Rex, 1970-1973 / 1985 / Warner Brothers ✦✦✦✦✦
This is it, T. Rex fans, the best of their greatest hits in a compilation. The only problem is, it's no longer in print. Unlike the T. Rex compilations currently available, *T. Rextasy* contains all the hits prior to *Electric Warrior*, as well as several tracks unavailable anywhere else. This is also the best sequencing job of the T. Rex hits, each song extending to the next, until you feel like you've taken an insightful journey through the dreamy and poetic world of Marc Bolan. You'll also find strong album tracks, like the guitar-fuzz freak-out "Jewel," which was one of T. Rex's first "rock" songs (after beginning as a straight folk duo), and an acoustic cover of "Summertime Blues." Also included are unedited versions of such classics as "Get It On (Bang a Gong)" and "Raw Ramp," with unreleased introductions. Every hit is here ("Metal Guru," "Telegram Sam," "Ride a White Swan," etc.), except for "Children of the Revolution," which would have made the anthology complete. If you don't want to buy all of T. Rex's early-'70s albums (which you really should—most of their album tracks were as good as their singles), hunt down *T. Rextasy: The Best of T. Rex 1970-1973*. It will supply you with nearly all of their prime cuts. *—Greg Prato*

The Definitive Tyrannosaurus Rex / Oct. 25, 1994 / Sequel ✦✦✦✦✦
Although several Tyrannosaurus Rex compilations appeared in the years following Marc Bolan and T. Rex's U.K. breakthrough in 1970, it was, remarkably, 1993 before anybody set about seriously evaluating their entire output with a set drawn from both the duo's album output and a surprisingly strong singles output. Seven of the 31 tracks featured on this aptly titled collection had never previously been anthologized, including the *Beard of Stars*-era outtakes and 1969's "Pewtor Suitor" and "Do You Remember" 45s. Programmed in strict chronological order, the album selections are fairly predictable: both the 1972 *Best of T. Rex* and the budget-priced *Ride a White Swan* compilation are represented in their near-entirety, while other cuts appear to have been selected as much for their diversity as for their quality. Even amid such familiar surroundings, there is ample cause for surprise; the almost classical magnificence of "Child Star" and "Cat Black" is clearly a template for the grandiose gestures which the superstar Bolan became so fond of delivering, and the deeper into the disc one delves, the more inevitable that superstardom becomes. Exemplary packaging and crystalline remastering complete *The Definitive*, and it would not be too far-fetched to say that, if and when the definitive Bolan box set materializes, the contents of one disc have already been sorted. Indeed, with this at your disposal, you could almost forego the purchase of the original albums. Almost. *—Dave Thompson*

Great Hits 1972-1977, Vol. 1: The A-Sides / Nov. 8, 1994 / Mercury ✦✦✦✦✦
Few other bands have had as many "Best Of" collections released over the years as T. Rex.

And for the most part, almost all are missing hits from their 1971 *Electric Warrior* album and before ("Bang a Gong," "Jeepster," "Ride a White Swan," "Hot Love," etc.). As confirmed by the title *Great Hits 1972-1977*, this 1994 collection is no different. While it does contain most of Bolan and company's biggest hits—"Metal Guru," "Solid Gold Easy Action," "Groover," "20th Century Boy" and others—it cannot be considered a definitive "Best Of." What makes this set different than others is the inclusion of A-sides from after 1973, something that most T. Rex compilations fail to do; hence, it's one of the few to contain their forgotten mid-'70s U.K. Top 20 hits "New York City" and "I Love to Boogie." But as most T. Rex fans know, Bolan peaked artistically and commercially in the early '70s, and the majority of his post-1973 work pales in comparison to his early hits. Hopefully one day a record company will finally collect T. Rex's true greatest hits from all eras. *—Greg Prato*

Great Hits 1972-1977, Vol. 2: B-Sides / Nov. 8, 1994 / Mercury ✦✦✦
From 1972-1977, Marc Bolan wrote an astonishing amount of non-album B-sides for his singles, which are all collected together for the first time on *Great Hits 1972-1977: The B-Sides*. And while not all of the tracks are winners, all of the selections from T. Rex's '72-73 glory period are outstanding—it's almost like discovering a long-lost T. Rex album. Standouts include the glam rockers "Cadilac," "Thunderwing," "Lady," "Jitterbug Love," "Sunken Rags," "Free Angel," and "Midnight," plus "Baby Strange" and "Born To Boogie" (although both appeared on T. Rex full-lengths), while a 12-second holiday greeting from Bolan entitled "Xmas Riff" can be skipped over. The album's 15 other tracks are not as consistent—some are worthwhile ("Sitting Here," "Explosive Mouth," "Space Boss"), while others are clearly not (disco covers of "Do You Wanna Dance" and "Dock of the Bay"). Also included in the CD booklet is info on each track (date of the recording, what Bolan was trying to accomplish, etc.), making it a great collection for the serious Marc Bolan/T. Rex fan. *—Greg Prato*

A Wizard, A True Star: Marc Bolan & T. Rex 1972-1977 / Nov. 5, 1996 / Edsel ✦✦✦✦✦
Back in the early '80s, EMI's Australian wing pulled off a remarkable coup, a three-LP Marc Bolan/T. Rex compilation which drew material from the length and breadth of his career, to serve up the most well-rounded portrait of the Bopping Elf that has ever been mustered. It disappeared from the racks pretty quickly, and fans have been praying for a similar gesture ever since. Well, it hasn't arrived yet, but the three discs here at least go halfway, covering the years during which Bolan operated his own record label, Hot Wax, and doing so with such precision that "perfect" is not too superlative a description for it. Quite simply, *A Wizard* offers the yardstick by which all box sets should be measured. The breakdown is breathtakingly straightforward, divided equally between the expected hits, the necessary album cuts, and the demanded rarities. Disc one follows Bolan through his period of greatest success, the 1972 to early-1973 era during which U.K. hits like "Telegram Sam" and "Metal Guru" trailed one of the most astonishing albums of the decade, *The Slider*. Disc two tracks the downhill-quickly years of 1973-1974; disc three catches the rebirth which was so cruelly curtailed by Bolan's September 1977 death. Each is superlative. The year 1972, in particular, passes in a blur of excitement; Bolan was at his vivacious best, and it matters not what he's doing, whether it's laying down the next monster hit single ("Children of the Revolution," "Solid Gold Easy Action") or strumming rudely through a demo that might never see the light of day ("Over the Flats," "Is It True?"). *—Dave Thompson*

Take That

f. 1990, **db.** Feb. 13, 1996
Teen Pop, Euro-Pop, Dance-Pop
As the most popular teen-pop sensation in Britain since the '60s, Take That ruled the UK charts during the first half of the '90s. In strict commercial terms, the band sold more records than any English act since the Beatles, though the cultural and musical importance was significantly less substantial. Conceived as a British answer to the New Kids on the Block, Take That initially worked the same territory as their American counterparts, singing watered-down new jack R&B, urban soul, and mainstream pop. Eventually, the group worked their way toward hi-NRG dance music, while also pursuing an adult-contemporary ballad direction. Take That's boyish good looks guaranteed them a significant portion of the teenybopper audience, but in a bizarre twist, most of their videos and promotional photos had a strong homosexual undercurrent—they were marketed to pre-teen girls and a kitschy gay audience simultaneously. Take That was also able to make inroads in the adult audience in Britain through Gary Barlow's melodic, sensitive ballads. For nearly five years, the group's popularity was unsurpassed in Britain, as they racked up a total of seven number one hits. By the middle of the decade, all of the members were entering their mid-'20s and became disenchanted with each other. Furthermore, the pop music tastes in Britain were shifting toward the classic guitar-pop sounds of Britpop bands like Blur and Oasis, who were able to appeal to both the indie-rock and teen-pop audience. Consequently, the group called it quits in 1996, as Oasis began to surpass Take That both in terms of sales and cultural impact. Nevertheless, Take That remained one of the most interesting and popular British teen-pop phenomenons not only of the '90s, but of the rock & roll era. *—Stephen Thomas Erlewine*

Take That & Party / 1993 / RCA ✦✦✦

Everything Changes / Oct. 18, 1993 / RCA ✦✦✦✦✦
British group Take That did not have the same worries about releasing *Everything Changes* as they had with their debut album. By this time they were giant superstars in Europe, and the question in their minds was not whether they could get a hit single, but how many and which would make it to number one. The album spawned six hit singles, four of which made number one, making it Record of the Year and one of the best-selling albums of the decade, proclaiming them the biggest male group since the Beatles. When the hype sets in, it is hard to distinguish the value of the material itself. It is an album of dance-pop and ballads sung by five young men, with a greater maturity than most boy band albums thanks to the writing by lead singer Gary Barlow. Boy bands have their share of skeptics, and getting those to tear down their defenses usually ends up competing with their struggle to please the fan base they already have. With saucy dance tracks like "Relight My Fire" (a hit for Dan Hartman in the '70s) and quality ballads like "Pray" and "Love Ain't Here Anymore," as well as pop tracks "Everything Changes" and "Whatever You Do to Me," Take That won over everyone they needed to. What they got in return was a reputation for being a fine group with real talent. *Everything Changes* marked the height of Take That popularity. *—Peter Fawthrop*

Nobody Else / Aug. 15, 1995 / RCA ✦✦✦✦
Presaging the teen-pop phenomenon of the late '90s, Take That took Great Britain by storm in 1993. They didn't, however, hit the States until this release, and even then they hardly made a dent, with only the single "Back for Good" getting any airplay. Where Hanson sparked the boy band craze in the U.S. with a tight band, assured songwriting, good vocals, and an appreciation for rock & roll, and the Backstreet Boys and *NSYNC gave us lush harmonies and production, Take That lacks the confidence or the style of even the weakest cut by the above-mentioned groups. With lyrics like "Love ain't here anymore / it's gone away to a town called yesterday," you almost snap out of the coma the rest of the album has induced—simply because the lines are laughable. Despite lilting vocals on "Back for Good" and the surprising, risqué "Babe," there isn't a cut that stands out on *Nobody Else*. Teen pop isn't always art, but it still needs to be well done and have a little bite. This album doesn't offer either. *—Bryan Buss*

● **Greatest Hits** / 1996 / RCA ✦✦✦✦✦
Take That disbanded just as they were on the verge of huge success in the U.S., but they never really needed American success—for all of the early '90s, they were undefeatable on the British pop charts. During their six years together, the band racked up seven number one hits, most of them between 1992 and 1996. Every member of Take That sang, but Robbie Williams, Mark Owen, and Gary Barlow were the main vocalists, and they have all of the best moments on the band's *Greatest Hits* collection. Weaving between dance-pop like "Relight My Fire," "Sure," and "I Found Heaven," and ballads like "A Million Love Songs," "Back for Good," and their farewell single, a cover of the Bee Gees' "How Deep Is Your Love," Take That's *Greatest Hits* is sugary, infectious pop that practically defines the term guilty pleasure. *—Stephen Thomas Erlewine*

Talk Talk

f. 1981, London, England, **db.** 1991
New Romantic, Post-Rock/Experimental, New Wave, Synth Pop
With the exception of a handful of common threads—chief among them the plaintive vocals and haunting lyrics of frontman Mark Hollis—there is little to suggest that the five studio LPs which make up the Talk Talk oeuvre are indeed the work of the same band throughout. After beginning their career with records which virtually epitomize the new wave era which spawned them, the British group never looked back, making significant strides with each successive album on their way to discovering a wholly unique and uncategorizable sound informed by elements of jazz, classical and ambient music; their masterful final recordings, while neglected commercially, possess a timelessness rare among music of any genre, and in retrospect they seem the clear starting point for the post-rock movement of the 1990s. For many casual listeners Eighties-era synth-pop hits like "It's My Life" and "Life Is What You Make of It" remain Talk Talk's enduring legacy, but among more serious fans the group's last two studio LPs, 1988's *Spirit of Eden* and 1991's *Laughing Stock*, are the real deal. *Spirit of Eden* is the breakthrough, rejecting pop conventions in favor of an unprecedented blend of ambient textures, jazz-inspired arrangements and avant-garde musings; complete with frontman Mark Hollis' plaintive vocals and heartfelt, deeply resonant lyrics, it's an album virtually without precedent, existing in its own world and its own time. *Laughing Stock*, meanwhile, refines the experiment, adopting a wider dynamic range while further moving outside the sphere of compositional structure. *—Jason Ankeny*

The Party's Over / 1982 / EMI ✦✦✦
Talk Talk began life as a slavishly derivative, Duran Duran-styled, new romantic synth-pop band, as their debut, *The Party's Over*, clearly shows. Much of the album seems to attempt to recreate Duran Duran's debut, but even with their most blatant ripoffs, like the single "Talk Talk," they do it with a naive charm that makes for some really enjoyable music, even if it isn't particularly innovative or groundbreaking. *—Chris Woodstra*

It's My Life / 1984 / EMI ✦✦✦✦
After an unremarkable debut, Talk Talk regrouped and refashioned themselves more in the style of sophisto-era Roxy Music while developing their own voice. *It's My Life* shows a great leap in songwriting, the band making highly personal statements with a sexy, seductive groove and a diversity that transcends the synth-pop tag. Synthesizers still play a dominant role, but the music is made far more interesting by mixing "real" instruments and challenging world music rhythms seamlessly with the technology. Still pulling off the catchy single (like "Dum Dum Girl" and the title track, as well as the simply sublime "Does Caroline Know?") on *It's My Life*, Talk Talk also proved themselves capable of achieving a cohesive album—a rare feat for the time and an unexpected surprise from a band that seemed to be simply a bandwagon-jumper. *—Chris Woodstra*

The Colour of Spring / 1986 / EMI ✦✦✦✦✦
With *It's My Life*, Talk Talk proved that they could pull off an entire album of strong material. With *Colour of Spring*, they took it one step further, moving to a near-concept song cycle, following the emotional ups and downs of relationships and pondering life in general. Musically, they built on the experimental direction of the previous album with

interesting rhythms, sweeping orchestration, complex arrangements, and even a children's chorus to create an evocative, hypnotic groove. Though the songs were catchier on the earlier efforts and the ambient experimentation was more fully achieved later on, *Colour of Spring* succeeded in marrying the two ideas into one unique sound for their most thoroughly satisfying album. —*Chris Woodstra*

Spirit of Eden / 1988 / EMI ✦✦✦✦✦
Compare *Spirit of Eden* with any other previous release in the Talk Talk catalog, and it's almost impossible to believe it's the work of the same band—exchanging electronics for live, organic sounds and rejecting structure in favor of mood and atmosphere, the album is an unprecedented breakthrough, a musical and emotional catharsis of immense power. Mark Hollis' songs exist far outside of the pop idiom, drawing instead on ambient textures, jazz-like arrangements, and avant-garde accents; for all of their intricacy and delicate beauty, compositions like "Inheritance" and "I Believe in You" also possess an elemental strength—Hollis' oblique lyrics speak to themes of loss and redemption with understated grace, and his hauntingly poignant vocals evoke wrenching spiritual turmoil tempered with unflagging hope. A singular musical experience. —*Jason Ankeny*

● **Natural History: The Very Best of Talk Talk** / Oct. 1990 / EMI America ✦✦✦✦
During the band's hiatus following *Spirit of Eden*, EMI issued a hits collection, compiling the singles from the first four albums as well as the non-LP "My Foolish Friend," a couple of live tracks, and an edit of "Desire." *Natural History* serves as a nice introduction to the band, showing them as an effective singles act despite their more recent album-concept experiments, and the added rarities make the package a necessary addition for fans as well. —*Chris Woodstra*

Laughing Stock / Nov. 19, 1991 / Polydor ✦✦✦✦✦
Virtually ignored upon its initial release, *Laughing Stock* continues to grow in stature and influence by leaps and bounds. Picking up where *Spirit of Eden* left off, the album operates outside of the accepted sphere of rock to create music which is both delicate and intense; recorded with a large classical ensemble, it defies easy categorization, conforming to very few structural precedents—while the gently hypnotic "Myrrhman" flirts with ambient textures, the percussive "Ascension Day" drifts toward jazz before the two sensibilities converge to create something entirely new and different on "New Grass." The epic "After the Flood," on the other hand, is an atmospheric whirlpool laced with jackhammer guitar feedback and Mark Hollis' remarkably plaintive vocals; it flows into "Taphead," perhaps the most evocative, spacious, and understated piece on the record. A work of staggering complexity and immense beauty, *Laughing Stock* remains an under-recognized masterpiece, and its echoes can be heard throughout much of the finest experimental music issued in its wake. —*Jason Ankeny*

The Very Best of Talk Talk / Jan. 27, 1997 / EMI ✦✦✦✦
The Very Best of Talk Talk is the most comprehensive retrospective assembled on the synth group to date, following the band from its new wave origins to its latter-day atmospheric new age recordings. Although the compilation features nothing from 1991's *Laughing Stock* and all of the songs from 1988's *Spirit of Eden* are presented in edited versions, the disc remains a good overview of the band's evolution and features all of their big hits, including "Talk Talk" and "Today." —*Stephen Thomas Erlewine*

Asides Besides / Apr. 1998 / EMI ✦✦✦✦
Asides Besides can certainly be seen as a cash-in release to coincide with Mark Hollis' first solo release and the reissue of Talk Talk's EMI catalog, but rarely does such a calculated industry move result in such a treat for fans. Over two discs, *Asides Besides* essentially ties up all of the loose ends for the band. Disc one is probably the least essential, bringing out all of the 12" remixes, which are of marginal interest, though all are superior to those found on the unauthorized *History Revisited*. Disc two however, reveals no shortage of prime rarities beginning with three demos from 1981 ("Talk Talk," "Mirror Man" and "Candy"). A handful of singles are included—the not-so-rare single, "My Foolish Friend," the ultra-rare "Why Is it So Hard" (from the film *First Born*), the U.S. remix of "Dum Dum Girl," and the edit of "Eden"—but the real gems are the B-sides, which are anything but "throwaways." In fact, the B-sides are not only in most cases as strong as the ones that made it onto the albums, but they also indicate the more experimental direction the band would take later on. *Asides Besides* may be of interest only to diehard Talk Talk fans, but for that audience this collection is absolutely essential. —*Chris Woodstra*

London 1986 / Apr. 20, 1999 / Blueprint ✦✦✦
To many, Talk Talk are not known as a "live band." They are known as a synth-pop dance band from the 1980s with a couple of radio hits. But in actuality Mark Hollis (founder and leader of Talk Talk) is a true musical genius who tried to alter that perception of Talk Talk by producing a number of superb albums that sadly have largely gone unnoticed. He also toured Talk Talk and managed to produce their sublime sound live. Recorded during the *Colour of Spring* tour (most of the songs performed are from that release), this would be the last time Talk Talk performed these "pop" titles, which makes this somewhat of a historical piece. Hollis went on to record the CDs *Spirit of Eden* and *Laughing Stock*, which were more jazz/experimental works. Some of the "jazz" sound can be heard in this performance. The playing is tight and flawless, and the songs take on a breath of fresh air from their album versions as the band sounds somewhat freer and not as produced. Hollis has done an admirable job putting this release together, and quite honestly it is required listening for Talk Talk fans to see what all of the fuss was, and is, about this band. Collectors note that the front sleeve is the design for the abandoned video release from the same tour. —*Aaron Bagdley*

Missing Pieces / 2001 / Pond Life ✦✦✦
Essentially for the most loyal Talk Talk fan only, *Missing Pieces* compiles the three singles released off the band's final LP, the boundlessly experimental and beautiful *Laughing*

Stock. It was odd that anything off that record was aimed at the pop charts, and it remains baffling when reminded of it ten years after the fact. It could be said that Talk Talk is to post-rock what Neil Young is to grunge, since they were one of the first to break free from rock constructs while maintaining the basic instrumental set-up. The album versions of "New Grass" and "Ascension Day" easily surpass the average single length, while a shortened "outtake" version of the hypnotic "After the Flood" remains otherworldly with five minutes trimmed from the original incarnation. Both of the proper B-sides—the only genuinely "new" Talk Talk material for most fans—are instrumentals. Neither one is too remarkable, but "5.09" is worth mentioning for its collage-like manipulation of random pieces from the album sessions. Elements of nearly every album track pop up, including some of the percussion from "Taphead" and contorted guitar snatched from "New Grass." A weird inclusion completes the disc: Mark Hollis' minimalist piano contribution to Allinson/Brown's *AV1* from 1998. (On that record, Hollis performed under the pseudonym of John Cope, named after the sound recordist who worked with the likes of Alfred Hitchcock and Cecil B. DeMille.) Time has been good to the material collected here, evident through the classic status accorded to *Laughing Stock* from critics and musicians alike, not to mention the outright sampling (Unkle's "Rabbit in Your Headlights") or worshipful cloning (Catherine Wheel's "Thunderbird" of Lee Harris' sensitive, tingly drumming. This collection might not be essential, but anything to satiate diehard cravings and increase the profile of *Laughing Stock* should be welcomed. —*Andy Kellman*

Talking Heads

f. 1974, db. 1991
College Rock, American Punk, New York Punk, Album Rock, Post-Punk, Pop/Rock, New Wave
At the start of their career, Talking Heads were all nervous energy, detached emotion, and subdued minimalism. When they released their last album about 12 years later, the band had recorded everything from art-funk to polyrhythmic worldbeat explorations and simple, melodic guitar-pop, becoming one of the most critically acclaimed bands of the '80s while still managing to earn several pop hits. While some of their music can seem too self-consciously experimental, clever, and intellectual for its own good, at their best, Talking Heads represents everything good about art-school punks. Vocalist/guitarist David Byrne, drummer Chris Franz, and bassist Tina Weymouth literally did meet at art school, adding keyboardist Jerry Harrison just after their New York debut. By 1977, the band had released their first album, *Talking Heads '77*. Working with Brian Eno on a trio of albums during the late '70s resulted in carefully constructed, arty pop songs, distinguished by extensive experimentation and flourishes of African-styled polyrhythms. With mid-'80s albums like *Speaking in Tongues* and *Little Creatures*, the band began emphasizing a more rigid pop-song structure, though they returned to the worldbeat explorations with 1988's *Naked*. Put on hiatus as Byrne pursued solo projects and Franz and Weymouth continued their Tom Tom Club side project, Talking Heads finally broke up in 1991. Five years later, Harrison, Franz and Weymouth formed the Heads for a reunion album; in 1999, all four original members worked together to promote a 15th-anniversary edition of *Stop Making Sense*. —*Stephen Thomas Erlewine*

☆ **Talking Heads: 77** / 1977 / Sire ✦✦✦✦✦
Though they were the most highly touted new wave band to emerge from the CBGB's scene in New York, it was not clear at first whether Talking Heads' Lower East Side art rock approach could make the subway ride to the midtown pop mainstream successfully. The leadoff track of the debut album, *Talking Heads: 77*, "Uh-Oh, Love Comes to Town," was a pop song that emphasized the group's unlikely roots in late-'60s bubblegum, Motown, and Caribbean music. But the "Uh-Oh" gave away the group's game early, with its nervous, disconnected lyrics and David Byrne's strained voice. All pretenses of normality were abandoned by the second track, as Talking Heads finally started to sound on record the way they did downtown: the staggered rhythms and sudden tempo changes, the odd guitar tunings and rhythmic, single-note patterns, the non-rhyming, non-linear lyrics that came across like odd remarks overheard from a psychiatrist's couch, and that voice, singing above its normal range, its falsetto leaps and strangled cries resembling a madman trying desperately to sound normal. Talking Heads threw you off balance, but grabbed your attention with a sound that seemed alternately threatening and goofy. The music was undeniably catchy, even at its most ominous, especially on "Psycho Killer," Byrne's supreme statement of demented purpose. Amazingly, that song made the singles chart for a few weeks, evidence of the group's quirky appeal, but the album was not a big hit, and it remained unclear whether Talking Heads spoke only the secret language of the urban arts types or whether that could be translated into the more common tongue of hip pop culture. In any case, they had succeeded as artists, using existing elements in an unusual combination to create something new that still managed to be oddly familiar. And that made *Talking Heads: 77* a landmark album. —*William Ruhlmann*

☆ **More Songs About Buildings and Food** / Jul. 14, 1978 / Sire ✦✦✦✦✦
The title of Talking Heads' second album, *More Songs About Buildings and Food*, slyly addressed the sophomore record syndrome, in which songs not used on a first LP are mixed with hastily written new material. If the band's sound seems more conventional, the reason simply may be that one had encountered the odd song structures, staccato rhythms, strained vocals, and impressionistic lyrics once before. Another was that new co-producer Brian Eno brought a musical unity that tied the album together, especially in terms of the rhythm section, the sequencing, the pacing, and the mixing. Where Talking Heads had largely been about David Byrne's voice and words, Eno moved the emphasis to the bass-and-drums team of Tina Weymouth and Chris Frantz; all the songs were danceable, and there were only short breaks between them. Byrne held his own, however, and he continued to explore the eccentric, if not demented persona first heard on 77, whether he was adding to his observations on boys and girls or turning his "Psycho

Killer" into an artist in "Artists Only." Through the first nine tracks, *More Songs* was the successor to *77*, which would not have earned it landmark status or made it the commercial breakthrough it became. It was the last two songs that pushed the album over those hurdles. First there was an inspired cover of Al Green's "Take Me to the River"; released as a single, it made the Top 40 and pushed the album to gold-record status. Second was the album closer, "The Big Country," Byrne's country-tinged reflection on flying over middle America; it crystallized his artist-vs.-ordinary people perspective in unusually direct and dismissive terms, turning the old Chuck Berry patriotic travelogue theme of rock & roll on its head and employing a great hook in the process. *—William Ruhlmann*

Fear of Music / Aug. 3, 1979 / Sire ♦♦♦♦♦
By titling their third album, *Fear of Music* and opening it with the African rhythmic experiment "I Zimbra," complete with nonsense lyrics by poet Hugo Ball, Talking Heads made the record seem more of a departure than it was. Though *Fear of Music* was musically distinct from its predecessors, mostly because of the use of minor keys that gave the music a more ominous sound. Previously, David Byrne's offbeat observations had been set off by an overtly humorous tone; on *Fear of Music*, he was still odd, but no longer so funny. At the same time, however, the music had become even more compelling. Worked up from jams (though Byrne received sole songwriter's credit), the music was becoming denser and more driving, notably on the album's standout track, "Life During Wartime," with lyrics that matched the music's power. "This ain't no party," declared Byrne, "this ain't no disco, this ain't no fooling around." The other key song, "Heaven," extended the dismissal Byrne had expressed for the U.S. in "The Big Country" to paradise itself: "Heaven is a place where nothing ever happens." It was also the album's most melodic song. Those were the highlights. What kept *Fear of Music* from being as impressive an album as Talking Heads' first two was that much of it seemed to repeat those earlier efforts, while the few newer elements seemed so risky and exciting. It was an uneven, transitional album, though its better songs were as good as any Talking Heads ever did. *—William Ruhlmann*

☆ **Remain in Light** / Oct. 8, 1980 / Sire ♦♦♦♦♦
The musical transition that seemed to have just begun with *Fear of Music* came to fruition on Talking Heads' fourth album, *Remain in Light*. "I Zimbra" and "Life During Wartime" from the earlier album served as the blueprints for a disc on which the group explored African polyrhythms on a series of driving groove tracks, over which David Byrne chanted and sang his typically disconnected lyrics. *Remain in Light* had more words than any previous Heads record, but they counted for less than ever in the sweep of the music. The album's single, "Once in a Lifetime," flopped upon release, but over the years became an audience favorite due to a striking video, its inclusion in the band's 1984 concert film *Stop Making Sense*, and its second single release (in the live version) because of its use in the 1986 movie *Down and Out in Beverly Hills*, when it became a minor chart entry. Byrne sounded typically uncomfortable in the verses ("And you may find yourself in a beautiful house, with a beautiful wife / And you may ask yourself—Well . . . how did I get here?"), which were undercut by the reassuring chorus ("Letting the days go by"). Even without a single, *Remain in Light* was a hit, indicating that Talking Heads were connecting with an audience ready to follow their musical evolution, and the album was so inventive and influential, it was no wonder. As it turned out, however, it marked the end of one aspect of the group's development and their last new music for three years. *—William Ruhlmann*

The Name of This Band Is Talking Heads / Mar. 24, 1982 / Sire ♦♦♦
For their first live album, Talking Heads devised a thorough retrospective, drawing material for the two-disc set from shows played between 1977 and 1981. The first disc chronicled the original quartet and its quirky new wave songs, including the previously unreleased "A Clean Break" and the previously single-only "Building on Fire." The album title was drawn from David Byrne's unadorned stage introductions ("The name of this band is Talking Heads. The name of this song is . . ."). On the second disc, the expanded '80s version of Talking Heads explored African rhythms and complex musical patterns, with each of the instruments doubled—Adrian Belew was on guitar, Bernie Worrell on keyboards, Busta Jones on bass, and Steve Scales on percussion, while Dolette McDonald and Nona Hendryx helped out on vocals. More than the typical live album, *The Name of This Band Is Talking Heads* was an intelligently programmed live history, but like nearly all live albums, it wasn't really essential. *—William Ruhlmann*

Speaking in Tongues / Jun. 1, 1983 / Sire ♦♦♦♦
Talking Heads found a way to open up the dense textures of the music they had developed with Brian Eno on their two previous studio albums for *Speaking in Tongues*, and were rewarded with their most popular album yet. Ten backup singers and musicians accompanied the original quartet, but somehow the sound was more spacious, and the music admitted aspects of gospel, notably in the call-and-response of "Slippery People," and John Lee Hooker-style blues, on "Swamp." As usual, David Byrne determinedly sang and chanted impressionistic, nonlinear lyrics, sometimes by mix-and-matching clichés ("No visible means of support and you have not seen nuthin' yet," he declared on "Burning Down the House," the Heads' first Top Ten hit), and the songs' very lack of clear meaning was itself a lyrical subject. "Still don't make no sense," Byrne admitted in "Making Flippy Floppy," but by the next song, "Girlfriend Is Better," that had become an order—"Stop making sense," he chanted over and over. Some of his charming goofiness had returned since the overly serious *Remain in Light* and *Fear of Music*, however, and the accompanying music, filled with odd percussive and synthesizer sounds, could be unusually light and bouncy. The album closer, "This Must Be the Place (Naive Melody)," even sounded hopeful. Well, sort of. Despite their formal power, Talking Heads' last two albums seemed to have painted them into a corner, which may be why it took them three years to craft a follow-up, but on *Speaking in Tongues*, they found an open window and flew out of it. *—William Ruhlmann*

Stop Making Sense / 1984 / Sire ♦♦♦
While there's no debating the importance of Jonathan Demme's classic film record of Talking Heads' 1983 tour, the soundtrack released in support of it is a thornier matter. Since its release, purists have found *Stop Making Sense* slickly mixed and, worse yet, incomprehensive. The nine tracks included jumble and truncate the natural progression of frontman David Byrne's meticulously-arranged stage show. Cries for a double-album treatment—a la 1982's live opus *The Name of This Band Is Talking Heads*—were sounded almost immediately; more enterprising fans merely dubbed the VHS release of the film onto cassette tape. So until a 1999 "special edition" cured the 1984 release's ills, fans had to make do with the *Stop Making Sense* they were given–which is, by any account, an exemplary snapshot of a band at the height of its powers. Even with some of his more memorable tics edited out, Byrne is in fine voice here: Never before had he sounded warmer or more approachable, as evidenced by his soaring rendition of "Once in a Lifetime." Though almost half the album focuses on *Speaking in Tongues* material, the band makes room for one of Byrne's *Catherine Wheel* tunes (the hard-driving, elliptical "What a Day That Was") as well as up-tempo versions of "Pyscho Killer" and "Take Me to the River." If anything, *Stop Making Sense*'s emphasis on keyboards and rhythm is its greatest asset as well as its biggest failing: Knob-tweakers Chris Frantz and Jerry Harrison play up their parts at the expense of the treblier aspects of the performance, and fans would have to wait almost 15 years for reparations. Still, for a generation that may have missed the band's seminal '70s work, *Stop Making Sense* proves to be an excellent primer. *—Michael Hastings*

Little Creatures / Jun. 10, 1985 / Sire ♦♦♦♦♦
Talking Heads' most immediately accessible album, *Little Creatures* eschewed the pattern of recent Heads albums, in which instrumental tracks had been worked up from riffs and grooves, after which David Byrne improvised melodies and lyrics. The songs on *Little Creatures*, most of which were credited to Byrne alone (with the band credited only with arrangements) sounded like they'd been written as songs. Perhaps as one result, the band had been streamlined, with extra musicians used only for specific effects rather than playing along as an ensemble. Byrne, who was singing in his natural range for once, frequently was augmented with backup singers. The overall result: ear candy. *Little Creatures* was a pop album, and an accomplished one, by a band that knew what it was doing. True, Byrne's lyrics were still intriguingly quirky, but even his subject matter was becoming more mature. "I've seen sex and I think it's okay," he sang on "Creatures of Love," and suddenly the geek had become a man. Where he had once pondered the hopes of boys and girls, he was now making observations about children. And even if his impulses remained strange—"I wanna make him stay up all night," he declared about a baby (presumably not his own) in "Stay Up Late"—he retained his charm and inventiveness. *Little Creatures* was, in a sense, Talking Heads lite. It was hard to think of this as the same band that produced "Psycho Killer." But for the band's expanding audience, who made this their second platinum album, that was okay. And their popularity was being accomplished with no diminution in their creativity. *—William Ruhlmann*

True Stories / 1986 / Sire ♦♦

Sounds from True Stories / 1986 / Luaka Bop ♦♦♦
This soundtrack to the Talking Heads film *True Stories* was the second release in a planned trilogy, the last of which—the film's actors covering the Talking Heads songs from the album—never surfaced. Fortunately, this second volume did, a selection of background music and non-Byrne tunes written for the film. Of the Byrne-penned selections, only a few borrow from Heads songs, and the original compositions, perched somewhere between Penguin Cafe Orchestra and a general Americana feel, are pleasant. Meredith Monk's "Road Song" does Byrne one better in this department, and Carl Finch's incredibly silly "Mall Muzak" suite pokes cockeyed fun. The only proper songs here are Terry Allen's "Cocktail Desperado" and Steve Jordan's Tex-Mex "Soy de Texas," both romping good fun. *—Ted Mills*

Naked / Mar. 1988 / Fly ♦♦

● **Popular Favorites 1984-1992: Sand in the Vaseline** / Oct. 13, 1992 / Sire ♦♦♦♦♦
Featuring material from every Talking Heads album except the live *The Name of This Band is Talking Heads*, *Sand in the Vaseline* is a terrific double-disc retrospective of the band's long and varied career. Featuring all of their hit singles and trademark songs ("Psycho Killer," "Take Me to the River," "Burning Down the House," "And She Was," "Once In a Lifetime," "Swamp," "Memories Can't Wait," "Crosseyed and Painless," "Road to Nowhere," "(Nothing But) Flowers," "Life During Wartime"), the set also includes five previously unreleased tracks. *—Stephen Thomas Erlewine*

Stop Making Sense [Special Edition] / Sep. 7, 1999 / Sire/Warner ♦♦♦
When the soundtrack for the classic Talking Heads movie *Stop Making Sense* was originally issued in 1984, it was only nine tracks in length, even though a total of 16 were performed on film. So when the film was rereleased in theaters and on home video in 1999, a new version of the soundtrack was issued as well, including all 16 songs and sporting an even better remastered sound. Recorded over three nights at Hollywood's Pantages Theatre in December 1983 (during the tour in support of *Speaking in Tongues*, the usual four-piece lineup was supplemented by Parliament-Funkadelic keyboardist Bernie Worrell, percussionist Steve Scales, guitarist Alex Weir, and backup singers Lynn Mabry and Ednah Holt. Songs from all eras of the band are featured. The first four tracks are early selections ("Psycho Killer," "Heaven") performed as bare renditions, plus full-band funky versions of such later hits as "Life During Wartime," "Burning Down the House," "Once in a Lifetime," and "Girlfriend Is Better." Also included are less-known album

tracks ("Swamp," "This Must Be the Place," "Crosseyed and Painless"), plus a track from David Byrne's 1981 *Catherine Wheel* album ("What a Day That Was"), and "Genius of Love" by the Tom Tom Club (a side project of drummer Chris Frantz and bassist Tina Weymouth). One of the greatest live albums ever, the 1999 version of *Stop Making Sense* captures the Talking Heads at the height of their powers. A quintessential purchase. *—Greg Prato*

Tall Dwarfs

f. 1979, **db.** 1988

College Rock, New Zealand Rock, Lo-Fi, Alternative Pop/Rock

Pioneers of the lo-fi aesthetic and towering figures of the New Zealand pop music scene, the Tall Dwarfs were formed in 1979 by singers/songwriters Chris Knox and Alec Bathgate, both former members of the popular New Zealand combo Toy Love. Tall Dwarfs' releases were deliberately primitive, the D.I.Y. ethic at its purest—songs were all recorded at home (performed in bedrooms, hallways and the like) and defiantly experimental in nature, presaging the rise of what was ultimately dubbed "lo-fi" as the sound began to grow in prominence and influence over the course of the decades to follow. With 1984's *SlugBucketHairyBreathMonster*, Tall Dwarfs scored their most successful record to date; the track "The Brain That Wouldn't Die" was a cult hit across New Zealand, and with its inclusion on the Flying Nun compilation *Tuatara*, it received significant international exposure as well. The 1988 EP *Dogma* saw the duo finally graduated to a proper studio, and the best-of collection *Hello Cruel World* was the first of their records to earn proper worldwide release; it won them considerable global media coverage as well. In 1990 they reconvened in the studio, emerging with so much material that the long-standing EP format was finally forsaken to release a full-length LP, dubbed *Weeville*. Despite frequent solo work by both Knox and Bathgate, Tall Dwarfs remained intact and issued *Stumpy* in 1997. *—Jason Ankeny*

Louis Likes His Daily Dip EP / 1982 / Flying Nun ♦♦♦

It wasn't heard to any significant degree in the Northern Hemisphere for a few years. But this seven-song 12-inch did a lot both to establish Tall Dwarfs as inheritors of sorts to the legacy of Syd Barrett, and to establish the direction for the Flying Nun/New Zealand indie scene in general. Daft pop songs with dabs of lo-fi noise. *—Richie Unterberger*

Canned Music / 1983 / Flying Nun ♦♦♦♦♦

Canned Music is the third piece of the Tall Dwarfs puzzle, and like the other key pieces of this stunningly beautiful and original tapestry, it shines with a homemade pop glory that is nearly matchless. From the giant-grub march of "Turning Brown and Torn in Two" to the drugged-up winter trance of "This Room Is Wrong" to the shimmering and righteous "Beauty" to the chill-bump-inducing "Shade For Today," the record overflows with the kind of ideals and standards that set the stage for the US indie movement of the early 1990's. One envies fans of Pavement and Sebadoh who have never heard these tracks, going giddy with the pure inventiveness of the craftsmanship here. The whole of *Canned Music* is available on the *Hello Cruel World* compilation, but hardcore fans will need to at least see the marvelous soup-can cover and the hilarious two-headed-monster drawing on the back of the vinyl original. *—Patrick Foster*

That's the Short and Long of It / 1985 / Flying Nun ♦♦♦

It's true, to a certain degree, that there isn't a great deal of variation in Tall Dwarfs' approach from record to record. It's also true, to a greater degree, that you can always count on a great deal of variation within any given record itself. That's the case with this hybrid LP-EP, which showed the group capable of expanding their template from their earliest releases. Side one, which plays at 45 rpm, has two related pieces, "Nothings Going to Happen" and "Nothings Going to Stop It," which sound sort of like a garage *Sgt. Pepper* with their lo-fi wall of orchestral psychedelia. It's back to 33 rpm for the ten songs on side two, a salad bar with samplings of pretty acoustic guitar, a bit of surf influence, some blasts of garage organ, nods to both Lennon and McCartney ("Woman" sounds like primal screamera Lennon backed by a sloppy San Francisco psychedelic act), and more. *—Richie Unterberger*

Throw a Sickie / 1986 / Flying Nun ♦♦♦

Although this 12-inch release has nine songs, it might be more properly classified as an EP due to its brief running time. It's one of their most marginal releases, both because of the relatively short slice of material, and because some of the tracks show the group's brand of lo-fi/psych at its most grating. Committed fans won't be disappointed, but non-completists would be far better off with one or some of their full-length discs. *—Richie Unterberger*

● **Hello Cruel World** / 1987 / Homestead ♦♦♦♦♦

The band's U.S. debut, *Hello Cruel World*, collects their legendary and most influential early recordings from 1981 to 1984—with selections from the ultra-rare *Three Songs* EP (1981), *Louis Loves His Daily Dip* EP (1982), *Canned Music* (1983), and *Slugbucket Hairybreath Monster* EP (1984). An excellent introduction to a truly unique and innovative band. *—Chris Woodstra*

Weeville / 1990 / Homestead ♦♦♦

As the liner notes proclaim, this is "the first straightforward LP by Tall Dwarfs ... in terms of having the same number of tracks on each side—both of which play at the same speed and which ain't a compilation." If Tall Dwarfs had only done one or two albums, this would have seemed like a more impressive document. But new ground isn't broken here—it's more of the same eclectic melange of homespun latter-day psychedelia. The converted will have no complaints. But for my money it's much better when it abandons the arty noise for acoustic-guitar driven and airy melodies, as it does here on a number of occasions. *—Richie Unterberger*

Fork Songs / 1992 / Flying Nun ♦♦♦♦

The acclaimed duo of Chris Knox and Alec Bathgate's 1980s output on the Flying Nun label was profoundly influential on a generation of lo-fi music. Their influence can be traced in the music of Yo La Tengo, Pavement, Smog, and others working with intimate and primitive songcraft. Legendary home recorders, *Fork Songs* continues to expand their self-built universe and deepen their songwriting partnership. Fearless assemblages of noisy loops, primitive guitars, and household objects are the instruments favored, and the ease with which they sculpt oblique elements into delicate upbeat songs is stunning. Like the Television Personalities, their low-tech methods prove that great songs will transcend recording methods, and *Fork Songs* is only another crucial chapter in the book of musical invention that the New Zealand duo wrote. *—Martin Walters*

3 EPs / 1994 / Flying Nun ♦♦♦♦♦

The *Hello Cruel World* compilation is the best way to get acquainted with Tall Dwarfs, but if you want just one of their other albums, this is probably the best choice. Recorded in 1992 and 1993, it has just as much variety as any other disc (compilation or otherwise) by the group, but doesn't wear out its welcome as much over the course of the merry-go-round. Some of their most spaced-out stuff is here: the fogged-over hurdy-gurdy waltz of "Bob's Yer Uncle," the stoner psychedelia of "Two Dozen Lousy Hours" (complete with warp-simulation sound effects), the white blues satire (how long has it been since you heard one of those?) "Postmodern Deconstructivist Blues." They can't resist succumbing to numbing repetitive lo-fi fuzz riffs from time to time [as on "Self-Deluded Dreamboy (In a Mess)"], but after a dozen years it seems unreasonable to expect that they'll grow up in this regard. *—Richie Unterberger*

Stumpy / Feb. 11, 1997 / Flying Nun ♦♦♦

Establishing the post-punk and independent scenes in New Zealand, Tall Dwarfs were arguably the first of indie rock's pioneers to take part in the home taping phenomenon. The styles and techniques of the creative collaboration of Chris Knox and Alec Bathgate have constantly changed since the Tall Dwarfs' inception in the early '80s, but experimentation has always been of first and foremost importance for them. After releasing a series of records on New Zealand's Flying Nun imprint, Knox and Bathgate began to take separate career routes but reunited for special occasions such as the compiling and recording of their 1997 release *Stumpy*. The record, released almost 20 years after their basement rock beginnings, was based on the idea that home tapers from around the globe would record bits and pieces of songs, send them to Knox and Bathgate, and the Dwarfs would then make songs from the basic structures of what they received. The result is an astoundingly fluid document of lo-fi weirdness, with its hand in every imaginable genre of music from folk to blues to punk to quirky out-rock to chamber pop. Of the 22 tracks, only a handful break the two-minute mark, so it is fair to assume that the Dwarfs did little in the way of adding much length to any of the pieces. The bulk of their toil was in the compiling and recording stages of the production. Strangely, there is very little clutter on the album and the flow of eclecticism runs extremely smoothly. More musicians should consider these concepts for future releases. A brilliant and successful undertaking. *—Ken Taylor*

Howard Tate

b. 1938, Macon, GA

Vocals / Pop-Soul, Soul

Highly regarded by soul music cultists, and virtually unknown by anybody else, Howard Tate had some minor success with the Verve label in the late '60s. The singer brought a lot of blues and gospel to his phrasing, but what made him palatable to the modern R&B (and, to a lesser degree, pop) audience was the Northeast soul production of Jerry Ragovoy, who also wrote much of Tate's material. Howard made the R&B Top 20 three times in the late '60s (with "Ain't Nobody Home," "Stop," and "Look at Granny Run Run"). However, he's most famous to rock audiences as the original performer of "Get It While You Can," which became one of Janis Joplin's signature tunes. Ragovoy recorded about ten singles with Tate between 1966 and 1969, the first for the small Utopia label, the rest for Verve. Tate moved on to Lloyd Price's Turntable label, for which he recorded a few singles in the late '60s and early '70s. From there he chalked up a short stint with Atlantic, which saw a few other 45s and a critically well-received album, but again little commercial success. A final 1974 single for Epic was his swan song. *—Richie Unterberger*

● **Get It While You Can: The Legendary Sessions** / Jun. 20, 1995 / Mercury ♦♦♦♦♦

Tate's entire Verve output, condensed into a tidy 17-track compilation, including all of his late '60s singles for the label, and one previously unreleased track. Solid period soul with a slight eclectic bent for the blues, gospel, and some pop influences. *—Richie Unterberger*

James Taylor

b. Mar. 12, 1948, Boston, MA

Vocals, Guitar / Folk-Rock, Soft Rock, Adult Contemporary, Singer/Songwriter

When people use the term "singer/songwriter" (often modified by the word "sensitive"), in praise or in criticism, it's James Taylor that they're thinking of. Yet in a career now extending three decades, Taylor's biggest hits have come with his cover versions of other people's songs. Go figure. He was signed as a solo artist by the Beatles' Apple label in 1968 and released his debut album, *James Taylor*. But it was his 1970 Warner Brothers LP, the triple-platinum *Sweet Baby James*, with its understated, autobiographical Top Ten hit "Fire and Rain," that was his commercial breakthrough. *Mud Slide Slim and the Blue Horizon* (1971) was another million-seller and contained the number one single "You've Got a Friend," written by Carole King. Taylor married Carly Simon in 1972, around the time that the gold *One Man Dog* was released. *In the Pocket* (1976) was Taylor's last album for Warner Brothers; he moved to Columbia Records for *JT* (1977), a double-platinum comeback that featured a Top Ten cover of Jimmy Jones' "Handy Man." *Flag* (1979) and *Dad Loves His Work* (1981) were Top Ten gold albums. *—William Ruhlmann*

James Taylor / Dec. 6, 1968 / Capitol ♦♦♦♦♦
On this self-titled debut album, James Taylor's reflective lyrics, containing his melancholic observations on life and love, were leavened by his attractive folk melodies, his acoustic guitar fingerpicking, and his warm, rich voice, which was unconsciously reminiscent of the calm crooning school of Bing Crosby and Perry Como. To these, producer Peter Asher added the accomplished but subdued string and brass arrangements, using a few pieces per track, with musical "links" between songs, building up to a full orchestra on the last two songs. The result was an amazingly distinctive effort, all in the service of Taylor's songs, which included "Knocking 'Round the Zoo" (a comic, bluesy reminiscence on life in a mental institution), "Something in the Way She Moves," "Rainy Day Man," and "Carolina in My Mind" (with Paul McCartney on bass), songs that have been concert favorites for decades. However personal Taylor's young angst may have been, it connected strongly with his generation's, and remains among his better efforts. *—William Ruhlmann*

☆ **Sweet Baby James** / Feb. 1970 / Warner Brothers ♦♦♦♦♦
The heart of James Taylor's appeal is that you can take him two ways. On the one hand, his music, including that warm voice, is soothing; its minor key melodies and restrained playing draw in the listener. On the other hand, his world view, especially on such songs as "Fire and Rain," reflects the pessimism and desperation of the 1960s hangover that was the early '70s. That may not be intentional: "Fire and Rain" was about the suicide of a fellow inmate of Taylor's at a mental institution, not the national malaise. But Taylor's sense of wounded hopelessness—"I'm all in pieces, you can have your own choice," he sings in "Country Road"—struck a chord with music fans, especially because of its attractive mixture of folk, country, gospel, and blues elements, all of them carefully understated and distanced. Taylor didn't break your heart, he understood that it was already broken, as was his own, and he offered comfort. As a result, *Sweet Baby James* sold millions of copies, spawned a Top Ten hit in "Fire and Rain" and a Top 40 hit in "Country Road," and launched not only Taylor's career as a pop superstar but also the entire singer/songwriter movement of the early '70s that included Joni Mitchell, Carole King, Jackson Browne, Cat Stevens, and others. A second legacy became clear two decades later, when country stars like Garth Brooks began to cite Taylor, with his use of steel guitar, references to Jesus, and rural and Western imagery on *Sweet Baby James*, as a major influence. *—William Ruhlmann*

Mud Slide Slim and the Blue Horizon / Apr. 1971 / Warner Brothers ♦♦♦♦
James Taylor's commercial breakthrough in 1970 was predicated on the relationship between the private concerns expressed in his songs and the larger philosophical mood of his audience. He was going through depression, heartbreak, and addiction; they were recovering from the political and cultural storms of the '60s. On his follow-up to the landmark *Sweet Baby James*, Taylor brought his listeners up to date, wisely trying to step beyond the cultural, if not the personal, markers he had established. Despite affirming romance in songs like "Love Has Brought Me Around" and the moving "You Can Close Your Eyes" as well as companionship in "You've Got a Friend," the record still came as a defense against the world, not an embrace of it; Taylor was unable to forget the past or trust the present. The songs were full of references to the road and the highway, and he was uncomfortable with his new role as spokesman. The confessional songwriter was now, necessarily, writing about what it was like to be a confessional songwriter: *Mud Slide Slim and the Blue Horizon* served the valuable function of beginning to move James Taylor away from the genre he had defined, which ultimately would give him a more long-lasting appeal. *—William Ruhlmann*

One Man Dog / Nov. 1972 / Warner Brothers ♦♦♦
A lot was riding on this album, James Taylor's follow-up to his two big hits, *Sweet Baby James* and *Mud Slide Slim and The Blue Horizon*; this was released 21 months after the latter, a long time between records in those days. And what a letdown. *One Man Dog* contained 18 tracks, some of them instrumentals, many of them running less than two minutes. A lot of it was sketchy and seemingly unfinished, and none of it had the impact of the best songs on the last two albums. *One Man Dog* spawned a Top 20 hit in "Don't Let Me Be Lonely Tonight," and it made the Top Ten and went gold itself largely on the momentum of Taylor's career. But it disappointed fans, and in the 19 months it took him to record another album, Taylor was bypassed by the singer-songwriter movement. *—William Ruhlmann*

Walking Man / Jun. 1974 / Warner Brothers ♦♦♦
One Man Dog drastically lowered expectations for a new James Taylor album, and those expectations were almost met by *Walking Man*, a more considered effort than its predecessor that managed to be just as trivial but even less interesting. As a result, it became the worst-selling album of Taylor's career. Somehow, a songwriter who had seemed in 1970 to have as precise an idea of the national mood as Bob Dylan had had in 1965 now seemed to be a man without a country. Instead, *Walking Man*, which began with Taylor asking, "Who is this walking man?" and ended with him commenting, "It's really not so bad to be fading away," sounded like the statement of a songwriter who either had nothing to say or didn't know how to say it. *—William Ruhlmann*

Gorilla / May 1975 / Warner Brothers ♦♦♦
Gorilla served notice to anyone expecting James Taylor to continue on in the personal, confessional vein of his first few albums that he did not intend to do so. Recording in Burbank with Warners staff producers Lenny Waronker and Russ Titelman, Taylor used a stellar backup band augmented by such guests as Graham Nash and David Crosby (who harmonized on the chart single "Mexico"), his wife Carly Simon, mandolinist David Grisman, saxophone player David Sanborn, Randy Newman on "hornorgan," and Little Feat slide guitarist Lowell George. This team worked on a set of light, pleasant songs that bordered on the generic—one was called "Music," another "Love Songs"—but were performed and sung with taste and care. Taylor was relentlessly upbeat; even "Angry Blues," which confessed, "I can't help it if I don't feel so good," didn't sound like things were that bad. But then, these songs didn't seem to be about Taylor, or if they were, as in the extended metaphor of the title track, the connection was so oblique that it was hard to say what the point was. Still, one could glide on Taylor's easy vocals and the band's competence, and *Gorilla* was an enjoyable listening experience. "How Sweet It Is (To Be Loved by You)," the first of a series of bleached R&B covers, became a Top Ten hit, and the album restored Taylor's commercial fortunes, setting him on the steady path he would follow for decades after. But who would have thought only a few years before that the king of the confessional song poets would turn into such a lightweight? *—William Ruhlmann*

In the Pocket / Jun. 1976 / Warner Brothers ♦♦♦
James Taylor's seventh album and last new recording for Warner Bros. is notable for producing his biggest self-written hit in four years, "Shower The People" (#22 pop, #1 easy listening). Bobby Womack's "Woman's Gotta Have It" was the album's only cover, and elsewhere Taylor took on a surprisingly rough set of issues in his typically gentle style, including "A Junkie's Lament" and "Money Machine." There were also reflections on being a "Family Man" even if, due to his peripatetic touring life, "Daddy's All Gone." Guest stars included Art Garfunkel, who harmonized on "Captain Jim's Drunken Dream," and Stevie Wonder, who co-wrote and played harmonica on "Don't Be Sad 'Cause Your Sun Is Down." On the whole, a respectable effort for an artist who was evolving into more of a craftsman than a virtuoso. *—William Ruhlmann*

★ **Greatest Hits** / Nov. 1976 / Warner Brothers ♦♦♦♦♦
James Taylor had scored eight Top 40 hits by the fall of 1976 when Warner Brothers marked the end of his contract with this compilation. One of those hits, the Top Ten gold single "Mockingbird," a duet with his wife Carly Simon, was on Elektra Records, part of the Warners family of labels and presumably available, but it was left off. "Long Ago and Far Away," a lesser hit (though it made the Top Ten on the Easy Listening charts) wasn't used either. In addition to the six hits—"Fire and Rain," "Country Road," "You've Got a Friend," "Don't Let Me Be Lonely Tonight," "How Sweet It Is (To Be Loved by You)," and "Shower the People"—that were included, the album featured a couple of less successful singles, "Mexico" and "Walking Man," the album track "Sweet Baby James," and three previously unreleased recordings—a live version of "Steamroller" and newly recorded versions of "Something in the Way She Moves" and "Carolina in My Mind," songs featured on Taylor's 1968 debut album, recorded for Apple/Capitol. The result was a reasonable collection for an artist who wasn't particularly well-defined by his singles. One got little sense of Taylor's evolution from the dour, confessional songs of his first two albums to the more conventional pop songs of his sixth and seventh ones. But one did hear isolated examples of Taylor's undeniable warmth and facility for folk/country-tinged pop. By the next summer, Taylor was back in the Top Ten on Columbia, and *Greatest Hits* was out of date. But it remains a good sampler of Taylor's more popular early work. And, decades later, it remained the only Taylor compilation in print in the U.S. *—William Ruhlmann*

JT / Jun. 1977 / Columbia/Legacy ♦♦♦♦
On his last couple of Warner Brothers albums, *Gorilla* and *In the Pocket*, James Taylor seemed to be converting himself from the shrinking violet, too-sensitive-to-live "rainy day man" of his early records into a mainstream, easy-listening crooner with a sunny outlook. *JT*, his debut album for Columbia Records, was something of a defense of this conversion. Returning to the autobiographical, Taylor declared his love for Carly Simon ("There We Are"), but expressed some surprise at his domestic bliss. "Isn't it amazing a man like me can feel this way?" he sang in the opening song, "Your Smiling Face" (a Top 40 hit). At the same time, domesticity could have its temporary depressions ("Another Grey Morning"). The key track was "Secret O' Life," which Taylor revealed as "enjoying the passage of time." Working with his long-time backup band of Danny Kortchmar, Leland Sklar, and Russell Kunkel, and with Peter Asher back in the producer's chair, Taylor also enjoyed the playing of music, mixing his patented acoustic guitar-based folk sound with elements of rock, blues, and country. He even made the Country charts briefly with "Bartender's Blues," a genre exercise complete with steel guitar and references to "honky tonk angels" that he would later re-record with George Jones. The album's Top Ten hit was Taylor's winning remake of Jimmy Jones' "Handy Man," which replaced the grit of the original with his characteristic warmth. *JT* was James Taylor's best album since *Mud Slide Slim and the Blue Horizon* because it acknowledged the darkness of his earlier work while explaining the deliberate lightness of his current viewpoint, and because it was his most consistent collection in years. Fans responded: *JT* sold better than any Taylor album since *Sweet Baby James*. *—William Ruhlmann*

Flag / May 1979 / Columbia/Legacy ♦♦♦
James Taylor followed his double-platinum Columbia Records label debut *JT* with this hodgepodge of a record. There are pointless covers of The Beatles' "Day Tripper" and The Drifters' "Up On The Roof" (#7 Adult Contemporary, #28 Pop), a remake of Taylor's own "Rainy Day Man," songs written for the failed Broadway musical *Working*, and a few inconsequential new Taylor compositions. The usual brain trust (producer Peter Asher) and the usual backup team (Danny Kortchmar, Dan Grolnick, Leland Sklar, Russ Kunkel) were on board, but the cruise was a snooze. *—William Ruhlmann*

Dad Loves His Work / Mar. 1981 / Columbia/Legacy ♦♦♦♦
James Taylor bounced back from the spotty *Flag* with this all-original album led by his collaboration with J.D. Souther on "Her Town Too" (#11 Pop, #5 Adult Contemporary), his biggest pop hit since "Handy Man" and biggest non-cover hit since his first, "Fire And Rain," in 1970. Also included were "Hard Times" (#72 Pop, #23 Adult Contemporary) and "Summer's Here" (#25 Adult Contemporary), not to mention the unusually impassioned

"Stand And Fight." After simmering this long, there wasn't much hope Taylor would ever come to a boil, but that track indicated he could at least heat up now and then. — *William Ruhlmann*

That's Why I'm Here / Oct. 1985 / Columbia/Legacy ✦✦✦
Taylor took four and a half years off from record-making in the early 1980s, returning with *That's Why I'm Here*, which suggested he had found his long-term niche with Baby Boomer fans now permanently tuned to soft-rock radio—this was Taylor's first record to spawn three Top Ten adult contemporary hits, with the title track, "Only One," and a cover of Buddy Holly's "Everyday." But those boomers just don't go to the record store as often as their children, and the album failed to go gold and was his lowest-charting effort since his debut. If, in the title song, he had reconciled himself to the notion that he was here to sing "Fire And Rain" at summer concerts, that also meant he was settling for a complacent position in which his new material was virtually irrelevant, and that being the case, why should people buy it? (Notwithstanding its initial commercial reception, *That's Why I'm Here* eventually went platinum.) — *William Ruhlmann*

Never Die Young / Jan. 1988 / Columbia/Legacy ✦✦✦
While his aging contemporaries took a variety of tacks to keep up with changing fashions, from adopting more synthesized, percussive production styles to assembling an orchestra and singing standards, James Taylor just kept playing a summer concert tour each year and periodically putting out another collection of similar-sounding songs. *Never Die Young* was unusual only in that there was no big oldies cover from the '50s or '60s—every song was written or co-written by Taylor—but otherwise it addressed the same audience in much the same terms as he always had. The title song and "Baby Boom Baby" (both Adult Contemporary hits) referred to the passage of time, and the rest floated on a sea of yuppie contentment. "I work hard to see that you remember my name," he sang, and that work seemed to consist of reminding his listeners why they had liked him in the first place. — *William Ruhlmann*

● **Classic Songs** / 1990 / Columbia ✦✦✦✦✦
Classic Songs is the only compilation to feature the original versions of all of James Taylor's classics from his debut up through 1985's *That's Why I'm Here*. Unfortunately, it's only available in Europe, yet it remains the best, most comprehensive collection of his work to date. — *Chris Woodstra*

New Moon Shine / Sep. 24, 1991 / Columbia ✦✦✦
James Taylor produced a typical collection of familiar-sounding songs on *New Moon Shine*, his concerns ranging from romance to the life of the working man to political issues like war and civil rights on which he took the expected liberal positions. The album was written, played, and sung with typical craft and care, and was a worthy addition to Taylor's catalog. Taylor's reliability means that his records do not disappoint his faithful audience, but neither do they provide any revelations. *New Moon Shine* provided four Adult Contemporary chart entries in "Copperline," "(I've Got To) Stop Thinkin' 'Bout That," a cover of Sam Cooke's "Everybody Loves to Cha Cha Cha," and "Like Everyone She Knows," and the album went gold, staying in the charts more than nine months, a good showing for a record that essentially repeated previous efforts. (*New Moon Shine* was eventually certified platinum.) — *William Ruhlmann*

Live / Aug. 10, 1993 / Columbia ✦✦✦✦
"A live James Taylor album has been suggested, demanded and contemplated for many years," writes Taylor's manager/producer Peter Asher in this album's liner notes, and the reasons are not hard to find. For one thing, Taylor has been a successful concert attraction for more than 20 years. For another, an artist who has scored in excess of 30 chart records (on four different labels) over those years is represented by only one, 20-year-old hits compilation. The 30-track, two-hour (*Live*), drawn from a tour staged specifically to record it, is an attempt to address those points. Fronting a typically top-notch band, Taylor ranges across his repertoire, back to 1968 for "Something in the Way She Moves" and "Carolina in My Mind," and up to 1991 for "Copperline," among other songs drawn from *New Moon Shine*. In between come most of his hits. (The most notable exception is "Her Town, Too," and there is a general paucity of later recordings like "That's Why I'm Here" and "Never Die Young.") Taylor treats the material in his relaxed, assured style, making occasional ironic or self-deprecatory remarks between songs and charming his audience even more. The effect of presenting the songs in a uniform manner is to imply an equality between them, as though the deeper material was less significant and the slighter songs more substantial. But that doesn't keep the set from being a consistently enjoyable listening experience. Taylor remains sorely in need of a retrospective that would bring his work into concise coherence, but this one at least presents most of his best-known material in effective performances. — *William Ruhlmann*

Original Flying Machine 1967 / Oct. 8, 1996 / Gadfly ✦✦
Original Flying Machine 1967 is comprised of recordings James Taylor with his band the Flying Machine made a year before he signed to Apple Records. At this stage, Taylor was still trying to find his voice, yet that is the very reason why these recordings are of interest to fans. Most of the material on *Original Flying Machine 1967* re-appeared on Taylor's eponymous debut album for Apple, while these originals stayed in the can. These arrangements are a bit more full-bodied, featuring the support of a full band, led by guitarist Danny Kortchmar. Though these are a bit more fleshed out, they aren't quite as strong as the later versions. Nevertheless, the album makes for a fascinating one-time listen for most fans. (The 1996 CD reissue features six of the original album's seven songs, adding the unreleased "Kootch's Song" as the seventh song.) — *Stephen Thomas Erlewine*

Hourglass / May 20, 1997 / Columbia ✦✦✦
James Taylor stopped pushing himself into new musical and lyrical territories in the late '70s, so it doesn't come as a great surprise that *Hour Glass*, his first studio album in six years, doesn't offer anything new—it's a collection of pleasant, melodic, simple songs about love, family and social activism. That's not necessarily a bad thing, since Taylor has a gift for such material, and on *Hour Glass*, he sounds as good as ever. The music, in many ways, has greater depth than previous records, since it features cameos from such heavy hitters as Stevie Wonder, Yo-Yo Ma, Shawn Colvin, Michael Brecker, Mark O'Connor and Branford Marsalis. There are a few songs that fall a little flat, failing to make much of an impression one way or the other, but on the whole, *Hour Glass* is a nice addition to his catalog. — *Stephen Thomas Erlewine*

Greatest Hits, Vol. 2 / Nov. 7, 2000 / Columbia/Legacy ✦✦✦✦✦
James Taylor's first *Greatest Hits* album, released in 1976 and consisting of his well-known early '70s recordings on Warner Bros. and re-recordings of some of the songs from his 1968 Apple Records debut, is in the rarefied sales category of double-digit millions, so a second volume, taking in his tenure at Columbia Records, was a no-brainer. The only wonder is why it took so long. But the second part of Taylor's recording career has been different from his first, especially when it comes to hits. All of Taylor's Columbia albums have been good sellers, hitting gold or platinum sales. But he has scored only four Top 40 hits on the pop charts: "Handy Man" (his only Top Ten single on Columbia), "Your Smiling Face," "Up on the Roof," and "Her Town Too." It's a different story on the adult contemporary charts, where he has been a mainstay. But *Greatest Hits, Vol. 2* is not so much a collection of Taylor's chart entries as it is a best-of. There are several tracks, among them "Secret O' Life," "Only a Dream in Rio," and "Song for You Far Away," that were never hits but have become audience favorites, frequently played in Taylor's concerts. And there are chart singles, notably "Only One," which got into the adult contemporary Top Ten, and "Hard Times" and "Honey Don't Leave L.A.," which made the pop charts, that have been omitted. That said, this is a well-balanced compilation that should please most of the singer/songwriter's fans and that serves as a good selection of his work, circa 1977-1997. — *William Ruhlmann*

Johnnie Taylor

b. May 5, 1938, Crawfordsville, AR, **d.** May 31, 2000, Dallas, TX
Vocals / Deep Soul, Southern Soul, Retro-Soul, Quiet Storm, Soul-Blues, Disco, Soul
Aptly dubbed the "Philosopher of Soul" by the Stax publicity department, Johnnie Taylor set the ladies' hearts aflutter during the early '70s with his tender brand of Memphis soul. Taylor wasn't always the sincere crooner he developed into. A Sam Cooke protégé who took over with The Soul Stirrers when Cooke went secular, and who retained a hint of his mentor's mellifluous delivery, Taylor took the same pop route via Cooke's SAR label in 1961. Once he got on the Stax label in 1966, the vocalist forged a sublime blues/soul synthesis with a series of absolutely gorgeous efforts. But there was nothing subtle about Taylor's first number one in 1968: "Who's Making Love" was an uncompromising treatise on cheating lovers, with storming brass and slashing guitar. The follow-ups "Take Care of Your Homework" and "Jody's Got Your Girl and Gone" pounded the same message home from different angles. As the decade turned, though, Taylor perceptibly mellowed, turning increasingly to ballads for inspiration—"I Believe in You (You Believe in Me)," "We're Getting Careless with Our Love." By the time he went platinum with the horribly repetitive "Disco Lady" in 1976, the rough edges that made his early work so absorbing were smoothed away, although his latter-day Malaco output sometimes managed to suggest Taylor's glory years. He died of an apparent heart attack on May 31, 2000. — *Bill Dahl*

● **Chronicle: The 20 Greatest Hits** / 1977 / Stax ✦✦✦✦✦
Johnnie Taylor's Stax hits were tailored to his gritty voice and tough manner. Taylor's nickname was "The Soul Philosopher," and few were better at dispensing romance formulas and fables, love, wit and wisdom. This collection rivals the two-record *Chronicle* as the best Taylor anthology, containing virtually every significant hit. "Who's Making Love," "Love Bones" and many others accent Taylor's swaggering delivery and the aggressive production and fine instrumental support that augmented his best material. There's no fluff here, just great textbook Southern soul. — *Ron Wynn*

The Best of Johnnie Taylor on Malaco, Vol. 1 / 1984-1992 / Malaco ✦✦✦✦
Given how much of a fixture Johnnie Taylor was on Black radio in the 1960s and early to mid-'70s, it's ironic that one of his best-of collections doesn't contain an abundance of hit singles. Rather, the focus of this CD is the veteran soul man's work for Malaco in the 1980s and '90s. Taylor may have been long past his peak commercially when these songs were recorded, but artistically, he still sounds like he's very much in his prime. Malaco's choices are generally excellent. Selections like "Don't Make Me Late," "Still Called the Blues" and "Everything's Out In the Open" show why Taylor has fared so well creatively at the label, which has encouraged him to continue taking a classic soul approach instead of catering to the urban contemporary market (something he has pretty much ignored). For listeners who haven't been exposed to his Malaco output, this collection is the logical starting point. — *Alex Henderson*

● **The Best of Johnnie Taylor: Rated X-Traordinaire** / Mar. 12, 1996 / Columbia/Legacy ✦✦✦✦✦
The 16-track *Rated X-Traordinaire* sets out to rescue the reputation of the Johnnie Taylor of 1976-1980, the period that began with his biggest smash, "Disco Lady," but that found him, so the conventional wisdom goes, a Southern soul man set adrift on the disco wave. Annotator Kalamu ya Salaam argues that "Disco Lady" is not a disco song, and backs this up by noting that the track actually was played by members of Parliament-Funkadelic. True enough, though that only applies to Taylor's debut Columbia album, *Eargasm*. Elsewhere, Taylor did drift, from Muscle Shoals tracks that updated his Stax Memphis sound to tracks that sounded like Marvin Gaye. The early years, 1976 and 1977, were more accomplished than the later ones, and that's where compilation producer Leo Sacks focuses,

with 12 of the 16 tracks coming from then. In so doing, he ignores R&B chart singles like "Keep on Dancing" and "Ever Ready," but he satisfies the "best of" title. *—William Ruhlmann*

Lifetime / Oct. 24, 2000 / Stax ♦♦♦
Taylor gets honored with a three-CD box set for this career retrospective. And it truly is a career retrospective: it spans 1956-1999 and includes a good deal of material that he did for other labels before and after his lengthy Stax stint. It's true that you have to be a pretty deep Taylor fan to commit to nearly four hours of his music. It's also true that even if you are a big Taylor fan, you're likely to need some patience to last through some of the average cuts, or his stylistic transition from gospel to soul to disco and retro-soul. Overall, however, it's a fine commemoration of an important if not quite great soul star. The most valuable components of the set are found on disc one, which kicks off with a half-dozen gospel tunes from his stints with the Highway Q.C.'s and the Soul Stirrers in the late '50s, moving into some of his soul sides for Sam Cooke's SAR label in the early '60s. For the remainder of disc one and some of disc two, there are plenty of fine soul-blues cuts from his early days at Stax in the mid-to-late '60s that will be familiar to relatively few listeners, his fine soul-blues-gospel vocal blend resulting in some of his finest work. As time wore on—even starting in the early '70s—Taylor's material got duller and more homogenized, though there were always some highlights to perk up your ears. Unsurprisingly, then, like most box sets, this gets less interesting the closer it draws to the finish line, although wisely his late-'70s Columbia era (yes, "Disco Lady" is here) and post-'70s Malaco output is represented by a mere four cuts each. Ultimately, it's a well-done summation of Taylor's legacy, with an accompanying 50-page booklet including essay, discography, and photos. *—Richie Unterberger*

Bram Tchaikovsky

b. Nov. 10, 1950
Power Pop, New Wave
Bram Tchaikovsky (born Peter Bramall) began playing in local pub-rock bands in Lincolnshire, England, in the late '60s. He joined The Motors in 1977 and was relegated to mere sideman status by the nucleus of the band, songwriters Andy McMaster and Nick Garvey. While waiting on pre-production work for the second Motors album, Tchaikovsky took the opportunity to do some recording of his own. The resulting single, "Sarah Smiles," drew enough interest for him to leave The Motors and form his own band. In addition to its leader, the band Bram Tchaikovsky consisted of Mike Broadbent (bass, keyboards) and Keith Boyce (drums). They signed to the new Radar label in 1978 along with Stiff expatriates Nick Lowe and Elvis Costello. The band showed a great deal of promise with their first album *Strange Man Changed Man*, fitting in nicely with the growing power-pop movement. The unforgettable "Girl of My Dreams," a true high point of the time, became a minor hit on both sides of the Atlantic. Tchaikovsky continued on through rapid personnel changes for two more albums, *The Russians Are Coming* (released in the U.S. as *Pressure*) in 1980 and *Funland* in 1981. A considerable drop in sales prompted Tchaikovsky to dissolve the band and retire from the music business. *—Chris Woodstra*

● **Strange Man, Changed Man** / 1979 / Polydor ♦♦♦♦♦
Strange Man Changed Man remains Bram Tchaikovsky's finest moment. Produced by his former Motors bandmate Nick Garvey on a shoestring buget, the resulting thin sound only serves to enhance the songs which owe as much to '60s pop as they do to pub/punk rock. The pure pop of "Girl of My Dreams" (a minor hit in the U.S.) perfectly encapsulates late-'70s Brit-pop and stands as one of the classic singles of the era. *—Chris Woodstra*

Pressure / 1980 / Polydor ♦♦♦
Pressure, released in the U.K. as *The Russians Are Coming*, is not quite as strong as the first album but still worthwhile. *—Chris Woodstra*

Funland / May 1981 / Arista ♦♦♦
By the time of the difficult third album, constant personnel changes and general lack of inspiration on the part of the band's leader had taken its toll. The deceptively titled *Funland* is a lackluster effort that effectively ended the band's career. *—Chris Woodstra*

Team Dresch

f. Portland, OR
Queercore, Riot Grrrl, Punk Revival, Indie Rock
Queercore revolutionaries Team Dresch formed in Portland, OR in late 1993, originally comprising bassist Donna Dresch (formerly of bands ranging from Dangermouse to Dinosaur Jr.), singer/guitarist Jody Bleyle (also of Hazel), singer/guitarist Kaia Wilson (ex-Adickdid) and Spinanes drummer Scott Plouf. The group played its first show on New Year's Day 1994 minus a name, considering Magic Animal and Dyke Access Road before finally agreeing on Team Dresch; after recording their Kill Rock Stars debut single "Hand Grenade," Plouf exited, with a series of short-lived drummers completing the lineup before the addition of onetime Calamity Jane member Marci Martinez. 1995's *Personal Best*, a brilliantly visceral fusion of punk-pop energy and lesbian empowerment, appeared jointly on Dresch's Chainsaw label and Bleyle's Candy-Ass imprint; following the record's completion Martinez left Team Dresch, and was replaced by former Vitapup drummer Melissa York for 1996's *Captain My Captain*. After issuing a self-titled solo LP Kaia left the group, with the revised foursome of Dresch, Bleyle, Martinez and guitarist Amanda Kelly releasing the Outpunk single "Deattached," credited to the New Team Dresch v.6.0 Beta. *—Jason Ankeny*

● **Personal Best** / 1995 / Chainsaw ♦♦♦♦♦
Of all the punk records to come out of the 1990s, *Personal Best* comes closest to actually recapturing the sheer passion and rage which originally spawned the movement two decades earlier; where other bands whine on endlessly about running out of beer money or losing the right to skateboard in the park, Team Dresch confront real issues—bigotry, oppression, religion, self-worth—with a sense of conviction and immediacy that lays to waste everything in their path. For an album that lasts less than 25 minutes, *Personal Best* is a draining, relentless experience—it explodes on contact, the cumulative result of years of pent-up anger, frustration and desperation finally allowed release. What distinguishes Team Dresch from the vast majority of their queercore compatriots is that they never put their politics ahead of their songs—each of these ten tracks is airtight, with melodies as blistering as the lyrics. And while some songs are explicitly polemical—"Hate the Christian Right!" would undoubtedly send Ralph Reed into apoplectic fits—and others like "Growing Up in Springfield" are deeply personal, there's ultimately no separating the two; *Personal Best* is above all a call-to-arms, which in the end is exactly what a great punk record should be. *—Jason Ankeny*

Captain My Captain / 1996 / Chainsaw ♦♦♦♦♦
Captain, My Captain, the sophomore album from the queercore band Team Dresch, resumes where *Personal Best* left off two years earlier. Like *Personal Best*, *Captain, My Captain* focuses on the struggle, angst, and confusion of being a lesbian. At the same time the album is able to transcend the lesbian cause making universally applicable statements about individual freedom, politics, and self-respect. The following quote illustrates the superior lyrics: "My mom says she loves me but I don't think its love 'cause she only loves me when I act just like she does and that's emotional blackmail." The fierce and biting lyrics are aided by raging, skilled punk rock sounds, creating one of the most intense and meaningful punk revival albums to date. Unfortunately, *Captain My Captain*, which yields few innovations, is unable to surpass the high standard set by *Personal Best*. However, Team Dresch is still able to accomplish more in this 35 minutes than many bands can in their entire career. *—John Hinrichsen*

The Teardrop Explodes

f. 1978, **db.** 1983
Post-Punk, New Wave
One of the pivotal groups to emerge from the Liverpool neo-psychedelia community during the late '70s, the Teardrop Explodes was a showcase for Julian Cope, a notoriously eccentric figure whose unfashionable love of Krautrock and hallucinogenic drugs set him distinctly apart from the prevailing punk mentality of the era. Cope formed the band in 1978, and recorded their 1979 debut single "Sleeping Gas," a surreal electro-pop effort distinguished by its swirling keyboard washes.

One year later, the Teardrop Explodes issued 1980's infectious "When I Dream," which hit the U.K. Top 50 and even garnered some airplay in the U.S. Finally, the band's debut LP *Kilimanjaro* appeared later that year, to rave reviews and respectable sales. The single "Reward" hit the Top Ten early in 1981, and the ambitious LP *Wilder* was highlighted by the smash "Passionate Friend." A tour of the States followed, with disastrous results to the band's fragile line-up. In the midst of recording their third LP, to be dubbed *Everybody Wants to Shag the Teardrop Explodes*, Cope finally dissolved the band; only a 1983 EP dubbed *You Disappear from View* appeared on schedule, although the unfinished sessions were finally released in full in 1990 under their projected title. In the wake of the Teardrop Explodes' breakup, Cope embarked on a successful and occasionally brilliant solo career. *—Jason Ankeny*

● **Kilimanjaro** / Oct. 1980 / Fontana ♦♦♦♦♦
Armed with trumpeters Ray Martinez and Hurricane Smith who add soaring flourishes and energetic blasts throughout, on *Kilimanjaro* the Teardrops explode in a torrent of creative, kicky and often downright fun songs that hotwire garage/psych inspirations into something more. Steering clear of ham-handed attempts to be commercially "new wave" while at the same time sounding young, bright and alive, the foursome go happily nuts with great results. Cope is already a commanding singer and frontman; his clever lyrics and strong projection result in a series of confident performances, whether his trading lines with himself on the motorik chug of "Sleeping Gas" or his yelps on "Books." For all the bad energy between himself and Balfe, the two sound like they're grafted at the hip throughout, the latter's keyboard washes and staccato melodies adding the fun, nervy vibe. Dwyer's spot-on drumming keeps the pace, while both guitarists, Finkler and his replacement Gill, don't drown the band in feedback to the exclusion of everything else. One listen to many of Gill's pieces, on songs like "Poppies," and Cope's oft-stated claim that early U2 was trying to rip off the Teardrops and other Liverpool/Manchester groups makes sense. Though it was assembled from a variety of different sessions *Kilimanjaro* still sounds cohesive. When it comes to the hit singles, it's no surprise songs like "Treason" and the brilliant "Reward," with its snarky opening line "Bless my cotton socks, I'm in the news today!" were such huge smashes. Perfectly hummable choruses, great arrangements and production and Cope's smiling vibe all add up with fantastic results. The sweet romance of "When I Dream" closes out this entertaining debut. *—Ned Raggett*

Wilder / Nov. 1981 / Mercury ♦♦♦
Despite the flux they were going through, the Teardrops somehow got it together to record the heavily-hyped *Wilder*, which unlike its predecessor did nothing in terms of sales or smash singles, outside of the semi-successful shimmering keyboard/crunch of "Passionate Friend." This isn't for lack of talent on the band's part, and the trademark kicky arrangements and horns appear throughout. However, unlike the joyous outpourings of *Kilimanjaro*, *Wilder* sounds distanced. Cope doesn't come across as the lead singer so much as he does someone singing with the music, ironic given that he wrote everything on this album. As a subtler pleasure, though, *Wilder* offers up some good stuff, with more cryptic compositions and performances throughout, while Clive Langer takes over full production after only doing a few on the first album. Strangely, some performances sound like where Sting eventually took the Police on *Synchronicity*, musically if not

vocally, like the layered attempts at tribal drumming on "Seven Views of Jerusalem." More measured, sometimes stiff songs like "Falling Down Around Me" make the overall mood more fragmented, while some of Balfe's keyboards sound like they're only there just because. When it connects, though, *Wilder* rocks just fine. The concluding track, "The Great Dominions," is one of Cope's all-time best, with a sweeping, epic sense of scope and sound. The angular funk of "The Culture Bunker" has both some fine guitar and a sharp lyric or two on Cope's part—the "crucial three" he refers to was his bedroom-only act with Ian McCulloch and Pete Wylie. Other high points include the moody synth shadings on "Tiny Children," where Balfe's work comes through best of all, and Dwyer's generally sharp drumming throughout, keeping the beat well. *—Ned Raggett*

Piano / 1990 / Document ♦♦♦
Piano collects The Teardrop Explodes' early recordings, featuring three singles and three tracks recorded for compilations. The songs make it clear the band was still trying to figure out their musical direction, but *Piano* is fascinating listening for dedicated fans of the group. *—Stephen Thomas Erlewine*

Everybody Wants to Shag the Teardrop Explodes / May 1990 / Fontana ♦♦♦
The title was originally intended for the band's debut, but attaching it to the long-unreleased third and final Teardrops album, an expansion of the four-track *You Disappear From View* EP, is as good a use as any. Cope trashed these sessions shortly after they were completed, but admitted years later that it wasn't all that bad. While this is a Balfe album more than anything else (he's credited with all the arrangements) with Cope on vocals, the rapidly collapsing band, augmented by a variety of other players, still manages to get in some good work. Cope certainly sounds like he's not entirely there at points—particularly on the lengthy opening number "Ouch Monkeys," where his voice is mixed in the background while Balfe's lounge-styled lead keyboards play against spectral choir sounds and echoed drums. Much of the percussion is a combination of Dwyer's suddenly arena-scaled pounding and rhythm box pulses, which, combined with the lack of guitars on all but two songs oftens transforms the Teardrops into something approaching New Romantic synth rock! "You Disappear From View" sounds like a reject from Spandau Ballet's early days. Often cuts sound like demos for fuller arrangements, which turned out to be the case for two of the songs, "Metranil Vavin" and "Sex (Pussyface)," which Cope recut on his solo debut *World Shut Your Mouth*. When Cope is fully engaged in the material, like on the charging "Count to Ten and Run For Cover," or the gently mysterious flow of "Soft Enough For You," it's a gentle revelation. A ringer concludes things—"Strange House in the Snow," an off-kilter, wiggy 1980-era cut with Gill on guitar. *—Ned Raggett*

Tears for Fears

f. 1981
College Rock, Pop/Rock, New Wave
Tears for Fears were always more ambitious than the average synth-pop group. From the beginning, the duo of Roland Orzabal and Curt Smith were tackling big subjects—their very name derived from Arthur Janov's primal scream therapy, and his theories were evident throughout their debut, *The Hurting*. Driven by catchy, infectious synth-pop, *The Hurting* became a big hit in their native England, setting the stage for international stardom with their second album, 1985's *Songs from the Big Chair*. On the strength of the singles "Everybody Wants To Rule the World" and "Shout," the record became a major hit, establishing the duo as one of the leading acts of the second generation of MTV stars. Instead of quickly recording a follow-up, Tears for Fears labored over their third album, the psychedelic and jazz-rock-tinged *The Seeds of Love*. While the album was a big hit, it was the end of an era instead of a new beginning. Smith left the group early in the '90s, and Orzabal continued with Tears for Fears, pursuing more sophisticated and pretentious directions to a smaller audience. *—Stephen Thomas Erlewine*

The Hurting / Mar. 1983 / Mercury ♦♦♦♦♦
Roland Orzabal and Curt Smith's debut featured the morose synth-pop hits "Pale Shelter" and "Mad World." *—Scott Bultman*

Songs from the Big Chair / 1985 / Mercury ♦♦♦♦♦
If *The Hurting* was mental anguish, *Songs From the Big Chair* marks the progression towards emotional healing, a particularly bold sort of catharsis culled from Roland Orzabal and Curt Smith's shared attraction to primal scream therapy. The album also heralded a dramatic maturation in the band's music, away from the synth-pop brand with which it was (unjustly) seared following the debut, and towards a complex, enveloping pop sophistication. The songwriting of Orzabal, Smith, and keyboardist Ian Stanley took a huge leap forward, drawing on reserves of palpable emotion and lovely, protracted melodies that draw just as much on soul and R&B music as they do on immediate pop hooks. The album could almost be called pseudo-conceptual, as each song holds its place and each is integral to the overall tapestry, a single-minded resolve that is easy to overlook when an album is as commercially successful as *Songs From the Big Chair*. And commercially successful it was, containing no less than three huge commercial radio hits, including the dramatic and insistent march, "Shout" and the shimmering, cascading "Head Over Heels," which, tellingly, is actually part of a song suite on the album. Orzabal and Smith's penchant for theorizing with steely-eyed austerity was mistaken for harsh bombasticism in some quarters, but separated from its era, the album only seems earnestly passionate and immediate, and each song has the same driven intent and the same glistening remoteness. It is not only a commercial triumph, it is an artistic *tour de force*. And in the loping, percolating "Everybody Wants to Rule the World," Tears for Fears perfectly captured the zeitgeist of the mid-'80s while impossibly managing to also create a dreamy, timeless pop classic. *Songs From the Big Chair* is one of the finest statements of the decade. *—Stanton Swihart*

The Seeds of Love / Sep. 1989 / Fontana ♦♦♦
Along with *Songs From the Big Chair, The Seeds of Love* was part of a one-two artistic punch in the late '80s that situated Tears For Fears as one of the decade's more ambitious pop groups. But at the time, Tears was more a platform for Roland Orzabal than a true band—Curt Smith is present only on the smash "Sowing the Seeds of Love" (his only co-writing credit), while Ian Stanley was replaced by Nicky Holland as a keyboardist and Orzabal's songwriting partner. Like their other albums, *The Seeds Of Love* continues the concept of moving from hurting to healing to beginning anew (the hit "Sowing the Seeds of Love") to growing apart. The songs feature expansive melodies instead of blatant hooks, and the sound is more grounded in soul and gospel on songs like "Woman in Chains," the updated Philly-soul strain of "Advice for the Young at Heart" and "Badman's Song." Orzabal's passionate vocals are well matched by Oleta Adams' fervent contributions. The group even dabbles in jazz on "Standing on the Corner of the Third World," the fabulous "Swords and Knives," and the slow-burning "Year of the Knife." As for the title track, it manages to be insanely intricate as well as catchy. Full of arcane references, lovely turns of phrase, and perfectly matched suite-like parts, it updates the orchestral grandiosity—though not the actual sound—of the Beatles' psychedelic period. It's completely different from the polished, atmospheric soul that surrounds it, but paradoxically, it's also the album's cornerstone. "Sowing the Seeds of Love" is the apotheosis of Orzabal and Smith's evolution together, and foreshadowed their impending split: the two parted on bad terms during the album, ensuring yet another change in the band's direction thereafter. *—Stanton Swihart*

Tears Roll Down: Greatest Hits 82-92 / Mar. 17, 1992 / Fontana ♦♦♦♦
Capturing some of their chart-topping smashes and other key tracks, Tears for Fears marks a monumental career with their collection *Tears Roll Down: Greatest Hits 82-92*. Toward the end of the praise surrounding their third album, 1991's *Seeds of Love*, Curt Smith left the band. Roland Orzabal was left to sail the ship alone, and the strong success dwindled years later. However, this dozen-track compilation showcases some of the band's early tracks heavily dominated by pulsating bass drops and heavy synth beats.
"Pale Shelter" and "Mad World" from their 1982 debut *The Hurting* moved toward the soul-defining musical maturation found on 1985's groundbreaking staple *Songs From the Big Chair*. The Top Ten hits are undoubtedly featured: "Everybody Wants to Rule the World," "Shout," and the more obscure "Mothers Talk." The luscious "Head Over Heels" cuts short of it's closing guitar work, a disappointment in the grand scheme of Tears for Fears' synth-dominated sound. Such layered riffs separated the rawness from the fluffy new wave aspect. "Sowing the Seeds of Love" marked the band's own branded progressive rock & roll, but "Woman in Chains," the gospel-tinged cut featuring guest vocals from Oleta Adams, was their most spiritual effort. Essentially, the dozen-track collection is a perfect look at what Tears for Fears did for music during the '80s until the mid-'90s. They made new wave sound cool and melodically beautiful. *—MacKenzie Wilson*

Elemental / Jun. 22, 1993 / Mercury ♦♦

Raoul and the Kings of Spain / Oct. 10, 1995 / Epic ♦♦
The second Tears for Fears album following Curt Smith's departure finds Roland Orzabel treading water (and self-consciously deep water at that). Long removed from the simple, melodic melancholy of the band's early work and abandoning the mid-period Beatles-influenced pop, *Raoul and the Kings of Spain* often borders on progressive rock. There's some genuinely pretty, if unexciting, music like the piano-driven ballad "Secrets," with it's soaring guitar line, and the gentle "Sketches of Pain." Unfortunately, everything is undone by Orzabel's lyrics (mostly co-written with guitarist/keyboardist Alan Griffiths). There seems to be a lack of ideas that cannot be concealed by the words, which are either inscrutable or embarrassingly silly ("What's the matter with your life/Did someone come and shoot your wife," he asks on "Sorry"). Listeners on both sides of the Atlantic couldn't be bothered and the act's commercial fortunes fell even further. *—Tom Demalon*

Saturnine Martial & Lunatic / Aug. 1996 / Mercury ♦♦♦
Spanning the group's prime period of 1983 to 1993, *Saturnine Martial & Lunatic* is an odd, incomplete collection of B-sides and rarities from Tears For Fears. Although this material is valuable for hardcore fans, it only scratches the surface of the group's B-sides. Nevertheless, several prime tracks—including the non-LP U.K. hit single "The Way You Are" and a cover of David Bowie's "Ashes to Ashes"—are featured, which makes it worthwhile for dedicated fans, even though its incompleteness (especially since it comes at the expense of several weaker latter-day cuts) will make *Saturnine Martial & Lunatic* a frustrating listen. *—Stephen Thomas Erlewine*

20th Century Masters—The Millennium Collection: The Best of Tears for Fears / Jun. 27, 2000 / Mercury ♦♦♦♦
The Millennium Collection: The Best of Tears for Fears mixes their biggest hits, including "Shout," "Everybody Wants to Rule the World," "Head Over Heels," and "Mothers Talk," with a sprinkling of rarities like the B-side "Pharoahs" and single versions of "Change" and "Advice for the Young at Heart." "Sowing the Seeds of Love," "Woman in Chains," and "Break It Down Again" complete this concise but worthwhile look at Tears for Fears' diverse, ambitious pop sound. *—Heather Phares*

● **Shout: The Very Best of Tears for Fears** / Sep. 25, 2001 / Uptown/Universal ♦♦♦♦

The Tee Set

f. 1966, Delft, Holland, **db.** 1971
AM Pop
The Tee Set—Peter Tetteroo (vocals), Dill Dennink (guitar, flute, banjo), Joop Bloom (drums), Franklin Madjid (bass), and Hans Van Eijck (keyboards)—was one of a handful of acts from Holland that made it onto the American charts in the late 1960s; others included the Shocking Blue ("Venus") and the George Baker Selection ("Little Green Bag"), both of whom had the same American representative, Jerry Ross. Recorded in 1969, "Ma

Belle Amie" was a pleasant piece of pop/rock first issued in Holland, where it sold 100,000 copies (a major hit in the small Dutch market). "Ma Belle Amie" was heard by Ross and licensed for release in America, where it became their only major hit. —*Bruce Eder*

● **Emotion** / 1994 / RPM ✦✦✦✦
A reissue of their 1966 debut album, doubled in length for CD with the addition of some 1966-67 singles and a solo 45 by lead vocalist Peter Tetteroo. Most of the material's original (although much of it was supplied by non-member Hans Van Eijck), but while the band plays competently and Tetteroo's a talented blue-eyed soulster, the songs are largely unmemorable mid-'60s soul pastiches (with some vague flower pop influence on some of the later sides). There *are* a couple standout tracks—the swampy "Play That Record" in particular is a buried treasure, and "Colours of the Rainbow" is the most dead-on emulation of Stevie Winwood in his Spencer Davis days that you'll ever come across. "Ma Belle Amie," released a few years after the era this compilation covers, ain't here; it can be found on Rhino's *Super Hits of the '70s: Have a Nice Day, Vol. 2* compilation. —*Richie Unterberger*

24 Carat / 1997 / Angel Air ✦✦✦✦
Betcha didn't know that the Tee Set had no less than 21 Dutch hits in the '60s and '70s. They're all here on this single-disc compilation, which also adds a couple of late-'60s singles by singer Peter Tetteroo. The packaging is exemplary—lengthy liner notes, reproductions of numerous vintage 45 sleeves, and a Tee Set family tree. The fact remains that nothing sounds as good as the one song which made it in the U.S., "Ma Belle Amie," which is included, of course, along with its soul-rock follow-up "If You Do Believe in Love," which just missed the U.S. Top 40. Otherwise, it's not terribly distinguished stuff, regardless of its considerable success in its homeland. It incorporates bits of blue-eyed soul, pop-rock, bubblegum, and progressive without adding up to anything too arresting, with the occasional tinge of something out of the ordinary, as in the Eurofolk-flavored "A Sunny Day in Greece," or "What Can I Do," which sounds like a mongrel of Eric Burdon and the Four Tops. RPM's *Emotion* compilation, which concentrates on their earliest and most R&B-influenced recordings, is actually a better listen, although it doesn't include "Ma Belle Amie." —*Richie Unterberger*

Teenage Fanclub

f. 1989, Glasgow, Scotland
Pop Underground, Indie Pop, Power Pop, Alternative Pop/Rock

Teenage Fanclub are three singer/songwriters from Glasgow and a drummer who make unearthly pop music but remain under-appreciated. So what else is new?

    Though Mersey Beat is at the core of their shimmering pop tunes, unlike the Beatles, it's often difficult to distinguish the voices of Norman Blake, Gerry Love and Raymond McGinley as their songs serve the band entity as one very pleasing whole. But like the Beatles, they sing with American accents. Even before their Matador debut, *A Catholic Education*, the indie sensation of 1990, the band had already made a splash as the pick to click in their native U.K.'s trendy music press. It was their second album, *Bandwagonesque* for Geffen that put the Scots on the pop music map. Long before the record was released, insiders talked of how this album was going to blow some minds. Indeed it did, and ended up on most critic's ten-best lists for the year. But not because it was a continuation of the dark and slow indie-trend formula they created for Matador, rather it sounded like a lost Big Star album. The Fanclub made no secret about their love for the obscure American pop band and it was a sound that stuck over the course of their next two albums, *Thirteen* and *Grand Prix.* —*Denise Sullivan*

A Catholic Education / 1990 / Matador ✦✦✦✦
Hard to believe now, but Teenage Fanclub first attracted critical attention for a record far removed from the sparkling power pop on which their fame largely rests—with its gloriously sloppy and sludgy sound, their debut album *A Catholic Education* instead prefigures the emergence of grunge, its viscous melodies and squalling guitars owing far more to Neil Young than Big Star. With not one but two songs dubbed "Heavy Metal," it's pretty obvious where *A Catholic Education* is coming from; the title track (also here in duplicate) is a surprisingly snarky attack on the church (at least for a band not exactly renowned for its political agenda), while the great "Everybody's Fool" is a merciless scenester put-down without any of the gentle sarcasm that characterizes similarly themed efforts like *Bandwagonesque*'s "Metal Baby." Regardless, for all its glaring differences in attitude and approach, there's no mistaking the effortless melodicism that remains the hallmark of all Teenage Fanclub records—in particular, the opening "Everything Flows," for all its meandering abrasiveness, is still as good as anything the band ever recorded, and that's saying something. —*Jason Ankeny*

● **Bandwagonesque** / Nov. 19, 1991 / DGC ✦✦✦✦✦
The gold standard of the early-'90s power pop revival, in its own way *Bandwagoneque* was as much a benchmark as contemporary records like *Nevermind* and *Loveless*; though not the generational rallying cry of the former nor the revolutionary sonic breakthrough of the latter, Teenage Fanclub's sophomore album nevertheless heralded the return of melody and craft, coupled with energy and spirit—hallmarks of much of the greatest rock & roll of the past, and virtues as rare as hen's teeth in the years immediately prior to the disc's release. Although its incandescent harmonies, lazily immediate songs, and crunching guitars earned it endless comparisons to vintage Big Star, *Bandwagonesque* is in every way a product of its own time—the thick, grungy sound of the Fannies' debut *A Catholic Education* remains intact for gems like "What You Do to Me" (arguably the most brilliantly simpleminded love song ever penned) and the instrumental "Satan," while the lyrics of other standout moments like "Star Sign" and "Alcoholiday" reflect a *laissez faire* irony and unassuming genius even more emblematic of the moment in question. —*Jason Ankeny*

Thirteen / Nov. 9, 1993 / DGC ✦✦✦✦
Unjustly savaged by fans and critics alike upon its initial release, with the benefit of hindsight *Thirteen* has revealed itself an eminently worthy follow-up to the classic *Bandwagonesque*; though not as consistent or refreshing as its predecessor, the album takes simultaneous steps backward and forward, retreating to a darker, sludgier guitar sound reminiscent of their debut effort *A Catholic Education* even as it blossoms to incorporate lilting string arrangements and glowing harmony vocals. Despite taking its title from Big Star's most gentle and optimistic moment, the record not only expands its horizons far beyond Alex Chilton-inspired pop but also maintains an emotional tenor that's largely bitter and disillusioned—titles like "Song to the Cynic," "120 Mins," and, especially, "Commercial Alternative" reflect the band's disenchantment with both its former flavor-of-the-month status and the growing creative malaise rampant throughout the alt-rock community (then at its commercial zenith). Although Gerard Love and Raymond McGinley make memorable contributions, *Thirteen* is first and foremost a showcase for the peerless pop genius of Norman Blake—the should-have-been hits "Norman 3" and "Ret Liv Dead" boast a crunchy, lumbering sound heavily indebted to Neil Young's records with Crazy Horse, while the soaring "Commercial Alternative" evokes vintage Byrds, a reference point further driven home by the epic closer "Gene Clark." [Original pressings of *Thirteen* included no fewer than six unlisted bonus cuts assembled from British singles—the material is consistently excellent, highlighted by the McGinley original "Golden Glades" as well as reverent covers of Phil Ochs' "Chords of Fame" and the Flying Burrito Brothers' "Older Guys."] —*Jason Ankeny*

Deep Fried Fanclub / 1995 / Paperhouse/Fire ✦✦

Grand Prix / Jul. 3, 1995 / DGC ✦✦✦✦
For all of the brilliance of records like *Bandwagonesque* and the underrated *Thirteen*, at times Teenage Fanclub seemed little more than a showcase for the laconic melodic genius of Norman Blake—fairly or not, the songwriting contributions of bandmates Gerard Love and Raymond McGinley suffered mightily by comparison, mere filler when stacked alongside Blake-penned marvels like "The Concept" and "Norman 3." That said, the superb *Grand Prix* is perhaps the truest group effort in the Fannies' catalog—more than ever before, their democratic approach truly bears fruit, and it's indicative of the disc's uniform excellence that the first Blake composition, the lovely "Mellow Doubt," doesn't even surface until track three, by which time McGinley's "About You" and Love's harmony-rich "Sparky's Dream" have already firmly established the set's ragged-but-right tenor. While new drummer Paul Quinn fails to recreate the buoyantly reckless abandon of the sacked Brendan O'Hare, *Grand Prix* otherwise captures complete creative synergy—in particular, "Don't Look Back" is Love's watershed moment, a gorgeously wistful love song highlighted by wittily lovelorn lyrics like "I'd steal a car to drive you home," as good a pick-up line as anything in the annals of rock & roll. Not everything works (McGinley's "Verisimilitude" goes nowhere fast) and Blake's contributions are still the highlights ("Neil Jung" and "I'll Make It Clear" are simply perfect pop songs), but *Grand Prix* is ultimately the product of a band at the peak of its collective powers, not as much a landmark as *Bandwagonesque* but every bit as good on its own terms. —*Jason Ankeny*

Songs From Northern Britain / Jul. 29, 1997 / Columbia ✦✦✦
Grand Prix's release was a shot in the arm for a Scottish quartet who had somehow survived all the obnoxious ephemeral fads the Brits inanely obsess about, but whose sound and style were wearing out a too-familiar welcome. TFC cut out the super-muff fuzz, vague metalisms, and (compost) heaps of grunge that had littered their backing tracks since the slow-hammering "Everything Flows" and the album *A Catholic Education* caught everyone's surprised ear. Yet they kept their (royal) flush of riffs, hooks, harmonies, and wistful melodies that have often made listeners sing along since "Starsign." In doing so, the eminently friendly gents gave the bums' rush to the Frankenstein-experiment meld of Big Star mania and Dinosaur Jr. worship on their better-known earlier work. They were more in the vein of the Byrds' timeless, starry-eyed pop. Along comes album number five and it's all but a replica of *Grand Prix*, like side three and four of a double LP. More slashing, enervated riffs, some of the nicest, deepest harmonies around, and one modest pop joy after another, none overdone. Songs such as "It's a Bad World," "I Don't Want Control of You," and the piano-brimming cool-shaker "Mount Everest" seem to melt into listeners' insides like butter on a pancake. Sure, Norman Blake and company are still too constricted (too many songs are alike, an old TFC bugaboo, despite the luxury of three songwriter/singers) and one can still picture their current pal, Alex Chilton, singing each of these songs. But with material, production, enthusiasm, and craftsmanship of this order, Teenage Fanclub makes a fine bid to make music commensurate with their heroes; they deserve to once again rule the alternative airwaves as they did in 1991-1992, though it doesn't seem like they will. —*Jack Rabid, The Big Takeover*

Howdy / Nov. 21, 2000 / Columbia ✦✦✦
For better or worse, the only thing that truly sticks out on Teenage Fanclub's sixth studio record is the title. It's the worst in rock & roll since *Ass*. However, "howdy" is a fitting way to sum up these 12 simple, humble pop songs, most of which are light-hearted and cheery. It would be easy—and understandable to a certain degree—if die-hard Fanclub fans felt letdown with the band flying in a stylistic holding pattern, though the influences on this one tend to point toward the hushed side of the Hollies more than the previous indebtedness to the Byrds and Big Star. Those feeling robbed should look at it this way: Just how many bands can last over a decade and continue to make completely non-cynical, non-cloying pop as well as Teenage Fanclub? Not many. There is zero flash. No blazing distortion, no extreme emotion, no showiness whatsoever. What's apparent is top-drawer craft, lovely three-part harmonies, delicately strummed guitars, and flawless arrangements. Nothing here is going to knock you off your feet, but is that such a bad thing? One of the best charms of *Howdy* is how you can put it on and have your mood improved

without having to put much thought into it. It doesn't take many plays to get your head around it, but it's anything but disposable or throwaway. They set out to make a good pop record, and they succeeded. It's by no means a landmark, and it's not close to their best; it's just well-done. There's nothing wrong with turning it up to five every now and then, is there? *—Andy Kellman*

Telegraph Avenue

Psychedelic, Prog-Rock/Art Rock

One of the few Peruvian groups from the early 1970s to have had their material reissued in the U.S., Telegraph Avenue were formed in 1970 after lead guitarist Bo Ichikawa had been exposed to hippie music and culture following a six-month stay in San Francisco. Singing in English, Telegraph Avenue were an average if competent amalgam of various strands of rock circa 1970—The Beatles, Californian psychedelia and soul-rock. They had a lighter and poppier feel than the heavy rock predominating in Northern Hemisphere bands in the early '70s, possibly because bands from South America tended to sound a little behind the trends due to their relative isolation from most of the rock world. Occasionally they incorporated Latin percussion, but the Peruvian and South American feel was never so audible to make average listeners automatically suspect that the music was South American in origin. They put out an album in 1971 and their second, final LP in 1975, and their material was reissued on CD in the States by Lazarus Audio Products in the late 1990s. *—Richie Unterberger*

Telegraph Avenue / 1997 / Lazarus Audio Products ♦♦♦

The liner notes are frustratingly vague on the origins of these 16 tracks. But because the first eight songs feature the lineup that played on their first album and the next eight songs the lineup that played on their second album, it seems reasonable to assume that this compiles most or all of the material from Telegraph Avenue's two LPs. It's pleasant if not engaging listening, and sometimes pretty easy to tell where the influence is coming from. "Lauralie" sounds like a variation of Tommy James' "Crystal Blue Persuasion," for instance, while "Happy" has enough late-Beatles pop ambience to please fans of Badfinger or the Nazz; "Sometimes in Winter" has some traits of Santana. Some slight South American folk elements cruise in on tracks like "Sungaligali." The final eight cuts, presumably taken from the 1975 album, are a little more hard rock guitar-oriented, but don't sound all that heavier than the previous ones (presumably taken from the 1971 album). These mid-'70s tracks have an anachronistic feel that makes them feel a few years behind the times, which is if anything a compliment, not a putdown. *—Richie Unterberger*

Television

f. 1973, New York, NY, **db.** 1978

American Punk, New York Punk, Proto-Punk, Punk

Television were one of the most creative bands to emerge from New York's punk scene of the mid-'70s, creating an influential new guitar vocabulary. While guitarists Tom Verlaine and Richard Lloyd liked to jam, they didn't follow the accepted rock structures for improvisation—they removed the blues while retaining the raw energy of garage rock, adding complex, lyrical solo lines that recalled both jazz and rock. With its angular rhythms and fluid leads, Television's music always went in unconventional directions, laying the groundwork for many of the guitar-based post-punk pop groups of the late '70s and '80s. Soon after forming, the band began to build up an underground following. After Television recorded an abortive demo tape in 1975 with Brian Eno for release on Island, bassist Richard Hell left to form the Heartbreakers and later mount a solo career. One year later the band released a British EP on Stiff, then signed with Elektra for their debut album, 1977's *Marquee Moon*. Released to great critical acclaim and a high position on the British charts, it failed to attract a wide audience in America. Television's second album *Adventure* was a Top Ten hit in Britain, though the group broke up scant months later, largely due to tensions between the two guitarists (who both pursued solo careers). Nearly 14 years after their breakup, Television recorded a new album for Capitol and toured to support it, but disbanded again in 1993. *—Stephen Thomas Erlewine*

★ **Marquee Moon** / 1977 / Elektra ♦♦♦♦♦

Marquee Moon is a revolutionary album, but it's a subtle, understated revolution. Without question, it is a guitar rock album—it's astonishing to hear the interplay between Tom Verlaine and Richard Lloyd—but it is a guitar rock album unlike any other. Where their predecessors in the New York punk scene, most notably the Velvet Underground, had fused blues structures with avant garde flourishes, Television completely strips away any sense of swing or groove, even when they are playing standard three chord changes. *Marquee Moon* is comprised entirely of tense garage rockers that spiral into heady intellectual territory, which is achieved through the group's long, interweaving instrumental sections, not through Tom Verlaine's words. That alone made *Marquee Moon* a trailblazing album—it's impossible to imagine post-punk soundscapes without it. Of course, it wouldn't have had such an impact if Verlaine hadn't written an excellent set of songs that conveyed a fractured urban mythology unlike any of his contemporaries. From the nervy opener "See No Evil" to the majestic title track, there is simply not a bad song on the entire record. And what has kept *Marquee Moon* fresh over the years is how Television fleshes out Verlaine's poetry into sweeping sonic epics. *—Stephen Thomas Erlewine*

Adventure / 1978 / Elektra ♦♦♦♦♦

Television's ground-breaking first album, *Marquee Moon*, was as close to a perfect debut as any band made in the 1970s, and in many respects it would have been all but impossible for the band to top it. One senses that Television knew this, because *Adventure* seems designed to avoid the comparisons by focusing on a different side of the band's personality. Where *Marquee Moon* was direct and straightforward in its approach, with the subtleties clearly in the performance and not in the production, *Adventure* is a decidedly softer and less aggressive disc, and while John Jansen's production isn't intrusive, it does round off the edges of the band's sound in a way Andy Johns' work on the first album did not. But the two qualities that really made *Marquee Moon* so special were Tom Verlaine's songs, and the way his guitar work meshed with that of Richard Lloyd, whose style was less showy but whose gifts were just as impressive, and if you have to listen a bit harder to *Adventure*, it doesn't take long to realize that both of those virtues are more than apparent here, and while one might wish the sound had a bit more bite on "Foxhole" or "Ain't That Nothin'," the quieter, more layered sound is just what the doctor ordered for "Glory" and "The Dream's Dream." Sure, *Marquee Moon* is a better album, but *Adventure* has one of the greatest guitar bands of all time playing superbly on a set of truly fine songs, and albums like this come along far too infrequently for anyone to ignore music this pleasurable simply on the grounds of relative evaluation; it's not quite a masterpiece, but it's a brilliant record by any yardstick. *—Mark Deming*

The Blow Up / 1982 / ROIR ♦♦♦

Double live albums frequently come off as redundant and indulgent, but in the case of Television, *The Blow Up* comes awfully close to being an essential document, simply because the band's studio albums didn't always capture the rawness and spontaneity that fueled their on-stage improvisations. Both of those qualities are present on *The Blow Up* in abundance; the sound quality is not exactly pristine, but the performances, recorded in 1978 on what proved to be the band's final tour, are exciting and frequently breathtaking, capturing a side of the band that will enlighten anyone wondering how Television's intricate, layered sound was ever tagged "punk." Six songs from *Marquee Moon* and two from *Adventure* appear, plus covers of "Satisfaction," "Knockin' on Heaven's Door," and the 13th Floor Elevators' "Fire Engine" (here renamed as the album's title track). It's interesting to hear the shorter songs outside of a studio setting, but the album's real treasures are the second half's nearly 15-minute versions of "Little Johnny Jewel" and "Marquee Moon," which are loaded with the improvisational fireworks that helped build Television's reputation. Anyone seeking a more complete, rounded picture of the band after digesting *Marquee Moon* should eventually find their way here. *—Steve Huey*

Television / Sep. 28, 1992 / Capitol ♦♦♦

After the breakthrough success of Nirvana's *Nevermind* in 1991, it seemed (at least for a while) that many of the tributaries of the American punk movement might finally have a chance to break through to a larger audience, and a number of seminal bands from the salad days of punk and new wave made reunion albums, imagining they might have a better chance to be heard than they did in the 1970s or '80s. Television were an especially strong example of a band whose influence and reputation far outstripped their commercial impact, so it's not that surprising that the group decided to reunite in 1992 and see if the mass audience might finally be prepared for them. However, Television's intricate guitar attack and elliptical melodies would have been a hard sell under ideal circumstances, and it didn't help much that the group's comeback disc, simply called *Television*, sounded even less approachable than the music of their masterpiece, *Marquee Moon*. With its skeletal melodies, starkly dynamic arrangements, and cryptically witty lyrics, *Television* sounds like one of Tom Verlaine's post-1982 solo albums more than anything else, but with one important difference—here, Verlaine is working with a second guitarist who is actually worth his while, and while on this set everyone seems to follow Verlaine's lead, with Richard Lloyd on hand to trade licks with Tom, and Fred Smith and Billy Ficca holding down the rhythm section with unobtrusive strength, it's easily the strongest record Verlaine made since *Dreamtime* in 1981. Anyone wanting to know why Television were one of the most important bands of their time needs to start with *Marquee Moon*, but if you want further proof that Tom Verlaine and Richard Lloyd truly bring out the best in each other's guitar work, this album will certainly help. *—Mark Deming*

Television Personalities

f. 1977, London, England, **db.** 1991

Indie Rock, Post-Punk, New Wave, Alternative Pop/Rock

Britain's Television Personalities enjoyed one of the new wave era's longest, most erratic, and most far-reaching careers. Over the course of a musical evolution which led them from wide-eyed, shambling pop to the outer reaches of psychedelia and back, the group directly influenced virtually every major pop uprising of the period, with artists as diverse as feedback virtuosos the Jesus and Mary Chain, twee pop titans the Pastels, and lo-fi kingpins Pavement readily acknowledging the TVPs' inspiration. Always a loose-knit group, the first relatively stable TVP line-up consisted of singer/songwriter Dan Treacy, organist vocalist Ed Ball, and guitarist Joe Foster, who recorded the band's 1980 debut *And Don't the Kids Just Love It*, a step into psychedelic pop typified by songs like "I Know Where Syd Barrett Lives." Treacy and Ball soon founded their own label, Whaam! to issue 1981's *Mummy You're Not Watching Me*, which made the Personalities one of the figureheads of a London psychedelia revival. Ball exited around the time of the release of 1982's *They Could Have Been Bigger Than the Beatles*, a collection of re-recordings. 1984's dark, moody *The Painted Word* was followed by the 1985 live set *Chocolat-Art*, by which point the TVPs were in dire straits; broke and without a label, the group could do little but infrequently perform live for several years. The band finally won a contract with Fire Records in 1989, eventually issuing the 1992 double LP *Closer to God*; despite critical approval, the album failed to find an audience, and Treacy reportedly fell prey to depression and drug problems. After several more years of occasional singles, they issued the harrowing *I Was a Mod Before You Was a Mod*. *—Jason Ankeny*

Bill Grundy / 1979 / Rough Trade ♦♦♦

And Don't the Kids Just Love It / 1980 / Razor & Tie ♦♦♦♦♦

The cover of... *And Don't the Kids Just Love It*—a collage bringing together supermodel

Twiggy and *The Avengers'* John Steed—is a strong indication of where the Television Personalities are coming from: their debut is a loving ode to sixties-era pop and pop culture, referencing movies ("Look Back in Anger"), Kinks-like class commentary ("Geoffrey Ingram") and psychedelic casualties ("I Know Where Syd Barrett Lives"). *—Jason Ankeny*

Mummy You're Not Watching Me / 1981 / Whaam! ♦♦♦♦
Where the TVPs merely tested the waters of psychedelia on their debut releases, they take the full plunge on the lo-fi *Mummy You're Not Watching Me*, which replaces the pop-culture references of the debut... *And Don't the Kids Just Love It* for the high culture of acid-pop excursions including "Lichtenstein Painting," "David Hockney's Diaries" and "Painting by Numbers." *—Jason Ankeny*

They Could Have Been Bigger Than the Beatles / 1982 / Whaam! ♦♦♦

The Painted Word / 1984 / Whaam! ♦♦♦
A more cleanly produced TVPs record than most of their previous efforts, *The Painted Word* is also a more serious album, less whimsical but no less charming; favoring a subtle, droning pop sound, tracks like the politically charged "Back to Vietnam" and the lovely "Someone to Share My Life With" are heartfelt and resonant, foreshadowing the more dramatic twists taken by Dan Treacy's songwriting following the band's long late-1980s layoff. *—Jason Ankeny*

Chocolat-Art / 1985 / Pastell ♦♦♦

● **Privilege** / 1989 / Fire ♦♦♦♦♦
Given that the crisp *Privilege* is the Television Personalities' first studio LP in four years, Dan Treacy has every right to be in a less-than-sunny mood—songs like "All My Dreams Are Dead," "This Time There's No Happy Ending" and "Sad Mona Lisa" are to be expected when a fertile songwriting talent finds himself without means of recording and releasing new material. The end result is one of the group's most personal and dark records, although the wonderful "Salvador Dali's Art Party"—which runs down all of the luminaries on the guest list—is a return to the psychedelic name-dropping of the group's formative years. *—Jason Ankeny*

Camping in France / 1991 / Overground ♦♦♦

Closer to God / 1992 / Seed ♦♦♦♦
The TVPs' most musically accessible album to date, *Closer to God* is also their most gloomy (although it's a ray of sunshine when compared to its follow-up, *I Was a Mod Before You Was a Mod*). Embellished by bright arrangements, strings and horns, tracks like "This Heart's Not Made of Stone" and "Coming Home Soon" are white lies, upbeat productions masking downbeat songs; more honest are "My First Nervous Breakdown" and "Very Dark Today," which make no bones about the depths of Dan Treacy's despair. *—Jason Ankeny*

Yes Darling, But is It Art? (Early Singles & Rarities) / Feb. 14, 1995 / Fire ♦♦♦♦♦
A superb, generous introduction to the Television Personalities' early years, *Yes Darling, But Is It Art?* assembles rarities and obscurities from singles, EPs and various-artists collections dating back to the group's debut "14th Floor" and including their lone hit, "Part-Time Punks." *—Jason Ankeny*

I Was a Mod Before You Was a Mod / Oct. 1995 / Overground ♦♦♦
Virtually a Dan Treacy solo record, *I Was a Mod Before You Was a Mod* strips away all remaining vestiges of the buoyancy long associated with the Television Personalities, leaving behind a harrowing portrait of alienation, desperation and self-loathing; "A Stranger to Myself," "Haunted," "Evan Doesn't Ring Me Anymore," "A Long Time Gone" and "I Can See My Whole World Crashing Down" are frighteningly bleak and painfully affecting. *—Jason Ankeny*

Temple of the Dog

f. 1990, **db.** 1990
Grunge, Alternative Pop/Rock, Hard Rock
Temple of the Dog was a one-album project conceived in 1990. The purpose of Temple of the Dog was to pay tribute to the late Andrew Wood, the lead singer of Mother Love Bone, who died of a heroin overdose in 1990. Following his death, Mother Love Bone broke up, but Wood's bandmates Jeff Ament (bass) and Stone Gossard (guitar) decided to continue working together. Before Ament and Gossard formed a new band, they assembled Temple of the Dog, recruiting Chris Cornell (vocals) and Matt Cameron (drums) from Soundgarden to form the core of the group. Temple of the Dog also featured contributions from then-unknown vocalist Eddie Vedder and guitarist Mike McCready.

Temple of the Dog recorded their eponymous album in 1990, releasing it at the end of the year on A&M Records. The album received positive reviews upon its release, but didn't chart until the summer of 1992, when Pearl Jam—a band Ament, Gossard, Vedder, McCready, and drummer Dave Krusen formed in late 1990 after the completion of the Temple of the Dog album—had a Top Ten album with their debut record, *Ten*. Following the success of *Ten*, A&M re-released "Hunger Strike"—a duet between Vedder and Cornell—as a video and single, and the album quickly scaled the charts, reaching the Top Ten and going platinum before the end of 1992. *—Stephen Thomas Erlewine*

Temple of the Dog / Dec. 1990 / A&M ♦♦♦♦♦
Featuring members of Soundgarden and what would soon become Pearl Jam, Temple of the Dog's lone eponymous album might never have reached a wide audience if not for Pearl Jam's breakout success a year later. Nearly every founding member of Pearl Jam appears on *Temple of the Dog* (including the then-unknown Eddie Vedder), so perhaps it isn't surprising that the record sounds like a bridge between Mother Love Bone's theatrical '70s-rock updates and Pearl Jam's hard-rocking seriousness. What is surprising, though, is that Cornell is the dominant composer, writing the music on seven of the ten tracks (and lyrics on all). Keeping in mind that Soundgarden's previous album was the overblown metallic miasma of *Louder Than Love*, the accessibly warm, relatively clean sound of *Temple of the Dog* is somewhat shocking, and its mellower moments are minor revelations in terms of Cornell's songwriting abilities. It isn't just the band, either—Cornell displays more emotional range than ever before, and his melodies and song structures are (for the most part) pure, vintage hard rock. In fact, it's almost as though he's trying to write in the style of Mother Love Bone—which makes sense, since *Temple of the Dog* was a tribute to that band's late singer, Andrew Wood. Not every song here is directly connected to Wood; once several specific elegies were recorded, additional material grew quickly out of the group's natural chemistry. The album's strength is its mournful, elegiac ballads, but thanks to the band's spontaneous creative energy and appropriately warm sound, it's permeated by a definite, life-affirming aura. That may seem like a paradox, but consider the adage that funerals are more for the living than the dead; *Temple of the Dog* shows Wood's associates working through their grief and finding the strength to move on. *—Steve Huey*

The Temptations

f. 1960, Detroit, MI
Smooth Soul, Pop-Soul, Motown, R&B, Soul
Thanks to their fine-tuned choreography—and even finer harmonies—the Temptations became the definitive male vocal group of the 1960s; one of Motown's most elastic acts, they tackled both lush pop and politically-charged funk with equal flair, and weathered a steady stream of changes in personnel and consumer tastes with rare dignity and grace. After a series of flop singles, the Temps' fortunes changed dramatically in 1964 when they entered the studio with writer/producer Smokey Robinson, emerging with the pop smash "The Way You Do the Things You Do," the first in a series of 37 career Top Ten hits. With Robinson again at the helm, they returned in 1965 with their signature song, "My Girl," a Number One pop and R&B hit; other Top 20 hits that year included "It's Growing," "Since I Lost My Baby," "Don't Look Back," and "My Baby." In 1966, the Temps recorded another Robinson hit, "Get Ready," before forgoing his smooth popcraft for the harder-edged soul of producers Norman Whitfield and Brian Holland for a string of hits including "Ain't Too Proud to Beg," "Beauty's Only Skin Deep" and "(I Know) I'm Losing You." Beginning around 1967, Whitfield assumed full production control, and their records became ever rougher and more muscular, as typified by the 1968 success "I Wish It Would Rain." The Temptations next entered a psychedelic-influenced soul period following the success of the single "Cloud Nine." As the times changed, so did the group, and as the 1960s drew to a close, their music became overtly political; in the wake of "Cloud Nine"—its title a thinly-veiled drug allegory—came records like "Run Away Child, Running Wild," "Psychedelic Shack," and "Ball of Confusion (That's What the World Is Today)." While the Temps hit the charts regularly through 1973 with "Masterpiece," "Let Your Hair Down," and "The Plastic Man," their success as a pop act gradually dwindled as the 1970s wore on, and by the 1990s they were essentially an oldies act. *—Jason Ankeny*

Hum Along and Dance: More of the Best (1963-1974) / Feb. 16, 1993 / Rhino ♦♦♦♦
This 18-track compilation contains Temptations B-sides, non-hit cuts and obscure sides recorded from 1963-1974. It includes such sumptuous ballads as "What Love Has Joined Together" and "Gonna Keep On Trying Till I Win Your Love," plus uptempo wailers and an occasional dud ("Stop The War Now"). The early tracks show the group evolving from its doo-wop roots into soul's premier group. While the cuts on this disc aren't the ones that made The Temptations popular music institutions, they're still a vital part of their legacy. *—Ron Wynn*

Emperors of Soul / Sep. 20, 1994 / Motown ♦♦♦♦♦
The Temptations were unquestionably one of Motown's greatest groups, recording a large number of classic singles. They were also one of the handful of Motown groups that were able to successfully make the transition from the '60s to the '70s, giving them a sizable amount of quality material from both decades. *Emperors of Soul*, a lavishly produced five-CD box set, draws from The Temptations' entire career, treating all aspects of it with equal respect. For the dedicated fan, the box set is a treasure—the sound is great and there are numerous rarities. However, for most listeners, it is simply too much music, featuring too many unfamiliar songs. *—Stephen Thomas Erlewine*

☆ **Anthology** / May 23, 1995 / Motown ♦♦♦♦♦
There were three versions of this collection (first released in 1973) that provided a comprehensive overview of their career at Motown. The second (1986) collection was an update that featured digitally remastered sound and some later hits that were not featured in the earlier incarnation, like "Shakey Ground" (1975), "Power" (1980), and the excellent "Treat Her like a Lady" (1983). Unfortunately, the updated 1995 collection (like the previous two incarnations) omits many fine tracks recorded and released before their 1964 breakthrough, like "I Want a Love I Can See" (1962) and "Check Yourself" (1963). Even so, *Anthology* is a conciser, less-expensive alternative to the box-set *Emperors of Soul*. *—John Lowe*

One by One: The Best of Their Solo Years / Mar. 19, 1996 / Motown ♦♦♦
An interesting concept for a compilation, devoted to the most significant solo tracks by Temptations vocalists David Ruffin, Eddie Kendricks, Dennis Edwards, and Paul Williams. In other words, this two-CD, 35-track compilation isn't really a Temptations CD at all, although it's more appropriate to list it under their entry than anywhere else. The ex-Temps' solo outings had their high points, like David Ruffin's Top Ten hit "My Whole World Ended (The Moment You Left Me)," and Eddie Kendricks's "Keep on Truckin'." But overall, this isn't anything special, with a pleasantly generic late-period Motown sound that sometimes begs the inevitable unfavorable comparisons with the Temptations' own work, from the perspectives of both material and execution. Kendricks comes off best here, but Motown fans will be interested in the chance to track down many obscure minor

hits and flops by the singers, and even a few unreleased cuts. It's too late to do anything about it, but the best of these solo hits would have been far more appropriate selections for the *Emperors of Soul* box than most of the group-performed post-"Papa Was a Rolling Stone" material that made the cut. *—Richie Unterberger*

★ **The Ultimate Collection** / Mar. 25, 1997 / Motown ♦♦♦♦♦
The Ultimate Collection is just that, a superb introduction to the Temps' greatest hits. Included are 16 of the group's Top Ten smashes, among them "My Girl," "Get Ready," "Ain't Too Proud to Beg," "(I Know) I'm Losing You," "You're My Everything," "I Wish It Would Rain," "I Can't Get Next to You," "Ball Of Confusion," "Just My Imagination," and "Papa Was A Rolling Stone." *—Jason Ankeny*

Lost and Found: You've Got to Earn It (1962-1968) / Sep. 28, 1999 / Motown ♦♦♦♦
As one of the entries in Motown's *Lost and Found* series, this is a 20-track major find of largely unreleased Temptations material. It all originates from the early golden period of the group's history, with Eddie Kendricks and David Ruffin finding their groove with each track, redefining soul history while searching for a hit. Several tunes would go through lyric and arrangement changes in Motown's rigid back-to-the-factory production methods, and some of the tunes aboard ("Last One Out Is Brokenhearted," "Camouflage," "Forever in My Heart," and "We'll Be Satisfied") are in their early incarnations. There are also alternate versions of the title track, "Ain't Too Proud to Beg," and a live performance at the Fox Theater of "My Girl," announced onstage as their newest single. Here's a treasure trove of rare Temps tracks from the good old days; far from a pack of leftovers, in all honesty it doesn't get much better than this. *—Cub Koda*

10cc

f. 1972, Manchester, England
Album Rock, Pop/Rock, Soft Rock, Prog-Rock/Art Rock
Deriving their name from the metric total of semen ejaculated by the average male, the tongue-in-cheek British art-pop band 10cc debuted in 1972 with "Donna." A sly satire of late-'50s doo wop, the single reached number two on the British charts and established not only a long-running string of major hits but also the quartet's fondness for ironic and affectionate reclamations of musty pop styles. The follow-up, "Rubber Bullets," topped the charts in 1973, and both the subsequent single "The Dean and I" and an eponymously titled debut LP further solidified 10cc as a major force in British pop. While 1974's *Sheet Music* continued 10cc's dominance of the UK charts, they found the American market virtually impenetrable prior to the release of 1975's "I'm Not in Love," which topped the charts at home and climbed as high as number two in the States. After vocalists Kevin Godley and Lol Creme exited the group in 1976, vocalist/guitarists Graham Gouldman and Eric Stewart continued 10cc's success with the 1977 perennial "The Things We Do for Love" and a number one reggae nod "Dreadlock Holiday" one year later. Following a series of unsuccessful efforts, including 1981's *10 Out of 10* and 1983's *Window in the Jungle*, the group disbanded. In 1992, the original lineup reunited for *Meanwhile*, while only Gouldman and Stewart remained for 1993's *Mirror Mirror*. *—Jason Ankeny*

10cc/Sheet Music / 1990 / DCC ♦♦♦♦♦
10cc's first two albums, recorded under the sponsorship of entrepreneur and one-time pop star Jonathan King, are combined on one disc for this CD reissue. 1973's *10cc* shows that from the start, the group had an uncommon command of recording studio technique; the performances are polished, the harmonies superb, and the production flawless and often witty (all the more remarkable from a new band producing themselves, albeit one comprised of music-biz vets). However, the group was still getting up to speed in terms of their songwriting at this point, and while the craft is fine, there isn't a lot of inspiration on hand. Except for the sardonic "Rubber Bullets" and sarcastically sprightly "The Dean and I," the '50s-inspired parodies on side one don't wear well, and most of side two is clever but not terribly distinguished. 1974's *Sheet Music* was where 10cc truly hit their stride; the album is full of effective barbed humor buffered by the superbly polished production, which leans toward pretension without quite falling into the pool. The band began dipping their toes into the elaborate extended narratives that would become Kevin Godley and Lol Creme's hallmark on "Somewhere in Hollywood" and "Hotel," while "Silly Love" and "The Wall Street Shuffle" proved the band could rock when they felt like it, and "The Sacro-Iliac" is one of the great non-dance craze tunes ever. This CD also features a liner essay from Jonathan King on working with the group and tacks on the non-LP single "Waterfall" as a bonus. *—Mark Deming*

The Original Soundtrack / 1975 / Mercury ♦♦♦
10cc's third album, *The Original Soundtrack*, finally scored them a major hit in the United States, and rightly so; "I'm Not in Love" walked a fine line between self-pity and self-parody with its weepy tale of a boy who isn't in love (really!), and the marvelously lush production and breathy vocals allowed the tune to work beautifully either as a sly joke or at face value. The album's opener, "Une Nuit a Paris," was nearly as marvelous; a sly and often hilarious extended parody of both cinematic stereotypes of life and love in France and overblown European pop. And side one's closer, "Blackmail," was a witty tale of sex and extortion gone wrong, with a superb guitar solo embroidering the ride-out. That's all on side one; side two, however, is a bit spottier, with two undistinguished tunes, "Brand New Day" and "Flying Junk," nearly dragging the proceedings to a halt before the band rallied the troops for a happy ending with the hilarious "The Film of Our Love." *The Original Soundtrack*'s best moments rank with the finest work 10cc ever released; however, at the same time it also displayed what was to become their Achilles' heel—the inability to make an entire album as strong and memorable as those moments. *—Mark Deming*

How Dare You? / 1976 / Mercury ♦♦♦
After scoring their commercial breakthrough with "I'm Not in Love" from 1975's *The Original Soundtrack*, 10cc continued to build on their good fortune with *How Dare You*. It didn't spawn another massive hit like "I'm Not in Love," but it is a well-crafted album that shows off 10cc's eccentric humor and pop smarts in equal measure. This time, the hit singles were "I'm Mandy Fly Me" and "Art for Art's Sake." The first tune is the fanciful tale of a plane crash victim saved from death by the stewardess of his dreams that plays out a poppy mock-exotica musical backdrop while the second is a tongue-in-cheek parody of commercial-minded artists set to a rocking, cowbell-driven beat. Elsewhere, *How Dare You* pursues a similar mix of zany humor and pop hooks: "Iceberg" brings its tale of a frigid romantic partner to life with an incredibly intricate and jazzy vocal melody, and "I Wanna Rule the World" is a witty tale of a dictator-in-training with enough catchy riffs and vocal harmonies for two or three songs. *How Dare You* loses a bit of steam on its second side when the songs' tempos start to slow down, but "Rock & Roll Lullaby" and "Don't Hang Up" keep the listener involved through a combination of melodic songwriting and typically well-crafted arrangements. In the end, *How Dare You* never hits the giddy heights of *The Original Soundtrack* but it remains a solid album of witty pop songs that will satisfy anyone with a yen for 10cc. *—Donald A. Guarisco*

Deceptive Bends / 1977 / Mercury ♦♦♦♦
When Kevin Godley and Lol Creme left 10cc in 1976 to pursue a solo career, many thought it was the death knell for the group. However, Eric Stewart and Graham Gouldman kept the group alive as a duo (with the assistance of percussionist Paul Burgess) and turned in a surprisingly solid album with 1977's *Deceptive Bends*. It may lack the devil-may-care wackiness that popped up on previous 10cc albums, but it makes up for it by crafting a series of lush, catchy pop songs that are witty in their own right. *Deceptive Bends* also produced a pair of notable hits for the group: "Good Morning Judge" told the comical tale of a career criminal over a hook-laden, surprisingly funky pop backing while "The Things We Do for Love" was an irresistible Beatles pastiche that showcased 10cc's mastery of pop vocal harmonies. "People in Love," a surprisingly straightforward ballad built on a gorgeous string arrangement, also became a modest chart success. The remainder of the material doesn't stand out as sharply as these hits, but each of the tracks offers up plenty of naggingly catchy pop hooks, oodles of catchy riffs, and surprising twists in their arrangements. Highlights among the non-hit tracks include "Marriage Bureau Rendezvous," a satire of dating services set to a lilting soft rock melody, and "You've Got a Cold," a portrait of illness-influenced misery set to a percolating pop melody. The only place where *Deceptive Bends* slips is on "Feel the Benefit," the lengthy medley that closes the album. Its excessive length and hazy lyrics make it less satisfying than the album's shorter tunes, but it is kept afloat by a catchy, mock-Spanish midsection and some lovely string arrangements. All in all, *Deceptive Bends* is the finest achievement of 10cc's post-Godley and Creme lineup and well worth a spin for anyone who enjoyed *Sheet Music* or *The Original Soundtrack*. *—Donald A. Guarisco*

● **The Very Best of 10 CC** / Jun. 17, 1997 / Mercury ♦♦♦♦♦
The Very Best of 10cc is a comprehensive collection, featuring all of the group's biggest hits and best-known songs—including "Neanderthal Man," "Donna," "Rubber Bullets," "The Dean & I," "I'm Not in Love," and "The Things We Do for Love," as well as Godley & Creme's solo hit "Cry"—making it a definitive retrospective and introduction. *—Stephen Thomas Erlewine*

10,000 Maniacs

f. 1981, Jamestown, NY
College Rock, Jangle Pop, Alternative Pop/Rock
10,000 Maniacs (named after the low-budget horror movie *2,000 Maniacs*) was formed in Jamestown, NY, in 1981 by singer Natalie Merchant and guitarist John Lombardo. Other members of the sextet were Robert Buck (guitar), Steven Gustafson (bass), Dennis Drew (keyboards), and Jerry Augustyniak (drums). The group gigged extensively and recorded independently before signing with Elektra and making *The Wishing Chair* in 1985. Cofounder Lombardo left the band in 1986, and they continued as a quintet, releasing the second album, *In My Tribe*, in 1987. This album broke into the charts, where it stayed 77 weeks, peaking at #37. *Blind Man's Zoo*, the 1989 follow-up, hit #13 and went gold.

After 1992's *Our Time in Eden* had finished its run on the charts, Natalie Merchant announced that she was leaving for a solo career. *MTV Unplugged* was released a few months after her departure. The remaining 10,000 Maniacs decided to continue performing, adding the folk-rock duo John & Mary (original member Lombardo and violinist/vocalist Mary Ramsey). The new lineup released *Love Among the Ruins*. Merchant released her first solo album, *Tiger Lily*, in the summer of 1995 and a follow-up, *Ophelia* in 1998. In 1999, the remaining Maniacs released *The Earth Pressed Flat* on Bar/None. Sadly a year later lead guitarist and founding member Robert Buck, who co-wrote some of the band's classics like "Hey Jack Kerouac" "What's The Matter Here?" and "These Are Days," died of liver failure. He was 42. *—William Ruhlmann*

The Wishing Chair / 1985 / Elektra ♦♦♦
Put simply, 10,000 Maniacs sound a lot like Fairport Convention with Sandy Denny, so it's appropriate that Fairport's original producer, Joe Boyd, was brought in to handle their major-label debut. The result is a gentle folk/rock record that highlights the haunting voice of Natalie Merchant. *—William Ruhlmann*

● **In My Tribe** / 1987 / Elektra ♦♦♦♦♦
The band's breakthrough album and creative high point, *In My Tribe* offers a survey in social concerns including child abuse ("What's the Matter Here"), illiteracy ("Cherry Tree"), war ("Gun Shy") and the environment ("Campfire Song")—all tackled subtly and tastefully without too much preaching or pretension and in believable, real-life situations. Producer Peter Asher, whose credits include James Taylor and Linda Ronstadt, provides the perfect sheen—the group's pleasant folk-pop lends itself nicely to the '70s-styled

singer/songwriter production. In the end, the album proves powerful not for the ideas (they've been covered before) but rather for the graceful execution and pure listenability. *In My Tribe* has served as one of the soundtracks for P.C. living and was required listening on college campuses in the late-'80s. *—Chris Woodstra*

Blind Man's Zoo / May 1989 / Elektra ♦♦♦
After the success of *In My Tribe*, it would be expected that hordes of bands would take a stab at the market with their own second-rate versions of the album—it's disappointing that 10,000 Maniacs would be one of them, churning out not only *In My Tribe, Pt. 2*, but an inferior copy at that. It's not that the album is bad—certainly they've perfected their sound and in many cases, the songs are catchier this time out—but in handling the issues (there's no shortage of them), Merchant has become more direct and obvious. For all of its earnestness and good-intentioned teachings, *Blind Man's Zoo* ultimately fails in its heavy-handed and generally uninteresting approach. *—Chris Woodstra*

Hope Chest: The Fredonia Recordings 1982-1983 / Oct. 1990 / Elektra ♦♦♦
Hope Chest collects the ultra-rare early recordings of the band—the *Human Conflict Number 5* EP from 1982 and *Secrets of the I Ching* from 1983—remastered and resequenced presumably for easier listening. While the songs are predictably unfocused and full of underdeveloped (though ambitious) ideas, these recordings give an interesting picture of the band's formative years. *—Chris Woodstra*

Our Time in Eden / Sep. 29, 1992 / Elektra ♦♦♦♦♦
Pushing through the sophomore jinx that gave *Blind Man's Zoo* its preachy feel, 10,000 Maniacs offer up a baker's dozen of wonderful folk-pop songs with hard-hitting messages, nearly matching the brilliance of their debut. Natalie Merchant is a few years older here, a few tribulations wiser, and a few shakes looser, although that's not to say she doesn't have a point (or 13) to make. Whether with old-school R&B horns ablaze or the simple elegance of a piano and strings, she glorifies, condemns, and cherishes the world she witnesses, not excusing herself or anyone else from the part they play. The rest of the band, Rob Buck, Dennis Drew, Steve Gustafson, and Jerome Augustyniak, gives her the superb musical roots and wings from which to grow and soar. The subject matter of the songs is sometimes subtle, sometimes overt, but always graceful. For instance, "These Are Days" is left open to interpretation, though the upbeat tone is unmistakable, while "I'm Not the Man" is a very pointed and poignant story of a jailed man falsely accused and awaiting his death. Merchant's poetry shimmers and tugs at your heart and head. The prophetically titled *Our Time in Eden* spawned modest hits with "These Are Days" and "Candy Everybody Wants," but turned out to be the final chapter for this maniacal five-some, as Merchant departed the band shortly after touring in support of the album. A finer swan song has seldom been heard. *—Kelly McCartney*

MTV Unplugged / Oct. 26, 1993 / Elektra ♦♦
When it was recorded, nobody knew that *MTV Unplugged* would be 10,000 Maniacs' last album with Natalie Merchant. As it stands, it's a quiet, gentle way for her to bow out, offering no new revelations but several solid versions of the group's signature songs (mainly concentrating on *Our Time in Eden*) and a cover of Patti Smith's "Because the Night." It's nothing new, but for fans it's a graceful way to say goodbye. *—Stephen Thomas Erlewine*

Love Among the Ruins / Jun. 17, 1997 / Geffen ♦♦
Most observers considered 10,000 Maniacs dead in the water following the departure of vocalist Natalie Merchant. Instead of calling it quits, the remaining members hired the jangle-folk duo John and Mary, whose guitarist, John Lombardo, played in one of the original incarnations of the Maniacs. The revamped group's first album, *Love Among the Ruins*, illustrated that the band could replicate their signature, gently jangly sound without too much effort, but it also illustrated that the group lacked focus without Merchant. *Love Among the Ruins* is a pleasant listen, but Mary Ramsey's thin voice occasionally grates, the songs are uniformly slight, and the cover of Roxy Music's "More Than This" is an outright embarrassment. Even with those flaws, the album isn't a disaster, and the surviving 10,000 Maniacs have demonstrated that they can continue with dignity, even if their inspiration is somewhat lacking. *—Stephen Thomas Erlewine*

The Earth Pressed Flat / Apr. 20, 1999 / Bar/None ♦♦♦
1999's *The Earth Pressed Flat* finds 10,000 Maniacs exploring similar musical terrain as their previous album, *Love Among the Ruins*, on which singer Mary Ramsey debuted. Ramsey sounds less like a stand-in and more like a frontwoman on *The Earth Pressed Flat*, which was released on the indie label Bar None. Fittingly, the album sounds more folky and down to earth than some of their previous albums. *The Earth Pressed Flat* was recorded over the course of four years at the group's home studio, on the road and in traditional studios; it also incorporates recordings of found sounds and rehearsals for a dreamlike, fluid continuity. Ramsey's vocals sound at home in *The Earth Pressed Flat*'s rustic, stripped-down settings, particularly on the Sandy Dennis cover "Who Knows Where the Time Goes." The title track and "On and On" also allow her vocals to breathe, with understated accompaniment from her fellow Maniacs on guitars and keyboards; Ramsey's own viola playing completes the picture. *The Earth Pressed Flat* blends old and new, ethereal and folky sounds into a style that is distinctively, yet differently, 10,000 Maniacs. *—Heather Phares*

Ten Years After

f. 1967, Nottingham, England, **db.** 1974
British Blues, Hard Rock, Blues-Rock
Ten Years After is a British blues-rock quartet consisting of Alvin Lee (b. Dec 19, 1944), guitar and vocals; Chick Churchill (b. Jan 2, 1949), keyboards; Leo Lyons (b. Nov 30, 1944) bass; and Ric Lee (b. Oct 20, 1945), drums. The group was formed in 1967 and signed to Decca in England. Its first album was not a success, but its second, the live *Undead* (1968) containing "I'm Going Home," a six-minute blues workout by the fleet-fingered Alvin hit the charts on both sides of the Atlantic. *Stonedhenge* (1969) hit the U.K. Top Ten in early 1969. Ten Years After's U.S. breakthrough came as a result of its appearance at Woodstock, at which it played a nine-minute version of "I'm Going Home." Its next album, *Ssssh*, reached the U.S. Top 20, and *Cricklewood Green*, containing the hit single "Love Like a Man," reached #14. *Watt* completed the group's Decca contract, after which it signed with Columbia and moved in a more mainstream pop direction, typified by the gold-selling 1971 album *A Space in Time* and its Top 40 single "I'd Love to Change the World." Subsequent efforts in that direction were less successful, however, and Ten Years After split up after the release of *Positive Vibrations* in 1974. They reunited in 1988 for concerts in Europe and recorded their first new album in 15 years, *About Time*, in 1989. *—William Ruhlmann*

Undead / 1968 / Deram ♦♦♦
Recorded live in a small London club, *Undead* contains the original "I'm Going Home," the song which brought Ten Years After its first blush of popularity following the Woodstock festival and film in which it was featured. However, the real strength of this album is side one, which contains two extended jazz jams, "I May Be Wrong But I Won't Be Wrong Always" and Woody Herman's "Woodchopper's Ball," both of which spotlight guitarist Alvin Lee's amazing speed and technique. Side two is less interesting, with an extended slow blues typical of the time, a drum solo feature, and the rock & roll rave-up of "I'm Going Home." *—Jim Newsom*

Ssssh / 1969 / BGO ♦♦♦♦
This was Ten Years After's new release at the time of their incendiary performance at the Woodstock Festival in August, 1969. As a result, it was their first hit album in the U.S., peaking at number 20 in September of that year. This recording is a primer of British blues-rock of the era, showcasing Alvin Lee's guitar pyrotechnics and the band's propulsive rhythm section. As with most of TYA's work, the lyrics were throwaways, but the music was hot. Featured is a lengthy cover of Sonny Boy Williamson's "Good Morning Little Schoolgirl," with reworked lyrics leaving little doubt what the singer had in mind for the title character. Also included was a twelve-bar blues song with the ultimate generic blues title, "I Woke Up This Morning." *Ssssh* marked the beginning of the band's two-year run of popularity on the U.S. album charts and in the "underground" FM-radio scene. *—Jim Newsom*

● **Cricklewood Green** / Apr. 1970 / Chrysalis ♦♦♦♦♦
Cricklewood Green provides the best example of Ten Years After's recorded sound. On this album, the band and engineer Andy Johns mix studio tricks and sound effects, blues-based song structures, a driving rhythm section, and Alvin Lee's signature lightning-fast guitar licks into a unified album that flows nicely from start to finish. *Cricklewood Green* opens with a pair of bluesy rockers, with "Working on the Road" propelled by a guitar and organ riff that holds the listener's attention through the use of tape manipulation as the song develops. "50,000 Miles Beneath My Brain" and "Love Like a Man" are classics of TYA's jam genre, with lyrically meaningless verses setting up extended guitar workouts that build in intensity, rhythmically and sonically. The latter was an FM-radio staple in the early '70s. "Year 3000 Blues" is a country romp sprinkled with Lee's silly sci-fi lyrics, while "Me and My Baby" concisely showcases the band's jazz licks better than any other TYA studio track, and features a tasty piano solo by Chick Churchill. It has a feel similar to the extended pieces on side one of the live album *Undead*. "Circles" is a hippie-ish acoustic guitar piece, while "As the Sun Still Burns Away" closes the album by building on another classic guitar-organ riff and more sci-fi sound effects. *—Jim Newsom*

A Space in Time / 1971 / Chrysalis ♦♦♦♦
A Space in Time was Ten Years After's best-selling album. This was due primarily to the strength of "I'd Love to Change the World," the band's only hit single, and one of the most ubiquitous AM and FM radio cuts of the summer of 1971. TYA's first album for Columbia, *A Space in Time* has more of a pop-oriented feel than any of their previous releases had. The individual cuts are shorter, and Alvin Lee displays a broader instrumental palette than before. In fact, six of the disc's ten songs are built around acoustic guitar riffs. However, there are still a couple of barn-burning jams. The leadoff track, "One of These Days," is a particularly scorching workout, featuring extended harmonica and guitar solos. After the opener, however, the album settles back into a more relaxed mood than one would have expected from Ten Years After. Many of the cuts make effective use of dynamic shifts, and the guitar solos are generally more understated than on previous outings. The production on *A Space in Time* is crisp and clean, a sound quite different from the denseness of its predecessors. Though not as consistent as *Cricklewood Green*, *A Space in Time* has its share of sparkling moments. *—Jim Newsom*

Alvin Lee & Company / 1972 / Deram ♦♦

Essential / 1991 / Chrysalis ♦♦♦♦♦
While it doesn't include all of their prime material, *Essential* features enough of their best songs to make it a fine introduction. *—AMG*

Tenpole Tudor

f. 1974, **db.** 1982
Pub Rock, New Wave
Tenpole Tudor was one the strangest and silliest groups on Stiff Records, a label that was known for its odd-balls. Led by Eddie Tudor (born Edward Tudorpole), a former actor that could barely carry a tune, the group played a mixture of punk, roots-rock, pop and British dance-hall music, developing a thoroughly entertaining and ridiculous style. Tudor formed the band in 1974 with guitarist Bob Kingston, bassist Dick Crippen, and drummer Gary Long. Before recording the band's first album, Tudor appeared in the Sex Pistols' movie *The Great Rock & Roll Swindle*, singing "Who Killed Bambi." After releasing a

single on Korova records, the group joined the Stiff roster, releasing "Three Bells in a Row." Tenpole Tudor released their debut album, *Eddie, Old Bob, Dick and Gary* in 1981; it sold well, launching two minor singles in addition to "Three Bells in a Row"—"Wunderbar" and "Swords of a Thousand Men." That same year, the group released their second album, *Let the Four Winds Blow*, which also performed well. The following year, Eddie Tudor broke up Tenpole Tudor; while he led a cajun-inspired version of Tenpole Tudor, the rest of the band became the Tudors. After the new incarnation of Tenpole Tudor failed, Tudor left Stiff Records and began performing in jazz and swing bands, as well as returning to acting; he has since concentrated on acting, although he has assembled new versions of Tenpole Tudor since. *—Stephen Thomas Erlewine*

● **Eddie, Old Bob, Dick & Gary** / 1981 / Stiff ✦✦✦✦✦
Tenpole Tudor's music is so defiantly silly and raucous that it would be easy to dismiss if it wasn't quite so fun. Taking the punk aesthetic to an extreme, no one in Tenpole Tudor, particularly lead vocalist Eddie Tudor, can sing *at all*, so each song turns into a drunken, noisy singalong. And most of these songs are singalongs, filled with rousing choruses, big hooks, and clattering chords that are messy and infectious. What's surprising about the group's debut album, *Eddie, Old Bob, Dick & Gary*, is how many flat-out excellent songs are on the record. Combining ridiculous swords-and-sorcery imagery with laddish party anthems, nearly half of the record is invigorating, noisy rock & roll, with the boozy "Swords of a Thousand Men," "Wunderbar," "Three Bells in a Row," "I Wish," and "There Are the Boys" standing out among the clatter. The rest of the album isn't quite as good, but it has reckless charm that makes *Eddie, Old Bob, Dick & Gary* a thrillingly primitive rock & roll record. *—Stephen Thomas Erlewine*

Let the Four Winds Blow / 1981 / Stiff ✦✦✦
Tenpole Tudor falters somewhat on their second album, *Let the Four Winds Blow*, partially in a wish to expand their musical reach. Instead of relying on the boozy, punky pub rock that dominated their debut, the band attempts to claim funk, music hall, pop, and country as their own, with mixed results. The record starts off with a great one-two punch of the title track and the ridiculous "Throwing My Baby Out With the Bathwater" before it quickly runs out of steam, making clear that the real problem with the record isn't patchy songwriting—the debut had that flaw as well—but a tamer performance, and when they play it calm, Tenpole Tudor isn't quite as endearing as when they rock out. Still, there's just enough good tracks to make the record necessary for the devoted, but without the relentlessly goofy and catchy appeal of *Eddie, Old Bob, Dick & Gary, Let the Four Winds Blow* simply won't be able to convert the uninitiated. *—Stephen Thomas Erlewine*

Swords of a Thousand Men / Apr. 21, 1998 / Recall ✦✦✦✦✦
To the average rock fan, Tenpole Tudor isn't remembered at all. To punk fans, they may be remembered as the group fronted by Eddie Tudorpole who stole the show singing "Who Killed Bambi?" in *The Great Rock & Roll Swindle.* For a select few—primarily Stiff Records collectors and punk/New Wave fetishists—the group was a strange, wonderful, supremely silly treasure. This was a band, after all, that came across as a gang of rockabilly toughs decked out in medieval garb, led by a gangly, goofy drama student that could sing but not carry a tune. This was a band that reveled in silly antics and sillier songs, stealing from old-time rock & roll, punk, novelty pop, and country, turning it into a joyous, catchy cacophony. They were misfits, classic British eccentrics making music that was a jumbled mess of American pop music, filtered through wry British humor and punk. If they were a footnote, at best, to rock history, some may wonder why the hell anyone would want *Swords of a Thousand Men*, a double-disc collection containing pretty much everything the band released. Well, once you fall in love with Tenpole Tudor you fall pretty hard and you never get out. You need everything they cut. Thankfully, it's all of pretty high quality, particularly their debut *Eddie Old Bob Dick and Gary*, a gleeful collection of raucous pop, sing-along choruses and utter nonsense. Admittedly, this is not music that everybody will like or maybe even tolerate. It's way too dumb and silly for hipsters, it rocks too hard for fans of geeky novelties, and Tudorpole's warbling can grate. But it also can be delirious, giddy fun, and, for those listeners, *Swords of a Thousand Men* is a pure delight. *—Stephen Thomas Erlewine*

● **The Best of Tenpole Tudor: Swords of a Thousand Men** / May 11, 2001 / Metro ✦✦✦✦✦

Tesla

f. 1985
Pop-Metal, Hair Metal, Heavy Metal, Hard Rock
With their first album, *Mechanical Resonance*, Tesla quickly established themselves as one of the better hard rock/heavy metal bands of the late '80s. Although they weren't utterly original, the band was tight and showed an ability for crafting melodic, driving riffs. What made Tesla different from other metal bands with pop inclinations was the fact that their music was grounded in gritty, bluesy hard rock instead of slick arena rock.

Although their debut climbed all the way to number 32 on the *Billboard* charts, their second album, 1989's *The Great Radio Controversy*, was an even greater success, scoring a Top Ten hit with the ballad "Love Song." Their follow-up album, *Five Man Acoustical Jam*, showed that the band didn't need overdriven amplifiers in order to play; it also showed that they had a fondness for sentimental hippie oldies, as their hit version of "Signs" proved. The record also turned out to be their biggest hit, reaching number 12 on the charts. While its follow-up, *Psychotic Supper*, wasn't as commercially successful, it captured Tesla branching into new musical territories; it proved that the band hadn't lost its creative spark. *—Stephen Thomas Erlewine*

Mechanical Resonance / 1986 / Geffen ✦✦✦
Sacramento's oddly named Tesla took the side door to '80s hard rock success, sneaking up on the charts and general public with their rock solid debut *Mechanical Resonance.* An interesting case of compromise, the album is clearly split into two quite different halves. The first (obviously intended for easy radio-friendly consumption) is chock full of throwaway, often clichéd arena anthems, like "Ez Come, Ez Go," "Cumin' Atcha Live," and "Rock Me to the Top," which offer few surprises but plenty of dumb testosterone. And though they do manage to sneak a little intelligence into the gritty strut of "Gettin' Better" and the bluesy balladry of "We're No Good Together," the band's true talents are saved for the album's second half, which quickly reveals an altogether more mature and accomplished group. It also properly introduces ace guitarist Frank Hannon, who takes charge with quiet assertiveness and establishes himself as the band's creative force and de facto leader on "Modern Day Cowboy." An epic of Led Zeppelin-like class and complexity, the song's highly technical and slightly lopsided main riff is so irresistible, nothing could keep it from becoming one of the most unexpected hits of the year. Another of the band's biggest early hits, "Changes," is next; introduced by a piano melody of striking beauty, it sets the stage for the delightful swagger and acoustic strums of "Little Suzi." And as a double parting shot, the band reveals even more weapons from their arsenal with the odd rhythms and clever economy of "Cover Queen" and the mysteriously moody "Before My Eyes." Overall, *Mechanical Resonance* offers a remarkably mature first glance at one of the most under-appreciated American rock bands of their time. *—Ed Rivadavia*

The Great Radio Controversy / 1989 / Geffen ✦✦✦✦✦
One of the band's best albums, *The Great Radio Controversy* retains the typical big-sounding production and anthemic hooks of '80s pop-metal, but Tesla adds a grittier, bluesier edge to their music than most of their peers. As on most of their records, Tesla's songwriting is consistently good but never quite great; however, "Love Song," "The Way It Is," and "Heaven's Trail (No Way Out)" are among their best, with melodies and riffs that aren't predictable, cookie-cutter product. *The Great Radio Controversy* broadens the sound of *Mechanical Resonance* somewhat with increased use of acoustic instruments, which provides more textural and dynamic contrasts, and the weaker moments are still enlivened by the twin-guitar attack of Frank Hannon and Tommy Skeoch. All in all, a fine effort. *—Steve Huey*

Five Man Acoustical Jam / Dec. 1990 / Geffen ✦✦✦
Comparisons to *MTV Unplugged* tend to be thrown around in an attempt to promote any pre-*Unplugged* acoustic music by linking it with a successful, more contemporary phenomenon, but Tesla's *Five Man Acoustical Jam* was actually a legitimate predecessor of the trend—it bears a strong resemblance to early *Unplugged* sessions in its informality and sense that the band is just having fun. Perhaps more importantly, the fact that a cover of the Five Man Electrical Band's "Signs" became a Top Ten hit demonstrated that acoustic *rock & roll*—not just ballads like Guns & Roses' "Patience" or Extreme's "More Than Words"—could find acceptance and commercial viability with rock audiences. As for the musical results, Tesla's originals generally translate well to the acoustic format, though some of the jams tend to ramble and lose focus, a fact underscored by the tightly melodic covers of '60s classics like "Lodi" and "Mother's Little Helper." Still, this adds to the informal atmosphere, and the album is a nice change of pace from the rest of Tesla's catalog. *—Steve Huey*

Psychotic Supper / Aug. 30, 1991 / Geffen ✦✦✦
Psychotic Supper benefits from a more stripped-down production than *The Great Radio Controversy*, using fewer overdubs and thereby enhancing Tesla's bluesy, acoustic-tinged rock & roll. Going over the top was never what Tesla did best, and *Psychotic Supper* shows enough variation and occasional understatement to retain the listener's interest. Many of the band's best songs are here, including "What You Give," "Call It What You Want," "Song and Emotion," and "Edison's Medicine"; the latter is perhaps the most typical of the pop-metal anthem sound, but its subject matter—the attention paid to Thomas Edison over lesser-known genius Nikola Tesla, to whom the band is obviously devoted—certainly qualifies it as distinctive. The guitar workout on "Don't De-Rock Me" is another highlight. *—Steve Huey*

Bust a Nut / Aug. 23, 1994 / Geffen ✦✦✦
When it came to honest-to-goodness hard-hitting rock & roll, Tesla were always miles ahead of their late '80s, early '90s brethren because they never relied on image or hype as much as, say Guns & Roses and Mötley Crüe. These guys could really write great songs and really play them, but in the end their fate was no different from the above-mentioned groups in the aftershock of the grunge invasion. Their fourth and final studio album, *Bust A Nut* is a natural proggression from *Psychotic Supper*, featuring classic rock riffs, acoustic passages (courtesy of guitar genius Frank Hannon), and memorable choruses. "Shine Away," "Need Your Loving," "Mama's Fool," and especially "Alot To Lose" are excellent tracks and could have done very well for the band in a less hostile musical climate, but this was not to be. Their record label Geffen, was probably too busy promoting Nirvana anyway, and the band called it a day following their next tour. *—Ed Rivadavia*

● **Time's Makin Changes: The Best of Tesla** / Nov. 1995 / Geffen ✦✦✦✦
Tesla's greatest hits and most popular album rock cuts are collected on *Time's Makin' Changes: The Best of Tesla.* In addition to hits like "Signs," "The Way It Is," and "Love Song," the compilation includes a new song, "Steppin' Over," which isn't particularly distinctive. Nevertheless, the record remains the one to get for casual fans—it has all the hits, in one place, after all. *—Stephen Thomas Erlewine*

Joe Tex (Joseph Arrington Jr.)

b. Aug. 8, 1933, Rogers, TX, **d.** Aug. 13, 1982, Navasota, TX
Vocals / Funk, Soul
Joe Tex made the first Southern soul record that also hit on the pop charts ("Hold What You've Got," in 1965, made number five in *Billboard*). His raspy-voiced, jackleg preacher style also laid some of the most important part's of rap's foundation. He is, arguably, the

most underrated of all the '60s soul performers associated with Atlantic Records, although his records were more likely than those of most soul stars to become crossover hits.

Tex was born Joseph Arrington in Rogers, TX, in 1933, and displayed his vocal talent quickly, first in gospel, then in R&B. By 1954, he'd won a local talent contest and come to New York, where he recorded a variety of derivative (and endlessly repackaged) singles for King, some as a ballad singer, some as a Little Richard-style rocker.

Tex's career didn't take off until he began his association with Nashville song publisher Buddy Killen, after Tex wrote James Brown's 1961 song "Baby You're Right." In 1965, Killen took him to Muscle Shoals, not yet a fashionable recording center, and they came up with "Hold What You've Got," which is about as close to a straight R&B ballad as Tex ever came. It was followed by a herd more, most of which made the R&B charts, a few cracking the pop Top 40.

Tex made his mark by preaching over tough hard soul tracks, clowning at some points, swooping into a croon at others. He was perhaps the most rustic and back-country of the soul stars, a role he played to the hilt by using turns of phrase that might have been heard on any ghetto street corner, "One Monkey Don't Stop No Show" the prototype. In 1966, his "I Believe I'm Gonna Make It," an imaginary letter home from Vietnam, became the first big hit directly associated with that war. His biggest hit was "Skinny Legs and All," from a 1967 live album, his rapping pure hokum over deeply funky riffs. "Skinny Legs" might have served as a template for all the raucous, ribald hip-hop hits of pop's future.

After "Skinny Legs," Tex had nothing but minor hits for five years until "I Gotcha" took off, a grittier twist on the funk that was becoming disco. He was too down-home for the slickness of the disco era, or so it would have seemed, yet in 1977, he adapted a dance craze, the Bump, and came up with the hilarious "Ain't Gonna Bump No More (With No Big Fat Woman)," his last Top Ten R&B hit, which also crossed over to number 12 on the pop chart.

In the early '70s, Tex converted to Islam and in 1972 changed his offstage name to Joseph Hazziez. He spent much of the time after "Ain't Gonna Bump" on his Texas farm, although he did join together with Wilson Pickett, Ben E. King, and Don Covay for a re-formed version of the Soul Clan in 1980. He died of a heart attack in 1982, only 49 years old. Killen, King, Covay, Pickett, and the great songwriter Percy Mayfield served as pallbearers. *—Dave Marsh*

I Believe I'm Gonna Make It / 1988 / Rhino ♦♦♦♦♦
First-rate country/soul, sung with the just the right blend of whimsy, worry, and relief. Joe Tex was routinely turning out excellent cuts throughout the mid-'60s, but it wasn't until his novelty/disco tunes of the mid-'70s that he finally attained any widespread recognition. Sadly, none of his great Dial albums are currently in print. *—Ron Wynn*

Show Me: The Hits . . . & More / Oct. 12, 1992 / Ichiban ♦♦♦♦
While he could spin a mean yarn, Tex was also a mournful, moving vocalist whose convincing delivery on country/soul ballads was sorely underrated. This 18-track collection includes some of Tex's biggest hits, fine covers of "Dark End Of The Street" and "You're Right," plus several Tex originals such as "I Want To Do Everything For You," "Same Old Soup," and "King Thaddeus." While there are some notable and surprising exclusions, it's a representative Tex collection, but isn't as complete as Rhino's single-disc anthology from 1988. *—Ron Wynn*

The Very Best of Joe Tex / 1996 / Rhino ♦♦♦♦♦
Excellent 16-track survey of Tex's best material, from the mid-'60s to the mid-'70s. It favors his country/soul period rather than the disco one, with all but three tracks originating from the '60s, but it does include his biggest '70s hits, "I Gotcha" and "Ain't Gonna Bump No More (With No Big Fat Woman)." *—Richie Unterberger*

• **25 All Time Greatest Hits** / Mar. 21, 2000 / Varese ♦♦♦♦♦
If you're set on having the best available Joe Tex CD anthology and you already have the 1996 16-track Rhino comp *The Very Best of Joe Tex*, it might vex you to learn that all 16 of those songs are on this 25-song anthology, making the Rhino disc redundant should you decide to upgrade. If you *don't* have a Joe Tex CD anthology yet, though, you're in luck, as this definitely supersedes others as the greatest-hits collection of choice. All but one of these songs (the 1965 B-side "Don't Let Your Left Hand Know") was a chart single, and aside from the 1977 hit "Ain't Gonna Bump No More (With No Big Fat Woman)," all are from his prime 1965-1972 period. Of the songs not on the Rhino disc, highlights are the 1965 slowies "You Better Get It" and "A Woman Can Change a Man," and the aforementioned "Don't Let Your Left Hand Know," an odd soul-pop tune with folky guitars and harmonies straight off a Rooftop Singers record. Also, "A Woman's Hands" (a small 1967 hit) is a good example of Tex's preaching style. Then there's 1968's "You Need Me Baby," in which Tex disses a stud who was the best athlete in town and left to become a big success, maintaining that he [Tex] is still a better catch for the woman whom the stud left behind, since he'll love her children. Heck, all of the songs not on the Rhino disc are worthwhile additions. There's no telling if this will remain the definitive Tex compilation if his catalog continues to get passed around, but there's a good chance that it won't be surpassed. *—Richie Unterberger*

Texas

f. 1986, Glasgow, Scotland
Adult Alternative Pop/Rock, Blue-Eyed Soul, Britpop, Pop/Rock, Alternative Pop/Rock
Texas was formed in Glasgow, Scotland in 1986 by Johnny McElhone, a veteran of the Scottish rock circuit who had been a part of two groups, Hipsway and Altered Images. Altered Images had considerable chart success in the U.S. and the U.K. in the mid-1980s, while Hipsway didn't become nearly so well known.

Texas is comprised of McElhone, bass, Eddie Campbell, keyboards, Ally McErlaine, guitar, Richard Hynd, drums and Sharleen Spiteri, vocals and guitar. The group made their performing debut as a band in March, 1988 at a local college in Glasgow. Texas took their name from the 1985 Wim Wenders film, *Paris, Texas*, for which Ry Cooder composed the soundtrack.

Their third album, *Rick's Road*, (1993) solidified the band's U.S. following, though their debut album was *Southside*, a 1989 release. After they added keyboardist Eddie Campbell, the group scored their first U.K. hit single, "I Don't Want A Lover," which went into Great Britain's Top Ten. *Southside* peeked at number three in England and then went on to sell 1.6 million units worldwide. Although their debut's eclectic mix of blues, soul, R&B and country-folk was well received by college radio stations, the band still hadn't made it over to the U.S. to tour. Their second album for Mercury, *Mother's Heaven*, followed with drummer Richard Hynd taking the place of the band's original drummer, Stuart Kerr.

The material on *Rick's Road* includes a cover of Al Green's "Tired of Being Alone," which landed in the U.K.'s Top 20 and restored a great deal of the band's credibility in their homeland, where they'd come on so strong with *Southside* and then followed it up with what many critics there thought was a mediocre sophomore release. Other highlights on *Rick's Road* include the vocal treatments of Sister Rose of Sly & the Family Stone. The group's influences are apparent on *Rick's Road*, and they include Spiteri's Janis Joplin styled vocals, McErlaine's blues-based guitar playing and Spiteri's country-styled vocals on "You Owe It All to Me."

In 1999, Texas released *Hush*, whose first single, "In Our Lifetime," became a hit on American alternative radio. Hynd later left the group. *—Richard Skelly*

Southside / 1989 / Mercury ♦♦♦♦
Intelligent, tuneful adult pop with terrific female vocals and bluesy slide guitar work. *—Steve Aldrich*

Mothers Heaven / 1991 / Mercury ♦♦♦
Texas is a good name for this band, whose sound is open, brooding and just a bit on the twangy side; if you can imagine a sound somewhere between the dour, minimalist bluesiness of Cowboy Junkies and the yearning, gospel-tinged bombast of early U2, you'll have a good idea what to expect. Singer Sharleen Spiteri has the perfect voice for this kind of thing: it's low-pitched and dark-hued, and is shown off to best effect when she's belting out big, cathartic numbers like the title track and "Why Believe in You." Ally McErlaine is a brilliant slide guitarist who can move from grungy, greasy rock to desolate acoustic Delta blues without missing a beat. It's true that the group still needs to digest its influences a bit—"Dream Hotel," in particular, sounds like a U2 reject—but most of the time, Texas does a good job of mapping out its own territory. And this is just their second album, remember. *—Rick Anderson*

Ricks Road / 1993 / Mercury ♦♦

White on Blonde / 1997 / Mercury ♦♦♦♦
Unexpectedly, Texas became a popular sensation prior to the release of *White on Blonde* when Chris Evans made the soulful single "Say What You Want" the de facto theme song on his morning program on Radio 1. On the strength of his support, Texas was catapulted to previously unthinkable success, and the majority of the fans who thought the number one single was fine shouldn't have been disappointed with the full-length album. A combination of roots-rock and soul, *White on Blonde* occasionally has more style than substance, but Sharleen Spiteri's gorgeous vocals and the band's professionalism make the record a charming, ingratiating listen. *—Stephen Thomas Erlewine*

The Hush / May 18, 1999 / Universal ♦♦♦♦
Blessed with a stylish production and sharp commercial songs, *White on Blonde* made Texas into superstars everywhere except America—a situation familiar to many British acts of the '80s and '90s. Like most of their peers, Texas failed to deliver in the U.S. because of bungled promotion, since singles like "Black Eyed Boy" could have easily fit onto adult alternative radio. Texas must have been aware of this, since they switched labels in America, releasing *White on Blonde's* sequel *The Hush* near-simultaneously in the U.S. and the U.K.—a sure sign that they were aiming for the big time. As it turns out, they pulled off a minor coup with *The Hush*—they build on the strengths of *White on Blonde*, creating a sophisticated, sexy pop album that manages to balance commercial and creative concerns, with seemingly very little effort. It won't please longtime fans, who might be pining for a return to the rock of their early records, but the album's lush blend of melody, blue-eyed soul, dance and pop is undeniably alluring. Wisely, the group takes their cue from Sharleen Spiteri's hushed vocals, which are sultry but never histrionic. Some could argue that the entire affair is too self-consciously mature—after all, the majority of the album is devoted to midtempo pop numbers, and even the uptempo cuts never work up much of a sweat—but the fact remains, few bands are capable of delivering a mainstream pop record as assured and listenable as this. *—Stephen Thomas Erlewine*

• **Song Book: Best of Texas** / Jan. 9, 2001 / Mercury ♦♦♦♦♦
Texas always seemed out of place, from the moment they released their debut 'til the time they hit the big-time with *White on Blonde* in the second half of the '90s. They may have been able to gain momentum from Brit-pop, but they didn't really belong, since their sensibility was far too soulful and classy, borrowing equally from the smooth soul of the '70s, Americana fascinations, and, in a roundabout way, the sophisti-pop of the '80s. Still, they were professional, stylish, and, thanks to Sharleen Spiterri, sexy, which meant they did make sense in the aftermath of Brit-pop, even if they were a bit out of step. As the splendid *Song Book* proves, they could even have made it into the American mainstream if they had received a push on adult alternative pop/rock radio, since they were melodic, classy, and solid. They never were groundbreaking, but they were professionals, and even if this hits collection has a couple of run-of-the-mill cuts, at its best—"Say What You Want,"

"Black Eyed Boy," "In Our Lifetime"—it's as good as mainstream post-alternative adult pop gets. For European listeners, this is certainly a snapshot of the times, and for Americans, this is a good way to get acquainted with a minor treasure. —*Stephen Thomas Erlewine*

that dog.

f. 1991
Alternative Pop/Rock
The lineup of the Los Angeles-based indie-pop quartet that dog. represented the flowering of a second generation of musical luminaries: singer/guitarist Anna Waronker was the daughter of famed producer and Warner Bros. head Lenny Waronker, while bassist Rachel Haden and her violinist sister Petra were two of the triplet daughters born to jazz titan Charlie Haden. Friends since high school, the trio first began playing music together in Waronker's bedroom in the early '90s. Joined by drummer Tony Maxwell in 1992, that dog. issued their debut double seven-inch on the tiny Magnatone Records, quickly becoming a staple of the L.A. club circuit; a flurry of label interest followed, and the group signed with DGC in 1993. that dog.'s self-titled debut LP appeared in 1994; an energetic and quirky punk-pop effort highlighted by sunny harmonies and the intriguing use of violin and cello, the record became a college radio hit, and the light-hearted video for the lead single "Old Timer" even garnered some MTV airplay. The follow-up, *Totally Crushed Out!*, was issued a year later; a concept album wittily exploring the teen angst of unrequited love (packaged to recall a *Sweet Valley High* romance novel), the record marked a significant maturity in Waronker's songwriting, evidenced by tracks like "Ms. Wrong" and "He's Kissing Christian." A planned Waronker solo project was scheduled to follow, but instead her more pop-oriented material became the basis for the third that dog. record; co-produced by Brad Wood, the stellar *Retreat From the Sun* appeared in 1997. The band's breakup was announced that September. —*Jason Ankeny*

that dog. / Mar. 1994 / DGC ♦♦♦
The group's debut is uneven but exciting. The mix of sweet harmonies, crunchy guitars and scratchy violins makes it an entertaining listen, especially on songs like "Raina" and "Punk Rock Girl." —*Heather Phares*

● **Totally Crushed Out!** / Jul. 18, 1995 / DGC ♦♦♦♦♦
An appealing concept album about crushes and puppy love, *Totally Crushed Out!* is full of tight punk-pop and pretty ballads. Tracks like "Ms. Wrong," "Silently" and "One Summer Night" capture the giddiness of first love with their three-part harmonies and sweet melodies. *Totally Crushed Out!* is cute and clever without being too cutesy or precious, and almost as memorable as a first crush. —*Heather Phares*

Retreat from the Sun / Apr. 8, 1997 / DGC ♦♦♦♦
Retreat from the Sun began its life as Anna Waronker's first solo album, and if you listen intently, those origins are apparent, particularly in the tenor of the songs themselves. that dog. previously veered toward cute-pop, and while there are remnants of that throughout the album, Waronker's songs are considerably more personal than before, which adds emotional depth to the record. Just as important, her songs are tighter and more melodic, demonstrating considerable growth in songcraft. Producer Brad Wood helps form these songs into shiny alterna-pop nuggets, making *Retreat from the Sun* into the best album Liz Phair never made. It comes at the expense of the raw, ragged and surprisingly hooky post-punk of *Totally Crushed Out*, which was quite charming in its own right, but with maturity do come greater rewards, as *Retreat from the Sun* proves. —*Stephen Thomas Erlewine*

That Petrol Emotion

f. 1984, Derry, Northern Ireland, **db.** Apr. 1994
Alternative Pop/Rock
After the Undertones broke up, Sean (formerly known as John) O'Neill and fellow Derry DJ Reámann O'Gormain formed That Petrol Emotion, with Sean's brother and Undertones bandmate Damian O'Neill joining on bass after the band moved to England. While they were more politically oriented and noisier than the Undertones, they managed to keep their former band's energetic, melodic kick. With their first album, *Manic Pop Thrill*, That Petrol Emotion became critics' favorites, as well as earning a respectable following in the U.K. Over the years, their music remained endlessly diverse, incorporating elements of every style of independent guitar rock. Occasionally, their albums were wildly uncohesive because of this, yet they managed to turn in several excellent songs on each record. Sean left the band after their third album, *End of the Millennium Psychosis Blues*. The album showed signs that That Petrol Emotion's exuberant diversity was beginning to wear thin; their next albums proved that they were running out of things to say. After eight years, That Petrol Emotion broke up in 1994. —*Stephen Thomas Erlewine*

Manic Pop Thrill / 1986 / Demon ♦♦

● **Babble** / 1987 / Polydor ♦♦♦♦♦
On their second album, That Petrol Emotion's electrifying mix of spiky guitar hooks, direct melodies, and righteous, socially conscious lyrics solidifies into a distinctive sound that's a little messy but completely invigorating. Although they released several records in the next seven years, the band were never able to replicate the sheer power and solid hooks of *Babble*. —*Stephen Thomas Erlewine*

End of the Millennium Psychosis Blues / 1988 / Virgin ♦♦♦
A flawed, but still enjoyable, album, *End of the Millennium Psychosis Blues* saw That Petrol Emotion take a step back from the headlong rush of their two previous efforts. If "The Price of My Soul" is just a little bit *too* worthy, then there are plenty of fine moments to counterbalance it, such as the whimsical "Candy Love Satellite" and "Groove Check" (indie dance five years before it happened). But the key track is Sean O'Neill's "Cello-

phane." People had always nagged him about writing about the Troubles when he was a member of the Undertones. You can catch his unmitigated, unabridged opinion about it here. —*Alex Ogg*

Chemicrazy / Mar. 1990 / Virgin ♦♦♦
Conventional wisdom would suggest that That Petrol Emotion peaked with their first two albums of cutthroat, frenetic garage pop, and that subsequent albums made too many concessions to pop currents and lost their charm. Piffle. *Chemicrazy* is the supreme statement by a band who could have gone on churning out excellent garage-rock songs from here till eternity, but chose not to. The results on *End of the Millennium Psychosis Blues* were patchy, but not here—especially on two of the finest singles never to grace the British charts: "Sensitize" and "Hey Venus." Vocalist Steve Mack's performance on the former, in particular, is stunning; and the rest of the album is almost as good. If you have any sort of appetite for pop music, you'd have to be dead from the neck up not to dance your legs off to this. —*Alex Ogg*

Fireproof / Feb. 15, 1994 / Rykodisc ♦♦

The The

f. 1979
College Rock, Post-Punk, Alternative Pop/Rock
The The was the guise of Matt Johnson, a mercurial singer/songwriter whose music ran the gamut from dance-pop to country. Johnson formed the first incarnation of The The in 1979; the group issued its first single, "Controversial Subject," on the 4AD label in 1980. A year later, contractual obligations forced Johnson to issue the LP *Burning Blue Soul* under his own name. In 1982, The The—now essentially a Johnson solo project, backed by a revolving coterie of musicians—recorded the album *The Pornography of Despair*, which a dissatisfied Johnson chose not to release; a 1983 single recorded with Orange Juice's Zeke Manyika, "This Is the Day," formed the centerpiece of The The's proper debut, 1983's *Soul Mining*, an excursion into dance-flavored pop. Illness sidelined Johnson for much of the following year, and The The did not return until 1986's *Infected*, an eclectic commentary on the state of Britain in the modern world that was accompanied by an ambitious album-length video. When The The returned with the dissonant *Mind Bomb* in 1989, they were once again a true band, with Johnson joined by ex-Smiths guitarist Johnny Marr, but 1995's *Hanky Panky* marked yet another new direction—the first in a series of occasional albums celebrating the work of legendary performers, it was a brooding covers collection honoring the music of country great Hank Williams. —*Jason Ankeny*

Burning Blue Soul / 1981 / 4AD ♦♦♦♦
Matt Johnson's work thrives on the tension between accessible pop and dissonant experimentation; between joyful wonder and despairing bleakness. *Burning Blue Soul* was a more disjointed solo album Johnson released under his own name in 1981 before these tensions were fully integrated. This reissue is a valuable sketchbook for The The fans interested in dissecting the early inner workings of Johnson's art, but the meandering tape-collages that serve as framework will leave most others cold. —*Roch Parisien*

Soul Mining / 1983 / Epic ♦♦♦
On The The's first album, Matt Johnson crafted a pleasant but unengaging set of dance-pop just barely hinting at the experimentalism he would develop on later records like *Infected* or *Mind Bomb*. —*Stephen Thomas Erlewine*

Infected / 1986 / Epic ♦♦♦♦♦
Infected is such a leap forward from *Soul Mining* that the album hardly seems like the work of the same band. Instead of the light, agreeable dance-pop of the previous album, *Infected* draws a dense, dark sonic landscape that accurately conveys the alienation and despair Matt Johnson sings about. —*Stephen Thomas Erlewine*

● **Mind Bomb** / Jun. 1989 / Some Bizarre/Epic ♦♦♦♦♦
With the addition of former Smiths guitarist Johnny Marr, The The attempted their most ambitious album yet with *Mind Bomb*. Instead of the darkly polished dance-pop stylings of *Infected*, *Mind Bomb* opens up the music to reveal a slow, winding textured world of sound that celebrates its rough edges instead of hiding them. It's serious, dance-influenced rock of the highest order. —*Stephen Thomas Erlewine*

Dusk / Jan. 5, 1993 / Epic ♦♦♦♦
As the follow up to the much acclaimed *Mind Bomb* LP, The The's sixth studio effort *Dusk* found Matt Johnson (and his varying crew of marauders) carving one of his most accomplished products to date. *Dusk* leaves behind the infected dance beats that served as the frame work for many of his previous albums and replaces them with steamy acoustic based rhythms that shimmer with red-orange warmth while the guitar work of Johnny Marr adds a touch of other worldliness that without, would have left the record to stand alone on its strange blend of honky-tonk gospel pop. Johnson's songs seem to be mostly uplifting tromps about standard subjects ranging from love, happiness, and helpfulness—while presented in over-the-top emotional grandeur ("Love is Stronger Than Death," "Helpline Operator," and the MTV "hit" "Dogs of Lust"). As quality reigns through these songs, the tempo can become overbearing and to solve that issue, Johnson shifts gears on the B-side to include some partially downtrodden numbers ("Bluer Than Midnight," "Lung Shadows"). In the end he points out (with an under-the-radar approach) that the songs and the major concept of the album are not so much rooted in the joy of love—but in the approching darkness of loneliness and seclusion that is just around the corner. —*Jack LV Isles*

Hanky Panky / Feb. 14, 1995 / 550 Music/Epic ♦♦

NakedSelf / Feb. 29, 2000 / Interscope ♦♦♦
It's never been easy to pin Matt Johnson down. He's always come across as intense and dark, but much of his music is melodic and airy. He managed to turn his gentle rage into

a masterpiece on 1990's *Mind Bomb*, and captured heat on record with *Dusk*. But there's no new ground broken on *NakedSelf*.

Overall, it is a hit-and-miss affair. The opener, "Boiling Point," is a slow build that never seems to hit stride, but "Shrunken Man" is a solid number with well-timed production. Matt has always had a good ear for melody, and most of the songs here are no exception. Tracks like "December Sunlight," "Global Eyes," and "Phantom Walls" float hand in hand with his airy vocals.

If the album proves anything, it's that Matt has learned that he should never work alone. The band he assembled here is tight and flows well with Johnson's melodic sensibilities. The strong points on *NakedSelf* are not hard to find, but they are subtle. And while it is a solid collection of songs, The The have shone brighter. *—Chris True*

Thee Midniters

f. 1964, **db.** 1972

Latin Rock, Brown-Eyed Soul, Frat Rock, Garage Rock, Rock & Roll

Indisputably the greatest Latino rock band of the '60s, Thee Midniters took their inspiration from both the British Invasion sound of the Rolling Stones and the more traditional R&B that they were weaned on in their native Los Angeles. Hugely popular in East Los Angeles, the group, featuring both guitars and horns, had a local hit (and a small national one) with their storming version of "Land of a Thousand Dances" in 1965. Much of their repertoire featured driving, slightly punkish rock/R&B, yet lead singer Willie Garcia also had a heartbreaking delivery on slow and steamy ballads. In the manner of other local phenomena like the Rationals (from Detroit), they were equally talented at whipping up a storm with up-tempo numbers and offering smoldering romantic soul tunes. After a few albums and an interesting detour into social consciousness with the single "Chicano Power," the group split in the early '70s, though their legacy is felt in later popular L.A. Latino rock acts like Los Lobos. *—Richie Unterberger*

Unlimited / 1967 / Whittier ✦✦✦

Except for the greatest-hits compilation, this is the group's most interesting album, as eight of the twelve songs were group originals. They favor a more straightforward blue-eyed soul approach than they do on many of their singles over the course of this LP, which also includes the unusually punky (for them) number "Never Knew I Had It So Bad." *—Richie Unterberger*

● **The Best of Thee Midniters** / 1983 / Rhino ✦✦✦✦✦

An excellent compilation of 14 of their best songs, including "Land Of A Thousand Dances" and "Chicano Power." They make a fair Latino Rolling Stones on "Empty Heart," "Everybody Needs Somebody," and "Whittier Blvd." (a thinly disguised reworking of The Stones' "2120 South Michigan Ave."); "That's All," "Dreaming Casually," and "Sad Girl" are exceptional slow R&B ballads, and "Jump, Jive And Harmonize" is a tough garage-punk original. *—Richie Unterberger*

Them

f. 1963, Belfast, Northern Ireland, **db.** 1971, Belfast, Northern Ireland

British Blues, British Invasion, Blues-Rock, Rock & Roll

Not strictly a British group, but packaged as part of the British Invasion, Them forged their hard-nosed R&B sound in Belfast, Ireland, moving to England in 1964 after landing a deal with Decca Records. The band's simmering sound was dominated by boiling organ riffs, lean guitars, and the tough vocals of lead singer Van Morrison, whose recordings with Them rank among the very best performances of the British Invasion. As a hit-making act, their résumé was brief—"Here Comes the Night" and "Baby Please Don't Go" were Top Ten hits in England, "Mystic Eyes" and "Here Comes the Night" made the Top 40 in the U.S.—but their influence was considerable, reaching bands like the Doors, who Them played with during a residency in Los Angeles just before Morrison quit the band in 1966. Their most influential song of all, the classic three-chord stormer "Gloria," was actually a B-side, although the Shadows of Knight had a hit in the U.S. with a faithful, tamer cover version. *—Richie Unterberger*

Them / 1965 / Decca ✦✦✦✦✦

The debut album by the group, also known as *The Angry Young Them*, and half its tracks make it a dead-on rival to the Stones' debut album. The reissue features the album's original British configuration ("Just a Little Bit," "I Gave My Love a Diamond," "Bright Lights, Big City," and "My Little Baby" are here; "One Two Brown Eyes" and "Here Comes the Night" are absent). "My Little Baby" was no huge loss, being a pale imitation of "Here Comes the Night," but the omitted "Just a Little Bit" features a Howlin' Wolf/"Spoonful"-style performance by Van Morrison that would have incinerated a lot of American teens. On the other hand, Morrison's soul-shouting performance on the deleted "I Gave My Love a Diamond," appropriated by Bert Berns from the public domain "Cherry Song," would have shocked any folkie familiar with the original. Morrison's "You Just Can't Win" isn't nearly as impressive, but even as a time-filler it isn't half bad. And then there's "Gloria," rock's ultimate '60s sex anthem, and one of the handful of white-authored songs that can just about hold its own against any blues standard you'd care to name. *—Bruce Eder*

Them Again / Apr. 1966 / Deram ✦✦✦

The group's second and, for all intents and purposes, last full album was recorded while Them was in a state of imminent collapse. To this day, nobody knows who played on the album, other than Van Morrison and bassist Alan Henderson, though it is probable that Jimmy Page was seldom very far away when Them was recording. The 16 songs here are a little less focused than the first LP. The material was cut under siege conditions, with a constantly shifting lineup and a grueling tour schedule; essentially, there was no "group" to provide focus to the sound, only Morrison's voice, so the material bounces from a surprisingly restrained "I Put a Spell on You" to the garage-punkoid "I Can Only Give You Everything." Folk-rock rears its head not only on the moody cover of Dylan's "It's All Over Now, Baby Blue" but also the Morrison-authored "My Lonely Sad Eyes," but the main thrust is soul, which Morrison oozes everywhere—while there's some filler, his is a voice that could easily have knocked Mick Jagger or Eric Burdon off their respective perches. *—Bruce Eder*

● **Them Featuring Van Morrison** / 1987 / London ✦✦✦✦✦

Not to be confused with the identically titled Parrot Records release, which is a 20-track double-LP set, this is a 13-track single CD set and a U.S. reissue of the Decca U.K. LP from 1982. It would have been less confusing if they had called it *Them's Greatest Hits*, since it is primarily a singles compilation. But then, only four of Them's singles were hits, either in the U.K. or the U.S.—"Baby, Please Don't Go," "Gloria," "Here Comes the Night," and "Mystic Eyes," all included here. Also featured are such non-charting singles as "Don't Start Crying Now," "One More Time," "(It Won't Hurt) Half As Much," and "Richard Cory." This is not the ideal Them compilation, but this is the one that contains Them's most familiar material. *—William Ruhlmann*

The Story of Them Featuring Van Morrison / 1997 / Deram ✦✦✦✦✦

Long-overdue double CD, collecting all but one of the 50 songs (only "Mighty Like a Rose" is missing) the legendary British blues band left behind in the English Decca and American London vaults. The sound is a significant improvement over prior reissues—really loud, the way it was meant to be heard—with little touches like "The Story of Them Parts 1 and 2" linked together. It doesn't follow chronological order of release, but the order is entertaining, with alternate takes (stereo single mixes, American single edits, etc.) broken up between the two discs. It would have been nice to have had recording dates and personnel, but considering the fact that the band's lineup, apart from Morrison and bassist Alan Henderson, seemed to change every month, it's conceivable that any session information would be suspect. And one wishes for a coherent essay on the history of the band to go with the spread of photographs of the different lineups that are reprinted here. *—Bruce Eder*

Therapy?

f. 1989, Belfast, Ireland

Alternative Metal, Heavy Metal, Alternative Pop/Rock

Belfast's Therapy? might have been amongst the vast number of bands who benefited from the rise of Nirvana and grunge in the early '90s, but they proved their worth by outlasting that trend and the sub-strains that followed throughout the remainder of that decade and the one that followed. They might have frustrated the unit shifters who banked on them to follow the pack and hit the charts, but they never felt the need to cash in. Constantly expanding upon a frame of influential references that included the usual suspects (Black Sabbath) and the not-so-usual for a metal band (Killing Joke, Hüsker Dü, Buzzcocks), Therapy? released a number of records that constantly challenged themselves and their fans. The band carried a melodic sensibility that also separated them from their alternative metal peers, and although the lyrical exorcisms were often clichéd, they were never innocuous. As a bridge between Metallica and Nirvana, they never played it straight or safe. Major labels came knocking on the strength of early indie releases, with A&M eventually winning out. The label expected something closer to a grunge record but received something that didn't sound too far removed from the earlier releases in *Nurse*. It slightly tweaked the band's sound, providing more focus on the rhythm and developing Andy Cairns' melodic vocal hooks. The band enjoyed its most commercial exposure with 1994's *Troublegum*, thanks to the poppy, teen angsty "Screamager." *Infernal Love* followed in early 1995, almost immediately after extensive touring. A bleak, cinematic effort that made the remainder of Therapy?'s records seem chirpy, it ruined their chances of ever making it to mainstream popularity. As a result, 1998's *Semi-Detached* came out without a Stateside label; in 2000, *Suicide Pact* was issued through Ark 21, as was a career retrospective. *—Andy Kellman*

Caucasian Psychosis / Mar. 1992 / Quarterstick ✦✦

Nurse / 1993 / A&M ✦✦✦

An expanded recording budget does wonders for Therapy? for their first proper studio record, released by new label A&M. But rather than record with a label-approved producer, the Irish band opted to go with their soundman to provide a grunge tinge to their punishing noise. So the band's fans rested easily knowing that *Nurse* was more than their band being courted off by the fairy princess, only to return a mutated band for the worse. *Nurse* expands on the basic gist of the *Caucasian Psychosis* compilation, benefiting from further focus on Michael McKeegan's bass and Fyfe Ewing's drumming. It still sounds dark and insular, but it casts off the lo-fi sludge factor that hampered the preceding EPs. Andy Cairns' lyrics don't develop a great deal, remaining straightforward and sometimes awkward. Aside from the line "Forget Columbus/Lost your culture," "Disgraceland" fails in societal commentary with its topical namedropping. But overall, the underlying theme of the record is "You're messed up, but I'm in worse shape." Everything tends to steam by, most notably on the "Ace of Spades"-like drive of "Accelerator." But where *Nurse* really hits its stride is when the trio doesn't play on top of each other, like on the screeching insomniac dub of "Deep Sleep," one of Therapy?'s best overall moments. Since *Nurse* is somewhere between the amateurish early compilation and the polished sounding, more melodic *Troublegum*, some Therapy? fans would argue that this is their best overall record. *—Andy Kellman*

● **Troublegum** / 1994 / A&M ✦✦✦✦✦

A high watermark of early alternative metal, *Troublegum* is a spectacular, powerful, clutter-free record. Densely packed at 14 songs in 40 minutes, there's sharpness on every level, demonstrating that the promise evidenced on *Nurse* was no mirage. Chris Sheldon's job on the boards provides separation among all the instruments, avoiding the mashed effect from Therapy?'s previous outings. Fyfe Ewing and Michael McKeegan basically do what they've been doing all along as a rhythm section, but the increased clarity really allows for one to fully appreciate their abilities. Andy Cairns' vocal range and ear for melody increase tenfold, and his guitar takes on countless tones and textures only hinted at before. Detractors might claim that the riffs are too predictable and too "metal," which is somewhat understandable but ultimately unfair. One could call them simple, and one could call them focused; it's more the latter. Since the songwriting is more direct and less concerned with merely knocking things out and stopping after three minutes or so, everything is fully formed and completely realized. It's the absolute opposite of aimless, which is something Therapy? was sometimes guilty of. There's much more variety, too. With each play, it becomes increasingly obvious that no two songs sound much like each other, yet each song hangs together to form a singular piece. Metal-phobes can't help but give in to the irresistible pop-punk hooks of "Screamager" and "Nowhere." An obvious influence is acknowledged in a storming version of Joy Division's "Isolation," which pays tribute and transforms at the same time. "Unrequited" can't be missed, featuring a rattling guitar riff that gets yanked away by a violent cello tug from Martin McCarrick. *—Andy Kellman*

Infernal Love / 1995 / A&M ♦♦♦♦

The final vocal line on *Infernal Love* might be "There is a light at the end of the tunnel," but there's no denying that *Infernal Love* is anything but optimistic; it's an unrelentingly dark and sometimes bluntly turgid record. Anyone familiar with the band had grown accustomed to Andy Cairns' spins on depression, anger, bitterness, and self-destruction, but even the most devoted listener probably screamed "Snap out of it!" while first listening to this third record. It's almost as if Therapy? went on a preemptive strike, just to make sure mainstream popularity slipped from its grasp. The band had a fair amount of momentum after the success of *Troublegum*, but *Infernal Love* seemed to leave that concept in the dust. Darker chords and slower tempos prevail, and the pop-punk hooks are all but washed away. The sequentially buried, bouncing "Loose" is an anomaly, sounding like a refugee from *Troublegum* that reads like a dystopian "Jack and Diane." Other than that, it's nothing but despair and heartache. What makes *Infernal Love* misunderstood is the musical depth, which is easy to miss from the endless doom. It's not one-dimensional at all, buoyed by mournful strings and stylistic curveballs. "Bad Mother" and "Stories" skank along in staccato rhythm, with the verses of the latter aided by swanky saxophones. "Bowels of Love" sounds like Andy Cairns and the Bad Seeds. If that's not enough of a departure, a cover of Hüsker Dü's "Diane" is nothing but voice and strings. David Holmes stitches everything together masterfully, employing numerous atmospheric effects and random trickery to give the record a cinematic flourish. If this is what Therapy? had in mind, the band hit the bullseye. *—Andy Kellman*

Semi-Detached / May 1998 / A&M ♦♦♦

If you convinced the staff at the psych ward to let you out after listening to *Infernal Love* for two weeks straight, you might have caught wind of Therapy?'s fourth studio record, released two years later. The U.S. branch of A&M opted not to release *Semi-Detached*, so odds are pretty good that some of the band's stateside fans found out about it much later on. Since Therapy? made no signs of crossing over into the rap-metal territory that was just beginning to prove profitable, the U.S. decision-makers likely felt that the band was no longer marketable. *Infernal Love*'s drab tone didn't help, though. Nonetheless, *Semi-Detached* deserved more ears upon release. The band would later admit to lacking direction and focus while recording it, but you really wouldn't know that when listening to it. Fyfe Ewing abandoned ship prior to recording, replaced by Graham Hopkins. Martin McCarrick, who had supplied cello for the band, was added as an official member on guitar and strings. Whether or not the transitional nature led to a perceived state of haziness is up for debate, but it's pound-for-pound a fine record. It's not as harrowing as *Infernal Love*, and it registers as 12 songs rather than a thematic slab. A return to defiantly anthemic melody is present, but there's nothing overtly poppy. The guitars gnaw and latch on. Andy Cairns' usual subject matter remains, but the songwriting is at its least clichéd. It's no masterpiece, but it's probably their second or third best record—hardly something to fret over. *—Andy Kellman*

Suicide Pact: You First / Feb. 8, 2000 / Ark 21 ♦♦♦

Very unapologetically, *Suicide Pact* says "Screw you if you don't like me." Shedding any sense of pop hooks, Andy Cairns and company resort to meat cleavers to reel you in. It's a big sloppy mess, which will likely appeal to fans of Therapy?'s older material—here's hoping they didn't lose them in the tar pit of *Infernal Love*. Those wanting a return to the tunefulness of "Screamager" and "Loose" will likely be disappointed. It's a warts-and-all record, which means it isn't short of its ugly bits ("Jam Jar Jail," "Six Mile Water"). Cairns' occasional Billy Gibbons-meets-Tom Waits warbling can get tiresome, especially when you're reminded of his fine singing voice. But when they really get their Irish blood pumping, the magic of *Troublegum*'s nastier bits ("Knives," "Trigger Inside") rears its demented head and Therapy? click on all cylinders. *Suicide Pact*'s greatest moment is the last track listed, "Sister"; it's the most rhythmic, bass-driven song on the record. Cairns' guitar allows room for the rhythm section to breathe a little, a rarity. If there's a running lyrical thread to Therapy?'s metallic miserablism throughout their decade-long existence, it's stated in that song: "Sister I'm lost/ And I'm taking you with me/ Wherever I go." Despite growing long in the tooth for a hard-rock band, they're still doing this music better than the majority of their younger ilk. *—Andy Kellman*

So Much for the Ten Year Plan: A Retrospective 1990-2000 / Oct. 3, 2000 / Ark 21 ♦♦♦♦

Therapy?'s sardonically-named retrospective *So Much for the Ten Year Plan* gathers singles, highlights from their albums, and two new tracks, "Bad Karma Follows You Around" and "Fat Camp." From their first single "Meat Abstract" to churning, angst-ridden pop like "Screamager" and "Nowhere" to darker, metal-tinged songs like "He's Not That Kind of Girl" and the Hüsker Dü cover "Diane," the hand-picked track selection covers all the bases of Therapy?'s sound, and provides fans and newcomers alike with an entertaining sampling of their best work. *—Heather Phares*

They Might Be Giants

f. 1983, Boston, MA

Pop Underground, College Rock, Post-Punk, Alternative Pop/Rock

Combining a knack for infectious melodies with a quirky, bizarre sense of humor and a vaguely avant-garde aesthetic borrowed from the New York post-punk underground, They Might Be Giants became one of the most unlikely alternative success stories of the late '80s and early '90s. Musically, the duo of John Flansburg and John Linnell borrowed from everywhere, but their free-wheeling eclecticism was enhanced by their arcane, geeky sense of humor. They would reference everything from British Invasion to Tin Pan Alley, while making allusion to pulp fiction and President Polk. Through their string of indie releases and constant touring as a duo, They Might Be Giants built up a huge following on college campuses during the late '80s, switching to a major label in the early '90s. With support from MTV, 1990's *Flood* became a gold album, and with it, the band began to reap commercial rewards, elevating them into the status of one of the most popular alternative bands before grunge. However, their whimsical outlook became buried in the avalanche of post-grunge groups that dominated MTV and modern rock radio in the mid-'90s, and the group retreated to its cult following. *—Stephen Thomas Erlewine*

They Might Be Giants / 1986 / Restless-Bar/None ♦♦♦♦♦

They Might Be Giants' eponymous debut album is a wild fusion of new wave pop and arty post-punk experiments borrowed from the New York underground. It runs through a head-spinning 19 songs in just over 45 minutes, running the gamut from the performance-art schtick of "Chess Piece Face" and "Youth Culture Killed My Dog" to the pure pop of "Don't Let's Start" and "Everything Right Is Wrong Again." While there are a lot of geeky jokes and barely developed ideas scattered throughout the album, the sheer kaleidoscopic array of styles is intoxicating, and it helps the best songs—the Costello-esque "Put Your Hand Inside the Puppet Head," the sighing "Hide Away Folk Family," the stomping "(She Was A) Hotel Detective" and the gorgeous "She's an Angel"—stand out in sharp relief. *—Stephen Thomas Erlewine*

● **Lincoln** / 1989 / Restless-Bar/None ♦♦♦♦♦

Cutting away some of the artier aspects of their debut, They Might Be Giants craft another wildly eclectic and geekily fun collection of alterna-pop with *Lincoln*. In general, the album displays greater musical ambition than its predecessor, especially since the duo have trimmed many of the weirder excesses of the debut. Without such arty trappings, their gift for irresistible pop hooks becomes all the more clear, with "Ana Ng," "Purple Toupee," the Latin shuffle of "The World's Address," "Santa's Beard," the surprisingly affecting "They'll Need a Crane" and the lounge jazz of "Kiss Me, Son of God" standing out among the 18 songs. And when They Might Be Giants don't go for the hooks, as on "Pencil Rain" or "Cage & Aquarium," they prove to be expert musical satirists, which means that *Lincoln* is every bit as infectious as the debut. *—Stephen Thomas Erlewine*

Flood / Jan. 1990 / Elektra ♦♦♦♦

On their major-label debut *Flood*, They Might Be Giants exchange quirky artiness for unabashed geekiness and a more varied and polished musical attack. Although the album contains two of the group's finest singles in "Birdhouse in Your Soul" and "Istanbul (Not Constantinople)," the overall record is uneven, since the group's hooks aren't quite as sharp as before and the humor is either too geeky or leavened with awkward social statements like "Your Racist Friend." Even with its faults, *Flood* has a number of first-rate songs, and it's a strong addition to their catalog, even if it isn't as weirdly intoxicating as its predecessors. *—Stephen Thomas Erlewine*

Miscellaneous T / Jul. 1991 / Restless-Bar/None ♦♦♦

Several of They Might Be Giants' finest songs were buried on B-sides, which makes the rarities compilation such a welcome addition to their catalog. While several of these songs are nothing but endearing jokes ("Mr. Klaw," "Lady is a Tramp," "For Science"), there are just as many gems. "We're the Replacements" is a fun homage to the Minneapolis legends, "The Famous Polk" is silly and infectious, "It's Not My Birthday" has a great hook, as does "Nightgown of the Sullen Moon," while "Hey Mr. DJ, I Thought You Said We Had a Deal" is a fun satire. Songs like these often capture the irreverent sense of humor that the group lost when they signed to a major label. *—Stephen Thomas Erlewine*

Apollo 18 / Mar. 24, 1992 / Elektra ♦♦♦

Although it lacks a standout single like "Birdhouse in Your Soul," *Apollo 18* is a more consistent album than *Flood*, overflowing with ideas and pop hooks. The most noteworthy idea may have been "Fingertips," a "suite" of 21 song fragments designed to make each random play a new experience, but the meat of the album lies in pop songs like "I Palindrome I," "My Evil Twin," "She's Actual Size" and "Which Describes How You're Feeling." The album has a slightly darker feeling than its predecessors, but that just gives the album a resonance that was missing on *Flood*. *—Stephen Thomas Erlewine*

John Henry / Sep. 13, 1994 / Elektra ♦♦♦

Just in case you thought that the only thing they were capable of was smart-aleck herky-jerk novelty tunes, on this album John Flansburgh and John Linnell put together an honest-to-goodness rock band and show that they know how to use it. And the result is one of the more satisfying TMBG projects, a crunchy yet sweet assortment of the usual bemusement ("Unrelated Thing"), weirdness ("Spy") and smart-aleck herky-jerk novelty tunes ("Meet James Ensor," "Extra Savoir Faire") bolstered by unusually hard-rocking accompaniment. Kudos to bass player (and Pere Ubu alumnus) Tony Maimone and to drummer Brian Doherty for coming up with the tectonic groove that powers "AKA Driver" and to everyone involved for the irresistible guitar pop of "Subliminal" and "I Should Be Allowed to Think." Skip over "O, Do Not Forsake Me" and the throwaway instrumental "Spy." *—Rick Anderson*

Factory Showroom / Oct. 8, 1996 / Elektra ✦✦

● **Then: The Earlier Years** / Mar. 25, 1997 / Restless ✦✦✦✦✦
Then: The Earlier Years is a double-disc set containing all of They Might Be Giants' original, independent records—the two albums *They Might Be Giants* and *Lincoln*, plus all of the B-sides and EP tracks that were compiled on *Misc. T*—adding nearly 20 previously unreleased tracks. While the bonus tracks are of varying quality—only "Now That I Have Anything" and demos of "Don't Let's Start," "Which Describes How You're Feeling" and "Hope That I Get Old Before I Die" are of interest to anyone but hardcore collectors—the official releases remain surprisingly fresh, a combination of melodic skills, inventive arrangements, self-consciously clever lyrics, and bizarre, geeky humor. For most listeners, *Then* is the definitive They Might Be Giants, encapsulating all of their charm and quirkiness and capturing them at the height of their career. *—Stephen Thomas Erlewine*

Severe Tire Damage / 1998 / Restless ✦✦✦
On their very first live album, *Severe Tire Damage*, intellectual rockers They Might Be Giants offer a "best of" set, which contains mostly radical re-workings of fan favorites. The reason for the emergence of a live album came about when TMBG played a successful radio session for the Spin Radio Network, where the duo was joined by their touring band as well as horn players and a rhythm section. They were so impressed with the results that they almost immediately went back and picked out versions of songs that sounded totally different live when compared to the original studio versions (especially the songs "She's Actual Size" and "Why Does the Sun Shine?"). Included are the 'hits' "Istanbul (Not Constantinople)" and "Particle Man," as well as the brand new track "Doctor Worm." To prove that they haven't lost their quirky edge, the album ends with 7 unlisted tracks that were written on the spot, in front of their audience. *—Greg Prato*

Thin Lizzy

f. 1970, Dublin, Ireland, **db.** 1983
Album Rock, British Metal, Heavy Metal, Hard Rock

Despite a huge hit single in the mid-'70s ("The Boys Are Back in Town") and becoming a popular act with hard rock/heavy metal fans, Thin Lizzy are still, in the pantheon of '70s rock bands, underappreciated. Formed in the late '60s by Irish singer/songwriter/bassist Phil Lynott, Lizzy, though not the first band to do so, combined romanticized working-class sentiments with their ferocious, twin-lead guitar attack. As the band's creative force, Lynott was a more insightful and intelligent writer than many of his ilk, preferring slice-of-life working-class dramas of love and hate influenced by Bob Dylan and Bruce Springsteen. As a black man, Lynott was an anomaly in the nearly all-White world of hard rock, and as such imbued much of his work with a sense of alienation; he was the outsider, the romantic guy from the other side of the tracks, a self-styled poet of the lovelorn and downtrodden. His sweeping vision and writerly impulses at times gave way to pretentious songs aspiring to cliched notions of literary significance, but Lynott's limitless charisma made even the most misguided moments worth hearing.

After a few records that hinted at their potential, Lizzy released *Fighting* in 1975, and the band had molded itself into a tight recording and performing unit. Lizzy's big break came with their next album, *Jailbreak*, and its first single, "The Boys Are Back in Town." Never the toast of critics, Lizzy toured relentlessly, building a reputation as a terrific live band, despite the lead guitar spot becoming a revolving door. The records came fast and furious, and Lynott began writing more ambitious songs, wrapping them up in vaguely articulated concept albums. The large fan base the band had built as a result of "Boys" turned into a smaller, yet still enthusiastic bunch of hard rockers. Adding insult to injury was the rise of punk rock, which Lynott vigorously supported, but made Lizzy look too traditional. By the mid-'80s, Thin Lizzy called it a career. Lynott recorded solo records and sadly, became a victim of his longtime substance abuse, dying in 1986 at age 35. *—John Dougan*

Thin Lizzy / 1971 / Deram ✦✦✦
Thin Lizzy were originally conceived as a power trio in the image of Cream and the Jimi Hendrix Experience, but Eric Bell lacked the charisma of these groups' guitarists, forcing vocalist/bassist Philip Lynott to take center stage from day one. Despite his already poetic, intensely personal lyrics, Lynott was only beginning to develop as a songwriter, and the band's unfocused, folk-infused early efforts are a far cry from their mid-'70s hard-rock glory. Recorded on a shoestring budget, their self-titled debut is surprisingly mellow; many songs, such as "Clifton Grange Hotel" and "The Friendly Ranger of Clontarf Castle," sound confused and unfinished. Quiet ballads like "Honesty is No Excuse," "Eire," and "Saga of the Ageing Orphan" abound, while supposed rockers such as "Ray-Gun" and "Return of the Farmer's Son" fall remarkably flat. In fact, Lizzy only bare their claws on "Look What the Wind Blew In," a gutsy rocker which hints at things to come. Four bonus tracks (originally released as singles) were added to the CD reissue, and of these "Things Ain't Working Out Down at the Farm" is quite memorable, while the mournful "Dublin" contains Lynott's first great lyric. *—Ed Rivadavia*

Shades of a Blue Orphanage / 1972 / Deram ✦✦✦
Named after the musicians' previous bands (Bell's Shades of Blue and Lynott and Downey's Orphanage), the disappointing *Shades of a Blue Orphanage* proved that Decca Records had absolutely no idea of what to do with *Thin Lizzy*. The complex arrangements of the title track and "The Rise and Dear Demise of the Funky Nomadic Tribes" are as overblown and disjointed as their titles. "I Don't Want to Forget How to Jive" is a lame, '50s-style rockabilly number, and "Call the Police" is only saved by Lynott's captivating tell-tale lyrics—something at which he would later excel. Lynott is equally eloquent and personal on the piano-led "Sarah," written about his grandmother and not to be confused with the song by the same name written for his daughter seven years later. The album's few, truly bright moments are confined to the aggressive hard rock of "Baby Face" and the charming, descending riff of "Buffalo Gal," a melancholy, mid-paced ballad in the style which would become a Lynott trademark. *—Ed Rivadavia*

Vagabonds of the Western World / 1973 / Deram ✦✦
After achieving a reluctant Top Ten hit with a rock version of the traditional Irish pub ballad "Whiskey in the Jar," Thin Lizzy began work on *Vagabonds of the Western World*—their third, and ultimately last album for Decca Records. The single's surprise success gave the band bargaining power to demand more money and time to record, resulting in their first sonically satisfying album. The environmentally-conscious R&B of "Mama Nature Said" kicks things off with Eric Bell leading the way on slide guitar. The overblown "The Hero and the Madman" and the tepid "Slow Blues" threaten to derail the proceedings, but all is well again when the band break into their first bona fide classic "The Rocker." Brimming with attitude and dangerous swagger, Lynott sets the tone, as drummer Brian Downey explodes into life for the first time on vinyl. Lizzy's Irish heritage permeates the title track, and the beautiful "Little Girl in Bloom" is absolutely flawless, featuring Lynott, the poet, in top form. In many ways, *Vagabonds*... actually rocks harder than Lizzy's next album, the soulful *Nightlife*—often considered the band's first "important" record. And with the inclusion of four non-LP singles, including the aforementioned "Whiskey in the Jar," this package becomes even more appealing. *—Ed Rivadavia*

Night Life / 1974 / Mercury ✦✦✦
Thin Lizzy's 1974 release, *Nightlife*, is not their best, but is an important release in the band's history nonetheless. It marked the first album to feature guitarists Scott Gorham and Brian Robertson, who joined Lizzy stalwarts Phil Lynott (bass/vocals) and Brian Downey (drums). Renowned hard rock producer Ron Nevison (the Who) was on hand but, surprisingly, the album does not rock nearly as hard as their more popular later releases would (*Jailbreak*, *Bad Reputation*, etc.). For the most part, the material is comparable to the laid back rock of Bob Seger and Steely Dan. But a couple of future concert crowd pleasers are included, such as the slow blues of "Still In Love With You" and one of the album's few true, hard rock tunes, "Sha-La-La." Some of the tracks are easily forgettable ("Frankie Carroll," "Philomena," etc.), while others turn out to be strong soft rock compositions ("Showdown," "She Knows," "Dear Heart," and the title track). Also included is one of Lizzy's most underrated rockers, "It's Only Money," which seems to have been forgotten over time. *Nightlife* is by no means a terrible album, it just wasn't the right one for Thin Lizzy, especially, since at pressing, they had two great rock guitarists in their fold. *—Greg Prato*

Fighting / 1975 / Mercury ✦✦✦✦
Musically, 1975's more hard rock-oriented *Fighting* was definitely a step in the right direction for Thin Lizzy (it's predecessor, *Nightlife*, was too rooted in laid back rock), yet compositionally, songwriter Phil Lynott was still developing. While the band was on tour with Bob Seger a year earlier, they were upset that Seger did not perform one of their favorite songs, "Rosalie." Lizzy took the matter into their own hands, covering the track for *Fighting*, and eventually making it their own concert staple (and eventual U.K. hit single when a live version was released in 1978). The muscular blues-groove of "Suicide" was another standout, as was the melodic "Wild One," the closing rocker "Ballad of a Hard Man," and two tracks paired back to back that create an underrated Lizzy epic, "King's Vengeance" and "Spirit Slips Away." Guitarists Gorham and Robertson have a more prominent role on the album, as their trademark dual guitar harmonies take center stage (and would inspire such future rock/metal bands as Metallica, Iron Maiden, and Def Leppard). *Fighting* did not prove to be the band's much sought-after commercial breakthrough (that was right around the corner, with 1976's *Jailbreak*), but it did introduce the band as a true hard rock force. *—Greg Prato*

Jailbreak / 1976 / Mercury ✦✦✦✦✦
On Lizzy's third album with new guitarists Gorham and Robertson, *Jailbreak*, the band perfected their hard rocking, storytelling, guitar-laden style, and was rewarded with worldwide breakthrough success. It also marked the first album where the band finally realized they were a true hard rock band, and put a stop to the soft rock that plagued such albums as 1974's *Nightlife*. Although vocalist/bassist Phil Lynott was unfairly criticized as being a Bruce Springsteen soundalike at the time, it was on *Jailbreak* that he came into his own, perfecting his storytelling lyric writing and becoming a true poet in the process. Songwise, the album was also Lizzy's first really consistent album, there is simply not a single weak track in the bunch. The hard rocking war tales of "Emerald" and "Warriors," the killer boogie of "Angel of the Coast," the country rocker "Cowboy Song," and a pair of rock's greatest anthems, the title track and the perennial radio favorite "The Boys Are Back in Town," are among Lizzy's best tracks ever. Add to it such strong album cuts as the Dire Straits-esque ballad "Fight or Fall" plus the heartbroken tales "Running Back" and "Romeo and the Lonely Girl," and you have one of the finest hard rock albums of all time. *—Greg Prato*

Johnny the Fox / 1976 / Mercury ✦✦✦
Instead of touring for a year solid behind their breakthrough *Jailbreak* album, Thin Lizzy had to cut the tour short when Phil Lynott became seriously ill with hepatitis. But the band didn't just sit around, they went directly back into the recording studio, and recorded a follow-up, *Johnny the Fox*. Although not as commercially successful as its predecessor, it was another classic Lizzy release—100% filler-free. Lynott's recurring tragic (and drug-addled) character, Johnny reappears in the album opener of the same name and the awesome funk rocker "Johnny the Fox Meets Jimmy the Weed," while a new character, Rocky, turns out to be a born rock & roll star. Also included is the U.K. hit single "Don't Believe

a Word," a pair of Lizzy's most gorgeous ballads—"Old Flame" and "Sweet Marie," and the grim war tale of "Massacre." Although Lizzy was effortlessly rolling off great albums, there was a lot of in-band bickering going on between guitarist Brian Robertson and Lynott, and *Johnny the Fox* would turn out to be the last studio album that Robertson would be a prominent part of. —*Greg Prato*

Bad Reputation / 1977 / Mercury ✦✦✦
Although Lizzy's last two albums, 1976's *Jailbreak* and *Johnny the Fox*, were hard rock classics laden with strong songwriting and playing, the production on both releases was anemic. On 1977's *Bad Reputation*, Lizzy hooked up with respected hard rock producer Tony Visconti (David Bowie, T. Rex), who finally helped the band fulfill their potential, sonically speaking. Lizzy had to record the majority of the album as a trio, since guitarist Brian Robertson was forced to bow out and recuperate from a hand injury sustained in a barroom fight. Hence, guitarist Scott Gorham performed double duty on almost all the tracks, and judging by the remarkable guitar harmonies, he rose to the occasion splendidly. Songwriter/singer/bassist Phil Lynott was again equipped with a fine batch of compositions, which comprise Lizzy's third classic album in a row. The tuneful epic "Soldier of Fortune" starts the album off, which quickly gives way to the furiously rocking title track. Lynott's storytelling lyrics take center stage on such tracks as "Opium Trail," "Southbound," and "Dear Lord," while the irresistible dirty funk of "Dancing in the Moonlight" was a U.K. hit single (and later covered by Smashing Pumpkins as a B-side in 1993). Other standouts include the vicious "Killer Without a Cause" and the reflective beauty of "Downtown Sundown." Yet another consistent, stellar Lizzy set. —*Greg Prato*

Live & Dangerous / 1978 / Warner Brothers ✦✦✦✦✦
Along with Kiss' *Alive*, the Who's *Live at Leeds*, and the Rolling Stones' *Get Yer Ya-Ya's Out*, Thin Lizzy's 1978 double album, *Live and Dangerous*, is one of the greatest live rock albums of all time. The band wisely hooked up with producer Tony Visconti, again, and although it's become known in later years that the tracks included extensive overdubbing, many of the performances outshine the original studio versions. Except for a few tracks, the majority of the material spans from 1974's *Nightlife* to 1977's *Bad Reputation*, while the concerts were recorded during Lizzy's last two major tours (1976 and 1977). Few bands have ever matched the explosive energy that Lizzy creates on such tracks as "Jailbreak," "Emerald," "Rosalie/Cowgirl's Song," "Don't Believe a Word," "Are You Ready," and "Sha-La-La," while their sing-along anthem "The Boys Are Back in Town" proves even more vivacious in a live setting. The more serene material—"Southbound" and "Dancing in the Moonlight"—is just as gripping, while the slow blues of "Still in Love with You" contains two of the most heartfelt and lyrical guitar solos ever (a trade-off between both Robertson and Gorham). Add to it such strong album cuts as "Massacre," "Johnny the Fox Meets Jimmy the Weed," "Warrior," "Suicide," and "The Rocker," and you have the ultimate Lizzy album. *Live and Dangerous* is a must-have for fans of powerful hard rock. —*Greg Prato*

Black Rose: A Rock Legend / 1979 / Warner Brothers ✦✦✦✦✦
Black Rose: A Rock Legend would prove to be Thin Lizzy's last true classic album (and last produced by Tony Visconti). Guitarist Brian Robertson was replaced by Gary Moore prior to the album's recording. Moore had already been a member of the band in the early '70s and served as a tour fill-in for Robertson in 1977, and he fits in perfectly with Lizzy's heavy, dual-guitar attack. *Black Rose* also turned out to be the band's most musically varied, accomplished, and successful studio album, reaching number two on the U.K. album charts upon release. Lizzy leader Phil Lynott is again equipped with a fine set of originals, which the rest of the band shines on—the percussion-driven opener "Do Anything You Want To," the pop hit "Waiting for an Alibi" and a gentle song for Lynott's newly born daughter, "Sarah." Not all the material is as upbeat, such as the funky "S&M," as well two grim tales of street life and substance abuse—"Toughest Street in Town" and "Got to Give It Up" (the latter sadly prophetic for Lynott). *Black Rose* closes with the epic seven-minute title track, which includes an amazing, complex guitar solo by Moore that incorporates Celtic themes against a hard rock accompaniment. *Black Rose: A Rock Legend* is one of the '70s lost rock classics. —*Greg Prato*

Chinatown / 1980 / Warner Brothers ✦✦✦
While Thin Lizzy's last release, *Black Rose*, was a focused, inspired hard rock masterwork, its follow-up, 1980's *Chinatown*, was a letdown. Guitarist Gary Moore was a major reason for the predecessor's success, but he quit during the subsequent tour (eventually replaced by ex-Pink Floyd touring guitarist Snowy White). Also, leader Phil Lynott and guitarist Scott Gorham were indulging heavily in hard drugs by this point, which was obviously taking its toll. And since producer Tony Visconti was not on board again, the lively production that played such a prominent part in the success of their past few releases was noticeably absent. The first side contains the best material: the anthemic "We Will Be Strong," the pop perfection of "Sweetheart," the obviously autobiographical drug tale of "Sugar Blues," plus the British hit singles "Killer on the Loose" and the title track. The second side, however, is comprised almost entirely of bland filler, such as "Having a Good Time," "Didn't I" and "Hey You." While it's not their worst album (that "honor" would go to their next studio album, 1981's *Renegade*), *Chinatown* should have been a lot better, especially coming off such a stellar release as *Black Rose*. —*Greg Prato*

Renegade / 1981 / Warner Brothers ✦✦

Thunder and Lightning / 1983 / Warner Brothers ✦✦✦

● **Dedication: The Very Best of Thin Lizzy** / Apr. 2, 1991 / Mercury ✦✦✦✦✦
Several Thin Lizzy "best of" collections have surfaced over the years (such as 1981's *Adventures of Thin Lizzy* and 1984's *Lizzy Lives!*), but the best two are undeniably 1996's *Wild One* and 1991's *Dedication*. While not as extensive as *Wild One* (only one track is featured from their '80s work), *Dedication* contains more early selections than the other

mentioned titles. But the real attraction for Lizzy buffs is the inclusion of the previously unreleased title track, which was completed by the other members years after Lynott's passing in 1986. Elsewhere, often-overlooked tracks like "She Knows," "Fighting My Way Back" and "Cowboy Song" get to share the spotlight with such familiar faves as "The Boys Are Back in Town," "Bad Reputation," "Jailbreak," "Waiting for an Alibi," "Dancing in the Moonlight" and "Don't Believe a Word." Also included is an essay in which Lynott is quoted as saying that he'd like Lizzy to be remembered as a great guitar band (in the tradition of the Yardbirds, etc.). After hearing the great tracks on *Dedication*, you'll be reminded that there was so much more to this legendary band. —*Greg Prato*

Peel Sessions / 1995 / Strange Fruit ✦✦✦✦✦
Better than the too-short, but still OK *Dedication* greatest hits compilation released by Mercury in 1991, *The Peel Sessions* features raw and wild versions of great Lizzy songs that provide a great historical overview of the band's development. For what it's worth, this is the only Peel session release with liner notes written by John Peel himself. —*John Dougan*

Thinking Fellers Union Local #282
f. 1986, San Francisco, CA
Experimental Rock, Indie Rock, Alternative Pop/Rock
With such a longwinded moniker, it seems likely that Thinking Fellers Union Local #282 could be nothing but a bunch of pretentious art-school rejects. Fortunately, that's pretty far from the truth—their sound is a hybrid of art rock and punk rock, based on noodling on organs, electric banjos, mandolins and heavy, fuzzed-out guitar blasts. The group formed in 1987 in San Francisco and released their first album *Wormed By Leonard* on their own label Thwart a year later. In 1991, the group made the jump to the Matador label, where they released 1991's critically acclaimed *Lovelyville*, 1992's *Mother Of All Saints* and 1994's *Strangers From the Universe*. They moved to Ajax for the following year's *Funeral Pudding* and then to Communion for 1996's *I Hope It Lands*, where they remained on the roster for the rest of the '90s despite their lack of further releases. However, they continued to play sporadic, spontaneous dates and a new album was rumored for a 2001 release. —*Heather Phares*

Wormed, By Leonard / 1988 / Thwart Productions ✦✦

Tangle / 1989 / Thwart Productions ✦✦✦
Tangle, the group's second album, contains more melodic but no less bizarre material than their debut. Both albums are released on the group's own aptly-named Thwart Productions record label. —*Heather Phares*

Lovelyville / 1991 / Matador ✦✦✦✦✦
The group's first album for Matador is also one of their more accessible ones, with the group's penchant for willful eccentricity colliding with some hummable melodies. However, this release also contains plenty of what TFUL #282 fans lovingly call "Feller-filler," i.e., noise-pieces that have no real beginning, or ending, or point for that matter. —*Heather Phares*

Mother of All Saints / 1992 / Matador ✦✦✦
Mother of All Saints is the Fellers' magnum opus. At 23 songs, it might be longer than most people's attention spans, but inside it lurks some of their finest moments, such as "Tell Me," "Hive," "Hummingbird in a Cube of Ice," and "Infection." True, there is plenty of "Feller-filler" on *Mother of All Saints* (an inspired piece called "Tuning Notes" attests to that) but the group's melodic sensibilities prevail on the actual songs on this album. —*Heather Phares*

● **Strangers from the Universe** / Sep. 12, 1994 / Matador ✦✦✦✦✦
The group's most subdued and melodic album yet, *Strangers* is ironically the Feller's least strange album. It's also their most diverse; the goofy "My Pal the Tortoise" shares space with the genuinely disturbing "The Operation" and the genuinely catchy weirdo-pop of "Socket," and "The Piston and the Shaft," "Noble Experiment," "February," and "Cup of Dreams" explore the group's rare sentimental side, and the result is the group's most complete and listenable album. —*Heather Phares*

Funeral Pudding / Jan. 1, 1995 / Ajax ✦✦✦

3rd Bass
f. 1987, Queens, NY, **db.** 1992
East Coast Rap, Alternative Rap, Golden Age
Along with the Beastie Boys, 3rd Bass stands as the rare white hip-hop act that's actually won respect and credibility among the rap hardcore. Pete Nice, one-time English major at Columbia whose radio program "Top of the Hip-Hop" was unceremoniously cancelled by the purportedly progressive WKCR-FM, teamed with MC Serch to offer devastating put-downs of the hip-hop lifestyle and worldview. They have since disbanded, but their two albums were definitive, if at times uneven. —*Ron Wynn*

● **The Cactus Album** / 1989 / Def Jam ✦✦✦✦✦
Besides the upper-middle-class frat-punks-in-rap-clothing shtick of the Beastie Boys and emissary/producer Rick Rubin, who both gained a legitimate, earned respect in the rap community, there were very few white kids in rap's first decade who spoke the poetry of the street with compassion and veneration for the form. That is, until *The Cactus Album*. Matching MC Serch's bombastic, goofy good nature and Prime Minister Pete Nice's gritty, English-trained wordsmithery (sounding like a young Don in training), 3rd Bass' debut album is revelatory in its way. For one, it is full of great songs, alternately upbeat rollers ("Sons of 3rd Bass"), casual-but-sincere disses ("The Gas Face"), razor-sharp street didacticism ("Triple Stage Darkness," "Wordz of Wizdom"), and sweaty city anthems ("Brooklyn Queens," "Steppin' to the A.M.," odes to day and night, respectively), with A-plus

production by heavyweights Prince Paul and Bomb Squad, as well as the surprising, overshadowing work of Sam Sever. The duo may not have come from the streets, but their hearts were there, and it shows. The album embodies New York life. Not every single idea plays out successfully—Serch's Louis Armstrong impression on "Flippin' Off the Wall..." is on the wrong side of the taste line, and "Desert Boots" is a puzzling Western-themed insertion—but they are at least interesting stretches that add to the dense, layered texture of the album. *The Cactus Album* was also important because it proved to the hip-hop heads that white kids could play along without appropriating or bastardizing the culture. It may not have completely integrated rap, but it was a precursor to a culture that became more inclusive and widespread after its arrival. *—Stanton Swihart*

Cactus Revisited / 1990 / Def Jam ♦♦♦
A bit of a between-album attempt to keep the band in people's sights, *Cactus Revisited* takes most of the biggest hits from 3rd Bass' debut and hands them over to such respected mixers as Marley Marl, Dave Darrell, and Prince Paul for them to play with. It is a patchy diversion. Some remixes such as the more danceable version of "The Cactus" or Prince Paul's terrifically energized take on "Gas Face" are mighty entertaining, but others seem to just sit on their thumbs and lengthen the original tracks. "Wordz of Wisdom," for instance, is clearly the worst delinquent because despite an absolutely delightful use of Depeche Mode samples, it quickly staggers as it tries to stretch out into its eight-minute entirety. Plus, to make matters worse, the previously unreleased "3 Strikes 5000" quickly loses its collector gem value since it later appeared on the band's superb *Derelicts of Dialect* full-length. In any case, for those desperately looking for anything new from a band cut too short in their career, *Cactus Revisited* might still placate such woes. Flaws and all. It's just unfortunate that while 3rd Bass might have been one of the most under-appreciated hip-hop acts around, this patchy remix collection too frequently gives their detractors more than enough ammo to fire back at them. *—Dean Carlson*

Derelicts of Dialect / 1991 / Def Jam ♦♦♦
Although 3rd Bass didn't fully realize their tremendous potential, the Brooklyn rappers offered enjoyable, if uneven, albums. Like the group's 1989 debut, their second and final album, *Derelects of Dialect*, makes it clear that the MCs weren't aiming for the pop charts—and were loyal only to the hip-hop hardcore. When MC Serch and Pete Nice tear into such aggressive and forceful declarations as "Pop Goes the Weasel" (an inflammatory attack on Vanilla Ice), "Portrait of the Artist as a Hood" and "Ace in the Hole," it's clear why they were among the few White MCs who were successful in the young Black community—someone who heard their rapping without seeing their picture could easily assume they were Black. Although the goofy "Herbalz in Your Mouth" shows some De La Soul and Tribe Called Quest influence, 3rd Bass doesn't allow itself to be nearly as lighthearted, and keeps things hardcore and intense. *—Alex Henderson*

Third Eye Blind

Adult Alternative Pop/Rock, Post-Grunge
Falling between Hootie & the Blowfish and Live, Third Eye Blind's catchy and melodic post-grunge made the group's first single, "Semi-Charmed Life," into a hit in the spring of 1997. The San Francisco-based quartet consisted of Stephan Jenkins (vocals), Kevin Cadogan (guitar), Arion Salazar (bass), and Brad Hargraves (drums). As Third Eye Blind was getting off the ground, Jenkins was earning major-label attention through his production of the Braids' 1996 cover of Queen's "Bohemian Rhapsody," which became an international hit. Shortly afterward, he signed a publishing deal, which was reported to be the largest ever for an unreleased artist. By playing the Bay Area frequently, Third Eye Blind cultivated a dedicated fan base, and the group's original 14-song demo attracted the attention of major labels. The buzz was continuing to build on Third Eye Blind when the group finagled their way to a prized opening slot for Oasis' April 1996 concert at San Francisco's Civic Auditorium. At the time of the concert, the group was unsigned, but following their well-received performance, the band became the subject of a bidding war. The band signed with Elektra/Asylum because the label offered the most artistic freedom, which included enlisting Jenkins as the album's producer. Upon signing to Elektra, he was offered a production deal to help develop new bands. Jenkins produced Third Eye Blind's eponymous debut, which was recorded in San Francisco with the assistance of Eric Valentine, an engineer who also worked on their early demos. *Third Eye Blind* was released in the spring of 1997, and by the summer, its first single, "Semi-Charmed Life," had become a number one modern rock hit. *Blue* followed in 1999. *—Stephen Thomas Erlewine*

● **Third Eye Blind** / Apr. 8, 1997 / Elektra ♦♦♦♦
Third Eye Blind's eponymous debut is catchier than the average post-grunge album, and that fact alone reveals a lot about the band. Instead of relying on standard, plodding grunge influences, Third Eye Blind draws heavily from the simple hook-laden traditions of classic arena rock, which makes the album more immediate. Unfortunately, this also makes it a little simplistic—the group can craft a naggingly memorable hook, as evidenced by the single "Semi-Charmed Life," but they aren't always able to fashion them into songs. Still, *Third Eye Blind* is easy on the ears, and its straight-ahead professionalism makes it a pleasurable listen for post-grungers. *—Stephen Thomas Erlewine*

Blue / Nov. 23, 1999 / Elektra ♦♦♦
By the 1999 release of *Blue*, Third Eye Blind's second album, many of their peers from 1997 had faded away. Stephan Jenkins must have been aware of the fleeting nature of fandom in the '90s, since he pushes his band hard throughout the album. It's as if he's trying to shake the ghost of "Semi-Charmed Life," the ingratiatingly hummable hit that gave TEB success but pegged them, in many observers' eyes, as a bubblegum one-hit wonder. *Blue* is certainly somber and serious, even with its moments of levity. Almost too much so. TEB sound a little strained when they earnestly try to rock, and the same problem occasionally plagues their slower songs, though they do sound more self-confident there. This problem surfaces because they sound natural when they're a little loose; at that point, they're not too self-conscious to avoid hooks, which they seem to do quite often on *Blue*. While this self-consciousness mars *Blue*, it doesn't ruin it, because it lifts often enough (on "Wounded," "An Ode to Maybe," "Anything," and "Never Let You Go," the album's highlight), and because it announces that they're stronger and more serious than many of their post-grunge peers. It also illustrates what TEB truly excel at—big, glossy alt-pop in the tradition of U2 and INXS. There's not quite enough of it this time around to make *Blue* the equal of its predecessor, but it should be enough to please devoted fans. *—Stephen Thomas Erlewine*

13th Floor Elevators

f. 1965, **db.** 1968
Garage Rock, Psychedelic
Featuring the yelping vocals and visionary, occasionally demented lyrics of Roky Erickson, the 13th Floor Elevators were one of the original acid-rock bands. Formed in Texas in the mid-'60s, the Elevators started as a garage rock outfit, scoring their one and only modest national hit with "You're Gonna Miss Me." While Erickson's loopy persona, along with Tommy Hall's odd "jug" percussion, were the band's most distinguishing features, several members of the group's original lineup contributed strong material to their albums. Although these inconsistent efforts sometimes wander off into a cloudy haze, they also include sturdy folk-rock tunes and driving psychedelic rockers. Trips to San Francisco established the group as up-and-coming underground favorites, but Erickson's drug problems led to the singer's commission to a state mental hospital in the late '60s, an ordeal from which he has never fully recovered. The band was really only at full power for a couple of albums, although all of their releases for the legendary International Artists label—produced by, of all people, Kenny Rogers' brother Leland—are revered among psychedelic collectors. Live recordings and outtakes of the Elevators continue to surface, though a cogent domestic compilation of the best of these erratic pioneers' work remains overdue. *—Richie Unterberger*

The Psychedelic Sounds of the 13th Floor Elevators / 1966 / Collectables ♦♦♦♦
Did the 13th Floor Elevators invent psychedelic rock? Aficionados will be debating that point for decades, but if Roky Erickson and his fellow travelers into inner space weren't there first, they were certainly close to the front of the line, and there are few albums from the early stages of the psych movement that sound as distinctively trippy—and remain as pleasing—as the group's groundbreaking debut, *The Psychedelic Sounds of the 13th Floor Elevators*. In 1966, psychedelia hadn't been around long enough for its clichés to be set in stone, and *Psychedelic Sounds* thankfully avoids most of them; while the sensuous twists of the melodies and the charming psychobabble of the lyrics make it sound like these folks were indulging in something stronger than Pearl Beer, at this point the Elevators sounded like a smarter-than-average folk-rock band with a truly uncommon level of intensity. Roky Erickson's vocals are strong and compelling throughout, whether he's wailing like some lysergic James Brown or murmuring quietly, and Stacy Sutherland's guitar leads—long on melodic invention without a lot of pointless heroics—are a real treat to hear. And nobody played electric jug quite like Tommy Hall—actually, nobody played it at all besides him, but his oddball noises gave the band a truly unique sonic texture. The 13th Floor Elevators were trailblazers in the psychedelic rock scene, and in time they'd pay a heavy price for exploring the outer edges of musical and psychological possibility, but along the way they left behind a few fine albums, and *The Psychedelic Sounds of the 13th Floor Elevators* remains a potent delight. *—Mark Deming*

Easter Everywhere / 1967 / Collectables ♦♦♦
This is a straight-up reissue of the group's second International Artists album. Roky Erickson's vocals sound as wonderfully drug-crazed as ever, and the music is trippy and as true to the psychedelic ideal as these types of records get. With the exception of a drifty version of Dylan's "Baby Blue," pretty much everything on here comes from band members' pens, with Roky and Tommy Hall's "Slip Inside This House," and "She Lives (In a Time of Her Own)" being particular standouts. Anyone wanting a real psychedelic album from the '60s should head right to the counter and grab this one. *—Cub Koda*

Bull of the Woods / 1968 / Collectables ♦♦♦
Guitarist Stacy Sutherland wrote most of the songs on the band's final studio album, as Roky was largely absent due to drugs and problems with the law. Decent psychedelic rock—pretty straight-ahead and disciplined for the genre, actually—that doesn't match the inspired heights of their previous material. The closing "May the Circle Be Unbroken," with its wads and wads of reverb, may be the strangest thing the band ever cut. *—Richie Unterberger*

Out of Order: Live at the Avalon, 1966 / 1978 / Lysergic ♦♦♦
This quasi-legal production has shown up in other packages (and titles) since its original issue. It's a fair-quality tape of a 1966 concert that's a decent document for fans. The versions don't differ a heck of a lot from the ones on the records, though "Splash I," given a more forceful and full-bodied folk-rock arrangement, is a notable exception. There are also a few somewhat unexpected covers, like "Roll Over Beethoven," "You Really Got Me," Buddy Holly's "I'm Gonna Love You Too," and the Beatles' "The Word." *—Richie Unterberger*

Fire in My Bones / 1985 / Texas Archive ♦♦♦
The best collection of previously unreleased Elevators. Side one has six songs from an early 1966 live Dallas TV broadcast, including "You're Gonna Miss Me" and "Fire Engine," as well as covers of hits by The Kinks, Them, and Chuck Berry. Side two has alternate versions of four songs from the first LP that are more uninhibited in spots than

the official versions, as well as the previously unreleased song "Fire in My Bones" and a live jam. —*Richie Unterberger*

Elevator Tracks / 1987 / Texas Archive ◆◆◆
More unreleased tracks. Side one has a previously unreleased acetate of "I Don't Ever Want to Come Down," and six alternate takes of officially released tunes (circa 1966) that are pretty close to the records, including "You're Gonna Miss Me," "Tried to Hide," and "Splash One." Side two is a fair-quality recording of a live summer 1966 gig in Houston, including covers of "Satisfaction," The Beatles' "I'm Down," and James Brown's "I Feel Good." Decent, but for completists. —*Richie Unterberger*

● **The Best of the 13th Floor Elevators** / 1994 / Eva ◆◆◆◆◆
Finally, a best-of compilation for one of the most popular cult psychedelic groups of all time. The 22 tracks draw most heavily upon the first LP, with choice bits from the second and third, as well as some material Roky Erickson cut with his pre-Elevators group the Spades. —*Richie Unterberger*

.38 Special

f. 1975, Jacksonville, FL
Album Rock, Arena Rock, Southern Rock, Hard Rock
Initially, .38 Special was one of many Southern rock bands in the vein of the Allman Brothers and Lynyrd Skynyrd; in fact, the band was led by Donnie Van Zant, the brother of Skynyrd's leader, Ronnie Van Zant. The band later revamped their sound to fall halfway between country-fried blues-rock and driving, arena-ready hard rock. The result was a string of hit albums and singles in the early '80s, beginning with their fifth album, 1981's *Wild-Eyed Southern Boys*. The group's first genuine hit, it went platinum and generated the Top 40 hit "Hold on Loosely." *Special Forces*, released in 1982, was even more popular, spawning the Top Ten single "Caught Up in You" and "If I'd Been the One." Though 1986's *Strength in Numbers* was quite popular upon release, it didn't stay on the charts as long as its predecessors. *Flashback*, the 1987 greatest-hits album, was moderately successful, but the band took precautions to retain their audience by recording the polished *Rock & Roll Strategy*. Released in 1989, the album slowly became a hit on the strength of "Second Chance," an adult-contemporary-oriented ballad that reached the Top Ten. .38 Special's popularity dipped soon after, and after one failed album in 1991, the group didn't release another until 1997's *Resolution*. —*Stephen Thomas Erlewine*

● **Flashback: The Best of .38 Special** / 1987 / A&M ◆◆◆◆◆
Flashback: Best of .38 Special is a terrific compilation of the Southern rock group's biggest hits, including "Caught Up in You," "If I'd Been the One," "Back Where You Belong," "Wild-Eyed Southern Boys" and the non-LP soundtrack contribution "Teacher Teacher." Since *Flashback* was released in 1987, it doesn't contain their biggest hit, 1989's syrupy ballad "Second Chance," but it remains a comprehensive overview of their best moments, and makes a convincing case that they were the last great Southern rock singles band. —*Stephen Thomas Erlewine*

20th Century Masters—The Millennium Collection: The Best of .38 Special / Jun. 27, 2000 / A&M ◆◆◆◆
The Millennium Collection: The Best of .38 Special focuses on the Southern rock group's original lineup and includes hits and radio staples like "Back Where You Belong," "Caught up in You," "Wild-Eyed Southern Boys," and "Rockin' Into the Night." Though it's not quite as comprehensive as *Flashback*, *The Best of .38 Special*'s dozen tracks provide a good starting point for casual fans. —*Heather Phares*

Anthology / Jun. 5, 2001 / Hip-O ◆◆◆◆
There's little question that Hip-O's 2001 double-disc set *Anthology* is a thorough, definitive overview of .38 Special's career, spanning from their hit-laden A&M albums, through their '90s albums for Charisma and Razor & Tie, and wrapping up with a studio cut from the CMC International release *Live at Sturgis*. This is a good thing, if you're just judging an album in terms of comprehensiveness, which just may be what the dedicated are looking for, but if you're not dedicated, this collection is awfully long. That's not to say it doesn't do a good job of summarizing the group's career, since it does, but the hits—"Rockin' in to the Night," "Hold On Loosely," "Caught Up in You," "If I'd Been the One," "Back Where You Belong"—are so good, that the rest of the material is shown as the good, but generic, material that it is. So, for the casual fans, it might be better to seek out a more concise collection, including the *20th Century Masters* disc, since they're almost all there. Yes, this collection contains a few gems not readily available on that disc or other collections—the *Teachers* theme "Teacher, Teacher" and the hit ballad "Second Chance"—but this still remains the province of the converted, not the casual. —*Stephen Thomas Erlewine*

This Mortal Coil

f. 1983, Wadsworth, London, England, db. 1991
Dream Pop, Indie Rock, Alternative Pop/Rock
This Mortal Coil is the brainchild of 4AD's president, Ivo Watts. It's not really a band, it's a way for Watts to explore different musical territory and cover his favorite artists, including Syd Barrett, Alex Chilton, Talking Heads, Tim Buckley, and Gene Clark. Over the years, the lineup has featured various stars from the record label's roster including Kim Deal, Tanya Donelly, Heidi Berry, and Robin Guthrie and Elizabeth Fraser from Cocteau Twins. Like most 4AD bands, This Mortal Coil is atmospheric, sometimes dreamy, other times haunting. Watts has said that 1991's *Blood* is the last album the outfit will release. —*Stephen Thomas Erlewine*

It'll End in Tears / 1984 / 4AD ◆◆◆
Features the Cocteau Twin's Elizabeth Fraser singing Tim Buckley's "Song to the Siren," Gordon Sharp singing Rema-Rema's "Fond Affections," and Howard Devoto singing Alex

Chilton's "Holocaust." Lisa Gerrard and Brendan Perry of Dead Can Dance are also included on this first collection of covers from 4AD. —*Heather Phares*

Filigree & Shadow / 1986 / 4AD ◆◆◆◆◆
The second album of This Mortal Coil interpretations includes the vocalist, Jean, doing a version of Van Morrison's "Come Here My Love," and Deidre and Louise Rutkowski singing Tim Buckley's "Morning Glory." Other songs include David Byrne's "Drugs" and Gene Clark's "Strength of Strings." —*Heather Phares*

● **Blood** / May 13, 1991 / 4AD/Warner Brothers ◆◆◆◆◆
The final This Mortal Coil album includes some of the project's finest moments, including a cover of The Byrds' "I Come and Stand at Every Door" by Louise and Deidre Rutkowski, Syd Barrett's "Late Night" sung by Caroline Crawley of Shellyan Orphan, a cover of Gene Clark's "With Tomorrow" and a standout performance of Chris Bell's "You and Your Sister" by the Breeders' Kim Deal and Belly's Tanya Donelly. —*Heather Phares*

1983-1991 / Mar. 30, 1993 / 4AD ◆◆◆
All three of This Mortal Coil's albums packaged in an expensive slipcase, along with a disc of the original versions of the songs they covered. Fans of 4AD bands like Throwing Muses, the Cocteau Twins, and Dead Can Dance will thoroughly enjoy This Mortal Coil's lush, haunting music; some members of these bands play on various tracks on the box, including a standout duet between Kim Deal and Tanya Donelly on Chris Bell's "You and Your Sister." Although the packaging is beautiful, there are no liner notes. —*Stephen Thomas Erlewine*

Carla Thomas

b. Dec. 21, 1942, Memphis, TN
Vocals / Memphis Soul, Southern Soul, Soul
In the glorious decade and a half of sound that was Stax in the '60s and early '70s, Carla Thomas was the Queen of Memphis Soul. She was born in Memphis in 1942, and 18 years later she recorded a duet with her father Rufus Thomas, giving the fledgling Satellite label its first taste of success with the regional hit "Cause I Love You." As her 18th birthday drew nigh, she cut her first solo single, the teen ballad "Gee Whiz (Look at His Eyes)." Written a few years earlier and rejected by Vee-Jay in Chicago, it gave Satellite its first national hit, breaking the Top Ten mark on both the R&B and pop charts. Shortly thereafter Satellite became Stax, and Carla proceeded to claw her way onto the national charts another 22 times with such immortal slices of soul as her answer song to Sam Cooke, "I'll Bring It on Home to You," as well as "Let Me Be Good to You," "B-A-B-Y," "Tramp" (with Otis Redding), and "I Like What You're Doing to Me." Carla released six solo albums and, with Otis Redding, one duet album on Stax between 1961 and 1971. —*Rob Bowman*

Hidden Gems / 1992 / Stax ◆◆◆
Twenty outtakes recorded for Stax between 1960 and 1968, a number of which are gems. In fact, it is really surprising just how good the unreleased Stax stuff was in the '60s. "Loneliness," "Sweet Sensation," and "It Ain't No Easy Thing" all could have been superb singles. —*Rob Bowman*

● **Gee Whiz: The Best of Carla Thomas** / Jul. 19, 1994 / Rhino ◆◆◆◆◆
Gee Whiz: The Best of Carla Thomas is a wonderful 22-track collection of her seminal recordings for Atlantic and Stax, featuring all of her biggest hits—"Gee Whiz," "I'll Bring It Home to You," "B-A-B-Y," "Tramp," "I Like What You're Doing (To Me)"—as well as a terrific selection of lesser-known singles and album tracks. —*Stephen Thomas Erlewine*

Sugar / Sep. 30, 1994 / Stax ◆◆◆
A collection of odds and ends from the late '60s and early '70s, including some obscure Stax singles, duets with Pervis Staples and Johnnie Taylor, and three live numbers from the *Wattstax* soundtrack. It's not the first (or second) Carla Thomas collection you should pick up, but it's solid material. Donny Hathaway and Chips Moman each produced a couple of the singles spotlighted here (A-sides and B-sides are included), adding moderately ambitious variations on the standard Stax sound. —*Richie Unterberger*

Irma Thomas

b. Feb. 18, 1941, Ponchatoula, LA
Vocals / New Orleans R&B, Soul
Radiating an outgoing joy that's inevitably at the heart of her infectious vocal delivery, Irma Thomas has no rivals as the Soul Queen of New Orleans. Working at a Crescent City nightery as a waitress in 1959, Thomas sat in one night with Tommy Ridgley's band and made such a favorable impression that the veteran bandleader hustled her into the studio shortly thereafter to wax her first hit for the Ron label, the driving "Don't Mess with My Man." She joined forces with producer Allen Toussaint to make some of her most moving outings for Minit Records during the early '60s, notably "It's Raining," "Ruler of My Heart," and "Cry On," before venturing to the West Coast, where she cut both her biggest seller, the lushly produced "Wish Someone Would Care," and her best-known song, the original "Time Is on My Side." The highly adaptable chanteuse also made some sizzling soul at Muscle Shoals studio for Chess in the summer of 1967 before cooling off for a while during the '70s. But she's back now, as radiant as ever—and for convincing proof, listen to her buoyant 1990 concert performance on Rounder, *Live! Simply the Best*. Now that's truth in packaging! Thomas finally fulfilled a lifelong ambition in 1993 by recording her first gospel release. *Walk Around Heaven* was as magnificently sung and emotionally convincing as any of her classic New Orleans soul cuts. —*Bill Dahl*

Time Is on My Side / 1983 / Kent ◆◆◆◆◆
Solid 16-song compilation of material from the mid-'60s. Most of this is duplicated by the more extensive CD compilations of the same era on EMI and Razor & Tie. But it's not entirely superfluous; five of the songs don't appear on either of the other collections. Those

tracks are worth hearing, particularly the gutsy soul-pop concoction "Baby Don't Look Down," one of Randy Newman's earliest compositions. —*Richie Unterberger*

Ruler of Hearts / 1989 / Charly ✦✦✦
Sides from her early-'60s Minit sessions. The most New Orleans R&B-influenced of Thomas' early work, it includes "Cry On," "It's Raining," and "Ruler Of My Heart," as well as lesser-known but equally moving cuts like "Two Winters Long" and "It's Too Soon To Know." —*Richie Unterberger*

★ **Time Is on My Side: The Best of Irma Thomas, Vol. 1** / Apr. 21, 1992 / EMI America ✦✦✦✦✦
Twenty-three sides representing the cream of Irma Thomas's brilliant Minit/Liberty years (1961-1966), when her reputation as "The Soul Queen of New Orleans" was built. Virtually all her best-known tunes are here—"Wish Someone Would Care," "Ruler of My Heart," "It's Raining," and "Time Is on My Side" (covered note-for-note by The Stones). Beautiful singing from one of the first ladies of soul music. Essential. —*Christine Ohlman*

Sweet Soul Queen of New Orleans: The Irma Thomas Collection / Feb. 20, 1996 / Razor & Tie ✦✦✦✦✦
23-track collection of early and mid-'60s sides largely duplicates the material on EMI's *Time Is on My Side* collection, with some additions and subtractions. The EMI set has a very slight edge, though for most listeners either compilation will do the job. It's too bad somebody doesn't take the plunge and issue an 80-minute CD documenting this era; as it is, serious Irma fans will need to get each best-of, as each contains tracks not on the other. —*Richie Unterberger*

The Story of My Life / Feb. 11, 1997 / Rounder ✦✦✦✦
The Story of My Life stands out among latter-day Irma Thomas albums not only because she gives a consistently excellent performance, but because the record boasts three new songs from Dan Penn, who wrote some of the greatest soul songs of the '60s. While his new songs ("Hold Me While I Cry," "I Count the Teardrops," "I Won't Cry for You") aren't quite as strong as his best, they are nevertheless wonderful contemporary soul numbers, and they help make the record, the remainder of which is comprised of covers and slightly weaker new numbers, one of Thomas' best latter-day albums. —*Stephen Thomas Erlewine*

Rufus Thomas

b. Mar. 26, 1917, Cayce, MS, **d.** Dec. 15, 2001, Memphis, TN
Vocals / Memphis Soul, Southern Soul, Electric Memphis Blues, Modern Electric Blues, R&B, Soul
Few of rock & roll's founding figures are as likable as Rufus Thomas. From the 1940s onward, he has personified Memphis music; his small but witty cameo role in Jim Jarmusch's *Mystery Train*, a film which satirizes and enshrines the city's role in popular culture, was entirely appropriate. As a recording artist, he wasn't a major innovator, but he could always be depended upon for some good, silly, and/or outrageous fun with his soul dance tunes. He was a crucial mentor to many important Memphis blues, rock, and soul musicians. Thomas recorded as early as 1941, but really made his mark on the Memphis music scene as a radio deejay. He had his first recording success in 1953 with the number three R&B hit "Bear Cat," the first national hit for Sun Records. Thomas recorded only sporadically during the 1950s, but then became one of the first and biggest stars—with his daughter Carla—on the Stax label during the '60s. On his own, Rufus wasn't as successful as his daughter, but issued a steady stream of decent dance/novelty singles. The biggest by far was "Walking the Dog," which made the Top Ten in 1963, and was covered by the Rolling Stones on their first album. He hit the R&B Top Five three times during the early '70s, though his recording career basically ended after Stax collapsed later in the '70s. —*Richie Unterberger*

Walking the Dog / 1964 / Rhino ✦✦✦✦✦
One of the artists who defined Memphis soul and put Stax Records on the map, Rufus Thomas is known for liking his R&B hard-edged, gritty and earthy. That approach served him impressively well on his debut album *Walking the Dog*. In contrast to the sleeker, more elaborate production style favored by the Northern soulsters of Motown, Thomas rejects pop elements altogether and thrives on rawness on his hits "Walking the Dog" and "The Dog," as well as inspired versions of "Land of 1000 Dances" (which became a major hit for Wilson Pickett), Lee Dorsey's "Ya Ya" and John Lee Hooker's "Boom Boom." Thomas was in his mid-40s when these fun, infectious recordings were made, and he definitely lives up to his title "The World's Oldest Teenager" (a title later given to Dick Clark as well). Reissued on CD in the early 1990s, *Walking the Dog* is an album Memphis soul aficionados shouldn't overlook. —*Alex Henderson*

Do the Funky Chicken / 1970 / Stax ✦✦✦
Rufus Thomas would storm the soul charts in 1970, scoring three hits, two of them in the Top 10. The title track and his number one smash "(Do The) Push and Pull" were identical—dance-based novelty tunes featuring Thomas' manic instructions and bluesy shouts backed by surging, horn-based soul and funk from the Stax band. It wasn't earth-shaking, just fun, brilliantly produced and arranged stuff. —*Ron Wynn*

Can't Get Away from This Dog / 1992 / Stax ✦✦✦
Can't Get Away from This Dog gathers 20 previously unreleased Rufus Thomas recordings from the Stax vaults. Stylistically, fans won't find any surprises—this is still hard-hitting, hard-driving Memphis soul—but they'll find a couple of hidden treasures, such as versions of "Wang Dang Doodle," "Reconsider Baby" and "Barefootin'," as well as alternates of "Walking the Dog," "Jump Back" and "Can Your Monkey Do the Dog?" Some of Thomas' original material is a little thin—there's only so many times you can work the word "dog" into a song title, after all—but this is a surprisingly successful collection of

rarities that will not only satiate diehards, but will entertain casual fans as well. —*Stephen Thomas Erlewine*

● **The Best of Rufus Thomas: Do the Funky Somethin'** / Apr. 1996 / Rhino ✦✦✦✦✦
Overdue career-spanning collection of his best material, centering around his Stax hits from the '60s and early '70s. The whole "dog" series of novelty dance songs from 1963-64 is here, as well as the hit "Jump Back" and a clutch of Stax singles that weren't hits, but became pretty well-known anyway, like "Sister's Got a Boyfriend" and "Sophisticated Sissy." There are also the early-'70s funk dance hits "Do the Funky Chicken," "(Do the) Push and Pull," "The Breakdown," and "Do the Funky Penguin," a couple of '60s duets with his daughter Carla, and his 1953 blues single "Bear Cat (The Answer to Hound Dog)," the first hit on Sun Records. A few other compilations have gone into specific phases of his career in greater depth, but this is certainly the best overview of a man who offered some of the funkiest and funniest Memphis soul around. —*Richie Unterberger*

Thompson Twins

f. 1977, **db.** 1993
Club/Dance, Pop/Rock, New Wave, Synth Pop, Dance-Pop
Neither a duo nor related, but simply named after the *Tin Tin* cartoon, the Thompson Twins were one of the more popular synth-pop groups of the early MTV era. While many of their contemporaries indulged in stylish variations on Roxy Music or robotic electronic funk, the Thompson Twins were more pop-oriented, even when they strayed into dance-pop. Despite their success—"Hold Me Now," "Lay Your Hands on Me," "King for a Day" all reached the U.S. Top Ten—the group couldn't expand their synth-pop sound; consequently, their audience disappeared by the late '80s. After several lineup changes and two largely-ignored albums—1981's *A Product Of* and 1982's *Set*, the group hit their stride when they became a trio. Tom Bailey, Joe Leeway and Alannah Currie released 1983's *Quick Step and Side Kick*, which reached number two on the UK charts; the singles "Love on Your Side" and "We Are Detective" made the Top Ten. In America, the record earned a cult following under the truncated title *Side Kicks*. They broke through in the US with 1984's *Into the Gap*, which featured "Hold Me Now," "Doctor Doctor" and "You Take Me Up." *Here's to Future Days* followed soon after; "Lay Your Hands On Me" and "King for a Day" hit the American Top Ten, but none of the singles became major hits in the U.K. After Leeway left the group in 1986, the Thompson Twins remained a duo on 1987's *Close to the Bone*, 1989's *Big Trash* and 1991's *Queer*, all of which did little to keep their audience. In 1994, Bailey and Currie formed Babble to explore newer electronic music styles. Working with programmer Keith Fernley, Babble released *The Stone* in 1994 on Reprise to little notice. —*Stephen Thomas Erlewine*

Side Kicks / 1983 / Arista ✦✦✦
Side Kicks is the American version of the Thompson Twins' third album, *Quick Step & Side Kick*, featuring the same songs in a different sequencing. The record was the first the group recorded as a trio and, not coincidentally, it finds them discovering their signature dance-inflected synth-pop sound. The singles "Love on Your Side" and "In the Name of Love" are the high points, but it's surprising how many of the remaining songs are enjoyable, cleverly crafted and catchy synth-pop gems. —*Stephen Thomas Erlewine*

Into the Gap / 1984 / Arista ✦✦✦✦
Their American breakthrough album featured the hits "Doctor Doctor" and "Hold Me Now." This is the best single album. —*Kenneth M. Cassidy*

Here's to Future Days / 1985 / Arista ✦✦✦✦
On their follow-up to the commercial breakthrough *Into the Gap*, The Thompson Twins attempt to toughen up their sound, but the results are only partially successful. In fact, the most infectious number, "Lay Your Hands on Me," sounds like it could have been an outtake from the previous album. —*Stephen Thomas Erlewine*

Close to the Bone / 1987 / Arista ✦✦

Big Trash / Mar. 1989 / Red Eye ✦✦✦
Big Trash was a successful attempt to add a stronger rhythmic sensibility to The Thompson Twins' sound, but the album failed to produce any hit bigger than the number 28 "Sugar Daddy," although there were several other strong numbers on the record. —*Stephen Thomas Erlewine*

Queer / Oct. 1991 / Warner Brothers ✦✦

● **Greatest Hits** / Oct. 1, 1996 / Arista ✦✦✦✦
During the '80s, Thompson Twins arguably produced the finest synth-pop singles, and *Greatest Hits* recollects their industrious years with Arista in clear, digitally remastered sound. Numerous collections exist in the Twins' catalog and nearly equal their studio albums, but *Greatest Hits* prevails as the most essential as it offers a definitive chronology from 1982's infectious debut "In the Name of Love" through 1987's reflective "Long Goodbye." Featuring 16 tracks, this brimming retrospective recalls MTV's formative years ("Lies"), those unforgettable Dr. Pepper commercials ("Doctor! Doctor!"), the anti-Apartheid movement ("The Gap"), and countless other '80s pop culture memories. Nearly flawless, this collection contains only one inferior single, the hokey electronic hoe-down "You Take Me Up," and it also excludes non-Arista releases, which means 1989's minor hit "Sugar Daddy," a Red Eye label recording, is absent. Nevertheless, Thompson Twins' *Greatest Hits*, along with Orchestral Manoeuvres in the Dark's *The Singles* and *The Best of Howard Jones*, remain indispensable for any '80s synth-pop enthusiast. —*Jacob N. Lunders*

The Master Hits: Thompson Twins / Jul. 27, 1999 / Arista ✦✦✦✦
Arista celebrated its 30th anniversary by releasing *The Heritage Series*, spotlighting the most popular artists on the label. The Thompson Twins' installment in *The Heritage Series* is pretty much a straight hits collection. While they were at Arista, the Thompson

Twins had such hits as "In the Name of Love," "Lies," "Hold Me Now," "Lay Your Hands on Me" and "King for a Day." All those songs are here, along with some highlights from their albums, providing a nice retrospective of their time with Arista. —*Stephen Thomas Erlewine*

Richard Thompson

b. Apr. 3, 1949, London, England

Vocals, Mandolin, Guitar, Guitar (Acoustic), Dulcimer / British Folk-Rock, Contemporary Folk, British Folk, Folk-Rock, Singer/Songwriter

Richard Thompson is among the most admired guitarists and songwriters in folk-rock music, and in the 1980s and '90s, he moved from a fervent cult following to broader exposure while maintaining critical accolades for his biting guitar work and sardonic songs. He was a founding member of Fairport Convention, the most important British folk-rock group to emerge in the 1960s, and he recorded five albums with them before quitting the group in January 1971. He made his debut solo album, *Henry the Human Fly*, before forming a duo with his wife Linda. The Thompsons released six albums, including the classics *I Want to See the Bright Lights Tonight*, *Pour Down Like Silver* and *Shoot Out the Lights* (1982) before breaking up personally and professionally. In 1981, Thompson had made a second solo album of instrumentals, *Strict Tempo!*; with 1983's *Hand of Kindness*, his first charting album, he relaunched his solo career. —*William Ruhlmann*

Henry the Human Fly / 1972 / Hannibal ✦✦✦✦✦

Fans and critics alike seemed to have a difficult time getting a handle on Thompson's new direction, which, for the most part, eschews the electric guitar that had been an integral part of the British folk-rock he had helped forge with his former band Fairport Convention. With the exception of a couple of short instrumental breaks and various electric shadings, Thompson's Stratocaster defers to accordions, fiddles, whistles, dulcimers, harps, and his own acoustic guitar. The songs, which are more idiosyncratic than his Fairport output, are the primary focus. Cuts such as "The Poor Ditching Boy," "The New St. George," and "The Old Changing Way" have the timelessness of the best traditional material Fairport had been mining in the past, while "Roll Over Vaughn Williams," with its swirling electric guitar, and the accordion and electric guitar interplay of the folk-rocker "The Angels Took My Racehorse Away" are prime examples of Thompson's vision of fusing the old and the new. At the time of its release, *Henry the Human Fly*, with its fresh, yet eccentric take on folk and rock, along with tales of "poor ditching boys," racehorses, tinkers, "painted ladies," and weddings where "nobody's wed" was not a fashionable record, but like the bulk of Richard Thompson's work, it transcends times and trends. Linda Peters (Thompson), Sandy Denny, Ashley Hutchings, and John Kirkpatrick guest. —*Bruce Eder*

☆ **I Want to See the Bright Lights Tonight** / Apr. 1974 / Hannibal ✦✦✦✦✦

In 1974, Richard Thompson and the former Linda Peters released their first album together, and *I Want To See The Bright Lights Tonight* was nothing short of a masterpiece, the starkly beautiful refinement of the promise of Thompson's solo debut, *Henry the Human Fly*. In Linda Thompson, Richard found a superb collaborator and a world-class vocalist; Linda possessed a voice as clear and rich as Sandy Denny's, but with a strength that could easily support Richard's often weighty material, and she proved capable of tackling anything presented to her, from the delicately mournful "Has He Got A Friend For Me" to the gleeful cynicism of "The Little Beggar Girl." And while Richard had already made clear that he was a songwriter to be reckoned with, on *I Want To See The Bright Lights Tonight* he went from strength to strength. While the album's mood is decidedly darker than anything he'd recorded before, the sorrow of "Withered and Died," "The End Of The Rainbow," and "The Great Valerio" spoke not of self-pity but of the contemplation of life's cruelties by a man who, at 25, had already been witness to more than his share. And though Thompson didn't give himself a guitar showcase quite like "Roll Over Vaughn Williams" on *Henry The Human Fly*, the brilliant solos that punctuated many of the songs were manna from heaven for any guitar enthusiast. While *I Want To See The Bright Lights Tonight* may be the darkest music of Richard & Linda Thompson's career, in this chronicle of pain and longing they were able to forge music of striking and unmistakable beauty; if the lyrics often ponder the high stakes of our fate in this life, the music offered a glimpse of the joys that make the struggle worthwhile. —*Mark Deming*

Hokey Pokey / 1975 / Hannibal ✦✦✦✦

With the release of their classic 1974 debut, *I Want to See the Bright Lights Tonight*, Richard and Linda Thompson set an unbelievably high standard for themselves. Although containing many of the same attributes, their follow-up, *Hokey Pokey*, doesn't quite reach the lofty heights of its predecessor, but then again not many records do. The Thompsons, from the opening Irish fiddle derivation of a Chuck Berry riff, through Linda's exquisite performance of "A Heart Needs a Home," to their cover of Mike Waterson's "Mole in a Hole" which closes the record, once again create a timeless amalgam of folk and rock. Recorded at the time of the Thompsons' conversion to Islam, *Hokey Pokey* comes across a bit lighter than *Bright Lights*. Songs such as the playfully suggestive title track, the jaunty "Georgie on a Spree" and the quirky tale of "Smiffy's Glass Eye" make *Hokey Pokey* seem downright cheery for Richard Thompson, although even at its sunniest, themes of sex, cruelty and avarice linger just below the surface. For those more accustomed to the usual straightforward doom and gloom from the Thompsons, there's the rueful "I'll Regret It All in the Morning," the sullen, traditional tone of "The Sun Never Shines on the Poor" and the mournful ballad "Never Again." *Hokey Pokey* is an often overlooked gem in the Thompsons' luminous catalog. —*Brett Hartenbach*

Pour Down Like Silver / 1975 / Hannibal ✦✦✦✦✦

Pour Down Like Silver was the last album Richard & Linda Thompson would release before beginning a self-imposed three-year retirement in order to join a communal Sufi

Muslim sect. The cover photographs show the Thompsons dressed in traditional Muslim garb, and while lyrically the album offers few clear signs of the Thompsons' new spiritual direction, the stark asceticism of the music marked a real change from the alcohol-fueled mood swings of *I Want to See the Bright Lights Tonight* and *Hokey Pokey*. The horns, accordion, and ancient instruments that had dotted Richard and Linda's previous albums were used far more sparingly on *Pour Down Like Silver*, and even Thompson's usually astounding electric guitar solos were pared down in favor of an emotionally intimate, bare-wired approach that sounds alternately like a confession and a plea for guidance. *Pour Down Like Silver* is downbeat even by Richard Thompson's less than joyful standards, but it also features some of his most beautiful and compelling songs—the ravaged plea for salvation of "Streets of Paradise," the mysterious and mesmerizing "Night Comes In," the mournful romantic meditations "Beat the Retreat" and "For Shame of Doing Wrong," and the spare but heartfelt love song "Dimming of the Day." And Linda (usually the more pragmatic of the two) breaks the mood near the end of side two with the cynically witty "Hard Luck Stories." *Pour Down Like Silver* is the most severe of the Richard & Linda Thompson albums, but those brave enough to look past its dark surface will find a startlingly beautiful album; it's not an easy album to listen to, but it greatly rewards the effort. —*Mark Deming*

Live (More or Less) / 1976 / Island ✦✦

Guitar & Vocal 1967-1976 / May 1976 / Hannibal ✦✦✦✦✦

A superb 68-minute collection of obscure and unreleased tracks from Thompson's career, covering late 1967 until April 1976. The album's first six tracks are devoted to Thompson's career with Fairport Convention—highlights include "Throwaway Street Puzzle" (the B-side of the single "Meet On the Ledge"), the BBC recording of "Mr. Lacey," the *Liege And Lief* session outtake "The Ballad of Easy Rider," the *Full House* session outtake "Poor Will And The Jolly Hangman," and "Sweet Little Rock & Roller" from the L.A. Troubadour (*House Full*) concert tapes. Thompson plays some sizzling guitar on these cuts, though "Ballad of Easy Rider"—played here the way Dylan might've covered it on *John Wesley Harding*—is more representative of Sandy Denny than Thompson. The post-Fairport material includes an alternate arrangement of "A Heart Needs A Home" from *Hokey Pokey*, a beautifully sung live rendition of "The Dark End of the Street" (featuring one of Linda Thompson's best performances); their hard-rocking live rendition of Jack Clement's "It'll Be Me"; the exquisite solo acoustic guitar instrumental "Flee As a Bird"; and two epics, "Night Comes In" and "Calvary Cross," featuring Thompson and his band stretching out on stage. Despite the existence of the triple-CD career retrospective, this disc still has enough prime rarities to rate as a must-own, even for casual fans. —*Bruce Eder*

First Light / 1978 / Hannibal ✦✦✦

After three years spent deeply pursuing their involvement in the Sufi Muslim faith, Richard & Linda Thompson returned to the recording studio in 1978 with *First Light*, and several of the songs clearly dealt with the couple's spiritual quest, most notably "Sweet Surrender," "Layla" (no, not the Eric Clapton hit), and the title song. However, Richard Thompson's grasp of worldly matters wasn't quite as sure as his perspective on Allah at this juncture, and the opening track, "Restless Highway," is one of the few songs in his catalog that sounds like a throwaway. The rest of the album's material was a good bit better, but one senses that Richard was still getting back on his feet in the studio; Linda's vocals are a lot stronger on this set, and Richard's usually fleet-footed guitar work is unusually subdued. Just as significantly, for *First Light* the Thompsons' usual band of British folk all-stars was augmented by Willie Weeks on bass and Andy Newmark on drums, a pair of first-call Los Angeles session heavyweights, and though they play with their usual effortless skill, their attempt to inject a country-rock undertow into Richard Thompson's very British melodies ends up pushing many of the performances into a strange middle ground that isn't especially interesting. The performances on *First Light* generally lack fire and personality, and several fine songs (most notably "Pavanne," "Died for Love," and "Don't Let a Thief Steal Into Your Heart") never really connect here as a result. Only on the penultimate track, "House of Cards," does this album really come alive; *First Light* is a long way from bad, but it's easily the least essential release in Richard & Linda Thompson's catalog. —*Mark Deming*

Sunnyvista / 1979 / Hannibal ✦✦✦

1978's *First Light* marked Richard & Linda Thompson's first time in a recording studio after three years away from music, and it suggested they were still getting warmed up as performers; a year later, *Sunnyvista* found them in much stronger form and a significantly more upbeat frame of mind. *Sunnyvista* is the wittiest and most joyous album Richard & Linda made together; while several of Richard Thompson's trademark meditations on romance at it's least successful are on hand, "Why Do You Turn Your Back" manages to generate an unusually soulful groove, "Lonely Hearts" captures the melancholy country feel that *First Light* never quite caught, and "Traces of My Love" finds a winning warmth in its sadness. Richard Thompson's satirical eye gets an airing on the darkly witty title cut, and he displays his rarely aired politically conscious streak on the rabble-rousing "Borrowed Time" and "Justice in the Streets." Linda Thompson's vocals are in superb form on "Sisters," a lovely duet with Anna McGarrigle. And you'd have to go back to *Hokey Pokey* to hear the Thompsons having as much fun as they do on the rollicking "Saturday Rolling Around" and the wildly passionate "You're Going to Need Somebody." With a big band of Fairport Convention and Albion Band associates and top UK session players on board, and Kate & Anna McGarrigle, Gerry Rafferty, and Glenn Tilbrook contributing vocals, *Sunnyvista* boasts the stylistic eclecticism of the Thompsons' best work, with a healthy dose of added enthusiasm. Anyone who thinks Richard & Linda Thompson's records are always depressing have obviously never heard *Sunnyvista*; if it isn't quite as resonant as *I Want to See the Bright Lights Tonight* and

Pour Down Like Silver, it still boasts great songs, great singing, *and* you can play it at a party. —*Mark Deming*

Strict Tempo! / 1981 / Hannibal ✦✦✦

While some listeners have expressed mixed degrees of enthusiasm with Richard Thompson's often down-beat work as a songwriter and his sometimes craggy vocals, no one has ever argued his gifts as an instrumentalist, and on *Strict Tempo!* Thompson lets loose on an instrumental collection of traditional British and Celtic jigs and reels, with a swinging Duke Ellington cover thrown in for variety and one new original offered as the finale. Thompson multi-tracks himself playing a variety of acoustic and electric guitars, basses, mandolins, and dulcimers with his usual (i.e., dazzling) degree of dexterity, with only percussionist Dave Mattacks for company on most of the tunes. If the performances don't quite match the head-spinning ferocity of the traditionally based folk-rock he pioneered with Fairport Convention on *Liege and Lief* and *Full House*, Thompson was certainly a better player in 1981 than he was when he left Fairport, and the arrangements reveal a degree of taste, imagination, and subtle wit that's second to none. *Strict Tempo!* was a pet project of Thompson's, originally released on his own label, and it sometimes sounds like it was created more for his own amusement than anything else, but even in its more esoteric moments, it shows one of the finest guitarists on Earth showing just how well he can play, and that's always a pleasure to hear. —*Mark Deming*

★ Shoot Out the Lights / 1982 / Hannibal ✦✦✦✦✦

Richard & Linda Thompson's marriage was crumbling as they were recording *Shoot Out The Lights* in 1982, and many critics have read the album as a chronicle of the couple's divorce. In truth, most of the album's songs had been written two years earlier (when the Thompsons were getting along fine) for an abandoned project produced by Gerry Rafferty, and tales of busted relationships and domestic discord were always prominent in their songbook. But there is a palpable tension to *Shoot Out The Lights* which gives songs like "Don't Renege On Our Love" and "Did She Jump Or Was She Pushed" an edgy bite different from the Thompsons' other albums together; there's a subtle, unmistakable undertow of anger and dread in this music that cuts straight down to the bone. Joe Boyd's clean, uncluttered production was the ideal match for these songs and their Spartan arrangements, and Richard Thompson's wiry guitar work was remarkable, displaying a blazing technical skill that never interfered with his melodic sensibilities. Individually, all eight of the album's songs are striking (especially the sonic fireworks of the title cut, the beautiful drift of "Just The Motion," and the bitter reminiscence of "Did She Jump Or Was She Pushed"), and as a whole they were far more than the sum of their parts, a meditation on love and loss in which beauty, passion, and heady joy can still be found in defeat. It's ironic that Richard & Linda Thompson enjoyed their breakthrough in the United States with the album that ended their career together, but *Shoot Out The Lights* found them rallying their strengths to the bitter end; it's often been cited as Richard Thompson's greatest work, and it's difficult for anyone who has heard his body of work to argue the point. —*Mark Deming*

Hand of Kindness / Jul. 1983 / Hannibal ✦✦✦✦✦

Richard & Linda Thompson's final album together, 1982's *Shoot Out the Lights*, was widely seen as a document of their collapsing relationship, despite the fact that both of them strongly denied that was ever their intention, and when Richard Thompson released *Hand of Kindness* in 1983, it was similarly read as a sad and bitter letter from a lovelorn divorcee, conveniently ignoring the fact that Richard left Linda (not the other way around), and was already involved in a new (and happy) relationship by the time he cut the album. While *Hand of Kindness* is dominated by songs about unhappy relationships, the truth is most of Thompson's albums are full of such songs; if you want to read an autobiographical slant into the album, Thompson's well of anger ("Tear Stained Letter," "A Poisoned Heart and a Twisted Memory") and regret ("How I Wanted To," "Hand of Kindness") seem to run especially deep. But the album's darkest track, "Devonside," is a tragic tale of a dysfunctional relationship that clearly does not involve himself, and the album has a number of solid up-tempo rockers, such as the witty horse-racing tale "Both Ends Burning" and the rollicking, Cajun-flavored "Two Left Feet." Thompson's vocals and guitar work are in splendid shape throughout, and his band is in particularly fine fettle, especially drummer Dave Mattacks and John Kirkpatrick on accordion. *Hand of Kindness* lacks a bit of the narrative depth and emotional push-and-pull that made *Shoot Out the Lights* an instant classic (and while "Both Ends Burning" and "Two Left Feet" are lots of fun, it's a stretch to call them great songs), but it certainly confirmed that Richard Thompson had a more than interesting solo career ahead of him. —*Mark Deming*

Small Town Romance / 1984 / Hannibal ✦✦✦✦

Small Town Romance was compiled from three warts-and-all live recordings (originally produced for radio broadcast) of Richard Thompson performing solo acoustic in New York City in 1982. The above-mentioned warts (a cough here and there, a very occasional flubbed note) are tiny and difficult to spot, but Thompson was quite aware of them—enough so that he persuaded Hannibal Records to delete the album from their catalog, though when the out-of-print album began fetching ridiculously high prices on the collectors market, he consented to a reissue in 1997. While the album is a hardly flawless recreation of the live Richard Thompson experience (and Thompson's solo acoustic shows would be noticeably stronger a few years down the line), it does capture Thompson's estimable charm as a stage performer with commendable accuracy, and the program is superb, featuring several Fairport Convention classics, a number of outstanding numbers from the Richard & Linda Thompson catalog, and a few otherwise unrecorded songs, most notably the devastating title track, which still stands as one of Richard's finest meditations on his favorite theme, love gone wrong. *Small Town Romance* may not be perfect, but it preserves a handful of passionate and impressive performances from one of the most gifted guitarists and songwriters around—which puts it far ahead of the vast majority of live albums that will cross your path. Hopefully, though, one of Richard Thompson's even more dazzling solo shows from the 1990s will find it's way onto a widely available, non-bootleg CD some time in the future. —*Mark Deming*

Across a Crowded Room / Feb. 1985 / Polydor ✦✦✦✦

Richard Thompson's 1985 album *Across A Crowded Room* (his first album for a major label since *Sunnyvista* in 1979) stylistically picked up where his previous set, *Hand of Kindness*, had left off, and while it didn't break much in the way of new ground, it also found Thompson doing plenty of what he does best—writing great songs and playing a lot of electric guitar. *Across A Crowded Room* takes a slightly more subtle approach than *Hand of Kindness*; the arrangements have been pared back a bit (there are fewer horn charts, and John Kirkpatrick's accordion is sadly absent), and Joe Boyd's production is roomier and more atmospheric, making the most of the album's broader soundscape. But for the most part Richard Thompson's formula remained the same here, and if that makes it sound like he's just treading water, that might be the case for an artist less consistently remarkable. "When The Spell Is Broken" and "Ghosts In The Wind" find Thompson revisiting his favorite theme, love gone awry (the latter boasting a beautifully delicate, ethereal arrangement), while "Fire In The Engine Room" and "Little Blue Number" are unusually hard-rocking numbers with Thompson laying into the songs fast and frantic. And "Love In A Faithless Country" is a striking sketch of love under difficult circumstances that recalls nothing so much as George Orwell's *1984*. There aren't many musicians who could make an album as strong as *Across A Crowded Room* and have it sound like business as usual, but given the consistent strength of Richard Thompson's body of work, this set sounds fairly typical…and typically splendid. —*Mark Deming*

Daring Adventures / Mar. 1986 / Polydor ✦✦✦

In 1986, Richard Thompson and his record label of the moment, Polydor, were eager to expand his audience, so Thompson parted ways with his long-time producer Joe Boyd and went into the studio with producer and keyboard player Mitchell Froom. While Froom's approach was noticeably different than Boyd's, he displayed an obvious respect for Thompson's gifts, and though *Daring Adventures* boasts a bit more aural sheen than the albums that preceded it, Richard Thompson's style as a guitarist and songwriter still shines through clear as day. Froom replaced Thompson's usual rhythm section with top-shelf session players Jerry Scheff on bass and Mickey Curry on drums (Jim Keltner sits in on three cuts), and if their style is less idiosyncratic than that of Dave Pegg and Dave Mattacks, they match the material far better than Willie Weeks and Andy Newmark did on *First Light*. And Froom kept his fondness for tape-loop keyboards and eccentric signal processing in check, giving the sessions an enjoyably warm, organic sound. If *Daring Adventures* has a flaw, it's the songs; while Thompson, as usual, has a handful of gems on board (among them the joyous near-rockabilly of "Valerie," the disquietingly atmospheric "Lover's Lane," and the two heart-rending tales of life during and after wartime that close the album, "How Will I Ever Be Simple Again" and "Al Bowlly's In Heaven"), there are also a few that don't go anywhere, and "Baby Talk" and "Dead Man's Handle" could have been left on the cutting room floor without disappointing anyone. If you're not familiar with Richard Thompson's music, you'll doubtless find that *Daring Adventures* has great songs played by a great band, with an amazing guitar player up front. But if you've already heard most of his records, you'll know he can do better. —*Mark Deming*

Amnesia / 1988 / Capitol ✦✦✦✦

Amnesia was Richard Thompson's second album with producer and keyboard player Mitchell Froom, and the two sounded a lot more comfortable with each other than they did on their previous project together, *Daring Adventures*. This being a Richard Thompson album, the high quality of the songs and the guitar playing is a given; while *Daring Adventures* had a few cuts that sounded like padding, Richard comes up aces this time out, and even sounds a bit more upbeat than usual, letting his political side rise to the surface on "Jerusalem on the Jukebox" and "Yankee, Go Home" and rocking out on "Don't Tempt Me" and "Gypsy Love Songs." (Be advised that the gloriously sad "I Still Dream" and "Waltzing's for Dreamers" are on hand to remind us this *is* a Richard Thompson album.) Froom's production makes more of a difference this time out; *Amnesia* sounds brighter and cleaner than *Daring Adventures*, with a sharp but glossy mix that truly flatters Thompson's fiery Stratocaster solos (not to mention Jim Keltner and Mickey Curry's drumming), and the blend of British folk-rock stalwarts (John Kirkpatrick, Phillip Pickett, Danny Thompson) and American session veterans (Keltner, Curry, Jerry Scheff, Tony Levin) makes for a set of tart and flavorful performances. *Amnesia* is one of Richard Thompson's best-sounding albums, and not a bad place for beginners; he hadn't sounded like he was having this much fun since *Sunnyvista* in 1979. —*Mark Deming*

Rumor and Sigh / May 1991 / Capitol ✦✦✦✦

While Richard Thompson's devotees will tell you the man is a triple-threat genius—passionate vocalist, compelling songwriter, and sterling guitarist—even his most loyal supporters will concede that the dour nature of his songs and the no-frills production of many of his albums make the bulk of his catalog tough sledding for the uninitiated. Given this, 1991's *Rumor and Sigh* is arguably the best album for those wanting to sample Thompson's work for the first time. It captures Thompson at the top of his form on all fronts, but also gives his songs just enough polish to make them approachable for the unconverted, and though it's several shades darker than the average adult-contemporary album, it honors Thompson's obsession with romantic despair and the less pleasant quirks of fate without sounding depressing in the process. Producer Mitchell Froom tricked up Thompson's sound a bit, but his approach added to the material rather than interfering with it; the topsy-turvy keyboards and sharp, snapping drum sound on "Gray Walls" and "You Dream Too Much" actually add to their narrative drama, and Froom coaxed some of Thompson's most soulful vocals on "Why Must I Plead" and "I Misunderstood." Thompson actually gets funny on "Don't Sit On My Jimmy Shands" and the darkly hilarious "Psycho Street," and Thompson fans who like his work straight with no chaser will be knocked flat by "1952 Vincent Black Lightning," perhaps the best traditional-style number in his songbook, and the harrowing "God Loves A Drunk," an unnerving tale of several kinds of addiction. While *Rumor and Sigh* is quite slick by Thompson's standards, its clean lines and bright mix serve both the songs and the bandleader quite well, and make Thompson's tunes sound like the radio hits they've always deserved to be. *—Mark Deming*

Watching the Dark / May 11, 1993 / Hannibal ✦✦✦✦✦
Multi-disc box-sets usually fall into two categories—they're either overstuffed "Greatest Hits" compilations, or packed with enough rarities to ensure loyal fans will part with their money. Since Richard Thompson's career hasn't sent him perilously close to worldwide stardom, the triple-disc anthology *Watching The Dark* was created with the latter market in mind, and if it falls short of being the perfect overview of Thompson's wildly varied career, it's a superb set that manages the not-inconsiderable feat of drawing an accurate picture of the height and breadth of Thompson's body of work, and offers enough buried treasures to leave jaded fans chuckling with glee. Sequenced thematically rather than chronologically, *Watching The Dark* covers Thompson's favorite themes well enough—there's enough spiritual mystery, mortal heartbreak, and British traditionalism to satisfy nearly anyone—and while the first priority appears to be Thompson the songwriter, Thompson the musician is documented with a similar degree of devotion. *Watching The Dark* gives relatively short shrift to Thompson's work with Fairport Convention and his experimental collaborations, but as an overview of his solo work (both with and without former wife and frequent collaborator Linda Thompson), it's remarkably thorough, and packed with fascinating and illuminating rarities. There are copious concert recordings, fascinating studio outtakes, and a handful of otherwise unavailable songs, along with an intelligently chosen selection of highlights from the first 25 years of his career in music. The sheer bulk of *Watching The Dark* (over three and a half hours of music) makes this a difficult introduction to Richard Thompson's work, but anyone with more than a passing familiarity with his music will be dazzled by it—few box set honor their subject with as much intelligence and depth as *Watching The Dark*. *—Mark Deming*

Mirror Blue / Feb. 8, 1994 / Capitol ✦✦✦
1991's *Rumor and Sigh* was among Richard Thompson's best-selling and most warmly received albums, even gaining a bit of radio and MTV exposure which introduced Thompson to a wider audience than ever before. But while Thompson has often expressed his desire to reach a greater number of listeners, he's (thankfully) unwilling to dumb his music down, and it's probably no coincidence that he followed up his most user-friendly album with the more difficult *Mirror Blue*. *Mirror Blue* was constructed on a more modest scale, with the arrangements scaled down and the mix putting the instruments in greater relief. While Mitchell Froom's production added both polish and punch to *Rumor and Sigh*, his work on *Mirror Blue* marked the point where he began to interfere more than he helped; the tinny, crashing sound he imposes on Thompson's guitar and Pete Thomas' drums soon wears out its welcome, and Froom's washes of retro-styled keyboards are more prominent than they need to be. And while song for song *Mirror Blue* boasts material just as strong as *Rumor and Sigh* (if not stronger), the tone is more dour, with the few rockers decidedly less friendly ("Mascara Tears" sounds downright mean) and the ballads more mournful (though "King Of Bohemia" and "Beeswing" are beautiful and affecting if you don't mind a good cry). But Thompson had a great set of songs here, and he performs them with typical fire and precision; his guitar work is glorious, and his vocals are passionate and unusually well controlled. *Mirror Blue* suggests that, after making an album with the mass audience in mind, Richard Thompson decided to make one for the fans—and himself—and if Froom's production sometimes gets in the way, loyalists will find plenty to revel in here. *—Mark Deming*

Live at Crawley 1993 / 1995 / Flypaper ✦✦✦
Accompanied by acoustic bassist Danny Thompson, acoustic guitarist Richard Thompson presents stripped-down versions of some of the songs featured on his recent albums. Thompson is an engaging performer, whose nuances and improvisations can be appreciated well in this intimate format. The album is a fan-club recording and "is part of our recent policy to regularly release live recordings... in an effort to stop inferior bootleg versions...," Thompson writes in the liner notes. Of course, hardcore fans will buy both, but it's nice to see Thompson joining the Grateful Dead in finding a way outside the usual record-company structure to address his fans' desires. Write to Flypaper, P.O. Box 516, Middle Village, NY 11379. *—William Ruhlmann*

You? Me? Us? / Apr. 16, 1996 / Capitol ✦✦✦
On the surface, *You? Me? Us?* appears to be a major statement from Richard Thompson. Spread out over two discs, the budget-priced album features 19 tracks, separated into an electric ("Voltage Enhanced") disc and an acoustic ("Nude") disc, which each run around 40 minutes; "Razor Dance" and "Hide It Away" appear on both discs. Despite its appearance, *You? Me? Us?* isn't one of Thompson's major works. What sinks the album isn't the songs—as always, Thompson has written a handful of gems—but Mitchell Froom's production. Froom's gauzy, pseudo-experimental approach masks the songs in an impenetrable haze, which neither Thompson's guitar or voice can cut through. There is no texture to the album's sound—it is mushy and colorless, which cuts away at the heart of Thompson's direct, emotional songs. If the songs on *You? Me? Us?* were given the simple, direct production they deserve, it would have been a completely different, more compelling experience. As it stands, it's a wildly uneven and unengaging listen, like the great majority of the Froom-produced Richard Thompson records. *—Stephen Thomas Erlewine*

Mock Tudor / Aug. 24, 1999 / Capitol ✦✦✦✦✦
Just how lost Richard Thompson lies under Mitchell Froom and Tchad Blake's direction during the '90s is made clear by *Mock Tudor*, the brilliant sequel to the botched *You? Me? Us?* Producers/engineers Tom Rothrock and Rob Schnapf keep the production clean and direct, allowing the songs to breathe and letting Thompson play guitar. That decision alone would have made *Mock Tudor* a satisfying listen, but what elevates it into the first rank of his albums is, naturally, the songs themselves. Thompson structured the album as a portrait of suburbia, tackling a different subject with each song. It's not all about desperation, although there certainly is a lot of that there. Instead, Thompson is at the top of his form, offering subtle shadings in his lyrics and remarkably catchy, memorable melodies throughout the album. As a matter of fact, it's a bit of a tour de force, opening with the rollicking "Cooksferry Queen" and closing with its polar opposite, the hushed, intimate black comedy of "Hope You Like the New Me." Between those two songs, Thompson covers all sorts of emotional textures, resulting in his most affecting effort in years. Since even on his uneven '90s efforts he demonstrated that he still was in full grasp of his talents, it can't be said that *Mock Tudor* is a comeback, but it's certainly the best album he's made in over a decade. *—Stephen Thomas Erlewine*

The Best of Richard & Linda Thompson: The Island Record Years / Jul. 25, 2000 / Island ✦✦✦✦
Since Richard and Linda Thompson's albums have been available through Hannibal Records for many years, it's easy to forget that they weren't all released by that label originally; in fact, only the last of the duo's six albums, *Shoot Out the Lights*, was a Hannibal album to begin with. The first three LPs (*I Want to See the Bright Lights Tonight*, *Hokey Pokey*, and *Pour Down Like Silver*) came out on Island Records, while the fourth and fifth (*First Light* and *Sunnyvista*) were on Chrysalis. This only becomes important when you consider the compilation *The Best of Richard & Linda Thompson: The Island Years*. That subtitle is important. It means the album collects material from only the first half of the Thompsons' recording career. The selection comes not just from those three Island duo albums, but also from Richard's first solo album, *Henry the Human Fly*, and from an earlier Thompson compilation, *Guitar, Vocal*, which featured alternate and live material from the Thompsons. It's hard to argue with the selections from that material made here. Appropriately, the masterful *I Want to See the Bright Lights Tonight* is the source of six cuts, the impressive *Pour Down Like Silver* provides four, and the weakest of the three albums, *Hokey Pokey*, only two. There is a good mixture of Linda-sung ballads and more up-tempo material, and "Night Comes In" and "Calvary Cross" feature extended examples of Richard's amazing guitar work. And the compilers have not shied away from featuring the often pessimistic tone of much of Richard's songwriting for the duo, from "Withered and Died" to "Beat the Retreat." But all this means that the album is a great half of a compilation of their career. *—William Ruhlmann*

Action Packed: The Best of the Capitol Years / Mar. 27, 2001 / Capitol ✦✦✦✦
Richard Thompson has been the archetypal critics' favorite since his days with Fairport Convention in the late '60s and early '70s, but he is also a man seemingly incapable of making any sort of peace with broad commercial appeal. But then, why should he, when record companies have lined up to release his work, even if they ultimately cut him loose after failing to get his account into the black? Thompson has successively signed to large independents Island and Chrysalis (when they were independents), then to major imprints Polydor and Capitol. Beginning in 1988, his Capitol sojourn has been the longest, spanning more than ten years and five regular studio albums, three of which actually nudged into the lower reaches of the charts. Certainly, *Action Packed* is not your typical best-of kiss-off, but rather a well-considered collection drawing on some of the most impressive recordings of Thompson's later career as well as including rarities. Thompson's Capitol catalog has been uneven occasionally, especially because of the inappropriate production style of Mitchell Froom on some of it, but by gathering together the best of each of his albums, Capitol here demonstrates that, especially as a songwriter, he has frequently matched the uncompromising style of his early work, particularly on "Turning of the Tide," "1952 Vincent Black Lightning," "I Misunderstood," "I Feel So Good," and "Beeswing," songs imbued with his dark, folk-informed sensibility, yet buoyed up by his stirring guitar work. *—William Ruhlmann*

George Thorogood

b. Dec. 24, 1950, Wilmington, DE
Slide Guitar, Vocals, Guitar / Slide Guitar Blues, Album Rock, Boogie Rock, Hard Rock, Blues-Rock

A blues-rock guitarist who draws his inspiration from Elmore James, Hound Dog Taylor, and Chuck Berry, George Thorogood never earned much respect from blues purists, but he became a popular favorite in the early '80s through repeated exposure on FM radio and the arena rock circuit. Thorogood's music was always loud, simple, and direct—his riffs and licks were taken straight out of '50s Chicago blues and rock & roll—but his formulaic approach helped him gain a rather large audience in the '80s, when his albums regularly went gold. Forming his first band in 1973, Thorogood later moved to Boston and became a regular on the blues club circuit. After signing to Rounder, Thorogood and the Destroyers' eponymous debut was released in early 1977. The group's second album, 1978's *Move It on Over*, entered the American Top 40 thanks to heavy FM airplay of the title track, a Hank Williams cover. A move to EMI brought his major-label debut, 1982's *Bad to the Bone*. The title track became his first major crossover hit, and helped the album go gold. (Its three follow-ups also went gold.) Despite declining record sales by the beginning of the '90s, Thorogood continued to tour and he usually drew large crowds. *—Stephen Thomas Erlewine*

George Thorogood & the Destroyers / 1977 / Rounder ✦✦✦✦✦
Contains Thorogood's crowd-pleasing rendition of John Lee Hooker's "One Bourbon, One Scotch, One Beer." Its basic approach—heavy on Thorogood's bluesy guitar playing—serves as the prototype for every Destroyers record that followed. *—William Ruhlmann*

Move It on Over / 1978 / Rounder ✦✦✦

In 1978, George Thorogood was just beginning to make some noise on the blues-rock circuit. This was his second album, and what's now almost a cliché then sounded fresh and vital. Thorogood's energy, rousing vocals and driving guitar playing came roaring through on inspired covers of Elmore James' "The Sky Is Crying," Bo Diddley's "Who Do You Love" and Chuck Berry's "It Wasn't Me." He even did a credible Piedmont blues on Brownie McGhee's "So Much Trouble." While Thorogood went on to make more commercially succesful albums, the spirit and innocence in his early releases has seldom been duplicated. This Rounder CD reissue returns him to a simpler, and in some ways superior, period. —*Ron Wynn*

More George Thorogood and the Destroyers / 1980 / Rounder ✦✦

Bad to the Bone / 1982 / EMI America ✦✦✦✦✦

Though songs such as"Back to Wentzville" are credited to G. Thorogood, he'd be the first to admit that they are proudly derivative of Chuck Berry and his other mentors. The title track, another Thorogood copyright, has become ubiquitous in *Terminator 2* and the *Problem Child* movies and elsewhere, but it's still terrific. —*William Ruhlmann*

● **The Baddest of George Thorogood and the Destroyers** / Jul. 28, 1992 / EMI America ✦✦✦✦✦

The aptly-titled *The Baddest of George Thorogood and the Destroyers* offers a dozen tracks that cleanse the church of rock & roll of all but its most basic elements: guitar, bass, drums, and a pile of Chuck Berry, Bo Diddley and Rolling Stone licks. Delaware's George Thorogood has never quite captured his wildman live presence in the studio, but having all his best material gathered on one disc—including "Bad to the Bone," "Move It on Over," and "One Bourbon, One Scotch, One Beer"—makes for a great party. Steve Morse's liner notes are brief but, like the songs, get right to the point … cut to the bone, you might say. —*Roch Parisien*

Haircut / Jul. 27, 1993 / EMI America ✦✦

Rockin' My Life Away / Mar. 25, 1997 / Capitol ✦✦

Anthology / Aug. 29, 2000 / Capitol ✦✦✦✦

Just because this double CD practically triples the tracks of 1992's *The Baddest of George Thorogood & the Destroyers*, features better fidelity, more informative liner notes, songs recorded for four more albums, and a handful of rarities, doesn't make it the better collection. A little bit of Thorogood's meat and potatoes mix of Chuck Berry riffs, Elmore James slide guitar, and stripped-down Hound Dog Taylor house rocking goes an awfully long way, and a double-disc dose of similar sounding, non-stop rocking becomes mind-numbing over the course of more than two hours of in your face boogie. As you'd expect, all of the Delaware pile-driving guitarist's recorded highlights are here, including six concert recordings that catch the band in their natural habitat. Thorogood and his road-hardened crew will bring any crowd to a frenzy, but having to wade through what amounts to the same three chords, albeit ones played with dogged enthusiasm and robust fervor, for 30 tracks without the sweat, beer, and infectious energy of actually being there, makes for a tiring and repetitious experience. Although you have to admire the guy for sticking to his guns for three decades, the lack of ballads, or really any change-ups chosen for this set, presents a limited, one-sided picture of this rugged rocker. Thorogood's individual albums include the occasional country or novelty tune, and his versions of Frank Zappa's "Trouble Everyday," Nick Lowe's "Half a Boy, Half a Man," or the trucking classic "Six Days on the Road," none of which are found here, would have made for a far more listenable and somewhat more eclectic compilation. Rough, tough, and unfailingly intense, *Anthology* is just too much reelin' and rocking for all but the most die-hard fan. —*Hal Horowitz*

Three Dog Night

f. 1968, Los Angeles, CA
AM Pop, Pop/Rock

Three Dog Night scored a succession of 21 hit singles, including eleven Top Tens, and twelve consecutive gold albums from 1969 to 1975, thanks to the slick, sometimes soulful vocal harmonies of singers Danny Hutton, Chuck Negron, and Cory Wells and an excellent ear for quality material. While often criticized as commercial, the band was noted for its creative arrangements and interpretations, and their cover choices gave exposure (and royalties) to several talented songwriters: Nilsson ("One"), Laura Nyro ("Eli's Coming"), Randy Newman ("Mama Told Me (Not to Come)"), Hoyt Axton ("Joy to the World"), Argent's Russ Ballard ("Liar"), and Leo Sayer ("The Show Must Go On"). "One" became the band's first Top Ten hit in 1969, while "Mama Told Me (Not to Come)" hit number one a year later. "Joy to the World" became the group's biggest hit in 1971, spending six weeks on top of the *Billboard* charts, and their streak continued with their final number one, 1972's "Black and White" (a U.K. reggae hit for Greyhound), and their final Top Ten, 1974's "The Show Must Go On." —*Steve Huey*

● **The Best of Three Dog Night** / 1983 / MCA ✦✦✦✦✦

Weighing it at a generous 20 tracks, *The Best of Three Dog Night* may be a little much for some casual listeners, yet it's unquestionably the definitive collection, featuring all of their hits, plus a nice selection of album tracks. There isn't anything major missing, and while some of the non-singles material isn't particularly strong, there are enough worthwhile moments to make this a fairly consistent, enjoyable listen, in addition to being the one Three Dog Night album most fans will need. —*Stephen Thomas Erlewine*

Celebrate: The Three Dog Night Story, 1965-1975 / Dec. 7, 1993 / MCA ✦✦✦✦

One of the better compilations of Three Dog Night material, *Celebrate* covers all the important bases in the popular trash-singles band's career. There's a brief hint of the pre-3DN material from co-lead singers Danny Hutton and Cory Wells (no Chuck Negron,

though) along with one stellar, tragically unreleased track from the band's brief Redwood incarnation, the Brian Wilson-penned "Time to Get Alone." The remainder of this two-CD collection is devoted to recapping the group's many Top 40 hits along with a few choice album tracks. The songs are judiciously chosen, and the liner notes provide glimpses of insight to the band's creative processes and internal skirmishes, but there's nothing in the way of remastered tracks or uncovered obscurities. Nevertheless, this is a better option for Three Dog Night fans than any of the numerous single-disc greatest hits collections available, simply because there are no glaring oversights in the song choices. The expanded selection also makes for great conversion material for people not yet warm to Three Dog Night's intricate harmony stylings: just play them the gorgeous non-singles "It's for You," "My Impersonal Life," and "I'd Be So Happy" back to back. —*Joseph McCombs*

20th Century Masters—The Millennium Collection: The Best of Three Dog Night / Oct. 19, 1999 / MCA ✦✦✦✦

All of Three Dog Night's staples are included on *The Millennium Collection: The Best of Three Dog Night*, including "Joy to the World," "One," "Mama Told Me Not to Come," "Eli's Coming," "Easy to Be Hard," and "An Old Fashioned Love Song." A compact and entertaining compilation of the group's biggest singles. —*Heather Phares*

The Three O'Clock

f. 1980, db. 1988
Neo-Psychedelia, Paisley Underground, Alternative Pop/Rock, American Underground

The Three O'Clock were the quintessential L.A. Paisley Underground band. Lead singer and bassist Michael Quercio in fact coined the term to describe the set of bands, including the Dream Syndicate, Rain Parade, Green On Red and the Bangles, who incorporated the chiming guitars of the Byrds and the Beatles into their pop songs with a psychedelic bent, and the clothes to match. Beginning as the Salvation Army in 1982 as a three-piece and forsaking the name due to a conflict with the actual organization, the Three O'Clock originally included Quercio, and guitarist Louis (formerly Gregg) Gutierrez. The band plied a garagey sound on their self-titled debut in 1982. When ex-Weirdos drummer Danny Benair and keyboardist Mickey Mariano joined for the follow-up EP *Baroque Hoedown* and the LP *Sixteen Tambourines* in 1983, the band found a more polished, perfect pop sound. In 1985 they released *Arrive Without Travelling* for IRS, followed by *Ever After* (IRS). Gutierrez departed in 1986. For their Warner Brothers/Paisley Park debut (Prince was a fan), *Vermillion*, Jason Falkner was added on guitar. Sadly, it proved to be their undoing, as they never really fulfilled the label's expectations and Quercio refused to be pigeonholed as a pretty-boy pop star or spokesperson for the premature retro revival. Quercio continues to play in L.A. pop bands, while Gutierrez became a principle member of Mary's Danish, and Falkner is a solo recording artist. —*Denise Sullivan*

The Salvation Army: Befour Three O'Clock / Feb. 1982 / Frontier ✦✦✦

A rough but engaging debut for this three-piece garage rock band with a '60s bent. Punk in spirit but filled in with near-psychedelic guitar swirls and pop vocals, the band forged the foundation of the Paisley Underground movement, a sound that incorporated the best of the '60s from the Beatles to the Byrds to the Velvet Underground. "She Turns to Flowers" and "While We Were in Your Room Talking to Your Wall," if only in their titles, send a clear message of where the band was coming from. —*Denise Sullivan*

Baroque Hoedown [EP] / Jun. 1982 / Frontier ✦✦

The band found its sound on this essential EP from L.A.'s influential Paisley Underground scene. "With a Cantaloupe Girlfriend" and "I Go Wild" capture the essence of the swirling psych-pop sound the band had naively mastered by this time, and their cover of the Easybeats' "Sorry" is worth the price of admission alone. Lead singer Michael Quercio's high, almost creepy voice could at times recall Syd Barrett, but was a unique instrument in its own right. —*Denise Sullivan*

Sixteen Tambourines / 1983 / Frontier ✦✦✦

As the band matured, they naturally got better technically, but in this case it wasn't necessarily a good thing. No longer a loose garage outfit, keen production by L.A. pop whiz Earle Mankey put the keyboards up front, and next to vocalist Michael Quercio's unusually high voice, the band ended up sounding a little twee. Still, "When Lightning Starts" is irresistibly cute, and their choice of cover material was always inspiring; the version of the Bee Gees' "In My Own Time" included here is a perfect fit. —*Denise Sullivan*

Arrive Without Travelling / 1985 / IRS ✦✦✦✦

Arrive Without Travelling is a record that typified the Paisley Underground sound. It also made The Three O'Clock a considerable talent. This record is made of track after track of quality, pop songwriting. The only problem is the production. muddy, reverberated, production brings down the greatness of a record that is consistently good. —*Zachary Curd*

Ever After / 1986 / IRS ✦✦✦

Another solid neo-psychedelic pop album. Though it fails to distinguish itself from previous releases, *Ever After* is still an interesting venture. —*Chris Woodstra*

● **Vermillion** / 1988 / Paisley Park ✦✦✦✦✦

The band's final album is also their strongest. No longer restricted to their "paisley underground" roots, they stretch out stylistically with rewarding results. Includes the wonderful "Neon Telephone" (written by Prince). —*Chris Woodstra*

Throbbing Gristle

f. Sep. 1975, London, England. db. 1981
Experimental, Industrial

Abrasive, aggressive and antagonistic, Britain's Throbbing Gristle pioneered industrial music; exploring death, mutilation, fascism and degradation amidst a thunderous cacophony of mechanical noise, tape loops, extremist anti-melodies and bludgeoning beats, the group's cultural terrorism—the "wreckers of civilization," one tabloid called them—raised the stakes of artistic confrontation to new heights, combating all notions of commerciality and good taste with a maniacal fervor.

Formed in London in the autumn of 1975, Throbbing Gristle consisted of vocalist/ringleader Genesis P-Orridge, his then-lover, guitarist Cosey Fanni Tutti, tape manipulator Peter "Sleazy" Christopherson and keyboardist Chris Carter. A performance art troupe as much as a band, their early live shows—each starting with a punch clock and running exactly 60 minutes before the power to the stage was cut—threatened obscenity laws; during their notorious premiere gig, P-Orridge even mounted an art exhibit consisting entirely of used tampons and soiled diapers.

Upon forming their own label, Industrial, the group issued their introductory release, *The Best of Throbbing Gristle, Vol. 2*, in 1976. A full-length debut, *2nd Annual Report* followed in 1977, in a pressing of only 500 copies; bowing to fan demand, the record was later reissued—cut from a master tape played backwards. The 1977 underground hit "United" marked a tiny step towards accessibility, thanks to the inclusion of a discernible rhythm. Typically, when the track reappeared on 1978's *D.O.A.: The Third and Final Report*, it was sped up to last all of 17 seconds; no less provocative was "Hamburger Lady" (inspired by the story of a burn-unit victim) or "Death Threats" (a compilation of murderous messages left on the group's answering machine).

20 Jazz Funk Greats, a harsh electro-pop outing, followed a year later, and after 1980's live-in-the-studio *Heathen Earth*, Throbbing Gristle called it quits. P-Orridge and Christopherson soon formed Psychic TV (though Christopherson split again to form Coil), while the remaining duo continued on as Chris and Cosey. As Throbbing Gristle's influence swelled, a seemingly endless series of posthumous releases followed, most of them taken from live dates; among the more notable were 1981's *24 Hours* (later reissued as *36 Hours*), 1983's *Once Upon a Time (Live at the Lyceum)* and 1986's *TG CD 1*. *—Jason Ankeny*

Second Annual Report / 1977 / Mute ✦✦✦
A proper debut of sorts, *Second Annual Report* includes several versions each (some live) of early Throbbing Gristle standards like "Slug Bait" and "Maggot Death," as well as an "Industrial Introduction" and the soundtrack work "After Cease to Exist." The music is relentless, grinding distortion, only occasionally leavened by vocal samples and percussion. *—John Bush*

D.O.A.: The Third and Final Report of Throbbing Gristle / Dec. 1978 / Mute ✦✦✦
Breaking from the live sound of the previous *Second Annual Report*, *D.O.A.* finds the group assembling collages of computer noise (before connecting to the internet sounded almost friendly), cassette tapes on fast forward, looped feedback and tape hiss, surreptitiously recorded conversation, threatening phone calls, and much more, all to a grand alienating effect, the sound of a gray day in a British tower block after all the drugs have run out. Of course, this was the intended effect and the band succeed well enough. "Weeping," Genesis P-Orridge's version of a love ballad, loses itself among delayed strings and drones, a barely enunciated vocal, and a violin like a squeaky door. "Hamburger Lady" (about a burn victim) is even more repellent, but in a good way—a genuinely scary listen. "AB/7A," on the other hand, approaches the pulsing electronics of Kraftwerk or early Yello. *—Ted Mills*

● **20 Jazz Funk Greats** / 1979 / Industrial ✦✦✦✦✦
It's a break in the clouds from Throbbing Gristle's pummeling noise and a first glimpse at the continuing pop influence on the TG/PTV axis, but *20 Jazz Funk Greats* still isn't best described by its title. If there is such a thing as a funky Throbbing Gristle LP, however, this could well be it. "Hot on the Heels of Love," "Hamburger Lady" and "Six Six Sixties" add only occasional bits of distortion between the rigid sequencer lines. *20 Jazz Funk Greats* is the best compromise between TG's early industrial aesthetic and the reams of industrial-dance and dark synth-pop groups that used the album as a stepping stone to crossover appeal. *—John Bush*

Heathen Earth / 1980 / Industrial ✦✦✦
Live in the studio, this combines the best of both harrowing worlds. *—Myles Boisen*

Mission of Dead Souls / 1981 / Mute ✦✦✦
Their final and perhaps most extreme musical assault was recorded live in San Francisco. *—Myles Boisen*

Greatest Hits / 1984 / Mute ✦✦✦✦
Like the title says (with irony), it's an industrial primer with song sensibility. *—Myles Boisen*

TG CD 1 / 1986 / Resonance ✦✦✦
A very raw studio session. *—Myles Boisen*

Throwing Muses

f. 1983, **db.** 1997
College Rock, Indie Rock, Alternative Pop/Rock
One of the quietly great college bands from the 1980s, Throwing Muses was formed in 1983 by guitarist/vocalist Kristin Hersh and her half-sister guitarist/vocalist Tanya Donelly. In 1986 the group's debut album was put out by the prestigious British label 4AD; Throwing Muses were the first American band to be released on that label. Throwing Muses' angular, anguished, mercurial sound had much to do with Hersh's mental illness (she suffered from a form of bipolarity that caused her to hallucinate), especially on the early albums like *House Tornado*. 1991's *The Real Ramona* marked a break from the heaviness of the previous albums, with lots of shimmery pop gems penned both by Hersh and Donelly. Creative tensions between the two songwriters rose until Donelly left in 1992 to play with The Breeders and ultimately form Belly. After 1992's *Red Heaven*, Hersh released a solo album and toured extensively, leaving fans to wonder about the status of The Muses. In 1995, however, the group released *University*, one of their most cohesive and accessible efforts; it was followed by *Limbo* in 1996. The group's dissolution was announced soon after, with Hersh continuing on as a solo artist. *—Heather Phares*

Throwing Muses / 1986 / 4AD ✦✦✦✦✦
Throwing Muses' self-titled, 1986 debut is still a startling collision of punk energy, folky melodicism, and Kristin Hersh's mercurial voice and lyrics. The violent, vibrant mood swings on songs like "Call Me" are a testament not only to Hersh's unique talent, but the elasticity of Tanya Donelly, David Narcizo, and Leslie Langston's playing. Even if the volatile moods on songs like "Hate My Way" aren't easily understood, they're easily felt; the twists and turns "Vicky's Box" and "Rabbits Dying" take are guided purely by the intense emotions they carry. *Throwing Muses* is almost as varied musically as it is emotionally, ranging from the scary punkabilly of "America (She Can't Say No)" to "Stand Up"'s angular, acoustic post-punk to the cathartic thrill of "Delicate Cutters"'s unsettling folk. Donelly contributes the surreal, ethereal love song "Green"; even at this early point in the Muses' career, it's clear that she is a more accessible, straightforward songwriter, despite the care taken to make the song sound more like the rest of the album. A powerful debut, *Throwing Muses* puts the work of most self-consciously "tortured" artists to shame; its fluid, effortless emotional shifts may not make for the most accessible music, but they're unquestionably genuine. *—Heather Phares*

Chains Changed / 1987 / 4AD ✦✦✦
This four-song EP is difficult to find, but is nevetheless worth the search. It contains some of Hersh's finest songs, including the rockabilly-tinged "Cry Baby Cry," the tumultuous "Finished" and "Snailhead." *Chain's Changed* combines the group's fiery intensity and moodiness with the pop prowess the band gradually developed. *—Heather Phares*

The Fat Skier / 1988 / 4AD/Sire ✦✦✦
Throwing Muses' 1988 *The Fat Skier* EP finds the group embracing an even more pop-oriented sound than that year's album, *House Tornado*. However, songs like the untamed, galloping "Soap and Water" and "Garoux des Larmes"—which sounds like it was influenced by the band's friendship with the Pixies—remain far outside the mainstream. "A Feeling" remains one of the band's hypnotic, sensual moments, while "And a She-Wolf After the War" reflects the increasing clarity of Hersh's songwriting. *The Fat Skier* ends with "You Cage," one of Hersh's simplest and most affecting ballads, reaffirming that what the Muses might have lost in volatility, they more than made up for with their work's new-found coherence. *—Heather Phares*

House Tornado / 1988 / 4AD/Sire ✦✦✦
On their second album and first major label release, Throwing Muses apply more polish, craft and melody to the challenging style they forged on their debut. The pop sheen on songs like "Colder" and "Saving Grace" makes their sudden dynamic shifts and tempo changes more accessible without dulling them. Kristin Hersh finds ways to mold her complex music into more straightforward song structures, particularly on "Juno" and "Run Letter." Tanya Donelly develops her own songwriting voice with "River" and "Giant," though both songs still feel like self-conscious attempts to blend with Hersh's material. "Marriage Tree" and "Mexican Women" flesh out the Muses' unique take on country-tinged post-punk; "Saving Grace" and "Walking In The Dark" are two of the group's best stream-of-consciousness meditations. *House Tornado* isn't quite as wild a ride as Throwing Muses' debut, but the album does prove that the band could expand on their unique sound without sacrificing any of its originality. *—Heather Phares*

Hunkpapa / Oct. 1990 / 4AD/Sire ✦✦

● **The Real Ramona** / Mar. 12, 1991 / 4AD/Sire ✦✦✦✦✦
The Real Ramona marked the perfect balance of the Muses' angular songwriting and latent pop tendencies. Where *Hunkpapa* tried, somewhat unsuccessfully, to mix these elements, this album succeeds with surreal pop songs like "Counting Backwards" and "Red Shoes." They're catchy and riveting, clearly linked to the band's early material yet more focused and accessible. "Graffiti" and "Two-Step" are two of Kristin Hersh's most appealing pop snippets, but dark, uncompromising tracks like "Say Goodbye," "Ellen West," and "Hook in Her Head" reaffirm that she can still write troubling, fascinating songs like nobody else. And just before she left the Muses to form Belly, Tanya Donelly finally arrived as a full-fledged songwriter with the giddy, gleeful "Not Too Soon" and "Honeychain," proving that she could be a charming foil to Hersh's more challenging style. Their final album as a quartet, *The Real Ramona* highlights the best points of the group's sound, making it a great starting point for new Throwing Muses fans. *—Heather Phares*

Red Heaven / Aug. 11, 1992 / 4AD/Sire ✦✦✦
Undaunted by the departure of Tanya Donelly to form her own group Belly, Kristen Hersh continued Throwing Muses as a trio on the band's fourth album, *Red Heaven*. The pared-down lineup gives rock songs like "Furious" and "Backroad" a more powerful, muscular sound, and pop tracks like "Dirty Water" and "Firepile" a crisp, spacious feel. Overall, *Red Heaven* is the Muses' most rock-oriented album since *House Tornado*, especially on songs like the Bob Mould duet "Dio," "The Visit," and "Rosetta Stone," but the band's pace has slowed into a slinky, winding groove that is more solid and forceful than the volatile tempo shifts of its early work. However, the ballad "Pearl" rivals anything on *Throwing Muses* with its spooky unpredictability, and the charming, delicate "Summer St." is one of Hersh's most endearing songs. One of Throwing Muses' finest albums, *Red Heaven* showcases Hersh's continuing development as a powerful and eclectic singer, songwriter, and guitarist. *—Heather Phares*

University / Jan. 17, 1995 / Sire/Reprise ✦✦✦✦✦
Possibly their finest album, Throwing Muses' fifth album *University* blends the rock

power of *Red Heaven*, their first effort as a trio, with the shiny, surreal pop of *The Real Ramona*. The result is a collection of songs, like the album opener "Bright Yellow Gun," that are as ferociously kinetic as they are insinuatingly melodic. At first, Tanya Donelly's departure from the group might have been seen as a liability, but on this dreamy yet direct album, it's an asset: it gives Kristin Hersh room for her most wide-ranging collection of songs yet. "Start," "Hazing," "Shimmer," and "Teller" are some of her most immediate, deceptively sweet punk-pop confections, rivalling previous Muses classics like "Counting Backwards" in their hooky intensity. Yet the delicate "Crabtown" and "Fever Few" reaffirm Hersh's finesse with brooding, folky melodies. "That's All You Wanted" and "Snakeface" remain two of the Muses' catchiest songs, and the driven "No Way in Hell" and "Flood" show that Hersh hasn't lost any of her edge. *University*'s smooth, streamlined production adds a bit of sheen to Hersh's jagged, elliptical guitar lines and keening vocals, but doesn't rob either of their impact; if anything, the album's polish just heightens its flowing yet diverse sound. The album the Muses had been trying to make since *Hunkpapa*, *University* is as hypnotic as it is accessible. *—Heather Phares*

Limbo / Aug. 13, 1996 / Rykodisc ♦♦♦♦
Their first release on their own Throwing Music label, Throwing Muses' *Limbo* is a strangely anticlimactic album. Though it should be a celebration of the Muses' liberation from a major label deal that ended up being a major disappointment, it lacks the shimmery spark of the band's best material. However, it's still a solid, well-written affair; the first three songs—"Buzz," "Ruthie's Knocking," and "Freeloader"—get *Limbo* off to a propulsive start, but on the whole, the album suffers from similar rhythms and progressions from song to song. "The Field" has an interesting riff; "Tango" and "Serene" are subtly edgy; dreamy ballads like "Mr. Bones," "Night Driving," and the hidden track "White Bikini Sand" are pleasantly eerie; and "Shark" closes the album on a driving, malevolent note, but few songs seem truly captivating. *Limbo*'s sequencing, which places most of the louder songs on the first half and lets the slower, quieter songs sink to the bottom, also works against the album. Strangely predictable, the effect that the Muses' seventh album achieves isn't so much *Limbo* as déjà vu; the band's once-mercurial twists and turns feel programmed and somewhat disappointing. *—Heather Phares*

In a Doghouse / Jul. 14, 1998 / Rykodisc ♦♦♦♦♦
Throwing Muses' classic first album was never released in the U.S., nor was their follow-up EP, *Chains Changed*. For well over a decade, the two records were only available as imports through 4AD, which meant that Throwing Muses, one of the most influential and individual albums of late-'80s alternative rock, was very hard for anyone outside of devoted record collectors to track down. Rykodisc fortunately remedied that situation in 1998 with the release of *In a Doghouse*, a double-disc set that provides a comprehensive overview of the Muses' early years. The first disc is devoted to *Throwing Muses* and *Chains Changed*, while the second disc contains the group's self-released demo tape *The Doghouse Cassette* and five recordings of Kristin Hersh's earliest songs that the final incarnation of the Muses cut in 1996. Usually, such material would be the province of hardcore collectors only, but the Muses were such an original, unpredictable band in their early days that even the early demos are fascinating. The re-recordings don't quite match the other recordings here, but it's fortunate that Hersh had the foresight to document these songs before they were forgotten. In this context, they are a nice bonus, but the quality of the remaining music—especially the idiosyncratic debut, which remains a fresh, unexpected listen—is why *In a Doghouse* is an essential compilation. *—Stephen Thomas Erlewine*

Thunderclap Newman

f. 1969, England, **db.** 1969
Psychedelic Pop, Prog-Rock/Art Rock, AM Pop
John "Speedy" Keene was an old crony of the Who, and had written "Armenia City in the Sky," which appeared on *The Who Sell Out* LP. The unlikely Andy Newman played terrific pub-style piano and looked much like a postal clerk, which in fact, he was. Jimmy McCullough, the guitarist, looked to be a mere teenager, and so he was. It was this combination, plus the production efforts of Pete Townshend, that offered the album, *Hollywood Dream*. As the now-classic single, "Something in the Air" had long preceded it, the album delivered the goods in a similar fashion, fueled by Keene's reedy vocals and Newman's charming honky-tonk piano. *Hollywood Dream* has remained an anglophile fave; sadly, it was to be Thunderclap Newman's only album. Even if you own the original LP, make sure to check out the recently expanded edition of the compact disc. *—Steve Aldrich*

• **Hollywood Dream** / 1969 / Polydor ♦♦♦♦♦
Thunderclap Newman seized the sound of an era with their 1969 hit, "Something in the Air," as beautiful a call for pacifism as you'll ever hear. That song is included on this expanded version of their Pete Townshend-produced debut, which features a strange but enticing mix of off-kilter originals and clever covers (such as the Dylan nugget "Open the Door Homer"). *—John Floyd*

Johnny Thunders (John Anthony Genzale, Jr)

b. Jul. 15, 1952, Leesburg, FL, **d.** Apr. 23, 1991, New Orleans, LA
Vocals, Guitar / New York Punk, Hard Rock, Punk, Rock & Roll
Following in the footsteps of his idol Keith Richards, Johnny Thunders (born John Anthony Genzale Jr.) lived the ultimate rock & roll life, spending most of his days wasted and churning out tough, sloppy three-chord rock & roll. He made his greatest impact as a member of the New York Dolls, the proto-punk glam rockers of the early '70s. During the late '70s, he was a familiar figure on the New York punk scene, both with the Heartbreakers and as a solo artist. Thunders went solo in 1978, recording *So Alone* with various rock and punk celebrities. After its release, Thunders and Sex Pistols bassist Sid Vicious played in the Living Dead for a short time. During the early '80s, Thunders reformed the Heartbreakers for various tours; the group recorded their final album in 1984. For most of the '80s, the only Johnny Thunders product available was haphazard compilations of live tracks and demos. Thunders kept performing and recording until his death in 1991, turning out a series of records that inadvertently documented his descent into heroin addiction. After years of abuse, Johnny Thunders was found dead in a New Orleans hotel room in April of 1991. While the autopsy didn't disclose the cause of death, most later reports claimed the guitarist died of a methadone overdose. Although it was a sad ending, it was appropriate—no other rock & roller ever lived as hard as Johnny Thunders. *—Stephen Thomas Erlewine*

• **So Alone** / 1978 / Real Music ♦♦♦♦♦
Following the drug-fueled implosion of the Heartbreakers, Johnny Thunders bounced back with his first solo outing, *So Alone*. Featuring a veritable who's who of '70s punk and hard rock—Chrissie Hynde, Phil Lynott, Peter Perrett, Steve Marriott, Paul Cook, and Steve Jones, among others—the record was a testament to what the former New York Dolls guitarist could accomplish with a little focus. Much like Thunders' best work with the Dolls and Heartbreakers, *So Alone* is a gloriously sloppy amalgam of R&B, doo-wop, and three-chord rock & roll. Despite the inevitable excesses that plagued every Thunders recording session, Steve Lillywhite's solid engineering job and a superb set of songs hold everything together. A cover of the Chantays' classic instrumental "Pipeline" leads things off, and is a teasing reminder of what a great guitarist Thunders could be when he put his mind to it. The record's indisputable masterpiece is "You Can't Put Your Arms Around a Memory," a wrenching, surprisingly literate ballad in which Thunders seems to acknowledge that his junkie lifestyle has doomed him to the abyss. Songs like "Leave Me Alone," "Hurtin'," and the chilling title track continue the theme of life inside the heroin balloon. Fortunately, all this back-alley gloom is leavened by some memorably animated moments. "London Boys" is a scathing reply to the Sex Pistols' indictment of the New York punk scene, "New York." The funky "Daddy Rolling Stone" features the inimitable Lynott on background vocals, while the raveups "Great Big Kiss" and "(She's So) Untouchable" are terrific examples of Thunders' raunchy take on classic R&B.

Sadly, Johnny Thunders never followed up on the promise of his solo debut. His subsequent records were a frustrating mix of drug-addled mediocrity and downright laziness. But for one brief moment, he seemed to put it all together. That moment is *So Alone*. *—Andy Claps*

'Til Tuesday

f. 1983, **db.** 1989
College Rock, Pop/Rock, New Wave
Remembered for their lone hit single "Voices Carry," 'Til Tuesday gradually evolved from a New Wave pop band into a vehicle for the songwriting of Aimee Mann. Emerging at the tail end of New Wave, 'Til Tuesday's commercial fortunes were helped dramatically by a stylish video for "Voices Carry," which quickly became an MTV favorite. Mann, involved in Boston's punk scene during the early '80s, formed 'Til Tuesday in 1983. The group signed to Epic one year later and their 1985 debut *Voices Carry* became a hit a few months after its release, as the title track climbed into the Top 10. The band quickly re-entered the studio to record their second album, 1986's *Welcome Home*, though it failed to produce any hits. 'Til Tuesday's third and final album, 1988's *Everything's Different Now*, sold even worse than *Welcome Home* but received strong reviews citing the growth of Mann's songwriting. The group broke up in 1989, though legal problems kept Mann from beginning her solo career until 1993. Her solo debut *Whatever* received strong critical reviews, and she enjoyed a successful cult following throughout the '90s. *—Stephen Thomas Erlewine*

Voices Carry / 1985 / Epic ♦♦♦
'Til Tuesday showed a lot of promise with this debut album, which focused on Aimee Mann's emotive singing, notably on the title track. *—William Ruhlmann*

Welcome Home / 1986 / Epic ♦♦♦♦♦
It took a lot of guts and integrity for 'Til Tuesday to record *Welcome Home*. Hitting big with 1985's *Voices Carry*, Tuesday became known for a sleek, high-tech style of new wave, and it would have been easy enough for the Boston band to come out with a similar album for a follow-up. But instead of playing it safe, Tuesday gambled with inspiration and moved from new wave to a less keyboard-driven, more folk-influenced approach. Listeners who knew Tuesday for "Love in a Vacuum," "No More Crying" and *Voices Carry's* hit title song found things to be a lot more organic on such personal pop-rock offerings as "David Denies" and "Welcome Home." Lead singer Aimee Mann sounds consistently inspired, and the writing is superb. From a commercial standpoint, the album was too radical a departure from its predecessor. But creatively, *Welcome Home* was quite a triumph for 'Til Tuesday. *—Alex Henderson*

Everything's Different Now / 1988 / Epic ♦♦♦♦♦
As commercially successful as 'Til Tuesday's debut album was, the Boston band could have easily slipped into formula and continued making infectious, synth-soaked pop-rock. But instead, Tuesday continued to challenge itself and grow with each album. *Everything's Different Now*, the group's third and final album, lacks the immediacy of *Voices Carry* and is even more intimate than *Welcome Home*, but is every bit as rewarding. An often poignant and moving singer/composer, Aimee Mann leaves no doubt that she's coming from the heart on such introspective and personal gems as "Long Gone (Buddy)," "Why Must I" and "(Believed You Were) Lucky." Comparing something as slick as "No More Crying" to much more organic and understated offerings like "Rip in Heaven" and "J for Jules," it becomes obvious just how much Tuesday evolved in the course of three albums. *—Alex Henderson*

• **Coming up Close: A Retrospective** / Sep. 24, 1996 / Epic/Legacy ♦♦♦♦
Just how radically 'Til Tuesday evolved during its three-album run is illustrated by *Coming Up Close: A Retrospective*. The superb CD kicks into high gear with three sleek, heavily produced new wave gems from the band's debut album of 1985, *Voices Carry*: "Love In a Vacuum," "You Know the Rest" and the hit title song. But as fresh-sounding and popular as that material was, lead singer Aimee Mann was dissatisfied. One hears Tuesday moving from keyboard-driven new wave to a more organic, less produced, folk-influenced sound on "Coming Up Close," "No One Is Watching You Now," "David Denies" and other songs from Tuesday's 1986 sophomore effort *Welcome Home*. And with its finale, *Everything's Different Now*, the Boston residents moved even further in that direction. "J For Jules," "Limits to Love," "Rip In Heaven," "Why Must I" and "Long Gone Buddy" have little in common with the tunes from *Voices Carry*, except for the fact that Mann & Co. always had a great melodic sense. All three of Tuesday's albums are worth having, but for novices, *Coming Up Close* would be the best starting point. *—Alex Henderson*

The Time

f. 1981, Minneapolis, MN
Urban, Funk
From their origins as Prince's first pet project to their self-produced funk-rock oeuvre, the Time has been a fascinating and outrageous congregation. Vocalist Morris Day infused his cocky, swaggering personality into dance hits that would make Rufus Thomas envious, and, unlike most of the competition, the band managed to do something unique with Prince's genre-busting innovations. The Time broke up in the late '80s, with Day going on to a somewhat disastrous solo career, Jesse Johnson crafting two dazzling solo albums, and Jimmy Jam and Terry Lewis becoming one of the most successful production teams this side of Gamble-Huff, working with everyone from Full Force and Janet Jackson to the S.O.S. Band and Human League. The group re-formed in 1990 and released the excellent *Pandemonium*. *—John Floyd*

The Time / 1981 / Warner Brothers ♦♦♦
The Time's 1981 debut album found the group of Minneapolis-based Prince affiliates in a formative stage, blending synthesizers with guitars, humor with sex, and rock with funk. This amalgam of seemingly juxtaposing elements wasn't anything incredibly innovative, particularly when one looks at '70s groups such as the Ohio Players or Funkadelic. But even if the Time are merely co-opting a '70s funk approach, they're instilling an undeniable '80s aesthetic—more studio polish, more prominent use of synthesizer, an emphasis on vanity, and more overt sexual innuendoes. So even if this self-titled debut isn't entirely realized in terms of musical direction, the Time has no doubt stumbled onto something exciting here, particularly given the album's 1981 release date. Furthermore, with "Give It Up," they offer a fully blossomed moment of brilliance among the other five formative songs; this song in particular sums up everything wonderful and worthy of praise about the Time and why they were so influential if not popular: the group's densely layered funk riffs anchored by Terry Lewis' bass lines, the dirty-minded lyrics, the catchy singalong chorus, Morris Day's quirky charisma, Jesse Johnson's manic guitar solos, the dual synthesizers, and the underlying near-mechanical drum sound. Furthermore, the song stretched itself to epic lengths, leaving plenty of time for jamming. Nothing else on this album quite compares, though "Cool" molds itself similarly, stretching itself to epic lengths. The shorter songs here aren't really that effective, particularly the ballads—it's clear even at this point that the group's strengths lie in their instrumentation and not Morris Day's songwriting. Though this isn't a perfect album, none of the Time's small handful of albums were. "Give It Up" by itself makes this self-titled debut worth seeking out; consider the other five songs a bonus. *—Jason Birchmeier*

• **What Time Is It?** / 1982 / Warner Brothers ♦♦♦♦♦
Despite only releasing three albums in the early '80s, the group thought of primarily as Prince's opening act by many at the time proved to be an influential group in retrospect. And if there is one album that illustrates why the Time deserve such praise, it's *What Time Is It?* First of all, the group only released a trilogy of early-'80s albums, with the other two—*The Time* (1981) and *Ice Cream Castle* (1984)—each somewhat flawed. Thankfully, *What Time Is It?* proves itself to be a perfect medium. The group's patented aesthetic that first became clear on "Give It Up" from their formative debut album blossoms here, and the ridge between Morris Day's wannabe-Prince megalomania and the musicians' enormous talents hasn't quite become an issue yet. Secondly, the group doesn't try anything too ambitious here; in fact, they almost seem to rewrite their debut album, fixing its flaws and expanding upon its strengths. Again, they offer six songs, this time going with more epic jam-orientated songs. Furthermore, Morris Day even manages to offer a respectable ballad with "Gigolos Get Lonely Too." But, for the most part, the Time are at their best when they're jamming—which they do plenty of here—and not when Day is singing or indulging in one of his many ideologically questionable skits. But what makes this album the Time's best isn't so much its highlights but rather its lack of poor moments. Both *The Time* and *Ice Cream Castle* have moments of brilliance that rival even this album's best; however, those two albums are burdened by lackluster moments—this album has none. From beginning to end, *What Time Is It?* is nothing but fun music, driven largely by brilliant funk riffing and also by some catchy hooks. *—Jason Birchmeier*

Ice Cream Castle / 1984 / Warner Brothers ♦♦♦
The final album released before the Time splintered into pieces for the remainder of the '80s, *Ice Cream Castle* provides ample evidence in regard to both the group's undeniable talents and also the personal issues that ultimately led to their demise. On the one hand, *Ice Cream Castle* finds the Time perfecting their patented style of synth-heavy funk-rock; while their previous two albums saw their music blossom, here it sounds fully realized. Never once does the band sound tentative, churning out densely layered riffs with near-reckless abandon when given the chance. In particular, Jesse Johnson steals the spotlight at times with his '80s-style guitar solos, complementing the rhythm section's synth funk with his rock aesthetic. Yet on the other hand, as tempting as it is to praise the Time for hitting their stride with *Ice Cream Castle*, Morris Day's egocentric indulgences ruin what very well could be the group's best album; you can feel the ridge dividing his megalomania from the remaining group's rapport. When Day keeps his antics to a minimum and lets the group jam—such as on "Ice Cream Castles," "My Drawers," and "Jungle Love"—it becomes quite clear why this group is so revered: at this point in their short-lived career, they can play circles around any other '80s funk band. But then there are the obvious Day vehicles—"Chili Sauce," "If the Kid Can't Make You Come," and "The Bird"—three songs that find the singer/songwriter's charismatic mania frustratingly eclipsing the band's efforts with his tasteless belligerence. In retrospect, this flawed album does have some brilliant moments worth seeking out; it's just unfortunate that a few self-centered moments on Day's part, and to a lesser degree overproduction, sour what could very well have been the Time's crowing achievement. *—Jason Birchmeier*

Pandemonium / Jun. 1990 / Paisley Park ♦♦♦

Tin Machine

Album Rock, Hard Rock
Even in a career defined by its detours and departures, it nevertheless raised eyebrows when David Bowie formed Tin Machine in 1989, briefly forgoing his long and successful solo career to work within the confines of a band. Featuring guitarist Reeves Gabrels and the sibling rhythm section of Tony and Hunt Sales—the sons of legendary television comic Soupy Sales—the group was ostensibly assembled to allow Bowie the opportunity to return to his roots, touring small clubs and collaborating in what he asserted was a truly democratic creative partnership. Indeed, Tin Machine's metallic, feedback-intensive sound set it distinctly apart from recent Bowie solo efforts, and their eponymous 1989 debut LP earned favorable reviews, scoring an MTV hit with the first single, "Under the God." *Tin Machine II* followed in 1991, but lacking the novelty and the attendant media coverage of its predecessor, the record failed to generate much excitement; the live *Oy Vey, Baby* appeared later that same year, but when Bowie resumed his solo career with 1993's *Black Tie White Noise*, the band quietly ceased to exist. *—Jason Ankeny*

• **Tin Machine** / 1989 / Virgin ♦♦♦♦♦

Tin Machine II / 1991 / Victory ♦♦♦
On their second album, Tin Machine streamlined their approach somewhat, trading the occasional noisy guitar flourish for a cleaner, more conventional lead line. However, that doesn't mean the group has abandoned the plodding dissonance that distinguished their debut—they've just made it more accessible. And that doesn't mean they've written better songs. Nothing on *Tin Machine II* compares with the highlights of the debut—it sounds like a collection of outtakes. It's not surprising that David Bowie chose to resume his solo career after the release of this collection. *—Stephen Thomas Erlewine*

Oy Vey, Baby / 1991 / Victory ♦♦
Tin Machine's live album *Oy Vey, Baby* features a looser performance than normal by the band, but it's still not enough to rescue the batch of underdeveloped songs that form the backbone of the record. *—Stephen Thomas Erlewine*

Tindersticks

f. 1992, Nottingham, England
Chamber Pop, Indie Rock, Alternative Pop/Rock
Tindersticks were one of the most original and distinctive British acts of the '90s, standing apart from both the British indie scene and the rash of Brit-pop guitar combos that dominated the UK charts. Where their contemporaries were often direct and to-the-point, Tindersticks were obtuse and leisurely, crafting dense, difficult songs layered with literary lyrics, intertwining melodies, mumbling vocals and gently melancholy orchestrations. Essentially, the group filtered the dark romanticism of Leonard Cohen, Ian Curtis and Scott Walker as filtered through the bizarre pop songcraft of Lee Hazlewood and the aesthetics of indie-rock. Though their music was far from casual listening, Tindersticks gained a dedicated cult following in the mid-'90s, beginning with their eponymous 1993 debut album. By the end of the year, the group and the album had won over most of the UK critics, and *Tindersticks* was named Album of the Year by *Melody Maker*. Tindersticks spent a quiet year in 1994, releasing a live album entitled *Amsterdam 1994*. In the spring of 1995, the group released their untitled second album, which received rave reviews and appeared on nearly every British Top Ten list of the Best of 1995. Late that year, the group released another live album, *Bloomsbury Theatre, 12.3.95*. Tindersticks were quiet for most of 1996, releasing the soundtrack to the Claire Denis film, *Nénette et Boni*. Finally, they re-emerged with 1997's *Curtains*. *—Stephen Thomas Erlewine*

Tindersticks / Oct. 1993 / Bar/None ♦♦♦♦♦
A thrilling, revelatory debut, *Tindersticks* is a chamber-pop masterpiece of romantic elegance and gutter debauchery. Within the framework of a remarkably consistent and mesmerizingly dank atmosphere, the group covers a stunning amount of ground—"Her" is a crashing flamenco number, "The Walt Blues" is a tipsy organ instrumental, and "Paco de Renaldo's Dream" is an impenetrable cinematic monologue punctuated by subdued guitars, pianos and strings. Stuart Staples' bacchanalian songs are obsessed with fluids, both bodily ("Blood," "Jism") and otherwise ("Nectar," "Whiskey and Water," "Raindrops"); no topic is too personal or too disturbing—"Piano Song" is frightening in its callousness, while "City Sickness" is an unflinching examination of emotional and physical desperation. Fascinatingly constructed and strikingly ambitious, *Tindersticks* is insidiously labyrinthine; the music speaks softly but carries tremendous weight, and its hold grows more and more unbreakable with each listen. *—Jason Ankeny*

● **Tindersticks [II]** / Mar. 1995 / This Way Up/London ✦✦✦✦✦

Tindersticks' second consecutive eponymously titled double-LP set refines the approach of their debut; while every bit as ambitious and adventuresome, it achieves an even greater musical balance, stretching into luxuriously long compositional structures and more intricate arrangements. While Stuart Staples' songs remain as obsessive and haunted as before, he wards off his demons with fits of pitch-black humor (the narrative "My Sister") and a more tender perspective; similarly, while his funereal vocals remain the focus, there's a new reliance on extended instrumental passages, and even a pair of duets (the centerpiece, "Travelling Light"—a gorgeous collaboration with the Walkabouts' Carla Torgeson—is akin to a Lee Hazlewood & Nancy Sinatra record trapped in emotional purgatory). Another awesome triumph of mood and atmosphere. —*Jason Ankeny*

Bloomsbury Theatre / Oct. 1995 / This Way Up ✦✦✦

Early in 1995, Tindersticks launched the release of their second album with a lavish concert at the Bloomsbury Theatre, performed with a full orchestra. In November, they released a limited-edition disc of the show. The grand, sweeping arrangements perfectly complement the lush, aching melancholy of their songs and, at times, even improve on the original album versions. —*Stephen Thomas Erlewine*

Nenette Et Boni / 1996 / This Way Up ✦✦✦

The plot of the 1996 film, *Nenette et Boni*, from French screenwriter and director Claire Denis, involves the rather downhearted premise of a 14-year-old girl who is in serious need of an attitude adjustment; she's also pregnant and runs away from her boarding school only to end up at the door of her preoccupied brother, who is fixated on the baker's seductive wife. As if that convoluted scenario was not melancholy enough, the soundtrack to the film, the subject matter of which is quite befitting a sort of downcast pop sound, was appropriately turned over to eternal-depressives Tindersticks. It was a perfect marriage. Of course, the soundtrack is not exactly a normal Tindersticks album; in some senses it is a radical departure. The obvious difference is that the album mostly lacks the bizarrely beautiful Leonard Cohen-on-valium croon of Stuart Staples (present only on the gorgeous "Petites Gouttes d'Eau"), and so some of their usual somber romanticism is inevitably lost. Also, not all of the individual pieces on the album are full-fledged songs, which is understandable given the album's primary responsibility as incidental music. It's a truly gorgeous piece of work, with the same lulling, shimmering, melancholy sheen that characterizes every Tindersticks album; together, the songs seem like a delusory, synesthetic oasis of sound. The music is absolutely sweeping at times, with string arrangements occasionally insinuating their way into a song almost as if from somewhere outside the piece. At other times, the music takes on a dark, insular complexion and vibe. Tindersticks can be simply creepy at times, as on "La Mort de Felix," but for the most part, their work here maintains enveloping, organic warmth, even when the sentiments are downhearted or chilling. —*Stanton Swihart*

Curtains / Jun. 24, 1997 / London ✦✦✦✦✦

Curtains finds Tindersticks exploring the same dark, string-drenched territory as their first two albums, and while it shares a surface similarity with its predecessors, there are subtle differences that make it a rewarding listen. The tone of *Curtains* is slightly brighter than that of the second album, with the songs unfolding into lush, affecting laments that recall Scott Walker at his finest. Though the sound is seductive, what is most impressive about *Curtains* is the songwriting. Tindersticks have become more assured writers, letting the songs gradually develop into intimate epics. Stuart Staples' lyrics are similarly textured and subtle, with alternating layers of pathos and humor. *Curtains*, in many ways, functions as the culmination of what Tindersticks set out to accomplish with their first two albums, and the results are appropriately stunning. —*Stephen Thomas Erlewine*

Donkeys 92-97 / Aug. 25, 1998 / London ✦✦✦✦

As indicated on the cover, *Donkeys* is a collection of singles, rarities, and unreleased recordings. For the hardcore Tindersticks fan on a budget, it might come as a bit of a disappointment, as the nearly endless well of Tindersticks B-sides from limited releases are barely touched upon here. The absolute gem on *Donkeys* is their (typically brooding) version of Otis Redding's "I've Been Loving You too Long," which was released as a B-side to "Travelling Light." Other highlights include the French version of "No More Affairs" ("Plus de Liaisons"), an orchestral version of Stuart Staples' duet with Isabella Rossellini on "A Marriage Made in Heaven," their single for Sub Pop (a cover of Pavement's "Here"), and their very Velvet Underground-inspired debut single. It's a solid chunk of music, and as an introduction to the band, it serves well. But since Tindersticks are a remarkably consistent band, the beginner can pick their starting point by blindfold and come out a winner every time. —*Andy Kellman*

Simple Pleasure / 1999 / Quicksilver/Island ✦✦✦✦✦

With a title like *Simple Pleasure* and songs like the disarmingly uptempo opener "Can We Start Again?," at first listen Tindersticks' fourth proper album seems buoyed by a guarded optimism totally absent from previous outings; dig deeper, however, and it's all a come-on—frontman Stuart Staples still inhabits a netherworld where nothing is ever simple, pleasure is an illusion, and starting again merely means making the same mistakes yet one more time. Nothing truly changes, which has been Tindersticks' point all along, of course—hopes are still meant to be dashed and hearts still meant to be broken, and *Simple Pleasure* is neither the time nor the place to begin pretending otherwise. Staples' songs remain the very essence of romantic despair, stunning in their funereal beauty and devastating in their tormented desperation; likewise, much of the record prowls familiar musical ground, although "Before You Close Your Eyes," "I Know That Loving," and the closing "CF GF" all draw heavily on long-simmering soul and gospel influences, while the disc's highlight, the achingly gorgeous "If You're Looking for a Way Out," transforms Odyssey's 1980 disco hit into a ballad of surprising tenderness. That same tenderness colors much of *Simple Pleasure*, in fact, making it not only Tindersticks'

most giving record, but also their most poignant, revealing a vulnerability even the bravest face can't mask. —*Jason Ankeny*

Can Our Love . . . / May 21, 2001 / Beggars Banquet ✦✦✦✦

A new label and a renewed sense of collaboration between the members of one of England's finest has resulted in *Can Our Love*, the loosest record yet in Tindersticks' decade-long existence. Here, they've lost all remaining self-consciousness. The listener is all the better for it. This lack of self-consciousness is the good kind—the kind derived from locking into place and letting things come naturally, chucking any degree of preconception out of the window. Between the spare instrumentation, crepuscular tempos, and somber coursing of Stuart Staples' voice throughout "Can Our Love" and "No Man in the World," one wouldn't have to be too inebriated to mistake parts of the album for Sam Cooke's *Night Beat* played at the wrong speed. On "People Keep Comin' Around" (their best moment yet?), it sounds as if they heard the Doors' "Riders on the Storm" and decided to speed up the tempo a notch and strip away the false dramatics, fashioning it into a seven-minute pearl custom fit for '70s soul radio. Staples effectively swaps verses in varying registers, one of them being a tinge higher than anything you've previously heard from him. (He'd still need several punches below the belt to attain a falsetto.) "Chilitetime" may not be a medley containing parts of "Have You Seen Her?" or "Are You My Woman?," but it's another extended slow dazzle warbler that doesn't outstay its welcome. And if "Dying Slowly" and "Don't Ever Get Tired" ring of garden variety quality, you're taking them for granted. There's no use in going into further detail—all the proper ingredients are in full effect. It's 3:00 AM somewhere, and no band is more aware of this than Tindersticks. They're a rare and reliable refuge in this mean old world. Here's to another ten years. —*Andy Kellman*

TLC

f. 1991

Club/Dance, Urban, Dance-Pop, Hip-Hop

Comprised of Tionne "T-Boz" Watkins, Rozonda "Chilli" Thomas, and Lisa "Left Eye" Lopes, the Atlanta, Georgia-based hip-hop trio TLC released their first album, *Oooooooh . . . On the TLC Tip*, in early 1992 to immediate success. Masterminded by the successful R&B producer/singer Pebbles, the group had three consecutive Top Ten hits in 1992, including "Ain't 2 Proud 2 Beg," "What About Your Friends," and "Baby-Baby-Baby." Shortly before the release of their second album, Lopes was arrested for burning down the house of her boyfriend, Andre Rison, then a member of the NFL's Atlanta Falcons. Lopes' arrest didn't affect the sales of their second album, 1994's *Crazysexycool*, which featured three number one singles and sold over four million copies. *FanMail* followed in 1999, launching a series of hits including "No Scrubs" and "Unpretty." —*Stephen Thomas Erlewine*

Ooooooohhh . . . On the TLC Tip / Feb. 25, 1992 / La Face ✦✦✦

TLC's debut album was a well-produced but inconsistent effort, with the three hit singles—"Ain't 2 Proud 2 Beg," "Baby-Baby-Baby," and "What About Your Friends"—being the catchiest and most memorable songs on the album. —*Sara Sytsma*

● **Crazysexycool** / 1994 / La Face ✦✦✦✦✦

On their second album, TLC downplays their overt rap connections, recording a smooth, seductive collection of contemporary soul reminiscent of both Philly soul and Prince, powered by new jack and hip-hop beats. Lisa Lopes contributes the occasional rap, but the majority of *CrazySexyCool* belongs to Tionne Watkins and Rozonda Thomas. While they aren't the most accomplished vocalists—they have a tendency to be just slightly off-key—the material they sing is consistently strong. As the cover of Prince's "If I Was Your Girlfriend" indicates, TLC favors erotic, midtempo funk. Yet the group removes any of the psychosexual complexities of Prince's songs, leaving a batch of sexy material that just sounds good, especially the hit singles. Both "Creep" and "Red Light Special" have a deep groove that accentuates the slinky hooks, but it's "Waterfalls," with its gently insistent horns and guitar lines and instantly memorable chorus, that ranks as one of the classic R&B songs of the '90s. —*Stephen Thomas Erlewine*

FanMail / Feb. 23, 1999 / La Face ✦✦✦✦

Crazysexycool was one of those records that defined an era. Few records before it combined hip-hop and classic soul songwriting quite as intoxicatingly or gracefully—the performances and productions were utterly seamless. It would have been difficult to top anyway, but TLC had it doubly bad, since a number of behind-the-scenes problems delayed a sequel for nearly five years. As with any eagerly anticipated record, that follow-up, *FanMail*, arrived with too many expectations. And initially, it may be disappointing to realize TLC doesn't forge new ground with *FanMail*, but after a few spins, it settles in that nobody else makes urban soul quite as engaging as this. Not that it was easy to make this record, as the head-spinning list of collaborators indicates. Almost ten producers worked on the record, all trying to replicate the easy, appealing sound of *Crazysexycool*. And "replicate" is the right word, since there are no new innovations on *FanMail*, apart from a few lifts from the Timbaland book of tricks. Nevertheless, that may be for the best, since TLC and their army of producers have spent time crafting the songs and productions, turning *FanMail* into a record that almost reaches the peaks of its predecessor. By the end of the record, it appears that they can do it all—funky, hip-hop-fueled dance-pop, seductive ballads, and mid-tempo jams—and they can do it all well. Other groups try to reach these heights, but they don't have the skills or the material to pull it off quite so well. True, the five-year wait felt interminable, and they're now standard-bearers instead of pioneers, but if takes TLC as long to make a sequel to *FanMail*, so be it—they have one of the best track records in '90s urban soul. —*Stephen Thomas Erlewine*

Toad the Wet Sprocket

f. 1986, Santa Barbara, CA, **db.** Jul. 27, 1998

College Rock, Adult Alternative Pop/Rock, Pop/Rock

So named in honor of a sketch by the Monty Python comedy troupe, Toad the Wet Sprocket's mellow, melodic folk-pop sound made them one of the most successful alternative rock bands of the early 1990s. Singer Glen Phillips, guitarist Todd Nichols, bassist Dean Dinning (the nephew of '50s hitmaker Mark "Teen Angel" Dinning) and drummer Randy Guss formed the group in 1986 in their native Santa Monica, CA, recording their 1988 debut LP *Bread and Circus* (reissued the following year on major label Columbia) in just eight days at a cost of $650. After years of persistent touring, Toad the Wet Sprocket's commercial breakthrough followed with 1991's *Fear*, as the single "All I Want"—quite nearly left off the album—became a Top 20 hit. Another single from the LP, "Walk on the Ocean," was also a success. Three years later, Toad returned with *Dulcinea*, which generated another Top 40 hit with the single "Fall Down." *Coil*, Toad the Wet Sprocket's fifth proper LP, followed in 1997. The group split in July 1998. *—Jason Ankeny*

Bread and Circus / Jul. 1989 / Columbia ✦✦✦

This is the first taste of Toad the Wet Sprocket's brand of California-flavored thinking man's pop. *Bread and Circus* is a collection of songs Toad had worked up over two years of playing the Santa Monica club circuit, and the album doesn't have the cohesive flow the band would find with later releases like *Pale* and *Fear*, but the songs are good from the get-go. "When We Recovered" and "One Little Girl" show two emotional sides to the band's songwriting, and the superb "Know Me" portends Toad's future efforts in one track—plaintive acoustic strumming, acerbic minor-key angst, and a soaring, defiant chorus. *—Troy Carpenter*

Pale / Jan. 1990 / Columbia ✦✦✦✦

Pale improved on the formula Toad The Wet Sprocket sketched out on their debut, *Bread and Circus*, since the band contributed a set of stronger songs with catchier melodies. *—Sara Sytsma*

Fear / Aug. 27, 1991 / Columbia ✦✦✦✦

Not only did *Fear* yield the Top 40 breakthrough hit "All I Want," but it also marked the emergence of a more refined Toad the Wet Sprocket. A far cry from their jangle pop, garage band sound of old, this album is full of smart and catchy pop/rock songs brought to life by four great musicians. Be it a tale of boyhood mischief ("Is It for Me") or a question of faith ("Pray Your Gods"), Glen Phillips shows himself to be one of the most literate and complex singer/songwriters around, layers of hidden subtext pouring from both his pen and voice. In fact, one of the finest lines ever found in a fare-thee-well song appears in "In My Ear": "Never meant half of the things that I said to you. So you know, there's a half that might be true." Enough said. The rest of the quartet—drummer Randy Guss, bassist/keyboardist Dean Dinning, and guitarist Todd Nichols—have merged together musically, defining what it really means to be a band. Their juxtaposition of accordions and mandolins against hard-hitting electric guitars amplifies the blend of ease and urgency that plays out from song to song, from the acoustic meandering of "Walk on the Ocean" to the aggressive commentary on rape in "Hold Her Down." The last tune, "I Will Not Take These Things for Granted," could have easily fallen into the abyss of cliché, but in Phillips' hands, it stands as a humble and poignant tribute to life's riches. With not a single weak song, wonderfully engaging performances, and amazing sonic precision, *Fear* is a wonderful welcome into the house of Toad. *—Kelly McCartney*

Dulcinea / May 24, 1994 / Columbia ✦✦✦✦

From the platform of success built by *Fear*, Toad the Wet Sprocket dove head first into their fourth release, *Dulcinea*. Without changing the formula too much, they conjured up 12 more hooks, stretching them ever so slightly to make the alternative tunes a bit edgier and the mellow ones a little folkier, and scoring a couple of modest hits along the way with "Something's Always Wrong" and "Fall Down." One of the thematic threads of Toad's music has always been a certain spirituality, a sense of awe and wonder in regard to life and death. *Dulcinea* exploits and explores that theme with reverence and humility, going so far as to close the album with "Reincarnation Song," a delicate examination of a soul's transition shrouded musically by a veil of electric guitar feedback. Counteracting that heaviness with an offbeat, country-tinged ditty about the pros of Nanci Griffith versus Loretta Lynn is pure Toad, never being pinned into a stylistic corner. One of the best songs on this album, and perhaps their entire catalog, is "Windmills," a moody look at the fragility and futility of existence that will cause not only the exquisite melody to linger with you, but contemplations of your own purpose in life. Framed by the flawless production of Gavin MacKillop, every song on this record creates a world of its own that is impossible not to be drawn into. *—Kelly McCartney*

In Light Syrup / Oct. 24, 1995 / Columbia ✦✦✦

Toad The Wet Sprocket's rarities and B-sides collection *In Light Syrup* works surprisingly well. Instead of sounding like a motley assortment of leftovers, the record forms a cohesive whole and highlights the group's considerable melodic talents. There aren't many departures from their gentle, R.E.M.-derived folk-rock, but that is the band's strongest point. No fan of Toad will be disappointed by *In Light Syrup*. *—Stephen Thomas Erlewine*

Coil / May 20, 1997 / Columbia ✦✦✦

Toad the Wet Sprocket illustrate that their ability to craft gentle, alternative folk-rock in the vein of R.E.M. continus to grow on *Coil*, a marginally darker record than the previous *Dulcinea*. Although the album is a little more somber, it is far from haunting, since Toad's talent is for pleasant, lightly melodic, acoustic pop, and *Coil* is no different from the rest of their catalog in that respect. In fact, it offers little new, but Toad is more reliable than predictable, since the record is quite well crafted. While it won't win the group any new fans, it's a solid effort that will certainly please fans. *—Stephen Thomas Erlewine*

● **P.S.: A Toad Retrospective** / Oct. 26, 1999 / Columbia ✦✦✦✦

Toad the Wet Sprocket was among the best and most popular of the adult alternative pop/rockers of the early '90s. They harnessed R.E.M.'s jangle pop, smoothed it out, and turned it into something pretty, melodic, and accessible to a wide audience. Toad the Wet Sprocket never was as idiosyncratic or edgy as R.E.M., so they could reach a totally different audience, comprised equally of politically correct collegiates and housewives. Their third album, *Fear*, arrived in the late summer of 1991 (after R.E.M.'s "Losing My Religion"), and they benefited from radio's new willingness to play alternative bands, as "All I Want" and "Walk on the Ocean" became staples on modern rock and adult contemporary stations alike. Their long-delayed follow-up *Dulcinea* appeared in 1994, and while it spawned the hit "Fall Down," it failed to capture the same audience as *Fear*. Their fifth album, 1997's *Coil*, did even worse, and the group disbanded the following year. Such a brief span of hitmaking years makes Toad the Wet Sprocket a perfect choice for a hits collection, which *P.S.: A Toad Retrospective* almost is. It has all the hits, plus many of the fan favorites, but not necessarily in the versions people know. There's a new version of the title track, remixes of "All I Want" and "Hold Her Down," the "non-album" version of "Jam," an edit of "Somethings Always Wrong"—not necessarily differences that are that noticeable, but are still a little disconcerting, and ultimately enough to make *P.S.* less than perfect. The alternate versions feel like misguided attempts to hook in die-hard fans (who may already own most of these takes), and while they're not alienating, they're not right, either. Nevertheless, it's still a good, basic collection—enough to satisfy most casual fans, since it has the hits on one disc. *—Stephen Thomas Erlewine*

The Tokens

f. 1960, Brooklyn, NY, **db.** 1971

Brill Building Pop, Doo Wop

This Brooklyn doo wop group was originally known as the Linc-Tones when they formed in 1955 at Lincoln High School. Hank Medress, Neil Sedaka, Eddie Rabkin, and Cynthia Zolitin didn't have much impact in their early days recording for Melba. They later disbanded, but Medress re-formed the group in 1960 as the Tokens. Brothers Phil and Mitch Margo and Jay Siegel were now the members. They recorded for Warwick in 1960, then had their one glorious hit in 1962, "The Lion Sleeps Tonight." It was based on the South African Zulu song "Wimoweh," and reached number seven on the R&B chart while topping the pop surveys. The Tokens formed their own label in 1964, B.T. Puppy, but weren't able to keep the hits coming very long, although "The Lion Sleeps Tonight" remains a standard. *—Ron Wynn*

● **Wimoweh: The Best of the Tokens** / 1994 / RCA ✦✦✦✦✦

The Lion Sleeps Tonight / 1994 / RCA ✦✦✦

Pretty short weight on this ten-track compilation of early-'60s material. After the title track, you get a few "Wimoweh" soundalikes, a couple of odd hot-rod numbers that try to imitate the Beach Boys, and a version of "Sincerely" arranged to sound as much as possible like their first hit, "Tonight I Fell in Love." That hit, by the way, isn't here, as it wasn't recorded for RCA. *—Richie Unterberger*

The All Time Greatest Hits / Jun. 30, 1998 / Taragon ✦✦✦✦✦

There are other hits collections out on the Tokens, but this release, a compact 35 minutes long but covering the proper bases, has virtues lacking in some of the competition. For one thing, it covers three decades of material, from the 1959 Warwick Records hit "Tonight I Fell in Love" through their 1970 cover of "Don't Worry Baby." In between are the shoulda-been-a-big-hit "When I Go to Sleep at Night," the requisite "The Lion Sleeps Tonight," the failed follow-ups "B'Wa Nina" and "La Bamba," their minimally successful attempt at a folk crossover, "Hear the Bells (Ringing Bells)," attempts at car songs ("Let's Go to the Drag Strip"), the middling mid-'60s single hits "I Hear Trumpets Blow" and "Portrait of My Love," and their re-recording of the Clairol jingle "She Lets Her Hair Down." The sound quality on most of this release rivals the best work done on the Beach Boys' classic Capitol CDs—not only clear and close (in glittering stereo on all but the first track), but loud; the only exceptions are the two late-'60s Warner Bros. tracks, which are merely clean and sharp, not awesome. The disc covers a wide range of styles as the group sought to adapt to changing public tastes. They weren't suited to car songs, singing well enough on "Let's Go to the Drag Strip" but sounding a bit too elegant, but they did capture the festive mood of the mid-'60s (in a manner similar to their West Coast rivals the Association) on numbers like "I Hear Trumpets Blow." The notes by Colin Escott explain a great deal about the group's history, although they have some minor holes. It's as much of the Tokens as anyone will ever want, but hardcore fans will need this disc, which restores some deserving recordings to the catalog. *—Bruce Eder*

Tom Tom Club

f. 1980

Alternative Pop/Rock, Dance-Pop

Tom Tom Club began life as a side project for Talking Heads members Chris Frantz and Tina Weymouth, who adopted a light, tropical dance style that won them a gold album in *Tom Tom Club* in 1981 and a Top 40 single in "Genius of Love." They continued to make albums under this moniker between Heads production projects: *Close to the Bone* (1983) and *Boom Boom Chi Boom Boom* (1989). They even toured as Tom Tom Club in the summer of 1989. When The Heads broke up in late 1991, Tom Tom Club became Frantz and Weymouth's main outlet. They released *Dark Sneak Love Action* in 1992 and eight years later they issued *The Good, The Bad, and the Funky*. *—William Ruhlmann*

● **Tom Tom Club** / Oct. 1981 / Sire ✦✦✦✦

"Who needs to think when your feet just go?" So sings Tina Weymouth on Tom Tom Club's debut album. And rightly so—this was the sunny break in the islands that the rhythm section of Talking Heads wanted and they got it, away from the art school intellectualism that had resulted in the classic, but understandably very un-sunny *Remain in Light*. This album, a collection of funky, spritely little tunes recorded in Barbados with Weymouth's sisters, hubbie and drummer Chris Frantz, and several of the members of the *Remain in Light* tour group: Adrian Belew, guitar, and Steven Stanley, percussion. Ironically, hoping to toss off a fun album under the radar, the group came out with an album, the best tracks of which, "Genius of Love" and "Wordy Rappinghood," became enormously influential throughout the '80s and '90s, eventually getting ripped off wholeheartedly for Mariah Carey's "Daydream." The album also marks a point in music history when the New York alternative scene and the burgeoning hip-hop scene were influencing each other, when both parties were on to something new. It's a snapshot of a time, and still holds together fairly well. *—Ted Mills*

Close to the Bone / 1983 / Sire ✦✦✦
Sure, it was tough to come up with a follow-up to their hit debut album, but *Close to the Bone* is quite a fine album in retrospect. There is a sense of repeating themselves, but then again, it's a formula that they created: a trio of female singers over bouncy reggae and hip-hop-inspired beats, with a dash of Talking Heads' art school sensibilities. "Pleasure of Love" rides the coattails of "Genius of Love," perked up with Wally Badarou's swirling keyboards. Lyrics are dionysian and silly paeans to love, equivalent to James Rizzi's artwork on the cover, with occasional dips into social commentary ("On the Line Again" spins a tale of the downside of club culture). Tina Weymouth and sisters Lani and Laura make good with the harmonies, smooth and icy. Fans of "Genius of Love" won't be disappointed. *—Ted Mills*

The Good, The Bad and the Funky / Sep. 12, 2000 / Rykodisc ✦✦✦✦
This aptly titled release from '80s art rockers and Talking Heads side project, Tom Tom Club is indeed good, bad, and funky. Tina Weymouth and Chris Frantz have explored a stunning amount of musical styles within the confines of this album, with every song sounding like it was produced by a different group. The use of a variety of vocalists, including Weymouth, who at times sounds like a 16-year-old Japanese girl instead of her more mature self, as well as Mystic Bowie and Charles Pettigrew only seems to heighten the variety of sounds offered. The lyrics are simple, yet clever, and laid over a variety of sampled tracks, scratching, and other turntablism and live instrumentation. The resulting sound ranges from dub to dance-pop to spacy funk. The variety does allow for some unevenness, however, though duds like the repetitive and spare "Time to Bounce," are more than balanced by gems like "Happiness Can't Buy Money" and the instrumental cleverness of "Lesbians by the Lake," among others. *—Stacia Proefrock*

Tommy Tutone

f. 1978, **db.** 1984
Pop/Rock, Power Pop, New Wave
Tommy Tutone were an early-'80s power-pop band led by vocalist Tommy Heath and guitarist Jim Keller. The group's first single, 1980's "Angel Say No," scraped the bottom of the American Top 40, yet it was 1981's "867-5309/Jenny" that sent the group to the top of the charts. Peaking in early 1982, the single hit number four and went gold. Tommy Tutone was never able to duplicate that success and the band broke up after the release of their third album, 1983's *National Emotion*.

In 1994, Heath returned using the name Tommy Tutone for a new release, *Nervous Love*, a collection of various post-Tommy Tutone recordings. *—Stephen Thomas Erlewine*

● **Tommy Tutone/Tommy Tutone 2** / Jul. 1, 1997 / Collectables ✦✦✦✦✦
Collectables reissued Tommy Tutone's first two albums, *Tommy Tutone* and *Tommy Tutone 2*, on this 1997 CD. It essentially acts as a greatest-hits collection, since it contains all of their big hits, but it also contains the majority of their best album tracks, thereby making it a definitive career overview. *—Stephen Thomas Erlewine*

Tomorrow

f. 1965, **db.** 1968
Freakbeat, British Psychedelia, Psychedelic Pop, Psychedelic
In the early days of British psychedelia, three bands were consistently cited as first-generation figureheads of the London-based underground sound: Pink Floyd, the Soft Machine, and Tomorrow. Pink Floyd became superstars and the Soft Machine influential cult legends, but Tomorrow is mostly remembered (if at all) for featuring Steve Howe as their lead guitarist in his pre-Yes days. Actually, Tomorrow was nearly the equal of the two more celebrated outfits. Along with the early Floyd and Soft Machine, they shared a propensity for flower-power whimsy. Though they were less recklessly innovative and imaginative, their songwriting was accomplished, with adroit harmonies, psychedelic guitar work, and adventurous structures and tempo changes. They never succumbed to mindless indulgence or jamming; indeed, their tracks were rather short and tightly woven in comparison with most psychedelic bands. A couple singles (especially "My White Bicycle") were underground favorites, but the group only managed to record one album before breaking up in 1968. Lead singer Keith West, even before the breakup, had a number two British hit with "Excerpt From a Teenage Opera," which helped inspire Pete Townshend's *Tommy*. Drummer Twink joined the Pretty Things and, later, the Pink Fairies. *—Richie Unterberger*

● **Tomorrow** / 1968 / See for Miles ✦✦✦✦✦
Tomorrow's sole album was a solid effort, with quite a few first-rate tracks. "My White Bicycle" was one of the first songs to prominently feature backwards guitar phasing, "Real Life Permanent Dream" has engaging English harmonies and sitar riffs, "Revolution" is an infectious hippie anthem, and "Now Your Time Has Come" features intricate riffing from Steve Howe. "Hallucinations," with its irresistible melody, gentle harmonies, and affectingly trippy lyrics, was perhaps their best track. The more self-conscious English whimsy—populated by jolly little dwarfs, Auntie Mary's dress shop, colonels, and the like—is less successful, although the band's craftsmanship is strong enough to avoid embarassment. The 1986 reissue of this album features detailed liner notes and the worthy B-side "Claremont Lake," though unfortunately West's sappy but influential "Excerpt From A Teenage Opera" was deleted. *—Richie Unterberger*

50 Minute Technicolour Dream / 1998 / RPM ✦✦✦
Tomorrow were one of the 1960s' best and most intriguing one-album artists, so this 16-track compilation of additional material comes as quite a welcome bonus to fans, even 30 years after their split. None of these demos, alternates, or live performances were issued in the '60s, although the two respectable mod-psych demos they did for *Blow Up* surfaced elsewhere in the '90s, and the BBC versions of "Revolution" and "Three Jolly Little Dwarfs" have long circulated among collectors. Studio rarities include a fine, slightly sinister unreleased cut "Caught in a Web," a cover of the Byrds' "Why," and considerably different versions of "Revolution" and "Real Life Permanent Dream." Eight songs from their late-1967 concert at the "Christmas on Earth Continued" psychedelic event in London are frustrating: the band plays well and the instruments are decently recorded, but Keith West's vocals suffer heavily from tinny distortion due to poor miking. Nonetheless, these are still interesting to hear, including versions of a bunch of songs from their album (among them "My White Bicycle"), "Why," and the otherwise unavailable "Shotgun & the Duck." The package is enhanced by detailed liner notes with comments from West and Steve Howe. *—Richie Unterberger*

Tone-Loc

Vocals / Pop-Rap, West Coast Rap
Tone-Loc (born Tony Smith) soared from obscurity into pop stardom in 1989 when his hoarse voice and unmistakable delivery made the song "Wild Thing" (using a sample from Van Halen's "Jamie's Cryin'") a massive hit. The song was co-written by Marvin Young, better known as Young MC, as was the second single smash "Funky Cold Medina." The album *Loc-ed After Dark* became the second rap release to top the pop charts. Tone-Loc expanded his horizons into acting in 1992 and 1993, appearing a few times on the Fox sitcom *Roc*. He was also in the films *Posse* and *Ace Ventura: Pet Detective*, and in 1991 returned to recording with *Cool Hand Loc*. *—Ron Wynn*

● **Loc-ed After Dark** / 1989 / Delicious Vinyl/Rhino ✦✦✦✦
A pop hit—however inventive—can be the kiss of death in hip-hop circles. When Tone Loc's incredibly infectious and highly original rap/rock hits "Wild Thing" and "Funky Cold Medina" took the pop world by storm, his reputation suffered considerably among b-boys. The Angelino maintained that those singles were the exception, not the rule—and that he was a hardcore rapper first and foremost. Indeed, most of *Loc-ed After Dark* bears that out. While this striking debut album does contain the above-mentioned hits, hardcore rap like "Next Episode," "Don't Get Close" and "Cheeba Cheeba" is in fact dominant. When "Cheeba Cheeba" was first released in 1987, the song took its share of criticism for promoting marijuana at a time when numerous rappers were vehemently protesting drug use. (Unfortunately, pro-drug songs would later become the norm in rap.) Deadpan and relaxed, the distinctive Loc isn't a rapper with much technique—though he certainly has a lot of personality. *—Alex Henderson*

Cool Hand Loc / 1991 / Delicious Vinyl/Rhino ✦✦✦
Aiming for credibility among hardcore hip-hoppers, Delicious Vinyl was careful not to include a lot of pop-influenced material on Tone-Loc's second album, *Cool Hand Loc*. But sadly, the inventiveness he displayed on "Wild Thing" continued working against Loc among b-boys and hip-hop's hardcore, who still resented the success he'd enjoyed in the pop market. Though not quite as strong as the triple platinum *Loc-ed After Dark*—either commercially or artistically—the album is a respectable and satisfying effort. The former L.A. gang member tends to overdo it with boasting lyrics—a problem he shares with quite a few other rappers—but his boasts are often quite clever. Sadly, Tone-Loc didn't have much longevity; after *Cool Hand Loc*, little was heard about him. *—Alex Henderson*

Tony! Toni! Toné!

f. 1987, Oakland, CA
Contemporary R&B, New Jack Swing, Urban, Soul, Hip-Hop
Brothers Dwayne and Raphael Wiggins and cousin Timothy Christian have proven themselves durable guardians of the soul and funk tradition, while also infusing their music with enough contemporary devices to remain popular. This Oakland trio scored a number one R&B hit right out of the box in 1988 with "Little Walter," a song that generated some criticism from gospel audiences for its use of the melody from "Wade in the Water." But they've since been able to keep things going on their own, as their LPs, *The Revival* in 1990 and *Sons of Soul* in 1993, have also been enormously successful. Tony! Toni! Toné! released their fourth album, *House of Music*, in the fall of 1996. *—Ron Wynn*

Who? / Jan. 1988 / Wing ✦✦✦
Dwayne and Raphael Wiggins, along with cousin Timothy Christian, made a quick and lasting impact with their 1988 debut album. The lead single, "Little Walter," used the melody from "Wade in the Water" and laid out in vivid detail the rise and fall of a comrade who lacked control and direction. It proved a huge R&B hit and got moderate pop attention, but it helped establish the trio and their creative mix of vintage soul and contemporary hip-hop and New Jack production. "Baby Doll" and "For the Love of You" also got sizable pop attention, and Tony! Toni! Toné! were on their way. *—Ron Wynn*

The Revival / Apr. 1990 / Wing ✦✦✦✦✦
One of the more distinctive R&B groups of the late 1980s and early 1990s, Tony! Toni! Toné! has managed to appeal to urban contemporary audiences while expressing its love

of 1970s soul and funk. As high-tech as things get on its sophomore effort *The Revival*, the Oakland trio never fails to sound organic and soulful. Funk smokers like "The Blues," "Oakland Stroke," "Let's Have a Good Time" and "Feels Good" (a major hit) may use technology extensively, but the soulsters always sound like they're in control of the technology (as opposed to it controlling them). Drawing on influences ranging from Sly & the Family Stone, Parliament/Funkadelic and Prince to Digital Underground, Tony! clearly likes its funk down and dirty. And yet, the group sounds equally inspired on such laidback, mellow slow jams as "I Care" and the hit "It Never Rains (In Southern California)." Many of the urban contemporary releases of 1990 were gutless and homogenized, but *The Revival* is an album that had commercial appeal, as well as artistic integrity. *—Alex Henderson*

Sons of Soul / Jun. 22, 1993 / Mercury ✦✦✦✦✦

With their third album, Tony! Toni! Toné! received their greatest chart success, without compromising their music; it was still the finely crafted, highly eclectic and funky pop-soul that distinguished their first two albums, while the band's songwriting and playing had improved. The result was the band's most successful album yet, both commercially and successfully. *—Stephen Thomas Erlewine*

House of Music / Nov. 19, 1996 / Mercury ✦✦✦✦

When Tony! Toni! Toné! finally delivered *House of Music*, their follow-up to their 1993 breakthrough *Sons of Soul*, their influence was beginning to be apparent, as younger soul singer/songwriters like Tony Rich and Maxwell began reaching the R&B charts. Like Tony! Toni! Toné!, Rich and Maxwell relied on traditional soul and R&B values of songwriting and live performances, discarding the synth-heavy productions of the late '80s and early '90s. But, as *House of Music* makes clear, the difference between the Tonies and their successors is that they know how to seamlessly incorporate hip-hop and new jack swingbeat into their essentially traditional sound. Embellishing soul and funk with slamming '90s beats, Tony! Toni! Toné! sounds modern, and they can successfully accomplish their fusion of the traditional and contemporary. More importantly, they can do this within the framework of memorable, catchy songs, whether its the party funk of "Let's Get Down" or the balladry of "Let Me Know." In short, *House of Music* continues the Tonies' tradition of excellence and demonstrates that the group is getting stronger and better all the time. *—Leo Stanley*

● **Greatest Hits** / Oct. 28, 1997 / Mercury ✦✦✦✦✦

Although it's a little early for Tony! Toni! Toné! to have a *Greatest Hits*, this single-disc compilation is nevertheless an excellent summary of their four albums, containing all of the trio's big hits ("If I Had No Loot," "Little Walter," "Feels Good," "It Never Rains (In Southern California)," "Anniversary," "Baby Doll," "The Blues," "Whatever You Want"), plus the new single "Boys and Girls." In the process, it makes a convincing argument that they were one of the best contemporary R&B bands of the early '90s. *—Stephen Thomas Erlewine*

20th Century Masters—The Millennium Collection: The Best of Tony Toni Toné / Aug. 14, 2001 / Mercury ✦✦✦✦

The 1997 collection *Greatest Hits* remains the definitive Tony! Toni! Toné! collection, but *20th Century Masters* still contains the great majority of their very best singles and songs—including "Little Walter," "Feels Good," and the peerless "If I Had No Loot"—which makes this an acceptable substitute for most listeners. *—Stephen Thomas Erlewine*

Too $hort (Todd Shaw)

b. Apr. 28, 1966, Los Angeles, CA

Vocals / West Coast Rap, Hardcore Rap, G-Funk, Gangsta Rap, Golden Age

Too $hort was the first West Coast rap star, recording four albums on his own before he made his major-label debut with 1986's gold album *Born to Mack*. Anticipating much of the later gangsta phenomenon, he restricted his lyrical themes to tales of sexual prowess and physical violence, with the occasional social-message track to mix things up. His second major album, 1988's *Life Is... Too $hort*, was his biggest success and earned double-platinum honors. The immense success of Too $hort that year made him much more viable for radio airplay, and "The Ghetto"—from 1990's *Short Dog's in the House* hit the R&B charts, and just barely missed the pop Top 40. He continued his hit track-record with 1992's *Shorty the Pimp* and 1993's *Get in Where You Fit In*, both of which went platinum. By the time of 1995's *Cocktails*, however, Too $hort began to be drowned out by a glut of similar-sounding West Coasters. Though *Gettin' It (Album Number Ten)* became his fifth platinum album by late 1996, he decided to retire, his status assured as one of the most successful solo rappers of the 1980s and early '90s. Just three years later, he returned with the aptly titled *Can't Stay Away*. *—John Bush*

● **Life Is... Too $hort** / 1988 / Jive ✦✦✦✦✦

Too $hort never had the skills or technique of LL Cool J or Big Daddy Kane, but what the Oakland rapper lacks in technique, he's always more than made up for with irresistible, '70s-inspired funk grooves that simply won't quit. When $hort—after enjoying a small cult following for a few years in Northern California—joined a major label with *Life Is... Too $hort's* predecessor, *Born to Mack*, too many East Coast MCs were inundating hip-hop with clichéd tracks consisting of only James Brown samples and a drum machine. Too $hort, however, presented an attractive alternative with highly melodic, danceable tracks that made no secret of his love of '70s funk heroes like Parliament, the Ohio Players and Cameo. This CD's X-rated, sexually explicit lyrics received their share of vehement criticism, and the MC responded that Too $hort is an outrageous character who shouldn't be taken too seriously. Be that as it may, his commanding reflection on the drug plague, "City of Dope," underscores the fact that he's cheating himself artistically by not devoting more time to social commentary and less time to exploiting sex. *—Alex Henderson*

Greatest Hits, Vol. 1: The Player Years, 1983-1988 / Nov. 10, 1993 / In-A-Minute ✦✦✦✦✦

If you've never read the collected works of Chester Himes or Iceberg Slim, simply run through this Too $hort anthology and you'll have the general idea. Although never an inventive rapper or clever composer of rhymes, Too $hort was smart enough to find his niche and stick to it. Most people who continually mined the pimp arena quickly become merely tedious; Too $hort became both tedious and profitable. *—Ron Wynn*

Tool

f. 1990

Alternative Metal, Heavy Metal

Tool's greatest breakthrough was to introduce dark, vaguely underground metal to the preening pretentiousness of art rock. Or maybe it was introducing the self-absorbed pretension of art rock to the wearing grind of post-thrash metal—the order really doesn't matter. Though Metallica wrote their multi-sectioned, layered songs as if they were composers, they kept their musical attack ferociously at street level. Tool didn't—they embraced the artsy, faux-bohemian preoccupations of Jane's Addiction while they simultaneously paid musical homage to the dark, relentlessly bleak visions of grindcore, death metal, and thrash. Even with their post-punk influences, they executed their music with the ponderous, anti-song aesthetic of prog rock, alternating between long, detailed instrumental interludes and tuneless, pseudo-meaningful lyrical rants in their songs. Tool, however, had a knack for conveying the strangled, oppressive angst that the alternative nation of the early '90s claimed as their own. So, the band was able to slip into the definition of alternative rock during the post-Nirvana era, landing a slot on the third Lollapalooza tour in 1993, which helped their debut album, *Undertow*, rocket into platinum status. By the time the band delivered their belated follow-up, *Aenima*, in 1996, alternative rock had lost its grip on the mainstream of America, and their audience had shaped up as essentially metal-oriented, which meant that the group and the record didn't capture as big an audience as their first album, despite debuting at number two on the charts. During their usual extended hiatus between albums, vocalist Maynard James Keenan decided to use his downtime productively by forming a side project, dubbed A Perfect Circle. May 2001 saw the release of Tool's third full-length release, *Lateralus*, which debuted at the number one position on the *Billboard* album chart. *—Stephen Thomas Erlewine & Greg Prato*

Undertow / 1993 / Zoo ✦✦✦✦

Just as grunge was reaching its boiling point and radio-friendly power punk loomed on the horizon, Tool released *Undertow*, which firmly reinforced metal's prominence as a musical style—but, for once, it had something worthwhile to say. At the forefront of Tool's commercial explosion were striking, haunting visuals that complemented the album's nihilistic yet wistful mood. Drawing equal inspiration from Black Sabbath, alternative theories of science, and Eastern religions, Tool's abrasive sonic assault begins from the opening notes and continues through the final moments of the last composition, an open mockery of organized religion and its incapacity for original thought. With its technical brilliance, musical complexities, and aggressive overtones, *Undertow* not only paved the way for several bands to break through to the mainstream adolescent mall-rage demographic, it also proved that metal could be simultaneously intelligent, emotional, and brutal. *—Rob Theakston*

★ **Aenima** / Oct. 1, 1996 / Volcano ✦✦✦✦✦

For its second full-length record, Tool explores the progressive rock territory previously forged by such bands as King Crimson. However, Tool is conceptually innovative with every minute detail of its art, which sets it apart from most bands. Make no mistake, this isn't your father's rock record. Sonically, the band has never sounded tighter. Long exploratory passages are unleashed with amazing precision, detail, and clarity, which only complements the aggressive, abrasive shorter pieces on the album. There is no compromise from any member of the band, with each of them discovering the dynamics of his respective instrument and pushing the physical capabilities to the limit. Topics such as the philosophies of Bill Hicks (eloquently eulogized in the packaging), evolution and genetics, and false martyrdom will fly over the heads of casual listeners. But those listening closely will discover a special treat: a catalyst encouraging them to discover a world around them to which they otherwise might have been blinded. If these aren't good enough reasons to listen to *Aenima*, then just trust the simple fact that Tool delivers the hard rock goods every time the band chooses to release something. *—Rob Theakston*

Lateralus / May 15, 2001 / Volcano ✦✦✦✦

After an exhaustive five-year litigation battle between the band and their label management, Tool offer up the latest chapter in their musical self-discovery in *Lateralus*. Make no mistake, this is a prog rock record, reminiscent back to the times of King Crimson and *Meddle*-era Pink Floyd, with a hint of Rush mutated with Tool's signature sonic assault on the ears. *Lateralus* demands close listening from the first piece onward, as it becomes quickly apparent that this is not going to be an album one can listen to and accept at face value. Complex rhythm changes, haunting vocals, and an onslaught of changes in dynamics make this an album other so-called metal groups could learn from. While some compositions seem out of place, others fit together seamlessly, such as the 23-minute song cycle serving as the climax and resolution of the album. However, the album's most disturbing moment arrives at the end, with dissonant electronic noises placed randomly with a drum solo over a phone call to a talk show discussing the secrets behind Area 51, once again serving as a symbolic gesture from the band encouraging people not to take things at face value and to think for themselves. Overall, a solid, well-produced album from a band that never fails to deliver with each release. *—Rob Theakston*

The Tornadoes

f. 1962, Redlands, CA

Surf, Instrumental Rock, Rock & Roll

Not to be confused with the British studio group that gave the world the Joe Meek-produced instrumental "Telstar," or the Midwest group that recorded "Scalping Party" on Cuca, *or* the Kennewick, Washington combo of the same name, this group of Tornadoes burst onto the national scene with one of the very first surf instrumentals, "Bustin' Surfboards," in 1962. A family band, their lineup consisted of two brothers (Gerald and Norman Sanders), their cousin Jesse Sanders and a friend, Leonard Delaney. They started out as an instrumental group in San Bernardino, CA called the Vaqueros. After adding sax man George White to the lineup, they changed their name to the Tornadoes. Their lone national chart entry was nonetheless an important one, with "Bustin' Surfboards" in 1962 making the playlists in cities that were far removed from any kind of surfing activity and signaling the beginnings of surf music as a national craze. Although using an off-brand echo unit in place of the Fender reverb unit (which hadn't been invented yet), the record had the prerequisite sound of this fledgling genre, utilizing a solid surfer's stomp drum beat and crashing wave sound effects throughout. More recordings followed, with a name change to the Hollywood Tornadoes for their next two singles in deference to their British namesakes, who had charted higher with "Telstar." Their fourth single, "Shootin' Beavers," was banned from radio play because of the so-called suggestive title. No more hits were forthcoming from the band, although they did release one excellent album that stands as one of the earliest—and best—examples of the genre. *—Cub Koda*

Bustin' Surfboards / 1963 / Sundazed ♦♦♦♦

The Tornadoes' biggest hit became the title track of this, their only album, which also includes acknowledged surf classics like "Shootin' Beavers" and "The Gremmie." The inclusion of three bonus tracks (including the previously unreleased "Charge of the Tornadoes") make this a must-own for fans of the surfin' sound. *—Cub Koda*

Bustin' Surfboards '98 / Mar. 10, 1998 / Garland ♦♦

● **Beyond the Surf: The Best of the Tornadoes** / Aug. 17, 1999 / Sundazed ♦♦♦♦

Compilation drawing principally from their Aertaun 45s and Josie LP, with the addition of three previously unissued cuts (including two Link Wray covers), a number ("Charge of the Tornadoes") previously available only on a Sundazed release, and a 25-minute interview with the group, conducted in the 1990s. The Tornadoes were an above-average, though not upper-echelon, Californian surf band, notable for writing much of their material and possessing one of the better early surf guitarists in Roly Sanders. The vocals are kept to a minimum, which is a good thing. The interview is pretty interesting, including a couple unexpected stories about how a young Frank Zappa helped out on some of their vintage recordings. *—Richie Unterberger*

The Tornados

f. 1961, **db.** 1964

Early British Pop/Rock, Instrumental Rock, Rock & Roll

One of the saddest stories in rock & roll history surrounds the Tornados, an instrumental group from Britain. Although there were other groups with the same name, this batch of Tornados were the creation of Joe Meek, England's first independent producer. Equal parts Thomas Edison, Phil Spector and Ed Wood, Meek pioneered such recording techniques as close miking of instruments, distortion and compression. He put together the original Tornados in late 1961 as a studio session group; after one single flopped, Meek had the group do one of his compositions, an instrumental called "Telstar." Utilizing willful distortion, cheap tape echo, beeping satellite sound effects, a cheesy-sounding Clavioline (a two-octave keyboard powered by a battery) and massive amounts of tube compression, the resulting production sounded like nothing else at the time, or since. It became the first number one record on the American charts by a British rock group and sold five million copies worldwide. But a French copyright infringement suit kept all royalties tied up for six years, and the Tornados were kept from touring the United States behind their international hit due to a contract employing them as a backup group to U.K. pretty boy Billy Fury. By the time the dust settled, the Tornados had gone hitless for several years, and so had Joe Meek. The copyright infringement suit was ruled in Meek's favor six years later, a year after he had blown his face off with a hunting rifle after murdering his landlady, ending his life in his beloved but debt-ridden studio. *—Cub Koda*

Away from It All / 1963 / Castle ♦♦

The only album recorded by the original lineup. Even if your interest in the Tornados extends beyond "Telstar," you may find this effort a humdrum affair, with weak material that can't overcome their trademark outer space roller rink organ and Meek's usual, at times cliched bag-of-tricks production. Has no overlap with their greatest hits CD on Music Club, if that is a concern. *—Richie Unterberger*

Yesterday's Pop Scene / 1972 / Decca ♦♦♦

When Tornados compilations were extremely scarce, this was one of the best bets around if you were determined to find *something* by the band. All of the 12 songs, though, were reissued on CD in the 1990s on Music Club's *Telstar* anthology in the U.K. *—Richie Unterberger*

● **Telstar: The Original Sixties Hits of the Tornados** / 1994 / Music Club ♦♦♦♦♦

All you could possibly want to hear: both sides of the nine singles they cut for Decca between 1962 and 1964, along with the small U.S. hit "Ridin' the Wind" and a cut from a soundtrack LP. A fun, if slight, document of one of the most distinctive instrumental rock groups of the early '60s, with thorough liner notes. *—Richie Unterberger*

The Very Best of the Tornados / May 20, 1997 / Music Club ♦♦♦♦

"Telstar" was a worldwide number one smash hit for the Tornados and maverick producer Joe Meek in 1962. But these so-called one-hit wonders left behind an overlooked legacy of catchy instrumentals, experimental 45s and pre-Moog and synthesizer rock. This 15-track compilation brings together the very best of their work on one disc. Meek's production on these tunes is equal parts control room freak genius and low-fi visionary. Although nothing packs the wallop of their lone mega-hit (and what really could?), Meek's use of heavy compression, freakish percussion effects and close miking earmark tracks like "Joystick," "Monte Carlo," "Jungle Fever," "Love and Fury," "Alan's Tune," and "Hymn For Teenagers." The Tornados may have been a studio creation of Meek's, but remain a marvelous creation nonetheless. *—Cub Koda*

Telstar: The Complete Tornados / 1998 / Repertoire ♦♦♦♦♦

Fifty-five Tornados tracks on two CDs may be 53 more than most casual listeners need, but this double-disc set justifies itself in the listening. To most Americans, and even most Britons, the Tornados were one-hit wonders, responsible for "Telstar" and not much else, but as this set shows, they did come up with some cool sounds and tunes under the guidance of producer/manager Joe Meek. "Robot" is nearly as pretty a tune as "Telstar" (it also charted in England at No. 17), and it sounds fresh, as something not nearly as widely heard for 36 years; "Life On Venus," the B-side, is a very close second, almost a "son of Telstar." "Ice Cream Man" was another British chart single, and offers the spectacle of Meek and the Tornados applying a Bo Diddley beat to their trademark sound. Other highlights include lots of television themes, both material for actual use on the air and the group's covers of such material as "Stringray" and "Aqua Marina" from the sci-fi kids' show *Stringray*. The material extends right into 1964 and the band's attempts to compete in the area of vocal records, when it became clear that the public wasn't too interested in instrumental rock & roll anymore. The annotation includes a beautifully detailed essay by Chris Welch, with extensive interview material on drummer Clem Cattini (the longest-tenured member of the Tornados) and Cattini's recollections on each of the tracks here. In the end, there's more to the Tornados' sound and history than most of us knew, all revealed here. *—Bruce Eder*

Tortoise

f. 1990, Chicago, IL

Experimental Rock, Indie Rock, Post-Rock/Experimental, Instrumental Rock

Tortoise revolutionized American indie-rock in the mid-'90s by playing down tried-and-true punk and rock & roll influences, emphasizing instead the incorporation of a variety of left-field music genres from the past 20 years, including Kraut-rock, dub, classical minimalism, ambient & space music, prog-rock, film music and British electronica. At odds as well with the shambling framework of alternative rock's normal song structure, the group—as large as a septet, with at times *two* vibes players—relied on a crisp instrumental aesthetic, tied to cool jazz, which practically stood alone in American indie-rock by actually focusing on instrumental prowess and group interaction. Although the group's unique vision is to an extent the creation of drummer and master producer John McEntire, most of the other members are well-connected—producers and/or participants—in Chicago's fraternal indie-rock community, which consists of numerous side projects and ongoing bands. After debuting in 1993 with several singles and an LP the following year, Tortoise's underground prestige emerged above terra firma with their second album *Millions Now Living Will Never Die*; the 21-minute opening track "Djed" was a sublime pastiche of Kraut-rock, dub and cool jazz. Tortoise then linked themselves with the cream of European electronica (Luke Vibert, Oval, U.N.K.L.E., Spring Heel Jack) to remix the album on a series of 12-inch singles. Despite the band's growing reliance on studio engineering, Tortoise began re-emphasizing their instrumentalist bent in 1998 for third album *TNT*. *—John Bush*

Tortoise / 1994 / Thrill Jockey ♦♦♦♦♦

One of the more original indie-rock albums, *Tortoise* takes its guitar inspiration from indie-rock bands like Slint, though the sound is much more laidback. As well, the group encompasses a wider range of music, including jazz and a twisted form of lo-fi electronics. With the great vibes of jazz and the cool chill of good ambience, the album rarely fails to please. *—John Bush*

Rhythms, Resolutions & Clusters / 1995 / Thrill Jockey ♦♦♦

Just after the release of their debut album, Tortoise invited several friends (including Steve Albini and Brad Wood) to dissect several tracks. The result is a 30-minute continuous mix, ranging from a hip-hop remix—with A Tribe Called Quest and Minnie Riperton samples—to environment-sound driftings. Most of the disc is on the experimental side, even compared to the original. *—John Bush*

★ **Millions Now Living Will Never Die** / Jan. 30, 1996 / Thrill Jockey ♦♦♦♦♦

Tortoise's production expertise hit an early peak with *Millions Now Living Will Never Die*, a work that not only references studio-centric forms like dub and electronica, but actively welds them to the group's aesthetic of sturdily constructed indie rock. The centerpiece is the 21-minute opener "Djed," a multi-part track which brought Tortoise's already impressive compositional abilities to a grand scale. It's almost a history of influences in miniature, first referencing tape music and dub for several minutes, then moving on to Krautrock with a chugging section incorporating wheezing organ and understated guitar chords. Halfway through, the band takes on minimalism with repeating figures of organ and vibes, then return to the green fields of their debut with a final few minutes of moody indie rock (though even this is spiced with a scratchy rhythm and various noise effects). With "Djed," Tortoise made experimental rock do double duty as evocative, beautiful music. The other songs on *Millions Now Living* are hardly afterthoughts, though; highlights "Glass Museum" and "The Taut and Tame" display the band quickly growing out of the angular indie rock ghetto with exquisite music, constructed with more thought and played with more emotion, than any of their peers. *—John Bush*

TNT / Mar. 10, 1998 / Thrill Jockey ✦✦✦✦✦

Expected by many to continue leading the post-rock brigade into a new fusion with dub and electronics, Tortoise instead turned yet another corner with their third album, *TNT*. Adding guitarist Jeff Parker to cement their musicianship as well as their connections to Chicago's fertile jazz/avant-garde scene, the band returned with a record of post-modern cool jazz, only slightly informed by the dub, Krautrock, and electronics of *Millions Now Living Will Never Die*. It shows from the first few seconds—a lazy, slightly free drum solo frames a few tentative guitar chords and some teased effects, before the band kicks in with a holds-barred jam that encompasses a tremulous solo from trumpeter Rob Mazurek. With engineer/mixer/drummer John McEntire and company adding only a few post-production frills to the mix—and those so complementary and subdued that they rarely even sound like effects—*TNT* comes off as a surprisingly organic record. The evocative Spanish-style guitar on "I Set My Face to the Hillside" plays over an assortment of playground sounds, while "The Suspension Bridge at Iguazú Falls" deconstructs a classically angular Tortoise groove and re-emerges with an evocative, deeply affecting groove over shimmering vibes and precision guitar lines. There are plenty of nods to post-rock touchstones like Krautrock ("Swing From the Gutters"), dub, and minimalism ("Ten-Day Interval"), but Tortoise hardly sounds like a difficult band here. Instead of forcing studio experimentation to become an end to itself, the band mastered—with a single, deft statement—the far more difficult lesson of making technology work for the music. *—John Bush*

Standards / Feb. 20, 2001 / Thrill Jockey ✦✦✦✦

Revered for their ineffably clean, precise playing, Tortoise couldn't help but mess with the formula slightly on their fourth album, *Standards*. And from the beginning of the first track it sounds like a major overhaul, with heavily over-miced drums and distorted guitars framing a pummeling groove from bassist Doug McCombs. On the second track "Eros," the phlegmatic synthesizer lines and clipped drums are more reminiscent of experimental electronica outfit Mouse on Mars than any fellow post-rock luminaries. When the band finally hits its stride, though, midway through the third track, "Benway," it's with a quintessential Tortoise groove, driven by repetitive bass figures and a vibraphone melody (plus a hilarious nod to prog-rock at the end, with several seconds of stop-start playing). *Standards* does return the group to the green fields of their last record, but only occasionally; John McEntire and company appear too restless to consider making the same album twice. Ironically, despite the range of sounds, Tortoise is still doing what they've been doing for nearly a decade: playing some of the most empathic, group-minded rock of their era, then indulging in much recomposition courtesy of the mixing desk and various effects. "Monica" is one of the least Tortoise-sounding tracks the group has ever recorded; it sounds like an early-'80s pop/R&B track (complete with talkbox guitar) filtered through the lens of British IDM, but then mutates into an intriguing stereo-separation drum workout. Overall, *Standards* has a few detours for fans conscious of any band's "progression," but plenty of interesting songs and great musicianship for less vested listeners. Though it doesn't develop the evocative or impressionistic side of Tortoise (as heard on *TNT*), the band is certainly as inventive as ever. *—John Bush*

Toto

f. 1978, Los Angeles, CA

Album Rock, Pop/Rock, Soft Rock, Adult Contemporary

Toto was formed in Los Angeles in 1978 by David Paich (keyboards, vocals), Steve Lukather (guitar, vocals), Bobby Kimball (vocals), Steve Porcaro (keyboards), David Hungate (bass), and Jeff Porcaro (drums). Paich was the son of arranger Marty Paich. The members had met in high school and at studio sessions in the 1970s, when they became some of the busiest session musicians in the music business. Paich, Hungate, and Jeff Porcaro wrote songs for and performed on *Silk Degrees*, Boz Scaggs' multi-million-selling 1976 album that combined pop, rock, and disco elements into a slick combination which heavily influenced mainstream pop music. Toto released its self-titled debut album in October 1978, and it hit the Top Ten, sold two million copies, and spawned the gold Top Ten single "Hold the Line." The gold-selling *Hydra* (1979) and *Turn Back* (1981) were less successful, but *Toto IV* (1982) was a multi-platinum Top Ten hit, featuring the number one hit "Africa" and the Top Tens "Rosanna" and "I Won't Hold You Back." At the 1982 Grammys, "Rosanna" won awards for Record of the Year, Best Pop Vocal Performance, and Best Instrumental Arrangement with Vocal, and *Toto IV* won awards for Album of the Year, Best Engineered Recording, and Best Producer. In 1984, a third Porcaro brother, Mike, replaced Hungate, then Kimball was replaced by Dennis "Fergie" Frederiksen. Toto's fifth album, *Isolation* (1984), went gold, but was a commercial disappointment. Frederiksen was replaced by Joseph Williams for 1986's *Fahrenheit*. Steve Porcaro quit in 1988, prior to the release of *The Seventh One*. In 1990, Jean-Michel Byron replaced Williams for the new recordings on *Past to Present 1977-1990*, then left, as Lukather became the lead singer. Jeff Porcaro died of a heart attack in 1992, but was featured on the group's next album, *Kingdom of Desire*. By this time, Toto was far more popular in Japan and Europe than at home. The group added British drummer Simon Phillips. *Tambu*, released in Europe in 1995, appeared in the U.S. in 1996. For 1999's *Mindfields*, Bobby Kimball returned to the lineup after a 15-year absence. *—William Ruhlmann*

Toto / Oct. 1978 / Columbia ✦✦✦✦

It's as easy to see why radio listeners loved Toto as it is to see why critics hated them. Toto's sessionman rock studio chops allowed them to play any current pop style at the drop of a hi-hat: one minute prog-rock, the next hard rock, the next funky R&B. It all sounded great, but it also implied that music-making took craft rather than inspiration and that the musical barriers critics like to erect were arbitrary. Then, too, Toto's timing couldn't have been much worse. They rode in in the middle of punk/new wave with its D.I.Y. aesthetic, and their sheer competence was an affront. Of course, there's always been an alternate history of popular music not available to rock critics (it's written in record stores and concert halls and on the radio), and in that story, Toto was a smash. Singles like "I'll Supply the Love" and "Georgy Porgy" (featuring Cheryl Lynn) made the charts, and "Hold the Line" hit the Top Ten and went gold. The members of Toto had already influenced the course of '70s popular music by playing on half the albums that came out of L.A. All they were doing with this album was going public. *—William Ruhlmann*

Hydra / Oct. 1979 / Columbia ✦✦✦

If Toto's musical advantage was that, since its members continued to play on many of the successful records made in L.A., its own music was popular almost by definition, its disadvantage was that it made little attempt to seek an individual musical signature—a particular style, say, or a distinctive singer (Bobby Kimball was not it) who could make its records immediately identifiable. "Hold the Line" had been a big hit, but who did it? Boston? Foreigner? As a result, Toto was less-well-positioned than most to come off a big debut album with the follow-up, and *Hydra* was unusually dependent on its lead-off single, "99." Maybe it was a tribute to the female lead on the old *Get Smart* TV show, but many listeners didn't get a song with a chorus that went, "Oh, 99, I love you," and the single stalled in the bottom half of the Top 40. The album went gold on momentum, but the songs, however well played, simply were not distinctive enough to consolidate the success Toto had achieved with its debut album. *—William Ruhlmann*

Turn Back / Jan. 1981 / Columbia ✦✦✦

Toto went from disappointment to disaster with its third album, the generic *Turn Back*. The group's ability to turn out highly competent studio rock was not translating into an individual sound, and since *Turn Back* had no memorable songs on it, one was left with nothing more than those famous chops that Toto possessed in abundance. The group would rally from this retreat, but for the moment a better title would have been *Fall Back*, as in, the studio jobs the band members had to fall back on. *—William Ruhlmann*

Toto IV / Apr. 1982 / Columbia ✦✦✦✦✦

It was do or die for Toto on the group's fourth album, and they rose to the challenge. Largely dispensing with the anonymous studio rock that had characterized their first three releases, the band worked harder on its melodies, made sure its simple lyrics treated romantic subjects, augmented Bobby Kimball's vocals by having other group members sing and bringing in ringers like Timothy B. Schmit, and slowed down the tempo to what came to be known as "power ballad" pace. Most of all, they wrote some hit songs: "Rosanna," the old story of a lovelorn lyric matched to a bouncy beat, was the gold, Top Ten comeback single accompanying the album release; "Make Believe" made the Top 30; and then, surprisingly, "Africa" hit number one ten months after the album's release. The members of Toto may have more relatives who are NARAS voters than any other group, but that still doesn't explain the sweep they achieved at the Grammys, winning six, including Album of the Year and Record of the Year (for "Rosanna"). Predictably, rock critics howled, but the Grammys helped set up the fourth single, "I Won't Hold You Back," another soft-rock smash and Top Ten hit. As a result, *Toto IV* was both the group's comeback and its peak; it remains a definitive album of slick L.A. pop for the early '80s and Toto's best and most consistent record. Having made it, the members happily went back to sessions, where they helped write and record Michael Jackson's *Thriller*. *—William Ruhlmann*

Isolation / Nov. 1984 / Columbia ✦✦✦

Having traded in lead singer Bobby Kimball for Fergie Frederiksen, a smooth tenor wailer in the tradition of Journey's Steve Perry, Toto proceeded to follow its power-ballad smash *Toto IV* with a Journey clone album, minus the aching ballads that had made Journey such a success. A workout for drummer Jeff Porcaro, keyboardist David Paich, and guitarist Steve Lukather, *Isolation* was anything but the kind of record those millions who had loved "Rosanna" were waiting for. It seemed intended to restore the band members' heady studio reputations as hard rock technicians, which it did by dispensing with the elements that finally had made the band a big success in 1982. *—William Ruhlmann*

Fahrenheit / Aug. 1986 / Columbia ✦✦

The Seventh One / Mar. 1988 / Columbia ✦✦

● **Past to Present 1977-1990** / Sep. 1990 / Columbia ✦✦✦✦✦

Toto's compilation is to be recommended in that it contains all four of the group's Top Ten hit singles—"Hold the Line," "Rosanna," "Africa," and "I Won't Hold You Back." It also contains four more of Toto's 14 pop chart singles—"Georgy Porgy," "99," "I'll Be over You," and "Pamela." But that means it leaves out six chart entries, including the Top 40 hits "Make Believe," "Stranger in Town," and "Without Your Love." In their place are an album track from the most recent album, *The Seventh One* and four newly recorded songs co-written and sung by the group's fourth lead vocalist, Jean-Michel Byron, who is more soulful than his predecessors, but no more memorable. As such, this is not the ideal Toto best-of and earns its "pick" designation over *Toto IV* only by virtue of its inclusion of the group's first hit, "Hold the Line." *—William Ruhlmann*

Tambu / May 1995 / Sony Legacy ✦✦

Toto XX: 1977-1997 / Dec. 8, 1998 / Sony Legacy ✦✦✦

Toto XX: 1977-1997 is hardly the definitive collection that its title suggests. Essentially, this is a reunion album, featuring nine new studio cuts and four live tracks, including a version of "Africa." The band sounds better than you might expect, but the material isn't all that different than that on *Tambu*—the performances are a little tighter, slicker and better. That said, it's not particularly interesting to anyone outside hardcore fans, who will probably be pleased to hear an approximation of the original lineup back in action, regardless if the tunes are memorable or not. —*Stephen Thomas Erlewine*

Allen Toussaint

b. Jan. 14, 1938, New Orleans, LA
Vocals, Keyboards, Piano / New Orleans R&B, R&B
His inherently funky piano work heavily influenced by his Crescent City forefathers—Professor Longhair, Huey "Piano" Smith, and Fats Domino—and with a heavy dose of Ray Charles, a young visionary named Allen Toussaint almost singlehandedly fashioned a fresh, vital New Orleans R&B sound for the early '60s. Earning a vaunted reputation as a session pianist, Toussaint debuted on vinyl in 1958 with an obscure RCA album whimsically billed as "A. Tousan." When Joe Banashak inaugurated his Minit label in 1960, Toussaint joined the firm as A&R man and quickly proved himself the ultimate behind-the-scenes wizard on the New Orleans scene. During the early to mid-'60s, Toussaint tirelessly wrote, arranged, produced, and played on hits by Ernie K-Doe, Irma Thomas, Jessie Hill, Chris Kenner, Barbara George, Lee Dorsey, Benny Spellman, the Showmen, and many more, his rolling keyboards vital to the charm of virtually all of them.

After unleashing The Meters on the world, Toussaint finally began to step out as a front man in 1970, although his low-key vocals have never achieved quite the same level of success as his previous productions for others. His brilliant compositions have been covered by everyone from Herb Alpert & the Tijuana Brass to Robert Palmer and Bonnie Raitt. Allen Toussaint's stature as a New Orleans musical giant endures. —*Bill Dahl*

The Wild Sound of New Orleans / 1958 / Edsel ✦✦✦✦
His debut album, featuring a killer beat, storming second-line instrumentals, and Toussaint's rolling 88s. —*Bill Dahl*

Toussaint / 1971 / Scepter ✦✦✦
New Orleans production and performing wizard Allen Toussaint launched his solo career with this early-'70s release. But for some strange reason, the same performer who's written and produced marvelous material for Irma Thomas, Lee Dorsey, Chocolate Milk, and General Johnson among others, was never able to score the same success working as a lead act. There was nothing on this album even in the same arena as his classic R&B tunes, and throughout Toussaint's run of solo releases, only the song "Southern Nights," which Glen Campbell made a hit, could be even mentioned in the same sentence with Toussaint classics like "Ride Your Pony" or "It Will Stand." —*Ron Wynn*

Life Love & Faith / 1972 / Reprise ✦✦✦
On this '70s Allen Toussaint album, he is backed by a sizable New Orleans studio cast, including The Meters and saxophonist Red Tyler. There are 12 cuts, which include "Victims of the Darkness," "Goin' Down," "Out of the City," "Soul Sister," "Fingers and Toes," "Gone Too Far," "Electricity," and more. —*Roots & Rhythm Newsletter*

Bomp City / 1973 / Reprise ✦✦✦

Southern Nights / 1975 / Reprise ✦✦✦✦✦
This CD reissue of Allen Toussaint's 1975 Reprise LP has ten beautiful cuts which flow like an extended suite, featuring Toussaint's grand piano chordings backed by The Meters and a seven-piece horn section. The title track became a big hit for Glen Campbell, and "What Do You Want the Girl to Do?" has often been covered. It also has "Last Train," "Worldwide," "Back in Baby's Arms," "Country John," "Basic Lady," "You Will Not Love," "When the Party's Over," and "Cruel Way to Go Down." —*Myles Boisen, Roots & Rhythm Newsletter*

Motion / Aug. 1978 / Reprise ✦✦✦
A nicely produced, competently performed, but disappointing album by New Orleans giant Allen Toussaint. He seemed unable to find a groove or a sound, dabbling in pop, light R&B, rock, and mild funk, but never coming close to duplicating prior magical productions or compositions. This was perhaps Toussaint's least impressive material, and was especially surprising in light of the artistic success of his prior Warner Bros. album *Homage*. —*Ron Wynn*

● **Allen Toussaint Collection** / Apr. 30, 1991 / Reprise ✦✦✦✦
R&B with some meat on its bones from New Orleans songwriter/producer Toussaint. This retrospective collection covers four albums since 1970, including his one album for Scepter, *From a Whisper to a Scream*. The music is often dark, without being depressing, horn driven and loosely propelled along by the rhythm section. It's the sort of music that may not be immediate, but given a few chances it'll work its way right under the skin and stay there. What's sad is that they rarely make music like this anymore—this is music out of blood and bone. —*Steven McDonald*

The Complete "Tousan" Sessions / 1992 / Bear Family ✦✦✦✦✦
A compilation of instrumentals from 1958 and 1959 featuring Toussaint at the top of his form, *The Complete "Tousan" Sessions* is a wonderful portrait of the seminal New Orleans pianist; it's also the first time this material has ever been available on CD. —*Stephen Thomas Erlewine*

A Taste of New Orleans / Mar. 9, 1999 / Nyno ✦✦✦
A 12-cut sampler of artists on Allen Toussaint's NYNO label, which is devoted to contemporary New Orleans music, and produced by Toussaint himself. All of these tracks are on single-artist NYNO albums, so it's more a promo for the company than a cohesive anthology. There's jazz from Amadee Castenell, gospel from Raymond Myles, reggae from Cool Riddims & Sista Teedy, updated old-time jazz from the New Birth Brass Band and good ol' New Orleans R&B from Toussaint, James Andrews and others. Toussaint is doing a noble service by recording New Orleans musicians, but this is not going to convince anyone that the city is headed for a new golden age. The traditional-style New Orleans

cuts are pleasantly familiar and unexceptional, while others seem to be trying too hard to add contemporary pop seasoning to New Orleans music, as if figuring that it might somehow help them get played on the radio. —*Richie Unterberger*

Tower of Power

f. 1967, Oakland, CA
Quiet Storm, Funk, Soul
Studio-session work has never lent itself to wide recognition except among other musicians, yet when not on the road as Tower of Power, the individuals who make up the critically acclaimed West Coast horn section might as well go by another name: "Backup to the World." Individually and in various incarnations, members of Tower of Power (fronted by Emilio Castillo) have recorded as sidemen for Elton John, Santana, Bonnie Raitt, Huey Lewis, Little Feat, David Sanborn, Michelle Shocked, Paula Abdul, Aaron Neville, and Riot. Tower of Power has had their share of personnel changes over the years, but the core group members (including Castillo on saxes and vocals, Stephen "Doc" Kupka on baritone sax, Greg Adams on trumpet and vocals, and Rocco Prestia on bass) have remained, giving the band a percussive horn-based sound that is not rooted in any one genre. —*Richard Skelly*

What Is Hip?: The Tower of Power Anthology / Aug. 31, 1999 / Rhino ✦✦✦✦✦
Having played on hundreds of hit records, it was only fitting that this Oakland-based group of studio hornmen should strike out on their own and this two-disc anthology from Rhino captures the ups, downs, ins, and outs of T.O.P.'s 30-year career. In many ways, the group retrospective is not just a document of the group's evolving sound, but a microcosm of the changing sound of R&B throughout the '70s and '80s. The soul band sound of early tracks like "Knock Yourself Out" sound as if the group is doing a muscular workout at a soul music revue and the oily R&B of "Back on the Streets Again" and "Down to the Nightclub" perfectly reflects the post-Motown pre-disco period of early-'70s rhythm and blues. As the songs progress the band goes on to dabble in funk ("You Got to Funkifize"), jazz soul ("Sparkling in the Sound"), and disco before ultimately (and unfortunately) giving way to the slick, hollow production standards of the '80s. Throughout the 35 tracks, however, singer Lenny Williams' voice sparkles and the group's tight musicianship, being honed through years of session work, is undeniable. At two discs, Rhino has made sure not to stretch the music thin and with a relative cost, the anthology is a good entrance to T.O.P.'s long career. —*Steve Kurutz*

Pete Townshend (Peter Dennis Blandford Townshend)

b. May 19, 1945, Chiswick, London, England
Vocals, Keyboards, Guitar (Electric), Guitar / Album Rock, Pop/Rock, Prog-Rock/Art Rock, Hard Rock, Singer/Songwriter
Pete Townshend was the guitarist and songwriter for the Who from 1964 to 1982; best known for his conceptual works, he wrote *Tommy* and *Quadrophenia* for the group. Townshend made his first, tentative solo album, *Who Came First*, in 1972. Dedicated to his guru, Meher Baba, the album continued themes pursued in the previous Who album, *Who's Next*, and contained material from an abortive conceptual work, *Lifehouse*. *Empty Glass* (1980) sold half a million copies and featured the Top Ten hit "Let My Love Open the Door," as well as the minor hits "A Little Is Enough" and "Rough Boys." Townshend followed this in 1982 with *All the Best Cowboys Have Chinese Eyes*. Following the demise of the Who, he released *Scoop*, a two-disc collection of demos, in 1983 (a second volume appeared in 1987). In 1985 he returned to thematic efforts with the album *White City—A Novel*, which included the Top 30 single "Face the Face." In 1989, Townshend released an album based on Ted Hughes' children's story, *The Iron Man*. Simultaneous with the album's release, Townshend embarked on a reunion tour with the Who. Four years later, he delivered *Psychoderelict* to mixed reviews and lukewarm sales. By that time, he had successfully reinvented himself as a Broadway tunesmith—the Broadway production of *The Who's Tommy* had become a runaway hit, earning Townshend a Tony and prompting him to pursue more stage musicals. —*William Ruhlmann*

Who Came First / Oct. 1972 / Rykodisc ✦✦✦✦
Pete Townshend's first solo album was a homespun, charming forum for low-key, personal songs that weren't deemed suitable for The Who, as well as spiritual paeans (direct and indirect) to his spiritual guru Meher Baba. Who fans will be immediately attracted by the presence of a couple of songs from the aborted Who concept album *Lifehouse* (much of which ended up on *Who's Next*), "Pure & Easy" and "Let's See Action." The Who did eventually release their own versions of both those songs. But Townshend's own versions aren't the highlights of this record, which shows a folkier and gentler side to The Who's chief muse than his albums with the group. "Sheraton Gibson" is a neat tune about rock & roll road life, and "Time Is Passing" takes very subtle inspiration from Baba. Most of the rest of the album contains some of the most unusual pieces Townshend has released: his acoustic cover of Jim Reeves' "There's A Heartache Following Me" (recorded because it was one of Baba's favorite tunes), "Evolution" (which is actually pretty much a solo track by his buddy Ronnie Lane of The Faces), "Parvardigar" (adapted from Baba's Universal Prayer), and "Content" (a philosophical poem by Maud Kennedy that Townshend put to music). The 1993 reissue of this LP for compact disc fleshes out the program considerably with six previously unreleased tracks, including Townshend's demo of The Who single "The Seeker." The other bonus cuts are by no means filler; meditative and melancholy originals, they're just as strong as the tracks on the original release. —*Richie Unterberger*

Rough Mix / Sep. 1977 / Atco ✦✦✦✦
Rough Mix, Pete Townshend's 1977 collaboration with former Small Faces and Faces

songwriter and bass player Ronnie Lane, combines the loose, rollicking folk-rock of Lane's former band Slim Chance with touches of country, folk and New Orleans rock & roll, along with Townshend's own trademark style. Lane's tunes, especially the beautiful "Annie," possess an understated charm, while Townshend, with songs such as "Misunderstood," the Meher Baba-inspired "Keep Me Turning," and the strange love song "My Baby Gives It Away," delivers some of the best material of his solo career. *Rough Mix* stands as a minor masterpiece and an overlooked gem in both artists' vast bodies of work. Eric Clapton, John Entwistle and Charlie Watts guest. *—Brett Hartenbach*

● **Empty Glass** / Apr. 21, 1980 / Atco ✦✦✦✦✦
Pete Townshend was heading toward collapse as the '70s turned into the '80s. He had battled a number of personal demons throughout the '70s, but he started spiraling downward after Keith Moon's death, questioning more than ever why he did what he did (and this is a songwriter who always asked questions). Signs of that crept out on *Face Dances*, but he saved a full-blown exploration of his psyche for *Empty Glass*, his first solo album since *Who Came First*, a vanity project released to little notice around *Who's Next* (so limited in its distribution that *Empty Glass* seemed like his solo debut). Some of the songs on *Empty Glass* would have worked as Who songs, yet this is clearly a singer/songwriter album, the work of a writer determined to lay his emotions bare, whether on the plaintive "I Am an Animal" or the blistering punk love letter "Rough Boys." Since this is Townshend, it can be a little artier than it needs to be, as on the pseudo-Gilbert & Sullivan chorus of "Keep on Working," but the joy of *Empty Glass* is that his writing is sharp, his performances lively, his gift for pop hooks as apparent as his wit. Though it runs out of steam toward the end, *Empty Glass* remains one of the highlights of Townshend's catalog and is one of the most revealing records he cut, next to his other breakdown album, *Who By Numbers*. *—Stephen Thomas Erlewine*

All the Best Cowboys Have Chinese Eyes / Jun. 1982 / Atco ✦✦✦✦✦
If *Empty Glass*, an album filled with songs that could have been performed by the Who, was a solo album because it was too revealing and personal, *All the Best Cowboys Have Chinese Eyes* was a solo record since it's impossible to hear anyone but Townshend wanting to indulge in this deliberately arty, awkwardly poetic bullshit. Where his other albums showed an inclination toward classical-influenced art rock, this is defiantly modern art, filled with stagey prose, synthesizers, drum machines, angular song structures, and a heavy debt to new wave—in short, Townshend's vision of what modern music should sound like in 1982. The problem is, this is Arty with a capital A and Pretentious with a capital P, yet Townshend never seems embarrassed, never shies away from indulging himself in his own ego. While autobiographical to a certain extent (how else to read "Somebody Saved Me" or "Stardom in Acton," which drops the Who's home borough?), it's hard to tell exactly what he's on about. So it's easy to see why many listeners are exasperated instead of intrigued (or even admire its damn impenetrability), but it's also easy to get fascinated by the album's very obtuseness. Indeed, separating *All the Best Cowboys* from its era is even difficult, since the album's surface glistens with new wave synths and guitars; this is clearly a record Townshend could only have made in 1982, emboldened by new wave, the reaction to *Empty Glass*, new sobriety, and general hubris. For these reasons, this is very much loved by a certain portion of Townsend's fan base—and for the same reasons many, many people despise it. And any record that fractures an audience so considerably is worth a spin. *—Stephen Thomas Erlewine*

Scoop / Apr. 1983 / Atco ✦✦✦✦✦
Pete Townshend's demos had grown legendary among Who collectors well before the official release of the double-album *Scoop* in 1983. On each demo, Townshend worked out full arrangements, which the Who would often follow exactly. He also recorded a wealth of songs and instrumental pieces that never made it to record. Over the course of two albums, *Scoop* features 25 of these demos, including both classic Who songs ("So Sad About Us," "Bargain," "Behind Blue Eyes," "Magic Bus," "Love Reign O'er Me") and unreleased gems ("Politician," "Melancholia," "To Barney Kessell," "Mary"). Occasionally, the songs sound better in their demo versions, particularly on latter-day Who songs, which were over-wrought in their official incarnations. But what makes *Scoop* so fascinating is its revelation of the depth and detail of Townshend's imagination, and how he refined his ideas. But even casual fans will find the sheer musicality of the record worthwhile—it's one of the most focused and impressive albums he has ever released. *—Stephen Thomas Erlewine*

White City: A Novel / Nov. 1985 / Atco ✦✦✦
After the experimental *All the Best Cowboys Have Chinese Eyes*, Pete Townshend returned to a more traditional form of concept album with *White City*. Built around a loose narrative concerning urban despair, the album doesn't work very well conceptually, yet a handful of the individual songs are among his finest solo work, including the punchy "Face the Face" and the anthemic "Give Blood." *—Stephen Thomas Erlewine*

Pete Townshend's Deep End Live! / Oct. 1986 / Atco ✦✦✦
An energetic live album featuring a handful of R&B classics (including "Barefootin'"), a few Who chestnuts, and some of his best solo work, *Pete Townshend's Deep End Live!* is the tightest rock & roll record he released as a solo artist. *—Stephen Thomas Erlewine*

Another Scoop / Jul. 8, 1987 / Atco ✦✦✦✦✦
Like its predecessor, *Another Scoop* is a collection of 27 demos Pete Townshend recorded for the Who and, if anything, it surpasses the first volume in terms of quality. *Another Scoop* has a greater percentage of familiar Who classics—including "You Better You Bet," "Pinball Wizard," "Happy Jack," "Substitute," "Long Live Rock," "Pictures of Lily" and "The Kids Are Alright"—and the outtakes are uniformly excellent, ranging from his takes on "Driftin' Blues" and "Begin the Beguine" to neglected gems "Girl In A Suitcase," "Holly Like Ivy" and "Ask Yourself," and even weird experiments like "Football Fugue." For any Townshend fan, *Another Scoop* is necessary listening, containing some of his best and most adventurous work. *—Stephen Thomas Erlewine*

The Iron Man: A Musical / Jun. 27, 1989 / Atlantic ✦✦
Pete Townshend adapted "The Iron Man," a children's fable written by the British poet Ted Hughes, for his sixth studio solo album, *Iron Man: A Musical*. Casting himself, Roger Daltrey, Nina Simone, and John Lee Hooker in leading roles, the album doesn't suffer from a lack of talent—it suffers from a lack of songs. Townshend has failed to come up with a set of compelling melodies for Hughes' poems and the arrangements are obvious and overblown, making *Iron Man* an overwrought, ambitious failure. *—Stephen Thomas Erlewine*

Psychoderelict / Jun. 15, 1993 / Atlantic ✦✦✦
In the past, Townsend has let his lyrics tell the story from within the music, and that has allowed much of his work to stand timeless both as individual songs and entire concept pieces. On *Psychoderelict*, songs and music fight the spoken word "drama" throughout. Some individual songs are interesting; many are forgettable. Townsend shoots for hip, self-deprecating irony with numbers like "Let's Get Pretentious" and "Outlive The Dinosaur," but the strategy is transparent. Throw in the added static of instrumental passages paying tribute to Townsend's spiritual mentor Meher Baba, and the overall effect is disjointed and most unsatisfying. *—Roch Parisien*

The Best of Pete Townshend: Coolwalkingsmoothtalkingstraightsmokingfirestoking / Apr. 23, 1996 / Atlantic ✦✦✦✦
Despite some unnecessary problems, *coolwalkingsmoothtalkingstraightsmokingfirestoking: The Best of Pete Townshend* is a good sampling of Townshend's biggest solo hits, as well as some of the songwriter's personal favorites. One of the major problems of the collection is Townshend's inability to leave the original mixes alone—for instance, there're two versions of "Let My Love Open the Door" and neither of them is the original version. Furthermore, some tracks have longer mixes, others are shorter and occasionally the mixes are significantly different than the album. Even with these problems, the album provides a good idea of the arc of Townshend's solo career, making it an adequate starting point for neophytes. For dedicated fans, it's a very frustrating release—not only is it baited with the unreleased *Pyschoderelict* outtake "Uneasy Street" and the "E. Cola mix" of "Let My Love Open the Door," the remixes and edits are awkward for those intimately familiar with the tracks. Which means *The Best of Pete Townshend* is best as a sampler, not as a definitive retrospective. *—Stephen Thomas Erlewine*

The Avatar Collection Box Set / 2000 / ✦✦✦✦
The limited-edition four-CD box set *Avatar* was released in an edition of 2,000 copies via Pete Townshend's Eel Pie Studios and quickly sold through its run. Some of the material has been reissued in a double CD. It contains the three collaborative devotional projects he recorded between 1970 and 1976 that were dedicated to his Indian spiritual teacher Meher Baba who had passed away in 1969. The first of these albums, *Happy Birthday*, was issued before *Who Came First*. The other three CDs in the package include two subsequent albums, *I Am* and *With Love*, 1972 and 1974 respectively, and the final disc in the set, *O Parvardigar*, is an eight-minute film with footage from the life and teachings of Meher Baba—an Indian guru who, in 1925, decided that everything had already been said, and took a vow of silence until his death in 1969. There are also two booklets, one, *Still Bites*, with an essay by Townshend on the history of the projects and who was involved with them. The other contains numerous artworks inspired by his teachings by one of the world's most well-known illustrators, Mike McInnerney; they are juxtaposed with excerpts from Baba's *Discourses*. Little would be compelling in this set were it not for the legend and myth surrounding the music it contains. Bootleg copies of some of these recordings have sold for hundreds of dollars over the last 25 years or so, and few except for the most ardent Who fans have ever heard them. This is an indispensable item in Townshend's catalogue as it reveals him at his most unguarded, open, and creatively playful and unburdened by his own stature as the "spokesman for his generation." *—Thom Jurek*

Lifehouse Chronicles / 2000 / ✦✦✦✦
Lifehouse was a rock opera Pete Townshend worked on feverishly and then abandoned—due to outside tinkering and betrayal—between the issues of *Tommy* and *Quadrophenia*. According to legend, Townshend couldn't get anybody interested in his allegedly disjointed ideas. The truth was all wrapped up in music and film-biz politics. Townshend's *Lifehouse* was to be a rock opera all right, but it was to be a musical for screen with footage of the Who performing the story's soundtrack. This contradicted the ambitions of the Who's then-manager Kit Lambert, who wanted to make a film of *Tommy* by any means necessary—even without the approval and participation of Townshend—as his first feature, a project Townshend wanted nothing to do with. In short, according to Townshend, who had made contact with Universal about *Lifehouse*, Lambert made his own film, the disastrous *Tommy*, by derailing the *Lifehouse* project using his influence with people at the band's label and elsewhere by telling them the entire thing was too big and unruly for pop music, that *Lifehouse* was unworkable. The project was abandoned, but never let go of. The Who recorded a number of the songs for *Lifehouse*, produced by Glyn Johns, who talked them out of a concept album and into a strong pop album. Those sessions, minus the classic "Pure and Easy" also recorded then, resulted in the record *Who's Next*. *The Lifehouse Chronicles* are six CDs of all the material associated with the project, past and present, including the original demos for the songs Townshend planned to include as he was developing it. It is a bit of rock history that finally gets its proper hearing and as a result begs the question in capital letters, "What if?" *—Thom Jurek*

Toy Love

f. 1979, **db.** 1980

New Zealand Rock, New Wave, Punk

Toy Love was a New Zealand new wave band that grew out of the country's first punk band of note, the Enemy. And while their small number of recordings were pretty much by-the-numbers new wave pop with a few moments of inspiration, Toy Love (and especially their founding member Chris Knox) proved to be an important starting point for New Zealand's alternative rock scene of the '80s. The Enemy was formed in 1977 in Dunedin by singer/songwriter Chris Knox, guitarist Alex Bathgate, drummer Mike Dooley, and guitarist Chris Pendergast. The band built a cult following, playing gigs throughout 1978 in Dunedin and Christchurch—Knox's reputation for wild onstage antics (such as self-mutilation) drew much attention. But the band decided to call it quits by January of 1979. Remaining members Knox, Bathgate, and Dooley recruited keyboardist Jane Walker and bassist Paul Kean to complete the lineup for their new band, Toy Love. WEA New Zealand signed the band for a single, "Rebel"/"Squeeze," in July 1979. The single received a lot of critical attention in New Zealand and probably stands as their finest recorded moment. In 1980, they recorded another single, "Don't Ask Me," for the independent Deluxe. The band were received well in their homeland, but an attempt to break in Australia failed, and constant touring took its toll on the band. They recorded one self-titled album before internal disputes forced the band to break up in late 1980. Though an artistic failure for the most part, the album and the single, "Bride of Frankenstein," saw some moderate success in New Zealand. The band broke up shortly after the release. Knox went on to a successful solo career and (along with Bathgate) formed Tall Dwarves, Flying Nun Records' first recording act. Kean later joined the Bats. *—Chris Woodstra*

Toy Love / 1980 / WEA ♦♦♦

Toy Love's sole album was recorded at a low point for the band during a hectic touring schedule and a failed attempt to break out of New Zealand into Australia. Predictably, the album lacked much of the live energy for which the band had come to be known, turning out instead to be pretty standard new wave fare. Though it didn't properly showcase what the band was capable of, it did hint at Knox's potential as a songwriter, and it proved to be influential to the emerging alternative scene in New Zealand, providing the blueprint for much of that scene's unique sound—fractured, off-kilter garage-pop owing as much to the '60s as it does to punk. *—Chris Woodstra*

Toystore

Indie Pop, Twee Pop

Toystore was the alias of the enigmatic twee-popster Jenky, a notoriously reclusive figure about whom almost nothing is known. According to legend, his demo tapes arrived unsolicited on the doorstep of the tiny Michigan-based indie label Janeane Records sometime in early 1998, accompanied only by a letter reading "At the very most, please release my music; at the very least, please do not make fun of it." Subsequent attempts to trace the package's origins proved fruitless, but undaunted the label issued Toystore's debut album *Jazz for Twee* later that same year in a very limited edition of only 100 copies; a small but fervent cult following now eagerly awaits Jenky's next move. *—Jason Ankeny*

Jazz for Twee / Jul. 28, 1998 / Janeane ♦♦♦♦

Already the stuff of legend in hipster circles, Toystore's debut—limited to a ridiculously small pressing of just 100 copies—clearly deserves a wider audience: main man Jenky is a compelling (albeit often unnerving) songwriter with a knack for sparkling pop hooks which shine even through the disc's no-fi production and Fisher-Price instrumentation. Although *Jazz for Twee*'s scant liner notes offer no insights into the Jenky enigma, the songs themselves reveal a confused and often disturbing personality lurking beneath the buoyant melodies—his obsession with "Girls Who Wear Glasses" borders on the pathological, and the food-and-sex metaphors of "Snickers Lips," "Frances Bacon" and "100% Cotton Candy" are all exceedingly kinky. Ultimately, however, it's the record's stark confessionalism which allows it to transcend its cuddle-core trappings—not merely twee-pop's darkest hour, it's also one of the genre's finest, and here's hoping Jenky graces us with his creepy genius once again. *—Jason Ankeny*

Trader Horne

Folk-Rock

One of the most interesting one-shots of the early '70s, this duo featured Irish multi-instrumentalist Jackie McAuley, who was responsible for some of those great organ lines on Them's early records, and Judy Dyble, who sang on Fairport Convention's first album before being replaced by Sandy Denny in 1968. Their sole LP, *Morning Way*, is nice if slightly precious British folk-rock with an Olde-English, fairy-tale air, and will appeal to fans of the early work of both Donovan and Fairport. *—Richie Unterberger*

● **Morning Way** / 1970 / Janus ♦♦♦♦♦

Jackie McAuley's original material dominates the group's only album (Judy Dyble also wrote or co-wrote a couple tunes), a nifty bit of British folk-rock with both traditional and pop influences. A British CD reissue adds a few bonus tracks. *—Richie Unterberger*

Traffic

f. 1967, Midlands, England, **db.** 1975

British Psychedelia, Album Rock, Jazz-Rock, Folk-Rock, Psychedelic, Prog-Rock/Art Rock, Blues-Rock

Though it ultimately must be considered an interim vehicle for singer/songwriter/keyboardist/guitarist Steve Winwood, Traffic was a successful group that followed its own individual course through the rock music scene of the late '60s and early '70s. At a time when electric guitars ruled rock, Traffic emphasized Winwood's organ and the reed instruments played by Chris Wood, especially flute. After Dave Mason, who had provided the band with an alternate folk-pop sound, departed for good, Traffic leaned toward extended songs that gave its players room to improvise in a jazz-like manner, even as the rhythms maintained a rock structure. The result was international success that ended only when Winwood finally decided he was ready to strike out on his own.

Traffic debuted in 1967 with *Mr. Fantasy*, a Top Ten hit. Though Mason left after its release, he later rejoined and contributed heavily to the band's second album, *Traffic*. After a temporary breakup, Winwood began work on a solo record in 1970, but quickly brought in Capaldi and Wood and turned it into the Traffic LP *John Barleycorn Must Die*. Traffic followed with 1971's *The Low Spark of High Heeled Boys*, which reached the American Top Ten, though it didn't even chart back home in Britain. *Shoot Out at the Fantasy Factory*, released in January 1973, also reached the American Top Ten. At the conclusion of a support tour for 1974's *When the Eagle Flies*, Traffic silently disbanded. In 1994, Winwood announced a reunion with Capaldi (Wood had died of liver failure). The two made a new album, *Far From Home*, and toured as Traffic during the summer. Though the album did not sell well, the 1967-1974 era band continued to enjoy significant status as a classic rock act, its albums earning CD reissues along with the release of compilations like *Smiling Phases* (1991) and *Feelin' Alright: The Very Best of Traffic* (2000). *—William Ruhlmann*

Mr. Fantasy / Dec. 1967 / Island ♦♦♦

Since Traffic's debut album *Mr. Fantasy* has been issued in different configurations over the years, a history of those differences is in order. In 1967, the British record industry considered albums and singles separate entities; thus, *Mr. Fantasy* did not contain the group's three previous Top Ten U.K. hits. Just as the album was being released in the U.K., Traffic split from Dave Mason. The album was changed drastically for U.S. release, both because American custom was that singles ought to appear on albums, and because the group sought to diminish Mason's presence; on the first pressing only, the title was changed to *Heaven Is in Your Mind*. In 2000, Island reissued *Mr. Fantasy* in its mono mix with the U.K. song list and five mono singles sides as bonus tracks; it also released *Heaven Is in Your Mind*, the American lineup in stereo with four bonus tracks. Naturally, the mono sound is punchier and more compressed, but it isn't ideal for the album, because Traffic was fashioned as an unusual rock band. Steve Winwood's primary instrument was organ, though he also played guitar; Chris Wood was a reed player, spending most of his time on flute; Mason played guitar, but he was also known to pick up the sitar, among other instruments. As such a mixture suggests, the band's musical approach was eclectic, combining their background in British pop with a taste for the comic and dance-hall styles of *Sgt. Pepper*, Indian music, and blues-rock jamming. Songs in the last category have proven the most distinctive and long-lasting, but Mason's more pop-oriented contributions remain winning, as do more light-hearted efforts. Interest in the mono mix is likely to be restricted to longtime fans; anyone wishing to hear Traffic's first album for the first time is directed to *Heaven Is in Your Mind*. *—William Ruhlmann*

★ **Traffic** / Feb. 1968 / Island ♦♦♦♦♦

After dispensing with his services in December 1967, the remaining members of Traffic reinstated Dave Mason in the group in the spring of 1968 as they struggled to write enough material for their impending second album. The result was a disc evenly divided between Mason's catchy folk-rock compositions and Steve Winwood's compelling rock jams. Mason's material was the most appealing both initially and eventually: the lead-off track, a jaunty effort called "You Can All Join In," became a European hit, and "Feelin' Alright?" turned out to be the only real standard to emerge from the album after it started earning cover versions from Joe Cocker and others in the 1970s. Winwood's efforts, with their haunting keyboard-based melodies augmented by Chris Wood's reed work and Jim Capaldi's exotic rhythms, work better as musical efforts than lyrical ones. Primary lyricist Capaldi's words tend to be impressionistic reveries or vague psychological reflections; the most satisfying is the shaggy-dog story "Forty Thousand Headmen," which doesn't really make any sense as anything other than a dream. But the lyrics to Winwood/Capaldi compositions take a back seat to the playing and Winwood's soulful voice. As Mason's simpler, more direct performances alternate with the more complex Winwood tunes, the album is well-balanced. It's too bad that the musicians were not able to maintain that balance in person; for the second time in two albums, Mason found himself dismissed from the group just as an LP to which he'd made a major contribution hit the stores. Only a few months after that, the band itself split up, but not before scoring their second consecutive Top Ten ranking in the U.K.; the album also reached the Top 20 in the U.S., breaking the temporarily defunct group stateside. *—William Ruhlmann*

Heaven Is in Your Mind / 1969 / Island ♦♦♦♦♦

In January 1968, United Artists Records released a reconfigured American version of Traffic's debut album *Mr. Fantasy* under the new title *Heaven Is in Your Mind*, but after the first pressing reverted to calling it *Mr. Fantasy*. In 2000, Island reissued two CD versions, one titled *Mr. Fantasy* containing the British track listing in mono, the other titled *Heaven Is in Your Mind* with the U.S. track listing in stereo. Both albums contained bonus tracks, making their contents similar (but not quite identical). Actually, the album originally called *Heaven Is in Your Mind* was the superior version even before this development brought the two editions into stark comparison, since the changes actually improved the record by adding strong singles. But just as important as the substitutions was the sequencing, which banished the British-flavored novelty songs to the middle of Side Two; "Dear Mr. Fantasy," which would turn out to be the best-remembered song on the album, was moved to a climactic position as the penultimate cut on Side Two. The result de-emphasized Traffic's pop-psychedelic style (a hangover from the influence of *Sgt. Pepper*) and promoted its abilities as a jamming blues-rock outfit, talents that were abetted by Jimmy Miller's production and that helped launch them as an album act in the U.S. The 2000 reissue includes as bonus tracks the two deleted Dave Mason songs and two songs from the *Here We Go 'Round the Mulberry Bush* soundtrack. Island's decision to reissue both versions could easily confuse consumers; the U.S. stereo version, once again known as *Heaven Is in Your Mind*, is really the one to own if you're only buying one. *—William Ruhlmann*

Last Exit / Jan. 1969 / Island ♦♦♦

Since Traffic originally planned its self-titled second album as a double LP, the group had extra material left over, some of which saw release before the end of 1968 (there was a new, one-off single released in December, "Medicated Goo"/"Shanghai Noodle Factory"). In January 1969, Steve Winwood announced the group's breakup. That left Island Records, the band's label, in the lurch, since Traffic had built up a considerable following. As far as Island was concerned, it was no time to stop, and the label quickly set about assembling a new album. The non-LP B-side "Withering Tree," "Medicated Goo," and "Shanghai Noodle Factory" were pressed into service, along with "Just for You," the B-side of a solo single by on-again, off-again member Dave Mason that had been released originally in February 1968 and happened to feature the rest of the members of Traffic as sidemen; a short, previously unreleased instrumental; and two extended jams on cover songs from a 1968 live appearance at the Fillmore West. It all added up to more than half an hour of music, and that was enough to package it as the posthumous Traffic album *Last Exit*. Actually, *Last Exit* isn't bad as profit-taking products go. "Just for You" is one of Mason's elegant folk-pop songs, including attractive Indian percussion. "Medicated Goo" has proven to be one of Traffic's more memorable jam tunes, despite its nonsense lyrics, and the equally appealing "Shanghai Noodle Factory" is hard not to interpret as Winwood's explanation of the band's split. And while the cover material seems unlikely, the songs are used as platforms for the band to jam cohesively. So, Traffic's third album, thought at the time of its release to be the final one, has its isolated pleasures, even if it doesn't measure up to its two predecessors. *—William Ruhlmann*

John Barleycorn Must Die / Jan. 1970 / Island ♦♦♦♦♦

At only 22 years old, Steve Winwood sat down in early 1970 to fulfill a contractual commitment by making his first solo album, on which he intended to play all the instruments himself. The record got as far as one backing track produced by Guy Stevens, "Stranger to Himself," before Winwood called his erstwhile partner from Traffic, Jim Capaldi, in to help out. The two completed a second track, "Every Mother's Son," then, with Winwood and Island Records chief Chris Blackwell moving to the production chores, brought in a third Traffic member, Chris Wood, to work on the sessions. Thus, Traffic, dead and buried for more than a year, was reborn. The band's new approach was closer to what it perhaps should have been back in 1967, basically a showcase for Winwood's voice and instrumental work, with Wood adding reed parts and Capaldi drumming and occasionally singing harmony vocals. If the original Traffic bowed to the perceived commercial necessity of crafting hit singles, the new Traffic was more interested in stretching out. Heretofore, no studio recording had run longer than the 5 1/2 minutes of "Dear Mr. Fantasy," but four of the six selections on *John Barleycorn Must Die* exceeded six minutes. Winwood and company used the time to play extended instrumental variations on compelling folk- and jazz-derived riffs. Five of the six songs had lyrics, and their tone of disaffection was typical of earlier Capaldi sentiments. But the vocal sections of the songs merely served as excuses for Winwood to exercise his expressive voice as punctuation to the extended instrumental sections. As such, *John Barleycorn Must Die* moved beyond the jamming that had characterized some of Traffic's 1968 work to approach the emerging field of jazz-rock. And that helped the band to achieve its commercial potential; this became Traffic's first gold album. *—William Ruhlmann*

Welcome to the Canteen / 1971 / Island ♦♦♦♦

Following the success of *John Barleycorn Must Die*, Traffic planned a concert album for the fall of 1970, and it got as far as a test pressing before being canceled. A recording was necessary to satisfy the terms of British label Island Records' licensing deal with American label United Artists, which had provided for five albums, of which four had been delivered. With Island starting to release its own albums in the U.S., the UA contract had to be completed, and hopefully not with the potentially lucrative studio follow-up to *John Barleycorn Must Die*. Thus, Traffic tried again to come up with a live album by recording shows on a British tour in July 1971. Joining for six dates of the tour was twice-dismissed Traffic singer/guitarist Dave Mason, who had subsequently scored a solo success with his *Alone Together* album. The resulting album, *Welcome to the Canteen* (which was technically credited to the seven individual musicians, not to Traffic), proved how good a contractual obligation album could be. Recording quality was not the best, with the vocals under-mixed and stray sounds horning in, but the playing was exemplary, and the set list an excellent mixture of old Traffic songs and recent Mason favorites. "Dear Mr. Fantasy" got an extended workout, and the capper was a rearranged version of Steve Winwood's old Spencer Davis Group hit "Gimme Some Lovin'." *Welcome to the Canteen*'s status as only a semi-legitimate offering was emphasized by the release, after a mere two months, of a new Traffic studio album on Island (*The Low Spark of High Heeled Boys*) that undercut its sales. But that doesn't make it any less appealing as a summing up of the Winwood/Mason/Traffic musical world. *—William Ruhlmann*

The Low Spark of High Heeled Boys / 1971 / Island ♦♦♦♦♦

The Low Spark of High Heeled Boys marked the commercial and artistic apex of the second coming of Traffic, which had commenced in 1970 with *John Barleycorn Must Die*. The trio that made that album had been augmented by three others (Ric Grech, Jim Gordon, and "Reebop" Kwaku Baah) in the interim, though apparently the *Low Spark* sessions featured varying combinations of these musicians, plus some guests. But where their previous album had grown out of sessions for a Steve Winwood solo album and retained that focus, *Low Spark* pointedly contained changes of pace from his usual contributions of midtempo, introspective jam tunes. "Rock & Roll Stew" was an uptempo treatise on life on the road, while Jim Capaldi's "Light up or Leave Me Alone" was another more aggressive number with an unusually emphatic Capaldi vocal that perked things up on side two. The other four tracks were Winwood/Capaldi compositions more in the band's familiar style. "Hidden Treasure" and "Rainmaker" bookended the disc with acoustic treatments of nature themes that were particularly concerned with water, and "Many a Mile to Freedom" also employed water imagery. But the standout was the 12-minute title track, with its distinctive piano riff and its lyrics of weary disillusionment with the music business. The band had only just fulfilled a contractual commitment by releasing the live album *Welcome to the Canteen*, and they had in their past the embarrassing *Last Exit* album thrown together as a commercial stopgap during a temporary breakup in 1969. But that anger had proven inspirational, and "The Low Spark of High Heeled Boys" was one of Traffic's greatest songs as well as its longest so far. The result was an album that quickly went gold (and eventually platinum) in the U.S., where the group toured frequently. *—William Ruhlmann*

Shoot Out at the Fantasy Factory / 1973 / Island ♦♦♦

After two exemplary releases, *Shoot Out at the Fantasy Factory* marked a fall-off in quality for Traffic. The problems lay in both composition and performance. Beginning with the title track, based on a guitar riff reminiscent of the recent Deep Purple hit "Smoke on the Water," and continuing through the lengthy "Roll Right Stones," the folkish ballad "Evening Blue," reed player Chris Wood's instrumental "Tragic Magic," and the uncertain self-help song "(Sometimes I Feel So) Uninspired," the material was far from the group's best. Lyricist Jim Capaldi was co-credited with Steve Winwood as the album's producer, and he may have contributed to the cleaner mix that made his words easier to understand. Easier, that is, in the technical sense, since the musing about a sort of minor-league Stonehenge "Roll Right Stones" didn't do much with the image, and, though it struggled for a more positive outlook, "(Sometimes I Feel So) Uninspired" seemed to come out on the side of despair. Winwood's music seemed to recycle his own ideas when it didn't borrow from others. Meanwhile, the rhythm section had been replaced by Muscle Shoals studio aces David Hood and Roger Hawkins, who proved proficient but not as kinetic as their predecessors, so that the playing often seemed mechanical. Capaldi sang no songs here, and Wood's flute and saxophone, so often the flavoring of Traffic songs, were largely absent. What was left was a competent, if perfunctory effort in the band's familiar style. They had built up enough of a following through touring that the album was a commercial success, but it sounds like an imitation of earlier triumphs. *—William Ruhlmann*

Traffic: On the Road / 1973 / Island ♦♦♦

Reportedly released as an effort to undercut bootleggers following a world tour, *Traffic: On the Road* was the band's second live album in three years. The album chronicled a late edition of the band in which original members Steve Winwood, Jim Capaldi, and Chris Wood were augmented not only by percussionist Reebop Kwaku Baah, but also by a trio of session musicians from the famed Muscle Shoals studio, Roger Hawkins, David Hood, and Barry Beckett. The studio pros lent a tightness and proficiency to their characteristic free-form jams, and though they sometimes sounded like they couldn't wait to get the songs over with, the tunes went on and on, four clocking in at over ten minutes. That might have been okay if the choice of material had been more balanced across the band's career, but 1971's *Welcome to the Canteen* had treated earlier efforts, and the 1973 tour was promoting *Shoot out at the Fantasy Factory*, from which three of the six selections were drawn. Unfortunately, that album was not one of Traffic's best, and the live versions of its songs were no more impressive than the studio ones had been. *Traffic: On the Road* featured plenty of room for soloing by some good musicians, but it was the logical extreme of the band's forays into extended performance, with single tunes taking up entire sides on the original LPs. It's not surprising that, after this, Traffic shrunk in size and returned to shorter songs. [Though best known in its two-LP version, *Traffic: On the Road* was initially released in the U.S. as a single LP containing only four tracks.] *—William Ruhlmann*

When the Eagle Flies / 1974 / Island ♦♦♦

In its second manifestation, Traffic displayed an affection for jazz-like improvisation over shuffling rhythms, and that tendency was never more indulged than on *When the Eagle Flies*. Having dispensed with the trio of session musicians who had accompanied them on tour, the remaining band members, led by Steve Winwood, jammed over long-lined musical structures. Still, this was nominally a rock album, with lyrics and vocals, and Winwood often seemed to be improvising his melodies over the music, paying little heed to the meaning of the words, especially on the title track. Jim Capaldi's lyrics touched on the ups and downs of romance and the vicissitudes of capitalism and politics, and warning of apocalypse. But he sounded most assured reflecting on his past and future in "Memories of a Rock & Rolla." The most intriguing lyric was a blank-verse effort from the Bonzo Dog Band's Vivian Stanshall, "Dream Gerrard," which took off from 19th-century French poet Gérard de Nerval's speculations about the relationship between dreams and reality. But Winwood treated the words and his singing as another musical element rather than fashioning the songs to emphasize them, so that *When the Eagle Flies*, not unlike previous Traffic albums, was really a mostly instrumental collection that happened to have vocals. That wouldn't have mattered if the music had been more compelling and effectively played, but rather than seeming like a fresh start for the band, the album was listless and remote. Although it became Traffic's fourth consecutive studio album to reach the Top Ten and go gold in the U.S., the group broke up following the American promotional tour in the fall of 1974. *—William Ruhlmann*

Smiling Phases / Nov. 19, 1991 / Island ♦♦♦♦♦

During their tumultuous existence between 1967 and 1974, Traffic had two distinct phases separated by a year (January 1969 to February 1970) during which the band was temporarily dissolved. In its first phase, Traffic was heavily influenced by the pop psychedelia of its time, but were also developing a distinctive blues-rock jam style. When Steve Winwood reconvened the group in 1970 without Dave Mason, he was ready to take the spotlight more forcefully, and Traffic evolved into a band that played long, largely instrumental songs. In constructing a two-CD retrospective of Traffic, compiler Kevin Patrick has taken the obvious step of devoting disc one to the early phase of Traffic and disc two to the later one. He faces different challenges in selecting tracks for each disc. The first CD is necessarily diverse; the early singles must be included, and so must some of Dave Mason's material, though his songs tend to sound more like solo tracks. The challenge for disc two is simply that the songs from 1970-1974 tend to be so long, and it's difficult to decide which ones to include. Patrick has met both of these challenges admirably. Though both discs are a bit short by CD standards, running a little over an hour each, there are few significant tracks that are missing. On disc two, Patrick has striven to be fair to the later Traffic albums, even though they are not as good as their predecessors from this phase, but he strikes a reasonable balance. Until 1991, Traffic had had no more than a few single-disc compilations, the most readily available being *The Best of Traffic*, which contained nothing from the group's later period. So, *Smiling Phases* was a welcome addition to the catalog, with solid selection and sequencing. *—William Ruhlmann*

Far from Home / May 3, 1994 / Virgin ✦✦✦
It could be argued that, in its most basic form, Traffic was a vehicle for the songs of Steve Winwood and Jim Capaldi, who wrote most of the material and on some tracks were the only musicians performing. But the question of whether Winwood and Capaldi could validly constitute Traffic by themselves was not addressed until 1994, 20 years after the group disbanded, when the two surprisingly announced they would be recording and touring under their old band name. The album they made together sounded for the most part like a Winwood solo album. He played most of the instruments and sang (Capaldi drummed and sang occasional backup vocals), and he didn't show much interest in the lengthy instrumental passages that characterized Traffic in its heyday. Winwood, the composer, had simply moved on from that old style, and since the new Traffic wasn't a band in any real sense, its sound reflected his contemporary concerns. But if you listened to the lyrics, written by Capaldi, you did hear traces of the old Traffic. Granted, lyrics were not among Traffic's strong suits, but Capaldi, in his sometimes roundabout way, did have certain continuing concerns—a generalized sense of spirituality, a tendency to give advice, and a rejection of the negative aspects of modern society. Winwood may have wished to return to music of greater substance, and if so, he got what he wanted; *Far from Home* certainly explored weightier topics than a Steve Winwood album. But Capaldi hadn't really improved as a writer over the years, and the final product still worked better musically than lyrically, and, to most ears, didn't really sound like a Traffic album. The resulting confusion kept the album from having much commercial impact. *—William Ruhlmann*

● **Feelin' Alright: The Very Best of Traffic** / Feb. 8, 2000 / Island ✦✦✦✦✦
Though the two-CD set *Smiling Phases* finally put a comprehensive Traffic compilation on the market in 1991, the only readily available single-disc collection had long been *Best of Traffic*, originally issued halfway through the band's career. Thus, *Feelin' Alright: The Very Best of Traffic*, a 77-minute sampler for the CD era, was long overdue. It combines the group's early singles hits like "Paper Sun" and "Hole in My Shoe" with lengthier album tracks like "Dear Mr. Fantasy" and "The Low Spark of High-Heeled Boys." Looking over the song list, any Traffic fan will be able to reel off omissions. But easy as it is to note what's missing, it's not so easy to figure out how such songs could be shoehorned into a single-disc set that is already packed with great material. Except in its first year in England, Traffic was not a band that made hit singles, but it did make a plethora of strong recordings, many of which were lengthy by the standards of the time. Several of the absolute necessities on a collection of their best work run longer than five minutes each; "The Low Spark of High-Heeled Boys" runs close to 12 minutes. Beyond those absolute musts are a bunch of other good songs, many more than could fit on one CD. Compilation producer Bill Levenson has made a reasonable choice among them to construct a well-balanced disc that shows off the band's many talents. Neophytes with a few extra dollars to spend are strongly urged to take the plunge and buy *Smiling Phases*, but as a one-CD collection of some of the highlights of Traffic's career, this album lives up to its title. *—William Ruhlmann*

Traffic Sound

f. 1968, **db.** 1972
Psychedelic, Prog-Rock/Art Rock
A popular Peruvian rock group in the late 1960s and early 1970s, Traffic Sound had a very British-influenced early progressive rock sound along the lines of Traffic and (more distantly) Jethro Tull. These similarities were evident in the band's use of flute and saxes, all played by Jean Pierre Magnet, who could also play vibes and percussion. What is surprising is that Traffic Sound, unlike other South American groups of the period that only came to light in the Northern Hemisphere in the 1990s, do not sound exotic or primitive. They simply sound like an accomplished minor-league 1970 rock band with considerable progressive, psychedelic, and soul influences informing their original material. There's a Latin feel to some of the rhythmic percussive grooves, sure, but no more, really, than you would find in a cut like Traffic's "Feelin' Alright." They disbanded in 1972 after four albums; some of their material found US release in 1997. *—Richie Unterberger*

Traffic Sound / 1970 / Lazarus Audio ✦✦✦✦

Lux / 1971 / Lazarus Audio ✦✦✦

● **Tibet's Suzettes** / 1997 / Lazarus Audio ✦✦✦✦
There's no solid information in the liner notes as to when the ten songs on this disc were originally released, although at least a couple of them, "Chicama Way" and "Tibet's Suzettes," are from their third album, *Traffic Sound* (1970). All of the material certainly does have a 1970 feel, and they sound like nothing so much as a good warm-up act for, say, Joe Cocker or Santana had they been able to tour in the Northern Hemisphere, with their soul-rock feel. Occasional bursts of jazzy flute indicate that they were probably fans of early Jethro Tull. Great typo in the liner notes: "In *1969* they recorded their second LP, *Virgin*, perhaps the finest rock album made in South America in the *seventies*." *—Richie Unterberger*

The Trammps

f. 1973, Philadelphia, PA, **db.** 1980
Disco, Soul
Disco's most soulful vocal group, the Trammps began in the '60s as the Volcanos, and were also called the Moods. A snappy revival of Judy Garland's '40s tune "Zing Went the Strings of My Heart" was their first chart single, reaching number 17 on the R&B list in 1972. Despite their well-deserved reputation and boisterous, jubilant harmonies and sound, the Trammps were never huge commercial successes even during disco's heyday. Indeed, they had only three R&B Top Ten hits from 1972 through 1978, and such wonderful records as "Soul Bones," "Ninety-Nine and a Half," and "I Feel Like I've Been Livin' (On the Dark Side of the Moon)" stiffed on the charts though they were beloved by club audiences and R&B fans alike. Their only huge hit was "Disco Inferno" in 1977, which was a number nine R&B single in 1977 and was also featured in *Saturday Night Fever*. Yet it missed the pop Top Ten, peaking at number 11. But the Trammps' prowess can't be measured by chart popularity; Jimmy Ellis' booming, joyous vocals brilliantly championed the celebratory fervor and atmosphere that made disco both beloved and hated among music fans. *—Ron Wynn*

● **This Is Where the Happy People Go: The Best of the Trammps** / 1994 / Rhino ✦✦✦✦✦
Due to all the great funk, R&B, and soul bands of the '70s, it's easy to overlook many of the lesser-known (but just as great) bands. Such is the case with the Trammps. Best known for their smash hit from the *Saturday Night Fever* Soundtrack, "Disco Inferno" (their only Top 20 appearance on the pop charts), the group had many other hits on the R&B charts, which were just as deserving of crossover success. Just about any track from the excellent *This Is Where All the Happy People Go: The Best of the Trammps* compilation is a solid example of '70s R&B at its finest and most expertly crafted. Many overlooked and forgotten gems reside here, such as "Hold Back the Night," "Trammps Disco Theme," "That's Where the Happy People Go," and "Zing Went the Strings of My Heart." Admittedly, the Trammps did seem to jump on the disco bandwagon, like so many other bands from this era, but the quality of the music never suffered. For a representation of some of the finest music the '70s had to offer, *The Best of the Trammps* simply can't be beat. *—Greg Prato*

Trans Am

f. 1990, Washington, DC
Experimental Rock, Indie Rock, Post-Rock/Experimental
Trans Am are loosely associated with the mid-'90s "post-rock" scene centered around Tortoise, Ui, Labradford, and Windy & Carl, among others, and the Thrill Jockey, Kranky, UHF, and Southern labels, among others. Although a vast distance separates Trans Am's albums, all of them are concerned with an extreme, somewhat humorous reorientation of the clichés and conventions of rock music, primarily through either technical (exaggerated displays of skill) or instrumental (electronics, effects) deviation. Formed in Washington, D.C., in 1990, the group didn't begin seriously recording until 1995, after its members (Phil Manley, Nathan Means, and Sebastian Thompson) finished college. Their self-titled debut, on the Chicago-based Thrill Jockey label, contained instrumental, largely improvised versions of simple rock-oriented figures based loosely (and, again, quite humorously) on '70s and '80s popular and progressive bands such as Boston, Bachman-Turner Overdrive, and Yes. Produced by Tortoise's John McEntire at Chicago's Idful Studios, the album was instantly (if somewhat ironically) lauded as an example of "post-rock," in turn leading to a short live tour as Tortoise's opening act. The group returned in the fall of 1996 with a self-titled EP of somewhat retro electro-funk experiments that brought to the fore an affectation for electronics previously reserved either for between-time studio distraction or the brief interludes separating the meatier segments of their debut. With 1997's *Surrender to the Night*, however, Trans Am expanded that approach to album length, with inadvertent tributes to Kraftwerk, Hashim, Can, and New Order dominating and only a few recognizably "rock" songs included. Also signaling a change in focus was the expanded role electronics would play in their live performances. Fourth album *Futureworld* followed in 1999, and a year later, the group returned with their most expansive album yet, *The Red Line*, which the group recorded in their own National Recording Studio. *—Sean Cooper*

● **Trans Am** / Jan. 30, 1996 / Thrill Jockey ✦✦✦✦✦
Trans Am play mostly Big Dumb Rock (of the tongue-in-cheek variety) on their Thrill Jockey debut, trading Boston and Foreigner licks with a talent for technique and not a little ironic displacement. Absent the irony this would be an absolutely horrendous record, but kept in mind it's an enjoyable, if somewhat expendable listen. *—Sean Cooper*

Surrender to the Night / Feb. 3, 1997 / Thrill Jockey ✦✦✦
Trans Am prove in one mildly amusing, backward-turned sitting that much of what defines "post-rock" sounds suspiciously like rock's longtime nemesis, the late-'70s pre-techno Euro-pop of Kraftwerk and New Order. With much of this record a simple meditation on the latter, *Surrender to the Night* is surprisingly slim on new ideas, sounding for the most part either like a self-defacing gambit or an updater course for those who missed

it the first time around. The group is at its best when they stumble onto the occasional square foot of new territory (as on "Cologne," "Tough Love," and the title cut, all of which wed live, more immediately rock-based instrumentation with electro-funk rhythms and synth figures), but much of *Surrender* lays on familiar, by now somewhat fallow soil. —*Sean Cooper*

The Surveillance / Mar. 10, 1998 / Thrill Jockey ✦✦✦✦
True artists find a voice and know how far they can stretch its ability to communicate. Trans Am have done just that with instrumental rock which relies on synthesizers almost as much as techno does. They can be at one moment abrasively digital, then quietly ambient by the end of the track. Such vacillation could be overly ambitious for many groups, but Trans Am manages to pull it off in a way that makes you think the song could have gone nowhere else. By working a contrasting harsh delivery and tranquil coda into a single piece naturally, Trans Am prove themselves deft masters of their craft. —*Thomas Schulte*

Futureworld / Mar. 23, 1999 / Thrill Jockey ✦✦✦✦
Trans Am's 1999 release, *Futureworld*, showcases the band's love of retro-futurism and above all, rock. Songs like "Television Eyes" and "City in Flames" feature a churning mix of drums, guitars and budget keyboards, giving the lie to Trans Am's "post-rock" label. More than anything, *Futureworld* is drummer Sebastian Thompson's album—his work on acoustic, electric and programmed drums propels the music, particularly on the Teutonic "AM Rhein." As the album progresses, however, it becomes increasingly melodic and keyboard-driven, as the relatively gentle "Runners Standing Still" and "Sad and Young" attest. Throw in the poppy title track and "Cocaine Computers"' sleazy, uptight disco, and the result is *Futureworld*, Trans Am's most diverse and accomplished work yet. —*Heather Phares*

You Can Always Get What You Want / May 2, 2000 / Thrill Jockey ✦✦✦
The Japanese collection *You Can Always Get What You Want* gathers 17 of Trans Am's singles, radio appearances, and B-sides, ranging from early tracks like "Man Machine" and "American Kooter" to *Futureworld*-era material. From the full-on, un-ironic rock of "Strong Sensations" to sparse tracks like "Illegal Ass" and the goofy sci-fi send-up "Now You Die, Thriddle Fool," the collection spans Trans Am's range. As a condensed timeline of the band's sound or a remedial course for fans who missed out on these singles the first time, this collection proves that *You Can Always Get What You Want.* —*Heather Phares*

The Red Line / Sep. 5, 2000 / Thrill Jockey ✦✦✦✦✦
Ranging from stripped-down percussion pieces to menacing electro/Krautrock to nimble, acoustic melodies, Trans Am's sprawling *The Red Line* encompasses all of the group's previous musical territory and stakes a few new claims. Though "Polizei (Zu Spat)" and "I Want It All," with their swarming synths and processed vocals, could have appeared on the group's earlier albums, the untreated singing on poppy songs like "Play in the Summer," "I'm Coming Down," and "Slow Response" is a first, and a welcome surprise. Mixed in are reflective pieces like "Village in Bubbles" and "Now and Forever," which recall the guitar atmospherics of Trans Am's early days, and minimal, completely electronic tracks such as "Talk You All Tight" and "Lunar Landing."

Best of all is the album's centerpiece, "The Dark Gift," which begins with subtle acoustic guitars, explodes in a sonic maelstrom, and then gallops away on an intricate yet propulsive synth and guitar counterpoint. On paper it might sound self-indulgent, but it anchors *The Red Line* and condenses its diversity into one piece. Likewise, the final track "Shady Groove" transforms from synth meanderings to a ferocious, sax and drums workout that cuts off abruptly, as if choked by its own momentum.

Even with all of the album's eclecticism, *The Red Line* doesn't forget Trans Am's sense of humor, as song titles like "Where Do You Want to Fuck Today?" and "Don't Bundle Me" prove. The guitar heroics on "Bad Cat" and "Ragged Agenda"'s impersonation of Suicide on speed and steroids reaffirm that the band can rock out in many different ways and still sound focused. At 21 wide-ranging tracks long, *The Red Line* is one of Trans Am's most impressive albums, but it's not their most immediately accessible one. However, after a few listenings, *The Red Line* reveals its full scope as an ambitious, diverse work from a group that never stands still. —*Heather Phares*

Translator

f. 1979, **db**. 1986
New Wave
Inspired by the Beatles, the four-piece Translator featured the talents of two singer/songwriters, Steve Barton (guitar) and Bob Darlington (guitar), and a sound that spanned Merseybeat to psychedelia. Formed in Los Angeles in 1979, the band relocated to San Francisco and were swiftly signed to Howie Klein's independent label, 415 Records, on the strength of their demo version of "Everywhere That I'm Not," the song that would remain the band's signature tune. *Heartbeats and Triggers* was a college-radio hit, but their second album, 1983's *No Time Like Now* didn't fare as well. The band was struggling to break away from the tight new wave formula and started to on their lush, third album from 1985, simply titled *Translator*. As the decade wore on, the band became increasingly interested in exploring psychedelia, and their live shows were often three-hour affairs that included lots of jamming. Their final album, *Evening of the Harvest* (1986), was the sound of a band that had matured and was their most realized statement. It was also the sound of a discontented band falling apart. —*Denise Sullivan*

Heartbeats and Triggers / 1982 / 415 ✦✦✦
The band's signature song, "Everywhere That I'm Not," a sweet slice of new wave guitar pop mourning the loss of John Lennon, is included here, along with nine other tracks that simultaneously celebrate love and alienation; naturally, it was critically embraced during the post-punk era. The recording is a completely apt portrayal of the San Francisco guitar

band sound from the era—shrouded in darkness and masked with a perky new wave drum sound. —*Denise Sullivan*

No Time Like Now / 1983 / CBS ✦✦✦
Translator took the new wave formula too far on this one, though "No Time Like Now" and "Un-Alone," ring through with the sound of chiming guitars, inspired by the Byrds, Beatles and the young R.E.M. —*Denise Sullivan*

Translator / 1985 / 415/Columbia ✦✦✦
Translator got the essential ingredients (solid songwriting, impeccable musicianship) back together on this one. "Fall Forever" and "Heaven By a String" are simply beautiful; "Another American Night" proves the guys can rock while taking on topical subjects, and "O Lazarus" became a fan favorite. Although it is unable to pass the blindfold test as to whether it was recorded in the '80s (clearly it was!), Ed Stasium's crisp production was a step in the right direction. —*Denise Sullivan*

Evening of the Harvest / 1986 / 415/Columbia ✦✦✦✦
Psychedelia, blues, folk and pop come home to roost on Translator's swan song. Finally finding their strength as a live band with supreme musicianship, this record comes closest to capturing what Translator really were: a great rock band that would have been recognized for the ages had their heyday not been during the early to mid-'80s. Sadly, because their three previous recordings were mostly unheralded, the band's demise was imminent upon this release. —*Denise Sullivan*

Translation / Aug. 15, 1995 / Oglio ✦✦✦
The adequete career compilation *Translation* includes beauties like the cover of the Jefferson Airplane's "Today" and the original "These Old Days," both culled from the brilliant *Evening of the Harvest* album. —*Denise Sullivan*

● **Everywhere That We Were: The Best of Translator** / Mar. 26, 1996 / Columbia/Legacy ✦✦✦✦✦
The Legacy collection is preferable to the *Translation* retrospective since it contains four more songs for the money, including the rare B-side and Beatles instrumental, "Cry For A Shadow," and the strident "When I Am With You" from *Heartbeats and Triggers*. Seek out *Evening of the Harvest* in addition to *Everywhere That We Were* and you'll have a fairly complete translation. —*Denise Sullivan*

The Trashmen

f. 1962, Minneapolis, MN, **db**. 1967
Frat Rock, Garage Rock, Surf, Rock & Roll
A Minneapolis rock & roll band, they evolved from Jim Thaxter & the Travelers, recording one single under that name ("Sally Jo"/"Cyclone"). The group comprises Tony Andreason (lead guitar), Dan Winslow (guitar/ vocals), Bob Reed (bass), and Steve Wahrer (drums/vocals). Unfairly depicted as a novelty act, the Trashmen were in actuality a top-notch rock & roll combo, enormously popular on the teen-club circuit, playing primarily surf music to a landlocked Minnesota audience. Drummer Steve Wahrer combined two songs by the Rivingtons ("The Bird's the Word" and "Pa Pa Ooh Mow Mow"), added freakish vocal effects and a pounding rhythm to the mix, and, by early 1964, the group was in the Top Ten nationwide with "Surfin' Bird." Though the group continued to release great follow-up singles and an excellent album, their moment in the sun had come and gone; they disbanded by late 1967/early 1968. They re-formed in the mid-'80s and continued to play locally until Wahrer's death. The Trashmen are revered by '60s collectors as one of the great American teen-band combos of all time, their lone hit exemplifying wild, unabashed rock & roll at its most demented, bare-bones-basic, lone-E-chord finest. —*Cub Koda*

Surfin' Bird / 1964 / Sundazed ✦✦✦✦✦
The only album released by the group during their lifetime actually outstrips most of the Southern California-based competition, due to the ferocious grit of the playing and a vaguely demented, go-for-broke recklessness. A good mix of instrumentals and vocals, though nothing else is on the level of the title cut; the CD reissue adds demos of "Surfin' Bird" and "Bird Dance Beat," and a couple rare singles. —*Richie Unterberger*

● **The Tube City!: The Best of The Trashmen** / 1992 / Sundazed ✦✦✦✦✦
The original *Surfin' Bird* album, plus all the original Garrett singles from that period. The perfect primer set. —*Cub Koda*

Comic Book Collector / 1994 / NPR ✦✦✦
This 11-song collection marks the final recording session of the original group, about a year before the untimely death of drummer-lead singer Steve Wahrer in 1989. While the recuts of their classics "Surfin' Bird" and "King of the Surf" don't hold a candle to the manic energy of the originals, the rest set list takes on "House of the Rising Sun," "Summertime Blues," "Believe What You Say," and "Love's Made a Fool of You" reveal a band that never lost its touch. The other three remaining tracks feature the current lineup with the drumming talent of Mark Andreason (brother of lead guitarist Tony) standing in for Steve, keeping the tradition alive and the heart of rock & roll still beating with a shot of fresh blood. This includes the title cut, a strong indication that this band still has a lot of gas left in the tank. —*Cub Koda*

The Great Lost Trashmen Album! / Oct. 21, 1994 / Sundazed ✦✦✦✦
The Great Lost Trashmen Album! features some fine unreleased studio recordings. —*Cub Koda*

Bird Call!: The Twin City Stomp of the Trashmen / Mar. 17, 1998 / Sundazed ✦✦✦
Over half of this collector's four-CD box set is previously unissued studio, demo, rehearsal, or live recordings. Nothing is duplicated in this material originally recorded from 1961-1967. The Trashmen are an amazing summary of contradictions when looked at from afar. In pictures, even live ones, they are four clean-cut chaps in suits. Their nationwide

1963 hit "Bird," the 1965 version of which is included here, is a deliriously silly, primitively noisy, and utterly infectious gem. It's like playing a Black Sabbath album and showing pictures of the Bee Gees and trying to get someone to believe they are one and the same. The Trashmen's arrangements are two guitars of clarion twang and garage crunch with harmony with lead vocals often moving from one member to another. While some of their covers are saccharine (for example, Buddy Holly's "Tell Me How"), they offer such glorious trash rock as the cartoonish analysis of Bo Diddley's signature sound in "Bird Diddley Beat." The Trashmen tap straight into a democratic and transforming American spirit that celebrates the Universal Goof, a sort of holy fool spreading pure joy through music. There you have the entertainment recipe of the Trashmen: surf, doo-wop, blues, and rock & roll motifs swirled together for either devastating hilarity or smooth, slow dancing ballads. *—Tom Schulte*

The Traveling Wilburys

f. 1988

Pop/Rock

Reversing the usual process by which groups break up and give way to solo careers, the Traveling Wilburys are a group made up of solo stars. The group was organized by former Beatle George Harrison, former Electric Light Orchestra leader Jeff Lynne, Bob Dylan, Tom Petty, and Roy Orbison, thus representing three generations of rock stars. In 1988, the five (who had known each other for years) came together to record a Harrison B-side single and ended up writing and recording an album on which they shared lead vocals. It turned out to be a way to transcend the high expectations made of any of them as individuals, and a delighted public sent the album to number three, with two singles, "Handle with Care" and "End of the Line," hitting the charts. Unfortunately, Orbison died of a heart attack only a few weeks after the album's release.

Two years later, the remaining quartet released a second album, inexplicably titled *Vol. 3*. Although it didn't match the success of the first Wilburys album, it was another million-selling hit. Throughout the '90s, there were rumors of another Traveling Wilburys record in the works, but no new albums from the group surfaced. Harrison and Lynne did reteam in 1995, when Lynne produced and reworked two John Lennon demos with the Beatles for their *Anthology* rarties collection. *—William Ruhlmann*

• **Traveling Wilburys, Vol. 1** / Oct. 1988 / Wilbury ♦♦♦♦♦

The Traveling Wilburys are the only supergroup that lives up to expectations because they underplay them. They never shoot for the moon on their 1988 debut, they simply lay back and have a little fun. Anyone expecting something monumental will be disappointed, yet that's precisely what's fun about it—Dylan, Petty, Harrison, Lynne, and Orbison are having such a good time that it's hard not to get caught up in the spirit of things. The songs? Well, the songs are on one level a mixed bag, a blend of easy rockers, folk-tunes, and silly jokes, but even if these might sound like throwaways on "serious" albums, they sound fresh, lively, funny, even heart-rending here. Apart from the two singles, "Handle With Care" and "End of the Line," the highlights belong to Dylan, who's having more fun here than he's had since *The Basement Tapes* (check out the Springsteen parody "Tweeter and the Monkey Man" for proof). If Lynne's production is a little lush and lavish for these roots rockers, it's nevertheless warm, welcoming, and appropriate, helping make *Traveling Wilburys, Vol. 1* a unique record, different than anything in any of the members' own catalogs. *—Stephen Thomas Erlewine*

Traveling Wilburys, Vol. 3 / Oct. 19, 1990 / Wilbury ♦♦♦

The Traveling Wilburys' second album, incongruously titled *Vol. 3*, sounds for all the world like a dead-ringer for their debut, but the feel is considerably different. It isn't that Roy Orbison sadly died shortly after the release of *Vol. 1* (which does make a slight difference), it's that the guys are sounding like they're trying very, very hard to have fun—how else to explain the exhortation to dance around with underwear on your head on "Wilbury Dance." No matter how silly the first Wilburys record got, it was frequently clever and never self-conscious—the polar opposite of its sequel, actually. Occasionally, these guys do get off a couple of good tunes—they're seasoned professionals, after all, and they can make a throwaway like "She's My Baby" infectious—but they don't do it a whole lot, and the rest of the record is padded out with songs that try hard to be fun, but never are. It's unfair to lay the blame on the absence of Orbison, since if he was around, the results would likely to have been the same. After all, it's nearly impossible to capture lightning in a bottle once, and it's a fool's game to try to do it twice. *—Stephen Thomas Erlewine*

Travis

f. Glasgow, Scotland

British Trad Rock, Post-Grunge, Britpop, Alternative Pop/Rock

Along with Cast, Ocean Colour Scene, Kula Shaker and Embrace, Travis were one of the most prominent British "trad-rock" bands in the mid-to-late '90s. Following Oasis' lead of crafting down-to-earth, heartfelt songs in the vein of classic British bands from the '60s, Travis were more successful and enduring than some of their peers due to their lively, impassioned songwriting and performances.

The group formed in Glasgow around 1990 as something of a lark for its members, singer/songwriter Francis Healy, guitarist Andy Dunlop, drummer Neil Primrose and bassist Douglas Payne. After finishing their studies at art school a few years later, the foursome became more serious about Travis' potential and moved to London in 1996. Their self-released debut EP, *All I Wanna Do Is Rock*, came out in the fall of that year; with its earnest vocals and soaring guitars, it captured the spirit of British rock at the time, which was retreating from some of Britpop's artiness to a back-to-basics sound. Their second single, 1997's "U16 Girls" was released by Independiente Records, the new label headed by former Go! Discs' director Andy MacDonald; a few months later, their critically-acclaimed full-length debut *Good Feeling* arrived. Recorded in a matter of days with top producer Steve Lillywhite, the album included hit singles like "Happy" and "Tied To The '90s" and immediately entered the Top 10 of the UK charts. The following year, Travis began sessions with star producer Nigel Godrich for the follow-up to *Good Feeling*, recording in six studios in as many months. Though it was a slower, darker affair, when *The Man Who* appeared in 1999, it eclipsed Travis' previous successes, going platinum six times in the UK and spawning more hit singles such as "Why Does It Always Rain On Me?" and "Writing To Reach You." Nominated *Select Magazine's* Album Of The Year (and finishing in the top 10 of many other publication's year-end lists), *The Man Who* appeared on US shores in early 2000, just in time for a tour with their musical big brothers, Oasis. Debuting at the number one spot on the UK album chart, *The Invisible Band* was issued in June 2001 just prior to stateside summer gigs with Dido. *—Heather Phares*

Good Feeling / Oct. 7, 1997 / Epic/Indepentente ♦♦♦♦

Like most post-Oasis bands, Travis is determined to be a classic band, which means they are decidedly classicist in their approach. Travis have the traditional Britpop influences—Beatles, Kinks, Small Faces, etc.—which are filtered through such '90s peers as the Stone Roses, Manic Street Preachers and, of course, Oasis. Fortunately, they aren't tied to the '60s, like Cast or Ocean Colour Scene; they try to revitalize the traditions with harder backbeats and louder guitars, and Fran Healy's voice often strains at the edge of screaming. That approach can keep their conventional aspects entertaining, but what makes *Good Feeling* a successful debut is that Healy can write hooks, whether it's the anthemic "All I Want To Do Is Rock" or the stompy "U16 Girls." There are several slow spots on *Good Feeling* which illustrate that the group's sound has its limits, but it's a promising debut that establishes Travis as one of the better British trad-rock groups. *—Stephen Thomas Erlewine*

• **The Man Who** / 1999 / Epic/Indepentente ♦♦♦♦

After their successful debut album of murky pop, Travis seemingly felt a need to tinker with the formula. The product of this change is *The Man Who*, a quiet album filled to the brim with atmospheric and introspective ballads. Acoustic guitars and tranquil melodies rule here, as this release is an entirely different affair than the band's revved-up debut. Fortunately for Travis, this disc became a massive U.K. hit, spawning no less than five hugely successful singles. The album highlight is "Why Does It Always Rain on Me?," a sweeping singalong that took England by storm and became one of the biggest hits of 1999. However, despite the public's warm embrace of this album, fans of the "old" Travis may be disappointed. Gone are the arena-ready stompers and the dirty, grimy singalong pop that comprised *Good Feeling*. Instead, what is left is merely adequate; *The Man Who* offers pleasant background music, but no truly gripping moments. It's lite-rock for late 1990s Britain that's, unfortunately, easily forgettable. [The U.S. release of this album, which came almost a year after its initial release, contains three bonus tracks.] *—Jason Damas*

The Invisible Band / Jun. 12, 2001 / Epic/Indepentente ♦♦♦♦

After the momentous success achieved with their sophomore effort (*The Man Who*), Travis' return to melodic rock & roll with *The Invisible Band* is once again personal and earnest. Having spent most of 2000 supporting Oasis and playing their own headlining gigs in the States, Travis remained humble while collecting a dozen solid tracks for another album, most of them plucked from Fran Healy's own humming and tinkering around with an acoustic. *The Invisible Band* finds Nigel Godrich (Radiohead, Beck, Neil Finn) mixing and mastering again, and vulnerability found within these songs is what makes Travis a decent band. They are not afraid to be catchy and they're certainly suckers for a sweet love tune. But Travis is conscious of the unconscious and reflects any kind of lyrical emotion. Debut single "Sing" is charming while addressing being inhibited within a relationship. The banjo is a nice touch, for it becomes a mainstay throughout and adds a slightly different touch versus the simplicities of an acoustic. "Side" and "Flowers in the Dirt" are instantly endearing with their Beatlesque hooks, but "The Humpty Dumpty Love Song" is Travis' finest moment of musical clarity with Healy's heart on his sleeve. Written while on tour with Oasis, "The Humpty Dumpty Love Song" reflects a hero's fading fervor of love lost—"All the kings horses and all the kings men/Couldn't pull my heart back together again/All the physicians and mathematicians too/Failed to stop my heart from breaking in two." Indeed, Travis is the basic man's poets and *The Invisible Band* plays toward the simplicities of humility. They've done it again, but with more internal charisma. *The Man Who* took them from indie angst to melodic humdrum. *The Invisible Band* perfects the ever-changing growth within the band for something great. *—MacKenzie Wilson*

The Tremeloes

f. 1958, Dagenham, Essex, England

British Invasion, Hard Rock, Rock & Roll

It's difficult for anyone who has heard them not to like—or even love—the Tremeloes. They were one of the more prodigiously talented British pop/rock bands of the 1960s, and they threw that talent into the making of amazingly catchy and well-crafted singles that lit up the charts and radio on both sides of the Atlantic for four years running, from 1966 through 1970. Their version of "Twist and Shout" managed to rise to number four on the English charts, despite running up head-to-head with the Beatles' recording. Their next record, a cover of the Contours' hit "Do You Love Me," was a classic of the era, an honest, authentic-sounding screamer of a single that hit number one in England once the Beatles' "She Loves You" vacated the spot, and managed to eclipse a rival version by the Dave Clark Five. In its wake, Brian Poole & the Tremeloes managed a series of respectable, even occasionally inspired hits over the next two years, including a U.K. Top Ten cover of Roy Orbison's "Candy Man" and a convincingly raucous rendition of the Strangeloves' Bo

Diddley-beat-driven anthem "I Want Candy." Yet, the Tremeloes are also one of the least known and least respected of 1960s English bands. The precise reason for the lack of respect is difficult to pin down, except perhaps that their timing was out, as far as making the most of their success—they generally didn't write their own material, and they cut their best singles long after the British Invasion (and the mystique surrounding the bands that were part of it) had ended. And, yet, ironically, the Tremeloes are also one of the longest surviving English rock & roll bands, still playing regularly more than 40 years after the group's founding. *—Bruce Eder*

● **The Best of the Tremeloes** / Feb. 25, 1992 / Rhino ✦✦✦✦
Back in the early 1990s, when this 20-song compilation came out, it was more music by the Tremeloes than had been seen in America in decades, and it was absolutely essential listening—the Tremeloes' music is so upbeat and enjoyable, that they could significantly improve the collective frame of mind of our society if their work was better known. Rhino's best-of is a decent cross-section of the band's work from early 1967 through 1974, covering their best and best-known singles. The sound here is a mix of late-era (almost retro) British beat ("Suddenly You Love Me," "Too Many Fish in the Sea"), white soul ("Ain't Nothin' But a House Party"), and Beatlesque pop/rock ("Here Comes My Baby," "Hello World"), all of it so catchy that even the most lethargic listener might well be moved to get up and dance to much of it. The hits are augmented by three album cuts and a pair of tracks ("You Can't Touch Sue," "Do I Love you") that never previously appeared in America, all mastered to Rhino's usual high standard by Bill Inglot. And the only reason that this disc doesn't get the highest rating is because the group's entire catalog has since been reissued, through Repertoire Records and Castle Communications, and there are equally good alternatives to this CD, though this disc remains competitive. *—Bruce Eder*

Good Day Sunshine (Singles A's & B'S) / 1999 / Sequel ✦✦✦✦
Fifty-one songs on two CDs by the post-Brian Poole quartet, and about as good a collection, at least for their U.K. output, as one is likely to find on this group, which is either highly underrated or a grotesquely lucky and long-lived middling ensemble of pop rockers. From the flowery pop/rock of "Good Day Sunshine" through the more self-consciously psychedelic "Let Your Hair Hang Down" and the catchy "Even the Bad Times Are Good," to their heavier recordings such as "Right Wheel, Left Hammer, Sham," and satirical ventures such as "Blue Suede Tie"—the latter a cutting send-up of the then burgeoning glam-rock sound—to their mid-1970s outings as the Trems, the group's history is documented with reasonable thoroughness. The relentlessly tuneful, singalong nature of the material can get to be tiresome in one sitting, like facing a plateful of cotton candy as the potential meal, but the group—especially guitarist Rick West—had a high degree of virtuosity in a pop vein, with West's abilities transcending that label, and their sound was always lively, making their stuff consistently entertaining in medium doses. The sound is state of the art and the contents go right up through "Words" and "I Will Return" from 1983, making this a very comprehensive collection, missing only some important album tracks and a handful of songs that were singles in America, a fact that may repel some stateside purchasers of this low-priced two-CD British import. *—Bruce Eder*

The Treniers

f. 1947

Jump Blues, R&B

Featuring twin brothers Cliff and Claude Trenier, the Treniers helped link swing music to rock & roll with their brand of hot jump blues in the late '40s and early '50s. To the latter-day listener, their early-'50s singles sound closer to swing than rock; indeed, Cliff and Claude had once sung with the Jimmie Lunceford Orchestra. The group did anticipate some crucial elements of rock & roll, though, with their solid, thumping beats, their squealing saxophone solos, and their song titles, such as "Rocking on Sunday Night," "Rockin' Is Our Business," and "It Rocks! It Rolls! It Swings!." The Treniers' brand of swing-cum-R&B was undoubtedly an influence on Bill Haley, who saw them when both acts were playing summer shows in Wildwood, NJ. They had work recorded for OKeh in the early '50s; by the middle of the decade, their sound was more R&B-oriented. Like many early R&B pioneers, they were unable to find success in the rock & roll era, though they appeared in a few of the first rock & roll films. *—Richie Unterberger*

● **They Rock! They Roll! They Swing!: The Best of the Treniers** / Feb. 28, 1995 / Epic/Legacy ✦✦✦✦✦
This 20-track compilation has all of their key early- and mid-'50s Okeh singles (only one of which, "Go! Go! Go!," was actually an R&B hit), five previously unreleased songs, and their 1953 version of Bill Haley's "Rock-A-Beatin' Boogie," which must rank as one of the first (if not the very first) covers of a White rock song by a Black artist. *—Richie Unterberger*

A Tribe Called Quest

f. 1988, Queens, NY, **db.** 1998

Jazz-Rap, East Coast Rap, Alternative Rap, Hip-Hop

Without question the most intelligent, artistic rap group during the '90s, A Tribe Called Quest jump-started and perfected the hip-hop alternative to hardcore and gangsta-rap. In essence, they abandoned the macho posturing which rap music had been constructed upon, and focused instead on abstract philosophy and message tracks. The "sucka MC" theme had never been completely ignored in hip-hop, but Tribe confronted numerous black issues—date rape, use of the word nigger, the trials and tribulations of the rap industry—all of which overpowered the occasional game of the dozens. Just as powerful musically, Quest built upon De La Soul's jazz-rap revolution, basing tracks around laid-back samples instead of the played-out James Brown-fests which many rappers had made a cottage industry by the late '80s. Comprised of Q-Tip, Ali Shaheed Muhammad, and Phife, A Tribe Called Quest debuted in 1989 and released their debut album one year later. Second album *The Low End Theory* was, quite simply, the most consistent and flowing hip-hop album ever recorded, though the trio moved closer to their harder contemporaries on 1993's *Midnight Marauders*. A spot on the 1993 Lollapalooza Tour showed their influence with the alternative crowd—always a bedrock of A Tribe Called Quest's support—but the group kept it real on 1996's *Beats, Rhymes and Life*, a dedication to the streets and the hip-hop underground. Soon after 1998's *The Love Movement* though, the group broke up. *—John Bush*

People's Instinctive Travels and the Paths of Rhythm / Apr. 17, 1990 / Jive ✦✦✦✦
With its superb debut album, A Tribe Called Quest established itself as leaders of alternative rap—a term also applied to De La Soul, Digable Planets and the Pharcyde. Though De La Soul had a strong influence on Quest, the experimental New York group projected a highly appealing personality of its own. Quirky, abstract and cerebral, the album lacks the immediacy of more hardcore rap and wasn't as big a seller as many of the gangster rap CDs released in 1990. In fact, much of its support came from alternative rock aficionados, who were drawn to its complexity. Jazz is a strong influence here, and like many jazz recordings, this is an album that necessitates several listenings in order to be fully appreciated and absorbed. *—Alex Henderson*

★ **The Low End Theory** / Sep. 24, 1991 / Jive ✦✦✦✦✦
While most of the players in the jazz-rap movement never quite escaped the pasted-on qualities of their vintage samples, with *The Low End Theory*, A Tribe Called Quest created one of the closest and most brilliant fusions of jazz atmosphere and hip-hop attitude ever recorded. The rapping by Q-Tip and Phife Dawg could be the smoothest of any rap record ever heard; the pair are so in tune with each other, they sound like flip sides of the same personality, fluidly trading off on rhymes, with the former earning his nickname (the Abstract) and Phife concerning himself with the more concrete issues of being young, gifted, and black. The trio also takes on the rap game with a pair of hard-hitting tracks: "Rap Promoter" and "Show Business," the latter a lyrical sound clash with Q-Tip and Phife plus Brand Nubian's Diamond D, Lord Jamar, and Sadat X. The woman problem gets investigated on two realistic yet sensitive tracks, "Butter" and "The Infamous Date Rape." The productions behind these tracks aren't quite skeletal, but they're certainly not complex. Instead, Tribe weaves little more than a stand-up bass (sampled or otherwise) and crisp, live-sounding drum programs with a few deftly placed samples or electric keyboards. It's a tribute to their unerring production sense that, with just those few tools, Tribe produced one of the best hip-hop albums in history, a record that sounds better with each listen. *The Low End Theory* is an unqualified success, the perfect marriage of intelligent, flowing raps to nuanced, groove-centered productions. *—John Bush*

☆ **Midnight Marauders** / Nov. 9, 1993 / Jive ✦✦✦✦✦
Midnight Marauders was an intriguing and smartly paced collection that ranged from descriptive verbal essays on city life to confrontational taunts, comic expositions, denunciations, and even quasi-religious theorizing. While their celebrated hip-hop/jazz roots were often evident, the group also utilized fusion, urban contemporary, Afro-Latin and funk samples, while Q-Tip's rap style could be cool and deadpan, reflective, analytical, satirical, or disgusted and angry. There was precious little gangsta posturing or sexist rhetoric, and such numbers as "Sucka Nigga," "God Lives Through," "Electric Relaxation" and "Award Tour" were cleverly delivered and brilliantly composed. *—Ron Wynn*

Beats, Rhymes & Life / Jul. 30, 1996 / Jive ✦✦✦
With their fourth album *Beats, Rhymes and Life*, A Tribe Called Quest manages to be one of the few hip-hop acts to successfully age by pushing both their music and their lyrics into new directions. Stylistically, the record is closest to its immediate predecessor, *Midnight Marauders*, in the sense that the group's jazz-rap fusion are downplayed and the beat stays surprisingly hard throughout the album. What distinguishes *Beats, Rhymes and Life* from *Marauders* is a deeper sense not only of eclectism, but of spirituality and maturity. Shortly before the album was written and recorded, Q-Tip converted to Islam and the religion's ideals are an undercurrent in nearly every track on the album. But what really stands out is Tip's unease with the transience of the youth-oriented hip-hop scene and his own urges to settle down. Unlike most rappers, he confronts these feelings in the music, by writing lyrics and helping to create music that illustrates the contradictions of growing old with hip-hop. And by tackling the issue head-on, A Tribe Called Quest sound fresh and suggest that it is possible to sustain a career in rap as you approach a full decade of recording, after all. *—Leo Stanley*

The Love Movement / Sep. 29, 1998 / BMG International ✦✦✦✦
Continuing with the subdued, mature stylistic flow of *Beats, Rhymes and Life*, *The Love Movement*, the fifth album from A Tribe Called Quest, is the group's most subtle album yet—which may just be a polite way for saying it's a little monotonous. Throughout the record, Tribe mines the same jazz-flavored, R&B-fueled beats that were the hallmark of *Beats*. Although the "love" concept provides a thematic cohesion to the album—almost all of the songs are about love, in one way or another—the overall effect is quite similar to its immediate predecessor: the music is enthralling for a while, but soon it all sounds a little too familiar. Part of the problem is that Tribe functions on a cerebral level, a point made painfully clear by Busta Rhymes and Redman's roaring, visceral cameos on "Steppin' It Up." On their own, Tribe favors craft over raw skills. That means there are plenty of pleasures to be had from careful listening, but they've reached a point where it's easier to admire Ummah's stylish production and the subtle rhymes of Q-Tip, Phife and Shaheed than it is to outright love them, which is ironic for an album bearing the title *The Love Movement*. *—Stephen Thomas Erlewine*

Anthology / Oct. 26, 1999 / Jive ✦✦✦✦✦
For those who haven't discovered that A Tribe Called Quest made several of the best LPs

in hip-hop history, *Anthology* is a perfect way to encapsulate the trio's decade-long career into one manageable portion. All of their best and biggest songs are here, from the early neglected joint "Luck of Lucien" to classic jazz-rap from *The Low End Theory* like "Jazz (We've Got)," and their 45-rpm peak with "Award Tour," all the way to their last big hit, "Find a Way," from 1998's *The Love Movement*. Yes, anyone who enjoys hip-hop needs to own at least *Midnight Marauders* and *The Low End Theory*, but *Anthology* succeeds in delivering all the highest points from a great hip-hop group's career. The collection also includes the first solo track from Q-Tip, 1999's "Vivrant Thing." *—John Bush*

Tricky (Adrian Thaws)

b. 1964, Knowle West, Bristol, Avon, England

Producer, Vocals / Electronica, Trip-Hop, Alternative Pop/Rock

Originally, Tricky was a member of the Wild Bunch, a Bristol-based rap troupe that eventually metamorphosed into Massive Attack during the early '90s. Tricky provided pivotal raps on Massive Attack's groundbreaking 1992 album *Blue Lines*. The following year, he released his debut single, "Aftermath." His debut album, *Maxinquaye*, appeared in the spring of 1995. Not only did the album receive overwhelmingly positive reviews when it was released, but it entered the UK charts at number two, despite the total lack of daytime radio airplay. Throughout 1995, Tricky was omnipresent in the UK, collaborating with and remixing for a wide variety of artists, including Björk, Luscious Jackson and Whale. At the end of the year, *Maxinquaye* topped many year-end polls in Britain, including *Melody Maker* and *NME*. In February of 1996, *Nearly God*—an album featuring Tricky's collaborations with artists as diverse as Terry Hall, Björk, Alison Moyet, and Neneh Cherry—was released, again to strong reviews; the album was released in the US six months later. Tricky's official second album, *Pre-Millenium Tension*, was released in 1996. Again, he received positive reviews, though there were a few dissenting opinions. *—Stephen Thomas Erlewine*

★ **Maxinquaye** / Apr. 18, 1995 / 4th & Broadway ♦♦♦♦♦

Though he hates the label of trip-hop, Tricky's debut album *Maxinquaye* is one of the finest that the genre has to offer. "Ponderosa," "Suffocated Love," and "Pumpkin" are disturbing and beautiful, with ominous background noises and Martine's soaring vocals, while tracks like the group's cover of "Black Steel" show off their harder side. A striking debut, Tricky's *Maxinquaye* is only the beginning for this innovative artist. *—Heather Phares*

Nearly God / Apr. 29, 1996 / 4th & Broadway ♦♦♦♦♦

Nearly God is Tricky's unofficial second album—he calls it a collection of brilliant, incomplete demos. When Tricky signed his contract with Island, it allowed him to release an album a year under a different name and *Nearly God* is the first of these efforts. Tricky recorded the record with a diverse cast of collaborators—in addition to his partner Martina, there's Terry Hall, Björk, Neneh Cherry, Cath Coffey, Dedi Madden, and Alison Moyet (Damon Albarn pulled his track just before the album's release). Building on the ghostly, dark soundscapes of Tricky's debut, *Maxinquaye*, *Nearly God* narrows the focus of his first record by making the music slower, hazier, and more distubing. It's not as coherent as *Maxinquaye*, but that's part of its appeal. *Nearly God* is a haunting, fractured, surreal nightmare that doesn't always make sense, but never fails to make an impact. Certain collaborators work better than others—Tricky understands the eeriness of Terry Hall's voice, but he does nothing to tame Alison Moyet's inappropriate bluesy shrieking—but the overall effect of the album is quietly devastating. It gets under your skin and stays there. It's a brilliantly evocative nightmare. *—Stephen Thomas Erlewine*

Tricky Presents Grassroots / Aug. 1996 / ffrr ♦♦♦

Perhaps in an effort to establish himself in the American hip-hop market—which largely ignored his groundbreaking debut, *Maxinquaye*—Tricky released the *Grassroots EP* in the summer of 1996. Recorded in early 1996, *Grassroots* consists primarily of one-off collaborations with a variety of underground and relatively undistinctive New York rappers and musicians, whose music is given weight by Tricky's menacing, hazy production. Tricky appears in the background of each song, murmuring indecipherably, but it's only when he takes the forefront on "Tricky Kid" that the EP matches the tense, psychotic soundscapes of *Maxinquaye* and *Nearly God*. The remaining four tracks have their moments—Drunkenstein's backing vocals are evocative, and "Devils Helper" is entrancing—but, for the most part, *Grassroots* consists of experiments that never quite reach their full potential. *—Stephen Thomas Erlewine*

Pre-Millennium Tension / Nov. 11, 1996 / 4th & Broadway ♦♦♦♦

Maxinquaye was an unexpected hit in England, launching a wave of similar-sounding artists, who incorporated Tricky's innovations into safer pop territory. Tricky responded by travelling to Jamaica to record *Pre-Millennium Tension*, a nervy, claustrophobic record that thrives in its own paranoia. Scaling back the clattering hooks of *Maxinquaye* and slowing the beat down, Tricky has created a hallucinatory soundscape, where the rhythms, samples, and guitars intertwine into a crawling procession of menacing sounds and disembodied lyrical threats. Its tone is set by the backward guitar loops of "Vent," and continued through the shifting "Christiansands," and the tense, lyrically dense "Tricky Kid," easily Tricky's best straight rap to date. Occasionally, the gloom is broken, such as when the shimmering piano chords of "Makes Me Want to Die" ring out, but nearly as often, it becomes bogged down in its own murk, as in the long ragga rant "Ghetto Youth." While the lyrics are often quite effective in conveying dope-addled paranoia, what ties the album together is its layered rhythms and soundscapes. Though it might not sound that way immediately, *Pre-Millennium Tension* is as much Tricky reaching back to his hardcore rap roots as it is a sonic exploration. As such, it stands as a transition record for Tricky, but its overall effect is only slightly less powerful than *Maxinquaye* or *Nearly God*. *—Stephen Thomas Erlewine*

Angels with Dirty Faces / Jun. 2, 1998 / Island ♦♦♦

Perhaps *Maxinquaye* was such a startling, focused, brilliant debut that Tricky's subsequent albums would have paled in comparison, regardless of their quality. Nevertheless, his desire to distance himself from the coffeehouse trip-hop that appeared after *Maxinquaye* forced him into a dark, paranoid corner. Determined to strip away all of his fair-weather fans, he delivered the claustrophobic *Pre-Millennium Tension*, a paranoid record that its follow-up, *Angels With Dirty Faces*, mirrors. Since it builds upon *Pre-Millennium* instead of breaking new ground, *Angels* may strike some listeners as merely a retread, but it gradually reveals new layers upon repeated listens. Tricky has been redefining his rhythms, adding skittering jungle loops and hardcore hip-hop beats to his trademark dub-warped trip-hop. On top of that, he's expanding his sonic palette, adding cheap synthesizers and avant-garde guitarists to create a nightmarish junk-pile of hip-hop, dub, electronica, rock, and gospel. Again, Martina is on board and her stylish croon adds moments of relief to the enveloping dread, as does Polly Harvey on the odd gospel-tinged "Broken Homes." Specific tracks work well individually—"Mellow," "Singing the Blues," "Angels With Dirty Faces," and the absurd, bile-ridden "Record Companies," in particular—but on the whole *Angels With Dirty Faces* is less than the sum of its parts. By being slightly different but essentially the same as *Pre-Millennium Tension*, *Angels With Dirty Faces* demands that listeners meet it on its own terms. Whether they'll want to is another matter entirely. *—Stephen Thomas Erlewine*

Juxtapose / Aug. 17, 1999 / Island ♦♦♦

Tricky's potential once seemed boundless, but by the time of his fifth album, *Juxtapose*, he hadn't expanded his trademark sound: a creeping, menacing blend of hip-hop, alternative rock, and ragga, all delivered with stoned paranoia. Perhaps Tricky realized that its rewards were smaller with each subsequent album, since he designed *Juxtapose* to be his most ambitious, eclectic album since *Maxinquaye*, and the one that finally broke him to the mainstream American hip-hop audience. So, he teamed with DJ Muggs (the architect of Cypress Hill's sound, a clear precedent for Tricky's) and DMX's producer, Grease. The end result is hardly a collaboration—in fact, it feels truncated, weighing in at a mere 35 minutes—but it works in other ways, since Tricky often seems revitalized. That much is evident on the stellar opening cut, "For Real"; the music is spaced-out, sexy, melodic, and appealing, even when it gets foreboding. It's a terrific beginning, suggesting that this will be the first album to offer significant variations on Tricky's signature sound. And it does, but it may not go far enough for some tastes, since a good portion of this brief album is devoted to retreads, which reveal his weaknesses all too well. Tricky remains unduly infatuated with ragga, letting British toaster Mad Dog run wild; his frenetic delivery single-handedly breaks the spell of each track he's featured on. But elsewhere, Tricky pushes forward in inventive ways that add weight to *Juxtapose*—"Contradictive" is his best pop move to date, blessed by Spanish guitars and elongated strings; the paranoid drums of "She Said" successfully deepen the menace; and "Scrappy Love" is a haunting blend of soul and trip-hop, with eerie piano reminiscent of DJ Shadow. *Juxtapose* is a qualified success, but it is a success since the moments that work are his best in years. *—Stephen Thomas Erlewine*

BlowBack / Jul. 2001 / Hollywood ♦♦♦

First, the bad news. There are no new tricks on *BlowBack*, the star-studded 2001 comeback by Tricky, the pioneering trip-hopper that wandered his way into the wilderness. He wandered so far that nobody really cared anymore if he had anything to say—particularly because he wound up saying the same thing, slightly differently, over and over again. He doesn't escape from this problem here, yet he's found a map—and that map is craft. He knew this before, since the best moments of *Angels With Dirty Faces* and *Juxtapose* were when he knew how to spin his signatures just right, so they jelled into something brilliant. He has the same gift here, and he extends it throughout the record, so this is the first record that really plays smoothly from start to finish since *Pre-Millennium Tension*. That, of course, isn't the same thing as being as good, since he has ceased to innovate, and he has a couple of annoying flaws, including his tendency to create one mood and sustain it without developing it, plus his love of dancehall toasting. So, it's a mixed bag, but it plays sharper than his albums of late. Yes, there are some astonishing slips—the backing track of "Something in the Way" sounds great, but Hawkman, the ragga bane of this album, castrates it of its power—but, at this point, that's a given with Tricky. Once you get past that, once you stop expecting genius—or at least something that matches *Maxinquaye* (or even *Tension*)—it's much easier to enjoy *BlowBack*. *—Stephen Thomas Erlewine*

Trip Shakespeare

Alternative Pop/Rock

Answering an ad for "wicked percussion hands," Harvard anthropology grad Elaine Harris hooked up with English major Matt Wilson, who would soon abandon school for music to relocate to his hometown of Minneapolis and found Trip Shakespeare, along with John Munson, a Chinese-language major at the University of Minnesota. After releasing a debut LP on Restless, *Applehead Man*, in 1988, the band expanded to include another Harvard student, Dan Wilson, a graduate student in Art and Matt's elder brother. With an arty sound that betrayed their intellectual pasts, the band continued to release albums for the next three years, including 1989's *Are You Shakesperienced?* on Twin/Tone. In 1990 the band signed with A&M, releasing *Across the Universe* the same year, followed by *Lulu* in 1991. These two major label albums showed off a bright melodic style, with increasingly tight production values, providing a nice package for their arcane lyrics and free-ranging instrumentation. The band broke up shortly after the release of *Lulu*, with Elaine Harris returning to the Boston area, Matt Wilson performing with several Minneapolis-area bands, and Dan Wilson and John Munson joining with Jacob Slichter to form Pleasure, later known as Semisonic. *—Stacia Proefrock*

Applehead Man / 1988 / Restless ✦✦✦

Although *Applehead Man* gives many indications of this band's bright future, it comes off merely as a collection of early Trip Shakespeare demos probably best left for collectors and hardcore fans. Its basement production and sheer lack of cohesion makes it a difficult listen for the average pop radio fan. In other words, it may be their first album, but don't start here. *Applehead Man* introduces the basic vision of bandleader Matt Wilson, but pines like a bedroom four-track for a more apt arena in which to present itself. The wistful trio wind their way through mythic rural fables, making apparent their penchant for extended '70s guitar solos and their strong melodic sense. Sadly, Wilson's songs suffer drastically under the gross misproduction and his unusual lyrics and hooks are almost ineffective. The band also has yet to define bassist John Munson's unique fretless sound and bring to the front drummer Elaine Harris' unorthodox playing style. A few standout tracks like "Applehead Man," "Pearle" (later re-recorded for their A&M debut, *Across the Universe*), and "Beatle" shine through the murky production and hint at the lush, romantic Midwestern pop that Trip Shakespeare would later define. In the two years following this release, the band found its true sound with the addition of Matt Wilson's younger brother Dan Wilson sharing guitar, piano, and vocal duties. —*Tim Monger*

Are You Shakespearienced? / 1989 / Twin/Tone ✦✦✦

The best of their early work. Features the great existential moving song "Two Wheeler, Four Wheeler" and the stupid "Toolmaster of Brainerd." —*John Dougan*

● **Across the Universe** / 1990 / A&M ✦✦✦✦✦

There are those enamored of Trip Shakespeare's independent-label work, but I'd recommend starting here. This is their strongest collection of tunes and tightest, most assertive playing. —*John Dougan*

Lulu / 1991 / A&M ✦✦✦

Trip Shakespeare's last full-length album comes off as a bit of a disappointment—as the band has honed its hooks and songwriting ability, the songs themselves just aren't horribly engaging. There's no doubt that there is a considerable amount of talent at work on *Lulu*, though most tracks do little to distinguish themselves from a lot of the more pop-oriented rock bands of the day, and the overall cheeriness of the record, when combined with rather vague lyrics, can be a little grating. All of the rough edges have been polished down to what has to be one of the most glossy recordings by a band with any indie rock leanings. Big melodies and rather nondescript arrangements somehow don't deliver songs that are really memorable in any way and end up seeming utterly out of step with the grunge movement that would soon dominate the rock scene. That, of course, would have been more acceptable if *Lulu* was a pop masterpiece. Instead, it remains only as pleasant listening and not a particularly inspiring finale. —*Matt Fink*

The Troggs

f. 1964, Andover, Hampshire, England

Frat Rock, British Invasion, Rock & Roll

Remembered chiefly as proto-punkers who reached the top of the charts with the "caveman rock" of "Wild Thing" (1966), the Troggs were also adept at crafting power-pop and ballads. Hearkening back to a somewhat simpler, more basic British Invasion approach as psychedelia began to explode in the late '60s, the group also reached the Top Five with their flower-power ballad "Love Is All Around" in 1968. While more popular in their native England than in the U.S., the band also fashioned memorable, insistently riffing hit singles like "With a Girl like You," "Night of the Long Grass," and the notoriously salacious "I Can't Control Myself" between 1966 and 1968. Paced by Reg Presley's lusting vocals, the group—which composed most of their own material—could crunch with the best of them, but were also capable of quite a bit more range and melodic invention than they've been given credit for. —*Richie Unterberger*

The Best of the Troggs [1988] / 1988 / PolyGram ✦✦✦✦

Polygram's *Best of the Troggs* is a basic primer, containing all of the group's best-known songs ("Wild Thing," "With a Girl like You," "I Can't Control Myself," "Love Is All Around"), as well as a smattering of some of their better obscurities, making it a fine introduction to the primitive British Invasion band. —*Stephen Thomas Erlewine*

Athens Andover / 1992 / Rhino ✦✦✦

Most comeback albums never work; *Athens Andover* is the rare exception that does. Backed by members of R.E.M. and the dB's, The Troggs make some of their best pop ever, full of ringing guitars and chiming melodies. [*Athens Andover* was reissued in 1996 by the Music Club label as *Athens, Georgia & Beyond* with additional tracks.] —*Stephen Thomas Erlewine*

Archeology (1967-1977) / Sep. 22, 1992 / Polydor/Chronicles ✦✦✦✦✦

A double-CD, 52-track box set that proves there was a lot more to The Troggs than "Wild Thing" and "Love Is All Around." This archetypally primitive British Invasion quartet scored many hits in the U.K. that barely dented the charts in the U.S., like "With A Girl Like You," "Night Of The Long Grass," and the notoriously racy "I Can't Control Myself." They're all here, along with notable album cuts, B-sides, and worldwide post-1968 flops. Primitive they may have been, but The Troggs—who wrote most of their own material—did not lack a flair for hard pop hooks, and could display a surprising delicacy in their ballads. Several of their obscure singles and album tracks are equal in worth to their hits, like the gothic but pretty "Cousin Jane," and the witty light psychedelia of "Maybe the Madman" and "Purple Shades." Some of the '70s hard rockers and glammish novelties are unimpressive, and 52 songs is arguably excessive. But there are a fair number of obscure gems to be found on this well-annotated package. —*Richie Unterberger*

● **The Best of the Troggs [1994]** / Oct. 4, 1994 / Fontana/Chronicles ✦✦✦✦✦

Trouble Funk

f. 1978, Washington, D.C., db. 1984

Go-Go, Disco, Funk

Miles off the radar of popular music during the early '80s, Trouble Funk energized their D.C. home with the sound of go-go music, an uproarious blend of swinging, uptempo '70s funk and a '60s-style horn section. The band formed in 1978, and quickly earned a loyal fanbase for their notoriously can't-miss live act, a raw, party-friendly version of dance and funk with few songs but plenty of extensive jams organized around audience-friendly vocal tags and call-out hooks.

The first go-go record released *outside* of D.C., Trouble Funk's 1982 debut *Drop the Bomb* appeared on Sugar Hill, the same label then championing early hip-hop. The band earned national distribution with a prescient concert record, 1985's *Saturday Night (Live from Washington, D.C.)*, released through Island. After taking the live act nationwide and even worldwide (they played the 1986 Montreux Jazz Festival), Trouble Funk returned in 1987 with the boundary-breaking *Trouble Over Here, Trouble Over There*, featuring sympathetic heads like Bootsy Collins and Kurtis Blow. It was a bit of a stylistic misstep, however, and Island released the group from its contract. Undeterred, Trouble Funk kept on grooving around the city, playing often, even into the '90s, for nostalgic party-goers as well as the musically curious. —*John Bush*

Drop the Bomb / 1982 / Sequel ✦✦✦✦✦

Masters of Washington, D.C.'s '80s go-go craze, Trouble Funk brought early hip-hop (the group was part of Sugarhill Records) to the dance floor with deep bass, propulsive rhythms, and party lyrics. Being even more inspired by '70s funk bands like Chic, Cameo, and the Gap Band than either the Sugar Hill Gang or Grandmaster Flash, Trouble Funk and other go-go acts like EU and Chuck Brown used the MC to conduct party-time call-and-response sessions and not generally for street poetry raps à la Melle Mel and Kurtis Blow. A celebratory atmosphere certainly prevails on Sequel Records' fine Trouble Funk collection *Drop the Bomb*, with many of the band's prime dance hits like the title track, "Get on Up," and "Let's Get Hot" being featured in their extended versions. The band's nasty synth licks, up-front percussion, and sinewy funk guitar lines keep the music pumping throughout, while both the go-go/rap hybrid "Pump Me Up" and Barry White-inspired soul ballad "Don't Try to Use Me" show off the group's musical flexibility. The set is rounded out with the ten-minute, bring-the-house-down jam "Supergrit," which nicely incorporates the funk of Kool & the Gang and Earth Wind & Fire into the go-go mix. This is a great introduction to both Trouble Funk's music and the go-go sound. —*Stephen Cook*

The Bomb Has Dropped / 1987 / Castle Communications ✦✦✦

One of the first CD compilations of Trouble Funk's classic sides for Sugar Hill, it has now been superseded by much better and more thorough retrospectives. However, there's no denying that all the essential tracks are here, in uncut form. "Pump Me Up," "Hey Fellas," and "Drop the Bomb" are all pure go-go, recognizable now as the source of numerous samples, and as funky as the genre got. On the other hand, the liner notes are scant, the sound tinny with very little bass, and the compilation ends on a ballad, "Don't Try to Use Me." Not terrible, but only serves to point out what they were really good at. —*Ted Mills*

● **Early Singles** / Mar. 11, 1997 / Warner Brothers ✦✦✦✦✦

The explosive singles of the Washington, D.C. go-go legends Trouble Funk are compiled on this essential collection, issued by the Infinite Zero label (which also lovingly re-released the group's seminal *Live* album in 1996). Among the highlights are "So Early in the Morning" and "Super Grit." —*Jason Ankeny*

Droppin' Bombs: The Definitive Trouble Funk / Aug. 25, 1998 / Harmless ✦✦✦✦✦

Doris Troy

b. Jan. 6, 1937, New York, NY

Vocals (Background), Vocals / Pop-Soul, Soul

Surely one of the most talented one-hit wonders of the rock era, Doris Troy hit the Top Ten with "Just One Look" in 1963, but also recorded many other fine pop-soul sides for Atlantic between 1963 and 1965. Unlike many soul performers of the time, Troy wrote most of her own material (under the pseudonym Payne), and had already written for other artists and sung backup for Dionne and Dee Dee Warwick and Cissy Houston on New York soul records before striking out on her own. More melodically ambitious and stylistically eclectic than many of her peers, her Atlantic sides blend elements of gospel, girl group, blues, and pop into a rich New York soul sound. Troy never reached the charts again after "Just One Look," but was more appreciated in England, where she toured occasionally and where the Hollies covered her "What'cha Gonna Do About It" on their first album. Moving to Britain, she recorded an album for Apple in 1970 with assistance from George Harrison and Billy Preston. In the early '70s, she sang backup vocals for British rock groups in addition to recording a couple more albums. In the '80s she starred in *Mama I Want to Sing*, a musical based on her life story. —*Richie Unterberger*

Doris Troy / 1970 / Capitol ✦✦✦

An all-star cast supported Troy on her lone Apple effort: George Harrison, Billy Preston, Peter Frampton, Stephen Stills, Klaus Voormann, Jackie Lomax, Eric Clapton, Leon Russell, and Delaney & Bonnie all contributed, and Harrison, Stills, Lomax, Preston, Voormann, and Ringo Starr pitched in on the songwriting, though Troy wrote or co-wrote most of the songs. Well-received by some critics, it really doesn't add up to the sum of its parts. Troy is in great voice, but much of the material is pedestrian, and the heavy rock/soul arrangements often have an over-beefy, early-'70s super-session feel. It works best when Troy puts the brakes on the hard rock to deliver emotional, slower soul tunes. The CD reissue adds five interesting cuts from non-LP singles and outtakes. —*Richie Unterberger*

● **Just One Look: The Best of Doris Troy** / Aug. 23, 1994 / Ichiban Soul Classics ✦✦✦✦✦
This 21-track anthology of her 1963-65 Atlantic sides is as comprehensive as one could ask for. It includes all of her singles, her rare album, three cuts only issued on British singles, and her rare 1965 single for the Calla label, "I'll Do Anything (He Wants Me To Do)." Besides "Just One Look," there are quite a few other downright excellent lost gems here: "What'cha Gonna Do About It," the bluesy "Draw Me Closer," the driving "You'd Better Stop" (with a fierce guitar break that sounds like a young Jimmy Page), and the soulful wall of sound on "I'll Do Anything." "How My Heart Aches" is a special standout that ranks among the very finest wrenching, melancholy soul ever waxed. Much more than a collector's item, this proves Troy to be a genuinely overlooked major talent. —*Richie Unterberger*

Tsunami
f. 1990
Indie Rock, Alternative Pop/Rock
Characterized by their muscular guitar sound and the powerful vocals of frontwoman Jenny Toomey, the aptly named Tsunami was among the most important and original bands to emerge from the American indie scene of the 1990s; the motivating force behind the highly regarded Simple Machines label, the group's sociopolitical activism and unwavering commitment to D.I.Y. principles established them among the most respected voices in the alternative community. Tsunami was formed in Arlington, VA, in 1990 by Toomey and guitarist Kristin Thomson, who together had founded Simple Machines as a result of their constant frustrations with music industry machinations. Toomey, a veteran of such groups as Geek and Slack, soon persuaded bassist pal Andrew Webster to relocate to Arlington and join the fledgling band, and with the addition of drummer John Pamer, the original Tsunami lineup was complete. In early 1991, Tsunami set out on their first tour, in support of the legendary Beat Happening. Upon returning to Arlington, they recorded a four-track demo called *Cow Arcade*; the 7" EP *Headringer*, the quartet's first official release, followed a short time later. Also in 1991, they recorded the brilliant "Genius of Crack" single, released to significant acclaim on the Homestead label. A series of 1992 releases raised the band's profile in the indie community. After so many 7"s, Tsunami finally issued their full-length debut, *Deep End*, in mid-1993. A tour on the support stage of Lollapalooza followed that summer. After a lengthy tour, Tsunami issued their stunning second LP, *The Heart's Tremolo*, in 1994; the road again beckoned, and in spring 1995 they issued *World Tour and Other Destinations*, a much-needed compilation of singles, B-sides, and compilation tracks. In 1997 Tsunami resurfaced with the excellent *A Brilliant Mistake*. Early in 1998, Toomey and Thomson announced the imminent demise of Simple Machines. —*Jason Ankeny*

Deep End / May 31, 1993 / Simple Machines ✦✦✦✦
The group's melodic, witty debut manages to be both heavy and catchy. Toomey and Thompson's vocal and guitar interplay make this an interesting listen. —*Heather Phares*

● **The Heart's Tremolo** / 1994 / Simple Machines ✦✦✦✦✦
The 11 songs on *The Heart's Tremolo* are more polished, complex, and accomplished than those of their debut. Toomey's torchy vocals and the group's trademark droning guitars make this album even better than *Deep End*. —*Heather Phares*

World Tour and Other Destinations / 1995 / Simple Machines ✦✦✦✦✦
This B-side compilation collects the group's plethora of singles in one place. These singles capture the bouncier, poppier side of Tsunami's sound, and this collection could be the starting point for the average listener. —*Heather Phares*

Brilliant Mistake / Sep. 23, 1997 / Simple Machines ✦✦✦
Tsunami's records are usually excellent, but on *The Brilliant Mistake*, Tsunami has truly reached their apex. This stroke of brilliance corresponds to the tragic end of the band's Simple Machines label after seven years of near-flawless production and indie rock mining. The band's earlier attempts at punk rock were often tedious at best, but with these 13 songs, they put aside their punk ambitions and create their cleanest, most cohesive record to date. On "Old Gray Mare," singer Jenny Toomey croons about the metaphorical, while two songs later, pulsing horns accompany her as she wails about struggling against the grain of mainstream society.
The Brilliant Mistake is pure, mellifluous indie rock, the place where a genuine DIY ethos meets pure pop sensibility. As expected, the album is strewn with literary references, from a song dedicated to David Foster Wallace to odd lyrics reworking elements of Allen Ginsberg's "The Howl." This record is often brilliant but never a mistake. —*Marc Ruxin*

The Tubes
f. 1972, San Francisco, CA, **db.** 1986
Album Rock, Arena Rock, Pop/Rock, Hard Rock
The Tubes were arch satirists of popular culture whose outrageous performance-art concepts—which swung wildly from soft-core pornography to suit-and-tie conservatism—frequently eclipsed their elusive musical identity. The Tubes earned a devoted cult following on the strength of guitarist Bill Spooner's parodic songs and the group's surreal live shows, which featured vocalist Fee Waybill adopting a variety of personas including the "crippled Nazi" Dr. Strangekiss, country singer Hugh Heifer, and Quay Lewd, a drug-addled British pop star. After signing to A&M in 1975, they released their self-titled debut, followed a year later by *Young and Rich*; while both failed to transfer the manic energy and theatrical complexity of their live set onto record, the single "White Punks on Dope" became a minor hit and a radio staple. After 1977's failed concept record *The Tubes Now*, the group toured England, where a series of banned performances made them a media sensation. However, during the recording of the concert LP *What Do You Want From*

Live? Waybill broke his leg onstage; the remainder of the tour was cancelled, and with it died the band's chart momentum. After returning to the U.S., they recruited producer Todd Rundgren and recorded 1979's *Remote Control*, a concept album exploring the influence of television; when it met a similar commercial fate as its predecessors, the Tubes were dropped by A&M. After signing to Capitol, they recorded 1981's *Completion Backwards Principle*, an album based on an actual sales training instruction manual; earning significant radio play, the LP became the Tubes' first Top 40 hit. Thanks to its provocative video, the single "She's a Beauty" reached the Top Ten, and pushed the 1983 LP *Outside/Inside* into the Top 20 Albums chart; after 1985's *Love Bomb* stiffed, however, the original lineup of the Tubes disbanded. —*Jason Ankeny*

The Tubes / 1975 / A&M ✦✦✦
Produced by Al Kooper, this debut by the notorious San Francisco group is best known for the blazing anthem "White Punks on Dope." Although the Tubes' *raison d'être* was their shock-rock stage dynamic, Bill Spooner, Fee Waybill, and company could, on occasion, deliver some offbeat pop splendor. A good example is the song "Haloes," co-written with Kooper, a tough power pop jewel that sounds like Todd Rundgren colliding with Roxy Music. Also of note is "Boy Crazy," which shows off Spooner's guitar skills. But for every "Haloes" and "Boy Crazy," there's a novelty number consciously created for the stage and that ultimately embarrasses, such as "Mondo Bondage" and "Space Baby." Kooper's production is faultless, however, as are the horn and string arrangements by Dominic Frontiere (Frontiere did the original score for the '60s cult sci-fi show *The Outer Limits*). —*Peter Kurtz*

Young & Rich / 1976 / A&M ✦✦✦
After knocking out an impressive debut with their self-titled 1975 release, The Tubes fell prey to the dreaded sophomore slump on their second album *Young And Rich*. Although this album contains a fistful of inspired and witty tracks, it simply lacks the coherence and consistent material that made *The Tubes* such a cheeky delight. *Young And Rich* finds the group trying to expand their satirical/theatrical rock style into new subgenres like disco and pre-Beatles pop and this material forms the best moments on this disc: "Slipped my Disco" effectively sends up the social rituals of the disco scene over a backing track that fuses the Tubes' pomp-rock excesses to a mocking dance beat while "Don't Touch Me There" is a hilarious, over-the-top send up of Phil Spector's "wall of sound" style built on a lascivious duet between Fee Waybill and Re Styles. However, the effect of these tracks is diluted by some less-inspired moments where the Tubes hedge their bets by trying to recycle some of the finer moments of their previous album. For instance, "Proud To Be American" tries to skewer the American Dream like "What Do You Want From Life" did but comes off as both toothless and overtly obvious while "Poland Whole/Madam I'm Adam" tries to recapture the orchestral sturm-und-drang of "Up From The Deep" but doesn't have enough riffs and hooks to fill its overtly-busy arrangement. Despite these problems, some other tracks manage to shine through the dull moments: "Tubes World Tour" and the title track is an effective send-up of children of privilege that plays out over a surprisingly elegant ballad-style arrangement. In the end, *Young And Rich* offers enough impressive tracks to satisfy the Tubes connoisseur but the casual listener would be better off sampling its highlights via a compilation. —*Donald A. Guarisco*

Now / 1977 / A&M ✦✦✦

What Do You Want from Live / 1978 / A&M ✦✦✦
Although their studio albums were often hit-and-miss affairs, the Tubes could always be counted on for a good live show during their mid-1970s heyday. In fact, they became a legend in the rock & roll world for the glitzy shows, which included half-nude women performing elaborate dance routines and a variety of characters invented by frontman Fee Waybill like punk rocker "Johnny Bugger" and blissed-out glam rock icon "Quay Lewd." *What Do You Want From Live* can't reproduce all this visual stimuli but it does show what many critics forgot to notice about the Tubes, i.e., the fact that they were a really sharp and exciting live band. Stripped of their outre visual surroundings, songs like "Mondo Bondage" and "I Was A Punk Before You Were A Punk" still pack a visceral punch thanks to their effective combination of gonzo humor and catchy melodies. Elsewhere, the Tubes get to show off their surprisingly impressive chops on "Overture," a fast-paced medley that transforms the instrumental highlights of six different songs into one head-spinning pomp-rock blitz, and "Crime Medley," a witty tapestry of crime jazz woven from television theme songs like "Theme From Peter Gunn" and "Theme From Dragnet." The downside of *What Do You Want From Live* is that some of the numbers are less potent without the choreographed routines surrounding them: "Smoke (La Vie In Fumer)" and "What Do You Want From Life" both feature Fee Waybill talking about the visual chaos surrounding him and this leaves the listener feeling like they're only witnessing part of the joke (if only someone would put out a video of one of the Tubes' shows from this era). Despite this caveat, *What Do You Want From Live* remains a witty and entertaining live album. It may not win any new converts to the Tubes' camp, but fans of the group will definitely want to check out this entertaining souvenir from the group's wildest era. —*Donald A. Guarisco*

Remote Control / 1979 / A&M ✦✦✦✦
After stunning the rock world with their memorable debut in 1975, the Tubes ran into trouble. Although *Young And Rich* and *Now* had fine moments, they were uneven and left many rock pundits wondering if the Tubes had anything to offer besides shock value. They got their answer with the release of *Remote Control*, a cohesive and surprisingly thoughtful concept album. On this 1979 outing, the Tubes enlisted the services of wunderkind producer Todd Rundgren to create a concept album that skewers the television generation. The choice was a wise one—Rundgren helped the group harness their satirical bite and love of pomp-rock excess to create a sharp and engaging collection of songs. As they chronicle the life of an average joe whose life and dreams are swallowed by his

television addiction, the Tubes lead the listener through a dazzling array of musical styles that include new-wave, lounge pop, reggae, and even full-throttle punk. Highlights include "Prime Time," a song that utilizes an effective combination of lounge-lizard atmosphere and new wave synthesizer textures to convey its portrait of television's seductiveness, and "Love's A Mystery (I Don't Understand)," a surprisingly straightforward ballad about romantic loss that features a truly heart-rending vocal from Fee Waybill. The group also gets a chance to show off their formidable instrumental chops on "Get-Overture," a tight instrumental that goes from atmospheric prog-rock to driving hard rock as it cleverly weaves together snippets of all the other songs' melodies. In short, *Remote Control* proves the Tubes were more than a bunch of musical jokesters. The end result is the band's finest hour and a treat for concept-album fanatics. *—Donald A. Guarisco*

T.R.A.S.H. (Tubes Rarities & Smash Hits) / 1981 / A&M ♦♦♦
The Tubes' reputation (or lack thereof) is built on their uninhibited '70s performances, and, to a much lesser extent, on the non-hits collected on *T.R.A.S.H.* Before ultra-clean David Foster production pushed the Tubes into the Top 40 in the '80s, this circus of the insane recorded with an eclectic array of talent, delivering bouncy, wavy Americana spitwads like the immortal "White Punks on Dope" and the materialistic "What Do You Want from Life?" Some funny stuff here ("Slipped my Disco"), but what works onstage, surrounded by naked women, doesn't always require repeat listening. The Tubes were definitely ahead (or outside) of their time, and "Don't Touch Me There" is the kind of looniness Jim Steinman would take to the top and beyond. The Tubes constructed many brilliant singles with wit and depth, but you-had-to-be-there for much of *T.R.A.S.H.* Still, this collection of their A&M work is easy access to the Tube's overlooked '70s stuff, and worth a few spins. *—Doug Stone*

The Completion Backward Principle / 1981 / Capitol ♦♦♦♦
The Completion Backward Principle was the first release on EMI/Capitol by San Francisco-based the Tubes. It found the outrageous septet working with producer David Foster, who gives the record a high-gloss sheen. It's a pairing that, while possibly surprising to fans of the band's earlier releases, actually works quite nicely. The ballads (the Top 40 hit "Don't Want to Wait Anymore" and the Toto-esque "Amnesia") don't suit the band, but most everything else does. There's a pair of catchy new wavish rockers in "Talk to Ya Later" and "Think About Me," the wacky "Sushi Girl," and the R&B-flavored "A Matter of Pride." *The Completion Backward Principle* rightfully earned the Tubes new fans and set the table for their commercial breakthrough, *Outside/Inside*, two years later. *—Tom Demalon*

Outside/Inside / 1983 / Capitol ♦♦

Love Bomb / 1985 / Capitol ♦♦

● **The Best of the Tubes** / Nov. 9, 1992 / A&M ♦♦♦♦♦
The Tubes were true American rock & roll originals who appeared to be headed for permanent cult-band status and a footnote for the minor hit "White Punks on Dope." However, having signed with Capitol at the beginning of the '80s, the group enjoyed a couple of successful albums, several radio hits, and a solid profile on the fledgling MTV. *The Best of the Tubes* culls material from the band's most commercially viable Capitol releases when the band worked with producers David Foster and Todd Rundgren. It contains such radio hits as the energetic Top Ten "She's a Beauty," the horn-laden "Tip of My Tongue," and the pop-crunch of "Piece By Piece." The set is fleshed out with some of the band's better album tracks like "Sushi Girl" and "Talk to Ya Later." The licensing and inclusion of some earlier tracks would have been nice, but for the casual fan, *The Best of the Tubes* is an excellent collection of their best-known and most accessible music. *—Tom Demalon*

The Best of the Tubes 1981-1987 / Mar. 21, 1995 / EMI-Capitol Special Markets ♦♦♦♦♦
The Tubes weren't album rockers in the classic sense, meaning that they didn't have the kind of devotion or mystery that served the likes of Pink Floyd or Yes so well. Nevertheless, there's no question that they were album rockers, crafting concept records about evils like television and receiving heavy, heavy airplay from AOR stations across the country. Ironically, it was that airplay alone that makes the Tubes seem less like the album rockers they actually were—they're better known by their singles, which makes them seem like an average arena-rock band. And they certainly could sound that way, but they were quite a bit stranger and quirkier than *The Best of the Tubes* suggests. Basically, *The Best of the Tubes* offers the basics—"She's a Beauty," "Talk to Ya Later," "Amnesia," "Tip of My Tongue," "The Monkey Time," "Don't Want to Wait Anymore"—without delving too deeply into their Capitol catalog for oddities or solid album tracks. And that's about what most casual listeners will want, since it certainly satisfies anyone's desire to hear the Tubes' greatest hits; but the dedicated will know that the collection just scratches the surface of their strangeness. *—Stephen Thomas Erlewine*

Goin' Down / 1996 / A&M ♦♦♦♦
Although they are known to modern listeners as the band behind the new wave gem "She's A Beauty," the Tubes had an entirely different career during their mid-to-late 1970s tenure on the A&M label. Working with gifted producers like Al Kooper and Todd Rundgren, the group created a body of work that fused prog-rock instrumental virtuosity, the sarcasm of new wave, and Frank Zappa-styled musical satire into a style all its own. Listeners get a great chance to sample the group's ambitious style on *Goin' Down*, a generous two-CD compilation that includes all the group's radio favorites, album tracks from each of their A&M releases (including the *Remote Control* album in its entirety), and most of the rarities that had previously appeared on *T.R.A.S.H. (Tubes Rarities And Smash Hits)*. The end result is one-stop shopping for any listener who wants to get all the highlights of the group's 1970s work without having to hunt down the group's often-inconsistent albums. Songs like "What Do You Want From Life" and "Don't Touch Me There" sound as eccentrically witty as ever, but the real surprises are the album tracks: "My Head Is My Only House Unless It Rains" is a surprisingly subtle ballad full of hypnotic synthesizer textures and "This Town" skewers big city life over a tune that recreates the vintage Frank Sinatra/Dean Martin lounge-pop sound with surprising faithfulness. The package is rounded out by brief but informative liner notes and a selection of provocative pictures from the group's notorious 1970s stage shows. All in all, *Goin' Down* may be a little too much Tubes for the casual listener but it remains the definitive portrait of the group's 1970s era for serious fans. *—Donald A. Guarisco*

20th Century Masters—The Millennium Collection: The Best of the Tubes / Oct. 17, 2000 / A&M ♦♦♦
There's no "She's a Beauty" or "Talk to You Later" on the Tubes' volume of *20th Century Masters: The Millennium Collection*, because those songs were recorded in the early '80s, while the group was on Capitol. This disc concentrates entirely on '70s material for A&M, when the group was at their strangest and artiest. True fans of this era will want to savor the full-length albums, of course, but for those that know the group only through album rock radio and want "White Punks on Dope," "Prime Time," and "Don't Touch Me There" in their collection, yet only want one disc, this is a good place to turn. Not for fans of the group's smoother material, of course, since this is just too weird, but it's still a good, surprisingly thorough sampler of the Tubes' A&M years. *—Stephen Thomas Erlewine*

Big Joe Turner

b. May 18, 1911, Kansas City, MO, **d.** Nov. 24, 1985, Inglewood, CA
Vocals / Jump Blues, Swing, Rock & Roll, R&B, Urban Blues
The premier blues shouter of the postwar era, Big Joe Turner's roar could rattle the very foundation of any gin joint he sang within—and that's without a microphone. Turner was a resilient figure in the history of blues—he effortlessly spanned boogie-woogie, jump blues, even the first wave of rock & roll, enjoying great success in each genre. Turner, whose powerful physique certainly matched his vocal might, was a product of the swinging, wide-open Kansas City scene, hooking up with boogie piano master Pete Johnson during the early '30s. Theirs was a partnership that would endure for 13 years. Atlantic picked up his recording contract in 1951, and Big Joe Turner's heyday commenced with a gorgeously world-weary reading to the moving blues ballad "Chains of Love" that restored him to the uppermost reaches of the R&B charts. From there, the hits came in droves: "Chill Is On," "Sweet Sixteen" and "Don't You Cry" were all done in New York, and all hit big. Big Joe Turner had no problem whatsoever adapting his prodigious pipes to whatever regional setting he was in: in 1953, he cut his first R&B chart-topper, the storming rocker "Honey Hush," in New Orleans, and before the year was through, he stopped off in Chicago to record with slide guitarist Elmore James' considerably rougher-edged combo and hit again with the salacious "T.V. Mama." Prolific Atlantic house writer Jesse Stone was the source of Turner's biggest smash of all, "Shake, Rattle and Roll," which proved his second chart-topper in 1954. Suddenly, at the age of 43, Big Joe Turner was a rock star. His jumping follow-ups—"Well All Right," "Flip Flop and Fly," "Hide and Seek," "Morning, Noon and Night," "The Chicken and the Hawk"—all mined the same goodtime groove. They called him the Boss of the Blues, and the appellation was truly a fitting one: when Big Joe Turner shouted a lyric, you were definitely at his beck and call. *—Bill Dahl*

☆ **Big, Bad & Blue: The Big Joe Turner Anthology** / Dec. 30, 1938-Jan. 26, 1983 / Rhino/ Atlantic ♦♦♦♦♦
This three-record anthology shows how Turner, without really ever changing his style, moved from strict Kansas City swing to pioneering rock & roll and back to basic jazzy blues. It contains 62 songs, everything from treasured hits to slow, sweltering ballads, strident uptempo wailers, moaning blues, novelty tunes and fiery pieces with lyrics and sentiments that wouldn't make it in today's environment. A comprehensive, well-written and lavishly prepared and illustrated booklet with numerous anecdotes and remembrances are the icing on a superb cake. *—Ron Wynn*

Have No Fear, Big Joe Turner Is Here / Feb. 2, 1945-Nov. 29, 1947 / Savoy Jazz ♦♦♦♦
Producer Herb Abramson's first encounters with Big Joe Turner weren't at Atlantic, but for the National logo, where Turner paused from 1945 to 1947 and cut the 26 swinging numbers on this collection. For once, the CD format limits the amount of selections rather than enlarging it; the original two-LP version of this package boasted a few more cuts. Pete Johnson returns to run the 88s on the first seven numbers (including a two-part cover of Saunders King's "S.K. Blues"), and familiar names like saxman Wild Bill Moore and drummer Red Saunders also turn up. "Sally Zu-Zazz," "I Got Love for Sale," and "My Gal's a Jockey" capture the peerless shouter at his ribald best. *—Bill Dahl*

Tell Me Pretty Baby / Nov. 1947-1949 / Arhoolie ♦♦♦♦
Lusty, romping jump blues and boogies from 1947-1949 that team Big Joe Turner with his longtime piano partner Pete Johnson and a coterie of solid L.A. sessioneers. The two dozen entries include party rockers like "Wine-O-Baby Boogie," "Christmas Date Boogie," "I Don't Dig It," and an incredibly raunchy two-part "Around the Clock Blues" (where Turner spends his time in a by-the-hour sexual tryst). *—Bill Dahl*

Rhythm & Blues Years / Apr. 17, 1951-Sep. 29, 1959 / Atlantic ♦♦♦♦♦
Picks up the rest of the 1950s Atlantic Records motherlode. The Chicago-cut double-entendre gem "TV Mama" (with Elmore James on guitar), the lighthearted rockers "Rock a While," "Morning Noon & Night," and "Lipstick, Powder & Paint," and a rip-snorting remake of Turner's classic "Roll 'Em Pete," here titled "(We're Gonna) Jump for Joy," that in its own way rivals the original (King Curtis' blistering sax solo doesn't hurt), are among the many highlights on the 28-song collection. *—Bill Dahl*

★ **Very Best of Big Joe Turner** / 1951-1959 / Rhino ♦♦♦♦♦
The Very Best of Big Joe Turner is an excellent 16-track collection that features his biggest hits from 1951-1959, including "Chains of Love," "Sweet Sixteen," "Honey Hush," "TV Mama," "Shake, Rattle and Roll," "Well All Right," "Flip Flop and Fly," "Hide and Seek,"

"The Chicken and the Hawk (Up, Up and Away)," "Boogie Woogie Country Girl," "Corrine Corrina" and "Midnight Special Train." All of his best-known songs in their hit versions are available on this concise, affordable disc, which makes for an ideal introduction to this legendary R&B vocalist. *—Stephen Thomas Erlewine*

☆ **Boss of the Blues** / Mar. 6, 1956-Mar. 7, 1956 / Atlantic ♦♦♦♦♦
During an era when Big Joe Turner recordings were often surprise hits with rock & roll fans (particularly "Shake, Rattle and Roll"), he occasionally recorded no-nonsense blues-oriented jazz dates too. This reissue album matched Turner for one of the last times with the veteran boogie-woogie pianist Pete Johnson and also includes a variety of top swing players: trumpeter Joe Newman, trombonist Lawrence Brown, altoist Pete Brown, tenor saxophonist Frank Wess, guitarist Freddie Green, bassist Walter Page and drummer Cliff Leeman. It is not surprising, considering the number of Basieites on the date, that the band often sounds like a Count Basie combo. Turner is in top form on remakes of some of his early tunes (including "Cherry Red," "Roll 'Em Pete" and "Wee Baby Blues"), a few traditional blues and a couple of swing standards. This music should appeal to many listeners. *—Scott Yanow*

☆ **Jumpin' with Joe: The Complete Aladdin & Imperial Recordings** / Jan. 11, 1994 / EMI America ♦♦♦♦♦
Big Joe Turner's remarkable recordings for Atlantic and Decca have been frequently reissued and evaluated. But his singles for other labels haven't gotten similar treatment, which makes this 18-cut single-disc anthology of Aladdin and Imperial material so welcome. These were recorded in the late '40s and early '50s and were closer to the Kansas City swing Turner had done earlier in his career; there was more emphasis on lyric interpretation, swing, and timing than sheer volume and volcanic, non-stop hollering. Although these songs aren't remembered as fondly as the landmark Atlantic numbers, they're just as important a part of Turner's legacy. *—Ron Wynn*

Ike Turner

b. Nov. 5, 1931, Clarksdale, MS
Producer, Vocals, Guitar (Electric), Songwriter, Piano, Guitar / Electric Memphis Blues, Soul-Blues, R&B, Soul

It is arguably true that Ike Turner would have never amounted to more than a footnote to rock history if he hadn't joined forces with Tina Turner in 1960. But as a solo artist, he's an important footnote. In 1951, he made a lasting contribution to music by playing piano on Jackie Brenston's "Rocket 88," which is often cited as one of the very first rock & roll records. That session was one of the first blues/R&B/rock & roll dates produced at Sun Studios in Memphis; Turner learned guitar shortly afterward, and backed up other R&B artists at Sun in the early '50s. Throughout the decade, the guitarist and piano player was a prolific session player, contributing to records by blues legends Elmore James, Howlin' Wolf, and Otis Rush.

Ike also backed a host of obscure R&B artists in his early years, occasionally issuing discs under his name. Not much of a singer, both his own records and the ones he contributed to and/or produced often showcased his stinging, bluesy licks, and the best of his solo outings tended to be his instrumentals. He continued to put out the occasional solo session and work with other artists after he hooked up with Tina, sometimes under the name Ike Turner's Kings of Rhythm. His career lurched along in obscurity after he broke up with Tina in the mid-'70s, though he remained active. *—Richie Unterberger*

Trailblazer / 1957 / Charly ♦♦♦♦♦
During 1956 and early 1957, Ike Turner's Kings of Rhythm recorded for the Cincinnati-based Federal label—the group's personnel included Raymond Hill and Eddie Jones on tenor sax, Jackie Brenston on baritone sax, Annie Mae Wilson and Fred Sample on piano, Jessie Knight, Jr. on bass, Eugene Washington on drums, and Turner on guitar, with vocalists including Brenston and Billy Gayles. This is some of the most solid material in Turner's output, with a rich, soulful sound, more polished than most of the group's output on Cobra. Some of the music is derivative—in seeking chart success, the group at various times sought to emulate the Coasters, Bill Justis, et al., but they almost always put their own spin on these numbers. Billy Gayles' impassioned vocals on "No Coming Back," Jackie Brenston's boisterous rendition of "The Mistreater," and the rest are all worth the price of admission, which is fairly low on this mid-priced import—but, surprisingly, some of the best stuff on here is by the Kings of Rhythm backing the vocal group the Gardenias ("Miserable," one of the best tracks among these 20, remained unreleased until 1991). And the real treat here is Turner's guitar pyrotechnics. He could strum along like most band guitarists, and occasionally did this, but he preferred to step out front and, having discovered the use of the tremelo arm on his guitar, he fairly tortures the instrument on several of these sides (check out the break on "No Comin' Back," and his accompaniment on "She Made My Blood Run Cold," itself an R&B track deserving of legendary status), and even gets a Hawaiian sound out of his instrument on "Trail Blazer." Fans of rock & roll guitar must own this record. *—Bruce Eder*

1958-1959 / May 13, 1993 / Paula ♦♦♦♦♦
Ever the hustler, Ike Turner found himself picking up some extra money on a road trip through Chicago recording for Cobra Records both as a bandleader and sideman. After contributing the sparkle to several Otis Rush classics (an alternate of one of them, "Keep On Loving Me Baby" is found here) and some early Buddy Guy sides, Turner also recorded a handful of sides, scant few of them seeing release until now. This CD collects them all up, including surviving alternate versions, and is a delightful fly on the wall invite to a 1950s Chicago blues session. *—Cub Koda*

● **I Like Ike! The Best of Ike Turner** / Nov. 15, 1994 / Rhino ♦♦♦♦♦
18 songs spotlighting Turner's work as a bandleader, guitarist, and solo artist from 1951 to 1972, concentrating heavily on his work in the 1950s and early '60s. Leading off with Jackie Brenston's classic "Rocket 88," it includes rare singles featuring Turner by Dennis Binder, the Sly Fox, Willie King, and others, along with rare Turner solo recordings, some under the pseudonym Icky Renrut, and a 1958 45 with Tina, then known as Annie Mae Bullock, on backing vocals. These singers are usually journeymen, frankly, and the material is rather standard-issue R&B; better are the instrumentals, which give Ike a chance to really strut his distinctive tone. *—Richie Unterberger*

Rhythm Rockin' Blues / Nov. 1995 / Ace ♦♦♦
This is the definitive early Ike Turner collection, at least until someone comes out with a box that assembles *everything.* The 21 tracks here are mostly drawn from Turner's early-'50s sessions with the Kings of Rhythm at the Clarksdale studio, done under the auspices of the Bihari Brothers' Modern, RPM, and Flair labels. Apart from a few well-known numbers like the classic "Rocket 88," much of the material here isn't in other collections, nor has it been assembled in one place before—some of it has shown up on vinyl, but never together on CD. It consists of Turner working with the Kings of Rhythm, evolving his guitar and piano technique and pumping up the volume and beat on R&B, pushing it toward rock & roll. The highlight for completists is the medley "All the Blues, All the Time," on which Turner, newly confident on the guitar, goes through an extended instrumental medley of B.B. King, Elmore James, Muddy Waters, and John Lee Hooker material. Also included is some hard R&B-cum-rock & roll by the Kings of Rhythm fronted by J. W. Walker, Little Johnny Burton, Dennis Binder, Lonnie "The Cat," and Billy Gayles. The interesting thing is that "Rocket 88," for all of its renown, is just one of the good tracks here—"Early Times" by Dennis Binder could just as easily have caught the public's fancy with its beat. The sound is somewhat compressed on some of the early material (and, especially, the Johnny Wright/Ike Turner orchestra numbers, although Turner's guitar is real sharp on "The World Is Yours"), but generally it is equal or superior to any other digital incarnation of the individual tracks, and the notes are extremely thorough. *—Bruce Eder*

Ike's Instrumentals / 2000 / Ace ♦♦♦
Taken from a variety of sources, this collects 22 of Ike Turner's instrumentals from 1954-1965, none of them vocals, none of them recorded with Tina Turner, and all of them highlighting his guitar work. Turner's really wild and uninhibited for much of this set, especially in his ferocious string-bending and use of the whammy bar. While the tunes themselves are mostly generic R&B with a touch of rock & roll, it's also fair to say that generic instrumental rock rarely sounds this good, mostly because Turner's guitar work is so much more inventive and passionate than the nominal songs to which they're tethered. About half of this consists of the tracks on his 1962 Sue album, *Dance With Ike & Tina Turner and Their Kings of Rhythm Band,* a good showcase for his crackling axework on a batch of mostly self-imposed wordless workouts. There are also a couple of numbers he cut in the late '50s under the pseudonym Icky Renrut; a 1965 single with brass that has a more soul-oriented arrangement than anything else here, albeit soul of a gutbucket kind; and a smattering of items dating back to his mid-'50s R&B days with Flair. There's also an odd nine-minute medley of instrumental blues covers, "All the Blues All the Time," which wound up on a 1963 Crown LP, *Rocks the Blues.* *—Richie Unterberger*

Ike and Tina Turner

f. 1959, **db.** 1976
R&B, Soul

There was a time when the Ike and Tina Turner Revue was one of the hottest, most durable, and potentially most explosive of all R&B ensembles. Fronted by Tina, with one of the rawest, most sensual and impossibly dynamic voices in black music, the Ike and Tina Revue was an ensemble that dripped musical discipline while manifesting nearly unbearable tension, eventually giving way to wave upon wave of catharsis. They met in 1959 in East St. Louis, where Ike's Kings of Rhythm were the reigning patriarchs of the local R&B scene; their most famous record, "Rocket 88," appeared under the moniker "Jackie Brenston with his Delta Cats" in 1951 and played an integral part in jump-starting the rock & roll revolution. Once Tina joined the Kings of Rhythm, life changed for all concerned. They recorded a demo of "A Fool in Love" in late 1959; by the autumn of 1960 the record was a number two R&B hit on Sue Records. "I Idolize You," "It's Gonna Work Out Fine," "Poor Fool," and "Tra La La La La" all quickly followed, giving the Revue five Top Ten R&B hits in two and a half years. All told, from 1960 to 1975 Ike and Tina Turner placed 25 records on the R&B charts for nine separate record companies. Their most successful pop recording was a reworking of Creedence Clearwater Revival's "Proud Mary" in 1971. *—Rob Bowman*

The Sound of Ike and Tina Turner / 1960 / Collectables ♦♦♦♦♦
Another early-'60s Ike and Tina Turner album, with Tina sounding tentative at times, and other times gaining confidence as the song progressed. They were far from a finished, polished act, especially in the studio. Tina was still determining how much power and sensuality she had in her voice and was developing her delivery and presentation, while Ike was honing the backdrop, and his band learning when to push and when to lay out behind Tina. *—Ron Wynn*

River Deep—Mountain High / 1966 / A&M ♦♦♦♦♦
These sessions, recorded in 1966, were produced by Phil Spector. Spector's production chops and Tina's voice were a match made in heaven. Tina possesses one of the strongest voices ever committed to wax; Spector envelops it in the grandest version of his Wall of Sound that he ever conceived. Besides the title track, Spector cut the Turners redoing their first three chart hits, "A Fool in Love," "I Idolize You," and "It's Gonna Work Out Fine." Although it's a sacrilege to say so, these versions are better than the originals. Finally, Turner's performance of the obscure Holland-Dozier-Holland ditty "A Love Like Yours" is another phenomenal highlight. *—Rob Bowman*

Workin' Together / 1970 / One Way ✦✦✦✦✦
Released late in 1970, a few months after *Come Together*, their first album for Liberty Records, *Workin' Together* was the first genuine hit album Ike & Tina had in years; actually, it was their biggest ever, working its way into Billboard's Top 25 and spending 38 weeks on the charts. They never had a bigger hit (the closest was their Blue Thumb release, *Outta Season*, which peaked at 91), and, in many ways, they didn't make a better album. After all, their classic '60s sides were just that—sides of a single, not an album. Even though it doesn't boast the sustained vision of such contemporaries as, say, Marvin Gaye and Al Green, *Workin' Together* feels like a proper album, where many of the buried album tracks are as strong as the singles. Like its predecessor, it relies a bit too much on contemporary covers, which isn't bad when it's the perennial "Proud Mary," since it deftly reinterprets the original, but readings of the Beatles' "Get Back" and "Let It Be," while not bad, are a little bit too pedestrian. Fortunately, they're entirely listenable and they're the only slow moments, outweighed by songs that crackle with style and passion. Nowhere is this truer than on the opening title track, a mid-tempo groover (written by Icky Renrut, Ike's brilliant inverted alias) powered by a soulful chorus and a guitar line that plays like a mutated version of Dylan's "I Want You" riff. Then, there's the terrific Stax/Volt stomper "(Long As I Can) Get You When I Want You," possibly the highlight on the record. Though they cut a couple of classics over the next few years, most notably "Nutbush City Limits," the duo never topped this, possibly the best proper album they ever cut. *—Stephen Thomas Erlewine*

Nutbush City Limits / 1973 / United Artists ✦✦✦✦✦
The album that marked the end of the Ike and Tina Turner alliance, although it wasn't their last album. But the turmoil that they were undergoing off-stage would soon shatter their personal and professional union. They scored a major international hit with the title cut, and also told their life story, although it turned out that this tale was a fantasy. Here's one of the few Ike and Tina Turner albums that deserves to be back in print. *—Ron Wynn*

● **Proud Mary: The Best of Ike & Tina Turner** / Mar. 18, 1991 / EMI America ✦✦✦✦✦
Proud Mary—The Best of Ike and Tina Turner is a fine 23-track collection that looks at the Turners' career at the beginning and the end. Their early-'60s hits on Juggy Murray's Sue label are included, as are their early- and mid-'70s successes on Liberty and United Artists. The mid- and late-'60s recordings for Kent, Loma, Modern, Innis, Blue Thumb, and Minit are not here, unfortunately. Superior liner notes round out a fine package. *—Rob Bowman*

Bold Soul Sister: The Best of the Blue Thumb Recordings / Jul. 15, 1997 / Hip-O ✦✦✦✦✦
Make no mistake about it, this 16-track collection culled from their two albums recorded for the Blue Thumb label in 1969 (*Outta Season* and *The Hunter*) is as much Ike's show as it is Tina's—truly the other half of the equation, the blues part of rhythm & blues. His stinging guitar matches Tina's voice lick for nasty lick, and the blues song choices ("Dust My Broom," "Three O'Clock Blues," "Please Love Me," "Five Long Years," "You Don't Love Me," "Mean Old World," "Rock Me Baby," "Honest I Do," "Reconsider Baby") were undoubtedly tunes he and the Kings of Rhythm knew in their sleep, playing them since they were new hits on the charts. These were the last truly pure R&B albums the two of them would ever make, and even the then-current stabs at R&B trends (the title track is little more than Ike's version of a James Brown groove with Tina babbling in true JB incomprehensibility in spots) shine brightly in the spotlight of hindsight. Subtitled *The Best of the Blue Thumb Recordings*, this makes a great document of what they must have sounded like in the clubs that dotted the landscape of the chitlin circuit way back when. *—Cub Koda*

The Kent Years / May 16, 2000 / Kent ✦✦✦✦
Twenty-six of the duo's 1964-1967 recordings (five previously unissued) for the Kent and Modern labels are on this compilation. Note, however, that this is just a partial retrospective of their mid-'60s work, since during this time the Turners were also releasing sides on several different other labels. It remains, though, a good sampling of their sound during this era, when their soul tracks still betrayed much of their blues/R&B roots, and before the arrangements had gotten as heavy and beefy as they would in the late '60s and early '70s. Tina Turner's vocals are unflaggingly enthusiastic and committed, if perhaps not as nuanced as they could be. What keeps this from the top rank of mid-'60s soul, however, is the largely average, occasionally below average material (mostly written by Ike Turner). It's often a collision of blues, chitlin circuit R&B, and brassy pop-soul that sounds a bit dashed off. There are some ace moments along the way, of course, like the infectious "I Can't Believe What You Say," the down-and-bluesy "Hurt Is All You Gave Me," and the swaggering soul-swing shuffle of "Chicken Shack." Ike Turner's twangy guitar seems underutilized for much of the set, and there's very little of the vocal sparring that would be such a big part of their act by the early '70s. Tina Turner goes into a big rap on the previously unissued "All I Could Do Was Cry" where she really overdoes the raspy breast-beating; Etta James' more famous version has a big edge. "Give Me Your Love" is minor-keyed blues/R&B that's not too far from Otis Rush territory; at the other extreme, "Makin' Plans Together" has gossamer strings typical of the New York pop-soul on the Scepter/Wand labels. *—Richie Unterberger*

Tina Turner

b. Nov. 26, 1938, Nutbush, TN
Vocals / Pop/Rock, R&B, Soul
The most dynamic female soul singer in the history of the music, Tina Turner oozed sexuality from every pore in a performing career that began the moment she stepped onstage as lead singer of the Ike & Tina Turner Revue in the late '50s. Her gritty and growling performances beat down doors everywhere, looking back to the double-barreled attack of gospel fervor and sexual abandon that had originally formed soul in the early '50s. Divorced from Ike in the mid-'70s, she recorded only occasionally later in the decade but resurfaced in the mid-'80s with a series of hit singles and movie appearances. Ike & Tina Turner began hitting the charts in 1960 and notched charting singles for over a decade, including the number four hit "Proud Mary." Increasingly frustrated by Ike's increasingly irrational behavior however, Tina walked out in 1974 and recorded several albums for United Artists, though with little attention. Turner returned in 1983, and hit with "What's Love Got to Do with It," one of the biggest singles of the following year. Her album *Private Dancer* included two more Top Ten singles, the title track and "Better Be Good to Me." She also found a number two hit with the theme to *Mad Max: Beyond Thunderdome*, "We Don't Need Another Hero." Though her chart success began to decline in the late '80s, her high-profile status was assured well into the '90s. *—John Bush*

● **Private Dancer** / Nov. 16, 1984 / Capitol ✦✦✦✦✦
In 1984, a 45-year-old Tina Turner made one of the most amazing comebacks in the history of American popular music. A few years earlier, it was hard to imagine the veteran soul/rock belter reinventing herself and returning to the top of the pop charts, but she did exactly that with the outstanding *Private Dancer*. And Turner did so without sacrificing her musical integrity. To be sure, this pop/rock/R&B pearl is decidedly slicker than such raw, earthy, hard-edged Ike & Tina classics as "Proud Mary," "Sexy Ida," and "I Wanna Take You Higher." But she still has a tough, throaty, passionate delivery that serves her beautifully on everything from the melancholy, reggae-influenced "What's Love Got to Do with It" to the gutsy "Better Be Good to Me" to heartfelt remakes of the Beatles' "Help," Al Green's "Let's Stay Together" and David Bowie's "1984." A reflection on the emptiness of a stripper's life, the dusky title song is as poignant as it is depressing. Without question, this was Turner's finest hour as a solo artist. *—Alex Henderson*

Break Every Rule / 1986 / Capitol ✦✦✦
Because it contains its share of memorable and inspired material—and even a few gems—it seems inappropriate to call *Break Every Rule* a disappointment. But because *Private Dancer* was so incredible a comeback, one greeted this anxiously awaited follow-up with such high expectations that anything less than outstanding would have been disappointing. And the album isn't outstanding—generally quite enjoyable and far from weak, but not outstanding. Be that as it may, there's a lot to savor here. "Two People" is forgettable, but Turner definitely has some gems in the power ballad "I'll Be Thunder," the driving rocker "Back Where You Started" and the haunting David Bowie piece "Girls." While *Private Dancer* would be a much better introduction to Turner's work as a solo artist, this has more pluses than minuses. *—Alex Henderson*

Tina Live in Europe / 1988 / Capitol ✦✦

Foreign Affair / Sep. 13, 1989 / Capitol ✦✦✦
Turner's last studio album for Capitol was produced by the late Dan Hartman of "Instant Replay" disco fame; however, this was not a retro '70s-style album. This set was comprised of 12 mature, middle-range, adult rock and pop songs. Turner tackled rock on "Steamy Windows" and "The Best," the latter a universal hit. She created fine club tracks such as "Falling Like Rain," "I Don't Wanna Lose You," and "Look Me in the Heart." Still, she cooled down long enough for a couple of gutbucket ballads in "Be Tender With Me Baby" and "Ask Me How I Feel." The most interesting cut was the scorching return to Turner's Delta roots on the flawless "Undercover Agent for the Blues," one of the finest pop-blues performances since B.B. King's "The Thrill Is Gone." Despite the slight musical style variations, the whole project was wrapped in an enticing pop style that gave it buoyancy and synthesis. *—Bill Carpenter*

Simply the Best / 1991 / Capitol ✦✦✦✦✦
A solid greatest-hits collection culled from her solo Capitol albums. Includes "Typical Male," "Steamy Windows" (written and produced by Tony Joe White), "I Can't Stand the Rain," and a duet with Rod Stewart on "It Takes Two." *—Cub Koda*

What's Love Got to Do with It / Jun. 15, 1993 / Virgin ✦✦✦
This is the soundtrack for the Tina Turner film that got Angela Bassett and Lawrence Fishburne Oscar nominations. There's little here that you couldn't get elsewhere in better versions, but if you only want a hint of the music Tina Turner made in various contexts, with and without Ike, this would be a serviceable purchase. Otherwise, get the film and hear the music in the correct setting. *—Ron Wynn*

The Collected Recordings—Sixties to Nineties / Nov. 15, 1994 / Capitol ✦✦✦
Over the course of three discs, *Collected Recordings—Sixties to Nineties* runs through most of Tina Turner's biggest hits, both with and without Ike Turner. However, the third disc comprises nothing but obscurities, making the collection a bit too much for anyone but the most devoted fans. *—Stephen Thomas Erlewine*

Wildest Dreams / Sep. 3, 1996 / Virgin ✦✦

Twenty Four Seven / Dec. 7, 1999 / Virgin ✦✦✦
The album is actually credited to just Tina, and no one has earned the right to a single moniker more than the former Mrs. Turner. Now over 60, Tina has picked a suite of songs about survival, a topic she knows well, and imbued them with as much soul as she can muster. Tina still puts Mariah Carey and Celine Dion to shame. But unfortunately, on *Twenty Four Seven*, the famous Turner passion is often submerged in glossy production that virtually defines "adult contemporary." In some transcendent moments, Tina reminds us of the woman who sang "River Deep, Mountain High"—like when she spits out "I've never been a winner but I still play the game" in "All the Woman," or during the powerful coda to "I Will Be There." As Tina sings in "Absolutely Nothing's Changed," she's lived to fight another day, and that's proof she ain't been broken. *—Mark Morgenstein*

The Turtles

f. 1963, Los Angeles, CA, **db.** 1970
Sunshine Pop, Folk-Rock, Pop

Though many remember only their 1967 hit "Happy Together," the Turtles were one of the more enjoyable American pop groups of the 1960s, moving from folk-rock inspired by the Byrds to a sparkling fusion of Zombies-inspired chamber-pop and straight-ahead good-time pop reminiscent of the Lovin' Spoonful, infused with beautiful vocal harmonies. Formed as early as 1963, the group's first single was a folk-rock cover of Bob Dylan's "It Ain't Me Babe" that followed the Byrds' own Dylan cover ("Mr. Tambourine Man") into the Top Ten during 1965. After hitting the Top 40 twice more, the Turtles appeared to run out of steam by the beginning of 1967 but stormed back with the infectious number one hit "Happy Together." The group made the expected leap into psychedelia with two Top Ten hits ("Elenore," "You Showed Me") during 1968, and produced an interesting concept LP (*The Turtles Present the Battle of the Bands*) but broke up before the end of the decade. Dual frontmen Howard Kaylan and Mark Volman later appeared with Frank Zappa's Mothers of Invention, and recorded on their own as Flo & Eddie. —*John Bush*

It Ain't Me Babe / Oct. 1965 / Sundazed ✦✦✦✦✦
The Turtles' first album presents them as a folk-rock group covering a lot of Dylan and P. F. Sloan material. They also found "It Was a Very Good Year" on a Kingston Trio album and cut it. Frank Sinatra heard their version and had one of his bigger hits with it, but their version is good too. —*William Ruhlmann*

You Baby / 1966 / Sundazed ✦✦✦
On their second album, The Turtles stuck to the same brand of sunny, commercial folk-rock as their debut. It's pleasant fare, but hardly in the same league as The Byrds, Lovin' Spoonful, or The Mamas & The Papas, and the group's original material is spotty and sometimes awkward. The best cuts are the ones penned by the Barri/Sloan songwriting team, including the hits "You Baby" and "Can I Get to Know You Better." —*Richie Unterberger*

Happy Together / Apr. 1967 / Sundazed ✦✦✦✦✦
The Turtles's best studio album includes the title hit, "She'd Rather Be with Me," "Guide for the Married Man," and then-unknown Warren Zevon's "Like the Seasons," among other songs. —*William Ruhlmann*

The Turtles Present the Battle of the Bands / Nov. 1968 / Sundazed ✦✦✦✦
Though the Turtles were rightfully known as an excellent pop-rock singles band, on this recording they let loose on humor, which was part of their act from the beginning. On the outside cover the group is dressed in conservative suits and bow ties, yet on the inside the group is clad in, shall it be tastefully said, less traditional attire. The Turtles (who wrote nine of the 12 songs on the original LP, two songs being added to the CD) basically mock the entire spectrum of music on this album, though elements of their pop-rock sound are contained even in the most country, psychedelic, and R&B elements of the music presented here. Two top ten hits are contained in this collection, Roger McGuinn's "You Showed Me" and the Turtles own subtly mocking "Elenore." Light psychedelia meets Booker T and the MG's in the instrumental "Buzzsaw." The Beach Boys sound shows up in "Surfer Dan" and the original album closer "Earth Anthem" is a hippie ecology, folk-pop anthem that is both very pretty and quite satirical—a listener could easily lose himself in the fine melody and atmospheric production, while laughing at the same time. The only potential problem with this album is that it is caught in the middle between two extremes: On the one hand, non-mainstream listeners will criticize the album for sounding too commercial, and on the other, typical Turtles fans will find the album too sophisticated, especially if they are looking for another album like "Happy Together." Between these two points of view falls an excellent album that is both commercial and comical, as if both of these elements couldn't coincide in one album. —*Michael Ofjord*

Turtle Soup / Nov. 1969 / Sundazed ✦✦✦
The group's final album, produced by Ray Davies, is a modestly enjoyable collection of good-time rock, occasionally with a slight progressive or satirical edge. The Turtles always seemed to harbor some serious ambitions, but the fact was that their only true forte was catchy pop/rock singles; when they aimed for more, the results were pleasant but unmemorable. There aren't any hit singles missing in action here, except maybe "You Don't Have to Walk in the Rain," so unless you're a dedicated fan you can pass without remorse. The CD reissue has a couple of bonus tracks. —*Richie Unterberger*

Wooden Head / 1970 / Sundazed ✦✦✦
In 1970, both White Whale Records and the Turtles, their biggest act, were on the verge of ending. This assortment of unreleased odds and ends from their early years was hastily assembled as a posthumous collection, although several of the tracks hadn't been properly finished. Surprisingly, it survives as one of their stronger albums, focusing almost exclusively on their early pop/folk-rock sound. Arguably, it's better than either of their first two official LPs, perhaps because they weren't able to sweeten the tracks with superfluous overdubs. Besides several strong originals, it features interesting compositions by P.F. Sloan, David Gates, and Peter & Gordon. The album, confusingly, has been reissued at various points by Rhino, Repertoire, and Sundazed, all with different bonus tracks. The Rhino configuration, which adds the nice folk-rocker "Is It Any Wonder?" and the odd, mordant, psychedelic-tinged 1966 flop single "Grim Reaper of Love," is a bit preferable to the Sundazed one. —*Richie Unterberger*

● **20 Greatest Hits** / 1983 / Rhino ✦✦✦✦✦
Rhino's *20 Greatest Hits* stands as the finest Turtles collection yet assembled, featuring not only all of their hits, but also providing good insight into why certain '60s fans believe

the group to be one of the most underrated pop groups of their time. The very nature of this kind of collection downplays the group's idiosyncratic nature and warped sense of humor—it's hard to tell that they're responsible for such a delightful detour as their *Battle of the Bands* album, where they assumed a different persona for each cut—but it does bring their music to the forefront. And while some of these songs, such as "Happy Together," may be overly familiar, the music still retains a bright freshness whether its through folky melodies, exuberant sunshine pop, or dreamy psych-pop. It's a dynamite summation of a fine band. —*Stephen Thomas Erlewine*

20/20

f. 1976, Tulsa, OK
Power Pop

20/20 was formed in Tulsa, Oklahoma, by high school friends Steve Allen (guitar, vocals) and Ron Flynt (bass, vocals). They relocated to Los Angeles in 1977, adding Mike Gallo on drums, and began playing local clubs. Greg Shaw, the head of Bomp! Records, was impressed with their highly charged power-pop and signed them to his label in 1978. The resulting single, "Under the Freeway," created enough interest in the band to secure a deal with Portrait Records. They added keyboardist Chris Silagyi and recorded their first LP, *20/20*. "Cheri" from the album saw some minor regional success but the album was virtually ignored apart from critical acclaim. The follow-up, *Look Out!* (1981), was equally strong but again failed. The band was dropped by Portrait in 1982 and effectively disbanded. They returned in 1982 with the independently released *Sex Trap*, but by this time, their sound was out of style and the band finally called it quits. A revived interest in the genre in the '90s inspired the band to reunite, contributing a few new songs to Big Deal's *Yellow Pills* compilations and recording a new album, *4 Day Tornado* for the fall of 1995 on Oglio Records. 20/20 returned in August of 1998 with *Interstate*. —*Chris Woodstra*

20/20 / 1979 / Portrait ✦✦✦✦✦
Released during the initial power-pop craze of the late '70s, the band's self-titled debut quickly stood out among the masses with its consistent quality, strict adherence to the melodic three-minute form, and tight, driving rhythm. Though the sales didn't reflect the strength of the album, songs like "Cheri" and "Yellow Pills" are considered classics of the period, the latter becoming the title for the premier power-pop fanzine, still in existence today. —*Chris Woodstra*

Look Out! / Jun. 1981 / Portrait ✦✦✦✦
An equally strong follow-up, *Look Out!*, is a pure pop artifact with its teen anthems discussing the "nuclear boys in the nuclear world," obsessing over girls (the haunting "Girl like You"), and telling the tale of a bizarre alien love affair (the silly "Alien"). *Look Out!* and *20/20* have been reissued as a two-fer CD on Oglio in 1995—an essential part of any power-pop collection. —*Chris Woodstra*

Sex Trap / 1982 / Teldec ✦✦✦
The mid-'80s were not kind to "skinny tie" bands like 20/20. By 1984, Portrait had dropped the band, forcing them to go independent with *Sex Trap*. As the title indicates, they shifted to a raunchier, harder-rocking band, with much of the gloss of the previous efforts removed. A slight misstep but still worth seeking out for completists. —*Chris Woodstra*

4 Day Tornado / Sep. 19, 1995 / Oglio ✦✦✦
During their brief existence in the early '80s, 20/20 represented all that was great about power-pop with their youthful exuberance and endlessly catchy melodies. *4 Day Tornado* marks the band's long awaited return, picking up right where they left off more than a decade earlier. The album serves as a gift to the loyal fans rather than attempting to break new ground or increase the band's small following. Those who loved the first two albums won't be disappointed with this one either. —*Chris Woodstra*

● **20/20/Look Out!** / 1997 / Oglio ✦✦✦✦✦
Oglio's pairing of *20/20* and *Look Out!*—the two finest albums in their catalog—on one CD remains one of the absolute essential American power-pop collections. —*Chris Woodstra*

Interstate / Aug. 11, 1998 / Oglio ✦✦✦
Throughout *Interstate*, 20/20 manages to never turn their instruments up all the way to 11. But this is a good thing as there's more of an emphasis on their country twang of guitar pop. With their use of slide guitars and slight influence of the Beatles, the melodic side of alternative country shines through as *Interstate* carries on this interesting hybrid. Not as gritty and dirty as the majority of acts that fit this genre, but enjoyable nonetheless. —*Mike DaRonco*

Dwight Twilley

b. Jun. 6, 1951, Tulsa, OK
Vocals, Keyboards / Album Rock, Power Pop

Though the Dwight Twilley Band only had one hit (Twilley had another on his own), Twilley and partner Phil Seymour created an enduring and highly memorable brand of power-pop that blended Beatlesque pop and Sun rockabilly "slapback" echo. Only a fraction of the band's early output was made available at the time, but these records are highly revered by power-pop aficionados. The two had recorded together for seven years before signing to the Shelter label in 1974. Their first single, "I'm on Fire," became a national hit in 1975, peaking at number 16, with relatively no promotion. Their follow-up single and completed album, *Sincerely*, went unreleased for 18 months due to label problems. *Twilley Don't Mind*, recorded for Arista in 1977, stiffed as well. Seymour left the band the following year, pursuing a brief solo career before lymphoma cut his life short in 1993. Twilley carried on as a solo act, releasing *Twilley* for Arista in 1979, *Scuba Divers* for EMI in 1982, and found success again with *Jungle* in 1984, when he scored his second hit with "Girls." Two newly recorded songs appeared on the "best of" collection *XXI* and he released an album titled *The Luck* in 2001. *The Great Lost Twilley Album* collects a fraction of the "hundreds" of unreleased songs Twilley and Seymour recorded in the early, ill-fated days. *—Chris Woodstra*

Sincerely / 1976 / The Right Stuff ✦✦✦✦✦
In power pop circles, the Dwight Twilley band's debut album is a classic, revered for its shiny, nervy blend of sparkling British Invasion pop and old-fashioned rock & roll. In other words, it sounds like Big Star, but with a swagger, a sneer, and a tough garage band mentality. Its rocking spirit is all the more remarkable when you realize that the band in question is simply Twilley and cohort Phil Seymour, and the two played every instrument and produced nearly every cut. Musically, the album is undeniably classicist, but there is so much spirit to the recording and songs that it's hard not to get caught up in the record, particularly when the music is as tight as "I'm on Fire" or as evocative as the lightly psychedelic title track. It's easy to see why this is a power pop touchstone—arriving after the twin titans of Badfinger and Big Star, this has sparkling tunes and a do-it-yourself spirit that isn't just great to listen to, it makes you think you can do it, too. Over the years, it has been proven that it's not that easy, and this record remains one of the greatest power pop platters precisely because of that. *—Stephen Thomas Erlewine*

Twilley Don't Mind / 1977 / The Right Stuff ✦✦✦✦
For their second record, Dwight Twilley and Phil Seymour expanded their sound, working with producer/engineer Bob Schaper, adding lead guitarist Bill Pitcock IV, and bringing in guest musicians, including Tom Petty, on occasion, in addition to adding horns and strings on various tracks. Given all these add-ons, it should come as no surprise that *Twilley Don't Mind* isn't as tight or rocking as *Sincerely*, even if the title track that kicks off the record is one of the hardest rocking things they ever cut. Also, the songs, while just a slight notch below those on the original, remain terrific retro-pop tunes, illustrating why this group is held in such high regard among power pop aficionados. Though it may not quite reach the heights of its predecessor, it's a worthy successor and is a large part of Twilley's legacy. *—Stephen Thomas Erlewine*

Twilley / 1979 / Arista ✦✦✦✦✦

Scuba Divers / 1982 / EMI ✦✦✦
1982's *Scuba Divers* continues the band's fine pop tradition though the material is not quite up to the standards of its predecessors. *—AMG*

Jungle / 1984 / EMI ✦✦✦
Twilley makes an unexpected return to the charts with the Top 20 hit single "Girls." The rest of *Jungle* is as enjoyable as that single. *—AMG*

Wild Dogs / 1986 / CBS ✦✦

The Great Lost Twilley Album / Apr. 1993 / DCC ✦✦✦✦
The rumor had always been that the original Dwight Twilley Band had completed four albums between 1974 and 1978 that were never released due to problems with their label, Shelter Records; the few writers and personal friends who heard the albums claimed the material was superior to much of their released work. *The Great Lost Twilley Album* collects the best "lost" tracks from this era, as well as prime material from the unreleased *Blueprint* album from 1980; true to the myth, the songs are easily as good as the band's classic early albums. The band especially shines on the proposed follow-up to the hit "I'm on Fire," "Shark," an infectious rocker that stands as one of the great "should-have-been-hits." *—Chris Woodstra*

● **XXI** / Mar. 19, 1996 / The Right Stuff ✦✦✦✦✦
Despite critical raves at the time and the undeniable high quality of the songs, the Dwight Twilley Band never quite achieved the success they so sorely deserved. *XXI* collects the finer moments of the band's brief recording career, which only ran from 1976 to 1978, as well as highlights from Twilley's solo work, spanning from 1979 to late 1995. This 21-track compilation offers a good sampling of album favorites, the hits ("I'm On Fire" and "Girls"—both peaked at number 16), some lost should-of-been hits ("Shark" and "Somebody to Love"), a never-before-released song from an aborted 1994 album and a newly recorded track, "That Thing You Do." For fans, the rarities and song-by-song commentary by Twilley make *XXI* an essential addition. For those unfamiliar with Twilley and company's perfect pop, there is no better place to start. *—Chris Woodstra*

Tulsa / Jun. 1, 1999 / Copper ✦✦✦
Tulsa, Dwight Twilley's seventh album—released on a tiny Houston record label just days before his 48th birthday—is as likely to make members of his fan club salivate as it is to keep record company executives from returning calls. As if no time at all has passed, Twilley once again presents his multitracked, heavily echoed vocals over driving rock rhythms and ringing guitars, sounding as urgent as he did on "I'm on Fire" (his other hit) in 1975. Here and there, his lyrics seem to refer to his struggles, especially "It's Hard to Be a Rebel," "The Luck" (some people have all of it), and "Miranda," with its chorus line, "Some things are worth waiting for." The eight-minute "Tulsa," Twilley's tribute to his hometown, is the album's centerpiece, a pull-out-the-stops tour de force that gives you everything Twilley can do in one exhaustive track. He sounds as good as ever, and, as usual, just from listening to his remarkable music, it's hard to understand why he isn't a million-selling star who made five albums like this between 1986 and 1999, instead of none. *—William Ruhlmann*

Between the Cracks, Vol. 1 / Jul. 1999 / Not Lame Archives ✦✦✦
Amazingly, star-crossed rocker Dwight Twilley, who had gone more than a decade between releases, put out two albums within seven weeks in 1999. In June came *Tulsa*, his first album of new material in 13 years, followed in July by the archival *Between the Cracks, Vol. 1*, subtitled, "a collection of rarities." Clearly, the reclusive Tulsa-based musician has been writing and recording all along, and he sifted through more than 20 years of tapes to compile this collection of outtakes, demos, and lost tracks from album projects that were never released. Kent Benjamin's liner notes reference unheard albums like *Blueprint* and *The Luck* that were the victims of record company machinations and bad luck, not to mention numerous recording sessions dating back to Twilley's teens. Twilley himself annotates the songs, some of which he has specific recollections about, others that he doesn't even remember writing. Dating from 1973 to 1994, they include polished pop/rock performances in the standard Twilley style, with its driving guitars and heavily echoed vocals, as well as oddities such as a Christmas song ("Christmas Love"), a near re-creation of the sound of Alvin & the Chipmunks called "Eli Bolack" ("I have no idea how, or why, this happened," Twilley writes), and a stately ballad that, as the artist notes, sounds like a song from a musical ("Where the Birds Fly"). Neophytes probably should pick up a copy of *XXI*, the Twilley best-of, before moving on to the arcana here, but initiates will welcome more of the pop sound the singer/songwriter/guitarist has been making since the mid-1970s. *—William Ruhlmann*

The Luck / Aug. 14, 2001 / Big Oak Recording ✦✦✦

Twinkle (Lynn Annette Ripley)

b. Jul. 15, 1948, Surbiton, Surrey, England
Obscuro, Indie Pop, Girl Group, British Invasion
A British one-hit wonder of the mid-'60s that never crossed over to the U.S., Twinkle made #4 in the U.K. at the end of 1964 with her self-penned debut "Terry," a maudlin disc about the death of a (fictional) biker boyfriend. "Leader of the Pack" it wasn't, yet the record caused a furor, accusations of bad taste leading to its ban from the BBC (and, most likely, aiding its rapid rise to popularity). Only 16 at the time, Twinkle owed her rapid entry into the studio to a then-boyfriend in the then-popular vocal group the Bachelors, who passed on her demo to his manager. Jimmy Page was among the high-profile session musicians who played on "Terry."

A lean mod blonde somewhat in the mold of Marianne Faithfull, Twinkle recorded several less successful follow-ups in the mid-'60s, most of which were light emulations of the New York girl group style. Vocally she bore a passing resemblance to Lesley Gore, though in an even Whiter style (if such a thing was possible), making Gore seem downright funky in comparison. Twinkle, whose real name was Lynn Ripley, wasn't a mere creation of the image factory, though; she wrote much of her own material, including "Golden Lights," her only other single to approximate hit status. After six singles for Decca, Twinkle retired from the studio in 1966, at around the time of her 18th birthday, although she did record a single for Andrew Loog Oldham's Immediate label in 1969. Her legacy was propogated in unexpected ways: Elton John and Cat Stevens were fans, and "Golden Lights" was covered in 1986 by the Smiths. *—Richie Unterberger*

● **Golden Lights** / 1993 / RPM ✦✦✦✦✦
Everything she recorded during the 1960s is on this 17-song compilation: both sides of her six 1964-66 singles, two tracks from a rare 1965 EP, her 1969 Immediate single, and a late-'60s outtake. Even by British '60s girl group standards, it's featherweight poppiness, but big fans of (for instance) Sandie Shaw could do worse than seek this out. *—Richie Unterberger*

Twisted Sister

f. 1973, **db.** 1987
Pop-Metal, Hair Metal, Heavy Metal
A product of New York City's early-'70s rock scene, Twisted Sister struggled for nearly a decade before getting their big break in the early '80s. And when this break finally came, the band would become one of the most gruesome examples of overexposure in the history of rock & roll, bringing an abrupt end to their brief moment in the sun. Founded in December 1972 by guitarist Jay Jay French, Twisted Sister was initially a glam-rock cover band modeled after the New York Dolls. The arrival of vocalist Dee Snider in early 1976 brought a strong Alice Cooper influence to the band, giving their by-then-antiquated glam sound a welcome kick in the ass and spurring a transformation into metallic hard rockers. Their first full-length album, 1982's *Under the Blade*, became a surprise underground success and created enough of a buzz to attract giant Atlantic Records. 1983's *You Can't Stop Rock & Roll* laid the groundwork for their success with its more polished production values and strong material. In 1984, Twisted Sister unleashed their definitive statement, *Stay Hungry*, which dug deep into Snider's pop and glam roots. With such monster hits as "We're Not Gonna Take It" and "I Wanna Rock" (and their hilariously tongue-in-cheek accompanying videos), the album would exceed the multi-platinum barrier. Of course the backlash, when it came, was equally quick and incredibly vicious. Overexposed to the breaking point, Twisted Sister had lost the edge of their dangerous image, not to mention their core metal fan base. To complicate matters, 1985's *Come Out and Play* album was very uneven, attempting to cater to both the band's harder elements and newfound pop constituency. With rumors running rampant about a rift between Snider and French, Twisted Sister returned to action with 1987's disappointing *Love is for Suckers*, and disintegrated shortly thereafter. Snider eventually re-emerged in the early '90s with a new band called Desperado (later Widowmaker). Snider would transition into a career as a nationally syndicated heavy metal DJ, before writing and starring in the 1998 terror flick *Strangeland*. *—Ed Rivadavia*

Under the Blade / 1982 / Secret ✦✦✦✦
Although Twisted Sister had been slugging it out on the New York-area bar/club scene for nearly a decade by the early '80s (developing a large following in the process), no major record label would sign the act. Noticing that England was in the midst of a heavy metal resurgence (dubbed the New Wave of British Heavy Metal), the quintet moved over

to the U.K., where they recorded their debut album, *Under the Blade*, issued in 1982 on the independent Secret Records. UFO bassist Pete Way produced the album, which featured many of the band's best compositions from their club days. The chilling title track remains one of the band's best and has became a perennial concert favorite, while other metallic highlights include the opening "What You Don't Know (Sure Can Hurt You)," "Sin After Sin," "Shoot 'Em Down," and "Tear It Loose." The band also brings the volume down a notch or two with the slow-burning tracks "Run for Your Life" and "Destroyer," while the 1999 CD re-issue on Spitfire included a bonus track not on the original record ("I'll Never Grow Up Now!"). *Under the Blade* remains one of Twisted Sister's hardest rocking albums and is highly recommended to lovers of early '80s British heavy metal. *—Greg Prato*

You Can't Stop Rock & Roll / 1983 / Atlantic ♦♦♦♦
From the solid sales of their independently released debut album, 1982's *Under the Blade*, New York's Twisted Sister were finally rewarded with a major record label contract (Atlantic), who issued their first domestic release, *You Can't Stop Rock & Roll*, a year later. The album followed the same raw heavy metal direction of their debut, and was even more consistent from a songwriting and performance standpoint. Several of Twisted Sister's best anthems reside here—the title track (which was one of the band's first videos to be aired on MTV), as well as "The Kids Are Back," "We're Gonna Make It," and "I Am (I'm Me)." But besides a ballad that vocalist Dee Snider wrote especially for his wife, "You're Not Alone (Suzette's Song)," the album is comprised of 100% heavy metal—"Like a Knife in the Back," "Ride to Live, Live to Ride," "I've Had Enough," and "I'll Take You Alive." The 1999 CD re-issue included three bonus tracks not included on the original: "One Man Woman," "Four Barrel Heart of Love," and "Feel the Power." Eventually certified gold in the U.S., *You Can't Stop Rock & Roll* set the stage perfectly for their next release, 1984's breakthrough *Stay Hungry*. *—Greg Prato*

Stay Hungry / 1984 / Atlantic ♦♦♦♦♦
After nearly a decade trying to make it to "The Show," Twisted Sister was finally up to bat. Their first album was a wild swing, their second had flown just barely foul, but with their third—the unstoppable *Stay Hungry*—the New York veterans finally hit one out of the park. And few bands were as deserving. Having paid their dues on the tough as nails N.Y.C. club scene (half of the band looked like the Ramones, the other half like the Dictators, and Dee Snider looked like, well, Dee Snider), Twisted Sister had finally worn down the opposition and truly arrived. With their comedic videos and bubblegum undertones, hit singles "We're Not Gonna Take It" and "I Wanna Rock" helped the band bridge the "beauty gap" into MTV acceptance, and a competent power ballad in "The Price" would cement their consumer-friendly status. But it was the irrefutable menace of tracks like "The Beast," "S.M.F.," and the massive "Burn in Hell" that connected with their loyal fans and displayed Twisted Sister's true power. Equally grim, "Captain Howdy" and "Street Justice"—the two songs comprising the "Horror-teria" suite (later the basis for Snider's ill-fated movie project *Strangeland*)—are a cross between Alice Cooper and its stated source of influence, Stephen King. And don't forget the all-out metal ambition of the title track. Ironically, the album's very mainstream appeal would alienate their core heavy metal fan base and spell the band's over-exposure-induced fall from grace, but for this brief moment, Twisted Sister was truly the "talk of the town, top of the heap." *—Ed Rivadavia*

Come Out & Play / 1985 / Atlantic ♦♦♦
Twisted Sister was left in a strange position after the massive breakthrough success of their 1984 album, *Stay Hungry*. While the album contained more of a pop edge than their more raw preceding albums (*Under the Blade* and *You Can't Stop Rock & Roll*), the heavy metal masses worldwide still embraced the album, as well as the lucrative MTV/pop audience. So for its follow-up, the band was faced with a question: Should they continue in a more pop-oriented direction or return to their early heavy metal? As the resulting album proved, 1985's *Come Out and Play*, the answer was a little bit of both. Behind the boards was Scorpions/Accept producer Dieter Dierks, and the compositions alternated between the ambitious (the title track), obvious ready-for-radio tracks (a cover of "Leader of the Pack," "Be Chrool to Your Scuel"), and songs custom-made for headbangers ("The Fire Still Burns," "Kill or Be Killed"). The aforementioned "Be Chrool to Your Scuel" contained such musical guests as Alice Cooper, Billy Joel, Clarence Clemons, and Brian Setzer, for which a humorous video was filmed, and ultimately banned by MTV. And although the album was certified gold shortly after its release, it soon slid from sight—eventually leading to Twisted Sister's demise a few years later. When originally released on Atlantic, the cassette version of *Come Out and Play* included a bonus track, "King of the Fools," which has been included on the Spitfire Records CD reissue in 1999. Strangely, the 1999 CD contained very muffled sonics. *—Greg Prato*

Love Is for Suckers / 1987 / Atlantic ♦♦

● **Big Hits and Nasty Cuts: The Best of Twisted Sister** / Mar. 17, 1992 / Atlantic ♦♦♦♦♦
Big Hits and Nasty Cuts: Best of Twisted Sister rounds up ten of the metal band's best-known songs, including "We're Not Gonna Take It" and "I Wanna Rock," adding five live tracks as an enticement for hardcore Sister collectors. Even though the live tracks are of questionable quality, the disc remains an excellent summation of the group's career. *—Stephen Thomas Erlewine*

2 Live Crew

f. 1986
Party Rap, Dirty Rap, Southern Rap, Bass Music, Hip-Hop
This Florida rap band was organized, supervised, and conceived by Luther Campbell, a promoter, record label owner, and rapper, as an updated version of old-time X-rated party performers. Campbell's production consists of heavy doses of booming synthesized bass, scratching effects, samples, and explicit sex raps and leers. From their beginnings in 1986, the notoriety of Campbell and the group grew in direct proportion to the lewdness of the material. As their songs attained more national prominence, Campbell has become part of a national controversy involving censorship and lyrics. 2 Live Crew hasn't found the going quite as smooth in the '90s. They've continued recording for Luke Records, but haven't scored as much success with such releases as *Move Somethin'* and *Sports Weekend*. Founder Luther Campbell issued both clean and dirty versions in an effort to defuse criticism, but 2 Live Crew's detractors have moved on to gangsta-rap and the group's later releases have been almost ignored. *—Ron Wynn*

● **2 Live Crew's Greatest Hits** / Sep. 29, 1992 / Luke ♦♦♦♦♦
Full of the low-minded humor that made this Miami outfit notorious throughout the country, *Greatest Hits* does contain the best material 2 Live Crew ever recorded; it is all the 2 Live Crew most will ever need to hear. *—Stephen Thomas Erlewine*

2Pac (Tupac Amaru Shakur)

b. Jun. 16, 1971, New York, NY, **d.** Sep. 13, 1996, Las Vegas, NV
Rap, Vocals / West Coast Rap, Hardcore Rap, G-Funk, Gangsta Rap
Tupac Shakur became the unlikely martyr of gangsta rap, and a tragic symbol of the toll its lifestyle exacted on urban Black America. At the outset of his career, it didn't appear that he would emerge as one of the definitive rappers of the '90s—he started out as a second-string rapper and dancer for Digital Underground, joining only after they had already landed their biggest hit. But in 1992, he delivered an acclaimed debut album, *2Pacalypse Now*, and quickly followed with a star-making performance in the urban drama *Juice*. Over the course of one year, his profile rose substantially, based as much on his run-ins with the law as his music. By 1994, 2Pac rivaled Snoop Doggy Dogg as the most controversial figure in rap, spending as much time in prison as he did in the recording studio. His burgeoning outlaw mythology helped his 1995 album *Me Against the World* enter the charts at number one, and it also opened him up to charges of exploitation. Yet, as the single "Dear Mama" illustrated, he was capable of sensitivity as well as violence. Signing with Death Row Records in late 1995, Shakur released the double album *All Eyez on Me* in the spring of 1996, and the record, as well as its hit single "California Love," confirmed his superstar status. Unfortunately, the gangsta lifestyle he captured in his music soon overtook his own life. While his celebrity was at its peak, he publicly fought with his rival the Notorious B.I.G., and there were tensions brewing at Death Row. Even with such conflicts, however, 2Pac's drive-by shooting in September 1996 came as an unexpected shock. On September 13, six days after the shooting, Shakur passed away, leaving behind a legacy that was based as much on his lifestyle as it was his music. *—Stephen Thomas Erlewine*

2Pacalypse Now / 1992 / Interscope ♦♦♦
Few expected former Digital Underground member Tupac Amaru Shakur to become hip-hop enemy number one when he made his solo debut with this 1992 album. Songs like "Crooked Ass Nigga" and "Tha' Lunatic" might have hinted that storm clouds were on the horizon, but there were also excellent advocacy numbers like "Words Of Wisdom" and "Young Black Male." This didn't make him a celebrity, but it put Tupac Shakur on the road to stardom. *—Ron Wynn*

Strictly 4 My N.I.G.G.A.Z. / Feb. 16, 1993 / Jive ♦♦♦♦
Released a year after *2Pacalypse Now*, *Strictly 4 My N.I.G.G.A.Z.* finds the young 2Pac further carving out his persona. Instead of seeming unsure of whether he wants to be a self-conscious poet or an iconic thug as he did on his debut album, he chooses the latter with this album, a choice that he would continue to define with successive albums. So even if *Strictly 4 My N.I.G.G.A.Z.* isn't even close to being as gangsta as Death Row-era 2Pac, it's still a harsh album filled with grim moments. Beginning with "Holler If Ya Hear Me," the hard stance cries for respect, highlighted on tough tracks such as "Last Wordz." Yet even if the rapper spends the majority of the album in thug poses, the standout moments, "Keep Ya Head Up" and "I Get Around," occur when 2Pac stops and raps from the heart. The sometimes shoddy, sometimes inconsistent production stands as one lingering problem with this album that makes it inferior to his two masterpieces, *Me Against the World* and *All Eyez on Me*. *—Jason Birchmeier*

☆ **Me Against the World** / Mar. 14, 1995 / Interscope ♦♦♦♦♦
As 2Pac's finest moment before being jailed and then being initiated into the gangsta world of the cultish Death Row camp, *Me Against the World* stands as a landmark rap album. It showcases a much different 2Pac than the more well-known 2Pac of *All Eyez on Me*—arguably a more sincere portrait of the rapper. Rather than spewing vengeful lyrics with no remorse or reservation, the 2Pac of *Me Against the World* seems uneasy with his hatred. Songs such as "Dear Mama" and "If I Die 2 Nite" remain some of the most heartfelt moments in rap history; in such a theatrical genre, rarely has a rapper spoke with such self-consciousness and sincerity. Yet the album isn't all confessional. Other songs such as "Fuck the World" and "Temptations" showcase another side of 2Pac, a thug persona driven by frustration and anger. Though stellar, this album's production isn't quite as rousing as that found on *All Eyez on Me*, and 2Pac isn't quite as charismatic as he would become on Death Row, but this is his most mannered album, a succinct portrait showcasing both the angry thug side of his character as well as a more heartfelt side which he would eventually suppress. *—Jason Birchmeier*

★ **All Eyez on Me** / Feb. 13, 1996 / Death Row ♦♦♦♦♦
Where most rappers would struggle to find enough subject matter to fill a double album, 2Pac uses the epic scope of *All Eyez on Me* as a forum for his seemingly never-ending rants. Whether ranting about his enemies ("Can't C Me"), women he hates ("Wonda Why They Call U Bytch"), women he loves ("Thug Passion"), his homies ("2 of Amerikaz Most Wanted"), the West Coast ("California Love"), his death ("Heaven Ain't Hard 2 Find"), or

himself ("Ambitionz Az a Ridah"), 2Pac never seems short on words. So even if this album features some truly amazing production by some of the West Coast's best producers circa 1996—Dr. Dre, Daz, DJ Pooh—2Pac's literate lyrics highlight this timeless album. It's a fitting farewell album for the artist, since it functions almost as an autobiography; furthermore, his well-crafted lyrics are only enhanced by his liquid flow, his aggression, and his clarity—few rappers will ever compare. Yet despite the amazing epic scope of this album and its no-holds-barred delivery, 2Pac seems almost *too* dramatic. After all, he was a talented actor, and one cannot forget that this is the same man who wrote heartfelt ballads such as "Dear Mama" and "Keep Ya Head Up"; yet this sort of emotion is nowhere to be found here, with the exception of a few foreboding moments where he raps about death. So if there can be any complaints about this otherwise amazing album, 2Pac's one-sided thug outlook and his suppressed emotions keep this album from being more revealing. —*Jason Birchmeier*

Don Killuminati: The 7 Day Theory / Nov. 5, 1996 / Death Row ✦✦
● **Greatest Hits** / Nov. 24, 1998 / Death Row/Interscope ✦✦✦✦✦
Greatest Hits is a strange release. Sure, Tupac Shakur had more than enough hits to make a terrific compilation, but its appearance in the fall of 1998 felt a bit like another opportunity to milk his catalog, simply because of the plethora of releases from previously unheard recordings to interview discs and bootlegs. Even with these misgivings taken into account, it has to be said that *Greatest Hits* does its job well. Given that it runs 25 tracks and two CDs, some may argue that it does its job a little too well, but the fact of the matter is, this contains all of his big hits, from "Keep Ya Head Up" and "Dear Mama" to "California Love" and "I Ain't Mad at Cha." Some may argue that it would have been more effective if it was sequenced in chronological order, but this remains the best place for casual listeners to get all the 2Pac they need. —*Stephen Thomas Erlewine*

U2

f. 1976, Dublin, Ireland
College Rock, Album Rock, Post-Punk, Pop/Rock, Alternative Pop/Rock
Through a combination of zealous righteousness and post-punk experimentalism, U2 became one of the most popular rock & roll bands of the '80s. Equally known for their sweeping anthems as for their grandiose statements about politics and religion, U2 were rock & roll crusaders during an era of synthesized pop and heavy metal. The Edge provided the group with a signature sound by creating sweeping sonic landscapes with his heavily processed, echoed guitars. Though the Edge's style wasn't conventional, the rhythm section of Adam Clayton and Larry Mullen Jr. played the songs as driving hard-rock, giving the band a forceful, powerful edge that was designed for arena rock. And their lead singer, Bono, was a frontman who had a knack of grand gestures that played better in arenas than small clubs. It's no accident that footage of Bono parading with a white flag with "Sunday Bloody Sunday" blaring in the background became the defining moment of U2's early career—there rarely was a band that believed so deeply in rock's potential for revolution as U2, and there rarely was a band that didn't care if they appeared foolish in the process. During the course of the early '80s, the group quickly built up a dedicated following through constant touring and a string of acclaimed records. By 1987, the band's following had grown large enough to propel them to the level of international superstars with the release of *The Joshua Tree*. Unlike many of their contemporaries, U2 was able to sustain their popularity in the '90s by reinventing themselves as a post-modern, self-consciously ironic dance-inflected pop-rock act, owing equally to the experimentalism of late '70s Bowie and '90s electronic dance and techno. By performing such a successful reinvention, the band confirmed its status as one of the most popular bands in rock history, in addition to earning additional critical respect. —*Stephen Thomas Erlewine*

Boy / 1980 / Island ◆◆◆◆
From the outset, U2 went for the big message—every song on their debut album *Boy* sounds huge, with oceans of processed guitars cascading around Bono's impassioned wail. It was an inspired combination of large, stadium-rock beats and post-punk textures. Without the Edge's echoed, ringing guitar, U2 would have sounded like a traditional hard rock band, since the rhythm section and Bono treat each song as an anthem. Of course, that's the charm of *Boy*: all of its emotions are on the surface, delivered with optimistic, youthful self-belief, yet the unusual, distinctive guitar textures give it an unexpected tension that makes it an exhilarating debut. The songs may occasionally show some weakness—the driving "I Will Follow," the dark "An Cat Dubh" and the shimmering "The Ocean" stand out among the sonic textures—yet the band's musical and lyrical vision keep *Boy* compelling until the finish. —*Stephen Thomas Erlewine*

October / 1981 / Island ◆◆◆
U2 sounded so confident and assured on their debut that perhaps it was inevitable they would stumble slightly on its follow-up, *October*. The record isn't weaker than its predecessor because it repeats the formula of *Boy*, it's because the band tries too hard to move forward. Bono, in particular, tries too hard to make big political, emotional, and religious statements, but the remainder of the band isn't innocent. In general, the music is too pompous, with the sound overwhelming the actual songs. But when U2 do marry the message, melody and sound together, as on "Gloria," "I Threw a Brick Through a Window" and "I Fall Down," the results are thoroughly impressive. —*Stephen Thomas Erlewine*

☆ War / Feb. 28, 1983 / Island ◆◆◆◆◆
Opening with the ominous, fiery protest of "Sunday Bloody Sunday," *War* immediately announces itself as U2's most focused and hardest-rocking album to date. Blowing away the fuzzy, sonic indulgences of *October* with propulsive, martial rhythms and shards of guitar, *War* bristles with anger, despair and, above all, passion. Previously, Bono's attempts at messages came across as grandstanding, but his vision became remarkably clear on this record, as his anthems ("New Year's Day," "40," "Seconds") are balanced by effective, surprisingly emotional love songs ("Two Hearts Beat As One"), which are just as desperate and pleading as his protests. He performs the difficult task of making the universal sound personal, and the band helps him out by bringing the songs crashing home with muscular, forceful performances that reveal their varied, expressive textures upon repeated listens. U2 always aimed at greatness, but *War* was the first time they achieved it. —*Stephen Thomas Erlewine*

Under a Blood Red Sky / Nov. 1983 / Island ◆◆◆
War turned U2 into arena-rock stars, and the EP *Under a Blood Red Sky* captures the band on its supporting tour as they adjusted to their larger audiences. Unsurprisingly for a band that always favored the grand statement, the group flourished in such a setting, as this mini-EP attests. Comprised of material recorded in America and Germany, *Under*

a Blood Red Sky draws equally from the band's first three albums, and these live versions, while less textured, are considerably tougher than their studio counterparts and illustrate quite effectively why U2 were considered one of the best, most exhilarating live bands of the '80s. —*Stephen Thomas Erlewine*

The Unforgettable Fire / 1984 / Island ◆◆◆◆
In many ways, U2 took their fondness for sonic bombast as far as it could go on *War*, so it isn't a complete surprise that they chose to explore the intricacies of the Edge's layered, effects-laden guitar on the follow-up, *The Unforgettable Fire*. Working with producers Brian Eno and Daniel Lanois, U2 created a dark, near-hallucinatory series of interlocking soundscapes that are occasionally punctuated by recognizable songs and melodies. In such a setting, the band both flourishes and flounders, creating some of their greatest music, as well as some of their worst. "Elvis Presley and America" may well be Bono's most embarrassing attempt at poetry, yet it is redeemed by the chilling and wonderful "Bad," a two-chord elegy for an addict that is stunning in its control and mastery. Similarly, the wet, shimmering textures of the title track, the charging "A Sort of Homecoming," and the surging Martin Luther King Jr. tribute "Pride (In the Name of Love)" are all remarkable, ranking among their very best music, making the missteps that clutter the remainder of the album somewhat forgivable. —*Stephen Thomas Erlewine*

Wide Awake in America / 1985 / Island ◆◆

★ The Joshua Tree / 1987 / Island ◆◆◆◆◆
Using the textured sonics of *The Unforgettable Fire* as a basis, U2 expanded those innovations by scaling back the songs to a personal setting and adding a grittier attack for its follow-up, *The Joshua Tree*. It's a move that returns them to the sweeping, anthemic rock of *War*, but if *War* was an exploding political bomb, *The Joshua Tree* is a journey through its aftermath, trying to find sense and hope in the desperation. That means that even the anthems—the epic opener "Where the Streets Have No Name," the yearning "I Still Haven't Found What I'm Looking For"—have seeds of doubt within their soaring choruses, and those fears take root throughout the album, whether it's in the mournful sliding acoustic guitars of "Running to Stand Still," the surging "One Tree Hill" or the hypnotic elegy "Mothers of the Disappeared." So it might seem a little ironic that U2 became superstars on the back of such a dark record, but their focus has never been clearer, nor has their music been catchier, than on *The Joshua Tree*. Unexpectedly, U2 have also tempered their textural post-punk with American influences. Not only are Bono's lyrics obsessed with America, but country and blues influences are heard throughout the record, and instead of using these as roots, they're used as ways to add texture to the music. With the uniformly excellent songs—only the clumsy, heavy rock and portentous lyrics of "Bullet the Blue Sky" fall flat—the result is a powerful, uncompromising record that became a hit due to its vision and its melody. Never before have their big messages sounded so direct and personal. —*Stephen Thomas Erlewine*

Rattle and Hum / 1988 / Island ◆◆◆
Functioning as both the soundtrack to the group's disastrous feature-film documentary and as a tentative follow-up to their career-making blockbuster, *Rattle & Hum* is all over the place. The live cuts lack the revelatory power of *Under a Blood Red Sky* and are undercut by heavy-handed performances and Bono's embarrassing stage patter; prefacing a leaden cover of "Helter Skelter" with "This is a song Charles Manson stole from the Beatles, and now we're stealing it back," is bad enough, but it pales next to Bono's exhortation "OK, Edge, play the blues!" on the worthy, decidedly unbluesy "Silver and Gold." Both comments reveal more than they intend—throughout the album, U2 sound paralyzed by their new status as "rock's most important band." They react by attempting to boost their classic rock credibility, they embrace American roots rock, something they ignored before. Occasionally, these experiments work: "Desire" has an intoxicating Bo Diddley beat, "Angel of Harlem" is a punchy, sunny Stax-soul tribute, "When Loves Come to Town" is an endearingly awkward blues duet with B.B. King, and the Dylan collaboration "Love Rescue Me" is an overlooked minor bluesy gem. However, these get swallowed up in the bluster of the live tracks, the misguided gospel interpretation of "I Still Haven't Found What I'm Looking For" and the shameful answer to John Lennon's searing confession "God," "God Part II." A couple of affecting laments—the cascading "All I Want Is You" and "Heartland," which sounds like a *Joshua Tree* outtake—do slip out underneath the posturing, but *Rattle & Hum* is by far the least-focused record U2 ever made, and it's little wonder that they retreated for three years after its release to rethink their whole approach. —*Stephen Thomas Erlewine*

☆ Achtung Baby / Nov. 19, 1991 / Island ◆◆◆◆◆
Reinventions rarely come as thorough and effective as *Achtung Baby*, an album that completely changed U2's sound and style. The crashing, unrecognizable distorted guitars that open "Zoo Station" are a clear signal that U2 have traded their Americana

pretensions for post-modern, contemporary European music. Drawing equally from Bowie's electronic, avant-garde explorations of the late '70s and the neo-psychedelic sounds of the thriving rave and Madchester club scenes of early '90s England, *Achtung Baby* sounds vibrant and endlessly inventive. Unlike their inspirations, U2 rarely experiment with song structures over the course of the album. Instead, they use the thick dance beats, swirling guitars, layers of effects and found sounds to break traditional songs out of their constraints, revealing the tortured emotional core of their songs with the hyper-loaded arrangements. In such a dense musical setting, it isn't surprising that U2 have abandoned the political for the personal on *Achtung Baby*, since the music, even with its inviting rhythms, is more introspective than anthemic. Bono has never been as emotionally naked as he is on *Achtung Baby*, creating a feverish nightmare of broken hearts and desperate loneliness; unlike other U2 albums, it's filled with sexual imagery, much of it quite disturbing, and it ends on a disquieting note. Few bands as far into their career as U2 have recorded an album as adventurous or fulfilled their ambitions quite as successfully as they do on *Achtung Baby*, and the result is arguably their best album. *—Stephen Thomas Erlewine*

Zooropa / May 1993 / Island ♦♦♦♦
U2 planned to record a new EP before launching the European leg of their ambitious Zoo TV tour in 1993, but the EP quickly turned into the full-length album *Zooropa*. Picking up where *Achtung Baby* left off, *Zooropa* delves heavily into U2's newfound affection for experimental music and dance clubs. While the title track marries those inclinations to the anthems of *The Joshua Tree*, most of the record is far more daring than its predecessor. While that occasionally means it's unfocused and meandering, it also results in a number of wonderful moments, like the quiet menace of "Daddy's Gonna Pay for Your Crashed Car," and the space-age German disco of "Lemon," Edge's droning mantra "Numb," and the gentle, heartbroken "Stay (Faraway, So Close!)," one of U2's very best love songs. As the album winds to a close, it drifts off track, yet the best moments of *Zooropa* rank among U2's most inspired and rewarding music. *—Stephen Thomas Erlewine*

Pop / Mar. 1997 / Island ♦♦♦
No matter which way you look at it, *Pop* doesn't have the same shock of the new that *Achtung Baby* delivered on first listen. Less experimental and more song-oriented than *Zooropa*, *Pop* attempts to sell the glitzy rush of techno to an audience weaned on arena rock. And that audience includes U2 themselves. While they never sound like they don't believe in what they're doing, they still remove most of the radical elements of electronic dance, which is evident to anyone with just a passing knowledge of the Chemical Brothers and Underworld. To a new listener, *Pop* has flashes of surprise—particularly on the rampaging "Mofo"—but underneath the surface, U2 relies on anthemic rockers and ballads. "Discotheque" might be a little clumsy, but "Staring at the Sun" shimmers with synthesizers borrowed from Massive Attack and a Noel Gallagher chorus. Similarly, "Do You Feel Loved" and "If You Wear That Velvet Dress" fuse old-fashioned U2 dynamism with a keen sense of the cool eroticism that makes trip-hop so alluring. Problems arise when the group tries to go for conventional rock songs, some of which are symptomatic of the return of U2's crusade for salvation. *Pop* is inflected with the desire for a higher power to save the world from its jaded spiral of decay and immorality, which is why the group's embrace of dance music never seems joyous—instead of providing an intoxicating rush of gloss and glamour, it functions as a backdrop for a plea of salvation. *Achtung Baby* also was a comment on the numbing isolation of modern culture, but it made sweeping statements through personal observations; *Pop* makes sweeping statements through sweeping observations. The difference is what makes *Pop* an easy record to admire, but a hard one to love. *—Stephen Thomas Erlewine*

Best of 1980-1990/B-Sides / Nov. 3, 1998 / Island ♦♦♦♦
Island and U2 realized that longtime fans of the band wouldn't need *The Best of 1980-1990*. Unlike the proposed *The Best of 1990-2000*, which would likely boast the non-LP "Hold Me, Thrill Me, Kiss Me, Kill Me" and the Passengers' "Miss Sarajevo," *1980-1990* contained nothing but material culled directly from the albums, which didn't exactly entice hardcore followers. So, the label and the band decided to pair the compilation with a collection of the group's B-sides from the '80s, none of which had ever appeared on an album before. For diehard U2 fans, this is something of a godsend—not necessarily a holy grail, which would have been a complete B-sides collection, including the long-missing early EPs—since many of these tracks have been out of print for years. That's not to say they'll be entirely pleased with what they hear. *The B-Sides* is wildly uneven, fluctuating between a handful of lost masterpieces ("Spanish Eyes," "Sweetest Thing," "Hallelujah Here She Comes," "Silver and Gold," "A Room at the Heartbreak Hotel," "Trash, Trampoline and the Party Girl"), a momentum-crushing triptych of mediocre karaoke ("Dancing Barefoot," "Everlasting Love," "Unchained Melody") and gormless filler (pretty much everything else). Despite the uneven music, fans will need *The B-Sides*, not just for the handful of worthy contenders, but for its sheer rarity. Not only have the B-sides themselves been difficult to locate, but the disc itself was designed as a collectors' item: after the first week of sales, *The B-Sides* was pulled from the market, and Island shipped only *The Best of 1980-1990*. Clearly, this was a tactic to raise press awareness and boost sales, but that doesn't mean that fans shouldn't take advantage of its limited release. *—Stephen Thomas Erlewine*

Best of 1980-1990 / Nov. 10, 1998 / Island ♦♦♦♦♦
As one of the most popular bands of the '80s, U2 didn't quite fit into any particular category. They were a post-punk band that quickly found acceptance from a hard rock audience, a group that made fully formed albums but often made their best statements on individual songs, especially during the '80s. Consequently, they're a very hard band to anthologize. Since they were most effective on single songs, it seems that throwing all of them together on one disc would work. The problem is, each of the albums, from *Boy* to *Rattle & Hum*, has a distinctive flavor that doesn't necessarily blend when combined, especially in the non-chronological form of *The Best of 1980-1990*. There's little quibbling with the featured tracks on U2's first compilation—a few important songs, such as "Gloria," "I Fall Down," "Seconds" and "Two Hearts Beat As One," may be missing, but everything else deserves to be here ("Pride," "New Year's Day," "With or Without You," "I Still Haven't Found What I'm Looking For," "Sunday Bloody Sunday," "Bad," "Desire," etc.). Even though the song selection is strong, the album winds up as less than the sum of its parts—each song is pretty great of its own accord (even the single mix of the B-side, "Sweetest Thing," which is, in truth, not much different at all), but the overall effect is a little underwhelming. On one hand, it may be a good choice for casual fans or nostalgia mongers, since it does contain everything they need to hear, but anyone who has more than a passing interest in the band will be better suited with individual albums. *—Stephen Thomas Erlewine*

All That You Can't Leave Behind / Oct. 31, 2000 / Interscope ♦♦♦♦
Nearly ten years after beginning U2 Mach II with their brilliant seventh album *Achtung Baby*, U2 eases into their third phase with 2000's *All That You Can't Leave Behind*. The title signifies more than it seems, since the group sifts through their past, working with Daniel Lanois and Brian Eno, all in an effort to construct a classicist U2 album. Thankfully, it's a rock record from a band that absorbed all the elastic experimentation, studio trickery, dance flirtations, and genre bending of *Achtung*, *Zooropa*, and *Pop*—all they've shed is the irony. U2 chooses not to delve as darkly personal as they did on *Achtung* or *Zooropa*, yet they also avoid the alienating archness of *Pop*, returnin to the generous spirit that flowed through their best '80s records. On that level, *All* may be reminiscent of *The Joshua Tree*, but this is a clever and craftsmanlike record, filled with nifty twists in the arrangements, small sonic details and colors. U2 take subtle risks, such as their best pure pop song ever with "Wild Honey"; they're so self-confident, they effortlessly write their best anthem in years with "Beautiful Day"; they offer the gospel-influenced "Stuck in a Moment," never once lowering it to the schtick it would have been on *Rattle & Hum*. Like any work from craftsmen, *All That You Can't Leave Behind* winds up being a work of modest pleasures, where the way the verse eases into the chorus means more than the overall message, and this is truly the first U2 album where that sentiment applies—but there is genuine pleasure in their craft, for the band and listener alike. *—Stephen Thomas Erlewine*

UB40

f. 1978, Birmingham, England
College Rock, Contemporary Reggae, Reggae-Pop, Pop/Rock, Adult Contemporary
Named after a British unemployment benefit form, pop-reggae band UB40 was formed in 1978 with a multiracial lineup that reflected the working-class community its members came from. The band consolidated its street credibility with political topics appealing to dissatisfied youth and got a boost from fans of the waning 2-Tone ska-revival movement. By 1980, their single "Food for Thought" reached the UK Top Ten. UB40's first two albums, *Signing Off* and *Present Arms*, were big sellers in Britain and addressed the political issues of the day with songs like "One in Ten," a Top Ten hit blasting Margaret Thatcher for the country's unemployment rate. 1983's *Labour of Love*, an album of reggae cover songs, gave the group its first chart album in America and first number one UK hit with Neil Diamond's "Red Red Wine." Five years after its initial release, the single entered the American charts and went all the way to the top. Finally having hit on a way to conquer the lucrative American market, UB40 responded with another covers album, *Labour of Love II*, which produced Top Ten singles with versions of the Temptations' "The Way You Do the Things You Do" and Al Green's "Here I Am (Come and Take Me)." The group scored a huge hit in America with Elvis Presley's "Can't Help Falling in Love," and spent seven weeks at number one. A third *Labour of Love* collection followed in 1999. *—Steve Huey*

Signing Off / Nov. 1980 / Virgin ♦♦♦
A hugely popular album in Britain, where it reached number two and stayed in the charts for months, *Signing Off* was the calling card of UB40, a multiracial Birmingham group who took their name from the administrative form used as proof of identity when collecting unemployment benefits. At the time, the post-punk Midlands scene was tinkering with reggae's forerunner, ska, which resulted in the swift rise of 2-Tone. However, the brothers Campbell and their colleagues decided there was a market for a modern Jamaican variant. After touring with the Pretenders, they released their debut single, "Food for Thought," which became an instant hit. The song was reprised on the album, alongside its B-side, "King," and a series of politically inclined, likeable, but musically sanitized cuts. When Graduate decided to excise the polemical "Burden of Shame" from South African copies of the album, UB40 quite rightly dumped the label. *—Alex Ogg*

Present Arms / Jun. 1981 / Virgin ♦♦♦
The popular perception of UB40 as a band who cling to the coattails of true reggae artists is partially merited, given their '90s karaoke-quality interpretations of popular standards in a Jamaican rub-a-dub style. But with albums such as their debut and this, admittedly a more uneven effort, their affection for the music was self-evidently genuine and generally well observed. Their conscience-driven lyrics ("One in Ten" especially) are heartfelt and convincing, though Ali Campbell's Rastabrummyfarian voice takes some getting used to. The bottom line? There are dozens of superior reggae albums, but this will do if you're too lazy to find them. *—Alex Ogg*

Present Arms in Dub / Oct. 1981 / Virgin ♦♦

● **Labour of Love** / Sep. 1983 / Virgin ♦♦♦♦♦
Named after the unemployment form in England, UB40 was never the most creative or

talented group of musicians. However, what they lacked in talent they made up for with an uplifting spirit and genuine affection for reggae music. This is never more apparent than on their breakthrough album, *Labour of Love*, in which they cover the songs of their heroes. They try to recapture the spirit of early reggae by singing songs originally released before the international success of Bob Marley. They manage to inject their own exuberance into every song; for example, they transform Jimmy Cliff's mournful "Many Rivers to Cross" into an uplifting song of empowerment. The song for which UB40 will always be known is their first number one hit in the U.S., "Red Red Wine," a Neil Diamond-penned tune given a full reggae makeover that miraculously turned the group into an international sensation. Although UB40 relies on standard reggae arrangements, this is their most enjoyable album as a result of the inspired vocal performances and the genuine joy they have for the music. A must-own for reggae fans. *—Vik Iyengar*

Geffery Morgan / 1984 / Virgin ✦✦✦✦✦

UB40 was faced with following up the surprisingly successful covers album *Labour Of Love* (which had topped the U.K. chart and become their U.S. chart debut) with this album of original material. Their own songs were good, but no match for what then seemed a one-of-a-kind collection. "If It Happens Again," which went to #9 in Britain, sounded like a song by The English Beat, while the second single, "Riddle Me" (#59), was a deeper reggae groove tune. It was a good set, but without a classic like "Red, Red Wine" suffered from a certain anonymity, especially in the U.S. *—William Ruhlmann*

Little Baggaridim / 1985 / Virgin ✦✦✦

UB40 scored their first Top 30 hit in the U.S. with a cover of Sonny And Cher's "I Got You, Babe," set to a reggae beat and sung with The Pretenders' Chrissie Hynde, heard on this mini-album. *—William Ruhlmann*

Rat in the Kitchen / 1986 / Virgin ✦✦✦✦✦

In the U.K., UB40 were major stars, and this album was their sixth Top 10 hit, featuring the singles "Sing Your Own Song" (#5), "All I Want To Do" (#41), and "Rat In Me Kitchen" (#12). In the U.S., the group remained a developing act with a modest following, only able to score a hit by covering a previous hit like "I Got You, Babe." *Rat In The Kitchen* did nothing to change that, although it was, as usual, a tuneful collection of reggae. *—William Ruhlmann*

UB40 / 1988 / Virgin ✦✦✦✦

UB40 was the first indication that the band was abandoning the political inclinations of their earlier work and concentrating solely on pop-reggae. Of course, pop informed all of their albums since *Labour of Love*, but on *UB40*, the group concentrates solely on the grooves, from the instrumental "Dance With the Devil" to a sultry cover of "Breakfast in Bed," featuring Chrissie Hynde on vocals. Even though the album and all of its mellow grooves are thoroughly enjoyable, it's hard not to long for something a little deeper, whether it's the tributes of *Labour of Love* or the edgy *Rat in the Kitchen*. *—Stephen Thomas Erlewine*

Labour of Love II / Nov. 1989 / Virgin ✦✦

Promises and Lies / Jul. 27, 1993 / Virgin ✦✦

The Best of UB40, Vol. 2 / Nov. 7, 1995 / Virgin ✦✦✦

The Best of UB40, Vol. 2 concentrates on the group's '90s recordings, when the band concentrated on pop-reggae crossovers instead of genuine reggae. There are a number of hits here—including "Here I Am (Come and Take Me)," "Kingston Town," "The Way You Do the Things You Do," "Where Did I Go Wrong?," "Until My Dying Day," "Higher Ground" and "Can't Help Falling in Love"—but fans of UB40's political edge and their genuine reggae roots won't find much of interest here. This is a collection for pop fans, not reggae fans, and in that sense, it is a good summation of the band's second decade indeed. *—Stephen Thomas Erlewine*

The Best of UB40, Vol. 1 / Nov. 14, 1995 / Virgin ✦✦✦✦

The Best of UB40, Vol. 1 is an adequate collection of the group's biggest '80s hits, including "Breakfast in Bed," "Red Red Wine," "Rat in My Kitchen," "Food for Thought," "Please Don't Make Me Cry," "Don't Break My Heart" and "Sing Our Own Song." Although it doesn't give enough weight to the group's earliest, edgiest (and best) recordings, it still offers a good sense of the band's evolution into a fine pop-reggae band, and it will satiate the needs of most casual fans. *—Stephen Thomas Erlewine*

Guns in the Ghetto / Jul. 1, 1997 / Virgin ✦✦

Labour of Love III / Nov. 17, 1998 / Virgin ✦✦

● **The Very Best of UB40 1980-2000** / Nov. 21, 2000 / Virgin ✦✦✦✦✦

While the two previous *Best of UB40* collections neatly divided the band's output between their more political early period and their later, covers-oriented pop success, they were also only ten tracks apiece. *The Very Best of UB40 1980-2000* is the first comprehensive single-disc overview of the band's career, and it's a lot more generous at 18 tracks (on the American version). It isn't arranged chronologically, which actually helps the programming by splitting up the covers over the course of the running order. There's a bit more toughness to the earlier songs, both in the lyrics and the punchier performances. Yet in the end, the sonic differences are subtle enough that casual fans should still be able to enjoy them (unless they *only* want to hear the band performing reggae-pop versions of oldies they already know). Skimpy though it is, *The Best of UB40, Vol. 1* is still the compilation for purists enamored of the band's early work, assuming they don't want to spend the money for the original albums. But with its fairly well-balanced selection and inclusion of all the band's U.S. hits, most American listeners who want a UB40 compilation will find *The Very Best of UB40 1980-2000* exactly what they're looking for. [The import version juggles the track listing and running order a bit, excising a couple of *Labour of Love II*'s American cover hits in favor of older songs and reggae covers of Jamaican origin. Also, the version of "Red Red Wine" is the shortened edit, without the toasting break at the end.] *—Steve Huey*

Ui

f. 1991, New York, NY

Experimental Rock, Indie Rock, Post-Rock/Experimental, Alternative Pop/Rock

Allied to the more organic, instrumental groovesters in the American post-rock scene led by Tortoise, Ui focuses on angular grooves provided by a dual-bass attack. The New York band was formed in 1991 by bassist Sasha Frere-Jones (formerly of the group Dolores and probably better known as a journalist than a musician) with drummer Clem Waldmann, additional bassist Alex Wright, and DJ/percussionist David Weeks. Wright and Weeks left the band by 1993, and were replaced by jazz bassist Wilbo Wright.

Ui's first release, the *2-Sided* EP, appeared later that year on the British Hemiola label. During 1995, the band recorded the *Unlike* EP in addition to another EP and single for Soul Static Sound. As part of a tour that year with Tortoise and Labradford, Ui signed a contract with Chicago's Southern Records. Their debut album, *Sidelong*, was released in 1996, followed by the *Dropplike* EP. The group collaborated with Techno Animal and Luke Vibert, among others in the experimental electronica underground, before teaming up with Stereolab for the *Fires* EP, released as Uilab. A second album, *Lifelike*, followed later that year. *—John Bush*

● **Sidelong** / 1996 / Southern ✦✦✦✦

Ui's first full-length is a set of grooves with the occasional mumbled vocal line and a sedate quality with links to the approaches of instrumentalists from John Fahey to Jim O'Rourke. The effect is similar to a Slint album with two bassists instead of two guitars. *—John Bush*

Lifelike / Apr. 7, 1998 / Southern ✦✦✦

Ui is a trio that pieces together instrumentals throughout *Lifelike*. The prefix "post" could be applied to the music, also to Ui's relationship with Stereolab in John McEntire's studio for Uilab. Ui falls into a nice groove at the beginning of the record, like something from an Isotope 217 record—mid-'70s jazz fusion feel with fewer solos and more electronics. The beginnings of all of the songs grab your attention, but do not have that something extra to keep your mind from wandering. The mixing of *Lifelike* is wonderful headphone music. Many instruments create rich layers, each complementing the other. Polyrhythms seem to be the backbone of *Lifelike*, creating the main pulse, while guitars and electronics sprinkle on top to add layers. The horns throughout the record add a nice contrast to the electronics, but those moments are few. "Laceria" is a track that stands out, having a dub feel with breakbeats. Rhythm is the concentration and moving force of the tune with guitars providing the subtle melody. The switch in listening action comes from the adding of small layers at a time. Ui is very consistent throughout, but has nothing to push it to the next level. Nothing really swings here. Bass lines with rhythms sound like marches. "Exeunt" is a drone soundscape, ambient music with tension created by the electronics in the background. Bottom tones rise up at the end of the song, giving *Lifelike* a quality finish to a solid record by Ui. *—David Serra*

U.K. Subs

f. 1976

British Punk, Oi!, Punk

Formed by R&B singer Charlie Harper in 1976, the London punk band U.K. may have tackled the occasional social or political topic, yet they were distinguished by their roaring, rocking three-chord ravers. In addition to Harper, the group featured guitarist Nicky Garratt, bassist Paul Slack, and drummer Pete Davies. The U.K. Subs released several singles in the late '70s, including "Stranglehold" and "Tomorrow's Girls," which managed to hit the British Top 40. As the '80s progressed, the band began to lose its audience as they incorporated heavy metal into the sound. Throughout their career the band's lineup has been fluctuating, with Harper being the only constant in the group's career. The U.K. Subs continued recording right into the '90s, although the audience for albums like 1995's *Punk Is Back* and 1997's *Riot* has decreased substantially. *—Stephen Thomas Erlewine*

Another Kind of Blues / 1979 / GEM ✦✦✦✦✦

The U.K. Subs' debut can easily stand alongside any other punk classics released during this time period. Musically, they are similar to the early Clash, but where the Clash spit out balls of fiery rage, the U.K. Subs leaven their bile with sardonic humor. "Tomorrow's Girls" imagines a futuristic Venus who "will be pre-programmed," and the music spits out a hilarious series of mock computer beeps. "Crash Course" promises staid executives that by just listening to the Subs' music and buying up the right clothes, they too can learn punk rock. Only the sneeringly sexist "All I Wanna Know" hits a sour note. The music is rooted in the typical punk influences: the New York Dolls, Velvet Underground, and early Who, but the band adds a twist of classic '60s British R&B groups like the Yardbirds. It's melodic, punchy, and fast, delivering the necessary bite without ever becoming too abrasive or sugary. *Another Kind of Blues* is an impressive debut from the classic punk era. *—Victor W. Valdivia*

Brand New Age / 1980 / Gem ✦✦✦✦✦

For their second album, *Brand New Age*, the U.K. Subs built on the frenzied, melodic assault of their debut by developing their songwriting skills. *Brand New Age* contains tracks that are more ambitious than those on the debut, with more variety and lyrical depth. Rather than the amusing teen angst rants of the debut, this album shows the Subs embracing a more political point of view. "Warhead" is a seething diatribe on nuclear war, delivered with the venom and ferocity such a topic deserves. "Organised Crime" rants about government oppression, and "Brand New Age" delivers a less than optimistic slant on the forthcoming privacy intrusions of the 1980s. There's no shortage of droll humor, though, with the hilarious "Teenage" and "Emotional Blackmail," the closest the Subs have come to a song about relationships. Musically, the band have grown as well. "War-head" has a more complex song structure than anything they did before, and "You Can't Take It Anymore" proves the band doesn't have to rely on simple velocity to get their point across. Far from falling prey to the sophomore slump, the U.K. Subs came of age on this album and proved they were one of the best, most promising acts of their era. *—Victor W. Valdivia*

● **Singles 1978-1982** / 1991 / Progressive ✦✦✦✦✦
Cramming 28 tracks into a lean 59 minutes, *Singles* compiles every A- and B-side released by U.K. Subs during the height of their influence. While the strictly singles format omits some classic album tracks such as "Emotional Blackmail" and "Down on the Farm," what remains is an hour of punchy, melodic punk rock. In fact, the album reveals the Subs as a true missing link between hardcore English punk and '60s music. It's not just the covers of the Zombies' "She's Not There" and the Velvet Underground's "I'm Waiting for the Man." The instrumental "The Harper," with its bluesy guitar licks and harmonica, sounds like a revved-up Yardbirds song, and "Keep on Running" could have fit on the legendary *Nuggets* anthology. The Subs also have an element that distinguishes them from too many other punk acts: a sense of humor. "New York State Police" is a hilarious swipe at police brutality, while "Teenage" is a dead-on satire of young consumerism. *Singles* is not only a worthy anthology for fans, who will be pleased that many difficult-to-find tracks are compiled in one place, but will also be the perfect intro to newcomers to one of the best, most underrated bands in punk history. *—Victor W. Valdivia*

The Punk Singles Collection / Jan. 1996 / Anagram ✦✦✦✦✦

Tracey Ullman

b. Dec. 30, 1959, Buckinghamshire, England
Vocals / Pop/Rock, New Wave
Before she became a famous TV comedienne, Tracy Ullman recorded two albums in the early '80s that effortlessly recalled the classic girl group sound of the '60s. Ullman covered everything from Doris Day ("Move Over Darling") to Blondie ["(I'm Always Touched By Your) Presence, Dear"], finding the underlying connections between classic pop songs of all eras. *You Broke My Heart in 17 Places*, her debut album, was a hit in the U.K., and she even managed to have a Top Ten hit in America with a version of Kirsty MacColl's "They Don't Know." Although it had some fine numbers, the follow-up, *You Caught Me Out*, wasn't as successful, prompting Ullman to return to television. By the end of the '80s, her comedy show, *The Tracy Ullman Show*, was one of the most critically acclaimed television shows in America; she hasn't recorded any music since. *—Stephen Thomas Erlewine*

You Broke My Heart in 17 Places / 1983 / Stiff/Repertoire ✦✦✦✦✦
Ullman's first album, recorded in the middle of the new wave and synth-pop movements, provided a refreshing break with its retro girl group sound. Includes her only U.S. hit, "They Don't Know" (written by Kirsty MacColl) as well as carefully chosen obscure oldies. One of the great lost classics of the new wave era. *—Chris Woodstra*

You Caught Me Out / 1984 / Repertoire ✦✦✦
The second album follows the same formula as the first—a well-chosen collection of covers from obscure oldies to contemporary favorites (Madness' "My Girl"—retitled here as "My Guy") and even another stab at a Kirsty MacColl song ("Terry")—all done in the classic '60s girl group sound. Though it failed to produce the smash hits of the debut, "My Guy" and "Sunglasses" were minor hits in the U.K., and the album is nearly as much fun. Repertoire has released a CD version with six bonus tracks. *—Chris Woodstra*

● **The Best of Tracey Ullman** / 1991 / Rhino ✦✦✦✦✦
This 20-track compilation provides an extensive look at the nearly forgotten singing career of this now famous actress. Combining the entire first LP, *You Broke My Heart in 17 Places*, the highlights from her second effort *You Caught Me Out*, and well chosen B-sides, it more than lives up to its name. Although this material was recorded in the early '80s, lovers of the classic '60s girl-group sound will find these retro-gems a familiar delight. *—Chris Woodstra*

Ultimate Spinach

f. 1967, Boston, MA, **db.** 1969
Acid Rock, Psychedelic, Hard Rock
Ultimate Spinach was one of the most well-known, and perhaps the most notorious, of the groups to be hyped as part of the "Bosstown Sound" in 1968. The name itself guaranteed attention, as one of the most ludicrous and heavy-handed "far out" monikers of the psychedelic era, even outdoing formidable competition such as the Peanut Butter Conspiracy. Although the group were competent musicians with streaks of imagination, their albums were generally poor third cousins to the West Coast psychedelic groups that served as their obvious inspirations. Ultimate Spinach was produced by veteran arranger Alan Lorber, a main architect of the "Bosstown Sound." On the first two of their three albums, Ultimate Spinach was utterly dominated by leader Ian Bruce-Douglas, who wrote all of the material, sang the majority of the lead vocals, and played a wide variety of instruments, most frequently electric keyboards. Their self-titled debut, released in 1967, was a seriously intended psychedelic stew, with inadvertent comically awkward results. Bruce-Douglas' songs tended to be either dippily, humorlessly cosmic, or colored by equally too-serious finger-pointing at mainstream society. *Behold and See*, also released in 1968, was similar to the debut album but a little more even-keeled. The mysterious Bruce-Douglas disbanded Ultimate Spinach after the second LP was recorded, leaving Lorber holding the bag, as a third Ultimate Spinach album had already been scheduled for release. An entirely different lineup was assembled for their third and last album, with only Barbara Hudson remaining from the one heard on the first LP. The record was an undistinguished jumble of psychedelic, hard rock, and pop styles that sounded like the work of several different bands. *—Richie Unterberger*

● **Ultimate Spinach** / 1967 / MGM ✦✦✦
Upon its release in early 1967, Ultimate Spinach's self-titled debut was derided by some as second-rate psychedelia, selling reasonably well only by virtue of its hype as part of the "Bosstown Sound." So how does it sound decades later, removed from that hype and standing on the music alone? It still sounds like bush league, bandwagon-riding psychedelia. Ian Bruce-Douglas dominates the record as lead singer, composer of all the songs, and multi-instrumentalist, and while he espoused a darker vision than many psychedelic songsmiths, he wasn't in remotely the same league as Jim Morrison, Grace Slick, or Country Joe McDonald. Such comparisons are not idly chosen; echoes of the Doors, Jefferson Airplane, and Country Joe & the Fish cross over into derivation more than once, sounding like a recombination of 1967 West Coast psychedelic music that was garbled on its journey across the continent. All the same, the record is their best, for what that's worth. It is not without some attractive aspects, the best of which are Bruce-Douglas' skittering, piercing organ lines heard to superior effect on "Sacrifice of the Moon," especially as that is unencumbered by his awkward, over-serious lyrics ("collapsed laughter, running, falling, drifting across the minefield of your thoughts, dissolve, wondering, who am I, why should I be alone, alone?"). He likely played Country Joe & the Fish's first LP over and over, as "Sacrifice of the Moon" and "Baroque #1" attest to; "Baroque #1" goes as far as to plagiarize Country Joe's "Masked Marauder," right down to the harmonica and scat vocals. Similarly, "Your Head Is Reeling" has grungy, distorted Doors guitar lifted straight out of Robby Krieger's intro to "The End." As Bruce-Douglas' vocals are only adequate, it's unfortunate more was not heard from guitarist and occasional lead singer Barbara Hudson, who has the kind of ice-cool style trendy among the female psychedelic singers of the era. *—Richie Unterberger*

Behold & See / Aug. 1968 / MGM ✦✦✦
Ultimate Spinach's second album the "Penultimate Spinach" (as they would make only one more LP) is a slightly more subdued continuation of the derivative psychedelia in their debut. Again, it's like a hack take on West Coast groups. There's Country Joe & the Fish in Ian Bruce-Douglas' electric keyboards (which don't play anything as good as his solos on "Sacrifice of the Moon" from the first album); Jefferson Airplane-like female vocals (by guest singer Carol Lee Britt) and songwriting on "Where You're At"; some Quicksilver Messenger Service-type guitar arrangements on "Mind Flowers"; a melody and vocal reminiscent of Kaleidoscope's "Keep Your Mind Open" on "Fragmentary March of Green"; and more. Songwriter Bruce-Douglas' lyrics are unintentional hippie parodies without any irony or humor, whether solemnly aspiring to a beatnik state ("take a trip to the center of your mind") or indicting the straight world ("he has an ulcer in his brain, from thinking of how to divorce his wife"). When the album turns to social critiques, it's uncertain whether the band is trying to mimic the Mothers of Invention without the wit, or whether they're unwittingly embodying the very kinds of groups whom the Mothers took the piss out of on *We're Only in It for the Money*. *—Richie Unterberger*

Ultimate Spinach III / 1969 / MGM ✦✦✦
The Ultimate Spinach were originally a psychedelic/underground band, but by the time of their third and last album, the group had changed personnel so much that their connection with the original lineup was tenuous in both sound and body. (Actually, the original band had broken up after their second album; the Ultimate Spinach heard on *III* included a couple of musicians that had recorded on the first two records, but was essentially an entirely different outfit.) They weren't that notable an act to begin with, and *III*, perhaps due to the somewhat ad hoc lineup, is so diffuse that it sounds like the work of a few different bands. There's an anachronistic (but actually okay) cover of the old pop-soul hit "(Just Like) Romeo & Juliet," pretty psych-pop ballads, and some annoying, decidedly un-tasty hard blues-rock jamming. Collectors may be interested to note the presence of guitarist Jeff Baxter (later to play with Steely Dan and the Doobie Brothers). But it's a pretty marginal effort, not particularly worth finding even if you're a psychedelic collector. *—Richie Unterberger*

● **The Very Best of Ultimate Spinach** / May 15, 2001 / Varese ✦✦✦✦

Ultramagnetic MC's

f. 1984, New York, NY [The Bronx], **db.** 1993
Underground Rap, East Coast Rap, Hip-Hop, Golden Age
Arising from the Boogie Down Bronx in the mid-'80s as a far-flung hip-hop trio with a heap of new ideas to try out, Ultramagnetic's Kool Keith, Ced Gee, and DJ Moe Love occupy something of a singular place in the old-school pantheon. Combining funk-heavy tracks with jeep-rocking beats and obscure lyrical references, Ultramagnetic MC's have a list of firsts to their credit: the first group to employ a sampler as an instrument, the first to feature extensive use of live instrumentation . . . the first to feature a former psychiatric patient (Keith) on the mic. Early singles like "Something Else" and "Space Groove" were block party staples and created waves in the underground, eventually landing the group on the disco-dominated Next Plateau label, where they released their underappreciated debut. The following years found the group shuffling from label to label, releasing albums on Mercury and Wild Pitch before splitting to pursue various projects. *—Sean Cooper*

★ **Critical Beatdown** / 1988 / Next Plateau ✦✦✦✦✦
Besides being an undeniable hip-hop classic, the first album by the cult crew Ultramagnetic MCs introduced to the world the larger-than-life, one-of-a-kind personality of Kool Keith. That alone would make this some sort of landmark recording, but it also happens to be one of the finest rap albums from the mid- to late-'80s "new school" in hip-hop that

numbered among its contributors Run-D.M.C., Public Enemy, and Boogie Down Productions. *Critical Beatdown* easily stands with the classic recordings made by those giants, and it is, in some ways, more intriguing because of how short-lived Ultramagnetic turned out to be. It would be wrong to assume that the finest thing about the album is its lyrical invention. Lyrically the group is inspired, to be sure, but the production is equally forward-looking. *Critical Beatdown* is full of the sort of gritty cuts that would define hip-hop's underground scene, with almost every song sounding like an instant classic. Although he turns in a brilliant performance, Kool Keith had not yet taken completely off into the stratosphere at this early point. He still has at least one foot planted on the street, and gives the album a viscerally real feel and accessibility that his later work sometimes lacks. His viewpoint is still uniquely and oddly individual, though, and he already shows signs of the freakish conceptualizing persona that would eventually surface fully under the guise of Dr. Octagon. If Kool Keith gives the album its progressive mentality and adrenaline rush, Ced Gee gives its street-level heft, and is, in many ways, the album's core. Somewhere in the nexus between the two stylistic extremes, brilliant music emanated. *Critical Beatdown* maintains all its sharpness and every ounce of its power, and it has not aged one second since 1988. —*Stanton Swihart*

Funk Your Head Up / Mar. 17, 1992 / Mercury ◆◆◆
Four years in the making, the follow-up was somewhat easy too ignore, overly crowded with half-thought ideas and water-treading glances back. Produced the radio hit "Poppa Large." —*Sean Cooper*

The Four Horsemen / Aug. 10, 1993 / Wild Pitch ◆◆◆◆
Back on track and on yet another label. The last album by the group before Keith would head off on his solo Doctor Octagon tangent. —*Sean Cooper*

Basement Tapes: 1984-1990 / May 17, 1995 / Tuff City ◆◆◆
Basement Tapes: 1984-1990 compiles a selection of Ultramagnetic MC's outtakes, rarities and demos. Considerably rougher than their official studio records, *Basement Tapes* has raw street vibe, and although it's clear why some of these tracks were never widely released, it's an exciting record, proving that the Ultramagnetic MC's were sorely neglected while they were active. —*Stephen Thomas Erlewine*

B-Side Companion / Oct. 7, 1997 / Next Plateau ◆◆◆◆
The Ultramagnetic MC's belong in the groundbreaking rap category (along with the likes of Run-D.M.C., Grandmaster Flash, etc.). Formed in the mid-'80s, the group rejected the fun rap style popular at the time (i.e., the Fat Boys and early Beastie Boys) and set out to create their own serious, funky, and bass-heavy groove style. The group definitely succeeded, but like many early rap artists, they did not meet with the commercial success they deserved for their trailblazing efforts.

    Back in the '80s, the 12" single was the main format for rappers to show their stuff (few rappers were granted full-length albums). So the Ultramagnetic MC's made the most of the 12", releasing many before their 1988 full-length *Critical Beatdown* appeared. An abundance of B-sides amassed after a while (with many as strong, if not better than, the featured A-side), so Next Plateau Records compiled the *crème de la crème* of these hard-to-find tracks on *The B-Side Companion*, remixing most to give them a more contemporary feel. Their first-ever release, "Ego Trippin'," is featured here as "Ego Trippin' 2000" and sets the tone for the rest of the album. You can't go wrong with tracks like "Watch Me Now," "MC's Ultra Part 2," and "Funky," all equally strong old-school rap that deserves to be heard. The seeds for today's rap stars were planted on the tracks included on *The B-Side Companion*. —*Greg Prato*

Ultravox

f. 1974, London, England, **db.** 1987
New Romantic, New Wave, Synth Pop
Rejecting the abrasive guitars of their punk-era contemporaries in favor of lushly romantic synthesizers, Ultravox emerged as one of the primary influences on the British electro-pop movement of the early '80s. Formed in London in 1974, the group was led by vocalist and keyboardist John Foxx; their obvious affection for the glam rock sound of David Bowie and Roxy Music brought them little respect from audiences caught up in the growing fervor of punk, but in 1977 Island Records signed the quintet anyway, with Brian Eno agreeing to produce their self-titled debut LP. Island dropped the band after 1978's *Systems of Romance*, at which time both Foxx and Simon quit, the former mounting a solo career and the latter joining Magazine. The remaining members of Ultravox tapped singer/guitarist Midge Ure; upon signing to Chrysalis, the new line-up recorded *Vienna*, scoring a surprise smash hit with the single "Sleepwalk," which reached the number two spot on the UK pop charts in 1981 and pushed the LP into the Top Five. Upon completing 1984's *Lament*, Ure left Ultravox to forge a solo career, topping the UK charts a year later with the solo smash "If I Was." —*Jason Ankeny*

Ultravox / 1977 / Island ◆◆◆
John Foxx proves to have an odd, Bowie-influenced vision, here aided and abetted by Brian Eno (then a Bowie crony) and Steve Lillywhite. "My Sex" and "I Want to Be a Machine" are standouts. —*William Ruhlmann*

Ha! Ha! Ha! / 1977 / Island/ ◆◆◆
There's something quite chilling and compulsive about the original model of Ultravox. Sure, lots of people were experimenting with synthesizers, but Ultravox married that sound to elements of glam rock and punk to produce a more affecting hybrid. You can feel the ghosts of Kraftwerk at play here, even more strongly than on the band's debut—and that's saying something. Twenty years on, some of it does sound a little corny; however, the album does include the one undeniable classic of early-period Ultravox: "Hiroshima Mon Amour." —*Alex Ogg*

Systems of Romance / Dec. 1978 / Island ◆◆◆◆
Systems of Romance, the high-water mark of pre-Midge Ultravox, also proved tremendously influential on the host of new romantic bands that followed in its wake. Produced by Conny Plank, the album divides into a rock-heavy first side and a synth-heavy second side. Though several songs lack a distinctive element and the record is occasionally dependent on a few rock & roll clichés, *Systems of Romance* is an important, intriguing album. —*John Bush*

Vienna / 1980 / Ariola ◆◆◆◆◆
The new Ultravox, under Midge Ure, has a dreamy, ethereal sound heard at its best on its debut album, which features the title song, "All Stood Still," "Passing Strangers," and "Sleepwalk," all UK hits. —*William Ruhlmann*

Rage in Eden / 1981 / Chrysalis ◆◆◆
This was another major U.K. chart hit, as Ultravox milked their "Vienna"-inspired success for all it was worth. Sadly, *Rage in Eden* is as pretentious and unwieldy as its title would suggest. Both "The Thin Wall" and "I Remember (Death in the Afternoon)" are stunningly overblown and self-satisfied. Midge Ure's lyrics are particularly at fault here—a shame, because the music itself is extremely good in parts. This was their last album produced in collaboration with Conny Plank; thereafter Ultravox would experience a steady commercial decline. —*Alex Ogg*

Quartet / 1982 / Chrysalis ◆◆◆
The single "Reap the Wild Wind" sets the tone for this hapless collection of songs, seemingly inspired by religious themes. Only "We Came to Dance" is of any value, with its nod to the earlier, less commercially successful (but more artistically satisfying) Ultravox sound. The producer? George Martin, no less. He's worked with better bands, allegedly. —*Alex Ogg*

Lament / 1984 / One Way ◆◆◆◆◆
Containing arguably their best work of the '80s, *Lament* showcases a band with confidence to match their commercial status (it was the first of their albums to be self-produced). The electro-synth workout "Dancing With Tears in My Eyes" actually works quite well, and is their best single since the epochal (for good and bad reasons) "Vienna." "White China," too, is impressive. —*Alex Ogg*

The Collection / 1984 / Chrysalis ◆◆◆◆◆
While Ultravox's commercial success was virtually nonexistent in the U.S., their singles were strewn across the British charts throughout the early half of the '80s. Led by Midge Ure's haunting but forceful vocal presence, sometimes reminiscent of U2's Bono, Ultravox used the keyboards to guide their sophisticated and intelligent pop style, resulting in some extremely intricate and provocative material. *The Collection* gathers the heartiest of Ultravox's repertoire, wisely ignoring any of their late-'70s albums in which John Foxx, the group's founder, inundated his darkened keyboard approach. Effectively desolate but rich in lyrical poetry and clever melodies, songs like "Vienna," "Reap the Wild Wind," and "The Voice" cast Ure's talents as a singer to the forefront, while livelier efforts, like the frantic forward thrust of "Love's Great Adventure," showcase the group's spirited synthesizer work. "Dancing With Tears in My Eyes" is a moody radio-dance track, and the hovering broodiness of "The Hymn" harbors its own brand of gothic charm. *The Collection* completes the task of covering the most crucial of Ultravox's material. —*Mike DeGagne*

U-Vox / 1986 / Chrysalis ◆◆

● **Dancing with Tears in My Eyes** / 1997 / EMI ◆◆◆◆◆
Dancing with Tears in My Eyes is a 15-track overview of Ultravox's early-'80s commercial peak, hitting most, but not all, of their biggest hits, including "Sleepwalk," "Vienna," "All Stood Still," and "Reap the Wild Wind." It's not a bad collection, but if it had included hits like "The Thin Wall," it could have been a definitive retrospective. —*Stephen Thomas Erlewine*

Uncle Kracker (Matt Shafer)

DJ / Rap-Rock, Turntablism, Rap-Metal, Alternative Pop/Rock
Slicing and dicing for his hometown chum, the foul-mouthed mainstream rap hero Kid Rock, Uncle Kracker (nee Matt Shafer) stepped out from behind the turntables to release his debut solo album, *Double Wide*, on Kid Rock's own Top Dog/Atlantic/Lava label. Yet another Detroit combination of funky post-grunge rock and hip-hop aesthetic, Uncle Kracker makes his predecessor proud.

    Kid Rock and Uncle Kracker are practically family. The two met in Clawson, Michigan in 1987, where Rock was spinning in an all-ages DJ contest at a popular night spot called Daytona's. The two had similar musical tastes (The Commodores, Run D.M.C., Lynyrd Skynyrd, and George Jones) and became fast friends. Kracker's first musical contribution was on Rock's 1991 debut, *Grits Sandwiches for Breakfast*, and he also co-wrote and performed on Rock's multi-platinum *Devil Without A Cause*. It was just a matter of time for Kracker to do his own thing.

    It's neither surprising that the media has tagged *Double Wide* as more radio friendly than *Devil Without A Cause*, nor that Rock and his band, Twisted Brown Trucker, come together to bang things up on *Double Wide*. Like his pal, Uncle Kracker wanted a maddening country growl woven into mainstream modern rock to create a mindblowing rap excursion; *Double Wide* was just that, released in summer 2000. —*MacKenzie Wilson*

● **Double Wide** / Jun. 13, 2000 / Atlantic ◆◆◆
With Kid Rock's "Only God Knows Why" playing in the background, Kid Rock's protégé Uncle Kracker poses his mentor a question: "What if I don't make it?" It's hard to believe that a musician would open his major-label debut CD with inspirational career advice from Kid Rock. But Kid Rock does know a thing or two about becoming a rock icon to legions of suburban teens and porn stars. As Kid Rock's self-proclaimed best

friend/DJ/backup singer/multi-platinum co-writer/sidekick thug boy, Uncle Kracker has Kid Rock's MTV-ready charisma and raunchy rock-rap fur-lined coattails to thank for the existence of this album. Maybe there is something in his native waters of Detroit, but Uncle Kracker definitely takes full advantage of the opportunity and delivers an amusing, party-ready debut CD of country-, rockabilly-, and hip-hop-infused rock & roll that is guaranteed to please. Each song drips with Uncle Kracker's laid-back, white-trash, Detroit-worshiping, beer-swilling attitude. Your opinion of Uncle Kracker, however, is largely dependent on your opinion of Kid Rock. Kid Rock's fingerprints are left all over the album, which is understandable considering he produced and co-wrote nearly every song. The album is even filled with samples from Kid Rock's *Devil Without a Cause*. If you loved *Devil Without a Cause* and *History of Rock*, you'll find *Double Wide* a welcome third helping. It's more of the same; however, Uncle Kracker provides an added dose of melody to the Kid Rock formula with his gravelly, mellow, and rather soulful voice. At times, the album does sound a bit recycled, but when you're having this much fun at a party, who really cares? Who knows how long the formula will remain fresh, but on *Double Wide*, Uncle Kracker hits like a full house of raucous dynamite. *—Brian Musich*

Uncle Tupelo

f. 1987, Belleville, IL, **db.** 1994

Americana, Alternative Country, Alternative Country-Rock, Alternative Pop/Rock

With the release of their 1990 debut LP *No Depression*, the Belleville, IL trio Uncle Tupelo launched more than simply their own career—by fusing the simplicity and honesty of country music with the bracing fury of punk, they kick-started a revolution which reverberated throughout the American underground. Thanks to a successful on-line site and subsequent fanzine which adopted the album's name, the tag "No Depression" became a catch-all for the like-minded artists who, along with Tupelo, signalled alternative rock's return to its country roots—at much the same time, ironically enough, that Nashville was itself embracing the slick gloss associated with mainstream rock and pop. Led by singers/songwriters Jay Farrar and Jeff Tweedy, Uncle Tupelo issued *No Depression* in 1990—a reflection of the band's disparate influences, ranging from everyone from Hank Williams to bluesman Leadbelly through to the famed postpunk trio Hüsker Dü, its songs were meditations on small-town, small-time life, candid snapshots of days spent working thankless jobs and nights spent in an alcoholic fog. With the acoustic *March 16-20, 1992*, the group plunged fully into country and folk; signing to Sire/Reprise, in 1993 Uncle Tupelo issued the LP *Anodyne*. Widely regarded as the group's definitive statement, it was a true country-rock hybrid which accented the power of both musical forms; however, the long-standing relationship between Farrar and Tweedy soon dissolved in bitter acrimony, and Uncle Tupelo disbanded. Shortly thereafter, Tweedy formed Wilco, while Farrar resurfaced in Son Volt. *—Jason Ankeny*

No Depression / 1990 / Rockville ✦✦✦✦

Uncle Tupelo's landmark opening salvo is the group's most rock-oriented album, steeped more in breakneck speed, punk crunch and guitar dissonance than any of their subsequent efforts. Indeed, despite the presence of mandolins, fiddles and banjos—as well as inclusion of the title track, a faithful cover of the A.P. Carter classic—the trio's vaunted country leanings are less musical than thematic on *No Depression*, thanks in large part to singers/songwriters Jay Farrar and Jeff Tweedy's acute depictions of rural, blue-collar life. Like the Replacements—never more obvious an influence than on this LP—Uncle Tupelo's songs paint grim, unrelenting portraits of aimless Midwestern existence, split between days working on the opening cut's "Factory Belt" and nights spent blurry-eyed and wasted ("Whiskey Bottle," "Before I Break"). Still, for all of the record's doleful cynicism—virtually every cut nods toward dashed hopes, broken promises and paralyzing fear—there's an undeniable electricity afoot as well; by channeling the mournful clarity of country into the crackling fury of punk, *No Depression* brings new life to both musical camps. *—Jason Ankeny*

Still Feel Gone / Sep. 17, 1991 / Rockville ✦✦✦

Still Feel Gone is Tupelo's transitional record; while it goes far in fusing the band's rock origins with their country aspirations, the alliance is often an uneasy, even schizophrenic, one. Writers Jay Farrar and Jeff Tweedy are rarely in synch; while the former's contributions embrace roots music wholeheartedly, Tweedy's songs journey more deeply into rock than ever before—his opening track, "Gun," is the most straightforward pop number the trio ever recorded, while "D. Boon," a tribute to the fallen leader of the legendary post-punk trio the Minutemen, borders on thrash. Still, while *Still Feel Gone* lacks the consistency of its predecessor *No Depression*, it's a more wide-ranging record, deeper in maturity, subtlety and texture—all clear evidence of things to come. *—Jason Ankeny*

March 16-20, 1992 / Aug. 3, 1992 / Rockville ✦✦✦✦✦

Produced by R.E.M.'s Peter Buck, *March 16-20, 1992* represents Uncle Tupelo's full evolution into a true country unit; with the exception of the eerie squalls of guitar feedback which haunt Jeff Tweedy's mesmerizing "Wait Up," there's virtually no evidence of the trio's punk heritage. Instead, the all-acoustic album—a combination of Tupelo originals and well-chosen traditional songs—taps into the very essence of backwoods culture, its music rooted in the darkest corners of Appalachian life. An inescapable sense of dread grips this collection, from the large-scale threat depicted in the stunning rendition of the Louvin Brothers' "The Great Atomic Power" to the fatalism of the worker anthems "Grindstone" and "Coalminers"; even the character studies, including a revelatory "Moonshiner," are relentlessly grim. A vivid glimpse at the harsh realities of rural existence, *March 16-20, 1992* is a brilliant resurrection of a bygone era of American folk artistry. *—Jason Ankeny*

● **Anodyne** / May 1993 / Sire ✦✦✦✦✦

Uncle Tupelo never struck a finer balance between rock and country than on *Anodyne*, their major-label debut and parting shot. For all of the ill will undoubtedly simmering throughout these sessions, Jay Farrar and Jeff Tweedy have never before been more attuned to each other musically; where earlier records often found the band's twin forces moving in opposing directions, *Anodyne* bears the full fruits of their shared vision. Recorded live in the studio, the album encompasses and reinterprets not only country-rock (evidenced by the group's pairing with Doug Sahm on his "Give Back the Key to My Heart") but also traditional country (the tribute to the songwriting legacy of "Acuff-Rose"), rock (the churning "The Long Cut," "Chickamauga") and folk ("New Madrid," "Steal the Crumbs"), the band's reach never once exceeding its grasp. *—Jason Ankeny*

Undertones

f. 1976, Derry, Northern Ireland, **db.** 1983

British Punk, New Wave, Punk

There are those who would disagree vehemently, but in my estimation the Undertones were Ireland's best rock band—ever. Roaring out of Northern Ireland in 1976, the Undertones fused speedy, loud Ramones-inspired walls of guitar racket with irresistible '60s pop hooks, with just a touch of mid-'70s glam rock for good measure. With the singular tenor vocals of frontman Feargal Sharkey making them instantaneously recognizable, Undertones songs tended to eschew punk vitriol for songs about teenage love, girls, snotty cousins, and summertime—life's simple joys (and pains). No more succinct a summation of their style, wit, and power can be found than on their out-of-print debut EP *Teenage Kicks*—a record of startling ebullience, the songs sound as exhilarating today as they did decades ago. However, the Undertones did not go into creative stasis with their winning punk-pop and simply replicate a proven formula over and over. As they grew as musicians, so did their albums change, incorporating some of the Tamla/Motown soul music they loved as kids. Sadly, the Undertones' story ended far too quickly. Growing up meant too much change too fast, and by the time they released their mediocre fourth album, restlessness and "musical differences" were splitting them apart. Sharkey went off to a short-lived solo career, while the guitar-playing O'Neill brothers put together the politically charged That Petrol Emotion. *—John Dougan*

● **The Undertones** / 1979 / Rykodisc ✦✦✦✦✦

An absolutely essential purchase. One of the best albums of the punk era, or any era. Song after song is infused with a liberating joy and intensity that only a handful of rock records at the time equalled. A crucial record, the 'Tones debut shows how influential '70s commercial pop was on the growing punk community, who embraced it and then tore it all to hell. A record that hasn't lost its luster after hundreds of plays and nearly two decades. Reissued on CD with seven bonus tracks by Rykodisc in 1994. *—John Dougan*

Hypnotised / 1980 / Rykodisc ✦✦✦✦✦

It's ridiculous to not encourage you to purchase the first three Undertones records, because they are such wonderful distillations of all that makes rock & roll great. *Hypnotised* picks up where the debut leaves off, but adds a slightly more sarcastic touch to some of the songs, especially the witty "My Perfect Cousin" and the goofy "More Songs About Chocolate and Girls" (a not-so-subtle parody of the title of Talking Heads' second LP *More Songs About Buildings and Food*). Reissued on CD with five bonus tracks by Rykodisc in 1994. *—John Dougan*

Positive Touch / 1981 / Rykodisc ✦✦✦

By this time, The Undertones had switched labels and recorded a challenging, slightly arty record that didn't sound much like their first two, and showed an amazing artistic development. There are musical elements not on the previous recordings (horns, Paul Carrack's keyboards); still, the band's creativity, intelligence and personality make this a tremendously rewarding record. Not where one unfamiliar with the 'Tones should start (get that guitar rush first), but once under their spell, *Positive Touch* will become almost as important as the first two albums. Reissued on CD with four bonus tracks by Rykodisc in 1994. *—John Dougan*

All Wrapped Up / 1983 / Rykodisc ✦✦✦

The Very Best of the Undertones / Oct. 25, 1994 / Rykodisc ✦✦✦✦✦

The Very Best of the Undertones collects the cream of the catalog. The group's earliest high-energy teenage anthems (themes of doubt, deceit, yearning, and infatuation) give way, over the course of 25 songs, to the sublime intimacy of "Wednesday Week" and "Julie Ocean," and then the sophisticated, Tamla/Motown layering of "Soul Seven." Group members discuss each track in the informative liner notes. Start here, fall in love, then go find the individual albums. *—Roch Parisien*

Underworld

f. 1988, London, England

Electronica, Techno, House, Progressive House

Underworld became one of the most crucial electronic acts of the 1990s via an intriguing synthesis of old and new. The trio's two-man frontline, vocalist Karl Hyde and guitarist Rick Smith, had been recording together since the early-'80s new wave explosion; after two unsuccessful albums released as Underworld during the late '80s, the pair finally hit it big when they recruited Darren Emerson, a young DJ hipped to the sound of techno and trance. Traditional pop song-forms were jettisoned in favor of Hyde's heavily treated vocals, barely-there whispering and surreal wordplay, stretched out over the urban break-beat trance ripped out by Emerson & Co. while Smith's cascade of guitar-shard effects provided a bluesy foil to the stark music. All in all, the decision to go pop was hardly a concession to the mainstream. The first Underworld album by the trio, *Dubnobasswithmyheadman*, appeared in late 1993 to a flurry of critical acclaim; the trio then gained U.S. distribution for the album with TVT. *Second Toughest in the Infants*, the group's sophomore LP, updated their sound slightly and received more praise than the debut. Unlike the first, the LP also sold well, thanks in part to the non-album single "Born Slippy," featured on the soundtrack to the seminal film *Trainspotting*. Though Underworld's 1999 LP *Beaucoup Fish* was a bit of a disappointment critically and commercially, the band continued to tour the world. *—John Bush*

• **Dubnobasswithmyheadman** / Dec. 1993 / Wax Trax! ♦♦♦♦♦
From the beginning of the first track "Dark & Long," Underworld's focus on production is clear, with songwriting coming in a distant second. The best tracks ("MMM Skyscraper I Love You," "Cowgirl") mesh Hyde's sultry songwriting with Emerson's beat-driven production, an innovative blend of classic acid house, techno and dub that sounds different from much that preceded it. In a decade awash with stale fusion, Underworld are truly a multi-genre group. *—John Bush*

Second Toughest in the Infants / Mar. 12, 1996 / Wax Trax! ♦♦♦♦♦
On their second album, Underworld continues to explore the fringes of dub, dance and techno, creating a seamless, eclectic fusion of various dance genres. *Second Toughest in the Infants* carries the same knockout punch of their debut, *Dubnobasswithmyheadman*, but it's subtler and more varied, offering proof that the outfit is one of the leading dance collectives of the mid-'90s. *—Stephen Thomas Erlewine*

Beaucoup Fish / Mar. 1, 1999 / Junior Boy's Own ♦♦♦♦
With the buzz almost completely died down from "Born Slippy," Underworld's *Trainspotting* hit of over two years before, *Beaucoup Fish* emerged to a distinctly uncaring public. And though it is a disappointing record compared to the group's high-flying previous albums, it displays Underworld's talents well—the trio is still the best at welding obtuse songcraft onto an uncompromising techno framework and making both sound great. Hyde's nasally vocals are a bit more obtrusive on tracks like the trance-rant "Moaner" and first single "Push Upstairs," but as before, impeccable production saves the day. While *Second Toughest in the Infants* showed Underworld were no mere novices at introducing super-tough breakbeats, here the focus is on throwback acid-house and trance. The effect is that Underworld have refused to compromise their artistic vision to anyone's view of commercialism; as such, the few excesses on *Beaucoup Fish* can be forgiven. *—John Bush*

Everything, Everything / Sep. 12, 2000 / JBO ♦♦♦♦
Underworld didn't become one of the biggest groups in the dance world by sitting in the studio all day, spending as much time making tea as producing tracks. Between records, the trio toured incessantly—playing rock venues, dancefloors, major festivals all over the world—and consistently made the single best case for techno working in a live (as opposed to club) context. So instead of a mix album (though alumnus Darren Emerson *did* record a volume in the *Global Underground* series), in mid-2000 Underworld released the live album *Everything, Everything*. And just like their studio LPs, this one works so well, not just because the tracks are so excellently produced, but because Underworld is so good at placing sympathetic tracks next to each other and creating effortless-sounding transitions. Each of the act's previous albums blended tracks so smoothly that new listeners were often forced to check the CD player just to see which track they're on at any second. Beginning here with "Juanita/Kiteless," the opening track(s) from 1996's *Second Toughest in the Infants*, Underworld tweaks the production slightly, then slides right into "Cups" and "Push Upstairs" from 1999's *Beaucoup Fish*. After pausing a few seconds to catch their breath (figuratively speaking) and accept some audience applause, the trio push onward into "Pearls Girl," perhaps the best production of their career and an obvious peak here. Granted, Underworld doesn't blend each transition on *Everything, Everything*, and Karl Hyde's vocals aren't always as perfect as on the LP. Still, excellent track selection (evenly distributed from all three LPs) and a winning performance let the band get nearly everything right on their first live album. *—John Bush*

Unit 4+2

f. 1963, Hertfordshire, England, **db.** 1967
Folk-Rock, British Invasion

Unit Four Plus Two was a one-hit wonder that probably deserved better. As one of the better acoustic-electric bands of the mid-'60s, the group stormed the charts with one memorable hit, "Concrete and Clay." With a memorable chorus, a bossa-nova beat, and pleasant, hook-laden acoustic guitars, "Concrete and Clay" was one of the finest pop records of 1965. Not only was it a U.K. number one, it was a worldwide hit, and the group was suddenly getting played on radio across the globe. It may have been too much, too soon. Like too many other groups of the period, the band had nothing remotely as good to serve as a follow-up release, as soon became apparent. Decca released an album to capitalize on their sudden success, but although a lot of what was there was pleasant, and their range was impressive—from Latin-based material to covers of current soul hits—little of it was as interesting or attractive as the single. Their next single, "You've Never Been in Love Like This Before," a more soul-influenced number, failed to match the chart performance of "Concrete and Clay," but made the English Top 20. By this time, music was changing rapidly around them, as British beat music began evolving into something more intense and virtuosic in nature. Unit Four Plus Two found themselves slipping behind the public, and unable to find a fresher approach to their music. *—Bruce Eder*

• **Unit 4+2 Featuring Concrete & Clay** / 1965 / London ♦♦♦♦
The sudden success of "Concrete and Clay" sent group and record company alike scrambling to do an LP. The sound is a mix of soft, harmony-based folk ("500 Miles," "Cotton Fields," "Wild Is the Wind"), folk-gospel ("Swing Down Chariot"), and Latin-flavored pop ("La Bamba" etc.), along with a rock number or two ("The Girl From New York City"). The repertory obviously reflects the group's live sets of the era. Strangely enough, it's all done in mono—one would think that stereo would've been standard by 1965—and all of it is pleasing, though the results are also slightly on the bland side. As musicians, the bandmembers were impeccable—especially notable are David Meikle's and Howard Lubin's guitars—and they harmonized well vocally. In the studio, at least, however, they just weren't that exciting, coming off as slightly more insipid competitors of Peter & Gordon and Chad & Jeremy. *—Bruce Eder*

Unit 4+2 / 1969 / Fontana ♦♦
A shift to another record label (Fontana) resulted in a new album after several failed singles. *Unit 4+2* is a more rocking effort than its similarly titled predecessor, but is still very rooted in harmony vocals. The playing is harder and more aggressive, with a kind of breezy quasi-psychedelic/pop air which, if they could've generated it in 1966 or 1967, might've made the group favorites on the club scene and the U.K. charts. By 1969, however, this material all sounded a bit passé, despite some superb playing on tracks like "I Will." For every good moment—like the dazzling acoustic guitar break on that number or the hook-laden chorus on "Too Fast, Too Slow"—there were slow, romantic string-laden pop ballads (such as "Face In My Head") to weigh down the record, and some of the material, such as "(Living In) The World of Broken Hearts," was just sappy. Without a hit single to drive its sales, the group's second LP sank without a trace, much as the band itself had called it quits by that time as well. *—Bruce Eder*

Concrete And Clay/Unit 4+2 / 1993 / Repertoire ♦♦♦
This 29-track CD combines the contents of both Decca Records LPs by the Hertfordshire, England sextet, plus seven additional tracks that were never on either of their albums. The result is a somewhat uneven collection that is melodious enough at various times but often lacking in excitement and drive. The group treads a fine line between delicacy and blandness as they go through various originals, spiced by covers of such familiar fare as "You've Lost That Loving Feeling," "Cotton Fields," "500 Miles," and "La Bamba." Their elegant vocal textures can be startling and even revelatory, as on their cover of the then-new Bob Dylan song "You Ain't Goin' Nowhere." They got better as they went along, but they were never able to come up with a song to match the attractiveness of "Concrete and Clay," from their own pens or in the form of covers of other authors' work. Their legacy, presented virtually in full here, is a body of soft acoustic pop/rock that's only interesting enough to sustain itself about half the time. The remastering is superior to the sound on Decca's vinyl collections of their material from the late 1970s, although—for reasons that are unclear—apparently everything that the group ever recorded, even as late as 1967, was issued in mono only. *—Bruce Eder*

The United States of America

f. 1967, Los Angeles, CA, **db.** 1969
Experimental Rock, Psychedelic

Despite releasing only one album, the United States of America was among the late '60s' most visionary bands. A mix of psychedelia and the avant-garde, their music predated modern ambient pop by several decades, eschewing guitars for strings, keyboards and haunting electronics. The group was led by composer/keyboardist Joseph Byrd, a Kentucky native raised in Tucson, Arizona. Byrd played in country, rock and jazz bands while in high school and attending the University of Arizona; though he won a fellowship to study music at Stanford, Instead, Byrd relocated to New York, intrigued by the avant-garde experiments of the city's downtown music scene. He earned international notoriety for his own compositions while working as a conductor, arranger, associate producer and assistant to critic Virgil Thomson.

Byrd eventually returned to the west coast, accepting an assistant teaching position at UCLA and moving into a beachfront commune populated by grad students, artists and Indian musicians. In the summer of 1967, Byrd left the university to write music and produce "happenings." To perform his new, Summer of Love-inspired material, Byrd recruited UCLA students (vocalist Dorothy Moskowitz, bassist Rand Forbes, electric violinist Gordon Marron and drummer Craig Woodson) to form the United States of America. The group's critically-acclaimed, 1968 self-titled LP on CBS owed much of its unique ambience to the ring modulator, a primitive synthesizer later popularized by the Krautrock sound. Despite the album's minor chart success, the United States of America disbanded later that year.

Byrd resurfaced in 1969 with *The American Metaphysical Circus*, credited to Joe Byrd and the Field Hippies, a twelve-piece band including vocalists Susan de Lange, Victoria Bond and Christie Thompson. A critical and commercial failure, the LP was his last until 1975's *Yankee Transcendoodle*, a collection of synthesizer pieces. Three years later, Byrd produced Ry Cooder's *Jazz* album; in 1980 he issued another synthesizer record, *Christmas Yet to Come*. He additionally wrote music for films, television and advertising. Fellow United States of America alum Dorothy Moskowitz later appeared with Country Joe McDonald's All-Star Band; the rest of the group disappeared from the music scene. *—Jason Ankeny*

• **The United States of America** / 1968 / Edsel ♦♦♦♦♦
Originally released on Columbia in 1968, this is one of the legendary pure psychedelic space records. Some of the harder rocking tunes have a fun-house recklessness that recalls aspects of early Pink Floyd and the Velvet Underground at their freakiest; the sedate, exquisitely orchestrated ballads, especially "Cloud Song" and the wonderfully titled "Love Song For The Dead Che," are among the best relics of dreamy psychedelia. Occasionally things get too excessive and self-conscious, and the attempts at comedy are a bit flat, but otherwise this is a near classic. The CD reissue adds two previously unreleased outtakes. *—Richie Unterberger*

Unrest

f. 1981, Washington, DC, **db.** 1994
Indie Rock, Alternative Pop/Rock, American Underground

The flagship act of frontman Mark Robinson's own TeenBeat label, Unrest was a towering pillar of the American indie rock community throughout the early '90s—from the tongue-in-cheek garage noise of their earliest efforts to the shimmering, manic pop thrills of their later, most enduring work, the band was a paragon of DIY virtue, perfecting a genre-hopping eclecticism and knowing, ironic lyrical outlook that virtually defined the sound and feel of college rock in the pre-grunge era. Robinson, bassist Tim Moran, and drummer Phil Krauth formed Unrest while students at Wakefield High School in Arlington, VA; borrowing their name from a Henry Cow record, the fledgling trio soon made its debut on the first TeenBeat release, the 1985 cassette compilation *Extremism in the Defense of Liberty Is No Vice.* TeenBeat itself would over time emerge as one of the most respected American indie labels of its period, evolving from the Xeroxed covers of early cassette releases to a prolific flow of beautifully designed releases inspired by Robinson's abiding affection for the lavish packaging of the British imprints Factory and 4AD; the company's ever-changing roster reflected its founder's diverse tastes, issuing recordings from artists spanning from Versus to Gastr del Sol to Blast Off Country Style. All of Unrest's releases cataloged Robinson's ever-shifting lyrical and musical obsessions, which (especially at the outset of the group's existence) often resulted in jarring track-to-track juxtapositions embracing everything from punk to funk. With the 1991 single "Yes, She Is My Skinhead Girl," Unrest achieved indie rock sainthood—a joint release with the K Records label, its skittering, oddly propulsive pop approach signaled the band's creative breakthrough, also earning strong critical notices. But at the peak of its success in 1994, Unrest disbanded. *—Jason Ankeny*

Imperial f.f.r.r. / Jul. 14, 1992 / TeenBeat/No. 6 ♦♦♦♦♦
Imperial is Unrest's full-length debut. It fleshes out the pop promise of their early singles, and expands on their pop and experimental background as well. "I Do Believe You Are Blushing," "Cherry Cream On," "Suki," "Isabel" and "June" are still some of the band's best songs, mixing high-energy guitars and subjects like girls and death to infectious effect. A near-perfect album of indie-pop. *—Heather Phares*

Isabel Bishop / May 11, 1993 / 4AD/Teenbeat ♦♦♦♦♦
This mini-album is Unrest's debut on 4AD. A re-recorded, lusher "Isabel" starts off this small but great collection, which includes "Teenage Suicide," "Yes She Is My Skinhead Girl," and "Like to Know." *—Heather Phares*

● **Perfect Teeth** / Aug. 24, 1993 / 4AD/Teenbeat ♦♦♦♦♦
Unrest's final and best album is both jangling and lush, and covers many styles of pop music, "Angel, I'll Walk You Home" is filled with pristine vocal harmonies, while "Cath Carroll" is flashy, thrashy punk-pop. "Light Brigade" is wistful and triumphant. "Breather x.o.x.o" is majestically melancholy, and "West Coast Love Affair" is breezy and tongue-in-cheek. Unrest's experimental and pop leanings come together with terrific success on *Perfect Teeth,* making it a high point in the band's too-brief recording career. *—Heather Phares*

Fuck Pussy Galore and All Her Friends / 1994 / Matador ♦♦♦
This aptly-titled album is a collection of the group's B-sides. If anything, it shows just how important bassist Bridget Cross was in shaping the group's sound. While it's a welcome addition to the Unrest fan's collection, not much here is absolutely vital. *—Heather Phares*

B.P.M. 1991-1994 / Jul. 25, 1995 / Southern ♦♦♦
B.P.M. (for "Bridget, Phil and Mark," or—if you prefer—"beats per minute") closed out Unrest's career in typically scattershot style, serving up a crazy quilt of classic singles, quirky remixes and unreleased sides. As the subtitle indicates, these 15 tracks cover only the Bridget Cross-era incarnation of the trio, a lineup that yielded the seminal *Imperial f.f.r.r.* and *Perfect Teeth* albums as well as a series of superb seven-inches; while the inclusion of hard-to-find tracks like the Miaow cover "When It All Comes Down" and "Bavarian Mods" makes the set essential for fans, it's a shame *B.P.M.* wasn't conceived as a more straightforward singles collection instead—remixes of favorites like "Cath Carroll" and "Imperial" are tedious, while the inclusion of two nearly identical versions of "Winona Ryder" (neither particularly worthwhile) is plain baffling. *—Jason Ankeny*

Urge Overkill

f. 1985
Alternative Pop/Rock, Hard Rock
Few bands ever lusted after rock stardom quite as blatantly as Chicago's Urge Overkill. Although they draped their quest for stardom in a cloak of ironic detachment, it was quite clear that the trio expected that if they acted like stars, they would become stars. For a while, their stylish, retro-'70s outfits, matching medallions, and heavy Cheap Trick homages earned the group a popular following in alternative rock circles. *The Super-Sonic Storybook* and the *Stull* EP were both underground hits in the early '90s, before alternative rock became big business. Once alternative rock entered the big leagues, it seemed likely that Urge Overkill, with their exceptionally accessible combination of arena rock, power-pop and underground punk, would follow Nirvana to the top of the charts, but mainstream America never quite understood their ironic outlook, embracing the group only after their cover of Neil Diamond's "Girl, You'll Be A Woman Soon" was used in a key scene in *Pulp Fiction.* Instead of breaking down the doors to stardom, the song proved to be a breaking point. *Exit the Dragon,* the first album released after the hit single, was a bomb, receiving little radio or MTV support, and the band soon fell prey to their widely-documented excesses. *—Stephen Thomas Erlewine*

Jesus Urge Superstar / 1989 / Touch & Go ♦♦

Americruiser/Jesus Urge Superstar / Oct. 1990 / Touch & Go ♦♦♦
Urge's first two albums were recorded at a time when their visions eclipsed their talents—while there is a lot of good indie-guitar bluster here, there aren't that many memorable songs. With its flat Steve Albini production, *Jesus Urge Superstar* is the weaker of the records. *Americruiser,* with production courtesy of Butch Vig, not only has a fuller sound, but also some real songs. "Ticket to L.A." is a classic rocker, with a locomotive riff and great lyrics. It was a sign of things to come. (The CD also includes their gonzo cover of Jimmy Webb's "Wichita Lineman.") *—Stephen Thomas Erlewine*

The Supersonic Storybook / 1991 / Touch & Go ♦♦♦♦
With the addition of drummer Blackie Onassis, Urge Overkill shapes up into a killer rock & roll combo. It also doesn't hurt that the songs are the finest they have written to date. Although the production is a little flat, there's no denying the force of the best tracks. "The Candidate" boasts a huge, stadium-size riff, "The Kids Are Insane" is a frenzied, frenetic rocker, "Today Is Blackie's Birthday" is gleefully stupid, and the band is surprisingly sexy on the old soul song "Emmaline." Things bog down a bit on the second side, but Urge is starting to sound like the rock stars they always knew they were. *—Stephen Thomas Erlewine*

Stull [EP] / Aug. 10, 1992 / Touch & Go ♦♦♦♦♦
It's not the full-throttle rock masterpiece that *Supersonic Storybook* suggested, but the *Stull EP* is almost as remarkable. Opening with a straight cover of Neil Diamond's "Girl, You'll Be a Woman Soon" (which fits Urge Overkill's image perfectly), the EP is an atmospheric guitar workout. While "Stitches" is a salute to their punk roots, the most impressive moments come during the stylish kiss-off to indie-rock "Goodbye to Guyville" and "Stull," with its sly, laidback groove. As the richness of *Stull* proves, Urge's vision was too large for the independents, and it was time to move on. *—Stephen Thomas Erlewine*

● **Saturation** / Jun. 8, 1993 / DGC ♦♦♦♦♦
When they hit the major labels, Urge Overkill followed through on their promise with the blistering *Saturation.* It's stadium rock by clever post-punkers who are smart enough to not let their carefully crafted image interfere with the music. Every one of the twelve songs is a killer, from the outlandish menace of "Stalker" to the moving ballad "Back On Me," as well as the tongue-in-cheek "Woman 2 Woman" and the radio hit "Sister Havana." *—Stephen Thomas Erlewine*

Exit the Dragon / Oct. 1995 / DGC ♦♦♦♦♦
Sonically falling somewhere between *Supersonic Storybook* and *Stull, Exit the Dragon* is a dark, lean album, the flipside of *Saturation*'s glossy celebration of '70s rock & roll excess and easily Urge Overkill's most haunting collection of songs. It kicks off with "Jaywalking," a terse, powerful rocker lamenting "all the evil in this world," which sets the album's tone. *Exit the Dragon* is dominated by Eddie "King" Roeser, with Nash Kato on only six of the 14 songs. As usual, Roeser's songs are more claustrophobic than Kato's, particularly the clenched riffs of "The Break" and the slow crawl of "Tin Foil." Although Kato contributes the flat-out rocker "Need Some Air," many of his songs are nearly as dark as Roeser's, whether it's the acoustic "View of the Rain" (previously released as "Take a Walk" on the *No Alternative* compilation), the skipping pop of "Somebody Else's Body," the power-pop of "Monopoly," or the soaring closer "Digital Black Epilogue," a duet with an uncredited female soul singer. But the heart of the record is Blackie Onassis' "The Mistake," an eerie tale of a drug overdose which helps *Exit the Dragon* take the form of a loose concept album about a rock & roll band beset by troubles on the road. While the subject is ripe for parody, Urge Overkill performs *Exit the Dragon* without much irony at all. Instead of being a fatal misstep, this choice proves that Urge is a tight, powerful rock & roll band blessed with first-rate songwriters, capable of more emotions than many listeners might have expected. *—Stephen Thomas Erlewine*

Uriah Heep

f. 1970, London, England
Album Rock, British Metal, Heavy Metal, Prog-Rock/Art Rock
Uriah Heep's by-the-books progressive heavy metal made the British band one of the most popular hard rock groups of the early '70s. Formed by vocalist David Byron and guitarist Mick Box in the late '60s, the group went through an astonishing number of members over the next two decades—nearly 30 different musicians passed through the band over the years. Uriah Heep released their debut album *Very 'eavy, Very 'umble* (called *Uriah Heep* in the U.S.) in 1970. Featuring a 16-minute title track recorded with a 26-piece orchestra, *Salisbury* showcased the band's more progressive tendencies. Beginning with 1972's *Demons and Wizards,* they released five albums between 1972 and 1975, after which the band's popularity began to slip. However, Uriah Heep soldiers on, continuing to release albums in the '90s. *—Stephen Thomas Erlewine*

Very 'eavy . . . Very 'umble / 1970 / Mercury ♦♦♦
This album was the debut of Uriah Heep, an English band that would become one of the Titans of the 1970s heavy metal sound. Despite their eventual hard-rocking reputation, *Very 'Eavy Very 'Umble* finds the band trying on different stylistic hats as they work towards finding their own sound. At this juncture, their music falls halfway between the crunch of heavy metal and the dramatic arrangements of prog rock. When this style jells, the results are quite powerful: "Dreammare" blends psychedelic lyrics and a complex vocal arrangement with a stomping beat from the rhythm section to create an effective slice of prog metal fusion while "I'll Keep On Trying" presents a head-spinning, complex tune with enough riffs, hooks, and tempo changes to fill three or four songs. However, the album's finest achievement is "Gypsy": this heavy metal gem nails the blend of swirling organ riffs, power chords, and leather-lunged vocal harmonies that would define the group's classic tunes and remains a staple of the band's live performances today. Unfortunately, the focus of the album is diluted by some unsuccessful experiments: "Lucy Blues" is a dull, unmemorable stab at a Led Zeppelin-style heavy blues tune and "Come Away Melinda" is an overproduced, melodramatic cover that tries to marry the band's full-throttle musical style to a message song. Despite these occasional moments of stylistic

schizophrenia, *Very 'Eavy Very 'Umble* is a likable album that shows the promise that Uriah Heep would soon realize. Those unfamiliar with Uriah Heep may want to try out *Demons and Wizards* or a compilation first, but anyone with a serious interest in Uriah Heep or the roots of heavy metal will find plenty to like on *Very 'Eavy Very 'Umble*. Collector's note: the American edition of this album was retitled *Uriah Heep* and omits "Lucy Blues" in favor of the track "Bird of Prey" from *Salisbury*. —*Donald A. Guarisco*

Salisbury / 1971 / Mercury ✦✦✦
On their second album, Uriah Heep jettisons the experiments that weighed down *Very 'Eavy Very 'Umble* and works toward perfecting their blend of heavy metal power and prog rock complexity. *Salisbury* tips the band's style in the prog direction, containing one side of songs and one side dominated by a lengthy and ornate epic-length composition. Highlights on the song-oriented side include "Bird of Prey," a soaring rocker that blends furious, power chord-fuelled verses with spacy, keyboard-drenched instrumental breaks, and "Lady in Black," a stylishly arranged tune that builds from a folk-styled acoustic tune into a throbbing rocker full of ghostly harmonies and crunching guitar riffs. The big surprise on this side is "The Park," a ballad-style song built on a light blend of acoustic guitars and ethereal keyboards. It has a gentle, appealingly psychedelic feel that is topped off by David Byron's falsetto vocal and some soaring harmonies from Byron and Ken Hensley. However, *Salisbury* is undone by its title track, the 16-minute track that dominates the album's entire second side: it feels more like a lengthy jam session instead of a prog epic with distinctive and carefully crafted sections. Another problem is that the overly busy brass and woodwind arrangements that have been grafted onto it intrude on the group's sound instead of fleshing it out. All in all, *Salisbury* is too unfocused for the casual listener but offers enough solid songs for the Uriah Heep completist. Collector's note: The American version of this album had different cover art (the tank on the British edition was replaced by a gruesome image of man tearing out of his own skin) and replaced "Bird of Prey" with a bluesy B-side entitled "Simon the Bullet Freak." —*Donald A. Guarisco*

Look at Yourself / 1971 / Mercury ✦✦✦✦
The third time proved to be the charm for Uriah Heep: On *Look at Yourself*, the group perfects their fusion of heavy metal power and prog rock majesty and the result is one of the best albums in their catalog. The gauntlet is thrown down by the title track, a powerful rocker that layers its relentless hard rock attack with ornate vocal harmonies and quicksilver organ runs before climaxing with a tribal-sounding drum jam. The remainder of *Look at Yourself*'s tracks present an effective blend of gutsy guitar rock and organ-fuelled prog excursions. In the rock arena, the gems are "Tears in My Eyes," a powerful rocker driven by an almost rockabilly-style riff that stops midway for a surprising vocal harmony break supported by smooth wah-wah guitar, and "Love Machine," a short, punchy slice of hard rock built on an infectious, stomping rhythm. However, the best track on the album is one of the more prog-oriented ones: "July Morning" starts with a pastoral organ riff then builds into a heavy yet symphonic rock tune that divides its time between gentle acoustic verses and emotional, organ-fuelled choruses before climaxing in a monstrous jam dominated by a swirling Moog synthesizer lead. Special note should also be taken of David Byron's vocal performance; his multi-octave, operatic style was no doubt an influence on later metal vocalists like Rob Halford. All in all, *Look at Yourself* is both one of Uriah Heep's finest, most cohesive albums and a high point of 1970s heavy metal. —*Donald A. Guarisco*

Demons & Wizards / Jan. 1972 / Mercury ✦✦✦✦✦
This is the album that solidified Uriah Heep's reputation as a master of gothic-inflected heavy metal. From short, sharp rock songs to lengthy, musically dense epics, *Demons and Wizards* finds Uriah Heep covering all the bases with style and power. The album's approach is set with its lead-off track, "The Wizard": It starts as a simple acoustic tune but soon builds into a stately rocker that surges forth on a wall of sound built from thick guitar riffs, churchy organ, and operatic vocal harmonies. Other highlights include "Traveller in Time," a fantasy-themed rocker built on thick wah-wah guitar riffs, and "Circle of Hands," a stately power ballad with a gospel-meets-heavy metal feel to it. *Demons and Wizards* also produced a notable radio hit for the band in "Easy Livin'," a punchy little rocker whose raging blend of fuzz guitar and swirling organ made it feel like a 1970s update of classic 1960s garage rockers like the Electric Prunes or Paul Revere and the Raiders. However, the top highlight of the album is the closing medley of "Paradise" and "The Spell": The first part of the medley starts in an acoustic folk mode and slowly adds layers of organ and electric guitar until it becomes a forceful slow-tempo rocker, while the second half is a punchy, organ-led rocker that includes an instrumental midsection where choral-style harmonies fortify a killer, Pink Floyd-style guitar solo from Mick Box. All in all, *Demons and Wizards* works both as a showcase for Uriah Heep's instrumental firepower and an excellent display of their songwriting skills in a variety of hard rock styles. As a result, it is considered by many fans to be their finest hour and is definitely worth a spin for anyone with an interest in 1970s heavy metal. —*Donald A. Guarisco*

Magician's Birthday / Feb. 1972 / Mercury ✦✦✦
After reaching an international level of success with *Demons and Wizards*, Uriah Heep continued to build their fan base by knocking out another album of prog-like metal before the year's end. The end result, *The Magician's Birthday*, is not as consistent or cohesive as *Demons and Wizards* but stills offers plenty of highlights. It starts dramatically with "Sunrise," a spooky power ballad that alternates quiet organ-led verses with an emotional chorus and guitar-fuelled instrumental breaks topped off by David Byron's operatic wail. The remainder of the album divides its time between punchy rockers and spacy balladry before climaxing with another prog-inflected epic. Highlights in the rock arena include "Blind Eye," an acoustic-flavored rocker whose galloping pace is firmly anchored by Gary Thain's melodic bass line, and "Sweet Lorraine," a stomping good-time rocker

that adds extra texture to its guitar-driven sound with some spacy synthesizer lines. As for the quieter moments, "Rain" is a lovely piano ballad that makes surprising and impressive use of a xylophone in its sound and "Echoes in the Dark" is an eerie mid-tempo song that alternates stark piano-led verses with an emotional chorus cemented by Mick Box's searing guitar leads. There is also another multi-part epic in the title track, a prog-ish piece with fantasy themes. It lacks a strong structure (it feels more like three songs grafted together than a true multi-part composition) and succumbs to a bit of aimless jamming in the middle, but it is redeemed by strong hooks in the opening and a spirited performance from the band on its space rock finale. All in all, *The Magician's Birthday* never quite hits the consistent heights of *Look at Yourself* or *Demons and Wizards* but remains a solid listen for Uriah Heep fans. —*Donald A. Guarisco*

Uriah Heep Live / 1973 / Mercury ✦✦

Sweet Freedom / 1973 / Roadrunner ✦✦✦
By 1973, Uriah Heep had progressed from an English heavy metal band to a worldwide success. They moved on to a new label (Warner Bros.) and began to explore new styles to flesh out their combination of prog complexity and heavy metal muscle. The band's desire to break new ground is established with the lead-off track, "Dreamer": while it riffs as hard as the band's past rockers, it adds a surprising element of funkiness into the band's sound. The gentle, acoustic guitar-dominated "Circus" is another change of pace that pushes the group's sound in a meditative, folky direction. The group also explores new avenues in the lyrical arena. Instead of the mystical tales that dominated albums like *Demons and Wizards*, *Sweet Freedom* offers lyrics designed to appeal to the listener on a personal level: The most stirring example is "Stealin'," a song about the regrets that come with living a self-obsessed life. These sentiments were combined with a stirring, soulful melody that helped make the song a radio favorite. Another highlight in this vein is the title track, a song that combines lyrics about the price of being free with an organ-fuelled, hymn-like melody. Despite these successful experiments, there are a few tracks that weigh the proceedings down: "Seven Stars" takes an exciting riff and runs it into the ground with a repetitive arrangement and "Pilgrim" is an over-the-top stab at an adventure tale that pushes the group's excesses to the level of self-parody. However, *Sweet Freedom* is likable enough to triumph over these missteps. While it isn't the group's finest record, it remains a solid listen for Uriah Heep fans. —*Donald A. Guarisco*

Wonderworld / 1974 / Castle Music America ✦✦✦
Wonderworld continues in the vein of *Sweet Freedom*, trying to bring Uriah Heep's appeal to a wider level while still retaining the grandiose trademark elements (the organ-guitar attack, David Byron's operatic shriek) that got them noticed. The result is an album that is solid but not as inspired as *Look at Yourself* or *Demons and Wizards*. The hard rock quotient is a little stronger on this album than it was on *Sweet Freedom*: "Something or Nothing" is a galloping stomp-rocker in the vein of past classics like "Love Machine" and "Suicidal Man" is an organ-fortified speed-rocker that is one of the band's finest hard rock tunes. On other tracks, the group continues in the experimental vein of *Sweet Freedom*: "The Shadows and the Wind" tacks a Queen-style round of a cappella harmonies onto its tag and "We Got We" marries one of the band's gothic melodies to a funky rhythm track that features some tasty clavinet jamming from Ken Hensley. However, the most successful experiment is "The Easy Road," an orchestrated romantic ballad that features a lovely, understated vocal performance from David Byron. Despite these highlights, the remainder of *Wonderworld* has trouble sustaining a similar level of inspiration: The title track is powerfully performed but feels like the band is going through the motions and "Dreams" lacks the strong melody necessary to prop up the song's interesting riffs. Ultimately, *Wonderworld* lacks the consistency and the high number of standout tunes that would help it win over new listeners but contains enough highlights to please the Uriah Heep fan base. —*Donald A. Guarisco*

Return to Fantasy / 1975 / Castle ✦✦✦
After two albums that downplayed their penchant for gothic sounds and mystical lyrics, Uriah Heep brought these elements back to the fore on 1975's *Return to Fantasy*. The resulting album retains the musical experimentation that marked *Sweet Freedom* and *Wonderworld* but has an overall harder-rocking feel that makes it more consistent than either one of those albums. *Return to Fantasy* throws down the gauntlet with the title track, which builds from a tapestry of spooky synthesizer and organ riffs into a thunderous rock tune where the guitar and organ duel over a galloping backbeat laid down by Lee Kerslake. It's bracing stuff and one of the finest rockers in the Uriah Heep canon. The rest of the first side continues in a similarly strong hard rock vein and its other key highlight is "Beautiful Dream," a song that marries stomping hard rock verses to a spooky, ethereal chorus that sounds like it could have been plucked from a mid-'70s Pink Floyd album. On the second side, Uriah Heep gives themselves over to experiments that, while listenable, cause the album to lose focus. For instance, "Prima Donna" is a sardonic commentary on the rock & roll world that features a prominent brass section and prominently overdubbed Beach Boys-style harmonies, while "Your Turn to Remember" is the kind of bluesy AOR ballad that would later be specialized in by groups like Journey. Both songs are fun listening but stray too far from the group's traditional sound and are too dissimilar to make *Return to Fantasy* a cohesive experience. Despite these problems, the group never turns in a less-than-engaging instrumental performance and the consistent quality of their work keeps the album from getting carried away by all the genre-hopping. In the end, *Return to Fantasy* lacks the coherence of a top-shelf Uriah Heep classic like *Demons and Wizards* but remains a strong and likable album that is guaranteed to please the group's fans. —*Donald A. Guarisco*

The Best of Uriah Heep / 1976 / Mercury ✦✦✦✦✦
Collecting the best moments of their sometimes inconsistent albums, *Best of Uriah Heep* is an effective introduction to the band. —*Daevid Jehnzen*

High and Mighty / 1976 / Bronze ✦✦

Firefly / 1977 / Castle ✦✦✦

Innocent Victim / 1977 / Castle ✦✦✦

Fallen Angel / 1978 / Castle ✦✦✦

A Time of Revelation / Aug. 5, 1996 / Castle ✦✦✦✦✦
A Time of Revelation is a four-disc box set spanning Uriah Heep's entire career. The bulk of the set draws from the Heep's '70s heyday, including album tracks, live cuts, and previously unavailable-on-disc rarities. For the die-hard collector, the set is a must-have for its obscure items, but the set is too much for casual fans, even those that want more than a simple greatest hits collection. After all, Uriah Heep were an album rock band that tailored individual albums, which means their songs often make more sense in the context of their original albums, not on compilations like these. —*Stephen Thomas Erlewine*

● **Classic Heep: An Anthology** / Sep. 15, 1998 / Mercury ✦✦✦✦✦
To irritate snobbish rock critics in the 1970s, all a band had to do was play heavy metal or progressive rock. Imagine their horror when Uriah Heep came along and consciously fused both styles. Uriah Heep was the subject of one vicious critic's infamous quote, "If this group makes it, I'll have to commit suicide." Well then, this critic is probably dead, because the British band did achieve widespread success. 1998's two-CD *Classic Heep: An Anthology* is a terrific compilation of Uriah Heep's 1970-1976 prime. The 30 songs are taken from nine studio albums: *Uriah Heep* (*Very 'Eavy, Very 'Umble* in the U.K.), *Salisbury*, *Look at Yourself*, *Demons and Wizards*, *The Magician's Birthday*, *Sweet Freedom*, *Wonderworld*, *Return to Fantasy*, and *High and Mighty*. It surely won't inspire a serious critical re-examination of Uriah Heep, but it should. The band was aggressively experimental, and while not everything worked, during its peak years vocalist David Byron, guitarist Mick Box, keyboardist/guitarist Ken Hensley, bass guitarists Gary Thain and John Wetton, and drummer Lee Kerslake tried it all. Musically, Uriah Heep relied on Byron's dramatic vocals, Box's gritty guitar crunch, Hensley's rumbling keyboards, and Thain's (later Wetton's) busy bass licks, and the band's harmony vocals and background "aah"s and "ooh"s were unique. Of course, Uriah Heep's two most famous songs, "Stealin'" and "Easy Livin'," are included. "Stealin'," a staple of classic rock radio, is the band's best: a powerfully tight, explosive lament from a penitent, ashamed outlaw. "Easy Livin'," the band's only U.S. Top 40 hit, is a catchy, full-bore rocker. Other notable cuts are "Gypsy," "Bird of Prey," "Lady in Black," "Rainbow Demon," "Blind Eye," "Sweet Lorraine," "Wonderworld," "Return to Fantasy," "Weep in Silence," and the ambitious epics "July Morning," "Paradise/The Spell," and "The Magician's Birthday." The detailed liner notes include an insightful essay by Hensley. —*Bret Adams*

20th Century Masters—The Millennium Collection: The Best of Uriah Heep / Aug. 21, 2001 / Mercury ✦✦✦
Uriah Heep wasn't really a band made for singles-and-songles-oriented collections like *20th Century Masters*, because they favored sweeping, heavy-prog epics that fit into their equally epic albums. And even in those terms, they were a bit of an acquired taste, since they melded those two excessive genres—metal and prog—in a particularly indulgent fashion. *20th Century Masters* certainly conveys that accomplishment, and it does contain many fan favorites, which is enough to make this an effective sampler, even if it's unlikely to win many converts. —*Stephen Thomas Erlewine*

U.S. Maple
f. 1995
Math Rock, Experimental Rock, Indie Rock, Experimental
In early 1995, the noisy, experimental rock group U.S. Maple rose from the ashes of two bands at Chicago's Northern Illinois University: lead singer Al Johnson and "high" guitarist Mark Shippy were in Shorty, while drummer Pat Samson and "low" guitarist Todd Rittman came from the Mercury Players. That fall, U.S. Maple recorded their first single, "When a Man Says Ow!"/"Stuck" at Doug Easley's Easley Recording Studios in Memphis, Tennessee. Chicago independent record label Skin Graft signed the band soon after and released the "Stuck" single. Soon after, U.S. Maple stepped into Solid Sound Studios at Hoffman Estates in Illinois to record their first full-length album *Long Hair in Three Stages*, which was released in October of 1995, with renowned indie producer Jim O'Rourke. The following year, they recorded an unrecognizable version of Dion and the Belmonts' 1961 hit "The Wanderer" for Sonic Bubblegum and contributed an equally different cover of AC/DC's "Sin City" for Skin Graft's tribute to the band, which also featured Shellac and Big'n. In early 1997, the group reconvened with O'Rourke at Solid Sound and recorded *Sang Phat Editor*, which was released in June.
   By 1998, U.S. Maple's extensive touring and recording schedule meant they needed a bigger label, and the group left Skin Graft that year. They signed to Drag City, one of Chicago's most prominent indies, a few months later and began recording their third full-length *Talker* in Brooklyn with former Swans leader Michael Gira; the album was released the following year. The group resumed their consistent touring that year and stayed on the road for a good part of 2000. Their fourth album was anticipated for a spring 2001 release. —*Stephen Howell*

● **Long Hair in Three Stages** / Oct. 24, 1995 / Skin Graft ✦✦✦✦
U.S. Maple's debut album is nothing short of stunning, combining angular guitar attacks, odd skronks, jazzy tones, and a generally deconstructive approach to music into a sound of unparalleled idiosyncrasy. The record's finest moments come when the slanted attack and fractured composition converge to simulate something approaching a conventional song ("Letter to ZZ Top," with lyrics like "Give my bones to Billy Gibbons," pretty much rules out any notion of normality). Between these off-kilter constructions and the group's even more off-kilter deconstructions, a truly amazing record is created, one that combines

hard-edged, "whiskey, no chaser" rock with exceptionally intelligent slants and fractures. —*Nitsuh Abebe*

Sang Phat Editor / Jun. 10, 1997 / Skin Graft ✦✦✦
Much more disjointed than their previous effort, every song on this record is full of pull-and-release tension. It contains everything from fleet-fingered, pseudo-southern guitar lines ("Coming Back to Damnit") to a song in which U.S. Maple sounds like a nightmarish rock band at a carnival gone wrong ("Through with Six Six Six"). Strange funk interplays with abrupt drum fills, restrained whoops and hollers by Johnson, and brittle, shaking guitars ("Songs That Have No Making Out," "Missouri Twist"). One of their best albums. —*Stephen Howell*

Talker / Jun. 8, 1999 / Drag City ✦✦✦✦
Talker, U.S. Maple's third album—and their debut for Drag City—features more of their melted, bluesy avant-rock. "Bumps & Guys," "Running from Kabob" and "Breeze, It's Your High School" feature droning, rubbery guitars, happenstance percussion and slow-burning tempos, creating the sonic equivalent of fresh tar: dark, hot and viscous. Abrasive and piercing guitars slice through the sludge on "More Horror" and "Apollo, Don't You Crust?" while raspy, warbling vocals push U.S. Maple even closer to the limits of listenability. For all its surface chaos however, *Talker's* noise has an underlying space and structure that makes it as compelling as it is initially inaccessible; once caught in its sonic tar pits, it's fascinating to hear what else is stuck in there. —*Heather Phares*

Acre Thrills / Apr. 24, 2001 / Drag City ✦✦✦

Gary Usher
Producer, Vocals, Songwriter / Surf
Gary Usher's importance in the history of California rock is considerable. He co-wrote several of the Beach Boys' early songs with Brian Wilson, including classics like "In My Room" and "409," and produced the Byrds' *Younger than Yesterday* and *Notorious Byrd Brothers* albums. He was also an occasional performer. —*Richie Unterberger*

Hot Rod U.S.A. / 1994 / Usher ✦✦✦✦✦
This quasi-legitimate release collects 30 tunes (mostly hot rod & surf) that Usher had a hand in as producer and/or performer between 1960 and 1965, most taken from rare collector 45s. While there are occasional touches of Buddy Holly, girl groups, or The Four Seasons, it sounds like nothing as much as a collection of Beach Boys/Jan & Dean outtakes from the early '60s. That's not to say, though, that they're on par with the average early Beach Boys albums; it's pretty innocuous (if not downright formulaic) stuff, and after a while you might start to wish it *was* The Beach Boys and not so relentlessly lightweight. Some of the better tracks are actually the ones on which he and/or his studio charges eschew the sub-Beach Boy approach altogether for raunchy, reverb-soaked surf instrumentals. This set includes some rare, virtually unknown cuts that Brian Wilson himself co-wrote, by the likes of The Super Stocks, the Timers, and Rachel & the Revolvers, but its appeal is really limited to surf/Beach Boy fanatics. —*Richie Unterberger*

● **Gary Usher Greats, Vol. 1: The Kickstands Vs. The Knights** / Feb. 27, 1996 / AVI ✦✦✦✦✦
Surf and hot rod genius Gary Usher was a budget-minded fellow—not unlike director Ed Wood—who could take a bunch of L.A. studio hotshot ringers into Gold Star studios for an afternoon and cut an album under any number of fake names and come up with something that not only was genre faithful, but pretty fine listening, too. A right-hand man in early times to Brian Wilson, Usher had hits on the charts and cranked this stuff out like sausage. This debut outing of his cut-'em-quick, cut-'em-cheap LP output combines two of his finer efforts, *Black Boots and Bikes* by the Kickstands and *Hot Rod High* by the Knights. The actual lineup of players and singers on these two albums reads like a first-call list on a Phil Spector or Jan & Dean session (Jerry Cole, Hal Blaine, Leon Russell, etc.) and the sound and style is a perfect match for any Capitol hot rod/surf album from that time period. —*Cub Koda*

Add Some Music To Your Day: 1970 Symphonic Tribute To Brian Wilson / 2001 / Poptones ✦

King Uszniewicz & His Uszniewicztones
f. 1969, **db.** 1979
Rock & Roll, Novelty
A hilariously inept Detroit bowling-alley/lounge band fronted by Ernie "King" Uszniewicz (b. 1945) from 1969 to 1979. The crudest tenor saxophonist in the history of rock & roll, King Uszniewicz (pronounced "you-snev-vitch") & the U-Tones had only one single, issued on a local label during the '70s. Dubbed by one critic as "the worst oldies band I ever heard in my life," they played with a bludgeoning energy, oblivious to the fact that they were woefully shy in the talent department. However, when the group's first album showed up on several college-radio playlists in 1989, they earned a minor cult following among both record collectors and young alternative-music fans. —*Stephen Thomas Erlewine*

Teenage Dance Party / 1989 / Norton ✦✦✦
Their first album, featuring both sides of their original and lone 45 ("Surfin' School"/"Cry on My Shoulder") and insane versions of "Papa Ooh Mow Mow," "Little Latin Lupe Lu," and "This Should Go On Forever." Raw, crude, tuneless and wonderful. —*Stephen Thomas Erlewine*

● **Twistin' and Bowlin'** / 1991 / Norton ✦✦✦✦✦
Subtitled "just when you thought it was safe to go back into the bowling alley," and more than living up to all that implies. Drunken, out-of-control versions of "Way Down Yonder in New Orleans," "Peppermint Twist," and Johnny Mathis' "Chances Are" are among the numerous highlights. Scary. —*Stephen Thomas Erlewine*

Doin' the Woo-Hoo / 1994 / Norton ♦♦♦♦♦
More oldies-band mayhem. "At the Hop," "G.T.O.," "Love Letters in the Sand," the title cut, and King Uszniewicz's wife Arlene belting out "It's My Party" are just a few of the standout tracks. Extremely potent stuff. *—Stephen Thomas Erlewine*

U.T.F.O.

f. 1983
Old School Rap, Hip-Hop
Doctor Ice, the Kangol Kid, and the Educated Rapper (later joined by Mix-Master Ice) formed the Brooklyn group Untouchable Force Organization (U.T.F.O.) by dreaming up a tune about a gorgeous woman oblivious to their charms and appeals. "Roxanne, Roxanne" dominated the airwaves for much of 1984 and 1985, yielding eventually over 100 answer versions. Their first albums included the hit single plus "Roxanne Part 2" and "The Real Roxanne." The group's popularity and influence waned as the Roxanne fad peaked, and subsequent releases had limited appeal. *—Ron Wynn*

UTFO / 1985 / Select ♦♦♦♦
The Brooklyn production/performance combo U.T.F.O. shot to fame in the mid-'80s with their story about "Roxanne, Roxanne." It generated a flood of answer songs, started the careers of both Roxanne Shante and the Real Roxanne, and for a moment put U.T.F.O. in the thick of hip-hop and urban contemporary music. Unfortunately, they really weren't that gifted, as they showed on such singles as "Bite It," "Beats and Rhymes," and "Lisa Lips." They're now rightly regarded as novelty/one-hit wonders. *—Ron Wynn*

Skeezer Pleezer / 1986 / Select ♦♦♦

Lethal / 1987 / Select ♦♦

Doin' It! / 1989 / Select ♦♦♦

● **The Best of U.T.F.O.** / Dec. 1996 / Select ♦♦♦♦♦
U.T.F.O. never had many hits. During the mid-'80s, the rap group released a series of singles, but only one stood out, and for good reason, because that song, "Roxanne, Roxanne," is one of the classic rap singles of all time. Though "Roxanne, Roxanne" only hit number ten on the R&B charts, it was far more popular than its chart position suggests, spawning a craze of answer records that ran for nearly two years. Unfortunately, U.T.F.O. never released anything else that quite matched the quality of "Roxanne, Roxanne," though their follow-up, "The Real Roxanne," was entertaining in its own right. Since the group had an uneven track record, *The Best of U.T.F.O.* is the best way to get acquainted with the group, even though it has a number of weak spots itself. Nevertheless, it has all the necessary items U.T.F.O. ever recorded, and "Roxanne, Roxanne" is a single that should be heard by all rap and hip-hop fans. *—Leo Stanley*

Utopia

f. 1974, New York, NY, **db.** 1986
Album Rock, Arena Rock, Pop/Rock, Power Pop, New Wave, Prog-Rock/Art Rock
Stardom was handed to him with *Something/Anything?*, but Todd Rundgren rejected it. He wanted to explore new musical territory instead, and his adventures led him to form Utopia in 1974. Initially, Utopia was a prog-rock septet featuring three keyboardists, but as the '70s progressed, the group evolved into a shiny mainstream rock quartet. As the group evolved, Rundgren retreated into the background, as each of his bandmates contributed songs and lead vocals to the albums. By the early '80s, Utopia had developed into a hit-making entity in their own right, even if much—if not all—of their audience were simply dedicated Rundgren fans, which highlights the problem with Utopia: although they did develop their own signature sound, they were nevertheless always perceived as Rundgren's folly. And to a certain extent that was accurate, since the band's musical evolution often mirrored his own—plus, once he decided he had enough of the group in 1985, it ceased to exist. At that point, Utopia was over a decade old, which made it something more than a folly, but even hardcore Rundgren fans will admit that it's impossible to view Utopia's career as being completely independent from his own. *—Stephen Thomas Erlewine*

Todd Rundgren's Utopia / Oct. 1974 / Bearsville/Rhino ♦♦
For much of the double album *Todd*, Todd Rundgren was exploring weird instrumental avenues, creating a warped, synth-fueled variation of prog-rock. This wasn't the culmination of the weirdness *A Wizard, A True Star* initiated—it was merely the beginning. Not long after completing *Todd*, Rundgren assembled Utopia, a prog-rock group with no less than three synth players, plus guitar, bass and drums. Ostensibly, the band was a collective effort, with Rundgren contributing no more than the remaining quintet, but the possessive nature of the title of their debut, *Todd Rundgren's Utopia*, illustrates who the driving force of the group was. And it is true that *TR's Utopia* picks up where *Todd* left off, expanding the already lengthy experimental instrumentals by adding layers of synthesizers that stretch on forever—which is no exaggeration, since only one track ("Freedom Fighters") is single-length, with the remaining three cuts clocking in between 10 and 30 minutes. For anyone who isn't a dedicated fan, slogging through these seemingly endless prog excursions is a little tedious, and even the devoted may find that these roads, while occasionally interesting, don't necessarily lead anywhere. *—Stephen Thomas Erlewine*

Another Live / Oct. 1975 / Bearsville/Rhino ♦♦♦
It's hard to say exactly why *Another Live* works better than either *Todd Rundgren's Utopia* or *Initiation*, Rundgren's two previous excursions into synth-heavy prog-rock. It's not that the music is more energetic or focused, since it isn't. Neither is the music more challenging or ambitious—it's simply better. It's true that the second half is devoted to covers (*West Side Story*'s "Something's Coming," the Move's "Do Ya") or Rundgren classics ("Heavy Metal Kids," "Just One Victory"), all of which are more song-oriented than anything on the first half, or anything on either *TR's Utopia* or *Initiation*. That said, the prog-rock epics that comprise the first half of the album cut deeper than before, possibly because the band has worked out the kinks in its style, developing a unified, provocative sound. It still tends to be a little excessive and impenetrable, but intriguing moments float to the surface alarmingly often. Too bad the hideous cover will prevent anyone but the most devoted Rundgren/Utopia fan from discovering that... *—Stephen Thomas Erlewine*

RA / Feb. 1977 / Bearsville/Rhino ♦♦♦
RA found Utopia moving away from the long, experimental instrumental jams that distinguished their first two albums, but what's surprising about it is how the group changed. Sure, the lineup was different but their approach changed on *RA*, as they moved away from prog rock and toward hard rock. In that regard, it makes sense that Rundgren's possessive has been stripped from Utopia's name, since the band no longer sounds like an indulgent spin-off of his own albums. *RA* has little to do with either Rundgren album that preceded or succeeded it. In fact, it's an anomaly in both the Utopia and Rundgren catalogs. Never before had Rundgren attempted what appears to be a full-fledged concept album, and never again did Utopia trade in pomp rock and all the grand, "important" themes that go with the territory. *RA* may not have a genuine narrative through line—with the exception, that is, of the closing 18-minute epic "Singring and the Glass Guitar," an "electrical fairy tale" Rundgren narrates in the voice of a mischievous elf—but all seven songs feel connected, largely because they're driven home with pure prog bombast. At times, the album feels like parody, particularly because all the sonic overhauls make Utopia sound like Queen. Despite all the indications that Utopia isn't taking this all that seriously—nobody could write the chorus of "Hiroshima" without having their tongue somewhat in cheek—but it's impossible to discern whether *RA* is satire since the murk of keyboards, guitar solos, and crushing chords is somberly played. Such quandaries and questions make *RA* intriguing, even if it's not particularly good, or listenable for that matter. *—Stephen Thomas Erlewine*

Oops! Wrong Planet / Sep. 1977 / Bearsville/Rhino ♦♦♦
Abandoning overt prog—thereby leaving behind the operas and extended instrumental sections, but not the organ solos—Utopia became a mainstream rock band with their fourth album, *Oops! Wrong Planet*. Since the group's first two albums were marginally listenable and *RA* flirted with outright parody, it comes as a shock to hear Utopia be outright accessible and listenable, two qualities virtually foreign to their previous work. The quartet has been revamped, redesigned as a mainstream arena rock band. And that means that the chores are spread a little more evenly—meaning, not only does everyone get to write, everyone gets to sing, occasionally on songs Todd wrote. Despite his efforts to democratize the group, Utopia still feels very much like Rundgren's baby, mainly because the only songs that really work are ones that he writes and sings. And since Utopia is now merely a hard rock band, Rundgren reserves his more ambitious ideas and complex songs for his solo records. The end result of all this is that *Oops! Wrong Planet* is more consistent than earlier Utopia records, but is not as sporadically brilliant or rewarding as Todd's solo albums. Even the bad moments, such as the very silly "Gangrene," aren't particularly unlistenable, yet there are simply too many average, undistinguished songs for the record to actually soar. Nevertheless, Rundgren turns in some fine moments—"Love in Action" is a terrific hard rocker, as is "Trapped," and "Love is the Answer" is an ideal stadium anthem—that make the record worthwhile for the cult, even if it will sound like little more than a period piece to most listeners. *—Stephen Thomas Erlewine*

Adventures in Utopia / Jan. 1980 / Bearsville/Rhino ♦♦♦
Oops! Wrong Planet wrote the blueprint for Utopia Mach II, but the group didn't deliver the polished, radio-ready follow-up *Adventures in Utopia* until two and a half years later. Granted, leader Todd Rundgren kept busy in the interim, but it was an abnormally long time between records. As it turns out, the wait didn't matter, since Utopia delivered a record that was quintessentially 1980—a shiny, buffed album every bit as pop as *The Hermit of Mink Hollow*, but considerably less introspective and altogether ready for action. It's a bid for the big seats, and Utopia, surprisingly, achieved their goals, as the record climbed into the Top 40 and spawned a hit single with "Set Me Free," a song sung by Kasim Sulton. That fact alone indicates that *Adventures* is the closest Utopia had yet come to its band ideal. It's no surprise that Todd Rundgren still dominates the proceedings, but his presence is not omnipresent, which is to the benefit of the album. Like its predecessor, *Adventures* is consistent but a little bland, but the shiny pop surfaces are more appealing than the arena rock bluster of *Oops!*, which makes the fact that it has about the same number of memorable songs—"You Make Me Crazy," "Second Nature," "Set Me Free," "The Very Last Time" (again, all top-loaded)—not quite as noticeable. It keeps things moving as the record is playing, and if the album as a whole isn't entirely memorable, at least the half that does take hold still sounds as if it was state-of-the-art pop-rock for 1980. *—Stephen Thomas Erlewine*

Deface the Music / Oct. 1980 / Bearsville/Rhino ♦♦♦♦
Having just scored their first big hits with *Adventures in Utopia*, Utopia inexplicably took a step into arcana with its follow-up, *Deface the Music*. Foregoing the radio-ready style of *Adventures*, Utopia delves deeply into Beatlemania, creating a swift, brutally funny and insanely catchy send-up of the Fab Four's entire career. Clearly, the high (nearly arty) concept makes *Deface the Music* the first Utopia album since *Another Live* to sound like it is solely the work of Todd Rundgren. The music is so savvy, it's clear that these songs are primarily the work of Todd, even if they're credited to Utopia. Rundgren is able to write songs that evoke specific eras of the Beatles' career and have them be funny without being a slave to parody. Like the Rutles, this music works well on its own merits and, unlike the Rutles, Rundgren is as credible with "Penny Lane" psychedelia ("Hoi Poloi") or "Eleanor Rigby" chamber-pop ("Life Goes On") as he is with Merseybeat ("I Just Want to

Touch You," "Crystal Ball"). Unlike the Rutles, it sounds like it was recorded in 1980, not the '60s, which intensifies the feeling that *Deface the Music* is merely a curiosity or an exercise for Rundgren, but since the entire thing is finished in just over a half hour, it feels more like a burst of cynical joy that is damn near impossible to resist. —*Stephen Thomas Erlewine*

Swing to the Right / Mar. 1982 / Bearsville/Rhino ✦✦✦
Utopia wandered into the wilderness with *Deface the Music*, losing much of the audience they won with *Adventures in Utopia*. If its follow-up *Swing to the Right* is any indication, the band didn't really care, since they doggedly pursue a weird fusion of new wave pop, arena rock, and soul, all spiked with social commentary. According to some reports, Bearsville didn't want to release the album, relenting only after considerable pressure from Rundgren, who defended it as the group effort it certainly is. In fact, *Swing to the Right* marks the beginning of Utopia Mach III, when each member pulled equal weight as composers and frontmen—at times, it's hard to tell who contributed what, or even who takes lead vocals. Admittedly, Rundgren's efforts are the strongest—"Lysistrata" condenses a Greek play into a three-minute pop gem, and "One World," a silly but catchy "love is all you need" chant. Both songs accentuate the anti-Reagan theme of *Swing to the Right*, which is clearly telegraphed by the album's title. True, the message can be a little fuzzy, yet each song has a loose anti-conservative theme, including their cover of the O'Jays' "For the Love of Money," which also provides a musical keynote for this new wave-soul-inflected record. Unfortunately, this all reads better than it plays. Apart from the aforementioned Rundgren numbers and (possibly) the title track, no songs make a lasting impression, as Utopia's pop instincts fail them for the first time since *Oops! Wrong Planet*. As a Reagan-era curiosity, however, it's intermittently fascinating. —*Stephen Thomas Erlewine*

Utopia / Sep. 1982 / Unidisc ✦✦✦
Utopia followed *Swing to the Right*, their first album for Elektra subsidiary Network, a mere six months after, dubbing the new album *Utopia*. Presumably, an eponymous release signaled a new beginning for the group, which is true to a certain extent. Utopia finally became a true collective here, with each member's contributions sounding remarkably similar, in performance and composition. Very few tunes bear an unmistakable Rundgren stamp, and even when they do, it's been processed into a signature Utopia sound—the first time they could truly be said to have a sound of their own. Strangely, this happens on an album where the group makes a self-conscious effort to sound contemporary, dressing in new wave gear for the cover shoot while molding the music after synthesized new wave pop. Granted, that quirkiness masks a fairly traditional set of Utopia arena pop, yet these songs wind up as the most consistent album in the group's catalog—which is saying a lot, considering that the album spreads over three sides. *Utopia* rarely sags in momentum, and even the weaker songs aren't far removed from the stronger material, highlighted by "Bad Little Actress," "Hammer in My Heart," "Princess of the Universe," and the excellent single "Feet Don't Fail Me Now." They had their moments before, but *Utopia* is where the band finally made a thoroughly enjoyable record; too bad they couldn't extend it through their final two records. —*Stephen Thomas Erlewine*

Oblivion / Jan. 1984 / Passport ✦✦✦
For *Oblivion*, their first album for the fledgling independent Passport, Utopia merged the new wave inclinations of *Utopia* with their previous hard rock sensibilities. In other words, it was a bid for chart success, as the quartet attempted to revamp themselves as mainstream rockers for the mid-'90s. Even if they were sharp enough to realize that synths, arena-sized hooks and big beats were all equally popular in 1984, they didn't assemble the components in a way that sounded contemporary. *Oblivion*, perhaps appropriately for an album with such a title, is a record out of time, one that sounds lost in a netherworld between the '70s and '80s. The sound of the record is disconcerting, but it would have been excusable if more than two songs—the opener "Itch In My Brain" and the excellent "Crybaby," which tries to ape Def Leppard and sounds like classic Todd—were memorable. Following the tight, focused *Utopia*, the lack of strong material is troubling and, in retrospect, it's clear that this was the beginning of the end for Utopia. —*Stephen Thomas Erlewine*

POV / Jan. 1985 / Passport ✦✦
POV was essentially *Oblivion, Pt. 2*, suffering from the same listless production and songwriting that sank their first effort for Passport Records. The main difference is that the performances lean toward hard rock instead of new wave, which only makes sense since new wave was passé by 1985. Nevertheless, the production remains stilted and unsatisfying, reigned in by drum machines and clumsy synthesizers that make the entire thing sound canned. That would have been a problem even if the material was strong, but unfortunately, the songs on *POV* are even less distinctive than those on *Oblivion*, highlighted only by "Mated," Todd Rundgren's power ballad valentine to his dedicated fans. Those hardcore followers turned out to be the only ones still paying attention to Utopia—*POV* bombed on the charts, peaking at #161. Congnizant of the commercial failure of the album, and perhaps realizing the group's well had run dry, Rundgren pulled the plug on Utopia after this record, and it's easy to see why. —*Stephen Thomas Erlewine*

Trivia / Jun. 1986 / Passport ✦✦✦
Released not long after the group's disbandment, *Trivia* rounds up highlights from Utopia's three post-Bearsville releases—*Utopia*, *Oblivion* and *POV*. In a way, its release was welcome, since *Oblivion* and *POV* were tremendously uneven, and their best moments sound better when paired with the highlights from *Utopia*, but—as Rhino's *Anthology* later proved—they still don't live up to prime Utopia. That said, *Trivia* is more listenable than either of the Passport releases and nearly as entertaining as *Utopia*, but once Rhino released *Anthology* two years later, it was pretty much useless for anyone outside of collectors. And that's because *Trivia* was baited with an outtake each from *Oblivion* and *POV*, presumably to make the collection enticing for the dedicated. "Fix Your Gaze" would have ranked as one of the better numbers on *Oblivion*, but "Monument" wasn't particularly interesting; they were both added as bonus tracks on Rhino's double-disc Passport collection, *Oblivion, POV & Some Trivia*. —*Stephen Thomas Erlewine*

● **Anthology** / May 1989 / Rhino ✦✦✦✦✦
For all their many attributes, Utopia was notoriously uneven on record. They were just as capable of turning out great pop tunes as they were to wander into meandering jams or directionless hard rock—and this applies not only to their earliest art-rock records, but also to their mainstream pop-rock albums. That's what makes Rhino's *Anthology* such a welcome addition to their catalog. There may be a few great songs missing ("Hammer in My Heart," for example) and the three prog-rock songs that appear toward the end of the album are a bit of a downer, but the remaining 13 tracks capture Utopia at their absolute best. The group may have attempted to cover more ground in their early prog-rock incarnation, but often those records meandered, which meant that the songs only made sense on the original albums. Once they gave themselves over to pop-rock with 1977's *Oops! Wrong Planet*, they were still uneven, but uneven pop-rock albums can be distilled into one dynamic collection. And that's what happens here. "Crybaby," "The Very Last Time," "Set Me Free," "Love in Action," "Love Is the Answer," "You Make Me Crazy," "Lysistrata," "Feet Don't Fail Me Now" and "I Just Want to Touch You" were undisputed highlights on their respective albums, and hearing them all in a row is a sheer delight. Taken together, they argue that Utopia's records were better and more consistent than they actually were, but the fact is, *Anthology* is "the definitive Utopia album," as Bud Scoppa writes in the liner notes. For Rundgren fans who love his solo records but never quite "got" Utopia, this is the only Utopia record they need. —*Stephen Thomas Erlewine*

Oblivion, POV & Some Trivia / Apr. 9, 1996 / Rhino ✦✦✦
Like *Utopia* before them, *Oblivion* and *POV* quickly went out of print after their initial release, since the fledging Passport label that initially released the records folded. As a result, the two records were out of print for nearly a decade, even as Rhino reissued the remainder of the Utopia catalog. It's likely that no one outside of hardcore Rundgren fans noticed they were missing, and it's just as likely that only hardcore fans rejoiced when Rhino finally released the two records, along with the two stray Passport cuts and the bonus track from the *POV* CD, as the double-disc set *Oblivion, POV & Some Trivia*. There's little question that Rhino did a superb job reissuing this material—it sounds terrific and it's blessed with exhaustive liner notes. Unfortunately, the music itself has dated particularly poorly, with only a handful of songs—"Itch in My Brain," "Crybaby," "Mated," "Fix Your Gaze"—making lasting impressions. Still, any hardcore Utopia/Rundgren fan will certainly need the set, if only as a way to fill in a major gap, and if they're disappointed with the music, they'll at least be pleased to know that the package is first-rate. —*Stephen Thomas Erlewine*

City in My Head / 1999 / Castle ✦✦✦✦
Even hardcore Todd Rundgren fans disagree on the merits of Utopia, his late-'70s/early-'80s band which fell halfway between vanity project and independent entity. Part of the problem is that the band were musically schizophrenic, embodying the extremes of both prog rock (in their earliest incarnation) and arena rock (in their latter-day phase). Rhino's 1989 collection *Anthology (1974-1985)* took a pop direction, which may have rewritten the group's history slightly, but it did an exceptional job of spotlighting the great majority of the group's best pop songs. Castle's double disc takes a different approach, somewhat out of necessity (it only covers the Bearsville years, meaning that such pop gems as "Crybaby" and "Feets Don't Fail Me Now" weren't even up for inclusion), but also out of purpose. The idea here is to emphasize Utopia's progressive nature. Much of the first disc is dedicated to the futuristic freak-outs of *Todd Rundgren's Utopia* and *Another Live*, and even when it moves toward pop on the second disc, it either emphasizes album-rock cuts like "Caravan" or arty moves like the Beatles parody of *Deface the Music* (nearly half of the album is featured here). Utopia beginners—mainly fans of Rundgren's maverick solo records—are advised to seek out Rhino's earlier disc first, because of its pop leanings. Once that's been absorbed, *City in My Head* is a good primer for the rest of the band's catalog. But for longtime followers, the comp's worth is marginal. There are no rarities, and Paul Lester's enthusiastic liner notes aren't as exhaustive as his work for the Rundgren compilations and reissues, but the remastered sound is very good. Of course, fans who care about that sort of thing may want to just get Castle's Utopia reissues instead. —*Stephen Thomas Erlewine*

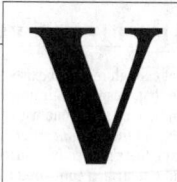

Steve Vai

b. Jun. 6, 1960, Long Island, NY

Arranger, Guitar / Guitar Virtuoso, Heavy Metal, Fusion, Hard Rock, Instrumental Rock
One of the top rock instrumentalists of the '80s and '90s, guitar virtuoso Steve Vai was a pupil of Joe Satriani as a teenager and studied at the Berklee School of Music before moving to Los Angeles at age 19. He was a huge fan of Frank Zappa, and joined Zappa's band after proving that he knew most of the repertoire and could transcribe orchestral pieces by ear. Zappa credited him on albums like *Ship Arriving Too Late to Save a Drowning Witch* as "stunt guitarist." He released the self-produced solo debut *Flex-Able* in 1984, combining his Zappa and Satriani influences. Vai next went on to play with Alcatrazz, David Lee Roth, Whitesnake, and Alice Cooper as well as landing a featured role as the devil's guitarist in the 1986 film *Crossroads*. Vai released his finest solo effort, the varied *Passion and Warfare*, in 1990. He then formed a backing group called VAI featuring vocalist Devin Townsend for 1993's *Sex & Religion*, and then returned to the solo format with 1995's *Alien Love Secrets*. *Fire Garden* followed in 1996, with the archival *Flex-Able Leftovers* appearing two years later, consisting of material from Vai's first sessions that had never been released on CD. Vai continued to maintain his impeccable skills with 1999's *The Ultra Zone*. In fall 2000, Vai issued a compilation of his instrumental ballads, *The 7th Song: Enchanting Guitar Melodies, Archives Vol. 1*, which recorded bonus tracks. *Alive in an Ultra World* appeared in summer 2001 and a month-long tour with Joe Satriani and Dream Theater's John Petrucci soon followed. —*Steve Huey*

Flex-Able / 1984 / Epic ✦✦✦✦✦
Steve Vai recorded his debut album, *Flex-Able*, at home on an eight-track studio and released it himself in 1984. Even though Vai is one of rock's most renowned guitar virtuosos, *Flex-Able* isn't really a typical "shred" album; playing with Frank Zappa for several years has rubbed off on Vai, and many of his compositions reflect both Zappa's musical influence and a skewed sense of humor that makes for some whimsically entertaining moments (i.e., "Little Green Men"). Make no mistake, there's still plenty of Satriani-esque technical virtuosity on display, but since Vai has a few other tricks in his bag, *Flex-Able* turns out to be much more enjoyable (and accessible to listeners other than guitar-technique fetishists) than the average '80s guitar shred-fest. —*Steve Huey*

● **Passion and Warfare** / Sep. 1990 / Epic ✦✦✦✦✦
Widely acclaimed as his best album, *Passion and Warfare* finds Steve Vai coming into his own as a composer, as well as bypassing vocals almost entirely. His style isn't quite as derivative of influences Frank Zappa and Joe Satriani as it was six years earlier on *Flex-Able*; while some of Vai's sense of humor is still evident on tracks like the cock-rock strut of "The Audience Is Listening," it is mostly replaced by a spiritual reflectiveness on ballads like "For the Love of God" and "Blue Powder" and dignified, committed rockers like "I Would Love To" and "Liberty." Vai is a more distinguished composer than most of his guitar-shredder contemporaries, and rather than simply showing off his technique, he isn't afraid to experiment or take chances in his playing. Thus, *Passion and Warfare* is arguably the richest and best hard rock guitar-virtuoso album of the '80s. —*Steve Huey*

Sex & Religion / Jul. 27, 1993 / Epic ✦✦

Alien Love Secrets / Mar. 21, 1995 / Epic ✦✦✦

Fire Garden / Sep. 17, 1996 / Epic ✦✦✦✦
Steve Vai offers the following words of advice about *Fire Garden*, his fifth solo album: "This is essentially a double-CD packed onto one. In this package there are over 74 minutes of music. Phase I (for the most part) is all instrumental music, and Phase II (for the most part) is all vocal selections, with the exception of 'Warm Regards.' … Being as dense as it is, this CD may best be experienced by devouring it in pieces, but those with a strong constitution may dare to consume it whole as it is." Seldom has an artist provided more telling liner notes for their own album. *Fire Garden* is indeed a dense album, filled with a never-ending arrray of sonic textures and guitar tones. Unlike most guitar heroes, Vai doesn't treat music as a way to demonstrate his technical skill. Instead, he channels his astonishing technical skill into creating soundscapes that will showcase his virtuosity as often as not. The result is a guitar album that is enjoyable for non-guitar freaks, as well. Vai's vocals still have a way to go before they are as expressive as his instrumental work, but this subtle and dense concept album is the closest he's ever gotten to integrating the two sides of his musical personality together. An impressive effort from a musician that continues to grow and stretch himself with each new release. —*Stephen Thomas Erlewine*

Flex-Able Leftovers / Nov. 10, 1998 / Epic ✦✦✦✦
Before his high-profile gigs with David Lee Roth and Whitesnake, Steve Vai served time as Frank Zappa's guitarist in the early '80s. And judging by Vai's first two solo albums released around this time, 1984's *Flex-Able* and *Flex-Able Leftovers*, he was heavily influ-

enced by Zappa's songwriting and compositional skills. Although there is definitely a noticeable Zappa stamp on the tunes, Vai's own personality and awe-inspiring guitar chops are what really make these two solo albums so impressive. Also, Vai was one of the few guitar heroes of the '80s to stress the importance of songwriting over mindless soloing. While *Flex-Able* was a full album, *Flex-Able Leftovers* was originally just an EP of material that didn't make it onto the debut. When *Flex-Able* was released on CD in 1988, a few tracks from *Leftovers* were included as a bonus, yet fans have wondered all along if the full EP would ever be released on CD. Ten years later, their wish came true. Not only has the EP been re-released, but unreleased tracks from that era are included, making up a full-length album. Vai's over-the-top humor can be sampled on the profanity-fest "#?@! Yourself" and the goofy "So Happy," while "Massacre" and "Natural Born Boy" feature his immense guitar skill. And Vai's unique songwriting talent is evident on such tracks as "Burnin' Down the Mountain," "The Beast of Love," and "Bledsoe Blvd." The 1998 version of *Flex-Able Leftovers* is highly recommended to guitar freaks everywhere, as well as lovers of completely original and cutting-edge rock music. —*Greg Prato*

The Ultra Zone / Sep. 7, 1999 / Epic ✦✦✦✦
This album contains two tributes to two other stellar guitarists. One of those is "Jiboom," which pays homage to Stevie Ray Vaughan, while "Frank" remembers Frank Zappa. Vai saw his career begin as a teenage stunt guitarist for Frank Zappa. Later, Mike Keneally performed the same role in a band backing Zappa. For this album, Keneally toured in Vai's band, but plays keyboards on the album. It is an amazing exhibition of six-string talent. —*Tom Schulte*

Ritchie Valens

b. May 13, 1941, Pacoima, CA, d. Feb. 3, 1959, Clear Lake, IA

Vocals, Guitar / Latin Rock, Rock & Roll
Ritchie Valens will forever be known primarily as one of the two rock stars (along with the Big Bopper) who perished with Buddy Holly when their plane crashed in the midst of a Midwest tour in 1959. At the time, Valens had just established himself as one of the most promising young talents in rock & roll; more than almost any other rock star who died prematurely, it's difficult to assess his unrealized potential—he was only 17 at the time of his death, and had just barely begun to make records. The first Hispanic rock star, Valens was discovered by producer Bob Keane in 1958. Keane signed the guitarist to his Del-Fi label, and they soon had a sizable hit with the brash "Come on Let's Go," which made number 42. It was the pensive, almost awkward "Donna" that got him to number two in early 1959. More innovative was the flipside, "La Bamba," sung entirely in Spanish, and featuring some fierce guitar work, as well as the thick sound of the Danelectro bass, which gave the instrument more electric presence than it had ever previously enjoyed on a rock & roll disc. —*Richie Unterberger*

In Concert at Pacoima Jr. High / 1960 / Rhino ✦✦✦
A bizarre piece of work: a home-made tape of a high school concert. Possibly rock's earliest "official" live album, padded with narration and unfinished studio tracks. In shaky sound, but unique. —*Bruce Eder*

The Best of Ritchie Valens / 1986 / Rhino ✦✦✦✦✦
The virtually complete recording legacy of an all-too-brief career. —*Bruce Eder*

The Ritchie Valens Story / Jun. 15, 1993 / Del-Fi ✦✦
While this compilation features the official versions of Ritchie's three biggest songs ("La Bamba," "Donna," and "Come on, Let's Go"), the bulk of it is turned over to recently unearthed rehearsal takes and demos of his better-known sides. Not the place to start your Valens collection, but a really good place to go after you've absorbed the hits. —*Cub Koda*

● **Rockin' All Night: The Best of Ritchie Valens** / Jan. 17, 1995 / Del-Fi ✦✦✦✦✦
There have been a few best-of packages for Valens over the last 20 years, and you're not necessarily better off with this one if you've picked up a collection in the past. As of the mid-'90s, though, this is the best anthology available. The 22 tracks cover all the important bases, including the few hits, several covers, and the best cuts from the remainder of his meager discography. —*Richie Unterberger*

Ritchie Valens: the Lost Tapes / Nov. 6, 1995 / Del-Fi ✦✦✦
The first major release of Ritchie Valens demos reveals his creative process in fragmentary form, with multiple outtakes of songs like "La Bamba" and "Cry Cry Cry," among others. The sound is somewhat shaky at times (none of this material was intended to be heard in public) but the variations on familiar songs show Valens' evolution as a musician and composer, as well as the contribution of session players and arrangers like Rene Hall (who also played on Sam Cooke's "You Send Me") and Carol Kaye. —*Bruce Eder*

Come On, Let's Go / May 5, 1998 / Del-Fi ✦✦✦✦✦
Considering Valens died about seven months after his first recording session, it's amazing

that enough material exists to piece together a three-CD, 62-song box set. It's also amazing that, despite a fair amount of inevitable filler, it's truly a worthwhile collection, recommended to anyone with a deep interest in '50s rock. Besides everything from his two LPs and the *In Concert at Pacoima Jr. High* set (which was actually only half live, anyway), there're a couple dozen home demos and studio outtakes; these are fragmentary and unpolished compared to the official stuff, but the enormous heart in his singing and guitar playing always shines through. While serious collectors probably already have most or all of this, it's never been packaged so thoroughly and thoughtfully: The 64-page booklet includes a long biographical essay and lots of photos, and a 12-page supplemental insert gives more technical notes about the recordings and session musicians. *—Richie Unterberger*

Frankie Valli (Francis Castelluccio)

b. May 3, 1937, Newark, NJ

Frankie Valli, the lead singer of the Four Seasons, launched a solo career in 1965 after several years of chart-topping success, while still continuing with the group, which was re-billed as "Frankie Valli and the Four Seasons." He had actually begun as a solo, releasing the 1953 single "My Mother's Eyes" under the name Frankie Valley. His debut solo single was "(You're Gonna) Hurt Yourself" at the end of 1965, but his first solo success came with the gold-selling "Can't Take My Eyes Off You" (June 1967), which appeared on his first solo album, *Frankie Valli—Solo* (July 1967). This was followed by *Timeless* (1968). Valli discontinued solo work for half a dozen years, concentrating on the group. But he returned to solo recordings in the mid-'70s. His subsequent solo hits included the number one "My Eyes Adored You" (November 1974), "Swearin' to God" (May 1975), "Our Day Will Come" (October 1975), and the number one "Grease" (May 1978). *—William Ruhlmann*

Greatest Hits, Vol. 1 / 1991 / Rhino ✦✦✦✦✦

The Four Seasons were never in a class with Frankie Lymon & the Teenagers or Little Anthony & the Imperials, and Franki Valli's voice tended to sound shrill. But despite their imperfections, Valli and friends came up with their share of fun, enjoyable teen pop in the early '60s. In fact, it's hard to imagine the early '60s without teen pop favorites like "Candy Girl" and "Big Girls Don't Cry." Spanning 1962-1965, *Greatest Hits, Vol. 1* boasts many of the Newark, NJ, group's definitive early hits, including "Stay," "Walk Like a Man," "Sherry," "Big Girls Don't Cry." and "Candy Girl." One hears the group maturing somewhat on 1965's classic, Beach Boys-influenced "Bye, Bye, Baby," which became a major hit for the Bay City Rollers in 1975. Obviously, *Greatest Hits, Vol. 1* isn't meant to be an in-depth study of Valli and the Four Seasons, but for the casual listener, this CD and its companion, *Vol. 2*, are easily recommended. *—Alex Henderson*

Greatest Hits, Vol. 2 / 1991 / Rhino ✦✦✦✦✦

The mid-'60s were a time of transition for Franki Valli and the Four Seasons. The teen market had put Valli on the map, but he knew that teenagers turn into adults, so he gradually shifted his focus from teen pop to a more mature and middle of the road (although still quite sugary) approach that incorporated influences ranging from Motown and the Beach Boys to the British Invasion. This new outlook would be reflected not only in his work with the Four Seasons, but also in the solo career he launched in 1965. Spanning 1964-1978, *Greatest Hits, Vol. 2* spotlights an edgier Valli than you'll generally find on *Vol. 1*. This CD ranges from Four Seasons hits such as 1964's "Rag Doll," 1966's "Working My Way Back to You" (which is so Motown-ish that it was a logical choice for the Spinners in 1979), and 1975's Beach Boys-influenced "Who Loves You" to solo favorites like "Can't Take My Eyes Off You" (1967), "My Eyes Adored You" (1974), the disco-ish "Swearin' to God" (1975), and the funky "Grease" (1978). Rock critics hated the fact that much of Valli's solo output was so unapologetically sentimental, but then, he never made records to please critics or intellectuals. Commercial pop was Valli's forte, and *Greatest Hits, Vol. 2* points to the fact that he could do it with likable if less-than-stunning results. *—Alex Henderson*

● **Anthology** / Rhino ✦✦✦✦✦

Van Halen

f. 1974, Pasadena, CA

Album Rock, Arena Rock, Heavy Metal, Pop/Rock, Hard Rock, Pop-Metal

With their 1978 eponymous debut, Van Halen simultaneously re-wrote the rules for rock guitar and hard rock in general. Guitarist Eddie Van Halen redefined what electric guitar could do, developing a blindingly fast technique with a variety of self-taught two-handed tapping, hammer-ons, pull-offs, and effects that mimicked the sound of machines and animals. It was wildly inventive and over-the-top, equaled only by vocalist David Lee Roth, who brought the role of a metal singer to near performance art standards. Roth wasn't blessed with great technique, unlike Eddie, but he had a flair for showmanship, derived as much from lounge performers as Robert Plant. Together, they made Van Halen into the most popular American rock & roll band of the late '70s and early '80s, and, in the process, set the template for hard-rock and heavy metal for the '80s. Throughout the '80s, it was impossible not to hear Van Halen's instrumental technique on records that ranged from the heaviest metal to soft-pop. Furthermore, Roth's irony-drenched antics were copied by singers who took everything literally. Once of those was Sammy Hagar, an arena-rock veteran from the '70s who replaced Roth after the vocalist had a falling out with Van Halen in 1985. Hagar stayed with the band longer than Roth, helping the group at the top of the charts through the late '80s and early '90s. However, the group's sales began to slide in the mid-'90s, just as tensions between Hagar and Eddie began to arise. In one of the most disastrous publicity stunts in rock history, Hagar was fired (or quit), Roth was brought back on, seemingly as a permanent member, but only for two songs on a greatest hits album. He was subsequently replaced by Gary Cherone, a former member of Extreme. *—Stephen Thomas Erlewine*

★ **Van Halen** / 1978 / Warner Brothers ✦✦✦✦✦

Van Halen's self-titled 1978 debut is undoubtedly one of the all-time best debuts by a hard rock/heavy metal band. All of the components for a classic are represented—excellent songs and high-octane performances (the excitement of their live show was captured perfectly by producer Ted Templeman) are used to create an invigorating, original sound. Like other acclaimed debuts (*Led Zeppelin I, Are You Experienced?*), Van Halen has a raw edge since it was recorded quickly, and every single song is a winner. It's also become one of the ultimate party albums over the years, since the overall mood is excited and celebratory. While singer David Lee Roth's bravado and the steady rhythm section of drummer Alex Van Halen and bassist Michael Anthony were both key ingredients, the main attraction was Eddie Van Halen's guitar playing. Few other guitarists have had such an instant impact on a generation of up-and-coming players, who copied his unorthodox, kamikaze style—especially his trademark tapping technique showcased on the album's legendary solo "Eruption." Almost all of the tracks on *Van Halen* have rightfully become radio staples, such as the scorching rockers "Runnin' With the Devil," "Ain't Talkin' 'Bout Love," "Jamie's Cryin'," "Atomic Punk," and "On Fire," while covers of "You Really Got Me" and "Ice Cream Man" remain awe-inspiring to this day. *Van Halen* proved to be the ultimate coming-of-age soundtrack to many a teenager since its release, resulting in sales of over 10 million in the U.S. alone. Everyone on the planet should own a copy of this landmark release. *—Greg Prato*

Van Halen II / 1979 / Warner Brothers ✦✦✦✦

Rather than take an extended break after spending nearly a year on the road promoting their exceptional 1978 debut, Van Halen went directly back into the studio to record another album. 1979's *Van Halen II* was just as intense as its predecessor, but wasn't as potent compositionally—which is forgivable since it was nearly impossible to top *Van Halen*. A very brief album (barely over 30 minutes in length), *Van Halen II* spawned the group's first true hit single, the aptly titled Top 20 hit "Dance the Night Away," while featuring another strong set of turbo-charged rock. A mid-paced cover of "You're No Good" (originally popularized by Linda Ronstadt) kicks things off, before the band's rowdy party rock regains shape—"Somebody Get Me a Doctor," "Bottoms Up!," "Outta Love Again," "Light Up the Sky," and "D.O.A." are all testosterone-heavy ragers. In addition to the aforementioned "Dance the Night Away," the album closer "Beautiful Girls" showed VH's burgeoning pop sensibilities, while Eddie Van Halen showcases his guitar chops again on the acoustic "Spanish Fly" and the exquisite intro to the sullen "Women In Love." *Van Halen II* confirmed that the band was fast becoming America's premier hard rock/metal band. *—Greg Prato*

Women & Children First / 1980 / Warner Brothers ✦✦✦✦✦

By Van Halen's third release, 1980's *Women and Children First*, the group was a bona fide arena headliner; hence, meaty guitar riffs and a huge, fat sound are featured throughout. While *Van Halen II* was closely rooted both compositionally and sonically to their self-titled debut, *Women and Children First* signaled the band's first (successful) attempt to branch out. The tracks may not have been as immediate as such previous favorites as "Runnin' With the Devil" or "Dance the Night Away," but they were much more ambitious from a songwriting standpoint, resulting in perhaps Van Halen's most underrated record. The anthemic album opener, "And the Cradle Will Rock...," was the first Van Halen track to ever feature keyboards (processed through a guitar amplifier for a heavy sound), while the massive yet spacious sound of such heavy hitters as "Everybody Wants Some!," "Fools," "Romeo Delight," and "Loss of Control" is simply awe-inspiring. Both the intro to "Take Your Whiskey Home" and "Could This Be Magic?" find the band in a loose and fun bluesy mode, while the album-closing epic ballad "In a Simple Rhyme" is one of Van Halen's all-time best and deserved to be a hit. An oft-overlooked hard rock classic. *—Greg Prato*

Fair Warning / 1981 / Warner Brothers ✦✦✦✦

Although Van Halen were enjoying an enormous amount of commercial success by 1981, not all was happy in the VH camp. While the public believed that the euphoric, party-hearty antics of their live show spilled into their personal lives, this proved not to be case. Edward Van Halen was feeling frustrated due to the group's unwillingness to branch out musically as much as he desired, resulting in the group's darkest album, *Fair Warning*. Unlike Van Halen's other Roth-era albums, not a single party anthem was included—in its place was an unmistakable feeling of strife and friction, both lyrically and musically. The album opener, "Mean Street," contains a furious guitar intro by Eddie, before leading into one of VH's funkiest grooves. While the mood is eased from time to time throughout ("Dirty Movies," "Hear About It Later," "Push Comes to Shove"), the album is simply an unapologetic ass-kicker—"Sinner's Swing!," "Unchained," "So This Is Love?," and "One Foot Out the Door" capture the band at their red-hot fiercest. Along with their self-titled debut and *1984*, *Fair Warning* is an undisputed Van Halen masterpiece. *—Greg Prato*

Diver Down / 1982 / Warner Brothers ✦✦✦

Although it went platinum, *Fair Warning* didn't match the multi-platinum standards of Van Halen's first three records, so the group revamped their sound slightly for the follow-up, *Diver Down*. Adding the slightest hints of synthesizers and streamlining both the guitar indulgences of Eddie Van Halen and the vocal excesses of David Lee Roth, the album contained some of the group's most pop-oriented performances—and they were all in the guise of covers. "(Oh) Pretty Woman" and "Dancing in the Street" had the traditional mechanical Van Halen rhythmic pulse, as well as concise solos from Eddie and restrained vocals from Diamond Dave, which helped them become the hits they were designed to be. If they were offset by more original material like "Hang 'Em High," the concessions would have been acceptable, but the rest of *Diver Down* is filled with covers, including

"Big Bad Bill," "Where Have All the Good Times Gone," and a closing "Happy Trails." All of the songs are professionally performed, and the music features more ideas than most previous Van Halen albums, but the lack of strong original material makes *Diver Down* less of an accomplishment than it appears. — *Stephen Thomas Erlewine*

☆ **1984** / 1984 / Warner Brothers ✦✦✦✦✦
Van Halen's *1984* is arguably the best and most defining rock release of the '80s. Eddie Van Halen's guest appearance on Michael Jackson's massive 1983 hit "Beat It" introduced VH to the pop audience, which the band attracted in droves with this expertly crafted set of hard rock with pop leanings, not to mention its imaginative accompanying videos. Musically, *1984* was a gamble that paid off massively—Eddie Van Halen was finally given the green light by his bandmates to incorporate keyboards into their sonic palette, resulting in the number one single "Jump" and the almost new wave-ish Top 15 love song "I'll Wait." But wisely, the keyboards weren't overpowering, and all of the other selections were typical VH hard-rocking heavies—the perennial radio favorites "Hot for Teacher" and "Panama," as well as the highly underrated album tracks "Top Jimmy," "Drop Dead Legs," "Girl Gone Bad," and "House of Pain." While the strong and instantly memorable songs were obviously the main ingredient for the album's success, a string of imaginative and humorous videos really introduced the band to a whole new audience (the hilarious clip for "Hot for Teacher" has to be one of the all-time best). *1984* also opened up the floodgates for many faceless, identical pop-metal bands (something VH was the complete opposite of), who suddenly realized that adding synths to heavy metal could increase their chances of commercial success. Still, it didn't tarnish the fact that *1984* is a timeless hard rock masterpiece, which eventually sold a staggering ten million copies. Unfortunately, the album would be the last Van Halen recording to feature David Lee Roth, who surprisingly left in 1985 at the height of the band's popularity. — *Greg Prato*

5150 / 1986 / Warner Brothers ✦✦✦✦
Few bands in rock history made as seamless a transition between lead vocalists as Van Halen. A platinum solo act in his own right, Sammy Hagar brought proven star power, a huge set of pipes, and an immediate air of confidence to the proceedings that no true newcomer could have ever hoped to deliver. On the down side, this seemingly perfect marriage would ignite a vicious feud between David Lee Roth loyalists, Hagar fans, and within the Van Halen creative/management camp as well. Thankfully, both sides would deliver in spades. *5150* (named after Eddie's home studio) became a number one blockbuster record with a sold-out tour to boot. Hagar ushered in the new era with an amazingly Roth-sounding squeal announcing the heavily sardonic "Good Enough"—a rousing number with all the classic VH trappings. The band set charts on fire with the massive first single "Why Can't This Be Love," equally loved and reviled by the band's old-school fans for its pervasively synth-laden sound. The band segues effortlessly from the frenzied "Get Up" into the soaring commercial anthem "Dreams," culminating with the stream-of-consciousness barroom chatter of album closer "Inside." In between, they serve up a trio of convincing rockers in "Summer Nights," "Best of Both Worlds," and the title track, as well as another outstanding power ballad, "Love Walks In." Even though *5150* sounded radically different from its predecessor, upon closer examination, its songs are clearly an extension of *1984*'s blueprint. The drums may sound different, the band may be mixed differently, but the intrinsic classic VH guitar attack remains intact. Technically a near-perfect collection of pop-minded rock anthems, *5150* still divides Van Halen fans to this day. Roth-era loyalists may balk at the album's contrived sleekness, but the overwhelming quality and consistency of its material is still undeniable. — *Ed Rivadavia & John Franck*

OU812 / 1988 / Warner Brothers ✦✦✦
Van Halen broke open the pop innovations of *5150* with *OU812*, their second album with Sammy Hagar. On *OU812*, Hagar's direct approach is fully incorporated into the group, as the band churns out straightahead heavy rockers like "Black and Blue" and pulsing power ballads like "Feels So Good." Under Eddie's direction, the group adds a couple of stylistic quirks—from the chicken-picking of "Finish What You Started" and the Hawaiian flourishes of "Cabo Wabo" to the driving, jazz-inflected metallic "Mine All Mine"—which make *OU812* one of the band's most intriguing and rewarding albums. — *Stephen Thomas Erlewine*

For Unlawful Carnal Knowledge / Jun. 17, 1991 / Warner Brothers ✦✦✦
The smirking title indicates the true nature of *For Unlawful Carnal Knowledge*, Van Halen's third album with Sammy Hagar. Backing away from the diversity of *OU812*, the band turns in some of the most basic, straightforward rock & roll of their career. At times, *F.U.C.K.* recalls the sleek hard rock of Hagar's early-'80s albums, and it's undeniable that his limited vocal power had a great deal to do with the obvious nature of most of this music. While the band is still tight and professional—and Eddie's guitar-work remains impressive—the songwriting is, by and large, undistinguished, with the anthemic "Right Now" standing out as the most memorable song of the batch, mainly because of its incessant chorus. — *Stephen Thomas Erlewine*

Van Halen Live: Right Here, Right Now / Feb. 23, 1993 / Warner Brothers ✦✦

Balance / 1995 / Warner Brothers ✦✦

The Best of Van Halen, Vol. 1 / Oct. 22, 1996 / Warner Brothers ✦✦✦✦✦
In theory, a Van Halen greatest-hits collection should be easy to assemble, but *The Best of Van Halen, Vol. 1* proves that isn't the case. By trying to give the David Lee Roth and Sammy Hagar eras equal space, they wind up not representing either particularly well. The first eight songs run through several of Diamond Dave's biggest songs—"Ain't Talkin' 'Bout Love," "Runnin' with the Devil," "And the Cradle Will Rock," "Jump" and "Panama." It's hard to argue with any of the choices, yet significant songs like "You Really Got Me," "Beautiful Girls," "(Oh) Pretty Woman," "I'll Wait" and "Hot for Teacher" are missing.

Similarly, the Sammy era has many big hits—"Why Can't This Be Love," "Dreams," "When It's Love," and "Right Now"—but skips over hits like "Love Walks In," "Black and Blue," and "Finish What Ya Started." Clearly, the collection would have been better served if it had been assembled as a double-disc set, with Dave and Sammy getting a disc apiece. Furthermore, the much-hyped reunion tracks with Roth, "Can't Get This Stuff No More" and "Me Wise Magic," are a slight disappointment; the band sounds good, but neither track contains a memorable hook. Also, the presence of "Humans Being," one of Van Halen's worst tracks, is an insult, considering how many great songs are missing. Nevertheless, *Best Of, Vol. 1* remains a good single-disc encapsulation of Van Halen's career, even if it isn't a definitive retrospective. — *Stephen Thomas Erlewine*

Van Halen III / Feb. 24, 1998 / Warner Brothers ✦✦
The "III" in the title of *Van Halen III* refers to the unveiling of the third incarnation of Van Halen, the post-Sammy Hagar lineup featuring former Extreme vocalist Gary Cherone as lead singer. According to the party line, Van Halen ditched Sammy because they wanted to try new musical and lyrical approaches that Hagar was reluctant to pursue. And it is true that *Van Halen III* makes a slight break from his dunderheaded party rock, but that's a difference that only hardcore fans will be able to hear. Less tired but no more inspired than *Balance*, *Van Halen III* suffers from the same problems as Hagar-era Van Halen—limp riffs, weak melodies, and plodding, colorless rhythms. On top of that, there are layers of pretensions, from portentous lyrics to segmented song structures that don't sound all that different from "Poundcake." Evidently, the group wanted to prove that they could still rock more than they wanted to stretch their musical muscle. There are a couple of new twists on the Van Halen format, whether it's funky breakdowns or political consciousness, but it's all too familiar, since Cherone sounds uncannily similar to Sammy, and Alex Van Halen and Michael Anthony remain the blandest rhythm section in all of hard rock. That would be a shame if Eddie had a clear idea of where he wanted to take the band, but he seems content to wallow in the big arena rock he has long since exhausted, churning out faceless riffs and technically proficient guitar solos that never expand the vocabulary he established 20 years ago. *Van Halen III* may showcase a new version of Van Halen, but that doesn't make it a new beginning. — *Stephen Thomas Erlewine*

Luther Vandross

b. Apr. 20, 1951, New York, NY [The Bronx]
Vocals / Quiet Storm, Urban, Soul

In R&B music, Luther Vandross ranked with Prince, Stevie Wonder, and Michael Jackson as one of the most successful singer-songwriters and producers of the '80s. Amazingly, unlike those peers, for the most part he did not cross over to widespread pop appeal, a situation that finally began to change at the end of the '80s. Vandross had an elastic tenor that made him a natural for backup singing and commercial work in the early '70s, when he became a top session vocalist. In 1981, he signed with Epic and released his debut album *Never Too Much*, which topped the R&B charts and sold two million copies. The title track was also an R&B number one hit single and reached the pop Top 40. His albums were all million-sellers that spawned major R&B hits, but Vandross' pop success was spotty until 1989, when Epic released *The Best of Luther Vandross…The Best of Love*, a greatest-hits album containing the new track "Here and Now," which became Vandross' first Top Ten pop hit. That proved his breakthrough, and Vandross' next album, *Power of Love* (1991), another million-seller, featured two pop hits, "Power of Love/Love Power" and "Don't Want to Be a Fool." — *William Ruhlmann*

Never Too Much / 1981 / Epic/Legacy ✦✦✦✦
The debut solo album from Luther Vandross featured one outstanding song after another. Vandross concocts a bouncy, vibrant flow on his up-tempo numbers and an intimate, emotional connection on his moderate grooves and his lone ballad. The title track stormed up the *Billboard* R&B charts to number one where it remained for two weeks. The mellow groove of "Don't You Know That," which checked in at number ten, was the second single. "Sugar and Spice" had less of an impact on the charts due to its short stay of six weeks. However, this feverish number gets all the juices flowing as does the unreleased "I've Been Working." Also featured on this set is the sentimental number "You Stopped Loving Me." The song was written by Vandross but initially released by Roberta Flack; both versions stand tall. "A House Is Not a Home" is the only ballad, and an elegant one it is, written by Burt Bacharach and Hal David and originally sung by Dionne Warwick nearly 20 years prior. Vandross orchestrates a contemporary masterpiece with this vintage number. Though it was never an official release by the label, it's a quiet storm jewel. In addition to his many music credits, Vandross was a featured guest vocalist with the progressive band Change. The same vocal savvy and smooth styling that the New York City native exhibited on songs like "Searching" and "Glow of Love" resurface here. This is one of the better R&B albums of the early '80s. — *Craig Lytle*

Forever, For Always, For Love / 1982 / Epic/Legacy ✦✦✦✦
New York City native Luther Vandross did not generate any number one hits with his second effort for the Epic imprint. Nonetheless, he presents another solid album. The smooth crooner has demonstrated a keen ability to attractively arrange remakes with such beauty and suspense as he did with three of the four featured releases. On the vintage ballad "If This World Were Mine," Vandross teams up with Cheryl Lynn. The single peaked at number four on the *Billboard* R&B charts. He lays his signature on a jammin' medley remake of "Bad Boy/Having a Party." The chandelier-swinging number stepped in at number three. He concludes with the Temptations' gem "Since I Lost My Baby." Penned by Smokey Robinson and Warren Moore, this mournful mid-tempo number tipped in at 17. "Promise Me," "Once You Know How," "She Loves Back," and the other selections are

supreme compositions. Luther Vandross' dominance of the R&B arena was beginning to surface. —*Craig Lytle*

Busy Body / 1983 / Epic ✦✦✦✦
Luther Vandross has acquired a reputation for releasing solid, quality albums. Whereas some artists, whether intentional or unintentional, release albums with one or two good songs, Vandross makes every recording count regardless if every song is released. This project falls in line with one superb composition after another. From the alluring arrangements to the striking melodies, every song glitters with a delightful spirit. The New York native did a remarkable job on the medley "Superstar/Until You Come Back to Me (That's What I'm Gonna Do)." Showing his appreciation for the Carpenters ("Superstar") and Aretha Franklin ("Until You Come Back to Me"), Vandross created a masterpiece with the combination of these two songs. It was a number five single on the *Billboard* R&B charts. "How Many Times Can We Say Goodbye," a duet with Dionne Warwick, is another work of art by the serenading tenor. It peaked at number seven. With a hurdling groove, "I'll Let You Slide" pranced it's way to number five on the *Billboard* R&B charts. From a supernatural lyric to a suspenseful string arrangement, "Make Me Believer" summed up the four releases cresting at 48. Only three selections remain, and all three could have easily charted. This is a splendid album. —*Craig Lytle*

The Night I Fell in Love / 1985 / Epic ✦✦✦✦
His fourth album under the Epic banner, and Luther Vandross still retains that freshness that is fulfilling to his audience and rightly so. This album spawned four *Billboard* R&B singles in "Til My Baby Comes Home," "It's Over Now," "Wait for Love," and "If Only for One Night." However, as superb as these songs are, any one of the remaining selections could have achieved comparable chart status. For starters, "The Other Side of the World" has that suspenseful rhythm and engaging lyric; "My Sensitivity" has a balmy arrangement enhanced with a bashful, yet mature, lyric. As for the title track and the remake of the Stevie Wonder classic "Creepin'," Vandross is witty with his vocal stylings. "If Only for One Night" was also a remake; it was written by Brenda Russell and covered by both her and Roberta Flack. The production skills of Vandross are commendable as he exhibits patience and acumen to know his boundaries. —*Craig Lytle*

Give Me the Reason / 1986 / Epic/Legacy ✦✦✦
Luther Vandross was riding high in the 1980s, dominating the R&B charts and slowly, but steadily, increasing his pop exposure. This was his fourth consecutive platinum smash and second straight double-platinum winner, but beyond that was a superbly sung, expressive triumph. "Stop To Love" and "Give Me The Reason" were beautifully produced, arranged, and performed numbers and huge R&B hits (the latter a chart topper), and deserved a better pop fate. —*Ron Wynn*

Any Love / 1988 / Epic ✦✦✦✦✦
There were some who felt that Vandross suffered a slight slump when this album only reached the platinum level after two consecutive double-platinum winners. But "Here And Now" was a huge smash, and by now the pop crowd was fully aware of Vandross' vocal charms and allure. "She Won't Talk To Me" was a bit on the posturing side, but still managed to do decently, while there were also fine album cuts like "I Wonder" and "Are You Gonna Love Me." —*Ron Wynn*

★ The Best of Luther Vandross / Sep. 1989 / Epic ✦✦✦✦✦
By the time this way-overdue double-record hits collection came out, Vandross had done many more R&B singles than could fit on it, so *The Best of Luther Vandross…The Best of Love* is inadequate to encompass him. It does, however, contain "Here and Now," which broke Vandross through to the pop Top Ten long after most people had given up hope that he'd ever cross over. —*William Ruhlmann*

Power of Love / Apr. 23, 1991 / Epic/Legacy ✦✦✦
Power of Love finds Luther Vandross at his peak, crafting immaculate urban R&B hits that are seductive and soulful. The singles "Power of Love / Love Power," "Don't Want to Be a Fool," "The Rush" and "Sometimes It's Only Love" are the high points, but the album is filled with songs that are nearly as powerful, including a wonderful cover of Ben E. King's "I (Who Have Nothing)." —*Stephen Thomas Erlewine*

Never Let Me Go / Jun. 1, 1993 / Epic ✦✦

Songs / Sep. 27, 1994 / Epic ✦✦

Your Secret Love / Oct. 1, 1996 / Epic ✦✦✦
Luther Vandross' tenth new studio album has much in common with its predecessors. It is filled with midtempo love ballads in which Vandross emotes over tasteful R&B gospel arrangements, mostly writing his own songs, but also finding room for a couple of pop favorites—in this case, Stevie Wonder's "Knocks Me Off My Feet" and the old Little Anthony and the Imperials hit "Goin' Out of My Head." As steeped as he is in the nomenclature of R&B vocal expressionism, Vandross as usual sounds more self-involved than romantically devoted. His references have always seemed not so much real emotions as other love songs, which makes him something of an anomaly: a formalist in a field at least nominally defined by excess of feeling. Of course, that's always been something of a conceit, which may be why the traditional R&B audience faithfully takes Vandross to its bosom each time out, while his relationship to the pop audience, after a flirtation in the early '90s, remains largely unconsummated. He may profess "Endless Love," but pop fans are only willing to believe him when he's singing with a diva like Mariah Carey. Give Vandross credit, he wants to be taken on his own terms, which is why he released his own songs, the title track and "I Can Make It Better," as the singles instead of going for a trendy R&B hit with "I Can't Wait No Longer (Let's Do This)," which features a rap by Deidra "Spin" Roper of Salt-N-Pepa, or trying to make "Goin' Out of My Head" a pop hit for the third time. Such integrity is probably what kept the album from selling beyond Vandross' existing fan base; lucky for him, there were a million of them. —*William Ruhlmann*

One Night With You: The Best of Love, Vol. 2 / Sep. 30, 1997 / Epic ✦✦✦✦
One Night With You picked up where Luther Vandross's first hits collection left off, including the R&B/pop Top Ten hits "Power of Love/Love Power," "Don't Want to Be a Fool," "The Best Things In Life Are Free," and "Endless Love," as well as the R&B Top Ten hits "Little Miracles" and "Your Secret Love." Also included was the Grammy-winning "Love the One You're With." Fans may have found the omission of some R&B hits in favor of Vandross's interpretation of Rodgers and Hammerstein's "My Favorite Things" questionable, and the four new songs, despite boasting the hot songwriting pens of Diane Warren, R. Kelly, and Jimmy Jam and Terry Lewis, did not generate any new hits of the kind that propelled Vandross's first hits album to triple-platinum status. Indeed, this second set was a sales disappointment. Maybe Vandross' fans already had these songs on the original albums. (More likely, the album marked the end of his sometimes stormy relationship with Epic, and the company didn't push it.) —*William Ruhlmann*

Always & Forever: The Classics / Sep. 22, 1998 / LV Records/Epic ✦✦✦✦
The title of *Always & Forever: The Classics* implies that its a collection of Luther Vandross' greatest hits of the mid- to late '90s. That's not the case. *The Classics* truly means classics, with each one of the featured songs (with an exception or two) ranking as a true pop classic. Since Vandross is an excellent, peerless contemporary R&B vocalist, this is an excellent opportunity for him to shine, and he does, particularly on "A House Is Not a Home," "Anyone Who Had a Heart," "Going Out of My Head" and "I (Who Have Nothing)." Occasionally, the production is a little too polished or smooth, but Vandross shines throughout the entire album, making it another treasure in his catalog. —*Leo Stanley*

Greatest Hits / Nov. 16, 1999 / Epic ✦✦✦✦✦
1999's *Greatest Hits* may not be as generous as 1989's *The Best of Luther Vandross*, which contained 20 tracks on two discs, but it's a good, concise 14-track collection that includes many of his very best songs. There is a lot of overlap with *The Best of*—it shares no less than nine tracks with that collection—but it also has such '90s hits as "Don't Want to Be a Fool" and "Power of Love / Love Power." It is a tight, single-disc collection, which may make it preferable to some listeners. However, *The Best of* does cover Vandross' prime period better, and since *Greatest Hits* covers much of that same territory while missing several big '90s hits, it isn't quite all it could be. Essentially, it's for casual fans that want all the big hits on one disc—serious listeners will want to stick with *The Best of*. —*Stephen Thomas Erlewine*

The Ultimate Luther Vandross / Aug. 7, 2001 / Epic ✦✦✦✦✦
Fans who prefer a little bit more material and/or Vandross' earlier era might be more satisfied sticking with the 20-song *The Best of Luther Vandross*, which only goes up to the late '80s in its coverage. However, *The Ultimate Luther Vandross* is his best single-disc compilation, with 17 songs from 1981-1994, 13 of which were Top Ten R&B hits. Naturally, his big Top Ten pop hits, "Here and Now," "Power of Love/Love Power," and "Don't Want to Be a Fool," are here. —*Richie Unterberger*

Vanilla Fudge
f. 1966, New York, NY, **db.** 1969
Psychedelic, Hard Rock
Specializing in thundering psychedelia, Vanilla Fudge gave the Supremes hit "You Keep Me Hangin' On" an ultra-serious, somewhat indulgent arrangement and hit big in 1968. The quartet was introduced to Atco by veteran producer Shadow Morton and fronted by keyboardist Mark Stein. "You Keep Me Hangin' On" was only a minor seller in 1967. Reissued a year later, it proved far more potent its second time around. Bassist Tim Bogert and drummer Carmine Appice later played with Jeff Beck and Rod Stewart. —*Bill Dahl*

● Psychedelic Sundae: The Best of Vanilla Fudge / 1993 / Rhino ✦✦✦✦✦
A generous compilation, *Psychedelic Sundae* includes the best of this heavy, progressive, psychedelic band from the late '60s. —*AMG*

Vanilla Ice
b. Oct. 31, 1968, Miami Lakes, FL
Vocals / Pop-Rap, Hardcore Rap
With his hit single "Ice Ice Baby" and its accompanying album, *To the Extreme*, Vanilla Ice became the second White rapper to top the charts. Unlike the Beastie Boys, he didn't have any street credibility, so the Miami-born rapper decided to invent some of his own, claming he had a seriously violent gangster past. Nevertheless, "Ice Ice Baby" became a number one hit late in 1990, thanks to the pulsating bass riff from David Bowie and Queen's "Under Pressure." *To the Extreme* also went to the top of the charts, spending 16 weeks at number one and selling over seven million copies. Ice began filming a feature film, *Cool as Ice*, in the spring of 1990, but by the time the film came out in the fall, his star had fallen dramatically; *To the Extreme* was at number one longer than the soundtrack to *Cool as Ice* was on the charts.
Sensing that his time had passed, Vanilla Ice took a couple years off, re-emerging in 1994 with *Mind Blowin'*. Dispensing with the pop-rap formula of his debut, the rapper adopted the lazy, rolling funk of Cypress Hill, as well as that trio's obsession with pot. The album was a commercial disaster, disappearing from sight immediately after its release. With 1998's *Hard to Swallow*, Ice attempted to reinvent himself as a hardcore, gangsta-styled rapper; again the public wanted no part of it. —*Stephen Thomas Erlewine*

● To the Extreme / 1990 / SBK ✦✦✦
Although *To the Extreme* remains the best-selling rap album of all time, Vanilla Ice's success was short-lived—and understandably so. The Dallas pop/rapper simply didn't have the rapping skills to sustain a long career. Sampling the groove from Queen and David Bowie's "Under Pressure," Ice's mega-hit "Ice Ice Baby" is catchy enough. But on the whole, this album suffers from weak, uneventful tracks and bland, lackluster rapping. It

should be stressed that the hostility hardcore rap audiences feel for pop/rap isn't always justifiable; in fact, pop/rappers ranging from Sir Mix-A-Lot to the Beastie Boys to Young MC are far more substantial and creative than some hardcore rappers would have us believe. But in the case of Vanilla Ice, the vehement criticism he took in the hood was indeed justified. —*Alex Henderson*

Extremely Live / Mar. 1991 / SBK ✦

Mind Blowin / 1994 / SBK ✦✦

Hard to Swallow / Oct. 20, 1998 / Republic ✦✦

The Vapors
....
f. 1978, **db.** 1981
Mod Revival, Power Pop, New Wave
Led by vocalist/guitarist Dave Fenton, the Vapors were a short-lived new wave guitar group that is best known for the spiky pop single "Turning Japanese." Fenton formed the first version of the Vapors in 1978, yet he was the only member to survive that lineup; in 1979, former Ellery Bops members Ed Bazalgette (lead guitar) and Howard Smith (drums) joined the band and bassist Steve Smith came aboard shortly afterward. One of the band's first concerts was seen by the Jam's Bruce Foxton, who asked them to perform on his group's *Setting Sons* tour. Before long, the Vapors were managed by Foxton and John Weller, the manager of the Jam, as well as the father of the group's leader, Paul Weller.

The Vapors signed to United Artists, releasing their first single, "Prisoners," at the end of 1979; it failed to chart. "Turning Japanese," the band's second single, became a major hit, reaching number three on the U.K. charts in March of 1980. *New Clear Days*, the band's debut album, was released two months later, which didn't sell as well as the single. In 1981, the Vapors released the more ambitious *Magnets*, yet it received lukewarm reviews and poor sales; the group disbanded shortly after its release. —*Stephen Thomas Erlewine*

New Clear Days / Jun. 1980 / Cargo ✦✦✦✦✦
It's easy to dismiss this band as a one-hit wonder—surely the album has nothing quite as infectious as the single, "Turning Japanese." *New Clear Days* is, however, a fine example of punchy Brit-pop in the vein of The Jam that holds up better than most albums from the period. —*Chris Woodstra*

Magnets / 1981 / Cargo ✦✦✦
David Fenton was obviously growing tired of being written off as lightweight after "Turning Japanese" and responded with the more ambitious and mature *Magnets*. Here he explores the darker side of life, discussing the Kennedy assasination ("Magnets"), police harrassment ("Civic Hall") and even cult leader/mass murder Rev. Jim Jones ("Jimmy Jones," the failed single). Musically the band is more sophisticated, taking the occasional misstep in the arrangements by adding an annoying sythesizer in songs like "Spiders." Virtually ignored by both critics and the buying public, this is a strong follow-up that deserved a better fate. —*Chris Woodstra*

Anthology / May 30, 1995 / One Way ✦✦✦✦
A somewhat misleading title, *Anthology* is a straight reissue of *New Clear Days* with four songs from *Magnets* tacked on the end. Since the band only made two albums it would have been nice to release both as a two-fer—or at least add some rare tracks to the anthology. Minor complaints aside, this is probably all The Vapors most people will ever need, though Collectable's *Vaporized*, which presents both albums in their entirety, is a better choice. —*Chris Woodstra*

Turning Japanese: The Best of the Vapors / 1996 / EMI ✦✦✦✦
A far better collection than its American counterpart (*Anthology*), *The Best of the Vapors* offers a bit more for the fans, combining all of the singles, five rare B-sides, and most of the best album tracks (though the *Magnets* album is still woefully underrepresented). As an introduction, there is no better place to start and for collectors, it's indispensable. —*Chris Woodstra*

● **Vaporized** / Apr. 7, 1998 / Collectables ✦✦✦✦✦
Vaporized is the third Vapors anthology in three years and, for a band who only released two proper albums, that's no small feat. This one rights the wrongs of earlier collections by finally putting out the two albums—1980's *New Clear Days* and 1981's *Magnets*—in their entirety on one CD. Collectors should still seek out the import, *Turning Japanese: The Best of the Vapors* as a supplement, but all but the obsessive can start and stop here. —*Chris Woodstra*

The Vaselines
....
f. 1986, **db.** 1990
Indie Pop, Twee Pop, Alternative Pop/Rock
Conventional wisdom dictates that the Vaselines might have been relegated to footnote status were it not for Nirvana's Kurt Cobain, who regularly cited the little-known Scottish quartet's influence in interviews with the music press. Cobain's gospel-spreading no doubt accelerated their rise to cult sainthood, but truth be told, the Vaselines would have gotten there sooner or later on their own accord—lewd but naïve and abrasive yet tender, the band's shambling, primitivist squall remains a perfect distillation of pop at its most guileless and euphoric. The group was formed in Edinburgh in 1987 by singers/guitarists Eugene Kelly and Frances McKee, who were later joined by Kelly's brother Charles on drums and James Seenan on bass; soon signing to Pastels frontman Stephan Pastel's newly-formed 53rd and 3rd label, the Vaselines' first-ever studio session yielded their debut single, 1987's fantastic "Son of a Gun." The follow-up, "Dying for It," appeared a year later, with the inclusion of viola player Sophie Pragnell plainly acknowledging the band's

debt to the Velvet Underground. The demise of 53rd and 3rd proved fatal to the Vaselines as well, however, and the group dissolved the same week their lone studio LP, 1989's *Dum Dum*, was released via Rough Trade, although the following year the original lineup briefly reunited to open for Nirvana in Edinburgh. Nirvana would go on to cover the Vaselines' "Molly's Lips" and "Son of a Gun" (both later compiled on their *Incesticide* collection) as well as performing "Jesus Doesn't Want Me for a Sunbeam" on their now-legendary *MTV Unplugged* appearance; renewed interest in the band resulted in the 1992 Sub Pop release of *The Way of the Vaselines*, an assemblage of all 19 of their official recordings. Eugene Kelly later went on to front Captain America (subsequently and rather unfortunately renamed Eugenius), while McKee spent the better part of the decade out of sight before finally resurfacing in Suckle. —*Jason Ankeny*

● **The Way of the Vaselines** / Jul. 31, 1992 / Sub Pop ✦✦✦✦✦
The Way of the Vaselines collects everything The Vaselines ever recorded; it's a rough gem of raw pop. —*Stephen Thomas Erlewine*

Stevie Ray Vaughan
....
b. Oct. 3, 1954, Dallas, TX, **d.** Aug. 27, 1990, East Troy, WI
Vocals, Guitar (Electric), Guitar / Album Rock, Modern Electric Texas Blues, Electric Texas Blues, Blues-Rock, Modern Electric Blues, Texas Blues
With his astonishingly accomplished guitar playing, Stevie Ray Vaughan ignited the blues revival of the '80s. Vaughan drew equally from bluesmen like Albert King, Otis Rush, and Muddy Waters and rock & roll players like Jimi Hendrix and Lonnie Mack, as well as the stray jazz guitarist like Kenny Burrell, developing a uniquely eclectic and fiery style that sounded like no other guitarist, regardless of genre. Vaughan bridged the gap between blues and rock like no other artist had since the late '60s. During the 1980s, he was the leading light in American blues, consistently selling out concerts while his albums regularly went gold. His tragic death in 1990 only emphasized his influence in blues and American rock & roll.

Vaughan began playing guitar as a child, and dropped out of high school to concentrate on playing music. After playing in a band called the Cobras during the early '70s, he formed Triple Threat in 1975, later to become Double Trouble. After the band's 1982 performance at the Montreux Festival caught the attention of David Bowie, Vaughan played on Bowie's *Let's Dance* in 1982. He signed to Epic and soon after, released his debut album *Texas Flood*, a blockbuster blues success and a crossover hit for rock radio. Vaughan's second album *Couldn't Stand the Weather* was even more successful than its predecessor, hitting the Top 40 and going gold.

Though 1985's *Soul to Soul* was also quite successful, Vaughan sank deep into alcoholism and drug addiction. He checked into a rehabilitation clinic in 1988, and performed only sparingly that year. Still, one year later *In Step* became his most successful album, earning a Grammy and going gold. In 1990, Stevie Ray recorded an album with his brother Jimmie, but was killed in a helicopter crash before the record was released. The album, *Family Style*, hit the Top Ten just two months after his death, beginning a series of posthumous releases that were as popular as the albums Stevie Ray released during his lifetime. —*Stephen Thomas Erlewine*

★ **Texas Flood** / 1983 / Epic/Legacy ✦✦✦✦✦
It's hard to overestimate the impact Stevie Ray Vaughan's debut *Texas Flood* had upon its release in 1983. At that point, blues was no longer hip, the way it was in the '60s. *Texas Flood* changed all that, climbing into the Top 40 and spending over half a year on the charts, which was practically unheard of for a blues recording. Vaughan became a genuine star and, in doing so, sparked a revitalization of the blues. This was a monumental impact, but his critics claimed that, no matter how prodigious Vaughan's instrumental talents were, he didn't forge a distinctive voice; instead, he wore his influences on his sleeve, whether it was Albert King's pinched yet muscular soloing or Larry Davis' emotive singing. There's a certain element of truth in that, but that was sort of the point of *Texas Flood*. Vaughan didn't hide his influences, he celebrated them, pumping fresh blood into a familiar genre. When Vaughan and Double Trouble cut the album over the course of three days in 1982, he had already played his set lists countless times; he knew how to turn this material inside out or power it up for maximum impact. The album is paced like a club show, kicking off with Vaughan's two best self-penned songs, "Love Struck Baby" and "Pride and Joy," then settling into a pair of covers, the slow-burning title track and an exciting reading of Howlin' Wolf's "Tell Me," before building to the climax of "Dirty Pool" and "I'm Crying." Vaughan caps the entire thing with "Lenny," a lyrical, jazzy tribute to his wife. It becomes clear that Vaughan's true achievement was finding something personal and emotional by fusing different elements of his idols. Sometimes the borrowing was overt, and other times subtle, but it all blended together into a style that recalled the past while seizing the excitement and essence of the present. —*Stephen Thomas Erlewine*

Couldn't Stand the Weather / 1984 / Epic/Legacy ✦✦✦✦
Stevie Ray Vaughan's second album, *Couldn't Stand the Weather*, pretty much did everything a second album should do: it confirmed that the acclaimed debut was no fluke, while matching, if not bettering, the sales of its predecessor, thereby cementing Vaughan's status as a giant of modern blues. So why does it feel like a letdown? Perhaps because it simply offers more of the same, all the while relying heavily on covers. Of the eight songs, half are covers, while two of his four originals are instrumentals—not necessarily a bad thing, but it gives the impression that Vaughan threw the album together in a rush, even if he didn't. Nevertheless, *Couldn't Stand the Weather* feels a bit like a holding pattern, since there's no elaboration on Double Trouble's core sound and no great strides forward, whether it's in Vaughan's songwriting or musicianship. Still, as holding patterns go, it's a pretty enjoyable one, since Vaughan and Double Trouble play spiritedly throughout the

record. With its swaggering, stuttering riff, the title track ranks as one of Vaughan's classics, and thanks to a nuanced vocal, he makes W.C. Clark's "Cold Shot" his own. The instrumentals—the breakneck Lonnie Mack-styled "Scuttle Buttin'" and "Stang's Swang," another effective demonstration of Vaughan's jazz inclinations—work well, even if the original shuffle "Honey Bee" fails to make much of an impression and the cover of "Voodoo Chile (Slight Return)" is too reminiscent of Jimi Hendrix's original. So, there aren't many weaknesses on the record, aside from the suspicion that Vaughan didn't really push himself as hard as he could have, and the feeling that if he had, he would have come up with something a bit stronger. *—Stephen Thomas Erlewine*

Soul to Soul / 1985 / Epic/Legacy ♦♦♦
By adding two members to Double Trouble—keyboardist Reese Wynans and saxophonist Joe Sublett—Stevie Ray Vaughan indicated he wanted to add soul and R&B inflections to his basic blues sound, and *Soul to Soul* does exactly that. It's still a modern blues album, yet it has a wider sonic palette, finding Vaughan fusing a variety of blues, rock, and R&B styles. Most of this is done through covers—notably Hank Ballard's "Look at Little Sister," the exquisitely jazzy "Gone Home," and Doyle Bramhall's impassioned soul-blues "Change It"—but Vaughan's songwriting occasionally follows suit, as well. Even if only the tortured blues wailer "Ain't Gone 'N' Give Up On Love" entered his acknowledged canon, he throws in some delightful soul-funk touches on "Say What!," the instrumental wah-wah workout that kicks off the album., and the Curtis Mayfield-inspired closer "Life Without You" captures Vaughan at his best as a composer and performer. It's such a seductive number—such a full realization of his soul-blues ambitions—that the rest of the album pales in comparison. In fact, for all of its positive attributes, *Soul to Soul* winds up being less than the sum of its parts, and it's hard to pinpoint an exact reason why. Perhaps it was because Vaughan was on the verge of a horrible battle with substance abuse at the time of recording or perhaps it just has that unevenness inherent in transitional albums. Still, he has good taste in covers, his originals are sturdy, and there's not a bad performance here, so *Soul to Soul* winds up enjoyable in spite of its flaws, and it clearly points the way to his 1989 masterpiece, *In Step*. *—Stephen Thomas Erlewine*

Live Alive / Jul. 1986 / Epic ♦♦♦
Live Alive is a magnificent double-length showcase for Stevie Ray Vaughan's guitar playing, featuring a number of extended jams on a selection of most of the best material from Vaughan's first three albums, plus covers of "Willie the Wimp," "I'm Leaving You (Commit a Crime)," and Stevie Wonder's "Superstition." The album may not be exceptionally tight or concise, but then again, that's not the point. The renditions here sound less polished than the studio versions, with Vaughan's guitar tone bitingly down and dirty and his playing spontaneous and passionate. *—Steve Huey*

☆ **In Step** / Jun. 1989 / Epic/Legacy ♦♦♦♦♦
Stevie Ray Vaughan had always been a phenomenal guitarist, but prior to *In Step*, this songwriting was hit-and-miss. Even when he wrote a classic modern blues song, it was firmly within the genre's conventions; only on *Soul to Soul*'s exquisite soul-blues "Life Without You" did he attempt to stretch the boundaries of the form. As it turns out, that was the keynote for *In Step*, an album where Vaughan found his own songwriting voice, blending blues, soul, and rock in unique ways, and writing with startling emotional honesty. Yes, there are a few covers, all well chosen, but the heart of the album rests in the songs he cowrote with Doyle Bramhall, the man who penned the *Soul to Soul* highlight "Change It." Bramhall proved to be an ideal collaborator for Vaughan; tunes like the terse "Tightrope" and the dense "Wall of Denial" feel so intensely personal, it's hard to believe that they weren't the product of just one man. Yet the lighter numbers—the dynamite boogie "The House Is Rockin'" and the breakneck blues of "Scratch-N-Sniff"—are just as effective as songs. Of course, he didn't need words to make effective music: "Travis Walk" is a blistering instrumental, complete with intricate fingerpicking reminiscent of the great country guitarist Merle Travis, while the shimmering "Riviera Paradise" is every bit as lyrical and lovely as his previous charmer, "Lenny." The magnificent thing about *In Step* is how it's fully realized, presenting every facet of Vaughan's musical personality, yet it still soars with a sense of discovery. It's a bittersweet triumph, given Vaughan's tragic death a little over a year after its release, yet it's a triumph all the same. *—Stephen Thomas Erlewine*

The Sky Is Crying / Nov. 5, 1991 / Epic ♦♦♦♦
The posthumously assembled ten-track outtakes collection *The Sky Is Crying* actually proves to be one of Vaughan's most consistent albums, rivaling *In Step* as the best outside of the *Greatest Hits* collection. These songs were recorded in sessions spanning from 1984's *Couldn't Stand the Weather* to 1989's *In Step* and were left off of the LPs for whatever reason (or, in the case of *Soul to Soul*'s "Empty Arms," a different version was used). What makes the record work is its eclectic diversity—Vaughan plays slide guitar on "Boot Hill" and acoustic on "Life By the Drop"; he smokes on the slow blues of "May I Have a Talk With You" and the title track just as much as on the uptempo Lonnie Mack cover "Wham"; and he shows the jazzy side of his playing on Hendrix's "Little Wing" and Kenny Burrell's "Chitlins Con Carne." But it's not just musical diversity that makes the record work, it's also Vaughan's emotional range. From the morbidly dark "Boot Hill" to the lilting "Little Wing" to the exuberant tributes to his influences—Lonnie Mack on "Wham" and Albert King on "The Sky Is Crying"—Vaughan makes the material resonate, and in light of his death, "The Sky Is Crying" and the touching survivor-story ballad "Life By the Drop" are two of the most moving moments in Vaughan's oeuvre. *—Steve Huey*

In the Beginning / Oct. 6, 1992 / Epic ♦♦

Greatest Hits / Nov. 21, 1995 / Epic ♦♦♦♦♦
Stevie Ray Vaughan was a great guitarist, but he had trouble making consistent albums. *Greatest Hits* rectifies that problem by collecting all of his best-known tracks, from "Pride and Joy" to "Crossfire." Not only is it a terrific introduction, it's his most consistent album, demonstrating exactly why he was one of the most important guitarists of the '80s. *—Stephen Thomas Erlewine*

Live at Carnegie Hall / Jul. 29, 1997 / Epic ♦♦♦♦
Live at Carnegie Hall captures Stevie Ray Vaughan on the supporting tour for his second album, 1984's *Couldn't Stand the Weather*. The Carnegie Hall concert was a special show, since it was the only time Vaughan and Double Trouble added a brass section to augment their sound; in addition, the concert featured guest appearences from Stevie's brother Jimmie and Dr. John. There might have been more musicians than usual onstage, but Stevie Ray remains the center of attention, and he is in prime form here, tearing through a selection of his best-known songs which generally sound tougher in concert than they do in the studio. It's the best live Stevie Ray record yet released. *—Thom Owens*

Real Deal: Greatest Hits, Vol. 2 / Mar. 23, 1999 / Epic/Legacy ♦♦♦♦
Stevie Ray Vaughan was one of a kind. Even his peers knew so. So many times, people like Eric Clapton and Buddy Guy have spoken publicly about Stevie Ray's gift, and it was a gift. His guitar leads would jet off into the stratosphere, return, reload and blast off again, time after time. *The Real Deal* is exactly what it says it is. This is a 16-song set that doesn't let up, not one time. Throughout classic Stevie Ray Vaughan tracks, like the full-speed-ahead instrumental "Scuttle Buttin'," "Love Struck Baby" and "Look at Little Sister," Stevie and the Double Trouble band consistently stand and deliver. Live tracks include the funky Stevie Wonder penned "Superstition," Vaughan favorite "Willie the Wimp," "Shake for Me" and the blues fire of "Leave My Girl Alone." It's Stevie Ray unleashed, live and without a net. One of the biggest crowd pleasers is included here, Stevie's retelling of the Jimi Hendrix standard, "Voodoo Chile (Slight Return)." Awesome. "Lenny" shows off Stevie's jazz influence with subtle phrasing that evokes memories of "Little Wing" or Chuck Leavell's coda on "Layla." No more perfect closer could have been chosen for this set than the solo acoustic number, "Life By the Drop." It's a touching tale of two old friends who become estranged, and then rekindle their old friendship. With *The Real Deal*, we are all in that same boat. Rekindling a friendship that never really died, but may have been forgotten by some for a while. The friendship we all have with the heart and soul of Stevie Ray Vaughan, his music. *—Michael B. Smith*

Blues at Sunrise / Apr. 4, 2000 / Epic/Legacy ♦♦♦
The concept behind *Blues at Sunrise* is a good one: collect ten of SRV's best slow blues numbers, primarily from the official studio albums but also a couple of unreleased cuts and rarities, and sequence them as if they were a lost studio album. It's a neat idea, especially when it's packaged in artwork that deliberately evokes memories of classic blues albums from the '60s (there's even a fake, faded record ring on the front and back covers), and it's hard to fault the music here. All the obvious selections are here—"Ain't Gone 'N' Give Up on Love," "The Things (That) I Used to Do," "Leave My Girl Alone." And the rarities are all worthwhile, including a live "Texas Flood" from the *Live at the El Macambo* video, a live duet with Johnny Copeland on "Tin Pan Alley" from 1985, an unreleased take of "The Sky Is Crying" from *Couldn't Stand the Weather*, and a duet with Albert King on "Blues at Sunrise" (also available on the Fantasy disc *In Session*). Still, some fans may complain, since this is the first posthumous release that feels as if it's trying to trick the hardcore into purchasing music they already have. That's a legitimate complaint, because there are only two songs that the hardcore won't have, and they very well may not want to sink down dollars for something that's just a reconfiguration of familiar tunes. But, as reconfigurations and repackagings go, *Blues at Sunrise* is strong and entertaining, working quite well as a mood piece. It may not be revelatory, but if you strip away your qualms and quibbles, it's enjoyable. *—Stephen Thomas Erlewine*

SRV / Nov. 21, 2000 / Epic/Legacy ♦♦♦♦
If you're gonna put out a box set that really offers something to the devoted fans of an artist, this four-CD package is the way to do it. It's not so much a best-of or career retrospective as a very generous pile of career-spanning material that will genuinely add a new dimension to the Stevie Ray Vaughan listener's library, as fully two-thirds of the 54 tracks were previously unreleased. In addition, of the songs that have been previously available, five of those are cuts on which Vaughan was a sideman or partner, so the Vaughan collector might have missed those in the past. Each of the first three discs clock in at more than 75 minutes, progressing from 1977 to 1990 and emphasizing live material, from soundchecks and radio programs to arena-headlining gigs and three solo acoustic tunes from a 1990 *MTV Unplugged* episode. As music, though, it's uneven. The earliest and leanest cuts are a valuable supplement to Vaughan's discography since he didn't have much opportunity to record until the early '80s. Yet sometimes these are too-long shuffles and boogies; his songwriting and singing are not nearly as impressive as his instrumental technique; and his occasional attempts to replicate Jimi Hendrix are inessential. A few familiar popular studio cuts like "Pride and Joy" and "Wall of Denial" are here, presumably to entertain the more casual Vaughan fans that need an extra push to spring for the box. The fourth disc is a DVD with five never-aired and never-issued performances from an episode of the television program *Austin City Limits*, recorded on October 10, 1989; the 72-page booklet of essays, appreciative quotes from several dozen peers, and more are other bonuses. *—Richie Unterberger*

Bobby Vee (Robert Thomas Velline)

b. Apr. 30, 1943, Fargo, ND
Vocals / Brill Building Pop, Teen Idol, Pop
His career launched as a fill-in for the recently deceased Buddy Holly, Bobby Vee scored several pop hits during the early '60s, that notorious period of popular music sandwiched between the birth of rock & roll and the rise of the British Invasion. Though a few of his singles—"Rubber Ball," for one—were as innocuous as anything else from the era, Vee had a knack for infectious Brill Building pop, thanks to his ebullient voice as well as the

cadre of songwriters standing behind him. His big break came at the expense of one of his musical idols; the Winter Dance Party package tour, with Buddy Holly, Ritchie Valens and the Big Bopper on their way to Fargo when their plane went down in Iowa, killing all three. Vee's band the Shadows were scheduled to play the date instead of Holly, and several months later, producer Tommy "Snuff" Garrett supervised their first recording session and the release of the single "Suzie Baby" on Soma Records. His third single, "Devil or Angel," hit the Top Ten in mid-1960, followed by "Rubber Ball" later that year. One year later, Vee's biggest hit, "Take Good Care of My Baby," spent three weeks at number one, followed by the number two "Run to Him." His fame appeared to wane after the 1962 Top Ten single "The Night Has a Thousand Eyes," due in large part to the success of the Beatles and other English acts. *—John Bush*

• **Legendary Masters** / 1990 / EMI America ♦♦♦♦♦
The most complete collection of Vee's recordings includes "Take Good Care of My Baby," "Rubber Ball," and "The Night Has a Thousand Eyes." *—Kenneth M. Cassidy*

Greatest Hits / Mar. 8, 1994 / Curb ♦♦♦
Ten of his biggest hits, including "Take Good Care of My Baby," "Run to Him," and "Come Back When You Grow Up," for those of you who are in a rush and have no time for nuances like liner notes and low-charting singles. These *are* all original recordings, though the minimal packaging and liner notes on Curb's *Greatest Hits* series might lead you to suspect otherwise. *—Richie Unterberger*

Suzanne Vega

b. Jul. 11, 1959, Santa Monica, CA
Vocals, Guitar / College Rock, Alternative Folk, Contemporary Folk, Adult Alternative Pop/Rock, Singer/Songwriter
Vega was born in Santa Monica, CA, and moved to New York City at age two. She attended the High School of Performing Arts, then Barnard College. Vega was still at Barnard when she began attracting attention at Greenwich Village folk clubs and was featured on several issues of the songwriters' magazine/record album *The CooP* (later *The Fast Folk Musical Magazine*) in 1982. She was signed to A&M Records in 1984 and released her first album, *Suzanne Vega* in 1985. It was a critical success and a moderate seller. Vega's second album, *Solitude Standing*, featured "Luka," a song about child abuse that became a surprise hit single in 1987. The album itself went gold. Vega took three years to release the follow-up, *Days of Open Hand* (1990), which was a commercial disappointment, though a few months later a couple of British DJs, under the name D.N.A., put out a dance version of her a cappella song "Tom's Diner" from the album *Solitude Standing*, and it became a hit.

On her next album, 1992's *99.9° F.*, Vega experimented with the dance rhythms that made "Tom's Diner" a hit; although the result was interesting, it didn't give her any hits. *—William Ruhlmann*

Suzanne Vega / May 1985 / A&M ♦♦♦♦
Though early comparisons were made to Joni Mitchell, Suzanne Vega's true antecedents were Janis Ian and Leonard Cohen. Like Ian, she sings with a precise, frequently half-spoken phrasing that gives her lyrics an intensity that seems to suggest an unsteady control consciously held over emotional chaos. Like Cohen, Vega observes the world in poetic metaphor, her cold urban landscapes reflecting a troubled sense of love and loss. The key track is "Small Blue Thing," in which the singer pictures herself as an object "Like a marble / or an eye," "made of china / made of glass," "lost inside your pocket" and "turning in your hand." The sharply picked acoustic guitar and other isolated musical elements echo the closely observed scenes—everything seems to be in tight closeup and sharp focus. Often, the singer seems to be using the songs to measure an emotional distance; sometimes, as in "Marlene on the Wall," she observes her own actions from a remove. In "Freeze Tag," she tells a companion, "I will be Dietrich / and you can be Dean"; in "Marlene," a poster of the aloof movie star "watches from the wall" observing the singer's succession of lovers, and she tries to emulate her heroine's persona, telling the current one, "Even if I am in love with you / All this to say, what's it to you?" The ten songs on *Suzanne Vega* constitute the self-analysis of a young woman who desires possession without offering commitment; no wonder that, upon its release, it was taken to heart by young women across the country and in Europe. *—William Ruhlmann*

• **Solitude Standing** / Apr. 1987 / A&M ♦♦♦♦♦
The songs on *Solitude Standing*, Suzanne Vega's second album, had years listed beside them on the lyric sheet, so you could see that some of them dated back to 1978. But that bold admission heralded the album's triumph—its diversity was what made it so good. Partially, that was because the old songs were the equal of anything on the first album—tunes like the a cappella slice-of-life "Tom's Diner" and the warmly romantic "Gypsy" simply wouldn't have fit thematically on the debut. On *Solitude Standing*, however, they became part of an album of story songs set in a variety of musical contexts; many had band arrangements, and in fact, members of Vega's touring band often were credited as co-writers. Additionally, Vega had developed more as a singer without losing the focused intonation that had made her debut—one of many compelling elements which helped make "Luka," a character song about domestic abuse, a fluke hit. *—William Ruhlmann*

Days of Open Hand / Apr. 1990 / A&M ♦♦
Suzanne Vega is a beautiful example of an artist excelling despite her limitations. While the singer-songwriter doesn't have much of a voice, she has no problem being incredibly expressive. Subtlety is the quality that defines *Days of Open Hand*, an album every bit as compelling as the superb *Solitude Standing*. Vega doesn't need to shout or preach in order to get her points across. On "Men in a War," the folk-pop-rock explorer examines the plight of disabled veterans without expressing the type of anger that Bruce Cockburn would when addressing such a subject. Restrained and understated, treasures like "Those Whole Girls (Run in Grace)," "Rusted Pipe" and "Room Off the Street" and the unsettling "Institution Green" show that for all their delicacy, Vega's songs can be quite meaty and give listeners a great deal to think about. *—Alex Henderson*

99.9° F. / Sep. 8, 1992 / A&M ♦♦♦
While this is not the techno album that Suzanne Vega was rumored to be making, *99.9° Fahrenheit* does offer a significant departure from her previous contemporary folk albums. Vega uses more synthesizers and drum machines, often evoking a bizarre carnival-esque atmosphere on the album. Still, *99.9° Fahrenheit* is a folk album at heart; every song is steeped in traditional song form, and Vega's writing is strong. Fans of Vega's previous work might be taken aback, but those willing to listen to the album will find that Vega has produced one of her strongest records yet. *—Stephen Thomas Erlewine*

Nine Objects of Desire / Sep. 10, 1996 / A&M ♦♦♦
Under the guidence of producer Mitchell Froom, who produced *99.9 Degrees Fahrenheit* and married her shortly after that album was completed, Suzanne Vega continues to explore more textured and vaguely experimental musical territory on *Nine Objects of Desire*. While it is less bold on the surface than its predecessor—most notably, there are no pseudo-industrial rhythms—*Nine Objects of Desire* still bears all the trademarks of a Mitchell Froom production. There is cheap, garage-yard percussion scattered throughout the record, layered keyboards and overly mannered, arty arrangements. It's not as extreme as Froom's work for Los Lobos, for instance, but it is still more self-consciously pretentious than any of Vega's albums, besides *99.9 Degrees Fahrenheit* Vega's songs manage to cut through the murky production more often than not and while the album doesn't boast her most consistent set of songs, they are on the whole stronger than the ones on her previous record. The songs on *Nine Objects of Desire* are more classically structured and inviting than the ones on its predecessor—it is only the production that keeps the listener at a distance. And that's ironic, since half of these songs rank among Vega's most personal work. *—Stephen Thomas Erlewine*

Best of Suzanne Vega: Tried and True / Dec. 14, 1999 / A&M ♦♦♦♦♦
This excellent overview of Vega's career contains all the hits and a fair sampling from each of her five albums, though *Days of Open Hand* receives a cold shoulder (only "Book of Dreams" represents it here), being a critical and personal failure. The CD as a whole shows that while Vega has stayed fairly consistent as a songwriter, her growth has been marked in the collaborations with various producers, from the spare, simplistic sound stages of Steve Addabbo and Lenny Kaye to the lush metallurgy of Mitchell Froom and Tchad Blake. The collection also features that bane of fans, the exclusive track, necessitating purchasing the CD when one owns all the other material. However, these two new songs—"Book & a Cover" and "Rosemary"—are quality entries in Vega's songbook, and once again feature the production skills of Froom and Blake. *—Ted Mills*

Songs In Red and Gray / 2001 / A&M ♦♦♦♦♦
In musical terms, it is less significant that Mitchell Froom is no longer Suzanne Vega's husband than it is that he is no longer her producer. Although Froom's experimental style helped the singer/songwriter fulfill her desire to expand beyond her folk-pop roots on her fourth and fifth albums, *99 F°* and *Nine Objects of Desire*, his approach actually worked against the material, cluttering her intimate, direct songs with inappropriate percussion tracks and various kinds of sound processing. So, listeners who responded strongly to her first three albums but found the Froom discs off-putting (and there were plenty of them) should be alerted that, sonically, *Songs in Red and Gray* is ready to welcome back old fans. Produced by Rupert Hine, it has the kind of carefully played acoustic guitar work and close-up vocal miking that characterized *Suzanne Vega* and *Solitude Standing*. That makes it easier to appreciate Froom's departure from Vega's personal life as well as her professional one, however. This is very much a divorce album, its songs frequently touching on romantic discord and the resulting fall-out. Vega is both precise and artful in describing the situation. She writes by metaphor, unafraid, on "Machine Ballerina," for example, to mix those metaphors and pile them up. That allows her some emotional distance, but never at the expense of meaning. Her concern with the dissolution of her marriage and its impact on her child is apparent in "Soap and Water" when she sings, "Daddy's a dark riddle/Mama's a headful of bees/you are my little kite /carried away in the wayward breeze," even though the lines make up a succession of metaphors. Her calm, hushed, clear singing only emphasizes the emotional torment the songs trace. The result is an album on a par with her best work. *—William Ruhlmann*

The Vejtables

f. 1964, **db.** 1966
Folk-Rock, Garage Rock, Psychedelic
A footnote of the dawn of San Francisco rock, the Vejtables scraped the bottom of the charts in 1965 with "I Still Love You," a pleasant, poppy folk-rocker. Their pair of singles for the San Francisco-based Autumn label strongly recalled a much poppier Beau Brummels, with their 12-string guitars, folky harmonies, and sparse harmonica. The similarity was quite understandable: The Beau Brummels were not only also from San Francisco, but also on the same label. The Vejtables' chief distinguishing mark and asset was one of the very few female drummers in a mid-'60s rock group, Jan Errico, who also sang and wrote much of their material (including "I Still Love You"). For a group with such a brief lifespan, the Vejtables' history was pretty tangled and twisting. Their tenure at Autumn was rudely interrupted when the label went bust. Errico, who had recorded a bit of solo material at Autumn (under, confusingly, the name of Jan Ashton), joined fellow embryonic S.F. band the Mojo Men, who had also had small hits on Autumn. In April of 1966 the Vejtables' guitarist, Jim Sawyers, joined the Syndicate of Sound, who had just hit it big with "Little Girl." Vejtables vocalist Bob Bailey kept the band going in 1966, however, with constantly shifting lineups. A couple more singles appeared on the Uptown and

Tower labels in 1966, finding the band probing a much more aggressive and psychedelic vein, sounding like an entirely different outfit from the "I Still Love You" lineup. "Feel the Music" was a legitimately outstanding effort from this time. But the band lacked either the songwriting depth or the instrumental finesse of the best acts on the then-burgeoning San Francisco psychedelic scene. The Vejtables finally withered on the vine around the end of 1966. —*Richie Unterberger*

Feel . . . The Vejtables / 1995 / Sundazed ✦✦✦

Although the Vejtables only released a few (very rare) singles in 1965 and 1966, this career retrospective has been fleshed out to album length with the addition of several unissued tracks. The 17 songs span both the folk-rock and psychedelic eras, switching abruptly from their soothing Autumn sides to slashing garage psychedelia. The folk-rock certainly outshines the psychedelic material, which (aside from "Feel the Music") are usually dirgeish and thinly written, the players trying to compensate for the weak songwriting with some too-feverish guitar meandering. Other than a few strong tracks, the Vejtables were really not a terribly interesting group; unless you're a heavy collector of the folk-psychedelic-garage style, the tracks that have surfaced on compilations (such as *Nuggets Vol. 7: Early San Francisco*) should be enough. —*Richie Unterberger*

Velvet Crush

f. 1989, Rhode Island
Indie Pop, Alternative Country-Rock, Power Pop, Alternative Pop/Rock, Pop Underground, Jangle Pop

A classic power-pop band in the tradition of the Raspberries and Big Star, Velvet Crush formed in Rhode Island in 1989, although their roots actually extended west to Champaign, Illinois, where vocalist/bassist Paul Chastain and drummer Ric Menck first met and began performing together. There Menck founded his own small label, Picture Book, on which he and Chastain recorded solo material as well as singles under various group names like the Springfields, Choo Choo Train, the Paint Set and Bag O'Shells. Picture Book also released records by the Milwaukee-based White Sisters, led by guitarist Jeffrey Borchardt, with whom Menck struck up a friendship. When Borchardt eventually moved to Providence, Rhode Island in 1988, he encouraged Menck and Chastain to follow; they did, and Velvet Crush soon began performing their first shows. In 1991, longtime friend Matthew Sweet produced their debut, *In the Presence of Greatness*, a hit with the British music press, the record earned the group a deal with the influential U.K. label Creation. For 1994's *Teenage Symphonies to God* (the title taken from Brian Wilson's description of the music intended for the Beach Boys' legendary *Smile* LP), Velvet Crush enlisted producer Mitch Easter, known for his work with R.E.M. and as the leader of Let's Active. The members of the group also continued working on solo projects, with Menck issuing the solo collection *The Ballad of Ric Menck* in 1996. The long-awaited third Velvet Crush LP, *Heavy Changes*, finally appeared on the band's own Action Musik imprint in 1998. Minus Borchardt, the group resurfaced in 1999 with *Free Expression. Rock Concert* was issued in fall 2000. —*Jason Ankeny*

In the Presence of Greatness / Oct. 18, 1991 / Ringers Lactate ✦✦✦✦✦

Velvet Crush's first and best album was mistakenly lumped in with the then-predominant shoegazer aesthetic upon its release in 1991, thanks to its British release on the shoegazer-central Creation label and the occasional washes of sparkly electric feedback and creamy-smooth harmonies that settle over some of the songs. However, this album, produced by the band and Matthew Sweet (who also added lead guitar and harmonies), is actually a straight-up piece of '90s power pop.

Considerably more electric and driving than Paul Chastain and Ric Menck's '80s recordings under a variety of band names (collected on the albums *Hey Wimpus!* and *The Ballad of Ric Menck*), thanks in large part to the contributions of guitarist Jeffrey Borchardt (confusingly known as Jeffrey Underhill when leading his own concurrent band Honeybunch) and Sweet, *In the Presence of Greatness* sounds like Big Star's *#1 Record* updated for a new decade. The general air of mildly anguished wistfulness is the same, as are the jangly guitars and high harmonies, but Velvet Crush play with a post-punk sprightliness and a less overtly British Invasion-inspired melodic sense.

The album was reissued in a new cover on Chastain and Menck's own Action Musik label in September 2001. The remastered sound is an improvement, but the three bonus tracks, the original "Circling the Sun" and covers of Teenage Fanclub's "Everything Flows" and Jonathan Richman's "She Cracked" are also available on the singles compilation *A Single Odessey* (sic). Folks happy with the original US release on Ringers Lactate or the Creation issue don't need to upgrade. —*Stewart Mason*

● **Teenage Symphonies to God** / Jul. 5, 1994 / Epic ✦✦✦✦✦

Velvet Crush's second album is an old-fashioned pop record: 12 songs in 40 minutes, filled with ultra-melodic guitar hooks and simple, memorable melodies. While it's traditional in form, the music on *Teenage Symphonies to God* isn't retro. Velvet Crush manage to inject a real enthusiasm and freshness in the standard three-minute pop song, whether they're playing originals that sound like forgotten classics ("Time Wraps Around You," "This Life is Killing Me," "My Blank Pages," "Hold Me Up") or forgotten classics themselves (Gene Clark's "Why Not Your Baby" and Matthew Sweet's "Something's Gotta Give"). With a crisp, warm production from Mitch Easter, *Teenage Symphonies to God* is one record that deserves to take its title from Brian Wilson. —*Stephen Thomas Erlewine*

Heavy Changes / 1998 / Action Musik ✦✦✦

Sadly forgoing the lush pop classicism which distinguished the preceding *Teenage Symphonies to God*, the aptly titled *Heavy Changes* is a looser, grittier effort closer in spirit to the early-'70s sound of bands like Badfinger and Big Star; despite the return of producer Mitch Easter, it lacks the effervescence and majesty of Velvet Crush's earlier work, aspiring instead for a noisy rock sound which often overwhelms the group's impeccable

melodies and superb harmonies. The banal, lumbering riffs of cuts like "Fear of Flying"—as well as the guitar solos which dominate seemingly every track—are jarring and most unwelcome, 180 degrees removed from the shimmering pop aesthetic which is Velvet Crush's true strength; there's much of value here, but it's hard to shake the sense that *Heavy Changes* is ultimately something of a wasted opportunity, an attempt to fix something that wasn't broken in the first place. —*Jason Ankeny*

Free Expresion / Oct. 26, 1999 / Bobsled ✦✦✦✦

Enlisting longtime friend Matthew Sweet as producer, Ric Menck and Paul Chastain (both are part of Matthew Sweet's backing band) rebounded greatly to produce one of Velvet Crush's most consistently engaging records with *Free Expression*. While it doesn't have any song as memorable as the hook-filled mania of 1994's "Hold Me Up," this release does expand considerably upon Velvet Crush's sound. The album as a whole is potentially their most consistent and the songs are of uniform quality, probably due to Sweet's production. Some horns are brought in on a few tracks to color the album even more, and, as usual, there are touches of country strewn throughout the song cycle. *Free Expression* proves that Velvet Crush are one of the finer pop acts out today, and that the band deserves more than merely a cult following. —*Jason Damas*

A Single Odessey / Aug. 28, 2001 / Action Musik ✦✦✦

A 20-track, 63-minute compilation named in honor of the Zombies' *Odessey and Oracle*, *A Single Odessey* collects all of the single and EP tracks from Velvet Crush's first 11 years. The chronological progression brings the listener through their sweetly jangly power pop early days that culminated in their excellent debut album, *In the Presence of Greatness*, to the country-tinged middle period of *Teenage Symphonies to God*, and then to the harder-edged material from the latter half of the '90s. Heard in bits and pieces like this, however, the progression sounds less like stylistic and personal development and more like aimless genre-hopping. That said, *A Single Odessey* has plenty of goodies to offer, particularly an excellent set of covers—including impressive takes on Teenage Fanclub's "Everything Flows" and a previously unreleased version of Gene Clark's "Elevator Operator." Paul Chastain and Ric Menck's attempt at the theme song for Tom Hanks' *That Thing You Do*, written and recorded with Mitch Easter, is another gem. This is probably not the best starting point for the Velvet Crush novice, but fans will find plenty to enjoy. —*Stewart Mason*

The Velvet Underground

f. 1964, New York, NY, **db.** 1973
Experimental Rock, Proto-Punk, Rock & Roll

Few rock groups can claim to have broken so much new territory, and maintain such consistent brilliance on record, as the Velvet Underground during their brief lifespan. It was the group's lot to be ahead of, or at least out of step with, their time. The mid-to-late '60s was an era of explosive growth and experimentation in rock, but the Velvets' innovations—which blended the energy of rock with the sonic adventurism of the avant-garde, and introduced a new degree of social realism and sexual kinkiness into rock lyrics—were too abrasive for the mainstream to handle. During their time, the group experienced little commercial success; though they were hugely appreciated by a cult audience and some critics, the larger public treated them with indifference or, occasionally, scorn. The Velvets' music was too important to languish in obscurity, though; their cult only grew larger and larger in the years following their demise, and continues to mushroom today. By the 1980s, they were acknowledged not just as one of the most important rock bands of the '60s, but one of the best of all time, and one whose immense significance cannot be measured by their relatively modest sales. Historians often hail the group for their incalculable influence upon the punk and new wave of subsequent years, and while the Velvets were undoubtedly a key touchstone of the movements, to focus upon these elements of their vision is to only get part of the story. The group were uncompromising in their music and lyrics, to be sure, sometimes espousing a bleakness and primitivism that would inspire alienated singers and songwriters of future generations. But their colorful and oft-grim soundscapes were firmly grounded in strong, well-constructed songs that could be as humanistic and compassionate as they were outrageous and confrontational. The member most responsible for these qualities was guitarist, singer, and songwriter Lou Reed, whose sing-speak vocals and gripping narratives have come to define street-savvy rock & roll. —*Richie Unterberger*

☆ **The Velvet Underground & Nico** / Jan. 1967 / Verve ✦✦✦✦✦

One would be hard pressed to name a rock album whose influence has been as broad and pervasive as *The Velvet Underground and Nico*. While it reportedly took over a decade for the album's sales to crack six figures, glam, punk, new wave, goth, noise, and nearly every other left-of-center rock movement owes an audible debt to this set. While The Velvet Underground had as distinctive a sound as any band, what's most surprising about this album is its diversity. Here, the Velvets dipped their toes into dreamy pop ("Sunday Morning"), tough garage rock ("Waiting for the Man"), stripped-down R&B ("There She Goes Again"), and understated love songs ("I'll Be Your Mirror") when they weren't busy creating sounds without pop precedent. Lou Reed's lyrical exploration of drugs and kinky sex (then risky stuff in film and literature, let alone "teen music") always received the most press attention, but the music Reed, John Cale, Sterling Morrison, and Maureen Tucker played was as radical as the words they accompanied. The bracing discord of "European Son," the troubling beauty of "All Tomorrow's Parties," and the expressive dynamics of "Heroin," all remain as compelling as the day they were recorded. While the significance of Nico's contributions have been debated over the years, she meshes with the band's outlook in that she hardly sounds like a typical rock vocalist, and if Andy Warhol's presence as producer was primarily a matter of signing the checks, his notoriety allowed The Velvet Underground to record their material without compromise, which would have been impossible under most other circumstances. Few rock albums are as important as *The Velvet Underground and Nico*, and fewer still have lost so little of their power to surprise and intrigue more than 30 years after first hitting the racks. *—Mark Deming*

☆ **White Light/White Heat** / Nov. 1967 / Verve ♦♦♦♦♦

The world of pop music was hardly ready for The Velvet Underground's first album when it appeared in the spring of 1967, but while *The Velvet Underground and Nico* sounded like an open challenge to conventional notions of what rock music could sound like (or what it could discuss), 1968's *White Light/White Heat* was a no-holds-barred frontal assault on cultural and aesthetic propriety. Recorded without the input of either Nico or Andy Warhol, *White Light/White Heat* was the purest and rawest document of the key Velvets lineup of Lou Reed, John Cale, Sterling Morrison, and Maureen Tucker, capturing the group at their toughest and most abrasive. The album opens with an open and enthusiastic endorsement of amphetamines (startling even from this group of noted drug enthusiasts), and side one continues with an amusing shaggy-dog story set to a slab of lurching mutant R&B ("The Gift"), a perverse variation on an old folktale ("Lady Godiva's Operation"), and the album's sole "pretty" song, the mildly disquieting "Here She Comes Now." While side one was a good bit darker in tone than the Velvets' first album, side two was where they truly threw down the gauntlet with the manic, free-jazz implosion of "I Heard Her Call My Name" (featuring Reed's guitar work at its most gloriously fractured), and the epic noise jam "Sister Ray," 17 minutes of sex, drugs, violence, and other non-wholesome fun with the loudest rock group in the history of Western Civilization as the house band. *White Light/White Heat* is easily the least accessible of The Velvet Underground's studio albums, but anyone wanting to hear their guitar-mauling tribal frenzy straight with no chaser will love it, and those benighted souls who think of the Velvets as some sort of folk-rock band are advised to crank their stereo up to ten and give side two a spin. *—Mark Deming*

☆ **The Velvet Underground** / 1969 / Verve ♦♦♦♦♦

Upon first release, The Velvet Underground's self-titled third album must have surprised their fans nearly as much as their first two albums shocked the few mainstream music fans who heard them. After testing the limits of how musically and thematically challenging rock could be on *The Velvet Underground and Nico* and *White Light/White Heat*, this 1969 release sounded spare, quiet, and contemplative, as if the previous albums documented some manic speed-fueled party and this was the subdued morning after. (The album's relative calm has often been attributed to the departure of the band's most committed avant-gardist, John Cale, in the fall of 1968, the arrival of new bassist Doug Yule, and the theft of the band's amplifiers shortly before they began recording.) But Lou Reed's lyrical exploration of the demimonde is as keen here as on any album he ever made, while displaying a warmth and compassion he sometimes denied his characters. "Candy Says," "Pale Blue Eyes," and "I'm Set Free" may be more muted in approach than what the band had done in the past, but "What Goes On" and "Beginning to See the Light" made it clear the VU still loved rock & roll, and "The Murder Mystery" (which mixes and matches four separate poetic narratives) is as brave and uncompromising as anything on *White Light/White Heat*. This album sounds less like The Velvet Underground than any of their studio albums, but it's as personal, honest, and moving as anything Lou Reed ever committed to tape. *—Mark Deming*

☆ **Loaded** / 1970 / Warner Brothers ♦♦♦♦♦

After The Velvet Underground cut three albums for the jazz-oriented Verve label that earned them lots of notoriety but negligible sales, the group signed with industry powerhouse Atlantic Records in 1970; label head Ahmet Ertegun supposedly asked Lou Reed to avoid sex and drugs in his songs, and instead focus on making an album "loaded with hits." *Loaded* was the result, and with appropriate irony it turned out to be the first VU album that made any noticeable impact on commercial radio—and also their swan song, with Reed leaving the group shortly before its release. With John Cale long gone from the band, Doug Yule highly prominent (he sings lead on four of the ten tracks), and Maureen Tucker absent on maternity leave, this is hardly a purist's Velvet Underground album. But while Lou Reed always wrote great rock & roll songs with killer hooks, on *Loaded* his tunes were at last given a polished but intelligent production that made them sound like the hits they should have been, and there's no arguing that "Sweet Jane" and "Rock & Roll" are as joyously anthemic as anything he's ever recorded. And if this release generally maintains a tight focus on the sunny side of the VU's personality (or would that be Reed's personality?), "New Age" and "Oh! Sweet Nuthin'" prove he had hardly abandoned his contemplative side, and "Train Around the Bend" is a subtle but revealing metaphor for his weariness with the music business. Sterling Morrison once said of *Loaded*, "It showed that we could have, all along, made truly commercial sounding records," but just as importantly, it proved they could do so without entirely abandoning their musical personality in the process. It's a pity that notion hadn't occurred to anyone a few years earlier. *—Mark Deming*

Live at Max's Kansas City / 1972 / Atlantic ♦♦♦

There's a certain amount of disagreement among Velvet Underground scholars regarding whether or not this album, recorded by Andy Warhol associate and longtime fan Brigid Polk on a portable cassette recorder on August 23, 1970, does in fact document Lou Reed's final appearance with the VU. If this wasn't his last stand with the group, it was certainly close to the end of the line, and while the performance is technically strong, it isn't especially inspired, with Reed sounding more than a bit weary. (At this point, the band was near the end of a three month residency at Max's, doing recording sessions for *Loaded* during the day, a schedule that would tax most performers.) The absence of Maureen Tucker on drums (who was pregnant and sitting out the Max's shows) makes an even bigger difference; the replacement of her steady, tribal pulse in favor of Billy Yule's busy, sometimes sloppy style does these songs no favors. But there are a few lovely moments, including rare live performances of "After Hours" and "Sunday Morning," and Reed and Sterling Morrison lock guitars with their usual authority on "Waiting for the Man" and "Beginning to See the Light." The audio quality isn't great, but given the circumstances it's better than you might expect (it's OK by the standards of an early '70s bootleg), though historical merit seems to be more the issue than high fidelity. And yes, that really is Jim Carroll ordering double Pernods and asking about the availability of Tuinol between songs. Fun for fans, but *1969: Velvet Underground Live* is a much stronger document of this band's onstage prowess. *—Mark Deming*

Squeeze / 1973 / Polydor ♦

After Lou Reed left the Velvet Underground, bassist Doug Yule took control of the group. Retaining the name "The Velvet Underground," Yule assembled several new lineups of the band and toured the U.S. By the time Yule's VU recorded their first album, the band featured Boston-based vocalist Willie Alexander and was playing a set of conventional pop/rock songs. *Squeeze*, the only album recorded with a bastardized version of the Velvet Underground, was released in 1973 to uniformly terrible reviews; Yule broke up the band shortly after its release. Over the years, *Squeeze* has not only become increasingly rare—after all, not many copies of the record were pressed—it has disappeared from the official Velvet Underground discography, and Yule's attempt to prolong the band's career has virtually been forgotten. *—Stephen Thomas Erlewine*

☆ **1969: Velvet Underground Live** / 1974 / Mercury ♦♦♦♦♦

Sadly, outside of a handful of audience tapes of extremely variable fidelity, no one thought to make a live recording of the Velvet Underground during their 1967-1968 peak period with John Cale prodding Lou Reed into remarkable flights of noise rock fancy. However, in 1969 a VU fan who was a recording engineer brought a reel-to-reel tape machine to two shows the band played during an engagement at a club in Dallas called the End of Cole Avenue; a few months later, the band played the Matrix in San Francisco, where a tape machine had been installed into the hall's sound system, and the band was allowed to record their set. Five years later, long after the Velvet Underground had collapsed and Lou Reed's solo career was on the rise, Mercury Records compiled highlights of the Dallas and San Francisco tapes into a two-record set, *1969: Velvet Underground Live*, and it is without question the best (legally released) document of this band's considerable strengths as a live act. Sounding tight, confident, and passionate on every cut, this set finds the band visiting highlights from all four of their studio albums, as well as a handful of previously unreleased numbers. From the delicacy of "New Age" and "I'll Be Your Mirror" to the rave-up energy of "What Goes On" and "White Light/White Heat," *1969: Velvet Underground Live* captures the many sides of their musical personality with commendable skill, and while it isn't their best album, it's one of the best places for a beginner to explore their body of work. (For CD release, Mercury has unfortunately divided it into two separate albums, *1969: Velvet Underground Live, Vol. 1* and *1969: Velvet Underground Live, Vol. 2*; thankfully, bonus tracks have been added to each.) *—Mark Deming*

1969: Velvet Underground Live, Vol. 1 / 1974 / Mercury ♦♦♦♦♦

The Velvet Underground were little more than a rumor when Lou Reed left the band in 1970, but by 1974, thanks to Reed's success as a solo artist, the Velvets had become a bona fide cult item, and that year Mercury Records released a two-record set compiled from tapes from shows in Dallas and San Francisco entitled *1969: Velvet Underground Live*. The album featured a generous 104 minutes of music, and when Mercury reissued it on CD in 1988, rather than edit the material or release a two-CD set, they put out the album as two separate discs. While this seemed like a rather curious move, the album's sequence was such that it divided in half quite cleanly, and while any VU fan will want both volumes, they don't work half bad as individual albums. *1969: Velvet Underground Live, Vol. 1* rocks a bit harder than its counterpart; it opens with a grooving version of "Waiting for My Man," moves on to a rave-up take of "What Goes On" that features some of Lou Reed's finest rhythm guitar work, and closes out with passionate renditions of "Rock & Roll" and "Beginning to See the Light." And where there are a number of ballads on hand (most notably a lovely take of "Lisa Says" and versions of "Sweet Jane" and "New Age" considerably different from those on *Loaded*), they sound just as committed and compelling as the rockers. While the Doug Yule-era edition of the Velvet Underground often gets short shrift from aficionados, the performances on *1969: Velvet Underground Live, Vol. 1* prove this band still had plenty of fire, and was playing at the top of their game. The CD also adds a final bonus track, an unreleased version of "Heroin"; while the same song appears on *Vol. 2*, this recording is a different (and considerably more aggressive) performance. *—Mark Deming*

1969: Velvet Underground Live, Vol. 2 / 1974 / Mercury ♦♦♦♦♦

Maureen Tucker once said that one of her greatest regrets about her tenure in the Velvet Underground is that the band didn't record their shows, and while the live tapes that do survive of the group's performances document an extraordinary band, sadly there aren't very many of them. *1969: Velvet Underground Live*, a two-record set released in 1974, is the best and most compelling (legally released) document of the band's powers in concert, but given its length (over 104 minutes), when Mercury Records reissued the set on CD in 1988, they opted to send it out as two separate single-disc albums, rather than as a two-disc set. The three long songs that open *1969: Velvet Underground Live, Vol. 2* (they were the whole of side three on the vinyl release) capture the Velvets at their most hypnotically beautiful, easing from the slow but dramatic ebb and flow of "Ocean," through the lovely melancholy of "Pale Blue Eyes," into the slow, unbearable build to manic frenzy of "Heroin." The disc's second half finds the band in more conventional but no less satisfying form, shifting back and forth between mid-tempo numbers like "Over You" and "Some Kinda Love" and charging rockers such as "White Light/White Heat" (a fine version of "I Can't Stand It" has been added for the CD issue). While Lou Reed's passionate vocals and guitar work are front and center throughout, the rest of the band is in equally superb form, especially Sterling Morrison, still the finest foil Reed ever had on guitar, and Maureen Tucker, whose subtle, highly musical drumming is at once minimal and superbly intelligent. If you care at all about the Velvet Underground, both volumes of *1969: Velvet Undergound Live* belong in your collection, but *Vol. 2* is the one to get if you want to know how much more this band could do than create bracing noise. *—Mark Deming*

☆ **VU** / 1985 / Verve ✦✦✦✦✦
Composed principally of songs that would have appeared on The Velvets' unreleased fourth MGM album, this is only slightly less impressive than their first three LPs, striking a balance between the searing pre-punk of their first two efforts and the calm eloquence of the third. "Lisa Says," "Ocean," and "Stephanie Says" are some of Reed's greatest ballads; "I Can't Stand It" is one of The Velvets' toughest and best conventional hard rock songs. Some of the other tunes are slight (if engaging) in comparison with The Velvets' prime work. Many of the tracks were re-recorded by Reed on his early solo albums, and in every instance, The Velvets' versions are better. *—Richie Unterberger*

Another View / 1986 / Verve ✦✦✦
After 18 years of having little or no idea of what to do with the Velvet Underground, sometime in 1985 it seems to have suddenly dawned on Verve Records that they had the back catalog of one of America's greatest and most influential rock bands languishing in their vaults, and they began to act accordingly; remastered (and budget-priced) versions of the group's first three albums were released, as well as *VU*, a superb collection of unreleased Velvet Underground tracks, most of which were recorded for a fourth Verve album that never saw the light of day. Commendably, the label went back to their tape archives a year later looking for more VU goodies, and *Another View* was the result. One thing that's obvious from the outset is the cream of the band's unreleased material had already been skimmed off for *VU*, and several of the tracks on *Another View* are rough demos for which the group never even recorded vocals ("Guess I'm Falling in Love," "Ride Into the Sun," and "I'm Gonna Move Right In" all have lyrics, but you don't hear 'em here). And while the non-bootleg emergence of "I Can't Stand It," "Foggy Notion," and "Temptation Inside Your Heart" made *VU* a major addition to the Velvet Underground's catalog, it's unclear how many fans were clamoring for an authorized release of second-string tunes like "Ferryboat Bill" and "Coney Island Steeplechase." But if *Another View* is marginalia, it's marginalia from a truly great band; the rough but rocking takes of "We're Gonna Have a Real Good Time Together" and "Rock & Roll" are great fun, and the two versions of "Hey Mr. Rain" are beautiful explorations of the band's psychedelic undercurrent. *Another View* isn't essential Velvet Underground, but it's still well worth a listen. *—Mark Deming*

● **The Best of the Velvet Underground** / Sep. 1989 / Verve ✦✦✦✦✦
The Best of the Velvet Underground: Words and Music of Lou Reed is a 15-track summary of The Velvets' career, borrowing heavily from the debut (six tracks) and featuring "Sweet Jane" and "Rock & Roll," licensed from Atlantic. *—William Ruhlmann*

What Goes On? / Aug. 9, 1993 / Raven ✦✦✦
An Australian box set covering their enormously influential career, *What Goes On?* covers nearly all of their most famous songs ("The Gift" is missing), but its real strength is in its rarities. Hardcore fans will adore the radio commercials for the band, as well the original mono mixes from *The Velvet Underground & Nico* and the alternate, "closet mixes" of the third album. Because of these tracks, diehard fans will need this box. *—Stephen Thomas Erlewine*

Live MCMXCIII / Oct. 26, 1993 / Warner Brothers ✦✦

☆ **Peel Slowly and See** / Sep. 26, 1995 / Polydor/Chronicles ✦✦✦✦✦
Does this five-CD box set feature an abundance of essential material? Certainly. It has all four of the studio albums released by the Lou Reed-led lineup, and a wealth of previously unreleased goodies. Is it an essential purchase? That depends on your level of fanaticism. Most serious Velvet fans have all four of the core studio albums already (although the third, self-titled LP is presented in its muffled, so-called "closet" mix), and will be most interested in the previously unavailable recordings, which do hold considerable fascination. The entire first disc is devoted to a drummer-less 1965 rehearsal tape in John Cale's loft, with radically different, almost folky run-throughs of most of the important songs from their classic debut, as well as a song that only made it onto Nico's first LP ("Wrap Your Troubles in Dreams"), and one which makes its first appearance anywhere (the Dylanesque "Prominent Men"). Other big bonuses include no less than seven outtakes from *Loaded* and other songs re-done by Reed on his early solo albums. And there are sundry other unreleased live and studio items, highlighted by a scorching live 1967 "Guess I'm Falling in Love" and the 1969 demo "Countess From Hong Kong." There are also highlights from *VU* and *Another View*, longer versions of *Loaded*'s "Sweet Jane" and "New Age," and an 80-page booklet. The thing is, though, that virtually everyone who's interested in this material has already bought the four studio albums, sometimes several times over. A separate release of the two discs or so of truly new material would have been welcomed by the many fans who aren't interested in paying for a five-CD box of stuff when they already have well over half of it. *—Richie Unterberger*

Loaded: Fully Loaded Edition / Feb. 18, 1997 / Rhino ✦✦✦✦✦
This does include the original *Loaded* album, with full-length versions of "Sweet Jane," "Rock & Roll," and "New Age" replacing the earlier edited ones. But that's less than half of the package; the rest of the two-disc, 33-track set is comprised of alternate mixes, alternate takes, and demos of the ten *Loaded* songs, as well as some songs that the group recorded during the *Loaded* era that didn't make it onto that LP. Some of this rare extraneous material surfaced on the *Peel Slowly and See* box, but a good half of this (17 tracks)

was previously unreleased anywhere. Basically, it presents an entirely alternate version of the album, plus more where that came from. Those who aren't serious fans may well want to stick with the regular album release; many of the alternate takes/mixes are only subtly different. There are some real goodies here, though: a Dylanish demo of "I Found a Reason," a clumsy early version of "Sweet Jane," a previously unavailable outtake of "I'm Sticking with You," a more basic demo version of "Rock & Roll," a previously unissued spooky take of "Ocean," and "Love Makes You Feel Ten Feet Tall," the one song on this set that has been previously unreleased by the Velvets in any way, shape, or form (although Reed would do it on his first album as "Love Makes You Feel"). With a lengthy essay by David Fricke, it's fascinating history, and pretty good listening on its own terms. *—Richie Unterberger*

The Ventures

f. 1959, Tacoma, WA
Surf, Instrumental Rock, Rock & Roll
Not the first but definitely the most popular rock instrumental combo, the Ventures scored several hit singles during the 1960s—most notably "Walk-Don't Run" and "Hawaii Five-O"—but made their name in the growing album market, covering hits of the day and organizing LPs linked thematically and musically. The band put their indelible stamp on each style of '60s music they covered, and they covered many—twist, country, pop, spy music, psychedelic, swamp, garage, TV themes. (In the '70s, the Ventures moved on to funk, disco, reggae, soft rock and Latin music.) And though the band's popularity in America virtually disappeared by the 1970s, their enormous contribution to pop culture was far from over; the Ventures soon became one of the most popular rock groups in the world, with dozens of albums recorded especially for the Japanese and European markets. They toured continually throughout the 1970s and '80s—selling 40 million records in Japan alone and influencing Japanese pop music of the time more than they had American music during the '60s. *—John Bush*

The Ventures Play Telstar, The Lonely Bull / Oct. 1962 / Dolton ✦✦✦

Ventures in Space / Aug. 1963 / Dolton ✦✦✦

The Ventures on Stage / May 1965 / Dolton ✦✦✦✦✦
Explosive live recordings from Japan, England, and the U.S., with a hot greatest-hits medley and a wild "Driving Guitars" being among the highlights. *The Ventures on Stage Around the World* is out of print but worth any search. *—Cub Koda*

★ **Walk—Don't Run: The Best of the Ventures** / 1990 / EMI America ✦✦✦✦✦
If one looks hard, there are so many CDs out on the Ventures, covering just about every phase of their history, that it's almost impossible to keep track of which numbers appear in what versions on which disc (and that's not even counting some superb Japanese-issued concert videos), but this is still the single best introduction to their work that one can buy. Starting with their second single (and career-establishing hit), "Walk—Don't Run," the 29 tracks on this CD bookend their history from 1960 through 1969, including every chart entry and also significant albums tracks such as the psychedelic era "Underground Fire," all in excellent sound. Producer Ron Furmanek has remixed most of the cuts from the original multi-tracks, but he's done it true to the originals, with results that transcend the best vinyl copies of much of this material. Understandably, much of the material is weighted toward the early '60s, but the group's hits right up through "Hawaii Five-O" are represented, and Furmanek has even included a few short 1960s-vintage radio spots featuring the band as an extra bonus for fans. *—Bruce Eder*

The Ventures Play Telstar/Ventures in Space / 1992 / EMI America ✦✦✦✦
Capitol released two early Ventures albums, *The Ventures Play Telstar—The Lonely Bull and Others* and *The Ventures in Space*, on one CD in 1992. A Top Ten album for the group in early 1963, *Telstar* really doesn't hold up today. Like many of their LPs, it demonstrates their versatility on faithful covers of a number of contemporary hits, ranging from rock to soul to easy listening. In every case, you're better off with the original versions. Few listeners need to dig deeper than a greatest-hits collection for the Ventures, but the early effort *Ventures in Space* is an arguable exception. The group embellished their trademark sleek guitar instrumentals with creepy, then-futuristic production effects, sounding at times like a mix of surf music and the incidental music to *Star Trek*. The ghostly, theremin-like sounds on several tracks are actually produced by top session player Red Rhodes on steel guitar. The British instrumental group the Tornados (of "Telstar" fame) did this kind of stuff better, if you're looking for this kind of thing. *—Richie Unterberger*

Live in Japan '65 / May 30, 1995 / Capitol ✦✦✦✦✦
Originally released in Japan as a double album, this live set was unavailable in the U.S. until 1995. So cleanly recorded (the drums are especially crisp) that one is tempted to believe these tracks might have actually been laid down in the studios, it has a speedy, frenetic, well-executed edge that makes this worth checking out by Ventures fans. Seventy minutes of material, including most of their big '60s hits, covers of then-contemporary surf and British Invasion tunes, and surprises like "The Pink Panther Theme" and a 10-minute version of Duke Ellington's "Caravan." *—Richie Unterberger*

Tele-Ventures: The Ventures Perform the Great TV Themes / Nov. 12, 1996 / EMI ✦✦

Tom Verlaine

b. 1949, Wilmington, DE
Vocals, Guitar / Alternative Pop/Rock
Famed for his trailblazing work as the singer and guitarist for the seminal New York punk band Television, Tom Verlaine also carved out an acclaimed and eclectic solo career. Born Thomas Miller in Wilmington, Delaware in 1949, Verlaine (who borrowed his name from the French symbolist poet) was trained as a classical pianist, but gravitated toward rock

music after an encounter with the Rolling Stones' "19th Nervous Breakdown." In 1968, he and bassist Richard Meyers (later Richard Hell) moved to New York's Lower East Side, where they and drummer Billy Ficca formed the group the Neon Boys. After the addition of second guitarist Richard Lloyd, the band renamed itself Television.

Beginning with their landmark 1975 debut single "Little Johnny Jewel," Television became one of the most renowned groups on the burgeoning New York underground scene; though lumped together with the punk phenomenon, the band's complex songraft—powered by Verlaine's strangled vocals, oblique lyrics and finely-honed guitar work—clearly set them apart from their peers. However, after only two albums, 1977's classic *Marquee Moon* and the disappointing 1978 follow-up *Adventure*, Television disbanded, and Verlaine started a solo career.

He resurfaced in 1979 with a self-titled debut which featured the song "Kingdom Come," later covered by avowed fan David Bowie. 1981's dense *Dreamtime* earned significant acclaim, and even hit the U.S. album charts. Both 1982's diverse *Words From the Front* and 1984's *Cover* drew raves from the British press, spurring Verlaine to take up residency in London. After a three-year hiatus, he returned with *Flash Light*, regarded as one of his best solo efforts. Following 1990's *The Wonder*, Television briefly reformed for a self-titled album and tour; the group again broke up, however, and in 1992 Verlaine issued his first instrumental LP, *Warm and Cool*. In 1994, he composed the score for the film *Love and a .45*. *—Jason Ankeny*

Tom Verlaine / 1979 / Elektra ♦♦♦♦♦

Tom Verlaine scores a solid winner on his first solo release. Not surprisingly, many of the songs here suggest the music of Television, his former band, especially in the use of vibrant and full guitar textures and frequent solo break sections in which to feature them. Verlaine's fey vocals surprisingly do not detract from the gutsiness of these numbers. Several of the songs here utilize hooky initial guitar riffs in the tradition of 1960s bands like the Rolling Stones, the Kinks, and the Beatles, most notably on "Flash Lightning," "Kingdom Come," and especially "Grip of Love." Two selections, "Red Leaves" and "Mr. Bingo," show mild swamper influence; the former also has subtle psychedelic touches in the chorus, while the latter (when Verlaine's vocal enters) suggests a Lou Reed number. Even more Lou Reed/Velvet Underground-oriented is the lengthy and wonderful "Breakin' in My Heart." "Last Night" is a noble slow-tempo number with unusually noticeable keyboard usage. And "Yonki Time" is a daffy, loping, bluesy selection with bizarre tongue-in-cheek lyrics and quirky production touches—a fun work to hear. This is a top-notch solo debut that bears repeated listenings. *—David Cleary*

• **Dreamtime** / 1981 / Warner Brothers ♦♦♦♦♦

This album serves up another helping of Television-style rocking numbers, featuring a by-now-stereotypical thick and ringing guitar sound. The platter contains chunky rockers such as "Always" (an especially toe-tapping selection) and "Future in Noise," as well as thumping midtempo numbers such as "Penetration" and "Down on the Farm." "The Blue Robe" is for all practical purposes a bluesy instrumental; vocals here enter very late in the selection and consist solely of the chanted phrase "Hi-fi." In general, these songs are decent and solid—but the fact is, they're not deathless music, either. Serious demerits go to the album's anonymous producer, who often allows the instrumental textures to swamp the vocals to the point of near inaudibility, particularly in "There's a Reason" and "Always." This release is not bad; fans will likely be interested, though newcomers to Verlaine's music might consider other albums to be of higher priority. *—David Cleary*

Words from the Front / Jun. 1982 / Warner Brothers ♦♦♦

Tom Verlaine's second solo album, *Dreamtime*, was easily the finest music he'd created since Television's *Marquee Moon*; it was so perfectly realized that one wondered what he could do to top it, and when 1982's *Words From The Front* was released, the obvious answer was that he hadn't—while it's hardly a bad album, the songs don't rank with Verlaine's best work, and though his guitar work is superb as always, he doesn't appear to be breaking much new ground, content for the most part to recycle ideas he'd worked through in the past. Of course, given the sterling quality of Verlaine's work, an album could be quite good and fall below his average, and that's certainly the case here; the butterfly solos on "True Story," the ominous but lyrical wartime tale of the title cut, and the loopy romanticism of "Postcard From Waterloo" are certainly a pleasure to hear. But most of the other tracks sound like Verlaine treading water, and overall the album lacks the cool but steely passion that made *Dreamtime* a high-water mark in his solo career. If you've never heard Tom Verlaine's work, *Words From The Front* may well dazzle you with it's fluid, atmospheric solos and brittle lyricism, but if you're a fan, you'll probably come to the conclusion that he can do better than this. *—Mark Deming*

Cover / 1984 / Warner Brothers ♦♦♦♦♦

Cover is easily Tom Verlaine's best platter since his first solo release. This album sports unusual, yet wonderfully effective and imaginative arrangements which are sparer, leaner, and more intricate than those on his earlier releases. Production values are top-shelf great. "Travelling" is a funk-flavored selection with dry screeching guitar sounds and some later slippery modulations. "Miss Emily" is a rollicking, jumpy number which (despite its quirky vocal and production touches) in places anticipates later-period songs by the Replacements. The other rocking number here is "Lindi-Lu," an uptempo, yet somehow lighter and less crunching selection. "Swim" begins with a spoken voiceover and then morphs into an eccentric, yet somehow expressive neo-1950s song. "Let Go to the Mountain" [sic] is equally quirky, an alternately ethereal/spooky and bouncy/sparkling song. Brian Eno-era Talking Heads is evoked on the kaleidoscopically nervous "Dissolve/Reveal." Most unusual of all is "O Foolish Heart," a synthesizer-dominated (yes, that's right) selection with a noticeable Lou Reed feel. This unusual, yet excellent album is well worth hearing. *—David Cleary*

Flash Light / 1987 / IRS ♦♦♦

The Wonder / 1990 / Fontana ♦♦

Warm and Cool / 1992 / Rykodisc ♦♦♦

The Miller's Tale: A Tom Verlaine Anthology / 1996 / Virgin ♦♦♦♦

The Verlaines

f. 1981, Dunedin, New Zealand

Indie Pop, New Zealand Rock, Alternative Pop/Rock

The literate and dramatic New Zealand guitar-pop band the Verlaines formed in 1981; led by singer/guitarist Graeme Downes, the group's original roster also included guitarist Craig Easton, keyboardist Anita Pillai, bassist Philip Higham and drummer Greg Kerr. Both Easton and Pillai quickly exited, and the Verlaines remained a three-piece for the remainder of the decade; the early lineup remained in a constant state of flux, however, and of the original group only Downes and Kerr remained by the time of their debut on the 1982 *Dunedin Double* compilation EP, recorded with bassist Jane Dodd. Drummer Alan Haig then replaced Kerr for the 1983 single "Death and the Maiden," for many fans the archetypal Verlaines song; the lineup finally cemented with the substitution of Haig for drummer Robbie Yeats, who first appeared on the 1984 EP *10 O'Clock in the Afternoon*.

The Verlaines' full-length debut, 1985's *Hallelujah All the Way Home*, was originally submitted as part of a composition project for Downes' honors-level music class; he received an "A" grade for the record, which bore the heavy influence of his classical background in its exacting compositions, as well as its orchestral and brass flourishes. After the 1986 "Doomsday" single, the Verlaines resurfaced a year later with the excellent *Bird-Dog* LP; a long layoff followed as Downes pursued his Ph.D, and the group—with new bassist Mike Stoodley—did not again appear until the 1990 album *Some Disenchanted Evening*. Yeats departed soon after, and was ultimately replaced by drummer Gregg Cairns. After recording 1991's *Ready to Fly*, the Verlaines swelled to a four-piece with the addition of second guitarist Paul Winders; after Cairns quit, new drummer Darren Stedman was enlisted in time for 1993's *Way Out Where*. Although Downes soon accepted a teaching position at the Auckland Institute of Technology, it was assumed that the Verlaines would continue with business as usual. *—Jason Ankeny*

Hallelujah All the Way Home / 1985 / Homestead ♦♦♦

Hallelujah All the Way Home finds the band looking for a style, somewhat aimlessly. Through epic-length complex compositions, the band sometimes loses its way, but in a few cases (such as "It Was Raining") a glimpse of potential is revealed. Not a great album, but a few very good songs. *—Chris Woodstra*

• **Bird Dog** / 1987 / Homestead ♦♦♦♦♦

Crafty New Zealand pop group lead by song craftsman Graham Downes that leaned heavily toward Baroque classicism on this exquisite collection of tales from 1987. Their art was in the subtlety of arrangements, and the group was pivotal in defining the complex simplicity of the Flying Nun sound alongside the Clean and the Chills. The Verlaines were certainly the first of the family in the '80s to embrace truly classical modality in their delicate pop sound, and the result is *Bird Dog* as a sophisticated and glorious album of Downes' distinct genius, whose only peers would be Robert Forster and Martin Phillips. Although his craft may be fastidious, the Verlaines have mastery of rendering it effortless on *Bird Dog*. Later their sound may have become a little more stilted, but for a group so ahead of their time, anything is forgivable, although many fans of this character and eccentricity displayed here may believe the edge was lost in the '90s when they pursued a straighter MOR sound. With *Hallelujah All the Way Home* and *Some Disenchanted Evening* on either side of this release, it is difficult to think of another group who made three albums of this quality in five years. *—Martin Walters*

Juvenilia / 1987 / Homestead ♦♦♦♦♦

A collection of singles from the band's early career which provides an adequate introduction to The Verlaines' unique style. *—Chris Woodstra*

Some Disenchanted Evening / 1990 / Homestead ♦♦♦

Some Disenchanted Evening returns with an approximation of its predecessor's brilliance. This time the band is more effective on the more traditional straight-ahead rock than on the experiments. While it's not as cohesive an effort, "Jesus What a Jerk" is probably their best pop song to date. *—Chris Woodstra*

Ready to Fly / Jul. 1991 / Slash ♦♦

Way Out Where / Sep. 14, 1993 / Slash ♦♦

Over the Moon / 1997 / Columbia ♦♦♦

A one-time Flying Nun act, Graham Downes' Verlaines produced some of the most sophisticated indie pop of the '80s while on the label, and made it to America all too ahead of their time. With *Over the Moon*, the Los Angeles production replaces the antipodean garage that gave their albums *Bird Dog* and *Hallelujah All the Way Home* such a distinctive character, which highlighted the eccentric songwriting sensibilities of Downes. His only peers in the craft being Go-Betweens frontman Robert Forster and fellow Kiwi Martin Phillips of the Chills for absolute mastery of the art. The collection here has all of the distinctive traits that made the Verlaines so special—quirky lyrics, Baroque string arrangements, and incessant guitar jangle, but somehow *Over the Moon* sounds a little lackluster with time. Ironically, though, it contains some of his most developed lyric writing and arranging skills, proving that it takes more than production trends to overshadow such genius. *—Sylvie Harrison*

Versus

f. 1992

Indie Rock

New York City indie rock favorites Versus evolved from the remnants of Flower, a band led by singer/guitarist Richard Baluyut. In the final months of Flower's existence, the group was joined by vocalist/guitarist Fontaine Toups, who remained with Baluyut in the short-lived Saturnine before the duo formed Versus (borrowing the name from an LP by Mission of Burma) with Baluyut's brother, Ed. After playing their first shows with a line-up comprising three guitars and a drum machine, Ed Baluyut relocated to the Phillipines, and Toups switched over to bass; upon Ed's return, he assumed drumming duties, and Versus issued its 1992 debut single, "Insomnia." In 1993, the trio issued the stellar EP *Let's Electrify!*, a taut, melodic collection spotlighting their intricate, dissonant guitar work and odd harmonies. After signing to the Teenbeat label, Versus issued their 1994 full-length debut, *The Stars Are Insane* (originally titled *Meat, Sports and Rock*, three subjects the band ardently supported, much to the dismay of the prevaling indie-scene mentality of the moment). A collection of singles, compilation tracks and demos titled *Dead Leaves* appeared in 1995, followed in early 1996 by the EP *Deep Red*. Another Baluyut brother, James, signed on for the 1996 LP *Secret Swingers*; the album was also Ed's last, with new drummer Patrick Ramos enlisting for 1998's *Two Cents Plus Tax*. The *Afterglow* EP followed on Merge Records a year later, and in mid-2000 Versus returned with the EP *Shangri-La* and the band's fifth studio effort *Hurrah*. *—Jason Ankeny*

Let's Electrify! / 1993 / Remora ✦✦✦✦✦

Issued on Richard Baluyut's own Remora label, Versus' six-cut opening salvo is the group's most viscerally exciting work; although the sameness of the production prompts the record to wear out its welcome by the closing "Sea Girl," much of *Let's Electrify!* is tense and wonderful—in particular, both the slow-burning "Noogie" and the dive-bombing title track rank among the trio's very best work. An auspicious debut. *—Jason Ankeny*

The Stars Are Insane / 1994 / Teen Beat ✦✦✦

The Stars Are Insane is a record that sticks to the similar jangly pop guitar rock that was common in the mid-'90s. Versus set themselves apart by playing with subtle repetition, dramatic dynamics, and varied instrumental intonation. Distorted guitar and bass play off one another, while the drums set the even tempo. Bass lines create melodies to the rhythm of the distorted guitar, switching from dreamy to a dry rock feel. The drums always have a good backbeat that creeps into the straight beat, changing things up a bit. Richard Baluyut and Fontaine Toups share vocal duties, both adding depths to the music. The vocals are sung with a sadness and pointed edge that brings a new dimension to the punch-ins of distorted guitar to clean tones. The mix of the record is of high quality; it allows you to enjoy both the music and the vocals equally. The songs may be a bit long for some, but they establish catchy grooves and creep a hummable melody in the jams at the end. "Blade of Grass" is the epic highlight of the record. The song is a jangly, three-chord progression with a haunting lead guitar jingle on top. *The Stars Are Insane* has the same pop/rock feel throughout, but if you focus on the individual tracks you will discover new delicate intricacies. *—David Serra*

Dead Leaves / Apr. 25, 1995 / Teen Beat ✦✦✦

Dead Leaves is a collection of singles, outtakes and demos featuring Versus' debut offerings "Insomnia" and "Bright Light" as well as "Tin Foil Star," their stunning contribution to the Simple Machines label's *Working Holiday* series. Energetic but erratic, it's by no means the best introduction to the group, but the abundance of obscure material makes it essential for fans. *—Jason Ankeny*

Deep Red / Mar. 12, 1996 / Teen Beat ✦✦✦

● **Secret Swingers** / Jul. 30, 1996 / Caroline ✦✦✦✦

The addition of second guitarist James Baluyut brings a new, more intricate dimension to the Versus sound on *Secret Swingers*, a superbly textured set more consistent and eclectic than anything else the band has done to date. While the *Deep Red* EP suggested that Versus had painted itself into a songwriting corner, each track here—from the taut "Glitter of Love" to the shimmering "Jealous"—sounds fresh and invigorated. Additionally, the group has learned the value of subtlety: the ethereal "One Million" is lovely, while "Ghost Story" achieves the haunting atmosphere promised by its title. Better still is the majestic "Angels Rush In," in which the point/counterpoint vocals of Richard Baluyut and Fontaine Toups stand firm against a slow-building but ultimately monolithic sound. *—Jason Ankeny*

Two Cents Plus Tax / May 5, 1998 / Caroline ✦✦✦✦

Two Cents Plus Tax continues the subtle refinements of the preceding *Secret Swingers*, moving Versus further away from the visceral indie rock of their earliest efforts toward a more evocative and spacious sound. Foregoing the blistering attack of before, here the group settles into a comparatively gentle, vaguely dreamy drift. Tracks like the opening "Atomic Kid" and "Dumb Fun" still crackle with energy, but at the same time they reflect a new melodic maturity, and are crafted with a greater focus on vocal and instrumental interplay. Similarly, while the brilliant centerpiece "Morning Glory" hits the ground running, as the song progresses it moves in unexpected directions, easing into a lovely atmospheric haze later resurrected for "Radar Follows You" and the sublime "Crazy-Maker (I'm Still in Love with Your Eyes)." And be sure not to miss the goofy hidden bonus cut "Oriental-American," found only by rewinding track one of the CD back to the –4:36 mark. *—Jason Ankeny*

Hurrah / Oct. 3, 2000 / Merge ✦✦

Veruca Salt

f. 1993, Chicago, IL

Grunge, Alternative Pop/Rock

Veruca Salt reshaped the jagged, abrasive punk-pop of the Pixies and Breeders into a more accessible, riff-driven formula that also borrowed from hard pop-rockers like Cheap Trick. Musically and commercially, they were successful, but at the expense of their indie-rock credibility; they became one of the most harshly criticized bands in post-Nirvana alternative rock.

Led by guitarists/vocalists Louise Post and Nina Gordon, and featuring bassist Steve Lack and drummer Jim Shapiro (Gordon's brother), Veruca Salt released their debut single, "Seether"/"All Hail Me," in 1994 on a Chicago-based independent label, Minty Fresh. Produced by Brad Wood (Liz Phair), the record became a word-of-mouth sensation, working its way to alternative and college radio stations.

While supporting Hole on their fall tour, Veruca Salt released their debut album, *American Thighs*, on Minty Fresh, yet they soon cut a deal with Geffen, who re-released the album. "Seether" became an MTV hit as well; however, the group was criticized by magazines and fanzines that claimed the band was derivative and used Minty Fresh as a way to gain credibility. Nevertheless, the group's popularity continued: *American Thighs* went gold, even though its other singles—"Number One Blind" and "All Hail Me"—attracted much less attention than "Seether."

After releasing the Steve Albini-produced, 1996 EP *Blow It Out Your Ass It's Veruca Salt*, the band returned in 1997 with the hard-rock inspired *Eight Arms to Hold You*. Critics' reactions were even more mixed, but the album still reached gold sales status. Rumors that Gordon and Post had been considering solo projects were confirmed in early 1998, when Gordon left the band for a solo career. Post regrouped Veruca Salt as her own project, with a new lineup of guitarist Stephen Fitzpatrick, bassist Suzanne Sokol, and drummer Jimmy Madla, and a new label, Beyond. In 2000, Veruca Salt and Nina Gordon returned with new albums—*Resolver* and *Tonight and the Rest of My Life*, respectively. *—Stephen Thomas Erlewine*

● **American Thighs** / Oct. 25, 1994 / Minty Fresh/DGC ✦✦✦✦

With their thin, sing-song vocals and fuzzed-out guitars, Veruca Salt may sound like the Breeders and the Pixies, but lack either band's talent for inverting pop conventions or taste for the bizarre. What Veruca Salt has instead is a raw talent for simple, infectious pop songs; the result is a surprisingly fresh fusion of alternative pop and bubblegum. Nina Gordon and Louise Post try hard to inject meaning into the sweet, distorted rush of "Seether," but all that sticks is the infectious melody and crushing guitars. That also applies to the slower songs, from the enchanting lust of "Spiderman '79" to "Forsythia," which is too close to the Breeders' *Pod* for comfort. But musically, *American Thighs* is surprisingly satisfying; it's a pure pop album masquerading as the next big thing. *—Stephen Thomas Erlewine*

Blow It out Your Ass It's Veruca Salt / Apr. 1996 / Minty Fresh/DGC ✦✦✦

Blow It Out Your Ass It's Veruca Salt is Veruca Salt's belated attempt for indie credibility. Recorded with Steve Albini, the four-song EP is a noisy, shrieking slice of indie guitar rock, featuring two songs apiece from Nina Gordon and Louise Post. Both of the songwriters contribute one pop song and one dirge-like grind; in both cases, the pop song is superior. However, the pop songs (Gordon's "Shimmer Like a Girl" and Post's "I'm Taking Europe with Me") are masked in shards of noise and screams, which tend to obscure the melodies. But that was the intent of the EP—to prove that Veruca Salt isn't a simpering little pop band. Unfortunately, they are at their best when they have strong, catchy hooks—something "New York Mining Disaster 1996" and "Disinherit" completely lack—and when they try to be nothing but a noise-rock band, they just aren't as powerful. *—Stephen Thomas Erlewine*

Eight Arms to Hold You / Feb. 11, 1997 / Outpost ✦✦✦

In case the AC/DC allusion in the title of *American Thighs* didn't clue you in, the balls-to-the-wall crunch of *Eight Arms to Hold You* makes it clear that Veruca Salt were always closet metal fans. Sure, the album's title was the working title for *Help!*, and there's an endearing love note to David Bowie on the record, but the album couldn't sound further from the British Invasion or gender-bending art-rock if it had been recorded by the Prodigy. Thanks to producer Bob Rock, every song on the record is powered by fully rounded heavy guitars and big, big drums—a sound that went out of style in 1990. Beneath it all, Nina Gordon and Louise Post still have a knack for charming, sing-song melodies, but only occasionally do these songs call for bombastic production. Those that do, like the infectious "Seether" re-write "Volcano Girls," qualify as guilty pleasures, but too often, the songs are buried by heavy guitars, since Veruca Salt sounds awkward when they try to rock out. *—Stephen Thomas Erlewine*

Resolver / May 16, 2000 / Beyond ✦✦✦

Veruca Salt was one of the greatest rock soap operas since Fleetwood Mac or Hüsker Dü, as longtime friends Louise Post and Nina Gordon had a bitter falling out over stolen boyfriends, stabbed backs, and general unpleasantness. Gordon set out on a solo career, while Post dug in her heels, retained the Veruca Salt name, assembled a new band, and recorded the third Veruca album, 2000's *Resolver*. The friendship with Gordon wasn't the only severed relationship Post endured between 1997's *Eight Arms to Hold You* and *Resolver*—she also broke up with Foo Fighters leader Dave Grohl. Now, the title of the record may suggest that she's trying to resolve her feelings toward these breakups, but the album plays as a relentless, unmitigated stream of bile. Never once does Post let up her attack on Gordon and Grohl, except for when it loses a little focus and becomes a vicious attack on the world in general. All of this is set to music that's halfway between *American Thighs* and *Blow it Out Your Ass* and completely dated in 2000. By any conventional yardstick, this does not result in a good album, but it surely is a fascinating listen. There's something unintentionally strange and perverse about the record, like being assaulted by a half-forgotten, half-drunken acquaintance, intent on filling you in on every single excruciating detail of their miserable life—at top volume, no less—after you haven't seen them in years. And it refuses to acknowledge any changes in music since 1994, which makes it even more unsettling and compelling. That is undoubtedly *not* what Louise Post had in mind when she made *Resolver*, but at least she made an album with some character, something that many of her peers can't claim. *—Stephen Thomas Erlewine*

The Verve

f. 1989, Wigan, Lancashire, England, **db.** Apr. 28, 1999

Dream Pop, Space Rock, Neo-Psychedelia, Britpop, Shoegazing, Alternative Pop/Rock, Noise Pop

Long acclaimed among the most innovative and spellbinding bands on the contemporary British pop scene, the Verve finally broke through to the mass international audience in 1997 with the instant classic "Bittersweet Symphony." By no stretch a study in overnight success, the group's rise was instead the culmination of a long, arduous journey which began at the dawn of the decade and went on to encompass a major breakup, lawsuits, and an extensive diet of narcotics; perfecting an oceanic sound fusing the exploratory vision of '60s-era psychedelia with the shimmering atmospherics of the shoegazer aesthetic, the Verve languished in relative obscurity while waiting for the rest of the music world to play catch-up, creating one of the most complex and rewarding bodies of work in modern rock & roll long before most listeners even learned of their existence—only to again fall apart at the peak of their success. Originally formed around vocalist Richard Ashcroft and guitarist Nick McCabe, the band scored with critics and the indie charts with their majestic debut LP, 1993's *A Storm in Heaven*. A lawsuit from the American jazz label also dubbed Verve forced the quartet to officially change their name to "The Verve," and after completing sessions for their 1995 follow-up *A Northern Soul*, Ashcroft exited. He quickly re-assembled the Verve a few weeks later, initially minus McCabe, though the guitarist came back to the fold in early 1997. The result, *Urban Hymns*, was their breakthrough LP, heralded by the smash singles "Bittersweet Symphony" and "The Drugs Don't Work." However, when McCabe pulled out of their 1998 US tour, the group suffered yet another blow, and after months of rumors they officially split the following spring. *—Jason Ankeny*

A Storm in Heaven / Jun. 21, 1993 / Vernon Yard ♦♦♦♦

Whereas future Verve masterpieces *A Northern Soul* and *Urban Hymns* would feature succinct song structures (for the most part) and instantly memorable verses and choruses, the group's 1993 full-length debut, *A Storm in Heaven*, was based on buoyant, extended psychedelic passages. Looking back today, it was an interesting and original musical direction, since at the time, angst-ridden Seattle bands (and their many copycats) were all the rage. While a few songs hint at the Verve's future penchant for composing pop gems ("Make It Till Monday," "Blue," "Butterfly"), many of the longer tracks are just as strong, especially the album's best track, the hauntingly beautiful "Already There." Also featured was the album-opening space rocker "Star Sail," the shifting moods of "Slide Away," the misty "Beautiful Mind," and the stark closer, "See You in the Next One (Have a Good Time)." A fine debut, *A Storm in Heaven* proved to be the important connection between the Verve's expansive early work (1992's self-titled EP) and their later worldwide pop hits. *—Greg Prato*

No Come Down / May 17, 1994 / Vernon Yard ♦♦♦

The Verve had amassed a substantial amount of non-album B-sides from British singles issued in light of their 1993 debut full-length, *A Storm in Heaven*, which remained largely unheard elsewhere in the world. To coincide with a spot on Lollapalooza 1994's second stage, a nine-track compilation of uncommon material was issued Stateside, entitled *No Come Down (B Sides & Outtakes)*. Some of the tracks were already issued on their aforementioned debut and their self-titled five-song EP from 1992, but the versions included here are completely different, such as a nearly ten-minute long live version of "Gravity Grave" from Glastonbury '93, stirring acoustic versions of "Make It Till Monday" and "Butterfly," plus a "USA Mix" of "Blue." The remaining selections are more obscure: the title track that gently opens the album, as well as several other soothing compositions (Where the Geese Go, "6 O' Clock," "One Way to Go," and "Twilight"). While the Verve's early B-sides aren't as exceptional as the ones that were included on the singles for 1995's *A Northern Soul* and '97's *Urban Hymns*, *No Come Down* is still recommended to the serious fan. *—Greg Prato*

A Northern Soul / Jul. 3, 1995 / Vernon Yard ♦♦♦♦♦

Though shorn of the more overtly shoegazer-styled elements of their debut *A Storm in Heaven*, the Verve's sophomore effort *A Northern Soul* is no less epic in scope, forging a heavier, more traditionally psychedelic sound infused with a chaotic energy which mirrors the emotional upheaval at the heart of Richard Ashcroft's songs. Reportedly produced under the influence of excessive drug use, the album is harrowingly intense, its darkly hypnotic momentum steered by Nick McCabe's spiraling guitar leads and Ashcroft's incantatory vocals; tracks like the remarkable "On Your Own," "So It Goes," and the majestically morose "History" are searing evocations of isolation and desperation, soaring yet heartbreaking anthems of disillusionment and loss. *—Jason Ankeny*

● **Urban Hymns** / Sep. 30, 1997 / Virgin ♦♦♦♦♦

Not long after the release of *A Northern Soul*, the Verve imploded due to friction between vocalist Richard Ashcroft and guitarist Nick McCabe. It looked like the band had ended before reaching its full potential, which is part of the reason why their third album, *Urban Hymns*—recorded after the pair patched things up in late 1996—is so remarkable. Much of the record consists of songs Ashcroft had intended for a solo project or a new group, yet *Urban Hymns* unmistakably sounds like the work of a full band, with its sweeping, grandiose soundscapes and sense of purpose. The Verve have toned down their trancy, psychedelic excursions, yet haven't abandoned them—if anything, they sound more muscular than before, whether it's the trippy "Catching the Butterfly" or the pounding "Come On." These powerful, guitar-drenched rockers provide the context for Ashcroft's affecting, string-laden ballads, which give *Urban Hymns* its hurt. The majestic "Bitter Sweet Symphony" and the heartbreaking, country-tinged "The Drugs Don't Work" are an astonishing pair, two anthemic ballads that make the personal universal, thereby sounding like instant classics. They just are the tip of the iceberg—"Sonnet" is a lovely, surprisingly understated ballad, "The Rolling People" has a measured, electric power, and many others match their quality. Although it may run a bit too long for some tastes, *Urban Hymns* is a rich album that revitalizes rock traditions without ever seeming less than contemporary. It is the album the Verve have been striving to make since their formation, and it turns out to be worth all the wait. *—Stephen Thomas Erlewine*

The Vibrators

f. 1976

British Punk, Punk

One of the great myths in rock & roll is that only serious, dedicated musicians can make great records; a philosophical tract dictating that great rock & roll is not the province of bandwagon jumpers, poseurs, fakes and commercially minded trend groupies. The reality is that great rock & roll can be made by anyone, even accidentally. Case in point, the Vibrators. If you saw a photograph of this "punk" band a few months before they signed a label deal with Columbia in 1976, you would have seen long hair, and bell-bottom trousers—they were bloody hippies! But, by the time they released their debut LP, *Pure Mania*, they had short hair, fake leopard-skin pants, safety pins, cheap sunglasses, all the accoutrements a good born-again punk band needed. Did that make them inherently bad? Not really, a tad disingenuous perhaps, but no worse than a punk band (e.g., Generation X) that professed to being real punks all the while secretly harboring the desire of being as commercially viable as the dinosaur bands they purportedly loathed. Sure, *Pure Mania* is a fake through and through, but hating it for that reason alone makes you the boring old fart. Besides, the speedy guitars, irresistible hooks and snappy songs are infectious. *—John Dougan*

Pure Mania / 1977 / Columbia ♦♦♦♦♦

Were the Vibrators real punks? Maybe not, but then again, were the Stranglers? Or Eddie and the Hot Rods? Even more to the point, was Steve Jones? Plenty of rock careerists jumped onto the punk/new wave bandwagon in the wake of the Sex Pistols' success (and more than a few folks, like Jones, stumbled into the new movement by accident), but unlike most of them, the Vibrators took to the fast/loud/stripped down thing like ducks to water, and both Knox (aka Ian Carnarchan) and Pat Collier had a genius for writing short, punchy songs with sneering melody lines and gutsy guitar breaks. If the Vibrators were into punk as a musical rather than a sociopolitical movement, it's obvious that they liked the music very much, and on that level their debut album stands the test of time quite well. *Pure Mania* boasts a bit more polish (and less politics) than many of the albums from punk's first graduating class (such as *Damned Damned Damned* or *The Clash*), but if you're looking for a strong, satisfying shot of chugging four-square punk, cue up "Yeah Yeah Yeah," "No Heart," "Petrol," or "Wrecked on You" and you'll be thrown into a gleeful pogo frenzy. Maybe *Pure Mania* isn't purist's punk, but it's pure rock & roll, and there's nothing wrong with that. *—Mark Deming*

V2 / 1978 / Epic ♦♦♦

As in their first album, *V2* shows the Vibrators taking the driving energy of punk and applying it to songs that have a subtle, pop-like quality; while it does not have the wonderfully brash and itchy cohesiveness of *Pure Mania*, it's a solid album well worth hearing. The songs are mostly catchy and listenable, the lyrics are as capable as those in the group's previous release, and the arrangements have much more variety and color than most punk records of the time do. "24 Hour People" sports Chuck Berry-style guitar licks and 1960s-derived backing vocals, "Public Enemy No. 1" and "Fall in Love" are less punky and more straightforward rockers, "Feel Alright" has a 1960s garage band-style chorus, and "Nazi Baby" audaciously adds strings to the fast, almost danceable music. The only really ineffective excursion on this album is "Troops of Tomorrow," a slow, menacing number that somehow gets too thick for its own good and is further marred by an excessively lengthy opening section. *—David Cleary*

Batteries Included / 1980 / CBS ♦♦♦♦♦

The first of several Vibrators compilation albums, this one has the advantage of concentrating heavily on the group's first two albums (with the exception of a couple of bonus cuts). If you think punk was just the Sex Pistols and the Clash, then you're missing out on a lot of fun. And the title is quite funny, too. *—Alex Ogg*

Guilty / 1983 / Anagram ♦♦♦

After Knox's unguarded comments about starting a solo career had ensured the death of the original Vibrators in 1980, they seemed destined to be remembered as underachieving also-rans from punk's first wave. However, in 1982 bass player Pat Collier, who had established the highly successful studio enterprise Alaska 127, decided to get the old gang back together, putting out a call to fellow original members John Ellis, Knox, and Eddie. Knox recalls the spirit behind the reunion: "They were initially saying, 'Oh, we can knock out any old rubbish and make some money.' But I said that we couldn't really; we had a history for being a good band, so we had to write good material." One thing his fellow band members did impress on Knox was that they wanted an equal share in songwriting. Not a good idea—the resulting *Guilty* suffers from a lot of uneven compositions. *—Alex Ogg*

Alaska 127 / 1984 / Ram ✦✦✦

The Vibrators' second album following their 1982 reunion. The title was taken from producer Pat Collier's studio, which had become their adopted home. It's actually a much better affair than its predecessor, *Guilty*. "Amphetamine Blue" starts things off and is typical of the 12 committed punk-pop efforts on display here. Sadly, there were precious few people prepared to take the Vibrators seriously the first time around; there were next to none now. —*Alex Ogg*

Fifth Amendment / 1985 / Ram ✦✦

The Power of Money: The Best of the Vibrators / Dec. 1991 / Continuum ✦✦✦

The title says it all. These are re-recorded versions of the Vibrators best tunes, performed by the '90s incarnation of the band. Buyer beware. —*Sean Westergaard*

The Independent Punk Singles / 1996 / Anagram ✦✦✦✦

The Vibrators, much maligned, often wholly dismissed, were nevertheless one of the better U.K. punk bands. Above and beyond anything else, they released a series of great singles—the real marker and currency of punk rock, lest we forget it in this era of digital archiving. This CD, presented in a nice chronological package, contains all of the group's post-reunion work with Cherry Red subsidiary Anagram, which began with 1982's "Baby Baby." Some may not consider that their peak, but there's some good stuff here. —*Alex Ogg*

● **We Vibrate: The Best of the Vibrators** / Aug. 19, 1997 / Cleopatra ✦✦✦✦✦

The title is deceptive. Though all the best early Vibrators tracks do appear here, from "Baby Baby" to "London Girls," these are not the famous, original 1977-1978 zippy punk versions. Instead, these 16 tracks are made up of 1991 re-recordings, 1977 demos, and live renditions from a 1977 London Marquee gig. On the other hand, those who were searching for a real best-of probably already found one of the greatest-hits collections that have already emerged, such as 1980's *Batteries Included* (issued on import when they initially split) or the reissued original LPs: 1977's *Pure Mania* and 1978's *V2*. Thus, for the demos and live stuff, this disc is somewhat more valuable than another oldies collection (newcomers, don't start here). The demos are rough and ready, and the in-concert looks at the exceptional "I Need a Slave," "Stiff Little Fingers" (an early B-side from which the Irish greats took their name), and "Whips and Furs" make this a viable purchase. Vintage U.K. punk was rarely this fun, funny, amphetamine-silly, and riffing-perfect, and it comes back in these versions. —*Jack Rabid, The Big Takeover*

Village People

f. 1977, New York, NY
Disco

Part clever concept, part exaggerated camp act, the Village People were worldwide sensations during disco's heyday and keep reviving like the phoenix. Producer Jacques Morali in 1977 assembled a group designed to attract gay audiences while parodying (some claimed exploiting) that same constituency's stereotypes. Songwriters Phil Hurtt and Peter Whitehead were tabbed to compose songs with gay underpinnings, and roles and costumes were carefully selected; among them were a cowboy, biker, soldier, policeman, and construction worker complete with hard hat. The group clicked first in England with the single "San Francisco (You Got Me)" in 1977, then reaped stateside honors with "Macho Man" in 1978. "Y.M.C.A." and "In the Navy" were worldwide smashes, both peaking at number two on the pop charts. After two more successful singles, "Go West" and "Can't Stop the Music," the group's fortunes plummeted, in large part due to their participation in the ill-fated film also titled *Can't Stop the Music*. —*Ron Wynn*

● **The Best of the Village People** / Mar. 22, 1994 / Casablanca ✦✦✦✦✦

Casablanca's *The Best of the Village People* is nearly identical to Rhino's *Greatest Hits*, since it contains all of the big hits, plus a similar selection of club hits. This 14-track collection contains only one remix ("Y.M.C.A.," which is also present in its original single version) and substitutes "Key West" for "Sodom and Gomorrah," and it also includes "In Hollywood (Everybody Is a Star)." These are such slight differences that the collection will be just as appealing as Rhino's to most fans, and both are first-rate retrospectives. —*Stephen Thomas Erlewine*

20th Century Masters—The Millennium Collection: The Best of the Village People / Aug. 21, 2001 / Mercury ✦✦✦✦

Gene Vincent

b. Feb. 11, 1935, Norfolk, VA, d. Oct. 12, 1971, Los Angeles, CA
Vocals / Rockabilly, Rock & Roll

Gene Vincent only had one really big hit, "Be Bop A Lula," which epitomized rockabilly at its prime in 1956 with its sharp guitar breaks, spare snare drums, fluttering echo, and breathless, sexy vocals. Yet his place as one of the great early rock & roll singers is secure, backed up by a wealth of fine smaller hits and non-hits that rate among the best rockabilly of all time. The leather-clad, limping, greasy-haired singer was also one of rock's original bad boys, lionized by romanticists of past and present generations attracted to his primitive, sometimes savage style and indomitable spirit. Vincent's backing unit the Blue Caps were one of the greatest rock bands of the '50s, anchored at first by the stunning silvery, faster-than-light guitar leads of Cliff Gallup. The slap-back echo of "Be-Bop-A-Lula," combined with Gene's swooping vocals, led many to mistake the singer for Elvis when the record first hit the airwaves in mid-1956, on its way to the Top Ten. Brilliant follow-ups like "Race with the Devil," "Bluejean Bop," and "B-I-Bickey, Bi, Bo-Bo-Go" failed to click in nearly as big a way, although these too are emblematic of rockabilly at its most exuberant and powerful. By the end of 1956, the Blue Caps were beginning to undergo the first of constant personnel changes that would continue throughout the '50s, the most crucial loss being the departure of Gallup. The 35 or so

tracks he cut with the band—many of which showed up only on albums or B-sides—were unquestionably Vincent's greatest work, as his subsequent recordings would never again capture their pristine clarity and uninhibited spontaneity. —*Richie Unterberger*

Bop That Just Won't Stop / 1974 / Capitol ✦✦✦✦✦

A good distillation of 12 of Vincent's best early tracks. Subsequent compilations have included this material and much more. But this is one of the most consistent of the lot, eliminating a lot of the average stuff and focusing exclusively on tracks cut with the band's first and best lineup (with guitarist Cliff Gallup). Beware of later editions of the LP that, inexcusably, eliminated a couple of the better songs. —*Richie Unterberger*

Greatest Hits / 1982 / Onyx Classix ✦✦

The bare bones of Vincent's best work, with ten tracks including "Be-Bop-A-Lula," "Lotta Lovin'," "Bluejean Bop," and "Race with the Devil." It gets a comparably low rating not for the quality of the music (which is good), but its brevity. There's a much more thorough, slightly more expensive Gene Vincent best-of available (on Capitol) that can be found with a minimum of effort. —*Richie Unterberger*

The Capitol Years 1956-63 / 1987 / Charly ✦✦✦✦

While Vincent recorded a fair number of overlooked gems during his prime, he also cut a greater number of uninspired tracks. This lavishly packaged and exhaustively annotated ten-album set inadvertently charts the rapidly plummeting quality of his recordings, even as it unearths worthy obscurities. It does manage to gather all of his classic 1956 sessions with guitarist Cliff Gallup in the same place, but Gene's subsequent efforts could have easily been boiled down to a supplementary disc or two. —*Richie Unterberger*

Capitol Collectors Series / 1990 / Capitol ✦✦✦✦✦

Breathless, unintelligible, and spirited rockabilly at its non-Sun best, this 21-track compilation covers Vincent's Capitol recordings (including "Be-Bop-A-Lula," "Race with the Devil," and "Lotta Lovin'") in admirable form. —*Hank Davis & Stephen Thomas Erlewine*

Gene Vincent Box Set / 1994 / EMI ✦✦✦✦✦

Six CDs containing the complete Capitol and EMI-Columbia recordings by Vincent, from 1956 through 1964. The 151 tracks may seem excessive, but the sound glitters, and since most of the post-1962 material was never issued in the United States, this stuff could be revelatory to serious fans. And the booklet is filled with detailed notes, sessionographies, and great photos. —*Bruce Eder*

★ **The Screaming End: The Best of Gene Vincent** / Jan. 21, 1997 / Razor & Tie ✦✦✦✦✦

The Screaming End: The Best Of Gene Vincent & His Blue Caps contains 20 of Gene Vincent's very best songs, including all of his hit singles ("Be Bop A Lula," "Race With the Devil," "Lotta Lovin'," "Wear My Ring," "Dance to the Bop") and several lesser-known but equally exciting singles and album tracks ("Bluejean Bop," "Crazy Legs," "Cruisin'," "Cat Man," "Who Slapped John," "Jump Back, Honey, Jump Back," "B-I-Bickey Bi, Bo-Bo Go," "Red Blue Jeans & a Ponytail"). *The Screaming End* may have one less song than *Capitol Collectors Series*, but it contains a stronger selection of material and the original mixes, plus a more infectious, listenable sequence, making it the definitive single-disc overview of this rock & roll pioneer. —*Stephen Thomas Erlewine*

Violent Femmes

f. 1982, Milwaukee, WI
College Rock, Post-Punk, New Wave, Alternative Pop/Rock

The textbook American cult band of the 1980s, the Violent Femmes captured the essence of teen angst with remarkable precision; raw and jittery, the trio's music found little commercial success but nonetheless emerged as the soundtrack for the lives of troubled adolescents the world over. The Violent Femmes formed in Milwaukee, WI in the early '80s, and comprised singer/guitarist Gordon Gano, bassist Brian Ritchie and percussionist Victor DeLorenzo; Ritchie originated the band's oxymoronic name, adopting the word "femme" from the Milwaukee area's slang for wimps. The trio signed to Slash and issued their self-titled 1983 debut, a melodic folk-punk collection which struck an obvious chord with young listeners who felt a strong connection to bitter, frustrated songs like "Blister in the Sun," "Kiss Off" and "Add It Up." Though never a chart hit, the album remained a rite of passage for succeeding generations of teen outsiders, and after close to a decade in release it achieved platinum status. With 1984's *Hallowed Ground*, Gano's lyrics began to reflect his devout Baptist upbringing, while the group's music approached more traditional folk and country structures; 1986's *The Blind Leading the Naked* advanced towards a more mainstream sound; a cover of the T. Rex chestnut "Children of the Revolution" even became a minor hit. —*Jason Ankeny*

★ **Violent Femmes** / 1983 / Slash/Rhino ✦✦✦✦✦

One of the most distinctive records of the early alternative movement and an enduring cult classic, *Violent Femmes* weds the geeky, child-man persona of Jonathan Richman and the tense, jittery, hyperactive feel of new wave in an unlikely context: raw, amateurish acoustic folk-rock. The music also owes something to the Modern Lovers' minimalism, but powered by Brian Ritchie's busy acoustic bass riffing and the urgency and wild abandon of punk rock, the Femmes forged a sound all their own. Still, the main reason *Violent Femmes* became the preferred soundtrack for the lives of many an angst-ridden teenager is lead singer and songwriter Gordon Gano. Naive and childish one minute, bitterly frustrated and rebellious the next, Gano's vocals perfectly captured the contradictions of adolescence and the difficulties of making the transition to adulthood. Clever lyrical flourishes didn't hurt either; while "Blister In the Sun" has deservedly become a standard, "Kiss Off"'s chant-along "count-up" section, "Add It Up"'s escalating "Why can't I get just one..." couplets, and "Gimme the Car"'s profanity-obscuring guitar bends ensured that Gano's intensely vulnerable confessions of despair and maladjustment came off as catchy and humorous as well. Even if the songwriting slips a bit on occasion, Gano's personality keeps the music engaging and compelling without overindulging in his seemingly willful naiveté. For the remainder of their career, the group would only approach this level in isolated moments. *—Steve Huey*

Hallowed Ground / 1985 / Slash/Rhino ♦♦♦
Though mistaken for a parody when it was released, *Hallowed Ground* features Gordon Gano's serious Christian convictions. The teenage angst is pushed aside on this more mature effort based, for the most part, in traditional American folk—of course, it's slightly skewed. *—Chris Woodstra*

Blind Leading the Naked / 1986 / Slash ♦♦♦♦♦
A more mainstream effort courtesy of producer Jerry Harrison (Talking Heads). Gano returns to his troubled teen persona and the band rocks harder than on the previous two releases. A nice cover of the T-Rex classic "Children of the Revolution" and the yearning "I Held Her in My Arms," complete with a horn section, are highlights. *—Chris Woodstra*

3 / 1989 / Slash ♦♦
The fourth album finds the band in somewhat of a rut creatively. Fans of the band's early days will appreciate the slightly stripped-back acoustic production but, without much energy and less focus on teen angst, the album falls flat in most places. Only the single, "Nightmares" and the confessional "See My Ships" leave any lasting impression. *—Chris Woodstra*

Debacle: The First Decade / 1991 / Slash ♦♦♦♦♦
This album is a compilation of all of their best recordings. Even though it contains a variety of The Femmes' changes in style, it doesn't live up to the standards of their first release. Still, enough highlights are covered to make this album the only other Violent Femmes album you'll need. *—Meredith Erlewine*

Why Do Birds Sing? / Apr. 30, 1991 / Reprise ♦♦♦
After a several-year absence, the Femmes make a comeback of sorts with the charming *Why Do Birds Sing?* Returning to their street-busking roots, the band plays stripped-back acoustic songs as a three-piece. Though they can't fight the fact that they have grown up, the songs show that they can still have fun. *—Chris Woodstra*

Add It Up (1981-1993) / Sep. 14, 1993 / Slash/Reprise ♦♦♦♦♦
Add It Up is not quite the definitive Violent Femmes compilation one might hope for, even if it does feature 23 tracks and adds essential later items missing from their first comp, *Debacle: The First Decade.* There are several charming rarities to hook dedicated fans, who will likely find several favorites missing (perhaps another song or two could have been substituted for the between-song bits). The group's self-titled debut does a better job of encapsulating why they were important, and remains the first Femmes album to buy; besides, no compilation that includes live versions of "Kiss Off" and "Add It Up" in place of the original studio cuts can claim to be definitive. However, even casual fans who enjoyed *Violent Femmes* will find post-debut songs like "American Music" and "I Held Her In My Arms" to be essential, so even if *Add It Up* is a little too imperfect to be a necessary first purchase, it's definitely a necessary second purchase. Unless you're a diehard fan, it will likely be the only other Violent Femmes disc you'll need. *—Steve Huey*

New Times / May 17, 1994 / Elektra ♦♦

Rock!!!!! / Jun. 30, 1998 / Cold Front ♦♦

Viva Wisconsin / Nov. 23, 1999 / Beyond ♦♦♦♦
Few bands have captured the angst, sexual frustration, and repressed rage of the '80s and '90s better than the Violent Femmes. Without falling prey to death, breakups, and commercial overexposure, the Femmes have maintained their simmering intensity with an ever-growing loyal fan base of former punks, Generation Xers, and their younger brothers and sisters. The Wisconsin trio captures nearly two decades of post-punk smarminess with *Viva Wisconsin,* a live retrospective recorded during a one-week tour of their home state in October 1998 that boasts a depth of song choices and performances. Whether playing their best-known hits or lesser-known classics, the band delivers great live performances with largely nothing more than the acoustic bass, drums, and guitar they are known for. The alternative radio staples "Blister in the Sun," "Gone Daddy Gone," and "Kiss Off" are here, of course, but longtime fans and new initiates will love the variety of songs spanning the bands' career. Dark gems like the twisted sagas "Country Death Song," "Gimme the Car," and "Hallowed Ground" showcase singer/songwriter Gordon Gano's capacity for spinning haunting tales. Creepy anthems of alienation like "Prove My Love" and "Confessions" show off the trio's musical virtuosity. Fans love the Femmes for their ability to merge punk, rockabilly, and roots rock with pain-ridden lyrics and pissed-off vibes. Their best anthems, like "American Music," "Black Girls," and the sublime "Add It Up" are played here with crackling intensity. This collection is a must for Femmes fans and a great way to introduce casual fans to the band's body of work. *—Theresa E. LaVeck*

Freak Magnet / Feb. 22, 2000 / Beyond ♦♦♦
The Violent Femmes' first album of new material to be released in the U.S. since 1994's muddled *New Times* (not counting the 1995 Australian import *Rock!!!*, reissued domestically in 1998), *Freak Magnet* is a pleasant surprise in its focus and consistency, marking yet another return to the group's folk-punk roots—the punk side of the equation in particular. Gordon Gano plays electric guitar for much (though not all) of the record, turning in a series of concise, catchy pop nuggets punctuated by a romp through free-jazz saxophonist Albert Ayler's R&B tune "New Generation." Although *Freak Magnet* doesn't really break new ground for the Femmes, it's a neat encapsulation of the most effective variations on their signature sound, featuring misfit anthems (the title track, "I'm Bad"), plaintive heartache ballads ("All I Want"), thrashy punk-pop ("Sleepwalkin'," "Mosh Pit"), gospel ("Rejoice and Be Happy"), and folk-pop ("Forbidden"). There's a bit of filler here, but it's agreeable and good-humored, and the memorable moments outweigh it by a wide margin. *Freak Magnet* isn't really an artistic rebirth for the Femmes, but it is a good, solid album and a welcome return to form. *—Steve Huey*

Visage

f. 1978, London, England, **db.** 1984
New Romantic, New Wave, Electronic
Pioneers of the New Romantic movement, the synth-pop group Visage emerged in 1978 from the London club Billy's, a neo-glam nightspot which stood in stark contrast to the prevailing punk mentality of the moment. Spearheading Billy's ultra-chic clientele were Steve Strange, a former member of the punk band the Moors Murderers, as well as DJ Rusty Egan, onetime drummer with the Rich Kids; seeking to record music of their own to fit in with the club's regular playlist (a steady diet of David Bowie, Kraftwerk and Roxy Music), Strange and Egan were offered studio time by another Rich Kids alum, guitarist Midge Ure. In late 1978, this trio recorded a demo which yielded the first Visage single, an aptly-futuristic cover of Zager & Evans' "In the Year 2525."

Adding Ultravox keyboardist Billy Currie as well as three members of Magazine—bassist Barry Adamson, guitarist John McGeoch, and keyboardist Dave Formula—Visage signed to Radar Records to release "Tar" in September 1979, followed a year later by their self-titled debut LP. The album yielded a major single in "Fade to Grey," an instant club classic which heralded synth-pop's imminent commercial breakthrough. The follow-up, "Mind of a Toy," was a Top 20 hit, but after releasing 1982's *The Anvil,* Visage began to disintegrate—first Ure exited to focus all of his energies on fronting Ultravox, then Currie and Formula broke ranks as well. 1984's *Beat Boys* was the group's final recording, although a remixed "Fade to Grey" was a UK Top 40 hit during the early '90s. *—Jason Ankeny*

Visage / Nov. 10, 1980 / One Way ♦♦♦

The Anvil / Mar. 8, 1982 / One Way ♦♦♦

Visage/The Anvil / 1983 / Polydor ♦♦♦♦♦
Polydor combined Visage's first two (and best) albums, *Visage* and *The Anvil,* on one cassette in the early '80s. It's not a bad way to collect all of this music at once, but the packaging and sound are a little shabby, and since it's out-of-print and quite rare anyway, it's best to go for the collection. *—Stephen Thomas Erlewine*

Beat Boy / 1984 / Polydor ♦♦
The third and final album from new romantic icons Visage found foppish frontman Steve Strange and drummer Rusty Egan almost completely without most of the high-profile sidemen—like Midge Ure, keyboardist Billy Currie and bassist Barry Adamson—who'd played such a big role in crafting the group's lush, haunting synth pop. Undeterred, Strange and Egan recruited a new lineup that gave a prominent role to saxophonist Gary Barnacle. But the real shock to fans was the shrieking, metallic guitar that appeared on most cuts, an intrusion that seemed completely at odds with the suave, continental image suggested by past hits like "Fade to Grey" and "The Damned Don't Cry." In fact, the guitar muscle worked surprisingly well when simply overlaid atop the group's familiar dance pulse, as on the title track and "The Promise." But straight-up rockers like the endless "Only the Good (Die Young)" and "Casualty" featured a lethal combination of ham-handed riffs and dumb lyrics, thoroughly alienating the blitz kids who'd once packed the London discos Strange and Egan ran. Those fans made a club hit of the melodic "Love Glove," the closest thing here to Visage's classic sound, but ignored the rest, making *Beat Boy* a disappointing swan song for the group. Yet despite the uneven songwriting, hindsight showed that Strange's ear for the next big trend hadn't deserted him. The next year, the success of Duran Duran offshoot the Power Station had synth poppers on both sides of the Atlantic scurrying to rough up their dance tracks with heavy guitar. Perhaps in this case, the colorfully-costumed Strange—who later displayed his sartorial sense in a new band, Strange Cruise, before largely bowing out of the music biz—was just too far in front of the fashion curve. *—Dan LeRoy*

● **Fade to Grey: The Singles Collection** / Feb. 22, 1994 / Polydor ♦♦♦♦♦
Fade to Grey includes the best of the band's Kraftwerk-inspired, post-disco synth-pop like "Fade to Grey" (of course), "Damned Don't Cry," "The Anvil" and "Night Train," as well as their cover of the Zager & Evans chestnut "In the Year 2525." There are only 12 tracks, but since it's the only collection available, it'll have to do. *—John Bush*

Vitamin C (Colleen Fitzpatrick)

Vocals / Teen Pop, Club/Dance, Dance-Pop
Vitamin C was the dance-pop alias of singer Colleen Fitzpatrick, the onetime frontwoman of the punk-pop band Eve's Plum as well as an actress whose resume includes performances in films including *Hairspray, The Naked Gun 2 1/2, Liar Liar* and *Dracula 2000.* Vitamin C's self-titled debut album appeared on Elektra in mid-1999, launching the summer hit "Smile." The sophomore effort *More,* which was issued after her monumental success with the summer single "Graduation," appeared in late 2000. *—Jason Ankeny*

● **Vitamin C** / Aug. 24, 1999 / Elektra ♦♦♦♦
Vitamin C is the nom de plume for singer Colleen Fitzpatrick who fronted Eve's Plum for two very good, and overlooked, albums released by 550 Music in the mid-'90s. Here, she steps out on her own for a self-titled solo debut that is every bit as engaging as those two releases and more so. The album shows a wider range stylistically from Fitzpatrick than she did with her former band, and the result is a stunning collection that mixes pop, alternative and dance music. Jamaican dancehall diva Lady Saw guests on the single "Smile," which fuses dancehall and alternapop to good effect on the opening track. There is no shortage of hooks on *Vitamin C.* "Turn Me On" is raucous pop with quiet spoken passages and a neat lyrical twist, and "Me, Myself and I" cops the vibe of War's "Lowrider." Fitzpatrick adopts a breathy delivery over electronic bursts and a hammering drumbeat

on "Not that Kind of Girl." She gets funky on "Do What You Want to Do" and explores role reversal on the electro-pop of "Girls Against the Boys." And just when it seems that she can't pull on more hooks from her bag of tricks, Fitzpatrick delivers the provocatively playful "About Last Night" and the nostalgic, string-laced "Graduation (Friends Forever)." She even takes an admirable stab at the Split Enz classic "I Got You." There's not a weak track on this stellar record. — *Tom Demalon*

More / Nov. 21, 2000 / Elektra ✦✦✦✦

Vitamin C's first album was pitched directly at junior-high and high-school kids, to the point that its breakthrough single, "Graduation (Friends Forever)," was pumped full of yearbook clichés. Perhaps it shouldn't be a surprise that she wanted to spice up her image with her second album, *More*, adding a little more sex and sophistication—two things that are only appropriate for a singer closing in on 30. While the title implies this is another ride on the teen pop merry-go-round, *More* winds up having more style and substance than its predecessor. Vitamin C isn't afraid to be either slyly witty or to celebrate her new wave roots, not just on the cover of the Waitresses' "I Know What Boys Like," but in the general frothy, synthesized approach of the entire album (highlighted by the near-robotic vocals on "She Talks About Love"). Much of this music is lightweight, but deliberately so, and, at its best, such as "Dangerous Girl," its bright, shiny attitude is utterly giddy. Vitamin C isn't content on making effervescent, featherweight pop singles; she wants to sex it up a bit, vamping on occasion (such as on the lead single, "The Itch"), and, with "Sex Has Come Between Us," she gives into a platonic friendship turned romantic (unlike Britney, who just teased on "Oops! I Did It Again"). There's no mistaking this for anything other than a dance-pop record, yet it's made by an artist that is (thankfully) a little too old for teen pop. She's in on the joke, playing with the conventions, adding a touch more wit, both in the music and lyrics, as well as more classicist pop songcraft. That doesn't mean that this is as purely pop as Fountains of Wayne, but it's easy to see this becoming a guilty pleasure for that group's fans. And they may even wind up embracing its knowing approach to teen pop more than teens themselves. — *Stephen Thomas Erlewine*

The Vogues

f. 1960, Turtle Creek, PA

Brill Building Pop, Pop

Harmony-pop vocal group the Vogues were formed in 1960 by lead baritone Bill Burkette, baritone Don Miller, first tenor Hugh Geyer, and second tenor Chuck Blasko, who were all high school friends from Turtle Creek, PA. Originally dubbed the Val-Aires, the foursome eventually signed to the tiny Co & Ce label, reaching the number four spot in the autumn of 1965 with "You're the One"; the Vogues' most memorable hit, the classic "Five O'Clock World," cracked the Top Five before the year ended as well. Two more Top 40 entries, "Magic Town" and "The Land of Milk and Honey," followed in 1966, and when the group resurfaced in 1968 with the Top Ten smash "Turn Around, Look at Me," they had jumped to major label Reprise. The single, the Vogues' lone million-seller, anticipated the lighter, more sophisticated approach of subsequent hits like "My Special Angel," "Till," and "No, Not Much." Despite no further chart action from 1970 onward, various Vogues lineups continued touring oldies circuits for years to come. — *Jason Ankeny*

● **Greatest Hits** / 1988 / Rhino ✦✦✦✦✦

● **You're the One: The Co & Ce Sessions** / Apr. 1996 / Varese Sarabande ✦✦✦✦✦

In the doo wop revival of the early '60s, the Vogues (formerly the Val-Aires on Dot and Cascade) from Pittsburgh were certainly not the definitive group from that time period, not even close. What gave them their slot in the immortality sweepstakes came a few years later when they laid their vocal-group harmonies over the emerging folk-rock sound of the mid-'60s and scored big with classics like "Five O'Clock World," "Magic Town," and the title cut. While this 16-track compilation contains neither their early sides as the Val-Aires or their later sides for Warner Brothers, it's all you'll ever need to own on this group. — *Cub Koda*

Wah!

f. Feb. 1979
Post-Punk, New Wave, Pop/Rock

Wah!, and its number of incarnations, was a vehicle for Liverpool post-punk enigma Pete Wylie. Whether viewed as a prolific genius or as a blowhard lunatic with no quality control, there's no denying that the larger-than-life Wylie was a steamroller of a character who did everything his way to the fullest possible extent. Wylie's recordings might have varied stylistically throughout the years, but they each share the qualities of being loud, proud, and heartfelt. Having cut his teeth in the short-lived bands the Crucial Three, the Mystery Girls, and the Nova Mob, Wylie wisely decided in the late '70s to form an outlet of his own to house his ideas. Having played with other strong-headed types like the Teardrop Explodes' Julian Cope and Echo & the Bunnymen's Ian McCullough, Wylie knew early on that he would have to be the center of things. Under various pseudonyms including Wah! Heat, the Mighty Wah!, Shambeko Say Wah!, Pete Wylie and Wah! The Mongrel, or just plain Wah!, Wylie released nearly 20 singles with the occasional studio LP or collection falling between most breaks in the release schedule. Throughout Wah!'s history, Wylie situated himself with a number of skilled support musicians who shifted in and out with great frequency. The studio albums morphed from manic new wave in the earlier days to patchwork fare of wild stylistic variety including soul, reggae, easy listening, electronic pop, and straight-ahead rock & roll. Most of the records garnered critical favor but didn't do terribly well on the U.K. charts. The 1982 single "The Story of the Blues" was the group's biggest hit, reaching number three. The career-spanning double-disc *Handy Wah! Hole* compilation appeared in late 2000, followed by Castle's reissuing of several Wah!-related full-lengths in 2001. —*Andy Kellman*

Nah Poo—The Art of Bluff / Jun. 1981 / Essential/Castle ✦✦✦✦
Pete Wylie's first album as/with Wah! is his finest work, filled to the brim with passionate post-punk and blitzkrieg funk that holds an impressive level of focused intensity from front to back—no doubt the result of having listened to Clash records over and over and over and over again. There's little of the Clash's melodic sensibility to be found, memorable guitar riffs might not be evident ever, but there's an infectiously blistered pace to the proceedings, if a bit overbearingly shouty and mushy mixing-wise. Wylie sing-shouts everything with ferocious vigor, giving the record a rare sense of immediacy. Wah! literally sounds like they're playing with the knowledge that there will be no tomorrow. Off to an iffy start, tribal drums and from the depths vocals on "The Wind Up" do exactly that. One gets wound up because they want the record to actually start. Maybe that was the point. After that, it refuses to let up, kicked off by the "Do It Clean"-meets-"Break on Through" of "Other Boys." An album sequenced for maximum impact, instrumental "The Seven Thousand Names of Wah!" (no kidding) sets the table for "Seven Minutes to Midnight," Wah!'s signature song. The instrumental serves the same purpose as Mission of Burma barnburners like "Secrets" and "All World Cowboy Romance," holding together the rest of the album's songs while upping the intensity (as if it needed upping). Castle's attractive 2001 reissue adds eight tracks, mostly alternate versions of *Nah* songs, including Ian Broudie's mix jobs on "Forget the Down" and "Somesay." The liner notes are littered with photos, as well as Wylie's thoughts on each song. —*Andy Kellman*

The Maverick Years 80-81 / Oct. 1982 / Essential/Castle ✦✦✦
The title of this compilation consisting of new and reworked songs is a bit misleading. One, Madonna's label had yet to exist, and there ain't a chance in hell that the Candlebox fan would have signed the Mighty Wah! to her label. Second, the title also implies that it could be a greatest hits or singles compilation, which also isn't the case. The title *Maverick Years* does prove to make sense within the context of this release, since Pete Wylie had grown restless with then-label Warner Bros.' clogged release schedule and higher priorities. So Wylie combined new demos with tweaked versions of older songs and released them on his own Wonderful World of Wah! label. Done without Warner Bros.' consent, it obviously upset Wylie's employers and resulted in his imminent disposal from the major label ranks. Most of the new material is stillborn or half-baked at best. The alternate versions are pointless to anyone but a devout fan. One glaring exemption from this rule is the optimistic blast "Remember," which would have been a surefire highlight of *Nah Poo*. "Shambeko" is a point of interest for its eerie keyboard structure and isolated chill. Reissued with re-vamped versions of *Nah Poo* and *A Word to the Wise Guy* in 2001, Castle's version adds ten additional tracks that should appeal to diehards. The nine-minute version of "The Story of the Blues Pts. 1 & 2" will be welcomed by *someone*, and a cover of the Three Degrees' "Year of Decision" hasn't aged well and sounds like a commercial. As with the other 2001 versions, the liner notes contain many photos and commentary by Wylie. —*Andy Kellman*

A Word to the Wise Guy / Jun. 1984 / Essential/Castle ✦✦✦
Becoming increasingly bored by the rock-based indie scene of the time, Pete Wylie started

with a rock & roll record and ended up with something entirely different for the proper follow-up to 1981's *Nah Poo*. Incorporating funk, soul, reggae, and gospel, in addition to lumping on brass and string sections of the real and synthetic varieties, it came as no surprise that *A Word to the Wise Guy* took a long time to complete and involved philosophical scraps between all of those in the studio. Dropped by Warner Bros. for not having any hit potential, Wylie and company wound up with a fresh start on Beggars Banquet. Attempts at gospel ("The Story of the Blues"), reggae (the incidental "Yuh Learn"s), soul ("Everwanna," "What's Happening Now"), flag waving Boss rock ("Come Back"), and inexplicable hybrids of any combination imaginable ("Papa Crack/God's Lonely Man") have all of the required spirit but none of the lasting value. Chalk it up to wanting to do too much, aiming to make a massive-sounding record that doesn't quite make it. Since it sounds very of its time, *A Word to the Wise Guy* is one of those "you had to be there" deals. For all his boastfulness and overbearing iconography, Wylie should be commended for never being a mope and also for never approaching complacency. Regardless of the mixed results here, Wylie has passion and intensity through his marrow. Like the other Wah! reissues released by Castle in 2001, numerous bonus tracks are scattered, as well as track-by-track commentary from Wylie and numerous photos and press clippings. —*Andy Kellman*

Infamy! Or How I Didn't Get Where I Am Today / 1991 / Siren ✦✦✦
Peter Wylie is not an artist who plays it safe. Following the success of *Sinful*, Wylie returned to his band name of Wah! (dropping the "Mighty" but adding "Mongrel") and created this somewhat difficult, angry album. Whereas on past releases Wylie wrote some very melodic tunes, this is not really the case here. He jams in words much like a rap artist, but this is not rap. This is angry rock & roll. Wylie's guitar work has never sounded so tight and loud, and the vocals are as strong as ever. The overall production is very hard and KLF's presence is felt throughout the songs, but through all of the sound, this is still a Peter Wylie album. —*Aaron Badgley*

Songs of Strength & Heartbreak / Apr. 2000 / When! / Castle Music ✦✦✦
Following the release of 1991's *Infamy, or How I Didn't Get Where I Am Today*, Pete Wylie and his several incarnations of Wah! or the Mighty Wah! seemed to disappear. In fact, he suffered a severe back injury and it took until 1999 for him to return to the studio. And return he did, with this batch of brilliant songs. This is classic Wylie. As usual, strong melodies are present and Wylie shouts out his typically angry lyrics. He has chosen to work with extremely talented producers who bring the fullness to the sound. However, for the most part, these producers made their mark during the 1980s and this CD has the overall feel of an '80s release. The only complaint with the CD is that it is too long, and a couple of the songs could have been put to better use as B-sides. Otherwise, this is a brilliant album, one that fans will love as well as anyone looking for classic '80s sound. —*Aaron Badgley*

● **The Handy Wah! Whole** / Oct. 2000 / Essential/Castle ✦✦✦✦
Despite the typically cumbersome title, *The Handy Wah! Whole* is indeed a handy and portable compilation of Pete Wylie's output from the late '70s through the late '90s. The two-disc set expertly selects the best-known moments of Wylie's scattered and occasionally great career. Early post-punk anthems like "Better Scream" and "Seven Minutes to Midnight" highlight the first disc, along with fine album tracks like the instrumental "Seven Minutes" lead-in "The Seven Thousand Names of Wah." The second disc covers the less productive years, including Wylie's solo single from 1986, "Sinful." (The 1991 hit remix of the same song also makes an appearance on the second disc.) 1998 comeback single "Heart as Big as Liverpool" is another bright spot, proving the artist to have just as much wide-eyed enthusiasm two decades into his career as he did when he first started. Even if you don't feel as if you need anything Wah!-related past 1982 and don't care for the genre hopping of the later periods (see the failed but ambitious gospel two-parter "The Story of the Blues"), the extensive compilation is priced as a single disc. Wylie might not have ever attained the creative or popular heights of former colleagues Ian McCullough (Echo & the Bunnymen) and Julian Cope (the Teardrop Explodes), but his productive career has resulted in its fair share of enthusiastic and powerful music that bleeds confidence and defiance. This might offer more of a complete picture, but fans of the late-'70s/early-'80s post-punk sound might be better served by Castle's 2001 reissue of *Nah Poo—The Art of Bluff*, the band's tough-as-nails debut. —*Andy Kellman*

The Wailers

f. 1958, **db.** 1969
Garage Rock, Instrumental Rock, Rock & Roll

The historical importance of the Wailers is undeniable. They were one of the very first, if not the first, of the American garage bands. Backing Rockin' Robin Roberts, they revamped an obscure R&B song called "Louie Louie" into a 1961 local hit that served as the prototype for the countless subsequent versions of the most popular garage song of the '60s. And their stomping, hard-nosed R&B/rock fusion inspired the Sonics, who took the Wailers' raunch to unimaginable extremes. While they anticipated the British Invasion bands with their brash, self-contained sound, their inability to write first-rate original material, as well as their rather outdated sax and organ-driven frat rock, put them in a distinctly lower echelon. As the decade progressed, the group did absorb mild folk-rock and psychedelic influences without great effect, either commercially or on their sound itself. *—Richie Unterberger*

● **Fabulous Wailers, The Boys From Tacoma: Anthology 1961-1969** / 1993 / Etiquette ✦✦✦✦✦

A 27-song anthology drawn from their many singles and albums. Whether backing other singers, playing instrumentals, or performing their own material, the group rarely escaped the classic three-chord progression. What must have been a revelation in the teen ballrooms of the early '60s is a rather flat and repetitious listening experience. This is a fun compilation, but it should not be mistaken for a work of major significance. *—Richie Unterberger*

Rufus Wainwright

Vocals / Chamber Pop, Adult Alternative Pop/Rock, Singer/Songwriter

A singer/songwriter whose lush, theatrical pop harked back to the traditions of Tin Pan Alley, cabaret and even opera, Rufus Wainwright was the son of folk music luminaries Loudon Wainwright III and Kate McGarrigle. Beginning his piano studies at age six, by thirteen he was touring with his mother, aunt Anna and his sister Martha in a group billed as the McGarrigle Sisters and Family; a year later, Wainwright was nominated for a Juno (the Canadian equivalent of a Grammy) as Most Promising Young Artist, while his "I'm A-Runnin'" was concurrently nominated for a Genie (the Canadian countepart to an Oscar) for Best Song in a Film. After attending the prestigious Millbrook School in upstate New York, he eventually turned away from classical performance towards pop and rock. Becoming a fixture on the Montreal club circuit, Wainwright soon cut a series of demos with producer Pierre Marchand; Loudon Wainwright III then passed a copy of the tape to friend Van Dyke Parks, who in turn handed it on to DreamWorks exec Lenny Waronker. The label signed him soon after, resulting in the release of *Rufus Wainwright* during the spring of 1998. *—Jason Ankeny*

● **Rufus Wainwright** / May 19, 1998 / DreamWorks ✦✦✦✦✦

What separates Rufus Wainwright and the other second-generation singers who sprang up at the same time (Sean Lennon, Emma Townshend and Chris Stills the most notable among them) is that Wainwright deserves to be heard regardless of his family tree; in fact, the issue of his parentage is ultimately as immaterial as that of his sexuality—this self-titled debut cares little for the rock clichés of an earlier generation, instead heralding the arrival of a unique and compelling voice steeped most solidly in the traditions of cabaret. Like his folks, Loudon Wainwright III and Kate McGarrigle, he's a superb songwriter, with a knack for elegantly rolling piano melodies and poignantly romantic lyrics; while the appearance of Van Dyke Parks and his trademark orchestral arrangements hints at an affinity for the pop classicism of Brian Wilson or Randy Newman, the vocals come straight out of opera, and although Wainwright is unlikely to be starring in *La Boheme* anytime soon, he conveys the kind of honest emotion sorely lacking in the ironic posing of many of his contemporaries. Maybe the kids are all right after all. *—Jason Ankeny*

Poses / Jun. 5, 2001 / DreamWorks ✦✦✦✦

While his self-titled first album was very much a work by Rufus Wainwright (aided by his contributing producers), *Poses* seems to be more of a group effort, with the young composer allowing the other performers on the album to lend their talents, creating an even fuller, more "live" sound. Produced by Pierre Marchand, the album continues the same outstretched, enveloping sound established by Wainwright's earlier work, but contributors like contemporary composer Damian le Gassick and Propellerheads' Alex Gifford push in different directions, adding understated drum loops and gritty beats in unexpected places. Above all of the studio gimcrackery and pedigreed guest stars floats Wainwright himself, whose introspective, wry, and heart-wrenching songwriting remains his true strength. The clunking, loping "Greek Song" evokes the sprawl of an impossible Ingmar Bergman spaghetti western, while the swaggering "California" shows a sunny exterior masking the song's satirical sneer. Amidst this sonic barrage, a high point comes in the cover of patriarch Loudon Wainwright III's "One Man Guy." Performed by Rufus, Martha Wainwright, and Teddy Thompson's simple acoustic guitar, these three grown children of the '70s folk movement embrace the song faithfully, basking in their own harmonies and offering a respite from the blissfully lush orchestral pop that surrounds it. While *Poses* shows growth and worthwhile exploration, the album's "group" feel suffers only slightly from being less intimate than Wainwright's first album. Although his contributors add much, there was something blushingly personal about his debut that may have gotten a little buried this time around. That being said, *Poses* is still a spectacular album, brimming over with Wainwright's trademark popera and young romantic wishes. At times the album is beautifully discordant and sonically chilling, but often hints at warm grins with mischievous winks. *—Zac Johnson*

John Waite

b. 1955, Lancashire, England

Vocals, Bass / Album Rock, Pop/Rock, Soft Rock

As a solo artist and as the lead singer of the Babys and Bad English, John Waite was a fixture on album-oriented rock radio stations during the '70s and '80s. Waite had a talent for power ballads and driving arena rock, occasionally touching on new wave-styled power pop, as well. Though he didn't consistently have hits, several of his songs—including "Missing You," the Babys' "Isn't It Time," and Bad English's "When I See You Smile"—became radio staples. Waite formed the Babys in London, England, in 1976. When Jonathan Cain left the Babys to join Journey in 1981, the group disbanded. Waite began his solo career the following year, releasing *Ignition* on Chrysalis. While the album generated the minor hit "Change," his second album, 1984's *No Brakes*, became a genuine Top Ten hit on the strength of the number one single "Missing You." While "Missing You" was an international smash, *No Brakes* produced only one other hit, the Top 40 "Tears." Its failure to produce another blockbuster was indicative of how Waite's solo career would proceed. *Mask of Smiles* (1985) barely managed a Top 40 entry ("Every Step of the Way") but *Rover's Return* (1987) produced no hits, bringing Waite's career to a standstill. With his career stalled, Waite formed the supergroup Bad English. The group's eponymous debut, released in 1989 on Epic Records, became a platinum success after the power ballad "When I See You Smile" became a number one hit. "Price of Love" was a Top Ten hit in the wake of "When I See You Smile," but their 1991 follow-up, *Backlash*, suffered from one. Bad English broke up shortly after the album's release. Waite resumed his solo career in 1995, releasing *Temple Bar* on Imago. *—Stephen Thomas Erlewine*

● **The Complete John Waite, Vol. 1: Falling Backwards** / Nov. 12, 1996 / EMI ✦✦✦✦✦

A 17-track career retrospective that not only spans the mid-1970s to the mid-1990s, but encompasses solo cuts and songs that he recorded with the Babys in the '70s, and Bad English in the '80s. For all that, it's remarkably inconsequential right-of-center mainstream commercial rock, whether he's playing guitar-based pop-rock with the Babys, or doing the power ballad thing with Bad English. Includes his 1984 #1 solo single "Missing You," and the Bad English smashes "When I See You Smile" and "Price of Love," and several smaller hits. *—Richie Unterberger*

Mask of Smiles/Rover's Return / Jul. 10, 2001 / One Way ✦✦✦

John Waite's second solo album, *No Brakes*, reached the Top Ten, almost entirely on the strength of "Missing You," a truly perfect single. It was a hell of an act to follow, and Waite couldn't quite deliver, at least until he re-teamed with former Baby Jonathan Cain in the late '80s with Bad English. During those years in the wilderness—roughly 1985 through 1990—he released two albums, 1985's *Mask of Smiles* and 1987's *Rover's Return*, which are combined on this CD reissue. No, *Mask of Smiles* doesn't have a great should-have-been-a-contender single as good as "Missing You," yet it's a surprisingly strong, tight little record. After *No Brakes*, it is the strongest album Waite ever recorded, and it even had a single—the insistent "Every Step of the Way"—that stood out amongst the rest. It was a great piece of mainstream popcraft, and that's really what the whole album is—professionally crafted mainstream rock that's engaging because of its sense of craft. It plays like a hit album that never was. Unfortunately, that's not the case with *Rover's Return*. It's like these two albums are the flip sides to one coin—the first illustrates how professional craft can be utterly engaging, the second illustrates that it can be a dead end. That's not to say that *Rover's Return* is a complete failure, because there are portions that work quite well—the surging opener "These Times Are Hard for Lovers" is good radio rock, and Waite's voice always sounds good in this polished setting. Still, it's a little stiff and predictable, never quite reaching a level that's interesting, either as a period artifact or a piece of professional craft. That's the fascinating thing about this reissue—it pairs the best of Waite with the worst, and throughout it all, he comes out shining. *—Stephen Thomas Erlewine*

Ignition/No Brakes / Aug. 14, 2001 / One Way ✦✦✦

John Waite's stardom as a member of the Babys was nothing compared to what would follow when Waite's solo career finally took off, yet it took a little effort for that career to gain momentum. Waite released his first solo album, *Ignition*, in the summer of 1982. Musically, the record certainly took its cues from the Babys, but it was also a product of its times, exhibiting a considerable new wave production sheen. The problem is that no matter how well-crafted *Ignition* is, none of its songs are total knockouts—the kind of single that would break down the doors to mainstream radio, regardless of whether it was given a push. And so, even though it was a very good solo debut, *Ignition* withered on the vine. Two years later, Waite returned with *No Brakes*, an album that had success in its sights. Cleverly, the record not only had an explicit commercial pop bent, featuring mid-tempo pop tunes and ballads, but it also rocked like a bastard, particularly on the opening cut "Saturday Night." Most importantly, it had a hit single in "Missing You." Perched perfectly between anthemic mainstream rock and sleek post-new wave pop, it was a minor miracle—a flawlessly written, classicist pop song, delivered with a stylish, MTV-ready flair. It deservedly became not just a number one hit, but one of those records that everybody knows, capturing a time yet transcending it to become part of the very fabric of pop culture. The rest of the record was as expertly crafted, constructed, and performed as the best of *Ignition*. In retrospect, it might sound a little bit too much like 1984, thanks to the big drums and clean production, but that's its charm: It's a prime example of fine mainstream rock circa the mid-'80s. *—Stephen Thomas Erlewine*

Figure in a Landscape / Aug. 21, 2001 / Gold Circle ✦✦

Like most singers, John Waite is only as good as the songs he sings, i.e., he still packs prime pipes, but Waite's quest for chart action often leaves him churning out demographically-inspired, clinical machinations. Why doesn't anyone ever return to power pop roots? At any rate, *Figure in a Landscape* goes for a mature, adult contemporary atmosphere, but comes across as competent countrified ennui. Opener "Keys to Your Heart" gets things going in a decent direction. "NYC Girl" oozes cool urban imagery, and "Thinking About You" isn't bad. "Special One" kicks up a little dust, but never gets dirty. Lone rocker "Godhead" smokes, ten years after Chris Cornell embodied the term. Classy torch closer "Masterpiece of Loneliness" holds some heartfelt sentiment, but the other songs (including a Vince Gill tune) are yawners. Waite's sole smash "Missing You" is a stigma that will forever haunt the singer, and that's apparent from the excessive amount of mellow numbers here. Like most stars from the '70s, Waite possesses a larger-than-life persona, and his particular style of verbosely turning bulky phrases (a la Meatloaf) remains an engaging trait. But the ever-present professional gloss doesn't make *Figure on the Landscape* any more distinctive, and, barring a miracle, this album won't make Waite any more of a star. Still, it's always a pleasure to hear that voice. *—Doug Stone*

The Waitresses

f. 1981, **db.** 1983
New Wave
The Waitresses existed for the purpose of performing the witty, often female-oriented songs of guitarist Chris Butler, who had previously led a series of new wave bands in Cleveland. The personnel of the band as of its 1982 debut album, *Wasn't Tomorrow Wonderful*, was, in addition to Butler, singer Patty Donahue, backup singer Ariel Warner, reed player Mars Williams, bassist David Horstra, drummer Billy Ficca (a once and future member of Television), and keyboardist Dan Klayman. The group recorded two albums and a mini-LP in the early '80s, stirring critical acclaim and international interest before both Donahue and Butler left. Ficca fronted the band for a while, then they broke up. Donahue died of cancer in 1996. *—William Ruhlmann*

Wasn't Tomorrow Wonderful? / 1982 / Polydor ✦✦✦✦✦
"No Guilt," in which Donahue's matter-of-fact voice details what a spurned lover has found out since the breakup ("I learned the reason for a three-pronged outlet"), and "I Know What Boys Like" are the standouts among these clever songs, but the whole album has an attitude that won't quit. *—William Ruhlmann*

Bruiseology / 1983 / Polydor ✦✦
By 1983, the band had all but fallen apart, and *Bruiseology* reflects much of the inner turmoil with a generally lackluster batch of songs—obviously the novelty hadn't held up well for the band and the fun had worn off. Nothing on the album approached "I Know What Boys Like" or even "Square Pegs," released slightly before the album. *—Chris Woodstra*

● **The Best of the Waitresses** / Oct. 1990 / Polydor ✦✦✦✦✦
Best of the Waitresses gives a good career overview of the band, collecting the bulk of the high points from their two albums, of course including the unforgettable "I Know What Boys Like," as well as some fun non-LP cuts like "Square Pegs" (the theme from the "valley girl" TV show *Square Pegs*) and the holiday rap "Christmas Wrapping." *Best of the Waitresses* offers ample proof that the band deserved more than one-hit wonder status, although this collection is probably all that most people need. The more ambitious should add the *King Biscuit Flower Hour* disc for a sampling of the band's truly inspired live shows. *—Chris Woodstra*

King Biscuit Flower Hour / Mar. 25, 1997 / King Biscuit ✦✦✦✦
Recorded live at My Father's Place in Roslyn, Long Island, New York, at the time of the release of their first album, this concert catches the Waitresses at the outset of their all-too-brief national career. Captured live for posterity are "I Know What Boys Like," "No Guilt," "Christmas Wrapping," and eight other songs, all jewels in the output of Chris Butler and catching the late Patty Donahue at her early peak—when she does the telephone monologue bit on "No Guilt" ("I'm just a busy girl . . . ") or the spoken/sung part on "Wise Up," she shows herself a better actress than Madonna. Mars Williams' stuttering sax is also a treat. The only thing missing is the title theme they did to the TV series *Square Pegs*. Better than their Polygram best-of. God bless King Biscuit for putting this out. *—Bruce Eder*

Tom Waits

b. Dec. 7, 1949, Pomona, CA
Vocals, Harmonium, Songwriter, Piano, Guitar, Organ / College Rock, Album Rock, Experimental Rock, Beat Poetry, Singer/Songwriter
In the 1970s, Tom Waits combined a lyrical focus on desperate, lowlife characters with a persona that seemed to embody the same lifestyle, which he sang about in a raspy, gravelly voice. From the '80s on, his work became increasingly theatrical as he moved into acting and composing. Waits' formal recording debut came with *Closing Time* (1973) on Asylum Records, an album that contained "Ol' 55," which was covered by labelmates the Eagles. Waits attracted critical acclaim and a cult audience for his subsequent late-'70s albums, *The Heart of Saturday Night*, *Small Change*, *Foreign Affairs* and *Heart Attack and Vine*. His music and persona proved highly cinematic, and starting in 1978 he launched parallel careers as an actor and as a composer of movie music. After moving to Island, Waits made 1983's *Swordfishtrombones*, which found him experimenting with horns and percussion and using more unusual recording techniques. In 1985, he released *Rain Dogs*. An album based on his theatrical debut, *Frank's Wild Years*, was released in 1987. In 1992, he scored the film *Night on Earth* and released the album *Bone Machine*, which won a Grammy Award for Best Alternative Music Album. In 1993, he released *The Black Rider*, the recording of a musical he had co-written with Beat novelist William Burroughs. A long absence from recording ended in 1999 with the release of *Mule Variations*. *—William Ruhlmann*

● **Closing Time** / 1973 / Asylum ✦✦✦✦✦
Tom Waits' debut album was a minor-key masterpiece filled with songs of late-night loneliness. Within the apparently narrow range of the cocktail bar pianistics and muttered vocals, Waits and producer Jerry Yester managed a suprisingly broad collection of styles, from the jazzy "Virginia Avenue" to the uptempo funk of "Ice Cream Man" and from the acoustic guitar folkiness of "I Hope That I Don't Fall in Love with You" to the saloon song "Midnight Lullaby," which would have been a perfect addition to the repertoires of Frank Sinatra or Tony Bennett. Waits' entire musical approach was stylized, of course, and at times derivative—"Lonely" borrowed a little too much from Randy Newman's "I Think It's Going to Rain Today"—and his lovelorn lyrics could be sentimental without being penetrating. But he also had a gift for gently rolling pop melodies, and he could come up with striking, original scenarios, as on the best songs, "Ol' 55" and "Martha," which Yester discreetly augmented with strings. *Closing Time* announced the arrival of a talented songwriter whose self-conscious melancholy could be surprisingly moving. *—William Ruhlmann*

The Heart of Saturday Night / 1974 / Asylum ✦✦✦
If *Closing Time*, Tom Waits' debut album, consisted of love songs set in a late-night world of bars and neon signs, its follow-up, *The Heart of Saturday Night*, largely dispensed with the romance in favor of poetic depictions of the same setting. On "Diamonds on My Windshield" and "The Ghosts of Saturday Night," Waits didn't even sing, instead reciting his verse rhythmically against bass and drums like a Beat hipster. Musically, the album contained the same mixture of folk, blues, and jazz as its predecessor, with producer Bones Howe occasionally bringing in an orchestra to underscore the loping melodies. Waits' songs were sometimes sketchier in addition to being more impersonal, but "(Looking For) The Heart of Saturday Night" and "Semi Suite" were the equal of anything on *Closing Time*. Still, with lines such as "... the clouds are like headlines / Upon a new front page sky" and references to "a 24-hour moon" and "champagne stars," Waits' imagery was beginning to get florid, and in material this stylized, the danger of self-parody was always present. *—William Ruhlmann*

Nighthawks at the Diner / Oct. 1975 / Asylum ✦✦✦
For his third album, Tom Waits set up a nightclub in the studio, invited an audience, and cut a 70-minute, two-LP set of new songs. It was an appropriate format for compositions that dealt even more graphically and, for the first time, humorously, with Waits' late-night world of bars and diners. The love lyrics of his debut album had long since given way to a comic lonely guy stance glimpsed in "Emotional Weather Report" and "Better off Without a Wife." But what really mattered was the elaborate scene-setting of songs like the six-and-a-half-minute "Spare Parts," the seven-and-a-half-minute "Putnam County," and especially the 11 1/2-minute "Nighthawk Postcards" that were essentially poetry recitations with jazz backing. Waits was a colorful tour guide of midnight L.A., raving over a swinging rhythm section of Jim Hughart (bass) and Bill Goodwin (drums), with Pete Christlieb wailing away on tenor sax between paragraphs and Mike Melvoin trading off with Waits on piano runs. You could call it overdone, but then, this kind of material made its impact through an accumulation of miscellaneous detail, and who was to say how much was too much? *—William Ruhlmann*

Small Change / Oct. 1976 / Asylum ✦✦✦✦✦
The fourth release in Tom Waits' series of skid-row travelogues, *Small Change* proved to be the archetypal album of his '70s work. A jazz trio comprising tenor sax player Lew Tabackin, bassist Jim Hughart, and drummer Shelly Manne, plus an occasional string section, backed Waits and his piano on songs steeped in whiskey and atmosphere in which he alternately sang in his broken-beaned drunk's voice (now deeper and overtly influenced by Louis Armstrong) and recited jazzy poetry. It was as if Waits was determined to combine the Humphrey Bogart and Dooley Wilson characters from *Casablanca* with a dash of *On the Road's* Dean Moriarty to illuminate a dark world of bars and all-night diners. Of course, he'd been in that world before, but in songs like "The Piano Has Been Drinking" and "Bad Liver and a Broken Heart," Waits gave it its clearest expression. *Small Change* is not Tom Waits' best album. It is, like most of the albums he made in the '70s, uneven, probably because he was putting out one a year and didn't have time to come up with enough first-rate material. But it is the most obvious and characteristic of his albums for Asylum Records. If you like it, you also will like the ones before and after it; otherwise, you're not Tom Waits' kind of listener. *—William Ruhlmann*

Foreign Affairs / Sep. 1977 / Asylum ✦✦✦
Tom Waits gave one side of his fifth album to his more structured, bluesy ballads and the other to his jazz raps. On side one, you got his duet with Bette Midler on the singles-bar dialogue "I Never Talk to Strangers" and his take on his Beat predecessors, Jack Kerouac and Neal Cassidy on "Jack Neal." On side two, you found the extended observations of "Potter's Field" and "Burma Shave." Waits' voice was becoming ever more gravelly, but his basic musical approach remained the same, and he had attracted a steady cult audience that enjoyed his verbal flights and boozy philosopher persona, even as critics began to complain that he was repeating himself. By the way, that's Waits' then-girlfriend, the then-unknown Rickie Lee Jones, on the cover with him. *—William Ruhlmann*

Blue Valentine / Oct. 1978 / Asylum ✦✦✦
Two welcome changes in style made *Blue Valentine* a fresh listening experience for Tom Waits fans. First, Waits had altered the instrumentation, bringing in electric guitar and keyboards and largely dispensing with the strings for a more blues-oriented, hard-edged sound. Second, though his worldview remained fixed on the lowlifes of the late night, he had expanded beyond the musings of the barstool philosopher who previously had acted as the first-person character of most of his songs. When Waits did use the "I," it was to write a "Christmas Card from a Hooker in Minneapolis," not the figure most listeners had associated with the singer himself. The result was a broadening of subject matter, a narrative discipline that made most of the tunes story songs, and a coherent framing for Waits' typically colorful and intriguing imagery. These were not radical reinventions, but Waits had followed such a rigidly stylized approach on his previous albums that for anyone who had followed him so far, the course correction was big news. *—William Ruhlmann*

Heartattack and Vine / Sep. 1980 / Asylum ✦✦✦
Heartattack and Vine, Tom Waits' first album in two years and his last of seven for Asylum Records, was a transitional album, with tracks like the rhythm-heavy title song

and "'Til the Money Runs Out" foreshadowing the sonic experiments of the Island albums, while piano with orchestra tracks like "Saving All My Love for You" and "On the Nickel" (written as a motion-picture title tune) harked back to Waits' Randy Newman-influenced early days. It was just as well that Waits never entirely gave up on the ballad material; "Jersey Girl," a Drifters-style song, was a winner, and it was appropriated by Bruce Springsteen on his 1981 tour. Also, at least at this point, the rougher tunes all tended to sound the same. *—William Ruhlmann*

☆ **Swordfishtrombones** / Sep. 1983 / Island ♦♦♦♦♦

Between the release of *Heartattack and Vine* in 1980 and *Swordfishtrombones* in 1983, Tom Waits got rid of his manager, his producer, and his record company. And he drastically altered a musical approach that had become as dependable as it was unexciting. *Swordfishtrombones* had none of the strings and much less of the piano work that Waits' previous albums had employed; instead, the dominant sounds on the record were low-pitched horns, bass instruments, and percussion, set in spare, close-miked arrangements (most of them by Waits) that sometimes were better described as "soundscapes." Lyrically, Waits' tales of the drunken and the lovelorn had been replaced by surreal accounts of people who burned down their homes and of Australian towns bypassed by the railroad—a world (not just a neighborhood) of misfits now had his attention. The music could be primitive, moving to odd time signatures, while Waits alternately howled and wheezed in his gravelly bass voice. He seemed to have moved on from Hoagy Carmichael and Louis Armstrong to Kurt Weill and Howlin' Wolf (as impersonated by Captain Beefheart). Waits seems to have had trouble interesting a record label in the album, which was cut 13 months before it was released, but when it appeared rock critics predictably raved: After all, it sounded weird and it didn't have a chance of selling. Actually, it did make the bottom of the bestseller charts, like most of Waits' albums, and, now that he was with a label based in Europe, even charted there. Artistically, *Swordfishtrombones* marked an evolution of which Waits had not seemed capable (though there were hints of this sound on his last two Asylum albums), and in career terms it re-invented him. *—William Ruhlmann*

★ **Rain Dogs** / Aug. 1985 / Island ♦♦♦♦♦

With its jarring rhythms and unusual instrumentation—marimba, accordion, various percussion—as well as its frequently surreal lyrics, *Rain Dogs* was very much a follow-up to *Swordfishtrombones*, which is to say that it sounded for the most part like *The Threepenny Opera* being sung by Howlin' Wolf. The chief musical difference was the introduction of guitarist Marc Ribot, who added his noisy leads to the general cacophony. But *Rain Dogs* was sprawling where its predecessor had been focused: Waits' lyrics here sometimes were imaginative to the point of obscurity, seemingly chosen to fit the rhythms rather than for sense. In the course of 19 tracks and 54 minutes, Waits sometimes went back to the more conventional music of his earlier records, which seemed like a retreat, though such tracks as the catchy "Hang Down Your Head," "Time," and especially "Downtown Train" (frequently covered and finally turned into a Top Ten hit by Rod Stewart five years later) provided some relief as well as variety. *Rain Dogs* could not surprise as *Swordfishtrombones* had, and in his attempt to continue in the direction suggested by that album, Waits occasionally bordered on the chaotic (which may only be to say that, like most of his records, this one was uneven). But much of the music matched the earlier album, and there was so much of it that that was enough to qualify *Rain Dogs* as one of Waits' better albums. *—William Ruhlmann*

The Asylum Years / Oct. 1986 / Asylum ♦♦♦♦♦

The second British Tom Waits compilation was a more extensive look at the 1973-1980 Asylum Records catalog than the first, *Bounced Checks* from 1981 (fourteen tracks vs. ten), but it was another idiosyncratic selection. Waits' stellar first two albums were better represented, with three strong tracks drawn from *The Heart of Saturday Night* and two from *Closing Time*, but "Ol' 55" was ignored again, and nothing was included from the third album, *Nighthawks at the Diner*, which is the favorite of many Waits fans. Three tracks were repeated from *Bounced Checks*—"Burma Shave," "I Never Talk to Strangers," a duet with Bette Midler, and "Tom Traubert's Blues"—and they were worthy, but where was "Jersey Girl"? The choices from the later albums were spotty: Why use Waits' questionable cover of "Somewhere" from *West Side Story* and leave out a brilliant story song like "Romeo Is Bleeding"? The overall unevenness of the Asylum albums cries out for a well-chosen compilation. After three attempts in the U.S. and U.K., it still hasn't been assembled. *—William Ruhlmann*

Franks Wild Years / Aug. 1987 / Island ♦♦♦♦

Tom Waits wrote a song called "Frank's Wild Years" for his 1983 *Swordfishtrombones* album, then used the title (minus its apostrophe) for a musical play he wrote with his wife, Kathleen Brennan, and toured with in 1986. The *Franks Wild Years* album, drawn from the show, is subtitled, "un operachi romantico in two acts," though the songs themselves do not carry the plot. Rather, this is just the third installment in Waits' eccentric series of Island Records albums in which he seems most inspired by German art song and carnival music, presenting songs in spare, stripped-down arrangements consisting of instruments like marimba, baritone horn, and pump organ and singing in a strained voice that has been artificially compressed and distorted. The songs themselves often are conventional romantic vignettes, or would be minus the oddities of instrumentation, arrangement, and performance. For example, "Innocent When You Dream," a song of disappointment in love and friendship, has a winning melody, but it is played in a seesaw arrangement of pump organ, bass, violin, and piano, and Waits sings it like an enraged drunk. (He points up the arbitrary nature of the arrangements by repeating "Straight to the Top," done as a demented rhumba in Act I, as a Vegas-style Frank Sinatra swing tune in Act II.) The result on record may not be theatrical, exactly, but it certainly is affected. It also has the quality of an inside joke that listeners are not being let in on. *—William Ruhlmann*

Big Time / Sep. 1988 / Island ♦♦♦

Big Time is an 18-track live album running nearly 68 minutes, its material drawn mostly from Tom Waits' trio of recent studio albums, *Swordfishtrombones*, *Rain Dogs*, and *Franks Wild Years*. (One track, "Falling Down," is a previously unissued studio recording. The performance of "Strange Weather" marks Waits' first recording of a song he and his wife, Kathleen Brennan, wrote for Marianne Faithfull.) It's challenging music, made somewhat more accessible in a live context. Waits' performances tended to be somewhat over the top on the studio versions of these songs, but before a live audience his theatrics seem more appropriate, and he even includes a mini-set of piano ballads. Still, it takes him until the seventh tune, "Way Down in the Hole," to bring the audience to life, and he rarely speaks, in marked contrast to the earlier live-in-the-studio album *Nighthawks at the Diner*. But *Big Time* makes a useful sampler of Waits' later work that might enable a listener to determine whether to invest in the studio recordings. *—William Ruhlmann*

The Early Years / Jul. 1991 / Bizarre/Straight ♦♦♦♦

This is an album of early demos recorded by a 21-year-old Tom Waits in 1971, two years before the release of his first album, *Closing Time*, and issued on the record label owned by his ex-manager. Waits accompanies himself on piano or guitar and sings in an unaffected nasal tenor. (One track, "Ice Cream Man," is given a full-band treatment.) Several of these songs, notably "Ice Cream Man," "Virginia Ave.," "Midnight Lullabye," and "Little Trip to Heaven," turned up on his later albums, but the overall level of writing and performance is well below Waits' usual standard. Clearly, his better early material was chosen for his Asylum albums. Hardcore fans will want to hear this album, of course, but others need not bother. *—William Ruhlmann*

Night on Earth / Apr. 1992 / Island ♦♦

Bone Machine / Aug. 1992 / Island ♦♦♦♦♦

Perhaps Tom Waits' most cohesive album, *Bone Machine* is a morbid, sinister nightmare, one that applied the quirks of his experimental '80s classics to stunningly evocative—and often harrowing—effect. In keeping with the title's grotesque image of the human body, *Bone Machine* is obsessed with decay and mortality, the ease with which earthly existence can be destroyed. The arrangements are accordingly stripped of all excess flesh; the very few, often non-traditional instruments float in distinct separation over the clanking junkyard percussion that dominates the record. It's a chilling, primal sound made all the more otherworldly (or, perhaps, underworldly) by Waits' raspy falsetto and often-distorted roars and growls. Matching that evocative power is Waits' songwriting, which is arguably the most consistently focused it's ever been. Rich in strange and extraordinarily vivid imagery, many of Waits' tales and musings are spun against an imposing backdrop of apocalyptic natural fury, underlining the insignificance of his subjects and their universally impending doom. Death is seen as freedom for the spirit, an escape from the dread and suffering of life in this world—which he paints as hellishly bleak, full of murder, suicide, and corruption. The chugging, oddly bouncy beats of the more uptempo numbers make them even more disturbing—there's a detached nonchalance beneath the horrific visions. Even the narrator of the catchy, playful "I Don't Wanna Grow Up" seems hopeless in this context, but that song paves the way for the closer "That Feel," an ode to the endurance of the human soul (with ultimate survivor Keith Richards on harmony vocals). The more upbeat ending hardly dispels the cloud of doom hanging over the rest of *Bone Machine*, but it does give the listener a gentler escape from that terrifying sonic world. All of it adds up to Waits' most affecting and powerful recording, even if it isn't his most accessible. *—Steve Huey*

The Early Years, Vol. 2 / Feb. 1993 / Bizarre/Straight ♦♦♦♦♦

Like its predecessor, *The Early Years, Vol. 2* consists of demos recorded by Tom Waits in 1971, two years before he released his debut album, *Closing Time*. "Hope I Don't Fall in Love With You," "Ol' 55," "Grapefruit Moon," and "Old Shoes" later turned up on that album, while "Shiver Me Timbers," "Diamonds on My Windshield," and "Please Call Me Baby" appeared on Waits' second album, *The Heart of Saturday Night*, in 1974. The release of the two *Early Years* albums demonstrates that Waits' better early material made it onto his regular releases—the previously unreleased stuff, while interesting, is not as good. And since Waits' albums were not overproduced, the main difference between these versions and the familiar ones is that the familiar ones are better. Still, Waits fans will enjoy hearing, for example, "Ol' 55" performed in a higher key and with an acoustic guitar backing. *—William Ruhlmann*

The Black Rider / Nov. 2, 1993 / Island ♦♦

Beautiful Maladies: The Island Years / Jun. 16, 1998 / Island ♦♦♦

Tom Waits' brilliance is messy—he has so many ideas that sometimes unrealized songs are juxtaposed with moments of greatness on his albums. That may make for the occasional uneven record, but each album has its own distinct tone that makes it a unique listening experience, whether it's a masterpiece or a missed opportunity. And that's the reason why his work, especially his sprawling Island albums, doesn't lend itself to retrospectives like *Beautiful Maladies: The Island Years*. On the surface, the collection looks promising. The single disc features 22 tracks from *Swordfishtrombones*, *Rain Dogs*, *Franks Wild Years*, *Big Time*, *Bone Machine* and *The Black Rider*, including such familiar and celebrated items as "Hang on St. Christopher," "Innocent When You Dream," "I Don't Wanna Grow Up," "16 Shells from a Thirty-Ought Six" and "Downtown Train." Some fans might spot missing favorites, but it's hard to fault the selections themselves—if it wasn't for the fact that they all sound somewhat disjointed when separated from the original albums. Because of this, *Beautiful Maladies* is a little odd—it's not a bad sampler, but it isn't necessarily a good introduction since the songs don't sound like they belong together. The curious may want this as a sampler, but if you wind up liking Tom Waits, you won't be satisfied with anything other than the original albums. —*Stephen Thomas Erlewine*

Mule Variations / Apr. 20, 1999 / Anti/Epitaph ✦✦✦✦
Tom Waits grew steadily less prolific after redefining himself as a junkyard noise poet with *Swordfishtrombones*, but the five-year wait between *The Black Rider* and 1999's *Mule Variations* was the longest yet. Given the fact that Waits decided to abandon major labels for the California indie Epitaph, *Mule Variations* would seem like a golden opportunity to redefine himself and begin a new phase of his career. However, it plays like a revue of highlights from every album he's made since *Swordfishtrombones*. Of course, that's hardly a criticism; the album uses the ragged cacophony of *Bone Machine* as a starting point, and proceeds to bring in the songwriterly aspects of *Rain Dogs*, along with its affection for backstreet and backwoods blues, plus a hint of the beatnik qualities of *Swordfish*. So *Mule Variations* delivers what fans want, in terms of both songs and sonics. But that also explains why it sounds terrific on initial spins, only to reveal itself as slightly dissatisfying with subsequent plays. All of Waits' Island records felt like fully conceived albums with genuine themes. *Mule Variations*, in contrast, is a collection of moments, and while each of those moments is very good (some even bordering on excellent), ultimately the whole doesn't equal the sum of its parts. While that may seem like nitpicking, some may have wanted a masterpiece after five years, and *Mule Variations* falls short of that mark. Nevertheless, this is a hell of a record by any other standard. Waits is still writing terrific songs and matching them with wildly evocative productions; furthermore, it's his *lightest* record in years—it's actually fun to listen to, even with a murder ballad here and a psycho blues there. In that sense, it's a unique item in his post-*Swordfish* catalog, and that may make up for it not being the masterpiece it seemed like it could have been. —*Stephen Thomas Erlewine*

Rick Wakeman

b. May 18, 1949, London, England
Keyboards, Arranger, Piano, Organ / Prog-Rock/Art Rock
By his late teens, pianist Rick Wakeman was an established sessionman, and one set of sessions with a folk-rock band called the Strawbs led to his joining the group in 1970. After two albums with the Strawbs, Wakeman joined Yes, a post-psychedelic hard rock band that had attracted considerable attention with their first three albums. Wakeman played a key role in the final shape of the group's fourth record, *Fragile*, creating a fierce, swirling sound on an array of synthesizers, Mellotrons, electric and acoustic pianos. Yes' next album, *Close to the Edge*, expanded his audience and his appeal, for his instruments were heard almost continually on the record. During the making of *Close to the Edge* in 1972, Wakeman also recorded his first solo album, an instrumental work entitled *The Six Wives of Henry VIII*. Released early in 1973 on A&M Records, it performed respectably on the charts. Public reception of Yes' 1974 album, *Tales From Topographic Oceans*, was mixed, and the critics were merciless in their attacks upon the record. Wakeman exited the group before the album's supporting tour. His next solo album, *Journey to the Center of the Earth*, adapted from the writings of Jules Verne, and featuring a rock band, narrator (David Hemmings), and full orchestral and choral accompaniment, was released to tremendous public response in both America and England, where it topped the charts. In 1977, Wakeman returned to Yes, with which he has continued recording and touring. Wakeman's audience and reputation survived the 1980s better than almost any progressive rock star of his era, as he continued releasing albums on his own label. He also remained associated with Yes into the '90s. —*Bruce Eder*

● **The Six Wives of Henry the VIII** / 1973 / A&M ✦✦✦✦✦
Not only did this album help pave the way for progressive rock, but it also introduced the unbridled energy and overall effectiveness of the synthesizer as a bona fide instrument. *Six Wives* gave Wakeman his chance to break away from the other instrumental complexities that made up Yes and allowed him to prove what a driving force the keyboard could truly be, especially in full album form. More than just synthesized wandering, Wakeman astoundingly conjures up a separate musical persona by way of an instrumental ode to each of Henry VIII's wives through his dazzling use of the Mellotron, Moog, and Hammond C3 organ. For example, Wakeman's fiery runs and fortissimo thwarting of the synthesizer throughout "Anne Boleyn" is a tribute to her feisty temper and valiant courage that she maintained while standing up to her husband. With "Jane Seymour," on the other hand, Wakeman's playing is somewhat subdued and gentile, which coincides with her legendary meekness and frailty, as well as her willingness to cater to Henry VIII. Wakeman's masterful use of his synthesizers is not only instrumentally stunning, but his talent of magically shaping the notes to represent behavioral idiosyncrasies of his characters is itself bewildering. Yes bassist Chris Squire lends a hand on "Catherine of Aragon," while guitarist Steve Howe and drummer Bill Bruford appear on a few tracks as well, as does former Strawbs member Dave Cousins, playing the electric banjo. *The Six Wives of Henry VIII* unleashes the unyielding power of the keyboard as a dominant instrument, but also displays Wakeman at the beginning of an extremely resplendent career as a solo musician. —*Mike DeGagne*

Journey to the Center of the Earth / Jan. 1974 / Mobile Fidelity ✦✦✦✦
Journey to the Center of the Earth is one of progressive rock's crowning achievements. With the help of the London Symphony Orchestra and the English Chamber Choir, Wakeman turns this classic Jules Verne tale into an exciting and suspenseful instrumental narrative. The story is told by David Hemmings in between the use of Wakeman's keyboards, especially the powerful Hammond organ and the innovative Moog synthesizer, and when coupled with the prestigious sound of the orchestra, creates the album's fairytale-like climate. Recorded at London's Royal Festival Hall, the tale of a group of explorers who

wander into the fantastic living world that exists in the Earth's core is told musically through Wakeman's synthesized theatrics and enriched by the haunting vocals of a chamber choir. Broken into four parts, the album's most riveting piece entitled "The Battle" involves Wakeman's most furious synthesized attack, churning and swirling the keyboards into a mass instrumental hysteria. With both "The Journey" and "The Forest," it's the effective use of the strings and percussion section of the London Symphony Orchestra that causes the elements of fantasy and myth to emerge from the album's depths. The gorgeous voice of Ashley Holt is effectively prominent, and some interesting guitar work via Mike Egan arises occasionally but meritoriously in amongst the keyboard fervor. The whole of *Journey to the Center of the Earth* still stands as one of the most interesting conglomerations of orchestral and synthesized music, and it is truly one of Wakeman's most flamboyant projects. —*Mike DeGagne*

Lisztomania / 1975 / A&M ✦✦

Myths and Legends of King Arthur and the Knights of the Round Table / 1975 / A&M ✦✦✦✦
Rick Wakeman's third solo album is among his best, as he employs his vast array of keyboards to their full extent, musically describing the characters pertaining to the days of King Arthur's reign. With orchestra and choir included, although a little less prevalent than on *Journey*, he musically addresses the importance and distinguishing characteristics of each figure through the use of multiple synthesizers and accompanying instruments. "Lady of the Lake" is given a mystical, enchanted feel, perpetrated by a more subtle use of piano and synthesizer, while the battle of "Sir Lancelot and the Black Knight" is made up of a barrage of feuding keyboard runs and staccato riffs, musically recounting the intensity of the duel. But it's on "Merlin the Magician" where Wakeman truly shines, as the whimsy and peculiarity of this fabled figure is wonderfully conjured up through the frenzy of the synthesizer. As one of Wakeman's most famous pieces, it is here that his astounding musicianship is laid out for all to hear, a marvelous bisque of keyboard artistry. The album's entirety is a sensational execution of Wakeman's adroitness, and with vocals from Ashley Holt and Gary Pickford Hopkins, it still stands along with *Journey to the Center of the Earth* and *The Six Wives of Henry VIII* as one of his most astute pieces. —*Mike DeGagne*

● **Voyage: The Very Best of Rick Wakeman** / 1997 / A&M ✦✦✦✦
Voyage is one of the best compilations available from keyboard wizard Rick Wakeman. Not only does this two-CD set include his most acclaimed pieces, but it also gathers material that is less renowned yet equally displays his instrumental prowess. Disc one starts off with four tracks from the famed *Six Wives of Henry VIII*, highlighted by the progressive weight of "Catherine Howard," followed by the synthesized mysticism of "Arthur" and the electronic whimsy of "Merlin the Magician" from *The Legend of King Arthur*. A well-deserved 40 minutes of the second disc is drawn from *Journey to the Center of the Earth*, with wonderful passages from "Recollection" and "The Battle" that emphasize Wakeman's keen approach of instrumentally narrating his music. The true value of *Voyage* lies in the lesser-known tracks that may only be familiar to die-hard fans, but are a must to uncover. Pieces like "Judas Iscariot," "After the Ball," and "Ice Run" are fabulous inclusions to this compilation, since they represent Wakeman's ability to play gorgeous, softly toned pieces as well as massive synthesized blitzes. Additions like "Searching for Gold" and "White Rock" from the album of the same name symbolize Wakeman's gift of producing both a setting and an atmosphere through his use of the keyboard, something that was evident in his days with the Strawbs. Detailed liner notes complete this best-of set, which would make a sound entry point for anyone interested in Rick Wakeman's musical craftsmanship. —*Mike DeGagne*

Recollections: The Very Best of Rick Wakeman (1973-1979) / Oct. 17, 2000 / A&M ✦✦✦✦
With all of his lengthy suites and unified concept albums, Rick Wakeman's solo work would appear to be very difficult to anthologize. As the first Wakeman compilation available domestically in the U.S., that's what *Recollections: The Very Best of Rick Wakeman (1973-1979)* sets out to do. The two tracks from *Journey to the Centre of the Earth* are edited excerpts, but otherwise all the material is present in its original, full-length form. Most of the other pieces (14 in all) are from *The Six Wives of Henry VIII*, *The Myths & Legends of King Arthur and the Knights of the Round Table*, *White Rock*, and *Rick Wakeman's Criminal Record*—most of them cohesive concept works that devoted fans will already have. By its very nature, *Recollections* can't be anything other than a sampler for casual fans, but in that respect it functions very well. —*Steve Huey*

The Walker Brothers

f. 1964, Los Angeles, CA, **db.** 1967
Baroque Pop, Experimental Rock, Blue-Eyed Soul, Soft Rock, British Invasion, Pop
They weren't British, they weren't brothers, and their real names weren't Walker, but Californians Scott Engel, John Maus, and Gary Leeds were briefly huge stars in England at the peak of the British Invasion. With surprising swiftness, they hit the top of the British charts with "Make It Easy on Yourself" in 1965, and "The Sun Ain't Gonna Shine Any More" the following year. While the Walkers looked the part of British Invaders with their shaggy moptops, in fact they were far more pop than rock and rarely played on their records. They favored orchestrated ballads that were a studied attempt to emulate the success of another brother act who weren't really brothers—the Righteous Brothers. Not quite as soulful, lead singer Scott Walker's deep croon wasn't chopped liver by any means, although it betrayed strong debts to non-rock vocalists like Tony Bennett and Frank Sinatra. In the intensely competitive days of 1967, the Walkers' brand of pop suddenly become passé, and the group disbanded in the face of diminishing success and Scott's increasingly fruitful solo career. Scott ran off a series of Top Ten British solo albums in

the late '60s, which have attracted a sizable cult. The Walkers reunited for a while in the mid-'70s, which produced a final British hit ("No Regrets") but disappointing music. —*Richie Unterberger*

Take It Easy with the Walker Brothers / 1965 / Fontana ✦✦✦✦✦
The track listing for the Walkers' first British album is similar to the one for their debut American LP (*Introducing the Walker Brothers*), except that it's missing their first single ("Pretty Girls Everywhere"/"Doin' the Jerk") and "My Ship Is Coming In," and adds three cuts not on the U.S. release. As it happens, these three tracks are worth having, particularly the David Gates-penned ballad "The Girl I Lost in the Rain" and "First Love Never Dies," another son-of-Righteous Brothers epic that would have made a reasonable single. The CD reissue is also much preferable to the American LP since it adds eight bonus cuts from the time, including the singles "Love Her" and "My Ship Is Coming In" and their B-sides, as well as the 1966 EP *I Need You*. A couple of the EP tracks are very strong: "Young Man Cried," another booming ballad with Spectoresque production, was one of Scott Walker's first good compositions (co-written with producer John Franz), and "Looking for Me" is a fine dramatic and little-known early Randy Newman song. Unfortunately "Pretty Girls Everywhere" and "Doin' the Jerk" weren't included on this (or any of the other Walker Brothers CD reissues) as bonus tracks; for those you'll still need to look for *Introducing the Walker Brothers*. —*Richie Unterberger*

Introducing the Walker Brothers / 1965 / Smash ✦✦✦
Their debut album was an erratic affair; they hit their trademark balladeering groove with the hits "Make It Easy On Yourself" and "My Ship Is Comin' In," but sound stiff on uptempo R&B numbers like "Land of 1,000 Dances" and "Dancing in the Street." It does include some interesting tracks which haven't been reissued, most notably the obscure early Randy Newman composition "I Don't Want to Hear It Any More" and the Scott Engel original "You're All Around Me," both of which are the kind of pop/rock ballads which were the Walkers' strongest suit. —*Richie Unterberger*

Portrait / 1966 / Fontana ✦✦✦
The Walkers' second U.K. album was their most commercially successful, reaching number three, yet its quality was quite erratic. Like some other pop/rock LPs of its time, it suffered from an apparent strategy to appeal to a wider demographic than those that typically bought pop/rock records, adding a cover of Louis Armstrong's "Just for a Thrill," the moldy standard "Old Folks," and the pedestrian white-boy soul workout on Curtis Mayfield's "People Get Ready." On the other hand, this had the dramatic "In My Room," a fine antecedent of Scott Walker's moody late-'60s solo outings. The two songs Scott actually wrote or co-wrote, "Saturday's Child" (which sounds too close to "River Deep, Mountain High" for comfort) and the easygoing crooner pop of "I Can See It Now," are okay but nothing more. The LP was filled out by a decent reading of "Summertime," covers of a couple of obscure Leiber/Stoller tunes ("Take It Like a Man" is very much in the Drifters style), and the melodramatic "No Sad Songs for Me" (the best tune that doesn't show up on the *After the Lights Go Out* compilation). The 1998 CD reissue essentially makes this into a whole new product by doubling the length to 24 songs, adding a dozen cuts from singles and EPs of the era. Some of the bonus tracks are among the Walkers' best, such as "The Sun Ain't Gonna Shine Anymore," "After the Lights Go Out," "Archangel," "Deadlier Than the Male," and "Mrs. Murphy." Yet all of these are available on *After the Lights Go Out*, and the rarer cuts aren't worthy of intense scrutiny. There's some excellent stuff on this disc, but as the best songs (from both the original *Portrait* LP and the extra tracks) are on *After the Lights Go Out*, it's only recommended to serious fans. —*Richie Unterberger*

Images / 1967 / Fontana ✦✦✦
The Walker Brothers' third and final album of the 1960s was as wildly uneven as their other pair. Affecting pop/rock ballads and operatic crooner vehicles were interspersed with absolutely inappropriate up-tempo blue-eyed soul (always a weak point for the group) and rock covers; the lugubrious reading of "Blueberry Hill" could be the worst track cut by the trio in the '60s. However, Scott Walker's songwriting and singing exhibited a growth that foreshadowed some of the more ambitious aspects of his early solo albums. The almost classical-sounding "Orpheus" was a standout in this arena, and his "Genevieve" was a fine ballad reflecting the encroaching influence of Jacques Brel. "Experience" was a real oddity, with a German oom-pah-like arrangement backing Scott's exhortation "here's to the people who live in a shell"; he also digs into Michel Legrand's "Once Upon a Summertime" and "I Will Wait for You." The gentle John Walker-written and -sung "I Can't Let It Happen to You" is one of the Walker Brothers' best songs, and undoubtedly the best thing John Walker contributed to their records. The CD reissue adds the four tracks from their 1967 singles, including their covers of "Stay With Me Baby" and "Walking in the Rain," and a good overlooked Scott Walker-penned B-side, "Turn Out the Moon." —*Richie Unterberger*

No Regrets / 1975 / Columbia ✦✦✦
The news that the Walker Brothers were preparing a comeback was not the hottest headline of 1975. Some seven years had passed since the trio parted—seven years during which all three members had essentially sunk from view, without even the benefit of a rabid cult following to set the pulse racing. Remember, this was pre-*Tilt*, pre-*Climate of Hunter*, pre-Julian Cope and Marc Almond, pre-all the subsequent developments which raised Scott Walker at least to semi-mythological status. In a nutshell, the Walkers were so washed up, there wasn't a towel in the world that could dry them. But somebody cared, and, by mid-summer, the Walkers were touring the British cabaret circuit and preparing to relaunch their recording career with "No Regrets," a gargantuan slab of maudlin sadness which wrung every last iota of pain from Scott's voice. Six minutes long, it defied almost every law of pop averages—even Queen's "Bohemian Rhapsody" and the Beatles' "Hey Jude" had variety on their side, as they slipped from movement to movement. "No

Regrets" was one long sulk from start to finish—and it was brilliant. The single shot up the U.K. chart, the Walkers were all over the TV, and the album of the same name was the most eagerly awaited of the season. It stunk. Okay, that's not strictly true. It had its moments—usually the Scott vocals, but occasionally John got a gem in as well. His reggae take on Curtis Mayfield's "He'll Break Your Heart" is a widescreen epic of echo-laden summertime, rivaled in punch only by Scott's closing "Burn Our Bridges." But "Boulder to Birmingham," so recently, sweetly, energized by Emmylou Harris, moldered by comparison with her version, while Janis Ian's "Lover's Lullaby" and Donna Weiss' "Hold an Old Friend's Hand" are the kind of turgid turkeys which the original band broke up to escape from. Had they followed suit this time around, no one could have blamed them in the slightest. —*Dave Thompson*

Lines / 1977 / Columbia ✦✦
The Walker Brothers intended recording the second of their comeback albums in Nashville. They returned from the sessions with just one demo and a burning hatred for everything they found there. "It's a place you go when you want to die," John Walker snapped, and the trio set to work in London instead. *Lines*, titled for the cocaine flavoring of the opening track, emerged a better balanced, but ultimately no more successful album than its predecessor, *No Regrets*. Still uncertain of their true role in the exciting world of mid-1970s pop, the Walkers remained torn between the big balladeering which had served them so well in the past, and the more experimental (or, at least, new) stylings which Scott, at least, was imbibing elsewhere. The end result erred on the side of caution, and painted the group firmly within the realms of middle-of-the-road radio fodder. The sacrifice, however, clearly rankled. Even on autopilot, Scott Walker can sing the pants off most other vocalists. But you can still tell that he is on autopilot, and so "Inside of You," Boz Scaggs' "We're All Alone," and "Lines" itself simply stumble around in search of some energy, then curl up and die before they reach the last chorus. Indeed, when the best song on a Walker Brothers album turns out to be one of John's efforts ("Taking It All in Stride"), you know you're in trouble. Maybe they should have stayed in Nashville after all. —*Dave Thompson*

Nite Flights / 1978 / Epic ✦✦✦
Whatever else they may have been, as their rebirth accelerated towards its gory end, the Walker Brothers remained a democracy, splitting vocals and songs between the three non-siblings, and only occasionally allowing any one the upper hand. But whereas John was still locked into the art-country balladeering which had always been his forte, and Gary was having trouble completing his allotment, Scott had finally realized that he had more to offer than another Kris Kristofferson outtake. As a writer, he had been all but silent since the late '60s, when his peculiarly twisted post-pop visions sent solo album after solo album hurtling into a commercial void. Now, however, he was reaching back into that abyss, and emerged with four songs—"Niteflights," "The Electrician," "Shut Out," and "Fat Mama Kick"—which not only realigned his entire future career, they also twisted the ongoing landscape of rock music itself. Electro-pumping soundscapes of grandiose synth, all four were clearly inspired by Bowie's then recent work with Iggy Pop and Brian Eno. In a perfect world, Scott would have completed the entire album himself, or at least been given an EP to himself. But of course that was not to be, and so *Nite Flights* appeared with the rest of the boys, the rest of the baggage, and, though both John and Gary at least tried to keep up with their bandmate, their failure was as painful as it was inevitable. Gary's "Death of Romance" and John's "Disciples of Death" are at least vindicated by their titles, but the songs are as thin as their composers' voices and could be outtakes from another album entirely. They're certainly from another planet. —*Dave Thompson*

● **After the Lights Go Out: The Best of 1965-1967** / 1990 / Fontana ✦✦✦✦
20 of their best songs, including all of their hit singles. On original compositions like "Mrs. Murphy," "Archangel," "Orpheus," and "Deadlier Than the Male," Scott Walker unveils the disturbed visions that would characterize his solo work, and John Walker's "Saddest Night In The World" and "I Can't Let It Happen To You" display a solid writing talent that he was sadly unable to develop into a solo career of his own. —*Richie Unterberger*

Anthology / Aug. 8, 1995 / One Way ✦✦✦✦✦
Although it contains The Walker Brothers' big hits from the '60s, *Anthology* is basically a resequenced version of the group's first album, adding a couple of bonus tracks. Nevertheless, it's a serviceable introduction to the group. —*Stephen Thomas Erlewine*

Junior Walker (Autry De Walt Mixon)
b. Jun. 14, 1931, Blytheville, AR, d. Nov. 23, 1995, Battle Creek, MI
Vocals, Saxophone / Pop-Soul, Motown, Rock & Roll, Soul
Of all the great musicians who played on scores of Motown records, none of them got label credit, much less a chance to bask in the spotlight. The lone exception was Junior Walker (born Audrey Dewalt), whose tenor sax wailings were made up of equal parts Illinois Jacquet high-note shrieks, Coleman Hawkins growls, and pure Midwest soul. Never much of a vocalist, Walker nonetheless scored hits with his rough-grained chops, though the sax solos remained the definite focal point. Highly influential on the Tom Scott/David Sanborn crowd, Walker should be close to the top of any list of rock & roll's great tenor saxophonists. —*Cub Koda*

Home Cookin' / 1969 / Motown ✦✦✦
Solid, mostly uptempo album, featuring some of his biggest late-'60s hits: "What Does It Take (To Win Your Love)," "Come See About Me," and "Hip City." Among the other tracks, the bittersweet instrumental "Sweet Soul" is a highlight. As with many Motown albums, the most noteworthy tracks are featured on best-of compilations. —*Richie Unterberger*

Nothing But Soul: the Singles / 1994 / Motown ✦✦✦✦✦
This 40-song double CD includes virtually every Walker track of significance, and then some. Walker is a great player and hits a great groove, but that groove can get tiring over

the course of several dozen tracks, especially the similar-sounding early instrumental cuts. Also, the post-'60s selections that take up much of disc two are hampered by material that is inferior to the best output of his '60s heyday. Excellent package and liner notes, but most listeners should be satisfied with the single-disc *Greatest Hits*, leaving this one for the collectors and specialists. *—Richie Unterberger*

• **The Ultimate Collection** / Oct. 7, 1997 / Motown ✦✦✦✦✦
The Ultimate Collection nearly lives up to its billing, featuring 25 tracks on a single disc, including all of Junior Walker & the All Stars' Top Ten pop and R&B hits ("Shotgun," "Do the Boomerang," "Shake and Fingerpop," "Cleo's Back," "(I'm A) Road Runner," "How Sweet It Is (To Be Loved By You)," "Come See About Me," "Hip City, Pt. 2," "What Does It Take (To Win Your Love)," "These Eyes," "Gotta Hold On To This Feeling," "Do You See My Love (For You Growing)," "Walk in the Night"). For most casual fans, those who just want the hits, this will be the definitive collection. *—Stephen Thomas Erlewine*

20th Century Masters—The Millennium Collection: The Best of Jr. Walker & the All Stars / Aug. 15, 2000 / Motown ✦✦✦✦
The Millennium Collection: The Very Best of Jr. Walker & the All Stars gathers highlights from the classic soul group's body of work, including "Shotgun," "What Does It Take (To Win Your Love)," "(I'm A) Road Runner," and "Shake and Fingerpop." Choice album tracks, radio favorites, and covers like the Guess Who's "These Eyes" and Marvin Gaye's "How Sweet It Is (To Be Loved By You)" make up the rest of this overview. While it's not as extensive as *The Ultimate Collection, The Very Best of Jr. Walker & the All Stars* is a concise, affordable hits collection from one of Motown's finest acts. *—Heather Phares*

Scott Walker

b. Jan. 9, 1943, Hamilton, OH
Vocals / Baroque Pop, Experimental Rock, Soft Rock, Pop, Avant-Garde
One of the most enigmatic figures in rock history, Scott Walker exited the Walker Brothers in 1967 to launch a hugely successful solo career in Britain with a unique blend of orchestrated, almost MOR arrangements with idiosyncratic and morose lyrics. At the height of psychedelia, Walker openly looked to crooners like Sinatra, Jack Jones, and Tony Bennett for inspiration, and to Jacques Brel for much of his material. None of those balladeers, however, would have sung about the oddball subjects—prostitutes, transvestites, suicidal brooders, plagues, and Joseph Stalin—that populated Walker's songs. His first four albums hit the Top Ten in the U.K.—his second, in fact, reached number one in 1968, in the midst of the hippie era. By the time of 1969's *Scott 4*, the singer was writing all of his material. Although this was perhaps his finest album, it was a commercial disappointment, and unfortunately discouraged him from relying entirely upon his own material on subsequent releases. After a long period of hibernation, he emerged with an album in 1984, *Climate of Hunter*, which drew critical raves for a minimalistic, trance-like ambience that showed him keeping abreast of cutting-edge '80s rock trends. This notoriously reclusive figure, who has rarely been interviewed or even seen in public since his days of stardom, emerged from hibernation in 1995 with a new album, *Tilt*. *—Richie Unterberger*

Scott / Sep. 16, 1967 / Fontana ✦✦✦✦✦
Scott Walker's success as a teen idol singer of Spectorish ballads with the Walker Brothers in no way prepared listeners for the mordant, despairing lyrics of his solo debut. To compound the surprise, he does his best to imitate the vocal girth of Tony Bennett and Frank Sinatra on this mix of original tunes and covers, which also features sweeping, bloated orchestral arrangements. It was hardly rock, and pop of a most oddball sort, but it found a surprisingly large audience—in Britain, anyway, where it reached the Top Three in 1967. Poke behind the velvet curtain of the languid MOR arrangements, and one finds a surprisingly literate existentialist at the helm of these proceedings. His lyrical nuances were probably lost on his audience of predominately teenage girls, though they've earned him a small cult audience that endures to this day. Besides presenting three of his own compositions, Walker covers tunes by Weill/Mann, Tim Hardin, and Andre & Dory Previn on this album, as well as three songs by his favorite writer, Jacques Brel. Highlights include his exquisitely anguished rendition of Brel's classic "Amsterdam" and his dramatic cover of the early-'60s Toni Fisher pop ballad "The Big Hurt." *—Richie Unterberger*

Scott 2 / 1968 / Fontana ✦✦✦✦✦
Although Walker's second album was his biggest commercial success, actually reaching number one in Britain, it was not his greatest artistic triumph. His taste remains eclectic, encompassing Bacharach/David, Tim Hardin, and of course his main man Jacques Brel (who is covered three times on this album). And his own songwriting efforts hold their own in this esteemed company. "The Girls From the Streets" and "Plastic Palace People" show an uncommonly ambitious lyricist cloaked behind the over-the-top, schmaltzy orchestral arrangements, one more interested in examining the seamy underside of glamour and romance than celebrating its glitter. The Brel tune "Next" must have lifted a few teenage mums' eyebrows with its not-so-hidden hints of homosexuality and abuse. Another Brel tune, "The Girl and the Dogs," is less controversial, but hardly less nasty in its jaded view of romance. Some of the material is not nearly as memorable, however, and the over-the-top show ballad production can get overbearing. The album included his first Top 20 U.K. hit, "Jackie." *—Richie Unterberger*

Looking Back with Scott Walker / 1968 / Ember ✦✦✦✦
When he was still in high school, Walker made his first ventures into the record business as a teen idol-type singer (under the name Scott Engel) for several small labels. All of them sank without a trace at the time, although some were reissued (along with tracks that hadn't previously seen the light of day) in the latter half of the 1960s, after Scott had reached stardom with the Walker Brothers. This has 27 cuts from the late '50s and early '60s, and the music betrays not a shred of the one-of-a-kind talent that would generate his avid cult following. It's putrid stuff that would hold no interest whatsoever for latter-day listeners if Walker had not developed into something else entirely. He does sing well for a teenager (in a much higher voice than he would employ in the '60s), but the material (none penned by Scott) is of strictly hold-your-nose stuff. Much of it, in fact, isn't really rock at all, but son-of-Eddie-Fisher-type pap, arranged with an oh-so-slight eye for the teen rock audience; some of it makes Paul Anka sound gritty by comparison. If you're a completist, it should be said, it's a well-assembled package, gathering most of his excruciatingly rare (and just plain excruciating) early sides in one place. Just beware that the relationship between this Scott Walker and the one that sang morose, complex ballads years later is nil. *—Richie Unterberger*

Scott 3 / 1969 / Fontana ✦✦✦
Scott Walker's final British Top Ten album was the first to be dominated by his own songwriting. Ten of the 13 tunes on this 1969 LP are originals; the remaining three, naturally, were written by one of his chief inspirations, Jacques Brel. There are some interesting moments here. "Big Louise" talks about a hefty prostitute with shocking explicitness for a pop star album of the era. "Copenhagen" (like much of Walker's '60s work) foreshadows David Bowie. "Funeral Tango" is a particularly vicious Brel song. "30 Century Man" is an uncommonly folkish and focused tune for Walker. "We Came Through" is an oddball cavalry charge featuring one of his occasional forays into Ennio Morricone spaghetti Western-like production. The tension between Walker's dense, foreboding lyrics and orchestral production is unusual, to say the least. But too often, it's too difficult to penetrate Walker's insights through Wally Scott's string-drenched production. It shrouds the lyrics in a fog that's often too syrupy to justify the effort needed to fight through it. *—Richie Unterberger*

Scott 4 / 1969 / Fontana ✦✦✦✦✦
Walker dropped out of the British Top Ten with his fourth album, but the result was probably his finest '60s LP. While the tension between the bloated production and his introspective, ambitious lyrics remains, much of the over-the-top bombast of the orchestral arrangements has been reined in, leaving a relatively stripped-down approach that complements his songs rather than smothering them. This is the first Walker album to feature entirely original material, and his songwriting is more lucid and cutting. Several of the tracks stand among his finest. "The Seventh Seal," based upon the classic film by Ingmar Bergman, features remarkably ambitious (and relatively successful) lyrics set against a haunting Ennio Morricone-style arrangement. "The Old Man's Back Again" also echoes Morricone, and tackles no less ambitious a lyrical palette; "dedicated to the neo-Stalinist regime," the "old man" of this song was supposedly Josef Stalin. "Hero of the War" is also one of Walker's better vignettes, serenading his war hero with a cryptic mix of tribute and irony. Other songs show engaging folk, country, and soul influences that were largely buried on his previous solo albums. *—Richie Unterberger*

Til the Band Comes In / 1970 / BGO ✦✦✦
Never regarded among Scott Walker's finest efforts, and a resounding flop when it first appeared in 1971, *Til the Band Comes In* is, retrospectively, the most shocking of all the singer's early albums. His first four, after all, are dramatic slabs of MOR noir, crucial experiences for anybody anxious to discover Brel, Bergman, and a taste for truly surreal pop tones; by their standards alone, shouldn't album number five surely have traveled even further astray? It doesn't. Two tracks culled for the *It's Raining Today* compilation, "Thanks for Chicago Mr James" and "Joe," are this album's sole concessions to such matters as reputation. A year earlier, the BBC gave Walker his own TV series, with the assurance that he would concentrate his tonsils on ballads and standards. He fulfilled the brief admirably, and released a soundtrack album to prove it. Unfortunately, *Til the Band Comes In* suggests he never got the saccharine out of his system. He even brings TV guest Esther O'Farim back into the action, but morbid curiosity and an incomprehensible fondness for "Cinderella Rockefeller" are surely the only reasons anyone could want to check out her solo contribution to the set. There is a reasonable rendering of Roy Orbison's "It's Over," aptly closing the album on a merciful note, but while Walker's first four albums remain essential listening, and the TV LP at least has its moments, *Til the Band Comes In* is best left waiting at the stage door. Some "lost classics" were lost with good reason. *—Dave Thompson*

The Moviegoer / 1972 / Philips ✦✦
Following the disappointing performance of *Til the Band Comes In*, Scott Walker returned to middle-of-the-road pop with *The Moviegoer*. Assembling a set of songs from his favorite films, including compositions from Michel Legrand and Henry Mancini, Walker essentially created a harmless mainstream pop album and delivered it without much care. The record did boast some nice arrangements by Johnny Franz, but the music was seldom noteworthy. *—Stephen Thomas Erlewine*

Stretch / 1973 / Columbia ✦✦

We Had It All / 1974 / Columbia ✦✦

Climate of Hunter / 1984 / Virgin ✦✦✦
Walker's only album of the 1980s was both a blow for artistic credibility, and a blow against most of his old fans. The voice of the balladeer was still intact, and still even crooned sometimes. But the arrangements backed brow-furrowing, obtuse lyrics with '80s-oriented rock that incorporated some quasi-classical structures. Walker was seemingly more interested in painting abstracts in which the textures counted more than the content. This made for an album which may have been a hell of a lot more interesting than '80s efforts by other '60s pop stars, but at the same time it was rather impenetrable, and one's attention tended to drift off over the course of the set. Yet it was not half as radical as the avant-garde direction he would stake out with his next album ten years later, *Tilt*. *—Richie Unterberger*

● **Boy Child: The Best of Scott Walker 1967-1970** / 1992 / Fontana ✦✦✦✦✦
This collection of "Scott's best self-composed songs" features 20 Walker originals from his 1967-1970 heyday. While he covered some interesting material on his albums during this period, paying tribute to Jacques Brel with special devotion and frequency, his original compositions are his most enduring achievements. Besides such highlights as "Big Louise," "We Came Through," "The Seventh Seal," "Plastic Palace People," and "The Old Man's Back Again," it includes half a dozen songs that were not included on the four other solo albums that Fontana UK has reissued on CD. Some of those cuts are very strong, especially "The Rope and the Colt," a dramatic Western ballad with an arrangement that would do Ennio Morricone proud, the positively eloquent despair of the ennui-ridden "Time Operator," and "The Plague," a representative sampling of Walker's taste for the disquieting and bizarre. This is a recommended starting point for those interested in checking out this singularly strange '60s phenomenon, who was a relatively unacknowledged and undetected, but nonetheless substantial, influence on David Bowie and other fashionably decadent British singers. — *Richie Unterberger*

No Regrets: The Best of Scott Walker & the Walker Brothers / 1992 / Fontana ✦✦✦✦✦
Including both of The Walker Brothers' big hits ("The Sun Ain't Gonna Shine Any More," "Make It Easy On Yourself") and highlights from Scott Walker's first four solo albums, *No Regrets: The Best of the Walker Brothers* is a fine overview of Walker's more pop-oriented music, containing the majority of his best-known songs including "Joanna," "Lights of Cincinnati," "Boy Child," "Montague Terrace in Blue," "Jackie" and "If You Go Away," plus one of the best songs from the Walkers' '70s reunion ("No Regrets"). — *Stephen Thomas Erlewine*

Tilt / 1995 / Drag City ✦✦✦✦✦
Tilt was Scott Walker's first album following over a decade of silence, and whatever else he may have done during his exile, brightening his musical horizon was not on the agenda. Indescribably barren and unutterably bleak, *Tilt* is the wind that buffets the gothic cathedrals of everyone's favorite nightmares. The opening "Farmer in the City" sets the pace, a cinematic sweep that somehow maintains a melody beneath the unrelenting melodrama of Walker's most grotesque vocal ever. Seemingly undecided whether he's recording an opera or simply haunting one, Walker doesn't so much perform as project his lyrics, hurling them into the alternating maelstroms and moods that careen behind him. The effect is unsettling, to put it mildly. At the time of its release, reviews were undecided whether to praise or pillory Walker for making an album so utterly divorced from even the outer limits of rock reality, an indecision only compounded by its occasional (and bloody-mindedly deceptive) lurches towards modern sensibilities. "The Cockfighter" is underpinned by an intensity that is almost industrial in its range and raucousness, while "Bouncer See Bouncer" would have quite a catchy chorus if anybody else had gotten their hands on it. Here, however, it is highlighted by an Eno-esque esotericism and the chatter of tiny locusts. The crowning irony, however, is "The Patriot (A Single)," seven minutes of unrelenting funeral dirge over which Walker infuses even the most innocuous lyric ("I brought nylons from New York") with indescribable pain and suffering. *Tilt* is not an easy album to love; it's not even that easy to listen to. First impressions place it on a plateau somewhere between Nico's *Marble Index* and Lou Reed's *Metal Machine Music*—before long, familiarity and the elitist chattering of so many well-heeled admirers rendered both albums mere forerunners to some future shift in mainstream taste. And maybe that is the fate awaiting *Tilt*, although one does wonder precisely what monsters could rise from soil so belligerently barren. Even *Metal Machine Music* could be whistled, after all. — *Dave Thompson*

It's Raining Today: The Scott Walker Story (1967-70) / Oct. 15, 1996 / Razor & Tie ✦✦✦
As the first Scott Walker album to be released in the U.S., *It's Raining Today: The Scott Walker Story* is an adequate 17-song overview of his solo career, containing many of the highlights from his first five albums ("Jackie," "Montague Terrace in Blue," "The Seventh Seal," "The Old Man's Back Again (Dedicated to the Neo-Stalinist Regime)," "Big Louise," "Lights of Cincinnati," "Joanna"), while overlooking some minor gems, including "Matilda" and the B-side "The Plague." Nevertheless, it remains a terrific introduction to Walker's music. — *Stephen Thomas Erlewine*

Stretch/We Had It All / Jun. 24, 1997 / BGO ✦✦
Neither *Stretch* nor *We Had It All* are major items in Walker's catalog, lacking the inspiration of his first albums, the adventure of his latter-day records or the technical mastery of his Walker Brothers recordings. Both albums are slight collections of contemporary country-pop and folk-rock covers, produced in an anemic, bloodless fashion where the strings don't soar, they limp. Walker sounds fine, yet he's singing without much passion or flair. Occasionally, such as "That's How I Got to Memphis," he connects with the song and the results are somewhat engaging, but they don't make this well-produced two-fer worthwhile to anyone outside of hardcore Walker fanatics. — *Stephen Thomas Erlewine*

Wall of Voodoo

f. 1977, **db.** 1988
Post-Punk, New Wave, Alternative Pop/Rock
Best known for their alternative radio classic "Mexican Radio," Wall of Voodoo formed in Los Angeles in 1977, originally as a soundtrack company. Led by singer/songwriter Stan Ridgway and rounded out by guitarist Marc Moreland, bassist/keyboardist Bruce Moreland, keyboardist Chas Gray, and drummer Joe Nanni, the group issued their self-titled debut EP in 1980. With the additions of bassist Bruce Moreland and his brother Marc on guitar (replacing Noland), the band's sound crystallized on 1981's full-length *Dark Continent*, which couched Ridgway's highly stylized and cinematic narratives—heavily influenced by Westerns and film noir, and sung in the vocalist's distinctively droll, narcoleptic manner—in atonal, electronically-based settings.

In 1982, following the exit of Bruce Moreland, Wall of Voodoo released their most successful effort, *Call of the West*, which featured "Mexican Radio," their biggest hit. After an appearance at the 1983 US Festival, Ridgway left the group for a solo career; the remaining members enlisted singer Andy Prieboy, and resurfaced in 1985 with the LP *Seven Days in Sammystown*. *Happy Planet* followed two years later, while 1988's live effort *The Ugly Americans in Australia** (the asterisk denoting that a few tracks were recorded in Bullhead City, Arizona) effectively closed out the Wall of Voodoo story. — *Jason Ankeny*

● **Call of the West** / 1982 / IRS ✦✦✦✦✦
Wall Of Voodoo's second full length album, *Call Of The West*, was a noticeably more approachable work than their debut, *Dark Continent*, and it even scored a fluke hit single, "Mexican Radio," a loopy little number about puzzled American tourists that's easily the catchiest thing on the album. But while Wall Of Voodoo's textures had gotten a bit less abrasive with time, the band's oddball minor-key approach was still a long way from synth-pop, and frontman Stan Ridgway's songs were Americana at it's darkest and least forgiving, full of tales of ordinary folks with little in the way of hopes or dreams, getting by on illusions that seem more like a willful denial of the truth the closer you get to them. There's a quiet tragedy in the ruined suburbanites of "Lost Weekend" and the emotionally stranded working stiff of "Factory," and the title song, which follows some Middle American sad sack as he chases a vague and hopeless dream in California, is as close as pop music has gotten to capturing the bitter chaos of the final chapter of Nathaniel West's *The Day Of The Locust*. In other words, anyone who bought *Call Of The West* figuring it would feature another nine off-kilter pop tunes like "Mexican Radio" probably recoiled in horror by the time they got to the end of side two. But there's an intelligence and wounded compassion in the album's gallery of lost souls, and there's enough bite in the music that it remains satisfying two decades on. *Call Of The West* is that rare example of a New Wave band scoring a fluke success with what was also their most satisfying album. — *Mark Deming*

The Wallflowers

f. 1990
American Trad Rock, Adult Alternative Pop/Rock
As part of the mid-'90s revival of roots-rock, the Wallflowers held a special connection to one of the original inspirations: vocalist/songwriter/guitarist Jakob Dylan. Though he is the son of a legend, Jakob's similarities to his father are occasional—in fact, the Wallflowers are more influenced by Tom Petty & the Heartbreakers than original '60s folk-rock, though lyrically, Jakob remains a close companion to the original Dylan. Released in August 1992, the Wallflowers' self-titled debut album sold poorly, and Virgin soon dropped their contract. Undaunted, the group signed to Interscope and recorded its second album with producer T-Bone Burnett, a long-time friend of the Dylan family. *Bringing Down the Horse* was released in May 1996, producing the alternative radio hit "6th Avenue Heartache." Late in 1996, the single "One Headlight" was released, and by the spring of 1997, it had become a Top 10 hit, pushing *Bringing Down the Horse* into the upper reaches of the charts, as well. Early in 1998, "One Headlight" won Grammys for Best Rock Song and Best Rock Performance by a Duo or Group With Vocal. — *John Bush*

The Wallflowers / Aug. 25, 1992 / Virgin ✦✦✦
The Wallflowers' eponymous debut album is a little too studied and underwritten to make much of an impression, yet there are enough promising moments to suggest that the group was capable of the lean, contemporary folk-rock that made *Bringing Down the Horse* such a winning record. — *Stephen Thomas Erlewine*

Bringing Down the Horse / May 21, 1996 / Interscope ✦✦✦✦✦
No sophomore jinx here. Of course, there are only two Wallflowers left from their first release, so this could be called a whole new band. No matter, because the music here is assured and contemporary with just enough of the past showing through to catch one's eye. Jakob Dylan has been polishing his compositional chops and it really shows on such cuts as "Invisible City," the hit "6th Avenue Heartache" and especially "One Headlight." A fine effort indeed. — *James Chrispell*

● **Breach** / Sep. 26, 2000 / Interscope ✦✦✦✦✦
When Jakob Dylan first debuted with the Wallflowers, nobody expected that he would ever escape the shadow of his famous father, and those doubts hung heavily above the band until their second album, *Bringing Down the Horse*, became an unexpected multiplatinum smash. In light of that success, Dylan became his own man, no longer seen as only Bob's kid. That freedom is evident on the Wallflowers' superb third album, *Breach*. At the time of its fall 2000 release, there was a lot of attention paid to Jakob finally writing about Bob, a subject he steadfastly ignored before, and it is true that several songs do clearly acknowledge his famous father. But that's not the most noteworthy thing about the album. What's remarkable about the album is that he is assured as a songwriter and bandleader. On the surface, there's not much different between this album and its predecessor, but the songs are stronger, sharper, and the performances are lean, muscular, and immediate. Andrew Slater and Michael Penn's clear, surprisingly varied production is a factor, but the credit goes to Jakob Dylan and the Wallflowers; the band has never sounded better and Dylan has never been as convincing as a writer or singer. The result is the finest straight-ahead rock album of 2000. — *Stephen Thomas Erlewine*

Joe Walsh

b. Nov. 20, 1947, Wichita, KS
Vocals, Guitar (Electric), Guitar, Synthesizer / Arena Rock, Pop/Rock, Hard Rock, Blues-Rock, Rock & Roll
From his early hits with the James Gang through to his tenure with the Eagles—as well

as a successful solo career—Joe Walsh remained one of the most colorful characters in rock & roll, lending his distinctively reedy vocals, off-the-wall lyrics, and expansive guitar leads to a series of AOR staples including "Funk #49," "Rocky Mountain Way," and "Life's Been Good." While attending Kent State University, Walsh first picked up the guitar, fronting the collegiate combo the Measles from 1965 to 1969. He then joined the Cleveland-based hard rock trio the James Gang, appearing on their debut LP, *Yer' Album*. The trio's 1970 album, *The James Gang Rides Again*, proved the group's commercial breakthrough, launching the FM radio favorite "Funk #49." While the follow-up, *Thirds*, was another success, Walsh found the James Gang's power-trio format too confining and left the group soon after. After relocating to Colorado, Walsh formed a new group, Barnstorm, recorded a self-titled 1972 LP before making his proper solo debut the following year with *The Smoker You Drink, the Player You Get*. The record cracked the Top Ten on the strength of the pop hit "Rocky Mountain Way." In the wake of 1976's *You Can't Argue With a Sick Mind*, Walsh replaced guitarist Bernie Leadon in the hugely popular West Coast rock quintet the Eagles, making his debut on their best-selling *Hotel California* album. He also continued his solo career, issuing *But Seriously, Folks* in 1978; the record's highlight, the hilarious "Life's Been Good" became his biggest pop hit, nearly reaching the Top Ten. Although 1981's *There Goes the Neighborhood* featured his final Top 40 entry, "A Life of Illusion," he continued recording steadily. —*Jason Ankeny*

Barnstorm / 1972 / Mobile Fidelity ◆◆◆◆
Here is where it all started. Walsh's hyper-productive solo career began with this album, *Barnstorm*. Featuring the would-be regular talents of Joe Vitale (drums, percussion, flute and backing vocals) and Kenny Passerelli (bass and vocals), *Barnstorm* led the way for subsequent Joe Walsh albums. The mix of slow, reserved tracks and heavy-rock riffs that lead into big, beefy solos was a much-similar formula to the style he would use throughout this era.

Barnstorm features many Joe Walsh classics, including the incredibly raucous "Turn to Stone." Walsh here performs one of his most incredible guitar solos, backed by multiple layers of heavily distorted guitar. "Mother Says," "Here We Go," and "Comin' Down" are all highlights of Joe's solo releases, and are all featured on *Barnstorm*. Indeed, this is one of the most enjoyable albums of the decade as well as being a benchmark for Joe Walsh. —*Ben Davies*

The Smoker You Drink, the Player You Get / 1973 / MCA ◆◆◆◆◆
The Smoker You Drink, the Player You Get, Walsh's second solo studio album, continues the heavy and light rock mix of tracks found on his previous release *Barnstorm*. Indeed, the opening two tracks bear this out. The first, perhaps Joe Walsh's most recognized track, "Rocky Mountain Way," comes replete with overly distorted guitars and the obligatory solo. The next song, "Bookends," is a tuneful ode to happy memories. Walsh's ability to swing wildly from one end of the rock scale to the other is unparalleled and makes for an album to suit many tastes.

Joe Vitale (drums, flute, backing vocals, keyboards and synthesisers—a talented man) and Kenny Passarelli (bass and backing vocals) are once again employed, and once again prove themselves adept at handling Walsh's various styles. The album sees an addition to the backing band in the form of Rocke Grace on keyboards and vocals. The legendary Bill Szymczyk works along with Walsh to handle the production, and takes care of the mixing. Szymczyk's work on this area is as always astounding.

The Smoker You Drink, the Player You Get features some of the most remembered Joe Walsh tracks, but it's not just these that made the album the success it was. Each of the nine tracks is a song to be proud of. This is a superb album by anyone's standards. —*Ben Davies*

So What / 1975 / MCA ◆◆◆
Walsh's catalog by this point was two albums strong and of a consistently high quality. Despite a change of staff for *So What*—a wide range of musicians is used, including the Eagles' Don Henley—the sound is very similar to previous releases. A number of classic Joe Walsh tracks are featured including a more polished version of "Turn to Stone," originally featured on Walsh's debut album *Barnstorm* in a somewhat more riotous style. "Help Me Thru The Night," Joe Walsh's mellowest song to date, is helped along by some fine lead and backing vocals from the band.

So What sees Joe Walsh in top gear as a guitarist. Most of the nine tracks feature solos of unquestionable quality in his usual rock style. The classic rock genre that the man so well defined with his earlier albums is present here throughout, and it is pulled off with the usual unparalleled Joe Walsh ability. —*Ben Davies*

You Can't Argue with a Sick Mind / 1976 / MCA ◆◆

But Seriously Folks / 1978 / Asylum ◆◆◆◆◆
As far as studio albums go, *But Seriously Folks* is Joe Walsh's most insightful and melodic. *But Seriously Folks*, released in 1978, was the album the Eagles should have made rather than the mediocre *The Long Run*. It captures a reflective song cycle along the same thematic lines of *Pet Sounds*, only for the '70s. The album's introspective outlook glides through rejuvenation ("Tomorrow," "Over and Over"), recapturing the simple pleasures of the past ("Indian Summer"), mid-career indecision ("At the Station," "Second Hand Store"), and a melancholy instrumental ("Theme From Boat Weirdos"). The disc's finale, "Life's Been Good," is a sarcastic and bittersweet ode to Walsh's "rock star-party guy" persona which reached the Top 10 on the pop charts and became a staple of FM rock radio. The only way *But Seriously Folks* could have been improved, was to include "In the City," essentially solo Walsh, which unfortunately ended up on *The Long Run* instead. —*Al Campbell*

There Goes the Neighborhood / 1981 / Asylum ◆◆◆◆◆

You Bought It: You Name It / 1983 / Warner Brothers ◆◆

The Confessor / 1985 / Full Moon ◆◆
Got Any Gum? / 1987 / Full Moon ◆◆
Ordinary Average Guy / Jan. 1991 / Epic ◆◆
Songs for a Dying Planet / May 1992 / Epic ◆◆◆
Night Riding / Jun. 30, 1992 / Castle ◆◆
Future to This Life / 1995 / Pyramid/Rhino ◆◆
Look What I Did!: The Joe Walsh Anthology / May 23, 1995 / MCA ◆◆◆◆◆
A double-disc set that draws from all of the phases of Joe Walsh's career, with the notable exception of The Eagles, *Look What I Did!* features almost every worthwhile song the guitarist ever recorded, even though it does contain pure dreck like "I.L.B.T.s," which is also known as "I Love Big Tits." —*David Jehnzen*

● **Greatest Hits: Little Did He Know** / Nov. 18, 1997 / MCA ◆◆◆◆◆
The double-disc *Look What I Did!* was simply too much for anyone but the dedicated Joe Walsh fan, which makes the release of the 15-song, single-disc *Greatest Hits: Little Did He Know* … so welcome. Drawing highlights from his solo career and his early records with the James Gang, *Greatest Hits* contains almost every song that most fans would want—"Funk #49," "Rocky Mountain Way," "Life's Been Good," "Meadows," "Turn to Stone," "All Night Long," "A Life of Illusion" and "Ordinary Average Guy." In other words, it's more definitive than *Look What I Did!*, even if it's shorter. —*Stephen Thomas Erlewine*

Travis Wammack
b. 1946
Vocals, Guitar / Rock & Roll
A guitarist, singer, and young instrumental genius from Memphis who cut his first record at the tender age of twelve, Travis Wammack is one of the great unheralded guitarists of rock & roll. A contemporary of Lonnie Mack, Wammack was simply the fastest guitar player in a town bursting at the seams with great guitarists. By the time he was 17, he appeared on the national charts with "Scratchy," a speed-burner instrumental featuring incredible distortion and dazzling technique. Several incredible singles followed, but none charted. By the late '60s, Wammack had moved into session work at the FAME Studios in Muscle Shoals, AL, playing on countless hits. He continues recording and touring to the present day (recently working as musical director for Little Richard), his hot and speedy guitar chops intact. —*Cub Koda*

● **That Scratchy Guitar from Memphis** / 1987 / Bear Family ◆◆◆◆◆
Wammack's best instrumental and vocal sides, 1964-1967. Simply incredible. —*Cub Koda*

Wang Chung
f. 1979, db. 1991
Pop/Rock, New Wave, Dance-Pop
The London-based new wave group Wang Chung had a handful of hits in the mid-'80s, achieving their greatest popularity in the U.S. Originally called Huang Chung, the band consisted of vocalist/guitarist Jack Hues, bassist Nick Feldman, and drummer Darren Costin. The band recorded four tracks for 101 Records in the late '70s, all of which appeared on a pair of compilation albums. Huang Chung released their first single, "Isn't It About Time We Were on Television?," in 1980; the record led to a contract with Arista Records. The group released their first album, *Huang Chung*, in 1982. By the time they recorded 1984's *Points on a Curve*, the band had changed their name to Wang Chung. "Dance Hall Days" was a small hit in Britain, yet the band hit the Top 40 twice in America—"Don't Let Go" made it to number 36, while "Dance Hall Days" reached number 16. From this point on, Wang Chung ignored the U.K. market, choosing to concentrate on the U.S. "To Live and Die in L.A.," the theme song from William Friedken's thriller, just missed making the Top 40 in 1985. That same year, Wang Chung switched from Geffen Records to A&M and Costin left the band. Hues and Feldman continued as a duo and released *Mosaic* in 1986. The album was their biggest hit, launching the number two hit "Everybody Have Fun Tonight" and the Top Ten "Let's Go!"

Wang Chung returned in 1989 with *The Warmer Side of Cool*, which spent a mere six weeks on the charts, spawning the minor hit, "Praying to a New God." After the relative disappointment of the album, the group quietly stopped touring and recording. —*Stephen Thomas Erlewine*

Huang Chung / 1982 / One Way ◆◆

Points on the Curve / 1984 / Geffen ◆◆◆◆
Wang Chung's second album became a moderate hit thanks to the hit singles "Dance Hall Days" and "Don't Let Go." While there was some pleasant new wave-influenced pop/rock on the rest of the album, none of the songs matched the inspired pop craft of the hits. —*Stephen Thomas Erlewine*

To Live and Die in L.A. / 1985 / Geffen ◆◆◆
Wang Chung provided the score for William Friedken's thriller *To Live and Die in L.A.*, contributing a set of atmospheric, moody synth-pop, highlighted by the hit single "To Live and Die in L.A." —*Stephen Thomas Erlewine*

Mosaic / 1986 / Geffen ◆◆◆
The incessantly catchy pop-funk number "Everybody Have Fun Tonight" illustrates the change in musical direction Wang Chung undertook on *Mosaic*. Backing away from the synth-laced pop/rock that characterized their earlier albums, the duo concentrated on dance-pop. Apart from the singles "Everybody Have Fun Tonight," "Let's Go!," and "Hypnotize Me," the band had trouble coming up with well-constructed pop songs, making *Mosaic* a checkered affair. —*Stephen Thomas Erlewine*

The Warmer Side of Cool / 1989 / Geffen ◆◆

● **Everybody Wang Chung Tonight: Wang Chung's Greatest Hits** / Mar. 25, 1997 / Geffen ✦✦✦✦✦

Everybody Wang Chung Tonight: Wang Chung's Greatest Hits does a good job in collecting all of Wang Chung's 1980s hits. In fact, this well-put-together collection doesn't miss a beat—it includes all eight of the duo's charted singles. At times, their music, which was a hybrid of 1980s post-punk pop/rock and new wave, was somewhat middle of the road (case in point—the top ten hit "Let's Go"), but when Wang Chung were at their edgy best, they produced some of the decade's most memorable hits. Among those is the swingin' 1984 top 20 smash "Dance Hall Days," the eerie, mid-tempo "To Live And Die In L.A.," and the unforgettable "Everybody Have Fun Tonight," one of 1986's biggest hits. Also included in this collection is the interesting "Fun Tonight: The Early Years," which is "Everybody Have Fun Tonight"'s original demo (in ballad form) and was the single's B-side (and is quite a good recording in its own right). "Space Junk" is a groovy, shuffling, hip-hop infused new track (at times reminiscent of Portishead) and one of the album's definite highlights. Finally, an updated and surprisingly good house/techno mix of "Dance Hall Days" rounds out this collection, which, for the casual fan, manages to include all of the duo's essential recordings and then some. If only all greatest hits albums could be this thorough! —*Jose F. Promis*

War

f. 1969, Long Beach, CA
Latin Rock, Brown-Eyed Soul, Funk, Soul
Freewheeling War mixed rock, jazz, and soul influences into a spicy stew throughout the '70s, resulting in a series of R&B and pop hits sporting funky melodies and politically aware messages. Born in Long Beach in 1969, the large combo initially served as rocker Eric Burdon's group, backing the ex-Animal on his 1970 million-seller "Spill the Wine." Bidding Burdon adieu, the band signed with United Artists in 1971 and enjoyed its first smash the next year with "Slippin' into Darkness." Tapping into a sizzling, horn-fueled rock/soul synthesis, "The World Is a Ghetto," "The Cisco Kid," and "Why Can't We Be Friends?" all went gold during the mid-'70s. Despite numerous personnel and label changes, War remained eminent throughout the '80s.

In the early '90s, War experienced a revival, partially due to the fact that all of their albums were reissued. But the group was also acknowledged as a primary influence on contemporary R&B and hip-hop. War returned to recording in 1994 to capitalize on their new-found popularity. While 1994's *Peace Sign* wasn't a blockbuster, it was a moderate success, enabling the group to continue recording into the late '90s. —*Bill Dahl*

Eric Burdon Declares War / 1970 / Rhino ✦✦✦

The debut effort by Eric Burdon & War was an erratic effort that hinted at more potential than it actually delivered. Three of the five tunes are meandering blues-jazz-psychedelic jams, two of which, "Tobacco Road" and "Blues For Memphis Slim," chug along for nearly 15 minutes. These showcase the then-unknown War's funky fusion and Burdon's still-impressive vocals, but suffer from a lack of focus and substance. "Spill The Wine," on the other hand, is inarguably the greatest moment of the Burdon-fronted lineup. Not only was this goofy funk shaggy-dog story one of the most truly inspired off-the-wall hit singles of all time, it was War's first smash—and Eric Burdon's last. The odd closing track, a short piece of avant-garde sentimentality called "You're No Stranger," was deleted from rereleases of this album for years due to legal complications, but was restored for its CD reissue. —*Richie Unterberger*

The Black-Man's Burdon / 1971 / Rhino ✦✦✦✦

Burdon's second and final album with War was a double set that could have benefited from quite a bit of judicious editing. Composed mostly of sprawling psychedelic funk jams, it does find War mapping out much of the jazz/Latin/soul grooves that, cut down to much more economical song structures, would shortly bring them success on their own. Highlights include the soulful vamps "Pretty Colors" and "They Can't Take Away Our Music"; the 13-minute "Paint It Black" medley is the height of their eccentricity, and not one, but two covers of "Nights In White Satin" are absurd low points. —*Richie Unterberger*

War / Jan. 1971 / Rhino ✦✦

All Day Music / Feb. 1971 / Rhino ✦✦✦✦

A great War album, the first where all their influences meshed. They blended gospel-tinged soul, funk, Afro-Latin, and light jazz, with enthusiastic group vocals and interplay, plus just the right amount of instrumental support and occasional solos by Lee Oskar on harmonica, Lonnie Jordan on keyboards, and Charles Miller on saxophones and flute. It also contained the fantastic "Slippin' Into Darkness," one of their best-arranged and performed numbers. —*Ron Wynn*

The World Is a Ghetto / 1972 / Rhino ✦✦✦✦

War hit its peak with this 1972 album, the only one they ever released that topped the pop charts. The title track was a triumphant blend of great exchanges and unison vocals, plus concise and spirited musical contributions all around. It also contained the delightful "Cisco Kid" and elaborate "City, Country, City," plus the curious "Beetles in the Bog." Harmonica player Lee Oskar and percussionist Papa Dee Allen were at their best, as were keyboardist Lonnie Jordan and saxophonist/flutist Charles Miller. —*Ron Wynn*

Deliver the Word / 1973 / Rhino ✦✦✦

War began to slide a bit from their early-'70s peak with this release. The best selection, "Gypsy Man," had to be edited for radio, and thus Lee Oskar's roaring harmonica solo wasn't heard by anyone who didn't purchase the album. "Me and Baby Brother" was another of their mock-humorous hits, but overall, this wasn't as sharp or effective an album as the ones they had been making. —*Ron Wynn*

War Live / 1973 / Rhino ✦✦

Why Can't We Be Friends / 1975 / Rhino ✦✦✦✦

War returned with a vengeance and new material in the mid-'70s, as the title hit was both a pop and R&B top 10 smash and "Low Rider" did even better, topping the two soul surveys and peaking at number seven pop. More importantly, they were once more a carefree, loose, jamming band. Unfortunately, it was the last definitive War album, as ego and production battles would soon undermine their success. —*Ron Wynn*

Love Is All Around / 1976 / ABC/Paramount ✦✦✦

When War debuted as Eric Burdon's backing band in the late '60s, they were on ABC-Paramount. The group was still hot in 1976, and ABC reissued vault material from their early days in a deceptive package trying to coast on the band's hitmaker status. The album deservedly flopped, and ABC's clumsy attempt failed. —*Ron Wynn*

Platinum Jazz / 1977 / Avenue Jazz ✦✦

Galaxy / 1977 / Rhino ✦✦✦

War had been on cruise control for over two years due to internal and record company troubles when they resurfaced in the late '70s on MCA. This album was a pleasant surprise, even though it had more disco production than their funk fans wanted. But they got a hit out of the title track, and the better tracks retained the old War grit and eclectic fire. —*Ron Wynn*

Youngblood / 1978 / United Artists ✦✦

The Best of War & More / 1991 / Rhino ✦✦✦✦

It's not a perfect compilation by any means—there's no "The World Is a Ghetto" and a bad remix of "Low Rider," for starters—but it's an important release from this influential band. The original vinyl was definitive. —*Stephen Thomas Erlewine*

Anthology (1970-1994) / Oct. 18, 1994 / Rhino/Avenue ✦✦✦✦✦

A two-disc set collecting the highlights from War's long, prolific career, *Anthology (1970-94)* is the definitive retrospective of the seminal funk band, containing all of their hits as well as most of their best album tracks. —*Stephen Thomas Erlewine*

The Best of War & More, Vol. 2 / Sep. 3, 1996 / Rhino ✦✦✦✦

Since Avenue botched War's *The Best of...and More* by neglecting to put on hit singles like "The World is A Ghetto" and "Gypsy Man"—although there was plenty of room for both songs, among others—the company needed to assemble a second compilation to take care of all the leftover singles and songs that didn't make the first volume. But, they managed to botch *The Best of War...And More, Vol. 2* as well. Sure, "The World Is A Ghetto," "Gypsy Man," "L.A. Sunshine," "Good, Good Feelin'," and several other R&B hit singles made the cut this time around, but the album is baited by an unnecessary remix of "Spill the Wine" by Junior Vasquez, plus selections from their latter-day albums (such as "Peace Sign") that could have been replaced by more first-rate album tracks in the vein of the killer "Don't Let No One Got You Down." Still, if you want to supplement the first *Best of* collection, *Vol. 2* is necessary. However, if you're going to spring for just two discs of War, you might as well go with the comprehensive double-disc collection, *Anthology*. —*Stephen Thomas Erlewine*

● **Grooves & Messages: Greatest Hits Of War** / Jun. 15, 1999 / Rhino ✦✦✦✦✦

Grooves & Messages is another compilation from Rhino that recycles War's greatest hits and, like the previous collections, it contains most of the hits, but not all of them. The difference is, it actually has all the Top 10 pop hits and the majority of the Top 10 R&B hits (only "LA Sunshine" is missing), and it's sequenced in chronological order—two important elements that were absent on *The Best of War* and its sequel, *The Best of War & More, Vol. 2*. Sounds perfect, doesn't it? The problem is, *Grooves & Messages* contains a bonus disc of remixes. There are a couple of big-name mixers here, including Armand Van Helden and Ganja Kru, but none of the mixes are of any interest. Furthermore, the casual fans that will want the first disc will have little use for the second. Still, that first disc is the best, most concise collection of War hits on the market, and *Grooves & Messages* is a specially priced double-disc set, so it may be worth the time of some casual fans, those willing to spend a little bit more to get a good hits collection. However, it would have been nicer if the first disc was available individually. —*Stephen Thomas Erlewine*

Billy Ward

b. Sep. 19, 1921, Los Angeles, CA
Vocals / R&B
The ultra-strict disciplinarian and bandleader of a seminal R&B group, Billy Ward ruled over the Dominoes in a tight-fisted manner. He attempted to regulate everything from onstage harmonies to offstage lifestyles. The group's ranks at one time included Clyde McPhatter and Jackie Wilson, but Ward's insistence on dictatorial control resulted in both of them soon bolting for solo status. The group remained active until the early '60s and scored ten Top Ten R&B hits and two colossal number one singles during its heyday from 1951 to 1957. "Sixty Minute Man" in 1951 was the ultimate innuendo hit, while "Have Mercy Baby" was a landmark uptempo stomper. Each topped the R&B charts for more than two months. All their hits were on either Federal or King, except for their final one, a cover of "Star Dust" in 1957 for Liberty that reached number five R&B and number 12 pop. —*Ron Wynn*

★ **Sixty Minute Men: The Best of Billy Ward & His Dominoes** / Nov. 16, 1993 / Rhino ✦✦✦✦✦

Billy Ward was neither a flamboyant vocalist nor a great instrumentalist; his success came directly from his ability to spot and nurture talent. Unfortunately, Ward was also a taskmaster and couldn't hold onto singers very long after discovering and recruiting them for his groups. But for a short period in the 1950s, Ward and the Dominoes ruled R&B by featuring two of its premier vocalists, Clyde McPhatter and Jackie Wilson. Neither stayed long, but were in the band enough time to make some seminal hits, included in this 20-cut anthology. Ironically, the song the group is remembered for the most featured bass vocalist Bill Brown doing the lead on the title track. *—Ron Wynn*

The Best of the 50's Masters: 1957-1959 / Mar. 21, 2000 / Varese ♦♦♦♦♦
This 19-song anthology covers Ward & the Dominoes' stint with Liberty. Although this was the period that saw them land two of their biggest hits—both "Star Dust" and "Deep Purple" made the Top 20—it's not remembered or written about nearly as much as are their recordings during the first half of the 1950s. That's because their late-'50s material was far less R&B-oriented than their discs for Federal and King, and also because the Dominoes' two best lead singers, Clyde McPhatter and Jackie Wilson, had departed the lineup. Indeed, by this time the group was walking pretty close to the middle of the road, covering numerous pre-rock popular standards and using lots of orchestration. There are still some doo wop and R&B elements involved, but it's far closer to pop than it is to rock & roll. Half a dozen different singers are on lead vocals, though most often taking lead is Eugene Mumford, the voice on "Star Dust" and "Deep Purple." It's not bad as far as harmonized pop vocals go, but often it's rather a throwback to the Ink Spots and the Mills Brothers, and certainly not as innovative as the group's earlier efforts. At times, there's a resemblance to the Platters (they even do "Smoke Gets in Your Eyes"), and for just one moment they turn into a straight R&B/rock group on an unexpected cover of the Jan & Arnie hit "Jennie Lee" that made the middle of the pop charts. Incidentally, five of the tracks (including an earlier vocal take of "Star Dust") were previously unreleased; on one of them, "These Foolish Things (Remind Me of You)," they totally lose the beat going into the second bridge. *—Richie Unterberger*

Warrant

f. 1984

Pop-Metal, Hair Metal, Heavy Metal, Hard Rock

With a pair of double-platinum albums, Warrant were one of the most popular pop-metal bands of the late '80s. Formed in Los Angeles in the mid-'80s, the group featured vocalist Jani Lane, guitarist Erik Turner, guitarist Joey Allen, bassist Jerry Dixon, and drummer Steven Sweet. They released *Dirty Rotten Filthy Stinking Rich* late in 1989; by the middle of 1989, it had climbed into the Top Ten and launched the hit singles "Down Boys," "Sometimes She Cries," and "Heaven," which reached number two. Released in the summer of 1990, *Cherry Pie* was an even bigger success, climbing into the Top Ten and featuring the Top Ten hits "I Saw Red" and "Cherry Pie." Warrant had some trouble continuing their multi-platinum success during the alternative explosion of 1992, although their third album, *Dog Eat Dog*, did go gold; 1995's *Ultraphobic*, however, failed to chart. *Under the Influence*, the band's first proper release in more than six years, was issued in spring 2001. *—Stephen Thomas Erlewine*

Dirty Rotten Filthy Stinking Rich / 1989 / Columbia ♦♦♦♦
Second-tier hair-metal bands like Warrant generally functioned primarily as singles acts, their albums containing perhaps a couple of attitude-laden hard rockers to hook the MTV metal audience while crossing over to the pop charts with a sensitive power ballad or two. *Dirty Rotten Filthy Stinking Rich* followed this formula to perfection; "Down Boys," arguably their best uptempo song, paved the way for the number two pop success of "Heaven"'s gigantic hooks. "Big Talk" and "Sometimes She Cries" were subsequently plugged into the same respective niches with a lesser degree of success, even though they were crafted nearly as well as their predecessors. Unfortunately, the same can't be said of the remainder of the album, which is by-the-numbers '80s metal without the strong hooks to keep it engaging; consequently, it's difficult to take the title track as anything but a crass statement of purpose. Fans of the genre will probably want the cream of this material on the *Best of Warrant* collection. *—Steve Huey*

Cherry Pie / 1990 / Columbia ♦♦♦♦
Cherry Pie, Warrant's second album, was a tighter, more consistent effort than their debut that managed to incorporate some blues into their pop-metal formula. Not only could they rock harder this time around, as the sleazy title track indicates, their ballads were better written, with "I Saw Red" standing as one of their finest moments. *—Stephen Thomas Erlewine*

Dog Eat Dog / Apr. 1992 / Columbia ♦♦♦
As a reaction to the grunge that had wiped pop-metal off the charts, Warrant spat out the tough *Dog Eat Dog*. While the majority of the record is more aggressive and powerful than their first two albums, the songwriting isn't as solid, suffering from a lack of memorable hooks. *—Stephen Thomas Erlewine*

Ultraphobic / Mar. 10, 1995 / CMC International ♦♦♦
Warrant's comeback album *Ultraphobic* was simply released at the wrong time. By 1995, the audience for the band's good-time, party-all-night pop-metal had evaporated, deserting them for the harder-edged sounds of grunge and alternative. Warrant try to sound harder on *Ultraphobic*, but all the grungy guitars sound forced. However, when the band sticks to their trademark metal, they turn in songs that are as good as anything they had ever done. But by the time the record was released, no one was listening anymore. *—Stephen Thomas Erlewine*

Rocking Tall / 1996 / Sony Special Products ♦♦♦

● **The Best of Warrant** / Apr. 2, 1996 / Sony Legacy ♦♦♦♦
The Best of Warrant collects all of the band's singles for Columbia, plus album tracks mostly culled from *Dirty Rotten Filthy Stinking Rich* and *Cherry Pie*. Since Warrant was primarily a singles band whose albums were often cluttered with unmemorable filler, this is the most consistent single disc in their catalog, even with the pointless remake of Queen's "We Will Rock You," and it's the most entertaining way to hear some of pop-metal's best singles, like "Down Boys" and "Sometimes She Cries." A case could be made for more material from *Cherry Pie*, which was more consistent than its predecessor, but *The Best of Warrant* is all that anyone but the devoted will need. *—Steve Huey*

Dee Dee Warwick

b. 1945

Vocals / R&B, Soul, Pop-Soul, Uptown Soul

Like Darlene Love and Cissy Houston, Dee Dee Warwick's considerable gifts as a soul singer were mostly confined to session work. And like Aretha Franklin's sisters, Dee Dee had to struggle with the shadow of a superstar sibling, Dionne Warwick. Certainly she had the talent to compete as an artist in her own right, but she only had a sporadic run of small hits in the 1960s and early '70s, and benefited from neither frequent recording opportunities nor substantial promotion from her labels. Dee Dee began singing with her older sister Dionne as a teenager in the 1950s, forming the Gospelaires. Like many gospel singers, Dee Dee moved into secular soul in the early '60s. Along with Dionne, Cissy, Doris Troy, and the Sweet Inspirations, she was one of New York's most in-demand session vocalists during the era, contributing to numerous pop/soul records by the likes of the Drifters, Chuck Jackson, Garnet Mimms, Aretha Franklin, Nina Simone, and Wilson Pickett. During her early career, Dee Dee was content to make a comfortable living as a backup singer. She began making her own records in 1963, however. She began treating her solo career more seriously in the second half of the 1960s, during which she released almost a dozen singles for Mercury, as well as a couple of albums. Dee Dee's 1960s recordings, while much less successful than Dionne's, were good New York pop/soul with a more pronounced R&B influence than her sister's. Warwick signed to Atco at the beginning of the 1970s, getting a Top Ten R&B single right off the bat with "She Didn't Know (She Kept on Talking)." Over the next couple of years she'd make several other singles and an album, all of which comprised her earthiest work to date. Only "Cold Night in Georgia" made a little commercial noise, however. *—Richie Unterberger*

I Want to Be with You / 1967 / Mercury ♦♦♦♦♦
Not too easy to find, but a strong album that features the original versions of "I'm Gonna Make You Love Me" (which would reach number two as a duet between The Supremes and the Temptations), "Gotta Get a Hold of Myself" (covered by The Zombies), and the Latin-tinged "House of Gold," which sounds like a super-soulful cover of a Jay & The Americans tune. *—Richie Unterberger*

She Didn't Know: The Atco Sessions / Feb. 1996 / Soul Classics ♦♦♦♦♦
In the early '70s, Warwick recorded for Atco with limited success, reaching the R&B Top Ten with "She Didn't Know (She Kept on Talking)," and gaining a couple of smaller R&B hits with "Cold Night in Georgia" and a cover of "Suspicious Minds." She did quite a bit of recording for Atco between 1970 and 1972 in a fairly down-home vein, sometimes with backing by the esteemed Dixie Flyers rhythm section, and backup vocals by the Sweet Inspirations, Cissy Houston, and Judy Clay. These sessions sounded something like a poppier variation on the Stax sound, though none of the songs had the arresting qualities necessary to break her to the pop audience. This 22-track compilation of her Atco work is a typically high-class Soul Classics production, including all the hits, non-LP singles, tracks from her 1970 LP *Turning Around*, and seven unreleased songs that are just as impressive as her official performances from the era. Dee Dee, incidentally, sounds nothing like her famed sister Dionne here, favoring far gutsier vocals, material, and arrangements. It's good late-period vintage soul, and more evidence that Warwick was one of the more unjustly neglected soul performers of her time. *—Richie Unterberger*

● **I Want to Be With You: The Mercury/Blue Rock Sessions** / Jun. 5, 2001 / Hip-O ♦♦♦♦♦
It wasn't for lack of talent that Dee Dee Warwick never approached the mainstream superstardom of her more famous older sister. As a sort of companion to *She Didn't Know: The Atco Sessions*, this generous 26-track collection compiles everything she recorded for the titular label from 1965-1969, with two tracks from a later 1973 session. Although revered by soul authorities as a great talent, when listening to these tracks it's easy to hear why she never clicked with the general public. For all her obvious vocal talents, there aren't enough great songs that draw attention to her fabulous gospel-driven voice. Additionally, like Dusty Springfield, her best assets are often buried behind a fussy and overbearing production that does neither her, nor these tunes, any favors. That said, there are enough gems scattered throughout to justify this disc's existence, especially since it marks the first CD appearance of many of these heretofore rare songs. Warwick lays into the bluesy "That's Not Love" like Etta James, causing distortion as she hauls off and wails with soul-searing power. The obscure Gerry Goffin/Carole King tune "Yours Until Tomorrow," best known from Gene Pitney's version, is a should-have-been hit, as is the original version of "I'm Gonna Make You Love Me," later a smash when the Temptations and the Supremes took it to the charts. Ultimately, Warwick was a substantial talent who didn't find her niche, or land songwriters of the Bacharach/David stature to guide her. This worthy collection—predominantly taken from the original masters but still sounding thin and sometimes shrill—is an important historical item for die-hard '60s soul fans, but disappointing for the casual listener. *—Hal Horowitz*

Dionne Warwick

b. Dec. 12, 1940, East Orange, NJ

Vocals / Pop-Soul, Brill Building Pop, Pop, Soul

The magically melodic voice of Dionne Warwick and the sophisticated pop compositions of Burt Bacharach and Hal David were the proverbial match made in heaven. Warwick proved the prolific songwriting team's favorite interpreter, scaling the pop and soul charts time and again with her soaring renditions of their memorable songs.

Warwick hailed from a musical brood with a strong gospel heritage, and her sister Dee Dee scored a few hits of her own. Dionne's sultry pipes stood out, even on the highly competitive background vocal scene in New York, and she got a chance to step out front in 1963, hitting big on Scepter with the uptown soul classic "Don't Make Me Over."

Under the expert tutelage of Bacharach and David, who doubled as her producers, Warwick's sound soon became smoother and more accessible to pop programming—a formula that resulted in the massive acceptance of her "Walk On By," "I Say a Little Prayer," "This Girl's in Love with You," and a slew of others.

Strangely, Warwick never made it to the top of the pop charts until she broke away from her mentors, traveling to Philadelphia to record the R&B-oriented "Then Came You" with the Spinners in 1974. As elegant and tasteful as ever, Dionne Warwick's breathy vocals still haven't gone out of style—she's managed to remain contemporary while never jeopardizing her appeal. —*Bill Dahl*

★ **The Dionne Warwick Collection: Her All-Time Greatest Hits** / 1989 / Rhino ✦✦✦✦✦
The finest collection of Warwick material compiled by anyone, this excellent set gathered every Warwick gem and smartly remastered them. It's a definitive CD, containing several landmark releases featuring the collaborative compositions of Burt Bacharach and Hal David. These songs underscored Warwick's ability to embody her pop tunes with a soulful, but also light and innocent, quality. It also has excellent liner notes and intelligent sequencing. This is by far the set to get if you want a comprehensive presentation of Warwick's pop/soul greatness. —*Ron Wynn*

Dionne Warwick Greatest Hits (1979-1990) / Oct. 1989 / Arista ✦✦✦
Dionne Warwick enjoyed a career revival in the late '70s and 1980s when she teamed with such producers as Barry Manilow, Barry Gibb, and even Luther Vandross. They returned her to the elaborately arranged and structured soul-tinged pop that had marked her finest hits, although the lyrics and compositions weren't as consistent as they were during the Burt Bacharach/Hal David period. This album collects the biggest hits from this second phase of Warwick's career, including such triumphs as "Deja Vu" and "I Know I'll Never Love This Way Again"; it also introduced a new tune, "Take Good Care of You And Me." —*Ron Wynn*

Hidden Gems: The Best of Dionne Warwick, Vol. 2 / Mar. 24, 1992 / Rhino ✦✦✦✦✦
Turning the spotlight on various rarities, B-sides, and album cuts, *Hidden Gems* reminds us that some of Dionne Warwick's best work with the prolific Burt Bacharach/Hal David team received little or no radio airplay. In retrospect, it's hard to believe that Warwick's versions of "What the World Needs Now Is Love," "The Look of Love" (also recorded by Isaac Hayes, Anita Baker, and countless others), and "Make It Easy on Yourself" (a smash for Jerry Butler) weren't major hits. They certainly deserved to be, as did the hauntingly pretty "Any Old Time of the Day" ("Walk on By"'s B-side) and "They Long to Be (Close to You)." For those who might have overlooked this fine material, *Hidden Gems* is quite a revelation. —*Alex Henderson*

Presenting Dionne Warwick/Anyone Who Had a Heart / 1995 / Sequel ✦✦✦✦
Her first two albums, combined onto one disc for CD reissue. While many of the songs are available on domestic reissue compilations, it's a superb package of early work that qualifies among her best and most soulful, enhanced by tasteful period New York orchestral pop/rock production. Includes her earliest hits ("Don't Make Me Over," "Anyone Who Had a Heart") and lesser-known but excellent songs by Bacharach/David and other composers. —*Richie Unterberger*

From the Vaults / Oct. 1995 / Ichiban/Soul Classics ✦✦✦
An anthology of 24 fairly obscure tracks, drawn from Warwick's 1963-1966 albums and B-sides. Although it has the look of something that would appeal primarily to serious fans and collectors, this is hardly any less satisfying than the greatest hits collections covering the same era. It's also just as good as Rhino's *Hidden Gems*, another anthology of little-known Warwick recordings from the '60s; what's more, it doesn't repeat any selections from that previous compilation. The first half of the CD (covering 1962-1964) shows Dionne at her most girl groupish and soulful, with arrangements that often recall those of her labelmates, the Shirelles (who in fact recorded their own versions of a few of these songs). "It's Love That Really Counts" and "Get Rid of Him" are highlights; "Mr. Heartbreak" is a wrenching, stately ballad, easily up to the standard of her hits of the period. The last half of the program covers material from 1965 and 1966, all of which (like most of the songs she sang in the late '60s) was penned by Bacharach/David. These show her going in a smoother, adult pop-oriented direction, and while the somewhat gutsier earlier sides are preferred, there are some good tunes that are impossible to come by otherwise, except on long out-of-print LPs. —*Richie Unterberger*

Definitive Collection / Apr. 13, 1999 / Arista ✦✦✦✦
Although the title might be stretching it a bit, *The Definitive Collection* is nevertheless a solid overview of Dionne Warwick's storied career; its greatest strength is that it encompasses the full breadth of the singer's catalog, assembling material not only from her peak-era Scepter tracks but also from her later hits on Arista. The vintage Burt Bacharach/Hal David-composed smashes have lost none of their lustre in the passing years, and many—"Walk on By," "Do You Know the Way to San Jose," "Don't Make Me Over" and "Anyone Who Had a Heart"—are presented in their definitive readings; Warwick's subsequent recordings can't help but suffer in comparison, although hits like "I'll Never Love This Way Again" and the Barry Gibb duet "Heartbreaker" possess a certain charm. —*Jason Ankeny*

The Very Best of Dionne Warwick / May 23, 2000 / Rhino ✦✦✦✦✦
Rhino's *The Very Best of Dionne Warwick* collects 16 of the singer's classic singles from 1962-74, the heyday of her collaboration with songwriters Burt Bacharach and Hal David. "Walk On By," "Alfie," "I Say a Little Prayer," and "This Girl's in Love With You" are some

of the hits that define Warwick's soulful, orchestral sound from that era, along with "(Theme From) Valley of the Dolls," "Do You Know the Way to San Jose" and "Then Came You," which also features the Spinners. A must for Warwick fans and worthwhile for anyone interested in classic singing and songwriting. —*Heather Phares*

Was (Not Was)

f. 1980, Detroit, MI, **db.** 1993
College Rock, Pop/Rock, Dance-Pop
Was (Not Was) plays contemporary R&B dance music, with lyrics that range from the satiric to the bizarre. The group is led by Detroit-natives David Weiss (David Was), who plays flute and writes those lyrics, and Don Fagenson (Don Was), who plays bass and writes music, but the group is fronted by singers Harry Bowens and Sweet Pea Atkinson. Was (Not Was) first gained notice for a dance single called "Wheel Me Out" in 1980. Their first album, *Was (Not Was)* (1981), did not reach the charts, but its follow-up, *Born to Laugh at Tornados* (1983), did. Then little was heard from the group for five years. They returned in 1988 with *What Up, Dog?*, which featured the #16 hit "Spy in the House of Love" and the number seven hit "Walk the Dinosaur." (During this period, Don Was had become a prominent record producer, handling the board for Bonnie Raitt's Grammy-winning *Nick of Time*, among many other mainstream pop records.) The fourth Was (Not Was) album, *Are You Okay?*, appeared in 1990.

Are You Okay? wasn't as commercially successful as the previous *What Up, Dog?* After the album's release, Don Was continued to pursue his production career, which began to increase tensions between him and David. In 1993, Was (Not Was) officially parted ways. —*William Ruhlmann*

Was (Not Was) / Aug. 1981 / Island ✦✦
Born to Laugh at Tornados / 1983 / Geffen ✦✦✦
The Was brothers provide a strange bunch of songs with irresistible dance beats, plus an array of guest singers that is, well, unusual to say the least: Mitch Ryder, Doug Fieger (of The Knack), Ozzy Osbourne, and, on the ballad "Zaz Turned Blue," Mel Tormé. —*William Ruhlmann*

● **What Up, Dog?** / 1988 / Chrysalis ✦✦✦✦✦
The guests are fewer (though Frank Sinatra, Jr., sings one song), but the oddities go on, with "11 MPH," a review of the JFK assassination, and "Dad I'm in Jail," a proud rant by David Was. Also included: the hits "Spy in the House of Love" and "Walk the Dinosaur." —*William Ruhlmann*

Are You Okay? / Jul. 1990 / Chrysalis ✦✦✦
The "hit" is a remake of "Papa Was a Rollin' Stone," but the album is more memorable for typically oddball tunes like "I Blew Up the United States" and "Elvis' Rolls Royce," which features a droll vocal by Leonard Cohen. —*William Ruhlmann*

The Waterboys

f. 1981, London, England, **db.** 1993
College Rock, Celtic Rock, Alternative Pop/Rock
Led by the literate singer/songwriter Mike Scott, the groups' sole constant member, the mercurial Waterboys were so named after a line in the Lou Reed song "The Kids," a moniker wholly appropriate given Scott's recurring lyrical fascination with sea imagery. The group issued their self-titled debut in 1983; keyboardist Karl Wallinger joined for the 1984 follow-up *A Pagan Place*, which expanded the group's rich, dramatic sound while further exploring Scott's interest in spirituality. With 1985's *This Is the Sea*, the Waterboys reached an early peak; a majestic, ambitious record, it earned the group a significant hit with the single "The Whole of the Moon." However, after the album's release, Wallinger departed to form World Party, which prompted Scott to relocate to Ireland and begin with a clean slate. When the Waterboys returned in 1988 with the acclaimed *Fisherman's Blues*, they were joined by traditional Irish players, resulting in a stripped-down, folky sound that was continued on 1990's *Room to Roam*. The release of 1993's *Dream Harder*, cut with session musicans, marked a return to an electric, more rock-oriented sound. Soon Scott began a lengthy stay at a spiritual commune; there he recorded the folk-tinged *Bring 'Em All In* under his own name, apparently putting the Waterboys to rest for good. —*Jason Ankeny*

The Waterboys / 1983 / Ensign/Chrysalis ✦✦✦✦
The Waterboys' eponymous debut album finds Mike Scott essaying his vision of "big music." Part Van Morrison, part U2, it was sweeping and romantic, with nearly every song stretched out to epic length. At this point, Scott's vision far exceeds his grasp, yet it's fascinating to hear him try to reconcile the two extremes. —*Stephen Thomas Erlewine*

A Pagan Place / 1984 / Ensign/Chrysalis ✦✦✦
On their second album, *A Pagan Place*, the Waterboys turn Celtic folk-rock into a monumental fusion of Van Morrison's poetry, arena rock, and Phil Spector's monolithic wall of sound. Mike Scott's ideas are simply too grand to be executed properly, yet *A Pagan Place* has enough thrilling moments to make his embarrassing missteps forgivable. —*Stephen Thomas Erlewine*

This Is the Sea / 1985 / Chrysalis ✦✦✦✦✦
Expanding the epic, multi-layered sound of *A Pagan Place*, *This is the Sea* is a more ambitious yet a more successful record, since it finds Mike Scott at his melodic peak. Consequently, the album has enough strong, accessible moments to make his indulgences forgivable. —*Stephen Thomas Erlewine*

Fisherman's Blues / 1988 / Ensign/Chrysalis ✦✦✦✦✦
Mike Scott had been pursuing his grandiose "big music" since he founded the Waterboys, so it came as a shock when he scaled back the group's sound for the Irish and English

folk of *Fisherman's Blues*. Although the arena-rock influences have been toned down, Scott's vision is no less sweeping or romantic, making even the simplest songs on *Fisherman's Blues* feel like epics. Nevertheless, the album is the Waterboys' warmest and most rewarding record, boasting a handful of fine songs ("And a Bang on the Ear," the ominous "We Will Not Be Lovers," "Has Anybody Here Seen Hank?," and the title track), as well as a surprisingly successful cover of Van Morrison's breathtaking "Sweet Thing." —*Stephen Thomas Erlewine*

Room to Roam / 1990 / Ensign/Chrysalis ✦✦✦

With *Room to Roam*, Mike Scott essentially expands the traditional folk of *Fisherman's Blues* by relying heavily on his Celtic leanings, but the record isn't quite as successful, since the record lacks the memorable songs that made its predecessor a surprising success. —*Stephen Thomas Erlewine*

● **The Best of the Waterboys: 1981-1990** / 1991 / Ensign/Chrysalis ✦✦✦✦✦

What separates The Waterboys' music from other bands of the same Celtic, folk-rock sound is the intricacies that lead singer Mike Scott puts into his work. His lyrics are forever tangled up in metaphors and philosophy, brightened by accompanying mandolins, saxophones, and even trumpets. Rich in its boatyard appeal and seaside caricature, *The Best of the Waterboys* harbors their most renowned pieces from 1981 straight through to 1990, bringing to light their dockside effervescence with songs like "Fisherman's Blues" and "Strange Boat." Superb at conveying atmosphere with their instruments, the Waterboys added depth and uniqueness to a decade that was being saturated with arena rock, synth pop, and heavy metal. The sweetness of tunes like "A Girl Called Johnny" and "Spirit" are blanketed with the comfort of Anthony Thistlethwaite's sax and upright bass strumming, and "A Bang on the Ear" loses itself in its cozy Englishness. The prettiest of all the songs is by far "The Whole of the Moon" from *This Is the Sea*, which has Scott singing his most passionate assortment of romantic lyrics to the relaxed pace of Karl Wallinger's synthesizer. The beauty of their music unfolds throughout their vivid collaboration of voice and instrument, heightened in tracks such as "A Man Is in Love" and "All the Things She Gave Me." Here, the small village idioms wrap themselves around the music to produce a certain innocence that forever binds itself to Scott's persona. It is this collaboration of esoteric lyricism and jovial harmonies that cast wonderment throughout each separate piece. This compilation is an excellent discovery point for anyone interested in the gorgeous complexity of the Waterboys' music. —*Mike DeGagne*

Dream Harder / May 25, 1993 / Geffen ✦✦

The Secret Life of the Waterboys 81-85 / 1994 / Ensign/Chrysalis ✦✦

Live Adventures of the Waterboys / Aug. 25, 1998 / Pilot ✦✦✦

The Whole of the Moon: The Music of the Waterboys & Mike Scott / Oct. 6, 1998 / Chrysalis ✦✦✦✦✦

This is the first American compilation to select most of the Waterboys' most memorable tracks and the first compilation to combine Waterboys tracks with songs from Mike Scott's solo albums. Combining all of the group's British chart singles except "And a Bang on the Ear" as well as live tracks, B-sides not previously on an album, and even one previously unreleased studio track, "Higher in Time," from 1991, it is in effect a "the best and the rest" selection of the work of Mike Scott from 1982 to 1997.

The sequencing pays no attention to chronology, instead moving back and forth between the Waterboys' early, ambitious rock creations, the effervescent neo-folk of the *Fisherman's Blues* era, and Scott's sometimes introspective solo work. Despite this, his impassioned singing holds things together better than might be expected, and the effect is not unlike a good Waterboys concert. Since the Waterboys were always more of a rumor than a real commercial threat in the U.S., there is always the chance for the band's music to be appreciated anew, and it didn't hurt that in the same season this album was released, "Fisherman's Blues" was used as the title music for the popular film *Waking Ned Devine*. The album makes an excellent sampler of Mike Scott's work so far. —*William Ruhlmann*

A Rock in the Weary Land / Nov. 7, 2000 / BMG International ✦✦✦

Through the years, the Waterboys have adopted whatever persona or fancy Mike Scott held at a given point in time. Hence, this band has fluctuated from the pop/rock of the early- to mid-'80s to the ensuing folk period to the aimless early '90s, which yielded *Dream Harder*. That was their swan song, which alienated Waterboys fans who grew to cherish the previous two releases, *Room to Roam* and *Fisherman's Blues*. That apparently didn't concern Scott too much, since he equates the individual (himself) with the band in no uncertain terms: "[T]o me there's no difference between Mike Scott and the Waterboys; they both mean the same thing. They mean myself and whoever are my current travelling musical companions." Appropriately, *A Rock in the Weary Land* fuses the complexity, grandeur, and simplicity that have characterized Scott's music in the past. This is the recording that the homogenous *Dream Harder* failed to become. It's ambitious, moody, surreal, and relevant. Scott terms the renewed sound of the Waterboys as "sonic rock," in which he incorporates all of the elements and possibilities of modern rock (which he finds compatible) into a uniform, technically updated body of work. Various distorted and synthesized effects are utilized throughout this album, but typically so are the psychedelic tendencies that Scott has always held dear. John Lennon influences seem to surface frequently, both vocally and compositionally, most notably on "Is She Conscious." And, as virtually all Mike Scott projects (both solo and group) will reveal, much of the content revolves around the struggle, confusion, and inspiration that his growing faith elicits. —*Dave Sleger*

Roger Waters (George Roger Waters)
....
b. Sep. 6, 1944, Great Bookham, Cambridge, England
Vocals, Guitar, Bass / Album Rock, Arena Rock, Psychedelic, Prog-Rock/Art Rock

Roger Waters was a primary creative force in Pink Floyd from 1965 to 1983. His first work outside Pink Floyd came in 1970, when he worked with Ron Geesin on the soundtrack for *The Body*. Pink Floyd's recordings had been moderately successful up to that time, but when Waters wrote all the lyrics and some of the music for 1973's *The Dark Side of the Moon*, it became a commercial breakthrough and one of the most successful albums in rock history. He took an increasingly dominant role in the writing of subsequent Pink Floyd albums, writing most of the lyrics and collaborating on the music for 1975's *Wish You Were Here*, 1977's *Animals*, 1979's *The Wall*, and 1983's *The Final Cut*.

Following the release of *The Final Cut*, Pink Floyd broke up and its members launched solo careers. Waters re-emerged with *The Pros and Cons of Hitchhiking* (April 1984), which went gold. He followed with *Radio K.A.O.S.* (June 1987) and went on tour to promote the release. Following the fall of the Berlin Wall, Waters organized an all-star performance of *The Wall* in Berlin in 1990, resulting in the album *The Wall—Live in Berlin*. He released a third solo album, *Amused to Death* (September 1992), and spent much of the 1990s working on an opera, *Ca Ira*, in French and English. But in 1999, he mounted his first U.S. tour in 12 years. It was so successful that he returned for a second leg in 2000, and the concerts served as the basis for the two-CD set *In the Flesh*. —*William Ruhlmann*

Music from "The Body" / 1970 / EMI ✦✦✦

This soundtrack album, credited to Ron Geesin and Roger Waters, contains various sound effects and musical fragments, plus a few folkish songs on which Waters accompanies himself on acoustic guitar and sings. The result is a precursor to some of Waters' and Pink Floyd's later work ("Breathe," for example, is suggestive of *The Dark Side Of The Moon*), but in an embryonic form. —*William Ruhlmann*

The Pros and Cons of Hitch Hiking / 1984 / Columbia ✦✦✦✦

When dissected carefully, *The Pros and Cons of Hitch Hiking* becomes a fascinating conceptual voyage into the workings of the human psyche. As an abstract peering into the intricate functions of the subconscious, Waters' first solo album involves numerous dream sequences that both figuratively and symbolically unravel his struggle with marriage, fidelity, commitment, and age at the height of a midlife crisis. While the songs (titled by the times in which Waters experiences each dream) seem to lack in musical fluidity at certain points, they make up for it with ingenious symbolism and his brilliant use of stream of consciousness within a subconscious realm. Outside from the deep but sometimes patchy narrative framework, the music slightly lacks in rhythm or hooks, except for the title track that includes some attractive guitar playing via Eric Clapton. David Sanborn's saxophone is another attribute, adding some life to "Go Fishing" and "The Pros and Cons of Hitch Hiking." But it's truly the imagery and the visual design of the album that is front and center, since the importance lies in what Waters is trying to get across to the audience, decorated somewhat casually by his singing and the music. With Pink Floyd, the marriage of Waters' concepts and ideas with the talented musicianship of the rest of the band presented a complete masterpiece in both thought and music, while his solo efforts lean more toward the conceptual aspects of his work. With this in mind, *The Pros and Cons of Hitch Hiking* continues to showcase Waters' unprecedented knack of addressing his darkest thoughts and conceptions in a most extraordinary fashion. —*Mike DeGagne*

Radio K.A.O.S. / 1987 / Columbia ✦✦

Roger Waters' second solo album is yet another conceptual narrative that tells the tale of a wheelchair-bound boy who tries to halt the threat of nuclear war through his use of the HAM radio. The story line isn't held together as tightly as his first album, and the whole fable seems a little too far fetched, even when taken lightly. Unlike *The Pros and Cons* album, the music here overrides the narrative, but not by much, highlighted by the upbeat pop single "Radio Waves." The last tune, entitled "The Tide Is Turning," is the only other focal point of the album, an honest-sounding ballad that relinquishes a glimmer of hope in an otherwise unpromising world. Waters' anti-war theme is stretched full across the album, but the music itself struggles to capture any attention, bogged down by half-whispers and flat-lined melodies that are only slightly resuscitated from time to time with some trumpet and saxophone. The novelty of Los Angeles disc jockey Jim Ladd wears off quickly, as he was obviously used to add some lightheartedness to the album's pessimistic undertones. Waters' use of imagery and thematic depth are absent from *Radio K.A.O.S.*, leaving his superficial spiel with barely any sustenance, which in turn hinders the moral of the album so that it fails to reach its fruition. While both *The Pros and Cons of Hitch Hiking* and *Amused to Death* convey his talented use of concept, imagination, and lyrical mastery, this album seems to be nothing more than a fictional tale with a blatantly apparent message. —*Mike DeGagne*

The Wall: Live in Berlin, 1990 / Aug. 1990 / Mercury ✦✦✦

Nobody really expected the Berlin Wall to come down in 1989, and so suddenly. Roger Waters especially, because he had once made a promise never to perform *The Wall* again after the 1980 tour until the bricks fell in Berlin. But they did, and Waters had no intention to renege on his promise. *The Wall* became a star-studded megaconcert to benefit the Memorial Fund for Disaster Relief, with larger bricks, bigger inflatable puppets, and a larger audience than any of the original Pink Floyd shows. There was always a contradiction in performing such a personal work in a stadium setting, but here it becomes especially acute when opening up the vocal tasks to a variety of artists. Bryan Adams is actually an astute choice for the cock-rock swagger of "Young Lust," but Cyndi Lauper ruins the spare funk of "Another Brick in the Wall Part Two" with over-enthusiastic yelping. And you'll definitely want to skip Jerry Hall's reading of the background dialog before "One of My Turns" ("Oh my gawd, what a fabulous room! Are all these your guitars?"—a piece known word for word by every Floyd fan out there), as she seems unaware that a microphone can be used for amplification. By running through the album track by track, a lot of the effect of the live versions wears thin, as it invites constant comparison to the studio album. But the trial scene is handled well, with Albert Finney, Tim Curry, Marianne Faithfull, Thomas Dolby, and Ute Lemper taking on the characters in Waters' psychological drama. It's fun, a nice document, but only makes you want to return to the original album. *—Ted Mills*

- **Amused to Death** / Sep. 1, 1992 / Columbia ♦♦♦♦

Amused to Death is a solid album both conceptually and musically, showcasing Waters as an artist who, like his work with Pink Floyd, conveys his thoughts and ideals with pinpoint accuracy so that they are engraved within his audience's mind. With this album, Waters touches heavily on the dangers of capitalism, the insensitivity of the human race, the ridiculousness of war, and the onslaught of mindless entertainment that encroaches on mankind on a day-to-day basis. Fitting all these aspects into 14 songs is a task in itself, but accomplishing this task alongside music that is forceful and appealing is extremely difficult, and still Waters succeeds in doing this throughout the duration of the album. "The Ballad of Bill Hubbard" is a moving spoken intro from Alf Razzell, a former member of Britain's Royal Fusiliers. A stab at the false sense of security that lies within religion is dealt with on the powerful "What God Wants, Pt. 1," and the cowardice of the world's leaders is addressed in "The Bravery of Being Out of Range," one of the albums most blatant tracks. Guest guitarist Jeff Beck rises to the occasion on a number of songs here, and both Rita Coolidge and Don Henley fill in behind and beside Waters on a couple of the longer tunes. Ending with the title track, a song that sums up the whole of the album with it's subtle yet hard-hitting demeanor, Waters proves that he can still reveal his conceptual ideas with pristine clarity, only on *Amused to Death*, the music is as equally entertaining and effective. *—Mike DeGagne*

In the Flesh Live / Dec. 5, 2000 / Columbia ♦♦♦♦

Roger Waters' tours of the U.S. during the summers of 1999 and 2000 were a pleasant surprise, since the reclusive rocker had not toured since 1987. In his liner notes to this two-CD set drawn from those performances, Waters does not shy away from discussing his antipathy to big concert venues. But he makes a distinction between stadiums and arenas, and he also notes that he found himself becoming more comfortable in the role of a frontman. This more personable Roger Waters isn't what comes across on the album, but the closer relationship he perceives to his audience is nevertheless palpable. As the man who wrote Pink Floyd's lyrics, he is far more concerned with their meaning than his old bandmates, and his singing is emphasized without robbing the music of its magisterial power. In fact, with a band boasting several guitarists to make up for the lack of David Gilmour, Waters effectively recreates the sound of his Pink Floyd work, which dominates the set list. The album contains only five selections out of 24 from Waters' solo albums: one track from *The Pros and Cons of Hitchhiking* and four from *Amused to Death*, with *Radio K.A.O.S.* left out completely. He does not choose the most obvious solo material, but he makes his selections work, especially "Perfect Sense (Parts I and II)" and "It's a Miracle" from *Amused to Death*. A new song, "Each Small Candle," finds him still obsessed with world problems, but seemingly more optimistic. Waters had seemed to allow his anger about Pink Floyd's continuance without him to keep him from claiming his own part of their legacy. His 1999-2000 touring changed that, and *In the Flesh* makes the point for those who couldn't get to the shows. *—William Ruhlmann*

Jody Watley

b. Jan. 30, 1959, Chicago, IL

Vocals / Club/Dance, Urban, Dance-Pop

Jody Watley got her start as a dancer on the TV show *Soul Train*. From 1977 to 1984, she was a singer in the group Shalamar. Her debut solo album, *Jody Watley* (1987), sold a million copies and produced three Top Ten hits—"Looking for a New Love," "Don't You Want Me," and "Some Kind of Lover." As a result of its success, Watley won the Grammy Award for Best New Artist of 1987. Her second album, *Larger than Life* (1989), went gold and contained the number two pop hit "Real Love" as well as the Top Tens "Friends" and "Everything." *You Wanna Dance with Me?*, released at the end of that year, contained dance remixes of her hits. Watley's third album, *Affairs of the Heart*, was released at the end of 1991; *Flower* followed in 1998. *—William Ruhlmann*

- **Greatest Hits** / Feb. 13, 1996 / MCA ♦♦♦♦

When Jody Watley was at the top of her game, she was truly a force to be reckoned with. Equipped with superior dancing skills, a keen sense of fashion, great looks, sultry vocals, and some of the catchiest pop/dance tunes of her time, Watley scored an impressive string of hit singles in the late '80s and early '90s. Unfortunately, her descent was just as dramatic as her success, and within a few years her hit parade completely stopped. This collection does a great job in compiling all of the singer's essential hits, and a few—including "Don't You Want Me" and "Some Kind Of Lover"—are included in their beefed-up single versions that weren't available on the original albums. Included here is the album-length version of her signature hit "Looking for a New Love," the unstoppable runaway smash "Real Love," the hip-hop club track "Friends" (which featured Eric B. & Rakim), the ballad "Everything," and "I'm the One You Need" (albeit in its original album version as opposed to the single mix). Minor hits, save for "Precious Love," also appear, including the guttural, bass-heavy dance hit "Still a Thrill," the jazzy, sophisticated "Your Love Keeps Working on Me" (which amazingly peaked at an embarrassing number 100), the R&B cut "I Want You," and the pop track "Most of All." Her largely spoken-word single "When a Man Loves a Woman" is also included, but in remixed form—the album version was much better. Finally, this compilation includes a sleek house remix of the album track "Ecstasy." For fans of late-'80s/early-'90s dance/pop/R&B, this stellar collection of irresistible songs is a must, and for new fans it provides a perfect introduction and summary of Jody Watley at her peak (since this album's release, Watley scored another minor hit with "Off the Hook" from the album *Flower*). *—Jose F. Promis*

20th Century Masters—The Millennium Collection: The Best of Jody Watley / Dec. 19, 2000 / MCA ♦♦♦♦

Some of the releases in MCA's *20th Century Masters: The Millennium Collection* series have been downright baffling, essentially just cutting a few tracks from an already-existing hits package. Jody Watley's installment is one of those—aside from the 1998 non-LP single "Off the Hook," which is only available here, every song on this compilation can be found on 1996's *Greatest Hits*, which also features four songs not present here (and is still in print). Granted, if you buy *The Millennium Collection*, you know you'll be getting the original single mixes (i.e., the ones that received radio airplay), whereas *Greatest Hits* did feature a few remixes, including one of the Top Ten hit "Some Kind of Lover" (which some fans may want in the original version). That and the slightly lower price may actually tip the scales in favor of *The Millennium Collection* for casual fans, but otherwise, it's kind of redundant. *—Steve Huey*

Mike Watt

Vocals, Bass / Alternative Pop/Rock, American Underground

Bassist Mike Watt was the living embodiment of the punk rock spirit. As a founding member of the highly influential Minutemen, he created one of the most important bodies of work in the American underground canon, delivering adventurous, fiercely polemical music informed by such disparate traditions as funk, folk, and free jazz. Watt's second group, fIREHOSE, carried on the Minutemen's spirit admirably, and after three indie releases they were signed to major label Columbia, where they debuted in 1991 with *flyin' the flannel*. fIREHOSE's tenure on Columbia was largely disappointing, and after 1993's album, the J. Mascis-produced *Mr. Machinery Operator*, failed to launch the group towards mainstream success, they quietly disbanded in early 1994. In 1995, Watt issued his first solo LP, *Ball-Hog or Tugboat?*, an all-star affair featuring guest appearances from members of Sonic Youth, the Beastie Boys, Nirvana, Soul Asylum, and the Screaming Trees. On a subsequent solo tour, Watt's standing within the alt-rock community was solidified by the roster of his backing band, which included Pearl Jam's Eddie Vedder and Nirvana alum Dave Grohl. A year later Watt played bass in Perry Farrell's band Porno for Pyros, appearing on their sophomore LP *Good God's Urge*; then in 1997 he issued his long-awaited second solo effort, *Contemplating the Engine Room*, an autobiographical "punk-rock opera" also based on the lives of his father, a chief in the navy, and D. Boon. Although his post-Minutemen material—most notably his records with the trio fIREHOSE, as well as his latter-day solo efforts—lacked the sheer impact of his earliest outings, Watt remained true to the D.I.Y. ethos which originally inspired him, emerging as one of the most highly respected figures in contemporary music. *—Jason Ankeny*

Ball-Hog or Tugboat? / 1995 / Columbia ♦♦♦♦

For his first solo album, Mike Watt assembled a different band for each track, creating a veritable who's-who of post-punk and alternative rock—Eddie Vedder, Dave Grohl, Thurston Moore, J. Mascis, Frank Black, Evan Dando, Dave Pirner, Henry Rollins, Flea, Lee Ranaldo, Mike D, and Pat Smear all appear, among others. Predictably, the sound is somewhat schizophrenic, but no more so than the average Minutemen album. *Ball-Hog or Tugboat?* is more polished than anything the Minutemen released, yet looser than fIREHOSE, filled with jazz-inflected breaks and sheer sonic freakouts, but dominated by a surprisingly large number of pop songs. On the power-pop rush of "Piss-Bottle Man," Dando sings with more emotion than on most Lemonheads records, and "Chinese Fire Drill" shows an effective folky side to Watt's music. And Watt's own vocals on "Big Train" are as big-hearted, sly and funny as the album itself. *—Stephen Thomas Erlewine*

- **Contemplating the Engine Room** / Oct. 7, 1997 / Columbia ♦♦♦♦

Mike Watt, recovering from his all-star alterna-rock debut solo album, returned in 1997 with what is perhaps the strongest album he has ever made. Of course, his earlier Minutemen albums will forever go down as landmarks, but in retrospect, many of the band's SST releases were brilliant but uneven affairs that put polemics (and great song titles) over consistent songwriting. Unfortunately, much of fIREHOSE's oeuvre is rife with inconsistency, and on Watt's first solo project, he and his songs were overshadowed by a boatload of high-profile musicians who contributed to the album. *Contemplating the Engine Room* is Watt's masterpiece, what he calls "a punk rock opera." This is a concept album that works on every level: musically, lyrically, and (most importantly) conceptually. Watt (who sings and plays his trusty bass guitar), drummer Steve Hodges, and guitarist Nels Cline form a psychic bond that allows them to dexterously maneuver the complex terrain Watt has laid out in his songs, which celebrate three guys playing together, punk rock, life, and his relationship with his dad. *—Kembrew McLeod*

We All Together

Obscuro, Foreign Language Rock, Pop/Rock, Power Pop, Prog-Rock/Art Rock

The Peruvian band We All Together, though unknown beyond a core cluster of cultists, was among the prime exponents of Beatlesque pop/rock in the early '70s. Led by singer and frequent composer Carlos Guerrero, who (along with some other members) had been in the Peruvian rock band Laghonia, they released two albums (singing in English) in the first half of the '70s. These were fashioned after the lighter side of the late-'60s Beatles, particularly in the vocal harmonies, melodic tunes and sophisticated arrangements blending keyboards, acoustic guitars and electric guitars in a graceful manner. Although Lennon, McCartney, and for that matter, Harrison's influence, show up in We All Together's work, they had more of an affinity for McCartney's engaging melodicism than for the other members of the Fab Four, to the point of covering some obscure, early

McCartney solo tunes. On their second album, they also reached into some British progressive rock riffs, although the Beatle vibe remained dominant. With the exception of Badfinger, they may have been the best band of their time to play in an avowedly Beatlesque style. Their albums, once all but impossible to find in the Northern Hemisphere, were reissued in the U.S. in the late '90s. —*Richie Unterberger*

We All Together / 1973 / Lazarus Audio Products ✦✦✦✦✦
No date of release is given in the liner notes of the CD reissue of We All Together's first album, but since it has a cover of a song from Paul McCartney's *Band on the Run* ("Bluebird") and since their second album came out in 1974, we can assume this is probably from 1973 or 1974. The Beatles, and particularly McCartney, fixation is obvious; they also cover a couple of obscure numbers from Wings' *Wildlife* album ("Tomorrow" and "Some People Never Know"), and throw in Badfinger's "Carry on Till Tomorrow" for good measure. Most of the album consists of original material, though, which is quite accomplished, well-arranged and melodic. What sets them apart from the leagues of other Beatle wannabes is that their song structures are usually not obviously derivative of well-known tunes by the real deal, and executed with a pretty unforced, natural ease. McCartney isn't the only one subject to tribute; "Dear Sally" has an echoey Lennon-esque hard rock vocal right from his Phil Spector-produced era, while "Ozzy" has a mock-Harrison slide guitar part. No, it doesn't get high marks for originality. But if you like late-'60s Beatles, early-'70s Beatles solo albums and Badfinger, you'd be a fool not to try this on for size. —*Richie Unterberger*

● **2** / 1974 / Lazarus Audio Products ✦✦✦✦✦
Their second and final album strongly echoes late-period Beatles, particularly Paul McCartney; in fact, it often seems pitched about midway between the 1969-70 Beatles and the beginning of McCartney's solo career. Although it's hard to shake the nagging feeling while listening to this CD that it's somehow been created by a cover band who got access to discarded early-'70s McCartney demos, it's a convincing and enjoyable emulation of Lennon & McCartney's pop-rock craftsmanship, if more lightweight, less cogent and personal, and lacking in truly world-class tunes. It's on a much higher plateau than Klaatu, for instance. And the Beatles aren't the sole point of reference; guitar riffs on "Follow Me If You Can," for instance, have been altered just enough from Yes' "Roundabout" to avoid plagiarism, while the full guitars and harmonies on many cuts will appeal to many a Badfinger fan. The CD reissue has five bonus cuts, some quite worthwhile. On "Rock of Ages," they offer a surprisingly convincing raunchy rocker, in contrast to their usual midtempo blends of voice, guitar, piano, and some orchestration; Carlos Guerrero's "Together Forever" and "It's Us Who Say Goodbye" are in the mold of folky *White Album* ballads like "I Will" and "Julia"; and there's a faithful version of McCartney's "Band on the Run," not exactly a common cover choice for bands of the time. —*Richie Unterberger*

Jimmy Webb

b. Aug. 15, 1946, Elk City, OK
Producer, Singer, Vocals, Keyboards, Arranger, Songwriter, Piano / Adult Alternative Pop/Rock, Pop, Singer/Songwriter
Jimmy Webb was that rarity in rock music, a professional songwriter; he was also a singer, but his performing career never eclipsed his success as a composer and producer. Indeed, Webb may well have kept the craft of the songwriter in popular music alive and kicking in a new generation, saving the profession from being ghetto-ized onto the Broadway stage and the world of the commercial jingle. In 1966, Johnny Rivers first recorded "By the Time I Get to Phoenix," which became a modest hit; Glen Campbell later cut it as well, and scored a gold record. Meanwhile, Webb was put in charge of the songs for the first album for a fledgling pop group called the Fifth Dimension; the result was a chart-topping million-selling single, "Up Up and Away." Between them, the two songs won eight Grammy Awards the following year, and turned Jimmy Webb into the most prominent songwriter of his generation. Like many of his peers, Webb had begun thinking of longer compositions and more coherent bodies of songs, and soon wrote "MacArthur Park," which fit into the new spirit of the era—the lyrics, although not remotely "psychedelic," were as rich and ornate as anything the Beatles or the Beach Boys were experimenting with, and the arrangement was a vast sonic canvas, filled with the combined sounds of a rock combo and a full orchestra and choir. It was placed with his friend, the actor Richard Harris; after Webb recorded the orchestral part in Los Angeles, Harris' voice was added on at a studio in Dublin. Webb tried selling "MacArthur Park" to several major labels, and was rejected—nobody felt that a seven-minute-plus single by an actor scarcely known as a singer had any chance of being played, much less becoming a hit. Instead, "MacArthur Park" climbed to Number Two on the American pop charts over a period of 13 weeks, and in the process shattered every preconception of air-time restrictions on AM radio. —*Bruce Eder*

Jim Webb Sings Jim Webb / 1968 / Epic ✦
A set of early demo recordings, redubbed and reorchestrated by the record company without Webb's participation or consent. None of his known hits or better songs are here, and the sound isn't terribly impressive either. Webb reportedly hated this release, which tried for the same effect as those early Randy Newman albums on Warner Bros. with far less success, artistic or commercial. Of purely historical interest. —*Bruce Eder*

Words & Music / Feb. 1970 / Reprise ✦✦✦
Words and Music marked Webb's official debut as a singer of his own songs. Though the second side's experiments (a suite in three movements and a song cycle/medley linking "Let It Be Me," "Never My Love," and "I Wanna Be Free") are a little too ambitious for comfort, side one features the concise, well-crafted pop (such as "P.F. Sloan" and "Love Song") that would feature heavily on later releases. —*Chris Woodstra*

And So On / 1971 / Reprise ✦✦✦
Webb's second album stripped down the excesses of its predecessor for a more consistently enjoyable set, featuring the haunting "Met Her on a Plane" (later covered by Ian Matthews) as well as the equally powerful "If Ships Were Made to Sail," "One Lady" and "All My Love's Laughter." —*Chris Woodstra*

Letters / 1972 / Reprise ✦✦✦
The most surprising, diverse, and possibly the most satisfying of all of Jimmy Webb's early solo LPs, *Letters* presents the singer/songwriter in an unexpectedly wide-ranging series of musical settings, all of which complement his somewhat restricted vocal abilities. There are surprises throughout, beginning with the opening cut, "Galveston." Sung by Webb with only a pair of acoustic guitars for accompaniment, this version of the song would never challenge Glen Campbell's recording for time of AM radio, but it is delivered with a quiet fervor and intimacy, and a close embrace of every word, that Campbell's version, for all of its polish, never gets near. Much of the rest of the album, however, has Webb working within a more conventional pop/rock setting, beginning with "Campo de Encino," which comes complete with flute courtesy of Skip Mosher. Webb brushes up against the outer boundaries of his vocal range and expressiveness on several of these numbers, yet, surprisingly, moves nimbly through a rendition of the classic "Love Hurts," which also benefits from a fairly inventive, slightly dissonant, and airy orchestration. Much of the album is hooked around lost or unrequited love on some level, but the sounds are sufficiently varied to hold one's interest. Lest one worry that the album is totally steeped in romantic angst, it isn't quite—one trio of songs deals with different sides of being a songwriter, "Catharsis" casting Webb in a lyrical, gently reflective mood in approaching the dark aspects of fame and creativity; while the hard-rocking, fuzz tone-laden "Song Seller" deals with the creative/business treadmill on which composers can find themselves trapped; and "Piano" is about the solitude that all creativity seems to entail, at some point. —*Bruce Eder*

Land's End / 1974 / Asylum ✦✦✦
While it is safe to say that very few people have heard *Land's End*, it is also a safe bet that some have heard a track or two. Most notable is "Crying In My Sleep," on which Art Garfunkel does such a fine job. Some folks might also remember "Alyce Blue Gown," but all in all, the rest of the music here hasn't found a wide fan base. Webb has quite a number of famous friends along to help him in his musical vision, but when all is said and done, *Land's End* generally falls just a bit short of the runway. —*James Chrispell*

El Mirage / 1977 / Atlantic ✦✦✦✦✦
Produced by George Martin, *El Mirage* is one of Webb's strongest albums. As always, the songs are perfectly constructed but this time sung with more confidence than ever before. Highlights include "If You See Me Getting Smaller" and "Christian No." —*Chris Woodstra*

Angel Heart / 1982 / Columbia/Legacy/Lorimar ✦✦

● **Archive** / 1993 / WEA International ✦✦✦✦✦
Archive is an excellent 20-track (U.K. import only) overview of Webb's criminally overlooked career as a performer from 1970 to 1977, his most productive period. While he is best remembered as the composer of hits for others, this collection offers proof that he was equally adept at interpreting his own songs—often times bringing more emotion to them. —*Chris Woodstra*

Suspending Disbelief / Sep. 7, 1993 / Elektra ✦✦✦
After a several year absence, Webb returns with one of his most polished efforts to date. His hook-filled melodies are instantly endearing, while he sings a love song to his sports car and remembers a meeting with Elvis. His voice, never one his strong points in the past, has aged particularly well. —*Chris Woodstra*

Ten Easy Pieces / Oct. 15, 1996 / Guardian ✦✦✦✦✦
The idea of releasing a collection of Jimmy Webb's best known songs sung by the author himself may seem like a no-brainer, but it's taken 20+ years for it to happen, apparently mostly because Webb needed to put some distance between himself and most of these numbers, in order to approach them in a fresh manner that makes this disc more than a mere exploitation effort. The result is the best and most accessible of all Webb's albums, featuring his 1990s' takes on "Galveston," "By The Time I Get to Phoenix," "Didn't We," "MacArthur Park," "The Moon Is a Harsh Mistress," "Wichita Lineman," and "All I Know," amongst others. His voice is more expressive than ever, and the performances are generally grittier, with more raw emotion than the better known hit versions display. The arrangements are generally very simple and straightforward, with Webb's piano the primary instrument, and several of the songs are performed in a deeply personal manner, more akin to home recording for Webb's own pleasure than to a commercial release—"Wichita Lineman," in particular, sounds here like the most personal and private of performances, filled with wrenching loneliness at which the Glen Campbell version only hints. The notes are very personal and revealing as well. —*Bruce Eder*

The Wedding Present

f. 1985, Leeds, England, db. 1997
C-86, Indie Rock, Post-Punk, Alternative Pop/Rock
Emerging in the wake of the Smiths' demise as the U.K.'s most successful indie-pop band during the late '80s, the Wedding Present were founded in Leeds, England in 1985. The Weddoes (as they were affectionately dubbed by fans) were essentially the vehicle of singer/songwriter David Gedge, the only constant member throughout the group's tumultuous history. The fledgling band quickly won a loyal following among university students, and released their remarkable debut *George Best* on their own Reception label in 1987. The group became the darlings of the British press overnight, winning acclaim for their distinct guitar-pop frenzy as well as Gedge's idiosyncratic vocal style and wittily

lovelorn, conversation-like lyrics. After the album established a foothold on the U.K. indie charts, *Tommy*—a hastily compiled overview of early singles, covers and radio broadcasts—followed in 1988. After reaching the Top 40 with the primal single "Kennedy," the Weddoes returned in 1989 with *Bizarro*, a more conventional effort highlighted by the single "Brassneck," produced by Steve Albini. 1991's aggressive *Seamonsters* returned Albini to the producer's seat.

Instead of recording a new studio LP, the Wedding Present spent the entirety of 1992 issuing a single on the first Monday of each month. Later compiled as the two-volume *Hit Parade* set, the singles featured original material on their A-sides and cover songs on the flipsides, among them interpretations of the Monkees' "Pleasant Valley Sunday," Neil Young's "Don't Cry No Tears," Isaac Hayes' "Theme from Shaft," and Julee Cruise's "Falling" (better known as the theme to *Twin Peaks*). The Weddoes resurfaced for 1994's *Watusi*, a nod towards the Amerindie love-rock scene produced by Steve Fisk. Following a rather uneventful 1995, the group returned in 1996 with a flurry of new material, including the *Mini* EP and the full-length *Saturnalia*. After a final Wedding Present show early in 1997, however, Gedge moved on to form the classic pop-oriented Cinerama. *—Jason Ankeny*

George Best + 9 / Oct. 1987 / Cooking Vinyl ✦✦✦✦✦
This huge collection summarizes the early portion of the Wedding Present's career, the C-86 era of jangly, revved-up indie-pop. The release compiles the band's first album and its first two singles ("Nobody's Twisting You Arm" and "Why Are You Being So Reasonable Now")—23 tracks worth of the hyper pop the band is known for. Apart from the dark and majestic *Seamonsters*, *George Best +* is easily the best possible introduction to the band's work; it's also a fine introduction to the entire C-86 scene that's had such an impact on British rock. It would be impossible to name the "standout" tracks, since the band's strength lies in the fact that every tune is so solid: it should suffice to mention "Everyone Thinks He Looks Daft," "My Favourite Dress," "Anyone Can Make a Mistake," a cover of the Beatles' "Getting Better," and a French version of "Why Are You Being So Reasonable Now?" (the last two featuring Heavenly/Talulah Gosh singer Amelia Fletcher)—then remember that nearly every song in the Wedding Present catalog is just as good as those that have been picked out as singles. This here is a definite classic. *—Nitsuh Abebe*

Tommy (1985-1987) / Jul. 1988 / Cooking Vinyl ✦✦✦
Just one year after releasing their debut album *George Best*, the Wedding Present compiled several early, hard-to-find singles and EPs onto *Tommy*. Not quite the best-of it should be, the album still is necessary for those interested in the band's complete discography. *—John Bush*

Bizarro / Oct. 1989 / RCA ✦✦✦✦
Two years on from their debut album, the Wedding Present delivered a proper sophomore effort, one quite distanced from the jangle-punk days of 1987's *George Best*. Though David Gedge's obsession with the lovelorn had by no means disappeared, the band finally found a way to frame his lyrics properly, resulting in a darker album with more emotional weight where needed. "Brassneck," the Weddoes' first collaboration with engineer Steve Albini, became their biggest hit yet, peaking at number 24 on the British charts. *—John Bush*

Seamonsters / May 1991 / Bizarre/Straight ✦✦✦✦
Steve Albini's production gives *Seamonsters* a noisy, discordant feel in some spots, but David Gedge's suberb songwriting lies just under the surface. He manipulates his limited vocal range into a rich, wistful voice just about to crack. The Wedding Present work best on this album when Gedge's plaintive love songs explode into a distorted fury, as on "Dalliance," and "Suck." *—John Bush*

The Hit Parade 1 / Jun. 1992 / First Warning ✦✦✦✦
The Wedding Present have been unanimously despised by the British music press following a brief honeymoon period in the mid-'80s. When they announced their desire to issue a single a month for a whole year, one particularly caustic *Melody Maker* journalist pointed out that she now had two low spots in her monthly cycle to endure. It must also be said that RCA were not too enamored of the projected release schedule when David Gedge first put his idea to them. For many, though—including discerning onlookers like long-standing friend and supporter John Peel—the Wedding Present's single-a-month blitz in 1992 was one of the highlights of that year. The band were at their peak: They'd just recorded their best record, *Seamonsters*, with Steve Albini, and they were beginning to stretch their sound beyond the coy romanticism of old. However, the real joy of the singles—good as they were—was Gedge's esoteric choices for B-sides, including the Go-Betweens' "Cattle and Cane," Altered Images' "Think That It Might" (Gedge was a huge fan of their overlooked *Love Bites* album), and the Monkees' "Pleasant Valley Sunday." Diverting, original, and great fun. *—Alex Ogg*

The Hit Parade 2 / Jan. 1993 / Bizarre/Straight ✦✦✦
The Wedding Present's second batch of 1992 singles, beginning with "Flying Saucer" and ending on the seasonal tirade "No Christmas." Once again, it's the B-sides that are the most fun. David Bowie's "Chant of the Ever Circling Skeletal Family" may well have been chosen because a band bearing a similar name stalked Leeds in the early '80s, when the city was Goth central. Gedge was also a huge fan of Gerry Anderson, the '60s/ '70s puppeteer and animator—hence the inclusion of "U.F.O." Bow Wow Wow are given overdue kudos via a cover of "Go Wild in the Country," and there's a gutsy attempt at "Theme From Shaft" (long before it became a fashionable nostalgia record). As this collection vividly proves, Gedge and the Wedding Present did a lot to brighten an otherwise moribund early-'90s alternative/indie rock scene. *—Alex Ogg*

● **Watusi** / Sep. 1994 / Island ✦✦✦✦✦
A year and a half after *Hit Parade*, the band released their Island debut. On *Watusi*, the noisy rhythms of *Seamonsters* are gone. Steve Fisk's production gives the LP a more varied musical feel; he lends his piano and organ skills over the crackling and popping of a turntable on the beautiful "Spangle." The first track, "So Long, Baby," begins as a normal, uptempo number, but then completely changes rhythm and melody for the chorus, a surprising and enjoyable move. "Yeah Yeah Yeah Yeah Yeah" is a high-powered, infectious sing-along. Although *Seamonsters* has more beautiful songs, *Watusi*'s diversity gives it an added edge. *—John Bush*

Saturnalia / Sep. 24, 1996 / Cooking Vinyl ✦✦✦
By the advent of this, their second album for Cooking Vinyl, the Wedding Present's career was in terminal decline. Perhaps not artistically, but certainly commercially. Not that such things bothered Gedge, who gave the impression he was pleased to have been able to abuse RCA's (and then Island's) generosity for as long as he had. It would be nice to report that the group survived the move from a major-label berth intact, but this album was a dour affair, lacking the gusto of previous releases. In fact, by the late '90s, Gedge's work with girlfriend Sally Murrell in Cinerama seemed to be of far more interest to everyone concerned, not least Gedge himself. *—Alex Ogg*

Singles 1989-1991 / Mar. 9, 1999 / Bizarre/Straight ✦✦✦✦
Besides the RCA singles released by the Wedding Present from 1989 to 1991 explicitly referred to in the title, this two-CD package also contains non-single material. CD one contains the group's first five RCA singles. CD two is a compilation of radio versions, tracks from compilations, live material, a previously unreleased song "Crushed," and extra tracks that only appeared on 10" versions of the singles. Britain's the Wedding Present is a jangly, power pop band that is diverse enough to recall the Pogues ("Cumberland Gap") and the Damned ("Blue Eyes"). The group also has an excellent sense for selecting material to cover. On *Singles* are their versions of such indie songs as Pell Mell's instrumental "Signal" and the Jean Paul Sartre Experience's "Mothers." Then, they also interpret such more widely known groups as the Velvet Underground with an acoustic "She's My Best Friend" and "Box Elder" from Pavement. On "Box Elder" and often elsewhere here, one may be reminded of the Fall by the voice of vocalist David Gedge (Cinerama) and the group's rollicking, noisy pop arrangements. The eight albums in the Wedding Present's discography and *Singles* are an excellent way to obtain an overview of their oeuvre or fill in the gaps in a fan's collection. *—Tom Schulte*

Registry / Jun. 22, 1999 / spinART ✦✦✦✦
Registry compiles the Wedding Present's first two albums (*George Best* and *Tommy*) with their last two (*Mini* and *Saturnalia*), which were previously out of print in the U.S.. The group's multi-faceted indie-rock shines on tracks like "My Favourite Dress," "Anyone Can Make a Mistake," "At the Edge of the Sea," "Mercury," "Jet Girl," and "Dreamworld." *Registry* is a handy and comprehensive set from an underrated band. *—Heather Phares*

Singles 1995-1997 / Oct. 5, 1999 / spinART ✦✦✦✦✦
CDs these days wrap up most of the Weddoes non-LP releases in neat bows. Their earliest 45s form *Tommy*. In 1999, Manifesto Records released *Singles 1989-1991*, the first five singles the group recorded after signing to RCA, with extra tracks. The band's "single a month" 1992 series of 12 originals and 12 covers can be found on two CDs, *Hit Parades 1 & 2*. There's also a *Peel Sessions* CD. And now the post-*Watusi* work is given the same treatment.

Those who already bought 1996's *Mini-Plus* will feel cheated, as that expanded version of the import *Mini* EP has merely been expanded again, in this case by another 11 songs, and given a new title. Maybe they should have called this *Mini-Ultra*, as that EP remains the centerpiece of this CD's early going. Yet it's the 11 "new" tracks that steal the show, suggesting that the *Saturnalia* period was even more of an inspired period for David Gedge and his latest lineup than the Fall-inspired *Mini*. Of all the hoppin' singles, compilation cuts, and tribute tracks, "2, 3, Go" and "Project Cenzo" positively cook with the speed, breakneck rush, and steamroller-falling-down-a-hill feel of the *George Best* days. Likewise, a cover of the *Cheers* theme is surprisingly great compared to the maudlin original. Live versions of the early single "My Favourite Dress" and *Bizarro* favorite "Brassneck" both slam and smack with in-the-pocket grooves. And, as usual, one always gets the benefit of Gedge's romantic war on himself. If his lyrics at all mirror his own experience, the sad sack singer has been left shaking in shattered silence and tattered nerves 100 times since 1985!

In the end, this argues that the Wedding Present is not an idea that's been exhausted over 12 years-plus. *—Jack Rabid, The Big Takeover*

Ween

f. 1984, New Hope, PA
Comedy Rock, Indie Rock, Alternative Pop/Rock, Lo-Fi
Ween was the ultimate cosmic goof of the alternative rock era, a prodigiously talented and deliriously odd duo whose work travelled far beyond the constraints of parody and novelty into the hallucinatory heart of surrealist ecstasy. Despite a mastery for seemingly every mutation of the musical spectrum, the group refused to play it straight; in essence, Ween were bratty deconstructionists, kicking dirt on the pop world around them with demented glee. Along with the occasional frat-boy lapses into misogyny, racism and homophobia, the band's razor-sharp satire cut to the inherently silly heart of rock & roll with hilariously acute savagery; fueled by psilocybin mushrooms and an all-consuming craving for hot meals, Ween created its own self-contained universe, a parallel dimension where the only sacred cow was their own demon god, the Boognish. *—Jason Ankeny*

GodWeenSatan: The Oneness / 1990 / Twin/Tone ✦✦✦✦
Dean and Gene Ween were barely out of their teens when they recorded *GodWeenSatan: The Oneness*, and it shows: it's juvenile in the best sense of the word, mixing their sprawling sense of humor with punk, heavy metal, and a surprising amount of pop literacy. At

a whopping 23 tracks long, the album features a lot of noodling and lots of whacked-out pop, including "Nan," a dweeby tale of unrequited love, and the jazzy "Never Squeal," which shows off Ween's musical prowess and versatility. *GodWeenSatan: The Oneness* also introduces many of the song styles the band included on their later releases, such as the prog-rock-inspired ballad "Squelch the Little Weasel," the Prince homage "L.M.L.Y.P.," the playful, helium-laced pop of "Don't Laugh" and the funky, soulful "Nicole." "El Camino"'s pseudo-flamenco, "Birthday Boy"'s surprising vulnerability, and the rambling, silly stoner-folk of "Puffycloud" also set the tone for Ween's future work. Though they'd released plenty of cassettes on their own by the time of *GodWeenSatan: The Oneness'* release, Ween still sounds like they're trying ideas on for size. Song snippets like "Cold & Wet," "Fat Lenny," and "I Gots a Weasel" are fun but less successful than some of the band's more developed songs or their more crazed outbursts, such as "You Fucked Up," "Wayne's Pet Youngin'," and "Papa Zit." Stomping rockers like "Old Queen Cole," the sparse weirdness of "I'm in the Mood to Move" and the gospel parody "Up on the Hill"—which introduces Ween's inspiration, the Boognish—make *GodWeenSatan* almost as eclectic and inspired as the albums that followed it. However, the fun Dean and Gene Ween had creating *GodWeenSatan: The Oneness* is palpable, making it more than just a promising debut. *—Heather Phares*

The Pod / 1991 / Elektra ♦♦♦

Another collection of inspired pop pastiche and four-track dementia, 1991's *The Pod* is nearly as long as *GodWeenSatan: The Oneness* but even weirder and more deranged, due in large part to the band's Scotchguard habit and the severe cases of mononucleosis Gene and Dean Ween contracted while recording the album. As a result, *The Pod* is dark and murky, with a slightly distant, fuzzy feel. On some songs, such as the cryptic, prog-inspired "Right to the Ways and the Rules of the World," the psych-tinged "Dr. Rock," and the mystic hard rock of "Captain Fantasy," this sound works well, but on others—like the opening track "Strap on That Jammypac"—it just doesn't fit. Ween flexes their stylistic chops a bit on "Sorry Charlie"'s country-rock, "Sketches of Winkle"'s crazed speed metal, "Oh My Dear"'s cute four-track, and "Pork Roll Egg and Cheese"'s Beatlesque psych-pop, but the majority of *The Pod*, for better or worse, focuses on sludgy weirdness like "Molly," "Awesome Sound," "Laura," and "Can U Taste the Waste?" That most of these songs are grouped together in the middle of the album makes them even more strange and impenetrable—though they may make more sense under the influence of Scotchguard or other, heavier, chemicals. Where *GodWeenSatan: The Oneness'* sense of fun and experimentation was contagious, *The Pod* is insular; you can tell that Dean and Gene had a fun—or at least bizarre—time making the album, but it doesn't translate. Though it does feature a few of Ween's best songs, *The Pod* is easily their most difficult work. However, hardcore fans will still find digging through its messy sprawl worthwhile. *—Heather Phares*

Pure Guava / Nov. 10, 1992 / Elektra ♦♦♦♦♦

By 1993's major label debut *Pure Guava*, Ween had distilled their unique mix of eclectic pop and crazed humor to its essence. *GodWeenSatan: The Oneness* and *The Pod* were fascinating, but occasionally frustrating albums; at 19 songs, *Pure Guava* is more polished and concise, but it's still sprawling and occasionally sick, featuring the fuzzed-out "Touch My Tooter" and the five-minute noise-burst "Mourning Glory," a tale of pumpkin-smoking gone horribly awry. Though "I Play It Off Legit"—a muttered conversation set to atmospheric keyboards—and the rhythmic, bass-heavy "The Goin' Gets Tough From The Getgo" could have appeared on *The Pod*, most of *Pure Guava*'s songs have a poppy, accessible sheen. Fragmented, distorted tracks like "Big Jilm," "Flies On My Dick" and the live favorite "Poop Ship Destroyer" benefit from the album's cleaner production, giddily mixing catchiness and silliness. If *The Pod* was influenced by the band's Scotchguard habit, *Pure Guava* sounds like it was recorded while Dean and Gene were huffing helium; it's fast, shiny and crisp, particularly on the hyper rant "Pumpin' 4 the Man" and the minor alternative rock hit "Push Th' Little Daisies." Ween's prog-rock fascination surfaces on "The Stallion, Pt. 3" and on "Don't Get 2 Close To My Fantasy," which sports wonderfully inane lyrics like "Stare into the lion's eyes / And if you taste the candy / You'll get to the surprise." In the midst of this weirdness, the sweet, seemingly genuine ballad "Sarah" feels like the album's strangest song. With *Pure Guava*, Ween moved away from the snippets of random craziness that defined their first two albums toward a more organized style. Considering Elektra released it, it's just as uncompromising as their previous work, but it hints at just how much further they could go with their music. *—Heather Phares*

• **Chocolate & Cheese** / Sep. 27, 1994 / Elektra ♦♦♦♦♦

A brilliant fusion of pop and gonzo humor, 1994's *Chocolate and Cheese* is arguably Ween's finest moment. Building on *Pure Guava*'s more focused approach, the album proved for once and all that, along with their twisted sense of humor and wide musical vocabulary, Dean and Gene are also impressive songwriters. Over the course of *Chocolate and Cheese*, Ween explore virtually every permutation of pop, rock, soul and funk, from the opening song "Take Me Away"'s rootsy rock to "Roses Are Free"'s homage to Prince's shiny Paisley Park era. On the dreamy, British psych-inspired "What Deaner Was Talking About," the Afro-Caribbean funk of "Voodoo Lady" and "Freedom of '76," their funny, sexy tribute to '70s Philly soul, Ween don't so much parody these styles as reinvent them. Indeed, "Drifter in the Dark"'s surprisingly traditional country and "Joppa Road"'s spot-on soft-rock—foreshadow *12 Golden Country Greats* and *White Pepper*, respectively. Despite *Chocolate and Cheese's* polish and prowess, Ween prove they're still proudly politically incorrect with "Spinal Meningitis (Got Me Down)" and "Mister Would You Please Help My Pony?," two of the creepiest songs about childhood ever recorded. "The HIV Song" revels in its questionable taste and "Don't Shit Where You Eat"'s laid-back pop is one of the album's subtler jokes. Old-school Ween weirdness surfaces on "Candi" (the shouting in the background was recorded from the trunk of Dean Ween's car) and the crazed stomp of "I Can't Put My Finger on It." "Buenas Tardes Amigo," an epic, spaghetti western-inspired tale of murder and revenge, and "Baby Bitch," a wry but stinging retort to an ex-girlfriend, show how good Ween are at taking silly things seriously and serious things lightly. That's exactly what makes *Chocolate and Cheese* such a fun, exciting album. *—Heather Phares*

12 Golden Country Greats / Jul. 1996 / Elektra ♦♦♦♦

The main problem with *12 Golden Country Greats* (which only contains ten songs, by the way) is that it's Ween's first album to concentrate on a single music genre and such concentration lends the impression that they consider themselves above the genre. But that isn't entirely the case. Ween recorded *12 Golden Country Greats* in Nashville with numerous legendary musicians, including the Jordanaires, Buddy Spicher, Charlie McCoy, Hargus "Pig" Robbins, and Russ Hicks. The presence of these musicians gives the music a very authentic feeling, even though the songs stick to '60s trends like country-pop, country-folk, and polished honky tonk. Some of Ween's songs fit this style perfectly, such as the rolling "You Were the Fool," "I'm Holding You," "Japanese Cowboy," "Fluffy," "Help Me Scrape the Mucus off My Brain," and "Pretty Girl." Even the vulgar honky tonk of "Piss up a Rope" works, turning into a truly delightful gem. The duo runs into trouble on the homophobic "Mister Richard Smoker," as well as with some of the vaguely elitist views that underpin the songs, such as on "I Don't Wanna Leave You on the Farm." Still, Ween's gift for songcraft and the talents of the Nashville musicians prevent the album from being just a joke. In fact, it's as satisfying as any of their records, and gutsier, too. After all, no country fan will want to hear this record and most of their fans are afraid of country music, and that's sort of an admirable move. *—Stephen Thomas Erlewine*

The Mollusk / Jun. 24, 1997 / Elektra ♦♦♦♦♦

On the surface, *The Mollusk* is a return to the panoramic, multi-genre extraganza of *Chocolate and Cheese*, but in its own way, it's as much of a concept album as *12 Golden Country Greats*. It just isn't as explicit about its intentions. Nearly every song on *The Mollusk* has a nautical theme, buoyed by a heavy progressive rock influence. Several songs deviate from the theme—the synthetic new wave pulse of "I'll Be Your Jonny on the Spot" and the frenzied pseudo-country of "Waving My Dick in the Wind" are neither seafaring nor prog—but there's an unmistakable watery undertow to the record. Perhaps the loose concept is the reason why *The Mollusk* is the most concise album in Ween's canon, but it's not what makes the record so impressive. Like *Chocolate and Cheese*, *The Mollusk* could seem like a comedy record to outsiders, but the songwriting and performances are so remarkably accomplished that it is just as listenable after the shock of the humor has faded away. "The Mollusk," "Mutilated Lips," "The Golden Eel" and "Buckingham Green" are all startlingly accurate send-ups of prog-rock, and they are better written than many of their inspirations. Similarly, the vulgar shanty "The Blarney Stone," the faux-Richard Thompson tragedy "She Wanted to Leave" and the sunny, Caribbean-flavored "Ocean Man" are terrific songs offering evidence that Ween are improving as songwriters and musicians with each record. Ironically, this array of silly jokes and musical parody is a richer and more diverse listen than most of its alternative rock contemporaries. *—Stephen Thomas Erlewine*

Paintin' the Town Brown: Ween Live 1990-1998 / Jun. 22, 1999 / Elektra ♦♦♦

Culled from some nine years worth of tapes, *Paintin' the Town Brown* comes close to approximating the full gonzo brilliance of a Ween live date—granted, there's nothing quite like the experience of being there in the flesh, watching Deaner and Gener guzzling Jack Daniels while the Scotchgard-addled masses look on adoringly, but it's a fine substitute. The two-disc set (also available on three chocolate-colored vinyl LPs, natch) covers all of the duo's stage incarnations, from their earliest appearances (backed only by a drum machine) to the full band assembled in support of *The Mollusk*; the set list is admirably eclectic, foregoing fan favorites like "Push th' Little Daisies" and "Buenos Tardes Amigo" in lieu of non-album obscurities including "Mountain Dew," "Cover It with Gas and Set It on Fire" and "Vallejo." The highlights are a string of tunes from the now-legendary 1996 tour featuring Bobby Ogdin and the Shit Creek Boys, a group of ace Nashville session men originally tapped to record Ween's classic *12 Golden Country Greats* album. *—Jason Ankeny*

White Pepper / May 2, 2000 / Elektra ♦♦♦♦

White Pepper is Ween's most accessible album to date, lacking their trademark flights of fancy and exuberant bizarreness. By any other standard, *White Pepper* is a weird, wild ride. Let's face it—no other band would even think of recording tracks as diverse as the Brit-pop-styled "Even If You Don't," the Jimmy Buffett parody "Bananas and Blow," a slamming hardcore punk song named after a Burt Reynolds flick ("Stroker Ace"), a tape-warped baroque instrumental called "Ice Castles," and the psych-prog-tinged soft-rock epic "Back to Basom," let alone sequencing all of them in a row. To neophytes, such whiplash shifts in mood may seem alienating (or intriguing, depending on their taste), but to any hardcore fan, it's not surprising and it might not even seem as funny as before. But, if you're listening to Ween just to chuckle, you're missing the point anyway, since they're not just consummate satirists—check out the wonderful "Pandy Fackler," which mimics Steely Dan's lush jazz-pop, down to Gene's deadly Donald Fagen imitation—they're consummate songwriters and musicians. Ween's music rewards multiple plays and *White Pepper* is ample proof. It may not be bracing, nor is it gonzo, yet it's a tight album filled with more pop gems than most bands can hope to achieve in their career. If that seems like hyperbole, especially for a duo that still indulges in silly dirty jokes, it's not. Yes, they may push the boundaries of good taste, but the music is always convincing, from the trippy "Exactly Where I'm At" and "Flutes of Chi" to the minor-key country stomper "Falling Out" and reflective ballad "She's Your Baby." If *White Pepper* isn't as crazy, funny, or sprawling as their previous albums, so be it—it's more satisfying than most records. *—Stephen Thomas Erlewine*

Weezer

f. 1993

Emo, Punk-Pop, Post-Grunge, Alternative Pop/Rock

As one of the most popular groups to emerge in the post-grunge alternative-rock aftermath, Weezer received equal amounts of criticism and praise for their hook-heavy guitar-pop. Drawing from the heavy power-pop of arena rockers like Cheap Trick and the angular guitar leads of the Pixies, Weezer leavened their melodies with doses of '70s metal learned from bands like Kiss. But what set the band apart was their geekiness. None of the members of Weezer, especially leader Rivers Cuomo, were conventional rockers—they were kids that holed up in their garage, playing along with their favorite records when they weren't studying or watching TV. As a result, their music was infused with a quirky sense of humor and an endearing awkwardness that made songs like "Undone (The Sweater Song)," "Buddy Holly" and "Say It Ain't So" into big modern rock hits during 1994 and 1995. All the singles were helped immeasurably by clever videos, which may have made the songs into hits, but they also made many critics believe that the band were one-hit wonders. Perversely, Cuomo began to feel the same way, and decided that the band would not rely on any visual gimmicks for the second album, 1996's *Pinkerton.* Simultaneously, Cuomo took control of the band, making it into a vehicle for his songwriting. While the album didn't sell as well as their 1994 eponymous debut, it did earn stronger reviews than its predecessor. *—Stephen Thomas Erlewine*

● **Weezer** / May 10, 1994 / DGC ✦✦✦✦✦

Weezer was disparaged from all corners when their 1994 debut became a hit. Hipsters and critics *hated* their raucous, melodic, Pixies-meets-metal geek-pop and the group's clever Spike Jonze-directed videos, proclaiming them as charlatans on the order of Stone Temple Pilots. Time has been kind to Weezer, since they not only turned out a second album that was (no joke) a masterpiece, they wound up being as influential on the emo scene as the purer Sunny Day Real Estate. To top it off, *Weezer* stands the test of time, standing as one of the great records of the post-grunge era. It's not as good or personal as *Pinkerton,* but this is a debut and it's a hell of a debut, too, capturing Rivers Cuomo's skills for effortlessly catchy, bone-crunching alt-pop, best heard on singles like "Buddy Holly," "Undone—The Sweater Song," and "Say It Ain't So," but much of the album is at a similar level of excellence. Also, there's something utterly charming about his sensibility and the band itself, who play with spirit, chiming in with tag-team harmonies. This, as much as grunge itself, is the music of outsiders. Specifically, it's the music of geeks, smart kids that loved comics, books, TV, metal, and girls, but were too afraid to talk to them directly. This spirit is what gave Weezer its character and it's the reason why the group remains beloved by a band of outsiders, years after this scaled to the top of the charts. *—Stephen Thomas Erlewine*

Pinkerton / Sep. 24, 1996 / Geffen ✦✦✦✦✦

From the pounding, primal assault of the opening track "Tired of Having Sex," it's clear from the outset that *Pinkerton* is a different record than the sunny, heavy guitar-pop of Weezer's eponymous debut. The first noticible difference is the darker, messier sound—the guitars rage and squeal, the beats are brutal and visceral, the vocals are mixed to the front, filled with overlapping, off-the-cuff backing vocals. In short, it sounds like the work of a live band, which makes it all the more ironic that *Pinkerton,* at its core, is a singer-songwriter record, representing Rivers Cuomo's bid for respectability. Since he hasn't changed Weezer's blend of power-pop and heavy metal (only the closing song, "Butterfly," is performed acoustically), many critics and much of the band's casual fans didn't notice Cuomo's signficant growth as a songwriter. Loosely structured as a concept album based on *Madame Butterfly,* each song works as an individual entity, driven by powerful, melodic hooks, a self-deprecating sense of humor ("Pink Triangle" is about a crush on a lesbian) and a touching vulnerability ("Across the Sea," "Why Bother?"). Weezer can still turn out catchy, off-beat singles—"The Good Life" has a chorus that is more memorable than "Buddy Holly," "El Scorcho" twists Pavement's junk-culture references in on itself, "Falling for You" is the most propulsive thing they've yet recorded—but their endearing geekiness isn't as cutesy as before, which means the album wasn't as successful on the charts. But, it's the better album, full of crunching power-pop with a surprisingly strong emotional undercurrent that becomes all the more resonant with each play. *—Stephen Thomas Erlewine*

Weezer (Green Album) / May 15, 2001 / Geffen ✦✦✦✦✦

Rivers Cuomo didn't want to record another album unless he knew somebody was listening, because he didn't know if there was a purpose otherwise. This is the quality that came shining through on *Pinkerton,* and it's also apparent on this Weezer album (which will inevitably be known as the *Green Album,* much like how fans dubbed the debut the *Blue Album,* due to its cover background), even if he consciously shies away from the stark autobiography that made their previous album. Sure, there may be clues tucked away in any of these songs, but for the most part, this is simply a collection of punk-pop songs in the now-patented Weezer style. And that, quite frankly, is more than enough. This may be a *very* short album—a mere 28:34, actually—but that just makes it bracing, a reminder of how good, nay great, this band can be. Especially since this is a conscious return to their debut, this may seem like nothing special—it's just punk-pop, delivered without much dynamic range but with a whole lot of hooks—but *nobody* else does it this well, no matter how many bands try. And, frankly, that's enough, because this band rocks tight and focused, with wonderful melodies, and songs that have enough little details to give them personality, even when Rivers is avoiding personality. This is a combination of great performances and great songwriting, something that puts to shame both the mainstream rockers and underground wannabes of the early 2000s. That's Weezer's great strength—they certainly are accessible, but they're so idiosyncratic within that realm, it's hard not to think of them as outsiders. *—Stephen Thomas Erlewine*

Paul Weller

b. May 25, 1958, Woking, Surrey, England

Vocals, Keyboards, Songwriter, Guitar / British Trad Rock, Pop/Rock, Singer/Songwriter

As the leader of the Jam, Paul Weller fronted the most popular British band of the punk era, influencing legions of English rockers that ranged from his mod-revival contemporaries to the Smiths in the '80s and Oasis in the '90s. During the final days of the Jam, he developed a fascination with Motown and soul, which led him to form the sophisti-pop group the Style Council in 1983. As the Style Council's career progressed, Weller's interest in soul developed into an infatuation with jazz-pop and house music, which eventually led to gradual erosion of his audience—by 1990, he couldn't get a record contract in the UK, where he had previously been worshipped as a demi-god. As a solo artist, Weller returned to soul music as an inspiration, cutting it with the progressive, hippie tendencies of Traffic. Weller's solo records were more organic and rootsier than the Style Council, which helped him regain his popularity within Britain. By the mid-'90s, he had released three successful albums which were both critically-acclaimed and massively popular in England, where contemporary bands like Ocean Colour Scene were citing him as an influence. Just as importantly, many observers, while occasionally criticizing the trad-rock nature of his music, acknowledged that Weller was one of the few rock veterans that had managed to stay vital within the second decade of his career. *—Stephen Thomas Erlewine*

Paul Weller / Oct. 6, 1992 / Go! Discs/London ✦✦✦✦

Humiliated by Polydor's rejection of the final Style Council album (it remained unreleased until the 1998 box set), Paul Weller retreated from the spotlight, licked his wounds, and redefined his music. He re-emerged with the Paul Weller Movement and the surging trad rock single "Into Tomorrow," a song that may not have been a big hit, but it signaled that he had begun a productive new phase. That same criticism applies to his 1992 solo debut (by this point, he had dropped "Movement," and decided to just be "Weller"). Heavily inspired by soul and classic rock (more early Humble Pie than Led Zeppelin, of course), it's a solid effort whose best songs—the opening triptych "Uh Huh Oh Yeh," "I Didn't Mean to Hurt You," and "Bull-Rush," plus "Into Tomorrow"—demonstrate the virtues of nostalgia, particularly when it's tempered with fine songwriting. If he drifts a bit toward the end, and winds up with some lightweight songs, it's still gritty and effective, displaying a focus absent in the Style Council's last few albums. It's not a full-fledged comeback (that would arrive next), but it's a fine start all the same. *—Stephen Thomas Erlewine*

● **Wild Wood** / 1993 / Go! Discs/London ✦✦✦✦✦

Paul Weller deservedly regained his status as the Modfather with his second solo album, *Wild Wood.* Actually, the album is only tangentially related to mod, since Weller picks up on the classicism of his debut, adding heavy elements of pastoral British folk and Traffic-styled trippiness. Add to that a yearning introspection and a clean production that nevertheless feels a little rustic, even homemade, and the result is his first true masterwork since ending the Jam. The great irony of the record is that many of the songs—"Has My Fire Really Gone Out?," "Can You Heal Us (Holy Man)"—question his motivation and, as is apparent in his spirited performances, he reawakened his music by writing these searching songs. Though this isn't as adventurous as the Style Council, it succeeds on its own terms, and winds up being a great testament from an artist entering middle age. And, it helped kick off the trad rock that dominated British music during the '90s. *—Stephen Thomas Erlewine*

Paul Weller Live Wood / 1994 / Go! Discs ✦✦✦

Weller's career was revitalized with *Wild Wood,* which sparked an equally successful world tour captured on the energetic *Live Wood.* The songs remain just as impressive, but what makes the live record worthwhile is the wonderful interplay of the band. They frequently launch into tight jams that never seem bloated, which is the mark of a good live album. *—Stephen Thomas Erlewine*

Stanley Road / Jun. 7, 1995 / Go! Discs/London ✦✦✦

In many ways, *Stanley Road* is *Wild Wood—Part Two,* a continuation of the laidback, soul-inflected rock that dominated his previous albums. Named after the street where he grew up, *Stanley Road* could be seen as a return to Paul Weller's roots, yet his roots were in The Who and the Kinks, not in Traffic. (At this point, the sound of The Jam matters little in what his music sounds like.) Weller's music has always had R&B roots—the major difference with both *Wild Wood* and *Stanley Road* is how much he and his band stretch out. *Stanley Road* in particular features more jamming than any of his previous work. That doesn't mean he has neglected his songwriting—a handful of Weller classics are scattered throughout the album. Unfortunately, too much of it is spent on drawn-out grooves that are self-conscious about their own authenticity. Still, he has the good sense to revive Dr. John's "I Walk on Gilded Splinters" and invite his disciple Noel Gallagher (Oasis) along to jam. *—Stephen Thomas Erlewine*

Heavy Soul / Aug. 5, 1997 / Go! Discs/London ✦✦✦

Like *Stanley Road* before it, *Heavy Soul* is more about vibe than songs. There are a few sharply written tracks here and there, but what's important is the rootsy, stripped-down atmosphere. Weller's soul and R&B influences reign supreme on *Heavy Soul,* yet they are filtered through late-'60s psychedelia, blues-rock and prog-folk, as he takes songs into extended instrumental jams. The band sounds tight, but Weller has suffered a bit of a songwriting slump, which is evidenced by the handful of keepers that form the core of the album. "Up in Suze's Room" is a hazy, folky gem, the soulful apology "I Should Have Been There to Inspire You" is affecting, and "Peacock Suit" is a fine "Changing Man" rewrite, but too much of *Heavy Soul* is concerned with texture instead of content. That doesn't make it a difficult listen—in fact, it's quite entertaining while it's playing—but there isn't much to explore on repeated plays. —*Stephen Thomas Erlewine*

Modern Classics: Greatest Hits / Nov. 24, 1998 / Go! Discs/London ◆◆◆◆
Wrapping up his contractual commitment to Go! Records, Paul Weller delivered *Modern Classics*, his first compilation of solo material, late in 1998. *Modern Classics* plays it safe, collecting all of his singles and adding a fine new song, "Brand New Start," which may not at first seem live up to its title, but eventually reveals itself to be a weightier ballad variation of the trad-rock of *Heavy Soul*. Regrettably, the album is not sequenced in chronological order, but there was a consistency to Weller's solo work that makes the compilation hold together well. And while it certainly confirms that his solo work is easily his most conservative music to date, it also proves that it wasn't slight—these singles are uniformly solid, whether it's the driving "Into Tomorrow," the rugged soul-pop of "Uh-Huh Oh-Yeh," the passionate "Sunflower," the ersatz ELO tribute "The Changingman," or ballads like "Broken Stones" and "Mermaids." Like *Snap!* and *The Singular Adventures of the Style Council*, *Modern Classics* is a testament to Weller's strength as a singles artist and a terrifically enjoyable listen in its own right. —*Stephen Thomas Erlewine*

Heliocentric / May 9, 2000 / Island ◆◆◆◆◆
Heliocentric is a lighter affair than the doggedly traditional *Heavy Soul*. It may be a subtle distinction, since he's using the same musical template he has since *Wild Wood*, plus the same producer and many of the same musicians. So, *Heliocentric* sounds very familiar, yet when it reaches its conclusion with the melancholy psychedelic sweep of "Love-Less," it's clear that it *feels* a lot different than its two immediate predecessors—it's of a similar quality and emotional tenor as *Wild Wood*. It's also his strongest record since then, a remarkably sturdy and varied set of songs and performances. Sadness and regret are scattered throughout the album, but there's also humor, affection, and, ultimately, optimism—three qualities missing on *Heavy Soul*. *Heliocentric* has many more musical quirks than its predecessor. Strings grace several songs, plus there are extended jams so psychedelic they're almost prog. There really aren't any rockers, but there's the wonderfully jaunty acoustic number "Sweet Pea, My Sweet Pea," one of his most unaffected and, well, sweetest songs. "A Whale's Tale" is his own spin on a sea ballad, while "Back in the Fire" rolls along on a nearly jazzy beat. Those ever-changing moods keep the record fresh and interesting, yet *Heliocentric* still winds up sounding part of a piece, since Weller is focused here, as a songwriter and a record-maker, which he hasn't been since *Wild Wood*. Like that latter-day Weller masterpiece, *Heliocentric* grows stronger with each spin, as the songs catch hold and details in the production and nuances in the performances reveal themselves. That may not constitute a new direction for Weller, but it's certainly a terrific record that signals a creative rebirth, which is the next best thing. —*Stephen Thomas Erlewine*

Mary Wells

b. May 13, 1943, Detroit, MI, **d.** Jul. 26, 1992, Los Angeles, CA
Vocals / Pop-Soul, Girl Group, Motown, Soul
Time and legions of other soul superstars have obscured the fact that for a brief moment, Mary Wells was Motown's biggest star. She came to the attention of Berry Gordy as a 17-year-old, hawking a song she'd written for Jackie Wilson; that song, "Bye Bye Baby," became her first Motown hit in 1961. The full-throated approach of that single was quickly toned down in favor of a pop-soul sound. Few other soul singers managed to be as shy and sexy at the same time as Wells, and the soft-voiced singer hit the Top Ten four times during the early '60s, including the number one hit "My Guy." She left Motown almost immediately afterwards, for a reported advance of over six figures from 20th Century Fox. Though Wells never remotely approached the success of her Motown years (entering the pop Top 40 only once), her '60s singles for 20th Century Fox (whom she ended up leaving after only a year), Atco, and Jubilee were solid pop-soul on which her vocal talents remained undiminished. She wrote and produced a lot of her late '60s and early '70s sessions, exploring a somewhat earthier groove than her more widely known pop efforts. She had trouble landing recording deals in the '70s and '80s, and succumbed to throat cancer in 1992. —*Richie Unterberger*

Complete Jubilee Sessions / 1993 / Sequel ◆◆◆◆◆
More proof that Wells still had what it took after leaving Motown. This 26-song collection assembles everything she recorded for the Jubilee label in the late '60s and early '70s: her 1968 LP *Servin' Up Some Soul*, a couple non-LP B-sides, and the entirety of a scrapped follow-up album (although some of the songs from that unreleased LP appeared on singles, seven were unreleased before this reissue). This is Wells' gutsiest period, with the majority of the material penned by her and husband Cecil Womack, who provides some excellent bluesy guitar licks. Wells is in top voice on both the fairly strong originals and a variety of well-done covers. The earlier *Servin' Up Some Soul* sessions have the edge over the later, slicker tracks, but almost all of it is well worth hearing. —*Richie Unterberger*

☆ **Looking Back 1961-1964** / Sep. 7, 1993 / Motown ◆◆◆◆◆
This two-CD, 43-track box set is the most comprehensive retrospective of Motown's biggest female star before Diana Ross. Although her first hit, "Bye Bye Baby," presented Wells as a blues belter, she quickly settled into a sly and sassy groove. Subsequent hits like "You Beat Me to the Punch," "Two Lovers," and "My Guy" (all included here) made the most of her shy, seductive voice by teaming her with some great songs and production by Smokey Robinson. Although many of these tunes were relegated to B-sides, album tracks, or even the can (11 were previously unreleased), the material—written by Motown stalwarts like Berry Gordy, Holland-Dozier-Holland, and Mickey Stevenson when Smokey was unavailable—is not far below the hits in quality. This is as much a testimony to Motown's overflow of prolific talent as Wells', but doesn't detract from the

consistency of this set, which includes her duets with Marvin Gaye (as well as a previously unreleased duet with Smokey Robinson). Includes a comprehensive essay in the photo-packed booklet, although the mysterious absence of the excellent "Was It Worth It" is a notable loss. —*Richie Unterberger*

Ain't It the Truth: The Best of Mary Wells 1964-1982 / Aug. 30, 1994 / Varese Sarabande ◆◆◆
It doesn't have anything from her 1965-67 years with Atco (those tracks are compiled on a separate collection), but otherwise this does a good job of assembling the highlights of her post-Motown career. The focus is on her handful of minor mid-'60s hits for 20th Century Fox (which were conscious or half-conscious attempts to emulate her Motown sound) and her grittier 1968-70 recordings for Jubilee (which she co-wrote and co-produced with guitarist and husband/producer Cecil Womack). A couple of unimpressive tracks from her 1981 Epic album round out the collection; Wells is in fine form throughout. —*Richie Unterberger*

Dear Lover: The Atco Sessions / Jan. 1995 / Ichiban Soul Classics ◆◆◆
In his autobiography, Jerry Wexler characterized Wells' tenure with Atlantic from 1965-67 as a failure for all parties concerned, but he's being too harsh. Commercially, it was certainly a fallow period; only the title track (a Top Ten R&B hit) paid off. But actually, her Atco singles were solid mid-'60s soul, usually recorded in Chicago and bearing the influence of that city's noted soul producer, Carl Davis (who produced some of these tracks). This collection includes both sides of all four of her Atco singles, five covers from her sole Atco LP, and a couple of decent previously unreleased tracks. —*Richie Unterberger*

Never, Never Leave Me: The 20th Century Sides / Feb. 1996 / Ichiban Soul Classics ◆◆◆
If Wells' brief stint with 20th Century had been a total misdirected failure, it would be easier to dismiss. It wasn't, though. Wells continued to deliver pop-flavored soul in just as good a voice as ever, and in fact had a few small hits. The problem is not so much approach as quality. Her material, though not bad, lacked the special magic of her best Motown classics; the production was somewhat thinner as well. This 18-track anthology assembles her best 20th Century performances, including her singles (some of them previously unavailable on album), songs from her first 20th Century LP, and three previously unreleased songs. Though it's principally of interest to Wells fans, it's better than you might expect, worth hearing for the pleasure of Wells' voice if not the average material. —*Richie Unterberger*

● **The Ultimate Collection** / Feb. 10, 1998 / Motown ◆◆◆◆◆
Motown is notorious for recycling their catalog as endless hit collections, but *The Ultimate Collection* is one of the finest series of greatest-hits CDs they have ever assembled. Each disc contains all of the major hits from an artist, plus important B-sides, album tracks and minor hits. Mary Wells' entry in the series is no exception to the rule, boasting all her Top Ten pop and R&B hits. Not only are the familiar Motown singles here—"Bye Bye Baby," "I Don't Want to Take a Chance," "The One Who Really Loves You," "You Beat Me to the Punch," "Two Lovers," "Laughing Boy," "Your Old Stand By," "What's Easy for Two Is So Hard for One," "You Lost the Sweetest Boy," "My Guy"—but also her Top Ten hit for Atco, "Dear Lover," a pair of singles from 20th Century and several minor Motown hits and B-sides, resulting in a total of 25 tracks. For anyone who wants a definitive hits collection but is hesitant to invest in the double-disc *Looking Back*, *The Ultimate Collection* is an ideal choice. —*Stephen Thomas Erlewine*

20th Century Masters—The Millennium Collection: The Best of Mary Wells / Oct. 26, 1999 / Motown ◆◆◆◆
The Mary Wells volume of MCA's *20th Century Masters: The Millennium Collection* may not be definitive, but the 11-track compilation contains all of her biggest hits—"Bye Bye Baby," "I Don't Want to Take a Chance," "The One Who Really Loves You," "You Beat Me to the Punch," "Two Lovers," "Laughing Boy," "You Lost the Sweetest Boy," and, of course, "My Guy"—which makes it the ideal choice for budget-minded fans. —*Stephen Thomas Erlewine*

Wendy & Lisa

f. 1986
Pop/Rock, Dance-Pop
When Prince broke up the Revolution in 1986, guitarist Wendy Melvoin and keyboardist Lisa Coleman, friends since childhood, decided to team up for a new musical project. The two had grown up together in Los Angeles, where both of their fathers were session musicians and encouraged their musical development from a young age. Coleman joined the Revolution in 1979 for *Dirty Mind*, and Melvoin signed on in 1984; in addition to their instrumental skills, the two also provided some of Prince's arrangements. Wendy and Lisa played almost all of the instruments on their self-titled debut and co-wrote most of the material with ex-Revolution drummer Bobby Z. After backing Joni Mitchell on *Chalk Mark in a Rainstorm* in 1988, the duo added Melvoin's twin sister Susannah and recorded *Fruit at the Bottom*, a song cycle about the ups and downs of romance. Several more family members joined up for the widely varied *Eroica*, which mixed Wendy & Lisa's disparate influences (funk, jazz, dance, pop, rock); k.d. lang also contributed vocals. *Eroica* followed in 1990, and though the duo were less busy during the decade, they returned in 1998 as the Girl Bros. —*Steve Huey*

Wendy & Lisa / 1987 / Columbia ◆◆◆◆
Wendy & Lisa's 1987 debut had very little in common with the sleek electronic funk they pioneered as members of Prince's backup band the Revolution. Simple, elegant pop-rock songs dominate here, from the shimmering "Waterfalls" to the gorgeous ballad "The Life." "White," an instrumental piece, has a jazzy feel, complete with sax playing by Tom Scott and Wendy Melvoin's spare guitar licks. Only "Blues Away" and "Light," with

harder-edged guitars and Prince-like drumbeats, have any connections to their previous work. Not only are Melvoin and Lisa Coleman gifted and articulate musicians, they also show a real talent for songwriting and arranging. There isn't anything truly groundbreaking here (those days seem behind them) but there is plenty of nicely crafted, beautifully played music that is definitely worth a listen. *—Victor W. Valdivia*

Fruit at the Bottom / 1989 / Columbia ✦✦

- **Eroica [Atlantic]** / 1990 / Atlantic ✦✦✦✦

After the disappointing *Fruit at the Bottom*, Wendy & Lisa hit a peak with their third album, *Eroica*. Containing some of the best music of their careers, it also is a perfect synthesis of the dance club beats of *Fruit* and the well-developed songwriting of their debut. "Staring at the Sun" and "Mother of Pearl" show compositional and arranging complexity that is positively breathtaking. What's more, the musicianship is at a peak, containing some of the best playing the duo have ever done, including a fiery Wendy Melvoin guitar solo in "Turn Me Inside Out." Lyrically, there is more depth as well. "Mother of Pearl," about broken relationships, and "Valley Vista," about a bittersweet childhood memory, have a far darker edge than the lighter material of *Fruit*. Even the love songs have more of a bite as well. *Eroica* is a perfect introduction to Wendy & Lisa's formidable talents. *—Victor W. Valdivia*

The West Coast Pop Art Experimental Band

Psychedelic

If a band could ever be called an average psychedelic group, the West Coast Pop Art Experimental Band fit the bill. This somewhat mysterious collection of L.A. players issued several albums in the late '60s that plugged into the era's standard folk-rock, freakouts, and trippy lyrics without establishing a solid identity of their own. But because the currents they were riding were themselves so inspired, average in this case doesn't necessarily mean bad. They cut a fair number of tracks, moving without rhyme or reason from straightforward Byrds and Kinks cops to zany orchestrated self-absorbed psychedelic pop to self-conscious exercises in hippy outrageousness (including, of all things, a cover of the Mothers' "Help I'm a Rock"). Though their legacy reeks of determined trendiness, the best of their output holds up reasonably well. *—Richie Unterberger*

West Coast Pop Art Experimental Band, Vol. 1 / 1966 / Sundazed ✦✦✦

Raw, sometimes sloppy material by this enigmatic psychedelic cult band appeared on an extremely rare debut album in 1966 (their first LP for Reprise, *Part One*, is usually considered their first recording). This 22-track compilation reissues that first album on CD, adding 11 other rare tracks from the '65-'67 era, most previously unreleased. West Coast Pop Art were always a strange act, and this collection does nothing to tarnish that perception. It's not so much the weirdness of the sound—they could be plenty weird *per se* on Zappaesque freakouts like "Insanity" (co-penned by Kim Fowley), but only occasionally. It's more the sheer unpredictable range of the material. One minute they're attacking "Louie, Louie" and the classic jazz instrumental "Work Song" with all the finesse of teenagers in their bedroom; the next they're doing pretty psych-pop tunes with a bizarre edge, like "I Won't Hurt You"; then there are the Dylan covers, which are approached as if they are Yardbirds tunes, with splashes of feedback and hard rock/R&B arrangements. And then there's an original baroque pop number worthy of the Left Banke or late-period Zombies ("She Surely Must Know"), a sharp, witty country-tinged rocker ("Sassafras"), and covers of the Left Banke's "She May Call You Up Tonight" and the mawkish "Funny How Love Can Be." No stylistic consistency whatsoever, in other words, but plenty of wacky energy, and occasional actual inspiration. Which makes this hard to recommend to anyone other than psychedelic junkies. But if you fit under that umbrella, it's not bad at all, though wildly erratic. *—Richie Unterberger*

West Coast Pop Art Experimental Band, Vol. 2: Breaking Through / 1967 / Reprise ✦✦

A Child's Guide to Good and Evil / 1968 / Reprise ✦✦

- **Transparent Day** / 1986 / Edsel ✦✦✦✦✦

Well-chosen collection of 16 tracks from their first two albums. "Transparent Day" is a ringing folk-rocker, the throbbing "I Won't Hurt You" a soundtrack to the beginning of an acid trip; "Shifting Sands" and the string-laden "Will You Walk With Me" are tremulous tunes with an odd undercurrent of fear and uncertainty. Other highlights are the early Kinks copy "If You Want This Love" and the P.F. Sloan cover "Here's Where You Belong." *—Richie Unterberger*

Paul Westerberg

b. Dec. 31, 1959

Vocals, Piano, Guitar / Adult Alternative Pop/Rock, Alternative Pop/Rock

After disbanding the Replacements in 1991, singer/songwriter Paul Westerberg resurfaced the following year with two songs on the *Singles* soundtrack. A year later, Westerberg released his first solo album, *14 Songs*, in the summer of 1993. Although the record received generally positive reviews and spawned the modern rock hit "World Class Fad," the album failed to break the songwriter into the mainstream. Three years later, Westerberg released his second solo album, *Eventually*. Like *14 Songs* and the entire Replacements catalog before it, *Eventually* received good reviews but failed to become a commercial success upon its spring 1996 release.

In the spring of 1997, Westerberg left Reprise Records. He recorded a one-off EP under the name Grandpaboy for the Boston-based indie label Soundproof/Monolyth Records; the label was co-owned by Darren Hill, who had previously played bass with Westerberg. By the time the EP was released in August of 1997, Westerberg had signed a new contract with Capitol Records, releasing *Suicaine Gratifaction*—widely acclaimed as his finest solo work to date—in early 1999. *—Stephen Thomas Erlewine*

- **14 Songs** / Jun. 15, 1993 / Sire/Reprise ✦✦✦✦

Westerberg's first solo album since the breakup of The Replacements is a strong yet incoherent collection of songs from one of the most influential songwriters of the 1980s. Falling somewhere between the sound of *All Shook Down* and the songwriting of *Tim*, *14 Songs* is a more mature effort from Westerberg, sounding like the optimistic brother of the last Replacements album. It's not as raw as *Let it Be* or *Tim* or as consistent as *Pleased to Meet Me*, but it is a solid collection of expertly crafted rock and pop songs. *—Stephen Thomas Erlewine*

Eventually / Apr. 30, 1996 / Reprise ✦✦

Suicaine Gratifaction / Feb. 23, 1999 / Capitol ✦✦✦

Paul Westerberg's solo career wasn't flourishing before he released his second album, *Eventually*, but that record effectively halted whatever momentum he had. Sinking into a deep depression and realizing it was time for a change, Westerberg left Reprise, signed with Capitol records and teamed with Don Was, the first time in years he worked with a heavyweight producer. *Suicaine Gratifaction*, the awkwardly-titled result, is a bit of a mess, at times seeming like the artistic comeback it was intended to be, at other times sounding as stilted as *Eventually*. To his credit, he doesn't rock out, a problem that plagued his two previous records, but he never sounds completely convincing as a confessional singer/songwriter. It could be because the depression that flows underneath his ballads provokes alienation, not empathy (especially since he sounds so tired throughout the record), or it could be that his slower numbers only occasionally boast melodies as memorable as his gently ambling mid-tempo pop-rockers. Either way, *Suicaine Gratifaction* is too mannered, not only in its presentation but within Westerberg's songwriting itself—there's little of the self-deprecating wit that was apparent as recently as *14 Songs* (it only surfaces on "Whatever Makes You Happy"), there's little of the disarming honesty that made his best work resonate so deeply. Since Was is a skilled recordmaker, the album holds together better than *Eventually*, even if the songs rarely eclipse the standard set by its predecessor—which is the reason why *Suicaine Gratifaction* ultimately feels unfulfilling, even if it doesn't sound half bad as it's playing. *—Stephen Thomas Erlewine*

Whale

Alternative Pop/Rock

Although they formed back in 1987 (originally as "The Southern Whale Cult"), the Swedish outfit Whale didn't hit the big time until 1995, with the MTV-hit "Hobo Humpin' Slobo Babe" (directed by Mark Pellington). Consisting of members Cia Soro (vocals), Henrik Schyffert (guitar) and Gordon Cyrus (bass), the band released several albums back home (such as *The 52nd State of America*, *In Style!*, *Whatever*, etc.) before signing a worldwide record deal in the mid-'90s. Their next album, *We Care*, failed to yield another hit like "Slobo Babe," and after opening for Blur on a North American tour, Cyrus left the band to form his own hip-hop record company. After a lengthy hiatus, new members Jorgen Wall (drums), Jon Jefferson Klingberg (2nd guitar), and Heikki Kiviaho (bass) joined in time to record their follow-up, 1998's *All Disco Dance Must End In Broken Bones*. Recorded in Chicago and London, the album was produced and engineered by two of today's top alternative producers—Chris Potter (the Verve) and Brad Wood (Veruca Salt, Placebo). An extensive U.S. tour with Tricky followed soon after the album's release. *—Greg Prato*

- **We Care** / 1995 / Virgin ✦✦✦✦✦

Whale isn't necessarily a band, it's a studio project by a pair of Swedish television personalities, who also happen to be ex-lovers. In other words, it's a highly stylized and manufactured album that is proud of its artificiality. Even more than that, Whale is about sex, particularly dirty, tawdry sex. From the blunt come-ons of "I'll Do Ya" to the lesbian fantasies about Saint Etienne's Sarah Cracknell on "Eurodog," *We Care* positively seethes with sex. No matter how dirty Whale gets ("Young, Dumb & Full of Cum" is about as far as they go), there is a jokey sense of good humor that keeps *We Care* from being an oppressively sleazy affair. What also helps is their wreckless mixture of styles. Taking elements of trip-hop beats, heavy metal guitars, sing-song pop, and football chants, the band creates a joyously noisy racket that emphasizes their humor and their sexiness. The sound might grow a little monotonous at various points on the album, but *We Care* succeeds on its raunchy charm. *—Stephen Thomas Erlewine*

Pay for Me / 1995 / Caroline ✦✦✦

All Disco Dance Must End in Broken Bones / Jul. 14, 1998 / Virgin ✦✦✦✦

After scoring a surprise MTV hit with "Hobo Humpin' Slobo Babe," Whale returns three years later as an older, wiser, and different band with *All Disco Dance Must End In Broken Bones*. By adding more members, Whale have strengthened their sound and manage to tackle more musical styles than their past releases. The band has toned down the unrefined trash-rock of their 1995 release *We Care* a notch or two, which results in an album that stands a much better chance of reaching a wider audience. It also doesn't hurt having not one, but two great rock producers (Brad Wood and Chris Potter) manning the controls. The album kicks off with the Portishead-esque "Crying at Airports," but the Whale of old returns with "Deliver the Juice," which contains a sound similar to the band's earlier releases. The album's first single, "Four Big Speakers," is a speedy dance track which contains a duet between singer Cia Soro and guitarist Henrik Schyffert, while the slow and sultry "Roadkill" features both Soro and second guitarist Jon Jefferson Klingberg on vocals. *All Disco Dance Must End In Broken Bones* is easily the band's most ambitious and best album. *—Greg Prato*

Wham!

f. 1981, **db.** 1986

Pop/Rock, New Wave, Adult Contemporary, Dance-Pop

Wham! sparked something of a pop revival in the mid-'80s and could arguably be held responsible for sparking off the boy band trend of the '90s. They were unashamedly pop, to the point of padding the front of their trousers for television appearances. At the heart, however, was a string of catchy singalong singles written by George Michael (born Georgios Kyrriacos Panayiotou in London to a Greek restauranting family).

George met Wham!'s other half, Andrew Ridgeley, at school in the London suburb of Bushey, and in 1979 they started performing together as part of the ska-based band the Executive. When that group dissolved, they wrote songs, made demos, and rushed into a recording contract with the equally eager independent label Innervision, scoring an instant hit with "Wham Rap!" (they thought that "wham" was the sound they made when Michael and Ridgeley performed together). In order to move to a recording contract with Sony label Epic, Wham! was forced to walk away from most of the royalties from their debut album, *Fantastic*. None of that mattered when their 1984 single, "Wake Me up Before You Go Go," became a worldwide hit, accompanied by a video of the pair cavorting in their sportswear. Almost immediately, George Michael started thinking of a solo career, and released "Careless Whisper," issued in the U.S. under George Michael of Wham!

Wham!'s end came suddenly two years later, in 1985, reputedly when the group's manager, Simon Napier-Bell (later to manage Take That), decided to sell a share of his management to a South African entertainment conglomerate. Supposedly, as part of a stand against South African politics, George Michael immediately announced Wham!'s breakup. They gave their farewell performance before a sold-out audience of 72,000 fans at London's Wembly Stadium.

George Michael comfortably stepped straight into his own highly successful solo performing and recording career. Andrew Ridgeley's post Wham! album, *Son of Albert*, sold poorly and produced just one minor hit, "Shake." —*Ed Nimmervoll*

Fantastic! / 1983 / Columbia ✦✦

Make It Big / 1984 / Columbia ✦✦✦✦✦
The title was a promise to themselves, Wham!'s assurance that they would make it big after struggling out of the gates the first time out. They succeeded on a grander scale than they ever could have imagined, conquering the world and elsewhere with this effervescent set of giddy new wave pop-soul, thereby making George Michael a superstar and consigning Andrew Ridgeley to the confines of Trivial Pursuit. It was so big and the singles were so strong that it's easy to overlook its patchwork qualities. It's no longer than eight tracks, short even for the pre-CD era, and while the four singles are strong, the rest is filler, including an Isley Brothers cover. Thankfully, it's the kind of filler that's so tied to its time that it's fascinating in its stilted post-disco dance-pop rhythms and Thatcher/Reagan materialism—an era that encouraged songs called "Credit Card Baby." If this dichotomy between the A-sides and B-sides is far too great to make this essential, the way *Faith* later would be, those A-sides range from good to terrific. "Wake Me Up Before You Go-Go" is absolute silliness whose very stupidity is its strength, and if "Everything She Wants" is merely agreeable bubblegum, "Freedom" is astounding, a sparkling Motown rip-off rippling with spirit and a timeless melody later ripped off by Noel Gallagher. Then, there's the concluding "Careless Whisper," a soulful slow one where Michael regrets a one-night stand over a richly seductive background and a yearning saxophone. It was an instant classic, and it was the first indication of George Michael's strengths as a pop craftsman—which means it points the way to *Faith*, not the halfhearted *Edge of Heaven*. —*Stephen Thomas Erlewine*

Music from the Edge of Heaven / 1986 / Columbia ✦✦✦
More of a hodgepodge of tracks than a coherent album, this still includes the Top Ten hits "I'm Your Man," "A Different Corner," and "The Edge of Heaven." —*William Ruhlmann*

● **The Best of Wham!: If You Were There . . .** / Nov. 1997 / Epic ✦✦✦✦✦
The Best of Wham!: If You Were There. . . is an excellent collection, featuring all the group's biggest hits, including "I'm Your Man," "Club Tropicana," "Wake Me Up Before You Go-Go," "Freedom," "The Edge of Heaven," "Wham Rap!," "Young Guns (Go for It!)," "Last Christmas" and "Everything She Wants '97." Apart from the original version of "A Different Corner" (which was credited to a solo George Michael) and "Everything She Wants," *The Best of Wham!* includes every worthwhile song the duo recorded and makes for a terrific overview for most fans. —*Stephen Thomas Erlewine*

Wheat

Indie Rock
Decidedly low-key band Wheat's dreamy sound owes a lot to the shoegazing bands of late '90s England. Formed in 1996, the band turned away from marketing themselves, instead exercising their creative whims in their live performances. A fan sent a tape to Chicago's Sugar Free Records, who signed the band immediately. Core members Scott Levesque, Brendan Harney and Ricky Brennan helped shape the band's sound across its first two albums, aided by Mike Flood, Kevin Camara, Ricky Brennan and Kenny Madaras. Their debut, *Medeiros*, issued in 1998, won critical praise for its ambient textures and far-ranging sound explorations. Flaming Lips producer David Frishman helped their follow-up, 1999's *Hope and Adams*, pull together far-reaching influences from alternative rock, slowcore and Brit-pop, resulting in an album that was even more ambitious than their first. —*Stacia Proefrock*

Wheat / 1997 / ✦✦✦

● **Medeiros** / Apr. 14, 1998 / Sugar Free ✦✦✦✦
Wheat's brand of hazy, unassumingly catchy music straddles the lines separating a slew of indie subgenres ranging from lo-fi to slowcore to ambient pop; ultimately, *Medeiros'* greatest strength is its refusal to sit still for too long, and although the album veers off in endless directions it all hangs together on the strength of its consistent songwriting and well-honed atmospheric sensibility. —*Chuck Donkers*

Hope and Adams / Oct. 26, 1999 / Sugar Free ✦✦✦✦
Any late-'90s band that refuses to pose for photo shoots, include the names of its members in its liner notes, or abstains for almost any type of promotion better have the goods to back up its stance. For the most part Wheat does. Borrowing from two decades worth of alternative rock, (including Brit-pop, ambient, shoegazer rock, and even a touch of *No Depression*), *Hope and Adams* revels in its own brand of detached melancholy and describes a world (or a small piece of one at least) populated by souls who feel they are far more important than they really are.

Across 14 tracks Wheat gives us well-constructed crunchy rock songs ("Raised Ranch Revolution"), as well as some curious soundscapes ("Body Talk Part 1"), and a handful of elegantly infectious pop exercises. The sparse, often inscrutable lyrics tell brief and sometimes uncomfortable tales. Co-producer Dave Fridmann (of Mercury Rev) doesn't quite reign all the loose, tattered ends into a cohesive whole, but regardless, this is an impressive debut. Despite the fact that we have no image of what this band is or who they are, the dusty, dark corners of *Hope and Adams* are made all the more intriguing. Certainly a band to watch. —*John Duffy*

Whiskeytown

f. 1994, db. 1999
Americana, Alternative Country-Rock, Alternative Pop/Rock
Alt-country upstarts Whiskeytown formed in Raleigh, NC, in 1994 when young singer/songwriter Ryan Adams grew tired of the limitations of punk and founded the country-leaning combo with violinist and vocalist Caitlin Cary, drummer Eric "Skillet" Gilmore, bassist Steve Grothman, and guitarist and vocalist Phil Wandscher. Their first release, a 7" EP entitled *Angels*, was released in 1995 by local indie label Mood Food Records and quickly followed by *Faithless Street*. The album drew considerable attention from *No Depression Magazine*, and their appearance at SXSW landed them a major-label deal with Outpost Records. Their major label debut, *Strangers Almanac*, followed in 1997, featuring replacement bassist Jeff Rice and new drummer Steven Terry. After sporadic (and volatile) touring, the band (now whittled down to a trio of Adams, Cary, and multi-instrumentalist Mike Daly) recorded their final album *Pneumonia* which remained in record label corporate merger limbo for three years. In that time, Cary subsequently released her solo album, *Walzie*, and Adams delved further into his anguished songwriting on 2000's sublime *Heartbreaker*. —*Zac Johnson*

Faithless Street / 1996 / Outpost ✦✦✦✦
Faithless Street serves as an interesting document in the history of alt-country upstarts Whiskeytown, showing 20-year-old bandleader and chief songwriter Ryan Adams' head-first leap from member of a high-school punk band into an emotionally charged, alcohol-fueled, traditional-minded country singer. The majority of the album was recorded in the summer of 1995 near Whiskeytown's hometown of Raleigh by Chris Stamey (dB's) and overflows with beer bottle, front porch, sun-drenched country anguish. Of the recording, Adams recalls: "All I remember is what we had to drink and Skillet and Ray Duffy's preoccupation with fireworks…the Roman candles and black cats sounded a lot like I'd hope we'd one day sound—pretty little things all set on fire waiting to get destroyed." Looking back on this statement, the band's history of lineup changes and well-documented onstage fights seems to fit into Adams' five-year plan perfectly. The music itself is often sparse and gritty, brutally honest, and quite beautiful, especially in the introspective "If He Can't Have You," "Desperate Ain't Lonely," and the achingly gorgeous "Excuse Me While I Break My Own Heart Tonight." For all of the attention surrounding Adams' songwriting and Gram Parsons-like self-destructive bluster, one of the album's highlights comes from violinist and vocalist Caitlin Cary's "Matrimony," sung with a fierce independence that is a far cry from Tammy Wynette's "Stand By Your Man," although with a similar heartfelt enthusiasm. Regarding his songwriting in the *Faithless Street*-era, the lead singer later confided: "In retrospect, I knew that was the last optimism I was gonna have for a long time," which sounds implausible regarding most of the album's subject matter, but later proved to be true. Overall, the album (re-released in 1998 by Outpost Recordings with several bonus tracks) stands as a terrific recording on its own, and also foreshadows many of the forthcoming troubles and achievements in the arc of the band's life span. —*Zac Johnson*

Rural Free Delivery / May 6, 1997 / Mood Food Records ✦✦✦
Independently released, *Rural Free Delivery* finds Whiskeytown in a bit of a transition from local heroes to national spotlight. Rockin' country pervades *R.F.D.*, especially on "Take Your Guns to Town," while the acoustic side comes to the fore on "Tennessee Square." While not essential, "Rural Free Delivery" is a fine batch of tunes that fans of Whiskeytown will love to hear. It's well worth seeking out. —*James Chrispell*

● **Stranger's Almanac** / Jul. 29, 1997 / Outpost ✦✦✦
Whiskeytown's first major label release, 1997's *Stranger's Almanac*, brought a lot of critical attention, particularly to the band's young singer and songwriter Ryan Adams. His world-weary drawl is pervasive throughout the album, with an honesty that belies his age (Adams was 22 at the time of recording, but many of the songs were written well before then). Credit must also be given to violinist and vocalist Caitlin Cary, whose good old-time fiddle sings above the rest of the band's crash and swagger, and whose vocal harmonies help to soothe Adams' gritty yowls and croons. The radio single "16 Days" is one of the stronger tracks, starting forlorn but quickly accelerating through the chorus, and "Everything I Do" pulls in some understated Hammond B3 organ and a Memphis-style horn section. Unfortunately, the album also drags in spots and often sounds like a studio creation, heavy with reverb and overdubs (unlike their collection of demos and indie release *Faithless Street*). One sure indicator of the notorious volatility of the band lies in the liner notes that read "This time Whiskeytown were as follows…,"

showing the signs of unrest that quickly burned out those around Adams' lifestyle and temperament. Alejandro Escovedo appears on three tracks, sounding rough and unprepared on a chorus of the otherwise sublime "Excuse Me While I Break My Own Heart Tonight," but adding subtle acoustic textures to "Dancing With the Women at the Bar." Overall, *Stranger's Almanac* is a good listen and a fine introduction to both the band's brash muscle and Adams bitterly tender songcraft. Listeners looking for something grittier might try their collection *Faithless Street*, and those in need of music on a grander pop scale should investigate *Pneumonia*, the band's third and final album. —*Zac Johnson*

Pneumonia / May 22, 2001 / Lost Highway ✦✦✦✦
Whiskeytown had ceased to be a band in the truest sense by the time they recorded their third (and final) full-length album, *Pneumonia*; the group began to collapse during the touring following *Strangers' Almanac*, with members coming and going at a remarkable pace, and for the *Pneumonia* sessions, the only musicians on hand who had appeared on *Faithless Street* three years earlier were lead vocalist and songwriter Ryan Adams and violinist and backing vocalist Caitlin Cary. Multi-instrumentalist Mike Daly and percussionist/producer Ethan Johns dominated the sessions' sprawling cast of players, with James Iha and Tommy Stinson popping up on some tracks. Ultimately, *Pneumonia* sounds more like an Adams solo project than anything else, and it walks a decidedly different path than the Whiskeytown albums that preceded it—there are no charging rockers and the country twang of "Too Drunk to Dream" or "Someone Remembers the Rose" has receded into the background. This is easily Whiskeytown's most ambitious and eclectic work, and proves that, despite his reckless public persona, Ryan Adams had gained a wealth of maturity and intelligence (at least as a songwriter and recording artist) since the last time he'd entered a recording studio. *Pneumonia* was recorded in 1999, but the closing of Outpost Records in the wake of that year's Polygram/Universal merger put the album on the shelf for two years; in the meantime, *Pneumonia* developed an underground reputation as a lost classic, and while that description is going a bit far to make a point, it is an undeniably striking and beautifully crafted set of songs, and it's interesting to imagine where this music would have taken Whiskeytown if the album had met its original release date—assuming that Whiskeytown was still a band by the time the record was finished. —*Mark Deming*

Ian Whitcomb

b. Jul. 10, 1941, Woking, Surrey, England
Vocals, Ukulele, Accordion, Songwriter, Piano / Music Hall, British Invasion, Nostalgia
An odd footnote to the British Invasion, English singer and pianist Ian Whitcomb formed his R&B group Bluesville in Dublin, Ireland. He never had a hit in the U.K. and wasn't all that wild about rock & roll in the first place, preferring traditional forms of blues, ragtime, and Tin Pan Alley. But "You Turn Me On"—a tongue-in-cheek three-chord knockoff at the end of a session with exaggerated falsetto vocals and an unforgettable orgasmic vocal hook—hit number eight in America in 1965, and Whitcomb was briefly a star. The bluesy follow-up, "N-N-Nervous," was a small hit, and that was the end of Whitcomb's hit-making days. Not much of a rock & roll singer, Whitcomb quickly turned to vaudevillian, British music hall-styled material on his subsequent releases, with meager commercial (and artistic) results. A dedicated archivist, Whitcomb's book, *After the Ball*, is a thorough history of pre-rock popular music forms. —*Richie Unterberger*

The Best of Ian Whitcomb / 1985 / Rhino ✦✦✦✦
15 songs from 1965-67, including "You Turn Me On," and the small hits "This Sporting Life" and "N-N-Nervous," and the protest song "Too Many Cars On The Road." The rockers are okay, but the post-1965 vaudevillian tunes that compose the bulk of this compilation are lame indeed, sounding almost unbearably quaint and stilted nearly 30 years later. Session players supporting Ian on these tracks (most recorded in Hollywood) include James Burton, Delaney Bramlett, Gerry Roslie of The Sonics, and Mitch Mitchell. Includes exhaustive liner notes by Whitcomb himself. —*Richie Unterberger*

You Turn Me On!/Mod, Mod Music Hall / Apr. 22, 1997 / Sundazed ✦✦✦
Whitcomb's first two albums, combined into one CD, with the addition of historical liner notes by the singer himself. The limp British R&B/pop of the debut is juxtaposed quite awkwardly with the yet limper ragtime retreads dominating the follow-up. Taken together, this has most of his best-known material, yet it's missing a couple of his best rock songs, the piano-driven "The End" (from 1965) and 1966's "Lover's Prayer" (with Mitch Mitchell on drums). Both of these tracks, as well as the best material from both of the first two albums, are featured on Rhino's *Best of Ian Whitcomb*, which remains the clear compilation of choice. —*Richie Unterberger*

● **You Turn Me On: The Very Best of Ian Whitcomb** / Feb. 24, 1998 / Varese ✦✦✦✦✦
Varese's *You Turn Me On: The Very Best of Ian Whitcomb* is a terrific 25-track single-disc collection that supplants Rhino's 1985 collection *The Best of Ian Whitcomb*. All of Whitcomb's hits—"You Turn Me On," "N-E-R-V-O-U-S," "Where Did Robinson Crusoe Go With Friday on Saturday Night," "The Sporting Life"—are featured, along with many singles, album cuts, and a handful of unreleased tracks. It's true that Whitcomb's jaunty music-hall romps and silly humor can wear thin on some listeners, but there's no argument that this disc is the best CD collection yet assembled of his career. —*Stephen Thomas Erlewine*

The White Stripes

Garage Rock Revival, Indie Rock
Detroit minimalist rock duo (specifically, southwest Detroit minimalist rock duo) the White Stripes—Jack White, guitar and vocals, Meg White, drums—formed in 1997 (Bastille Day, to be precise) with the idea of making simple rock & roll music. From the

red and white peppermint candy motif of their debut singles, self-titled album, and stage show to their on-the-surface rudimentary style, they succeeded wildly and immediately with that mission. Their first recordings were a mix of garage rock, blues, and the occasional show tune. In frontman Jack (a former drummer for Detroit country outfit Goober & the Peas), the White Stripes have a formidable songwriter, guitar player, and vocalist capable of both morphing between styles and changing the musical styles themselves (from the folk blues of Blind Willie McTell to soaring Kinks-esque pop and narrative pop tunes worthy of Cole Porter and into deepest Captain Beefheart territory within the span of 15 minutes is not an uncommon listening experience with either the White Stripes live show or on record). In drummer Meg, the White Stripes have a minimalist percussionist who seems to sense intuitively exactly when to not play. The White Stripes are grounded in punk and blues, but the undercurrent to all of their work has been the aforementioned striving for simplicity, a love of American folk music and a careful approach to intriguing, emotional, and evocative lyrics not found anywhere else in the modern punk, or garage rock (or amongst post-modern "blues" practitioners such as Jon Spencer, for that matter).

While they may have sprung from the Detroit rock scene (and they remain regular fixtures on the Detroit club circuit with Jack producing or working with many Detroit-area bands), the White Stripes quickly gained a national following after two successive tours with indie rockers Pavement and Sleater-Kinney in 1999 and 2000. The White Stripes released their second LP, *De Stijl*, in 2000 and it further spread the group's reputation. They followed its release with successful tours of Japan and Australia and entered the Memphis studio of renowned producer Doug Easley for 2001's *White Blood Cells*. —*Chris Handyside*

The White Stripes / Jun. 15, 1999 / Sympathy for the Record Industry ✦✦✦✦
Minimal to the point of sounding monumental, this Detroit guitar-drums-voice duo makes the most of its aesthetic choices and the spaces between riffage and the big beat. In fact, the White Stripes sound like arena rock as hand-crafted in the attic. Singer/guitarist Jack White's voice is a singular, evocative combination of punk, metal, blues, and backwoods while his guitar work is grand and banging with just enough lyrical touches of slide and subtle solo work to let you know he means to use the metal-blues riff collisions just so. Drummer Meg White balances out the fretwork and the fretting with methodical, spare, and booming cymbal, bass drum, and snare cracks. In a word, economy (and that goes for both of the players). The Whites' choice of covers is inspired, too. J. White's voice is equally suited to the task of tackling both the desperation of Robert Johnson's "Stop Breakin' Down" and the loneliness of Bob Dylan's "One More Cup of Coffee." Neither are equal to the originals, but they take a distinctive, haunting spin around the turntable nevertheless. All D.I.Y. punk-country-blues-metal singer/songwriting duos should sound this good. —*Chris Handyside*

De Stijl / Jun. 20, 2000 / Sympathy for the Record Industry ✦✦✦✦
Despite their reputation as garage rock revivalists, the White Stripes display an impressive range of styles on their second album, *De Stijl*, which is Dutch for "the style." Perhaps the album's diversity—which incorporates elements of bubblegum, cabaret, blues, and classic rock—shouldn't come as a surprise from a band that dedicates its album to bluesman Blind Willie McTell and Dutch artist Gerrit Rietveld. Nevertheless, it's refreshing to hear the band go from the Tommy James-style pop of "You're Pretty Good Looking" to the garagey stomp of "Hello Operator" in a one-two punch. It's even more impressive that the theatrical, piano-driven ballad "Apple Blossom" and a cover of Son House's "Death Letter" go so well together on the same album. Jack White's understated production work and versatile guitar playing and vocals also stand out on the languid, fuzzy "Sister, Do You Know My Name?" as well as insistent rockers like "Little Bird" and "Why Can't You Be Nicer to Me?" As distinctive as it is diverse, *De Stijl* blends the Stripes' arty leanings with enough rock muscle to back up the band's ambitions. —*Heather Phares*

● **White Blood Cells** / Jul. 3, 2001 / Sympathy for the Record Industry ✦✦✦✦✦
Despite the seemingly instant attention surrounding them—glowing write-ups in glossy magazines like *Rolling Stone* and *Mojo*; guest lists boasting names like Kate Hudson and Chris Robinson and appearances on national TV—the White Stripes have stayed true to the approach that brought them this success in the first place. *White Blood Cells*, Jack and Meg White's third effort for Sympathy for the Record Industry, wraps their powerful, deceptively simple style around meditations on fame, love and betrayal. As produced by Doug Easley, it sounds exactly how an underground sensation's breakthrough album should: bigger and tighter than their earlier material, but not so polished that it will scare away longtime fans. Admittedly, *White Blood Cells* lacks some of *The White Stripes*' blues influence and urgency, but it perfects the pop skills the duo honed on *De Stijl* and expands on them. The country-tinged "Hotel Yorba" and immediate, crazed garage-pop of "Fell In Love With a Girl" define the album's immediacy, along with the folky, McCartneyesque "We're Going to Be Friends," a charming, school days love song that's among Jack White's finest work. However, White's growth as a songwriter shines through on virtually every track, from the cocky opener "Dead Leaves and the Dirty Ground" to vicious indictments like "The Union Forever" and "I Think I Smell a Rat." "Same Boy You've Always Known" and "Offend in Every Way" are two more quintessential tracks, offering up more of the group's stomping riffs and rhythms and us-against-the-world attitude. Few garage-rock groups would name one of their most driving numbers "I'm Finding It Harder To Be a Gentleman" and fewer still would pen lyrics like "I'm so tired of acting tough / I'm gonna do what I please / Let's get married," but it's precisely this mix of strength and sweetness, among other contrasts, that makes the White Stripes so intriguing. Likewise, *White Blood Cells*' ability to surprise old fans and win over new ones makes it the Stripes' finest work to date. —*Heather Phares*

White Zombie

f. 1985

Alternative Metal, Alternative Pop/Rock

All garish colors and trashy noise, White Zombie brought some sleazy fun back to heavy metal, celebrating the sheer schlock of cheap sex and bad horror movies. Although they gathered a cult following with a series of independent albums in the late '80s, it wasn't until their video for "Thunder Kiss '65" was aired on MTV's *Beavis & Butt-Head* in 1993 that the band crossed over to a large audience. And they were the rare metal band that could appeal to jaded, postmodern hipsters; with their campy lyrics and theatrics, it was clear that the band didn't take themselves seriously.

White Zombie consolidated their success in 1995 with *Astro Creep: 2000—Songs of Love, Destruction*, which sold over two million copies. In the summer of 1996, the group released a collection of remixes from *Astro Creep* called *Supersexy Swingin' Sounds*. —*Stephen Thomas Erlewine*

● **La Sexorcisto: Devil Music, Vol. 1** / Mar. 17, 1992 / Geffen ♦♦♦♦♦

Perhaps co-defining the future of heavy metal, White Zombie's major label debut nearly equals fellow classics Guns & Roses' *Appetite for Destruction*, the Cult's *Electric*, and Soundgarden's *Badmotorfinger* in significance. With a funky, rap-metal undercurrent, these metal monsters combine Black Sabbath's riff sludge and Metallica's rhythmic intensity that would again resurface in the late '90s. On *La Sexorcisto: Devil Music, Vol. 1*, Zombie and Co. take listeners on a hokey carnival ride capable of inducing vomit yet provide an exhilarating, heart-throbbing metal experience. Tactless and continuously shocking, lyricist Rob Zombie reveals blatant tales of muscle cars, sleazy encounters, and *Fangoria*-mustered fantasy, clearly paying homage to vintage trash culture. Complemented by Russ Meyer film soundbites and demonic aura, Zombie ridicules middle American *Leave It to Beaver* values and insolently challenges the politically correct. Diabolical manifestos such as the barbaric "Soul-Crusher," macabre "Spiderbaby (Yeah-Yeah-Yeah)," and sexually indiscreet "Thrust!" will intrigue those yearning for lewd explicitness but may offend traditional hard rock enthusiasts. "Thunder Kiss '65," an ode to Russ Meyer's 1965 busty B-movies *Faster, Pussycat! Kill! Kill!* and *Mudhoney*, remains this album's most listenable and enduring highlight. Along with perverted lyrics, Rob Zombie's vocal snarls and the band's muscular metal thunder produce the furious concoction that secures, *La Sexorcisto: Devil Music, Vol. 1*'s place in heavy metal history. Weak appetites for raunchy, tongue-in-cheek decadence need not apply. —*Jacob N. Lunders*

Astro Creep: 2000—Songs of Love, Destruction / Apr. 11, 1995 / Geffen ♦♦♦♦

Following the belated surprise success of *La Sexorcisto, Astro-Creep: 2000—Songs of Love, Destruction and Other Synthetic Delusions of the Electric Head* carried the weight of high expectations, something that White Zombie was never familiar with before. Unsurprisingly, White Zombie plays it safe on *Astro-Creep*, never straying from their white-trash-on-acid metal. While it's undeniably campy, the band genuinely loves the trash they sing about, so they fit right into the tradition of tongue-in-cheek heavy metal bands from Alice Cooper to Kiss. Where those bands relied on songcraft beneath their schtick, White Zombie relies on a full-throttle roar. Borrowing such techniques as distorted vocals and drilling riffs from pseudo-industrial metal like Ministry, the band beefs up their basic sound, making it powerful enough to disguise the lack of solid song structures and memorable riffs. Sonically, *Astro Creep* delivers the initial goods, yet it never develops into trash as substantial as "Thunder Kiss '65." —*Stephen Thomas Erlewine*

Supersexy Swingin' Sounds / Aug. 1996 / Geffen ♦♦♦

With *Supersexy Swingin' Sounds*, White Zombie offer a collection of ten remixes of songs from *Astro-Creep 2000*, plus a new mix of their cover of KC & the Sunshine Band's "I'm Your Boogie Man" (which was originally on *The Crow II* soundtrack). Not quite as experimental or dance-oriented as they would like to be, the band has always flirted with industrial and disco, but at their core they are a metal band. Granted, they're a metal band that reconfigures the kitschy pleasures of pop culture much in the vein of the Cramps and the B-52's. However, with *Supersexy Swingin' Sounds* the weaknesses in their approach become clear. Despite the presence of remixers like the Dust Brothers, P.M. Dawn, and Charlie Closer (among several others), there simply isn't enough interesting original material to make the reconfigured versions compelling. Furthermore the album artwork—featuring pseudo-exotica design and an array of scantly-clad or naked models, all dressed like '60s pin-ups—seems like the band is hopping on the bandwagon, instead of carving out new camp territory of their own. It's not a bad listen, but it is a surprisingly unengaging one. —*Stephen Thomas Erlewine*

Barry White

b. Sep. 12, 1944, Galveston, TX

Vocals, Keyboards, Arranger / Smooth Soul, Urban, Disco, Soul

Barry White has been involved in the popular music industry since age 11, when he played piano on Jesse Belvin's hit single "Goodnight My Love." He recorded with the Upfronts for Lumntone in 1960, then as a lead vocalist for Atlantic in 1964 and for Downey and Veep in 1965 under the name of Lee Barry. He was an A&R man for Mustang/Bronco Records in 1966 and 1967. White formed the female trio Love Unlimited in 1969, and also became leader of the 40-piece Love Unlimited Orchestra. His solo career was revitalized in the early '70s as his formidable, deep, captivating bass, coupled with pseudo-sophisticated strings and elaborate productions, helped him rack up five number one hits and seven other Top Ten R&B hits from 1973 until 1978 for 20th Century Records. He also scored five Top Ten pop singles and one number one in that same stretch. "I'm Gonna Love You a Little More Baby" started the string in 1973, and his final Top Ten R&B single was "Your Sweetness Is My Weakness," which peaked at number two in 1978. White continued recording for United Gold, 20th Century again, United Gold, and A&M. He scored a mild comeback by being one of the featured vocalists on Quincy Jones' single "The Garden" in 1989 and continues recording for A&M in the '90s. *The Icon Is Love* (1994) marked White's return as a potent commercial force. —*Ron Wynn*

Greatest Hits, Vol. 1 / 1975 / Casablanca ♦♦♦♦♦

Before a definitive multi-disc boxed set was issued in the 1990s, there were two single-album volumes of Barry White hits released by Casablanca in the 1970s. The first edition was the best, with sweeping versions of such disco classics as "Can't Get Enough of Your Love, Babe" and "You're the First, The Last, My Everything." White's productions and arrangements were never as intricate as they seemed, but his booming baritone and romantic dialogue sounded convincing when underscored by the lush backgrounds. If you only want a little Barry White, this is the album to grab. —*Ron Wynn*

Greatest Hits, Vol. 2 / 1981 / Casablanca ♦♦♦♦

This second set of Barry White hits isn't quite as impressive or essential as its predecessor. White's arrangements and compositions grew stale as the 1970s wore on, and he recycled the romantic dialogue and exploited the robust baritone until he became a caricature of himself. Put this one in the "for fans only" category. —*Ron Wynn*

Just for You / Nov. 17, 1992 / Casablanca ♦♦♦♦♦

With 1970s nostalgia being quite the rage in the early 1990s, Mercury set out to cash in on the trend with this three-CD box set by one of the top soul/disco men of that decade. Though three CDs is a bit much for novices (who would be better off with the 1995 single-CD anthology *All Time Greatest Hits*), more seasoned White devotees will find that there's a lot to admire about this comprehensive package. Essential '70s hits like "I'm Gonna Love You Just a Little More, Baby," "Can't Get Enough of Your Love, Babe" and "It's Ecstasy" are included along with gems he produced for the female group Love Unlimited (including the sexy "Walking In the Rain With the One I Love" and the sweet "I Belong to You") and his instrumental-oriented Love Unlimited Orchestra ("Love's Theme" and "Satin Soul," among other hits). And the set also contains some of White's more recent work, such as 1989's "L.A. My Kinda Place" and a remake of Lisa Stansfield's "All Around the World" that finds him forming a memorable duo with the British singer. Despite the fact that some of the newer selections aren't essential, *Just for You* does a fine job of summarizing White's many post-1971 accomplishments. —*Alex Henderson*

★ **All Time Greatest Hits** / 1995 / Mercury Funk Essentials ♦♦♦♦♦

Condensing the best moments from the two *Greatest Hits* collections onto one disc, *All Time Greatest Hits* contains all of Barry White's biggest hits, including "I'm Gonna Love You Just A Little More Baby," "Never, Never Gonna Give Ya Up," "Can't Get Enough of Your Love, Babe," "You're the First, the Last, My Everything," and "It's Ecstasy When You Lay Down Next to Me." *All Time Greatest Hits* is the definitive collection of Barry White's '70s heyday, containing all of his truly essential songs. —*Stephen Thomas Erlewine*

Under the Influence of Love: The Very Best of Barry White / Jan. 5, 1998 / Collectables ♦♦

Boss Soul: The Genius of Barry White / Aug. 4, 1998 / Del-Fi ♦♦♦

In 1966-67, long before he attained seventies superstardom as a growling bedroom funkster, Barry White gained valuable experience as an A&R man for the Del-Fi label in Los Angeles. This compilation has 16 tracks that he was involved with as producer, engineer, songwriter, and/or session musician, the results appearing on Del-Fi's Bronco and Mustang subsidiaries; note, however, that only five of the cuts are by White himself (including one instrumental and a pre-Del Fi 1965 single released under the pseudonym of Lee Barry). At this time, White was very much under the spell of Motown both as producer and songwriter (he wrote or co-wrote all but two of these tunes). The material, whether by White or other Mustang/Bronco artists Felice Taylor, Viola Wills, and Johnny Wyatt, consists for the most part of very derivative, but nonetheless enjoyable and professional, Motown variations. Felice Taylor's "It May Be Winter Outside," a #42 pop hit in 1966, is the most accurate mid-'60s Supremes imitation bar none, both for Taylor's uncanny Diana Ross-like vocals and the dead-on Motownesque arrangement. Her only slightly less Supremish "Under the Influence of Love," though unreleased in the U.S., was a #11 hit in the U.K. in 1967; an instrumental version (credited to White) is also on the CD. As for White's own performances, it's a shock to hear that familiar hoarse voice applied to much lighter, poppier songs than we're accustomed to hearing from the singer, and though they're okay efforts, it's easy to see why they may not have been considered commercial properties in the '60s. An interesting document of White's little-heard formative years, and a decent pickup for aficionados of little-heard '60s soul in general. —*Richie Unterberger*

The Ultimate Collection / Jan. 25, 2000 / Polygram ♦♦♦

The Ultimate Collection gathers two discs' worth of Barry White's greatest hits and definitive tracks, as selected by White himself. Along with the title track from his 1999 album *Staying Power*, the set collects '70s hits like "I'm Gonna Love You Just a Little More Baby," "Can't Get Enough of Your Love Babe," "You're the First, the Last, My Everything," and "Never, Never Gonna Give You Up" and highlights of his work with the Love Unlimited Orchestra such as "My Sweet Summer Suite," "Midnight and You," and "Love's Theme." Later tracks like "Sho' You Right," "Put Me in Your Mix," and "Practice What You Preach" round out this worthwhile overview of White's career highlights. —*Heather Phares*

Tony Joe White

b. Jul. 23, 1943, Oak Grove, LA

Vocals, Songwriter, Harmonica, Guitar / Pop-Soul, Pop/Rock, Country-Pop, Country-Rock, Rock & Roll

Tony Joe White has parlayed his songwriting talent into a modestly successful country and rock career in Europe as well as America. He began working clubs in Texas during the mid-'60s, and moved to Nashville by 1968. White's 1969 debut album for Monument, *Black and White*, featured his Top Ten pop hit "Polk Salad Annie" and another charting single, "Roosevelt and Ira Lee (Night of the Moccasin)." That same year, Dusty Springfield reached the charts with his "Willie and Laura Mae Jones." Brook Benton recorded a version of White's "Rainy Night in Georgia" that hit number four early in 1970; the song has since become a near-standard with over 100 credits. White's own "Groupie Girl" began his European success with a short stay on the British charts in 1970. White moved to Warner Brothers in 1971, but success eluded him on his three albums—*Tony Joe White*, *The Train I'm On* and *Homemade Ice Cream*. Other stars, however, continued to keep his name on the charts during the '70s: Elvis charted with "For Ol' Times Sake" and "I've Got a Thing About You Baby" (Top Five on the country charts), and Hank Williams Jr. took "A Rainy Night in Georgia" to number 13 country. White himself recorded *Eyes* for 20th Century Fox in 1976, but then disappeared for four years. He signed to Casablanca for 1980's *The Real Thang* but moved to Columbia in 1983 for *Dangerous*, which included the modest country hits "The Lady in My Life" and "We Belong Together." White was inactive through much of the '80s. He released *Closer to the Truth* in 1990 for his own Swamp label, and toured with Eric Clapton and Joe Cocker to very receptive French crowds. —*John Bush*

● **Polk Salad Annie: The Best of Tony Joe White** / 1994 / Warner Archive ✦✦✦✦✦
Twenty tracks from 1969-73, the period of White's greatest success, including "Polk Salad Annie" and White's own version of his composition, "Rainy Night in Georgia." Most of this is quality swamp-rock with pop-soul-conscious production; on cuts like "High Sheriff of Calhoun Parrish," it sounds very much like he was trying to achieve a groove in the mold of Bobbie Joe Gentry's "Ode to Billie Joe." Sometimes he gets real downhome in a stomping backwoods blues style that makes him sound a little like a White counterpart to John Lee Hooker, as on "Stockholm Blues." If there's any criticism to be levied against this music, it's in its occasional lack of variety, White mining staple swamp rock boogie riffs for all they're worth. However, few, if any, performers and writers were as skilled as White in doing so, and he has a fine knack for sharp storytelling lyrics. —*Richie Unterberger*

Whitesnake

f. 1977, London, England
Hair Metal, Heavy Metal, Hard Rock, Pop-Metal
After recording two solo albums, former Deep Purple vocalist David Coverdale formed Whitesnake around 1977. In the glut of hard rock and heavy metal bands of the late '70s, their first albums got somewhat lost in the shuffle, although they were fairly popular in Europe and Japan. During 1982, Coverdale took some time off, so he could take care of his sick daughter. When he re-emerged with a new version of Whitesnake in 1984, the band sounded revitalized and energetic. *Slide It In* may have relied on Led Zeppelin and Deep Purple's old tricks, but the band had a knack for writing hooks; the record became their first platinum album. Three years later, Whitesnake released an eponymous album which was even better. Portions of the album were blatantly derivative—"Still of the Night" was a dead ringer for early Zeppelin—but the group could write powerful, heavy rockers like "Here I Go Again" that were driven as much by melody as riffs, as well as hit power ballads like "Is This Love." *Whitesnake* was an enormous international success, selling over six million copies in the U.S. alone. —*Stephen Thomas Erlewine*

Ready An' Willing / 1980 / EMI ✦✦✦✦
Come An' Get It / 1981 / Geffen ✦✦✦
Saints & Sinners / 1982 / Geffen ✦✦✦✦
Slide It In / 1984 / Geffen ✦✦✦✦✦
Following up the splendid *Saints & Sinners* album was no easy task, but 1984's *Slide It In* turned out to be an even greater triumph for David Coverdale's Whitesnake. From the boisterous machismo of "Spit It Out" and "All or Nothing" to the resigned despair of "Gambler" and "Standing in the Shadow," and the embarrassingly silly title track, everything seems to click. For hit singles, look no further than the twin guitar attack of "Guilty of Love" and the sheer poetry and emotion of "Love Ain't No Stranger," one of the decade's greatest power ballads, bar none. Not to be outdone, "Slow an' Easy" is a masterpiece of sexual tension and the kind of power-blues which no one does as well as Whitesnake. On a quirky historical note, Coverdale fired most of the band soon after the album's release, replacing them with younger, prettier faces with which to better conquer America. For that purpose, Geffen Records even released a re-recorded version of *Slide It In* with flashy soloing from new guitarist John Sykes, sparking an ongoing debate as to which version is better. —*Ed Rivadavia*

Whitesnake / 1987 / Geffen ✦✦✦✦✦
David Coverdale built Whitesnake's commercial breakthrough on a collection of loud, polished hard rockers, plus the band's best set of pop hooks. The Led Zeppelin-ish "Still of the Night" offered headbanger appeal, but it was the big chorus of "Here I Go Again"—one of the very small number of non-power ballad '80s hard rock singles to actually top the pop charts—and the quiet ballad "Is This Love" that really sold the album in spades. The rest of the album generally holds interest as well, and it's easily the band's best. —*Steve Huey*

Slip of the Tongue / Feb. 1989 / Geffen ✦✦✦
A replica of the mega-hit *Whitesnake*, *Slip of the Tongue* wasn't as successful because the band's songs weren't as catchy and the riffs weren't as powerful. Not even the presence of guitar superhero Steve Vai could add excitement to the band's bland, futile attempt at keeping its pop audience. —*Stephen Thomas Erlewine*

● **Whitesnake's Greatest Hits** / Jul. 19, 1994 / Geffen ✦✦✦✦✦

Whitesnake's Greatest Hits collects the cream of the band's later '80s efforts, gathering most of its material from *Slide It In*, *Whitesnake*, and *Slip of the Tongue*. Bigger fans will find worthwhile album tracks on the former two efforts, but this collection of Zeppelin-ish rock anthems and hooky power ballads are all most fans will need. —*Steve Huey*

20th Century Masters—The Millennium Collection: The Best of Whitesnake / Jun. 27, 2000 / Geffen ✦✦✦✦
The Millennium Collection: The Best of Whitesnake revisits the group's biggest hits, including "Here I Go Again," "Still of the Night," "Is This Love," and "Fool for Your Loving." Album tracks from their later releases, such as *Slip of the Tongue*'s "The Deeper the Love" and *Slide It In*'s "Love Ain't No Stranger" give a good overview of the band's '80s heyday. Though it's not quite as comprehensive as *Whitesnake's Greatest Hits*, *The Best of Whitesnake* does provide a good selection of hits for casual fans. —*Heather Phares*

The Who

f. 1964, London, England, **db.** 1983
British Psychedelia, Album Rock, Mod, Pop/Rock, British Invasion, Hard Rock, Rock & Roll
Few bands in the history of rock & roll were riddled with as many contradictions as the Who. All four members had wildly different personalities, as their notoriously intense live performances demonstrated. The group was a whirlwind of activity, as the wild Keith Moon fell over his drum kit and Pete Townshend leaped into the air with his guitar, spinning his right hand in exaggerated windmills. Vocalist Roger Daltrey strutted across the stage with a thuggish menace, as bassist John Entwistle stood silent, functioning as the eye of the hurricane. These divergent personalities frequently clashed, but these frictions also resulted in a decade's worth of remarkable music. As one of the key figures of the British Invasion and the mod movement of the mid-'60s, the Who were a dynamic and undeniably powerful sonic force. They often sounded like they were exploding conventional rock and R&B structures with Townshend's furious guitar chords, Entwistle's hyperactive bass lines and Moon's vigorous, chaotic drumming. Unlike most rock bands, the Who based their rhythm on Townshend's guitar, letting Moon and Entwistle improvise wildly over his foundation, while Daltrey belted out his vocals. This was the sound the Who thrived on in concert, but on record they were a different proposition, as Townshend pushed the group toward new sonic territory. He soon became regarded as one of the finest British songwriters of his era, as songs like "The Kids Are Alright" and "My Generation" became teenage anthems, and his rock opera *Tommy* earned him respect from mainstream music critics. Townshend continually pushed the band toward more ambitious territory, incorporating white noise, pop art and conceptual extended musical pieces into the group's style. At their peak, the Who were one of the most innovative and powerful bands in rock history. —*Stephen Thomas Erlewine*

☆ **The Who Sings My Generation** / 1965 / MCA ✦✦✦✦✦
An explosive debut, and the hardest mod pop recorded by anyone. At the time of its release, it also had the most ferociously powerful guitars and drums yet captured on a rock record. Townshend's exhilarating chord crunches and guitar distortions threaten to leap off the grooves on "My Generation" and "Out in the Street"; Keith Moon attacks the drums with a lightning, ruthless finesse throughout. Some "Maximum R&B" influence lingered in the two James Brown covers, but much of Townshend's original material fused Beatlesque hooks and power chords with anthemic mod lyrics, with "The Good's Gone," "Much Too Much," "La La La Lies," and especially "The Kids Are Alright" being highlights. "A Legal Matter" hinted at more ambitious lyrical concerns, and "The Ox" was instrumental mayhem that pushed the envelope of 1965 amplification with its guitar feedback and nonstop crashing drum rolls. While the execution was sometimes crude, and the songwriting not as sophisticated as it would shortly become, the Who never surpassed the pure energy level of this record. —*Richie Unterberger*

A Quick One (Happy Jack) / 1966 / MCA ✦✦✦✦✦
The group's second album is a less impressive outing than their debut, primarily because, at the urging of their managers, all four members penned original material (though Townshend wrote more than anyone else). The pure adrenaline of *My Generation* also subsided somewhat, as the band began to grapple with more complex melodic and lyrical themes, especially on the erratic mini-opera, "A Quick One While He's Away." Still, there's some great madness on Moon's instrumental "Cobwebs and Strange," and Townshend delivered some solid mod pop with "Run Run Run" and "So Sad About Us." John Entwistle was also revealed to be a writer of considerable talent (and a morbid bent) on "Whiskey Man" and "Boris the Spider." The 1995 CD reissue adds ten bonus tracks: some 1966-67 B-sides, their U.K.-only 1966 *Ready Steady Who!* EP, an acoustic version of "Happy Jack," and a previously unreleased cover of the Everly Brothers' "Man with the Money." —*Richie Unterberger*

☆ **The Who Sell Out** / 1967 / MCA ✦✦✦✦✦
Townshend originally planned this as a concept album of sorts that would simultaneously mock and pay tribute to pirate radio stations, complete with fake jingles and commercials linking the tracks. For reasons that remain somewhat ill-defined, the concept wasn't quite driven to completion, breaking down around the middle of side two (on the original vinyl configuration). Nonetheless, on strictly musical merits, it's a terrific set of songs that ultimately stands as one of the group's greatest achievements. "I Can See For Miles" (a Top Ten hit) is the Who at their most thunderous; tinges of psychedelia add a rush to "Armenia, City in the Sky" and "Relax"; "I Can't Reach You" finds Townshend beginning to stretch himself into quasi-spiritual territory; and "Tattoo" and the acoustic "Sunrise" show introspective, vulnerable sides to the singer-songwriter that had previously been hidden. "Rael" was another mini-opera, with musical motifs that reappeared in *Tommy*. The album is as perfect a balance between melodic mod pop and powerful instrumentation as the Who (or

any other group) would achieve; psychedelic pop was never as jubilant, not to say funny (the fake commercials and jingles interspersed between the songs are a hoot). The 1995 CD reissue has over half a dozen interesting outtakes from the time of the sessions, as well as unused commercials, the B-side "Someone's Coming," and an alternate version of "Mary Anne with the Shaky Hand." *—Richie Unterberger*

Magic Bus / 1968 / MCA ✦✦✦
A ripoff of sorts even upon its original release, with a few senseless repeats of tracks from *Quick One* and *Sell Out*, as well as a sleeve that erroneously implied a live recording. This mish-mash of singles, B-sides, and stray tracks from past British releases did have some fine moments, particularly the singles "Call Me Lightning" and the Bo Diddley-influenced "Magic Bus," which became one of their most popular concert numbers. Other highlights are the fine '66 pop-art tune "Disguises" and Entwistle's hysterical "Doctor, Doctor," but these (and a few of the other cuts) are now available as bonus tracks on the *Quick One* and *Sell Out* reissues. Completists should know that one song, Entwistle's typically black-humored "Dr. Jekyll & Mr. Hyde," is unavailable on any other U.S. release, so it's not time to throw away your copy of *Magic Bus* just yet. *—Richie Unterberger*

Tommy / 1969 / MCA ✦✦✦✦✦
The full-blown rock opera about a deaf, dumb, and blind boy that launched the band to international superstardom, written almost entirely by Townshend. Hailed as a breakthrough upon its release, it's critical standing has diminished somewhat in the ensuing decades, because of the occasional pretensions of the concept, and the insubstantial nature of some of the songs that functioned as little more than devices to advance the rather sketchy plot. Nonetheless, the double album has many excellent songs, including "I'm Free," "Pinball Wizard," "Sensation," "Christmas," "We're Not Gonna Take It," and the dramatic ten-minute instrumental, "Underture." Though the album was slightly flawed, Townshend's ability to construct a lengthy conceptual narrative brought new possibilities to rock music. Despite the complexity of the project, he and the Who never lost sight of solid pop melodies, harmonies, and forceful instrumentation, imbuing the material with a suitably powerful grace. *—Richie Unterberger*

☆ **Live at Leeds** / 1970 / MCA ✦✦✦✦✦
A loud, raunchy concert showcase for the group, with surprisingly little material from *Tommy*. The group's R&B roots are showcased here far better than on their post-*My Generation* studio albums, and the only problem for some listeners is the lack of the sophisticated studio sound they'd developed on previous releases. The 1995 CD reissue doubles the length of the original LP, with plenty of additional material from the same performance, including versions of some more of their early singles and unexpected items like "Tattoo" and the R&B standard "Fortune Teller." *—Bruce Eder*

★ **Meaty Beaty Big and Bouncy** / 1971 / MCA ✦✦✦✦✦
Meaty, Beaty, Big & Bouncy has the distinction of being the first in a long line of Who compilations. It also has the distinction of being the best. Part of the reason why it is so successful is that it has an actual purpose. *Meaty* was designed as a collection of the group's singles, many of which never appeared on albums. The Who recorded their share of great albums during the '60s, but condensing their highlights to just the singles is an electrifying experience. "The Kids Are Alright" follows "I Can't Explain," "I Can See for Miles" bleeds into "Pictures of Lily" and "My Generation," "Magic Bus" gives way to "Substitute" and "I'm a Boy"—it's an extraordinary lineup, and each song builds on its predecessor's power. Since it was released prior to *Who's Next*, it contains none of the group's album rock hits, but that's for the best—their '60s singles have a kinetic, frenzied power that the louder, harder AOR cuts simply couldn't touch. Also, there is such a distinct change in sound with *Who's Next* that the two eras don't quite sound right on one greatest-hits collection, as *My Generation* and *Who's Better, Who's Best* proved. By concentrating on the early years—when the Who were fresh and Pete Townshend was developing his own songwriting identity—*Meaty, Beaty, Big & Bouncy* is musically unified and incredibly powerful. *This* is what the Who sounded like when they were a great band. *—Stephen Thomas Erlewine*

★ **Who's Next** / 1971 / MCA ✦✦✦✦✦
Much of *Who's Next* derives from *Lifehouse*, an ambitious sci-fi rock opera Pete Townshend abandoned after suffering a nervous breakdown, caused in part from working on the sequel to *Tommy*. There's no discernable theme behind these songs, yet this album is stronger than *Tommy*, falling just behind *Who Sell Out* as the finest record the Who ever cut. Townshend developed an infatuation with synthesizers during the recording of the album, and they're all over this album, adding texture where needed and amplifying the force, which is already at a fever pitch. Apart from *Live at Leeds*, the Who have never sounded as LOUD and unhinged as they do here, yet that's balanced by ballads, both lovely ("The Song Is Over") and scathing ("Behind Blue Eyes"). That's the key to *Who's Next*—there's anger and sorrow, humor and regret, passion and tumult, all wrapped up in a blistering package where the rage is as affecting as the heartbreak. This is a retreat from the '60s, as Townshend declares the "Song Is Over," scorns the teenage wasteland, and bitterly declares that we "Won't Get Fooled Again." For all the sorrow and heartbreak that runs beneath the surface, this is an invigorating record, not just because Keith Moon runs rampant or because Roger Daltrey has never sung better or because John Entwistle spins out manic bass lines that are as captivating as his "My Wife" is funny. This is invigorating because it has all of that, plus Townshend laying his soul bare in ways that are funny, painful, and utterly life-affirming. That is what the Who was about, not the rock operas, and that's why *Who's Next* is truer than *Tommy* or the abandoned *Lifehouse*. Those were art—this, even with its pretensions, is rock & roll. *—Stephen Thomas Erlewine*

Quadrophenia / 1973 / MCA ✦✦✦✦✦
Pete Townshend revisited the rock opera concept with another double-album opus, this time built around the story of a young mod's struggle to come of age in the mid-'60s. If anything, this was a more ambitious project than *Tommy*, given added weight by the fact that the Who weren't devising some fantasy, but were re-examining the roots of their own birth in mod culture. In the end, there may have been *too* much weight, as Townshend tried to combine the story of a mixed-up mod named Jimmy with the examination of a four-way split personality (hence the title *Quadrophenia*), in turn meant to reflect the four conflicting personas at work within the Who themselves. The concept might have ultimately been too obscure and confusing for a mass audience. But there's plenty of great music anyway, especially on "The Real Me," "The Punk Meets the Godfather," "I'm One," "Bell Boy," and "Love, Reign O'er Me." Some of Townshend's most direct, heartfelt writing is contained here, and production-wise it's a tour de force, with some of the most imaginative use of synthesizers on a rock record. Various members of the band griped endlessly about flaws in the mix, but really these will bug very few listeners, who in general will find this to be one of the Who's most powerful statements. *—Richie Unterberger*

Odds & Sods / 1974 / MCA ✦✦✦
This compilation of outtakes and rarities from the Who's first decade was a rather jumpy listen that harbored few songs that could be termed top-of-the-line. Also, since its 1974 release, several of the tracks have been issued on other compilations, or as bonus tracks to CD reissues of legitimate Who albums. Setting your expectations at the appropriate level, you'll find much of this worthwhile. "Pure and Easy," "Naked Eye," and "Long Live Rock" were all concert favorites of the group in the 1970s; "Glow Girl" introduced some riffs that would resurface in *Tommy*; and "Postcard," Entwistle's tale of rock life on the road, was one of his better compositions. This also has their very first single, "I'm the Face," recorded in 1964 when the group were known as the High Numbers. The 1998 CD reissue is a must-have even if you've got the original LP, as it doubles the album size with a dozen bonus tracks, most previously unreleased. These include some real interesting items: the Motown covers "Leaving Here" and "Baby Don't You Do It" are taken from demos circa late 1964, the latter track featuring some early guitar distortion freakout in the solo; "Mary Anne with the Shaky Hand" is the rare U.S. B-side version; there are late-sixties studio versions of *Live at Leeds* faves "Summertime Blues" and "Young Man Blues"; the Rolling Stones' cover "Under My Thumb" and "Water" are B-sides that weren't on an album for a long time; and there are less exciting alternates and outtakes from *Tommy*, *Who's Next* and *Quadrophenia*. *—Richie Unterberger*

The Who By Numbers / 1975 / MCA ✦✦✦✦
The Who by Numbers functions as Pete Townshend's confessional singer-songwriter album, as he chronicles his problems with alcohol ("However Much I Booze"), women ("Dreaming from the Waist" and "They Are All in Love"), and life in general. However, his introspective musings are rendered ineffective by Roger Daltrey's bluster and the cloying, lightweight filler of "Squeeze Box." In addition, Townshend's songs tend to be underdeveloped, relying on verbosity instead of melodicism, with only the simple power of "Slip Kid," the grace of "Blue Red and Grey," and John Entwistle's heavy rocker "Success Story" making much of an impact. The 1996 CD reissue adds three live tracks from a 1976 concert. *—Stephen Thomas Erlewine*

Who Are You / 1978 / MCA ✦✦✦
On the band's final album with Moon, their trademark honest power started to get diluted by fatigue and a sense that the group's collective vision was beginning to fade. As instrumentalists, their skills were intact. More problematic was the erratic quality of the material, which seemed torn between blustery attempts at contemporary relevance ("Sister Disco," "New Song," "Music Must Change") and bittersweet insecurity ("Love Is Coming Down"). Most problematic of all were the arrangements, heavy on the symphonic synthesizers and strings, which make the record sound cluttered and over-anxious. Daltrey's operatic tough-guy braggadocio in particular was beginning to sound annoying on several cuts. Yet Townshend's better tunes—"Music Must Change," "Love Is Coming Down," and the anthemic title track—continued to explore the contradictions of aging rockers in interesting, effective ways. Whether due to Moon's death or not, it was the last reasonably interesting Who record. The 1996 CD reissue adds five previously unreleased alternate takes and demos. *—Richie Unterberger*

The Kids Are Alright / 1979 / MCA ✦✦✦✦
Like the film itself, the soundtrack to the Who's *Kids Are Alright* documentary is frustrating even as it pleases, since it falls short of being definitive. If the film was supposed to explain the excitement and history of the Who, tracing their evolution from mod superstars to arena rock gods, it somehow failed by just not quite gelling together. Similarly, the soundtrack attempts to gather a bunch of live rarities, thereby capturing the band at the peak of their powers, but it falls a little bit short of the mark by hopping all over the place chronologically, adding a couple of studio cuts (including live-in-the-studio tracks), along the way. So, you can view this as a missed opportunity or treasure what's here—and, really, the latter is the preferred method of listening to this album, since there is a lot to treasure here. There's the epochal performance of "My Generation" from the 1967 *Smothers Brothers* show, three performances from Woodstock, terrific television performances of "Magic Bus" and "Anyway, Anyhow, Anywhere," a blistering "Young Man Blues," and the definitive performance of "A Quick One, While He's Away," the version they played at the Rolling Stones' *Rock & Roll Circus*. Then, there are some really fine latter-day versions of "My Wife," "Baba O'Riley," and "Won't Get Fooled Again," along with a medley of "Join Together/Roadrunner/My Generation Blues" from 1975, that may not be era-defining, like those mentioned above, but they're pretty damn great all the same. So, it's a bit too haphazard to really be definitive, but the Who were always a bit haphazard, and if you love them, that's something you love about them. And, in turn, it's hard not to love this album, if you love them. *—Stephen Thomas Erlewine*

Face Dances / 1981 / MCA ✦✦✦
Without Keith Moon, the Who may have lacked the restless fire power that distinguished their earlier albums, but *Face Dances* had some of Pete Townshend's best, most incisive compositions since *Quadrophenia*. "Don't Let Go the Coat" was one of his better odes to Meher Baba, "You Better You Bet" was a driving rocker, as was the rueful "Cache Cache," while "How Can You Do It Alone" was a solid ballad. While Townshend's songs were graceful and introspective, Roger Daltrey delivered them without any subtlety, rendering their power impotent. The new compact disc reissue adds five tracks to the original nine-song lineup, including three tracks that didn't make the album's final cut (Townshend's "I Like Nightmares," "It's In You" and "Somebody Saved Me") and two live tracks, a rough jam of "How Can You Do It Alone" and Entwistle's "The Quiet One," from 1979 and 1982, respectively. —*Stephen Thomas Erlewine and Cub Koda*

It's Hard / 1982 / MCA ✦✦
Driven by Pete Townshend's arching musical ambitions, *It's Hard* was an undistinguished final effort from the Who. Featuring layers of synthesizers and long-winded, twisting song structures, the album featured few memorable melodies and little energy, with only the anthemic "Athena" and the terse "Eminence Front" making a lasting impression. The new compact disc reissue adds four bonus tracks to the original 12-song lineup, all of them live. These alternate versions of "Eminence Front," the title song and "Cry If You Want," along with John Entwistle's "Dangerous," all come from performances at the Maple Leaf Gardens in Toronto, Canada. Although no specific recording dates are given in the booklet, these bonus tracks give us far more lively versions of these songs than their original studio counterparts. —*Stephen Thomas Erlewine and Cub Koda*

Who's Missing / 1985 / MCA ✦✦✦
A dozen B-sides, UK-only singles, and other oddities from the 1960s and early '70s. Some of these are really good: the raucous 1965 cover of James Brown's "Shout and Shimmy," "Heaven and Hell" (one of John Entwistle's better tunes), the 45 version of "Mary Anne with the Shaky Hand," the obscure Roger Daltrey tune "Here for More." Other cuts are pretty peripheral, like the lame '65 R&B of "Lubie (Come Back Home)," or the live version of "Bargain." Also, a few of these have since been tacked onto CD reissues of proper Who albums as bonus tracks. It's not bad, but it's really only for fans of the band. —*Richie Unterberger*

Two's Missing / 1987 / MCA ✦✦✦
Like *Who's Missing*, this is an assortment of B-sides, UK-only tracks, outtakes, and live cuts from the 1960s and early '70s. Again, there's some notable, even terrific, material here: the fiery 1967 covers of the Rolling Stones' "The Last Time" and "Under My Thumb," the strange 1968 UK single "Dogs," the heavy R&B of the '65 British B-side "Daddy Rolling Stone." Yet much of the rest of the album is extraneous to all but diehards, like a sluggish 1965 cover of Martha & the Vandellas' "Motoring," Keith Moon's novelty B-side "Wasp Man," or the 1969 instrumental "Dogs, Part 2" (which *does* have some slick guitar runs and manic drumming). The record's haphazardly sequenced as well. Also, *Who's Missing* and *Two's Missing* still manage to miss a couple '60s B-sides that Who fanatics might want (Entwistle's "I've Been Away" and Keith Moon's "In the City"), although those two cuts are now available on the CD reissue of *A Quick One*. In fact, the well-known bootleg *Who's Zoo* does a much better job of assembling most of the group's early rarities into two albums. —*Richie Unterberger*

Who's Better Who's Best / Nov. 14, 1988 / MCA ✦✦✦✦
Who's Better, Who's Best is a compilation of the Who's best-known songs, containing all of the familiar items—"I Can't Explain," "I Can See for Miles," "Pinball Wizard," "My Generation," "Substitute"—but presented without much care. The album is further plagued by the presence of some filler tracks that really don't deserve to be on any best-of. *Who's Better, Who's Best* is, however, in its finer moments a fine compilation. Indeed, the first half of this 1988 release collects nine of the most interesting rock tracks ever. Unfortunately, the compilation falters as it comes to a close. A more forthright compilation is perhaps a better option for most (*Meaty Beaty Big and Bouncy* springs to mind). Nevertheless, *Who's Better, Who's Best* is a solid career overview and is useful for both casual and hardcore fans. —*Ben Davies*

Thirty Years of Maximum R&B / Jul. 5, 1994 / MCA ✦✦✦
One of the more overblown recent box sets, this four-CD collection does include all of their big hits and the lion's share of their key album tracks. Previously unreleased rarities include some interesting selections (the '60s outtakes "Early Morning Cold Taxi" and "Melancholia"), but these bits and pieces, which include some live versions, commercials, Keith Moon sketches, and the like, are mostly inessential. The post-Keith Moon cuts that bring us up to the present are out of the league of the body of The Who's work. As most of The Who's '60s and '70s albums are very strong, cohesive works in and of themselves, this can't be recommended as either a starting point or a necessary addition. —*Richie Unterberger*

● **My Generation: The Very Best of the Who** / Aug. 27, 1996 / MCA ✦✦✦✦✦
The Who have issued more greatest hits collections than any other major artist, releasing a vast array of compilations while they were together and in the years following their breakup. Released in 1996, *My Generation: The Very Best of the Who* was intended to be the definitive single-disc collection, replacing all the others that preceded it. While it is a very good collection, it just misses being a definitive sampler. Essentially, *My Generation* is a replica of *Who's Better, Who's Best* that adds four tracks that were missing from the previous compilation, including the seminal post-*Tommy* single "The Seeker" and the original single mix of "Magic Bus." *My Generation* isn't strictly a singles collection, since it contains such album rock staples as "Baba O'Riley" and the full-length version of "Won't Get Fooled Again." It also spans the group's entire career, so it has a bit of a scatter-shot feel to it—"You Better You Bet" sounds a little odd next to tense early singles like

"Substitute" and "I Can See for Miles." The career-spanning approach doesn't make for as cohesive a collection as *Meaty, Beaty, Big and Bouncy*, but it does mean that *My Generation* is an excellent—even necessary—introduction. There's a lot more in the Who's catalog that needs to be heard, but *My Generation* does boil down the most essential items (even though the abominable "Squeeze Box" is included) to a fine single-disc set. —*Stephen Thomas Erlewine*

Live at the Isle of Wight Festival 1970 / Oct. 29, 1996 / Columbia/Legacy ✦✦✦✦✦
This double CD is pretty similar in sound and content to the expanded *Live at Leeds* album, except there's much more from *Tommy*, and a few semi-obscure numbers like "I Don't Even Know Myself," "Water," and "Naked Eye." Hardcore Who fanatics seem to prefer *Live at Leeds*, which was recorded only a few months before this material. That viewpoint is understandable: the performances are sharper on *Leeds*, and if you're not a big-league fan, that single-disc set is a more economical survey of the band in concert during this era. If you *do* like the Who a lot, though, *Isle of Wight* is worth having. The sound and performances are decent, although be aware that the band's onstage version of *Tommy* omits some decent songs from the opera, such as "Sensation" and "Underture." —*Richie Unterberger*

The Blues to the Bush / 2000 / Musicmaker.com ✦✦✦
To many Who fans, the band was never the same after original drummer Keith Moon's death in 1978. After trying to fill the vacancy with ex-Faces drummer Kenney Jones didn't work out, the band called it a day in 1982. But during their *Quadrophenia* tour of 1996, the Who found a drummer that finally filled Moon's void properly—Zak Starkey (son of Ringo Starr). While not as flashy as Moon, Starkey is more solid and powerful, as proven by his playing on the Who's 2000 live album, *The Blues to the Bush*, only available through the website Musicmaker.com. Recorded during four shows during late 1999 (the House of Blues in Chicago and the Empire Theatre in Shepherds Bush), the compilation mixes favorites with obscure material. While original Who members Pete Townshend, Roger Daltrey, and John Entwistle may be getting up there in the age department, the band (with longtime keyboardist John "Rabbit" Bundrick in tow) hasn't sounded this vibrant and energetic in ages. While the double-CD's 20 tracks are all outstanding, the album-closing rendition of "My Generation" is an absolute must-hear—few bands of the era can sound as fierce and vicious as the Who does here. You can't miss with great renditions of Who standards such as "I Can't Explain," "Pinball Wizard," "Baba O'Riley," "You Better You Bet," "Who Are You," "5:15," and "Won't Get Fooled Again," but lesser-known tracks like "Pure & Easy," "Getting in Tune," and "The Real Me" shine brilliantly as well. *The Blues to the Bush* shows that the Who's late 1999/2000 reunion wasn't just going through the motions—they had something to prove. —*Greg Prato*

The BBC Sessions / Feb. 15, 2000 / MCA ✦✦✦✦✦
A fine compilation of 1965-73 BBC performances, the majority of the tracks hailing from 1965-67, although some are drawn from 1970 and 1973. As one of the best live bands ever, the Who as expected come through pretty well in the live-in-the-studio environment, although the arrangements usually stick close to the records. Most of the songs were done by the group for studio releases as well, but there are a few covers that they never put on their albums or singles at the time, making this essential for the fan. Those numbers include the obscure James Brown tune "Just You and Me, Darling," "Dancing in the Street," "Good Lovin'," and "Leaving Here" (although a mid-1960s studio version of that last song was eventually released). Of the other tracks, particularly worthwhile are "Anyway, Anyhow, Anywhere," with its extensive feedback solo, quite a challenge to do live in May 1965; "The Good's Gone," which has a fuzz solo not on the studio version; and the 1970 performance of "Shakin' All Over," which might be the best rendition of that concert staple that they ever did. This does not have a few BBC songs that have shown up on bootlegs; particularly unfortunate exclusions are "So Sad About Us," "Summertime Blues," and their 1966 cover of the Everly Brothers' "Man with Money." —*Richie Unterberger*

Whodini

f. 1981
Old School Rap, Hip-Hop, Golden Age
Coming out of the fertile early-'80s New York rap scene, Whodini was one of the first rap groups to add a straight R&B twist to their music, thus laying the groundwork for the new jack swing movement. The group consisted of rappers Jalil Hutchins and John "Ecstasy" Fletcher, adding legendary DJ Drew "Grandmaster Dee" Carter, known for being able to scratch records with nearly every part of his body, in 1986. Whodini made its name with good-humored songs like "Magic's Wand" (the first rap song to feature an accompanying video), "The Haunted House of Rock" (a rewrite of "Monster Mash"), and "Freaks Come Out at Night," and their live shows were the first rap concerts to feature official dancers (U.T.F.O. members Dr. Ice and Kangol Kid). Following 1987's *Open Sesame*, Whodini went on hiatus due to problems with their record company, as well as to concentrate on new families. The group attempted a comeback in 1991 with *Bag-A-Trix* without much success, despite receiving their due as rap innovators. Five years later, Whodini returned with their sixth album, appropriately titled *Six*. The album disappeared shortly after its release. —*Steve Huey*

Whodini / 1983 / Jive ✦✦✦

Escape / 1984 / Jive ✦✦✦
Their best release, containing "Friends," "Freaks Come out at Night," and "Big Mouth." Memorable tunes and state-of-the-art (for that time) production. —*Ron Wynn*

Back in Black / 1986 / Jive ✦✦✦
As one of the first successful rap acts, Whodini's albums quickly became standard bearers and necessities. The Brooklyn-raised trio of Jalil Hutchins, Ecstasy, and DJ Grandmaster

Dee first came to national attention with the single "The Haunted House of Rock." This effort is the follow-up to the multi-platinum album, 1984's *Escape*. Those expecting a by-the-numbers sequel of sorts to that effort won't be too let down here. Although *Back in Black* does revisit lyrical and musical themes of previous efforts, it also offers a few new tricks or two. The first track and single release, "Funky Beat" features monster bass and drums, the one-two punch of Hutchins and Ecstasy, as well as a rare rap from Grandmaster Dee. The well-produced "One Love" has great synth signatures and the guys dispensing their brand of pithy and pragmatic advice. They seem to unlearn those lessons by the time the hilarious "I'm a Ho" rolls around. The slow scratch-laden track has the boastful chorus "I rock three different freaks after every show" and Hutchins' life-threatening rhyme, "How your wife and my kid." Despite the group's best efforts, *Back in Black* does often seem to be style over substance. Luckily the producer Larry Smith knew how to keep things sonically interesting. On the lyrically foggy "Fugitive," the hard rock guitars and clanging cymbals mesh especially well with Ecstasy's droll and abrupt delivery. "Echo Scratch" is also all over the road, but it was a great chance for Grandmaster Dee to show off his turntable skills. Recorded at Battery Studios in London, *Back in Black* wasn't as influential as *Escape*, but it's nearly as enjoyable. *—Jason Elias*

Open Sesame / 1987 / Jive ✦✦

★ **Greatest Hits** / Jun. 1990 / Jive ✦✦✦✦✦
When funksters and soulsters who reached adulthood in the 1960s and '70s criticize rap, their #1 complaint is usually that too much of it isn't melodic enough. But they seldom make that complaint about Whodini, which in the mid-'80s, enjoyed a lot more support from R&B fans than the more forceful and abrasive sounds of Run-D.M.C. or LL Cool J. While those artists rocked hard, Whodini grooved. Many of Whodini's early albums are well worth acquiring—including *Escape* and *Back in Black*—but for the more casual listener, *Greatest Hits* serves as a fine introduction. From the poignant rap ballad "One Love" to such addictive and highly danceable grooves as "Five Minutes of Funk" and "Freaks Come Out at Night," *Greatest Hits* makes it clear why Whodini was so successful in the mid-'80s. *—Alex Henderson*

Bag-A-Trix / Mar. 19, 1991 / MCA ✦✦

Jive Collection Series, Vol. 1 / Jun. 27, 1995 / Jive ✦✦✦✦✦
Whodini's installment of the *Jive Collection Series* contains all of the group's groundbreaking singles from the early '80s, plus a selection of lesser-known album tracks and singles, making it an ideal introduction to the group. *—Stephen Thomas Erlewine*

Six / Sep. 17, 1996 / So So Def/Columbia ✦✦✦

Wilco

f. 1994
Adult Alternative Pop/Rock, Alternative Country-Rock, Alternative Pop/Rock
The alternative country band Wilco rose from the ashes of the seminal roots-rockers Uncle Tupelo, who disbanded in 1994. While Jay Farrar, one of the group's two singer/songwriters, went on to form the band Son Volt, his ex-partner Jeff Tweedy established Wilco along with the remaining members of Tupelo's final incarnation, which included drummer Ken Coomer as well as part-time bandmates John Stirratt (bass) and Max Johnston (mandolin, banjo, fiddle and lap steel). Guitarist Jay Bennett rounded out the group, which in 1995 issued their debut album, *A.M.*, a collection of spry country-rock tunes that followed the course established in Tweedy's earlier work. Wilco's sophomore effort, 1996's two-disc set *Being There*, marked a radical transformation in the group's sound; while remaining steeped in the style that earned Tweedy his reputation, the songs took unexpected detours into psychedelia, power-pop and soul, complete with orchestral touches and R&B horn flourishes. Shortly after the release of *Being There*, which most critics judged to be among the year's best releases, Johnston left the group to play with his sister, singer Michelle Shocked, and was replaced by guitarist Bob Egan of the band Freakwater. At the same time, while remaining full-time members of Wilco, Stirratt, Bennett and Coomer also began performing together in the pop side project Courtesy Move. In 1998, Wilco collaborated with singer-songwriter Billy Bragg on *Mermaid Avenue*, a collection of performances based on unreleased material originally written by Woody Guthrie.

Their stunningly lush third album, *Summer Teeth*, followed in 1999 and met with critical acclaim but only average sales, initiating tensions with their label Warner Bros. 2000 saw the release of *Mermaid Avenue, Vol. 2*, which featured more selections from the band's collaborations with Bragg on Woody Guthrie's unfinished songs. Following this release, longtime drummer Ken Coomer decided to amicably leave the band and was replaced by the Chicago-based Glenn Kotche. The band then focused on recording their fourth album, *Yankee Hotel Foxtrot*, which ultimately led to the departure of guitarist Jay Bennett, and further tensions with their label. Unwilling to change the album to make it more "commercially viable," Wilco bought the finished studio tapes from Warner/Reprise for a reported $50,000 and left the label altogether. Leaked tracks from the album surfaced on the internet in late 2001, and the stripped-down lineup of Tweedy, Kotche, Stirratt and multi-instrumentalist Leroy Bach embarked on a small tour to support (or drum up support for) their unreleased album. *—Jason Ankeny & Zac Johnson*

A.M. / Mar. 28, 1995 / Sire/Reprise ✦✦✦
Not surprisingly, Wilco's debut album, *A.M.*, isn't a great departure from Uncle Tupelo. Wilco's music rocks in a more conventional way than Uncle Tupelo, rolling along with a loping beat that swings more than it rocks. "Casino Queen" is a shambling, bluesy honky-tonk number that's boozier than anything Tupelo recorded, which is indicative of the major difference between the bands. Wilco wears its heart on its sleeve, writing songs that fit into the conventions of country-rock, not ones that rework the rules. "Box Full of Letters" doesn't deviate from the standard midtempo country-rock number, yet it's done so well, it doesn't matter. Still, the opener, "I Must Be High"—a clever love song that subtly tweaks both lyrical and musical cliches, as well as featuring a killer melody—casts a shadow over *A.M.*, offering the knowledge that Wilco can subvert the genre without losing its accessibility. In its light, all the very good songs that follow seem somewhat disappointing. *—Stephen Thomas Erlewine*

● **Being There** / Oct. 29, 1996 / Sire/Reprise ✦✦✦✦✦
While Wilco's debut *A.M.* spread its wings in an expectedly country-rock fashion, their sophomore effort *Being There* is the group's great leap forward, a masterful, wildly eclectic collection shot through with ambitions and ideas. Although a few songs remain rooted in their signature sound, here Jeff Tweedy and band are as fascinated by their music's possibilities as its origins, and they push the songs which make up this sprawling two-disc set down consistently surprising paths and byways. For starters, the opener "Misunderstood" is majestic psychedelia, built on studio trickery and string flourishes, while "I Got You (At the End of the Century)" is virtual power-pop, right down to the handclaps. The lovely "Someone Else's Song" borrows heavily from the Beatles' "Norwegian Wood," while the R&B-influenced boogie of "Monday" wouldn't sound at all out of place on *Exile on Main Street*; and on and on. The remarkable thing is how fresh all of these seeming clichés sound when re-imagined with so much love and conviction; even the most traditional songs take unexpected twists and turns, never once sinking into mere imitation. "Music is my savior/I was named by rock & roll/I was maimed by rock & roll/I was tamed by rock & roll/I got my name from rock & roll," Tweedy sings on "Sunken Treasure," the opener of the second disc, and throughout the course of these 19 songs he explores rock as though he were tracing his family geneology, fervently seeking to discover not only where he came from but also where he's going. With *Being There*, he finds what he's been looking for. *—Jason Ankeny*

Summer Teeth / Mar. 9, 1999 / Warner Brothers ✦✦✦✦✦
Jeff Tweedy once blazed the trail for the American rock underground's embrace of its country and folk roots, but as the decade draws to its close he's spearheading the return of classic pop; simply put, what once were fiddles on Wilco records are now violins—the same instrument, to be sure, but viewed with a radical shift in perception and meaning. While lacking the sheer breadth and ambition of the previous *Being There*, *Summer Teeth* is the most focused Wilco effort yet, honing the lessons of the last record to forge a majestic pop sound almost completely devoid of alt-country elements; the lush string arrangements and gorgeous harmonies of tracks like "She's a Jar" and "Pieholden Suite" suggest nothing less than a land-locked Brian Wilson, while more straightforward rockers like the opening "I Can't Stand It" bear the influence of everything from R&B to psychedelia. Still, for all of the superficial warmth and beauty of the record's arrangements, Tweedy's songs are perhaps his darkest and most haunting to date, bleak domestic dramas informed by recurring themes of alienation, adultery and abuse—even the sunniest melodies mask moments of devastating power. If *Summer Teeth* has a precedent, it's peak-era Band; the album not only possesses a similar pastoral sensibility, but like Robbie Robertson and company before them, Wilco seems directly connected to a kind of American musical consciousness, not only rejuvenating our collective creative mythology, but adding new chapters to the legend with each successive record. *—Jason Ankeny*

Wild Tchoupitoulas

f. Louisiana
New Orleans R&B, Zydeco, Creole
The Wild Tchoupitoulas—Spy Boy (Amos Landry), Trail Chief (Booker Washington), Big Chief Jolly (George Landry), Flag Boy (Carl Christmas), The Third Chief (Thomas Jackson), and Second Chief (Norman Bell)—are a Mardi Gras ceremonial parade group and "Black Indian tribe" based in New Orleans. George Landry is an uncle to the Neville brothers. *The Wild Tchoupitoulas* is their only album. *—William Ruhlmann*

★ **Wild Tchoupitoulas** / 1976 / Mango ✦✦✦✦✦
The Wild Tchoupitoulas—a group of Mardi Gras Indians headed by George "Big Chief Jolly" Landry—only released one album, but that one record caused a sensation upon its initial 1976 release. It was one of the first records of the album-rock generation that captured the heady gumbo of New Orleans R&B and funk. Landry may have fronted the Wild Tchoupitoulas, but the key to the record's success was his nephews, Charles and Cyril Neville, who headed the rhythm section. They drafted in their brothers, Art and Aaron, to harmonize, and thereby unwittingly gave birth to the band that became the Neville Brothers. Still, the fact that *The Wild Tchoupitoulas* ranks among the great New Orleans albums isn't because of the Nevillles themselves, but the way the Tchoupitoulas lock into an extraordinary hybrid that marries several indigenous New Orleans musics, with swampy, dirty funk taking its place in the forefront. There are only eight songs, and they are all strung together, as if they're variations on the same themes and rhythms. That's a compliment, by the way, since the organic, flowing groove is the key to the album's success. *—Stephen Thomas Erlewine*

The Wilde Flowers

f. 1963, **db.** 1969
Canterbury Scene, Psychedelic, British Invasion
The Wilde Flowers never released a record during their existence, but their influence exceeds that of many groups with lengthy discographies. The band served as the wellspring of the so-called Canterbury sound: future Soft Machine members Robert Wyatt, Kevin Ayers, and Hugh Hopper all played with the Wilde Flowers before the Soft Machine were founded, and Pye Hastings, David Sinclair, Richard Sinclair, and Richard Coughlan played in the group at various points before forming Caravan. The musicians who wandered through the Wilde Flowers (who went through several lineups between 1963 and

1969) came from a far more intellectual, artistic, and jazz-oriented background than was the norm for pop musicians in the mid-'60s. Thus, although the group played beat fare much like thousands of other British combos in their formative days, when they began to write their own material, it betrayed the bemused whimsy—replete with odd jazzy flourishes, droll obtuse lyrics, and adventurous chord changes—that would come to characterize the Canterbury bands, and prove influential on the development of psychedelia and progressive rock. At long last, a wealth of the Wilde Flowers' demos and unreleased recordings was released in 1994. —*Richie Unterberger*

● **Tales of Canterbury: The Wilde Flowers Story** / Dec. 8, 1994 / Voiceprint ✦✦✦✦✦
Twenty-two tracks, recorded between 1965 and 1969 by various aggregations of the band. Some of the fidelity is primitive, and the performances are much more tentative and less virtuosic than what the musicians would tender on their Soft Machine and Caravan records. But the songs are playful and melodic, pushing the boundaries of the British Invasion pop they began with toward something more idiosyncratic and adventurous. Several of the songs, like "Memories" (three versions, considerably different from each other, are included here), ended up in the Soft Machine's early repertoire. Indeed, it's a shame that the Softs didn't record more of them; the chief flaw of these tracks is that the arrangements and instrumental proficiency are underdeveloped, and the Soft Machine could have transformed them into prime stuff. A few of the cuts were recorded in late 1969, and could have easily slotted in on the Wyatt-era Soft Machine albums. Wyatt and Hugh Hopper appear on most of the 22 tracks; to a lesser extent, Kevin Ayers, Pye Hastings, and even Mike Ratledge also pop up. Comes with an excellent booklet of photos and an extensive history by Wilde Flowers guitarist Brian Hopper, brother of Hugh. —*Richie Unterberger*

Kim Wilde

b. Nov. 18, 1960, Chiswick, England
Vocals / Club/Dance, New Wave, Hi-NRG
The daughter of '50s British pop singer Marty Wilde, Kim Wilde had several pop hits during the '80s. Initially, her synth-driven pop fit in with the new wave movement, but as the decade progressed, it became clear that her strength was mainstream pop.

In 1980, Kim Wilde signed with producer Mickie Most's Rak Records, releasing her first single, "Kids in America" early in 1981. "Kids in America" climbed to number two on the British charts that spring, while her second single, "Chequered Love" made it into the Top Ten; her self-titled debut album performed as well as her singles. The following year, "Kids in America" became a Top 40 hit in America, while *Select* kept her in the British charts. However, Wilde wasn't able to keep her momentum going and it wasn't until late 1986 that she had another hit with a dance cover of the Supremes' "You Keep Me Hangin' On," which charted in the Top Ten on both sides of the Atlantic. Wilde never had another hit in America, yet she was back in the charts in the summer of 1987 with "Another Step (Closer to You)," a duet with Junior Giscombe. After the single's success, she began changing her image, becoming sexier. The approach didn't entirely pay off, though she had a handful of hit singles from her 1988 album, *Close*, including "You Came," "Never Trust a Stranger" and "Four Letter Word." Wilde has continued to record in the '90s, scoring the occasional hit, either in the dance or adult contemporary field. —*Stephen Thomas Erlewine*

● **The Singles Collection 1981-1993** / Nov. 9, 1993 / MCA ✦✦✦✦
Kim Wilde's number one cover of the Supremes' "You Keep Me Hangin' On" gave her a number one hit back in 1987, but she gained chart life five years earlier with the glitzy bounce of "Kids in America," allied with the new decade's keyboard-laden pop sound and peaking at number 25 on *Billboard's* Top 40. *The Singles Collection 1981-1993* is easily the most opportune avenue available to investigate the rest of Wilde's material. While video may have been her best friend throughout her career, sporting her attractive looks and modest Brit attitude, Wilde's music does contain some pleasing dance hooks and catchy melodies. "Another Step (Closer to You)" and "Love Is Holy" are bright and lively with typical yet congenial pop melodies, while "You Came" mixes a clean, keyboard-aided backdrop to Wilde's sheer vocal style. "Chequered Love" and "Water on Glass" aren't genius, but their arrant pop melodies and simplistic beats are anything but standstill. Even minor efforts like "Rage to Love" and "Never Trust a Stranger" find a way of hurdling clichéd '80s pop/rock fabrications so that they sound slightly fresh and breezy. Only the unbecoming "Cambodia" and the hollowed out "Child Come Away" should be avoided on this collection, as both lack the spirit that Wilde usually packs. —*Mike DeGagne*

Andre Williams

b. Nov. 1, 1936, Chicago, IL
Vocals, Guitar / Detroit Blues, R&B, Soul
Multi-talented Zeffrey "Andre" Williams has worn many musical hats during his long career: recording artist, songwriter, producer, road manager, among others. The R&B legend is best known for co-writing and producing "Twine Time" for Alvin Cash & the Crawlers, "Shake a Tailfeather" by the Five Dutones, and a greasy solo recording "Bacon Fat," where Andre talked over a funky, crude rhythm. Andre starting talking instead of singing because he knew he couldn't compete vocally with the Nolan Strongses, Clyde McPhatters, Little Willie Johns, Jackie Wilsons, and others. He created a new style that was later adapted by Harvey Fuqua ("Any Way You Wanna"), Jerry-O, Shorty Long, Bootsy Collins, and others. He originally ventured to Detroit in his late teens and befriended Jack and Devora Brown, the owners of Fortune Records. At Fortune, Andre started singing with the Don Juans and became adept at putting songs together. In 1956, Fortune issued seven singles by Andre Williams, all but two with co-billing with the Don Juans: "Going Down to Tia Juana," "It's All Over," "Bacon Fat," "Mean Jean," "Jail Bait," "The Greasy

Chicken," and "Country Girl." Andre later sang with the Five Dollars who released records on Fortune from 1956 to 1957, and were billed as Andre Williams & the Five Dollars on a 1960 release. After Fortune, Andre languished with Berry Gordy and Motown from 1961 to 1965. By 1965 he left Motown for good to sign with Chicago's Chess Records and had a string of R&B releases including "The Stroke," "Girdle Up," "Humpin' Bumpin' & Thumpin'," and "Cadillac Jack." His biggest period as an artist was around 1960 when Fortune released the LP *Jail Bait.* —*Andrew Hamilton*

● **Jail Bait** / 1960 / Fortune ✦✦✦✦✦
Good (though not complete) overview of Andre's Fortune period. —*Cub Koda*

Fat Back & Corn Liquor / Jun. 23, 2000 / St. George ✦✦✦
Andre Williams, the man who was rappin' three decades before they had a name for it, is back after a much too long sabbatical, with the kind of comeback album that would do any R&B legend proud. With a tight little band and the El Dorados providing crackerjack support, producer George Paulus has managed to restoke some of the fires that burned so brightly on a spate of brilliant, creative singles for Fortune and Checker in the '50s and '60s. The big plus here is that Williams can still deliver that deadpan badass turn of the phrase better than anybody. Although I personally find the recuts here of his old Fortune classics like "Jail Bait" ill-advised (to quote Rocky, the Flying Squirrel, "That trick never works!"), there's just so much great stuff on this biscuit that it's a minor niggling point at best. By far and away, my favorite track on here is one simply titled "Gin." Recalling one of his legendary Fortune sides, "Please Pass the Biscuits," without Xeroxing it, this is four minutes plus of Williams at his nutzo best. A winner. —*Cub Koda*

Larry Williams

b. May 10, 1935, New Orleans, LA, d. Jan. 7, 1980, Los Angeles, CA
Vocals, Saxophone, Keyboards, Songwriter, Piano / Pop-Soul, Rock & Roll, R&B, Soul
A rough, rowdy rock & roll singer, Larry Williams had several hits in the late '50s, several of which—"Bony Maroney," "Dizzy, Miss Lizzy," "Short Fat Fannie," "Bad Boy," "She Said Yeah"—became genuine rock & roll classics and were recorded by British Invasion groups; John Lennon, in particular, was a fan of Williams, recording several of his songs over the course of his career. Singer Lloyd Price hired the teenaged Williams as his valet and introduced him to Robert "Bumps" Blackwell, the Specialty label's house producer. Soon, the label's owner, Art Rupe, signed Williams to a solo recording contract. Just after Specialty signed Larry Williams, the company lost Little Richard, their biggest seller; the label then put all of its energy into making Williams a star, giving him an image makeover and a set of material—ranging from hard R&B, rock & roll, to ballads—that were quite similar to Richard's hits. Williams' first post-Little Richard single was the raucous "Short Fat Fannie," which shot to number one on the R&B charts and number five on the pop charts in the summer of 1957. It was followed in the fall by "Bony Maronie," which hit number four on the R&B charts and number 14 on the pop charts. Williams wasn't able to maintain that momentum, however. "You Bug Me, Baby" and "Dizzy Miss Lizzy," his next two singles, missed the R&B charts but became minor pop hits in late 1957 and early 1958. Despite the relative failure of these singles, Williams' records became popular import items in Britain; the Beatles would cover both sides of the "Dizzy Miss Lizzy" single (the B-side was "Slow Down") in the mid-'60s. However, Williams' commercial fortunes in America continued to decline, despite Specialty's release of a constant stream of singles and one full-length album. —*Stephen Thomas Erlewine*

Unreleased Larry Williams / 1986 / Specialty ✦✦✦
This deeper look into the obscure and alternate takes of Williams' work is mostly for collectors. —*Hank Davis*

★ **Bad Boy** / Apr. 6, 1992 / Specialty ✦✦✦✦✦
Bad Boy compiles 23 tracks Larry Williams recorded between 1957 and 1958. The core of the collection are his hit singles—"Bony Maronie," "She Said Yeah," "Lawdy Miss Clawdy," "Just Because," "Dizzy Miss Lizzy," "Short Fat Fannie," "Bad Boy," "Slow Down"—many of which became standards. —*Stephen Thomas Erlewine*

Lucinda Williams

b. Jan. 26, 1953, Lake Charles, LA
Vocals, Guitar / Alternative Folk, Heartland Rock, Americana, Contemporary Folk, Alternative Country-Rock, Singer/Songwriter
Lucinda Williams isn't the kind of artist who caves in easily. Faced with label executives and producers who want to shape her music into clean-cut, radio-friendly rock or country numbers, Williams has time and again proven herself to be as stubborn as she is talented. She has released a limited amount of material since her debut partly because she's had such a hard time finding a label whose demands don't get in the way of the music as she hears it. Her 1979 debut for Folkways, *Ramblin' on My Mind,* was followed by *Happy Woman Blues* on Smithsonian/Folkways, though it was another eight years before Williams' eponymous third album appeared on the indie-rock label Rough Trade. It immediately stood out for its integration of traditional folk, country, and blues influences into a rock & roll format. An ill-fated association with RCA followed, and her next album, 1992's *Sweet Old World,* was released on another indie label, Chameleon. Since then Williams has switched labels again, this time to American Recordings, where after a brief stay she landed at Mercury, which in 1998 finally released her long-delayed *Car Wheels on a Gravel Road.* —*Kurt Wolff*

Ramblin' / 1979 / Smithsonian/Folkways ✦✦

Happy Woman Blues / 1980 / Folkways ✦✦✦✦
Williams' first collection of original material—recorded with a full band—is stunning for its mixture of blues, folk, and country traditions with her captivating, complex, and visceral approach to writing and singing. Songs like "Lafayette," "King of Hearts," and

"Sharp Cutting Wings" are classics: structurally solid and emotionally intense. A gutsy, refreshingly rootsy album. Re-released by Smithsonian/Folkways in 1990. —*Kurt Wolff*

Lucinda Williams / 1988 / Rough Trade ✦✦✦✦✦

Lucinda Williams took eight years to write and record her second album of original songs. While some producers and record executives have said that she is difficult to work with, one can never argue with the finished product. She crafts each song meticulously and deftly blends country, blues, and folk to create a unique sound that cannot be pigeonholed into any particular format. Her voice contains a heartache comparable to Emmylou Harris, but she has a darker side and a toughness that allows her to live inside the blues or rock with abandon. Re-released with bonus tracks after receiving long overdue commercial acclaim for *Car Wheels on a Gravel Road*, *Lucinda Williams* is an album that has been long been recognized as a classic. It has been mined for hit songs over the years by such artists as Mary Chapin Carpenter, who turned "Passionate Kisses" into a country hit, and Tom Petty, who included "Changed the Locks" on his soundtrack album *She's the One*. In addition to writing strong melodies, Lucinda Williams is an amazing songwriter with a knack at writing a lyric that acknowledges the complicated nature of relationships while cutting right to the heart of the matter. Every song packs an emotional punch line and rewards the listener each time with something new. The bonus tracks mostly feature Williams accompanied only by her guitar, and it adds emotional weight to the album's highlight, "Side of the Road," which expresses the delicate balance of giving up oneself in a relationship without losing one's own identity. A must-own for country and blues fans that appreciate great songwriting. — *Vik Iyengar*

Passionate Kisses / 1989 / Rough Trade ✦✦✦

The title track of this EP comes from Williams' 1988 album. Also included are four live acoustic cuts—"Side of the Road" and three blues covers. —*Kurt Wolff*

● Sweet Old World / Aug. 25, 1992 / Chameleon ✦✦✦✦✦

After seemingly coming out of nowhere to be hailed as a major songwriter and roots music stylist, it took Lucinda Williams four years to prepare the follow-up to her masterful 1988 eponymous album. When it finally arrived, *Sweet Old World* proved to be every bit the equal of its predecessor, if not even better. Although *Sweet Old World* isn't really a concept album, it often feels like one. Its first half is dominated by the title track and "Pineola," two stunning meditations on suicide. Their sense of tragedy is reinforced with the closing cover of Nick Drake's "Which Will," and their shadow hangs heavy over the rest of the album. Several character portraits ponder where and why their subjects' lives went wrong; in this context, the dead-end situations seem that much more tragic and final. Moreover, when Williams offers an emotionally complex love ballad or a sexy blues strut, it's hard to take them as truly celebratory; here, the singer sounds as though she wants to appreciate who she has while she still can. That's also why "Little Angel, Little Brother" doesn't come off as remotely sentimental; the affectionate tribute works so well that, sandwiched between "Sweet Old World" and "Pineola," Williams' brother sounds like the suicide victim (it was actually a family friend). Williams' voice glows with the same warmth, for although it's limited in range, it's also a gorgeous instrument that Williams has learned to manipulate for maximum impact. Stylistically, *Sweet Old World* is similar to *Lucinda Williams*, juggling both the sounds and instruments of country, folk, blues, and rock & roll. It might not explode with confidence in the manner of *Lucinda Williams*, but *Sweet Old World* is no less vital; it's a gorgeous, elegiac record that not only consolidates but expands Williams' ample talents. —*Steve Huey*

Car Wheels on a Gravel Road / Jun. 30, 1998 / Mercury ✦✦✦✦✦

It isn't surprising that Lucinda Williams' level of craft takes time to assemble, but the six-year wait between *Sweet Old World* and its 1998 follow-up, *Car Wheels on a Gravel Road*, still raised eyebrows. The delay stemmed both from label difficulties and Williams' meticulous perfectionism, the latter reportedly over a too-produced sound and her own vocals. Listening to the record, one can understand why both might have concerned Williams. *Car Wheels* is far and away her most produced album to date, which is something of a mixed blessing. Its surfaces are clean and contemporary, with something in the timbres of the instruments (especially the drums) sounding extremely typical of a late-'90s major-label roots-rock album. While that might subtly alter the timeless qualities of Williams' writing, there's also no denying that her sound is punchier and livelier. The production also throws Williams' idiosyncratic voice into sharp relief, to the point where it's noticeably separate from the band. As a result, every inflection and slight tonal alteration is captured, and it would hardly be surprising if Williams did obsess over those small details. But whether or not you miss the earthiness of *Car Wheels*' predecessors, it's ultimately the material that matters, and Williams' songwriting is as captivating as ever. Intentionally or not, the album's common thread seems to be its strongly grounded sense of place—specifically, the Deep South, conveyed through images and numerous references to specific towns. Many songs are set, in some way, in the middle or aftermath of not-quite-resolved love affairs, as Williams meditates on the complexities of human passion. Even her simplest songs have more going on under the surface than their poetic structures might indicate. In the end, *Car Wheels on a Gravel Road* is Williams' third straight winner; although she might not be the most prolific songwriter of the '90s, she's certainly one of the most brilliant. —*Steve Huey*

Essence / Jun. 5, 2001 / Lost Highway ✦✦✦✦

Subtle and often stark, *Essence* is an unusually quiet and frequently downbeat set that depicts a fragile emotional vulnerability which rarely makes its presence felt in Lucinda Williams' music; there's an unadorned longing in songs like "Blue" and "Lonely Girls" that's new and deeply affecting, and the leaf-in-the-breeze quaver of Williams' voice on "I Envy the Wind" is as heart-rending as anything she's ever committed to tape. But while a blue mood dominates *Essence*, this isn't an album about the blue funk of heartbreak, but a chronicle of the search for transcendence over sorrow in our lives, as her characters

look for a path out of isolation ("Out of Touch"), try to find answers through faith ("Get Right With God"), or reconcile love with the desires of the flesh ("Essence"). As a songwriter, Williams has long shown a knack for charting the human heart and mind with intelligence and economy, and *Essence* finds her at the peak of her form; the delicacy of this music does not speak of weakness, but of the passion and bravery it takes to bare one's soul. And while Williams has gained a certain infamy for her obsessive perfectionism in the studio, the quality of her work speaks for the wisdom of her decision-making process, and *Essence* proves how well she understands the art of recording; the album sounds full and rich even in its quietest moments, and her sweet-and-sour voice blends with the arrangements with subtle perfection. Those hoping for another dose of the bluesy roots rock of *Car Wheels on a Gravel Road* may be disappointed, but if you want to take a deep and compelling look into the heart and soul of a major artist, then you owe it to yourself to hear *Essence*. —*Mark Deming*

Maurice Williams

b. Lancaster, SC
Doo Wop, R&B

Although Maurice Williams & the Zodiacs only had one big hit, the song became one of the classic singles in the history of rock & roll and R&B. The song, "Stay," was a number one hit upon its release in 1960. Williams and the Zodiacs' career didn't prove to be as popular as the song itself. They only had two more minor pop hits before they disappeared from the charts, but over the course of the next three decades, "Stay" remained one of the most popular songs of the era and it was played constantly on oldies radio stations. "Stay" was covered by numerous other artists and has enjoyed a few revivals in mass popularity, most notably when it was featured in the hit 1987 film, *Dirty Dancing*. After the single charted nationally, the Zodiacs constantly toured America, playing revues with artists like James Brown. The group released a follow-up single titled "I Remember" at the end of the year, but it didn't make it past 86 on the pop charts and didn't appear on the R&B charts at all. Neither did "Come Along," which was released in the spring of 1961 and only climbed to number 83 on the pop charts. Maurice Williams and the Zodiacs continued to release singles until the late '60s, but none of the records received any attention. Throughout the '70s and '80s, Williams led various incarnations of the Zodiacs on oldies tours, primarily on the Beach Music circuit on the U.S. east coast. —*Stephen Thomas Erlewine*

Maurice Williams and the Zodiacs Anthology / 1992 / Ripete ✦✦✦✦✦

One would have expected Maurice Williams & the Zodiacs to have their work represented by a good Rhino anthology, but they don't. Instead, Ripete Records out of Columbia, SC, has released this 25-song compilation, which includes material going back to "Little Darlin'" by the Gladiolas (which appears here in an alternate take) and the original demo version of "Stay." There are very few stones left unturned here, as the disc features a mixture of rare outtakes ("Stay" with punchier rhythm instruments and an organ) and brilliant Williams originals, of which the most fascinating is "May I," produced by Marshall Sehom and Allen Toussaint. The overview provided by this anthology doesn't include background notes on every track, but the tracks justify themselves. Four numbers from a 1965 live album cut at Myrtle Beach, SC, show off Williams and company doing superb covers of other peoples' songs ("The In Crowd," "Sherry," "Stubborn Kind of Fellow," "It's Not Unusual"), the mix of band and backing vocals startlingly good for what should be one of the great mid-'60s live soul albums. The big surprise, however, is the quality of Williams' 1987 recordings—when he doesn't fall into the nostalgia trap, he still has the same gift for rich, memorable melodies and inventive, clever lyrics that he had in the late '50s, a voice that's even more expressive if not quite as rich, and a great sense of how to phrase a lyric; coupled with tasteful arrangements, the results are as compelling as anything in Williams' output. —*Bruce Eder*

Paul Williams

Vocals / Pop/Rock, Singer/Songwriter

Pop songwriter, singer, and actor Paul Williams' early movie career was largely frustrating, despite landing a major role in the 1965 satire *The Loved One*. He eventually formed the band Holy Mackerel, which issued a self-titled LP in 1968. The record went nowhere, and in 1970 Williams resurfaced as a solo artist with the album *Someday Man*. It too fared poorly, and he next landed as a staff songwriter at A&M; paired with composer Roger Nichols, he quickly co-authored the hit "Out in the Country" for Three Dog Night. Williams and Nichols were next hired to write theme music for a local bank commercial advertising services for newlyweds; the resulting "We've Only Just Begun" became a blockbuster hit when later covered by the Carpenters. Williams returned to recording with the 1971 A&M effort *Just an Old Fashioned Love Song*, the title track becoming a smash for Three Dog Night; in between 1972's *Life Goes On* and 1974's *Here Comes Inspiration*, he also earned his first Academy Award nomination, teaming with composer John Williams on "Nice to Be Around" from the film *Cinderella Liberty*. He finally won the Oscar—as well as a Grammy and a Golden Globe—for "Evergreen," the love theme to the 1976 Barbra Streisand film *A Star Is Born*. By the late '70s, Williams was a true celebrity, known not only for his music but also for regular guest appearances on television and occasional film work. Williams' profile declined sharply in the decade to follow, however, and as the hits dried up he concentrated less on music than acting. He returned to music in 1992 with the Grammy-nominated soundtrack to *The Muppet Christmas Carol*, and in 1997 issued *Back to Love Again*, his first new studio LP since 1979's *A Little on the Windy Side*. —*Jason Ankeny*

Just an Old Fashioned Love Song / 1971 / A&M ✦✦✦✦✦

Here Williams came into his own, writing the bulk of his material single-handedly. *Just An Old Fashioned Love Song* boasts "We've Only Just Begun"—one of his signature compositions—and finds him in wistful, melancholic form. The uncluttered arrangements, and the fact that Williams has learned to use his weak voice for emotional effect make his second album a comparative success. While it's not really right to assess him in singer/songwriterly terms (he never played piano, guitar, or indeed any instrument, and is more accurately termed an easy-listening tunesmith), *Just an Old Fashioned Love Song* is a worthy addition to the genre. "Waking Up Alone," "A Perfect Love," and "Gone Forever" form a touching triptych of moving, and surprisingly subtle love-gone-wrong songs. Each adequately displays Williams' growth as both a performer and composer. —*Charles Donovan*

Someday Man / 1971 / Reprise ✦✦✦✦✦
Williams, a jobbing songwriter and actor, only provided lyrics on his debut album—all the music was composed by producer Roger Nichols. Williams' vocal limitations are immediately clear; his voice is thin, inarticulate and markedly stunted of range—it takes considerable getting used to. The ten songs here roll along merrily enough in a soft-rock vein, but none is particularly mesmerising. The plaintive "I Know You" is a touching moment and "Roan Pony" reveals a penchant for the kind of greeting-card whimsy that would later spawn some of Williams' big songwriting hits ("Rainy Days and Mondays," "Evergreen"). The rest is stuff that no one would object to hearing, principally because they're more than likely to have forgotten it a few minutes after the disc stops spinning. —*Charles Donovan*

Life Goes on / 1972 / A&M ✦✦✦
"I Won't Last A Day Without You" was leapt upon by the Carpenters (and recorded by Barbra Streisand for her *Butterfly* album), but despite the inclusion of Williams' own version, *Life Goes On* isn't in the same league as *Just An Old Fashioned Love Song*. Too much of it is unutterably bland. "Park Avenue," with its patronizing lyric that takes cheap pot shots at ladies who lunch, signposts one of Williams' weaknesses; he's not one of life's wits or sharp observational writers, and is better sticking to introspective autobiographical material. The songs here are arranged similarly to his other recordings of the period, with assistance from slick sidemen like Leland Sklar and Russell Kunkel, but there's none of the bittersweet quality Williams had evinced before. His heart-felt performance on the standard "That Lucky Old Sun" is the one tender spot in an otherwise dull, unengaging collection. —*Charles Donovan*

Here Comes Inspiration / 1974 / A&M ✦✦✦
Here Comes Inspiration is one of Williams' better albums. It revisits all of his strongest artistic points, and includes dreamy, whimsical high points like "Rainy Days and Mondays," "Driftwood," and "You And Me Against the World." His voice is certainly still a weak, bleating non-instrument, but here it's never dishonest or insincere. As usual, he's supported by the finest session musicians money can buy and an orchestra whose subtle arrangements never overpower the songs. Most of the material is written by Williams alone (with occasional co-writes from producer Ken Asher). Listeners may prefer the more professional performances of the Carpenters and Helen Reddy, who've recorded a number of the titles (Reddy recorded no less than four of them), but there's a more raw, affecting quality to these original renditions. —*Charles Donovan*

A Little Bit of Love / 1974 / A&M ✦✦

Ordinary Fool / 1975 / A&M ✦✦

● **Classics** / 1977 / A&M ✦✦✦✦✦

Robbie Williams

b. Feb. 13, 1974, Tunstall, Stoke-on-Trent, Staffordshire, England
Vocals / Britpop, Pop/Rock, Alternative Pop/Rock, Dance-Pop

Out of all the members of Take That, Robbie Williams never really seemed to fit in. Roguishly handsome where his bandmates were merely cute, Williams was tougher and sexier than the rest, which made him more distinctive. He also fought regularly with the other members and their management, primarily because he was occasionally adverse to being so heavily packaged. So it didn't come as a surprise that he was the first to leave the band, departing early in the summer of 1995 and attempting to boost his credibility by tagging along with Oasis, hoping that Noel Gallagher would give him a couple of songs. He never did, but all of his time with Oasis launched Williams into a world of heavy partying, drinking and drugging. Over the course of 1996, he was only heard from in gossip columns, and occasionally, he was quoted as saying his new music would abandon lightweight dance-pop for traditional Brit-pop, but his first single was a cover of George Michael's "Freedom '90." Released late in 1996, the single was a disaster, but his second single, 1997's "Old Before I Die," was more in the vein of his early pronouncements, featuring a distinct Oasis influence. Williams released his first solo album, *LIfe Thru a Lens*, in 1997. The album became a big hit in Britain, prompting his second *I've Been Expecting You*, in 1998. *The Ego Has Landed*, a US-only compilation designed for breaking Williams to American audiences, was released in the US in 1999. —*Stephen Thomas Erlewine*

● **Life Thru a Lens** / 1997 / Chrysalis ✦✦✦✦✦
One of the best U.K. debuts of the '90s, *Life Thru a Lens* is an uninhibited joyride through all manner of British music, from glam to alternative to soft-rock to dance-pop. Beginning with the joyous "Lazy Days," the album continually betrays overt influences from Oasis and other Britpop stars, but triumphs nevertheless due to gorgeous production, Williams' irresistible personality, and the overall flavor of outrageous, utterly enjoyable pop music. Whether he's romping through aggressive burners like "Ego A Go Go" and "South of the Border," crooning on the ballad "Angels," or offering a slice of life—working-class style—on the title track and "Lazy Days," Williams is a pop star through and through.

For those who appreciate great pop with plenty of cheek, *Life Thru a Lens* is an excellent album. —*John Bush*

I've Been Expecting You / Aug. 25, 1998 / Chrysalis ✦✦✦✦
If *Life Through a Lens* crowned England's highly worshipped star, then *I've Been Expecting You* adds the super-glue. Despite all of his popularity in England, Robbie Williams has yet to make a big impression on America. Here is a British artist who could tell the Queen of England where to sit at the table, and on U.S. *Billboard* charts he can't crack the top ten. Status is not everything, however, quality is. *I've Been Expecting You* is comprised of pop songs with thought-provoking lyrics and snide observations. He makes references to Oprah Winfrey and Ricki Lake on the hit single "Strong" and wrote what was probably the official song for 2000 and first single from the album, "Millennium." "No Regrets" is dark and brooding with Pet Shop Boys on chorus. His attempts at "Angel"-size ballads don't pan out completely, "She's the One" and "Heaven From Here" are sweet and soft, but not soaring like his former hit. What Williams has is the amazing ability to completely throw himself into other mindsets (characters, if you will) and weave the listener into his world with surprises rather than tacking listeners along on predictability. "Karma Killer" makes the best case, a haunting, screaming song with dog-barking that is not so subtly packaged between the two previously mentioned ballads. Is it Williams in Williams mode? Is it Williams in a past life? You don't know, and you don't care, it's just part of the ride. Egotistical charm intact, he even tops his "Speech for a Teacher" hidden track on *Life* with a hidden song called "Stalker's Day Off," in which "he" apologizes over his victim's answering machine for calling too much and the "newspaper with blood on it." Quite cheeky. —*Peter Fawthrop*

● **The Ego Has Landed** / May 4, 1999 / Capitol ✦✦✦✦
Robbie Williams was an international superstar at the end of the millennium, a recognizable icon in all countries but one—the United States. Traditionally, this is a problem for British superstars, who are able to amass a large global following but are hard pressed to break down the doors to America for a variety of reasons, many of which are inexplicable. For Williams, it was because his records weren't released in the U.S., probably because his former band, Take That, never developed into a commercial powerhouse in America. Once the group split, conventional wisdom suggested that lead singer Gary Barlow would become the star, but after Williams delivered back-to-back smashes (*Life Thru a Lens*, *I've Been Expecting You*), he seemed like the genuine star. It was time for America to become acquainted with the lovable rock & roll rascal, hence the brilliantly titled *The Ego Has Landed*. Containing six songs from *Life* and eight from *I've Been*, *The Ego Has Landed* isn't a perfect compilation, but it's not half bad either. Since it's culled from just two records, it doesn't have great momentum or pacing, but it does contain a very good cross section of his two albums, leaning a little toward the mid-tempo and ballad side. The pacing is a little off, but the songs are there: the clever showmanship of "Let Me Entertain You," the endearingly silly "Old Before I Die," the crooning "No Regrets," the propulsive "Man Machine," and "Millennium," Willliams' bid for sampadelic hipness—everything that illustrates why he is a perfect post-alternative, post-Brit-pop, post-ironic pop star. —*Stephen Thomas Erlewine*

Sing When You're Winning / Oct. 3, 2000 / Capitol ✦✦✦✦
Poised for global domination with his third album, Robbie Williams and producer Guy Chambers hardly dared mess with the formula of their 1998 crossover hit *I've Been Expecting You*. As such, *Sing When You're Winning* has plenty of introspective balladry akin to "Angels," and a few irresistible party-time tracks in similar company to "Millennium." The album also moves Williams farther away from the increasingly dated visions of Oasis-style Brit-pop to embrace post-millennial dance-pop, complete with the bruising beats and extroverted productions to match. And Chambers certainly knows his production playbook well, conjuring a panoply of classic British rock touchstones like psychedelia, slick country-rock, Ian Dury, the Who, Elton John, and Madchester. Despite a small drop in songwriting from its predecessor, *Sing When You're Winning* ultimately succeeds, and most of the credit must go to Williams himself. Amidst a few overly familiar arrangements and lyrical themes, Williams proves the consummate entertainer, delivering powerful, engaging vocals—no matter the quality of the material—and striking the perfect balance between tongue-in-cheek, self-mocking humor ("Knutsford City Limits") and genuine feeling (tender ballads like "Better Man" and "If It's Hurting You"). The radio-ready single "Rock DJ" is a piece of immediately gratifying pop candyfloss with a surprisingly endless shelf life, though "Kids," a vivacious, vacuous vamp of a duet with Kylie Minogue, doesn't even hold its own after one listen. Toss in a few beautiful album tracks (the opener "Let Love Be Your Energy," "Love Calling Earth," "Singing for the Lonely"), but then counter them with a few bland singalongs ("Supreme," "Forever Texas"), and the result is a scattered, entertaining album whose real star is Robbie Williams' personality. —*John Bush*

Vanessa Williams

b. Mar. 18, 1963, Tarrytown, NY
Vocals / Adult Contemporary, Urban, Dance-Pop

When Vanessa Williams lost her Miss America crown in 1984, it seemed like her career was over. Actually, the truth was quite different. Four years later, she re-emerged as an urban R&B vocalist with *The Right Stuff*, which featured the Top Ten hit "Dreamin'." Her next album was an even bigger success, thanks to the smash hit "Saving the Best for Last"; it confirmed her status as one of urban R&B's most popular vocalists. *The Sweetest Days* followed in 1995, and Williams returned three years later with *Greatest Hits*. —*Stephen Thomas Erlewine*

The Right Stuff / Feb. 1988 / Wing ✦✦✦✦✦
The disc is evenly divided between dance-floor fodder and AOR fluff, and it ain't half bad.

Despite the fact that Williams works with six producers and eight songwriters, the disc has a consistent feel, and while Vanessa doesn't have a voice suited to belting out raunchy R&B, she's smart enough to stay within her limitations and let her personality take up the slack. *—J. Poet*

The Comfort Zone / Aug. 20, 1991 / Wing ♦♦♦♦
Typically, Vanessa Williams' albums are mixed bags. She's at her most exciting when taking chances and coming from the heart, and at her worst when recording frightfully dull material that is designed strictly for commercial radio airplay. This is certainly true of her sophomore effort, *The Comfort Zone*. Williams is at her best on the sexy, alluring title song and a striking remake of the Isley Brothers' "Work to Do," and at her worst on the hit adult contemporary ballad "Save the Best For Last." The song isn't genuinely romantic, only corny and insipid. One wishes Williams would stick to songs that are worthy of her, but when artists are under pressure from labels to sell as many albums as possible, artistic considerations easily fall by the wayside. *—Alex Henderson*

Sweetest Days / 1995 / Wing ♦♦♦
More diverse than Vanessa Williams' two previous albums, *The Sweetest Days* finds the singer exploring jazz-influenced songs without giving up the type of boring, radio-minded fluff that had enabled her to sell millions of albums. The CD's standout track is "Ellamental," an irresistible R&B/jazz/hip-hop tribute to Ella Fitzgerald. (Much to her credit, Williams was insightful enough to praise the jazz legend while she was still alive instead of waiting until after her death.) She's almost as appealing on "Sister Moon" (a torchy Sting gem) and the Babyface contributions "You Can't Run" (which has a Sade-ish quality) and the haunting "Betcha Never." But sadly, Williams doesn't hesitate to waste her talent on such contrived, hopelessly dull adult contemporary fluff as the title song—a song that's every bit as clichéd and insipid as "Save the Best For Last." *—Alex Henderson*

Star Bright / Nov. 5, 1996 / Mercury ♦♦♦♦
With the help of some talented friends, charming pop vocalist Vanessa Williams blends in the beauty of jazz, gospel, and soul music to create a portrait of Christmas songs. The record, entitled *Star Bright*, is genuinely filled with a glistening appeal, and the songs that it contains encompass a rich tapestry of the best and brightest seasonal music. The setting changes via each song, some tunes filled with Williams' rich voice backed by an assertive, charismatic gospel choir. The collection is filled with such traditionals as "Do You Hear What I Hear" and "What Child Is This?" A brilliant rendition of Rob Mathis' "Star Bright" is featured, and "Angels We Have Heard on High" draws the listener to the feeling of a wintry landscape of hope and joy during this festive season. Perhaps the most romantic tune featured in this collection is Williams' duet with Bobby Caldwell, a flavorful jazz singer in his own right. These arrangements make good soup for the casual holiday music listener and should be favorites for a long time to come in the holiday section at one's local retail music store. Just a side note—the packaging is quite festive and appealing, decorated with snowflakes and blue-type lettering in the credits. Williams looks quite radiant by herself on the cover, enough to appease the listener to buy the record. Other uplifting, praiseworthy tunes such as "Go Tell It on the Mountain" and "Gracious Good Shepherd" deserve a listen. The final track, "I'll Be Home for Christmas," is the most reflective piece, and should spark one to ponder on holidays and years past, and reminisce on precious times with family or without. *—Shawn M. Haney*

● **Greatest Hits: The First Ten Years** / Nov. 17, 1998 / Wing/Mercury ♦♦♦♦♦
When former Miss America/Penthouse poser Vanessa Williams picked up a microphone in 1988 with *The Right Stuff*, her managers did the business-smart, and expected, thing: They buried her beneath a coat of glossy production and dance floor beeps and bips to disguise whatever vocal shortcomings this walking mannequin might have. But a funny thing happened within a few years. It turned out that Williams, when given the right material, could actually sing. And when handed torch songs that emphasized her natural slow burn—like on the glorious ballad "Save the Best for Last"—Williams was a genuinely sexy and capable performer. *Greatest Hits: The First Ten Years* gathers the biggest 13 songs from her first decade. The club tunes are generic and could be served just as well by anyone, but the finest tunes here ("Save the Best for Last," "Love Is," and "Colors of the Wind") are smoldering slices of R&B that certify Williams is more than just a pretty face. *—Michael Gallucci*

Victoria Williams

b. Dec. 23, 1958, Shreveport, LA
Vocals, Guitar / Alternative Folk, Contemporary Folk, Adult Alternative Pop/Rock, Alternative Country-Rock, Folk-Rock, Singer/Songwriter

Despite a successful career as a idiosyncratic country-folk performer, Victoria Williams was perhaps best known as a songwriter—thanks, ironically enough, to a tribute album recorded in her honor. Williams made her solo recording debut in 1987 with *Happy Come Home*, a collection showcasing her vivid songcraft as well as her off-kilter, squeaky vocal style; a follow-up record, *Swing the Statue!*, appeared in 1990. Two years later, while opening for Neil Young, Williams was diagnosed with the degenerative neurological disorder multiple sclerosis. The medical bills quickly piled up, and like many musicians, she was not covered by health insurance. In response, her manager began assembling friends and fans to record Williams' songs for a benefit album; the result, 1993 *Sweet Relief: A Benefit for Victoria Williams*, featured the likes of Pearl Jam, Lou Reed and Soul Asylum, whose rendition of "Summer of Drugs" was the record's first single. Due to its all-star line-up, *Sweet Relief* far outsold any of Williams' own efforts. In 1994 Williams issued *Loose*, a varied collection featuring duets with Soul Asylum's Dave Pirner and the Jayhawks' Mark Olson, Williams' second husband. *—Jason Ankeny*

Happy Come Home / 1987 / Geffen ♦♦♦
This debut album by Victoria Williams is as wonderful as it is eclectic. Van Dyke Parks' arrangements give the collection a carnival feel, while Anton Fier's pop productions never let this become anything close to an ordinary singer/songwriter album. But how could it, with Williams's elastic vocals and trippy lyrics? This is a great record to play when anyone says that all L.A. pop albums are slick and sanitized. *—Richard Meyer*

● **Swing the Statue** / 1990 / Mammoth ♦♦♦♦♦
Victoria Williams' second album was her most accomplished set of folk-rock, featuring the remarkable "Summer of Drugs." *—Stephen Thomas Erlewine*

Loose / 1994 / Mammoth ♦♦♦♦♦
What a great collection. Victoria Williams has put together a fine-tuned tight but loose band, as expressed in the title. Her folk-rock Carol Channing voice is perfectly suited to the arrangements, some of which were written by Van Dyke Parks, and include players such as Greg Cohen, Peter Buck, and Don Heffinton. Her originals are quirky and beautiful. Williams's choice of covers is also refreshing. She does a heartbreaking take on "What a Wonderful World" and revives the psychedelic chestnut "Nature's Way," making it her own. *Loose* is a wonderful album, full of life. *—Richard Meyer*

This Moment: Live in Toronto / Nov. 7, 1995 / Atlantic ♦♦♦

Musings of a Creek Dipper / Jan. 13, 1998 / Atlantic ♦♦♦

Water to Drink / Aug. 15, 2000 / Atlantic ♦♦♦♦
Williams is an innovative and adventurous songwriter and performer, but many find her folky antics and unique voice to be a bit much. Certainly *Water to Drink*, her first solo album since 1998's critically acclaimed *Musings of a Creek Dipper*, will add quite a few new souls to each camp. Here Williams stretches herself artistically and scores more than a few creative triumphs, but her personal mannerisms color their share of songs as well.

The opening song swings along in somewhat self-indulgent ramblings about personal freedom, forgiveness, and her grandmother's hat pin, backed up by an instrumental soup of buzzy psychedelic guitars and Carole King-inspired piano. The result is a muddy mess that doesn't seem to go anywhere in particular. The rest of the album truly is a joy, however. The hippie vibe works better on "Joy of Love," where a breezy chorus seems more like a rallying cry than a repetitive drone. The title track "Water to Drink" is even better. An English version of Antonio Carlos Jobim's "Agua de Beber," the song allows Williams a fun vehicle for her vocal creativity. Here her voice seems more in its element, gaining a kind of Betty Boop coy sexiness instead of the croony qualities that seem to pervade elsewhere. Indeed, two of the other strongest performances on the album, on "Until the Real Thing Comes Along" and "Young at Heart," are standards, proving that Williams may be strongest when interpreting the songs of other people. Perhaps her lyrical quirkiness and eccentric tone and phrasing is a little too much all at once and the constraints of performing another composer's songs tone down the blur of her ideas, giving her space where she can spread out and share her immense talent. *—Stacia Proefrock*

Chuck Willis (Harold Willis)

b. Jan. 31, 1928, Atlanta, GA, **d.** Apr. 10, 1958, Atlanta, GA
Vocals / R&B

There were two distinct sides to Chuck Willis. In addition to being a convincing blues shouter, Willis harbored a vulnerable blues balladeer side. In addition, he was a masterful songwriter who penned some of the most distinctive R&B numbers of the 1950s. He wrote such gems as "I Feel So Bad" (later covered by Elvis Presley), the anguished ballads "Don't Deceive Me (Please Don't Go)" and "It's Too Late" (the latter attracting covers by Buddy Holly and Otis Redding), and his swan song, "Hang Up My Rock & Roll Shoes." He first recorded in 1951, issuing one single for Columbia before he was shuttled over to its recently reactivated OKeh R&B subsidiary. One year later, he crashed the national R&B lists for OKeh with a typically plaintive ballad, "My Story." He followed up with his own "Don't Deceive Me" and the surging Latin-beat "I Feel So Bad" in 1954. After moving over to Atlantic in 1956, he immediately enjoyed another round of hits with "It's Too Late" and "Juanita." His 1957 revival of the ancient "C.C. Rider" became his first R&B number one hit and a huge pop seller. But the turban-wearing crooner's time was growing short—he had long suffered from ulcers prior to his 1958 death from peritonitis. *—Bill Dahl*

My Story / 1980 / Columbia ♦♦♦♦
Not as exhaustive as Legacy's subsequent look at Willis' early- to mid-'50s hitmaking stint at OKeh, but this 14-tracker still gets the job done with the smooth ballads "Going to the River," "Don't Deceive Me," and "My Story" and Willis' surging, Latin-tempoed original "I Feel So Bad." *—Bill Dahl*

Let's Jump Tonight! The Best of Chuck Willis: 1951-1956 / 1994 / Epic/Legacy ♦♦♦♦♦
Before his brief turn as a rock & roll star with Atlantic, Willis cut a lot of material for OKeh in much more of an R&B/jump blues vein. This 26-cut collection includes all of his early and mid-'50s R&B hits—"My Story," "Goin' to the River," "Don't Deceive Me," "You're Still My Baby," and his most famous number from this period, "I Feel So Bad" (revived by Elvis Presley, among others). The influence of Joe Turner, Charles Brown, early Lloyd Price, and similar performers is strongly felt; Willis could shout competently, but was much better on the emotional R&B ballads. Not as strong or distinctive as his Atlantic material, this includes several cuts that were previously unreleased or previously unavailable in the U.S. *—Richie Unterberger*

★ **Stroll On: The Chuck Willis Collection** / Oct. 19, 1994 / Razor & Tie ♦♦♦♦♦
All 25 of the versatile Atlanta-bred singer's Atlantic Records sides, presented beautifully (every R&B reissue on CD should be packaged so well, with plenty of brilliant stereo). Willis really hit his stride at Atlantic, doing the Stroll with his easy-going "C.C. Rider" and "Betty and Dupree" (both boasting darting sax breaks from Gene Barge), baring his tender soul on a devotional "What Am I Living For," and taking R&B into fresh directions

with a jumping "Kansas City Woman," the relentless "Keep A-Drivin'," and a buoyant "Hang Up My Rock & Roll Shoes." *—Bill Dahl*

Wilson Phillips

f. 1989, **db.** 1993

Adult Contemporary

A female vocal trio consisting of Carnie and Wendy Wilson (daughters of Beach Boy Brian Wilson) and Chynna Phillips (daughter of John and Michelle Phillips of the Mamas & the Papas). They broke through to enormous pop success with their debut album, which sold four million copies. The follow-up, *Shadows and Light*, got off to a fast start in the spring of 1992. Although the album was successful, selling over a million copies, it didn't have the staying power of their debut. Wilson Phillips broke up the following year. *—William Ruhlmann*

● **Wilson Phillips** / 1990 / Capitol ♦♦♦♦

Sugary, commercial pop/rock isn't necessarily a bad thing, and in fact can be fairly enjoyable in the right hands. But Wilson Phillips is much too sweet for its own good. This debut album—which amazingly went quadruple platinum—is about as lightweight and sophomoric as it gets. Chynna Phillips' weak singing on such homogenized, mundane fluff as "Impulse," "The Dream Is Still Alive" and the hit "Hold On" isn't even remotely convincing. Compared to Phillips' saccharine performances on "You're In Love" (another major hit) and "A Reason To Believe," even Tiffany and Debbie Gibson's debut albums have some bite. *—Alex Henderson*

Shadows & Light / Jun. 2, 1992 / SBK ♦♦♦

This is a big step forward for Carnie and Wendy Wilson and Chynna Phillips. Their first album, which was a phenomenal success, was shiny and happy and upbeat for the most part; this follow-up is murkier, with denser arrangements and hooks that aren't quite as obvious on first listen. This works both for and against the group. With their soaring harmonies, they bring a joyful brassiness to the hopeful "It's Only Life," which is this album's "Hold On"—though it is far from being a blueprint. The affirmation of love on track nine, "All the Way From New York," juxtaposed with track ten, the sexy rocker "Fueled for Houston," works, and it is the brightest spot on the album. Unfortunately, though, while their hearts seem to have been in the right place, much of this material just doesn't work. In fact, they even sing in "Goodbye, Carmen": "We're convinced our intentions are good/but we live in this world often misunderstood." This certainly applies to that cut, about a maid. It's odd subject matter, and it doesn't quite fly. The girls end up sounding pretentious and condescending. Though the group teamed again with Glen Ballard, who produced their first album, something got lost in the translation this time around. Their angelic voices still mesh seamlessly, but stepping forward toward maturity, the trio seems to have lost some of the fun that made them click in the first place. *Shadows & Light* is far from being a disaster, but it is a misstep, though worth checking out if you enjoy girl groups or are a fan of Wilson Phillips. *—Bryan Buss*

● **Greatest Hits** / May 23, 2000 / Capitol ♦♦♦♦

Wilson Phillips may have been nearly ubiquitous during the dawning years of the '90s, but they really didn't have that many big singles—only four, actually: "Hold On," "You're in Love," "Impulsive," and "Release Me," plus the minor hit "The Dream Is Still Alive." That's not a lot to build a collection on, much less a 15-track retrospective, so it's only natural that Capitol had to pad this out with a variety of rarities—album cuts, songs contributed to tribute albums, live cuts, and, best of all, a 90-second "Conversation With Wilson Phillips." In other words, it's a bit much, and it would have been much better if it were ten tracks, since the filler wouldn't stand out as much, and that filler really does slow it down quite a bit, even if this is a fairly representative overview of the group's short-lived time in the sun. *—Stephen Thomas Erlewine*

Brian Wilson

b. Jun. 20, 1942, Hawthorne, CA

Vocals, Keyboards, Songwriter, Piano, Guitar, Bass / Pop/Rock

Brian Wilson is arguably the greatest American composer of popular music in the rock era. Born and raised in Hawthorne, CA, Wilson formed the Beach Boys, with his two younger brothers, cousin Mike Love, and school friend Alan Jardine, and they became the most successful American rock band in history by performing his songs, which initially combined the rock urgency of Chuck Berry with the harmonies of the Four Freshmen. Wilson's musical imagination expanded during the '60s to the point of such remarkable works as "Good Vibrations," a chart-topping Beach Boys single of 1966. Wilson retreated from his dominance of the Beach Boys after 1967, as their popularity declined. He made sporadic contributions to their records, returning briefly as a songwriter and producer in the mid-'70s. Wilson issued a debut solo album in 1988, but his second one, *Sweet Insanity*, was rejected by Sire Records. In 1995, he reunited with longtime collaborator Van Dyke Parks for *Orange Crate Art*; that same year, Wilson was the subject of a documentary feature, *I Just Wasn't Made for These Times*. *Imagination* followed in 1998. *—William Ruhlmann*

● **Brian Wilson** / 1988 / Rhino ♦♦♦♦

Brian Wilson's first solo album created a good share of media hoopla upon its release. This was not necessarily because of the music, but simply because his very existence—or, at least, proof of his existence via his first fully engaged recording project in about a decade—was greeted as a cause for celebration. Although it did not shift tons of units, it did spark a landslide of ecstatic-to-charitable reviews, largely because so many critics were eager to latch on to any evidence that Wilson's musical genius was intact. Viewed more coldly after the hype has faded, this self-titled release is an odd, flawed creation, certainly leagues above the Beach Boys' post-1970s output, yet certainly leagues below Wilson's best work with that group in the 1960s. While he retained his gift for catchy melodies and dense, symphonic production, there was a forced stiffness to both the songwriting and execution. Much of the blame for the album's mixed success can be laid upon its sterile, synthesizer-laden arrangements and echoing percussion, which epitomized some of the less attractive aspects of late-1980s production. However, the songs were not among Wilson's best either, their hooks pleasant but easily fading from memory, the lyrics full of ambiguous romantic optimism that was totally belied by the nervous, mannered vocals. The concluding eight-minute suite, "Rio Grande," was a self-conscious and, again, only partially successful attempt to match the grandeur of the miniature conceptual pieces Wilson was penning in the *Smile* era. For all that, it remains the best album of Wilson's solo career, principally because he has recorded so little material since then, and written even less. The 2000 Warner Archives/Rhino reissue adds more than a dozen bonus tracks, including demos, backing tracks, and alternates of songs from the album. *—Richie Unterberger*

Sweet Insanity / 1990 / Sire ♦♦♦

Some unreleased albums are better left unreleased, and this one, quite frankly, is a good example. Recorded and written after Brian Wilson's fine 1988 Sire debut, *Sweet Insanity* is almost more of a Eugene Landy album than a Brian Wilson effort. Landy has been described as both the man who saved Brian's life as well as a man who was a Svengali who exerted an overkill of control to "rehabilitate" this gifted musician. Most of the record is overbaked both lyrically and musically, with a feeling of sitting in on a therapy session rather than a recording. Some of it is unlistenable, and the mark of Brian Wilson only surfaces rarely. For diehard collectors and the brave of heart. *—Matthew Greenwald*

I Just Wasn't Made for These Times / Oct. 1995 / MCA ♦♦♦

The soundtrack for a Don Was-produced documentary about the life and music of Brian Wilson, *I Just Wasn't Made for These Times* is a collection of new versions of Wilson's classic Beach Boys material. While most of the versions don't compare with the original recordings, the album remains a testament to the beauty of his work. *—Stephen Thomas Erlewine*

Orange Crate Art / Nov. 7, 1995 / Warner Brothers ♦♦

Imagination / Jun. 16, 1998 / Giant ♦♦♦♦

As his second official solo album, *Imagination* is a stronger record than its predecessor. Brian Wilson is singing better and his writing is more assured, filled with gorgeous arrangements that others may replicate but never quite match. That doesn't quite erase the suspicion that it could have been better, however. Sessions with the respected power pop producer Andy Paley were hailed as Wilson's best material in years, though the collaboration didn't happen. Wilson, allegedly on the advice of his wife, decided to work with Joe Thomas, a former wrestler determined to make inroads in the music business. Thomas steered Wilson toward a slick, overly produced sound straight out of the late '80s, filled with sterile surfaces and synthesizers that hide the genuine musical attributes of the album. Listen closely and it's possible to hear a handful of songs that are startlingly beautiful. Wilson's writing may not be as magical as his '60s peak, but there are moments that soar, from the lovely "Cry" to the sunny choruses of "South America" to the affecting "Lay Down Burden" to the layered, avant-pop "Happy Days." Songs such as these, however, accentuate the weaknesses of other parts of the album—namely the lyrics. Such lyricists as Jimmy Buffet, Carole Bayer Sager, and J.D. Souther collaborated with Wilson on these songs, contributing surpassingly banal words, perhaps in an attempt to capture the sweet naïveté of classic Beach Boys songs. They didn't need to try so hard—Wilson can come close enough on his own. All he needs is collaborators that realize that and not force him into areas, whether it's musical or lyrical, that he needn't tread. The best parts of *Imagination* prove that he can spin enough magic on his own terms. *—Stephen Thomas Erlewine*

Live at the Roxy Theatre / May 2000 / BriMel ♦♦♦♦

As if to emphasize that Brian Wilson is really in charge of his solo career, *Live at the Roxy Theatre*, his first live solo album, begins with him instructing to his band and halting a false start before launching into "The Little Girl I Once Knew." And the choice of that lead-off song, a relative commercial disappointment in 1965, alerts listeners that the set will be an attempt to reclaim gems from Wilson's extensive catalog, not necessarily the string of golden oldies that Wilson's former group does at its concerts. *Live at the Roxy Theatre* certainly boasts Beach Boys favorites, but it touches on all phases of Wilson's career, from the early surf music to the sophisticated compositions that made *Pet Sounds* a landmark, solo songs from the 1980s and '90s, and even a couple of new tunes and covers (including the Barenaked Ladies' "Brian Wilson"). Wilson's ten-piece backup band, anchored by the members of the Wondermints, effectively recreates the elaborate Beach Boys studio performances and also sings in Beach Boys-like style. One is reminded of the discovery Wilson and the Beach Boys made in the mid-'60s, when they began touring and recording without each other: the Beach Boys' sound is really more a function of the vocal arrangements than of particular singers. And listening to the mix of selections, one must recognize that this is music of a single sensibility. *Live at the Roxy Theatre* presents Wilson in good voice for a 57 year old (even the falsetto is pretty sturdy), with a strong band and an enthusiastic audience, performing some of the best compositions of his career. It makes both a good introduction to Wilson's work and a satisfying summation for longtime fans. *—William Ruhlmann*

Dennis Wilson

b. Dec. 4, 1944, Inglewood, CA, **d.** Dec. 28, 1983, Marina del Rey, CA

Vocals, Drums / Pop/Rock

The most obviously untalented Wilson brother at the beginning of the Beach Boys, Dennis Wilson later matured into an excellent songwriter, producer, and vocalist. Though he only released one LP before drowning at the age of 39, his assortment of heart-rending ballads and pop curios were major assets to the Beach Boys' late-'60s and early-'70s output.

Born in 1944, Dennis was the youngest of the three Wilson brothers, also including Brian and Carl. An obvious target of female enthusiasm, Dennis delivered his first lead vocal on a Beach Boys hit with 1965's "Do You Wanna Dance," and began writing his own songs during the late '60s. After the Beach Boys '60s peak, he began rating a few songs on each album, often tender ballads flaunting his gruff voice and emotionally naked persona. His solo album, 1977's *Pacific Ocean Blue*, even charted inside the Top 100—higher than either of the Beach Boys' next two LPs. Though a few of his songs ended up on later Beach Boys albums, a projected second solo work never materialized. Wilson drowned in December 1983 while diving around his boat in California. *—John Bush*

● **Pacific Ocean Blue** / 1977 / Caribou ♦♦♦♦♦

Though the roots of this 1977 album go back to the early '70s, Dennis Wilson's one issued solo project is certainly a product of its time musically and texturally. The set's 12 songs reveal a songwriter who was looking to stretch out on his own and engage a vision of music that stood far outside what the Beach Boys were capable of handling or executing. Wilson himself panned the album, claiming it had no substance and looked forward to the release of *Bamboo*, a record that remained unfinished and unreleased at the time of his death. Brother Brian, however, loved the album and celebrated it with his usual childlike intensity. *Pacific Ocean Blue* is a moody view of the SoCal landscape, and of Wilson's own interior life—or his struggle to have one. From the environmental lament "River Song" that opens the disc, a new kind of West Coast music emerges. It's not steeped in the weighty philosophical and political concerns that other Angelinos such as Jackson Browne were penning. Instead, it's a wispy rock tune revolving around a beautiful piano figure, shuffling guitars, and a lyric that takes a personal concern for the state of the nature crumbling around it. Mostly, however, *Pacific Ocean Blue* is a diary. Given that it was recorded over nearly seven years, the songs reflect a snapshot quality of Wilson's life in the studio, what he was capable of, what he learned, and how he stretched himself. This album is a classic, blissed-out, coked-up slice of '70s rock and pop that is as essential as Fleetwood Mac's *Rumours*. *—Thom Jurek*

Bamboo [Unreleased] / 1996 / Bootleg ♦♦♦♦♦

Bamboo was the working title of Beach Boy Dennis Wilson's second solo album, an album that was, for many reasons, not completed at the time of his death by drowning on December 28, 1983. The folks at the Bamboo Archive Project (http://www.denniswilson-dreamer.com) have lovingly and professionally assembled what they consider the definitive issue of the *Bamboo* sessions. This is, thus far, the only authoritative collection of tracks—with fine sound and a couple of remastered and remixed cuts—that exists. The sessions for *Bamboo* began, reportedly, before those for *Pacific Ocean Blue*. For various reasons they were shelved as that album came to fruition, and after *POB* was released and the Beach Boys sold their studios and came to a slow, debilitating, frustrating halt amid personal problems and internal conflicts within the Beach Boys organization. Along with rarities, like "He's a Bum," remixed with a vibes backing track, and a gorgeous reprise of "Love Surrounds Me," there are four bonus tracks that include live versions of "Angel Come Home" and "Good Timin'" as well as studio takes of "10,000 Years" and "New Orleans." In all, this set showcases more than any of the posthumous Dennis Wilson outings how wildly inventive in a studio he was, and how his songwriting had taken a turn for the adventurous—note the Brazilian rhythms in "Companion," and the slippery profundity of "It's Not Too Late"—and the experimental. We'll never know what ultimately would have been on *Bamboo*, but this version is the best yet for imagining. *—Thom Jurek*

Jackie Wilson (Jack Leroy Wilson)

b. Jun. 9, 1934, Detroit, MI, **d.** Jan. 21, 1984, Mount Holly, NJ

Vocals / Chicago Soul, Uptown Soul, Pop-Soul, R&B, Soul

Jackie Wilson was one of the most important agents of Black pop's transition from rhythm & blues into soul. In terms of vocal power (especially in the upper register), few could outdo him; he was also an electricfying onstage showman. He was a consistent hitmaker from the mid-1950s through the early 1970s, although never a crossover superstar. His reputation isn't quite on par with Ray Charles, James Brown, or Sam Cooke, however, because his records did not always reflect his artistic genius. Indeed, there is a consensus of sorts among critics that Wilson was something of an underachiever in the studio, due to the sometimes inappropriately pop-based material and arrangements that he used. Wilson would score his first big R&B (and small pop) hit in late 1956 with the brassy, stuttering "Reet Petite," which was co-written by an emerging Detroit songwriter named Berry Gordy, Jr. Gordy would also help write a few other hits for Jackie in the late '50s, "To Be Loved," "Lonely Teardrops," "That's Why (I Love You So)," and "I'll Be Satisfied"; they also crossed over to the pop charts, "Lonely Teardrops" making the Top Ten. Most of these were upbeat, creatively arranged marriages of pop and R&B that, in retrospect, helped set the stage both for '60s soul, and for Gordy's own huge pop success at Motown. In the early '60s, Wilson maintained his pop stardom with regular hit singles that often used horn arrangements and female choruses that have dated somewhat badly. At the same time, he remained capable of unleashing a sweaty, uptempo, gospel-soaked number: "Baby Workout," which fit that description to a T, was a #5 hit for him in 1963. In 1966, his career was briefly revived when he teamed up with Chicago soul producer Carl Davis, who had been instrumental in the success of Windy City performers like Gene Chandler, Major Lance, and Jerry Butler. Davis successfully updated Wilson's sound with horn-heavy arrangements, getting near the Top Ten with "Whispers," and then making #6 in 1967 with "Higher and Higher." *—Richie Unterberger*

He's So Fine / 1958 / Brunswick ♦♦♦♦

In 1957, Jackie Wilson left the Dominoes and released this debut album on Brunswick Records a year later. The new songwriting team of Berry Gordy Jr. & Tyran Carlo (a.k.a. Billy Davis) wrote six of the 12 songs. Backed by a big band, Wilson belts out "Reet Petite" like it's an Olympic event, displaying his irresistible vocal gymnastics; "Etcetera" treads the same path, but lacks the dynamics. "To Be Loved" and "Danny Boy," the old standard, are heartfelt, stately ballads. Wilson wrote "Come Back to Me," a rather bland jump tune. An overblown big band sound mars all but the most crafted creations, and there's no denying Wilson's fantastic takes, but the Brunswick sound may be a bit too full for diehard soul lovers. *—Andrew Hamilton*

Jackie Wilson at the Copa / 1962 / Brunswick ♦♦♦

The only live album of Wilson's career was recorded in the early '60s at New York's famous Copacabana nightclub. It was an almost obligatory rite of passage for early soul stars breaking into the mainstream, one also enacted by Sam Cooke and several Motown stars. As you'd expect, the cirumstances don't exactly lend themselves to showing Wilson at his greatest advantage, particularly if you're principally a fan of Wilson the soul singer, not Wilson the all-around entertainer. He sounds like an over-the-top lounge lizard throughout much of the proceedings, zipping through standards like Leonard Bernstein's "Tonight," "Body and Soul," "St. James Infirmary," and Cole Porter's "Love for Sale," occasionally pausing for some corny between-song patter. He does interject a few of his R&B hits ("That's Why," "Doggin' Around," "To Be Loved," "Lonely Teardrops"), but these too get the casino band treatment, complete with strings and strident female backup vocalists. No, it's not what you play as exhibit A to showcase Jackie Wilson, Rock & Roll Hall of Famer. But taken on its own terms it's enjoyably cheesy entertainment, Wilson's astounding vocal prowess always in evidence. Out of print since 1967, it was reissued on CD in 1995. *—Richie Unterberger*

Higher and Higher / Nov. 1967 / Brunswick ♦♦♦♦

Driven by Jackie Wilson's biggest latter-day hit, "(Your Love Keeps Lifting Me) Higher and Higher," this 1967 LP offers great performances (from vocalist and band) and a variety of material. Though original LPs surely aren't the best place to start for Wilson, fans of the nearly irresistible Brunswick sound will find much here to like, from the propulsive "You Can Count on Me" and "Open the Door to Your Heart" to the classy Impressions-style "When Will Our Day Come" and the ballad "Those Heartaches." Wilson's performances are excellent as usual, making *Higher and Higher* one of the better original albums of his career. *—John Bush*

Mr. Excitement / Nov. 10, 1992 / Rhino ♦♦♦♦♦

A three-CD box from the experts of reissue at Rhino, *Mr. Excitement* takes Wilson's career from his first sides with Billy Ward & the Dominoes in 1956 through his final recordings in the early '70s. The former Detroit boxer hit either the R&B or pop chart over 50 times, making him one of the most successful R&B artists ever, in chart terms at least. Every one of those recordings is contained in this set, including such classics as "Reet Petite," "Lonely Teardrops," and "(Your Love Keeps Lifting Me) Higher and Higher." Wilson had an explosive falsetto and a downright weird sense of phrasing that made him utterly unique. Some of his productions were a little overwrought but even in the most extreme cases, that voice was a gift from God. Seminal. *—Rob Bowman*

☆ **The Very Best of Jackie Wilson [Ace]** / Feb. 4, 1993 / Ace ♦♦♦♦♦

Similar to the U.S. greatest-hits collection of the same name (on Rhino), but with substantially more tracks. This 24-song anthology has all the familiar big singles on the Rhino compilation, but goes into his late-'60s-early-'70s material in greater depth. His best stuff was recorded before that, though, so you're not much (if at all) worse off by sticking to the cheaper, more easily available domestic collection. *—Richie Unterberger*

★ **The Very Best of Jackie Wilson [Rhino]** / Jan. 18, 1994 / Rhino ♦♦♦♦♦

This 16-song overview of Wilson at the peak of his career at Brunswick Records was the best CD of his work available during the 1990s, with the usual care for sound and choice of master tape sources that Rhino is known for. It was also far more entertaining than Rhino's less-than-edifying triple-CD set on Wilson. As of the year 2000, however, it had been deleted and supplanted by Brunswick's own greatest-hits CD, a straight reissue of its 1969 compilation, although anyone finding the Rhino disc as an out-of-print item should have no reservations about purchasing it. *—Bruce Eder*

This Love Is Real/You Got Me Walking / Jun. 29, 1999 / Edsel ♦♦♦♦

This brings together two of Wilson's best latter-day albums onto one CD. Both of these LPs were produced by Carl Davis for Brunswick in 1970 and the following year and draw heavily from Davis' writing pool of talent, including Eugene Record, leader of the Chi-Lites. This is Jackie Wilson making a cutting edge batch of recordings for the 1970s soul market and although these recordings weren't big sellers, they stand as some of his best and most inspired work before the oldies circuit beckoned. Highlights include "Say You Will," "Love Changed Her Face," "Where There Is Love," "Think About the Good Times," "Love Uprising" and "The Fountain." *—Cub Koda*

Beautiful Day/Nobody But You / Sep. 27, 1999 / Diablo ♦♦♦♦

This outstanding 1999 two-LP single CD from U.K. label Edsel Records pairs two of Jackie Wilson's best latter day albums. Both were produced by Chicago soul icon Carl Davis. 1974's *Beautiful Day* was co-produced by arranger Sonny Sanders and features songs co-written by Jeffree Perry, whose credits also include hits by various Motown artists and 100 Proof (Aged In Soul). Speaking of Motown, the label's tight studio band, The Funk Brothers, can be heard throughout the album. The inspiring title track shimmers from Wilson's emotive vocals. Other highlights include "Because of You," "Go Away," and "I Get Lonely Sometimes." *Nobody But You* was Wilson's final album and had superb arrangements by David Van De Pitte. There are several poignant moments. The dreamy opening track "Where Is Love" is a heartfelt plea for racial equality. The singer's fiery vocal sparks his duet with the Chi-Lites on the energetically majestic "Don't Burn No Bridges." Other standouts are "You're The Song I Can't Stop Singing," the Sam Dees ballad "Just As Soon As the Feeling's Over," the light and brisk "It Only Happens When I Look At You," and the big, brassy horn-laced "Satisfy My Soul." As Wilson sings on the album's final track, "I've learned about life/whatever will be will be for me," you might get a lump in your throat when you consider the singer's tragic end. *—Ed Hogan*

Wimple Winch

f. 1963, **db.** 1969

Freakbeat, British Psychedelia, Psychedelic, British Invasion

Despite the silly name and their near-total lack of commercial success, Wimple Winch was an interesting British '60s group, weaving soul, intricate harmonies, and unusual whimsical lyrics into their original material. Starting out as Just Four Men, the Liverpool-area outfit was initially just one of the dozens of Merseybeat groups riding the Beatles' coattails, although they cut a couple of fair singles. Changing their name to Wimple Winch, they released three much more progressive singles that were popular locally, including the explosive raver "Save My Soul" and the dramatic story-song "Rumble on Mersey Square South." Arguably the most creative group to work from Liverpool after the Merseybeat boom dried up, they broke up in the late '60s, leaving a wealth of unreleased material. Much of that material, as well as their rare singles, eventually appeared on compilations of British Invasion and British psychedelic rarities in the '80s. *—Richie Unterberger*

The Wimple Story 1963-1968 / 1992 / Bam Caruso ♦♦♦

Just Four Men are responsible for 12 of the 28 tracks on this compilation, which also includes 16 later songs by the group into which they evolved, Wimple Winch. All four songs from their 1964-65 singles are here, the standout being "Things Will Never Be the Same," on which the guitars chug along at a really jittery, propulsive tempo. The rest of the songs are higher on potential than impact, as the band seems to be struggling with their ambitions: some unexpected minor chords and odd, moody lyrical twists that wouldn't get realized until the Wimple Winch era. The unreleased cuts are erratic, and sometimes thinly produced and derivative of typical Merseybeats melodies and harmonies. The Just Four Men tracks are totally outclassed by the Wimple Winch segment of the disc, which is an interesting blend of crunching mod pop, psychedelia, and soul, with unexpected rhythmic shifts, fine harmonies, strong melodies, and unusual lyrics (although they sometimes get a little fruity). *—Richie Unterberger*

Jesse Winchester

b. May 17, 1944, Shreveport, LA

Vocals, Keyboards, Guitar / Contemporary Folk, Folk-Rock, Singer/Songwriter

Jesse Winchester was the music world's most prominent Vietnam War draft-evader, though his renown came from a body of wry, closely observed songs. After growing up in Memphis, Winchester received his draft notice in 1967 and moved to Montreal, Canada, rather than serve in the military. In 1969, he met Robbie Robertson of the Band, who helped launch his recording career. In the same way that James Taylor's history of mental instability and drug abuse served as a subtext for his early music, Winchester's exile lent real-life poignancy to songs like "Yankee Lady." Despite critical acclaim, his inability to tour in the U.S. prevented him from taking his place among the major singer/songwriters of the early '70s, but he made a series of impressive albums before President Jimmy Carter instituted an amnesty that finally allowed him to play in his homeland. By that time, the singer/songwriter boom had passed, though Winchester continued to record and even scored a Top 40 hit with "Say What" in 1981. His most prominently covered songs include "The Brand New Tennessee Waltz," "Biloxi," "Mississippi, You're on My Mind," "Defying Gravity," "Rhumba Girl," "Well-A-Wiggy" and "I'm Gonna Miss You, Girl." *—William Ruhlmann*

Jesse Winchester / 1970 / Stony Plain ♦♦♦♦♦

Jesse Winchester first gained notice as a protégé of the Band's Robbie Robertson, who produced and played guitar on his debut album and brought along bandmate Levon Helm to play drums and mandolin. The album had much of the rustic Southern charm and rollicking country-rock of the Band. Winchester's other immediate appeal was a certain sense of mystery. A Southern American expatriate living in Canada, he was unable to appear in the U.S. to promote the album, which was released in a fold-out LP jacket that featured the same sepia-toned portrait (which looked like one of those austere Matthew Brady photos from the Civil War era) on each of its four sides. Winchester emphasized the dichotomy between his southern origins and his northern exile in songs like "Snow" (which Robertson co-wrote), "The Brand New Tennessee Waltz" ("I've a sadness too sad to be true"), and "Yankee Lady." *Jesse Winchester* was timely: it spoke to a disaffected American generation that sympathized with Winchester's pacifism. But it was also timeless: the songs revealed a powerful writing talent (recognized by the numerous artists who covered them), and Winchester's gentle vocals made a wonderful vehicle for delivering them. (Originally released by Ampex in 1970, *Jesse Winchester* was reissued by Bearsville Records in 1976 and again in 1988 by Rhino/ Bearsville). *—William Ruhlmann*

Third Down, 110 to Go / 1972 / Stony Plain ♦♦♦♦♦

If Jesse Winchester's debut album was an auspicious introduction to a powerful new songwriting talent, his two-and-a-half-years-in-the-making follow-up was in some ways even more impressive. Without the influence of Robbie Robertson, Winchester, who produced most of the album himself (three tracks were handled by Todd Rundgren), gave it a homemade feel, using small collections of acoustic instruments, an appropriate setting for a group of short, intimate songs that expressed a deliberately positive worldview set against an acknowledgement of desperate times. Winchester found hope in religion and domesticity, but the key to his stance was a kind of good-humored accommodation. "If the wheel is fixed," he sang, "I would still take a chance. If we're skating on thin ice, then we might as well dance." The album was littered with such examples of aphoristic folk wisdom, adding up to a portrait of a man, cut off from his very deep roots and yet determined to maintain his dignity with grace and even occasionally a goofy sense of humor. *—William Ruhlmann*

Learn to Love It / 1974 / Stony Plain ♦♦♦

As the title suggests, making a virtue of necessity had always been a goal of Jesse Winchester's, and by the time of the release of his third album, the American expatriate had gone ahead and assumed Canadian citizenship. This seemed to free him to comment explicitly on his anti-war exile in "Pharaoh's Army" and especially a version of the old campaign song "Tell Me Why You Like Roosevelt" updated with new lyrics: "In the year of 1967, as a somewhat younger man, the call to bloody glory came, and I would not raise my hand." Elsewhere, Winchester continued to write love songs to his lost South ("L'Air De La Louisiane," "Mississippi, You're on My Mind") and, to a lesser extent, to pursue the wistful philosophizing found on *Third Down, 110 to Go* ("Defying Gravity"). The sense that he was repeating himself was inescapable, however, and with one-third of the album written by others and two of the originals in French Canadian, it was also obvious that Winchester was straining to come up with material. Interestingly, the two Russell Smith songs included, "Third Rate Romance" (which Smith sang uncredited) and "The End Is Not in Sight," went on to become Top 40 country hits for Smith's group, the Amazing Rhythm Aces, in the next two years. Stoney Edwards took "Mississippi, You're on My Hind" into the country Top 40 in 1975. *—William Ruhlmann*

Let the Rough Side Drag / 1976 / Stony Plain ♦♦♦

At his best, Jesse Winchester is an inspired songwriter with a unique worldview. But even at less than his best, he is a craftsman, capable of turning out an album's worth of well-written songs like those here that, now and then, suggest his personal viewpoint. The title track, another of Winchester's reflections on the importance of persevering under difficult circumstances, and "Damned If You Do," which suggests that you might as well follow your heart because you're in trouble either way, are up to his usual standard. But even slight songs like "Everybody Knows But Me" are clever and enjoyable, and overall, *Let the Rough Side Drag*, with its accomplished mixture of country and R&B, was Winchester's most accessible album so far, even if it was his least ambitious. *—William Ruhlmann*

Nothing But a Breeze / 1977 / Stony Plain ♦♦♦

Jesse Winchester regularly took two years between record releases, but he brought in his fifth album, *Nothing but a Breeze*, a mere nine months after its predecessor, *Let the Rough Side Drag*. The impetus for such speed seems to have been the potential commercial bonanza to be gained by Winchester's first U.S. appearances since he moved to Canada to avoid the draft in 1967, due to President Jimmy Carter's amnesty program. Winchester also used a real producer, Brian Ahern (known for his work with Emmylou Harris), for the first time, and augmented his usual backup band with session stars such as Ricky Skaggs and James Burton, plus supporting vocalists like Harris and Anne Murray. The result was an Ahern-style country-pop album, but, perhaps predictably, a rather light effort for Winchester, who performed three covers among the ten tracks and included among the originals such comic trifles as "Twigs and Seeds" and "Rhumba Man." The title track, which became his first singles-chart entry, and "My Songbird," which Harris later covered, were effective songs, but the significance of *Nothing but a Breeze*, which enjoyed a media buzz and became Winchester's highest-charting album (which isn't saying much), was in inverse proportion to the attention it received. *—William Ruhlmann*

A Touch on the Rainy Side / 1978 / Stony Plain ♦♦♦

With American recording studios open to him for the first time, Jesse Winchester traveled to Nashville and enlisted producer Norbert Putnam, who assembled the elements of the Nashville Sound, with its strings and horns and backup choruses, to make an album that moved him more toward lush country and especially R&B. Winchester's flexible voice, capable of gliding into a sweet falsetto, made the latter more successful than might have been expected. What kept the album from being one of his better collections was not the slick production, it was the material. A year after a media blitz had failed to make him a star, Winchester was starting to show signs of strain. He led the album off with the title track, an explicit expression of devotion to his wife, who he mentioned by name. This was followed by a sour on-the-road song, "A Showman's Life," and later on there were tributes to driving and drinking. In fact, the most heartfelt song was "Little Glass of Wine," an alcoholic's love song. None of this was up to his songwriting standard. *—William Ruhlmann*

Talk Memphis / 1981 / Stony Plain ♦♦♦

Humour Me / 1988 / Sugar Hill ♦♦♦

● **The Best of Jesse Winchester** / 1989 / Rhino ♦♦♦♦♦

Jesse Winchester wrote and recorded more than enough great songs for Bearsville to fill a single-disc compilation, which means that some of them were bound to be left off. The trick was to balance the material from the brilliant first two albums with a careful selection from the subsequent five albums, each of which had its virtues. This 14-track album chooses four from *Jesse Winchester*, including the essential "Yankee Lady," "Biloxi," and "The Brand New Tennessee Waltz," and three from its follow-up, *Third Down, 110 to Go*. There are three from *Learn to Love It*, one each from *Nothing but a Breeze* and *A Touch on the Rainy Side*, and two from *Talk Memphis*. Lesser material such as "Tell Me Why You Like Roosevelt" and "Rhumba Man" could have been excised in favor of more from *Third Down*, but the selection is good enough to give a reasonable representation of

Winchester's seven Bearsville albums, which contain some of the most impressive songwriting of the 1970s. —*William Ruhlmann*

Gentleman of Leisure / Jun. 22, 1999 / Sugar Hill ✦✦✦✦

From the opening vocals of the almost rockabilly "Club Manhattan," the undeniably excellent songwriting of Jesse Winchester makes its way back into our collective psyche. Backed by an unparalleled group of musicians, and with guest appearances from such musical dignitaries as the Fairfield Four, Jerry Douglas, Steve "The Colonel" Cropper, and Vince Gill, Winchester has assembled a highly enjoyable album, filled with the same magic his past releases all possessed. The kind of musical and lyrical genius that has caused dozens of artists to record his music gets into some funky blues territory with "Sweet Little Shoe," and downright beautiful with "That's What Makes You Strong," featuring the lap steel guitar work of Jerry Douglas, who also acts as producer for the album. The title track is a rocking blues number with some out-in-front drums from John Gardner and more of Jerry Douglas' excellent lap steel. "Wander My Way Back Home," a gospel tune, backed by the fabulous Fairfield Four, is one of the album's best tracks, and is reprised at the very end of the record. "Just Because I'm in Love With You" brings some Roy Orbison feeling, with flawless harmonies from country superstar Vince Gill. "Sweet Loving Daddy" features some fine dobro picking from Douglas, but the absolute finest track on the album has to be the final cut, "I Wave Bye Bye." *Gentleman of Leisure* is an album 11 years on coming, and it was well worth the wait. —*Michael B. Smith*

Windy & Carl

f. 1991, Dearborn, MI
Space Rock, Indie Rock, Post-Rock/Experimental
A leading light of the Michigan space-rock scene, the Dearborn-based duo Windy and Carl comprised guitarist Carl Hultgren and bassist Windy Weber. Hultgren first began recording instrumental guitar-drone pieces in 1992, self-releasing a cassette, *Portal*, before teaming with Weber; by the end of 1993 they issued a single, "Watersong," on their own Blue Flea label. From 1994 to 1995 Windy and Carl expanded to a quartet with the inclusion of guitarist/keyboardist Randall Nieman and percussionist Brenda Markovich; the reconfigured group later issued an EP, *Drifting*, which was credited to Once Dreamt. After the departures of both Nieman (who went on to form Füxa) and Markovich, Windy and Carl continued as a duo, reissuing *Portal* complete with new material in 1994; the LP *Drawing of Sound* followed a year later, and in 1998 the duo resurfaced with *Depths*. The following year, the duo collaborated with synthesist Greg Gasiorowski and released the album *Five Way Mirror*; in 2000, they appeared at Terrastock and recorded their fourth album *Consciousness*. Windy & Carl also run a record store in Dearborn, MI called Stormy Records. —*Jason Ankeny*

Portal / Nov. 1994 / Blue Flea ✦✦✦

The reissued version of Windy & Carl's debut album includes a full hour of shimmering aural concrete and guitar-feedback ambience, with a focus on space travel indicated by track titles "Preparation," "Sound Ignition," and "Exploration." —*John Bush*

Drawing of Sound / Mar. 1996 / Blue Flea ✦✦✦✦

Dream of Blue / Oct. 1997 / Ochre ✦✦✦

● **Depths** / Mar. 23, 1998 / Kranky ✦✦✦

Though it's another album of slow-building textural ambience, *Depths* is quite organic-sounding compared to the duo's debut. Besides the spacious noise that remains a focus, there are several tracks of faraway guitar pop ("Silent Ocean" and "Undercurrent" are highlights) that include vocals (by Windy) much closer to singing than their previous work. —*John Bush*

Windy & Carl & The Lothars / 2000 / Blue Flea ✦✦✦

Consciousness / 2001 / Kranky ✦✦✦✦

The world of experimental rock is crowded with musicians seeking to add more and varied sounds to their growing body of recorded work, while restlessly seeking to diversify their approach by absorbing more and more from outside their musical universe in terms of form, source, and stylistic considerations. Dearborn, MI, duo Windy & Carl tread a different path: They are interested—no—obsessed with creating a musical aesthetic based solely on digging ever deeper into the sub-subbasement of drone-based guitar music. As evidenced by this, their fourth long-player, they've accomplished that. Windy & Carl, with their deceptively spare production mannerisms and subtle shadings of guitars, barely audible vocals, some keyboards, and employed sounds from other spheres, have developed a manner of letting the music speak for itself through them. By getting out of the way, they have developed a signature that belongs to them (apart from stealing an Archie Shepp album cover from the 1970s to illustrate this small wonder). While the tone of their music is always contemplative, it is never static: Movement happens at different speeds, in odd ebbs and flows, but travel is inherently what the music on *Consciousness* is all about. *Consciousness* is humble, moving, and brilliant. It's an achievement when a band creates an aesthetic, holds beauty as a goal in and of itself, and knows how endless the pursuit of it is. —*Thom Jurek*

Winger

f. 1986, New York, NY
Pop-Metal, Hair Metal, Heavy Metal, Hard Rock
A former member of Alice Cooper's band, bassist Kip Winger formed his own group in 1986; in addition to vocalist/bassist Winger, the group featured guitarist Reb Beach, bassist Paul Taylor, and drummer Rod Morgenstein, formerly of The Dixie Dregs. Taking its name from its leader, Winger specialized in the stylish pop-metal that sent Bon Jovi and Poison to the top of the charts. The band's eponymous debut sold over a million

copies on the strength of the rocker "Seventeen" and the ballad "Headed for a Heartbreak." Winger's second album, 1990's *In the Heart of the Young*, was equally successful, selling over a million copies and featuring the hit power-ballad "Miles Away." However, the band didn't outlast the post-alternative pop-metal backlash and the group faded away after the release of its 1993 album *Pull*. Kip Winger launched a solo career at the tail end of the '90s. —*Stephen Thomas Erlewine*

● **Winger** / 1988 / Atlantic ✦✦✦✦✦

Since Winger was marketed largely on the looks of lead singer Kip Winger, and since their sleazy rockers and lovelorn ballads cover the same old pop-metal territory, the band's high-quality musicianship tended to get overlooked. Guitarist Reb Beach earned wide praise from other musicians, and he, ex-Dixie Dregs drummer Rod Morgenstein, and keyboardist Paul Taylor bring a distinct progressive-metal influence to many of the tunes on *Winger*. Even if the lyrics are standard-issue, the album is impeccably composed, crafted, and played, with melodies, riffs, and guitar solos taking off in unexpected directions and keeping the listener slightly off balance—no easy task in the cookie-cutter hair-metal genre. The only misstep is an overdone, tight-assed, totally misguided recasting of "Purple Haze." Otherwise, *Winger* is a surprisingly accomplished debut. —*Steve Huey*

In the Heart of the Young / 1990 / Atlantic ✦✦✦

Winger's second album, *In the Heart of the Young*, continues in the same vein of slick, progressive-tinged, radio-ready pop-metal featured on their debut—almost what Asia or *90125*-era Yes might sound like as hair bands. The melodies and guitars still twist and turn in unpredictable directions, but the material on *In the Heart of the Young* isn't always as musically interesting as the songs on *Winger*. Plus, the inclusion of more ballads detracts from the overall energy. Still, there's enough here to make the album worthwhile for anyone who enjoyed its predecessor, especially in the absence of a best-of collection. "Miles Away" became a Gulf War love anthem, while "Can't Get Enuff" and "Easy Come Easy Go" are fine rockers that nevertheless failed to make much of a dent in the charts. —*Steve Huey*

Pull / May 18, 1993 / Atlantic ✦✦

The Winkies

Pub Rock
Of all the songwriters and performers who were thrown into the spotlight during the early to mid-'70s, yet never attained more than a modicum of mainstream success, few proved as accomplished as Phil Rambow. Author of such modern classics as "Night Out" and "Young Lust" (for Ellen Foley) and "There's a Guy Works Down the Chip Shop Swears He's Elvis" with Kirsty MacColl, Rambow himself also emerged as a major player on two of the most important underground scenes of the era: the British pub rock boom of the early to mid-'70s and the near-concurrent New York proto-punk explosion. Forming his band, the Winkies, with ex-Holy Rollers guitarist Guy Humphreys and the rhythm section of Brian Torrington and Mike Desmaris, Rambow's outrageous stage persona immediately attracted attention—a pub rock band in glam rock clothing, they were everything that their compatriots on the bar scene weren't: blatant, theatrical, and flashy as hell. It was this which drew the interest of Eno, as he prepared to launch his first solo album, *Here Come the Warm Jets*. Impressed by the Winkies' performance, he adopted them as his backing band. The brevity of the union notwithstanding, the Winkies time with Eno slammed them into the limelight; by late spring 1974, the band had signed with Chrysalis and was recording their debut album with producer Leo Lyons of Ten Years After. Sadly, the album was never completed; instead, the Winkies began work on another set, this time with maverick Guy Stevens at the helm. *The Winkies* finally appeared in spring 1975. Unfortunately, much of the fervor surrounding the group had dissipated. The record did nothing and by early summer, the Winkies had disbanded. —*Dave Thompson*

● **The Winkies** / 1975 / Chrysalis ✦✦✦✦

Time has done *The Winkies* considerably more favors than contemporary critics ever did. It does still sound like vintage Mott, but that's something to be celebrated now—imagine if Ian Hunter and Co. had not gone off with David Bowie following 1971's madcap *Brain Capers* album, but if Ariel Bender had joined the group regardless. *The Winkies* is edgy urban rock, as distinctly Dylan influenced as its role model, but shot through with Philip Rambow's chiming, scything guitars and strained, emotional vocals. There're hints of the Heavy Metal Kids in the mix, and that's a grand thing as well—side by side, their debut and *The Winkies* illuminate the future direction of British street rock as brightly as any other period albums you could name. True to the pub rock template, there are occasional glances towards beery country ("North to Alaska"), and a nod towards heartland Americana (Bob Seger's "Long Song Comin'"). But the heart of *The Winkies* is carved out between Rambow's slow-burning "Red Dog" and Guy Humphreys' "Put Out the Light," tough blues stompers with a Stonesy grind and an enviably dissolute lurch. While everyone else was doing the greasy boogie shuffle, here come the Winkies sounding sexy as your sister. In a way, the mid-'70s critics were right. *The Winkies* isn't the album it could have been; may not be the record it should have been. But all that really means is, the band didn't trot obediently off down the path they were meant to and looked instead to their own needs and instincts. The future would thank them for their indulgence. —*Dave Thompson*

Winter Hours

Folk-Rock, Alternative Pop/Rock
Strongly influenced by early Buffalo Springfield, Bob Dylan and Gene Clark-era Byrds, Winter Hours' rootsy, aggressive style put them in sharp contrast with their late '80s rock brethren. A quintet consisting of Joseph Marques on vocals, Michael Carlucci on guitar, Bob Perry on guitars and vocals, Bob Messing on bass and Stanley Demeski on drums,

the band built up a presence on college radio after opening for artists like the Bongos, the Godfathers, Let's Active, the Hoodoo Gurus and Marshall Crenshaw. By the time they had signed with Link Records and issued their first EP, 1985's *Churches*, they had a new drummer, John Albanese. Four more EPs followed in 1986 on Link, *Wait till the Morning*, The *Confessional*, *Leaving Time* and *Say the Word* (which featured another new drummer, Frank Fiannini). The same endless touring that helped build their fan base also brought them to the attention of Chrysalis Records, who signed the band and issued a self-titled LP in 1989. Their final personnel change came with that album, with yet another drummer, Dave Scheff. This lineup would release one last single in 1989, "Roadside Flowers," before officially deciding to split two years later. *—Stacia Proefrock*

Leaving Time / 1985 / Link ♦♦♦
... *Leaving Time* is more of the same: ringing guitars, clearly articulated Stipe-like lyrics, and polite but firm rhythmic support. I did find myself falling for "The Confessional," "Waiting for the Thunder," and "Up There Again," but... I seriously doubt if my interest will ever become more than nominal. *—John Dougan*

Wait 'Till the Morning / 1986 / Link ♦♦♦♦
Compilation of two early EPs and some singles. It lacks the punch of Chrysalis's release but is a very tuneful and engaging record, with some pleasing rough edges. *—Bruce Eder*

● **Winter Hours** / 1989 / Chrysalis ♦♦♦♦
Self-titled album resounds with echoes of Neil Young, Pete Townshend, and Phil Ochs, haunting melodies, and dazzling guitar by Mike Carlucci. A must-own for anyone who ever cared about any of those three influences. *—Bruce Eder*

Johnny Winter

b. Feb. 23, 1944, Beaumont, TX
Slide Guitar, Vocals, Harmonica, Guitar / Slide Guitar Blues, Album Rock, Modern Electric Texas Blues, Boogie Rock, Arena Rock, Hard Rock, Blues-Rock, Modern Electric Blues
Blues guitarist Winter became a major star in the late '60s and early '70s. Since that time he's confirmed his reputation in the blues by working with Muddy Waters and continuing to play in the style, despite musical fashion. Born in Beaumont, TX, Winter formed his first band at 14 with his brother Edgar in Beaumont, and spent his youth in recording studios cutting regional singles and in bars playing the blues. His discovery on a national level came via an article in *Rolling Stone* in 1968, which led to a management contract with New York club owner Steve Paul and a record deal with Columbia. His debut album (there are numerous albums of juvenilia), *Johnny Winter*, reached the charts in 1969. Starting out with a trio, Winter later formed a band with former members of The McCoys, including second guitarist Rick Derringer. It was called Johnny Winter And. He achieved a sales peak in 1971 with the gold-selling *Live/Johnny Winter And*. He returned in 1973 with *Still Alive and Well*, his highest-charting album. His albums became more overtly blues-oriented in the late '70s and he also produced several albums for Muddy Waters. In the '80s he switched to the blues label Alligator for three albums, and has since recorded for the labels MCA and Pointblank/Virgin. *Back In Beaumont* was released in 2000. *—William Ruhlmann*

Johnny Winter / 1969 / Columbia ♦♦♦♦♦
Winter's debut album for Columbia was also arguably his bluesiest and best. Straight out of Texas with a hot trio, Winter made blues-rock music for the angels, tearing up a cheap Fender guitar with total abandon on tracks like "I'm Yours and I'm Hers," "Leland Mississippi Blues," and perhaps the slow blues moment to die for on this set, B.B. King's "Be Careful With a Fool." Winter's playing and vocals have yet to become mannered or clichéd on this session, and if you've ever wondered what the fuss is all about, here's the best place to check out his true legacy. *—Cub Koda*

The Progressive Blues Experiment / 1969 / Razor & Tie ♦♦♦
Although his early Columbia albums brought him worldwide stardom, it was this modest little album (first released on Imperial before the Columbia sides) that first brought Johnny Winter to the attention of guitarheads in America. It's also Winter at the beginning of a long career, playing the blues as if his life depends on it, without applying a glimmer of rock commercialism. The standard classic repertoire here includes "Rollin' & Tumblin'," "Got Love If You Want It," "44," "It's My Own Fault," and "Help Me," with Winter mixing it up with his original Texas trio of Red Turner on drums and Tommy Shannon (later of Stevie Ray Vaughan's *Double Trouble*) on bass. A true classic. *—Cub Koda*

● **Second Winter** / 1969 / Columbia ♦♦♦♦♦
Johnny's second Columbia album shows an artist in transition. He's still obviously a Texas bluesman, recording in the same trio format that he left Dallas with. But his music is moving toward the more rock & roll sounds he would go on to create. The opener, "Memory Pain," moves him into psychedelic blues-rock territory, while old-time rockers like "Johnny B. Goode," "Miss Ann," and "Slippin' and Slidin'" provide him with familiar landscapes on which to spray his patented licks. His reworking of Dylan's "Highway 61 Revisited" is the high spot of the record, a career-defining track that's still a major component of his modern-day set list. This was originally released back in the day as a three-sided vinyl double album, by the way. *—Cub Koda*

Johnny Winter And... / 1970 / DCC ♦♦♦♦♦
Winter puts together a new band and takes on the assistance of Rick Derringer, who co-produces and provides such great songs as "Rock & Roll, Hoochie Koo." *—William Ruhlmann*

Johnny Winter And... Live / 1971 / Columbia ♦♦♦
Winter and his new band turn out hard-rock versions of "Jumpin' Jack Flash," "Johnny B. Goode," and other rock & roll favorites. *—William Ruhlmann*

Still Alive and Well / 1973 / Columbia ♦♦♦
Still Alive and Well proved to the record buying public that Johnny Winter was both. This is a truly enjoyable album, chock full of great tunes played well. Johnny's version of the Rolling Stones' "Silver Train" shows us the potential this song has and what the Stones failed to capture. Everything here is good, so get it and dig in. *—James Chrispell*

Saints & Sinners / 1974 / Columbia ♦♦♦
Johnny Winter's sixth Columbia album was also his second since his comeback from drug addiction. Its predecessor, *Still Alive and Well*, had been his highest charting effort. *Saints & Sinners* was just as energetically played, but its mixture of material, including 1950s rock & roll oldies like Chuck Berry's "Thirty Days," Larry Williams' "Bony Moronie," and Leiber and Stoller's "Riot in Cell Block #9," recent covers like the Rolling Stones' "Stray Cat Blues," and a couple of originals, was more eclectic than inspired. (Van Morrison completists should note that the album also contains Winter's cover of Morrison's "Feedback on Highway 101," a typical bluesy groove song that Morrison recorded for his 1973 *Hardnose the Highway* album but dropped. Winter's is the only released recording of the song.) Abetted by the members of the old Johnny Winter And band, Rick Derringer, Randy Hobbs, and Richard Hughes, plus his brother Edgar and Dan Hartman, Winter produced forceful hard rock focused on his searing lead guitar runs and rough-edged voice. It was the less-impressive choice of material that kept this collection from matching its predecessor. (Originally released in February 1974, *Saints & Sinners* was reissued on February 27, 1996 with the previously unreleased song "Dirty," a Winter original, added. The slide guitar-and-flute track is not consistent with the rest of the album, but it is interesting to hear. Wonder who played the flute?) *—William Ruhlmann*

Nothin' But the Blues / 1977 / Blue Sky ♦♦♦♦
After a long period making rock records, Winter fronts the Muddy Waters band (with Waters singing) on this Chicago blues workout. He sounds happier than ever before. *—William Ruhlmann*

Guitar Slinger / 1984 / Alligator ♦♦♦♦
The first of three blues albums recorded after a four-year studio hiatus finds Winter as fleet-fingered as before and sounding more vocally involved than in some of the later Columbia material. *—William Ruhlmann*

Birds Can't Row Boats / 1988 / Relix ♦♦♦♦
Aside from "Ice Cube" (a 1959 instrumental), these tracks date from 1965-68. Many are previously unissued or only available on rare 45s. Those accustomed to his more famous recordings are in for a jolt, as this shows Johnny in several unexpected settings: grinding Texas psych-punk, the British Invasion-cum-folk-rock garage single "Gone for Bad," blue-eyed R&B/soul, an Everly Brothers cover, a *Highway 61*-era Dylan imitation, and even a shit-kickin' C&W tune. There are also some straight, predominantly acoustic blues numbers. *—Richie Unterberger*

Let Me In / Aug. 1991 / Pointblank ♦♦♦♦
Let Me In is a star-studded all-blues set from Johnny Winter, featuring cameos from Dr. John, Albert Collins, and several others. Though the set focuses on blues material, Winters can never leave his rock roots behind—the sheer volume and pile-driving energy of his performances ensures that. For most of the record, his enthusiasm is contagious, but there are a couple of bland, generic exercises that fail to work up a head of steam. But there is a lovely acoustic number called "Blue Mood," which shows Winter trying to stretch a bit by playing jazzy licks. It's a refreshing change of pace. *—Thom Owens*

Scorchin' Blues / Jun. 16, 1992 / Epic/Legacy ♦♦♦
Scorchin' Blues marries tracks from Johnny Winter's early Columbia albums—including the classic National steel-driven "Dallas" from his 1969 debut—with material from his return-to-roots Blue Sky period in the late '70s. The aggressive playing and raunchy vocals will appeal to both blues and rock fans, and Ben Sandmel crams an authoritative biography into seven pages, complete with interesting Winter quotes. The one downside: a miserly ten tracks spread over only 45 minutes of playing time. *—Roch Parisien*

Collection / Jun. 30, 1992 / Castle ♦♦♦

Hey, Where's Your Brother? / Jul. 1992 / Pointblank ♦♦♦

A Rock & Roll Collection / 1994 / Columbia/Legacy ♦♦♦♦♦
A two-CD survey of Winter's recordings for Columbia between 1969 and 1979, the era of his greatest commercial success. This collects many of his most popular tracks, though it doesn't do much to argue a case for artistic diversity. Includes two otherwise unavailable songs: an alternate take of "30 Days," and a previously unreleased 1973 cover of Robert Johnson's "Come on in My Kitchen." *—Richie Unterberger*

Relix's Best of the Blues, Vol. 2 / Apr. 15, 1997 / Relix ♦♦♦

Deluxe Edition / Jan. 30, 2001 / Alligator ♦♦♦♦♦
Johnny Winter joined Chicago's Alligator Records in 1984 after a four-year recording hiatus. Following 12 generally spotty albums and 11 years associated with Columbia, either on their label or his own Blue Sky imprint (which they distributed), Winter was itching to get back to the sparse, house-rocking, rough Texas blues on which he made his name, and forego the flashy rock & roll which dominated many of his patchy albums. His three albums for the label were released in three consecutive years: *Guitar Slinger*, *Serious Business*, and *Third Degree* were slam-bang affairs that provided an ideal forum for Winter's gritty voice and edgy, quicksilver guitar firepower. This 14-track compilation of these years rounds up the best of those releases and is a testament to the albino bluesman's substantial talents musically and as an interpreter of other artists' material. He sounds positively enthusiastic throughout, whooping and hollering like it's his first time in the studio, and when he whips out his nasty slide the searing intensity of his tone practically rips through the speakers. Winter does a bit of fast country-blues on "Broke and Lonely"

and pulls out his National steel on Memphis Willie B's "Bad Girl Blues," but generally these cuts find the guitarist in fine boogie form. The collection closes with *Guitar Slinger*'s "Kiss Tomorrow Goodbye," a smoking slice of '50s R&B that proved all too prophetic; he was to release only two more studio albums of original material through the end of the century. Winter's subsequent work in the '90s was sporadically energized, seldom matching the ground-rumbling yet uncluttered approach he favored during these crucial years. *—Hal Horowitz*

Steve Winwood

b. May 12, 1948, Birmingham, England
Vocals, Keyboards, Guitar, Organ / Album Rock, Blue-Eyed Soul, Pop/Rock, Adult Contemporary

Singer/songwriter, keyboardist, and guitarist Steve Winwood was a well-known musician long before he finally embarked on a solo career in the second half of the '70s. Born in Birmingham, England, Winwood joined the Spencer Davis Group with his older brother Muff when he was only 15 years old. His was the soulful, Ray Charles-like voice on such hits as "Gimme Some Lovin'" and "I'm a Man," songs he also co-wrote. In 1967 he formed Traffic, which he led, with time off for the supergroup Blind Faith in 1969, until 1974. Winwood finally released his first solo album in 1977 and, in 1981 had his first million-seller with his second album, *Arc of a Diver. Talking Back to the Night* (1982) was not as much of a success, and Winwood spent four years preparing *Back in the High Life* (1986), which sold three million copies. *Roll with It* (1988) went to number one, but *Refugees of the Heart* (1990) was not up to his usual standard.

After the relative failure of *Refugees of the Heart*, Winwood and Jim Capaldi re-formed Traffic in 1994; although their record and tour were well-received, the reunion wasn't as successful as expected, and Winwood began work on a solo album in 1995. Two years later he presented the result: *Junction Seven. —William Ruhlmann*

Steve Winwood / Jun. 1977 / Island ◆◆◆
Rock fans had been waiting for a Steve Winwood solo album for more than a decade, as he made his way through such bands as the Spencer Davis Group and Traffic. When Winwood finally delivered with this LP, just about everybody was disappointed. Traffic had finally petered out three years before, but Winwood, using such former members as Jim Capaldi and Reebop Kwaku Baah, failed to project a strong individual identity outside the group. That great voice was singing the songs, that talented guitarist/keyboardist was playing them, and that excellent songwriter had composed them, but nothing here was memorable, and the long-awaited debut proved a bust. *—William Ruhlmann*

Arc of a Diver / Jan. 1981 / Island ◆◆◆◆◆
Utterly unencumbered by the baggage of his long years in the music business, Winwood reinvents himself as a completely contemporary artist on this outstanding album, leading off with his best solo song, "While You See a Chance." Winwood also plays all the instruments. *—William Ruhlmann*

Talking Back to the Night / Aug. 1982 / Island ◆◆◆
Okay, so after missing with his first solo album, Steve Winwood had hit the jackpot with his second, *Arc of a Diver*, finally fulfilling his enormous promise. What did he do next? He returned to the record racks only a year and a half later with this retread, which attempted to turn the "While You See a Chance" sound into a formula and to a large extent succeeded, unfortunately. "Valerie" (number 70 U.S., number 51 U.K.), the leadoff track, had that same keyboard sound and tempo, and Winwood kept it up for much of the rest of the record, including the album's biggest U.S. single, "Still in the Game" (number 47). Fans were dismayed, and *Talking Back to the Night* had an even lower chart peak than *Steve Winwood. —William Ruhlmann*

● **Back in the High Life** / Jun. 1986 / Island ◆◆◆◆◆
Turning to involved percussion tracks and horns, Winwood turns another musical corner on this sophisticated album, which contains echoes of everything from gospel to Caribbean music. Contains the number one hit "Higher Love." *—William Ruhlmann*

Chronicles / Nov. 1987 / Island ◆◆◆◆◆
This isn't an adequate compilation of the years 1977-1986, but it does manage to gather some of the better songs of the period. *—William Ruhlmann*

Roll with It / Jun. 1988 / Virgin ◆◆◆
Winwood manages to reintroduce some of the R&B elements of the Spencer Davis Group and some of the psychedelic effects of early Traffic here, though this is also an effective follow-up to the directions indicated on *Back in the High Life*. Contains the number one title track and "Don't You Know What the Night Can Do?" *—William Ruhlmann*

Refugees of the Heart / Nov. 1990 / Virgin ◆◆◆
The key to Steve Winwood's solo career is inconsistency; *Refugees of the Heart* was a letdown. The distinction between a great Winwood album and one that's only okay is dangerously small—it has more to do with performance than composition—and on *Refugees of the Heart*, as on *Talking Back to the Night*, Winwood was unable to invest Will Jennings' pedestrian lyrics with the soulful feeling of which he's capable. The album's standout is a collaboration with ex-Traffic partner Jim Capaldi, "One and Only Man," which topped *Billboard*'s Album Rock Tracks chart. Perhaps noting this exception, Winwood next teamed with Capaldi in a 1994 reunion of Traffic. *—William Ruhlmann*

The Finer Things / Mar. 21, 1995 / Island ◆◆◆◆◆
Steve Winwood has led a long and varied career, recording everything from straight R&B and jazz-flavored rock to folk and pop. Over the course of four discs, *The Finer Things* chronicles the entirety of his career, beginning with The Spencer Davis Group, through Traffic and Blind Faith, right until his successful solo career. It includes all of the hits and many of his finest album tracks, yet the overall approach is rather exhausting—the

rarities are rarely illuminating, they're just there for the sake of being there. Nevertheless, it is a worthwhile purchase for anyone wanting a comprehensive picture of Winwood in all of his various guises. *—Stephen Thomas Erlewine*

Junction Seven / Jun. 3, 1997 / Virgin ◆◆

20th Century Masters—The Millennium Collection: The Best of Steve Winwood / Oct. 19, 1999 / Island ◆◆◆◆
This volume of *20th Century Masters: The Millennium Collection* may have been released under Steve Winwood's name, but that's slightly misleading. True, he does sing lead on all these songs, but there are no solo recordings here—just Spencer Davis Group, Traffic, and Blind Faith numbers. In that sense, it's actually a welcome compilation, since it's the first of its kind. True, this isn't definitive, but it has all the major songs here—"Gimme Some Lovin'," "I'm a Man," "Paper Sun," "Dear Mr. Fantasy," "Pearly Queen," "Can't Find My Way Home," "John Barleycorn," "Low Spark of High Heeled Boys"—that will make it a good choice for casual fans looking to supplement a solo recordings collection. *—Stephen Thomas Erlewine*

The Wipers

f. 1978, Portland, OR
Indie Rock, Hardcore Punk, Alternative Pop/Rock, Punk, American Underground
By bridging the gap between hard rock and punk, the Wipers managed to create a surprisingly influential style of post-punk. Led by guitarist Greg Sage, the band melded the furious rage and independent punk ethic with a fondness for loud, long guitar workouts. Sage was one of the few immediate post-punk guitarists that played by the conventional rules of a guitar hero, including several long guitar solos, without losing his indie edge.

The Wipers formed in Portland, OR, in the late '70s; the group released their first album in 1979. Two years later, the band delivered the *Youth of America* EP, which featured a slightly different lineup than the debut. The group recorded five more albums during the '80s (Sage also released a solo record, *Straight Ahead*, in 1985), before breaking up in 1988. While they never gained much more than a cult audience while they were recording, the Wipers managed to influence a number of musicians, including Nirvana's Kurt Cobain and J. Mascis of Dinosaur Jr. Consequently, the band was arguably better known in the early '90s than in the early '80s, when they were active.

Greg Sage assembled a new lineup of the Wipers in 1995, releasing *The Herd*—his first studio album in eight years—early in 1996. *—Stephen Thomas Erlewine*

Is This Real? / 1980 / Sub Pop ◆◆◆◆
The production leaves much to be desired with its tinny-sounding drums, but, fortunately, the negatives don't outweigh the positives on this album. Guitarist/vocalist Greg Sage writes fairly simplistic songs with power chords, but each melody infects your brain like a fever. Even though Sage is from Oregon, he sings in a New York-style slur not dissimilar to Joey Ramone. Throughout the album, there is a very dark and ominous feel to the material (e.g., "D-7"), but it's made interesting on tracks like "Alien Boy," which changes from 4/4 time to 2/4 time. Sage also has a unique guitar style where he strums chords and lets them sustain into feedback, which creates rich textures in the songs (e.g., "Potential Suicide" and "Don't Know What I Am"). *—Stephen Howell*

Over the Edge / 1983 / Restless ◆◆◆◆◆
By far their best. Aggressive and direct, this burns! *—John Dougan*

● **The Best of Wipers and Greg Sage** / 1990 / Restless ◆◆◆◆◆
The Wipers have a long-standing reputation as sounding like "Jimi Hendrix fronting a garage band," and while Greg Sage's nimble fretwork might draw comparisons to Hendrix, the Wipers prove on this disc that they're far more proficient than any garage band. The pulsating rhythm section manages to sound vibrant but subdued, allowing Sage's squelching guitar noise to dominate the palette. Unlike other guitar luminaries whose popularity is restrained to a specific audience (e.g., gearheads for Joe Satriani, stoners for Kyuss), Sage's fretboard ramblings made him the favorite guitar hero of the late-'80s underground rock scene. From the deadly riff of "Taking Too Long" to the textured frustration of "Way of Love" to the ringing desire of "Just a Dream Away," Sage proves he is both a versatile and unique talent. Not just among the best of the U.S. post-punk wave, but an enormously influential act that made an indelible mark on styles as disparate as the noise rock of Sonic Youth and Pavement's slacker indie pop. *—Ari Wiznitzer*

Wire

f. 1976, London, England, **db.** 1991
British Punk, Experimental Rock, Post-Punk, Alternative Pop/Rock, Punk, College Rock
Wire's brief, fractured songs and minimalistic sound made the band the artiest of all punk bands, as well as one of the most influential. Unlike most other punk bands, their stripped-down approach was not an attempt to get back to rock's roots; it was cutting the music to its raw nerve, so nothing extraneous was left. Their nervy, dissonant avant-pop sound was more art experiment than rock & roll and as a result, their 1977 debut *Pink Flag* was a revolutionary album, a collection of 21 brief songs that displayed a blinding array of ideas. The two follow-ups to *Pink Flag, Chairs Missing* and *154*, were more measured and detailed records, boasting layered productions. Though they weren't as visionary as the band's debut, they refined and expanded the group's sound, earning great critical praise in the process. Just as the group's cult following was growing, Wire suddenly broke up in late 1979. After spending several years pursuing various solo projects, the band members reunited in 1986. For the next five years, Wire released a series of experimental pop records which generally received popular reviews. However, their cult was slowly shrinking, and the group disbanded for good in 1991. All three main members, Colin Newman, Bruce Gilbert and Graham Lewis, pursued solo projects. *—Stephen Thomas Erlewine*

☆ **Pink Flag** / Dec. 1977 / Restless ✦✦✦✦✦

Perhaps the most original debut album to come out of the first wave of British punk, Wire's *Pink Flag* plays like *The Ramones Go to Art School*—song after song careens past in a glorious, stripped-down rush. However, unlike the Ramones, Wire ultimately made their mark through unpredictability. Very few of the songs followed traditional verse/chorus structures—if one or two riffs sufficed, no more were added; if a musical hook or lyric didn't need to be repeated, Wire immediately stopped playing, accounting for the album's brevity (21 songs in under 36 minutes on the original version). The sometimes dissonant, minimalist arrangements allow for space and interplay between the instruments; Colin Newman isn't always the most comprehensible singer, but he displays an acerbic wit and balances the occasional lyrical abstraction with plenty of bile in his delivery. Many punk bands aimed to strip rock & roll of its excess, but Wire took the concept a step further, cutting punk itself down to its essence and achieving an even more concentrated impact. Some of the tracks may seem at first like underdeveloped sketches or fragments, but further listening demonstrates that in most cases, the music is memorable even without the repetition and structure most ears have come to expect—it simply requires a bit more concentration. And Wire is full of ideas; for such a fiercely minimalist band, they display quite a musical range, spanning slow, haunting texture exercises, warped power pop, punk anthems, and proto-hardcore rants—it's recognizable, yet simultaneously quite unlike anything that preceded it. *Pink Flag's* enduring influence pops up in hardcore, post-punk, alternative rock, and even Brit-pop, and it still remains a fresh, invigorating listen today: a fascinating, highly inventive rethinking of punk rock and its freedom to make up your own rules. *—Steve Huey*

☆ **Chairs Missing** / Aug. 1978 / Restless ✦✦✦✦✦

Chairs Missing marks a partial retreat from *Pink Flag's* austere, bare-bones minimalism, although it still takes concentrated listening to dig out some of the melodies. Producer Mike Thorne's synth adds a Brian Eno-esque layer of atmospherics, and Wire itself seems more concerned with the sonic textures they can coax from their instruments; the tempos are slower, the arrangements employ more detail and sound effects, and the band allows itself to stretch out on a few songs. The results are a bit variable—"Mercy," in particular, meanders for too long—but compelling much more often than not. The album's clear high point is the statement of purpose "I Am the Fly," which employs an emphasis-shifting melody and guitar sounds which actually evoke the sound of the title insect. But that's not all by any means—"Outdoor Miner" and "Used To" have a gentle lilt, while "Sand in My Joints" is a brief anthem worthy of *Pink Flag*, and the four-minute "Practice Makes Perfect" is the best result of the album's incorporation of odd electronic flavors. In general, the lyrics are darker than those on *Pink Flag*, even morbid at times; images of cold, drowning, pain, and suicide haunt the record, and the title itself is a reference to mental instability. The arty darkness of *Chairs Missing*, combined with the often icy-sounding synth/guitar arrangements, help make the record a crucial landmark in the evolution of punk into post-punk and goth, as well as a testament to Wire's rapid development and inventiveness. [The CD reissue contains three bonus tracks: the fine non-LP single "A Question of Degree" and the B-sides "Go Ahead" and "Former Airline."] *—Steve Huey*

154 / 1979 / Restless ✦✦✦✦✦

Named for the number of live gigs Wire had played to that point, *154* refines and expands the innovations of *Chairs Missing*, with producer Mike Thorne's synthesizer effects playing an even more integral role; little of *Pink Flag's* rawness remains. If *Chairs Missing* was a transitional album between punk and post-punk, *154* is squarely in the latter camp, devoting itself to experimental soundscapes that can sound cold and forbidding at times. However, the best tracks retain their humanity thanks to the arrangements' smooth, seamless blend of electronic and guitar textures and the beauty of the group's melodies. Where previously some of Wire's hooks could find themselves buried or not properly brought out, the fully fleshed-out production of *154* lends a sweeping splendor to "The 15th," the epic "A Touching Display," "A Mutual Friend," and the gorgeous (if obscurely titled) "Map Ref. 41°N 93°W." Not every track is a gem, as the group's artier tendencies occasionally get the better of them, but *154's* best moments help make it at least the equal of *Chairs Missing*. It's difficult to believe that a band which evolved as quickly and altered its sound as restlessly as Wire did could be out of ideas after only three years and three albums, but such was the case according to its members, and with their (temporary, as it turned out) disbandment following this album, Wire's most fertile and influential period came to a close. [The CD reissue features four bonus tracks from an experimental EP issued with some copies of the vinyl LP.] *—Steve Huey*

Document and Eyewitness / 1981 / Mute ✦✦

The Ideal Copy / 1987 / Mute ✦✦✦

Wire's first new full-length effort in eight years is a stunning comeback picking up where *154* left off while also reflecting the strides made by the members' solo work. Finding its footing in dark, edgy dance rhythms and ominous digital textures, *The Ideal Copy* is experimental and forward-thinking, spanning from the buzzing melodies of "Ahead" and "Ambitious" to the taut minimalism of "Feed Me"; the record has its flaws, but its restless creative spirit and refusal to rest on past glories make it one of the few reunion efforts which actually matters. *—Jason Ankeny*

A Bell Is a Cup ... Until it Is Struck / 1988 / Mute ✦✦✦

Like *The Ideal Copy*, *A Bell Is a Cup...Until It Is Struck* continues to push Wire into avant-dance territory, tempering the music's digital rhythms with an increasingly strong sense of melodic ingenuity. More inviting and accessible than the previous recording (or, for that matter, the vast majority of the group's prior work), the album relies heavily on textured guitar patterns to create a warm, dreamy sound; the songs follow suit, spinning

surreal, densely free-associative narratives which further enhance the record's abstract allure. *—Jason Ankeny*

● **On Returning (1977-1979)** / 1989 / Restless ✦✦✦✦✦

On Returning (1977-1979) is a generous 31-song overview of Wire's punk heyday, covering the albums *Pink Flag*, *Chairs Missing*, and *154*, plus several songs that appeared only on non-album singles. Subsequent CD reissues by Restless have added nearly all of those rarities to the original albums as bonus tracks (the sole exception is the fine "Dot Dash"), so the compilation isn't quite as useful for devoted fans as it once was. Furthermore, even if *On Returning* is a handy way to chart Wire's rapid musical development, their progression is better heard on the individual albums, all of which create their own distinct musical moods. However, *On Returning* does have its advantages: first and foremost, it culls *nearly* all of the group's best songs from the time period ("Mannequin" is missing, and the selection from *154* is somewhat botched—omitting the brilliant "Map Ref. 41°N 93°W," among others, is inexcusable). And listeners with a low tolerance for artiness may find this a more concise and acceptable way to familiarize themselves with this important band; make no mistake, Wire's experiments with sonic texture and song structure are willfully challenging, although ultimately well worth the effort. So, the bottom line is that *On Returning (1977-1979)* is a pretty good overview and likely all the Wire a casual fan will need; however, if you're a neophyte and Wire sounds highly intriguing to you, chances are you'll end up with all three 1977-1979 albums anyway, rendering this compilation redundant. In the latter scenario, the classic *Pink Flag* is the better starting point. *—Steve Huey*

It's Beginning To & Back Again / May 1989 / Enigma ✦✦✦

Begun as a collection of live recordings cut in Chicago and Portugal, the songs which comprise *IBTABA* were subsequently reconstructed in the studio to the point of becoming virtually unrecognizable. The material largely reprises tracks from *A Bell Is a Cup*...along with a number of new cuts, highlighted by the single "Eardrum Buzz"; while the record is respectable on its own terms, it's impossible to discern its relevance—neither a true live album nor a remix collection, its original intentions remain lost in the translation. *—Jason Ankeny*

Manscape / May 1990 / Restless ✦✦

The First Letter / Oct. 29, 1991 / Mute ✦✦

1985-1990: The A List / May 18, 1993 / Mute ✦✦✦✦

Wire 1985-1990: The A List is a fine 16-track compilation of the highlights from Wire's surprising and successful comeback. This material isn't quite as essential as their early output—Wire doesn't sound as revolutionary on these sides, although the music is still high-quality. It bears some similarities to the sort of '80s college-radio synth/guitar-pop being produced by the likes of New Order and the Cure, although it isn't as danceable, and it retains Wire's signature love of dissonance and pure sonic oddity. The more controlled, polished sound of this material may tone down the heady excitement of their early albums, or seem a bit mechanical at times, but it's intriguing to hear the high-tech production values that were missing from their initial attempts at creating layers of detail in their arrangements, and there are some fine pop songs here as well. *The A List* could have been sequenced better—its track listing was determined through a poll of fans, various critics, and band associates, and the selections were simply arranged according to which ones received the largest number of votes, meaning that the compilation loses a little steam since many of the best songs appear toward the beginning. Still, that's a minor flaw, especially since *The A List* is such a handy overview of their uneven comeback albums. It's the best way to hear catchy slices of post-punk avant-pop like "Ahead," "Kidney Bingos," "Eardrum Buzz," and "In Vivo," and for all but the most devoted, *The A List* is probably all that's necessary from this period. *—Steve Huey*

Behind the Curtain / 1995 / EMI ✦✦✦

Behind the Curtain collects live tracks and demos from *Pink Flag*, *Chairs Missing* and *154*. *—John Bush*

Turns and Strokes / Apr. 1996 / WMO ✦✦

Wire Train

f. Apr. 1983, db. 1993
New Wave

Wire Train was formed as the Renegades in April 1983 in San Francisco by San Francisco State University students and guitarists Kevin Hunter and Kurt Herr with the rhythm section of Anders Rundblad (bass) and Frederico Gil-Sola (drums). The group signed to the local 415 label, also home to acts like Romeo Void and Translator, all of which found themselves with national distribution when 415 entered into a deal with Columbia Records. Wire Train's first album,...*In a Chamber*, made the national charts in 1984, but the group began to suffer personnel changes. Gil-Sola was replaced by Brian Macleod for the second album, *Between Two Words*, after which Herr left, to be replaced by Jeffrey Trott. A third album, *Ten Women*, charted in 1987. The group's last two albums, *Wire Train* (1990) and *No Soul No Strain* (1992), appeared on MCA. *—William Ruhlmann*

In a Chamber/Between Two Words / Jan. 31, 1995 / Oglio ✦✦✦✦

Compiling Wire Train's earliest and best LPs onto one disc, *In a Chamber/Between Two Words* solidifies the group's standing as one of the more criminally overlooked acts of the mid-1980s—their brand of guitar pop, though clearly a product of its era, has aged remarkably well, with standouts like "I'll Do You," "Chamber of Hellos," "Last Perfect Thing" and "Skills of Summer" still bearing the bittersweet taste of should-have-been hits even all these years later. *—Jason Ankeny*

● **Last Perfect Thing: A Retrospective** / Mar. 26, 1996 / Columbia/Legacy ✦✦✦✦✦

Wire Train's musical style reflected the cross-breeding between post-new wave power-pop and post-disco dance music that characterized the early '80s. The guitars jangled and there were hooks and catchy choruses with harmony vocals, just like the mid-'60s (not to mention covers of Bob Dylan and Buffalo Springfield), but the tempos were unusually quick and the drummer even pushed the beat, while touches of keyboard sometimes shimmered on the edges of the sound picture. More popular bands such as U2 and R.E.M. were doing roughly the same thing at the same time, if with a bit more distinction. But Wire Train frontman Kevin Hunter had an ear for a good melody and an adequate voice to express his pop sentiments, so there's no real answer to the question, why didn't Wire Train make it? This hour-long, 16-track compilation selects the highlights from the group's three Columbia albums (but not its two MCA albums), along with a few rarities. (Amazingly, early copies mistakenly substituted the B-side "Half a Lifetime" for the title song. The problem was to be corrected, but meanwhile an interesting collector's item had been created.) —*William Ruhlmann*

Mark Wirtz

b. 1943, Cologne, Germany
Keyboards, Instrumental / Exotica

"Easy listening" isn't really an appropriate classification for Mark Wirtz; "instrumental pop" may suit him better. An EMI staff producer in the late '60s, Wirtz's most enduring contributions to contemporary music were as producer of Tomorrow, one of the finest overlooked British psychedelic groups (featuring guitarist Steve Howe in his pre-Yes days). (It's also been reported that Wirtz turned down a chance to work with Pink Floyd in the Syd Barrett days.) Wirtz also made some "mood music" albums on his own, the most ambitious of which was a "Teenage Opera" song cycle of sorts that he began working on in 1967. Tomorrow lead singer Keith West was enlisted as lyricist, and one piece developed into West's 1967 "Excerpt from a Teenage Opera" single. A grandiose, multi-part orchestrated narrative, it became an unexpectedly huge (#2) hit in Britain in the summer of 1967.

This led to reports that an entire "Teenage Opera" was in the works, and indeed West did record a marginally successful follow-up ("Sam") in the same vein. The entire opera, however, never appeared, partly because West wasn't entirely keen on the project, and far more eager to continue playing underground psychedelic rock with Tomorrow (which would break up in 1968 anyway) than sing far more pop-oriented material as a solo act. Wirtz continued to work as a producer and issue more rock-influenced easy-listening albums; dribs and drabs of songs that may have been earmarked for the "Teenage Opera" project would appear under the names of both himself and non-entities like Sweetshop and Zion de Gallier. While the "Teenage Opera" and "Sam" singles sound as much like kiddie rock as grand concepts in the making, it's possible that their suite-like construction influenced the Who's *Tommy* and the Pretty Things' *S.F. Sorrow*, both of which are usually referred to as the first full-blown rock concept albums that followed a storyline. In 1996, a mock-up of what the "Teenage Opera" album may have sounded like was built from tracks by Wirtz, West, Tomorrow, and others, and issued on the RPM label. —*Richie Unterberger*

● **A Teenage Opera: the Original Soundtrack Recording** / 1996 / RPM ✦✦✦
"A Teenage Opera," like the Beach Boys' infinitely more celebrated *Smile*, was never truly completed as such; collectors have always wondered, however, if the project exists as a "lost" album of sorts. This 23-track sequence of tracks by Keith West, Tomorrow, Wirtz, Kippington Lodge, the Sweetshop, Zion de Gallier, and Steve Flynn (some previously unissued), is as close an approximation as can be delivered. The psychedelically influenced baroque rock-cum-easy listening arrangements are interesting, but really this is too twee and precious to qualify as anything like a lost masterpiece. Nor is it much of an orchestral pop suite; it's more a grouping of songs with a similar sunny fairyland vibe, sounding like an in-progress version of a children's rock record. You're far better off hearing "Teenage Opera," "Sam," and the Tomorrow cuts—which are the gutsiest and most durable selections here by a wide margin—on RPM's *The Complete Keith West* compilation, or the original (and only) Tomorrow album. —*Richie Unterberger*

The Go-Go Music of Mark Wirtz, His Orchestra & Chorus / 1997 / RPM ✦✦
Twenty-three track compilation of material overseen by Wirtz between 1965 and 1969, assembled from a few LPs and singles. Revisionist claims to the contrary, this is European easy listening at its most trivial—lightened-up covers of contemporary pop and rock hits for the middle-aged crowd, and background music that, as the title implies, was entirely suitable for go-go scenes in B-movie soundtracks. There is fun easy-listening trash from the '60s, and then there is simply meaningless easy-listening trifles from the same era. This compilation falls much closer to the latter. It's not even amusing for camp value; it's just dumb and boring, appealing only to those whose tastes are irredeemably immature, or collectors convincing themselves that this stuff merits investigation by virtue of its very obscurity. —*Richie Unterberger*

Wishbone Ash

f. 1966, Devon, England
Prog-Rock/Art Rock, Hard Rock, Album Rock, Boogie Rock

During the early and mid-'70s, Wishbone Ash were among England's most popular hard rock acts. The group's roots dated to the summer of 1966, when drummer Steve Upton formed a band called Empty Vessels with bassist/vocalist Martin Turner and guitarist Glen Turner. Empty Vessels soon changed their name to Tanglewood and moved to London. Glen Turner left the band at that point, and an advertisement for a guitarist resulted in the addition of both David Alan "Ted" Turner and Andy Powell, who provided the basis for the sound of the new lineup with intertwining riffs and phrases drawn from both soul and blues, coupled with Martin Turner's melodic bass sound and Upton's jazz-influenced drumming. A new name was called for; "Wishbone Ash" was chosen from two

lists of words. Their self-titled first album appeared in 1970; *Pilgrimage* and *Argus* followed over the next two years, and each showed a major advance in the band's sound. The release of 1973's *Wishbone Four* reflected a greater maturity to the group, and was their first fully developed album, with songwriting that didn't hide behind a progressive pose but luxuriated in the members' folk music inclinations, without compromising the harder edge of their music. The album also saw the departure of Ted Turner, who was replaced by Laurie Wisefield. *Locked In* and *New England* followed; Martin Turner departed after 1979's *Just Testing*, to be replaced by ex-King Crimson bassist/singer John Wetton. Wishbone Ash's history came full circle in the 1980s with the reunion of Powell, Upton, Ted Turner, and Martin Turner, and the recording of three albums for I.R.S. They remained a working band into the 1990s, led by Andy Powell and Ted Turner and touring and recording regularly. —*Bruce Eder*

● **Time Was: The Wishbone Ash Collection** / 1993 / MCA ✦✦✦✦✦
A two-disc snapshot of this band's more vital work, from the meat-and-potatoes rock of their eponymous 1970 debut, the thematic, progressive-minded peak of *Pilgrimage* and *Argus*, and a return to more basic structures for *Wishbone 4*. Mercifully, their less "enduring" albums from the later '70s and early '80s are touched on only sporadically. The set includes a pair of previously unreleased tracks and a good booklet with interviews; somehow the digital remastering has left the sound a little thin. —*Roch Parisien*

The Best of Wishbone Ash / Jul. 1, 1997 / MCA ✦✦✦✦
The twin-guitar-jam-infested ramblings of Wishbone Ash are for some the place where British rock and Southern rock meet in an unholy alliance, both influencing the other. This 11-track collection of this British group's best starts features nine classic tracks, plus two previously unreleased versions of a pair of Wishbone Ash favorites. The album, which was compiled and co-produced by founding member Andy Powell, includes "Blind Eye," "Phoenix," "The Pilgrim," "Sometime World," "Warrior," "Throw Down the Sword," "Persephone," "F.U.B.B." and "Living Proof." Also included is a live version of "Lorelei," recorded at a Liverpool concert back in 1976, and an acoustic version of "Blowin' Free," recorded specifically for this compilation in 1997 by the band. —*Cub Koda*

Distillation / 1998 / Repertoire ✦✦✦✦
While it's certainly too much for the average Wishbone Ash fan, *Distillation* is an excellent three-disc, 56-track box set that features the best of the band's heavy boogie from the '70s. None of the group's essential tracks are missing, and it contains a few fine rarities, making this an essential overview for the collector or serious fan. —*Stephen Thomas Erlewine*

Bill Withers

b. Jul. 4, 1938, Slab Fork, WV
Vocals / Smooth Soul, Urban, Soul

Songwriter/singer/guitarist Bill Withers is best remembered for the classic "Lean on Me" and his other million-selling singles "Ain't No Sunshine" and "Use Me," but he has a sizable cache of great songs to his credit.

Born July 4, 1938, in Slab Folk, WV, Withers was the youngest of six children. After a nine-year stint in the Navy, Withers moved to Los Angeles to pursue a music career in 1967. He recorded demos at night while working at the Boeing aircraft company where he made toilet seats. His debut album, *Just As I Am* included his first charting single, "Ain't No Sunshine" which went gold and made it to number six R&B and number three pop in summer 1971, also winning a Grammy as Best R&B Song. Withers wrote "Lean on Me" based on his experiences growing up in a West Virginia coal mining town. His second gold single, "Lean on Me," landed at number one R&B and number one pop for three weeks on *Billboard*'s charts in summer 1972. After a legal battle with his label, Sussex, Withers signed with Columbia Records. Columbia later bought his Sussex masters when the label went out of business. His releases on Columbia included *Making Music*, and *Menagerie 'Bout Love* from spring 1979. Teaming with Elektra Records artist Grover Washington Jr., Withers sang the crystalline ballad "Just the Two of Us." It went to number three R&B and held the number two pop spot for three weeks in early 1981. Withers' last charting LP was *Watching You, Watching Me* in spring 1985. He also occasionally did dates with Grover Washington Jr. during the '90s. His songs and recordings have been used as both the source of numerous covers and sampled by a multitude of hip-hop/rap groups. —*Ed Hogan*

Still Bill / 1972 / Sussex ✦✦✦✦✦
Bill's West Virginia drawl was the perfect vehicle to sell his compositions laden with down-home lyrics and Bo Diddley inspired rhythms. "Use Me," will remind you of the old hambone, where you made rhythms by slapping your legs and thighs with your hands. The lyrics, however, are universally sad; he's so love-struck he begs his woman to use him as her personal door mat. Diddley's famous beat is even more evident on "Kissing My Love," an up-tempo ditty that's ideal for hand jiving. The accusing "Who Is He (And What Is He to You)" is self-explanatory; the track is more advanced than many of Wither's compositions, and has been re-recorded by a slew of artists. His heart's on his sleeve on "Lean on Me," which is closer to old school country than anything, but the passion and sincerity in Bill's voice make it palatable to music lovers of any genre. This is Bill's most popular album, nothing phoney or jive, just real Bill. —*Andrew Hamilton*

Live at Carnegie Hall / 1973 / Columbia ✦✦✦✦
A wonderful live album that capitalizes on Withers' trademark melancholy soul sound while expanding the music to fit the room granted by a live show. Lovely versions of "Grandma's Hands" and "Lean on Me" are balanced by heartfelt downbeat numbers like "Better Off Dead" and "I Can't Write Left-Handed," the latter being an anti-war song with a chilling message. The set finishes off with the lengthy "Harlem/Cold Baloney," with lots

of audience-pleased call-and-response going on. One of the best live releases from the '70s. *—Steven McDonald*

Lean on Me: The Best of Bill Withers / Aug. 9, 1994 / Columbia/Legacy ✦✦✦✦✦
18 tracks, from the early '70s to the mid-'80s, including his early Top Ten singles, but also minor hits like "Grandma's Hands," "Kissing My Love," and "Lovely Day." Those who admire songs like "Lean on Me" and "Ain't No Sunshine" are advised to approach this best-of with caution; from the mid-'70s onward, Withers forsook his folky singer-songwriter soul for more anonymous, slick MOR soul and urban contemporary. His early sound was far more distinctive, and his early-'70s Sussex albums are recommended alternatives to this compilation. *—Richie Unterberger*

● **The Best of Bill Withers: Lean on Me** / May 30, 2000 / Columbia/Legacy ✦✦✦✦✦
Collectors note: This is *not* the same as the very similarly titled *Lean on Me: The Best of Bill Withers*, a 1994 best-of that also came out on Sony (catalog #5294). Each disc has 18 tracks and includes his biggest and best hits, yet only 13 of the songs are found on both CDs, and the 2000 compilation has a new set of liner notes by David Ritz. This is still too light on his earliest Sussex material, which is his best work and is represented by just seven of the tunes. It's also messily sequenced, with six less impressive and poppier mid-1970s Columbia outings leading off the program before you get to the early '70s goodies, including "Ain't No Sunshine," "Lean on Me," and "Use Me." Still, this would have to get the nod over the 1994 best-of just for the inclusion of one of those Sussex tunes alone, the uplifting and earthily bluesy 1971 cut "Harlem." *—Richie Unterberger*

Peter Wolf

b. Mar. 7, 1946, New York, NY [The Bronx]
Vocals, Keyboards / Pop/Rock, Rock & Roll, Album Rock
Best known for his tenure fronting the J. Geils Band, singer Peter Wolf was born and raised in the Bronx. Wolf's earliest passion was painting, and he was accepted on a scholarship to the Museum of Modern Art's Special Studies for Children, and later to the High School of Music and Art, just blocks from the Apollo Theatre, where the young Wolf would make weekly visits. Seeing performers like Jackie Wilson, Dinah Washington, Otis Redding, and James Brown sparked his early interest in blues and R&B. In Chicago, he became involved in a couple of blues and folk music societies while studying painting at the University of Chicago. While there, he visited the southside blues clubs, drawing influence from the musicians he saw there. With a grant to study at the Boston Museum School of Fine Arts, he became a disc jockey on WBCN-FM. In 1967, he formed the group that would go on to become the J. Geils Band, who became known for their marathon live performances, with Wolf establishing a reputation as a particularly dynamic frontman. In 1983, the group was at the height of their popularity, and had gone 17 years without a personnel change. Finally, the J. Geils Band went their separate ways and Wolf went on to produce numerous film soundtracks and run art exhibits of his original paintings. In 1984, he released his first solo album, *Lights Out*, followed in 1987 by *Come As You Are*, which spurred the hit single of the same name. In between albums he worked on duets with Mick Jagger and Aretha Franklin, who recruited him specifically for her *Who's Zoomin' Who* album. In 1989, after a six-month songwriting retreat in Nashville, he recorded his third solo album, *Up to No Good*, which appeared the following year. *—Richard Skelly*

● **Lights Out** / 1984 / EMI America ✦✦✦✦✦
On his own, Wolf achieves a more contemporary pop sound than that of the bluesy J. Geils Band and scores three chart hits: "Lights Out" (#12), "I Need You Tonight" (#36), and "Oo-Ee-Diddley-Bop!" (#61). *—William Ruhlmann*

Come As You Are / 1987 / EMI America ✦✦✦✦
Wolf gets back in the Top 15 with the title track, but the best song is the leadoff, an R&B raveup ironically called, "Can't Get Started." *—William Ruhlmann*

Up to No Good / 1990 / MCA ✦✦✦

Long Line / May 14, 1996 / Reprise ✦✦✦✦
Long Line is Peter Wolf's '90s comeback album and it does everything that it should do. It demonstrates that Wolf has matured without abandoning his love for greasy R&B and loud rock & roll. Although the songs are slightly uneven throughout *Long Line*, he demonstrates humor and compassion even on the weak numbers. With it's energetic rockers and, especially, heart-felt ballads, *Long Line* ranks as one of Wolf's most engaging and consistent albums. *—Stephen Thomas Erlewine*

Fool's Parade / Sep. 29, 1998 / Mercury ✦✦✦✦
Peter Wolf lost his mainstream audience long before he released *Fool's Parade* in the fall of 1998. By the time the album hit the stores, it had been ten years since he had graced the Top 40, when "Come as You Are" reached number 15. To his credit, Wolf realized he no longer was a pop star, so he decided to continue in the vein of his comeback record, 1996's *Long Line*. Which is to say, *Fool's Parade* is a collection of rock & roll, R&B, blues and soul, all delivered with professional showmanship from Wolf, along with a surplus of true heart and passion. It's a mature album in the best sense of the word—it's clear that Wolf has lived the life he sings about, and he exhibits a sense of craft that only veterans can convey. Following the equally accomplished *Long Line*, *Fool's Parade* is proof that veteran rockers need not be washed up or written off, even if they are no longer playing to stadium-sized crowds. *—Stephen Thomas Erlewine*

Wolfie

f. 1996
Indie Pop, Twee Pop
Another product of the indie-pop hotbed of Champaign-Urbana, Illinois, Wolfie's origins date to the fall of 1991, when bassist/singer Joe Ziemba and singer/guitarist Mike Downey first met while attending high school together. Despite common musical interests, both played in separate bands for the next few years, with Downey soon joining drummer R.J. Porter in Plain Jane; at age 17, Ziemba also issued a self-released solo tape called *Slackjawed*. In 1995, he recruited both Downey and Porter to perform live in a band also called Slackjawed; originally a one-off project, the trio ended up releasing a pair of home recordings, with Downey also issuing the solo cassette *A Fire Breathing Dinosaur by Tim*. In late 1996 Ziemba's girlfriend, singer/keyboardist Amanda Lyons, joined the group, and with her arrival the quartet rechristened themselves Wolfie; debuting a year later with the single "Don't Turn It Off," in 1998 they released the effervescent full-length *Awful Mess Mystery*. *Where's Wolfie* followed in the spring of 1999; a year later, the group moved to the Kindercore label to issue the EP *Wolfie, and the Coat and the Hat*. The full-length *Tall Dark Hill* followed in 2001. *—Jason Ankeny*

● **Awful Mess Mystery** / 1998 / Mud ✦✦✦✦
What's great about Wolfie is that their music isn't out to change the world; with song titles like "Hey It's Finally Yay," "Yeah Yeah You" and "Life Saver Socks," it's tough to take *Awful Mess Mystery* too seriously, which is precisely the point. Although the crunchy guitars and adenoidal vocals make comparisons to Superchunk inevitable, Wolfie still sounds fresh, investing new life and energy into their time-tested boy-girl harmonies, cheesy synth lines and classic pop songs which average under the two-minute mark. Effervescent, guileless and relentlessly charming, *Awful Mess Mystery* is ultimately about nothing more than good, clean fun, and even if it won't change the world, it can't help but make it a better place to live. *—Jason Ankeny*

Where's Wolfie / Apr. 6, 1999 / Parasol ✦✦✦✦
It's undoubtedly something of a misnomer to call a Wolfie disc "mature"—the group still possesses a childlike wonder with the very concept of pop music that is hopelessly endearing, and one rues the day it finally does disappear—but there's no denying that *Where's Wolfie* is a major leap forward, expanding on the keyboard-powered, new wave-influenced sound of before to showcase an increasing debt to Zombies-like, late-'60s popcraft. Where at times Wolfie's debut, *Awful Mess Mystery*, suffered from sameness from song to song, each track on this sophomore effort bears its own distinctive stamp—the boy-girl harmonies that were such a delight last time out are even more prominent here, and the melodies are consistently crisp and catchy. Irresistible. *—Jason Ankeny*

And The Coat and The Hat / 2000 / Kindercore ✦✦✦✦
And the Coat and the Hat marks a different direction for the normally gleeful Wolfie. Instead of the sugarcoated indie pop and cutesy lyrics on which they built themselves, this EP uncovers a new maturity that scraps their original three-chord structure. Here, there's a foundation of new wave, Weezer-esque esthetics and dual male-female vocals. Resulting in a playful tone of upbeat pop, Wolfie's change is definitely a progression for the better. *—Mike DaRonco*

Tall Dark Hill / 2001 / March ✦✦✦✦
For a band as superficially simple as Wolfie, charting their creative development is much trickier than it might seem—with each successive record, the band's grown progressively more mature and sophisticated, two adjectives which seemingly run in direct opposition to the youthful euphoria and childlike innocence their music so wonderfully captures. *Tall Dark Hill* is their best—and, accordingly, most contradictory—effort to date; the melodies are stronger, the harmonies tighter, and the lyrics more meaningful, yet somehow the music maintains the same "Hey, kids, let's put on a show!" effervescence which made their earlier records so engaging. Abandoning the Casio-dominated sound of old in favor of a more straightforward power pop approach, *Tall Dark Hill* also draws influence from the classic sunshine pop of the late 1960s; Joe Ziemba's songs are more full-bodied than before, and his adenoidal vocals remain perfectly complemented by the cotton-candy harmonies of keyboardist Amanda Lyons, who also takes on a welcome number of lead duties. Proof positive that even indie-pop can age gracefully. *—Jason Ankeny*

Bobby Womack

b. Mar. 4, 1944, Cleveland, OH
Vocals, Guitar / Blaxploitation, Smooth Soul, Quiet Storm, R&B, Soul
Few careers in American popular music have been as consistently productive and influential as that of singer/songwriter and guitarist Bobby Womack. Sam Cooke, for whom Womack played guitar, financed his first recordings in the early '60s. With his brothers as the Valentinos, he cut two R&B classics, "It's All Over Now" (later a hit for the Stones) and "Lookin' for a Love" (a mega-hit for J. Geils). The Valentinos' combination of shouting lead vocals and blues/gospel harmonies predated late-'60s soul music. Womack knew and championed Jimi Hendrix early on, befriending him during a 1962 soul package tour. Womack's lean, groundbreaking guitar work, so similar in flavor to that of his contemporary Curtis Mayfield, influenced Hendrix. Later, Hendrix would return the favor by popularizing the wah-wah—an effect Womack would use to chilling effect on Sly Stone's *There's a Riot Goin' On* album and its smash single, "Family Affair" (he doubled here on bass). In fact, Womack himself was one of the legendary "wild" soul men, friend and partying companion of Wilson Pickett, for whom he wrote "Midnight Mover" and "I'm in Love." He even scored a movie, *Across 110th Street*, which came out at the same time as the landmark blaxploitation film *Shaft*. He made a stunning 1981 comeback with the number one R&B album *The Poet* and reunited with old Memphis studio friends and producer Chips Moman on 1986's *Womagic*. *—Christine Ohlman*

Communication / Sep. 15, 1971 / The Right Stuff ✦✦✦✦

Understanding / May 30, 1972 / The Right Stuff ✦✦✦✦✦
As compelling as Bobby Womack's lacerating baritone may be, it still has that uncanny ability to be an engaging voice. This album has that timeliness appeal. It features the chart-buster in the mid-tempo number "Woman's Gotta Have It." It was a number one

single on the *Billboard* R&B charts. In addition to the aforementioned song, Womack also features a host of other granite numbers like "Ruby Dean" and "I Can Understand It." The latter, penned by Womack, was also covered by New Birth. Both versions are excellent. However, Womack's version has a soothing effect as it employs a sensuous string arrangement while New Birth's rendition is rather funky, retaining a spirited horn arrangement. Womack's version was never a release. "Harry Hippie" is a narrative about his brother and former bandmate Harris Womack. It checked in at number eight. The Ohio native's unique trait to calm a song with his blistering baritone re-surfaces on "Sweet Caroline," the album's third and final release. For a song to be so sweet and gentle, Womack enhances the flavor of this sentimental number with a heartfelt, soulful approach. It slipped into the Top 20 at 16. By all standards, this album is stirring. *—Craig Lytle*

Across 110th Street / Dec. 16, 1972 / Charly ♦♦♦
The soundtrack to a relatively little-known 1972 blaxploitation film featured songs written and performed by Bobby Womack, as well as a musical score by J.J. Johnson. Although the inconsistency of the approach precluded a musical statement along the lines of *Superfly*, it's an interesting find for those looking for little-heeded early-'70s soul with funk and rock influences. Womack's cuts count among his better material, and even if the title track cops much of its attitude from *Superfly*, it has a satisfyingly tough soul-rock groove of its own. "If You Want My Love" is a good grainy ballad, "Quicksand" a propulsive number well-suited for action scenes, and "Do It Right" in the mold of James Brown, but more rock-oriented. Johnson's instrumental contributions, while not as interesting, set a nice period soul-jazz mood, and there are nifty periodic washes of electronic effects in both composers' contributions. *—Richie Unterberger*

The Facts of Life / Jun. 8, 1973 / The Right Stuff ♦♦♦♦♦
Womack is one of the most prolific and influential acts in R&B and rock. With songs like "I Can Understand It," "Harry Hippie," and "Woman Got to Have It," Womack often displayed a depth, candor, and an expert turn of phrase that helped him outpace his contemporaries. *Facts of Life* is the follow-up to the 1972 classic *Communication.* This album is even better. Womack is known for his often uncomfortably real takes on love, life, and relationships, and *Facts of Life* expertly deals with a myriad of subjects. The only released single is his revamped take of the standard "Nobody Wants You When You're Down and Out." The song has been done *ad infinitum*, but Womack put a nasty edge on it that made it sound like a song he wrote himself. "I'm Through Trying to Prove My Love to You" is punctuated by his great guitar riffing and plaintive vocal and lyrical gems like, "See when you take my heart/I can't let you take my soul." "He'll Be There When the Sun Goes Down" benefits from more witticisms and a strong string arrangement from Womack and Rene Hall. Perhaps the most surprising thing about *Facts of Life* is that Womack is so adept at taking others' material and making it his own. "Natural Man," a cover of "You Make Me Feel Like a Natural Woman," is the biggest shock here. Where Aretha Franklin's version had her skillfully shouting from the rooftops, Womack brings tenderness to the lyric and is believable. Produced by Womack and recorded in Muscle Shoals with its renowned players, *Facts of Life* is an album of undeniable craft. *—Jason Elias*

Lookin' for a Love Again / Jan. 11, 1974 / The Right Stuff ♦♦♦♦
Bobby Womack can arguably be billed the quintessential soul singer (along with a few others). From his testimonial pleas to his lacerating deliveries, Womack truly brings his songs to life. The title track gave the Cleveland, OH, native his second number one song. It held that position on the *Billboard* R&B charts for three consecutive weeks and scaled the Top Ten on the pop charts as well. (His other number one song was "Woman's Gotta Have It.") "You're Welcome, Stop on By" was the second single. As with most of this soulman's numbers, this one has that irresistible, percolating rhythm augmented by Womack's wailing delivery. Whether Womack is strokin' country & western rhythms, burnin' a blues melody with his guitar or expressing a painful confession with his trademark baritone, rest assured that the outcome is going to be nothing short of sizzlin'. *—Craig Lytle*

The Poet [Razor & Tie] / 1981 / Razor & Tie ♦♦♦♦
Eschewing the orchestrated sound that dominated much of his 1970s output, the *Across 110th St.* soundtrack being the definitive example, with *The Poet* Womack stays in that slick vein, but this time does so with a soft jazz feel. Workouts like "Where Do We Go From Here" contain long intros and codas with Womack's gruff vocal style trading off with the silky voices of a female choir; on "So Many Sides of You," one of the more rollicking songs on the record, the piano, drums, and Nathan East's bass are as crisp as a new dollar bill. A bonus, aside from the songs, is the great cover art, which shows Womack decked out in a lavender sportcoat and a pair of sunglasses, which only someone of his soulful grace could pull off. *—Steve Kurutz*

Poet 2 / 1984 / Razor & Tie ♦♦♦
Though Womack's in great voice, there's only one major thing wrong with *The Poet II*: it's an inferior follow-up to *The Poet*, which successfully executed ideas Womack had been tinkering with since 1979's *Roads of Life.* This seeks the success *The Poet* got by surprise. Womack's skill is his pragmatic take on relationships but on *The Poet II*, his aim is a little off. "Love Has Finally Come at Last" is the first of three duets with Patti LaBelle. The song is OK, but a fan might want to hear him sing all by himself. The duet idea works better on "It Takes a Lot of Strength to Say Goodbye"; it sounds better suited for two singers, and the dramatic arrangement and chemistry between Womack and LaBelle are strong but not that exciting. *The Poet II* also features some over-produced though skillful dance tracks. "Tell Me Why" is effective and has Womack asking why his relationship is failing and uses his children as pawns when he sings, "You don't have to do it for me/But do it for the sake of the kids." By the end of the album, Womack's lack of winning premises starts to catch up with him. "I Wish I Had Someone to Come Home To" has him sounding a little phony with lyrics like "Ain't no way this lonely man can seem to win." Fans of Womack know he'd think up something to do. The effort's last track "American Dream" features snippets of Martin Luther King's "I Have a Dream" speech. With its so-so lyrics and plodding arrangement, it just falls apart within the first two minutes. *The Poet II* is no doubt a good Bobby Womack album, but it is clear that he can do much better. *—Jason Elias*

● **Midnight Mover** / Feb. 1993 / EMI America ♦♦♦♦♦
Midnight Mover is a double-disc set that offers 44 tracks from Bobby Womack's 1968-1976 stint with United Artists and its related labels. Tracks like "I'm a Midnight Mover," "I'm in Love," and "Broadway Walk" have Womack feeling his way with producer Chips Moman. After parting ways with Moman, Womack himself became one of the more skilled and inventive producers in the Muscle Shoals tradition. "That's the Way I Feel About Cha" and "I Can Understand It" both have plaintive melodies and are punctuated by Womack's guitar skills and his ever-broadening and felt vocals. The poignant "Harry Hippie" had him flawlessly singing each line. Disc two covers the years 1973-1976. During this time he had become an even bigger star as his albums became sagacious ruminations on love and life. This set takes six tracks from his classic 1973 album, *Facts of Life.* From his effortlessly revamped and rock-fueled "Nobody Wants You (When You're Down and Out)" to his perfect cover of Sam Cooke's "That's Heaven to Me," Womack's interpretive skills were only matched by his rootsy yet polished productions. After the frisky "Check It Out," Womack seemed preoccupied with the darker side of love with a little religion on the side to confuse things. Tracks like "Jealous Love" and "Interlude #1/I Don't Know" have the message and meaning slipping through his fingers. *Midnight Mover* is a flawless anthology. *—Jason Elias*

Lookin' for a Real Love: The Best of Bobby Womack / 1994 / Razor & Tie ♦♦♦♦♦
At 14 tracks, Razor & Tie's *Lookin' for a Real Love: The Best of Bobby Womack* isn't particularly comprehensive, and it does miss some excellent, even important tracks, but as a sampling, it still works very well since it contains such classics as "That's the Way I Feel About 'Cha," "Woman's Gotta Have It," "Harry Hippie," "It's All Over Now," and "Across 110th Street," while whetting the appetite to hear more. So, while it might not be the definitive word on Womack's great solo career, it does work as an effective introduction. *—Stephen Thomas Erlewine*

● **Greatest Hits** / Oct. 5, 1999 / The Right Stuff ♦♦♦♦♦
This overview of Womack's solo career features his R&B and pop classics: "Lookin' for a Love," "Welcome Stop on By," "Women Gotta Have It," and "That's the Way I Feel About Cha'." Even versions of the folkish "Sweet Caroline" and "Harry Hippie" come out gritty. The price is right too, a good opportunity to add some gritty, uncut soul to your collection. *—Andrew Hamilton*

The Wombles

Psychedelic Pop, Bubblegum

Hugely popular for awhile in the UK, the Wombles are creatures whose whole mission is to help clean up the world, carrying their "tidy bags" with them wherever they go, picking up the trash left behind by humans, and reusing it. Created in the late '60s by children's book author Elisabeth Berseford, the Wombles books caught on and were translated into several languages. In the '70s, the furry, pointy-snouted characters then became the stars of their own live action (instead of animated) children's television series, and added music-making to their list of talents. The show featured the music of the multi-talented composer and musician Mike Batt, who garnered his first eight hit singles with his Wombles' music. With the amount of Wombles music released in the '70s—six albums and over a dozen singles in the UK, and an album and a handful of singles making their way to Canada and the U.S.—compilations of Wombles material have been periodically surfacing ever since, intriguing collectors with a wide array of musical styles, and catchy tunes including "Remember You're a Womble," and "Non Stop Wombling Summer Party." Some of the more recent compilations include Columbia's *The Best Wombles Album So Far, Vol. 1* (1998), and *The Wombles Collection*, a double-disc set released in 2000 on Dramatico. The Wombles television show was also revived for a brief time in the late '90s, when over a dozen new episodes aired. *—Joslyn Layne*

● **The Best Wombles Album So Far, Vol. 1** / May 1998 / Columbia ♦♦♦♦♦
The Best Wombles Album So Far, Vol. 1 is an excellent single-disc collection showcasing 17 of their finest songs. Though on the surface the music may seem more a novelty than anything else, this collection is ample proof of the brilliance of their recordings. Mike Batt's songs cover a broad musical canvas, offering a survey of many styles ranging from whimsical music hall-inspired British pop and over-the-top orchestral prog-rock to country, blues, and even barbershop quartet—all songs chronicling the furry creatures' never-ending quest to rid the land of trash. *—Chris Woodstra*

● **Wombles Collection** / Nov. 2000 / Dramatico ♦♦♦♦♦
The Wombles Collection manages to outdo even *The Best Wombles Album So Far* by adding another disc's worth of material. The additional 18 tracks include "I Wish It Could Be a Wombling Merry Christmas Every Day," with Roy Wood reprising his biggest hit in a new Wombling version. Of course, two discs of the Wombles may seem excessive by normal standards, but those in the know will certainly be thrilled by more—and the second disc matches the first in quality. A complete recorded works is certainly in order. *—Chris Woodstra*

The Wonder Stuff

f. 1988, Stourbridge, England, **db.** 1994
Alternative Pop/Rock

When the Wonder Stuff released their first album, *The Eight Legged Groove Machine*, in

1988, the British press wrote scores of articles about the band, mainly because of the arrogant self-confidence of their leader, vocalist/guitarist Miles Hunt. Hunt's brash public image was the Wonder Stuff personified—mean, self-satisfied, self-serving, and scathingly witty. Accordingly, their colorful mixture of pop melodies, loud guitars, sneering lyrics, and touches of dance music was sometimes brilliant and sometimes banal. Between 1988 and 1993, the band kept incorporating more stylistic flourishes to their basic, punk- and new wave-inspired pop/rock. The Wonder Stuff were instant stars in England; America never warmed to their music. After trying to gain a worldwide audience for five years, the band broke up in 1994. *—Stephen Thomas Erlewine*

The Eight Legged Groove Machine / 1988 / Polydor ✦✦✦✦✦
A brash, scattershot debut driven by the band's sheer arrogance as much as their catchy, but erratic, guitar hooks. *—Stephen Thomas Erlewine*

Hup! / 1989 / Polydor ✦✦✦
The Wonder Stuff's second album isn't as snotty as their first, but it's more ambitious, adding bits of folk, psychedelia, and art-rock to their self-involved punk-pop. Unfortunately, they didn't bring as many hooks and melodies this time around, leaving *Hup!* an admirable but failed experiment. *—Stephen Thomas Erlewine*

Never Loved Elvis / 1991 / Polydor ✦✦✦✦✦
The Wonder Stuff's carefully constructed melodies, endless ambition, spiky guitars, and self-confidence combined into a consistently engaging sound on their third album. *—Stephen Thomas Erlewine*

Construction for the Modern Idiot / Oct. 5, 1993 / Polydor ✦✦✦
With *Construction for the Modern Idiot*, The Wonder Stuff rebounds from a somewhat lackluster streak of records with an album of brash guitar pop rivaling its earlier releases. *—Stephen Thomas Erlewine*

● **If the Beatles Had Read Hunter . . . The Singles** / 1994 / Polydor ✦✦✦✦✦
The Wonder Stuff's albums were wildly incoherent, which makes this British collection of their U.K. hit singles not only their most consistent album, but also their most entertaining. *—Stephen Thomas Erlewine*

Love Bites & Bruises: Wonder Stuff Anthology / Jan. 9, 2001 / Polydor ✦✦✦✦
This solid two-disc live/rarities collection gleaned from the not-so-long history of the band not only shows how underrated they were, but that they were genuinely concerned with musical and artistic growth. The first disc starts with short blasts of snide pop, before moving into the brilliant "Our New Song." Disc two is where the magic really happens, and right from the get go. "Professional Disturber of the Peace" may be one of the best songs in their catalog. Also included are highlights from the last tour and their big UK hit, "Dizzy" which is performed with Vic Reeves at the Phoenix festival. It's nice to finally get the rest of the picture with this band, but unfortunate that they're not still making new music together. *—Chris True*

Stevie Wonder (Steveland Morris)

b. May 13, 1950, Saginaw, MI
Vocals, Piano (Electric), Keyboards, Piano, Harmonica / Smooth Soul, Album Rock, Pop-Soul, Pop/Rock, Motown, Urban, Funk, Soul
When Stevie Wonder began recording in 1962, he was only eleven years old. Even then, his talent was evident, although there was no sign of how deep it was. After all, the music was the work of a startlingly gifted child; it was all exuberant flash, with few complexities. Soon, Wonder would go far beyond the infectious energy of "Fingertips (Part 2)." In two years, he became one of Motown's finest artists, recording a series of brilliant singles, the overwhelming majority of which he wrote himself. With his creativity growing by leaps and bounds, Wonder soon felt limited by Motown's strict production and publishing contracts. After recording two full albums of material by himself, he gained total artistic control of his career and helped usher in a new era of soul/R&B. Along with Sly Stone and Marvin Gaye, Wonder was responsible for making soul and R&B albums not just collections of singles, but cohesive artistic statements, where artists could extend their music beyond the confines of a three-minute hit single. With the *Talking Book* and *Innervisions* albums, Wonder's music became richly complex and inventive. He sustained his creative peak through the '70s, then moved into more straightforward pop with 1980's *Hotter than July*, his first platinum album. Although his records sold well and he scored the occasional hit—including the smash hit ballad "I Just Called to Say I Love You"—his albums weren't as focused as they were a decade earlier. By the '90s, he was still an immensely respected musician, but his music was no longer on the cutting edge. *—Stephen Thomas Erlewine*

The 12 Year Old Genius / May 21, 1963 / Motown ✦✦✦
Recorded live, this includes the full seven-minute version of his number one hit "Fingertips." The rest of the album shows him as a young prodigy fixated on Ray Charles; indeed, the final three songs are covers of the early Charles tunes "Hallelujah I Love Her So," "Drown in My Own Tears," and "Don't You Know." A couple jams and a cover of "(I'm Afraid) The Masquerade Is Over" fill out this seven-song LP. *—Richie Unterberger*

Greatest Hits / Mar. 25, 1968 / Motown ✦✦✦✦✦
When it was released, Stevie Wonder's first hits collection, a 12-track disc tracing his work from 1963 to 1967, served a common function of compilations: It gathered together stray, disparate pieces, from "Fingertips—Pt. 2" to "I Was Made to Love Her," and focused attention on the artist. Wonder had a spotty singles record: five Top Ten hits, but only two of them in succession over the four-and-a-half years, yet *Greatest Hits* made him seem like a consistent hitmaker with an astounding range, from those early harmonica instrumentals to soulful wailers like "Uptight (Everything's Alright)" and even oddball ballads like "A Place in the Sun." By now this set has long since been eclipsed, notably by the *Looking Back* album, but as a demonstration of Wonder's early promise, it is notable. *—William Ruhlmann*

For Once in My Life / Dec. 6, 1968 / Motown ✦✦✦
Rather than rushing out an album in the spring of 1968, when "Shoo-Be-Doo-Be-Doo-Da-Day" (#9 Pop, #1 R&B) hit, Motown waited, through the modest summer success of "You Met Your Match" (#35 Pop, #2 R&B) until "For Once in My Life" (#2 Pop and R&B) became Wonder's next mammoth single, to release an album. As a result, this album contained all three hits, making it one of Wonder's more consistent albums of the '60s, even with filler like "Sunny" and "God Bless the Child." The real find, however, is the driving "I Don't Know Why," which, when placed on the B-side of Wonder's next single, "My Cherie Amour," became a hit on its own, going #39 Pop, #16 R&B. *—William Ruhlmann*

My Cherie Amour / Aug. 29, 1969 / Motown ✦✦✦
Notable for containing Wonder's then-most recent Top Ten hit, the title track, and its follow-up, "Yester-Me, Yester-You, Yesterday," this album otherwise contains contemporary filler like "Light My Fire," plus a peculiar arrangement of "Hello, Young Lovers" from *The King and I* that makes it sound like "For Once In My Life." *—William Ruhlmann*

Signed, Sealed & Delivered / Aug. 7, 1970 / Motown ✦✦✦
Stevie Wonder was beginning to rebel against the Motown hit factory mentality in the early '70s. While he certainly hadn't lost his commercial touch, Wonder was anxious to address social concerns, experiment with electronics and not be restricted by radio and marketplace considerations. Still, he gave the label another definitive smash with the title track, while sneaking in a cover of the Beatles' "We Can Work It Out" and penning more intriguing tunes like "I Can't Let My Heaven Walk Away" and "Never Had a Dream Come True." *—Ron Wynn*

Where I'm Coming From / Apr. 12, 1971 / Motown ✦✦✦✦✦
Released one month before Stevie Wonder's 21st birthday, *Where I'm Coming From* is really his first adult album, and although it was not a massive hit, it anticipated the musical approach of his commercial breakthrough, *Talking Book*, by a year and a half. The lovely "Never Dreamed You'd Leave in Summer," as the B-side to a cover of the Beatles' "We Can Work It Out," has become a Wonder standard, and the album's real hit, "If You Really Love Me" (number eight pop, number four R&B), marked the first rewards of his alliance with then-wife Syreeta Wright. Elsewhere, Wonder, who produced and composed all the tracks, introduced the funky keyboard style that would take him through the next few years, as well as the social concerns that would absorb him later on. This album was a shot across the bow, fair warning that a major, nearly mature talent had arrived. *—William Ruhlmann*

Greatest Hits, Vol. 2 / Oct. 21, 1971 / Motown ✦✦✦
Stevie Wonder's second hits collection, gathering together his singles from 1968 to 1971, traces his development into a virtuoso talent, from upbeat Motown numbers like "For Once In My Life" to the emergence of Wonder's own style in songs like "Never Dreamed You'd Leave In Summer" and "If You Really Love Me." Along the way, he demonstrates an amazingly broad pop sensibility that allows him to handle soul, pop/rock, and ballads, all with equal ease. And, of course, the remarkable thing is that this set was obselete the day it came out, the summing up of what turned out to be only the first phase of Wonder's remarkable career. This album has been superseded by the *Looking Back* compilation. *—William Ruhlmann*

Music of My Mind / Mar. 3, 1972 / Motown ✦✦✦✦✦
When Wonder turned 21, he renegotiated his Motown contract; the key issue was control. Stevie Wonder had a vision that veered far away from that of the Motown hit-making machine. Influenced by the work of Isaac Hayes in 1969 and 1970 and labelmate Marvin Gaye in 1971, Wonder was no longer content with putting out albums that were a collection of two or three hit singles plus filler; he wanted to record full-length albums that had an integrity unto themselves. *Music of My Mind* was the first such effort. Wonder produced, wrote the songs, and played the majority of the instruments. At the time it was a revelation. Compared with Wonder's subsequent efforts, it pales just slightly. *—Rob Bowman*

★ **Talking Book** / Oct. 27, 1972 / Motown ✦✦✦✦✦
Stevie Wonder came into his own with *Music of My Mind*, but *Talking Book* is where he hit his stride, developing a signature blend of sweet pop, spacy studio experimentation, and hard funk. This wasn't just far removed from what his Motown labelmates were doing, this was far removed from anything his peers were making either, due to his meticulous studiocraft. With a few exceptions, Wonder played everything on the album, relying largely on synthesizers, then piecing it together meticulously in his studio. This gave the music a unique character, warm but insular—this was certainly music of his mind, self-contained and idiosyncratic, yet inviting and generous. Take "I Believe (When I Fall in Love It Will Be Forever)," a psychedelic love song that drifts though its verses before it reaches its anthemic chorus. It's a head trip, yet it pulls the listener in and that's the album—"You Are the Sunshine of My Life" and "Superstition" pull the listener in, setting the stage for such wonderful opposites as the dreamy "You've Got It Bad Girl" or the ominous, funky "Maybe Your Baby." Wonder isn't just a master of mood, he's a tremendous songwriter, and those two elements blend together seamlessly here, kicking off a series of albums that remain among the most impressive in rock, pop, or soul. *—Stephen Thomas Erlewine*

☆ **Innervisions** / Aug. 3, 1973 / Motown ✦✦✦✦✦
The political undercurrents long simmering in Stevie Wonder's work reached their boiling point on the masterful *Innervisions*, a record as potent and insightful in its exploration of contemporary life as Marvin Gaye's *What's Going On* two years earlier. The opening "Too High," an acute condemnation of drug use, quickly establishes the record's

forceful yet vibrant tone, which alternates between utopian dreamscapes ("Visions") and tough-minded realism ("Jesus Children of America"); the record's dueling concerns converge on the hit "Living for the City," which is both a brilliant examination of the myriad social ills so endemic to the ghetto experience and a stirring celebration of African-American resilience. And on "Higher Ground," Wonder even points a finger at himself to detail a sinner's second chance at life—a song which took on even greater resonance in the wake of the car crash which nearly killed him just months after the LP's release. *—Jason Ankeny*

Fulfillingness' First Finale / Jul. 22, 1974 / Motown ♦♦♦♦♦
With *Innervisions*, Stevie Wonder eclipsed his peers not just as a musician, but as a social commentator, and it was a hard record to top. If *Fulfillingness' First Finale* doesn't top it, it's nevertheless a fascinating move forward, as Wonder starts to deepen his eclecticism. Despite the portrait of MLK on the back cover, he tempers his social criticism somewhat, though the scathing "You Haven't Done Nothin'" is perhaps his fiercest song. The rest of the record is a little sweet and trippy, a sentiment that infects even such groovers as "Boogie on Reggae Woman." This characteristic means that *Fulfillingness* is perhaps the most idiosyncratic record he released during his classic period, and it demands some serious attention from the listener, since it can drift off in an insular haze. Yet, it's a fascinating, intricate, albeit slightly stoned, record that does reward that bit of intense, concentrated listening. *—Stephen Thomas Erlewine*

☆ **Songs in the Key of Life** / Sep. 28, 1976 / Motown ♦♦♦♦♦
Stevie Wonder's classic period peaked with *Songs in the Key of Life*. Not coincidentally, it's also the peak of his ambition and excess, spreading out over two albums, plus a bonus EP (now part of the last disc on a two-CD set), which gives him plenty of space to explore (or indulge, depending on your charity). And there are some superbly indulgent moments here, yet this is the kind of double album where those excesses add to the overall effect, making the immediate songs—"Sir Duke," "I Wish," "Isn't She Lovely"—shine all the more brightly, and providing little detours to explore on repeated listens. Musically, this is more consolidation than progression, adding elements of the direct *Talking Book* to the pseudo-psychedelic *Fulfillingness' First Finale*, leaving the record as a grand, sprawling demonstration of Wonder at his very peak. Though he tried to move further and farther, he never equaled this, which shines as brightly on its hits as it does in its eccentricities. *—Stephen Thomas Erlewine*

★ **Looking Back** / Nov. 30, 1977 / Motown ♦♦♦♦♦
Between 1963 and the end of 1971, Stevie Wonder placed 25 songs on *Billboard*'s charts. Twenty-four of those—including such radio staples as "Fingertips—Pt. 2," "Uptight (Everything's Alright)," "I Was Made to Love Her," "For Once in My Life," "My Cherie Amour," and "Signed, Sealed, Delivered, I'm Yours"—appear on *Looking Back*. Wonder's recordings in the '60s stand apart from most Motown acts partially because he was paired with producers and writers who very rarely worked with the Temptations, Supremes, et al. In the beginning Wonder was often produced by Clarence Paul and/or William Stevenson; during the golden years, Henry Cosby was usually manning the controls. Then in 1970, Wonder started producing himself, beginning with "Signed, Sealed, Delivered." Most of Wonder's singles were written by Wonder himself in tandem with a variety of others, or by Ron Miller. The hits alternated between stomping barn-burners and mid-tempo, understated ballads. *—Rob Bowman*

Journey Through the Secret Life of Plants / Oct. 30, 1979 / Motown ♦♦♦
Perhaps the most curious album in Stevie Wonder's career, this was ostensibly a soundtrack for a film few people saw (if indeed it was ever released). These were mostly instrumentals, plus a few oddball vocals, but most observers didn't know what to make of it at the time. Wonder was so hot that the record peaked at number four on the pop albums chart, despite the lack of any real singles and confounding almost everyone who heard it. Though "Send One Your Love" and "Outside My Window" both made the pop charts, the R&B community ignored the entire album. *—Ron Wynn*

Hotter Than July / Sep. 29, 1980 / Motown ♦♦♦♦♦
Hotter Than July was Wonder's real follow-up to *Songs in the Key of Life*, even if it took him the then-unconscionably long four years to release it. Wonder had been perhaps the most accomplished and successful pop artist of the years 1972-1977, but his absence had cooled him off commercially, and this album demonstrated that, artistically, he was also past his peak. Individual moments suggested his earlier triumphs, and Wonder remained a remarkably facile singer/player/composer, but he had lost his ability to amaze his listeners. The album's biggest single was "Master Blaster (Jammin')" (#5 pop, #1 R&B), an adequate but unremarkable reggae number, but the standout track was "Happy Birthday," the theme song for the ultimately successful campaign to make Dr. Martin Luther King, Jr.'s birthday a national holiday. *—William Ruhlmann*

★ **Original Musiquarium I** / May 4, 1982 / Motown ♦♦♦♦♦
Released in 1982, the double-album *Original Musiquarium I* summarizes Stevie Wonder's classic period of the '70s, concentrating primarily on the hits, but adding a few album tracks to hint at the depth of his albums, as well as four new songs (one for each side, all pleasant, none particularly remarkable). Though there could be some dispute about the album tracks, this does wind up as an excellent overview of Wonder's period of greatest activity, and it's a terrific listen to boot—any record that sports such hits as "Superstition," "You Haven't Done Nothin'," "Living for the City," "You Are the Sunshine of My Life," "Higher Ground," "Sir Duke," "Boogie on Reggae Woman," and "I Wish" is guaranteed to be a great listen, and it is. Wonder remains a quintessential album artist, but this record is a terrific snapshot of the highlights. *—Stephen Thomas Erlewine*

The Woman in Red / Aug. 28, 1984 / Motown ♦♦♦
Stevie Wonder's career in the 1980s was a source of frustration to the fans he had earned in the '60s and '70s. In 1982, there were a few new songs on a greatest-hits album and a duet with Paul McCartney. Then came this soundtrack to a Gene Wilder comedy that was simultaneously more of a pop vocal album than most soundtracks and yet less than a full-fledged Wonder record. The gold-selling #1 hit that resulted was the sappy "I Just Called To Say I Love You," a formulaic TV commercial-in-the-making. "Love Light In Flight" also hit, and the album featured Dionne Warwick on two duets and one solo. This was a pleasant record, but slight, and after four years, Wonder fans wanted more than that. *—William Ruhlmann*

In Square Circle / Sep. 13, 1985 / Motown ♦♦♦
Although it went platinum, nothing stands as better evidence of how cyclical the pop experience is than the response to *In Square Circle*. Wonder actually wrote some superb songs, and several, like "Overjoyed" and "I Love You Too Much," were superior to the hit single "Part-Time Lover." But that one zoomed to the top spot and became the album's definitive tune in the minds of many. *—Ron Wynn*

Characters / Nov. 6, 1987 / Motown ♦♦♦
Wonder shocked fans by taking only two years to release his next new non-soundtrack studio album, *Characters*. Unfortunately, it had long since become clear that Wonder was willing to settle for good pop music without challenging himself to make great pop music. And by now, a big chunk of his formerly mass audience had gotten the message: this was Wonder's first new album to miss the pop Top Five in 15 years. (The Black music audience, however, responded far more favorably, as the album topped the R&B charts for seven weeks.) The biggest single was the "Superstition"-like dance track "Skeletons" (#19 Pop, #1 R&B), and Wonder also charted with the pretty "You Will Know" and an uptempo duet with Michael Jackson, "Get It." *—William Ruhlmann*

Jungle Fever / May 22, 1991 / Motown ♦♦♦
Despite all of the hype surrounding it, the soundtrack to *Jungle Fever* is Stevie Wonder's best work in years. Although it can't compare to Wonder's glory days, *Jungle Fever* is a considerable improvement from his bland late-'80s albums. Wonder still borders on saccharine on his ballads, although even the sappiest of them ("These Three Words") is never as sickening as "I Just Called to Say I Love You." While the keyboard funk of "Chemical Love," "Gotta Have You" and "Queen in the Black" doesn't sound new, it does sound alive, which is better than Wonder has sounded in years. *—Stephen Thomas Erlewine*

Conversation Peace / Mar. 21, 1995 / Motown ♦♦♦
Stevie Wonder's albums have not caught the public's attention since the mid-'80s, and *Conversation Peace* did not change that, although it wasn't for lack of trying. Wonder's gift for melody is still in place, and he incorporates understated hip-hop rhythms into his music well, yet he isn't able to make music that fits into the rigid playlists of '90s urban contemporary radio. *—Stephen Thomas Erlewine*

Natural Wonder / Nov. 21, 1995 / Motown ♦♦♦
Following the relative commercial failure of *Conversation Peace*, Stevie Wonder rushed out this double-disc live album drawn from an international tour during which he was backed by different symphony orchestras, his older songs featuring string parts in place of the synthesizer lines. He introduced several new songs—"Dancing to the Rhythm," and the instrumental "Stevie Ray Blues," "Stay Gold," and "Ms. & Mr. Little Ones"—which demonstrated that his melodic muse was still with him and that he remained an awkward lyricist when he was more interested in the political stance than the poetical scansion. But for most of the running time, he acted as a human jukebox, pumping out his bits with enthusiasm and humor before an audibly enthralled audience. That made *Natural Wonder* entertaining, but inessential. *—William Ruhlmann*

Song Review: Greatest Hits / Dec. 10, 1996 / Motown ♦♦♦♦♦
While it's not quite the definitive compilation it could have been, the double-disc *Song Review: Greatest Hits* is still a good overview of Stevie Wonder's long, prolific career. Skipping over "Fingertips, Pt. 2" and picking up with "Uptight (Everything's Alright)" and "I Was Made to Love Her," *Song Review* runs through the next three decades, hitting most of his biggest hits along the way, including "Signed, Sealed, Delivered I'm Yours," "Superstition," "You Are the Sunshine of My Life," "Higher Ground," "Living for the City," "I Wish," "Master Blaster (Jammin')," "Ebony and Ivory," "I Just Called to Say I Love You," and "Part-Time Lover." Unfortunately, none of the songs are presented in chronological order. It begins in the '80s, switches to the '70s, hits the '80s again before going back to the '60s—in other words, it's not really coherent. Nevertheless, most of Wonder's best-known and a good cross-section of his very best songs are included, making *Song Review* a fine, but not perfect, introduction to his career. *—Stephen Thomas Erlewine*

☆ **At the Close of the Century** / Nov. 23, 1999 / Motown ♦♦♦♦♦
He's been called one of the most influential performers and songwriters of the century, but until 1999 Stevie Wonder didn't even have a box set to call his own. Such was the reissue campaign at Motown that, until very recently, some of the best pop music of the '60s sounded poorer in reissue form than when it was first played on AM radio. In 1996, the long-awaited Stevie Wonder digital-age hits package *Song Review* reached the shelves, but it didn't even follow compilation etiquette (that is, chronological order). Finally, *At the Close of a Century* made everything right—complete with digital remastering, near-perfect sound, complete coverage of his epic career, an attractive design, and copious liner notes and pictures. The box, a four-disc set spanning 1962 to 1996, debuts with "Fingertips, Pts. 1 & 2," the long-unheard seven-minute version of his first hit. The first disc includes every hit that fans can remember, including great-sounding versions of "Uptight (Everything's Alright)" and "Hey Love," plus plenty of moderate hits they may not remember, like his definitive cover of the Beatles' "We Can Work It Out." Disc two features more than a dozen of his biggest hits, including "Superstition," "You Are the Sunshine of My Life," "Living for the City," "Higher Ground," and "Boogie On Reggae Woman." Disc

three begins with no less than nine tracks from *Songs in the Key of Life*, his standout double album from 1976. Right into the '80s and '90s, Stevie Wonder remained at the top of the charts, with hits like "Rocket Love," "Master Blaster (Jammin')," "Happy Birthday," "I Just Called to Say I Love You," and "Part-Time Lover." It took far too long, but Motown finally issued a box set worthy of Stevie Wonder's continuing artistry. *—John Bush*

The Wondermints

Power Pop, Pop Underground

The Wondermints were formed in Los Angeles in 1991 by guitarists/vocalists/songwriters Darian Sahanaja and Nick Walusko, drummer/vocalist Mike D'Amico, and bassist Brian Kassan. They recorded three demo cassettes from 1992 to 1994, which got them a deal with the Japanese label Toy's Factory. Their self-titled 1995 debut on Toy's Factory was re-released in the U.S. on Big Deal and attracted notice in power-pop circles for its wide array of classic pop influences. Kassan then left to form Chewy Marble and was replaced by Probyn Gregory, who handled bass and horn work on the song the Wondermints contributed to the soundtrack of the 1997 Mike Myers comedy *Austin Powers: International Man of Mystery*. The band also recorded a Japanese-only all-covers album, *The Wonderful World of the Wondermints*, and backed Brian Wilson on tour before resurfacing with *Bali*, which received a proper release in 2000. *—Steve Huey*

● **Wondermints** / 1995 / Toy's Factory ✦✦✦✦✦

Throughout the early '90s, the Wondermints recorded a bevy of exceptional homemade demos and small indie singles primarily in co-founder Darian Sahanaja's bedroom studio. Slowly but surely that music circulated through the Los Angeles underground music scene on a series of semi-legendary tapes identified solely by their colors. The band's music, however, still flew under the radar of the music business until the Japanese label Toy's Factory picked up the slack, releasing an eponymous debut in 1995 that cherry-picked the very best songs from those original tapes. It is hard to imagine a more auspicious and stunning debut of pop/rock accomplishment than *Wondermints*. The album is primarily the baby of Sahanaja and co-founder Nick Walusko, who wrote all the songs between them. They owe a huge debt to Brian Wilson, both in song construction and melodies as well as in the production on the bulk of the songs. The sunfried ambience of '70s power pop and classic FM rock holds an equally powerful sway over their sound. What the album comes down to, however, is not the references from which it was constructed, but rather how amazingly fresh and dynamic it manages to sound even while sonically name-checking those artists. It is state-of-the-art '90s pop/rock, at once reverential and ambitious. And it only grows more inventive as it goes, hitting its most original (not to mention psychedelic and spacy) peak during the second half of the album on remarkable songs like "Global Village Idiot" and "Playtex Aviary." It is a rare first attempt on which the band's reach and grasp are virtually identical. *—Stanton Swihart*

Wonderful World of the Wondermints / 1996 / Toy's Factory ✦✦✦

Technically, this second album from the Wondermints isn't *their* wonderful world at all, since it consists entirely of cover songs. Figuratively, however, this is exactly the world that gave birth to and nourished the band, the great pop records of the 1960s and 1970s from which they learned their chops, and a legacy the band had not only absorbed but also taken into the future and elevated to new heights on their debut album. At the same time, although an enjoyable exercise, it is not really the artistic statement that the band had envisioned recording for their second album. It was recorded on the insistence of their Japanese label, Toy's Factory. Regardless of its genesis, though, it is undoubtedly a stellar and revealing effort, a valuable window into the building blocks that created the band. They better virtually every song here, with the exceptions of the indomitable Five Stairsteps classic "Ooh Child," Pink Floyd's brilliant "Arnold Layne," and ABBA's "Knowing Me, Knowing Me," which is really apples-and-oranges anyway. That isn't to depreciate any of the original artists, but instead says volumes about the brilliance of the Wondermints, not only their interpretive powers but also the resonance of their artistry. In a way, although it is an oblique step sideways rather than forward from their original work, *Wonderful World* goes further towards defining what is special about the band than their previous album had. What could have been a loose run-through or soundcheck for the "real" work turns into an album that is not only wholly enjoyable, but also stands on its own quite admirably. The music is not a pastiche of past influences; it is a refining of and advancement on them. *—Stanton Swihart*

Bali / 1998 / EMI ✦✦✦✦

Long unavailable in America, the record that snagged a support slot for Brian Wilson's 1999 solo tour features a parade of classic '60s pop influences, from the Left Banke ("Hypnolove") to the Zombies ("Sting O'Luv") to late-period Beatles ("In and Around Greg Lake") and, of course, the Beach Boys ("Spoke of a Wheel Whirled"). The songwriting could be a bit stronger, and the vintage production tricks don't always come off, but overall *Bali* is an excellent album that ably reaches out to fans of classic rock and power-pop as well as the mid-'90s offerings by the Elephant 6 indie collective. *—John Bush*

Brenton Wood

b. Jun. 26, 1941, Shreveport, LA

Vocals / Brown-Eyed Soul, Pop-Soul, Soul, Beach

Brenton Wood's charmingly unpredictable phrasing and his infectious sense of good times made the smooth uptown soul of "The Oogum Boogum Song" and "Gimme Little Sign" into hits in 1967. Despite his skill as a pop-soul vocalist, Wood was never able to match such heights again, yet those two songs became genuine R&B classics of their era. Wood formed the Quotations during college, but soon after graduation he became a solo act. Signing with Double Shot Records, Wood had a hit single in the spring of 1967 with "The Oogum Boogum Song," which reached number 19 on the R&B charts and number 34 pop. It was quickly followed by "Gimme Little Sign," which climbed to number nine pop and matched its predecessor's R&B position. It was a promising start to a career, but Wood wasn't able to follow it through. "Baby You Got It" stalled in the bottom reaches of the pop and R&B Top 40 in early 1968 and "Some Got It, Some Don't" failed to make the pop charts later that year. Wood continued to perform and even recorded a duet with Shirley Goodman, but he wasn't able to reach the charts again until 1977, when "Come Softly to Me" registered in the lower reaches of the R&B Top 100. Following its release, Wood faded away, becoming part of the oldies soul circuit. *—Stephen Thomas Erlewine*

● **Brenton Wood's 18 Best** / Jun. 5, 1992 / Original Sound ✦✦✦✦✦

It's hard not to hear Brenton Wood's biggest hit "Gimme Little Sign" and not be convinced that it very well might be the greatest single ever cut. It relies on no one thing—the song is slinky, surprising and seductive, blessed with a perfect production (the organ break in the middle is positively, eerily beautiful) and a wonderful, understated performance by Wood, who proves with his smooth, sure-handed delivery that he is one of the finest soul singers of his generation. Apart from "Gimme Little Sign" and the cheerful, infectious "Oogun Boogum," he had few blockbusters, but those were two of the best singles of the '60s, and the rest of his canon was uniformly enjoyable, even if lacking songs as undeniable as that pair. Sadly, his catalog still lacks a truly convincing overview of his career, but, in a pinch, *18 Best* will have to do. Doggedly non-chronological, lacking liner notes or cohesion, and not necessarily spotlighting his best, it still does make a strong case for Wood's talents as a singer and even the weaker material is enjoyable, thanks to his voice and production. It may not be perfect, but it does have a perfect single, one nearly as good, and a bunch of other songs that prove Wood was at the forefront of uptown soul in the '60s. *—Stephen Thomas Erlewine*

18 More of the Best, Vol. 2 / Oct. 5, 1999 / Original Sound ✦✦✦✦

Brenton Wood's biggest hits were covered on Original Sound's first collection, *18 of the Best*, which leaves this collection without any easy hook into its treasures. But, make no mistake, even with this shoddy packaging, indifferent mastering, and haphazard sequencing (including some songs that might not have made the cut in a more carefully considered collection), this still has a number of wonderful, easygoing, classy pop-soul gems that offer convincing evidence that Wood is one of the most underrated soul singers of his time. And, considering that so little of his material is easily available on CD, you take these kind of pleasures wherever you can find them. *—Stephen Thomas Erlewine*

This Love Is for Real / Apr. 10, 2001 / Varese ✦✦

On his first collection of all-new recordings in a decade, Brenton Wood presented mostly new songs, along with remakes of "Boogum Boogum Boogum/The Oogum Boogum Song" and "Baby You Got It." It's always a bad sign on comebacks by soul veterans when you see keyboard programmers credited on most of the songs. True to suspicions, this is mellow soul updated with contemporary arrangements, with synthesizers and ultra-sweet backup vocals. Whether intentionally or not, the impression is that of songs calculated to pick up adult contemporary radio airplay. The best that can be said is that Wood's voice is good, and still expert at hitting the high silky notes. But the material is dull, and the production worse. *—Richie Unterberger*

Ron Wood

b. Jun. 1, 1947, Hillingdon, London

Vocals, Guitar, Bass / Rock & Roll

U.K. guitarist Ron Wood has spent most of his career in groups—the Creation, the Jeff Beck Group, Faces, and, since 1976, the Rolling Stones—but he's found time to make a variety of non-group albums, including duet albums with Ronnie Lane and with Bo Diddley, and even a few solo albums that serve as assemblages of his friends. *—William Ruhlmann*

I've Got My Own Album to Do / 1974 / Warner Brothers ✦✦✦✦✦

For his first album, Ron Wood enlisted Keith Richards and the Faces' pianist Ian McLagan as support and turned in a loose, good-humored album that catches fire on the swaggering "Take a Look at the Guy," the earnest cover of "If You Gotta Make a Fool of Somebody," and the grinding R&B workout "Crotch Music." *—Stephen Thomas Erlewine*

Now Look / 1975 / Warner Brothers ✦✦✦✦

Now Look, Ron Wood's second solo album, was a tighter affair than his debut, yet it lost none of its predecessor's off-the-cuff charm, thanks to convincing, ragged covers of Ann Peeble's "I Can't Stand the Rain" and "I Got Lost When I Found You," which was written by the album's producer, Bobby Womack. *—Stephen Thomas Erlewine*

Mahoney's Last Stand / 1976 / Atlantic ✦✦✦

Billed as an "Original Motion Picture Soundtrack," fellow Faces Wood and Lane come up with various stabs at instrumental music for film, as well as a few songs too. Backed by various other Faces, a member of the Who, a Fairport Conventioner, and a violinist from Family and/or Blind Faith, Wood and Lane ham things up like one could only do on a movie soundtrack back in the '70s. *—James Chrispell*

● **Gimme Some Neck** / 1979 / Columbia ✦✦✦✦✦

Wood leads a pickup band that includes, on various cuts, fellow Rolling Stones Charlie Watts, Mick Jagger, and Keith Richards, plus Mick Fleetwood, Dave Mason, and other notables. The highlight is a then-unreleased Bob Dylan song called "Seven Days," where the rough-voiced Wood sounds uncannily like Mr. D himself. *—William Ruhlmann*

1234 / 1981 / CBS ✦✦

Slide on This / Sep. 1992 / Continuum ✦✦✦

Ron Wood's first solo album in over ten years is a relaxed, rocking, star-studded affair, including appearances by Charlie Watts, Hothouse Flowers, Joe Elliott from Def Leppard, and the Edge. Nothing here is earth-shaking, but the quality of "Knock Yer Teeth Out,"

"Show Me," and a cover of The Parliaments' "Testify" makes *Slide on This* Wood's best solo album. —*AMG*

Slide on Live / 1994 / Continuum ♦♦

Roy Wood

b. Nov. 8, 1946, Birmingham, England

Multi Instruments, Wind, Vocals, Keyboards, Horn, Cello, Songwriter, Guitar, Bass, Bagpipes / Album Rock, Pop/Rock, Glam Rock, Prog-Rock/Art Rock, Hard Rock, Rock & Roll

Roy Wood has long been regarded as one of the most important, if eccentric, rock musicians to come out of Birmingham, primarily for his role as the leader/cofounder of both the Move and the Electric Light Orchestra. He organized the Move in 1964, and the group hit big three years later with the number two hit "Night of Fear." By 1971 though, Wood had developed ideas and ambitions that were too wide to be embraced by any one band, so he formed an offshoot of the Move called the Electric Light Orchestra. The new band soon attracted more serious attention than the Move, though Wood soon left both groups to form Wizzard. Singles like "Ballpark Incident" and "See My Baby Jive" did very well on the British charts, though the band's first album, *Wizzard's Brew*, didn't fare nearly as well. Wood continued recording and releasing records under his own name in addition to his work with Wizzard, and found hits with 1973's "I Wish It Could Be Christmas Everyday" and "Forever." Meanwhile, Wood's own solo albums, *Boulders* (1973) and *Mustard* (1975) were too idiosyncratic to achieve major followings. After the demise of Wizzard in 1974, his subsequent solo records, *On the Road* (1979) and *Starting Up* (1987) failed to achieve anything like the success of his early-'70s work. —*Bruce Eder*

Wizzard Brew / Mar. 1973 / EMI/Harvest ♦♦♦

Roy Wood designed Wizzard's singles to be hooky, accessible propositions. The "real art" was saved for the albums...or at least that's the impression their debut, *Wizzard Brew*, leaves. It's hard to tell what to make of *Wizzard Brew*, actually, and it seems all the stranger since it was released the same year as four jubilant, sparkling pop singles, all deliberately left off of the LP. Stylistically, the album isn't all that different from the hits—four of the six songs are firmly rooted in '50s rock & roll, while the other two hearken back to the Move at their most self-consciously British—but the music sounds as if it was performed by a different band. In a way, *Wizzard Brew* picks up where "Brontosaurus" left off, since its foundation is heavy on guitars and complicated riffing, yet that still doesn't explain the strangeness of the album. Despite its Chuck Berry/Eddie Cochran roots, the record plays like sonic terrorism—a bizarre blend of boogie riffs and old-time rock & roll, spiked with traces of British psychedelia and music hall, all filtered through sheer white noise. *Wizzard Brew* is easily the noisiest damn record of its era—compressed, processed, and flattened within an inch of its life. It's possible that this is all the result of a studio mishap, but it doesn't feel that way. The noise feels like an artistic decision, a way to push Wizzard's blend of retro rock and art into uncharted territory. It's the polar opposite of ELO—consciously primitive art-rock. Only two songs clock in at under five minutes; the rest beat the listener into submission with their pummeling riffs, unbridled boogie, and sheets of noise. It leaves you dazed and senseless, yet not necessarily satisfied. —*Stephen Thomas Erlewine*

● **Boulders** / Jul. 1973 / BGO ♦♦♦♦♦

An intricate, deliberately idiosyncratic record, assembled piece by piece, *Boulders* perfectly captures Roy Wood's peculiar genius, more so than anything else he recorded. All of his obsessions are here—classical music, psychedelia, pre-Beatles pop, pastoral folk ballads, absurdist humor, studio trickery, and good old-fashioned rock & roll—assembled in a gracefully eccentric fashion. Some listeners may find that eccentricity a little alienating, but it's the core of Wood's music. He wrote tuneful, accessible songs, but indulged his passions and weird ideas, so even the loveliest melodies and catchiest hooks are dressed in colorful, odd arrangements. The marvelous thing is, these arrangements never sound self-consciously weird—it's the sound of Wood's music in full bloom. Never before and never again did his quirks sound so charming, even thrilling, as they do on *Boulders*. As soon as "Songs of Praise" reaches its chorus, a choir of sped-up, multi-tracked Roys kick in, sending it into the stratosphere. All nine tunes unwind in a similar fashion, each blessed with delightfully unpredictable twists. It's easy to spot the tossed-off jokes on the goofy "When Gran'ma Plays the Banjo," but it may take several spins to realize that the percussion on "Wake Up" is the sound of Roy slapping a bowl of water. *Boulders* is a sonic mosaic—you can choose to wonder at the little details or gaze at the glorious whole, enjoying the shape it forms. Wood has an unerring knack for melodies, whether they're in folk ballads, sweet pop or old-fashioned rock & rollers, yet his brilliance is how he turns the hooks 180 degrees until they're gloriously out of sync with his influences and peers. *Boulders* still sounds wonderfully out of time and it's easy to argue that it's the peak of his career. —*Stephen Thomas Erlewine*

Introducing Eddy & the Falcons / Aug. 1974 / Edsel ♦♦♦

Since Roy Wood loves music more than the nostalgia, on Wizzard's early rock & roll tribute *Introducing Eddy & the Falcons* he doesn't offer an oldie pastiche, a la Sha Na Na. Wood takes this project very seriously even when he's offering gentle satire. He wrote eight different stylistic and artistic tributes, summarizing with the closing "We're Gonna Rock & Roll Tonight," a song that recalls such latter-day Move rockers as "California Man"—a neat way of illustrating what Roy learned, actually. The rest of the album is deliberately self-conscious, as Wood labors to reconstruct specific sounds—Phil Spector on "This Is the Story of My Love (Baby)," Del Shannon's "Runaway" on "Everyday I Wonder," Elvis on "I Dun Lotsa Cryin' Over You," teen idol pop on "You Got Me Runnin'." The trick is, Wood's writing retains much of its character no matter what suit he tries on. Depending on your point of view, this is a fun stylistic exercise—either in Wood's musicality or in

nostalgic almost-camp—or it's a little contrived and irritating. *Eddy & the Falcons* divides audiences in two because it's too easy to hear the wheels turning on certain songs. This may not bother listeners looking for a straight-up rock & roll record, especially since a handful of songs are pretty good, yet Wood fans that cherish his eccentricity and ability to fuse disparate strands into something distinctive will likely appreciate *Eddy & the Falcons* as a conceptual coup rather than truly enjoy it. [Edsel Records reissued *Introducing Eddy & the Falcons* on CD in 1999 with five bonus tracks; they don't jibe with the rest of the record, but they are interesting, even if there are no real classics among them.] —*Stephen Thomas Erlewine*

Mustard / Nov. 1975 / Edsel ♦♦♦♦♦

Unlike *Boulders*, *Mustard* is designed as a full-fledged album instead of a collection of pop vignettes. Outside of Wood's love for Brian Wilson there's no concept, yet it flows smoothly and attractively, since each song sounds like an epic pop extravaganza in miniature. In a typically perverse turn, Wood opens the record with a scratchy parody of the Andrews Sisters, tackling the harmonies with sped-up vocal tapes, but as soon as "Any Old Time Will Do" kicks off, it's clear that this is a shining, glittering pop record. There isn't much of his signature absurdist humor or quirky studio effects, apart from the jaw-dropping "You Sure Got It Now," a masterwork that Wood claims "sounds like the Andrews Sisters backed by John Mayall," yet it isn't missed since the studiocraft on *Mustard* is quite alluring. Where *Boulders* felt homemade, almost pastoral, *Mustard* is unabashedly grand, bolstered by endlessly layered harmonies, chiming keyboards, and cavernous productions. The Beach Boys influences shine brightly on "Why Does a Pretty Girl Sing Those Sad Songs" and "Look Thru' the Eyes of a Fool," and are inescapable on the gorgeous ballad "The Rain Came Down on Everything." Wood never really rocks out until the multi-segmented closer, "Get on Down Home" and even if it's the one misstep, it hardly detracts from the pop wonders that precede it. *Mustard* might not equal the brilliantly maverick *Boulders*, yet it's easily one of the best, most cohesive records Wood ever made and one of the few to capture him as a (relatively) focused pop craftsman. [Edsel's 1999 CD reissue of *Mustard* is graced by no less than seven bonus tracks, all A- and B-sides of non-LP singles, highlighted by "Oh What a Shame" and "Indiana Rainbow."] —*Stephen Thomas Erlewine*

The Roy Wood Years 1971-73 You Can Dance the Rock & Roll / 1979 / EMI/Harvest ♦♦♦♦♦

The finest compilation of Wood's work to date, drawing on his closing years with The Move, his sole album with ELO, the biggest hits of Wizzard, and Wood's official solo albums and singles. —*Bruce Eder*

Singles / Aug. 11, 1995 / Repertoire ♦♦♦♦♦

If there's anything wrong with Repertoire's *Singles A's & B's*, it's that Wizzard peaked early, albeit brilliantly, and their B-sides never capitalized on their dazzling, Spector/Beach Boys-tinted rock & roll. It's no coincidence that those B-sides were written by everybody else in the band but Wood, and that most of those were instrumentals. Some are amusing (the mild ELO send-up "Bend Over Beethoven"), some are interesting ("Rob Roy's Nightmare"), but they're all disposable, especially when compared to the A-sides, which are uniformly enchanting. True, they're a little similar—the core is straight-ahead, old-fashioned rock & roll, sort of like Dave Edmunds, graced with wildly ornate arrangements and vocal harmonies—but "Ball Park Incident," "See My Baby Jive," "Angel Fingers," "Rock & Roll Winter," "This Is the Story of My Love (Baby)," and "I Wish It Could Be Christmas Everyday" are all giddy entertainments. The three remaining singles were recorded when Wizzard was trucking as the oldies outfit Eddy & the Falcons, a silly but enjoyable trek into nostalgia highlighted by the *Grease*-soundalike "You Got Me Running." Considering the quality of the nine A-sides, it's easy to wish that they had been combined with Wood's solo A-sides on a dynamite single disc, but that's not what happened—and, perhaps that's appropriate, since with the preponderance of B-sides on both discs are accurate representations of how idiosyncratic Wood is. Even if it is a bit uneven, there's little argument that *Singles* is much, much better and considerably more logical than most Wood/Wizzard compilations. —*Stephen Thomas Erlewine*

● **Exotic Mixture** / Oct. 12, 1999 / Repertoire ♦♦♦♦

Even though it spans two discs and nearly 40 songs, *Exotic Mixture* is hardly the definitive word on Roy Wood. Part of the problem is that it excludes Wizzard recordings (featured on *Singles A's & B's*), but the real problem is that it, like Wood, simply covers too much ground. *Exotic Mixture* is evenly divided, with the first disc devoted to *Boulders* through *Mustard* (plus assorted singles), the second running from 1977's *Super Active Wizzo* to 1987's *Starting Up* (plus assorted singles). The second disc has some fine moments—Roy's duet single with Annie Haslam, "I Never Believed in Love"/"Inside My Life," isn't bad; "Dancing at the Rainbow's End" is strong; and even 1985's "Sing Out the Old—Bring in the New" is a solid piece of Wizzard-styled Spector/Wilson pop—but, by and large, it's forgettable in comparison to the first disc. Although Wizzard singles are sadly absent from the first disc and the inclusion of instrumental B-sides hurts its momentum, it remains terrific. Over half of *Boulders* is here, as is over half of *Mustard*, as are such spectacular non-LP singles as "Going Down the Road," the Beach Boys tribute "Forever," and "Indiana Rainbow." These songs capture Wood at a pinnacle, and even if they're surrounded by filler when they should be surrounded by Wizzard, no other compilation has managed to summarize his solo work as well as the first disc of *Exotic Mixture*. —*Stephen Thomas Erlewine*

Main Street / May 2, 2000 / Edsel ♦♦

Recorded in 1976, but not released until 2000 because the record label considered it uncommercial, *Main Street* proves the record company right—there was no way in hell this collection of winding jazz-influenced instrumentals, studio experimentation, and dense post-Beach Boys pop would have gotten onto the charts, particularly in 1976. That doesn't mean that it should have sat on the shelves for nearly 25 years, either, since Roy Wood's cult is of the kind that will purchase anything he cut. Still, this can be pretty tough sledding even for that cult, since it isn't so much eccentric as it is messy. There are a few nice moments here and there, particularly on the terrific "Indiana Rainbow," but that's better heard on *Exotic Mixture*. This is for Roy fanatics and historians; interesting to hear once, but unlikely to find its way back to the stereo too often. *—Stephen Thomas Erlewine*

Very Best Of Roy Wood: Through The Years / May 20, 2000 / EMI Gold ✦✦✦✦

Given that Roy Wood scored a lot of hits during the late '60s to the early '80s in groups like the Move and Wizzard or recording as a solo artist, it's impossible that a single-disc retrospective could capture all the highlights from this era but *The Very Best of Roy Wood: Through The Years* provides a solid sampler of Wood's songwriting and performing skills. It starts with the latter-day Move hits like "Down on the Bay" and "California Man" but spends most of its time on Wood's early- to mid-'70s era, dividing its time between his glam rocking hits with Wizzard and his solo exercises in retro-pop. In the Wizzard category, the combination of power chords and pomp-rock instrumentation that dominate Phil Spector-influenced stompers like "See My Baby Jive" and "Ball Park Incident" remains bracing today. The solo hits cover a more impressive, diverse swath of stylistic territory, including everything from Beach Boys-style harmonic pop like "Forever" to the unlikely but listenable fusion of Scottish folk and reggae rhythms on "Goin' Down the Road." This set also throws in some rarities for the hardcore fan, mainly fun, impressively arranged instrumentals like the harpsichord-dominated "Carlsberg Special" and the quirky yet majestic "Premium Bond Theme." Despite this engaging collection of material, *Through the Years* fails to live up to its ambitious title because it is too short (two discs would have worked better) and it omits crucial early Move songs like "I Can Hear the Grass Grow" and "Hello Suzie" due to licensing restrictions. Just the same, the quality of what was included can't be denied and *Through the Years* makes a fine sampler of Wood's prodigious talents for the uninitiated listener. *—Donald A. Guarisco*

The Woodentops

f. 1983, **db.** 1992

Alternative Pop/Rock

Taking punk's D.I.Y. ideals and applying it to stripped-down acoustic pop, the Woodentops achieved a great deal of critical success in the short time they were together. Formed in the early '80s in Northhampton, England, the group consisted of Rolo McGinty (vocals, guitar), Frank de Freitas (bass), Simon Mawby (guitar), Benny Staples (drums), and Alice Thompson (keyboards). The band released their debut single "Plenty" on Food Records; the record led to a contract with Rough Trade. Throughout 1985, the Woodentops released a series of singles, all written by McGinty, that began to attract an audience in the U.K. The group released their acclaimed debut album, *Giant*, in 1986. The following year, the band began experimenting with their sound, adding tougher guitars and electronics. These changes were particularly evident in their live show, as shown by their 1987 live recording, *Hypno-Beat*. Featuring the contributions of professional studio musicians Bernie Worrell and Doug Wimbish among others, 1988's *Wooden Foot Cops on the Highway* continued the group's experimentations with rhythmic and sonic textures.

While the band managed to keep creative, they weren't able to gain much of an audience anywhere outside Japan. In 1991 and 1992, they toured the world without ever becoming any bigger than a cult band. Soon after, the Woodentops broke up. *—Stephen Thomas Erlewine*

Well Well Well: The Unabridged Singles Collection / 1986 / Upside ✦✦✦✦✦

While the Woodentops' music obliquely shows influences as diverse as Devo, Talking Heads, and 1950s rockabilly (this last sped up to double-even triple-time), they are primarily a pure pop band—perhaps the most manic one ever. This album, a collection of early singles and B-sides, is their most diverse. "Move Me," "Get It On," and the title cut are all itchy, frantic, and wonderful pop tunes with more raw energy than a roomful of hyperactive toddlers. "It Will Come" exhibits a broader-breathed line than the other selections of this type, while "Do It Anyway" ratchets the tempo even faster to a truly dizzying speed. The other three numbers (all B-sides) are totally unlike anything else in the band's oeuvre. All are highly experimental pop-derived numbers with definite psychedelic touches, imaginatively produced and quite lengthy. The standout track of these three is "Steady Steady," a chilling, reverb-drenched song about terminal illness with ominous bass/low synthesizer underpinnings and imaginatively tasteful use of guitar feedback that sounds like screaming. This is an excellent release well worth hearing. *—David Cleary*

• **Giant** / 1986 / Columbia ✦✦✦✦✦

This album, the group's best, explores a wide range of variations on the band's signature manic pop style, here adding occasional marimba, trumpet, accordion, and strings to the mix. The nervous single "Get It On" is presented in an intricately redone version, an improvement over its appearance on *Well Well Well*. Other great jittery numbers here include the frantic "Love Train" and "Travelling Man," as well as the stun-level manic "Shout" and "Hear Me James." The midtempo numbers here are generally excellent, especially the warmly expressive "Good Thing" and the lovely, loping "Give It Time." "Last Time" is a sadly yearning number with some odd touches that nearly undermine its mood, while "So Good Today" is a breezy, accordion-dominated selection that shamelessly flirts with wimpiness and only partially escapes. "Everything Breaks" manages to combine martial drums, funk guitar touches, a ringing arrangement, and production-number aspirations into one very effective package. There are also two songs that are just plain wacky fun, the nerdy Devo-inspired number "History" and the hiccuping fiddle-flecked song "Love Affair with Everyday Living." Production values here are utterly inspired. If you like pure, bouncy pop, you'll love this release. *—David Cleary*

Hypno Beat Live / 1987 / Upside ✦✦

Wooden Foot Cops on the Highway / 1988 / Columbia ✦✦✦

The Woodentops' last album to date shows the group experimenting with different styles in their own eccentrically nervous way. "They Can Say What They Want" is best described as infectiously nerdy funk, while "Wheels Turning" is a lengthy song that's as close to a danceable number as the group ever produced. "In a Dream" is a manic, poppish, rap-tinged number, while "You Make Me Feel" is a capable selection that exhibits discreet country influences. Other experiments are less successful. "Heaven" is a slow, synthesizer-dominated number with gospel touches that is marred by haphazardly jumbled text setting. "Tuesday Wednesday" is a bizarre folkish number with mild Latin coloration and odd beeping interjections. "What You Give Out" is a barely disguised ripoff of the Talking Heads song "The Great Curve"—listenable, to be sure, but unbelievably derivative. For those hoping to find attractively manic, pure pop numbers like those on prior releases, there are two excellent examples here, "Maybe It Won't Last" and "Stop the Car." Production values are again intricate and often clever, though at times they seem at cross-purposes with the musical mood the band is trying to create. This album is not bad, though not on a par with previous releases. *—David Cleary*

World Party

f. 1986

College Rock, Adult Alternative Pop/Rock, Pop/Rock, Alternative Pop/Rock

World Party began as an outlet for the pop infatuations of vocalist and multi-instrumentalist Karl Wallinger, previously best known for his tenure with the Waterboys. Born October 19, 1957 in Prestatyn, Wales, Wallinger grew up enamored not only of the Beatles but also of the Motown and Merseybeat sounds, and made his professional debut in 1976 as a member of the group Quasimodo. (Years later, after Wallinger had exited to move to London to work as a clerk for ATV/Northern Songs, Quasimodo evolved into the Alarm.)

Following a tenure as the musical director of a West End performance of *The Rocky Horror Picture Show*, Wallinger joined a funk band dubbed the Out before signing on with Mike Scott's Waterboys in 1984 to record the LP *A Pagan Place*. After 1985's superb *This Is the Sea*, Wallinger amicably departed to form World Party, a one-man project heavily indebted to *Revolver*-era Beatlesque pop; recorded in Wallinger's home studio, the 1987 debut *Private Revolution* scored a Top 40 hit with the infectious lead single "Ship of Fools."

After a long-layoff (during which time Wallinger aided Sinead O'Connor in recording her 1988 debut *The Lion and the Cobra*), World Party returned in 1990 with *Goodbye Jumbo*, another successful collection offering the minor hits "Way Down Now" and "Put the Message in the Box." After the 1991 stop-gap EP *Thank You World* (including a cover of the Beatles' "Happiness Is a Warm Gun"), Wallinger recruited guitarist Dave Caitlin-Birch and drummer Chris Sharrock as full-fledged members for 1993's *Bang!*, which reached the number two position on the British album charts. In the late '90s, Wallinger took a three-year break from World Party, returning in 2000. *—Jason Ankeny*

Private Revolution / Mar. 1987 / Papillon ✦✦✦

This debut album from World Party is a solid release, even if it is a bit heavy on the synthesized sounds (what can you expect from a one-man band?). Wallinger's insightful songs deal primarily with the responsibility of the individual to recognize and cope with the problems of the world. Features mainly original songs like "Private Revolution," "World Party," and "It's All Mine," as well as a cover of Dylan's "All I Really Want to Do," which remains surprisingly true to the original version. *—Iotis Erlewine*

• **Goodbye Jumbo** / Apr. 1990 / Papillon ✦✦✦✦✦

This excellent follow-up album from World Party is much tighter than the debut. Dealing with issues from the environment ("Take It Up," "Put the Message in the Box") to relationship woes ("And I Fell Back Alone"), these tracks manage to maintain a hopeful, positive mood without becoming trivial. In these songs, Wallinger has developed his own distinct style. A great album, worth checking out just for the uptempo groove of "Way Down Now." *—Iotis Erlewine*

Bang! / Apr. 20, 1993 / Papillon ✦✦✦

On his previous releases, Wallinger has displayed a social conscience, but never has it taken prominence like it does on *Bang!*, World Party's third album. *Bang!* does contain some glorious music that equals his masterpiece *Goodbye Jumbo*, but the album slows down when he tries to say too much (as in the quasi-operatic "And God Said"). Even then, Wallinger's preaching doesn't obliterate the considerable pleasures of the music. Wallinger has often been accused of recycling the Beatles, but the truth is that he can combine the Beatles, Beach Boys, Sly Stone, Dylan, and Prince into a musical style that is distinctive and unique yet familiar. *Bang!*, for all of its shortcomings, is as strong an album as any Wallinger has released. *—Stephen Thomas Erlewine*

Egyptology / Jun. 17, 1997 / Papillon ✦✦✦✦

Karl Wallinger defined the ornate, Beatlesque World Party sound on their debut *Private Revolution*, and he never strayed from that blueprint over the next decade, even if he augmented it with other '60s and '70s pop flourishes. *Egyptology* finds Wallinger at his most conservative, sticking to the basic late-'60s pop and psychedelia that distinguished *Private Revolution* and *Goodbye Jumbo*. As always, his production is tasteful and subtle, revealing new layers of sonic detail on each listen, and his songcraft is sturdy and tuneful, if not remarkable. Few of the songs jump out upon the first few listens, yet there are no weak moments on the record, which makes *Egyptology*, of all things, a workmanlike release. It's not flashy or extravagant, and it may not have the inspiration of

Goodbye Jumbo, but it does deliver a collection of fine pop tunes without pretension, and that alone makes it a better album than the overly ambitious *Bang!*. *—Stephen Thomas Erlewine*

Dumbing Up / Oct. 31, 2000 / Papillon ♦♦♦♦
After a three-year absence, *Dumbing It Up* marks the return of leader Karl Wallinger, and he manages to recapture the magic of previous efforts such as *Goodbye Jumbo* and *Bang*. During Wallinger's hiatus, interest in the band had grown after their song "She's The One" became a hit for British pop star Robbie Williams. For the most part, Wallinger delivers, ably demonstrating his considerable strengths as a writer, arranger, and lyricist. The album is a mix of influences, but chief among them is Bob Dylan. Several songs, such as "Who Are You," feature bare-boned guitar arrangements that let the wordplay stand out. Other '60s influences abound. The lead single, "Here Comes the Future," is an intriguing bit of retro soul while "Another 1000 Years" plays like a Beatles ballad. After a lackluster 1997 release, *Egyptology*, Wallinger redeems himself with an agreeable album that is more comforting than it is groundbreaking. *—Jon Azpiri*

Link Wray (Frederick Lincoln Wray)

b. May 2, 1929, Dunn, NC
Vocals, Guitar (Electric), Guitar / Instrumental Rock, Rock & Roll
Link Wray may never get into the Rock & Roll Hall of Fame, but his contribution to the language of rockin' guitar would still be a major one, even if he had never walked into another studio after cutting "Rumble." Quite simply, Link Wray invented the power chord, the major modus operandi of modern rock guitarists. Listen to any of the tracks he recorded between that landmark instrumental in 1958 through his Swan recordings in the early 1960s and you'll hear the blueprints for heavy metal, thrash, you name it. Though rock historians always like to draw a nice, clean line between the distorted electric guitar work that fuels early blues records to the late-'60s Hendrix-Clapton-Beck-Page-Townshend mob, with no stops in between, a quick spin of any of the sides Link recorded during *his* golden decade punches holes in that theory right quick. If a direct line from a black blues musician crankin' up his amp and playing with a ton of violence and aggression can be traced to a young, white guy doing a mutated form of same, the line points straight to Link Wray, no contest. Pete Townshend summed it up for more guitarists than he probably realized when he said, "He is the king; if it hadn't been for Link Wray and 'Rumble,' I would have never picked up a guitar." *—Cub Koda*

Missing Links, Vol. 1: Hillbilly Wolf / 1990 / Norton ♦♦♦♦♦
Unlike many early cult rock & roll greats, Link Wray recorded dozens upon dozens of sides that are good (and diverse) enough to make the search for his rarities worthwhile. This is the first volume of a three-part series of way-obscure sides from his early days, some previously unreleased. Some, indeed, aren't credited to Link himself, though he plays a prominent role on the tracks here credited to Lucky Wray (actually Link's brother Vern), Ray Vernon, the Wraymen, and Marvin Rainwater. Much of this is as unhoned as early rockabilly and instrumental rock got, the mid-'50s exposing Wray's hillbilly roots like raw nerve endings. It's a fine collection, worth getting if you have enough interest in Link to fish beyond a best-of compilation. *—Richie Unterberger*

Missing Links, Vol. 2: Big City After Dark / 1990 / Norton ♦♦♦
A mix of super-rare cuts, a couple of unissued outtakes, and live material, all from the 1960s. It's rawer than Link's norm (which is durned raw indeed), but not necessarily any less exciting than all but the best of his material in wide circulation. "Big City After Dark" and "Rawhide '63," for instance, have some of the best Wray string-bending you're likely to hear; "Hold It" is pre-Beatles garage rock at its most ferocious. This compilation gets a slightly lower rating than its companion volumes in the *Missing Links* series because the live material that takes up most of side two is of a somewhat lower standard than the other rarities, in both musical quality and audio fidelity. *—Richie Unterberger*

Missing Links, Vol. 3: Some Kinda Nut / 1990 / Norton ♦♦♦♦♦
Another great grab bag of hideously rare Link, all from the 1960s on this volume, including tracks that Wray issued under his own name, and side projects that he lent his guitar to (by the Fender Benders, Moon Men, and Bunker Hill). "Baby Doll" and "Please Please Me" are surprisingly cool fusions of Wray raunch with Merseybeat; the primitive late-'60s recordings from the rare *Yesterday and Today* LP were some of his most menacing cuts ever. On the lighter side are the hot rod-flavored instros by the Fender Benders, and the wild R&B/rock outings of Bunker Hill, a singer that Link backed who made Little Richard sound like Ricky Nelson. *—Richie Unterberger*

Walkin' with Link / Apr. 1992 / Epic/Legacy ♦♦♦♦♦
After cutting the anthemic instrumental "Rumble" for Cadence Records, Link took his follow-up "Rawhide" over to Epic Records, and this 20-track compilation is the most excellent distillation of his tenure at the label. The honchos at Columbia were trying their level best to tame Link down for mass consumption (Duane Eddy twanged for White teenage America; Link Wray played for hoods). Fortunately here we're spared having to hear "seemed like a good idea at the time" atrocities like "Trail of the Lonesome Pine" and "Clare De Lune" in favor of 20 tracks of solid rockin' mayhem. Casual fans who only think of Wray as a wild-ass guitarist (his tone on the title track is pure, detuned, hacking filth) will be very surprised to find that rebel nature also applies to his vocal cords on such raucous outings as Jimmy Reed's "Ain't That Lovin' You Baby" (in two different takes here), Ray Charles' "Mary Anne," and the previously unissued rocker "Oh Babe Be Mine." This compilation may lack some of the big hits that a best-of collection would have to offer (thus denying it first-purchase status), but as another essential piece in building the perfect Link Wray (or rock & roll guitar gods) collection, one would be very hard-pressed to imagine it *not* residing in the pile. Link at his best, and that's just about as wild and crazy as original rock & roll guitar gets. *—Cub Koda*

★ **Rumble! The Best of Link Wray** / May 18, 1993 / Rhino ♦♦♦♦♦
Finally, a multi-label Link Wray collection spanning his lengthy career is available. Starting, appropriately enough, with "Rumble," *Rumble! The Best of Link Wray* illustrates through its 20 tracks (15 on cassette) that Wray was indeed one of the pioneering guitarists of rock & roll, expanding the sonic possibilities of the instrument with a variety of effects. All of the tracks feature some truly warped, genius-caliber fretboard work from Wray, and a few also feature his equally demented vocals. *Rumble! The Best of Link Wray* is the definitive Wray collection. *—Stephen Thomas Erlewine*

Mr. Guitar / Jun. 20, 1995 / Norton ♦♦♦♦♦
While Link cut some great records in the late '50s and early '60s, he really reached his peak during his stay with the Swan label in the early and mid-'60s. This double-CD, 63-song set documents this period with as much thoroughness as anyone is likely to attempt, including great singles like "Jack The Ripper," "Mr. Guitar," "Ace Of Spades," and "The Fat Back," where Link let loose with his dirtiest and most groundbreaking fuzz tones. Including quite a few rarities and tracks that were never previously released in the U.S., as well as a good number of vocal performances (which were never Wray's forte), this is perhaps too exhaustive for the average fan. A single-disc distillation of his best Swan sides would be absolutely killer, but this is still one of the greatest collections of instrumental rock out there, despite its unevenness. *—Richie Unterberger*

Guitar Preacher: The Polydor Years / Aug. 22, 1995 / Polydor ♦♦♦
Wray's image as leather-clad, fuzz-drenched cowpunk is so indelibly etched into the minds of most fans that it's been convenient to overlook the fact that in the early '70s, he eschewed grungy instrumentals for laid-back, homespun roots rock. He wrote lyrics and sang on these albums as well, some of which were recorded in a three-track studio built in a converted chicken coop on his family farm. Reflecting the pastoral, rural influence of the Band and other groups of the day, Link also largely abandoned his electric guitars for acoustic ones on some of the albums, though he returned to harder-rocking electric sounds by the middle of the 1970s. This double-CD box set collects 37 songs from five albums spanning 1971 to 1974. One of these LPs only surfaced in England (*Beans and Fatback*), and another was an odd effort by one Mordecai Jones on which Link played most of the instruments and wrote most of the material. The anthology rightfully emphasizes his self-titled 1971 comeback album, the best of these recordings, which has an enigmatic backwoods ambience and spiritual lyrics, and contains a couple tunes later covered by the Nevilles ("Fire and Brimstone" and "Fallin' Rain"). The later albums, some of which featured high-profile guests like Jerry Garcia and Tower of Power, had a more generic early-'70s AOR rock feel; not so on the Mordecai Jones tracks, though, on which rustic arrangements back Jones' vocals, which sound like a more subdued Robert Plant. As a whole, the work assembled here isn't nearly as important as Wray's instrumental recordings from the '50s and '60s—and Wray's wracked, tense vocals are something of an acquired taste—but it's rather intriguing stuff with little relationship to the rest of his catalog. *—Richie Unterberger*

Missing Links, Vol. 4: Streets of Chicago / 1997 / Norton ♦♦♦
Considering Norton had already issued no less than three previous Link Wray rarities volumes (in addition to a 63-song CD with entirely different material from the 1960s), it's a bit of a miracle that they even managed to assemble enough material for a fourth installment. Only one of these songs (a version of "Lillian" from the *Great Guitar Hits* LP) has been released before. As you would expect, at this point the well is starting to run a little dry, though this 17-track compilation of stray items from the early and mid-'60s has its moments. The studio outtakes are mostly original, with detours into covers of Gene Vincent and Elvis; they're typical Wray guitar-grinders, with occasional vocals, but not as compelling as his greatest material. There are also half a dozen live recordings, including more Elvis covers and versions of classics like "Rumble" and "Ace of Spades"; the performances on these are suitably energetic, though the fidelity is average at best, and rather poor at worst. The best track is probably "Bluebeard," an early demo of a growling instrumental that ended up being retitled "Mustang" for its official release. For those of us who love the Linkster, this is a worthwhile disc, but even more than the previous *Missing Links* volumes, its appeal is limited to aficionados. *—Richie Unterberger*

Wreckless Eric

b. Newhaven, England
Vocals, Guitar / British Punk, Pub Rock, New Wave
Wreckless Eric gained notoriety as part of Stiff Records' highly eccentric roster of punk and New Wave artists during the late '70s. With his whiny, slurred cockney voice, Eric couldn't carry a tune, but that didn't prevent him from being an enjoyable, if limited, rock & roller. With his early Stiff singles "Whole Wide World," "Semaphore Signals," and "Take the Cash (K.A.S.H.)," Eric bashed out a series of ragged, chaotic, three-chord punk-pop singles driven by his pent-up energy and a knack for melodic pop hooks. Though his he never had a big pop hit, his engaging sense of humor and fondness for simple rock & roll helped make him a cult figure that continued to have a following into the '90s. After signing to Stiff in 1977, Eric's debut single was "Whole Wide World," a moderate hit in the punk underground. His 1978 eponymous debut had a boozy sense of charm, though his second album *The Wonderful World of Wreckless Eric* demonstrated a previously unknown musical versatility. He fashioned his third album *Big Smash* as a commercial breakthrough, though when it failed he quit the music industry. Eric returned to music during the mid-'80s with two groups, Captains of Industry and the Len Bright Combo, then released the solo album *Le Beat Group Electrique* in 1989. He continued releasing records and performing during the '90s, mostly in France. *—Stephen Thomas Erlewine*

Wreckless Eric / 1978 / Repertoire ♦♦♦♦♦
Wreckless Eric's eponymous debut is a ragged, endearing collection of crude rock & roll.

In a way, crude doesn't even begin to describe Eric's music. A muddle of scratchy guitars, pounding drumming, and snarled, indecipherable vocals, the record is pure, primal garage rock in the old-fashioned sense. Although Wreckless Eric has the demeanor of a punk, his music is straight-out rock & roll in the old-fashioned sense—there's even saxophones and organs popping out of the mix. What makes *Wreckless Eric* such fun is its combination of catchy hooks, spirited playing, and downright rudeness. Only a handful of songs are fully formed, and those—"Whole Wide World" and Ian Dury's "Rough Kids"—are punk-inflected pub rock classics, pure pop songs in every sense of the term. The remainder are off-kilter, idiosyncratic pop songs—about everything from "Personal Hygiene" and "Waxworks" to "Telephoning Home" and "Brain Thieves"—performed with sloppy, drunken abandon. Too punk for pub rockers, too straightforward for punk, and too weird for everybody else, Wreckless Eric's debut album is one of the small gems of the punk era. —*Stephen Thomas Erlewine*

The Wonderful World of Wreckless Eric / Nov. 1978 / Stiff ✦✦✦✦
Wreckless Eric had already begun to tire of Stiff's promotion of him as a drunken rebellious lout by the time of his second album, *The Wonderful World of Wreckless Eric*. He hadn't grown strong enough to break free of Stiff's hold, but he was able to clean up his sound enough for *The Wonderful World* to make his music slightly more accessible—which means it just doesn't sound as messy as his debut. Wreckless Eric still has an odd, idiosyncratic point of view, but the sound is streamlined enough to make his snarls and growls palatable. Also, his hooks are getting stronger overall, and while only "Take the Cash" is on the level of "Whole Wide World," the rest of the record is comprised of rockers (and two pointless covers of Tommy Roe and Buddy Holly) that are quite enjoyable. —*Stephen Thomas Erlewine*

The Whole Wide World / 1979 / Stiff ✦✦✦✦✦
The Whole Wide World was an American-only collection of Wreckless Eric singles that provided an excellent distillation of his best moments, from "Whole Wide World" to "Semaphore Signals" and "Take the Cash (K.A.S.H.)." The album was added as a bonus LP to the original pressings of Eric's third album, *Big Smash!* —*Stephen Thomas Erlewine*

Big Smash / 1980 / Stiff ✦✦✦
Big Smash was Wreckless Eric's big crossover attempt, designed to bring him closer to the mainstream. However, the polished production and tempered performances remove much of his charm. While the music may be more accessible, Eric simply doesn't have a voice suited for careful productions, and that undercuts even the best songs on the record. And that's a shame, because it's clear that he is continuing to grow as a songwriter, finding more and better hooks, as well as sharp, clever lyrics. But without the rough, ragged music that made his first two records so exciting, *Big Smash* is a disappointment. The songs are there, but the record is not as fun as his first pair of albums. —*Stephen Thomas Erlewine*

Le Beat Group Electrique / 1989 / New Rose ✦✦✦✦
This overlooked comeback effort was an unheralded triumph for Eric, on which he fronted a guitar-bass-drums trio (he also plays his usual cheesy organ) on a stripped-down set of strong songs with a live production feel. With his strangled, yearning vocals, basic melodic hooks, and songs about messed-up relationships, Wreckless recalls Lou Reed and Syd Barrett's better solo work, as he makes his confusion a cause for infectious celebration instead of gloomy moping. —*Richie Unterberger*

Donovan of Trash / 1991 / Sympathy for the Record Industry ✦✦✦

● **Greatest Stiffs** / Mar. 20, 2001 / Metro ✦✦✦✦✦
There's one complaint with Metro's *Greatest Stiffs* collection—Wreckless Eric's unhinged version of Devo's "Be Stiff," the song that the British indie Stiff made all their second-wave artists record, isn't here. It was the best out of all the versions of "Be Stiff," and it would have been a highlight of his Stiff recordings even if he'd been the only one to cut it there. Apart from that, and maybe the absence of his smashing version of Ian Dury's "Rough Kids," this is a flawless collection of his terrific recordings for Stiff, drawing highlights from those three full-length albums, including songs that haven't been easily available on CD. And while Wreckless' incoherent, slurred growl may be an acquired taste, it's totally rock & roll, and the best early songs here—"Whole Wide World," "Reconnez Cherie," "Semaphore Signals," "Take the Cash (K.A.S.H.)," among others—are wild, terrific rock & roll, while the songs toward the end of the record prove that he's a fine pop songwriter as well. Wreckless Eric may be a cult act, but this record proves why he has a cult. —*Stephen Thomas Erlewine*

Wreckx-N-Effect

f. 1989
Party Rap, Pop-Rap, New Jack Swing, Hip-Hop
Wreckx-N-Effect earned a huge crossover smash with the single "Rump Shaker" off their 1992 album *Hard or Smooth*. The accompanying video with its array of shapely women following the directions of the lead singer generated nearly as much heat as Sir Mix-A-Lot's "Baby Got Back." It also helped the group secure a platinum certification, something it hardly seemed they'd earn from their Motown debut *Wrecks-N-Effect* in 1991. Markell Riley, brother of super-producer Teddy Riley, was part of the rap ensemble along with Aquil Davidson and Brandon Mitchell; Mitchell was killed in a 1990 shooting. Following the success of "Rump Shaker," the group resurfaced in 1996 with *Rap's New Generation*. —*Ron Wynn*

● **Wrecks-N-Effect** / 1991 / Atlantic ✦✦✦✦
A striking mix of go-go funk and new jack swing is highlighted by "New Jack Swing," an

anthem for the new beat. Produced by Teddy Riley, who created that new beat with Guy. —*John Floyd*

Hard or Smooth / 1992 / MCA ✦✦✦✦
Although nothing else on *Hard or Smooth* compares to the monster groove of "Rump Shaker," the rest of the album offers enough beats to satisfy most fans of the hit singles. —*AMG*

Rap's New Generation / Sep. 24, 1996 / MCA ✦✦✦
Wreckx-N-Effect's fusion of party hip-hop and soulful urban R&B was a revelation on its first two albums, but it has grown tired and predictable on its belated third album *Rap's New Generation*. Few of the tracks demonstrate any lyrical or musical imagination, and the good-time grooves all fall flat—in short, it sounds like a party you can't wait to leave. —*Leo Stanley*

Betty Wright

b. Dec. 21, 1953, Miami, FL
Vocals / Quiet Storm, Soul
A consistently strong presence on the Miami music scene throughout the '70s and '80s, Betty Wright was just 15 when she cut the Top 40 "Girls Can't Do What the Guys Do." A child gospel star who switched to R&B at age 13, she put the Miami scene on the map in 1971 with the #6 hit "Clean Up Woman," notable for its prominent guitar riff and Wright's swaggering lead vocal. She won a Grammy in 1974 for "Where Is the Love?" (not to be confused with the Roberta Flack/Donny Hathaway tune of the same name). She collaborated with Stevie Wonder in 1981 on the Epic hit "What Are You Gonna Do with It?" Betty continues to live and work in the Miami area. —*Christine Ohlman*

The Best of Betty Wright: The T.K. Years / 1995 / Sequel ✦✦✦
The T.K. years were lucrative for Ms. B; this was Stage 2 of Betty Wright's career, sandwiched by early hits on Alston Records, e.g., "Girl's Can't Do What The Guys Do" and "Clean Up Woman," and career winders on various labels. The T.K. years cuts came in Wright's prime, past the teen years–though this set does include "Tonight Is The Night" a tune about a virgin losing her virginity–and before middle-age spread. These tracks are more elaborate than the sparse Alston recordings and they include crossovers: "Shoorah! Shoorah!, Slip And Do It," a remake of Brainstorm's "Lovin' Is Really My Game" and "Where Is The Love." The 18-track disc also features slow southern burners like "That's When I'll Stop Loving You," "If I Ever Do Wrong" and "You Can't See For Looking"; Wright co-wrote many of the songs. —*Andrew Hamilton*

● **The Very Best of Betty Wright** / Jun. 20, 2000 / Rhino ✦✦✦✦✦
Rhino's *Very Best of Betty Wright* collects some of the soul diva's definitive tracks, including her first Top 40 hit "Girls Can't Do What the Guys Do," her 1971 Top 10 hit "Clean Up Woman," "Let Me Your Lovemaker," her 1974 Grammy winner "Where Is the Love," and "I'm Gettin' Tired Baby." Though it's not as extensive as the label's earlier compilation *The Best of Betty Wright*, this album does present most of her major singles as well as a few representative album tracks. —*Heather Phares*

Charles Wright

b. 1942, Clarksdale, MS
Vocals, Guitar / Smooth Soul, Funk, Soul
Charles Wright headed one of the late '60s and early '70s great funk groups, the Watts 103rd Street Rhythm Band. Wright, who was born in Clarksdale, MS, was a singer, pianist, guitarist, and leader of the eight-member band, recruited from Watts in Los Angeles. They were originally known as the Soul Runners. Bill Cosby helped get the band off the ground by giving them appearances at his gigs. They began recording for Keyman in 1967, then moved to Warner Bros. in 1969. While "Do Your Thing" and "Till You Get Enough" were Top 20 R&B hits, their finest selection was "Express Yourself," a song that expressed the urge for freedom as adroitly as the Isley Brothers' "It's Your Thing" had in the '60s. It has also been among the most sampled funk tracks for hip-hop and rap groups. "Your Love (Means Everything to Me)" was their final R&B hit in 1971, peaking at number nine R&B and number 12 pop. The group's best ballad, "Love Land," did better pop-wise than among R&B fans, many of whom saw it as a bit soft. They continued recording for Dunhill in 1973 before disbanding. Drummer James Gadson and guitarist Al McKay, who later joined Earth, Wind & Fire, were among the instrumental corps of the Watts 103rd Street Rhythm Band. —*Ron Wynn*

● **Express Yourself: The Best of Charles Wright** / 1993 / Warner Archive ✦✦✦✦✦
A definitive, 16-track collection of Charles Wright's best material. —*Stephen Thomas Erlewine*

In the Jungle Babe/Express Yourself / Apr. 8, 1997 / Warner Brothers ✦✦✦✦✦
Released in 1997, this two-fer collects Charles Wright and the Watts 103rd Street Rhythm Band's third and fourth records, 1969's *In the Jungle, Babe* and the following year's *Express Yourself*. A transitional work, *In the Jungle, Babe* captures a group struggling to find its own identity; for every superb workout like the shimmering "Love Land" or the propulsive "I'm a Midnight Mover," there's a redundant cover of the Doors' "Light My Fire" or Sly and the Family Stone's "Everyday People" which falls flat on its face. *Express Yourself*, on the other hand, is the group's masterpiece, a remarkable fusion of funk attitude and soul conviction. Highlighted by the classic title hit—one of the most powerful declarations of independence in the canon, as well as one of the most sampled records of all time—*Express Yourself* is a whirlwind tour through the spectrum of R&B; from the poignance of the Otis Redding-worthy ballad "Tell Me What You Want Me to Do" (arguably Wright's best vocal turn ever) to the supple funk-jazz jam session "High as Apple Pie–Slice I and II," the record is assured and muscular, a primal blast of soul power. —*Jason Ankeny*

Gary Wright

b. Apr. 26, 1943, Creskill, NJ

Vocals, Keyboards, Violin, Piano / Pop/Rock, Soft Rock, Prog-Rock/Art Rock

Most closely associated with his atmospheric 1976 smash "Dream Weaver," singer Gary Wright was born April 26, 1943 in Creskill, NJ; a former child actor who appeared on Broadway in a production of *Fanny*, he fronted a number of local rock bands during his high school years before turning his attention to psychology, completing his studies in Berlin at Frei University. In 1967, Wright's band, the New York Times, opened for Traffic, bringing him to the attention of Island Records honcho Chris Blackwell, who in turn introduced the singer to the members of the band Art; relocating to London, Wright joined the band, soon renamed Spooky Tooth and later emerging among the UK's premier hard rock outfits. When Spooky Tooth temporarily disbanded in 1970, Wright jumped ship to form Wonderwheel, concurrently playing keyboards on George Harrison's *All Things Must Pass*; the two eventually became close friends and collaborators, together taking a trip to India which inspired the mystical themes of Wright's subsequent solo efforts. He returned to Spooky Tooth in 1973, but when the band again dissolved the following year he returned to his solo career, scoring his greatest success with 1975's *The Dream Weaver*; both the title track and "Love Is Alive" reached number two on the *Billboard* pop charts, and the album—one of the first created solely via synthesizer technology—achieved platinum status. Follow-ups including *Light of Smiles*, 1977's *Touch and Gone*, and 1979's *Headin' Home* failed to repeat *The Dream Weaver*'s success, however, and in 1981 Wright notched his final chart hit with "Really Wanna Know You," from *The Right Place*. From there he composed a series of film scores, including 1985's *Fire and Ice*, which topped the German charts; Wright's first solo album in seven years, *Who Am I*, featured contributions from Indian classical greats Lakshmi Shankar and L. Subramanium. In 1991, he remade "Dream Weaver" for the soundtrack of the hit film comedy *Wayne's World*, and in 1995 issued his first world music effort, *First Signs of Life*. *Human Love* followed five years later. *—Jason Ankeny*

Extraction / 1971 / A&M ♦♦♦

While lacking the heaviness of Spooky Tooth, Gary Wright's first solo effort was not all that different in structure from his parent band. "The Wrong Time" was predominantly riff-oriented, with a catchy, melodic chorus. Also of note was "Sing a Song," with nice falsetto vocals. Altogether, a good first showing. *—James Chrispell*

Footprint / 1972 / A&M ♦♦♦♦

Following a year after his first solo release, Gary Wright put out this superstar-filled record, boasting amongst the credits one George O'Hara, also known as George Harrison. Harrison lent his slide guitar stylings to several of the tracks, most notably "Two-Faced Man," which he also performed with Wright on the *Dick Cavett Show*. A much stronger effort, it still failed to set the charts on fire. That's a shame, because there's some fine music to be found here. If you get a chance, check out *Footprint* for yourself. *—James Chrispell*

Dream Weaver / 1975 / Warner Brothers ♦♦♦♦♦

No one expected the success of *Dream Weaver* when it was released, but it sailed to the top of the charts, and with good reason. Backed with only drums and a wide assortment of keyboards, Wright crafted instantly recognizable tunes such as the title cut and "Love Is Alive," which caught on and remain staples of classic rock stations around the country. All very revolutionary and new at the time, *Dream Weaver* hasn't lost any of its magic over time. *—James Chrispell*

● **Best of the Dream Weaver** / Sep. 15, 1998 / Rhino ♦♦♦♦♦

Rhino usually does these archive collections right, and *Best of the Dream Weaver* hits the essential bits of Gary Wright's solo career (bypassing the smoky Spooky Tooth), plus the disc plays chronologically. The early-'70s stuff seems likable enough and sounds fine. Wright's considerable pipes wrap around above-average rock proceedings with George Harrison, Alan White, and other luminaries traipsing through "Get on the Right Road" and "Two Faced Man." These tracks give no indication of the hovering phenomenon that was to follow. The obvious draw here is the classic "Dream Weaver" (actually written on acoustic guitar), and the original version roosts on *Best of the Dream Weaver* as the sensational centerpiece. Erie disco follow-up "Love Is Alive" also appears in all its shimmering brilliance. Both fall from 1975's smash *Dream Weaver* LP, one of the most insular and unique records in history. Naturally, bizarre synth effects affect the remainder of the keyboardist's catalogue. "Time Machine" is very cool, one of those obscure dandies the artist disavows because it had the unenviable task of following a breakthrough. Wright's last chart appearance, the glistening "Really Wanna Know You" (co-written with Ali Thomson), luckily makes the cut. "Don't Try to Own Me" apes Peter Gabriel. The accompanying booklet is graphically detailed. This appears to be as much solo Gary Wright as the average human needs. *—Doug Stone*

O.V. Wright

b. Oct. 9, 1939, Leno, TN, **d.** Nov. 16, 1980

Vocals / Memphis Soul, Deep Soul, Southern Soul, Soul

A truly incendiary deep-soul performer. O.V. Wright's melismatic vocals and Willie Mitchell's vaunted Hi Rhythm Section combined to make classic Memphis soul during the early '70s. Overton Vertis Wright learned his trade on the gospel circuit with the Sunset Travelers before going secular in 1964 with the passionate ballad "That's How Strong My Love Is" for Goldwax in Memphis. Otis Redding liked the song so much that he covered it, killing any chance of Wright's version hitting. Since Wright was already under contract to Houston-based Peacock as a gospel act, owner Don Robey demanded his return, and from then on, Wright appeared on Robey's Backbeat subsidiary. Wright's sanctified sound oozes sweet soul on the spine-chilling "You're Gonna Make Me Cry," a 1965 smash, but it took Memphis producer Willie Mitchell to wring the best consistently from Wright. Utilizing Mitchell's surging house rhythm section, Wright's early-'70s Backbeat singles "Ace of Spades," "A Nickel and a Nail," and "I Can't Take It" rank among the very best Southern soul of their era. No disco bandwagon for O.V. Wright—he kept right on pouring out his emotions through the '70s, convincing his faithful that "I'd Rather Be (Blind, Crippled & Crazy)," that he was "Into Something (Can't Shake Loose)." Unfortunately, he apparently was—drugs have often been cited as causing Wright's downfall; the soul great died at only 41 years of age in 1980. *—Bill Dahl*

● **The Soul of O.V. Wright** / Dec. 22, 1992 / MCA ♦♦♦♦♦

O.V. Wright epitomized gospel-based soul singing. He screamed, roared, belted, hollered, and wailed, proclaiming his need for love. His songs were simple; they were often anguished remembrances of lost loves or pleas that this time things might be different. Occasionally, he did an uptempo dance or novelty number, but Wright was at his best on slow burners. This collection of 1960s and '70s material for Don Robey's Back Beat label includes evocative ballads, lightweight but enjoyable numbers, and songs which returned him to his gospel days. While several foreign anthologies spotlighting Wright have been issued, this 18-track CD stands as the most complete domestic reissue package currently available. *—Ron Wynn*

Hi Masters / Sep. 15, 1998 / Hi ♦♦♦

The *Hi Masters* compiles 15 studio recordings, all from 1977 and 1978 with the exception of the two songs that comprised O.V. Wright's first release on Hi, the 1976 single "Rhymes" (which charted in the R&B Top 100 that year) and it's B-side, "Without You." The collection kicks off strong with the gospel-drenched delivery, decidedly secular subject, and driving momentum of "Into Something (Can't Shake Loose)," his sole hit in 1977 (it reached the Top 50). The following year brought the last two songs by Wright to hit the charts, "Precious, Precious" (R&B Top 50, early 1978) and "I Don't Do Windows" (Top 100). Besides the inclusion of his last four hits, the *Hi Masters* is a collection of the lesser-known material from late in Wright's career. It's not his prime period, but the soft-moving numbers and ballads from this time, including standouts "I Don't Know Why" and "Your Good Thing Is About to End," make *Hi Masters* a relaxed listen that is second priority—but a nice complement—to O.V. Wright's key earlier recordings. *—Joslyn Layne*

The Complete O.V. Wright on Hi Records, Vol.1: In the Studio / Aug. 24, 1999 / Hi ♦♦♦♦♦

The first volume of the two-disc set *The Complete O.V. Wright on Hi Records* concentrates on *In the Studio*, which means this is the stuff that hit the charts and the stuff that made the albums. Wright was one of the gutsiest vocalists on the tight, smooth, soulful Hi label, as this collection proves, and he often had material to match his talents, thanks to such fine songwriters as the Mitchell/Randle team. It is true that 30 tracks may be a bit much for a certain breed of listener, since there are some cuts that are merely good genre pieces, but for the soul aficionado, this is a welcome addition to the library. *—Stephen Thomas Erlewine*

The Complete O.V. Wright on Hi Records, Vol. 2: On Stage / Oct. 26, 1999 / Hi ♦♦♦♦

O.V. Wright was a hell of a performer, one of the highlights of Hi's roster, but that doesn't necessarily mean that the second volume of *The Complete O.V. Wright on Hi Records* is necessary for anyone outside of the hardcore. The reason for this? It's because it concentrates entirely on live performances he cut for the label. He was a fine live performer, as several of these selections prove, but these recordings are primarily for the dedicated—especially because the disc has a rather abbreviated running time. They will find this collection pleasing, but it's likely too specialized for anyone outside of the devoted. *—Stephen Thomas Erlewine*

Shannon Wright

Sadcore, Indie Pop, Experimental Rock, Indie Rock, Singer/Songwriter

The onetime frontwoman for the acclaimed indie pop combo Crowsdell, singer/songwriter Shannon Wright was born and raised in Jacksonville, FL. A product of the area's thriving all-ages punk scene, she formed Crowsdell with bassist Paul Howell and drummer Laurie Anne Wall, debuting in 1995 with the underground favorite *Dreamette* and soon after relocating to New York City. However, when relations with label Big Cat soured in the wake of 1997's *Within the Curve of an Arm*, the group dissolved, and an embittered Wright sold most of her belongings and moved to rural North Carolina, where she began recording a series of deeply personal, folk-inflected songs to four-track. A handful of solo singles followed before she recorded the full-length *Flightsafety*, issued on Quarterstick in 1999. *Maps of Tacit* appeared a year later. *—Jason Ankeny*

● **Flightsafety** / Apr. 20, 1999 / Quarterstick ♦♦♦♦♦

Sequestering herself in North Carolina after the dissolution of her previous band Crowsdell, Shannon Wright emerged with several single releases and finally the impressive full-length solo debut *Flightsafety*. It's a gentle, melancholy affair on which Wright plays nearly all of the instruments (including drums), augmenting the songs' piano and guitar bases with cello, harmonium, and organ. Wright's musical milieu is haunting indie folk-rock, of the type that's been tagged "sadcore" due to its intense, despondent introspection. In that vein, *Flightsafety* often resembles a mildly dissonant version of early Elliott Smith; Wright has fully mastered the contrast inherent in the gentle sense of swing that propels some of Smith's saddest tunes (see "All These Things"). However, Wright has her own tactics, creating tension through dissonant harmonies and angular chord changes (as on "Rich Hum of Air") rather than projecting outright bitterness. She can also be lilting and catchy, as on the indie single "Captain of Quarantine," which fortunately made the cut here. The elliptical, imagistic poetry of her lyrics is richly personal, conveying its meanings more through impression and feel than literal interpretation; Wright's restrained yet impassioned performances and tight melodicism supply all the subtext that's needed. Overall, *Flightsafety* is an extremely promising debut from a bright, accomplished songwriter. *—Steve Huey*

Maps of Tacit / May 9, 2000 / Quarterstick ✦✦✦✦✦
Shannon Wright's debut album, *Flightsafety*, positioned her as a sensitive, talented purveyor of melancholy, Elliott Smith-styled indie folk. The quiet intensity underpinning *Flightsafety* bubbles to the surface on its follow-up, *Maps of Tacit*, a bold and startling leap into uncharted territory. Although the album begins in a relatively similar style, by the halfway point it's apparent that Wright is drawing just as much on the dissonant art-song of theatrical composer Kurt Weill and the minimalist instrumentation of latter-day Tom Waits (sans junkyard percussion); the more carnival-esque work of Lisa Germano is perhaps the best comparison, and the wilder moments might even recall German art rock chanteuse Dagmar Krause for some. The differences are apparent on the re-recording of *Flightsafety*'s "Heavy Crown," now overtly rather than vaguely unsettling; where the original relied on its creeping chordal lines for impact, here Wright wails the chorus with a newfound power, climaxing in an apocalyptic scream that provides one of the record's most intense moments. Yet that shouldn't be taken to mean that Wright has thrown off all restraint or nuance; quite the contrary, she simply sounds more confident, her live performances having informed the sharper emotional contrasts in her music. The intensity of *Maps of Tacit* feels cathartic rather than tortured, and it makes Wright's experiments with sonic texture all the more exciting and fresh. That's especially true of the pieces utilizing harmonium or Wurlitzer organ; their frequently aggressive dissonance hangs in the air behind Wright with an eerie, almost spectral quality. If the album has a flaw, it's that the second half's shorter, sometimes instrumental pieces could perhaps have been fleshed out into something more complete-sounding; still, they at least fit the atmosphere well. Overall, *Maps of Tacit* finds Wright growing more adventurous both as a composer and performer; it's a dark and challenging work, yet it isn't off-putting or overly harrowing, and its bracing experimentalism and originality suggest even greater things to come. *—Steve Huey*

Dyed in the Wool / Aug. 21, 2001 / Quarterstick ✦✦✦✦
As indie rockers go, Shannon Wright is something special. After disbanding Crowsdell and embarking on a solo career, she released two wildly different but extremely high-quality solo recordings, the stark, acoustically haunted *Flight Safety* and the set of rage-rock excess that was *Maps of Tacit*. On *Dyed in the Wool*, Wright changes her direction by freeing herself of the constraints of having to play everything on her own records. She enlists help from mates in bands like Rachel's, the Boxhead Ensemble, the Lofty Pillars, Edith Frost, and the Rock*A*Teens, and the engineering help of Steve Albini and Andy Baker. The tracks range from the haunted chamber pop of "Vessel for a Minor Malady," with its sweeping string and piano choruses and broken lyric, to the screaming rawness of "Less Than a Moment," with its angular melody line and deconstructed rock chorus, to the gothically shambolic title track done in waltz time, which has the protagonists singing with a loss so total it upsets the balance of the world: "There goes your body in a box/But it's all I have left/Now this odor lines my shaking bed/There's no order to you/Come with me you dirty wretch/How does this duty send me relief/When I've been cheated of you." The seam of the track splits, allowing for the singer's contradictions to meet with the downpour of emotion and musical fragmentation like a surprise rainstorm in a desert. The lyrics here reflect Wright's precise yet poetic way of mapping the emotional landscape as it careens from pain and loss to hope and then rage. With a band of musical collaborators to free up her musical vision, Wright has given listeners her finest outing so far—and that's saying plenty. *—Thom Jurek*

Wu-Tang Clan

f. 1992
Hardcore Rap, East Coast Rap, Hip-Hop
Emerging in 1993, when Dr. Dre's G-funk had overtaken the hip-hop world, the Staten Island, New York-based Wu-Tang Clan proved to be the most revolutionary rap group of the mid-'90s and only partially because of their music. Turning the standard concept of a hip-hop crew inside out, the Wu-Tang Clan was assembled as a loose congregation of nine MCs almost as a support group. Instead of releasing one album after another, the Clan was designed to overtake the record industry in as profitable a fashion as possible—the idea was to establish the Wu-Tang as a force with their debut album, and then spin off into as many side projects as possible. In the process, the members would all become individual stars, as well as receive individual royality checks. Surprsingly, the plan worked. All of the various Wu-Tang solo projects elaborate on the theme the group laid out on their 1993 debut, the spare, menacing *Enter the Wu-Tang: 36 Chambers*. Taking their group name from an powerful, mythical kung fu sword wielded by an invincible congregation of warriors, the crew is a loose collective of nine MCs. All nine members work under a number of pseudonyms, but they are best known as: RZA (b. Robert Diggs), Genius/GZA (Greg Grice), Ol' Dirty Bastard (Russell Jones), Method Man (Clifford Smith), Raekwon the Chef (Corey Woods), Ghostface Killa (Dennis Coles), U-God (Lamont Hawkins), Inspecta Deck (Jason Hunter) and Masta Killa (E. Turner) Although he wasn't one of the two founding members—Genius/GZA and Ol' Dirty Bastard were the first—the vision of the Wu-Tang Clan is undoubtedly due to the musical skills of RZA. Under his direction, the group—through its own efforts and the solo projects, all of which he produced or co-produced—created a hazy, surreal and menacing soundscape out of hardcore beats, eerie piano riffs and minimal samples. Over these surrealistic backing tracks, the MCs rapped hard, updating the old school attack with vicious violence, martial arts imagery, and a welcome warped humor. By 1995, the sound was one of the most instantly recognizable in hip-hop. *—Stephen Thomas Erlewine*

★ **Enter the Wu-Tang (36 Chambers)** / Nov. 1993 / Loud/RCA ✦✦✦✦✦
The Wu-Tang Clan's debut album *Enter the Wu-Tang (36 Chambers)* wasn't an across-the-boards blockbuster like Dr. Dre's *The Chronic*, the other seminal hip-hop record of the early '90s, but its impact was just as widespread. Where Dr. Dre was loose, hedonistic and funky, the Wu-Tang was tense, scary and funny. *Enter the Wu-Tang* is a series of intense, surrealistic soundscapes that draws equally from pop culture, martial arts, and gangsta traditions. Other hardcore gangstas simply boasted about their hardness—the Wu-Tang clan boasted, but they supported their inventive rhymes with stripped-down samples and lean, menacing beats that evoked their gritty, urban surroundings more effectively than their words. And that's what makes *Enter the Wu-Tang* so effective—the group's unique lyrical obsessions and the distinctive, innovative production techniques of Prince Rakeem. After releasing this pioneering debut, all the members pursued solo careers that explored various elements of *Enter the Wu-Tang* in more depth—and, occasionally, with more effective results—but this contains the roots of everything that followed. *—Stephen Thomas Erlewine*

Wu-Tang Forever / Jun. 3, 1997 / Loud/RCA ✦✦✦✦
The Wu-Tang Clan's long-awaited second album *Wu-Tang Forever* arrived to great anticipation, and the double-disc set does not disappoint. Where contemporaries like 2-Pac and the Notorious B.I.G. issued double-discs cluttered with filler, *Wu-Tang Forever* is purposeful and surprisingly lean, illustrating the immense depth of producer RZA and the entire nine-piece crew. Each rapper has a different lyrical style, from Ol' Dirty Bastard's bizarre rants to Raekwon's story sketches, and RZA subtly shifts his trademark style for each song, creating an album of cinematic proportions. There are no great musical innovations on the album, since the Wu-Tang's signature blend of skeletal beats, scratchy samples, eerie pianos and spectral strings remains intact. Yet the music is more nuanced and focused than ever before, balanced equally between scary soundscapes and darkly soulful tracks. The result is an intoxicating display of musical and lyrical virtuosity, one that reveals how bereft of imagination the Wu-Tang's contemporaries are. *—Stephen Thomas Erlewine*

Wu-Chronicles / Mar. 23, 1999 / Wu-Tang ✦✦✦
The continuing marketing of Wu-Tang Clan product hit a new low with the release of *Wu-Chronicles*. Though the concept of a Wu-Tang compilation—in effect, spanning the dozen or so albums released by members and cutting away the dross—is perfect for the legion of fans who haven't been able to keep up with the collective's hectic release schedule, this disc stretches everything a bit thin, including tracks by fringe-of-the-fringe groups like Heltah Skeltah, Ras Kass, Killarmy and some artist known as Wu-Syndicate. Yes, it's hard to argue with any album that features some great productions by RZA, and *Wu-Chronicles* does include some good collaborations—notably Ol' Dirty Bastard with Tha Alkaholiks on "Hip Hop Drunkies" and Cocoa Brovaz (formerly Smif-N-Wessun) with Raekwon on "Black Trump"—but for the most part it's a wasted attempt at releasing an excellent collection. *—Keith Farley*

The W / Nov. 21, 2000 / Columbia ✦✦✦✦✦
After a host of disappointing solo albums and quickly diminishing celebrity (most of the latter devoted to the continuing extra-legal saga of Ol' Dirty Bastard), Wu-Tang Clan returned, very quietly, with 2000's *The W*. The lack of hype was fitting, for this is a very spartan work, especially compared to its predecessor, the sprawling and overblown *Wu-Tang Forever*. While the trademark sound is still much in force, group mastermind RZA jettisoned the elaborate beat symphonies and carefully placed strings of *Forever* in favor of tight productions with little more than scarred soul samples and tight, tough beats. The back-to-basics approach works well, not only because it rightly puts the focus back on the best cadre of rappers in the world of hip-hop, but also because RZA's immense trackmaster talents can't help but shine through anyway. Paranoid kung fu samples and bizarre found sounds drive the fantastic streets-is-watching nightmare "Careful (Click, Click)."

Unfortunately, though, *The W* isn't quite the masterpiece it sounds like after the first few tracks. It falls prey to the same inconsistency as *Forever*, resulting in half-formed tracks like "Conditioner," with Snoop Dogg barely saving Ol' Dirty Bastard's lone appearance on the LP, a phoned-in vocal (in terms of sound *and* quality). When they're hitting on all cylinders though, Wu-Tang Clan are nearly invincible; "Let My Niggas Live," a feature with Nas, isn't just claustrophobic and dense but positively strangling, and singles material like "Protect Ya Neck (The Jump Off)" and "Do You Really (Thang, Thang)" are punishing tracks. Paring down *Wu-Tang Forever*—nearly a two-hour set—to the 60-minute work found here was a good start, but the Wu could probably create another masterpiece worthy of their debut if they spent even more time in the editing room. *—John Bush*

Robert Wyatt

b. Jan. 28, 1945, Bristol, England
Vocals, Drums / Canterbury Scene, Prog-Rock/Art Rock
An enduring figure who came to prominence in the early days of the English art-rock scene, Robert Wyatt has produced a significant body of work, both as drummer and vocalist for art-rockers the Soft Machine and as a radical political singer/songwriter. It was not long after his first solo release, 1971's *End of an Ear*, that Wyatt fell from an open window during a party, fracturing his back and permanently paralyzing him from the waist down. After months of painful recuperation, Wyatt re-emerged with the harrowing recorded *Rock Bottom*, which dealt explicitly with his post-accident life. Wyatt shockingly recorded a straight version of the Monkees "I'm a Believer" in 1974 that became a big British hit. Despite his success, Wyatt recorded sparingly during the '70s and released only a handful of singles for the indie label Rough Trade. He returned in the '80s with albums that were lush, at times almost meditative. Wyatt's voice—clear, emotionally charged and

always on the verge of breaking—brought great depth and soul to songs that, if recorded by a lesser artist, would have sounded terse and tired. He recorded several albums during the '90s as well, also devoting time to political work. Despite his occasionally strident political posture, he has recorded some stunning music, full of wonder, possibility and pure emotion, that remains undiscovered by many. *—John Dougan*

The End of an Ear / 1971 / CBS ♦♦♦♦

Of all the projects Robert Wyatt created apart from his tenure with Soft Machine and Matching Mole, *The End of an Ear* has to be the strangest, and among the most beautiful and misunderstood recordings of his career. Recorded near the end of his membership in Soft Machine, *End of an Ear* finds Wyatt experimenting far more with jazz and avant-garde material than in the jazz-rock-structured environment of his band. The Wyatt on *The End of an Ear* (a play on words for the end of the SM era, and another session called *Ear of the Beholder*) is still very much the fiery drummer and percussionist who is interested in electronic effects and jazz and not the composer and interpretive singer of his post-accident years. Influenced by Miles Davis' electric bands and the fledgling Weather Report who did their first gigs in the U.K., Wyatt opens and closes the album with two readings of Gil Evans' "Las Vegas Tango, Pt. 1." These are the most structured pieces on the recording, and the only ones not dedicated in some way: "To Mark Everywhere," "To Caravan and Brother Jim," "To Nick Everyone," "To the Old World (Thank You for the Use of Your Body, Goodbye)," "To Carla, Marsha, and Caroline (For Making Everything Beautifuller)," and others. The titles reveal how personal the nature of these sound experiments can be. *—Thom Jurek*

• **Rock Bottom** / 1974 / Thirsty Ear ♦♦♦♦♦

Rock Bottom, recorded with a star-studded cast of Canterbury musicians, has been deservedly acclaimed as one of the finest art rock albums. Several forces surrounding Wyatt's life helped shape its outcome. First, it was recorded after the former Soft Machine drummer and singer fell out of a five-story window and broke his spine. Legend had it that the album was a chronicle of his stay in the hospital. Wyatt dispels this notion in the liner notes of the 1997 Thirsty Ear reissue of the album, as well as the book *Wrong Movements: A Robert Wyatt History*. Much of the material was composed prior to his accident in anticipation of rehearsals of a new lineup of Matching Mole. The writing was completed in the hospital, where Wyatt realized that he would now need to sing more, since he could no longer be solely the drummer. Many of *Rock Bottom*'s songs are very personal and introspective love songs, since he would soon marry Alfreda Benge. Benge suggested to Wyatt that his music was too cluttered and needed more open spaces. Therefore, Robert Wyatt not only ploughed new ground in songwriting territory, but he presented the songs differently, taking time to allow songs like "Sea Song" and "Alifib" to develop slowly. Previous attempts at love songs, like "O Caroline," while earnest and wistful, were very literal and lyrically clumsy. *Rock Bottom* was Robert Wyatt's most focused and relaxed album up to its time of release. In 1974, it won the French Grand Prix Charles Cros Record of the Year Award. It is also considered an essential record in any comprehensive collection of psychedelic or progressive rock. Concurrently released was the first of his two singles to reach the British Top 40, "I'm a Believer." *—Jim Powers*

Ruth Is Stranger Than Richard / 1975 / Thirsty Ear ♦♦♦♦

There was no way that Wyatt's follow-up to *Rock Bottom* could be as personal and searching, but this album that came barely a year later instead collects some earlier material to be revamped for this release. "Soup Song," for instance, is a rewrite of "Slow Walkin' Talk," written before the forming of Soft Machine. "Team Spirit," written with Phil Manzanera and Bill MacCormick of Quiet Sun, would turn up the same year as "Frontera" on Manzanera's *Diamond Head*. While some of the songs tend to plod along, the dirge-like "Five Black Notes and One White Notes," a lethargic cover of Offenbach's "Baccarole," Charlie Haden's "Song for Che," and Fred Frith's piano team-up with Wyatt on "Muddy Mouth" are magical. As usual, the assembled band, including the underrated Gary Windo on sax and Mongezi Feza on trumpet, never dissapoint. *—Ted Mills*

Nothing Can Stop Us / 1981 / Thirsty Ear ♦♦♦♦♦

This compilation of early-'80s singles includes some of Wyatt's finest work. Aside from "Born Again Cretin" (whose vocals recall the Beach Boys at their most experimental), all of it's non-original material that Wyatt makes his own with his sad, haunting vocals. You could hardly ask for a more diverse assortment of covers: Chic's "At Last I Am Free" (given an eerie treatment with especially mysterious, spacy keyboards), the a cappella gospel of "Stalin Wasn't Stallin'," political commentary with "Trade Union," the Billie Holiday standard "Strange Fruit," Ivor Cutler's "Grass," and a couple of songs in Spanish. The tracks have since been reissued a few times, with bonus tracks such as the "Shipbuilding" single; the best option for U.S. consumers is *Compilation*, which pairs *Nothing Can Stop Us* with *Old Rottenhat*. *—Richie Unterberger*

Old Rottenhat / 1985 / Thirsty Ear ♦♦♦

Wyatt has been quoted as declaring that this record was "a conscious attempt to make unmisusable music," i.e., music that couldn't be appropriated by the Right or broadcast on Voice of America. VOA doesn't broadcast uncommercial music such as this in any case, but Wyatt did succeed in stating some of his political concerns—imperialism, the carnage in East Timor, the flaws of rigid political ideology—in an understated manner. He went back to writing his own material for this album, after having focused on eclectic "covers" in the early '80s, with fair success. It's perhaps an even moodier outing than usual for Wyatt, his melancholia amplified by the foggy, spooky keyboards. It was reissued on CD in 1990 as half of *Compilation*, which also includes the entirety of *Nothing Can Stop Us Now*. Somewhat confusingly, it was *also* reissued on CD as half of *Mid-Eighties*, an entirely different Gramavision release which adds eight tracks from assorted EPs, singles, and compilations of the time. *—Richie Unterberger*

Dondestan / 1991 / Gramavision ♦♦♦♦

For half of these songs, Wyatt put music to the poetry of his wife Alfreda Benge; he wrote both words and music for the remainder (with the exception of "Lisp Service," whose music was written by ex-Soft Machine bassist Hugh Hopper). Roughly speaking, the collaborations with Benge are more abstract, and the other compositions more politically oriented, dealing with concerns such as Palestine, privatization, and the Communist Party (the wittily titled "CP Jeebies"). If you're worried that this is agit-prop, don't fret; it's all delivered with Wyatt's typical understated melancholy, subtle humor, and trademark eerie keyboards. Indeed, the mix of jazz, pop, and progressive rock—owing, as ever, little to contemporary trends—is appealing enough that it may take a while for the subversive lyrical ideas to make themselves apparent. *—Richie Unterberger*

Mid-Eighties / 1993 / Gramavision ♦♦♦♦♦

Basically, this is an expanded version of the 1985 album *Old Rottenhat*, with the addition of eight extra tracks from the period: the four-song *Work in Progress* EP, two songs from the B-side of "Shipbuilding," and a couple of cuts from various-artist compilations. These bonus tracks are hardly extraneous, containing as they do some of his strongest work from the time, especially his covers of Peter Gabriel's "Biko" and Monk's "'Round Midnight," which are further evidence of Wyatt as one of contemporary music's most imaginative interpreters. *—Richie Unterberger*

Floatsam Jetsam / 1994 / Rough Trade ♦♦♦

Not for the neophytes, this is a spectacular collection of unreleased oddities that span the years 1968-1990. Included are Wyatt's work with Jimi Hendrix (Soft Machine toured America as Hendrix's opening act in 1968) and his work with veteran avant-gardists Lol Coxhill and Dagmar Krause. Nothing here matches Wyatt's most important work, but for those so inclined, this is a unique opportunity to explore some of the hidden nooks and crannies of an always-interesting artist's career. Caveat emptor: as with *Going Back a Bit*, this is an expensive English import. *—John Dougan*

• **Going Back a Bit: A Little History of Robert Wyatt** / 1994 / Virgin ♦♦♦♦♦

A wonderfully compiled 28-track, two-CD set that includes some of Wyatt's work with Soft Machine and his short-lived band of radical politicos Matching Mole (who, frankly, are not very interesting). Also, this generous set includes some outtakes and unreleased material. As for a basic overview of Wyatt's career that's doesn't skimp on the strong stuff and provides a sense of chronology, you can't do much better. The lone drawback is that the set is only available as a pricy English import. But if you've got the time and money, it's well worth the investment. *—John Dougan*

Short Break / Oct. 8, 1996 / Resurgent ♦♦♦

When Robert Wyatt followed up his welcome return of a CD (*Dondestan*) with this EP "only" two years later, some fans thought a new era of productivity had hit the reclusive singer. (Alas, it took until 1998 for a full-length follow-up to appear.) *A Short Break* is a musical scrapbook, a glimpse of half-thought ideas and hints of melody—atmospheres, not songs. Armed with a lone piano, a set of cymbals, some rudimentary percussion, an organ, and his plaintive voice, Wyatt's pieces are melancholy, sad, and contemplative. They are also, it must be added, not that interesting, and worth listening to only because the man is capable of so much more (it would not have even been released if it was anybody else). Only "Unmasked" could have made it onto *Dondestan*, and sounds like an outtake. More fascinating are the childhood photos and short essay by Wyatt that accompany the CD. *—Ted Mills*

Shleep / Nov. 1997 / Thirsty Ear ♦♦♦♦♦

Wyatt continues to follow his singular musical path with the lovely *Shleep*, delivering another album of considerable quirky charm and understated beauty; a less melancholy affair than much of his recent work, the record is informed by a hazy, dreamlike quality perfectly in keeping with the elements of subconsciousness implicit in the title. *—Jason Ankeny*

Dondestan Revisited / Nov. 3, 1998 / Thirsty Ear ♦♦♦♦

The original issue of *Dondestan*, one of Robert Wyatt's later, signature recordings, ran over budget, prompting him to release the album without an authoritative final mix. Wyatt, unlike many of the artists of his era, has often been in the unenviable position of having the original unmixed tapes of his records either disappear or get erased. *Dondestan* was the lone exception and he took full advantage. Where the original recording was a seamless whole, full of spare, haunting, keyboard and percussive textures, *Revisited* showcases the collaborations with his wife, poet Alfreda Benge, his own songs, and a collaboration with former Soft Machine bandmate Hugh Hopper, as separate entities, standing on their own as songs, rather than as episodes in a drifting non-narrative of poetics ("Sight of the Wind"), communism ("C.P. Jeebies"), and abstract reflections on post-modern life ("N.I.O."). It's fitting that, even though the original order of the songs hasn't been changed, his and Benge's songs being placed squarely in the middle of the recording act as bridges to Wyatt's political notions. It humanizes the ideology, rather than the other way around. Also, on certain tracks, such as "Sight of the Wind" and "Worship," as well as "Lisp Service," Wyatt was able to bring the ambient textures that were all but inaudible on the original, into prominent hearing, changing, in effect, the timbre and flavor of these songs and others, making something already somewhat ethereal—if very humorous in places—into a work almost ghostly with its hovering presence. When this project was first announced, many of Wyatt's faithful were apprehensive, this writer included—after all, why tamper with a masterpiece? There was no need for concern. The result made a great work of art a sublime one. *—Thom Jurek*

Steve Wynn

b. Feb. 21, 1960, Los Angeles, CA

Vocals, Guitar / Paisley Underground, Indie Rock, Alternative Pop/Rock, Singer/Songwriter, American Underground

Born February 21, 1960 and raised in Los Angeles, Steve Wynn, as founder of the Dream Syndicate in the early '80s, almost single-handedly made college-age rock fans open their eyes to two decades' worth of the guitar-drenched rock that inspired him.

After graduating from the University of California in Davis and a stint with his new wave band, Suspects, Wynn took a cross-country trip in search of Alex Chilton, one of his spiritual mentors, who had been sorely missed on the music scene since his days with the seminal pop band Big Star. When he returned to California, almost simultaneously the underground rock scene was experiencing a guitar-rock revival, aided by fellow Chilton devotees R.E.M. and the Replacements. Wynn abruptly did an about face and embraced the feedback-flooded sounds of the Velvet Underground for his new band Dream Syndicate. Heralded as the leaders of the Paisley Underground, a neo-'60s scene out of Los Angeles that included the Bangles and the Three O'Clock, Dream Syndicate were by far the most "outside" band in the bunch, often challenging their audiences to three-hour sets built around endless jams and feedback sessions. After four albums on four labels and a change in direction (Wynn traded in his Lou Reed fixation for Neil Young), the Syndicate called it quits and Wynn embarked on his solo career. Out of the gate with *Kerosene Man* (Rhino, 1990) and followed by *Dazzling Display* (Rhino 1992), Wynn relied on his keen songwriting skill, unique vocal style and a bunch of friends (including Peter Buck) for the recordings. 1994's *Fluorescent* (Mute) took Wynn even further out of the spotlight due to the difficulty of finding the record in shops and his subtle stylistic variance from rocker to semi-folkie. With Gutterball, his side project with the House of Freaks and Bob Rupe of the Silos, Wynn used the opportunity to cut loose and unleash his most drunken rambler material in the context of a very unserious rock & roll band; the solo efforts *Melting in the Dark* (1996), *Sweetness and Light* (1997) and *My Midnight* (1999) followed. —*Denise Sullivan*

Kerosene Man / Apr. 1990 / Rhino ♦♦♦

Wynn's solo debut is a logical extension of his work with the now-legendary Dream Syndicate. "Tears Won't Help," "Carolyn" and "Killing Time" are fairly straightforward pop. "Something to Remember Me By" and "Kerosene Man" are in more familiar Wynn territory—a mean-spirited character and his professional persona respectively spit out some handy lyrics set to neo-roots music. —*Denise Sullivan*

Dazzling Display / 1992 / Rhino ♦♦♦

For those who wondered what Wynn would sound like orchestrated, everything including the kitchen sink went into the making of this record. Peter Buck co-wrote "A Dazzling Display," and there's a Serge Gainsbourg cover and a hymn by Wynn's granddad. John Wesley Harding's harmonica was left uncredited on the over-the-top "Tuesday," on which Flo & Eddie and Susan Cowsill also sing while violins, cello and Buck's 12-string ring out like the bells of Rhymney. Johnette Napolitano, Russ Tolman and Chris Cacavas also guest. —*Denise Sullivan*

Kerosene Man [EP] / 1991 / RNA ♦♦♦♦

For those who never made it to the end of Wynn's solo debut to hear the nifty title cut, this disc sticks it up front. Followed by the Jim Thompson-esque "Something to Remember Me By," the reason to own this EP is for the covers: Sonic Youth's "Kool Thing" and Paul Simon's "Boy in the Bubble" reveal Wynn's love of all music and his ability to share his wealth of enthusiasm. —*Denise Sullivan*

Take Your Flunky and Dangle / 1993 / Return to Sender ♦♦♦

Hard to explain this one, other than that a bunch of his cronies got together and fooled around in the studio. Wynn likes to record quickly, and it's a sure bet that this collection of spare, unused songs written between 1987-1993 took the time it takes to play the CD to lay down. Still, it cuts to the heart of Wynn's love of pure, indigenous music. —*Denise Sullivan*

● **Fluorescent** / Mar. 29, 1994 / Mute ♦♦♦♦♦

No longer does Wynn allow his various bands to crash and burn or his producers to drown out his fire. With some subtle shifts in instrumentation, Wynn takes on Dylan's *Nashville Skyline* voice (a tone that suits him) and turns out pop and folk ("That's Why I Wear Black") and even Victoria Williams on "Layer by Layer." —*Denise Sullivan*

Melting in the Dark / Jul. 29, 1996 / Zero Hour ♦♦♦

Out on his own since the 1989 breakup of highly influential paisley underground act the Dream Syndicate, Steve Wynn spent the 1990s pursuing a solo career. While 1991's *Dazzling Display* found the singer incorporating both strings and horns into the mix, and 1994's self-produced *Fluorescent* seemed at times to head for the country, *Melting in the Dark* is a stylistic regression of sorts. Back in the production seat, Wynn is joined by Boston's Come, for a batch of songs propelled by layers of gritty guitar rather than a delicate strum. The album announces its intentions from the opening snarl of "Why," a near rockabilly number with drummer Arthur Johnson pounding away at his kit beneath the clamor. A guitar solo opts for a series of fractured textures over a conventional melody. The set opener is followed by the icy pop of "Shelley's Blues, Pt. 2" and the feedback trails and train-like rhythms of "What We Call Love." Wynn's admiration for Lou Reed and the Velvet Underground is made explicit on a handful of occasions. On both "The Angels" and "Silence is Your Only Friend" he even sounds like the man himself. The former could be an outtake from *New York*, Wynn adopting Reed's dry, half-spoken/half-sung delivery, while the latter resembles the Velvets circa 1969. More often than not however, such influences are better disguised and, as a result, more natural. The lack of tunefulness begins to wear as the album progresses, but otherwise the return to a stark, visceral, guitar-driven sound suited Wynn well. —*Nathan Bush*

Sweetness & Light / Sep. 9, 1997 / Zero Hour ♦♦♦

Sweetness & Light follows the same blueprint as its predecessor, *Melting in the Dark*, finding Steve Wynn exploring the feedback-drenched, psychedelicized rock that was his signature with the Dream Syndicate. While it's not as heavy as *Melting in the Dark*, *Sweetness & Light* has a grander array of sonic textures and a number of well-crafted songs that make it worthwhile for longtime fans. —*Stephen Thomas Erlewine*

My Midnight / Mar. 23, 1999 / Zero Hour ♦♦♦♦

Here Comes the Miracles / Apr. 24, 2001 / Innerstate ♦♦♦♦♦

Steve Wynn defines the phrase "What goes around comes around" on this double-disc, psychedelic set that recalls his groundbreaking bash-and-drone halcyon days with the '80s group the Dream Syndicate, yet is completely original and of the moment in its own right. Grunging and crunching out on blues-based riffs on songs like "Strange New World" and "Crawling Misanthropic Blues," Wynn has hardly sounded better or just plain more alive and at home in the garage rock setting. Recorded during a ten-day studio session in Tucson, AZ, Wynn called in his usual group of suspects and amigos: Linda Pitmon on drums, Chris Cacavas on keyboards, Chris Brokaw on guitar, and locals John Convertino and Howe Gelb (Giant Sand). The sprawling epics ("Good and Bad," "Butterscotch"), another one of Wynn's strong suits, coexist with the full-on rockers (riff monsters "Watch Your Step" and "Smash Myself to Bits"). The varied songs slide over, under, and sideways, between the grooves, while adding to the essence of the entirely freewheeling project. Wynn just may have painted his masterpiece. —*Denise Sullivan*

X

f. 1977

American Punk, L.A. Punk, Alternative Pop/Rock, Punk, College Rock, American Underground

X were the quintessential L.A. punk rockers before they grew into a world-class rock & roll band and live band; however, enthusiasm for their unique, intelligent and humorous work never quite reached critical mass. Formed in 1977 by John Doe and Exene Cervenka, the band garnered an immediate following via their discovery by ex-Doors keyboardist Ray Manzarek, who recorded their album debut *Los Angeles* in 1980. The record's across-the-board raves earned them stature as California's preeminent punk band, while 1982's *Under the Big Black Sun* began what would be a long career merging hard rock, country and folk into their fiery mix. The band successfully began to mix in their populist politics with an eye toward matters of the heart. As the band began to reach wider audiences, both Doe and Cervenka enjoyed outside careers in the arts—he as an actor in films like *Great Balls of Fire* and *Roadside Prophets*, and she as a poet and spoken-word artist, collaborating with Lydia Lunch and Wanda Coleman. Though the band never broke up, X took some much-needed time off after 1987's *See How We Are*, with Doe and Cervenka continuing their work as solo artists. By 1993, the band got together for the recording of *Hey Zeus!*, a collection of new songs, but the response was underwhelming, and it was back to solo work. X occasionally performed during their frequent hiatuses, recording the live album *Unclogged* in San Francisco in 1995. —*Denise Sullivan*

☆ **Los Angeles** / 1980 / Slash ♦♦♦♦♦

By the late '70s, punk rock and hardcore were infiltrating the Los Angeles music scene. Such bands as Black Flag, the Germs, and, especially, X were the leaders of the pack, prompting an avalanche of copycat bands and eventually signing record contracts themselves. X's debut, *Los Angeles*, is considered by many to be one of punk's all-time finest recordings, and with good reason. Most punk bands used their musical inability to create their own style, but X actually consisted of some truly gifted musicians, including rockabilly guitarist Billy Zoom, bassist John Doe, and frontwoman Exene Cervenka, who, with Doe, penned poetic lyrics and perfected sweet yet biting vocal harmonies. *Los Angeles* is prime X, offering such all-time classics as the venomous "Your Phone's Off the Hook, but You're Not," a tale of date rape called "Johnny Hit and Run Paulene," and two of their best anthems, "Nausea" and the title track. While they were tagged as a punk rock act from the get-go (many felt that this eventually proved a hindrance), X are not easily categorized. Although they utilize elements of punk's frenzy and electricity, they also add country, ballads, and rockabilly to the mix. [In 1988 *Los Angeles* and *Wild Gift* were combined as part of a CD reissue by Slash Records.] —*Greg Prato*

☆ **Wild Gift** / May 1981 / Slash ♦♦♦♦♦

For X's second release, 1981's *Wild Gift*, the quartet followed the same path they had taken a year earlier on their debut, *Los Angeles*, creating another batch of timeless compositions that merged the energy of punk rock with other musical styles. Former Doors keyboardist Ray Manzarek reprised his role as producer on what would turn out to be X's last independent release before signing to Elektra. Included are such eventual punk standards as "We're Desperate," the melodic hookfest "White Girl" (sampled years later by the Red Hot Chili Peppers in their song "Good Time Boys"), and "Beyond and Back" (which would serve as a title for their 1997 two-CD anthology). Other highlights include the '50s-prom feel of "Adult Books," the punk-pop composition "In This House That I Call Home," and the rapid "Back 2 the Base." While it may be a shade less exceptional than its predecessor, *Wild Gift* is nonetheless a classic effort. [In 1988 *Los Angeles* and *Wild Gift* were combined as part of a CD reissue by Slash Records.] —*Greg Prato*

Under the Big Black Sun / Jul. 1982 / Elektra ♦♦♦♦♦

X's first album issued on a major label, 1982's *Under the Big Black Sun*, is arguably their finest record. All 11 songs are exceptional, from both a performance and compositional point of view. Ray Manzarek's production is more akin to hard rock bands than their earlier punk works, but the songs still pack quite a punch. Before the recording of the album, singer Exene Cervenka's sister was killed by a drunk driver, and the band decided to work out their grief in the music, as evidenced by two of the album's best tracks: the melodic "Riding With Mary" and the vintage '50s sound of "Come Back to Me." The highlights don't stop there, however; also included are the Led Zeppelin-esque "The Hungry Wolf" (an early video favorite of MTV), the accelerating "Motel Room in My Bed," the rocker "Blue Spark," the spacious title track, and the album closer "The Have Nots." Again, Cervenka and John Doe supply some great vocal harmonies (perhaps the only punk band to ever do so), while Billy Zoom shows off great rockabilly chops throughout. *Under the Big Black Sun* is one of the quintessential rock records from the '80s. —*Greg Prato*

More Fun in the New World / 1983 / Elektra ♦♦♦♦♦

Coming off their 1982 masterpiece *Under the Big Black Sun*, X offered their follow-up *More Fun in the New World* one year later. While its predecessor won the band a slew of new fans, it didn't serve as the major breakthrough that it so deservedly should have. Rightfully, they didn't fool with their already winning formula; they issued another solid set of songs produced, again, by Ray Manzarek. The anthemic album opener "The New World" is still powerful years later, as is the absolutely beautiful ballad "I Must Not Think Bad Thoughts," which perfectly captures the paranoid feeling of Reagan's America in the '80s. X achieved new rough and rocking heights with the vicious "Devil Doll," "Painting the Town Blue," and "Make the Music Go Bang," while returning once again to their retro '50s roots with "Poor Girl." *More Fun in the New World* would prove to be Manzarek's final production credit with X, who would hook up with renowned heavy metal veteran Michael Wagener for their next release two years later, *Ain't Love Grand!* —*Greg Prato*

Ain't Love Grand! / 1985 / Elektra ♦♦♦♦

After several exceptional (but commercially underappreciated) classic albums, X decided to change their approach on the fifth album, 1985's *Ain't Love Grand*. The most noticeable difference is in the production. Renowned heavy metal producer Michael Wagener was on board (whose credits include Mötley Crüe, Dokken, and Great White), replacing longtime X-ally Ray Manzarek. As usual, the songwriting and performances shine, but the raw sound of their earlier work is noticeably absent—instead of changing his approach for X, Wagener produced them as he would a metal band of the '80s, smoothing out the rough edges. Still, the band scored perhaps their biggest radio and MTV hit ever with "Burning House of Love," and they composed such other highlights as "What's Wrong With Me," "All or Nothing," and "My Soul Cries Your Name." *Ain't Love Grand* would also mark guitarist Billy Zoom's last album with X, retiring from the music biz entirely until a brief X reunion in the late '90s. Not exactly on par with the classics *Under the Big Black Sun* and *More Fun in the New World*, *Ain't Love Grand* still manages to offer a few X standards. —*Greg Prato*

See How We Are / 1987 / Elektra ♦♦♦

X's 1987 release *See How We Are* saw the band hook up with new guitarist Tony Gilkyson, who replaced original member Billy Zoom. Since the two guitarists had a similar style (punk and rockabilly), Gilkyson fit in quite well. Instead of returning to their previous producer Michael Wagener, the group enlisted the help of newcomer Alvin Clark, who merges the punk sound of X's earlier work with Wagener's glossy approach. Included as the title track is one of X's all-time best ballads—proof of how beautiful and affecting John Doe and Exene Cervenka's vocal harmonies can be. Also featured are the anthemic rocker "4th of July" (written by ex-Blasters and sometimes X fill-in guitarist Dave Alvin), and the standouts "In the Time It Takes," "I'm Lost," and "Surprise Surprise." Although they were still penning fine tunes and giving good concerts (as evidenced by the 1988 live set *Live at the Whiskey a Go-Go*), X would take several years off after wrapping up the tour for *See How We Are*, not issuing a new studio album until 1993. —*Greg Prato*

Live at the Whiskey a Go-Go / 1988 / Elektra ♦♦♦

X were undeniably not just one of the greatest punk bands, but one of the greatest live rock acts of all time. Although they never issued a true live set featuring the stellar, original lineup with guitarist Billy Zoom, X's one and only live album, 1988's *Live at the Whiskey a Go-Go*, is still a great sample of the band in concert. Recorded during the tour in support of their album *See How We Are* (with new addition Tony Gilkyson on the six-string), the quartet sounds ferocious playing at one of their favorite early venues. Many of the versions found here come pretty close to topping the originals, especially in terms of energy, most notably the classics "Los Angeles," "The New World," "Burning House of Love," "Hungry Wolf," "Riding With Mary," "White Girl," "Unheard Music," and "Johnny Hit & Run Pauline." Also included are plenty of the solid, oft-overlooked album cuts such as "Surprise, Surprise," "Because I Do," "Blue Spark," "Devil Doll," and "The World's a Mess," as well as several more country-flavored tunes performed as X's alter ego, the Knitters (including the great "The Call of the Wreckin' Ball"). *Live at the Whiskey a Go-Go* is essential X. [Due to time limitations, the tracks "In the Time It Takes," "Just Another Perfect Day," and "True Love" were not included on the CD version]. —*Greg Prato*

★ **Los Angeles/Wild Gift** / Sep. 20, 1988 / Slash ♦♦♦♦♦

Since X's first two classic releases—1980's *Los Angeles* and 1981's *Wild Gift*—were relatively short albums, and since they were also released independently, both were combined as a CD reissue in 1988. *Los Angeles/Wild Gift* presents 22 tracks of indispensable X. Recorded just as the L.A. punk scene was gaining worldwide attention, you can hear the excitement in the band's inspired playing and fine songwriting. Numerous highlights are included, such as "Johnny Hit and Run Pauline," "Nausea," "Los Angeles," "We're Desperate," "White Girl," and "Beyond and Back." While the quartet's sound would expand even further on such future releases as *Under the Big Black Sun* and *Ain't Love Grand!*

(touching upon hard rock, to be exact), *Los Angeles/Wild Gift* contains X's most straightforward compositions. It is an essential purchase for fans of punk, and for admirers of fine rock & roll in general. *—Greg Prato*

Hey Zeus! / Jun. 8, 1993 / Big Life ♦♦♦
From the opening notes of the record, one would be hard-pressed to guess this was an X album. Perhaps giving to the six years between studio recordings, contemporary music had changed, and X, always at the forefront, were in the unenviable position of having to play catch-up. It's not that the songs are bad; they're simply tainted by production maestros Tony Berg and Tchad Blake and the lack of focus drawn from a band who'd ceased to continue working as a family unit. "Big Blue House" is as close to the real John and Exene as it gets. *—Denise Sullivan*

Unclogged / Jun. 13, 1995 / Infidelity/Sunset Boulevard ♦♦♦♦
Perhaps referring to the staid forum known as contemporary "unplugged music," or their own aging arteries, *Unclogged* successfully reprises X's finest work in an electro-acoustic live set. No worse for the wear, John Doe and Exene Cervenka are in perfect voice, while Tony Gilkyson and D.J. Bonebrake play the songs they played a million times with the renewed spirit of a band that can finally relax and rest on its laurels. If there was ever anything to prove—that X was a supreme live band or that Doe and Cervenka were two of the most talented songwriters to come out of punk—this is the evidence. *—Denise Sullivan*

Beyond & Back: The X Anthology / Oct. 28, 1997 / Elektra ♦♦♦♦♦
X cannot be praised enough. The legendary L.A. band wrote countless classics, released consistent albums, and have influenced many along the way (just check out the raves fellow rockers give the band in *Beyond & Back's* liner notes). It's a testament to their greatness that the material on *Beyond & Back (The X Anthology)* sounds original and fresh in the present day. The group touched on many styles, such as rockabilly, folk and punk, and successfully made each one their own. This two-CD release is a hefty two hours long, and is 50% hits and 50% rarities/unreleased material (demos, outtakes, live takes, etc.). Highlights include the riff-heavy "Hungry Wolf," the beautiful vocal harmonies of "I Must Not Think Bad Thoughts," and the Nirvana-pop of "White Girl." Some interesting oddities include a cover of the Doors' "Soul Kitchen," a remixed version of their "Blue Spark," and a live take of "Nausea" (a song Jane's Addiction covered). If you're unfamiliar with (or don't own) X's albums, do yourself a favor and get *Under the Big Black Sun, More Fun in the New World,* and/or *Los Angeles/Wild Gift.* Then work your way to *Beyond And Back.* You won't regret it. *—Greg Prato*

X-Ray Spex

f. 1976
British Punk, Punk
One of the great English punk bands of the late '70s, there is only one thing wrong with the careers of X-Ray Spex and lead singer Poly Styrene—they didn't record enough music. X-Ray Spex exploded onto the punk scene with one of the era's great singles, the feminist punk rallying cry "Oh Bondage, Up Yours."—along with the early Sex Pistols and Clash singles, this was one of punk rock's defining moments. So, too, was X-Ray Spex's debut LP *Germ Free Adolescents,* which was great in spite of "Oh Bondage" not being on it (a situation that would be rectified with the 1993 CD reissue). The songs were guitar-driven punk-pop that combined outrage and aggression with a sense of alienation and disenfranchisement about rampant commerciality and an increasingly sterile and artificial world. Poly's songs were more likely to be about drowning in a sea of corporate-designed consumer fantasies than straight-out attacks against the government. This didn't mean the songs were any less political; they simply attacked the zeitgeist from a different vantage point. Tragically, there was no immediate second X-Ray Spex record. But there was Poly Styrene's only full-length solo record, *Translucence.* *—John Dougan*

● **Germ Free Adolescents** / Nov. 1978 / Blue Plate/Caroline ♦♦♦♦♦
Perhaps the most utopian aspect of the U.K. punk scene was that it offered creative, articulate young people the opportunity to express themselves, and to kick up an exuberantly noisy racket in the process. X-Ray Spex certainly came from this wing of the movement, the brainchild of two female schoolmates who re-christened themselves Poly Styrene and Lora Logic. X-Ray Spex was far from the only female-centered British punk act, but they were arguably the best, combining exuberant energy with a cohesive worldview courtesy of singer and songwriter Poly Styrene. As her *nom de punk* hinted, Styrene was obsessed with the artificiality she saw permeating Britain's consumer society, linking synthetic goods with a sort of processed, manufactured humanity. Styrene's frantic claustrophobia permeates the record, as she rails in her distinctively quavering yowl against the alienation she feels preventing her from discovering her true self. *Germ Free Adolescents* is tied together by Styrene's yearning to be free not only from demands for consumption, but from the insecurity corporate advertisers used to exploit their targets (especially in women)—in other words, to enjoy being real, imperfect, non-sterile humans living in a real, imperfect, non-Day-Glo world. Fortunately, the record is just as effective musically as it is conceptually. It's full of kick-out-the-jams rockers, with a few up-tempo thrashers and surprisingly atmospheric pieces mixed in; the raw, wailing saxophone of Rudi Thomson (who replaced Lora Logic early on) gives the band its true sonic signature. The CD reissue of *Germ Free Adolescents* appends both sides of the classic debut single "Oh Bondage Up Yours!," one of the most visceral moments in all of British punk—which means everything you need is right here. *—Steve Huey*

Conscious Consumer / Oct. 24, 1995 / Receiver ♦♦♦
When the original X-Ray Spex disbanded and Poly Styrene joined the Hare Krishnas, rather wild speculation ensued among some fans that she'd gone off the deep end. She's still in the Hare Krishna sect, but this unexpected comeback effort demonstrates that her worldview hasn't changed all that much since the punk era, though the music (much of which was written over ten years before this was recorded) has mellowed somewhat. She's still examining the crassness of consumer culture on cuts like "Cigarettes" and "Junk Food Junkie," but her experiences as an adult are reflected in more subdued cuts like "India" and "Prayer for Peace." Original group members Lora Logic and Paul Dean are still on board for this outing, which finds Styrene in just as good a voice as the old days, though the brash exuberance has been toned down. It might not be all that old-school punk fans would wish for, but it's worth checking out, and the languid "Crystal Clear" may be the catchiest tune she's ever laid down. *—Richie Unterberger*

XTC

f. 1976, Swindon, England
College Rock, Pop/Rock, New Wave, Alternative Pop/Rock
XTC was one of the smartest—and catchiest—British pop bands to emerge from the punk and new wave explosion of the late '70s. From the tense, jerky riffs of their early singles to the lushly arranged, meticulous pop of their later albums, XTC's music has always been driven by the hook-laden songwriting of guitarist Andy Partridge and bassist Colin Moulding. While popular success has eluded them in both Britain and America, the group has developed a devoted cult following in both countries that remains loyal over two decades after their first records.

Critics praised the angular yet melodic pop of XTC's first two records, *White Music* and *Go 2,* both released in 1978. One year later, the band recorded their first charting single ("Life Begins at the Hop") and released a calmer, more pop-oriented album, *Drums and Wires.* XTC continued to smooth out their edges on 1980's *Black Sea* and 1982's *English Settlement,* featuring more complex arrangements and intellectual lyrics. Nevertheless, *English Settlement* was their biggest success in the U.K., reaching number five on the charts and launching the Top Ten single, "Senses Working Overtime."

After cancelling a tour in 1982, Partridge announced that XTC would never play live again. The first albums recorded by the studio-bound band, *Mummer* and *The Big Express,* were more detailed, well-produced efforts than previous LPs. After a difficult recording session with producer Todd Rundgren, the pastoral *Skylarking* (1986) was hailed as a masterwork by critics and spent over six months on the American charts. *Oranges and Lemons* (1989) featured reworked psychedelia with a Ray Davies-inspired sense of nostalgia, and the single "Mayor of Simpleton" became XTC's only charting U.S. single. Three years later, the group released *Nonsuch,* an album that recalled both *Pet Sounds* and *Revolver.* Years of internal difficulties and label battles kept the group from releasing any new material for much of the decade, however, and not until 1999 did the next XTC album, *Apple Venus, Pt. 1,* finally appear. *Wasp Star (Apple Venus, Pt. 2* followed in mid-2000. *—Stephen Thomas Erlewine*

White Music / Jan. 20, 1978 / Geffen ♦♦♦
XTC's first full album shows the band going full-throttle in true punk spirit. More dissonant than their latter period, the young band shines with directionless energy and a good sense of humor. Highlights include the catchy singles, "This Is Pop" and "Radios in Motion" as well as a jumpy version of "All Along the Watchtower." Their first release, *3D EP,* has been appended to the CD version. *—Chris Woodstra*

Go 2 / Oct. 13, 1978 / Geffen ♦♦
Recorded in a rush, less than a year after *White Music, Go 2* predictably suffered. The album, while slightly more melodic, reprises much of the quirky, high-energy playing of *White Music,* but the material is considerably weaker this time out. Aside from a couple of standout tracks like "Mechanic Dancing," *Go 2* is probably most memorable for its witty, word-heavy cover art. *—Chris Woodstra*

Drums & Wires / Aug. 17, 1979 / Virgin ♦♦♦♦♦
Following *Go 2,* keyboardist Barry Andrews left the band and, rather than finding a replacement keyboard player, the band opted to recruit another guitarist (who could also play keyboards), Dave Gregory. The album that followed the lineup change, *Drums and Wires,* marked a turning point for the band, with a more subdued set of songs that reflected an increasing songwriting proficiency. The aimless energy of the first two albums was focused into a cohesive statement with a distinctive voice that retained their clever humor, quirky wordplay and decidedly British flavor. Musically, *Drums and Wires,* titled to reflect the big drum sound they developed for the album, is certainly driven by the powerful rhythms and angular, mainly minimalistic arrangements, but the addition of a second guitarist also allowed for some inventive and interesting guitar work (the "wires") that made up for the lack of Andrews' odd flourishes—the tension between the two sounds creates some truly inspired, nervy pop. Colin Moulding also came into his own as a songwriter, penning their first substantial hit, the new wave classic "Making Plans for Nigel." [The CD reissue contains tracks from the bonus single originally included with the LP—"Limelight" and "Chain of Command"—as well as "Life Begins at the Hop."] *—Chris Woodstra*

Black Sea / Sep. 12, 1980 / Geffen ♦♦♦♦♦
XTC continued on with the big drum sound of *Drums and Wires,* adding more polish and an even heavier-hitting approach for *Black Sea*—their arrangements are fuller and they rock harder than ever before. Where *Drums and Wires* implied social commentary, *Black Sea* more directly addressed sociopolitical concerns, handling them not strictly in a theoretical sense, but rather showing a human response to the circumstances. Of course, the band's skewed outlook and mid-'60s pop sense keeps things from becoming too heavy—included are some of their finest songs, like "Respectable Street," "Generals and Majors," and "Towers of London," as well as the thoroughly enjoyable pop fluff throwaway, "Sgt. Rock (Is Going to Help Me)," to keep the mood light. All in all, there isn't a bad song in the bunch—*Black Sea* was their most consistent album up to that point—and although

XTC always operated on the fringes, the album is their most commercial-sounding, fitting in perfectly with the new wave of the late '70s/early '80s. [The CD reissue adds three tracks—"Smokeless Zone," "Don't Lose Your Temper," and "The Somnambulist"—to the middle of the album. And while the extras are welcomed (especially "Don't Lose Your Temper"), they really should have been tacked on to the end rather than disrupting the original.] —*Chris Woodstra*

English Settlement / Feb. 12, 1982 / Geffen ✦✦✦✦
Andy Partridge's discovery of the 12-string guitar set the tone for *English Settlement*, an album which moved away from the pop gloss of *Black Sea* in favor of lighter, though still rhythmically heavy, acoustic numbers with more complex and intricate instrumentation. There are plenty of pop gems —"Senses Working Overtime" stands as one of their finest songs—but the main focus seems to be the more expansive sound; most of the songs are drawn out to near-epic length, ultimately taking some of the impact of the songs away. Despite several terrific tracks, *English Settlement* seems more a transitional album than anything else, although the textural sound of the album is quite remarkable, indicating the direction they would take in their post-touring incarnation. —*Chris Woodstra*

• **Waxworks: Some Singles 1977-1982** / Nov. 1982 / Geffen ✦✦✦✦✦
Though it has been since supplanted by more comprehensive collections—the most notable being *Fossil Fuel*, which repeats all of the *Waxworks* tracks plus the later singles—*Waxworks—Some Singles 1977-1982* remains the classic compilation of the band's first, pre-studio-bound period. Originally, the album was packaged with a second record, *Beeswax—Some B-Sides 1977-1982*, later made available separately. —*Chris Woodstra*

Beeswax: Some B-Sides 1977-1982 / Nov. 1982 / Virgin ✦✦✦
A nice companion to *Waxworks*, *Beeswax* does a fine job of collecting the B-sides to the singles up to 1982. While these songs were often as engaging as the A-sides, their addition to the CDs as bonus tracks now makes this collection redundant. —*Chris Woodstra*

Mummer / Aug. 30, 1983 / Geffen ✦✦✦
Mummer, the first album to follow Andy Partridge's mental breakdown which led to the band's retirement from touring, is very much the work of an eccentric in isolation. The album is a collection that builds on the groundwork of *English Settlement* with gentle, acoustic songs that evoke pastoral images and peaceful times. There are moments of real inspiration, resulting in some of their finest songs to date—"Love on a Farmboy's Wages," "Great Fire," and "Lady Bird"—and the sound sets a pleasingly consistent mood, although the sameness tends to work against the lesser material. Only the out-of-place afterthought of "Funk Pop A Roll," a tirade against the music industry, breaks things up, recapturing the abrasive Partridge of past. [When *Mummer* was reissued on CD, six tracks were added to the middle of the album. While "Jump," "Toys" and "Desert Island" are welcome additions of pop confection, the atmospheric instrumentals "Frost Circus" and "Processions Toward the Learning Land," from the simply bizarre *Homo Safari Series*, serve to disrupt the album's flow.] —*Chris Woodstra*

The Big Express / Oct. 15, 1984 / Geffen ✦✦✦✦
XTC took full advantage of their studio-bound status with *The Big Express*, creating their most painstakingly detailed, multi-layered, sonically dynamic album to date. The more upbeat material and brighter sound recall some of the band's earlier moments, but most of all, *The Big Express* signals a turning point for the band, setting the blueprint for their later approach—a combination of studio perfection matched with impeccable songcraft that results in a thoroughly consistent and enjoyable album beginning to end. *Skylarking*, the album that followed, gets much more glory, and certainly its impact was greater (this one was virtually ignored), but really, *The Big Express* covers much of the same territory and is just as strong an album in many ways. [Three songs were added to the middle of the CD reissue—"Red Brick Dream," "Washaway," and "Blue Overall"—but they fit seamlessly into the complete picture.] —*Chris Woodstra*

★ **Skylarking** / Oct. 27, 1986 / Geffen ✦✦✦✦✦
Working with producer Todd Rundgren didn't necessarily bring XTC a sense of sonic cohesion—after all, every record since *English Settlement* followed its own interior logic—but it did help the group sharpen their focus, making *Skylarking* their tightest record since *Drums and Wires*. Ironically, *Skylarking* had little to do with new wave and everything to do with the lush, post-psychedelic pop of the Beatles and Beach Boys. Combining the charming pastoral feel of *Mummer* with the classicist English pop of *The Big Express*, XTC expands their signature sound by enhancing their intelligently melodic pop with graceful, lyrical arrangements and sweeping, detailed instrumentation. Rundgren may have devised the sequencing, helping the record feel like a song cycle even if it doesn't play like one, but what really impresses is the consistency and depth of Andy Partridge's and Colin Moulding's songs. Each song is a small gem, marrying sweet, catchy melodies to decidedly adult lyrical themes, from celebrations of love ("Grass") and marriage ("Big Day") to skepticism about maturation ("Earn Enough for Us") and religion ("Dear God"). Moulding's songs complement Partridge's songs better than before, and each writer is at a melodic and lyrical peak, which Rundgren helps convey with his supple production. The result is a pop masterpiece—an album that has great ambitions and fulfills them with ease. [The initial release of *Skylarking* didn't feature "Dear God," which was originally the B-side of "Grass." After "Dear God" became an unexpected hit, "Mermaid Smile" was pulled from the album so the hit single could be added to the record.] —*Stephen Thomas Erlewine*

Compact XTC: The Singles 1978-85 / 1987 / Virgin ✦✦✦✦✦
Taking the *Waxworks* collection one step further, this 18-track disc collects all of the pre-*Skylarking* singles. Not a bad place for beginners to start though the two-disc *Fossil Fuel* offers a more complete picture of the band. —*Chris Woodstra*

Oranges & Lemons / Feb. 27, 1989 / Geffen ✦✦✦✦

Skylarking was an ambitious yet concise record, one that recalled such graceful concept albums as *Pet Sounds* and *Sgt. Pepper*, so it wasn't entirely a surprise that XTC embraced psychedelia on its double-album follow-up *Oranges and Lemons*, especially if their celebrated Dukes of Stratosphear side project was taken into consideration as well. *Oranges and Lemons* lacks the singular focus of *Skylarking*, but at its best, it's just as impressive as its predecessor. Instead of revelling in the form of psychedelic pop, as they did with the Dukes, XTC bring the genre's sensibility to the mature pop of *Skylarking*, spiking it with a wry, occasionally absurd, sense of humor missing from its predecessor. The result is a record exploding with detail, not the least of which are backward guitars, sound effects and head-spinningly eclectic arrangements. It's sonically rich and filled with immaculately crafted songs, but *Oranges and Lemons* falls just short of being a tour-de-force, since each song feels like an island—they work well as individual tracks, but they don't form a cohesive statement. However, that's a minor complaint, because Colin Moulding and Andy Partridge in particular are in peak form, contributing some of their very finest songs in "Garden of Earthly Delights," "The Loving," "One of the Millions," "Merely a Man," "Pink Thing" and the elegiac "Chalkhills and Children." Such songs make the relative weaknesses of the album well worth enduring. —*Stephen Thomas Erlewine*

Explode Together: The Dub Experiments 78-80 / Aug. 1990 / Virgin ✦✦
Between 1978 and 1980, Andy Partridge experimented with the power of the studio—the results were the puzzling releases of *Go+* (an EP of dub remixes of the *Go 2* album) and *Take Away/Lure of the Salvage* (an electronic collage based on the *Drums and Wires* album and credited under the name Mr. Partridge). *Explode Together* combines the two unusual projects. This is purely experimental music for the curious completists only. —*Chris Woodstra*

Rag 'N' Bone Buffet / Sep. 24, 1990 / Geffen ✦✦✦
Rag 'N' Bone Buffet collects 24 rarities, B-sides, and side projects, including "Too Many Cooks in the Kitchen" (released under the pseudonym the Colonel), "Thanks for Christmas" (by the Three Wise Men), "Mermaid Smiled," the song dropped from *Skylarking* to make room for "Dear God," "Take This Town," from the film *Times Square*, and a handful of BBC sessions. Finding the complete recorded works of XTC is a collector's nightmare, and *Rag 'N' Bone Buffet* really only scratches the surface of what's out there, but it is a start. Even though these songs were thrown away by the band, there is really some terrific music to be found here—the collection is just as essential as the proper albums. —*Chris Woodstra*

Nonsuch / Mar. 30, 1992 / Geffen ✦✦✦✦✦
Since *Skylarking*, each XTC album was carefully composed and crafted, and *Nonsuch* is no different. Working with producer Gus Dudgeon (Elton John), XTC crafted their most immaculate album to date with *Nonsuch*. A measured and reflective record, recalling the Beach Boys more than the Beatles, the album retains some of their late-'80s psychedelic flourishes, but those have been integrated into an elaborate, lush pop setting that falls somewhere between *Skylarking* and *Oranges and Lemons*. While it lacks the thematic unity of *Skylarking*, as well as the grandstanding eclecticism of *Oranges and Lemons*, *Nonsuch* is in many ways more musically consistent, presenting a set of 17 wonderfully detailed and immediately catchy pop songs, ranging from the relatively rocking "The Ballad of Peter Pumpkinhead" to the sweet "Holly Up on Poppy." Occasionally, the album dips slightly lyrically—Moulding's "The Smartest Monkeys" and "War Dance" are a little too preachy—but never musically, making *Nonsuch* a modest, minor masterpiece. —*Stephen Thomas Erlewine*

Drums and Wireless: BBC Live / 1994 / Virgin ✦✦✦
Drums and Wireless does a good job of collecting the bulk of the band's BBC appearances from 1977 to 1989—many of which have previously been available only on inferior bootlegs. While many band's BBC sessions differ only slightly from the studio recordings, XTC was able to stretch out on their sessions for significantly different interpretations. This is a necessary addition to any fan's collection. —*Chris Woodstra*

★ **Fossil Fuel: The XTC Singles 1977-1992** / 1996 / Virgin/EMI ✦✦✦✦✦
Fossil Fuel: The XTC Singles 1977-1992 is a splendid double-disc set that runs through every one of the group's 31 A-sides, from the nervy "Science Friction" to the lush, sighing "Wrapped in Grey." Between those two songs, XTC's craftsmanship grows remarkably fast—based on the edgy pop of their new wave singles "Statue of Liberty," "This Is Pop," "Are You Receiving Me?," and "Life Begins at the Hop," it's hard to believe that they would later write the subtle, near-pastoral Beatles, Kinks, and Beach Boys pastiches of "Love on a Farmboy's Wages," "Great Fire," and "Grass." And those songs just scratch the surface of the terrific pop singles available on *Fossil Fuel*—"Making Plans for Nigel," "Ten Feet Tall," "Generals and Majors," "Towers of London," "Respectable Street," "Sense Working Overtime," "This World Over," "Dear God," "The Mayor of Simpleton," "King for a Day," and "The Ballad of Peter Pumpkinhead" are wonderful songs and forgotten classics. Although XTC continually made carefully constructed albums, they were a dynamite singles band, releasing songs that were tightly constructed and impossibly catchy. They never had hits, because their unabashed pop was never in fashion; plus, Andy Partridge's voice was too pinched and his lyrics frequently too cerebral. But XTC's music stands as some of the best and most influential pop of their era, and nowhere is that more evident than on *Fossil Fuel*. —*Stephen Thomas Erlewine*

Upsy Daisy Assortment / Jun. 17, 1997 / Geffen ✦✦✦✦
Instead of releasing the complete double-disc set *Fossil Fuel: The XTC Singles 1977-92*, the American division of Geffen decided to assemble *Upsy Daisy Assortment*, a 19-track budget-priced collection that follows XTC from 1979's *Drums & Wires* to 1992's *Nonsuch*. Such a decision was conceivably driven by the idea that casual fans and the curious will want all of the band's familiar songs—"Making Plans for Nigel," "Generals & Majors," "Respectable Street," "Senses Working Overtime," "Dear God," "The Mayor of Simpleton,"

"King for a Day," "The Ballad of Peter Pumpkinhead"—on one disc, and on that level *Upsy Daisy Assortment* works. However, it's not the compilation it should have been, since it bypasses such essential early singles as "Statue of Liberty," "Science Friction," "Are You Receiving Me?" and "This is Pop," which captured the band at their nerviest. It also contains several idiosyncratic selections like "Seagulls Screaming Kiss Her, Kiss Her," "Chalkhills and Children" and "The Disappointed," which were album tracks that worked better on their original albums. But, given its budget price and generous selection, *Upsy Daisy Assortment* makes a good introduction for indiscriminate listeners. —*Stephen Thomas Erlewine*

Transistor Blast: Best of the BBC Sessions / Nov. 24, 1998 / TVT ✦✦✦
XTC finally shook loose of Virgin Records in early 1998, freeing themselves to finally begin recording and releasing records. The first album out the door was not the long-anticipated sequel to *Nonsuch*, but *Transistor Blast: The Best of the BBC Sessions*, a four-disc set chronicling the majority of the group's BBC recordings, from *White Music* through *Oranges and Lemons*. There have been a handful of limited releases of this material, most notably on *Drums and Wireless*, but usually these tracks haven't been seen anywhere outside of bootlegs—and a significant number of cuts on the collection haven't even appeared there. All of this makes *Transistor Blast* seem like an ideal release for collectors, and it is. However, it's a little more than that, since the performances here are often exhilarating. Essentially, the earliest material—and much of this dates from the pre-stage fright years, meaning *White Music* to *English Settlement*—boasts identical arrangements to the recorded versions, but quite a few live cuts crackle with nervous energy which is undeniably exciting. Similarly, the acoustic arrangments of latter-day songs from *Skylarking* and *Oranges and Lemons* aren't necessarily revelatory, but they do present familiar songs from a welcome, different angle. And that's what's neat about *Transistor Blast*—nothing here is essential to understanding XTC, but it only enhances a dedicated fan's appreciation of the group. —*Stephen Thomas Erlewine*

Apple Venus, Pt. 1 / Feb. 23, 1999 / TVT ✦✦✦✦✦
Seven years is a long time between records, so it shouldn't come as a surprise that *Apple Venus* is a significant step forward from *Nonsuch*, but the sparse strings and circular arrangements of "River of Orchids" nevertheless come as a shock, especially since its slow build-up feels as ominous and intellectual as 20th century classical music. It provides the keynote for the album, setting the stage for an ambitious, unpredictable, and strangely beautiful record. Although there are similarities with the pastoral *Skylarking* or parts of *Nonsuch*, there is really no comparable record in XTC's canon, given its sustained mood, experimentalism, and glimpses of confession. Colin Moulding wrote the brightest tunes on the record, and while the bouncy "Frivolous Tonight" and "Fruit Nut" will be endearing to any longtime XTC fan, they don't fit the tone of *Apple Venus*, which feels like an Andy Partridge solo album—not just a confessional, but a grand outpouring of ideas. Partridge insisted that *Apple Venus* be released in two parts—Gregory left partially because he believed the album would be stronger if it was consolidated into one record—presumably because all his songs on *Pt. 1* are of a piece, sharing similar lyrical and musical themes. Split between orchestral and acoustic pop, *Apple Venus* is alternately lush and melancholy, sometimes within one song. Some of Partridge's darkest work is here, such as the vindictive "Your Dictionary," yet the album overall has a hopeful note—the perfect aural encapsulation of their long, bitter struggle of the '90s. The strike was frustrating for the band and fans alike, but perhaps the extended layoff paid off in sharpening Partridge's focus, since *Apple Venus, Pt. 1* easily ranks as one of XTC's greatest works. —*Stephen Thomas Erlewine*

Homespun / Oct. 5, 1999 / TVT ✦✦✦
After a seven-year recording hiatus induced by contract strife, XTC returned with a vengeance: Just a few months after the release of *Apple Venus, Vol. 1*, and a few months before *Vol. 2*, the band issued *Homespun*, a collection of demo recordings laid down at bassist Colin Moulding's home. Its track list and sequence are nearly identical to *Apple Venus Vol. 1*; most of these recordings are so close to the finished products that a casual listener might not even be able to tell the difference. However, closer examination yields revealing glimpses into the band's creative process. For instance, the Moulding tune "Frivolous Tonight," performed on piano in the album version, receives a brisk and choppy acoustic guitar treatment on *Homespun*. As expected, "Greenman" was improved significantly by the presence of a full orchestra on *Apple Venus*, but the demo contains its own subtle pleasures, including a vigorous rhythm guitar backing (provided by a Romanian nylon-string guitar belonging to Andy Partridge's daughter) and a sort of Hari Krishna-esque background melody at song's end that didn't make the final cut. The CD also contains extraordinarily detailed liner notes and handwritten drafts of each song's lyrics with some illuminating discarded phrases. But *Homespun*'s most valuable nuggets are brief, embryonic takes of "I'd Like That" and "Harvest Festival" recorded hastily by Partridge in the process of writing the songs. The tunes are there but the lyrics are still fragmentary, and in both cases he sounds like he's doing a Paul McCartney impression. These "mumbled mono cassette sketches" are far more intriguing than the demos and are worthy of a *Homespun* release unto themselves. —*Evan Cater*

Wasp Star (Apple Venus, Pt. 2) / May 23, 2000 / TVT ✦✦✦
Anyone expecting *Wasp Star: Apple Venus, Vol. 2* to continue the majestic acoustic-orchestral blends of *Apple Venus* will be disappointed, because it's a straightforward collection of sharp, witty, well-constructed pop songs. Directness is perhaps the oddest thing about *Wasp Star*—it's unassuming pop from a band that operated on a conceptual plain for nearly 20 years. It could be argued that all the songs that fit a dark, introspective mood went to *Apple Venus*, XTC's first album after seven years in exile, while *Wasp Star* wound up as a clearinghouse for everything else. If that is true, it ignores a basic fact—XTC's leftovers are better than most band's keepers. "Leftovers" isn't quite an accurate term, either. These songs are orphans, tunes without a particular project, which may mean that *Wasp Star* is an album of moments, but there's plenty to cherish here. Colin Moulding is in fine shape, with the spare "Boarded Up" and the clever "Standing in for Joe." Andy Partridge has a few tricks up his sleeve—his compositions are heavy on electric guitars, he builds "Wounded Horse" around a blues riff, and "You and the Clouds Will Still Be Beautiful" is just about the breeziest thing he's ever written—but for the most part, he's in pop craftsman mode, turning out expert, layered tunes that may not push his talents but certainly exploit his capabilities to their fullest. After all, most pop bands would give their eyeteeth to have songs as smart, melodic, and memorable as "Playground," "Stupidly Happy," "My Brown Guitar" and "I'm the Man Who Murdered Love" as their *orphans*—and if these constitute an average XTC album, that's a testament to what a terrific band they are. —*Stephen Thomas Erlewine*

Homegrown / May 22, 2001 / TVT ✦✦✦
It goes without saying that a collection of demos is only for the diehard, only for the cult, but XTC has the kind of cult that ravenously seeks this material out, craving every note the group has recorded. So, it makes perfect sense for XTC and TVT to release collections of demos of the two *Apple Venus* albums, since it not only makes them easier to find, they get to profit from it, as well. Where *Homespun*, the companion volume to *Apple Venus*, revealed that the songs were essentially finished when the demos were recorded, thereby only sounding like a slightly less elaborate version of the final product, *Homegrown*, the demo companion to *Wasp Star*, takes great lengths to show how the songs were written. Several songs are presented in "early cassette ideas," sometimes followed by a finished demo (the most fascinating of these are for "The Man Who Murdered Love" which went through two separate incarnations, including a bizarre Tamla/Motown version, before arriving at the finished product—and that demo is looser, slightly different than the one on the finished album). Though there are some songs that are quite similar to those on *Wasp Star* (such as the opener "Playground") there are a lot of little things that are different, not just in the stated early and alternate versions, but in the final demos, that make this utterly fascinating for the devoted. And that fascination is only enhanced by Andy Partridge's brilliant, self-deprecating, funny, revelatory liner notes that help make this already worthwhile package essential for the collectors that would have bought this album in bootleg form. —*Stephen Thomas Erlewine*

Yachts

f. 1978, Liverpool, England, **db.** 1981
Power Pop, New Wave, Rock & Roll

Power-pop/new wave group the Yachts was formed in 1978 by Liverpool art-schoolmates Henry Priestman (vocals, keyboards), Martin Watson (guitar, vocals), Martin Dempsey (bass, vocals), Bob Bellis (drums, vocals) and J.J. Campbell (vocals). They signed to Stiff Records after a supporting spot for Elvis Costello in 1977, releasing the endlessly catchy "Suffice to Say" single (produced by Will Birch) before following Costello to Radar Records. They released two power-pop classics, *Yachts* (1979) and *Yachts Without Radar* (1980), before disbanding in the early '80s when power-pop fell from favor. —*Chris Woodstra*

● **Yachts** / 1979 / Radar ✦✦✦✦✦

On the Yachts' self-titled debut (also known as *S.O.S.* due to the misleading cover art), the former art-school students couldn't completely leave behind their arty pretentions, but power-pop eventually prevails. Frontman Henry Priestman's tacky organ flourishes surprisingly complement the typical power-pop arrangements. Includes "Suffice to Say," the striking debut single, as well as the infectious "Yachting Type" and "Look Back in Love." —*Chris Woodstra*

Yachts Without Radar / 1980 / Radar ✦✦

The Yardbirds

f. 1963, Surrey, England, **db.** Jul. 1968, London, England
British Psychedelia, British Blues, Psychedelic, British Invasion, Blues-Rock, Rock & Roll

The Yardbirds are mostly known to the casual rock fan as the starting point for three of the greatest British rock guitarists—Eric Clapton, Jeff Beck, and Jimmy Page. Undoubtedly these three figures did much to shape the group's sound, but throughout their career, the Yardbirds were very much a unit, albeit a rather unstable one. And they were truly one of the great rock bands—one whose contributions went far beyond the scope of their half dozen or so mid-'60s hits ("For Your Love," "Heart Full of Soul," "Shapes of Things," "I'm a Man," "Over Under Sideways Down," "Happenings Ten Years Time Ago"). Not content to limit themselves to the R&B and blues covers they concentrated upon initially, they quickly branched out into moody, increasingly experimental pop/rock. The innovations of Clapton, Beck, and Page redefined the role of the guitar in rock music, breaking immense ground in the use of feedback, distortion, and amplification with finesse and breathtaking virtuosity. With the arguable exception of the Byrds, they did more than any other outfit to pioneer psychedelia, with an eclectic, risk-taking approach that laid the groundwork for much of the hard rock and progressive rock from the late '60s to the present. —*Richie Unterberger*

Five Live Yardbirds / Dec. 1964 / Rhino ✦✦✦✦✦

Five Live Yardbirds was the first important—indeed, essential—live album to come out of the 1960s British rock & roll boom. In terms of the performance captured and the recording quality, it was also the best such live record of the entire middle of the decade. Cut at a Marquee Club show in 1964, *Five Live Yardbirds* was a popular album, especially once Eric Clapton's fame began to spread after leaving the band. Although the album didn't appear officially in the United States until its CD release by Rhino in the late 1980s, four of its tracks—"Smokestack Lightning," "Respectable," "I'm a Man," and "Here 'Tis"—made up one side of their classic U.S. album *Having a Rave Up*, and the British EMI LP became a very popular import during the early 1970s as a showcase for both the band and the playing of Eric Clapton. That album had astonishingly good sound, which was not the case with any of the reissues that followed, on vinyl or CD—even Rhino's compact disc suffered from blurry textures and noise, though it was an improvement over any release since the original EMI LP. The 1999 Repertoire Records reissue is the first CD that matches the clarity and sharpness of the original LP, and along with that improvement, their original concert has been very sensibly expanded with a half-dozen live cuts from roughly the same period, recorded at the Crawdaddy Club. Among them is a killer live version of the Billy Boy Arnold classic "I Wish You Would." There's also a pair of live tracks from German television in 1967—"I'm a Man" and "Shapes of Things"; the two, in a flash, make up for what they lack in perfect fidelity. —*Bruce Eder*

For Your Love / 1965 / Epic ✦✦✦

Back in 1965, this album seemed like a real mess, which was understandable, because *For Your Love* wasn't a "real" album, in the sense that the Yardbirds ever assembled an LP of that name or content. Rather, it was the response of their American label, Epic Records, to the band's achieving a number six single with the title track, with manager Giorgio Gomelsky selecting the cuts. The quasi-progressive "For Your Love," dominated by guest artist Brian Auger's harpsichord, is juxtaposed with hard-rocking blues-based

numbers, almost all of which featured departed lead guitarist Eric Clapton (who is mentioned nowhere on the LP), with current lead guitarist Jeff Beck on just three tracks. The Clapton cuts, although primitive next to the material he was soon to cut with John Mayall, have an intensity that's still riveting to hear four decades later, and was some of the best blues-based rock & roll of its era. The three Beck sides show where the band was really heading, beyond the immediate success of "For Your Love"—"I'm Not Talking" and "I Ain't Done Wrong" were hard, loud, blazing showcases for Beck's concise blues playing, while "My Girl Sloopy" was the first extended jam to emerge on record from a band on the British blues scene; the source material isn't ideal, but Beck and company make their point in an era where bands were seldom allowed to go more than four minutes on even an album track—these boys could play and make it count. The 13 bonus tracks are mostly blues-rock and are mostly scintillating, and the Repertoire CD has the best sound that any of this music has ever displayed. —*Bruce Eder*

Having a Rave-Up with the Yardbirds / Nov. 1965 / Epic ✦✦✦✦

In its original U.S. vinyl release, this album, comprised of several singles and B-sides plus excerpts off of *Five Live Yardbirds*, was one of the best LPs of the entire British invasion, ranking on a par with the greatest mid-1960s work of the Beatles and the Rolling Stones; it was also just a step away from being a best-of the Yardbirds as well. The contents have reappeared numerous times in many different configurations, but no collection has ever outdone the sheer compactness and high quality of *Having a Rave Up*. One major problem since the 1960s, as with all of the Yardbirds material owned by Charly Records, has been the sound—for years, Charly only had substandard master materials to offer. That situation improved significantly in the mid- to late 1990s, and Repertoire Records is working from sources that are the cleanest and most impressive to have surfaced on these tracks during the CD era; one suspects that there might still be room for improvement, but not nearly as much as was previously the case—a quick comparison of tracks between this and the contents of *Train Kept A-Rollin'* reveals somewhat superior sound here. The Repertoire reissue also adds 11 songs that cut across the group's history: principally outtakes from later in their careers and some odd studio sides from much earlier, plus the B-side "New York City Blues" (a rewrite of "Five Long Years"), the single "Shapes of Things, and their featured number from the Antonioni movie *Blow Up*, the "Train Kept A-Rollin'" rewrite "Stroll On," featuring Jeff Beck and Jimmy Page in the lineup. There are new notes by Chris Welch that, although structured somewhat haphazardly, give a good account of the history of the varied (and overall stunning) contents of this CD. —*Bruce Eder*

Sonny Boy Williamson & the Yardbirds / 1966 / Mercury ✦✦

An exploitative album, released in 1966 shortly after the Yardbirds had their first American hits. This is a live show from late 1963, on which Chicago blues great Sonny Boy Williamson is backed by an extremely green Yardbirds. Yes, Eric Clapton is on here; no, he doesn't play well, managing some thin, extremely tentative solos that find him stumbling occasionally. It's really not that bad, though, as Sonny Boy himself sings well. But it should really be treated as a Sonny Boy Williamson release that happens to have a soon-to-be-famous-but-still-embryonic band in the background, in the manner of the sides the Beatles cut in Hamburg supporting Tony Sheridan. All of the material, and even some unreleased/alternate takes from the same dates, has since shown up on anthologies that are much easier to find than this instant collector's item. —*Richie Unterberger*

Roger the Engineer / Jul. 15, 1966 / Edsel ✦✦✦✦✦

Once Jeff Beck joined the Yardbirds, the group began to explore uncharted territory, expanding their blues-rock into wild sonic permutations of psychedelia, Indian music and avant-garde white noise. Each subsequent single displayed a new direction, one that expanded on the ideas of the previous single, so it would seem that *Roger the Engineer*—Beck's first full album with the group and the band's first album of all original material—would have offered them the opportunity to fully explore their adventurous inclinations. Despite a handful of brilliant moments, *Roger the Engineer* falls short of expectations, partially because the band is reluctant to leave their blues roots behind and partially because they simply can't write a consistent set of songs. At their best on *Roger*, the Yardbirds strike a kinetic balance of blues-rock form and explosive psychedelia ("Lost Woman," "Over, Under Sideways, Down," "The Nazz Are Blue," "He's Always There," "Psycho Daisies") but they can also bog down in silly eastern drones (although "Happenings Ten Years Time Ago" is a classic piece of menacing psychedelia) or blues tradition ("Jeff's Boogie" is a pointless guitar workout that doesn't even showcase Beck at his most imaginative). The result is an unfocused record that careens between the great and the merely adequate but the Yardbirds always had a problem with consistency—none of their early albums had the impact of the singles, and *Roger the Engineer* suffers from the same problem. Nevertheless, it is the Yardbirds' best individual studio album, offering some of their very best psychedelia, even if it doesn't rank among the great albums of its era. *—Stephen Thomas Erlewine*

★ **Greatest Hits, Vol. 1: 1964-1966** / 1986 / Rhino ✦✦✦✦✦
Greatest Hits, Vol. 1: 1964-1966 falls short of being a truly definitive compilation, stopping shortly after Jeff Beck joined the group and thereby leaving off anything from *Roger the Engineer* on. Still, as a collection of early singles, plus highlights from *Five Live Yardbirds*, this is first-rate, containing their tough blues-rock ravers and their first forays into psychedelia. Yes, it would have been stronger if it had post-1966 material, but considering there is no compilation that does, this remains the most essential, accessible overview of the Yardbirds' classic material. *—Stephen Thomas Erlewine*

Vol. 1: Smokestack Lightning / Oct. 1, 1991 / Columbia ✦✦✦✦
This two-CD set was part of the first serious attempt to assemble the early Yardbirds material in a coherent form, mastered from decent sources. As the first Yardbirds release to come from Columbia Records' offices (by then part of Sony Music) in more than a decade, it was also the first CD set to be made from something resembling master tape sources on at least some of the tracks—up to that point, most of the CDs (apart from Rhino's somewhat limited *Greatest Hits, Volume 1*), had come from vinyl sources and other less than optimum masters. The results were respectable in their time, although since then further research and digging in vaults has yielded superior sources, available from Charly Records directly in their four-CD Yardbirds box and, even better and more recently, from Repertoire Records' expanded reissues of the original Yardbirds albums. The emphasis on this volume is on the chart hits, coupled with the early blues-based recordings, both live and in the studio, making this a good starter set for anyone just discovering the group and its reputation, as well as anyone seeking insights into Eric Clapton's earliest official studio sides or his work on stage circa 1963-1964. The material featuring Jeff Beck, which is essentially all of the charted songs represented here apart from "For Your Love," is also very impressive, and focuses on his surprisingly advanced technique from very early on as Clapton's successor. *—Bruce Eder*

Vol. 2: Blues, Backtracks and Shapes of Things / Oct. 1, 1991 / Columbia ✦✦✦✦
The second volume of Sony Music Special Products' attempt to make coherent sense of the early Yardbirds catalog is just about a match for the first. This material had been circulating in one form or another since the early '80s, mostly in very substandard versions on vinyl and CD, which this set and its *Vol. 1: Smokestack Lightning* companion sought to correct. Concentrating on the 1965-vintage studio material, this double-CD set is a celebration of Jeff Beck's early tenure with the group, including outtakes of their classic singles ("Heart Full of Soul" played with a sitar, etc.) and working versions of songs that later turned up on *The Yardbirds* (aka *Roger the Engineer*), coupled with one groundbreaking single ("Shapes of Things") and a Jimmy Page-era cut ("Stroll On"), both mastered from what were then the best sources used for a CD. *—Bruce Eder*

Little Games [1996 Expanded] / Nov. 12, 1996 / EMI ✦✦✦
A curious release that basically condenses 1992's *Little Games Sessions & More* 32-track double CD into a 26-song, single-disc package. Six of the less essential cuts from the expanded version were dropped, with all of the group's principal 1967-68 material (from the *Little Games* LP and a few non-LP singles) remaining, along with a few alternates and outtakes. You don't lose that much in the transition, but it's annoying because anybody who bothers to track down this stuff in the first place is probably a collector who would prefer the double CD with everything, rather than a slightly abridged version. *—Richie Unterberger*

Live at the BBC / Oct. 7, 1997 / Warner Archives ✦✦✦✦
The Yardbirds recorded several live sessions for the BBC between 1965 and 1968, following Eric Clapton's departure from the band. These recordings have previously been released on bootlegs and small independent labels but Warner Archives' *The Yardbirds BBC Sessions* marks the first big-budget, official release of the material. The disc contains 26 tracks—20 featuring Jeff Beck, six featuring Jimmy Page—which is slightly less than some editions of this same material, but that won't matter to anyone but completists since the gist is the same: the Yardbirds were a tough live band that essentially recreated its studio recordings on the BBC stage. There are slight differences in the guitar solos but the songs are so short, neither Beck or Page have the opportunity to completely tear loose. Nevertheless, hardcore Yardbirds fans will relish the few rarities here, which mainly are covers the band never recorded in the studio: "Dust My Broom," "Most Likely You Go Your Way (And I'll Go Mine)," "My Baby" and "The Sun is Shining." *—Stephen Thomas Erlewine*

★ **Ultimate!** / Jul. 17, 2001 / Rhino ✦✦✦✦✦
It had to happen sometime, and after about 30 years of piecemeal Yardbirds compilations, here it is: a lengthy best-of anthology that manages to cross-license material from the Clapton, Beck, and Page eras. The result is a two-CD, 52-song anthology that includes all of their big hits, most of their outstanding albums tracks and non-hit singles, and a few rarities. If you're looking for one Yardbirds compilation, either as a starter or a summary, this is it. Previous anthologies almost always had to be divided in early 1966 after the "Shapes of Things" single for licensing reasons, but finally you can hear early blues-derived Clapton sides, 1965 initial British Invasion hit singles, "Shapes of Things," "Over Under Sideways Down," "Happenings Ten Years Time Ago," and the (comparatively slight) highlights of the 1967-1968 Page lineup all in one place. As quite minor quibbles, one could argue that some of the album tracks that were passed over—like "Respectable," "Ever Since the World Began," and "Glimpses"—would have been better choices than some of the cuts that did make it. A few relatively obscure items are included—the late 1963 recording "Boom Boom"/"Honey in Your Hips," the 1965 B-side "Steeled Blues," the 1966 B-side "Psycho Daises," the *Blow-Up* soundtrack item "Stroll On," the weird Italian pop single "Questa Volta"/"Pafff... Bum," and particularly the three pop-folky 1966 songs from Keith Relf's solo singles. Some of those lesser rarities are at cross-purposes with the overall tone of a set largely selected on the basis of quality, rather than collectability. Still, with fine liner notes and packaging, overall it gives the music of one of the greatest rock bands the respectful, high-class presentation it deserves. *—Richie Unterberger*

Yaz

f. 1981, **db.** 1983
New Wave, Synth Pop, Dance-Pop
Yaz was the American name taken by Yazoo, a British duo made up of former Depeche Mode synthesizer player Vince Clarke and singer Alison Moyet (b. Jun 18, 1961). The two stayed together only about a year and a half (1982-1983), but that was long enough to score four British hit singles and two top-selling albums. Moyet then went solo and Clarke eventually formed another successful duo, Erasure. *—William Ruhlmann*

Upstairs at Eric's / 1982 / Sire ✦✦✦✦
Yaz's music is spare, striking electronic backup contrasted with full-throated, emotional singing, but one shouldn't discount some remarkable songwriting, especially the hits "Don't Go," "Only You," and "Situation." *—William Ruhlmann*

You and Me Both / 1983 / Sire ✦✦✦✦
Perhaps a more consistent collection overall than the first album, this one demonstrates that the duo was anything but played out. While both have gone on to successful careers, you can't help regretting that this is the end of Yaz. *—William Ruhlmann*

● **Best of Yaz** / Sep. 14, 1999 / Mute/Reprise ✦✦✦✦
The Best of Yaz does an excellent job of summarizing the synth-pop duo's singles, containing such hits as "Only You," "Ode to Boy," "Nobody's Diary," "Midnight," "Don't Go," "Mr. Blue," "Tuesday," "Winter Kills," and "Goodbye Seventies," plus a couple of rarities—the American 12" mix of "Situation" and Richard Stannard's 1999 remix of "Only You"—to attract longtime followers. That might be enough for some hardcore fans, who will already have the bulk of this material, but the collection remains an excellent choice for neophytes and casual fans. *—Stephen Thomas Erlewine*

Yello

f. 1979, Zurich, Switzerland
Club/Dance, Prog-Rock/Art Rock, Synth Pop
The ambitious Swiss electronic duo Yello comprised vocalist/conceptualist Dieter Meier—a millionaire industrialist, professional gambler and member of Switzerland's national golf team—and composer/arranger Boris Blank. After signing with the Residents' label Ralph Records, Yello issued their 1980 debut LP, *Solid Pleasure*, which spawned the dance hit "Bostitch." With 1981's *Claro Que Si*, Yello made its first forays into music video; their clip for the single "Pinball Cha Cha," directed by Meier, garnered considerable acclaim and in 1985 was selected as one of 32 works included in the Museum of Modern Art's Music Video Exhibition. Visual accompaniment remained a pivotal component of the duo's work after they signed to Elektra in 1983 for the LP *You Gotta Say Yes to Another Excess*, as the videos for "I Love You" and "Lost and Found" received heavy airplay on MTV. 1985's *Stella* proved to be Yello's commercial breakthrough: while the singles and videos "Desire" and "Vicious Games" found success upon their initial release, the duo enjoyed a delayed hit with the album track "Oh Yeah," which reached the U.S. singles chart after being prominently featured in countless films. *—Jason Ankeny*

Solid Pleasure / Nov. 1980 / Mercury ✦✦✦✦
The most varied and accomplished of any synth-pop debut, Yello's first album presents a few irresistible pop songs (the hit "Bostich," plus "Bimbo," and "Eternal Legs"), Boris Blank's synthesizer interpretations of several different forms of music ("Downtown Samba," "Bananas to the Beat," "Rock Stop," "Coast to Polka"), and even a three-song suite of atmospheric industrial music that functions as a miniature invisible soundtrack. The dark lyrical concerns and futurist electronics immediately lifted Yello above the rut of Kraftwerk imitators. *—John Bush*

Claro Que Si / 1981 / Ralph ✦✦✦
Another leap in musical sophistication made Yello's second album another high point in the development of synth-pop. The future of Eurodisco and dance-pop are easily audible from the opener "Daily Disco" and other tracks like "Pinball Cha Cha," "The Evening's Young," and "Cuad el Habib." Though *Claro Que Si* is slightly more pop-oriented than the group's debut, with Boris Blank's electronics just as innovative and obtuse as before, that's hardly a step backward. *—John Bush*

You Gotta Say Yes to Another Excess / 1983 / Mercury ✦✦✦✦
The seeds of Euro-dance sown on *Claro Que Si* reached fruition on Yello's next record, naturally titled *You Gotta Say Yes to Another Excess*. There are fewer novelty synth tracks than before, those being replaced by a series of sleazy, deep-throated vocals on "I Love You," "Lost Again," "Heavy Whispers," and the title track. There are also a few exercises in worldbeat synth-pop, with heavy percussion on the title track as well as the closing number "Salut Mayoumba." Though Blank's production doesn't sound as consistently innovative as on the first two Yello records, that's probably due more to other synth-pop groups catching up than any comedown on his part. *—John Bush*

Stella / 1985 / Mercury ✦✦✦✦✦
Yes, *Stella* is the album that includes Yello's biggest hit, "Oh Yeah." It's also their best single LP, an excellent production throughout by Boris Blank, from the theatric instrumentals "Stalakdrama" and "Ciel Ouvert" to the frenetic pitched percussion on "Let Me Cry." As well, Dieter Meier proves he's at his best vocally, whether it's the seamy side of life on "Desert Inn" or an exaggerated leer for "Koladi-ola." Both hit their peak on the

same album, and *Stella* is a complete joy for fans of the vocal or production side of the group. —*John Bush*

One Second / 1987 / Mercury ✦✦✦
One Second expands the Eurodisco approach of *Stella*, and while it's considerably less adventurous than Yello's earlier works, it's engaging dance music, highlighted by some clever uses of Latin rhythms and vocal cameos from Billy Mackenzie and Shirley Bassey. —*Stephen Thomas Erlewine*

Flag / 1988 / Mercury ✦✦✦
Flag was a watershed album for the group. On one hand, it is a refinement of all the ideas the band had been following through the '80s, on the other, in the wake of their high-profile success with "Oh Yeah," Yello had reached the point where ideas turned into self-parody—the cover art of Deiter Meier and Boris Blank pulled together into a human knot is horrifically appropriate. Nothing is a surprise here, apart from how "The Race" is a Xerox of their own 1981 song "Bostich." Tracks like "Of Course I'm Lying" are empty exercises in suave, like late-period Roxy Music without the pedigree. Billy Mackenzie returns to provide backup vocals on the more romantic tunes. This isn't to say that the album is a dull listen—"Tied Up," repeated here three times on a nine-track album, is a fascinating collage of Afro-Cuban rhythms, rain storm effects, drums nicked from a Broadway revue, monkey chatter, basso-profundo lyrics, and screams. Similar thick, eclectic production dogs each track like cologne on a lounge lizard—too much of a good thing. Yello saw the decade out with *Flag*—they haven't found their way back since. —*Ted Mills*

Baby / 1991 / Mercury ✦✦✦
The Swiss act Yello began as an avant-garde electronic trio, releasing two critically acclaimed albums (1980's *Solid Pleasure* and 1981's *Claro Que Si*) before scoring major U.S. club success (and MTV exposure) with 1983's more accessible *You Gotta Say Yes to Another Excess*. Following the departure of Carlos Peron, founding members Boris Blank and Dieter Meier toned down the more experimental touches while successfully keeping Yello's quirky club/dance sensibilities intact. In 1985, Yello released the more pop-oriented *Stella*, which included the song that would be a major turning point in the group's career. "Oh Yeah" became a sensation, appearing in major motion pictures and countless commercials before belatedly hitting the U.S. pop chart in 1987. With the release of 1988's *Flag*, Yello achieved its greatest commercial and critical success. *Baby*, the 1991 follow-up to *Flag*, predictably sounds quite similar to its predecessor. With *Flag*, Yello began to heavily incorporate Latin rhythms into its signature sound, and *Baby* continues this approach, although with less success. *Baby* is not without its share of strong tracks, however. "Jungle Bill" and "Who's Gone" are as delightful as anything on *Flag*, and the wonderfully weird "Rubberbandman" proves Yello definitely has a sense of humor. With *Baby*, however, Yello faces the task of following its strongest album, and the material is too slight to scale the heights of the complex and often brilliant *Flag*. But *Baby* is, for the most part, frothy and fun, and definitely a worthy addition to the Yello catalog. —*William Cooper*

● **Essential** / 1992 / 4th & Broadway ✦✦✦✦✦
Essential is a fine 16-track compilation that features all of Yello's best-known Eurodance hits including, of course, their signature song, "Oh Yeah" as well as earlier material like "Bostich," "Pinball Cha Cha," "Tied Up" and "Vicious Games." —*Stephen Thomas Erlewine*

Zebra / 1994 / 4th & Broadway ✦✦

Yes

f. 1968, Birmingham, England
British Psychedelia, Album Rock, Pop/Rock, Prog-Rock/Art Rock
Far and away the longest lasting and the most successful of the 1970s' progressive rock groups, Yes has proved one of the lingering success stories from that musical genre. The band, founded in 1968, has overcome a generational shift in its audience and the departure of its most visible members at key points in its history to reach the end of the century as the definitive progressive rock band. Where rivals such as Emerson, Lake & Palmer withered away commercially after the mid-'70s, and Genesis and King Crimson altered their sounds so radically as to become unrecognizable to their original fans, Yes—singer Jon Anderson, guitarist Steve Howe, bassist Chris Squire, keyboardist Rick Wakeman and drummer Bill Bruford in their most celebrated incarnation—has retained the same sound, and performs much of the same repertory that they were doing in 1971—and for their trouble, they find themselves being taken seriously a quarter of a century later. Their audience remains huge because they've always attracted younger listeners drawn to their mix of daunting virtuosity, cosmic (often mystical) lyrics, complex musical textures, and powerful yet delicate lead vocals. Today, their music of almost every era is regarded by fans with undiminished enthusiasm, and by their critics as respectable attempts at doing something serious with rock music. —*Bruce Eder*

Yes / Oct. 15, 1969 / Atlantic ✦✦✦
Yes' debut album is surprisingly strong, given the inexperience of all those involved at the time. In an era when psychedelic meanderings were the order of the day, Yes delivered a surprisingly focused and exciting record that covered lots of bases (perhaps too many) in presenting their sound. The album opens boldly, with the fervor of a metal band of the era playing full tilt on "Beyond and Before," but it is with the second number, a cover of the Byrds' "I See You," that they show some of their real range. The song is highlighted by an extraordinary jazz workout from lead guitarist Peter Banks and drummer Bill Bruford that runs circles around the original by Roger McGuinn and company. "Harold Land" was the first song on which Chris Squire's bass playing could be heard in anything resembling the prominence it would eventually assume in their sound and anticipates in its structure the multi-part suites the group would later record, with its extended introduction and its myriad shifts in texture, timbre, and volume. And then there is "Every Little Thing," the most daring Beatles cover ever to appear on an English record, with an apocalyptic introduction and extraordinary shifts in tempo and dynamics, Banks' guitar and Bruford's drums so animated that they seem to be playing several songs at once. This song also hosts an astonishingly charismatic performance by Jon Anderson. There were numerous problems in recording this album, owing to the inexperience of the group, the producer, and the engineer, in addition to the unusual nature of their sound. Many of the numbers give unusual prominence to the guitar and drums, thus making it the most uncharacteristic of all the group's albums. Its first decent-sounding edition anywhere came with the 1997 remastering by Atlantic. —*Bruce Eder*

Time and a Word / Nov. 2, 1970 / Atlantic ✦✦

The Yes Album / Mar. 19, 1971 / Atlantic ✦✦✦✦
The album that first gave shape to the established Yes sound, build around science-fiction concepts, folk melodies, and soaring organ, guitar, and vocal showpieces. "Your Move" actually made the U.S. charts as a single, and "Starship Trooper," "Perpetual Change," and "Yours Is No Disgrace" became much-loved parts of the band's concert repertory for many tours to come. Remastered in 1995 with significantly improved sound. —*Bruce Eder*

★ **Fragile** / Jan. 4, 1972 / Atlantic ✦✦✦✦✦
The band's breakthrough album, dominated by science-fiction and fantasy elements and new member Rick Wakeman, whose organ, synthesizers, Mellotrons, and other keyboard exotica added a larger than life element to the procedings. Ironically, the album was a patchwork job, hastily assembled in order to cover the cost of Wakeman's array of instruments. But the group built effectively on the groundwork left by *The Yes Album*, and the group had an AM radio sucker punch, aimed at all of those other progressive bands who eschewed the notion of hit singles, in the form of "Roundabout," the edited version (sort of "highlights" of the album version) of which pulled in millions of young kids who'd never heard them before. The single clicked, most album buyers liked the long version and all of the rest of what they found, and the band was made. Remastered in much improved sound and graphics in 1995, look for the version of this CD with a reference to "digital remastering" across the top back of the jewel case. —*Bruce Eder*

☆ **Close to the Edge** / Sep. 13, 1972 / Atlantic ✦✦✦✦✦
For most fans, this album represents the peak of Yes' work. Side-length suites allowed Jon Anderson even more opportunity for vocal acrobatics and Rick Wakeman an even bigger canvas on which to paint his electronic synthesizer swirls, organ arpeggios, and great swathes of Mellotron-generated color. Steve Howe's playing took on a particularly urgent quality here, but never lost sight of its lyricism, while Chris Squire's bass is practically another lead instrument, and Bill Bruford—in his then seeming swan song with the band—contributed some of his most elegant drumming. The 1995 remastering, referred to on the top back of the jewel box, was especially welcome on this album, the new CD version being many steps superior to the old one in terms of sound. —*Bruce Eder*

Yessongs / May 4, 1973 / Atlantic ✦✦✦✦✦
The best live album to emerge from the entire early-'70s art-rock scene, a compendium of blazing performances covering the previous three studio albums by the group and the accompanying solo career of Rick Wakeman. Some of the performances are superior to their studio originals, most notably "Siberian Khatru," although "And You and I" is something of a disappointment next to the version on *Close to the Edge*. Virtually a live "best-of" album. The 1995 remastered version, in the narrow double jewel box with the label stating that it is the remastered version on the top of the back of the jewel box, is the version to own, being far superior to the old edition. —*Bruce Eder*

Tales from Topographic Oceans / Jan. 9, 1974 / Atlantic ✦✦✦✦
Either the finest record or the most overblown album in Yes' output. When it was released, critics and fans raved over its 20-minute-long tracks, each taking up one side of a double album, and it sold very well. By the 1980s, it was being derided by critics as one of the worst examples of progressive rock's over-indulgent nature. Jon Anderson's fascination with Eastern religions never manifested itself more clearly or broadly, but one needn't understand any of that to appreciate the many sublimely beautiful moments on this album, some of the most gorgeous passages ever recorded by the band. The newly remastered version, in the narrow double jewel box, with a reference to the remastering on the top back of the jewel case, is the version to own, with crisp textures, vivid sound, and excellent reproductions of the original art. —*Bruce Eder*

Relayer / Dec. 5, 1974 / Atlantic ✦✦✦
Yes had fallen out of critical favor with *Tales from Topographic Oceans*, a two-record set of four songs that reviewers found indulgent. But they had not fallen out of the Top Ten, and so they had little incentive to curb their musical ambitiousness. *Relayer*, released 11 months after *Tales*, was a single-disc, two-song album, its music organized into suites that alternated abrasive, rhythmically dense instrumental sections featuring solos for the various instruments with delicate vocal and choral sections featuring poetic lyrics devoted to spiritual imagery. Such compositions seemed intended to provide an interesting musical landscape over which the listener might travel, and enough Yes fans did that to make *Relayer* a Top Ten, gold-selling hit, though critics continued to complain about the lack of concise, coherent song structures. —*William Ruhlmann*

Yesterdays / Feb. 27, 1975 / Atlantic ✦✦✦
A pleasant but minor compilation of early Yes cuts. Howe and Wakeman put in an appearance on an uptempo art-rock reworking of Paul Simon's "America"; listen for Bruford's wah-wahed bongos. The rest of this record is largely a showcase for the shunned talents of Tony Kaye and Peter Banks, although the song selections pass over the edgier

material in favor of hazy tunes like "Survival." The previously unreleased "Dear Father" is a wonderful, if heavily orchestrated, evocation of youthful angst. *—Paul Collins*

Going for the One / Jul. 7, 1977 / Atlantic ✦✦✦
Going For the One is perhaps the most overlooked item in the Yes catalog. It marked Rick Wakeman's return to the band after a three-year absence, and also a return to shorter song forms after the experimentalism of *Close to the Edge*, *Tales from Topographic Oceans* and *Relayer*. In many ways, this disc could be seen as the follow-up to *Fragile*. Its five tracks still retain mystical, abstract lyrical images, and the music is grand and melodic, the vocal harmonies perfectly balanced by the stinging guitar work of Howe, Wakeman's keyboards, and the solid rhythms of White and Squire. The title track features Howe on steel guitar (he's the only prog-rocker who bothers with the instrument). "Turn of the Century" and the album's single, "Wonderous Stories" are lovely ballads the way only Yes can do them. "Parallels" is the album's big, pompous song, so well done that in later years the band opened concerts with it. Wakeman's stately church organ, recorded at St. Martin's Church, Vevey, Switzerland, sets the tone for this "Roundabout"-ish track. The concluding "Awaken" is the album's nod to the extended suite. Again, the lyrics are spacy in the extreme, but Anderson and Squire are dead-on vocally, and the addition of Anderson's harp and White's tuned percussion round out this evocative track. *—Ross Boissoneau*

Tormato / Sep. 20, 1978 / Atlantic ✦✦

Drama / Aug. 18, 1980 / Atlantic ✦✦✦
For this one album, ex-Buggles Geoff Downes and Trevor Horn were drafted in to replace Anderson and Wakeman. It rocks harder than other Yes albums, and for classically inclined fans was a jarring departure; but it was a harbinger of Yes and Asia albums to come. A newly emboldened Squire lays down aggressive rhythms with White, and Howe eschews his usual acoustic rags and flamenco licks for a more metallic approach, opting for sheets of electric sound. Prime cuts include the doom-laden "Machine Messiah" and the manic ska inflections of "Tempus Fugit." Despite the promise of this new material, the band soon fell apart; Horn went into production, Howe and Downes joined Asia, and Squire and White toyed and then gave up on a pair-up with Robert Plant and Jimmy Page, which was to be titled XYZ (i.e., Ex-Yes and Zeppelin). *—Paul Collins*

Yesshows / Nov. 24, 1980 / Atlantic ✦✦✦
Not *Yessongs* in terms of comprehensiveness of the material, and at just under 80 minutes, this could have been put on one CD. But this budget-priced double-disc set, newly remastered for its first CD release in the U.S., does feature key elements of the group's mid- and late-'70s repertory, including an excellent performance of "The Gates of Delirium," and along with "Parallels," "Don't Kill the Whale," "Ritual," and "Wonderous Stories," and their live reconsideration of "Time and a Word." Rick Wakeman is mostly featured, with a few Moraz tracks. The group is a good deal noisier on this record than they were on *Yessongs*, but the performances are reasonably urgent, and the sound is considerably improved over the old imported version from Japan. Only flaw is the indexing on disc two, which doesn't match the label. *—Bruce Eder*

Classic Yes / Nov. 30, 1981 / Atlantic ✦✦✦✦✦
Classic Yes collects the group's biggest radio hits, which were frequently their most accessible and catchy songs. Nevertheless, Yes made albums, not singles, in the '70s, so these songs make more sense in their original context than they do on this compilation. *—Stephen Thomas Erlewine*

90125 / Nov. 7, 1983 / Atco ✦✦✦✦✦
A stunning self-reinvention by a band that many had given up for dead, *90125* is the album that introduced a whole new generation of listeners to Yes. Begun as Cinema, a new band by Squire and White, the project grew to include the slick production of Trevor Horn, the new blood (and distinctly '80s guitar sound) of Trevor Rabin, and eventually the trademark vocals of returning founder Jon Anderson. His late entry insured that Rabin and Horn had a heavy influence on the sound. The album also marked the return of prodigal keyboardist Tony Kaye, whose crisp synth work on "Changes" marked the band's definitive break with its art-rock roots. "Owner of a Lonely Heart" was a huge crossover hit, and its orchestral break has been relentlessly sampled by rappers ever since. The vocal harmonies of "Leave It" and the beautifully sprawling "Hearts" are additional high points, but there's nary a duff track on the album. *—Paul Collins*

Big Generator / Sep. 17, 1987 / Atco ✦✦

Union / Apr. 30, 1991 / Arista ✦✦✦
With the exception of Peter Banks and Trevor Horn, virtually all the major contributors to Yes in its various incarnations over the previous 23 years, including both of its drummers, threw their hands into the making of *Union*, which was supported by a massive tour that filled arenas with at least two generations of fans. So even if *Union* had been as good as one hoped, this was an album that couldn't possibly have met the expectations inherent in the array of talent involved.

The material is reasonably solid, and under ordinary circumstances this album would have been considered just fine, if not exceptional. "I Would Have Waited Forever" shows off the group's vocalizing (by Chris Squire and Jon Anderson) at its most melodic and Steve Howe has one of the most beautiful classical guitar showcases of his Yes career on "Masquerade." But the Trevor Rabin/Chris Squire-composed "Lift Me Up" seems a forced exercise in heaviness, and "Without Hope You Cannot Start" seems more like a composed-by-numbers piece than a truly inspired song. None of the material here would rate alongside the better (forget the best) tracks from any of the group's 1971-1974 albums. Perhaps the defects revealed the real purpose of this album, which wasn't so much to make a definitive statement by any of the participants, but rather to show the flag of the reunited band, which it did. The single "Lift Me Up" topped *Billboard*'s Album Rock Tracks chart for six weeks, with two other cuts also making the list. But the single also only limped to number 86 on the Hot 100, and although the album shot to number 15 and went gold, this was a serious falloff from previous sales. *—Bruce Eder & William Ruhlmann*

Yesyears / Aug. 6, 1991 / Atco ✦✦✦✦✦
It would be really easy for someone to complain about this song or that not being included on this four-disc set. However, when you consider the amount of material in Yes' catalog by the point of this release, such arguments are somewhat silly. There is no way that all the songs everyone wanted included could be here. The disc includes a nice balance of original release material and alternate takes, unreleased songs, etc. Of course, for the die-hard Yes fans, probably the main audience for this box set, the rarities are the true selling point of the compilation. There are some very interesting ones represented here. "Vevey" parts one and two are instrumental cuts performed by Jon Anderson and Rick Wakeman. They are songs that were recorded during the "Going for the One" sessions. "Montreux's Theme" is another from that same time. "Money," a humorous track with a raunchy spoken word voiceover by Rick Wakeman, is a sure winner. "Run With the Fox," although not truly a Yes song, but rather a recording by Alan White and Chris Squire, is a great Christmas-oriented piece. Of course, Yes' live take on the Beatles' "I'm Down" is another great addition to any Yes collection. The comprehensive booklet that accompanies the set is very well done. All in all, this set should please both the die-hard fans and those wanting a quick immersion in the works of this classic progressive rock outfit. *—Gary Hill*

Yesstory / 1992 / Atco ✦✦✦✦✦
Despite the seeming overabundance of Yes compilations and live recordings, this two-CD release does fill an important niche—it's the definitive Yes set for fans who demand more than a single disc, *The Very Best of*, but don't want to spring for the bulky box set. Essentially a distillation of the *Yesyears* box set, it benefits from the fine remastering job, while at the same time trimming away less vital tracks like the Tormato B-sides and the tepid '80s live performances. Still, it's shocking that the fine album *Drama* was left out entirely, or that *Relayer* was whittled down to the unsatisfying excerpt of "Soon." And only picking the two hit singles from *90125* and *Big Generator* won't fool many true fans of their later work—both could have been passed over for better cuts that didn't pull in the teenyboppers. Still, despite its post-1980 lapses, fans of early Yes may find this an entirely satisfactory compilation. *—Paul Collins*

The Very Best of Yes / Sep. 21, 1993 / Atlantic ✦✦✦✦✦
If you view *The Very Best of Yes* as a singles sampler, not an attempt to offer a thorough overview of Yes' doggedly album-oriented career, this 11-track collection is actually quite successful, offering the bulk of the band's best-known songs, from "I've Seen All Good People," "Roundabout," and "Long Distance Runaround" to "Owner of a Lonely Heart" and "Leave It." It's sequenced chronologically, too, which gives some sense of the band's development. Therefore, for the curious, this offers a nice snapshot of what Yes did throughout the '70s and into the mid-'80s. *—Stephen Thomas Erlewine*

Family Album / 1994 / Connoisseur ✦✦✦✦✦
Given the dizzying array of solo albums released by Yes members, a compilation of their best solo work really is a splendid idea. This collection focuses on their halcyon days of the 1970s; and while one might quibble with the track selections, the songs themselves are well-chosen and represent the high points of each member's solo output. And in a refreshing change, less acknowledged alumni like Kaye, Moraz, and Banks get their due on here. It's especially gratifying to hear the long-absent Banks getting the one '90s cut on this disc—although it would be even better to also include a sample of his '70s work with Flash or Empire. *—Paul Collins*

Talk / Mar. 22, 1994 / Victory ✦✦

Keys to Ascension / Oct. 29, 1996 / CMC International ✦✦✦✦
Yes, this time consisting of Jon Anderson, Chris Squire, Steve Howe, Rick Wakeman, and Alan White got together for three nights in March of 1996 at San Luis Obispo, California to cut this, the group's fourth live album in 28 years, which is rounded out with two new studio creations. Four of the seven live tracks are covers of songs that the band originally recorded between 1970 and 1974. The group has aged well, and *Keys To Ascension* is a more satisfying album than 1980's *Yesshows*. "Siberian Khatru" has less intensity, but more lyricism than it did 23 years ago, making it slightly less dramatic—the ending lacks some necessary attack, replacing it instead with more articulate guitar. *Tales From Topographic Oceans* is represented by "The Revealing Science of God," which shows off some superb ensemble playing on a 20-minute piece that is most difficult to bring off on stage, with Rick Wakeman the standout among the instrumentalists. Jon Anderson's falsetto has lowered slightly with age, and lost a bit of its power in the process as well, but the ensemble carries the piece successfully to its conclusion. Nearly as surprising is the presence of Paul Simon's "America," a song they cut back in the early '70s, which comes off as a lot more engaging here than it did back when. "Onward" and "Awaken," from the late 1970's, are well represented, in beautiful live covers. The new songs featured as studio recordings on the second disc are superior to anything on the recent *Union* "mega-Yes" album, with soaring harmonies and very spacious song construction. *—Bruce Eder*

Open Your Eyes / Nov. 25, 1997 / Beyond ✦✦

Beyond & Before: BBC Recordings 1969-1970 / Apr. 28, 1998 / Cleopatra ✦✦✦✦✦
Yes' early years, up until *The Yes Album*, are usually perceived as a formative period, primarily of interest to hardcore fans. This double-CD set of live BBC and other radio-related tracks from 1969-70, however, forces the listener to take this era of the group's history on its own terms. The performances and repertory all date from the tail end of the psychedelic era, and a time when the Nice were the only fully functioning progressive rock unit in England—one can hear the early incarnation of Yes catching up fast with Keith

Emerson and company, throwing in progressive influences of their own and generally playing like there was no tomorrow. The fact that the BBC sessions never permitted retakes, and were never intended for commercial release, gave them a raw, spontaneous quality that was missing from the studio equivalents. The drawback is that the singing is sometimes a lot rougher than the group would have preferred—so "Dear Father," for example, is vibrant but a little raw; on the other hand, "Every Little Thing" is practically worth the price of the disc by itself, as the most exciting track here. Disc two features more live performances of the era off of radio, including a completely different but equally impressive version of "Every Little Thing" and more amazing work by Bill Bruford. Overall, it's the perfect early Yes companion to *Yessongs*, with notes by Peter Banks, the band's co-founder and lead guitarist during this era, that reveal a lot about what the band was like during this era and some of the rivalries and alleged unfairness in the divvying up of credits and revenues. *—Bruce Eder*

The Ladder / Sep. 28, 1999 / Damian ♦♦♦
You'd probably need a mainframe computer to keep track of all the personnel changes in Yes over the years, and the quality of the prog-rock giant's music has fluctuated nearly as much as the lineups. *The Ladder* is a synthesis of the best traits of the experimental *Fragile* era and the pop-oriented *90125* era. Producer Bruce Fairbairn completed *The Ladder* shortly before his death in 1999, and unlike some of his work with Bon Jovi, Aerosmith, Kiss, and others, he didn't overproduce it. Vocalist Jon Anderson, lead guitarist Steve Howe, and bass guitarist Chris Squire all have fine moments and drummer Alan White is consistent. The roles of keyboardist Igor Khoroshev and, in particular, guitarist Billy Sherwood, are less clear. It occasionally seems the purpose of Khoroshev's keyboards is providing a variety of sonic textures instead of functioning as a lead instrument. Sherwood's second guitar tends to flesh out the sound. "Homeworld (The Ladder)" is a tight band performance, but the supple vocals/acoustic guitar/piano coda is the best part. Howe's bouncy acoustic guitar drives "Lightning Strikes," yet the biggest surprise is the addition of a horn section. The energetic "Face to Face" is the strongest track, and Squire lets loose with a sputtering bass line. "If Only You Knew" is a sweet, straightforward love song Anderson wrote for his wife. "The Messenger" has a smooth, funky feel—a remarkable feat considering prog-rock is usually considered the "whitest" rock genre. "New Language" is the best long song on *The Ladder*, thanks to a clever arrangement giving all six members an opportunity to demonstrate their talents. *—Bret Adams*

Yo La Tengo

f. 1984, Hoboken, NJ
Noise Pop, Dream Pop, Indie Rock, Alternative Pop/Rock
Yo La Tengo was in many respects the quintessential critic's band: in addition to their adventurous eclecticism, defiant independence and restless creative ambition—three qualities which virtually guarantee music press acclaim—the group's frontman, Ira Kaplan, even tenured as a rock scribe prior to finding success as a performer. So frequently compared to the Velvet Underground that they even portrayed the legendary group in the 1996 film *I Shot Andy Warhol*, the Hoboken, New Jersey-based unit explored the extremes of feedback-driven noise-rock and sweetly melodic pop, shading their work with equal parts scholarly composure and fannish enthusiasm; prolific and mercurial, Yo La Tengo ultimately transcended its myriad influences to ensconce itself as a beloved institution of the indie community. *—Jason Ankeny*

Ride the Tiger / 1986 / Matador ♦♦♦♦
Anyone who encountered Yo La Tengo's first album, *Ride the Tiger*, upon its original release in 1986 can be forgiven if they didn't immediately recognize that the band would become one of the most consistently interesting American acts of the next 15 years. Yo La Tengo's debut is a decidedly modest affair, and Ira Kaplan often sounds as if he's still finding his feet as a singer and guitarist, though Dave Schramm does more than his share to take up the slack (in his liner essay for the 1993 reissue of *Ride The Tiger*, Kaplan went so far as to write that "Dave's guitar playing is inarguably the best thing about the record"). However, Kaplan already knew where he was going as a songwriter, as "The Cone of Silence," "The Forest Green," and "The Pain of Pain" make clear, and if the group's bracing blend of tuneful eclecticism and creatively applied noise was still gestating, Kaplan's lovely melodic sense and the haunting blend of his reedy tenor and Georgia Hubley's slightly fragile soprano marked Yo La Tengo as a band with real potential. Clint Conley made a rare post-Mission of Burma appearance on *Ride the Tiger* as producer (he also takes over from bassist Mike Lewis for three cuts), and he had the smarts not to impose a *Vs.*-style hard guitar sound on the band, instead making the most of the band's roomy jangle and giving the sound plenty of body when it needs it. *Ride the Tiger* is Yo La Tengo's juvenilia, and they'd create much stronger work a few years down the line, but on its own terms, it's an intelligent and engaging set, and any band that can cover the Kinks and Pete Seeger on the same album and make them both work must be doing something right. *—Mark Deming*

New Wave Hot Dogs / 1987 / Coyote/Twintone ♦♦♦♦
Ira Kaplan once described the first lineup of Yo La Tengo as "a band of timid folk-rockers," but the departure of guitarist Dave Schramm forced Kaplan to develop a stronger backbone, and he certainly put it to splendid use on the group's second album, *New Wave Hot Dogs*. The opener, a snappy dose of uptempo angst called "Clunk," was decidedly more aggressive than anything on YLT's debut, *Ride The Tiger*, and if Kaplan hadn't exactly become an expert guitarist (in the purist's sense, he never would), his enthusiastic bashing and joyous embrace of feedback gave the song a passionate edge much of his earlier work had lacked, and his vocal displayed the fire and conviction of a true rock and roller. While *New Wave Hot Dogs* moves back and forth between skronk-friendly rockers and quieter, more poppy material (including a lovely cover of the Velvet Underground's then-unreleased "It's Alright [The Way That You Live]"), the band sounds firmer and more assured throughout the disc (even though the band was already on their third bassist by this time), and the songs showed Kaplan was coming into his own as a songwriter, with a gift for stick-in-the-ear melodies (both upbeat and contemplative) and witty lyrical conceits (how many albums can get laughs by listing America's greatest hits and name-checking Steve Albini?). Yo La Tengo hadn't reached full musical maturity on *New Wave Hot Dogs*, but it was a quantum leap over the sound of their debut, and set the stage for the music that would make them one of the most satisfying American bands of their time. (*New Wave Hot Dogs* is available on CD in tandem with the later EP *President Yo La Tengo*.) *—Mark Deming*

President Yo La Tengo / 1989 / Coyote ♦♦♦♦
With the feedback loop that opened "Barnaby, Hardly Working," Yo La Tengo announced that they'd finally truly arrived as a band. Though ostensively just a seven-song EP, *President Yo La Tengo* far outstripped the group's first two albums in both ambition and accomplishment, embracing inventive musical structures (the opening cut), showing off their wit and their smarts (both on abundant display in "Drug Test"), running the gamut from folkie simplicity to furious thrash ("Alyda" and "Orange Song," respectively), and sounding more tighter and more potent than ever. The ten-minute skronk-fest "The Evil That Men Do (Pablo's Version)" was a stunning showcase for Ira Kaplan, whose feedback-drenched wailing suggested a meeting of the minds between Neil Young and Mission Of Burma, and while Georgia Hubley's drumming is rarely flashy, here she displays an intuitive grace and intelligence that most percussionists would do well to study. And the modest but heartfelt cover of "I Threw It All Away" that closes the set is as affecting a Dylan cover as you're likely to run across. Yo La Tengo had great ideas from the start, but *President Yo La Tengo* was their first record where their execution was every bit as strong as the thinking behind it, and it stands as the group's first unqualified triumph. (*President Yo La Tengo* is available on CD in tandem with *New Wave Hot Dogs*.) *—Mark Deming*

President Yo La Tengo/New Wave Hot Dogs / 1989 / Matador ♦♦♦♦♦
Two records now available as a single CD, these really show off Yo La Tengo's ability to create musical extremes. *New Wave Hot Dogs* has the firm pop sense and strong songwriting of the debut, but *President Yo La Tengo* offers up a little more free-form skronk in the ten-minute live version of "The Evil That Men Do," a gloriously squalling, over-the-top crash-and-bash session which proves how liberating and fun sonic dissonance can be. Just in case you don't like that sort of thing, "Evil" also shows up as a straight-ahead folk-rock track. This is a great collection of material that, as well as anything else they have recorded, gets to the heart of what makes this band tick. *—John Dougan*

Fakebook / 1990 / Bar/None ♦♦♦♦♦
Recommending *Fakebook* as the best place to begin a relationship with Yo La Tengo is slightly disingenuous, mainly because Yo La Tengo has never made another record like it, and perhaps never will. So, as completely wonderful as this record is (and believe me, it is), it's an accurate representation of one side of Yo La Tengo, and assuming that everything sounds like *Fakebook* might be disappointing. A collection of cover songs that lean toward the idiosyncratic (e.g., Peter Stampfel, Daniel Johnston, Jad Fair), *Fakebook* is warm, low-key and lovely, with heartfelt singing and playing that never flags after hundreds of replays. It's impossible to imagine playing this record and not smiling and singing along. A big bonus is a great version of The Flamin' Groovies "You Tore Me Down." *—John Dougan*

May I Sing with Me / Feb. 28, 1992 / Alias ♦♦♦
With song titles like "Mushroom Cloud of Hiss" and "Five-Cornered Drone (Crispy Duck)," *May I* is classic Yo La Tengo merging pop and noise in an awesome aural display. Songs start with Kaplan's repetitive (and very simple) chord changes, as Hubley and (at this juncture) regular bassist James McNew add layer after layer of supportive sound. During the noisier tracks (especially the aforementioned "Mushroom Cloud of Hiss"), the song explodes in paroxysms of feedback and drops the rhythmic pulse altogether, eventually returning the backbeat after a few minutes of white noise. That may not be everybody's cup of tea, but for those who like this adventurousness and recklessness, it's a lot of fun. *—John Dougan*

Painful / Oct. 5, 1993 / Matador ♦♦♦♦♦
Yo La Tengo has released several fine albums before, but only *Painful* encapsulates their folky guitar experimentalism perfectly. Alternating between dreamy Velvet Underground-style ballads and raving, Sonic Youth guitar squalls, *Painful* also finds the group improving their songwriting skills immeasurably. Before, they relied on soundscapes; now, the sound fleshes out their songs, from the trance-like "Nowhere Near" to the dense "From A Motel 6" and the two versions of "Big Day Coming," which cover both ends of the spectrum. A subtly addicting album. *—Stephen Thomas Erlewine*

Electr-O-Pura / May 2, 1995 / Matador/Atlantic ♦♦♦
After the noisy but dream-like drift of *Painful*, *Electr-O-Pura* found Yo La Tengo in livelier and more outwardly enthusiastic form; while they had hardly abandoned their more subdued and contemplative side, as evidenced by the lovely "The Hour Grows Late" and "Pablo and Andrea," they seemed eager to once again explore the grittier textures they'd unearthed on *President Yo La Tengo* and *May I Sing With Me* with tunes like the gleefully manic "False Ending" and the bizarre horn-blasted "Attack on Love." Yo La Tengo also served up one of the most perfectly realized pop tunes in their repertoire with "Tom Courtenay" (which not only name checks the Beatles, but boasts a tune the Fab Four would have been happy to come up with themselves), and revisited the concept of the noisy groove jam (which they pioneered on "The Evil That Men Do [Pablo's Version]") with the acetone-powered "False Alarm" and the joyous "Blue Line Swinger." Throughout, Ira Kaplan's simple but forceful guitar lines, Georgia Hubley's steady, subtly inventive drumming, and James McNew's solid, supportive bass add up to a group that prizes

intelligence and imagination over flash, and makes it work over and over. Few bands have consistently better ideas than Yo La Tengo, and they make 14 of them work like a charm on *Electr-O-Pura*. (By the way, those incongruous comments about the songs were lifted from an obscure book on the Blues Project, and don't trust those timings on the back cover—they're deliberately inaccurate.) —*Mark Deming*

Genius + Love = Yo La Tengo / Sep. 10, 1996 / Matador ♦♦♦
Making their debut in 1985 with a 45 that paired the group's own "The River of Water" with a take on Love's "A House is Not a Motel," Yo La Tengo established their love of both the single format and the eclectic cover version from the get-go. Subsequent years produced a steady stream of between-album releases, tour-only singles, compilation appearances and of course, more memorable covers. Beginning in 1988, with the group on the cusp of unleashing their *President Yo La Tengo* album, *Genius + Love = Yo La Tengo* gathers 30 rarities, selected and annotated by the band themselves and divided into vocal and instrumental discs. John Cale's "Hanky Panky Nohow," the Velvet Underground's "I'm Set Free" and Beat Happening's "Cast a Shadow" are all spared by fairly faithful renditions. Elsewhere the group infuse Jackson Browne's "Somebody's Baby" with new, anthemic life, play the Ramones' "Blitzkreig Bop" as a surf instrumental, find themselves joined by a phoned-in Daniel Johnston for a radio performance of the singer's "Speeding Motorcycle" and nearly lose the reins on a blistering live-in-studio version of Wire's "Too Late." Housed on the vocal disc are a handful of originals that rival the band's official output. "Evanescent Psychic Pez Drop" rides a motorik drumbeat and organ drone, fractured by Ira Kaplan's splintering guitar. Georgia Hubley takes the lead on the dreamy "Demons" (whose working title, the band admits, was "White Rabbit") and the trio set their sound adrift on the languid "Up to You": a song that would have fit comfortably on the stunning *And Then Nothing Turned Itself Inside Out* six years later. Though the instrumental disc isn't nearly as impressive (comprised largely of failed experiments and song sketches), it's still well worth looking beyond YLT's studio albums for the hidden gems packaged here. —*Nathan Bush*

• **I Can Hear the Heart Beating as One** / Apr. 22, 1997 / Matador ♦♦♦♦♦
Functioning as a virtual catalog of mid-'90s indie-rock trends, *I Can Hear the Heart Beating as One* is an astonishing tour de force from Yo La Tengo, establishing their deep talents as songwriters and musicians. Although the album may run a little long for some tastes, there are very few throwaways on the record—even the shoegazer cover of the Beach Boys' "Little Honda" is a revelatory gem. But what truly impresses is the way the songs, ranging from hypnotically droning instrumentals to tightly written and catchy pop songs, hold together to form what is arguably Yo La Tengo's finest and most coherent album to date. —*Stephen Thomas Erlewine*

And Then Nothing Turned Itself Inside-Out / Feb. 22, 2000 / Matador ♦♦♦♦
After years as one of indie rock's standard-bearing groups, Yo La Tengo surpasses itself with *And Then Nothing Turned Itself Inside-Out*. A culturally literate, emotionally rich album, on songs like "Let's Save Tony Orlando's House," "The Crying of Lot G," and "The Last Days of Disco," it alludes to *The Simpsons*, enigmatic author Thomas Pynchon and independent films while exploring the comforting, confining, complex aspects of relationships. "Our Way to Fall" sets Ira Kaplan's recollection of falling in love to a dreamy, down-to-earth backdrop of gently brushed drums, luminous organs and vibes; "The Crying of Lot G" transforms the syrupy sweetness of '50s ballads into a monologue about a relationship's shortcomings. "Madeline"'s shimmery indie bossa-nova and the countrified ballad "Tears Are in Your Eyes" showcase Georgia Hubley's buttery, empathetic voice; her singing makes these vignettes universal as well as personal. Like mature indie rock records such as Pavement's *Terror Twilight* and Jim O'Rourke's *Eureka*, *And Then Nothing*... favors mellow songwriting, detailed arrangements, and eclectic influences, such as the Silver Apples-like drum machines and doo wop backing vocals that adorn many of the songs. The wintry, implosive "Everyday" uses both of these elements, along with a plaintive guitar and hushed, hypnotic vocals, to begin the album on a surprisingly somber note. Similarly, the off-kilter beats, odd piano bursts, and harmonies on "Saturday" add to the song's awkward, uneasy beauty. Finally, nine songs into the album, Yo La Tengo breaks out the whammy and feedback action on "Cherry Chapstick," their most incandescent song since "Sugarcube." Easily one of 2000's most accomplished albums, *And Then Nothing Turned Itself Inside-Out* isn't as immediate as some of the group's earlier work, but it's just as enduring, proving that Yo La Tengo is the perfect band to grow old with. —*Heather Phares*

Young Marble Giants

f. 1978, Cardiff, Wales, **db.** 1981
Indie Pop, Post-Punk, New Wave
One of the quirkiest and most idiosyncratic groups to emerge from the early British new wave indie scene, Young Marble Giants (from Cardiff, Wales) were not so much new wave in sound as in strategy. They subverted conventional pop/rock methods by stripping both song construction and instrumentation to its essence. A reverberant funky bass, a shrill organ, short choppy bursts of guitar chords, a softly clicking drum machine—that was all the trio needed. The hauntingly spacious sound was made both more intimate and foreboding by Alison Statton's coolly intoned, almost neutral vocals. The words were more important for their mood than their content. Pop minimalism of the first order, it now stands as one of the first fully formed expressions of the sub-genre that would be called post-punk.

Needless to say, it was also quite resistant to widespread commercial success, although it quickly attracted a cult following. Almost the whole of their output is contained on their debut and, as it turned out, only album, *Colossal Youth* (1980). After an EP in 1981, the group broke up. Alison Statton went into a more jazz-lounge-pop direction with Weekend and solo recordings. YMG guitarist and principal YMG songwriter Stuart Moxham formed the Gist, and in the 1990s, after a series of personal setbacks, began regularly releasing solo product with fuller and more traditional rock arrangements than those identified with the Young Marble Giants. —*Richie Unterberger*

• **Colossal Youth** / 1980 / Rough Trade ♦♦♦♦♦
Young Marble Giants' one album is a collection of sparse, evocative tunes emphasizing Statton's floating vocals and minimal guitar/organ/bass/drum machine arrangements. Comparable to little else from its time or since, this is rock music at its most austere. The original album had 15 songs; a subsequent CD added a few more. But the 1994 edition on Crepuscule is the one to get, pushing the total to 24 tracks with additions from the *Testcard* EP, the 1979 "Final Day" single, and a compilation cut—everything they ever did, in fact. —*Richie Unterberger*

Salad Days / Jun. 6, 2000 / Vinyl Japan ♦♦♦♦
It's rare for any band's earliest recordings to warrant attention outside of their most fanatical followers, but in the case of the Young Marble Giants' *Salad Days*—a collection of 15 songs dating back to their very first home studio sessions—such interest is rewarded; although nowhere near as brilliant as their *Colossal Youth* album, the set is an even purer distillation of the group's true essence, with the inherent primitivism of the demo process providing the perfect context for their consciously minimalist pop. It's remarkable to consider how fully formed and distinctive Stuart Moxham's reductivist musical vision was even in its infancy—these early stabs at classic YMG songs like "N.I.T.A.," "Constantly Changing," and "Eating Noddemix" are intimate and mysterious at the same time, distinguished by the austere spaciousness of their ingenious arrangements and the icy allure of Alison Statton's vocals. —*Jason Ankeny*

Young MC

b. May 10, 1967, London, England
Vocals / Pop-Rap, West Coast Rap, Hip-Hop
Intelligent and middle-class, rapper Marvin Young earned a degree in economics from USC, where he met Michael Ross and Matt Dike, co-founders of the fledgling Delicious Vinyl rap label. He made his debut as Young MC on the single "I Let 'Em Know." In 1989, Young collaborated with Tone Loc on "Wild Thing," the first Top Ten pop hit for a Black rapper, and the follow-up smash "Funky Cold Medina." Young MC stepped out on his own later in the year with the Top Ten smash "Bust a Move," a good-natured examination of romantic successes and failures spiced by his sense of humor and quick-tongued rapping. The song won a Grammy for Best Rap Performance, and its strong pop appeal helped the attendant album *Stone Cold Rhymin'* go platinum. The follow-up, "Principal's Office," was a humorous, everyday high school tale resembling a Chuck Berry plot and also climbed into the Top 40.

Following Young MC's success, he split acrimoniously from Delicious Vinyl, citing restrictions on his work and unwanted tinkering with his album; the label sued him for breach of contract and eventually settled out of court. Young signed with Capitol and released *Brainstorm* in 1991, expanding into message tracks promoting personal responsibility. The album didn't fare as well, and by 1993, audience tastes had shifted towards harder-edged hip-hop, rendering *What's the Flavor?* a flop. In late 2000, he attempted a return with *Ain't Going Out Like That* on the indie label, Young Man Moving.—*Steve Huey*

• **Stone Cold Rhymin'** / 1989 / Delicious Vinyl/Rhino ♦♦♦♦♦
Young MC wasn't given props at the time and he wasn't respected in the years following the release of his debut *Stone Cold Rhymin'*, largely because he worked entirely in the pop-rap/crossover vein. All the same, that's what's great about his debut, since it's exceptionally clever and effective, a wonderful combination of deft rhymes and skillful production. And there's no discounting Matt Dike, Michael Ross, the Dust Brothers, and engineer Mario Caldato Jr. (the latter two names are members of the Beastie Boys' inner circle), who make this record easily accessible, without a trace of guilt, even if it does sample from familiar sources. And, really, Young MC is a gifted rapper, spinning out rhymes with a deft touch and turning out rhymes much more clever than they should be. Yes, *Stone Cold Rhymin'* is a product of its time, particularly in its sound and lyrical references, but divorced from the Bush era, it comes off as one of the catchiest, friendliest pop-rap records and it's still an infectious party record years after its release. —*Stephen Thomas Erlewine*

Brainstorm / 1991 / Capitol ♦♦♦
In hardcore hip-hop circles, more commercial rappers generally aren't thought of as having a lot of technique—the consensus is that they're getting over on their pop or R&B appeal rather than their rapping skills. After "Bust a Move" became a major hit in the R&B market, Young MC was viewed suspiciously by b-boys. But make no mistake: the clean-cut L.A. rapper has considerable technique and could no doubt hold his own in a microphone battle. While his second album wasn't the hit that *Stone Cold Rhymin'* was, it's a decent, enjoyable effort with strong hooks and definite dancefloor appeal. Such congenial, R&B-ish fare as "That's the Way Love Goes," "Listen to the Beat of the Music," and "After School" obviously wasn't aimed at hardcore rap audiences, but leaves no doubt that Young MC could flow with the best. —*Alex Henderson*

Jesse Colin Young

b. Nov. 22, 1941, New York, NY
Vocals, Songwriter, Guitar, Bass / Singer/Songwriter
Jesse Colin Young got his start as a folksinger in Greenwich Village coffeehouses in the early '60s, releasing two major-label albums, *The Soul of a City Boy* (April 1964) and *Young Blood* (March 1965). He met guitarist Jerry Corbitt in Cambridge, MS, and with

keyboardist/guitarist Lowell "Banana" Levinger and drummer Joe Bauer, they formed the Youngbloods, initially playing in the jug band, good-time style of the Lovin' Spoonful. Signed to RCA, they released their debut single, Corbitt's "Grizzly Bear," a chart entry, in November 1966, followed by their self-titled debut album in February 1967. By the time of *Elephant Mountain* (April 1969), they had moved to the San Francisco Bay Area and Corbitt had dropped out. Forming their own Raccoon Records label with distribution by Warner Brothers, they released the live albums *Rock Festival* (October 1970) and *Ride the Wind* (July 1971), followed by the studio album *Good and Dusty* (November 1971). Young recorded a solo album, *Together* (March 1972), and due to its success he disbanded the Youngbloods after their final album, *High on a Ridge Top* (November 1972). He then made a number of solo albums, all of which charted in the Top 100. He moved to Elektra Records for the less successful *American Dreams* (November 1978) and *The Perfect Stranger* (July 1982). Like most folk-rock singer/songwriters, he was abandoned by the major labels in the '80s, but he continued to tour in an acoustic format, also appearing with a reformed Youngbloods lineup. He returned to recording in 1987 with *The Highway Is for Heroes* on the short-lived Cypress Records label. He launched his own Ridgetop Music label, releasing several albums in the 1990s. Meanwhile, he had acquired the rights to his Mercury, Warner Brothers, and Elektra albums and began to reissue them. *— William Ruhlmann*

● **The Best of Jesse Colin Young: The Solo Years** / 1991 / Rhino ✦✦✦✦✦
Since Jesse Colin Young never enjoyed a chart single, the selection of a best-of might seem potentially problematic. But Young's fans have their favorites, and most of them are likely to be on this 16-track, 73-plus minute disc. Representative tracks are lifted from Young's two acoustic albums of the mid-'60s, followed by the key tracks from his '70s solo albums *Together, Song for Juli, Light Shine, Songbird,* and *On the Road.* There's nothing from the unimpressive *American Dreams* album, and only one track from the obscure *The Perfect Stranger.* Four songs are remakes of Youngbloods tunes. One can easily trace Young's development from his folk-blues roots to the rural hippie sentiments of songs like "Good Times" and "Ridgetop," and sample the range of concerns from the intimate family celebration of "Song for Juli" to the sober political reflections of "Before You Came." Throughout, Young uses his attractive high voice for hopeful encouragement and optimism, reflected in sunny imagery—song titles include "Morning Sun," "Light Shine," and "Sunlight." Young's individual albums are often inconsistent, so this well-chosen compilation does him a particular favor: It is the great album his fans always thought he had in him, but that he never quite made. *— William Ruhlmann*

Neil Young

b. Nov. 12, 1945, Toronto, Ontario, Canada
Vocals, Ukulele, Songwriter, Piano, Harmonica, Guitar / Heartland Rock, Album Rock, Folk-Rock, Hard Rock, Singer/Songwriter, Country-Rock

After Neil Young left the Californian folk-rock band Buffalo Springfield in 1968, he slowly established himself as one of the most influential and idiosyncratic singer-songwriters of his generation. Young's body of work ranks second only to Bob Dylan in terms of depth, and he was able to sustain his critical reputation, as well as record sales, for a longer period of time than Dylan, partially because of his willfully perverse work ethic. From the beginning of his solo career in the late '60s until the late '90s, he never stopped writing, recording and performing; his official catalog only represented a portion of his work, since he kept countless tapes of unreleased songs in his vaults. Just as importantly, Young continually explored new musical territory, from rockabilly and the blues to electronic music. But these stylistic exercises only gained depth when compared to his two primary styles—gentle folk and country-rock, and crushingly loud electric guitar rock, which he frequently recorded with the Californian garage band Crazy Horse. Throughout his career, Young alternated between these two extremes, and both proved equally influential; there were just as many simpy singer-songwriters as there were grunge and country-rock bands claiming to be influenced by Neil Young. Despite his enormous catalog and influence, Young continued to move forward, writing new songs and exploring new music in his fourth decade as a performing artist. That restless spirit ensured that he was one of the few rock veterans as vital in his old age as he was in his youth. *—Stephen Thomas Erlewine*

Neil Young / Jan. 1969 / Reprise ✦✦✦
On his songs for Buffalo Springfield, Neil Young had demonstrated an eclecticism that ranged from the rock of "Mr. Soul" to the complicated, multi-part arrangement of "Broken Arrow." On his debut solo album, he continued to work with composer/arranger Jack Nitzsche, with whom he had made "Expecting to Fly" on the *Buffalo Springfield Again* album, and together the two recorded a restrained effort on which the folk-rock instrumentation, most of which was by Young, overdubbing himself, was augmented by discreet string parts. The country & western elements that had tinged the Springfield's sound were also present, notably on the lead-off track, "The Emperor of Wymoning," an instrumental that recalled the Springfield song "A Child's Claim to Fame." Still unsure of his voice, Young sang in a becalmed high tenor that could be haunting as often as it was listless and whining. He was at his least appealing on the nine-and-a-half-minute closing track, "The Last Trip to Tulsa," on which he accompanied himself with acoustic guitar, singing an impressionistic set of lyrics seemingly derived from Bob Dylan's *Highway 61 Revisited.* But double-tracking and the addition of a female backup chorus improved the singing elsewhere, and on "The Loner," the album's most memorable track, Young displayed some of the noisy electric guitar work that would characterize his recordings with Crazy Horse and reminded listeners of his ability to turn a phrase. Still, *Neil Young* made for an uneven, low-key introduction to Young's solo career, and when released it was a commercial flop, his only album not to make the charts. (Several months after the album's release, Young remixed it to bring out his vocals more and added some overdubs. This second version replaced the first in the U.S. from then on, though the original mix remained available overseas.) *— William Ruhlmann*

☆ **Everybody Knows This Is Nowhere** / May 1969 / Reprise ✦✦✦✦✦
Neil Young's second solo album, released only four months after his first, was nearly a total rejection of that polished effort. Though a couple of songs, "Round Round (It Won't Be Long)" and "The Losing End (When You're On)," shared that album's country-folk style, they were altogether livelier and more assured. The difference was that while *Neil Young* was a solo effort, *Everybody Knows* marked the beginning of his recording association with Crazy Horse; with them, Young quickly cut a set of loose, guitar-heavy rock songs—"Cinnamon Girl," "Down by the River," and "Cowgirl in the Sand"—that redefined him as a rock & roll artist. The songs were deliberately underwritten and sketchy as compositions, their lyrics more suggestive than complete, but that made them useful as frames on which to hang extended improvisations and to reflect the ominous tone of his singing. Additionally, it set a musical pattern Young and his many musical descendants have followed ever since; almost 30 years later, he was still playing this sort of music with Crazy Horse, and a lot of contemporary bands were playing music clearly influenced by it. *— William Ruhlmann*

☆ **After the Gold Rush** / Aug. 1970 / Reprise ✦✦✦✦✦
In the 15 months between the release of *Everybody Knows This Is Nowhere* and *After the Gold Rush,* Neil Young issued a series of recordings in different styles that could have prepared his listeners for the differences between the two LPs. His two compositions on the Crosby, Stills, Nash & Young album *Déjà Vu,* "Helpless" and "Country Girl," returned him to the folk and country styles he had pursued before delving into the hard rock of *Everybody Knows*; two other singles, "Sugar Mountain" and "Oh, Lonesome Me," also emphasized those roots. But "Ohio," a CSNY single, rocked as hard as anything on the second album. *After the Gold Rush* was recorded with the aid of Nils Lofgren, a 17-year-old unknown whose piano was a major instrument, turning one of the few real rockers, "Southern Man" (which had unsparing protest lyrics typical of Phil Ochs), into a more stately effort than anything on the previous album and giving a classic tone to the title track, a mystical ballad that featured some of Young's most imaginative lyrics and became one of his most memorable songs. But much of *After the Gold Rush* consisted of folk-country love songs, which consolidated the audience Young had earned through his tours and recordings with CSNY; its dark yet hopeful tone matched the tenor of the times in 1970, making it one of the definitive singer/songwriter albums, and it has remained among Young's major achievements. *— William Ruhlmann*

Harvest / Feb. 1972 / Reprise ✦✦✦✦✦
Neil Young's most popular album, *Harvest* employs a number of jarringly different styles. Much of it is country-tinged, although there is also an acoustic track, a couple of electric guitar-drenched rock performances, and two songs on which Young is accompanied by the London Symphony Orchestra. But the album does have an overall mood and an overall lyric content, and they conflict with each other: The mood is melancholic, but the songs mostly describe the longing for and fulfillment of new love. Young's concerns are perhaps most explicit on the controversial "A Man Needs a Maid," which contrasts the fears of committing to a relationship with simply living alone and hiring help. Over and over, he sings of the need for love in such songs as "Out on the Weekend," "Heart of Gold," and "Old Man," and the songs are unusually melodic and accessible; the rock numbers "Are You Ready for the Country" and "Alabama" are in Young's familiar style and unremarkable, and "There's a World" and "Words (Between the Lines of Age)" are ponderous and overdone. But the love songs and the harrowing portrait of a friend's descent into heroin addiction, "The Needle and the Damage Done," remain among Young's most affecting and memorable songs. *— William Ruhlmann*

Journey Through the Past / Nov. 1972 / Reprise ✦✦

Time Fades Away / Oct. 1973 / Reprise ✦✦✦
In his concerts of the early '70s, the prolific Neil Young frequently played new, unrecorded songs, sometimes for half the show or more. This tendency found its expression on his fifth album, *Time Fades Away,* a live record consisting of previously unreleased songs, most recorded during his national concert tour during the first quarter of 1973. The album also represented the culmination of Young's desire to present his music in as raw a state as possible: not only was it mastered direct to disc from the 16-track tape, but also the performances were anything but polished. The approach was consistent with the unvarnished nature of the songs: *Time Fades Away* was an album by a man who seemed to have lost something and was determinedly trying to regain it. Both its sound and its songs were alien to much of the mass audience Young had gained with "Heart of Gold" and *Harvest.* Ultimately, his escape from the commercial trap into which he had fallen would seem a healthy development in his career, and *Time Fades Away* was the first (mis)step. *— William Ruhlmann*

☆ **On the Beach** / Jul. 1974 / Reprise ✦✦✦✦✦
Following the 1973 *Time Fades Away* tour, Neil Young wrote and recorded an Irish wake of a record called *Tonight's the Night* and went on the road drunkenly playing its songs to uncomprehending listeners and hostile reviewers. Reprise rejected the record, and Young went right back and made *On the Beach,* which shares some of the ragged style of its two predecessors. But where *Time* was embattled and *Tonight* mournful, *On the Beach* was savage and, ultimately, triumphant. "I'm a vampire, babe," Young sang, and he proceeded to take bites out of various subjects: threatening the lives of the stars who lived in L.A.'s Laurel Canyon ("Revolution Blues"); answering back to Lynyrd Skynyrd, whose "Sweet Home Alabama" had taken him to task for his criticisms of the South in "Southern Man" and "Alabama" ("Walk On"); and rejecting the critics ("Ambulance Blues"). But the barbs were mixed with humor and even affection, as Young seemed to be emerging from the grief and self-abuse that had plagued him for two years. But the

album was so spare and underproduced, its lyrics so harrowing, that it was easy to miss Young's conclusion: He was saying goodbye to despair, not being overwhelmed by it. *— William Ruhlmann*

☆ **Tonight's the Night** / Jun. 1975 / Reprise ✦✦✦✦✦
Written and recorded in 1973 shortly after the death of roadie Bruce Berry, *Tonight's the Night* was Young's musical expression of grief, combined with his rejection of the stardom he had achieved in the late '60s and early '70s. The title track, performed twice, was a direct narrative about Berry, while the late Crazy Horse guitarist Danny Whitten was heard singing "Come on Baby Let's Go Downtown," a live track recorded years earlier. Performing with the remains of Crazy Horse, bassist Billy Talbot and drummer Ralph Molina, along with Nils Lofgren and Ben Keith, Young performed in the ragged manner familiar from *Time Fades Away*—his voice was often hoarse and he strained to reach high notes, while the playing was loose, with mistakes and shifting tempos. But the style worked perfectly for the material, emphasizing the emotional tone of Young's mourning; it was the work of a man trying to turn his torment into art and doing so unflinchingly. *— William Ruhlmann*

Zuma / Nov. 1975 / Reprise ✦✦✦✦✦
Having apparently exorcised his demons by releasing the cathartic *Tonight's the Night*, Neil Young returned to his commercial strengths with *Zuma* (named after Zuma Beach in Los Angeles, where he now owned a house). Seven of the album's nine songs were recorded with the reunited Crazy Horse, in which rhythm guitarist Frank Sampedro had replaced the late Danny Whitten, but there were also nods to other popular Young styles in "Pardon My Heart," an acoustic song that would have fit on *Harvest*, his most popular album, and "Through My Sails," retrieved from one of Crosby, Stills, Nash & Young's abortive recording sessions. Young had abandoned the ragged, first-take approach of his previous three albums, but Crazy Horse would never be a polished act, and the music had a lively sound well-suited to the songs, which were some of the most melodic, pop-oriented tunes Young had crafted in years, though they were played with an electric-guitar-drenched rock intensity. The overall theme concerned romantic conflict, with lyrics that lamented lost love and sometimes longed for a return ("Pardon My Heart" even found Young singing, "I don't believe this song"), though the overall conclusion, notably in such catchy songs as "Don't Cry No Tears" and "Lookin' for a Love," was to move on to the next relationship. But the album's standout track (apparently the only holdover from an early intention to present songs with historical subjects) was the seven-and-a-half-minute epic "Cortez the Killer," a commentary on the Spanish conqueror of Latin America that served as a platform for Young's most extensive guitar soloing since his work on *Everybody Knows This Is Nowhere*. *— William Ruhlmann*

Long May You Run / Sep. 1976 / Reprise ✦✦✦
Long May You Run is not a Neil Young solo album. It is credited to "The Stills-Young Band," which is to say, Stephen Stills and his band with Young added, and the two divide up the songwriting and lead vocals, five for Young, four for Stills. The pairing, though it proved short-lived and had, in fact, ended before this album was released, must have seemed commercially logical. Like Young, Stills had seen his record sales decline after a successful period following the 1970 breakup of CSNY. So had erstwhile partners David Crosby and Graham Nash, but they had returned to Top Ten, gold-selling status in the fall of 1975 with their *Wind on the Water* duo album. Why couldn't Stills and Young do the same thing? Maybe they could have (and, actually, this was the first gold album for either in two years) if they had made a better record together. Young's songs were pleasant newly written throwaways with the exception of the title track, a trunk song he had written as a tribute to an old car. Stills' compositions seemed more seriously intended, but still were not substantial. The playing, largely handled by the professional session man types in Stills' band, was far smoother than what one was accustomed to in a Young album. The result was a listenable record, but not a compelling one, and thus well below Young's usual standard and Stills' best. (As of mid-1996, *Long May You Run* had not been released in the U.S. on CD.) *— William Ruhlmann*

American Stars 'N Bars / Jun. 1977 / Reprise ✦✦✦
Neil Young made a point of listing the recording dates of the songs on *American Stars 'N Bars*; the dates even appeared on the LP labels. They revealed that the songs had been cut at four different sessions dating back to 1974. But even without such documentation, it would have been easy to tell that the album was a stylistic hodgepodge, its first side consisting of country-tinged material featuring steel guitar and fiddle, plus backup vocals from Linda Ronstadt and the then-unknown Nicolette Larson, while the four songs on the second side varied from acoustic solo numbers like "Will to Love" to raging rockers such as "Like a Hurricane." Just as apparent was the album's unevenness: side one consisted of lightweight compositions, while side two had more ambitious ones, with "Will to Love," for example, extending the romantic metaphor of a salmon swimming upsteam across seven minutes. The album's saving grace was "Like a Hurricane," one of Young's classic hard rock songs and guitar workouts, a perennial concert favorite. Without it, *American Stars 'N Bars* would have been one of Young's least memorable albums, and since it turned up the following year on the compilation *Decade*, the LP was rendered inessential. (As of mid-1996, *American Stars 'N Bars* had not been released on CD in the U.S.) *— William Ruhlmann*

★ **Decade** / Nov. 1977 / Reprise ✦✦✦✦✦
Given the quirkiness of Neil Young's recording career, with its frequent cancellations of releases and last-minute rearrangements of material, it is a relief to report that this two-disc compilation is so conventional and so satisfying. A 35-track selection of the best of Young's work between 1966 and 1976, it includes songs performed by Buffalo Springfield, Crosby, Stills, Nash & Young, and the Stills/Young Band, as well as solo work. In addition to five unreleased songs, *Decade* offers such key tracks as the Springfield's "Mr. Soul," "Broken Arrow," and "I Am a Child"; "Sugar Mountain," a song that had appeared only as a single before; "Cinnamon Girl," "Down by the River," and "Cowgirl in the Sand" from *Everybody Knows This Is Nowhere*; "Southern Man" and the title track from *After the Gold Rush*; and "Old Man" and the chart-topping "Heart of Gold" from *Harvest*. This is the material that built Young's reputation between 1966 and 1972, although he is more idiosyncratic with the later material, including the blockbusters "Like a Hurricane" and "Cortez the Killer" but mixing in more unreleased recordings as the set draws to a close. He seems intent on making the album a listenable one that will appeal to a broad base of fans, and he succeeds despite the exclusion of much of the harrowing work of 1973-1975. Nevertheless, the album is an ideal sampler for new listeners, and since there is no one-disc Young compilation covering any significant portion of his career, this lengthy chronicle is the place to start. *— William Ruhlmann*

Comes a Time / Oct. 1978 / Reprise ✦✦✦✦✦
Six and a half years later, *Comes a Time* finally was the Neil Young album for the millions of fans who had loved *Harvest*, an acoustic-based record with country overtones and romantic, autobiographical lyrics, and many of those fans returned to the fold, enough to make *Comes a Time* Young's first Top Ten album since *Harvest*. He signaled the album's direction with the leadoff track, "Goin' Back," and its retrospective theme augmented with an orchestral backup and the deliberate beat familiar from his number one hit "Heart of Gold." Of course, Young remained sly about this retrenchment. "I feel like goin' back," he sang, but added, "Back where there's nowhere to stay." Doubtless he had no intention of staying with this style, but, for the length of the album, melodies, love lyrics, lush arrangements, and steel guitar solos dominated, and Young's vocals were made more accessible by being paired with Nicolette Larson's harmonies. Larson's own version of Young's "Lotta Love," released shortly after the one heard here, became a Top Ten hit single. Other highlights included the reflective "Already One," which treats the unusual subject of the nature of a divorced family, the ironic "Field of Opportunity," and a cover of Ian Tyson's folk standard "Four Strong Winds" (a country Top Ten hit for Bobby Bare in 1965). *— William Ruhlmann*

☆ **Rust Never Sleeps** / Jul. 1979 / Reprise ✦✦✦✦✦
Rust Never Sleeps, its aphoristic title drawn from an intended advertising slogan, was an album of new songs, some of them recorded on Neil Young's 1978 concert tour. His strongest collection since *Tonight's the Night*, its obvious antecedent was Bob Dylan's *Bringing It All Back Home*, and, as Dylan did, Young divided his record into acoustic and electric sides while filling his songs with wildly imaginative imagery. The leadoff track, "My My, Hey Hey (Out of the Blue)" (repeated in an electric version at album's end as "Hey Hey, My My [Into the Black]" with slightly altered lyrics), is the most concise and knowing description of the entertainment industry ever written; it was followed by "Thrasher," which describes Young's parallel artistic quest in an extended metaphor that also reflected the album's overall theme—the inevitability of deterioration and the challenge of overcoming it. Young then spent the rest of the album demonstrating that his chief weapons against rusting were his imagination and his daring, creating an archetypal album that encapsulated his many styles on a single disc with great songs—in particular the remarkable "Powderfinger"—unlike any he had written before. *— William Ruhlmann*

Live Rust / Nov. 1979 / Reprise ✦✦✦✦✦
All the kudos Neil Young earned for *Rust Never Sleeps* he lost for *Live Rust*, the double-LP live album released four months later. *Live Rust* was the soundtrack to Young's concert film, *Rust Never Sleeps* (he had wanted to give it that title, but Reprise vetoed the idea, fearing confusion with the earlier album), and likewise was recorded Oct. 22, 1978, at the Cow Palace in San Francisco. But much of the *Rust Never Sleeps* album had been recorded on the same tour, and *Live Rust* repeated four songs from that disc; besides, since Young had released the career retrospective *Decade* in 1977, critics felt he was unfairly recycling his older material and repeating his new material. In retrospect, however, *Live Rust*, now a single 74-minute CD, comes off as an excellent Neil Young live album and career summary, starting with the early song "Sugar Mountain" and running through then-new songs like "My My, Hey Hey (Out of the Blue)" and "Powderfinger." Young is effective in both his acoustic folk singer and hard-rocking Crazy Horse bandleader modes. The various distractions of the concert itself and the film, such as the pretentious props and cowled roadies, are absent, and what's left is a terrific Neil Young concert recording. *— William Ruhlmann*

Hawks & Doves / Nov. 1980 / Reprise ✦✦✦
Following the triumph of *Rust Never Sleeps*, *Hawks & Doves* benefited from the enormous critical goodwill Neil Young had amassed, though fans and critics nevertheless were baffled by its set of obscure acoustic and country-tinged songs. The seven-plus-minute "The Old Homestead" (copyright 1974) was interpreted by some as an allegory for Young's relationship to CSNY, perhaps because that was the only way to make any sense of the most mysterious Young lyric since "The Last Trip to Tulsa." In retrospect, now that we know Young was distracted by domestic medical concerns while working on the album, its theme of perseverance in the face of adversity, both in a personal context of family commitment ("Stayin' Power," "Coastline"), and in a national context of hard work and patriotism ("Union Man," "Comin' Apart at Every Nail," "Hawks & Doves") seems more apparent, as does the sense that Young may have been trying to fulfill his recording contract (even with the inclusion of trunk songs like "The Old Homestead," the album runs less than half an hour) while devoting a bare minimum of his time and attention to the effort. The result is correspondingly slight. *— William Ruhlmann*

Re-ac-tor / Nov. 1981 / Reprise ✦✦

Trans / Jan. 1983 / Geffen ✦✦
When it was released, *Trans* was Neil Young's most baffling album. He had employed a

vocoder to synthesize his voice on five of the album's nine tracks, resulting in disembodied singing, the lyrics nearly impossible to decipher without the lyric sheet. And even when you read the words, "Computer Age," "We R In Control," "Transformer Man," "Computer Cowboy," and "Sample and Hold" seemed like a vague mishmash of high-tech jargon. Later, Young would reveal that some of the songs expressed a theme of attempted communication with his disabled son, and in that context, lines like "I stand by you" and "So many things still left to do / But we haven't made it yet" seemed clearer. But the vocoder, which robbed Young's voice of its dynamics and phrasing, still kept the songs from being as moving as they were intended to be. And despite the crisp dance beats and synthesizers, the music sounded less like new Kraftwerk than like old Devo. A few more conventional Young songs (left over from an earlier rejected album) seemed out of place. *Trans* had a few good songs, notably "Sample and Hold" (which seemed to be about a computer dating service for robots), a remake of "Mr. Soul," and "Like an Inca" (an intended cross between "Like a Hurricane" and "Cortez the Killer"?), but on the whole it was an idea that just didn't work. (*Trans* has been released in the U.S. on CD. The European CD release replaces the original 5:09 take of "Sample and Hold" with the 8:04 alternate take later used on the *Lucky Thirteen* compilation.) *—William Ruhlmann*

Everybody's Rockin' / Aug. 1983 / Geffen ✦✦

By following the hi-tech *Trans* after only seven months with a rockabilly album, Neil Young baffled his audience. Just as he had followed the sales peak of *Harvest* in 1972 with a series of challenging, uncommercial albums, Young had now dissipated the commercial and critical acceptance he had enjoyed with 1979's *Rust Never Sleeps* with a series of mediocre albums and inexplicable genre exercises. *Everybody's Rockin'*, credited to "Neil and the Shocking Pinks," represented the nadir of this attempted career suicide. Running less than 25 minutes, it found Young covering early rock evergreens like "Betty Lou's Got a New Pair of Shoes" and writing a few songs in the same vein ("Kinda Fonda Wanda"). If he had presented this as a mini-album at a discount price, it would have been easier to enjoy the joke Young seemed to intend. As it was, fans who already had their doubts about Young dropped off the radar screen; *Everybody's Rocking* was his lowest-charting album since his 1969 solo debut, and he didn't release another album for two years (his longest break ever between records). *—William Ruhlmann*

Old Ways / Aug. 1985 / Geffen ✦✦✦

In 1984, Geffen Records sued Neil Young on the grounds that he had submitted uncharacteristic, uncommercial records to the label. By the time a settlement had been reached, Young had been on the road with a country band called the International Harvesters for over a year and recorded a revamped version of *Old Ways*, a 1982 recording originally rejected by Geffen which was cut in the style of *Harvest* and *Comes a Time*, but with a stronger country leaning. Young depends heavily on friends, especially for vocals—Waylon Jennings sings harmony on six out of the ten tracks, and one of the others is a duet with Willie Nelson. Though populated by cowboys and country references, Young's take on the genre is typically idiosyncratic, including a reworked version of his autobiography in "Get Back to the Country," a cover of the 1956 Gogi Grant hit "Wayward Wind," and the uncategorizable "Misfits," which portrays astronauts watching Muhammad Ali fights on television in space. *Old Ways* is not a great Neil Young album and at the time of its release served to alienate him even further from his audience, but it has its moments. *—William Ruhlmann*

Landing on Water / Jul. 1986 / Geffen ✦✦

Life / Jul. 1987 / Geffen ✦✦✦

Life, Young's first album with Crazy Horse since 1981's *Re-ac-tor*, was not one of his best albums. It was, however, better than most of the other albums he made in the 1980s, and the first really interesting record he'd made in a long time. Despite the return to Crazy Horse, Young continued to use some of the production techniques from *Landing on Water*, especially the loud drums and synthesizers. But he mixed things up, including acoustic-based songs such as "Long Walk Home" and "Inca Queen." It could be argued that Young was repeating himself on much of this material and that the album was typically uneven, but *Life* was an encouraging step back to the tried and true for an exploratory artist who finally seemed to have realized that he had experimented too much for his own good. *—William Ruhlmann*

This Note's for You / Apr. 1988 / Reprise ✦✦✦

A collective groan from Neil Young fans could be heard when it was announced that, as his return to Reprise Records, Young was engaging in yet another genre experiment, this time recording blues and R&B with a six-piece horn section. If *Landing On Water* and *Life* had been lackluster, at least they hadn't been as embarrassing as Young's forays into rockabilly (*Everybodys Rockin'*) and techno (*Trans*). And if you took *This Note's For You* on its own genre terms, it could be just as laughable. A song like "Sunny Inside," with its marching rhythm and charging horn charts, seemed to demand a forceful, gritty singer on the order of Wilson Pickett, and Young's watery tenor just didn't cut it. But the album was only half uptempo numbers; the other half was bluesy ballads for which Young's singing was effective and on which he sounded more personally involved than he had in years. And even on the rockers, his sense of humor often carried the day. *This Note's For You* was the best of Young's stylistic sidetrips because it was the only one in which the style augmented his own instead of overwhelming him. The songs were mediocre, but the playing was spirited. The album earned much better reviews than Young had gotten lately, largely because critics tend to stand in awe of The Blues in whatever form it appears. And Young got further kudos due to his contretemps with MTV when the video channel first declined to program a clip for the title song because it featured parodies of popular MTV artists and commercial sponsors, then caved in and named it Best Video of the Year. Lost in all that hoopla, however, was that record buyers never came to the party. *This Note's For You* was another commercial failure for Young, and it was apparent that, to lure back his audience, he would have to go back to making the kind of music his fans had liked a decade before. *—William Ruhlmann*

Eldorado / 1989 / Reprise ✦✦✦

When this five-song, 25-minute EP was released in Japan in 1989, it served notice that Neil Young was capable of writing powerful songs and playing fierce rock & roll again, a fact confirmed by the subsequent release of the *Freedom* album. Three of the songs on *Eldorado* turned up on that record ("Don't Cry" in a different version), but "Cocaine Eyes" and "Heavy Love" did not, making this disc a necessary purchase for Young completists. *—William Ruhlmann*

Freedom / Oct. 1989 / Reprise ✦✦✦✦✦

Neil Young is famous for scrapping completed albums and substituting hastily recorded ones in radically different styles; *Freedom*, a major critical and commercial comeback, seemed to be a selection of the best tracks from several different unissued projects. First and foremost was a hard rock album like the material heard on Young's recent EP *Eldorado* (released only in the Far East), several of whose tracks were repeated on *Freedom*. On these songs—especially "Don't Cry" and a cover of the Drifters' "On Broadway"—Young played distorted electric guitar over a rhythm section in an even more raucous fashion than on his Crazy Horse records. Second was a follow-up to *This Note's For You*, which had featured a six-piece horn section; they were back on the lengthy "Crime in the City" and "Someday," each of which contained a series of seemingly unrelated, mood-setting verses. Third, there were tracks that harked back to acoustic-based, country-tinged albums like *Harvest* and *Comes a Time*, including "Hangin' on a Limb" and "The Ways of Love." What made it all work was that Young had once again written a great bunch of songs, bookended by acoustic and electric versions of one of Young's greatest anthems, "Rockin' in the Free World." *—William Ruhlmann*

Ragged Glory / Oct. 11, 1990 / Reprise ✦✦✦✦✦

Having re-established his reputation with the musically varied, lyrically enraged *Freedom*, Neil Young returned to being the lead guitarist of Crazy Horse for the musically homogenous, lyrically hopeful *Ragged Glory*. The album's dominant sound was made by Young's noisy guitar, which bordered on and sometimes slipped over into distortion, while Crazy Horse kept up the songs' bright tempos. Despite the volume, the tunes were catchy, with strong melodies and good choruses, and they were given over to love, humor, and warm reminiscence. They were also platforms for often extended guitar excursions: "Love To Burn" and "Love And Only Love" ran over ten minutes each, and the album as a whole lasted nearly 63 minutes with only ten songs. Much about the record had a retrospective feel—the first two tracks, "Country Home" and "White Line," were newly recorded versions of songs Young had played with Crazy Horse but never released in the '70s; "Mansion On The Hill," the album's most accessible track, celebrated a place where "psychedelic music fills the air" and "peace and love live there still"; there was a cover of the Premiers' garage rock oldie "Farmer John"; and "Days That Used To Be," in addition to its backward-looking theme, borrowed the melody from Bob Dylan's "My Back Pages" (by way of the Byrds' arrangement), while "Mother Earth (Natural Anthem)" was the folk standard "The Water Is Wide" with new, environmentally aware lyrics. Young was not generally known as an artist who evoked the past this much, but if he could extend his creative rebirth with music this exhilarating, no one was likely to complain. *—William Ruhlmann*

Weld / Oct. 1991 / Reprise ✦✦✦✦✦

Weld, Neil Young's two-hour-plus double-CD chronicle of his 1991 Ragged Glory/Smell the Horse Tour with Crazy Horse, was received with only mild enthusiasm from Young's fans and rock critics, perhaps because it seemed redundant. Such warhorses as "Like a Hurricane" and "Cortez the Killer" were making their fourth appearances on a Young album, and the five songs from the *Ragged Glory* album were basically unchanged from their studio versions. Containing only 16 tracks, the album's songs averaged over seven and a half minutes in length, and that length was given over to extended guitar improvisations, which often were filled with feedback and distortion. Where Young's previous double live album, *Live Rust*, which bore some similarities to this one, was a career retrospective including some acoustic numbers, *Weld* was all electric rock with Crazy Horse. The one previously unreleased song was a Gulf War-era cover of Bob Dylan's "Blowin' In the Wind," complete with gunshots and exploding bombs. In retrospect, *Weld* seems like an excellent expression of one part of Young's musical persona, putting some of his best hard rock material onto one album. [Initially, *Weld* was released in a 25,000-copy limited edition called *Arc Weld* (Reprise 26746) containing a third disc made up of guitar feedback and called *Arc*.] *—William Ruhlmann*

Arc / Oct. 1991 / Reprise ✦✦

A 35-minute "compilation compositor" by Neil Young, *Arc* consists of a series of excerpts from 1991 concerts by Young & Crazy Horse strung together. Young has taken the tune-ups and outros, the guitar feedback and random playing and singing from various songs and shows, and constructed a nearly atonal sound collage. Now and then, he is heard singing a verse or two from "Like a Hurricane" or another song, but for the most part, *Arc* sounds like a band preparing to play a song that never actually begins or trying to end one that has not been heard. As such, the album ranks with such studies in noise as Lou Reed's *Metal Machine Music*. [Initially, *Arc* was released in a 25,000-copy limited edition called *Arc Weld* (Reprise 26746) containing the two discs making up the live album *Weld*.] *—William Ruhlmann*

Harvest Moon / Oct. 27, 1992 / Reprise ✦✦✦

The year of the 20th anniversary of the release of his most popular album, *Harvest*, Neil Young released a new album that harked back to that recording, employing many of the same musicians, again dubbed the Stray Gators, as well as arranger Jack Nitzsche and background singers Linda Ronstadt and James Taylor. He also used a similar folk-country acoustic style and sang songs that often had a personal, confessional tone. But the similarities were more of form than of content because, while *Harvest* was the statement of a confused, if earnest, 26-year-old, *Harvest Moon* embodied the ruminations of a somewhat regretful 46-year-old. Indeed, the greatest comparison to be made between the two records was that Young tried to use the passage of time as a confirmation of continuity. In the first several songs, he seemed to be trying to reconcile with his wife and revive their love, though he was uncertain that was possible. In "One of These Days," he regretted the loss of friendships over the years. "War of Man" and the long and ponderous "Natural Beauty" concerned environmental preservation, and even the rollicking banjo tune "Old King" was a lament for the death of a faithful dog. "I never tried to burn any bridges," sang an artist whose contradictory instincts to move on and to return found him, by the time of his 27th solo album, trying to get back to the feel of his fourth. If the attempt was not completely successful, nevertheless it was well and honestly made, and Young wasn't alone in his desire. As Hollywood has long-since learned, sequels have a built-in audience, and *Harvest Moon* became Young's best-selling album in 13 years. *—William Ruhlmann*

Lucky Thirteen / Jan. 5, 1993 / Geffen ✦✦✦

Geffen Records seems to have intended a straightforward best-of compilation containing the singles released from Neil Young's five albums with the label between 1982 and 1987. Then Young himself became involved, and his version of a Geffen sampler naturally turned out to be more unusual. There were four songs never before released on a Young album—"Depression Blues," "Get Gone" and the bluesy "Don't Take Your Love Away From Me" (live recordings with the Shocking Pinks) and "Ain't It the Truth" (a live track cut with the Bluenotes). There were also an alternate version of *Trans'* "Sample and Hold" and a live take of "This Note's for You," the title song from Young's 1988 return to Reprise Records. None of these were revelatory, and Young's choices from his Geffen era failed to represent his best work; given that he veered wildly from synth-pop to rockabilly to country to rock during this period, assembling a coherent compilation was something of a challenge, and Young didn't even try, just picking his favorites and sequencing them chronologically. There were some interesting songs here to be sure, notably "Hippie Dream" and "Mideast Vacation," but this summing up of Young's least impressive, most bizarre era, instead of rehabilitating that era, was itself bizarre and unimpressive, too. *—William Ruhlmann*

Unplugged / Jun. 15, 1993 / Reprise ✦✦✦✦✦

The virtue of the "unplugged" concept pioneered by MTV was that it provided a forum for rock musicians to re-interpret their work without using rock's favorite instrument, the electric guitar. But by 1993, the *Unplugged* sessions were serving as another way of creating product without coming up with anything really new, thus joining live albums, greatest hits albums, and covers albums. Neil Young, who has always alternated between rock and folk approaches to his music anyway, would not seem like an ideal candidate for an "unplugged" session, but in a few of the 14 selections in this 65-and-a-half-minute recording, he did give his audience new ways to listen to his repertoire. Particularly notable were a pump-organ and harmonica arrangement of his guitar rock classic "Like a Hurricane" and an acoustic guitar rendition of his Buffalo Springfield hit "Mr. Soul." For the most part, however, Young's *Unplugged* was simply an acoustic live album drawn from a show that was part of his *Harvest Moon* promotional tour. Songs like "Pocahontas" and "The Needle and the Damage Done" had been in his acoustic set lists for years, played exactly as they were here. While Young ranged across his career, picking songs from as far back as 1967 and including three *Harvest Moon* songs, the set did not function as a live acoustic greatest hits selection since favorites like "Heart of Gold" and "Old Man" were missing. The choices seemed nearly arbitrary: Popular songs like "Helpless" (first heard on the 1970 Crosby, Stills, Nash & Young album *Déjà Vu*) shared space with relatively obscure album tracks like "World on a String" (from *Tonight's the Night*) and the never-before released 20-year-old song "Stringman." It may be that a random selection of 14 Neil Young songs gives as accurate a representation of his work as a more carefully compiled one would, but it does not show Young off at his best. *Unplugged* is an enjoyable record that with greater care in arrangement, performance, and song selection could have been considerably better. *—William Ruhlmann*

Sleeps With Angels / Aug. 16, 1994 / Reprise ✦✦✦✦

Though it once again reunited him with Crazy Horse and included such typical rock workouts as the lengthy "Change Your Mind" and the raucous "Piece of Crap," *Sleeps With Angels* was more musically varied than most of Neil Young's albums with his erstwhile backup group, ranging from piano-based ballads like the album opener, "My Heart" and closer, "A Dream That Can Last," which might have fit on *After the Gold Rush*, to the country-folk "Train of Love," which sounded like a leftover from *Harvest Moon*, and the hard-edged grunge of the title track. The Crazy Horse influence came in the songs' structural simplicity and the unpolished playing. Though musically diverse, *Sleeps With Angels* was a song cycle in which Young repeated the same themes and images. To put it simply, the album was about death, presumably primarily the suicide of Nirvana's Kurt Cobain, which occurred while it was being recorded. From "My Heart," which declared, "It's not too late" and "Somehow, someone has a dream come true" to "A Dream That Can Last," which declared, "There's a better life for me someday," Young began and ended with a shaky, uncertain optimism, even though his language was riddled with references to violence, especially gunfire, and desperation. As in the album's title, even the references to sleep and dreams were about death. Young repeated some of the same lines from song to song and sometimes the same music ("Western Hero" and "Train of Love" have the same tune). The album thus has a tired, mournful feel that is both compelling and off-putting. Young had not investigated such forbidding territory since the days of *Tonight's The Night* and *On The Beach*, and *Sleeps With Angels* was on a par with those often harrowing works. *—William Ruhlmann*

Mirror Ball / Jun. 27, 1995 / Reprise ✦✦✦

Neil Young uses Pearl Jam on *Mirror Ball* much as he has used his perennial backup band Crazy Horse, looking for feel and spontaneity. At the start of the record, he can be heard instructing them: "No tuning, nothing," and the take of "I'm the Ocean" is an obvious run-through that became a master take. But Pearl Jam is not Crazy Horse; in place of the latter's primitive, non-swinging sound, the former boasts spirited rhythms and dense guitar interplay that Young makes excellent use of in a series of songs built out of simple, melodic rifts. Those songs come mostly in pairs: "Song X" and "Act of Love," the first two tracks, both seem to be about abortion, especially in its religious aspect, each containing a reference to "the holy war"; "What Happened to Yesterday" and "Fallen Angel" are song fragments on which Young plays the pump organ; and "Downtown" and "Peace and Love" find Young addressing the musical and philosophical concerns of hippies and contain name checks of Jimi Hendrix, John Lennon, and Led Zeppelin. The songs also share highly imagistic lyrics that are allusive and frequently just obscure. At their best, notably on "I'm the Ocean" and "Scenery," they provide intriguing portraits of the artist—"People my age/They don't do the things I do," Young sings in "Ocean"—while "Scenery" is one of his bitter denunciations of celebrity. Such subject matter is not new for Young, and *Mirror Ball* is typically uneven. But it is always interesting musically, suggesting that he has found another catch-up that works. Probably due to the commercial power of Pearl Jam, the album became Young's highest charting record since *Harvest* 23 years earlier, though it had a relatively short chart life. *—William Ruhlmann*

Dead Man / Feb. 27, 1996 / Vapor ✦✦

Broken Arrow / Jul. 2, 1996 / Reprise ✦✦✦

In many ways, *Broken Arrow* follows the same path as Neil Young's other '90s albums with Crazy Horse. *Broken Arrow* floats on waves of lumbering guitars and cascading feedback, ebbing and flowing with winding solos and drifting melodies. In a typical display of artistic perversion, Young has front-loaded the album with three epics with a combined running time of just over 25 minutes. Following the three epic-length songs come four concise tunes that range from the country-rock stomp of "Changing Highways" to the reflective "Music Arcade." Like the three songs that preceded them, these songs are uneven, with hazy melodies and under-developed lyrics. Finally, a long live workout of Jimmy Reed's "Baby What You Want Me To Do"—which sounds like it was taken from an audience recording—is tacked on to the end of the album. Although the song is a standout, it raises the question of: What is the purpose of *Broken Arrow?* The album floats from song to song, with the guitars drowning out the sound of Young's voice. There are some fine songs buried admist the long jams but the album is directionless, and that lack of direction never manages to develop a consistent emotional tone. *—Stephen Thomas Erlewine*

Year of the Horse / Jun. 17, 1997 / Reprise ✦✦✦

As Neil Young's second double live album of the '90s, *Year of the Horse* could seem a little redundant to anyone who isn't a diehard fan. After all, *Weld* was useful, since it appeared ten years after the release of *Live Rust*, their first double live album, and it captured Young and Crazy Horse at their peak. *Year of the Horse*, however, appeared merely five years after *Weld*, and in between those two records, Young had only released two albums' worth of material that suited these high-voltage, improvised performances. These factors didn't matter, since Young decided to allow Jim Jarmusch to make a film documentary about his 1996 tour, and *Year of the Horse* is the album that was released to coincide with the movie. (It's not really a soundtrack, since these performances don't appear in the film.) It is true that there are many songs here that haven't made Young's previous live albums, but the performances themselves aren't particularly remarkable—they sound like tired, meandering variations of *Weld*. There are enough strong moments to make *Year of the Horse* worthwhile for diehard fans, but it's too predictable to appeal to anyone else. *—Stephen Thomas Erlewine*

Silver & Gold / Apr. 25, 2000 / Reprise ✦✦✦

Silver & Gold went through a number of incarnations before it was finally released in the spring of 2000. The endless delays raised hopes for the album, as did superstition—dedicated Neil Young fans believed he was creatively reborn at the end of each decade. *Everybody Knows This is Nowhere, Rust Never Sleeps*, and *Freedom* added credence to this theory, but those records were knocked out quickly, appearing a year after their predecessors. In contrast, *Silver & Gold* appeared four years after *Broken Arrow*. During those four years, all sorts of projects were in the works for Neil, including a 1999 reunion with Crosby, Stills & Nash. Young's three songs on their comeback *Looking Forward* were pleasant acoustic numbers that often seemed a little slight. It was easy to assume that Young was saving the real treasures for his solo record, but *Silver & Gold* doesn't confirm that theory. Instead, it's a continuation of his *Looking Forward* contributions, performed with the warm, amiable ramble of *Harvest Moon*. A pleasant sound, to be sure, but not exactly what Young followers were expecting. They also may be a little dismayed to realize that two of its best songs, "Silver & Gold" and "Razor Love," date from 1982 and 1987, respectively, suggesting that Neil may not be at the top of his game. Still, there are no truly bad songs here, although the light-hearted, light-headed reminiscence "Buffalo Springfield Again" treads close to the borderline. It's a low-key, charming, *comfortable* record, which is hardly a bad thing at all—it just doesn't quite live up to the abnormally high expectations. Fortunately, those expectations fade upon repeated plays, and *Silver & Gold* reveals itself as a nice Neil Young record. Nothing particularly special, but nice all the same. *—Stephen Thomas Erlewine*

Road Rock, Vol. 1 / Nov. 21, 2000 / Reprise ✦✦✦

For some reason, Neil decided that his 2000 tour was particularly hot, so he decided to record a live album and rush release it by the end of the year. So, that explains the appearance of *Road Rock, Vol. 1*, an eight-song collection recorded with an ensemble featuring Spooner Oldham on keyboards, Duck Dunn on bass, Jim Keltner on drums, and Astrid and Pegi Young on vocals—thereby explaining the "Friends and Relatives" subtitle. This band is pretty good, even supple, but this doesn't feel necessary at any time and suffers from indulgence. And it doesn't shy away from this indulgence, either, opening with an 18-minute "Cowgirl in the Sand" that only diehards could sit through. And, in a sense, that summarizes this album, since only diehards will thrill to an 11-minute "Words," a previously unreleased "Fool for Your Love," a 10-minute "Tonight's the Night," or an "All Along the Watchtower" featuring opener Chrissie Hynde on guitar. This isn't bad, but it's not really good, either, and as the third live album in one decade, it's not just anticlimatic, it's unnecessary even for diehards, who probably would find this more exciting as a bootleg than an official album. —*Stephen Thomas Erlewine*

Paul Young

b. Jan. 17, 1956, Luton, Bedfordshire, England
Vocals / Pop/Rock, New Wave
A soulful U.K. interpretive singer who gained fame in his native country in 1983 with a cover of Marvin Gaye's "Wherever I Lay My Hat (That's My Home)" and in the U.S. with Daryl Hall's "Everytime You Go Away" in 1985. Young found less success writing his own songs, then returned to the U.S. Top Ten with a cover of the Chi-Lites' "Oh Girl" in 1990. In 1992, he left Columbia and moved to MCA. —*William Ruhlmann*

No Parlez / 1983 / Columbia ♦♦♦♦
Paul Young's debut album was a strong set of soulful covers of forgotten classics ("Love of the Common People," "Wherever I Lay My Hat [That's My Home]") and contemporary classics ("Love Will Tear Us Apart"), as well as the occasional made-to-order original, like the hit "Come Back and Stay." —*Stephen Thomas Erlewine*

The Secret of Association / 1985 / Columbia ♦♦♦♦
In 1984 Paul Young scored a couple of medium-sized U.S. hits with "Come Back And Stay" and "Love Of The Common People" from his album *No Parlez*. In 1985, however, with his stellar album *The Secret Of Association*, the British singer gained his highest level of commercial success with several hit singles, most notable his chart-topping cover of Daryl Hall's "Every Time You Go Away," which was miles better than the original. Featuring lush orchestration and Young's signature, soulful vocals, this album remains the singer's best, and one of the better albums of the 1980s. Other notable tracks include his wicked take on "I'm Gonna Tear Your Playhouse Down," the gorgeous "Everything Must Change" (which almost sounds like a country song), and the popular album tracks "Soldier's Things" and "Tomb Of Memories." Note, however, that the radio versions of all three singles released from this album are not the versions included here. Those versions can be found on his hits collection *From Time To Time*. —*Jose F. Promis*

Between Two Fires / 1986 / Columbia ♦♦

Other Voices / Jun. 1990 / Columbia ♦♦♦
Other Voices marked a comeback from the tepid *Between Two Fires*, featuring a set of lush, soulful covers (the Top Ten hit "Oh Girl") and several harder-rocking numbers, including a cover of Free's "A Little Bit of Love." —*Stephen Thomas Erlewine*

● **From Time to Time: The Singles Collection** / Nov. 1991 / Columbia ♦♦♦♦
Paul Young's retrospective *From Time To Time: The Singles Collection* brings together all his major U.S. and European hits from the 1980s and early 1990s. Some of these, including his only U.S. number one "Every Time You Go Away," were remixed when released as singles and to radio—this collection intelligently includes those versions. Young's music, which bridged new wave, British soul, and adult contemporary, always sported state-of-the-art production, and, coupled with his soulful, yearning voice, has gone on to become some of the finest and most timeless the 1980s had to offer. This sound just as lush and energetic as when first released. Highlights include his bewitching breakthrough U.S. single "Come Back And Stay," its reggae-flavored follow-up "Love Of The Common People," his massive "Every Time You Go Away," the electrifying "I'm Gonna Tear Your Playhouse Down," the timeless and sadly underrated "Everything Must Change," his breakthrough U.K. cover of Marvin Gaye's "Wherever I Lay My Hat (That's My Home)," his last U.S. top ten hit "Oh Girl" and the international smash "Senza Una Donna" (with Italian star Zucchero). Paul Young was a superb interpreter of other people's hits, evident here by two new tracks—his stirring renditions of Crowded House's "Don't Dream It's Over" and Joni Mitchell's "Both Sides Now." The only hit missing is his smash from *Fried Green Tomatoes*, "What Becomes of The Brokenhearted," but, then again, that song was released the year after this collection. —*Jose F. Promis*

Reflections / 1995 / Vision Music ♦♦♦

The Youngbloods

f. 1965, New York, NY, **db.** 1972
Folk-Rock, Pop
The Youngbloods could not be considered a major '60s band, but they were capable of offering some mighty pleasurable folk-rock in the late '60s, and produced a few great tunes along the way. One of the better groups to emerge from the East Coast in the mid-'60s, they would temper their blues and jugband influences with gentle California psychedelia, particularly after they moved to the San Francisco Bay Area. For most listeners, they're identified almost exclusively with their Top 10 hit "Get Together," but they managed

several respectable albums as well, all under the leadership of singer/songwriter Jesse Colin Young. Comparisons between the Youngbloods and the Lovin' Spoonful are inevitable—both groups offered good-timey folk-rock with much stronger jugband influences than West Coast rivals like the Byrds, though the Youngbloods made greater use of electric keyboards than the Spoonful, courtesy of the enigmatically named Lowell "Banana" Levinger. The Youngbloods didn't craft nearly as many brilliant singles as the Lovin' Spoonful, but (unlike the Spoonful) endured well into the hippie/psychedelic era. The group broke up in 1972, and Jesse Colin Young had a long and moderately successful career as a solo singer/songwriter. —*Richie Unterberger*

The Youngbloods / 1967 / Edsel ♦♦♦♦
The New York quartet come off as a mini-Lovin' Spoonful on their engaging debut, with a deeper touch of melancholy and more prominent electric keyboards. As with the Spoonful, they would have been better off leaving the blues alone, but the rest of the material is good, highlighted by "Get Together" and the achingly tuneful "All Over the World (La-La)." —*Richie Unterberger*

Earth Music / 1967 / Edsel ♦♦♦
Similar but a bit inferior to their debut, with the same division between accomplished folk-rock, good-timey ragtime-influenced romps, and pedestrian blues-rock. Includes one of the best versions of Tim Hardin's oft-covered standard "Reason to Believe." —*Richie Unterberger*

Elephant Mountain / 1969 / RCA ♦♦♦♦
By the time they made this album, the group had relocated to Northern California from New York and guitarist Jerry Corbitt had departed, leaving the songwriting chores almost exclusively in the hands of Jesse Colin Young. The mellower, more psychedelic sound reflected the group's new surroundings, and despite some weak moments, it remains their strongest and most cohesive LP. Young's acoustic love song "Sunlight" is his best original composition, and the Youngbloods' best track besides "Get Together"; "Darkness, Darkness" and "Smug" are also outstanding. —*Richie Unterberger*

● **The Best of the Youngbloods** / 1970 / RCA ♦♦♦♦
It's a bit short at ten songs, but this collection offers a nice overview of this '60s band's growth from good-time ragtimers to laid-back jammers. —*Jeff Tamarkin*

Timi Yuro

b. Aug. 4, 1941, Chicago, IL
Vocals / Brill Building Pop, Pop
Known as "the little girl with the big voice," Timi Yuro's booming, resonant vocals were sometimes mistaken for being black, being a man's, or both. Her voice was indeed mammoth, and her delivery astonishingly mature, on her debut single, "Hurt." This 1961 version of the pop standard reached number four and was followed by a brief period of stardom in the early '60s. Too pop in orientation to be called a rock singer, too conscious of rock and soul trends to be pigeonholed into what was then called the adult market, Yuro's undoubted talents never fully jibed with her material. While there was soul in her voice, it was of the Dinah Washington or Nancy Wilson sort, with perhaps more of a bend for straight pop than pop/rock. Over the course of the few years following "Hurt," she actually found her greatest success on the easy listening charts, but also dabbled in girl group pop, R&B, Gene Pitney-like ballads, and Patsy Cline-like country. She scored several minor hits during this time, the biggest of which was the most soulful: "What's a Matter Baby (Is It Hurting You)"; reaching number 12 in the U.S., it was covered by the Small Faces a few years later as the B-side of their first single. Continuing to record throughout the '60s and into the '70s, she experienced little success after leaving the Liberty label in 1964. —*Richie Unterberger*

● **The Hurt: The Best of Timi Yuro** / 1992 / EMI ♦♦♦
25-song compilation of her Liberty work, all but one dating from her commercial and artistic peak in 1961-64. Includes all of her chart singles, and some of her more memorable LP tracks, as well as an informative history by Dawn Eden. A jumpy document of an impressive talent whose material was not always up to her skills, with early-'60s orchestral arrangements ranging from effective to dated. —*Richie Unterberger*

The Lost Voice of Soul / 1993 / RPM ♦♦♦
26-track British import best-of is perhaps a shade less MOR-oriented than the American EMI *Best of Timi Yuro* compilation. Both have the biggest hits, but *The Lost Voice of Soul* isn't a redundant purchase if you're a serious Yuro fan, as about half the songs don't appear on the EMI anthology. It's difficult to make an argument over which disc's track selection is better; what you prefer, if you want just one, will depend very much on your individual taste, although North American listeners will have an easier time locating the U.S. anthology. —*Richie Unterberger*

The Voice That Got Away / 1996 / RPM ♦♦♦
If you want more Yuro than what you can find on the greatest-hits collections, this 26-track compilation is the next stop. Drawn primarily from her Liberty material (from both the early and late '60s), it also has a few obscure '70s sides that hold up much better than expected. B-sides, non-hit singles, and album tracks abound, and the songs are of nearly equal quality to her more celebrated performances. It also showcases her remarkable versatility, which may have been both an asset and a hindrance, as listeners found it difficult to match a solid musical identity with that magnificent voice. She does blue-eyed soul, orchestral pop ballads, pop-rock, and country with assurance, but rarely latches onto a classic bit of material. —*Richie Unterberger*

Zakary Thaks

Garage Rock

One of the best garage bands of the '60s, and one of the best teenage rock groups of all time, Zakary Thaks released a half-dozen regionally distributed singles in 1966 and 1967; some were hits in their hometown of Corpus Christi, TX, but none were heard elsewhere until they achieved renown among '60s collectors. Heavily indebted (as were so many bands) to R&B-influenced British heavyweights like the Stones, the Kinks, and the Yardbirds, the group added a thick dollop of Texas raunch to their fuzzy, distorted guitars and hell-bent energy. Most importantly, they were first-rate songwriters, with the breakneck "Bad Girl" (later compiled on *Pebbles, Vol. 2*), "Won't Come Back," the smoking "Face to Face," "Can't You Hear Your Daddy's Footsteps," and the folk-rock/Merseybeat hybrid "Please" ranking among the top echelon of American '60s garage rock. Their 1967 singles found the group moving into psychedelic territory; some songs betrayed a Moby Grape influence, and some good melodic numbers were diluted by poppy arrangements that recalled the Buckinghams and Grass Roots. Lead singer Chris Gerniottis, only 15 when Zakary Thaks began making records, joined another interesting Corpus Christi garage/psychedelic group, the Liberty Bell. —*Richie Unterberger*

● **Texas Band** / 1980 / Moxie ✦✦✦✦✦

Both sides of all six of their singles, marred only by some subpar sound quality (the tracks were mastered from rare singles). —*Richie Unterberger*

Texas Reverberations / 1982 / Texas Archive ✦✦✦

Side one has a couple of alternate takes (an instrumental version of "Daddy's Footsteps," a longer cut of "Face To Face") and some songs by The Liberty Bell. Side two is a subpar fidelity live recording (though the performances are rabble-rousing) of cover versions the band performed in a promotional film. For collectors only. —*Richie Unterberger*

J-Beck Story 2 / 1984 / Eva ✦✦✦

All 12 of their officially released songs, plus a couple rarities. Remastered from tape, this would displace *Texas Band* as the definitive Zakary Thaks collection, except that the remixes have actually diluted the punch of several of the tracks. —*Richie Unterberger*

Frank Zappa

b. Dec. 21, 1940, Baltimore, MD, **d.** Dec. 4, 1993, Los Angeles, CA

Vocals, Guitar (Electric), Guitar / Album Rock, Experimental Rock, Comedy Rock, Jazz-Rock, Experimental, Prog-Rock/Art Rock, Fusion, Hard Rock, Computer Music, 20th Century Classical/Modern Composition, Progressive Big Band, Proto-Punk

Frank Zappa was one of the most accomplished composers of the rock era; his music combines an understanding of and appreciation for such contemporary classical figures as Stravinsky, Stockhausen, and Varese with an affection for late-'50s doo wop rock & roll and a facility for the guitar-heavy rock that dominated pop in the '70s. But Zappa was also a satirist whose reserves of scorn seemed bottomless and whose wicked sense of humor and absurdity have delighted his numerous fans, even when his lyrics crossed over the broadest bounds of taste.

A band he joined in 1964 evolved into the Mothers by 1966, the year of the group's first album for MGM, a two-LP set called *Freak Out!* Subsequent albums extended the musical and lyrical themes of the debut, and they came frequently. Toward the end of the '60s, Zappa expanded the Mothers lineup, turning more toward instrumental jazz-rock. Zappa assembled a new edition of the Mothers in 1970, moving the group more in the direction of X-rated comedy. During a London performance however, he was pushed from the stage by a demented fan and seriously injured. After he recovered, Zappa re-formed the Mothers with himself as lead singer and made pop/rock albums, such as *Over-nite Sensation*, which were among his best-selling records ever. In the '80s, Zappa gained the rights to his old albums and began to reissue them, at first on his own and then through the pioneering Rykodisc CD label. Zappa died in 1993, two years after he was confirmed as being seriously ill with cancer. —*William Ruhlmann*

☆ **Freak Out!** / Jul. 1966 / Rykodisc ✦✦✦✦✦

One of the most ambitious debuts in rock history, *Freak Out!* was a seminal concept album that somehow foreshadowed both art rock and punk at the same time. Its four LP sides deconstruct rock conventions right and left, eventually pushing into territory inspired by avant-garde classical composers. Yet the album is sequenced in an accessibly logical progression; the first half is dedicated to catchy, satirical pop/rock songs that question assumptions about pop music, setting the tone for the radical new directions of the second half. Opening with the nonconformist call to arms "Hungry Freaks, Daddy," *Freak Out!* quickly posits the Mothers of Invention as the antithesis of teen-idol bands, often with sneering mockeries of the teen-romance songs that had long been rock's commercial stock-in-trade. Despite his genuine emotional alienation and dissatisfaction with pop

conventions, though, Frank Zappa was actually a skilled pop composer; even with the raw performances and his stinging guitar work, there's a subtle sophistication apparent in his unorthodox arrangements and tight, unpredictable melodicism. After returning to social criticism on the first song of the second half, the perceptive Watts riot protest "Trouble Every Day," Zappa exchanges pop song structure for experiments with musique concrète, amelodic dissonance, shifting time signatures, and studio effects. It's the first salvo in his career-long project of synthesizing popular and art music, high and low culture; while these pieces can meander, they virtually explode the limits of what can appear on a rock album, and effectively illustrate *Freak Out!*'s underlying principles: acceptance of differences and free individual expression. Zappa would spend much of his career developing and exploring ideas—both musical and conceptual—first put forth here; while his myriad directions often produced more sophisticated work, *Freak Out!* contains at least the rudiments of almost everything that followed, and few of Zappa's records can match its excitement over its own sense of possibility. —*Steve Huey*

Absolutely Free / May 26, 1967 / Rykodisc ✦✦✦✦✦

Frank Zappa's liner notes for *Freak Out!* name-checked an enormous breadth of musical and intellectual influences, and he seemingly attempts to cover them all on the second Mothers of Invention album, *Absolutely Free*. Leaping from style to style without warning, the album has a freewheeling, almost schizophrenic quality, encompassing everything from complex mutations of "Louie, Louie" to jazz improvisations and quotes from Stravinsky's *The Rite of Spring*.

It's made possible not only by expanded instrumentation, but also Zappa's experiments with tape manipulation and abrupt editing, culminating in an orchestrated mini-rock opera ("Brown Shoes Don't Make It") whose musical style shifts every few lines, often in accordance with the lyrical content. In general, the lyrics here are more given over to absurdity and non sequiturs, with the sense that they're often part of some private framework of satirical symbols. But elsewhere, Zappa's satire also grows more explicitly social, ranting against commercial consumer culture and related themes of artificiality and conformity.

By turns hilarious, inscrutable, and virtuosically complex, *Absolutely Free* is more difficult to make sense of than *Freak Out!*, partly because it lacks that album's careful pacing and conceptual focus. But even if it isn't quite fully realized, *Absolutely Free* is still a fabulously inventive record, bursting at the seams with ideas that would coalesce into a masterpiece with Zappa's next project. —*Steve Huey*

Lumpy Gravy / Dec. 1967 / Rykodisc ✦✦✦✦

Lumpy Gravy, Frank Zappa's first solo album, was released months before the Mothers of Invention's third LP (even though its back cover asked the question: "Is this phase two of *We're Only in It for the Money?*") and both were conceptualized and recorded at the same time. *We're Only in It for the Money* became a song-oriented anti-flower power album with one contemporary/musique concrète/sound collage hybrid piece by way of conclusion. *Lumpy Gravy* collaged bits of orchestral music, sonic manipulations, spoken words, and occasional pop ditties into two lumps of 16 minutes each. This album presents Zappa's first recordings with a decent orchestra, the 50-piece Abnuceals Emuukha Electric Symphony Orchestra. His symphonic writing was very much influenced by Stravinsky and Varèse. It still had to loose its sharp edges and find the lushness found in *200 Motels*. The segments of music are loosely tied together by bits of dialogue from inside the piano. MOI members and friends were invited to talk with their head inside a grand piano with the sustain pedal depressed (the technique was immortalized in the song "Evelyn, A Modified Dog"). The reverberating space gave the voices an eerie quality, but made it very difficult to convincingly edit the material. Thus, the plot emanating from these portions remains very vague (it was clarified 25 years later in *Civilization Phaze III*). The song bits include "Oh No," "Theme From Lumpy Gravy" (aka "Duodenum"), "King Kong," and "Take Your Clothes off When You Dance," all in instrumental versions, all making their first appearance on record. The starting point of Zappa's "serious music," *Lumpy Gravy* suffers from a lack of coherence, but it remains historically important and contains many conceptual continuity clues for the fan. The opening line of part one ("The way I see it, Barry, this should be a dynamite show") became a classic reference. —*François Couture*

★ **We're Only in It for the Money** / Sep. 1968 / Rykodisc ✦✦✦✦✦

From the beginning, Frank Zappa cultivated a role as voice of the freaks—imaginative outsiders who didn't fit comfortably into any group. *We're Only in It for the Money* is the ultimate expression of that sensibility, a satirical masterpiece that simultaneously skewered the hippies and the straights as prisoners of the same narrow-minded, superficial phoniness. Zappa's barbs were vicious and perceptive, and not just humorously so: his seemingly paranoid vision of authoritarian violence against the counterculture was borne out two years later by the Kent State killings. Like *Freak Out*, *We're Only in It for the*

Money essentially devotes its first half to satire, and its second half to presenting alternatives. Despite some specific references, the first-half suite is still wickedly funny, since its targets remain immediately recognizable. The second half shows where his sympathies lie, with character sketches of Zappa's real-life freak acquaintances, a carefree utopia in "Take Your Clothes Off When You Dance," and the strident, unironic protest "Mother People." Regardless of how dark the subject matter, there's a pervasively surreal, whimsical flavor to the music, sort of like *Sgt. Pepper* as a creepy nightmare. Some of the instruments and most of the vocals have been manipulated to produce odd textures and cartoonish voices; most songs are abbreviated, segue into others through edited snippets of music and dialogue, or are broken into fragments by more snippets, consistently interrupting the album's continuity. Compositionally, though, the music reveals itself as exceptionally strong, and Zappa's politics and satirical instinct have rarely been so focused and relevant, making *We're Only in It for the Money* quite probably his greatest achievement. [Rykodisc's 1987 reissue restored passages censored on the LP, but included re-recorded rhythm tracks and sounded quite different. Their 1995 re-reissue contains both the original music and content edits.] *—Steve Huey*

Cruising With Ruben and the Jets / Oct. 1968 / Rykodisc ♦♦♦

Frank Zappa loved '50s doo wop music. He grew up with it, collected it, and it was the first kind of pop music he wrote (like "Memories of El Monte," recorded by the Penguins in 1962). *Cruising With Ruben & the Jets*, the Mothers of Invention's fourth LP, is a collection of such music, all Zappa originals (some co-written with MOI singer Ray Collins). To the unexperienced, songs like "Cheap Thrills," "Deseri," and "Jelly Roll Gum Drop" can sound like an average doo wop song. A closer look reveals unusual chord sequences, Stravinsky quotes, and hilariously moronic lyrics—all that wrapped in four-way harmony vocals and linear piano triplets. A handful of songs from the group's 1966 debut, *Freak Out*, were rearranged ("How Could I Be Such a Fool" and "Anyway the Wind Blows" give the weirdest results), old material predating the Mothers was recycled ("Fountain of Love"), "Love of My Life" and "You Didn't Try to Call Me" became live staples. For the album's first CD reissue in 1985, Zappa had bassist Scott Thunes and drummer Chad Wackerman re-recording rhythm tracks for all but one song. Since then, all reissues have followed the 1985 mix, leaving "Stuff up the Cracks" the only surviving example of what *Cruising With Ruben & the Jets* really sounded like. Unless listeners are particularly fond of soul music, this album is definitely not the best place to start in Zappa's catalog. *—François Couture*

Burnt Weeny Sandwich / Feb. 1970 / Rykodisc ♦♦♦♦♦

Burnt Weeny Sandwich is the first of two albums by the Mothers of Invention that Frank Zappa released in 1970, after he had disbanded the original lineup. While *Weasels Ripped My Flesh* focuses on complex material and improvised stage madness, this collection of studio and live recordings summarizes the leader's various interests and influences at the time. It opens and closes on '50s pop covers, "WPLJ" and "Valarie." "Aybe Sea" is a Zappafied sea shanty, while "Igor's Boogie" is named after composer Igor Stravinsky, the closest thing to a hero Zappa ever worshipped. But the best material is represented by "Holiday in Berlin," a theme that would become central to the music of *200 Motels*, and "The Little House I Used to Live In," including a virtuoso piano solo by Ian Underwood. Presented as an extended set of theme and variations, the latter does not reach the same heights as "King Kong." In many places, and with the two aforementioned exceptions in mind, *Burnt Weeny Sandwich* sounds like a set of outtakes from *Uncle Meat*, which already summarized to an extent the adventures of the early Mothers. It lacks some direction, but those allergic to the group's grunts and free-form playing will prefer it to the wacky *Weasels Ripped My Flesh*. *—François Couture*

Uncle Meat / Jun. 1969 / Rykodisc ♦♦♦♦♦

Just three years into their recording career, the Mothers of Invention released their second double album, *Uncle Meat*, which began life as the largely instrumental soundtrack to an unfinished film. It's essentially a transitional work, but it's a fascinating one, showcasing Frank Zappa's ever-increasing compositional dexterity and the Mothers' emerging instrumental prowess. It was potentially easy to overlook Zappa's melodic gifts on albums past, but on *Uncle Meat*, he thrusts them firmly into the spotlight; what few lyrics there are, Zappa says in the liner notes, are in-jokes relevant only to the band. Thus, *Uncle Meat* became the point at which Zappa began to establish himself as a composer and he would return to many of these pieces repeatedly over the course of his career. Taken as a whole, *Uncle Meat* comes off as a hodgepodge, with centerpieces scattered between variations on previous pieces, short concert excerpts, less-realized experiments, doo wop tunes, and comedy bits; the programming often feels as random as the abrupt transitions and tape experiments held over from Zappa's last few projects. But despite the absence of a conceptual framework, the unfocused sprawl of *Uncle Meat* is actually a big part of its appeal. It's exciting to hear one of the most creatively fertile minds in rock pushing restlessly into new territory, even if he isn't always quite sure where he's going. However, several tracks hint at the jazz-rock fusion soon to come, especially the extended album closer "King Kong"; it's his first unequivocal success in that area, with its odd time signature helping turn it into a rhythmically kinetic blowing vehicle. Though some might miss the gleeful satire of Zappa's previous work with the Mothers, *Uncle Meat's* continued abundance of musical ideas places it among his most intriguing works. *—Steve Huey*

Hot Rats / Oct. 10, 1969 / Rykodisc ♦♦♦♦♦

Aside from the experimental side project *Lumpy Gravy*, *Hot Rats* was the first album Frank Zappa recorded as a solo artist sans the Mothers, though he continued to employ previous musical collaborators, most notably multi-instrumentalist Ian Underwood. Other than another side project—the doo wop tribute *Cruising With Ruben and the Jets*—*Hot Rats* was also the first time Zappa focused his efforts in one general area, namely jazz-rock. The result is a classic of the genre. *Hot Rats'* genius lies in the way it fuses the compositional sophistication of jazz with rock's down and dirty attitude—there's a real looseness and grit to the three lengthy jams, and a surprising, wry elegance to the three shorter, tightly arranged numbers (particularly the sumptuous "Peaches en Regalia"). Perhaps the biggest revelation isn't the straightforward presentation, or the intricately shifting instrumental voices in Zappa's arrangements—it's his own virtuosity on the electric guitar, recorded during extended improvisational workouts for the first time here. His wonderfully scuzzy, distorted tone is an especially good fit on "Willie the Pimp," with its greasy blues riffs and guest vocalist Captain Beefheart's Howlin' Wolf theatrics. Elsewhere, his skill as a melodist was in full flower, whether dominating an entire piece or providing a memorable theme as a jumping-off point. In addition to Underwood, the backing band featured contributions from Jean-Luc Ponty, Lowell George, and Don "Sugarcane" Harris, among others; still, Zappa is unquestionably the star of the show. *Hot Rats* still sizzles; few albums originating on the rock side of jazz-rock fusion flowed so freely between both sides of the equation, or achieved such unwavering excitement and energy. *—Steve Huey*

Weasels Ripped My Flesh / Aug. 1970 / Rykodisc ♦♦♦♦♦

A fascinating collection of mostly instrumental live and studio material recorded by the original Mothers, complete with horn section, from 1967-69, *Weasels Ripped My Flesh* segues unpredictably between arty experimentation and traditional song structures. Highlights of the former category include the classical avant-garde elements of "Didja Get Any Onya," which blends odd rhythmic accents and time signatures with dissonance and wordless vocal noises; these pop up again in "Prelude to the Afternoon of a Sexually Aroused Gas Mask" and "Toads of the Short Forest." The latter and "The Eric Dolphy Memorial Barbecue" also show Zappa's willingness to embrace the avant-garde jazz of the period. Yet, interspersed are straightforward tunes like a cover of Little Richard's "Directly From My Heart to You," with great violin from Sugarcane Harris; the stinging Zappa-sung rocker "My Guitar Wants to Kill Your Mama," and "Oh No," a familiar Broadway-esque Zappa melody (it turned up on *Lumpy Gravy*) fitted with lyrics and sung by Ray Collins. Thus, *Weasels* can make for difficult, incoherent listening, especially at first. But there is a certain logic behind the band's accomplished genre-bending and Zappa's gleefully abrupt veering between musical extremes; without pretension, Zappa blurs the normally sharp line between intellectual concept music and the visceral immediacy of rock and R&B. Zappa's anything-goes approach and the distance between his extremes are what make *Weasels Ripped My Flesh* ultimately invigorating; they also even make the closing title track—a minute and a half of squalling feedback, followed by applause—perfectly logical in the album's context. *—Steve Huey*

Chunga's Revenge / Oct. 23, 1970 / Rykodisc ♦♦♦

Chunga's Revenge marks the debut of Mark Volman and Howard Kaylan (among several other musicians) with the Mothers, and while their schtick has not reached the graphic proportions it later would, the thematic obsessions of the *200 Motels* period are foreshadowed on tracks like "Road Ladies" and "Would You Go All the Way?" Other vocal numbers include the hard-rocking "Tell Me You Love Me," the musicians' union satire "Rudy Wants to Buy Yez a Drink," and the doo-wop-influenced "Sharleena." Meanwhile, Zappa's strong instrumental music incorporates Eastern European influences ("Transylvania Boogie"), cocktail jazz ("Twenty Small Cigars"), and the percussion-only "The Clap." Zappa's guitar tone is wonderfully biting and nasty throughout; George Duke provides another musical highlight by scat-singing a "drum solo." But while there are plenty of fine moments, *Chunga's Revenge* is in the end more of a hodgepodge transitional album, with less coherence than Zappa's other 1969-70 works. Still, it will appeal to fans of that creatively fertile period in Zappa's oeuvre. *—Steve Huey*

Fillmore East: June 1971 / Jun. 1971 / Rykodisc ♦♦♦

As an enduring work, *Fillmore East: June 1971* is a mixed bag, but it does represent the peak of the Flo & Eddie edition of the Mothers. Most of the songs are essentially comedy routines set to music, often dealing with the life of a touring rock musician and, of course, the various opportunities for sexual adventure therein; in one scenario, Mark Volman and Howard Kaylan reprise their Turtles hit "Happy Together" in exchange for sexual favors. The humor is often glib and juvenile, marking the beginnings of Zappa's tactic of making complex music more accessible with half-sardonic arena-frontman antics and crowd-pleasing dirty jokes. Whether one considers the results funny and parodic or crass and pandering, the band is undeniably good, especially as showcased on "Little House I Used to Live In," "Willie the Pimp Part One," and "Peaches en Regalia." *—Steve Huey*

200 Motels / Oct. 1971 / Rykodisc ♦♦♦♦

The soundtrack to Zappa's strange early-'70s film was always doomed to be a peripheral entry in his discography. The movie's story was not easy to follow, and neither is the record (not that plot was ever a big focus of the production). It's typically wacky Zappa of the era, with unpredictable sharp turns between crunchy rock bombast, orchestration, and jazz/classical influences, as well as interjections of wacky spoken dialogue. Those who like his late-'60s/early-'70s work—not as song-oriented as his first albums, in other words, but not as "serious" or as silly as his later records—will probably like this fine, although it's not up to the level of *Uncle Meat*. It's funny in spots as well, especially the part where a disgruntled sideman gets tempted away from the band to do his own thing (a libretto that was, apparently, based on real-life incidents concerning Zappa sideman Jeff Simmons, who left during the project). On the other hand, there's a growing tendency to deploy the smutty, cheap humor that would soon dominate much of Zappa's work. Originally released in 1971, this didn't make it onto CD until 1997, in a two-disc package that included a bit of bonus material, although this was merely four promotional radio spots for the film and the single edit of "Magic Fingers." *—Richie Unterberger*

Just Another Band From L.A. / Apr. 1972 / Rykodisc ♦♦

Waka/Jawaka: Hot Rats II / Jul. 5, 1972 / Rykodisc ✦✦✦

When Frank Zappa found himself stuck in a wheelchair for most of the year 1972 (after a "fan" pushed him off stage on December 10 of the previous year), he relieved his then-current band (including singers Flo & Eddie) of its duties and turned to studio work. One of the first things he tried was to write fusion jazz music scored for wider instrumentations than an average rock band. *Waka/Jawaka* was conceived in parallel to *The Grand Wazoo*, but with less players. The album, released in July 1972, is comprised of two extended instrumental pieces and two shorter songs. "Big Swifty," a theme-and-solos showcase would become a live favorite, but the highlight came in the form of the orgiastic title track, recorded with ex-Mothers of Invention Don Preston, trumpter Sal Marquez, trombonists Bill Byers and Ken Shroyer, saxophonist Mike Altschul, bassist Erroneous and drummer Aynsley Dunbar. The songs, never performed live, feel like filler material. *Waka/Jawaka* was Zappa's second solo album and is occasionally referred to as "Hot Rats II" (the handles of the faucets on the cover artwork show the words "hot" and "rats" instead of "hot" and "cold"). His writing and recording technique had matured a lot in very little time. The dirty blues jamming of the 1970 LP has been replaced by clean, crisp jazz improvisations—no need to say this was also an abrupt change in style from the Mothers' 1969-1971 incarnation. But this album was only transitional: Zappa's big band stylings would really flourish in *The Grand Wazoo* a few months later. *—François Couture*

The Grand Wazoo / May 1973 / Rykodisc ✦✦✦✦✦

Like its immediate predecessor, *Waka/Jawaka*, *The Grand Wazoo* was a largely instrumental jazz fusion album recorded during Zappa's convalescence from injuries sustained after being pushed off a concert stage. While Zappa contributes some guitar solos and occasional vocals, the focus is more on his skills as a composer and arranger. Most of the five selections supposedly form a musical representation of a story told in the liner notes about two warring musical factions, but the bottom line is that overall, the compositions here are more memorably melodic and consistently engaging than *Waka/Jawaka*. The instrumentation is somewhat unique in the Zappa catalog as well, with the band more of a chamber jazz orchestra than a compact rock unit; over 20 musicians and vocalists contribute to the record. While *Hot Rats* is still the peak of Zappa's jazz-rock fusion efforts, *The Grand Wazoo* comes close, and it's essential for anyone interested in Zappa's instrumental works. *—Steve Huey*

● **Over-Nite Sensation** / Sep. 1973 / Rykodisc ✦✦✦✦✦

Love it or hate it, *Over-Nite Sensation* was a watershed album for Frank Zappa, the point where his post-'60s aesthetic was truly established; it became his first gold album, and most of these songs became staples of his live shows for years to come. Where the Flo and Eddie years were dominated by rambling, off-color comedy routines, *Over-Nite Sensation* tightened up the song structures and tucked sexual and social humor into melodic, technically accomplished heavy guitar rock with jazzy chord changes and funky rhythms; meanwhile, Zappa's growling new post-accident voice takes over the storytelling. While the music is some of Zappa's most accessible, the apparent callousness and/or stunning sexual explicitness of "Camarillo Brillo," "Dirty Love," and especially "Dinah-Moe Humm" leave him on shaky aesthetic ground. Zappa often protested that the charges of misogyny leveled at such material missed out on the implicit satire of male stupidity, and also confirmed intellectuals' self-conscious reticence about indulging in dumb fun; however, the glee in his voice as he spins his adolescent fantasies can undermine his point. Indeed, that enjoyment, also evident in the silly wordplay, suggests that Zappa is throwing his juvenile crassness in the face of critical expectation, asserting his right to follow his muse even if it leads him into blatant stupidity (ironic or otherwise). One can read this motif into the absurd shaggy-dog story of a dental floss rancher in "Montana," the album's indisputable highlight, which features amazing, uncredited vocal backing from Tina Turner and the Ikettes. As with much of Zappa's best '70s and '80s material, *Over-Nite Sensation* is ideologically problematic and musically terrific. *—Steve Huey*

Apostrophe / Mar. 1974 / Rykodisc ✦✦✦✦✦

The musically similar follow-up to the commercial breakthrough of *Over-Nite Sensation*, *Apostrophe* became Frank Zappa's second gold and only Top Ten album with the help of the "doggy wee-wee" jokes of "Don't Eat the Yellow Snow," Zappa's first chart single (a longer, edited version that used portions of other songs on the LP). The first half of the album is full of nonsensical shaggy-dog story-songs that segue into one another without seeming to finish themselves first; their dirty jokes are generally more subtle and veiled than the more notorious cuts on *Over-Nite Sensation*. The second half contains the instrumental title cut, featuring Jack Bruce on bass; "Uncle Remus," an update of Zappa's critique of racial discord on "Trouble Every Day"; and a return to the album's earlier silliness in "Stink Foot." *Apostrophe* has the narrative feel of a concept album, but aside from its willful absurdity, the concept is difficult to decipher; even so, that doesn't detract from its entertainment value. *—Steve Huey*

Roxy & Elsewhere / Sep. 10, 1974 / Rykodisc ✦✦✦✦

The double-length *Roxy & Elsewhere* captures the 1973 edition of the Mothers in concert with a rich, full-sounding recording. This lineup was one of the most technically accomplished versions of the band, as their interplay on complex, intricate compositions like "Echidna's Arf (Of You)," "Don't You Ever Wash That Thing," and "Bebop Tango (of the Jazzman's Church)" amply indicates. Other highlights include the typical Zappa humor of "Penguin in Bondage" and "Cheepnis," plus the revisited "More Trouble Every Day" and "Son of Orange County" (a revamped "Oh No"). *—Steve Huey*

One Size Fits All / Jun. 25, 1975 / Rykodisc ✦✦✦

The first Mothers of Invention studio album since the group's biggest hit, *Over-Nite Sensation* (although the Zappa solo album *Apostrophe* and the live group album *Roxy & Elsewhere* came in between), *One Size Fits All* found Frank Zappa retreating from the frontman position he took on the previous album, sharing lead vocals with keyboard player George Duke, reed man Napoleon Murphy Brock, and guitarist Johnny "Guitar" Watson. The lyrics are the usual mix of scorn, absurdity, humor, and local references ("San Ber'dino"), and the music leans toward heavy metal and fusion, although with the usual Zappa signature elements of sudden rhythmic changes and short, startling passages, many of them provided by vibes player Ruth Underwood. The album's standout is the stately "Sofa No. 2," which is sung in German. *—William Ruhlmann*

Bongo Fury / Oct. 2, 1975 / Rykodisc ✦✦✦

Except for two instrumental studio tracks, *Bongo Fury* was recorded live in Austin, Texas on a reunion tour between Zappa and Captain Beefheart, the latter of whom takes most of the vocals. Many of the tracks feature Beefheart's surreal poetry with musical backing from the Mothers reminiscent of the Flo and Eddie band; Zappa also takes a few guitar solos and pushes some songs into bluesier territory, revisiting the music that originally cemented his and Beefheart's friendship. On this album, Zappa and Beefheart are a decent, if not quite inspiring pairing, with such highlights as "Carolina Hardcore Ecstasy," the Zappa-sung "Muffin Man," and the country-tinged bicentennial satire "Poofter's Froth Wyoming Plans Ahead." *—Steve Huey*

Zoot Allures / Oct. 29, 1976 / Rykodisc ✦✦✦✦

Frank Zappa's albums could be incredibly self-indulgent—something that would be off-putting coming from others, but worked to the rocker's artistic advantage. Zappa was often so insanely clever and uniquely humorous that one could excuse his excesses (or even enjoy them). *Zoot Allures*, one of the best albums Zappa recorded in the mid-'70s, is about as self-indulgent as it gets. From "The Torture Never Stops" (a very twisted ode to a medieval-type S&M dungeon) to "Disco Boy" (which lampoons disco culture) to the infectious "Ms. Pinky," everything on the album is an eccentric, delightfully unorthodox classic. Zappa was quite a risk-taker, and those risks pay off in a major way on this CD. *—Alex Henderson*

Zappa in New York / Mar. 3, 1978 / Rykodisc ✦✦✦✦

This album was recorded in December 1976 at the Palladium in New York and originally intended for release in 1977. It was held up due to arguments between Frank Zappa and his then-record label, Warner Bros. When the two-LP set finally appeared in March 1978, Warner had deleted "Punky's Whips," a song about drummer Terry Bozzio's attraction to Punky Meadows of Angel. When Zappa reacquired the album and released it as a double-CD in 1991, he restored "Punky's Whips" and added four bonus tracks. The Zappa band, which includes bassist Patrick O'Hearn, percussionist Ruth Underwood, and keyboard player Eddie Jobson, along with a horn section including the two Brecker brothers, was one of the bandleader's most accomplished, which it had to be to play songs like "Black Page," even in the "easy" version presented here. Zappa also was at the height of his comic stagecraft, notably on songs like "Titties & Beer," which essentially is a comedy routine between Zappa and Bozzio, and "The Illinois Enema Bandit," which features TV announcer Don Pardo. *—William Ruhlmann*

Studio Tan / Sep. 15, 1978 / Rykodisc ✦✦

Sleep Dirt / Jan. 19, 1979 / Rykodisc ✦✦✦

The material on this album originally was intended to be part of a four-record set called *Läther*, prepared for release in 1977. Then Frank Zappa got into a disagreement with his record company, Warner Bros., and *Läther* was split up into several different releases as part of a contractual agreement. The results were dumped on the market during 1978 and 1979, while Zappa moved on to his own record label. *Sleep Dirt* consists of miscellaneous tracks recorded between 1974 and 1976, including "Flambay," "Spider Of Destiny," and "Time Is Money," songs that apparently were part of an unissued Zappa musical/rock opera from 1972 called *Hunchentoot*. They are sung by soprano Thana Harris. It's impossible to say what the entire work would have been like, but this album is little more than musical fragments. *—William Ruhlmann*

Sheik Yerbouti / Mar. 3, 1979 / Rykodisc ✦✦✦✦

In order to finance his artier excursions, which increasingly required more expensive technology, Frank Zappa recorded several collections of guitar- and song-oriented material in the late '70s and early '80s, which generally concentrated on the bawdy lyrical themes many fans had come to expect and enjoy in concert. *Sheik Yerbouti* (two LPs, one CD) was one of the first and most successful of these albums, garnering attention for such tracks as the Grammy-nominated disco satire "Dancin' Fool," the controversial "Jewish Princess," and the equally controversial "Bobby Brown Goes Down," a song about gay S&M that became a substantial hit in European clubs. While Zappa's attitude on the latter two tracks was even more politically incorrect than usual for him, it didn't stop the album from becoming his second highest-charting ever. Social satire, leering sexual preoccupations, and tight, melodic songs dominated the rest of the record as well, as Zappa stuck to what had been commercially successful for him in the past. The "dumb entertainment" (as Zappa liked to describe this style) on *Sheik Yerbouti* was some of his dumbest, for better or worse, and the music was undeniably good—easily some of his best since *Apostrophe*, and certainly the most accessible. Even if it sometimes drifts a bit, fans of Zappa's '70s work will find *Sheik Yerbouti* on nearly an equal level with *Apostrophe* and *Over-Nite Sensation*, both in terms of humor and musical quality. *—Steve Huey*

Orchestral Favorites / May 4, 1979 / Rykodisc ✦✦✦

The material on this album originally was intended to be part of a four-record set called *Läther*, prepared for release in 1977. Then Frank Zappa got into a disagreement with his record company, Warner Bros., and *Läther* was split up into several different releases as part of a contractual agreement. The results were dumped on the market during 1978 and 1979, while Zappa moved on to his own record label. *Orchestral Favorites* consists of material recorded on September 17 and 18, 1975, with a 37-piece orchestra and includes such familiar Zappa themes as "Duke of Prunes" (from *Absolutely Free*) and "Strictly Genteel" (from *200 Motels*); "Bogus Pomp" also consisted largely of *200 Motels* music. The themes are melodic and often majestic, with various startling juxtapositions and changes. This was the first release of Zappa orchestral material since *Lumpy Gravy* and a precursor of things to come. *—William Ruhlmann*

Joe's Garage: Acts 1-3 / Nov. 19, 1979 / Rykodisc ✦✦✦✦✦

Joe's Garage was originally released in 1979 in two separate parts; *Act 1* came first, followed by a two-record set containing *Acts 2-3*. Rykodisc's reissue puts all three acts together on two CDs. *Joe's Garage* is generally regarded as one of Zappa's finest post-'60s conceptual works, a sprawling, satirical rock opera about a totalitarian future in which music is outlawed to control the population. The narrative is long, winding, and occasionally loses focus; it was improvised in a weekend, some of it around previously existing songs, but Zappa manages to make most of it hang together. *Acts 2-3* give off much the same feel, as Zappa relies heavily on what he termed "xenochrony"—previously recorded guitar solos transferred onto new, rhythmically different backing tracks to produce random musical coincidences. Such an approach is guaranteed to produce some slow moments as well, but critics latched onto the work more for its conceptual substance. *Joe's Garage* satirizes social control mechanisms, consumerism, corporate abuses, gender politics, religion, and the rock & roll lifestyle; all these forces conspire against the title protagonist, an average young man who simply wants to play guitar and enjoy himself. Even though Zappa himself hated punk rock and even says so on the album, his ideas seemed to support punk's do-it-yourself challenge to the record industry and to social norms in general. Since this is 1979-era Zappa, there are liberal applications of his trademark scatological humor (the titles of "Catholic Girls," "Crew Slut," "Why Does It Hurt When I Pee?," and "Keep It Greasey" are self-explanatory). Still, in spite of its flaws, *Joe's Garage* has enough substance to make it one of Zappa's most important '70s works and overall political statements, even if it's not focused enough to rank with his earliest Mothers of Invention masterpieces. *—Steve Huey*

Shut Up 'N Play Yer Guitar / May 11, 1981 / Barking Pumpkin ✦✦✦✦

Shut Up 'N Play Yer Guitar Some More / May 11, 1981 / Barking Pumpkin ✦✦✦✦

Return of the Son of Shut Up 'N Play Yer Guitar / May 11, 1981 / Barking Pumpkin ✦✦✦✦

These three albums of guitar solos by Frank Zappa were released simultaneously by his mail order record company, Barking Pumpkin, and subsequently released to retail by Rykodisc on September 1, 1986, as part of a two-CD set called *Shut Up 'N Play Yer Guitar*. The tracks were recorded, mostly in concert, in 1979 and 1980, and they demonstrate Zappa's mastery of the electric guitar, establishing him as the peer of the other guitar heroes of his generation. *—William Ruhlmann*

Tinsel Town Rebellion / May 17, 1981 / Rykodisc ✦✦✦

An uneven, nearly all-live double-record set, *Tinsel Town Rebellion* mixes new material and versions of Zappa oldies like "Love of My Life," "I Ain't Got No Heart," "Tell Me You Love Me," "Brown Shoes Don't Make It," and a reworked "Peaches En Regalia," titled "Peaches III." These songs, as well as the band's stellar instrumental work, provide the album's best moments. Elsewhere, the title track is an only partially accurate satire of punk; Zappa's intentionally smarmy crowd banter is featured on "Dance Contest" and "Panty Rap," the latter a bit involving the collection of female audience members' underwear. More problematic is the sometimes violent sexual juvenilia of songs like "Fine Girl," "Easy Meat," "Pick Me, I'm Clean," and "Bamboozled By Love"; if, as Zappa insisted, this part of his oeuvre simply mixes dumb fun and satire of both sexes' peccadilloes, with no underlying misogyny, it's rather difficult to tell. *—Steve Huey*

You Are What You Is / Sep. 1981 / Rykodisc ✦✦✦✦

You Are What You Is was another of Zappa's periodic post-*Over-Nite Sensation* efforts that concentrated on tight songwriting supported by satirical lyrics. Originally a two-record set featuring 20 songs, *You Are What You Is* skewered a variety of targets, from teenagers, punk rock, disco, and country music to the media, yuppies, the beauty and fitness industry, upper-class vice, religious hypocrisy, suicide, and the military draft—all the trappings of Reagan-era America. Occasionally, Zappa's satirical points seem ill-thought-out, if not unnecessarily malicious; "Jumbo Go Away" is perhaps the most offensive song in Zappa's huge canon of potentially offensive songs, a tale of a whining, VD-riddled groupie who is portrayed as deserving the punch in the face she gets from an irritated musician. Despite that misstep, though, *You Are What You Is* is quite ambitious in scope and in general one of Zappa's most accessible later-period efforts; it's a showcase for his songwriting skills and his often acute satirical perspective, with less of the smutty humor that some listeners find off-putting. *—Steve Huey*

Ship Arriving Too Late to Save a Drowning Witch / May 1982 / Rykodisc ✦✦✦

Ship Arriving Too Late to Save a Drowning Witch is perhaps most notable for the inclusion of the novelty hit "Valley Girl," Zappa's first Top 40 single, which featured a 14-year-old Moon Unit doing a deadly accurate impersonation of the spoiled rich girls in the neighboring San Fernando Valley; the song triggered a national fad and myriad catch phrases and helped the LP into the Top 30. The rest of the album isn't quite as memorable, with standard but not incredibly distinguished Zappa compositions covering familiar instrumental ("Drowning Witch") and thematic ("Teenage Prostitute") ground. Steve Vai is credited with "impossible guitar." *—Steve Huey*

Baby Snakes / Mar. 1983 / Rykodisc ✦✦

Man from Utopia / Mar. 1983 / Rykodisc ✦✦

Them or Us / Oct. 1984 / Rykodisc ✦✦✦

Featuring a caution against the dangers of traveling "In France," a tribute to "Sharleena," and a cover of the Allman Brothers Band's "Whipping Post," the double-LP set *Them or Us* (subsequently reissued on a single CD) found Frank Zappa repeating himself with his usual scorn and formidable musicianship, but not breaking any new ground. *—William Ruhlmann*

Thing-Fish / Nov. 1984 / Rykodisc ✦✦✦

A three-record box set (subsequently reissued as a double-CD), *Thing-Fish* purported to be the cast album for an unproduced Broadway show, but was in fact a savage satire on theater and several other things that could not have been produced theatrically. Ike Willis' *Amos 'n' Andy* patois had long since passed into the objectionable by this point, and the composer's preoccupation with sexual and excretory functions had become extreme. This was something of a culmination of Zappa's tendencies over the last decade, and their most complete expression. Certainly, he retreated from such works in the future, in fact releasing relatively little new material in the last nine years of his life. *—William Ruhlmann*

Jazz From Hell / Nov. 15, 1986 / Rykodisc ✦✦✦✦

This is an album of jazz-rock-oriented instrumental music that, with the exception of the track "St. Etienne," was recorded on the Synclavier music synthesizer. As an expression of Frank Zappa's more popular music styles, it ranks in execution with such albums as *Hot Rats*. It is the winner of a Grammy Award for Best Rock Instrumental Performance (Orchestra Group or Soloist). *—William Ruhlmann*

London Symphony Orchestra 2 / 1987 / Rykodisc ✦✦✦

This is a CD reissue of *Zappa Volume I* with the addition of the 24 1/2-minute "Bogus Pomp" and the deletion of "Pedro's Dowry" and "Envelopes." Common to both LP and CD are "Sad Jane" and "Mo 'N Herb's Vacation." These are orchestral works by Frank Zappa, played by The London Symphony Orchestra, conducted by Kent Nagano. Although Zappa himself has criticized these recordings, they represent the best rendition so far of his orchestral ambitions, more accomplished than *Lumpy Gravy* or *Orchestral Favorites*. The music is moody and ponderous, slow with sudden dramatic passages, in the manner of Stravinsky, and exhibits little of Zappa's usual melodic invention and humor. *—William Ruhlmann*

Guitar / Apr. 1988 / Rykodisc ✦✦✦✦

Frank Zappa's follow-up to *Shut Up 'N Play Yer Guitar*, this double-CD (there is also a double-LP on Barking Pumpkin with fewer tracks) again excerpts Zappa's guitar solos from live performances, recorded between 1979 and 1984. Guitar aficionados will have another field day. (Release date is for the LP; the CD was released on May 23, 1988.) *—William Ruhlmann*

You Can't Do That on Stage Anymore, Vol. 1 / May 16, 1988 / Rykodisc ✦✦✦✦✦

This two-LP set provides a curtain-raiser on the massive *You Can't Do That On Stage Anymore* series and is typical of the approach of the series in that it jumps from one time and band and location to another, leading off, for example, with a version of "Plastic People" recorded by the Mothers of Invention in 1969 and moving immediately to a version of "The Torture Never Stops" by Frank Zappa's band in 1977. Some of Zappa's more entertaining numbers are here, such as "Montana," "King Kong" (a short version from 1982), and "Cosmic Debris," but, as with most of the series, the jumping around gives the album an unfocused feel. *—William Ruhlmann*

You Can't Do That on Stage Anymore, Vol. 2 / Oct. 1988 / Rykodisc ✦✦✦✦✦

Unlike the other volumes in Frank Zappa's giant reissue series of concert recordings, *Volume 2* chronicles a single performance, "The Helsinki Concert," which occurred on September 22, 1974. At the time, Zappa was leading a relatively small band consisting of himself on guitar and vocals, Napoleon Murphy Brock on sax and vocals, George Duke on keyboard and vocals, Ruth Underwood on percussion, Tom Fowler on bass, and Chester Thompson on drums. "The repertoire is basically the same as the *Roxy* album," Zappa writes in the liner notes, referring to *Roxy & Elsewhere*, which is true, although the 20 tracks include material from earlier (such as "The Idiot Bastard Son") and later, as well as some unreleased material. As Zappa suggests, the band, which had been on the road a year, is tight, and this is a strong, coherent live performance. *—William Ruhlmann*

Broadway the Hard Way / Oct. 1988 / Rykodisc ✦✦✦✦✦

The first live album compiled from various performances on Zappa's 1988 world tour (his final outing), the double-LP/single-CD *Broadway the Hard Way* is composed mostly of new, vocal-oriented material. The tone throughout is highly political, with Zappa taking potshots at such targets as Elvis Presley, Michael Jackson, Richard Nixon, Ronald Reagan, Pat Robertson and other televangelists, Jesse Jackson, C. Everett Koop, and so on. Despite Zappa's well-deserved reputation as an acute satirist, his sarcasm is often surprisingly humorless here, leaning toward didacticism; his choice to name names and address his subjects explicitly, rather than through metaphor, also renders the album instantly dated, almost like a late-'80s stand-up comedy routine. Despite these flaws, many of Zappa's political observations hit the mark, as do some of the jokes, easily making *Broadway the Hard Way* one of his best and most intellectually stimulating post-1960s political efforts. The CD features a memorable guest appearance from Sting, singing his Jimmy Swaggart-condemned Police tune "Murder By Numbers." *—Steve Huey*

You Can't Do That on Stage Anymore, Vol. 3 / Nov. 1989 / Rykodisc ✦✦✦✦✦

On the third volume of his live reissue series, after devoting *Volume 2* to a single concert, Frank Zappa returned to his policy of mixing times, bands, and repertoire from throughout his career from one track to the next. The first disc, however, is drawn entirely from Zappa's 1984 tour, which gives it more musical coherence than the second disc, which ranges from 1971 to 1984. Many familiar tunes are featured, notably a 24-and-a-half-minute version of "King Kong" that is edited from performances in 1982 and 1971, and there are several previously unreleased compositions. *—William Ruhlmann*

Frank Zappa Meets the Mothers of Prevention / May 1990 / Rykodisc ✦✦✦
This album mixes the usual Frank Zappa instrumentals and satire with excerpts from Zappa's testimony before Congress in opposition to censorship and to the Parents Music Resource Center (PMRC). The album was issued in three different forms. The U.S. LP version (Barking Pumpkin ST 74203) contains seven tracks. The European LP version (EMI EMC 3507), released in February 1986, eliminated the 12-minute track "Porn Wars" on the grounds that it "would not have been interesting to listeners outside the U.S.," as a sleeve note explained, and substituted three new tracks, "I Don't Even Care," "One Man—One Vote," and "H.R. 2911." The U.S. CD version (Rykodisc RCD 10023), released September 1, 1986, added "I Don't Even Care" and "One Man—One Vote" to the U.S. LP track listing. *—William Ruhlmann*

The Best Band You Never Heard in Your Life / Apr. 1991 / Rykodisc ✦✦✦✦✦
This is the second album that Frank Zappa culled from live performances on his final 1988 world tour, the first being *Broadway the Hard Way.* That release contained newly written material; this one, in contrast, contains, as Zappa puts it in his liner notes, "big-band arrangements of concert favorites and obscure album cuts, along with deranged versions of cover tunes and a few premiere recordings." In practice, that means you have the opportunity to hear Zappa treatments of such surprising songs as "Ring of Fire," "I Left My Heart In San Francisco," "Bolero," "Purple Haze," and "Stairway to Heaven." In other words, even for an idiosyncratic artist, this is an idiosyncratic album. (The title derives from Zappa's note that the band "self-destructed" before most of the U.S. could hear it play.) *—William Ruhlmann*

Make a Jazz Noise Here / Jun. 1991 / Rykodisc ✦✦✦
This is the third album Frank Zappa culled from his final 1988 world tour. The first, *Broadway the Hard Way,* featured new material, and the second, *The Best Band You Never Heard In Your Life,* offered many unusual cover songs. This album displays the band's musical acuity on various demanding Zappa compositions, such as "The Black Page (new age version)" and even includes snatches of Stravinsky and Bartok. *—William Ruhlmann*

You Can't Do That on Stage Anymore, Vol. 4 / Jun. 21, 1991 / Rykodisc ✦✦✦✦✦
The fourth volume in Frank Zappa's series of CD compilations of live material is typical in that it features recordings made between 1969 and 1988, including such familiar songs as "My Guitar Wants to Kill Your Mama," "Willie the Pimp," and "Disco Boy." There is, however, an unusually large complement of previously unreleased songs here, including a cover of "Take Me Out to the Ball Game," and the first performance of "The Torture Never Stops," running more than nine minutes, is a highlight. *—William Ruhlmann*

You Can't Do That on Stage Anymore, Vol. 5 / 1992 / Rykodisc ✦✦✦✦
One of Frank Zappa's avowed purposes in compiling his series of archival live recordings under the *You Can't Do That On Stage Anymore* rubric was to demonstrate to fans that, despite what they thought, his bands after the original Mothers of Invention were an improvement over that legendary outfit. On *Volume 5,* however, he seems to have dropped this effort, devoting the first disc to '60s material. And what do you know? It proves him wrong, at least on an emotional level. Maybe the Mothers weren't great technical musicians and maybe these tapes aren't as high-tech as later ones, but the first disc here is more fun than the rest of the series combined. Disc two is given over to a 1982 European concert tour distinguished by Zappa's threat in Geneva to end the concert if anyone else threw something. Can you guess what happened then? *—William Ruhlmann*

You Can't Do That on Stage Anymore, Vol. 6 / Oct. 23, 1992 / Rykodisc ✦✦✦✦
Frank Zappa ended his series of albums of previously unreleased concert recordings with this volume, which features one disc given over to "songs dealing generally with the topic of sex (safe and otherwise)," as Zappa puts it in the liner notes. Actually, with songs like "Alien Orifice," "Crew Slut," and "Take Your Clothes Off When You Dance," the same theme pervades disc two, also. *—William Ruhlmann*

Ahead of Their Time / Mar. 23, 1993 / Rykodisc ✦✦✦
This album contains a previously unreleased live concert by the Mothers of Invention recorded October 28, 1968, at the Royal Festival Hall in London. It finds the band still playing some of its familiar repertoire ("Help, I'm a Rock," "Sleeping in a Jar," "Let's Make the Water Turn Black") from its early albums, but also looking forward to the more ambitious *Uncle Meat,* which would be released the following spring ("King Kong"). Members of the BBC Symphony Orchestra accompany the Mothers on some of Frank Zappa's early orchestral efforts. This is a recording from a key point in the Mothers' history. *—William Ruhlmann*

The Yellow Shark / Nov. 2, 1993 / Rykodisc ✦✦✦✦
Released only a month before Frank Zappa's death, *The Yellow Shark* is an album of orchestral treatments of Zappa's compositions done by the 25-piece Ensemble Modern orchestra, conducted by Peter Rundel. It features vintage material like "Dog Breath Variations" as well as more recent work, played with more sensitivity and verve than previous orchestras have brought to Zappa's music. Hence, this is a great choice for fans who want to hear the orchestral Zappa—this is the best executed and most varied of the albums Zappa devoted to his "serious" music. *—William Ruhlmann*

Strictly Commercial: The Best of Frank Zappa / Aug. 22, 1995 / Rykodisc ✦✦✦✦✦
For all of his many attributes, one thing Frank Zappa most certainly was not is commercial. Presumably, the title of this collection is ironic. *Strictly Commercial: The Best of Frank Zappa* is a compilation not of the composer's hits—he only broke the Top 40 on one occasion, with "Valley Girl"—but rather, a collection of his best-known material, from "Don't Eat the Yellow Snow" to "Sexual Harassment in the Workplace." Zappa's albums often function as individual works, but the disc offers an intelligent selection of songs, serving as an introduction to the maverick musician. *—Stephen Thomas Erlewine*

Lost Episodes / Feb. 27, 1996 / Rykodisc ✦✦✦✦
A 30-track compilation of rarities, spanning much of his career, but in the main confined to the 1960s and early '70s (some date from as early as the late '50s!). Much of it's previously unreleased, or extremely hard to locate. It's not just a collection of fan-oriented odds and ends, though. The material, for one thing, is extremely diverse, ranging from collaborations with Captain Beefheart and primitive teenage garage recordings to comic dialog to progressive instrumentals and orchestral pieces. The pre-*Freak Out* stuff in particular is revelatory, in the sense that it finds Zappa's sophisticated compositional and arrangement skills in full bloom years before he made his proper debut. There's also good old rock & roll, in an early version of "Any Way the Wind Blows," and an early '60s take of "Fountain of Love" with explosive fuzz bass. The cuts range in duration from 11 seconds to 11 minutes, often connected by amusing bits of spoken patter or nifty instrumental links. The effect is somewhat like *Uncle Meat* or *Lumpy Gravy,* meaning that those who appreciate that period of Zappa's evolution will find an immediate affinity with this anthology. *—Richie Unterberger*

Läther / Sep. 24, 1996 / Rykodisc ✦✦✦
The full saga of *Läther* (pronounced leather) is tangled enough to give a migraine to all but committed Zappaphiles. Basically, what you need to know is that this project was originally conceived of as a four-record box set. When record company politics prevented its release in that format, much of the material was spread over the albums *Live in New York, Sleep Dirt, Studio Tan,* and *Orchestral Favorites.* This three-CD set presents the album as it was originally conceived, with the addition of four bonus tracks at the end. It mixes previously available material, alternate mixes, and edits, and previously unissued stuff, though only the most serious Zappa fans will have a good grip on exactly what has appeared where (the liner notes are surprisingly unexact in this regard). And the music? It's almost like a résumé of Zappa's bag of tricks: *Uncle Meat*-like experimentation, intricate jazz-rock, straight hard rock, orchestral composition, and comedy. Some of those comedy tracks became some of his most notorious routines, like "Punky's Whips" and "Titties 'n Beer," which amounted to avant-rock for drunk frat boys and pot smoking, underachieving junior high school students. The juvenile humor, ham-fisted parody of hard rock clichés, and the shaggy-dog opera of the 20-minute "The Adventures of Greggery Peccary" are outshone by the lengthy, more experimental instrumental passages. It's interesting, but exhausting to wade through all at once, and the avant-garde/composerly cuts are not as exceptional as his earlier work in this vein in the late '60s and early '70s. That means that this will appeal far more to the Zappa cultist than the general listener, though the Zappa cult—which has been craving *Läther* in its original format for years—is a pretty wide fan base in and of itself. *—Richie Unterberger*

Have I Offended Someone? / Apr. 8, 1997 / Rykodisc ✦✦✦✦
As the title suggests, *Have I Offended Someone?* contains all of Zappa's notoriously tasteless parodies and satires, from "Bobby Brown Goes Down," "Catholic Girls" and "Jewish Princess" to "He's So Gay," "Titties N' Beer," and "Dinah-Moe Humm." Nearly all of the tracks are presented in new remixed versions, and two songs, "Dumb All Over" and "Tinsel-Town Rebellion," have never been released before. Tinkering with the sound of the songs doesn't change their impact at all—this is the material that made Zappa into an adolescent favorite during the late '70s and early '80s and, in a sense, that makes *Have I Offended Someone?* a best-of collection, even though only "Valley Girl" was a hit. In other words, for some Zappa fans, this collection is everything they loved about him, and for most of his detractors, it's everything they always hated about him. *—Stephen Thomas Erlewine*

Strictly Genteel: A Classical Introduction to Frank Zappa / May 20, 1997 / Rykodisc ✦✦✦✦
A more than adequate introduction to the world of Frank Zappa's instrumental music. A great deal of attention was focused on Zappa's often infantile lyrics, sometimes to the extent that the quality of Zappa's music was ignored. From a performance standpoint, the music was often a challenge (becoming almost impossible once Zappa was composing for the Synclavier); from a compositional standpoint, Zappa's instrumental music shows its 20th century influences in no uncertain terms. *Strictly Genteel* serves up music performed by orchestral ensembles as well as pieces performed on Synclavier and in a band context, with the common thread being Zappa's overall brilliance—while sometimes an imperfect composer, his drive and talent resulted in a huge body of excellent work that may one day come to be appreciated by classicists. *—Steven McDonald*

Cucamonga / 1998 / Del-Fi ✦✦✦✦
Before forming the Mothers of Invention, Zappa made numerous recordings at small studios. Several tracks that he had a hand in, as producer, instrumentalist, or writer, were issued on extremely rare singles in the early and mid-1960s. This collects 14 such numbers that found their way to the L.A. Del-Fi label, including items by Paul Buff, the Rotations, the Pauls, Mr. Clean, the Heartbreakers, and Baby Ray & the Ferns, the last of which featured future Mother Ray Collins on vocals. It's largely eccentric—but not *that* eccentric—doo wop and R&B with a humorous/novelty bent, though there's also a surf single by the Rotations. You can hear the seeds of the production techniques of the Mothers albums occasionally, particularly on Bob Guy's weird horror-rock ditties, "Dear Jeepers" and "Letter From Jeepers"; a snippet of the Rotations' "Heavies" even showed up on the Mothers' *We're Only in It for the Money.* Yet this stuff wasn't outrageously funny enough to be novelty hits, or original or hooky enough to be straight pop or R&B successes. Put another way, in hindsight they show elements of Zappa's later work, but at the time no one could have guessed that he would develop into a major force in experimental rock. About half of this has shown up on reissues before, but the rest can't be found elsewhere on CD, so it's useful to Zappa collectors. It does not, however, collect all of his pre-Mothers releases, notable omissions being the Penguins' "Memories of El Monte" (which he co-wrote with Ray Collins) and

"Drums A-Go-Go," the go-go-rock-in-a-harem instrumental by the Hollywood Persuaders. *—Richie Unterberger*

Warren Zevon

b. Jan. 24, 1947, Chicago, IL

Vocals, Keyboards, Piano, Guitar, Bass / Album Rock, Hard Rock, Singer/Songwriter

One of the most acute and savagely satiric songwriters of his era, as a youth Warren Zevon focused primarily on classical material, even studying under the tutelage of Igor Stravinsky. However, a disintegrating home life led him into pop music, as well as a few run-ins with the law, and at 16 he hopped into the Corvette his father won in a card game and headed for New York to become a folksinger. His music found little response, however, and he returned to California, eventually releasing his first recordings as part of the duo Lyme and Cybelle. Session work followed before Zevon issued his solo debut *Wanted—Dead or Alive* in 1969; the LP received a poor reception, and so he returned to session gigs and composing advertising jingles. With longtime friend Jackson Browne in the producer's seat, Zevon returned with a self-titled offering which was met with lavish critical praise upon its 1976 release. His 1978 follow-up *Excitable Boy* established him as a wholly unique talent, and earned a sizable hit with its wry single "Werewolves of London." However, Zevon had fallen prey to alcoholism, and his personal demons sidelined him for the next two years; the promise of his early work was finally restored on 1982's brilliant *The Envoy*. The album fared miserably on the charts, however, and Zevon again fell off the wagon. A long period of therapy and counseling followed before, newly sober and revitalized, he issued *Sentimental Hygiene* in 1987. *—Jason Ankeny*

Wanted Dead or Alive / 1969 / One Way ✦✦✦

The first Zevon album certainly sounds like it. Containing some of the fire that was to shine on releases to come, *Wanted Dead or Alive* shows Zevon as a bluesy singer-songwriter trying to find a voice in the L.A. scene. Of note is his version of "Iko-Iko," done dancehall style, and his own "Hitch-Hikin' Woman." Of note for the curious. *—James Chrispell*

Warren Zevon / 1976 / Asylum ✦✦✦✦✦

Warren Zevon was a ten-year music industry veteran who had written songs for the Turtles, backed up Phil Everly, done years of session work, and been befriended by Jackson Browne by the time he cut his self-titled album in 1976 (which wasn't his debut, though the less said about 1969's misbegotten *Wanted Dead or Alive* the better). Even though Warren Zevon was on good terms with L.A.'s Mellow Mafia, he sure didn't think (or write) like any of his pals in the Eagles or Fleetwood Mac; Zevon's music was full of blood, bile, and mean-spirited irony, and the glossy surfaces of Jackson Browne's production failed to disguise the bitter heart of the songs on *Warren Zevon*. The album opened with a jaunty celebration of a pair of Old West thieves and gunfighters ("Frank and Jesse James"), and went on to tell remarkable, slightly unnerving tales of ambitious pimps ("The French Inhaler"), lonesome junkies ("Carmelita"), wired, hard-living lunatics ("I'll Sleep When I'm Dead"), and truly dastardly womanizers ("Poor Poor Pitiful Me"), and even Zevon's celebrations of life in Los Angeles, long a staple of the soft rock genre, had both a menace and an epic sweep his contemporaries could never match ("Join Me in L.A." and "Desperados Under the Eaves"). But for all their darkness, Zevon's songs also possessed a steely intelligence, a winning wit, and an unusually sophisticated melodic sense, and he certainly made the most of the high-priced help who backed him on the album. *Warren Zevon* may not have been the songwriter's debut, but it was the album that confirmed he was a major talent, and it remains a black-hearted pop delight. *—Mark Deming*

Excitable Boy / 1978 / Asylum ✦✦✦✦

Warren Zevon's self-titled 1976 album announced he was one of the most striking talents to emerge from the Los Angeles soft rock singer/songwriter community, and Linda Ronstadt (a shrewd judge of talent if a sometimes questionable interpreter) recorded three of its songs on two of her biggest selling albums, which doubtlessly earned Zevon bigger royalty checks than the album itself ever did. But if *Warren Zevon* was an impressive calling card, the follow-up, *Excitable Boy*, was an actual hit, scoring one major hit single, "Werewolves of London," and a trio of turntable hits ("Roland the Headless Thompson Gunner," "Lawyers, Guns and Money," and the title track). But while *Excitable Boy* won Zevon the larger audience his music certainly deserved, the truth is it was a markedly inferior album; while it had all the bile of *Warren Zevon*, and significantly raised Zevon's dark-humor factor, it was often obvious where his previous album had been subtle, and while all 11 tracks on *Warren Zevon* were strong and compelling, two of the nine tunes on *Excitable Boy*—"Johnny Strike Up the Band" and "Nighttime in the Switching Yard"—sound like they're just taking up space. Musically, most of *Excitable Boy* is stuck in a polished but unexceptional FM pop groove, and only "Veracruz" hints at the artful intelligence of *Warren Zevon*'s finest moments. It's hard to say if Zevon was feeling uninspired or just dumbing himself down when he made *Excitable Boy*, but while it made him famous, it lacks the smarts and substance of his best work. *—Mark Deming*

Bad Luck Streak in Dancing School / 1980 / Elektra ✦✦✦✦✦

Excitable Boy earned Warren Zevon a hit single ("Werewolves of London") and the mainstream success he richly deserved, but his new fame came with a price; the hard-living Zevon did not react well to the temptations that come with rock stardom, and in the wake of *Excitable Boy* he had developed a severe drinking problem. *Bad Luck Streak in Dancing School* was cut as Zevon was working hard to stay clean and sober and put his career back on track, and it projects an ambition and strength of focus that was decidedly absent from *Excitable Boy*. The album's rockers hit harder and cut deeper than any of his previous work, especially the twisted Southern gothic of "Play It All Night Long" and the mercenary's anthem "Jungle Work," while "Bed of Coals" and "Wild Age" found Zevon bravely addressing his own failings and expressing his need for a greater maturity in his life. While the album was still short on subtlety compared to 1976's *Warren Zevon*, "Empty Handed Heart" proved Zevon could still write a straightforward song about love (not a happy one, but no one expected that from him anyway), and the two interludes for orchestra gave credence to Zevon's claims that he planned to write a symphony some day (and that it might even be worth hearing). And if "Gorilla You're a Desperado" was a throwaway, it was a better waste of time than "Midnight at the Switching Yard" on *Excitable Boy*. While *Bad Luck Streak in Dancing School* didn't quite return Zevon to the top of his game, it made clear that the quality of *Warren Zevon* was no fluke, and is a stronger effort than *Excitable Boy* in nearly every respect. *—Mark Deming*

Stand in the Fire / 1981 / Asylum ✦✦✦

After the release of Warren Zevon's fourth album, *Bad Luck Streak in Dancing School*, he was clean and sober for the first time in years, and on stage he was determined to make the most of his newfound strength and self-control. While his songs long had a dark and frantic undercurrent, Zevon was now capable of playing a no-holds-barred rock show where he could bring the sharper edges of his music to the forefront. *Stand in the Fire*, recorded during a five-night stand at L.A.'s Roxy near the end of the tour, captures Zevon and his band at their peak. The musicians (anchored by flashy lead guitarist David Landau) pour out these tunes with plenty of fire, and the songs rock a lot harder than anything Zevon had summoned in the studio at that point. And the artist proved he was a superb rock & roll frontman on this tour, singing with mean-spirited glee (for a change, "Werewolves of London" and "I'll Sleep When I'm Dead" sound just as menacing as they were meant to be) and spewing hilarious bile at every turn (his ad-libbed "the Ayatollah has his problems, too" on "Mohammed's Radio" alone is worth the price of admission). The set list is dominated by Zevon's better-known tunes of the period, though there are two otherwise unrecorded originals (the OK title cut and the blazing "The Sin"), and a rave-up encore on "Bo Diddley's a Gunslinger" that revels in the joyous surrealism of the lyrics. No one argues that Zevon is a gifted singer and songwriter, but *Stand in the Fire* proves that, when he wants to, he can also rock with the best of 'em. *—Mark Deming*

The Envoy / 1982 / Asylum ✦✦✦

On *The Envoy*, Warren Zevon's reflective side came to the forefront, as he created a set of songs that were more carefully-crafted and subtle than his previous work, particularly the wistful "Looking for the Next Best Thing," but also had time for grinding rockers like "Ain't That Pretty at All." *—Stephen Thomas Erlewine*

A Quiet Normal Life: The Best of Warren Zevon / 1986 / Asylum ✦✦✦✦✦

Warren Zevon's body of work is a good bit more diverse and intelligent than you might imagine if you only know his music from the radio; while his relative hits ("Werewolves of London," "Excitable Boy," "Lawyers, Guns and Money") play more like novelty songs than anything else, his best albums display a melodic sophistication that never gets in the way of his desire to rock out, and a lyrical perspective that's unusually literate, witty, and brutally cynical. As one might expect, *A Quiet Normal Life: The Best of Warren Zevon* focuses on the artist's best known stuff from his tenure at Asylum Records, and leans more towards "Crazy Warren" tunes (like the above-mentioned trio) over superior if more difficult material like "The French Inhaler" or "Frank and Jesse James," with no rare or unreleased material for completists. It doesn't even honor the hits as well as one might hope (the remastering is a bit on the flat side, and "Lawyers, Guns and Money" appears in a radio edit that deletes the final verse), and there isn't a single song from *Stand in the Fire*, Zevon's superb live album. But you do get the most famous songs, which are invariably worth hearing (his own hits and a couple tunes that were made famous by Linda Ronstadt, though "Hasten Down the Wind" is curiously absent), along with a few pleasant surprises, including the incendiary "Play It All Night Long" and one of Zevon's finest meditations on life in L.A., "Desperados Under the Eaves." *A Quiet Normal Life: The Best of Warren Zevon* will satisfy those with a casual interest in the artist, but for a better one-stop introduction to this songwriter's body of work, try *I'll Sleep When I'm Dead (An Anthology)*. *—Mark Deming*

Sentimental Hygiene / 1987 / Virgin ✦✦✦✦✦

After a rather well-publicized fall off the wagon following the release of *The Envoy*, Warren Zevon went five years without releasing an album, but his time in the woodshed seemed to have done him good, as *Sentimental Hygiene* was his strongest album since *Warren Zevon* in 1976. While a few members of the L.A. Mellow Mafia (David Lindley, Waddy Wachtel, Don Henley) made cameo appearances on the album, for most of the sessions Zevon worked with Peter Buck, Mike Mills, and Bill Berry of R.E.M., who were about a year away from their mainstream commercial breakthrough; they made for a solid, no-nonsense rhythm section, and gave the music a passionate, forceful backbone that was largely absent from *The Envoy* (not to mention rocking harder than one might expect from the kings of jangle pop). Zevon put his newly muscular sound to good use; the songs on *Sentimental Hygiene* are Warren Zevon at his flintiest, as he indulges in his usual obsessions with machismo ("Boom Boom Mancini") and bad love (the title cut) while also exploring the media's skewed perspective on his addiction problems ("Detox Mansion," "Trouble Waiting to Happen"), his disgust with the music business ("Even a Dog Can Shake Hands"), and errors in both personal and political judgement ("Bad Karma," "Leave My Monkey Alone"). And Zevon scored three inspired musical guest shots on the album—Neil Young, whose jagged guitar runs embroider the title cut; Bob Dylan, whose howling harmonica is the ideal punctuation for the Springsteen-gone-psychotic "The Factory"; and George Clinton, who adds a bed of menacing funk to "Leave My Monkey Alone." *Sentimental Hygiene* proved that Warren Zevon was still an artist to be reckoned with, and that which didn't kill him had only made him stronger (and more bitterly funny). *—Mark Deming*

Transverse City / Oct. 1989 / Virgin ✦✦✦✦
Warren Zevon, the "Excitable Boy," followed his comeback *Sentimental Hygiene* with 1989's *Transverse City*, an album that was another creative success but met with the same commercial yawn as its predecessor. It was unfortunate because *Transverse City* is glorious documentation of social, and personal, decay, delivered with the acerbic wit that Zevon had made his reputation with. Many of Zevon's usual musical crew are aboard like guitarists Waddy Wachtel and David Lindley, but Zevon also makes good use of cameos by everyone from Chick Corea and Neil Young to Jerry Garcia and David Gilmour. "Run Straight Down" sets the tone early on, with its moody lyrics detailing urban collapse, and the jangly upbeat "Splendid Isolation" finds the protagonist surrendering to the chaos of it all. Zevon also addresses gridlock, consumerism, and even finds room for the bittersweet ballad "Nobody's in Love This Year." Sometimes the lyrics are stretched a bit thin ("Long Arm of the Law"), but the level of musicianship is impressive and *Transverse City* is another strong entry in Zevon's catalog. *—Tom Demalon*

Mr. Bad Example / Oct. 15, 1991 / Giant ✦✦

Learning to Flinch / Apr. 13, 1993 / Giant ✦✦✦
Warren Zevon recorded the acoustic *Learning to Flinch* at various venues all over the world. All of his best-known songs are here, in riveting, rough acoustic forms. Longtime Zevon fans will find this essential, and it may win him a few new ones too. *—Stephen Thomas Erlewine*

Mutineer / May 23, 1995 / Giant ✦✦

● **I'll Sleep When I'm Dead (An Anthology)** / Sep. 17, 1996 / Rhino ✦✦✦✦✦
I'll Sleep When I'm Dead (An Anthology) covers the bulk of Warren Zevon's career, conviently skipping over his long-forgotten first album and concentrating heavily on his Asylum records, as well as his albums for Virgin and Giant. Over the course of the double-disc set's 44 songs, nearly every one of Zevon's greatest songs is featured, including six songs each from *Warren Zevon* and *Excitable Boy*, as well as a number of songs only featured on soundtrack albums, a handful of outtakes, and Hindu Love Gods' cover of Prince's "Raspberry Beret." The quality of Zevon's music declines somewhat as his career progresses, but the compilation captures most of the highlights from his latter-day records. For casual fans that want to dig deeper than *Warren Zevon* or *Excitable Boy, I'll Sleep When I'm Dead (An Anthology)* is an ideal purchase. *—Stephen Thomas Erlewine*

Life'll Kill Ya / Jan. 25, 2000 / Artemis ✦✦✦
Life hasn't killed Warren Zevon yet. Witty hits like "Werewolves of London" and "Excitable Boy" made Zevon the clown prince of the hard-living L.A. music set in the late '70s. More than 20 years later, he's cleaned up his living a lot, but only toned down his lyrics a bit. The title track and "My Shit's Fucked Up" showcase Zevon's ironic pessimism. It's uncertain exactly what "Porcelain Monkey" is about, but this much is certain: once it gets inside your head, good luck trying to get it out. Zevon also does well with others' songs. A wonderfully understated "Back in the High Life Again" eclipses Steve Winwood's original. "For My Next Trick I'll Need a Volunteer" is great, too, but Zevon ought to be paying Bruce Springsteen residuals for copping "The Promised Land." *—Mark Morgenstein*

The Zombies

f. 1962, St. Albans, Herts, England, **db.** 1967
British Psychedelia, Psychedelic Pop, Psychedelic, British Invasion, Pop
Aside from the Beatles and perhaps the Beach Boys, no mid-'60s rock group wrote melodies as gorgeous as those of the Zombies. Dominated by Colin Blunstone's breathy vocals, choral backup harmonies, and Rod Argent's shining jazz- and classical-influenced organ and piano, the band sounded utterly unique for their era. Indeed, their material—penned by either Argent or guitarist Chris White, with unexpected shifts from major to minor keys—was perhaps too adventurous for the singles market. To this day, they're known primarily for their three big hit singles, "She's Not There" (1964), "Tell Her No" (1965), and "Time of the Season" (1969). Most listeners remain unaware that the group maintained a remarkably high quality of work for several years. Argent's composition "She's Not There" got them a deal with Decca, and the song ended up being their debut release. It was a remarkably confident and original first-time effort, with a great minor melody and the organ, harmonies, and urgent, almost neurotic vocals that would typify much of their work. The tragedy was that throughout 1965 and 1966, the Zombies released a string of equally fine, intricately arranged singles that flopped commercially, at a time in which chart success on 45s was a lot more important to sustain a band's livelihood than it would be a few years down the road. *Odessey and Oracle* was their only cohesive full-length platter (the first album was largely pasted together from singles and covers). A near-masterpiece of pop/psychedelia, it showed the Zombies reaching new levels of sophistication in composition and performance, finally branching out beyond strictly romantic themes into more varied lyrical territory. The album passed virtually unnoticed in Britain, and was only released in the States after some lobbying from Al Kooper. By this time it was 1968, and the group had split for good. *—Richie Unterberger*

The Zombies (Featuring She's Not There and Tell Her No) / Dec. 1964 / Parrot ✦✦✦
The Zombies' first American LP was a rushed, somewhat schizophrenic affair, mixing first-rate originals ("It's Alright," "Sometimes," and the two big hits) with sloppy, ill-suited R&B covers. There's some very good stuff here, but you're much better advised to pick it up on a number of CD reissue compilations than track down the pricy original vinyl. *—Richie Unterberger*

Begin Here / Apr. 1965 / Decca ✦✦✦
The group's British debut LP repeated a lot of the same tracks from the American version, but as was the habit in those days, deleted some cuts and substituted some others. Unlike the U.S. record, it was reissued, and thus became much easier to find. But as with the American version, you can find all of the tracks on other CD compilations, and almost all of the important ones on the anthologies that concentrate only on their best material. The 1999 CD reissue on Big Beat expands the track lineup substantially with the addition of three songs from their 1965 U.K. EP *The Zombies* and, more interestingly, alternate takes of "Sticks and Stones" and "It's Alright With Me," as well as demos of "I Know She Will" and "I'll Keep Trying." The demos of these last two tunes are notable in that they don't have the overdubs on the versions available on other albums. *—Richie Unterberger*

☆ **Odessey & Oracle** / 1968 / Rhino ✦✦✦✦✦
Odessey & Oracle was one of the flukiest (and best) albums of the 1960s, and one of the most enduring long-players to come out of the entire British psychedelic boom, mixing trippy melodies, ornate choruses, and lush Mellotron sounds with a solid hard rock base. Ironically, at the time of its recording in the summer of 1967, permanency was not much on the minds of the band members. *Odessey & Oracle* was intended as a final statement, a bold last hurrah, having worked hard for three years only to see the quality of their gigs decline as the hits stopped coming. The results are consistently pleasing, surprising, and challenging: "Hung Up on a Dream" and "Changes" are some of the most powerful psychedelic pop/rock ever heard out of England, with a solid rhythm section, a hot Mellotron sound, and chiming, hard guitar, as well as highly melodic piano; "Changes" also benefits from radiant singing. "This Will Be Our Year" makes use of trumpets (one of the very few instances of real overdubbing) in a manner reminiscent of "Penny Lane"; and then there's "Time of the Season," the most well-known song in their output and a white soul classic. Not all of the album is that inspired, but it's all consistently interesting and very good listening, and superior to most other psychedelic albums this side of the Beatles' best and Pink Floyd's early work. Indeed, the only complaint one might have about the original LP is its relatively short running time, barely over 30 minutes, but even that's refreshing in an era where most musicians took their (and our) time making their point, and most of the CD reissues have bonus tracks to fill out the space available. *—Bruce Eder*

Early Days / 1969 / London ✦✦✦
Mish-mash of mid-'60s tracks, including "She's Not There," "Tell Her No," and several fine cuts that had not been available on U.S. LPs before. Every song but one ("Kinda Girl") is on *Singles A's & B's*, making this compilation largely obsolete. *—Richie Unterberger*

Time of the Zombies / 1973 / Epic ✦✦✦
This double LP, containing the entire *Odessey and Oracle* and another disc of hits and outtakes, is not recommended as an overall sampler; there are other compilations that do a much better job. Zombie collectors, though, will be interested in finding this; side two contains eight songs that have rarely been available anywhere else, comprised mostly of late-'60s outtakes and a rare single, some of which may have been recorded in the post-Zombies, pre-Argent days without Blunstone. This material doesn't rank among their best (though Dusty Springfield did cover "If It Don't Work Out" in the mid-'60s), but the piano-dominated "I'll Call You Mine" would have been easily strong enough to fit into *Odessey and Oracle*. *—Richie Unterberger*

Rock Roots / 1976 / Decca ✦✦✦
16 tracks from 1964-67, including their most popular singles and a couple of LP tracks. It's good material, but it's now available on better, more extensive compilations. *—Richie Unterberger*

Live on the BBC / 1985 / Rhino ✦✦✦
While this compilation of 14 BBC airshots has barely different versions of their self-penned singles "Tell Her No," "Just Out of Reach," and "Whenever You're Ready," it concentrates on their covers of a surprisingly wide array of soul and R&B standards that the group never released on record. Unlike, say, the Stones, the Zombies were much more noted for their compositional prowess than their original interpretations of American rock and soul; the group's tasteful, melodic restraint could make them sound twee and out of their depth when they tackled chestnuts like "I've Got My Mojo Working" on their first LP. But the covers here, emphasizing the band's harmonies and Rod Argent's keyboards, are reasonably well done. Includes songs originally performed by the Isley Brothers, Aretha Franklin, Gene Vincent, the Supremes, Curtis Mayfield, and others, some of them quite obscure even in their original incarnations. Excellent sound rounds off an album that gives some unexpected insight into the Zombies' influences. *—Richie Unterberger*

The Best & the Rest of the Zombies / 1986 / Back-Trac ✦✦✦
This half-baked compilation, with only eight songs, is noteworthy only in that it includes three previously unreleased songs, two of which were actually recorded by Rod Argent and Chris White in the late '60s without Colin Blunstone. One of those, "Girl Help Me," is a really fine ballad, and the mid-'60s outtake "I'll Keep Trying" is a decent, characteristic uptempo number. *—Richie Unterberger*

★ **The Singles A's & B's** / 1990 / See For Miles ✦✦✦✦✦
While "She's Not There" and "Tell Her No" are the only well-remembered mid-'60s Zombies singles, they recorded quite a few great non-hit 45s as well during this period. This outstanding collection (now available on CD) features all 22 of the sides they released on singles between 1964-67, and shows the group to be among the most superbly inventive pop-rock composers of their era, exploring moody minor-key melodies more than anyone before or since. Colin Blunstone's delicate, neurotic vocals and Rod Argent's biting electric keyboards pace the band on this set, which features the two big hits and such great lost classics as "Remember When I Loved Her," "I Want You Back Again," "I Must Move," "Indication," and "Gotta Get a Hold of Myself." Essential British Invasion music. *—Richie Unterberger*

Zombie Heaven / Nov. 18, 1997 / Big Beat ✦✦✦✦✦
After years of being under-recognized as the true geniuses that they were, the Zombies finally started getting their due in the 1990s. Artists such as Eric Matthews, Jason Faulkner, and others have been profoundly influenced by the group. Lovingly compiled by longtime fan and journalist Alec Palao, this four-CD set offers everything that this fine group ever cut, with numerous outtakes, live versions, and alternate mixes. The sound alone is awesome, especially on the *Odessey and Oracle* album and the outtakes that came from it. The early material such as "I Remember You," "Tell Her No," and "She's Not There" sparkle as well. Add to that that this is essentially a template for *any* box set, and you have one of the finest rock or pop releases of the 1990s. *—Matthew Greenwald*

● **Absolutely the Best** / Jul. 13, 1999 / Varese ✦✦✦✦✦
At the time of its release, *Absolutely the Best* was, indeed, absolutely the best single-disc Zombies collection available in the U.S. Of course the big hits "She's Not There," "Tell Her No," and "Time of the Season" were included, along with the group's minor U.S. chart entries "She's Coming Home," "I Want You Back Again," "Just out of Reach," and "Imagine the Swan," and some good album tracks. With 16 cuts in just over 40 minutes, this is not a comprehensive compilation, but for most fans who know only the three big hits and would welcome some similar sounding material, it's plenty. *—William Ruhlmann*

The Singles Collection: A's & B's, 1964-1969 / Mar. 14, 2000 / Big Beat ✦✦✦✦✦
This presents, in chronological sequence, both sides of all 14 of the Zombies' British singles. The Zombies were one of the most consistent British '60s bands, so it's no surprise that this is a great compilation, containing nothing mediocre and little that's even average. In addition to the three well-known hits "She's Not There," "Tell Her No," and "Time of the Season" (all present), there's an abundance of gems from B-sides and flop singles: "I Must Move," "Indication," "She's Coming Home," "Gotta Get a Hold of Myself," and "Beechwood Park" are just the very best of those. However, the absence of the great U.S.-only 1965 single "I Want You Back Again"/"I Remember When I Loved Her" and, to a lesser degree, some standout LP-only tracks (particularly "Changes" from *Odessey & Oracle*) prevents this from being the definitive single-disc best-of. Collectors should note that all tracks are presented in their mono versions, as they were originally issued. The differences between these and other versions in circulation are usually minor, but occasionally noticeable, as in the strange guitar reverb on "I Must Move" and the more prominent organ lines in "Time of the Season," although in the latter case the mono mix is actually inferior to the more familiar one. There are no liner notes, but the insert contains lots of press clippings and reprints of original press reviews of the singles, if you're looking for another reason to buy tracks that you might already have. *—Richie Unterberger*

ZZ Top

f. 1970, Houston, TX
Album Rock, Boogie Rock, Arena Rock, Southern Rock, Hard Rock, Blues-Rock
A sturdy American blues-rock trio from Texas, ZZ Top consists of Billy Gibbons (guitar), Dusty Hill (bass), and Frank Beard (drums). Their first two albums reflected the strong blues roots and Texas humor of the band. Their third album (*Tres Hombres*) gained them national attention with the hit "La Grange," a signature riff tune to this day, based on John Lee Hooker's "Boogie Chillen." Their success continued unabated throughout the '70s, culminating with the year-and-a-half-long Worldwide Texas Tour. Exhausted from the overwhelming work load, they took a three-year break, then switched labels and returned to form with *Deguello* and *El Loco*, both harbingers of what was to come. By their next album, *Eliminator*, and its worldwide smash follow-up, *Afterburner*, they had successfully harnessed the potential of synthesizers to their patented grungy blues-groove, giving their material a more contemporary edge while retaining their patented Texas style. As genuine roots musicians, they have few peers; Gibbons is one of America's finest blues guitarists working in the arena rock idiom—both influenced by the originators of the form and British blues-rock guitarists like Peter Green—while Hill and Beard provide the ultimate rhythm section support. ZZ Top's music is always instantly recognizable, eminently powerful, profoundly soulful, and 100 percent American in derivation. *—Cub Koda*

ZZ Top's First Album / 1970 / Warner Brothers ✦✦✦
ZZ Top's First Album may not be perfectly polished, but it does establish their sound, attitude, and quirks. Simply put, it's a dirty little blues-rock record, filled with fuzzy guitars, barrelhouse rhythms, dirty jokes, and Texan slang. They have a good, ballsy sound that hits at gut level, and if the record's not entirely satisfying, it's because they're still learning how to craft records—which means that they're still learning pacing as much as they're learning how to assemble a set of indelible material. Too much of this record glides by on its sound, without offering any true substance, but the tracks that really work—"(Somebody Else Been) Shaking Your Tree," "Backdoor Love Affair," "Brown Sugar," and "Goin' Down to Mexico," among them—show that ZZ Top was that lil' ol' blues band from Texas from their very first record on. *—Stephen Thomas Erlewine*

Rio Grande Mud / 1972 / Warner Brothers ✦✦✦
With their second album, *Rio Grande Mud*, ZZ Top uses the sound they sketched out on their debut as a blueprint, yet tweak it in slight but important ways. The first is heavier, more powerful sound, turning the boogie guitars into a locomotive force. There are slight production flares that date this as a 1972 record, but for the most part, this is a straight-ahead, dirty blues-rock difference. Essentially like the first album, then. That's where the second difference comes in—they have a much better set of songs this time around, highlighted by the swaggering shuffle "Just Got Paid," the pile-driving boogie "Bar-B-Q," the slide guitar workout "Apologies to Pearly," and two Dusty Hill-sung numbers, "Francine" and "Chevrolet." There are still a couple of tracks that don't quite gel and their fuzz-blues still can sound a little one-dimensional at times, but *Rio Grande Mud* is the first flowering of ZZ Top as a great, down-n-dirty blooze rock band. *—Stephen Thomas Erlewine*

Tres Hombres / 1973 / Warner Brothers ✦✦✦✦✦
Tres Hombres is the record that brought ZZ Top their first Top Ten record, making them stars in the process. It couldn't have happened to a better record. ZZ Top finally got their low-down, cheerfully sleazy blooze-n-boogie right on this, their third album. As their sound gelled, producer Bill Ham discovered how to record the trio so simply that they sound indestructible, and the group brought the best set of songs they'd ever have to the table. On the surface, there's nothing really special about the record, since it is just a driving blues-rock album from a Texas bar band, but that's what's special about it. It has a filthy groove and an infectious feel, thanks to Billy Gibbons' growling guitars and the steady propulsion of Dusty Hill and Frank Beard's rhythm section. They get the blend of bluesy shuffles, gut-bucket rocking, and off-beat humor just right. ZZ Top's very identity comes from this earthy sound and songs as utterly infectious as "Waitin' for the Bus," "Jesus Just Left Chicago," "Move Me on Down the Line," and the John Lee Hooker boogie "La Grange." In a sense, they kept trying to remake this record from this point on—what is *Eliminator* if not *Tres Hombres* with sequencers and synthesizers?—but they never got it better than they did here. *—Stephen Thomas Erlewine*

Fandango / 1975 / Warner Brothers ✦✦✦
Blessed with their first full-fledged hit album, ZZ Top followed it up with *Fandango*, a record split between a side of live tracks and a side of new studio cuts. In a way, this might have made sense, since they were a kick-ass live band, and they do sound good here, but it's hard not to see this as a bit of a wasted opportunity in retrospect. Why? Because the studio side is a worthy successor to the all-fine *Tres Hombres*, driven by "Tush" and "Heard it on the X," two of their greatest songs that build on that album by consolidating their sound and amplifying their humor. If they had sustained this energy and quality throughout a full studio album, it would have been their greatest, but instead the mood is broken by the live cuts. Now, these are really good live cuts—and "Backdoor Medley" and "Jailhouse Rock" were fine interpretations, making familiar songs sound utterly comfortable in their signature sound—and *Fandango* remains one of their better albums, but it's hard not to think that it could have been even better. *—Stephen Thomas Erlewine*

Tejas / 1976 / Warner Brothers ✦✦

● **The Best of ZZ Top** / 1977 / Warner Brothers ✦✦✦✦✦
ZZ Top closed out their tenure with London records in late 1977 with *The Best of ZZ Top*, a basic but terrific ten-song retrospective of highlights from their first five albums (well, four, actually, since the underwhelming *Tejas* is ignored). There are no surprises here, just album rock favorites, which means it does draw heavily on *Tres Hombres* (four songs, total), adds *Fandango*'s "Tush," "Blue Jean Blues," and "Heard it on the X" for good measure, then rounds it out with two songs from *Rio Grande Mud* and a selection from the debut. Yeah, there are a couple good album tracks missing, but as a ten-song summary of their early years, this can't be beat. *—Stephen Thomas Erlewine*

Deguello / 1979 / Warner Brothers ✦✦✦✦✦
ZZ Top returned after an extended layoff in late 1979 with *Deguello*, their best album since 1973's *Tres Hombres*. During their time off, ZZ Top didn't change much—hell, their sound never really changed during their entire career—but it did harden, in a way. The grooves became harder, sleeker, and their off-kilter sensibility and humor began to dominate, as "Cheap Sunglasses" and "Fool for Your Stockings" illustrate. Ironically, this, their wildest album lyrically, doesn't have the unhinged rawness of their early blooze rockers, but the streamlined production makes it feel sleazier all the same, since its slickness lets the perversity slide forth. And, let us not forget, the trio is in fine shape here, knocking out a great set of rockers and sounding stylish all the time. Undoubtedly one of their strong suits. *—Stephen Thomas Erlewine*

El Loco / 1981 / Warner Brothers ✦✦✦
El Loco follows through on the streamlined, jet-engine boogie-rock of *Deguello*, but kicking all the ingredients up a notch. That means that the grooves are getting a little slicker, while the jokes are getting a little sillier, a little raunchier. The double entendres on "Tube Snake Boogie" and "Pearl Necklace" are barely disguised, while much of the record plays as flat-out goofy party rock. Not necessarily a bad thing, but much of it is a little too obvious to be totally winning. Still, the most telling thing about *El Loco* may be the rhythm of "Pearl Necklace," its biggest single and best song, which clearly points the way to the new wave blues-rock of *Eliminator*. *—Stephen Thomas Erlewine*

Eliminator / 1983 / Warner Brothers ✦✦✦✦✦
ZZ Top had reached the top of the charts before, but that didn't make their sudden popularity in 1983 any more predictable. It wasn't that they were just popular—they were *hip*, for God's sake, since they were one of the only AOR favorites to figure out to harness the stylish, synthesized grooves of new wave, and then figure out how to sell it on MTV. Of course, it helped that they had songs that deserved to be hits. With "Gimme All Your Lovin," "Sharp Dressed Man," and "Legs," they had their greatest set of singles since the heady days of *Tres Hombres*, and the songs that surrounded them weren't bad either—they would have been singles on *El Loco*, as a matter of fact. The songs alone would have made *Eliminator* one of ZZ Top's three greatest albums, but their embrace of synths and sequencers made it a blockbuster hit, since it was the sound of the times. Years later, the sound of the times winds up sounding a bit stiff. It's still an excellent ZZ Top album, one of their best, yet it sounds like a mechanized ZZ Top thanks to the unflaggingly accurate grooves. Then again, that's part of the album's charm—this is new wave blues-rock, glossed up for the video, looking as good as the omnipresent convertible on the cover and sounding as irresistible as Reaganomics. Not the sort the old-school fans or blues-rock purists will love, but ZZ Top never sounded as much like a band of its time as they did here. *—Stephen Thomas Erlewine*

Afterburner / 1985 / Warner Brothers ✦✦✦

Well, if you just had your biggest hit ever, you'd probably try to replicate it, too. And if you were called visionary because you played your blues to a slightly sequenced beat, you'd probably be tempted to turn on the drum-machine and graft on synthesizers, too, since it'll all signal how futuristic you are. While you're at it, you might as well visualize how space age this all is by turning your signature car into a space shuttle. From this viewpoint, *Afterburner* makes perfect sense—ZZ Top are just giving the people *more* of what they want. Problem is, no matter how much you dress 'em up, they're still ZZ Top, they're still that li'l ol' blues band from Texas, and blues-rock just doesn't have a kick when it's synthesized, even if ZZ Top's grooves always bordered on robotic. So, *Afterburner*, their most synthetic album, will not please most ZZ Top fans, even if it did go platinum several times over. That's just a sign of the times, when even hard rock bands had to sound as slick as synth-pop, complete with clanging DX-7s and cavernous drums. As an artifact of that time, *Afterburner* is pretty good—never has a hard rock album sounded so artificial, nor has a blues-rock album sounded so devoid of blues. Apart from the chugging "Sleeping Bag," not even the singles sound like ZZ Top: the terrific post-new wave rocker "Stages" is the poppiest thing they ever cut, the ballad "Rough Boy" is far removed from slow blues, and the full-fledged synth-dance of "Velcro Fly" is a true mind-bender. Above all, *Afterburner* is merely an album of its time—the only record ZZ Top could have made in 1985, and it remains forever tied to that year. *—Stephen Thomas Erlewine*

Recycler / 1990 / Warner Brothers ✦✦

● **Greatest Hits** / Apr. 14, 1992 / Warner Brothers ✦✦✦✦✦

This isn't a perfect roundup of ZZ Top's superstar years of the '80s, but it comes pretty close. It dips back into the '70s for "Pearl Necklace" and "La Grange," with a couple of selections from the post-peak '90s, but this does offer the MTV-era basics: "Gimme All Your Lovin'," "Sharp Dressed Man," "Rough Boy," "Tush," "My Head's in Mississippi," "Doubleback," "Cheap Sunglasses," "Sleeping Bag." What slows this record down are some new cuts and album tracks that don't deserve to be here, along with a remix, not the original version, of "Legs." Still, that may just be quibbling for some listeners, since the basics are all here, making this a good complement to the '70s-focused *The Best of ZZ Top* (although it would be nice if a definitive disc, with all the hits, would appear on the market). *—Stephen Thomas Erlewine*

Antenna / Jan. 18, 1994 / RCA ✦✦✦

Like precious few bands from the '70s whose best work is mummified daily thanks to classic rock radio, ZZ Top just keeps rolling on into the next decade. There's much to love here, from the downright nasty stomp of "Fuzzbox Voodoo," the powerhouse slow blues of "Cover Your Rig," the bass-pumping looniness of "Girl in a T-Shirt," to the slow grind of "Breakaway." While Billy Gibbon's guitar tones on this album are highly reminiscent of *Tres Hombres* (an early high-water mark for the band), the high production sheen from their '80s albums remains intact. But Gibbons hasn't played with this much over-the-top abandon since their pre-beard 'n' babes days, and that's what separates this album from the three that came before it. *—Cub Koda*

One Foot in the Blues / Nov. 22, 1994 / Warner Brothers ✦✦

Rhythmeen / Sep. 17, 1996 / RCA ✦✦✦

XXX / Sep. 28, 1999 / RCA ✦✦

Various Artists

25 All-Time Greatest Bubblegum Hits: The Ultimate Bubblegum Collection / Jun. 27, 2000 / Varese ✦✦✦✦✦

25 All-Time Greatest Bubblegum Hits is subtitled "The Ultimate Collection," and it's hard to argue with that claim. It certainly qualifies as the most comprehensive collection on a single disc. The set is an overview of the entire bubblegum movement from the mid-'60s until its nominative demise in the early '70s. It includes most of the key tracks from the Kasenetz & Katz hit factory, such as "Indian Giver," "Yummy Yummy Yummy," and the sublime "Quick Joey Small." Flesh-and-blood TV idols such as the Monkees and Bobby Sherman are represented alongside their cartoon-and-costume counterparts: the Archies, Josie & the Pussycats, and the Banana Splits. Rounding out the collection are British classics of the genre such as "My Baby Loves Lovin'," "Smile a Little Smile for Me," and "Love Grows Where My Rosemary Goes." This set is a primer on the manufacture of teenybopper singles in the era of Top 40 radio. It's infectious fun from start to finish, and it may dawn on the listener that this music's influence reverberates to this very day. —*Mary Grady*

Ace Story, Vol. 1 / Ace ✦✦✦✦✦

With five separate volumes, *Ace Story* is the most comprehensive portrait of the seminal New Orleans R&B record label. Over the course of the series, each of the label's hits are featured, including "Sea Cruise," "Rockin' Pneumonia," "Pop Eye," among others, as well as many lesser-known gems. During the late '50s and early '60s, Ace's roster featured such R&B giants as Huey "Piano" Smith, Eddie Bo, Joe Tex, Lightnin' Hopkins, Charles Brown, Amos Milburn, and Earl King; each artist is featured on at least one disc of *Ace Story*, along with several acts that didn't have hits, but recorded some outstanding tracks. Start with the first volume, then proceed to the other discs; every one is filled with timeless R&B. —*Stephen Thomas Erlewine*

● **Acid Visions: Best of Texas Punk/Psychedelic, Vol. 1** / 1991 / Collectables ✦✦✦✦✦

One of the very best '60s garage compilations, a high compliment given the thousands of competitors, and the very best Texas '60s garage anthology. With the possible exception of California, Texas was home to more fine obscure garage records than any other state, and these 14 cuts are among the finest. Roy Head delivers a fine Johnny Winter tune, "Easy Lovin' Girl," and Winter himself sings a prime slice of folk-rock-acid-punk, "Birds Can't Row Boats" (this version, incidentally, is much better than the one found on the early Winter compilation of the same name). The other names are totally obscure, and some of the tracks weren't even released until the 1980s. But the Things and the Bad Roads come through with fine pop-punk numbers, and A-440's "Torture," Satori's "Time Machine," and the Pandas' "Walk" have been belatedly recognized as some of the best garage psychedelia ever, combining sharp melodic hooks and songwriting with out-and-out dementia. —*Richie Unterberger*

Ain't I'm a Dog: 25 More Rockabilly Rave-Ups / 2000 / Columbia/Legacy ✦✦✦✦

Like its simultaneously released companion volume *Whistle Bait!*, this rescues 25 obscure rockabilly tracks of the 1950s from the CBS vaults. Not that every name here is obscure: Carl Perkins, Marty Robbins, Link Wray, Rose Maddox, and Johnny Horton are pretty well known, while the Collins Kids, Ronnie Self, and Ronnie Dawson (heard here under the pseudonym Commonwealth Jones) have pretty sizable cult followings. When you get down to a previously unreleased 1956 tune by one Werly Fairburn, though, you're getting as arcane as any white-label European rockabilly bootleg comp. At any rate, this isn't quite as impressive as *Whistle Bait!*, but it has a similar mix of good crazed out-and-out rockabilly and country hillbillies trying to adapt, more or less, to the rockabilly sound. High points are Joe Maphis and Larry Collins' sizzling instrumental duet "Hurricane," Johnny Horton's two contributions (from the overlooked period when he was a nearly rockabilly honky tonker), Link Wray's typically overdriven instro "New Studio Blues," and Ronnie Self's "You're So Right for Me," where his hoarse vocals must have made the dignified major-label execs reach for the smelling salts. Talk about raw: Commonwealth Jones' 1961 single "Who's Been Here?"/"Do Do Do" (both songs are included) was likely the crudest slab of rock issued on a big label that year. Some of the rest is just okay, and Rose Maddox does sound like she would have rather been sticking with country swing than getting to grips with the new music on "Hey Little Dreamboat," with its odd combination of electric guitar and fiddles. —*Richie Unterberger*

AK79 / 1993 / Flying Nun ✦✦✦✦

AK79 is probably the best compilation of New Zealand's entries for punk rock and new wave of the late '70s. While most of this material was released on small independent labels like Ripper, Propeller, Flying Nun, and Mushroom and never saw any exposure outside of New Zealand, the quality of the songs and raw energy behind them should appeal to genre specialists and certainly deserves discovery. Included are rarities from the brilliant yet underrated Swingers, Suburban Reptiles, and Toy Love, among others. —*Chris Woodstra*

★ **Ambient, Vol. 1: A Brief History of Ambient** / Aug. 9, 1993 / Virgin ✦✦✦✦✦

Although it seemed to arrive out of nowhere in the early '90s, ambient music actually has a long and varied history, leading back to Brian Eno and Kraftwerk's electronic experiments in the 1970s right up to Aphex Twin's textural techno soundscapes. As an introduction and history lesson, the two-disc *A Brief History of Ambient Music* can't be beat; it shows that the ambient-techno trend has roots that most fans wouldn't even realize existed. —*Stephen Thomas Erlewine*

★ **Artificial Intelligence** / 1992 / Wax Trax! ✦✦✦✦✦

The premier listening-techno label for the early '90s, Warp (distributed by TVT) released seminal albums by Polygon Window (aka Aphex Twin), Black Dog, B12, and Autechre. Great tracks from all these artists appear on *Artificial Intelligence*, along with contributions from Richie Hawtin, Speedy J, and the Orb's Dr. Alex Paterson. The B12 track "Telefone 529" (as Musicology), Black Dog's "Clan" (as I.A.O.) and Autechre's "Crystel" are three of the best here. The cover display, of a robotic humanoid relaxing in a futuristic living room with copies of Kraftwerk and Pink Floyd LPs on the floor, is quite appropriate: Warp virtually pioneered the concept of applying the concepts of '70s ambience to '80s techno. The result is a superb collection of electronic listening music, and it's a great place to start for the newly interested. —*John Bush*

Artificial Intelligence, Vol. 2 / 1994 / Wax Trax! ✦✦✦✦

With more artists than the previous *Artificial Intelligence* compilation, this second installment is a bit more sonically experimental, though it suffers from a lack of enjoyable tracks. Besides contributions from *AI* regulars (Autechre, Speedy J, B12, Polygon Window, the Black Dog's Balil project), tracks by newer names like Beaumont Hannant, Mark Franklin, and Higher Intelligence Agency water down the quality somewhat. The Global Communication project Link contributes what is quite possibly the highlight, the almost progressive house number "Arcadian." While the British edition includes a limited second disc (including an unreleased Richard D. James track named "My Teapot"), the American version of *Artificial Intelligence, Vol. 2* is single-disc only. —*John Bush*

☆ **Atlantic Rhythm & Blues 1947-1974 [Box]** / 1991 / Atlantic ✦✦✦✦✦

This eight-CD set should be a part of any collection that presumes to take American music—not just rock & roll or rhythm & blues—seriously. Atlantic Records was one of dozens of independent labels started up after the war by neophyte executives and producers, but it was different from most of the others in that the guys who ran it were honest and genuinely loved music. Coupled with a lot of luck and some good judgment, the results trace a good chunk of the history of American music and popular culture. Disc one opens with cuts which slot in somewhere midway between jazz, bop, and "race" music (as the term was used then). Disc two is pure, distilled R&B, the stuff filling the airwaves of black radio and the jukeboxes in the "wrong" parts of town in 1952-54. Surprisingly, the material on Disc three, covering 1955-57, isn't very different in content or character from Disc two, despite the fact that it covers the period when white teenagers were starting to listen to and buy these records in large numbers. It's only with Disc four that one sees the consequences of the late '50s—Ray Charles in his final days with the label, juxtaposed with the Drifters in their post-1958 incarnation and the start of the company's relationship with Stax/Volt Records. Disc six (1965-67) is practically a mini-tribute to Stax/Volt, filled with the best-known sides of Eddie Floyd, Otis Redding, Sam & Dave, and Booker T. & the MG's. Discs seven and eight run from the late '60s and the heyday of Aretha Franklin to some great early-'70s soul, including Roberta Flack and the Spinners. The booklet, with a full sessionography and biographical notes on each artist, would be worth 20 bucks on its own. —*Bruce Eder*

Bad Boy's Greatest Hits / Sep. 29, 1998 / Bad Boy ✦✦✦✦✦

Though albums by Bad Boy Records artists always sold incredibly well, the single productions of Sean "Puffy" Combs lit up the charts. Collected here is the essence of Bad Boy, including all of the label's best tracks: the remix of Craig Mack's "Flava in Ya Ear" that practically made the label, the Notorious B.I.G.'s "One More Chance/Stay With Me," Puff Daddy's "It's All About the Benjamins," and Mase's "Feel So Good." Unless you're a big fan, that's about all the Bad Boy you need. It's a bit of a shame that it doesn't include the B.I.G. tribute "I'll Be Missing You," but *Bad Boy's Greatest Hits* is still an excellent summation of the label's hit production. —*John Bush*

The Beat Generation / 1992 / Rhino ✦✦✦✦✦

A three-CD box set featuring recordings from titans including William S. Burroughs, Allen Ginsberg, and Kenneth Rexroth, *The Beat Generation* works in tandem with Rhino's earlier compilation *The Jack Kerouac Collection* to paint a definitive audio portrait of one of the seminal literary uprisings of the 20th century. Because the Beats were so heavily influenced by jazz, their work ranks among the most rhythmic and lyrical in all of literature and lends itself perfectly to spoken word recordings; Kerouac's insistence that Beat stood for "beatific" aside, the name's musical implications are undeniable, with the writers' free-flowing, improvisational wordplay—what Ginsberg dubbed "spontaneous bop prosody"—echoing the radical innovations of Charlie Parker and Dizzy Gillespie. The set also charts the Beats' own influence on musicians spanning from Lambert, Hendricks, and Ross to Perry Como to Tom Waits, at the same time embracing kindred spirits including Ken Nordine, Lord Buckley, and Lenny Bruce; the inclusion of some of the material is questionable at best—the box would probably work as effectively at two discs instead of three—but in recapturing the singular spirit of its time, *The Beat Generation* is an essential document of cool. —*Jason Ankeny*

Beats & Rhymes: Hip-Hop of the 90's, Vol. 1 / Oct. 28, 1997 / Rhino ♦♦♦
With the three-volume *Beats & Rhymes: Hip-Hop of the '90s*, Rhino attempts to sketch a history of rap in the early '90s, before gangsta rap dominated the marketplace. Hip-hop was thriving between 1990 and 1993, as both veteran artists like Boogie Down Productions and new crews like A Tribe Called Quest began pursuing adventurous territory, fusing hip-hop with jazz and pop, among other things. There aren't many big crossover hits on any of the three volumes, but there are big names and cuts that were important in the underground. Unfortunately, there's some mediocre stuff mixed in with the prime cuts, but the bulk of each disc is so strong—and the set's budget-line price is so attractive—that the entire series functions as an excellent primer, especially when the liner notes by Harry Allen are added into the equation. Among the highlights on the 15-track *Beats & Rhymes: Hip-Hop of the '90s, Vol. 1* are cuts by A Tribe Called Quest ("Bonita Applebum"), the D.O.C. ("It's Funky Enough"), Main Source ("Looking at the Front Door"), Poor Righteous Teachers ("Rock Dis Funky Joint"), Big Daddy Kane ("I Get the Job Done"), and Jungle Brothers ("Doin' Our Own Dang"). —*Stephen Thomas Erlewine*

Beats & Rhymes: Hip-Hop of the 90's, Vol. 2 / Oct. 28, 1997 / Rhino ♦♦♦
Beats & Rhymes: Hip-Hop of the '90s, Vol. 2 picks up where its predecessor left off, running through a number of rap classics and underappreciated gems from the early '90s. Cut for cut, the 15-track *Vol. 2* isn't as consistent as its predecessor, but there are still plenty of terrific moments on the disc—including tracks by Leaders of the New School ("Case of the P.T.A."), A Tribe Called Quest ("Check the Rhyme"), Brand Nubian ("Slow Down"), Eric B. & Rakim ("What's On Your Mind"), DJ Jazzy Jeff & the Fresh Prince ("Summertime"), and the UMC's ("Blue Cheese")—that make it an essential history lesson. That said, there's still no reason why there are no less than three Chubb Rock cuts on this disc. —*Stephen Thomas Erlewine*

Beats & Rhymes: Hip-Hop of the 90's, Vol. 3 / Oct. 28, 1997 / Rhino ♦♦♦
The third and final volume of *Beats & Rhymes: Hip-Hop of the '90s* is as effective as its two predecessors, chronicling the period in the early '90s before gangsta rap became the dominant form of hip-hop. Several years after its original release, much of this music retains the excitement and spirit of adventure, and it shames much of the music that followed it in the mid-'90s. *Vol. 3* rivals *Vol. 1* for sheer consistency, boasting cuts by A Tribe Called Quest ("Hot Sex," "Scenario"), Grand Puba ("360 Degrees (What Goes Around)"), Main Source ("Fakin' the Funk"), Naughty By Nature ("Guard Your Grill"), the Pharcyde ("Ya Mama"), Fu-Schnickens ("La Schmoove"), Del tha Funkee Homosapien ("Mistadobalina"), and Digital Underground ("No Nose Job"). Not only does it capture the depth and range of the era, it's also an excellent listen. —*Stephen Thomas Erlewine*

Beg Scream & Shout: The Big Ol' Box of '60s Soul / Aug. 5, 1997 / Rhino ♦♦♦♦
Six CDs, and 144 songs, of classic '60s soul, including selections by every major performer in the idiom (except for Sam Cooke and Sly Stone, who were unavailable for licensing reasons), as well as numerous influential minor performers, one-shot artists, and just plain unknowns. The music is classic, and the packaging is an event in itself, with the discs enclosed in a mock briefcase for carrying 45 singles, and trading cards for each song on the volume that have photos and trivia questions on front and mini-essays on the back. Yet it ultimately occupies a rather perplexing space on the collector's shelf. Anyone who's enough of a soul lover to fork over the dough for this production will no doubt have a good many of the tunes already, particularly the Hall of Fame hits like "Sweet Soul Music," "(I Know) I'm Losing You," "Don't Make Me Over," and "La-La-Means I Love You." There are numerous great rarities here—Jay Wiggins' magnificent melancholy ballad "Sad Girl," and the rare original versions of "Shake a Tail Feather" (the Five Du-Tones), "Tainted Love" (Gloria Jones), "Mustang Sally" (Sir Mack Rice), and "Piece of My Heart" (Erma Franklin). Yet the tracks used to represent some superstars—"You've Been in Love Too Long" for Martha & the Vandellas, or "Fly Me to the Moon" for Bobby Womack—seem almost deliberately idiosyncratic, even though this method also yields underrated off-the-beaten-tracks by Ray Charles ("In the Heat of the Night"), Al Green ("Back Up Train"), and others. It's almost as if some guys stayed up several nights running trying to make the ultimate '60s soul party tape—one which demonstrated both their impeccable taste and the depth of their record collection—and got so carried away with the idea that a box set resulted. Like all well-made party tapes, the content is excellent, but the sum is neither a definitive '60s soul box (an impossible task in any case), nor one which offers quite enough lost classics to justify its hefty price tag for those who already have half or more of the tunes. —*Richie Unterberger*

☆ **The Best of Chess Rock & Roll** / Chess ♦♦♦♦♦
Over two separate volumes, *Best of Chess Rock & Roll* gives a good portrait of the seminal record label's massive contributions to rock & roll. Not only are landmarks like Chuck Berry's "Johnny B. Goode" and Bo Diddley's "Bo Diddley" covered, but cult favorites like the Moonglows and the Students are also featured. With "Johnny B. Goode," "Maybelline," "Who Do You Love," "Ain't Got No Home," "Rocket 88," and "Susie Q" all on the first volume, it is one of the most essential single-disc rock collections ever assembled; the second volume is nearly as important, with "Book of Love," "High Heel Sneakers," "No Particular Place to Go," "Ten Commandments of Love," and "Road Runner" among the featured tracks. —*Stephen Thomas Erlewine*

☆ **Best of Doo Wop Ballads** / 1989 / Rhino ♦♦♦♦♦
The companion volume to Rhino's *Best of Doo-Wop Uptempo* checks out the ballad side of the aisle and comes up with 18 smoothies in the bargain. Highlights include Dion and the Belmonts' "Where or When," the Five Satins' "In the Still of the Nite," the Cadillacs' "Gloria," the Moonglows' original of "Sincerely," the Velvetones' "Glory of Love," the Crests' "16 Candles," the Flamingos' evocative "I Only Have Eyes for You," and Lee Andrews and the Hearts' "Teardrops." Selections from the Pastels, the Skyliners, the Jive Five, the Dells, the Blue jays, the Penguins, the Spaniels, and the Heartbeats complete the set. —*Cub Koda*

☆ **Best of Doo Wop Ballads, Vol. 2: Golden Archive Series** / 1991 / Rhino ♦♦♦♦♦
The Best of Doo Wop Ballads, Vol. 2: Golden Archive Series is an excellent supplement to the first volume, featuring 14 classic doo wop songs, including the Flamingos' "I Only Have Eyes for You," the Cadillacs' "Gloria," the Clovers' "Devil or Angel," the Heartbeats' "A Thousand Miles Away," Shep & the Limelites' "Daddy's Home," Lee Andrews' "Tear Drops," the Jive Five's "What Time is It?," and the Skyliners' "Since I Don't Have You." It's an excellent single disc, but doo wop connoisseurs may prefer to invest in Rhino's excellent pair of doo wop boxes instead of this collection. —*Stephen Thomas Erlewine*

☆ **Best of Doo Wop Uptempo** / 1989 / Rhino ♦♦♦♦♦
Part of a two-volume set, this brings together 18 classic performances from rock & roll's ground floor era. in addition to mega hits like "Gee," "Come Go With Me," "Speedo," "I Wonder Why," "Blue Moon," "Book of Love," and "Why Do Fools Fall in Love," the collection also features some more obscure sides like "Denise" by Randy and the Rainbows, "I Love You" by the Volumes, "Hushabye" by the Mystics, and "Foot Stomping-Part 1" by the Flares. Although this material gets recycled quite a bit on other compilations, this one's a nicely assembled set and a fine addition to anyone's rock & roll collection. —*Cub Koda*

☆ **Best of Doo Wop Uptempo, Vol. 2: Golden Archive Series** / 1991 / Rhino ♦♦♦♦♦
The Best of Doo Wop Uptempo, Vol. 2: Golden Archive Series is a good supplement to the first volume, containing a number of classic doo wop singles, but true collectors would be better served by Rhino's pair of doo wop boxes. —*Stephen Thomas Erlewine*

☆ **Sound of the Swamp: The Best of Excello, Vol. 1** / 1991 / Rhino ♦♦♦♦♦
The Nashville-based Excello label specialized in obscure blues, R&B, and rock & roll from the '50s and early '60s. This first volume of *Sound of the Swamp: The Best of Excello, Vol. 1* covers the best from Crowley, LA, producer Jay Miller's blues, rockabilly, and swamp-pop sides. —*John Floyd*

The Southern Rhythm 'n' Rock: The Best of Excello, Vol. 2 / 1991 / Rhino ♦♦♦♦♦
The Best of Excello Records, Vol. 2 doesn't have the high percentage of classics and interesting obscurities that made the first volume essential, but it does have some fine cuts that will be of interest to fans of swamp R&B, including the Gladiolas' "Little Darlin'," Rudy Green's "My Mumblin' Baby," Louis Brooks & His Hi-Toppers' "It's Love Baby (24 Hours A Day)," Ray Batts' "Stealin' Sugar," Robert Garrett's "Quit My Drinkin'," Arthur Gunter's "Baby Let's Play House," the King Crooners' "Now That She's Gone," Hooks Coleman's "Fine Young Girl," and Shy Guy Douglas' "Long Gone." —*Stephen Thomas Erlewine*

★ **The Best of New Orleans Rhythm & Blues, Vol. 1** / 1988 / Rhino ♦♦♦♦♦
The Best of New Orleans Rhythm & Blues, Vol. 1 is an incredible collection of 18 of the greatest Crescent City R&B singles ever released. Divided equally between classics ["Mother-In-Law," "It Will Stand," "I Hear You Knocking," "I'm Gonna Be a Wheel Someday," "Lipstick Traces (On a Cigarette)," "A Certain Girl," "One Night," "Ooh Poo Pah Doo (Pt. 1)"] and terrific but frequently underappreciated singles from the likes of the Spiders, Irma Thomas, Aaron Neville, Earl King, and Dave Bartholomew, the collection is a concise and utterly intoxicating overview of New Orleans R&B, one that appeals not only to neophytes, but also to collectors. —*Stephen Thomas Erlewine*

☆ **The Best of New Orleans Rhythm & Blues, Vol. 2** / 1988 / Rhino ♦♦♦♦♦
The Best of New Orleans Rhythm & Blues, Vol. 2 is just as thrilling as its predecessor, featuring 18 tracks of classic, funky R&B from the likes of Frankie Ford ("Sea Cruise"), Shirley & Lee ("Let the Good Times Roll"), Lee Dorsey ("Ride Your Pony," "Working in a Coal Mine"), the Meters ("Cissy Strut"), Irma Thomas ("Ruler of My Heart," "It's Raining"), the Dixie Cups ("Iko Iko"), Lloyd Price ("Just Because," "Lawdy Miss Clawdy"), Barbara George ("I Know (You Don't Love Me No More)"), Guitar Slim ("The Things That I Used to Do"), Chris Kenner ("I Like It Like That"), and Clarence "Frogman" Henry ("Ain't Got No Home"). There are no bad cuts here, and nearly every song is a classic, making it an essential edition to any library, as well as one of the definitive overviews of New Orleans R&B. —*Stephen Thomas Erlewine*

The Best of Sugar Hill Records / Oct. 6, 1998 / Rhino ♦♦♦♦♦
If Rhino's massive five-disc summation of the crucial old-school label Sugar Hill makes you cringe, this single-disc set is a much better distillation of the label (and the period) than much else out there. It covers the three tracks that are hands-down classics—"Rapper's Delight" by the Sugarhill Gang plus "The Message" and "White Lines" by Grandmaster Flash & the Furious Five. In addition, there are at least a half-dozen minor standouts like the Sugarhill Gang's "8th Wonder" and "Apache," the Funky 4 + 1's "That's the Joint," Kevie Kev's "All Night Long (Waterbed)," and Grandmaster Flash's "Scorpio" and "New York New York." —*John Bush*

Best of the Colpix-Dimensions Story / 1994 / Rhino ♦♦♦
In the first half of the 1960s, Colpix and Dimension were record label offshoots of Columbia Pictures; Colpix tended toward teen idols, while Dimension was mainly an outlet for the compositions of the Gerry Goffin/Carole King songwriting team. This 40-song double CD includes all the major hits on the labels by the Marcels, James Darren,

Shelley Fabares, Paul Petersen, Little Eva, the Cookies, and Carole King herself, as well as quite a few rarities. Although the compilers have done a thorough job, the jumble of disparate styles—sappy teen-idol pop, rhythm and blues, girl groups, soul, even a garage band—makes for tough end-to-end listening. Several of the sides by Darren and Petersen are unbearably cloying; the ones by Fabares, Teddy Randazzo, and Sandy Stewart are barely any better. The hits by Little Eva and the Cookies, on the other hand, are great dynamic girl-group performances. And some of the rarities are pretty cool—Carole King's odd, almost folk-rockish flop single "He's a Bad Boy," Earl-Jean's original version of "I'm Into Something Good" (covered for a hit by Herman's Hermits), the Girlfriends' "My One and Only, Jimmy Boy" (the best Wall of Sound girl-group record not produced by Phil Spector), the little-anthologized Top Ten soul hit "Hey Girl" by Freddie Scott, rare sides by Lou Christie and Duane Eddy, a silly Beatle parody by Sonny Curtis, and extremely rare (if not terribly good) singles by David Jones and Michael Nesmith before they joined the Monkees. *—Richie Unterberger*

The Best of the Girl Groups, Vol. 1 / Rhino ♦♦♦♦
Rhino's *Best of the Girl Groups, Vol. 1* collects 18 of the greatest girl group singles, including the Ad Libs' "The Boy From New York City," Betty Everett's "The Shoop Shoop Song (It's In His Kiss)," the Exciters' "He's Got the Power," and Claudine Clark's "Party Lights." The Shangri-Las have no less than three of their singles—"Leader of the Pack," "Remember (Walking in the Sand)," and "Give Him a Great Big Kiss"—included here, while two of the Shirelles' finest, "Baby It's You" and "Will You Love Me Tomorrow," and the Chiffons' "He's So Fine" and "One Fine Day" reaffirm why all three acts are among the best girl groups. Most of the style's big hits, such as the Dixie Cups' "Chapel of Love," are featured, but the lesser-known tracks, like the Jaynetts' "Sally, Go Round the Roses," Evie Sands' "I Can't Let Go," and Skeeter Davis' "I Can't Stay Mad at You," keep the collection interesting for more serious fans of girl group pop. A solid, entertaining album, *Best of the Girl Groups, Vol. 1* is a must for anyone interested in one of the most distinctive sounds of the '60s. *—Heather Phares*

The Best of the Girl Groups, Vol. 2 / 1990 / Rhino ♦♦♦♦♦
Picking up where the first volume left off, *The Best of the Girl Groups, Vol. 2* contains 18 classics from the golden age of girl groups. These are hardly leftovers; if anything, it feels like a greatest hits collection, thanks to songs such as "My Boyfriend's Back," "Sweet Talkin' Guy," "The Loco-Motion," "A Lover's Concerto," "Chains," "Popsicles and Icicles," "Tell Him," "Don't Say Nothin' Bad (About My Baby)," "Easier Said than Done" and "Johnny Get Angry." A few of these tunes may sound a little dated, but the startling thing about *The Best of the Girl Groups, Vol. 2* is that the majority of the music sounds as fresh and exuberant as it did when it was originally released. Which only reiterates the fact that this isn't just some of the best girl-group pop ever made—it's some of the best pop of any era. *—Stephen Thomas Erlewine*

The Best of the Teen Idols / 1987 / Rhino ♦♦♦♦♦
The teen idol style probably gets more abuse than any other genre in rock history. But it was a significant, if often lamentable, transitional period in the development of rock & roll. This 14-song compilation presents everything that most listeners will need to know/hear about the teen idols. It has the biggest hits by Fabian, Paul Anka, Frankie Avalon, and Bobby Vee, and one-shots by Tab Hunter and Troy Shondell. There are also dynamic classics by Dion and Del Shannon that are probably too good to be lumped into the teen idol category, but are present because those singers, accurately or inaccurately, were often thought of as teen idols at the peak of their success. There are also excellent liner notes to put the music in its proper context. *—Richie Unterberger*

Black Box Waxtrax! Records: The First 13 Years / 1994 / Wax Trax! ♦♦♦♦♦
Wax Trax was the definitive industrial label and the four-disc box set *Black Box* is the definitive overview of their peak years. The label's artists—including Ministry, Trent Reznor, and KMFDM—developed the corrosive guitars, synths, distorted vocals, and jackhammer beats that became the signature sound of industrial. *Black Box* gathers nearly every worthwhile song to emerge from the Chicago label, including many rare singles, and provides an excellent summary of some of the most cutting-edge dance music of the 1980s and '90s. *—Stephen Thomas Erlewine*

Bosstown Sound, 1968: The Music & the Time / 1996 / Big Beat ♦♦
The Bosstown (Boston) sound was pushed as a next big thing in the late '60s, but failed to take off, mostly because, as Gertrude Stein might say, there was no "there" there. This double CD features tracks by most of the area's biggest groups—Ultimate Spinach, Orpheus, Earth Opera, Rockin' Ramrods, Bagatelle, Eden's Children—as well as even smaller footnoes, like Ill Wind and Chamaeleon (sic) Church. Mostly it's rather dreary, second-rate psychedelia, heavy on the sub-Cream blues-rock jamming, sub-Airplane mystical riffing, and pretentious wordplay. The poppier acts, in contrast, sound like psychedelicized variants of the Association, a rather ill-advised recipe. Points of interest: Earth Opera's lineup included Peter Rowan and David Grisman (their epic "The American Eagle Tragedy" is featured); the Rockin' Ramrods had a dynamite local pop-rock smash with "Bright Lit Blue Skies" (which has been compiled elsewhere); and the Lost, featuring Willie Alexander and Walter Powers (who would show up in the post-Lou Reed Velvet Underground), offer a couple raw 1965 folk-rockers that aren't bad. *—Richie Unterberger*

The Songs of Tommy Boyce & Bobby Hart / Oct. 24, 1995 / Varese Saraband ♦♦♦
Boyce & Hart, best known as frequent songwriters for the Monkees, were among the more successful West Coast pop/rock composers of the late '60s, also landing some material with other artists and making some records of their own, including the hit "I Wonder What She's Doing Tonight." Only six of these 18 tracks were recorded by the Boyce & Hart duo (another was recorded by Dolenz, Jones, Boyce & Hart). But since Boyce & Hart's principal importance came from their songwriting rather than their performing, this compilation—which matches the most notable Boyce & Hart recordings with the best and most famous cuts by other artists covering Boyce-Hart compositions—is the best representative sampling of their most important music. Other than "I Wonder What She's Doing Tonite," Boyce & Hart's own tracks pale next to the cover versions on this disc, which include the Monkees' "Last Train to Clarksville" and "Valleri"; "(I'm Not Your) Stepping Stone" in its pre-Monkees version by Paul Revere & the Raiders; and relatively rare, gritty versions of "Words" (from 1966, by the Boston Tea Party) and "Tomorrow's Gonna Be Another Day" (from 1965, by the Astronauts), both of which would later be done by the Monkees as well. There are also a bunch of hits that Boyce & Hart did not write on their own, or to which only Boyce or only Hart contributed, like Freddie Cannon's "Action," Curtis Lee's "Pretty Little Angel Eyes," Jay & the Americans' "Come a Little Bit Closer," and Little Anthony & the Imperials' "Hurt So Bad." Overall, it's a decent compilation of the best work of a composing team with a knack for the peppy and catchy melodies typical of the form of LA '60s rock known as sunshine pop, although their songs were usually on the lightweight side. *—Richie Unterberger*

Brill Building Sound / 1993 / Era ♦♦♦♦♦
Although Phil Spector's songs weren't available due to licensing restrictions, the four-CD box set *Brill Building Sound* remains an important and entertaining collection, featuring many of the songs that made the Brill Building a pop music institution in the early '60s. *—Stephen Thomas Erlewine*

British Beat Before the Beatles [Series Overview] / 1994 / EMI ♦♦♦
As the title says, there was British rock before the Beatles, but it wasn't particularly great—it was often stiff and stilted, sounding tentative. Still, there were some gems amidst the mediocrity, and the best thing about this seven-disc series is that it captures both the good and the bad, providing a thorough retrospective of this little-acknowledged (especially to American collectors) period of rock & roll. While that is certainly a valuable service, be forewarned that this does not make for engaging listening. Essentially, this is a curiosity, even for serious rock & roll collectors, and for every great song by Billy Fury, Cliff Richard, or Johnny Kidd & the Pirates, there are many, many songs that don't hold up except as historical curiosities that simply aren't that interesting—even for those who buy rarities as a way of life. *—Stephen Thomas Erlewine*

☆ **British Invasion: History of British Rock [Series Overview]** / 1992 / Rhino ♦♦♦♦♦
Rhino's *The British Invasion: The History of British Rock* is the most comprehensive series assembled on the style. It's also the best, not just because it's so exhaustive, but because it's done right, following from the exciting early days of Merseybeat all the way through swinging London to the end days of the '60s, dominated by psychedelic pop. It's not strictly chronological, especially since the final five volumes were released three years after the initial four, but the groupings of songs do make sense—it never ricochets between the Beatles' "Ain't She Sweet" and Donovan's "Sunshine Superman," even when they're on the same volume; instead, it builds to that conclusion. Yeah, there are no Stones, Who, or prime-period Beatles, but that doesn't matter, because the selections by the Kinks, the Yardbirds, the Hollies, and the Zombies provide a solid foundation for the one-hit wonders, singles acts, and cult favorites that comprise the rest of the collection. It's a fantastic representation of one of the great movements in pop history, and this makes it still sound exciting and fresh. *—Stephen Thomas Erlewine*

The British Psychedelic Trip 1966-1969 / 1986 / See For Miles ♦♦♦
A compilation of late '60s British psychedelic rarities from the Decca label sounds rather more enticing than the end product. Much of this is British psych at its fruitiest; at what other time could a band called the Muffin Man release a song called "World of Oz" on a major label? (Ditto for Turquoise's "Tales of Flossie Fillett.") This is too tilted toward fey romanticism for comfort, and the best tracks had already appeared on other compilations (although it must be admitted that the sound quality is often notably better here). It does have some endring moments: the Accent's "Red Sky at Night" has some fine thunder-of-doom guitars, the End's dainty "Shades of Orange" bears production and co-songwriting credits from Bill Wyman, and Tintern Abbey's "Beeside" is one of the most melodic, graceful slices of Mellotron-soaked pop-psych ever. *—Richie Unterberger*

British R&B Explosion: '62-'68, Vol. 1 / See For Miles ♦♦♦
There really isn't any thread tying this 20-track compilation together, other than the fact that all of them originally appeared on Decca Records. It does offer the British Invasion collector a convenient way to gather up some loose ends, including rare early singles by Rod Stewart and Joe Cocker; three Graham Bond rarities that only appeared on an EP and a compilation; obscure 45s by cult artists Graham Gouldman, Duffy Power, and Zoot Money; and garage-cum-R&B cuts by Blues by Five, the Fairies, and others. The problem is, most of it's fairly humdrum: the really good selections (by the Fairies and Them) are easily available elsewhere, and much of the rest is pedestrian, even strained, British R&B. The top find is Tony Knight's "I Feel So Blue," which is not exactly R&B, but sounds like a Joe Meek production with its hyperventilating tempo and brilliant nervous guitar line. *—Richie Unterberger*

Brown Eyed Soul: The Sound of East L.A., Vol. 1 / Sep. 16, 1997 / Rhino ♦♦♦
Rhino's three-disc series *Brown Eyed Soul* intends to document the underappreciated Chicano soul scene of East Los Angeles in the '60s. Although many of the artists featured on *Brown Eyed Soul* are indeed Hispanic, many of the cuts on the series are by artists, such as Brenton Wood, that were simply popular in East L.A. and weren't Chicano. Throughout the late '50s and '60s, East L.A. was vibrant, filled with excellent R&B, soul and rock & roll that was rarely heard outside of the city. Regrettably, *Brown Eyed Soul* is not sequenced chronologically—on this first volume, it jumps from 1956 to 1980 to 1971 to 1954—but there's a wealth of terrific music scattered throughout the series, even if none of the volumes make for cohesive listening. On this first volume, there are cuts from War ("All Day Music"), the Penguins ("Hey Senorita"), Tony Clarke ("The Entertainer"),

Van McCoy ("Mr. D.J."), Brenton Wood ("Me and You"), Chuck Higgins ("Pachuko Hop"), and the Five Satins ("Our Anniversary"). *—Stephen Thomas Erlewine*

Brown Eyed Soul: The Sound of East L.A., Vol. 2 / Sep. 16, 1997 / Rhino ♦♦♦
Since *Brown Eyed Soul: The Sound of East L.A.* doesn't follow any chronological order, *Vol. 2* doesn't really pick up where its predecessor left off. Instead, it simply follows the pattern of *Vol. 1*, compiling forgotten singles from the '50s, '60s, '70s, and '80s with no particular rhyme or reason. There are a few familiar songs on *Vol. 2*—including Ritchie Valens' "We Belong Together," War's "Why Can't We Be Friends?," and the Premiers' "Farmer John"—but its main strength is that it gathers regional soul, R&B, and rock & roll hits from the likes of the Blendells ("La La La La La"), McKinley Travis ("Baby, Is There Something on Your Mind"), the Gallahads ("I'm Without a Girl Friend"), Cannibal & the Headhunters ("Please Baby Please"), Brenton Wood ("Baby You Got It"), and Hank Jacobs ("East Side"). *—Stephen Thomas Erlewine*

Brown Eyed Soul: The Sound of East L.A., Vol. 3 / Sep. 16, 1997 / Rhino ♦♦♦♦
An enjoyable compilation of diverse R&B recordings released between 1959 and 1975 that were popular plays on East Los Angeles radio stations. Many were also popular in other localities, like the Olympics' "Mine Exclusively," a hard, bouncy R&B vocal that proved they could do more than just dance tunes. The little-known ballad "I Fooled You This Time" (by Gene Chandler) and a song many used for weddings, "Forever" (by the Marvelettes), were R&B chart-dwellers that never crossed over ("Forever" was the B-side of "Locking Up My Heart"). Smashes like "Land of 1,000 Dances" by Cannibal & the Headhunters, Leon Haywood's "It's Got to Be Mellow," and "Natural High" by Bloodstone are balanced by local favorites such as Brenton Wood's "Catch You on the Rebound," El Chicano's "Tell Her She's Lovely," and Rosie & Ron's "Bring Me Happiness." *—Andrew Hamilton*

Bubblegum Classics, Vol. 3 / Aug. 27, 1996 / Varese ♦♦♦
Bubblegum music could be fun stuff, but it wasn't *that* deep in the content arena, and the third volume of Varese Sarabande's fine series lags a bit behind the first couple in terms of top-notch tunes. It does have some of the core classics of the genre with the Archies' "Sugar, Sugar," and Ohio Express' "Chewy, Chewy," and Mac & Katie Kissoon's "Chirpy Chirpy Cheep Cheep." The Monkees (arguably not bubblegum) weigh in with "A Little Bit Me, A Little Bit You," Bobby Sherman represents the teen idol wing with "Little Woman," and Sweet play bubblegum at its hardest and most glam-influenced with "Little Willy." The cuts by the likes of Robin McNamara, Tony Burrows, the Clique, and Salt Water Taffy may be way more obscure, but hearing them all at once is as ill-advised as chewing three packs of the pink stuff a day. Song titles include "Ricky Ticky Ta Ta Ta," "Wham! Bam! Ala Cazam," and Kasenetz-Katz Super Cirkus' immortal "Dong-Dong-Diki-Di-Ki Dong"; they really *don't* write 'em like that anymore. *—Richie Unterberger*

Bubblegum Classics, Vol. 4 / Feb. 10, 1998 / Varese ♦♦♦♦
Bubblegum Classics, Vol. 4 is a retitled reissue of Varese's Tony Burrows compilation *Love Grows (Where My Rosemary Goes)*. It never was a Tony Burrows album proper, but an 18-song compilation of records that he sang lead on from 1969 through 1985 (mostly from the first half of the 1970s), for Edison Lighthouse, First Class, White Plains, the Brotherhood of Man, the Pipkins, the Flowerpot Men, and others. All the big hits are here ("Love Grows," "Gimme Dat Ding," "My Baby Loves Lovin'," "United We Stand," "Beach Baby"), as well as quite a few misses. It's candy-floss early-'70s pop of the most disposable variety, many of the flops being pale Beach Boys imitations. *—Richie Unterberger*

Bubblegum Classics, Vol. 5 / Feb. 10, 1998 / Varese ♦♦♦♦
Bubblegum Classics, Vol. 5 is a retitled reissue of Varese's *Soulful Pop* collection. This is the kind of compilation that doesn't attract much critical attention, but is a pretty nifty concept: 17 songs from 1966-76 that are soul-pop at its poppiest and most commercial, running the scale from R&B-grounded cuts to near-bubblegum. It's a good mix of classics of the micro-genre (the Foundations' "Build Me Up Buttercup" and "Baby, Now That I Found You," Jay & the Techniques' "Keep the Ball Rollin'," Maxine Nightingale's "Right Back Where We Started From"), minor half-forgotten hits (James & Bobby Purify's "Let Love Come Between Us," Chairmen of the Board's "You've Got Me Dangling on a String"), singles that were only big in England (Blue Mink's "Melting Pot," the Love Affair's cover of Robert Knight's "Everlasting Love"), and total flops (by the Groove and the People's Choice). Especially ingratiating are the Five Stairsteps' "O-oh Child" and Chee-Chee & Peppy's "I Know I'm in Love," a forgotten Jackson 5 imitation (and minor hit) from 1971. *—Richie Unterberger*

● **Bubblegum Classics, Vols. 1 & 2** / 1995 / Varese Vintage ♦♦♦♦♦
Although they're missing a few key tracks (notably the Archies' hits and Kasenetz-Katz's "Quick Joey Small"), these are the best collections of late-'60s and early-'70s bubblegum hits ever assembled, including most of the major hits and a fair number of enticing rarities. In their favor, they encompass not just the most infantile, pre-teen smashes of the genre (1910 Fruitgum Co., Tommy Roe, Bobby Sherman), but also quite a few cuts that could just as easily be classified as enjoyable, highly polished mainstream pop/rock (the Monkees, Tommy James, the Cuff Links, Keith, the Five Americans, the Flying Machine). Running at 20 tracks each, they're maybe a bit much all at once, but they're the best overview of a significant chapter in rock history. *—Richie Unterberger*

Buddah Box / 1993 / Essex ♦♦♦♦
This remarkable three-CD box set recaps the biggest hits spawned by the Buddah record label and its distributed labels (Kama Sutra, Team, Pavilion, Hot Wax, Sussex, and Curtom). While the Buddah label was best known for its role in the 1967-1970 bubblegum genre and for giving rise to one surprise hit after another, it also was responsible for more substantive work from such acts as Curtis Mayfield, Gladys Knight & the Pips, early Captain Beefheart, and Charlie Daniels. The latter two are unfortunately not represented in this collection; even so, the sheer breadth of material covered here is astonishing. Unlike better-known labels of the period like Motown, Stax, and Philles, there is no unifying sonic trait in the artists under the Buddah umbrella. Consequently, listening to the entire collection in one sitting is a schizophrenic endeavor in its bouncing from bubblegum (1910 Fruitgum Company, Ohio Express, et al.) to Jesus-freakdom (Ocean's "Put Your Hand in the Hand," the Edwin Hawkins Singers' "Oh Happy Day") to '70s soul balladry (the elegant "Dream Merchant" from New Birth and "You Are My Starship" by Norman Connors) to disco oddities (Andrea True Connection's "More, More, More," the bizarre "Wide Receiver" by Michael Henderson). Despite the stylistic inconsistency, *The Buddah Box* is a worthwhile investment for music collectors, as its liner notes tell a fascinating story of the label's evolution, and there are a number of hard to find gems represented. It might have benefited from a few more obscurities—the collection sticks to Top 40 hits wherever it can—but it makes a good argument that the story of a trash-singles label can be just as interesting, and the tunes nearly as compelling, as that of the more respected labels of the '60s and '70s. *—Joseph McCombs*

The Burt Bacharach Songbook / Feb. 24, 1998 / Varese ♦♦♦♦♦
The Burt Bacharach Songbook is an excellent single-disc collection of 17 hits Bacharach penned for other artists. While it isn't as sublime as the British-only *The Look of Love*—often, the familiar versions are not present, like when Andy Williams' version of "Close to You" is substituted for the Carpenters' hit—most of the disc is absolutely excellent, featuring such classics as Jackie DeShannon's "What the World Needs Now Is Love," Dusty Springfield's "I Just Don't Know What to Do With Myself," Sandie Shaw's "(There's) Always Something There to Remind Me," and Gene Pitney's "Only Love Can Break a Heart." The disc also suffers from not having any songs by Dionne Warwick, arguably the foremost interpreter of Bacharach-David's work, but for its midline price it's an excellent bargain, especially considering there is no comprable collection currently available on the American market. *—Stephen Thomas Erlewine*

Casablanca Records Story / 1994 / Casablanca/Mercury ♦♦♦♦♦
Even though it includes four discs, *The Casablanca Records Story* ignores the record label's biggest success, Kiss. But that doesn't matter; Kiss didn't fit into the rest of the label's roster. Driven by the massive success of Donna Summer, Casablanca was arguably the definitive disco label in the late '70s, scoring a string of hit singles that have become classics of the era. Featuring four discs of original single versions and 12" mixes, *The Casablanca Records Story* features most of the best music the label released, even though it probably could have been more effectively compiled on two or three discs. Nevertheless, there is plenty of fine, even seminal, music here, which makes it essential for serious disco collectors. *—Stephen Thomas Erlewine*

Chartbusters: The Best of Beserkley Years, 1975-1978 / Rhino ♦♦♦♦♦
Beserkley never scored any chart hits, but they were one of the best American independent record labels of the late '70s and early '80s, featuring such cult favorites as Jonathan Richman and Greg Kihn. *Best of the Beserkley Years* gathers up some of the label's best stripped-down rock & roll, offering a good overview of the indie label. *—Stephen Thomas Erlewine*

☆ **Chess Blues-Rock Songbook: The Classic Originals** / Aug. 26, 1997 / Chess ♦♦♦♦♦
While Chess Records' legacy as a dominating and shaping force on rock & roll is well chronicled, you don't really get the full range of it until you're ultimately confronted with the music itself. This two-disc, 36-track compilation drives that point home with an almost numbing intensity. Whether they're blues tunes that have been covered so many times they now are staples of everyone's set list (Muddy Water's "I'm Your Hoochie Coochie Man," "I Just Want to Make Love to You"; Bo Diddley's "I'm a Man"; or Howlin' Wolf's "Back Door Man"), classics waiting to be covered ("More and More," "Bring It On Home," "Ice Cream Man"), or early rock classics themselves ("Rock & Roll Music," "Johnny B. Goode," "Susie-Q," "See You Later Alligator"), Chess seems to have laid the first set of musical footprints in the snow. No mere publishing sampler, this is an essential piece of rock & roll history and a great primer for ground-floor roots-music enthusiasts. *—Cub Koda*

Chess Rhythm & Roll / 1994 / MCA ♦♦♦♦♦
A four-disc set chronicling the more rockin' sides in this landmark label's catalog. Here we have the landmark early recordings by Chuck Berry, Bo Diddley, the Moonglows, the Flamingos, marvelous one-shot hit artists like the Monotones ("Book of Love"), Dale Hawkins ("Susie-Q"), the Sensations ("Let Me In"), as well as seminal soul sides from Etta James, Billy Stewart and Tommy Tucker's original "High Heel Sneakers." Essential doesn't even begin to describe this box; music from a landmark label that changed the world. *—Cub Koda*

Chess Uptown Soul / Mar. 25, 1997 / Kent ♦♦♦
If you're trying to differentiate what was specifically "uptown" about these '60s Chess soul sides, you're getting into a game of serious hairsplitting. Basically this 24-track comp offers material—mostly non-hits—from 1963-67 that leans toward sophisticated, brassy soul borrowing much from Motown and Curtis Mayfield, but not matching the peaks of either. It's still pretty enjoyable, if sometimes generic, material, including efforts by some stars (Gene Chandler, Billy Stewart, Etta James, Ramsey Lewis, Little Milton, the Dells, Fontella Bass), Jan Bradley's great one-shot "Mama Didn't Lie," Tony Clarke's fine Top 40 ballad "The Entertainer," and barely heeded names like Jackie Ross, the Radiants, and Marlena Shaw (there's also an early non-hit by Johnny Nash). There's also the occasional song that deserved a much wider hearing than it got, like Nash's "Love Ain't Nothin'," the Radiants' infectious "It Ain't No Big Thing," and Mitty Collier's "I Had a Talk With My Man," which was covered by Dusty Springfield. *—Richie Unterberger*

● **Chicano Power: Latin Rock in the USA 1968-1976** / Dec. 14, 1999 / Soul Jazz ♦♦♦♦♦
These two CDs contain 17 tracks by Latin bands throughout the U.S. who fused rock, jazz,

and Latin music in the late 1960s and 1970s. The title is a trifle misleading; although Mexican-American bands from Los Angeles and San Francisco are well represented on the set, it also includes Puerto Rican-American artists and groups from New York and Miami. There are also a couple cuts from the Peruvian band Black Sugar, included to illustrate the influence of U.S. Latin rock in Latin America itself. At any rate, it's a solid collection of a genre that, other than the hit records by Santana of course, is largely overlooked by mainstream rock history and poorly represented on reissues. It should be noted that the tracks by larger ensembles with several horn players and percussionists can sound rather more like salsa music with a rock influence, rather than the other way around (not that that's a bad thing). Cuts like Black Sugar's "Viajecito," for instance, could fit well on a salsa radio station but for the obvious touches of contemporary rock, usually in the guitar. In "Viajecito," for example, there's a wild "Shaft"-like psychedelic guitar that runs through the entirety of what otherwise is a fairly standard Latin pop-jazz song; Tierra's "Sun God" kicks off with crazy synthesizers reminiscent of those heard on Pink Floyd's "On the Run." The influence of Santana is felt mightily throughout, particularly in the more rock-oriented bands, like Miami's the Antiques, whose "Chauca" is like early Santana with a dash of the Yardbirds, and a real highlight of the collection. The Santana comparisons are not always coincidental: Carlos Santana's brother Jorge Santana played guitar in Malo, and onetime Santana member Coke Escovedo founded Azteca. At its best, this collection, like early Santana, is an intoxicating mix of rock, R&B, psychedelia, jazz, and Latin music; even at its least impressive, it's still pretty enjoyable. Santana themselves are represented by the song that's probably the apex of the whole musical movement, "Soul Sacrifice." The only major complaint one could offer is that 75 minutes of music is spread throughout two discs, and could have been combined onto one CD. As compensation, there's a 40-page booklet with information on the groups and the sociopolitical factors that gave birth to the style. *—Richie Unterberger*

Chitlin Circuit Soul! The Best of Today's Southern Blues / May 15, 2001 / Wea/Atlantic/Rhino ♦♦♦♦♦

This is the soul record people have been looking for for a long time, but may not have known it. Alongside the Stax/Volt and Motown compilations that keep selling, and every rarities collection from the soulful '50s and '60s that's issued in Europe or Japan and disappears upon release, exists a soul music every bit as vital and pure as those venerable recordings have offered us. Apparently, soul music is now a secret music in America, where in urban centers, on weekends, large groups of folks get together and clap, shout, and dance for their favorite performers—some of whom have been making music for decades and some younger people who are making vital, exciting soul music now because it's the only music that moved them when they were coming up. This compilation aims to showcase a number of these current artists by juxtaposing their music against some of the genre's greats. The folks at Rhino, who do some of the best reissues in the world, are also committed to new explorers. The set opens with the illustrious silver-tongued angel Bobby Blue Bland with his deeply moving "Members Only," cut for Malaco in 1985 (and reached number 43 in the R&B chart). Bland is the consummate soul singer, and the arrangement is classic Chicago gospel croon à la Curtis Mayfield. When Bland sings "Members only, it's a private party/don't need no money to qualify/don't bring your checkbook, bring your broken heart/cause it's member's only tonight/say you lost your woman, say you lost your man/you got a lot of problems in your life/they're throwin' a party for the broken hearted/it's members only tonight," the melody is straight from "People Get Ready," and the strings swirl into the spare horn arrangements as the female vocals enter at the chorus. With a flute solo in the bridge, it's as deep and moving a song as there exists today. Johnnie Taylor, Bobby Rush, Clarence Carter (forget about "Patches"; his "Strokin'" is a racy, sensual extrapolation of "Givin' It Up for Your Love"), Little Milton, Shirley Brown—whose "Woman to Woman" is as marvelous, feminine, and tough a ballad as any ballad ever recorded—Betty Wright, and Millie Jackson are among the legends on the 16-track set. And so what—right, these are all stalwarts who are the current soul dudes and divas that carry the torch for a music that seems impossible to make in the current cultural climate. Okay. First of all, there's the remarkable Sterling Harrison & the New Breed doing the classic "There's a Rat in My House"—given such a stinging wrangling guitar treatment by Buddy Guy in the '80s that the song was lost—is a blues that comes from the Magic Sam School of Blues & R&B. His growling, roaring gospel-preacher moans open the door for the backbone to slip on out the back door. Newcomer Ronnie Lovejoy's chitlin circuit jukebox hit (remember those), the cocky "Still Wasn't Me," is a deeper-than-blue study in romantic denial and deceit. His mix of righteous indignation and soulful pleading are infectious and reaching. The drums are a bit thin, but the tune's story, his killer voice—Solomon Burke meets Wilson Pickett—with Philly soul production and a huge chorus of female backing vocals are convincing evidence that deep soul is still alive and kicking. Sterling Meadows, whose spoken beginning is another tale of denial: the protagonist's former woman is hanging out steady with someone else, and he's refusing to buy it as authentic. When he croons with the backbeat: "She can fool her friends, that's the easy part/Just wait she can't fool her heart/You're still my love… You can't turn it off when you want to/Love don't work that way/For eyes that weep, there's a heart that yearns/And soon he'll learn/She's still my love…." Echoes of Al Green, Brook Benton, Cecil Womack, and David Ruffin slip through the mix unabashedly, but the tune has it all anyway. The delivery could be anyone because the groove is so deep. There isn't a dog in this 16-track bunch; I can hardly wait for the second volume. *—Thom Jurek*

Chocolate Soup for Diabetics, Vol. 1-3 / 1980-1982 / Relics ♦♦♦♦♦

These three volumes of obscure '60s British psychedelic treasures are slightly tainted by dubbed-from-disc sound quality; the transfers also made the records play faster than their actual speed. The music, however, is mostly terrific, the cream of a very fertile U.K. scene that gave birth to dozens of little-known classics and near classics during its brief apogee in 1966-68. The influence of the Who, Syd Barrett—era Pink Floyd, and 1967 Beatles runs rampant, but most of it's too idiosyncratic to be dismissed as imitative. You could actually say that this was the genre of rock music that most effectively balanced exuberant melodies/harmonies with imaginative experimentation. If that nutshell description sounds appealing, you won't be disappointed by the gems on offer from Tintern Abbey, Dantalian's Chariot, One in a Million, Big Boy Pete, Mike Stuart Span, Syn, and numerous others. A lot of the tracks have been since reissued in better fidelity on sanctioned re-releases, but some are hard to find anywhere else but on these anthologies, which are now themselves sought-after collector's items. *—Richie Unterberger*

Chuck D Presents: Louder Than a Bomb / Aug. 31, 1999 / Rhino ♦♦♦

The idea behind *Chuck D Presents: Louder Than a Bomb* is sound. After all, Chuck D may not have invented political and socially conscious rap, but he sure became the spokesman for it during the peak years of his groundbreaking outfit, Public Enemy. Therefore, he was the perfect choice to present this 17-track compilation, containing many of the greatest protest songs in hip-hop history, including Run-DMC's "Proud to Be Black," Boogie Down Productions' "You Must Learn" (available in a "Live From Caucus Mountains Remix [single edit]"), Grandmaster Flash & the Furious Five's "The Message," Ice-T's "Freedom of Speech," and Public Enemy's "Fight the Power." Most of this dates from hip-hop's golden age, which gives the album some sort of thematic consistency, but not all the tracks are right; for instance, Ice-T's "Freedom of Speech" is the Body Count re-recording with Jello Biafra, not the original from *The Iceberg*. Little differences like this, along with a somewhat tiring sequencing, means that *Louder Than a Bomb* falls short of its promise, but it's still an admirable effort to chronicle the best protest hip-hop in one collection and is thus worth a listen. *—Stephen Thomas Erlewine*

☆ **The Complete Stax-Volt Singles 1959-1968** / 1991 / Atlantic ♦♦♦♦♦

At nine discs and 244 tracks, *The Complete Stax-Volt Singles: 1959-1968* is far too exhaustive for casual fans, but that's not who the set is designed for—it's made for the collector. Featuring every A-side the label released during those nine years, as well as several B-sides, the set is a definitive portrait of gritty, deep Southern soul. Many of the genre's major names—Otis Redding, Sam & Dave, Carla Thomas, Booker T & the MG's, William Bell, Rufus Thomas, the Bar-Kays, Albert King—plus many terrific one-shot wonders are showcased in terrific sound and augmented with an in-depth booklet. For any serious soul or rock collector, it's an essental set, since Stax-Volt was not only was a musically revolutionary label, their roster was deep with talent, which means much of the music on this collection is first-rate. But if you only want the hits, you'll be better off with a smaller collection, since too much of this set will sound too similar, and sorting through the nine discs will be a monumental task if you only want to hear Otis, Rufus, Carla and Sam & Dave. *—Stephen Thomas Erlewine*

The Complete Stax-Volt Soul Singles, Vol. 2: 1968-1971 / 1993 / Stax ♦♦♦♦♦

The first Stax-Volt box was a monolith, standing as the definitive document of the labels and, therefore, gritty Southern soul. Its sequel, *The Complete Stax-Volt Soul Singles, Vol. 2: 1968-1971* is considerably more problematic. Covering only four years compared to its predecessor, which showcased nine years, *Vol. 2* contains 216 tracks, including all of the A- and B-sides released during that era. Most critics consider these four years to be substantially less interesting than Stax's earlier years, and in a sense, they're right. There's no Otis Redding or Sam & Dave, and the music doesn't have the same innovative, kinetic spark of the early years. There's still a lot of great, great music here, but it's difficult to sort it out among these nine discs. About three or four discs' worth of material is truly essential, and it might have been better to boil this era down to a smaller box set, since that would have made for a necessary purchase. As it stands, it's too sprawling and comprehensive to be an essential purchase for anyone other than soul fetishists and hardcore collectors, but those listeners should find much of this fascinating. *—Stephen Thomas Erlewine*

The Complete Stax-Volt Soul Singles, Vol. 3: 1972-1975 / 1994 / Stax ♦♦♦

As the last installment in the three-volume document of the complete Stax-Volt singles, *Vol. 3: 1972-1975* is by far the weakest of the series. During those four years, the label was winding down, since it was unable to successfully make the transition from gritty soul to smoother soul and disco. Their older artists couldn't handle the newer sound, and the newer artists were generally saddled with undistinguished songs. In other words, there weren't many great singles from this era, which is what makes listening to *The Complete Stax-Volt Soul Singles, Vol. 3: 1972-1975* such a chore. While the sound of the set is pleasant, evoking both the funky and smooth soul of the early '70s quite well, the songs and the performances aren't particularly noteworthy. There's about a disc and a half worth of prime material scattered across this set, and only die-hard collectors and fetishists will have the patience to find them. Still, those dedicated listeners will find the box a nice way to conclude the series, since it is a well-produced and comprehensive set, even if the music itself is uneven. *—Stephen Thomas Erlewine*

Cowabunga! The Surf Box / May 21, 1996 / Rhino ♦♦♦♦♦

Massive, though not quite definitive, four-CD, 82-track box set of surf music. The first three discs are devoted to material from the genre's '60s prime, and the fourth devoted to revivalists from 1977 to 1995. Most listeners are still better off with the several excellent single-disc surf compilations available (the best of which, like this one, are on Rhino). If your interest runs very deep, this should satisfy, placing most of the emphasis on instrumentals rather than vocals (though significant efforts in the latter vein by the Beach Boys, Jan & Dean, and others are included). It has most of the big hits, and quite a few of the ones which were principally popular in Southern California, as well as some neat rarities that are hard to find anywhere, like the Illusions' storming "Jezebel," and the Surfmen's "Paradise Cove," the Latin-surf hybrid of Dave Myers's "Moment of Truth," the Sandals' "Theme From Endless Summer," and the Sunrays' pale Beach Boys Xerox, "I Live for the

Sun." The fourth disc of modern-day revivalists, alas, was probably unnecessary in the minds of everyone except the compilers; it's the first three that really deal with the heart of the matter, with voluminous annotation in the 66-page booklet. *—Richie Unterberger*

Creation Records: International Guardians of Rock & Roll 1983-1999 / Oct. 2000 / Creation/Sony ♦♦♦♦♦

Modest title, eh? While it's true that Creation became the U.K.'s most important independent record label, the self-serving praise grows as tiresome as Liam Gallagher's umpteenth boastful comment. What were the other great indies between the period covered here? Chopped liver? With the corpse of Alan McGee's label still fresh, their distribution outlet via Sony released this two disc set in late 2000, compiling 30 highlights of the label's lifespan. McGee selected these tracks, thankfully balancing the known hit with the buried gem rather well. Some of his choices are questionable, like choosing early acts like Slaughter Joe and Meat Whiplash over Revolving Paint Dream and his own Biff Bang Pow. Choosing Ride's "Drive Blind" over the more representative "Vapour Trail" and favoring the House of Love's "Shine On" over "Christine" is a bit bizarre. Pop elitists will chuckle at Teenage Fanclub's two inclusions over Oasis' lone entry. Many don't realize that the label had a history prior to Oasis' *Definitely Maybe*, and even more don't realize that the label had a history prior to Primal Scream's *Screamadelica*, which *International Guardians* illustrates. It does trace something of a timeline in trendsetting British music, from the Jesus and Mary Chain's Velvet Underground-with-daggers, then Primal Scream's dancefloor hedonism, and on to Oasis' retro polishing. The biggest omission is clearly My Bloody Valentine's otherworldly dream pop; allegedly, Kevin Shields pulled his band's three tracks just prior to release. Later acts aren't forgotten, such as Super Furry Animals and Bernard Butler's first solo single. Like the label's ascension from the gutters to the penthouse, *International Guardians* is a thrilling, bumpy ride. Frustrating but ridiculously accomplished. *—Andy Kellman*

☆ **Creole Kings of New Orleans** / 1992 / Specialty ♦♦♦♦♦

Creole Kings of New Orleans is a splendid 26-track sampler of Specialty Records' numerous R&B legends, including Professor Longhair, Percy Mayfield, Lloyd Price, Joe Liggins, and Guitar Slim. Although only a couple of big hits are included, the material is consistently strong, making the disc an excellent purchase. *—Stephen Thomas Erlewine*

☆ **Crescent City Soul: The Sound of New Orleans** / Apr. 2, 1996 / EMI ♦♦♦♦♦

The new king of the hill as far as retrospectives of early New Orleans R&B/rock go. This four-CD, 119-song box has hits by all of the major artists and hits and misses by most of the important minor ones as well. The standards for inclusion are flexible and reasonable: Although New Orleans residents usually carry the day, important records that were recorded in New Orleans by non-natives are also featured. Fats Domino, Little Richard, Irma Thomas, Lee Dorsey, Smiley Lewis, Chris Kenner, Barbara George, Ernie K-Doe, Clarence "Frogman" Henry, Lloyd Price, Aaron Neville, Professor Longhair, Shirley & Lee, and Dr. John are all here, as are one-shots and regional figures like the Showmen, Earl King, Benny Spellman, Dave Bartholomew, and the Spiders. There are plenty of hits, but also plenty of fine songs that most listeners won't be aware of: the original versions of "My Ding-A-Ling" (two of them!), "I'm Gonna Be a Wheel Someday," and "One Night," for instance, which were covered for huge smashes by Fats Domino, Chuck Berry, and Elvis Presley. It's not perfect: the absence of Frankie Ford's "Sea Cruise" is absolutely inexcusable, and the omission of hits like "Blueberry Hill," "Ya Ya," and "Rocking Pneumonia" only slightly less mystifying. It's still the best chunk of New Orleans rock/R&B in one place, with more than enough variety to make the lengthy set a pleasure all the way through. *—Richie Unterberger*

★ **D.I.Y.: Anarchy in the UK: UK Punk I (1976-77)** / Jan. 19, 1993 / Rhino ♦♦♦♦♦

With the exception of the Clash, who could not be included because of licensing obstacles, this 19-song collection includes all of the major originators of British punk music. The Sex Pistols are here, of course, with somewhat rawer demo versions of "Anarchy in the U.K." and "God Save the Queen" that have previously appeared on various quasi-legitimate albums. Otherwise, you get the major singles from a posse of leading bands of the movement, including the Damned, the Saints, the Jam, and the Buzzcocks. Cult acts of nearly equal importance, like X-Ray Spex, the Adverts, the Only Ones, Generation X, and Wire also weigh in with trailblazing singles like "Orgasm Addict" and "One Chord Wonders." Major punk fans and collectors won't find anything here that they don't already have. But for those who didn't pick up everything the first time around, or weren't even around the first time around, it's as ideal an introduction as can be imagined to a sound that totally realigned rock with its emphasis on brittle guitars, amphetamine rhythms, and socially charged songwriting. The booklet includes a lengthy, informative essay by Jon Savage, author of the British punk history *England's Dreaming*. *—Richie Unterberger*

★ **D.I.Y.: Blank Generation: The New York Scene (1975-78)** / Jan. 19, 1993 / Rhino ♦♦♦♦♦

From the outset, New York punk rock had more subgenres and styles than its British counterparts. Even the Ramones, who were seemingly the most straightforward band on the scene, had a distinctly arty conceit behind their fusion of garage-rock, bubblegum, and pop-culture kitsch. Most of their contemporaries had similar attitudes, whether it was Blondie with their sexy, ironic revision of '60s pop, Television's cerebral guitar rock, Richard Hell's jaggedly atonal rock, Patti Smith's punk poetry, or Suicide's eerie synthesizers. All of those bands are collected on the superb overview *D.I.Y.: Blank Generation: The New York Scene (1975-78)*, along with such cult favorites as the Dictators ["(I Live for) Cars and Girls"], Mink DeVille ("Let Me Dream If I Want To"), Wayne County, the Dead Boys, the Heartbreakers, and the Mumps. While Talking Heads are missing from the collection, *Blank Generation* nevertheless is an accurate and nearly flawless portrait of the heyday of New York punk. *—Stephen Thomas Erlewine*

★ **D.I.Y.: Come Out and Play: American Power Pop (1975-78)** / Feb. 16, 1993 / Rhino ♦♦♦♦♦

Power pop benefited from the punk explosion, since it had as much to do with the rock & roll mainstream as with the punks. In the wake of the Ramones and Sex Pistols, straightforward, guitar-driven power-pop bands had a greater audience than before, since more listeners were aware of the existence of such music. And if the ringing pop on *D.I.Y.: Come Out and Play: American Power Pop (1975-78)* has more to do with the British Invasion than the Damned, it shares the same kinetic energy and vital spirit as punk, especially since many of the bands on this collection were doggedly releasing independent records and touring in the late '70s to a dedicated cult following. There are no hits on *Come Out on Play*—Cheap Trick, the one marquee name on the compilation, is represented by the dynamic album track "Southern Girls"—but that doesn't mean it's a collection of also-rans and mediocrities. Instead, these songs are the foundation of the first wave of power pop, and many of the artists here—Pezband ("Baby It's Cold Outside"), the Nerves ("Hanging on the Telephone"), Artful Dodger ("Wayside"), Chris Stamey ("Summer Sun"), Tommy Hoehn ("Blow Yourself Up"), the Paley Brothers ("Come Out and Play"), Fotomaker ("Where Have You Been All My Life"), and Chris Bell ("I Am the Cosmos"—have become legendary in certain circles. As a result, *Come Out and Play* serves as a terrific introduction to the world of power pop, but it's better seen as a collection of some of the best and catchiest pop singles that slipped through the cracks in the late '70s. *—Stephen Thomas Erlewine*

D.I.Y.: Mass. Ave.: The Boston Scene (1979-83) / Feb. 16, 1993 / Rhino ♦♦♦♦♦

Like the Los Angeles installment of the series, *D.I.Y.: Mass. Ave.: The Boston Scene (1979-83)* is weaker than its predecessors because the music it covers simply isn't as diverse, energetic or interesting as the music from New York and England. Boston did have some great bands, yet their second-level groups weren't particularly interesting, and they pale considerably when placed next to the paranoid punk of Mission of Burma ("That's When I Reach for My Revolver"), the garage rock of the Lyres ("I Want to Help You Ann"), the rootsy Del Fuegos ("I Always Call Her Back"), and the Cars' raw demo of "You're All I've Got Tonight." There are a few cool obscurities, such as Willie Alexander's "Mass. Ave," Nervous Eaters' "Loretta," Unnatural Axe's "They Saved Hitler's Brain," Neighborhood Threat's "No Place Like Home," and the Neats' "Six," but they aren't enough to make *Mass. Ave.* worthwhile for anyone but punk and new wave fetishists. *—Stephen Thomas Erlewine*

D.I.Y.: Shake It Up: American Power Pop (1978-80) / Feb. 16, 1993 / Rhino ♦♦♦♦♦

In general, the songs on *D.I.Y.: Shake It Up: American Power Pop (1978-80)* are a little lighter and bouncier than those on its predecessor *Come Out and Play*, but since there was always an element of sweetness in power pop anyway, that difference will matter to only a handful of listeners. *Shake It Up* still shares many of the same characteristics of *Come Out and Play*—namely, it's a collection of 19 dynamic, hook-laden singles from the first wave of American power-pop bands. Again, only a couple of these songs are well known outside of power-pop circles—the Romantics' "What I Like About You" had become a frat-rock anthem by the end of the '80s—but within those circles, the Rubinoos ("I Wanna Be Your Boyfriend"), Chris Stamey & the dB's ["(I Thought) You Wanted to Know"], the Shoes ("Tomorrow Night," "Too Late"), 20/20 ("Yellow Pills," "Giving It All"), Off Broadway USA ("Stay in Time"), Holly and the Italians ("Tell That Girl to Shut Up"), and the Beat ("Work-A-Day World," "Walking Out on Love") and their songs became semi-legendary. With the exception of *Come Out and Play*, there's no better overview of the early-'80s power-pop movement than *Shake It Up*, even with the absence of such major players as Dwight Twilley, Phil Seymour, and Great Buildings. *—Stephen Thomas Erlewine*

☆ **D.I.Y.: Starry Eyes: UK Pop, Vol. 2** / Jan. 19, 1993 / Rhino ♦♦♦♦♦

Picking up where *Teenage Kicks* left off, *D.I.Y.: Starry Eyes: U.K. Pop, Vol. 2* is even more pop-oriented than its predecessor, and that's taking the Buzzcocks' searing "Ever Fallen in Love (With Someone You Shouldn't've?)" into consideration. Although it includes a handful of great singles from artists that were on *Teenage Kicks* (the Undertones' "Get Over You," XTC's "Life Begins at the Hop," Squeeze's "Up the Junction," the Revillos' "Where's the Boy for Me?"), plus Joe Jackson's familiar "Is She Really Going Out With Him?," *Starry Eyes* shines in rounding up terrific singles from under-appreciated artists like Bram Tchaikovsky ("Girl of My Dreams"), the Jags ["Back of My Hand (I've Got Your Number)"], the Records ("Starry Eyes"), the Searchers ("Hearts in Her Eyes"), and Purple Hearts ("Millions Like Us"). These are sparkling pop songs, with ringing guitars and immediate, catchy melodies. Very few of these songs were actual hits, but they are the cornerstone of British new wave and power pop, which has rarely sounded as energetic and vital as it does here. *—Stephen Thomas Erlewine*

★ **D.I.Y.: Teenage Kicks: UK Pop (1976-79)** / Jan. 19, 1993 / Rhino ♦♦♦♦♦

Punk helped restore a nervy, stripped-down sensibility to rock that was quickly filtered through a number of more pop-oriented bands that were labeled as new wave. Not surprisingly, many of these new wavers were holdovers from pub-rock, whose unpretentious, anti-star attitude foreshadowed punk rock. These pub-rockers were devoted to the three-minute pop single, but they also had a biting wit and kinetic energy that separated them from conventional pop-rock bands, and the best of this first wave of new wavers are collected on the dynamic *D.I.Y.: Teenage Kicks: U.K. Pop (1976-79)*. Beginning with Nick Lowe's explosive "So It Goes," the collection runs through a series of classic singles from Eddie & the Hot Rods ("Do Anything You Wanna Do"), Wreckless Eric ("Whole Wide World"), the Motors ("Dancing the Night Away"), Tom Robinson Band ("2-4-6-8 Motorway"), Squeeze ("Take Me, I'm Yours"), the Only Ones ("Another Girl, Another Planet"), XTC ("This is Pop?"), the Rezillos ("Top of the Pops"), and the Undertones ("Teenage Kicks"), throwing in a number of forgotten gems along the way. Although the collection doesn't feature Elvis Costello due to licensing restrictions, he isn't missed—in fact, the collection plays better without him, since focusing on overlooked artists demonstrates what an amazing era new wave was for smart, catchy guitar pop. Few various-artist collections capture their subject as well, or as infectiously, as *Teenage Kicks* does. *—Stephen Thomas Erlewine*

★ **D.I.Y.: The Modern World: UK Punk II (1977-78)** / Jan. 19, 1993 / Rhino ♦♦♦♦♦
Picking up where the first volume of *D.I.Y.: U.K. Punk* left off, *D.I.Y.: The Modern World: U.K. Punk II (1977-78)* captures the moment when punk began to fracture into post-punk, hardcore, and new wave. There are still some straightforward punk anthems from the Jam ("The Modern World"), the Buzzcocks ("What Do I Get?"), the Rezillos ("(My Baby Does) Good Sculptures"), Generation X ("Wild Youth"), and Stiff Little Fingers ("Alternative Ulster," "Suspect Device"), but the collection finds punk turning dark, noisy, paranoid, and weird through Siouxsie & the Banshees ("Hong Kong Garden"), the Fall ("Bingo Master"), Wire ("I Am the Fly"), X-Ray Spex ("The Day the World Turned Day-Glo"), the Soft Boys ["(I Want to Be An) Angleploise Lamp"], and Magazine ("Shot By Both Sides"). There's also some loutish rock from Sham 69 and 999, but *The Modern World* on the whole is much more interesting than that. Despite missing a few major figures like the Clash, it is a definitive portrait of the last days of the original British punk movement, and it works both as an introduction and a great, listenable overview. *—Stephen Thomas Erlewine*

D.I.Y.: We're Desperate: The L.A. Scene (1976-79) / Feb. 16, 1993 / Rhino ♦♦♦♦♦
If *D.I.Y.: We're Desperate: The L.A. Scene (1976-79)* is one of the weakest installments in the *D.I.Y.* series, it's only because the Los Angeles scene wasn't nearly as rich and diverse as those in New York and London. New wave pop didn't have a stronghold in the L.A. punk community, which tended to favor raw, hard, amateurish punk. Essentially, Los Angeles was one of the first towns to embrace hardcore, and almost all of *We're Desperate* plays as proto-hardcore punk. Of all the bands on the collection, X displays the greatest songcraft and style with their edgy guitars and tag-team vocals. No other group has their finesse, but then again, they don't attempt to write songs, they just want to make noise; on that level the collection works, even if it may get tedious to listeners who have just a passing interest in this style of punk. Still, *We're Desperate* is a good overview of the L.A. scene, featuring its handful of major players—the Germs ("Forming," "Lexicon Devil"), the Dickies ["You Drive Me Ape (You Big Gorilla)"], the Weirdos ("We Got the Neutron Bomb," "A Life of Crime"), the Dils ("I Hate the Rich")—plus many lesser-known acts like the Zeros, the Furys, Eyes, Bags, the Last, Alley Cats, the Plugz, and the Dogs, as well as a demo from the Motels. There's not enough variety or substance to make it as essential as the New York and U.K. collections, but that means *We're Desperate* is an accurate representation of Los Angeles punk. *—Stephen Thomas Erlewine*

Death Row Greatest Hits / Dec. 1996 / Death Row/Priority ♦♦♦♦
More than any other label, Death Row defined gangsta rap and hip-hop in the early '90s, and the double-disc *Death Row Greatest Hits* captures nearly all of the label's biggest hits from artists like Dr. Dre, Snoop Doggy Dogg, and 2Pac. Although the disc bends some rules by including cuts that weren't released on Death Row and containing an abundance of previously unreleased songs, the compilation sums up the feeling of the early and mid-'90s. A single disc would have provided more consistent thrills—and it would have eliminated the annoying remixes on disc two—but the sprawl is also indicative of the self-indulgence of gangsta rap, which is essential to understanding the genre. And *Death Row Greatest Hits* has a string of great songs—"Let Me Ride," "What's My Name," "Gin and Juice," "Nothin' But a G Thang" (but no "California Love")—making it an excellent summation of gangsta rap's glory days. *—Stephen Thomas Erlewine*

☆ **Def Jam Music Group—Ten Year Anniversary** / 1995 / Def Jam ♦♦♦♦♦
In the '80s, Def Jam Records became the leading rap and hip-hop label in America. Featuring a roster filled with superstars—including Public Enemy, L.L. Cool J, the Beastie Boys, Slick Rick, and EPMD—Def Jam released many of the most innovative and groundbreaking records of the late '80s and, as the four-CD box *Ten Year Anniversary* proves, the music has lost none of its impact over the years. Over the course of the four discs, the set runs through a number or hip-hop classics, including "I Can't Live Without My Radio," "Fight the Power," "(You Gotta) Fight for Your Right (To Party)," "Slam," "Don't Believe the Hype," "Rock the Bells," "Regulate," "Crossover," and over 50 other tracks. The one (minor) drawback of the set is the fact that it isn't sequenced chronologically; nevertheless, each disc in the box is compulsively listenable. In sheer musical terms, *Ten Year Anniversary* is one of the best box sets ever compiled and is essential to any popular music collection. *—Stephen Thomas Erlewine*

Def Jam Recordings Greatest Hits / Sep. 9, 1997 / Def Jam ♦♦♦♦
Although it doesn't follow any chronological order and doesn't always gel musically, *Def Jam Recordings Greatest Hits* is a good cross section of the pioneering hip-hop label's biggest hits, featuring such classics as Onyx's "Slam," the Beastie Boys' "Brass Monkey," L.L. Cool J's "Around the Way Girl," 3rd Bass's "Gas Face," Domino's "Getto Jam," Slick Rick's "Children's Story," and Warren G's "Regulate." *—Stephen Thomas Erlewine*

The Del-Fi & Donna Story / 1994 / Del-Fi ♦♦♦
In the late '50s and early '60s, Del-Fi was an interesting, eclectic L.A.-based independent rock label, recording surf, rockabilly, R&B, and pop, occasionally landing a national hit. Precisely because of that eclecticism, though, a survey disc of notable tracks from the Del-Fi vaults isn't the smoothest listen. This 31-disc compilation does include good sides by Ritchie Valens, Chan Romero (famous for "Hippy Hippy Shake"), Ron Holden (who had a one-shot with the New Orleans R&B-like "Love You So"), teen idol Johnny Crawford, and surf combo the Lively Ones. Serious collectors will also appreciate the CD availability of rare sides by Dick Dale, Rene Hall (who played guitar on Valens' classic "La Bamba"), a pre-Bread David Gates, and other unknown tracks in the surf, R&B, and instrumental vein. Valens, Romero, Crawford, and the Lively Ones are better appreciated in the context of their own best-of compilations, however. *—Richie Unterberger*

Diggin' in the Crates, Vol. 1: Profile Rap Classics / 1994 / Profile ♦♦♦♦
When hip-hop became huge in the early '80s, its popularity put quite a few independent labels on the map. One of the most important was Profile, which was founded in 1981 and went on to become one of the top indie labels in the U.S. Profile never recorded rap exclusively (the company also provided its share of dance classics), but it was hip-hop more than anything that brought attention to the label. In 1994, Profile looked back on its rap output of the early to mid-'80s with this gem-laden collection. The CD's oldest track is Dr. Jeckyll & Mr. Hyde's "Genius Rap"—a 1981 classic that finds the hip-hop pioneers rapping to the Tom Tom Club's "Genius of Love"—and its most recent is Dana Dane's quirky "Nightmares" from 1986. Gems like Run-D.M.C.'s "Sucker MCs," Pebblee-Poo's "A Fly Guy" (a female's response to the Boogie Boys' "A Fly Girl"), and Pumpkin's "Here Comes That Beat!" transport the listener back to a classic era in hip-hop—a time when New York still dominated the genre, breakdancers were doing their thing on the sidewalks of major American cities, gangsta rap had yet to become popular, and MCs used the term "fresh" to praise things that excited them. *Diggin' in the Crates* reminds us that Profile's contributions to rap were sizable. *—Alex Henderson*

Dischord 1981: The Year in Seven Inches / 1993 / Dischord ♦♦♦
Dischord 1981: The Year in Seven Inches tells the story of the origins of the one of the first hardcore punk labels and the early D.C. hardcore scene. When the Teen Idles had no one to release their posthumous record, Ian MacKaye and Jeff Nelson took $600 in the band's gig money and made it themselves. Like every band on this album, the Teen Idles were meagerly recorded on a four-track, giving them a raw sound that came to characterize the early hardcore scene. The album kicks off with "Teen Idles," a 44-second anthem that ends with the memorable line "We're as idle as teens can get." Debuts of four other D.C. bands follow. A young Henry Garfield (later known as Henry Rollins) is heard chanting with S.O.A. (State of Alert). With the breakup of the Teen Idles, Nelson and MacKaye went onto form Minor Threat, whose classics "Straight Edge" and "Minor Threat" appear along with "In My Eyes" and "Out of Step" from its second EP. The hard-driving, super-fast songs of Government Issue and Youth Brigade bring the record's total to 48 tracks, all for eight bucks. *—Ron DePasquale*

☆ **Disco Box** / Feb. 16, 1999 / Rhino ♦♦♦♦♦
Rhino's four-CD *Disco Box* is the most impressive disco retrospective yet assembled, featuring 80 tracks and exhaustive liner notes which chronicle the music's history, artists, innovations, and subsequent influence. Like many of the best Rhino anthologies of this sort, *The Disco Box* is a mixture of acknowledged classics and neglected yet surprisingly high-quality lesser-knowns (although the emphasis here is more on the former). The result is an enormously infectious, entertaining package that makes the best case yet for the importance and creative viability of disco in its heyday. There are a couple of minor flaws—most disco fans will be able to name a few absent favorites (none of the Bee Gees' historically crucial *Saturday Night Fever* tracks were available for licensing, for example), and others may bemoan the lack of extended 12" club versions, which simply wouldn't fit into a compilation of this scope. At any rate, *The Disco Box* is still as definitive and well-done an overview as we're ever likely to see, and even at four CDs, it's the perfect introduction. *—Steve Huey*

☆ **The Disco Years, Vol. 1: Turn the Beat Around** / 1990 / Rhino ♦♦♦♦♦
A comprehensive series featuring many of the greatest disco songs ever recorded, Rhino's five-volume *Disco Years* set accurately chronicles *the* pop music sensation of the mid-'70s. The first two volumes are the places to start; the other three are necessary for devoted disco fans and pop music historians. *—Stephen Thomas Erlewine*

☆ **The Disco Years, Vol. 2: On the Beat** / 1990 / Rhino ♦♦♦♦♦
Disco Years, Vol. 2: On the Beat continues the fine tradition of its predecessor, offering 16 classic disco singles, plus a handful of interesting obscurities. Of course, there are more hits than rarities here, and the hits are what make this one of the handful of definitive disco compilations. Among the highlights are "I Want Your Love," "Ring My Bell," "I Will Survive," "Ain't No Stoppin' Us Now," "Funkytown," "Celebration," "YMCA," "Heart of Glass," "Last Night a DJ Saved My Life," and "Got to Be Real." They're all songs that defined an era, and there's no better place to hear them than this collection. *—Stephen Thomas Erlewine*

☆ **The Disco Years, Vol. 3: Boogie Fever** / 1992 / Rhino ♦♦♦♦♦
Disco Years, Vol. 3: Boogie Fever isn't quite as consistent as its two predecessors, but it has enough seminal singles—"Rock the Boat," "Get Down Tonight," "Boogie Fever," "I Love the Nightlife (Disco 'Round)," "Macho Man," "Dancing Machine," "Soul Makossa," "Le Freak," "We Are Family," "Knock on Wood," "Bad Girls"—to make it an essential disco collection. *—Stephen Thomas Erlewine*

The Disco Years, Vol. 4: Lost in Music / 1992 / Rhino ♦♦♦♦♦
Another good installment in Rhino's comprehensive five-volume overview of the disco era. For disco fans, each volume is worth purchasing. *—Stephen Thomas Erlewine*

The Disco Years, Vol. 5: Must Be the Music / 1992 / Rhino ♦♦♦♦♦
Another good installment in Rhino's comprehensive five-volume overview of the disco era. For disco fans, each volume is worth purchasing. *—Stephen Thomas Erlewine*

The Disco Years, Vol. 6: Everybody Dance / Jul. 18, 1995 / Rhino ♦♦♦♦
Rhino's six-volume *The Disco Years* is the best, most comprehensive overview of disco's late-'70s heyday, featuring all of the genre's biggest hits with the exception of the Bee Gees' singles from *Saturday Night Fever*. The first four volumes—*Turn the Beat Around, On the Beat, Boogie Fever,* and *Lost in Music*—are essential additions to any comprehensive pop library, since they contain the biggest and best hits: "The Hustle," "Never Can Say Goodbye," "That's the Way (I Like It)," "Car Wash," "Disco Inferno," "Love Hangover," "Turn the Beat Around," "Boogie Oogie Oogie," "You Make Me Feel (Mighty Real)," "Ring

My Bell," "I Will Survive," "Funkytown," "Celebration," "Y.M.C.A.," "Heart of Glass," "Get Down Tonight," "Macho Man," "Le Freak," "We Are Family," "Bad Girls," "Hot Stuff," "He's the Greatest Dancer," "In the Bush," and "Good Times," among others. The next three—*Must Be the Music, Everybody Dance,* and *The Best Disco in Town*—aren't nearly as consistent, but for listeners with a deep interest in disco, they have enough obscurities and interesting tracks to make them worthwhile. Still, the first four volumes of *The Disco Years* are what's really necessary for most listeners, since that's where all the true classics are. *—Stephen Thomas Erlewine*

The Disco Years, Vol. 7: The Best Disco in Town / Jul. 18, 1995 / Rhino ✦✦✦
The Weather Girls, Hot Chocolate, and Chic all pop up on the seventh volume of this disco collection. Also included in the glitter of the disco ball are Kool & the Gang, Evelyn King, and Ashford & Simpson. *—Jonathan Ball*

☆ **Doo Wop Box** / 1994 / Rhino ✦✦✦✦✦
The four-disc set *The Doo Wop Box* is a superb collection of 101 classic doo wop songs from the genre's golden era. Not only are the classic hit singles presented in crystal clear sound, but so are a number of forgotten treasures. It's the rare box set that's equally appealing to both novices and collectors. *—Stephen Thomas Erlewine*

The Doo Wop Box, Vol. 2 / Oct. 1, 1996 / Rhino ✦✦✦✦✦
Rhino's first box set of doo wop classics was obviously successful enough to bring about this second, four-CD set. This time around, with all of the hits covered on the first box, the compilers have dug deep into the genre's history to put together a selection of some of the music's great sides, lesser-known hits, and rarities. Highlights on disc one include "Fool, Fool, Fool" by the Clovers, "A Thousand Stars" by the Rivileers, "I Love You So" by the Crows, "I'll Be Forever Loving You" by the El Dorados, "Smokey Joe's Cafe" by the Robins, "Life Is But a Dream" by the Harptones, and "Ling Ting Tong" by the Five Keys. Disc two covers a two year period (1955-1957) and features "Eddie My Love" by the Teen Queens, "Ruby Baby" by the Drifters, "Zoom" by the Cadillacs, "Ka-Ding Dong" by the G-Clefs, "The ABC's of Love" by Frankie Lymon and the Teenagers, "Guided Missiles" by the Cuff Links, "Glory of Love" by the Velvetones, and "Mr. Lee" by the Bobettes. Disc three covers sides from 1957 to 1960, including "Could This Be Magic" by the Dubs, "Zoom Zoom Zoom" by the Collegians, "We Belong Together" by Robert & Johnny, "You're So Fine" by the Falcons, "Island OF Love" by the Sheppards, "Bad Girl" by the Miracles, and "Love Potion No. 9" by the Clovers. The final disc covers 1960 to 1963, when doo wop had its last great renaissance on the pop charts, with "Valarie" by the Starlites, "Those Oldies But Goodies (Remind Me of You)" by Little Caesar and the Romans, "Pretty Little Angel Eyes" by Curtis Lee, "I Love You" by the Volumes, "Duke of Earl" by Gene Chandler, "What Time Is It?" by the Jive Five, and "Rip Van Winkle" by the Devotions. A sumptuous booklet also provides much important info on the artists, the sound and the style. An important addition to anyone's doo wop or '50s music collection. *—Cub Koda*

Doo Wop Box, Vol. 3: 101 More Vocal Group Gems from the Golden Age of Rock & Roll / Aug. 1, 2000 / Rhino ✦✦✦✦
The first two Rhino doo wop box sets were straightforward anthologies of the best music in the style, concentrating on big and small hits and the best overlooked rarities. The third installment is also a worthy chunk of the genre's better moments, yet it is definitely a notch or two below its predecessors. Part of the reason is that, as many doo wop records as there were, the lion's share of the great hits were already used up on the first two boxes. Thus, Rhino took a different strategy for this four-disc set, devoting the first CD to hits (many of which weren't *that* big, or have certainly escaped oldies rotation); disc two to "should-have-been hits"; disc three to "celebrity picks" of the favorite doo wop tunes by star musicians, comedians, and record executives; and disc four to modern doo wop post-dating the early '60s. Overall, it's still a nice package, but it's probably an idea that has finally come to the end of its line. *—Richie Unterberger*

The Ego Trip's the Big Playback / Apr. 11, 2000 / Priority ✦✦✦✦✦
The soundtrack to *Ego Trip's Book of Rap Lists* salutes its namesake by offering a dozen classic tracks from the mid-'80s golden age of hip-hop. Still, rap fans may be a bit surprised at the track list; there's nobody here with the name recognition of the period's heroes (Eric B. & Rakim, Public Enemy, EPMD, L.L. Cool J) or even those with renewed underground cred during the late '90s (Ultramagnetic MC's, Kool G. Rap & DJ Polo). Instead, this compilation focuses on *real* obscurities, not necessarily the best tracks of all time, but top-rate cuts that never got the attention they deserved. Obviously, it's required listening for readers of the book, the perfect way to actually *hear* some of the out of print classics mentioned in sections like "Quarter Pound of Underacknowledged Hip Hop Cuts" and "Disses You Might Have Missed." Even for fans who aren't interested in a book of rap lists, *Ego Trip's the Big Playback* is a stellar compilation, providing a couple of the original tracks whose samples might sound very familiar to '90s fans: "Holy War (Live)" by Divine Force (used by DJ Premier on a Jeru the Damaja cut) and "Get Retarded" by MC EZ & Troup (used by Dr. Dre on "Zoom" from the *Bulworth* soundtrack). Other highlights among these rarities include "Marly Marl Scratch," the first solo-billed track by Marly Marl, and "Get Down Grandmaster" by Grandmaster Caz, a great latter-day cut by the old-school legend. *—John Bush*

Electric Sugar Cube Flashbacks / AIP ✦✦✦✦✦
When AIP upgrades its catalog to CD, there's a lot of confusion; the same title is usually kept as the vinyl edition, but the tracks are taken from various volumes of a series, and lots of previously uncompiled bonus tracks are tacked on. The CD version of *Electric Sugar Cube Flashbacks* draws from a few volumes of the multi-LP series of British '60s psychedelic rarities that went under that name, especially volume four. About a dozen of the cuts, though (over half the CD), didn't appear on any of the vinyl compilations. There are a few moderately well-known groups among the 21 tracks (the Smoke, Family) and rarities by big-time artists (the Dave Clark Five, Sweet). But mostly these are no-names who caught the lightning for a track or two on hopelessly obscure singles. Not everything here's great, but a lot of it's good, or better than that, fusing melodic pop crunch with experimentation better than virtually any other subgenre of rock. Highlights are the contributions by the Smoke, Big Boy Pete, Andy Ellison, Svensk, and Mike Stuart Span (represented by a rare BBC version of their glorious flop single, "Children of Tomorrow"). *—Richie Unterberger*

Electric Sugar Cube Flashbacks, Vol. 1-4 / AIP ✦✦✦
In comparison to U.S. bands, obscure British groups of the mid- and late '60s have been ill-served by compilations; there are dozens of Pebbles volumes and hundreds of American garage rock compilations in the same vein, but comparatively few for their British counterparts. There are some, however, and the *Electric Sugar Cube Flashbacks* series is probably the best of them, spotlighting rare early British R&B, "beat," and psychedelic recordings from impossibly rare 45s, many of which were never released in the States. The British bands tended to be somewhat more accomplished, tuneful, and imaginative in their lyrics and arrangements than their American counterparts; those looking for obscure music in the classic British '60s R&B/rock and power-pop style should check these out, with the awareness that they're generally more crudely performed, written, and produced than the material by the British Invasion giants we know and love. As is the case with all AIP series, the volumes tend to get worse as the series progresses; Volume One, if you can find it, is by far the best. *—Richie Unterberger*

English Freakbeat, Vols. 1-5 / AIP ✦✦✦
Like its cousin series *Electric Sugar Cube Flashbacks*, this focuses on way-obscure British "beat," R&B, and early psychedelia, circa 1964-1968. There are some great cuts to be found on these, as well as super-rare singles by groups that featured future stars like Steve Howe, Mick Ronson, and Graham Gouldman, and even famous never-weres like Pete Best. They're very uneven anthologies, though, more so than the *Electric Sugar Cube Flashbacks* volumes; one gets the feeling that the tracks were sometimes selected as much or more for their rarity than their actual musical value. *—Richie Unterberger*

Epitaph for a Legend / 1980 / Collectables ✦✦✦✦✦
The Texas-based International Artists label recorded some intriguing, slightly off-the-wall psychedelic-garage-pop in the 1960s, their most famous act being the 13th Floor Elevators. This is an erratic but extremely interesting double-LP compilation of IA oddities and rarities, much of it previously unreleased. The five Red Krayola demos (some of which would be re-recorded for their first LP) are prime acid folk, especially "Hurricane Fighter Plane," one of the closest American approximations of Syd Barrett-era Pink Floyd. The Chapparrals' "I Tried So Hard" is gutsy punk-pop, Thursday's Children's "A Part of You" is reminiscent of the mid-period Zombies, and the Emperors' "I Want My Woman" is growling garage punk. Side four is devoted entirely to 13th Floor Elevators/Roky Erickson rarities, including a beautiful acoustic version of "Splash I" and the rare single by Roky's pre-Elevators group the Spades. In this company, side three—which has unexceptional straight blues material, including a song by Lightnin' Hopkins—is a misfit, but psychedelic collectors will want the record for the rock material. *—Richie Unterberger*

Everything Is Nice: Matador Records 10th Anniversary Anthology / Sep. 14, 1999 / Matador ✦✦✦✦
Founded by Gerard Cosloy and Chris Lombardi in the autumn of 1989, Matador Records emerged as one of the most important and influential American independent labels of the decade to follow, largely defining the sound and spirit of indie rock through seminal releases from artists including Pavement, Liz Phair, Yo la Tengo, and Guided by Voices. The three-disc *Everything Is Nice* celebrates Matador's tenth anniversary by compiling key singles, live tracks, and rarities, spotlighting the label's vaunted eclecticism by assembling material by everyone from grrrl-punk icons Sleater-Kinney to Japanese pop savant Cornelius to drone merchants Bardo Pond. Some of the inclusions are questionable at best—Pavement's "Stereo" over "Summer Babe"? For shame—but as an introduction the set more than serves its purpose, with the abundance of unreleased tracks making it worthwhile for longtime fans as well. *—Jason Ankeny*

Faster & Louder: Hardcore Punk, Vol. 1 / 1993 / Rhino ✦✦✦✦✦
Faster & Louder: Hardcore Punk, Vol. 1 overlooks a handful of classic singles in favor of several novelties and rarities, yet the 17-track collection remains a first-rate introduction to hardcore, featuring two absolute classics in the Dead Kennedys' "Holiday in Cambodia" and Bad Brains' "Pay to Cum," plus cuts from such major figures as the Circle Jerks, Suicidal Tendencies, Angry Samoans, Meatmen, Government Issue, and Hüsker Dü. *—Stephen Thomas Erlewine*

Faster & Louder: Hardcore Punk, Vol. 2 / 1993 / Rhino ✦✦✦
Considered unimaginably over-the-top and atonal at the time, the early sounds of hardcore punk don't sound nearly as noisy 15 years later. Dare we say, they even sound a bit poppy and tightly conceived in comparison with the uncompromisingly bleak, rushed, and amelodic sounds of today's underground hardcore groups. That's not to take away from the undeniable influence and power of first-generation hardcore. *Faster & Louder: Hardcore Punk, Vol. 2* does a good job of assembling some of the most enduring and accessible moments of the genre's genesis. This 17-song compilation includes the first singles by Husker Du and X, who went on to transcend hardcore's limitations pretty rapidly. It also includes seminal tracks by Agent Orange and Wire, as well as influential bands with smaller cults like the Wipers, the Dils, and Zero Boys, down to nearly forgotten acts (Dys, Stranglehold). The bleakest and most vicious strand of early hardcore is represented by Fear, the Germs, the Subhumans. Not a bad package for those who want to sample the genre's highlights and limit its representation in their collection to this fairly small and manageable dose. *—Richie Unterberger*

☆ **Fiddling While Romo Burns** / 1996 / Melody Maker ✦✦✦✦✦

For a brief, shining moment in the mid-'90s, the world was captured by the sounds of Romo, a fey, arty offspring of Brit-pop who pointedly revived the sounds of early-'80s new romantic synth-pop crossed with a touch of irony, modernist art, a healthy love of the Style Council and the Spice Girls, inspiration from Pulp, jealousy of Menswear, a vague idea of Roxy Music, heritage in the Smiths and the Manics, and a minor obsession with *Dead Poets Society*. Actually, they didn't really take over the world, they were pushed relentlessly by *Melody Maker* (more accurately, journalists Simon Price and Taylor Parkes) and embraced by less than 100 people in the U.K. and a handful of pop obsessives in the States (most of them likely located in western Michigan at the time, all two of them working for the same company). Melody Maker pushed the imagined movement to an extreme, putting several fops on a glorious cover as a way to introduce the movement, then assembling a tour to push Romo, issuing *Fiddling While Romo Burns*, a five-song promotional tape attached to Melody Maker, as a way to hype it all. Even though it was the height of Brit-pop—with patriotism permeating every inch of the British Isles and every band outside of Bush being hailed as continuing the great British guitar band tradition (yes, even 60 Foot Dolls and Heavy Stereo)—it was a monumental disaster, with barely anybody attending shows. It's estimated that only 100 people attended the shows throughout the United Kingdom, a shockingly small number for a tour so heavily hyped by a leading music publication. Not surprisingly, Melody Maker bailed from Romo shortly afterward. A few singles still trickled out from the likes of DexDexter and Plastic Fantastic, along with Orlando's *Passive Soul* (the only full-fledged Romo album), leaving *Fiddling While Romo Burns* as the unexpected last will and testament of this aborted movement. That's not much of a recorded legacy, but listening to the tape years after the hype failed to launch is an utterly fascinating experience, especially if you were one of the 102 people who were into it at the time. Romo essentially boiled down to a cross between Adam Ant, Roxy Music, Pulp, and Blur, with a hint of an idea of what Bowie may have meant. They were theatrical and sillier than the perpetrators imagined, and while they certainly captured the more ridiculous aspects of the new romantics, anybody who supported this overlooked one crucial fact—nobody on God's green earth wanted to hear this stuff except those 102 people. Why? Well, there's nothing but style and artifice here, and at crushing levels, particularly since the groups are reveling in unabashed silliness without even realizing it. And that's the joy of it—this is good pop. True, it's filled with affectation and pretension, but there's a giddy, hedonistic joy from the bands themselves as they get carried away with their plastic infatuation, turning out the most ridiculous choruses you could hope to hear, whether it was in the service of style or sincerity. Based on this tape, Romo was fun, stylish, goofy, and invigorating. If you shared their viewpoint—whether you were postmodern art students in London or pub rockers with affection for Adam Ant—this was a thrilling extension of the promise of new wave, and even if it never caught on, it's hard not to cherish it all the same. —*Stephen Thomas Erlewine*

Frat Rock, Vol. 1 / 1991 / Rhino ♦♦♦♦

Rhino's *Frat Rock, Vol. 1* is a near-perfect collection of consistently fun rock, pop, and soul from the '60s, including such classics as the Kingsmen's genre-defining "Louie Louie," Sam the Sham & the Pharaohs' "Woolly Bully," the Surfaris' "Wipe Out," the Gentrys' "Keep on Dancing," and the Human Beinz' "Nobody but Me." The Dynatones' "Shout," the Isley Brothers' "Twist and Shout," and the Swinging Medallions' "Double Shot (Of My Baby's Love)" keep the party vibe going strong, while the stomping rhythms of the Trogg's classic "Wild Thing," the McCoys' "Hang on Sloopy," and the Strangeloves' "I Want Candy" make them frat rock staples. If *Frat Rock, Vol. 1* featured Mitch Ryder's incendiary version of "Little Latin Lupe Lu" instead of the Righteous Brothers' slightly less intense (but still worthy) rendition, it would be the perfect collection of joyously dumb frat rock classics, but as it stands, it's merely an excellent collection of some of the '60s most vibrant, energetic singles. —*Heather Phares*

Frat Rock, Vol. 2 / 1991 / Rhino ♦♦♦♦♦

Though it's not quite the nonstop party of *Frat Rock, Vol. 1*, *Vol. 2* of the series comes close to matching its predecessor's energy with '50s and '60s classics like Sly & the Family Stone's "Dance to the Music," Ritchie Valens' "La Bamba," the Champs' "Tequila," and the Spencer Davis Group's "Gimme Some Lovin'." Technically, several of the songs on this volume aren't really frat rock, though Chuck Berry's "Reelin' and Rockin'" and the Marathons' "Peanut Butter" are fun and energetic enough to hold their own against frat rock classics like the Premiers' "Farmer John," the Music Explosion's "Little Bit O' Soul," the Blendells' "La La La La La," and the Bobby Fuller Four's "I Fought the Law." Nitpicking aside, *Frat Rock, Vol. 2* is nearly as much of a blast as the first volume, even if it isn't quite as focused on true frat rock. —*Heather Phares*

Frat Rock, Vol. 3 / 1991 / Rhino ♦♦♦♦♦

Frat Rock, Vol. 3 continues in the tradition of the rest of the *Frat Rock* series, mixing true frat rock classics like Cannibal & the Head Hunters' "Land of 1000 Dances" with other up-tempo '50s and '60s hits such as Chuck Berry's "Johnny B. Goode" and Del Shannon's "Do You Want to Dance?" *Volume 3* also traces frat rock's progression into garage rock with tracks like the Standells' classic "Dirty Water" and the Castaways' "Liar Liar." James Purify's "Shake a Tailfeather," the Beach Boys' "Barbara Ann," the Guess Who's "Shakin' All Over," and the Kingsmen's "Jolly Green Giant" are some of the album's other highlights, along with tracks from Ray Charles and the Midniters. *Frat Rock, Vol. 3* manages to expand the definition of the genre while delivering nearly as many great singles as the series' first two volumes. —*Heather Phares*

Frat Rock, Vol. 4 / 1991 / Rhino ♦♦♦

The final volume in the *Frat Rock* series, *Frat Rock, Vol. 4*, gathers more fun, party-minded singles like Mitch Ryder & the Detroit Wheels' "Devil With a Blue Dress On/Good Golly Miss Molly," Tommy James and the Shondells' "Mony Mony," and Wilson Pickett's "In the Midnight Hour." Jimmy Gilmer's "Bottle of Wine" and Roger Miller's

"Chug-A-Lug" deliver a one-two punch of drinking music, while the Isley Brothers' "Shout, Pts. 1 & 2" and the Capitols' "Cool Jerk" add a soulful, danceable air to the mix. The Rivieras' "California Sun" and Gary "U.S." Bonds' "Quarter to Three" are some of the other highlights of this exuberant collection, which captures the fun of '60s party music, even if most of the tracks aren't technically frat rock. —*Heather Phares*

Frat Rock: More of the '70s / 1995 / Rhino ♦♦♦

Like the first volume of *Frat Rock: The '70s*, *More of the '70s* functions more as a sampler of album-rock hits than frat-house rock, but it still contains a number of good songs, including Golden Earring's "Radar Love," and Deep Purple's "Smoke on the Water," The Kinks' "Sleepwalker," Joe Walsh's "Life's Been Good," Foghat's "Slow Ride," Bad Company's "Can't Get Enough," and Gary Glitter's anthemic "Rock & Roll, Part 2." —*Stephen Thomas Erlewine*

Frat Rock: The '70s / 1995 / Rhino ♦♦♦

A fun, but haphazard, collection of album-rock rave-ups from the '70s, this disc contains highlights like Alice Cooper's "School's Out," and Grand Funk Railroad's "We're an American Band," Foreigner's "Hot Blooded," and the Knack's "My Sharona." —*Stephen Thomas Erlewine*

Frat Rock: The '80s / 1995 / Rhino ♦♦♦

The '70s editions of the *Frat Rock* series concentrated on album-rock crossover hits. *Frat Rock: The '80s* is more schizophrenic. Most of the disc concentrates on new wave hits like Madness' "Our House," Adam Ant's "Goody Two Shoes," Devo's "Whip It," Stray Cats' "Rock This Town," and Tommy Tutone's "867-5309/Jenny Jenny," but it also has album-rock tracks like the J. Geils Band's "Centerfold" and Top 40 cuts like Robert Palmer's "Addicted to Love," Glenn Frey's "The Heat Is On," and Poison's "Nothin' but a Good Time." —*Stephen Thomas Erlewine*

Freestyle Explosion, Vols. 1-5 / May 2, 2000 / Thump ♦♦♦♦♦

Thump's *Freestyle Explosion* compilation series was an excellent, definitive overview of the Latin-influenced dance-pop style born and bred in the clubs of Miami. Thump repackaged all five volumes of the series into a limited-edition slipcased box set, giving devoted freestyle fans a handy way to pick them all up at once. While some of the artists here scored bigger pop-chart successes with ballads, these collections concentrate only on the dance floor; some of those artists include Stevie B, TKA, Sweet Sensation, the Cover Girls, Exposé, Taylor Dayne, Sa-Fire, Lisette Melendez, Lisa Lisa & Cult Jam with Full Force, Dino, Will to Power, Nu Shooz, and Pretty Poison. —*Steve Huey*

Funk Box / Nov. 21, 2000 / Hip-O ♦♦♦♦

At four discs and 55 tracks, Hip-O's *Funk Box* seems to want to be the last word on funk, and while it's a pretty good set, it ends up more representative than definitive of its chosen genre. Virtually all of funk's most important artists are featured, but not always by their most significant singles—sometimes the collection gets it right, and sometimes it's disappointing (leaving out Curtis Mayfield's "Superfly," the Average White Band's "Pick Up the Pieces," War's "Low Rider," and "Why Can't We Be Friends," and the Ohio Players' "Fire" and "Love Rollercoaster" in favor of alternate selections). Still, the *Funk Box* does have a generous helping of full-length funk classics, including several rare 12" versions; moreover, it's been digitally remastered, and it features a 48-page booklet. It's just too bad the set doesn't completely hit the mark. —*Steve Huey*

Funky Broadway Stax Revue Live at the 5/4 Ballroom / 1992 / Stax ♦♦♦♦♦

Nearly an hour of previously unreleased Stax soul recorded at a Los Angeles venue in August 1965, including cuts by Booker T. & the MGs, Carla Thomas, Rufus Thomas, William Bell, and the Mar-Keys; a couple of relatively little-known Stax vocal groups, the Mad Lads and the Astors, round out the program. This isn't just of interest to soul completists. Good live mid-'60s soul records, in decent fidelity, are fairly rare items. This is genuinely galvanizing stuff, with a rawer, more party-oriented feel than the classic Stax studio sides of the same era. Especially good are Booker T. & the MGs, who really burn throgh classics like "Green Onions" and "Soul Twist," and Rufus Thomas, who clowns his way through a nine-minute version of "Do the Dog." —*Richie Unterberger*

G.S. I Love You Too: Japanese Garage Bands of the '60s / Nov. 9, 1999 / Big Beat ♦♦

Like its predecessor *G.S. I Love You*, this compiles unheard-in-the-West cuts by 1960s Japanese garage-psych bands. All 27 songs were released on Philips in Japan between 1966-69; the "G.S." of the title is an abbreviation for "Group Sounds," as this genre was termed in Japan. Sure, you'd be challenged to find many (any?) collectors outside of Japan who had all of this stuff. This does not mean, though, that this is any less generic than many a standard '60s garage/psych/punk compilation from the U.S. or Europe, though the fidelity is certainly way better than the standard. In most respects these Japanese bands were the same as those from other lands in their catalog of fuzz riffs and basic variations of R&B-influenced rock patterns. It's a little strange to English-reared ears because of the accents, frequent mangling of English phrases, and off-kilter, bizarrely energetic transmutations of American and British rock cliches. The truth is, the songwriting and instrumentation aren't too imaginative, and attention tends to wander often during the course of the lengthy disc. Yes, you can pick out odd touches to numerous arrangements—the television drama horns that mix with fuzz guitars on the Carnabeats' "Chu! Chu! Chu!," the verbatim quote of the guitar riff from the Byrds' "Here Without You" that opens the Tempters' "Himitsu No Rikotoba" (after which it goes right into a totally unrelated, basic garage-psych tune), the quasi-San Francisco blues-rock groove of the Tempters' "Tell Me More," the D'Swooners' eccentric translation of "Stone Free," and the Shadows-meet-Joe Meek instrumental "Space Express" by the Savage. But, to trot out a reviewer cliché to match the musical ones, little sticks in the memory. The most entertaining cuts actually tend to be the ones in which raunchy '60s rock meets incongruously poppy, brassy production (as in Lind & the Linders' "Koi Ni Shiberete"), if only for the novel admixture. *—Richie Unterberger*

G.S. I Love You: Japanese Garage Bands of the '60s / 1996 / Big Beat ♦♦♦
Japan, like many non-English-speaking countries, was home to a thriving garage/beat band scene in the 1960s. The Japanese scene, at least to Western ears, was more peculiar than most: for one thing, it didn't really kick into gear into 1966, and Japanese groups were still playing in an early British Invasion-influenced style until the end of the decade. Singing in both Japanese and heavily accented English, the guitars (as a result of the Ventures' huge popularity there) were surfish Mosrites, and the material was often a strange fusion of Merseybeat, punk, and over-the-top weirdness. *G.S. I Love You* is a 28-track compilation of songs originally released on the Crown and Teichiku labels, and while it's no match for the real British groups (or, for that matter, the best beat/punk groups from Holland and Sweden), it's truly like no other '60s rock you've heard. The guitar work is often frenzied and imaginative; the vocals walk the line between tough raunch and low comedy, particularly when they mangle English phonetics (the Swing West's version of Arthur Brown's "Fire," as well as the Out Cast's butchering of "Long Tall Sally," defy printed description). Sound quality and liner notes (in English) are excellent, and cuts like the Blue Jeans' "One More Please" are genuinely good fusions of pop and punk, making this a good pickup for the more adventurous '60s collector. *—Richie Unterberger*

Get Hot or Go Home: Vintage RCA Rockabilly '56-'59—Vols. I & II / Country Music Foundation ♦♦♦♦♦
Get Hot or Go Home: Vintage RCA Rockabilly, '56-'59 is an expertly assembled double-disc collection of rare rockabilly from the RCA vaults. After Elvis Presley became a star, RCA decided to sign a number of new acts to their label, as well as revamp some older country artists to fit the new rockabilly sound. It didn't matter that they bought out Elvis' contract from Sun—they didn't want to risk missing the next Elvis, so they signed anyone they could find. Of course, none of the artists on *Get Hot or Go Home* (including an early Roy Orbison) could have followed Presley's footsteps—they were either too hillbilly (Pee Wee King, Homer & Jethro, Tommy Black) or too slick to cut it. That doesn't mean that the compilation makes for bad listening; in fact, the unevenness of the material makes the set all the more appealing, because the failures are nearly as entertaining as the successful cuts. Out of all the artists on *Get Hot or Go Home*, only Joe Clay sounds as if he should have had a full-fledged career, but the also-rans, one-hit wonders, and the country guys trying to go rockabilly are all fascinating and frequently fun. It's a great purchase for avid rockabilly and country fans. *—Stephen Thomas Erlewine*

★ **Golden Age of American Rock & Roll, Vol. 1** / 1991 / Ace ♦♦♦♦♦
For many years, Original Sound's *Oldies But Goodies* series was acknowledged as the best source for catching up on the many great early rock & roll hits by artists who had only one (or two, or three, or even a few more) classics to offer. Ace's *Golden Age of American Rock & Roll* series, however, has surpassed *Oldies But Goodies* as the series of choice in the CD age. Even at an import price, they offer better value (with 30 songs each!); they use the best possible available source tapes for remastering; they also offer lengthy, intelligent liner notes and some photos, where Original Sound have historically offered none. Most important, they offer a wealth of great hits from rock & roll's first decade as a widespread phenomenon (1954-63), some of which are very difficult to find on other recordings, CD or not. There are some huge hits represented, but an equal amount of attention is paid to lower-charting items that have fallen out of rotation at oldies stations, as well as some slight/regional hits that you might not have heard even if you grew up during the era. Volume One, like each installment, reflects the incredible diversity and excitement of rock's first decade: doo wop, primitive rockabilly, girl groups, instrumental rock, proto-soul, pop-rock, and more, ranging from famous one-shots (the Jaynetts' "Sally Go Round the Roses," the Penguins' "Earth Angel") to semi-forgotten treasures like the Fendermen's "Mule Skinner Blues" and Toni Fisher's "The Big Hurt." *—Richie Unterberger*

★ **The Golden Age of American Rock & Roll, Vol. 2** / 1993 / Ace ♦♦♦♦♦
No volume of the *Golden Age of American Rock & Roll* series is more essential than any other one. As all have a good range of styles, and a mix of big and small hits, none is particularly recommended more than others; all are worth acquiring if you want to build a serious rock & roll collection. Volume Two has plenty of classics (the Silhouettes' "Get a Job," Maurice Williams' "Stay," Lonnie Mack's "Memphis," the Rivieras' "California Sun," Link Wray's "Rumble") to go along with some neat one-shots (the Bell-Notes' "I've Had It," Barbara George's "I Know," Harold Dorman's "Mountain of Love"). Just as interesting are the minor hits, like the Eternals' ridiculous "Rockin' in the Jungle" (up-tempo doo wop with side-splitting bird calls) and the Gladiolas' original version of "Little Darlin'" (covered with much bigger success by the Diamonds). *—Richie Unterberger*

★ **The Golden Age of American Rock & Roll, Vol. 3** / 1994 / Ace ♦♦♦♦♦
More good, classic stuff. Everyone will have different favorites according to their tastes, which is an advantage of having such a diverse collection on CD—you can skip around as you like. The roll call here includes many classic one-shots, by Wilbert Harrison ("Kansas City"), Bill Parsons ("The All American Boy," sung by Bobby Bare, although Parsons got the label credit), the Teddy Bears ("To Know Him Is to Love Him," Phil Spector's first classic), the Turbans ("When You Dance"), Skip & Flip ("It Was I"), the Olympics ("Western Movies"), and the Castells ("Sacred"). *—Richie Unterberger*

★ **The Golden Age of American Rock & Roll, Vol. 4** / 1994 / Ace ♦♦♦♦♦
Another reliably well-packaged collection of major and minor pre-Beatle rock hits. Besides the hits by stars like Dion, Gary U.S. Bonds, Jan & Dean, and Buddy Knox, you have plenty of one-shots by the likes of the Edsels ("Rama Lama Ding Dong"), Little Caesar & the Romans ("Those Oldies but Goodies"), Barbara Lynn ("You'll Lose a Good Thing"), and Ray Sharpe (the classic R&B/jump rocker "Linda Lu"). The further the series goes, the deeper it gets into the lower rungs of the charts, so even rock scholars may not have previously heard cuts by the likes of Nat Kendrick, Nappy Brown, or the Royaltones. Others you may have only heard once or twice, like the ones by Tommy Facenda, the Rip Chords, and Billy & Lillie. *—Richie Unterberger*

★ **The Golden Age of American Rock & Roll, Vol. 5** / 1995 / Ace ♦♦♦♦♦
It's been said before, but it bears repeating: much of the history (and soul) of early rock & roll resides not only in the recordings of giants like Elvis, Little Richard, Chuck Berry, and Buddy Holly, but in the literally hundreds of acts who managed to produce one or two great singles, in an incredible variety of styles. You can't claim to have a comprehensive rock & roll collection without seeking these out, and you'll have a surprising amount of fun doing so. The fifth volume of the *Golden Age of American Rock & Roll* series shows no signs of flagging in its mission to document these important sounds. Big hits by stars (Freddie Cannon, Jan & Dean, Gene Chandler); huge one-shot hits like Dale & Grace's "I'm Leaving It Up to You," and Johnnie & Joe's "Over the Mountain, Across the Sea," and Jimmy McCracklin's "The Walk"; treasured cult classics by the Showmen ("It Will Stand") and Eddie Fontaine ("Nothin' Shakin'," covered by the Beatles on *Live at the BBC*); all are here, and more. *—Richie Unterberger*

☆ **Grandson of Frat Rock!, Vol. 3** / 1991 / Rhino ♦♦♦♦♦
Like the first two volumes of *Frat Rock*, *Grandson of Frat Rock* contains 18 terrific rock & roll and R&B singles from the '60s. There are a few singles from major artists—Chuck Berry's "Johnny B. Goode," and Del Shannon's "Do You Want to Dance?," Ray Charles' "What'd I Say, Pt. 1," the Isley Brothers' "Twist and Shout" and "Shout, Pts. 1 & 2," and, inexplicably, Roger Miller's "Chug-a-Lug"—but the primary value of the set is that it collects one-hit wonders like "Hang on Sloopy," "I Want Candy," "Surfin' Bird," "Tequila," "Liar, Liar," "Dirty Water," "Bread and Butter," "Gimme, Gimme Good Lovin'," and "Shake a Tail Feather," great singles by artists who never made great albums. And while this disc has its flaws, it's still one of the best ways to collect all of these songs at once. *—Stephen Thomas Erlewine*

Groove 'N' Grind: 50's & 60's Dance Hits / Rhino ♦♦♦♦♦
This dance-oriented collection of 18 tracks brings together records from the late 1950s and early '60s, the height of dancefloor mania until the dreaded coming of disco. Kicking off with Cannibal and the Headhunters' "Land of 1,000 Dances," the set also features great one-hit wonders like "Cool Jerk" by the Capitols, "The Loco Motion" by Little Eva, "The Jerk" by the Larks, and "C'mon and Swim" by Bobby Freeman. Also aboard are classics like "The Walk" by Jimmy McCracklin, "Georgia Slop" by Big Al Downing, "Harlem Shuffle" by Bob and Earl (later covered by the Rolling Stones), and "The Monkey Time" by Major Lance. The only clinker is a re-recorded version of "The Twist" by Chubby Checker, a real anomaly on a Rhino package, a label that usually loathes such tacky, cash-grabbing motives. *—Cub Koda*

Growin' up Too Fast: The Girl Group Anthology / 1996 / Mercury ♦♦♦
A two-CD, 50-song collection of girl-group hits and misses originally released on the MGM, Smash, Philips, Fontana, 20th Century Fox, and Mercury labels in the early and mid-'60s. It's nice to have some of these rarities easily available in state-of-the-art fidelity, but it's not one of the best girl-group compilations around, in terms of either thematic coherence or consistent quality. The hits by the Shangri-Las, Lesley Gore, Dusty Springfield, the Angels, and the Royalettes are good to great, but are better heard in the context of their own compilations. Much of the rest—by obscure singers like Ginny Arnell, the Pixies Three, and Beverly Washburn—is pleasant but rather forgettable. There are some really neat one-shots and lost classics here, though, like Diane Renay's Top Ten hit, "Navy Blue," and her flop follow-up, "Watch Out, Sally!," is one of the toughest white girl-group records ever. Also cool are the Secrets' "The Boy Next Door" (an Angels sound-alike) and the two songs by Sadina, which are among the best unknown Wall-of-Sound-type productions ever. *—Richie Unterberger*

The Grunge Years: Sub Pop Compilation / 1994 / Sub Pop ♦♦♦♦♦
Thirteen-track, sardonically packaged (completed with suited, briefcase-toting executive types on the front cover) compilation of material from Sub Pop's late-'80s/early-'90s period, when the company had just been tagged (and saddled) with the grunge label. Much of it was originally released on vinyl 45, and some has subsequently resurfaced on CD; indeed, only dedicated collectors could probably tell you which of these tracks are truly rare by now. In any case, it's a decent sampler, with cuts by Nirvana, Tad, L7, Mark Lanegan, Screaming Trees, Mudhoney, Afghan Whigs, Babes in Toyland, and less expected entries like Beat Happening and the decidedly un-grunge Walkabouts. The *Hype!* soundtrack—which includes material by several of these acts, and adds songs by many Seattle-area bands not represented here—is actually a better genre overview, at least until the inevitable day when the grunge box sets start appearing. *—Richie Unterberger*

Happy Together: Very Best of White Whale Records / Aug. 10, 1999 / Varese ♦♦♦
White Whale was one of the better independent Los Angeles rock labels of the mid-to-late 1960s. Its only consistent hitmakers were the Turtles, and most of its releases were also in a good-time rock vein, although some got a little weirder, and some delved into bubblegum. This is a pretty fair 21-song compilation of hit and flop White Whale singles from 1965-70, less interesting for the three Turtle smashes included than for the rarities. The Matthew Moore Plus Four's 1965 single "Codyne" [sic], for instance, is probably the first rock version of Buffy St. Marie's oft-covered "Codeine." Warren Zevon was in the male-female folk-rock duo Lyme & Cybelle, represented not just by the small hit "Follow Me," but also the much rarer cover of Bob Dylan's "If You Gotta Go, Go Now." To the left of these folk-rockers were the off-the-wall mod-psychedelia of John's Children's "Smashed! Blocked!," and the 1968 single by the Rockets, who would soon become Crazy Horse. Efforts by the Clique, the Committee, and others are far more lightweight; the Latino easy listening of Rene & Rene's "Lo Mucho Que Te Quiero," though a big hit, is a

pretty ill fit on this disc. The easygoing pop of Liz Damon's Orient Express' 1970 Top 40 single "1900 Yesterday" and Nino Tempo & April Stevens' Phil Spector-soundalike hit "All Strung Out" are more stylistic variations to round out the compilation. Interesting stuff more often than not, but because of its emphasis on singles exclusively, this misses the most interesting White Whale rarity of all: J.K. & Co.'s mysterious album *Suddenly One Summer*, a cross between *All Things Must Pass*-era George Harrison and Donovan. *—Richie Unterberger*

★ **Hardcore Doo-Wop: In the Hallway-Under the Street Lamp** / 1993 / Specialty ♦♦♦♦♦
This compact disc collects 25 doo wop collector's classics from a variety of small West Coast R&B labels who dabbled in the genre. The California version of the streetcorner vocal group phenomena had stronger leanings toward bluesier harmonies and vocal performances bordering on madness. As best exemplified here by groups like Arthur Lee Maye & The Crowns and Byron "Slick" Gipson & the Sliders, the West Coast doo wop movement definitely had a sound all its own. *—Cub Koda*

☆ **Harvest Festival** / 1999 / EMI/Harvest ♦♦♦♦♦
Harvest Festival is a genuinely comprehensive and thorough look at the one British major label venture into psychedelia and progressive rock that actually worked, commercially and artistically; it's a panoramic journey though a major part of British rock as it developed over a period of just under a decade. Over the five CDs and 119 songs, more than two dozen acts are featured, ranging from purely English phenomena like Michael Chapman, Quatermass, and Pete Brown to mega-arena acts like Pink Floyd, and the set comes complete with a built-in 120-page book that would be worth 35 dollars by itself. Beginning with the Edgar Broughton Band's Jimi-Hendrix-meets-the-Crazy-World-of-Arthur-Brown track "Evil," the programming goes a long way to explaining why Harvest worked while other attempts at forming psychedelic and progressive labels in England failed—in contrast to the slick, commercial psychedelic ventures at rival Deram Records, Harvest always gave its artists the freedom to be louder (or softer) than the norm, and to be bold in their expressions. Moreover, the diversity of form was astonishing, from the acoustic instrumental chamber music rock of the Third Ear Band, to the lively acoustic psychedelia of Syd Barrett and Kevin Ayers, to the high-energy attack of Deep Purple, Quatermass, and Bakerloo—it all sounds amazingly strong, well crafted, and exciting. Harvest had room for jugband music, traditional acoustic folk, progressive folk-rock, spoken word, and, full-circle commercially from Harvest's late-'60s origins, psychedelic Beatles-influenced commercial rock by way of ELO. Harvest also grew to embrace sounds that would have been inconceivable for EMI to have signed when they started, including Be-Bop Deluxe (versions 1 and 2), Bill Nelson's Red Noise, the reggae outfit Matumbi, the Shirts with Annie Golden, and the punk band Wire. It's all fascinating stuff, told in great detail in the accompanying book, but ultimately, a set like this stands or falls on the music. The archivists have dug deeply enough to find material that makes Barrett's output look tame and conventional, specifically Tea & Symphony, whose "Maybe My Mind (With Egg)" is a truly dissonant and strange journey into thought processes bent by the prism of drugs and meditation. Not everything on this set will be to everyone's liking, but anyone inclined to enjoy Pink Floyd or Syd Barrett's solo stuff will be entranced by most of the content. The sound has been treated first-class, with new state-of-the-art 1999 remasterings. The other measure of success of this box is that there's a huge amount of material here that leaves the listener wanting more from a lot of the acts featured. *—Bruce Eder*

Hey Drag City / Oct. 24, 1994 / Drag City ♦♦♦♦♦
Hey Drag City collects songs from Drag City's early-'90s roster, which included bands like Desert Storm, King Kong, Burnout, Fruitcake, and Mantis. Many of the label's better-known bands contribute the album's highlights; Pavement's "Nail Clinic" shows off the group's early, unraveled art-punk sound, and Smog's "Your Face" is one of Bill Callahan's creepiest, yet most affecting, songs. Palace's shambling "For the Mekons Et Al," the Silver Jews' "Famous Eyes," and Royal Trux's untitled piece also rank among the best songs from this snapshot of Drag City's early years. *—Heather Phares*

Hi Records: Early Years, Vols. 1 & 2 / May 11, 1999 / HI ♦♦♦
Hi Records is usually identified with such R&B artists as Al Green and Ann Peebles, but this 57-track double-CD reveals the early pop, country, rockabilly, and rock & roll roots of the label. Drawn mainly from the late '50s and 1960s, *Hi Records: The Early Years* includes contributions by such recognizable names as Ace Cannon, Narvel Felts, Gene Simmons (whose 1964 hit "Haunted House" is here), and the Bill Black Combo. Other interesting items include seven tracks by the Johnny Cash-influenced Tommy Tucker, seven tracks by one-hit wonder Jerry Jaye (whose "My Girl Josephine" charted in 1967 and is included on this compilation), and a handful of recordings by Carl McVoy, one of Jerry Lee Lewis' many musical cousins. Much of this music is marginal but enjoyable, and the compilation is clearly aimed at collectors and specialists. Enthusiasts of country, rock, and rockabilly from this period might look for *Hi Records: The Early Years* in the R&B racks, where it will inevitably be misfiled. *—Greg Adams*

Hi Records: The 45's Collection Vols.1-2 / Cream-Hi ♦♦♦
Hi Records became famous for a brace of Southern soul recordings by folks like Al Green and Ann Peebles, both produced by Willie Mitchell and expertly played by the Hi house band. This is a two-disc set of rarities from that same Hi soul team, simply loaded with breathtakingly raw but elegant soul gems. In addition to stray tracks from Peebles, O.V. Wright, and Otis Clay, we're also treated to true rarities from James Fry, David Duke, Eddie McGee, Norm West, Syl Johnson, Bobo Mr. Soul, T-99, Willie Walker, George Jackson, Erma Coffee, Phillip Mitchell, the Masqueraders, and Teacher's Edition. An important chunk of Memphis musical history. *—Cub Koda*

Hi Times: Hi Records R&B Years [Box] / Feb. 21, 1995 / Capitol ♦♦♦♦♦
Hi Times: Hi Records R&B Years is a superb three-disc box set covering all of the label's greatest hits, plus a number of forgotten gems. Al Green understandably dominates the set, since he not only was Hi's biggest artist, he also defined the label's sound with producer Willie Mitchell. As a result, the music on these three discs can sound a little similar at times, but the songwriting and performances from the likes of Green, Ann Peebles, and Joe Clay is first-rate, making *Hi Times* a necessary addition to any serious soul collection. *—Stephen Thomas Erlewine*

☆ **Hip Hop Greats: Classic Raps** / Rhino ♦♦♦♦♦
Although it's far from perfect, the ten-track *Hip Hop Greats: Classic Raps* offers a good overview of the first national rap hits. Since it contains the majority of hip-hop's early classics—Sugarhill Gang's "Rapper's Delight," and UTFO's "Roxanne, Roxanne," Kurtis Blow's "The Breaks," Run-D.M.C.'s "It's Like That," and both "White Lines (Don't Don't Do It)" and "The Message" from Grandmaster Flash—it's an excellent primer and introduction, even though it's a bit too brief to be a definitive overview. *—Stephen Thomas Erlewine*

Hitsville USA, Vol. 2: The Motown Singles Collection 1972-1992 / Oct. 19, 1993 / Motown ♦♦♦
Hitsville USA was such a success that it was little wonder that Motown decided to issue the sequel, *Hitsville USA, Vol. 2: The Motown Singles Collection 1972-1992.* Certainly, these four discs couldn't help but suffer in comparison to their predecessor—the first volume contained some of the greatest pop singles in history—since Motown was following trends during these 20 years instead of setting them. Nevertheless, there are a surprising number of classic singles here, from "Papa Was a Rolling Stone," "Let's Get It On," and "Dancing Machine" to "Easy," "Brick House," and "Super Freak." Unfortunately, there are too many mediocre songs on this set to make searching for these gems a pleasurable experience. If the compilers had limited themselves to a two-disc set, they would have been able to fit all the highlights on a consistent, listenable collection. As it stands, *Hitsville USA, Vol. 2* simply contains too much middling music to make it useful for anyone but dedicated Motown fans. *—Stephen Thomas Erlewine*

☆ **Hitsville USA: The Motown Singles Collection 1959-1971** / 1992 / Motown ♦♦♦♦♦
Instead of following Stax/Volt's pattern and delivering an exhaustive box set containing all of their singles, Motown decided to limit their singles box, *Hitsville USA: The Motown Singles Collection 1959-1971*, to four discs that concentrated on the hits. There are a handful of wonderful lesser-known songs here, such as the Contours' "First I Look at the Purse," but the main strength of the 103-track box is that it features all of the biggest songs from Motown's golden era in one place. Collectors could have used a more comprehensive set, and the box itself could have been packaged with a little more care (there are no artists listed on the back of the individual discs, only songs), but *Hitsville USA* stands as a definitive overview and introduction to one of the most groundbreaking labels in pop music history. *—Stephen Thomas Erlewine*

Hut Recordings: 1991-2001 / Jun. 26, 2001 / Hut ♦♦♦
Hut Recordings hasn't necessarily stood at the forefront of the vanguard as far as independents are considered, but they have had their fair share of major successes without the benefit of standard major-label business practices. Owned by the massive Virgin machine, Hut nonetheless receives their distribution through Rough Trade, qualifying their releases for the U.K. indie charts. *Hut Recordings: 1991-2001* celebrates a decade of the label's existence (well, if you want to get technical, 11 years) in addition to including a small batch of songs from some of their newer, promising acts. Commercial successes like the Smashing Pumpkins (the stomping "I Am One") and the Verve (the tearjerking ballad "History") are included with critical favorites the Auteurs (the uncharacteristically aggressive but taut "Lenny Valentino"), Gomez (a version of "Whippin' Piccadilly"), and Dave Matthews fave David Gray ("Wisdom"). Other notable inclusions come from glam/grunge fusionists Placebo ("Nancy Boy"), David McAlmont and Bernard Butler's hit collaboration ("Yes"), Whale's unlikely semi-fluke hit ("Hobo Humpin Slobo Babe"), and one of Embrace's better Verve/Spiritualized approximations ("All You Good Good People"). One major grumble is the exclusion of Moose, who released a trio of spectacular shoegaze singles in 1991 and an equally great pop record on Hut the following year. There aren't that many people walking the earth hunter-gathering each of the label's releases as one would for labels like 4AD or Creation, so the compilation's "priced to sell" nature helps. The disc also boasts some spiffy graphic design in the spirit of *Harvest Festival.* *—Andy Kellman*

If You're Ready! The Best of Dunwich Records, Vol. 2 / 1994 / Sundazed ♦♦♦♦♦
This second volume investigating the history of Chicago's best—and most influential—teen band label of the mid-'60s comes up with 28 tracks of classic Windy City garage band genius with more emphasis on rarities and unissued material than its initial volume, *Oh Yeah!* Dunwich was a small concern, run by three jazz heads, who nonetheless managed to tap into Chicago's fertile teen scene of the mid-'60s and get the very best groups down on tape at the city's best studio, Universal. Although "Gloria" by the Shadows of Knight was their only major national hit, they were one of the few labels that steadily catered to this kind of teenage racket; the quality of their releases was very high and many of them have reached legendary status. The Pride and Joy (actually the Del-Vetts) kick things off with the title track and rare Dunwich 45s from the Shadows of Knight ("I'm Gonna Make You Mine," which starts out with a four-chord guitar blast dripping with reverb, distortion, and rock & roll), Things to Come, the Luv'd Ones, Saturday's Children ("You Don't Know Better"), the Rovin' Kind (great covers of "Girl" and John Sebastian's "Didn't Want to Have to Do It"), and the Wanderin' Kind all keeping the disc stuck in high gear. Seven of the tracks here are previously unissued masters, and these, along with radio spots by H.P. Lovecraft and the American Breed—one of them for Ban deodorant!—and a rare alternate session take of the Shadows of Knight creaming "I Got My Mojo Working" (originally released on a vinyl album of Dunwich outtakes in the '70s called *Early Chicago*)

make this fine collection a worthwhile addition to anyone's '60s garage band collection. This one literally screams of teen clubs, Rickenbacker guitars, and fake IDs. —*Cub Koda*

Immediate Singles Collection, Vols. 1-5 / Line ✦✦✦

This six-CD 162-song set is the most comprehensive look yet at the complete singles output of Andrew Loog Oldham's Immediate Records from its beginnings in 1965 through its end in bankruptcy in the spring of 1970. This is probably the best way to trace the history of the company on a day-to-day basis, as opposed to their albums, which were fewer and farther between. The range of sounds runs from folk and pop/rock to experimental progressive rock and psychedelia with serious detours into folk-rock and blues-rock (a separate body of work, represented in other collections); Oldham, thanks to his social and business connections, probably gave Immediate an advantage over most other start-up labels, in that artists were eager to get into an orbit somewhere in the vicinity of the Rolling Stones, or at least their manager. In contrast to past Immediate collections, the producers of this box have dug up B-sides as well as A-sides so that one gets to hear genuine rarities such as "The Last Mile," the punchier flip side of the Nico Immediate single "I'm Not Sayin'"; both sides of Glyn Johns' only single as a recording artist; and the Marquis of Kensington's Minstrels' track "Reverse Thrust" that have gone virtually unheard anywhere for more than 30 years. More to the point, one gets to hear such otherwise forgotten representatives of swinging London as the Warm Sounds, Joey Vine, and the Hill. Coupled with these rarities are the best sounding masters of most of the rest that have yet been heard; some of the latter is a product of some decently thorough tape research, coupled with modern analog-to-digital transfers. If the music is a tour through a good-sized cross section of swinging London's musical environment, the annotated booklet is a cornucopia of background and behind-the-scenes information about the artists and their era, which ought to be worth the price of two additional CDs. As a cautionary note, one should be aware that Immediate's blues output is not represented here, that material having been reserved for a separate compilation; on the other hand, the material that is here features several good Jimmy Page productions (most notably involving the Fifth Avenue) that are seldom mentioned anywhere and of which few people are aware. —*Bruce Eder*

The In Crowd: UK Mod R&B Beat,1964-1967 / May 15, 2001 / RPM ✦✦✦

There's a decent amount of good stuff on this anthology, but it does represent the second to third rung of artists and tracks in this immensely exciting genre. It's something to investigate only after you've digested the Who, the Small Faces, Creation, and the Pretty Things, especially as there are no tracks by any of those groups on this 26-track anthology. And the songs by the biggest names are rather peripheral to their core discographies: The Yardbirds' "Stroll On" is the reworking of "The Train Kept A-Rollin'" that they did for the *Blow-Up* film, while the Spencer Davis Group's "Keep on Running" is a live radio version, not the original hit single. Getting past these considerations, almost everything here is fair to excellent British R&B-mod, including cuts by some of the better second-division acts on the scene (Brian Auger, Julie Driscoll, the Artwoods, John's Children, the Untamed, the Eyes, Graham Bond) and early recordings by some future superstars like Rod Stewart, Steve Howe (as part of the In Crowd), and David Bowie (as part of the Manish Boys). The Action's blue-eyed soul masterpiece "I'll Keep Holding On," Gary Farr & the T-Bones' R&B cover of Mongo Santamaria's "Get the Money," and Les Fleur Des Lys' "Mud in Your Eye," in fact, are great cuts, and John's Children's "The Love I Thought I'd Found" (also known as "Smashed Blocked") is mod on the verge of dissolving into psychedelia. "It's Alright," by the Rocking Vickers, is an oddity in that it's basically Pete Townshend's "The Kids Are Alright" with different lyrics and song structure (though Townshend still gets the songwriting credit). This is really more of a first purchase for listeners just beginning to investigate obscure mod music than one for the specialists, though, since many people interested in these sounds in the first place will already have many or most of the songs on other reissues. There's an extraordinary bonus, however: An enhanced CD track has a three-minute video clip from a 1964 documentary focusing on the Four + 1 (with future members of the psychedelic band Tomorrow), including a snippet of a live performance of Bo Diddley's "Nursery Rhyme." —*Richie Unterberger*

The In Crowd: The Story of Northern Soul / 2001 / Sanctuary ✦✦✦✦

Issued in conjunction with the acclaimed book of the same name, the two-disc *The In Crowd: The Story of Northern Soul* assembles 50 dancefloor classics rediscovered and resurrected thanks to the energy and passion of the DJs and revelers packing underground British clubs during the R&B and mod revival of the 1970s. While Dobie Gray's classic title cut is the most recognizable entry here, die-hard Northern soul aficionados will likely own most if not all of the tracks on 7" or other CD collections; the set is instead more of a primer and history lesson, packed with perennial crowd favorites which together comprise a fairly definitive portrait of what the otherwise nebulous "Northern soul" tag actually constitutes. It may seem like hyperbole to suggest that out of 50 songs there's not a dud in the bunch, but each and every moment of *The In Crowd* is deserving of inclusion—for a rundown of highlights, just look at the track listing. —*Jason Ankeny*

In Tha Beginning . . . Tha Originals / Nov. 25, 1997 / Priority ✦✦✦

The *In Tha Beginning* project seems like a good idea in theory. Take some of the greatest hip-hop singles from the '80s, have some hot '90s stars record new versions, then release companion albums, one containing the originals, the other the covers. It's an excellent marketing scheme that has one major flaw—there's no way that the new versions could match the originals. After all, NWA's "Dopeman" and "Fuck tha Police," Ice-T's "6 in the Mornin'," Doug E. Fresh's "The Show," BDP's "I'm Still #1," Biz Markie's "Make the Music with Your Mouth," L.L. Cool J's "Big Ole Butt," EPMD's "Knick Knack Patty Wack" and Rock Master Scott's "The Roof Is on Fire" are all seminal singles in their own way, showcasing some of the greatest musical and lyrical talents of their time. Which means, of course, that *In Tha Beginning…Tha Originals* is a great listen, since it contains 12

timeless tunes. There are better hip-hop comps, of course, but this is still a great primer in the roots of hard-core hip-hop. —*Stephen Thomas Erlewine*

In Yo' Face! (The History of Funk), Vol. 1 / 1993 / Rhino ✦✦✦✦✦

Funk fans eagerly anticipated Rhino's five-part series, thinking that they would get something equivalent to the label's wonderful 1970s soul line. While the final results are good, things are not quite as rosy as earlier reports indicated. The most disappointing thing was the decision to settle for single versions of tracks rather than extended ones. This was how the songs sounded on radio, but the results are truncated versions of "Sex Machine" and "Keep On Truckin'," rather than the glorious full cuts with complete musical interludes. Otherwise, most song choices are great, especially the JB's, Funkadelic, and Lyn Collins. —*Ron Wynn*

In Yo' Face! (The History of Funk), Vol. 2 / Rhino ✦✦✦✦✦

Volume two of Rhino's funk series offers 15 more mostly strong cuts, although it is disappointing to hear edited versions of great anthems. The marvelous trumpet solo and additional chorus from the O'Jays' "For the Love of Money" has been trimmed, and although they don't tell you, only part of B.T. Express' "Do It ('Til You're Satisfied)" is included. There's still plenty of wonderful funk, including classics by Sly & the Family Stone, James Brown, Kool & The Gang, Rufus, Parliament, AWB, and the Temptations. —*Ron Wynn*

In Yo' Face! (The History of Funk), Vol. 3 / Rhino ✦✦✦✦✦

By the third volume of Rhino's generally solid funk series, it has become apparent who did and did not permit their songs to be licensed. Once more there are songs from James Brown, Sly & the Family Stone, Parliament, Funkadelic, the O'Jays, and AWB, and it's great that George McCrae's delightful "I Get Lifted" made the cut, as well as Graham Central Station's "The Jam." Cameo's "Funk Funk" reveals how close to Parliament they were early in their career, while the Brothers Johnson, Kool & the Gang in their great pre-J.T. Taylor phase, and one-hit wonders Wild Cherry complete the disc. —*Ron Wynn*

In Yo' Face! (The History of Funk), Vol. 4 / 1993 / Rhino ✦✦✦✦✦

Familiar names comprise the bulk of the final volume in Rhino's funk series. There are more tracks by James Brown, Sly & the Family Stone and AWB, plus numbers from repeat entries the Isley Brothers, Earth, Wind & Fire, Kool & the Gang and Graham Central Station. But new acts offer prototype funk on some smoking numbers such as Slave's "Slide," the Bar-Kays' "Shake Your Rump to the Funk," Brick's "Dazz," and George Duke's "Reach For It." Bootsy's "The Pinocchio Theory" was a classic, and the same is true for Marvin Gaye's "Got to Give It Up, Part 1." Only Brass Construction's "L-O-V-E-U" falls below the standard. —*Ron Wynn*

In Yo' Face! (The History of Funk), Vol. 5 / 1993 / Rhino ✦✦✦

The fifth volume of *In Yo' Face! (The History of Funk)* features more stellar performances from funk greats like the Ohio Players, Fatback, the Gap Band, and Chuck Brown. Sly & the Family Stone's "Loose Booty," Parliament's "Flash Light," Zapp's "More Bounce to the Ounce," and Rick James' "Bustin' Out (On Funk)" are among the many highlights of this collection, which also includes the Brides of Funkenstein's "Disco to Go" and Cameo's "I Just Want to Be." As with all of the volumes of the *In Yo' Face!* series, *Vol. 5* offers a wonderful introduction to—or reminder of—funk's vibrant, sexy sound. —*Heather Phares*

In Yo' Face! (The Roots of Funk), Vol. 1/2 / 1994 / Rhino ✦✦✦✦

Since the five-volume funk series *In Yo' Face* proved successful, Rhino decided to release a collection of gritty, funky R&B and soul from the late '60s and early '70s as *In Yo' Face! (The Roots of Funk), Vol. 1/2*. It's certainly possible to hear the funk in Lowell Fulson's "Tramp," Dyke & the Blazers' "Funky Broadway," Archie Bell's "Tighten Up," the Meters' "Cissy Strut," and Lee Dorsey's "Everthing I Do Gonh Be Funky," but what makes this such good listening are the obscurities from the likes of Wilson Pickett, Watts 103rd Street, Laura Lee, and Betty Wright, plus lesser-knowns like 8th Day, Fugi, Fantastic Johnny "C," and Tami Lynn. That's what gives the album depth and makes it far more interesting than the average soul or funk collection. —*Stephen Thomas Erlewine*

Industrial Strength Machine Music: Framework of Industrial Rock 1978-1995 / Sep. 14, 1999 / Rhino ✦✦✦

Rhino's AP Presents *Industrial Strength Machine Music: The Framework of Industrial Rock 1978-1995* presents 16 tracks from the heyday of industrial, when the music was part of the underground and progressing at a rapid speed. Actually, the title is a bit misleading, since the disc doesn't contain all that much from the late '70s, or even the mid-'90s—it concentrates on the salad days of the late '80s and early '90s, when the music ruled college airwaves. Any industrial fan or anyone that followed college radio during those days will recognize many of the names here—Throbbing Gristle, Cabaret Voltaire, Coil, Einsturzende Neubauten, Skinny Puppy, Scraping Foetus Off the Wheel, Front 242, Clock DVA, Meat Beat Manifesto, Ministry, My Life with the Thrill Kill Kult, KMFDM, Revolting Cocks, Nine Inch Nails. Most of the groups are represented by their most familiar material and when they're not, such as the previously unreleased RevCo cover of "Physical" or the previously unreleased live version of NIN's "Gave Up," they're sops to collectors who already have all this material in their collection. Does that mean that *Industrial Strength Machine Music* is only for collectors. Hardly. As a matter of fact, there's probably enough rarities here to make it truly of interest to them, but for casual fans or neophytes, this is a good basic primer. Sure, it might have been nicer to have "Head Like a Hole" instead of "Gave Up," but that's only one minor flaw in an otherwise strong collection. —*Stephen Thomas Erlewine*

It's Bigger Than the Both of Us—N.Z. Singles 1979-82 / 1989 / Festival ✦✦✦

It's Bigger Than the Both of Us offers two discs worth of rare singles and stray tracks from New Zealand's often overlooked underground from 1979 to 1981 with releases not only from the better known Flying Nun label but also from Propeller, Ripper, and R.E.M. Featuring some legendary tracks from the Clean, Toy Love, Tall Dwarves, and the Swingers this is essential listening for anyone interested in the development of New Zealand rock. *—Chris Woodstra*

☆ **Just Can't Get Enough: New Wave Hits of the 80's [Series Overview]** / 1994 / Rhino ✦✦✦✦✦
Following their landmark *Soul Hits of the '70s* by a couple years, Rhino's *Just Can't Get Enough* is an exhaustive 15-volume overview of new wave, arguably the last great singles era. Though there are hints of post-punk scattered throughout this series (appropriately, those with pop concessions), this pretty much subscribes to the idea that new wave was quirky, invigorating, stylish pop, and follows it from 1979 through the early years of MTV. Some may complain that stars like Elvis Costello and the Clash are absent, but they're not terribly missed, since a series like this gains its greatest strength by collecting hits from singles-oriented artists or one-hit wonders. Like many Rhino compilations of the mid-'90s, this does tend to include maybe three too many novelties, and some of these singles haven't aged well, but for the most part there is an abundance of great songs here. That could mean novelties like Trio's "Da Da Da," but it also means full-fledged pop masterpieces like Spandau Ballet's gorgeous "True," Nick Lowe's "Cruel to Be Kind," Charlie Sexton's coolly stylish "Beat's So Lonely," or Men at Work's "It's a Mistake." Several of the volumes could have used a little tightening in their sequencing, but each disc boasts so many highlights and is so essential for new wave and pop libraries that that little quibble hardly matters. *—Stephen Thomas Erlewine*

Kill Rock Stars / 1991 / Kill Rock Stars ✦✦✦✦✦
Kill Rock Stars is an excellent 18-track various-artists collection capturing the essence of early-'90s indie-rock pop underground. It's divided equally between amateurish indie-pop, abrasive punk and riot grrrl, featuring many of the best underground bands of that time, including Bratmobile ("Girl Germs"), Mecca Normal ("Narrow"), Bikini Kill ("Feels Blind"), Heavens to Betsy ("My Red Self"), Unwound ("You Speak Jealousy"), Nation of Ulysses ("N.O.U. Cooking with Gas"), Some Velvet Sidewalk ("Loch Ness"), Nirvana ("Beeswax"), and Lois performing under the name Courtney Love ("Don't Mix the Colors"). *—Stephen Thomas Erlewine*

Kindercore Fifty: We Thank You / 2000 / Kindercore ✦✦✦✦
Since first surfacing in 1996, the Athens, GA-based indie Kindercore has emerged as arguably the most consistently entertaining and appealing label in the new American underground. Records as diverse as Dressy Bessy's *Pink Hearts, Yellow Moons*, Kitty Craft's *Beats and Breaks From the Flower Patch*, and Japancakes' *If I Could See Dallas* compare favorably with anything issued in the late 1990s, and while much of the company's focus remains devoted to the resurgent Athens scene, releases like Etienne Charry's *36 Erreurs* and the *Just Another Taste of Electronic Watusi Boogaloo* comp reveal an increasing international outlook all too often absent from the insular Amerindie community. *Kindercore Fifty: We Thank You* celebrates the label's success in grand style, serving up three discs of brand new material, rarities, and remixes spanning from obscurities like the Catskills' cover of the Phil Spector classic "Christmas (Baby Please Come Home)" and the hilariously-named Nipples for Days' "Cows in a Tornado" to tracks from indie icons like the Olivia Tremor Control and the Apples in Stereo. The remix disc is entirely superfluous, but the rarities disc is a godsend for collectors and the new recordings are consistently great recent signings like Tuesday Weld, C.A.R., and the Four Corners bode well for Kindercore's future. No, thank you. *—Jason Ankeny*

Kurtis Blow Presents the History of Rap, Vol. 1: The Genesis / Aug. 19, 1997 / Rhino ✦✦✦✦
The first volume of the three-part *Kurtis Blow Presents the History of Rap* is subtitled *The Genesis*, which means that it covers a period of time when rap was strictly a live art form and rarely made it to record. That means, of course, that the disc is filled with funk records—specifically ones with extended rhythm breaks and grooves that provided ideal instrumental backdrops for rappers. *The Genesis* leans toward the obscure, where even the most familiar names (James Brown, the Isley Brothers, Booker T. & the M.G.'s, the Jackson 5) are represented with unfamiliar songs, and the remainder of the compilation is filled with cult artists (Baby Huey, Michael Viner's Incredible Bongo Band, Black Heat, Rhythm Heritage). While many of these songs may be unfamiliar, there are beats and samples that have been popularized through sampling, which makes listening to the disc fascinating. Unfortunately, it never becomes truly intoxicating, since it's a historical recording that's designed for education, not entertainment, but anyone interested in the birth of hip-hop will find it necessary listening. *—Stephen Thomas Erlewine*

Kurtis Blow Presents the History of Rap, Vol. 2: The Birth of the Rap Record / Aug. 19, 1997 / Rhino ✦✦✦✦✦
As the second installment of Kurtis Blow Presents the History of Rap, *The Birth of the Rap Record* chronicles the moment that hip-hop entered the popular consciousness. The record that broke the doors down was "Rapper's Delight," which is represented here, like the ten other tracks on the compilation, in an extended version that allows both the beats and the rhymes to flourish. Where most early rap compilations focus on records that made an impact on the R&B charts, *The Birth of the Rap Records* is devoted to the underground. There are a number of familiar songs here—"The Breaks," "The Message"—but the majority of the disc is devoted to underappreciated artists like the Sequence, Spoonie Gee, "Love Bug" Starski, Davy DMX and Funky Four Plus One More, or unfamiliar songs by artsits like Afrika Bambaataa and the Treacherous Three. Unlike its predecessor, *The Genesis, Vol. 2: The Birth of the Rap Record* plays smoothly, making it a rare historical release that is as entertaining as it is educational. *—Stephen Thomas Erlewine*

Kurtis Blow Presents the History of Rap, Vol. 3: The Golden Age / Aug. 19, 1997 / Rhino ✦✦✦✦✦
Where *Kurtis Blow Presents the History of Rap, Vol. 2: The Birth of the Rap Record* chronicled rap's first forays into the mainstream, *Vol. 3: The Golden Age* documents the point when hip-hop culture became an undeniable part of popular culture. There are more hits on *The Golden Age* than on any other disc in *The History of Rap*, featuring classics by such artists as Run-D.M.C. ("Rock Box"), Whodini ("Friends"), the Fat Boys ("Jail House Rap"), UTFO ("Roxanne, Roxanne"), Public Enemy ("Rebel Without a Pause"), Boogie Down Productions ("Criminal Minded"), Big Daddy Kane ("Raw"), Rob Base & DJ E-Z Rock ("It Takes Two"), and Biz Markie ("Vapors," "Just a Friend"). At that time, rap was becoming more diverse, boasting different rhyming and production styles—where early rap was similiar stylistically, there was a world of difference between the dizzying hardcore of Public Enemy and the comedy shenanigans on Biz Markie. The musical depth of rap is evident on *The Golden Age*—it certainly does not all sound the same—and while it does overlook some artists, it nevertheless is an invaluable sampler, capturing the essence of the era. *—Stephen Thomas Erlewine*

Land of 1000 Dances / Feb. 26, 1999 / Ace ✦✦✦✦✦
Thirty-song compilation of big and small hits from 1958-1965 based around a rock & roll dance. Although it's imperfect and the smaller, more obscure hits simply aren't as good as the familiar smashes, it's about as good an anthology of the sort as you're going to get, due to the length and quality of the presentation. How to argue with "The Loco-Motion," "Ride Your Pony," "Peppermint Twist," "Walking the Dog," "Cool Jerk," "Twist and Shout," "The Monkey Time," "The Nitty Gritty," "Let's Dance," "The Walk," "The Monster Mash," "The Stroll," and Cannibal and the Headhunters' version of "Land of 1,000 Dances"? You also get almost a dozen cuts that hardly show up on any collections, like Russell Byrd's "Hitch Hike Part 1," Ray Barretto's "El Watusi," Al Brown's "The Madison," Tony and Joe's "The Freeze," and Steve Alaimo's "Mashed Potatoes," which add some enticement to the collection even if they're not among the disc's musical highlights. Presumably because of licensing restrictions, some obvious contenders from the Cameo-Parkway catalog are not here, like Chubby Checker's "The Twist" and Dee Dee Sharp's "Mashed Potato Time." *—Richie Unterberger*

Listen to the Music: '70s California Sound / Jun. 18, 1996 / Rhino ✦✦✦
Sixteen tracks epitomizing the mellower aspects of the singer/songwriter sound, a genre that either serves as a comfortable home base or a symbol of all that was most repellent about the '70s, depending upon your tastes. It's been selected with care, though, mixing critical favorites like the Flying Burrito Brothers, Little Feat, Crazy Horse, Gram Parsons, and Warren Zevon with much cornier outings by the Doobie Brothers, Linda Ronstadt, and Nicolette Larson (her lousy cover of Neil Young's "Lotta Love"). Few of these are little-heard, although it does sneak on the Burritos' cover of Jagger-Richards' "Wild Horses" (released a year before the Rolling Stones' version) and Spirit's "Nature's Way." Those somewhat offbeat selections are balanced, though, by sappy tunes from Kenny Rankin, Walter Egan, Livingston Taylor, Bob Welch ("Sentimental Lady"), and others. *—Richie Unterberger*

Listen to the Music: '70s Females Singer / Jun. 18, 1996 / Rhino ✦✦✦
The best volume of the '70s singer/songwriter *Listen to the Music* series. This has less nightmare mellow archetypes (although there's some of that as well), and is more inclined toward serious, dignified statements. There are some expected dentist office staples here (Joan Baez' "Diamonds and Rust," and Karla Bonoff's "Someone to Lay Down Beside Me"), as well as the mammoth "Poetry Man" single by Phoebe Snow. Most of the rest, however, are less clichéd, with quality selections by Jackie DeShannon, Emmylou Harris, Joan Armatrading, Laura Nyro (the downright brassy "Beads of Sweat"), and Melanie (the surprisingly serious "Leftover Wine"). It also stretches the time frame a bit with Buffy Sainte-Marie's mid-'60s classic, "Until It's Time for You to Go," and a Rosanne Cash cut from the early '80s, "Seven Year Ache." *—Richie Unterberger*

Listen to the Music: '70s Male Singer/Songwriters / Jun. 18, 1996 / Rhino ✦✦✦
Sixteen archetypal sensitive male performances from the dawn of the age of mellow. There are some exceptions, like Warren Zevon's "Carmelita," and Leonard Cohen's "Bird on the Wire," Leon Russell's "A Song for You," and Todd Rundgren's "Hello It's Me." But generally the sentimental airhead quotient is unreasonably high, including adult contemporary radio standards that us rock critic types love to make fun of by the likes of Stephen Bishop, Rupert Holmes, Dan Fogelberg, Dave Mason, and Paul Davis. Falling somewhere in between the poles are James Taylor ("Fire and Rain"), Leo Sayer ("Giving It All Away"), Harry Chapin ("Taxi"), and John Sebastian ("She's a Lady"), as well as the odd obscure name like Jake Holmes. *—Richie Unterberger*

Live Stiffs / Edsel ✦✦✦✦✦
In order to promote their label and their roster, Stiff Records devised the Live Stiffs package tour as way to showcase all of their key artists (Elvis Costello, Nick Lowe, Ian Dury, Wreckless Eric, Lew Lewis Reformer), as well as themselves. The Live Stiffs shows became notorious for their intoxicatingly (and intoxicated) ragged performances, which the live album *Live Stiffs* captures particularly well. Elvis Costello's torchy version of Bacharach-David's "I Just Don't Know What to Do With Myself" is a highlight, as are Nick Lowe's two cuts, the otherwise-unavailable "Let's Eat" and a rocking version of "I Knew the Bride," which he never released during the late '70s. Dury and Wreckless Eric are nearly as good, and the entire record captures the wild, careening spirit of Stiff—it's fun, trashy rock & roll. *—Stephen Thomas Erlewine*

★ **The Look of Love: The Classic Songs of Burt Bacharach** / 1996 / Polygram ✦✦✦✦✦
Although it doesn't contain every great song Burt Bacharach ever wrote, the various-artists collection *The Look of Love: The Classic Songs of Burt Bacharach* is a wonderful sampling of his best moments. Over the course of 23 tracks, the album includes the most familiar Bacharach songs, all of them presented in their original hit versions, which means there is Dionne Warwick's "Walk on By," and Dusty Springfield's "I Just Don't Know What to Do With Myself," the Walker Brothers' "Make It Easy on Yourself," Sandie Shaw's "(There's) Always Something There to Remind Me," Gene Pitney's "Twenty Four

Hours From Tulsa," Aretha Franklin's "I Say a Little Prayer," B.J. Thomas' "Raindrops Keep Fallin' on My Head," and the Carpenters' "(They Long to Be) Close to You," among many others. Perhaps the collection could have featured all the key moments over the course of two discs, but as it stands, *The Look of Love* is an indispensable sampler of one of the greatest pop music composers of the '60s. *—Stephen Thomas Erlewine*

☆ **Loud, Fast & Out of Control: The Wild Sounds of the '50s [Box]** / May 18, 1999 / Rhino ✦✦✦✦✦
If anyone wanted to prove that original '50s rock & roll was a lot more than just white guys trying to sound black, this deluxe box set would be the perfect flag-waver. Loaded up heavy from top to bottom with the kind of discs that rockabilly collectors consider their personal epiphany, along with obvious hits from Elvis Presley, Jerry Lee Lewis, Little Richard, Bo Diddley and others, this collection burrows right into the heart of what made the first edition of rock & roll so upsetting to staid adults back in the '50s. This is loud, noisy, *dangerous* music, as far away from malt-shop memories and wedding-reception drivel as you could possibly ask for. Encompassing rockabilly, jump R&B, crazed instrumentals, hits and classics that have earned their rep over the intervening decades, this should be a major cornerstone of anyone building a sensible rock & roll collection. *—Cub Koda*

☆ **Machine Soul: An Odyssey Into Electronic Dance Music** / Mar. 14, 2000 / Rhino ✦✦✦✦✦
An effective compilation of electronic pop with a narrow scope and an overly safe track listing but with plenty of highlights, *Machine Soul: An Odyssey Into Electronic Dance* sets out to cover the goal stated in the title. As such, the two-disc set begins with the logical choice: Kraftwerk. From there, the album moves into disco (the Giorgio Moroder-produced "I Feel Love" by Donna Summer), synth-pop (Sparks, OMD, Gary Numan), industrial electronics (Throbbing Gristle, Cabaret Voltaire), electro (Afrika Bambaataa, Newcleus), and Detroit techno (Juan Atkins' Cybotron, Derrick May's Rythim Is Rythim, Kevin Saunderson's Inner City). Moving seamlessly from electronic progenitors to the rave-era explosion, *Machine Soul* continues on the second disc with sampladelic and acid-house anthems from M/A/R/R/S, the KLF, the Orb, the Shamen, and Moby before hitting electronica with Prodigy, Underworld, and the Chemical Brothers, then ending with epic trance producers Paul Van Dyk and BT. The journey takes over two hours, but the *Machine Soul* odyssey presents an unfailingly straight line from the early '70s to the end of the century, with no speedbumps or problems with weak licensing (for the latter, thank Rhino's corporate cousin, Time/Warner). For listeners unfamiliar with the genre, caveats here are practically non-existent. A few electronic-dance fans, however, may quibble with the direction of the compilation; practically *every* track here is led by vocals, whereas the vast majority of electronic-dance tracks have none. And given a style that focuses so much on the underground, the compilers would have been wise to insert tracks from at least one or two recent independent producers. Besides focusing on the "soul" of the "machine" rather than the reverse, *Machine Soul* is an excellent definition of the genre. *—John Bush*

Max's Kansas City 1976 / Aug. 27, 1996 / ROIR ✦✦✦✦✦
Originally released in 1976 on the tiny label RAM (fronted by Tommy Dean, who also owned Max's), *Max's Kansas City* is a great compilation of almost all the influential and charismatic bands that frequently played there in the early to mid-'70s. Recently re-released with four extra tracks not on the original, the album serves as a reminder and souvenir of punk's early days, featuring the known (Pere Ubu, Suicide, Wayne County) along with the lesser-known (the Fast, the Brats, Harry Toledo). Unlike many compilations of punk's early days, these rare tracks are all great-sounding studio recordings, with absolutely no lo-fi live tracks (which are usually commonplace on punk anthologies). You'll be treated to great, early versions of the classics "Final Solution" by Cleveland experimentalists Pere Ubu, as well as "Rocket U.S.A." by New York's confrontational electronic duo Suicide. Wayne County's title track lists just about every band that was playing the venue at the time of song's writing, many of them reaching legendary status (Talking Heads, Ramones, Johnny Thunders, etc.). If you want to re-experience the New York punk of yesteryear, *Max's Kansas City 1976* is the ultimate ticket. *—Greg Prato*

Mellow Rock Hits of the '70s: Summer Breeze / Feb. 4, 1997 / Rhino ✦✦✦
Rock's long and winding road from Woodstock to the waiting room at the doctor's office was paved with '70s staples such as these. "A Horse With No Name" (America), "Summer Breeze" (Seals & Crofts), "Dreams" (Fleetwood Mac), "How Much I Feel" (Ambrosia)—you get the idea. If you want these for home listening as well, there are some advantages to this 16-track compilation. The liner notes are intelligent and informative, and a bit of sly progressivism sneaks in via the Flying Burrito Brothers "Hot Burrito #1." Other artists include James Taylor, Linda Ronstadt, and Joe Walsh, as well as vanished easy rockers like Terence Boylan and Jack Tempchin. *—Richie Unterberger*

Mellow Rock Hits of the 70's: Sundown / Feb. 4, 1997 / Rhino ✦✦✦
The most artistically credible volume of Rhino's *Mellow Rock Hits of the '70s* series focuses on male singer/songwriters. Most of these cats have (or had, at any rate) pretty high critical reps, though this tends to be their most familiar/commercial work: Gordon Lightfoot, Don McLean, Kris Kristofferson, Arlo Guthrie, Steve Goodman, John Prine, Steve Forbert. The second tier includes Cat Stevens, Jim Croce, and John David Souther; Gram Parsons slips in, counterbalanced by Breadman David Gates. Some of the merits of these songs have been dulled by overexposure, but it's certainly one of the more respectable anthologies likely to surface for this sort of thing. *—Richie Unterberger*

Mellow Rock Hits of the '70s: Ventura Highway / Feb. 4, 1997 / Rhino ✦✦✦
Mellow rock at its most easygoing and cheerful is the focus of this 16-track comp, with entries by Seals & Crofts, America, Steve Miller, the Doobie Brothers, and adult-contemporary forerunners that you may not want to revisit: Pure Prairie League's "Amie," Pablo Cruise's "Love Will Find a Way," Player's "Baby Come Back," Orleans' "Still the One." The selections by Little Feat ("Dixie Chicken"), Dr. Hook, and Poco may be a bit unexpected, but aren't nearly radical enough to upset the even-tempered flow of the disc. The crumb tossed to pot-smokers, the Grateful Dead's "Uncle John's Band," is without doubt the CD's high-water mark. *—Richie Unterberger*

Mercury Blues 'n' Rhythm Story 1945-1955 / Sep. 24, 1996 / Polygram ✦✦✦✦✦
Mercury R&B Story 1945-55 is a four-disc, 211-track collection covering Mercury's first decade as a label. Each of the four discs is arranged thematically according to region—East Coast, West Coast, Midwest, and Southwest—and each features a number of blues and R&B classics, including cuts from Professor Longhair, Johnny Otis, Eddie "Cleanhead" Vinson, Dinah Washington, Lightnin' Hopkins, Jimmy Witherspoon, and Big Bill Broonzy. Twenty-two unreleased performances are mixed into the compilation, making the set enticing for collectors, but the main value of *Mercury R&B Story 1945-55* is as a concise overview of one of the most influential R&B labels in history. *—Stephen Thomas Erlewine*

Metal Age: The Roots of Metal / 1992 / Rhino ✦✦✦✦✦
Actually, *Roots of Metal* comes closer to representing the heyday of heavy metal. From Status Quo to Motorhead, all kinds of '70s arena hard rock and metal are covered; over the course of the disc, it becomes clear that metal does *not* all sound the same—there's quite a difference between the thuggish Wishbone Ash, the melodic Cheap Trick, snarling Runaways, and the bloated blues of Beck, Bogert and Appice. Some of it holds up surprisingly well and some of it is embarrassing, but there's no question that it captures its era particularly well. *—Stephen Thomas Erlewine*

☆ **Millennium Party: Funk** / Jul. 14, 1998 / Rhino ✦✦✦✦✦
After offering comprehensive overviews of funk with the multi-volume series *In Yo' Face* and *Phat Trax*, Rhino wisely distilled those two sets into one indispensable single disc, *Millennium Party: Funk*. Boasting 20 songs, all of which are indisputable classics, *Millennium Party* is the best single-disc sampler of '70s and early '80s funk available. There's no James Brown or Sly Stone on the collection—instead, the earliest music on the disc is Curtis Mayfield's 1972 masterpiece, "Superfly." From there, the disc winds through a head-spinning series of classics, including "Brick House," "Love Rollercoster," "Tear the Roof Off the Sucker (Give Up the Funk)," "Jungle Boogie," "I'll take You There," "Best of My Love," "Atomic Dog," "Fantastic Voyage," "More Bounce to the Ounce," "Rapper's Delight," and "You Dropped a Bomb on Me." Although the disc isn't presented in chronological order, it doesn't matter since the sequencing makes for better listening. Besides, it's hard to find flaws with a collection that contains as many flat-out great songs as this. Essential for both casual listeners and funk fanatics. *—Stephen Thomas Erlewine*

The Minit/Instant Story / Jan. 1, 1996 / Charly ✦✦✦✦✦
This 52-song collection doesn't entirely overlap EMI's *Minit Records Story* box set, which has a few rarities and obscure tracks, but it's a good overview of some of the best and most interesting of the label's output, and also the sheer diversity of the company's output, from the hard blues of Jessie Hill to the smooth, near-pop stylings of Allen & Allen. Joe Banashak, who founded Minit and Instant, was truly in love with the sounds he heard from the clubs in New Orleans, and he seldom seems to have heard any artists expressing confidence and inspiration who he didn't want to release. Thus, hard-rocking numbers like Lee Dorsey's "Lottie Mo" share space on this set with harmony numbers like "The Owl Sees You" by the Showmen (aka the Humdingers) and the sultry, seductive soul of Irma Thomas ("It's Too Soon to Know," "Ruler of My Heart," "It's Raining"). British Invasion fans will find a lot to keep them busy as well, given the originals by several Brit-rock favorites, including "Fortune Teller," "Something You Got," and "I Like It Like That" represented here. Throughout both of these discs, Allen Toussaint is represented as producer, arranger, and frequently songwriter as well; if anyone needed convincing that Banashak had a resident genius under contract, the first few tracks do the job. The second disc moves up through later, post-Toussaint Instant and Seven B label tracks that feature Eddie Lang, Skip Easterling, and Eddie Bo, as well as Bo's production work from the mid- and late '60s. The sound is excellent as well, and one only wishes that a bit more material from Minit's early history was present and that a few more details were available on some of the lesser-known artists. *—Bruce Eder*

The Mod Scene / 1998 / Deram ✦✦✦✦✦
This 25-song CD is much more than just an excursion into the farther reaches of English Decca Records' vaults—it's also a de facto tour of the playlists of some of England's hottest mod clubs of the middle-late 1960's; hardly a sound on this collection ever made it anywhere near a chart listing, anywhere in the U.K. (much less the U.S.), but a lot of what is here did get picked up locally in London among the mods that made up the audiences of most of these bands. Considering how badly England's Decca Records fared in the middle-late 1960's (apart from the Rolling Stones, the Small Faces, and the Moody Blues) in signing really solid acts, this is an astonishingly good collection of soul-influenced, mod-oriented singles from the company's vaults. A few of the acts included, such as the Small Faces, Tom Jones, St. Louis Union, Chris Farlowe, and the Amen Corner, made some kind of splash on the charts, but most of the musicians here got their chance on these single sides, failed to find success, and disappeared into the mist of musical history. The CD jumps headfirst into the kind of hard-rocking, intense soul numbers that were played to death in London' mod clubs, even if they never scraped even the lower reaches of the charts. The sound on these singles tells you right away why most of these groups were never going to make it as world-class recording acts, being too raw and direct—without the distinctive hooks to get more than a listen from any radio deejays. By themselves, the Ronnie Jones track, coupled with those by Tom Jones, Steve Aldo, Graham Gouldman, Poets, the Eyes of Blue, and the Quik, justify the cost of this $20 import. The sound is excellent throughout, and it's also reassuring on some level to learn from the

notes that Decca is digging so deeply into its vaults that these acts are nearly as obscure to the people producing this compilation as they are to us. *—Bruce Eder*

Modern Rock 1986: Hang the DJ / Sep. 1996 / Rhino ✦✦✦
Rhino's college-radio series *Modern Rock 1986: Hang the DJ* is inherently flawed, concentrating more on crossover hits than college radio hits. Though *Modern Rock 1986: Hang the DJ* features selections by the Smiths and Guadalcanal Diary, most of the album is comprised either of Top 40 hits like the Bangles' "Walk Like an Egyptian," Eurythmics' "Missionary Man," and Bananarama's "Venus," or album rock crossovers like INXS, the Divinyls, the Alarm, and the Pretenders. Much of this music is tangentially related to the modern rock of the mid- and late '80s, yet it doesn't draw an accurate picture of what was happening that particulary year. Furthermore, the album doesn't hold together very well, with the highlights sticking out like sore thumbs among the tamer selections. In all, it's a weak way to begin the series. *—Stephen Thomas Erlewine*

Modern Rock 1987: Hang the DJ / Sep. 1996 / Rhino ✦✦✦✦
Although it suffers from some of the same problems as its predecessor, *Modern Rock 1987: Hang the DJ* is a much stronger volume than the *1986* disc. Primarily, it benefits from the lack of crossover hits. Many of these songs—most notably R.E.M.'s "It's the End of the World as We Know It (And I Feel Fine)"—have become radio hits in the years since their release, but all of the cuts here intially were played on college radio. In fact, with songs by the Sugarcubes, the Smiths, Hoodoo Gurus, Julian Cope, and Public Image Limited, *Modern Rock 1987: Hang the DJ* offers a representative sampling of what American alternative rock sounded like in that particular year. *—Stephen Thomas Erlewine*

Modern Rock 1988: Hang the DJ / Sep. 1996 / Rhino ✦✦✦✦✦
Modern Rock 1988: Hang the DJ is the strongest installment in Rhino's college rock series, offering the best sampling of popular alternative rock favorites of the late '80s. A few Top 40 hits have been included—the Bangles' "Hazy Shade of Winter" and INXS' "Need You Tonight"—that perhaps shouldn't have been present, but the majority of the collection concentrates on songs by Jane's Addiction, the Fall, Ministry, Erasure, the Primitives, the Mission UK, the Smithereens, R.E.M. and the Church that were primarily heard on college radio stations. It's a diverse collection that offers the roots of the alternative rock breakthrough of the early '90s. *—Stephen Thomas Erlewine*

Mods Mayday '79 / May 27, 1997 / Dojo ✦✦✦✦✦
Since the British music market was flooded with mod-revivalists in the late '70s, the only effective way to promote the bands was through package tours—several like-minded (and like-sounding) bands playing short sets on the same night. *Mods Mayday '79* is a classic collection which compiles the highlights of one of these tours. Most of the second wave revivalists—bands who received their inspiration directly from the Jam's early albums—are represented: Secret Affair, Beggar, Small Hours, the Mods, Squire, and the Merton Parkas. The one glaring omission is the Lambrettas, who where unable to attend the tour due to contractual obligations. Nevertheless, this provides the best look at the genre and is the only place to hear some of the bands who, despite their derivative nature, wrote some excellent pop songs that hold up pretty well even when removed from their context. *—Chris Woodstra*

Monterey International Pop Festival Box Set / Jun. 1967 / Rhino ✦✦✦✦✦
A sumptuous, four-CD box set with all the deluxe trimmings celebrating the grandaddy of all outdoor rock concerts. With legendary performances by Otis Redding, the Who, Jimi Hendrix, Janis Joplin, the Byrds, and Paul Butterfield all taken from the mobile-unit multi-track masters (not to mention an album-sized booklet that'll knock your eyes out), this box evokes a sound and an era the way few (if any) retrospectives of like material ever do. Important music from a turning point in rock's history. *—Cub Koda*

☆ **More Girl Group Greats** / Mar. 6, 2001 / Rhino ✦✦✦✦✦
More Girl Group Greats boasts a track listing that's nearly as essential as that of its predecessor, *Girl Group Greats*. Though none of the album's 20 tracks could be called obscure, songs like the Chiffons' "One Fine Day" and "Sweet Talking Guy," the Dixie Cups' "People Say," and the Shangri-Las' "Remember (Walking in the Sand)" provide a more well-rounded look at the styles and personalities of each of these groups. Likewise, singles such as the Marvelettes' "Beachwood 4-5789" and "Too Many Fish in the Sea," Martha and the Vandellas' "Nowhere to Run," and the Supremes' "Baby Love" are nearly as strong as the smash hits that appeared on *Girl Group Greats*; slightly smaller hits like the Chantels' "Maybe," the Cookies' "Chains," the Paris Sisters' "I Love How You Love Me," and the Angels' "Til" make this a consistently fun, entertaining testament to how great the girl group era was. Though the album isn't really intended for die-hard fans of the genre, who should have all of these tracks already, *More Girl Group Greats* is exactly the kind of collection that makes casual listeners want to discover what other treats the girl group sound has in store for them. *—Heather Phares*

☆ **More Nuggets** / 1987 / Rhino ✦✦✦✦✦
Picking up where the first *Nuggets* CD left off, *More Nuggets* contains 18 wonderfully raw garage-rockers, which are intercut with some trippy psychedelia and folk-rock. The selection on *More Nuggets* is a little more unpredictable than on its predecessor, since it doesn't just feature hits like "Liar Liar," "I Wonder What She's Doing Tonight," "Talk Talk," "(We Ain't Got) Nothin' Yet," "Western Union," and "The Little Black Egg," but also cult classics from the likes of the Merry-Go-Round ("Live," "You're a Very Lovely Woman"), Captain Beefheart ("Diddy Wah Diddy"), the Chocolate Watch Band ("Are You Gonna Be There [At the Love-In]?," "Sweet Young Thing"), the Left Banke ("Desiree"), the Standells ("Sometimes Good Guys Don't Wear White"), and Mouse & the Traps ("A Public Execution"). *—Stephen Thomas Erlewine*

Motown: The Classic Years / Aug. 29, 2000 / Motown ✦✦✦✦✦
Even if you're not an avid fan of classic Motown music, you will probably recognize almost every song on this two-disc, 40-track compilation. These insanely catchy and indefatigably peppy tunes, all of which hit Billboard's pop Top 40 between 1959 and 1972, proved remarkably durable throughout the remainder of the 20th century and figure to maintain their high public profile well into the 21st. This is thanks in large part to their enduring popularity with producers of movies and television commercials. Nearly every one of these songs has been used in the media for some purpose over the last few decades, whether it be to sell raisins ("I Heard It Through the Grapevine") or baked goods ("I Can't Help Myself (Sugar Pie, Honey Bunch)") or to add an energetic backdrop for a film montage sequence ("Do You Love Me," "War"). *Motown: The Classic Years* does an excellent job of covering the major songs of the era, from the late-'50s rock & roll rumble of Barrett Strong's "Money (That's What I Want)" through the early-'70s disco groove of the Temptations' "Papa Was a Rolling Stone." Along the way, the collection manages to draw general outlines of the career development of major artists like Marvin Gaye and Stevie Wonder. The latter is heard in his debut as a teen star ("Fingertips Pt. 2," 1963) and in his first efforts as a songwriter ("Uptight [Everything's Alright]," 1965), and as a producer ("Signed, Sealed and Delivered I'm Yours," 1970). *Motown: The Classic Years* is an outstanding resource for casual listeners looking for a comprehensive introduction to the Motown sound. For many, it will be all the Motown they ever need. *—Evan Cater*

MTV Presents: Hip-Hop Back in the Day / Feb. 17, 1998 / Priority ✦✦✦✦
Released to coincide with the first showing of MTV's program *This Is Music: Hip-Hop Back in the Day, MTV Presents: Hip-Hop Back in the Day* is an excellent collection of early rap hits. While a handful of the songs stretch past old school and into the late '80s (Boogie Down Productions' "South Bronx," L.L. Cool J's "Rock the Bells," Tone Loc's "Funky Cold Medina," MC Shan's "The Bridge"), the majority of the collection is devoted to early and mid-'80s hits like Kurtis Blow's "The Breaks," Grandmaster Flash's "The Message," Afrika Bambaataa's "Planet Rock," the Fat Boys' "Fat Boys," UTFO's "Roxanne, Roxanne," Doug E. Fresh's "The Show," Whodini's "Freaks Come Out at Night," and Heavy D's "The Overweight Lover's in the House." Almost every one of these tracks was a hip-hop milestone, and this isn't a bad way to pick them up on one disc, even if the presence of the bonus 1998 remix of "The Message" leaves a bitter aftertaste. *—Stephen Thomas Erlewine*

Mule Milk 'N' Firewater / Aug. 15, 2000 / West Side ✦✦✦
This is an outstanding collection from the vaults of King and its subsidiary labels, Federal and Deluxe. These 24 tracks collect jump blues, doo wop, piano boogie, and outright bizarre novelties stretching from the late '40s through the early '60s. There is not a bad track on *Mule Milk 'N' Firewater*, featuring plenty of well-known names on mainly wild up-tempo songs by Roy Brown, Big Jay McNeely, Little Willie John, Hank Ballad & the Midnighters, and Jack Dupree. There are a few standouts amongst these rarities that may raise a few eyebrows. "Ring a Ling Dong" is from 1955 by Rudy Moore aka Rudy Ray Moore of Dolomite fame, and "Davy, You Upset My Home" finds a young Joe Tex vividly describing how his domestic situation is being torn apart by his girlfriend's unhealthy obsession with all things Davy Crockett! Unbelievable! *—Al Campbell*

The Muscle Shoals Sound / Rhino ✦✦✦✦✦
In a series of nondescript studios in tiny towns tucked in the corner of northwest Alabama, a small band of musicians, singers, and producers sculpted a sound that revolutionized rhythm and blues in the 1960s. Dubbed the "Muscle Shoals Sound" after one of those towns, this region gave birth to the grittiest and funkiest Southern soul music of the era. The 18-song compilation *The Muscle Shoals Sound* presents a cross section of some of the most influential grooves laid down in these studios during its golden decade (1962-1972). Besides hits by soul giants like Otis Redding, Aretha Franklin, and Wilson Pickett, it includes influential sides by lesser stars like Percy Sledge ("When a Man Loves a Woman"), Etta James ("Tell Mama"), Arthur Conley ("Sweet Soul Music"), and Clarence Carter ("Patches"). It also includes the very first hit cut in the region, Arthur Alexander's "You Better Move On." Behind the scenes, songwriters and musicians like Spooner Oldham, Dan Penn, and Duane Allman were equally important in crafting a style distinguished by rock-solid rhythms and passionate performances. With thorough liner notes about the songs, performers, and musicians, this is a fine introduction to the "deep soul" music that was envied by such heavyweights as the Rolling Stones. *—Richie Unterberger*

☆ **Naughty Rhythms: The Best of Pub Rock** / Apr. 1996 / EMI Premier ✦✦✦✦✦
Pub rock is the frequently forgotten forefather of punk rock, although on the surface the two genres don't appear to have much in common. Punk rock was about revolution and pub rock was about tradition, at least superficially. But place pub rock in its proper context, and it was nearly as revolutionary as punk. In the early '70s, rock & roll was dominated by heavy metal, art rock, and blues-rock, all genres that required skill. The simple, laid-back three-chord shuffles of pub rock—ranging from straight-ahead rock & roll, to country and blues-rock—didn't require much skill, but it was a working class, do-it-yourself movent that took rock & roll back to its roots, which is essentially what punk rock did. Furthermore, pub rock bands established a circuit of nightclubs within England, which is where all the original punk bands played. *Naughty Rhythms: The Best of Pub Rock* is the first comprehensive colllection of the scene, featuring every major pub rock band, as well as nearly every minor band. Compiled by former Kursaal Flyer Will Birch with Paul Bradshaw, the double disc set effectively traces the development of the genre, from its country-rock roots with Brinsley Schwarz to the pounding, proto-punk of Eddie & the Hot Rods. In between, there are 34 other songs that cover all the aspects of pub rock, from the relaxed acoustic rock of Eggs Over Easy and the Stonesy groove of Ducks Deluxe and Dr. Feelgood to the commercial gloss of Ace and the eccentric rock of Kilburn and the High Roads. The double-disc set provides all the worthwhile songs from almost every band featured on the collection, with the notable exception of Brinsley Schwarz,

who were already represented with five tracks. *Naughty Rhythms* is the definitive document of pub rock and for most listeners, it will be all they need to know. *—Stephen Thomas Erlewine*

☆ **The New Orleans Hit Story** / Oct. 21, 1997 / Charly ✦✦✦✦✦
A 54-track marathon of songs cut in New Orleans and released and distributed on various labels. The Crescent City was unique in that it didn't follow national trends; runaway hits in other cities often never aired in New Orleans. Starting with four cuts by Fats Domino on disc one, the collection ends with a 14-song battle royal between the Meters and Johnny Adams. Sandwiched between is a musical gumbo of entrees from Ernie K Doe, Chris Kenner, Lee Dorsey, Benny Spellman, the Dixie Cups, Robert Parker, Aaron Neville, and others. Spellman and Doe's tunes include "Lipstick Traces" and "I've Cried My Last Tear"; both were redone by the O'Jays on Imperial Records. Little Richards' "I Don't Know What You Got but Its Got Me" is an emotional, drenching declaration that shows the flamboyant singer in a different light. The thick soul only lightens on the smooth, choral singing Dixie Cups cuts, a group you normally don't associate with New Orleans. Contains enough hits to interest casual fans, including Robert Parker's "Barefootin'," the Showmen's "It Will Stand," "Mother-in-Law" by Ernie K-Doe, Chris Kenner's monsters, Aaron Neville's "Tell It Like It Is," and Lee Dorsey's unforgettable "Working in a Coal Mine." An exiting CD by a talented cast of characters. *—Andrew Hamilton*

New Romantics / Aug. 14, 1996 / Alex ✦✦✦
New Romantics is a decent, if somewhat flawed look at the theatrical, Roxy Music/David Bowie-influenced new wave subgenre. There are a number of obscurities and/or questionable selections—the robotic synth-pop of Kraftwerk and Devo don't really fit the definition of "new romantic," for example—and the artists here aren't always represented by one of their better-known tracks. But most of the movement's standout bands are here, like Duran Duran ("Girls on Film"), Spandau Ballet ("Lifeline"), Heaven 17 ("We Don't Need This Fascist Groove Thing"), OMD ("Messages"), Japan ("Quiet Life"), the Human League ("Empire State Human"), Ultravox ("The Voice"), and China Crisis ("African and White"). It isn't definitive, since acts like ABC, Talk Talk, A Flock of Seagulls, and Naked Eyes are missing, but the collection will ultimately clue listeners in on what the new romantic movement was all about. *—Steve Huey*

Northern Soul Spectrum / Apr. 22, 1997 / Kent ✦✦✦✦
Taken from the vaults of EMI Records, *Northern Soul Spectrum* brings together soul styles from the vaults of many of the company's small label holdings, including classics from Roulette, Jubilee, Josie, Port, J2, Satin, Calla, and Rust. With 28 tracks covering the years 1962 to 1968 with a stray track from the '70s (Magic Night's soul-disco "If You and I Had Never Met") that atmospherically fits in, this is no mere R&B hodgepodge compilation, but instead a well-programmed and diverse selection of a wide variety of Northern Soul styles. From the pop-flavored offerings of Annabelle Fox's "Lonely Girl" and Frankie & the Classicals' "What Shall I Do" to the minor-key Motown-on-fire romp of Brenda Lee Jones' "You're the Love of My Life" to the classic soul balladry of Scotty Williams on "I've Got to Find Her (and Tell Her)," the sheer emotionalism, musicality, and danceability of the genre is here for the listening. For those who want to investigate further than the hit packages of Motown and Stax/Atlantic material, here's a big chunk to digest in one sitting that's grade-A soul music from the classic era. *—Cub Koda*

Nuggets From Nuggets: Choice Artyfacts From the First Psychedelic Era / Nov. 7, 2000 / Rhino ✦✦✦✦✦
Nuggets From Nuggets: Original Artyfacts From the First Psychedelic Era is a single-disc, 20-track distillation of Rhino's stellar, similarly titled four-disc box. Nearly all of the biggest hits included on that larger set have also made their way here, plus a few signature tunes from significant cult bands, making for an extremely solid sampler. The Kingsmen's "Louie Louie," Sam the Sham & the Pharaohs' "Wooly Bully," the Count Five's "Psychotic Reaction," the Standells' "Dirty Water," Strawberry Alarm Clock's "Incense and Peppermints," and the Seeds' "Pushin' Too Hard" are just some of the '60s garage rock and psychedelic classics present, and for those without the time and/or money to sift through the full box, this is a necessary purchase. *—Steve Huey*

Nuggets, Vol. 2: Original Artyfacts From the British Empire & Beyond / Jun. 19, 2001 / Rhino ✦✦✦✦✦
Nuggets, Lenny Kaye's original 1972 compilation of garage and psych, loomed large in the record collectors consciousness, canonizing a portion of rock that was originally laughed off while setting the standard for reissues. Rhino's 1998 box set of the same name expanded the scope of that record, replicating most of the original while gloriously spilling forth over three additional discs—and, in doing so, it spurred a minor revolution, becoming one of the most talked-about reissues of the last half of the '90s. Rhino knew there was an audience thirsting for a sequel, and they gave them one in 2001, but they didn't take the easy way out. Instead of offering another round of American garage rockers, they decided to take the road less traveled, compiling four discs of hidden treasures from non-American garage and psych bands. Most of these cuts are from British bands, but there are also selections from a pre-fame Guess Who, the New Zealand act the Smoke, the Brazilian psychedelia of Os Mutantes, the exceptional Merseybeat stylings of Uruguay's Los Shakers, and the extraordinary Peruvian combo We All Together, among other non-Brit acts. It's a brilliant, even necessary, move, since most of these bands and songs have been only heard only by the most dedicated collectors—the kind that are willing to risk money based on just hearing a band mentioned, not to hear the group themselves. Let's face it—apart from the Status Quo's "Pictures of Matchstick Men," the Small Faces' "Here Comes the Nice," and the Pretty Things' "Rosalyn," the most familiar song here is the opener, the Creation's "Making Time," simply because it provided the indelible soundtrack to Max Fischer's yearbook in *Rushmore*. That's four songs out of 109—a ratio that should simply entice most die-hard rockers and record collectors, especially since the familiar names (the Move, Them, the Easybeats, the Troggs) are represented by songs that aren't heard all that often. So, the big question is, does *Nuggets, Vol. 2* deliver and is it worth spending the money for 100-plus songs you've never heard before? Well, if you're even slightly interested in this, the answer is yes. That doesn't mean this isn't without its faults—like any garage rock, if it's listened to in once concentrated burst, it becomes a little samey, which is also a by-product of its biggest flaw, namely how the compilers favor songs that sound like American garage and downplaying the delirious, precious frutiness of British psych. Still, that's a minor complaint, because the simple fact of the matter is this—there's no better way to fall in love with this music, not just because it does its job so well, it just simply doesn't have any peers. Furthermore, a lot of this stuff is pretty hard to come by (personally, I spent about 150 dollars on a complete Idle Race collection, and it's much better to get their two best songs here). Also, much of the bands here are best heard in this context, since they have a song, maybe three, that were stunners—and all of these stunners in one place is stunning. *—Stephen Thomas Erlewine*

☆ **Nuggets: A Classic Collection From the Psychedelic Sixties** / 1986 / Rhino ✦✦✦✦✦
In its time, in the mid-'80s, Rhino Records' first volume of its *Nuggets* series was one of the basic starting points for a collection of mid-'60s psychedelic and garage punk music, and it still holds up for content. Almost everything here is a musical touchstone of the genres, either a major chart hit or an underground classic, and the little that doesn't really fit entirely into those categories, such as "Friday on My Mind" by the Easybeats and "Laugh Laugh" and "Just a Little" by the Beau Brummels, is still catchy enough to fit in seamlessly with the rest. The main drawback for new purchasers may be the sound—Rhino's mastering standards were always higher than those of virtually every other company, which means that their '80s CDs have held their value a very long time, but there are better things being done with the sound on most of this material in the early 21st century. As of 1998, thanks to a new licensing agreement, Rhino was able to issue a much-expanded version of that double album as a four-CD box and put out *Nuggets From Nuggets*, a 20-song highlights CD that includes five of the cuts from this CD and 15 choice additions; of the missing tracks, the Chocolate Watch Band's "Let's Talk About Girls" is the only hugely glaring omission, the others being a matter of subjective choice, some of which is dictated by their availability elsewhere and changing perceptions of the music. This remains a superb starting point, however, and even fits in well alongside *Nuggets From Nuggets*. *—Bruce Eder*

Nuggets: Even More Nuggets / 1989 / Rhino ✦✦✦✦✦
Even More Nuggets, the third volume of Rhino's garage rock and psychedelic-pop series, is equally divided between hits ("I Had too Much to Dream Last Night," "Gloria," "Incense and Peppermint," "Just Dropped in [To See What Condition My Condition Was In]," "Who Do You Love," "Red Rubber Ball," "Time Has Come Today," "Let's Live for Today") and cult favorites from the Barbarians, Third Rail, the Sunshine Company, and the E-Types. It doesn't have quite as many classics as its two predecessors, yet it remains one of the more satisfying collections of mainstream garage-rock assembled. *—Stephen Thomas Erlewine*

☆ **Nuggets: Original Artyfacts From the First Psychedelic Era 1965-1968 [Box]** / Sep. 15, 1998 / Rhino ✦✦✦✦✦
Compiled by rock critic and future Patti Smith Group guitarist Lenny Kaye, 1972's *Nuggets* was the anthology responsible for reviving interest in mid-'60s American garage rock. After the proliferation of specialized volumes with the *Nuggets* title by reissue label Rhino, this four-CD box set is intended as the ideal summation/expansion of the *Nuggets* concept. The first CD reproduces, track-by-track, the original 27-song *Nuggets*, while the other three CDs add what may be considered 91 bonus tracks, from the biggest-selling garage hits ("Louie Louie," "Wooly Bully") to some cuts that only devout '60s specialists will know. All important permutations of the mid-'60s garage style are present: primitive fuzz, folk-rock, horn rock, psychedelic dementia, protest rock, etc. Major heroes the Music Machine, the Seeds, the Shadows of Knight, the Electric Prunes, the Standells, the Sonics, the Chocolate Watch Band, and many others are all represented, often by more than one song. If it's possible to give a five-star rating with reservations, it's tempting to do so here. No one could have possibly satisfied all rabid garage collectors with a mere 118 songs, but that's not really the point here; the object was to provide a wide-ranging box set of '60s garage rock that would entertain, represent the considerable span of garage styles, and be massive—yet affordable—for the committed rock fan who nonetheless doesn't want everything. Rhino has succeeded, while also presenting the songs in the best possible quality (in mono), whether from the master tapes or best existing copies. With a 100-page booklet of new liner notes (Kaye's original annotation is also included), it is the best investment possible for those who thirst for more '60s garage rock than is available on the best single-volume compilations, with a track selection geared toward cream-of-the-crop quality and variety rather than narrow collector prejudices. *—Richie Unterberger*

Oh Yeah! The Best of Dunwich Records / 1992 / Sundazed ✦✦✦✦✦
The Chicago-based Dunwich Records was the leading Midwestern garage-rock label, turning out countless great singles from the likes of Shadows of Knight, American Breed, the Rovin' Kind, and H.P. Lovecraft. *Oh Yeah! The Best of Dunwich Records* is an excellent 31-track collection that contains the label's best-known hits, plus several fine unreleased cuts, radio commercials, and interviews. Anyone interested in delving into garage-rock any deeper than the *Nuggets* compilations should start here—it gives a good idea of both the treasures and the mediocrities to be found in the multitudes of compilations, and few other collections are quite as consistently listenable as this one. *—Stephen Thomas Erlewine*

Oh, Merge: Merge Records 10 Year Anniversary Compilation / Jul. 6, 1999 / Merge ✦✦✦✦
The respected indie label Merge Records celebrated its ten-year anniversary with *Oh, Merge*, a collection of mostly rare and unreleased tracks from some of its finest artists.

The album displays Merge's diversity, showcasing old-school indie rock from Guv'ner, Spent, and label founders Superchunk along with the post-rock of Ganger and lo-fi electronica of Third Eye Foundation, while still finding room for the pop classicism of East River Pipe, Neutral Milk Hotel, and the Ladybug Transistor, who turn in a rendition of the Bee Gees' "Massachusetts." The Mad Scene, the Magnetic Fields, Lambchop, Pipe, and Portastatic also contribute worthy tracks to *Oh, Merge*, making it a fine retrospective of a distinctive and accomplished label. *—Heather Phares*

☆ **OHM: The Early Gurus of Electronic Music** / Apr. 25, 2000 / Ellipsis Arts ✦✦✦✦✦
This three-CD, 42-track compilation, spanning 1937-1982 (though largely comprised of performances from the '60s and '70s), includes pieces by many of the big names in experimental electronic music: John Cage, Pauline Oliveros, Steve Reich, Terry Riley, Karlheinz Stockhausen, Milton Babbitt, Laurie Spiegel, Robert Ashley, LaMonte Young, Morton Subotnick, and Iannis Xenakis. That alone would make this anthology impressive, but there are also contributions from composers who have made some impact with rock and pop recordings (Brian Eno, Klaus Schulze, Holger Czukay of Can, Jon Hassell), along with some names that are not commonly discussed in highbrow serious music circles (Raymond Scott), some composers not always associated with electronic music (Olivier Messiaen, Edgard Varese), and a host of names that aren't too well known beyond the avant-garde community. What is most impressive about this set, however, is that is not only serves as a reasonable overview of pre-1980 electronic music, but also is much more accessible in content to non-experts than many such compilations would have been. Contrary to the stereotype of serious electronic music as being difficult to listen to, many of the pieces are quite engaging for novices and electronic specialists alike. That's not to say there aren't plenty of more jarring or abstract pieces with minimal ambience or cut-up assemblages, or even occasional tracks that most listeners might find downright annoying (such as MEV's cacophonous "Spacecraft," mercifully placed at the very end of the first disc). On the whole, however, the set achieves the effect of both educating and entertaining, and is likely to expand the audience for a music that is too often unwilling to offer inviting introductions that might incite listeners to explore further. The 98-page booklet includes detailed track descriptions and comments, usually by the composers/performers themselves. *—Richie Unterberger*

☆ **The OKeh Rhythm & Blues Story 1949-1957** / 1995 / Epic/Okeh/Legacy ✦✦✦✦✦
The three-CD set is a real eye opener. As the most straight-laced and self-consciously upscale of the major labels, Columbia Records isn't usually thought of as having had much to contribute to the history and development of rhythm & blues. That impression was never more than partly true, however, as every track on this three-disc set reminds us. The postwar OKeh label was Columbia's attempt to grab a piece of a market that, as early as 1948, it knew it was losing, and the music is as solid a representation of R&B of the era as that of any major label of the period. It's true that OKeh had only sporadic success and developed a relative handful of R&B stars: Chuck Willis, Big Maybelle, the Treniers, and Screamin' Jay Hawkins. A great many other notable artists passed through, however, either after their biggest successes or in the years prior to their emergence, including LaVern Baker (known at the time as Bea Baker) singing with Maurice King & His Wolverines, Marvin Gaye as a member of the Marquees (working with Bo Diddley), Hadda Brooks, Annie Laurie, and the Ravens. They're all represented here, and there's not a second-rate song anywhere on this set, which also features some of the cleanest, richest remastering heard on a Columbia CD set of truly vintage material up to that time. The booklet is also pretty impressive in its details, listing individual band members and filled with concise encapsulated biographies (where known) of the artists. *—Bruce Eder*

☆ **On Broadway: Hit Songs and Rarities From the Brill Building Era** / Mar. 2, 1999 / West Side ✦✦✦✦✦
There's like two weeks of dazzling analytical listening to be found on this double-CD set, unless you want to try it for the pure pleasure, which is practically infinite. *On Broadway* is a magnificent idea for a multi-artist compilation, and one that no U.S. label could do, because the licensing fees would be too high. The primary focus is the work of the Brill Building-based songwriting teams of Gerry Goffin and Carole King, Barry Mann and Cynthia Weil, and Jeff Barry and Ellie Greenwich, which hardly makes it restrictive. There are at least a dozen revelations for the casual listener among the 25 songs on each CD in this set. One gets to hear alternate (but equally valid) performances, sometimes predating the hits by months, of several dozen songs that became pop standards in other hands. The talent represented here includes period pop music icons (Little Eva) and up-and-coming talent (pre-Phil Spector Ronettes), pop culture footnotes (Vince Edwards, Paul Petersen, Shelley Fabares), sibling acts (Idalia Boyd, sister of Little Eva), forgotten performers (the James Boys, Myrna March), one future jazz success (Birdie Green), and a future pop/rock superstar (Carole King). There aren't any new horizons in pop music to be discovered here, just some beautiful and mostly forgotten moments, and established hits as well. The Raindrops are here, of course, as are Carole King and a handful of Barry Mann solo numbers, just to give the performing side of their early careers a nod. The notes are thorough and then some, although they're weighted toward the songwriters rather than the performers, especially where the genuinely obscure acts are concerned. And the sound is good to excellent, though a couple of the Freddie Scott numbers (but not "On Broadway") seem slightly compressed. *—Bruce Eder*

On the Charts: I.R.S. Records 1979-1994 / 1994 / IRS ✦✦✦
IRS Records was one of the giants of the post-punk era. They cultivated a roster filled with groundbreaking underground rockers, from the English Beat to R.E.M. Like most great labels, they stayed around a little too long, so their message was diluted toward the end of their life, but in their prime, they were a diverse, exceptional label. Since it sticks to the label's crossover hits, *On the Charts: IRS Records 1979-1994* doesn't quite give an accurate portrait of the label's history (important bands like Let's Active never had a hit, so they're absent from this compilation), but it does have a good cross section of the label's finest singles. In the process, it paints an accurate portrait of post-punk's evolution from new wave to alt-rock. Because it takes its subtitle seriously, the collection does contain a few duds—dada's "Dizz Knee Land" happens to be the newest thing here, but it already sounds more dated than Wall of Voodoo's "Mexican Radio"—but the best moments—the Go-Go's' "Our Lips Are Sealed," Timbuk 3's "The Future's So Bright, I Gotta Wear Shades," Fine Young Cannibals' "She Drives Me Crazy," General Public's "Tenderness," R.E.M.'s "The One I Love" and the English Beat's perfect "Save It For Later"—illustrate what a great label IRS was, which is reason enough to hear this collection. *—Stephen Thomas Erlewine*

Dick Bartley Presents: One Hit Wonders of the '60s, Vol. 1 / Oct. 15, 1990 / Rhino ✦✦✦✦✦
One Hit Wonders of the '60s, Vol. 1 collects 12 hit singles from '60s artists who never had more than one hit, so it's a terrific way to collect a number of wonderful pop singles—"You Were on My Mind," "I Wonder What She's Doing Tonight," "Last Kiss," "Walk Right In," "If You Wanna Be Happy"—that are better heard on a various-artists collection than a greatest-hits compilation. *—Stephen Thomas Erlewine*

● **Dick Bartley Presents: One Hit Wonders of the '60s, Vol. 2** / Oct. 15, 1990 / Rhino ✦✦✦✦✦
If anything, the second volume of *One Hit Wonders of the '60s, Vol. 2* is even better than the first, boasting a stronger selection of songs from artists that never had more than one hit, including the Hombres ("Let It Out [Let It All Hang Out]"), Crazy Elephant ("Gimme, Gimme Good Lovin'"), Robert Knight ("Everlasting Love"), Merrilee Rush ("Angel of the Morning"), the Neon Philharmonic ("Morning Girl"), Derek ("Cinnamon"), the Casinos ("Then You Can Tell Me Goodbye"), and the McCoys ("Hang on Sloopy"). *—Stephen Thomas Erlewine*

Paisley Pop: Pye Psych (& Other Colors), 1966-1969 / 1994 / Collectables ✦✦✦
As the liner notes say, English paisley pop "sat around in gray municipal libraries doodling until closing time, or bus station cafes drawing patterns on the misted up windows of our Technicolor mindscapes." Here are Pye's more obscure contributions to the genre, highlighted by a couple of hitmaking bands (the Flying Machine, the Status Quo), but otherwise featuring those who never quite.... Still, this is a strong set of tunes ranging from the fey meanderings of "The Bitter Thoughts of Little Jane" by Timon (complete with small orchestra) to raucous pop-punk from the Montanas. There is indeed much variety here: the trance-like electric folk musings of Trader Horne, sunnier sounds from the likes of the Rainbow People, and the proto-Morrissey ravings of Schadel. The common denominator is that it is all tinged with a slightly off-kilter wistfulness and given to lyrical flights of fancy. The two best songs are "Tamaris Khan" by the Onyx, driven by a menacing guitar and a smashing chorus, and "I Wonder Where My Sister's Gone" by the unheard of Anan, featuring many mixing effects in its brutally surreal beauty. Some of the rest cloy even the keenest sweet tooth, but for those who enjoy British psychedelia with a definite Syd Barrett stamp, here's the place to find it. Non-completist '60s collectors will find this album a convenient collection of often rare songs of the genre on one compact disc. *—Stephen Constantelos*

Palatine: The Factory Story/1979-1990 / Nov. 1991 / Factory ✦✦✦✦✦
Palatine: The Factory Story/1979-1990 is a box set that combines the four separately released discs that distill the history of Manchester, England's Factory Records. Thanks to a roster that included the likes of Joy Division, New Order, Cabaret Voltaire, the Durutti Column, and (later) the Happy Mondays, Factory is regarded along the same level as Rough Trade, Postcard, Mute, 4AD, and Creation as one of the most important indie labels—U.K. or otherwise—to have broken the mold of the large company-based music industry during the late '70s and early '80s. Aside from the aforementioned acts, Factory never really became much of a force on the charts, save for the occasional hit. However, these four discs are impressive in gathering a good percentage of quality music that varies from post-punk to synth pop to Madchester to just plain weird. Each of the discs holds a particular theme, whether it's the mood or the time period covered. (Beware: The title of the box is deviously similar to the third volume, titled *Palatine: The Factory Story, Vol. 3/1979-1989*). There aren't any major omissions throughout these 49 songs; a healthy amount of attention is paid to the label's biggest acts, and smaller notables like A Certain Ratio, ESG, and the Stockholm Monsters are thankfully represented. While it could be argued that Crispy Ambulance and the Names could have been included instead of the nth New Order inclusion or arguably lesser acts like Kalima or Quando Quango, there aren't any true gripes to be had with this package. It also comes with a thick booklet. *—Andy Kellman*

Pebbles, Vols. 1-28 / AIP ✦✦✦✦✦
Though 1972's *Nuggets* compilation reawakened listeners to the sounds of mid-'60s garage rock, it only focused on the tip of the iceberg. Behind those forgotten hits and semi-hits lurked hundreds, if not thousands, of regional hits and flops from the same era, most even rawer and cruder. In the late '70s, the *Pebbles* compilations came along to fill in the gap and then some. Each volume gathered 15 to 20 obscure 45s, originally issued on tiny labels and remastered right from the excruciatingly rare original vinyl. The featured acts were unknown to anyone but collectors and those who happened to have lived in the areas where the bands played. More than any other factor, these compilations were responsible for the resurgence of interest in garage rock, which remains high among collectors to this day. Though the lyrics are at times downright juvenile and sexist, the main attraction is the sound and stance, which anticipates the outrage of punk rock, but tempers it with tough British Invasion-inspired melodies, harmonies, and hooks, as well as fuzz-toned guitars, Farfisa organs, and wildly manic songwriting and performances. There are a lot of great unknown songs on *Pebbles*, but there are also a fair number of

generic tunes that have little to recommend them beyond an excess of energy, which can make listening to an entire volume at once as much a challenge as a joy. Listeners approaching this series for the first time should search for the first ten volumes; after this initial burst, the well ran increasingly dry, and the later volumes can be a chore. Most of the individual installments don't have themes, but those looking for a concentration of certain items should check out the third (psychedelia) and sixth (British R&B/mod) volumes. Of special interest among the later volumes are installments devoted to wide-ranging obscurities from the European continent. —*Richie Unterberger*

Pepperisms: Around the World / Nov. 17, 1998 / QDK Media ✦✦✦
The idea of this compilation is to gather obscure music from the late 1960s styled after, or inspired by, the Beatles' *Sgt. Pepper's Lonely Hearts Club Band*. It's a refreshing idea for an anthology, since so many collections of rare '60s rock focus on garage or fairly raw psychedelia; relatively refined and polished psychedelia that was just as out-of-the-way is much harder to find on reissues. And *Pepperisms* certainly does go out of the way to assemble little-heard tracks, not just from the U.S. and U.K., but also from South America, Canada, Australia, and even Czechoslovakia, Hong Kong, Hungary, South Africa, and Malaysia. The title might be a little misleading to Beatles or even general '60s fans, though, because this is more a general compilation of obscure ornate, elaborate late-'60s psychedelia than tracks which are specifically derivative of *Sgt. Pepper*. You can hear the Pepperisms in some cuts, like the Rockadrome's "Ain't It a Shame" and Quentin E. Klopjaeger's "Weatherman" (with their bouncing McCartneyesque piano) and "When the Alarm Clock Rings" by England's Blossom Toes (the best, and actually best-known, group on the CD). But the songs are more clever and pleasant than outstanding, and occasionally draw more from a *White Album* sound (as on the cuts by Jade and the October Cherries) than a *Sgt. Pepper* one. As a friend of mine noted in a nice way, it sounds kind of like listening to the Dukes of Stratosphear (who were actually XTC), except that these songs are actually from the late 1960s, and not uncanny re-creations. —*Richie Unterberger*

☆ **Phat Trax, Vols. 1-5** / 1994 / Rhino ✦✦✦✦✦
Phat Trax is a seven-volume series (all discs are available individually) that chronicles the late-'70s and early-'80s heyday of funk. Each disc is filled with classic cuts, rarities and 12" mixes, giving an excellent overview of every element of funk. The series begins to lose some steam on its later volumes, as it spends too much time on mediocrities, but the set remains the definitive overview of funk. —*Leo Stanley*

Philly Sound: Kenny Gamble, Leon Huff and the Story of Brotherly Love (1966-1976) / Sep. 30, 1997 / Epic/Legacy ✦✦✦✦✦
Along with Thom Bell, Kenny Gamble and Leon Huff defined the sweet, smooth Philadelphia Sound in the early '70s, producing hit records by the O'Jays, Harold Melvin & the Blue Notes, and Joe Simon, among many others. Spanning three discs, *The Philly Sound (1966-1976): Kenny Gamble & Leon Huff* is a stunning chronicle of the team at their peak, featuring all of their biggest hits, plus a generous selection of neglected gems. For some tastes, the three discs may be a bit too much of a good thing—often, these songs sound more remarkable when they're heard in small doses—but for a definitive overview of Gamble & Huff's accomplishments, this can't be beat. —*Stephen Thomas Erlewine*

Pimps, Players & Private Eyes / Jan. 14, 1992 / Warner Brothers ✦✦✦✦✦
Pimps, Players & Private Eyes gathers ten theme songs from early-'70s blaxploitation films, including Curtis Mayfield's "Pusherman," Willie Hutch's "Theme of Foxy Brown" and "I Choose You," Isaac Hayes' "Theme From Shaft," Bobby Womack's "Across 110th Street" and Marvin Gaye's "Trouble Man." Although "Superfly" should have been on the album, these funky, soulful cuts effortlessly evoke their era and make for a highly entertaining listen. —*Stephen Thomas Erlewine*

Platinum Breakz / Jul. 8, 1996 / ffrr ✦✦✦✦✦
The first compilation of Goldie's Metalheadz label is a roll call of jungle's most crucial artists: Photek, Source Direct, Dillinja, J. Majik, Alex Reece, Peshay, and Lemon D. Released around the same time as L.T.J. Bukem's *Logical Progression*, *Platinum Breakz* proves that Bukem has no business talking about intelligent jungle; though the styles of Metalheadz and Bukem's Looking Good/Good Looking imprints are quite similar—that is, somewhat house-influenced breakbeats—most of the contributions on *Logical Progression* have simple rhythms and are usually drowned out by extra, unneeded effects. The beats and percussion work on *Platinum Breakz* stand alone, besides spare synth lines and the occasional diva vocal. The rhythms constantly shift around, stopping and restarting. While *Logical Progression* begins to sound same, the artists on *Platinum Breakz* are easily differentiated. Highlights are difficult to define, though Source Direct, Photek, Dillinja, and J Majik's contributions are a very small step above the rest. Goldie's only contribution—recorded as the Rufige Kru—is okay but gets overshadowed. —*John Bush*

Poptopia! 70's Power Pop Classics / May 27, 1997 / Rhino ✦✦✦✦✦
Named after an annual power-pop festival in the Los Angeles, Rhino's three-disc *Poptopia! Power Pop Classics* series attempts to chronicle power pop's evolution from its '70s roots to its '90s incarnation as a cult genre. Power pop, in many ways, is the ultimate cult music: it has a specific sound, a strict songwriting formula, and a small number of classic artists. In other words, it's a genre that lends itself easily to an anthology—it's possible to feature both the classics and a number of obscure gems on one compact disc. The first volume of *Poptopia* proves this point, as it skillfully balances the familiar with the relatively unknown. Over the course of 18 tracks, the album features all of the key power-pop bands, from the Raspberries ("Go All the Way") and Big Star ("September Gurls") to Cheap Trick ("Come On, Come On") and 20/20 ("Yellow Pills"). Nearly every artist is represented by one of their big songs, with the notable exception of Badfinger, whose Capitol material wasn't available due to licensing restrictions. As a result, *Poptopia! Power Pop Classics of the '70s* is a basic primer on the genre, offering every major artist and many of the great

songs that provided power pop with its foundation, including Nick Lowe ("Cruel to Be Kind"), the Dwight Twilley Band ("I'm on Fire"), Flamin' Groovies ("Shake Some Action"), Todd Rundgren ("Couldn't I Just Tell You"), the Knack ("Good Girls Don't"), Bram Tchaikovsky ("Girl of My Dreams"), the Shoes ("Too Late"), Pezband ("Baby It's Cold Outside"), the Rubinoos ("I Wanna Be Your Boyfriend"), and the Records ("Starry Eyes"). Any serious power pop fan, and many casual listeners as well, will have everything here, but this is where the curious should start. —*Stephen Thomas Erlewine*

Poptopia! Power Pop Classics of the '80s / May 27, 1997 / Rhino ✦✦✦✦
Poptopia! Power Pop Classics of the '70s presented the roots of power pop, and its successor, *Power Pop Classics of the '80s*, finds the genre slowly mutating into a classicist style. In the '80s, power pop didn't have as dedicated an audience as it did in the previous decade (or that it would have in the '90s), and the place to hear catchy guitar pop was in the ringing jangle pop of the American underground. As a result, about half of the bands on this collection—including Let's Active, the Bangles, the DB's, Tommy Keene, the Smithereens, Hoodoo Gurus, and the La's—had more in common with jangle pop than power pop, but they shared the same love of the three-minute single and the pure, catchy melody. Also, their presence makes *Power Pop Classics of the '80s* a bit more diverse than its predecessor, since there's a greater variety of pop styles, from the punchy rock of the Romantics' "What I Like About You" and the British Invasion stylings of the Sponge Tones ("She Goes Out With Everybody") to the AOR of Utopia ("Crybaby") and the new wave of Holly & the Italians ("Tell That Girl to Shut Up") and the Plimsouls ("A Million Miles Away"). On the whole, the collection doesn't deliver as many thrills as *Power Pop Classics of the '70s*, but that's only by a slight margin, since among these 18 tracks are some of the finest pop singles of the '80s. —*Stephen Thomas Erlewine*

Poptopia! Power Pop Classics of the '90s / May 27, 1997 / Rhino ✦✦✦
The compilers of *Poptopia!* were on solid ground when they assembled the '70s and '80s editions of their series, since there was already an established canon of power pop greats for those decades. However, they ran into problems with *Power Pop Classics of the '90s*; first, the album was released in 1997, three years before the decade was finished. It's quite likely that all the significant power pop bands of the '90s had already appeared, but the major hurdle the compilers faced was the possibility that some artists might not be available for licensing. That certainly is the case with *Power Pop Classics of the '90s*; there's even a disclaimer in the liner notes that apologizes for the absence of Material Issue, the Gin Blossoms, and Teenage Fanclub. It's hard to believe that Material Issue and Teenage Fanclub were unavailable, considering that Matthew Sweet, the Lemonheads, and the Posies—three acts that sold more than those bands—are present, but their absence accentuates how uneven this collection actually is. There are some wonderful songs on *Power Pop Classics of the '90s*, but the remainder of the record proves that '90s power pop was a classicist genre, caring more about form than content. Most of these songs sound good but just aren't that memorable, an especially frustrating situation in the case of Velocity Girl, the Rembrandts, and the Posies, bands that all have better songs in their catalogs. And that draws attention to the fact that many of the liveliest and best pop bands of the '90s—from Sloan and Sugar to Cast and Fountains of Wayne—are not here. Consequently, *Power Pop Classics of the '90s* can only be seen as an admirable effort, not a definitive collection. —*Stephen Thomas Erlewine*

Poptronica: Dance / Aug. 10, 1999 / Buddha ✦✦✦✦
Buddha's *Poptronica* series boasts a title that's a play on the prevalent term for techno in the '90s, electronica. In the early '80s, however, synth-pop was often called techno—something that the compilers of *Poptronica* remembered when it came time to assemble a three-disc series of synth-pop hits from the '80s. Though *Poptronica* has a bit of a jokey title, the discs themselves are excellent new wave retrospectives. *Dance* focuses on dance hits, including a number of hits that had "dance" in the title ("Dance Hall Days," "The Politics of Dancing," "Safety Dance"). Essentially, these are almost all pop hits that had strong beats—"Who's That Girl?," "Too Shy," "Rock Me Amadeus," "Poison Arrow," Fun Boy Three's original "Our Lips Are Sealed"—with a couple of selections that are just slightly off the beaten track (EBN-OZN's "AEIOU [And Sometimes Y]," Thompson Twins' "Love on Your Side," Nina Hagen's "New York, New York," INXS' "I Send a Message"). There's not quite enough unusual selection to make it of interest to serious new wave collectors, but it plays remarkably well, which is the reason why it's one of the better examples of this breed. —*Stephen Thomas Erlewine*

Poptronica: Romance / Aug. 10, 1999 / Buddha ✦✦✦✦
Buddha's *Poptronica* series boasts a title that's a play on the prevalent term for techno in the '90s, electronica. In the early '80s, however, synth-pop was often called techno—something that the compilers of *Poptronica* remembered when it came time to assemble a three-disc series of synth-pop hits from the '80s. Though *Poptronica* has a bit of a jokey title, the discs themselves are excellent new wave retrospectives. *Romance* focuses on hits about love, even if it stretches the definition of a love song (Laurie Anderson's "O Superman" isn't most people's idea of a romantic tune). It also stretches its synth-pop boundaries somewhat, adding Love and Rocket's 1989 smash "So Alive," which had no discernable synths, but at its core are several great new wave hits—"The Metro," "Words," "Here Comes the Rain Again," "In the Name of Love," "Lucky Number," "Love Plus One." There are more offbeat selections here than on the other *Poptronica* discs—Japan's "Gentlemen Take Polaroids," the Fixx's "Stand or Fall," the Parachute Club's "Love Is Fire," Classic Nouveaux's "Guilty"—which might make it of interest to serious new wave collectors. Nevertheless, the main attribute of *Poptronica: Romance* is that it plays remarkably well, which is the reason why it's one of the better examples of this breed. —*Stephen Thomas Erlewine*

Poptronica: Sci-Fi / Aug. 10, 1999 / Buddha ✦✦✦✦
Buddha's *Poptronica* series boasts a title that's a play on the prevalent term for techno in

the '90s, electronica. In the early '80s, however, synth-pop was often called techno—something that the compilers of *Poptronica* remembered when it came time to assemble a three-disc series of synth-pop hits from the '80s. Though *Poptronica* has a bit of a jokey title, the discs themselves are excellent new wave retrospectives. *Sci-Fi* focuses on new wave songs about science—or at least songs that sound like the product of mad scientists. Indeed, it may be hard to discern what the theme of the compilation is without glancing at the title, but it's actually the most cohesive of the three *Poptronica* discs. That may be because it's filled with hits—"Weird Science," "She Blinded Me With Science," "Sweet Dreams (Are Made of This)," "Cars," "Oh Yeah," "Lies," "Rock Lobster," After the Fire's "Der Kommissar," a live version of "Whip It"—or it could be that the relative obscurities (A Flock of Seagull's "Space Age Love Song," Missing Person's "Destination Unknown," Q-Feel's "Dancing in Heaven [Orbital Be-Bop]") are all first-rate. Either way, it's not really of interest to serious new wave collectors, since there aren't a lot of rarities, but *Poptronica: Sci-Fi* plays remarkably well, which is the reason why it's among the better new wave comps. *—Stephen Thomas Erlewine*

Postpunk Chronicles: Going Underground / Jan. 12, 1999 / Rhino ✦✦✦✦✦
For the most part, *Going Underground* is a coronation of the guitar in the post-punk ethic. With a couple exceptions—like Throbbing Gristle—this volume in the *Postpunk Chronicles* series demonstrates the fusion of distortion and power with rediscovered pop melody. A dollop or two of romantic angst doesn't hurt either. A handful of punk and alternative's most important all-time artists show up here, such as the Smiths, Sonic Youth, Gang of Four, Pere Ubu, and the Jam; much of the second tier is represented as well. Highlights are all over the map: the Smiths' still-rousing "What Difference Does It Make?," troubadour Billy Bragg's wistful "A New England," and two of nihilism's all-time greatest hits, the Soft Boys' "I Wanna Destroy You" and Pere Ubu's "Final Solution." The "title track" from the Jam closes the set as both an epitaph and a hint of where this music was largely headed: to the American underground, until bands like Nirvana proclaimed its importance to a wider audience. *—Paul Pearson*

Postpunk Chronicles: Left of the Dial / Jan. 12, 1999 / Rhino ✦✦✦✦✦
One of three initial releases in Rhino's survey of the pop music landscape after it had been redefined by the punk aesthetic. Series producer Jim Neill's goal with each 16-song volume in the series was to simulate "how a typical college radio show might have played out" circa 1979 to 1984.

Left of the Dial concentrates on the architects of dark avant-rock and moody, synthesized new wave. The lineup on this installment omits some key tracks because of licensing snags acknowledged in the liner notes, but the end result is no less enchanting. Key tracks are the original single version of R.E.M.'s "Radio Free Europe," Wire's "Outdoor Miner," and the Church's cover of Paul Simon's "I Am a Rock," an ideally revised anthem for the disenfranchised underground of the '80s. These songs quietly linger long after they've ended. *—Paul Pearson*

Postpunk Chronicles: Scared to Dance / Jan. 12, 1999 / Rhino ✦✦✦✦✦
Of the three initial entries in Rhino's *Postpunk Chronicles*, this volume might sound the most dated, but in its own way it's the most enjoyable. *Scared to Dance* skews toward faster-tempo landmarks of the early-'80s college underground, particularly the prototypes of synth-pop and dance music. You can hear bands trying to figure out where keyboards and dance might fit in the punk aesthetic, especially in Heaven 17's wry "(We Don't Need This) Fascist Groove Thang" and Pigbag's jungle instrumental "Papa's Got a Brand New Pigbag." These songs were largely created just before MIDI and sampling improved synthesizers' flexibility, and their joyful innocence is retroactively stunning. Other highlights include Magazine's amazing "The Light Pours Out of Me," Iggy Pop's jagged "New Values," and cuts from Orchestral Manoeuvres in the Dark ("Enola Gay") and Simple Minds ("Life in a Day") before they broke it big thanks to contributions to John Hughes movies. *—Paul Pearson*

Psychedelia at Abbey Road: 1965-1969 / Aug. 25, 1998 / EMI ✦✦✦✦
A 22-track single CD seems a bit paltry given the scope of the title—except, of course, that the 1969 cutoff date here puts the material from Harvest (a label started late that year and containing the lion's share of EMI psychedelia) out of reach. Of course, there are no Beatles tracks and, likewise, no Pink Floyd here, but we do get cuts by the Hollies, Donovan, Tomorrow, the Fingers, Focus 3, the Tales of Justine, Simon Dupree & the Big Sound, the Pretty Things, the Aquarian Age, the Koobas, the Nocturnes, Locomotive, the Gods, Mandrake Paddle Steamer, Mark Wirtz, and Syd Barrett. Most of this stuff, apart from "Sunshine Superman," "My White Bicycle," and "King Midas in Reverse," isn't exactly routine material, and two tracks—"Delighted to See You" by the N'Betweens and "Why" by Tomorrow—are previously unissued. The latter, a cover of the Byrds' song, features a *tour de force* guitar break by future Yes member Steve Howe. Just as revelatory is "Monday Morning," a 1967 single by the largely forgotten the Tales of Justine, featuring David Daltrey, with arrangement and production by Tim Rice and Andrew Lloyd Webber, respectively. Everything on the album has been remastered in 24-bit digital sound, and the long version of Donovan's "Sunshine Superman" has been remixed, bringing out extraordinary detail in the percussion section, from the choppy rhythm guitars and harpsichord down to the exceptionally busy drumming. The annotation by Brian Hogg is detailed without going overboard on trivia, and the entire collection turns out to be great fun. *—Bruce Eder*

The R&B Box: 30 Years of Rhythm & Blues / 1994 / Rhino ✦✦✦✦
The concept behind the six-disc *The R&B Box: 30 Years of Rhythm & Blues* is admirable, but it's really too difficult to execute. Rhino wanted to tell the history of R&B's golden era of 1944-1974 by including one cut by each of the major artists in the genre, from Louis Jordan to the Spinners. Licensing restricitions prevented the label from including such heavy hitters as Sam Cooke and Sly Stone, which stops the set from being definitive. They also chose to include questionable cuts by some artists (Smokey Robinson is represented by "Mickey's Monkey"), and the one-song-per-artist rule prevents the collection from being truly representative. That said, *The R&B Box* is still worthwhile for neophytes, since it gives a general idea of the evolution of R&B, and features many great songs in one convenient place. It may leave just as many great songs off, but for listeners unfamiliar with the genre it's a good, if costly, primer. *—Stephen Thomas Erlewine*

Radio Daze: Pop Hits of the 80's, Vols. 1-5 / 1995 / Rhino ✦✦✦✦✦
Rhino's *Radio Daze: Pop Hits of the '80s* is a five-volume series culling the hits and highlights from early-'80s adult contemporary radio. Each disc is equally divided between guilty pleasures and bland, tedious dreck, but that only means that the series captures the feeling and sound of adult contemporary radio. In fact, it's surprising how many genuinely good songs are scattered throughout the collection. Although one volume is no better than the next—making any of the five discs an equally representative starting point—there is just as much schlock as there are worthwhile songs and entertaining kitsch on each collection. Because of this, *Radio Daze* may not be consistently entertaining, but it's hard to imagine a better collection of early-'80s adult contemporary than this. And that's even acknowledging the absence of Air Supply. *—Stephen Thomas Erlewine*

Rarest Rockabilly & Hillbilly Boogie: The Best of Ace Rockabilly / Ace ✦✦✦✦✦
This compact disc combines two Ace Records vinyl compilations of choice 1950s material. *Rarest Rockabilly & Hillbilly Boogie* anthologizes rockabilly history through the prism of the vanity pressing. For a hundred dollars or so, an Elvis wannabe could cut a couple songs and get back a small pressing for their efforts. Once copies were distributed to nearby radio stations, promoters, and juke box operators, the remaining stash was given away to fans and relatives or sold at dances. Texas-based Starday Records was a hotbed for this; in a period of six years, they issued over 500 titles on their Dixie label or vanity labels, and these are this basis for this compilation. As primitive as some of these are, the music is just fine. Most of the artists collected here are just names on labels of a phonograph record company, yet the inclusion of two early rockin' sides from Jimmie Dale Gilmore are most illuminating. This compilation errs on the side of hillbilly boogie but if cowboy boots stand in for blue suede shoes, there's still pep aplenty in selections like Bill Mack's "It's Saturday Night" and Buddy Shaw's "Don't Sweep That Dirt on Me." *Best of Ace Rockabilly* returns to the classic sound and is loaded with collector's prizes. Sonny Fisher's "Rockin' Daddy" and "Sneaky Pete" are raw Texas style rockabilly at its best, while Louisiana is represented by Link Davis' "Trucker From Tennessee" and Jimmy Johnny's "I Can't Find the Doorknob." The big ticket items are two of George Jones' rare excursions into the deep waters of the big beat, "Rock It" and "How Come It." All in all, a superlative compilation that truly gives a sense of rock & roll's ground-floor incarnation in the wake of Elvis. *—Cub Koda*

● **The Red Bird Story** / 1991 / Charly ✦✦✦✦✦
Red Bird was a great label in the mid-'60s, releasing some excellent soul/pop hybrids and some of the greatest girl group records of all time, especially those by the Shangri-Las and the Dixie Cups. This four-CD, 96-track compilation is a frustratingly mixed attempt to enshrine its legacy. There are lots of great sides here: all the Shangri-Las and Dixie Cups hits, many of their rarities, one-shots by the Ad Libs, Jelly Beans, Butterflies, and Tradewinds, and cool rarities by Bessie Banks, Dee Dee Warwick, Evie Sands, Ellie Greenwich, the Soul Brothers, Cathy Saint, Linda Jones, and Andy Kim. But the programming is unnervingly jumpy and haphazard, the liner notes surprisingly fuzzy (no information whatsoever is given about many of the lesser-known artists), and, in the absence of master tapes, some of the cuts were obviously taken from records. And for all its length, it's not even a complete collection of Red Bird's output; some songs that were excluded had even surfaced on previous Charly vinyl anthologies. There's still a lot of great music here, but the execution could have been a lot better. *—Richie Unterberger*

Risque Rhythm: Nasty '50s R&B / 1991 / Rhino ✦✦✦✦✦
Risque Rhythm: Nasty '50s R&B contains 18 raw, raunchy R&B and jump blues records from the likes of Moose Jackson, Dinah Washington, the Five Royales, Billy Ward & the Dominoes, Wynonie Harris, Roy Brown, and the Swallows. It's remarkable how explicit these double-entrendre-laced singles were, but what really makes *Risque Rhythm* worth acquiring is its gritty, pounding rhythms, which are just as sexy as the lyrics. *—Stephen Thomas Erlewine*

The Rock & Roll Fever!: The Wildest From Specialty / 1994 / Specialty ✦✦✦
Excellent 25-track compilation featuring '50s sides that appeared on the Specialty label. Highlights include Jerry Byrne's "Lights Out" and "Carry On" (both featuring a young Dr. John on piano), Bob "Froggy" Landers' surreal "Cherokee Dance," Don and Dewey's original take of "Justine," the Pentagons' "It's Spring Again," and Roddy Jackson's "Moose on the Loose." From the label that brought you Little Richard, this is piano-poundin', shack-shakin', borderline-nuts first-generation rock & roll. For once, a compilation that truly reflects its title. *—Cub Koda*

Rock Instrumental Classics, Vol. 3 / 1994 / Rhino ✦✦✦
Rhino's third rock instrumentals volume covers the '70s, a period that found disco, funk, and fusion joining the formula alongside one-shot concept works and the usual novelty numbers. The 18 cuts include stomping club/funk from B.T. Express and Brass Construction, King Curtis' updated honking sax cover of Led Zeppelin's "Whole Lotta Love," very stylized material from the Electric Light Orchestra and Deodato, and memorable outings by Billy Preston, Edgar Winter, and AWB. Gary Glitter, Edgar Winter, the Chakachas, Rhinoceros, and Van McCoy offer lighter pop variations, and "Sun Goddess" was a musically adventurous excursion into fusion by Earth, Wind & Fire. *—Ron Wynn*

Rock Instrumental Classics, Vol. 4 / 1994 / Rhino ✦✦✦
While the material on volume four of Rhino's rock instrumentals set chronologically

preceded what was on the third volume, no soul, R&B, or even soul-jazz and funk fan should mind these 18 genuine classics, including two superb numbers from Booker T. and the MGs, seminal tracks by the Mar-Keys, Bar-Kays, and Cannonball Adderley, and great Latin tunes from Ray Barretto and Mongo Santamaria. There's absolutely no fluff, and the presence on CD of rare cuts like the Young Holt Trio's "Wack Wack" and Alvin Cash & the Crawlers' "Twine Time" is most welcome. *—Ron Wynn*

Rock Instrumental Classics, Vol. 5 / 1994 / Rhino ♦♦♦♦
Rhino closes its five-volume rock instrumentals series with an 18-track outing devoted to surf guitar. This fast-paced, prickly, and frequently exciting form may not be among the most diversified structurally, but if does offer some surging playing from its practitioners. They range from founding father Dick Dale to its most popular bands, the Surfaris, Belairs, Ventures, and Chantays. While not particularly a hardcore surf collection, this disc certainly outlines its virtues, and the tunes were long enough to display guitar proficiency, but short enough to prevent self-indulgence and repetition. *—Ron Wynn*

Rock Instrumental Classics, Vol. 1 / 1994 / Rhino ♦♦♦♦
Rhino begins yet another concept line with 18 tasty instrumentals from the rock era. It's the first of a five-volume set devoted to this genre, and they certainly picked the right era to launch it. From Duane Eddy's shuddering guitar riffs and Link Wray's rumbling licks to Lee Allen's honking sax lines and bleating phrases, Dave "Baby" Cortez's distorted organ, and Ernie Fields' swing/boogie, this anthology shows how early rock & roll emerged through the union of seemingly disparate musical elements. Besides big-band jazz and shouting blues, there were also bits of rockabilly, pop, novelty tunes, and country, reworked and presented in short, captivating ditties. *—Ron Wynn*

Rock Instrumental Classics, Vol. 2 / 1994 / Rhino ♦♦♦♦
The second release in Rhino's rock instrumentals series moves into the 1960s, again presenting a wide array of material. There's jazz-tinged fare by pianist Ray Bryant, roadhouse blues/boogie from Lonnie Mack, the Ventures' signature surf tune "Walk Don't Run," and another Duane Eddy floor-shaker, "Because They're Young." This collection also shows that the novelty and silly tunes weren't quite as inspired in the 1960s; neither the Fireballs' "Bulldog" or the T-Bones' "No Matter What Shape (Your Stomach's In)" will ever make anyone forget the Coasters. There are several interesting gimmicks and odd period pieces, from Mason Williams' "Classical Gas" to Jorgen Ingmann's "Apache" and "(Ghost) Riders in the Sky" by the Ramroads. It's shorter than the first volume and has a bit more fluff, but is still quite valuable. *—Ron Wynn*

☆ **Rock This Town: Rockabilly Hits, Vol. 1** / 1991 / Rhino ♦♦♦♦♦
Rock This Town: Rockabilly Hits, Vol. 1 is a stellar, 18-track collection that contains such classic rockabilly singles as Johnny Burnette's "The Train Kept a-Rollin," Bill Haley's "Rock the Joint," Roy Orbison's "Ooby Dooby," Carl Perkins' "Blue Suede Shoes," Billy Riley's "Red Hot," Dale Hawkins' "Susie-Q," Buddy Knox's "Party Doll," Gene Vincent's "Lotta Lovin'," Buddy Holly's "Oh Boy!," Jerry Lee Lewis' "High School Confidential," and Ritchie Valens' "Come On, Let's Go." Not only does it contain those hits, but there are terrific obscurities from Jimmy Lloyd, Nicky Nelson, Sonnee West, Janis Martin, and Sanford Clark, making *Rock This Town* and its companion volume a definitive collection for the average listener. *—Stephen Thomas Erlewine*

☆ **Rock This Town: Rockabilly Hits, Vol. 2** / 1991 / Rhino ♦♦♦♦♦
For its first half, the second volume of *Rock This Town: Rockabilly Hits* is as strong as its predecessor, running through such classic singles as Eddie Cochran's "C'mon Everybody," Wanda Jackson's "Let's Have a Party," Conway Twitty's "Danny Boy," Ronnie Hawkins' "Mary Lou," Johnny Horton's "Honky Tonk Hardwood Floor," Jack Scott's "The Way I Walk," and the Rock-a-Teens' "Woo-Hoo." The latter half contains rockabilly revival numbers ranging from Commander Cody ("Hot Rod Lincoln"), Dave Edmunds ("I Hear You Knocking"), and Billy Swan ("I Can Help") to the Blasters ("Flattop Joint"), Robert Gordon ("Red Hot"), and Stray Cats ("Rock This Town"). While these latter-day recordings have merit, they would have been better heard on a third volume, leaving the second volume to additional cuts from the '50s and '60s. So, that does mean *Rock This Town* is an imperfect collection, but there's enough good stuff to make it necessary for anyone who purchased *Vol. 1*. *—Stephen Thomas Erlewine*

Rockin' From Coast to Coast, Vol. 1 / 1996 / Ace ♦♦♦
Garage rock wasn't a concept that originated in the mid-'60s. In the aftermath of the initial rock & roll explosion, young rockabilly and R&B singers brought their unhoned talents into tiny studios throughout the country. This is a compilation of 26 of those efforts, mostly from the late '50s (mostly from 1958, in fact), and mostly for small independent labels, although some of these were leased to major labels, and a few were even recorded for major labels directly. Only one of these was a chart hit (Freddy Cannon's "Buzz Buzz A-Diddle-It"), and it's easy to see why, from two points of view. The approaches were too uncompromisingly raw, and the production too crude. On the other side of that coin, the songs themselves were rarely anything special, usually being standard three-chord knockoffs with little to make them stand out besides the ferocious energy of the performances. It's not great art, but it's certainly entertaining. That's especially true when the energy spills over to mania, as on the legendary Tyrone Schmidling's shambling sides, the incredibly sloppy rendition of "Good Golly Miss Molly" by Sam Cooke proteges the Valiants, or the echoed-to-infinity Tex-Mex-cum-Jerry Lee Lewis of the Rio Rockers (released on Capitol!). There are some unexpected appearances by stars as well, such as Eddie Cochran (who plays guitar on Lee Denson's "New Shoes"), Brenda Lee (the early rockabilly track "Rock the Bop"), a teenaged Joe South, and Roy Clark (heard as a rockabilly singer). The collection's also educational in its own way, as an illustration of just how extreme and far-flung the rock & roll revolution had become at the grass-roots level just a few years after its birth. *—Richie Unterberger*

Rockin' From Coast to Coast, Vol. 2 / May 11, 1999 / Ace ♦♦♦
Another volume of raw 1950s rock where obscurity fights it out with quality. The former trait getting the upper hand more often than not, although you might have heard a few of the names here, particularly Wanda Jackson and Ronnie Dee (aka Ronnie Dawson). Like the first volume, it's an OK sampler of the range of unbridled sounds recorded in the wake of the original rock & roll explosion, from both white and (less often) black artists. Joe Clay's "Duck Tail," Big T Tyler's "King Kong," and Tarheel Slim's "No. 9 Train" are big enough cult favorites that they—along with the Jackson and Dawson cuts—are on Rhino's *Loud, Fast & Out of Control* '50s rock box set. The remainder of the CD consists of about 20 other high-octane performances that are, more often than not, quite derivative of Elvis Presley, Gene Vincent, Jerry Lee Lewis, and Little Richard, to name the most obvious targets. Sometimes the imitation is blatant enough to actually preclude even casual enjoyment; why listen to the Catalinas' "Speechless" when it's obvious as hell that it would not have existed if not for "Breathless" by Jerry Lee Lewis? On the other hand, some of the unknown tracks have their share of thrills, like Joyce Harris' screams-her-throat-raw version of "Got My Mojo Working." Some reasonably well-known names are scattered throughout the rest of the set: Roy Brown trying New Orleans rock & roll on "Saturday Night," Ersel Hickey doing "Goin' Down the Road," future soul singer Sugar Pie DeSantos duetting with Peewee, and Jerry Reed and Joe South playing the stormy acoustic guitars powering Ric Cartey's "Scratchin' on My Screen." *—Richie Unterberger*

Rockin' on Broadway: The Time, Brent, Shad Story / Jun. 6, 2000 / Ace ♦♦♦
What do the small Time, Brent, and Shad labels have in common? Aside from being minor indies of the late 1950s/early 1960s, they were all run by producer Bob Shad. Like a bunch of indie entrepreneurs of the era, his didn't subscribe to a set vision. Doo wop, primeval guitar rock & roll, rockabilly, novelty, ballads, girl group: all and more got a shot with Shad. And some succeeded: the Bell Notes' "I've Had It," a pretty cool mid-tempo song juxtaposing winsome lamenting harmonized vocals against growling guitars, made number six in 1959, while Skip and Flip almost made the Top Ten with both the catchy rockaballad "It Was I" and the slicker "Cherry Pie." All of those are on this 30-song compilation, which has some other interesting moments along the way. The Genies' "Who's That Knocking" is exuberant up-tempo doo wop; "The People Hater" is a disagreeable novelty about a misanthrope (really); the Beau-Marks were among the first Canadian rockers to make an impact in the States with their generic 1960 rocker "Clap Your Hands"; and the Donays made a girl-group classic with their only single, "Devil in His Heart," covered by the Beatles in 1963 (the B-side, "Bad Boy," is also here). Strangest of all are no less than four songs graced by the presence of a young Lou Reed—yes, *the* Lou Reed. As a teenager he sang on the Jades' unremarkable 1958 doo wop single "So Blue"/"Leave Her for Me." More remarkably, this CD also unearths two previously unreleased (and previously unknown) 1962 solo tracks, credited to "Lewis Reed," which are typical commercial 1962 rock (penned by Reed himself) that would be utterly undistinguished if not for his unmistakable vocals. Still, about half of this CD is unmemorable period filler, making it a hit-and-miss listen. *—Richie Unterberger*

Rough Trade Shops: 25 Years / Apr. 10, 2001 / Mute ♦♦♦♦♦
Rough Trade's story began in 1976 with a shop in Notting Hill, branching out within a couple years to become a label and a distributor. Beginning with Pere Ubu and concluding with Tindersticks, *Rough Trade Shops: 25 Years* chronologically distills the history of the pioneering independent outlet into four discs and 56 tracks, concentrating on old and new favorites that have graced the shop's new release racks. Just about every style associated with U.K.-based independent and underground music between 1975 and 2000 is accounted for. The first half concentrates on the punk and post-punk staples of the Buzzcocks ("Boredom"), the Birthday Party ("Mr. Clarinet"), the Cocteau Twins ("Sugar Hiccup"), and the Smiths ("Hand in Glove"), throwing in the occasional pleasant surprise like the short-lived Native Hipsters ("Look There Goes Concord Again") and diversions into reggae (Lee "Scratch" Perry, the Congos). The second half does a lot more hopping around stylistically. Spacemen 3 ("Revolution"), the Pixies ("Bone Machine"), the Chills ("Pink Frost"), and Clinic ("Monkey on Your Back") represent the guitar-based efforts, while Gescom ("Sciew Spoc"), Boards of Canada ("Everything You Do Is a Balloon"), and Plastikman ("Plastique") hit upon more electronic and experimental terrain. Since this compilation includes acts distributed and sold by the like-named shop, label, and distributor, there are major gaps with the Rough Trade bands proper—no Galaxie 500, Scrawl, AR Kane, or This Heat. Since the label itself released nearly 300 singles, no package short of complete would avoid such a pitfall. But quite successfully, *25 Years* provides a fantastic skip through Rough Trade's existence. Many great artists have Rough Trade to thank for bin space, recording costs, and retail distribution. Here's hoping for 25 more years—and here's hoping that they're less turbulent financially. *—Andy Kellman*

The Roulette Story / Nov. 10, 1998 / West Side ♦♦♦♦♦
This three-CD, 84-track box set brings together the hits and rarities from Morris Levy's New York indie label that closed down in 1977, after being in business for a 20-year period spanning the history of rock & roll's ascendancy to the top of the charts. Starting off with two million sellers on its first two releases (Buddy Knox's "Party Doll" and Jimmy Bowen's "I'm Sticking With You"), Roulette also made inroads in the folk and pop fields with the success of Jimmie Rodgers and artists like Valerie Carr and Georgia Gibbs. The label also released some of the very best in rockabilly, doo wop, and rock & roll with Ronnie Hawkins' "Forty Days" and "Who Do You Love," Tiny Tim and the Hits' "Wedding Bells," and Jimmy Lloyd's "Rocket in My Pocket." But Roulette was much more than just another indie rock & roll label, as the second disc amply proves with stellar jazz offerings from Count Basie, Joe Williams, Sarah Vaughan, Sonny Stitt, Louis Armstrong, and Duke Ellington peppering the catalog. The third disc picks up the pop/rock story from the early '60s to the label's demise in the late '70s, with hitworthy selections from Lou Christie, the

Hullabaloos, Tommy James, and Alive and Kicking. The label also knew a good novelty record when it heard one, as all three discs are peppered with items like the Playmates' "Beep Beep" and the Detergents' "Leader of the Laundromat." For true surrealism, one is directed to Jim Nabors doing a rock & roll version of "There's No Tomorrow," an early stab at what Elvis later turned into "It's Now or Never." Excellent notes, stellar sound; this is one great label overview that tells the story of rock & roll and its place in the pop music scheme of things in microcosm. —*Cub Koda*

Ruffhouse Records Greatest Hits / May 4, 1999 / Ruffhouse/Columbia ✦✦✦✦
Although it never gained the notoriety of Def Jam, Death Row, or No Limit, Ruffhouse had its share of excellent artists during the '90s, most notably Cypress Hill, the Fugees, Lauryn Hill, Wyclef Jean, and Kris Kross. As a celebration of nearly ten years in the business—or at least as a way of celebrating the massive success of Hill's debut solo album—the label released *Ruffhouse Records Greatest Hits*, a generous compilation that contains 14 of their biggest hits, along with an interesting but superfluous Jason Nevins remix of "Insane in the Brain." Perhaps that mix was added as incentive to collectors, but the reason to pick up the compilation are the hits themselves; the best of these—"How I Could Just Kill a Man," "Fu-Gee-La," "Killing Me Softly With His Song," "Insane in the Brain," "Doo Wop (That Thing)," "Gone Till November" and "Jump"—sound like contemporary classics, while such lesser numbers as Tim Dog's silly, silly "Fuck Compton" are great nostalgia trips. It's not perfect, of course—although the Fugees and their side projects are rightly emphasized, it's at the expense of some good music by other artists—but it still is a first-class portrait of the label. —*Stephen Thomas Erlewine*

☆ **Saturday Night Fever** / 1977 / Polydor ✦✦✦✦✦
Saturday Night Fever is the point where disco turned from a fad into a phenomenon, crossing over into the mainstream and infiltrating every area of pop culture. Based on the film's soundtrack, it's not hard to see why. Where most disco albums were weighed down by endless grooves, *Saturday Night Fever* is relatively concise; only two tracks are longer than five minutes, and one of those, the Trammps' "Disco Inferno," actually showed how intoxicatingly good extended disco could be. But the real key to the album's success isn't "Disco Inferno," or the silly instrumentals "A Fifth of Beethoven" and "Night on Disco Mountain"; it's that the Bee Gees were able to mold disco into a pop form on "Stayin' Alive," "How Deep is Your Love," "Night Fever," "More Than a Woman," "Jive Talkin'," "You Should Be Dancing" and Yvonne Elliman's "If I Can't Have You." These are the songs that kept *Saturday Night Fever* on the charts for months on end, and these are the songs that defined an era. Portions of *Saturday Night Fever* now sound dated, but at its best, it was a peak that most disco albums could not reach. —*Stephen Thomas Erlewine*

☆ **The Scepter Records Story** / May 26, 1992 / Capricorn ✦✦✦✦✦
During the '50s and early '60s, NYC-based Scepter Records and its subsidiary Wand were part of a group of independents whose artists churned out hit after hit, defining the sound of the day and shaping the sound of the future. The Shirelles, Dionne Warwick, and the Isley Brothers all got their start there; if you love tough, pre-soul-era records like "Will You Still Love Me Tomorrow," "Twist and Shout," and "Walk on By," then this is for you. The label's roster also included singers Chuck Jackson, Maxine Brown, and Tommy Hunt; instrumentalist King Curtis; proto-pop/country artists B. J. Thomas and Ronnie Milsap; and punksters Kingsmen. That's right—"Louie Louie" is here, along with lots of other truly great music. Even though the three discs could have been condensed to a killer two, this box gets high marks. —*Christine Ohlman*

● **Searchin' for Shakes: Swedish Beat 1965-1968** / 1984 / Amigo Musik ✦✦✦✦✦
One of the very best compilations of '60s rock from a non-English-speaking country, with excellent fidelity (usually not the case with these productions). With their barely accented English vocals and the heavy mod rock flavor (with a pinch of Merseybeat thrown in), a bunch of these Swedish bands could pass for overlooked British Invasion groups. The Who's brand of auto-destruct guitar noise seemed to hit home particularly hard in Sweden, and the cuts by the Steampacket II, Lee Kings, Tages, Namelosers, and Boot-jacks will appeal to anyone who reveres the early Who and Creation. Other highlights include the Mascots, whose track is one of the best early Merseybeat imitations to be found anywhere, and the Lea Riders, whose "Dom Kellar Dos Mods" (previously issued on a *Pebbles* volume) is one of the prime demented psychedelic obscurities of all time. —*Richie Unterberger*

A Shot of Rhythm & Blues: R&B Era, Vol. 1 / 1990 / Sequel ✦✦✦✦
There are some pretty valuable tracks here, all dating from between 1963 and 1965. The stars include Cyril Davies & His Rhythm and Blues All-Stars ("Country Line Special"), Tony Jackson & the Vibrations ("Fortune Teller"), the Undertakers ("If You Don't Come Back"), and the Kinks ("Milk Cow Blues"), but they're augmented by a brace of worthwhile songs by unknown acts, including the Riot Squad ("Jump"), Felders Orioles ("Turn on Your Lovelight"), Jimmy Powell & the Dimensions ("I'm Looking for a Woman"), and the Chosen Few ("Today Tonight and Tomorrow"). Along the way are glimpses of the early work of future members of Lindisfarne and the Blockheads (the Chosen Few) and the Rutles (Felders Orioles), among other bands from the '70s and '80s. The producers have become a bit too ambitious at 22 tracks, however; Wayne Gibson & the Dynamic Sounds' "Portland Town" is way too folky and Van Dyke & the Bambis' "All I Want Is You" is pretty forgettable. As a result, about half of this CD is priceless, a third is edifying, and about 20 percent fills space and takes your time. —*Bruce Eder*

Singles / Jun. 30, 1992 / Epic ✦✦✦✦✦
The romantic comedy *Singles*, in part a homage to director Cameron Crowe's hometown of Seattle, was released at exactly the right time (summer 1992). Nirvana's *Nevermind* had symbolically knocked Michael Jackson off the top of the album charts at the beginning of the year, and the underground buzz about Seattle bands like Alice in Chains, Soundgarden, and Pearl Jam was beginning to find its way past circles of indie

aficionados and open-minded hard rock fans and into the mainstream. *Singles* helped crystallize the idea of the "Seattle scene" in the mainstream public's mind, and it was also one of the first big-selling '90s movie soundtracks (it went platinum and reached the Top Ten) to feature largely new work from contemporary artists. The soundtrack's strength was the way it was so firmly rooted in place—where future soundtrack extravaganzas simply contrived to gather as many big-name acts as possible, *Singles* focused specifically on Seattle-area music (quite logically, given the film's plot and setting), which gave the album the feel of a cohesive document. It didn't hurt that nearly all the bands involved contributed high-quality material—although Nirvana is absent, scene stalwarts Soundgarden, their lead singer Chris Cornell (the haunting acoustic ballad "Seasons"), Alice in Chains ("Would?," which showed up on their subsequent album *Dirt*), Mudhoney, Pearl Jam (two tracks), and Screaming Trees all weigh in with strong new cuts, as well as stylistic compatriots Smashing Pumpkins (Chicago) and Minneapolis alt-rock god Paul Westerberg (his first two charmingly playful solo songs). The vaults are mined for chestnuts by Mother Love Bone (the epic "Chloe Dancer/Crown of Thorns," perhaps their strongest moment) and Seattle native Jimi Hendrix (the shimmering "May This Be Love," which fits the mood of the album perfectly), and Seattle sisters Ann and Nancy Wilson, leaders of Heart, appear as the Lovemongers on a stellar acoustic cover of Led Zeppelin's "The Battle of Evermore." Despite Mudhoney's gripe that the whole early-'90s Seattle scene was "Overblown," *Singles* illustrates through its marvelous consistency the richness and wealth of the city's musical talent, as well as the alternative scene in general; meanwhile, the Lovemongers and Hendrix cuts demonstrate the city's past musical heritage, and along with the Westerberg numbers, provide a handy template of several major (albeit more mainstream) grunge-scene influences—Hendrix's guitar-heavy psychedelia, Led Zeppelin's epic hard rock, the Replacements' post-hardcore power pop—that sit very well next to their followers. So *Singles* isn't just an entertaining sampler of Seattle grunge in its prime; it's a milestone in the breakthrough of alternative rock into mainstream popular culture, neatly and effectively packaging the Seattle phenomenon for the wider national consciousness. —*Steve Huey*

Smooth Grooves: A Sensual Collection, Vols. 1-9 / 1995 / Rhino ✦✦✦✦✦
Rhino's *Smooth Grooves: A Sensual Collection, Vols. 1-9* is an excellent overview of late-'70s and early-'80s urban R&B ballads; in other words, it features the biggest hits and best-known quiet storm songs. Each disc contains 12 tracks, some presented in their 12" mixes never before available on CD. But the primary strength of *Smooth Grooves* is that it proves there were many classic soul songs released during this often-overlooked era. While there are a few tediously bland cuts on nearly every volume, there are more keepers than throwaways, including such classics as "Shining Star," "Sexual Healing," "Float On," and "Something He Can Feel." The curious should start with the first volume, which gives an accurate idea of what the series is about, but any quiet storm fan will find every volume worth acquiring. —*Stephen Thomas Erlewine*

☆ **Son of Frat Rock** / 1991 / Rhino ✦✦✦✦✦
Son of Frat Rock continues the pattern of its father, *Frat Rock*, by providing 18 infectious, danceable rock & roll and R&B oldies. There are a couple of big names here—the Kinks ("You Really Got Me"), Tommy James ("Mony Mony"), Mitch Ryder ("Devil With a Blue Dress"), Ritchie Valens ("La Bamba"), Bobby Fuller ("I Fought the Law")—but the main attraction of the disc is that it collects one-hit wonders like "Little Bit O' Soul," "Farmer John," "Cool Jerk," "Shout! Shout! (Knock Yourself Out)," "If You Wanna Be Happy," "Peanut Butter," "Bottle of Wine," "California Sun," "Quarter to Three" and "Hot Pastrami." There's no better place to get these classic rock & roll singles—which are some of the greatest rock & roll ever recorded—in one place than *Son of Frat Rock*, no matter how silly the title and the packaging may be, and that's why it's essential. —*Stephen Thomas Erlewine*

Songs Lennon & McCartney Gave Away / 1979 / EMI ✦✦✦✦
This British import isn't easy to find these days, but it's essential for Beatles and British music fans, collecting almost every Lennon-McCartney song that was not recorded by the Beatles, but that did appear on releases by other artists. The bulk of the material dates from 1963 and 1964 and, indeed, most of these were British and/or American hits, some of them quite huge. The tracks by Peter & Gordon and Billy J. Kramer are probably the best known, but you also get the more obscure compositions they donated to Cilla Black, the Applejacks, the Fourmost, P.J. Proby, Tommy Quickly, and Mike Shannon & the Strangers (who?). As in almost everything else they did, John and Paul displayed shrewd judgment in the tracks they passed on to others; most of them are far more lightweight and sappy than the Beatles' typical material. And so are most of the interpretations; in cases where the Beatles recorded unreleased versions (as with "Hello Little Girl," "Love of the Loved," and "That Means a Lot"), the Fab Four's versions are vastly superior. That said, this is irresistibly melodic and jaunty British Invasion pop, with a few late-'60s tracks thrown in by Cilla Black, Carlos Mendes, and Chris Barber. The only notable absentees are the hits by Mary Hopkin ("Goodbye") and Badfinger ("Come and Get It," which actually bears a McCartney solo composition credit). —*Richie Unterberger*

☆ **Soul Hits of the 70s: Didn't It Blow Your Mind [Series Overview]** / 1991 / Rhino ✦✦✦✦✦
As soul music moved into the early '70s, it became dominated by smoother sounds and polished productions, picking up its cues from Motown, Chicago soul, and uptown soul. By the beginning of the decade, soul was fracturing in a manner similar to pop/rock, as pop-soul, funk, vocal groups, string-laden Philly soul, and sexy Memphis soul became just a few of the many different subgenres to surface. Often the productions on these records were much more polished than '60s production, boasting sound effects, synthesizers, electric keyboards, echoes, horn sections, acoustic guitars, and strings. It was one of the most ambitious eras in the history of soul, but it was often overlooked because only a handful

of superstars—Stevie Wonder, Al Green, Marvin Gaye, the Spinners, Sly Stone, the O'Jays, and James Brown—emerged, and they didn't dominate the charts like Otis Redding, Aretha Franklin, and Smokey Robinson did just a few years back. However, there was an astonishing string of one-hit wonders and artists, like the Chi-Lites, who had a handful of hits. Those are the artists who are spotlighted on Rhino's *Soul Hits of the '70s: Didn't It Blow Your Mind*, a wonderful 20-disc series that contains many of the greatest singles and forgotten hits from the early '70s. The first 15 volumes are the heart of the series, capturing the golden age of '70s soul, filled with smooth soul, items from Philly, proto-disco, and gorgeous, lush masterpieces of production, performance, and song. Though there are few of the above-mentioned superstars here, there is no shortage of great singles, and part of the joy of the series is discovering little-heard gems. The last five volumes aren't as interesting since they capture the post-disco, funk, and quiet storm; they do their job as well as the previous 15, but the music itself isn't as good. Still, that's hardly an embarrassment and overall *Soul Hits of the '70s* is perhaps the finest soul series ever assembled. *—Stephen Thomas Erlewine*

☆ **Soul Shots [Series Overview]** / 1988 / Rhino ♦♦♦♦♦
Originally released as a stellar vinyl series, Rhino's *Soul Shots* changed drastically when it went over to CD. Where the vinyl editions concentrated on specific styles, the CDs tended to focus on just the hits and the brightest little-known gems—which is by no means a bad thing. In fact, in this format the *Soul Shots* series is one of the best soul collections available, offering a healthy dose of wonderful, pure unadulterated soul on each disc. *—Stephen Thomas Erlewine*

Soul Train: Hall of Fame, 20th Anniversary / 1974-1991 / Rhino ♦♦♦♦
Soul Train, the longest-running weekly syndicated program in television, gave black artists and dancers a forum when there was no interest from the major networks. This fine three-disc boxed set celebrates the show's two decades and serves as a good overview of how contemporary black pop has changed during its run. The opening disc is by far the most diverse; during the mid-'70s, there was still room for Southern soul and blues, stylish pop, funk, and vocal groups. The second disc mirrors the turn toward more sophisticated production, a less soulful sound, and the coming of disco. The final CD begins with light soul and pop-tinged fare, then slides into rap, hip-hop, and new jack swing. Most of these songs are available elsewhere, but this collection gives listeners a consistently entertaining tour. Rhino deserves bonus points for using all original versions throughout. *—Ron Wynn*

Space Box: 1970 & Beyond—Space, Krautrock & Acid Trips / Aug. 20, 1996 / Cleopatra ♦♦♦
The Space Box contains four discs of prog rock and art rock, as well as trance-inducing Krautrock, from the early '70s. Most of this music was inspired by the sonic experimentalism of late '60s Pink Floyd—it builds on the long, free-form coda to "Interstellar Overdrive." There are subtle differences between the bands—for instance, Hawkwind tends to lean toward hard rock more than their contemporaries, who explore psychedelia and classical music flourishes. Even though the set is well compiled and contains some fine songs (Faust and Gong sound particularly good), there's no denying that there is a limited audience for this, even among prog-rock fans. It's experimental music that is oddly limited, working the same vibe, if not the same sound. If you're not a fanatic of space-rock, then the four discs of *The Space Box* will simply be too much to digest. *—Stephen Thomas Erlewine*

Specialty Legends of Jump Blues, Vol. 1 / 1994 / Specialty ♦♦♦
Ranging from major hits to little-known rarities, this 1994 CD looks back at Specialty's jump blues output of the late '40s and early '50s. Specialty, which was founded in L.A. in 1945, was one of the most prolific independent labels when it came to jump blues, the music that ruled the dance floor in the African-American community after the swing era and before the emergence of soul music. A blend of swing and blues that started in the 1930s, jump blues was especially hot in the post-World War II years, when big bands were fading in popularity and it was clear that an innovative new form of jazz called bebop was great for listening but hardly great for dancing. The undeniable king of jump blues was Louis Jordan, who was a major influence on Joe Liggins, Jimmy Liggins, Roy Milton, Percy Mayfield, Joe Lutcher, and others on this CD. Some of the collection's better-known recordings include Joe Liggins' "Pink Champagne" (1950) and his 1950 remake of his 1945 hit "The Honeydripper," while its rarities include King Perry's amusing and previously unreleased "I Wonder Who's Boogin' My Woogie" and Mayfield's alternate takes of "I Dare You, Baby" and "The Hunt Is On." Though most of the material is decent, only some of it is essential or superb; this is a disc that contains too many rarities for the casual listener. So if you need a taste of Introductory Jump Blues 101, it's best to look elsewhere. But if you're a collector, this CD is certainly enjoyable. *—Alex Henderson*

Specialty Records Greatest Hits / May 15, 2001 / Specialty ♦♦♦♦♦
The Specialty label was one of the leading companies of both postwar rhythm & blues and early rock & roll. This 20-song anthology is a concise and well-selected survey of their biggest hits and most important performers, including cuts by Little Richard, Larry Williams, Sam Cooke (the early solo performance "I'll Come Running Back to You"), Percy Mayfield, Lloyd Price, Roy Milton, Joe Liggins, and Jimmy Liggins. Some might complain that this is missing representative samples of other R&B notables on Specialty, from Camille Howard and Marvin & Johnny to Floyd Dixon and Jessie Belvin. But then, if you want to go that deep, there's the five-CD box *The Specialty Story*, as well as numerous single-artist Specialty compilations. This is a good introduction, the most familiar items by far being Little Richard's five hits (and, of course, there are several other of his hits that *aren't* here), Larry Williams' "Bony Moronie" and "Short Fat Fanny," and Lloyd Price's "Lawdy Miss Clawdy." Not as well known, but still massively influential in the just-pre-rock R&B world, were Percy Mayfield's ballad "Please Send Me Someone to Love," Joe Liggins' romp "Pink Champagne," and Jimmy Liggins' even more raucous "Drunk." *—Richie Unterberger*

The Specialty Story [Box] / 1994 / Specialty ♦♦♦♦♦
Label-owner Art Rupe was a savvy businessman who knew the black jukebox industry and what made it tick when he started his Specialty label in the late-'40s. This sumptuous five-disc box set contains a bevy of highlights from this seminal R&B/rock & roll label. Over the years, Rupe recorded a little bit of everything; early big band jump (the Liggins brothers), down-home blues and zydeco (Guitar Slim, Frankie Lee Sims, Clifton Chenier), gospel (early Sam Cooke and the Soul Stirrers), and doo wop (the Pentagons, Jesse Belvin). But with the discovery of the label's biggest star, Little Richard, in 1955, here is where the real story of rock & roll begins. A box set that no lover of the real thing can be without. *—Cub Koda*

Starday Dixie Rockabilly, Vol. 1 / Feb. 26, 1999 / Ace ♦♦♦
This is Texas rockabilly served up raw and honest on this 24-track collection that also features many of the custom pressed singles that came out on Starday's Dixie subsidiary, roping in out of state hopefuls. Tracks like Tony & Jackie Lamie's "Wore to a Frazzle," Mack Banks' "Be-Boppin' Daddy," the Hi-Tombs' "Sweet Rockin' Mama," Warren Robbe's "My Chicken Penn" are rockabilly with one foot still doing a square dance, hillbilly artists giving this new music a shot with surprisingly wild results. The quality and approaches vary wildly from rocked-out strokes like Rudy Grayzell's "Let's Get Wild" and Jay Richards' "Gosh Dog Baby" to straight-up Elvis wannabes like Gene Terry's "The Woman I Love" and Carl Trantham's "Where There's a Will (There's a Way)." You'd be hard-pressed to find a cruder bopper than "Boogie Woogie All Night" by Bill Willis, just as you'd be equally hard-pressed to find a better Jerry Lee tribute than Groovy Joe Poovey's "Ten Long Fingers." Bottom line, this is one '50s rockabilly collection that delivers the goods big time and would make an essential addition to anyone's rockabilly must-have list. No major hits, but much major music. *—Cub Koda*

Starday Dixie Rockabilly, Vol. 2 / Jul. 11, 2000 / Ace ♦♦♦
Ace's second volume of rare rockabilly cuts for the Starday-Dixie operation in the late '50s focuses to a large degree on custom pressings, essentially pay-to-play vinyl with emerging artists paying for Starday to press a very small quantity of discs. When an archive compilation is entirely devoted to such material, the result is often something that is best left in the closet, but actually this 24-song disc is pretty respectable. Like much Starday rockabilly, it often has far more of a country hillbilly flavor than the well-known rockabilly of the era did. That's certainly the case with the most famous (by far) artist represented, Buck Owens, who did a couple of nice rockabilly numbers under the pseudonym Corky Jones on a 1957 single. He redid one of them ("Hot Dog"), in fact, in 1988 as a duet with Dwight Yoakam. As for other highlights, Joe Poovey's "Careful Baby" is like hillbilly with a Bill Haley rick-a-tick beat and (like "Hot Dog") is one of the relatively few items here that you could imagine having some commercial success. That accusation certainly could not be levied at Eddie Seacrist's "Dancing to the Rhythm of a Rock & Roll Band," with a moronic cowbell-anchored nonsense chorus and ham-fisted drums that make you wonder whether the performance was authentically comically inept or a deliberate rock & roll parody. As for other names you might actually recognize, Lucky Wray's slightly raw country-nearing-rockabilly 1956 single is by one of Link Wray's brothers, and Link himself plays on those two songs, with barely a trace of the wildman guitar rock for which he would become known. The anthology's fidelity is usually pretty good, and although some numbers are obviously mastered from wobbly sources, in this case that adds to the amateurish appeal. *—Richie Unterberger*

Stars Kill Rock / Kill Rock Stars ♦♦♦
Stars Kill Rock is a collection of largely unreleased material from one of the '90s preeminent American indie labels, Kill Rock Stars, operated by Bikini Kill's Tobi Vail. While there are a few clinkers, most of the material is top-shelf; the music generally leans toward punk, and in keeping with the label's riot-grrrl aesthetic, most of the artists involved are female. Among the highlights are contributions from the cuddle-core quartet Tiger Trap, the British sexual terrorists Huggy Bear, and Boston folkie Mary Lou Lord. *—Jason Ankeny*

Stax Story / Oct. 24, 2000 / Stax ♦♦♦♦♦
The legendary Memphis soul label Stax's legacy is well represented by this four-CD box set, which manages to do what many similar box retrospectives don't. That is to provide a well-balanced overview of a genre of music that mixes the essential hits with many noteworthy yet lesser-known singles and rarities, coming about as close as possible to pleasing both the collector and the less intense soul fan. The first disc alone, subtitled "The Hits," takes care of most of the consensus classics most listeners would demand from such a box, including hits by Carla Thomas, Otis Redding, the Staple Singers, Sam & Dave, Booker T. & the MGs, Rufus Thomas, Albert King, and Johnnie Taylor. Disc two and disc three chronologically survey lower-profile chart hits and flops, taking in additional material by all of the stars, as well as great songs that have escaped the net of oldies radio: William Bell's "You Don't Miss Your Water," Albert King's "Crosscut Saw," Mable John's "Your Good Thing (Is About to End)." Disc four is entirely devoted to live recordings, most by the company's biggest acts, that sometimes give a rawer sense of the performers' charisma than was evident on their studio efforts. Some pretty minor reservations might keep this box from getting awarded the highest possible score: some of the non-hit cuts aren't that exciting (particularly from the label's later years), the track annotation doesn't make it clear whether some of the live cuts were previously unreleased in any form, Booker T. & the MGs' "Hang 'Em High" is represented by a live 1993 reunion recording rather than the original hit single, and some good mid-level hits by the biggest Stax acts aren't here. Still, it's a very worthy summation of the label's highlights, augmented by detailed liner notes. *—Richie Unterberger*

☆ **Stax: Top of the Stax, Vol. 1: Twenty Greatest Hits** / Stax ✦✦✦✦✦

The opening gun in this series collects 20 of the label's biggest hits—a veritable treasure trove of soul classics. Nice transfers of "Green Onions," "Knock on Wood," "Theme From 'Shaft,'" "Sittin' on the Dock of the Bay," "B-A-B-Y," and "Hold On, I'm Comin'" make this a set that's well worth adding to the collection. Tracks from William Bell, Shirley Brown, the Dramatics, the Emotions, Jean Knight, Frederick Knight, Little Milton, the Soul Children, the Staple Singers, Rufus Thomas, and Johnnie Taylor round out this topnotch collection. —*Cub Koda*

☆ **Stax: Top of the Stax, Vol. 2: Twenty Greatest Hits** / Stax ✦✦✦✦✦

This second entry into Stax's greatest hits rounds up another 20 greats that first saw life as singles on the Stax, Volt, Enterprise, We Produce, and Satellite labels. With the exception of Otis Redding's "Respect," the Bar-Kays' "Soul Finger," William Bell's "You Don't Miss Your Water," and the Mar-Keys' "Last Night," all the material compiled here comes from Stax's later period. Tracks like the Dramatics' "Whatcha See Is Whatcha Get," Little Milton's "Behind Closed Doors," and the Staple Singers' "Touch a Hand, Make a Friend" show the direction soul music and R&B were moving, with the label moving right with the times. If you can't pop for the Stax box set, this series makes a right fine alternative. —*Cub Koda*

☆ **The Stiff Records Box Set** / 1992 / Rhino ✦✦✦✦✦

Stiff Records was a maverick among British independent record labels, partially responsible for starting the punk and new wave revolution of the late '70s. Under the guidance of house producer Nick Lowe, Stiff turned out an enormous number of seminal punk and new wave singles in their first years, including classic tracks by the Damned, Elvis Costello, Graham Parker, the Adverts, Ian Dury, and Lowe himself. But what really gave the label its wild, original flavor were minor artists like Ian Dury, Wreckless Eric, Tenpole Tudor, the Yachts, Lene Lovich, Rachel Sweet, and Mickey Jupp, who turned out a series of raw pop gems that were everything good rock & roll singles should be—catchy, energetic, and memorable. Over 100 of Stiff's finest tracks are collected on this wonderful four-disc box set. While most of these songs weren't hits, they are classic rock & roll. The first three discs are excellent; the fourth disc contains some bright moments, but by that time, their artists were pretty much spent. However, the box remains one of the most compulsively listenable sets ever assembled, providing the definitive retrospective of arguably the most important and influential British record label of the late '70s. —*Stephen Thomas Erlewine*

Street Corner Serenade: The Greatest Doo Wop of the '50s and '60s / Jul. 20, 1999 / Rhino ✦✦✦✦

For those unable or unwilling to shell out for Rhino's exemplary four-disc *Doo Wop Box*, *Street Corner Serenade: Greatest Doo Wop Hits of the '50s and '60s* is a terrific single-disc substitute, featuring 22 of the very biggest hits and especial highlights from that set. In fact, it's arguably the best single-disc doo wop compilation on the market, although *The Doo Wop Box* is still a more highly recommended purchase. —*Steve Huey*

Street Jams: Back 2 the Old Skool, Vol. 1 / Aug. 20, 1996 / Rhino ✦✦✦✦

The *Back 2 the Old Skool* volumes of Rhino's *Street Jams* series concentrates on late '70s and early '80s funk, always presented in their full-length versions. Where the *Hip-Hop From the Top* and *Street Funk* editions are more closely related to hip-hop, these songs provided the basis for many hip-hop records, either as the source for samples or as the scratched grooves. *Street Jams: Back 2 the Old Skool, Vol. 1* features songs by Bootsy Collins, Dazz, Fatback, and several other artists. Rhino has presented these songs on other collections—most notably *Phat Trax*—before, but *Back 2 the Old Skool* remains an entertaining and informative listen. —*Leo Stanley*

Street Jams: Electric Funk, Vols. 1-4 / Jul. 16, 1996 / Rhino ✦✦✦✦✦

Available either as a box set or as individual discs, *Street Jams: Electric Funk, Vols. 1-4* is an excellent, comprehensive overview of the groundbreaking electro-funk of the early '80s. Over the course of four discs, most of the genre's major players, including Afrika Bambaataa and Grandmaster Flash, are represented by their biggest hits and best-known remixes; many of its one-hit wonders are here as well, adding depth and context. Much of this music is presented in 12" mixes, which gives a more accurate portrait of electrofunk and how it stretched and played with rhythms and electronics. For casual listeners, the sheer length of some of these songs may be intimidating—some push the ten-minute mark—but any serious collector or listener of hip-hop, urban R&B, electronica, or modern music should be familiar with many of these songs and mixes. —*Stephen Thomas Erlewine*

Street Jams: Hip-Hop From the Top, Vols. 1-4 / Aug. 20, 1996 / Rhino ✦✦✦✦

Available either as a box set or as four individual discs, *Street Jams: Hip-Hop From the Top, Vols. 1-4* is a superb collection of old-school rap, featuring most of the major singles and artists from the genre's formative years. Over the course of the series, such classics as "Rapper's Delight," "The Breaks," "The Message," "It's Like That," "The Roof Is on Fire," "Roxanne, Roxanne," "The Real Roxanne," "The Show," "Freaks Come Out at Night," "Nightmares," and "La-Di-Da-Di" are presented, usually in their full-length 12" mix. It's comprehensive and surprisingly listenable, illustrating that even from the start all hip-hop did not sound the same. It's an essential collection for any comprehensive urban, rap or pop library. —*Stephen Thomas Erlewine*

Sub-Pop-200 / 1988 / SUB ✦✦✦✦

With the exception of the Melvins, at the point this album was released Sub Pop had virtually every important Seattle band on its roster. On *Sub-Pop-200*, 20 bands get to strut their stuff in the pre-mainstream alternative rock world. And many of the bands that helped alternative rock reach its popularity are represented here, including Soundgarden, Nirvana, Screaming Trees, and Green River (which would mutate into Pearl Jam).

Strangely enough, most of these bands do not have the standout tracks on the album. The Fastbacks try to steal the show with their charged cover of Green River's "Swallow My Pride," but the Walkabouts might have the best song here with their folk-rocker "Got No Chains." Mudhoney covers the Bette Midler torch song "The Rose," while Chemistry Set has an impressive entry with "Underground." The Thrown Ups also show up with the best song in their catalog, "You Lost It." The album as a whole is really good; there are few standouts but everything is solid. Many will buy the album for the Nirvana track "Spank Thru," which is decent, but hopefully those listeners will stick around for the good obscure grunge tracks included. —*Bradley Torreano*

★ **The Sugar Hill Records Story** / Feb. 4, 1997 / Rhino ✦✦✦✦

Sugar Hill Records was the first rap and hip-hop label, giving many listeners their first exposure to the urban rhyming and scratching that transformed pop music during the '80s. Like most indie labels, they had troubles with finances and distribution; eventually, that situation resulted in their records remaining out of print during the rise of the hip-hop during the late '80s and '90s. The five-disc *Sugar Hill Records Story* remedies this situation by collecting all of the label's classic A-sides, many in their full-length mixes, on one set. Tracks by the Sugarhill Gang, Grandmaster Flash, and the Treacherous Three are commonplace and remain excellent, but the true revelation of the box set is how strong largely forgotten cuts by Spoonie Gee, the Funky Four Plus One, Trouble Funk, the Sequence, Super-Wolf, and West Street Mob are—these are supremely funky, infectious and inventive cuts, which have been made familiar through samples and quatations on modern rap records. Another surprise is how integrated this music is—male and female rappers trade lines without hesitation, and there is none of the misogyny or violence that characterized gangsta rap. But that doesn't mean the old-school rap on *The Sugar Hill Records Story* sounds dated—much of this bright, elastic electro-funk has provided the foundation for '90s hits by the likes of the Beastie Boys and Dr. Dre. But the most surprising thing of all is how *The Sugar Hill Records Story* barely loses momentum over the course of five discs. There is the occasional dull spot or oddity (check out the bizarre B-52's rip-off "At the Ice Arcade" by the Chilly Kids) that interrupts the flow, but the music is consistently strong, even on the fifth disc. It was inevitable that *The Sugar Hill Records Story* would be an important historical document, but what makes it truly essential is how rich, diverse, and timeless the music actually is. —*Stephen Thomas Erlewine*

Sun Country Collection / 1990 / Rhino ✦✦✦

This might be more country-oriented than the rockabilly the Sun label was most famous for, but it's not exactly straight country either. Hints of rockabilly abandon lie just below (and sometimes not even below) the surface of these 18 mid-'50s cuts. Includes country-oriented tracks by Carl Perkins, Jerry Lee Lewis, and Johnny Cash, as well as great country boogie by Hardrock Gunter, uniquely raw and goofy sounds by Harmonica Frank, a pre-Elvis appearance by Scotty Moore as part of Doug Poindexter & the Starlite Wranglers, and many other interesting obscurities. —*Richie Unterberger*

☆ **The Sun Records Collection** / 1994 / Rhino ✦✦✦✦✦

There have been a lot of Sun compilations over the years; this three-CD, 74-song compilation strikes the medium ground between abridged single-disc highlights and overkill ten-album box sets. What this means is that you get virtually all the key sides of this vastly influential blues, country, and rockabilly label, including the biggest Sun hits cut by Elvis, Carl Perkins, Jerry Lee Lewis, Johnny Cash, Charlie Rich, and Roy Orbison. There's also a lot of the pioneering electric blues cut by label head Sam Phillips before he made rockabilly Sun's focus, including sides by Howlin' Wolf, B.B. King, Rufus Thomas, Junior Parker, and James Cotton. Then there are the interesting small hits and flops by minor rockabilly figures like Warren Smith, Billy Lee Riley, Malcolm Yelvington, Onie Wheeler, and Carl Mann. There aren't any previously unreleased songs, so the Sun specialist most likely already has everything here; it's a better buy for the avid, knowledgeable fan who isn't a completist. —*Richie Unterberger*

☆ **The Sun Story** / 1987 / Rhino ✦✦✦✦✦

Summing up the history of one of America's most important record labels in 20 songs is a task that borders on the impossible, and *The Sun Story* is hardly the final or definitive word on the subject of Sam Phillips and the nearly seismic impact his label wrought on popular music. While Sun Records is usually cited for (a) giving birth to rock & roll, (b) creating a home for rockabilly, or (c) bringing Elvis Presley into the recording studio for the first time, producer and label founder Sam Phillips had a broader vision than any of those descriptions would imply, embracing in one way or another the full range of the music of the American South—blues, R&B, hard country, gospel, and even a dash of pop. Rhino Records' original two-LP vinyl edition of *The Sun Story* offered a solid introduction to the superb and eclectic roster of talent that recorded for Phillips' little label; sadly, the current single-CD version shortchanges Phillips' vitally important R&B recordings (Jackie Brenston, Roscoe Gordon, and the Prisonaires) in favor of the better-known rock & roll performers who followed them. But as a convenient and affordable collection of Sun's best-known hits and better-known also-rans, *The Sun Story* more than fills the bill, packed to the brim with great, groundbreaking music from Elvis Presley, Jerry Lee Lewis, Carl Perkins, Johnny Cash, Billy Lee Riley, Roy Orbison, Charlie Rich, and many others. As is the norm with a collection from Rhino, the remastered audio is superb (something that hasn't always been the case with earlier Sun reissues), and the liner notes are informative, intelligent, and entertaining. *The Sun Story* is hardly the complete Sun story, but it's not bad as a starter, and if you're looking for a disc with some of the greatest and most satisfying American rock & roll ever committed to tape, this is just what you need. —*Mark Deming*

Sunshine Days, Vol. 1: 60's Pop Classics / Jul. 29, 1997 / Varese ✦✦✦✦

The opening gun in this three-volume set collects up 14 tracks from the sunshiney '60s with a strong pop leaning to the entire set. Obvious hits (Dennis Yost and the Classics IV's

"Stormy," the 5th Dimension's "Go Where You Wanna Go," the Happenings' "I Got Rhythm," and Spanky and Our Gang's "Sunday Will Never Be the Same") sit alongside not so obvious ones [the Critters' "Mr. Dieingly Sad," the Arbors' "A Symphony for Susan," Mercy's "Love (Can Make You Happy)" and Tommy Roe's "It's Now Winter's Day"] from the period, making this lightweight but fun listening that fills more than a few holes in the collection. *—Cub Koda*

Sunshine Days, Vol. 2: 60's Pop Classics / Jul. 29, 1997 / Varese ✦✦✦✦
The second volume in this set features 14 more tracks from the poppiest, most non-psychedelic side of the 1960s. Although there are drivetime hits galore on here (the Buckinghams' "Don't You Care," Keith's "98.6," the Mamas & the Papas' "Dedicated to the One I Love," the Friends of Distinction's "Grazing in the Grass," and the Monkees' "Daydream Believer" for starters), the real surprises come with off-the-wall chart fodder like "Mind Excursion" by the Trade Winds, "There's Got to Be a Word!" by the Innocence, "The Disadvantages of You" by the Brass Ring, and the never-ending beauty of "Sandy" by Ronny and the Daytonas. Nice transfers throughout in this series, too. *—Cub Koda*

Sunshine Days, Vol. 3: 60's Pop Classics / Jul. 29, 1997 / Varese ✦✦✦✦
The final installment in this three volume series delivers another 14 tracks of '60s pop sugar in a big way. This is probably the most hit-laden entry of the bunch, sporting the likes of "Monday, Monday" by the Mamas & the Papas, "Did You Ever Have to Make Up Your Mind" by the Lovin' Spoonful, "Workin' on a Groovy Thing" by the 5th Dimension, and "Don't Sleep in the Subway" by Petula Clark. But the less than standard-issue inclusion of "Tomorrow" by the Strawberry Alarm Clock, "Beautiful People" by Kenny O'Dell, "Yellow Balloon" by the Yellow Balloon, and "Kissin' My Life Away" by the Hondells make this volume just as much of a left-field delight as the other two volumes in the series. *—Cub Koda*

Sunshine Days, Vol. 4: 60's Pop Classics / Jul. 28, 1998 / Varese ✦✦✦✦
Well, the title says it all: another in a series of Varese Sarabande's fine collections of sunshine pop. As usual, these are a great way for fans of some obscure '60s pop hits to pick up some hard-to-find titles at a convenient, mid-line price. Tunes like Petula Clark's "I Couldn't Live Without You," Don & the Goodtimers' "I Could Be So Good to You" (with an awesome Jack Nitzsche arrangement), and several others make volume four a tasty little disc to pick up. Many of these aren't the tunes that you usually hear on oldies radio, and this is a great way to get 'em. The obscurities on this disc are buttressed by some bigger this like "Pleasant Valley Sunday" and "Feelin' Groovy" (and boy, has that aged well), so you have plenty to enjoy here. The one thing that might make these volumes better is if they were to cover a specific period (i.e., spring 1968). This is a minor point, however. If you enjoy one of the titles, you're likely to have a good time listening to the entire disc. *—Matthew Greenwald*

Sunshine Days, Vol. 5: 60's Pop Classics / Jul. 28, 1998 / Varese ✦✦✦✦
Volume five of *Sunshine Days* is another excellent buy for the pop music CD fan on the never-ending search for obscure '60s titles. Some of the cooler titles on volume five are "Back on the Street Again" (the Sunshine Company), "Pretty Ballerina" (the Left Banke) and the Monkees' excellent version of the Paul Williams/Roger Nichols composition "Someday Man." One of the cuts on here has really aged remarkably well, that being the Turtles' "Elenore." Boosted by drummer Johnny Barbata's unbelievable marriage of hard rock and swing, along with nimble conga overdubs, this song is an absolute joy to rediscover; the vocal performance carries it over the goal line. It's the feel that counts on records like this, and "Elenore" has it. As usual, the tracks by the Mamas & the Papas and the Lovin' Spoonful are completely ageless. To be sure, there's some crap (like the Buckinghams' abominable "Hey Baby," among others), but if you like any of the records mentioned above, you'll love volume five. *—Matthew Greenwald*

Super Hits of the '70s: Have a Nice Day / 1990 / Rhino ✦✦✦✦✦
Mainstream pop began catching up with the innovations of the late '60s sometime in the early '70s, incorporating watered-down versions of psychedelia, soul, prog rock, country-rock, and folk-rock. The result was well-produced and crafted schlock that gleefully corrupted countercultural values. Along with the schlock was pure trash ranging from bubblegum epics like "The Night Chicago Died" and "I Think I Love You" to soft rock ("Precious and Few"), Jesus rock ("One Toke Over the Line," "Spirit in the Sky"), hard rock ("Mississippi Queen"), and songs like "Gimme Dat Thing" that are simply uncategorizable. What they all had in common was their utter lack of seriousness and big, catchy hooks, which made them perfect singles for AM radio. Rhino's multi-volume various-artists set *Have a Nice Day: Super Hits of the '70s* (available as individual discs) is an exhaustive overview of such hit singles, containing 12 tracks on each disc. To be sure, there are some outright dogs on some of these discs, but it's remarkable how entertaining the entire series is. Initially, the label intended to only compile ten or 15 collections, taking the set into the mid-'70s, but *Have a Nice Day* proved so successful that it ran a full 25 volumes and extended right until 1979. Consequently, there's a lot of variety here, and every volume may not be entertaining to all listeners, especially since Rhino predictably leans a little too heavily on novelties. Still, it's a terrific series to pick and choose from, and each disc has several "classics" as well as several fun obscurities; it's impossible to imagine a better, more thorough chronicle of this era than *Have a Nice Day*. *—Stephen Thomas Erlewine*

Supernatural Fairy Tales: The Progressive Rock Era / Aug. 20, 1996 / Rhino ✦✦✦
Right down to the Roger Dean-designed sleeve, this five-CD box set overview of 1967-1976 progressive rock is as grandiose as the music itself, which is not necessarily an unconditional recommendation. But give the compilation points for diversity and thoughtful selection. The expected superstars (Yes, Genesis, ELP, Procol Harum) are usually represented by unexpected cuts that haven't been played to death on FM radio. A lot of ground is covered, from Krautrock (Can, Amon Düül II) and symphonic keyboards (Rare Bird, Argent, the Nice's "America") to the Canterbury sound (Caravan, Hatfield & the North) and pop hits with prog overtones (Traffic's "Paper Sun," Golden Earring's "Radar Love," Roxy Music's "Virginia Plain"). A lot of the Continental bands—like Le Orme, Lard Free, Wigwam, Ange, and Samla Mammas Manna—will be fuzzy or unfamiliar names even to progressive rock fans, making cult faves like Van Der Graaf Generator, Curved Air, the Pretty Things, Savage Rose, and Gong (all here as well) famous by comparison. Will the music cause those who dislike prog rock to re-evaluate their feelings? Absolutely not; the more accessible and poppy cuts are balanced by flashy instrumental workouts that—as even the musicians themselves may admit—do not exhibit a trace of humor. And no box that fails to include selections by Pink Floyd, King Crimson, Jethro Tull, Soft Machine, Kraftwerk, Mike Oldfield, early Brian Eno, and Kevin Ayers (in at least some cases for licensing reasons) can claim to be comprehensive. It *is* an interesting, carefully assembled, and *extremely* wide-ranging and catholic survey of the much-maligned genre. It's just a bit too much to take in all at once, and its very eclecticism ensures that many listeners (even dedicated prog fans) will feel the urge to skip around to concentrate on the subgenres they find most appealing. *—Richie Unterberger*

Surf & Drag, Vol. 1 / 1989 / Sundazed ✦✦✦✦✦
All the great surf and hot-rod sides from the Challenge label. Features Gary Usher, the Four Speeds, the Knickerbockers, Jan and Dean, the Royal Coachmen, Donna Loren, and the Rhythm Rockers. Powerful genre material—this is as good as it gets. *—Cub Koda*

Surf & Drag, Vol. 2 / 1993 / Sundazed ✦✦✦
Featuring more rare tracks from the second tier of surf and hot-rod performers, this volume is no less potent than the first. Highlights include the original version of "She Rides With Me" by Paul Petersen, "Bustin' Surfboards" by the Tornadoes, and "GeeTO Tiger" by the Tigers. *—Cub Koda*

The Swingtime Records Story / May 17, 1994 / Capricorn ✦✦✦✦✦
A black entrepreneur named Jack Lauderdale, for a period of a half-dozen years, ran the Swingtime label—and its myriad subsidiaries—and his story is nicely told through the music on this wonderful two-disc box set. Lauderdale was no two bit hustler; he had both vision and ambition. He recorded everything from big band jump blues to piano trios to gospel groups. He released the first major recordings of guitarist Lowell Fulson and discovered a young Ray Charles when he was still in his Nat King Cole phase, although starting to find his own style. Nineteen of the 50 tracks included here are either by Fulson or Charles, the twin historical peaks of Lauderdale's empire. Add to that mix delightful work from Big Joe Turner, pianist Lloyd Glenn, a young Jimmy McCracklin, Percy Mayfield, Johnny Otis, and Charles Brown and you're beginning to get the big picture. In many ways, the tracks included here could easily represent the breadth of late '40s to early '50s in vogue sounds of African-American music. It's that far-reaching in its scope. *—Cub Koda*

Teen Beat, Vol. 1 / 1993 / Ace ✦✦✦✦
30 instrumentals from the late '50s and early '60s, the era when instrumental rock was at its peak. Most of these were hits, though a few of them didn't make the Top 20, and some didn't even make the Top 100. Hence the selections are often more obscure than what you'll find on Rhino's *Rock Instrumentals* series. The Rhino series, however, remains not only a much better introduction to this nifty genre, but considerably higher in overall quality. The best songs on *Teen Beat* are often on the Rhino series as well (the Ventures' "Walk Don't Run," Preston Epps' "Bongo Rock," Link Wray's "Rumble"); the lesser-known ones, though a boon to collectors, simply aren't as good or imaginative. It's a serviceable supplement, though, if you're looking for more of the style, and the best cuts are certainly dynamite. *—Richie Unterberger*

Teen Beat, Vol. 2 / 1994 / Ace ✦✦✦
This digs way deeper into the cobwebs of history than the first volume of the series. Although a few of these were big hits, over half of the 30 tracks didn't even make it into the Top 100. That doesn't mean they should be dismissed. But in the case of these selections at least, they're simply not nearly as memorable as the best early rock & roll instrumentals, whether hits or flops. There are some nifty highlights, like two raw, bluesy '61 cuts by a young Roy Buchanan, uncommonly rocking items by Chet Atkins, and the early Danelectro bass workout by the Fireballs ("Carioca"). But a lot of these are standard-issue three-chord instrumentals by no-names like the Atmospheres, or forgettable flop followups by one-hit wonders like Dave Cortez, Floyd Cramer, and the Champs. The energy level is always high, but that in itself isn't a high recommendation, although devotees of instrumental rock will certainly find a lot of cuts here that are hard to locate on CD. *—Richie Unterberger*

Teen Beat, Vol. 3 / 1996 / Ace ✦✦✦
Devoted wholly to rock instrumentals of the late '50s and early '60s, this 30-track disc is a good investment for collectors looking for hits in the genre that didn't crack the Top 20 (and hence don't get played on oldies radio today), or missed the charts entirely. A couple smashes ("Wipe Out," "Pipeline") slip through, but otherwise there's a variety of forgotten hot wordless platters here, like the Astronauts' "Baja" (some of the best instrumental surf to originate outside out of California), the New Orleans-cum-Philly R&B of saxophonist Lee Allen, the creepy organ of the Wailers' "Mau Mau," the minimalist rockabilly of the Rock-a-Teens' "Woo-Hoo," the Ramrods' wacky adaptation of "Ghost Riders in the Sky," and the hard guitar of Duane Eddy associate Al Casey. When all is said and done, though, these aren't as good as the most famous vintage instrumental hits—stick with the more prominent compilations unless you're deeply into the sound. *—Richie Unterberger*

Teen Beat, Vol. 4 / 1997 / Ace ✦✦✦
In some ways this series actually gets more interesting with the fourth volume, possibly because the need to fill up so much space (another 30 tracks worth) with instrumental

rock oldies meant that more unusual items had to be excavated. There are a few big hits (Bill Justis' "Raunchy," Bill Black's "Smokie"), yet most of these are singles that didn't even make it into the Top 100; over half missed the listings altogether. Not all of these are rock, either; Hank Levine's "Image" is a lost exotica single, Moe Koffman's "The Swingin' Shepherd Blues" is light jazz, and Kokomo's "Asia Minor" is classical boogie. While some of the selections are only average, there are some good nuggets here, like the Megatons' scorching variation of "You Don't Love Me" ("Shimmy, Shimmy Walk"), Travis Wammack's innovative guitar work on "Scratchy" (which has a snatch of backwards vocals that was way ahead of its time for 1964), the Centurians' moody surf instro "Bullwinkle Pt. II" (used in the *Pulp Fiction* soundtrack), and Lonnie Mack's "Chicken Pickin'." There's also the peculiar belly-dance rock of the Hollywood Persuaders' "Drums-a-Go-Go," which was created by a pre-Mothers Frank Zappa with Paul Buff. *—Richie Unterberger*

Teen Beat, Vol. 5 / Jun. 26, 2000 / Ace ♦♦♦♦♦

The fifth and final installment of Ace's series of early rock instrumental compilations is one of the best *Teen Beat* volumes, in large part because about half of these are acknowledged classic hits. Booker T. & the MG's' "Green Onions," Sandy Nelson's "Let There Be Drums," the Pyramids' "Penetration," Link Wray's "Raw-Hide," the Routers' "Let's Go (Pony)," Jack Nitzsche's "The Lonely Surfer," Bill Doggett's "Honky Tonk," the Mar-Keys' "Last Night," Paul Revere & the Raiders' "Like Long Hair": they're all dynamite tunes, and even if they might not be that hard to find on other reissues, it's good to have them all in one place. The 30-track disc is filled out by lesser hits that haven't made it into oldies radio formats, although all but a couple at least entered the charts. Some of them, frankly, are highly derivative and forgettable, even if they actually did quite well. What, then, are the relative rarities here to keep an eye on? There's "Week End" by the Kingsmen, not the "Louie Louie" folks but an entire different outfit comprised of Bill Haley's Comets playing under a different name. New Orleans pianist legend James Booker almost made the Top 40 in 1960 with the highly atypical (for him) "Gonzo," with its organ and flute. Ray Bryant Combo's big band-cum-rock "The Madison Time (Part 1)" was used in the soundtrack of John Waters' *Hairspray.* Phil Spector did the rare , non-charting Duane Eddy-like tune "Bumbershoot" in 1959, under the pseudonym Phil Harvey. There's even a leap back to the pre-rock era with Arthur Smith's "Guitar Boogie," a 1948 hit that pointed the way to the hillbilly-boogie fusion that would lay a major foundation for rock & roll, and was redone as a fully rock & roll hit in 1959 by the Virtues (as "Guitar Boogie Shuffle"). *—Richie Unterberger*

Teen Riot / Aug. 22, 2000 / Razor & Tie ♦♦♦♦

It's impossible not to compare Razor & Tie's *Teen Riot* compilation to Rhino's *Heartthrob Hits*; after all, both concentrate on slick teen idol pop from the '80s, from bubbly dance numbers to sentimental ballads. Unfortunately, overall, the two are quite similar in execution as well as concept, containing many of the same artists and in some cases the exact same songs. In other words, if you have one, you probably won't want the other. In its favor, though, *Teen Riot* does add a few artists not present on *Heartthrob Hits* whose contributions fit the theme perfectly (New Edition's "Cool It Now," Stacey Q's "Two of Hearts," and Martika's number one hit "Toy Soldiers"). Plus, taken as a listen unto itself, *Teen Riot* evokes the same sort of nostalgia for its era that *Heartthrob Hits* does; these songs are unmistakably products of the '80s, and they'll be surprisingly infectious for many people who grew up while this music dominated MTV and, especially, pop radio. It's just a shame that this territory was already covered in very similar fashion. *—Steve Huey*

Teenage Crush / 1997 / Ace ♦♦♦

28 rock and pop ballads from the late '50s and early '60s, most (though not all) falling into the teen idol mold. Now that rock itself is no longer under direct threat from being emasculated by this kind of stuff, we can enjoy quality material like Brian Hyland's "Sealed With a Kiss" without a twinge of guilt. But for every "Sea of Love" by Phil Phillips, there are drippy melodramas by Paul Anka, Bobby Vee, Ray Peterson, Frankie Avalon, and Tommy Sands. There are also a few cuts that are adult pop rather than pop/rock, by Julie London, Tommy Edwards, and Johnny Mathis. It's a decent compilation of a kind of pop music that played a big part in its era, but much of it hasn't aged well at all. *—Richie Unterberger*

Teenage Crush, Vol. 2 / Feb. 12, 1999 / Ace ♦♦♦

Twenty-eight more of what Ace refers to as "rockaballads" from the late 1950s and early 1960s—that is, the very poppiest and most ballad-oriented shade of early rock & roll, or tracks that are essentially pop songs but had enough rock or teen idol influence to appeal to a teen audience. It's a bit hard to figure which fans might want to pick this up. The best and most famous tracks—Eddie Cochran's "Sittin' in the Balcony," Ritchie Valens' "Donna," Jimmie Rodgers' "Honeycomb," and Skeeter Davis' "The End of the World"—have been easily available on reissues for decades. So have hits like Frankie Avalon's "Venus," George Hamilton IV's "A Rose and a Baby Ruth," the Fleetwoods' "Come Softly to Me" and others. Almost half of these are lesser-known cuts, several of which only charted in the 20s or so, and are hard to find on reissues (and indeed rarely played even on oldies radio). The problem is, these cuts have been neglected for a reason; they're often facile teen pop songs that aren't very good, like Tony Bellus' "Robbin' the Cradle," Bobby Curtola's "Fortune Teller," Dale Ward's abominable "Letter From Sherry," and Garry Miles' "Look for a Star." About the most interesting off-the-beaten-path item is Jimmy Elledge's version of Willie Nelson's "Funny How Time Slips Away," which hit number 22 in 1961. This isn't that bad a listen, and points to Ace for including a wide spectrum of light early ballad rock—including black artists like Brook Benton and one-shots like singer Ed Townsend, who made the Top 20 in 1958 with "For Your Love"—but it's no great shakes either. *—Richie Unterberger*

Teenage Crush, Vol. 3 / Dec. 27, 2000 / Ace ♦♦♦

The third installment of this series has 28 more big and small chart hits from 1957-1964, exemplifying the most clean-cut aspects of early rock & roll. The adjective "clean-cut" is not a pejorative presumption; it's taken right from the banner on the back sleeve. There are a few teen idols here (Fabian, Johnny Crawford), but actually the sounds take in much more than teen idol rock, covering string-drenched early soul (Little Willie John's "Talk to Me, Talk to Me" and Dee Clark's "Raindrops"), Elvis Presley impersonations (Terry Stafford's "Suspicion" and Ral Donner's "Girl of My Best Friend"), a Buddy Holly impersonation (Tommy Roe's "Sheila"), and group vocal hits with a dab of doo wop (the Echoes' "Baby Blue" and Donnie & the Dreamers' "Count Every Star"). Most of the best songs on the disc are mentioned in the preceding sentence, but for collectors, the main attractions might be the relative abundance of high and low chart hits that don't often make it onto compilations, like Donnie Brooks' "Mission Bell," Jerry Wallace's "Primrose Lane," Ken Copeland's "Pledge of Love" (covered in the early '60s by Bobby Fuller), Glen Campbell's original small hit version of "Turn Around, Look at Me" (from a 1961 Crest single), and Kenny Chandler's "Heart" (also a low-charting single for Wayne Newton). It's certainly true that, other than the odd classic, this is certainly innocuous and lightweight fluff. But as such compilations (including some others on Ace) go, it has more variety than most, and can therefore be recommended for those who want to dig into these kinds of sounds and pick up some material to which they might not have been overexposed. *—Richie Unterberger*

Teenage Rock & Roll Party / 1995 / Ace ♦♦♦

This 30-track compilation draws the majority of its contents from 1950s-era West Coast and Southern labels both great and small, including selections from Specialty, Modern, Era, Excello, Goldband, and Johnny Otis' Dig label. While labeled a "rock & roll party," the majority of contents compiled here are straight-up rockin' R&B: "Old Folks' Boogie," by Al Simmons with Slim Green and the Cats From Fresno, takes John Lee Hooker's "Boogie Chillen" and Junior Parker's "Feelin' Good" and reduces them down to a single riff that's even more elemental than those two bare-bones boogies, if such an artistic notion is possible. Several artists right on the edge between rhythm and blues and rock & roll are featured here, including Little Richard, Larry Williams, Young Jessie, and Richard Berry, and blues artists with some rockin' in their blood get their due here as well with Slim Harpo, Johnny "Guitar" Watson ("Those Lonely Lonely Nights," with its famous one note solo), and Hop Wilson all making appearances. Honking West Coast sax men Joe Houston and Chuck Higgins contribute a track apiece, while the doo wop side of the equation primarily comes from selections released by the East Coast-based Old Town Records, with the Harptones, Jive 5, and the Cleftones all contributing to the mix. This collection shows considerable depth and breadth, and brings together tracks that seldom make it onto packages like this. Well done. *—Cub Koda*

Texas Music, Vol. 3: Garage Bands & Psychedelia / 1994 / Rhino ♦♦♦

Texas arguably produced the most manic and raunchiest garage rock of any state during the 1960s. While seasoned collectors will find little on this 18-song compilation that they don't already have, it's a decent intro to some of the Lone Star State's shining moments. In a state long renowned as a melting pot of sounds, Texas groups often flavored their records with R&B, blues, and Tex-Mex, which means that in addition to classic garage sides by the Bobby Fuller Four, the 13th Floor Elevators, Kenny & the Kasuals, and Mouse & the Traps, you get blues-rock (Steve Miller, Johnny Winter), blue-eyed soul (Roy Head's "Treat Her Right"), Tex-Mex-flavored rock (Sam the Sham & the Pharoahs, the Sir Douglas Quintet), and all-out weirdness (the Legendary Stardust Cowboy's "Paralyzed"). There are also garage singles by the Chessmen, Scotty McKay, and Nobody's Children that were quite rare in their day, though they've appeared on easy-to-find garage compilations. The real find is the Ron-Dels' (featuring Delbert McClinton) "If You Really Want Me To, I'll Go," a country-flavored beat ballad strongly reminiscent of the Beatles' similar material from 1964 and 1965. *—Richie Unterberger*

That'll Flat Git It! [Series Overview] / 199 / Bear Family ♦♦♦♦♦

Rockabilly collectors are a hearty, fanatical breed with little compunction about seeking out rare, rarely heard singles based on legend or label. Not everybody has the time or patience to find original pressings, even if they love the music, so for the average collector, Bear Family's multi-volume *That'll Flat Git It!* series is the way to dig deep into the rockabilly arcana. The series is divided by label, spotlighting the forgotten sides and smaller hits for labels as well-known as Decca and RCA, along with lesser-known regional labels. This is not everything that was released on a label, of course, but it is a fairly thorough overview of what kinds of rockabilly the label released, and it hits almost all of the high points, at least as far as rockabilly collectors are concerned (and when the label can't fit everything on one disc, it breaks it up in two parts). Like many multi-part series, this is strongest on the earlier volumes, but if you're a dyed-in-the-wool collector, any of these volumes are worthwhile. Some of them are loaded with generic mediocrities, but they all have a couple of dynamite gems, plus they're presented lovingly, with wonderful sound and detailed, well-researched liner notes. This is essentially a collector's series, but it's a collector's series in the best sense—filled with rare gems worth seeking out and presented in a luxurious fashion. *—Stephen Thomas Erlewine*

☆ **There's a Riot Goin' On! The Rock & Roll Classics of Lieber and Stoller** / 1991 / Rhino ♦♦♦♦♦

Sure, you can spend a lot of dough buying CD reissues by all the bands Leiber & Stoller wrote songs for. And while that would give you a great record collection (especially of Drifters and Coasters material), you might want to start with this indispensable 18-track collection. All the big hits are here, as are the songs that show off Leiber & Stoller's melodramatic way with a song ("I Who Have Nothing") and their deft comic touch ("Charlie Brown"). The essence of Leiber & Stoller's genius is here, and you'll likely recognize nearly all of these songs as soon as they start. Memory can be a wonderful thing. —*John Dougan*

This Are Two Tone / 1983 / Chrysalis ✦✦✦✦✦
This Are Two Tone is a classic collection of the label's seminal ska-revival hits, highlighted by cuts from Madness ("Madness"), Selecter ("On My Radio," "Too Much Pressure"), the [English] Beat ("Ranking Full Stop," "Tears of a Clown"), Bodysnatchers ("Too Experienced"), and several singles from the Specials ("Gangsters," "Rudy, A Message to You," "Stereotype," "Ghost Town"). Although the double-disc *Two Tone Compilation: A Checkered Past* is a more comprehensive set, *This Are Two Tone* remains an excellent, 16-song primer. —*Stephen Thomas Erlewine*

This Is Mod, Vol. 1: The Rarities 1979-1981 / 1995 / Anagram ✦✦✦
The British mod revival may have been a fad, driven by fashion and most of the time too derivative, but it did produce some fun singles. Since many of the bands that jumped on the bandwagon only released singles or poorly distributed albums for independent labels, much of this music has been hopelessly lost over the years; *This Is Mod, Vol. 1* collects many of the admittedly third-rate (though enjoyable) revival bands for the first time on CD. In 21 tracks, this disc provides the nearly complete recorded output of the Circles, the Amber Squad, the Cigarettes, the Deadbeats, the Letters, the Nips, the Odds, and the Sussed (whose novelty record, "I've Got Me Parka" takes a fun look at the fad)—with each band receiving detailed biographical sketches. For specialists and fetishists, this disc is essential. For most, it's simply excessive. —*Chris Woodstra*

This Is Mod, Vol. 2: More Rarities 1979-81 / 1996 / Anagram ✦✦✦✦
The second volume of the *This Is Mod* series covers more mod revivalists: the Killermeters, the Exits, the V.I.P.'s, the Crooks, the Same, Teenage Filmstars, Terry Tonik, and the Purple Hearts. Only the Purple Hearts came close to being major contenders, but all provide a fascinating look at the short-lived genre. —*Chris Woodstra*

This Is Mod, Vol. 3: A Diamond Collection / 1996 / Anagram ✦✦✦
Volume three of the *This is Mod Series* focuses on the short-lived Diamond Records, a London-based label which sought to keep the mod revival on life support during the mid-'80s—and nearly all of the label's output is here with the exception (thankfully) of the obscure Oi! band, the Business. Most of the bands, which includes the Scene, Long Tall Short, the Moment, the B Team, the Way Out, and the Rage, were more '60s purists than the Jam, but it's not much of a stretch to lump these groups in with their late-'70s predecessors. It is, however, hard to believe this stuff was being done as late as 1986. —*Chris Woodstra*

This Is Mod, Vol. 4: Modities / 1996 / Anagram ✦✦✦
Modities continues the series' exhaustive mining of mod revival rarities, ranging from the more distinctive and noteworthy Lambrettas, Merton Parkas, and the Accidents to the hopelessly obscure Directions, the Nightriders, the Onlookers, the Reputation, and the Untouchables (U.K.). As with the first three installments, this may be excessive but it sure is fun. —*Chris Woodstra*

TK Deep Soul: Sunshine Girls / May 30, 1995 / Sequel ✦✦✦✦
Five female Southern soul artists tell it like it is, was, and gonna be on a slew of salty love sagas. Jackie Moore cranks out eight of the 15 tracks warming them with her golden alto and no-nonsense approach. Ann Sexton does only one track ("Loving You, Loving Me"), which is a shame since her distinctive, sexy soprano is an ice-breaker. Paulette Reeves smokes on four tracks, including "Jazz Freak," a song about her love of jazz music; it has a Southern feel, and it's also the only album track that's not about relationships. Reeves' jazzy, soulful rendition of "Your Good Thing Is About to End" is classy and well done. Brandye contributes "One Woman's Trash Is Another Woman's Treasure," a song where the music and the lyrics don't equal the title. Ruby Wilson contributes "I'll Be Right Here (When You Return)" (with help from the Blue Chips) and "Man and a Baby Boy." —*Andrew Hamilton*

Tommy Boy's Greatest Beats 1981-1996 / Oct. 27, 1998 / Tommy Boy ✦✦✦✦
Only one label, Tommy Boy, spans hip-hop's entire recorded history with no loss of hits or perfect beats over the course of those ten years. The five-disc box released to commemorate the label's 15th anniversary includes a wealth of hip-hop classics, everything from "Planet Rock" to "Plug Tunin'" to "Humpty Dance" to "Jump Around" to "Play at Your Own Risk" to "Hip Hop Hooray" to "Gangsta's Paradise." The addition of a few dance cuts—from Information Society, Coldcut, and 808 State—don't work quite as well as they should, but on the whole *Tommy Boy's Greatest Beats 1981-1996* is an excellent collection that sums up hip-hop better than any other label could. The fifth disc includes nine Tommy Boy classics given the remix treatment, resulting in intriguing combinations like Grooverider with Jonzun Crew's "Pack Jam," Dimitri From Paris with Stetsasonic's "Talkin' All That Jazz," and DJ Premier with Queen Latifah's "Wrath of My Madness." —*Keith Farley*

Tony the Tyger Presents Fuzz Flaykes & Shakes, Vol. 1: 60 Miles High / Oct. 12, 1999 / Bacchus ✦✦✦
Bacchus' *Fuzz Flaykes & Shakes, Vol. 1* is a terrific collection of obscure pop/rock and psychedelia. This is certainly not for safe, careful listeners, but those with a taste for the strange, the weird, and the unheard of will delight in this sampler featuring cuts by the Glass Sun, the Shaggs, the Odyssey, Time of Your Life, the Thyme, the Countdown Five, the Society, the Rites, the Gregorians, the Magic Mushroom, the Stained Glass, the Humane Society, and the Bedpost Oracle. Basically, if the name of the group sounds intriguing to you, it's worth giving this one a try. —*Stephen Thomas Erlewine*

Tony The Tyger Presents Fuzz Flaykes & Shakes, Vol. 2: The Day Breaks at Dawn / Nov. 16, 1999 / Bacchus ✦✦✦
If anything, the second volume in *Fuzz, Flaykes, & Shakes* is superior to its predecessor

on purely musical terms, emphasizing bands with harder, more frantic, soulful psychedelic sounds. Dave Travis Extreme's "Last Night, the Flowers Bloomed" is a lost artifact of the Sunset Strip riots that is a match for the Standells' classic on the same subject; the Chicago-based Traces of Time's "Oh Bob" is an even harder and better-paced piece of psych-punk, and it only gets better from there. John English & Lemon Drops ("Just Don't Complain") and Zorbra & the Greeks ("One and Only Girl") are incredibly cool, frantic dance numbers with a hard psych edge, but the real revelation is track number five, "I Saw Her Yesterday" by the Sunrisers; these guys came from Whitestone, Queens (and nearby Little Neck), and they delivered up one of the smoothest, coolest, most well-played pieces of psychedelic rock ever to come out of New York City, period, with a great beat, memorable hooks, and mournfully frustrated teen vocals; this jewel from October of 1966 was, alas, their only recorded venture in the psych-punk vein. Soul Inc's "Stronger Than Dirt" is a funny psychedelic take on a pop-culture theme. The Amoeba ("Lost Love") out of McAllen, TX, may well have gotten tarred and feathered for pushing a sound this punked out in 1965—even the 13th Floor Elevators had to blow relatively cosmopolitan Houston, after all—and these guys were just as direct in their punk sensibilities. The Deepest Blue, the Last Chapter, the Graven Image ("Take a Bite of Life," with a Bo Diddley-beat), the Hackers ("Keep On Running, Girl"), the Tracers ("Who Do You Love," with a pumping organ in the mix), the Denims, Flowers, Fruits & Pretty Things ("Take Me Away"), and the Search ("Mr. Custer") all acquit themselves well, but there are a handful of acts here that could easily have competed in the larger musical arena with the material or the talent they offer up here: the Druids with "Cool, Calm & Collected" (not the Rolling Stones song), and its catchy choruses and solid guitar hooks; the Other Four with "Searching for My Love," crunchy rhythm guitars (and one great lead player) and surging organ beneath an achingly beautiful melody, especially on the choruses; and the title track of this compilation by the Backgrounds, which is a great song handled by a lead singer who's trying just a little too hard to sound like Arthur Lee of Love. The sound on this CD is very slightly shakier than the quality of its predecessor, but the music is the purest, distilled psych-punk, with barely a mellow or reflective moment anywhere on this disc. —*Bruce Eder*

Tony the Tyger Presents Fuzz Flaykes & Shakes, Vol. 3: Stay Out of My World / Nov. 16, 1999 / Bacchus ✦✦✦
There are 18 more obscurities from the mid- to late '60s on the third volume of this garage rock series, falling squarely in the middle of the pack as far as worth and interest. For some that might qualify as a ringing recommendation. Others might be put off by the relatively unexceptional songwriting and the limited melodic and creative range, often sticking to brooding minor keys, topped off with some fuzz guitar and folk-rock trimmings. This isn't wonderful stuff, but there are some songs here and there that stick out. The Soul Survivors' "Can't Stand to Be in Love With You," which is like a mating of a Zombies-type tune with U.S. garage raunch, was a number one hit in Denver in late 1965 (and if you're wondering, they were not the Soul Survivors who had a huge hit with "Expressway to Your Heart," but an entirely different band). The Tikis' "Somebody's Son," a first-person tale of an abandoned orphan, is pretty strong stuff for a teen-oriented 1966 single. The Merseybeats USA's "Nobody Loves Me That Way" is more in the typical teen rock mold, but is one of the few cuts here to feature (somewhat) name performers, as Terry Adams and Steve Ferguson went on to NRBQ. The Camel Drivers' "The Grass Looks Greener" is another effective utilization of a Zombies-type sheen to the songwriting. —*Richie Unterberger*

Tony the Tyger Presents Fuzz Flaykes & Shakes, Vol. 4: Experiment in Color / Mar. 6, 2001 / Bacchus ✦✦✦
More 1960s psych-punk-garage for the treadmill is found on volume four of this series, assembling 17 rare sides from 1965-1969 singles by American bands. There's not much to make you sit bolt-upright in delight or surprise; it's the expected melange of fuzz guitar, organ, and surly attitude, leavened by some poppy influences from folk-rock and British Invasion music (especially in the harmonies). The Primates' "She," the best cut, leaps out in this company almost as much as a high-quality Zombies single would, with its compelling, brooding minor-key melody. As for other tracks of above-average interest, the Canterbury Fair's "The Man" is not found on the Sundazed CD reissue of the band's material and shows a possible Music Machine influence in the ominous circus-like fuzz guitar-organ riffing. The Soultans' "Rain Down Soul," if you're looking for more evidence that '60s cult bands actually exerted during the time they were around, has an obvious debt to Love's "Signed D.C.," though using a far fuller electric approach. The only musician here of some renown is a real misfit in this company: Joey Welz, once a member of Bill Haley's Comets, is backed by the Time Machine on the 1967 garage-psych ballad "Caught By Love," actually one of the better songs with its sad melody, harmonies, and eerie organ. —*Richie Unterberger*

Tony the Tyger Presents Fuzz Flaykes & Shakes, Vol. 5: Keep Right on Living / Mar. 6, 2001 / Bacchus ✦✦✦
The fifth volume of this 1960s garage-psychedelic compilation series is above-average when judged against the other installments, with a slightly better standard of material, although it's usually in the same generic '60s punk mold. As such generic workouts go, though, the Continentals' "Sick & Tired" is tastier than usual, if only for the supremely confident vocal. Other items that are enjoyable, though not brilliant, include the Noblemen's "She Still Thinks I Love Her" with its full harmonies, organ-driven arrangement, and nice double-time break; the Insects' "Girl That Sits There," with another good organ part, and welcome pop harmony influence; and the Creatures' "Letter of Love," which bears traces of the sort of minor-key melodies Ray Davies used on many early Kinks songs. The cut most deserving of the "killer" adjective is "Baby Show the World" by the Sons of Adam, one of the best obscure Los Angeles psych-punk bands. While this,

the B-side of their third single, was done after guitarist Randy Holden (the Other Half, Blue Cheer) and drummer Michael Stuart (Love) departed, it still has some fine distorted sustain/feedback-laden guitar and raw, tense psychedelic dynamics. *—Richie Unterberger*

The Toussaint Touch / Aug. 1, 2000 / RPM ✦✦✦✦

This is a good if rather scattershot compilation of early Allen Toussaint productions for various artists, focusing solely on his 1960-65 work, when he was at the helm of the best rock and soul recordings to come out of New Orleans. About half of the 22 tracks are devoted to the most well-known artists in his charge, including a few well-known cuts, like Benny Spellman's "Fortune Teller," Ernie K-Doe's "A Certain Girl," and Irma Thomas' "Ruler of My Heart." The rest of the names might be strange even to New Orleans experts, encompassing as they do the likes of Curly Moore, Willie West, and Zilla Mayes. So it's almost as though this can't make up its mind whether to be a best-of for his vintage years, or an overview mixing classics with rarities. Nonetheless, it's a good if slightly uneven patchwork, usually boasting Toussaint's inimitable blend of fine pop melodies, lazy bluesy funk, and a certain light production touch in which the music sounds both spontaneous and cleverly arranged. If you've already picked up the best early sides by Thomas, Aaron Neville, Spellman, K-Doe, and Hill, you're likely to be most intrigued by the dozen cuts by the no-names, some of them quite good, and most of them with a more modern soul sound, indicating that they were cut in the mid-1960s rather than the dawn of the decade. John Williams' "Blues Tears Sorrow" is a typically melancholy yet melodic Toussaint ballad, while Willie Harper's "Here Comes the Hurt Again" is exuberant southern pop-soul with an over-recorded lead vocal. Most of those secondary cuts are fetching combos of blues and pop-soul sass, even if some have an oddly unfinished feel. Overall it's a nice secondary pickup for the 1960s New Orleans soul fan. *—Richie Unterberger*

Trainspotting / Feb. 1996 / Capitol ✦✦✦✦✦

Trainspotting concerns the adventures of a group of young, nearly criminal, drug-addicted Scottish friends. The novel, written by Irvine Welsh, became one of the most popular books in the British indie scene in the early '90s and was adapted to film in 1996 by the makers of *Shallow Grave*. Appropriately, an all-star collection of British pop and techno stars—everyone from Blur, Pulp, and Elastica to Leftfield, Primal Scream, and Underworld—contributed to the soundtrack, which also features a couple of oldies by veteran punk godfathers like Lou Reed ("Perfect Day") and Iggy Pop ("Lust for Life," "Nightclubbing"). The entire soundtrack holds together surprisingly well, as the techno tracks balance with the pop singles. Every song, whether it's Pulp's deceptively bouncy "Mile End" or Brian Eno's lush "Deep Blue Day," is quite melancholy, creating an effectively bleak, but oddly romantic, atmosphere for the entire record. With the exception of the oldies, every song is rare or especially recorded for the soundtrack, and nearly every one is superb. Primal Scream's title track sees them returning to the dub/dance experiments of *Screamadelica* with grace, while Damon Albarn's first solo song, "Closet Romantic," is as good as any of Blur's waltzes. But the finest new song is Pulp's "Mile End," with its jaunty, neo-dancehall melody and rhythms and Jarvis Cocker's evocative, haunting lyrics. That song, more than anything else on the soundtrack, captures the feeling of the film. *—Stephen Thomas Erlewine*

☆ **The Two Tone Compilation: A Checkered Past** / Nov. 16, 1993 / Chrysalis ✦✦✦✦✦

Two Tone Compilation: A Checkered Past is a sublime double-disc set containing all of the ska-revival label's greatest singles, not only from superstars like the Specials, Madness, the [English] Beat, Bodysnatchers, and the Selecter, but also the Special A.K.A., Swinging Cats, Higsons, and Apollinaires. Not one of the label's great songs are missing, and several cuts reveal themselves as forgotten gems. It's a comprehensive and compulsively listenable set, illustrating the kinetic energy of ska-revival as well as the depth of the label's roster. [In England, *A Checkered Past* was released as a four-disc box containing all of the label's A- and B-sides.] *—Stephen Thomas Erlewine*

Ugly Things, Vols. 1-3 / Raven ✦✦✦

U.S. and U.K. audiences were totally unaware at the time, but Australia was home to a thriving garage-punk scene in the mid-'60s. The scope and output of these groups were limited by the country's population, which was only about 15 million or somewhat less, after all. But there was a surprisingly large number of fine singles, some of which measured up to the manic, over-the-top R&B-derived energy of anything coming from Texas, California, or London. *Volume 1* is by far the best of the series and, indeed, one of the best '60s garage compilations ever, filled with good hooks, screams, and crunching riffs. The second and third volumes aren't nearly as good, peppered with undistinguished covers and unmemorable tracks, although some excellent ones do surface, including some from neighboring New Zealand; the best of these two LPs should have been combined into one. Raven has put out a best-of compilation CD from the *Ugly Things* series that draws from all of the volumes and adds some other cuts. *—Richie Unterberger*

Uptown Down South / 1995 / Excello ✦✦✦✦

The title implies that these are recordings cut south of the Mason-Dixon Line, but with an uptown sound; the concept is flawed. Just as you can't make a silk purse out of a sow's ear, if you use southern musicians and producers, the product is going to sound likewise. If Diana Ross used these same hookups, she would sound like Ann Sexton or Betty Wright. However, the compilation deserves kudos despite its gray area because its selections are so scarce. To have them accessible on one CD is a musical godsend. Highlights among the 24-tracks include Roger Hatcher's glorious "Sweetest Girl in the World"; Marva Whitney's tumultuous "Don't Let Our Love Fade Away"; Skip Mahoney & the Casuals' "Running Away From Love"; Bits 'N' Pieces' "Keep On Running Away"; the Wallace Brothers' "Thanks a Lot"; and ZZ Hill's "Our Love Is Getting Better." Other saucy entrées include tracks by the Kelly Brothers, the Avons (a little-known female group), and Lucille Mathis. *—Andrew Hamilton*

The Vee-Jay Story: Celebrating 40 Years of Classic Hits 1953-1993 / 1993 / Rhino Handmade ✦✦✦✦

Most conversations about Vee-Jay Records will usually be limited to a few salient facts: that they put out great, influential blues and R&B records during the '50s and '60s. That they became the most successful African-American-owned record company in the United States, breaking into the pop field with hits by Gene Chandler, Dee Clark, and the early sides by the Four Seasons. That they were the first American company to have the Beatles. And that, with all that success, they went bankrupt by 1966. But the Vee-Jay Records story is, for all its twists and turns, a true American success story that went sour. Admittedly, this three-disc retrospective *does* leave out some important chunks of the company's history due to licensing restrictions; the Four Seasons' masters aren't aboard, as their original appearance on the label was a lease deal. What *is* here are all the important sides, 75 of them, that moved Vee-Jay from a Gary, IN, storefront to a major corporation. Much of Vee-Jay's reputation rests as much on the records that weren't hits and many of them are here. Disc one takes us back to the beginning of the label, with the label's first two artists, the Spaniels and bluesman Jimmy Reed. Disc two starts in blues and soul land, and brings aboard Dee Clark—the label's first African-American artist to cross over consistently into the pop field—and Jerry Butler, Curtis Mayfield, and the Impressions. The third disc runs the hits and classics from 1961 to the label's impending demise in 1965, including quite a few pop-chart successes and even some great jazz sides. Producer/compiler/annotator Billy Vera deserves special mention for a job well done, given the size constraints and licensing restrictions. An important chunk of American musical history served up classy. *—Cub Koda*

The Warmth of the Sun: Songs Inspired by the Beach Boys / May 23, 2000 / Varese ✦✦✦

Subtitled *Songs Inspired by the Beach Boys*, this 19-track collection is an odd-duck assortment of new and old tracks that somehow all fit under this surf, hot rod, Brian Wilson-influenced umbrella. From the obvious ("G.T.O.," "New York's a Lonely Town," "Hot Rod High," and "Competition Coupe" to First Class' "Beach Baby") to the not so obvious ("Yellow Balloon," "My World Fell Down," and "Channel Surfing" to Eric Carmen's "She Did It"), this is a set of tunes that actually extend the musical ideas of Wilson and the group into modern times, showing the utter timelessness of their work. An interesting idea, an even better compilation. *—Cub Koda*

☆ **Warp 10+1: The Influences** / Oct. 12, 1999 / Matador ✦✦✦✦✦

Not only the world's premiere label for forward-thinking electronic dance, Sheffield's Warp celebrated its tenth anniversary with a historic compilation series, the first of which includes more than 20 techno classics from the '80s that influenced the imprint's founders and its many artists. And as compilations of obscure but important techno go, this could be the best ever produced. *Warp 10+1: The Influences* balances only the best tracks from the early Chicago house, Detroit techno, and British scenes, including undeniable classics from Mr. Fingers aka Larry Heard ("Can U Feel It"), Adonis ("No Way Back"), Reese & Santonio aka Kevin Saunderson ("The Sound"), Model 500 aka Juan Atkins ("Off to Battle"), Rhythim Is Rhythim aka Derrick May ("Nude Photo"), Phuture ("Acid Tracks"), 808 State ("Let Yourself Go"), and A Guy Called Gerald ("Voodoo Ray"). Most of these have been anthologized several times, but where *Warp 10+1* really shines is the inclusion of a few incredibly rare tracks—"Bang Bang You're Mine" by Bang the Party, "The Theme" by Unique Three, "My Medusa" by K-Alexi Shelby, "Computer Madness" by Steve Poindexter—that techno fans have often heard about, but never heard. Electronic music has progressed so much over the course of ten years that later Warp heroes like Autechre and Aphex Twin sound nothing like these producers, but the energy and power of mid- to late-'80s techno is undiminished with time. *—John Bush*

Warp 10+2: The Classics 1989-1992 / Oct. 12, 1999 / Matador ✦✦✦✦✦

The second installment in Warp's ten-year anniversary campaign recycles the first four years in the label's history, times when Warp specialized in what's become known as bleep techno. Unlike the electronic listening music later developed by Warp acts Black Dog, Aphex Twin, and B12, and the more experimental approach to electronics that has become the label's forte thanks to Autechre and Squarepusher, early Warp records were Spartan productions. Classics like "LFO" by LFO, "Aftermath" by Nightmares on Wax, and "Testone" by Sweet Exorcist were heavy on the polar extremes of sound frequency: low-signal bass designed to rattle all but the most high-end sub-woofers, chirpy treble effects that focused on a cleaner, more precise angle to Chicago's trademark acid tracks, and complex percussion programs learned from classic Detroit producers. Instead of a collection charting the entire decade of its history, Warp chose to appease hardcore fans by focusing on its earliest, rarest tracks. Since Warp is such a collector-driven label anyway, it's a perfect match—fans can finally own the tracks that in some cases they've only heard about, including the first Warp release (Forgemasters' "Track With No Name") plus tracks by Warp one-shots like Sweet Exorcist, Tricky Disco, and DJ Mink. Although the format may not work well for those unfamiliar with the label's complete history, it's a fitting tribute to the beginning of electronic dance's move from the club floor to the living room. *—John Bush*

Warp 10+3: The Remixes / Oct. 12, 1999 / Matador ✦✦✦✦✦

The final volume in Warp Records' ten-year anniversary celebration looks at the immense influence the label has had on experimental and electronic music the world over. An assortment of indie rock and electronic figures take on their favorites from the label's surprisingly large back catalog, beginning with Pram's garage rock rendering of LFO's "Simon From Sydney" and continuing on through Stereolab's shuffling remake of "Kid for Today" by Boards of Canada, Jim O'Rourke's version of "Characi" by Autechre, Tortoise-frontman John McEntire's reworking of "Playtime" by Nightmares on Wax, and Spiritualized's pure-phased wave-of-sound redux of "Tied Up" by LFO. There are plenty of remixes by electronic artists though, and a few by Warp acts themselves (Autechre, Plaid, Mira Calix, Jimi Tenor, Plone). Always a forward-thinking label, Warp also showcases some newer names in the electronic world. The remixes by new signings (as of 1999) Isan and Four Tet are among the best of the two-disc set. And the new wave of stateside neo-electro producers Push Button Objects and Richard Devine pump up the beats on their contributions, Boards of Canada's "An Eagle in Your Mind" and Aphex Twin's "Come to Daddy." Though it might be too sprawling for fans of just one or two of the acts included, *Warp10+3: The Remixes* is an effective statement of the electronic/dance world circa the end of the millennium. *—John Bush*

Wax, Board and Woodie / Jul. 29, 1996 / Varese Sarabande ♦♦♦
Subtitled "a collection of rare and unreleased surf and hot rod songs," this 14-track compilation hits the intended target in a big way. Culling its contents primarily from the MCA/Dot Records vaults, one of the big tickets here is a bone-chilling unreleased moment when we hear the Surfaris attempting to take on the Rolling Stones with their swipe at "Route 66," way cooler than it sounds. A couple of silly but great fun anyway P.F. Sloan sides, including a unreleased sloppy-as-hell song demo, compliment one-off instrumentals like "El Gato" by the Chandelles and "Tremble" by the Galaxies. And in true Dot Records tradition (the label that made their rep inflicting Pat Boone on an unsuspecting world) there's even a "cover" version on here by a Milt Rogers of Dick Dale's "Let's Go Trippin'!!" Not the most essential set of tunes, but one hell of a fun compilation. *—Cub Koda*

The West Coast East Side Sound, Vol. 1 / Jul. 13, 1999 / Varese ♦♦♦
This 16-song collection may be a little too diverse for its own good. Overall, it's a nicely assembled opening volume of a four-CD series devoted to the music of Faro, Rampart, and other labels owned and operated by Eddie Davis in Los Angeles from the '50s through the mid-'70s. It opens with the biggest single that Faro ever issued, "Land of 1,000 Dances" by Cannibal & the Headhunters. The rest of the CD jumps around throughout the history of Davis' various labels, back a year earlier for the Romancers' "Don't Let Her Go," and then on to "Darling (Please Bring Your Love)," a doo wop throwback from 1961, and so it goes. One wants to say that the emphasis is on early-'60s dance and novelty tunes ("Olive Oyl" by the Mixtures being the only annoying example of the latter), but then there's the Village Callers' version of "Evil Ways" from 1969, which nearly hit in place of the Santana version. The CD then jumps back to Ron Holden's early-'60s soul showcase "Girl I Love You"; further along is the Motown-flavored "Crazy Little Things" by the Souljers. There's very little sense to much of the order, although it plays great. The producers' apologies for some supposedly substandard sources seems uncalled for, since the sound is good to excellent throughout. The majority of the material on this CD will be unfamiliar to all but the most serious West Coast music buffs. One just wishes that it could've been assembled in a more coherent manner, so that the discoveries could be more orderly. *—Bruce Eder*

The West Coast East Side Sound, Vol. 2 / Jul. 13, 1999 / Varese ♦♦♦
If anything, this CD is an improvement over the initial volume in the series, although it shares similar flaws. The emphasis here is almost completely on dance numbers, with no novelty tracks intruding, and it's all to the credit of bands like the Blendells ("La La La La"), the Romancers ("Take My Heart"), the Premiers ("Get Your Baby"), and the Mixtures ("Rainbow Stomp") that their stuff holds up magnificently today. What's more, the mastering is so good that one really gets to appreciate the playing as well as the songs. And even the one odd track, "Hector" by the Village Callers, fits in perfectly on a stylistic level with everything else, although it's about four years newer than most everything else here. Being slow romantic numbers in these surroundings, the ballads "Karen" by Little Ray & the Mixtures, "My Heart Cries" by the Romancers, and "Girl of My Dreams" by the Majestics have the hardest time fitting in, and 1962's "Destiny" by Larry Tamblyn has him sounding a little too much like Frankie Avalon, but these songs only change the mood without breaking it. The notes are a little fragmentary and, as with this entire series, one must read the insert booklets of all four volumes to get a decent picture of Eddie Davis and his record labels. *—Bruce Eder*

The West Coast East Side Sound, Vol. 3 / Jul. 13, 1999 / Varese ♦♦♦♦
This volume in the series is more cohesive than most, opening with the Premiers' 1964 hit "Farmer John" and generally confining itself to eminently danceable rockers from that same period by the likes of the Atlantics, Larry Tamblyn & the Standells ("The Girl in My Heart"), the Jaguars, the Romancers, the Soul-jers ("Gonna Be a Big Man"), and Sammy Lee & the Summits. As with the other three parts of this series, there's not a weak song here, whether it's Cannibal & the Headhunters (backed by the King Curtis band) doing "Follow the Music," the edgier, less lyrical, but more rousing "Sloop Dance" by the Atlantics, or the soul rave-up "That's Why I Love You" by the Romancers. Maybe the most interesting tracks here are two covers: the instrumental "Chinese Checkers," a piano-dominated version of the Booker T. and the MG's track cut by the Mixtures, and the extroverted rendition of "Love Is Strange" by the Salas Brothers and the Jaguars. And, oddly enough, the Standells, who were more influenced by doo wop in the early '60s, are outclassed in the garage band department by the Romancers' "She Took My Oldsmobile." The sound is excellent throughout. *—Bruce Eder*

The West Coast East Side Sound, Vol. 4 / Jul. 13, 1999 / Varese ♦♦♦
This last volume in the four-CD series is confusing in its content and programming. Opening with a pair of very ethnic sounding numbers, El Chicano's "Viva Tirado" and the Salas Brothers' "Leaving You" (which owes a bit to "Blue Moon"), it has a split personality from the start. The Majestics' "Everything Is Gonna Be Alright" is also a loud, upbeat dance number, but then comes the Romancers' smoothly romantic "She Gives Me Love." And these numbers bounce back and forth across a half-decade or more in terms of recording dates—and are then closely followed by the Premiers' fuzz-laden "Get on This Plane," which deserved a place on the *Nuggets* box. Somewhere after that comes the smooth soul sound of the East Side Kids' "Listen to the Wise Man" and the Santana-like "Con Safos" by Tocayo. It makes for a very confusing if rewarding 16 songs, linked in the most general terms, some of them very enlightening and all of it good listening. *—Bruce Eder*

West Coast Rap: The First Dynasty, Vol. 1 / 1992 / Rhino ♦♦♦♦♦
Although it contains too many obscurities and novelties to make it absolutely essential for casual listeners, *West Coast Rap: The First Dynasty, Vol. 1* is an excellent compilation of early-'80s hip-hop from the likes of Ice-T ("The Coldest Rap"), Egyptian Lover ("Egypt, Egypt"), L.A. Dream Team ("Rockberry Jam"), World Class Wreckin' Cru ("Slice"), 2 Live Crew ("2 Live") and Bobby Jimmy & the Critters ("We Like Ugly Women"). Only Timex Social Club's "Rumors" stands out as a stone-cold classic, but the rest of the record is first-rate old-school rap, and worth the time of any serious hip-hop fan. *—Stephen Thomas Erlewine*

West Coast Rap: The First Dynasty, Vol. 2 / 1992 / Rhino ♦♦♦♦♦
Like its predecessor, *West Coast Rap: The First Dynasty, Vol. 2* is short on indisputable classics, yet the overall quality of the material is quite high. Over the course of 13 tracks, *West Coast Rap* runs through several funky old-school highlights from the likes of Ice-T ("Body Rock"), D.J. Matrix ("Feel My Bass"), Kid Frost ("Rough Cut"), L.A. Dream Team ("Calling on the Dream Team"), Darkstar ("Sexybaby") and Egyptian Lover ("Freak-a-Holic"). Most of this is simply party music, but it's good party music, and the collection is worthwhile for any devoted rap listener, even though its momentum occasionally sags. *—Stephen Thomas Erlewine*

☆ **West Coast Rap: The First Dynasty, Vol. 3** / 1992 / Rhino ♦♦♦♦♦
Like the other two collections of *West Coast Rap: The First Dynasty, Vol. 3* promises more than it delivers, since it is short on genuine classics and long on novelties. Despite its flaws, *Vol 3.*, like the rest of the *West Coast Rap* series, remains one of the best old-school hip-hop compilations on the market, since it was put together with some care and the overall quality of the music is quite high, even if certain names (Ice-T, Egyptian Lover, Kid Frost, 2 Live Crew, Bobby, Jimmy & the Critters) are a little too familiar from the disc's predecessors. Nevertheless, there are enough solid cuts to make this a strong addition to any comprehensive hip-hop collection. *—Stephen Thomas Erlewine*

What's Shakin' / 1966 / Elektra ♦♦♦
An odd, erratic, but interesting anthology of rare performances recorded by Elektra in the mid-'60s, when it was just getting its feet wet with rock. Leading the way are the Paul Butterfield Blues Band, whose five tracks are very much in the style of their first LP; the Butterfield original "Lovin' Cup" is about as good as anything he ever did. Eric Clapton & the Powerhouse are a most interesting aggregation, also featuring Stevie Winwood, Paul Jones, Jack Bruce, and Spencer Davis Group drummer Pete York; their three tracks include early versions of "Steppin' Out" and "Crossroads," which Clapton would record with the Bluesbreakers and Cream, respectively. The Lovin' Spoonful's four tracks date from before reaching stardom with the Kama Sutra label; here they concentrate on blues and early rock & roll-style songs, which frankly don't measure up to their folk-rock. Rare tracks by Tom Rush and Al Kooper (who reworked his contribution, "Can't Keep From Crying Sometimes," with the Blues Project) round out the set. *—Richie Unterberger*

What's Up Matador / Jul. 1997 / Matador ♦♦♦♦
Once Sub Pop's roster broke through to the mainstream in the early '90s, its reign as America's premier independent label drew to a close, leaving Matador Records as the definitive indie label of the decade. Matador's period of greatest impact was between 1991 and 1997, which is the time that the double-disc set *What's Up Matador* chronicles. The budget-priced compilation is designed as both an introduction and as a collector's dream, containing one disc called Favorite Tracks and one disc of unreleased songs. Matador didn't have a signature sound, preferring to cultivate a loose aesthetic that permitted its artists to do whatever the hell they wanted. So, there's the nervous punk of Superchunk, the jangling pop of Bettie Serveert, the fractured pop of Pavement, pure weirdness from the Frogs, mathematical rock from Chavez, disco from the Pizzicato Five, the avant rock of Silkworm, hardcore punk from Unsane, psycho-blues from the Jon Spencer Blues Explosion and Railroad Jerk, and lo-fi from Guided By Voices and Spoon, along with singer/songwriters like Liz Phair, Helium's Mary Timony, Cat Power, and Barbra Manning/SF Seals. It's an eclectic roster, but it's a rich one, containing many of the best and most important bands of the decade. The first disc runs through the hits quite effectively; for anyone curious about Matador specifically and American indie rock in general, it's an excellent primer. The second disc is for collectors and fanatics, and it does not disappoint. Many of the bands on disc one contribute unreleased songs that never sound like throwaways, and some of the label's newer bands that didn't make the first disc—Run On, The For Carnation, and Bardo Pond—are included. With its abundance of strong music and its complete Matador discography, *What's Up Matador* is an essential purchase for anyone curious about '90s indie rock. *—Stephen Thomas Erlewine*

When a Man Cries / Nov. 9, 1999 / Kent ♦♦♦
The soul music issued by the Scepter/Wand and Musicor/Dynamo labels tended to be the most pop-oriented, "uptown" sort of 1960s New York soul, as sung by stars on their roster like Dionne Warwick, Chuck Jackson, Maxine Brown, and the Shirelles. However, from the mid-'60s through the early '70s, the labels did license material from other sources, often from the South, that was in much more of a "deep soul" or "sweet soul" style, with gospel-derived vocals and brassy production. *When a Man Cries* has 27 of those releases from 1965-73. A lot of these names are unknown; with the exception of Lloyd Price, even the recognizable artists are minor ones, such as Jackie Moore, Judy Clay, Tommy Hunt, LC Cooke (Sam Cooke's brother), and Johnny Copeland. Like so many of these collector-targeted anthologies, it's the second or third tier of the genre, not the cream

of it. The imprint of the Stax ballad approach (with horns and bluesy guitars and organs), as well as fainter echoes of the Philadelphia and Chicago "sweet soul" vibe, is audible on many of the cuts. By and large they're emotionally sung and well produced—and not possessed of that special something, particularly that special songwriting, needed to elevate the cut to major durability. There are occasional lifts from more famous songs—let's not try to pretend these don't exist—such as Murge's "How Long Must This Fool Pay," whose opening piano is pretty close to Brenda Holloway's classic "Every Little Bit Hurts." Guess what the punchline of Marvin Preyer's previously unissued "You Don't Have to Be Crazy to Love Her" is? (Yep: "But it sure helps a lot.") *—Richie Unterberger*

Where the Girls Are / 1997 / Ace ♦♦

24 girl-group rarities from all over the place, released between 1961 and 1968 (the track by Reparata and the Delrons was previously unissued). This will have pretty limited appeal beyond the hardline girl-group collecting market. The level of production expertise is high—indeed, there are little-known efforts by Leiber & Stoller, David Gates, Goffin-King, and future early Byrds producers Terry Melcher and Allen Stanton. Yet the songs aren't really too special, with a higher innocuousness quotient than is the norm in an already innocuous genre. It does have a couple of semi-forgotten classics (though they actually hit the Top 40) in Ruby & the Romantics' 1963 original of "Hey There Lonely Boy" (which would be reworked into a number two hit by Eddie Holman in 1970 as "Hey There Lonely Girl"), and Patty & the Emblems brassy'n'sassy "Mixed-Up, Shook-Up Girl" (co-written by Leon Huff). Curiosity seekers, it must be said, will find plenty here, including barely known girl-group-style singles by Joey Heatherton, Doris Day, and Dolly Parton; a 1961 single by Erma Franklin, Aretha's sister; and a 1962 single by Idalia Boyd, sister of Little Eva of "Loco-Motion" fame. *—Richie Unterberger*

Where the Girls Are, Vol. 2 / Jul. 27, 1999 / Ace ♦♦♦♦

A 30-song collection of early and mid-'60s girl group rarities, some previously unreleased, from the vaults of the New York-based Scepter and Musicor labels. This is ephemera that can only be recommended to hard-bitten girl group fans, but if you're in that category there are probably enough goodies here to merit a spin. Chief among these is Diane & Annita's tentative 1965 version of "A Groovy Kind of Love" (previously only on a French EP), which according to the liners is the original, even predating the one by Patti LaBelle & the Blue Belles (which is usually presumed to be the original that was covered by the Mindbenders for a huge hit). There's a rare 1962 cut by Tammy Montgomery, who became Tammi Terrell at Motown, and unreleased cuts by Maxine Brown, Goldie & the Gingerbreads, and Marie Knight. The songs by the Shirelles and the Shangri-Las, though not well known, have been easy to find on other compilations. As for the contributions by no names, these are often pleasant and well produced but largely inconsequential; one bright spot is Ernestine Eady's perky "The Change," which has an uptown bounce typical of many quality New York soul-pop productions of the period. *—Richie Unterberger*

Where the Girls Are, Vol. 3 / Jul. 11, 2000 / Ace ♦♦♦

Starting in the 1990s, a cluster of CD reissues have served to remind us that Chess was not just a blues label, in fact recording a great deal of worthwhile (and often successful) soul in the 1960s. *Where the Girls Are, Vol. 3* is not the best of these, but it puts an interesting spin on the concept by focusing exclusively on women pop-soul-girl-group singers who recorded for Chess during the decade. There are a few name artists here—Etta James, Sugar Pie de Santo, Tammy Montgomery (soon to be renamed Tammi Terrell), and (to a lesser degree) Jackie Ross, Mitty Collier, Jan Bradley, and a teenaged Minnie Riperton (as part of the Gems and under the pseudonym Andrea Davis)—though most of these are only known to those fanatical, often British, soul collectors. The same comments that you could direct toward Chess' '60s soul in general apply to this anthology in particular: while well produced, it sometimes came off as derivative of both Motown and other Chicago soul competitors, without as much standout material as the best competition. That makes this 26-song CD second-division, but certainly not second-rate. For one thing, there is a certain consistency of sound that makes it more listenable than many other similar archive CDs are. There are also some pretty good songs amidst the so-so ones. Geraldine Hunt's 1962 single "I Let Myself Go" is an incredibly blatant yet enjoyable and accurate Mary Wells imitation; Timiko's "Is It a Sin?," which is just marginally less Wells-like, has some fetching hooks; while the Clickettes' "I Just Can't Help It" is cool and catchy soul-tinged girl-group pop. Everything else wilts, however, besides Etta James' compelling "Pushover," an actual 1963 Top 30 hit that was one of her poppiest, yet gutsiest, and best singles. *—Richie Unterberger*

Where the Girls Are, Vol. 4 / 2001 / Ace ♦♦♦

This series of girl group rarities and oddities turns its focus to the Atlantic vaults for its fourth volume. Actually, some of these might tread closer to soul, pop/rock sung by female solo vocalists, or even doo wop than the standard girl group sound. But that shouldn't bother people looking for some reasonably interesting rock in this vein of the early and mid-1960s, which is here in quantity on this uneven but generally worthwhile anthology. None of these were big hits, and in fact only a few of the performers (Doris Troy, Patti LaBelle & the Bluebelles, April Stevens) will ring bells for most non-specialist listeners. There are some quite good tracks here, though: the original version of "A Groovy Kind of Love" by Patti LaBelle; Shirley Matthews's "Big Town Boy" (a fine Phil Spector sound-alike and a big hit in her native Canada); Troy's customarily excellent soul-pop/rock on her two tracks; more son-of-wall-of-sound on the Goodnight Kisses' "If He Kissed Me"; Shirelles-style stuff by Carol Shaw (later of Goldie & the Gingerbreads) on "Jimmy Boy"; and a rare 1956 doo wop/pop outing by the Cookies (the only track here not from 1960-67). Sometimes the cuts are obviously imitative, like the Dorelles' "Heat Wave" knockoff "The Beating of My Heart," or the Meantimes' "Friday Kind of Monday" (produced and written by Jeff Barry and Ellie Greenwich), an answer record to the Mamas & the Papas' "Monday, Monday." Atlantic's high standard of production and arrangements makes this sound better and more accomplished than many such odds-and-ends compilations, and there are some big names among the producers of these tracks, like Barry-Greenwich, Bob Crewe, Nino Tempo, and Bert Berns. *—Richie Unterberger*

Whistle Bait: 25 Rockabilly Rave-Ups / 2000 / Columbia/Legacy ♦♦♦♦

Culled from the CBS vaults, *Whistle Bait* is a very good anthology of 25 rockabilly numbers—or, if not quite rockabilly, tracks by country artists veering close to rockabilly—that for the most part will be unfamiliar to all but the most dedicated rockabilly collectors. Sure, there are some stars and cult faves here, like the Collins Kids, Link Wray, the post-Sun Carl Perkins, the post-Sun Johnny Cash, and Ronnie Self, whose "Bop-a-Lena" (included here) was one of the most certifiably insane rockers ever put out by a major label. You also get a generous helping of country artists trying to board the rockabilly wagon, and actually, they usually acquit themselves quite well. Don't believe it? Listen to Lefty Frizzell's "You're Humbuggin' Me," Rose Maddox's "Wild Wild Young Men," and Little Jimmy Dickens' "I Got a Hole in My Pocket" for evidence. Then there are the cats you've never heard of that managed to put out something quite hep, like Jaycee Hill on his 1956 single "Romp Stompin' Boogie." Johnny Horton draws from the best of both honky tonk and rock & roll on his two numbers, which are a far cry from the corny Americana that would land him big pop hits at the end of the '50s. Although there's undeniable aesthetic purity in collecting anthologies of crude rockabilly by no-hopers on some tiny label operating out of a small Texas oil town, the truth is that this big company vault-clearing exercise is way better than the average such rockabilly collection. It may not be too popular to say so, but one of the reasons is that major label production values usually delivered far better-sounding, tighter performances and secured better material. Put this on your shopping list if you want quality rare rockabilly. *—Richie Unterberger*

Wild Surf! / 1996 / Del-Fi ♦♦♦

In the early and mid-1960s, Del-Fi recorded a good deal of surf music. This compilation brings together 24 tracks recorded by acts whose impact was strictly regional, including the Lively Ones, the Centurions, Dave Myers, the Sentinals, the Impacts, the Surfman, the Original Surfaris (not the "Wipe Out" guys), the Pharos, and the Gonzos. Some of the best tunes have shown up on surf compilations (like Rhino's *Surf Box*). But if your interest in surf runs deeper than the usual greatest hits collections, this is one of the more solid secondary anthologies out there, many of the tracks exhibiting a distinct Latin influence in the melodies and rhythms. *—Richie Unterberger*

Wild Things: Wild Kiwi Garage 1966-1969 / 1991 / Flying Nun ♦♦♦♦♦

New Zealand, a tiny country with a population less than the metropolitan San Francisco Bay Area, nevertheless had a fairly prolific and interesting garage/beat scene in the mid-'60s. This collects 16 singles that, with one or two exceptions, were obscure even in the land of their release. Like the bands from neighboring Australia, the Kiwis compensated for their isolation with crude mania, and this has some ferocious sub-Stones pounders from the likes of the La De Da's, Chants R&B, and the Bluestars. An above-average garage collection, well worth checking out by '60s aficionados. *—Richie Unterberger*

Wild Wild Young Women / Roulette/Rounder ♦♦♦♦♦

Rockabilly was largely a male domain; except for Wanda Jackson and Brenda Lee, no female rockabilly singers made a notable national impact. But there were a few other women rockabilly vocalists making some good records, and this is the best basic collection of them. Janis Martin, known as "the female Elvis," checks in with three cuts, including "My Boy Elvis"; the Davis Sisters (one of whom was Skeeter Davis) and Rose Maddox are represented by some mid-'50s sides which illustrate rockabilly's close links to country boogie. The Collins Kids recorded some of the most hyper-tempo rockabilly of any sort, and Sparkle Moore, from Nebraska, had a great over-the-top, swooping delivery. You also get some even more obscure, but also worthy, cuts from the Nettles Sisters, Jean Chapel, Joan King, Linda and the Epics, and Alvadean Coker. More sides are available on single-artist compilations by some of these acts, particularly the Collins Kids, the Davis Sisters, Janis Martin, and Rose Maddox, but the compilers have done a good job of selecting first-rate tracks for a general overview. *—Richie Unterberger*

Wired Magazine Presents: Music Futurists / Feb. 16, 1999 / Rhino ♦♦♦♦

Covering 38 years, *Music Futurists* is a compilation of tracks from pop artists "on the cutting edge of technology in music," according to the liner notes. That premise would probably make a great multi-disc box set. As a single-disc, 15-track release, though, *Music Futurists* runs into conceptual trouble despite having more than enough to recommend it. Arranged chronologically, these 15 songs move from space-age bachelor Esquivel to avant-garde trumpeter Ben Neill. The commonalities linking the selections are deliberately obscure, and that's fine. Some of the inclusions, however, have to be questioned. No doubt Devo belongs here, for example, but why the relatively uneventful "Beautiful World" instead of one of the songs from *Q: Are We Not Men?* Godley & Creme's "Cry" is a sublime pop moment, but how much more innovative was it from other select Top 40 songs that came before? Most mysterious is the inclusion of Beck's "Total Soul Future (Eat It)." With the already rich backlog of work Beck had by this album's 1999 release, the appearance of this very short song feels arbitrary, as if the compilers needed to attach a bigger, contemporary name to the project. Ignore the concept, though, and this music takes subtle and entrancing effect. Better-known innovators like Todd Rundgren and Brian Eno refine their reputations by being heard side by side with less heralded heroes like composer Steve Reich and the painfully underappreciated German experimentalists Can. Laurie Anderson's "O Superman" is a turning point that's good to hear wherever it shows up. *Wired Magazine* wanted to make both a historical artifact and a great mix tape with this album. They've at least made the latter, but it's begging for a lot of sequels. *—Paul Pearson*

Woodstock: Three Days of Peace & Music [25th Anniversary] / 1995 / Atlantic ♦♦♦♦

This four-disc box set was released commemorating the 25th anniversary of the original

Woodstock festival that took place in August 1969 and combined both of the Woodstock albums released in 1970 and 1971 with previously unreleased material. It's a well-known part of the festival's history that many of the participants played self-confessed lackluster sets. However, considering the surrounding circumstances in which this music was conceived—not enough food or water, an abundance of drugs, and thunderstorms—these artists manage to rise above it more often than not. What is most interesting about this box set are the unreleased tracks by the Band, Tim Hardin, Johnny Winter, Creedence Clearwater Revival, Jefferson Airplane, Jimi Hendrix, Janis Joplin, and Ritchie Havens. A whittled down single-disc sampler featuring many of the aforementioned unreleased tracks are also available on *Woodstock Diary* containing Mountain's "Southbound Train," Sly and the Family Stone's "Love City," and CS&N's "Blackbird" which aren't included on the box set. —*Al Campbell*

Working Holiday! / Dec. 12, 1994 / Simple Machines ✦✦✦✦
During 1993, Jenny Toomey and Kristin Thomson decided to try a project with their Simple Machines label; they formed a record club, putting out a seasonally themed 7" single each month featuring two bands, and then wrapping the year up with a three-day concert festival featuring most of the involved bands. Thankfully, the majority of the music lived up to the inspired concept—the singles featured tracks from lauded independent acts like Versus, Scrawl, the Coctails, Eggs, Veronica Lake, My Dad Is Dead, Nothing Painted Blue, Lois, Small Factory, Superchunk, and Tsunami, among many others. As such, the two-disc *Working Holiday!* collection serves as a sort of time capsule of indie rock in the early to mid-'90s, before electronica, post-rock, and *Pet Sounds* imitation took the focus away from this vein of music. The collection's second disc compiles 17 performances from the year-ending concert festival, including excellent tracks from Archers of Loaf, Superchunk, Franklin Bruno and Versus—even better, the concert material and extensive liner notes document the year-long, shoestring-budget process of getting the records out, and the indie scene they were aimed at. Toomey and Thomson certainly deserved some sort of medal for putting together such a project and for tapping in to everything that was appealing about the indie scene of this period—the *Working Holiday!* collection, more than a lot of "seminal" albums, documents the entire scene, attitude, and aesthetic that made an initially underground phenomenon such an important force and influence in music. —*Nitsuh Abebe*

Youth Gone Wild: Heavy Metal Hits of the '80s, Vol. 1 / Mar. 26, 1996 / Rhino ✦✦✦✦✦
Rhino's three-volume set *Youth Gone Wild: Heavy Metal Hits of the '80s* nearly chronicles the excesses of '80s metal accurately, but the set falls just short of being definitive. None of the three discs (available separately) has a logical or chronological sequencing, seemingly throwing all of the songs together in random order. Also, several big stars and definitive songs are missing in favor of negligible cult favorties. Even with these two significant flaws, the series is terrific and captures the essence of the era. *Vol. 1* concentrates on early-'80s hits like the Scorpions' "Rock You Like a Hurricane," Twisted Sister's "We're Not Gonna Take It," Accept's "Balls to the Wall," Motörhead's "Ace of Spades," Judas Priest's "Parental Guidance," Ratt's "Lay It Down," and Quiet Riot's "Cum on Feel the Noize," throwing in cuts like Poison's "Talk Dirty to Me" for good measure. It might not make for coherent listening, and several cuts (including Krokus' "Screaming in the Night" and Dio's "The Last in Line") have dated poorly, but the set nevertheless has many metal

classics. And if you want to know what mainstream '80s metal and hard rock sounded like, *Youth Gone Wild* can't be beat. —*Stephen Thomas Erlewine*

Youth Gone Wild: Heavy Metal Hits of the '80s, Vol. 2 / Mar. 26, 1996 / Rhino ✦✦✦✦✦
The second installment of Rhino's *Youth Gone Wild: Heavy Metal Hits Of The '80s* is divided between mid-'80s hits by David Lee Roth ("Goin' Crazy!"), Great White ("Rock Me"), Europe ("The Final Countdown") and Yngwie Malmsteen ("Heaven Tonight") and late-'80s cuts from Winger ("Seventeen"), Vixen ("Edge of a Broken Heart"), and Faster Pussycat ("Poison Ivy"). More than any other entry in the series, *Vol. 2* suffers from cutesy, ironic selections—there's no reason Sam Kinison's "Wild Thing" should have been included, and Helloween only gained fame after being showcased on *Beavis & Butt-Head* in the '90s—and a few cuts, like King's X's "Over My Head," appear to be on the disc simply because they were personal favorites of the compilers. Nevertheless, *Youth Gone Wild, Vol. 2* remains a good purchase, especially for fans who want to replace their worn cassettes with only the hits, not full albums. —*Stephen Thomas Erlewine*

Youth Gone Wild: Heavy Metal Hits of the '80s, Vol. 3 / Mar. 26, 1996 / Rhino ✦✦✦✦✦
The third and final volume of *Youth Gone Wild: Heavy Metal Hits of the '80s* has fewer hits than either of its predecessors, and it suffers as a result. Of all the cuts, only a handful—Whitesnake's "Still of the Night," Cinderella's "Gypsy Road," White Lion's "Wait," Kingdom Come's "Get it On," Bulletboys' "Smooth Up In Ya," Britny Fox's "Girlschool"—were actually hits, while the rest all seem to be randomly selected. Mr. Big's "Addicted to That Rush" has the virtuosity of Paul Gilbert and Billy Sheehan to reccomend it, and D.A.D. has some dark glamour, but Bang Tango, Raging Slab, Love/Hate, Dangerous Toys, Fastway, and Helix are all faceless and nearly interchangeable, making *Vol. 3* considerably less entertaining than its predecessors. Still, the hits alone make the disc worthwhile for any nostalgic metalhead. —*Stephen Thomas Erlewine*

Youth Gone Wild: Heavy Metal Hits of the '80s, Vol. 4 / Jun. 16, 1998 / Rhino ✦✦✦
Even though Rhino established on the first three volumes of its *Youth Gone Wild: Heavy Metal Hits of the '80s* series that there would be no power ballads and no material from pop superstars like Def Leppard, Mötley Crüe, and Bon Jovi, there were still a few key items indispensable to a definitive hair metal retrospective that went missing. *Vol. 4* begins to remedy that, including Slaughter's "Up All Night," and Warrant's "Down Boys," and Autograph's AOR hit "Turn Up the Radio," but those tracks seem to be the only licensing coups the producers could pull off, as *Vol. 4* proves the weakest outing in the series to date. Hardcore viewers of late-'80s MTV programs like *Dial MTV* and *Headbanger's Ball* might find faint flickerings of memories stirred by tracks from Danger Danger ("Naughty Naughty"), Tora Tora ("Walkin' Shoes"), Junkyard ("Hollywood"), Stryper ("To Hell With the Devil"), Shotgun Messiah ("Heartbreak Blvd."), and Enuff Z'Nuff ("New Thing"), but aside from the latter item, an overlooked classic of the genre, most of what's here is a generic, manufactured blend of slickly produced AOR and L.A. sleaze-rock. One could argue that Metal Church, a serious, progressive thrash outfit influenced by Metallica, doesn't really belong here, either; however, listeners who own the remainder of this series and don't mind sorting through the chaff, or who take pleasure in locating items by these more obscure bands, will find it enjoyable enough to add it to their collections. —*Steve Huey*

Essays

Birth of Rock & Roll

For those of us born too late to experience the birth of rock & roll firsthand, an unlikely parallel might be drawn to the Internet. It has been written that no one planned the Internet; it just happened. And the same could be said of rock & roll. No one planned rock & roll, and it overtook the musical culture of America and then the world, with a sudden impact that revolutionized popular music as surely as the Internet is revolutionizing telecommunications.

It has often been said that rock & roll was the result of cross-breeding between rhythm & blues and country & western music. That's a large part of the equation, of course, but hardly the entire picture. Gospel music, swing jazz, jump blues combos, country swing bands, Tin Pan Alley publishers—they were just some of the other key building blocks of the music.

Few would dispute that rock & roll owes most of its origins to the musical traditions of America's black population. From Africa, blacks brought a strong oral musical tradition of music for storytelling, recreation, and work. Continued and modified in the United States under incredibly harsh conditions, these elements would provide the backbone of blues music. As segregated as American society has been, there has been constant personal interchange and cultural exchange between races throughout the nation's history. The white southern population of the United States had its own musical conventions: Anglo-Saxon folk songs, Appalachian music, and religious music for the church. African-Americans absorbed influences from whites in their use of stringed instruments and harmonies. The development of jazz around the turn of the 20th century introduced larger bands and stronger rhythmic elements.

Just as technological developments affected the pace and complexity of life in the early 20th century, so did it accelerate the growth of popular music. The phonograph record enabled artists to reach and influence an exponentially larger audience of listeners and fellow musicians. Huge numbers of blacks from the south migrated to urban communities, where music and dancing took place in considerably more crowded and hectic environments. And to be heard in these venues, musicians eventually had no choice but to use electronic amplification and, eventually, electric instruments.

As early as the 1930s, strong intimations of rock & roll can be found in rhythmic, increasingly riff-driven swing jazz music, as well as blues-influenced country recordings by the Delmore Brothers, Bob Wills, Jimmie Rodgers, the Maddox Brothers, and others. Charlie Christian pioneered the use of the electric guitar in the early 1940s, at the same time as jazz musicians like Lionel Hampton were putting out riff-heavy hits like "Flyin' Home." As the '40s progressed, jazz musicians like Illinois Jacquet, Big Joe Turner, Louis Jordan, Jay McShann, and others upped the R&B quotient with honking saxes, "shouter" vocals, and pounding boogie-woogie piano.

Big bands became increasingly less economically viable after the second World War, and smaller combos became more in vogue. They still had to play just as loudly as ever, though, and riffs, electric guitars, "shouting" R&B vocals, and prominent beats were usually the ticket. So it was that jump blues came into style, paced by Louis Jordan and singers like Wynonie Harris, Tiny Bradshaw, and Roy Brown.

Jump blues itself wasn't far removed from rock & roll, and there were several other major changes afoot as the '50s began. The Delmore Brothers recorded frenetic country-boogie that anticipated the spirit of rockabilly. Vocal groups like the Orioles took the smooth popular stylings of black harmony ensembles like the Mills Brothers and the Ink Spots and added a more pronounced R&B and gospel feel. After Delta musicians like Muddy Waters amplified their guitars and added rhythm sections, a fullbodied electric blues sound was born in Chicago, Memphis, and other urban centers. Fats Domino, Lloyd Price, and others pioneered the keyboard-and-horn driven grooves of New Orleans R&B. Les Paul took electric guitar wattage to new heights with his innovative multi-track recordings.

There were also major rumblings in the music industry and American society itself. Independent companies like Atlantic, King, Sun, Specialty, Chess, and numerous others recorded R&B and hillbilly music, catering to audiences that the major labels deemed too specialized and uncouth to service. Young white listeners began tuning in radio stations that played music for these supposed minority tastes. And the increasingly affluent economy meant that these young listeners had more time and money than ever to spend on records.

These disparate strands began to collide and merge as the '50s progressed. There are a great number of opinions as to what could be called the first "rock & roll" record; indeed, an entire book (the fine *What Was the First Rock & Roll Record?*) has been written on the subject. Certainly, early sides by Jackie Brenston ("Rocket 88"), Bill Haley, Lloyd Price, Hank Ballard, Fats Domino, and others have strong claims. Whatever it was, and whenever it became a style, by 1954 there were several records in the Top 30 that couldn't, from a latter-day vantage point, be called anything but rock & roll: Bill Haley's

primitive rockabilly ("Shake, Rattle, and Roll"), the joyous doo wop of the Crows and the Chords ("Gee" and "Sh-Boom"), the saucy R&B of Hank Ballard ("Work With Me Annie"). The music needed a name, and several theories have been advanced as to how the term "rock & roll" came about. Influential Cleveland and New York DJ Alan Freed's claim to have originated the phrase is probably the most widely circulated, though rocking and rolling had long been a euphemism, especially in the black community, for dancing, partying, and more private pleasures.

In 1955, Bill Haley's "Rock Around the Clock" became the first number one rock & roll hit; Little Richard and Chuck Berry had their first national smashes that year with "Tutti Frutti" and "Maybellene," songs which put electric guitar leads, honking vocals, and lyrics about cars and girls to the forefront in a glorious package. In early 1956, Elvis Presley's number one hit "Heartbreak Hotel" ended any doubt (or hope by the more conservative factions of the music business) that rock & roll would fade.

An emerging regional sensation, Elvis pioneered rockabilly on his legendary recordings for Sun records in 1954 and 1955 by marrying the feels of the blues and country boogie with his hard-driving rhythms and frenetic vocals. His jump to a major label—and assimilation of slightly more pop-oriented values into his recordings that didn't diminish his genius in the slightest (at least at first)—made rock & roll an international phenomenon. His massive success, and the success of the countless rock & rollers who followed, was the end of the line in the evolution of the forces that gave birth to rock music—and the beginning, of course, of much more.

15 Most Essential Recordings Leading to the Birth of Rock & Roll:

The Delmore Brothers, *The Best of the Delmore Brothers* (Starday). Country boogie with a reckless feel, close harmonies, and pounding backbeat, separated from rockabilly only by the level of electric instruments and a rhythm section. This collection of their late 1940s sides continues much of their most raucous work.

Bill Haley & His Comets, *Rock the Joint!* (Schoolkids). A collection of his early 1950s singles, prior to his breakthrough to mass success with "Shake, Rattle, and Roll" and "Rock Around the Clock." The earliest white rock & roll ever recorded, combining country swing, electric guitars, saxophones, and R&B rhythms to come up with something different altogether.

Louis Jordan, *The Best of Louis Jordan* (MCA). A crucial bridge from swing jazz to jump blues, and a major influence upon Chuck Berry

The Maddox Brothers & Rose, *Vol. 1* (Arhoolie). Another hillbilly band that anticipated elements of rockabilly with their rumbling boogie and slap-back bass. This has 27 of their songs from 1946-51.

Various Artists, *Hillbilly Music Vol. 1 ... Thank God!* (Capitol). A double album of rowdy hillbilly music from the late '40s to the mid-'50s, featuring such country giants as Tennessee Ernie Ford, Merle Travis, Buck Owens, and the Louvin Brothers. No other compilation illustrates the white country roots of rock & roll as well.

Various Artists, *Atlantic R&B: 1947-1952* (Atlantic). The Atlantic label was arguably the greatest and most influential record company specializing in rhythm & blues in rock & roll's formative years. This is the first volume of a seven-part series, also available as part of a box set.

Various Artists, *Atlantic R&B: 1952-1955* (Atlantic). More classic performances from the early Atlantic roster, edging closer to rock & roll from its more blues- and R&B-based beginnings.

Various Artists, *Blues Masters Volume 5: Jump Blues Classics* (Rhino). The best jump blues compilation, with classics by Big Jay McNeely, Wynonie Harris, Tiny Bradshaw, Big Joe Turner, and others. A second volume in the Blues Masters series (More Jump Blues Classics) is of equally high quality.

Various Artists, *Blues Masters Volume 6: Blues Originals* (Rhino). Many of these songs helped form the backbone of the rock repertoire. Often popularized to a larger audience by white performers from Elvis Presley and the Rolling Stones down, here is where you'll find the original versions of classics like "That's All Right," "Back Door Man," "Love in Vain," and a lot of others.

Various Artists, *A History of New Orleans Rhythm and Blues Vol. 1* (Rhino). The first part of this three-volume series features key performances from the early and mid-1950s by artists who laid the foundations for the New Orleans sound, such as Lloyd Price and Guitar Slim.

Billy Ward, *Sixty Minute Men: The Best of Billy Ward & His Dominoes* (Rhino). One of the first great black harmony groups of rhythm & blues, featuring lead vocals by two singers who would go on to become early rock & roll stars in their own right, Clyde McPhatter and Jackie Wilson

Muddy Waters, *The Best of Muddy Waters* (Chess). The cream of the prolific output of the man who did more than any other performer to shape the course of modern electric blues, one of the primary currents feeding into the rock of both the past and present.

Various Artists, *A Sun Blues Collection* (Rhino). Excellent single-disc survey of the

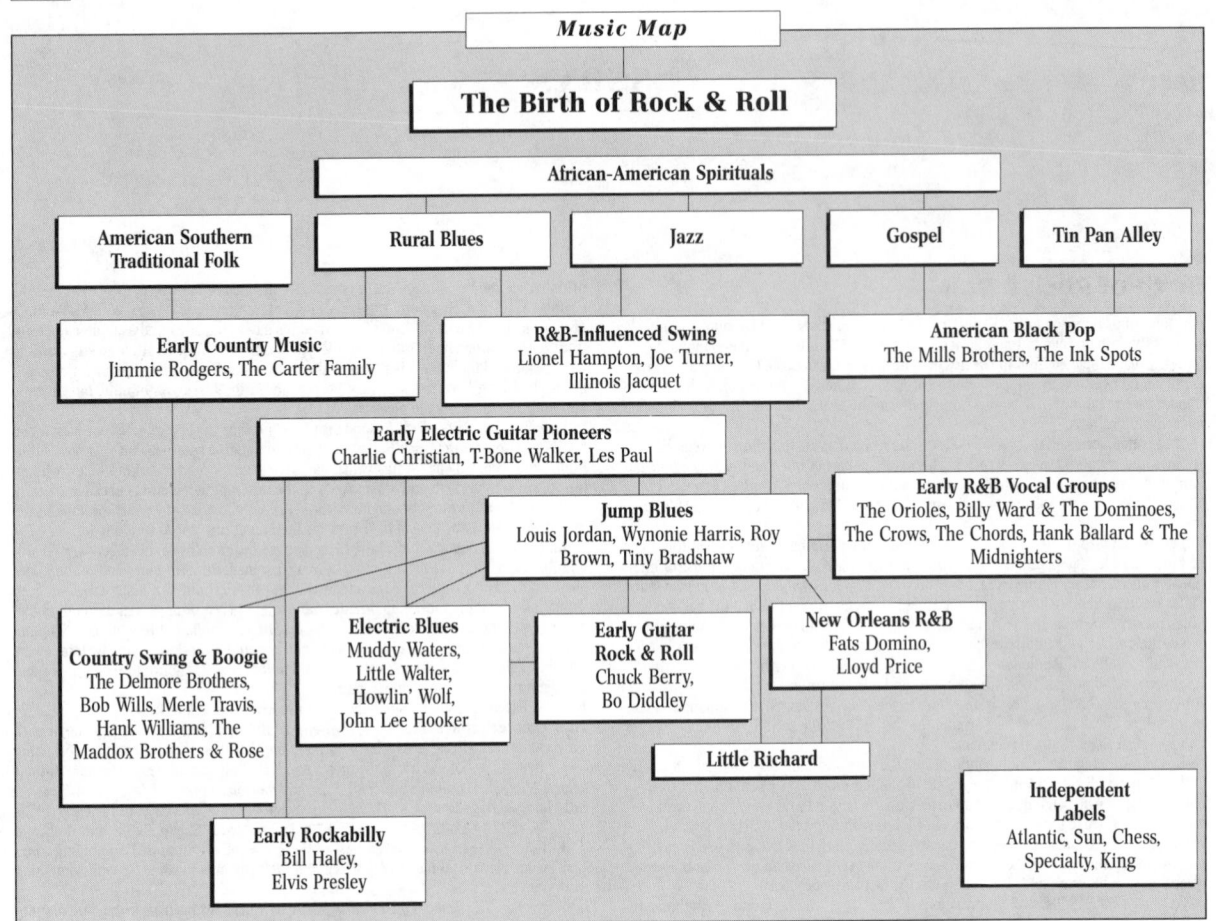

Music Map

The Birth of Rock & Roll

African-American Spirituals

American Southern Traditional Folk | **Rural Blues** | **Jazz** | **Gospel** | **Tin Pan Alley**

Early Country Music
Jimmie Rodgers, The Carter Family

R&B-Influenced Swing
Lionel Hampton, Joe Turner, Illinois Jacquet

American Black Pop
The Mills Brothers, The Ink Spots

Early Electric Guitar Pioneers
Charlie Christian, T-Bone Walker, Les Paul

Early R&B Vocal Groups
The Orioles, Billy Ward & The Dominoes, The Crows, The Chords, Hank Ballard & The Midnighters

Jump Blues
Louis Jordan, Wynonie Harris, Roy Brown, Tiny Bradshaw

Country Swing & Boogie
The Delmore Brothers, Bob Wills, Merle Travis, Hank Williams, The Maddox Brothers & Rose

Electric Blues
Muddy Waters, Little Walter, Howlin' Wolf, John Lee Hooker

Early Guitar Rock & Roll
Chuck Berry, Bo Diddley

New Orleans R&B
Fats Domino, Lloyd Price

Little Richard

Independent Labels
Atlantic, Sun, Chess, Specialty, King

Early Rockabilly
Bill Haley, Elvis Presley

---

electrified country blues that the Sun label specialized in before moving to rockabilly, with great early and mid-'50s sides by Rufus Thomas, B.B. King, James Cotton, and others.

Various Artists, *A Sun Country Collection* (Rhino). The other side of the Sun equation has the country side of the Sun equation by Johnny Cash, Carl Perkins, Jerry Lee Lewis, Warren Smith, Charlie Feathers, and more obscure performers.

Elvis Presley, *The Complete Sun Sessions* (RCA). The full-fledged birth of rockabilly on Elvis' legendary 1954-55 recordings, which in the eyes of some critics have never been surpassed in the entire history of rock & roll.

Books:
What Was the First Rock & Roll Record?, by Jim Dawson & Steve Propes (1992, Faber & Faber)
Unsung Heroes of Rock & Roll, by Nick Tosches (1984, Charles Scribner's Sons)
The Sound of the City, by Charlie Gillett (1983, Pantheon)

—*Richie Unterberger*

Early Rhythm & Blues

When rhythm & blues began in the mid-'40s, it didn't even have a name. When the term caught on, though, it caught on in a big way. Right up until the present day, R&B has come to refer to the entire world of black popular music, although it's mostly identified as R&B—rather than rap, soul, or urban contemporary—by specialized audiences and music industry insiders, not general fans.

In its earliest form, rhythm & blues was among the most important precursors of rock & roll, if not THE most important. Early rock & roll is basically R&B blended with country & western and pop influences. R&B wasn't only a crucial bridge between blues and rock & roll, but between blues and soul, R&B's longest-lived and most important offshoot.

The blues, of course, was a big part of rhythm and blues, but jazz was nearly as important. The earliest rhythm & blues artists emerged from the big-band and swing-jazz era. Before World War II, jazz, much more so than today, was a dance-oriented music, often featuring vocalists. Around World War II, many major jazz players began developing bebop and cool jazz, a decidedly less danceable (though equally worthy) style; economic

factors, as well as the draft and wartime restrictions on travel, made big bands less viable. Audiences, especially the rapidly growing metropolitan African-American communities, still wanted dance music. The musicians accomodated them by playing louder, more electric instruments, and accentuating riffs, boogies, and vocals.

The first popular style of rhythm & blues is often referred to as "jump" blues. From jazz, jump blues took its horn-driven lineup and swing rhythms; from blues, it took its general riffs and chord structures. Cab Calloway was perhaps the most important precursor of the style, but in jump blues, the vocals were harsher, the rhythms faster. The instrumentation was different, too; the pianos pounded harder, and, most important, the saxes didn't just blow, but honked and squealed.

The most important and popular jump blues star was Louis Jordan, whose records, unusually for the era, enjoyed success with both black and white audiences; he was a particularly big influence on Chuck Berry. Many of the early jump blues performers emerged from Los Angeles, where a large black community had been growing during the Depression and the war; most other big cities had jump blues stars of their own by the end of the 1940s. Independent labels such as L.A.'s Specialty and Alladin jump-started their success with the jump blues sound, filling a demand that the majors were basically unaware of. Joe Liggins, Tiny Bradshaw (the original performer of "The Train Kept a-Rollin'"), Amos Milburn, Camille Howard—all are largely forgotten except by record collectors, but all had huge R&B successes in the jump blues style, and ranked among the most popular black musicians of their time.

Jump blues itself came in several different styles. There were the vocalists that came to be known as the "shouters," adding energy, soul, and gospel to the more restrained brand of big-band singing. Big Joe Turner, who got his start with Kansas City jazz bands, was the most legendary link between the eras, shifting into the R&B era with ease, and even scoring some early rock & roll hits. Wynonie Harris, Roy Brown, Roy Milton, and Nappy Brown were a few of the most popular "shouters" of the late '40s and early '50s, although they aren't nearly as well remembered by history as Turner. There were also showmen, usually saxophonists, whose appeal was primarily instrumental: Big Jay McNeely, Illinois Jacquet, and Joe Houston with strong roots in jazz, drove dance crowds crazy with their acrobatic honking. And there were smoother, more urbane singers, like Charles Brown, Percy Mayfield, and Cecil Gant, who were as adept at ballads as up-tempo material.

By the time the '50s started, "race" music, as it was known within the industry, had been renamed the more appropriate "rhythm & blues" by *Billboard* magazine staff member Jerry Wexler. As an A&R man at Atlantic Records, Wexler helped shape jump blues into something with more appeal to pop listeners and teenagers. The recordings by early Atlantic stars like Ruth Brown, LaVern Baker, the first incarnation of the Drifters, and Chuck Willis (who actually began at the Okeh label) retained a strong jump blues flavor, but their rhythms, riffs, and lyrics point more clearly toward rock & roll. Indeed, Baker, and Willis managed to enjoy some success in the early rock & roll era with material that was tailored toward a younger audience. As rock & roll began to emerge in the early and mid-'50s, several distinct branches of R&B had developed that would each exert a large influence on popular music in their own rights: doo wop groups, electric blues, and New Orleans rhythm & blues. All of these subgenres are examined in greater depth in this book in essays of their own, and all would prove to have a greater and more lasting impact on rock & roll than the earlier, jazzier forms of R&B.

Still, there were quite a few performers who survived through the 1950s, and sometimes thrived, recording music that could not be called anything but R&B. Ike Turner, Ivory Joe Hunter, Faye Adams, Wynona Carr, Big Mama Thornton, Big Maybelle—none of these were straight blues artists, but their music wasn't rock & roll either. Blues singers like Bobby "Blue" Bland, Junior Parker, and Little Milton bridged electric blues and soul, but they couldn't be pigeonholed as straight rock & roll singers. Occasionally R&B performers like Johnny Otis, Screamin' Jay Hawkins, and Wilbert Harrison crossed over to the rock & roll audience with their most hook-savvy songs; Harrison's *Kansas City* audience is largely jump blues with a shuffle beat, at least until it gets to the searing electric guitar break.

Several 1950s singers began as more or less straight R&B performers, but added an earthier, more pronounced gospel and church influence than had ever been heard before. Today, we recognize the greatest of these vocalists—Ray Charles, James Brown, Jackie Wilson, Little Willie John, Johnny Ace, Jessie Belvin, and Clyde McPhatter—as the forefathers of soul. Some of them, like Charles and Brown, would indeed become soul superstars in the '60s. Others, like McPhatter and John, were unable to make the transition, due to a combination of inability to grow with the times and personal problems that proved insurmountable. R&B, though it has changed greatly since its birth, remains a crucial part of rock, soul, and rap, just below or very much above the surface.

For all of its monumental significance, and the vast critical acclaim it has belatedly received, early R&B recordings can be tough to swallow in large lumps for the neophyte. The R&B performers and labels of the '40s and '50s were concerned with entertaining, not establishing diverse artistic oeuvres, and the similar chord patterns and arrangements can be wearing on a compact disc rather than a juke box or dance floor, which is where the songs were often played in their heyday. Those investigating the genre in depth for the first time are advised to start with some general various artist samplers, and move on from there according to their degrees of interest.

15 Recommended Recordings (omitting doo wop, electric blues, New Orleans R&B, or soul collections):

Various Artists, *Blues Masters, Volume 5: Jump Blues Classics* (Rhino). The best jump blues introduction, with key cuts by Joe Turner, Wynonie Harris, Roy Brown, Tiny Bradshaw, Jay McNeely, Big Mama Thornton, Ruth Brown, and others.

Various Artists, *Blues Masters, Volume 14: More Jump Blues* (Rhino). Up to the same level as Jump Blues Classics, with tracks by Louis Jordan, LaVern Baker, Big Maybelle, Faye Adams, and many more.

Big Joe Turner, *Big, Bad & Blue: The Big Joe Turner Anthology* (Rhino). As mammoth as the man himself, this three-disc set encompasses several decades, reflecting R&B's evolution from the days of big-band jazz through rock & roll. Too extensive for the casual fan; as alternatives, there are other Turner anthologies that focus on specific phases of his career.

Louis Jordan, *The Best of Louis Jordan* (MCA). Jordan recorded a great deal of material in the 1940s and 1950s, and no collection satisfactorily encompasses all of his classics; this one is the best.

Various Artists, *Atlantic Rhythm & Blues Vol. 1-4* (Atlantic). The most important label in the development of modern R&B, this is part of a seven-volume series that goes up to 1974. There's a whole box set of them if you want to go whole hog, but the first four cover 1947-1962, before R&B had been fully renamed rock and soul.

Various Artists, *Specialty Story* (Specialty). At five discs, this is too much for non-specialists, if you'll pardon the pun. But it does offer a comprehensive survey of one of early R&B and rock & roll's most important labels, with tracks by such greats as Joe Liggins, Percy Mayfield, Roy Milton, and Lloyd Price up through early rock stars like Little Richard and Larry Williams.

Ruth Brown, *Rockin' in Rhythm: The Best of Ruth Brown* (Rhino). The singer on whom much of Atlantic's early fortune was built, this double disc contains her most popular 1950s sides.

LaVern Baker, *Soul on Fire: The Best of LaVern Baker* (Rhino). One of the most important singers to lead the transition from R&B to rock & roll.

The Drifters, *Let the Boogie-Woogie Roll: Greatest Hits (1953-1958)* (Atlantic). The first lineup of the Drifters, featuring Clyde McPhatter, could be called a doo wop group as well, but also had strong early R&B/jump blues influences.

Ike Turner, *I Like Ike: The Best of Ike Turner* (Rhino). Before joining Tina, Ike was an important talent scout, sideman, and bandleader. This collection of odds'n'ends is mostly from the 1950s, and often walks the edge between R&B and electric blues.

Ray Charles, *Birth of Soul* (Rhino). Aptly titled three-disc box of Charles' work for Atlantic in the 1950s.

Johnny Otis, *The Capitol Years* (Capitol). An enormously popular figure in R&B as a bandleader, musician, and talent scout, Otis crossed over to success in the rock market in the late '50s by adding a Bo Diddley beat. Although Otis himself preferred straight R&B, this collection of late-'50s sides is his best.

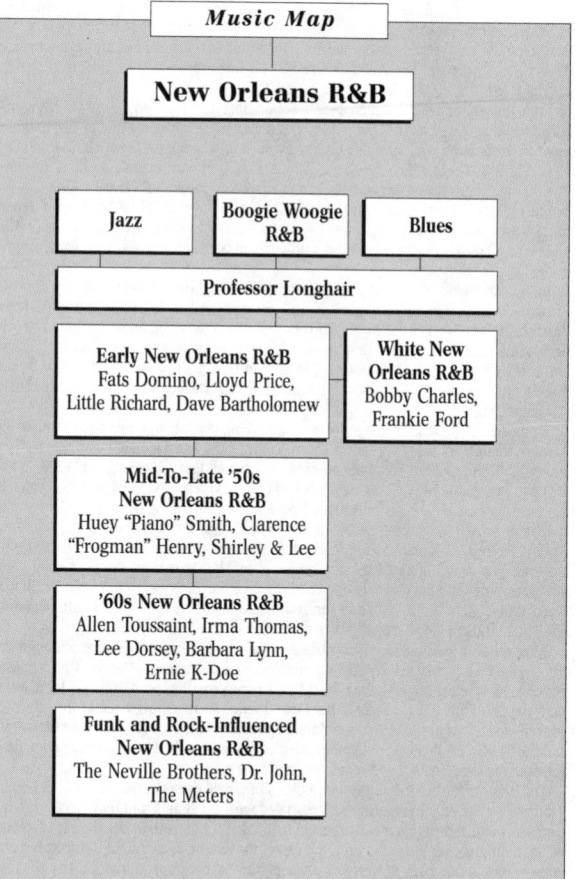

Music Map

New Orleans R&B

Jazz	Boogie Woogie R&B	Blues

Professor Longhair

Early New Orleans R&B Fats Domino, Lloyd Price, Little Richard, Dave Bartholomew	**White New Orleans R&B** Bobby Charles, Frankie Ford

Mid-To-Late '50s New Orleans R&B Huey "Piano" Smith, Clarence "Frogman" Henry, Shirley & Lee

'60s New Orleans R&B Allen Toussaint, Irma Thomas, Lee Dorsey, Barbara Lynn, Ernie K-Doe

Funk and Rock-Influenced New Orleans R&B The Neville Brothers, Dr. John, The Meters

Little Willie John, *Fever: The Best of Little Willie John* (Rhino). One of R&B's most versatile vocalists and a huge influence on James Brown.

Clyde McPhatter, *Deep Sea Ball: The Best of Clyde McPhatter* (Rhino). His biggest hits for Atlantic in the late '50s, after he left the Drifters.

James Brown, *Roots of a Revolution* (PolyGram). A double-CD retrospective of 1956-1964 recordings, bringing us from hardcore R&B to the verge of the birth of funk.

—Richie Unterberger

New Orleans R&B

When it comes down to naming which American city contributed most to the birth of rock & roll, it really only comes down to two: Memphis and New Orleans. New Orleans, of course, already occupied a rarefied place in the legacy of American popular music for its crucial role in the birth of jazz music. Its contribution to rock & roll was nearly equal in stature, supplying the music with many of its bedrock rhythms, as well as much of its playful humor. Its population, a vibrant mix of Creole, Cajun, black, and white cultures, cultivated precisely the kind of melting pot of music that led to the early styles of rock & roll.

The early New Orleans sound was characterized by boogie piano, honking saxes, and relaxed, unfettered performances. Pianist Professor Longhair embodies the true sound of New Orleans for some listeners, but it wasn't established as a major commercial force until the emergence of Fats Domino. His 1950 single "The Fat Man" is one of the dozens of performances routinely cited as one of the first rock & roll records. It took a while for Fats to cross over to the pop audience, but once he did, starting with 1955's "Ain't That a Shame," he became one of the most popular early rock & roll performers, rolling off hit after hit for the next half-dozen years.

Another Crescent City candidate for the title of first rock & roll record was Lloyd Price's "Lawdy Miss Clawdy," a 1952 number one R&B hit. Price's late-'50s hits had a much more commercial sound, but his early work was much rawer and influenced his label, the L.A.-based Specialty Records, to move its focus from jump blues to rock & roll. Their biggest star was Little Richard, a Georgia native who didn't find his groove until he started recording in New Orleans, reeling off a batch of hugely influential hit singles in the mid-'50s that helped define early rock & roll with their wooly vocals, pounding piano, and shrieking horns.

The chief behind-the-scenes architect of the New Orleans sound was Dave

Bartholomew, a trumpeter, songwriter, and producer who graced many early classic New Orleans R&B/rock sessions, not the least of which were those of Fats Domino (whose hits Bartholomew co-wrote). Session players like drummer Earl Palmer and saxophonists Alvin "Red" Tyler and Lee Allen also played on numerous sessions, and were instrumental in putting the stamp on the early New Orleans sound.

Little Richard and Fats Domino were the only superstars to emerge from the city's rock & roll scene in the 1950s, but there were also many artists with only one or two national hits that recorded a wealth of fine material (much of which gave them sizable regional hits). Shirley & Lee ("Let the Good Times Roll"), Huey "Piano" Smith ("Rocking Pneumonia & the Boogie-Woogie Flu"), and Clarence "Frogman" Henry ("Ain't Got No Home") all recorded classics which continue to live at the heart of the rock & roll repertoire. Most of the music was recorded by blacks, but Bobby Charles ("See You Later Alligator") and Frankie Ford ("Sea Cruise") proved that whites could also rock convincingly in the New Orleans style.

In the early '60s, the New Orleans sound updated slightly to reflect trends in the still-young soul scene. Pianist, songwriter, and producer Allen Toussaint inherited Dave Bartholomew's crown as the city's chief rock & roll visionary. Again, while there were no stars of the magnitude of Fats Domino or Little Richard there were many classic hits and non-hits by the likes of Ernie K-Doe ("Mother-In-Law"), Chris Kenner ("I Like It Like That"), the Showmen ("It Will Stand"), Barbara George ("I Know"), and Benny Spellman ("Fortune Teller").

Some of the New Orleans performers emerging during this period proved to be durable, though not superstars. Irma Thomas may be the finest female New Orleans R&B singer of all time, not to mention one of the finest soul-R&B singers of any kind; in addition to her classic early New Orleans ballads, she also recorded great pop/rock sides in L.A. and "deep soul" tracks with the Muscle Shoals rhythm section. Lee Dorsey had charming novelty-tinged hits with "Ya Ya," "Working in a Coal Mine," and "Ride Your Pony." Clarence "Frogman" Henry roared back into the charts in the early '60s with several singles in a sort of updated Fats Domino style. The Dixie Cups ran off several great girl group singles in the mid-'60s, one of which, "Iko Iko," was a variation on a traditional Mardi Gras Indian chant. Barbara Lynn recorded many early soul singles, although only one, "You'll Lose a Good Thing," was a big national smash.

After the mid-'60s, national New Orleans R&B hits were relatively rare, although the city continued to house a lively music scene. The most influential latter-day Crescent City performers were the Meters, who mixed New Orleans rhythms with funk; Dr. John, a session player with extensive roots in the New Orleans scene dating back to the late '50s, who created a sort of mystic voodoo-tinged updating of the vintage New Orleans sound; and the Neville Brothers, a prodigiously talented family who had been releasing fine R&B and soul records, together and separately, since the mid-'50s.

The New Orleans sound may not be a big commercial presence nowadays—the Neville Brothers are the only big touring act associated with the sound, and they've never delivered the classic record that critics expect of their talents. But truth to tell, the city can carry on its traditions with little help from the rest of the nation, as many R&B musicians continue to base themselves in New Orleans and play to a regional audience. The city also continues to feature dozens of its R&B, blues, and rock performers in the massive New Orleans Jazz festival, which attracts huge crowds from around the world every year.

13 Most Essential New Orleans R&B Recordings:
Various Artists, *A History of New Orleans Rhythm & Blues Vol. 1-3* (Rhino)
Fats Domino, *My Blue Heaven: Best of Fats Domino* (EMI)
Little Richard, *18 Greatest Hits* (Rhino)
Lee Dorsey, *Holy Cow!: Best of Lee Dorsey* (Arista)
Dr. John, *Anthology* (Rhino)
Irma Thomas, *Time Is on My Side (The Best Of Irma Thomas), Vol. 1* (EMI)
Lloyd Price, *Lawdy!* (Specialty)
The Neville Brothers, *Treacherous—A History of the Neville Brothers (1955-1985)* (Rhino)
The Meters, *Funkify Your Life: The Meters Anthology* (Rhino)
Professor Longhair, *Fess: Professor Longhair Anthology* (Rhino)
Dave Bartholomew, *Spirit of New Orleans* (EMI)
Huey "Piano" Smith, *Rock & Roll Revival* (Ace, UK)
Various Artists, *Crescent City Soul: The Sound of New Orleans* (EMI)

—Richie Unterberger

Doo Wop

"Doo wop"—the words bring smiles to the faces of most knowledgeable rock listeners. In some cases, they're smirks of derision, from those who feel that the form exemplifies rock & roll at its most innocuous, silliest, and embarrassingly quaint. From those who grew up during the '50s, it's more likely a smile of pleasure from someone who treasures the exquisite vocal harmonies and mourns the loss of the utter lack of pretension and guile that characterized great doo wop recordings.

Love it or hate it, doo wop is a major part of rock & roll's lexicon. The rhythm & blues ballads and up-tempo numbers of doo wop are characterized by those harmonies, of course, but also by the nonsense syllables that often formed the backbone of the backup vocals. "Doo wop" was just one of those common phrases; "bop-bop, dip-dip," "bomp-a-bomp-bomp-bomp, bum-dang-a-dang-dang," "wah wah, shoop shoop," "dooby dooby doo," and "yip-yip-yip-yip-yip-yip-yip-yip" were just a few of the others. Usually they were love songs, but often they were outrageous comic novelty tunes as well. They were early rock & roll at its most sentimental and humorous. Doo wop—like all great African-American music—has much of its roots in the harmonies and emotive phrasing of gospel. The more pop-oriented side of the equation was provided by the first popular American black vocal

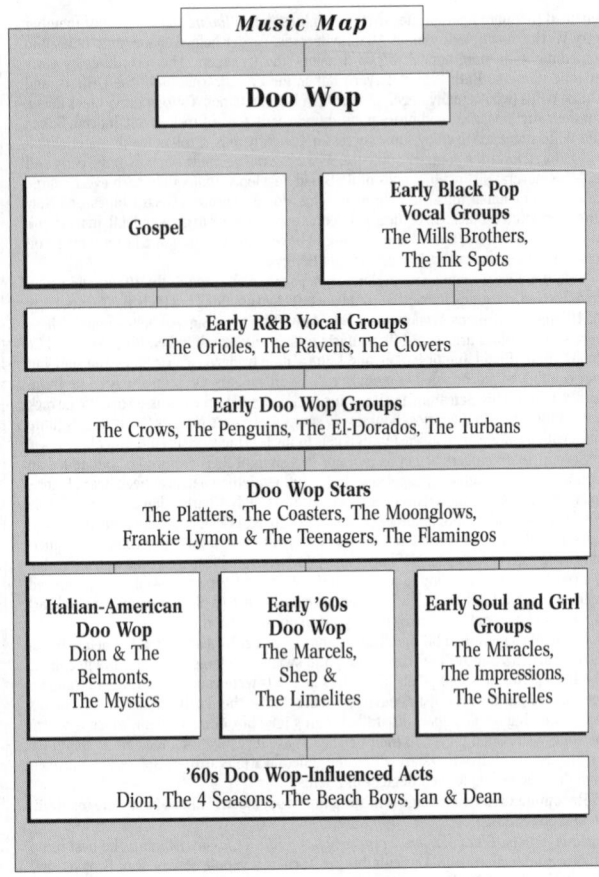

Music Map

Doo Wop

Gospel	Early Black Pop Vocal Groups The Mills Brothers, The Ink Spots

Early R&B Vocal Groups
The Orioles, The Ravens, The Clovers

Early Doo Wop Groups
The Crows, The Penguins, The El-Dorados, The Turbans

Doo Wop Stars
The Platters, The Coasters, The Moonglows, Frankie Lymon & The Teenagers, The Flamingos

Italian-American Doo Wop Dion & The Belmonts, The Mystics	Early '60s Doo Wop The Marcels, Shep & The Limelites	Early Soul and Girl Groups The Miracles, The Impressions, The Shirelles

'60s Doo Wop-Influenced Acts
Dion, The 4 Seasons, The Beach Boys, Jan & Dean

groups, the Ink Spots and the Mills Brothers Adding a rhythm & blues flavor to this blueprint, as well as a strong "church" feel, the Orioles had a number one R&B hit in 1948 with "It's Too Soon to Know," which is often cited as the first doo wop (and sometimes, even the first rock & roll) record.

Several groups followed in the Orioles' style over the next few years, including the Ravens the Cardinals, and the Larks (many of the early doo wop acts named themselves after birds). The Clovers drew more explicitly from rhythm & blues, and the snappier rhythms and saucier lyrics of jump blues infiltrated the form in recordings by the Dominoes (featuring Clyde McPhatter) and Hank Ballard & the Midnighters.

By 1954, singles by the Crows ("Gee"), Dominoes, Orioles and Hank Ballard had crossed over from the R&B market to become bona fide pop chart hits. Numerous urban vocal groups sprang up—a lot of them probably did start on the street corner, as legend would have it—and numerous record companies rushed to get a piece of the action. As rock & roll gained momentum, doo wop become brassier, with more honking sax solos, outrageous stuttering vocal interplay, and more explicitly teenage and young adult themes.

There were probably over a thousand groups that eventually cut a doo wop record over the next decade, leading to a vociferous collector community that probably ranks as the most devoted of its kind in rock & roll. A great many of the records originated in New York, though Los Angeles and Philadelphia were also active centers, and scattered doo wop acts were active, in the studio and otherwise, across the country.

Most of the doo wop groups, if they made it onto the charts at all, were one or two-shot acts, quickly fading into obscurity after failing to secure follow-ups. The Penguins, the Five Satins, the Monotones, the El Dorados, the Dell Vikings, the Silhouettes—these are just a few of those glorious names, though in some cases they recorded some non-hit efforts that were nearly as fine as their smashes.

There were also a few groups that managed to maintain a presence on the R&B and pop charts for a few years running, sometimes with numerous personnel changes. The Clovers the Flamingos, Little Anthony & the Imperials, and the Moonglows were a few of the best. With the Teenagers, Frankie Lymon pioneered a brand of pre-teen soul that was rightfully pinpointed as an influence on Michael Jackson when the Jackson 5 emerged many years later. Before Clyde McPhatter left to become a solo act, the first incarnation of the Drifters was one of the most popular R&B acts of the mid-'50s.

At the top of the pyramid were a couple groups that ranked among the most popular early rock & rollers. The Platters were one of the most pop-oriented of all of the doo wop

```
                          ┌─────────────────────────┐
                          │       Music Map         │
                          └─────────────────────────┘

                          ┌─────────────────────────┐
                          │       Rockabilly        │
                          └─────────────────────────┘

┌────────────────────────┐  ┌───────────────────────┐  ┌──────────────────────┐
│ Country Swing and Boogie│  │  Jump Blues Shouters  │  │    Electric Blues    │
│ Bob Wills, The Delmore  │  │ Wynonie Harris, Roy   │  │ Howlin' Wolf, Junior │
│  Brothers, The Maddox   │  │        Brown          │  │ Parker, Arthur "Big  │
│    Brothers & Rose      │  │                       │  │    Boy" Crudup       │
└────────────────────────┘  └───────────────────────┘  └──────────────────────┘

┌───────────────────────────────────────────────────────────────────────────┐
│                       Bill Haley and His Comets                            │
└───────────────────────────────────────────────────────────────────────────┘

┌───────────────────────────────────────────────────────────────────────────┐
│                            The Sun Sound                                    │
│ Elvis Presley, Carl Perkins, Jerry Lee Lewis, Billy Lee Riley, Roy Orbison  │
└───────────────────────────────────────────────────────────────────────────┘

┌──────────────────────────────────┐  ┌──────────────────────────────────────┐
│       Early Rockabilly Stars     │  │           L.A. Rockabilly            │
│ Gene Vincent, Buddy Holly, Wanda │  │       Eddie Cochran, Ricky Nelson    │
│ Jackson, Dale Hawkins, Johnny    │  │                                      │
│           Burnette               │  │                                      │
└──────────────────────────────────┘  └──────────────────────────────────────┘
```

groups, and appealed to the adult audience more than almost any of the early major rock & roll acts. The Coasters were among the wittiest rock groups of any era, courtesy of Jerry Lieber and Mike Stoller who penned and produced many classic songs for the singers, including "Searchin'," "Young Blood," "Yakety Yak," and "Poison Ivy."

As the '50s progressed, more and more white performers sang doo wop, sometimes in integrated ensembles (such as the Dell Vikings and the Impalas), sometimes as all-White groups (the Mystics, Dion & the Belmonts). Often Italian-American in origin, by the time the '60s began, these white singers were a major part of the form, which was becoming less of a commercial force.

But before doo wop vanished from the charts altogether, it underwent a revival of sorts in the early '60s, which saw huge doo wop hits by the likes of the Marcels the Capris, Maurice Williams and Shep & the Limelites. By the time of the British Invasion, though, there was barely a ripple of pure doo wop to be found on the charts.

Doo wop did not vanish so much as become permanently absorbed into rock and soul. Early soul giants like the Miracles and the Impressions owed huge debts to doo wop; indeed, their early records pretty much are doo wop. A lot of doo wop could be heard in the girl groups of the early '60s. Many hits by the Four Seasons and Dion were doo wop in construction, if not always in production. In vocal surf music, there's no doubt that doo wop was a prime influence on the ensemble singing of the Beach Boys and Jan & Dean. You can also hear it in the early records by the Beatles and several other British Invasion groups, as well as many of Frank Zappa's satirical efforts. And right on up to Boyz II Men soul music has built upon the harmonies and vocal arrangements of doo wop music.

12 Most Essential Doo Wop Recordings:

Various Artists, *The Doo Wop Box, Vol. 1-2* (Rhino)

Billy Ward & the Dominoes, *Sixty Minute Men: The Best of Billy Ward & His Dominoes* (Rhino)

Hank Ballard & the Midnighters, *Sexy Ways: The Best of Hank Ballard & the Midnighters* (Rhino)

The Drifters, *The Boogie Woogie Roll—Greatest Hits (1953-1958)* (Atlantic)

The Platters, *Magic Touch: An Anthology* (Mercury)

Frankie Lymon & the Teenagers, *Best of Frankie Lymon & the Teenagers* (Rhino)

Dion & the Belmonts, *Everything You Always Wanted to Hear by Dion & the Belmonts* (Laurie)

The Coasters, *50 Coastin' Classics* (Rhino)

The Clovers, *Down In The Alley: The Best of the Clovers* (Atlantic)

The Moonglows, *Blue Velvet: The Ultimate Collection* (Chess)

Various Artists, *The Best of Doo Wop Uptempo Vol. 1, The Best of Doo Wop Uptempo Vol. 2* (Rhino)

Various Artists, *The Best of Doo Wop Ballads Vol. 1, The Best of Doo Wop Ballads Vol. 2* (Rhino):

Books:

Doo Wop: The Forgotten Third of Rock & Roll, by Dr. Anthony Gribin & Dr. Matthew Shiff (Krause Publications, 1992)

They All Sang on the Corner, by Phillip Groia (Phillie Dee Enterprises, 1983)

                                          —*Richie Unterberger*

Rockabilly

If rock & roll can be called the child of rhythm and blues and country & western music, no style is a purer blend than rockabilly. The first form of rock & roll performed by white

musicians, its duration of mass popularity was brief, but the best of it remains among the most exciting and frenetic rock & roll ever waxed.

Even in the segregated American South of the early 20th century, blacks and whites often had cause to interact with each other on a daily basis. The interaction carried over to music, and White hillbilly country performers have reflected the influence of the blues and other African-American music since they began recording, as a listen to Jimmie Rodgers will attest to. Just as blues became jazzier, faster, and more electric throughout the 1940s and early '50s, so did country, through swing bands like Bob Wills and the Maddox Brothers. The Delmore Brothers, starting as a more traditional hillbilly harmony act, anticipated much of rockabilly's mania when they added a thumping country boogie beat to the equation on their finest recordings in the late '40s. Nearly forgotten performers like Arthur Smith and Hardrock Gunter laid down country boogie sides that brought the guitar to the forefront.

Considering that most rockabilly musicians of importance came from the South, it's ironic that the first records that could be termed as honest-to-god rockabilly were issued by a Northerner, Bill Haley. The Philadelphian had been pursuing a hillbilly career with generally dismal results until 1951, when he covered Jackie Brenston's "Rocket 88" (which is itself often cited as one of the very first rock & roll records). Although they aren't nearly as well known as his huge rock & roll hits like "Rock Around the Clock," the sides he cut for the small Essex label between 1951 and 1954 are groundbreaking early rockabilly; the 1952 single "Rock the Joint," in fact, is almost identical in melody and arrangement to "Rock Around the Clock." Haley was no Elvis vocally, and the steel guitars and jump beats of his Comets betrayed lingering influences of hillbilly and swing music. But he was undoubtedly the first to bring together R&B and C&W with such force, although nobody knew quite what to call the music at the time.

There were certainly numerous musicians in the South experimenting with primitive rockabilly-like sounds by mid-1954. Sam Phillips and his Memphis record label, Sun Records, were chiefly responsible for honing the sound and capturing it on vinyl.

Often quoted as having said that he could make a fortune with a White singer who sounded Black (though he has denied saying this in such explicit terms), he found the perfect vehicle for doing so with Elvis Presley, who recorded five singles for Sun between mid-1954 and the end of 1955. Supported by guitarist Scotty Moore and bassist Bill Black, this was rockabilly, if not rock & roll, at its best and purest; as great as his subsequent achievements were, by critical consensus this handful of 45s ranks as Elvis' finest work. Presley didn't set off a mass wave of imitators right away; he was primarily a regional sensation until his contract was bought by RCA. Sam Phillips used the money from the sale to develop his own formidable stable of rockabilly performers. Carl Perkins's "Blue Suede Shoes" almost beat Elvis's "Heartbreak Hotel" to the top of the charts, and although Perkins was never able to duplicate the success, Sun generated a wealth of great rockabilly hits and misses over the next few years by Jerry Lee Lewis, Billy Lee Riley, Sonny Burgess, Carl Mann, and Roy Orbison. The Sun Sound—echo-chamber vocals, crisp electric guitar leads, and slap-back bass—became the standard of rockabilly excellence, often imitated, never recaptured. Presleymania overran the country in 1956, setting off a wave of rockabilly recordings, nationally and (more often) regionally distributed, that was similar in some respects to the garage band explosion of a decade later. Hundreds of performers found their way into studios in Tennessee, Texas, California, and other locales, embracing the new sound with a hepped-up enthusiasm that often bordered on mania. The singles were usually crudely recorded and extremely basic and derivative, their not inconsiderable saving grace being their infectious energy.

While the Sun Sound was the pinnacle of rockabilly, several performers established legends of their own outside of Sam Phillips's studio. Gene Vincent's 1956 sides, featuring his breathy vocals and the speed-of-light guitar of Cliff Gallup from his backing band the Blue Caps, were usually brilliant. Eddie Cochran brought a sophisticated brand of teenage rebellion to his rockabilly hits, which helped pioneer the use of overdubbed guitars and vocals. Ricky Nelson recorded first-class rockabilly pop in Hollywood with the help of ace guitarist James Burton. Johnny Burnette and his trio recorded some of the raunchiest Elvis-derived rock & roll of the time, including the first rock version of "The Train Kept A-Rollin'." Dale Hawkins cut a crackling classic with "Suzy Q," and Wanda Jackson's raspy rockabilly sides rank as the finest rock & roll recorded by a female singer in the 1950s.

Rockabilly began to fade as a commercial force around 1958, not just because of fickle popular taste, but because of the rapid evolution of rock & roll itself. One of the greatest rockabilly singers, Buddy Holly, displayed a facility for melodic invention that branched into all forms of pop/rock, and had a far-reaching influence on all of pop that extended to the British Invasion. Along with the Everly Brothers and Ricky Nelson, he began gravitating towards a more gentle, melodic sound that was not as structurally limited, if not as energetic, as pure rockabilly. Elvis himself was moving toward more straightforward rock material, and then toward pop after his hitch in the Army.

Those performers that stuck with the basic rockabilly sound faced diminishing returns. Some, like Gene Vincent, simply vanished from the charts, although they maintained loyal audiences, especially overseas. Roy Orbison, never comfortable as a rockabilly singer in the first place, reinvented himself as a masterful crooner of pop/rock ballads. Jerry Lee Lewis's career was crippled by scandal. Eventually he would find success in the country & western mainstream, a path followed by many other singers who had achieved limited success with rockabilly.

Rockabilly never returned to the charts in a significant way after the '50s, though several acts have scored big hits in the style, such as Billy Swan and the Stray Cats. A huge influence on the early Beatles, Creedence Clearwater Revival, and others, rockabilly was instrumental in establishing the focus of rock & roll on the electric guitar-bass-drums combination, with a simple joy and force that has helped inspire generations of musicians.

12 Essential Rockabilly Recordings:

Elvis Presley, *King of Rock & Roll: Complete '50s Masters*
Buddy Holly, *Buddy Holly Collection*
Gene Vincent, *Capitol Collectors Series*
Carl Perkins, *Original Sun Greatest Hits*
Jerry Lee Lewis, *18 Original Sun Greatest Hits*
Johnny Burnette, *Tear It Up*
Eddie Cochran, *Legendary Masters*
Ricky Nelson, *Legendary Masters*
Wanda Jackson, *Rockin' with Wanda*
The Collins Kids, *Introducing Larry and Laurie*
Bill Haley and His Comets, *Rock the Joint!*
Various Artists, *Rock This Town Vol. 1, Rock This Town Vol. 2*

Books:

Good Rockin' Tonight: Sun Records and the Birth of Rock & Roll, by Colin Escott with Martin Hawkins (1991, St. Martin's)
Last Train to Memphis, by Peter Guralnick (1994, Little, Brown & Co.)
Elvis: The Illustrated Record, by Roy Carr & Mick Farren (1982, Harmony)
Remembering Buddy: The Definitive Biography Of Buddy Holly, by John Goldrosen and John Beecher (1987, Penguin)
The Day the World Turned Blue: A Biography of Gene Vincent, by Britt Hagarty (1984, Blandford Press, U.K.)
Ricky Nelson: Idol for a Generation, by Joel Selvin (Contemporary, 1990)

—Richie Unterberger

Rock & Roll

Ask 20 people for a definition of rock & roll and you'll get 20 different answers, for everyone has their own idea of what the music is and what it should do. And that's good, because if rock & roll could be defined with a simple, concise description, it would've died sometime in the mid-'60s. Rock & roll defies categorization: you can't trace its origins back to one particular source, you can't define its content with words like "rebellion" or "sexuality," and you can't pinpoint its sensibility with one clever catch phrase.

More than any other genre of 20th century music, rock & roll has stood the test of time on the strength of its diversity—the diversity of the countless producers, engineers, songwriters, vocalists, and musicians who create the stuff. The hierarchy in anyone's personal history of rock & roll is predestined to include dozens of eclectic names and song titles. And the things people think rock & roll should do vary as wildly as the artistic approaches of the Beatles and the Rolling Stones Some think it should be full of rebellion, anger, and venom, and they point to the early work of the Who, the Rolling Stones, or the Sex Pistols or to the rantings of some contemporary agit-popster. Others may see it as a vehicle for romantic expoundings, positing their arguments with an armful of doo wop singles and the complete works of Phil Spector. Still others may argue that the music is simply a white bastardization of black blues and R&B; these people can point to just about any post-'50s group and make a convincing argument.

But rock's origins aren't so easily defined. Many critics and historians credit Jackie Brenston's "Rocket 88," recorded in 1951 at Sam Phillips's Sun Studio in Memphis, TN, as the first "rock & roll" record. Its driving beat, over-amped guitar riffs, blaring horns, and automobile-as-sexual-metaphor theme lend weight to this theory. What about the blues-laced prewar country work of Jimmie Rodgers or the vivid imagery and pathos in the oeuvre of Hank Williams? What about the prewar and postwar gospel that provided much of the foundation for not only rock & roll but for blues, R&B, and soul? What about the swaggering jump-blues that proliferated in the Midwest and on the West Coast during the '40s and early '50s? What about the Delmore Brothers' choogling, revved-up acoustic country? What about the high, mournful wail of Bill Monroe and the Stanley Brothers? What about the raucous assault of blues pioneers such as Howlin' Wolf, Muddy Waters, Little Walter Jacobs, and Sonny Boy Williamson?

The diversity of rock's origins may explain why the Rock, Pop, & Soul chapter of the AMG is the most variegated section of the book. With over 20 critics applying their opinions and critical idiosyncrasies to the canon of 20th century popular music, the variety of music highlighted is certain to be eclectic, to say the least. Whatever your personal definition of rock & roll may be, that eclecticism is necessary, if only to give an accurate overview of what's out there. It also means, however, that not every starred or bulleted album is going to fill everyone's needs. Someone may think Michael Bolton is a pockmark on the face of contemporary pop; someone else may think he's inherited the white soulman traditions of Van Morrison or the Rascals. Whatever your opinion, in the pages of this section there's a bulleted album recorded by Bolton. We realize no one is going to agree with every critical assessment found in this chapter, and no one should; if they do, they probably aren't asserting their own personality quite as strongly as they should. And some may squabble that we've included contemporary and vintage soul, doo wop, and jump blues within the rock and pop section. But without the artists who've worked and continue to work in those genres, the rock & roll section of any book (or record store) would be considerably smaller—and far less interesting.

What this chapter should do, however, is act as a guidepost for the curious, a map to guide readers through areas of music they may not find on their own. You may already know about a lot of the music discussed here, but maybe you'll find a record that somehow slipped through the cracks of popularity. Or maybe you're interested in tracking down the finest album by an obscure New York noise band or an overlooked doo wop quintet. Odds are, you'll find them both somewhere within these pages. Keep in mind, though, that regardless of how painstakingly the All-Music editors have worked at making this a definitive portrait of what's good in rock, pop, and soul, it is not definitive—there's no way any one book ever could attain that goal. But if it makes one person purchase an album by an artist they've never heard of, if it makes somebody decide once and for all to dig into the roots of American music to find out where the Rolling Stones got all those cool old songs, the AMG has accomplished its task. You, the reader, will be the final judge of its success.

—John Floyd

Instrumental Rock

Except for a brief period at the end of the '50s and the early '60s, instrumental rock hasn't been a major commercial force. There have always been instrumental rock hits, of course, and the best instrumental rockers have acted as key inspirations to many of the best rock & roll musicians.

Even before rock & roll became the nation's dominant popular music in the mid-'50s, instrumentals were common in the R&B, jump blues, and country boogie that ranked as rock's chief ancestors. Raunchy R&B saxophonist Joe Houston and lightning-fast country boogie steel guitarist Speedy West were just two of the primarily instrumental musicians who were key influences on first generation rock & rollers. In 1956, organist Bill Doggett's "*Honky Tonk*" became the first massive instrumental hit of the rock era, although it was more notable for the sax riffs of Clifford Scott than the playing of bandleader Doggett.

The earliest rock & roll instrumental hits, such as the Champs' "Tequila," featured the sax as the lead instrument, but in 1958 Duane Eddy was responsible for changing the emphasis of instrumental rock to the guitar. With his distinctively low, twanging leads (augmented by Steve Douglas's superb saxophone), Eddy was one of the most popular singles artists of his era. His material can sound somewhat repetitious and dated these days, but he was a major influence on the next generation of rock guitarists, from George Harrison on down.

The Ventures were perhaps even more influential, offering a sleek sound with dual lead guitars and crisp drumming. A key building block of instrumental surf music, the group inspired countless nascent guitarists and were extremely popular, especially overseas, where the English language wasn't as key a component of rock music.

Link Wray, although nowhere near as successful as Eddy or the Ventures, may have been the most innovative guitarist of the era. On his 1958 hit "Rumble" and numerous excellent non-hit follow-ups, he pioneered guitar fuzz and distortion on vicious rockers. He was cited as an influence by Pete Townshend, who with several other British guitarists would take Wray's sound a few steps further in the distortion and feedback-riddled guitar leads of British Invasion and psychedelic rock.

In Southern California, Dick Dale developed a reverb-heavy sound with his Fender Telecaster that became known as "surf music."

Though relatively few surf instrumentals were big national hits (the Surfaris' "Wipe Out" and the Chantays' "Pipeline" were the biggest), the surf scene was huge in California, and of course a big influence on the Beach Boys, who (along with Jan & Dean) developed a vocal surf sound that became an important part of early- and mid-'60s rock & roll.

The years 1958-1963 were also riddled with many exciting hits, big and small, by performers who were never heard from again, or only managed to run off two or three big tunes. Besides guitarists like Santo & Johnny and Lonnie Mack drummers (Sandy Nelson, Preston Epps, Cozy Cole), organists (Dave "Baby" Cortez), saxophone-driven combos (Johnny & the Hurricanes), and even bass players (ex-Elvis Presley sideman Bill Black) got in on the act with memorable hit tunes.

Instrumental rock was already decreasing in popularity when the British Invasion overran the States, making vocalists a near necessity. In the years between the initial rock & roll explosion and the Beatles, however, instrumental performers were responsible for

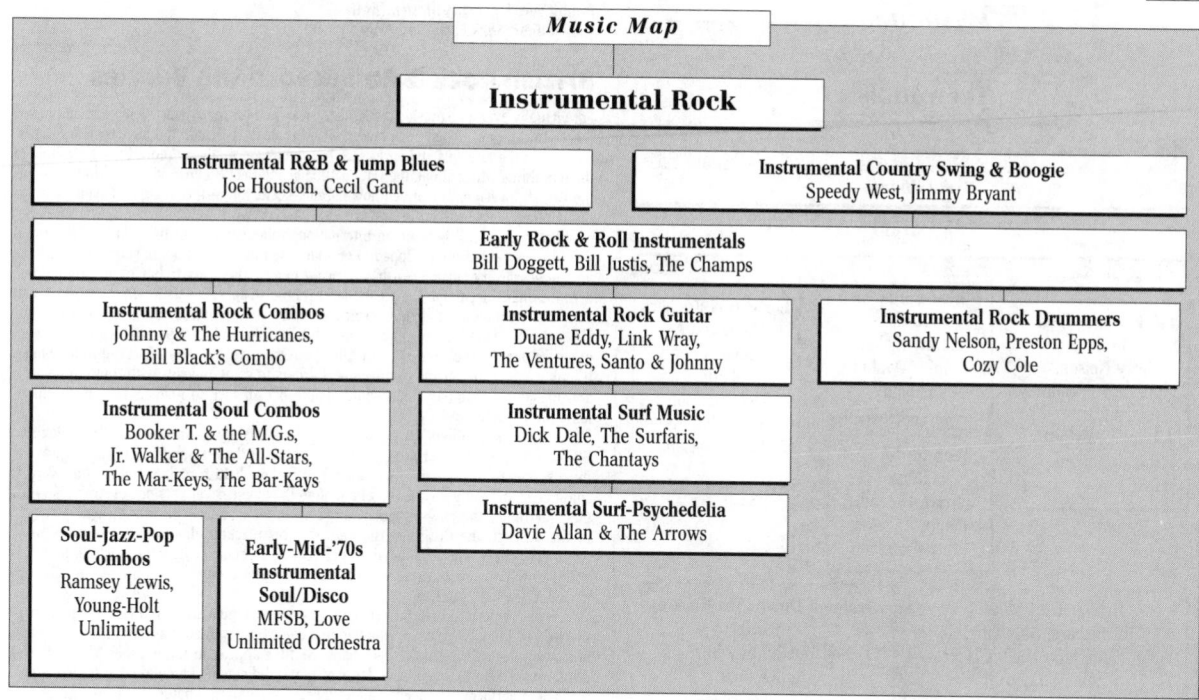

Music Map

Instrumental Rock

Instrumental R&B & Jump Blues
Joe Houston, Cecil Gant

Instrumental Country Swing & Boogie
Speedy West, Jimmy Bryant

Early Rock & Roll Instrumentals
Bill Doggett, Bill Justis, The Champs

Instrumental Rock Combos
Johnny & The Hurricanes,
Bill Black's Combo

Instrumental Rock Guitar
Duane Eddy, Link Wray,
The Ventures, Santo & Johnny

Instrumental Rock Drummers
Sandy Nelson, Preston Epps,
Cozy Cole

Instrumental Soul Combos
Booker T. & the M.G.s,
Jr. Walker & The All-Stars,
The Mar-Keys, The Bar-Kays

Instrumental Surf Music
Dick Dale, The Surfaris,
The Chantays

Soul-Jazz-Pop Combos
Ramsey Lewis,
Young-Holt
Unlimited

Early-Mid-'70s Instrumental Soul/Disco
MFSB, Love
Unlimited Orchestra

Instrumental Surf-Psychedelia
Davie Allan & The Arrows

some of the most exciting and gutsy rock & roll available. A key force in the preservation of rock's most exciting elements, instrumental rock was also hugely popular at a local level, and many musicians who wet their chops in instrumental combos went on to join, or develop into, important '60s rock groups. In any case, mid- and late-'60s rock groups never neglected instrumental rock entirely—Paul Butterfield's *East West*, the Rolling Stones' "2120 South Michigan Avenue," the Who's "Underture," Quicksilver Messenger Service's "Gold and Silver," the Yardbirds' "Jeff's Boogie," Pink Floyd's "Interstellar Overdrive," and Country Joe & the Fish's "Section 43" are only a few of the great hard rock and psychedelic instrumentals of the era. While the British Invasion is often thought of as a death knell for instrumental rock, instrumentals remained a key strand of soul music for the next decade. The most popular and influential instrumental soul combo were Booker T. & the M.G.'s. In addition to backing most of the greatest performances on the Stax/Volt label, the Memphis group also ran off a long string of marvelously taut instrumental hits of their own. The Mar-Keys and the Bar-Kays were also popular instrumental exponents of the Memphis soul sound. Saxophonist Junior Walker took Motown to its grittiest extremes on his instrumentals (though he often used vocals as well).

There was also no shortage of one-shot soul instrumental hits. Cliff Nobles ("The Horse"), jazzman Hugh Masekela ("Grazing in the Grass"), Billy Preston ("Outa-Space"), Love Unlimited Orchestra ("Love's Theme"), MFSB ("TSOP"), and the Average White Band ("Pick up the Pieces") all had mammoth pop hits with soul instrumentals, although these groups by and large didn't limit their material to instrumentals exclusively. Ramsey Lewis developed a breed of soul-jazz-pop in the mid-'60s, as did his ex-sidemen Young-Holt Unlimited who hit the Top Ten when they added a lot of straight funk and came up with "Soulful Strut."

While rock and soul instrumentals haven't been nearly as prevalent in the 1980s and '90s as they were in earlier decades, instrumentals will always be a presence in the music, as surprise hit singles and a testament to the power of guitars, saxophones, drums, and other instruments to move listeners without the benefit of vocals.

12 Most Important Instrumental Rock Albums:
Various Artists, *Rock Instrumental Classics, Vol. 1: The '50s* (Rhino)
Various Artists, *Rock Instrumental Classics, Vol. 2: The '60s* (Rhino)
Various Artists, *Rock Instrumental Classics, Vol. 3: The '70s* (Rhino)
Various Artists, *Rock Instrumental Classics, Vol. 4: Soul* (Rhino)
Various Artists, *Rock Instrumental Classics, Vol. 5: Surf* (Rhino)
Duane Eddy, *Twang Thang: The Anthology* (Rhino)
Link Wray, *Rumble! The Best of Link Wray* (Rhino)
The Ventures, *Walk, Don't Run: The Best of the Ventures* (EMI)
Booker T. & the M.G.'s, *The Very Best of Booker T. & the M.G.'s* (Rhino)
Booker T. & the M.G.'s, *Best of Booker T. & the M.G.'s* (Fantasy)
Dick Dale, *King of Surf Guitar: Best of Dick Dale* (Rhino)
Various Artists, *Guitar Player Presents Legends of Guitar, Surf: Vol. 1* (Rhino)
—Richie Unterberger

Teen Idols

To many avid rock historians, the teen idols—who were firmly entrenched on the top of the charts between the death of Buddy Holly and the rise of the Beatles—represent the greatest threat to rock's survival that the music ever weathered. Wimpy, overwhelmingly bland and safe, their connection to rock & roll was often tenuous, and their commercial ascendancy has even been discussed as a conspiracy by the music business and sundry other moral authorities to rob rock & roll of its vitality.

In retrospect, that seems fairly unlikely, though there's no doubt that the more conservative elements of the entertainment industry and the status quo as a whole felt more comfortable with these performers. Owing as much or more to traditional Tin Pan Alley and middle-of-the-road values than pure rock & roll, their massive success nonetheless didn't come close to stamping out the forces that gave birth to the explosive soul, surf, and British Invasion sounds that reclaimed the airwaves after only a few years.

"Teen idols" were by no means a phenomenon that began with the rock & roll era; bobbysoxers had been pining to the sound of mainstream pop crooners for a good decade or more before Elvis hit the scene. As far as rock was concerned, the original teen idol was Pat Boone, whose first hits were bowdlerized versions of classic rockers by Little Richard and Fats Domino. As Greg Shaw wittily pointed out in *The Rolling Stone Illustrated History of Rock & Roll*, Boone "began as a safe alternative to Elvis, and is still a safe alternative to just about everything."

The first two teen idols to achieve mass success after Boone could hardly have possibly defined the polar extremes of the genre better. There was Paul Anka, whose early hits were mainstream ballads with mild rock & roll trimmings, and who exemplified the style at its most operatic and melodramatic. Then there was Ricky Nelson, whose success was virtually guaranteed by his popular weekly TV series, and whose rockabilly records were better than they had any right to be.

The Philadelphia teen idols of the late '50s—Bobby Rydell, Frankie Avalon, and Fabian—patterned themselves after Anka much more than Nelson. Recorded on the local Cameo-Parkway, Chancellor, and Swan labels, they were launched into national success with regular appearances on American Bandstand, hosted by Dick Clark, who sometimes held financial interests in the record companies of the singers he pushed in this manner. Rydell, at least, could sing; few would contest that Avalon and Fabian were promoted more on their appearance than their limited vocal abilities, and both would move into movies and television work as their chief focus after their initial musical success.

It worked the other way around as well, of course; established teenage television stars with meager vocal abilities were hustled into recording studios to capitalize on their screen images. Ex-Mouseketeer Annette Funicello became one of the first big female teen idols in this fashion, and Ed "Kookie" Byrnes, Connie Stevens, Johnny Crawford, James Darren, and Shelley Fabares also got onto the hit parade after they were already established TV performers. Artistically, this was the weakest wing of the teen idol genre; unsuited for singing in the first place, their material often sank to the level of drivel, with a few unexpected choice items thrown in, usually from Brill Building songwriters.

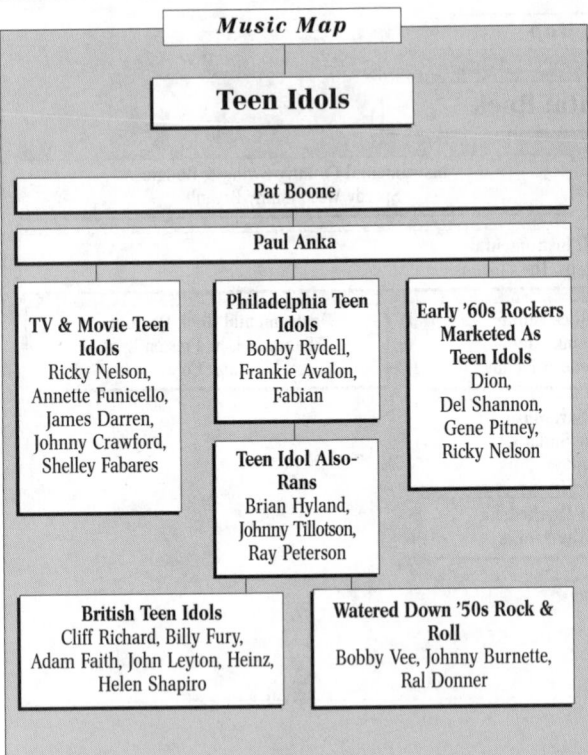

Music Map

Teen Idols

Pat Boone

Paul Anka

TV & Movie Teen Idols
Ricky Nelson, Annette Funicello, James Darren, Johnny Crawford, Shelley Fabares

Philadelphia Teen Idols
Bobby Rydell, Frankie Avalon, Fabian

Early '60s Rockers Marketed As Teen Idols
Dion, Del Shannon, Gene Pitney, Ricky Nelson

Teen Idol Also-Rans
Brian Hyland, Johnny Tillotson, Ray Peterson

British Teen Idols
Cliff Richard, Billy Fury, Adam Faith, John Leyton, Heinz, Helen Shapiro

Watered Down '50s Rock & Roll
Bobby Vee, Johnny Burnette, Ral Donner

Bobby Vee, *Legendary Masters* (EMI)
Ral Donner, *She's Everything* (Murray Hill)

—*Richie Unterberger*

British Rock & Roll Before the Beatles

For virtually everyone outside the British Isles—and for many who were born and raised there—the story of British rock begins with the Beatles. Britain did have rock & roll performers in the late '50s and early '60s, but they were really no more than a footnote to the real thing, which shook the U.K. in 1963 as the Beat Boom, and the world in 1964 as the British Invasion. This little-known scene has its interest, though, and even its gems, though they're few and far between.

When rock & roll became an international phenomenon in the mid-'50s, Britain, it would seem, was more equipped to emulate the music on its home shores than almost any other country outside North America. After all, the primary barrier to singing rock & roll is linguistic, and as the second-largest English-speaking nation in the world, Great Britain at least didn't have that obstacle to worry about. But the indigenous music of the U.K., with the possible exception of British Isles folk, had little parallel with the stew of blues, country, gospel, and Tin Pan Alley pop that gave birth to rock & roll in the States. It took a long time for the country's performers to come to grips with these influences, and master a vocabulary that would enable British rock to hold its own in the international marketplace.

British rock & rollers sprang up almost immediately in the wake of Bill Haley and Elvis Presley, Wee Willie Harris is usually credited as the first, and Tommy Steele was the most successful of the very first batch. The earliest British rock & roll records were, it could be said, hardly rock & roll at all; often they were cover versions of American rock hits that framed the songs in much more conventional and saccharine pop arrangements. In this respect, the British music industry was reacting along similar lines as some American labels, who responded to rock & roll's ascendancy by whitewashing R&B hits with sterile pop covers, or developed teen idols whose music was only marginally connected to the real thing.

A more important British development was the popularity of skiffle, principally popularized by Lonnie Donegan, who had first come to prominence as a traditional jazz and blues performer in Chris Barber's band. Skiffle's appeal, in the manner of garage and punk music right to the present day, was that it didn't take a great deal of technical proficiency to perform: you needed a few chords on guitar and banjo, a washboard for percussion, and a repertoire of a few folk songs. Donegan was a hugely successful singer in the late '50s in Britain (his "Rock Island Line" was also a big hit in the States), and many of the skiffle groups he inspired, such as the Quarrymen (soon to become the Beatles), would become key players in the British Invasion. Another Chris Barber sideman, Alexis Korner, would become mentor to key figures of blues and R&B-based rock groups of the Rolling Stones, Kinks, Yardbirds, and others, though his contributions really fall beyond the scope of pre-Beatle British rock.

In the meantime, however, the teenagers in these skiffle bands had to suffer through bland pop/rock, or a bland facsimile of such, on their own hit parade. The most popular of the early British rock singers was Cliff Richard, a sort of mini-Elvis who actually managed some respectable rock & roll on his earliest singles in the late '50s, especially on his debut hit, "Move It." He was backed by the Shadows, a tight unit who scored many instrumental hits on their own, emphasizing spare, precise (one might even say clean-cut) riffs.

Cliff Richard and the Shadows are remembered fondly by many in British rock circles, and Shadows guitarist Hank Marvin is cited as an influence by many British guitar heroes. But listening to their peak output several decades later, one suspects that this may be more due to nostalgia than quality; the overwhelming majority of their repertoire consists of watered-down derivations of American pop, pop/rock, and instrumental rock. Shadows bassist Jet Harris, sometimes in collaboration with Shadows drummer Tony Meehan, did have some nifty, growling instrumental hits just before the Beatles broke.

There were quite a few British teen idols in the late '50s and early '60s, usually with fanciful show-business names such as Johnny Gentle, Marty Wilde, Vince Eager, Adam Faith, and Duffy Power (the last of which, surprisingly, turned out to be a decent cult blues-rock performer in the '60s). Like their American cousins, they were innocent and harmless to the point of dopiness. The best of them, Billy Fury, managed to cut some fair, and self-penned, approximations of American rockabilly on his 1960 LP *Sound of Fury* with the help of guitarist Joe Brown (who would have some hits of his own in the early '60s). Fury was also an inspiration to Malcolm McLaren when he was casting about to form the Sex Pistols, but again, one suspects nostalgia as an ingredient for this latter-day respect; Fury was a competent singer, but he too went heavy on the drippy ballads for the hit parade, and as a rockabilly singer, he would have been an also-ran in the States.

Amidst all the dross, there were some genuine fierce British rockers in these dark days. Tony Sheridan, though he never got a chance to adequately showcase his talents on record, was of course an inspiration to the early Beatles, who backed him on several German recordings. Vince Taylor managed a couple respectable Gene Vincent-type numbers, most notably "Brand New Cadillac."

The best by far, though, and indeed the best pre-Beatle British rockers by a wide margin, were Johnny Kidd & the Pirates. Their late-'50s and early-'60s singles were tough, rockabilly-influenced performances that came off as a cross between Jerry Lee Lewis and Gene Vincent. Kidd was also an underappreciated factor in establishing the dominance of guitar in '60s British rock; several of his songs featured superbly menacing riffs from session players like Joe Moretti that were quite advanced for their time, especially the one from "Shakin' All Over," perhaps the only true pre-Beatle classic of British rock, and the only one which became a rock standard (in versions by the Who, Guess Who, and others).

A great many teen idol singers had one or two big hits in this era without establishing a long recording career. Mark Dinning ("Teen Angel") and Ray Peterson ("Tell Laura I Love Her") capitalized on the short-lived vogue for teen death melodrama; Troy Shondell, Johnny Tillotson, Brian Hyland, and even a young Tony Orlando were merely some of the more successful of the legions of young faces who were packaged for the young, middle-class, white, predominantly teenage audience in this era.

Then there were the singers who happened to be packaged as teen idols, but who were probably good enough to have succeeded anyway. Dion, Gene Pitney, and Del Shannon, as well as Ricky Nelson, all fall in this category; their music sometimes contained the melodramatic hallmarks of the teen idol style, but they were genuine pop/rock innovators each and every one, and have too often been dismissed as superfluous by listeners more concerned with these performers' images than their actual accomplishments.

And there were also teen idols whose music was obviously a watered-down version of early rock & roll forms. Bobby Vee was a transparent Buddy Holly clone, though much softer; Ral Donner was the most accurate Elvis Presley sound-alike, though he took after Elvis's pop/rock ballads rather than the King's rockers; and Johnny Burnette had a brief career as a mainstream teen idol after moderate success as one of the best early rockabilly singers. Finally, there was an entire wing of British teen idols, although they had virtually no success in the States. Cliff Richard was by far the biggest, followed by a stable of singers with unlikely movie-star names, most managed by British impresario Larry Parnes; Billy Fury was the best of them; Adam Faith, John Leyton, Heinz, Helen Shapiro, and others were also big in their homeland before they largely sank into irrelevance after the rise of the Beatles in 1963.

The teen idol style was already on the wane before the Beatles landed in America in early 1964; Motown and other forms of soul music were on the rise, girl groups were big, surf sounds were at their crest. The manufacturing of face and image over content and ability that characterized the teen idol era has repeated itself, to a smaller extent, ever since, though one may call them the preteen idols now. Bobby Sherman and David Cassidy, the Bay City Rollers, Tiffany, Debbie Gibson, Milli Vanilli, New Kids on the Block—all strongly echoed the teen idol era, and sold millions of records despite the wrath of rock critics the world over, as other teen idols will do in the future.

Ten Most Essential Teen Idol Records:
Various Artists, *Teen Idols* (Rhino)
Dion, *24 Golden Greats* (Arista)
Gene Pitney, *Anthology 1961-1968* (Rhino)
Del Shannon, *Greatest Hits* (Rhino)
Pat Boone, *Greatest Hits* (MCA)
Paul Anka, *30th Anniversary Collection* (Rhino)
Ricky Nelson, *The Best of Rick Nelson Vol. 1 & 2* (EMI)
Annette Funicello, *Annette: A Musical Reunion with America's Girl Next Door* (Disney)

Music Map

British Rock & Roll Before the Beatles

First British Rock Singers
Wee Willie Harris, Tommy Steele, Cliff Richard

British Teen Idols
Billy Fury, John Leyton, Adam Faith, Helen Shapiro

Early '60s British Instrumental Groups	**Early '60s British Rockers**
The Shadows, The Tornados, The Outlaws	Vince Taylor, Johnny Kidd & The Pirates, Screaming Lord Sutch

---

Joe Meek Productions
John Leyton, The Tornados, The Outlaws, Screaming Lord Sutch, Mike Berry

Kidd, alas, was already in a decline phase when the Beat Boom hit, and died in a car crash in 1966.

Besides the Pirates, the hardest rocking British band of the early '60s was Screaming Lord Sutch and the Savages. Sutch, a colorful figure who wore long hair years before it was fashionable, shamelessly emulated Screamin' Jay Hawkins, and ran for Parliament advocating such causes as the right of teenagers to vote and pirate radio, wasn't much of a singer. But his band did play real rock & roll of the hard-driving sort, at a time when that was rarely done in the British Isles, and his early-'60s singles (most recorded after the Beatles had debuted), though hardly classics, had a sense of hard-driving reckless fun that anticipated the spirit of the British Invasion. His bands also provided early schooling for such mainstays of British rock as Nicky Hopkins and Ritchie Blackmore (who also recorded some sides as a teenager in the early '60s as part of the instrumental group the Outlaws).

Sutch and the Outlaws were both produced by Joe Meek, a major figure who has merited an entire biography. Meek was the very first British producer to establish his own production company for leasing masters to labels, ensuring control over his product. A legendary eccentric obsessed with the occult and UFOs, Meek imprinted his recordings with as distinctive a sound as any other producer. Compression, sped-up vocals, otherwordly organs, howling wind, and ghostly choruses combined into a sort of space-age sound which was quite futuristic for its era, and is best heard on the Tornadoes' instrumental "Telstar," which topped the charts on both sides of the Atlantic over a year before the Beatles broke in America.

Had Meek only been working with more talented acts and better material, there would be no question of his important stature. As it was, he usually favored simpering teen-idols, anonymous instrumental groups, and cringingly dippy material, though he almost always added adventurous production that made the records stand out in the vapid early-'60s British scene. He did manage some tough-rocking sides with the Outlaws, Heinz, Tornadoes, and especially Screaming Lord Sutch, and sustained his success into the early British Invasion with the Honeycombs. As a producer he was ahead of his time, but his taste in material was rendered hopelessly passe by the Beat Boom, and he died in sordid circumstances (a combination murder-suicide) in early 1967.

The weakness of pre-Beatle rock is reflected in the near-total lack of cover versions of early British rock tunes by British Invasion bands. Though most of those group's early repertoires were dominated by rock & roll covers, they rarely looked to their own countrymen. *The Complete Beatles Chronicle*, for example, documents the hundreds of songs the group were known to have performed on-stage before 1963; only about ten odds and ends by British performers appear, by singers like Lonnie Donegan and Joe Brown.

What was happening, really, was that it was necessary for an entirely new generation of musicians, one which had grown up listening and playing rock & roll, to emerge to really play the music properly. The Beatles, and hundreds of other beat combos, looked to the U.S. for inspiration, not their own land. And when they had mastered their instruments, performance, and finally songwriting enough to offer quality material on record, the result turned the British music industry on its head literally within months. The old guard hung on for a few more hits; in some cases, such as Cliff Richard's, they maintained a reasonable degree of popularity.

In the U.S., British pop hits only crossed over very occasionally. When they did make it into the American hit parade, they tended to be rather quaint pop novelty items, such as Laurie London's "He's Got the Whole World in His Hands," the Caravelles' "You Don't Have to Be a Baby to Cry," and Frank Ifield's "I Remember You" ("Telstar," though real

instrumental rock, was also a novelty). Early British rock never meant a thing in the States, and that's why the Beatles and other British groups couldn't get a foothold in the U.S. in 1963; the industry had no reason to expect anything that they couldn't find, cheaper and better, in their own backyard. With "I Want to Hold Your Hand" in early 1964, that all changed—for which we can all be thankful, on both sides of the Atlantic.

Ten Most Essential Pre-Beatle British Rock & Roll Recordings:
Lonnie Donegan, *Collection* (Castle, UK)
Cliff Richard, *20 Rock & Roll Hits* (EMI, UK)
Various Artists, *Roots of British Rock* (Sire)
Billy Fury, *Sound of Fury Plus 10* (PolyGram)
Jet Harris & Tony Meehan, *Diamonds & Other Gems* (Deram, UK)
Johnny Kidd & the Pirates, *Complete Johnny Kidd* (EMI, UK)
Screaming Lord Sutch, *Story* (no label)
The Tornados, *Telstar: The Original Sixties Hits of the Tornados* (Music Club, UK)
The Shadows, *20 Golden Greats* (EMI, UK)
The Outlaws, *Ride Again (The Singles As & Bs)* (See for Miles, UK)

—Richie Unterberger

Brill Building Sound

Rock & roll is usually thought of as a hybrid of several types of American roots music—the blues, country & western, R&B, gospel, and others. The influence of mainstream American popular songwriting, embodied by the conglomerate of professional composers and publishers dubbed Tin Pan Alley, on rock's early development is sometimes overlooked. While rock & roll was to a significant degree a reaction against the overly professional, sentimental, and sterile conventions of pre-rock American pop, the best of Tin Pan Alley's melodic and lyrical hallmarks were incorporated into rock & roll to raise the music to new levels of sophistication.

The songwriters most crucial to this process congregated in the early '60s in a New York block known as the Brill Building. Home to leading music industry publishers, it also bred a stable of young songwriters who were just as steeped in rock & roll and rhythm and blues as Tin Pan Alley, if not more so. Several of the most prominent worked for Aldon Music, a publishing firm headed by Al Nevins and Don Kirshner, the same Don Kirshner who would later mastermind the Monkees' hits and act as a legendarily bland master of ceremonies for network TV rock specials.

Many pop/rock songwriters worked in the Brill Building in the early '60s, but several teams carved a legendary legacy, including Gerry Goffin & Carole King, Barry Mann & Cynthia Weil, Jerry Leiber & Mike Stoller, Jeff Barry & Ellie Greenwich and Doc Pomus & Mort Shuman. Responsible for literally pages worth of hits in the late '50s and first half of the '60s, they matched Tin Pan Alley's highest standards of inventive melodies and lyrics, but they were clearly different from their predecessors. The rock & roll market demanded tunes targeted at teenagers, with earthier concerns than the classics of the '30s and '40s. For many of these songwriters, the task hardly required an adjustment; they were barely out of (or even still in) their teens, and they were going through the pangs of young love and searches for identity themselves. For good measure, Goffin-King, Mann-Weil and Barry-Greenwich were married to each other, infusing their work with a passion that was actually grounded in their real-life romances.

Brill Building compositions were placed all over the pop/rock map, but had their greatest impact and success with girl groups. It was a heavenly match: girl groups sang about young love with forlorn and passionate innocence, and were largely based near New York City, but very few were songwriters, and they needed suitable material; young Brill Building songwriters wrote about young love with forlorn and passionate innocence, and were largely based near New York City, but needed suitable performers. Most of the classic hits of the Ronettes, Chiffons, Shangri-Las, Dixie Cups and Little Eva originated at the Brill Building, as well as a few classic one-shots and misses.

Other prime outlets for Brill Building material were teen idols like Connie Francis, Bobby Vee, James Darren and Neil Sedaka (the last of whom was one of the most successful Brill Building songwriters himself, often in collaboration with Howard Greenfield). These tended to be the most lightweight Brill Building confections, at times even approaching disposable, as a listen to a James Darren greatest hits compilation confirms. Uneven quality couldn't be helped; the songwriters were under tremendous pressure to deliver tunes in a near-assembly-line fashion, and couldn't be expected to come up with "Will You Love Me Tomorrow" or "On Broadway" every time out.

Leiber-Stoller and Pomus-Shuman however, usually wrote for pop-flavored R&B and early soul acts. Leiber-Stoller wrote (and produced) most of the Coasters' classic comic vignettes, and Pomus-Shuman penned several of the Drifters' hits. Both teams also wrote some of the greatest Elvis Presley songs of the late '50s and early '60s; Goffin-King and Mann-Weil for their part, would supply songs for the Drifters and Phil Spector's great productions with the best blue-eyed soul act of the '60s, the Righteous Brothers.

Other notable Brill Building mainstays included Phil Spector, a great songwriter and even greater producer; Bert Berns, who also wore both songwriting and production hats, though he worked in a more of a pop-soul vein; and Bacharach-David, who probably owed the most to Tin Pan Alley classic traditions, although that didn't prevent them from writing some great pop/rock songs for the Shirelles, Dionne Warwick and others. And for every Goffin-King it must be remembered that there were dozens of much less successful hopefuls scuffling around the edges of the Brill Building crowd, including future folk-rock stars Paul Simon and Jim McGuinn, and future disco king of the "hustle," Van McCoy.

Though Phil Spector is by far the most legendary producer with Brill Building associations, most of the great Brill Building songwriters were also great producers, although they weren't always credited on the label. Several of them were also great performers,

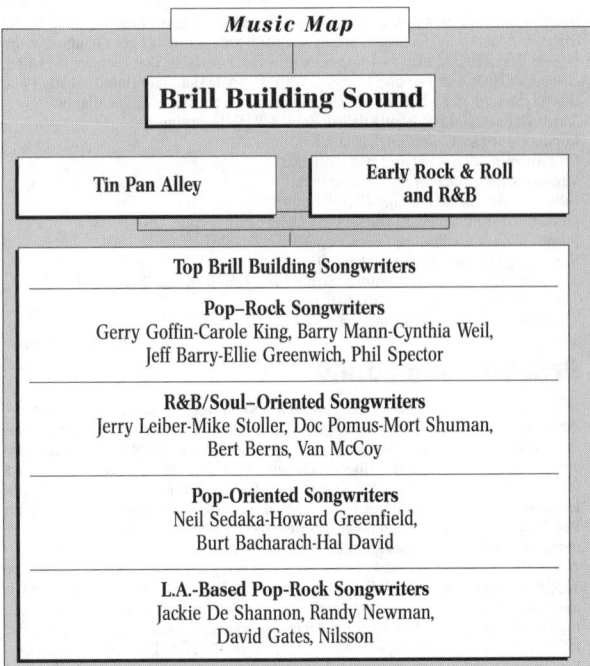

Music Map

Brill Building Sound

Tin Pan Alley	Early Rock & Roll and R&B

Top Brill Building Songwriters

Pop–Rock Songwriters
Gerry Goffin-Carole King, Barry Mann-Cynthia Weil,
Jeff Barry-Ellie Greenwich, Phil Spector

R&B/Soul–Oriented Songwriters
Jerry Leiber-Mike Stoller, Doc Pomus-Mort Shuman,
Bert Berns, Van McCoy

Pop-Oriented Songwriters
Neil Sedaka-Howard Greenfield,
Burt Bacharach-Hal David

L.A.-Based Pop-Rock Songwriters
Jackie De Shannon, Randy Newman,
David Gates, Nilsson

and it has been said that the demos they cut were often as good or better than the versions recorded by the performers to whom they were given. Barry Mann, Carole King and Jeff Barry & Ellie Greenwich (the latter pair as the Raindrops) actually had some hit records on their own, though they much preferred to run things behind the scenes.

There were also quite a few Los Angeles-based songwriters who, though not based at the actual Brill Building, operated in an almost identical fashion. David Gates, Jackie De Shannon, Randy Newman and Nilsson were some of the best; eventually, each of them would become singing-songwriting stars in their own right.

The British Invasion turned the focus of rock & roll on performers that wrote their own material, and while that didn't spell the end of the success of the great Brill Building songwriters, it meant some adjustments were in order. Girl group records were still hugely successful in 1964, the first year of the British Invasion, but it was soon obvious that their time was coming to an end. The irony was that John Lennon and Paul McCartney owed a great deal to the Brill Building, openly declaring Goffin and King as their greatest songwriting influences, and covering Brill Building classics by the Shirelles, Cookies and Isley Brothers. Manfred Mann ("Do Wah Diddy Diddy"), Herman's Hermits ("I'm into Something Good"), and other British Invasion groups also took Brill Building covers into the top of the charts.

Occasionally Brill Building songwriters actually managed to supply fresh material to British Invasion groups, as Mann-Weil did with the Animals and Bert Berns did with Them and Lulu. But inevitably, the proliferation of self-contained rock groups, not to mention soul songwriters who wrote their own material, meant less of a need for professional tunesmiths. And the fact was, both the world and the songwriters were changing as fast as everything else was in the '60s; the composers wanted to express more mature concerns, and much of the rock audience had progressed beyond adolescent love affairs.

The principal architects of the Brill Building coped with these changes in varying fashions. Some became jingle writers; some (Ellie Greenwich) eventually wrote musicals; some (Jeff Barry) wrote and produced bubblegum for the Archies; some (Phil Spector) retired; some (Bacharach-David) moved from pop/rock to MOR pop. The most resourceful became singer/songwriter stars themselves; not only the aforementioned L.A. composers, but also Carole King who became a superstar as a solo act. The legacy of the Brill Building was enormous, setting the standard for pop/rock songwriting that has been emulated ever since, by everyone from the Beatles on down.

Ten Most Essential Brill Building Albums:
Various Artists, *Brill Building Sound* (Era)
Phil Spector, *Back to Mono* (ABKCO)
The Drifters, *All-Time Greatest Hits & More: 1959-1965* (Atlantic)
The Coasters, *50 Coastin' Classics* (Rhino)
Various Artists, *The Colpix-Dimension Story* (Rhino)
The Shangri-Las, *Golden Hits of the Shangri-Las* (Polygram)
Neil Sedaka, *All-Time Greatest Hits* (RCA)
Various Artists, *The Red Bird Story* (Charly, UK)
Various Artists, *The Best of the Girl Groups, Vol. 1* (Rhino)
Various Artists, *The Best of the Girl Groups, Vol. 2* (Rhino)

—*Richie Unterberger*

Girl Groups

The story of the "girl group" sound—which reached its commercial and artistic peak in the early and mid-'60s—is not just the story of the performers. More than any other style in rock & roll, it was the product of more or less equal partnerships between the singer/performers, songwriters, and producers. The result was one of the most vital links between the birth of rock & roll and the British Invasion, the arrival of which gradually eroded the presence of girl groups on the charts even as it acknowledged enormous debts to the genre.

Girl groups were more polished than the early rock & roll pioneers, more innocent than the soul music that was originating at the same time, and as firmly planted in Tin Pan Alley as rhythm and blues. While it wasn't the rawest or most artistically expressive pop music, few forms of rock were as affecting, romantic, and tuneful. They also provided the forums and mouthpieces for some of pop/rock's most talented songwriting teams, as well as laying the foundation for groundbreaking orchestral production that lent an increased sophistication to rock & roll.

The Chantels led by the heart-wrenching vocals of Arlene Smith are generally acknowledged as the first girl group. Their Top 20 hit "Maybe" (1958) had obvious roots in gospel and doo wop, but also displayed yearning, innocent, and vulnerable qualities not apparent in the suaver male doo wop outfits.

It was the Shirelles however, who really established girl groups as a major force with their number one hit, "Will You Love Me Tomorrow?," in 1960. Significantly, that hit also featured many of the classic girl group trademarks—sweeping orchestral strings, full background harmonies, and a lead vocal that projected soul, warmth, hope, and uncertainty. The Shirelles scored a half-dozen Top 20 singles in the next couple years (along with several memorable lesser hits), and ranked as the most successful female vocal group of the era.

The song was written by Gerry Goffin and Carole King who would go on to write many girl group classics in the next few years, and were one of the hottest songwriting teams of the "Brill Building" sound. Named after a complex of music publishing offices on Broadway in New York, it also gave birth to the partnerships between Jeff Barry and Ellie Greenwich and Barry Mann and Cynthia Weil These teams were responsible for the lion's share of the best girl group recordings, investing rock & roll with the best melodic and lyrical qualities of classic pop, while retaining a feel for the rhythm and blues roots of the performers. Less celebrated writers like Luther Dixon (who wrote several songs for the Shirelles) and a pre-discoton Van McCoy also contributed timeless classics to the genre.

It took Phil Spector to launch the girl group sound to its pinnacle. The producer set material from the cream of the Brill Building crop (as well as his own original compositions) to grandly majestic, orchestral arrangements that achieved an unheard-of density without sacrificing any of the music's passion and melody. The Crystals, the Ronettes, and Darlene Love (who sang uncredited vocals on some of the Crystals' biggest smashes) were the most talented pilots of Spector's grandoise "Wall of Sound" productions, most of which were released on his own label, Philles.

While the Shirelles and Phil Spector's acts were the most prominent girl groups in the years preceding the British Invasion, the sound was emulated by several one- or two-shot groups, and less-celebrated producers, with great success. The Chiffons, Claudine Clark the Cookies, the Jaynetts, Little Eva and the Exciters all contributed timeless classics. And there were dozens—if not hundreds—of worthy singles in the style that, for one reason or another, didn't become blockbusters, although they had most or all of the essential elements.

Most of the great girl groups were black, with clear affinities for R&B and doo wop, but the most innocent qualities of the sound (and occasionally the most soulful ones) were projected in many records by white teen girl singers as well. Lesley Gore was the most renowned of these performers, who also included the Angels the Raindrops (with Ellie Greenwich on lead vocals), and one-shot artists like Diane Renay and the Murmaids.

While the arrival of the Beatles in 1964 is often thought of as the beginning of the end for the girl groups, girl group records were actually as successful as ever during that year. The rise of the Red Bird label, featuring the Dixie Cups and the Shangri-Las (who both scored number one hits in 1964), did much to boost the style's commercial fortunes.

Although financial problems caused the Red Bird label to fold within a few years of its founding, the years 1964 and 1965 saw the label shine brightly indeed, and found songwriters like Jeff Barry, Barry Mann, Ellie Greenwich, Jerry Lieber and Mike Stoller overseeing most of its output from the producer's booth. Producer and songwriter Shadow Morton—almost as idiosyncratic a talent as Phil Spector—created some of the greatest girl group records with the Shangri-Las. These tough-talking but tender-hearted Queens Teens may have made the sassiest and most heart-wrenching girl group mini-operas of all.

Although the burgeoning Motown empire wasn't heavily rooted in the girl group sound, 1964 saw the release of breakthrough discs by Mary Wells, the Supremes, and Martha & the Vandellas that owed heavy debts to the style. Relying heavily on the production and songwriting talents of Smokey Robinson and Berry Gordy Jr. (among others), their sound was nonetheless grittier and bluesier than the New York school, and their personas (on record and in performance) more distinctive.

There's no doubt that girl groups were among the British Invasion groups' chief influences. John Lennon has stated for the record that he and Paul McCartney hoped to duplicate the success of Goffin and King with their songwriting partnership, and the Beatles' early albums included covers of hits by the Shirelles, the Cookies, and the Marvelettes. Manfred Mann, despite their R&B roots, scored their biggest U.S. hits with covers of songs by the Exciters ("Do Wah Diddy Diddy") and the Shirelles ("Sha La La"), and several other British groups, ranging from Herman's Hermits and the Searchers to the

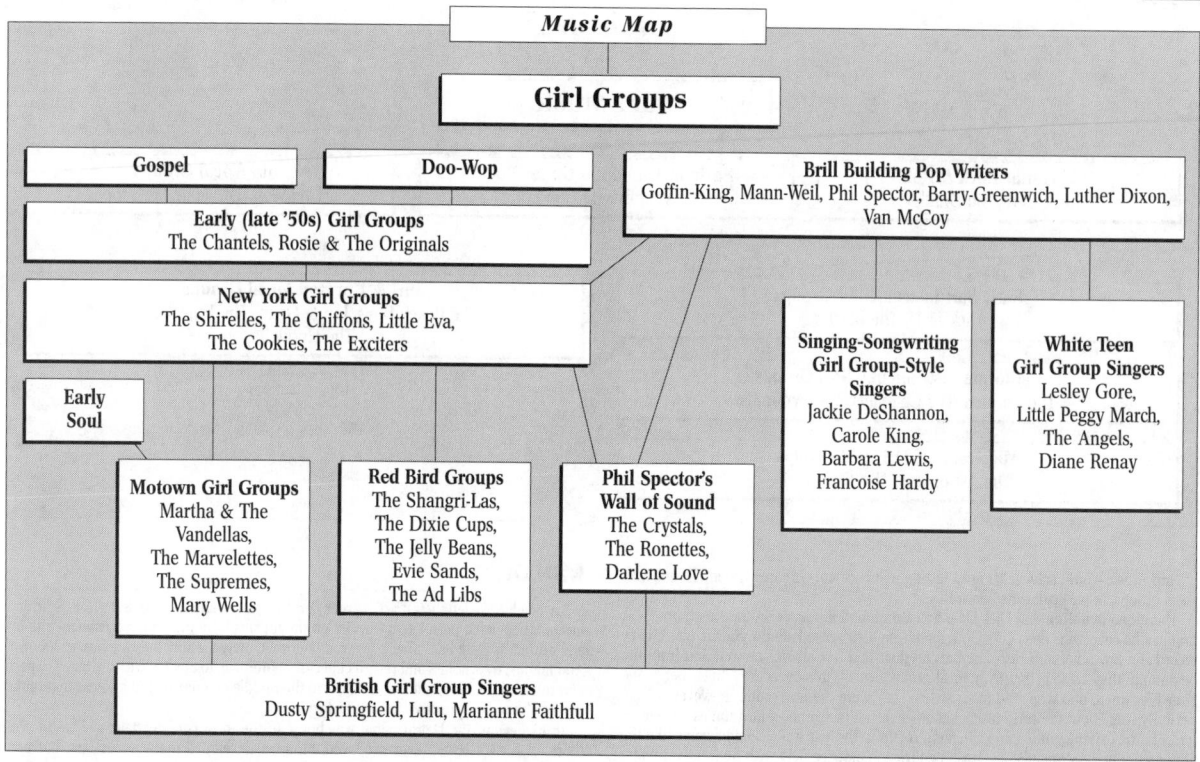

Music Map

Girl Groups

Gospel

Doo-Wop

Brill Building Pop Writers
Goffin-King, Mann-Weil, Phil Spector, Barry-Greenwich, Luther Dixon, Van McCoy

Early (late '50s) Girl Groups
The Chantels, Rosie & The Originals

New York Girl Groups
The Shirelles, The Chiffons, Little Eva, The Cookies, The Exciters

Singing-Songwriting Girl Group-Style Singers
Jackie DeShannon, Carole King, Barbara Lewis, Francoise Hardy

White Teen Girl Group Singers
Lesley Gore, Little Peggy March, The Angels, Diane Renay

Early Soul

Motown Girl Groups
Martha & The Vandellas, The Marvelettes, The Supremes, Mary Wells

Red Bird Groups
The Shangri-Las, The Dixie Cups, The Jelly Beans, Evie Sands, The Ad Libs

Phil Spector's Wall of Sound
The Crystals, The Ronettes, Darlene Love

British Girl Group Singers
Dusty Springfield, Lulu, Marianne Faithfull

Mindbenders also made it big with girl group covers. However, the most successful British groups—the Beatles first and foremost among them—were those that relied primarily upon their own material. And it was this shift in emphasis toward self-contained rock groups that played their own instruments that spelled the end of the girl groups as a major force, although singers like Jackie DeShannon, Dusty Springfield, Lulu, Evie Sands, Barbara Lewis and others continued to produce classic recordings (and sometimes score major hits) in the girl group vein throughout the '60s.

The girl group sound, though, never really went away. You can hear it in many female vocal groups, self-contained and otherwise, through the present day. In the case of some soul groups (such as the Pointer Sisters) or new wave bands (the Bangles, Blondie and the Go-Go's), the influence is worn quite cheerfully on the sleeve. More subtly, its echoes are heard in all rock that relies upon orchestral production, harmonies, and/or crafty, melodic compositions to send its message.

12 Most Essential Girl Group Albums:
The Shirelles, *The World's Greatest Girl Group* (Tomato/Rhino)
The Shangri-Las, *The Best of the Shangri-Las* (PolyGram)
The Ronettes, *Best of the Ronettes* (ABKCO)
The Crystals, *Best of the Crystals* (ABKCO)
The Chiffons, *Best of the Chiffons* (Laurie)
The Supremes, *Anthology* (Motown)
Martha & the Vandellas, *Live Wire! The Singles 1962-1972* (Motown)
Mary Wells, *Looking Back 1961-1964* (Motown)
Lesley Gore, *It's My Party: Mercury Anthology* (Mercury)
The Marvelettes, *Deliver: The Singles 1961-1971* (Rhino)
Various Artists, *The Best of the Girl Groups, Vol. 1, The Best of the Girl Groups, Vol. 2* (Rhino)
The Exciters, *Tell Him* (EMI)
Recommended Reading:
Girl Groups: The Story of a Sound, by Alan Betrock (Delilah, 1982)
Will You Still Love Me Tomorrow? Girl Groups From the 50s On ..., by Charlotte Greig (Virago, 1989, UK)

—*Richie Unterberger*

Surf Music

In terms of commercial impact, surf music was a short-lived phenomenon. The vast majority of popular surf recordings were waxed between 1961 and 1965; even then, their success was often confined to an isolated region (more often than not, Southern California). Yet its influence upon the course of rock & roll is incalculable. Felt by hundreds of artists, it continues to surface, in a much modified form, to this very day.

Between the time when the initial explosion of rock & roll died down in the late '50s and the British Invasion, instrumental rock was more responsible for keeping alive the raunchiest and wildest aspects of the music than any other style. It was also responsible for keeping the electric guitar at the forefront of the music, and surf music was certainly the most guitar-oriented style of instrumental rock & roll, though splashing drums and honking saxes were also prime features of the sound.

Southern California guitarist Dick Dale is roundly acknowledged as the father of surf music. In the late '50s, he developed its trademark reverb sound. Whether intentionally or otherwise, the "wet," full echo of surf guitars evoked the rides and waves of surfing, which in the early '60s was still an emerging teenage sport that was little known outside of Southern California and Hawaii. Ironically, Jimi Hendrix, who intoned "you'll never hear surf music again" on "Third Stone from the Sun" on his debut album, has been said to have been influenced by Dale, who like Hendrix played his guitar left-handed and upside-down.

"For most surf instrumentals," wrote surf music authority John Blair in his liner notes to *Guitar Player Magazine Presents Legends of Guitar: Surf, Vol. 1,* "a small electronic device called a reverberation unit, or 'reverb' for short, was used to create the distinctive 'surf' guitar sound. Although several companies had reverbs on the market, the one made by the Fender Musical Instrument Company (introduced in the summer of 1961) was the popular choice of most surf bands ...

"[Dick Dale] used Fender amplifiers and even had the company customize a special left-handed (he played upside-down and left-handed) gold metalflake Stratocaster guitar, which he still plays. In fact, Dale's close association with Fender enabled him to 'roadtest' new equipment for the company. The powerful Dual Showman amplifier, introduced in late 1962, was developed with Dale's help."

On vinyl, the surf craze kicked off with Dale's late-1961 single, "Let's Go Trippin'." Although it was only a regional hit, its influence was tremendous, and within months, dozens of bands—virtually all of them based in Southern California—were playing surf music. Hundreds would record surf singles and albums before the fad started to fade in the mid-'60s. Although they were not Californian, and would certainly not identify themselves as a surf group, the dark, reverberant guitars of the Ventures—then reaching the peak of their massive popularity—were also formidable influences on these groups.

On a national level, the impact of instrumental surf bands was notable, but much slighter. The Chantays ("Pipeline") and the Surfaris ("Wipe Out") scored huge national hits, but few others dented the Top 40, let alone the Top Ten. The Pyramids' early-1964 single "Penetration" was the last big national instrumental surf hit.

While most surf groups were based in Southern California, the genre was not strictly isolated to the region. The Astronauts (from Colorado) and the Trashmen (from Minneapolis) were the most successful of the not inconsiderable number of landlocked bands who played surf music, or at least made a few stabs at it. The Trashmen, indeed, went to the Top Five with "Surfin' Bird" in early 1964; only the Beatles, then hitting the U.S. with full force, kept them from the top spot. One of the very best instrumental surf groups, the Atlantics, were not even from the U.S., but from Australia, where they scored some massive hits in 1963 and 1964.

Music Map

Surf Music

'50s Guitar Rock & Roll Chuck Berry, Bo Diddley	**Early Instrumental Guitar Rock** The Ventures, Duane Eddy	**'50s Vocal Groups** Doo-Wop, The Four Freshmen

Early Surf Instrumental Groups
Dick Dale, The Belairs

Surf & Hot Rod Vocal Groups
The Beach Boys, Jan & Dean, The Rip-Chords,
The Hondells

California Instrumental Surf Groups
The Surfaris, The Chantays, The Pyramids

Midwest Surf-Oriented Groups
The Astronauts, The Trashmen

Surf music would achieve its most lasting influence not with instrumentals, but with vocal groups, in particular the Beach Boys.

There's no doubting that Dick Dale was a profound influence on the Hawthorne, CA group, who covered Dale's "Let's Go Trippin'" on their second album, *Surfin' U.S.A.* They recorded a few other surf instrumentals on their first few albums as well, but from the beginning, they were primarily a vocal group, heavily influenced by Chuck Berry, the Four Freshmen, doo wop, and other styles. They were the first group, however, to successfully sing about the surf music phenomenon, adding complex harmonies and clever lyrics to the driving guitars and chugging rhythms. In their wake, some groups like the aforementioned Astronauts and Trashmen tried to play the field with both instrumental and vocal numbers.

Other California vocal acts were quick to jump on the bandwagon, but besides the Beach Boys, only Jan & Dean (who were occasionally beneficiaries of songs and harmonies by Beach Boy leader Brian Wilson) were a significant success, commercially or artistically. Jan & Dean had been a modestly successful duo for years before latching onto the surf fad, and—like the Beach Boys—they would soon adapt the surf sound to hot rod lyrics emphasizing cars and drag racing. Acts like Ronny & the Daytonas ("G.T.O.") and the Rip Chords ("Hey Little Cobra") hit the Top Ten with one-shot hits in the same style, but were out of their depth when they tried to mine it for memorable followups.

Indeed, after 1963, the Beach Boys—still remembered by many listeners primarily as a surf group—left the subject behind for good. They soon broadened their scope leagues beyond even hot rods and girls to create challenging, personal pop/rock on a competitive level with the British Invasion groups that sounded the death knell for surf music at the beginning of 1964. Even Jan & Dean's hits were not solely limited to surf and hot rod tunes, though their career came to a skidding halt with—ironically—severe injuries suffered by Jan Berry in a car crash in 1966 on Sunset Boulevard in Los Angeles.

The Beach Boys' harmonies, though, left their stamp on countless other groups. The Who's Keith Moon was a huge surf music fan, and the manic splashing of his drum kit owes something to the bashing rumble of surf ensembles; the Who's own harmonies owed surprisingly large debts to the Beach Boys. The lineups of several obscure surf groups included members who went on to fame in surprisingly different contexts. The Crossfires, for example, evolved into the Turtles, and the Jesters, led by Jim Messina, also featured Glenn Frey of the Eagles.

Three decades later, few groups play surf music, although Dick Dale made a surprisingly strong comeback on record and as a national touring act in the early '90s. Echoes of the style, however, live on whenever you heard a reverbed guitar or sweet, high vocal harmonies in a rock & roll song.

12 Most Essential Surf Records:
The Beach Boys, *Good Vibrations* (Capitol)
The Beach Boys, *Surfin' U.S.A.* (Capitol)
The Beach Boys, *Surfer Girl* (Capitol)
Jan & Dean, *The Legendary Master Series* (EMI)
Dick Dale, *King of the Surf Guitar: The Best of Dick Dale* (Rhino)
The Astronauts, *Surf Party* (RCA)
The Trashmen, *Best of the Trashmen* (Sundazed)
Various Artists, *Guitar Player Presents Legends of Guitar—Surf, Vol. 1* (Rhino)
Various Artists, *The History of Surf Music, Vol. 1* (Rhino)
Various Artists, *Surfin' Hits* (Rhino)
The Atlantics, *The CBS Singles Collection 1963-1965* (Canetoad, Australia)
The Surfaris, *Wipe Out! The Best of the Surfaris* (Varese Sarabande)
Most essential book:
The Beach Boys, by David Leaf (1985, Courage)

                                    —Richie Unterberger

Motown

Many labels have left their mark on rock & roll—Sun, Atlantic, Chess, Stax/Volt, Stiff, and lots of others left a permanent imprint on the music's legacy by honing distinctive styles and attitudes. Only one label, however, is immediately identified as a genre of its own. And not just by scholars and record collectors—Motown, to anyone who's listened to popular music since 1960, is not just a label in the middle of a record, but a sound that ranks among the most distinctive in rock history.

In its heyday, the Detroit label was home to the most commercially successful synthesis of R&B and pop ever produced. Motown developed many superstars, but performers were only part of the story. Equally important were the songwriters, including such masters as Smokey Robinson and the Holland-Dozier-Holland team; producers (who often doubled as songwriters); the (often uncredited) backing musicians, like bassist James Jamerson and drummer Benny Benjamin who gave the music its rock-solid foundation; and the vision of owner Berry Gordy Jr. You could almost always identify a Motown Record: instantly hummable melodies, pulsing bass lines, punchy tambourines and handclaps, rousing horns and violins, and vocals that evoked a gospel flavor with the call-and-response lines between the lead and backup singers.

The Motown empire, which eventually grew into the biggest black-owned business in America, was a success story as unlikely as those of Elvis or the Beatles A former boxer and failed jazz record-store owner, Gordy was a struggling hustler on the edges of the R&B music business in the late '50s, writing some hits for Jackie Wilson In 1959, he borrowed money from his family to start an independent production company. After leasing hits by Marv Johnson and Barrett Strong to other labels, Gordy formed his own labels. The releases would appear both on Motown and other imprints like Tamla, Gordy, and Soul.

Motown quickly established itself in the early '60s with hits by the Miracles, the Marvelettes, and Mary Wells. It was Gordy's increasingly refined and systematic production techniques, however, that would ensure that the label continued to succeed and grow. The Motown sound has often been compared to an assembly line, drawing upon the influence of Detroit's automobile plants, with performers, songwriters, producers, and musicians embellishing a basic tried-and-true blueprint. If it were indeed true that Motown's formula was nothing more than an assembly line, it most likely would have exhausted itself quickly. Gordy and Motown's genius was that it was able to spin almost infinite variations on its hugely appealing recipes, while still retaining an instantly recognizable sound, endearing itself to millions of listeners through both innovation and familiarity.

Motown releases might have shared many general similarities, but in time its superstars would develop strong identities of their own. The Miracles paced by Smokey Robinson (who wrote many of Motown's best songs, both for the Miracles and other artists) handled both romantic ballads and up-tempo dance tunes; the Temptations were the most polished soul group of their day; the Four Tops were gritty and emotional; Mary Wells and the Marvelettes recorded the most soulful girl group singles around; child prodigy Stevie Wonder developed into a magnificently gifted songwriter and instrumentalist; Martha Reeves & the Vandellas were Motown at its most feverish and gospel-influenced; Diana Ross & the Supremes were, aside from the Beatles the most successful pop group of the '60s; Marvin Gaye along with Stevie Wonder would prove to be the most eclectic and innovative singer/songwriter on the Motown roster, not even reaching his maturity as an artist (like Wonder) until the 1970s; Junior Walker cut the label's earthiest, most party-oriented R&B.

These were the superstars; there were other fine performers who recorded a notable body of work for Motown in the 1960s, including Gladys Knight, Brenda Holloway, Edwin Starr, Kim Weston, Tammi Terrell and the Contours. The label's roster was so deep, in fact, that some illustrious artists were neglected; the Spinners didn't do much of

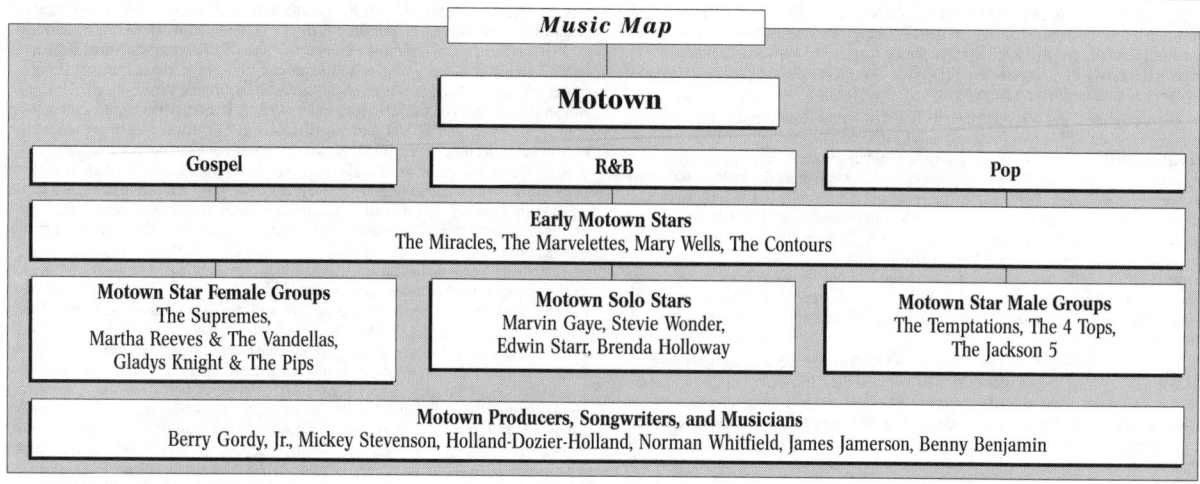

Music Map

Motown

| Gospel | R&B | Pop |

Early Motown Stars
The Miracles, The Marvelettes, Mary Wells, The Contours

Motown Star Female Groups
The Supremes,
Martha Reeves & The Vandellas,
Gladys Knight & The Pips

Motown Solo Stars
Marvin Gaye, Stevie Wonder,
Edwin Starr, Brenda Holloway

Motown Star Male Groups
The Temptations, The 4 Tops,
The Jackson 5

Motown Producers, Songwriters, and Musicians
Berry Gordy, Jr., Mickey Stevenson, Holland-Dozier-Holland, Norman Whitfield, James Jamerson, Benny Benjamin

anything until they left Motown in the early '70s, the Isley Brothers had only one big hit during their several years there (perhaps because of their inability to truly adapt to the Motown formula), and early-'60s soul star Chuck Jackson had only minimal success after moving to Motown.

Even the stars sometimes expressed dissatisfaction about how they were promoted and directed by Motown, but they most likely knew that their success was at least equally attributable to the label as to their own talents. The point was underscored by Mary Wells' surprise decision to leave Motown in 1964 just after her number one hit, "My Guy." Lured away by a big contract and the promise of a movie career, Wells never had another big hit; without the estimable Motown team, she was just another soul singer.

The loss of Wells was covered by the burgeoning careers of other Motown stars, but Gordy faced a much more serious problem in late 1967, when the songwriting and production team of Brian Holland, Lamont Dozier and Eddie Holland demanded an accounting of their royalties. After initiating a suit against Motown, the trio left the label to establish a company of their own. For a few years, Motown's fortunes were unaffected; they launched the Jackson 5 as superstars, and producers such as Norman Whitfield infused Motown with contemporary funk, psychedelia, and social commentary on tracks like the Temptations' "Cloud Nine," "Psychedelic Shack," and "Ball of Confusion."

Motown's golden age truly ended, however, in 1971, when the company moved from Detroit to Los Angeles. Around this time, the careers of some of Motown's mainstays, such as Martha Reeves and the Marvelettes had petered out; Diana Ross had already left the Supremes, Marvin Gaye and Stevie Wonder recorded some stupendous album-length statements in the 1970s that showed their full gifts as songwriters and performers for the first time, as well as expanding their lyrical concerns beyond the romantic themes that Motown had largely stuck to. But Motown no longer bred scads of stars, or honed a distinctive sound; they were simply a soul/R&B record label, albeit a very big and successful one.

When people talk about the Motown sound, they're referring to those 1960s and early '70s recordings. The most successful label of its day, and the most successful independent label of all time (it's now part of MCA), it was the most influential factor in establishing African-American music as an integral part of mainstream U.S. culture.

15 Most Essential Motown Recordings:
Smokey Robinson & the Miracles, *Anthology*
Mary Wells, *Looking Back 1961-1964*
Martha & the Vandellas, *Live Wire! The Singles 1962-1972*
The Marvelettes, *Marvelettes' Greatest Hits*
Marvin Gaye, *Anthology*
Stevie Wonder, *Looking Back*
The Supremes, *Anthology*
The Temptations, *Emperors of Soul*
The Four Tops, *Anthology*
The Jackson 5, *Anthology*
Junior Walker, *Greatest Hits*
Gladys Knight & the Pips, *Anthology*
Brenda Holloway, *Greatest Hits & Rare Classics*
Edwin Starr, *Motown Superstar Series Vol. 3*
Various Artists, *Hitsville USA: The Motown Singles Collection 1959-1971*
Book:
Where Did Our Love Go?: The Rise and Fall of the Motown Sound, by Nelson George (St. Martin's, 1985)

—Richie Unterberger

Early British R&B

The margin between early British blues and early British R&B is not a wide one—important figures like the Rolling Stones and Eric Clapton have feet in both camps. It's

a fairly big gap between Alexis Korner and the Yardbirds, though, and the distinction between R&B and blues is a meaningful one, not just a hairsplitter. The early British R&B bands were far more rock- and pop-oriented than the blues purists. It would be the British R&B bands that would capture the wide pop audience, and indeed turn out by and large to be the most durable acts that emerged from the British Invasion.

The British R&B scene had its roots in London in the early '60s, where teenage enthusiasts were eagerly discovering American pioneers via hard-to-come-by import recordings. The story is often told of how the Rolling Stones' partnership was sparked when Keith Richards spotted Mick Jagger carrying a stack of imported Chess Records album on a train. This music was by no means unknown by the bands that would spearhead the first wave of the British Invasion in Liverpool. But for those groups, R&B was one aspect of the rock and soul music they loved to cover, not the main course. Their earthier counterparts to the south were more purist in their orientation—they reserved most of their enthusiasm for rhythm and blues by black Americans, although they weren't entirely ignorant of the rockabilly, girl group, and early Motown sounds that formed a much larger building block of the Mersey repertoire.

When the first wave of British R&B groups began performing in the early '60s, they stuck mostly to blues of the 12-bar variety. Much of this purism is attributable to British blues father Korner, who at various points acted as a mentor to members of the Rolling Stones, the Yardbirds, Manfred Mann, the Graham Bond Organization, and even Ray Davies of the Kinks. Even in their embryonic days, though, there was a split in the Rolling Stones (who had yet to name themselves) along these lines, when guitarist Geoff Bradford left because he felt that playing songs by Bo Diddley and Chuck Berry would be too blatantly commercial.

In retrospect, Berry and Diddley were the two biggest influences upon the Stones, and maybe on the British R&B scene as a whole. Berry and Diddley owed a lot to the blues, but they were not blues singers; they were rock & roll originators. In Britain, some musicians felt more comfortable calling them R&B performers than rock & rollers, though the distinction seems a bit academic now. What they really meant, it seems, was that Berry and Diddley were not commercial music, and apparently rock & roll was a lot more likely to be dismissed as commercial pap than R&B.

The Stones may have started out trying to earnestly imitate Berry, Diddley, and other R&B/blues performers, but what actually came out was inevitably different. The Stones were white, younger, and though not exactly privileged, didn't come from nearly as hardbitten backgrounds as their black idols. The music was accordingly more innocent, though just as raw. The arrangements were more guitar-oriented, and the tempos became more accelerated, as the groups were more concerned with whipping up energy than refining their finesse.

And the fact was, the beat boom—ignited by the Beatles and other Mersey groups as 1963 began—could not be ignored. The more pop-based sound of Liverpool left room for (and, some would say, needed) a grittier counterpoint. It was that breach that the Stones stepped into when they began recording in 1963, and by mid-1964, they had firmly established themselves as the second most popular group in the U.K.

The Stones were in the vanguard of a legion of British R&B groups that moved beyond the purist circuit of small clubs into the pop charts. 1964 saw a wave of groups that found big British (and often American) success with a heavily R&B-oriented sound. Chief among these were the Pretty Things, perhaps the rawest of the lot, whose guitarist, Dick Taylor, had been in an early version of the Stones; Manfred Mann, perhaps the smoothest, who had one of the scene's best vocalists in Paul Jones; and the Yardbirds, whose Eric Clapton did much to establish the role of the guitar hero in rock & roll, although the group wouldn't actually break commercially until he left, to be replaced by Jeff Beck.

Some of the best and biggest British R&B groups came from outside of London. The Animals, from Newcastle, seared ears with both Eric Burdon's wailing vocals and Alan Price's organ. Organs were also featured prominently in the Spencer Davis Group, which despite their name were primarily a vehicle for the teenage Stevie Winwood, and Them, which featured the young Van Morrison, and are commonly identified as a British Invasion act although they hailed from Belfast, Ireland. A couple of the other best British groups, the Kinks and the Who, also had strong roots in the R&B scene, although they had for the most part progressed to writing their own, more rock- and pop-based material by the time they began recording.

There was also a sub-wing of British R&B that was more explicitly jazz-influenced, including keyboardist Georgie Fame (an eclectic who actually had quite a bit of pop success), the Graham Bond Organization (whose rhythm section featured future Cream members Jack Bruce and Ginger Baker), and Zoot Money (whose lineup included future Policeman Andy Summers for a time). There were also blues purists that delved into R&B more than is generally realized, such as John Mayall's Bluesbreakers, who presented a set of live, original material on their first (pre-Clapton) album in 1965 that sounds closer to the early Rolling Stones than B.B. King or Freddie King. And there were also scores of energetic British R&B bands who pounded out a single or two, some cringingly sloppy, some classic; they offered a rough parallel to the garage rock scene of the United States, and some of the musicians surfaced in prominent psychedelic and progressive rock bands of the late '60s.

Some rock historians have griped that British R&B groups did nothing more than imitate American black music, selling it to British (and then, ironically, back to American) listeners who could only handle a diluted version of the real thing, and/or were too ignorant to seek out the original article. It's true to a large extent that the groups were capitalizing on a huge backlog of classic material that was virtually unknown in the U.K. (and in large pockets of the U.S.), selling it to listeners (and an industry) more willing to embrace young white musicians than older black ones.

The assertion that the British groups merely photocopied or watered down the original versions is much harder to support, although it certainly happened sometimes. The songs were attacked with a reckless energy that made them fresh, and at times were radically revised, or even redefined. Whether they were improved or not is a matter of personal taste, but it's undeniable that the results were often exciting, and clearly different than the models they were built upon. The Yardbirds, for one, used R&B songs as a template upon which to jam and improvise on guitar "rave-ups" that transformed them into something else entirely. Jagger, Winwood, Burdon, Jones, Morrison, and others were also top-notch singers that had distinctive styles of their own, and were not just flailing wanna-be blacks.

It should be noted that none of these acts could really be termed R&B purists upon close inspection. Start with the biggest of them, the Stones. Their first big British hit was "I Wanna Be Your Man," written for them by John Lennon and Paul McCartney. Their second was "Not Fade Away," a Bo Diddleyization of a Buddy Holly song. On an early album, they covered Dale Hawkins' rockabilly hit "Suzy Q." None of this is to intimate that the Stones were hypocrites, proclaiming themselves to be hardcore R&B men but turning commercial when it suited them; what it means is that even then the Stones were eclectic in their choice of material, and not limiting themselves to what could or couldn't be classified as R&B.

Look at some other groups, and you can find other trangressions into pop/rock. Manfred Mann had their two biggest American hits with covers of girl-group singles. The Animals had two of their biggest hits with songs that were written for them by Brill Building composers. Them had their biggest hit with a song written by an American producer that had previously been recorded by Lulu ("Here Comes the Night"); the Spencer Davis Group had their first big singles with songs written for them by Jackie Edwards, a West Indian steeped in ska music. For that matter, many of the Liverpool groups, for all their supposed lightweightedness, often covered the same hardcore R&B classics as their southern rivals (though it's certainly more satisfying to hear the Beatles rip into "Money" than Freddie & the Dreamers). While many groups identified themselves as R&B for a time to distinguish themselves from the pop mainstream, their main concern was making good music (and, not incidentally, becoming successful), whether it was explicitly R&B-based or not.

The groups had firmer artistic grounds to stand upon when they began penning their own material. Virtually all of them did this at least occasionally from the start, if for no other goal than to pick up some royalties on B-sides and stray album tracks. Many of these early efforts were shamelessly derivative; check out a number of the Stones' first compositions ("Stoned," "Little By Little," "Grown Up Wrong") for evidence. Quite quickly, though, virtually all of the bands would pick up a knack for writing songs that were nearly as strong as, or even just as strong as, the ones they were covering. Groups like the Animals or Manfred Mann would never really develop into first-rate songwriters, despite coming up with some good originals; others, like the Rolling Stones and the Yardbirds, took a year or two before they really found their compositional voices. Once they did, though, the Stones and Yardbirds—and for that matter the Spencer Davis Group, Them, and the Pretty Things—found themselves capable of writing enough good songs to become self-sufficient.

In the process of learning to rely upon their own material, though, a change was taking place, one which was in all likelihood not deliberate. When the Stones came up with "Satisfaction," or Them with "Gloria," or the Yardbirds with "Shapes of Things," the sound had obvious R&B connotations, but it wasn't R&B. It was, whether the groups felt comfortable with the label or not, rock music. The musicians, after all, didn't grow up in black urban centers, but several thousand miles away, in a slightly later age. When they drew upon their own experiences to create their own vocabulary, the results were inevitably different. With the pervasive influence of the likes of the Beatles, Bob Dylan, the Byrds, Motown, Stax-Volt, and other currents in the mid-'60s maelstrom, it would have been a difficult—and rather pointless—exercise to stick to R&B purism. At any rate, everybody was coming out a winner here, as the group's more rock-oriented self-penned material was just as good, or better, than their R&B covers, and on the whole more innovative.

This was really the end of the golden age of British R&B. It wasn't mourned at the time, either, because all of the groups were still around, and still producing their best stuff; it just didn't happen to be only R&B anymore. Virtually without exception, all of the good British R&B groups had made the leap from covering American material to writing most of their own by the end of 1965, much as virtually every American folk singer/songwriter of note made the leap from acoustic to electric arrangements in the wake of Dylan's success. It's sometimes noted that the shift in public tastes from gutbucket R&B to contemporary soul music was also responsible for ending the trend, and while this was a factor, it primarily damaged club bands that had to change their live sound to provide dance fodder, or third-division acts (such as the Downliners Sect) that lacked the smarts to evolve a style of their own.

There had been those British acts that had doggedly stuck to a more purist vision, such as the Graham Bond Organization, but by 1966 sticking to this prototype would have been a laughable anachronism. By this time, for instance, Bond was messing around with a Mellotron on his albums, and Jack Bruce and Ginger Baker were getting ready to expand their horizons with Cream. John Mayall achieved considerable success when Eric Clapton, remarkably, became the most prominent musician by far to turn his back on the pop/rock that the original British R&B groups were gravitating towards, leaving the Yardbirds after "For Your Love" because he wanted to play straight blues riffs rather than (as he saw it) commercial pop. Mayall's Bluesbreakers would be the bastion of British blues purism throughout much of the '60s, though ironically his three star lead guitarists would leave the band for more rock-oriented outfits (Clapton for Cream, Peter Green for Fleetwood Mac, and Mick Taylor to replace Brian Jones in the Rolling Stones). In a further irony, Cream and Fleetwood Mac had started out as pretty much straight blues-rock groups, but quickly evolved into quite versatile rock ensembles that played blues only some of the time.

As preserved on record, however, British R&B is not an anachronism; it remains exciting, and at its best, ground-breaking. Responsible for some of the best music of the British Invasion, it also gave crucial schooling to many of the best British rock musicians of the '60s, and the lessons they learned continued to echo strongly when they moved on to hard rock, mod, psychedelia, and progressive rock.

15 Most Essential British R&B Recordings:
The Rolling Stones, *England's Newest Hitmakers* (ABKCO)
The Rolling Stones, *12 X 5* (ABKCO)
The Rolling Stones, *The Rolling Stones Now!* (ABKCO)
The Rolling Stones, *Bright Lights, Big City* (bootleg)
The Pretty Things, *Get A Buzz: The Best Of The Fontana Years* (Fontana)
The Yardbirds, *Five Live Yardbirds* (Rhino)
Them, *Them Featuring Van Morrison* (Deram)
The Animals, *The Complete Animals* (EMI, UK)
The Spencer Davis Group, *The Best Of* (Rhino)
John Mayall, *John Mayall Plays John Mayall* (Deram)
Manfred Mann, *The R&B Years* (Charly, UK)
The Graham Bond Organization, *The Sound Of '65* (Edsel, UK)
Various Artists, *The Demention Of Sound* (Feedback)
Various Artists, *Pebbles Vol. 6: The Roots Of Mod* (BFD)
The Belfast Gypsies, *Them Belfast Gypsies* (Sonet, Sweden)

—Richie Unterberger

British Invasion

Of all the movements that have shaken the world of rock & roll in the last 40 years, the British Invasion ranks among the very most exciting and important. Only the music's actual birth as a popular phenomenon with the rise of Elvis Presley is comparable; the punk/new wave explosion of the mid-'70s, while equally unexpected and revolutionary, lacked the British Invasion's across-the-board impact on mainstream popular music and culture.

The British Invasion has sometimes been unfairly disparaged as a bunch of white guitar groups re-selling secondhand, vintage American rock & roll and R&B to a public that had forgotten it, or had never been exposed to it in the first place. While it's true that early American rock and soul were the performers' chief inspirations, the best of the groups broke immense ground as performers, songwriters, and stylists, introducing many of the attitudes and innovations that are taken for granted as part and parcel of rock music today.

The British Invasion had its roots in the country's skiffle craze of the mid-'50s, sparked by Lonnie Donegan. Innumerable British teenagers were inspired to form groups based on the simple (and cheap) instrumentation of guitars and washboards. The watered-down folk and blues sound of skiffle can sound unbearably stilted today, but many of those teenage musicians quickly graduated to electric guitars and drums as the focus of their interest shifted to classic early American rock & roll.

There was a homegrown British rock & roll scene in the late '50s and early '60s, but it was overpopulated by pale imitations of American rock, clean-cut instrumentals, and teen idols who offered little more than slightly reworked MOR ballad fare. Tours by American rock & rollers were uncommon, and rock & roll itself was only played on the radio a few hours per week. Which meant that young British musicians and listeners devoted to rock & roll had no alternative but to create a grass roots scene themselves.

While Liverpool was by far the biggest breeding ground for the "beat boom," with hundreds of bands in action by the early '60s, groups were sprouting up all over the British Isles—in Manchester, London, Belfast, and elsewhere. While early pioneers of rock were

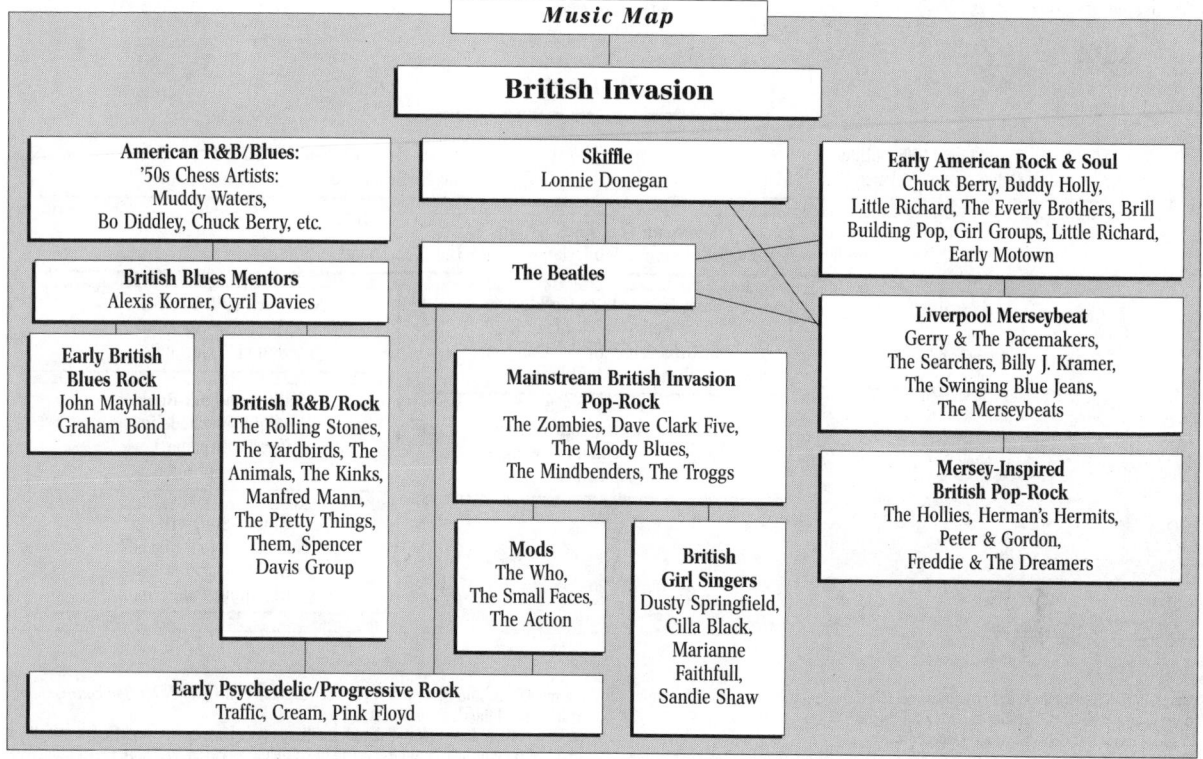

Music Map

British Invasion

American R&B/Blues:
'50s Chess Artists:
Muddy Waters,
Bo Diddley, Chuck Berry, etc.

Skiffle
Lonnie Donegan

Early American Rock & Soul
Chuck Berry, Buddy Holly,
Little Richard, The Everly Brothers, Brill
Building Pop, Girl Groups, Little Richard,
Early Motown

British Blues Mentors
Alexis Korner, Cyril Davies

The Beatles

Liverpool Merseybeat
Gerry & The Pacemakers,
The Searchers, Billy J. Kramer,
The Swinging Blue Jeans,
The Merseybeats

**Early British
Blues Rock**
John Mayhall,
Graham Bond

British R&B/Rock
The Rolling Stones,
The Yardbirds, The
Animals, The Kinks,
Manfred Mann,
The Pretty Things,
Them, Spencer
Davis Group

**Mainstream British Invasion
Pop-Rock**
The Zombies, Dave Clark Five,
The Moody Blues,
The Mindbenders, The Troggs

**Mersey-Inspired
British Pop-Rock**
The Hollies, Herman's Hermits,
Peter & Gordon,
Freddie & The Dreamers

Mods
The Who,
The Small Faces,
The Action

**British
Girl Singers**
Dusty Springfield,
Cilla Black,
Marianne
Faithfull,
Sandie Shaw

Early Psychedelic/Progressive Rock
Traffic, Cream, Pink Floyd

dying, retiring, crippled by scandal, or falling into commercial disfavor in the United States, these British musicians maintained a fanatical devotion to their idols' music. Chuck Berry and Buddy Holly were arguably the most influential heroes to this generation of musicians, but the British also revered a wide range of other great American performers, including the Everly Brothers, Elvis, Gene Vincent, girl groups, the early Motown acts, and many more.

A listen to the Beatles' early recordings leaves no doubt about their adulation for, and mastery of, the styles of their heroes, but they added a lot more of themselves. They were pioneers in so many areas: writing most of their material at a time when that was rarely done; devising melodies and harmonies that were more inventive than any others that had been used in rock & roll; writing and performing as a self-contained group with distinctive individual talents and personalities, rather than a star with anonymous backing musicians; and embodying the spirit of rebellious youth with their energetic performances, humor, and nonconformist attitudes. They, and the best of their fellow British groups, did this with a giddy exuberance which has rarely been matched in the history of rock & roll.

The impact of Beatlemania—which blanketed Britain in 1963, and the United States the following year—could not be overestimated, not only in terms of commercial success (as in the oft-quoted statistic of the Beatles claiming the top five singles in the U.S. one week in early 1964), but in how it changed rock & roll itself. Sometimes unfairly criticized as a "safe" alternative to the moodier and blacker Rolling Stones, the Beatles displayed an enormous versatility that refutes such categorizations. They could rock as hard as anyone when that suited them, but more important, they were pop's greatest eclectics, constantly evolving and experimenting in their successful quest to create the most diverse and innovative body of work ever produced by a rock group.

The first flush of "beat" bands, as they were called initially, to overtake Britain and (slightly later) the United States were often from Liverpool, and tended to emulate the Beatles' lightest, most innocuous features. Dubbed "Merseybeat," guitars and harmonies were to the fore, as were bouncy, irresistible melodies (sometimes in the form of actual Lennon-McCartney compositions that the Beatles had rejected for their own recordings). Cute and clean-cut, the recordings of Gerry & the Pacemakers, Billy J. Kramer, Freddie & the Dreamers and Herman's Hermits have fared poorly in latter-day jaded rock critiques for their lightweight, at times insipid content. But this shouldn't obscure the glittering harmonies and chiming guitars of the Searchers, the Hollies, and Peter & Gordon, who were probably the best bands that followed the mold of the Beatles' most pop-oriented recordings.

The Beatles' greatest challenge came from the London-based R&B scene, by groups who drew from American electric bluesmen like Muddy Waters, and tended to emulate the Beatles' lightest, most innocuous features. Schooled by early British bluesmen like Alexis Korner and Cyril Davies, the Rolling Stones, the Yardbirds, Manfred Mann, the Kinks, the Pretty Things, the Who, and non-London acts like the Animals, the Spencer Davis Group, and Them took

the bulk of their early repertoires from obscure blues and R&B recordings, investing them with accelerated tempos and a reckless guitar-based approach. As personalities, they took the Beatles' anti-Establishment stance further, rebelling against society more openly and wearing their hair even longer.

The difference between these R&B cultists and the Beatles is not nearly as great as it has sometimes been portrayed. The Beatles and the R&B groups often covered the same songs, not just by Chuck Berry but by many others; the Beatles, the Stones, and for that matter, Freddie & the Dreamers—all recorded the early Motown tune "Money." The Stones' first big British hit was a cover of Lennon-McCartney's "I Wanna Be Your Man"; their second was a cover of a Buddy Holly song. Manfred Mann covered obscure girl group tunes for their biggest hits, and the Kinks would draw upon British music hall traditions for their most creative work. All the groups from this earthier faction would come to pen their own material, often placing a premium upon melodic invention and harmonies.

Sometimes overlooked in this battle of supposed opposites were the groups that favored neither the R&B or dippy pop approach, instead focusing their efforts on masterful straightforward rock. The Zombies were probably second only to the Beatles in their breathtakingly adventurous melodies; the Dave Clark Five pounded out tuneful rockers with glorious abandon; the first incarnation of the Moody Blues sang haunting pop/rock tunes that borrowed from R&B, soul, and the Brill Building.

In 1964 and 1965, the march of the British Invaders seemed endless, but in the face of a volatile rock scene, it became clear that only the bands that could both write their own material and evolve stylistically would survive. The Beatles, Stones, Who and Kinks were the only British bands to maintain a high standard of work throughout the '60s, expanding their songwriting talents and instrumental resources at a dizzying pace. Bands like the Yardbirds and Zombies briefly exhibited similar resources for pioneering psychedelia and experimentation before folding due to internal and external pressures. Groups like Gerry & the Pacemakers, the Dave Clark Five and the Searchers fell off the map commercially due to their inability to write top-notch material or evolve with the times. And a few, like the Hollies and Manfred Mann survived by incorporating enough progressive elements into their brand of pop/rock to remain hip (and commercially successful).

While a few first-rate bands like the mod Small Faces and the crude Troggs emerged in 1966, that year saw the impetus of the original British Invasion start to fade. A second generation of bands sprung up that took progressive experimentation, cohesive albums, and self-contained songwriting as a given. Some (Traffic, Cream) featured veterans of the first wave of the invasion; others (Pink Floyd) owed little to the movement at all.

In reality, though, the British Invasion has never stopped. Artists from the British Isles continue to invade the American, and indeed the international, audience at a rapid pace, if not nearly as phenomenal a rate as the heady days of 1964 and 1965. Folk-rock, garage-rock, and psychedelia grew directly out of the innovations of the best British Invasion groups. And rock & roll owes much of its climate for artistic freedom and individual

Music Map

Folk-Rock

Early '60s Folkies	British Invasion Groups
Bob Dylan (acoustic), Peter, Paul & Mary	The Beatles, the Searchers, The Animals

American Folk Rock Groups
The Byrds, The Beau Brummels, Bob Dylan (electric), The Blue Things

Commercial L.A. Folk Rock	Early '60s Folkies Go Electric	New York Folk Rock Groups
The Mamas & the Papas, Sonny & Cher, The Turtles	Fred Neil, Gordon Lightfoot, Phil Ochs, Ian & Sylvia, Donovan, Richard & Mimi Farina	The Lovin' Spoonful, Simon & Garfunkel

Late '60s British Folk-Rockers
Fairport Convention, Pentangle, Nick Drake

California Folk-Rockers Gone Psychedelic
Jefferson Airplane, Love, Buffalo Springfield

Singer/Songwriters
Neil Young, Joni Mitchell, Tim Buckley, Jackson Browne, Carole King, Paul Simon

---

expression—not to mention its harmonies, melodies, and guitar-based ensemble sound—to the road paved by the Beatles and their followers.

15 Most Essential British Invasion Recordings:
The Beatles, all of their albums, though *The Beatles 1962-66* (Capitol) has their biggest early hits.
The Rolling Stones, *The Singles Collection* (ABKCO)
The Who, *Meaty, Beaty, Big and Bouncy* (MCA)
The Kinks, *Greatest Hits* (Rhino)
The Yardbirds, *Greatest Hits, Vol.-1* (Rhino)
The Animals, *The Complete Animals* (EMI, UK)
The Zombies, *Singles As & Bs* (See For Miles, UK)
Manfred Mann, *Best of the EMI Years* (Griffin)
The Dave Clark Five, *The History of the Dave Clark Five* (Hollywood)
The Hollies, *30th Anniversary Collection* (EMI)
Them, *Them Featuring Van Morrison* (Parrot)
Various Artists, *The British Invasion Vol. 1-9* (Rhino)
The Pretty Things, *Get A Buzz: The Best of the Fontana Years* (Fontana)
The Small Faces, *The Small Faces* (PolyGram)
The Spencer Davis Group, *The Best of the Spencer Davis Group* (Rhino)
Recommended reading:
The British Invasion, by Nicholas Schaffner (McGraw Hill)
Videos:
A Hard Day's Night (also available as CD-ROM from Voyager)
The Compleat Beatles

—Richie Unterberger

Folk-Rock

In the early '60s, any suggestion that the folk and rock & roll worlds would intertwine to create a hybrid called folk-rock would have met with utter disbelief from both camps. The folk community prided itself on its purity, which meant acoustic instruments and songs of substance; they regarded rock & roll as vulgar and commercial. Rock & rollers, for the most part, were utterly ignorant of folk traditions, and unconcerned with broadening their lyrical content beyond tried-and-true themes of romance and youthful partying. Yet within a few years, folk and rock not only combined into a new form of popular music, but became hugely successful and influential.

By 1964, Bob Dylan had already done much to revolutionize contemporary folk music by singing about topical issues and (after a couple years) abstract personal and romantic concerns in a poetic and uniquely expressive fashion. Dylan harbored a secret admiration for the Beatles and other major British Invasion bands, a fascination which was mutual. It was only a matter of time before each started to influence the other.

The roots of folk-rock can be detected in a few pre-1965 recordings by the Searchers and Jackie DeShannon (who helped introduce the ringing, circular 12-string guitar riffs that became one of the music's major trademarks), as well as the Beau Brummels, the Animals' superb bluesy interpretation of the traditional folk standard "The House of the Rising Sun," and the Beatles' own "I'm a Loser." It took the Byrds however, to really kick the movement into gear with their electric version of Dylan's "*Mr. Tambourine Man,*" which topped the charts in mid-1965.

The first and best folk-rock band, the Byrds may have been comprised of ex-folkies who had only picked up their electric instruments a year or so before they became superstars. But they were, if anything, influenced more by the Beatles than Dylan; as they were once quoted (albeit tongue in cheek), they based their sound on "21% Beatles, 11% Zombies, 8% Dillards, 18% Dylan, 14% Pete Seeger, 16% Searchers, and 12% trial and error/ignorance/accident/originality." Leader Roger McGuinn's chiming 12-string guitar set the sonic standard for the new genre, as did the group's beautiful choral harmonies and superb interpretations of songs by Dylan and Seeger, traditional folk ballads, and their own first-rate original material.

Dylan himself moved into folk-rock around the same time as the Byrds on his *Bringing It All Back Home* album, divided into electric and acoustic sides. The subsequent *Highway 61 Revisited* and *Blonde on Blonde* were full-bore electric rock records, marrying Dylan's intense, at times surrealistic poetry to a tough beat, provided by soon-to-be-stars in their own right like Mike Bloomfield, Al Kooper and the Band. His conversion to rock & roll outraged much of his original constituency, which was more than offset by his legions of new fans; indeed, all three of his albums from 1965 and 1966 made the Top Ten, as did the singles "Like a Rolling Stone," "Positively 4th Street," and "Rainy Day Women #12 & 35."

The success of the Byrds and Dylan ignited a firestorm of emulators and imitators. The Lovin' Spoonful, from Dylan's own stomping ground of Greenwich Village, were the era's greatest exponents of good-time folk-rock; the Mamas & the Papas, led by ex-folkie John Phillips, were at the head of a slickly produced L.A. variation of the sound; Sonny & Cher, the most commercial of the bunch, latched on to a few of folk-rock's most saleable attributes on their first batch of smashes, and went on to highly successful careers in pop's mainstream. Donovan, one of the most talented mid-'60s folkies to follow in Dylan's footsteps, went not only electric, but psychedelic. Producers added 12-string guitars and a rhythm section to an old track by Simon & Garfunkel; after "Sound of Silence" became a number one hit, the duo became one of the most successful folk-rock acts of all. Obscure regional groups like the Leaves (from L.A.) and the Blue Things (from Kansas) recorded some wonderful folk-rock singles and even albums that were in the same class as the hits by the top folk-rock stars.

The "rock" in folk-rock was always more prominent than the "folk"; all of the above acts had a highly commercial sense of melody, grafting guitar patterns and somewhat more personal, topical lyrical concerns from folk music into their own superb pop/rock creations. Performers approaching the hybrid from the folk side were less frequent and less commercially successful, but singer/songwriters like Fred Neil, Phil Ochs, Gordon Lightfoot, Ian & Sylvia, Richard & Mimi Farina, and others proved willing and able to electrify their sound with positive commercial and artistic results.

Folk-rock was not only a tremendous success on the charts in 1965 and 1966, but tremendously influential in expanding the sonic and lyrical vistas of rock as a whole. The Beatles were already addressing more personal concerns on the mid-1965 tunes "Help" and "You've Got to Hide Your Love Away"; *Rubber Soul,* issued at the end of the year, was one of folk-rock's greatest triumphs. Many of the early psychedelic bands from San Francisco were comprised of renegade folkies, and while groups like the Jefferson

Airplane and the Beatles themselves would move beyond folk-rock to psychedelia fairly quickly, there's no doubt that folk-rock whetted their appetites for lyrical and instrumental experimentation and innovation.

While folk-rock's commercial heyday was in 1965 and 1966, in truth it has been a strong presence in rock ever since, fading only as a marketing term for a sound that was initially perceived by the industry as a fad, not a permanent addition to the rock & roll lexicon. In 1967, L.A. bands Buffalo Springfield and Love would release classic recordings that drew upon folk-rock as their core, adding elements of eclecticism and psychedelia. In the late '60s, British groups like Fairport Convention and Pentangle achieved perhaps the purest folk-rock blend, with nearly equal balances between the electric and the acoustic, and between modern compositions and traditional numbers. The singer/songwriter movement of the late '60s and early '70s was not as prone to electric guitars and group ensembles, perhaps, but also took folk-rock as its chief inspiration. The harmonies, ringing guitars, and chord patterns of classic folk-rock live on in countless contemporary acts, ranging from bands like R.E.M. to singers like Tracy Chapman.

15 Most Essential Recordings:

The Byrds, *Mr. Tambourine Man* (Columbia)
The Byrds, *Greatest Hits* (Columbia)
Bob Dylan, *Blonde on Blonde* (Columbia)
Bob Dylan, *Highway 61 Revisited* (Columbia)
The Lovin' Spoonful, *Anthology* (Rhino)
The Beatles, *Rubber Soul* (Capitol)
Donovan, *Troubadour: The Definitive Collection 1964-1976* (Epic)
Simon & Garfunkel, *Collected Works* (Columbia)
Buffalo Springfield, *Buffalo Springfield* (1973 double-LP compilation) (Atco)
Love, *Forever Changes* (Elektra)
The Mamas & The Papas, *Creeque Alley* (MCA)
The Blue Things, *The Blue Things Story Vol. 1-3* (Cicadelic)
The Beau Brummels, *Best of the Beau Brummels* (Rhino)
Richard & Mimi Farina, *The Best of Richard & Mimi Farina* (Vanguard)
The Leaves, *1966* (Panda)

Recommended reading:

Timeless Flight: The Definitive Biography of the Byrds, by Johnny Rogan (1990, Square One, U.K.)

—Richie Unterberger

Merseybeat

Merseybeat, the first form of British rock & roll to make international waves, is recalled by some rock historians as happy but sappy music, quickly rendered passe by both the increased sophistication of Merseybeat champs the Beatles and the tougher, more R&B-based sounds of the Rolling Stones and their ilk. It was innocent stuff, to be sure, but dismissing it as a lightweight phase in rock's evolution fails to acknowledge its downright revolutionary qualities. In its 1963-1964 heyday, Merseybeat brought the stale and stuffy British music industry to life, and was instrumental in establishing the self-contained guitar group as the rock & roll norm—a prototype which remains in place, to a large extent, over 30 years later.

Merseybeat, sometimes spelled Mersey Beat, centered around the British industrial port city of Liverpool, which is situated on the Mersey River. As late as 1962, had anyone suggested that the British (and, slightly later, American) charts would be overrun by Liverpudlians, the very idea would have been scorned at as unthinkably ridiculous. The British music industry was very much centered in London, in terms of its performers, studios, and publishers. In the annals of popular culture, Liverpool was mostly known for its comedians. While it's difficult to compare because of differences in culture and size, an explosion of talent from Liverpool seemed about as unlikely as a fountain of American pop issuing forth without warning from St. Louis, Tampa Bay, or Buffalo.

Liverpool, however, was an unusual British city in some important respects. As an industrial port, it was exposed to rather more international influence than most towns in the U.K., particularly from America and Ireland. Partially because of this influx, earthy folk and country music already enjoyed a large audience in Liverpool even before rock & roll was first heard in England in the mid-1950s. When rock & roll did make it over there—first with Bill Haley, then with Elvis—it found an immediate, enthusiastic audience in the city's youth. And throughout the 1950s and early 1960s, American rock & roll of all sorts made its way into Liverpool via the tastes of American sailors, who would sometimes bring imported singles that were all but impossible to find in the shops or hear on the BBC airwaves (which accorded precious little airtime to pop music of any kind).

Many of these teenagers were galvanized into picking up their own instruments, not only by rock & roll, but by the skiffle music of Lonnie Donegan and others. Skiffle can sound like a corny variation on British folk today, but made a key contribution to the British music scene by making it easy for young people to form their own groups. The reasons were simple: skiffle music, with a few basic chords, was easy to play, and many of its instruments (simple guitars, banjos, and washboards) were inexpensive, an important consideration in postwar Britain, where living standards weren't high.

When the musicians got a little older, a little more proficient, and a little more ambitious, it was just another step to upgrade their guitars and drums, and add amplifiers. By the late 1950s, there were already quite a few groups active on the Merseyside. There weren't, however, many places for them to play locally, where the young musicians encountered stiff resistance from clubs used to booking antiquated "trad" jazz bands. There were parties or tiny clubs to play (one located in the basement of the home of early Beatle drummer Pete Best), but an entirely unexpected factor would help set the scene into overdrive.

Local entrepreneur Allan Williams, through a series of fascinating and comical coincidences (detailed in several Beatle biographies), got a Hamburg clubowner interested in booking local bands. The long-forgotten Derry & the Seniors were the first to go, and after that engagement was a success, Williams was asked to provide others. He didn't want to send the Beatles—a very raw group who lacked even a drummer—but in the absence of other bands qualified or willing to make the journey, he relented, on the condition that they find a permanent drummer. After Pete Best was enlisted, they went to Germany in August, 1960, and when they returned four months later, they were improved almost beyond recognition. Throughout the early '60s, other Liverpool bands, such as Gerry & the Pacemakers, the Searchers, and Rory Storm & the Hurricanes (with Ringo Starr on drums) would also play extensive Hamburg jaunts.

As Lester Bangs wrote in *The Rolling Stone Illustrated History of Rock & Roll*, "Hamburg was a crucible, a proving ground, a place where groups were required to play loud and fast and raw all night, hour after hour, using stimulants to maintain the pace, forcing members of the band who had thought they could not sing to take the mike when the leader's lungs gave out. Things got wild, and the sound took on a mania that became a crucial factor in the coming assault on the United States."

When the Liverpool bands returned to their stomping grounds, their audiences were astounding by the wild energy that the musicians had cultivated overseas. Clubs began opening their doors to rock & roll (then called "beat") groups, most notably the legendary Cavern Club, where the Beatles played roughly 300 shows. Bill Harry, an art college pal of John Lennon's, fed the boom by establishing *Mersey Beat*, a tabloid that covered the local music scene with enthusiasm.

In those days, the groups' repertoires were usually derived almost wholly from American rock & roll and R&B of a much tougher sort than the wimpy, homegrown derivatives of the early British rock performers (who were few in number in any case). The best American rock & rollers retained fierce followings even when they fell from commercial grace in the United States, or had tamed their music. In particular, Chuck Berry, Buddy Holly, the Everly Brothers, Little Richard, Elvis Presley, Jerry Lee Lewis, and Gene Vincent were revered. But the taste of many Liverpool groups was eclectic, also encompassing early soul and girl groups, and many rare, even cult-like items by performers that never even made it big in the States, such as Chan Romero, Eddie Fontaine, the Jodimars, and the Donays.

There were probably several hundred or so combos active in the Liverpool area by 1962, but the thriving local scene remained unknown beyond the region, and may have remained an isolated phenomenon if not for the efforts of Brian Epstein. The owner of the city's biggest record shop, located just around the corner from the Cavern, he claimed to have been unaware of the Beatles before late 1961. Whether that's true or not, he was bowled over by the group's magnetism when he saw them at the Cavern. Taking over their management almost immediately, he determined to do what then seemed almost impossible: make them a national act. He set up an audition with Decca within weeks (the results of that January 1, 1962 session are readily available on numerous bootlegs), but was told, unbelievably, that groups of guitars were on the way out.

What Decca and other companies that rejected the Beatles failed to perceive was that the group were not just another collection of musicians. They were the cutting edge of a British generation that had grown up with rock & roll, and played it with as much authentic heart as their American idols. They didn't just happen to sing and play guitars at the same time: the guitars, rhythm especially, were fast and way up front, and the vocals and harmonies were unabashedly enthusiastic. And, in the case of the Beatles (and a few other Merseybeat groups), they even wrote some of their own material. To be fair to Decca, these qualities weren't quite in full bloom at the Beatles' audition, and it's to Epstein's enormous credit that he persevered for months against a stodgy, parochial British music industry that was disinterested in anything from Liverpool, or for that matter little beyond the vicinity of London. EMI producer George Martin also deserves enormous credit for recognizing the Beatles' potential and signing them in mid-1962.

So much has been written about the Beatles that it's difficult to add much about the significance of their early records, but it's no exaggeration to say that their early hits turned the British music business—and, more importantly, the British audience—on their heads in early 1963. The number one hit "Please Please Me" and the album of the same name were British pop of an entirely different kind, sung, played, and harmonized with enormous freshness, melodic invention, and energy. The big British labels immediately realized that there might be a lot more of that where it came from, and descended upon the Merseyside to scoop up groups by the handful.

Epstein had already been greasing the wheels for the Merseybeat Boom by signing some of the region's top acts, including Gerry & the Pacemakers, Billy J. Kramer & the Dakotas, the Fourmost, Cilla Black, and several much more obscure acts. Gerry & the Pacemakers actually seriously rivaled the Beatles in popularity for a while in 1963, as their first three singles (including "How Do You Do It," which had been rejected as a possible debut single for the Beatles) made number one in the U.K. While Epstein did manage to corral most of the city's most successful performers into his stable, a few others also reached national success, particularly the Searchers, the Merseybeats, and the Mojos.

While the Beatles and Merseybeat were almost synonymous for a brief period, the other Liverpool acts were, ironically, far more typical of what came with time to be thought of as the Mersey sound. The rhythms were fast, choppy, and bouncy. Rhythm guitars and simple bass-drum patterns dominated the arrangements. The songs were attacked with an utter lack of self-consciousness, and harmonies and backup vocals were often to the fore, particularly in the Beatles and the Searchers. The melodies were irresistibly catchy, often combining major and minor chords in unusual fashions, and the lyrics simple and romantic, sometimes almost mindlessly so. The trivial words and relentlessly happy-go-lucky sentiments can strike some listeners as dated and quaint.

Good Merseybeat is not mere period music, though. The lightweight factors are redeemed by a positively giddy enthusiasm, and a naive, all-things-are-possible energy. It's "feel good" music, and far from the earthiest rock & roll variant of that time or any other. But few rock & roll styles provide such an immediate lift, due to those damn catchy melodies, harmonies, and a positive joy that comes through even when the groups were running through overplayed oldies, or music hallish numbers written for them by British songwriters from the old school.

The Searchers were undoubtedly the best Merseybeat band besides the Beatles, with glittering harmonies and 12-string guitars that helped inspire folk-rock. Gerry & the Pacemakers, though equally popular, have not aged as well, epitomizing some of the almost-too-jaunty cheer of lightweight Merseybeat. Billy J. Kramer, also big in 1963-64, was actually one of the tamer regional acts, and had most of his hits with innocuous Lennon-McCartney discards that the Beatles usually didn't record themselves.

Other Merseybeat groups were much more successful in the U.K. than the U.S., and are worth checking out by British Invasion aficionados who might have missed them the first time around. The Swinging Blue Jeans, who did have an American hit with "Hippy Hippy Shake" (although the Beatles did a much better version on the BBC), were the best of these, sounding like a Gerry & the Pacemakers with far more guts. The same could also be said to some degree of the Mojos, who had a big British hit with "Everything's Alright" (covered by David Bowie on *Pinups*), though their material wasn't as strong as the Blue Jeans'. The Merseybeats, who had a few British hits, weren't as raucous, and some of their repertoire was pretty ordinary, though their harmonies and mid-tempo material retain some appeal.

The British Beat Boom was hardly limited to the Mersey River, though it was by far the most active hotbed. Nearby Manchester in particular was also home to groups that could have easily been classified as genuine Merseybeat acts with their guitar- and harmony-dominated approach. Freddie & the Dreamers, in fact, were the first non-Liverpool group to have a big hit in England after the Beatles broke, although for many they and fellow Mancunians Herman & the Hermits (justifiably) represent the British Invasion at its corniest. More palatable were the Hollies, who ranked with the Beatles and the Searchers as the best groups which placed a premium on Everly Brothers-like harmonies. The influence of Merseybeat was felt throughout Britain as well, though not to such a blatant extent; heavy echoes of the sound can be heard in the Dave Clark Five, Peter & Gordon, and others, and even some of the early compositions of Mick Jagger and Keith Richards betray a distinct Merseybeat flavor.

Merseybeat reigned supreme on the British charts in 1963, and seemed to be actually getting bigger in early 1964. The Beatles conquered America in February, making Merseybeat an international term, and opening the gate for U.S. success for several other groups from the area. During one week in that same month, six of the top ten singles on the British chart were from the Merseyside—none of those, amazingly, by the Beatles. Yet within a year, Merseybeat was yesterday's papers, and all of the groups except the Beatles were on a rapid downslide.

There were a couple of major reasons for this downturn. On one hand, the Liverpool groups faced tough competition from other bands in other parts of the country that had begun recording after the success of the Beatles. Mostly from London—with exceptions such as the Animals (from Newcastle), the Spencer Davis Group (Birmingham), and Them (Belfast)—these groups by and large favored a grittier, less pop-based sound that was far more oriented towards raucous blues, R&B, and soul. Manfred Mann, the Pretty Things, the Yardbirds, the Kinks, the Who, and of course the Rolling Stones were some of the most threatening. Ironically, none of them may have gotten as far as a recording contract if the Merseybeat explosion hadn't awakened the industry to the general existence of thousands of young bands throughout the nation.

The harder truth to swallow was that other than the Beatles—who were in any case by far the most talented band on the Merseyside—the groups simply didn't have what it took to compete in the rapidly evolving international pop and rock climate. For one thing, despite the Beatles' sterling example, many of them wrote little of their own material (although some may be surprised to learn that Gerry Marsden did write most of the Pacemakers' hits). Indeed, a lot of the Merseybeat bands you've never heard never learned to inject a lot of themselves into their covers, as the collection *This Is Merseybeat* (stuffed with tepid material by a host of no-names) demonstrates.

They also failed to follow the Beatles' lead in that they didn't, or couldn't, change with the times, sticking with basic tuneful pop-rock when the Beatles continued to expand their sound with increasingly sophisticated songwriting, experimentation in the studio, and a willingness to absorb all manner of contemporary influences. In marked contrast, groups like the Stones, Yardbirds, Kinks, and Who—and even some more pop-oriented acts, like the Zombies and the Moody Blues—displayed a daring ability to take risks and experiment, often successfully, without compromising the qualities that had made their success possible in the first place. And all of them came to write most or all of their own material, realizing that old rock and R&B chestnuts couldn't be recycled forever.

The British Invasion enabled groups like Gerry & the Pacemakers to extend their run a bit with hits in America in 1964 and 1965, at a time when they were already wobbling on their home turf. But by the end of 1965, none of the Merseybeat stars were stars anymore, although they in some instances managed to produce some good records in '66. The Beatles themselves had begun to move beyond Merseybeat way back in 1963 on their second album, and by 1966 were never identified with Merseybeat, but with the cutting edge of rock as a whole. Unbelievably, considering the wealth of bands generated by the Merseyside in 1963 and 1964, no other Liverpool group of major significance emerged during the last half of the 1960s.

Latter-day revivalists can't recreate the sound of Merseybeat without sounding excruciatingly sappy and self-conscious, an irony considering that one of Merseybeat's most enduring qualities was its lack of self-consciousness. Its legacy, however, is enormous, felt in the whole of British pop, in American folk-rock groups the Byrds and the Beau Brummels (both of whom looked to Merseybeat for much of their harmonic blend, early songwriting acumen, and guitar sound), and indeed in the aspirations of any band who doesn't let the fact that they don't happen to be located in a fashionable city deter them from playing and writing just for the sake of doing it. Groups of guitars will never be on the way out again.

13 Recommended Recordings:
The Beatles, *Please Please Me* (Capitol)
The Beatles, *Live At The BBC* (Capitol)
The Beatles, *With The Beatles* (Capitol)
Various Artists, *The Songs Lennon & McCartney Gave Away* (EMI, UK)
The Searchers, *Greatest Hits* (Rhino)
The Swinging Blue Jeans, *Hippy Hippy Shake: The Definitive Collection* (EMI)
Gerry & the Pacemakers, *Best Of: The Definitive Collection* (EMI)
Billy J. Kramer & the Dakotas, *Best Of* (EMI)
The Mojos, *Working* (Edsel, UK)
The Merseybeats, *Beat... And Ballads* (Edsel, UK)
Honorary Mentions (from Manchester):
The Hollies, *30th Anniversary Collection* (EMI)
Freddie & the Dreamers, *Best Of* (EMI)
Herman's Hermits, *Their Greatest Hits* (ABKCO)

—Richie Unterberger

Garage Rock

For those who prize adolescent, primitive energy as one of rock & roll's best features, the garage rock bands of the '60s rank at or near the top of the rock & roll pyramid. Ignored or even scorned by critics in its heyday, garage rock proved an influential inspiration for the punk rock explosion of the '70s, and experienced a renaissance of sorts in the '80s, among the rock underground and collector community if nowhere else.

Largely a North American phenomenon, the garage band movement began in the wake of the British Invasion in 1964. There were already plenty of young, white rock groups throughout the U.S., but they were usually found playing instrumental (sometimes surf) rock or heavily R&B-influenced "frat rock," and largely unconcerned with writing their own songs or making individualistic, rebellious statements. The Beatles, Rolling Stones, Kinks, Animals and others changed that overnight. Caught off-guard by this unexpected onslaught, teenage groups put the focus on loud electric guitars and grew their hair long in attempts to emulate their heroes.

What emerged was a distinctly cruder and more adolescent variation on the British Invasion sound (which itself had been largely inspired by American rock and R&B in the first place). It is not accurate to say that the garage groups matched the talents of their British idols, or of American outfits like the Byrds; they were usually considerably younger and less sophisticated, and lacked the songwriting skills or instrumental finesse of the era's major groups. By way of compensation, perhaps, they placed a premium on sheer outrageousness: over-the-top vocal screams and sneers fought it out with loud guitars that almost always had a fuzztone attached. Garage bands were so named after the habitual practice space of the musicians, which were overwhelmingly white, suburban, and teenaged. While scattered 1964 recordings by groups like the Gestures and the Barbarians served as early blueprints for the sound, it didn't blanket the country properly until 1965, when virtually every major city (and many minor ones) became home to dozens of new guitar groups hungering for a piece of the action—which meant parties, girls and, of course, records.

These records were usually pressed on tiny local labels, and usually only heard within a 50-100 mile radius (if they were heard on local radio at all). Occasionally they were picked up for nationwide distribution by a larger company; more occasionally still, they became bona fide national hits. The Shadows of Knight, The Count Five, the 13th Floor Elevators, The Standells, The Seeds, ? & The Mysterians, and the Gentrys were among the lucky few who hit this jackpot, although their time in the spotlight was brief.

An enormous amount of records were released by garage bands in the '60s, particularly between 1965 and 1967. California and Texas were probably home to more of these bands per capita than any other state, but the number of groups that recorded, let alone played, was staggering. Detroit, Boston, Chicago, Minneapolis, Seattle, Pittsburgh, Cleveland, Phoenix; they all were home to large local scenes supporting several dozens of bands, much in the manner of today's alternative rock and punk communities.

There are a great many generic garage band recordings: fuzzy variations of the "Satisfaction" or "You Really Got Me" riffs, simplistic lyrics about cheating girlfriends, inept guitar solos and cheesy organ riffs. There are also a great many great garage band records by bands that combined their energy with sharp songwriting skills, compelling hooks, or sheer unpredictable mania.

The Texas bands favored galloping rhythms with bigger-than-life fuzztones; the California bands often copped folk-rock and psychedelic licks from their own local heroes; Midwest groups sometimes drew upon trends in soul music; New England groups were more prone to use Zombies-like keyboards and melodies; Cleveland acts showed a strong affinity for Merseybeat and British power-pop.

But the bands from these far-flung territories had a lot more in common than not; all of them kept abreast of the latest trends in British rock, folk-rock, and psychedelic music.

A number of factors conspired to slow the momentum of the garage phenomenon around 1967 and 1968. Facing college, lack of national success and, worst of all, the military draft, many of the bands simply didn't stay together for very long. Increasingly homogenous national radio airplay and distribution meant less of a chance for regional

---

Garage Rock

Instrumental and Surf Groups The Ventures, Dick Dale, The Trashmen, The Astronauts	**British Invasion Groups** The Beatles, The Rolling Stones, The Animals, The Kinks, The Yardbirds	**Frat Rock Groups** The Kingsmen, the Rivieras

Early Garage Bands
The Gestures, the Barbarians, the Chartbusters

British Pop-Rock Influenced Garage Bands The Remains, New Colony Six	**Raunchy R&B-Influenced Garage Bands** The Chocolate Watchband, The Standells, The Shadows of Knight, The Count Five

Garage Psychedelia
The Music Machine, The Electric Prunes, The Seeds,
The 13th Floor Elevators

---

labels to succeed or get their records played, and hence less opportunities for local talent to enter the studio. And the fact was, a lot of the garage bands were outgrowing the pop/rock of the first wave of the British Invasion, and moving—as their inspirations were—towards more progressive and psychedelic sounds, with lyrics that, for better or worse, addressed more mature concerns than picking up girls and adolescent rebellion.

Almost immediately forgotten by rock historians, garage music began its comeback when future Patti Smith Group guitarist Lenny Kaye compiled the original Nuggets album in 1972. This double set featured the most popular garage band recordings by the likes of the Standells, Seeds, Chocolate Watch Band and others; Kaye helped coin the term "punk rock" in his liner notes, in reference to bands such as these that celebrated rock & roll at its most primal and unself-conscious. Adding a measure of contemporary lyrical content and attitude, bands like the Sex Pistols would embellish this prototype and give birth to modern punk rock a few years later.

The *Pebbles* series of the late '70s took the Nuggets approach several steps further, unearthing even rarer and rawer garage band recordings from across the nation. Eventually numbering dozens of volumes, *Pebbles* in turn kicked off a deluge of '60s garage band reissues and compilations; often great, sometimes awful, these numbered in the hundreds by the late '80s. Contemporary groups like the Fuzztones, the Pandoras, Thee Fourgiven and dozens of others played garage revival music in the 1980s, though in truth they never approached the authentic qualities of the best of the '60s garage, and never made a significant impact on either the mainstream or underground rock scenes.

The reissues introduced young and old listeners to scores of fine bands, ironically giving them their greatest international exposure decades after they broke up. Some, like the Remains or the Music Machine were arguably too talented and innovative to be lumped in with the garage crowd in the first place. Others, like Zakary Thaks, the Chocolate Watch Band and the Rising Storm personified teenage rock & roll at its most enjoyable. All of the above-mentioned groups—and quite a few others—were nearly as good as the more accomplished and more famous British and American hitmaking bands of the era, and deserve belated recognition as first-rate '60s rock & rollers.

13 Most Essential '60s Garage Rock Records:
Various Artists, *Nuggets Vol. 1-12* (Rhino)
Various Artists, *Pebbles Vol. 1-10* (AIP)
The New Colony Six, *At the River's Edge* (Sundazed)
The Chocolate Watch Band, *Best of the Chocolate Watchband* (Rhino)
The Standells, *Best of the Standells* (Rhino)
Zakary Thaks, *Texas Band* (Moxie)
The Music Machine, *Best of the Music Machine* (Rhino)
The Rising Storm, *Calm Before* (Arf Arf)
The Remains, *The Remains* (Epic)
We the People, *Declaration of Independence* (Eva, France)
The Shadows of Knight, *Dark Sides: The Best of the Shadows of Knight* (Rhino)
The Mystic Tide, *Solid Sound* (Distortions)
The Lemon Drops, *Crystal Pure* (Cicadelic)

—Richie Unterberger

Mod

The prime of British mod rock was very short—almost all of the key recordings were made in 1965 and 1966. Only two pure "mod" groups, the Who and the Small Faces, could be said to have had a substantial commercial and artistic impact. And even then, this impact was largely limited to Britain at the time; not only that, by the time they'd been recording for a couple of years, each of those groups had largely moved beyond mod

music entirely. Yet mod remains a durable part of rock's fabric, providing the key link between the British Beat Boom and British psychedelia, and fusing melodic harmonies, power guitar chords, soul/R&B, and a distinctly British breeziness into a genuinely new and exciting style that typified British pop at its most energetic and effervescent.

Because mod was such a short-lived and elastic label, it can be surprisingly hard to pin down which groups were truly "mod," which weren't, or which were, sort of, at times. The movement was certainly based in London, where hundreds of bands had sprung up in the wake of the initial success of the Beatles and the Rolling Stones. The orientation of these acts tended to be more R&B-based than the Mersey groups (though these boundaries were fluid, not absolute). They were also in the main guitar-oriented, and when the repertoires of role models like the Stones started to slide away from blues and hard R&B, and towards soul and self-penned material, the scene followed suit.

Some of these groups, however, belonged to (or at least often played to) a subculture with strong roots in fashion and attitude as well as music. The mods were extremely style-conscious, placing a premium on sharp and flashy clothes that found a mirror in the exploding London fashion community and trends in modern pop art. They also placed a premium on independent social values that walked a delicate line between rebellion and hedonism, developing a lifestyle based around dancing to live music, taking (mild, by latter-day standards) amphetamines, buying cool threads, and going mobile on small scooters (fancy cars being beyond the economic reach of most of them). They sometimes clashed with another British subculture, the more '50s-minded (in both dress and musical taste) "rockers," in rumbles which made national headlines in England. These sharp divisions between subcultures have always been hard to comprehend in the United States, where a) these subcultures didn't exist, and b) many listeners paid little heed to the boundaries separating, say, rockabilly and the Kinks, certainly not enough to fight about it. The film *Quadrophenia*, based upon the Who's concept album about the mod era, is the best evocation of the period for novices wishing to get a flavor of the time, diluted and distorted though it might be by latter-day hindsight.

Musically, the mods favored American R&B and soul, particularly the kind being pumped out by Motown in the mid-'60s. Live R&B and soul music of the genuine African-American sort, however, was a rarity in the U.K. in the mid-'60s, when black soul stars hardly ever toured Britain, and in any case would have been unlikely to play the sort of small clubs the mods usually went to. When they needed live music of their own, they had to turn to guitar-wielding rock bands composed of their peers. The first group they could truly call their own were the Who.

It's often been pointed out that the Who were no more genuine mods than Brian Wilson was a genuine surfer. Much as this didn't prevent the Beach Boys from being the best surf group, though, it didn't prevent the Who from being the best mod group. The Who, like most of the important London bands of the mid-'60s, looked to American R&B for the bulk of their early repertoire. They weren't proficient enough at that game, though, to compete on the level of the Stones or Animals, despite the fact that famous early posters extol the Who for their "Maximum R&B." Their real talents lay in building a ferocious wall of pop-rock sound, and in songwriter Pete Townshend's ability to celebrate the mod lifestyle, and articulate the mods' hopes and insecurities, with original material. In this respect, Townshend echoed Brian Wilson: an outsider of the culture he wrote about, he nonetheless evoked its spirit better than anyone else.

The Who had already played the club circuit for a few years (sometimes as the High Numbers) by the time they scored their first British hit, "I Can't Explain," in early 1965. They may have been steeped in R&B, but they hardly sounded like a Motown act. Their first burst of hits featured chunky, slashing power chords, played as if they were riffs in and of themselves. Townshend was borrowing considerably from Steve Cropper, the Kingsmen's "Louie Louie," and the Kinks' "You Really Got Me" in his early days, but the sound was even more frenetic and wilder, sometimes bursting into blasts of feedback and distortion that had no precedent in rock & roll. Sometimes called "auto-destruct," the guitar was a sonic equivalent of pop art and action painting in its bold lightning flashes, and the group also reflected pop art trends in its visual and performance style, smashing their instruments and wearing brightly colored clothes of posters and flags. Keith Moon's crashing, speed-of-light drums were also an important element in the mix, as were Townshend's anthemically rebellious lyrics, on their next pair of singles, "Anyway, Anyhow, Anywhere," and "My Generation," and their debut album, *The Who Sing My Generation.* This was mod at its apex, also laying the groundwork for power pop and aspects of psychedelia.

The Who, or indeed British mod music as a whole, made little impact in the United States at its peak. The Who's records were poorly promoted stateside (where their American label had initially rejected "Anyway, Anyhow, Anywhere" for release because they thought the guitar feedback was a tape defect), and the group were only known on a very underground, cultish level until they began to tour the U.S. in 1967. This wasn't the case in England, though, where they were a sensation, their influence soon felt in the work of the Beatles (particularly "Paperback Writer" and *Revolver*), the Kinks (who were already mods of a sort anyway, and had influenced the Who quite a bit as well), and even a young David Bowie, who released a blatant early Who imitation in 1965 ("You've Got a Habit of Leaving") when he was still known as Davy Jones. There were also other previously unknown mod outfits springing up, virtually all of which (like the Who) had started off playing straight R&B. Many would make fine records, but only one would become big stars—the Small Faces.

For those who wanted the soul influence much more upfront in their mod music, the Small Faces provided the ticket, particularly in the richly wailing vocals of their guitarist, Steve Marriott. They weren't exactly a blue-eyed soul act, however; they wrote most of their own songs, and from their first hit ("What'cha Gonna Do About It") they utilized the crunching power chords that are perhaps mod's most distinguishing feature. Like the Who, the Small Faces were virtually unknown in the United States; unlike the Who, they never toured there, and by the time they had their one and only American hit ("Itchycoo Park") they were no longer a mod band.

There were a few other fine mod bands in the mid-'60s that had some degree of success in the U.K.; in the U.S., they are known only to collectors. Prominent among these were the Creation, who emulated the Who's feedback screeches and drones, though their material was actually quite poppy. Creation guitarist Eddie Phillips pioneered the use of violin bow on electric guitar before Jimmy Page adapted the device for the Yardbirds and Led Zeppelin; Pete Townshend even asked him to join the Who as second guitarist. Another group who took inspiration from the Who's marriage of auto-destruct frenzy to smart pop riffs were the Eyes, although the value of that group's output was limited to no more than about three singles before they themselves autodestructed.

Those who liked their mod dipped in heavy soul batter could find none better than the Action, who followed the path of the early Small Faces, but took much more of a blatantly blue-eyed soul tack. Despite a run of singles produced by George Martin, the last of which found them starting to find a greater voice through original material and the absorption of non-soul influences, they never had anything close to a hit. At the more pop-oriented end of the spectrum were the Smoke, who made some of the cheeriest mod music, or indeed some of the cheeriest British rock of the '60s; their classic "My Friend Jack" was on its way to becoming a hit when it was banned by the BBC for supposed drug references. John's Children, who emerged after the mod area had peaked, represented a triumph of image over content. The group (which briefly counted Marc Bolan as a member) could barely play their instruments when they started, but attracted attention through a series of over-the-top publicity stunts, and reportedly upstaged the Who with their own version of auto-destruct during a German tour. For all their supposed ineptness, they managed a few decent fey mod-pop singles.

The strongest common thread linking all of these groups was their attitude. The loud guitars, catchy melodies, and anthemic lyrics weren't just a celebration of good times; rock & roll had always delivered that. They were also a declaration of independence, and a celebration not just of dancing the night away, but of a whole independent youth subculture. The groundwork for this had already been laid by the initial burst of the British Invasion, but the mods took it to bolder, more sophisticated, and more confident extremes.

Mod's influence was pervasive on the cutting edge of British rock in the mid-'60s, and the boundaries between who was mod and who was not are sometimes blurry. The Beatles and Rolling Stones were popular among many mods (as they were among most rock listeners), but could not be called mod groups by any stretch. Innovative British R&B groups like the Yardbirds boasted strong mod followings at one time, but their music couldn't be properly called mod either. The Kinks didn't evolve out of the mod scene, but their bashing early material fit the label well, and their work on 1966's *Face To Face* and singles like "Dedicated Follower of Fashion" and "Well Respected Man" were some of the period's strongest evocations of Swinging London—in which mod played a large role. Then there's a group like the Sorrows, whom are never referred to in accounts of the mod era, although their music—replete with stomping beats, catchy riff-chords, and a British Invasion bounce—would seem to fit the genre well.

In other countries, the influence of mod was small, but could be detected, even if most of the world would have to wait until limited edition compilations of the '80s and '90s to hear it. Quite a few Scandinivian bands, for instance, plugged into the mod vibe with confidence; the best of these were the Tages, but a number of others can be heard on those collector compilations, especially *Searchin' For Shakes,* which is devoted to Swedish bands entirely. In the United States, where genuine mod records were nearly impossible to come by, bands that played explicit mod music were virtually unknown, though collectors have stumbled across one (Northern California's Powder) that sound like a genuine Who Jr. And for some reason, a few mod groups—notably the Creation and the Smoke—found much greater success in Germany, where they were full-blown stars, than their native England.

It was, perhaps, in the cards that mod wouldn't last long. The whole mod ethic, after all, was built upon flash, sensation, and living for the moment. It was the type of adrenaline rush that was difficult to sustain, particularly as the movement's leaders, the Who and the Small Faces, quickly evolved into psychedelic-influenced hard rock bands in 1967. The evolution from mod to psychedelia, actually, was fairly natural, as many of the bands were already pioneering the guitar distortion that would be one of psychedelia's hallmarks, and moving towards more ambitious and personal lyrical statements. Even some of the lesser known mod groups, such as the Creation, the Smoke, John's Children, and even Wimple Winch (from Liverpool) were moving in a decisively psychedelic direction by 1967, and in each case produced work in the idiom that was just as impressive as their mod outings.

It may have thus seemed like mod was almost over before it started, but its influence has been enduring. The Who, for one, never shook off the musical or lyrical influence of mod, returning to the subject for a full-length opera in 1973. The numerous power-pop boomlets of the last 30 years are often grounded in mod; the form's influence can be heard in the Easybeats, the Raspberries, Elvis Costello, and many others. As an adjunct to the punk-new wave movement of the late '70s, there was a mod revival, spearheaded by the Jam (who took most of their initial inspiration from the My Generation-era Who). And many British bands have emulated mod's blend of cool and rebellion, as well as its catchy riffs, since mod's demise, running from the Move (who were sometimes tagged as Who copyists when they started in 1967), to current-day darlings of the pages of NME like Oasis, Blur, and the Boo Radleys.

Ten Essential Mod Recordings:
The Who, *The Who Sing My Generation* (MCA)
The Who, *A Quick One* (MCA)
The Small Faces, *Small Faces* (PolyGram)
The Creation, *How Does It Feel To Feel* (Edsel, UK)
The Eyes, *Blink* (Bam Caruso, UK)
The Smoke, *It's Smoke Time* (Repertoire, Germany)
The Action, *The Ultimate Action* (Edsel, UK)
John's Children, *Midsummer Night's Scene* (Bam Caruso, UK)
The Sorrows, *The Sorrows* (Sequel, UK)
Various Artists, *Searchin' For Shakes: Swedish Beat 1965-1968* (Amigo, Sweden)

—Richie Unterberger

Psychedelic Rock

Psychedelia represented rock & roll at its most breathtakingly adventurous and innovative—and sometimes, at its most foolish. While the most self-conscious experiments of the mid- and late '60s have dated badly, the best psychedelic rock had an exhilarating recklessness that has been difficult to recapture in the ensuing decades.

Psychedelic music was fed by many sources. The desire to emulate the state of mind-altering drugs in sound is its most sensational feature. But the musicians who pioneered psychedelia were equally driven by a hunger to expand rock's boundaries and enhance its eclecticism by incorporating influences from middle eastern music and improvisational jazz. This went hand-in-hand with exploring the frontiers of amplified sound and instrumental textures (primarily on the electric guitar), as well as lyrics that addressed the burning social and psychological issues of the day.

Trying to pin down the first psychedelic record is nearly as elusive as trying to name the first rock & roll record. Far-fetched claims have been advanced for songs running from the Tornados' futuristic 1962 number one instrumental "Telstar" to the Dave Clark Five's massively reverb-laden "Any Way You Want It." In 1964, the Beatles introduced guitar feedback on "I Feel Fine"; a year later, they introduced the sitar to rock on "Norwegian Wood." But two groups from different sides of the Atlantic with somewhat similar names, the Yardbirds and the Byrds, were really the most responsible for sounding the psychedelic siren.

With their ominous minor key melodies, hyperactive instrumental breaks (called "rave-ups"), unpredictable tempo changes, and use of Gregorian chants (most notably on the single "Still I'm Sad"), the Yardbirds helped define the manic eclecticism that would characterize early psychedelic rock. Jeff Beck's fuzzy, distorted guitar sustain laid the blueprint for psychedelic guitar.

Their early '66 hit "Shapes of Things" was arguably the first out-and-out psychedelic rock song, with its blistering feedback breaks, veering tempos, and stream-of-consciousness lyrics that owed nothing to traditional romantic themes. The Yardbirds' psychedelic peak was brief, but subsequent 1966 recordings—*Over Under Sideways Down* and "Happenings Ten Years Time Ago" especially—found them approximating speed-of-light trips, drug-induced or otherwise, with nervy but taut daring.

Jst a couple months after "Shapes of Things," the Byrds flew into uncharted territory with "Eight Miles High." While the group always claimed that the title referred to an airplane flight, the impressionistic lyrics were taken by many to reflect the psychedelic drug experience, while the furious guitar and bass breaks reflected the group's assimilation of John Coltrane's free jazz and Ravi Shankar's Indian music. The single's B-side ("Why") and many of the songs on their 1966 album *Fifth Dimension* crashed through similar sonic frontiers. Although the Byrds would trade in their spacesuits for cowboy threads in just a couple years, they continued to produce exciting psychedelic-influenced music through the end of 1967.

Ideas traveled fast in the crucible of 1966 rock, and within a few months many of the era's top bands were flashing psychedelic colors on their recordings. The Beatles' mid-'66

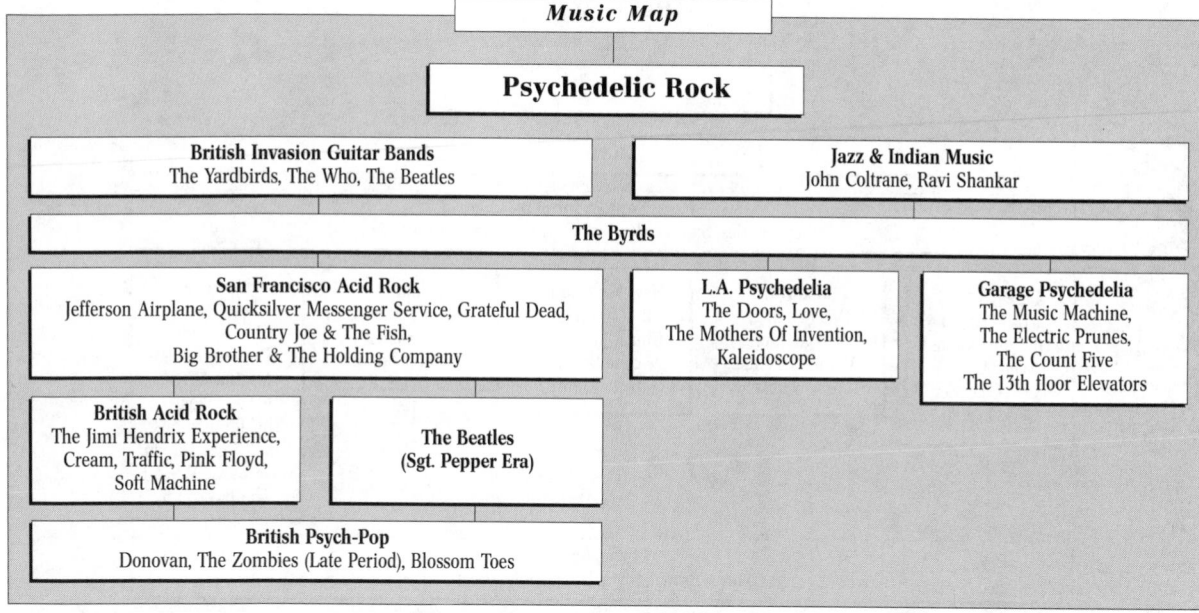

Music Map

Psychedelic Rock

British Invasion Guitar Bands	**Jazz & Indian Music**
The Yardbirds, The Who, The Beatles	John Coltrane, Ravi Shankar

The Byrds

San Francisco Acid Rock
Jefferson Airplane, Quicksilver Messenger Service, Grateful Dead, Country Joe & The Fish, Big Brother & The Holding Company

L.A. Psychedelia
The Doors, Love, The Mothers Of Invention, Kaleidoscope

Garage Psychedelia
The Music Machine, The Electric Prunes, The Count Five The 13th floor Elevators

British Acid Rock
The Jimi Hendrix Experience, Cream, Traffic, Pink Floyd, Soft Machine

The Beatles
(Sgt. Pepper Era)

British Psych-Pop
Donovan, The Zombies (Late Period), Blossom Toes

---

single "Rain" used backwards guitars and vocals, and their *Revolver* album was by far their most eclectic pre-'67 work, imbued with churning, distorted guitars, coy references to drug trips, and even quotes from Timothy Leary's version of the *Tibetan Book of the Dead*. The Rolling Stones used the sitar—perhaps to its greatest effect in a rock & roll song—on "Paint It Black," and constructed a dense morass of psychedelic sound and lyrics on "Have You Seen Your Mother, Baby, Standing in the Shadow?" Donovan forsook his acoustic guitar for storybook wanderings in densely orchestrated musical arrangements that drew from both Indian sitars and fog-bound British moors. Garage bands, already attuned to distorted guitars via their attempts to emulate the fuzz riffs on Stones classics like "Satisfaction," went the extra nine yards into all-out freakouts on cuts like the Magic Mushrooms' "It's-a-Happening."

In the United States, psychedelic music took root most firmly in California, particularly San Francisco, where an increasingly large bohemian community had been living the psychedelic lifestyle or a year or two before it infiltrated rock & roll. In 1965 and 1966, disaffected folk musicians formed the Grateful Dead, the Jefferson Airplane, the Charlatans, the Great Society, Country Joe & the Fish, Big Brother & the Holding Company, Quicksilver Messenger Service, and many other less famous combos with equally (for the time) outrageous names. It took them a while to get a handle on their electric instruments, as some of their tentative and awkward pre-'67 recordings can attest to. But after honing their chops on the fertile Haight-Ashbury scene, they introduced a whole new spacy element into the psychedelic brew with their searing guitars and euphoric melodies.

The British strain of psychedelia tended to be more whimsical and fairytale-ish than the west coast brand of acid-rock. Ethereal organs and Mellotrons often set the tone of the generally more symphonic arrangements; the lyrics, occasionally wry to the point of surrealism, were often populated with eccentric British character types, or took a storybook, child's-eye perspective. The Beatles' brilliant early '67 "Strawberry Fields"/"Penny Lane" single was the apex of this genre, and newly emerging bands like Pink Floyd and Traffic, as well as less successful but equally intriguing underground acts like the Soft Machine and Tomorrow, also mined this field with great success.

1967's summer of love saw psychedelic music at its pinnacle. The Beatles released their definitive psychedelic statement, *Sgt. Pepper*; the San Francisco groups made an international impact via the Monterey Pop Festival; Pink Floyd, the Jefferson Airplane, and Traffic issued their best psychedelic albums. Jimi Hendrix and Cream became international superstars with guitar-based acid-rock that had its roots in the Yardbirds' innovations. The Doors' first album explored the dark and mysterious crannies of psychedelia with an impact that neither they nor anyone else would match. Even the Rolling Stones joined the psychedelic bandwagon, with an underappreciated LP, *Their Satanic Majesties Request*, that was accused by many of being an ersatz Sgt. Pepper despite including several first-rate songs.

Psychedelic music was a strong presence in rock & roll throughout the rest of the '60s, but there's no doubt that the genre began to become tired and self-indulgent as the decade approached its end. Following the lead, perhaps, of Bob Dylan's calm and simple *John Wesley Harding*, the Beatles, Byrds, and Rolling Stones all released albums in 1968 with a decidedly earthy and back-to-basics tone (although they didn't eschew progressive experiments altogether). Cream, Traffic, and the original Jimi Hendrix Experience broke up; Pink Floyd's leader, Syd Barrett, became the era's first acid casualty after their brilliant

debut album; the Doors peaked early and couldn't repeat the fluid consistently of their own debut, despite releasing several worthy attempts. Pre-heavy metal groups like Iron Butterfly and Blue Cheer emulated the roar of psychedelic guitar growl without paying any heed to the style's more subtle attractions. And quite a few groups presented psychedelic cliches—long guitar solos, florid lyrics, effects-happy production—without saying much of anything original.

Many of the trimmings of psychedelic rock would form the backbone of progressive rock and heavy metal, which devoted themselves to the most extreme ends of the genre—ambitious, neo-classical epics on the one hand, mind-melting guitar distortion on the other. While groups ranging from Echo & the Bunnymen to Sonic Youth have (usually erroneously) been termed neo-psychedelic at one time or another, psychedelia has retreated from the front of rock's collective consciousness since about 1970 or so.

In its time, however, the psychedelic sound fueled some of the '60s' finest moments, influencing most of the top rock acts to some degree. While groups like the Who, the Beach Boys, Love, and Buffalo Springfield could not exactly be called "psychedelic," some of their finest recordings—"I Can See For Miles," "Good Vibrations," Love's *Forever Changes LP*, Buffalo Springfield's "Expecting to Fly" and "Broken Arrow"—betray a strong psychedelic influence, and could not have been made without the inspiration of their more overtly trippy peers. And the intricate arrangements and heavily amplified/distorted guitars of psychedelic productions broke ground that has been utilized routinely in rock recordings from the late '60s to the present day.

15 Most Essential Psychedelic Albums:
The Beatles, *Sgt. Pepper's Lonely Hearts Club Band* (Capitol)
The Beatles, *Magical Mystery Tour* (Capitol)
The Yardbirds, *Roger The Engineer* (Edsel)
The Byrds, *Fifth Dimension* (Columbia)
The Doors, *The Doors* (Elektra)
The Jefferson Airplane, *Jefferson Airplane Loves You* (RCA)
Pink Floyd, *Piper At The Gates Of Dawn* (Capitol)
The Jimi Hendrix Experience, *Are You Experienced?* (Reprise)
The Great Society, *Collector's Item* (Columbia)
The Mothers Of Invention, *We're Only It In For The Money* (Rykodisc)
The Rolling Stones, *Their Satanic Majesties Request* (ABKCO)
Donovan, *Sunshine Superman* (Epic)
Cream, *Disraeli Gears* (Polydor)
Traffic, *Mr. Fantasy* (Island)
The Misunderstood, *Before The Dream Faded* (Cherry Red)

—Richie Unterberger

Soul

More than almost any other genre of the rock era, soul is a wide-ranging and immensely diverse style that can only be delineated in the sketchiest manner in a few paragraphs. Peaking in the 1960s, it helped define the African-American experience in America with a passion, pride, and optimism rare in any art form.

Broadly speaking, soul was the combination of rhythm & blues, gospel, and pop. The gospel ingredient was most evident in the supremely emotional, pleading, and jubilant

Music Map

Soul

Pop	R&B	Gospel

Early Soul Performers
Ray Charles, Sam Cooke, Jackie Wilson, James Brown

Chicago Soul	Stax/Volt	New York Soul	Atlantic	Motown
Curtis Mayfield & The Impressions, Major Lance, Gene Chandler, Betty Everett	Otis Redding, Sam & Dave, Wilson Pickett, Carla Thomas	Ben E. King, Chuck Jackson, Maxine Brown, Garnett Mimms	Aretha Franklin, Percy Sledge, Solomon Burke	The Miracles, Mary Wells, The Supremes, Martha & The Vandellas, The Temptations, The 4 Tops, Marvin Gaye, Stevie Wonder, The Jackson 5

Early Funk
James Brown, Sly & The Family Stone

Disco & Dance-Pop

Philly Soul
Jerry Butler, The Intruders, The O'Jays, The Spinners, Harold Melvin & The Blue Notes, The Stylistics

'70s Memphis Soul/Hi Records
Al Green, Ann Peebles

vocals and harmonies. Rock-solid rhythm sections, punchy horn arrangements, and tight instrumental and vocal ensemble work were also frequent hallmarks of the classic soul sound.

The forefathers of soul were veterans of 1950s rhythm & blues. Ray Charles was perhaps the first to merge gospel, pop, and rhythm and blues in a style that we recognize as a direct ancestor of soul with his 1954 hit "I Got a Woman." Other important pioneers were Jackie Wilson, Sam Cooke, and James Brown. They came from somewhat different backgrounds—Wilson from the R&B vocal group tradition, Cooke from straight gospel as the lead singer of the Soul Stirrers, Brown from the "chitlin" circuit—but they shared an appetite for constantly modernizing their sound with both pop crossover material and R&B-based work that put their emotions at the fore with an arresting grit, naked emotion, and increasingly mature lyrical concerns.

As R&B grew into soul in the early '60s, the arrangements became more intricate, as did the harmonies (though they were often rooted in doo wop, as is obvious from listening to the early work of the Miracles and the Impressions). Romance was usually the subject, but it often was a more complex, adult, and bittersweet form of love than the adolescent fare of much early rock & roll and R&B. Songwriter/performer/producers like Smokey Robinson and Curtis Mayfield put a greater personal stamp on their product than was customary in the 1950s. The session players at labels like Stax/Volt and Motown, though sometimes uncredited on the releases, set a level of instrumental discipline and virtuosity that remains among the benchmark standards of musical excellence in contemporary popular music. Starting with the Drifters, strings were often used to tastefully embellish the material without detracting from the performers' gutsy power.

There were literally hundreds of soul performers who laid down bodies of work that endure several decades later. In many cases, the artists themselves grew enormously over the course of their career, and cannot be conveniently pigeonholed into a certain subgenre or peak output—Marvin Gaye, Aretha Franklin, Curtis Mayfield, and Stevie Wonder are only a few of those. There were certain regional styles that developed, although soul was such a nationwide, overlapping phenomenon that these too cannot be categorized too rigorously, and great acts like the Isley Brothers couldn't be conveniently pigeonholed into any certain school.

By far the most successful style of soul was the kind that came to be identified with Motown Records in Detroit. Emphasizing melodic hooks, bright, clear production, and an extraordinary roster of talented vocalists, Motown was the most successful independent label of its era, crossing over to the pop charts for literally hundreds of Top 20 hits during the 1960s. Instrumental in bringing the sounds of Black America into mainstream American life, Motown has been disdained by some latter-day critics for a formulaic approach, and for appealing to whites, teenagers, and pop listeners more than other kinds

of down-home soul music. These are really fairly ridiculous assertions. Motown was if anything more popular with black audiences than white ones, and its legendary performers—Smokey Robinson, the Temptations, Martha & the Vandellas, Marvin Gaye, Stevie Wonder, the Supremes, Mary Wells, the Four Tops, the Jackson Five, and many others—released an astonishingly large and diverse body of classic work in the 1960s and beyond.

Motown's most serious rival for soul supremacy was the Stax/Volt label, based in Memphis. With Booker T. & the MG's (stars in their own right) usually providing the backing, these records offered a funkier, rootsier brand of soul, with generally rawer vocals and a heavier reliance on horn riffs. Otis Redding, Wilson Pickett, Carla Thomas, and Sam & Dave were the biggest stars to emerge from the Stax/Volt label, which was absorbed into Atlantic in the late '60s. Atlantic Records itself was one of the most influential soul labels, with gritty soul sensations like Solomon Burke and Percy Sledge. A great deal of soul with a similarly down-home Southern sensibility also emerged from the legendary studios in Muscle Shoals, Alabama; Muscle Shoals-players backed Aretha Franklin on many of her greatest sides.

In Chicago, performers like the Impressions, Jerry Butler, Betty Everett, Major Lance, and Gene Chandler established their own distinctive regional sound, prominently featuring blaring horn charts and smooth harmonic interplay. New York had a somewhat more pop-oriented, "uptown" sound, typified by Chuck Jackson and Maxine Brown, although as always there were rootsier exceptions like Garnett Mimms, and artists who combined the best of both worlds, like Ben E. King (both as lead singer of the Drifters and as a solo artist). Philadelphia soul records leaned toward doo wop-like group harmonies, eventually evolving into a serious rival to Motown's production machines with the ascendance of Gamble & Huff and Thom Bell.

By the late '60s, soul was changing with the times. Motown-producer Norman Whitfield expanded the label's lyrical scope into psychedelia and social consciousness with songs like the Temptations' *Cloud Nine*. James Brown pioneered funk music with his incredible churning rhythms backing increasingly assertive statements of black pride. Sly & the Family Stone merged hippie concerns and funk on a string of hit singles and albums. In the early '70s, Motown veterans Marvin Gaye and Stevie Wonder broke free of the label's hit-oriented production process to issue vastly influential, album-length statements. The Philadelphia sound, string-drenched and impeccably produced and harmonized, took soul to another level of slickness. In Memphis, Al Green established himself as an heir to Otis Redding with Hi Records and the Memphis Horns.

Soul diminished as a commercial presence in the mid-'70s, as funk and disco began to put more emphasis on danceable rhythms than songwriting and the singing. Al Green, seen by some fans as the standardbearer of the classic soul sound, turned to gospel; the once-thriving Stax/Volt empire collapsed in a confusing mess. Much black soul music became increasingly middle-of-the-road, leading to the new genre of urban contemporary music. Soul is still very much alive, of course, in the harmonies and production that continue to inform contemporary African-American popular music, whether in funk, disco, dance-pop, or rap. The "classic" soul style lives on in different ways—old stars continue to release and record new material for a specialized audience, and veteran performers like Tina Turner and Patti LaBelle have achieved new levels of superstardom with their updated brand of contemporary soul.

15 Most Essential Soul Recordings (omitting Motown releases, listed in separate music map):
Various Artists, *Soul Shots series* (Rhino)
Various Artists, *The Complete Stax-Volt Singles 1959-1968* (Atlantic)
James Brown, *Star Time* (PolyGram)
Otis Redding, *Otis! The Definitive Otis Redding* (Rhino)
Aretha Franklin, *Queen of Soul: The Atlantic Recordings* (Rhino)
Curtis Mayfield & the Impressions, *Anthology 1961-1977* (MCA)
Sam Cooke, *Man & His Music* (RCA)
Ray Charles, *Birth of Soul* (Rhino)
Ben E. King, *Anthology* (Rhino)
Sly & the Family Stone, *Anthology* (Epic)
Al Green, *Al Green's Greatest Hits* (Hi)
The Isley Brothers, *The Isley Brothers Story, Vol. 1* (Rhino)
Wilson Pickett, *A Man and a Half: The Best of Wilson Pickett* (Rhino)
Jackie Wilson, *Mr. Excitement* (Rhino)
Solomon Burke, *Home in Your Heart* (Rhino)

Books:
The Blackwell Guide to Soul Recordings, edited by Robert Pruter (Blackwell, 1993)
Where Did Our Love Go? The Rise and Fall of the Motown Sound, by Nelson George (St. Martin's Press, 1985)
Sweet Soul Music, by Peter Guralnick (Harper & Row, 1986)
Nowhere to Run: The Story of Soul Music, by Gerry Hirshey (Times Books, 1984)
—*Richie Unterberger*

Blue-Eyed Soul

"Can white men sing the blues?" That's been a point of contention in the worlds of rock and soul since white musicians began singing music with heavy debts to rhythm & blues. White attempts to sing African-American-derived music have often been embarrassing (if sometimes touching in their naivete). But at the same time, some whites have crossed into the world of R&B and soul with a natural ease that proves that music, like all good things in life, is color-blind. During soul music's heyday, a handful of whites handled the challenge with confidence, giving rise to the relatively small but important subgenre of soul music called blue-eyed soul.

The roots of blue-eyed soul could probably be traced back as far as Elvis Presley's legendary Sun singles, on which he masterfully interpreted a handful of blues and R&B classics. It can also be detected in the many Italian-American doo wop singers during that music's last phase, as well as early '60s acts like Dion and the Four Seasons who borrowed heavily from R&B phrasing and harmonies.

The first of the classic blue-eyed soul acts, and one which was instrumental to defining the genre, were the Righteous Brothers. Hailing from Orange County, CA, of all places, Bill Medley and Bobby Hatfield looked very white, but sounded black. After teaming up with Phil Spector in the mid-'60s, they reeled off a brief string of huge hits that were as soaked with gospel feeling as any African-American soul, but were unable to maintain their artistic or commercial momentum after their association with Spector ended.

The most successful blue-eyed soul group of the '60s were the Rascals. Young veterans of New York's Italian-American rock & roll scene, they flavored their strong (and mostly original) material with horns, harmonies, and a touch of British Invasion energy. Although they worked within the self-contained rock band format, playing their own instruments and writing their own songs, their sound owed as much, if not more, to soul as '60s rock trends. They were also one of the relatively few blue-eyed soul acts to successfully change with the times, writing increasingly reflective and sophisticated material, culminating with the rabble-rousing anthem "People Got to Be Free" in 1968.

Blue-eyed soul acts tended to spring up in the proximity of regions with active soul scenes. Detroit's biggest contribution to the genre were Mitch Ryder and the Detroit Wheels, who served up some of the sweatiest soul-rock hybrids ever waxed. Motown couldn't help but influence a lot of the city's white rock and garage bands, and the Motor City sound is reflected in fine regional Michigan rock hits of the time by the Rationals and the early singles of Bob Seger.

White Southern performers also absorbed the inflections of deep soul into their own earthy sounds. John Fred and Tony Joe White displayed the influence of New Orleans and Louisiana R&B and soul in their brand of swamp pop; Bill Deal and the Rhondels played a kind of soul frat-rock that drew from the "beach music" cult of the Carolinas; Roy Head drew upon the melting pot of Texas blues and R&B for one of the mid-'60s best one-shot hits, "Treat Her Right." In Memphis, Dan Penn, a white Alabaman who helped write many great deep soul records, produced hits by the Box Tops; teenage lead singer Alex Chilton's vocals were so unnaturally gravelly that many listeners were convinced he was black. In Los Angeles, there were several Latin soul-rock-R&B acts, the best of which were Thee Midniters (although the group also played convincing Rolling Stones-styled garage rock).

The line between R&B-influenced rock & roll and blue-eyed soul is a thin one that was skirted by many of the British Invasion's finest performers. Certainly Eric Burdon (of the Animals), Stevie Winwood (of the Spencer Davis Group and Traffic), and Van Morrison

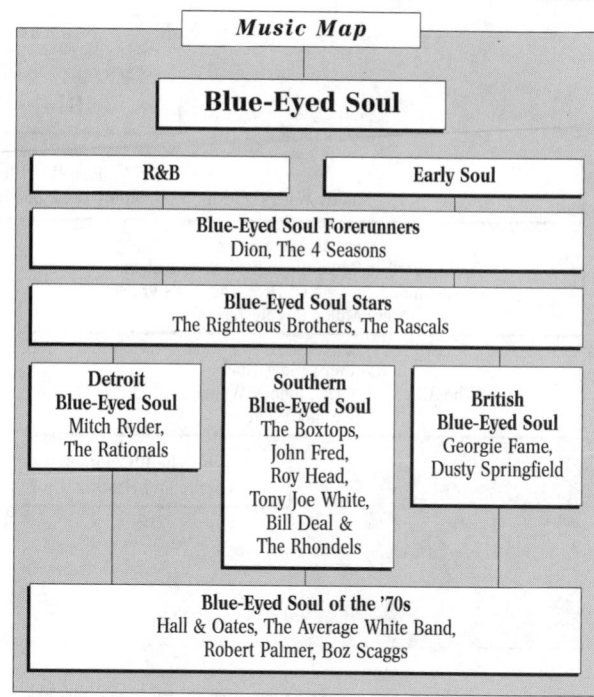

Music Map

Blue-Eyed Soul

R&B	Early Soul

Blue-Eyed Soul Forerunners
Dion, The 4 Seasons

Blue-Eyed Soul Stars
The Righteous Brothers, The Rascals

Detroit Blue-Eyed Soul Mitch Ryder, The Rationals	**Southern Blue-Eyed Soul** The Boxtops, John Fred, Roy Head, Tony Joe White, Bill Deal & The Rhondels	**British Blue-Eyed Soul** Georgie Fame, Dusty Springfield

Blue-Eyed Soul of the '70s
Hall & Oates, The Average White Band, Robert Palmer, Boz Scaggs

were extremely soulful singers, even if their material and the sound of their backing groups were more rock-oriented than classic soul grooves. Georgie Fame probably fit the classic blue-eyed soul mold more than any other British Invasion performer, although he also owed quite a bit to Mose Allison's brand of jazz. Dusty Springfield was the best female blue-eyed soul singer of the '60s, though she also sang girl group, rock, and pop ballad material; at the end of the '60s, she traveled to Stax studios in Memphis to cut *Dusty in Memphis*, considered by many listeners as one of the finest white soul albums of all time.

It's worth pointing out that many classic soul records of the '60s by black performers featured white musicians. Booker T. & the MG's, an integrated ensemble featuring the economic, biting licks of white guitarist Steve Cropper played on most of the great Stax/Volt soul hits of the '60s, as well as cutting a lot of instrumental soul smashes on their own. Stax/Volt's strongest rival in the field of deep Southern soul was the Muscle Shoals Studio in Alabama, which also featured white musicians on many of their sessions, backing soul greats from Aretha Franklin on down. Duane Allman may be mostly known for helping to found Southern rock with the Allman Brothers but he also played guitar on sessions by Franklin, Wilson Pickett, Clarence Carter and King Curtis.

The heyday of blue-eyed soul, like soul music itself, was in the 1960s; after that decade, it was a more scattered presence, although acts like Hall & Oates, the Average White Band, Boz Scaggs, Robert Palmer, David Bowie (in one of his many phases), the latter-day Bee Gees and Billy Swan all carried the blue-eyed soul torch to large degrees. Contemporary acts like Michael Bolton and George Michael have also been labeled as blue-eyed soul, although their material owes more to classic MOR pop than the original pioneers of the style.

Ten Most Essential Blue-Eyed Soul Albums:
Various Artists, *Soul Shots Vol. 6: Blue-Eyed Soul* (Rhino)
The Righteous Brothers, *Anthology 1962-74* (Rhino)
The Rascals, *Anthology (1965-1972)* (Rhino)
Mitch Ryder, *Rev-Up: The Best of Mitch Ryder & the Detroit Wheels* (Rhino)
The Box Tops, *Ultimate Box Tops* (Warner Brothers)
Dusty Springfield, *Dusty in Memphis* (Rhino)
John Fred & the Playboys, *The History of John Fred & the Playboys* (Paula)
Tony Joe White, *The Best of Tony Joe White* (Warner)
Georgie Fame, *20 Beat Classics* (RSO)
Thee Midniters, *The Best of Thee Midniters* (Rhino)
—*Richie Unterberger*

Blues Rock

The blues and rock & roll are often divided by the thinnest of the margins. Blues, more than any other musical style, influenced the birth of rock & roll, and the amplified electric blues of Chicago, Memphis, and other cities during the 1950s was separated from the new music only by its more traditional chord patterns, cruder production values, and narrower market. The term "blues-rock" came into being only around the mid-'60s, when white musicians infused electric blues with somewhat louder guitars and flashy images that helped the music make inroads into the white rock audience.

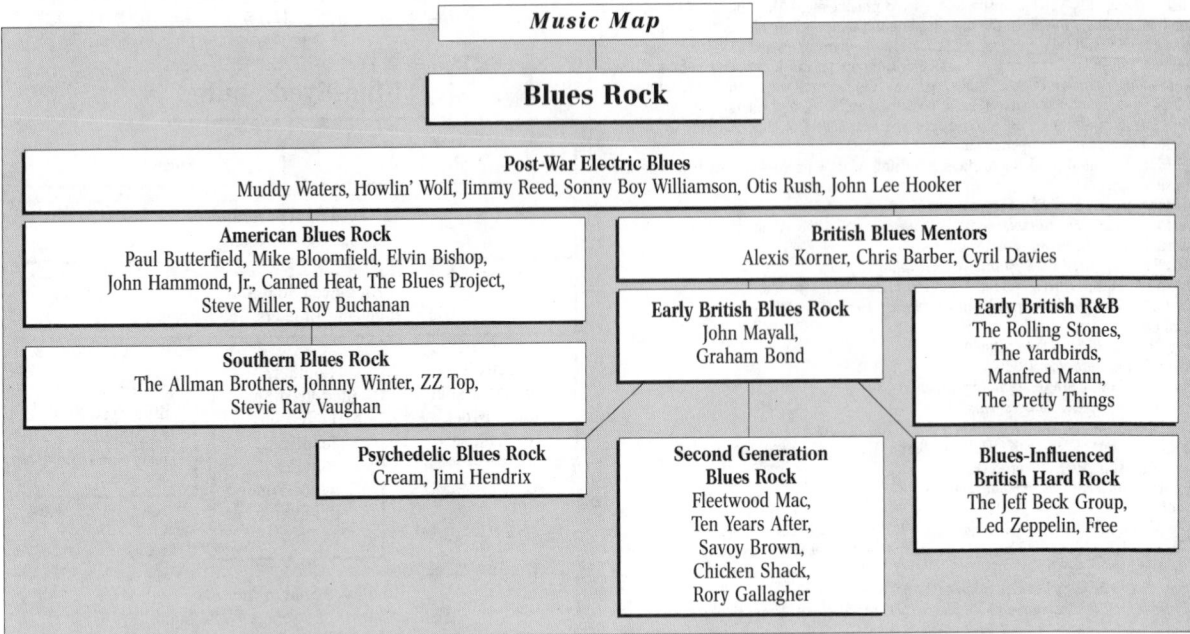

Music Map

Blues Rock

Post-War Electric Blues
Muddy Waters, Howlin' Wolf, Jimmy Reed, Sonny Boy Williamson, Otis Rush, John Lee Hooker

American Blues Rock
Paul Butterfield, Mike Bloomfield, Elvin Bishop,
John Hammond, Jr., Canned Heat, The Blues Project,
Steve Miller, Roy Buchanan

British Blues Mentors
Alexis Korner, Chris Barber, Cyril Davies

Early British Blues Rock
John Mayall,
Graham Bond

Early British R&B
The Rolling Stones,
The Yardbirds,
Manfred Mann,
The Pretty Things

Southern Blues Rock
The Allman Brothers, Johnny Winter, ZZ Top,
Stevie Ray Vaughan

Psychedelic Blues Rock
Cream, Jimi Hendrix

**Second Generation
Blues Rock**
Fleetwood Mac,
Ten Years After,
Savoy Brown,
Chicken Shack,
Rory Gallagher

**Blues-Influenced
British Hard Rock**
The Jeff Beck Group,
Led Zeppelin, Free

Many of the early blues rockers were British musicians who had been schooled by Alexis Korner. Helping to organize the first overseas tours by many major American bluesmen, Korner—as well as his former boss Chris Barber, and his early collaborator Cyril Davies—was more responsible than any other musician for introducing the blues to Britain. More important, he acted as a mentor to many younger musicians who would form the R&B-oriented wing of the British Invasion, including Jack Bruce, members of Manfred Mann, Eric Clapton and, most significantly, the Rolling Stones, whose lead vocalist, Mick Jagger sang with Korner before the Stones were firmly established.

The Rolling Stones featured a wealth of stone cold blues in their early repertoire. They and other British groups like the Yardbirds and Animals brought a faster and brasher flavor to traditional numbers. They would quickly branch out from 12-bar blues to R&B, soul, and finally, original material of a much more innovative and rock-oriented nature, without ever losing sight of their blues roots.

Several British acts, however, were more steadfast in their devotion to traditional blues, sacrificing commercial success for purism. These included the early Graham Bond Organisation (who featured future Cream members Jack Bruce and Ginger Baker) and, more significantly, John Mayall's Bluesbreakers. In early 1965, Mayall's group provided a refuge for Eric Clapton who left the Yardbirds on the eve of international success in protest to their forays into pop/rock. His sole album with Mayall, *Bluesbreakers With Eric Clapton* (1966), was an unexpected Top Ten hit in the U.K. Clapton's lightning-fast and fluid leads were vastly influential, both on fellow musicians and in introducing tough electric blues to a wide audience.

While Clapton would rapidly depart the Bluesbreakers to form Cream (who took blues-rock to more amplified and psychedelic levels), Mayall continued to be Britain's foremost exponent of blues-rock, as a bandleader of innumerable Bluesbreakers line-ups. Many musicians of note were schooled by Mayall, the most prominent being Clapton's successors, Peter Green and future Rolling Stone Mick Taylor. Like Clapton, Green left Mayall after just one album, forming the first incarnation of Fleetwood Mac with a couple members of Mayall's rhythm section, John McVie and Mick Fleetwood. Under Green's helm, Fleetwood Mac were the finest British blues-rock act of the late '60s. They invested electric Chicago blues with zest and humor, but their own material—featuring Green's icy guitar tone, rich vocals, and personal, often somber lyrics—was more impressive, and extremely successful in Britain, where they racked up several hit albums and singles.

As a bandleader of rotating lineups featuring budding guitar geniuses, Chicago harmonica player Paul Butterfield was Mayall's American counterpart; the two even recorded a rare EP together in the late '60s. The Paul Butterfield Blues Band's first pair of albums featured the sterling guitar duo of Mike Bloomfield and Elvin Bishop, as well as bona fide African-American Chicago bluesmen in the rhythm section. Willing to tackle soul, jazz, and even psychedelic jams in addition to Chicago blues, they were the first American blues-rock band, and perhaps the best.

While blues-rock was less of a commercial or artistic force in the U.S. than the U.K., several other American blues-rockers of note emerged in the '60s. Canned Heat were probably the most successful, reaching the Top 20 with "On the Road Again" and an electric update of an obscure rural blues number, "Going up the Country." Steve Miller played mostly blues, with Barry Goldberg and as the leader of his own band, in his early days before tuning into the psychedelic ethos of his adopted base of San Francisco. Captain

Beefheart was briefly a white counterpart to Howlin' Wolf before heading off on a furious avant-garde tangent.

In New York, Bob Dylan used Mike Bloomfield on much of his *Highway 61 Revisited* album, and teamed with the Butterfield Band for his enormously controversial electric appearance at the 1965 Newport Folk Festival. John Hammond recorded blues-rock in the mid-'60s with future members of the Band and Dion cut some overlooked blues-rock sides after being exposed to classic blues by Hammond's father, the legendary Columbia A&R man John Hammond, Sr. The Blues Project led by Al Kooper often reworked blues songs with rock arrangements, although their vision was too eclectic to be pigeonholed as blues-rock, also encompassing folk-rock, pop/rock, and psychedelia.

The influence of the first generation of blues-rockers is evident in the early recordings of Jimi Hendrix, and indeed Jimi would always feature a strong element of the blues in his material.

Albert King and B.B. King couldn't exactly be called blues-rockers, but their late-'60s material betrays contemporary influences from the worlds of rock and soul that found them leaning more in that direction. Early hard rock bands like Led Zeppelin, Free and the Jeff Beck Group played a great deal of blues, though not enough for purists to consider them actual blues acts.

The blues-rock form became more pedestrian and boogie-oriented as the '60s came to a close. From Britain, Ten Years After, Savoy Brown, the Climax Blues Band, Rory Gallagher, Chicken Shack, Juicy Lucy and Foghat all achieved some success. In the U.S., blues-rock was the cornerstone of the Allman Brothers' innovative early-'70s recordings (which in turned spawned the blues-influenced school of Southern rock), and Johnny Winter had success with a much more traditional approach.

While blues-rock hasn't been a major commercial force since the late '60s, the style has spawned some hugely successful acts, like ZZ Top and Foghat as well as influencing all hard rock since the late '60s to some degree. The success of Stevie Ray Vaughan in the 1980s, and groups like Blues Traveler and Spin Doctors in the 1990s, shows that its audience is far from dead. And it is a cliche, but it is often true, that many white listeners would be unaware of black blues performers if they hadn't been led to them through the work of white blues-rock bands.

12 Essential Blues Rock Recordings:
John Mayall, *Bluesbreakers with Eric Clapton* (PolyGram)
John Mayall, *London Blues (1964-1969)* (PolyGram)
The Paul Butterfield Blues Band, *East-West* (Elektra)
Fleetwood Mac, *Black Magic Woman* (Epic)
Fleetwood Mac, *Then Play On* (Reprise)
Jimi Hendrix, *Blues* (MCA)
The Graham Bond Organisation, *The Sound of '65* (Edsel)
Canned Heat, *Best of Canned Heat* (EMI)
Cream, *Fresh Cream* (Polydor)
John Hammond, Jr., *So Many Roads* (Vanguard)
The Allman Brothers, *At Fillmore East* (Polydor)
Duffy Power, *Little Boy Blue* (Demon/Edsel)
Books:
Blues—The British Connection, by Bob Brunning (1986, Blandford Press)
—*Richie Unterberger*

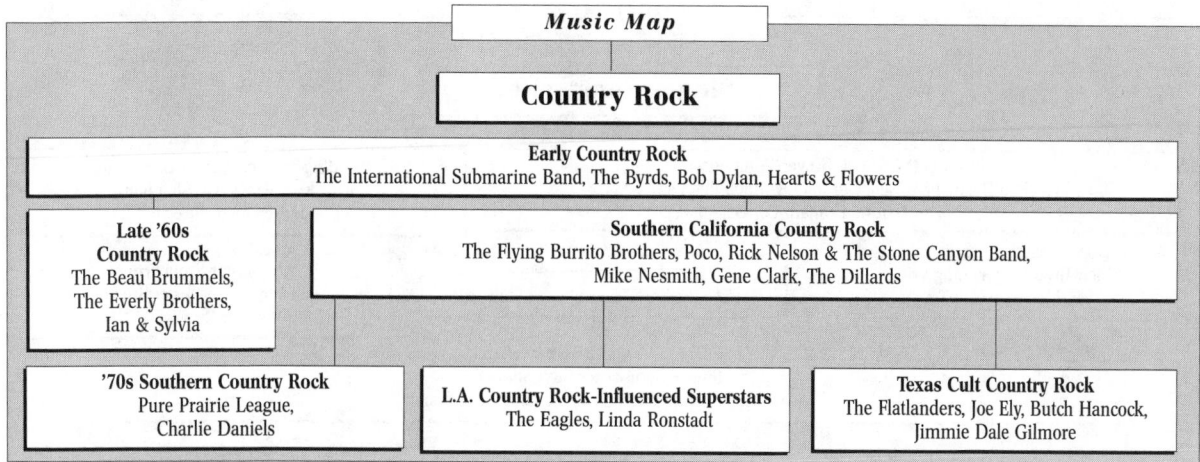

Music Map

Country Rock

Early Country Rock
The International Submarine Band, The Byrds, Bob Dylan, Hearts & Flowers

Late '60s Country Rock
The Beau Brummels, The Everly Brothers, Ian & Sylvia

Southern California Country Rock
The Flying Burrito Brothers, Poco, Rick Nelson & The Stone Canyon Band, Mike Nesmith, Gene Clark, The Dillards

'70s Southern Country Rock
Pure Prairie League, Charlie Daniels

L.A. Country Rock-Influenced Superstars
The Eagles, Linda Ronstadt

Texas Cult Country Rock
The Flatlanders, Joe Ely, Butch Hancock, Jimmie Dale Gilmore

Country Rock

Country-rock is one of the hardest rock & roll styles to map and define. Country music, of course, was integral to the birth of rock & roll, and has continued to exert a huge influence on rock until the present. You can find innumerable examples of rock & roll performers that are heavily soaked with country, from Elvis Presley to Elvis Costello. As a label and as a movement, however, country-rock is primarily identified with a school of bands in the late '60s and early '70s that brought the modern and irreverent qualities of rock to the more traditional musical values of country music.

There are many antecedents to country-rock; the close harmonies and acoustic guitars on much of the Everly Brothers' material foreshadows much of it. In the mid-'60s, Del Shannon recorded an entire album of Hank Williams tunes, George Jones and Gene Pitney teamed up for an LP of duets, and the trashy British R&B/punk band the Downliners Sect recorded a bizarre straight country album that was unnoticed commercially and unsuccessful artistically. Several of the '60s top groups dallied successfully with countrified rock & roll at times, such as the Beatles (especially around the *Beatles for Sale* period, on tracks like "I Don't Want to Spoil the Party"), the early Byrds ("Satisfied Mind," "Mr. Spaceman," "Time Between"), and Buffalo Springfield ("Go and Say Goodbye," "Kind Woman"); all of these bands placed a premium on close harmonies, and could incorporate country signatures into their sound with natural ease when the spirit moved them.

The term "country-rock" actually began to get used and thrown around in 1968, when most of the major rock acts were retreating from their psychedelic experiments into a "back to basics" approach. Bob Dylan, who had never embraced psychedelia in the first place, led the way with his *John Wesley Harding* album. Dylan had recorded in Nashville before, but this early 1968 effort was far more basic in instrumentation and far more country in tone. In 1969, he would largely eschew his inscrutable wordplay for basic homilies on *Nashville Skyline*, as well as recording an entire unreleased LP with one of his chief mentors, Johnny Cash.

The true god of country-rock, though, was guitarist and singer Gram Parsons. As the leader of the International Submarine Band, he recorded an album in 1967, *Safe at Home*, that prominently used pedal steel guitar. The LP is seen by some scholars as the first true country-rock record, although it was little noticed upon its release. Shortly afterwards, Parsons joined the Byrds and was almost single-handedly responsible for altering the band's focus from folk-rock to country-rock. Byrds leader Roger McGuinn had been entertaining the idea of an ambitious double album with heavy use of electronics, but the project was scuttled in favor of *Sweetheart of the Rodeo*. The 1968 release is almost universally hailed as one of the first and best country-rock efforts.

The Byrds' country-rock era was short; Parsons left the band after a year. Longtime Byrds bassist Chris Hillman left the group around the same time, and the pair quickly teamed to form the nucleus of the Flying Burrito Brothers; Parsons only stayed with the band for a couple albums, but these works, also prominently featuring Sneeky Pete Kleinow on pedal steel, are the purest and most influential country-rock hybrids, and among the few major country-rock recordings that are not in reality closer to rock than country.

Country music may have sprung from the southern states, but country-rock primarily flourished in southern California. Other country-rock acts of note in the late '60s included the little-known Hearts & Flowers, who actually surfaced before 1968, but were classified as folk-rock at the time, and Poco, featuring former Buffalo Springfield members Richie Furay and Jim Messina. In northern California, the New Riders of the Purple Sage established themselves as a more countrified and laidback cousin of the Grateful Dead in the early '70s.

Some veteran acts primarily associated with other forms of rock and folk became country-rockers for a time in the late '60s. Folk-rock pioneers the Beau Brummels went to Nashville to record *Bradley's Barn* at the legendary studio of the same name; the Everly Brothers' *Roots* was their most critically acclaimed post-early-'60s work; Ian & Sylvia

moved from contemporary folk to country as a duo and leaders of the band Great Speckled Bird; Rick Nelson had an artistic renaissance while fronting the Stone Canyon Band, which featured future Eagle Randy Meisner. Former Byrd Gene Clark recorded country-rock on his own and as part of Dillard & Clark. The Dillards themselves, primarily known as a bluegrass act before the late '60s, had already acted as important figures in folk-rock by helping teach the Byrds harmony vocals, and employing Dewey Martin on drums before he left to join Buffalo Springfield. On 1968's *Wheatstraw Suite*, they became one of the few noted country-rock performers to move into the style from country rather than rock.

Country-rock wasn't big commercially, and may have made its greatest impact as an influence on other performers. The Band, the Grateful Dead, Creedence Clearwater Revival and George Harrison for instance, could not be called country-rock performers by any means, but all recorded some impressive country-rock material on their late-'60s and early-'70s albums. Gram Parsons was a big influence on the Rolling Stones around this time, and on Keith Richards in particular, though it should be pointed out that the Stones had fused country and rock as far back as 1966 on "High and Dry." Still, their *Let It Bleed* and *Sticky Fingers* albums had quite a few country licks, most famously on "Wild Horses" (which appeared as a cover by the Flying Burrito Brothers before the Stones released their own version).

Country-rock hasn't gotten much attention as a movement since the early '70s. Commercially, it found its greatest success in the mid-'70s on hits by the Eagles (who featured ex-members of the Burritos, Poco, and the Stone Canyon Band) and Linda Ronstadt, who absorbed country-rock into their brands of soft rock and pop. Southern bands like Pure Prairie League and Charlie Daniels had some success with more Southern-fried sounds, and Southern rock bands like the Allman Brothers, the Ozark Mountain Daredevils, and Lynyrd Skynyrd recorded some country-influenced material, although their focus remained blues-rock and hard rock. In the 1980s and 1990s, it could be argued that Nashville has been a lot more successful in borrowing from rock than the other way around.

Country-rock arguably never recovered from the death of Gram Parsons in 1973, but it's remained alive and kicking, if hardly omnipresent. Elvis Costello made an all-out country album, albeit a commercial flop, in 1981 with *Almost Blue*; country music informs much of Neil Young's work, in whatever decade he's working in; alternative rockers like the Meat Puppets and the Jayhawks have leaned heavily on country-rock at times. Texas eccentrics Joe Ely, Butch Hancock and Jimmie Dale Gilmore (all of whom have played with each other at some point) have formed a sort of extended family for their brand of maverick country-rock. Once in a while a country-rock band will get a big push, like Lone Justice, but the hybrid seems to resist huge commercial success.

12 Essential Country Rock Albums:
The Byrds, *Sweetheart of the Rodeo* (Columbia)
The Flying Burrito Brothers, *Farther Along: The Best of the Flying Burrito Brothers* (A&M)
The International Submarine Band, *Safe at Home* (Rhino)
Hearts & Flowers, *Now Is the Time* (Bam Caruso, UK)
The Beau Brummels, *Bradley's Barn* (Edsel, UK)
Poco, *Pickin' up the Pieces* (Epic)
The Everly Brothers, *Roots* (Warner)
The Dillards, *Wheatstraw Suite* (Elektra)
Bob Dylan, *John Wesley Harding* (Columbia)
Various Artists, *Hillbilly Fever, Vol. 5* (Rhino)
The Flatlanders, *More a Legend than a Band* (Rounder)
Neil Young, *Harvest Moon* (Reprise)
Books:
Gram Parsons: A Music Biography, by Sid Griffin (Sierra, 1985)
Hickory Wind: The Gram Parsons Story, by Ben Fong-Torres

—Richie Unterberger

Music Map

Singer/Songwriters

Mid-'60s Folk-Rock Singer-Songwriters
Bob Dylan, Fred Neil, Gordon Lightfoot, Phil Ochs,
Tim Hardin, Leonard Cohen

Brill Building-Trained Singer-Songwriters
Carole King, Jackie De Shannon,
Randy Newman, Nilsson

Rock-Bred Singer-Songwriters
Van Morrison, Neil Young

British Singer-Songwriters
Cat Stevens, Nick Drake, Al Stewart

L.A. Singer-Songwriters
Joni Mitchell, Jackson Browne,
Tim Buckley

Singer-Songwriter Superstars
James Taylor, Carole King, Paul Simon, Carly Simon

Cult Singer-Songwriters
Steve Forbert, John Hiatt, Peter Case

Singer-Songwriter Stars of the '80s
Rickie Lee Jones, Suzanne Vega, Tracy Chapman

Singer/Songwriters

The definition of a rock singer/songwriter is elusive. Chuck Berry, the Beatles, Marvin Gaye, Patti Smith, Elvis Costello, Paul Westerberg, Liz Phair—are they not all singers and songwriters of the first degree? Of course they are, but none of them fit the label of a singer/songwriter that has been applied since the form's heyday in the late '60s and early '70s. Generally speaking, singer/songwriters put the emphasis on their material, rather than their vocal delivery, stylistic signatures, or musical backing (although those factors were certainly important). Both the compositions and the arrangements are written primarily as solo vehicles, rather than with full rock & roll bands in mind. Singer/songwriters almost exclusively play guitar and piano; quite a few play both. More than most rock styles, singer/songwriter records draw from folk and acoustic music. There are a higher percentage of women using the singer/songwriter format than you'll find in almost any other form of rock. The material tends toward the introspective, sensitive, romantic, and confessional, though it is not as wholly self-absorbed as some critics claim. They are not singles-oriented artists (though there have been quite a few massive singer/songwriter hit singles), but craft albums as complete, flowing statements.

The golden age of singer/songwriters was in many respects a blend of American contemporary folk and professional pop/rock songcraft. In the early '60s, Bob Dylan was more responsible than any other songwriter for pioneering personal expression and idiosyncratic lyrics; when he moved from acoustic folk arrangements to folk-rock, many of his peers followed. In the mid- and late '60s, Fred Neil, Tim Hardin, Phil Ochs, and Gordon Lightfoot were some of the more notable folkies who followed Dylan into singer/songwriter territory.

There was also a school of songwriters who came to the singer/songwriting camp from the opposite direction of pop/rock. Composers like Randy Newman, Jackie DeShannon, Nilsson, and Carole King began their professional careers primarily as songwriters supplying material for pop acts, not as performers in their own right. DeShannon—an extremely underrated pioneer of the singer/songwriter genre—was the first of these to become a recording star on her own. By the late '60s, many others had stepped out from behind the scenes to begin singing their own songs, even if their voices and images didn't conform to normal commercial music business standards of what was marketable.

Not all came from one wing or the other, of course. Leonard Cohen was already an established poet when he ventured into the musical arena with material that ranks among the most literary rock ever committed to vinyl. Laura Nyro, one of the first critically acclaimed singer/songwriters, drew upon soul and Tin Pan Alley. Neil Young and Van Morrison were seasoned rock & roll performers as members of influential '60s bands, although Young's work has been too eclectic and, at times, fiercely rocking for him to be classified as a singer/songwriter in the classic mold. Paul Simon, as many have pointed out, drew equally from pop and folk traditions, and was a veteran folk-rock star as half of Simon & Garfunkel before moving into more personal territory as a solo act.

Singer/songwriters were overwhelmingly White, middle-class, and well-educated; unsurprisingly, perhaps, many were based in Southern California or the Northeast, particularly Los Angeles or New York City. Los Angeles was always a chief well-spring of folk-rock, and in the late '60s, many talented singer/songwriters emerged that helped define the sound's folk-pop, laid-back milieu. The best of these, Joni Mitchell, actually (like Neil Young) hailed from Canada, but was based in L.A. by the time she began recording.

Mitchell's acoustic guitar- and piano-based sound, along with her intimate vocals and largely romantic themes, was a prototype of sorts for the singer/songwriter genre, although she moved on to experiment with jazz in both her vocals and arrangements after reaching superstardom in the mid-'70s.

Other important Southern California singer/songwriters were Randy Newman, who infused the form with humor and (occasionally bitter) satire, and Jackson Browne, whose even-tempoed, easygoing ruminations have defined, for better or worse, the mellow L.A. rock sound in the minds of many listeners. A more eclectic singer/songwriter from the region was Tim Buckley, who dovetailed with psychedelia, jazz, soul, and just plain strange vocal experimentation within the singer/songwriter format.

As far as bringing singer/songwriters to Middle America, no performer was more influential than Carole King, who had already enjoyed a long career dating back to the early '60s as one of America's most successful songwriters. Her 1971 album *Tapestry* remains one of the best-selling recordings of all time. James Taylor, perhaps, was King's closest counterpart; his cover version of King's "You've Got a Friend" (from *Tapestry*) made it to number one, and his 1970 album *Sweet Baby James* epitomized the calming soft rock trends of the early '70s.

Singer/songwriters weren't as big a deal in Britain, but several did emerge that put their own spins on the form. Al Stewart took a more narrative, fanciful, and third-person approach; Nick Drake delved into dark and ambiguous themes that the stars found uncomfortable, or were unwilling to explore. Cat Stevens, the most successful British singer/songwriter of the '70s, was also the most similar in sound and content to his American counterparts.

Singer/songwriters—like almost everything else, but even more so—were a target of early punk and new wave performers, who disdained what they viewed as the genre's self-satisfied, complacent hippie homilies. The style, however, had already crested by the time punk arrived. The huge stars remained popular, sometimes at the same plateau (Paul Simon), more often at steady but diminishing levels. New crops of talent, however, did not arrive; there were occasional waves from performers like Rickie Lee Jones, and critical cults for artists like Steve Forbert, Peter Case, and John Hiatt, whose sheafs of good press never translated into major record sales.

Suzanne Vega and Tracy Chapman were by far the biggest singer/songwriter stars to emerge after 1980, and others like Shawn Colvin, Joe Henry, and Luka Bloom continue to make their mark, although usually more with the critics than the masses. And the influence of the singer/songwriter is strongly felt in dozens, if not hundreds, of artists not strictly identified with the style, ranging from Stevie Wonder and Bruce Springsteen to Mary-Chapin Carpenter and Bob Mould.

12 Most Essential Singer/Songwriter Albums:
Joni Mitchell, *Clouds* (Reprise)
Carole King, *Tapestry* (Epic)
Tim Buckley, *Goodbye & Hello* (Elektra)
Paul Simon, *Negotiations & Love Songs 1971-1986* (Warner Brothers)
Leonard Cohen, *Songs of Leonard Cohen* (CBS)
Nick Drake, *Fruit Tree* (Rykodisc)
James Taylor, *Sweet Baby James* (Warner Brothers)
Jackson Browne, *Late for the Sky* (Asylum)
Randy Newman, *12 Songs* (Reprise)
Neil Young, *After the Gold Rush* (Reprise)
Suzanne Vega, *Suzanne Vega* (A&M)
Tracy Chapman, *Tracy Chapman* (Elektra)

—*Richie Unterberger*

Jazz Rock

More than most such subgenres, jazz-rock is a hybrid that has resisted true alchemy. The impulse to blend the basic drive of rock with the improvisational verve and rhythmic

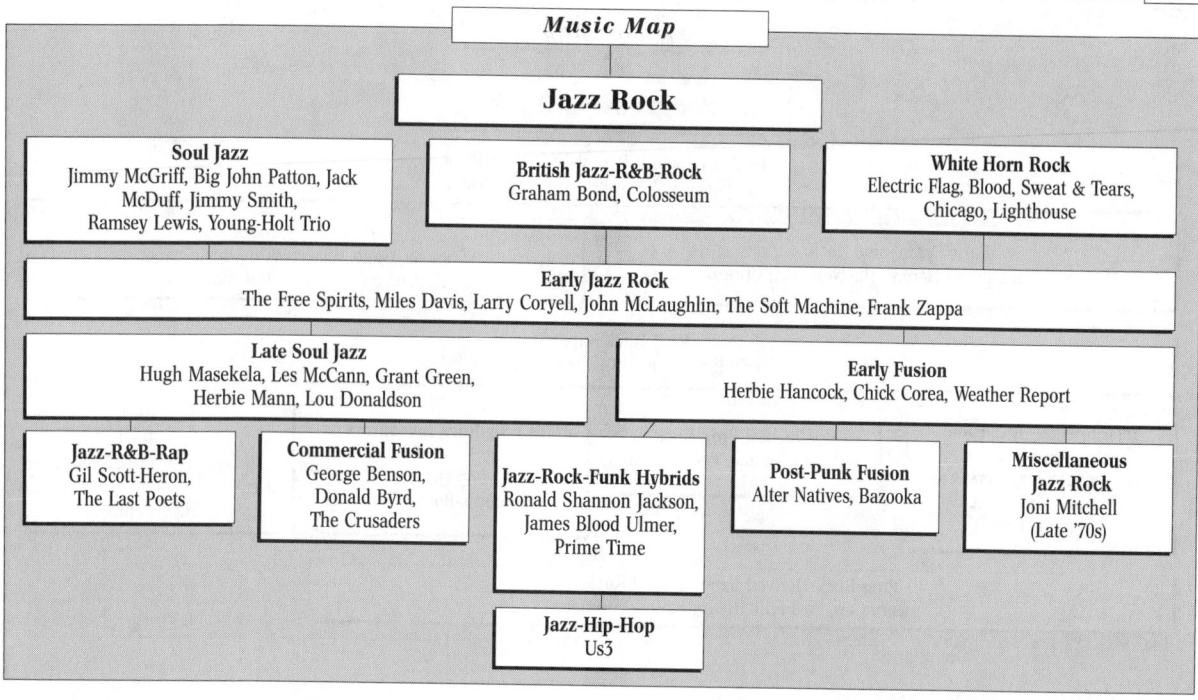

Music Map

Jazz Rock

Soul Jazz
Jimmy McGriff, Big John Patton, Jack McDuff, Jimmy Smith, Ramsey Lewis, Young-Holt Trio

British Jazz-R&B-Rock
Graham Bond, Colosseum

White Horn Rock
Electric Flag, Blood, Sweat & Tears, Chicago, Lighthouse

Early Jazz Rock
The Free Spirits, Miles Davis, Larry Coryell, John McLaughlin, The Soft Machine, Frank Zappa

Late Soul Jazz
Hugh Masekela, Les McCann, Grant Green, Herbie Mann, Lou Donaldson

Early Fusion
Herbie Hancock, Chick Corea, Weather Report

Jazz-R&B-Rap
Gil Scott-Heron, The Last Poets

Commercial Fusion
George Benson, Donald Byrd, The Crusaders

Jazz-Rock-Funk Hybrids
Ronald Shannon Jackson, James Blood Ulmer, Prime Time

Post-Punk Fusion
Alter Natives, Bazooka

Miscellaneous Jazz Rock
Joni Mitchell (Late '70s)

Jazz-Hip-Hop
Us3

---

complexity of jazz is a challenge that has been taken up by many. Not only has it been successfully faced by few, but the results often prove more weighted toward either rock or jazz than a true fusion of the styles.

Half a century ago, rock and jazz were much more closely intertwined than they were today. In the big-band and swing era, jazz was a much more dance-oriented music; early R&B and jump blues acts that helped lay the foundation for rock & roll drew much of their boogies, riffs, and rhythms (as well as instrumentalists) from jazz. Artists like Joe Turner and Jay McShann could have been classified as either jazz or R&B, but as rock & roll grew into a full-grown giant and jazz evolved toward bebop, the styles took substantially divergent paths.

Jazz's influence on rock & roll during the '50s and '60s wasn't negligible. Lots of R&B and soul bands, including those of Little Richard, Ray Charles and James Brown, featured musicians from jazz backgrounds. Respected jazz musicians like Barney Kessel played on many rock & roll sessions to help pay the rent, and drummer Cozy Cole crossed over to the rock & roll market with his instrumental smash *Topsy*. In the mid-'60s, the Byrds openly credited John Coltrane as an influence on early psychedelic landmarks like "Eight Miles High," and used South African jazz trumpeter Hugh Masekela as a prominent session man on a couple of their singles. Notable '60s groups like the Doors, Zombies, Blues Project, Paul Butterfield, Manfred Mann, Traffic and Santana clearly displayed important secondary jazz influences. Jazz was also an important element in Van Morrison's late-'60s album *Astral Weeks*, which featured the rhythm section of noted jazz players Richard Davis on bass and Connie Kay of the Modern Jazz Quartet on drums.

Not to be overlooked, either, is '60s soul-jazz, a form which attracts little critical attention today, but was quite popular in its day—indeed, it might have been the most popular form of jazz with urban, African-American audiences. Using organs, vocals, and R&B riffs with greater frequency than other jazz musicians, the most popular performers in this subgenre would include Jimmy Smith, Jimmy McGriff, Big John Patton and Jack McDuff. Ramsey Lewis and the spinoff combo Young-Holt Trio (later to become Young-Holt Unlimited) had a more pop-oriented take on soul-jazz that led to substantial Top 40 success.

"Jazz-rock" as a self-conscious label, however, didn't evolve until the late '60s. The first acts to be widely identified as jazz-rock bands (and, to this day, the most successful) weren't so much jazz-rockers as R&B-oriented White rock bands with jazzy horn sections. The Electric Flag featuring Mike Bloomfield, Buddy Miles and Nick Gravenites were the first of these; Blood, Sweat & Tears and Chicago became huge stars, although the MOR nature of their hits led some critics to dub them as "wedding band" or "bar mitzvah" soul.

A more ambitious, although extremely obscure, jazz-rock record that predates any of the bands in the above paragraph was the sole album by the New York-based Free Spirits featuring the young Larry Coryell on guitar. This interesting but erratic effort came much closer to truly striking a midpoint between rock song forms and jazz instrumentation, although the songs remained in the neighborhood of three minutes, and the vocals were fairly weak. Concentrating more on the jazz and instrumental side of things, Coryell became one of the leading early jazz-rock and fusion performers as the leader of Eleventh House and as a solo artist.

Several British '60s bands featured players that emerged from a jazz background, most notably the Graham Bond Organization. Besides the leader, they featured Jack Bruce and Ginger Baker in their pre-Cream days, and, for a time, guitarist John McLaughlin, although they quickly gravitated toward the R&B and blues sounds of the day. Bruce and Baker have occasionally recorded respectable jazz albums right up to the present, and Bond-John Mayall spinoff-band Colosseum were probably the best jazz-oriented act to emerge from the British R&B-blues scene. The most successful British jazz-rock band of all, and indeed the one act that could be termed to have truly fused the two styles more than any other, were the Soft Machine. Starting as an underground psychedelic group (and a very good one), their late-'60s and early-'70s albums turned toward an increasingly improvisational and instrumental sound, retaining rock elements in Mike Ratledge's buzzing organ and Robert Wyatt's brilliant drumming and soulful vocals.

For most critics, though, the true peak of jazz-rock was reached by Miles Davis on his early-'70s recordings. Impressed by Jimi Hendrix and other late-'60s rock musicians, Davis brought electric guitars and keyboards into his band, culminating in the landmark 1970 LP *Bitches Brew*, roundly acclaimed as one of the most influential jazz recordings of all time. That record featured guitarist John McLaughlin, who would immediately become a leading jazz-rock figure himself, on his own, with Davis, with the Mahavishnu Orchestra, and in collaborations with ex-Davis drummer Tony Williams and Carlos Santana.

Other jazz musicians took the cue from Davis, always a leader and innovator, and added electric instruments and rock-influenced rhythms to their sound. Herbie Hancock, Chick Corea and Weather Report were the best of these groups, although it's fair to say that, even more than Davis, they were really "rock-influenced jazz," not "jazz-rock." The compositions were usually instrumental, the melodic themes and improvisations clearly from the jazz tradition; the rock influence was felt in the electric instruments and the forceful funk of the arrangements.

Not unsurprisingly, jazz-rock quickly turned in a more commercial, watered-down direction that resulted in the style known as "fusion." As work became harder to find in the struggling jazz scene of the late '60s, notable jazzmen like Lou Donaldson, Herbie Mann, Les McCann, Hugh Masekela and Grant Green had already been turning in a jazz-soul direction as a means of both broadening their horizons and survival. Many jazz players, usually for brief periods, brought electric instruments and funk rhythms into their arrangements during the 1970s, resulting by and large in unimpressive, at times embarrassing, results. Guitarist George Benson and trumpeter Donald Byrd, to name two of the most obvious examples, found much greater commercial success as pop-fusioneers than with their more critically respected straight jazz efforts of the '60s.

Jazz-rock hasn't been a big critical or commercial deal since the mid-'70s, but occasional innovators have produced interesting efforts along the lines of the best jazz-rock pioneers. Frank Zappa couldn't properly be considered a jazz-rock musician, but several of his '70s recordings, most notably *Hot Rats*, rank among the most ambitious blends of rock and jazz principles. Guitarist James Blood Ulmer and drummer Ronald Shannon Jackson (whose band, the Decoding Society, featured future Living Colour guitarist Vernon Reid) were both students of the Ornette Coleman school of harmolodics. The best

Music Map

Progressive Rock

British Late '60s Psychedelia-Prog-Rock
Pink Floyd, Soft Machine, The Pretty Things

Early Symphonic Rock
Moody Blues, Procol Harum, The Nice, King Crimson

Canterbury Scene
Caravan, Gong, Robert Wyatt, Kevin Ayers,
Hatfield & The North, Matching Mole

Prog-Rock Superstars
Jethro Tull, Genesis, Yes, Emerson, Lake & Palmer

Instrumental / Electronic Prog-Rock
Mike Oldfield, Kraftwerk, Can,
Amon Düül, Faust,
Tangerine Dream

Continental Prog-Rock
Aphrodite's Child, Focus, P.F.M.

'70s Prog Rock Innovators
Roxy Music, Eno,
Be-Bop Deluxe,
Bill Nelson, Robert Fripp

Pop-Rock Prog-Rock
Boston, Foreigner, Kansas,
Electric Light Orchestra, Journey,
Supertramp

Prog-Rock-Derived Experimental Rock
Henry Cow, Fred Frith, Henry Kaiser, Material

---

of their records have melded jazz improvisation, funk rhythms, and visceral electric drive as well as anyone. Coleman himself drew on jazz-rock innovations with his Prime Time band. Streetwise jazz poets Gil-Scott Heron and the Last Poets helped lay the foundation for rap music. Defunkt merged jazz and funk rhythms without, at least at the beginning, pandering to watered-down commercial fusion interests. And, most unpredictably, folk-rock star Joni Mitchell delved heavily into jazz improvisation in the late '70s with the help of sidemen Jaco Pastorius and Pat Metheny and put lyrics to Charles Mingus' last compositions (at his request) on the 1979 album, *Mingus*.

The jazz-rock fusion continues to tempt musicians intermittently in the '90s. Several bands on the alternative rock label SST, most notably Alter Natives and Bazooka, played what was essentially improvisational jazz with fierce electric guitar-driven arrangements. The downtown New York avant-rock-whatchamacallit scene is too eclectic to be figured easily into the jazz-rock equation, but many of its performers are clearly strongly influenced by both worlds. Under the pseudonym Buckshot LeFonque, leading contemporary jazz musician Branford Marsalis took a stab at jazz-funk-R&B-soul-hip-hop. British act Us3 grafted hip-hop samples onto classic Blue Note jazz recordings, sparking some occasionally inspired jazz-hip-hop crossover recordings in the jazz community itself.

15 Recommended Jazz-Rock Recordings:

Various Artists, *Blue Funk: The History of the Hammond Organ* (Blue Note). More quality soul-jazz was recorded on the Blue Note label than any other, and this compilation includes tracks by most of the biggest stars of the genre: Jimmy Smith, Jimmy McGriff, Jack McDuff, Grant Green, Big John Patton, Lou Donaldson.

The Free Spirits, *Out of Sight, Out of Sound* (ABC). Pretty hard to find these days, this stakes a strong claim as the first jazz-rock record.

The Electric Flag, *A Long Time Comin'* (Columbia). The best of the records by late-'60s White rock groups to be classified as "jazz-rock."

Miles Davis, *Bitches Brew* (Columbia). Still the most influential and respected jazz-rock recording.

The Soft Machine, *Third* (Columbia). Their most successful pure jazz-rock outing, although their earlier, more psychedelic rock-flavored albums weren't too shabby either.

John McLaughlin, *Devotion* (Restless). It's really a matter of taste as to which early-'70s McLaughlin album stands as his best, but rock listeners might find this one of the more approachable ones, as it uses Jimi Hendrix's Band of Gypsies rhythm section.

Frank Zappa, *Hot Rats* (Rykodisc). One of his most jazz-rock-oriented recordings, this largely instrumental 1970 effort features some of his best guitar playing.

Herbie Hancock, *Headhunters* (Columbia). The album that broke fusion as a commercial force, though those looking for something a bit more adventurous in the jazz-rock vein might try the early-'70s LPs he released just prior to this effort.

Gil-Scott Heron, *The Revolution Will Not Be Televised* (Flying Dutchman). The leading jazz-R&B-rock poet.

Miles Davis, *Pangaea* (Columbia). Arguably the most recklessly electric of Davis's fusion sessions, featuring the guitar pyrotechnics of Pete Cosey. Those looking for something slightly less experimental should try *Agharta*, recorded on the same day.

Joni Mitchell, *Mingus* (Asylum). The central recording of Mitchell's jazz-rock phase, a period which inspired much debate among both fans and critics.

James Blood Ulmer, *Are You Glad to Be in America?* (Artists House). None of Ulmer's records could exactly be termed accessible, but this strikes the best balance between funk-R&B-rock and harmolodics.

Ronald Shannon Jackson, *Decode Yourself* (Island). None of Jackson's albums particularly stands out as his most influential; this 1985 Bill Laswell-produced session is one of the more accessible.

Bazooka, *Blowhole* (SST). A group that, like others on the SST label, pursues the elusive goal of wedding Ornette Coleman to post-punk attitude and eclecticism.

Various Artists, *Stolen Moments: Red, Hot & Cool* (GRP). The best jazz-hip-hop compilation, featuring some of the top talents from both worlds.

—Richie Unterberger

Progressive Rock

Devotees of progressive rock have to fend off more vilification than fans of almost any other rock genre. Pure-bred rock & rollers scorn it for lacking rock's earthier and poppier elements; scholars of classical and serious music find it too simple and undemanding to merit attention; latter-day punks and new wavers held it aloft as a target, painting it as the embodiment of the self-satisfied dinosaur that the music business had become, and one which needed to be deflated (in the days when John Lydon joined the Sex Pistols so the story goes, he wore a T-shirt emblazoned with the logo "I hate Pink Floyd"). Nonetheless, progressive rock was one of the defining styles of '70s rock, and responsible for some of rock's most ambitious—and pretentious—efforts.

Progressive rock came in many shapes and sizes, but it can be loosely defined as music that attempted to combine rock and psychedelia with classical, symphonic, and literary elements. Most of the groups placed instrumental virtuosity at a premium, used keyboards rather more than the typical rock group, and used synthesizers a lot more than the typical rock group. Electric guitars were also important, sometimes battling it out with the keyboards, sometimes taking off for lofty, lengthy solos on their own. Lyrically, prog-rockers didn't neglect love songs entirely, but were usually more concerned with weighty philosophical matters, which were often influenced by psychedelic drugs, science fiction, and fantasy, sometimes on an epic scale. Virtually all of the major prog-rock groups were British in origin, some hailing from the European continent as well.

Progressive rock—sometimes called "art-rock"—has its origins in the British psychedelic scene of the late '60s. The Moody Blues were the first group to combine rock with classical symphonic music on their 1967 album *Days of Future Passed*. On subsequent albums, they dispensed with the actual orchestra and used synthesizers and sophisticated studio techniques to create symphonies by themselves. Few groups have endured as much frenzied adulation and vituperative criticism as the Moodies; undeniably pretentious, they were also one of progressive rock's most infectiously melodic acts.

Also massively popular were the Pink Floyd who turned increasingly serious-minded after the departure of their original leader, Syd Barrett in early 1968. Many thought the band was dead with the loss of Barrett, their original songwriter, guitarist, and singer, whose inimitable sense of whimsy made the group's 1967 debut, *Piper at the Gates of Dawn*, one of the greatest psychedelic rock albums. The Floyd surprised their critics by getting bigger and bigger, with increasingly lengthy and spacious experimental epics whose electronic eerieness defined early "head music" for many listeners.

While their big international breakthrough was 1973's *Dark Side of the Moon*, which remains one of the best-selling albums of all time, their earlier output contained some of their most original work, and the group never entirely lost sight of their pop and blues roots.

Other key British bands of the late '60s were the Soft Machine who incorporated jazz and Dadaism into their psychedelic hard rock; Procol Harum who used multi-layered keyboards, melodies with strong echoes of classical music, and the consciously literary lyrics of Keith Reid; the Nice who featured Keith Emerson's virtuosic, classical-inspired keyboards and flamboyant showmanship; the Pretty Things whose rock opera *S.F. Sorrow* predated the Who's *Tommy* by about a year; and Jethro Tull whose early mixes of blues-rock and Rahsaan Roland Kirk soon metamorphosed into inscrutable album-length epic poems with strong hints of traditional English folk music.

For many aficionados, the first true progressive rock band were King Crimson whose 1969 debut was a groundbreaking synthesis of stately virtuosity and fierce guitars and Mellotrons. Although some critics would be loathe to concur, early reviewers often compared King Crimson's first lineup to the similarly melodic and Mellotron-laden excursions of the early Moody Blues. With guitarist Robert Fripp at the helm, the group endured several rapid changes of personnel and quickly became a less song-oriented outfit, with increasing emphasis on flights of instrumental virtuosity and dense, challenging material with strong jazz and avant-garde influences.

Even as early as 1970, there were striking subdivisions within the progressive rock school. Several of the most critically respected bands clustered around the banner of the Canterbury sound; spearheaded by the Soft Machine these also included Caravan, Hatfield & the North, and Soft Machine-offshoots like Matching Mole, Gong and the solo work of ex-Softs, Robert Wyatt and Kevin Ayers. Lighter in tone than the most commercially successful exponents of the genre, they also frequently exhibited a sense of humor that the superstars were not exactly prone to display.

While these bands may have gotten critical accolades, it was up to Emerson, Lake & Palmer, Yes, Pink Floyd, Jethro Tull and Genesis to shift serious units. While Pink Floyd used fairly economic licks on their epics, the other stars tended to brandish flashy instrumental passages by guitar and keyboard heroes like Steve Howe, Rick Wakeman and Keith Emerson. All their considerable bombast couldn't mask a firm grasp of songwriting hooks and tasty instrumental riffs that the masses found most palatable.

When they deigned to examine art-rock, critics reserved a lot of their enthusiasm for Roxy Music whose ironic pop was flavored with unnerving synthesizer blasts from Brian Eno. After a short time with Roxy, Eno split for a solo career and recorded increasingly abstract, and increasingly instrumental, rock-flavored compositions that rank among the most well-respected art-rock and avant-rock recordings of all time, although Eno would largely forsake rock by the late '70s for contemporary composition (he continues to work with many rock performers as a producer).

Then there was a wing of progressive rock that was primarily instrumental. Unsurprisingly, many of these acts came from the European continent, and used the instrumental format as a way to circumvent their limited grasp of English, the lingua franca of popular music. Germany's Kraftwerk had a surprise Top Ten album in the mid-'70s with *Autobahn*; their foreboding, electronic textures, as well as those of fellow German bands like Can, Amon Düül, Faust, and Tangerine Dream, gave rise to the school of "Kraut rock" (dubbed as such by England's Virgin Records, who marketed the bands to an international audience), and had a considerable influence on new wave acts several years later. Holland's Focus featuring guitar wizard Jan Akkerman, Greece's *Aphrodite's Child* (featuring a young Vangelis), and Italy's P.F.M. also made international inroads. And in the U.K., Mike Oldfield (who had played guitar with Kevin Ayers) had a huge international hit with the instrumental suite *Tubular Bells*.

Progressive rock's influence declined after the mid-'70s; the punk/new wave and disco explosions were factors, but more important, a lot of the bands broke up, moved toward more pop-oriented fare, or simply played themselves out. The British Harvest and Virgin labels, instrumental in exposing the music to a wide audience, wound down their activities (Harvest) or moved on to the larger pop/rock market (Virgin). Groups like Electric Light Orchestra, Boston, Foreigner, Journey, Asia, Kansas and Supertramp became massively successful by incorporating progressive rock's flashiest attributes into their brands of mainstream pop/rock.

With a more modified symphonic lens, bands like the Moody Blues and Pink Floyd remain superstar concert attractions and big record sellers whenever they reassemble to work in the studio or hit the road, and scattered modern bands like Marillion pursue the original prog-rock ideal. From the other side of the spectrum, performers like Fred Frith, Henry Kaiser, Robert Fripp, Material and Public Image Limited took progressive rock into more avant-garde territory than it ever dared to tread during its heyday. And there's no doubt that the loftier excursions of performers like the Who, Led Zeppelin, the Mothers of Invention, Peter Gabriel and David Bowie owe not a little to the better values of progressive rock.

12 Essential Progressive Rock Albums:
Pink Floyd, *Dark Side of the Moon* (Capitol)
Procol Harum, *Procol Harum* (Deram)
The Moody Blues, *Days of Future Passed* (Polydor)
Yes, *Fragile* (Atlantic)
Brian Eno, *Here Come the Warm Jets* (EG)
The Soft Machine, *The Soft Machine Volumes 1 & 2* (Big Beat, UK)
Caravan, *Canterbury Tales* (Polydor)
Mike Oldfield, *Tubular Bells* (Virgin)

Music Map
Bubblegum

Bubblegum Forerunners
The Monkees, Tommy James, Tommy Roe

Kasenetz-Katz Productions
The Ohio Express, The 1910 Fruitgum Co.

TV Bubblegum Stars
The Archies, The Banana Splits

Pre-Teen Idols
The Partridge Family, The Osmonds, Bobby Sherman, The DeFranco Family

King Crimson, *Frame by Frame* (Caroline)
Kraftwerk, *Autobahn* (Warner Brothers)
The Pretty Things, *S.F. Sorrow* (Edsel)
Jethro Tull, *20 Years of Jethro Tull: Highlights* (Chrysalis)
Various Artists, *Supernatural Fairy Tales: The Progressive Rock Era* (Rhino)
                                       —*Richie Unterberger*

Bubblegum

Considering bubblegum's fairly meager legacy—a few dozen hits in the late 1960s and early 1970s—it inspired a lot of heated discussion and revisionism. It arose at a time when the listener demographic for rock was expanding rapidly; originally marketed almost exclusively to teenagers, those teenagers were now growing up, leaving their teens, and continuing to buy and play rock & roll. At the same time, the purchasing power of pre-teens was growing. Too young in most cases to appreciate the subtleties of *Tommy* or "Cloud Nine," they needed a simple form of rock & roll to identify with, and bubblegum was created to satisfy their desires.

While 1967 was a year that saw rock and soul shake with paroxysms of change, it also saw million-selling singles by the Monkees who starred in a show whose audience was composed more of small kids than any other type of viewer. It also saw hits by singers like Tommy James whose simple but catchy pop/rock was probably vastly more popular with pre-teens than post-adolescents. Although the Monkees' and Tommy James' best work holds up today as outstanding pop/rock, at the time it pointed the way for even more simple and naive music. And although the Monkees eventually played their own instruments on their records, industry insiders were well aware that their early hits were crafted by studio musicians, and knew that bona fide self-contained groups weren't strictly necessary to create smash records.

Most of the early bubblegum records were manufactured at Buddah Records by the production team of Jerry Kasenetz and Jeff Katz. Emphasizing repetitive, throbbing bass lines, simple singalong lyrics, cheesy organs, and insinuatingly (some would say obnoxiously) catchy melodies, their hit singles by the Ohio Express and the 1910 Fruitgum Co. were played by sessionmen—the "groups" didn't exist outside of the studio. Dubbed "bubblegum" for its childish qualities, mass production values, and instant disposability, it was celebrated as such in the minor 1969 hit single "Bubble Gum Music," released by the unforgettable Rock & Roll Dubble Bubble Trading Card Co. of Philadelphia 19141.

It didn't take long for the Archies, masterminded by brilliant Brill Building tunesmith and producer Jeff Barry, to establish themselves as the most successful bubblegum group. "Jingle Jangle" and particularly the number one hit "Sugar Sugar" were unavoidable if you were within earshot of a radio in 1969; the latter song's qualities were recognized by Wilson Pickett, who made the tune his own in a soul cover version. Another studio-only group, the Archies' records were tied in to a cartoon series based on the famous comic book, with Archie, Jughead, and the gang playing the songs on the program.

The cross-promotion value of the Monkees' and the Archies' television programs was duplicated by the Partridge Family, the Banana Splits, and to some degree by Bobby Sherman, a pre-teen idol. The Partridge Family themselves were picking up a fumble by the Cowsills, a clean-cut pop/rock family act that the Partridges were loosely based upon (although the Cowsills' arrangements were somewhat more sophisticated than the bubblegum norm). When the Partridges peaked, they in turn were supplanted by the Osmonds, a bubblegum version of the Jackson 5 (who, naturally, also had their own TV cartoon series around this time). The Partridges and Osmonds even inspired the briefly successful imitators, the DeFranco Family.

In bubblegum's prime, there were also several huge one-shot hits by "artists" destined never to be heard from again. The Cuff Links' "Tracy," from 1969, featured the same singer

Southern Rock

Founders
The Allman Brothers Band

Southern Country Rock Charlie Daniels, The Outlaws	**Descendants** Lynyrd Skynyrd, Wet Willie, Ozark Mountain Daredevils	**Jazzy Southern Rock** Sea Level, Dixie Dregs	**Pop-Influenced Southern Rock** Atlanta Rhythm Section

Southern Bar Band Rock
Marshall Tucker Band,
.38 Special, Molly Hatchet

Contemporary Southern Rock
The Georgia Satellites,
The Black Crowes,
The Dave Matthews Band,
Widespread Panic

who took the lead for the Archies. Daddy Dewdrop ("Chick-A-Boom"), the Pipkins ("Gimme Dat Ding"), and Crazy Elephant ("Gimme Gimme Good Lovin") were some of the others whose tunes continued to echo in the brain long after their equally silly monikers had faded from memory. A few pop/rock veterans got some mileage out of bubblegum, like Tommy Roe, who cut bubblegum hits with "Dizzy" and "Jam up Jelly Tight"; the Troggs even recorded a bubblegum single, "Hip Hip Hooray," modeled after the Ohio Express.

Bubblegum was savaged by the rock press, who were outraged that simple clap-trap like "Yummy Yummy Yummy"—records by groups that didn't even exist outside of the studio—could sell millions of copies while sensitive, literate efforts of progressive rockers and singer/songwriters struggled to be heard. After bubblegum had faded and punk emerged in the late '70s, some critics took a revisionist stance, hailing bubblegum for its innovative production techniques and for boiling pop/rock down to its irreducible essence. It's often been pointed out that one of the first songs the Talking Heads performed was the 1910 Fruitgum Co.'s "1-2-3 Red Light," and the simple throbbing rhythm and lyrics of numbers like "Psycho Killer" have a distant relation to bubblegum, although no one's going to confuse *Remain in Light* with music aimed at pre-teens.

Bubblegum's influence continues to hover in all music aimed at the record-buying public's youngest segment, who don't care if their heroes wrote the songs or even played on the records. Bubblegum was hardly one of the high points of rock history, but even the most serious-minded listeners are probably fooling themselves if they can't admit to the ingratiating catchiness of hits like "Tracy" and "Sugar, Sugar."

5 Most Essential Bubblegum Recordings:
Various Artists, *The Best of the Ohio Express & Other Bubblegum Smashes*
Various Artists, *The Best of the 1910 Fruitgum Company & Other Bubblegum Smashes*
Various Artists, *Bubblegum Classics Vol. 1-3* (Varese Sarabande)
The Archies, *The Archies' Greatest Hits*
Tommy Roe, *Greatest Hits*

—*Richie Unterberger*

Heavy Metal

Heavy metal, in simple terms, is rock & roll music played with a little more intensity than normal. The guitar, which is a major factor of the music, may be played with a bit more vengeance and perhaps a little louder than usual. The bass was also put up in the front, which may be partly due to the Who and to John Entwistle's performance in "My Generation" and "Magic Bus." Only in jazz had the bass been used as a lead instrument, but now it became as important as the singing. The drums had to be played harder and sometimes faster than normal pop music, and this made an impact on the listener. And then there's the vocalist—the one who carries the listener through emotions, feelings, and story lines that can range from death to the discovery of sex, drugs, or alcohol and the impact of discovering something new. Many of the topics were new, and those that had been told before in pop music were made more realistic, more believable, maybe even more frightening in heavy metal.

The band that possibly started the ball rolling was England's Black Sabbath. The name was evil; it brought an immediate image of what the music could be like: dark, mysterious, vulgar, rebellious. And without fear of the unknown, maybe the music could be fun.

The band's self-titled debut album, released in 1970, featured all of those aspects and led many to call this group outrageous. Regardless of what people thought, Black Sabbath struck a chord with anybody who was willing to listen. Its songs, often dealing with the discovery of the unknown, appealed to many teenagers, who could easily relate with the band's struggle to find who they really were. The music was strong, it was loud, it was heavy, and it was heavy metal. Since then the music has gone through a lot of changes, and for those who could not understand it, it got into a lot of trouble.

When punk rock bloomed in the latter half of the '70s (at a time when disco was all the rage), there were people from both sides of the Atlantic who were fed up with playing in basements while others took the spotlight. In England, there seemed to be an enormous number of bands waiting to be heard, and a few of them got noticed in America. This became known as the New Wave of British Heavy Metal, or NWOBHM. Over in America, young musicians who were brought up on Led Zeppelin, Aerosmith, Deep Purple, and Yes started forming their own bands, and thus the genre became official. And it wasn't only in the States or England; Australia and Germany also had bands that could easily compete with the best.

The younger kids in England got a bit more uptight with what they heard, and they chose to make things darker and maybe faster. One of the first bands to do this was Motörhead. Then there were the adventurous American kids who sought out imported albums from their favorite NWOBHM bands and, rather than emulate what they heard, played it the way it felt to them. Some of these bands took a cue from punk rock, and what was heard was louder, harder, and faster. This became thrash-metal, a form that started around 1982. A few bands made the rhythm the essential part of their recipe, and a young musician from southern California named Jeff Dahl is considered the first individual to coin the phrase "speed-metal." Thrash-metal and speed-metal are essentially the same thing, with thrash sometimes being slightly slower and emphasizing the guitar.

From there, everything goes crazy. Bands who sang about the end of the world were called death-metal bands. Those who spoke about hell and the devil were labeled black-metal bands. Soon young British bands were doing grindcore, which is superfast music with almost unintelligible lyrics and as heavy as possible. Then there are the heavy metal bands who stuck with their roots and came out as strong and as daring as those who explored the possibilities. Loud, disgusting, meaningful, powerful, gross, fast, faster, destructive, innovative, intelligent, a way of life: that's heavy metal.

—*John Book*

Southern Rock

While the South, more than any other American region, was responsible for breeding rock & roll, it lacked a readily identifiable white rock band sound after the decline of rockabilly. Southern rock groups were hardly unknown in the 1960s; John Fred & the Playboys, the Boxtops, and Bill Deal & the Rondels rank among the most talented blue-eyed soul performers, and there were occasional bands following the British Invasion and folk-rock trends, such as the underappreciated Gants. Soul music, of course, thrived in Memphis, New Orleans, and other southern regions throughout the '60s, and white session musicians (especially the white half of Booker T. & the MG's) contributed mightily to the sounds crafted at Stax/Volt Records and the Muscle Shoals and Fame studios.

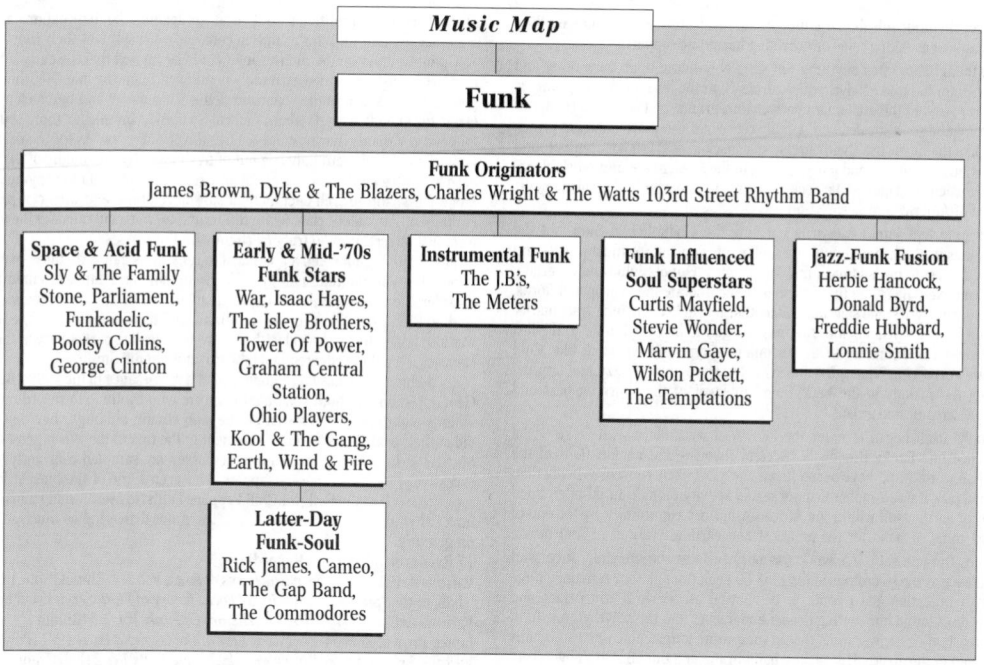

Music Map

Funk

Funk Originators
James Brown, Dyke & The Blazers, Charles Wright & The Watts 103rd Street Rhythm Band

Space & Acid Funk
Sly & The Family Stone, Parliament, Funkadelic, Bootsy Collins, George Clinton

Early & Mid-'70s Funk Stars
War, Isaac Hayes, The Isley Brothers, Tower Of Power, Graham Central Station, Ohio Players, Kool & The Gang, Earth, Wind & Fire

Instrumental Funk
The J.B.'s, The Meters

Funk Influenced Soul Superstars
Curtis Mayfield, Stevie Wonder, Marvin Gaye, Wilson Pickett, The Temptations

Jazz-Funk Fusion
Herbie Hancock, Donald Byrd, Freddie Hubbard, Lonnie Smith

Latter-Day Funk-Soul
Rick James, Cameo, The Gap Band, The Commodores

But southern rock, as an identifiable style, didn't come into its own until about 1970. Like many sub-genres of rock & roll, southern rock peaked very early in its development. Its story is more tragic than most, perhaps, because it fell from grace not so much from the usual reasons of flagging inspiration and rampant imitation, but from sudden tragedies that tore the heart out of its two flagship groups.

Southern rock proper began with the Allman Brothers, who had already made some recordings in California as the Hourglass; lead guitarist Duane Allman was a respected session player, contributing to records by Aretha Franklin, Boz Scaggs, and (after the Allmans were established) Eric Clapton. The Allman Brothers established the blueprint for southern rock in their heavy debts to roots music forms: the blues was foremost, as were boogie, soul, and hints of country. They weren't at all like either the early rockabilly performers or the contemporary soul musicians, however, in that the guitar-dominated thrust of their arrangements were clearly inspired by the leading hard rock and psychedelic bands of the day, such as Cream and Jimi Hendrix.

While the Allmans were to some degree responsible for some of southern rock's lesser attributes—the endless jams, the repetitive boogie riffs—they executed these with much more subtle polish than any of their descendents, and at their best demonstrated a real facility for combining muscular rock with improvisation. Anchored by Gregg Allman's soulful vocals and the twin lead guitars of Duane Allman and Dickey Betts, the group became stars after the release of the double LP *Live At The Fillmore East*, still one of the most popular live rock recordings of all time. Duane Allman was killed in a motorcycle accident in late 1971, shortly after the release of *Fillmore East*, and bassist Berry Oakley died in eerily similar circumstances a year later. The band has continued to record to the present day, at times with great commercial success, but has never approached the artistic heights of their original lineup.

In the wake of the Allmans' success, several other southern bands arose to mine the same territory of rootsy boogies and guitar-driven stomp, usually with considerably less subtlety. The most successful, both critically and commercially, were Lynyrd Skynyrd. Attracting important and influential fans in Al Kooper (who produced their debut) and Pete Townshend (who had the group open for the Who during a tour in the early '70s), Lynyrd Skynyrd boasted three lead guitarists. As songwriters and performers, they helped establish the good ol' boy (or, as some would put it less kindly, redneck) image of southern rock, and helped define '70s guitar rock with "Freebird," which vies with "Stairway To Heaven" as the most overplayed classic rock song of all time. At the same time, they could show uncommon lyrical subtlety for the genre, as well as economic hook-savvy smarts. They were one of America's most popular bands by 1977, when lead singer Ronnie Van Zandt and guitarist Steve Gaines died in a plane crash. Subseqent recordings by the group, as well as the spinoff Rossington-Collins Band, didn't measure up to those by the Van Zandt-fronted lineup.

While no other southern rock bands of the '70s approached the Allmans or Lynyrd Skynyrd in popularity or influence, quite a few of them were big. The Charlie Daniels Band and the Outlaws were the most country-influenced; the Dixie Dregs and Sea Level (both of whom recorded for the Allmans' label, Capricorn) the jazziest; Wet Willie the most R&B and gospel-influenced; the Ozark Mountain Daredevils and the Atlanta Rhythm Section, briefly stars, the most pop-influenced. American blues-rock performers with southern roots like Johnny Winter, Edgar Winter, ZZ Top, and Elvin Bishop were sometimes lumped in the southern rock school, although they were really on the edge of the style both geographically and stylistically.

The bar band boogie hallmarks of southern rock always go over big live, and several fairly generic bands rose to a level of considerable popularity without offering anything particularly valuable, and, at their worst, perpetuating the worst "redneck rock" stereotypes of brawling, good-time southern boys. Included in this category would be .38 Special and Molly Hatchet. The Marshall Tucker Band, originators of a seemingly endless stream of competently indistinguishable southern rock albums, epitomized the common denominator of the genre.

As a big commercial force, southern rock didn't last into the 1980s. Many notable alternative rock groups, such as R.E.M. and the B-52s, came from the south, but their allegiance was to punk, pop, and new wave, not the blues, country, soul, and hard rock of the '70s southern rock groups. The Georgia Satellites and the Black Crowes had big chart albums in the '80s and '90s, though their hard rock was less identifiably southern than their '70s ancestors. Like most rock styles, southern rock will continue to command a significant audience that occasionally results in artists that break out nationally. The mid-'90s success of Widespread Panic and the Dave Matthews Band proved its current viability, though these groups do not so much develop the southern rock tradition as keep it alive.

12 Recommended Recordings:
The Allman Brothers Band, *Beginnings* (Polydor)
The Allman Brothers, *Live At The Fillmore East* (Polydor)
Lynyrd Skynyrd, *Gold & Platinum* (MCA)
Various Artists, *Rebel Rousers: Southern Rock Classics* (Rhino)
The Ozark Mountain Daredevils, *The Best* (A&M)
The Dixie Dregs, *The Best Of The Dixie Dregs* (Grand Slamm)
The Charlie Daniels Band, *A Decade Of Hits* (Epic)
The Atlanta Rhythm Section, *A Rock And Roll Alternative* (Polydor)
Sea Level, *Sea Level* (Capricorn)
Wet Willie, *The Best Of Wet Willie* (Polydor)
The Georgia Satellites, *The Georgia Satellites* (Elektra)
The Black Crowes, *Shake Your Money Maker* (Def American)

—Richie Unterberger

Funk

Bridging the classic soul era and the dawn of disco, funk was R&B at its most rhythmic, earthy, and (occasionally) wild and experimental. Not as hugely successful with the masses as soul or disco, it has proven to be about as influential, strongly affecting not just all post-1970 R&B, but also contemporary rap and alternative rock music.

What exactly puts the "unk" into "funk" can be hard to pigeonhole, but there are some basic traits which distinguish it from mainstream soul and rock music. The emphasis, above all, is on the rhythm, and the accent is often placed on the downbeat, or the first and third beats of 4/4 patterns. The function of the guitar becomes more rhythmic than melodic, often employing what has been called "scratch" or even "chicken scratch" staccato bursts of percussive strings; the horns also take a stronger rhythmic role than traditional soul music, used for percussive riffing and punctuation as well as taking solos or providing harmonic support.

The rhythms, though, are often anything but simple, building upon each other and playing in counterpoint to build a polyrhythmic drive. Both the lead and backup singers often do their part to add to the excitement with chants, grants, and screams. The lyrics have at times been quite sophisticated and socially conscious, but more often are principally concerned, like the music itself, with stream-of-consciousness grooves, built around slogans and exhortations to dance and party. Adding to the ferment are unpredictable influences from psychedelic and hard guitar rock, Latin music, doo wop, and other elements of the melting pot of American rock, soul, and pop.

Few would dispute that James Brown is not only the Godfather of Soul, but the Godfather of Funk as well. The ignition of the funk explosion can for most intents and purposes be boiled down to his landmark mid-'60s singles "Out of Sight" and especially "Papa's Got A Brand New Bag," the first smashes to incorporate the syncopated horns, stream-of-consciousness lyrics, and staccato guitars that would become funk trademarks. Although it would be a few years before the music began to be called funk, in the last half of the '60s Brown would continue to lay the funk prototype with workouts like "Cold Sweat" and "There Was a Time" that grew increasingly polyrhythmic, jazzy, and improvisational, pushing the melody to the background in favor of the churning beat and Brown's inimitable screams and groans.

The word "funk" itself began to enter the R&B/soul vocabulary with Dyke & the Blazers' R&B dance hit "Funky Broadway." Several theories and explanations of the origins of the actual word "funk" have been offered, the most likely consensus being that, like rock & roll and jazz, it was a euphemism for sexual activity, though "funk" often stood for smelly, gritty, or earthy stuff within the African-American community. By the end of the 1960s, it had come to stand for the greasiest and earthiest variant of soul music.

Although James Brown's early-'70s work was not nearly as commercially successful with the pop audience as the recordings of his 1965-69 peak (though they remained huge R&B sellers), with time they have come to be viewed as nearly as important and influential. These discs found him getting deeper and deeper into the polyrhythmic funk groove, with increasingly basic workouts that in time came to resemble one continuous (if often compelling) performance. His backup band of the era, the J.B.'s, are now recognized as some of funk's greatest musicians, particularly guitarist Jimmy Nolen and hornplayers Fred Wesley, Pee Wee Ellis, Maceo Parker, and Clair Pinckney; they also cut many underappreciated instrumental funk workouts on their own.

Another influential Brown sideman, although he was only with the band for about a couple years, was bassist Bootsy Collins, who was instrumental in boosting his instrument's importance in the funk mix. After leaving Brown in the early '70s, Bootsy teamed up with George Clinton to become a vital cog in what many funk fans regard as the finest exponents of the genre, Parliament-Funkadelic. Clinton was a veteran R&B/soul performer who changed gears radically around 1970, constructing elaborate funk heavily influenced by the acid rock of Jimi Hendrix, as well as touches of jazz and psychedelia. Almost anything went with Clinton and his troops, including extended spacy jams, inscrutable self-mythologizing and unfathomable concept opuses about spaceships and funk itself, though the bands never lost their slightly absurd sense of humor.

The Parliament-Funkadelic family tree is among the most twisted and difficult to follow in rock history, with a revolving door of musicians who often played in both Parliament and Funkadelic (for tangled contractual reasons, Clinton led similar groups recording under both names, sometimes simultaneously). It grew more complex when Bootsy Collins became a solo star in his own right with a similarly (perhaps even more excessive) cosmic vision, as a solo act and leader of Bootsy's Rubber Band. Both Clinton and Collins remain active and influential musicians to this day, as both individual artists and collaborators with other heavyweights.

Although they are usually categorized as a soul act rather than a funk one, Sly & the Family Stone also did a great deal to cross-fertilize soul and psychedelia to come up with some of the most adventurous funk of the early '70s. Larry Graham's distinctive finger-popping bass sound has become perhaps *the* most single identifying characteristic associated with funk, and Sly Stone's commentaries on racial injustice and people power rank as some of the genre's most sophisticated lyrics. While their early, more soul- and pop-flavored work of the late '60s is equally important, their 1971 album *There's a Riot Goin' On* is their deepest foray into hardcore funk, and remains one of the few funk LPs that hits as deep with its words as its grooves.

The late '60s and early '70s saw several other less important but interesting groups make their mark in the funk parade. Dyke & the Blazers and the Watts 103rd Street Rhythm Band (most famous for "Express Yourself") were among the style's earliest practitioners. After an apprenticeship with Eric Burdon, War stormed the charts in the early and mid-'70s with a series of hits that incorporated Latin rhythms, loose, jazzy grooves, and vague social pontifications. The Meters took the sound of New Orleans R&B, already a bedrock of much post-1950 R&B, soul, and rock, into the funk era, largely on instrumentals (at least at first). Isaac Hayes took endless bubbling funk monologues onto both album and single charts, as his *Shaft* took the wah-wah guitar signatures often found in funk to their limit.

There were also quite a few funk classics in the early '70s committed to vinyl by performers who are really best categorized as soul musicians, but were deeply influenced by the funk groove. These years certainly saw some of the best work of soul giants Curtis Mayfield, Stevie Wonder, Wilson Pickett, and Marvin Gaye, all of whom drew heavily upon the expanded lyrical and musical grooves opened up by funk. The Isley Brothers, always one of soul's most eclectic stars, became close to an out-and-out funk band after beefing up their guitars and arrangements under the influence of Jimi Hendrix and Sly Stone. Even more traditional soul vocal groups like the Temptations and O'Jays delved quite heavily into funk for a time to come up with some of their most memorable hits.

Opinions differ on the matter, but it could be argued that the early '70s saw funk at its peak. The music remained extremely popular through the mid-'70s, though, with less sophisticated acts who either concentrated on the dance-and-party element (Kool & the Gang, the Ohio Players, Graham Central Station) or the slicker, more soul- and harmony-influenced variants (Earth, Wind & Fire, Tower of Power). As for the original innovators, James Brown had seemingly run out of fresh ideas by the middle of the decade, accused even by his backup musicians of not only repeating himself but copying his imitators. Sly Stone fell victim to well-documented substance abuse and financial problems, and the Parliament-Funkadelic clan, while continuing to churn out music at the top of their game, were just too eccentric to truly catch on with the masses.

Disco, although it owed a great deal to funk in its dance rhythms, overran its ancestor in popularity in the mid- and late '70s. Some pop- and dance-oriented acts that owed a considerable debt to funk did enjoy great success in the late '70s and '80s, though, including Rick James, Cameo, the Gap Band, and the Commodores. The influence of funk was also felt in the jazz world with the advent of fusion, particularly in the work of Herbie Hancock, Donald Byrd, Freddie Hubbard, and Lonnie Smith.

If anything, funk has undergone a bit of a renaissance in the 1990s. Bootsy Collins and George Clinton are both venerated pioneers who continue to record critically respected albums and draw huge crowds on the club circuit, although they don't chart like they did at their peak. Funk was a big element in the mix of the '80s biggest black superstars, Michael Jackson and Prince, and funk classics are sampled constantly (some would say excessively) by contemporary rappers. And even some of the biggest White alternative rock acts, such as the Red Hot Chili Peppers, Faith No More, and Primus, draw heavily on funk's rhythms and in-your-face attitudes, if not delivering as much soul as its original progenitors.

17 Recommended Funk Recordings:

Various Artists, *In Yo' Face! The Roots of Funk, Vol. 1/2* (Rhino) [Note: this is volume one-half, or the "prequel" to the *In Yo' Face History of Funk Series* listed below]

Various Artists, *In Yo' Face! The History Of Funk, Vol. 1-5* (Rhino)

James Brown, *Love Power Peace: Live at the Olympia Paris 1971* (PolyGram)

Various Artists, *James Brown's Funky People Parts 1 & 2* (PolyGram)

The J.B.'s, *Funky Good Time* (PolyGram)

Dyke & the Blazers, *Dyke's Greatest Hits* (Original Sound)

Charles Wright & the Watts 103rd Street Rhythm Band, *Express Yourself: The Best Of* (Warner Brothers)

Sly & the Family Stone, *There's a Riot Goin' On* (Epic)

Parliament, *Tear the Roof Off* (Casablanca)

Funkadelic, *Music for Your Mother* (Westbound)

Bootsy Collins, *Back in the Day: The Best Of* (Warners)

War, *Anthology (1970-1994)* (Rhino)

The Meters, *Funkify Your Life: The Meters Anthology* (Rhino)

Curtis Mayfield, *Superfly* (Curtom)

James Brown, *Foundations of Funk: A Brand New Bag: 1964-1969* (Polydor)

James Brown, *Funk Power 1970: A Brand New Thang* (Polydor)

James Brown, *Make It Funky: The Big Payback: 1971-1975* (Polydor)

—Richie Unterberger

Philly Soul

The last major movement of the classic soul era to make a wide impact, Philadelphia soul represented the style at its sweetest, and soul production at its most sophisticated. Its severest critics would contend that much of the genre was overly slick, the most lightweight of which helped set the ground for the more mechanized elements of disco and urban contemporary. Others would praise the music for almost exactly the same reasons, seeing the Philly sound as soul at its most romantic, ushering in an era of elaborate instrumental and vocal arrangements that continue to play a large part in black pop music today.

The hallmarks of Philadelphia soul—the lush, buoyant strings and horns, the smooth group harmonies with a touch of street corner a cappella, the insistent danceable rhythms and smoldering ballads—were often the handiwork of an extremely small clique of producers. Most of the classic Philly soul recordings of the late '60s and first half of the '70s were devised by the producers Kenny Gamble and Leon Huff (who worked as a team), as well as producer Thom Bell (who sometimes arranged material for Gamble-Huff). Their extremely prolific output, maintaining enough diversity to ensure continuing public interest while stamping each record with distinctive Philly soul qualities, was reminiscent in some respects of Motown's production line during their 1960s glory days. Gamble & Huff, like Motown, also used a house band of sorts, a core group of musicians that contributed mightily to establishing a sound that could be identified with their records.

None of this could have been accomplished without first-rate singers, both soloists and groups, and the Philly soul stars, like those of Motown, were distinctive talents in their own right. They did differ from their counterparts in that while Motown's stars were largely tapped from their Detroit base, the Philadelphia performers were often (though not by any means always) transplants. Indeed, after the Philly sound had become a major industry force, established soul stars like Wilson Pickett, Dionne Warwick, and Lou Rawls would travel to the city specifically to record with top producers. There was generally less grit involved in the Philadelphia studios, and though it's a matter of conjecture whether the performer's role was more or less limited than it was at Motown or other soul centers, there's no doubt that production was just as important, if not more, as material or performance.

Gamble and Huff were young veterans of the Philly music scene who began scoring their first big national hits in the late '60s with smooth vocal groups like the Intruders and Delfonics and more raucous, dance-oriented records with Archie Bell & the Drells. It was a long-running association with Jerry Butler, already a star with many popular Chicago soul recordings under his belt, that really got them on a roll. The team rode high through the mid-'70s with hits by the aforementioned acts and Joe Simon, Harold Melvin & the Blue Notes (featuring Teddy Pendergrass), and above all the O'Jays, who may have done more than any other act to define the Philadelphia soul sound.

Thom Bell oversaw a smaller roster, and generally pursued a smoother (though only slightly smoother) sound. His big acts were the Stylistics, whose creamy harmonies sailed on top of the frothiest Philly soul hits, and the Spinners, who found massive success in Philadelphia studios after years of recording as also-rans for Motown and other labels.

While Gamble-Huff and Bell dominated the Philly scene, they didn't produce every last hit of the era by any means. In particular, Bunny Sigler helped produce some successes for Gamble-Huff's Philadelphia International label, and Peter DeAngelis (who cut his teeth with, of all people, Frankie Avalon and Fabian) arranged and produced Philly soul records for Eddie Holman that both recalled and stood up to the best that Gamble-Huff were churning out at the same time.

Philadelphia soul hits occasionally boasted strong, socially aware lyrics, especially on some of the O'Jays hottest sellers; "Back Stabbers" in particular is often cited as one of the hardest- itting reflections of urban street life in soul music. By and large, though, they focused on the joys and sorrows of romance, not civil rights or expanding consciousness. That didn't affect commercial sales in the least, but did perhaps limit their impact upon the world of rock at a time when the pressure for lyrical significance was high. David Bowie, always looking for something new to sink his teeth into, brought a lot of Philadelphia soul into his work in the mid-'70s when he unpredictably terminated his arty glam rock phase and traveled to Sigma Sound Studios, where many classic Philly soul hits were recorded, to cut some of his most commercially (though not critically) successful work.

With a rhythmic and elaborate production line already in place, the Philadelphia sound was more equipped than any other soul scene to face the disco era. Indeed, the mid-'70s saw many of the biggest early disco hits emerge from Philadelphia, including recordings which found stalwarts like the O'Jays adapting to the new trend, and new disco acts like the Trammps. Not as critically esteemed as the earlier Philadelphia soul productions, they were nonetheless extremely successful in the marketplace.

But the Philadelphia sound, as practiced by Gamble-Huff and their brethren, had spent most of its power as a major artistic force by the end of the '70s, much as Motown lost most of its impetus after the '60s. Unlike Motown, though, the Philadelphia producers didn't maintain a respectable sales profile, largely dropping from sight after the early 1980s. Philadelphia soul lingers, however, in almost all urban contemporary soul and R&B, both by veterans like Patti LaBelle and newcomers like Boyz II Men.

10 Recommended Philadelphia Soul Recordings:
The Delfonics, *Best Of The Delfonics* (Arista)
The Intruders, *Super Hits* (Philadelphia International)
Archie Bell & The Drells, *The Best Of* (Rhino)
Jerry Butler, *Iceman: The Mercury Years* (PolyGram)
The O'Jays, *The O'Jays In Philadelphia* (Philadelphia International)
Eddie Holman, *I Love You* (Varese Sarabande)
The Stylistics, *Best Of The Stylistics* (Amherst)
The O'Jays, *Greatest Hits* (Philadelphia International)
The Spinners, *One Of A Kind Love Affair—The Anthology* (Atlantic)
Harold Melvin & the Blue Notes, *Collector's Item* (Philadelphia International)

—Richie Unterberger

Pub Rock

Defiantly unpretentious and unfazed by the zeitgeist, pub rock, despite being a short-lived permutation of British rock, was in essence a roots-rock retrenchment that flew in the face of British glam/glitter rock of the early and mid-'70s. Many of pub rock's proponents came from a mixture of mid-'60s British R&B, hippie folk-blues, and country backgrounds, and this conflation of similar styles led to some wonderfully spirited rock & roll that, somewhat unintentionally, turned into a subtle rebellion by musicians against the machinations of the pop music industry. Pub rock never caught on in a big way; in fact some critics assert its heyday was only between 1971-74. Nonetheless, there were plenty of excellent pub rock bands, and many musicians who cut their teeth during this time went on to join some of the seminal English bands of the late '70s.

Although it shares many common elements with American roots-rock, pub rock is distinctly British; the result of a small but supportive community-based scene that focused in pubs around London. The scene coalesced around a former London jazz club, the Tally Ho, and soon spread to dozens of other pubs in the city keen to book rock bands. With glitter/glam rock dominating the British charts, pub rock musicians, fans, and the pub owners who booked them regarded this music as a way to reject the egregious trappings and slavish attempts at pop superstardom for something that was more honest, direct, and communal.

Ironically, the band that gets credit for jumpstarting pub rock is an obscure American R&B band, Eggs over Easy, who in 1972 gigged at the Tally Ho. Despite this jarring piece of history, it should be known that the English musicians inspired by the Eggs had been playing in mid-to-late-'60s blues, folk, and R&B bands such as the Action and Kippington Lodge (the latter featuring Brinsley Schwarz and Nick Lowe). British rock critic Pete Frame, who has written definitively about pub rock, notes three periods in the genre's development roughly spanning the years 1972-1975: first was the early Tally Ho period featuring bands such as Bees Make Honey (their moniker a tribute to Eggs over Easy), Brinsley Schwarz, and Ducks Deluxe; the second wave of bands included Kilburn and the High Roads (featuring Ian Dury), Chilli Willi and the Red Hot Peppers, and Ace; the third and final bunch of pub rockers were led by the Winkies, Sniff and the Tears, and the great Dr. Feelgood.

Of the aforementioned bands, the one perhaps most familiar to American audiences is Brinsley Schwarz. Named after their great lead guitarist, they more than any other band, defined all that was good about pub rock. And, unlike many of their ilk (up until Dr. Feelgood), had the longest and most successful recording career and managed to get many of their LPs released in America. Despite a storied public-relations disaster wherein the band was flown to the Fillmore East for a showcase gig and slammed by American rock critics (effectively ending stateside interest in pub rock), Brinsley Schwarz set up a two-gigs-a-week residency at the Tally Ho, providing the inspiration for literally every pub rock band that came in their wake. Brinsley Schwarz broke up in 1975, bassist Nick Lowe went on to a solo career, as did guitarist Ian Gomm, while Schwarz and keyboardist Bob Andrews joined forces with ex-Ducks Deluxe guitarist Martin Belmont to form Graham Parker's phenomenal backing band, the Rumour.

Lowe's success and the rise of Graham Parker and the Rumour are a small indication of the kind of influence pub rock had on the next generation of British rock & rollers. After Kilburn and the High Roads, Ian Dury embarked on a wonderful, if inconsistent, solo career; Elvis Costello's earliest musical days were with pub rockers Flip City and he found future Attractions drummer Pete Thomas in Chilli Willi and the Red Hot Peppers; Clash frontman Joe Strummer made his first records in a late-period pub rock band, the 101'ers; even enigmatic avant-gardists the Residents had significant musical contributions made to their records by pub rock vet, the late Phil "Snakefinger" Lithman, another ex-member of Chilli Willi. And lest one think that pub rock had no impact on the American Top Ten, remember the song "How Long" reached number three in 1975 by pub rock veterans Ace, featuring vocalist/keyboardist Paul Carrack.

Pete Frame argues (and he's right) that after the breakup of Brinsley Schwarz and Ducks Deluxe in 1975, pub rock was, for all intents and purposes, over. However, a wild, high-energy blues/R&B band from Canvey Island in Essex named Dr. Feelgood was the most vital band of the late pub rock era and served as a crucial link to early punk rock. Fronted by the late great Lee Brilleaux (who succumbed to cancer in 1994), and the inspired guitar playing of Wilko Johnson, the Feelgoods released their first LP, *Down by the Jetty* (recorded in mono) in 1975 and released four great LPs before Johnson's departure in 1977. The band soldiered on until Brilleaux's death, (at the end Brilleaux was the lone original member) made some good records, but lacked the panache that Wilko supplied. What's important to note is that the members of Feelgood lent the necessary cash for pub rock-fan Dave Robinson to start his great independent label Stiff and give artists like Nick Lowe, Elvis Costello, Ian Dury, Wreckless Eric, the Damned, and Dave Edmunds a place to record.

In many ways, pub rock, because of its insularity, smallness, and disinterest in becoming an international pop phenomenon, was destined to last only a short while. And although it remains somewhat of a mystery to many American ears, the music that resulted from this scene retains its vigorous, uncorruptable spirit. It was the music of the moment, played by musicians who cared more about sincerity and less about fame.

Eight Essential Pub Rock Recordings:
Ace, *Five a Side*
Bees Make Honey, *Music Every Night*
Brinsley Schwarz, *Brinsley Schwarz* and *Silver Pistol*
Chilli Willi and the Red Hot Peppers, *Bongos over Balham*
Ducks Deluxe, *Don't Mind Rockin' Tonight*
Dr. Feelgood, *Malpractice* and *Stupidity*
The 101'ers, *Elgin Avenue Breakdown*
The Winkies, *The Winkies*

—John Dougan

Punk Music

English critic Jon Savage noted that history is made by those who say "No," and in 1976 there was no louder "No" than that of punk rock. Dismissed by the shortsighted as crude anti-musicality, punk dared to place itself in direct confrontation with the then-ruling rock hegemony: generally thirty-something pop stars content to reinvent and regurgitate clichés in a sort of stylistic stasis, a dire situation exacerbated by the tightly controlled mid-to-late-'70s FM programming style known as AOR (album-oriented rock) and glutted with a seemingly endless array of not-so-hard-rock and not-quite-so-heavy-metal bands that sounded as if they'd been created by record-label marketing departments.

From the start, punk angrily stood in direct contrast to the zeitgeist. Still, as with all rock genres and sub-genres, it was hardly an organic movement. Its antecedents included the noisy primitivism of the Velvet Underground, the mega-loud working-class anger of the Who, the high-energy guitar spuzz of the MC5 and the Stooges, and the androgyny of the New York Dolls (with a few dollops of Bowie and early Roxy Music for good measure). Of course as punk developed (Note: The first known use of "punk rock" as a genre identifier goes back to the early '70s, *Creem* magazine, and critics Dave Marsh and Lester Bangs), it metamorphosed into numerous subgenres that championed a host of influences as disparate as reggae, mid-'60s bubblegum, early psychedelic rock, art-rock, free jazz, and musique concrète. Literally anything fit the equation; it was just a matter of attitude and presentation.

In a purely historical sense, punk's timeline is 1975-1978, and even that's somewhat generous. But with its supernova long since faded and its style co-opted by greedy major labels who turned it into the more sanitized "new wave," punk's impact is still being felt in the '90s. It almost single-handedly revived the independent record-label network and

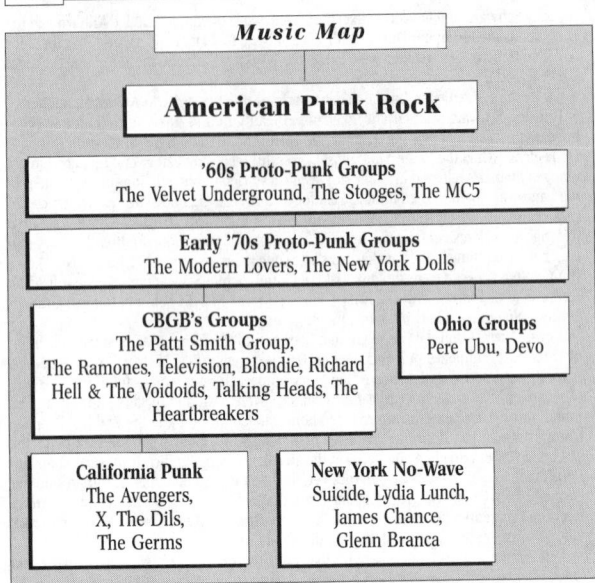

Music Map

American Punk Rock

'60s Proto-Punk Groups
The Velvet Underground, The Stooges, The MC5

Early '70s Proto-Punk Groups
The Modern Lovers, The New York Dolls

CBGB's Groups
The Patti Smith Group,
The Ramones, Television, Blondie, Richard
Hell & The Voidoids, Talking Heads, The
Heartbreakers

Ohio Groups
Pere Ubu, Devo

California Punk
The Avengers,
X, The Dils,
The Germs

New York No-Wave
Suicide, Lydia Lunch,
James Chance,
Glenn Branca

helped start a legitimate network of underground journals and a new style of music criticism. Most importantly, it imbued a younger generation with the spirit that they too could become part of the great rock & roll whatsis, thereby planting the seeds for the future development of many successful U.S. and U.K. regional alternative rock scenes (e.g., Los Angeles; Minneapolis; Seattle; Athens, GA; Manchester, England). It's hard to imagine bands like the Replacements, Nirvana or even R.E.M. existing without the contributions of the Sex Pistols, Clash, the Ramones and the Buzzcocks.

These days, the term "punk" seems almost quaint. And truth be told, the story of punk and its pervasive influence is only now being told. But as with rap and current heavy metal (two genres that share punk's attitude), punk always seemed to be about the unencumbered joy of self-expression: total, unequivocal and often unedited. If you listen to a handful of the records listed in the following sections, you'll soon hear that, even today, punk never seems too far from the pop zeitgeist, a range of influence far greater than its originators had in mind.

Book:
Punk Diary, by George Dimarc (St. Martin's, 1994)

—John Dougan

American Punk Rock

American punk rock was actively brewing years before the U.K. scene. The trade-off, perhaps, was that it was less explosive, less of a broad-based movement, less confrontational, and less concerned with disowning time-honored rock & roll traditions. Still, it was not only a crucial source of inspiration for Britain's more volatile brand of punk, but a more diverse (though diffuse) movement whose effects were just as influential and long-reaching.

Some have argued that the true source of American punk rock lies in the incredibly active garage rock scene of the mid-'60s, and indeed the term "punk rock" was originally coined by critics like Dave Marsh, Lester Bangs, and future Patti Smith Group guitarist Lenny Kaye to refer to these bands. In the late '60s, Detroit groups the MC5 and the Stooges played amphetamined rock driven by fuzzed-out guitars and baldly outraged (and outrageous) lyrics that sound all but indistinguishable from early punk records.

An equally important, artier strand of raw rock & roll minimalism was pioneered in New York in the late '60s by the Velvet Underground. Not all of their work foreshadowed punk, but even their songs that didn't feature street-life vignettes and overamped guitars (and there were plenty of both, especially on their early albums) had a no-frills, unembellished attitude that acted as the standard for the many groups, in New York and elsewhere, that looked to them for inspiration.

Two American acts blazed lonely trails in the early '70s that midwifed the birth of punk. In Boston, the Modern Lovers led by Jonathan Richman added youthful naiveté to the Velvets' glorious primitivism. Their early-'70s recordings rank among the most joyous and affecting proto-punk/new wave efforts, although, tragically, the original and best lineup of the band released nothing during their lifetime. The New York Dolls affected a trashy, sub-early Rolling Stones glam rock image that attracted raves from local critics, but made little national impact, although Malcolm McLaren's brief association with the band in their dying days gave him many ideas to pass on to the Sex Pistols.

The American punk scene coalesced around New York City's Lower East Side and, specifically, at Hilly Kristal's Bowery club, CBGB's. By late 1975/early 1976, bands such as the Patti Smith Group, the Ramones, Talking Heads, Blondie, Television and the Heart-

breakers (featuring former New York Doll Johnny Thunders) had pretty much made this dive their home, and complacent old American rock now faced a significant challenge.

Suddenly there was a scene that offered cultural solidarity, if little in the way of stylistic unanimity: the fast, loud, tuneful minimalism of the Ramones was offset by Patti Smith's poetic incantations, Television's spiraling guitar duels, Blondie's sexy neo-Spector pop, the egghead pop of the Talking Heads and the fierce synthesizer minimalism of Suicide. What connected these bands was a sense of purpose and community; they were angry outsiders who insisted that the only way to change rock & roll was to dismantle it and rebuild it, thereby reclaiming it. That didn't actually mean they weren't cognizant of rock's best traditions: "Hey Joe," "Surfin' Bird," "1-2-3 Red Light," and old songs by the 13th Floor Elevators, Al Green and Randy & the Rainbows were featured prominently in the early repertoires of one or the other of the bands listed above.

At the outset, these bands were more influential than popular on a national level, though Patti Smith did fairly well, and Blondie and the Talking Heads would eventually break through to superstardom. In fact, Television were far more popular in the U.K., where their second album even made the Top Ten. The Ramones were also more popular there, and extremely influential; indeed, their "1-2-3-4!" brand of accelerated rock & roll made them one of the only early CBGB's bands to fit most listeners' basic conceptions of punk rock. It's been claimed that Malcolm McLaren took the prototype safety pin and torn T-shirt punk look from Richard Hell, who helped ignite the scene with Tom Verlaine in the original Television lineup before fronting the Voidoids. Outside of New York, the U.S. lacked a strong punk scene. With innovative but impossibly uncommercial groups like the Electric Eels, as well as more accessible acts like Rocket from the Tombs and Mirrors, Cleveland had an active proto-punk scene that lacked the exposure, either in a renowned club or on national record labels, necessary to spread its influence. Devo (not actually from Cleveland, but from the Ohio town of Akron) and Pere Ubu eventually broke through to widespread recognition with a style of new wave that was bleaker and more mechanized than most anything happening in New York. Many Boston bands would appear by the late '70s, on the whole more identified with power-pop than punk.

In 1977, active punk scenes quickly sprang up in California, particularly in Los Angeles, which owed considerably more to the influence of early British punk—just making its inroads in the States via import records—than the New York bands. Generally, these groups played a harder, nastier, faster, more jaded type of punk. Not as commercial as either the London or New York punk acts—not that any of the California bands would have cared—the Dils, the Germs, the Avengers, and the Dickies laid the foundation for thrash/hardcore. X, very much a part of the early L.A. scene, would be one of the few to break out into any sort of large-scale success, by which time they'd tempered and diversified their original sound.

Isolated pockets of punk activity took hold in quite a few U.S. cities, mainly ones with large youthful, artistic-leaning populations, such as Seattle and Austin. But the fact of the matter is, punk never seized the collective consciousness in the States, partly because of industry resistance to the music, and at least equally because many (perhaps most) rock listeners didn't like it. Nonetheless, American punk bands were a bedrock of much of the music of the 1980s and 1990s: the Athens, GA, new wave scene; alternative rock; the "no-wave" of New York avant-rockers ranging from Lydia Lunch and James Chance to Glenn Branca and Sonic Youth; hardcore; grunge—all of these developments derived key inspiration from the original punk bands.

12 Most Essential U.S. Punk Recordings:
The Modern Lovers, *Modern Lovers* (Bomp)
The Patti Smith Group, *Horses* (Arista)
The Ramones, *All the Stuff & More, Vol. 1* (Warner Brothers)
Television, *Marquee Moon* (Elektra)
Blondie, *Blondie* (Chrysalis)
The Talking Heads, *Talking Heads '77* (Sire)
Various Artists, *Blank Generation—The New York Scene* (Rhino)
Various Artists, *We're Desperate—The L.A. Scene* (Rhino)
Richard Hell & the Voidoids, *Blank Generation* (Sire)
The Avengers, *Avengers* (CD Presents)
Suicide, *Suicide* (Restless)
Pere Ubu, *Terminal Tower* (Twintone)
Book:
From the Velvets to the Voidoids, by Clinton Heylin (Penguin, 1993)

—Richie Unterberger

British Punk

Taking cues from some American bands, as well as the English mini-phenomenon known as "pub rock," English punk transmogrified into an entirely different beast, one that also valued stripped-down, primal guitar rock and a DIY (do-it-yourself) attitude, but one that openly embraced multiculturalism (e.g., ska and reggae), politics (a dysfunctional late-'70s government), and radical philosophy (e.g., the French Situationists). With the galvanic Sex Pistols leading the way, English rock would never be the same, as the sybaritic excesses of the post-hippie era were replaced by angry kids yelling "no future" and referring to successful rock stars as "boring old farts."

Punk took Great Britain—both its entertainment industry and its general citizenry—by surprise. In the mid-'70s, the massive tornado of the British Invasion was a fading memory whose survivors sat atop the charts with pale echoes of their best work. Disco and soft pop/rock were the trends of the day, as they were in the U.S. The nation's economy was flailing, and more and more teenagers left school to go straight on the dole (a British equivalent of welfare), with little hope for financial success or social stimulation in the near future.

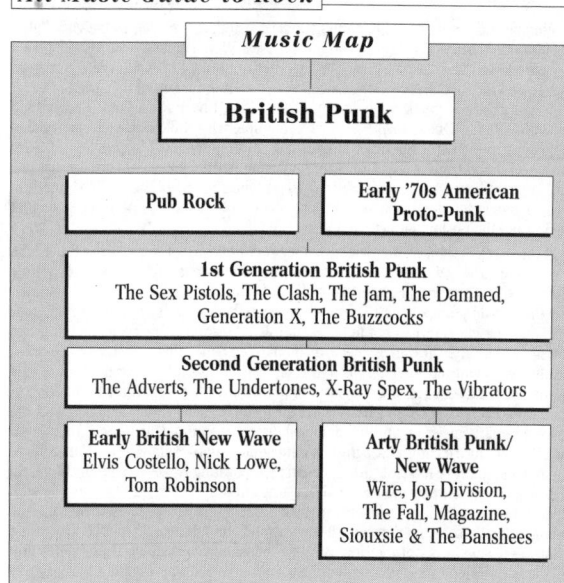

Music Map

British Punk

Pub Rock	Early '70s American Proto-Punk

1st Generation British Punk
The Sex Pistols, The Clash, The Jam, The Damned, Generation X, The Buzzcocks

Second Generation British Punk
The Adverts, The Undertones, X-Ray Spex, The Vibrators

Early British New Wave Elvis Costello, Nick Lowe, Tom Robinson	**Arty British Punk/ New Wave** Wire, Joy Division, The Fall, Magazine, Siouxsie & The Banshees

Malcolm McLaren who with his wife Vivienne Westwood ran a boutique that catered to an ever-changing clientele seeking alternative fashions, was on the lookout for a band of loutish post-adolescents to use as a platform for his loosely held anarchist and Situationist ideas. He harbored aspirations to take over the New York Dolls' management, but when that band splintered, he looked to even scruffier, younger musicians that frequented his store. In late 1975, the Sex Pistols began to perform, with McLaren as their manager.

An "alternative" scene (though they didn't call it as such at the time) did exist in Britain on a small level, as "pub rock." In truth, bands like Dr. Feelgood, Eggs over Easy, Ducks Deluxe and even the acclaimed Brinsley Schwarz sound pretty tame and unrevolutionary. What they shared with punk was a disdain for contemporary pop and progressive rock trends, and a love for basic, stripped-down, guitar-oriented music. Besides supplying punk with some of its early figureheads, such as the principal movers of Stiff Records and Joe Strummer (who left his pub rock band the 101'ers to join the Clash), the pub rock performance circuit provided crucial live venues for punk acts when the music was struggling to get off the ground.

Throughout 1976, the Sex Pistols built up a fierce underground reputation with their incendiary live shows (which were often as not, violence-ridden, chaotic affairs). In late 1976, their debut single "Anarchy in the U.K.," established punk's modus operandi: scabrous guitars, hyperkinetic rhythms, and inflammatory, venomous lyrics, with crude energy carrying the day.

The Pistols endured a complicated tangle of personnel, management, and label problems in 1977 that kept them from releasing a full-length album for about a year (although a couple more key singles appeared in the meantime). Other groups were already following their blueprint, however, and stepped into the breach that Johnny Rotten had opened. The most famous members of what has come to be called "The Class of '77" include the Damned; the Clash who infused punk with revolutionary politics and reggae rhythms; the Jam post-mods who modeled themselves after the early Who; and the Buzzcocks whose nervous, accelerated rhythms didn't hide a keen grasp of pop hooks.

As with all momentous musical movements, these figureheads (they would have disdained the label "stars" at the time) were the tip of an explosion that saw many minor but important groups adding their voices to the clamor, as well as interesting one- and two-shots leaping into the volcano. Generation X, the Adverts, the Vibrators and the Saints (actually from Australia) recorded important early punk records; X-Ray Spex did a lot to smash rock stereotypes by featuring a half-black teenage female with braces as their lead singer. Groups like Chelsea, Eater, Johnny Moped, and Slaughter & the Dogs are esteemed by collectors for the one or two memorable songs they had in them.

Today, early British punk records still sound exciting, but hardly the epitome of nihilistic shock. At the time, however, they could not have caused more of a sensation, inspiring equal measures of fervent praise and outright hostility. The tempo was FAST (although hardcore made it go even faster), the guitars and vocals slashing and LOUD, and the lyrics—much, though by no means all, negative in nature—addressed politics, sex, depression, and society with a frank realism that had rarely been heard in pop music, and never as part of a broad-based movement. The performers were not seasoned virtuosos, valuing inspiration and attitude above professionalism. Some listeners viewed the results as unbearably crude; others welcomed them as a necessary shot of air to blast rock & roll out of its complacency.

Punk never took hold in the U.S. as it did in Britain, although those who were con-

verted took up the music with a passion that equaled their U.K. counterparts. The Sex Pistols found this out the hard way, with John Lydon (aka Rotten) leaving the group in early 1978 after the last show of a brief, legendarily chaotic tour of the States, where their album stopped just short of the Top 100.

British punk did not so much die out as mutate and diversify, as any vital musical style needs to do in order to survive. As liberating as the first wave of punk was, it was impossible to perform an endless loop of hyper-fast, bile-filled anthems, as the musicians' ambitions broadened and their skills improved. The Jam remained huge stars in their homeland through the early '80s. Like the Clash who become stars in the U.S. at long last after 1979's *London Calling*, they refined their sound and incorporated R&B, soul, and pop into their compositions without compromising their integrity. While original British punkers like Generation X and Sham 69 played themselves out almost immediately, others went into arty minimalism (Wire, the Fall), post-psychedelia (the Soft Boys), pop-punk (the Undertones from Northern Ireland), or new wave (Siouxsie & the Banshees).

A fertile, more techno-oriented scene developed in the Buzzcocks' home territory of Manchester, spearheaded by Joy Division and other acts on Factory Records. And pub rock veterans like Nick Lowe, Elvis Costello and Tom Robinson tapped into punk's energy to midwife new wave, which by 1980 had become the new label for a modified, tamed, but innovative offspring of the original punk explosion.

12 Most Essential British Punk Recordings:
The Sex Pistols, *Never Mind the Bollocks* (Warner Brothers)
Various Artists, *Anarchy in the UK—UK Punk I (1976-77)* (Rhino)
Various Artists, *The Modern World—UK Punk II (1977-78)* (Rhino)
The Clash, *The Clash* (Epic)
The Jam, *Snap!* (Polydor)
The Buzzcocks, *Singles Going Steady* (IRS)
The Adverts, *Crossing the Sea with the Adverts* (Link Classics, UK)
X-Ray Spex, *Germ-Free Adolescents* (EMI)
The Vibrators, *Power of Money: The Best of the Vibrators* (Continuum)
The Undertones, *The Undertones* (Rykodisc)
Generation X, *Generation X* (Chrysalis)
The Damned, *Damned Damned Damned* (Frontier)
Book:
England's Dreaming: Sex Pistols and Punk Rock, by Jon Savage (St. Martin's, 1991)
—*Richie Unterberger*

Post-Punk

For many artists and musicians, punk rock represented the relaxation of artistic conventions and restraints. While some musicians interpreted this relaxation as a cue to be vulgar and anti-social—and thereby laying the groundwork for the nihilistic hardcore movement—just as many interpreted it as a way for them to push musical boundaries. These artists were initially categorized as part of the New Wave, but it became clear that the post-punk bands were more ambitious, serious and challenging than the pop-oriented New Wave groups. As a result, they rarely had the same commercial success as New Wave, but their records received greater critical acclaim and large cult followings that eventually turned into musicians themselves.

Post-punk was artier and darker than punk. It was less concerned with rock, preferring to concentrate on alternately haunting and abrasive textures, incorporating elements of the avant-garde, funk and worldbeat into their minimalistic rock & roll. Essentially, it was assaultive art-rock, one that had little connection with the bloated prog-rock of the '70s but owed a great deal to the experimental music of the Velvet Underground, the Who, Frank Zappa, the Stooges and Captain Beefheart. This esthetic was alive and well before the New York strains of punk rock burst to life in the late '70s, as the Cleveland, Ohio-based Pere Ubu illustrates.

Pere Ubu were post-punk before punk even existed. Basing their weird, noisy urban blues-rock on British bands like the Yardbirds and the Who, Pere Ubu moved into dark, claustrophobic and strange directions with their first singles and 1978 debut album *The Modern Dance*. Their music was too odd for most listeners, yet its arty eclecticism and bleak tone set the pace for much of American post-punk, not the least of which was their Akron, Ohio contemporaries Devo. Appearing a few years after Pere Ubu, Devo married their concept of humankind's "devolution" to noisy, herky-jerky synthesized pop and a striking visual style, where the band all looked like robotic clones of each other. Of all the post-punk bands, Devo tended to be a little catchier, yet their hooks were geeky, introverted, and entirely arty and claustrophobic.

Since Devo had a clever visual concept, they were able to translate to MTV, thereby giving them a significantly larger audience. Not all of their American peers were as lucky. The Residents' performance-art avant-operas were nearly as old as Pere Ubu, yet they were barely noticed outside of metropolitan circles. All of New York's abrasive, nearly-unlistenable "no wave" scene, led by James Chance & the Contortions, remained obscure outside of the Big Apple. The Feelies were rarely heard outside of underground circles, yet their nervy, jangly pop would have great impact in the American indie-rock world during the '80s. One of the only American post-punk bands to reach both a large cult audience and the mainstream were Talking Heads, who had played both punk and New Wave before they worked with Brian Eno on the groundbreaking, African-influenced *Remain in Light*.

On the whole, the Americans were defiantly, self-consciously arty and detachedly intellectual. Their British counterparts were just as arty, yet their music was darker and more emotional; it was angst, not intellectualism. The first wave of post-punks—Gang of Four, Siouxsie & the Banshees, Joy Division, Adam & the Ants—formed immediately after the Sex Pistols, and instead of following through on Johnny Rotten's unbridled rage, they turned it inward, creating gloomy, atmospheric soundscapes that bristled with tension and claustrophobic angst. Gang of Four's blend of leftist politics, abrasive guitar noise and funk rhythms was invigorating, acclaimed and influential, yet they were rarely heard outside of small circles. Both Siouxsie & the Banshees and Adam & the Ants mined similar territory at first, making records that were dense with dissonant keyboards and angular guitars, and giving theatrical concerts. Joy Division and their lead Ian Curtis weren't as explicitly arty, but their music was even more introverted. Their two haunting, monolithic albums *Unknown Pleasures* and *Closer*, functioned as the touchstone for goth-rock, which was the subgenre that the Cure became known for. Initially, the Cure's music was jagged and fractured, yet quite catchy, but as their career progressed, they slowed their tempos down and began languishing in long, synth-driven soundscapes. But if any band was known for goth, it was Bauhaus, a quartet that specialized in slow, atmospheric textures punctuated by phased guitar and Bowie-esque vocals.

By the early '80s, post-punk had distinguished itself from New Wave, which had begun to break into the pop mainstream. Post-punk didn't aim for such success, yet it proved to be a mercurial phenomenon anyway. Many of the groups were short-lived, and those that did continue—Talking Heads, Adam & the Ants, Siouxsie & the Banshees, the Cure—altered the sound and attack as they grew artistically. Two other bands, Joy Division and Bauhaus, continued in new guises—New Order and Love & Rockets, respectively—and started to explore new stylistic ground. Most of these groups began moving away from the claustrophobic doom that distinguished early post-punk, moving toward cleaner, dissonant attacks. The Birthday Party and its leader Nick Cave picked up the gloomy slack, but other groups—such as the fractured Fall, the agit-rock Pop Group, the ringingly anthemic U2, the twisted roots-punk of the Mekons, and the stark, cool neo-pschedelia of Echo & the Bunnymen and the Teardrop Explodes—fit into the newly redefined sound of post-punk.

Post-punk never died out, but it faded away in the mid-'80s, as its offspring began making records. By that time, the jangle-pop of R.E.M., the post-hardcore punk-pop of Hüsker Dü and the avant-rock of Sonic Youth had all taken centerstage in the American underground, while the self-absorbed pop of the Smiths and the swirling noise of the Jesus & Mary Chain divided the British indie scene into two camps. While these groups were active, several of their forefathers were enjoying their greatest success. The Cure, New Order, Siouxsie & the Banshees, Nick Cave, Love & Rockets, and the Fall continued to be major players into the early '90s, by which time their music had lost some of its initial shock. Some of the records now sound dated and precious, but the best post-punk retains its power, and it's possible to hear its impact throughout contemporary rock, particularly in the epic soundscapes of Radiohead.

Recommended Recordings:

Joy Division, *Unknown Pleasures* (Qwest)
Joy Division, *Closer* (Qwest)
The Cure, *Staring at the Sea* (Elecktra)
Pere Ubu, *The Modern Dance* (Blank/Rough Trade)
Talking Heads, *Remain in Light* (Sire)
Adam & the Ants, *Dirk Wears White Socks* (Do It/Epic)
Siouxsie & the Banshees, *Once Upon a Time* (Geffen)
The Feelies, *Crazy Rhythms* (A&M)
Gang of Four, *Entertainment!* (Infinite Zero)
Bauhaus, *In the Flat Field* (4AD)
U2, *Boy* (Island)
The Fall, *458489 A-Sides* (Beggars Banquet)
Birthday Party, *Hits* (4AD)
Mekons, *Mekons Rock & Roll* (A&M)
Echo & the Bunnymen, *Songs to Learn and Sing* (Sire)
New Order, *Movement* (Qwest)
The Pop Group, *The Pop Group* (Radar)
X, *Los Angeles/Wild Gift* (Slash)
The Slits, *Cut* (Antilles)
The Residents, *Meet the Residents* (East Side Digital)
Devo, *Are We Not Men? We Are Devo!* (Warner Brothers)

—Stephen Thomas Erlewine

New Wave

Punk rock may not have had the all-encompassing revolutionary effect that it originally was supposed to—after all, disco and pop still reigned on the charts after the Sex Pistols' disbandment—but it left a number of musical upheavals in its wake. At the time, every musical genre that followed punk was termed "New Wave," in homage to the generation of French filmmakers that revolutionized the cinema in the '50s. Many hardline punk fans and critics complained about the term New Wave and the music itself, claiming that it was designed to defuse the danger of punk, but in retrospect, the commercialization and broadening of punk culture was inevitable. Also, it seems that New Wave is quite different than post-punk, which tended to be more adventurous and self-consciously arty, as well as hardcore, which took the amateurish, thuggish tendencies of punk to an extreme. So where does that leave New Wave? It is a catch-all term, collecting a variety of pop-oriented musics that weren't part of the mainstream, yet were melodic, catchy, idiosyncratic and quirky. New Wave applied to everything from synthesized dance-pop to Mod and Ska revivalists—as long as it relied on hooks and was disregarded by the pop mainstream, it was called New Wave. There wasn't a specific sound, but there was a sensibility, one that was humorous, quirky and, most of all, not dangerous. It had a left-of-center sensibility, but none of the revolutionary danger, of punk rock.

In America, some of the very first punk bands indicated how the music would transform into New Wave. With their ironic reworkings of '60s pop, bubblegum and garage rock, Blondie and the Ramones had the melodic sensibilities, as well as the visual gimmicks that would prove to be key to commercial New Wave success. However, Blondie—who were blessed with Debbie Harry's sexy, photogenic looks—made the commercial crossover, and the Ramones remained a cult act, no matter how hard they tried to break into the pop charts with buzzingly catchy rockers like "Sheena is a Punk Rocker" and "Rock & Roll Radio." One of their New York contemporaries, Talking Heads, managed to become stars in the early '80s, after albums like *Talking Heads '77*, *More Songs About Buildings and Food* and *Remain in Light* had established their geeky, intellectual pop sense. Through these early records, Talking Heads became one of the leading American New Wave bands, but their influence was overshadowed by the Athens, Georgia quartet the B-52's and the Boston quintet, the Cars.

With their celebration of B-movie kitsch, dissonant harmonies and jerky hooks, the B-52's developed a new rock & roll lexicon. They were defiantly strange and weirdly funny, with distinctive visual gimmicks and aural hooks that were easily as revolutionary as the speedy guitars of the Ramones. Their esthetic was borrowed by numerous bands, many of which turned out to be one-hit wonders, but there were a handful that took it as rallying cry. These generally turned out to be bands that were major players in alternative rock—during the late '70s and early '80s, the sound of the B-52's was only heard in clubs and colleges, since mainstream radio accepted New Wave in the form of the Cars. For a band that cribbed heavily from the Velvet Underground and Iggy Pop, the Cars were remarkably straightforward; their pulsating, minimalistic rock & roll played like arena-rock since it emphasized the hook and loud guitars. Following the Cars, album-rock radio and many of its staple artists began incorporating New Wave production techniques in an attempt to stay modern, and it resulted in some trashy, fun hits from veteran rockers that were generally clueless about punk. Of course, there were also bands like the Motels, Missing Persons and the Fixx whose sensibility was more akin to AOR than punk, but they were able to co-opt the New Wave sound quite successfully. These bands provided the backdrop for the true sound of New Wave, the multitudes of quirky, edgy pop singles that incorporated punk sensibility and culture within the confines of a three-minute pop single. The first to essay this idea successfully was Elvis Costello, a pub-rock singer-songwriter that became a sensation with his 1977 debut album *My Aim is True*. A smart, nervy collection of tight pop songs and ballads, *My Aim is True* illustrated that punk's energy could be harnessed in more accessible, straightforward styles and it also established that the music could be the province of geeky outsiders instead of stylish hipsters or brutish thugs. Costello's geeky persona would echo throughout the New Wave years, yet his initial impact was how he pushed older pub rockers like Nick Lowe and Graham Parker into the limelight. These pub-rockers, whose initial rejection of rock stardom conventions paved the way for punk, favored pop, rock and folk, and helped usher in an explosive era of singles that covered a wide spectrum of sounds and styles. During the late '70s and early '80s, there were countless bands that mined the catchy, quirky guitar-pop vein of New Wave. There were conventional power-pop bands like Bram Tchaikovsky, the Romantics, 20/20 and the Knack, as well as the revitalized rock & roll of the Pretenders, the jittery pop of XTC, the inspired songcraft of Squeeze, the Police's savvy pop-reggae and the spruced-up retro-rock of Rockpile and its two leaders, Nick Lowe and Dave Edmunds. Almost simultaneously, the ska and mod revivals surfaced in England. The Specials, Madness and the English Beat spearheaded the ska revival, which had a stronger dance rhythm than most New Wave variations, along with more humor. The Jam updated the stridently British rock of the Who and the Kinks, and countless bands tried to mimic the band's punchy attack and lead singer/songwriter Paul Weller's biting lyricism. Soon, such guitar-oriented bands gave way to the synthesized, danceable territory of synth-pop and New Romantics like ABC, Duran Duran and Spandau Ballet. Inspired by David Bowie and Roxy Music's detached glamor and robotic soul, the New Romantics had cool electronic surfaces, crooning vocals and a distinctive visual style, which incorporated teased hair and flamboyant clothing. Such striking visuals made them naturals for MTV, a cable television network that debuted in 1981.

MTV needed videos to fill their 24 hours of programming, and New Wave, particularly New Romantics, became their key to success. Soon, these groups, who had already had significant success in England, began making inroads across America, not only in New York and Los Angeles, but also in the midwest. Elvis Costello, the Clash, the Go-Go's, the Police, the Cars, the Pretenders and Talking Heads became stars thanks to MTV and mainstream radio play, but MTV's most significant contribution was fueling the last great era of one-hit wonders. The network did play the Jam, XTC and the Specials, but these only became major cult acts in America. Instead, the US audience favored A Flock of Seagulls, Haircut 100, the Joboxers, the Buggles—an endless stream of bands that were united only by the fact that they had great videos and one or two hits.

Within a few years, MTV was a major force in the music industry, and they had helped make bands like Duran Duran and the Australian pop-rock combo Men At Work into international stars. But by that point, New Wave was beginning to run out of steam. Several major bands, including the Clash, the Specials and the Jam broke up, while others, such as Squeeze, Elvis Costello and Madness had taken time off to restructure their sound. Furthermore, the record industry had pushed too many bands like the Motels that simply co-opted New Wave, which helped the public reach a saturation point. Also, MTV began airing videos from veteran stars that successfully negotiated the music video, which meant they didn't have to air New Wave all the time. So, New Wave quickly disappeared, since only the major players were able to sustain careers. During much of the late '80s, it was ridiculed for its silly fashion and disposable music, but in the mid-'90s, it not only became the subject of a wave of nostalgia, but it became clear that many artists had been inspired by the music. A critical re-evaluation of the period, however, was far from immanent, since it remained a subject for easy ridicule. And that just ignores that New Wave, for all of its crass tendencies, was a stellar time for pop singles.

Recommended Recordings:
Various Artists, *Just Can't Get Enough: New Wave Hits of the '80s, Vols. 1-15* (Rhino)
Various Artists, *DIY: UK Pop, Vols. 1 & 2* (Rhino)
Various Artists, *DIY: US Power Pop, Vol. 1 & 2* (Rhino)
Various Artists, *A Checkered Past: The 2-Tone Story* (Chrysalis/2-Tone)
The Specials, *The Specials* (Chrysalis/2-Tone)
Madness, *Complete Madness* (Stiff)
The Pretenders, *Pretenders* (Sire)
Elvis Costello, *Armed Forces* (Rykodisc)
The Jam, *Snap!* (Polydor)
Squeeze, *Singles: 45's and Under* (A&M)
XTC, *Waxworks* (Geffen)
Talking Heads, *Sand in the Vaseline* (Sire)
Blondie, *Parallel Lines* (Chrysalis)
Duran Duran, *Decade* (Capitol)
Nick Lowe, *Labour of Lust* (Columbia)
The Go-Go's, *Return to the Valley of the Go-Go's* (IRS)
Adam & the Ants, *Antics in the Forbidden Zone* (Epic)

—Stephen Thomas Erlewine

Power Pop

While there is nothing inherently wrong with power-pop, it's often seen as a post-punk major-label marketing scam, helped along by greedy do-anything-to-make-it musicians who were willing to trade in their spiky haircuts and alienation for skinny ties and sunny dispositions. As true as this is, it represents only a fraction of what can accurately be described as power-pop. While it's very easy (and tempting) to dismiss this subgenre as egregious, market-driven dross, the fact remains that power-pop, even at its sleaziest and most manipulative, had a longer history than many people realize, producing some terrific bands and equally terrific music.

The musical sourcepoint for nearly all power-pop is the Beatles. Virtually all stylistic appropriations begin with them: distinctive harmony singing, strong melodic lines, unforgettable guitar riffs, lyrics about boys and girls in love; they created the model that other power-poppers copied for the next couple of decades. Other profound influences include the Who, the Kinks, and the Move, bands whose aggressive melodies and loud distorted guitars put the "power" in power-pop. Actually, in order to be complete, it's safe to say that an authoritative genealogical tree of power-pop influences would include virtually all of the bands of the British Invasion and Mod era. Which brings up a subtle, yet essential facet of nearly all (era notwithstanding) American power-pop bands—they seem, vaguely, British. That is, they sing with a slight English lilt to their voices, are likely to cover songs by British bands and, as was the case with many British mod bands, dress up rather than down. Even the most prominent American power-pop influence, the jangly folk-rock of the mid-'60s Byrds, had a British tinge to it a la the Searchers and the Hollies.

American power-pop's first heyday (ironically, before it was called power-pop) was the early '70s. Few American bands encapsulated the commercial popularity and influential cult status of early power-pop better than the Raspberries and Big Star. Both recorded great records, and while Big Star's entire recorded output (thanks mainly to the talents of Alex Chilton) remains inarguably the best of the bunch, both bands approached their craft with a similar intent: to write smart, punchy, hook-filled songs. For the Raspberries, a Cleveland-based band built around the Brit-rock obsessions of vocalist Eric Carmen and guitarist Wally Bryson, it was a string of huge hits like "Go All the Way," "Tonight" and the autobiographical "Overnight Sensation (Hit Record)" that made them one of the best commercial rock bands of the early '70s. Granted, their songs were hardly deep, but as heartfelt evocations of romantic teen angst and the naiveté of young love, they remain unbeatable. Memphis natives Big Star, on the other hand, did record deep, emotionally complex songs on three amazing records (*#1 Record, Radio City* and *Third/Sister Lovers*) that went unheard in their day but contained the best songs of American power pop ("Ballad of El Goodo," "Mod Lang," and the stunning "September Gurls"). Rediscovered by a later generation of pop-loving rockers (most notably the Replacements' Paul Westerberg), Big Star, though never touching the commercial success enjoyed by the Raspberries, became significantly more influential and revered.

By the mid- to late '70s, power-pop's lifeline continued with fluke hits like Dwight Twilley's 1975 Top 20 smash "I'm on Fire." Twilley, a native of Tulsa, OK, along with partner Phil Seymour, recorded a wonderful debut record, *Sincerely*, that along with containing the aforementioned hit, is an excellent example of ebullient, tuneful, rockabilly-tinged power-pop. Around the same time, Cheap Trick, a hard rock/pop quartet from Rockford, IL, capitalized on the strong vocals and good looks of lead singer Robin Zander, and the bizarre antics and the surreal lyrical narratives of guitarist Rick Nielsen, recording some of the finest pop/rock of the time. After three undeniably great records, the worldwide success of a so-so live album signalled the beginning of the end as Cheap Trick began living up to its name, their greatness reduced to formula.

Power-pop, however, was not solely the province of American bands who wanted to sound British; there was a British power-pop "invasion" of sorts in the '70s. Badfinger was the most blatantly Beatles-influenced (they even recorded for the Beatles' Apple label and had Paul McCartney as a producer), but they produced some excellent, occasionally thrilling songs such as "No Matter What," "Baby Blue," and "Day After Day," all three Top 20 hits in 1970-71. Loaded with lush guitars, instantly recognizable melodies and two fine singers in Pete Ham and Joey Molland (a fellow Liverpudlian who bears a strong resemblance to McCartney), Badfinger was the model of a great power-pop band. Sadly, guitarist and songwriter Pete Ham committed suicide in 1975, effectively ending the band's career. By the mid-'70s English power-pop was essentially the music of glam rock: stiff,

boot-stomping rhythms that sounded like football (i.e., soccer) chants. Glam rock cranked up the guitars while sweetening the melodies, thereby making loud, bubblegum rock fodder perfect for radio. With artists such as Gary Glitter, the Sweet, Slade, and Suzi Quatro (an American who found great success in England), leading the way, glam rock produced a handful of good songs, one great band (Slade) and the obsequious marketing of negligibly talented teen idols (e.g., Bay City Rollers) that would become common practice in the early-'80s power-pop sweepstakes.

Power-pop's nadir was reached, ironically, during an amazingly fertile period in its history. In the wake of Cheap Trick, excellent Midwestern power-pop bands like the Pezband and the Shoes (both from Illinois) made great records. On the West Coast, Jack Lee, Peter Case and Paul Collins formed the punk-pop Nerves; in Boston, the Real Kids released their debut LP; in Athens, GA, R.E.M. released the *Chronic Town* EP, a gem of Byrdsian power-pop; and in New York, Chris Stamey and Peter Holsapple formed the dB's and released two of the smartest and most ambitious power-pop records ever made. Even in England, former pub rocker Will Birch of the Kursaal Flyers formed the Records, a snazzy little combo that released a couple of fine records and an unforgettable single, "Starry Eyes." However, power-pop of the late '70s/early '80s is also remembered for the slavish imitators and skinny-tie-wearing no-talents, writing second-generation Raspberries ripoffs, pouting and posing on destined-for-the-cutout-bin album covers that major labels vomited at an alarming rate.

Although most people are loathe to use the term these days, power-pop still exists. Alternarock bands like the Posies, Belly, Throwing Muses, Elastica, Echobelly, Urge Overkill and the Gin Blossoms are not too far removed from the power-pop days of yore. There are flashes of it in Nirvana, and even retro-punk bands such as the Offspring and Green Day. Inevitably, there are also bands like Material Issue and Jellyfish, who are merely the next generation of Cretones and Jags, fobbing off style and mechanical reproduction as substance. Ultimately power-pop is much better than the term implies, and it seems as though it's not willing to go away anytime soon. Which is fine, just as long as skinny ties never make a comeback.

16 Essential Power Pop Records:
Badfinger, *Straight Up*
Big Star, *#1 Record* and *Radio City*
Cheap Trick, *In Color* and *In Black and White*
The dB's, *Stands for Decibels* and *Repercussion*
Flamin' Groovies, *Shake Some Action*
Go-Go's, *Greatest*
Nick Lowe, *Pure Pop for Now People*
Pezband, *30 Seconds over Shaumburg*
Raspberries, *The Raspberries' Best* (featuring Eric Carmen)
The Real Kids, *The Real Kids*
The Records, *The Records*
Scruffs, *Wanna Meet the Scruffs?*
Shoes, *Black Vinyl Shoes*
Slade, *Best of Slade*
Sweet, *Best of Sweet*
Dwight Twilley Band, *Sincerely*

—John Dougan

Hardcore & Thrash

Few rock listeners have noncommittal, or even mixed, opinions about hardcore and thrash. The substantial majority will not only never develop a fondness for the music, but will always view it with active dislike; quite a few figuratively cover their ears and run as fast as they can in the opposite direction. On the other hand, its "core" audience, if you will, forms one of the most fiercely loyal and zealous subcultures in all of rock & roll. The hardcore scene, love it or hate it, has exerted a substantial influence on rock & roll, one that is felt in today's Top 40 more than it was in its early-'80s heyday.

Hardcore, to use what by now has become a cliché, was harder, louder, and faster than its direct ancestor, early punk music. As shocking an assault as first-generation punk was on the heart of the rock industry, hardcore turned on the heat and tightened the screws. Lots of listeners already found the Ramones, Buzzcocks, the Clash and other early punk giants impossibly fast, loud, and abrasive. Hardcore took the Ramones' trademark "1-2-3-4!" kickoff countdown and sped up the tempos as fast as humanly possible, sticking largely to monochrome guitars, bass, and drums, and favoring half-shouted lyrics venting the most inflammatory sentiments the singers and songwriters could devise.

Hardcore's roots could be traced to the early American reaction to the supernova of 1977 British punk. In somewhat of the same manner as garage bands reacting to the British Invasion in the mid-'60s, American groups came up with an even cruder and rawer variation. A great many of these bands were based in California, particularly Southern California and the San Francisco Bay Area. Outfits like the Avengers, Dils and Germs played a more jaded and nastier version of British punk. Very shortly afterwards, other bands (who were often peers of the aforementioned acts) went the last nine yards into hardcore, although the line between "straight-ahead" punk and hardcore/thrash could often be (and often still is) thin.

The giants of early hardcore were mostly Californians: the Dead Kennedys, Black Flag, Flipper, the Circle Jerks. Just as almost every city or university town had its punk scene, so they soon had their hardcore bands. Washington, D.C., home of Minor Threat, the Bad Brains and many other groups, was arguably the biggest hotspot outside of the Golden State, but there were many groups in cities like Vancouver and Boston, to cite just the tip of the iceberg. British hardcore bands were not unknown—early records by Wire and the Fall were certainly hardcore keystones with their melodically minimal, percussive

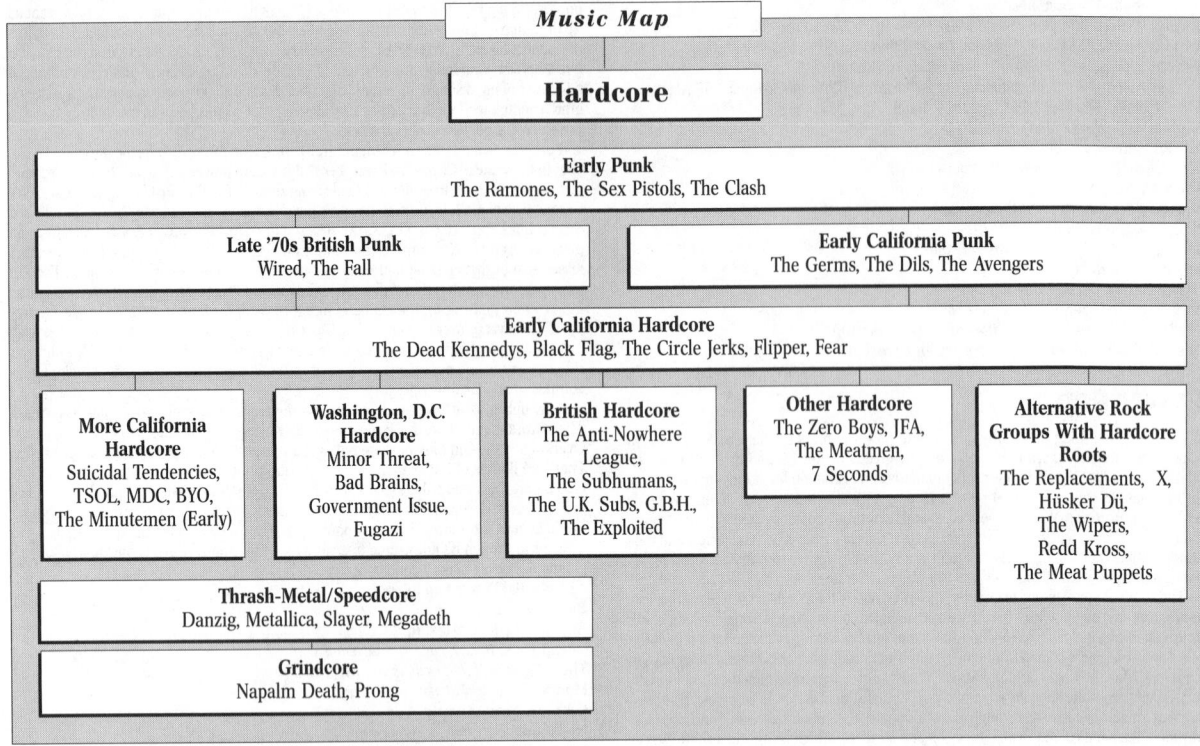

Music Map

Hardcore

Early Punk
The Ramones, The Sex Pistols, The Clash

Late '70s British Punk
Wired, The Fall

Early California Punk
The Germs, The Dils, The Avengers

Early California Hardcore
The Dead Kennedys, Black Flag, The Circle Jerks, Flipper, Fear

More California Hardcore
Suicidal Tendencies, TSOL, MDC, BYO, The Minutemen (Early)

Washington, D.C. Hardcore
Minor Threat, Bad Brains, Government Issue, Fugazi

British Hardcore
The Anti-Nowhere League, The Subhumans, The U.K. Subs, G.B.H., The Exploited

Other Hardcore
The Zero Boys, JFA, The Meatmen, 7 Seconds

Alternative Rock Groups With Hardcore Roots
The Replacements, X, Hüsker Dü, The Wipers, Redd Kross, The Meat Puppets

Thrash-Metal/Speedcore
Danzig, Metallica, Slayer, Megadeth

Grindcore
Napalm Death, Prong

---

structures, and groups like the Anti-Nowhere League, the Subhumans, G.B.H., the Exploited, and the U.K. Subs had big international followings. Indeed, there were scads of hardcore bands all over the globe, but North America was always the chief breeding ground. Melody, it's fair to say, wasn't uppermost in the minds of most thrashers. Not infrequently, it wasn't a consideration at all. Energy and, much more often than not, outrage were paramount. As in rap music, the lyrics and the message took precedence, though hardcore never matched the textural and sonic variety of rap. The lyrics were often more pointedly sociopolitical than anything else around, and often pointed fingers: at the government, institutions, teachers, employers, and authority figures of every kind. There was always sexism, racism, the arms race, yuppies, and conformists of all kinds to share the blame as well. A lot of hardcore bands lacked a sense of humor, as people who dwell on such topics are wont to do, but a lot of them could also be quite funny. The Dead Kennedys, Black Flag, Suicidal Tendencies and many other groups managed the difficult act of lambasting their targets with considerable humor, and songs such as "TV Party" (Black Flag) and "Institutionalized" (Suicidal Tendencies) provoked some honest-to-god belly laughs, and not exclusively from punks.

What is striking when listening to early hardcore is how melodic and poppy it can sound in comparison to later recordings in the genre, although it seemed unimaginably fast and devoid of melody at the time. Hardcore, more than the typical rock genre, didn't require much in the way of traditional instrumental and songwriting skills; virtually all hardcore records were released on small independent labels, often by the bands themselves. Given these low hurdles, the scene was soon crowded with generic bands. Some of the slightly later-than-first-generation hardcore outfits garnered substantial followings: TSOL, the Wipers, MDC (which stood for Millions of Dead Cops, Multi-Death Corporation, and Millions of Damn Christians, and other such phrases during various points in their existence), JFA (an acronym for Jodie Foster's Army), and Redd Kross (barely in their teens when they became nationally known) were some of the most famous. Each month (at its peak, each week) saw cheapo albums, singles, and tapes unleashed on the marketplace, many poorly recorded and virtually indistinguishable from track to track; any back issue of the international flagship punk zine, *Maximum Rock & Roll*, yields dozens of tiny reviews of bands from all over the place that are virtually forgotten, or were not even known at the time.

Hardcore, even more than most subcultures, was a sea of contradictions. It placed a premium on non-conformism, but a great deal of the music adhered to extremely clichéd conventions (the number of hardcore songs starting with a blast of guitar distortion, a shouted "1, 2, 1-2-3-4," followed by a dog-pulls-the-tablecloth-off-the-kitchen-during-dinner blur of chords, must number in the thousands). Its politics were generally well to the left of center (sometimes openly proclaiming anarchy), yet its fashions and sometimes even music were picked up by some Fascist and neo-Nazi youth. It placed great value on the message of the lyrics, which were often shouted so throatily as to be indecipherable. The music was played violently, confrontationally; the lyrics often preached tolerance, unity, and peace. Laudably, it championed racial and sexual equality; its performers and

audience were usually White and male. It preached against apathy, and advocated social change, but often reduced larger society to cartoon stereotypes, and was defiantly inaccessible and uncommercial, ensuring that the vast majority of rock listeners (let alone the population) would never hear the music. And when performers with roots in the thrash community did attract a larger audience, they were invariably accused by large segments of said community of selling out.

While it may be true that such performers were attracted by the prospects of commercial success, the more difficult truth to swallow was that they also felt constrained by the melodic, lyrical, and stylistic limits of hardcore, which are more severe than most any other subgenre of rock. The Replacements, X, the Meat Puppets and Hüsker Dü all started out as more or less hardcore acts; none broadened their success beyond a cult level until they broadened the scope of their music (and, it must be pointed out, all eventually betrayed the original punk/hardcore ideal by signing with major labels). All of these groups helped lay the foundation for "alternative rock," though none achieved the multi-platinum success of Green Day and Nirvana who likely listened to hardcore quite vociferously at some points in their youth. In the mid-'90s, early hardcore "stars" like Henry Rollins (of Black Flag), Bob Mould (of Hüsker Dü), and Mike Watt (of the Minutemen, so-named for the brevity of their songs, and later of fIREHOSE) are genuine rock stars; they don't play hardcore anymore, but their music shows debts to the form, and they've rarely if ever compromised their product in exchange for sales. There are even rare cases of also-ran hardcore bands that radically changed their game plan and hit the commercial jackpot; the Beastie Boys are the example that towers above all others that could be placed in this category.

Unexpectedly, hardcore and thrash also had a substantial influence on some of the '80s and '90s biggest metal bands, who combined the guitar octane of metal with a degree of the faster tempos and lyrical consciousness of hardcore. Metallica, Slayer, Danzig (whose lead singer, Glenn Danzig started out in the late '70s with punk/hardcore band the Misfits), and Megadeth have all done this to a large degree; the hybrid is sometimes called "thrash-metal," "death-metal" (actually not often an accurate designation), or "speedcore," among other terms. Prong, Napalm Death and others mixed punky nihilism with grinding metal to come up with "grindcore." Groups like Helmet have achieved critical acclaim with artsy punk-metal blends that, like bleached hair, show hardcore roots if you listen hard enough. On the fairly rare occasions that hardcore stars (like Suicidal Tendencies) or groups with hardcorish leanings (like Social Distortion) were signed to major labels, they probed, or were urged into, a more hard rock, metalish direction.

When the hardcore community is noticed by the outside world, unfortunately, the consequences can be severe. No one knows this more than Dead Kennedys lead singer Jello Biafra who also helps run the Alternative Tentacles label. In association with a poster included in a Dead Kennedys album, he and others were prosecuted by the Los Angeles City Attorney's office for distributing material harmful to minors. He was eventually acquitted, but the long and exhausting legal defense helped break up the Dead Kennedys. Hardcore records are all but ignored by the media (even most of the alternative publications), but hardcore has retained a significant audience in the last decade, linked by a tight (some would say insular) network of zines, skateboarder cliques, and tiny performance spaces. Some acts, like 7 Seconds, the deliberately offensive Meatmen, and the long-gone BYO, were huge within the hardcore community while passing virtually unnoticed by the larger rock world. Very occasionally, bands like Fugazi (led by Ian MacKaye formerly with "straight-edge" pioneers Minor Threat) achieve wide acclaim in the rock underground by broadening the hardcore base of their sound without alienating the hardcore base of their fans. *Maximum Rock & Roll*, the monthly punk journal, continues to review hardcore recordings by the boatload, and espouse a fervently radical sociopolitical view that some feel to be unhealthily rigid. When Jello Biafra had his leg mangled by slam-dancing thugs (who accused him of being a sellout rock star as they stomped on him) at a Berkeley, CA punk club with strong ties to the magazine in 1994, it was not so much the end of an era as a reflection of the long, strange road this most uncommercial breed of rock music has taken, and the contradictions it continues to embody.

12 Recommended Recordings:

Various Artists, *Faster & Louder: Hardcore Punk, Vol. 1* (Rhino)
Various Artists, *Faster & Louder: Hardcore Punk, Vol. 2* (Rhino)
The Dead Kennedys, *Fresh Fruit for Rotting Vegetables* (IRS)
Black Flag, *The First Four Years* (SST)
The Wipers, *Over the Edge* (Restless)
Bad Brains, *Rock for Light* (Caroline)
Hüsker Dü, *Metal Circus* (SST)
The Replacements, *Sorry Ma, Forgot to Take out the Trash* (Twin/Tone)
The Minutemen, *Double Nickels on the Dime* (SST)
Minor Threat, *Complete* (Dischord)
Suicidal Tendencies, *Suicidal Tendencies* (Frontier)
Fugazi, *Repeater* (Dischord)

—*Richie Unterberger*

Australian Rock

In 1975, most Americans' relationship with Australian rock consisted of maybe being able to sing the Easybeats' (who weren't native Australians) "Friday on My Mind." A geographically isolated continent, Australia's impact on the global rock & roll market seemed tangential at best; touring was difficult, most people carelessly lumped you in with English bands, and there was a strong feeling that no matter how good you might be, your career was limited to the Western Hemisphere.

In fact, rock & roll has been produced in Australia since the music made its first international impact in the mid-'50s. In 1957, Gene Vincent, Eddie Cochran and Little Richard became the first rock & roll stars to tour the continent (in fact, it was during this tour that Richard declared his intention to renounce rock & roll for the ministry). Australia had its homegrown rockers in the late '50s and early '60s, like Johnny Rebb who were unknown elsewhere in the world, and remain little-heard to this day even among rabid collectors and historians. The best of the pre-Beatles groups were the Atlantics, who recorded quite a few storming surf records that match the best instrumental surf music issued in Southern California around the same time.

Beatlemania had as great an impact in Australia as the U.K. or U.S., and after the Beatles swept through Australia on a mid-1964 tour, many British Invasion-inspired combos sprung up throughout the country. One of the first, and the most famous by far, were the Easybeats who created a mini-Beatlemania of their own (dubbed "Easyfever") on their home turf. Actually composed of musicians who had emigrated from Britain and Holland to Australia during their childhood or teens, the Easybeats boasted prolific writers in guitarists George Young and Harry Vanda. Much of their output during their mid-'60s prime bears a great deal of similarity to the Kinks, Small Faces and of course the Beatles, with a bouncier, more pop-oriented feel. After moving to Britain in 1966, they had an international smash with "Friday on My Mind," as well as some lesser U.K. hits, and dallied in increasingly sophisticated studio concoctions before packing it up at the end of the decade. They ultimately do not measure up to the level of greatness of the best British Invasion bands, but were indisputably the most original and influential Australian group of their time.

Australia was still something of a backwater in the '60s—major American and British groups didn't tour there often, sophisticated equipment and studios were hard to come by, and albums were a rarity, reserved for big stars like the Easybeats. Lacking first-hand exposure to their idols, or easy access to an international audience, Australian groups had to generate their own scene, much in the manner of regional garage groups in the United States. As with the garage bands, the result was often a rawer, less professional variation of the British Invasion sound.

At their best, the Australian garage groups were a match for the best American ones, compensating for their lack of virtuosity with an overdose of outrage. They're represented on a variety of compilations, which (as with American garage comps) mix gems with tedious genre exercises and unimaginative covers, although *Ugly Things Vol. 1* is recognized as one of the very best '60s garage anthologies from anywhere. Albums and compilations by some of the better and more prolific groups, like the Loved Ones, the Twilights and the super-raw Missing Links are spotty, but worth checking out for '60s collectors. The best '60s Australian group bar the Easybeats were the Master's Apprentices, who issued some terrific power-pop-garage singles in their early years, and evolved with the times through psychedelia and progressive rock, attaining some modest recognition in the U.K. after moving there for a time in the early '70s. Reissues of work by all of the bands mentioned in this paragraph, as well as *Ugly Things* and various other compilations, are available on the Raven label, the company primarily responsible for bringing some measure of belated acclaim to '60s Australian rock. (The Strangeloves though billed as Australian when they hit with "I Want Candy" in 1965, were not the genuine article; they were in fact New York session musicians/songwriters, using the fake nationality as an attention-grabbing gimmick.)

The most successful Australian rock act of the '60s are not often classified as Australian. The Bee Gees were composed of three brothers who had emigrated from Britain as children; in 1967, they would move to England and successfully invade the British and American markets as lightweight Beatles emulators, becoming even bigger in the 1970s as they moved into disco. They'd been stars in Australia for some time before 1967, though. Their underappreciated 1964-66 work, though rarely heard, reveals them to be among the best British Invasion-wannabes from anywhere in the globe, often recalling the Hollies' best mid-'60s recordings.

Australian rock, like much rock from outside of North America or the British Isles, was extremely derivative and imitative of American and British trends, and the late '60s and early '70s produced many Australian clones of psychedelia, soul, progressive, glam, and other rock trends, almost without exception unworthy of close scrutiny. And Australian bands never rated more than a footnote until ex-Easybeats Harry Vanda and George Young decided to record the band started by George's younger brothers Angus and Malcolm. Ridiculed from the start by critics, and passionately loved by their fans, AC/DC went on to become (and continues to be) a hugely popular heavy metal band. Driven by Angus Young's spastic, mega-loud guitar playing and exhausting stage antics (while dressed up in a schoolboy's uniform), and Bon Scott's screeching tenor voice (Scott died in 1980, his spot filled by Scottish shrieker Brian Johnson), AC/DC stripped away all artifice, laying down a thudding, insistent, riff-driven, feral assault that was as catchy as it was simple. In many ways AC/DC's no-frills faster-and-louder approach to rock & roll anticipated what was to be a defining element of the early punk rock scene.

AC/DC, despite a "punky," anti-authoritarian attitude, were never truly a punk band (nor for that matter were they really Australian: Malcolm and Angus like older brother George were born in Scotland). They were more precisely the most successful practitioners of Australia's popular working class hard rock/heavy metal scene, which included influential but lesser known bands such as the Angels (known later as Angel City) and Rose Tattoo. And while the aggressive attitude of these bands made a significant impact on young Australian punks-to-be, another important ingredient precipitating this genesis came in the early '70s when Ann Arbor, MI native Deniz Tek emigrated to Sydney. A guitarist and fan of the hyped-up, loud and direct, proto-punk motor sound of the Stooges and MC5, Tek joined forces with blond, gruff-voiced Aussie native Rob Younger and formed the seminal (and arguably first) Australian punk band, Radio Birdman. In 1976, Radio Birdman released a scorching EP, *Burn My Eye*, following it up with a terrific steeped-in-the-Stooges debut LP, *Radios Appear* (the title taken from a Blue Öyster Cult song). But despite beating everyone else in getting a record out, and providing the critical impetus that influenced other bands, Radio Birdman were not the center of media attention (especially in the English rock press) for the then nascent Aussie punk movement. That recognition went to a quartet from Brisbane called the Saints.

Co-led by Ed Kuepper and Chris Bailey, the Saints' debut, "(I'm) Stranded" was every inch a classic late '70s punk rock record: Bailey's snarling, petulant vocals; the speedy, superdistorted guitars; the (mostly) brief songs; and one of the punk era's best tunes (one that could only be written by an Aussie band) about alienation, "(I'm) Stranded." Because they were the first of their ilk to get to England, the U.K. pop press enthusiastically dubbed them the Aussie punk band to be reckoned with, thereby cementing their reputation and causing "(I'm) Stranded" to be a hit single. The Saints became the band that (almost) singlehandedly informed the rest of the world that there was a thriving and interesting alternative rock & roll scene in Australia. Unlike Radio Birdman who were finished by 1981 (Tek did, however, live out a dream by forming the short-lived New Race with ex-Stooges guitarist Ron Asheton and ex-MC5 drummer Dennis Thompson), the Saints (despite Kuepper's departure in 1978 to form the arty, psychedelic Laughing Clowns) continued to record into the '90s as Bailey took them from raw, blitz-speed punk into more deliberate, tuneful, and far less confrontational pop/rock.

As Australia's largest city, Sydney was the putative focal point of the burgeoning Aussie punk scene. However, many interesting, innovative bands were popping up all over the continent. Especially in Melbourne, a city with a rock tradition that went back to the mid-'60s and the much loved Loved Ones. Its large student population formed the sympathetic core for a more arty, avant-garde brand of punk that was less interested in fast guitars, and more interested in free-form musical and literary explorations. Seminal Melbourne underground musicians such as llie Olsonin and his bands Whirlywind and No created a churning din of sound, punctuated by vituperative lyrical broadsides, culminating in extreme performances that sometimes included self-inflicted violence and bloodshed. Still, with much of the student community supporting this sound, Melbourne was soon producing bands unlike anywhere else on the continent. (For an interesting fictional account of the early days of the Melbourne scene see the 1987 film *Dogs in Space* which surprisingly features a fine performance by INXS lead singer Michael Hutchence)

Few bands from the Melbourne scene were more interesting, and exhibited more promise, than did the Boys Next Door. Led by the doomy baritone voice and poetically-inclined pen of Jim Morrison acolyte Nick Cave and the twisted, noisy, gnarled guitar playing of Rowland S. Howard, the Boys released *Door Door* in 1979 and almost immediately became one of Melbourne's most influential punk bands. However, Melbourne wasn't big enough, nor centrally located to international audiences, for the Boys. By 1980, they had changed their name to the Birthday Party, moved to London, and become one of the post-punk era's most enduring and copied bands. Cave after going solo in 1984, has had success that eclipses that of the Birthday Party and the Boys combined. With and without his backing band the Bad Seeds, Cave has pursued the darker impulses of rock & roll, incorporating Delta blues and country music into his cauldron of musical ideas.

Cave (with the Bad Seeds) was a featured act on the Lollapalooza tour, published a novel, became a dad, and kicked a long-standing heroin addiction. His career spans dozens of recordings.

By the early '80s, the punk-inspired deluge of bands had given Australia more musical recognition than ever before. New bands, influenced by Anglo and American punk rock, Radio Birdman, the Saints, and the Melbourne scene, sprang up everywhere, embracing punk's DIY ethos while replicating and reinventing rock & roll. From the remote western city of Perth came the Kim Salmon-led, Scientists; '60s psychedelic garage rock was reinterpreted by the Lime Spiders; hook-filled pure pop was the calling card of the Hoodoo Gurus; and a melancholic take on Beatles-inspired pop was offered up by Marty-Willson Piper, Steve Kilbey, and Peter Koppes in the popular Church. There were art-punks Feedtime (who sounded like Flipper); the Melbourne-influenced King Snake Roost and Hunters and Collectors; the commercial hard rock of the Divinyls (great first record, everything else is worthless); the criminally overlooked Died Pretty; the over-amped pop of the Screaming Tribesmen; the extremely popular, but negligibly interesting, dance-rock of INXS (featuring Michael Hutchence); Rob Younger's post-Birdman outfit, the New Christs; hardcore punks the Cosmic Psychos and the delicately named Hard Ons; Brisbane's brilliant the Go-Betweens featuring Grant McLennan and Robert Forster; and two very important Sydney-based bands: the Celibate Rifles and Midnight Oil.

Midnight Oil began as a punk-influenced band big with Sydney's sizable surfing community. Led by the imposing figure of surfer/lawyer Peter Garrett, the Oils as they were affectionately dubbed by fans, began recording in 1978, but it wasn't until five years later, when they released *10, 9, 8, 7, 6, 5, 4, 3, 2, 1*, that (thanks to its huge success in Australia) they established a toehold in the international rock marketplace. Early Oils music is loud, technically adept, and very aggressive, indicative of their fondness for punk. Also it was the kind of assertive, boisterous rock that went down well with the surfer crowds they played to in Sydney-area bars. By the time they recorded *10, 9, 8...* the Oils' music was becoming more polished and pop-oriented, but not so much so that it sacrificed the guitar-driven mania from whence they sprang. Longtime advocates for the environment and aboriginal land rites, and with the articulate Garrett acting as band spokesman, it wasn't long before Midnight Oil became the biggest Aussie rock act since AC/DC. Much of it was due to the enormous success of the single and video "Beds Are Burning" (from the 1987 album *Diesel and Dust*) and ferocious live shows. Although their recent efforts have not yielded a hit single the magnitude of "Beds Are Burning," the Oils have developed a devoted fan base, and continue to make solid, if much less aggressive, records that consistently sell in the millions.

The stripped-down, loud and fast, Ramones-inspired rock of the Celibate Rifles deserves special mention, for this Sydney-based band proved to be the best Australian rock band to emerge from the Radio Birdman/Saints era. With droll, deadpan lead vocals supplied by Damien Lovelock the core of the Rifles was built around the rampaging guitars of Kent Steedman and Dave Morris. And while they valued power, speed, and volume, they weren't shy about tastefully adding horns, acoustic instruments, and slowing down the tempo. Perhaps too extreme and enigmatic to make a big splash in America, the Rifles did, however, develop a solid, supportive fan base in indie rock circles. However, they toured America sporadically, and as the '80s ended they seemed content to spend much of their time in Australia. Since they released their first EP in 1982, the Rifles' output has been frequently stunning, proving them to be the best Australian rock band you've never heard.

Aussie rock music is more diverse than the hard rock and punk-influenced rock that dominates American and British rock. Unfortunately, there are plenty of standard issue types like gruff-voiced Bob Seger wannabe Jimmy Barnes; hugely popular teenage soap star ("Neighbors") turned sexpot dance-pop singer Kylie Minogue; so-so hard rockers Cold Chisel; and worthless, radio/MTV panderers like '80s popular one-shots Men at Work. Far more interesting are recent performers such as blues guitarist Dave Hole and aboriginal singer/songwriter Archie Roach who have recorded exciting, very different sounding records than what emanates from both the Aussie mainstream and alternative rock communities. The success of Archie Roach and the band Yothu Yindi (whose influences include mid-'80s aboriginal rock bands such as Goanna and the Warumpi Band) has created a new focus on music made by Australia's aboriginal population, resulting in other established, yet heretofore unknown, Australian performers finding more acceptance (and more fans) in the global pop community, and on previously monochromatic Aussie pop music radio. Artists such as Ruby Hunter, Kev Carmody (the Australian Bob Dylan), and Blek Bela Mujik send a clear signal that there is much more to contemporary Australia rock & roll than simply White boys flailing away at guitars.

As more and more bands receive international acclaim, the Aussie music scene has been accorded more respect and, as a result, is more vigilantly watched by label executives for marketable bands. So, the next generation of Aussie bands, populated by up-and-comers like Silverchair, Spiderbait, the Mark of Cain, and the Joy of Noise, will have a much larger ready-made audience than did their predecessors. Even an old-timer like Deniz Tek has returned to the fray, teaming up with Celibate Rifle Kent Steedman in a part-time project that recaptures the high energy Detroit rock sound that played such a pivotal role in the development of punk and post-punk Australian rock. Despite being on the other side of the planet, the truth is, since the late '70s, rock & roll has helped bring Australia a lot closer to the rest of the world and made it a lot more influential than anyone would have guessed.

20 Essential Australian Rock Recordings:

The Easybeats, *Absolute Anthology* (EMI, Australia)
Various Artists, *Ugly Things Vol. 1* (Raven, Australia)
The Bee Gees, *The Early Years Vol. 1, The Early Years Vol. 2* (Excelsior)
The Master's Apprentices, *Hands of Time 1965-72* (Raven, Australia)
AC/DC, *Back in Black* (Atlantic)
Radio Birdman, *Radios Appear* (Sire)
The Saints, *(I'm) Stranded* (Sire)
Midnight Oil, *10, 9, 8, 7, 6, 5, 4, 3, 2, 1* (Columbia)
The Celibate Rifles, *Roman Beach Party* (What Goes On)
The Celibate Rifles, *Blind Ear* (EMI-True Tone, Australia)
Feedtime, *Shovel* (Aberrant/Rough Trade)
The Go-Betweens, *1978-1990* (Beggars Banquet/Capitol)
Divinyls, *Desperate* (Chrysalis)
Archie Roach, *Charcoal Lane* (Hightone)
Yothu Yindi, *Freedom* (Hollywood)
Birthday Party, *Hits* (Warner Brothers)
Nick Cave & the Bad Seeds, *The First Born Is Dead* (Mute)
Died Pretty, *Free Dirt* (What Goes On)
The Hoodoo Gurus, *Stonage Romeos* (A&M)
The Scientists, *Weird Love* (Big Time)
Film:
Dogs in Space (1987)

—John Dougan & Richie Unterberger

New Zealand Rock

New Zealand's influence upon the international rock & roll scene has been limited by its size and isolation. The total population of the two islands that comprise the nation is about three million; considerably less than, for instance, the population of the San Francisco Bay Area. The country didn't even have a recording studio until 1948, and as recently as 1989, it took only 7500 units of sales to qualify for a gold record. Yet its very size and isolation have also helped foster a brand of rock that may have been too idiosyncratic to flourish elsewhere.

The very first New Zealand rock & roll record was cut way back in August 1955, when John Cooper recorded a version of "Rock Around the Clock." Much in the manner of its much larger neighbor Australia, there was plenty of homegrown Kiwi rock & roll in the late '50s and '60s, especially after the British Invasion sparked the formation of self-contained guitar bands. Some of this was fairly good: Ray Columbus & the Invaders (British Invasion-styled pop) and the La-De-Das (British Invasion-styled R&B/rock) were about the best, and the best of the handful of outrageous New Zealand garage bands can be heard on the compilation *Wild Things*, which holds its own with most international '60s garage reissues of the sort.

The great majority of New Zealand rock and pop, however, was extremely, at times slavishly, derivative of British and American rock trends. To a large degree, this was also characteristic of Australian rock, but the best '60s Australian rock had a more distinctive flavor, and occasional international successes. Few listeners outside the Antipodes heard New Zealand rock until the moderate success of Split Enz beginning in the mid-'70s.

At various times characterized as art-rock, new wave, or comedy-rock, Split Enz attracted the attention of Roxy Music guitarist Phil Manzanera who produced one of their early albums. Big stars at home, they also made splashes, in progressively smaller order, in Australia, the U.K., and the U.S. Outside of New Zealand and Australia, they remain very much a cult item, despite their frequent pop/rock focus; listeners tend to either find them intriguingly offbeat, or gimmicky performers who epitomized some of new wave's sillier aspects. In the mid-'80s, Split Enz-mainstay Neil Finn (eventually joined by his brother Tim) led Crowded House to international success with tuneful, just-left-of-mainstream pop/rock.

To this day, there continue to be a good many mainstream New Zealand rockers who are popular, or even stars, in their native country. Almost without exception, they are lesser variations on mainstream rock trends originating in the U.K. or U.S. There are several bands featuring blends of rock and the music of the indigenous Maori people of the islands, but these are rarely distributed internationally, and often lean more toward the tame pop/rock side of things than ethnic roots. Of much more interest to the inquisitive rock fan are the many alternative Kiwi bands, which emerged from a scene that really didn't get going until the late '70s and early '80s.

If there could be said to be a founding father of New Zealand alternative rock, the title would probably be awarded to Chris Knox. Singer in one of the country's first punk bands, the Enemy, he subsequently fronted the energetic new wave group Toy Love, probably the first alternative rock group of its sort to gain a lot of success in the islands. He subsequently teamed with Alec Bathgate to form half of Tall Dwarfs who have produced quite a few albums of determinedly individual, eccentric, and funkily recorded punk- and new wave-influenced rock that set the tone for the New Zealand underground of the 1980s. Knox has also recorded some similar albums on his own, and remains quite active in the scene to this day.

Tall Dwarfs were one of the first bands to record for the Flying Nun label, the company which has become almost synonymous with New Zealand underground/alternative rock. The small Kiwi punk scene of the late '70s had given birth to a few independent labels (Ripper and Propeller were the best known); those releases have rarely been heard overseas, and then usually on obscure compilations. Flying Nun, begun in 1981 by record-store manager Roger Shepherd, almost immediately placed a couple singles on the country's charts, and acted as a magnet for the best non-mainstream Kiwi rock talent. By the late '80s, it seemed as though virtually every alternative Kiwi rock act of note was affiliated with the company.

Although Flying Nun has become home to a fairly diverse roster of artists, there are certain attributes which could be broadly applied to their sound, and by association the New Zealand alternative scene as a whole. The bands were very much of the D.I.Y. generation spawned by punk and new wave, but placed high premium on tuneful melodies and a sprinkling of pop hooks. They eschewed in-your-face booming hi-tech production, usually sticking to classic guitar-organ-bass-drums lineups. At the same time, however, they weren't averse to embellishing their products with all manner of odd production touches, often in the four-track manner pioneered by the Tall Dwarfs. Without being slavishly reverent, their music betrayed strong debts to the psychedelia of the '60s, as well as the jangle-pop of the Byrds; the ghost of Syd Barrett's brilliant pop-psychedelia fusions is particularly strong, hovering over many if not most of the NZ groups.

An equally important factor in the warm reception granted New Zealand bands by alternative rock fans worldwide was the innocence, naiveté, and humility of the music. New Zealand is a modern society, but it is the most isolated of the English-speaking territories; overseas records, books, and films take months and years to arrive in the islands, if they become available there at all. In its low-key lifestyle, it's closer to the America of the 1950s than the 1990s. This relative lack of overwhelming outside influence, as well as the tight-knit camaraderie of a scene which remains a minority taste on its home turf, accounts to some degree for the originality of the Flying Nun product, right down to the artful, colorful, at times seemingly hand-drawn sleeves.

One could be forgiven for viewing the Flying Nun label as a sort of extended family of New Zealand rock groups; the groups tend to change personnel quite frequently, often joining or rejoining each other's bands, or forming spinoffs of their own. The label is based in New Zealand's largest city, Auckland, yet many of the musicians hail from the relatively small south island town of Dunedin, as well as its bigger south island neighbor Christchurch. Considering the rather limited population pool, Flying Nun cultivated an impressively lengthy roster of bands that made an international impression of sorts in the 1980s: the Chills, the Bats, the Clean, the Jean-Paul Sartre Experience, the Verlaines, Straightjacket Fits, and Bailter Space on down to more cultish acts like Able Tasmans, Headless Chickens, and the Cake Kitchen.

On an international level, the most successful of these bands were the Chills who have gone through a dozen or so lineups under the leadership of Martin Phillipps, and the Bats whose guitar-dominated sound fits in most readily with the music favored by college radio in the late '80s. The Verlaines, the Jean-Paul Sartre Experience and Straightjacket Fits also landed overseas licensing deals; Homestead, Rough Trade, and Communion were the prime outlets for NZ product in the U.S. Since the mid-'80s, appreciation for the Flying Nun sound had grown steadily overseas, especially in the United States. Granted these fans tended to cluster in big cities and university towns; San Francisco has a particularly large clique of Flying Nun aficionados, as do Los Angeles, New York, and Chicago. If one were to judge by the large amounts of ink devoted to Flying Nun bands in underground rock publications and fanzines, one would assume that they were stars. They're not, actually, outside of the fairly small community of listeners who read them. Mainstream audiences have not so much never warmed to these groups as never heard them, although a couple (most notably the Chills) had major-label deals. The bands at least gathered enough of a following to enable them to tour the U.S., although in most cases these were limited to the East and West Coasts.

Lest one be tempted to think that Flying Nun remains the first and last word in New Zealand indie rock, other Kiwi indies such as Xpressway and IND have also released a few albums that have achieved international recognition, the excruciating noise-rock of the Dead C and the Syd Barrettisms of Alastair Galbraith being two of the more widely known examples. Flying Nun remains as active as ever in the mid-'90s, even though its roster seems increasingly static, the new acts often composed of spinoffs of groups that first recorded with the label in the 1980s. In judging the health of the New Zealand indie scene, one runs up against the isolation problem in reverse: it can take years for bands to get heard overseas, if they get heard at all. The islands can retain considerable pride, though, in schooling a brand of alternative rock that rarely bowed to commercial pressures from the mainstream or the underground, while remaining accessible to all who managed to find it.

12 Most Essential New Zealand Rock Recordings:
Various Artists, *Wild Things* (Flying Nun)
Split Enz, *History Never Repeats: The Best of Split Enz* (A&M)
Toy Love, *Toy Love* (WEA, New Zealand)
Various Artists, *Tuatara* (Flying Nun)
The Tall Dwarfs, *Hello Cruel World* (Homestead)
The Chills, *Kaleidoscope World* (Homestead)
The Clean, *Compilation* (Homestead)
The Bats, *The Law of Things* (Communion)
The Jean-Paul Sartre Experience, *Love Songs* (Communion)
The Verlaines, *Juvenilia* (Homestead)
Straightjacket Fits, *Hail* (Flying Nun)
Alastair Galbraith, *Seely Girn* (Feel Good All Over)
Book:
Stranded in Paradise: New Zealand Rock & Roll 1955-1988, by John Dix (1988, Paradise Publications, New Zealand)

—Richie Unterberger

Jangle Pop

In the early '80s, once punk rock spawned New Wave and launched a move toward mostly English electronic and synth-pop bands, American jangle-rock, (the sound characterized by the chiming acoustic and electric guitars of the Beatles, Byrds, Soft Boys and Big Star, and made famous in the '80s by R.E.M.), was the antidotal reaction. A new generation of folk-based guitar bands were born, but commercial radio, a new invention called MTV, and the baby-boomer dominated staffs at the mainstream rock press were slow to catch on to the sounds. College radio and fanzines were the only available outlets for the new music and consequently, it would take years before the new generation of guitar-wielding musicians would be recognized as cornerstones to the foundation of what would become modern, melody-driven, alternative rock.

The word "jangle" was a reference to Bob Dylan's lyric in the Byrds greatest hit, "Mr. Tambourine Man"; "in the jingle-jangle morning." Accompanied by the chiming guitar sound and luscious harmonies, also in evidence in the Byrds' (and Robyn Hitchcock's) version of Pete Seeger's "Bells of Rhymney," the terms "jangling," "ringing" and "chiming" were added to budding rock critic parlance to describe the sound. Fanzines like *The Bob, Matter, Tasty World* and the U.K.'s *Bucketfull of Brains,* all paid great attention to covering the genre. It was also the golden age of college radio, independent record stores, and tiny clubs all of which served a large part in spreading the good word about the R.E.M. and Big Star-related bands, (the dB's, Let's Active, Game Theory) and regional artists. The new bands were welcomed into the regional folks' hearts as well as literally into their homes, as the music inspired an unusual passion among record lovers.

R.E.M. were known as the leaders of the movement (if it could be called one) due to their higher profile, and guitarist Peter Buck was free with his endorsements of the aforementioned bands—as he proselytized on his cross-country trips, sleeping on people's couches, granting interviews to small fanzines and combing record stores—telling anyone who would listen about the new guitar rock and the records that excited him, past and present. Independent record stores were the hub of much of this type of exchange as store clerks and owners were also responsible for turning their customers on to the rich guitar-rock canon.

Buck's rudimentary style, at his own admission inspired by Roger McGuinn's Rickenbacker, offered the chance to anyone who could hold a guitar the opportunity to play one (not so unlike punk rock) and the ensuing guitar-rock revival was often heralded as the "Return of the Rickenbacker."

Hard to believe that a little-known band from North Carolina sparked the '80s guitar rock revolution, but all signs point toward the dB's reinventing "jangle-rock," before R.E.M. made it famous. The dB's, led by songwriters Chris Stamey and Peter Holsapple, cut two records (*Stands For Decibels* and *Repercussion*, the latter not coincidentally produced by Scott Litt who would later become R.E.M.'s producer) but had relocated from the South to New York, as regional bands at the time were wont to do. R.E.M. stayed and broke out of the tiny college town of Athens, GA, perhaps making theirs a more interesting story. They recorded their highly praised debut single, "Radio Free Europe" and *Chronic Town* EP at Mitch Easter's Drive-In studio in Winston-Salem, North Carolina and *Murmur* and *Reckoning* at Reflection Studios in Charlotte. Subsequently, industry attention became focused on the burgeoning scenes that were developing outside of the obvious urban centers and Easter and his recording partner Don Dixon got pretty busy on the heels of R.E.M.'s early, underground success. Though not all of the bands who recorded there—like Easter's own Let's Active, Athens' Art in the Dark, Mississippi's Windbreakers and New York's Bongos—were makers of the shimmering guitar rock, they often got lumped into the category. Basically, anytime a band with a good pop hook added harmonies or acoustic guitars into the mix, they were given the guitar-rock subhead as there was no other place to put these bands during the dawn of MTV and the era of new technology that spawned synth-rock; it was a convenient catch-all.

Consequently, rougher bands like the punk Hüsker Dü and the drunk Replacements were also beneficiaries of the jangle-rock tag from time to time no doubt due to Buck's perpetual endorsement of their virtues in the press, his guitar work on the 'Mats jangly 1984 single, "I Will Dare," and Replacement Paul Westerberg's and the Hüsker's Bob Mould's own abilities to write great pop hooks. Early records by singer-songwriters Matthew Sweet and Tommy Keane were also influenced by the R.E.M./Drive-In sound.

Meanwhile on the West Coast, the Dream Syndicate were experimenting with guitar rock of a different sort, more along the lines of the sonic type as practiced by the Velvet Underground and Neil Young—though both artists held some sway with the janglers; The Velvets "There She Goes Again" and Young's "Mr. Soul" were covered by bands too numerous to mention. But it was the Syndicate's brethren in the Los Angeles Paisley Underground like the Three O'Clock and Bangles who were paying homage to the soaring, harmony and guitar-driven sound of Alex Chilton and Big Star's *#1 Record* and *Radio City.* LA's The Long Ryders, particularly the group's leader Sid Griffin, were Byrds and Gram Parsons devotees, so country-rock and folk-rock became part of the package, as did good old American rock & roll as played by LA's Green on Red and Nashville's Jason and the Scorchers.

The attendant Hoboken scene sparked by the dB's and revolving around the club Maxwell's included the Richard Barone and James Mastro-led Bongos, and Doug and Janet Wygal's The Individuals. Their forbearers in New York-based guitar pop were the Feelies.

Power-pop was another cross-over influence as groups like the Plimsouls had their greatest success with a shimmering guitar song, "A Million Miles Away" in 1983. Jules and the Polar Bears (Jules Shear), Cheap Trick and Badfinger are cousins to the sound, as on closer inspection, the jangle bands were pulling inspiration from a variety of pure pop sources. For example, the songs Lenny Kaye compiled on the first *Nuggets* record were also informing these bands—if it was guitar-driven and hooky, it qualified, and the pop and garage-rock side of '60s psychedelia was definitely embraced, as heard in LA's Rain Parade and Boston's Lyres.

Perhaps the most significant development of all was that the jangle-rock movement was taking place in America, and the college rock charts were suddenly dominated by homegrown bands as opposed to the U.K. acts which they'd previously helped introduce to U.S. audiences. (Though early records by Australia's The Church also fit the bill; the Smiths' Johnny Marr jangled, but Morrissey was too English). It also opened the door for local bands in each region that were practicing guitar rock, by garnering them airplay, record contracts and occasionally the ever-so-important Buck endorsement during R.E.M.'s countless cross-country treks. Northern California's Game Theory, New Haven's Miracle Legion and Minneapolis' Reverbs gained notoriety during the second wave of guitar rock. San Francisco's Translator and Wire Train had their jangle moments, particularly Translator with its 1982 college hit, "Everywhere That I'm Not," but faulty production left the bands saddled with the New Wave tag. Perhaps they should have checked into the Drive-In.

Jangle-rock finally put to rest the notion that the only rock that emanated from the South was the vaguely racist and sexist blues-derived boogie that bands typically referred to as Southern Rock produced in the '70s. Bands appeared to grow on tress in Athens, like Kilkenny Cats, Oh-OK and Dreams So Real (refer to the soundtrack to the film, *Athens, GA—Inside/Out*). It also shot down the idea that alternative and underground rock was inaccessible noise; akin to punk rock and not suitable for the masses.

Like punk, mixed-gender bands were common as the groups aped the era of the Mama's and the Papa's, the Mojo Men and the Velvets and fused the male-dominated seventies rock with female singer-songwriter rock. It's no coincidence that once bands like the Natalie Merchant-led 10,000 Maniacs experienced a modicum of popularity, it made way for the emergence of Suzanne Vega, Tracy Chapman, and the Indigo Girls later in the decade who paved the way for the '90s wave of female singer-songwriter rock. Once Peter Case, formerly jangling with his Plimsouls, took a cue from John Hiatt and put down his electric guitar in favor of a subdued, coffeehouse-style delivery, more rockers followed suit and lightened up their attack. The move toward bands performing "unplugged" was partially due to the jangle rock bands whose folk-rock melodies lent themselves to acoustic renditions that were performed mid-set, at college radio stations and in-stores, long before it became the standard (check *Rainy Day*, a 1983 compilation of Paisley Undergrounders doing acoustic covers).

By the mid-'80s, even mainstream rockers like John Mellencamp had incorporated the jangle sound into their music; in particular, Mellencamp's folksy, *1985 Scarecrow* album which was arguably influenced by R.E.M. To be fair, there was an exchange going on— R.E.M. recorded *Lifes Rich Pageant* at Mellencamp's Belmont Mall studio the year after, partially inspired by an acoustic version of Mellencamp's "Small Town" which appeared as a B-side. As in any important movement—such exchange is key and leads to a number of other strings and tangents. *Lifes Rich Pageant* was a turning point for R.E.M. as a case could also be made for them borrowing the instrumental border-ska of Camper Van Beethoven (who accompanied them on tour) for their track "Underneath the Bunker" from the same LP. It also had them dabbling in the political-rock arena with their "Flowers of Guatemala."

Lyrics were not exactly at the forefront of jangle (after all, it was named for the guitars), unlike the folk-rock sounds of the '60s—but they weren't as simple and trite as its other cousin, power-pop; such timeless rock and roll themes as love and alienation cropped up often. Though their tenure was during the cold Reagan era, few bands engaged in the political arena as mixing politics with rock was considered foolish at the time (perhaps due to a gaffe made by Neil Young who seemingly endorsed Reagan).

However, there was an unspoken thread of political correctness that ran throughout— as if to say all jangle-rock devotees came from a left-wing perspective. After keeping their mouths shut for years, R.E.M. became the most cause-concerned band around and their ever-present, offstage green politics contributed toward bands in general becoming more politically aware.

Additionally, Michael Stipe's mumble gave way to a more ethereal sound that was lost in the mix, rather than pointed lyrical accounts. Both factors partially explain why the genre was generally ignored and completely lost on the old-school writers at the mainstream music publications. Few had anything positive to say regarding this portion of the underground, relegating most coverage to fanzines and word of mouth, which is partially why by today's standards it took R.E.M. and others so long to break (in the case of R.E.M. it took six years!). Tight formats at MTV and commercial radio also contributed to the lock-out as they did not allow for experimentation. Thus, airplay was confined to specialty programming (like IRS Record's "The Cutting Edge" weekly hour on MTV, wherein bands like R.E.M., Let's Active and Hüsker Dü were allowed to develop previously unseen on-camera personalities. Mid-decade radio opened up to incorporate "modern rock," (which would soon be coined "alternative") programming, but save for the latest records by R.E.M., their playlists were mostly comprised of the synth-pop songs college radio made popular in years prior.

As the decade wore on, it was taken for granted that the guitar had returned as the key instrument in rock and roll and the world at large was ready for the takeover, while the media pretended to have been there all along. By the time Nirvana burst onto the scene, though they'd claimed R.E.M. as a prime influence, Kurt Cobain and other more melodious grunge rockers had turned the form upside down, cashing in the harmonies and delicate vocals, but retaining the guitar-driven spirit behind the melodies. What they also retained was R.E.M.'s take no prisoners, D.I.Y. model of how to be an "alternative" band, by ceaseless touring, retaining artistic control and supporting humanist causes. Ironically, it was right around this time that R.E.M. became the biggest jangle-rock band in the world with their 1991 single "Losing My Religion" from the *Out of Time* record and subsequently traded in the chime for a darker sound, reclaiming their earliest influences, the Velvet Underground and the Stooges. Entering their second decade as a band, they released the moody *Automatic For the People*, and the thundering, metallic *Monster*.

In the '90s, The Velvets continued to be an overriding influence. However, it was the sound of Big Star's *Third/Sister Lovers* that became favored by former jangler David Roback (Rain Parade) who formed Opal (with the Dream Syndicate's Kendra Smith) then Mazzy Star with Chilton's record as his blueprint. Traces of Chilton's jangle from the first

two Big Star album's, along with power pop and hard rock were heard in the records of the Seattle-based Posies.

The Posies proved their love of jangle when Jon Auer and Ken Stringfellow served as one half of the reformed Big Star with Chilton and Jody Stephens for a 1993 live album, *Columbia* and tour. Scotland's Teenage Fanclub turned out an album in 1990, *Bandwagonesque*, that was wholly inspired by Big Star, and continue to work and refine their guitar-driven sound. In San Francisco, Scott Miller (ex-Game Theory) still pines at inflecting his music with authentic jangle sounds in his Loud Family.

Brit-pop, though supposedly British to the core, has traces of the jangle. Along with their obvious debt to the Beatles, Oasis' Manchester jangle, inspired by the Smiths, came to them via Marr who probably picked it up from Buck and the Byrds before the Smiths' 1984 debut.

Both the lo-fi and American indie-rock movements of the '90s were heavily indebted to jangle-rock. The three leading figures of lo-fi—Pavement, Sebadoh and Guided By Voices—used jangle as a foundation, capturing its spirit, if not necessarily its sound. Not coincidentally, all three bands were either of college age or in their early 20s during the mid- and late '80s, and they took the do-it-yourself, self-sustained sense of community of jangle-rock to heart, staying on independent labels when they could have moved to the majors.

The Americana, occasionally jangling sounds of Wilco, Son Volt and Jayhawks can be traced immediately back to the Parsons-lovin' Long Ryders and raw, rockin' Jim Dickinson, Memphis productions by Green on Red (*Here Come The Snakes*), and the Replacements (*Pleased to Meet Me*). The Gin Blossoms owe a great debt to Paul Westerberg and the Replacements; R.E.M. begat Live and Todd the Wet Sprocket, ad nauseam. But everyone should tip their hat to Bob Dylan, who though never a favorite among jangle rockers, was the first to fuse rock with folk, and he gave the Byrds "Mr. Tambourine Man" to add their chiming harmonies and jangling guitars, making it accessible to the world.

Recommended Recordings:

Big Star, *#1 Record/Radio City* (Fantasy)
The Soft Boys, *Underwater Moonlight* (Rykodisc)
The dB's, *Repercussion* (IRS)
R.E.M., *Chronic Town* (IRS)
R.E.M., *Murmur* (IRS)
R.E.M., *Reckoning* (IRS)
Let's Active, *Afooot/Cypress* (IRS)
The Plimsouls, *Everywhere At Once* (Geffen)
Bangles, *Bangles EP* (Faulty)
Rain Parade, *Emergency Third Rail Power Trip/Explosions in the Glass Palace* (Enigma)
Dream Syndicate, *Tell Me When It's Over: The Best of the Dream Syndicate* (Rhino)
Three O'Clock, *Baroque Hoedown EP* (Frontier)
Richard Barone/James Mastro, *Nuts and Bolts* (Passport)
Various Artists, *Rainy Day*
Long Ryders, *10-5-60 EP* (PVC)
The Replacements, *Let It Be* (Twin/Tone)
Robyn Hitchcock & the Egyptians, *Fegmania!* (Rhino)
Game Theory, *Real Nighttime* (Alias)
Camper Van Beethoven, *Telephone Free Landslide Victory* (IRS)
Miracle Legion, *The Backyard EP*

                         —Denise Sullivan

American Alternative Rock / Post-Punk

Like new wave before it, "alternative" is basically a meaningless term. Punk, heavy metal, funk, rap, pop, rock & roll, singer/songwriter—everything fits under the term. Essentially, "alternative" is a catch-all for post-punk bands that appeared as new wave began to die out in 1983-84, and runs all the way into 1995, when alternative pop/rock is the mainstream. Although there's nothing alternative about Live and Silverchair, their inspiration by R.E.M. and Nirvana were decidedly part of an underground, anti-mainstream rock & roll movement. But what really distinguishes alternative pop/rock is how it reprocesses and reworks rock history, bringing together diverse strands into a whole. Alternative followed somewhat different paths in America and Britain; although the two countries have had bands that were big on both continents, like R.E.M., certain phenomena like Pearl Jam or the Stone Roses haven't translated particularly well between the two. In addition, entire subgenres are isolated to either the U.S. or the U.K. (funk-metal, for instance, has never been very popular in Britain).

Alternative pop/rock has its basic roots in punk, new wave and hardcore; it does recall other genres, particularly '60s pop and heavy metal, but the entire subculture first emerged from the punk movement. To over-simplify things, the first American alternative bands were R.E.M. and Hüsker Dü. Both bands formed in the early '80s or late '70s, releasing records on small independent labels before moving to bigger indies and then the majors. In their wake, thousands of bands followed, both musically and ideologically. Hüsker Dü broke up without achieving any mainstream success, while R.E.M. soldiered on into the '90s, becoming one of the most popular rock & roll bands in the world.

For most of the '80s, alternative rock remained the province of small clubs, independent labels, fanzines, and college radio, with the occasional song breaking into MTV and Top 40, or the occasional album receiving critical praise in mainstream publications like *Rolling Stone*. However, the commercial appeal of most alternative bands was nearly nonexistent. Instead, the bands built underground followings by touring constantly and releasing a low-budget album every year. New bands would form in their wake, and soon there was a sizable underground circuit in America, with different parts of the country having different scenes.

R.E.M. immediately had the most impact, both commercially and musically. *Murmur*, the band's 1983 debut album, received enormous critical praise, helping the album chart in the Top 40. Legions of jangling imitators followed, and the group's success helped other Southern guitar-pop bands like the dB's and Let's Active get exposure. Also, they helped kick off a group of bands dubbed "the Paisley Underground" that drew from the Velvet Underground and '60s psychedelia. R.E.M. toured non-stop throughout the decade, releasing a record each year and slowly expanding their following, which set the stage for their Top Ten breakthrough in 1987 with *Document* and "The One I Love." By that time, the group's ringing, chiming guitars and Michael Stipe's mumbling vocals had become commonplace on college radio.

While R.E.M.'s success provided a blueprint for many bands of the late '80s and '90s, Hüsker Dü's music had an equally large impact. Starting as a blistering hardcore band, the trio soon moved away from the confines of their subgenre. Without abandoning the loud guitars and furious tempos of hardcore, Hüsker Dü created a music that was both abrasive and melodic, filled with shards of noise and catchy hooks. *Zen Arcade*, a double album released in 1984, was their creative breakthrough, filled with concise pop and noisy, winding instrumental stretches. The group's last album, 1987's *Warehouse: Songs and Stories*, had a more polished sound than their earlier records, but it provided a template for the shiny punk-pop production of Nirvana's seminal *Nevermind*.

Hüsker Dü was signed to SST Records, the label founded by Black Flag leader Greg Ginn in the early '80s. SST was the most influential American independent label of the '80s, not only featuring Black Flag and Hüsker Dü, but also Sonic Youth, the Minutemen, the Meat Puppets, and Dinosaur Jr., among others. While they didn't necessarily pave the way for Sonic Youth—the New York band was already recording when Hüsker came to prominence—Hüsker Dü's albums prepared both critics and audiences for Sonic Youth's all-out noise experiments. Sonic Youth was more self-consciously arty than either R.E.M. or Hüsker Dü, with their lyrics sounding like performance-art poetry and their songs essentially being long, winding, dissonant soundscapes.

Hüsker Dü were also the leaders of the loose Minneapolis scene, which also included the Replacements and Soul Asylum, both of whom initially sounded a great deal like the Hüskers. However, the Replacements wound up providing a link between punk and traditional Stones/Faces rock & roll, as well as narrowing the gap between R.E.M.'s pop and Hüsker Dü's noise. At that point in time, Hüsker Dü had broken up, R.E.M. had made a commercial breakthrough, the Minutemen were crippled by the death of D. Boon, and Sonic Youth were inactive between 1988 and 1990, as they were preparing to move to a major label. Consequently, several different subgenres that had thrived underneath the reign of the SST bands and R.E.M. came to the forefont. In addition to the loud, sloppy punky rock & roll of the Replacements and Soul Asylum, quirky alternative pop and noisy industrial rock dominated the late-'80s American alternative scene.

Much of the alternative guitar-pop of the late '80s had its roots in the awkward, jangly music of the Feelies and the nervous, geeky folk-rock of the Violent Femmes, who both released their debut albums in the early '80s. The Feelies never sold many records at the time, yet their chiming guitar riffs helped pave the way for R.E.M. Unlike R.E.M., the Feelies' melodies and lyrics were twitchy and uptight, quite similar to the songs that Gordon Gano wrote for the Violent Femmes' self-titled debut. Both of the bands began a trend of geeky guitar-pop groups that emphasized strangeness and bizarre humor. Since they were actively recording and touring at the time quirky guitar-pop became prominent, the Violent Femmes and the Feelies were part of the movement as well as being its forefathers. However, there were many other bands, from the jokey duo They Might Be Giants to the warped eclecticism of Camper Van Beethoven, that kept the music alive on the college charts. A number of off-kilter British guitar-pop bands fit into this trend as well, finding a larger following on American college radio stations than in their homeland. Robyn Hitchcock, the leader of the Soft Boys (who were an acknowledged influence on R.E.M.), was one of the British pop musicians who was warmly welcomed in the U.S. By this point in their career, XTC had a larger fan base in America than they had in Britain, which meant that their intelligent, meticulously crafted pop was prominently featured on American college radio.

In direct contrast to the good-natured, quirky pop of the Violent Femmes and XTC stood the legions of industrial and post-hardcore noise bands. While many industrial bands had their roots in European electronic groups, both the industrial and post-hardcore bands owed a great debt to Chicago's Big Black. Led by guitarist Steve Albini, Big Black created bleak, scathing, noisy soundscapes with two guitars, a bass, and a drum machine. The group's thin, tinny guitar roar became part of the indie-rock musical vocabulary, as did its shards of white noise. Their records, particularly 1986's *Atomizer*, prepared alternative audiences and college radio audiences for the jarring guitar grind of the Butthole Surfers, Scratch Acid and its offspring, the Jesus Lizard, and countless bands that appropriated the same noise as their own. Most of these bands were also produced by Steve Albini, who continued to be a prominent figure in underground rock into the '90s.

Big Black's records also paved the way for industrial groups that spliced together noisy guitars, dense samples, and relentless drum-machine driven beats. European bands like Front 242, Einstürzende Neubauten, and KMFDM were pioneers in the music and gained a significant amount of American college airplay, but it was Chicago's Ministry that popularized the genre. Originally a synth-pop band in the early '80s, the group, led by guitarist/keyboardist Al Jourgensen, changed direction in the mid-'80s, incorporating elements of dance, heavy metal, electronic music and hip-hop. Ministry's artistic breakthrough, and the record that helped establish industrial music as a staple of alternative rock, was 1988's *The Land of Rape and Honey*. As the years progressed, Ministry began leaning toward heavy metal, helping to make industrial techniques part of mainstream rock. Just as important was Cleveland's Nine Inch Nails, led by Trent Reznor. Nine Inch Nails were more pop-oriented than any other industrial band, which meant they were the ones that brought the music to a wider audience. But by the time that their 1989 debut, *Pretty Hate Machine*, became popular in 1991, industrial music had become passé in most alternative circles.

What had replaced industrial rock as a favored source of noise were revamped versions of Stooges-style punk and heavy metal. After the rise of industrial and quirky guitar pop, the spiky punk-pop of the Pixies and heavy grandeur of Jane's Addiction were the two most popular sounds in alternative rock. The Pixies returned a sense of punk brevity to alternative music, as well as working raw noise into pop song structures that were deliberately off-center. Their fractured, stripped-down punk-pop provided a blueprint for groups as diverse as Nirvana, Pavement, Weezer, and Radiohead, who all appropriated portions of the Pixies' music into their rock & roll. Although the Pixies were stars in most of Europe, they never achieved commercial success in America. Jane's Addiction were among the first to break down the walls between alternative and AOR radio, which wasn't surprising, given their affection for ponderous heavy metal. Perry Farrell's lyrics may have had the performance-art shock of Sonic Youth, but the band's music was heavy metal in the vein of Led Zeppelin. Similarly, Seattle's Soundgarden reworked Zeppelin/Black Sabbath heavy metal territory, yet they injected a raw, punkish intensity to the familiar sludge. Both Jane's Addiction and Soundgarden received positive reviews in mainstream publications like *Rolling Stone*, earning them a sizable cult following.

Soundgarden was the first of the Seattle bands to earn widespread acclaim in America. In England, Mudhoney was the first Seattle band to earn positive reviews. Mudhoney's Stooges-soaked, fuzz-toned 1988 single "Touch Me, I'm Sick" received a significant amount of acclaim in Britain, and the band earned a cult following in the U.K. by constant touring. To varying degrees, the success of Soundgarden, Mudhoney, the Pixies, and Jane's Addiction, as well as R.E.M., set the stage for Nirvana's breakthrough in late 1991.

Nirvana was the turning point for alternative rock as a commercially viable genre. Other bands had hits before them—particularly R.E.M. and Jane's Addiction—but Nirvana broke down the doors forever with their brand of punk-pop, which took equally from the Pixies, Sonic Youth, Soundgarden, and the Beatles. Following the number one success of *Nevermind*—which symbolically knocked Michael Jackson's *Dangerous* off the top of the charts—bands that had been on the fringe became multi-platinum stars, including the funk-metal of the Red Hot Chili Peppers and Primus, the industrial rock of Ministry and Nine Inch Nails, and the revamped arena-rock of Pearl Jam.

Although Nirvana's success did help send scores of bands, from Pearl Jam and Stone Temple Pilots to Green Day and the Offspring, to the top of the charts, it didn't eliminate the underground—this just gave it more exposure. Initially, this resulted in a flood of Seattle bands achieving considerable commercial success, including Pearl Jam, Alice in Chains, and Offspring. Nirvana's breakthrough also popularized so-called "Generation X" and "slacker" culture. Slackers came in many forms, but no band embodied the aesthetic quite as well as the Beastie Boys. Initially a hardcore band, the Beasties turned to rap in the early '80s, recording *Licensed to Ill*, one of hip-hop's major commercial breakthroughs. In 1989, the group released *Paul's Boutique*, a dense collage of pop and literary references that virtually defined the multi-culturalism and junk culture aesthetic that dominated much of the popular alternative rock of the '90s. However, *Paul's Boutique* was a commercial failure. When the Beastie Boys released *Check Your Head* in 1992, they had returned to playing their instruments and created a record that fused punk culture with hip-hop culture.

While the Beastie Boys presented another commercially successful alternative to heavy alternative rock, a number of female rockers began to gain attention both in the rock press and, occasionally, on MTV. During the '80s, women had prominent roles in important bands like Sonic Youth (bassist Kim Gordon) and the Pixies (bassist Kim Deal). In the late '80s, a number of new female singer/songwriters emerged, particularly Michelle Shocked, Tracy Chapman, Sinéad O'Connor, and Kristin Hersh of the Throwing Muses. While Shocked and Chapman were essentially folkies, O'Connor and Hersh bent the rules of rock & roll. O'Connor experimented with folk, punk, dance, and art-rock, creating a creative amalgam of styles that paid off with her 1990 commercial breakthrough, *I Do Not Want What I Haven't Got*. Under the direction of Kristin Hersh—and occasionally her stepsister, Tanya Donelly—Throwing Muses created a bracing music that had unpredictable lyrical and song structures which placed the band somewhere between punk, pop and folk.

The late-'80s female singer/songwriters prepared the rock media for the onslaught of the early '90s, as well as directly influencing several musicians. In particular, the songs on Liz Phair's 1993 debut *Exile in Guyville* recall music that was made in the late '80s, but her music included elements of rock & roll, power-pop, Joni Mitchell-styled folk-rock, and lo-fi alternative rock. There were other singer/songwriters similar to Phair, particularly the blues-punk of England's P.J. Harvey, but most of the female rock & roll acts of the early '90s were punk rock bands, with the occasional fusion of punk and heavy metal which recalled the music of Nirvana and Soundgarden. L7, Babes In Toyland, and Hole fit into this category, but there were underground bands like Bikini Kill and Bratmobile that sketched out an amateurish and politically confrontational form of punk labeled riot grrrl. There were also guitar-pop acts like Belly and Juliana Hatfield which were decidedly sunnier than their counterparts, but there were bands like the Breeders, led by Kim Deal, that straddled the line between arty punk and pop without surrendering to either side.

Because of a media-created desire to lump all of these acts under the banner of "women in rock," most of these bands received a fair amount of press, but only a handful—Belly, Breeders, Hole, and Liz Phair—sold many records. After the initial onslaught of Nirvana, Pearl Jam, Soundgarden, Smashing Pumpkins, and Red Hot Chili Peppers, the groups that sold the most records were neo-punk rockers Green Day and the Offspring. Although it didn't sound much different than their two previous indie releases, Green Day's third album, *Dookie*, and the singles "Long View" and "Basketcase," sent the group to the top of the charts in the summer of 1994; by the summer of 1995, *Dookie* had sold over eight million copies. Green Day's music essentially was revamped power-pop with hints of the Clash and the Jam, but the band's success led to the multi-platinum breakthrough of the metallic punk band the Offspring, who adopted the look of a punk group and the attack of a metal band. In their wake, Green Day and the Offspring focused attention on the hundreds of punk bands that played on the West Coast, particularly Rancid and Pennywise.

For all their ties with independent rock & roll and the underground, Green Day and the Offspring had little to do with alternative music by the time they broke into the mainstream. After Nirvana's breakthrough, the American underground divided into several factions that were all united by their desire to remain underground. There were neo-punk bands like North Carolina's Superchunk, which developed devoted followings but never had any desire to break beyond the level of an indie-rock band. There were arty, minimalist pop bands like Unrest which were knowingly clever, post-modern and ironic, but made melodic catchy songs that were never destined to break out of their cult following because the band never intended them for anything larger than their cult audience. There were handfuls of country-rockers like Uncle Tupelo, who imploded before they could reach any success.

Most important to the '90s American underground were the group of pop-rockers that were lumped under the "lo-fi" label, named after the poor sound of the band's generally homemade recordings. Beck helped popularize the subgenre with his debut album, *Mellow Gold*. However, *Mellow Gold* was not strictly a lo-fi record—it was too well-produced to fit that label. Nevertheless, Beck acted like a scavenger, much like the Beastie Boys, taking bits and pieces from different musical genres and recording songs that alternately recalled hip-hop, folk, garage-rock, and psychedelia. Beck's other records, the noisy *Stereopathetic Soul Manure* and the folky *One Foot in the Grave*, were genuine lo-fi records, but the success of *Mellow Gold* helped draw attention to the leaders of the movement, Sebadoh and Pavement. Both bands had earned a significant amount of critical acclaim, as well as sizable cult followings, before Beck, but his success began a trend in the rock press to lump all of the bands together. If any band embodies everything that is good and bad about lo-fi, it is Sebadoh. Led by former Dinosaur Jr. member Lou Barlow, Sebadoh isn't so much a band as it is a collective, with each individual member turning in their own songs. Barlow became the figurehead for the lo-fi movement, as he released an amazing amount of recordings in the early '90s under Sebadoh's name, as well as Sentridoh, the Folk Implosion, and his own name. Essentially, Barlow is a post-punk singer/songwriter, writing fairly conventional pop songs that are distinguished by his recording techniques and the occasional burst of pop noise. Nevertheless, the aesthetic is as important as the songs for many lo-fi fans, and Lou Barlow's work provides plenty of good songs and bad songs, all characterized by the thin recording techniques.

The one band that transcends the label of lo-fi is Pavement. What was important about Pavement's music was not the aesthetics, but the concepts. The group reassembled a variety of different rock & roll genres—from noise-rock to country-rock, hitting on power-pop, folk-rock, rock & roll, soul, etc. along the way—into a fractured, but tuneful, kaleidoscope of pop music. Unlike Beck's eclecticism, Pavement's songs—mainly written by guitarist/vocalist Stephen Malkmus—not only recontextualize familiar rock genres, they frequently subvert conventional pop structures. Pavement's three albums and numerous singles have earned them a sizable cult following as well as a wealth of critical praise, in effect, establishing the band as a leader of the post-Nirvana American alternative underground. Currently, they don't seem poised for a commercial breakthrough, but many observers felt that way about R.E.M. in 1985.

Recommended Albums:

The Feelies, *Crazy Rhythms*
Violent Femmes, *Violent Femmes*
R.E.M, *Murmur*
Replacements, *Let It Be*
Hüsker Dü, *New Day Rising*
Big Black, *The Rich Man's Eight-Track*
Throwing Muses, *Throwing Muses*
Dinosaur Jr., *You're Living All Over Me*
R.E.M., *Document*
10,000 Maniacs, *In My Tribe*
Ministry, *The Land of Rape and Honey*
Sonic Youth, *Daydream Nation*
Michelle Shocked, *Short Sharp Shocked*
Jane's Addiction, *Nothing's Shocking*
Soundgarden, *Louder than Love*
Mudhoney, *Superfuzz Bigmuff*
Pixies, *Doolittle*
Nine Inch Nails, *Pretty Hate Machine*
Nirvana, *Nevermind*
Pearl Jam, *Ten*
Liz Phair, *Exile in Guyville*
Pavement, *Slanted & Enchanted*
Beastie Boys, *Check Your Head*
Beck, *Mellow Gold*

—Stephen Thomas Erlewine

British Alternative Rock

Two things separate British alternative rock from its American counterpart. By and large, it's considerably more pop-oriented. Of course, there are some exceptions, particularly goth-rock and shoegazing, but most of the bands concentrate on singles as well as albums. Secondly, it acknowledges dance and club culture freely, with pop/rock groups frequently experimenting with dance rhythms and textures. Both of these factors are part of the reason why very few British alternative bands were successful in America between 1984-1995. The other major factor is a tendency to write about specifically British concerns. From the Smiths to Blur, the lyrics of many British groups are dense with British references. However, 1994 and 1995 showed that the success of American alternative rock had begun to break down the barriers in the U.S. for British bands, as Blur had a Top 60 hit, Oasis had a gold album, and Elastica had two charting hits, as well as a prime spot on Lollapalooza.

Like R.E.M. in the U.S., the Smiths functioned as the turning point between new wave and alternative rock. Hailing from Manchester, the group's layered guitar-pop recalled the Beatles and the Kinks, as well as various girl groups and less-celebrated '60s pop groups. Johnny Marr's innovative, ringing guitar riffs were offset by the literate, self-deprecating and viciously intelligent lyrics of Morrissey. In addition to his distinctive, clever lyrics, Morrissey's voice was unusual, alternating between mild crooning and abrupt yelps, particularly on the band's earlier records. Although the Smiths had only two Top Ten hits, the band's influence loomed large over the next decade, as various bands appropriated Marr's riffs and neo-'60s look. Morrissey's lyrical preoccupations became familiar as well, particularly his tales about English life. The Smiths' lifespan was quite short—their first album was released in 1984, their last in 1987—but no other British band since the Sex Pistols had as large of a musical impact as the Manchester quartet.

For the latter half of the '80s, British alternative pop/rock was dominated by the goth rock of the Cure, the dance-rock of New Order, and the noisy, neo-psychedelia of the Jesus and Mary Chain. The Cure had formed during the heyday of punk rock, yet their cult began to expand in 1983 and 1984, after which they had a series of best-selling albums and singles. Driven by slow tempos, droning guitars and keyboards, and Robert Smith's self-absorbed, morbid lyrics, the Cure appealed to some of the Smiths' audience, yet they were decidedly gloomier and less pop-oriented. Bands that copied the music of the Cure and Joy Division were quite popular in the late '80s, particularly Sisters of Mercy and Mission (UK).

Joy Division was arguably more important to goth rock than the Cure, but after the band's lead vocalist, Ian Curtis, committed suicide in 1980, the group moved in a different direction under the name New Order. Instead of relying on rock rhythms, New Order experimented with dance, disco, and club beats, creating a fusion between rock and dance which proved to be commercially successful and musically influential. Although not many bands immediately imitated the sound, it laid the groundwork for the Manchester scene of the early '90s.

Although they used a drum machine on their earliest recordings, the Jesus and Mary Chain were as far away from the dance textures of New Order as possible. Instead, the band unearthed the droning noise of the Velvet Underground, adding more distortion, tighter song structure, and floating harmonies. The Jesus and Mary Chain, along with the gargantuan guitar roar of America's Pixies and Sonic Youth, instigated a flood of bands in the '90s that relied on shatteringly loud guitars and ethereal, Beach Boys-derived harmonies.

During this time, a number of British acts found greater success in America than they did at home. While artists like the Cure and the Smiths were popular in both countries, certain musicians were virtually ignored in the U.K. but thrived on American college radio. Foremost among these groups was XTC. Although the group had hits when they first appeared at the height of punk and new wave, they failed to have more than one hit between 1984 and 1989. Nevertheless, the band's late-'80s albums of lush, psychedelic pop found a home in the American alternative scene, particularly 1987's *Skylarking*. Like XTC, Robyn Hitchcock was a new wave survivor, although his former group the Soft Boys were never anywhere near as popular as XTC. However, the Soft Boys' tough, ringing guitar-pop had an influence on many alternative bands of the '80s, particularly R.E.M. Once Hitchcock went solo, he gained a cult following in his native England and America, but had considerably more success in the U.S., thanks to support from college radio. His 1988 major-label debut, *Globe of Frogs*, marked the peak of his popularity, spending 15 weeks on the American charts. In addition to the off-center pop of XTC and Robyn Hitchcock, there were guitar bands that refined the jangling, multi-layered pop of the Smiths, making it smoother, more laidback and sophisticated. These bands, particularly the Housemartins, managed to sustain popularity on the British charts as well as American college radio.

However, the most significant British band of the late '80s and early '90s was the Stone Roses. Like their fellow Mancunians the Smiths, the Stone Roses specialized in an updated version of '60s guitar-pop. Unlike the Smiths, the Stone Roses were in debt to neo-psychedelic guitar-pop and experimented with club textures, particularly on the singles "Fool's Gold" and "One Love." But the key to the band's success was guitarist John Squire, who crafted songs that sounded like forgotten classics but were driven by an urgent energy and cocksure arrogance. The success of the Stone Roses opened the gates for a flood of bands that reworked the same territory, like the Charlatans and Inspiral Carpets. Of these bands, the Happy Mondays—who were also based in Manchester, giving way to the nickname "Madchester" for the entire pseudo-psychedelic dance scene—were the most noteworthy. Where the Stone Roses only flirted with dance music, the Happy Mondays immersed themselves in it, particularly the funky rhythms and psychedelic drugs like Ecstasy. Shaun Ryder, the band's lead vocalist, wrote lyrics that were cryptically surreal and melodies that appropriated hooks from other pop songs (the Mondays' "Kinky Afro" had the same melody as Labelle's "Lady Marmalade").

At the beginning of the '90s, it appeared as if the Stone Roses and Happy Mondays would be the leading figures in British pop music for the next few years. However, the Madchester scene quickly collapsed. The Stone Roses became embroiled in a debilitating lawsuit with their record company which took two years to resolve; after the case was settled, they took another three years to deliver a follow-up album, ruining any chances of world domination. The Happy Mondays ran out of steam quickly, mainly due to Ryder's drug addictions. Within a year, British alternative rock was robbed of its two most popular bands, leaving the legions of the Jesus and Mary Chain imitators to come to the forefront. Well, initially they were imitators of the Jesus and Mary Chain. However, by the time the so-called "shoegazers"—so dubbed by the British music press for their tendency to do nothing but stare at the floor during concerts—came to popularity in 1991, they were mining the territory My Bloody Valentine established in the late '80s.

My Bloody Valentine formed before the Jesus and Mary Chain, but their records didn't gain attention until 1987, when they released a series of EPs, culminating in 1988's album *Isn't Anything*. MBV's music was louder and more ethereal than JMC's records, creating shimmering soundscapes constructed from dissonance, distortion and detached vocals. Soon, the band's influence eclipsed that of the Jesus and Mary Chain, with numerous bands forming in its wake, including Ride, Lush and the Boo Radleys. Out of all the shoegazing records released in 1991, My Bloody Valentine's *Loveless* was the one that defined the entire scene.

Apart from shoegazing, the other major British musical development of 1991 was the release of Primal Scream's third album, *Screamadelica*. Compared to *Screamadelica*, the dance-oriented music of the Happy Mondays was positively tentative. Primal Scream employed a number of dance and techno producers, particularly Andrew Weatherall, to help them create their album. The group's basic compositions were clearly rock songs—the single "Movin' On Up" recalled both the Rolling Stones and Stephen Stills' "Love the One You're With"—but the producers took the songs into new territory with the inclusion of dance-club production techniques. The result was one of the most critically acclaimed albums of the year, as well as a commercial hit. More importantly, *Screamadelica* helped open the doors for techno and club music to be discussed seriously in the British music press, which helped the careers of such techno and ambient musicians like the Orb and the Aphex Twin, as well as dance-oriented bands like Massive Attack, Portishead, and Tricky.

However, neither Primal Scream nor the legions of shoegazers provided as much good copy as the Stone Roses and Happy Mondays, which is crucial for an industry with weekly music newspapers. For all of 1991 and most of 1992, the two trends dominated British alternative rock, as well as the presence of American groups like Nirvana and Pearl Jam. The arrival of Suede in late 1992 kick-started a revival of British guitar-pop that reached a fruition two years later. Under the leadership of vocalist Brett Anderson and guitarist Bernard Butler, Suede created a pop-savvy fusion of glam-rock and the Smiths' guitar-pop. The band was praised by the music weeklies as the "Best Band in Britain" before their first single was even released, and Morrissey began covering "My Insatiable One" in concert, setting the stage for enormous expectations. By and large, Suede fulfilled the expectations, as they had a series of hit singles that all charted higher than the first, and their 1993 self-titled debut became the fastest-selling record in British history. The band single-handedly knocked the shoegazers off the front cover of *Melody Maker* and *NME*, setting the stage for British alternative rock's breakthrough into the mainstream in 1994.

Suede may have become British stars in 1993, but they couldn't find a niche in America. During 1994, the band's star began to fade, as Butler left the group before the completion of their second album. That alone wouldn't have been enough to dim their stardom, but the band had created a monster with their debut album that soon outgrew the band itself. Over the course of 1994, no less than three bands emerged as massively popular artists, both commercially and critically. Of these bands, Blur was the first and most successful.

Blur had originally emerged during the height of shoegazing in 1991 with *Leisure*, a record that combined strands of shoegazing with the Madchester craze. Initially, they were popular, but they quickly fell out of favor. The group returned in 1993 with *Modern Life Is Rubbish*, a record that recalled the glory days of British pop, featuring elements of the Kinks, Small Faces, the Jam, and Madness. It was a moderate success, but its performance did nothing to indicate the magnitude of Blur's 1994 breakthrough with *Parklife*. Although it was as fiercely British as its predecessor, *Parklife* was more focused and featured stronger songs, several of which added elements of '80s synth-pop and new wave. "Girls and Boys," the album's opening dance-pop number, entered the charts at number five upon its release in the spring of 1994, opening the doors for a year where British alternative rock became the dominating musical force in the country. By the end of the year, *Parklife* had gone triple platinum in the U.K., establishing Blur as arguably the most popular band in the country.

As *Parklife* was beginning to take off in the spring of 1994, a new Manchester-based quintet called Oasis began receiving overwhelmingly positive reviews in the weeklies. By the end of the summer, Oasis had a genuine hit with "Live Forever," and their debut album, *Definitely Maybe*, had unseated *Suede* as the fastest-selling debut album in U.K. history. Oasis quickly became as popular as Blur, scoring a number one single in the spring of 1995 with "Some Might Say"; by summer 1995, *Definitely Maybe* had gone triple platinum. In addition to Oasis and Blur, a flood of independent and alternative bands began ruling the British pop charts. The spiky new wave revivalism of Elastica, the elegantly wasted synth-pop of Pulp, the youthful exuberance of Supergrass, the streamlined Smiths guitar-pop of Gene, the Boo Radleys, and Shaun Ryder's new band, Black Grape, all enjoyed Top Ten hits on the pop charts, including several number ones. It was the equivalent of Nirvana's American breakthrough, as nearly every one of Britain's most popular bands had its roots in the alternative pop/rock scene of the past decade.

16 Essential Records:
The Smiths, *Singles*
The Smiths, *The Queen Is Dead*
The Cure, *Staring at the Sea*
The Jesus and Mary Chain, *Psychocandy*
New Order, *Substance*
XTC, *Skylarking*
Robyn Hitchcock, *Globe of Frogs*
The Housemartins, *London 0 Hull 4*
The Stone Roses, *The Stone Roses*
The La's, *The La's*
Happy Mondays, *Pills 'n' Thrills & Bellyaches*
My Bloody Valentine, *Loveless*
Primal Scream, *Screamadelica*
Suede, *Suede*
Blur, *Parklife*
Oasis, *Definitely Maybe*

—Stephen Thomas Erlewine

Rap

The most popular and influential form of African-American pop music of the 1980s and 1990s, rap is also one of the most controversial styles of the rock era. And not just among the guardians of cultural taste and purity that have always been counted among rock & roll's chief enemies—Black, White, rock, and soul audiences continue to fiercely debate the musical and social merits of rap, whose most radical innovations subverted many of the musical and cultural tenets upon which rock was built.

Antecedents of rap are easy to find in rock and other kinds of music. Music is often used to tell a story, often with spoken rhymes over instruments and rhythms. Talking blues, spoken passages of sanctified prose in gospel, and numerous hits that call out slogans and rhymes, from Bo Diddley's "Say Man" to Shirley Ellis' *The Name Game* to Jerry Reed's *"When You're Hot, You're Hot"*—you can find pre-raps in material by performers as diverse as Lou Reed, the Shangri-Las, and the Jimmy Castor Bunch, if you want to stretch it.

More direct paths leading to rap, though, can be found in a few of the trends of the late '60s and '70s. In R&B music, funk and disco stripped soul down to its most basic rhythms, foregoing much of the instrumentation and vocals habitually used as embellishments. James Brown in particular is often cited as a forefather in his use of stream-of-consciousness raps over elemental funk backup, and he (and some other funk giants) have been sampled by modern-day rappers on innumerable occasions.

Two much more overlooked influences originated from outside of the R&B and rock mainstream. The Last Poets, Gil Scott-Heron, and Jayne Cortez set highly politicized tales of African-American and urban life against percussive jazz tracks in the early '70s. In reggae, the use of DJs, or "toasters," to rap over basic instrumental backing tracks when they took their mobile sound systems to dances became widespread. New York City, particularly Brooklyn and (more importantly in terms of rap's birth) the Bronx, was home to a large Jamaican community. Jamaican DJs (DJ Kool Herc has been credited as the first) mixed sounds from several turntables, a device which would become one of rap's trademarks.

Although mixing from large sound systems began to be employed at New York house parties in the 1970s, it didn't really emerge as a recorded sound until the Sugarhill Gang's "Rapper's Delight" in 1979. While many critics and listeners shrugged the song aside as a fluke novelty hit, the early rap sound—usually composed of slangy, boastful spoken rhymes over basic bass and percussion grooves—continued to spread in the early '80s, due in large part to the efforts of the Sugarhill label itself. Grandmaster Flash's hard-hitting 1982 single, "The Message," really stands as rap's watershed mark, with a massive impact belied by its relatively modest peak on the pop charts. No longer could rap be ignored as a frivolous micro-genre; here was straight-up social comment, reporting from the front lines of the ghetto with more immediacy than almost any newspaper or television broadcast.

From its inception, rap endured a lot of hostility from listeners—many, but not all, White—who found the music too harsh, monotonous, and lacking in traditional melodic values. However, millions of others—often, though not always, young African-Americans from underprivileged inner-city backgrounds—found an immediate connection with the style. Here was poetry of the street, directly reflecting and addressing the day-to-day reality of the ghetto in a confrontational fashion not found in any other music or media. What's more, you could dance to it, rhyme to it, bring it most anywhere on increasingly ubiquitous portable cassette players (dubbed "ghetto blasters"), and, in the best rock & roll tradition, form your own band without much in the way of formal training.

The basic workouts of early rappers like Kurtis Blow and the Fat Boys (eventually referred to as "old school" rap) can sound a bit tame today, although the productions of veterans like Afrika Bambaataa and Keith LeBlanc have lost none of their luster. Many were still expecting the music to peter out before Run-D.M.C. came along. Rap was, and to a large degree still is, a singles-oriented medium, but these Queens men proved that rappers could maintain interest and diversity over the course of entire full-length albums. Combining hard beats and innovative production with strong material that emphasized positive social activism without ignoring the cruel realities of urban life, they found as much favor with the critics as the street. Among the first rap groups to climb the pop

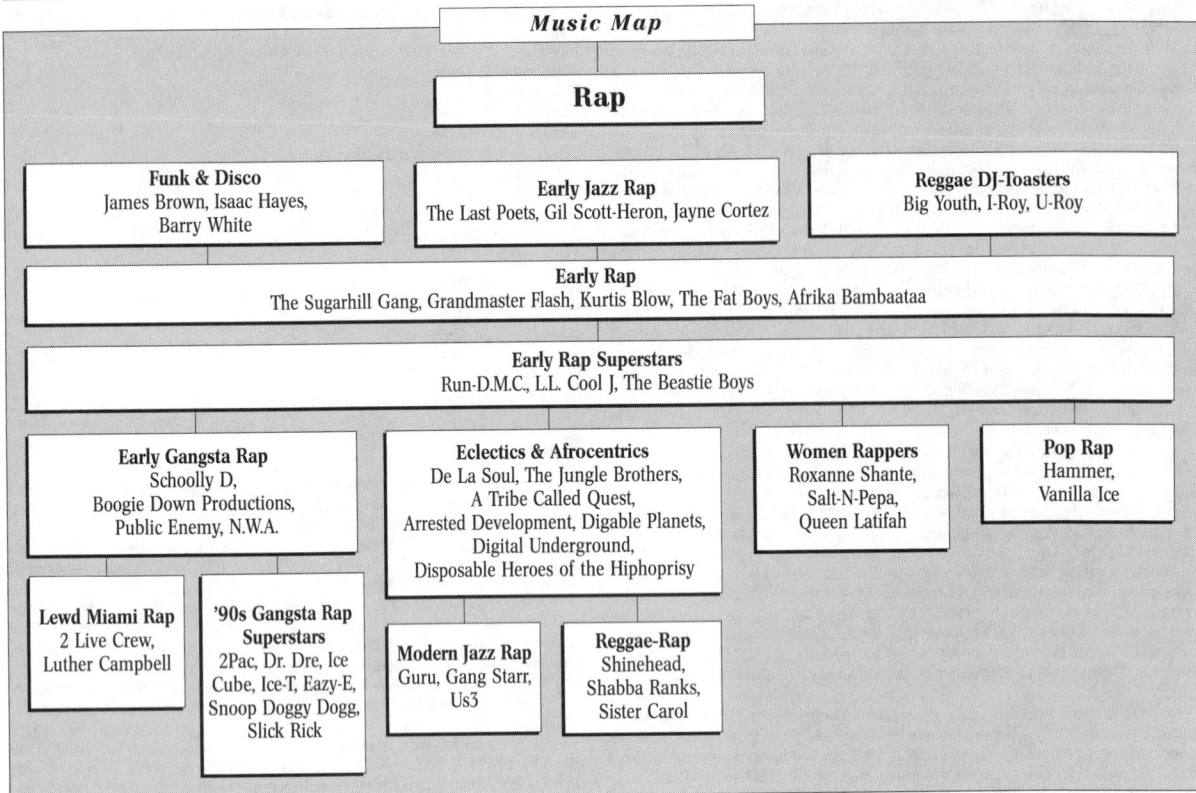

Music Map

Rap

Funk & Disco	Early Jazz Rap	Reggae DJ-Toasters
James Brown, Isaac Hayes, Barry White	The Last Poets, Gil Scott-Heron, Jayne Cortez	Big Youth, I-Roy, U-Roy

Early Rap
The Sugarhill Gang, Grandmaster Flash, Kurtis Blow, The Fat Boys, Afrika Bambaataa

Early Rap Superstars
Run-D.M.C., L.L. Cool J, The Beastie Boys

Early Gangsta Rap
Schoolly D,
Boogie Down Productions,
Public Enemy, N.W.A.

Eclectics & Afrocentrics
De La Soul, The Jungle Brothers,
A Tribe Called Quest,
Arrested Development, Digable Planets,
Digital Underground,
Disposable Heroes of the Hiphoprisy

Women Rappers
Roxanne Shante,
Salt-N-Pepa,
Queen Latifah

Pop Rap
Hammer,
Vanilla Ice

Lewd Miami Rap
2 Live Crew,
Luther Campbell

'90s Gangsta Rap Superstars
2Pac, Dr. Dre, Ice Cube, Ice-T, Eazy-E, Snoop Doggy Dogg, Slick Rick

Modern Jazz Rap
Guru, Gang Starr, Us3

Reggae-Rap
Shinehead,
Shabba Ranks,
Sister Carol

charts in a big way, they also were among the first to make big inroads into the White and Middle American audiences when they teamed up with Aerosmith's Steven Tyler and Joe Perry for the hit single "Walk This Way."

The mid- and late '80s saw rap continuing to explode in popularity, with the ascendancy of superstars like L.L. Cool J and Hammer (the latter of whom is often accused of providing a safe rap-pop alternative). Although most early rap productions originated in New York City and its environs, the music took hold as a national phenomenon, with strong scenes developing in other East Coast cities like Philadelphia, as well as West Coast strongholds in Los Angeles and Oakland. Production techniques became increasingly sophisticated; electronics, stop-on-a-dime editing, and—most importantly—sampling from previously recorded sources became prominent (although turntable mixing, along with the "scratching" produced by wiggling records back and forth, continued to be a strong ingredient). The increased emphasis on electronic beats led to the popularization of the term "hip-hop," a designation which is by now used more or less interchangeably with rap. The Beastie Boys, obnoxious white ex-punks from New York, brought rap further into the Middle American mainstream with their vastly popular hybrids of hip-hop, hard rock, and in-your-face braggadocio.

While rap had always forthrightly dealt with urban struggle, the late '80s saw the emergence of a more militant strain of the music. Sometimes dubbed "gangsta rap," the hotbed of this school was found in the disadvantaged neighborhoods of South Central Los Angeles, although performers like Philadelphia's Schoolly D proved that the genre was not specific to the area. Boogie Down Productions laid down a prototype that was taken to more extreme measures by N.W.A. (Niggaz with Attitude), who reported on the crime, sex, and violence of the ghetto with an explicit verve that some viewed as verging on celebration rather than journalism. Enormously controversial, and enormously popular with record buyers, several N.W.A. members went on to stardom as solo acts, including Ice Cube, Eazy-E, and Dr. Dre. Other boys from their 'hood also made their mark with inflammatory works, such as Ice-T and Snoop Doggy Dogg.

The most popular and controversial of the militant rappers, the New York-based Public Enemy, were perhaps the most political as well. Their brand of activism, like that of Malcolm X's two decades earlier, made a lot of people, including liberals, pretty uncomfortable, with their emphasis upon black nationalism and careless anti-Semitic, homophobic, and sexist references.

Groups such as Public Enemy ignited an ongoing debate in the media. Activist-oriented critics and audiences found a lot to praise in their music: powerful articulations against social and racial injustice, uncompromising portraits of realities that mainstream media shy away from, exhortations to the disadvantaged to empower themselves, and the sometimes overlooked fact that rap generated most of the few massive-selling independent releases produced outside of the corporate major-label machine. At the same time,

they could not let the xenophobic tendencies of these acts pass unnoticed, or ignore the frequent quasi-celebration in much rap music of misogyny, drugs, and violence, and the status to be gained in the urban community by the practice thereof. Many rap and rock & roll fans were also concerned parents, torn almost against their will between wanting to support the struggle against race and class oppression, and wanting to protect their children against possible identification with the violence- and obscenity-riddled content of the records themselves. Passionate advocates of civil liberties and free speech wondered, sometimes aloud, whether rappers were taking those privileges too far.

It's a conundrum that remains unresolved. The apolitical, over-the-top explicit sexual boasting of 2 Live Crew and the several acts propogated by the group's mastermind and label entrepreneur, Luther Campbell, seemed too comically overdrawn to really inspire serious controversy. Some government authorities felt otherwise, subjecting the Miami-based Campbell to serious legal pressure and harassment. First Amendment champions found themselves in the awkward position of defending his and other rappers' rights to spew content that they found morally reprehensible. Newly emerging gangsta rappers like Snoop Doggy Dogg and 2Pac not only take the violent subject matter of their lyrics to new extremes (and to the top of the charts), but have been accused of enacting their scenarios in real life, landing in jail for manslaughter or fighting similarly grave charges. These performers often unrepentantly contend they are only reporting things as they happen in the 'hood, of a culture that not only shoots people, but is being shot at. Many critics find their line between art and reality too thin, and are loath to see them spreading their gospel from the top of the charts (2Pac's 1995 album *Me Against the World* debuted at number one even as he was serving a prison sentence), or serve as role models for international youth.

Gangsta rap may have gotten a lot of the headlines in recent years, but the field of rap as a whole remains diverse, and not as dominated by the shoot-'em-out minidramas of gangsta rap as many would have you believe. De La Soul took rap and hip-hop productions to new heights with their 1989 debut *Three Feet High & Rising*, an almost psychedelic melange of sampling and editing of a wildly eclectic pool of sources that would do Frank Zappa proud. Their humorous and cheerful vibe inspired a mini-school of "Afrocentric" acts, the most notable of which were the Jungle Brothers and A Tribe Called Quest. Arrested Development, Digable Planets, and Digital Underground also pursued playful, heavily jazz- and funk-oriented paths to immense success and high critical praise. Rap is a highly macho (some would say sexist) environment, but some female performers arose to provide a much-needed counterpoint, from various perspectives: the saucy (the various Roxannes), the pop (Salt-N-Pepa), and the feminist (Queen Latifah).

It is a measure of rap's huge influence that the style has infiltrated mainstream soul and rock as well. Producer Teddy Riley gave urban-contemporary performers like Bobby Brown a vaguely hip edge with his brand of "New Jack Swing"; White alternative rockers like G. Love, Bobby Sichran, and most notably Beck devised a strange hybrid of rap, blues, and rock. Vanilla Ice proved that whitebread pop-rap could top the charts, though he was unable to sustain his success.

More than most genres, rap and hip-hop have become a culture with their own sub-genres and buzzwords, which can seem almost impenetrable to the novice. "Dope" and "fresh" beats, "old school," "new school," East Coast and West Coast tips, B-boys and fly-girls, Miami bass, phat bass, G-style funk—all are terms thrown around in rap magazines, differentiated by small gradations which can seem almost trivial to the outsider. Despite this proliferation of schools of production and performance, many rap records can appear virtually indistinguishable from each other to the novice listener. And there's no getting around the fact that a lot of them are—the market is saturated with repetitive beats and monotonously uncompromising slices of urban street life, to the point that they've lost a lot of both their musical novelty and shock value.

Rap music has lost none of its momentum or its capacity to inspire outrage in society as a whole. Scenes continue to proliferate, not just on the coasts, but in Atlanta, Houston, and such unlikely locales as Paris (home of leading French rapper MC Solaar). It may appeal more to inner-city adolescents than anyone else, but gangsta rap may be bigger than anything else in R&B music commercially, and there are more multi-platinum rap/hip-hop acts than you can shake a stick at, far too many than could be specifically cited in this brief essay. Shinehead, Shabba Ranks, and less-heralded performers like Sister Carol have fused reggae and rap. And the jazz and rap worlds are being brought closer together than ever through the efforts of Gang Starr and their leader Guru, Us3, and the landmark *Stolen Moments: Red, Hot + Cool* compilation, which united many of the top names of hip-hop and jazz.

21 Essential Rap Albums:
Various Artists, *Street Jams—Hip-Hop from the Top, Vol. 1-4* (Rhino)
Various Artists, *Street Jams—Electric Funk, Vol. 1-4* (Rhino)
Various Artists, *Hip-Hop Greats—Classic Raps* (Rhino)
Afrika Bambaataa, *Planet Rock* (Tommy Boy)
Run-D.M.C., *Together Forever: Greatest Hits* (Profile)
L.L. Cool J, *Radio* (Def Jam)
The Beastie Boys, *Licensed to Ill* (Def Jam)
Public Enemy, *It Takes a Nation Of Millions to Hold Us Back* (Def Jam)
Boogie Down Productions, *Criminal Minded* (Sugar Hill Rap)
N.W.A., *Straight Outta Compton* (Priority)
De La Soul, *Three Feet High & Rising* (Tommy Boy)
Queen Latifah, *All Hail the Queen* (Tommy Boy)
Shinehead, *Unity* (Elektra)
Digable Planets, *Reachin': A New Refutation.* (Pendulum)
Various Artists, *Stolen Moments: Red, Hot + Cool* (GRP)
Ice-T, *O.G. Original Gangster* (Sire)
Salt-N-Pepa, *Blacks' Magic* (London)
Digital Underground, *Sex Packets* (Tommy Boy)
Arrested Development, *Three Years, Five Months & Two Days in the Life Of...* (Chrysalis)
Guru, *Jazzmatazz, Vol. 1* (Chrysalis)
Dr. Dre, *The Chronic* (Priority)

—Jimmie James

Non-Rock Styles that Influenced Rock

Acoustic Blues

The blues is only one of the foundations of rock & roll music, but it may be the sturdiest and most central. Even in its earliest forms, it pointed toward rock & roll in its reliance upon guitar, piano, and percussion, its raw energy, and its classic chord patterns. Embellished with instruments, fuller arrangements, and electricity, it provided building blocks for jazz, R&B, and electric blues, from which it was just a few more steps to rock music. Rock itself has always looked back to the blues, both electric and acoustic, for inspiration and regeneration.

The history of the blues is a long, complicated, and often fascinating one, examined in detail in many scholarly treatises and college courses. It's beyond the scope of this brief overview, in which we'll just note its roots in African chants and rhythms, plantation work songs and field hollers, gospel, ragtime, and minstrel. Largely a Southern-based music, it had been around for decades, if not centuries, before it began to be widely recorded in the 1920s. Even then, there were several distinct schools of blues music.

The most popular were the early female blues vocalists, who were closely tied to jazz and even pop/vaudeville. Mamie Smith, Ma Rainey, Bessie Smith and Victoria Spivey were stars with a wide audience, one which was hardly confined to a rural base, enjoying great popularity in the cities. Not enormously influential on the course of R&B and rock, the singers were nonetheless greatly admired by Janis Joplin and Tracy Nelson (who recorded an entire album of Ma Rainey and Bessie Smith songs in her folkie days), which in turn influenced numerous rock performers who never heard the originals.

After its rediscovery by fanatics in the 1960s, the early blues acquired a romantic image as a musical reflection of suffering and hard times that was unrivaled in its authenticity. It comes as a surprise to some modern listeners to find that there were plenty of early blues performers that didn't conform to that stereotype. There were blues singers with strong shades of ragtime, vaudeville, and gospel. Many were entertainers, able indeed to perform hard-bitten tales of toil when the spirit moved them, but also able to sing all types of music, ranging from country to pop, when their audience required it. There were also quite a few jug bands, several in Memphis alone, frequently using fiddles, banjos, kazoos, and other instruments that hardly fit the blues stereotype.

Unquestionably, however, it was the Southern solo guitarists of the first generation of recorded bluesmen that cast the greatest shadow over rock, and held the greatest mystique for listeners that weren't around (or, usually, even born) when the blues first became available on record. Many of them came from the Mississippi Delta—Son House, Charley Patton, Bukka White, Fred McDowell, Skip James and, above all, Robert Johnson have all acquired mythic stature. There were also blues legends active throughout the South, especially Texas (Blind Lemon Jefferson), Atlanta (Blind Willie McTell), Memphis (Furry Lewis, Memphis Minnie), and Southeastern performers who came to be referred to as the Piedmont School (Blind Blake, Blind Boy Fuller).

Not all major blues artists were guitarists—there were also quite a few pianists in the barrelhouse and boogie styles, such as Peetie Wheatstraw, Cow Cow Davenport and a host of incredibly obscure names that usually only turn up on obscure import compilations. But the guitarists, understandably, were the source of greatest influence and fascination for subsequent generations of rock & rollers. The guitar, after all, is rock's premier instrument, and quite a few of the picking styles, riffs, and even songs can be traced directly back to rural blues. Rockers past and present have been equally enamored with its raw vocals and personal lyrics, a direct, personal, and supremely earthy expression of their joys and struggles.

Numerous examples could be used of old blues songs that have taken new lives as rock hits. A particularly colorful example is "Matchbox," originally performed by Blind Lemon Jefferson. The song, which may well have been traditional in origin, was spruced up into rockabilly in the mid-'50s by Carl Perkins (who claimed the writing credits); ten years later, it was transformed yet again into full-bore rock & roll by the Beatles who learned the song from the Perkins version, and may not have even been aware that Jefferson recorded it in the 1920s.

Acoustic blues records were quite popular with Black listeners when they first appeared, but the Depression meant that many of them—poor to begin with—couldn't afford any records at all. Hence many blues performers rarely recorded, or never got to record at all, during much of the 1930s and 1940s. When the blues became popular again, it was a new kind of blues, played with electric guitars and drums, in cities like Chicago and Memphis. Many of these performers, such as Muddy Waters, Elmore James and Johnny Shines had moved to the city from the Delta, where they had already perfected their craft as acoustic performers. They electrified as a matter of professional survival, and updated the classic rural blues sound as much as they changed it—you can hear strong echoes of the Delta in everything they did, down to the 12-bar structure that was established as the classic blues form.

Many of the original country blues performers were forgotten until the blues revival of the early 1960s. Not everyone went to the lengths of guitarist John Fahey who located Bukka White by writing a letter to "Bukka White, Old Blues Singer, c/o General Delivery, Aberdeen, Mississippi" (a town mentioned in one of his songs), but many blues singers, unknown and obscure even in their hometowns, were rediscovered and coaxed out of retirement by White enthusiasts. They found an entire new audience, mostly young and collegiate, waiting for them, and were often, as White was, able to tour and record internationally to considerable acclaim in their remaining years. Singers like Mississippi John Hurt, Skip James and Fred McDowell may have reached more listeners by touring the folk circuit in the '60s than they did during their prime.

The rediscovery and reappreciation of these early blues legends saw some major rock bands, who had already plundered electric blues for much of their inspiration, going back even further to the earlier acoustic blues. The Rolling Stones were the most successful; their late '60s and early '70s albums often tap into the Delta spirit without sounding like a slavish imitation or bad parody, both on original material like "Salt of the Earth" and covers of classics by Robert Wilkins, Robert Johnson and Fred McDowell, McDowell himself toured with Bonnie Raitt who has openly credited the bluesman as a major influence. Canned Heat updated a Henry Thomas panpipe number, "Bull Doze Blues," into the Top 20 single "Going up the Country." The Allman Brothers revived Blind Willie McTell's "Statesboro Blues." Cream recorded exciting electric versions of Skip James' "I'm So Glad" and Robert Johnson's "Crossroads." So it continues until today: Nirvana's posthumous *Unplugged* release included a version of Leadbelly's "Where Did You Sleep Last Night?"

Acoustic blues will always be an element of rock & roll, although not nearly as much as electric blues, both as an influence and as a source of cover material. Acoustic blues itself isn't recorded or performed much these days; it is the modern age, after all, and the great majority of blues performers are working in the electric format both out of choice and necessity. The surprise success of Robert Johnson's 1990 box set, which sold several hundred thousand copies in the days of synthesizers and 64-track production, proves that acoustic blues will always strike listeners with its power and passion, no matter what the era.

Despite its undisputed importance, the unseasoned listener is urged to ease her or his way into the classic blues repertoire. The primitive sound (on which the guitar and vocals sometimes appear to be in the process of being fried on the skillet), the limited melodic variation, and the harsh execution can disappoint those led by enthusiastic critics to expect an instantly transforming experience. Rather than jump into the legacy of legendarily challenging legends like Robert Pete Williams it might be best to start with more accessible collections, such as the ones listed below.

15 Recommended Recordings:

Various Artists, *Blues Masters, Vol. 10: Blues Roots* (Rhino). Just what it says, focusing on forms like prison songs, work songs, and native African music.

Various Artists, *Blues Masters, Vol. 11: Classic Blues Women* (Rhino). The early female blues stars: Bessie Smith, Mamie Smith, Sippie Wallace, Billie Holiday, Ma Rainey.

Various Artists, *Roots of Robert Johnson* (Yazoo). An interesting concept: the performances that can be seen, with hindsight, to have influenced Johnson by fellow Mississippi Delta bluesmen like Skip James, Charley Patton, Son House and Lonnie Johnson.

Various Artists, *Slide Guitar—Bottles Knives & Steel, Vol. 1 & 2* (CBS). The slide guitar is many people's favorite feature of early blues, and these collections have cuts by major practitioners like Bukka White, Tampa Red, Blind Willie Johnson and Leadbelly.

Skip James, *The Complete Early Recordings* (Yazoo). The most thorough collection of his 1930s sides, including the original version of "I'm So Glad."

Mississippi John Hurt, *1928 Sessions* (Yazoo). One of the finest fingerpicking early blues guitarists. For those who find remastered 78s tough listening, the Vanguard albums he recorded in the 1960s following his rediscovery are a recommended alternative.

Blind Willie McTell, *The Definitive Blind Willie McTell* (Columbia). Double disc of 1929-33 material by the versatile performer, an innovator of 12-string guitar playing.

Leadbelly, *King of the 12-String Guitar* (CBS). Through his popularization of "Goodnight, Irene," "Midnight Special," and others, Leadbelly's influence was also felt in the folk and pop worlds.

Memphis Minnie, *Hoodoo Lady (1933-37)* (CBS). Singer-guitarist roundly considered to be the greatest pre-World War II blueswoman.

Robert Johnson, *The Complete Recordings* (CBS). More may have been written and analyzed about this set of tracks than those found on any other blues collection.

Bukka White, *The Complete Bukka White* (Columbia). One of the most hard-bitten and starkly personal blues singers, these 1937 and 1940 sessions are considered to be his best work.

Muddy Waters, *The Complete Plantation Recordings* (MCA). Recorded for the Library of Congress in the early 1940s, when Muddy lived in Mississippi, and had yet to plug in an electric guitar. A fascinating link between the old and new guard, even if no one could have been aware at the time.

Mississippi Fred McDowell, *Mississippi Delta Blues* (Arhoolie). Although he was born shortly after 1900, this bottleneck slide guitarist wasn't discovered and recorded until 1959; these mid-'60s recordings are considered among his best.

J.B. Lenoir, *Down in Mississippi* (L&R, Germany). A second-division electric Chicago bluesman who recorded for Chess and other labels, Lenoir made a couple little-known European albums in the mid-'60s shortly before his death. These found him expanding the acoustic blues traditions in interesting ways, writing topical songs about contemporary issues like segregation and Vietnam, and using African-derived percussive rhythms. This is recommended above the similar *Alabama Blues* for its greater accessibility.

Ted Hawkins, *Happy Hour* (Rounder). A street performer on the Venice Beach boardwalk in Los Angeles for many years, Hawkins was one of the few acoustic blues musicians to achieve widespread recognition in the 1980s and 1990s, though his material and vocals actually owed as much to soul and R&B as straight blues. Hawkins released his first major label album at the age of 58, shortly before his death in 1995; this 1987 effort uses sparer instrumentation.

Recommended Reading:

Deep Blues, by Robert Palmer (1981, Viking Press)

The Blackwell Guide to Blues Records, edited by Paul Oliver (1989, Blackwell)

The Story of the Blues, by Paul Oliver (Chilton, 1970)

—Richie Unterberger

Gospel

Gospel music has rarely been a significant presence in the commercial mainstream, and indeed its fervent religious concerns will most likely always limit it to a specialized audience. Rock and pop fans often find pure gospel rough going, both due to its intensely spiritual focus and its melodic and compositional strictures. Yet even for those rock fans who never develop a passion for the form, it's worth appreciation as one of rock and soul's bedrock influences.

There are strong gospel traditions, reaching back through several centuries, in both the Black and White population of America. The Black tradition, a combination of indigenous African music with Western religious influences, found its expression in both "work songs" and the church, one of the few places where the Black community could openly express itself in the days of segregation. When black gospel traditions began to mix with the music of the secular world, the combinations that resulted were pivotal in the birth of R&B and soul.

The groaning, moaning, pleading, and supplicating qualities of gospel are easy to hear in the vocals of jump blues artists like Percy Mayfield, Roy Brown and Wynona Carr as well as early soul pioneers like Ray Charles, James Brown, Clyde McPhatter and Little Willie John even if they may be singing about raucous and romantic joys. Likewise, the harmonies and call-and-response interplay of the classic doo wop groups, from the Orioles through the early work of the Impressions, were refined in the chapel as well as on the street corner.

The connection between gospel and soul, however, is often far more direct. A few of soul's greatest singers, including Wilson Pickett and Little Johnny Taylor got their starts in gospel quartets. Taylor had been in the Soul Stirrers, also the breeding ground for Sam Cooke, the most famous singer to cross over to pop after establishing himself as a gospel star. Gospel fans were outraged when Cooke abandoned the circuit for pop stardom in the late '50s, but pop and rock fans were enriched immeasurably, as Cooke's work until his death in 1964 was immensely important in paving the road for modern soul music.

Notable female soul and pop singers who began as gospel vocalists include Dionne Warwick and Whitney Houston, whose mother Cissy directed the Sweet Inspirations, who sang backup vocals on some of Aretha Franklin's early hits. Franklin herself was the daughter of noted preacher and gospel singer C.L. Franklin, and recorded some gospel as a teenager. When she reached superstardom with a burst of soul smashes in 1967, listeners were responding to a voice letting loose the unbridled passion of gospel on contemporary pop-R&B. Franklin's vision is really too wide to be categorized as a gospel offshoot, but she has always remained cognizant of her roots, occasionally immersing herself in them, as on her acclaimed 1972 live album, *Amazing Grace*.

Other notable gospel-soul crossovers include the Chambers Brothers, who were one of the few Black groups to become favorites with the psychedelic crowd; the Edwin Hawkins Singers, who landed a surprise Top Five hit in 1969 with "Oh Happy Day"; and the Staple Singers, whose Memphis soul-gospel approach yielded some of the most inspirational hits of the early '70s. Also from Memphis is Al Green, the most famous singer to travel in the reverse direction, abandoning pop superstardom for gospel. The music world was shocked when Green embraced gospel in the late '70s after a reign of five years or so as soul's most popular performer, and though he's largely a memory for the masses, he's been very active in the studio and as a performer in the gospel world.

In the world of White rock & roll, gospel has been a less prominent but nevertheless important influence. The church was a focal point of White Southern rural culture, and often offered the easiest place to sing and play music, as it did in the early African-American community. Most of the first White rock & rollers were Southern, and they were also schooled in gospel harmonies and spiritual standards. Many early country acts, like the Carter Family, Bill Monroe and Tennessee Ernie Ford, took a large part of their repertoire from gospel. The close harmonies of acts like the Delmore Brothers often derived from, and were sometimes actually used on, sacred songs, in turn influencing early rock & rollers who didn't actually perform gospel, the Everly Brothers being the most famous example.

Many early rockabilly stars may have been set on raising hell onstage and in the studio, but gospel was a big part of their background, even in the most unlikely of cases—Jerry Lee Lewis, for instance, is Jimmy Swaggart's cousin, and can be heard debating spiritual matters with Sam Phillips on a famous outtake from Sun Studios. When Lewis, Elvis Presley, Carl Perkins and others gathered in the same studio in 1956 for the famous *Million Dollar Quartet* session, they jammed on the songs they all shared and knew by heart—many of which, to the surprise of some latter-day listeners, were gospel tunes. Elvis counted gospel groups like the Statesmen and the Blackwood Brothers among his biggest influences, and employed a gospel group, the Jordanaires, to harmonize and sing backing vocals on most of his biggest hits. He also recorded a good deal of straight gospel himself, from 1957 on through to the 1970s.

Rock stars without direct gospel influences have occasionally called on gospel singers to record appropriate embellishments to particular recordings; Paul Simon was never one to let a good ethnic flavor pass unnoticed, and his use of the Dixie Hummingbirds on the 1973 hit "Loves Me Like a Rock" is one of the most famous examples. Occasionally, rockers have embraced religion long after establishing themselves as secular pop stars, recording gospel-influenced albums that have by and large not been well received, Bob Dylan being the most famous of these. Dylan was outraged at the audience for, as he saw it, dismissing his music because of its religious values; this may have been partly true, but the audiences were also turning a cold shoulder to the records because spiritual music was not his strongest suit, and because they didn't enjoy being hammered over the head with a message, fundamentalist or otherwise. When Violent Femmes leader Gordon Gano recorded a gospel album with his side group the Mercy Seat, the reaction was not so much hostility as indifference, partly because Gano wasn't nearly as mythological a figure as Dylan.

In contemporary music, gospel usually isn't a visible factor, not because its influence is negligible, but because it permeated the rock and soul mainstream so deeply that it's become permanently absorbed into its structure. It continues to permeate urban contemporary R&B in the smooth harmonies and lead vocals, even if the singers are no longer as directly steeped in the church as they were in the 1950s and 1960s. And there are still instances of singers moving from spiritual music to secular pop/rock, as Amy Grant has done on a superstar level, and singer/songwriter Sam Phillips has done as a cult alternative rock favorite.

12 Recommended Recordings:

Various Artists, *Jubilation Vol. 1-3* (Rhino). Anthologies of classic gospel. The first two volumes cover black artists like the Soul Stirrers, the Swan Silvertones, Aretha Franklin, Mahalia Jackson, the Staple Singers, and the Five Blind Boys; the third focuses on white country gospel, with sides by the Carter Family, the Louvin Brothers, Kitty Wells, George Jones and Tammy Wynette, Bill Monroe, Johnny Cash and Hank Williams.

The Soul Stirrers, *The Gospel Soul of Sam Cooke, Vol. 2* (Specialty). An entire disc of Cooke's sides with the gospel group during the first half of the 1950s. Other Soul Stirrers discs, if you want to go further, include performances by Johnnie Taylor and other noteworthy singers who took the leads when Cooke wasn't in the group.

Various Artists, *Something Got a Hold of Me* (RCA). Classic country gospel by the Carter Family, Bill Monroe, the Blue Sky Boys, Uncle Dave Macon and other less celebrated acts.

Elvis Presley, *The Million Dollar Quartet* (RCA). Actually Elvis, Carl Perkins and Jerry Lee Lewis plus a few other musicians (Johnny Cash was present for the photo but not for the recording, apparently), jamming on rock, R&B, and not a little gospel. The double-CD *Amazing Grace* is the most wide-ranging compilation of Presley's gospel recordings, but will have considerably less appeal for the rock fan.

Mahalia Jackson, *Gospels, Spirituals & Hymns* (CBS). Often rated as the best gospel singer of all.

Various Artists, *Sam Cooke's SAR Records Story 1959-1965* (ABKCO). Cooke acted as label owner and frequent producer and songwriter for SAR, recording gospel, soul, and combinations of the two by performers like the Womack Brothers, Johnnie Taylor, and the Valentinos.

The Chambers Brothers, *Time Has Come: the Best of the Chambers Brothers* (Columbia). An erratic group whose funk and psychedelic excesses never hid their gospel roots.

The Staple Singers, *Greatest Hits* (Fantasy). A compilation of early-'60s material that gives listeners a sampling of their gospel roots as it was being tempered by contemporary influences. No Staple Singers collection surveys their entire career, which stretches across several decades; try Vee Jay compilations for their earliest and purest gospel material, and *The Best of the Staple Singers* (on Stax) for their soul hits.

Aretha Franklin, *Amazing Grace* (Atlantic). Her 1972 gospel album, also featuring James Cleveland and the Southern California Community Choir.

The Dixie Hummingbirds, *Live* (MCA). A 75-minute live set from the mid-'70s.

Al Green, *The Belle Album* (Hi). His last album (from 1977) before his conversion to full-time gospel, catching him bridging secular soul music with personal spiritual concerns.

Sweet Honey in the Rock, *Live at Carnegie Hall* (Flying Fish). Not purely a gospel group, though heavily gospel-influenced, this all-woman African-American a cappella group is proof that music can both draw on gospel traditions and comment on contemporary political, social, and personal concerns. Active since the mid-'70s, with various lineups under the leadership of Bernice Reagon, this is a 1988 concert recording.

—Richie Unterberger

Electric Blues

Of all the many forms of music that contributed to the birth of rock & roll, electric blues has arguably exerted the most fundamental and durable influence. It's not just that electric blues helped establish the prototype of the basic rock lineup—electric guitars and a rhythm section—and that much early rock & roll, from both America and Great Britain, was an embellishment of electric blues with somewhat different rhythms and song construction. It's also that electric blues, in sound, spirit, and execution, is separated from rock & roll by only the thinnest of boundaries. It's rare indeed to find a rock & roll fan who doesn't have the same visceral response to electric blues, even though the music isn't nearly as dominant a presence in the media and the marketplace.

The blues started to become electrified shortly before World War II, as a direct result of major shifts in the lives of millions of African-Americans. Masses of Black migration from rural areas to urban factories, in search of better employment opportunities and living conditions, resulted in a swelling of the Black communities in America's inner cities. A great many of these blacks came from the South, settling in metropolises like Chicago, St. Louis, Detroit, and Los Angeles. They brought their musical tastes with them, but rural blues had to be adapted to city life to survive. The pace of urban life was faster, the performance venues larger and more lively. To cut through the noise of the crowds, electric instruments and drums were a necessity.

It's unclear exactly who the first electric blues guitarist was, but most likely bluesmen began to try amplified instruments in the late '30s; there have even been rumors that Robert Johnson was playing electric guitar with a band shortly before his death in 1938. Early electric jazz guitar pioneers Eddie Durham and, especially, Charlie Christian mapped out the single-string solo style that early electric blues guitarists would build upon. Guitarist T-Bone Walker, a Texan who relocated to Los Angeles, is almost universally credited as the first electric blues master. Starting around 1940, he combined electric blues with elements of R&B and jazz, enjoying a prolific career that stretched over several decades.

What most people think of as the classic electric blues sound, however, developed in Chicago shortly after World War II. Many of the great Chicago blues musicians had relocated from the Mississippi Delta, long a fountain of great blues performers, and indeed many of the new arrivals had already perfected their craft on acoustic instruments. A brasher, faster electric style was required for professional survival in the Windy City. By the 1950s, Chicago electric blues was thriving, in a small combo format established by bandleaders like Muddy Waters.

Waters was not the first notable electric blues musician in Chicago; John Lee Williamson (the first "Sonny Boy" Williamson), Johnny Shines and a few others had already used amplification by the time he arrived in the city in 1943. Waters himself was already a blues performer of some note, recording acoustic sessions for the Library of Congress in the early '40s at the Mississippi plantation where he worked. He knew he needed to adapt, though, and assembled a powerhouse band that would, at various points, feature performers who were stars in their own right, including Little Walter, Jimmy Rogers, Otis Spann, Junior Wells and James Cotton. Driven by compelling riffs on guitar and harmonica, a forceful rhythm section, and strong original material that derived from and updated the classic Delta blues Waters had already mastered, his band was the prototype for Chicago electric blues.

Waters recorded for Chess Records, which quickly became the city's most successful blues and R&B label, with a roster including Little Walter, Howlin' Wolf, Sonny Boy Williamson, and Jimmy Rogers, as well as (for brief periods) Elmore James, John Lee Hooker, Otis Rush and many interesting minor performers. The Chess sound, spare, clear, and reverberant, did a lot in its own right to refine and solidify the music without sacrificing its raw power. A lot of the credit for Chess' success belongs to arranger, bassist, songwriter, and occasional performer Willie Dixon, who perhaps wrote more classic blues songs than any other songwriter.

A lot of classic Chicago blues from this era was recorded on other labels by greats like Rush, James, Billy Boy Arnold and Jimmy Reed. And while Chicago had by far the greatest concentration of talent, the blues became electrified in similar patterns in other cities. Memphis had Howlin' Wolf before he moved to Chicago, as well as B.B. King, Ike Turner and Junior Parker; before he moved into rockabilly, Sam Phillips of Sun Records was often responsible for recording the best Memphis blues musicians. Detroit had John Lee Hooker, the king of boogie; Guitar Slim and Slim Harpo recorded swamp blues in Louisiana; and there were strong scenes in Houston, St. Louis, and California.

Blues didn't only adapt the classic 12-bar, three-chord pattern when it became electrified; it also combined with jazz, pop, and gospel to feed into rhythm & blues, in the form of jump blues "shouters" like Big Joe Turner, Tiny Bradshaw, Ruth Brown and Jimmy Witherspoon. R&B, of course, eventually fed into rock & roll and early soul pioneers like Ray Charles, James Brown and Little Willie John, all of whom were strongly influenced by the blues. Bobby "Blue" Bland was the most prominent vocalist who borrowed in fairly equal measures from blues, R&B, and soul. Guitarists like Chuck Berry and Bo Diddley took the electric blues foundation and pioneered rock & roll by adding R&B, jump blues, and pop elements. And ironically (more so considering that Berry and Diddley actually recorded for Chess), rock & roll cut deeply into the blues audience by the end of the 1950s, and electric blues, a huge commercial success on the R&B charts in the early and mid-'50s, was relegated to a small corner of the record-buying public once again.

Electric blues still thrived in the local clubs, and came roaring back into the public consciousness again in the mid-'60s, as British Invasion bands like the Rolling Stones and Yardbirds popularized electric blues classics for the mass audience, and folk festivals and European tours introduced living legends like Waters to White listeners who would never have come across the music otherwise. Some of the best electric blues dates from this decade, when some greats leavened their sound with contemporary R&B and soul influences without removing their blues foundations. Junior Wells, Magic Sam, Buddy Guy and Albert King recorded their best work in this era; B.B. King even crossed over to the pop charts, a feat that has remained rare for electric blues of all kinds.

It's the Chicago sound of the 1950s that remains the most influential form of electric blues on rock. Jazzed up with faster tempos and more flexible melodies, it was a primary foundation for a great deal of early rockabilly and rock & roll. Many British bands, and a few American ones, built their early chops by covering classics from this time, and built their original material around blues riffs (see separate sidebar on blues-rock). Hundreds of classic songs from this era, by Dixon, Waters, James, Reed and many others, remain at the heart of the rock & roll repertoire.

Blues has not been a significant commercial presence in the past few decades, but continues to thrive, albeit fitfully, on a local level, and via a worldwide network of enthusiasts, festivals, and independent labels. A lot of the Chicago legends are very much alive and active, joined by younger masters like Son Seals and Robert Cray, the latter of whom proved that blues could still sell to the masses on his albums of the late '80s and '90s. Electric blues is a huge and diverse field, with literally hundreds of noteworthy performers. The list below is not meant to be a definitive distillation of the cream of the crop—there are entire books devoted to that purpose—but some top-notch ports of entry.

20 Recommended Albums:

Various Artists, *Blues Masters, Vol. 1-15* (Rhino). The most comprehensive introductory history to all forms of electric and acoustic blues, including special volumes for Memphis, Texas, Chicago, urban, and jump blues. *Volume 6, Blues Originals*, illustrates the connection between blues and rock most vividly, with original versions of blues classics made popular by rock performers.

T-Bone Walker, *The Complete Imperial Recordings* (EMI America). A double CD of early-'50s sides; a more wide-ranging, but more expensive and hard-to-find compilation, is the six-CD set *The Complete T-Bone Walker Recordings*.

Muddy Waters, *The Best of Muddy Waters* (Chess). The best single-CD collection; to dip deeper into his huge repertoire, try the three-CD *Chess Box*.

Little Walter, *The Essential Little Walter* (MCA). Double CD of the greatest and most influential blues harmonica player of all time.

Howlin' Wolf, *Howlin' Wolf/Moanin' in the Moonlight* (MCA). This combination of Wolf's first and second albums on one CD is chock full of blues classics that would later became rock & roll staples, including "Little Red Rooster," "Wang Wang Doodle," "Spoonful," and "Back Door Man." Those with a deeper interest and bigger budget should go for the three-CD *Chess Box*.

Elmore James, *The Sky Is Crying* (Rhino). The best single-disc CD of the best blues slide guitarist. This prolific artist has several good compilations available; this is the most wide-ranging, and hence a recommended starting point.

John Lee Hooker, *The Ultimate Collection (1948-90)* (Rhino). The singer whose low, booming voice and stomping rhythms defined electric blues boogie has recorded a staggering quantity of material; this double disc is not so much the best as the most wide-ranging.

Jimmy Reed, *Speak the Lyrics to Me, Mama Reed* (Vee Jay). 25 tracks on a single disc of the singer whose lazy, shuffling blues-R&B yielded several blues-rock classics, including "Big Boss Man," "Baby What You Want Me to Do?," and "Bright Lights, Big City."

Sonny Boy Williamson, *Essential Sonny Boy Williamson* (MCA). Probably the least famous and striking of the four Chess blues superstars (Waters, Little Walter, and Howlin' Wolf were the others), but an outstanding harmonica player and songwriter.

Various Artists, *A Sun Blues Collection* (Rhino). Important early and mid-'50s Memphis blues sides by Howlin' Wolf, Rufus Thomas, Little Milton, James Cotton, Junior Parker, B.B. King, and others.

Otis Rush, *Cobra Recordings, 1956-58* (Flyright). Minor-key blues with a gospel moan and chilling, stinging guitar runs.

Slim Harpo, *The Best of Slim Harpo* (Rhino). The best swamp-bluesman, influential on the Rolling Stones, Kinks and Yardbirds including his Top 40 hits "Baby, Scratch My Back" and "Rainin' in My Heart," as well as the original versions of "I'm a King Bee" and "Got Love If You Want It."

B.B. King, *Live at the Regal* (MCA). This 1965 album is almost universally regarded as the best live blues recording. The four-CD box set *King of the Blues* is the most comprehensive anthology of this major blues legend.

Bobby "Blue" Bland, *I Pity the Fool* (MCA). Double-CD compilation of the most respected performer to bridge blues with soul and R&B.

Junior Wells, *Hoodoo Man Blues* (Delmark). One of the greatest blues albums, enlivened by soul, R&B, and Latin influences, this enthralling 1965 session also features Buddy Guy on guitar.

Magic Sam, *West Side Soul* (Delmark). The best album by a bluesman who was just reaching his peak when he died at the end of the 1960s.

Koko Taylor, *What It Takes—The Chess Years* (Chess). The best of the early sides by the premier modern female blues singer.

Albert King, *Ultimate Collection* (Rhino). Double CD of the great soul-influenced bluesman, a big influence on Eric Clapton among others.

Son Seals, *The Son Seals Blues Band* (Alligator). A fiery guitarist, Seals is the most respected Chicago bluesman to achieve national recognition after the 1960s.

Robert Cray, *Strong Persuader* (Mercury). The 1986 album that brought blues back to the commercial spotlight, adding modern rock influences to the classic electric blues prototype.

Recommended Reading:

Deep Blues, by Robert Palmer (1981, Viking Press)

I Am the Blues, by Willie Dixon with Don Snowden (1989, Da Capo)

The Blackwell Guide to Blues Records, edited by Paul Oliver (1989, Blackwell)

—Richie Unterberger

American Folk

American folk music, like most everything else American, is not so much an indigenous sound as it is a melting pot of traditional forms and songs from Europe (especially the British Isles) and Africa, honed in the U.S., especially in the South, since the 17th century. Usually (but not exclusively) played on acoustic string instruments, the folk repertoire passed from generation to generation, influencing the birth of rock & roll less directly than blues, country, gospel, and jazz, although it was part of the collective consciousness of all American musicians. Folk's revival after the second World War, culminating in an all-out boom in the early '60s, was safeguarded from commercial corruption by zealous traditionalists, who insisted on reverent interpretation and acoustic instruments. For a while, that is; by the mid-'60s, it would alter the course of rock and pop in ways that no one foresaw just a few short years earlier.

In the early days of the record business, traditional folk music was a small corner of the market indeed. Certainly the early acoustic blues musicians, and country stars such as Jimmie Rodgers and the Carter Family owed a great deal to folk music, although they weren't classified and marketed as such. The folk that was recorded was often being preserved for historical, scholarly purposes (as with the extensive Library of Congress catalog), or commercialized almost beyond recognition, or geared toward extremely specialized audiences (as with early Yiddish and Klezmer recordings directed toward the Jewish immigrant community).

Woody Guthrie more than any other performer, was responsible for linking traditional American folk forms to concerns of the present day. Although he often drew upon classic folk melodies, he was the first major folksinger to develop an extensive repertoire of original material that drew upon his personal experiences and commented directly on contemporary life and social conditions. Contemporaries like Cisco Houston and Oscar Brand also followed this model, but Guthrie who recorded hundreds of sides in the 1940s and early 1950s, was by far the most influential, on both slightly younger performers like Pete Seeger and Jack Elliott and singers of the next generation, especially Bob Dylan.

In the late 1940s, the Weavers a harmonizing folk group featuring Pete Seeger brought folk to the masses. Although hugely successful—their 1950 #1 hit "Goodnight Irene" topped the charts for 13 weeks—their left-leaning politics did not escape the attention of certain government authorities in the Communist-fearing early '50s, and their career was prematurely snuffed by blacklists. In the latter half of the decade, the Weavers resumed activity and, along with other veteran performers and newly emerging interpreters of traditional material like Joan Baez (who was instrumental in exposing Bob Dylan to a wide audience), Dave Van Ronk, and Judy Collins spearheaded a folk revival.

The folk music that was actually on the charts, however, was usually a highly commercial, watered-down variant of traditional sounds and material. The Kingston Trio, Harry Belafonte, the Rooftop Singers, and the Limeliters were the most popular of these, and they deserve some credit for at least making many Americans aware of folk music in the first place, although they should in no way be taken as its most authentic ambassadors. Other performers, like Bob Gibson and more particularly Peter, Paul & Mary, combined commercial appeal with more passion and material that ran closer to the motherlode of traditional folk.

Small independent labels, chiefly Elektra, Vanguard, and Folkways, did their part to record the era's most earnest interpreters. The audience for these more "authentic" sounds was usually found on campuses and cities with large intellectual, politically progressive populations, like Boston, Berkeley, and New York, where the scene was centered in Greenwich Village. Large festivals, like the ones staged at Newport, were important showcases for the era's best talent. And so the music might have stayed for some time—a popular, if minority, taste, nurtured by a large alternative community—if not for a new generation of performers intent on combining folk with contemporary musical and social influences.

Chief among these was Bob Dylan who was inspired to become a folk performer after becoming enamored of Woody Guthrie. Dylan assimilated a wide variety of American traditional folk music as well as anyone of his time, as he demonstrated on his debut album (consisting mostly of folk standards) and the astonishingly extensive repertoire of trad material that he ran through, and to a large extent continues to run through, in live performances and on oodles of bootlegs. His second LP, *Freewheelin' Bob Dylan* (1962), was his true groundbreaker, consisting mostly of original material that commented specifically on contemporary political issues and the feelings of his generation.

Dylan was initially embraced as a savior by the folk community, who howled in protest when he quickly moved away from protest material to personal, romantic tunes and surrealistic poems. The howls became battle cries when, with the British Invasion in full swing, he embraced electric instruments and rock & roll, creating the hybrid folk-rock along with the Byrds and others. The old guard crucified Bob as a sellout, but virtually all of his contemporaries—Phil Ochs, Fred Neil, Tim Hardin, Judy Collins, Joan Baez, Gordon Lightfoot, Ian & Sylvia, Buffy Sainte-Marie—followed suit, sooner rather than later. And it wasn't done just to make money and keep pace with the times; to a man and to a woman, every contemporary folk performer knew that original material (or, at least, covers of contemporary songwriters) and electric instruments paved the way for wider expression and, hence, greater art, unfettered by the now outdated demands for purism in the folk community.

All of the performers mentioned in the above paragraph retained a great deal of folk's strength in their folk-rock; the primacy of guitars, the earnest passion and commitment, the incorporation of time-honored American traditional forms. Some more than others; Phil Ochs, for instance, inherited Dylan's mantle as the day's premier protest singer, and while he recorded a lot of non-political material, he never wholly abandoned his left-leaning political consciousness. The folk-rock movement is covered in detail in a separate sidebar, but it's important to point out that many of the '60s' leading folk-rock and psychedelic musicians were ex-folkies, led back to the rock & roll of their youth by the Beatles and Dylan. The Byrds, the Jefferson Airplane, the Buffalo Springfield, the Grateful Dead, and many others were populated by ex-folk musicians who would have probably remained obscure, and never reached artistic heights of note, if they hadn't realized that the social consciousness of folk could be expressed with far more vitality in rock arrangements.

The interplay between folk and rock has never been nearly as intense as it was in the mid-'60s, probably because the attributes of folk music were absorbed into rock's framework so quickly and deeply. The singer-songwriter movement of the late '60s and early '70s owes a lot to folk music—indeed, some of its most popular practitioners started out as acoustic folkies. But no one would mistake singer-songwriter albums for traditional American folk; the accent was on individual expression and original material, and the arrangements, if somewhat softer than much other rock, did not eschew electric instruments and rhythm sections, although acoustic guitars, harmonicas, and pianos were often prominent in the mix.

While you might hear, say, Nirvana covering a Leadbelly song, or John Cougar Mellencamp and Bruce Springsteen paying lip service to Woody Guthrie, and all manner of bands showing up with acoustic instruments on MTV's *Unplugged* show, the influence of traditional folk on today's rock is pretty small. The "anti-folk" scene of the late 1980s, an attempt by New York musicians to provide an acoustic-based heir of sorts to the hootenannies of the '50s and '60s, had minimal impact; the Washington Squares attempting to mimic the "beatnik folk" of Peter, Paul & Mary, were a failure on all counts.

Many fine performers of the last couple decades have been labeled as folk because their arrangements are largely acoustic, but really belong more in the singer-songwriter camp than traditional music; their category is often more a function of the audiences they play for, or the fact that acoustic guitars are at the forefront of their arrangements. Hence you might find Kate Wolf, Lucinda Williams, Tish Hinojosa, Mary McCaslin, Peter Stampfel, the McGarrigle Sisters, Townes Van Zandt and Bill Morrissey in folk sections, although they sing original, at times compelling material about the here and now, and are often not adverse to using some electric instruments. Indeed, the music of the above performers is not terribly dissimilar from some artists commonly marketed as rock and pop musicians, such as Joni Mitchell.

Some performers that are in many respects troubadours in the folk tradition, like Michelle Shocked or Phranc, are marketed as rock because that is where their audience is perceived to be; the Eleventh Dream Day offshoot Freakwater was marketed to alternative/indie rock listeners more because of their pedigree than the music, which hearkens in spirit back to the Carter Family.

Nanci Griffith has been increasingly directed towards a country market, although she's as much a contemporary folk singer-songwriter as anything else, and has attracted such decidedly rock fans as Paul Westerberg.

Such separation of performers into folk or non-folk categories approaches arbitrariness at times, which is unfortunate. Contemporary folk continues to produce interesting performers and songwriters that share rock's impulse to reflect and affect the times we live in, although it will often be necessary to check out the folk circuit and the specialized programming of non-commercial and college radio stations to find them.

16 Recommended Albums:

Various Artists, *The Sounds Of The South* (Atlantic). A four-CD box set of field recordings made by premier folklorist Alan Lomax in 1959, this captures the wide variety of American southern folk traditions, white and black, in about as authentic a context as modern times allow, including black gospel, white spirituals, Appalachian music, rural blues, and traditional children's songs.

Woody Guthrie, *The Greatest Songs Of Woody Guthrie* (Vanguard). Guthrie has many discs available; this 23-song collection has the most famous, and is thus the best starting point, though *Dust Bowl Ballads* was the album that specifically inspired Bob Dylan more than any other.

The Weavers, *Weavers At Carnegie Hall* (Vanguard). Their 1955 comeback concert from their McCarthy-imposed hiatus, unfettered by the orchestration that appears on some of their hits.

Various Artists, *Troubadours Of The Folk Era, Vol. 1, Troubadours Of The Folk Era, Vol. 2, Troubadours Of The Folk Era, Vol. 3* (Rhino). Encompassing Woody Guthrie, Pete Seeger, the Weavers, and the Kingston Trio, up through '60s singer-songwriters like Tim Hardin, Richard Farina, Fred Neil and Buffy Sainte-Marie, this is the best delineation of folk's evolution from traditional to modern forms.

Peter, Paul & Mary, *Peter, Paul & Mary* (Warner Brothers). Sounds dated now, but this was the act with the soaring harmonies that was responsible for popularizing folk in the early '60s more than any other, and the first to bring Dylan to the attention of the mass audience via their covers of "Blowin' In The Wind" and other songs.

Joan Baez, *First Ten Years* (Vanguard). Both traditional and contemporary folk material recorded by Baez during the 1960s, remaining her most influential work.

Dave Van Ronk, *Inside Dave Van Ronk* (Fantasy). A CD repackage of two early '60s albums by this gruff and moving acoustic interpreter of traditional blues and folk, whose impassioned delivery was a big influence on Dylan among others.

Bob Dylan, *Freewheelin' Bob Dylan* (Columbia). Plenty of Bob Dylan albums have a strong folk influence, but this was the one which established his territory as a contemporary songwriter and performer.

Ian & Sylvia, *Greatest Hits* (Vanguard). This Canadian duo played a large, if somewhat unheralded role, in updating trad folk and paving the way for folk-rock by being among the first to cover material by Dylan and Gordon Lightfoot, being among the first to use bass on their recordings, and writing strong material of their own, like "You Were On

My Mind." Their wide repertoire of original and traditional material, as well as their blend of male and female harmonies, was an overlooked influence on the Jefferson Airplane, the Mamas & the Papas, and Fairport Convention.

Judy Collins, *#3* (Elektra). Another overlooked link from folk to folk-rock, this 1963 album mixed standards with covers of material by Dylan, Bob Gibson, Pete Seeger and Shel Silverstein. Future Byrd, Roger McGuinn contributed arrangements, second guitar, and banjo, and may have gotten the idea to revamp Seeger's "Turn! Turn! Turn!" (which was a #1 hit for the Byrds in 1966) from Collins, who recorded a fine version on this LP.

John Fahey, *Return Of The Repressed* (Rhino). A master of the acoustic guitar, Fahey twisted blues and folk with an adveturous spirit and irreverence that anticipated the innovations of psychedelic rock. This is a double-CD of selections from his huge catalog, spanning the late 1950s to the mid-1980s.

Phil Ochs, *Chords Of Fame* (A&M). Double-LP compilation of the best acoustic and electric work by the finest topical songwriter of the '60s, at ease in both folk and rock settings.

The Holy Modal Rounders, *The Moray Eels Eat The Holy Modal Rounders* (Elektra). Greenwich village folkies Peter Stampfel and Steve Weber were determined to take acoustic traditional music to its most bizarre limits, and were a chief inspiration for the Fugs (on whose albums the Rounders sometimes played). This late-'60s album is perhaps the ultimate psychedelic folk fusion, and while not for everybody (certainly not for traditionalists), is a humorous and vibrant example of the '60s folk scene at its most wacked-out.

Mary McCaslin, *The Best Of Mary McCaslin* (Rounder). Not a household name by any means, McCaslin was one of several outstanding folk-based contemporary singer-songwriters to emerge during the '70s, along with Kate Wolf, the McGarrigle Sisters, and several others. This album was selected because she is arguably the most accessible of these to rock listeners, and because she has recorded some of the best Beatles covers with folk arrangements.

Nanci Griffith, *The Last Of The True Believers* (Philo). Perhaps the most widely known songwriter of recent years with clear roots in traditional American folk music, her major label albums have been more country-oriented than this 1986 recording, her last before signing with MCA.

Freakwater, *Dancing Underwater* (Amoeba). Featuring Eleventh Dream Day drummer/singer Janet Bean (who primarily plays guitar with Freakwater), this acoustic side project, with Appalachian overtones and close country harmonies, is proof that post-punk alternative rockers can draw upon American folk traditions with conviction. This CD includes both the 1991 album *Dancing Underwater* and their starker, self-titled 1989 debut.

Recommended Reading:

Bringing It All Back Home, by Robbie Wolliver (1986, Pantheon)

Dylan, by Anthony Scaduto (1971, Grosset & Dunlap)

Death Of A Rebel: A Biography Of Phil Ochs, by Marc Eliot (1989, Franklin Watts)

—Richie Unterberger

British Isles Folk Music

Since the British began to colonize North America, the indigenous folk music of the British Isles has been a notable factor in American folk music, informing the development of Appalachian and Southern folk sounds and thus, by extension, country and rock. Rock wouldn't really feel the direct influence of British folk until the mid-'60s, though, and then primarily on its native soil, although hybrids of British folk and contemporary rock enjoy a strong cult in the U.S.

In the early '60s, Britain had a traditional folk scene that was comparable to the United States in its strength, though it was smaller. Both communities were increasingly straight-jacketed by an overly insular and reverent attitude that demanded traditional instrumentation and interpretation—demands that seemed increasingly stultifying as contemporary society grew increasingly turbulent and electric. The emergence of Bob Dylan, a performer who wrote his own songs and directly commented on the here and now, was welcomed as much in the U.K. as the U.S.; he toured Britain several times in the early and mid-'60s, and even his acoustic albums were Top Ten sellers.

Dylan himself had been influenced by British Isles folk, as he had by most kinds of folk music; indeed, top Irish traditional band the Clancy Brothers were pals of Dylan's in his Greenwich Village days. Dylan had also learned some tunes from British guitarist Martin Carthy (he adapted one of them for "Girl from the North Country"), a seminal figure in preserving and arranging tunes from the British folk heritage, and one who remains very much a figurehead of the British folk scene up to the present.

It wasn't long before Britain had produced an answer of sorts to Bob Dylan in Donovan, who made his mark (and even had a few hits) with acoustic material in 1965 before moving into pop-psychedelia. The Scottish singer has been unfairly disparaged by those who remember him primarily as a blissed-out hippie that couldn't match the sophistication of Dylan; his early work was quite bound in British folk, and his earliest albums are littered with old British folk songs made relevant to the day's young generation with lively interpretations.

The earliest records of British folkies of the era like Shirley Collins and Martin Carthy hardly sound groundbreaking several decades later, but they were important in how they opened up the British folk repertoire to imaginative interpretations instead of ossifications. Carthy's influence indirectly extended to the masses when Paul Simon moved to Britain for about a year in the mid-'60s, before Simon & Garfunkel had taken off. Carthy taught Simon "Scarborough Fair," which became one of S&G's most popular early tracks.

Simon learned another of his popular early album tracks, "Anji," from guitarist Davey Graham. Though he wasn't much of a vocalist, Graham was vastly influential in synthesizing and extending various traditional folk styles into something new and progressive, though still acoustic, blending blues, folk, jazz, and Middle Eastern music. A more widely heralded British guitarist was Bert Jansch, also a talented songwriter and singer, whose early recordings were reminiscent of the early efforts of fellow Scotsman Donovan. Jansch's presence was also felt on the rock world via his impact on the styles of Neil Young and Jimmy Page, both of whom have cited Jansch as an important influence.

Jansch began recording as a solo artist, but would soon team up with guitarist John Renbourn to form Pentangle. While Pentangle used almost exclusively acoustic instrumentation, they performed, wrote, and interpreted with an energy and flexible imagination that was unquestionably derived, at least in part, from rock, making them one of Britain's greatest folk-rock hybrids. Though they peaked early, it's no exaggeration to note that the talented ensemble were a Beatles of sorts in how their different but complementary talents expanded British folk into uncharted horizons, drawing from jazz, blues, and classical as well as rock.

The British folk community was certainly aware of psychedelia, and though you wouldn't find its performers using mellotrons and backwards tapes, the influence was reflected in their willingness to expand its boundaries and incorporate more adventurous lyrics, arrangements (sometimes electric), and instruments. The most psychedelic-oriented of the British folk acts were the Incredible String Band, a duo of colorful Scotsmen who acted as psychedelic minstrels of sorts with their whimsical songs and unpredictable combinations of sounds, though they remained largely acoustic-based.

For many listeners, the foremost exponents of British folk-rock were Fairport Convention. Starting out as a straight folk-rock group, the group began to veer towards more and more traditional material without altering their forceful electric guitars and rhythm section. Their 1969 album *Liege and Lief* was perhaps the ultimate fusion between electric rock instrumentation and traditional British folk. Equally important, the group acted as the springboard for an astounding range of spin-offs that came to dominate the British folk-rock scene, including Fotheringay, Steeleye Span, the Albion Band, and the solo careers of Richard Thompson, Sandy Denny and Ian Matthews.

The early half of the 1970s was probably the golden age of British folk-rock. Fairport Convention and their spin-offs, as well as groups like Lindisfarne and the Strawbs, not only continued to electrify British folk fundamentals, but were actually quite commercially successful in the U.K., landing several albums in the Top Ten. Their repertoire varied from heavily traditional to mostly self-penned, sharing a general commitment to, as a member of Steeleye Span once put it, "put traditional music back into current musical language—to make folk music less esoteric." And this wasn't a scene limited to the young upstarts; veterans Shirley Collins and Martin Carthy showed up for a time in the Albion Band and Steeleye Span. Nick Drake and the solo recordings of Richard Thompson owe more to the singer/songwriter tradition than traditional British Isles fare, but their work did reflect its influence, Thompson's much more so than Drake.

These bands never made it big in the States, although several achieved enough underground acclaim and FM radio exposure to tour there. By the late '70s, they were no longer stars at home, but the musicians, whether they stuck with their bands or headed to other projects, maintained a fairly solid audience.

The British folk-rock scene wasn't moribund as an artistic force, reviving in the 1980s under the banner of "rogue folk." Due to the efforts of Britain's *Folk Roots* magazine and others, appreciation of acoustic and roots music in the U.K. began to rise. In the mid-'80s, a couple bonafide stars emerged: the Pogues infused Irish traditional folk with punk energy, and Billy Bragg delivered articulate political and social commentary using (on his early records, at least) little more than a guitar. Bragg's guitar was electric, though, and his rough-hewn attitudes and vocals marked him as a clear product of the post-punk revolution, though he was also a folk troubadour in the best sense of that tradition.

There were other acclaimed "rogue folk" performers that combined folk traditions with modern (often electric) instruments and attitudes, most of whom (unlike Bragg or the Pogues) remain virtually unknown in the States. Scottish guitarist Dick Gaughan sang both traditional material and contemporary political fare, and songwriter Leon Rosselson has been compared to Phil Ochs. The Oyster Band drew from traditional material and contemporary political commentary in their rock-influenced modern folk dance music. In the United States, a society somewhat more removed in everyday life from acoustic musical traditions than the British or Irish, these artists will probably never achieve much more than college and community radio exposure. American bands that actually follow the British folk-rock mold are quite rare; Boiled in Lead, from Minneapolis, is the only one to attain even a modest level of recognition.

On the commercial airwaves, however, you can hear the strains—usually indirect, sometimes fairly evident—of Irish traditional music in that country's most successful rock stars, like Van Morrison, Sinéad O'Connor and U2. The Levellers, stars in the U.K. and thus far a flop stateside, derive much of their influence from British traditional music. And performers from British folk-rock's most successful phase, such as Richard Thompson and June Tabor, continue to record and tour to considerable acclaim in their middle age.

15 Recommended Recordings:

Donovan, *Spotlight on Donovan* (Pye, UK). Donovan's early mid-'60s acoustic recordings are frustratingly scattered and haphazardly reissued; this double-LP import is the best collection, though it's getting harder to find.

Davey Graham, *Folk Blues and All Points in Between* (See For Miles, UK). A reissue of the eclectic guitarist's groundbreaking 1965 album, with additional bonus cuts from the best of his late-'60s recordings.

Bert Jansch, *Bert Jansch/Jack Orion,* (Demon/Transatlantic, UK). His first and third albums, from the mid-'60s, combined onto a double-CD, demonstrate his facility with both original and traditional material.

The Incredible String Band, *The Hangman's Beautiful Daughter* (Rykodisc). This 1967 album was the ISB's most acclaimed effort. Those looking for a wide-ranging sampler should try to find the two-record Relics compilation.

The Pentangle, *Sweet Child* (Reprise). This late-'60s double set, a mixture of studio and live material, is only given the nod because of its length and variety; their self-titled debut and *Basket of Light* are equally worthy.

Fairport Convention, *Liege and Lief* (Hannibal). Not their best album—their previous, more rock-oriented efforts, *What We Did on Our Holidays* and *Unhalfbricking*, were better—but in terms of rock and British folk fusion, this was their most influential. Or, for a compilation with greater breadth, try to find *Chronicles*.

Sandy Denny, *Who Knows Where the Time Goes* (Hannibal). Three-CD box set of Britain's finest folk-rock singer, featuring both solo tracks and performances with Fairport Convention, the Strawbs and Fotheringay

Richard Thompson, *Watching the Dark* (Hannibal). Another three-CD compilation, including solo work and cuts with Fairport and his ex-wife Linda.

Steeleye Span, *The Steeleye Span Story: Original Masters* (Chrysalis). Getting harder to find, but this double album is the widest-spanning collection of a prolific group that changed personnel quite a few times.

Clannad, *Clannad* (Boot, Canada). Most of this famous Irish group's releases have leaned towards either the traditional or the pop; on this overlooked 1973 debut, they came off as a sort of Irish Pentangle. Has been issued on different labels, depending upon which country has a copy to be found.

Billy Bragg, *Back to Basics* (Elektra). A compilation of his first two albums, as well as an early EP. Bragg subsequently added fuller rock arrangements without diluting his integrity, but these initial tracks—many only featuring him and his electric guitar—are the recordings most closely tied to British folk sounds.

The Pogues, *Rum, Sodomy & the Lash* (MCA). Their second album, produced by Elvis Costello, blends punk and Irish folk without compromising either form, and includes their best-known tune, a cover of Ewan MacColl's "Dirty Old Town."

The Oyster Band, *From Little Rock to Leipzig* (Rykodisc). With quite a few albums to their credit, it's hard to single out one as the best starting point. This live outing was chosen because it includes versions of material from several of their releases.

The Chieftains, *Long Black Veil* (RCA). The foremost Irish traditional folk band performs folk, pop, and country & western with the Rolling Stones, Sting, Ry Cooder, Marianne Faithfull, Sinead O'Connor, Tom Jones, Mick Jagger and Van Morrison. In 1988, Morrison recorded an entire album of traditional Irish songs with the Chieftains, *Irish Heartbeat* (Mercury).

June Tabor, *Against the Stream* (Green Linnet). Britain's most acclaimed contemporary folk singer interprets traditional tunes and songs by Richard Thompson and her big fan, Elvis Costello on this elegantly subdued and moody 1994 record, demonstrating the continued flexibility of modern British folk.

Various Artists, *Troubadours of British Folk Vol. 1-3* (Rhino). Excellent three-volume survey of British folk and folk-rock from the 1950s through the 1980s, from its traditional roots through its electrification, with key cuts from almost all of its major performers (Fairport Convention, Steeleye Span, Pentangle, the Incredible String Band, Richard Thompson, Nick Drake, Billy Bragg, Oyster Band, etc.)

—Richie Unterberger

Reggae

No form of popular music from the third world has made as much of an international impact as reggae. It has borrowed from rock & roll, and rock in turn has borrowed from it, but it remains a minority, specialty taste for much of the rock audience. That's nothing for reggae proponents to be ashamed of; that the tiny island of Jamaica has produced a wealth of musicians that affected the course of international rock and pop music is astounding.

Reggae had its beginnings in the late '50s, when Jamaican popular musicians combined their indigenous folk music with jazz, African and Caribbean rhythms, and New Orleans rhythm & blues to come up with a music of their own, ska. An oft-repeated folk legend has it that the frenetic, offbeat rhythm was created when islanders listened to New Orleans R&B stations on their transistor radios, the static garbling the rhythms so much that the musicians bastardized the sound into something else altogether when they tried to imitate it. Most likely that's a fanciful tale, but there's no doubt that R&B, particularly the New Orleans variety, was a dominant influence on early ska, and that the ska rhythm never quite locked into a reproduction of its inspiration.

Ska was a relentlessly joyous and upbeat music, finding great popularity not only in Jamaica, but in Britain, which had a large West Indian population. Lots of ska records were imported and licensed for release in Britain, and some British-based musicians recorded ska of their own. One of these productions, Millie Small's *My Boy Lollipop*, became a huge hit in both the U.K. and the U.S. in 1964, bringing ska to an international audience, and remaining—incredibly—one of the very best-selling Jamaican discs ever. This single was produced by White Jamaican expatriate Chris Blackwell, whose label, Island, licensed and produced many ska singles in the '60s, and would be instrumental in exposing reggae to a worldwide audience over the next few decades.

By around 1966, the hyper-rhythms of ska began to give way to the slower, loping beats of rocksteady. Dreamy and ideal for romantic dancing, harmonies (which had often been a prominent ingredient of ska already) came to the forefront, and the squeaky, jazzy horns that characterized ska were muted and pushed down in the mix. It's obvious from the passionate vocals on classic rocksteady that Jamaican performers of this era were heavily attuned to American soul, as heavy echoes of Motown, Memphis, and harmonizing R&B groups are obvious in the recordings.

Reggae, as much Jamaican popular music came to be known at the end of the 1960s, embellished the bedrock rhythms of ska and rocksteady with political and social lyrics, often informed by Rastafarianism, racial pride, and the turbulent Jamaican political climate. The rhythms ebbed and flowed with the hypnotic, jerky pulse that has become reggae's most identifiable trademark, and the bass and choppy rhythm tracks became not just prominent, but dominant. For many fans, this is reggae's golden age, as many of the music's greatest legends emerged or cut their prime work during this period, including Toots & the Maytals, Burning Spear, and above all the Wailers.

The Wailers' Bob Marley would become reggae's towering figure, revered in many Third World countries with a zeal on par with American and British fanaticism for the Beatles; fellow-Wailers Peter Tosh and Bunny Wailer also established influential solo careers.

The influence of reggae was felt in rock almost immediately, but usually surfaced as a tangential reference in some stars' isolated songs. The early Beatles song "I Call Your Name," for instance, has a ska break; a few years later, they would appropriate the reggae rhythm for "Ob-La-Di, Ob-La-Da." Jamaican singer Jackie Edwards wrote a couple ska-flavored rock-soul hits for the Spencer Davis Group, "Keep on Running" and "Somebody Help Me"; Paul Simon, never one to let a good ethnic sound pass unnoticed, put a reggae beat behind one of his first solo hits, "Mother and Child Reunion." Paul McCartney went full-tilt into reggae on his early solo track "C Moon," and Eric Clapton had a number one hit with his cover of Bob Marley's "I Shot the Sherriff." Stevie Wonder sometimes flirted with reggae rhythms, as on his hit "Boogie on Reggae Woman." But aside from Johnny Nash, a Texan soul singer who actually did some recording in Jamaica and landed big hits with reggae-soul concoctions like "Hold Me Tight," "I Can See Clearly Now," and Marley's "Stir It Up," hardly any rock or soul performers made reggae an integral component of their work.

Occasionally reggae performers would cross over to the rock and pop audience, as with Jimmy Cliff's "Wonderful World," "Beautiful People," and Desmond Dekker's "The Israelites," but international reggae hits remained a rare phenomenon. When artists like the Wailers began to get wide international distribution in the early and mid-'70s (usually on Island), the music garnered a sizable cult following on both sides of the Atlantic, primarily with White audiences. Reggae's greatest attributes—its spare power, its outspoken (sometimes militant) commentary on politics, class strife, and religion, its idionsyncratic production flourishes—may also have been what kept it from gaining anything close to the commercial foothold enjoyed by rock and soul.

Reggae itself continued to evolve, not always in accordance with the preferences of its overseas audience. The operators of mobile "sound systems" in Jamaica had often embellished their presentations with voiceovers, and this was eventually practiced in the studio as the art of DJing or toasting, wherein the artist chanted, rhymed, and expounded over a musical backing track. There was also dub music, which erased vocals and stripped tracks to their bones of bass and rhythm, over which all manner of strange and wonderful echo, reverb, and miscellaneous sound effects were overlaid to create spacy and pulsating instrumentals.

Towards the end of the 1970s, reggae's influence made itself felt on a couple of the era's rock and R&B trends. Punk and new wave performers were often big reggae fans, particularly in Britain; the West Indian population was much larger there than in the U.S., and punks felt a kinship with their struggles as an oppressed minority. The Clash sometimes used reggae rhythms and production touches, even enlisting top dub reggae artist Lee Perry to produce some tracks, and punk bands like the Slits incorporated reggae signatures into their music. Top new wave bands Blondie, and more particularly the Police, built some of their hits around watered-down reggae flourishes. British reggae group Steel Pulse built its following by playing punk venues, and Bob Marley himself encouraged the alliance with a British single, "Punky Reggae Party." The Ruts (who evolved into Ruts D.C.) blended reggae and punk in the late '70s and early '80s, a fusion which the Bad Brains would also attempt throughout the 1980s. In the early '80s, producer Adrian Sherwood used early punk musicians like the Slits, Public Image Ltd. , the Raincoats, and the Pop Group to enhance his edgy, hard-to-classify excursions into dub reggae with the New Age Steppers.

At the tail end of the decade, Britain experienced an all-out ska revival. Bands like the Specials, Madness, the Selecter, and the English Beat enjoyed huge popularity at home—and cult popularity in the U.S.—with their hybrid of ska and new wave. Sometimes called the Two-Tone sound (in honor of the label on which many of the bands appeared), this brand of ska-cum-rock is still kicking today, albeit on a much smaller level.

In the United States around this time, young African-Americans—by and large in New York, home to a fairly large Jamaican community—began to build upon the DJs and toasters to come up with their own stream-of-consciousness poems. The connection between reggae and rap has never gotten a lot of attention, but there's no doubt that reggae contributed to the genesis of what became the most flamboyant African-American music of the 1980s and '90s. Of course, the backing tracks of American rap are usually harsher and starker than reggae, and with isolated exceptions like Shinehead, few have tried to bridge the styles, perhaps because reggae never had an appreciable audience among American blacks.

With the death of Bob Marley in 1981, as well as the murder of Peter Tosh in 1987, many listeners feel that the golden age of reggae has gone forever. It continues to thrive in Jamaica, where more records are released per capita than any other country in the world. DJing and toasting has produced the spinoff dancehall, which has a more electronic-driven rhythm and, sometimes, risque or "slack" vocals and lyrics. Reggae itself continues to exert a tangential influence on rock and pop—many stars from the Rolling

Stones down have occasionally appropriated reggae rhythms, top Jamaican rhythm section Sly & Robbie guest on albums by major figures like Bob Dylan, and reggae-pop hybrids like UB40 and Aswad even have chart success with pop-conscious adaptations of reggae sounds.

Recommended Listening—15 Albums:

Various Artists, *Tougher than Tough: The Story of Jamaican Music* (Mango). This four-disc box set documents the evolution of reggae from its beginnings to the present, from ska and rocksteady up through dub and dancehall. Of course no box set can cover the music definitively, and this one doesn't claim to, but it's the best retrospective of reggae as a whole, including tracks by most of its major performers.

Various Artists, *Scandal Ska* (Mango). Because it was a soundtrack tie-in to a movie about the 1963 British Profumo scandal, this superb anthology was pretty much ignored by critics. It's probably the best introductory ska sampler, though, with early-'60s sides by Jimmy Cliff, Bob Marley, Desmond Dekker, Laurel Aitken, Ernest Ranglin, Roland Alphonso and others.

Alton Ellis, *Alton & Hortense* (Heartbeat). There are more wide-ranging rocksteady anthologies available, but this collection of late-'60s sides, featuring solo performances by one of Jamaica's premier vocalists (Alton) and his much less famous but similarly talented sister (Hortense), is enchanting romantic music that makes clear the influence of American '60s soul on reggae.

Johnny Nash, *The Reggae Collection* (Epic/Legacy). 20-track collection spanning the late '60s to the mid-'70s, focusing on the reggae-inspired work of the first (and, still, one of the few) musicians to fuse rock and soul with reggae for commercial success. Includes the big hits and several less famous songs.

Bob Marley, *Legend* (Tuff Gong). 14 of his most famous tracks. If you want to dig deeper after this, there are many albums to choose from; the Wailers' *Burnin'* and *Catch a Fire* are the most celebrated single LPs, and the four-CD box *Songs of Freedom* the most extensive career retrospective.

Various Artists, *The Harder They Come* (Island). This cult film deserved a lot of credit for introducing worldwide audiences to reggae, both via its gritty picture of Jamaican culture and its top-notch soundtrack, which featured music by Jimmy Cliff (who starred in the film as well), the Maytals, the Melodians, Desmond Dekker, and others.

Toots & the Maytals, *Funky Kingston* (Mango). The most acclaimed album by Toots Hibbert, widely acknowledged as reggae's most soulful singer.

Lee Perry, *The Greatest* (Mango). Vintage productions by dub's top exponent, featuring the Heptones, Junior Murvin, Max Romeo, Prince Jazzbo, and Perry himself. Those looking to go deeper should look for *The Upsetter Compact Set*; actually issued under the name of Perry's studio band, the Upsetters, this is a three-CD package of some of his best work.

Burning Spear, *Marcus Garvey* (Mango). The mid-'70s record that brought them to international attention remains one of reggae's most powerful album-length statements.

Various Artists, *The Best of Punky Reggae* (Rhino). 17-track anthology illustrates the cross-fertilization of punk and reggae, with tracks by Patti Smith, Graham Parker, Devo, Pere Ubu, Blondie, Steel Pulse, the Specials, Selecter, the English Beat, UB40, Madness, Keith Levene and others. Missing influential cuts by the Clash and Bob Marley, presumably because of licensing hurdles.

Various Artists, *Two Tone Compilation: A Checkered Past* (Chrysalis). Double CD of the best tracks from the premier British ska revival label, including hits by the Specials, the English Beat, Madness, the Selecter, and various spinoffs.

Various Artists, *Inna Reggae Style* (EMI). Not one of the greatest reggae albums of all time, it's included on this list because it illustrates connections between rock and reggae with covers of rock and soul songs by reggae performers like Peter Tosh, the Heptones, and Toots & the Maytals, reggae cuts by rock acts like Blondie and Boy George, pop-reggae hybrids by Aswad, the English Beat, and Third World, and a duet between Peter Tosh and Mick Jagger.

Shinehead, *Unity* (Elektra). The 1988 debut by one of the few performers to successfully bridge reggae with rap.

Divination, *Ambient Dub Vol. 1 & 2.* Bassist Bill Laswell is the heaviest contributor to these explorations by top experimental rock musicians into dub music, twisting it into more sinister and electronic forms.

Various Artists, *Mash up the Place—The Best of Reggae Dancehall* (Rhino). There are a lot of reggae dancehall compilations; Rhino gets the nod because, typically, it provides the most cohesive and informative packaging. Includes tracks by Shabba Ranks, Ninja Man, Macka B. and others.

—Richie Unterberger

Index

A
A Bones 410
A House 238
A., Donna 329
Aaliyah **1**, 362, 782
Aaronson, Kenny 1086, 1087
ABBA **1**, 2, 5, 32, 34, 373, 688, 1240
Abbott, Jacqueline 81, 82
ABC **2**, 3, 157, 208, 695, 986, 1288, 1338
Abdul, Paula **3**, 49, 602, 983, 1151
Able Tasmans 1343
Abney, Terence 'Tramp Baby' 861
Abong, Fred 91
Abrahams, Mick 587
Abrams, Joshua 879
Abramson, Herb 1162
AC/DC **3**, 4, 5, 52, 76, 107, 128, 188, 190, 252, 273, 274, 425, 459, 484, 495, 497, 537, 561, 590, 606, 635, 668, 768, 1032, 1178, 1192, 1341, 1342
Accents 1275
Accept 1167, 1302
Accidents 1298
Ace [1] **5**, 6, 186, 187, 735, 1287, 1335
Ace of Base **5**, 781
Ace, Johnny **5**, 6, 883, 1305
Acker, Kathy 722
Ackles, David **6**, 254, 533
Acklin, Barbara 198, 208
Acland, Chris 680
Acquaviva, John 867
Act [1] 336
Action 656, 735
Action [1] **6**, 734, 735, 1284, 1322, 1335
Ad Libs 1275
Adam & the Ants 30, 31, 133, 358, 684, 756, 948, 1337, 1338, 1339
Adams, Arthur 1217
Adams, Billy 307
Adams, Bronwyn 268
Adams, Bryan **6**, 7, 124, 230, 914, 915, 1081, 1209
Adams, Carl 513
Adams, Craig 743, 1017
Adams, Donn 896
Adams, Faye 1305
Adams, Greg [2] 1151
Adams, Johnny 302, 1288
Adams, Mark [1] Antone 1020
Adams, Oleta 1122
Adams, Ryan 1217, 1218
Adams, Terry 386, 668, 805, 806, 1298
Adamson, Barbara 97
Adamson, Barry 7, 99, 192, 193, 687, 688, 1195
Adamson, Stuart 96, 97, 1019
Add N to X **7**, 8, 471, 638
Addabbo, Steve 1187
Adderley, Cannonball 44, 152, 694, 1292
Adderley, Nat 44, 317
Addrisi, Don 327, 793
Adkins, Hasil **8**, 262, 263
Adkins, Jim 591
Adler, Danny 956, 957
Adler, Larry 956
Adler, Lou 304, 620, 690, 944, 1056
Adler, Steven 494
Adolescents 1037
Adonis [1] 860, 1299
Advert, Gaye 9
Adverts **8**, 9, 997, 1087, 1278, 1295, 1337

Aerosmith **9**, 10, 11, 32, 217, 486, 494, 495, 735, 767, 906, 920, 930, 962, 963, 1087, 1257, 1332, 1348
Afanasieff, Walter 318, 978
Afghan Whigs **11**, 35, 1282
Afrodiziak 255
After Seven 278
After the Fire 1291
AFX 33
Agent Orange 1280
Agnello, John 581
Agnetha & Frida 373
Agnew, Pete 783
Agnew, Rikk 1037
Aguado, Dionysio 634
Aguilar, David 213
Aguilera, Christina **11**, 12, 531, 760, 781, 1014, 1051
a-ha **12**
Ahern, Brian 1230
Ainge, Gary 399
Air [1] 278
Air [2] **12**, 13
Air Supply **13**, 50, 406, 978, 1291
Aitchison, Dominic 750
Aitken, Laurel 1356
Akil 608
Akkerman, Jan 420, 1331
Akyroyd, Dan 38
Alaimo, Jim 752
Alaimo, Steve 1285
Alarm **13**, 14, 97, 1242, 1287
Albarn, Damon 120, 121, 334, 475, 726, 1159, 1299
Albert, Howard 448
Albert, Ron 448
Alberti, Dorona 627
Albertine, Viv 1023
Albin, Peter 96
Albini, Steve 35, 43, 94, 96, 139, 141, 161, 281, 434, 510, 521, 586, 587, 616, 744, 803, 836, 864, 983, 984, 1000, 1001, 1006, 1053, 1104, 1149, 1176, 1192, 1212, 1246, 1257, 1345
Albion Band 388
Albion Country Band 1138
Alcatrazz 1181
Alcivar, Bob 403
Alden, Gene 197
Aldo, Steve 1286
Aldridge, Tommy 832
Alexakis, Art 205, 379, 380
Alexander Nevermind 349
Alexander, Arthur **14**, 80, 1287
Alexander, Dave [1] 1086
Alexander, Dave [2] 1085, 1086
Alexander, Dottie 484, 815
Alexander, Gary [1] 'Jules' 41
Alexander, Geoffrey 136
Alexander, Gregg 793
Alexander, James 64
Alexander, Sharon 253
Alexander, Tim 888
Alexander, Tim [1] 'Herb' 888
Alexander, Willie [1] 'Loco' 1189, 1278
Ali, Muhammad 1261
Ali, Muhammad [1] 938
Alice in Chains **14**, 15, 774, 848, 984, 1067, 1085, 1293
All [1] 302, 303
All About Eve **15**, 16
All City 823
All Fellas Band 444

All Saints **16**, 781
Allan, Cameron 726
Allan, Chad 50, 491
Allan, Davie **16**
Allcock, Martin 388, 589
Allen & Allen 1286
Allen Brothers 104
Allen, Colin 708
Allen, Daevid 473, 474, 1038, 1039
Allen, Dave [1] 196, 448, 548
Allen, Dave [2] 448
Allen, Dave [Bass] 448
Allen, Frank 987
Allen, Harry [1] 1274
Allen, Joey 1207
Allen, Kevin 27
Allen, Lee 21, 67, 109, 148, 328, 1292, 1296, 1306
Allen, Peter 50
Allen, Richard [Rock] 1035
Allen, Rick [1] 294
Allen, Steve 1165
Allen, Terry 154, 1117
Allen, Woody 35, 676
Alley Cats [1] 1279
Alley, Kirstie 890
Allinson/Brown 1116
Allison, Clay 823
Allison, Darren 320
Allison, Jerry 535
Allison, Joe 1032
Allison, Mose 764, 864, 1325
Allison, Vern 298
Allman Brothers **16**, 17, 18, 19, 57, 103, 104, 185, 330, 346, 501, 681, 682, 699, 735, 834, 961, 1136, 1267, 1325, 1326, 1327, 1333, 1350
Allman Joys 17
Allman, Duane 17, 18, 19, 220, 297, 301, 302, 430, 980, 1287, 1325, 1333
Allman, Gregg 17, **18**, 19, 188, 1333
Allom, Tom (Colonel) 674
Allum, Rob 8
Almond, John 708
Almond, Marc **19**, 20, 234, 243, 863, 1018, 1038, 1202
Almstead, Derek 484, 815
Alomar, Carlos 134, 874
Alpert, Herb 50, 430, 757, 801, 1013, 1043, 1151
Alpha Band 159
Alphonso, Roland 1356
Alston, Barbara 272
Alston, Gerald 692
ALT [1] **21**, 405
Alter Natives 1330
Altered Images 1129, 1212
Alternative TV 897
Alvarez, Karl 302
Alvin & the Chipmunks 1088, 1166
Alvin, Dave [1] **21**, 109, 158, 1249
Alvin, Dave & The Guilty Men 21
Alvin, Phil 21, 109
Always, Billy 1095
Aly, Brandon 143
Amato, Buzz 710
Amazing Blondel **21**, 22
Amazing Rhythm Aces **22**, 1230
Ambel, Eric 296
Amber Squad 1298
Amboy Dukes 807, 1067
Ambrose Slade 1019

Ambrosia **22**, 23, 1286
Amen Corner **23**, 1286
Ament, Jeff 486, 767, 848, 1125
America [1] **23**, 24, 406, 917, 1286
American Analog Set **24**, 232
American Breed 1283, 1288
American Flyer **24**
American Music Club **24**, 25, 175, 356, 357, 640, 922, 984
American Spring 537
Ames, Joe 196
Amil 581
Amm 829
Ammons, Gene 44
Amon Duul **25**, 26, 131, 463, 1331
Amon Duul II 25, 26, 252, 1296
Amos, Tori **26**, 27, 82, 161, 236, 761, 814
Amp [1] 420
Amphlett, Christina 321, 322
Amps **27**
Anarchy Six 923
Anastasio, Trey 859, 860
And You Will Know Us by the Trail of Dead **27**
Anders, Allison 21, 256
Andersen, Eric 119, 238, 814
Anderson, Al [1] 354, 805, 806
Anderson, Bill [1] 787
Anderson, Brett 162, 190, 358, 713, 1098, 1099, 1347
Anderson, Carleen 401, 402
Anderson, Dave [02] 26
Anderson, Emma 680
Anderson, Eric 955
Anderson, Gary 125
Anderson, Ian [1] 176, 507, 587, 588, 589
Anderson, Ike 589
Anderson, John [1] 722, 1256, 1257
Anderson, Jon 157, 617, 1255, 1256, 1257
Anderson, Jon [1] 842
Anderson, Laurie **28**, 369, 736, 1005, 1290
Anderson, Lindsay 887
Anderson, Lynn 1046
Anderson, Paul Thomas 693
Anderson, Pete 117, 423, 720, 1002
Anderson, Signe 583
Anderson, Simon [1] 244
Andersson, Benny 1, 2, 373
Andes, Mark 405, 1056
Andre [1] 834
Andre Three Thousand 833
Andreason, Tony 1156
Andrews Sisters 1043, 1051, 1241
Andrews, Barry 874, 1250
Andrews, Bob [1] 324, 962, 1335
Andrews, Chris 999
Andrews, James 1151
Andrews, Lee 1274
Andrews, Reggie 286
Andy, Horace 701
Ange 1296
Angel [1] 304, 1266
Angels [1] **28**, 125, 978, 1087, 1282, 1312, 1341
Angevin, Monique 794
Anglin, Jack 1224
Angry Samoans 735, 1280
Angus [1] 3
Animals **29**, 30, 137, 324, 425, 432, 532, 595, 694, 745, 752, 886, 887, 936, 949, 1016, 1019, 1029, 1054, 1067, 1206, 1312, 1315, 1316, 1318, 1320, 1321, 1325, 1326

Anka, Paul **30**, 475, 610, 945, 1203, 1275, 1297, 1309, 1310
Ann-Margret 80
Annisette 979
Anonymous, Rodney 289, 290
Another Bad Creation 88
Ansani, Ted 703
Anselmo, Philip 839
Ant, Adam **30**, 31, 132, 439, 802, 1014, 1048, 1281
Antenna 108, 511
Anthony, Dee 428
Anthony, Marc 669, 1014
Anthony, Michael [1] 1183
Anthony, Michael [2] 1182
Anthrax **31**, 32, 632, 898, 1020
Anti Nowhere League 997, 1340
Anton, Alan 259
Antoni, Robert 784
Antonioni, Claude 1253
Any Trouble **32**, 489, 866
Apartments [1] **32**, 33
Aphex Twin 12, **33**, 101, 771, 774, 911, 972, 990, 1029, 1064, 1273, 1299, 1300, 1347
Aphrodite [1] 776
Apollo Four Forty 478
Apollo Nine 948
Apollo Nine [1] 948
Appell, Dave Applejacks [UK] 1293
Appice, Carmine 84, 1184
Appice, Vinny 316
Apple, Fiona **33**, 34, 483, 608
Apples in Stereo **34**, 362, 484, 790, 821, 1285
April Wine 484
Aqua [1] **34**
Aquabats 111
Aquarium Rescue Unit 871
Aquarius [1] 860
AR Kane 680, 838, 1292
Arab Strap **34**, 35
Araya, Tom 1021
Arbors 1296
Archer, John 548
Archers of Loaf 1058, 1302
Archia, Tom 507
Archies [1] **35**, 60, 212, 1273, 1276, 1312, 1331, 1332
Arden, Jann 831
Ardoin, Chris 433, 850
Ardolino, Tom 805, 806
Arduser, Chris 76
Argent **35**, 913, 1270, 1296
Argent, Rod 35, 878, 1059, 1270
Argentina 749
Arlen, Harold 1091, 1093
Arlin, Bobby 643
Arm, Mark 417, 486, 774, 775
Armando [1] 860
Armatrading, Joan **35**, 36, 37, 1285
Armoury Show 1019
Armstead, Joshie 148, 380, 569
Armstrong, Billie Joe 485
Armstrong, Craig 701
Armstrong, Harry 268
Armstrong, Kevin 327
Armstrong, Louis 341, 652, 983, 1135, 1199, 1200, 1292
Armstrong, Roger 279
Armstrong, Tim 823, 917
Arnaert, Geike 538, 539
Arnaz, Desi Jr. 315
Arnell, Ginny 1282
Arnold [1] 830, 834
Arnold, Billy Boy 1253, 1352
Arnold, Bruce 830
Arnold, Eddy 203, 1032, 1046
Arnold, Gary 982
Arnold, Harvey Dalton 834
Arnold, Jerome 163
Arnold, Joe 924
Arnold, Kokomo 883
Arnold, Larkin 453
Arnold, P.P. 37, 797, 812, 1028, 1081
Aronoff, Kenny 267, 719
Arrested Development 37, 1348, 1349
Arrington, Steve 1020
Arrogance 322

Arrows [1] 16
Art [1] 433, 1245
Art Attacks 756
Art Bears 261
Art Collection 240, 878
Art Ensemble of Chicago 68, 638, 830
Art In the Dark 1343
Art of Noise **37**, 38, 602
Artery [1] 743
Artful Dodger [1] 1278
Artwoods 1284
Ash [1] **38**, 673
Ash Ra Tempel 419
Ash, Daniel 69, 70, 71, 672, 673, 776, 876, 897
Ashcroft, Richard 55, 1193
Asher, Jane 855
Asher, Peter 309, 855, 955, 956, 1046, 1119, 1120, 1126
Asher, Tony 198
Asheton, Ron 305, 875, 910, 1085, 1086, 1341
Asheton, Scott 1085, 1086
Ashford & Simpson **39**, 957, 962, 1061, 1280
Ashford, Chris 461
Ashford, Nickolas 39, 148, 380, 569, 699
Ashley, Robert 936, 1289
Ashly, Phil 458
Ashman, Matthew 132
Ashton, Jack 1187
Ashton, John 896
Ashworth, Audie 173
Asia **39**, 40, 157, 687, 899, 1231, 1256, 1331
Askew, Steve 609
Askey, Gil 709
Assembly 372
Associates **40**
Associates [1] 40, 776
Association **40**, 41, 122, 433, 736, 752, 788, 830, 960, 990, 1054, 1089, 1146, 1275
Assunto, Frank 1037
Astaire, Fred 616
Astbury, Ian 273, 274, 338
Asthana, Shivika 840
Astley, Rick **41**, 678, 740
Astors 1281
Astronauts 1275, 1296, 1314
Aswad 1356
Asylum Choir 968
At the Drive In 28, **41**, 42, 783
Atkin, James 365
Atkins, Chet 599, 853, 1296
Atkins, Juan 383, 560, 1286, 1299
Atkins, Martin 616, 898, 899
Atkinson, Damon 139
Atkinson, Sweet Pea 1208
Atlantics [1] 1313, 1314
Atlas, Natacha 559
Atmospheres 1296
Atom [3] 948
Attaway, Murray 491
Attila **42**, 593
Attractions [1] 211, 254, 255, 256, 504, 841, 1335
Au Go Go Singers 1082
Au Pairs **42**
Auchinvole, Liz 827
Audio Two [1] 16
Auer 877, 878
Auer, Jon 877, 878, 924, 1344
Auger, Brian 473, 1253, 1284
Augeri, Steve 604
Augustyniak, Jerome 1127
Aukerman, Milo 302, 303, 760
Aurobindo 990
Aurra 1020
Austin, Dallas 431
Austin, Derek 182
Austin, Patti 560, 1077
Autechre 911, 990, 1019, 1273, 1299, 1300
Auteurs 13, **42**, 43, 102, 1283
Autoclave 520
Automatics 1052
Automator 327, 631, 892
Autry, Gene 203
Avalon, Frankie **43**, 946, 1275, 1297, 1300, 1309, 1335
Avengers [1] **43**, 543, 1336, 1339

Average White Band 41, **43**, 565, 980, 981, 1281, 1284, 1291, 1309, 1325
Avery, Eric 579
Avons 1299
Avory, Mick 622
Avsec, Mark 562
Axelrod, David **43**, 44
Axton, Hoyt 150, 519, 696, 1070, 1141
Ayers, Kevin **44**, 45, 216, 474, 476, 974, 1038, 1039, 1223, 1224, 1283, 1296, 1331
Ayers, Kevin & the Whole World 45
Ayers, Roy 56, 348, 495
Aykroyd, Dan 118
Ayler, Albert 1195
Ayres, Ben 252
Aznavour, Charles 20, 256, 371, 1060
Azoff, Irving 420
Aztec Camera **45**, 46, 235, 238, 489

B
B Fifty Two's **47**, 126, 187, 491, 559, 602, 665, 673, 775, 875, 902, 915, 931, 994, 1219, 1333
B Real 277, 380
B Team 1298
B Twelve 1273, 1299
B-52s 130
B., Eric 374, 915
B., Howie 101, 946
B., Jon 50
B., Malik 957
B.B. Blunder 114
Ba Duong 160
Baah, Rebop Kwaku 1154
Babbitt, Milton 1289
Babble 1137
Babes In Toyland **47**, 48, 259, 1282, 1345
Babies [1] 1198
Babjak, Jim 1032
Baby Animals 978
Baby Bam 608
Baby Bird [1] **48**, 49, 1076
Baby Bird 1285
Baby Huey 440, 1285
Babyface [1] **49**, 50, 110, 140, 145, 220, 544, 569, 581, 613, 861, 1227
Babys **50**, 53, 1198
Bach, Johann Sebastian 158, 212, 893, 1072
Bach, Sebastian 1018
Bacharach, Burt 12, 37, **50**, 106, 151, 183, 185, 203, 235, 256, 303, 304, 422, 430, 471, 528, 569, 637, 638, 672, 705, 728, 760, 781, 787, 811, 829, 865, 868, 882, 962, 969, 986, 1001, 1033, 1059, 1060, 1068, 1094, 1109, 1183, 1203, 1207, 1208, 1276, 1285
Bacharach/Bayer Sager 1060
Bacharach/David 389, 403, 404, 551, 956, 1208
Bachelors 1166
Bachman Turner Overdrive **50**, 51, 491, 611, 1155
Bachman, Randy 50, 302, 491, 492
Bachman, Robbie 50
Bachman, Tim 50, 404, 405, 827
Backstreet Boys 51, 781, 1052, 1115
Backstreet Boys [1] **51**, 760, 781, 1014
Bacon, Kevin [1] 243, 244
Bad Boy Bill 260
Bad Brains 51, 52, 663, 1280, 1339, 1341, 1355
Bad Company [1] **52**, 53, 432, 491, 769, 770, 1281
Bad English 50, **53**, 604, 1198
Bad Manners **53**
Bad Religion **53**, 54, 218, 804
Bad Roads 1273
Bad Seed 7, 99
Bad Seeds 7, 99, 192, 193, 194, 268, 356, 1132, 1341, 1342
Badalamenti, Angelo 7, 102, 390
Badalementi, Angelo 390
Badarou, Wally 684, 1147
Badfinger **54**, 55, 97, 370, 417, 501, 544, 566, 799, 820, 921, 964, 1087, 1090, 1124, 1166, 1188, 1211, 1290, 1293, 1339, 1343
Badly Drawn Boy **55**, 476
Badu, Erykah **55**, 56, 495

Baermann, Carl 1229
Baerwald, David 271, 283
Baez, Joan **56**, 57, 395, 605, 813, 892, 1285, 1353
Bagdasarian, Ross 806
Bags 1279
Bahamadia 1018
Bailey Brothers 974
Bailey [1] 227
Bailey, Bob [1] 1187
Bailey, Buddy 227
Bailey, Chris 973, 974, 1341
Bailey, Derek 829
Bailey, Paul 210, 211
Bailey, Philip 348
Bailey, Richard [1] 369
Bailey, Tom 425, 1137
Baillie, Mike 1019
Bailter Space **57**, 58, 1343
Bain, Jimmy 316
Bain, Pete 1047
Bainbridge, Harvey 515
Baines, Una 391
Baird, Alex 574
Baird, Dan 459, 460
Baker, Andy 579, 1246
Baker, Anita **58**, 59, 1208
Baker, Arthur [1] 60, 84
Baker, Bea 1289
Baker, Bill 408
Baker, Brian 740
Baker, Chet 45
Baker, Dale 1017
Baker, David [Trombone] 728
Baker, David [Vocals] 728
Baker, Duck 477
Baker, Gary 724
Baker, George **59**
Baker, George Selection 59, 1122
Baker, Ginger 110, 124, 264, 702, 878, 893, 899, 1316, 1326, 1329
Baker, Glenn A. 636, 702
Baker, James 537
Baker, John 201
Baker, LaVern **59**, 104, 149, 1289, 1305
Baker, Lefty 1049
Baker, Lennie 996
Baker, Mickey **59**, 108, 338, 513, 733
Baker, Richard 976
Baker, Ron [1] 536
Baker, Roy Thomas 187, 306, 505, 1087
Baker, Steve [2] 904
Baker-Knight, Thomas 787
Bakerloo 1283
Balance, John 234, 897
Baldry, Long John 1081
Baldursson, Siggi 1099
Baldwin, Dave 554
Baldwin, Terry 560
Balfa, Tony 1144
Balfe, David 351
Balil 1273
Balin, Marty 583, 584, 585, 908
Ball 43
Ball, Dave [1] 20, 897, 1038
Ball, Dave [2] 897
Ball, Ed 1124
Ball, Gini 193
Ball, Ian 472
Ball, James A. 415
Ball, Roger 43
Ballads 453
Ballance, Laura 1104
Ballard, Clint Jr. 532
Ballard, Florence 423
Ballard, Glen 10, 209, 704, 761, 1228
Ballard, Hank **59**, 60, 146, 147, 357, 450, 1186, 1303, 1306, 1307
Ballard, Hank & the Midnighters 60, 205
Ballard, John 5
Ballard, Russ 35, 913, 976, 1071, 1141
Ballew, Chris 879, 880
Ballroom 736
Ballroom [1] 737
Ballroom [2] 737
Balough, Bill 960
Baluyut, Ed 1192

Baluyut, James 476, 1192
Baluyut, Richard 1192
Bambaataa, Afrika 60, 147, 607, 633, 647, 766, 1285, 1286, 1287, 1295, 1347, 1349
Bambaataa, Afrika & the Soul Sonic Force 60
Banana Splits 60, 1273, 1331
Bananarama 60, 439, 1287
Banashak, Joe 1151, 1286
Banbury, James 43
Band [1] 23, 61, 62, 117, 143, 175, 218, 257, 308, 342, 343, 424, 450, 513, 546, 647, 653, 721, 840, 945, 946, 1223, 1230, 1243, 1326
Band [3] 432
Band Aid 129, 214
Band of Gypsies [1] 523, 976
Band of Susans 62, 63
Bang Tango 1302
Bang the Party 1299
Bangalter, Thomas 278
Bangham, Kid 384
Bangles 63, 253, 537, 668, 912, 999, 1000, 1141, 1248, 1287, 1290, 1313, 1343, 1344
Bangs, Lester 196, 423, 492, 722, 1319
Banks, Bessie 1291
Banks, Homer 560
Banks, Peter [1] 1255, 1256, 1257
Banks, Ron 336
Banks, Tony 456
Baptista, Arnaldo 778, 876
Baptista, Sergio 778
Bar Kays 63, 64, 515, 516, 696, 711, 1277, 1284, 1292, 1295, 1309,
Bar-B-Q Killers 241
Barbara [1] 537
Barbarians 64, 1288, 1320
Barbarossa, Dave 132
Barbata, John 585, 733
Barbe, David 1099
Barber, Chris 329, 1293, 1326
Barber, Samuel 540
Barber, Tony 164, 166
Barbero, Lori 47, 48
Barbieri, Richard 579
Barbot, Bill 160, 580
Barclay James Harvest 64
Bardens, Pete 176
Bardo Pond 64, 65, 1280, 1300
Bardot, Brigitte 445, 446, 679
Bare, Bobby 1260, 1282
Barenaked Ladies 65, 66, 289, 1050, 1228
Barge, Gene 1227
Bargeld, Blixa 192, 193, 194, 268, 356
Barham, Meriel 837, 838
Bark Psychosis 66
Barker, Andrew 355
Barker, Paul 739
Barker, Phil 164
Barker, Philip 166
Barker, Rocco 415
Barlow, Barriemore 588
Barlow, Bruce 241
Barlow, Gary 781, 1115, 1226
Barlow, Lou 315, 334, 422, 423, 705, 914, 987, 988, 1018, 1023, 1346
Barnacle, Gary 1195
Barnes, Alan 234, 815
Barnes, James [1] 854
Barnes, Jimmy 234, 1342
Barnes, Kevin [1] 484, 699, 815, 816
Barnes, Kevin [2] 815
Barnes, Patrick 319
Barnes, Prentiss 759
Barnes, Ted 830
Barnes, Tim 376, 1008
Barnett, Spot 972
Barnstorm 576
Barocas, Zach 580
Baron [1] 376
Baron, Jeff 376
Baron, Jennifer 637, 638
Barone, Richard 125, 322, 601, 1343, 1344
Barre, Martin 587, 588, 589
Barrere, Gabriel Paul 659
Barrere, Paul 659, 660
Barrett, Marcia 125
Barrett, Mike 376

Barrett, Richard 198
Barrett, Richard [1] 198, 199
Barrett, Russell 200
Barrett, Syd 19, 45, 66, 67, 79, 120, 211, 225, 250, 251, 281, 292, 305, 355, 374, 375, 506, 507, 530, 531, 599, 745, 794, 816, 835, 861, 862, 886, 1039, 1053, 1118, 1136, 1141, 1235, 1244, 1277, 1280, 1283, 1289, 1291, 1323, 1330, 1343
Barretto, Ray 1285, 1292
Barri, Steve 108, 480, 578, 1024, 1165
Barron, Chris 1054
Barrow, Geoff 877, 971
Barry & the Remains 67
Barry, Jeff 35, 67, 260, 617, 754, 755, 830, 955, 998, 1060, 1289, 1301, 1311, 1312, 1331
Barry, John 20, 39, 307, 389, 688, 748, 826
Barry, Len 67, 680
Barson, Mike 685, 686
Barthol, Bruce 258
Bartholomew, Dave 67, 68, 148, 327, 328, 425, 652, 653, 661, 887, 1274, 1278, 1306
Bartlett, Homer Newton 646
Bartley, Jock 405, 846
Bartok, Bela 1268
Barton, Lou Ann 375
Barton, Steve 1156
Bartos, Karl 361
Base, Rob 1285
Basement Jaxx 68
Basement Wall 68
Basie, Count 44, 202, 831, 994, 1163, 1292
Basil, Toni 498
Baskin, Don 1112
Baskin, Richard 1093
Bass, Fontella 68, 402, 1276
Bass, Martha 68
Bassey, Shirley 20, 1255
Bastro 232, 451, 1023
Bates, Ashley 200
Bathgate, Alec 629, 1118, 1153, 1342
Batoh, Masaki 463, 464
Bators, Stiv 287
Bats 69, 1018
Bats ['60s] 224
Bats ['80s] 69, 1343
Batt, Mike 1072
Battin, Skip 167, 168
Battiste, Harold 459
Battlecat 1036
Batts, Ray 1274
Batty, Coby 126
Bauer, Joe [1] 1259
Bauer, Judah 1053
Bauer, Mireille 473
Baughn, David 338
Bauhaus 69, 70, 71, 288, 402, 672, 673, 776, 777, 1338
Bauman, John 996
Baxter, Jeff 331, 1172
Bay City Rollers 71, 234, 613, 1310, 1339
Bayer, Carole 754
Bayley, Blaze 564
Baylor, John 560
Bazalgette, Edward 1185
Bazilian, Eric 736
Bazooka [1] 1330
Beach Boys 1, 23, 34, 41, 71, 72, 73, 74, 75, 79, 92, 95, 107, 108, 122, 128, 151, 161, 166, 168, 174, 180, 208, 225, 226, 252, 254, 255, 262, 273, 278, 280, 290, 296, 302, 315, 339, 346, 358, 379, 397, 410, 411, 412, 413, 414, 426, 427, 433, 472, 501, 525, 527, 528, 529, 537, 544, 560, 577, 578, 585, 637, 663, 671, 705, 713, 734, 736, 772, 773, 780, 787, 790, 797, 821, 842, 852, 858, 867, 876, 897, 916, 923, 931, 944, 952, 956, 964, 971, 973, 1003, 1008, 1024, 1030, 1074, 1102, 1103, 1105, 1107, 1146, 1165, 1178, 1188, 1211, 1228, 1229, 1235, 1240, 1241, 1242, 1247, 1251, 1258, 1270, 1276, 1277, 1281, 1307, 1314, 1321, 1323
Beach, Reb 327, 1231
Beach-Nuts 1087
Beachwood Sparks 75
Beacon Street Union 75
Bean, Janet Beveridge 361, 432, 1354

Bear, Booga 207
Beard, Annette 986
Beard, Dean 986
Beard, Frank 1271
Bears [1] 76, 88
Beastie Boys 51, 76, 100, 101, 191, 271, 277, 365, 376, 397, 439, 440, 444, 462, 573, 591, 615, 679, 892, 926, 952, 962, 1035, 1101, 1134, 1173, 1184, 1185, 1210, 1258, 1279, 1295, 1340, 1345, 1346, 1348, 1349
Beat Farmers 77
Beat Happening 77, 157, 273, 1161, 1282
Beat Rodeo 981
Beat [US] 366, 367, 404, 788, 1278
Beatle Barkers 1024
Beatles 6, 10, 14, 22, 23, 24, 26, 31, 34, 43, 47, 54, 55, 56, 60, 61, 63, 64, 67, 68, 71, 72, 74, 77, 78, 79, 80, 81, 84, 85, 86, 87, 88, 89, 92, 93, 97, 106, 117, 118, 120, 124, 125, 126, 127, 128, 129, 132, 143, 144, 148, 152, 155, 161, 165, 166, 167, 168, 184, 185, 190, 195, 198, 200, 203, 204, 205, 206, 212, 213, 216, 220, 221, 222, 227, 230, 233, 240, 252, 255, 256, 260, 267, 270, 272, 277, 279, 280, 282, 288, 290, 293, 294, 296, 300, 310, 317, 319, 327, 328, 330, 339, 341, 346, 349, 350, 358, 359, 360, 370, 371, 375, 380, 383, 389, 399, 401, 403, 405, 410, 411, 412, 424, 426, 427, 429, 430, 432, 442, 446, 450, 460, 462, 465, 470, 472, 476, 477, 482, 488, 489, 491, 492, 499, 508, 509, 515, 516, 518, 527, 531, 532, 533, 534, 535, 539, 543, 544, 555, 556, 565, 566, 574, 582, 585, 589, 592, 594, 595, 598, 599, 602, 612, 614, 615, 617, 619, 621, 624, 625, 626, 627, 628, 630, 631, 636, 643, 644, 645, 647, 648, 649, 659, 690, 693, 694, 695, 697, 703, 704, 713, 714, 715, 716, 720, 725, 726, 728, 731, 734, 736, 743, 754, 755, 758, 771, 772, 773, 777, 778, 784, 787, 790, 799, 805, 811, 814, 815, 816, 820, 821, 823, 846, 850, 853, 855, 858, 864, 869, 873, 876, 877, 878, 884, 894, 903, 907, 916, 918, 919, 924, 925, 931, 932, 934, 935, 936, 938, 939, 940, 945, 949, 950, 959, 962, 964, 965, 968, 969, 973, 979, 986, 987, 990, 996, 997, 998, 999, 1001, 1002, 1003, 1008, 1014, 1015, 1016, 1017, 1024, 1025, 1027, 1030, 1033, 1034, 1035, 1054, 1057, 1058, 1065, 1070, 1071, 1077, 1082, 1087, 1090, 1104, 1105, 1106, 1107, 1109, 1110, 1113, 1115, 1116, 1119, 1122, 1123, 1124, 1126, 1135, 1136, 1141, 1156, 1157, 1158, 1161, 1164, 1165, 1169, 1179, 1180, 1187, 1191, 1202, 1210, 1211, 1212, 1220, 1223, 1224, 1230, 1238, 1239, 1240, 1241, 1242, 1243, 1251, 1253, 1255, 1256, 1257, 1270, 1275, 1277, 1282, 1283, 1290, 1291, 1292, 1293, 1297, 1299, 1307, 1308, 1309, 1310, 1311, 1312, 1313, 1314, 1316, 1317, 1318, 1319, 1320, 1321, 1322, 1323, 1327, 1328, 1339, 1341, 1342, 1343, 1344, 1346, 1350, 1353, 1354, 1355
Beatless 485
Beatmasters 37
Beatnik Beatch 585
Beatnuts 464
Beats by the Pound 702
Beau Brummels 80, 81, 117, 118, 381, 407, 676, 1187, 1288, 1319, 1320, 1327
Beau Marks 1292
Beauford, Carter 704
Beaumont, Jimmy 1019
Beautiful South 81, 82, 235, 542, 654
Beauvoir, Jean 916
BeBop Deluxe 82, 808, 1019, 1283
Becher, Curt 74
Bechirian, Roger 1065
Beck 55, 82, 83, 84, 252, 355, 380, 472, 693, 781, 952, 973, 1028, 1053, 1101, 1253, 1346, 1349
Beck, Bogert, Appice 1286
Beck, Jeff 84, 85, 123, 330, 410, 521, 537, 574, 644, 663, 696, 743, 745, 857, 1035, 1079, 1080, 1106, 1184, 1210, 1243, 1253, 1254, 1315, 1322, 1326
Beck, Jeff Group 84, 85, 330, 1081, 1240
Becker, Walter 35, 182, 385, 602, 870, 1072, 1073, 1092

Beckett, Barry 57, 829, 868, 976
Beckett, Larry 153
Beckett, Peter 868
Beckley, Gerry 23
Bedford, David 45
Bedhead 232
Bee Gees 74, 85, 86, 87, 186, 206, 213, 249, 318, 389, 396, 409, 456, 465, 582, 603, 679, 705, 999, 1093, 1115, 1141, 1157, 1279, 1289, 1293, 1325, 1341, 1342
Beebe, David 606
Beecher, Michael 175, 176
Been, Michael 175, 176
Bees Make Honey 87, 1335
Beethoven, Ludwig Van 594
Bef 999
Beggar 1287
Beggs, Nick 609
Beginning 619
Beiderbecke, Bix 246
Beinhorn, Michael 532, 698
Bel Airs [1] 195, 1292
Belafonte, Harry 205, 1353
Belew, Adrian 28, 36, 76, 88, 134, 618, 801, 1117, 1147
Belew, Audie 88
Belfast Gypsies 1316
Belgrave, Marcus 202
Believers 375
Bell Biv Devoe 88, 89, 137, 145, 442, 792
Bell Notes 1282, 1292
Bell [1] 97, 297, 376, 793, 818, 1096
Bell, Al 90, 418, 1069
Bell, Andy [1] 372, 373, 374, 942, 943
Bell, Archie 89, 794, 1284, 1335
Bell, Chris [1] 89, 97, 98, 212, 878, 1136, 1278
Bell, Eric 1133
Bell, Maggie 473
Bell, Marc 301, 520
Bell, Mark 101, 301
Bell, Norman 1223
Bell, Pedro 441
Bell, Richard 62
Bell, Ricky 88, 89, 792
Bell, Rico 722
Bell, Robert 115
Bell, Sasha 376
Bell, Steve 144, 439
Bell, Thom 169, 297, 536, 597, 598, 793, 794, 819, 1017, 1055, 1096, 1290, 1334, 1335
Bell, Todd 139
Bell, Vince 675
Bell, William 89, 90, 224, 418, 1277, 1281, 1294, 1295
Belladonna, Joey 31, 32
Bellamy, Howard 336
Belle & Sebastian 90, 334, 402, 459
Bellis, Bob 1253
Bellotte, Pete 597
Belltower 566
Belly 90, 91, 141, 1136, 1142, 1339, 1345
Belmont, Martin 338, 962, 1335
Belmonts 316, 317, 1178
Belshaw, Brian 114
Belushi, James 118
Belushi, John 31, 118
Belvin, Jesse 700, 850, 1219, 1294, 1305
Benair, Danny 1141
Benante, Charlie 31
Benatar, Pat 91, 92, 133, 296, 465, 635, 767, 919
Bender, Ariel 770, 1231
Benediktsson, Einar Orn 1099, 1100
Benet, Eric 983
Benge, Alfreda 1247
Benitiz, John Jellybean 367
Benjamin, Andre 833
Benjamin, Bennie 1314
Benjamin, Kent 1166
Bennett, Bob [1] 1042
Bennett, Bob [3] 1295
Bennett, Estelle 955
Bennett, Jay 138, 1223
Bennett, Joe 1050
Bennett, Mike 394

Bennett, Nedra 955
Bennett, Ronnie 955
Bennett, Tony 1199, 1201, 1203
Bennett, Veronica 955
Bennett, Will 21
Benning, Sadie 643
Benson, George [Guitarist] 512, 524, 1329
Benson, John 16
Bentley Rhythm Ace 874
Bentley, Taz 938
Benton, Brook 92, 514, 925, 1220, 1297
Berberich, Bob 665
Berenyi, Miki 680
Berg, Alban 579
Berg, Eric 579
Berg, Tony 1065, 1250
Bergeron, Shirley 846
Bergman, Alan 1093, 1094
Bergman, Marilyn 1094
Berlin [1] 36, 92, 244
Berlin, Irving 6, 50, 450, 1091
Berlin, Steve 109, 831
Berline, Byron 160, 418, 706, 845
Berliner, Jay 762
Berman, David 272, 821, 1007, 1008
Berman, Shelley 1007
Bernick, Andy 1110, 1111
Berns, Bert 159, 565, 566, 650, 1131, 1301, 1312
Bernstein, Elmer 292, 1070
Bernstein, Leonard 264, 430, 552, 797, 1062, 1094, 1229
Berry, Bill [2] 931, 1269
Berry, Chu 1232
Berry, Chuck 29, 30, 59, 61, 68, 71, 74, 78, 80, 92, 93, 94, 103, 119, 136, 137, 150, 158, 172, 178, 205, 227, 257, 268, 296, 310, 311, 317, 324, 334, 338, 353, 354, 358, 385, 410, 459, 461, 472, 513, 515, 532, 540, 630, 652, 661, 677, 712, 715, 787, 794, 852, 882, 892, 944, 949, 951, 976, 991, 992, 1062, 1087, 1117, 1135, 1138, 1140, 1141, 1193, 1228, 1241, 1258, 1274, 1276, 1278, 1281, 1282, 1303, 1304, 1314, 1315, 1317, 1319, 1328, 1352
Berry, Dave 623
Berry, Heidi 680, 1136
Berry, Jan 578, 1314
Berry, John [Country] 258
Berry, Mike 720
Berry, Richard 94, 451, 620, 1297
Berryman, Guy 235
Bertei, Adele 197
Bertolucci, Bernando 538
Bess, Carlos 464
Bessman, Jim 841
Best, Beatrice 591
Best, Pete 1280, 1319
Beta Band 55, 548
Bethea, Ken 820
Betinis, Mimi 857
Bettencourt, Nuno 383
Bettie Serveert 94, 95, 914, 1300
Bettis, John 304
Betts, Dickey 17, 18, 19, 1333
Betty Boop 139, 305
Beulah 95
Bevan, Alonza 358
Bevan, Bev 358
Beverly, Frankie 58, 711
Bevis Frond 669
Bevoir, Paul 589
Bewley, Randy 902
Bex 668
Bez 104
Bhatt, Vishwa Mohan 247
Bhosle, Asha 252
Biafra, Jello 103, 289, 553, 900, 993, 1277, 1340, 1341
Bialik, Louise 978
Bichel, Kenneth 1087
Bickers, Terry 541
Bid [1] 756
Bielli, Nick 579
Biff Bang Pow 1278
Big Apple Band 793
Big Audio 95

Big Audio Dynamite 45, 95
Big Audio Dynamite II 95
Big Bad Voodoo Daddy 994
Big Black [1] 95, 96, 510, 1000, 1345, 1346
Big Boi 362, 833, 834
Big Bopper 51, 87, 96, 534, 1181, 1187
Big Boy Pete 211, 671, 1277, 1280
Big Brother & the Holding Company 96, 410, 603, 653, 1323
Big Brother [1] 96, 603
Big Country 96, 97, 1019
Big Daddy Kane 97, 376, 892, 1076, 1148, 1274, 1285
Big DS 822
Big F 92
Big in Japan 654
Big in Japan [1] 429, 654
Big Maybelle 59, 1289, 1305
Big Rig 823
Big Star 89, 97, 98, 136, 205, 211, 212, 286, 426, 447, 671, 703, 834, 877, 878, 921, 934, 1024, 1045, 1066, 1107, 1123, 1166, 1188, 1248, 1290, 1339, 1343, 1344
Big Three [US] 691
Big Wheeler 38
Bikel, Theodore 239
Bikini Kill 98, 590, 643, 921, 1021, 1285, 1294, 1345
Billie [1] 98
Billingslea, Joe 246
Billy and Lillie 1282
Binder, Dennis 1163
Bingenheimer, Rodney 335
Biogen 1005
Biohazard 520
Birch, Martin 105, 563
Birch, Rob 1074
Birch, Will 325, 634, 667, 921, 1253, 1287, 1339
Bird, Andrew 502
Bird, Jeff 258
Bird, Jez 639
Bird, Ronnie 59, 449
Birdman [1] 195, 910
Birds [1] 98, 1035
Birdsong, Cindy 636
Birdsongs of the Mesozoic 744
Birdstuff 691
Birgisson, Jon Thor 1005
Birkin, Jane 445, 1101
Birthday Party 99, 192, 193, 268, 356, 463, 1292, 1338, 1341, 1342
Bis 99, 100
Biscoe, Joey 296
Biscuits, Chuck 282
Bishop [1] 415
Bishop, Dickie 329
Bishop, Elvin 100, 163, 1333
Bishop, Glen 415
Bishop, Jeb 451, 829, 1104
Bishop, Stephen [1] 100, 270, 1285
Bishops [1] 257
Bisi, Martin 130
Bissonette, Gregg 958
Bitch Magnet 232, 1023
Bitney, Dan 566
Bittan, Roy 718, 1062
Bivins, Michael 88, 89, 137, 792
Biz Markie 76, 100, 101, 287, 647, 820
Bizet, Georges 673
Bjelland, Kat 47, 48
Bjork 16, 101, 102, 301, 355, 602, 935, 971, 1023, 1044, 1099, 1100, 1159
Bjork, Brant 634
Black Box Recorder 102
Black Crowes 102, 103, 337, 385, 717, 738, 943, 1333
Black Dog 1273, 1299
Black Flag 43, 103, 104, 217, 302, 406, 740, 742, 921, 923, 924, 953, 954, 1249, 1339, 1340, 1341, 1345
Black Grape 104, 952, 1347
Black Heat 1285
Black Oak Arkansas 104
Black Rob 900
Black Sabbath 14, 32, 53, 104, 105, 106, 116,

126, 131, 144, 163, 164, 183, 232, 241, 252, 277, 281, 292, 294, 310, 316, 358, 389, 397, 417, 432, 506, 518, 553, 563, 605, 634, 702, 784, 802, 831, 832, 913, 962, 984, 1029, 1044, 1045, 1131, 1148, 1157, 1219, 1332, 1345
Black Satin 408
Black Sheep [2] 106, 477
Black Sugar 1277
Black Swan Network 821
Black Thought 957
Black, Alan 182
Black, Bill 1297, 1307, 1308
Black, Bobby 241
Black, Cilla 50, 106, 107, 999, 1293, 1319
Black, Frank 107, 281, 864, 1059, 1210
Black, Jay 581
Black, Pauline 992
Black, Robin [1] 588
Black, Stuart 726
Blackburn, Ade 225
Blackburn, Paul 472
Blackburn, Sean and Liz Masterson 225
Blackburn, Tony 1078
Blackeyed Susans 319
Blackfoot 16, 107, 108, 682
Blackhawk 834
Blackjack [1] 123
Blackman, Nicole 470, 471
Blackmon, Larry 145, 177, 1032
Blackmore, Ritchie 122, 292, 293, 327, 506, 832, 913, 1106, 1311
Blackmore, Ritchie Rainbow 316
Blackstreet 108, 324, 496
Blackwell, Bumps 661
Blackwell, Chris [1] 284, 390, 1154, 1245, 1355
Blackwell, Otis 108, 390, 880
Blackwell, Robert 1224
Blackwell, Scrapper 114
Blackwood Brothers 1351
Bladd, Stephen 454
Blades, Jack 799
Blades, Ruben 160
Blaikley, Alan 536
Blaine, Hal 108, 185, 196, 450, 517, 801, 939, 1011, 1061, 1178
Blair, John 516, 1313
Blair, Michael 929
Blake Babies 108, 109, 511
Blake, Cicero 537
Blake, Ginger 537
Blake, Norman [2] 1123
Blake, Tchad 271, 405, 641, 670, 796, 820, 915, 995, 1043, 1140, 1187, 1250
Blake, Tim 473, 474
Blake, Tommy 394
Blake, William 44, 364, 393
Blakey, Art 313, 1064
Blanchard, Terence 571
Bland, Bobby 147, 148, 514, 535, 981, 1277, 1305
Blank 1254
Blank, Boris 1254, 1255
Blasters [1] 21, 109, 493, 1292
Blatt, Melanie 16
Blauvelt, Howard Arthur 511
Blaze [1] 854
Bledsoe, Carroll 1110
Blendells 1276
Bley, Carla 470, 696, 805
Bley, Paul 260, 834
Blige, Mary J. 109, 110, 140, 323, 379, 464, 581, 731, 804, 899, 1076, 1081
Blind Blake [1] 1350
Blind Faith 110, 218, 219, 220, 264, 302, 432, 776, 899, 1233, 1240
Blind Melon 110
Blink One Eighty Two 111
Blitz, Johnny 287
Bloch 396
Bloch, Kurt 396
Block, Alan 245
Block, Kurt 396
Block, Rory 988
Blockheads 340
Blonde Redhead 111, 112

Blondie 40, 112, 113, 133, 187, 335, 352, 358, 465, 703, 727, 775, 788, 878, 896, 954, 1001, 1029, 1087, 1172, 1278, 1313, 1336, 1338, 1339, 1355, 1356
Blood Sweat & Tears 24, 113, 127, 195, 358, 512, 534, 555, 587, 809, 919, 1329
Blood, Dave 289, 290
Bloodstone [1] 43
Bloodvessel, Buster 53
Bloom, Bobby 113, 577
Bloom, Eric 116
Bloom, Luka 559, 1328
Bloomfield, Michael 114, 141, 163, 341, 358, 450
Blossom Toes 114, 1290
Blossoms 272, 674
Blotzer, Bobby 920
Blow Monkeys 567
Blow, Kurtis 115, 397, 1160, 1283, 1287, 1347
Blue Caps 1194, 1308
Blue Cheer 115, 411, 463, 634, 775, 1299, 1323
Blue Chips 1298
Blue Diamonds 609
Blue Jays [1] 759
Blue Magic 700, 1096
Blue Men 720
Blue Nile 115, 116, 235
Blue Notes [2] 724
Blue Orchids 391
Blue Oyster Cult 116, 117, 194, 222, 324, 406, 515, 730, 910, 1341
Blue Ridge Rangers 117, 421
Blue Rodeo 117, 995
Blue Shadows 260
Blue Sky 1232
Blue Sky Boys 1351
Blue Things 117, 118, 1318, 1319
Blue Zone [1] U.K. 1068
Blue, Buddy 77
Blue, David 688
Blue, Pamela 720
Bluenotes 1262
Blues Brothers 118, 594, 974
Blues By Five 1275
Blues Explosion 131
Blues Magoos 24, 118, 646, 786
Blues Project 113, 119, 213, 657, 1258, 1326, 1329
Blues Traveler 119, 120, 506, 704, 1326
Blues, Elwood 118
Bluestars 1301
Bluetile Lounge 773
Bluetones 120
Blumenfeld, Roy 119
Blunstone, Colin 35, 844, 845, 1270
Blunt, Martin 201
Blur 100, 120, 121, 190, 475, 500, 649, 686, 695, 726, 779, 811, 940, 1022, 1076, 1104, 1115, 1216, 1299, 1322, 1346, 1347
BMX Bandits 846, 1045, 1046
Bo, Eddie 1273, 1286
Boards of Canada 1292, 1299, 1300
Bob & Earl 121, 285, 535, 952
Bob B. Soxx & the Blue Jeans 536, 674, 1052
Bobby Z 1215
Bobo, Willie 977
Bocelli, Andrea 318
Bodean, Sammy 122
BoDeans 121, 122, 159, 267
Bodeco 361
Bodine [1] 139
Bodine, Michelle 139
Bodnar, Andrew 841, 962
Body Count 553, 554, 1277
Bodysnatchers 1298, 1299
Boettcher, Curt 40, 41, 122, 226, 736, 737, 971
Bogart, Humphrey 527
Bogart, Neil 624, 646, 996, 1070
Bogdan, Henry 520
Bogert, Tim 84, 1318
Boiled in Lead 388
Bolan, Marc 133, 212, 279, 336, 359, 466, 595, 600, 770, 1070, 1113, 1114, 1115, 1322
Bolick, Earl 776
Bolin, Tommy 122, 123, 292, 293, 576, 577
Bolles, Don 461
Bolotin, Michael 123

Bolton, Michael **123**, 230, 560, 625, 719, 953, 1094, 1308, 1325
Bomb Squad [1] 324, 376, 552, 897, 898, 1135
Bomb Squad [2] 130
Bomb the Bass 355
Bon Jovi **123**, 124, 217, 249, 459, 675, 793, 805, 872, 1066, 1231, 1257, 1302
Bond [1] 124
Bond, Graham **124**, 125, 264, 477, 878, 1275, 1284, 1326, 1329
Bond, Graham Organization 124, 587, 1315, 1316
Bond, James E. 28
Bond, Jimmy 153
Bond, Victoria 1175
Bonds, Gary 'U.S.' 107, **125**, 205, 661, 662, 1281, 1282
Bondy, Egon 900
Bone Thugs N Harmony 702, 805
Bone, Ponty 154
Boner, Freda 108, 109, 511
Boney M **125**
Bonfa, Luiz 158
Bonfanti, Jim 919
Bongos **125**, 126, 601, 981, 1343
Bongwater 82, **126**
Bonham 645
Bonham, John 76, 200, 367, 644, 645
Bonin, Paul 589
BonJovi, Jon 124, 217, 798, 805, 1047
Bonnar, John 461
Bonner, Gary 283, 688
Bonner, Graham 1108
Bonner, Joe 688, 1108
Bonner, Leroy 'Sugarfoot' 818
Bonnet, Graham 913
Bonney, Simon 268
Bonnie Prince Billy 821
Bonniwell, Sean 777
Bono 116, 159, 160, 175, 722, 825, 1169, 1170
Bono, Sonny 18, 206, 328, 769, 770, 1042
Bonoff, Karla 955, 1285
Bontemps Roulez 211, 962
Bonzo Dog Band **126**, 127, 476, 509, 968, 1154
Boo Radleys **127**, 128, 680, 778, 1347
Boo Yaa TRIBE 389
Boogie Boys 1279
Boogie Down Productions **128**, 324, 892, 897, 962, 1173, 1274, 1277, 1284, 1285, 1287, 1348, 1349
Booker T. & Priscilla 1013, 1069
Booker T. & the MG's 90, **128**, 129, 253, 418, 696, 925, 976, 1273, 1277, 1281, 1285, 1292, 1294, 1297, 1309, 1324, 1332
Booker, James 1297
Boomtown Rats **129**, 130
Boon 742
Boon, Clint 561
Boon, D. 217, 406, 740, 741, 742, 1174, 1210
Boone, Debby 185
Boone, Larry 305
Boone, Pat **130**, 148, 268, 357, 787, 796, 1300, 1309, 1310
Booth, Tim 575, 576
Boquist, Dave 1039
Borchardt, Jeffrey 1188
Borden, Barry 'B.B.' 834
Bordin, Mike 389
Boredoms **130**, 131, 216, 259, 927
Borland, Wes 656
Borrell, Craig 1101
Boss Hog **131**
Boss Tones 67
Bossi, Benjamin 954
Bostaph, Paul 1021
Boston 52, **132**, 425, 611, 757, 1109, 1150, 1155, 1331
Boston Tea Party 1275
Boston, Anne Richmond 1109
Bostrom, Derrick 719
Botnick, Bruce 152, 712
Bottle Rockets 935
Bottler, Mitchell 226
Bottrell, Bill 271, 572
Bottum, Roddy 388, 389, 557
Bouchard, Albert 116

Bourgeois Tagg **132**
Bourgeois, Brent 132
Bourke, Pieter 461, 462
Bovell, Dennis 130, 238, 1023
Bow Street Runners **132**
Bow Wow Wow 30, **132**, 133, 257, 1212
Bowen, Jimmy 315, 629, 1292
Bower, Mick 702
Bowers, Bryan 702
Bowers, Tony 1013
Bowie 133
Bowie, Ash 520
Bowie, David 2, 19, 25, 31, 40, 70, 82, 88, 102, 107, 120, 121, 124, 126, **133**, 134, 135, 136, 152, 162, 187, 190, 252, 306, 315, 327, 335, 339, 354, 355, 368, 369, 401, 409, 444, 451, 463, 479, 482, 486, 500, 505, 526, 547, 554, 556, 579, 601, 633, 643, 647, 649, 679, 687, 695, 698, 716, 729, 769, 776, 789, 794, 799, 803, 804, 807, 808, 834, 865, 874, 875, 886, 896, 900, 901, 904, 923, 926, 929, 973, 1015, 1045, 1072, 1081, 1086, 1093, 1098, 1104, 1114, 1122, 1134, 1144, 1164, 1169, 1170, 1173, 1184, 1185, 1191, 1192, 1195, 1202, 1203, 1204, 1212, 1231, 1284, 1288, 1320, 1322, 1325, 1331, 1335, 1338
Bowie, Joseph 197
Bowie, Lester 68, 197
Bowman, Rob 61, 62, 129, 442
Box Tops 97, **136**, 137, 198, 211, 212, 230, 328, 1325
Box, Mick 1176, 1177, 1178
Boxhead Ensemble 1246
Boy George 37, 196, 274, 275, 1356
Boyce & Hart 1275
Boyce, Keith 1121
Boyce, Mark 131
Boyce, Tommy 754
Boyd, Joe 187, 334, 335, 930, 1126, 1139
Boyfriends 189
Boykins, DeAndre 613
Boylan, Jeffrey 544
Boylan, John 787
Boylan, Terence 1286
Boyle, Danny 38
Boyle, Jeremy 592
Boymerang 66
Boys Next Door [1] 99, 1341
Boys [1] 51
Boyz 327
Boyz II Men 49, 88, **137**, 184, 278, 592, 664, 939, 1307, 1335
Bozulich, Carla 460
Bozzio, Dale 743
Bozzio, Terry 628, 743, 1266
Brackman, Jacob 1010
Bracy, Timothy 725, 726
Bradfield, James Dean 355, 740
Bradford, Geoff 1315
Bradley, Balfe 1121, 1122
Bradley, Carrie 27
Bradley, Jan 1276, 1301
Bradley, Owen 81, 191, 535
Bradshaw, Paul 1287
Bradshaw, Tiny 1303, 1304, 1305, 1352
Brady Bunch 433
Brady, Paul 270, 915
Bragg, Billy **137**, 138, 360, 504, 1223, 1354, 1355
Braid **139**, 160, 462, 977
Brainiac **139**
Braithwaite, Stuart 750
Bralove, Bob 481
Bramah, Martin 391
Bramhall, Doyle 1186
Bramlett, Bekka 414
Bramlett, Bonnie 297
Bramlett, Delaney 159, 173, 218, 297, 1218
Bramley, Clyde 537
Branca, Glenn 62, 1336
Brand New Heavies **139**, 140, 495
Brand Nubian 1158, 1274
Brand, John 467
Brand, Oscar 1353
Brandy **140**
Branigan, Laura 123, **140**, 901
Brant, Jon 204

Brant, Marley 845
Brashear, Todd 837
Brass Construction 151, 1284, 1291
Brass Ring 1296
Bratmobile 139, 1021, 1285, 1345
Brats 1286
Braxton, Toni 50, **140**, 940
Brayfield, Buddy 835
Bread [1] **140**, 141, 181, 413, 430, 1060, 1279, 1286
Breakbeat Era 1018
Bream, Julian 311
Breathless [UK] 562
Brebner, Asa 942
Brecht, Bertolt 160, 288, 390
Brecker Brothers 1070, 1266
Brecker, Michael 382, 747, 1120
Brecker, Randy 113
Bredice, Richard 606
Breeders 27, 90, 91, 95, **141**, 838, 864, 994, 1023, 1136, 1142, 1192, 1345
Brel, Jacques 6, 19, 20, 102, 239, 308, 753, 999, 1202, 1203, 1204
Bremner, Billy 677, 949
Brenda & The Tabulations 700
Brennan, Kathleen 1200
Brennan, Stan 870
Brenner, Simon 534
Brenston, Jackie 498, 1163, 1295, 1303, 1307, 1308
Bressanutti, Daniel 435
Bretch, Bertolt 390
Brewer & Shipley **141**, 142
Brewer, Don 478
Brewer, Michael 141
Brian Jonestown Massacre **142**, 656
Brice, Fanny 1092
Bricheno, Tim 15
Brick **142**, 244, 1284
Brickell, Edie **142**, 143, 188, 313, 1089
Brickell, Edie & New Bohemians 143
Bricker, Gene 697
Brides of Funkenstein 348, 1284
Bridgewater, Joe 202
Brigati 918
Brigati, David 385
Brigati, Eddie 385, 918
Briggs, Billy 67
Briggs, David [1] 490
Briggs, David [2] [Producer] 193
Briggs, She'kspere 861
Bright, Kevin 931
Bright, Tim 664
Brightman, Sarah 940
Brill, Rob 92
Brilleaux, Lee 324, 325, 338, 1335
Brinsley Schwarz 143, 144, 210, 230, 241, 254, 324, 353, 355, 472, 673, 677, 678, 1335, 1337
Brion, Jon 33, 355, 357, 483, 484, 531, 585, 693
Brisco Hay, Vanessa 902
Bristol, Johnny 980, 1095
Britny Fox 1302
Broach, Chris 139
Broadbent, Micky 1121
Broadcast 638, 771
Brock, Dave 515
Brock, Issac 750
Brock, Jeremy 405
Brock, Napoleon Murphy 1266, 1267
Brock, Timothy 750
Brock, Tony 50
Brodsky Quartet 101, 256
Brody, Bruce 602
Brokaw, Chris 232, 241, 1248
Brokeback 361
Bronski Beat **144**, 243, 1100
Brook, Michael 401, 419, 776, 816, 1005
Brook, Rachel 419, 773
Brooker, Gary 100, 162, 219, 608, 893, 894
Brookes, Jon 201
Brooklyn Bridge 268, 403, 687
Brooks, Don 1297
Brooks, Garth 307, 595, 624, 738, 831, 948, 1119
Brooks, Hadda 1028, 1289

Brooks, Harvey [1] 551
Brooks, La La 272
Brooks, Meredith 556
Broonzy, Big Bill 477, 587, 953, 1002, 1286
Brotherhood of Lizards 224, 795
Brotherhood of Man 161, 353, 1276
Brothers Four 560
Brothers Johnson **144**, 242, 832, 1284
Brothers [1] 144, 206
Brotzmann, Peter 867
Broudie, Ian 351, 501, 554, 654, 935, 1197
Broughton, Edgar **144**
Broughton, Edgar Band 1283
Broughtons 145
Browder, Stony 323
Brown Dots 560
Brown [1] 451
Brown, Al 1285
Brown, Amanda 468
Brown, Arthur [1] **145**, 1282
Brown, Arthur [1] Crazy World 363, 364
Brown, Bill 1207
Brown, Billy [1] 752
Brown, Bobby [1] 88, 89, 109, **145**, 496, 792, 1348
Brown, Bruce [2] 727
Brown, Bundy K. 241, 451
Brown, Buster 1112
Brown, Carlinhos 993
Brown, Carter 636
Brown, Charles [1] 202, 385, 915, 1227, 1273, 1296, 1304
Brown, Chuck 1160, 1284
Brown, Clarence [1] 'Gatemouth' 895, 1002
Brown, Danny [1] Joe 752
Brown, David [1] 976
Brown, Errol 540, 1086, 1087
Brown, Foxy [Rap] 581
Brown, Gerald 997
Brown, Greg [1] 240
Brown, Greg [2] 172
Brown, Ian 1084
Brown, Ian [1] 1074, 1084
Brown, James [1] 60, 118, 121, 129, 134, 139, **145**, 146, 147, 148, 191, 197, 198, 208, 212, 237, 282, 323, 333, 340, 341, 347, 374, 407, 408, 426, 433, 442, 475, 516, 536, 582, 607, 615, 627, 631, 644, 662, 663, 730, 742, 771, 814, 842, 860, 874, 890, 921, 925, 935, 936, 1025, 1026, 1029, 1043, 1069, 1112, 1135, 1136, 1148, 1158, 1164, 1220, 1222, 1225, 1229, 1236, 1284, 1285, 1286, 1305, 1324, 1325, 1334, 1347, 1351, 1352
Brown, James [1] & His Famous Flames 145
Brown, Jimmy 142
Brown, Joe [1] 442, 1310, 1311
Brown, John [01] 793, 794
Brown, Lawrence [1] [Trombone] 1163
Brown, Mark [8] 253
Brown, Marty 766
Brown, Maxine **148**, 569, 1324, 1293, 1300, 1301
Brown, Mel 850
Brown, Michael [1] 646
Brown, Michael [Keyboards] 645, 1086, 1087
Brown, Mick 327, 743
Brown, Nappy 171, 1282, 1304
Brown, Nick 1071
Brown, Oscar Jr. [1] 317, 558
Brown, Pete [1] 1163, 1283
Brown, Phill 534
Brown, Ray [1] 59
Brown, Richard [3] 749
Brown, Rick [1] 963
Brown, Roy [1] 147, **148**, 363, 507, 883, 1291, 1292, 1303, 1304, 1305, 1351
Brown, Ruth 59, **148**, 149, 629, 915, 1305, 1352
Brown, Shirley 1295
Brown, Steve [Producer] 273
Brown, Terry 967
Brown, Tim [1] 127
Brown, Timothy 128
Brown, Tom [1] 544
Brown, Vinnie 783
Brown, Walter 93
Brown, William [Memphis Soul] 752

Browne, Colleen 837, 838
Browne, Ivan 646
Browne, Jackson 18, 57, 125, **149**, 150, 230, 346, 559, 569, 606, 657, 658, 662, 705, 706, 798, 829, 914, 915, 955, 1119, 1269, 1328
Brownson, Derry 365
Brownstein, Carrie 1021, 1022
Brownsville Station **150**, 296, 630, 767
Brubeck, Dave 627
Bruce, Bobby 1032
Bruce, Buddy 197
Bruce, Denny 384, 385, 433
Bruce, Jack 124, 264, 330, 470, 490, 707, 708, 771, 878, 927, 1266, 1300, 1316, 1326, 1329
Bruce, Lenny 210, 503, 813, 927, 928, 953, 1274
Bruford 1255
Bruford, Bill 473, 617, 618, 1201, 1255, 1257
Brunetti, Richard 328
Bruni, Jebin 899
Bruno, Franklin 1302
Brute 207
Bruton, Stephen 375
Bruton, Turner Stephen 375, 376
Bryan, David 123
Bryan, Mark 538
Bryan, Robert 82
Bryans, Richard 55
Bryant, Boudleaux 381, 983
Bryant, Don 849
Bryant, Felice 381, 983
Bryant, Marty 1096
Bryant, Ray 1292
Bryant, Ray Combo 1297
Bryars, Gavin 368, 1005
Brydon, Mark 752
Bryson, Jeanie 919
Bryson, Peabo 317, 409, 692
Bryson, Wally 919, 1339
Brzezicki, Mark 97
BT 1286
BT Express **150**, 151, 1284, 1291
Bubble Puppy **151**
Buchanan, Bill 403
Buchanan, Bob 561
Buchanan, Paul 115, 116
Buchanan, Roy 84, **151**, 512, 513, 1296
Buchanan, Wallis 577
Buck, Mike 384, 665
Buck, Peter 138, 245, 357, 399, 415, 531, 612, 665, 930, 931, 1174, 1227, 1248, 1269, 1343, 1344
Buck, Rob 1127
Buck, Robert 1126
Buckingham Nicks 151
Buckingham, Lindsey **151**, 152, 412, 413, 414, 796, 797, 798, 857, 1007
Buckinghams **152**, 1264, 1296
Buckland, Jon 234
Buckley, Jeff **152**, 235, 506
Buckley, Robert 591
Buckley, Tim 113, **152**, 153, 154, 288, 760, 785, 786, 1084, 1136, 1328
Buckmaster, Paul 233, 235, 596, 597, 598, 950, 952
Buckner, Richard **154**, 175
Budd, Harold 231, 368
Budgie [1] 729, 730, 1014
Budgie [Drums] 1014, 1015
Budgie [Metal] 1023
Buell, Bebe 965
Buff, Paul 1268, 1297
Buffalo Daughter **154**, 155
Buffalo Springfield 44, 75, 117, 127, 143, **155**, 270, 576, 646, 665, 667, 668, 752, 754, 869, 870, 898, 943, 1082, 1235, 1259, 1260, 1262, 1319, 1323, 1327
Buffalo Tom **155**, 156, 246
Buffalo, Norton 242
Buffett, Jimmy **156**, 157, 917, 1228, 1213
Buffett, Jimmy & the Coral Reefer Band 156
Buggles 39, **157**, 1256, 1338
Bugnel, Jim 411
Buhne, Lorenzo 310
Buick MacKane 375, 376
Buie, Buddy 223

Built to Spill **157**, 158
Bukem, LTJ 471, 860, 1018, 1290
Bull [1] 158
Bull, Martyn 211
Bull, Richard 634
Bull, Sandy **158**, 477
Buller, Ed 128, 1025, 1099
Bullet LaVolta 203
Bulletboys 1302
Bulloch, Martin 750
Bultitude, Paul 589
Bundrick, John 'Rabbit' 1222
Bunford, Huw 1103
Bunker Hill 1243
Bunker, Clive 587
Bunnell, Dewey 23
Bunnell, George 1089
Bunnymen 351
Bunskoeke, Herman 94
Bunton, Emma 98
Bunyan, John 1090
Buoys 535
Burch, Rick 591
Burchill, Charlie 1012, 1013
Burdon, Eric 29, 30, 324, 432, 1123, 1131, 1206, 1315, 1316, 1325, 1334
Burdon, Eric & the Animals 30
Burdon, Eric & the New Animals 29, 281
Bureau [1] 307
Burgess, Anthony 519
Burgess, Dave 197, 788
Burgess, Iain 580
Burgess, Mark 196
Burgess, Paul 554, 1126
Burgess, Sonny **158**, 944, 1307
Burgess, Sonny [1] 158
Burgess, Tim 201, 475, 972
Burke, Betty 408
Burke, Clarence 408
Burke, Clarence Jr. 408
Burke, Clem 336
Burke, Gary 571
Burke, Solomon 118, **159**, 224, 245, 450, 895, 996, 1106, 1324, 1325
Burlison, Paul 160
Burn, Malcolm 460, 875
Burnett, Larry 405
Burnett, T-Bone 122, **159**, 160, 175, 229, 230, 255, 257, 267, 415, 470, 524, 600, 601, 612, 858, 859, 1204
Burnette, Billy 262, 414
Burnette, Dorsey 460, 788
Burnette, Johnny **160**, 787, 1070, 1292, 1308, 1310
Burnette, Johnny & Roll Trio 160
Burnette, Patrick 461
Burnette, Smiley 311
Burnham, Hugo 448
Burning Airlines **160**
Burning Spear 1355, 1356
Burns, Bob [Drums] 175
Burns, Gary 971
Burns, Jake 1082
Burns, Joey 175
Burns, Karl 391, 392, 394
Burns, Ralph 202
Burns, Scott 993
Burnstein, Cliff 852, 967
Burr, Clive 564
Burrage, Harold 285
Burrell, Boz 52, 617
Burrell, Kenny 203, 430, 1185, 1186
Burroughs, William S. 821, 929, 1273
Burrows, Tony **161**, 353, 1276
Burt-Martin, Wes 143
Burton, Barry 22
Burton, Cliff 729
Burton, James 122, 155, 238, 256, 267, 494, 512, 517, 786, 787, 789, 801, 845, 846, 882, 883, 1090, 1218, 1230, 1308
Busch, Neil 27
Bush [1] **161**
Bush [2] 161
Bush Tetras 954
Bush, Dave 393, 394
Bush, David 393
Bush, George 32, 160

Bush, John [Vocals] 32, 143
Bush, Kate 26, 27, 82, **161**, 162, 236, 445, 507, 707, 747
Bush, Roger 418
Bush, Sam 893
Busher, Jerry 437
Bushwick Bill 462
Business 1298
Butcher, Blinda 315, 779
Butler, Antonia 162
Butler, Artie 998
Butler, Bernard **162**, 693, 713, 1098, 1278, 1283, 1347
Butler, Billy [2] 442, 558, 709
Butler, Chris 1199
Butler, Floyd 433
Butler, Geezer 105
Butler, Jerry **162**, 163, 197, 380, 418, 512, 514, 516, 557, 558, 709, 819, 1208, 1229, 1299, 1324, 1335
Butler, Richard 896
Butler, Tim 896
Butler, Tony [1] 97
Butlers 711
Butterfield Blues Band 163
Butterfield, Paul 100, 114, **163**, 179, 630, 708, 754, 1287, 1300, 1309, 1326, 1329
Butterfield, Paul Blues Band 100, 163, 358, 711
Butterflies [1] 1291
Butterfly Train 157
Butterfly [1] 314
Butters, Steve 451
Butthole Surfers 24, 130, 131, **163**, 164, 290, 375, 406, 599, 924
Buttrey, Kenneth A. 81, 653
Buxton, Felix 68
Buzzcocks 9, 38, 39, **164**, 165, 166, 302, 358, 396, 484, 485, 510, 548, 574, 581, 687, 688, 753, 874, 1001, 1003, 1045, 1061, 1104, 1131, 1278, 1279, 1292, 1336, 1337, 1339
Bykowski, Ron 441, 842
Byrd, Bobby 121, 146, 147
Byrd, Donald 495
Byrd, Joe & the Field Hippies 1175
Byrd, Joseph 246, 1175
Byrd, Roy 895
Byrds 22, 75, 78, 80, 81, 97, 98, 117, 118, 125, 141, 142, 155, **166**, 167, 168, 214, 215, 221, 222, 238, 239, 253, 254, 269, 270, 272, 304, 337, 351, 395, 405, 406, 410, 418, 419, 426, 432, 465, 480, 491, 519, 525, 531, 555, 556, 561, 580, 643, 667, 672, 676, 691, 693, 704, 735, 736, 760, 761, 772, 773, 834, 845, 846, 855, 856, 869, 878, 913, 931, 932, 941, 971, 979, 1038, 1071, 1077, 1123, 1136, 1141, 1147, 1156, 1165, 1178, 1216, 1253, 1255, 1261, 1263, 1281, 1287, 1291, 1301, 1316, 1318, 1319, 1320, 1322, 1323, 1327, 1329, 1339, 1343, 1344, 1353, 1354
Byrne, David 47, 88, 126, 168, 169, 190, 208, 225, 252, 368, 439, 618, 778, 953, 1116, 1117, 1118, 1136
Byrne, Peter [1] 781
Byrne, Sean 257
Byron, David 1176, 1177, 1178
Byron, Jean-Michel 1150

C

C & C Music Factory **170**
C., Joe [1] 615
CA Quintet **170**
Cabaret Voltaire 8, **170**, 171, 205, 355, 1019, 1284, 1286, 1289
Cable, Stuart 1076
Cacavas, Chris 337, 485, 1248
Cacophony 31, 721
Caddy, Alan 615
Cadets [1] 171, 794
Cadillacs **171**, 172, 264, 697, 793, 850, 1274, 1280
Cadogan, Kevin 1135
Cafe Society [2] 947
Cafferty, John **172**, 490
Cafferty, John & the Beaver Brown Band 172
Cage, John 62, 633, 935, 1041, 1289
Cahn, Elliot 996

Cahn, Sammy 848, 1091
Cain, Jonathan 50, 604, 1198
Cain, Randy 297
Cain, Sim 954
Caine, Michael 192, 321, 685
Cairns, Andy 1131, 1132, 1191
Cairns, David 988
Cairns, Gregg 1191
Cake [1] **172**, 440
Cakekitchen 1343
Calamity Jane 1121
Calder, Jeff 1109
Caldwell, Bobby [Guitar] 123, 471, 1227
Caldwell, Ronnie 63
Caldwell, Tom 699
Caldwell, Toy 682, 699
Cale, J.J. 5, **172**, 173, 174, 218, 219, 220, 318, 450, 451, 682, 976
Cale, John 20, **173**, 174, 175, 319, 334, 369, 547, 798, 929, 941, 1031, 1045, 1065, 1085, 1188, 1189, 1190
Calexico **175**
Calhoun, Andrew 286
Calhoun, Dave 133
Calhoun, Will 663
California, Randy 1056
Calix, Mira 1300
Call **175**, 176
Call, John 901
Callahan, Bill [1] 837, 1034, 1035
Callas, Maria 367
Callier, Alex 538, 539
Callier, Terry 830, 831
Calloway, Cab 118, 324, 571, 614, 1304
Calvert, Bob 515
Calvert, Craig 675
Calvert, Phill 99
Calvert, Robert [1] 26
Calvi, Eric 45
Camel **176**, 181, 697
Cameo 145, **177**, 1148, 1160, 1284, 1334
Cameron, Doug [1] 321
Cameron, G.C. 1055
Cameron, John [1] 330, 331
Cameron, Matt 767, 849, 906, 1045, 1125
Camp, Greg 1028
Camp, Hamilton 653, 907
Camp, Jon 932
Campagne, Carmen 919
Campbell, Al [1] 1211
Campbell, Ali 1170
Campbell, Brian 225
Campbell, Eddie 1129
Campbell, Glen 197, 745, 787, 1151, 1211
Campbell, Glen [1] 122, 882, 1211, 1297
Campbell, Isobel 90, 459
Campbell, J.J. 1253
Campbell, Luther [1] 1167, 1348
Campbell, Mike [1] 667, 798, 856, 857, 956
Campbell, Mike [2] 1107
Campbell, Stan 1052
Campbell, Tevin 278, 890
Campbell, Vivian 316
Camper Van Beethoven **177**, 178, 261, 262, 281, 804, 1344, 1345
Can 8, 100, 131, 165, **178**, 179, 301, 392, 440, 460, 463, 548, 668, 771, 789, 898, 1108, 1111, 1155, 1289, 1296, 1301, 1331
Candelario, Benji 68
Candlebox 1197
Canned Heat 116, **179**, 1024, 1075, 1326, 1350
Cannibal & the Headhunters 636, 1276, 1300
Cannon, Ace 1283
Cannon, Brian 94
Cannon, Freddy 74, **179**, 205, 1282, 1292
Cannon, Joe 517
Canterbury Fair 1298
Cantrell, Jerry 14, 15
Canty, Brendan 436, 437, 690, 783, 944
Canty, Jimmy 689, 783
Cap'n Jazz 139, 592, 895
Capaldi, Jim 701, 1153, 1154, 1155, 1233
Capehart, Jerry 227
Capital Q 337
Capitols **179**, 336, 1281, 1282
Capote, Truman 842, 1091
Cappadonna 464

Capps, Andy 157
Capris [1] **179**, 180, 1307
Captain 279
Captain & Tennille **180**, 185, 917, 989
Captain America 1185
Captain Beefheart 107, 114, 130, 144, 145, 164, **180**, 181, 246, 395, 459, 501, 520, 557, 688, 773, 867, 898, 900, 935, 1265, 1266, 1268, 1276, 1287, 1326, 1337
Captain Beefheart & the Magic Band 180, 181
Captain Sensible 279, 795, 804
Captains Of Industry 1243
Car 1285
Caravan [1] 176, **181**, 182, 183, 703, 1038, 1223, 1224, 1296, 1331
Caravelles 1311
Carbo, Chuck 1054
Carbo, Leonard 1054
Cardigans **183**, 321, 630, 671, 1050
Cardinal **183**, 235, 284, 705
Cardinals 1306
Care [1] 654
Carey, Bob 785
Carey, Jake 118, 412
Carey, Mariah 49, 88, 140, **183**, 184, 291, 305, 442, 543, 837, 978, 1014, 1147, 1164, 1184
Carey, Zeke 412
Carla 1277
Carlisle, Cliff 1158
Carlo, Tyran 1229
Carlos, Wendy 8
Carlson, Charles 248
Carlton, Larry 57, 1061
Carlucci, Michael 1232
Carmassi, Denny 757
Carmen [1] 184
Carmen, Eric **184**, 190, 304, 919, 1299, 1339
Carmichael, Arnell 841
Carmichael, Darren 841
Carmichael, Hoagy 202, 1200
Carmichael, James [2] 242
Carmody, Kev 1110
Carmody, Seana 1193
Carnes, Kim **184**, 303, 304, 1093
Carney, Ralph 446
Carnochan, Ian 1193
Carpenter, John [1] 116
Carpenter, Karen 185, 186, 297, 876, 1040
Carpenter, Mary-Chapin 1225, 1328
Carpenter, Richard 185, 186
Carpenter, Richard [1] 185, 186
Carpenter, Richard [Rock] 185, 186
Carpenter, Stephen 295
Carpenters [1] **185**, 186, 626, 1003, 1226, 1276, 1286
Carr, Eric 624, 625
Carr, James **186**
Carr, Leroy 329
Carr, Martin 127, 128
Carr, Valerie 1292
Carr, Wynona 1305, 1351
Carrack, Paul 5, **186**, 187, 598, 601, 735, 736, 1065, 1174, 1335
Carrasco, Joe 'King' **187**
Carrasco, Joe 'King' & the Crowns 907
Carrasco, Joe 'King' Y Las Coronas 187
Carrier, Lori 726
Carrion, Doug 302
Carroll, Earl [2] 'Speedo' 171
Carroll, Jack 1091
Carroll, Jim [1] 1189
Carroll, Ted 257
Carruthers, William 1047, 1048
Cars **187**, 188, 306, 747, 922, 942, 999, 1029, 1088, 1278, 1338
Carson, Lori **188**, 470, 471
Carter Dimmock, Sheila 371
Carter Family 56, 432, 1351, 1353
Carter the Unstoppable Sex Machine 874
Carter, A.P. 1174
Carter, Andrew 673
Carter, Betty 203
Carter, Carlene 187, 354, 962
Carter, Chris [1] 1142
Carter, Chris [2] 335, 336
Carter, Clarence 186, **188**, 189, 195, 1277, 1287, 1325

Carter, John [2] 298
Carter, Larry 954
Carter, Laura 362
Carter, Mel 247
Carter, Melvin 244
Carter, Nick [2] 51
Carter, Ron 430, 918, 983, 1011
Carter, Sam 1020
Carter, Shawn 581
Carthy, Martin 1071, 1072, 1354
Carty, Ric 1292
Caruso, Enrico 824
Cary, Caitlin 1217, 1218
Cary, Dick 1217
Casady, Jack 540, 583, 585
Casale, Bob 306
Casale, Gerald V. 306
Casale, Jerry 306
Case, Byron 1102
Case, Neko **189**
Case, Peter 160, **189**, 267, 788, 868, 1328, 1339, 1344
Casey, Al [1] 191, 518, 1296
Casey, Harry Wayne 'K.C.' 611, 612
Cash, Alvin 1292
Cash, Alvin & the Crawlers 1224
Cash, Fred 408, 557, 558
Cash, Johnny 8, 77, 126, 174, 193, 287, 331, 342, 344, 398, 517, 551, 642, 678, 702, 722, 772, 773, 787, 806, 820, 824, 853, 854, 921, 1014, 1037, 1283, 1295, 1301, 1304, 1351
Cash, Rosanne 526, 786, 956, 1000, 1285
Cash, Steve 835
Cashman & West **189**
Cashman, Pistilli & West 189
Cashman, Terry 189
Casinos 1289
Cassidy, David 190, 544, 846, 1004, 1310
Cassidy, Ed 246, 1056
Cassidy, Shaun **190**
Cassius 278
Cast [1] 1157, 1290
Cast [2] **190**
Castaways 190, 1281
Castells 1282
Castillo, Emilio 1151
Castillo, Joey 281
Castor, Jimmy **190**, 191, 977, 1347
Castronovo, Deen 604
Cat Power **191**, 1035, 1300
Catalinas 1292
Cataline, Glen 469
Catatonia **191**, 192, 1076
Catching, Dave 906
Catherine Wheel **192**, 244, 680, 1025, 1116
Catherine [1] 86
Catherine, Philip 420
Catholics 107
Cats [2] 994
Cattini, Clem 1149
Cauley, Ben 64
Caustic Resin 157
Cauty, Jimi 626, 627
Cavalera, Igor 993
Cavalera, Max 993
Cavaliere, Felix 809, 918
Cavazo, Carlos 909
Cave, Nick 7, 99, 174, **192**, 193, 194, 268, 356, 510, 511, 730, 1338, 1341, 1342
Cave, Nick & the Bad Seeds 194
Cecil, Malcolm 983
Ced Gee 1172, 1173
Cee, Bob 87
Celibate Rifles **194**, 195, 910, 1342
Celtic Frost 993
Cenac, Ben 'Cozmo-D' 794
Centurions 1301
Cerrone 676
Certain Ratio 1289
Cervenka, Exene 361, 921, 1249, 1250
Cesare, Giovanni Martino 1074
Cetera, Peter 208, 209
Chad & Jeremy **195**, 990, 1175
Chad, Dominic 695
Chadwick, Guy 541, 542, 761

Chairmen of the Board **195**, 645, 822, 1004, 1276
Chakachas 1291
Chali Twona 608
Challengers **195**, 196
Challengers [Surf] 195
Chamberlain, Dean 766
Chamberlain, Matt 142, 143
Chamberlin, Jimmy 1029
Chambers Brothers **196**, 1351
Chambers, Guy 740, 1226
Chambers, Martin 885
Chambers, Roland 732
Chameleons UK **196**, 197, 215, 1061
Champion, Will 234
Champlin, Bill 209
Champs **197**, 210, 310, 986, 1281, 1296, 1308
Chan, Al 962
Chance [1] 197
Chance, James **197**, 1336
Chance, James & the Contortions 197, 1337
Chance, Slim 1152
Chandler, Chas 29, 355, 523, 1019
Chandler, Eric 642
Chandler, Gene **197**, 198, 258, 558, 573, 709, 722, 949, 1229, 1276, 1280, 1282, 1299, 1324
Chandler, Kenny 1297
Chandler, Knox 470
Chandler, Len 785
Change 208, 1183
Channel Light Vessel 336
Channel, Bruce 198, 512, 635, 636, 1070
Channing, Carol 800, 1227
Chantays 32, **198**, 1143, 1292, 1308, 1313
Chantels **198**, 199, 1287, 1312
Chants 631
Chants R&B 1301
Chapel, Jean 1301
Chapin Brothers 199
Chapin, Harry **199**, 1285
Chapin, Tom 472, 878
Chaplin, Blondie 73, 1025
Chaplin, Nick 1025
Chapman 394, 774
Chapman, Michael [Folk] 112, 628, 703, 1106
Chapman, Mike [Producer] 133, 465, 774
Chapman, Roger 394
Chapman, Tracy 143, 199, 200, 1328, 1344, 1345
Chapman, Tracy [1] 199, 559
Chapparrals 1280
Chappell, Les 676
Chappell, Ray 979
Chapter Eight 58, 1049
Chapterhouse **200**, 680, 751, 778, 1006
Chaquico, Craig 584, 585
Charig, Marc 618
Charlatans **200**, 201, 202, 410, 475, 972, 1323, 1346
Charlatans UK 199, **200**, 201, 334, 811
Charlemagne, Diane 471
Charles, Bobby 524, 1306
Charles, Charlie 340
Charles, Dave [1] 515
Charles, Denis [1] 434
Charles, Pee Wee 653
Charles, Ray [1] 29, 39, 118, 123, 148, **202**, 203, 224, 248, 254, 381, 407, 430, 477, 512, 517, 548, 559, 562, 569, 594, 614, 711, 943, 948, 1022, 1151, 1229, 1233, 1238, 1243, 1273, 1274, 1281, 1282, 1296, 1305, 1324, 1325, 1329, 1351, 1352
Charlton, Manny 783
Charmels 262
Charry, Etienne 1285
Chase [1] 555
Chase, Andy 566, 567
Chase, Peter 842
Chasez, JC 11, 781
Chastain, Paul 1188
Chatfield, Mark 469
Chatham, Rhys 62
Chavez **203**, 204, 1300
Cheap Trick 76, 96, 116, **204**, 205, 245, 272, 310, 335, 370, 465, 469, 474, 475, 493, 649,

703, 802, 857, 877, 878, 966, 984, 1176, 1192, 1214, 1278, 1286, 1290, 1339, 1343
Checker, Chubby 59, 60, **205**, 397, 697, 804, 1282, 1285
Cheech & Chong 329
Chelsea 1337
Chemical Brothers 201, **205**, 206, 278, 397, 503, 638, 748, 771, 811, 830, 895, 971, 972, 1170, 1286
Chemistry Set 1295
Cheng, Chi 295
Chenier, Clifton 1294
Cher [1] 18, **206**, 674, 718, 1042
Cherone, Gary 959, 1182, 1183
Cherry, Don [1] 126, 207, 524, 928
Cherry, Eagle-Eye 977
Cherry, Neneh 16, **207**, 612, 873, 1159
Cheslin, Matt 785
Chesnutt, Vic 175, **207**, 208, 1049
Chessmen 1297
Chevron, Philip 871
Chewy Marble 1240
Chi-Lites 208, 712, 1229, 1230, 1263
Chic 135, **208**, 339, 401, 448, 686, 743, 793, 898, 958, 962, 983, 1017, 1044, 1100, 1160, 1247, 1280
Chicago 195, **208**, 209, 358, 745, 973, 1329
Chicago Underground Duo 879
Chickasaw Mudd Puppies **210**
Chicken Shack 1326
Chiefs of Relief 133
Chieftains 253, 764, 1355
Chiffons **210**, 619, 620, 955, 1275, 1287, 1311, 1312, 1313
Child, Desmond 10, 123, 124, 249
Child, Jane **210**
Childish, Billy **210**, 775
Childress, Ross 236
Childs, Euros 476
Childs, Megan 476
Chill [1] 1343
Chilli Willi & the Red Hot Peppers **210**, 1335
Chilliwack 211
Chills **211**, 541, 679, 1191, 1292, 1343
Chilton, Alex 63, 89, 97, 98, 136, 137, **211**, 212, 262, 486, 543, 934, 935, 1045, 1123, 1136, 1248, 1325, 1339, 1343, 1344
Chimes [1] 1044
Chin, Brian 612
Chin, Clive 908
China Crisis 1288
Chinmoy, Sri 975
Chinn, Nicky 774, 1106
Chinn, Nicky & Mike Chapman 429
Chipmunks 134, 393, 720, 794
Chipping, Tim 828
Chocolate Milk 1151
Chocolate Watchband 142, **212**, 213, 346, 360, 600, 918, 1287, 1288, 1321
Choice 861
Choir [2] **213**
Chomsky, Noam 214
Choo Choo Train 1188
Chopin, Frederic 23
Chordettes 353
Chords [1] 268, 1303
Chosen Few [Detroit] 1067
Chowning, Randle 835
Chris & Cosey 1142
Christ, John 281, 282
Christgau, Robert 867
Christian, Arlester 'Dyke' 340
Christian, Charlie 1303, 1352
Christian, Tim 1147
Christie Front Drive 591
Christie, Lou **213**, 214, 804, 1275, 1292
Christina, Fran 385
Christopher, Gretchen 415
Christopherson, Peter 234, 896, 897, 1142
Chrome [1] 170
Chrome, Cheetah 287
Chronic [1] 314
Chubb Rock 1274
Chuck Wagon 309
Chumbawamba **214**
Chung, April 250

Chung, Mark 356
Church 15, 16, **214**, 215, 216, 1000, 1287, 1342, 1343
Church, Bill [1] 757
Churchill, Chick 1127
Churilla, Scott 938
Chusid, Irwin 997
Chyskillz 822
Ciancia, Keith 631
Ciaran, Cian 1103
Ciarlante, Randy 62
Cibo Matto **216**, 217, 475, 501
Ciccone Youth **217**
Ciccotelli, Lou 638
Cieka, Rob 127, 128
Cigarettes 1298
Cima, Andrea 253
Cinderella [1] **217**, 1302
Cinelu, Mino 473
Cinema 1256
Cinerama 1212
Cipollina, John 907, 908
Circle Jerks **217**, 218, 742, 921, 923, 1280, 1339
Circles [1] 1298
Clan 464, 819, 1246
Clancy Brothers 1354
Clannad 370, 371, 1355
Clapton, Eric 7, 8, 17, 49, 50, 62, 84, 85, 93, 100, 110, 124, 127, 162, 172, 173, **218**, 219, 220, 251, 264, 291, 297, 301, 302, 318, 337, 384, 430, 508, 509, 521, 587, 701, 707, 708, 848, 898, 940, 951, 977, 1005, 1070, 1081, 1138, 1152, 1160, 1186, 1209, 1220, 1243, 1253, 1254, 1300, 1315, 1316, 1326, 1333, 1352, 1355
Claridge, Eric 985
Clark [1] 642
Clark, Alan 318
Clark, Allen [1] 642
Clark, Alvin 1249
Clark, Andrew 82
Clark, Andy 82
Clark, Bernard 467
Clark, Claudine 1275, 1312
Clark, Dave Five 87, **220**, 221, 285, 938, 969, 1058, 1157, 1280, 1317, 1318, 1320, 1322
Clark, Dee 108, **221**, 1297, 1299
Clark, Dick [1] 384, 560, 887, 935, 1137
Clark, Gene [1] 81, 166, 167, 168, **221**, 222, 346, 388, 410, 519, 667, 705, 1136, 1188
Clark, Glen 159
Clark, Guy 173, 363, 675, 917, 1002, 1106
Clark, Keith 217
Clark, Louis 359
Clark, Michael [1] 393
Clark, Petula 39, 190, **222**, 389, 505, 627, 776, 1296
Clark, Robin 1013
Clark, Roy 573, 1292
Clark, Sanford 1292
Clark, Shellie 536
Clark, Steve [1] 294
Clark, W.C. 1186
Clarke, Allan 533, 844
Clarke, Andy 372
Clarke, Bruce 996
Clarke, Diana 537
Clarke, Eddie [2] 768
Clarke, Mark 771
Clarke, Michael 167, 221, 405, 406, 418
Clarke, Stanley 650, 889
Clarke, Steve [2] 294
Clarke, Tony [1] 1275, 1276
Clarke, Vince 300, 372, 373, 374, 503, 1254
Clash 9, 14, 45, 51, 62, 95, 104, 165, 175, **222**, 223, 289, 314, 358, 362, 372, 456, 485, 547, 574, 667, 692, 725, 734, 740, 769, 822, 855, 871, 898, 917, 918, 994, 997, 1023, 1032, 1037, 1082, 1095, 1171, 1193, 1197, 1250, 1279, 1335, 1336, 1337, 1338, 1339, 1346, 1355, 1356
Classic Nouveaux 1290
Classics IV **223**, 1295
Claudette 946
Clay, Andrew Dice 441, 953
Clay, Joe 1282, 1283, 1292

Clay, Judy 89, 90, **224**, 1106, 1207, 1300
Clay, Otis 151, **224**, 1283
Claypool, Les 210, 237, 888, 889
Clayton, Adam 1169
Clayton, Buck 59
Clayton, Sam 660
Clayton-Thomas, David 113, 533
Clean 57, 69, 211, 224, 1191, 1284, 1343
Clean, Dean 289
Cleaners from Venus 224, 225, 795
Clearmountain, Bob 7, 215, 235, 547
Clearwater, Eddy 630
Cleaves, Jessica 348, 433, 434
Cleaves, Slaid 434
Cleftones 1297
Clegg, Johnny 57
Clemens, Jeffrey 444
Clement, Jack 893
Clement, Steven 8
Clements, Rod 657
Clements, Terry [2] 653
Clements, Vassar 513
Cleminson, Zal 783
Clemons, Clarence 431, 1167
Clemson, Clem 546
Cleveland, James 430, 431, 1351
Cliff, Jimmy 150, 255, 782, 1171, 1355, 1356
Clifford, Doug 117
Clifford, James 253
Clifford, Linda 709
Clifford, Mark 990
Clift, Montgomery 223
Climax Blues Band **225**, 1326
Climax Chicago Blues Band 225
Climie Fisher 781
Climie, Simon 220
Cline, Alex 673
Cline, Mark 673
Cline, Nels 460, 1210
Cline, Patsy 258, 259, 853, 943, 1032, 1263
Clinic [1] 1292
Clinic [2] **225**
Clinton, George [1] 130, 177, 208, **226**, 237, 314, 324, 327, 348, 440, 441, 442, 577, 833, 834, 842, 843, 844, 889, 890, 892, 921, 926, 1269, 1334
Clique [1] **226**, 227, 1276
Clivilles & Cole 170
Clivilles, Robert 170
Clock DVA 494, 1284
Cloud Nine 752
Cloudberry Jam 630
Clover [1] 254
Clovers **227**, 629, 737, 1274, 1280, 1306, 1307
Clowney, David 253
Club Nouveau 366
Club, Billy 309
Cluster 25, 368, 369, 790
Clyde, Jeremy 195
Coal Porters 667
Coasters 52, 171, **227**, 284, 337, 535, 560, 619, 642, 772, 821, 822, 986, 1046, 1163, 1292, 1297, 1307, 1311, 1312
Coates, Odia 30
Cobain, Kurt 27, 251, 337, 423, 532, 599, 639, 640, 643, 669, 802, 803, 913, 1067, 1185, 1233, 1262, 1344
Cobb, Arnett 198
Cobb, Ed 213, 346, 600, 1068
Cobb, James 223
Cobb, Margaret 198
Cobham, Billy 122, 123, 975
Cobra Verde 493
Cochran Brothers 227, 228
Cochran, Eddie 115, **227**, 228, 411, 645, 772, 773, 805, 948, 1004, 1090, 1241, 1292, 1308, 1341
Cochran, Hank 227
Cochran, Wayne 121
Cochrane, Tom 479
Cockburn, Bruce 175, **228**, 229, 230, 450, 1187
Cockburn, Howard 825
Cocker, Jarvis 7, 35, 102, 307, 680, 900, 901, 968, 1299
Cocker, Joe **230**, 231, 394, 701, 733, 796, 968, 1153, 1155, 1220, 1275

Cockney Rebel 505
Cockrell, Bud 836
Cocoa Brovaz 1246
Coconuts 614
Coctails 886, 1302
Cocteau Twins **231**, 232, 238, 287, 400, 494, 676, 680, 701, 760, 761, 778, 779, 837, 1005, 1025, 1101, 1136
Code of Practice 860
Codeine **232**, 241, 607
Codename John 471
Codenys, Patrick 435
Coffee, Erma 1283
Coffey, Cath 1074, 1159
Coffey, Dennis 998
Coffey, King 24, 163, 164
Cogbill, Tommy 937
Cohen, Alan 272
Cohen, Andy [1] 272, 1006, 1007
Cohen, David [1] 258
Cohen, Greg 1227
Cohen, Jem 437
Cohen, John 450
Cohen, Leonard 32, 33, 57, 140, 193, 230, **232**, 233, 234, 236, 238, 239, 245, 308, 316, 376, 388, 504, 523, 602, 654, 849, 900, 956, 1017, 1049, 1052, 1144, 1145, 1187, 1208, 1285, 1328
Cohen, Tony 99, 194
Cohn, Marc 270
Coil **234**, 802, 897, 1142, 1284
Colbert, Loz 942, 943
Colbourn, Chris 155, 156
Colburn, Richard 90
Cold Blood 512
Cold Chisel **234**, 1342
Cold Crush Brothers 608
Coldcut 374, 1068, 1298
Coldplay **234**, 235
Cole, B.J. 352
Cole, Cozy 1308, 1329
Cole, David 170
Cole, Isaac 512
Cole, Jerry 517, 1178
Cole, Lloyd **235**, 236, 1107
Cole, Lloyd & the Commotions 235, 236
Cole, Mike 776
Cole, Nat King 92, 93, 98, 202, 573, 1296
Cole, Natalie 59, 994
Cole, Paula **236**, 556, 1000
Coleman, Cy 1091
Coleman, Gene 451
Coleman, Hooks 1274
Coleman, Jaz 367, 616
Coleman, Kevin 1028
Coleman, Lisa 747, 1215, 1216
Coleman, Ornette 17, 103, 197, 806, 892, 1329, 1330
Coleman, Ray [1] 220
Coleman, Steve [1] 957
Coleman, Wanda 1249
Coles, Richard 243
Coletta, Kim 160, 580
Coley, Byron 305, 447
Collective Soul **236**
Colley, Dana 762
Collie, Shirley 1032
Collier, Mitty 1276, 1301
Collier, Pat 531, 1193, 1194
Collingwood, Chris 426
Collins Kids **237**, 1273, 1301, 1308
Collins, Aaron 171
Collins, Albert [1] 1232
Collins, Allen 682, 683
Collins, Betty 171
Collins, Bootsy 146, 147, 226, **237**, 291, 292, 350, 397, 440, 441, 449, 470, 471, 497, 842, 843, 956, 1160, 1224, 1284, 1295, 1334
Collins, Carter 153
Collins, Catfish 147, 237
Collins, Dolly 558
Collins, Edwyn **237**, 238, 554, 823, 824
Collins, Glenda 720
Collins, Judy 185, 233, **238**, 239, 298, 299, 558, 1353, 1354
Collins, Larry 237, 476, 1273
Collins, Lorrie 237

Collins, Lyn 147, 1284
Collins, Mark 201
Collins, Mel [1] 176, 401, 617, 618, 845, 1111
Collins, Paul [1] 367, 788, 1339
Collins, Paul [1] Beat 788
Collins, Peter 249, 559
Collins, Phelps 147
Collins, Phil 31, 100, 122, 174, 176, 219, 220, **239**, 270, 318, 368, 456, 457, 458, 735, 736, 866
Collins, Ray 1265, 1268
Collins, Rob 200, 201
Collins, Rosie 171
Collins, Shirley 477, 558, 1354
Collins, Victor 634
Collins, William 'Bootsy' 147
Collister, Christine 32, 489
Color Me Badd 379
Color Me Gone 601
Colosseum 477, 1329
Colourfield **240**, 500, 501
Colquhoun, Andy 306
Colter, Jessi 835
Colter, Wendie 1065
Coltrane, Alice 918
Coltrane, John 128, 898, 975, 976, 983, 1322, 1329
Columbus, Ray 240, 878, 1342
Colvin, Shawn **240**, 241, 539, 543, 669, 1120, 1328
Combs, Sean 'Puffy' 109, 184, 585, 654, 655, 669, 899, 900, 1273
Come **241**
Commander Cody **241**, 242, 1292
Commander Cody & His Lost Planet Airmen 241, 242
Commandos 511
Commodores **242**, 243, 287, 389, 940, 941, 1173, 1334
Common [1] 957
Common Ground [1] 766, 983
Communards 144, **243**
Como, Perry 130, 1119, 1274
Company Flow 608
Compton's Most Wanted 962
Comsat Angels **243**, 244, 1007
Con Funk Shun **244**, 245, 711
Concrete Blonde 53, **245**
Congo Ashante Roy 598, 599, 793
Congos 1292
Conley, Arthur 159, **245**, 1287
Conley, Clint 744, 1257
Connell, Andy 1109
Connell, David 245
Connell, Michael 245
Connells **245**, 246, 974
Connelly, Chris 938
Connelly, Chris [1] 938
Conner, Gary Lee 77, 984
Conner, Tom 969
Conner, Van 906
Connolly, Brian 683
Connolly, Jeff 683
Connor, Michael 901
Connor, Tony 540
Connors, Norman 577, 1276
Conolly, Jeff 683
Conrad, Tony 397, 452, 728
Conroy, Mick 749
Contardo, Johnny 996
Continental Drifters 260, 536
Continentals [Rock] 1298
Contortions 197
Contours **246**, 822, 1157, 1283, 1314
Contrera, Al 780
Convertino, John 175, 1248
Conway, Billy 762
Conway, Gerry 388, 589, 1071
Cooder, Ry 158, 159, 180, 186, 189, 219, **246**, 247, 353, 505, 526, 637, 653, 654, 658, 659, 662, 786, 795, 796, 842, 1089, 1129, 1175, 1355
Cook, Kyle 702
Cook, Louis 53
Cook, Murray 727
Cook, Norman 397
Cook, Paul 60, 238, 590, 994, 1143

Cook, Stu 117
Cook, Yvette 'Lady E' 794
Cooke, L.C. 247
Cooke, Sam 22, 49, 145, 159, 186, 187, 202,
   245, **247**, 248, 338, 401, 412, 418, 430, 451,
   486, 514, 560, 662, 707, 718, 782, 791, 841,
   920, 924, 925, 942, 949, 1004, 1027, 1047,
   1120, 1121, 1136, 1145, 1181, 1229, 1236,
   1237, 1274, 1291, 1292, 1294, 1300, 1324,
   1325, 1351
Cooke, Sam & the Soul Stirrers 1095
Cookies **248**, 619, 1275, 1287, 1301, 1312
Cool Riddims 1151
Cooley, Eddie 108
Coolidge, Rita 297, 701, 1210
Coolio 226, **248**
Coombes, Rod 1090
Coomer, Ken 1223
Cooper, Alex 611
Cooper, Alice [1] 92, 150, **248**, 249, 250, 279,
   495, 624, 698, 831, 866, 1166, 1181, 1219,
   1231, 1281
Cooper, Buster 203
Cooper, Chris [1] 837
Cooper, Colin 225
Cooper, Gary [1] 237
Cooper, John [1] 1342
Cooper, Les 619
Cooper, Martin 826, 827
Cooper, Michael [1] 244, 245
Cooper, Neil 52
Cooper, Ray 302, 598
Cooper, Ryan 678
Cooper, Ted 573
Coots, J. Fred 1094
Cop Shoot Cop **250**
Cope, Julian **250**, 251, 252, 397, 789, 1121,
   1122, 1197, 1202, 1287
Copeland, Johnny 1186, 1300
Copeland, Ken 1297
Copeland, Stewart 872, 873, 889
Copland, Aaron 23, 364
Copping, Chris 893
Corbijn, Anton 31
Corbitt, Jerry 1258, 1259, 1263
Corby, Mike 50
Cordell, Denny 917
Cordell, Ritchie 916
Cordes, Attrell 868
Cordes, Jarrett 868
Corea, Chick 59, 1270, 1329
Corgan, Billy 205, 370, 434, 532, 698, 904,
   1028, 1029
Cormega 748
Corndolly 977
Corneal, Jon 561
Cornelius [2] **252**, 433, 528
Cornell, Chris 249, 767, 984, 1044, 1045,
   1125, 1293
Corner, Chris 1035
Cornershop **252**, 253
Cornick, Glen 587
Cornish, Gene 918
Cornwell, Hugh 1088
Corr, Andrea 253
Corr, Caroline 253
Corr, Jim 253
Corr, Sharon 253
Corrs **253**
Cortez, Dave 'Baby' 191, 253, 1292,
   1296, 1308
Cortez, Jayne 1347
Cortinas 997
Coryell, Larry 1329
Cosby, Bill 1244
Cosby, Henry 534, 1239
Cosby, Rooster 251, 252
Cosloy, Gerard 434, 1006, 1280
Cosmic Psychos 1342
Cosmic Rough Riders **253**, 254
Costa, Gal 778
Costell, Dave 651
Costello, Elvis 32, 45, 50, 159, 190, 208, 211,
   254, 255, 256, 266, 295, 354, 378, 382, 392,
   399, 443, 489, 492, 504, 525, 526, 571, 601,
   612, 677, 678, 693, 715, 726, 728, 795, 806,
   840, 850, 858, 870, 915, 947, 955, 962, 995,

1016, 1052, 1059, 1065, 1105, 1121, 1132,
   1253, 1278, 1285, 1295, 1322, 1327, 1328,
   1335, 1337, 1338, 1339, 1355
Costello, Elvis & the Attractions 907, 1065
Coster, Tom 976
Costin, Darren 1205
Cotten, Elizabeth 450, 481
Cotton, James 1295, 1304, 1352
Cotton, Jeff 395, 557, 773
Cotton, Josie 467
Cotton, Paul 870
Couch Flambeau 434
Cougar, John Band 724
Coughlan, Cathal 527
Coughlan, Richard 181, 1223
Coultas, Kevin 241
Coulter, Clifford 613
Coulter, Phil 613
Count Bishops 257
Count Five 257, 262, 1320
Counting Crows 159, 188, **257**, 258
Country Gazette 418
Country Joe & the Fish 170, **258**, 1172,
   1309, 1323
County, Jayne 592
County, Wayne 1278, 1286
Courtney, David 980
Courtney, Zephan 511
Cousin, Andy 15
Cousins, Dave 298, 299, 1089, 1090, 1201
Covay, Don 67, 159, 245, **258**, 285, 860
Cover Girls 1281
Coverdale, David 192, 292, 293,
   920, 1220
Covington, Joey 583
Cowan, Blair 235
Coward Brothers 255
Coward, Noel 321, 390, 621
Cowboy Junkies 230, **258**, 259, 751, 1129
Cowboys 18
Cowe, Simon 657
Cows **259**, 260
Cowsill, Barbara 260
Cowsill, Bill 260
Cowsill, Susan 536, 1248
Cowsills 185, **260**, 433, 846, 1331
Cox 151, 404
Cox, Alex 1095
Cox, Andy 367, 404
Cox, Billy 522
Cox, Carl 292, 748
Cox, Dave 404
Cox, Deborah 544
Cox, Irv 584
Cox, Paul 515
Cox, Roy 151
Cox, Terry 851, 878
Coxhill, Lol 44, 45, 1247
Coxon, Graham 120, 121
Coyne, Kevin 210, **260**, 261, 607
Coyne, Wayne 411, 412
Crabb, Graham 874
Cracker 177, **261**, 262
Cracknell, Sarah **262**, 972, 973, 1018, 1216
Cracolici, Albee 780
Cracolici, Phil 780
Cradle 903
Crafton, Bob 'Chilly B.' 794
Craig, Carl 383, 748, 1064
Cramer, Floyd 881, 883, 964, 1296
Cramps 77, 193, **262**, 263, 279, 775, 937, 1219
Cranberries 253, **263**, 760
Crane, Tony 728
Crash [1] 461
Crash, Darby 461
Crass 234, 826
Craswell, Denny 190
Craven, Joe 450
Crawford, Ed 406
Crawford, Hank 203
Crawford, John 92
Crawford, Johnny 1279, 1297, 1309
Crawford, Michael [1] 1094
Crawford, Stuart 609
Crawford, Sugar Boy 326
Crawley, Caroline 1136
Cray, Robert 93, 219, 1352

Crazy Elephant 264, 1289, 1332
Crazy Horse **264**, 337, 361, 527, 665, 913,
   1123, 1259, 1260, 1261, 1262, 1282, 1285
Creach, Papa John 540, 541, 584, 585
Cream [1] 73, 84, 110, 124, 135, 218, 219, 220,
   264, 265, 432, 490, 515, 522, 551, 577, 644,
   702, 707, 708, 771, 776, 784, 785, 878, 944,
   967, 1133, 1300, 1316, 1317, 1323, 1326,
   1329, 1333, 1350
Creamer, Mark 304
Creation **265**, 1035, 1240, 1284, 1288,
   1293, 1322
Creation Rebel 1024
Creatures [1] 1298
Creedence Clearwater Revisited 1007
Creedence Clearwater Revival 117, 210, 218,
   265, 266, 272, 324, 364, 421, 467, 472, 533,
   991, 1163, 1302, 1308, 1327
Creeggan, Andy 65
Cregan, Jim 114
Creme, Lol 608, 1126
Crenshaw, Marshall 14, 159, 246, **266**, 267,
   465, 601, 820, 1089
Crenshaw, Robert [1] 267
Creole, Kid 614
Crescents 1019
Crests **268**, 687, 1274
Cretones 1339
Cretu, Michael 367
Crew Cuts 268
Crewe, Bob 427, 969, 1301
Crickets [1] 534, 535
Crime & the City Solution **268**, 1108
Crippen, Dick 1127
Crispy Ambulance **268**, 269, 1289
Criss, Peter 624, 625
Criss, Treach 783
Critters 676, 1296
Croce, Giovanni 189, 190
Croce, Jim 189, **269**, 1286
Crofts, Dash 197, 787, 986
Crombie, Noel 606, 981
Cronin, Kevin 933
Cronk, Charles 1090
Cronley, T.J. 150
Crooks 1298
Crooks, Richard [1] 988
Cropper, Steve 84, 100, 128, 129, 208, 407,
   418, 696, 860, 892, 924, 925, 1069, 1231,
   1321, 1325
Crosby & Nash 658
Crosby, Bing 130, 269, 1119
Crosby, David 149, 166, 167, 168, 222, 269,
   270, 369, 746, 785, 786, 915, 1119, 1260
Crosby, David [1] 253, **269**, 559, 1082
Crosby, Robbin 920
Crosby, Stills & Nash 24, 143, 149, 253, 269,
   270, 395, 448, 521, 565, 583, 735, 773, 932,
   1082, 1259, 1260, 1262
Crosby, Stills, Nash & Young 52, 253, 1262
Croslin, John 930, 1059
Cross, Bridget 1176
Cross, Christopher 50, **270**, 271, 599, 899
Cross, David 617, 618
Cross, Reuben 620
Crossfires 1314
Croucier, Juan 920
Crow 271
Crow, Sheryl **271**, 405, 556, 559, 798, 891,
   914, 1089
Crowded House **271**, 272, 404, 405, 831, 915,
   1057, 1058, 1263, 1342
Crowe, Cameron 445
Crowe, Curtis 902
Crowe, J.D. 756
Crowell, Rodney 337, 992
Crowley, Aleister 234
Crowley, J.C. 868
Crowns 187, 1283
Crows [1] 1303, 1306
Crowsdell 1245
Crucial Three 1197
Crudup, Arthur 'Big Boy' 880, 883
Cruise, Julee 102, 539
Cruisers 562
Crump, Bruce 752
Crunch, Star 691

Crusaders [1] 382
Crust Brothers 272
Cryan' Shames 272
Crystals 190, **272**, 273, 674, 705, 863, 946, 955,
   1052, 1312, 1313
Cua, Rick 834
Cub [1] **273**, 296, 977
Cuccurullo, Warren 743
Cuckston, Rosie 420
Cuddy, Jim 117
Cuff Links 1276, 1280
Cuff Links [1] 1331
Cullimore, Stan 542
Cullinan, Tom 908
Cullum, Jim Jr. 756
Cullum, Ross 371
Cult **273**, 274, 1219, 1278
Culture Club 74, **274**, 275, 545, 1054
Culver, Joe 64
Cummings, Burton 491, 492
Cummings, George 325
Cummings, John 750
Cunha, Rick 519
Cunniff, Jill 679
Cunningham, Abe 295
Cunningham, Blair 498
Cunningham, Carl 63
Cuomo, Rivers 1214
Cupid Car Club 783
Cups, Dixie 1288
Curb, Mike 16
Cure 19, 40, 196, **275**, 276, 287, 295, 315, 320,
   393, 400, 409, 467, 501, 556, 579, 581, 631,
   876, 901, 1015, 1234, 1338, 1346, 1347
Curley, John [1] 11
Curmin, Cy 408
Curnin, Cy 408
Currie, Alannah 753, 1137
Currie, Billy 1195
Currie, Cherie 963
Currie, Jim 329
Currie, Justin 295
Currie, Nick 752, 753
Curry, Mickey 160, 1139
Curry, Tim 1210
Curtis, Chris 987
Curtis, Ian 269, 580, 604, 793, 1144,
   1338, 1346
Curtis, Jon 200
Curtis, Sonny 381, 535, 787, 1275
Curve **276**, 277, 449
Curved Air 474, 588, 1296
Cusano, Vinnie 625
Cuscuna, Michael 914
Cut Chemist 608
Cuthbert, Gary 253
Cuthbert, Scott 379
Cutler, Bill 337
Cutler, Chris 935
Cutler, Ivor 1247
Cybotron 1286
Cypress Hill **277**, 912, 1159, 1184, 1293
Cyrkle **277**
Cyrus [1] 1216
Cyrus, Gordon 1216
Czerwinec, Jaro 258
Czukay, Holger 178, 898, 1111, 1289

D
D Rock 647
D Train 374
D'Angelo **278**
D., Chris 493, 642
D., Chuck 128, 226, 552, 570, 615, 641, 891,
   897, 898, 912, 915, 1040, 1277
D., Mike 55
D'Angelo 278, 529, 707
Da Brat 362
Dacus, Donnie 209
DAD [1] 1302
Dada [1] 38
Daddy Dewdrop 1332
Daddy O 906, 1076
Dade, Sushil 1045
DAF 171
Daft Punk 68, **278**
Dahl, Jeff 1332

Dahlquist, Michael 272, 1006, 1007
D'Albuquerque, Michael 358
Dale & Grace 328, 1282
Dale, Dick [1] **278**, 663, 761, 1279, 1292, 1300, 1308, 1309, 1313, 1314
Daley, Richard 823
Dali's Car 776
Dall, Cindy 1034
Dallin, Sarah Elizabeth 60
Dallon, Miki 570
Daltrey, David 1291
Daltrey, Roger 99, 797, 1027, 1152, 1220, 1221, 1222
Daly, Mike 376, 1217, 1218
Daly, Steven 823
Dalyrimple, Desiree 365, 552
Dambuilders 236
Damiani, Victor 172
D'Amico, Mike 1240
Dammers, Jerry 1052
Damn Yankees 799
Damned 9, 165, **278**, 279, 280, 352, 677, 804, 899, 969, 1107, 1212, 1278, 1335, 1337
Damon & Naomi 446, 463
Damon, Liz Orient Express 1283
Damon, Matt 994
Dando, Evan 109, 511, 646, 647, 1210
D'Andrea, Richard 766
Dandrieu, Jean-Francois 304
Dandy Warhols **280**
Dandy, Jim 104, 105
Dane, Dana 1279
Danell, Dennis 1037
Danger Danger 1302
Dangerous Birds 241
Dangerous Toys 1302
Daniel, Britt 1058, 1059
Daniel, Davis 1058
Daniels, Billy 997
Daniels, Charlie 682, 1276
Daniels, Jeffrey 997
Daniels, Phil 121
Danielson Family **280**, 281
Danko, Rick 61, 62, 218, 513
Danny & the Juniors 996
Danny Ray 542
Dantalian's Chariot **281**, 1277
Danzig **281**, 282, 1340
Danzig, Glenn 281, 282, 742, 1340
D'Arby, Terence Trent **282**, 519, 707, 986
Darbyshire, Keith 269
D'Arcy 205, 1029
Darin, Bobby **282**, 283, 503, 610, 1093
Darkstar [1] 1300
Darlington, Robert 1156
Darnell, August 323, 324, 614
Darnells 699
Darrell, Diamond 839
Darren, James 1274, 1275, 1309, 1311
Darroch, James 195
Darrow, Chris 610
Darryl 51
Das EFX **283**
Dasch, David 1079
Dash, Sarah 636, 809, 940
Dashut, Richard 1003
Date, Terry 984, 1067
Daugherty, Jay Dee 1031
Daughtry, Dean 223
Davenport, Charles 'Cow Cow' 1350
Davenport, N'Dea 140, 495
Davenport, Robert 269
Davey, Alan 515
David & David **283**
David J 69, 70, 71, 672, 673, 876
David [1] 962
David, Craig 1068
David, Hal 50, 151, 185, 203, 304, 451, 471, 569, 672, 728, 781, 829, 1059, 1183, 1203, 1207, 1208, 1285
David, John 325, 987
David, Stuart 90, 459
Davidowski, Stephen 322
Davidson, Aaron 749
Davidson, Aqil 1244
Davies, Alan 402
Davies, Alun 1077

Davies, Annemari 402
Davies, Cliff 807
Davies, Cyril 324, 776, 1326
Davies, Dave [1] **283**, 284, 621, 622, 623
Davies, Dennis Russell 390
Davies, Jeff 142
Davies, Lynn 252
Davies, Pete 1171
Davies, Ray 43, 55, 114, 121, **283**, 320, 340, 349, 536, 566, 574, 621, 622, 623, 693, 702, 722, 794, 815, 885, 913, 957, 986, 1033, 1050, 1071, 1090, 1165, 1250, 1298, 1315
Davies, Rhett 401
Davies, Richard 183, 235, **284**, 705
Davies, Rick 1105
Davies, Roy 354
Davis Sisters [1] 1301
Davis, Andrea 944, 1301
Davis, Angela 647
Davis, Art 551
Davis, Billy [4] Jr. 403
Davis, Carl [1] 197, 198, 573, 639, 1215, 1229
Davis, Clive 308, 544, 834, 891, 977
Davis, Delissa 997
Davis, Don [1] 336
Davis, Eddie [1] 1300
Davis, Gary [1] 540, 541
Davis, Hal 452
Davis, Jesse Ed 114, 221
Davis, John [01] 422, 423
Davis, John [02] 422
Davis, Jonathan 632, 993
Davis, Josh 322, 323
Davis, Kerry 241
Davis, Larry 1185
Davis, Link 1291
Davis, Mac 159, 882
Davis, Martha [2] 736, 766, 767
Davis, Maxwell 711
Davis, Michael [1] 305
Davis, Michael [MC5] 712
Davis, Miles 7, 128, 152, 173, 175, 617, 639, 706, 728, 846, 898, 976, 1064, 1247, 1329, 1330
Davis, Noel 992
Davis, Paul [1] **284**, 1285
Davis, Reverend Gary 238, 477
Davis, Richard [1] 762, 1329
Davis, Rob 336
Davis, Sammy Jr. 948
Davis, Skeeter 806, 1275, 1301
Davis, Spencer 284, 562, 636, 1123, 1154
Davis, Spencer Group 118, **284**, 285, 381, 542, 700, 1233, 1281, 1284, 1300, 1316, 1318, 1325, 1355
Davis, Tyrone **285**
Davison, Brian 797
Davy DMX 1285
Dawn [1] 829
Dawson, David 519
Dawson, Ronnie 1273, 1292
Day, Bobby 37, **285**, 535
Day, Bobby [1] 121, 285, 424
Day, Bruce 836
Day, Doris 782, 1172, 1301
Day, Morris 1144
Daye, Cory 323
Dayne, Taylor 543, 1281
Dayron, Norman 114
Dayton, Kelli 1035
Daz 1168
Dazz Band **286**, 1295
DB [1] 1290, 1343, 1344
dB's 211, **286**, 536, 601, 981, 1036, 1160, 1217, 1278, 1339, 1345
De La Soul 45, 60, **286**, 287, 314, 441, 442, 501, 607, 608, 766, 865, 869, 892, 903, 906, 1076, 1135, 1158, 1348, 1349
Deacon, John 904
Dead Boys **287**, 310, 520, 836, 1278
Dead C 224, 1343
Dead Can Dance 71, **287**, 288, 461, 462, 1136
Dead Kennedys 103, **289**, 438, 553, 1280, 1339, 1340, 1341
Dead Milkmen **289**, 290
Dead or Alive 41, 743

Dead [Group] 261
Deadbeats [Mod] 1298
Deal, Bill 27, 1325, 1332
Deal, Kelley 1, 27, 141, 207, 304, 305
Deal, Kelley 6000 141
Deal, Kim 27, 141, 493, 863, 864, 1059, 1136, 1345
Dean, Aki 236
Dean, Elton 1039
Dean, Johnny 726
Dean, Paul 674, 675, 1250
Dean, Roger 708, 1296
Dean, Tommy 1286
Deaner 1213
DeAngelis, Peter 1335
Deary, Joan 883
Death Cult 273
DeBurgh, Chris **290**, 291
Debussy, Claude 1093
DeCaro, Nick 653, 654
Deck, Brian 750
DeCloedt, Mark 365
DeCurtis, Anthony 302
Dederer, Dave 879
Dedrick, Bruce 433
Dedrick, Stefanie 433
Dee Dee [1] 917, 1208
Dee, Jay [1] 56
Dee, Joey **291**
Dee, Ronnie 1292
Deebank, Maurice 399, 400
Deee Lite 237, **291**, 292
Deele 49
Deep Purple 105, 116, 122, 123, 144, 201, 234, **292**, 293, 294, 327, 371, 411, 432, 576, 605, 613, 869, 913, 1046, 1154, 1220, 1281, 1283, 1332
Dees, Bill 824
Dees, Sam 1230
Def Leppard 188, **293**, 294, 316, 547, 563, 768, 805, 816, 872, 1133, 1180, 1240, 1302
Defever, Warren 529, 530, 555, 834
DeFleur, Zenon 257
DeFranco Family **294**, 1331
DeFranco, Anthony 294
DeFranco, Benjamin 294
DeFranco, Marisa 294
DeFranco, Nino 294
DeFreitas, Frank 1242
DeFreitas, Pete 251, 350, 351
Deftones **294**, 295, 521, 656
Defunkt 1330
DeGarmo, Chris 907
DeGrate, Dalvin 592, 593
DeGrate, Donald Jr. 592, 593
DeHarrison, Double 250, 251
DeHeredia, Sebastian Aguilera 11, 12
DeHomem-Christo, Guy-Manuel 278
Deily, Ben 646
DeJohnette, Jack 580
Dekker, Desmond 367, 1355, 1356
Dekker, Desmond & The Aces 782
Del Amitri **295**
Del Fuegos **295**, 1278
Del Lords **295**, 296
Del Satins 687
Del Tha Funkee Homosapien 475, 501, 1274
Del Tino's **296**
Del Vetts 1283
Del-Vikings [1] **296**, 297, 1306, 1307
Delaney & Bonnie 5, 56, 172, 218, **297**, 302, 414, 701, 1160
Delaney & Bonnie & Friends 218, 301
Delaney, Leonard 1149
DeLange, Susan 1175
DeLaParra, Fito 179
DeLaRocha, Zack 912
DelBarrio, George 831
Delegates 221
DeLeo, Dean 1085
Delfonics 137, **297**, 464, 700, 1096, 1335
Delgatto, John M. 845
DeLisle, Paul 1028
Delisle, Wayne 727
Delivery 181, 182
Dells **297**, 298, 650, 1079, 1095, 1274, 1276
Delmonas 210

Delmore Brothers 1303, 1307, 1308, 1351
Delonge, Tom 111
DeLorenzo, Victor 1194
Delp, Bradley 132
Deltron Thirty Thirty 475
DeLuca, Anthony 1110
DeMachaut, Guillaume 158
DeMarrais, Caithlin 913, 914
Dement, Iris 893
Demeski, Stanley 399, 679
Demetrius, Claude 881
DeMeyer, Jean-Luc 435
Demian 151
Demille, Cecil B. 1116
Deming, Mike 854
Demme, Jonathan 531, 564, 1117
Demps, Larry 336
Dempsey, Martin 1253
Demudd, Pierre 286
Dench, Ian 365
DenElzen, Michael 606, 981
Denison, Duane 586, 587
Denman, Paul S. 971
Dennert, Paul 945
Dennink, Dill 1122
Dennis, Sandy 1127
Denny, Martin 886, 1075
Denny, Sandy **298**, 299, 386, 387, 388, 426, 433, 477, 543, 644, 705, 706, 831, 1071, 1089, 1126, 1138, 1153, 1354, 1355
Densmore, John 332
Denson, Lee 1292
Denver, John **299**, 515
Deodato 631
Deodato, Eumir 631
DePace, Steve 416
Depeche Mode 277, 292, **300**, 301, 351, 372, 435, 466, 539, 627, 824, 826, 837, 1029, 1038, 1135, 1254
Deppler, Paul 725
Deprijck, Lou 867
Depth Charge 971
Derakh, Amir 282
Deram 134, 135
Derby, Dave 236
Derek & the Dominos 218, 219, 220, 297, **301**, 302, 432
Derek [1] 1289
Derelicts [1] 822
Derrah, Jay 954
Derringer, Rick **302**, 624, 716, 1232
Des'ree **302**
Desanto, Sugar Pie 1301
DeSario, Teri 612
Descendants 446
Descendents **302**, 303
Deschamps, Kim 117
Desert Storm 1283
DeShannon, Jackie 50, 166, 168, 184, 206, 246, **303**, 304, 389, 403, 424, 601, 610, 955, 986, 1276, 1285, 1312, 1313, 1318
Designer [2] 566
Desjardins, Chris 642
Desperado 1166
Destiny's Child **304**, 305, 1014
Destri, Jimmy 112
Destroy All Monsters **305**
Detergents 1293
Detroit 969
Deupree, Taylor 465, 502, 999
Deviants [UK] **305**, 306
Deviants IXVI 306
Devine, Richard 1300
DeVito, Liberty 595
DeVito, Tommy 427
Devlin, Shawn 520
Devo 187, 303, **306**, 307, 562, 775, 802, 803, 807, 808, 878, 888, 902, 994, 1051, 1088, 1109, 1242, 1261, 1281, 1288, 1301, 1336, 1337, 1338, 1356
DeVoe, Ronnie 88, 89, 792
Devoto, Howard 164, 165, 543, 687, 688, 1136
Dewees, James 462
Dexy's Midnight Runners **307**, 308, 899
DeYoung, Dennis 1097
Diablos 1095

Diamond D. 1158
Diamond Dogs 615
Diamond Head 729, 730
Diamond, David [1] 92
Diamond, Lance 474
Diamond, Neil **308**, 309, 679, 754, 755, 772, 773, 777, 882, 1093, 1171, 1176
Diamonds [Canada] 127, 1282
Diamonds [US] 57
Dianno, Paul 563, 564
Dias, Allan 899
Dickens, Charles 693
Dickens, Hazel 1121
Dickens, Little Jimmy 1301
Dickenson, Vic 59
Dickerson, Lance 241
Dickies **309**, 310, 880, 1336, 1279
Dickins, Rob 371
Dickinson, Bruce [1] 563, 564
Dickinson, Bruce [2] 1054
Dickinson, Jim 246, 399, 486, 934, 949, 1344
Dickinson, Rob 192
Dicks 163, 557
Dickson, Jim 168
Dickson, Sean 1045
Dictators 218, 222, 296, **310**, 311, 1167, 1278
Diddley, Bo 18, 59, 99, 119, 137, 150, 181, 254, 257, 296, 311, 312, 324, 334, 360, 423, 630, 643, 695, 732, 733, 885, 886, 892, 907, 942, 949, 950, 976, 996, 1079, 1085, 1087, 1141, 1149, 1157, 1169, 1221, 1235, 1240, 1274, 1276, 1284, 1286, 1289, 1298, 1305, 1315, 1347, 1352
Didier, Dan 895
Dido **312**, 1157
Died Pretty 1342
Dierks, Dieter 1167
Diesel M 774
Dietrich, Marlene 45, 390, 643
Dif Juz 231
Dif, Rene 34
Difford & Tilbrook 949
Difford, Chris 187, 531, 693, 1065, 1066
DiFiore, Vince 172
DiFranco, Ani **312**, 313
Digable Planets **513**, 314, 337, 442, 607, 1158, 1348, 1349
Diggle, Steve 164, 165, 166
Diggs, Robert 970
DiGiovanni, Marty 1102
Digital Underground **314**, 1148, 1167, 1274, 1348, 1349
Digital [1] 860
Dike, Matt 1258
Diken, Dennis 315, 1032
DiLando, Ross 1066
Dillard & Clark 168, 221, 222, 1327
Dillard, Doug 157, 168, 221, 222
Dillards 155, 519, 1327
Dillenger, Daz 1036
Dillinja 101, 471, 1290
Dillon, Jay 469
Dillon, John 835
Dillon, Mavis 214
Dils **314**, 1279, 1280, 1336, 1339
Dimitri from Paris 278, 1298
Dimitri [Netherlands] 291
DiMucci, Dion 316, 547, 610
Dinger, Klaus 789, 790
DiNizio, Pat 1032, 1033
Dinning, Dean 1146
Dinning, Mark 801, 1310
Dino [2] 994
Dino, Desi & Billy **315**
Dinosaur Jr. 11, 38, 155, 156, 259, **315**, 316, 585, 639, 640, 906, 987, 1108, 1109, 1121, 1233, 1346
Dio 106, **316**, 1302
Dio, Ronnie James 105, 106, 293, 316, 913
Dion **316**, 317, 687, 697, 769, 1052, 1059, 1275, 1282, 1307, 1310, 1325, 1326
Dion & the Belmonts 317
Dion, Celine 140, 156, 183, 253, **317**, 318, 613, 978, 1014, 1030, 1164
Dire Straits 5, 57, 173, 240, **318**, 319, 1133
Directions 1298
Dirnt, Mike 484

Dirt Eaters 529
Dirty Dozen Brass Band 168, 255
Dirty Looks [1] **319**
Dirty Three 191, 194, **319**, 320, 677, 821, 963
Discharge 32
Disciples of Soul 661
Disco Four 1074
Disjecta 990
Dismemberment Plan **320**
Disreali Gears 264
DiStefano, Peter 777, 876
Ditchum, Martin 19
Divination 1356
Divine Comedy **320**, 321, 554, 779
Divine Force 1280
Divine Styler 1074
Divinyls **321**, 537, 1287, 1342
Dix, David 834
Dixie Chicks 798
Dixie Cups 74, 1274, 1275, 1287, 1288, 1306, 1311, 1312,
Dixie Dregs **322**, 585, 682, 1231, 1333
Dixie Flyers 430, 679, 975, 1207
Dixie Hummingbirds 1011, 1351
Dixon, Bill 197
Dixon, Don 245, 267, **322**, 470, 601, 612, 930, 1032, 1036, 1343
Dixon, Floyd 1294
Dixon, George 1055
Dixon, Jerry 1207
Dixon, Jessy 1011
Dixon, Luther 1001
Dixon, Willie 17, 84, 94, 108, 159, 210, 264, 317, 358, 371, 477, 628, 673, 694, 721, 755, 872, 944, 980, 996, 1352
Dizek, John Edward 511
Dizz, Lefty 630
DJ Ani 291
DJ Bonebrake 461, 1250
DJ Cam 383
DJ Clue [1] 323, 581
DJ Die 1018
DJ Dmitry 291, 292
DJ Eric B 915
DJ Food 1064
DJ Jazzy Jeff & the Fresh Prince **322**, 1032, 1274
DJ Krush 323
DJ Lethal 380, 542, 656
DJ Matrix 1300
DJ Minutemix 868
DJ Moe Love 1172
DJ Muggs 277
DJ Muggs [1] 277, 542, 1159
DJ Nu-Mark 608
DJ One 292
DJ Pooh 1168
DJ Premier 278, 337, 449, 495, 581, 585, 782, 805, 915, 1280, 1298
DJ Q Bert 323, 327, 631
DJ Shadow 38, 44, **322**, 323, 327, 501, 631, 898, 1159
DJ Shok 323
DJ Silver 292
DJ Sneak 68
DJ Suv 1018
DMC 805
DMX [1] **323**, 1016, 1159
DMZ [1] 683
DNA [1] 250
Dobson, Mark [1] 402
DOC [1] **323**, 1274
Docko, Joe 780
Doctor Buzzard's Original Savannah Band **323**, 324
Doctor Delecto 691
Doctor Demento 247, 740
Doctor Dooom 326, 631
Doctor Dre [1] 140, 248, 263, 277, 314, 323, **324**, 350, 365, 437, 552, 553, 613, 631, 701, 782, 808, 809, 981, 1036, 1168, 1246, 1279, 1280, 1295, 1348, 1349
Doctor Feelgood 143, 257, **324**, 325, 338, 340, 352, 526, 608, 678, 776, 822, 1287, 1335, 1337
Doctor Hook [1] **325**, 1286
Doctor Hook & The Medicine Show 325

Doctor Ice 1179, 1222
Doctor Jeckyll & Mr. Hyde 1279
Doctor John 18, 114, **326**, 390, 430, 444, 765, 801, 895, 972, 999, 1056, 1070, 1186, 1214, 1232, 1278, 1291, 1306
Doctor Know [1] 51, 1021
Doctor Know [2] 51, 52
Doctor Octagon 323, **326**, 327, 365, 608, 631, 1173
Doctor West's Medicine Show & Junk Band 488
Dodd, Dick 1068
Dodd, Jane 1191
Doe, John 21, 361, 1037, 1089, 1249, 1250
Dogbowl 126
Dogg, Nate 1036
Doggett, Bill 1297, 1308
Dogs [2] 1279
Doherty, Brian 1133
Doherty, Denny 690, 691
Dokken **327**, 1249
Dokken, Don 327
Dolby, Thomas 226, **327**, 676, 879, 1210
Dolemite 324
Dolenz, Micky 754, 755
Domino [1] 1279
Domino, Fats 30, 61, 67, 68, 74, 130, 147, 148, 230, **327**, 328, 425, 524, 613, 715, 731, 795, 796, 887, 895, 1151, 1278, 1288, 1303, 1305, 1306, 1309
Dominoes [1] 1206, 1229, 1306
Don & Dewey **328**, 821, 1291
Don & Juan **328**, 723, 793
Don Caballero 165
Donahue, Dan 484
Donahue, Jerry 387, 426
Donahue, Jonathan 411, 506, 728
Donahue, Patty 1199
Donald, Ann 1003
Donald, Barbara 1003
Donald, Chris 996
Donaldson, Bo 267, **328**
Donaldson, Bo & the Heywoods 328
Donaldson, Bobby 328
Donaldson, Lou 287, 1329
Donato, Chris 267
Donays 1292
Donegan, Lonnie **328**, 329, 986, 1310, 1311, 1319
Donelly, Tanya 90, 91, 141, 1136, 1142, 1143
Donna, Jim 190
Donnas **329**
Donne, Robert 636, 637
Donner, Ral 1297, 1310
Donnie & the Dreamers 1297
Donovan [1] 57, 119, **329**, 330, 331, 334, 506, 507, 519, 539, 549, 583, 591, 618, 643, 724, 999, 1153, 1319, 1323, 1354
Donovan, Bazil 117
Donovan, Dan [1] 95
Doobie Brothers 23, 180, **331**, 385, 421, 470, 565, 716, 799, 1172, 1285, 1286
Dooley, Mike 1153
Doom, Lorna 461
Doors 26, 31, 103, 132, 152, 170, 248, 273, 274, 289, **332**, 333, 337, 350, 351, 394, 438, 556, 577, 672, 702, 711, 767, 780, 798, 823, 900, 973, 979, 1031, 1085, 1089, 1131, 1145, 1172, 1244, 1249, 1250, 1323, 1329
DoReen 1044
Dorn, Joel 790
Dorney, Tim 935
Doroschuk, Ivan 725
Doroschuk, Stefan 725
Dorough, Bob 1049
Dorough, Howie 51
Dorset, Ray 776
Dorsey, Lee 307, **333**, 415, 730, 731, 1046, 1137, 1151, 1274, 1278, 1284, 1286, 1288, 1306
Doss, Alan 790
Doss, Bill 34, 790, 821
Dotson, Ward 494
Double Trouble [1] 1185, 1186
Doucette, Paul 702
Doucette, Salvadore Jr. 68
Doughboys 725

Dougher, Sarah 914
Doughty, M. 1043
Douglas, Alan [1] 522, 523
Douglas, Alan [2] 640
Douglas, Chip 754
Douglas, Graeme 352, 634
Douglas, Jack 9, 840, 1031
Douglas, Jerry 160, 1231
Douglas, Shy Guy 1274
Douglas, Steve [1] 196, 1308
Dovells 661
Doves [1] **333**, 334
Dowd, Tom 17, 18, 219, 666, 682, 1060, 1080
Down, Tom 17
Downchild Blues Band 284
Downes, Geoffrey 39, 40, 157, 1191, 1256
Downes, Graeme 1191
Downey, Brian 1133, 1236
Downey, Tyrone 506
Downfall 823
Downing, Big Al 1282
Downing, K.K. 605, 606
Downliners Sect **334**, 1327
Download [1] 1019
Dowson, Scott 668
Doyle, John [Drums] 687, 688
Dozier, Lamont 219, 427, 536, 645, 699, 822, 841, 1163, 1215, 1315
Dozier, Tim 1020
Dragon, Darryl 180
Drake, John 807
Drake, Nick 299, **334**, 335, 336, 403, 476, 507, 543, 555, 655, 705, 751, 831, 922, 963, 1030, 1225, 1328, 1354, 1355
Drake, Pete 883, 1046
Drakoulias, George 717, 857, 943
Dramarama **335**, 336
Dramatics 297, **336**, 1295
Draper, Paul 695, 696
Draper, Ray 695
Draper, Terry 626
Dre [1] 833
Dre [2] 809, 833, 834
Dream Academy **336**, 337
Dream Command 244
Dream Six 245
Dream Syndicate 63, **337**, 361, 485, 541, 667, 823, 912, 913, 1141, 1248, 1343, 1344
Dream Theater 1181
Dream Warriors **337**
Dreams So Real 1344
Dres [1] 106
Dresch, Donna 1021, 1121
Dresden, Martin 420
Dressy Bessy 1285
Drew, Dennis 1126, 1127
Drew, Nicholas 82
Drewery, Corinne 1109
Drifters [US] 50, 59, 227, 248, 272, 317, **337**, 338, 535, 581, 619, 651, 718, 986, 1046, 1106, 1119, 1200, 1207, 1261, 1273, 1297, 1305, 1306, 1307, 1311, 1312, 1324
Drifting Cowboys 998
Driggins, Tony 150
Drinkard Singers 224, 1106
Driscoll, Julie 1284
Driscoll, Rick 613
Drive Like Jehu 320, 948
Droge, Pete 669
Drozd, Steven 411
Dru Hill 1016
Drucker, Ben 1110
Druids 1298
Drummond, Bill 250, 351, 626
Drummond, Billy 626, 627
Drummond, Burleigh 22, 23
Dryden, Spencer 583
Dryden, Tim 478
Dub Narcotic Sound System 77, 750
Dubbe, Berend 94
DuBrow, Kevin 1020
Dubs 568, 1280
Ducanes 1052
Duchene, Frank 538
Duck, Dennis 337
Ducks 338

Ducks Deluxe 143, 241, 319, **338**, 608, 769, 822, 962, 1287, 1335, 1337
Duckworth, John 1112
Dudanski, Richard 822, 898, 913
Dudgeon, Gus 37, 597, 1251
Dudley, Anne 37, 38, 367, 429
Dudley, Dave 846
Duffy [1] 655
Duffy, Billy 273, 274
Duffy, Martin 201, 399, 400
Duffy, Nick 655
Duffy, Stephen 655
Dufort, Dave 45
Dugmore, Dan 893
Duhig, Tony 607
Dukays 197, 198
Duke, David 1283
Duke, George 68, 831, 1265, 1266, 1267, 1284
Dukes of Stratosphear 279, **338**, 339, 1251, 1290
Dulfer, Candy 764
Dulli, Greg 11, 35
Dump 639
Dunbar, Aynsley 547, 707, 927
Dunbar, Aynsley Retaliation 1081
Dunbar, Sly 340
Dunbar, Tommy 749, 961
Duncan, Gary 907, 908
Duncan, Malcolm 43
Dunckel, Jean-Benoit 13
Dunford, Michael 932, 933
Dunlop, Andy 1157
Dunlop, Ian 561
Dunlop, Russell 727
Dunn, Bob 696
Dunn, Brian 432
Dunn, Donald 'Duck' 219, 418, 696
Dunn, Monte 551, 786
Dunton, Brian 520
Dupree, Simon & The Big Sound 458, 1291
Duprey, Rob 775
Dupri, Jermaine 1, 184, 304, 431, 581
Duran Duran 12, 43, 132, 208, 273, 339, 601, 609, 666, 743, 749, 808, 828, 838, 875, 1003, 1048, 1115, 1195, 1288, 1338, 1339
Durand, Dominique 566, 567
Durango, Santiago 96
Durante, Mark 627
Durham, Eddie 1352
Duritz, Adam 257, 258
Durst, Fred 656, 657, 889, 1067
Durutti Column 765, 1013, 1289
Dury, Ian **339**, 340, 429, 686, 1226, 1244, 1285, 1295, 1335
Dury, Ian & The Blockheads 340
Dust Brothers 76, 83, 272, 502, 952, 977, 1101, 1219, 1258
Duvall, Shelley 842
Dvorak, Antonin 758
Dwarves 906, 1118
Dweeb 750
Dwyer, Damon 1122
Dwyer, Gary 250, 1121, 1122
Dyble, Judy 298, 586, 387, 1153
Dyke & the Blazers 340, 341, 956, 1284, 1334
Dylan [1] 1259
Dylan, Bob 6, 13, 48, 56, 57, 61, 62, 66, 76, 78, 81, 82, 92, 114, 117, 118, 119, 123, 125, 129, 137, 149, 159, 166, 167, 168, 172, 177, 191, 195, 201, 213, 218, 219, 221, 222, 230, 233, 234, 238, 239, 254, 256, 271, 272, 286, 298, 299, 301, 304, 308, 316, 317, 318, 325, 329, 330, 331, **341**, 342, 343, 344, 345, 354, 380, 385, 386, 387, 388, 390, 395, 401, 406, 418, 423, 424, 426, 427, 434, 450, 463, 467, 468, 477, 479, 480, 495, 498, 504, 505, 507, 508, 513, 521, 522, 526, 531, 533, 540, 547, 551, 559, 565, 582, 595, 603, 606, 621, 643, 653, 654, 657, 660, 669, 694, 701, 704, 709, 751, 769, 770, 771, 783, 786, 787, 790, 795, 801, 811, 812, 813, 814, 819, 831, 848, 855, 856, 887, 912, 921, 922, 927, 945, 946, 950, 952, 964, 972, 992, 999, 1000, 1008, 1016, 1037, 1042, 1046, 1052, 1062, 1064, 1069, 1072, 1073, 1078, 1080, 1081, 1090, 1119, 1131, 1133, 1138, 1143, 1157, 1165, 1169, 1175,

1190, 1204, 1216, 1218, 1232, 1235, 1240, 1242, 1243, 1248, 1259, 1260, 1261, 1269, 1282, 1316, 1318, 1319, 1323, 1326, 1327, 1328, 1342, 1343, 1344, 1351, 1353, 1354, 1356
Dylan, Bob & the Rolling Thunder Revue 143, 343
Dylan, Jakob 1204
Dynamics [1] 336
Dynasty [1] 49
Dyrason, Orri Pall 1005
DYS 1280
Dzidzornu, Rocky 334

E
E [1] 355
E Types **546**, 1288
E., Sheila 375, 376
Eager, Allen 508
Eager, Brenda Lee 162
Eager, Vince 1310
Eagle 418
Eagles [1] 22, 24, 52, 149, 187, 234, 241, 253, **346**, 347, 387, 418, 421, 486, 519, 523, 576, 661, 788, 796, 834, 835, 901, 955, 1046, 1199, 1204, 1205, 1269, 1314, 1327
Eagles [2] 523, 1205
Eaglin, Snooks 895
Eakle, Matt 450
Earl, Colin 776
Earl, Richard 1108
Earl, Roger 421, 979
Earl-Jean 1275
Earle, Steve [1] 675, 995
Earle, Steve [2] 11
Earth Opera 1275
Earth Wind & Fire **347**, 348, 349, 366, 454, 457, 711, 1020, 1079, 1093, 1160, 1244, 1284, 1291, 1334
Earth, Wind & Fire **347**, 348, 365, 434, 453
Earthtones 834
Easdale, Brian 336
Easdale, John 335, 336
Easley, Doug 1178
East Bay Ray 289
East River Pipe 639, 1289
East, Nathan 219, 247, 1237
Easter 1036
Easter, Mitch 246, 267, 322, 447, 601, 649, 650, 671, 673, 760, 950, 1036, 1188
Easterling, Skip 1286
Eastern Dark 195
Easton, Elliot 999, 1191
Easton, Sheena 49, **349**
Eastwood, Clint [Actor] 129, 409
Easybeats 56, 134, **349**, 350, 734, 742, 1141, 1288, 1322, 1341, 1342
Eater 997, 1337
Eaton, Gerald 442
Eaton, Wally 223
Eazy E 323, **350**, 552, 809, 1348
Echeverria, Rob 520
Echo & the Bunnymen 48, 58, 251, **350**, 351, 542, 554, 654, 837, 1197, 1323, 1338
Echobelly **352**, 1339
Echoes 511, 1297
Eckstine, Billy 427
Eddie & the Hot Rods **352**, 534, 634, 822, 1278, 1287
Eddie and The Tide 1193
Eddie [2] 1193
Eddy, Duane 37, 38, 263, **353**, 517, 564, 663, 945, 1243, 1275, 1292, 1296, 1297, 1308, 1309
Edelman, Randy 304
Eden, Dawn 1263
Eden, Sean 679
Eden's Children 1275
Edgar, Ron 777
Edge [1] 122, 243, 825, 896, 899, 1169, 1170, 1240
Edge, Graeme 758, 759
Edison Lighthouse 161, **353**, 1276
Edmonds, Kenneth 'Babyface' 49
Edmonds, Lu 899
Edmonton Symphony Orchestra 894
Edmunds, Dave 317, 338, **353**, 354, 380, 381,

384, 410, 608, 668, 673, 677, 678, 914, 949, 962, 986, 987, 999, 1065, 1090, 1091, 1241, 1292, 1335, 1338
Edmunds, Dave & Rockpile 354
Edsels 354, 1282
Educated Rapper 1179
Edward, Greg 286
Edward, John 1055
Edwards, Bernard 208, 743, 793, 898, 958, 1017, 1080
Edwards, Chico 1055
Edwards, Dennis 246, 1125
Edwards, Dickon 828
Edwards, George 544
Edwards, Gordon 366
Edwards, Jackie 284, 285, 1316, 1355
Edwards, John [1] 1055
Edwards, Jonathan [1] **354**, 355
Edwards, Ken 1084
Edwards, Kenny [1] 1046
Edwards, Mike 586
Edwards, Richard 692
Edwards, Stoney 1230
Edwards, Teddy 507
Edwards, Todd 278
Edwards, Tommy 1297
Edwards, Vincent 1289
Eels **355**, 484
Egan, Bob 1223
Egan, Mike 1201
Egan, Rusty 939, 1195
Egan, Walter 1285
Egerton, Stephen 302
Egg Hunt 740
Egg [1] 8
Eggs over Easy 87, 143, **355**, 1287, 1335, 1337
Egyptian Lover 553, 1300
Ehart, Phil 610
Eight O Eight State 101, **355**, 1298, 1299
Eightball 748
Eighth Day 1284
Ein Heit 1006
Einheit, F.M. 356
Einsturzende Neubauten 178, 192, 193, 268, 300, **355**, 356, 902, 1284, 1345
Eisentrager, Thor 260
Eitzel, Mark 24, 25, 334, **356**, 357, 922
Eklund, Greg 379
El Chicano 1276, 1300
El Dorados 357, 1224, 1280, 1306
El P 501
El Rays 298
Elam, Keith 495
Elastica 121, 280, 352, **358**, 393, 680, 726, 1299, 1339, 1346, 1347
Elastica [1] 358
Eldritch, Andrew 743, 1017
Electrafixion 280, 350
Electric Company 24
Electric Eels 1336
Electric Flag 114, **358**, 561, 976, 1329, 1330
Electric Light Orchestra 88, 234, 320, 354, **358**, 359, 360, 509, 544, 555, 626, 772, 773, 796, 856, 1107, 1157, 1241, 1283, 1331
Electric Prunes 44, 279, **360**, 778, 804, 1177, 1288
Electrifying Mojo 752
Electronic 360, 361
Electronic Eye 170
Elefante, John 610
Elephant Six Orchestra 376
Elevators 375
Eleventh Dream Day 361, 432, 436, 1353, 1354
Eleventh House 1329
Elf 105, 293, 316
Elf Power 95, **362**, 376, 815
Elfman, Danny 112, 730, 818
ElHadi, Suliaman 640, 641
Eli, Bobby 536
Eliot, T.S. 456, 587
Ellenis, Theothorous Athanasious 335
Eller, James 250, 251
Elliman, Yvonne 87, 1293
Ellington, Duke 202, 216, 450, 831, 885, 1139, 1190, 1292
Ellington, Marc 705

Ellington, Robert 336
Elliot, Bobby 533
Elliot, Cass 690, 691
Elliot, Chad 305
Elliott, Brad 50
Elliott, Cassandra 701
Elliott, Dennis 426
Elliott, Joe 294, 1240
Elliott, Lol 224
Elliott, Louise 638
Elliott, Missy 305, 362, 805, 926
Elliott, Missy Misdemeanor **362**, 544
Elliott, Ramblin' Jack 1353
Elliott, Ron [1] 81, 381
Elliott, Ron [2] 81
Ellis [1] 582
Ellis, Barbara 415
Ellis, Bill 411
Ellis, Jimmy 1155
Ellis, John [1] 320, 1193
Ellis, Mark [1] 639
Ellis, Pee Wee 147, 582, 1334
Ellis, Rob 638
Ellis, Robert 511
Ellis, Shirley 1347
Ellis, Terry [1] 366
Ellis, Timo 216
Ellis, Warren 194, 319
Ellison, Andy 595, 1280
Ellison, Jim 703, 704
Elm, Bill 175
Elmhirst, Tom 161
Elmore, Elizabeth 977
Elmore, Greg 908, 977
Elph 234
Elsey, Bob 1109
Elston, Harry 433
Elton, Bobby 534
Ely 363
Ely, Claude 896
Ely, Jack 620
Ely, Joe 154, **362**, 363, 1327
Ely, Vince 896
Embarrassment 295, 399
Embrace [1] 580, 740, 1157
Embrace [2] 1283
Emerick, Geoff 54, 89, 255, 612
Emerson, Darren 1174, 1175
Emerson, Keith 124, 363, 364, 394, 420, 797, 1256, 1331
Emerson, Lake & Palmer 39, 40, 292, **363**, 364, 365, 394, 458, 617, 797, 1049, 1255, 1296, 1331
Emery, James 591
EMF 39, **365**, 1074
Eminem 324, 362, **365**, 699
Emmons, Buddy 835, 893, 1106
Emo, Brian 1058
Emotions [1] 348, **365**, 366, 1037
Emperors 1280
Empire, Alec 154, 501
En Vogue 366, 554, 1001, 1081
Enchanters 738
End [1] 1275
Endino, Jack 47, 486, 639, 803
Enemy 224, 629, 1153, 1342
Energy [1] 122
Engel, Scott 1201, 1202, 1203
England Dan & John Ford Coley 366
England's Glory 366
Engle, John 232
English Beat **366**, 367, 404, 455, 1052, 1171, 1289, 1298, 1299, 1338, 1355, 1356
English Chamber Choir 1201
English, Joe 714
English, Richard 411
Enigk, Jeremy 1102
Enigma 38, **367**
Eno 70
Eno, Brian 28, 40, 70, 133, 134, 135, 136, 160, 168, 173, 174, 176, 197, 231, 256, 306, **367**, 368, 369, 389, 401, 402, 545, 555, 575, 576, 674, 688, 703, 798, 807, 824, 959, 960, 1005, 1025, 1041, 1116, 1117, 1124, 1169, 1170, 1173, 1191, 1202, 1231, 1234, 1273, 1289, 1296, 1299, 1301, 1331, 1337
Eno, Jim 1059

Eno, Roger 336, 369, 545
Eno/Cale 369
Ensemble Modern 1268
Entwistle, John 1070, 1152, 1220, 1221, 1222, 1332
Enuff Z'nuff **370**, 1302
Enya **370**, 371
Episode Six **371**
EPMD **372**, 912, 926, 1279, 1280, 1284
Epps, Preston 1296, 1308
Epstein, Brian 79, 106, 462, 1319
Epstein, Howie 856, 892, 956
Equals **372**
Erasure 300, **372**, 373, 374, 824, 827, 1100, 1254, 1287
Erdelyi, Tommy 916, 934
Eric B & Rakim **374**, 752, 912, 1274, 1280
Eric's Trip **374**
Erickson, Roky 126, 250, 251, **374**, 375, 411, 485, 599, 923, 1135, 1136, 1280
Erikson, Duke 449
Erlandson, Eric 532
Errico, Greg 1187
Errico, Jan 751, 752, 1187
Erskine, Fred 607
Ertegun, Ahmet 227, 537, 1042, 1189
Erwin, Ken 170
Esch, En 627
Escobar, Nas 782
Escorts [2] **375**
Escorts [3] 375
Escott, Colin 228, 237, 338, 398, 399, 854, 1146
Escovedo, Alejandro **375**, 376
Escovedo, Coke 1277
Escovedo, Javier 375
Escovedo, Pete 375
Escovedo, Sheila 376
ESG [1] **376**, 655
Esham 631, 632
Esposito, Enzo 1066
Esquerita **376**
Esquivel 1075
Essex Green **376**, 377, 484
Estefan, Emilio Jr. 669
Estefan, Gloria 16, **377**, 988
Estefan, Gloria & Miami Sound Machine 377
Estes, Sleepy John 189, 219, 246, 645, 988
Estrada, Roy 459, 659, 661
Eternals [3] 1282
Etheridge, Melissa **377**, 378, 831
Ethridge, Chris 418, 561
Ethyl Meatplow 460
Etzioni, Marvin 667
EU **378**
Eugenius 1185
Europe **378**, 1302
Eurythmics 276, **378**, 379, 431, 574, 649, 984, 1287
Evan, John 587, 588, 589
Evans, Bill [Piano] 540
Evans, Chris 1129
Evans, Faith **379**, 899, 906
Evans, Gil 778, 976, 1083, 1247
Evans, Joel 484
Evans, John [1] 588
Evans, Mal 566
Evans, Mark 3, 151
Evans, Mike 6, 734
Evans, Nate 558
Evans, Pete 541
Evans, Rod 292
Evans, Shane 236
Evans, Tom 55, 501
Evans, Tom [Badfinger] 54, 55, 232
Eve's Plum 1195
Even Dozen Jug Band 988
Everclear **379**, 380
Everett, Betty 148, 162, **380**, 1110, 1275, 1324
Everett, Matt 726
Everlast **380**, 542, 892
Everly Brothers 12, 80, 85, 122, 189, 221, 228, 317, 319, 346, 353, 354, **380**, 381, 382, 383, 401, 451, 491, 509, 532, 610, 783, 784, 787, 824, 855, 892, 932, 949, 1050, 1220, 1222, 1232, 1308, 1317, 1319, 1327, 1351

Everly, Don 381, 382, 893
Everly, Phil 381, 382, 661, 1269
Everything But the Girl **382**, 383, 571, 1013, 1109
Ewen, Christopher 443
Ewing, Fyfe 1131, 1132
Ewing, Roy 139
Ex 677, 722
Ex Cat Heads 635
Exceptions [1] 208
Exciters **383**, 1275, 1312, 1313
Excuse Seventeen 1021
Exiles [1] 557
Exits 1298
Experimental Audio Research 636
Exploited 997, 1340
Extreme [1] **383**, 1128, 1182, 1183
Eye [1] 130, 131
Eye, Yamantaka 131
Eye, Yamatsuka 130, 131
Eyes of Blue 1286
Eyes [1] 415, 1279, 1284, 1322
Ezrin, Bob 50, 92, 248, 249, 611, 624, 625, 626, 741, 926, 927, 969

F

Fabares, Shelley 1275, 1289, 1309
Fabian 43, **384**, 1275, 1297, 1309, 1335,
Fabio [Dance] 471
Fabulous Thunderbirds **384**, 385, 915, 976
Facenda, Tommy 1282
Faces 84, 93, 98, 102, 103, **385**, 455, 459, 795, 888, 934, 1027, 1079, 1080, 1081, 1087, 1151, 1222, 1240
Factory [1] 459, 659, 661
Fadyl, San 637
Fagen, Donald 35, **385**, 594, 870, 1072, 1073, 1092, 1213
Fagenson, Don 1208
Fahey, John 159, 419, 451, 452, 477, 923, 1171, 1350, 1354
Fahey, Siobhan 60
Fair, David 210, 386, 498, 499
Fair, Jad 210, **385**, 386, 498, 499, 599, 1257
Fair, Ron 251
Fairbairn, Bruce 10, 674, 1257
Fairburn, Werly 1273
Fairchild, Jim 478
Fairfield Four 256, 1231
Fairfield Parlour 610
Fairies 1275
Fairport Convention 36, 298, 299, 334, **386**, 387, 388, 395, 426, 551, 588, 589, 657, 705, 706, 707, 728, 851, 1071, 1072, 1090, 1126, 1138, 1139, 1140, 1153, 1240, 1319, 1354, 1355
Fairweather-Low, Andy 23
Faith No More **388**, 389, 557, 632, 656, 744, 745, 921, 1050, 1051, 1334
Faith, Adam 999, 1310
Faithfull, Marianne 261, **389**, 390, 572, 638, 657, 727, 730, 863, 1166, 1200, 1210, 1355
Faithless 312
Fakes 783
Falco 498
Falconer, Andy 897
Falconer, Doug 548
Falconi, Ted 260, 416
Falcons [1] 418, 822, 828, 860, 861
Falkner, Jason 13, **390**, 391, 483, 484, 585, 1141
Fall 178, 358, **391**, 392, 393, 394, 400, 448, 561, 654, 776, 1212, 1279, 1287, 1337, 1338, 1339
Fallen Angels [1] 845
Fallen Angels [4] 846
Faloon, Brian 1082
Faltermeyer, Harold 1051
Faltskog, Agnetha 1
Faludi, Susan Schiff 559
Fambrough, Henry 1055
Fame, Georgie 432, 764, 887, 1079, 1316, 1325
Fame, Herb 848
Family [1] 394, 1042, 1240, 1280
Family Fantastic 374
Famous Flames 121
Fanatics 812

Fancher, Lisa 310
Fankhauser, Merrell **395**, 557, 773, 774
Fankhauser, Merrell & HMS Bounty 395
Fanny [1] 253
Fantastic Baggys 1024
Fantastic Johnny C. 1284
Fapardokly **395**, 557, 773
Faragher, Davey 527
Fardon, Don 1042, 1043
Farian, Frank 125, 738
Farina, Mimi 57, 395
Farina, Richard 238, 239, 298, 395, 705, 1353
Farina, Richard & Mimi **395**, 1318, 1319
Farinas 394
Farley, Nate 493
Farley, Terry 395
Farlow, Billy C. 241, 242
Farlowe, Chris 950, 1286
Farm [1] **395**, 396
Farmer, Frances 382
Farmer, Steve 807
Farndon, Pete 885
Farner, Mark 115, 478
Farnham, John 661
Farr, Gary & The T-Bones 1284
Farrar, Jay 1039, 1174, 1223
Farrar, Jimmy 752
Farrell, Bobby [1] 125
Farrell, Joe 86, 918
Farrell, Perry 578, 579, 876, 1210, 1345
Farrell, Wes 793
Farren, David 53
Farren, Mick 305, 306
Farris, Steve 745
Farrow, Mia 330
Fast 439
Fast, Larry 36
Fastbacks **396**, 486, 1295
Faster Pussycat 1302
Fastway 1302
Fat Boys 205, **396**, 397, 696, 1173, 1285, 1287, 1347
Fat Mike 804
Fataar, Ricky 73
Fatback 191, 1284, 1295
Fatboy Slim 76, **397**, 748, 781, 959
Fateman, Johanna 643
Father MC 899
Father Shaheed 915
Fatheringale, Hermione 135
Fatima Mansions 527
Fatone, Joey 781
Fattoruso, Hugo 997
Faulkner, David 537
Faulkner, Jason 1271
Faust [1] 126, **397**, 398, 829, 1074, 1294, 1331
Fay, Bob 284, 987, 988
FBI 41
Fear of Pop 422
Fear [1] 1280
Fearing, Charles 841
Fearman, Eric 286
Feather, Leonard 508
Feathers [1] 135
Feathers, Bubba 398
Feathers, Charlie **398**, 399, 1090, 1304
Feedtime 1342
Feelies **399**, 470, 673, 679, 1337, 1338, 1343, 1345, 1346
Fehlmann, Thomas 373, 824
Feinberg, Jon 664
Feinstein, Harvey 1050
Felber, Dean 538
Felder, Don 346, 347, 798
Felder, Wilton 57
Feldman, Bob 1087
Feldman, Eric Drew 107, 181
Feldman, Lee 28, 716
Feldman, Nick 1205
Feldman, Richard 219
Felice, John 942
Feliciano, Jose 86, 504
Felix, John 568
Fellini, Federico 233
Fellini, Valeria 273
Fellows, Graham 591
Fellows, Mike 821, 1008

Fellows, Stephen 243, 244
Felt [1] **399**, 400
Felts, Narvel 1283
Fender Benders 1243
Fender, Freddy 1015
Fendermen 1282
Fennelly, Gere 924
Fennelly, Michael 736
Fenner, Kate 313
Fenner, Tom 419
Fenstein, Herb 279
Fenton, David 1185
Fenwick, Ray 285
Ferguson, Doug 176
Ferguson, Jay [1] 1024, 1056
Ferguson, Jay [2] 1024
Ferguson, Jim [1] 671
Ferguson, Keith 384
Ferguson, Larry 540
Ferguson, Paul 616
Ferguson, Steve [1] 805, 1298
Fergusson, Alex 897
Fergusson, Bill 671
Fernley, Keith 1137
Ferrante, Bob 780
Ferrante, Russell 382
Ferre, Leo 20
Ferrer, Ibrahim 475
Ferrier, Tom 175
Ferrone, Steve 43, 219, 402, 831
Ferry, Bryan 2, 327, 356, 368, **400**, 401, 402, 468, 505, 514, 579, 900, 959, 960, 1112
Fetters, Rob 76
Feza, Mongezi 1247
Ficca, Billy 1124, 1191, 1199
Fichter, Morgan 177
Fiedler, Margaret 638
Fieger, Doug 628, 1208
Field Mice **402**
Field, John 607
Field, Tim 1059
Fielding, Dave 196, 197
Fielding, Eddie 196
Fields of the Nephilim **402**, 403
Fields, Ernie 1292
Fields, Frank 68, 609
Fiend One 750
Fier, Anton 188, 399, 470, 471, 852, 1088, 1107, 1227
Fifth Dimension [1] 41, **403**, 404, 475, 687, 736, 788, 809, 830, 846, 1211, 1296
Fifth Dimension [2] 480, 690, 1025
Fifty Four Forty 538
Fifty Seventh Dynasty 1074
Fig, Anton 36, 625
Fight 605
Figi, Baird 361
Figures on a Beach 443
Filer, 'Cripple' Jim 250
Files, Christina 1110
Fileti, Donn 519
Finch, Carl 1117
Finch, Jennifer 47, 635
Finch, Richard 611
Fincher, David 554
Fine Young Cannibals 367, **404**, 1076
Fine, Jon 232
Finer, Jem 871
Fingers Inc. 860
Fini Tribe 938
Finkler, Michael 1121
Finn Brothers **404**
Finn [1] 404, 405
Finn, Jason 396, 879
Finn, Mickey [1] 1113
Finn, Neil 271, 272, **404**, 405, 1057, 1058, 1157, 1342
Finn, Tim 21, 272, 404, **405**, 1057, 1058
Finney, Albert 1210
Finns 404
Fire Engines 575
Fireballs [1] 535, 1292, 1296
Firefall 366, 387, **405**, 406, 448, 835, 1056
Firehose **406**, 740, 876, 1210
Firewater 250
First Choice 1001
First Class 161, 1276, 1299

First Family 582
First National Band 755, 789
Fischer, Kyle 913, 914
Fish & Roses 963
Fish [1] 697, 698
Fish, Alan 170
Fishbone 406, 407
Fishburne, Larry 1164
Fisher 781
Fisher, Charles 978
Fisher, Dean 511
Fisher, Eddie [1] 130
Fisher, Matthew 893, 894
Fisher, Norwood 407
Fisher, Rob [2] 781
Fisher, Sonny 1291
Fisher, Toni 1203, 1282
Fisk, Steve 77, 460, 676, 1212
Fitch, John 620
Fitzgerald, Alan 799
Fitzgerald, Ella 1227
Fitzgerald, Kevin 460
Fitzgerald, Patrik 799
Fitzpatrick, Colleen 1195
Five Americans 68, 407, 512, 1276
Five Blind Boys 1351
Five Crowns 619
Five Du Tones 901, 1224, 1274
Five Keys 1280
Five Man Electrical Band 1128
Five Royales 59, 407, 1291
Five Satins 408, 535, 793, 794, 1046, 1306, 1274, 1276
Five Stairsteps 408, 1240, 1276
Fixsen, Guy 638, 760
Fixx 408, 409, 1338, 1290
Flack, Roberta 409, 437, 512, 846, 1183, 1184, 1244, 1273
Flames [1] 145, 535
Flamin' Groovies 262, 353, 396, 409, 410, 411, 612, 911, 1257, 1290, 1339
Flaming Ember 411
Flaming Lips 284, 411, 412, 1049, 1050
Flamingos 412, 1274
Flamingos [1] 130, 412, 1306
Flanders, Tommy 119
Flansburgh, John 1132
Flanz, Neil 846
Flares 171, 1274
Flash [1] 270, 1256
Flatlanders 362, 363, 1327
Flatley, Michael 371
Flavor Flav 226, 897
Flea 579, 921, 922, 1210
Fleck, Bela 539
Fleetwood Mac 151, 152, 234, 257, 270, 304, 412, 413, 414, 432, 605, 627, 701, 707, 708, 797, 798, 975, 1007, 1015, 1029, 1192, 1269, 1286, 1316, 1326
Fleetwood, Mick 151, 412, 413, 414, 707, 708, 1240
Fleetwoods 415
Fleming, Don 253, 386, 498, 532, 877
Fleming, Stephen 253
Flemion, Dennis 434
Flemion, Jimmy 434
Flesh 415
Flesh Eaters 642
Flesh for Lulu 415
Fleshtones 195, 415, 416
Fletcher, Alan 301
Fletcher, Amelia 1212
Fletcher, John [2] 'Ecstasy' 1222, 1223
Fletcher, Justin 990
Fleur de Lys 416, 1035
Flint, Hughie 708
Flint, Keith 894, 895
Flipper 260, 416, 417, 1339, 1342
Flo & Eddie 417, 896, 1047, 1165, 1248, 1265
Float Up CP 207
Flock of Seagulls 36, 92, 244, 417, 472, 808, 1288, 1338
Flood [1] 201, 276, 301, 372, 373, 510, 511, 1029
Flop 396
Flores, Rosie 21
Flouride, Klaus 289

Flower Pot Men 161
Flower [1] 1192
Flowered Up 935
Flowers, Cornelius 'Snookey' 114
Floyd, Eddie 418, 575, 860, 1273
Flying Burrito Brothers 75, 81, 117, 167, 221, 222, 299, 405, 406, 418, 519, 525, 667, 668, 845, 846, 869, 1123, 1285, 1286, 1327
Flying Lizards 155
Flying Machine [1] 1120, 1276, 1289
Flying Saucer Attack 419, 420, 636
Flynt, Ron 1165
Foad, Paul 42
Focus [1] 420, 1331
Foetus 99, 234, 250, 874
Fogel, Andy 927
Fogelberg, Dan 420, 421, 1285
Fogerty, John 117, 265, 266, 354, 375, 421, 460, 472, 485, 494, 786
Fogerty, Tom 421
Foghat 421, 432, 979, 980, 1281, 1326
Folds, Ben 421, 422, 602
Folds, Ben Five 422, 805
Foley, Ellen 1231
Foley, Zac 365
Foljahn, Tim 191
Folk Implosion 422, 423, 987, 988
Folschow, Bob 190
Fonda, Peter 16
Fonfara, Michael 927, 928
Fong, Lincoln 760
Fontaine, Eddie 80, 1282, 1319
Fontana, D.J. 513, 881
Fontana, Wayne 423
Fontana, Wayne & the Mind Benders 423
Foo Fighters 423, 1102, 1192
For Carnation 1023, 1300
Forbert, Steve 158, 423, 424, 1286, 1328
Forbes, Derek 1013
Forbes, Rand 1175
Force MD's 424, 425, 608
Force [1] 378
Ford, Doug 742
Ford, Eric 330
Ford, Frankie 67, 421, 425, 432, 1030, 1274, 1278, 1306
Ford, Jim [1] 143
Ford, John 1089, 1090
Ford, Lita 767, 963
Ford, Penny 1044
Ford, Robben 602
Ford, Tennessee Ernie 1303
Ford, Willie 336
Fore, David 151
Foreigner 425, 426, 432, 477, 478, 584, 595, 1150, 1155, 1281, 1331
Forester, Kim 141
Forgemasters 1299
Fork, Rick 948
Formby, Richard 1048
Formula, Dave 687, 688, 1195
Fornatale, Mike 756
Forrester, A.C. 815
Forrester, Alan 751
Forsey, Keith 455, 556
Forshe 556
Forster, Robert 467, 468, 1191, 1342
Fortson, Marty 945
Fortuna, Nick 152
Forty Five Grave 337
Forty Five King 895, 915
Foster, David 140, 209, 318, 1094
Foster, David [1] 309, 544, 1162
Foster, Denzil 366
Foster, J.D. [1] 982
Foster, Joe 1124
Foster, Radney 158
Foster, Stephen 6, 842
Fotheringay 298, 299, 387, 426, 705, 1354, 1355
Fotomaker 919, 1278
Foundations 426, 1276
Fountains of Wayne 426, 566, 1196, 1290
Four Aces [Vocal] 268
Four Corners 1285
Four Freshmen 71, 72, 268, 427, 691, 1102, 1228, 1314

Four Hero 471
Four Lads 560
Four Pennies 210
Four Preps 213
Four Seasons 1, 71, 426, 427, 594, 867, 1055, 1072, 1178, 1182, 1299, 1307, 1325
Four Speeds 1296
Four Tet 1300
Four Tops 89, 100, 123, 195, 292, 427, 434, 822, 1093, 1123, 1314, 1315, 1324
Fourmost 1293, 1319
Fowler, Simon 812
Fowler, Tom 1267
Fowley, Kim 804, 941, 963, 990, 1216
Fox, Dave 877
Fox, Jim 576
Fox, Jim [1] 576
Fox, Mark 498
Fox, Paul 531
Fox, Samantha 41
Fox, Simon 82
Foxton, Bruce 574, 575, 1185
Foxx, John 1173
Foxx, Redd 417
Foxx, Vikki 370
Fraboni, Rob 914
Frame, Pete 387
Frame, Roddy 45, 46, 238
Frampton, Peter 123, 315, 427, 428, 546, 592, 966, 1027, 1070, 1160
Francis, Barrington 973
Francis, Bill 325
Francis, Black 107, 280, 478, 712, 863, 864
Francis, Connie 428, 429, 1311
Francis, Panama 780
Frank & Walters 238
Frankie Goes to Hollywood 157, 429, 986
Franklin, Adam 1108, 1109
Franklin, Aretha 57, 118, 137, 149, 186, 224, 258, 304, 378, 407, 409, 430, 431, 512, 619, 636, 732, 745, 850, 860, 882, 919, 924, 975, 1013, 1036, 1046, 1106, 1108, 1184, 1207, 1236, 1237, 1270, 1273, 1286, 1287, 1301, 1324, 1325, 1333, 1351
Franklin, C.L. 431
Franklin, Carolyn 430
Franklin, Erma 1301
Franklin, Farrah 304
Franklin, Kirk 1014
Franklin, Kirk & the Family 846
Franklin, Mark 1273
Franklin, Melvin 700
Franks, Clive 597
Frantz, Chris 368, 475, 1116, 1117, 1118, 1146, 1147
Franz, John 1202, 1203
Fraser, Andy 707
Fraser, Elizabeth 231, 232, 400, 701, 760, 761, 1005, 1136
Frayne, George 241, 242
Frazier Chorus 654
Freakwater 361, 432, 1223, 1353, 1354
Fred, John 432, 1325, 1332
Freddie & the Dreamers 432, 1317, 1320
Frederick, Kevin 286
Frederickson, Christian 910
Frederiksen, Fergie 1150
Frederiksen, Lars 917
Frederiksen, Marti 11
Fredriksson, Marie 959
Fredro 822
Free [1] 52, 53, 108, 234, 432, 433, 601, 708, 1263, 1326
Free Design 433
Free Spirits [1] 1329, 1330
Free, Mickie 997
Freebairn-Smith, Ian 813
Freed, Alan 425, 658, 681, 759, 944, 1303
Freehill, Sean 245
Freeman, Arthur 823
Freeman, Bobby 116, 433, 1026, 1282
Freeman, Lee 1089
Freeman, Matt 917
Frehley, Ace 624, 625
Frehley's Comet 625
Freiberg, David 585, 907, 908

French, J.J. 1166
French, John 181, 395
Frenett, John 638
Frenette, Matthew 674
Frere-Jones, Sasha 1171
Fresh Prince 322, 1032
Fresh, Doug E. 663, 1023, 1284, 1287
Freud, James 467
Frey, Glenn 149, 346, 347, 581, 661, 1046, 1281, 1314
Fricke, David 917, 1190
Fricke, Janie 366
Fricker, Sylvia 551
Friction [1] 139, 900
Frida 1, 373
Friday, Gavin 234, 301
Fridmann, Dave 362, 751, 1050
Friedland, Mitch 1061
Friedman, David [1] 153
Friedman, Kinky 1106
Friedman, Marty 721
Friend, Ali 830
Friends of Dean Martinez 175
Friends of Distinction 433, 434, 1296
Friese-Greene, Tim 192, 327, 534, 680
Friesen, David 868
Friesen, John 868
Frigo, Derek 370
Frigo, Johnny 370
Fripp, Robert 88, 134, 368, 369, 500, 617, 618, 703, 723, 893, 1111, 1331
Fripp, Robert & Eno 1111
Fripp/Eno 779
Frischmann, Justine 121, 358
Frisell, Bill 256
Frith, Fred 126, 470, 498, 1247, 1331
Fritz, Gaspard 797
Frizzell, Lefty 1301
Froese, Howard 211
Frogs [1] 434, 435, 1300
Front Two Four Two 171, 435, 739, 1284
Frontiere, Dominic 129, 1161
Froom, Mitchell 25, 63, 160, 189, 255, 256, 271, 272, 295, 405, 641, 670, 717, 796, 831, 885, 915, 995, 1139, 1140, 1187
Frost [2] 1067
Frost, Edith 435, 436, 1246
Frost, Richard 878
Frost, Thomas 878
Frosty [1] 732, 733
Frumholz, Steve 675
Frusciante, John 921, 922
Fry, Martin 2, 3, 779
Fryer, John 200, 837, 838
Fryer, Terry 837
Fu Manchu 906
Fu Schnickens 1274
Fucking Champs 783
Fuentes, Miguel 732
Fuentes, Sasha 1101
Fugazi 41, 112, 436, 437, 448, 740, 783, 873, 944, 953, 1341
Fugees 437, 528, 529, 582, 585, 906, 1013, 1293
Fugitives [1] 1067
Fugs 305, 437, 438, 469, 900, 1354
Full Force 658, 1144
Full Time Men 415
Fuller & Kaz 24
Fuller, Blind Boy 1350
Fuller, Bobby 151, 267, 338, 438, 439, 1293, 1297
Fuller, Bobby Four 439, 1297
Fuller, Craig 24, 660, 901
Fuller, Dolores 881
Fuller, Jerry [1] 787
Fuller, Jerry [2] 788
Fuller, Jesse 776
Fuller, Randy 439
Fuller, Randy Four [Group] 439
Fulson, Lowell 1284, 1296
Fulwood, Ramon Tiki 440
Fun Boy Three 60, 121, 240, 439, 500, 501, 1052, 1290
Fun Da Mental 873, 874
Fun Lovin' Criminals 439, 440

Funaro, Frank 296
Funches, Johnny 298
Funicello, Annette 43, 1309, 1310
Funichello, Ross 'The Boss' 310
Funk Brothers 1229
Funkadelic 131, 177, 226, 237, 251, 314, 324, 389, 418, **440**, 441, 442, 582, 818, 842, 843, 1020, 1117, 1120, 1144, 1148, 1284, 1334
Funky Four Plus One 1274, 1285, 1295
Funky Kings 606, 999, 1000
Fuqua, Charlie 560, 759
Fuqua, Harvey 759, 793, 1055, 1224
Furay, Richie 117, 155, 869, 870, 1046, 1327
Furious, Danny 43
Furmanek, Ron 855, 990, 1190
Furs 896
Furtado, Nelly **442**
Furtado, Tony 442
Furuholmen, Magne 12
Furuya, Setsuko 463
Fury, Billy **442**, 1149, 1310, 1311
Furys 1279
Fuse [3] 867
Futter, Brian 192
Future Bible Heroes **442**, 443, 689
Futures [1] 297
Fuxa 1231
Fuzztones 1321

G
G Clefs 1280
G Dep 900
G, Warren 324
G. Love 433, 444, 689
G. Love & Special Sauce 439, **444**
G., Kenny 123
G., Lisa 273
G., Mike 608
G., Warren 1036, 1279
Gaar, Gillian 239
Gabay, Yuval 1043
Gabrels, Reeves 1144
Gabriel, Gilbert 336
Gabriel, Pascal 776
Gabriel, Peter [1] 28, 57, 64, 81, 116, 175, 236, 239, 251, 364, **444**, 445, 456, 457, 458, 588, 697, 706, 717, 746, 747, 814, 889, 945, 946, 947, 966, 1013, 1247, 1331
Gadler, Frank 805
Gadson, James 1244
Gaffney, Chris 21
Gaffney, Eric 987, 1243, 1244
Gage, Pete 325
Gahan, David 300, 301
Gaines, Steve 682, 683, 1333
Gaines, Walter 828
Gainsbourg, Serge 32, 233, **445**, 446, 679, 753, 897, 1101, 1248
Gaither, Tommy 828
Galas, Chris 738
Galas, Diamanda 7, 373
Galaxie Five Hundred 24, 126, 232, **446**, 447, 555, 671, 676, 679, 751, 773, 837, 1292
Galaxies 1300
Galbraith, Alastair 69, 1343
Galdames, Andres 725
Galfo, George 780
Gallagher & Lyle 539, 1070
Gallagher, Liam 351, 811, 812, 1109, 1278
Gallagher, Mick 428
Gallagher, Noel 206, 334, 471, 726, 811, 812, 1170, 1214, 1217, 1226
Gallagher, Rory 1326
Gallahads 1276
Gallico, Paul 176
Gallo, Mike 1165
Gallucci, Don 1085
Gallup, Cliff 1090, 1194
Galuten, Albhy 87, 1093
Gamble & Huff 89, 208, 568, 732, 809, 1017, 1060, 1290
Gamble, Kenneth 89, 336, 380, 536, 568, 724, 732, 819, 920, 1010, 1106, 1144, 1290, 1334, 1335
Gamble, Terry 678
Gamboa, Steve 689, 783
Game Theory **447**, 671, 672, 775, 1343, 1344

Gamson, David 985
Gane, Tim 1074
Gang of Four 42, 96, 100, 160, 252, 409, 436, **448**, 449, 510, 548, 580, 587, 744, 749, 873, 1059, 1082, 1291, 1337, 1338
Gang Starr 314, 337, **449**, 495, 585, 774, 1349
Ganja Kru 1206
Gannon, Craig 501
Gano, Gordon 1194, 1195, 1345, 1351
Gant, Cecil 1304
Gant, Don 788
Gants 1332
Gap Band [1] **449**, 496, 673, 674, 1284, 1334
Garay, Val 36, 976
Garbage 183, 277, **449**, 935
Garbo, Greta 764
Garcia, Dean 276, 277
Garcia, Jerry 141, 177, 369, **449**, 450, 451, 480, 481, 482, 539, 583, 660, 1243, 1270
Garcia, Jerry Band 450
Garcia, John 634
Garcia, Kevin 478
Garcia, Willie 1131
Gardener, Mark 942, 943
Gardiner, Paul 808
Gardner, Bunk 153
Gardner, Carl 227
Gardner, Freddy 1010
Gardner, John 1231
Gardner, Mark [1] 942
Gardner, Rick 874
Garfield, Henry 1279
Garfunkel 451
Garfunkel, Art 100, 270, **451**, 594, 1008, 1011, 1012, 1119, 1211
Gargiulo, Lulu 396
Garland, Hank 881, 883
Garland, Judy 19, 1092, 1094, 1155
Garner, Erroll 963
Garner, Sue 963
Garnes, Sherman 680
Garnett, Gale 920
Garrett, Bobby 121
Garrett, Donald Rafael 451
Garrett, Leif **451**
Garrett, Nick 1171
Garrett, Peter 733, 734, 1342
Garrett, Robert 1274
Garrett, Snuff 651, 1042
Garrett, Tommy 'Snuff' 650, 1187
Garrison, Al 620
Garrity, Freddie 432
Garson, Mike 134
Garth, Al 666
Gartside, Green 985
Garvey, Nick 319, 338, 769, 1121
Garvey, Steve 165, 166
Gastr del Sol 436, **451**, 452, 592, 636, 821, 829, 879, 985, 1023, 1041
Gates, David 140, 141, 181, 434, 754, 1165, 1202, 1279, 1286, 1301
Gates, David [1] 140, 141, 1312
Gatlin, Larry 882
Gaudet, Mark 374
Gaudio, Bob 427
Gaugh, Bud 1098
Gaughan, Dick 1354
Gauvin, Mickey 561
Gavurin, David 1101
Gawenda, Tommy 857
Gaye, Anna Gordy 453
Gaye, Marvin 39, 61, 89, 90, 99, 148, 207, 258, 266, 278, **452**, 453, 486, 506, 512, 549, 569, 600, 602, 613, 628, 641, 687, 699, 707, 709, 711, 712, 759, 817, 828, 869, 924, 937, 940, 949, 957, 958, 1013, 1027, 1069, 1095, 1120, 1164, 1203, 1215, 1238, 1263, 1284, 1287, 1289, 1290, 1314, 1320, 1324, 1328, 1334
Gayles, Billy 1163
Gaynor, Adam 702
Gaynor, Gloria 243, **453**
Gayol, Danny 122
GBH [1] 1340
Gean, Doug 945
Geddes, Chris 90
Gedge, David 1211, 1212
Geerts, Raymond 538, 539

Geesin, Ron 1209
Geffen, David 342, 746, 751
Gehman, Don 539, 930, 931
Gehman, Pleasant 461
Geils, J. 454, 1236
Geils, J. Band **454**, 455, 490, 1236
Gelb, Howe 175, 207, 1248
Geldof, Bob 129, 130
Geller, Herb 848
Gems [1] 944, 1301
Gendel, Keith 840
Gene [1] **455**, 1103
GENE [3] 455, 1347
Gene Loves Jezebel 15
General Degree 337
General Public 367, 404, **455**
Generation X **455**, 456, 556, 932, 1193, 1278, 1279, 1337
Genesis [1] 186, 187, 239, 336, 338, 369, 444, 445, **456**, 457, 458, 611, 697, 735, 736, 1105, 1255, 1296, 1331
Geneva [1] 235
Genies 793, 1292
Genius [1] **458**, 731, 1246
Gentile, Katie 963
Gentle Giant **458**, 459
Gentle Waves **459**
Gentry, Bobbie 460
Gentry, Chris 726
Gentrys 71, 1320, 1281
Geordie [1] 616
George & Teddy 1026
George, Barbara **459**, 1151, 1274, 1278, 1282, 1306
George, Lowell 167, 173, **459**, 460, 470, 481, 659, 660, 661, 914, 1119, 1265
George, Sam 179
George, Steve [1] 745
Georgia Satellites **459**, 460, 1333
Geraci, Sonny 835
Geraldine Fibbers **460**
Geraldo, Neil 91, 296
Germano, Lisa 175, 188, 405, **460**, 461, 559, 1246
Germs **461**, 1249, 1279, 1280, 1336, 1339
Gerniottis, Chris 1264
Gerrard, Lisa 287, 288, **461**, 462, 1136
Gerritsen, Rinus 470
Gerry & The Pacemakers 106, 349, **462**, 986, 1317, 1319, 1320
Gersh, Gary 946
Gershwin, George 50, 198, 439, 494, 539, 540, 571, 1036, 1079, 1091, 1092, 1094
Gershwin, Ira 539
Gescom 1292
Gessle, Per 959
Get Up Kids **462**
Geto Boys **462**, 463, 981
Getz, Stan [1] 382
Ghost [2] 131, **463**, 464, 868
Ghost Dance 1017
Ghostface Killah 458, **464**, 731, 911, 912, 970, 1246
Giammarese, Carl 152
Giannini, Frank 125
Giant Sand 175, 1248
Gibb, Andy 85, 87
Gibb, Barry 85, 86, 87, 1093, 1094, 1208
Gibb, Maurice 85, 86, 87, 679, 1070
Gibb, Robin 85, 86, 87
Gibbons, Beth 877
Gibbons, Billy 719, 773, 1132, 1271, 1272
Gibbons, Michael 65
Gibbons, Mike [2] 55
Gibbs, Georgia 149, 268, 1292
Gibbs, Melvin 954
Gibson, Bob 238, 1353, 1354
Gibson, Charlene 433
Gibson, Debbie 217, 218, **464**, 864, 1052, 1228, 1310
Gibson, Don 203, 705
Gibson, Jill 690
Gibson, Wayne 1293
Giddings, Andy 589
Giessmann, Brent 295
Giessmann, Woody 295

Gifford, Alex 608, 1198
Gift, Roland 404
Giger, H.R. 281
Gil, Gilberto 778, 876
Gil-Sola, Federico 1234
Gilbert & Sullivan 955, 964, 965, 1152
Gilbert, Bruce 62, 1233
Gilbert, Gillian 793
Gilbert, Kevin 962
Gilbert, Paul 1302
Gilbert, Ronnie 56
Gilberto, Astrud 382
Gilchrist, Chad 530, 834
Gilder, Nick **464**, 465
Giles, Giles & Fripp 618
Giles, Michael 617, 618
Giles, Peter 617
Gilkyson, Tony 1249, 1250
Gill **448**
Gill, Alan 1121, 1122
Gill, Andrew 100, 448
Gill, Johnny 792, 939
Gill, Peter [1] 429
Gill, Vince 901, 1231
Gillan, Ian 292, 293, 327, 371
Gillard, Doug 493
Gillespie, Bobby 726, 887, 888, 1081
Gillespie, Dizzy 872, 888, 1274
Gillis, Brad 799, 832
Gilmer, Jimmy 1281
Gilmore, Jimmie Dale 154, 362, 363, 484, 917, 1291, 1327
Gilmore, Jimmie Dale & the Flatlanders 363
Gilmour, David 66, 67, 162, 336, 337, 401, 507, 715, 861, 862, 863, 1210, 1270
Gin Blossoms 266, **465**, 1290, 1339, 1344
Ginastera, Alberto 364
Ginger [1] **465**, 479
Ginn, Greg 103, 104, 217, 953, 1345
Ginsberg, Allen 223, 252, 437, 438, 814, 867, 1041, 1161, 1273
Ginsberg, Jennifer 627
Ginsburg, Arnie 578
Ginuwine 362, **465**, 466
Gion, Joel 142
Giordano, Lou 474, 1102
Giorno, John 171
Gira, Michael 1178
Giri, Michael 655
Girl Brothers 1215
Girlfriends 536, 1275
Girls 1053
Girls Against Boys 139
Girlschool 768
Giscombe, Junior 1224
Gist 1258
Gladiolas 1225, 1282
Gladwin, John 21, 22
Glaisher, Mik 243, 244
Glascock, Brian 766
Glascock, John 588
Glaser, Gabrielle 679
Glass, Philip 936, 1011, 1035
Glass, Preston 297
Glaze, Brian 142
Glenn, Lloyd 1296
Glenn, Will 913
Glide 351
Glimmer Twins 952, 961
Glitter Band **466**
Glitter, Gary 8, 126, 204, 294, 338, 393, 415, 439, **466**, 497, 519, 577, 590, 1004, 1281, 1291, 1339
Global Communication 200, 1273
Gloria Mundi 756
Glover, Corey 663
Glover, Henry 291
Glover, Leroy 376
Glover, Roger 292, 293, 371
Glover, Tony 344
Gnewikow, Jason 895
Go [2] **466**
Go Go's [1] 439, **466**, 467, 635, 775, 902, 1087, 1313, 1338, 1339
Go Sailor 1039
Go-Betweens **467**, 468, 542, 680, 1191, 1212, 1342

Goanna 1342
Goat, Johnny 434
Goats 131
God [1] 638
God Bullies 259
God Lives Underwater 1019
God's Property 1014
Godchaux, Donna 51, 190, 450
Godchaux, Keith 450, 482
Goddess, Tony 840
Godding, Brian 114
Godfrey, John 776
Godin, Nicolas 13
Godley & Creme 608, 1126
Godley, Kevin 608, 1126
Godrich, Nigel 83, 321, 391, 556, 847, 1157
Godspeed You Black Emperor! 468, 469, 636, 1005
Godz [1] **469**
Godz [2] **469**
Goese, Mimi 545
Goettel, R. Dwayne 1019
Goffey, Danny 256
Goffin & King 248, 1060
Goffin, Gerry 143, 166, 210, 248, 273, 360, 380, 381, 430, 475, 524, 619, 658, 659, 754, 887, 1001, 1059, 1274, 1289, 1301, 1311, 1312
Gok 827
Gold, Andrew **469**
Goldberg, Barry [1] 1326
Goldberg, Barry [Keyboards] 737
Goldberg, Michael 417
Goldberg, Neil 1099
Golden Earring **470**, 1281, 1296
Golden Palominos 188, **470**, 471, 1068, 1088, 1089
Golden, Annie 1283
Golden, Rusty 296
Goldfrapp **471**
Goldfrapp, Allison 471, 826
Goldie 101, **471**, 1290
Goldie [1] 471, 860, 1018
Goldie & the Gingerbreads 1301
Golding, Lynval 439, 1052
Goldman, Steve 409
Goldmark, Andy 837
Goldner, George 198, 412
Goldsboro, Bobby **471**, 472
Goldsmith, Jerry 821, 1102
Goldsmith, William 423, 1102
Goldstein, Jerry 28, 716, 1087
Goldstein, Mark 998
Goldy, Craig 316
Golliwogs 421, **472**
Gomelsky, Giorgio 114, 473, 1039, 1253
Gomez [1] **472**, 1283
Gomez, Alice **472**
Gomm, Ian 143, 144, **472**, 1335
Gong [1] 201, **473**, 474, 1038, 1294, 1296, 1331
Gongzilla 473
Gonsalves, Paul 202
Gonson, Claudia 443
Gonzales, Andy 699
Gonzalez, Andy 699
Gonzalez, Bob 1112
Gonzos 1301
Goo Goo Dolls **474**, 475
Good Liars 504
Gooden, Sam 557, 558
Goodfriend, Steve 910
Goodie Mob 833
Gooding, Cuba 689
Goodman, Al [2] 569, 752
Goodman, Benny 450
Goodman, Dave 995
Goodman, Jerry 322
Goodman, Ray 1067
Goodman, Shirley 569, 1001, 1240
Goodman, Steve [1] 156, 496, 892, 1286
Goodmanson, John [1] 112, 510
Goodroe, Michael 766
Goodwin, Bill 1199
Goodwin, Jim [1] 175
Goodwin, Jimi 333, 334
Googe 702

Googe, Deb 779
Gordon, Alan 283, 688, 1093
Gordon, Billy 246
Gordon, Bob [1] 665, 688, 1192
Gordon, Chris 846
Gordon, James [2] 297
Gordon, Jay [2] 282
Gordon, Jim [Drums] 297, 1154
Gordon, Karl 16
Gordon, Kim 217, 532, 1022, 1040, 1041, 1045
Gordon, Marc 58
Gordon, Nina 1192
Gordon, Robert [1] 266, 944
Gordon, Robert [2] 1292
Gordons 57, 58
Gordy, Berry Jr. 246, 426, 427, 452, 453, 534, 549, 568, 680, 699, 828, 946, 959, 1095, 1215, 1229
Gore, Lesley 401, **475**, 590, 1166, 1282, 1312, 1313
Gore, Martin L. 300, 301
Gorham, Scott 1133, 1134
Gorillaz **475**
Gorky's Zygotic Mynci **476**
Gorman, Chris 91
Gorman, David 267
Gorman, Fred 133, 828
Gorman, Leigh 132
Gorman, Tom 91
Gorrie, Alan 43
Gosdin Brothers 221
Gosdin, Rex 221
Gosdin, Vern 221
Goshorn, Larry 901
Gospelaires 1207
Goss, Chris 634, 702
Gossard, Stone 486, 767, 848, 1125
Goswell, Rachel 751, 1025
Gothic Archies 689
Gottehrer, Richard 28, 36, 37, 112, 125, 325, 716, 727, 1087
Gotti, Irv 820
Goudreau, Barry 132
Gough, Damon 55
Gould, Bill 389
Gould, Boon 650
Gould, Philip 650, 684
Goulding, Steve 962
Gouldman, Graham 423, **476**, 534, 817, 916, 989, 1126, 1275, 1280, 1286
Gourdine, Anthony 658
Government Issue 160, 1279, 1280
Grabham, Mick 894
Grace, Rocke 1205
Gradney, Kenny 660
Graff, Gary 807
Graffin, Greg 53
Graham Central Station 1284, 1334
Graham, Billy [Country] 100, 799, 975, 976
Graham, Bobby 477
Graham, Davey 477, 1354
Graham, Larry 433, 565, 1334
Graham, Leo 285
Graham, Terry 493
Gramm, Benny 478
Gramm, Lou 425, 426, **477**, 478, 758
Granahan, Gerry 28
Grand Funk 115, 478
Grand Funk Railroad 115, 469, **478**, 964, 1281
Grand Puba 109, 501, 1274
Granda, Michael 835
Grandaddy **478**
Grandmaster Caz 1280
Grandmaster Dee 1222, 1223
Grandmaster Flash **479**, 962, 1160, 1173, 1274, 1283, 1287, 1295, 1347
Grandmaster Flash & the Furious Five 479, 608, 1274, 1277
Grandmaster Melle Mel 479
Grange, Rob 807
Grant Lee Buffalo **479**
Grant, Amy 831, 858, 1351
Grant, Arthur 144
Grant, Eddy 216, 372, 993, 1083
Grant, Gogi 1261
Grantham, George 869, 870
Grapes of Wrath [1] 465, **479**, 480

Grappelli, Stephane 1011
Grass Roots 40, 63, 227, **480**, 1024, 1264
Grasshopper [1] 506
Grassroots 286
Grateful Dead 119, 143, 177, 344, 369, 409, 410, 449, 450, **480**, 481, 482, 521, 539, 540, 541, 646, 657, 660, 704, 711, 719, 735, 749, 773, 843, 859, 907, 965, 975, 1054, 1140, 1286, 1323, 1327
Gravediggaz 892, 970, 1076
Gravenites, Nick 114, 450, 1329
Graves, Alexander 759
Graves, Michael 742
Gravity Kills 808
Gray, Andrew 483
Gray, David [1] **482**, 483, 826, 1283
Gray, Dobie 267, **483**, 1071, 1284
Gray, James [1] 117
Gray, Les 774
Gray, Macy 1, 397, **483**, 495, 798
Gray, Nigel 873
Gray, Paul 279
Gray, Tom 472
Grays [1] 390, **483**, 484
Grease Band 230, 501
Grease, Dame 323
Great Buildings 931, 1278
Great Lakes **484**
Great Society **484**, 583, 1323
Great Speckled Bird 551, 1327
Great Unwashed 57
Great White **484**, 1249, 1302
Grech, Rik 394, 1154
Greco, Juliette 20
Green Day 38, 111, 303, 309, 462, **484**, 485, 510, 917, 1098, 1339, 1340, 1345, 1346
Green Jelly 994
Green on Red 337, **485**, 486, 1141, 1343, 1344
Green River 486, 767, 1044, 1295
Green, Al 21, 90, 278, 401, 464, 486, 487, 488, 613, 654, 662, 663, 707, 718, 849, 850, 943, 980, 1117, 1129, 1164, 1274, 1283, 1324, 1325, 1336, 1351
Green, Alex 1047
Green, Birdie 1289
Green, Carl 700
Green, Derrick 993
Green, Freddie 1163
Green, Gary 458
Green, Grant 1329, 1330
Green, Jeremiah 750
Green, Jerome 311, 312
Green, Mick 338
Green, Peter [1] 412, 413, 414, 707, 708, 1039, 1271, 1316, 1326
Green, Rudy 1274
Green, Tim 783
Greenbaum, Norman **488**
Greenberg, Florence 1001
Greenbriar Boys 56
Greene, Dennis 996
Greene, Jessy 460
Greene, Larry 354
Greene, Richard 221
Greenfield, Howard 989, 1311
Greentree, Richard 94
Greenwich, Ellie 35, 112, 475, 617, 830, 955, 1289, 1291, 1301, 1311, 1312
Greenwood, Gail 91
Greer, Big John 507
Gregory, Byron 262
Gregory, David 338, 1250
Gregory, Glenn 3, 519
Gregory, Probyn 1240
Gregory, Will 471
Gregson, Clive 32, 388, **489**, 601, 866
Grein, Paul 186
Greller, Allan 982
Grey, Paris 560
Grey, Robbie 749
Grid [1] 20, 401
Grieg, Edvard 1067
Griffey, Dick 49, 997
Griffin [1] 140, 141
Griffin, Alex 785
Griffin, Bob 121
Griffin, Gene 496

Griffin, James [1] 140, 141
Griffin, Patty 956
Griffin, Reggie 49
Griffin, Sid 138, 222, 667, 668, 1343
Griffith, Nanci 1146, 1353, 1354
Griffiths, Alan 1122
Griffiths, Mark [3] 705, 706
Grifters [1] **489**, 490
Griggs, Nigel 606, 981
Grimaldi, John 35
Grimes, Howard 487
Grimes, Rachel 910
Grimes, Tiny 513
Grin **490**, 665
Grin [1] 490, 665
Grindersswitch 173
Grisman, David 449, 450, 1119, 1275
Grissom, David 363
Grohl, Dave 423, 803, 1102, 1192, 1210
Groia, Phil 519
Grolnick, Don 1119
Groom, Mick 338
Groothuizen, Chris 541
Grooverider 471, 1018, 1298
Gross, Henry 159, 190, 996
Gross, Jason 656
Grosse, Ben 277
Grossman, Albert [1] 421
Grossman, Bill 1007
Grossman, Stefan 477, 1011
Grothman, Steve 1217
Groundhogs 26, **490**
Grunt, Blind Boy 395
Grushecky, Joe **490**
Guadalcanal Diary **491**, 974, 1109, 1287
Guaraldi, Vince 44
Guercio, James William 113, 195, 208, 209
Guerrero, Carlos 1210, 1211
Guess Who [1] 50, 164, **491**, 492, 576, 1203, 1288, 1310
Guess, Anthony 177
Guess, Stacy 1067
Guest, Christopher 1065
Guevara, Che 239
Guibert, Mary 152
Guida, Frank 125
Guided by Voices 27, 489, **492**, 493, 771, 1058, 1280, 1300, 1344
Guitar Shorty [1] 1178
Guitar Slim [Alec Seward] 1274
Guitar Slim [Eddie Jones] 147, 1030, 1278, 1303, 1352
Guitar, Johnny 257
Gulliksen, Eric 830
Gulliver 500
Gumball 386
Gun Club 193, 376, **493**, 494, 1017
Gunn, Ben 1017
Gunn, Tommy 836
Gunn, Trey 618, 1111
Gunnarsson, Rutger 1
Gunnels, Gene 1089
Guns N Roses 9, 102, 238, 249, 396, **494**, 495, 523, 640, 692, 742, 767, 875, 1051, 1087, 1128, 1219
Gunter, Arthur 883, 892, 1274
Gunter, Hardrock 1295, 1307
Guralnick, Peter 399, 883
Gurewitz, Brett 53
Guru [1] 287, 337, 449, **495**, 496, 585, 1349
Guru Guru 789
Gurus 538
Gus Gus [1] 1005
Guss, Randy 1146
Gustafson, Steve 1126, 1127
Guster, Keith 416
Guthrie, Arlo **496**, 519, 680, 1286
Guthrie, James 23
Guthrie, Nora 138
Guthrie, Robin 200, 231, 232, 238, 287, 399, 400, 494, 680, 1136
Guthrie, Woody 56, 137, 138, 139, 166, 246, 317, 329, 341, 432, 496, 529, 1016, 1049, 1223, 1353
Gutierrez, Louis 1141
Gutkowski, Mark 802

Gutterball 541, 667, 673, 1248
Gutteridge, Peter 224
Guy 89, 109, 145, 496, 1044
Guy [1] 108, **496**, 1244
Guy Called Gerald 355, 1299
Guy, Buddy 8, 219, 708, 1163, 1186, 1352
Gwar 994
GZA 458, 464

H

Haack, Bruce 8
Haas, Chris 268
Hacke, Alexander 268, 356
Hackett, Steve 456, 457, 697
Haden, Charlie 539, 602, 1130, 1247
Haden, Petra 1130
Haden, Rachel 1130
Hafler Trio 20
Hagar, Sammy **497**, 719, 757, 758, 799, 1061,
    1182, 1183
Hagen, Nina 100, **497**, 498, 1290
Hagerty, Neil 689, 960, 961
Haggard, Merle 21, 166, 167, 381, 480, 813,
    820, 846, 893, 901
Haglof, Karen 62
Hague, Stephen 200, 243, 373, 606, 607, 852,
    899, 946
Haig, Al 1191
Haig, Alan 1191
Hailey, Cedric 'K-Ci' 592, 609
Hailey, Joel 'Jo Jo' 609
Hain, Enoch 310
Haines, Julia 43, 102
Haines, Luke 13, 42, 43, 102
Haircut One Hundred **498**, 1338
Hakim, Omar 1083
Hale, Andrew 971
Hale, Corky 101
Hale, Malcolm 1049
Halee, Roy 451, 1008
Haley, Bill 328, **498**, 652, 880, 1158, 1292,
    1294, 1303, 1307, 1308, 1310, 1319
Haley, Bill & His Comets 1297, 1298
Half Japanese 210, 386, 469, 489, **498**,
    499, 599
Halfnelson 1050
Halford, Rob 605, 606, 907, 1177
Halifax Three 691
Hall & Oates 160, 187, 287, **499**, 500,
    835, 1325
Hall, Aaron 496
Hall, Andy 179
Hall, Arsenio 712
Hall, Bob 979
Hall, Bobbye 619
Hall, Damion 496
Hall, Daryl 255, 499, **500**, 1263
Hall, Earl P. 788
Hall, Janine 973
Hall, Jerry 401, 1209
Hall, John [1] 829
Hall, Pete 252
Hall, Rene 1181, 1237, 1279
Hall, Rick 14, 224, 645, 718, 901, 949
Hall, Terry 121, 240, 439, 466, **500**, 501,
    1052, 1159
Hall, Tom T. 524
Hall, Tommy 1135
Hall, Wesley 150
Halliday, Toni 276
Hallman, Mark 620, 706, 707
Halloran, Jack Choir 203
Halo Benders 77, 157, 158
Halo of Flies 165, 259
Halstead, Neil 751, 1025
Halvorsen, John 57
Ham, Bill 1271
Ham, Greg 725
Ham, Pete 54, 55, 232, 501, 1339
Hamburg, Dan 438
Hamer, Harry 214
Hamilton [1] 38
Hamilton, Andy [2] 339
Hamilton, Chico 287, 977
Hamilton, Mark 38
Hamilton, Page 62, 63, 520, 521, 524
Hamlisch, Marvin 475, 1092, 1094

Hamm, Stuart 978
Hammer, Jack 108
Hammer, Jan 84, 122, 975
Hammerstein, Oscar II 1091
Hammett, Kirk 729, 977
Hammill, Peter 19, 1056
Hammond, Albert [1] 451
Hammond, John [1] Jr. 1326
Hammond, John [2] Sr. 114, 395
Hammond, Murry 820
Hammond-Hammond, Jeffrey 588
Hampson, Robert 668, 669
Hampton Grease Band **501**
Hampton, Bruce 501
Hampton, John 612
Hampton, Lionel 508, 570, 831, 1303
Hampton, Michael 441, 442, 843
Hampton, Mike 441
Hancock, Butch 154, 362, 363, 1327
Hancock, Herbie 495, 496, 574, 895, 1329,
    1330, 1334
Handel, George Frideric 461, 462, 1093
Handful of Dust 419
Handsome Boy Modeling School **501**, 892
Handsome Family **501**, 502
Handy, W.C. 884
Haney, J.D. 756
Hani 292
Hankes, Doug 296
Hanks, Tom 38, 416, 1188
Hanley, Paul 391, 392
Hanley, Steve 391, 392, 393, 394
Hanna 643
Hanna [1] 643
Hanna, Jerome 591
Hanna, Kathleen 98, 643
Hannant, Beaumont 1273
Hanneman, Jeff 1020, 1021
Hannett, Martin 269, 376, 503, 687
Hannibal, Chauncey 108
Hannon, Frank 1128
Hannon, Neil 320, 321, 554, 779
Hansen, Barret 247
Hansen, Mary 528, 771, 1075
Hansen, Steve 740
Hanson [1] 51, **502**, 1115
Happenings 1296
Happy Family [1] 753
Happy Mondays 104, 200, 201, 365, **502**,
    503, 541, 561, 887, 1046, 1074, 1099,
    1346, 1347
Harbach, Otto 1092
Harbin, Mike 160
Harburg, E.Y. 1091
Hard Ons 1342
Hardesty, Herbert 328
Hardin, Eddie [1] 285
Hardin, Mel 722
Hardin, Tim 283, 304, 390, **503**, 507, 519, 551,
    582, 785, 787, 995, 1080, 1203, 1263, 1302,
    1328, 1353
Harding, John Wesley 375, **504**, 943, 1248
Harding, Scott 892
Hardy, Francoise **504**, 505, 893, 1074
Hardy, Joe 486, 612
Hardy, Thomas 451
Hargrett, Charlie 107, 108
Hargrove, Roy 56, 278
Harket, Morten 12
Harlem Boys Choir 612
Harley, Steve **505**, 506
Harley, Steve & Cockney Rebel 505
Harmonia [1] 790
Harmony Rockets **506**
Harp 697
Harp, Cornelius 697
Harper [1] 506, 507
Harper, Ben **506**
Harper, Charlie 1171
Harper, Roy **506**, 507, 530, 531
Harper, Willie 1299
Harpers Bizarre 41, 433, **507**, 842
Harpo, Slim 212, 1297, 1352
Harptones 1280, 1297
Harrell, Andre 593
Harrell, Tom 59
Harrington, Jeremy 756

Harrington, Tim 702
Harris [1] 286, 536
Harris, Betty 333
Harris, Bobby [1] 286
Harris, Corey 138
Harris, David 57
Harris, Don [1] Sugarcane 328, 1265
Harris, Don [3] 1265
Harris, Eddie 76
Harris, Elaine 1160
Harris, Emmylou 67, 232, 355, 667, 675, 845,
    846, 893, 955, 956, 1202, 1225, 1230, 1285
Harris, Hi Tide 708
Harris, James III 352
Harris, Jet 1310, 1311
Harris, Jody 197, 470
Harris, Joey 77
Harris, Lee 534, 1116
Harris, Major 297
Harris, Micky 655
Harris, Muscle Shoals 1237
Harris, Norman 536, 732
Harris, Paul 551
Harris, Richard 591, 1211
Harris, Ross 1101
Harris, Steve 563, 564
Harris, Thana 1266
Harris, Thurston 285, 945
Harris, Webster 591
Harris, Wee Willie 1310
Harris, Wynonie 148, **507**, 508, 1291, 1303,
    1304, 1305
Harrison, Donald 314
Harrison, George [1] 42, 54, 78, 79, 80, 88, 210,
    264, 297, 302, 330, 349, 353, 446, **508**, 509,
    591, 592, 701, 758, 801, 853, 1052, 1070,
    1157, 1160, 1211, 1245, 1308, 1327
Harrison, Jerry 121, 404, 455, 662, 663, 941,
    942, 1116, 1117, 1195
Harrison, Keith 286
Harrison, Nigel 112
Harrison, Noel 293
Harrison, Wilbert 401, **509**, 1305, 1282
Harry, Debbie 112, 113, 133, 493, 494,
    954, 1338
Harshe, Sue 983, 984
Hart, Bobby 754
Hart, Freddie 893
Hart, Grant [1] **510**, 548, 549
Hart, Lorenz 1091, 1096
Hart, Mark 271
Hart, Mickey 482, 497
Hart, Tim 1071
Hart, Wilbert 297
Hart, William 297
Hartford, Jamie 827
Hartford, John 430
Hartley, Keef 708
Hartley, Mathieu 225
Hartman, Dan 1115, 1164, 1232
Hartnall, Paul 826
Hartnoll, P. & P. 826
Hartnoll, Paul 825, 826
Hartnoll, Phil 825, 826
Hartridge, Jimmy 1108
Harvest [1] 64
Harvey & The Moonglows 759
Harvey Danger **510**
Harvey, Alex 783
Harvey, Bryan 541
Harvey, Mick 99, 192, 193, 194, 268
Harvey, P.J. 194, 510, 511, 638, 1159
Harvey, Phil 1297
Harvey, PJ 95, 161, **510**, 511, 1050
Harvey, Ted 630
Harvie, Ian 295
Harwell, Steve 1028
Harwood, Justin 211, 679
Hash Jar Tempo 65
Hashian, Sib 132
Hashim 1155
Haskell, Gordon 416, 617
Haskett, Chris 954
Haskins, Clarence 'Fuzzy' 842
Haskins, Kevin 69, 70, 71, 672, 673, 876
Haslam, Annie 932, 1241
Haslam, Geoffrey 712

Hasselhoff, David 953
Hassell, Jon 313, 368, 369, 1289
Hassinger, David 360
Hassinger, J.D. 251
Hassles **511**, 593
Hastings, Jimmy 181, 182, 1039
Hastings, Pye 181, 182, 183, 1223, 1224
Hatch, Tony 222
Hatcher, Roger 1299
Hated 555
Hatfield & the North 703, 1296, 1331
Hatfield, Bobby 943, 1063, 1325
Hatfield, Juliana 108, 109, **511**, 512,
    646, 1345
Hatfield, Juliana Three **511**
Hathaway, Donny 380, 383, 409, **512**,
    1136, 1244
Hatherley, Charlotte 38
Hatori, Miho 216, 217, 475, 501
Haughland, Ian 378
Havens, Richie **512**, 787
Havermanns, Cyril 420
Havoc [1] 748, 805
Havranek, Pete 139
Hawes, Bruce 1096
Hawes, Dave 192
Hawes, Hampton 44
Hawke, Ethan 664
Hawken, John 1090
Hawkes, Chesney 614
Hawketts 790
Hawkins, Coleman 983, 1202
Hawkins, Dale 151, 265, 407, **512**, 513, 1276,
    1292, 1308, 1316
Hawkins, Edwin 57, 723
Hawkins, Edwin Singers 1276
Hawkins, Elizabeth 514
Hawkins, Nick 95
Hawkins, Roger 219, 829, 1154
Hawkins, Ronnie 62, **513**, 737, 945, 1292
Hawkins, Ronnie & The Hawks 945
Hawkins, Screamin' Jay 145, 256, 265, 401,
    513, 636, 1106, 1289, 1305, 1311
Hawkins, Sophie B. **514**, 831
Hawkins, Ted **514**, 515, 1351
Hawkins, Xian 1007
Hawks [1] 61, 62, 341, 513
Hawkwind 216, 305, **515**, 668, 768, 1294
Hawtin, Richie 867, 868
Hay, Barry 470
Hay, Colin 725
Hay, Ivor 973
Haycock, Peter 225
Hayes, Bonnie 868
Hayes, Darren 978
Hayes, David 707
Hayes, Isaac 365, 452, 495, 496, **515**, 516,
    517, 974, 975, 981, 1106, 1208, 1212, 1238,
    1290, 1334
Hayes, Liam 837, 868
Hayes, Peter 142
Haynes, Gibby 163, 164
Haynes, Richard 653
Haynes, Rick 654
Haynes, Warren 17, 18, 380
Hayward, Charles 399
Hayward, Justin 758, 759
Hayward, Lawrence 399, 400
Hayward, Martin 846
Hayward, Rick 659
Haywood, Kitty 431
Haywood, Leon 560, 1276
Haza, Ofra 1017
Hazel, Eddie 440, 441, 442, 842, 843
Hazlewood, Lee 13, 20, 90, 142, 222, 356, **517**,
    518, 680, 761, 1014, 1144, 1145
Head [2] 1074
Head, Murray 1108
Head, Roy **518**, 924, 1273, 1297, 1325
Headless Chickens 1343
Headliner 37
Headon, Topper 580
Heads [1] 1116, 1146
Healey, Jay 662
Healey, Jeff 527
Healy, Francis 246, 1157
Heard, Larry 824, 1299

Heart [1] 425, **518**, 519, 674, 1056
Heart [2] 245
Heart Throbs 837
Heartbeats [1] **519**
Heartbreakers [1] 520, 855, 856, 857, 892, 1124, 1143, 1268, 1278, 1336
Hearts & Flowers **519**, 1327
Heasley, Kurt 656
Heath, Jim 937
Heath, Tommy 1147
Heatherton, Joey 1301
Heaton, Paul 81, 82
Heatwave 242
Heaven Seventeen 3, 373, 374, 422, **519**, 545, 999, 1288
Heavenly [1] 977
Heavens To Betsy 1021, 1285
Heavy D 519, 520
Heavy D & the Boyz **519**, 520, 593, 1287
Heavy Metal Kids 1231
Hebb, Bobby 224, 326, 920
Hecker, Robert 923
Heckstall-Smith, Dick 124, 477, 707
Hedayat, Dashiell 473
Hedford, Eric 280
Hedgecock, Ryan 667
Hedges, Michael [1] 230, 270
Hedges, Mike 19, 680
Hefe, El 804
Heffington, Don 667, 1227
Heggie, Will 231
Heidorn, Michael 1039
Height, Donald 535
Heinemann, Larry 1061
Heinz 720, 1310, 1311
Helium 27, **520**, 815, 1018, 1022, 1300
Helium, Bryan 362, 815
Helix [1] 1302
Hell, Richard **520**, 916, 1124, 1191, 1278, 1336
Hell, Richard & the Voidoids 235
Hellerman, Fred 56
Helloween 1302
Helm, Levon 61, 62, 513, 915, 945, 1230
Helmet 62, 63, 250, 259, **520**, 521, 524, 632, 1340
Help Yourself **521**
Heltah Skeltah 1246
Hemmings, David 168, 1201
Hemmingway, Dave 81, 82, 542
Hempsall, Alan 268, 269
Henderson, Alan 1131
Henderson, Andy 352
Henderson, Bernard 544
Henderson, Bill [Vocals] 211
Henderson, Billy 1055
Henderson, Joe [1] 602
Henderson, Peter 967
Henderson, Willie 285
Hendrix, Jeff 164
Hendrix, Jimi 29, 42, 56, 73, 84, 115, 166, 219, 226, 258, 278, 291, 306, 316, 364, 413, 440, 442, 506, **521**, 522, 523, 529, 531, 565, 602, 605, 617, 618, 624, 627, 633, 634, 644, 661, 663, 737, 745, 772, 773, 780, 784, 835, 848, 885, 918, 944, 964, 976, 1004, 1005, 1016, 1080, 1185, 1186, 1233, 1236, 1243, 1247, 1262, 1283, 1287, 1293, 1302, 1313, 1323, 1326, 1329, 1330, 1333, 1334
Hendrix, Jimi Experience 85, 521, 522, 523, 1133
Hendrix, Margie 248
Hendry, Rob 932
Hendryx, Nona 636, 809, 1117
Henley, Don 271, 346, 347, **523**, 539, 747, 796, 797, 798, 1035, 1046, 1205, 1210, 1269
Henneghan, Greg 678
Henrit, Robert 35
Henry Cow 126, 261, 393, 867, 935
Henry, Clarence 'Frogman' 61, **524**, 1274, 1278, 1306
Henry, Joe **524**, 1328
Henry, Pierre 8
Henrys [1] 816
Hensley, Harold 1032
Hensley, Ken 107, 1177, 1178
Hensley, Roy 190

Henson, Ronnie 678
Heptones 1356
Herald, John 551
Herbert [1] 610
Herbert, Vincent 1
Herd & Luke 546
Herd [1] 427, 428, 546
Herman's Hermits 235, 389, 476, **524**, 525, 532, 533, 1275, 1312, 1317, 1320
Herman, Gus 53
Herman, Maureen 47
Herman, Pee Wee 744
Herman, Tom 851, 852
Herman, Woody 114, 1127
Hermann, John 207
Hernandez, Alfredo 634, 906
Hernandez, Andy 'Coatimundi' 324, 614
Hernandez, Patrick 324, 634, 906
Herndon, John 566
Heron, Mike 558
Herr, Kurt 1234
Herrema, Jennifer 689, 960, 961
Herrera, Fred 1108
Herring, Dennis 258, 541
Herrmann, Bernard 7
Herron, Cindy 366
Hersh, Kristin 207, **524**, 525, 774, 1142, 1143, 1345
Hesitations [2] 296
Hester, Carolyn 395
Hester, Paul [1] 271, 272
Heston, Charlton 63
Hetfield, James 729, 730, 889
Hetson, Greg 217, 218, 923
Heukamp, Andrea 541
Hewett, Howard 127, 997
Hewitt, Steve 127, 865
Hewson, Richard 932
Heylin, Clinton 299
Heyman, Richard X. **525**, 612
Heyward, Dubose 1079
Heyward, Nick 498
Heywood, Eric 376
Hi Lo's 560
Hi Rhythm 380, 486, 487, 850
Hiatt, John 3, 19, 62, 267, 270, 354, 504, **526**, 527, 601, 662, 678, 786, 956, 995, 1328, 1344
Hibbert, Toots 914
Hickey, Ersel 1292
Hickman, Johnny 207, 261
Hicks, Bill [1] 927, 1148
Hicks, Dan 327
Hicks, Mark 1020
Hicks, Russ 1213
Hicks, Tony 533
Hidalgo, David 21, 160, 189, 641, 668, 670
Higgins, Bertie **527**
Higgins, Billy 158
Higgins, Chuck 1276, 1297
High Llamas 8, 235, 433, 436, **527**, 528, 931, 973, 1075, 1103
High Numbers 1221
Higher Intelligence Agency 1273
Highway QC's 247, 1121
Highwaymen [Folk] 56
Hill, Bob 469
Hill, Brendan 119
Hill, Dan **528**
Hill, Darren 1216
Hill, Dave [Slade] 1020
Hill, Dusty 1271
Hill, Jessie **528**, 1151, 1286
Hill, Joel Scott 733
Hill, Lauryn 110, 278, 431, 437, **528**, 529, 544, 582, 977, 983, 1293
Hill, Raymond 1163
Hill, Stuart 1004
Hillage, Steve 44, 201, 473, 790, 824
Hillier, Ben 352
Hillman, Chris 166, 167, 221, 222, 418, 419, 519, 870, 1046, 1327
Hillman, Dwayne 'Bones' 1110
Hillmen 168
Hills, Cliff 197
Hine, Rupert 176, 408, 736, 967
Hinkler, Simon 743, 744

Hinojosa, Tish 1353
Hinsche, Billy 315
Hinshaw, Chris 167
Hinsley, Harvey 540
Hipsway 1129
Hirsch, Beth 13
Hirsch, Larry 189, 267
Hirsh, Chicken 258
His Name Is Alive 529, 530, 555, 834
Hiscock, Michael 402
Hiseman, Jon 477
Hitchcock, Alfred 1116
Hitchcock, Robyn 48, 67, 244, 375, 443, **530**, 531, 1037, 1038, 1343, 1345, 1346, 1347
Hitchcock, Robyn & The Egyptians 530, 531, 954, 1344
Hitchcock, Russell 13
Hite, Bob 179
Hlavsa, Milan 900
Hlubek, Dave 752
Ho, Don 531
Hobbs, Mick 499
Hobbs, Randy Jo 1232
Hodge 882
Hodge, Charlie 882
Hodge, Gaynell 850
Hodges, Charles [2] 883
Hodges, Mabon 'Teenie' 487
Hodges, Stephen 1210
Hodges, Warner 580
Hoehn, Tommy 1278
Hoerner, Dan 1102
Hoffman, Guy 121
Hoffman, Kristian 775
Hoffman, Peter 725, 726
Hoffman, Steve 198, 535
Hoffman, Steven 93, 498
Hoffs, Susanna 63
Hofmann, Pete 43
Hogan, Annie 19, 20
Hogan, Kelly 189, 504
Hogan, Lance 288
Hogan, Noel 263
Hogarth, Steve 697, 698
Hogg, Brian 331, 519, 987, 990, 1067, 1291
Hoh, Eddie 733
Hoku **531**, 760
Hokum, Suzi Jane 517
Hold, Ashley 1201
Holden, Randy 115, 1299
Holden, Ron 1279, 1300
Holder, Gene 286, 536, 963
Holder, Noddy 743, 1020
Holdsworth, Allan 473, 474, 650
Hole 47, 48, 413, 510, **531**, 532, 635, 1192, 1345
Hole, Dave 1342
Holiday, Billie 40, 56, 98, 202, 390, 402, 483, 512, 602, 747, 787, 831, 957, 958, 1066, 1247, 1350
Holiday, Eddie 822
Holiday, Jimmy 304
Hollaender, Friedrich 390
Holland Dozier Holland 195, 427, 536, 565, 699, 828, 841, 974, 1314
Holland, Brian 645, 822, 1125, 1315
Holland, Dexter 816
Holland, Eddie 99, 427, 536, 566, 645, 699, 822, 1163, 1215, 1315
Holland, Jools 404, 1065
Holland, Nicky 1122
Holland, Steve 752
Holliday, Jennifer 425
Hollies 54, 85, 235, 239, 270, 273, 360, 371, 375, 381, 476, **532**, 533, 534, 555, 636, 728, 844, 877, 987, 1112, 1123, 1160, 1291, 1317, 1318, 1339, 1341
Hollis, Ed 534
Hollis, Mark **534**, 1115, 1116
Hollister, Dave 108
Holloway, Brenda 284, 297, **534**, 1028, 1301, 1314, 1315
Holly & the Italians 1278, 1290
Holly, Buddy 30, 80, 96, 110, 118, 130, 159, 198, 205, 227, 237, 266, 267, 298, 304, 311, 314, 363, 375, 439, 442, 513, 532, **534**, 535, 540, 546, 629, 642, 717, 774, 786, 787, 813,

825, 855, 901, 940, 949, 1004, 1028, 1050, 1120, 1135, 1157, 1178, 1181, 1186, 1187, 1227, 1244, 1282, 1292, 1297, 1308, 1309, 1310, 1316, 1317, 1319
Hollywood Flames 285, **535**
Hollywood Persuaders 1269, 1297
Hollywood Tornadoes 1149
Hollywood, Matt 142
Holm, Georg 1005
Holman, Eddie 1301, 1335
Holmberg, Marcus 630
Holmes, David 34, 1132
Holmes, Jake 1285
Holmes, Richard 'Groove' 76
Holmes, Rupert **535**, 1093, 1285
Holmstrom, Peter 280
Holocaust 729
Holroyd, Les 64
Holsapple, Peter 211, 286, 536, 1339, 1343
Holsapple-Stamey **536**
Holst, Gustav 617, 618
Holt, Ashley 1201
Holt, Derek 225
Holt, Ednah 1117
Holt, John 225
Holvay, Jimmy 152
Holy Barbarians 273
Holy Mackerel 1225
Holy Modal Rounders 469, 503, 1354
Holy Rollers 1231
Holzman, Jac 152
Hombres 723, 1289
Homer & Jethro 1282
Homme, Josh 634, 906
Honda, Yuka 216, 217
Hondells 71, 1296
Honey & The Bees **536**
Honey Cone 195, **536**, 645, 822
Honeycombs **536**, 720, 1311
Honeydrippers [1] **536**
Honeyman, Suzie 722
Honeyman-Scott, James 884, 885
Honeys **537**
Hood [2] 26
Hood, David 1154
Hoodoo Gurus **537**, 538, 910, 1287, 1290, 1342
Hook, Peter 269, 604, 605, 793
Hooker, John Lee 17, 30, 118, 193, 284, 432, 450, 454, 565, 660, 764, 977, 1117, 1137, 1140, 1152, 1163, 1220, 1271, 1297, 1352
Hoon, Shannon 110
Hooper, Chris 465, 479, 480
Hooper, Nellee 16, 101, 701, 899, 1044
Hooper, Tom 465, 479, 480
Hooper, Tony 1089
Hooters 660
Hootie & The Blowfish 207, 506, **538**, 704, 1135
Hooton, Peter 395
Hoover, Susan 176
Hooverphonic **538**, 539
Hope, Dave 610
Hopkin, Mary 1, **539**, 1293
Hopkins, Claude 465, 829
Hopkins, Doug 465
Hopkins, Gary [1] Pickford 1201
Hopkins, Graham 1132
Hopkins, Lightnin' 316, 1273, 1280, 1286
Hopkins, Mike 556
Hopkins, Nicky 141, 336, 428, 583, 907, 1106
Hopkins, Nicky [1] 84, 737, 1007, 1081, 1311
Hopkins, Telma 829
Hoppen, Lance 829
Hoppen, Larry 829
Hopper, Brian 1224
Hopper, Dennis 1074
Hopper, Hugh 66, 1038, 1039, 1223, 1224, 1247
Hoppus, Mark 111
Hord, Eric 551
Horn, Trevor 20, 38, 157, 429, 985, 986, 1256
Horne, Alan 823
Hornsby, Bobby [Producer] 539
Hornsby, Bruce 523, **539**, 540, 798, 915, 968, 1065
Hornsby, Bruce & The Range 539
Horny Horns 237, 291, 292, 842, 843

Horowitz, Jimmy 932
Horton, Big Walter 163
Horton, Johnny 1273, 1292, 1301
Horvath, Russ 977
Hosford, Larry 346
Hoskins, Davey 203
Hosono, Haruomi 865
Hot Band [1] 355
Hot Chocolate **540**, 1086, 1280
Hot Chocolate [UK] 540, 1087
Hot Monkey 489
Hot Snakes 948
Hot Tuna **540**, 541, 583
Hothouse Flowers 21, 405, 559, 1002, 1240
Hott, Johnny 541
Houghton, Michael 251
Houndog 670
Hour Glass 1333
Housden, Janet 923
House of Freaks **541**, 673, 1248
House of Love **541**, 1278
House of Love [1] **541**, 542, 761
House of Pain 380, **542**, 656
House, Simon 515
House, Son 1218, 1350
Housemartins 81, 397, **542**, 543, 1346, 1347
Houser, Brad 142, 143
Houser, Michael 207
Houserockers 296, 490, 630
Houston, Cisco 496, 1353
Houston, Cissy 224, 409, 543, 1106, 1160, 1207, 1351
Houston, Joe 1297, 1304, 1308
Houston, Penelope 43, **543**
Houston, Stephen 436
Houston, Thelma 243
Houston, Whitney 49, 145, 183, 184, 409, **543**, 544, 627, 1106
Howard, Camille 1294, 1304
Howard, Harlan 203, 1010
Howard, James Newton 1094
Howard, Ken 536
Howard, Oliver 1054
Howard, Rowland S. 99, 193, 268, 1341
Howe, Bones 41, 403, 1199
Howe, Brian 53
Howe, Liam 1035
Howe, Steve 39, 40, 429, 926, 1147, 1201, 1235, 1255, 1256, 1257, 1280, 1284, 1291, 1331
Howell, Jeff 834
Howlett, Liam 894, 895
Howlett, Mike 36, 244, 417, 473
Howlin' Wolf 84, 179, 180, 181, 220, 311, 324, 481, 526, 610, 630, 659, 745, 883, 953, 1043, 1067, 1131, 1163, 1185, 1200, 1265, 1276, 1295, 1308, 1326, 1352
Hozier, Vince 1102
HP Lovecraft 141, **544**, 1283, 1288
HR [1] 51, 52
Huang Chung 1205
Hubbard, Freddie 495, 594, 1334
Hubbard, Leonard 957
Hubble Bubble 867
Hubley, Georgia 1018, 1257, 1258
Hucknall, Mick 1013
Hudson Brothers **544**
Hudson, Barbara 1172
Hudson, Earl 51, 52
Hudson, Garth 61, 62, 390, 513, 559
Hudson, Jon 389
Hudson, Mark 11
Hudson, Mike [1] 836
Hudson, Raymond 126
Hudson, Richard 1089, 1090
Huerta, Ed 642
Hues Corporation **544**
Hues, Jack 1205
Huff, Leon 67, 89, 336, 380, 536, 568, 724, 732, 819, 1290, 1301
Huffman, Aaron 510
Hugg, Mike 694
Huggy Bear 98, 99, 100, 1294
Hughart, Jim 1199
Hughes, Andy 824
Hughes, Brian 658
Hughes, Chris 371

Hughes, Glenn [1] 106, 293
Hughes, Howard 40, 776
Hughes, John [1] 896, 1291
Hughes, Michael 658
Hughes, Richard 1232
Hughes, Ted 1151, 1152
Hugo Largo **545**
Hugo, Victor 310
Huidor, Sergio 446
Hula [1] 170
Hull, Alan 657
Hultgren, Carl 1231
Human Beans 673
Human Beinz 565
Human League 128, 131, 300, 373, 519, **545**, 739, 1144
Human Rich Vox Y 130
Human Switchboard **545**, 546, 981
Humble Pie 66, 428, 432, **546**, 812, 1027, 1214
Humblebums 912
Hummell, Andy 97
Humperdinck, Engelbert [1] 535
Humphrey, Ross 57
Humphreys, Paul 826, 827
Humphreys, Steve 19
Humphries, John 57
Humphries, Simon 485
Humphries, Tony 68, 1099
Hungate, David 1150
Hunt, Darryl 871
Hunt, Geraldine 1301
Hunt, Miles 1238
Hunt, Tommy 1293, 1300
Hunter, Charlie [1] 278
Hunter, Faye 649
Hunter, Ian 190, 335, 376, 456, 484, 490, **546**, 547, 769, 770, 886, 1231
Hunter, Ivory Joe 130, 147, **547**, 548, 566, 678, 699, 880, 1305
Hunter, James 764
Hunter, Kevin 1234, 1235
Hunter, Matt 1008
Hunter, Robert 344, 450, 480, 481
Hunter, Russell 305
Hunter, Steve 927
Hunter, Tab 1275
Hunter, Ty 730, 828
Hunters & Collectors **548**, 1342
Huntley, George 245, 246
Hurley, George 406, 740, 741, 742, 923
Hurley, Michael 175, 191
Hurst, Mike 37, 1004
Hurt, Mississippi John 114, 450, 1350
Hurtt, Phil 1194
Husband, Gary 650
Husick, Anne 62
Husker Du 103, 164, 259, 510, 542, **548**, 549, 559, 580, 646, 671, 719, 740, 770, 771, 934, 1040, 1043, 1085, 1099, 1104, 1131, 1132, 1174, 1192, 1280, 1338, 1340, 1341, 1343, 1344, 1345, 1346
Hussey, Wayne 743, 744, 1017
Huston, Paul 892
Hutch, Willie 206, **549**, 1290
Hutchence, Michael 561, 1341, 1342
Hutchings, Ashley 386, 388, 1071, 1138
Hutchins, Jalil 1222, 1223
Hutchinson, Jeanette 365
Hutchinson, John [1] 135
Hutchinson, Sheila 365
Hutchinson, Wanda 365
Hutson, LeRoy 558
Hutter, Ralf 632
Hutton, Danny 842, 1141
Hyatt, Walter 675
Hyde, Bob 990
Hyde, John 1175
Hyde, Karl 1174, 1175
Hyland, Brian **549**, 550, 1297, 1310
Hymas, Tony 84
Hynd, Richard 1129
Hynde, Chrissie 91, 94, 511, 562, 884, 885, 1031, 1143, 1171

I

Ian & Sylvia **551**, 552, 654, 1318, 1327, 1353
Ian, Janis 233, **552**, 601, 625, 1061, 1187, 1202

Ian, Scott 31
Ice Cube 226, 350, 374, 463, **552**, 553, 805, 809, 962, 981, 1348
Ice T 374, 380, 462, 463, **553**, 554, 615, 663, 664, 709, 808, 915, 962, 1277, 1284, 1300, 1348, 1349
Iceberg Slim [1] 553
Icicle Works **554**, 654
Ida [1] **555**
Ides of March 555
Idle Race 555, 556
Idle, Eric 968
Idol, Billy 455, 456, **556**, 577, 747
Ierace, Dominic 562
Ifield, Frank 127, 1311
Iggy & the Stooges 1086
Iggy [1] 1086
Iglauer, Bruce 151
Iglesias, Enrique 544
Iha, James 567, 1029, 1218
Ikettes 37, 536, 1266
Ill Wind 1275
Illusions [1] 1277
Imbruglia, Natalie **556**
Immergluck, David 527
Immerwahr, Stephen 232
Impacts [1] 395, **557**, 1301
Impalas [1] 1307
Imperial Teen **557**
Imperials [1] 658, 882
Impressions 162, 198, 408, 549, 550, **557**, 558, 565, 573, 709, 710, 722, 1299, 1307, 1324
In Crowd [2] 1284
In the Nursery 234, 971
Incredible Casuals 806
Incredible String Band 394, 530, 531, **558**, 609, 851, 1354, 1355
Indigo Girls **558**, 559, 1344
Indigos 559
Individual Fruit Pie 637
Individuals [1] 1343
Indrizzo, Victor 702
Infamous Mobb 748
Infectious Grooves 1100
Infinite Arkatechz 912
Information Society 470, 899, 1298
Ingber, Elliot 459
Ingle, Doug 563
Inglot, Bill 918, 1158
Ingmann, Jorgen 16, 1292
Ingram, James **559**, 560, 831, 955
Ingram, John 218
Ingram, Luther 543, **560**
Ink Spots 227, 298, 560, 759
Ink Spots [1] **560**, 828, 1207, 1303, 1306
Inner City **560**, 1286
Innes, Neil 126, 127, 446, 968, 969
Innocence [1] 1296
Innocent Criminals 506
Insects 1298
Inspectah Deck 458, 970, 1246
Inspiral Carpets 355, **561**, 1346
Interior, Lux 262, 263
International Submarine Band 81, 166, 168, 418, **561**, 845, 846, 1327
Intruders [1] 198, 732, 1335
Invaders [2] 240
Invisibl Skratch Piklz 76, 608, 631
INXS 537, **561**, 562, 1135, 1287, 1290, 1341, 1342
Iommi, Tony 105, 106, 832, 913
Iovine, Jimmy 97, 667, 797, 798, 840, 856, 1013, 1031
Iris, Donnie **562**, 563
Iris, Donnie & The Cruisers 562
Iron Butterfly **563**, 1323
Iron City Houserockers 490
Iron Maiden 105, 294, 310, 486, **563**, 564, 605, 606, 729, 768, 906, 907, 1133
Irons, Eddie 142
Irons, Jack 849, 921
Irving, Matt 1065
Irwin, Big Dee 532
Irwin, Bob 432
Irwin, Catherine Ann 432
Isaak, Chris **564**, 565, 727
ISAN 1300

Islam, Yusuf 1076, 1078
Isles, Bill 818
Isley Brothers 1, 123, 267, 291, 348, 543, **565**, 566, 710, 804, 976, 1217, 1227, 1244, 1270, 1281, 1282, 1284, 1285, 1293, 1312, 1315, 1324, 1325, 1334
Isley Jasper Isley 557
Isley, Ernie 565
Isley, Marvin 565
Isley, OKelly 565
Isley, Ronald 549, 565
Isley, Rudolph 565
Isotope Two Seventeen **566**, 1171
It's a Beautiful Day 836
Iveys [1] 54, **566**
Ivo [1] 751, 837
Ivy 426, **566**, 567
Iwata, Robynn 273
Iyall, Deborah 954, 955

J

J Live 501
Ja Rule 731
Jabs, Matthias 982
Jack the Lad 657
Jackie & the Starlites **568**
Jackman, David 829
Jacks 171
Jacks, Susan 876
Jacks, Terry 875, 876
Jackson Five 89, 502, **568**, 569, 570, 572, 680, 792, 1017, 1285, 1306, 1315, 1324, 1331
Jackson, Al 129
Jackson, Al Jr. 90
Jackson, Andy 403
Jackson, Bob [1] 501
Jackson, Bull Moose 1291
Jackson, Charles 569
Jackson, Chris [2] 607
Jackson, Chuck [1] 50, 148, **569**, 1019, 1207, 1293, 1300, 1315, 1324
Jackson, Eddie 907
Jackson, Freddie **569**, 570, 760
Jackson, George 1283
Jackson, Henry 1100
Jackson, J.J. 418, **570**
Jackson, Jackie 568, 569
Jackson, Janet 108, 140, 145, 545, **570**, 939, 1144
Jackson, Jermaine 544, 568, 569, 570, 947
Jackson, Jerome 689
Jackson, Joe 32, 422, 568, **571**, 572, 602, 994, 1278
Jackson, Lee 797
Jackson, Mahalia 884, 1351
Jackson, Marlon 568, 569
Jackson, Martin 687, 1109
Jackson, Michael [1] 87, 187, 197, 271, 274, 282, 496, 499, 543, 568, 569, 570, **572**, 573, 613, 680, 713, 714, 804, 940, 1150, 1183, 1239, 1267, 1293, 1306, 1334, 1345
Jackson, Millie 645
Jackson, Milt 203, 287, 694
Jackson, Pervis 1055
Jackson, Python Lee 742, 1081
Jackson, Randy [1] 568
Jackson, Randy [Jacksons] 568
Jackson, Ray 1071
Jackson, Roddy 1291
Jackson, Roger 530
Jackson, Ronald [1] Shannon 197, 1329, 1330
Jackson, Steve 90
Jackson, Stevie 90, 459
Jackson, Thomas 1223
Jackson, Tito 568, 569
Jackson, Tony [2] 987
Jackson, Walter 558, **573**
Jackson, Wanda **573**, 1292, 1301, 1308
Jackson, Wayne 696, 924
Jacksons 3, 569, 572
Jacobites 1108
Jacobs, Hank 1276
Jacobs, Paul [1] 718
Jacobsen, Erik 200
Jacquet, Illinois 507, 1202, 1303, 1304
Jacquet, Russell 760

Jade Warrior 607
Jades [1] 1292
Jagger, Mick 11, 37, 142, 153, 201, 205, 324, 327, 336, 389, 390, 401, 410, 561, 569, **573**, 574, 663, 749, 793, 840, 863, 885, 924, 949, 950, 951, 952, 1027, 1081, 1086, 1131, 1236, 1240, 1285, 1315, 1316, 1320, 1326, 1355, 1356
Jaggerz 562
Jags **574**, 1339, 1278
Jaimoe 18
Jake [1] 118
Jalal 640
Jale 374
Jam [1] 97, 120, 121, 156, 222, 455, 484, 485, **574**, 575, 639, 685, 729, 811, 988, 989, 1066, 1095, 1096, 1104, 1185, 1214, 1278, 1287, 1298, 1322, 1337, 1338, 1339, 1346, 1347
Jam Band 9
Jam Master Jay 822, 962
Jam, Jimmy 58, 88, 110, 424, 545, 570, 571, 1081, 1144, 1184
Jamerson, James 376
Jamerson, James Jr. 1314
James [1] 33, **575**, 576
James Gang [1] 122, 123, **576**, 577, 1204, 1205
James Gang [2] 576
James, Alan 607
James, Alex 120
James, Bob [1] 666, 757
James, Bob [2] 758
James, Brian 9, 279, 456
James, Eddie 507
James, Elmore 92, 93, 412, 413, 414, 833, 1140, 1141, 1162, 1163, 1350, 1352
James, Ethan 741
James, Etta 93, 149, 189, 658, 1080, 1164, 1207, 1276, 1287, 1301
James, Fred 158
James, Mark 883
James, Richard [1] D. 33, 774, 1064, 1273
James, Richey 476, 692, 693
James, Rick 145, 453, **577**, 712, 820, 1284, 1334
James, Simon 476
James, Skip 193, 1350
James, Tommy [Rock] 227, 577, 1218, 1276, 1293
James, Tommy [Rock] & the Shondells 226, 541, **577**, 590, 961, 1331
James, Tony 455, 456
Jamie Wednesday 874
Jamiroquai 495, **577**, 578
Jan & Arnie 578, 1207
Jan & Dean 6, 72, 354, 537, **578**, 663, 1178, 1277, 1282, 1296, 1307, 1308, 1314
Jandek 507
Jane's Addiction 63, **578**, 579, 632, 663, 802, 895, 922, 1044, 1148, 1250, 1287, 1345, 1346
Janes, Roland 944
Janicek, Josef 900
Jankel, Chas 340
Janney, Eli 139
Janovitz, Bill 155, 156, 175
Jansch, Bert 330, 477, 506, 507, 851, 1354
Jansen, John 125, 1124
Jansen, Steve 1111
Janssen, Bill 88
Japan 243, **579**, 776, 1111, 1112, 1288, 1290
Japancakes **579**, 580, 1285
Jardine, Alan 71, 73, 74, 1228
Jarmels 780
Jarmusch, Jim 1095, 1137, 1262
Jarre, Jean Michel 12, 373
Jarrett, John Tribe 235
Jars of Clay 88
Jarvis, Felton 789, 882
Jason & the Scorchers **580**
Jasper, Chris 565
Jawbox 42, 160, **580**, 581
Jawbreaker 42
Jay & the Americans **581**, 669, 780, 1207, 1275
Jay & the Techniques 1276

Jay Z 323, **581**, 582, 805
Jaye, Jerry 1283
Jayhawks [1] 254, 524, **582**, 717, 1227, 1327, 1344
Jaynetts 1275, 1282, 1312
Jazz [1] 1016
Jazz Is Dead 585
Jazzie B. 1044
Jazzy Jeff 322
JB [2] 1164
JB's 146, 147, 237, 582, 608, 843, 895, 1284, 1334
JBs 536, **582**
JC Two Thousand 948
Jean 1136
Jean, Donna 482
Jean, Wyclef 304, 437, 529, 544, **582**, 1013, 1293
Jean-Paul Sartre Experience 1343
Jeckell, Frank 802
Jefferies, Peter 191
Jefferson Airplane 41, 132, 168, 200, 330, 388, 409, 463, 470, 484, 491, 540, 544, 551, 577, **582**, 583, 584, 585, 603, 646, 711, 749, 752, 785, 786, 867, 876, 907, 908, 975, 979, 1049, 1053, 1108, 1156, 1172, 1302, 1318, 1323
Jefferson Starship 416, 582, 583, **584**, 585
Jefferson, Blind Lemon 1350
Jefferson, Joe 1096
Jefferson, Marshall 170
Jeffreys, Garland 173
Jelly Beans [1] 1291
Jelly Roll 1036
Jellyfish 390, 391, **585**, 1071, 1339
Jenifer, Darryl 51, 52
Jenkins, Barry 29
Jenkins, Gordon 800
Jenkins, Leroy 836
Jenkins, Stephan 1135
Jenkinson, Tom 1064
Jenky 1153
Jenner, Peter 507
Jennings, Waylon 699, 835, 882, 917, 1106, 1261
Jennings, Will 1233
Jensen, Harry 191
Jerden, Dave 578, 1037
Jerkins, Rodney 140, 305, 781, 1054
Jerks 217, 218
Jeru the Damaja 585, 898, 1280
Jesperson, Peter 665
Jesse [2] 335
Jessie, Young 1297
Jesters [1] 1314
Jesus & Mary Chain 102, 142, 224, 262, 263, 375, 541, 542, **585**, 586, 673, 778, 779, 837, 864, 887, 990, 999, 1003, 1124, 1278, 1347
Jesus Jones 365, **586**
Jesus Lizard 241, 250, **586**, 587, 607, 1345
Jet Set [1] 168
Jeter, Claude 1011
Jethro Tull 338, 386, 394, 420, 491, 564, **587**, 588, 589, 611, 657, 852, 952, 1072, 1077, 1155, 1296, 1331
JetSet [1] 269, **589**
Jett, Joan 98, 273, 296, 461, 577, **590**, 635, 963
Jett, Joan & The Blackhearts 133, 590
Jewel [1] 531, **590**
Jewels [1] 1079
Jez [1] 333, 1108
Jezzard, Ralph 200
JFA 1340
Jillette, Penn 935
Jilted John **591**
Jim & Jean 386
Jim & Jesse 866
Jimenez, Flaco 246
Jimmy Eat World **591**
Jimmy, Bobby & the Critters 1300
Jinks, Nial 985
Jirous, Ivan 867
Jive Five 267, **591**, 1274, 1280, 1297
Jivin' Gene 198
JJ Seventy Two 38
JK & Co. **591**, 592
Jo Jo Gunne 405, 1056
Joan of Arc 592

Jobe, Rivers 979
Jobim, Antonio Carlos 216, 382, 755, 999, 1060, 1075, 1227
JoBoxers 1338
Jobriath 592
Jobson, Eddie 474, 588, 618, 1266
Jobson, Richard 1019
Jodeci 49, 442, **592**, 593, 609, 899
Jodimars 80, 1319
Joe, Billie 485
Joel, Billy 42, 128, 422, 511, **593**, 594, 595, 666, 831, 1093, 1167
Joffe, Ritch 996
Johansson, Johann G. 20
Johanson, David 20, **595**, 794
Johansson, Glenn 352
John 596
John & Mary 816, 1126, 1127
John Disco 99, 100
John's Children 595
John, Elton 31, 45, 230, 284, 291, 298, 422, 482, 495, 544, 593, **596**, 597, 598, 659, 647, 732, 940, 989, 1061, 1070, 1079, 1080, 1104, 1151, 1166, 1226, 1251
John, Mable 1294
John's Children 1282, 1284, 1322
Johnnie & Joe 1282
Johnny & the Hurricanes 1308
Johnny & the Self Abusers 1012
Johns, Andy 432, 1124, 1127
Johns, Ethan 1218
Johns, Glyn 36, 57, 91, 219, 223, 270, 346, 387, 486, 546, 734, 835, 956, 980, 1152, 1284
Johns, John 338
Johnson, Al 1178
Johnson, Alan 697
Johnson, Alphonso [1] 976
Johnson, Arthur [1] 241
Johnson, Bert 419
Johnson, Billy [1] 711, 759
Johnson, Blind Willie 193, 230, 1350
Johnson, Bob [1] 1071, 1072
Johnson, Brian 4
Johnson, Brian [1] 3, 4, 274, 1341
Johnson, Calvin 77, 83, 157, 689, 750, 1039
Johnson, Claude [1] 328
Johnson, Claude [2] 328, 793, 794
Johnson, Corinthian 'Kripp' 296
Johnson, Denise 361
Johnson, Don [1] 349, 1094
Johnson, Doug [1] 674
Johnson, Doug [2] 675
Johnson, Earl 981
Johnson, Eric [1] **598**, 599
Johnson, Freddy 697
Johnson, Gene 1004
Johnson, General 195, 1004, 1151
Johnson, George [2] 144
Johnson, Holly 429
Johnson, Hubert 246
Johnson, Jesse 1144
Johnson, Johnnie 93
Johnson, Kevin [1] 1020
Johnson, Linton Kwesi 571
Johnson, Lonnie 114, 329, 1350
Johnson, Louis 144, 565, 831
Johnson, Marcus 'Benjy' [Bass] 109
Johnson, Marv 1314
Johnson, Matt [The The] 19, 1130, 1131
Johnson, Michael [Engineer] 640
Johnson, Mike [1] 315, 639, 640, 906
Johnson, Nate 396
Johnson, Norman 591
Johnson, Pat 543
Johnson, Paul [1] 196
Johnson, Pete 1162, 1163
Johnson, Ralph [1] 558
Johnson, Rob 1072
Johnson, Robert [01] 258, 259, 264, 317, 494, 540, 587, 645, 950, 1072, 1218, 1232, 1350, 1352
Johnson, Robert [02] 220
Johnson, Robert [03] 237
Johnson, Scott 465
Johnson, Syl [1] 1283
Johnson, Terry [1] 696
Johnson, Tom [1] 331

Johnson, Wilko 324, 338, 340, 1335
Johnston, Bob 233, 657, 936
Johnston, Bruce 71, 73, 74, 122, 451
Johnston, Daniel [1] 290, 386, **599**, 1257
Johnston, Freedy **600**, 669, 1000
Johnston, Max 432, 1223
Johnston, Tom [2] 331
Johnstone, Davey 597, 598
Johnstone, Phil 866
Jojo [1] 49, 593
Jolson, Al 202, 308, 994, 998
Jones [1] 95, 129, 425, 560, 949
Jones, Allen 23
Jones, Billy [1] 834, 1109
Jones, Bob [Drummer] 114
Jones, Booker T. 90, 129, 229, 418, 924, 976
Jones, Brenda 1288
Jones, Brian [1] 724, 897, 949, 950, 952, 953, 1316
Jones, Brian [7] 897
Jones, Busta Cherry 1117
Jones, Commonwealth 1273
Jones, Corky 1294
Jones, Daniel [1] 978
Jones, David [01] 1275
Jones, Davy 754, 755, 1322
Jones, Donell 495
Jones, Eddie 1163
Jones, George [1] 8, 96, 117, 460, 820, 883, 1119, 1173, 1291, 1327, 1351
Jones, George [5] Jr. 354
Jones, Gloria [1] 450, **600**, 1038, 1274
Jones, Graham 498
Jones, Howard **600**, 601
Jones, Hugh 455, 554, 749, 837, 838
Jones, Jack [1] 1203
Jones, Jim 853, 897
Jones, Jimmy [1] 1119
Jones, Jimmy [2] 127
Jones, John Paul 504, 518, 519, 679, 743, 836
Jones, John Paul [1] 164, 215, 330, 369, 644, 743
Jones, John Paul [2] 331
Jones, Kelly 1076
Jones, Kendall [1] 407
Jones, Kenney [1] 1222
Jones, Kenny [1] 93, 138, 1027
Jones, Linda 1291
Jones, Malcolm 66
Jones, Marti 266, 322, **601**
Jones, Matt 773
Jones, Maxine 366
Jones, Michael [Nuage] 150
Jones, Mick [Clash] 95, 222, 223, 477
Jones, Mick [Foreigner] 45, 95, 425, 426, 547, 595, 1095
Jones, Mordicai 1243
Jones, Neil 23
Jones, Nic 504
Jones, Paul [01] 137, 191, 694, 695, 1300, 1315, 1316
Jones, Pearce 420
Jones, Percy 368
Jones, Phalon 63
Jones, Quincy 144, 202, 203, 475, 560, 572, 1070, 1219
Jones, Richard [3] 225, 1076
Jones, Rickie Lee 459, **601**, 602, 1199, 1328
Jones, Robin 94
Jones, Ronald 284, 411
Jones, Ronald [Guitar] [1] 284
Jones, Ronnie 1286
Jones, Shirley [1] 190, 846
Jones, Spike 127
Jones, Stephen 48, 49
Jones, Stephen [1] 48
Jones, Steve [1] 590, 875, 994, 1014, 1143, 1193
Jones, Steven 48
Jones, Steven A. 48
Jones, Tom [1] 30, 38, 41, 423, **602**, 603, 883, 893, 1286, 1355
Jones, Vince 480
Jones, Vincent 465, 479
Jones, Will [1] 'Dub' 171, 227
Jonze, Spike 101, 1214

Jonzun Crew 1298
Joplin, Janis 57, 96, 123, 233, 297, 377, 482, **603**, 739, 745, 772, 773, 778, 979, 1037, 1118, 1129, 1287, 1302, 1350
Joplin, Janis & the Full Tilt Boogie Band 603
Joplin, Scott 593
Jordan 410
Jordan, Cyril 410
Jordan, Lonnie 1206
Jordan, Louis 1294
Jordan, Louis [1] 68, 147, 571, 700, 994, 1291, 1303, 1304, 1305
Jordan, Steve [2] 1117
Jordan, Steve [3] 93
Jordanaires 109, 159, 376, 429, 787, 880, 883, 1213
Josef K 823
Joseph, Quinton 732
Josie & the Pussycats 1273
Josie & the Pussycats [1] 60
Jourard, Jeff 766
Jourgensen, Alain 295, 739, 938, 1019, 1345
Jourgensen, Patty 739
Journey 10, 50, 53, 184, 416, 425, **603**, 604, 799, 909, 933, 948, 965, 1150, 1177, 1198, 1331
Jowe Head 1108
Joy Division 40, 243, 269, 376, 392, 510, 545, 580, **604**, 605, 676, 687, 688, 749, 790, 793, 902, 984, 1014, 1015, 1132, 1289, 1337, 1338, 1346
Joyce, Chris 1013
Joyce, James 583
Joyce, Jay 405
Joyce, Mike 766
Juarez, Martin 827
Judas Priest 23, 170, 294, 329, 563, **605**, 606, 729, 768, 799, 831, 907, 920, 1302
Judd, Phil 405, **606**, 981, 1057, 1110
Judds 853, 883
Judge, Buddy 483, 484
Judy, Eric 750
Jugg, Roman 279
Juicy Lucy 1047, 1326
Jules & the Polar Bears **606**, 607, 706, 999, 1000
Julian [Rock] 649
Julian, Ivan 520
July [1] **607**
Jun, Rose Marie 1091
June of Forty Four **607**
Jungle Brothers 60, **607**, 1076, 1274, 1348
Junior, Marvin 297, 298
Junior MAFIA 655, 899
Junkyard Love 485, 1248
Jupp, Mickey 354, **608**, 677, 678, 1295
Jurassic Five **608**
Jurgensen, Jens 131
Just Four Men 1230
Justified Ancients of Mu Mu 626
Justis, Bill 1163, 1297
Justman, Seth 454, 455
Juston, Sidney 997

K
K Ci 49
K Ci & Jo Jo 593, **609**
K-Doe, Ernie **609**, 1053, 1151, 1278, 1299, 1306
Ka-Spel, Edward 234
Kaballero, Karlos 309
Kabes, Jira 900
Kahn, John 114, 450
Kahne, David 63, 954
Kaiser, Henry 658, 829, 1331
Kaja 609
Kajagoogoo **609**
Kakoulli, Harry 366
Kalb, Danny 119, 238, 813
Kaleidoscope [UK] **609**
Kaleidoscope [US] 459, 519, 609, **610**, 657
Kalin Twins **610**
Kalin, Harold 610
Kalodner, John 10
Kalwa, Eddie 913
Kamanski, Paul 77
Kamen, Michael 162, 219, 559, 906

Kanal, Tony 803
Kandanes, Andy 222
Kane, Chris 53
Kane, J. Saul 971
Kane, Kevin 465, 479, 480
Kangol Kid 1179, 1222
Kannberg, Scott 690, 847, 1007
Kansas [1] 322, 324, 515, **610**, 611, 1331
Kantner, Paul 583, 584, 585
Kaphan, Bruce 357
Kaplan, Ira 963, 1257, 1258
Karie, Kahimi 753
Karlsson, Lena 630, 631
Karn, Mick 579, 776
Karoli, Michael 165, 178
Karrer, Chris 25, 26
Karydes, Terry 981, 982
Kasenetz, Jerry 646, 777, 802, 817, 1331
Kasenetz-Katz 264, 1273, 1276
Kashif 150, 151, 620
Kasper, Adam 423
Kassan, Brian 1240
Katche, Manu 747, 1083
Kath, Terry 209
Kato, Nash 1176
Katrina & the Waves **611**
Katz, Bruce 802
Katz, Gary 385, 1072
Katz, Jeff 646, 777, 802, 817, 1331
Katz, Matthew 749
Katz, Steve 24, 113, 119
Kaufman, Matthew King 615
Kaukonen, Jorma 410, 540, 541, 583, 584, 603, 646
Kavanagh, Chris 95
Kavanagh, Lydia 470
Kay, Connie 203, 762, 1329
Kay, Jason 577, 578
Kay, Jay [1] 578
Kay, John 1073, 1074
Kay, Matthew 985
Kaye, Carol 1181
Kaye, Danny 592
Kaye, John 592
Kaye, Lenny 228, 257, 525, 1031, 1043, 1187, 1288, 1321, 1336, 1343
Kaye, Thomas Jefferson 221
Kaye, Tony 55, 1255, 1256
Kaylan, Howard 417, 1113, 1165, 1265
Kaz, Eric 24, 914
KC & the Sunshine Band 87, **611**, 612, 817, 1219
Ke'No 702
Keagy, Kelly 799
Kean, Paul 1153
Keane, Bob 1181
Keane, John 207, 210
Keane, Tommy 1343
Keating, Matt 669
Keays, Jim 702
Keegan, David 846, 1003
Keegan, Tim 531
Keelor, Greg 117, 995
Keely, Conrad 27
Keen, John 'Speedy' 607, 769
Keen, Robert Earl Jr. 363, 675
Keenan, Brian 196
Keenan, Daniel 460
Keenan, Maynard James 295
Keene, Barry 1056
Keene, Tommy 322, **612**, 1143, 1290
Keifer, Tom 217
Keister, Shane 366
Keith [1] 1276, 1296
Keith, Ben 1260
Kelis 495, **612**, 613
Kelleher, Dan 822
Keller, James 1147
Kellett, Tim 1013
Kelley, Kevin 167
Kelley, Mike 305
Kelley, Mike [1] 305
Kellichan, Tom 1019
Kellogg, Ralph Burns 115
Kelly Brothers 1299
Kelly, Carey 613
Kelly, Eugene 846, 1185

Kelly, Jo Ann 210
Kelly, John [1] 81
Kelly, Jon [1] 82
Kelly, Kevin [1] 153
Kelly, R. 1, 110, 140, 278, 318, 573, **613**, 664, 805, 1055, 1184
Kelly, Roger 1071
Kelly, Todd 579
Kelly, Tom 63
Kelly, Wells 829
Keltner, Jim 151, 175, 196, 246, 247, 256, 526, 662, 981, 1139, 1263
Kember, Pete 1048
Kemp, Gary 1048
Kemp, Martin 1048
Kemp, Rick 1071, 1072
Kemper, David 159
Kempner, Scott 296, 310, 311
Kendall, Alan 86
Kendrick, Nat 1282
Kendricks, Eddie 1125, 1126
Keneally, Mike 1181
Keneipp, Kelly 208, 665
Keneipp, Nikki 207, 208
Kennedy, Bill 281
Kennedy, Brian 764
Kennedy, Ray [1] 995
Kenner, Chris 67, 387, **613**, 636, 1151, 1274, 1278, 1284, 1306
Kennibrew, Dee Dee 272, 273
Kennington, Fido 827
Kenny [1] **613**
Kenny & The Kasuals 1297
Kenny, Bill 560, 613
Kenny, Claire 238
Kent, Clark 915
Kenton, Stan 44
Keringer, Leonard 642
Kermit 104
Kern, Jerome 84, 1091, 1092, 1094
Kerner, Kenny 624, 1087
Kerouac, Jack 76, 1199
Kerr, Anita 1191
Kerr, Greg 1191
Kerr, Jim 175, 1012, 1013
Kerr, Stuart 1129
Kershaw, Andy 514
Kershaw, Doug 787
Kershaw, Nik **613**, 614
Kershenbaum, David 267, 840, 1077
Kerslake, Lee 1177, 1178
Kerwin, Jim 450
Kesh, Abe 'Voco' 115
Kessel, Barney 1329
Kessel, Kenny 671, 672
Kessler, Larry 469
Kevie Kev 1274
Key, Cevin 1019
Key, Ted 542
Keys, Bobby 93
Keyser, Alex 352
Khachaturian, Aram Il'yich 673
Khadaroo, Eshan 133
Khan, Ali Akbar 477
Khan, Chaka 109, 110, **614**
Khan, Nusrat Fateh Ali 442
Khoroshev, Igor 1257
Kick Horns 128, 373
Kicking Giant 783
Kickstands 1178
Kid Capri 581
Kid Creole & the Coconuts 324, **614**
Kid Frost 1300
Kid Koala 475
Kid Loco 528
Kid N Play **614**, 615
Kid Rock 277, **615**, 1067, 1173, 1174
Kid Six O Six 234
Kid Spatula 774
Kidd, Johnny **615**, 1110, 1310, 1311
Kidney, Robert 470, 471
Kiedis, Anthony 921, 922
Kiely, Kevin 775
Kier, Lady Miss 291, 292
Kihn, Greg **615**, 616, 1276
Kilbey, Russell 215
Kilbey, Steve 214, 215, 216, 1342

Kilburn & The High Roads 339, 1287, 1335
Kilburn, Duncan 896
Kilgore, Merle 512
Kilgour, David 57, 224
Kilgour, Hamish 57, 224
Kilkenny Cats 241, 1344
Killarmy 970, 1246
Killen, Buddy 1129
Killen, Kevin 236, 255
Killermeters 1298
Killing Joke 96, 272, 520, **616**, 617, 729, 824, 1131
Kim, Andy **617**, 1291
Kimball, Bobby 1150
Kimball, Jim 587
Kimble, Paul 479
Kimbrough, Junior 399
Kimmel, Bob 1084
Kimsey, Chris 697
Kincaid, Jesse Lee 519
Kinchla, Chan 119
King Adora 38
King Buzzo 260
King Crimson 39, 52, 88, 182, 363, 364, 398, 416, 420, 425, 445, 457, 458, 473, 500, 588, **617**, 618, 668, 797, 801, 893, 1039, 1089, 1111, 1148, 1235, 1255, 1296, 1331
King Crooners 1274
King Curtis 59, 430, **619**, 733, 918, 1001, 1162, 1291, 1293, 1300
King Diamond 605, 606
King Kong [1] 1023
King Lou 337
King Missile 126, 643
King Perry 1294
King Snake Roost 1342
King Tee 553
King [1] 210, 448, 650
King, Alan [1] 734, 735
King, Albert 90, 128, 129, 219, 264, 430, 522, 1185, 1186, 1277, 1294, 1326, 1352
King, B.B. 93, 148, 220, 227, 346, 430, 599, 662, 712, 804, 833, 924, 1163, 1164, 1169, 1232, 1295, 1304, 1316, 1352
King, Ben E. 159, 245, 246, 338, 526, **619**, 694, 908, 924, 1184, 1324, 1325
King, Carole 143, 166, 184, 185, 212, 248, 273, 304, 380, 409, 411, 430, 475, 519, 524, 565, **619**, 620, 658, 659, 745, 754, 829, 868, 887, 955, 964, 1000, 1001, 1059, 1060, 1081, 1092, 1096, 1118, 1119, 1227, 1274, 1275, 1289, 1301, 1311, 1312, 1328
King, Earl 67, 68, 333, 522, 1030, 1273, 1274, 1278
King, Ed 683, 1089
King, Evelyn Champagne 620, 1280
King, Freddie 265, 673, 696, 708, 1316
King, Jimmy 63
King, Jon 448
King, Jonathan 1126
King, Kerry 1020, 1021
King, Mark 650
King, Martin Luther Jr. 898, 1237
King, Martin Luther Sr. 60
King, Maurice and His Wolverines 1289
King, Paul [3] 776
King, Pee Wee 1282
King, Reg 6, 734, 735
King, Rob 305
King, Saunders 976, 1162
King, Stephen 4, 31, 529, 1167
King, Stove 695
King, Tom 835
King, Will 1163
King's Singers 987
King's X 1302
Kingdom Come [1] 145, 1302
Kings of Rhythm 1163, 1164
Kingsmen 257, 415, 416, 477, 545, **620**, 913, 943, 1042, 1085, 1086, 1087, 1281, 1288, 1293, 1297, 1321
Kingsmill, Mark 537, 538
Kingston Trio 56, 57, 990, 1165, 1353
Kingston, Bob [2] 1127
Kinison, Sam 1302
Kinks 34, 35, 42, 54, 98, 99, 114, 120, 121, 134, 135, 177, 213, 220, 222, 283, 284, 332, 349,

350, 377, 393, 405, 410, 416, 470, 476, 485,
520, 532, 536, 544, 574, 606, **620**, 621, 622,
623, 628, 656, 683, 685, 742, 752, 769, 784,
795, 811, 815, 885, 893, 949, 950, 1027,
1028, 1033, 1042, 1057, 1065, 1087, 1104,
1112, 1125, 1135, 1157, 1191, 1214, 1216,
1251, 1257, 1264, 1281, 1293, 1298, 1310,
1315, 1316, 1317, 1318, 1320, 1322, 1338,
1339, 1341, 1346, 1347, 1352
Kinky 373
Kinman, Chip 314
Kinman, Tony 314
Kinsella, Mike 592
Kinsella, Tim 592
Kinsley, Billy 728
Kinsman Dazz 286
Kipling, Rudyard 240
Kippington Lodge 144, 1235
Kirby, Robert 334
Kirchen, Bill 241, 242
Kirk, Andy 170, 823
Kirk, James 823
Kirk, Rahsaan Roland 587, 873, 1331
Kirk, Richard H. 170, 171
Kirke, Simon 52, 53, 432
Kirkland, Kenny 1083
Kirkman, Terry 41
Kirkpatrick, Chris 781
Kirkpatrick, John 1138, 1139
Kirkwood, Curt 719, 720
Kirshner, Don 35, 659, 755, 1311
Kirwan, Danny 413, 414
Kiss 32, 35, 252, 556, **624**, 625, 626, 767, 923,
924, 934, 963, 1018, 1024, 1219, 1276
Kiss [Rock] 302, 469, 624, 625, 626, 866, 903,
906, 922, 963, 966, 1018, 1134, 1214, 1257
Kisser, Andreas 993
Kissoon, Mac & Katie 1276
Kitchen, Steve 128
Kitt, Eartha 20
Kitty Craft 1285
Kiwi 1191
Klaatu 186, **626**, 1211
Klayman, Dan 1199
Klebe, Gary 1002, 1003
Kleenex 656
Klein, Alan 205
Klein, Gary 424, 1093
Klein, Larry 240, 747
Kleinow, Sneaky Pete 298, 418
KLF 206, 250, 351, **626**, 627, 1286
Kluster [1] 771
KMFDM **627**, 628, 640, 938, 1019, 1275,
1284, 1345
Knack [1] 289, 628, 703, 962, 1208, 1290, 1338
Knaup, Renate 25
Knaup-Kroetenschwanz, Renate 26
Knaves 415
Kneale, Sarah 1003
Knechtel, Larry 403, 939, 1011
Knickerbockers **628**, 771, 1296
Knight, Baker 787, 788
Knight, Cheri 1
Knight, Frederick [1] 639
Knight, Gladys 1, 39, 258, 624, **628**, 629, 710,
841, 1087, 1095, 1314
Knight, Gladys & the Pips 512, 629,
1276, 1315
Knight, Jean 1295
Knight, Jerry 841
Knight, Jesse 1163
Knight, Jonathan [1] 792
Knight, Jordan 792
Knight, Marie 1301
Knight, Peter 185, 758, 1071, 1072
Knight, Robert 1276, 1289
Knight, Steve 771
Knight, Suge 324, 899
Knight, Terry & the Pack 478
Knight, Tony 1275
Knights 1178
Knights, David 893
Knitters 21, 1249
Knopfler, David 318, 319
Knopfler, Mark 45, 172, 173, 220, 318,
319, 795

Knowland, James 759
Knowles, Beyonce 305
Knox 1153, 1193
Knox, Buddy 148, **629**, 1118, 1282, 1292
Knox, Chris 629, 630, 1018, 1118, 1153, 1342
Knox, Nick 262, 263
Koda, Cub 150, 197, 296, **630**, 1068
Koehler, Ted 848
Koerner, John 623
Koffman, Moe 1297
Kogel, Michael 669
Kokane 1036
Kokomo [1] 956
Kolderie, Paul Q. 156, 735
Kolotkin, Glen 916
Komeda **630**, 631
Komputer 8
Kongos, John 503
Konishi, Yasuharu 252, 865
Koobas **631**
Kool & the Gang **631**, 1160, 1280, 1284, 1334
Kool G Rap 748
Kool G Rap & DJ Polo 1074, 1280
Kool Gents 221
Kool Keith 326, 327, 501, **631**, 632, 892, 895,
1172, 1173
Kool Moe Dee **632**, 664
Kooner, Jagz 971
Kooper, Al 113, 114, 119, 650, 681, 863, 1161,
1162, 1270, 1300, 1318, 1326, 1333
Kootch, Danny 438
Kooymans, George 470
Koppel, Thomas 979
Koppes, Peter 215, 216, 1342
Korn [1] 295, 521, 553, **632**, 656, 839, 888,
993, 1067
Korner, Alexis 329, 414, 477, 522, 776, 878,
1310, 1315, 1317, 1326
Kornfeld, Artie 260
Kortchmar, Danny 214, 523, 595, 600, 620,
798, 1119, 1120
Kossoff, Paul 432
Kottke, Leo 158, 476
Kowalczyk, Edward 662, 663
Kozelek, Mark 922, 923
Kraftwelt 8
Kraftwerk 8, 60, 96, 134, 155, 171, 300, 360,
361, 378, 545, 548, 553, 628, **632**, 633, 638,
688, 753, 771, 789, 790, 793, 807, 826, 827,
962, 1048, 1142, 1155, 1173, 1195, 1254,
1261, 1273, 1286, 1288, 1296, 1331
Kral, Ivan 874
Krall, Diana 602
Kramer [1] 126, 280, 446, 447, 676, 712
Kramer, Amanda 470, 471
Kramer, Billy J. 80, 106, **633**, 1293, 1319, 1320
Kramer, Eddie 522, 523, 592, 624, 1087
Kramer, Wayne 712
Krasnow, Bob 180
Krause, Bernie 508
Krause, Dagmar 261, 1246, 1247
Kraushaar, Bob 19
Krauss, Alison 852
Krauss, Scott 851, 852
Kravitz, Lenny 126, 164, 209, 625, **633**, 634
Kreidler 772
Kreutzmann, Bill 482
Krieger, Robbie 332
Kris Kross 1293
Kriss, Tom 576
Kristofferson, Kris 401, 480, 487, 653, 654,
892, 1010, 1093, 1106, 1202, 1286
Krokus 1302
Krokus [1] 40
Kroner, Steve 783
Kronos Quartet 389, 704
KRS One 128, 585, 615, 906, 931
Kruder & Dorfmeister 1018
Krugman, Murray 116
Krukowski, Damon 446, 447
Krummenacher, Victor 177, 178
Krusen, Dave 848, 1125
Krust 1018
Krust [1] 1018
Kuehn, William 913, 914
Kuepper, Ed 973, 974, 1341
Kula Shaker 895, 1157

Kulberg, Andy 119
Kulick, Bob 624
Kulick, Bruce 624
Kunkel, Russ 1046, 1119, 1226
Kupferberg, Tuli 437, 438
Kupka, Stephen 'Doc' 1151
Kurihara, Michio 463
Kuroko, Shigeru 463
Kurosky, Miles 95
Kursaal Flyers 352, **634**, 921, 1287, 1339
Kurupt 1036
Kustow, Danny 947
Kweli, Talib 766
Kweskin, Jim Jug Band 988
Kyuss **634**, 702, 906, 1233

L

L Seven 47, 48, 295, 590, **635**, 895, 1282, 1345
La De Das **635**, 636, 1342
LA Dream Team 553, 1300
La Dusseldorf 790
LA Express 746
La Magia 19, 20
La Rue 568
La's 190, **636**, 1290, 1347
Labelle 503, 602, **636**, 872, 1347
Labelle, Patti **636**, 809, 1019, 1237, 1301,
1325, 1335
Labelle, Patti & the Bluebelles 636, 1301
Labradford 468, **636**, 637, 1155, 1171
LaBranch, Jackie 450
Lachey, Nick 1014
Lachowski, Michael 902
Lack, Steve 1192
Lacy, Jay 789
Ladanyi, Greg 414
Ladd, Jim 1209
Lady Luck 372
Lady Saw 1195
Lady Soul 430
Ladybug Transistor 376, **637**
Ladytron [1] **638**
Ladytron [2] 638
LaFreniere, Shelley 447
Laguna, Kenny 133
Laibach 288
Laidlaw, Ray 657
Laika **638**, 760, 1007
Laine, Denny 714, 758, 759
Laine, Frankie 289
Laing, Corky 771
Laird-Clowes, Nick 336
Lake, Greg 363, 364, 491, 617, 618, 797
Lakeside 248
Lally, Joe 436, 437
LaLonde, Larry 888, 977
Lamb [2] 355
Lambchop 207, 507, **638**, 639
Lambert, Dave [1] 1090
Lambert, Dennis 243
Lambert, Hendricks & Ross 433
Lamble, Martin 386, 388
Lambrettas **639**, 1287, 1298
Lamm, Robert 209
Lampe, Hans 790
Lampkin, Tyrone 441
Lamplighters 945
Lance, Major 558, 573, **639**, 709, 1229,
1324, 1282
Land, Harold 44, 807
Landau, David 1269
Landau, Jon 149, 712
Landreth, Sonny 267, 526, 527
Landry, Amos 1223
Landry, George 1223
Lane, Anita 99
Lane, Burton 1092
Lane, Cristy 385
Lane, Danny 789
Lane, Gary 1028
Lane, Jani 1207
Lane, Jeff 150
Lane, Ronnie 1027, 1081, 1151, 1152, 1240
Lanegan, Mark 77, **639**, 640, 906, 984,
985, 1282
Lang, Eddie [1] 1286
Lang, Jonny 502

Lang, k.d. 189, 678, 825, 1215
Lange, Robert John 'Mutt' 4, 188, 294,
327, 840
Langer, Clive 161, 235, 255, 307, 685,
765, 1121
Langford, Jon 376, 721, 722
Langston, Leslie 1142
Langton, Huw-Lloyd Group 515
Lanham, Jim 901
Lanier, Allen 116
Lanois, Daniel 344, 368, 369, 524, 679, 790,
791, 945, 946, 995, 1089, 1169, 1170
Lantree, Honey 536
Lard Free 1296
Larkey, Charles 620
Larks [1] 1306
LaRock, Scott 128
Larson, Joel 733, 939
Larson, Nathan 1004
Larson, Nicolette **640**, 1260, 1285
LaRue, Dave 322
Larue, Florence 403
LaSalle, Denise 645
Laskanich, Katrina 611
Last 1279
Last Poets [1] 479, **640**, 641, 983,
1330, 1347
Lastie, Dave 528
Lastie, Mel 918
Lastie, Melvin 459
Laswell, Bill 368, 470, 471, 769, 875, 899,
1330, 1356
Latimer 176
Latimer, Andy 176
Latimore **641**
Latimore, Benny 641
Latin Playboys 271, **641**, 670, 831
Lauderdale, Jack 202, 1296
Laughing Clowns 973, 1341
Laughner, Peter 287, 669, 851, 852
Launay, Nick 734
Lauper, Cyndi 239, 302, 318, 382, 594, **641**,
642, 743, 751, 999, 1209
Laurie, Annie 1289
Lavelle, James 323
Lavey, Anton 698
Lavin, Christine 543
Lavis, Gilson 840
Lavitz, T. 322, 585
Law, Don 237
Law, Jude 994
Lawrence, Claire 211
Lawrence, D.H. 821
Lawrence, John 476
Lawrence, Pete 1002
Lawrence, Ron [1] 'Amen-Ra' 915
Laws, Hubert 918, 983
Laxo, Rob 1110
Lay, Sam 163
Layhe, Chris 554
Lazie, Josh 281
Lazy Cowgirls **642**
Le Orme 1296
Le Tigre **643**
Lea, Jim 743, 1020
Leadbelly 193, 246, 329, 496, 640, 765, 828,
1002, 1174, 1350, 1353
Leaders of the New School 939, 1274
Leadon, Bernie 346, 347, 418, 486, 519,
956, 1205
Leaf, David 74
Leake, Lafayette 311
Leander, Mike 389, 390, 466
Lear, Amanda **643**
Lear, Graham 976
Leary, Paul 163, 164, 375, 599, 720, 938
Leary, Timothy 758, 1323
Leavell, Chuck 17, 18, 93
Leaves 166, **643**, 1318, 1319
Leblanc, Keith 1347
Lebon, Simon 339
Leckie, John 190, 259, 338, 392, 400, 655,
877, 943
Led Zeppelin 9, 10, 11, 26, 27, 52, 84, 85, 119,
126, 152, 164, 177, 234, 243, 273, 274, 290,
292, 293, 310, 338, 358, 367, 389, 411, 444,
484, 504, 506, 507, 518, 519, 536, 538, 563,

578, 579, 605, 627, **643**, 644, 645, 663, 679, 682, 702, 733, 734, 743, 767, 811, 819, 836, 848, 866, 886, 888, 903, 904, 912, 933, 963, 967, 980, 994, 999, 1027, 1028, 1044, 1045, 1056, 1084, 1087, 1090, 1128, 1176, 1214, 1220, 1249, 1262, 1291, 1322, 1326, 1331, 1332, 1345
Lee Kings 1293
Lee [1] 672
Lee, Adrian 735
Lee, Albert 219, 220
Lee, Alvin 115, 1127
Lee, Arthur 672, 694, 1298
Lee, Barry 1219
Lee, Ben 679
Lee, Bill [1] 238, 239, 551
Lee, Billy & the Rivieras 969
Lee, Brenda 298, 679, 1292, 1301
Lee, Bruce 192
Lee, Byron 782
Lee, Curtis 1052, 1275, 1280
Lee, Freddy Fingers 547
Lee, Geddy 966, 967, 1007
Lee, Jack 112, 189, 788, 1339
Lee, Jackie [1] 121
Lee, Jake 832
Lee, Larry 835
Lee, Laura 195, **645**, 1284
Lee, Leonard 1001
Lee, Marty 562
Lee, Mary 395
Lee, Michael 351
Lee, Peggy [1] 131, 662
Lee, Ric 1127
Lee, Rita 778
Lee, Sara 448
Lee, Sarah 313
Lee, Spike 449, 551, 898
Lee, Stan 309, 310
Lee, Tracy 923
Lee, Will [1] [Bass] 625
Leech, Mike 937
Leeds, Alan 237
Leeds, Gary 1201
Leeman, Cliff 1163
Leen, Bill 465
Lees, Gene 64
Lees, John 64
Leeway, Joe 1137
Left Banke 183, 602, **645**, 646, 706, 707, 728, 736, 830, 840, 1086, 1087, 1216, 1240, 1287, 1296
Left Hand Frank 630
Leftfield 1299
LeGassick, Damian 1198
Legend [1] 608
Legendary Stardust Cowboy 1297
Legrand, Michel 1092, 1093, 1202, 1203
Lehning, Kyle 366
Lehrer, Lucky 217, 218
Leiber & Stoller 59, 227, 401, 639, 794, 1297, 1301
Leiber, Jerry 108, 227, 383, 513, 581, 619, 880, 894, 1232, 1311
Leibezeit, Jaki 178, 179, 898
Leigh, Caroline 1091
Leigh, Michael 642
Leigh, Mike 391, 824
Leisz, Greg 21
Leitch, Donovan 330, 331
Leka, Paul 646
Lemmy 305, 515, 768, 769, 832
Lemon D 471, 1290
Lemon Drops 1321
Lemon Pipers **646**, 817
Lemonheads 511, **646**, 1045, 1210, 1290
Lemper, Ute 1210
LEN 647
Len Bright Combo 1243
Lennear, Claudia 701
Lennon, John 28, 34, 57, 76, 77, 78, 79, 80, 88, 98, 119, 127, 135, 196, 198, 205, 214, 222, 336, 346, 358, 359, 365, 370, 389, 423, 456, 477, 479, 480, 491, 508, 530, 541, 544, 556, 565, 591, 594, 597, 598, 603, 626, 628, 629, 633, 634, **647**, 648, 649, 658, 713, 714, 715, 716, 799, 800, 801, 813, 849, 855, 858, 868,

886, 952, 968, 986, 1003, 1011, 1015, 1044, 1065, 1070, 1082, 1092, 1118, 1156, 1157, 1169, 1209, 1210, 1211, 1224, 1262, 1293, 1312, 1316, 1317, 1319, 1320
Lennon, Julian 93, 115, **649**, 1032
Lennon, Sean 216, 217, 501, 850, 948, 1198
Lennox, Annie 378, 379, **649**, 667
Lenoble, Martyn 876
Lenoir, J.B. 630, 1351
Leon, Craig 393, 415, 468
Leon, Michael 47, 48
Leonard, Patrick 401, 590
Lerma, Luis 27
Lerner & Loewe 256
Lerner, Alan Jay 1092
Lerner, Michael 1007
LeRoi Brothers 290
Lesh, Phil 481, 482
Leskiw, Greg 491, 492
Leslie, Chris 388
Lessard, Stefan 704
Lester, Bobby 759
Lester, Paul 1180
Lester, Wally 1019
Let's Active 246, 286, **649**, 760, 1036, 1188, 1289, 1290, 1343, 1344, 1345
Letta 44
Letterman, David 953
Lettermen 830
Letters 1298
Letts, Don 95
Leuan, Dafydd 191, 1103
Levan, Larry 376
Level Forty Two **650**
Leven, John 378
Levene, Keith 898, 899, 1023, 1356
Levenson, Bill 1155
Leventhal, John 240, 241
Lever, John 196, 197
LeVert 58, **650**
Levert, Eddie 818, 819
LeVert, Gerald 58, 278, 650
Levin, Drake 936, 939
Levin, Tony [Bass] 36, 160, 618, 927, 1139
Levine, Hank 1297
Levine, Joey 802, 817
Levine, Steve 74
Levinger, Lowell 1259, 1263
Levy, Alison Faith 672
Levy, Arthur 117
Levy, Morris 974, 1292
Lewie, Jona 707
Lewis, Aaron 1067
Lewis, Anthony 16, 1067
Lewis, Barbara **650**, 1313
Lewis, C.S. 575
Lewis, Chuck 759
Lewis, Furry 212, 696, 851, 1350
Lewis, Gary 315, 650, 651
Lewis, Gary & The Playboys **650**, 651
Lewis, Graham 1233
Lewis, Heather [1] 77
Lewis, Huey 254, 354, 497, 539, **651**, 1151
Lewis, Huey & the News 651
Lewis, James [3] Mingo 975
Lewis, Jerry 650
Lewis, Jerry Lee 108, 109, 148, 150, 263, 439, 513, **652**, 765, 772, 773, 782, 783, 787, 825, 853, 883, 944, 968, 1062, 1283, 1286, 1292, 1295, 1304, 1307, 1308, 1310, 1319, 1351
Lewis, John [01] 684
Lewis, Lew 338
Lewis, Lew & Reformer 1285
Lewis, Linda Gail 765
Lewis, Margaret 513
Lewis, Mel Orchestra 994
Lewis, Mike [1] 981, 1257
Lewis, Pete [2] 'Guitar' 749
Lewis, Peter 749
Lewis, Ramsey 495, 1276, 1309, 1329
Lewis, Rudy 338
Lewis, Sam M. 1094
Lewis, Shaznay 16
Lewis, Smiley 67, 68, **652**, 653, 1278
Lewis, Terry 58, 88, 110, 424, 545, 570, 571, 1081, 1144, 1184
Lewis, Tony 833

Lewthwaite, Alistair 196
Lewy, Henry 667
Leyton, John 720, 1310
LFO [1] 101, 301, 971, 1064, 1299
Lhooq 20
Liberty Bell 1264
Licher, Bruce 177, 978
Licht, Alan 963
Licht, David 126
Lieber, Jerry 1307, 1312
Liebezeit, Jaki 178, 301
Liesz, Greg 1107
Lifeson, Alex 966, 967
Ligertwood, Alex 43
Liggins, Jimmy 1294
Liggins, Joe 1278, 1294, 1304, 1305
Light, Enoch 433
Lightfoot, Gordon 221, 238, 246, 342, 387, 551, **653**, 654, 1078, 1092, 1286, 1318, 1328, 1353
Lightman, John 98
Lightnin' Rod 640
Lightning Seeds 361, 501, **654**, 935
Lil Kim 581, **654**, 655, 748, 805, 899, 1016
Lil' Louis 655
Lil' Mo' Yin Yang 68
Lilac Time **655**
Liles, Brent 1037
Liliput **655**, 656, 1023
Lilker, Dan 31
Lillywhite, Adrian 724
Lillywhite, Steve 36, 37, 97, 196, 250, 267, 684, 704, 859, 870, 896, 1012, 1143, 1157, 1173
Lilys **656**
Limahl 609
Lime Spiders 910, 1342
Limeliters 1353
Limerick, Alison 554, 776
Limp Bizkit 277, 295, 554, 632, **656**, 657, 849, 912, 1067
Lind, Bob 430, **657**
Lind, Rob 1042
Lind, Zach 591
Lindisfarne **657**, 1071, 1354, 1293
Lindley, David 149, 215, 267, 506, 610, **657**, 658, 706, 875, 1269, 1270
Lindley, David & El Rayo-X 658
Lindsay, Arto 217, 470
Lindsay, Mark 936, 937
Lindup, Mike 650
Link [1] 1273
Linkous, Mark 1049, 1050
Linn, Roger 219
Linna, Miriam 410, 1042
Linnell, John 1132
Linton, Tom 591
Linzell, Peter 981
Lipsius, Fred 113, 716
LiPuma, Tommy 382, 701
Liquid Liquid 376, 655
Liquorice 555
Lironi, Stephen 502
Lisa Lisa 658
Lisa Lisa & Cult Jam 658
Lisher, Greg 177
Lister, Hovie & the Statesmen 1351
Lithman, Phil 'Snakefinger' 210, 211
Lithops 772
Litt, Scott 511, 931, 1343
Litter 67, 1027
Little Anthony & the Imperials 658, 1182, 1184, 1275, 1306
Little Anthony [1] 782
Little Caesar & the Romans 1282
Little Eva 210, 248, 619, **658**, 659, 739, 1275, 1282, 1289, 1301, 1311, 1312
Little Feat 103, 173, 246, 261, 299, 459, 481, **659**, 660, 661, 699, 838, 894, 901, 914, 981, 1082, 1119, 1151, 1285, 1286
Little Green Men [2] 944
Little Milton 68, 1305, 1352, 1276, 1295
Little Richard 80, 93, 94, 109, 130, 146, 148, 221, 241, 256, 258, 265, 293, 297, 328, 338, 375, 376, 381, 439, 631, 652, **661**, 663, 715, 801, 880, 884, 924, 969, 1042, 1110, 1129, 1205, 1224, 1243, 1278, 1282, 1286, 1291,

1292, 1294, 1297, 1303, 1305, 1306, 1309, 1319, 1329, 1341
Little River Band **661**
Little Steven & the Disciples of Soul **661**, 662, 665
Little Village 527, **662**
Little Walter 384, 1352
Little Willie John 147, **662**, 1287, 1297, 1305, 1351, 1352
Little, Levi 108
Littleton, Dan 555
Littleton, Michael 555
Littrell, Brian 51
Live [1] **662**, 663, 1135, 1344
Live Skull 203, 241
Lively Ones [1] **663**, 1279, 1301
Liverbirds 311
Livesey, Warne 734
Livgren, Kerry 610
Living Colour **663**, 664, 921, 977, 1329
Livingston, Bob 977
LL Cool J 323, 372, 376, 462, 615, 632, **664**, 696, 702, 712, 731, 895, 974, 1020, 1148, 1223, 1279, 1280, 1284, 1287
Llanas, Samuel 122
Lloyd Webber, Andrew 37, 255, 1094, 1291
Lloyd, Ian 1086, 1087
Lloyd, Richard 1107, 1124, 1191
Lloyd, Robert [1] 504
Lloyd, Tom 295
Lo, James 203
Locke, John 783, 1056
Lockett, Tom 1020
Locorriere, Dennis 325, 326
Locust [3] 751
Lodge, John 758, 759
Loeb, Lisa 555, 556, **664**, 665
Loesser, Frank 1094
Loewenstein, Jason 837, 987, 988
Lofgren, Nils 478, 490, **665**, 1259, 1260
Lofgren, Tom 665
Lofty Pillars 1246
Logan, Jack 208, **665**
Loggins & Messina **665**, 666, 869, 872
Loggins, Dave 666
Loggins, Kenny 665, **666**, 667, 691
Logic, Lora 1250
Lois 1285, 1302
Lomas, Barbara Joyce 150
Lomax, Alan 1353
Lomax, Jackie 1160
Lombardo, Dave 1021
Lombardo, John 1126, 1127
Lombardo, Tony 302, 303
Lonberg-Holm, Fred 1104
London Community Gospel Choir 373, 1056
London Festival Orchestra 758
London Symphony Orchestra 64, 351, 715, 932, 1201, 1259, 1267
London, John 788, 789
London, Julie 1091, 1297
London, Laurie 1311
London, Mark 679
Lone Justice 667, 716, 717
Lonergan, Mark 62
Loney, Roy 409, 410
Long Ryders 667, 668, 1343, 1344
Long Tall Short 1298
Long, Avon 620
Long, Dee 626
Long, Gary [2] 1127
Long, Shorty [1] 1224
Longacre, Kim 930
Loop 65, 142, 637, **668**, 669
Looper 90
Loose Ends [1] 37
Loose Gravel 200
Loose, Bruce 416
Lopes, Dick 1145
Lopes, Joe 296
Lopes, Lisa 'Left Eye' 1145
Lopez Capillas, Francisco 669
Lopez, Jennifer **669**, 988
Lopez, Vincent [1] 1062
Lopez, Vini 1062
Lorber, Alan 830, 1172
Lorber, Jeff 1172

Lord 669
Lord Buckley 1274
Lord Jamar 1158
Lord, Jon 292, 293
Lord, Mary Lou **669**, 1294
Lord, Peter 3
Lords of the New Church 287
Loren, Bryan 305
Loren, Cary 305
Loren, Donna 1296
Lorimer, Pete 282
Lorimer, Roddy 128
Lorre, Peter 82
Los Angeles Philharmonic 22
Los Bravos **669**, 724
Los Lobos 109, 159, 375, 450, 641, 668, **670**,
    671, 831, 915, 1131, 1187
Los Super Seven 670
Lose, Bruce 417
Lost Souls [2] [US] 511
Lothar & the Hand People **671**
Lotion **671**
Loud Family 447, **671**, 672
Loud, Lance 775
Loudermilk, John D. 227
Louris, Gary 524, 582
Louvin Brothers 166, 582, 837, 845, 1174,
    1303, 1351
Love 48, 63, 109, 152, 403, 485, 532, 636, 643,
    672, 694, 772, 773, 991, 1109, 1123, 1298,
    1299, 1319, 1323
Love and Rockets 69, 70, 274, 280, **672**, 673,
    776, 876, 897, 1338
Love As Laughter 158
Love Battery 879
Love Child 963
Love Sculpture 353, 354, 371, **673**
Love Spit Love 896
Love Tractor **673**, 674
Love Unlimited 1219
Love Unlimited Orchestra 1219, 1309
Love, Andrew 696, 924
Love, Barbara 434
Love, Courtney 47, 388, 413, 531, 532, 669,
    814, 1285
Love, Courtney [1] 48, 532
Love, Darlene 272, 536, 601, **674**, 946, 1052,
    1207, 1312
Love, Duma 216
Love, Freda 108, 109
Love, Gerard 1123
Love, Mike 71, 73, 74, 1228
Love, Steve 1086, 1087
Love/Hate 1302
Loved Ones [Australia] 1341
Lovegrove, Florence 773
Loveland 328
Loveless, Patty 893
Lovell, Steve 250, 417
Lovelock, Damien 194, 195, 1342
Lovemongers 518, 1293
Loverboy **674**, 675
Lovering, David 863, 864
Lovetro, Gary 1089
Lovett, Lyle 488, **675**, 795, 917, 1084
Lovich, Lene 327, **676**, 1295
Lovin' Spoonful 87, 200, 283, 409, 410, **676**,
    688, 691, 785, 960, 988, 999, 1165, 1259,
    1263, 1296, 1300
Low [1] 232, **676**, 677
Lowe, Chris 360, 855, 1059
Lowe, James 1050
Lowe, Nick 143, 144, 186, 254, 255, 256, 322,
    325, 338, 353, 354, 355, 380, 384, 432, 472,
    504, 526, 541, 608, 628, 662, 673, **677**, 678,
    727, 820, 840, 949, 962, 1065, 1081, 1121,
    1141, 1278, 1285, 1290, 1295, 1335, 1337,
    1338, 1339
Lowe, Nick & His Cowboy Outfit 678
Lowery, Bill 223
Lowery, David 177, 178, 207, 258, 261, 1049
Lowry, Roame 711
LOX 805
Lozaga, Bon 474
LTD 609, **678**
LTD [1] 678, 831
Lubin, Howard 1175

Lucas, Carrie 49
Lucas, Gary 152, 181, 816
Lucas, George 478
Lucas, Harold 227
Lucas, Paulina 617
Lucas, Trevor 298, 299, 387, 426
Luckett, L.C. 304
Luckett, LeToya 304
Luckey, Sharon Marie 73
Ludacris 362
Ludovico, Vinnie 702
Lukather, Steve 40, 523, 1150
Lukin, Matt 775
Lulu 106, **679**, 999, 1313, 1316
Luna [1] 446, **679**, 1018
Lunceford, Jimmie 1158
Lunch, Lydia 99, 197, 1040, 1249, 1336
Lundin, Kristian 781
Lundy, Antoine 425
Lupper, Kenneth 431
Luscious Jackson 216, 440, 559, **679**, 1159
Lush 192, 200, **680**, 751, 778, 837, 838, 1347
Lutcher, Joe 1294
Lutz, Michael 150
Luv'd Ones 1283
Lux, Matt 566
Lwin, Annabella 30, 132, 133
Lyall, Susan 62
Lydon, John 60, 470, 471, 896, 898, 899
Lyman, Steve 1067
Lyme & Cybelle 1269, 1282
Lymon, Frankie 191, 568, 658, **680**, 681,
    1306, 1307
Lymon, Frankie & the Teenagers 680, 681,
    958, 1182
Lynch Mob 327
Lynch, David [Director] 102, 390, 564, 745
Lynch, David [Rock] 7, 564
Lynch, George 327
Lynch, Tim 409
Lyngstad, Anni-Frid 1
Lynn, Barbara **681**, 949, 1282, 1306
Lynn, Cheryl 1150, 1183
Lynn, Loretta 189, 1146
Lynn, Tamiya 1284
Lynne, Gloria 358, 555, 556, 1157
Lynne, Jeff 67, 353, 354, 358, 359, 360, 381,
    508, 509, 555, 556, 772, 773, 825, 856,
    998, 1157
Lynne, Shelby 914
Lynott, Phil 1133, 1134, 1143
Lynyrd Skynyrd 16, 52, 104, 107, 173, 272,
    615, **681**, 682, 683, 730, 821, 834, 1089,
    1136, 1173, 1259, 1327, 1333
Lyon, Johnny 1046
Lyons, Leo 1127, 1231
Lyons, Toby 240
Lyres **683**, 907, 1278, 1343
Lytle, Jason 478

M
M [1] **684**
Ma, Yo-Yo 1120
Mabry, Lynn 1117
Maby, Graham 267, 571
Macaulay, Tony 426
Macaulay, Tony 353
MacColl, Ewan 238, 653, 654, 684, 813,
    1079, 1355
MacColl, Kirsty 138, **684**, 870, 1172, 1231
MacColl, Neill 483
MacCormick, Bill 703, 1247
MacDonald, Andy 1157
Macdonald, Eddie 13
MacFarlane, Lora 1021
MacGowan, Shane 870, 871
Machine Head 1021
Maciejak, Rafa 566
Mack, Bill 1291
Mack, Craig 248, 899, 1273
Mack, James 285
Mack, Lonnie 122, 212, 518, 1185, 1186, 1205,
    1282, 1292, 1297, 1308
Mack, Steve 1130
Mackay, Andy 368, 401, 959
Mackay, Andy [Sax] 173, 174, 668
MacKay, Neil 668

MacKaye, Ian 436, 437, 740, 944, 953, 1279
MacKenzie, Ali 99
MacKenzie, Billy 40, 1255
Mackenzie, Ian 1341
Mackey, Steve 102
MacKillop, Gavin 1146
MacLean, Bryan 672
Maclean, John 94
MacLeod, Brian [1] 211, 335, 1234
Maclure, Andy 1022
MacManus, Declan 255
MacMillan, James 536
Macon, Uncle Dave 1351
MacPherson, Fraser 141
MacPherson, Jim 27, 141
MacRae, Dave 703
Macrocosmica 750
Mad Dog [1] 1159
Mad Dogs & Englishman 230
Mad Dogs & Englishmen 230
Mad Lads [1] 287, 1281
Mad Professor 701, 824, 1023
Madan, Sonya Aurora 352
Maddox Brothers & Rose 1303, 1307
Maddox, Rose 1032, 1273, 1301
Maddox, Walt 697
Madeley, Gary 269
Madey, James 153
Madison, James 153
Madness [1] 120, 161, 367, 404, **685**, 686, 729,
    992, 1052, 1104, 1172, 1281, 1298, 1299,
    1338, 1339, 1347, 1355, 1356
Madonna 31, 49, 97, 112, 207, 208, 217, 274,
    373, 401, 464, 499, 663, **686**, 687, 732, 740,
    932, 1044, 1053, 1081, 1197, 1199
Mae, Michelle 689
Mael, Fon 1051
Mael, Ron 1050, 1051
Mael, Russell 1050, 1051
Maestro, Johnny 268, **687**
Magazine 7, 40, 164, 192, 268, **687**, 688, 776,
    899, 969, 1014, 1195, 1279
Magic Dick 454
Magic Mushroom Band 1323
Magic Sam [1] 1352
Magicians **688**
Maginnis, Tom 155, 156
Magma 473
Magnetic Fields 443, **688**, 689, 1018
Magnum, Jeff 287
Magnuson, Ann 82, 126
Maguire, Andy 1058
Mahal, Taj 114, 246, 506, 602, 914, 952
Mahavishnu Orchestra 322, 473, 975, 1064
Maher, Fred 235, 520, 928, 985
Maher, John 164, 165, 166
Mahler, Gustav 292
Maimone, Tony 852, 853, 981, 1132
Main 65, 420, 637, 668
Main Ingredient **689**, 791
Main Source [1] 140, 781, 1274
Maines, Lloyd 154, 363
Maines, Natalie 798
Majik, J. 471, 860, 1290
Make Up **689**, 690, 783
Makino, Kazu 111, 112
Makowski, Pete 366
Malcolm X [1] 1348
Malherbe, Didier 473, 474
Malins, Steve 808
Malkmus, Stephen 272, **690**, 847, 1007, 1008
Mallinder, Stephen 170, 171
Mallon, Tom 25
Malmsteen, Yngwie 1302
Malo, Raul 309, 363
Malone, Kenny 893
Malone, Marcus 977
Maltby, Richard Jr. 1092
Mama Cass 701
Mamas & the Papas 63, 290, 403, 407, 480,
    551, 597, 676, **690**, 691, 736, 752, 1048,
    1049, 1108, 1165, 1228, 1296, 1318, 1319,
    1344, 1354
Man or Astro Man? **691**, 993
Manassas 418, 1082
Mancha, Steve 822
Manchester, Melissa 518, **691**, 1061, 1070

Manchild [1] 49
Mancini, Henry 994, 1203
Mandalaband 1072
Mandel, Harvey 179
Mandell, Steve 239
Manfreds 694, 695
Mangano, Diana 585
Mangrum, James 104
Mangrum, Jim 'Dandy' 104
Mangum, Jeff 34, 790
Manhattan Transfer 185, 190, 946, 994
Manhattans **692**
Mani [1] 888, 1084
Manic Street Preachers 206, 355, 476, **692**,
    693, 695, 740, 828, 1076, 1157
Manigault, Bobby 191
Manilow, Barry 174, 547, 691, **693**, 1208
Manish Boys 1284
Manitoba, Handsome Dick 310, 311
Mankey, Earle 1050, 1141
Mankey, James 245, 1050
Mann, Aimee 33, 484, 543, **693**, 694, 956,
    1143, 1144
Mann, Barry 381, 528, 754, 860, 936, 955,
    1203, 1289, 1311, 1312
Mann, Carl 1307, 1295
Mann, Groovie 779
Mann, Herbie 1075, 1329
Mann, Manfred [Individual] **694**
Mann, Manfred Earth Band 694
Mann, Manfred [Individual] 137, 381, 383,
    694, 695, 1001, 1312, 1315, 1316, 1317,
    1318, 1320, 1326, 1329
Manne, Shelly 694, 1199
Manning, Barbara 175, **695**, 1018, 1300
Manning, Chris 585
Manning, Leo 979
Manning, Roger [1] 585
Manning, Roger [2] 585
Mansell, Clint 874
Mansfield, David 159
Manson, Charles 73, 495, 698, 727, 897, 923,
    924, 1169
Manson, Shirley 449
Mansun **695**, 696
Mantia, Brian 888
Mantovani 235
Mantronik, Kurtis 696
Mantronix **696**
Mantz, Nancie 360
Manuel, Richard 61, 62, 513
Many, Trey 555
Manyika, Zeke 823, 1130
Manzanera, Phil 40, 173, 174, 368, 401, 402,
    798, 959, 1057, 1247, 1342
Manzarek, Ray 332, 1249
Mapes, Jo 785
Maphis, Joe 237, 1273
Mapplethorpe, Robert 1031
Mar Keys 129, 515, **696**, 1281, 1295,
    1297, 1309
Marascalco, John 801
Marathons 1281
Marc & the Mambas 19
Marc Seven 608
Marcarian, Myrna 546
Marcellino, Jocko 996
Marcello, Kee 378
Marcels **697**, 1274, 1307
March Violets 749
March, Little Peggy 222
March, Myrna 1289
March, Richard 874
Marchan, Bobby 425, 1030
Marchand, Pierre 717, 1198
Marcum, Mark 913
Marcus, Floyd 802
Marcus, Greil 913, 979
Marder, Marlene 655, 656
Mardi Gras 1223
Mardin, Arif 87, 1060, 1070
Maresca, Ernie 780
Maresh, Chris 599
Margaret, Ann 994
Margarita 1003
Margo, Mitch 1146
Margo, Phil 1146

Mariano, Mickey 1141
Marie, Teena 577, 658, 1068
Marillion 696, **697**, 698, 1331
Marilyn Manson 33, 323, 632, **698**, 699, 767, 802, 831, 865
Marimba, Ed 180
Marinos, Jimmy 954
Mark Four [1] 265
Mark of Cain 1342
Mark Two 293
Mark, Jon 708
Marker, Steve 449
Markie, Biz 76, **100**, 287, 1284, 1285
Markovich, Brenda 1231
Marks, Larry 813
Marl, Marley 372
Marley Marl 97, 101, 664, 1135
Marley, Bob 51, 218, 437, 506, 735, 782, 969, 976, 1082, 1093, 1171, 1355, 1356
Marley, Bob & the Wailers 1296
Marley, Rita 409, 778
Marley, Stephen 56
Marmalade 705
Marnie 638
Marquees 1289
Marquis De Tren 821
Marr, Johnny 40, 104, 138, 162, 263, 350, 352, 360, 361, 400, 401, 455, 684, 765, 885, 999, 1033, 1034, 1130, 1343, 1346
Marr, Lisa 273
Marriott 1027
Marriott, Steve 6, 190, 385, 428, 546, 797, 1027, 1028, 1143, 1322
Marron, Gordon 1175
MARRS 1286
Mars [1] 250
Mars, Chris 934
Marsalis, Branford 481, 482, 495, 1083, 1120, 1330
Marsalis, Wynton 1083
Marsden, Gerry 462, 1320
Marsh, Dave 189, 884, 1022
Marsh, Fergus 229
Marsh, Helena 638
Marsh, Hugh 777
Marsh, Ian Craig 519, 545
Marsh, Nick 415
Marshall Tucker Band 16, 682, **699**, 1333
Marshall, Bob 198
Marshall, Chan 191, 1035
Marshall, Dana 983, 984
Marshall, Sherman 793
Marshmallow Coast **699**
Marsicek, Lisa 432
Marson, Andrew 53
Martha & the Vandellas 210, 475, 536, 612, **699**, 1001, 1222, 1274, 1312, 1313, 1324
Martin, Barrett 906
Martin, Barry [1] 634
Martin, Bill 613
Martin, Billy 217
Martin, Chris [3] 234, 235
Martin, Dean 130, 315, 881, 1162
Martin, Dewey 155, 1327
Martin, Dino Jr. 315
Martin, Fred 659
Martin, George 6, 24, 78, 79, 84, 106, 204, 241, 539, 626, 638, 661, 714, 734, 1070, 1173, 1211, 1319, 1322
Martin, Janis 1292, 1301
Martin, Jim [1] 388, 389, 889
Martin, Marilyn 100
Martin, Mary 1037
Martin, Max 51, 760, 781, 1052
Martin, Moon 996
Martin, Ricky 12, 988
Martin, Sarah 90
Martin, Skip 286
Martin, Steve [1] 645, 646
Martin, Steve [2] 646
Martin, Steve [Comedy] 830
Martin, Tony [1] 106, 881
Martin, Vince 785
Martina 889
Martine [1] 1159
Martinez, Anthony 104
Martinez, Claude 131, 1121

Martinez, Cliff 181, 310
Martinez, Cristina 131
Martinez, Marci 1121
Martinez, Ray [1] 1121
Martinez, Rudy 907
Martsch, Doug 157, 158
Martyn, John 228, 830
Marvelettes 6, 60, **699**, 700, 828, 1001, 1276, 1287, 1312, 1313, 1314, 1315
Marvin & Johnny 700, 1294
Marvin, Hank 1310
Marx, Gary 1017
Marx, Groucho 314
Marx, Richard **700**
Mary Jane Girls 577
Mary's Danish 1141
Masciarelli, Scott 203
Mascis, J. 155, 156, 315, 316, 386, 646, 779, 865, 1045, 1210, 1233
Mascots 818
Mase 140, 323, 805, 900, 1273
Masekela, Hugh 1013, 1309, 1329
Mason 1153
Mason, Barbara **700**
Mason, Barry 353
Mason, Dave [1] 297, 403, 414, **700**, 701, 1035, 1153, 1154, 1155, 1240, 1285
Mason, Nick 279, 411, 861
Mason, Stephen 94
Mason, Stephen [1] 94
Mason, Steve [1] 455
Mason, Steve [Guitar] 455
Mass Production 151
Massenberg, George 956
Massenburg, George 914
Massey, Bobby 818
Massey, Graham 101, 355
Massi, Nick 427
Massive Attack 16, 48, 382, 383, 687, **701**, 752, 876, 877, 1035, 1044, 1159, 1170, 1347
Masta Killa 970, 1246
Mastelotto, Pat 618, 745
Master Gee 1100
Master P **701**, 702, 748, 981, 1036
Master's Apprentices **702**, 742, 1342
Masterettes 383
Masters 837
Masters at Work 68
Masters of Reality 634, **702**
Masters, Ian 837, 838
Mastro, Jim 125
Masuak, Chris 911
Matare, Vitus 337
Matassa, Cosimo 328
Matchbox Twenty 502, **702**, 703
Matching Mole 181, 182, **703**, 1038, 1247, 1331
Material 470, 543, 824, 1331
Material Issue **703**, 704, 858, 1290, 1339
Mathematics [1] 731
Mathematics, Allah 464
Mathers, Marshall 365
Mathis, Johnny [1] 451, 658, 782, 1094, 1178, 1297
Mathus, Jim 1066, 1067
Matlock, Glen 874, 939, 994, 995
Matmos 636, 910
Mattacks, Dave 334, 382, 387, 1071, 1139
Matthew [1] 866
Matthewman, Stuart 707, 971
Matthews, Cerys 191, 192
Matthews, Chris 1004
Matthews, Dave [1] 191, **704**, 705, 952, 1283, 1333
Matthews, Dave [3] 704
Matthews, David [4] 146
Matthews, Eric 183, 284, 390, 567, **705**, 1271
Matthews, Eric [1] 284, 390, 705
Matthews, Ian 388, **705**, 706, 707, 866, 1211
Matthews, Ian Southern Comfort 706, 707
Matthews, Scott 526
Matthews, Shirley 1301
Mattis, David 5
Mattock, Jon 1048
Matumbi 1283
Matz, Peter 1091, 1092

Maurer, John 1037
Maurice, Margaret 725, 726
Maurizio 868
Maus, John 1201
Mavericks 309
Mavers, Lee 190, 636
Mawby, Simon 541, 1242
Maxim 895
Maxon, Joe 1054
Maxwell **707**, 1148
Maxwell, Tom 1067
Maxwell, Tony 1130
May, Billy 282, 1091
May, Brian [1] 905, 1029
May, Derrick 12, 560, 1286, 1299
May, Phil 885, 886
Mayall, Gaz 355
Mayall, John 124, 125, 220, 225, 230, 328, 355, 413, 414, 635, 636, **707**, 708, 1241, 1253, 1316, 1326, 1329
Mayall, John & the Bluesbreakers 413, 708, 709, 1316
Maye, Arthur Lee 1283
Mayell, Norman 115
Mayer, John [2] 364
Mayes, Lenny 336
Mayfield, Curtis 90, 163, 197, 313, 366, 407, 408, 418, 431, 452, 488, 506, 512, 514, 516, 532, 534, 549, 553, 557, 558, 573, 633, 634, 639, 700, **709**, 710, 819, 919, 976, 1036, 1053, 1069, 1186, 1202, 1236, 1270, 1276, 1277, 1281, 1286, 1290, 1299, 1324, 1325, 1334
Mayfield, Curtis & The Impressions 557, 558
Mayfield, Percy 203, 430, **710**, 711, 786, 1278, 1294, 1296, 1304, 1305, 1351
Mayhew, John 456
Mayo, John 325
Mayorga, Lincoln 813
Mays, Lyle 747
Mays, Marcy 11, 983, 984
Maytals 1356
Maze [1] **711**
Maze [2] 711
Mazer, Elliot 337
Mazurek, Rob 566, 829, 879, 1150
Mazzy Star 586, **711**, 751, 823, 838, 913, 1344
MC Five 115, 194, 248, 268, 279, 305, 311, 627, 668, **711**, 712, 757, 834, 910, 911, 912, 919, 942, 948, 991, 992, 1031, 1044, 1067, 1335, 1336, 1341
MC Hammer 244, 577, **712**, 713, 1348
MC Lyte 892
MC Ren 350, 553, 809
MC Serch 1134, 1135
Mc Shan 128, 608, 1287
MC Solaar 1349
MC Tee 696
MC Tunes 355
McAlmont 713
McAlmont & Butler **713**
McAlmont, David 162, 713, 1283
McAloon, Paddy 878, 879
McArdle, Shannon 726
McAuley, Jackie 1153
McBrain, Nicko 564
McCabe, Nick 94, 1193
McCabe, Zia 280
McCafferty, Dan 783, 784
McCall, C.W. 823
McCann, Chris 465
McCann, Dan 465
McCann, Les 409, 786, 920, 1329
McCarl, Scott 919
McCarrick, Martin 19, 20, 1132
McCarroll, Dan 483, 484
McCarthy [1] 667
McCarthy, Gavin 1110
McCarthy, Jim 469
McCarthy, Steve 222, 667
McCartney, Linda 506, 713, 714, 715, 731, 1210, 1211
McCartney, Paul 24, 28, 43, 54, 76, 78, 79, 80, 82, 86, 98, 106, 126, 127, 128, 160, 206, 214, 222, 255, 299, 353, 359, 375, 381, 385, 423, 477, 480, 501, 506, 507, 508, 509, 539, 544, 566, 593, 594, 626, 633, 647, 649, 695, 701,

713, 714, 715, 716, 728, 730, 731, 737, 799, 800, 811, 855, 886, 912, 919, 922, 938, 939, 964, 967, 986, 995, 999, 1003, 1015, 1065, 1070, 1118, 1119, 1211, 1239, 1252, 1293, 1312, 1316, 1317, 1320, 1339, 1355
McCartney, Paul & Wings 713, 714
McCarty, Jim [UK] 969
McCaslin, Mary 1353, 1354
McCaughan, Mac 69, 876, 1103, 1104
McCaughey, Scott 504
McClain, Albritton 562
McClain, Marlon 286
McClary, Thomas 243
McClintock, Scott 827
McClinton, Delbert 151, 159, 198, 915, 1297
McClure, Bobby 68
McCluskey, Andy 826, 827
McClymont, David 823
McCollum, Rick 787
McCombs, Douglas 361, 1150
McCoo, Marilyn 403
McCoy [Band] 402, 403
McCoy, Carl 402, 403
McCoy, Charlie [1] 883, 1213
McCoy, Charlie [2] 653, 737
McCoy, Van 195, 380, 409, 475, 512, 573, 629, 718, 848, 1001, 1276, 1291, 1311, 1312
McCoys 302, **716**, 792, 1087, 1232, 1281, 1289
McCracken, Hugh 409, 426
McCracklin, Jimmy 109, 1282, 1296
McCraw, Lloyd 171
McCrea, Ethel 'Earl-Jean' 248
McCrea, John 172
McCready, Mike 848, 1125
McCreary, Mary 968
McCulloch, Andy 1045
McCulloch, Ian 251, 350, 351, 355, 1122
McCulloch, Jim 1045
McCulloch, Jimmy 464, 714
McCullough, Henry 678
McCullough, Ian 1197
McCurdy, Xan 172
McCutcheon, Ian 751, 1025
McDaniel, Elias 312
McDaniels, Gene 558
McDonald, Country Joe 258, 1172
McDonald, Dollette 1117
McDonald, Ian 425, 617, 618
McDonald, Jeff 1003
McDonald, Jeff [1] 923
McDonald, Jeff [2] 923
McDonald, Michael [1] 271, 331, 385, 560, 666, **716**, 1037
McDonald, Roy 923
McDonald, Steve [Bass] 923
McDonald, Steven [1] 924
McDougal, Don 492
McDowell, Gary 749
McDowell, Mississippi Fred 914, 1053, 1350, 1351
McDuff, Jack 570, 1330
McDuffie, Joanne 'Jojo' 593
McElhone, Johnny 1129
McElrath, John 1110
McElroy, Solly 412
McElroy, Thomas 366
McEntee, Mark 321
McEntire, John 361, 451, 829, 879, 923, 985, 1035, 1075, 1149, 1150, 1155, 1171, 1299
McErlaine, Ally 1129
McFarlane, Elaine 'Spanky' 1049
McGarrigle, Anna 956, 1138
McGarrigle, Kate 956, 1198
McGee 541
McGee [1] 238
McGee, Alan 238, 541, 1025, 1278
McGee, Billy 19, 20, 234
McGeeney, Ross 1071
McGeoch, John 687, 688, 776, 899, 1014, 1195
McGhee, Howard 507
McGhee, Johnny 678
McGill, Michael 298
McGinley, Raymond 1123
McGinty, Joe 638
McGinty, Rolo 1242
McGovern, Maureen 766

McGovern, Tim 766
McGriff, Edna 828
McGriff, Jimmy 1329, 1330
McGuinn, Clark & Hillman 168
McGuinn, Roger 166, 167, 168, 221, 222, 238, 255, 480, 667, 855, 876, 999, 1165, 1255
McGuinness, Tom 694
McGuire Sisters 268
McGuire, Barry 310, **716**, 1024, 1025
McGuire, Brenndan 1024
McIntosh, Carl 43
McIntosh, Greg [1] 827
Mcintosh, Heather 579
McIntosh, Robbie [1] 43
McIntyre, Jim 34
McIntyre, Joe 792
McIntyre, Onnie 43
McKagan, Duff 'Rose' 396, 494, 495, 875
McKay, Al 1244
McKay, John 1014
Mckay, Scotty 1297
McKean, Michael 1065
McKee, Frances 1185
McKee, Maria 602, 667, **716**, 717
McKeegan, Michael 1131, 1132
McKeever, Steve 983
McKenes, Jack 830
McKenna, Mae 176
McKenna, Paul 267
McKenzie, Derrick 577
McKenzie, Scott 551
McKeown, Susan 388
McKillop, K.J. 'Moose' 761
McKnight, Brian 184, 781
McKuen, Rod 102, 788
McLachlan, Brent 57
McLachlan, Sarah 117, 188, 236, 377, **717**, 798, 814
McLagan, Ian 93, 1240
McLaine, Shirley 1095
McLaren, Malcolm 30, 132, 133, 237, 684, 866, 1310, 1336, 1337
McLaughlin, John 878, 975, 976, 1330
McLaughlin, Ollie 179, 650
McLean, A.J. 51
McLean, Don **717**, 718, 770, 1286
McLean, Rene 34
McLemore, Lamonte 403
McLennan, Andrew 1110
McLennan, Grant 467, 468, 1342
McMahan, Brian 1023
McMahon, John 157, 158
McManus Gang 715
McManus, Gary 715
McMaster, Andy 338, 769, 1121
McMurray, Rick 38
McMurtry, James 322
McNabb, Ian 554
McNair, Harold 330
McNally, John 986, 987
McNamara, Robin 1276
McNeely, Big Jay 1287, 1303, 1304, 1305
McNeilly, Mac 241, 587
McNew, James 357, 1257
McNicol, Steve 485
McPhatter, Clyde 337, 338, 498, 662, **718**, 1106, 1206, 1207, 1303, 1305, 1306, 1351
McPherson, Donald 689
McPherson, Graham 'Suggs' 685, 686
McPherson, Tim 722
McQuater, Matthew 227
McQueen, Mike 793
McQueen, Tim 793, 794
McShann, Jay 1303, 1329
McShee, Jacqui 298, 477, 851
McTell, Blind Willie 17, 21, 988, 1218, 1350
McTell, Ralph 388, 489, 539
McVann, Andy 395
McVea, Jack 507
McVie, Christine 412, 413, 414
McVie, John 412, 413, 414, 707, 708, 709, 1326
McVoy, Carl 1283
MDC 1002, 1340
Meadows, Punky 1266
Meadows, Sean 607
Mean Street 756

Means, Nathan 1155
Meat Beat Manifesto 206, 1284
Meat Loaf 302, 318, **718**, 719, 807, 964, 1093
Meat Puppets 411, 472, **719**, 720, 740, 802, 983, 1327, 1340
Meat Whiplash 1278
Meatmen 836, 1341, 1280
Meaux, Huey P. 518, 681, 972, 1015
Mecca Normal 1285
Medallions 1110
Medeiros, Glenn 145
Medeski, John 217
Medeski, Martin & Wood 217
Medley, Bill 628, 943, 969, 1325
Medlocke, Rick 108, 682
Medlocke, Shorty 107
Medora, Eddie 1102
Medress, Hank 829, 1146
Meehan, Tony 1310
Meek, Joe 8, 536, **720**, 1106, 1149, 1275, 1281, 1311
Mega City Four 38
Megadeth 632, 635, **720**, 721, 768, 993, 1020, 1021, 1340
Mehta, Zubin 22
Meid, Lothar 25, 26
Meier, Dieter 1254, 1255
Meine, Klaus 982
Meisel, Steven 686
Meisner, Randy 346, 347, 869
Mekons 42, 131, **721**, 722, 744, 1338
Mel & Tim **722**
Melanie 317, **723**, 769, 770, 1018, 1285
Melberg, Rose 1039
Melcher, Terry 167, 936, 1301
Melendez, Lisette 1281
Mellencamp, John Cougar 6, 7, 91, 96, 363, 375, 377, 424, 460, 490, 539, **723**, 724, 784, 930, 969, 1093, 1344, 1353
Mello, Dave 823
Melodians 1356
Melouney, Vince 85, 86
Melton, Barry 258
Meltzer, Richard 116, 311
Melvin, Eric 804
Melvin, Harold **724**, 732, 850, 1013, 1335
Melvin, Harold & the Blue Notes 724, 1013, 1290
Melvins 115, 486, 802, 803, 1295
Melvoin, Mike 1199
Melvoin, Susannah 1215
Melvoin, Wendy 747, 1215, 1216
Members **724**
Members [1] 724
Memphis Bleek 581
Memphis Horns 696, 1069, 1324
Memphis Minnie 92, 1350
Memphis Slim 147, 477
Memphis Symphony Orchestra 937
Memphis Willie B. 1233
Men at Work **725**, 1338, 1342
Men in a Suitcase 214
Men Without Hats **725**, 1051
Menck, Ric 1188
Mendel, Nate 1102
Mendes, Carlos 1293
Mendes, Sergio 778
Mendoza Line **725**, 726
Mendoza, Vince 101, 747
Mengede, Peter 520
Menswear 82, **726**
Menta, Dean 389
Mental As Anything **726**, 727
Menton, Todd 642
Menza, Nick 721
Mercer, Chris 401
Mercer, Glenn 399
Mercer, Johnny 571, 693
Merchant, Jimmy 680
Merchant, Natalie 138, 259, **727**, 728, 858, 1126, 1127, 1344
Mercurius, S. Flavius 507
Mercury Rev 506, 671, 679, **728**, 1049, 1050, 1217
Mercury, Freddie 214, 429, 495, 903, 904, 905, 1004
Mercy [1] 1296

Merman, Ethel 1092
Merrick 31
Merrick, Bryn 279
Merrill, Bob 1091
Merritt, Jymie 1018
Merritt, Stephin 443, 680, 688, 689, 1018
Merriweather, Big Maceo 93
Merry Go Round 63, **728**, 938, 1287
Merseybeats 349, 716, **728**, 1230, 1319, 1320
Merseys 134
Merton Parkas **729**, 1095, 1287, 1298
Mesaros, Mike 1032
Mesmerize, Eric 875
Messiaen, Olivier 1289
Messina, Jim 665, 666, 869, 870, 1314, 1327
Metal Church 1302
Metallica 31, 131, 194, 274, 591, 605, 615, 616, 720, 721, **729**, 730, 735, 742, 768, 816, 834, 839, 889, 903, 904, 977, 993, 1020, 1021, 1067, 1131, 1133, 1148, 1219, 1302, 1340
Metcalfe, Andy 530, 531, 930
Meters 131, 139, 326, 333, 436, **730**, 731, 791, 838, 871, 1151, 1274, 1284, 1288, 1306, 1334
Metheny, Pat 747, 1330
Method Man 278, 362, 372, 458, 464, **731**, 911, 926, 970, 1018, 1246
Metoff, Mike 'Tommy Gun' 836
Metro [1] 135
Metz, Ron 981, 982
Metzger, Bob 706
MEV 1289
Meyer, Mandy 40
Meyer, Russ 262, 774
Meyer, Skip 1002, 1003
Meynell, Kevin 1066
Meynell, Tony 1066
MFSB **732**, 1309
MG's 696
Miall, Terry Lee 31
Miami Horns 1046
Miami Sound Machine 377
Mic Geronimo 323
Michael [1] 982
Michael, George 431, 597, 696, **732**, 837, 869, 905, 1217, 1325
Michaeli, Mic 378
Michaels, Bret 823, 872
Michaels, Dave 544
Michaels, Hilly 1050
Michaels, Jesse 823
Michaels, Lee **732**, 733
Michel, Prakazrel 'Pras' 437, 529, 582
Mickey & Sylvia 59, **733**, 752
Mickey Finn 1113
Microdisney 527
Microstoria 771
Middleton, Andy 35
Middleton, Malcolm 34, 35
Middleton, Mark 108
Middleton, Max 84
Midgett, Tim 272, 1006, 1007
Midler, Bette 266, 302, 602, 691, 693, 790, 849, 892, 1199, 1200, 1295
Midnight Oil 576, **733**, 734, 865, 1110, 1342
Midnight Star 49
Midnighters [1] 59
Mighty Baby 6, 210, **734**, 735
Mighty Mighty Bosstones 686, **735**
Mighty Wah! 1197
Miguel, Luis 1098
Mihm, Danny 409
Mike & The Mechanics 186, 187, **735**, 736
Mike D [Michael Diamond] 1210
Mike Stuart Span 1277, 1280
Milburn, Amos 1273, 1304
Milchem, Glenn 117
Miles, Buddy 522, 976, 1329
Miles, John 844, 986
Milhizer, Bill 415, 416
Milkshakes 210
Milla **736**
Milla, Roger 736
Millennium [1] 41, 122, **736**, 737
Millennium [2] 737
Miller Brothers 305
Miller, Adam 173

Miller, Ben 305
Miller, Billy 8
Miller, Charles [2] 1206
Miller, Daniel 327, 1038
Miller, Donald 149
Miller, Floyd 1020
Miller, Gene 924
Miller, Glenn [1] 211
Miller, Jay 1274
Miller, Jerry 749
Miller, Jimmy 297, 768, 888, 1153
Miller, John 153
Miller, Mark [1] 470
Miller, Phil 182, 703
Miller, Rhett 820
Miller, Robin 404, 618
Miller, Roger [Country] 308, 744, 893
Miller, Roger [Rock] 744
Miller, Ron [2] 1239
Miller, Scott [1] 447, 671, 672, 1344
Miller, Steve [1] 181, 182, 715, **737**, 738, 980, 1286, 1297, 1326
Miller, Steve [1] Band 737, 980
Miller, Vern 67
Milli Vanilli 125, **738**, 1310
Milligan, Malford 599
Million Bill 399
Million, Bill 399
Mills Brothers 227, 355, 1207, 1303, 1306
Mills, Crispian 895
Mills, Gordon 602
Mills, Kevin 415
Mills, Mike [1] 930, 931, 1269
Mills, Russell 1111
Mills, Ted [1] 1096
Milne, A.A. 588
Milsap, Ronnie 526, 1293
Milton, Roy 1304, 1305, 1294
Mimms, Garnet 514, **738**, 739, 1106, 1207, 1324
Mindbenders 423, 475, 1301, 1313
Miner, David 159, 484
Miner, Tim 487
Ming, Leslie 150
Mingus, Charles 84, 256, 477, 747, 851, 1330
Ministry 164, 295, 435, 627, 640, **739**, 938, 1019, 1021, 1219, 1275, 1284, 1287, 1345, 1346
Mink DeVille 1278
Minnear, Kerry 458
Minogue, Kylie 194, **739**, 740, 1226, 1342
Minor Threat 580, 735, **740**, 742, 804, 823, 912, 918, 1021, 1279, 1339, 1341
Minutemen 217, 406, 719, 740, 741, 742, 830, 876, 1005, 1007, 1174, 1210, 1340, 1341
Miracle Legion 1344
Miracles 184, 427, 534, 700, 946, 947, 1280, 1307, 1314, 1324
Mirwais 687
Misfits 281, 729, 730, **742**, 1340
Missing Links [1] **742**, 1341
Missing Links [2] **742**
Missing Persons [1] **743**, 1029, 1338
Mission [UK] **743**, 744, 1017, 1287, 1346
Mission of Burma 612, **744**, 930, 1006, 1192, 1197, 1257, 1278
Mista Lawnge 106
Mister Big [1] 958, 1302
Mister Bungle 389, **744**, 745
Mister Cee 97
Mister Clean [2] 1268
Mister Dibbs 647
Mister Fingers 1299
Mister Mister 1212 ... **745**
Mister Scruff 971
Misty in Roots 969
Misunderstood **745**, 1323
Mitchell, Blue Richard 179
Mitchell, Bobby 227
Mitchell, Brandon 496, 1244
Mitchell, Chad 299
Mitchell, Elizabeth 555
Mitchell, James [Sax] 415, 487
Mitchell, Joni 26, 57, 62, 149, 238, 239, 240, 270, 284, 298, 299, 308, 316, 327, 342, 386, 388, 477, 518, 551, 558, 559, 601, 654, 705,

717, **745**, 746, 747, 751, 869, 914, 963, 980, 986, 1036, 1037, 1092, 1093, 1119, 1187, 1215, 1263, 1328, 1330
Mitchell, Keith 823
Mitchell, Liz 125
Mitchell, Mitch [1] 521, 720, 1106, 1218
Mitchell, Phillip 1283
Mitchell, Willie 224, 408, 486, 487, 488, 849, 850, 981, 1245, 1283
Mix Master Mike 647
Mixmaster Morris 76
Mixtures [1] 1300
Mobb Deep **747**, 748
Moby 638, **748**, 1286
Moby Grape 191, 200, 331, 470, **748**, 749, 772, 773, 975, 1053, 1264
Mockers **749**
Mockers [1] 749
Mockingbirds [2] 476
Model Five Hundred 383, 1299
Modern English 680, **749**
Modern Jazz Quartet 694, 1329
Modern Lovers 173, 468, 941, 942, 1194, 1336
Modest Mouse 158, **750**
Mods 1287
Moebius 369
Moebius, Dieter 368, 790
Moerlen, Benoit 473
Moerlen, Pierre 473, 474
Moerlen, Pierre's Gong 473, 474
Moffat, Aidan 35
Moffatt, Katy 21
Moffett, Peter 160
Mofungo 981
Mogwai 65, **750**, 751, 1023
Mohawk, Essra **751**
Mojave Three **751**, 1025
Mojo Men **751**, 752, 1026, 1187, 1344
Mojos 631, 1319, 1320
Mokran, Peter 412
Mole, Adam 874
Moles [1] 183, 284, 705
Molina, Ralph 264, 1260
Molko, Brian 865
Molla, Chris 177
Molland, Joey 54, 55, 566, 1339
Molloy, Mick 87
Molly Hatchet **752**, 1333
Molo, John 539
Moloko 501, **752**
Moman, Chips 136, 186, 696, 882, 937, 1136, 1236, 1237
Mombassa, Reg 726, 727
Moments 569, **752**, 1027, 1028, 1096
Momus 687, **752**, 753, 754, 1018
Monahan, Thom 854
Monasterio, Juan 139
Money Mark 154
Money, Eddie **754**
Money, Zoot 45, 281, 1316, 1275
Money, Zoot Big Roll Band 281
Monger, Jamie 827
Monger, Timothy 827
Monica [1] 140
Monk, Meredith 1117
Monk, Thelonious 1247
Monkees 35, 60, 126, 136, 152, 216, 226, 308, 310, 315, 491, 619, 726, 727, **754**, 755, 788, 789, 846, 932, 937, 1084, 1212, 1246, 1273, 1275, 1276, 1296, 1298, 1311, 1331
Monkey Mafia 278
Monks [1] **756**
Monks [2] 393
Monks of Doom 177
Monn, Anthony 643
Monochrome Set **756**
Monotones 1306
Monroe, Bill 8, 432, 715, 1308, 1351
Monroe, Bill [1] 820
Monroe, Marilyn 159
Monroe, Vaughn 453, 834
Monster Magnet **757**, 906
Montage [60's] 645, 1086
Montana, Country Dick 21, 77
Montana, Vince 732
Montanas 1289

Montand, Yves 1092
Montez, Chris **757**, 916
Montgomery, Andrew 235
Montgomery, Bob 534
Montgomery, Little Brother 114, 1049
Montgomery, Melba 893
Montgomery, Roy 65, 420
Montoya, Craig 379
Montrose 396, 497, **757**, 758, 799
Montrose, Ronnie 497, 757
Monty Python 127, 225, 229, 968, 1146
Monty Python's Flying Circus 127
Mood Six 759
Moodists 319
Moods 1155
Moody Blues 22, 64, 85, 86, 185, 290, 310, 330, 364, 456, 515, 555, 617, 673, **758**, 759, 772, 782, 883, 893, 1089, 1090, 1286, 1317, 1320, 1330, 1331
Moody, James 59
Moog, Bob 7
Moon, Keith [1] 279, 474, 797, 1062, 1105, 1152, 1220, 1221, 1222, 1314, 1322
Moon-Eye 251
Moondog 96
Mooney, Malcolm 178
Mooney, Ralph 1032
Moonglows 535, **759**, 793, 1274, 1306
Moonlighters 759
Moonshake 638
Moorcock, Michael 515
Moore, Angelo 406
Moore, Ben 901
Moore, Dudley 126
Moore, Eric [1] 469
Moore, Gary [1] 1134
Moore, Jackie 819, 1298, 1300
Moore, John [2] 102
Moore, John [Drums] 102
Moore, Johnny [2] 338
Moore, Kid Prince 21
Moore, Larry 732
Moore, Leroi 704
Moore, Mandy **759**, 760
Moore, Melba 732, **760**
Moore, Merrill 410
Moore, Paul Joseph 115
Moore, Pete 946
Moore, Phil 59
Moore, R. Stevie 127
Moore, Rudy Ray 97, 1287
Moore, Sam [1] 974, 975, 1063
Moore, Samuel 975
Moore, Scotty 159, 512, 853, 880, 881, 882, 883, 1090, 1295, 1307
Moore, Sean 740
Moore, Sparkle 1301
Moore, Terry 211
Moore, Thurston 63, 217, 305, 319, 927, 1040, 1041, 1210
Moore, Wild Bill 1162
Moors Murderers 1195
Moose 200, **760**
Moose [1] 760, 761, 1283
Moped, Johnny 1337
Morali, Jacques 1194
Moran, Pat 478
Moraz, Patrick 759, 1256
Morcheeba 168, 567
Moreland, Bruce 1204
Moreland, Marc 1204
Morello, Tom 889, 912
Moreno, Chino 295
Moretti, Joe 1510
Morgan, Ed 245, 246
Morgan, Hite 75
Morgan, Scott [1] 919
Morgan, Scott [1] Band 919
Morgenstein, Rod 322, 1231
Mori, Romi 494
Morillo, Erick 'More' 68
Morissette, Alanis 10, 313, 377, 538, 556, 612, 704, **761**, 814, 1071
Morley, Paul 429
Morning Mist 190
Moroder, Giorgio 373, 497, 498, 545, 1050, 1051, 1101, 1286

Morphine **761**, 762
Morricone, Ennio 7, 164, 175, 216, 279, 288, 745, 761, 1203, 1204
Morris, Chris [1] 416
Morris, Dave [1] 194, 1342
Morris, Joe [1] 1110
Morris, Keith [1] 217, 218
Morris, Kenny 1014
Morris, Kevin 325
Morris, Owen 38
Morris, Roger 896
Morris, Stephen 604
Morris, Walter 569
Morris, Wiley 1017
Morrison, Jim 103, 153, 170, 193, 249, 281, 332, 333, 350, 492, 556, 698, 763, 767, 798, 802, 1031, 1172, 1341
Morrison, Lindy 467, 468
Morrison, Patricia 1017
Morrison, Sterling 679, 1188, 1189, 1190
Morrison, Van 61, 62, 152, 257, 261, 295, 307, 326, 334, 336, 375, 403, 420, 451, 526, 530, 582, **762**, 763, 764, 765, 840, 973, 980, 989, 992, 996, 1037, 1061, 1062, 1081, 1106, 1131, 1136, 1208, 1209, 1232, 1308, 1316, 1325, 1328, 1329, 1354, 1355
Morrison, Walter 'Junie' 226
Morrissey 40, 90, 135, 236, 252, 263, 307, 320, 352, 455, 501, 575, 592, **765**, 766, 803, 816, 828, 999, 1033, 1034, 1099, 1343, 1346, 1347
Morrissey, Bill 1353
Morse, Steve 292, 322, 611, 682, 1141
Mortimer 183
Morton, Jelly Roll 540
Morton, Jelly Roll Red Hot Peppers 1335
Morton, Rockette 180
Morton, Shadow 552, 794, 998, 1184, 1312
Mos Def 140, 608, **766**, 957
Moscheles, Gary 774
Mosely, Chuck 388, 389, 658
Moses, Pirkle Lee Jr. 357
Mosher, Skip 1211
Moskowitz, Dorothy 1175
Mosley, Bob 733, 749
Mosley, Ian 697
Moss, Buddy 868
Moss, David 470
Moss, Ian 234
Moss, Jennie 720
Moss, Joel 1037
Moss, Ronn 868
Mosser, Jonell 230
Mosson, Cordell 441, 843
Most, Mickie 29, 30, 330, 331, 524, 774, 903, 1224
Motels [1] 766, 767, 1279, 1338
Mother Gong 473
Mother Love Bone 486, **767**, 848, 1125, 1293
Mothersbaugh, Bob 306
Mothersbaugh, Mark 306
Motley Crue 249, **767**, 768, 872, 1128, 1249, 1302
Motorbass 278
Motorcycle Boy 1003
Motorhead 195, 305, 563, 635, 729, **768**, 769, 832, 866, 875, 1100, 1286, 1302, 1332
Motors 204, 319, 338, **769**, 1121, 1278
Mott the Hoople 52, 134, 190, 216, 293, 294, 335, 484, 546, 547, **769**, 770, 904
Mottola, Tommy 184, 500
Mould, Bob 470, 479, 492, 510, 548, 549, 671, 761, **770**, 771, 1018, 1043, 1099, 1142, 1328, 1340, 1343
Moulder, Alan 277, 586, 680
Moulding, Colin 338, 1250, 1251, 1252
Moulton, Tom 612, 838
Moulton, Victor 64
Mountain 411, **771**, 1302
Mouse & the Traps **771**, 1287, 1297
Mouse on Mars 528, **771**, 772, 790, 1150
Moutenot, Roger 600
Mouzon, Alphonse 123
Move 204, 405, 525, 544, 745, **772**, 773, 784, 1241

Move [1] 204, 358, 555, 556, **772**, 773, 1057, 1241, 1242, 1288, 1322, 1339
Move [2] 773
Mover, Jonathan 697, 978
Movietone 419, **773**
Moving Pictures [80s] 978
Moving Sidewalks **773**
Moxham, Stuart 1258
Moxy 123
Moyet, Alison 372, 373, 1159, 1254
Mozart, Wolfgang Amadeus 797
Mu 395, 557, **773**, 774
Mu Ziq **774**, 990
Mud [1] **774**
Mudcrutch 856, 857
Mudhoney 11, 115, 396, 486, 510, **774**, 775, 924, 1048, 1282, 1293, 1295, 1345, 1346
Mueller, Jeff 607
Muggleton, Paul 979
Muggs [1] 277, 552
Mugwumps 584, 691
Muir, Jamie 617
Muir, Mike 1100
Muldaur, Jenni 965
Mullen, Larry Jr. 1169
Mullins, Larry 875, 896
Mumps [1] **775**, 1278
Mundi, Coati 614
Mundy, Ronald 697
Mungo Jerry 556, **776**
Munky 632
Munson, John 1160
Murdoch, Stuart 90
Murmaids 1312
Murph 315
Murphey, Michael Martin 675, 933
Murphy, Alan 650
Murphy, Chris [1] 1024
Murphy, Chris [Sloan] 1024
Murphy, Daniel 1043
Murphy, Eddie 953
Murphy, Jeff 703, 1002, 1003
Murphy, John [1] 1002, 1003
Murphy, Peter 69, 70, 71, **776**, 777, 1112
Murphy, Rian 1008, 1034
Murphy, Roisin 501, 752
Murphy, Shaun 660
Murray, Anne 666, 1230
Murray, David [2] 563, 564
Murray, Juggy 1164
Murray, Larry 519
Murrell, Sally 1212
Murvin, Junior 223, 1356
Musburger, Mike 396
Muscle Shoals Horns 430, 639
Muse, David 405
Music Explosion **777**, 802
Music Machine **777**, 1321, 1288, 1298
Music Tapes 699
Musick, Scott 175
Musicology 1273
Musselwhite, Charlie 114
Mussorgsky, Modest Petrovich 364
Mustaine, Dave 720, 721, 729
Mutantes **777**, 778, 876, 1288
MX Eighty 232
MX Eighty Sound 232
My Bloody Valentine 65, 120, 127, 128, 142, 200, 205, 235, 252, 276, 315, 419, 449, 538, 585, 656, 671, 680, **778**, 779, 837, 864, 911, 942, 943, 990, 1005, 1024, 1025, 1110, 1278, 1347
My Dad Is Dead 1302
My Life Story 779
My Life with the Thrill Kill Kult **779**, 780, 1284
Mydland, Brent 481, 539
Myers, Dave [1] 1277, 1301
Myers, Mike 1240
Myhr, Ken 259, 1005
Mylar, Marc 642
Myrick, Don 348
Mystery Girls 1197
Mystic Tide **780**, 1321
Mystics [1] **780**, 1307

N

N Joi 935
N Sync 11, 12, 51, 377, 760, **781**, 849, 1014, 1052, 1115
Nabors, Jim 1293
Naftalin, Mark 114, 163, 711, 908
Nagano, Kent 1267
Nagel, Ron 526
Nagle, Chris 269
Nagle, Julia 394
Nails 207
Nakamura, Dan 475, 501
Naked City 130
Naked Eyes 609, **781**, 1288
Naked Raygun 580
Names 1289
Namlook, Pete 867
Nanan, Angus 589
Nance, Todd 207
Nanna, Bob 139
Napalm Death 1340
Napier-Bell, Simon 595, 1217
Napolitano, Johnette 53, 245, 934, 1248
Narcizo, David 1142
Nas 248, 323, 747, **781**, 782, 911, 1023, 1246
Nascimento, Milton 1013
Naser, Hani 658
Nash, Graham 269, 270, 375, 533, 534, 829, 1082, 1093, 1119, 1260
Nash, Johnny 291, **782**, 1276, 1355, 1356
Nash, Leigh 1017
Nashville Teens 350, **782**, 783, 1090
Nastanovich, Bob 1007, 1008
Nasty Nas 782
Nathan, David 39, 430, 711
Nathan, Syd 145
Nation of Ulysses 100, 689, **783**, 1285
National Health 703, 1038
Native Hipsters 1292
Natz 250
Naughty by Nature **783**, 1274
Navarro, Dave 63, 579, 876, 922
Navetta, Frank 302, 303
Naysmith, Graeme 837, 838
Nazareth 495, **783**, 784, 1020
Nazz 249, **784**, 964, 965, 1124
NdegeOcello, Me'Shell 559, 614, **784**, 785
NDour, Youssou 207
Neal X 20
Neats 1278
Ned's Atomic Dustbin **785**
Needs, Kris 278
Neel, Johnny 17
Neff, John 579
Negativland 397
Negoescu, Craig 707
Negron, Chuck 1141
Negroni, Joe 680
Neil, Christopher 736
Neil, Fred 81, 126, 138, 153, 168, 308, 316, 395, 503, 544, 583, **785**, 786, 799, 800, 830, 1053, 1082, 1318, 1328, 1353
Neil, Linda 216
Neil, Vince 370, 767
Neill, Ben 1301
Neilson, John 171
Nelsen, Wayne 661
Nelson [1] 121
Nelson, Bill 82, 171, 336, 417, 808, 1019, 1111
Nelson, Bill Red Noise 1283
Nelson, Brett 157
Nelson, Chris 981
Nelson, Earl 121, 535
Nelson, Gabe 172
Nelson, Jeff 740, 1279
Nelson, Mark 636
Nelson, Mark [1] 637
Nelson, Mark [2] 637
Nelson, Nate 412
Nelson, Oliver 1070
Nelson, Rick [1] 241, 262, 310, 395, **786**, 787, 1308, 1309, 1310, 1327
Nelson, Rick [1] & the Stone Canyon Band 786
Nelson, Ricky 148, 227, 263
Nelson, Sandy 1308, 1297
Nelson, Sean 510

Nelson, Shara 701
Nelson, Tracy [1] 1350
Nelson, Willie 56, 203, 376, 401, 460, 487, 747, 787, 930, 968, 972, 976, 1261
Nemcova, Michaela 900
Neme, Tom 991
Nemes, Les 498
Neon Boys 520
Neon Philharmonic **788**, 1289
Neotropic 1019
Neptunes [2] 582, 820
Neruda, Pablo 1017
Nerves [1] 189, **788**, 1278, 1339
Nervosa, Theresa 163
Nervous Eaters 1278
Nesmith, Michael 126, 705, 706, 754, 755, **788**, 789, 1084, 1275
Nesmith, Michael & the First National Band 788, 789
Ness, Mike 1037
Nessa, Chuck 753
Netson, Brett 157
Nettlebeck, Uwe 398
Nettles Sisters 1301
Neu 131, 211, 771, **789**, 790, 827, 1074
Neumann, Kurt 121, 122
Neumeier, Mani 369
Neutral Milk Hotel 34, 362, **790**, 821, 1289
Neuwirth, Bob 159, 189
Neville Brothers 526, **790**, 791, 792, 1223, 1306
Neville, Aaron 731, 790, **791**, 956, 1151, 1223, 1243, 1274, 1278, 1288, 1299
Neville, Art 730, 790, 946, 1223
Neville, Charles 790, 1223
Neville, Cyril 790, 1223
Neville, Naomi 144
Nevin, Mark E. 765
Nevins, Al 1311
Nevins, Jason 1108, 1293
Nevins, Nanci 1108
Nevison, Ron 50, 519, 719, 1133
New Age Steppers 1023, 1355
New Bohemians 142
New Bomb Turks 642
New Christs 910, 1342
New Christy Minstrels 184, 221, 716, 990
New Colony Six 272, **792**, 1321
New Duncan Imperials 8
New Dylans 424
New Edition 88, 89, 145, **792**
New Edition [US] 696, 792
New Grass Revival 892, 968
New Jersey Mass Choir of the GMWA 425
New Kids on the Block **792**, 1052, 1115, 1310
New Kingdom 892
New Lost City Ramblers 450
New Model Army 993
New Order [UK] 7, 100, 128, 290, 351, 360, 361, 604, 654, **793**, 827, 935, 1015, 1099, 1155, 1234, 1338, 1346, 1347
New Order [US] 446
New Power Generation 890, 891
New Race 910, 1341
New Radiant Storm King 1008
New Radicals **793**
New Riders of the Purple Sage 241, 470, 1327
New York City **793**, 794
New York Dolls 9, 20, 335, 415, 495, 520, 579, 595, 624, 770, 775, **794**, 822, 896, 916, 942, 964, 969, 1087, 1143, 1166, 1171, 1335, 1336, 1337
New York Rock & Roll Ensemble 385
New, Steve 874, 939
Newberry, Mickey 56
Newbury, Mickey 136
Newcleus 725, **794**, 1286
Newcombe, Anton 142
Newell, Martin 224, 225, 629, **794**, 795
Newey, Jon 366
Newgarden, David 963
Newley, Anthony 133, 134, 135, 1059
Newman, Andy 1143
Newman, Carl 189
Newman, Colin 1233, 1234
Newman, David 'Fathead' 202, 203, 430
Newman, Floyd 924

Newman, Joe 508, 1163
Newman, Randy 6, 137, 231, 246, 254, 304, 308, 422, 451, 507, 544, 599, 600, 653, 654, 675, 705, 787, **795**, 796, 799, 800, 801, 842, 863, 887, 914, 962, 1002, 1059, 1060, 1070, 1092, 1119, 1137, 1141, 1198, 1199, 1200, 1202, 1211, 1312, 1328
Newman, Tom 607
Newmark, Andy 401, 1138, 1139
Newsham, Sean 908
Newsome, George 225
Newsted, Jason 729, 993
Newton, Adi 519
Newton, Juice 354
Newton, Wayne 1297
Newton-Howard, James 209, 597, 1081, 1094
Newton-John, Olivia 358, 359, 796, 797, 940
Nice [1] 363, 364, 394, 458, 617, **797**, 893, 1256, 1296, 1331
Nice, Pete 1134, 1135
Nicely, Ted 580, 1004
Nicholas, J.D. 243
Nicholls, Billy **797**
Nicholls, Sheila 797
Nichols, Bobby 676, 1225
Nichols, Geoff [1] [Black Sabbath] 105, 106
Nichols, Jay 678
Nichols, John 676
Nichols, Roger [Songwriter] 1225, 1226
Nichols, Todd 1146
Nicholson, Hugo 887
Nicks, Stevie 151, 412, 413, 414, 666, 691, 759, 797, 798, 1013
Nico [1] 19, 102, 149, 173, 503, **798**, 799, 1074, 1188, 1189, 1190
Nicol, Simon 386, 387, 388
Nicole [1] 376
Nicolette 701
Niedringhaus, Derek 977
Nielsen, Rick 204, 205, 335, 370, 396, 625, 703, 877
Nieman, Randall 1231
Nieve, Steve 254, 841, 1065
Night Ranger **799**, 805, 832
Night Train Clemons 514
Nighthawk, Robert 114
Nightingale, Maxine 1276
Nightmares on Wax 971, 1299
Nightriders 1298
Nilsson, Harry 54, 55, 113, 390, 417, 501, 507, 519, 535, 679, 736, 754, 761, 785, 787, **799**, 800, 801, 939, 1003, 1070, 1141
Nine Below Zero 613
Nine Inch Nails 33, 88, 234, 277, 301, 434, 435, 627, 698, 739, **801**, 802, 904, 912, 1019, 1021, 1284, 1345, 1346
Nine Nine Nine 1279
Nineteen Ten Fruitgum Company 646, 777, **802**, 816, 817, 1276
Ninety Eight Degrees 1014
Ninjaman 1356
Nips 1298
Nirvana [US] **802**
Nirvana [UK] 335, 396, 434, 449, 510, 757, 888, 1067, 1148, 1210
Nirvana [US] 14, 27, 38, 69, 95, 130, 160, 161, 164, 195, 235, 263, 301, 365, 379, 423, 472, 474, 484, 485, 520, 532, 542, 548, 599, 635, 639, 640, 662, 705, 719, 770, 774, 775, 802, 803, 816, 848, 863, 913, 924, 935, 984, 1018, 1020, 1021, 1024, 1028, 1029, 1040, 1044, 1059, 1085, 1124, 1128, 1131, 1176, 1185, 1192, 1233, 1262, 1282, 1285, 1293, 1295, 1336, 1339, 1340, 1344, 1345, 1346, 1347, 1350, 1353
Nitty Gritty Dirt Band 640, 665, 666, 1049
Nitzsche, Jack 153, 264, 304, 527, 657, 1259, 1261, 1296, 1297
Nix, Bern 197
Nix, Don 84, 696
Nixey, Sarah 102
Nixon, Mojo 21
Nkishi, Dodo 772
No Doubt 107, 407, 686, 735, **803**, 804, 1028
No.1 Y 130
Noble, Jason 910
Noble, Reggie 731

Noblemen 1298
Nobles, Cliff 1309
Nobody's Children 1297
NOFX 111, **804**
Nolan, Bob 747
Noland, Bill 1204
Nomad, Naz 804
Nomi, Klaus **804**
Nomiya, Maki 865
Noodles [1] 816
Noone, Peter 524, 525
Nordine, Ken 280, 1274
Norman, Chris [1] 903
Norman, Don And The Other Four 179
Norman, Larry 863
Norman, Max 832
Norris, Richard 401, 402, 897
Norris, Robbie 125
Nort 171
North, Christopher 22, 23
Northern Picture Library 402
Norton, Butch 355
Norton, Gil 91, 192, 352, 423, 837, 838, 864
Norton, Greg 510, 548
Norum, John 378
Norwood, Brandy 140
Nothing Painted Blue 1302
Notorious BIG 379, 581, 655, **804**, 805, 899, 900, 1167, 1273
Nova Mob 510
Nova, Aldo **805**
Novak, Todd 981
Novoselic, Chris 635, 639, 640, 803
Nowell, Brad 1098
Nowels, Rick 798
NPG 890
NRBQ 93, **805**, 806, 854, 896
Nu Shooz 1281
Nuese, John 561
Nugent, Ted 92, 116, 757, 799, **806**, 807, 934
Nuggets 70, 1343
Null, K.K. 829
Numan, Gary 68, 178, 300, 327, 369, 633, 688, **807**, 808, 838, 973, 1018, 1286
Numbers Band 470
Nunley, Chris 960
Nunn, Terri 92
Nuns 375
Nuriddin, Jalaluddin Mansur 640
Nuss, Otto 945
Nutter, Alice 214
NWA 323, 324, 350, 372, 463, 552, 554, 632, 664, **808**, 809, 811, 898, 962, 1284, 1349
Nyasuma, Mamadi 678
Nye, Steve 1111
Nyman, Michael 162, 320, 368
Nyro, Laura 113, 403, 404, 475, 552, 602, 751, 784, **809**, 810, 958, 1084, 1092, 1141, 1285, 1328
Nystrom, Lene Grawford 34
Nyswonger, Bob 76

O

Oakenfold, Paul 503, 696
Oakes, Richard 1098, 1099
Oakey, Philip 519, 545
Oakland Symphony Chamber Chorus 763
Oakley, Berry 17, 1333
Oasis 38, 94, 120, 190, 235, 334, 351, 358, 360, 442, 466, 472, 503, 562, 575, 649, 695, 726, 740, **811**, 812, 1081, 1103, 1109, 1115, 1157, 1214, 1226, 1278, 1322, 1346, 1347
Oates, John 499, 500
O'Bannon, Matthew 361
O'Bannon, Wink 361
O'Brien, Brendan 611, 850, 1059, 1107
O'Brien, Deke 87
O'Brien, Derek 1037
O'Brien, Sean [1] 241
Ocasek, Ric 51, 112, 187, 188, 493, 942, 1101
Ocean Colour Scene 333, **812**, 1157, 1214
Ocean, Billy 560, **812**
Ochs, Michael 813
Ochs, Phil 222, 238, 341, 386, 390, 504, 551, 653, **812**, 813, 814, 1123, 1232, 1259, 1318, 1328, 1353, 1354
O'Conner, Jimmy 979

O'Connor, Frank [2] 814
O'Connor, Mark 160
O'Connor, Sinead 232, 288, 312, 559, **814**, 815, 890, 956, 1006, 1242, 1345, 1354, 1355
O'Day, Alan 1061
Odds [1] 1298
O'Dell, Dennis 536
O'Dell, Kenny 1296
O'Doherty, Peter 726, 727
Of Montreal 376, 484, 699, **815**, 816
O'Farrill, Chico 1070
Off Broadway 1278
Offspring 303, 804, **816**, 917, 1037, 1098, 1339, 1345, 1346
Ogermann, Claus 475
Ogilvie, Dave 698, 1019
Ogilvie, Gordon 1082
Ogino, Kazuo 463
Ogoin, Bobby 1213
O'Gormain, Reamann 1130
Ogre, Nivek 295, 1019
Oh OK 1107, 1344
O'Hagan, Sean 527, 528, 1075
O'Hara, Catherine 816
O'Hara, Mary Margaret 207, 383, **816**
O'Hare, Brendan 750, 1123
O'Hearn, Patrick 743, 1266
Ohio Express 646, 777, 802, **816**, 817, 1276, 1332
Ohio Players **817**, 818, 1144, 1148, 1281, 1284, 1334
Ohno, Yumiko 154
Oingo Boingo **818**
O'Jays 336, 340, 341, 650, 732, **818**, 819, 831, 1096, 1180, 1284, 1288, 1290, 1334, 1335
O'Keefe, Danny 149, 834
O'Keefe, Frank 834
O'Keefe, Johnny 875
Ol' Dirty Bastard 184, 464, 612, **819**, 820, 939, 970, 1246
Old & In the Way [1] 449
Old Ninety Sevens **820**
Oldfield, Mike 44, 45, 474, 607, 974, 1296, 1331
Oldfield, Sally 736, 974
Oldham, Alan 645
Oldham, Andrew Loog 37, 389, 1027, 1166, 1284
Oldham, Andrew Loog Orchestra 37, 999
Oldham, Ned 837
Oldham, Spooner 136, 245, 645, 901, 937, 1263, 1287
Oldham, Will **820**, 821, 837, 868
O'Leary, Carolyn 983, 984
O'List, Davy 797
Olive, Pat 540
Oliver, Gwen 536
Oliver, Karin 529
Oliver, Troy 465
Oliver, Vaughan 161
Oliveri, Nick 634, 906
Oliveros, Pauline 368, 1041, 1289
Olivia Tremor Control 34, 95, 362, 376, 790, **821**, 1285
Olney, David 956
O'Lochlainn, Ruan 87
Olsdal, Stefan 865
Olsen, Keith 50, 777
Olsen, Rick 92
Olson, Carla 221, 222, 996
Olson, Gary 637, 638
Olson, Mark 582, 1227
Olson, Mark [Jayhawks] 582
Olympics [1] 328, **821**, 822, 919, 1276, 1282
Omaha Sheriff 979
O'Maonlai, Liam 21, 405
Omartian, Michael 666
Onallee 1018
Onassis, Blackie 1176
Once Dreamt 1231
Ondras, Charlie 131
One Hundred and One Strings Orchestra 1074
One Hundred Proof (Aged in Soul) 195, 645, **822**, 828
One In A Million 1277
One O Oners **822**, 1335, 1337
One Twelve 861, 899

One [US] 227, 357, 665
O'Neil, Tara Jane 241
O'Neill, Damian 1130
O'Neill, Jimme 1130
O'Neill, Keith 190
O'Neill, Sean 1130
O'Neill, Tina 1163
Onlookers 1298
Only Ones [1] 366, **822**, 1278
Ono, Yoko 47, 131, 255, 365, 446, 447, 647, 648, 649, 979
Onyx **822**, 823, 1279
Onyx [1] 822, 823
Opal 711, **823**, 913, 1344
Operation Ivy **823**, 917
Opitz, John 537
Oppenheimer, Rusty 802
Optical [1] 471
Orange Juice 45, 82, 235, 237, 238, 467, **823**
Orange Nine mm 520
Orb 373, 579, **824**, 874, 971, 1273, 1286, 1347
Orbison, Roy 159, 193, 198, 233, 263, 296, 381, 471, 487, 532, 534, 564, 565, 785, 786, **824**, 825, 863, 881, 882, 955, 982, 1112, 1157, 1203, 1231, 1282, 1292, 1295, 1307, 1308
Orbison, Roy [1] 508
Orbit [1] 687
Orbit [2] 687
Orbit, William 121, 687, 830
Orbital 373, 471, **825**, 826
Orchestral Manoeuvres in the Dark 244, **826**, 827, 1137, 1286, 1291
Orff, Carl 367
Organisation 632
Organization 124
Organized Noize 833, 834
Organum 829
Orgy [1] 282
Origin Unknown 1018
Original Brothers and Sisters of Love **827**, 828
Original Mirrors 654
Original Surfaris 1301
Originals [1] **828**
Orioles 608, **828**, 1303, 1306, 1351
O'Riordan, Cait 160, 870
O'Riordan, Dolores 263, 760
Orlando [1] **828**
Orlando, Tony **829**, 1310
Orleans **829**, 1286
Ormsby, Buck 1042
O'Rourke, Jim 398, 451, 452, 528, 580, 751, **829**, 830, 879, 923, 1041, 1075, 1104, 1171, 1178, 1258, 1299
Orphanage 1133
Orpheus [1] **830**
Orr, Benjamin 747
Orrall, Frank 871
Orridge 1142
Orton, Beth 383, 602, 701, **830**, 831
Orwell, George 1139
Orzabal, Roland 1122
Os Mutantes **777**, 778
Osborn, Joe 185, 186
Osborne, Billy 678
Osborne, Gary 597
Osborne, Jeffrey 678, **831**
Osborne, Joan 559, **831**, 1089
Osborne, Joe 1011
Osborne, Steve 276, 503
Osbourne, Ozzy 105, 106, 183, 249, 632, 799, **831**, 832, 939, 1208
Osgood, Chris 1043
Oskar, Lee 1206
Osman, Diid 1022
Osmond Brothers 328
Osmond, Donny 620, 837
Osmonds 16, 294, 495, 1331
O'Snodaigh, Ronan 288
O'Sullivan, Gilbert 101, **832**
Other Four 1298
Other Half 392, 1299
Otis, Clyde 92
Otis, Johnny 6, 218, 219, 507, 832, 833, 1286, 1296, 1297, 1305
Otis, Shuggie **832**, 833

O'Toole, Mark 429
Ottewell, Ben 472
Otto, John 656
Ouimet, Dave 250
Outfield **833**
OutKast 362, **833**, 834, 1023
Outlaws [1] **834**, 1333
Outlaws [UK] 1311
Outrageous Cherry **834**, 835
Outsiders [Cleveland] 565, **835**
Outsiders [Netherlands] **835**
Oval 1149
Owen If 1074
Owen, Gorwel 476
Owen, Malcolm 969
Owen, Mark 1115
Owens, Buck 21, 167, 487, 938, 1032, 1294, 1303
Owens, Donnie 517
Owens, Robert 860
Owens, Tim 'Ripper' 605
Owens, Wilson 969
Oyewole, Abiodun 640
Oysterband 1354, 1355
Ozark Mountain Daredevils **835**, 1327, 1333
Ozomatli 608

P
P Funk 237, 441, 843
P Funk All Stars 226, 314, 442, 833, 843, 844
P-Orridge, Genesis 896, 897, 1142
P-We YY 130
P. Diddy 900
Pablo Cruise **836**, 1286
Pablo, Augustus 1064
Pace, Amedeo 111
Pace, Simone 111
Pacers 158
Pachelbel, Johann 842
Pack, David 22, 23
Packers 696
Padgham, Hugh 271, 336, 873
Pagans [1] **836**
Page & Plant **836**, 837
Page, Ian 988, 989, 1066
Page, Jimmy 84, 103, 115, 177, 230, 304, 389, 416, 477, 484, 506, 507, 537, 644, 645, 660, 662, 745, 836, 866, 932, 1029, 1078, 1106, 1131, 1161, 1166, 1243, 1253, 1254, 1256, 1284, 1322
Page, Patti 149
Page, Richard 745
Page, Steven 65, 66
Page, Walter 1163
Pahinui, Gabby 246
Paice, Ian 292, 293
Paich, David 1150
Paich, Marty 203, 1150
Paige, Jennifer **837**
Pailhead 740
Pajo, David 821
Pakula, Lenny 732
Pakulski, Jan Marek 416
Palace [1] 436, 820, 821, **837**, 1023
Palace Brothers 820, 837, 868
Palao, Alec 1271
Pale Saints **837**, 838
Paley Brothers 1278
Paley, Andy 504, 525, 942, 1228
Palm Fabric Orchestra 871
Palmer, Bruce 155
Palmer, Carl 39, 40, 363, 364, 797
Palmer, David [1] 588, 1072
Palmer, David [Jethro Tull] 588
Palmer, Earl [1] 44, 67, 68, 609, 1306
Palmer, Robert [1] 62, 240, 217, 244, 250, 660, 730, 731, 819, **838**, 839, 849, 1151, 1281, 1325
Palmolive 1023
Pamer, John 1161
Pandoras 1321
Pankow, James 209
Panozzo, Chuck 1097
Panozzo, John 1097
Pansy Division 557
Pantera 521, 632, **839**
Papa M 636

Papas Fritas **839**, 840
Pape, Ben 160
Pappalardi, Felix 395, 551, 771, 785
Parachute Club 1290
Paradinas, Mike 774
Pardo, Don 1266
Pariah [1] 720
Paris Sisters 1052
Parish, John 95, 511
Park, Sooyoung 232
Parker, Alan [1] 445
Parker, Alister 57
Parker, Charlie 706, 846, 1064, 1274
Parker, Clive 97
Parker, Graham 211, 230, 354, 571, 601, 678, 786, **840**, 841, 962, 1002, 1081, 1295, 1335, 1338, 1356,
Parker, Jeff [1] 566
Parker, Jeff [2] 1150
Parker, Junior 425, 883, 1295, 1297, 1305, 1352
Parker, Maceo 146, 147, 226, 287, 291, 313, 582, 663, 843, 1334
Parker, Maceo & All the King's Men 582
Parker, Maceo & the Macks 147, 582
Parker, Mimi 676, 677
Parker, Peter [2] 319
Parker, Ray [1] Jr. 841
Parker, Robert [1] 67, **841**, 842
Parker, Roger 1020
Parker, Tom [1] 881, 882, 883
Parkin, Ian 82
Parks, Van Dyke 73, 81, 153, 160, 189, 211, 246, 247, 403, 507, 528, 653, 654, 752, 788, **842**, 858, 1198, 1227
Parks, VanDyke 842
Parliament 177, 226, 237, 248, 314, 324, 418, 434, 440, 441, 442, 582, 631, **842**, 843, 844, 926, 1020, 1117, 1120, 1148, 1241, 1284, 1334
Parliaments 226, 894
Parr, John 745
Parris, Fred 408
Parrish, Man 804
Parrish, Mark 322
Parsons, Alan 23, 659, **844**, 845
Parsons, Alan Project 23, 176, 359, 844, 845
Parsons, Bill 1282
Parsons, Dave 998
Parsons, Gene 167, 168
Parsons, Gram 57, 67, 75, 117, 166, 167, 168, 255, 346, 406, 418, 419, 524, 525, 561, 582, 646, 667, 668, 721, 788, **845**, 846, 1217, 1282, 1285, 1286, 1327, 1343
Partch, Harry 935
Partington, Darren 355
Parton, Dolly 189, 349, 543, 667, 955, 956, 1301
Partridge Family 417, 433, 535, **846**, 924, 1331
Partridge, Andy 225, 327, 338, 655, 794, 795, 1250, 1251, 1252
Parypa, Andy 1042
Parypa, Larry 1042
Pasemaster Mase 286, 287
Passarelli, Kenny 1205
Passenger 233
Passion Killers 214
Passions [US] 822
Pastels [1] 77, **846**, 1003, 1004, 1124
Pastorius, Jaco 547, 746, 747, 1330
Pate, Johnny 557
Paterson, Alex 824, 1273
Patino, Juan 664
Patrick, Kevin 1155
Patterson, Jim 307
Pattinson, Les 350, 351
Patton, Big John 1329, 1330
Patton, Charley 193, 1069, 1350
Patton, Mike [1] 388, 389, 744, 745, 993
Patty & the Emblems 1301
Paul, Alan 17
Paul, Billy 700, **846**, 847
Paul, Clarence 1239
Paul, Henry 834
Paul, Les 353, 428, 1303
Paul, Steven 1232
Pauling, Lowman 407

Paulus, George 1224
Pavarotti, Luciano 501
Pavement 95, 158, 177, 191, 272, 319, 478, 492,
    671, 690, **847**, 1007, 1058, 1108, 1118, 1124,
    1145, 1212, 1218, 1233, 1258, 1280, 1283,
    1300, 1344, 1345, 1346
Pawlett, Yvonne 391
Paxton, Tom 57, 238, 298, 308, 317, 772, 990
Paycheck, Johnny 289, 394
Payne, Bill 18, 659, 660, 914
Payne, Christopher 724
Payne, Davey 799
Payne, Freda 11, 195, 645, 822, **847**
Payne, John 39, 762
Peach Cobbler 963
Peaches & Herb **847**, 848
Peacock, Adam 545
Peacock, Olly 472
Peacock, Sarah 990
Peake, Andy 243, 244
Peanut Butter Conspiracy 1172
Pearce, Dave 420
Pearcy, Stephen 920
Pearl Jam 161, 434, 472, 479, 484, 486, 542,
    611, 703, 704, 767, 774, 775, **848**, 849, 1021,
    1028, 1085, 1125, 1210, 1227, 1262, 1293,
    1295, 1344, 1345, 1346, 1347
Pearlman, Louis J. 51
Pearlman, Sandy 51, 116, 222
Pearls 253
Pearls Before Swine 464, **849**
Pearson, Jack 19
Peart, Neil 966, 967
Peaston, David 68
Pebbles [1] 49, 50, 379, 1145
Pedder, JOhn 48
Pedersen, Chris 177
Peebles, Ann 459, **849**, 850, 1240, 1283
Peel, John 31, 70, 127, 153, 165, 225, 244, 269,
    392, 419, 468, 581, 657, 745, 756, 864, 1024,
    1134, 1212
Peeples, Philip 820
Pegg, Bob 191
Pegg, Dave 334, 386, 387, 388, 588, 589, 1139
Pegrum, Nigel 588, 1072
Pela, Mike 971
Peligro, D.H. 289
Pellington, Mark 1216
Peluso, Tony 185
Pender, Mike 987
Pendergrass, Teddy 620, 724, **850**, 1013, 1335
Penguin Cafe Orchestra 1117
Penguins 268, **850**, 1268, 1274, 1275,
    1282, 1306
Penn, Dan 136, 137, 159, 186, 245, 645, 901,
    1106, 1137, 1287
Penn, Leo 850
Penn, Michael 391, **850**, 851, 1065, 1204
Pennebaker, D.A. 29, 301
Pennell, Joe 945
Penney, John 785
Pennywise 111, 1346
Pentagons 787, 1291
Pentangle 153, 334, 477, **851**, 878, 974, 1090,
    1319, 1354, 1355
Pentland, Patrick 1024
People's Choice 1276
Peppas, Mel 543
Peppers 921, 922
Peraza, Armando 975, 976
Pere Ubu 107, 252, 287, 305, 470, 545, 618,
    744, 776, 789, **851**, 852, 853, 923, 981,
    1109, 1132, 1286, 1291, 1292, 1336, 1337,
    1338, 1356
Perez, Danilo 641
Perez, Louie 670, 831
Perfect Disaster 141
Perfect, Christine 412, 413
Periz, Louie 641
Perkins Brothers 854
Perkins, Al [1] [Guitar] 418, 796
Perkins, Al [2] 845
Perkins, Carl [Jazz] 806, 1050, 1295
Perkins, Carl [Rock] 78, 80, 263, 714, 786, 805,
    824, 825, **853**, 854, 883, 944, 994, 1273,
    1292, 1295, 1301, 1304, 1307, 1308,
    1350, 1351

Perkins, James 1110
Perkins, Jay 854
Perkins, Stephen 579, 876
Perko, Lynn 557
Perlman, Marc 524
Pernice Brothers **854**
Pernice, Joe 854
Peron, Carlos 1255
Perrett, Peter 366, 822, 1143
Perrey, Al 700
Perrson, Hans 415
Perry, Brendan 287, 288, 461, 1136
Perry, Doane 589, 928
Perry, Guy 766
Perry, Jeffree 1229
Perry, Joe 9, 10, 11, 625, 962, 1348
Perry, Joe Project 10
Perry, Lee [1] 'Scratch' 76, 824, 1355, 1356
Perry, Lee [2] 898
Perry, Lee [3] 393
Perry, Richard 451, 741, 800, 1010, 1070,
    1092, 1093
Perry, Robert 288
Perry, Steve [1] 603, 604, 666, 1150
Persson, Nina 183, 321, 1050
Persuaders [1] **854**
Peshay 471, 860, 1290
Pet Shop Boys 68, 144, 243, 360, 592, 654,
    852, **854**, 855, 935, 986, 1051, 1059, 1226
Peter & Gordon 195, 222, 349, 755, **855**, 990,
    1165, 1175, 1293, 1317, 1320
Peter Paul & Mary 299, 532, 534, 653, 1084
Peter, Paul & Mary 299, 341, 990, 1353
Peterik, Jim 555
Peters, Adam 235
Peters, Bernadette 963
Peters, Dale 576
Peters, Dan 396, 775
Peters, Joey 479
Peters, Jon 1093
Peters, Linda 298, 387, 1138
Peters, Mike 13, 14
Petersen, Paul 1275, 1289, 1296
Peterson, Debbi 63
Peterson, Dickie 115
Peterson, John 507
Peterson, Oscar 694
Peterson, Ray 1297, 1310
Peterson, Robert 716
Peterson, Vicki 63
Petersson, Tom 204, 205, 245
Petrucci, John 1181
Pettibone, Shep 793
Pettiford, Oscar 202, 203, 507
Pettigrew, Charles 1147
Pettus, Kenny 286
Petty, Norman 534, 535
Petty, Tom 7, 52, 97, 132, 166, 335, 343,
    380, 490, 508, 525, 703, 723, 747, 786,
    797, 798, 825, 840, **855**, 856, 857, 892,
    996, 998, 999, 1007, 1071, 1081, 1157,
    1166, 1225
Petty, Tom & the Heartbreakers 855, 856, **857**,
    1107, 1204
Peverett, Lonesome Dave 421, 979, 980
Pew, Tracy 99, 193
Pezband 857, 1278, 1290, 1339
Pfeifer, Bob 545, 546
Pfeifer, Rob 546
PFM [1] 1331
Phair, Liz 191, 543, 638, 693, 761, 814, **857**,
    858, 1130, 1192, 1280, 1300, 1328,
    1345, 1346
Phantom Tollbooth 126
Phantom, Slim Jim 1090
Pharcyde 140, 1158, 1274
Pharos 1301
Phelps, Joel 1006, 1007
Phife 766, 903, 1158
Phife Dawg 1158
Philadelphia 289
Philidor, Andre Danican 1224
Philip, Lynott 1133
Philippe, Louis 433
Phillinganes, Greg 219
Phillipps, Martin 211, 1343
Phillips, Anthony 456, 700

Phillips, Brewer 630
Phillips, Chynna 1228
Phillips, Doug 642
Phillips, Eddie 265, 1322
Phillips, Esther 14
Phillips, Glen 1146
Phillips, Glenn [1] 501
Phillips, Grant Lee 479, 531
Phillips, Jerry 892
Phillips, John [1] 690, 691, 945, 1228
Phillips, Knox 892
Phillips, Leonard Graves 309, 310
Phillips, Leslie 159, 858
Phillips, Martin 211, 1191
Phillips, Marvin 700
Phillips, Michelle 690, 1228
Phillips, Phil 191, 1297
Phillips, Ricky 50
Phillips, Sam [Singer] 159, 230, **858**, 859,
    1307, 1351, 1352
Phillips, Sam [Producer] 398, 652, 883,
    892, 1295
Phillips, Shawn 330
Phillips, Simon 1150
Phillips, Todd 511
Phillips, Utah 363
Philosopher Kings 442
Phiri, Ray 1012
Phish 506, 521, 660, 704, **859**, 860, 871
Photek 383, 471, **860**, 1018, 1290
Phuture 1299
Piano Red 652, 776
Piazza, Sammy 540, 541
Picciotto, Guy 112, 436, 437, 944
Pickerel, Mark 639, 984
Pickering, Mike 503
Pickett, Nick 414
Pickett, Philip 1139
Pickett, Wilson 128, 186, 224, 245, 258, 265,
    418, 549, **860**, 861, 919, 975, 1046, 1106,
    1137, 1207, 1236, 1261, 1281, 1284, 1287,
    1324, 1325, 1331, 1334, 1351
Pickup, Howard 9
Pieces of Eight 1110
Pierce 1048, 1057
Pierce, Adam 1110
Pierce, Jason 1047, 1048, 1056, 1057
Pierce, Jeffrey Lee 493, 494
Pierce, Nat 59
Pierce, Webb 514, 820
Pierson, Kate 47, 667, 875, 931
Pigpen [1] 482
Pilot, Felton 244
Pilson, Jeff 327
Pin Group 57
Pinchevsky, Jorge 473
Pinckney, Saint Clair 146, 147, 1334
Pinder, Michael 758, 759
Pine Valley Cosmonauts 722
Pink 861, 1081
Pink Fairies 211, 305, 306, 768, 1147
Pink Floyd 23, 34, 45, 52, 64, 65, 66, 67,
    134, 176, 177, 192, 211, 269, 279, 281,
    292, 305, 403, 411, 419, 463, 506, 515,
    605, 624, 726, 735, 745, 780, 784, 790,
    824, 835, **861**, 862, 863, 885, 886, 906,
    907, 910, 911, 979, 1038, 1039, 1089,
    1134, 1147, 1148, 1162, 1175, 1177, 1209,
    1210, 1235, 1240, 1270, 1273, 1277, 1280,
    1283, 1291, 1294, 1296, 1309, 1317, 1323,
    1330, 1331
Pinkerton, Peyton 1008
Pinkus, Jeff 164
Pion, Renaud 288
Pioneers 1027
Piper 98
Piper, Billie 98
Pipkins 161, 1332
Pippen, Lovetta Sharie 529, 530
Pips 628, 629
Pirates 338, 1311
Pirner, Richard 1043, 1210, 1227
Pirroni, Marco 30, 31
Pistilli, Gene 189
Pitcock, Bill 1166
Pitman, Jimmy 1089
Pitmon, Linda 1248

Pitney, Gene 19, 50, 193, 310, 535, 536, 610,
    669, 786, 788, **863**, 893, 994, 1052, 1207,
    1263, 1276, 1285, 1310, 1327
Pitt, Eugene 591
Pittman, Fred 297
Piucci, Matt 913
Pixies 27, 91, 95, 107, 141, 160, 161, 181, 280,
    315, 361, 467, 478, 479, 510, 548, 586, 690,
    802, 837, **863**, 864, 911, 1058, 1059, 1099,
    1192, 1214, 1292, 1345, 1346
Pixies Three 1282
Pizzaman 397
Pizzarelli, Bucky 780
Pizzarelli, John 602
Pizzicato Five 252, 433, **864**, 865, 1300
Place, Pat 197
Placebo **865**, 866, 1216, 1283
Plaid 1300
Plain Jane 1236
Plainsong 705, 706, 707, **866**
Plamondon, Luc 318
Planet Gong [1] 473
Planet, Janet 763
Plank, Conrad 369, 378, 548, 789, 1173
Plant, Robert 152, 367, 484, 491, 492, 518,
    537, 644, 767, 836, **866**, 1053, 1087, 1182,
    1243, 1256
Plasencio, J.J. 1017
Plasmatics [1] **866**
Plaster Caster, Cynthia 754
Plastic Bertrand **866**, 867
Plastic Fantastic 828
Plastic People of the Universe **867**, 900
Plasticland 867
Plastikman **867**, 868, 1273, 1292
Platt, John 114, 773
Platters 337, 535, **868**, 1070, 1207, 1306, 1307
Play [1] 615
Playboys 650
Player [1] **868**, 1286
Playford, Rob 471
Playmates 1293
Plaza, Martin 726, 727
Pleasure Barons 21
Plimsouls 189, 474, 788, **868**, 1290, 1343, 1344
Plone 1300
Ploog, Richard 215, 216
Plouf, Scott 157, 1121
Plugz 1279
Plunk, Jerry 411
Plush [1] **868**
Plytas, Nick 957
PM Dawn **868**, 869, 1219
Pobo, Kenneth 577
Poco 22, 68, 117, 155, 241, 406, 665, 666, 835,
    869, 870, 1286, 1327
Poe, Edgar Allan 70, 844, 936
Poets [1] 689, 1286
Pogues **870**, 871, 1212, 1354, 1355
Poi Dog Pondering **871**
Poindexter, Buster 595
Poindexter, Doug 1295
Poindexter, Steve 1299
Pointer Sisters 303, **872**, 1001, 1313
Pointer, Anita 872
Pointer, Bonnie 872
Pointer, June 872
Pointer, Mick 697
Pointer, Ruth 872
Poison 370, 793, **872**, 1067, 1231, 1281, 1302
Poison Idea 183
Poison Ivy 262, 263
Pole [2] 636
Polhemus, Art 688
Police 49, 240, 260, 281, 336, 618, 725, **872**,
    873, 889, 899, 969, 1083, 1084, 1102, 1109,
    1121, 1267, 1316, 1338, 1355
Politicians 196
Pollard, Robert 492, 493
Pollard, Russ 988
Pollock, Jackson 898, 1084
Polvo 520
Polygon Window 1273
Pomus, Doc 7, 381, 384, 619, 780, 999, 1311
Poncia, Vini 625, 1070
Pons, Jim 643
Ponty, Jean-Luc 76, 1265

Poole, Brian 1158
Poole, Brian [1] 1071
Poole, Brian & the Tremeloes 574, 1076
Poole, Brian [1] & the Tremeloes 1157, 1158
Poole, Tony 1071
Poor Righteous Teachers 1274
Poovey, Joe 1294
Pop Group 96, 668, **873**, 899, 1023, 1338, 1355
Pop Rivets 210
Pop Will Eat Itself 785, **874**, 895
Pop [1] 875
Pop [U.S.] 766
Pop, Denniz 781
Pop, Iggy 42, 45, 66, 70, 107, 187, 188, 216,
    238, 306, 461, 486, 510, 526, 776, 858,
    874, 875, 973, 1021, 1085, 1086, 1202,
    1299, 1338
Pope John Paul II 814
Popp, Markus 771
Popper, John 119, 120, 502
Poppies 874
Poppy Family **875**, 876
Porcaro, Jeff 523, 1063, 1150
Porcaro, Steve 1150
Porch 889
Porno for Pyros 579, 777, **876**, 1210
Portastatic **876**, 1104
Porter, Cole 329, 581, 789, 848, 946, 999,
    1091, 1229
Porter, David 365, 515, 516, 860, 974, 975,
    981, 1106
Porter, John 138, 401
Porter, R.J. 1236
Porter, Sam 711
Portishead 357, 383, 442, 472, 556, 602, 638,
    701, 752, **876**, 877, 971, 1035, 1216, 1347
Portius, Bryce 979
Posdnuos 287
Posey, Sandy 678
Posies 396, 426, **877**, 878, 924, 1071, 1290,
    1339, 1344
Poss & Stenger 63
Poss, Robert 62, 63
Post, Louise 1192, 1193
Potak, Steve 246
Potatomen 273
Potter, Chris [Saxophone] 1216
Potter, Cipriani 151
Potter, Todd 151
Potts, Sylvester 246
Pound, Ezra 913
Powder [1] **878**
Powell, Andrew [1] 23
Powell, Andy [2] Jay 932, 1235
Powell, Bill [1] 683
Powell, Bud 540
Powell, Cozy 106
Powell, George 901
Powell, Jeff 984
Powell, Michael 431
Powell, Michael J. 58
Powell, Richard [Bass] 940
Powell, Roger [1] 734, 965
Powell, Scott 996
Powell, William 818, 819
Power Station 838, 839, 1080, 1195
Power, Duffy **878**, 1275, 1310, 1326
Power, J. 190
Power, John 190
Powerhouse [1] 1300
Powers, Kid Congo 193, 262, 493, 494
Powers, Walter 1275
Powles, Tim 216
Pram 420, 1299
Prarie Prince 585
Prater, Dave 974, 975
Prater, David 974, 975
Precoda, Karl 337, 361
Prefab Sprout 235, **878**, 879
Prekop, Sam 829, **879**, 985
Prelude Baroque 556
Premiers 328, 1261, 1276, 1281, 1300
Prescott, Jimmy 444
Prescott, Peter 744
Presence, Orson 756
Presidents of the United States of America
    396, **879**, 880, 1028

Preslar, Lyle 740
Presley, Elvis 8, 14, 18, 43, 59, 80, 84, 92, 108,
    130, 137, 139, 148, 159, 160, 174, 177, 193,
    198, 202, 203, 204, 212, 227, 233, 255, 259,
    263, 268, 281, 295, 328, 329, 341, 342, 376,
    401, 421, 429, 442, 450, 456, 498, 513, 534,
    535, 564, 569, 573, 595, 598, 610, 627, 652,
    661, 662, 715, 774, 786, 787, 789, 804, 813,
    824, 825, 828, 846, 853, 854, 879, **880**, 881,
    882, 883, 884, 892, 893, 904, 937, 940, 973,
    982, 983, 994, 1106, 1107, 1194, 1211, 1227,
    1241, 1243, 1267, 1278, 1282, 1286, 1291,
    1292, 1293, 1295, 1297, 1303, 1304, 1307,
    1308, 1309, 1310, 1311, 1314, 1316, 1317,
    1319, 1325, 1327, 1351
Prestia, Francis 1151
Preston, Billy 247, 428, **884**, 1026, 1070, 1160,
    1291, 1309
Preston, Johnny 96
Preston, Nigel 273
Pretenders [1] 94, 245, 360, 382, 621, 677, **884**,
    885, 1031, 1171, 1287, 1338, 1339
Pretty Face 1039
Pretty Poison 1281
Pretty Things 99, 134, 135, 144, 216, 257, 305,
    334, 387, 570, 702, 716, 835, **885**, 886, 1042,
    1067, 1147, 1235, 1284, 1288, 1291, 1296,
    1315, 1316, 1318, 1320, 1331
Previn, Andre 1203
Prevost, Eddie 829
Prewitt, Archer 829, 879, **886**, 985
Price, Alan 29, 30, **887**, 1315
Price, Lloyd 67, 532, 534, 647, 788, **887**, 1118,
    1224, 1227, 1274, 1278, 1294, 1300, 1303,
    1305, 1306
Price, Lon 36
Price, Mark 15
Price, Martin 355
Price, Rick 358
Price, Rod 421
Price, Steve [1] 836
Pride & Joy 1283
Pride, Charley 514, 971, 1015
Prieboy, Andy 245, 956, 1204
Priest, Maxi 409
Priestman, Henry 1253
Prima, Louis 994
Primal Scream 201, 400, 440, 726, 779, 824,
    887, 888, 971, 1081, 1278, 1299, 1347
Primates 1298
Prime Minister Pete Nice & Daddy Rich 1134
Prime Time 262, 1330
Primitives [1] 1287
Primrose, Neil 1157
Primus 27, 210, 656, **888**, 889, 977, 1334, 1345
Prina, Stephen 923
Prince 63, 68, 83, 122, 151, 162, 184, 208, 226,
    237, 256, 274, 278, 282, 314, 349, 375, 440,
    444, 465, 474, 499, 504, 506, 570, 593, 599,
    613, 614, 633, 634, 639, 665, 695, 707, 712,
    743, 747, 784, 808, 814, 869, **889**, 890, 891,
    892, 893, 940, 969, 983, 1141, 1144, 1145,
    1148, 1183, 1213, 1215, 1216, 1242, 1334
Prince & the New Power Generation 689
Prince & the Revolution 890, 1215
Prince Be 868, 869
Prince Buster 367, 1052
Prince Jazzbo 1356
Prince Markie Dee 396
Prince Paul 97, 286, 287, 501, **892**, 1076, 1135
Prince Rakeem 464, 819, 970, 1246
Prince, Prairie 965
Prince, Rod 151
Prine, John 57, 189, 259, **892**, 893, 914, 1286
Prior, Maddy 298, 477, 588, 1071, 1072
Priore, Domenic 663
Prisonaires 1295
Proby, P.J. 80, 420, **893**, 1293
Procol Harum 20, 162, 219, 416, 584, **893**,
    894, 1067, 1296, 1331
Prodigy [1] 37, 68, 85, 638, 747, **894**, 895, 1192
Prodigy [2] 748, 1286
Professor Longhair 326, 731, 841, **895**, 946,
    1151, 1278, 1286, 1305, 1306
Promise Ring 139, 462, 592, **895**, 896
Prong 1340
Propellerheads 608, 1198

Prophet, Billy 591
Prophet, Chuck 485, 486
Provost, Joe 711
Prudence, Steve 574
Pruter, Robert 298, 636
Pryce, Guto 1103
Pryor, Matthew 462
Pryor, Richard 953
Prysock, Red 507
Psi Com 578
Psychedelic Furs 156, 335, 470, **896**
Psychic TV 234, 752, **896**, 897, 1142
Psychodots 76
Public Affection 662
Public Announcement 613
Public Enemy 31, 32, 37, 128, 205, 226, 277,
    287, 324, 367, 372, 376, 406, 552, 554, 570,
    632, 664, 808, 834, **897**, 898, 899, 906,
    962, 1040, 1173, 1277, 1279, 1280, 1285,
    1348, 1349
Public Image Limited 178, 269, 376, 388,
    668, 822, 875, **898**, 899, 984, 1023, 1287,
    1331, 1355
Puckett, Gary & the Union Gap 533
Puente, Tito 975
Puerta, Joe 22
Puff Daddy 248, 379, 431, 581, 655, 766, 805,
    898, **899**, 1083, 1084, 1273
Puffy 748
Puleo, Philip 250
Pulnoc 867, **900**
Pulp 7, 35, 102, 320, 321, 442, 726, 752, 779,
    828, **900**, 901, 1299, 1347
Pulusha 990
Pumpkin 1279
Purcell, Henry 804
Purdie, Bernard 'Pretty' 641
Purdy, Bernard 409
Pure Morning 225
Pure Prairie League 24, 699, **901**,
    1286, 1327
Purify, Bobby 901
Purify, James 901, 1281
Purify, James and Bobby **901**
Purple Hearts [1] 988, 1278, 1298
Pursey, Jimmy 997, 998
Push Button Objects 1300
Push [1] 985
Pussy Galore 63, 83, 131, **902**, 960, 1053
Putnam, Jim 910
Putnam, Norbert 526, 1230
Pyke, M. 327
Pyle, Artimus 682, 683
Pyle, Pip 473, 474
Pylon 491, 673, **902**, 930, 1109
Pynchon, Thomas 671
Pyramids 1313, 1297

Q
Q [1] 1109
Q Bert 631
Q Tip 140, 278, 291, 544, 766, 782, **903**,
    1158, 1159
Quackenbush, Gary 1067
Quackenbush, Glenn 1067
Quando Quango 1289
Quarrymen 80, 1310
Quarterflash 903
Quasimodo Brothers 1242
Quatermass 1283
Quatro, Suzi **903**, 1339
Queen 187, 208, 252, 293, 383, 455, 495, 547,
    592, 605, 626, 730, 886, **903**, 904, 905, 906,
    956, 1005, 1050, 1087, 1177, 1179, 1184,
    1202, 1207
Queen Latifah 60, 607, 612, 663, 783, 892,
    905, 906, 1076, 1298, 1348, 1349
Queens of the Stone Age 28, 634, **906**
Queens, Hollis 131
Queensryche **906**, 907
Queralt, Steve 943
Quercio, Michael 1141
Quest, J. 245
Question Mark 907
Question Mark & the Mysterians 262, 683,
    907, 1087, 1320
Questlove 56, 957

Quickly, Tommy 1293
Quicksilver Messenger Service 521, 646, **907**,
    908, 1172, 1309, 1323
Quickspace **908**
Quiet Riot 831, **909**, 1020, 1302
Quiet Sun 1247
Quigley, Joe 664
Quik [2] 1286
Quine, Robert 235, 369, 520, 928, 929, 1107
Quinichette, Paul 59
Quinn, Brad 612
Quinn, Paul [1] 238, 1123
Quiver 705
Quotations 1240

R
Ra, Sun 103, 442, 508, 794, 805, 806, 824, 935
Rabbit, Jimmy 771
Rabid, Jack 1061
Rabin, Trevor 986, 1256
Rabkin, Eddie 1146
Race, Hugo 193
Rachel's 241, 530, **910**
Rachell, Yank 988
Rachmaninov, Sergei 184, 292
Radar Brothers 910
Rademaker, Brent 75
Radiants 1276
Radio Birdman 194, 195, **910**, 911, 1341, 1342
Radiohead 13, 83, 94, 225, 235, 321, 333, 334,
    442, 472, 478, 483, 556, 697, 847, **911**, 1005,
    1157, 1345
Radle, Carl 297
Radley, Kate 1056
Raekwon 458, 464, 731, 748, **911**, 912,
    1023, 1246
Raelettes 248
Rafferty, Gerry **912**, 1138, 1139
Ragamuffins 777
Rage Against the Machine 32, 448, 632, 873,
    888, **912**
Rage [1] 612, 1298
Raging Slab 1302
Ragnarok [1] 617
Ragogna, Mike 37, 841
Ragovoy, Jerry 57, 576, 914, 1059, 1118
Rahzel 957, 1018
Raiders [2] 937
Railroad Jerk 1300
Rain Parade 667, 668, 711, 823, **912**, 913,
    1141, 1343, 1344
Rain Tree Crow 579, 1111
Rainbow [1] 105, 292, 293, 316, 529, **913**
Rainbow, Chris 844, 845
Rainbows 258
Raincoats 655, 802, 822, **913**, 1023, 1355
Raindrops 1289, 1312
Rainer Maria **913**, 914
Raines, Annie 988
Rainey, Chuck 409
Rainey, Ma 1350
Rainford, Phil 16
Rainwater, Marvin 1243
Raisins 76, 88
Raitt, Bonnie 24, 66, 375, 526, 660, 806, 829,
    892, **914**, 915, 1151, 1208, 1350
Rakim 374, 615, 712, **915**
Ralphs, Mick 52, 53, 335, 769, 770
Ralske, Kurt 566
Ram Jam 646
Ram, Buck 868
Rambow, Philip 1231
Ramone, Dee Dee 916
Ramone, Joey 916, 917, 1233
Ramone, Johnny 396, 916, 917
Ramone, Phil 270, 594, 595, 666, 732, 1036
Ramones 45, 69, 107, 112, 165, 194, 195, 273,
    309, 310, 311, 324, 329, 396, 468, 486, 520,
    538, 554, 590, 635, 642, 668, 683, 742, 775,
    822, 855, 910, **915**, 916, 917, 921, 932, 934,
    954, 973, 1003, 1037, 1052, 1106, 1114,
    1167, 1174, 1234, 1278, 1286, 1336, 1338,
    1339, 1342
Ramos, Michael 122
Ramos, Patrick 1192
Ramrods 1296
Ramsay, Andy 8

Ramsey, Al 651
Ramsey, Mary 1126, 1127
Ramsey, Willis Alan 180, 240, **917**
Ranaldo, Lee 47, 599, 1040, 1041, 1210
Rancid 823, **917**, 918, 1037, 1346
Randazzo, Teddy 1275
Randolph, Boots 881
Random, Eric 171
Randy 795
Randy & the Rainbows 1336
Randy [1] 273
Raney, Jerry 77
Ranglin, Ernest 1356
Rank & File 314, 375
Rankin, Billy 783
Rankin, Kenny 1285
Rankin, Ned E. 490
Rankine, Alan 40
Ranking Roger 367, 404, 455
Ranks, Shabba 1349, 1356
Ransom, Ray 142
Rapeman 95, 1000
Rapp, Anthony 849
Rapp, Tom 464, 849
Rare Bird 1296
Rare Earth 264, 426, 989
Ras Kass 1246
Rascals 136, 328, 385, 511, 716, 822, **918**, 919,
    1060, 1308, 1325
Rashbaum, David 123
Raspberries 50, 55, 88, 184, 213, 417, 784,
    873, 877, **919**, 921, 961, 1002, 1188, 1290,
    1322, 1339
Raspberries [1] 919, 1002
Raspberries [2] 97
Rasputina 671
Rasted, Soren 34
Rat 785
Ratcliffe, Simon 68
Rathke, Mike 929
Rationals **919**, 990, 1067, 1131, 1325
Ratledge, Mike 66, 1038, 1039, 1224, 1329
Ratt 767, **920**, 1302
Ravan, Genya 287
Raven, Paul 616
Raven, Paul [1] 616, 617
Raven-Symone 362
Ravenstine, Allen 851, 852, 853
Ravishing Beauties 336
Raw Soul 711
Rawls, Lou 44, 568, **920**, 1334
Ray, Amy 558, 559
Ray, Andre 678
Ray, Gil 447, 672
Ray, Glen 668
Ray, Goodman & Brown 752
Ray, Harry 569, 752
Ray, Larry 834, 1112
Ray, Oliver 1031
Raydio 841
Raye, Don 93
Raymonde, Simon 231, 232, 494
Raynor, Scott 'Mad Dog' 111
Razaf, Andy 1091
Razzell, Alf 1210
Rea, Chris **920**
Rea, David 551
Rea, Jimmy Lloyd 1292
Reagan, Ronald 1180
Real Kids 942, 948, 1339
Real Roxanne 1179
Reb, Johnny 1341
Rebels 945
Rebennack, Mac 326, 763
Reckless Sleepers 999, 1000
Recoil [1] 301
Record, Eugene 208, 1229
Records 634, **920**, 921, 1278, 1290, 1339
Red Aunts 921
Red Cross 923
Red Hot Chili Peppers 63, 237, 314, 389, 407,
    573, 587, 656, 818, 876, 888, **921**, 922, 1076,
    1249, 1334, 1345
Red House Painters 676, **922**, 923
Red Krayola 171, 411, 852, **923**, 1280
Red Lorry Yellow Lorry 743

Red Noise 82
Red Rider 479
Red Snapper 771, 830
Redbone 191
Redbone, Leon 321
Redd Kross 217, **923**, 924, 1003, 1340
Redding, Noel 521
Redding, Otis 63, 90, 102, 118, 128, 148, 151,
    186, 196, 245, 264, 404, 418, 445, 486, 515,
    532, 569, 570, 860, 893, **924**, 925, 949, 973,
    975, 1027, 1035, 1069, 1070, 1079, 1136,
    1145, 1227, 1236, 1244, 1245, 1273, 1277,
    1287, 1294, 1295, 1324, 1325
Reddy, Helen 453, 625, 1226
Redman 278, 362, 372, 731, **926**
Redus, Richard 181
Redwood 1141
Reece, Alex 471
Reece, Christopher 1037
Reece, Jason 27
Reed, A.C. 336
Reed, Al 326
Reed, Bob 1156
Reed, Brett 917
Reed, Dizzy 495
Reed, Francine 675
Reed, Jerry 81, 889, 1347, 1292
Reed, Jimmy [1] 324, 334, 430, 540, 636, 643,
    745, 981, 996, 1243, 1262, 1299, 1352
Reed, Jimmy [3] 29
Reed, Larry 336
Reed, Lou 19, 28, 77, 135, 150, 173, 174, 235,
    258, 259, 317, 334, 337, 355, 357, 366, 399,
    400, 415, 438, 446, 468, 499, 546, 612, 638,
    679, 764, 798, 799, 846, 863, 923, **926**, 927,
    928, 929, 941, 969, 1048, 1088, 1107, 1188,
    1189, 1190, 1191, 1204, 1208, 1227, 1244,
    1248, 1261, 1275, 1292, 1299, 1347
Reeder, Scott 634
Reegs 196
Rees, John 725
Reeves, Jim [1] 1151
Reeves, Jim [2] 642
Reeves, Martha 699, 1314, 1315
Regal, Mara 142
Regan, Julianne 15, 16
Rego, Howard 979
Reich, Steve 320, 632, 935, 1056, 1289, 1301
Reid, Brenda 383
Reid, Jim 585, 586
Reid, Keith 893, 894, 1331
Reid, L.A. 140, 145, 569, 861
Reid, LA 861
Reid, Matt 92
Reid, Steve [3] 40
Reid, Terry 724
Reid, Vernon 663, 977, 1329
Reid, William 585
Reilly, Jim 1082
Reilly, Michael 901
Reilly, Mike 901
Reilly, Vini 350, 765
Reis, John 948
Reis, Kevin 948
Reisman, Marc 490
Reivers **930**
Rekow, Raul 976
Relf, Bob 121
Relf, Jane 932
Relf, Keith 657, 932
REM 97, 108, 109, 166, 199, 207, 208, 210,
    215, 227, 245, 246, 257, 286, 322, 337, 351,
    357, 375, 415, 465, 479, 491, 493, 511, 525,
    538, 541, 545, 548, 559, 562, 576, 580, 612,
    649, 665, 671, 673, 740, 760, 770, 775, 803,
    834, 858, 902, 911, **930**, 931, 934, 973, 984,
    1004, 1036, 1037, 1038, 1040, 1071, 1088,
    1089, 1107, 1109, 1146, 1156, 1160, 1174,
    1188, 1235, 1248, 1269, 1287, 1333, 1336,
    1338, 1343, 1344, 1345, 1346
Rema Rema 1136
Remains 67, 117, 222, 1321
Rembrandts 931, 932, 1290
Renaissance 932, 933
Renaldo & the Loaf 936
Renaldo, Don 732
Renay, Diane 1312, 1282

Renbourn, John 477, 506, 737, 851, 974, 1354
Renegade Soundwave 206, 874
Renegades [1] 1234
Reni 1084
Reno, Mike 674, 675
Rentals 107
Renwick, Tim 1078
REO Speedwagon 420, 745, 799, **933**
Reparata & The Delrons 1301
Replacements 11, 128, 212, 375, 385, 411, 474,
    475, 492, 548, 646, 665, 840, **934**, 935, 1037,
    1038, 1174, 1191, 1216, 1248, 1336, 1339,
    1340, 1341, 1343, 1344, 1345, 1346
Republica 895, **935**
Reputations 1298
Residents 211, 307, **935**, 936, 1254, 1335, 1338
Resnick, Randy 708
Retsin 241
Rev, Martin 1100, 1101
Revell, Graeme 188
Revell, Mark 554
Reverbs 1344
Revere, Paul & the Raiders 328, 360, 620, 804,
    936, 937, 1042, 1275, 1297
Reverend Horton Heat **937**, 938
Revillos 938, 1278
Revolting Cocks 739, **938**, 1019, 1284
Revolution 889
Revolver [1] 359
Revolving Paint Dream 1278
Rew, Kimberley 63, 531, 611, 1038
Rex [1] 607
Rexroth, Kenneth 1273
Reyes, Ronnie 923
Reynolds, Barry 390
Reynolds, Ben 210
Reynolds, Burt 1213
Reynolds, Debbie 210, 336
Reynolds, James 354
Reynolds, John [1] 814
Reynolds, Malvina 56, 238
Reynolds, Paul 417
Reynolds, Simon 66, 637
Reynolds, Tim 704
Rezillos 131, 257, 396, 691, **938**, 1278, 1279
Reznor 802
Reznor, Trent 234, 274, 625, 698, 801, 802, 874,
    1275, 1345
Rhinoceros 1291
Rhoads, Randy 831, 832
Rhodes, David 160
Rhodes, Emitt 386, 706, 728, **938**, 939
Rhodes, Louise [1] 355
Rhodes, Nick 339, 609
Rhodes, Phillip 465
Rhodes, Red 706, 788, 789, 1190
Rhodes, Robert 75
Rhodes-Chalmers-Rhodes 487
Rhymes, Busta 372, 805, 926, **939**, 1158
Rhys, Gruff 751, 1103
Rhythim Is Rhythim 1299
Rhythm Heritage 1285
Rhythm Method 687
Rhythm Orchids 629
Rhythm Rockers 1296
Rhythmx 631
Ribot, Marc 256, 390, 859, 1111, 1200
Rice, Jeff 1217
Rice, Mack 919, 1274
Rice, Ross 88
Rice, Tim 597, 1291
Rice, Tony 450
Rich Kids **939**, 1195
Rich, Buddy 126, 651, 921
Rich, Charlie 22, 212, 299, 787, 1295
Rich, Tony 140, **939**, 940, 1148
Richard Twenty Three 435
Richard, Cliff 198, 214, 381, 433, 762, 764,
    940, 1310, 1311
Richard, Cliff & the Shadows 240
Richards, Alec 191
Richards, Dave 866
Richards, Keith 4, 93, 102, 142, 312, 327, 335,
    389, 390, 415, 418, 573, 749, 863, 885, 924,
    940, 949, 950, 951, 952, 961, 1033, 1081,
    1086, 1143, 1200, 1240, 1285, 1315, 1320
Richards, Rick 460

Richards, Tom 960
Richardson, Barry 87
Richardson, Barry Band 87
Richardson, Colin 196
Richardson, Dawn 671
Richardson, Jack 492
Richardson, John [Drums] 612
Richardson, Karl 87
Richardson, Kevin [1] 51
Richardson, Scott 1067
Richbourg, John 1010
Richie, Lionel 242, 243, 700, **940**, 941
Richman, Jonathan 174, 210, 386, 446, 447,
    498, 616, **941**, 942, 995, 1188, 1194,
    1276, 1336
Richmond, Fritz 988
Richmond, Michael 673
Rick, Dave 126
Ricketts, David 271, 283
Rickfors, Mikael 533
Riddle, Nelson 955, 956
Ride 192, 510, 680, 778, **942**, 943, 1278, 1347
Ridgeley, Andrew 732, 1217
Ridgley, Andrew 1217
Ridgley, Tommy 1136
Rieger, Andrew 362
Rifkin, Joshua 238
Rigby, Amy **943**, 1000
Rigby, Will 286, 943, 981, 1036
Rigg, Diana 817
Righteous Brothers 6, 74, 121, 136, 328, 505,
    628, 918, 919, **943**, 944, 1052, 1063, 1078,
    1201, 1202, 1281, 1325
Riley, Billy 1292
Riley, Billy Lee 129, **944**, 1295, 1307
Riley, Dave 96
Riley, Marc 391, 392
Riley, Markell 1244
Riley, Paul 210, 211
Riley, Teddy [1] 108, 496, 572, 581, 632, 1016,
    1244, 1348
Riley, Terry 173, 174, 632, 1289
Riley, Timothy Christian 1147
Rin, Manda 99, 100
Ringenberg, Jason 580
Rio, Chuck 197
Riot Squad [1] 720
Riot [1] 1151
Rip Chords 1282, 1314
Rip Rig & Panic 207, 873, 899
Riperton, Minnie **944**, 1149, 1301
Ripley, Larry 802
Risbrook, Bill 150
Risbrook, Louis 150
Rising Sons [1] 246
Rising Storm 979, 1321
Rison, Andre 1145
Ritchie, Brian 1194
Rites of Spring [1] 112, 320, 580, **944**
Ritter, Rob 493
Ritter, Tex 237
Rittman, Todd 1178
Ritz, David 453, 819, 1236
Ritz, James 787, 788
Rivers, John [Producer] 672
Rivers, Johnny 403, 472, 678, 788, **944**, 945,
    1024, 1025, 1212
Rivers, Sam [2] 656
Rivieras [1] **945**, 1282
Rivileers 1280
Rivingtons 72, **945**, 1156
Rizzo, Rick 361
Roach, Archie 1342
Rob B. 1074
Roback, David 711, 823, 913, 1344
Roback, Steven 913
Robb Brothers 156
Robbins, Dennis 160
Robbins, Hargus 'Pig' 1213
Robbins, Ira 455, 773, 1003
Robbins, J. 160, 580
Robbins, Marty 50, 653, 1046, 1273
Roberson, Latavia 304
Robert & Johnny 1280
Roberton, Sandy 706
Roberts, Andy [1] 706, 707, 866
Roberts, Bob 191

Roberts, Greg 95
Roberts, Kim 720
Roberts, Mark [1] 191
Roberts, Matt 667
Roberts, Rick 405, 406, 418
Roberts, Rick [70's] 418
Roberts, Rocker 1197
Robertson, B.A. 736
Robertson, Brian 1133, 1134
Robertson, Ed 65, 66
Robertson, Justin 1099
Robertson, Robbie 56, 57, 61, 62, 115, 121, 175, 218, 219, 221, 257, 258, 308, 341, 342, 513, **945**, 946, 1070, 1081, 1223, 1230
Robey, Don 6, 1245
Robillard, Duke 384
Robins [1] 227
Robinson, Bert 87, 397
Robinson, Bob 333, 509
Robinson, Bobby 333, 568, 1059
Robinson, Chris 102, 103, 337
Robinson, Claudette 946, 947
Robinson, Dave [Drums] 87
Robinson, Dave [Producer #1] 319, 325, 1335
Robinson, David [Drums] 941, 942
Robinson, Dawn 366
Robinson, Fenton 980
Robinson, Mark [1] 517
Robinson, Rich 102
Robinson, Richard [1] 102, 103, 409, 410
Robinson, Ross 42, 656
Robinson, Sharon 233
Robinson, Simon 293
Robinson, Smokey 67, 129, 238, 246, 255, 278, 333, 367, 418, 427, 430, 450, 475, 534, 566, 569, 577, 680, 699, 709, 718, 924, 925, 940, **946**, 947, 1125, 1183, 1215, 1291, 1312, 1314, 1315, 1324
Robinson, Smokey & the Miracles 367, 401, 568, 918, 947
Robinson, Sylvia 569, 733, 752, 1100
Robinson, Tom [1] 597, **947**, 948, 1337
Robinson, Tom [1] Band 948, 1278
Roby, Dick 190
Roches 559
Rock A Teens [1] 1292, 1296
Rock Master Scott and the Dynamic 1284
Rock, Bob 274, 493, 615, 730, 767, 1173, 1192
Rock, Chris 892
Rock, Pete 782, 912, 915
Rock, Pete & C.L. Smooth 109
Rockenfield, Scott 907
Rocker, Lee 1090
Rocket from the Crypt 416, **948**, 949, 973
Rocket from the Tombs 287, 851, 853
Rocket [1] 287
Rockin' Ramrods 1275
Rockin' Vickers 410
Rockpile 353, 354, 472, 608, 673, 677, 678, 684, 726, 727, **949**
Rodan 241, 607, 910
Roddenberry, Gene 758
Rodford, Jim 35
Rodgers & Hammerstein 1091
Rodgers & Hart 259, 353, 690, 697, 1091, 1092
Rodgers, Jimmie [1] 381, 450, 765, 787, 980, 1292, 1303, 1307, 1308, 1353
Rodgers, Nile 47, 84, 135, 208, 339, 401, 402, 537, 561, 686, 958, 983, 1011, 1017
Rodgers, Paul 52, 53, 432, 491
Rodgers/Hart 603
Rodrigues, Amalia 442
Rodriguez, David [1] 675
Roe, Tommy 122, 144, 223, 424, 527, **949**, 1244, 1276, 1296, 1297, 1332
Roedelius 369
Roedelius, Hans Joachim 368, 790
Roemans 527
Roeser, Donald 116
Roeser, Eddie 'King' 1176
Roessler, Kira 103, 104, 406
Rogers, Bobby 946
Rogers, Jimmy 1352
Rogers, Kenny [1] 184, 349, 788, 941, 1135
Rogers, Kenny [1] & First Edition 876
Rogers, Lelan 1135

Rogers, Milt 1300
Rogers, Nile 208, 793
Rogers, Simon 392, 393, 654, 776
Rogerson, Roger 217, 218
Roland, Duane 752
Roland, Ed 236, 237
Rolie, Gregg 976
Rolling Stones 9, 10, 11, 14, 27, 29, 30, 37, 54, 56, 63, 66, 67, 84, 86, 92, 93, 98, 102, 103, 107, 114, 115, 116, 121, 124, 128, 129, 130, 135, 142, 146, 155, 163, 166, 181, 191, 195, 196, 200, 201, 213, 216, 217, 220, 233, 241, 244, 246, 258, 261, 267, 271, 272, 273, 284, 296, 311, 319, 322, 324, 327, 328, 329, 334, 336, 341, 343, 352, 360, 379, 384, 385, 387, 389, 390, 399, 401, 410, 415, 416, 418, 426, 454, 459, 460, 463, 468, 470, 475, 484, 489, 494, 495, 532, 534, 546, 547, 561, 562, 568, 573, 574, 576, 578, 580, 590, 624, 625, 635, 636, 642, 643, 659, 665, 672, 681, 683, 689, 694, 707, 708, 716, 723, 724, 728, 731, 737, 745, 749, 751, 752, 768, 769, 770, 784, 793, 794, 811, 840, 855, 856, 857, 863, 865, 871, 878, 885, 886, 887, 888, 889, 897, 912, 923, 924, 935, 936, 940, **949**, 950, 951, 952, 953, 954, 955, 960, 961, 968, 974, 989, 990, 996, 999, 1006, 1007, 1014, 1027, 1028, 1037, 1046, 1052, 1053, 1054, 1068, 1079, 1080, 1085, 1086, 1087, 1104, 1131, 1134, 1137, 1141, 1191, 1221, 1222, 1232, 1236, 1240, 1253, 1264, 1270, 1282, 1284, 1285, 1286, 1298, 1300, 1301, 1303, 1308, 1309, 1310, 1315, 1316, 1317, 1318, 1319, 1320, 1321, 1322, 1323, 1326, 1327, 1336, 1347, 1350, 1352, 1355
Rollins Band 663, 953, 954
Rollins, Henry 103, 104, **953**, 954, 1210, 1279, 1340
Rollins, Sonny 313, 477, 571, 951
Rollo 312
Rollo, Zoot Horn 180
Romancers 433, 1300
Romanski, Chad 977
Romanthony 278
Romantics [1] **954**, 1278, 1290, 1338
Romberg, Sigmund 1091
Rome, Harold 1091
Romeo Void **954**, 955, 1234
Romeo, Max 1356
Romeo, Tony 846
Romero, Chan 80, 1279, 1319
Romero, Tony 214
Romweber, Sara 649
Ron-Dels 1297
Rondinelli, Jim 361
Ronettes 291, 946, **955**, 998, 1052, 1289, 1311, 1312, 1313
Ronga, Bob 866
Ronnie & the Delinquents 326
Ronny & the Daytonas 1296, 1314
Ronson, Mick 70, 133, 134, 135, 136, 159, 294, 335, 490, 547, 595, 765, 770, 901, 926, 1280
Ronstadt, Linda 24, 93, 186, 254, 284, 309, 346, 380, 560, 658, 667, 788, 789, 791, 800, 855, 914, **955**, 956, 1046, 1084, 1110, 1126, 1182, 1260, 1262, 1269, 1285, 1286, 1327
Rooftop Singers 990, 1129, 1353
Roogalator 684, **956**, 957
Roomful of Blues 384, 385
Rooney, Corey 465
Rooney, Herb 383
Rooney, Jim 893
Roots [1] 56, 495, **957**, 1018
Roots, The 440, **957**, 983
Roper, Deidra 'Spin' 1184
Roper, Skid 172
Roper, Tim 338
Roper, Todd 172
Ropers 656
Rosas, Cesar 670
Rose Royce 686
Rose Tattoo 734
Rose, Axl 494, 495, 523, 963, 1087
Rose, Tim 137, 193, 356, 371, 673, 679, 772, 773
Roseman, Josh 957
Roses [1] 120

Rosie & Ron 1276
Roslie, Gerry 1042, 1218
Rosolino, Frank 44
Ross, Diana 39, 40, 304, 403, 453, 568, 600, 680, **957**, 958, 1105, 1215, 1219, 1299, 1314, 1315
Ross, Jackie 1276, 1301
Ross, Jerry 1049, 1122
Ross, Kirk 1068
Ross, Lucius Tawl 442
Ross, Malcolm 823
Ross, Michael 1258
Ross, Michael C. 1258
Rossdale, Gavin 161
Rosselson, Leon 1354
Rossington Collins Band 1333
Rossington, Gary 682, 683
Rossiter, Martin 455
Rotary Connection 944
Rotations 1268
Roth, David Lee 497, **958**, 959, 1181, 1182, 1183, 1302
Roth, Uli Jon 982
Rothchild, Paul 152, 914
Rother, Michael 789, 790
Rothery, Steve 698
Rothrock, Tom 1140
Rotten, Johnny 898, 994, 995, 1023, 1337
Rough Trade 127
Roulettes [1] 631
Roundabout 293
Rourke, Andy 999
Routers 1297
Rovell, Barbara 537
Rovell, Marilyn 537
Rovin' Kind 1283, 1288
Rowan, Peter 450, 1275
Rowberry, Dave 29, 30
Rowe, Dennis 150
Rowe, Hahn 545
Rowe, Hanny 474
Rowe, Keith 829
Rowe, Simon 200, 751
Rowland, Bruce 387
Rowland, Kelly 304
Rowland, Kevin 307, 308
Rowlands, Euros 476
Rowlands, Tom 205, 206, 476
Roxette **959**, 978
Roxy Music 2, 5, 8, 40, 102, 173, 186, 187, 339, 368, 369, 400, 401, 402, 579, 588, 638, 643, 687, 688, 797, 896, 900, **959**, 960, 1012, 1048, 1057, 1115, 1127, 1137, 1161, 1173, 1195, 1255, 1288, 1296, 1331, 1335, 1338, 1342
Roxy [1] 401
Roxy [2] 2, 401
Royal Coachmen 1296
Royal Crown Revue 994
Royal Guardsmen **960**
Royal Trux 489, 689, **960**, 961, 1053, 1283
Royal, Billy Joe 223, 666, 1046
Royalettes 1282
Royals 59, **407**
Royaltones 1282
Royer, Casey 1037
Royer, Robb 141
RTZ 132
Rubalcaba, Mario 948
Rubber Band 237
Rubicon [1] 403
Rubin, Jon 961, 962
Rubin, Rick 5, 273, 274, 281, 331, 416, 462, 463, 573, 574, 664, 702, 856, 857, 922, 1020, 1134
Rubinoos 961, 962, 1278, 1290
Rubinson, David 749, 976
Ruby & The Romantics 1301
Rucker, Darius 538
Rucker, Dwight 538
Rudolph, Paul 306
Rue, Jackie 568
Ruffin, David 246, 483, 569, 1125, 1126
Rufige Kru 1290
Rufus [1] 614, **962**, 1284
Ruin, Clint 234
Ruiter, Bert 420

Rumour 338, 840, **962**, 1107, 1335
Run DMC 10, 32, 664, 696, 754, 794, 822, **962**, 963, 1020, 1173, 1223, 1277, 1279, 1283, 1285, 1347, 1349
Run On **963**, 1300
Runaways [1] 329, 590, **963**, 1286
Rundblad, Anders 1234
Rundgren, Todd 54, 55, 88, 117, 132, 190, 204, 422, 478, 499, 501, 718, 784, 794, 838, 896, 947, 961, **964**, 965, 966, 999, 1031, 1050, 1161, 1162, 1179, 1180, 1230, 1250, 1251, 1285, 1290, 1301
Runt 964
RuPaul 598
Rupe, Art 661, 711, 887, 1224, 1294
Rupe, Bob 541, 673, 1248
Rupert's People 416
Rush [1] 103, 123, 441, 865, 888, **966**, 967, 968, 1024, 1148
Rush, Billy 1047
Rush, Bobby 1277
Rush, Joe 776
Rush, Merrilee 1289
Rush, Otis 414, 454, 708, 1163, 1164, 1185, 1352
Rush, Tom 1300
Rushakoff, Harry 245
Rushent, Martin 40, 165, 545, 1088, 1107
Rushton, Joe 897
Russell, Brenda 1184
Russell, Bruce 419
Russell, Graham 13
Russell, Jack [1] 484
Russell, Karl 544
Russell, Leon 5, 185, 221, 230, 297, 449, 512, 650, 651, 701, 801, **968**, 991, 1060, 1160, 1178, 1285
Russell, Mike 1004
Russell, Tom 21, 189, 363
Rutherford, Mike 186, 187, 456, 457, 735, 736
Rutherford, Paul [2] 429
Rutkowski, Deirdre 1136
Rutkowski, Louise 1136
Rutles 446, 589, **968**, 969, 1179, 1180, 1293
Rutmanis, Kevin 260
Rutner, Paul 775
Ruts 436, **969**, 1355
Ruts DC 969, 1023
Ryan, Jay 139
Ryan, Mark 908
Ryan, Nicky 371
Ryan, Roma 371
Rydell, Bobby 43, 624, 1309
Ryder, Mitch 918, 943, **969**, 970, 1208, 1281, 1293, 1325
Ryder, Mitch & the Detroit Wheels 969, 1281
Ryder, Shaun 104, 502, 503, 1074, 1346, 1347
Ryders 668
RZA 458, 464, 731, 805, 819, 820, 892, 911, 912, **970**, 1246
Rzeznik, Johnny 474, 475

S

Saadiq, Raphael 278
Saber, Danny 952
Sabres of Paradise **971**, 1078
Sacks, Leo 1120
Sacred Mushroom 901
Sad Cafe 735
Sadat X 501, 1158
Sade 382, 707, 877, **971**, 1109, 1227
Sadier, Laetitia 679, 771, 1074, 1075
Sadkin, Alex 425
Sadonius, Liesje 538
Saffery, Anthony 252
Saffron 895, 935
Safka, Melanie 723
Sage, Greg 1233
Sager, Carole Bayer 50, 691, 1094, 1228
Sagittarius [1] 41, 122, 736, **971**
Sahanaja, Darian 1240
Sahm, Doug 769, **972**, 1015, 1016, 1174
Saint Etienne 102, 262, 865, **972**, 973, 1216
Saint Holmes, Derek 807
Saint John, Chris 771
Saint John, Kate 250, 336, 337
Saint Louis Union 1286

Saint Victor, Sandra 3
Saint Werner, Jan 771, 772
Saint-Saens, Camille 804
Sainte-Marie, Buffy 308, 330, 643, 908, 1014, 1285, 1353
Saints [1] 194, 195, 279, 394, 467, 642, 910, **973**, 974, 1278, 1337, 1341, 1342
Sakamoto, Hiromichi 463
Sakamoto, Ryuichi 46, 579, 899, 1111
Salaam, Kalamu Ya 1120
Salazar, Arion 1135
Salem Sixty Six 834
Salem, Freddie 834
Salen, Jeffrey 1050
Sales, Hunt 874, 1144
Sales, Soupy 1144
Sales, Tony 874
Saliers, Emily 558, 559
Salley, Roly 892
Sally [Group] 974
Sally, Zak 676
Sallyangie **974**
Salmon, Kim 1342
Saloman, Nick 669
Salt N Pepa 366, 442, **974**, 1184, 1348, 1349
Salt Water Taffy 1276
Salvation Army 1141
Sam & Dave 121, 123, 128, 254, 401, 511, 515, 532, 817, **974**, 975, 1063, 1273, 1277, 1294, 1324
Sam the Sham & the Pharaohs 187, 1281, 1288, 1297
Sambora, Richie 124
Same 1298
Samhain 281
Samla Mammas Manna 1296
Sampedro, Frank 'Poncho' 264, 1260
Sample, Fred 1163
Sample, Joe 57, 382
Samson [1] 563
Samson, Pat 1178
Samwell-Smith, Paul 1076, 1077, 1078
San Francisco Symphony Orchestra 730
Sanborn, David 1119, 1151, 1202, 1209
Sanchez, Junior 68
Sanchez, Roger [1] 68, 397
Sancious, David 1062
Sandals [1] 1277
Sanders, Ed 437, 438, 813
Sanders, Jesse 1149
Sanders, Norman 1149
Sanders, Pharoah 348, 494, 641, 983
Sanders, Ric 388
Sanders, Richard 388, 589
Sanders, Sonny 1229
Sanderson, Nick 494
Sandin, Erik 804
Sandler, Harry 830
Sandman, Mark 761, 762
Sandmel, Ben 1232
Sandoval, Andrew 119, 755
Sandoval, Hope 586, 711, 823
Sandoz [2] 170
Sandpipers 842, 990
Sands, Evie 1275, 1291, 1313
Sands, Tommy [Pop] 1297
Santamaria, Mongo 1284, 1292
Santana 100, 162, 375, 420, 470, 474, 603, 708, 798, 799, 871, **975**, 976, 977, 1124, 1151, 1155, 1277, 1300, 1329
Santana, Carlos 380, 701, 891, 975, 976, 1277
Santana, Jorge 1277
Santiago, Herman 680
Santiago, Joey 107, 863, 864
Santo & Johnny 750, 1308
Sarge [1] **977**
Sargeant, Bob 448, 498
Sarzo, Rudy 832
Sasaki, Mamiko 865
Satan, Buck & the 666 Shooters 938
Satellites 285
Satellites [2] 459
Satie, Erik 368
Satori 1273
Satriani, Joe 292, 599, 959, **977**, 978, 1181, 1233
Saturday's Children 1283

Saturnine 376
Saunders, Doug 639
Saunders, Fernando 267, 390, 928, 929
Saunders, Mark [2] 196, 642
Saunders, Merl 449, 450
Saunders, Red 1162
Saunders, Ric 388
Saunderson, Ann 560
Saunderson, Kevin 560, 1286, 1299
Sausage 889
Saussy, Tupper 788
Sauter, Brenda 399
Savage Garden **978**
Savage Republic **978**, 979
Savage Rose **979**, 1296
Savage, Donna 211
Savage, Jan 989
Savage, Jon 449, 605, 1278
Savages [1] **979**
Savakus, Russ 551
Save Ferris 307
Savill, Christian 1025
Savoy Brown 210, 421, 683, **979**, 980, 1326
Savoy, Marc 12
Sawyer, Phil [2] 285
Sawyer, Ray 325, 326
Sawyers, Jim 1112
Saxa 367
Saxon, Sky 989, 990
Sayer, Leo 797, **980**, 1081, 1141, 1285
Sayles, Johnny 151
Sbragia, Jen 1039
Scabies, Rat 279, 804
Scaggs, Boz 385, 454, 737, **980**, 981, 1150, 1202, 1325, 1333
Scala 990
Scala, Ralph 118
Scales, Steve 1117
Scandal [1] 703, 1035
Scanlon, Craig 391, 392, 393, 394
Scarface [1] 462, 553, **981**
Scarlett, Willow 540
Scarnella 460
Scarpantoni, Jane 536, 559
Scene 1298
Scene Is Now **981**
Scenic 637
Schacher, Mel 478
Schaffer, Janne 1
Schaper, Bob 1166
Scharf, Stuart 1049
Scharin, Douglas 232, 607
Scheff, Jason 209
Scheff, Jerry 151, 160, 882, 1139
Schekeryk, Peter 723
Schellenbach, Kate 559, 679
Schenker, Michael 982
Schenker, Rudolf 982
Schermerhorn, Eric 875
Schickele, Karla 555
Schiff, Klaudia 655
Schifrin, Lalo 477, 865, 877, 920
Schilla, Tomas 900
Schilling, Peter 408, 867
Schlatter, Beat 656
Schlesinger, Adam 426, 566, 567
Schloss, Zander 217
Schmersal, John 139
Schmid, Robert 1109
Schmidt, Irmin 178
Schmit, Timothy B. 270, 346, 347, 523, 870, 1150
Schnapf, Rob 493, 1140
Schneider, Florian 632, 790
Schneider, Fred 47, 126
Schneider, Robert [1] 34, 484, 790
Schnell Fenster 606, **981**, 1110
Schnell, Claude 316
Schoenbeck, Scott 895
Schofield, Brian 196, 197
Schofield, Marcia 393
Scholz, Tom 132
Schon, Neal 53, 603, 604
Schoolly D 206, 1348
Schools, Dave 207
Schramm, Dave 536, 981, 982, 1257

Schramms **981**, 982
Schultzberg, Robert 865
Schulz, Mark 899
Schulze, Klaus [1] 1289
Schumann, Robert 1093
Schwalm, Jan Peter 369
Schwartz, Glenn 576
Schwartz, Will 557
Schwarz, Brinsley **143**, 144, 354, 472, 677, 678, 840, 841, 962, 986, 1287
Schwitters, Kurt 368
Schyffert, Henrik 1216
Sci-Fi Steven 100
Scientists [1] 1342
Scoppa, Bud 660, 1009, 1180
Scoppettone, Dick 507
Scorchers 580
Score, Mike 417
Scorpions [1] 107, 327, **982**, 1302
Scorsese, Martin 440
Scott Four 55
Scott [1] 224
Scott, Andrew 1024
Scott, Bon 3, 4, 5, 1341
Scott, Clifford 1308
Scott, Doc 471, 860
Scott, Douglas [1] 854
Scott, Freddie 620, 1275, 1289
Scott, Gloria 1026
Scott, Jack **982**, 983, 1292
Scott, Jack [1] 982, 983
Scott, Jill 1, **983**
Scott, Julian 684
Scott, Ken [1] 743
Scott, Luke 48
Scott, Mike [1] 97, 1208, 1209, 1242
Scott, Raymond 1289
Scott, Robert 69, 224, 1018
Scott, Robin 684, 956
Scott, Sherry 348
Scott, Tom 509, 746, 1093, 1202, 1215
Scott, Tom & the L.A. Express 57, 509
Scott, Wally 1203
Scott, Winfield 108
Scott-Heron, Gil 380, 479, **983**, 1330, 1347
Scottsville Squirrel Barkers 519
Scraping Foetus off the Wheel 1284
Scratch Acid 586, 1345
Scrawl 11, **983**, 984, 1292, 1302
Screaming Target 95
Screaming Trees 77, 379, 639, 640, 906, **984**, 985, 1210, 1282, 1293, 1295
Screaming Tribesmen 910, 1342
Scritti Politti **985**
Scroggins, Marie 376
Scroggins, Renee 376
Scroggins, Valerie 376
Scruffs 1339
Scud Mountain Boys 854
Sea and Cake 451, 829, 879, 886, **985**
Sea Level [1] 322, 1333
Seahorses 1084
Seal **985**, 986
Seals & Crofts 197, 565, 566, **986**, 1286
Seals, Jim 197, 366, 986
Seals, Melvin 450
Seals, Son 1352
Seaman, Dave 740
Searchers 106, 118, 227, 272, 349, 378, 513, 598, 631, 636, 643, 728, 921, 979, **986**, 987, 990, 1278, 1312, 1317, 1318, 1319, 1320, 1339
Sears, Al 383
Sears, Pete 416, 584, 585
Sebadoh 48, 284, 315, 422, 771, 803, 837, 847, 908, **987**, 988, 1344, 1346
Sebastian, John 230, 238, 653, 654, 676, 785, 786, 809, **988**, 1283, 1285
Secada, Jon 377, **988**
Secret Affair 589, **988**, 989, 1066, 1287
Secret Square 34, 790, 821
Secrets 1282
Sedaka, Neil 180, 248, 329, 403, 428, 754, **989**, 1146, 1311, 1312
Seeds 193, 212, 485, 654, 683, 804, 907, **989**, 990, 1288, 1320, 1321
Seefeel **990**

Seeger, Pete 166, 238, 239, 496, 717, 995, 1257, 1343, 1353, 1354
Seekers 193, **990**
Seenan, James 1185
Segel, Jonathan 177, 178
Seger, Bob 224, 295, 490, 615, 625, 723, 730, 786, **990**, 991, 992, 1133, 1231, 1342
Seger, Bob & the Last Heard 991
Seger, Bob System 990, 991
Seiter, John 1049
Selberg, Shannon 259
Selby, Hubert Jr. 929
Selecter **992**, 1052, 1298, 1299, 1355, 1356
Self, Ronnie 1273, 1301
Seligman, Matthew 327
Sellers, Peter 566
Sen 277
Sen Dog 277
Sendak, Maurice 240, 619
Senior, Russell 900
Sentinals 1301
Sentinel [1] 860
Sentridoh 987
Seol, Randy 1089
Sepultura 521, **992**, 993
Sequel 557
Sequence 1059, 1285, 1295
Sergeant, Will 350, 351
Sergent, Rex 393
Sergent, Will 350, 351
Serletic, Matt 1035
Sermon, Erick 372, 731, 926
Servotron **993**, 994
Sessions, Angel 297
Setzer, Brian 853, **994**, 1090, 1167
Setzer, Brian Orchestra 994
Seven Mary Three 1085
Seven Seconds 1341
Seven, Barry 8
Sever, Sam 1135
Severin, Steve 1014, 1015
Sevilla, Mickey 324
Sewell, Marshall 354
Sex Pistols 51, 60, 132, 133, 164, 210, 222, 238, 268, 278, 279, 289, 328, 339, 352, 448, 456, 482, 520, 543, 556, 590, 668, 692, 767, 768, 794, 804, 811, 822, 865, 875, 895, 896, 898, 916, 939, 973, **994**, 995, 997, 1014, 1018, 1037, 1082, 1085, 1086, 1087, 1099, 1143, 1193, 1250, 1278, 1308, 1310, 1321, 1330, 1336, 1337, 1338, 1346
Sexsmith, Ron 189, 956, **995**, 996, 1000, 1081
Sexton, Ann 1298, 1299
Sexton, Charlie 290, 375
Seymour, Daren 990
Seymour, Mark 548
Seymour, Nick 271, 272
Seymour, Phil **996**, 1165, 1166, 1278, 1339
SF Seals 695, 1300
Sha Na Na **996**, 1004, 1241
Shacklefords 517
Shad, Bob 807, 1292
Shades of Blue 1133
Shadow King 478
Shadows of Knight 251, **996**, 1131, 1283, 1288, 1320
Shadows [1] 240, 940, 996, 1310, 1311
Shadowy Men on a Shadowy Planet 189
Shaefer, Kelly 993
Shaffer, J. Munky 632
Shaffer, Paul 632
Shaggs 469, **996**, 997, 1288, 1298
Shakers [3] **997**
Shakers [Uruguay] 997
Shakespeare, Robbie 340
Shalamar 50, **997**, 1210
Shale, Karl 240
Sham Sixty Nine 307, **997**, 998, 1279, 1337
Shambeko Say Wah! 1197
Shamen 935, 1286
Shams 981
Shams [1] 943
Shanahan, Tony 1031
Shangri Las 71, 112, 552, 751, 923, **998**, 1001, 1275, 1282, 1287, 1301, 1311, 1312, 1313, 1347

Shank, Barry 667
Shankar, Lakshmi 1245
Shankar, Ravi 477, 1322
Shannon, Del 198, 359, 550, 797, 855, 882, 914, **998**, 999, 1027, 1241, 1275, 1281, 1282, 1310, 1327
Shannon, Tommy 1232
Shante, Roxanne 1179
Shapiro, Helen 98, 1310
Shapiro, Jim 1192
Sharkey, Feargal 372, 1174
Sharkey, John 1112
Sharp, Cecil 551
Sharp, Dave 13
Sharp, Dee Dee 1285
Sharp, Elliott 981
Sharp, Gordon 1136
Sharp, Joel 'Razor' 237
Sharpe, Ray 1282
Sharpley, Cedric 808
Sharps 945
Sharrock, Chris 554, 1242
Sharrock, Sonny 361
Shatner, William 422
Shatter, Will 416, 417
Shaver, Billy Joe 363, 1106
Shaw, Artie 305
Shaw, Carol 1301
Shaw, Greg 998, 1002, 1165, 1309
Shaw, Jim 305
Shaw, Marlena 1276
Shaw, Sandie 50, 519, 678, **999**, 1166, 1276, 1285
Shaw, Tommy 799, 1097
Shea, Red 653, 654
Shear, Jules 62, 63, 541, 606, 607, 706, 707, **999**, 1000, 1343
Sheehan, Billy 119, 958, 1302
Sheehan, Bob [1] 119, 120
Sheehan, Fran 132
Sheeley, Sharon 304
Shelby, Kaay Alexi 1299
Sheldon, Chris 1131
Shell, Ed 794
Shellac **1000**, 1001, 1178
Shelley, Pete 164, 165, 166, 687, 688, **1001**
Shelley, Steve 111, 191, 357, 599, 913, 1040
Shelleyan Orphan 1136
Shelton, Louie 986
Shelton, Seb 988
Shenton, Ann 8
Shep & the Limelites 1307
Shep and the Limelites 519
Shepard, Sam 343
Shephard, Bill 86
Shepherd, Ben 640, 1045
Shepherd, Brad 537
Shepp, Archie 1231
Sheppard, Andy 519
Sheppards 1280
Sherba, Glenn 55
Sheridan, Mike & the Nightriders 555
Sheridan, Tony 79, 80, 1253, 1310
Sherman, Bobby 1273, 1276, 1310, 1331
Sherman, Jack 921
Shernoff, Andy 310, 311
Sherriff, Andrew 200
Sherrill, Billy 638, 718
Sherwood, Adrian 171, 393, 873, 888, 1019, 1023, 1024, 1355
Sherwood, Billy 1257
Shider, Gary 226, 441, 842, 843
Shields, Kevin 58, 128, 315, 778, 779, 1005, 1278
Shields, Rhonda 694
Shillingford, Jake 779
Shilos 845
Shinehead 1349, 1355, 1356
Shines, Johnny 1350, 1352
Shipley, Tom 141
Shipp, Horace Jr. 89, 90
Shippy, Mark 1178
Shire, David 1092
Shirelles 28, 50, 407, 569, 619, 955, 998, **1001**, 1208, 1275, 1293, 1300, 1301, 1311, 1312, 1313

Shirley & Lee 67, 68, **1001**, 1002, 1274, 1278, 1306
Shirley, Jerry 66
Shirley, Kevin 10
Shirts 1283
Shock G 314
Shockabilly 126
Shocked, Michelle 117, **1002**, 1151, 1223, 1345, 1346, 1353
Shocking Blue 59, 61, 1122
Shoes [1] 370, 703, **1002**, 1003, 1058, 1278, 1290, 1339
Sholes, Steve 880
Shondell, Troy 1275, 1310
Shondells 577
Shonen Knife **1003**
Shop Assistants 846, **1003**, 1004
Shorrock, Glenn 661
Shorter, Wayne 539
Shortkut 608
Shotgun Express 1081
Shotgun Messiah 1302
Showaddywaddy **1004**
Showbiz, Grant 391
Showmen [1] 742, **1004**, 1151, 1278, 1282, 1286, 1306
Shrapnel 757
Shrat 25
Shriekback 448, 548
Shrimp Boat 985
Shudder to Think 580, **1004**, 1005
Shulman, Derek 458
Shulman, Phil 458
Shulman, Ray 458, 559
Shuman, Mort 7, 381, 384, 576, 619, 780, 1311
Shurtleff, Jeffrey 57
Shuttleworth, Paul 634
Shyne 900
Shyster 416
Sibelius, Jean 292, 797
Siberry, Jane 559, **1005**
Sice 127, 128
Sichran, Bobby 1349
Sick Things [1] 319
Sidewinder [1] 518
Sidney, Hilarie 34
Sidran, Ben 737, 764
Siebel, Paul 706
Siegel, Jay 1146
Sigel, Beanie 581
Sigler, Bunny 819, 1335
Sigsworth, Guy 687
Sigue Sigue Sputnik 20, 422, 455, 456
Sigur Ros **1005**, 1006
Silagyi, Chris 1165
Silence [2] 547
Silhouettes [1] 1306, 1282
Silk [2] 939
Silkworm 272, **1006**, 1007, 1058, 1300
Silos 541, 1248
Silver Apples **1007**, 1258
Silver Beatles 80
Silver Bullet Band 990, 992
Silver Jews 272, **1007**, 1008, 1283
Silverchair 10, 1342, 1344
Silveria, David 632
Silverstein, Shel 238, 326
Simenon, Tim 301
Simeon 1007
Simins, Russell 216, 1053
Simmonds, Kim 979, 980
Simmons, Al 1297
Simmons, Chester 759, 1096
Simmons, Daryl 140, 305, 431, 710, 861
Simmons, Gene [1] 624, 625, 866
Simmons, Jeff 1265
Simmons, Luther Jr. 689
Simmons, Patrick 331
Simmons, Russell 1020, 1023
Simms, Nick 252
Simon & Garfunkel 41, 90, 277, 380, 451, 477, 646, 702, 772, 922, **1008**, 1009, 1011, 1012, 1030, 1046, 1318, 1319, 1328, 1354
Simon, Carly 44, 518, **1009**, 1010, 1118, 1119
Simon, Joe [1] **1010**, 1335, 1290
Simon, John [1] 277, 424, 653, 988
Simon, Lucy 1009

Simon, Paul 90, 142, 277, 308, 310, 342, 451, 477, 507, 532, 594, 614, 691, 704, 746, 772, 780, 787, 796, 821, 990, 1008, **1011**, 1012, 1030, 1248, 1255, 1311, 1328, 1351, 1354, 1355
Simon, Robin 1173
Simon, Screamin' Scott 996
Simone, Nina 33, 183, 483, 598, 1152, 1207
Simonon, Paul 223
Simons, Ed 205, 206
Simper, Nick 292
Simple Minds 201, 556, 871, **1012**, 1013, 1048, 1291
Simply Red **1013**, 1109
Simpson [1] 39
Simpson, Bernice 846
Simpson, Gerald 355
Simpson, Graham 400
Simpson, Homer 478
Simpson, Jessica [1] 760, **1013**, 1014
Simpson, Paul 654
Simpson, Valerie 39, 148, 380, 569, 699, 1107
Simpson, William 1019
Sims, David [1] Wm. 586, 587
Sims, Frankie Lee 1294
Sims, Joyce 191
Sims, Neil 192
Sims, Zoot [1] 1036, 1061
Sin, Marco 319
Sinatra, Frank 108, 118, 130, 174, 282, 315, 318, 429, 438, 528, 593, 598, 671, 747, 796, 896, 994, 995, 1014, 1066, 1091, 1162, 1165, 1199, 1200, 1201, 1203
Sinatra, Frank Jr. 1208
Sinatra, Nancy 90, 356, 459, 517, 518, 680, 721, 935, **1014**, 1145
Sinclair, Dave 181, 182, 703, 1223
Sinclair, John [1] 647
Sinclair, Richard 176, 181, 182, 1223
Sinclair, Richard Caravan of Dreams 182
Sinclair, Ross A. 1045
Sinfield, Peter 64, 364
Singer, Eric [1] 625
Singer, Hal 507
Singh, Avtar 252
Singh, Satwan 875
Singh, Talvin 252, 1111
Singh, Tjinder 252
Singleton, David 723
Singleton, Shelby 1059
Sioux, Siouxsie 290, 1014, 1015
Siouxsie & the Banshees 19, 40, 899, 902, **1014**, 1015, 1023, 1025, 1087, 1279, 1337, 1338
Sir Douglas Quintet 187, 224, 681, 972, **1015**, 1016, 1297
Sir Menelik 608
Sir Mix A Lot 372, 879, 904, **1016**, 1185, 1244
Sisqo **1016**, 1017
Sista 362
Sista Teedy 1151
Sister Carol 1349
Sister Double Happiness 557
Sister Rose 1129
Sister Sledge 393, **1017**
Sisterhood 743, 1017
Sisters Love 549
Sisters of Mercy 15, 95, 743, **1017**
Sixpence None the Richer **1017**
Sixth Great Lake 376
Sixths 443, 688, 689, **1018**
Sixty Foot Dolls 1076
Size [1] **1018**
Size, Roni 1018
Size, Roni & Reprazent 1018
Skaggs, Ricky 1230
Skeletons 942, 1089
Skeoch, Tommy 1128
Skewbald 740
Skid Row [1] **1018**
Skids 97, **1019**
Skillings, Muzz 663
Skinner 250, 251
Skinner, Donald Ross 250, 251
Skinner, Frank 654
Skinny Puppy 295, 435, 627, **1019**, 1101, 1284
Skip & Flip 1282, 1292
Sklar, Leland 235, 1119, 1226

Skold, Tim 627
Skopelitis, Nicky 470
Skunk [Rock] 203
Sky, Patrick 119
Skyliners [1] **1019**
Skyscraper 1108
Slab 971
Slack [1] 555, 1161
Slack, Paul 1171
Slade [1] 743, 909, **1019**, 1020, 1339
Slade, Sean 156, 352, 735
Sladich, Joe 411
Slam [1] 824
Slant Six 689
Slapp Happy 126, 261
Slash [1] 205, 494, 495, 497, 875, 1087
Slater, Andrew 33, 483, 1204
Slaughter & The Dogs 1337
Slaughter Joe 1278
Slave 448, 711, **1020**, 1284
Slayer 605, 993, 1020, 1021
Slayer [1] 462, 702, **1020**, 1021, 1340
Slazenger, Jake 774
Sleater-Kinney 467, 468, 977, **1021**, 1022, 1218, 1280
Sledge, Kathy 1017
Sledge, Kim 1017
Sledge, Percy 14, 123, 186, **1022**, 1287, 1324
Sleeper 352, **1022**
Slick Rick 383, 712, 1020, **1022**, 1023, 1279
Slick, Darby 484
Slick, Grace 484, 583, 584, 585, 1108, 1172
Slik 613
Slim, T.V. 668
Slint 141, 232, 451, 607, 750, **1023**, 1149, 1171
Slits 42, 155, 207, 655, 684, 1014, **1023**, 1024, 1338, 1355
Sloan 374, 391, 784, **1024**, 1290
Sloan, Allen 322
Sloan, P.F. 108, 380, 480, 578, **1024**, 1025, 1165, 1216, 1300
Slocum, Matt 1017
Sloski, Michael 229
Slovak, Hillel 921, 922
Slowdive 192, 200, 751, 778, **1025**
Sluggett, John 499
Sly & Robbie 1356
Sly & The Family Stone 37, 90, 196, 287, 347, 348, 407, 433, 440, 569, 590, 688, 730, 817, 842, 932, 1025, **1026**, 1027, 1129, 1148, 1244, 1281, 1284, 1324, 1325, 1334
Sly Fox 1163
Sly Stone & the Mojo Men 634, 728
Small Faces 6, 98, 120, 121, 190, 349, 350, 385, 417, 428, 546, 574, 615, 636, 656, 812, 867, **1027**, 1028, 1035, 1042, 1079, 1104, 1151, 1157, 1263, 1284, 1286, 1288, 1317, 1318, 1321, 1322, 1341, 1347
Small Factory 1302
Small Hours 1287
Small, Jon 42, 511
Small, Jonathan 511
Small, Millie 782, 1355
Smalley, Dave [1] 303, 919
Smalls, Biggie 379, 805, 899
Smalltown Parade 589
Smart, N.D. II 67, 846
Smart, Norman D. 771
Smash Mouth **1028**
Smashing Pumpkins 115, 205, 207, 434, 449, 532, 635, 760, 865, 903, 984, **1028**, 1029, 1134, 1283, 1293, 1345
Smear, Pat 461, 1210
Smee, Phil 1035, 1067
Smif-N-Wessun 1246
Smith [1] 391, 393, 394, 692
Smith, Adrian 563, 564
Smith, Annette 198
Smith, Arlene 198, 1312
Smith, Arthur [1] 1297, 1307
Smith, Barry 8
Smith, Bessie 59, 1350
Smith, Bobbie 1055
Smith, Bobby 1055
Smith, Bobby [2] 1055
Smith, Brix 391, 392, 393, 394
Smith, Bruce [3] 899
Smith, Chad [1] 921, 922

Smith, Connie 893
Smith, Curt 1122
Smith, Daniel [1] 280, 281
Smith, Debbie 352
Smith, Dennis [Bass] 988
Smith, Elliott 669, **1030**, 1245, 1246
Smith, Fred [1] 'Sonic' 712, 1031
Smith, Fred [Bass] 822, 919, 1124
Smith, Fred [Guitar] 'Sonic' 712
Smith, Fred [Sax] 712
Smith, Gary [1] 863, 983
Smith, George [1] Harmonica 692
Smith, George [2] 'Smitty' 692
Smith, Giles 224, 225
Smith, Greedy 726, 727
Smith, Harry [4] 438
Smith, Howard 1185
Smith, Huey 'Piano' 421, 425, 439, 609, 895, 946, **1030**, 1031, 1052, 1151, 1273, 1306
Smith, Huey 'Piano' & the Clowns 1030, 1053
Smith, Hurricane 1121
Smith, James [11] Herb 732
Smith, Jimmy [1] 145, 253, 314, 865, 1329, 1330
Smith, Kendra 337, 711, 823, 913, 1344
Smith, Larry [2] 1223
Smith, Legs Larry 127, 509
Smith, Lonnie Liston 495
Smith, Lonnie [Organ] 1334
Smith, Mamie 1350
Smith, Mark [1] E. 25, 238, 391, 392, 393, 394, 448, 561, 936
Smith, Mark [2] 392
Smith, Martin 476
Smith, Matt 835
Smith, Matthew 834
Smith, Megan 280
Smith, Mike [Dave Clark Five] 936
Smith, Mike [Drums] 936
Smith, Mike [Sax] 23
Smith, Neil 866
Smith, Parrish 372
Smith, Patti 103, 116, 173, 241, 390, 468, 511, 520, 525, 575, 743, 840, 916, 927, 931, 983, **1031**, 1064, 1127, 1278, 1321, 1328, 1336, 1356
Smith, Patti Group 1031, 1288
Smith, Philip [1] 498
Smith, Rex 1107
Smith, Rick [1] 1174
Smith, Robert [01] 287
Smith, Robert [Cure] 334, 501, 1346
Smith, Ron [1] 711
Smith, Russell [1] 22, 1230
Smith, Samuel 311
Smith, Sara P. 566
Smith, Scott 674, 675
Smith, Simon [1] 729
Smith, Smitty [1] 692
Smith, Steve [Drums] [Rock] 604
Smith, Steve [Vapors] 1185
Smith, T.V. 9
Smith, Tab 508
Smith, Tim 585
Smith, Toby 577
Smith, Tony [1] 1147
Smith, V. Jeffrey 3
Smith, Warren [Percussion] 762, **1031**
Smith, Warren [Rockabilly] **1031**, 1032, 1304
Smith, Will [1] 322, 983, **1032**
Smith, Will [2] **1032**
Smith, Zachary 671
Smithereens 315, 322, **1032**, 1033, 1287, 1290
Smithies, Reg 196, 197
Smiths 40, 42, 90, 104, 120, 162, 263, 279, 295, 334, 351, 352, 360, 361, 400, 401, 402, 455, 467, 501, 510, 538, 541, 542, 575, 576, 580, 636, 638, 684, 765, 766, 811, 999, **1033**, 1034, 1098, 1101, 1130, 1166, 1211, 1214, 1287, 1291, 1292, 1338, 1343, 1346, 1347
Smog 191, 830, 837, **1034**, 1035, 1118, 1283
Smoke [Rap] 1035, 1280
Smoke [UK] **1035**, 1322, 1288
Smooth, C.L. 109
Smoothies 691
Smothers, Otis Smokey 163
Smyth, Gilli 473

Smyth, Patty **1035**
Snakefinger 211, 936, 1335
Snap 545
Sneaker Pimps 277, 567, 701, 877, **1035**
Sneakers **1036**
Sneakers [1] 1036
Snell, Lester 700
Snider, Dee 1167
Sniff 'n' the Tears 1335
Snoop Dogg 324, 350, 582, 805, 1023, **1036**, 1246, 1348
Snoop Doggy Dogg 323, 324, 941, 1036, 1167, 1279
Snoopy 324
Snow, Hank 202, 398, 949
Snow, Phoebe 385, **1036**, 1037, 1285
Snow, Tom 914
Snyder, Richard 181
Sobule, Jill 236
Social Distortion **1037**, 1340
Soft Boys 63, 217, 218, 244, 290, 530, 531, 611, **1037**, 1038, 1279, 1337, 1343, 1344, 1346
Soft Cell 19, 20, 40, 92, 600, 897, **1038**, 1100
Soft Machine 44, 45, 66, 114, 126, 181, 182, 281, 398, 473, 476, 703, 780, **1038**, 1039, 1147, 1223, 1224, 1246, 1247, 1296, 1323, 1330, 1331
Softies [1] 1039
Softies [2] 1039
Solem, Phil 931
Soles, J. Steven 189
Soles, Steven 159
Solinger, Johnny 1018
Sollenberger, Isobel 64, 65
Some Velvet Sidewalk 1285
Somerville, Jimmy 86, 144, 243, 1051
Something Else 349
Sommer, Bert 646
Sommer, Timothy 545
Son Volt 485, 541, **1039**, 1040, 1043, 1174, 1223, 1344
Sondheim, Stephen 238, 1010, 1094
Sonefeld, Jim 538
Sonic Boom [1] 1047, 1048
Sonic Youth 27, 34, 47, 62, 63, 65, 83, 111, 112, 130, 177, 191, 217, 280, 315, 319, 357, 361, 374, 411, 449, 489, 510, 520, 599, 635, 668, 740, 750, 775, 778, 789, 790, 864, 865, 913, 927, 961, 1024, **1040**, 1041, 1045, 1058, 1108, 1210, 1233, 1248, 1257, 1291, 1323, 1336, 1338, 1345, 1346
Sonic's Rendezvous Band 919
Sonics [1] 67, 262, 683, **1042**, 1198, 1218, 1288
Sonny & Cher 206, 326, 865, 878, **1042**, 1171, 1318
Sonora Pine 607
Sons of Adam 1298
Sons of Champlin 209
Sons of the Pioneers 880
Soopafly 1036
Sorrows [UK] **1042**
Sorum, Matt 274
SOS Band 1144
Sosebee, Scott 579
Soul Asylum 475, 1043, 1210, 1227, 1345
Soul Brothers [1] 1291
Soul Children 515
Soul Clan 159
Soul Coughing 217, **1043**
Soul II Soul 208, 701, 1013, **1044**
Soul Runners 1244
Soul Stirrers 247, 1120, 1121, 1294, 1324, 1351
Soul Survivors 1298
Soul, Inc. 1298
Soul, Jimmy 614, **1044**
Soultans 1298
Sound [1] 1061
Soundgarden 14, 110, 216, 249, 355, 486, 640, 698, 757, 767, 774, 775, 802, 848, 849, 906, 984, **1044**, 1045, 1085, 1108, 1125, 1219, 1293, 1295, 1345, 1346
Soundtracks, Epic 268, **1045**, 1108
Soup Dragons 846, **1045**, 1046
Source Direct 471, 1290
Sousa, John Philip 935

Soussan, Simon 997
South, Joe 292, 401, **1046**, 1292
Souther, J.D. 523, **1046**, 1119, 1228, 1286
Southern California Community Choir 430, 431
Southern Death Cult 273, 274, 402
Southside Johnny 661, **1046**, 1047
Southside Johnny & the Asbury Jukes 661, 662, 1046, 1047
Space [3] 824
Spacemen Three 65, 131, 142, 200, 251, 637, 668, 1007, 1047, 1048, 1056, **1057**, 1108, 1292
Spades 375, 1136, 1280
Spaeth, Gordon 416
Spain [1] 33
Spake, Jim 212
Spampinato, Joey 93, 805, 806
Spampinato, Johnny 806
Spandau Ballet 273, 339, 869, **1048**, 1122, 1288, 1338
Spaniels 1274, 1299
Spanky & Our Gang 185, **1048**, 1049, 1296
Spann, Otis 311, 1352
Sparhawk, Alan 676, 677
Sparklehorse 478, **1049**, 1050
Sparkletones **1050**
Sparks [1] 310, 535, 775, 1015, **1050**, 1051, 1286
Sparks, Brett 501, 502
Sparks, Darrell 502
Sparks, Rennie 501, 502
Sparrow [1] 1073
Spear, Roger Ruskin 127
Spears, Billie Jo 1051
Spears, Britney 11, 12, 51, 531, 638, 760, 781, 1014, **1051**, 1052, 1054, 1107, 1196
Special Pillow 963
Special Sauce 444
Specials 53, 240, 367, 439, 475, 500, 501, 685, 823, 917, 992, **1052**, 1298, 1299, 1338, 1339, 1355, 1356
Spector, Phil 2, 28, 37, 72, 79, 108, 225, 233, 272, 273, 316, 353, 373, 410, 508, 537, 585, 593, 619, 624, 637, 647, 674, 677, 688, 689, 699, 705, 720, 787, 797, 802, 830, 876, 916, 943, 946, 955, 968, 986, 998, 1035, **1052**, 1056, 1060, 1062, 1107, 1149, 1161, 1163, 1178, 1208, 1211, 1241, 1242, 1275, 1282, 1283, 1285, 1289, 1297, 1301, 1308, 1311, 1312, 1325
Spector, Ronnie 955, 1046, 1052
Spectre [1] 892
Spectrum [Easy] 185
Spectrum [UK] 1007, 1047, 1048
Spedding, Chris 20, 36, 174, 401
Speech 37
Speedy J 1273
Speiser, Jerry 725
Spellman, Benny 609, **1052**, 1053, 1070, 1151, 1306, 1278, 1288, 1299
Spence, Joseph 246
Spence, Skip 84, 251, 583, 749, 834, **1053**
Spencer, Casey 591
Spencer, Jeremy 131, 257, 412, 413, 414
Spencer, Jon [Rock] 131
Spencer, Jon [Rock] Blues Explosion 83, 131, 216, 472, 902, 960, **1053**, 1300
Spencer, Lee 830
Spencer, Mike 257
Spencer, Robert 264
Spenner, Alan 401
Spent Poets 95
Sperske, Aaron 75, 854
Spice Girls 16, 51, 98, 235, 377, 781, 959, **1053**, 1054
Spicher, Buddy 737, 1213
Spickard, Bob 198
Spiders [1] **1054**
Spiders [2] **1054**
Spiders from Mars 134, 136
Spiders [1] 134, 249, 1054, 1274, 1278
Spiders [2] 1054
Spiegel, Laurie 1289
Spielberg, Steven 1109
Spill 830
Spillane, Davy 371

Spillane, Scott 484
Spin Doctors 704, **1054**, 1326
Spinal Tap 96, 143, 393, 968, 1032, 1065
Spinanes 914
Spindrift 179
Spindt, Donn 961, 962
Spinks, John 833
Spinners 427, 526, 718, 732, 759, 794, **1054**, 1055, 1096, 1182, 1208, 1273, 1291, 1314, 1335
Spinners [US] 841
Spiral Stairs 847
Spires, Jakson 107
Spirit [1] 246, 405, 783, **1056**, 1285
Spirit, Astrid 655
Spiritualized 206, 472, 1006, 1047, 1048, **1056**, 1057, 1283, 1299
Spiteri, Sharleen 1129
Spitz, Dan 31
Spitzer, Ron 62
Spivey, Victoria 1350
Split Enz 21, 271, 272, 404, 405, 606, 981, **1057**, 1058, 1110, 1196, 1342, 1343
Spongetones **1058**, 1290
Spontaneous Combustion 50
Spooky Tooth 425, 426, 473, 477, 605, 772, 1245
Spoon [1] 930, **1058**, 1059, 1300
Spooner, Bill 1161
Spoonie Gee 76, **1059**, 1285, 1295
Sports 194
Spot [1] 549, 741
Spring Heel Jack 1149
Springer, Jerry 365
Springfield, Dusty 50, 71, 106, 206, 254, 262, 679, 728, 854, 987, 999, **1059**, 1060, 1061, 1207, 1220, 1270, 1276, 1282, 1285, 1313, 1325
Springfield, Rick **1061**
Springfields [1] 1059, 1060, 1188
Springhouse **1061**
Springsteen 593
Springsteen, Aden 123
Springsteen, Bruce 6, 7, 62, 123, 124, 125, 129, 132, 158, 172, 189, 257, 258, 259, 302, 311, 317, 324, 354, 363, 377, 382, 424, 429, 475, 480, 490, 498, 594, 606, 616, 661, 662, 665, 694, 718, 723, 786, 840, 872, 879, 892, 956, 957, 990, 992, 994, 1013, 1031, 1046, 1047, **1062**, 1063, 1064, 1082, 1133, 1157, 1200, 1269, 1270, 1328, 1353
Springsteen, Bruce & the E Street Band 36, 125, 423, 424, 490, 661, 662, 718, 719, 1046, 1062, 1063, 1064
Sprout, Tobin 492, 493
Spruance, Trey 745
Spruill, Jimmy 253, 509
Spruill, Stephanie 44
Square Roots [1] 957
Square, Lester 756
Squarepusher 33, **1064**, 1065, 1299
Squeeze [UK] 5, 76, 88, 173, 186, 187, 366, 404, 489, 585, 601, 727, 735, 932, 962, **1065**, 1278, 1338, 1339
Squier, Billy **1066**
Squire [1066], 1084, 1287
Squire, Chris 1201, 1255, 1256, 1257
Squire, John 1084
Squires 328
Squirrel Bait 232, 451, 607, 1023
Squirrel Nut Zippers 502, **1066**, 1067
SRC [1] **1067**
Ssd 735
Stacey Q 1297
Staehely, Al 1056
Staehely, Chris 1056
Stafford, Terry 424, 1297
Staind **1067**
Staley, Layne 14, 15
Staley, Tom 805
Stalling, Carl 101
Stamey, Chris 286, 322, 376, 536, 1036, **1067**, 1068, 1107, 1217, 1278, 1339, 1343
Stampfel, Peter 126, 1257, 1353, 1354
Stampfel, Peter & the Bottle Caps 981
Standells 213, 257, 346, 360, 600, 636, **1068**, 1320, 1321, 1281, 1287, 1288, 1298, 1300

Stanier, John 520, 521
Stanley Brothers 1308
Stanley, Bob 972
Stanley, Ian 1122
Stanley, Paul 624, 625
Stanley, Richard 698
Stanley, Steven 1147
Stannard, Richard 1254
Stansfield, Lisa 50, 1044, **1068**, 1219
Stanshall, Viv 126, 127, 1154
Stanton, Allen 1301
Stanton, Harry Dean 175
Staple Singers 455, 512, 839, **1069**, 1294, 1295, 1351
Staples 1069
Staples, Benny 1242
Staples, Cleo 1069
Staples, Mavis 89, 418, 890, 1069
Staples, Neville 439, 1052
Staples, Pervis 1069, 1136
Staples, Pops 1002, 1069
Staples, Roebuck 1106
Staples, Roebuck 'Pop' 1069
Staples, Stuart 1145
Staples, Yvonne 1069
Stardrive 979
Starkey, Zak 554, 654, 1222
Starks, John 'Jabo' 147
Starliters 291
Starlites 568, 1280
Starr, Brenda K. 184
Starr, Edwin 429, **1069**, 1070, 1095, 1314, 1315
Starr, Fredro 823
Starr, Maurice 792
Starr, Ringo 78, 79, 132, 177, 428, 508, 554, 566, 654, 665, 714, 800, 877, **1070**, 1071, 1160, 1222, 1319
Starry Eyed & Laughing **1071**
Stars of Faith [1] 979
Starship 583
Starski, Lovebug 1285
Starz 469
Stasium, Ed 251, 537, 1032, 1156
State Of Alert 1279
State of Play 276
Statham, David 776
Statham, Paul 776
Static X 521
Statton, Alison 1258
Status Quo [UK] 177, 190, **1071**, 1286, 1288
Stax, Mike 265
Steaks, Chuck 908
Stealers Wheel 912
Steampacket [1] 1081, 1293
Stebbings, Jone 557
Stec, Joey 736
Stecklein, Val 117, 118
Stedman, Darren 1191
Steed, Mike 415
Steedman, Kent 194, 910, 1342
Steel Mill 661
Steel Pulse 1355, 1356
Steel, Dave 367
Steel, John 29
Steele, David [1] 404
Steele, Jeff 404
Steele, Tommy 1310
Steeler, Bob 540
Steeleye Span 21, 588, 851, **1071**, 1072, 1354, 1355
Steely Dan 16, 182, 287, 331, 385, 594, 706, 835, **1072**, 1073, 1092, 1133, 1172, 1213
Stefani, Gwen 803, 804, 891, 994
Steig, Jeremy 122
Stein, Andy 241
Stein, Chris 112, 493, 494, 874
Stein, Mark 1184
Stein, Seymour 987
Steinberg, Billy 63
Steinberg, Sebastian 217, 1043
Steinhardt, Robbie 610, 611
Steinman, Jim 318, 718, 719, 1017, 1093, 1162
Stench, John 954
Stenger, Susan 62, 63
Stent, Mark 'Spike' 101, 687, 811

Stephens, Bruce 115
Stephens, Carlos 702
Stephens, Jody 97, 1344
Stephens, Leigh 115
Stephenson, James 211
Stepney, Charles 366
Steppenwolf 115, 116, 274, 741, **1073**, 1074
Stereo MC's **1074**
Stereolab 8, 24, 178, 433, 528, 630, 636, 679, 760, 771, 789, 847, 908, 985, 1024, **1074**, 1075, 1171, 1299
Stereophonics **1076**
Sterling, Scott 128
Stern, Thomas 268
Stern, Toni 619
Sternberg, Liam 63
Stetsasonic 286, 287, 892, 906, **1076**, 1298
Steve, Miami 125
Stevens, April 1301
Stevens, Cat 37, 208, 390, 413, 506, 525, 539, 599, 607, 631, 636, 976, **1076**, 1077, 1078, 1080, 1119, 1166, 1286
Stevens, Connie 1309
Stevens, Guy 769, 1154, 1231
Stevens, Steve 556
Stevens, Tony 421, 979
Stevenson, Bill 103, 302, 303
Stevenson, Mickey 534, 699, 700, 1215
Stevenson, William 'Mickey' 1239
Stewart, Al [1] 506, 507, 558, **1078**, 1079, 1328
Stewart, Billy 258, **1079**, 1276
Stewart, Dave [1] 276, 378, 379, 500, 574, 649, 856, 916
Stewart, Dave [Guitar, Producer] 378, 379
Stewart, Eric 423, 476, 1126
Stewart, Gary [1] 267
Stewart, Gary [2] 427
Stewart, Jamie 273
Stewart, John 6, 77
Stewart, Jon 1022
Stewart, Mark [1] 592, 668, 873
Stewart, Martin 53
Stewart, Ralph 925
Stewart, Rod 37, 84, 102, 377, 385, 394, 503, 570, 624, 722, 854, 938, 986, 1027, **1079**, 1080, 1081, 1087, 1164, 1184, 1200, 1275, 1284
Stewart, Sandy [1] 1275
Stewart, Sylvester 'Sly Stone' 633, 921, 1026, 1274, 1291
Stewart, Tyler 65
Stewkey 784
Sticky Fingaz 822, 823
Stielow, John 923
Stiff Little Fingers **1082**, 1279
Stigwood, Robert 86, 115
Still, Stephen 546
Stills 1082
Stills, Chris 1198
Stills, Stephen 114, 155, 238, 254, 269, 270, 430, 565, 731, 785, 786, 888, 991, 1069, 1070, **1082**, 1160, 1260
Stills-Young Band 1260
Stiltskin 457
Sting [1] 594, 704, 725, 746, 872, 873, 1081, **1083**, 1084, 1121, 1227, 1267, 1355
Stinson, Bob 934
Stinson, Tommy 934, 1218
Stipe, Michael 138, 207, 208, 210, 245, 315, 406, 470, 525, 545, 580, 676, 930, 931, 1088, 1089, 1344, 1345
Stirratt, John 1223
Stitt, Sonny 1292
Stochansky, Andy 313
Stock, Aitken & Waterman 41, 60, 61, 740, 1069
Stock, Hausen & Walkman 740
Stocker, Wally 50
Stocker, Walt 50
Stockhausen, Karlheinz 1264, 1289
Stodghill, Charles 854
Stoecklein, Val 118
Stoller, Mike 108, 227, 383, 513, 581, 619, 880, 894, 1232, 1307, 1311, 1312
Stonadge, Gary 95
Stone Poneys 519, 788, 955, **1084**

Stone Roses 120, 190, 200, 201, 334, 400, 502, 503, 541, 561, 785, 811, 887, 888, 940, 1006, **1084**, 1085, 1157, 1344, 1346, 1347
Stone Temple Pilots 611, **1085**, 1214, 1345
Stone, Al 578
Stone, Fred 228
Stone, Henry 641, 974
Stone, Jesse 248, 1162
Stone, Martin [1] 210, 211, 338, 735, 979
Stone, Matt 889
Stone, Mike [1] 39
Stoneground 836
Stones 217, 723, 949, 1232
Stoney [1] 719
Stoodley, Mike 1191
Stooges 14, 41, 99, 107, 115, 131, 173, 194, 218, 248, 279, 305, 310, 311, 337, 356, 399, 416, 448, 486, 495, 498, 538, 585, 668, 683, 711, 719, 744, 757, 767, 774, 775, 794, 803, 853, 863, 874, 875, 910, 911, 915, 919, 923, 924, 942, 948, 973, 984, 992, 1040, 1044, 1047, 1067, **1085**, 1086, 1108, 1109, 1114, 1335, 1336, 1337, 1341, 1344
Storch, Scott 957, 1036
Stories **1086**, 1087
Storm, Gale 652
Stormtroopers of Death 32
Storyville 599
Stotts, Richie 866
Stradlin, Izzy 494, 495, **1087**
Stradlin, Izzy & The Ju Ju Hounds 1087
Strafe 376
Strait, George 524
Straitjacket Fits 1343
Strange Cruise 1195
Strange Fruit 886
Strange, Billy 222, 315, 1014
Strange, Steve 1195
Strangeloves 70, 133, 311, 716, **1087**, 1157, 1281, 1341
Stranglehold 1280
Stranglers 358, **1087**, 1088, 1193
Stratton, Dennis 563
Stratton-Smith, Tony 631
Stravinsky, Igor 1264, 1265, 1267, 1268, 1269
Straw, Syd 21, 267, 470, 600, **1088**, 1089
Strawberry Alarm Clock 377, 646, **1089**, 1288, 1296
Strawbs 22, 298, **1089**, 1090, 1201, 1355
Stray Cats 354, 725, 853, 994, **1090**, 1091, 1281, 1292, 1308
Stray Gators 1261
Strayhorn, Billy 602
Streep, Meryl 377
Street, Stephen 121, 263, 765, 1022, 1034
Streetwalkers 394
Streisand, Barbra 100, 302, 308, 309, 318, 349, 357, 424, 535, 544, 719, 800, 809, 935, 978, 999, **1091**, 1092, 1093, 1094, 1095, 1225, 1226
Streng, Keith 415
Stretch [1] 782
Strictly Ballroom 75
Strider 50
Stringfellow, Ken 877, 878, 1344
Stroffolino, Chris 1008
Strohm, John P. 108, 109, 511
Strong, Barrett **1095**, 1287, 1314
Strong, Keith 415
Strong, Nolan **1095**
Strummer, Joe 9, 45, 95, 104, 222, 223, 822, 871, 994, **1095**, 1335, 1337
Strykert, Ron 725
Stryper 1302
Stuart, Chad 195
Stuart, Dan 485, 486
Stuart, Hamish 43
Stuart, Marty 893
Stuart, Michael 1299
Stubblefield, Clyde 146, 147
Stubbs, Joe 822, 828
Stubbs, Levi 195, 427, 822
Stuckey, Scott 207
Students 1274
Studio Pressure 860
Sturgis, Michael 12
Sturmer, Andy 585

Style Council 571, 729, **1095**, 1096, 1214
Styles, Re 1161
Stylistics 297, 572, 700, 732, **1096**, 1335
Styne, Jule 1091
Styrene, Poly 1250
Styx **1097**
Styx [1] 799, 1097
Su, Cong 168
Suave Dre 822
Sub Sub 333
Subhumans [UK] 1340
Sublett, Joe 1186
Sublime 407, 735, **1098**
Subotnick, Morton 1289
Suburban Reptiles 1273
Sucherman, Todd 1097
Sudden, Nikki 142, 1045, 1108
Suede [1] 42, 120, 162, 358, 419, 575, 692, 695, 696, 713, 726, 779, 811, 847, 865, **1098**, 1099, 1103, 1347
Suga Bear 702
Sugar [1] 770, 771, **1099**, 1290
Sugar Hill 441, 479, 1059
Sugar Ray 1028
Sugarcubes 101, 392, 458, **1099**, 1100, 1287
Sugarfoot 818
Sugarhill Gang 208, **1100**, 1274, 1283, 1295, 1347
Suicidal Tendencies **1100**, 1280, 1340, 1341
Suicide [1] 8, 96, 170, 225, 251, 668, 669, 1007, 1019, **1100**, 1101, 1156, 1278, 1336
Suicide Commandos 1043
Sukia **1101**
Sullivan, Darcy 212
Sullivan, Ed 311, 884
Sullivan, Terence 932
Sullivan, Terry 932
Sult, Evan 510
Sultans [2] 948
Sulton, Kasim 719, 1179
Summer, Donna 140, 144, 625, 804, 1051, 1093, **1101**, 1276, 1286
Summers, Andy 260, 281, 872, 1316
Summers, Jazz 1045
Sumner, Bernard 355, 360, 361, 503, 605, 793
Sumner, J.D. 883
Sun & The Moon 196
Sun City Girls 451
Sun Electric 824
Sun Rhythm Section 158, 160
Sun, Ahaguna G. 711
Sundays 458, **1101**, 1102
Sunny Day Real Estate **1102**, 1214
Sunrays **1102**, 1103
Sunset Travelers [Miami] 1245
Sunshine Company 1288, 1296
Sunz of Man 970
Super Furry Animals 191, 475, 476, 716, 751, 1076, 1103, 1278
Super Stocks 1178
Super Wolf 1295
Superchunk 69, 406, 548, 876, 948, 987, **1103**, 1104, 1236, 1289, 1300, 1302
Supergrass 256, **1104**, 1105, 1347
Supernova 993
Supertramp 967, 980, **1105**, 1331
Supporting Actress 977
Supreme Dicks 676
Supremes 11, 39, 292, 304, 376, 423, 427, 628, 636, 699, 947, 957, 958, 974, 1001, 1070, 1079, 1091, **1105**, 1184, 1207, 1219, 1224, 1239, 1270, 1287, 1312, 1313, 1314, 1315, 1324
Suptic, Jim 462
Sure, Al B. 135, 379, 488
Surfaris 557, **1105**, 1281, 1300, 1308, 1313, 1314
Surfers [1] 163
Surfmen 1277, 1301
Surftones 864
Susan 876
Susans [1] 63
Suspects [1] 1248
Sussed [1] 1298
Sust, David Navarro 288
Sutch, Screaming Lord 720, 938, **1106**, 1311
Sutherland, Stacy 1135

Sutton, Graham 66
Suzuki, Damo 178
Suzuki, Keiichi 824
Sveinsson, Kjartan 1005, 1006
Sveningsson, Magnus 183
Svenonius, Ian 689, 783
Svensson, Peter 183
SWA 302
Swaggart, Jimmy 160
Swales, Julian 1005
Swallow, Roger 705
Swallows 1291
Swan Silvertones 1351
Swan, Billy 189, **1106**, 1292, 1308, 1325
Swans 259, 1178
Swarbrick, Dave 298, 386, 387, 388
Swayze, Patrick 745
Sweat, Keith 496, 1016
Swedien, Bruce 572
Sweeney Todd 464, 465
Sweeney, Matt [1] 203
Sweet Exorcist 1299
Sweet Honey in the Rock 1351
Sweet Inspirations 431, 576, 882, **1106**, 1207
Sweet Things 848
Sweet [1] 290, 294, 338, 396, 703, 767, 938, **1106**, 1276, 1280, 1339
Sweet, Darrell 783
Sweet, Matthew 235, 272, 391, 426, 470, 654, 878, **1107**, 1188, 1290, 1343
Sweet, Rachel 962, **1107**, 1108, 1295
Sweet, Steven 1207
Sweetshop 1235
Sweetwater **1108**
Swell Maps 268, 1045, **1108**
Swenson, Rod 866
Swervedriver 244, **1108**, 1109
Swift, Kay 1091
Swimming Pool Q's **1109**
Swing Out Sister **1109**
Swing, DeVante 593
Swingers [NZ] 606, **1109**, 1273, 1284
Swingin' Medallions **1110**
Swinging Blue Jeans 375, 857, **1110**, 1320
Swinging Cats 240, 1299
Swingle Singers 185, 778
Swirl Three Sixty 878
Swirlies **1110**, 1111
Switzky, Rachel 977
Swizz Beatz 323
SWV 496
Sykes, John 1220
Sylvain, Sylvain 794
Sylvester, Terry 375, 533, 844
Sylvia [Soul] 569
Sylvian, David 579, **1111**, 1112
Syn 1277
Syndicate of Soul 1112
Syndicate of Sound **1112**, 1187
Syrup USA 1110
System 58, 991
System Seven 473
Szymczyk, Bill 346, 347, 576, 834, 1205

T

T Bones [US] 1292
T Life 620
T Rex 70, 94, 124, 125, 187, 216, 293, 294, 434, 465, 492, 595, 600, 673, 735, 794, 823, 864, 890, 1090, **1113**, 1114, 1115, 1134, 1195
T. Life 620
T., Booker 128, 129, 598
T., Tommy [1] 335
Tabackin, Lew 1199
Tabor, June 298, 1072, 1355
Tackett, Fred 659, 660, 981
Tackhead 873
Tad 1282
Tages 1293, 1322
Tagg, Larry 132
Tajima, Takao 865
Takac, Robby 474, 475
Takahashi, Maki 111
Take Six 523
Take That 365, 781, 1053, **1115**, 1217, 1226
Takeda, Clint 64
Takizawa, Taishi 463

Talas 958
Talbot, Billy 264, 1260
Talbot, Danny 729
Talbot, Mick 1095, 1096
Talcum, Joe Jack 289, 290
Talk Talk 100, 192, 534, 1025, **1115**, 1116, 1288
Talking Heads 88, 112, 121, 168, 169, 187, 240, 252, 306, 320, 368, 401, 404, 439, 618, 655, 662, 663, 859, 864, 915, 916, 942, **1116**, 1117, 1136, 1146, 1147, 1174, 1191, 1195, 1242, 1278, 1286, 1332, 1336, 1337, 1338, 1339
Tall Dwarfs 629, **1118**, 1153, 1284, 1342, 1343
Tallent, Garry 158, 423, 424
Tallman, Susie 62
Talmy, Shel 135, 265, 349, 507, 621, 783, 974
Talton, Tommy 18
Talulah Gosh 1039, 1212
Tamarkin, Jeff 358, 584
Tamblyn, Larry 1300
Tampa Red 92, 188, 776, 1350
Tams 223, 949
Tandy, Richard 358, 359
Tandy, Sharon 416
Tangerine Dream 25, 252, 545, 824, 1331
Tarheel Slim 513, 1292
Tarplin, Marvin 946
Tartachny, Paul 75
Tarver, Clay 203
Tashian, Barry 67
Tashian, Barry and Holly 67
Tate, Billy 609
Tate, Geoff 906, 907
Tate, Grady 59, 430
Tate, Howard **1118**
Tater Totz 923
Taub, Melvyn J. 589
Taupin, Bernie 544, 596, 597, 598
Tavares 87
Tax Free 835
Taylor, Alex 1003
Taylor, Andy 339, 1080
Taylor, Billy [1] 960
Taylor, Chad 663, 879
Taylor, Chip 573
Taylor, Clive [1] 23
Taylor, Courtney 280
Taylor, Danny 1007
Taylor, Dean 142
Taylor, Delburt 1020
Taylor, Derek 331
Taylor, Dick [1] 1315
Taylor, Dick [Pretty Things] 885
Taylor, Dolphin 1082
Taylor, Eric 675
Taylor, Felice 1219
Taylor, Hound Dog 296, 630, 1140, 1141
Taylor, Jack [1] 1019
Taylor, James [1] 113, 149, 240, 388, 390, 451, 526, 565, 593, 619, 620, 657, 746, 855, 1010, 1118, 1119, 1120, 1126, 1262, 1285, 1286, 1328
Taylor, James [3] 'J.T.' 631, 1284
Taylor, John [Piano] 339
Taylor, Johnnie 247, 515, **1120**, 1121, 1136, 1277, 1294, 1295, 1351
Taylor, Koko 1352
Taylor, Larry 708
Taylor, Little Johnny 1351
Taylor, Livingston 1285
Taylor, Mick 114, 336, 343, 470, 474, 665, 707, 708, 709, 950, 951, 1316
Taylor, Paul 1231
Taylor, Phil 768, 769
Taylor, R. Dean 392, 393
Taylor, Roger [1] 339, 904
Taylor, Sam [1] 'The Man' 108, 338, 513
Taylor, Ted 171
Taylor, Tim [1] 139
Taylor, Vince 1310
Taylor, Vince & the Playboys 996
Tchaikovsky, Bram 769, **1121**, 1278, 1290, 1338
Tchaikovsky, Pyotr Ilyich 797
Tea & Symphony 1283
Team Dresch 977, 1021, **1121**

Teardrop Explodes 250, 251, 455, 554, 654, **1121**, 1122, 1197, 1338
Teardrops 1122
Tears for Fears 82, 695, 1122
TEB 1135
Techno Animal 1171
Teddy Bears [1] 1052, 1282
Tee Set 59, **1122**, 1123
Tee, Richard 409
Teel, Jerry 131
Teen Idles 740, 1279
Teen Kings 825
Teen Queens 1280
Teenage Fanclub 212, 426, 750, 878, 943, 1046, 1107, **1123**, 1188, 1278, 1290
Teenage Filmstars 1298
Teenage Jesus and the Jerks 250
Teenagers 191, 680, 681, 1306
Tei, Towa 291, 292, 865
Tek, Deniz 910, 911, 1341, 1342
Telefunken Blues 419, 420
Telegraph Avenue **1124**
Television 63, 216, 399, 400, 520, 775, 834, 916, 1006, 1022, 1024, **1124**, 1190, 1191, 1199, 1278, 1336
Television Personalities 225, 1108, 1118, 1124, 1125
Telligman, Keith 642
Telstar Ponies 750
Tempchin, Jack 346, 1286
Tempest, Joey 378
Temple of the Dog **1125**
Temple, Michael 853
Templeman, Ted 180, 219, 507, 659, 1182
Tempo, Nino 1301
Tempo, Nino & April Stevens 1283
Temptations 32, 198, 246, 336, 347, 427, 431, 440, 442, 486, 514, 577, 628, 694, 841, 946, 947, 951, 1055, 1079, 1080, 1095, **1125**, 1126, 1170, 1183, 1207, 1239, 1284, 1287, 1314, 1315, 1324, 1334
Ten CC 423, 476, 489, 608, 817, 989, **1126**
Ten Thousand Maniacs 7, 143, 199, 259, 559, 727, **1126**, 1127, 1344, 1346
Ten Years After 115, 394, 702, **1127**, 1231, 1326
Tench, Benmont 335, 336, 369, 667, 856, 1089
Tench, Bob 84
Tennant, Neil 360, 854, 855, 1059
Tennille, Toni 180
Tenniswood, Keith 971
Tenor, Jimi 771, 1300
Tenpole Tudor 995, **1127**, 1128, 1295
Tepper, Jeff Moris 181
Terenzi, Fiorella 327
Terminator X 898
Terrell, Tammi 39, 453, 1301, 1314
Terry, Blair & Anouchka 500
Terry, Dewey 328
Terry, Helen 274
Terry, Sonny & Brownie McGhee 247
Terry, Steven 1217
Terry, Todd 68, 292, 382
Tesco, Nicky 724
Tesla **1128**
Tetteroo, Pete 1122, 1123
Tex, Joe 14, 145, 159, 245, 601, 718, 949, **1128**, 1129, 1273, 1287
Texans 160
Texas Is the Reason 895
Texas Playboys 607
Texas Tornados 1015
Texas [1] 1015, **1129**
Textones 996
Teye 363
Tha Alkaholiks 1246
Tha Dogg Pound 1036
Thain, Gary 1177, 1178
Tharp, Twyla 168
That Dog 84, **1130**
That Petrol Emotion **1130**, 1174
Thatcher, Betty 932
Thayer, Donnette 447
Thayil, Kim 1044
the Nazz **784**
The 360, **1130**, 1131
The Wild Tchoupitoulas 1223

Thee Fourgiven 1321
Thee Headcoats 210
Thee Midniters **1131**
Thee Mighty Caesars 210
Thee Slayer Hippy 183
Them [1] 73, 284, 472, 679, 742, 751, 762, 763, 764, 780, 792, 949, 989, 996, **1131**, 1135, 1153, 1275, 1288, 1312, 1315, 1316, 1317, 1318, 1320
Theodore, Mike Orchestra 1074
Therapy [1] **1131**, 1132
These Immortal Souls 268
Thewlis, David 824
They Might Be Giants 65, 107, 127, 426, 880, 1050, 1051, **1132**, 1133, 1345
Thiele, Bob 983
Thighpaulsandra 251, 252
Thin Lizzy 245, 324, 704, 730, 991, **1133**, 1134
Thin White Rope 460
Things 1273
Things To Come 1283
Thinking Fellers Union Local Two Eight Two **1134**
Third Bass 892, **1134**, 1135, 1279
Third Ear Band 1283
Third Eye Blind 703, **1135**
Third Eye Foundation 419, 1289
Third Rail [1] 1288
Third World 716, 1356
Thirteenth Floor Elevators 126, 151, 374, 375, 411, 778, 1047, 1048, 1124, **1135**, 1136, 1280, 1297, 1320, 1336
Thirty Eight Special 555, 682, 683, **1136**, 1333
This Heat 1292
This Mortal Coil 222, 231, 816, **1136**
Thistlethwaite, Anthony 1209
Thoman, John 913
Thomas, Alton 568
Thomas, B.J. 50, 1286, 1293
Thomas, Banner 752
Thomas, Bruce 256, 504
Thomas, Carla 89, 128, 148, 212, 418, 512, 515, 569, 645, 850, 924, 925, **1136**, 1137, 1277, 1281, 1294, 1324
Thomas, Chris [Guitar #1] 173
Thomas, Chris [Producer] 55, 715
Thomas, Dave [1] 853
Thomas, David 852, 853
Thomas, David [11] 287, 851, 852
Thomas, David [Pere Ubu] 545, 851, 852, 853
Thomas, Dawn 142
Thomas, Dylan 174
Thomas, Fred [Bass] 146
Thomas, Gerry 191
Thomas, Grady 842
Thomas, Henry [1] 1350
Thomas, Irma 304, **1136**, 1137, 1151, 1274, 1278, 1286, 1299, 1306
Thomas, Joe [Keyboards] 1228
Thomas, John [06] 145
Thomas, Leon 976
Thomas, Mary [1] 272
Thomas, Mickey 584
Thomas, Nigel 115
Thomas, Pete [1] 210, 211, 256, 504, 841, 1065, 1140, 1335
Thomas, Ray 758
Thomas, Richard [1] 231, 760
Thomas, Rob 702, 703
Thomas, Rozonda 1145
Thomas, Rufus 696, 817, 1028, **1136**, **1137**, 1144, 1277, 1281, 1294, 1295, 1304, 1352
Thomas, Terry 53
Thomas, Wayne 711
Thomasson, Hughie 834
Thompkins, Russell Jr. 1096
Thompson Twins 425, 601, **1137**, 1290
Thompson, Alice 1242
Thompson, Bob [4] 813
Thompson, Bobby [1] 737
Thompson, Chester [Drums] 976, 1267
Thompson, Chris [1] 374
Thompson, Christie 1175
Thompson, Chucky 109
Thompson, D. Clinton 942

Thompson, Danny [Bass] 153, 334, 515, 851, 878
Thompson, Danny [Guitar] 851, 1139
Thompson, Danny [Sax] 382, 477, 878, 1140
Thompson, Dennis 712, 910, 1341
Thompson, Hank 573
Thompson, Hank & His Brazos Valley Boys 573
Thompson, Linda 298, 1138, 1139, 1140
Thompson, Linda [1] 489, 1138, 1140
Thompson, Mayo 171, 391, 852, 923
Thompson, Paul 245
Thompson, Paul [Drums] 401
Thompson, Richard [1] 158, 159, 255, 267, 298, 334, 335, 382, 386, 387, 388, 405, 470, 489, 705, 706, 707, 771, 915, 1071, 1089, **1138**, 1139, 1140, 1213, 1354, 1355
Thompson, Richard [1] & Linda 973, 1138, 1139, 1140
Thompson, Rick 150
Thompson, Rudi 1250
Thompson, Stephen 708
Thompson, Teddy 1198
Thompson, Tony [1] 898
Thompson, Wayne 136
Thompson, Wayne Carson 136, 137, 198
Thomson, Kristin 1161, 1302
Thomson, Virgil 1161, 1175
Thorn, Tracey 382, 383, 701
Thornalley, Phil 556
Thorne, Mike 20, 174, 243, 776, 1234
Thorngren, Eric 'ET' 899
Thornhill, Claude 1158
Thornton, Big Mama 1305
Thornton, Billy 893
Thornton, Paul 469
Thorogood, George **1140**, 1141
Thorogood, George & the Destroyers 1140
Three D [4] 701
Three Degrees 199, 732, 1001, 1197
Three Dog Night 35, 426, 480, 526, 610, 799, 801, 842, 980, **1141**, 1225
Three Eleven 632
Three Johns 722
Three Mustaphas Three 899
Three O'Clock 390, 912, **1141**, 1248, 1343, 1344
Three Peeps 1039
Throbbing Gristle 170, 234, 269, 355, 627, 896, 897, 1019, 1100, **1141**, 1142, 1284, 1286, 1291
Thrower, Stephen 234
Throwing Muses 90, 91, 141, 524, 525, 671, 864, 1136, **1142**, 1143, 1339, 1345, 1346
Thrown Ups 1295
Thunderclap Newman 856, **1143**
Thunders, Johnny 494, 495, 520, 794, 875, 961, **1143**, 1286, 1336
Thurber, James 246
Thurston, Scott 874
Thyme 1298
Tibet, David 234
Tice, Dave 257
Tichy, John 241
Tiers, Wharton 1041
Tiffany [1] 577, 1228, 1310
Tiger Trap 1039, 1294
Tijuana Brass 175, 208
Tikaram, Tanita 35
Tikis 507, 1298
Til Tuesday 693, **1143**, 1144
Til, Sonny 828
Tilbrook, Glenn 531, 693, 962, 1065, 1138
Tiller, Jay 434
Tillinghast, Josh 827
Tillis, Mel 667, 1106
Tillman, Floyd 203
Tillman, Martin 336
Tillotson, Johnny 1310
Tilston, Steve 388
Tim Dog 1293
Timbaland 1, 362, 465, 581, 631, 782, 1017, 1036, 1145
Timberlake, Justin 11, 781
Timbrell, Tiny 880, 1292
Timbuk Three 541
Time [1] 570, 890, **1144**

Time Machine [1] 1298
Time of Your Life 1298
Timelords 626
Timers 1178
Timex Social Club 1300
Timko, Greg 1301
Timmins, Margo 230, 258, 259
Timmins, Michael 258, 259
Timmins, Peter 259
Timms, Daniel 722
Timms, Sally 721, 722, 1018
Timony, Mary 520, 1018, 1300
Timperley, Clive 822
Tin Machine 88, **1144**
Tin Pan Alley 1198
Tin Tin [1] 655
Tindersticks 33, **1144**, 1145, 1292
Tinsley, Boyd 704
Tintern Abbey 1277
Tiomkin, Dimitri 292
Tippett, Keith 617
Tipton, Glenn 605, 606
Titelman, Russ 1119
Tito, Duke 114
Titus, Andre 'Dres' 106
Tka 1281
TLC 140, 366, 376, 442, 781, 833, 861, 940, 1081, **1145**
Toad the Wet Sprocket **1146**
Toad the Wet Sprocket [1] **1146**, 1344
Toad [1] 1146
Tobler, John 912
Tod A. 250
Todd, Andy 211, 935
Todd, David 620
Todd, Pat 642
Todd, Terry 244
Toddy Tee 553
Toiling Midgets 357
Tokens 371, 1102, **1146**
Tolbert, Larry 841
Toledo, Harry 1286
Toler, Dan 17
Tolman, Russ 1248
Tolson, Pete 886
Tom & Jerry [1] 1012
Tom Tom Club 88, 475, 643, 1116, 1118, **1146**, 1147, 1279
Tom Tom Eighty-Four 285
Toma, Andi 771, 772
Tomcats [1] 607
Tomita 12
Tommy Tutone **1147**, 1281
Tommy [1] 699
Tomorrow [1] **1147**, 1235, 1284, 1323
Tone Loc **1147**, 1258, 1287
Tones on Tail 776
Toney, Norma 700
Tonik, Terry 1298
Tonio K. 160
Tony Toni Tone 278, **1147**, 1148
Too Short 805, **1148**
Took, Steve Peregrin 1113
Tool [1] 274, 295, 839, 1067, **1148**
Toomey, Jenny 555, 1161, 1302
Toots & the Maytals 1355, 1356
Topley-Bird, Martina 1159
Topping, Ray 507
Tora Tora 1302
Torbert, Dave 480
Torian, Reggie 558
Tork, Peter 754, 755
Torme, Mel 19, 203, 1208
Tornadoes [1] **1149**, 1311
Tornados 720, **1149**, 1190, 1311, 1322
Tornados [1] 1149
Torquays 756
Torrance, Dean 6
Torrence, Dean 72
Tortelli, Joe 297
Tortoise 8, 66, 241, 361, 566, 677, 751, 772, 829, 879, 923, 963, 985, 1023, 1035, 1041, 1075, **1149**, 1150, 1155, 1171, 1299
Tosh, Peter 1355, 1356
Total [1] 449, 899
Toto [1] 40, 523, 745, **1150**, 1162
Totten, Brennan 942

Toups, Fontaine 1192
Tourists 378, 923
Toussaint, Allen 61, 62, 298, 326, 333, 450, 459, 528, 609, 613, 659, 730, 791, 838, 872, 895, 914, 980, 1052, 1053, 1136, **1151**, 1225, 1286, 1299, 1306
Tout, John 932, 933
Tower of Power 314, **1151**, 1243, 1334
Townes, Jeff 983, 1032
Townsend, David 844
Townsend, Devin 1181
Townsend, Ed 1297
Townshend, Emma 1198
Townshend, Paul 145, 797
Townshend, Pete 99, 119, 159, 190, 220, 265, 319, 410, 521, 574, 576, 585, 797, 879, 885, 1143, 1147, **1151**, 1152, 1220, 1221, 1222, 1232, 1243, 1284, 1321, 1322, 1333
Townson, Ron 403
Toy Love 629, 1118, **1153**, 1273, 1284, 1342, 1343
Toystore **1153**
Trackmasters 782
Tracks, Gordon 13
Tracy Chapman **199**
Trade Winds 1296
Tradewinds 1291
Traffic 5, 110, 113, 181, 182, 284, 285, 481, 511, 694, 700, 701, 812, 1042, 1056, 1072, **1153**, 1154, 1155, 1214, 1233, 1245, 1296, 1317, 1323, 1325, 1329
Traffic Sound **1155**
Trainer, Todd 1000
Trammps **1155**, 1293, 1335
Trance Atlantic Airwaves 367
Trans Am [1] 1007, **1155**, 1156
TransGlobal Underground 874
Translator 351, **1156**, 1234, 1344
Trapeze 293
Trash Can Sinatras 654
Trashmen 262, 263, 296, 945, **1156**, 1157, 1313, 1314
Traveling Wilburys 88, 508, 825, 856, **1157**
Travers, Pat 564
Travis [1] 246, **1157**
Travis [UK] **1157**
Travis, Chuck 802
Travis, Geoff 171, 391
Travis, Malcolm 1099
Travis, McKinley 1276
Travis, Merle 235, 787, 853, 1157, 1186, 1303
Travis, Scott 606
Travolta, John 745
Traynor, Chris 520
Traynor, Jay 581
Treacherous Three 608, 632, 1285, 1295
Treacy, Dan 1124, 1125
Treepeople 157
Trehus, Mark 836
Trembling Blue Stars 402
Tremeloes 85, **1157**, 1158
Tren Brothers 821
Trenier, Claude 1158
Treniers **1158**, 1289
Trent Reznor 802
Trent, Tyler 139
Trepte, Uli 789
Tresvant, Ralph 792
Tribe Called Quest 60, 291, 314, 607, 608, 766, 903, 1135, 1149, **1158**, 1274, 1348
Tricky [1] 101, 301, 383, 471, 500, 602, 701, 861, 876, 1035, **1159**, 1216, 1347
Tricky Disco 1299
Trimble, Vivian 679
Trip Shakespeare **1159**, 1160
Triple Threat 1185
Tritsch, Christian 473
Triumphs [1] 818
Troggs 212, 742, 1047, 1085, **1160**, 1288, 1317, 1332
Troiano, Domenic 122, 576
Trone, Roland 328
Tropea, John 809
Trott, Jeff 1234
Trouble Funk 252, **1160**, 1295

Troubleneck Brothers 1074
Trouser Enthusiasts 973
Troutman, Roger 171
Trower, Robin 401, 402, 893, 894
Troxell, Gary 415
Troy, Doris 1106, **1160**, 1161, 1207, 1301
Troy, Roger 114
Trucks, Derek 18
True Believers 375
True Believers [1] 375
Trueblood, Paul 390
Trugoy the Dove 286, 287
Trujillo, Robert 1100
Trust [1] 32
Tsangarides, Chris 245
TSOL 1340
Tsunami [1] 555, **1161**
Tubb, Ernest 189
Tube Bar 336
Tubes 498, 585, 965, **1161**, 1162
Tubeway Army 807, 808
Tuca [1] 504
Tucker, Alonzo 59
Tucker, Annette 360
Tucker, Corin 1021, 1022
Tucker, Maureen 498, 799, 834, 1188, 1189, 1190
Tucker, Tanya 638
Tucker, Tommy [Rock] 1276
Tucker, William 627
Tudor, Eddie 1128
Tudorpole, Eddie 1127, 1128
Tudors 1128
Tufano, Dennis 152
Tuggle, Brett 958
Tumahai, Charlie 82
Tungsten, Drake 1058, 1059
Turbans 1282
Turgon, Bruce 478
Turks 125, 850
Turner, Big Joe 507, 508, **1162**, 1163, 1296, 1303, 1304, 1305, 1352
Turner, Big Joe [50s] 59, 1162
Turner, C.F. 50
Turner, Charles 868
Turner, Eric 1207
Turner, Glen 1235
Turner, Ike 59, **1163**, 1164, 1305, 1352
Turner, Ike & His Kings of Rhythm 1163
Turner, Ike and Tina 37, 59, 284, 373, 694, 968, 1052, **1163**, 1164
Turner, Joe 68, 248, 1227, 1329
Turner, Joe Lynn 913
Turner, Martin 1235
Turner, Mick 191, 319, 821
Turner, Nakeisha 678
Turner, Red 1232
Turner, Rick 551
Turner, Scott 801
Turner, Steve [1] 486
Turner, Steve [2] 775
Turner, Steve [3] 486
Turner, Ted 1235
Turner, Tina 7, 37, 219, 519, 751, 766, 849, 915, 946, 986, 991, 1163, **1164**, 1266, 1325
Turner, Titus 662
Turney, Carl 225
Turney, Ross 211
Turpin, Will 236
Turrentine, Stanley 1275
Turtles 225, 283, 286, 287, 346, 349, 380, 417, 480, 643, 755, 1024, 1025, 1049, 1113, **1165**, 1265, 1269, 1282, 1296, 1314
Tusken Raiders 774
Tutt, Ron 450, 789, 846, 882
Tutti, Cosey Fanni 896, 1142
Tutton, William 460
Tuva 627
Twain, Shania 294
Tweedy, Jeff 138, 502, 1039, 1174, 1223
Twenty Twenty [1] 996, **1165**, 1278, 1290, 1338
Twiggy [1] 539, 1125
Twilights 1341
Twilley, Dwight 336, 855, 996, **1165**, 1166, 1278, 1339
Twilley, Dwight Band 996, 1165, 1166, 1290

Twink [1] 1147
Twinkle 1033, **1166**
Twist, Nigel 13
Twisted Brown Trucker 615, 1173
Twisted Sister **1166**, 1167, 1302
Twitty, Conway 432, 526, 1106, 1292
Two Dollar Guitar 191
Two K 626
Two Live Crew 59, 462, 631, **1167**, 1300, 1348
Two Lone Swordsmen 971
Two Pac 314, 323, 449, 581, 609, 805, 899, 981, **1167**, 1168, 1246, 1279, 1348
Tyla, Sean 338
Tyla, Sean Gang 338
Tyler, Alvin 'Red' 67, 1151
Tyler, Red 425
Tyler, Steven 9, 10, 11, 217, 962, 1348
Tyner, McCoy 712
Tyner, Rob 712
Tyrannosaurus Rex 556, 1113, 1114
Tyson, Ian 239, 551, 1260
Tyson, Liam 190
Tyson, Sylvia 551
Tzuke, Judie 979

U

U Two 12, 13, 14, 48, 57, 97, 121, 122, 158, 170, 175, 216, 243, 273, 335, 361, 368, 377, 415, 442, 548, 554, 562, 575, 576, 662, 667, 673, 722, 732, 825, 848, 858, 886, 896, 911, 945, 1012, 1013, 1044, 1121, 1129, 1135, **1169**, 1170, 1208, 1235, 1338
UB Forty 309, 355, 455, **1170**, 1171, 1356
UFO [1] 982
Ui 1155, **1171**
Uilab 1171
UK Subs 917, **1171**, 1172, 1340
Ulaky, Wayne 75
Ullman, Tracey 684, **1172**
Ulmer, James Blood 104, 741, 1329, 1330
Ulrich, Lars 729
Ulrich, Peter 288
Ultimate Spinach 830, **1172**, 1275
Ultramagnetic MC's 326, 327, 631, 1074, **1172**, 1173, 1280
Ultravox 178, 216, 339, 939, **1173**, 1195, 1288
Ulvaeus, Bjorn 1, 2, 373
UMC's 1274
Ummah 903, 1158
Umphred, Neal 881
Unclaimed 667
Uncle Kracker **1173**, 1174
Uncle Tupelo 154, 246, 1039, **1174**, 1223
Uncool 995
Undertakers [UK] 1293
Undertones 485, 1130, **1174**, 1278, 1337
Underwood, George 136
Underwood, Ian 1265
Underwood, Lee 153
Underwood, Ruth 474, 1266, 1267
Underworld [1] 33, 101, 1170, **1174**, 1175, 1286, 1299
Unique Three 1299
Unit Four Plus Two **1175**
United States of America **1175**
Unitt, Victor 144
UNKLE 44, 55, 154, 1116, 1149
Unnatural Axe 1278
Uno, Conrad 775
Unrest [1] 376, **1175**, 1176, 1346
Unruh, N.U. 356
Unsane [1] 1300
Untamed [1] 1284
Untouchables [UK] 1298
Unwound 1285
Up, Ari 1023, 1024
Upchurch, Phil 221
Upsetters [Reggae] 1356
Upton, Steve 1235
Ure, Midge 613, 939, 1173, 1195
Urge Overkill 95, 236, 309, 843, 857, **1176**, 1339
Uriah Heep 107, **1176**, 1177, 1178
Urubamba 1011
US Maple **1178**
US Three 1330, 1349
Usher 972

Usher, Gary 122, 166, 226, 537, 736, 971, 1105, 1106, **1178**, 1296
Usher, George 981, 982
Uszniewicz, King **1178**, 1179
UTFO **1179**, 1222, 1283, 1285, 1287
Utley, Adrian 877
Utopia 964, 965, **1179**, 1180, 1290
Utvous, Bjorn 1
Uzi [1] 241

V

Vagrants [1] 771
Vai 899
Vai, Steve 571, 599, 899, 958, 959, 977, **1181**, 1220, 1267
Vail, Tobi 1294
Valens, Ritchie 96, 424, 534, 670, 716, 757, **1181**, 1187, 1276, 1279, 1281, 1292, 1293
Valente, Dino 583, 907, 908
Valentine, Eric 1135
Valentine, Gary 112
Valentine, Hilton 29
Valentine, Kevin 562
Valentino, Bobby 121
Valentino, Sal 81
Valentinos 247, 1236
Valenzuela, Jesse 465
Valiants 1292
Vallance, Jim 10
Vallee, Rudy 127
Valley, Jim 936
Valli, Frankie 67, 213, 426, 427, **1182**
Valli, Frankie & the Four Seasons 427
Valory, Ross 965
Van Der Graaf Generator 1296
Van Halen 14, 180, 314, 383, 497, 615, 640, 719, 735, 741, 757, 831, 903, 906, 920, 958, 959, 1066, 1147, **1182**, 1183
Van Zant 681
VanAcker, Luc 938
Vanda [1] 3
Vanda, Harry 4, 349, 350, 1341
Vandellas 536
VanDePitte, David 1229
VanDerLynden, Pierre 420
Vandermark, Ken 1104
VanDijk, Carol 94, 95
Vandross, Luther 431, 569, **1183**, 1184, 1208
VanDyk, Paul 1286
VanDyke, David 507
VanEaton, J.M. 944
VanEijck, Hans 1122, 1123
Vangelis 12, 1331
VanHalen, Alex 1182, 1183
VanHalen, Eddie 124, 177, 383, 572, 831, 832, 958, 1182, 1183
VanHelden, Armand 1206
VanHoen, Mark 751, 771, 990
VanHooke, Peter 735
Vanian, Dave 279, 804
Vanilla Fudge 84, 144, 264, 292, 751, **1184**
Vanilla Ice 712, 1135, **1184**, 1185, 1349
VanLeer, Thijs 420
VanOsten, Carson 784
VanPoppel, Bart 494
VanRonk, Dave 503, 1353
VanSant, Gus 1030
VanTieghem, David 368
VanVliet, Don 180
VanZandt, Steven 125, 490, 661, 719, 1046, 1047
VanZandt, Townes 173, 259, 363, 675, 917, 1353
VanZant, Donnie 1136
VanZant, Ronnie 681, 682, 683, 1136, 1333
Vapors 858, **1185**
Varese, Edgard 7, 1264, 1289
Vaselines 802, 803, 846, **1185**
Vasquez, Junior 724, 1206
Vaughan, Frankie 50
Vaughan, Jimmie 312, 384, 1185, 1186
Vaughan, Sarah 58, 1292
Vaughan, Stevie Ray 278, 384, 994, 1181, **1185**, 1186, 1232, 1326
Vaughan, Stevie Ray & Double Trouble 1186
Vaughn, Ben 267
Vaughn, Jimmy 384

Vaughn, Stephen 511
Vedder, Eddie 53, 396, 703, 767, 848, 849, 1125, 1210
Vee, Bobby 620, 651, **1186**, 1275, 1297, 1310, 1311
Vee, Tesco 836
Vega, Alan 668, 1100, 1101
Vega, Suzanne 312, 525, 543, 646, 831, 915, **1187**, 1328, 1344
Vegas [1] 500
Vejtables 751, **1187**, 1188
Velez, Lisa 658
Vells 699
Velocity Girl 656, 1290
Veloso, Caetano 217, 778, 876
Velvelettes 60
Velvet Crush 222, 612, 650, **1188**
Velvet Underground 19, 20, 24, 83, 94, 102, 120, 171, 173, 178, 179, 187, 191, 193, 211, 224, 225, 232, 238, 258, 280, 311, 334, 335, 337, 339, 351, 352, 397, 399, 401, 402, 415, 438, 446, 447, 463, 467, 468, 498, 545, 546, 578, 585, 604, 633, 634, 668, 679, 711, 712, 744, 778, 780, 798, 799, 817, 834, 846, 847, 867, 879, 887, 900, 907, 926, 927, 928, 929, 930, 941, 942, 959, 1009, 1024, 1040, 1056, 1074, 1085, 1114, 1124, 1141, 1145, 1172, 1175, **1188**, 1189, 1190, 1191, 1212, 1248, 1257, 1275, 1278, 1335, 1336, 1337, 1338, 1343, 1344, 1345, 1346
Velvetones 1274, 1280
Velvets 173, 174, 585, 927, 1188
Venable, Kim 223
Venet, Nick 519
Venom P. Stinger 319
Ventures 598, 691, 865, **1190**, 1282, 1292, 1296, 1308, 1309, 1313
Venuto, Joe 1061
Vera, Billy 224, 661, 786, 1299
Verbal Abuse 1021
Verity, John 35
Verlaine, Tom 152, 399, 400, 520, 679, 1031, 1124, **1190**, 1191, 1336
Verlaines **1191**, 1343
Vermouth, Apollo C. 126
Verne, Jules 1201
Vernon, Mike 414, 708
Vernon, Ray 1243
Veronica Lake 1302
Versatiles [2] 403
VerScharen, Joe 1019
Versus [1] **1192**
Versus [2] **1192**
Veruca Salt **1192**, 1216
Verve 86, 94, 333, 334, 442, 472, 506, 760, **1193**, 1216, 1283
Vestine, Henry 179
Vibert, Luke 1149, 1171
Vibrators 1082, 1087, **1193**, 1194, 1337
Vicious, Sid 461, 498, 898, 994, 995, 1014, 1023, 1143
Vickers, Carle 678
Vickers, Howie 211
Vickers, Mike 694
Vickers, Robert 467
Victorian Philharmonic Orchestra 461
Vie, Donnie 370
Vienna Radio Symphony Orchestra 390
Vig, Butch 38, 449, 600, 635, 753, 802, 1028, 1029, 1040, 1041, 1176
Vilato, Orestes 976
Village Callers 1300
Village People 855, **1194**
Vincent [1] 829, 1194
Vincent, Gene 84, 227, 267, 376, 381, 647, 881, 983, 1028, 1090, 1091, 1101, **1194**, 1243, 1270, 1292, 1307, 1308, 1310, 1319, 1341
Vincent, Johnny 425, 1031
Vincent, Joyce 829
Vincent, Stan [1] 408
Vincent, Vinnie 63, 625, 626
Vinegar Joe 838
Viner, Michael 1285
Vines, Adi 1108
Vinson, Eddie 'Cleanhead' 1286
Vinyl Devotion 650
Viola, Mike 566

Violent Femmes 459, 863, **1194**, 1195, 1346, 1351
VIP's 1298
Vipers [1] 715
Virtues 1297
Visage 939, 1038, **1195**
Visconti, Tony 13, 31, 133, 458, 526, 539, 979, 1050, 1051, 1113, 1134
Visser, Peter 94, 95
Vitale, Joe 1205
Vitamin C [1] **1195**, 1196
Vito, Rick 414
Viva Saturn 913
Vivino, Jimmy 988, 1037
Vixen [1] 1302
Voelz, Susan 871
Vogel, Janet 1019
Vogues 222, 1062, **1196**
Volcanos 1155
Volebeats 834
Volk, Phil 'Fang' 936
Volman, Mark 417, 1113, 1165, 1265
Volume Ten 912
Volumes 1274, 1280
Von, Eerie 282
Vonbohlen, Davey 895
VonSchmidt, Eric 395
VonSneidern, Chris 504
Voorman, Klaus 428, 1070
Voormann, Klaus 694, 1160
Votel, Andy 55
Votel, Freddy 260
Vozniak, Jaroslav 867

W

Waaktaar, Pal 12
Wachtel, Richard 151
Wachtel, Waddy 214, 215, 401, 875, 956, 1046, 1269, 1270
Waco Brothers 722
Waddy 237
Waddy, Frankie Kash 237
Wade, Adam [1] 580
Wade, Adam [Shudder to Think] 1004
Wade, Colin 197
Wagener, Michael 1249
Wagner, Dick 927
Wagner, Kurt 507, 638, 639
Wagner, Richard 1060
Wagner, Richard [Classical] 288
Wagon Christ 1075
Wagon, Chuck 310
Wah! 654, **1197**
Wah! Heat 1197
Wahl, Terri 921
Wahlberg, Donnie 792
Wahres, Steve 1156
Wailer, Bunny 1355
Wailers [1] 1042, **1197**, 1198, 1355, 1356
Wailers [2] 1042, 1197
Wainwright, Loudon III 98, 388, 432, 601, 1007, 1198
Wainwright, Martha 1198
Wainwright, Rufus **1198**
Waite, John 50, 53, **1198**, 1199
Waitresses 1196, **1199**
Waits, Tom 346, 382, 446, 511, 513, 524, 541, 675, 706, 717, 848, 889, 935, 942, 1050, 1053, 1081, 1132, **1199**, 1200, 1201, 1246, 1274
Wakeling, Dave 367, 455
Wakeman, Rick 105, 133, 135, 157, 842, 852, 926, 1078, 1089, 1090, **1201**, 1255, 1256, 1331
Walcott, Derek 1012
Walden, Narada Michael 431, 710
Walden, Phil 100, 501
Waldmann, Clem 1171
Walford, Britt 141
Walkabouts 337, 1007, 1145, 1282, 1295
Walker Brothers 50, 121, 1000, **1201**, 1202, 1203, 1204, 1285
Walker [1] 1201
Walker, Charlie 1032
Walker, Dave 556, 651
Walker, Don 234
Walker, Greg T. 107

Walker, Jane 1153
Walker, Jerry Jeff 308, 342
Walker, Jim [Flute] 898
Walker, Jimmy [3] 628
Walker, John 1202
Walker, John [1] 1202
Walker, Junior 425, **1202**, 1309, 1314, 1315
Walker, Junior & the All-Stars 1203
Walker, Phillip 514
Walker, Scott 19, 20, 40, 121, 189, 193, 225, 321, 463, 503, 779, 900, 1098, 1144, 1145, 1201, 1202, **1203**, 1204
Walker, Scott [1] 193, 320, 321, 1201, 1202, 1203, 1204
Walker, Simon 541
Walker, Stephen 749
Walker, T-Bone 68, 109, 694, 833, 981, 1015
Walker, Willie 1283
Walkie Talkies 743
Walking Wounded 981
Wall of Voodoo 245, **1204**
Wallace, Andy 953, 1004
Wallace, Chris 804
Wallace, Ian [1] 617, 658
Wallace, Jerry 1297
Wallace, Jimbo 938
Wallace, Sippie 914, 1350
Wallace, Voletta 805
Walle, Rune 835
Waller, Fats 1091
Waller, Gordon 855
Waller, Mickey 84, 1080
Wallert, Charles 569
Wallflowers [1] 159, **1204**
Wallinger, Karl 1208, 1209, 1242, 1243
Wallis, Larry 306, 768
Walmsley, Steve 646
Walsh, Joe 122, 302, 346, 347, 364, 523, 576, 1070, 1071, **1204**, 1205, 1281, 1286
Walsh, Peter 32
Walsh, Peter [1] 33, 215
Walsh, Steve 610, 611
Walter, Tommy 355
Walusko, Nick 1240
Wammack, Travis **1205**, 1297
Wanderin' Kind 1283
Wandscher, Phil 1217
Wang Chung **1205**, 1206
Wansel, Dexter 37, 568, 732
War [1] 29, 68, 119, 153, 1087, **1206**, 1275, 1276, 1281, 1334
Warburton, Damien 760
Warburton, Reginald 1011
Ward, Alastair 279
Ward, Andy [1] 176, 697
Ward, Billy 147, **1206**
Ward, Billy & The Dominoes 1207, 1291
Ward, Billy [1] 1206, 1303, 1307
Ward, Billy [1] & The Dominoes 718, 1229
Ward, Carlos 150
Ward, Ed 395, 552
Ware, John 788, 789
Ware, Leon 452, 707
Ware, Martyn 373, 519, 545
Wareham, Dean 446, 447, 676, 679, 751, 1018
Warford, Robert 789
Warhol, Andy 174, 290, 756, 798, 929, 1188, 1189
Wariner, Steve 640
Warner, Ariel 1199
Warner, Brian 698
Warner, Les 274
Warnes, Jennifer 230, 231, 233, 376
Warnick, Kim 396
Waronker, Anna 1130
Waronker, Lenny 81, 219, 507, 1119, 1130, 1198
Warrant [1] 370, **1207**
Warren Zevon 1270
Warren, Andrew 756
Warren, Diane 123, 140, 230, 719, 738, 1032, 1093, 1094, 1184
Warren, Patrick 850
Warsaw 605
Warton, Dan 785
Warwick, Dee Dee 1106, 1160, **1207**, 1291

Warwick, Dionne 50, 106, 148, 256, 304, 543, 569, 831, 863, 986, 1055, 1059, 1106, 1160, 1183, 1184, **1207**, 1208, 1239, 1276, 1285, 1293, 1300, 1311, 1334, 1351
Was (Not Was) **1208**
Was Not Was 875, 915, 1208
Was, David 1208
Was, Don 3, 47, 65, 66, 270, 344, 528, 602, 874, 875, 915, 952, 1071, 1089, 1208, 1216, 1228
Washburn, Beverly 1282
Washington Squares 1353
Washington, Booker T. 1223
Washington, Dinah 92, 846, 1236, 1263, 1286, 1291
Washington, Eugene 1163
Washington, Frank 297
Washington, Grover Jr. 1235
Washington, Steve 1020
WASP 1006
Wasserman, Rob 792, 929
Wasserman, Ron 929
Waterboys 575, 999, **1208**, 1209, 1242
Waterman, Paul 41
Waterman, Pete 41
Waters [1] 862, 1209, 1232
Waters, John 779, 1107, 1297
Waters, Muddy 17, 93, 119, 220, 334, 522, 745, 951, 1048, 1053, 1163, 1185, 1232, 1276, 1303, 1308, 1317, 1350, 1352
Waters, Roger 66, 861, 862, 863, **1209**, 1210
Waterson, Jack 485
Waterson, Mike 1138
Watkins, Martin 20
Watkins, Tionne 1145
Watley, Jody 997, **1210**
Watson Family 735
Watson, Bruce [guitar] 97
Watson, Chris 170
Watson, Deek 560
Watson, Doc 1002
Watson, Jeff 799
Watson, Johnny [1] 'Guitar' 380, 610, 1266, 1297
Watson, Martin J. 1253
Watson, Pete 734
Watson, Wah Wah 707
Watt, Ben 217, 382, 383, 831
Watt, Mike 217, 406, 740, 741, 742, 876, **1210**, 1340
Watts One Hundred-Third Street Rhythm Band 1244, 1284, 1334
Watts, Charlie 949, 1152, 1240
Watts, Ivo 1136
Watts, Louis Thomas 214
Watts, Michael 251
Watts, Raymond 627
Watts-Russell, Ivo 460, 529, 776, 922
Wavy Gravy 668
Wax Doctor 471
Waxman, Franz 292
Way Out 1298
Way, Darryl 474, 588
Way, Pete 1167
Waybill, Fee 1161, 1162
Wayne, Carl [1] 773
Wayne, John [1] 517
We All Together **1210**, 1211, 1288
We the People 18
Weather Girls 1280
Weather Report 348, 473, 660, 1064, 1247, 1329
Weatherall, Andrew 887, 888
Weatherly, Jim 629
Weaver, Blue 23, 1090
Weaver, Ken 438
Weavers 56, 57, 126
Webb, Jimmy [1] 193, 270, 285, 304, 403, 404, 409, 451, 459, 600, 705, 730, 788, 945, 1060, 1176, 1295
Webb, Joe 794
Webb, Paul 534
Webb, Russell 1019
Webber, Harry 511
Webber, Mark 511
Weber, Steve 503, 1354
Weber, Windy 1231
Webster, Andrew 1161

Webster, Ben 979
Webster, Danny 1020
Weckerman, Dave 399
Wedding Present 94, 510, 837, 1006, **1211**, 1212
Weddoes 1212
Wedren, Craig 320, 1004
Weeds 100
Weekday, D.D. 642
Weekend 1258
Weeks, David 1171
Weeks, Willie 1138, 1139
Ween 847, 1051, **1212**, 1213
Ween, Dean 1212, 1213
Ween, Gene 1212, 1213
Weezer 107, 462, 478, 511, 865, **1214**, 1236, 1345
Weider, Jim 62
Weil, Cynthia 381, 754, 860, 936, 955, 1203, 1289, 1311, 1312
Weiland, Scott 1071, 1085
Weill, Kurt 2, 6, 390, 965, 1200, 1246
Weinberg, Max 718, 1062
Weinger, Harry 244
Weinzierl, John 26
Weir, Alex 1117
Weir, Bob 480, 481, 482, 660
Weir, Graham 826
Weir, Neil 826
Weird Summer 665
Weirdos 461, 1141, 1279
Weisberg, Tim 421
Weisburg, Richard 75
Weiss 771
Weiss, Andrew 953
Weiss, David [1] 1208
Weiss, Donna 1202
Weiss, Janet 1021, 1022
Weiss, Ronnie 'Mouse' 771
Weissberg, Eric 238, 239, 551
Weisser, Michael 369
Weitz, Mark 1089
Weize, Richard 825
Welch, Bob 413, 1285
Welch, Brian 632
Welch, Chris 1149, 1253
Welch, Gillian 432
Welding, Pete 202
Wellander, Lasse 1, 2
Weller, John 1185
Weller, Paul [1] 216, 307, 340, 574, 575, 812, 989, 1095, 1096, **1214**, 1215, 1338
Weller, Paul [1] Movement 1214
Welles, Orson 844
Wellford, Armistead 673
Wells, Cory 1141
Wells, Junior 764, 973, 1074, 1352
Wells, Kitty 573, 1351
Wells, Mary 197, 198, 453, 614, 699, 946, **1215**, 1301, 1312, 1313, 1314, 1315, 1324
Wells, Meech 1036
Welnick, Vince 965
Welz, Joey 1298
Wenders, Wim 179, 268
Wendy & Lisa 405, 599, **1215**, 1216
Wener, Louise 1022
Wenner, Jann 980
Werman, Tom 116, 204, 580, 807
Wertz, Kenny 418
Wesley, Fred 146, 147, 226, 291, 536, 582, 843, 1334
Wesley, Fred & The JB's 582
Wesolowski, Nick 756
Wess, Frank 430, 1163
West 189, 190, 1147
West Coast Pop Art Experimental Band 371, **1216**
West Coast Vocaleers 433
West Street Mob 1295
West Virginia Creeper 241
West, Andy 322
West, Brian 442
West, Bruce & Laing 771
West, John 651
West, Keith 1147, 1235
West, Leslie 771
West, Norm 1283

West, Rick 1158
West, Sonnee 1292
West, Tommy 189
West, Willie [2] 1299
Westerberg, Paul 375, 411, 474, 486, 612, 934, 935, **1216**, 1293, 1328, 1339, 1343, 1344
Westermark, Greg 43
Western, Johnny 1032
Westlake, Kevin 114
Westlife 235
Weston 1000
Weston, Bob [1] 462, 1000
Weston, Bob [2] 451, 1000
Weston, Kim 453, 699, 924, 1314
Weston, Kris 824
Wet Willie 1333
Wetton, John 39, 40, 401, 617, 1178, 1235
Wexler, Jerry 430, 650, 1060
Weymouth, Lani 1147
Weymouth, Laura 1147
Weymouth, Tina 475, 1116, 1118, 1146, 1147
Whale 1159, **1216**, 1283
Whalen, Katharine 1066, 1067
Whaley, Paul 115
Wham! 732, 811, 871, 1045, **1216**, 1217
Whatnauts 569
Wheat **1217**
Wheeler, Billy Edd 238
Wheeler, Carl 1044
Wheeler, Caron 373, 1044
Wheeler, Harriet 1101
Wheeler, Kenny 1111
Wheeler, Onie 1295
Wheeler, Robert 853
Wheeler, Tim 38
Wheels [1] 969
Whelan, Gavan 575
Whippersnapper [1] 388
Whirlywind 1341
Whisker, Gary 402
Whiskeytown **1217**, 1218
Whispers 49
Whitaker, Hugh 542
Whitcomb, Ian **1218**
White Lion 470, 1302
White Plains 161, 1276
White Sister 1188
White Stripes **1218**
White Zombie 281, 1019, **1219**
White, Alan [1] 811, 1256
White, Alan [Yes] 366, 1256, 1257
White, Andy [1] 21, 405, 442
White, Barry 97, 121, 321, 843, 1068, 1160, **1219**
White, Bukka 1350
White, Charlie 227
White, Chris [1] 1270
White, Clarence 167, 168, 221, 795
White, David [Producer] 606
White, George 1149
White, J. 1218
White, Jack 1218
White, James 197
White, Jim [1] 319, 821
White, Jim [Dirty Three] 191, 319
White, Josh 29
White, Mark [1] 2
White, Maurice 347, 348, 365, 366, 1079, 1093
White, Meg 1218
White, Rick 374
White, Ronnie 946
White, Simon 726
White, Snowy 1134
White, Tony Joe 92, 882, 1164, **1219**, 1220, 1325
White, Verdine 347
Whitehead, Peter 1194
Whiteman, Ian 735
Whites 1218
Whitesnake 105, 292, 293, 316, 1181, **1220**, 1302
Whitfield, Norman 109, 453, 628, 629, 1095, 1125, 1315, 1324
Whitford, Brad 10
Whitlock, Bobby [1] 297, 302
Whitman, Slim 6
Whitman, Walt 119

Whitney, Charlie 394
Whitney, John [2] 'Charlie' 394
Whitney, Lou 296, 942
Whitney, Marva 147, 1299
Whitten, Chris 250
Whitten, Danny 665, 706, 1080, 1260
Who [1] 6, 8, 28, 84, 97, 98, 99, 115, 120, 134,
    135, 141, 190, 204, 223, 257, 265, 310, 336,
    338, 349, 350, 396, 397, 410, 416, 455, 470,
    525, 574, 576, 578, 595, 612, 615, 621, 628,
    656, 716, 728, 734, 739, 742, 773, 778, 784,
    797, 811, 815, 878, 885, 886, 949, 952, 996,
    1003, 1027, 1028, 1035, 1067, 1072, 1077,
    1087, 1090, 1103, 1104, 1110, 1133, 1134,
    1143, 1151, 1152, 1171, 1214, **1220**, 1221,
    1222, 1226, 1235, 1240, 1277, 1284, 1287,
    1293, 1308, 1309, 1310, 1314, 1316, 1317,
    1318, 1320, 1321, 1322, 1323, 1331, 1332,
    1333, 1335, 1337, 1338, 1339
Whodini 962, **1222**, 1223, 1285, 1287
Wicked Lester 624
Wickham, Vicki 636
Wicks, John 921
Widespread panic 207, 1333
Widowmaker [US] 1166
Wiedlin, Jane 439, 466, 1050, 1051
Wieneke, Paul 671
Wiggins, DWayne 305, 1147
Wiggins, Jay 1274
Wiggins, Raphael 1147
Wiggs, Johnny 141
Wiggs, Josephine 141
Wiggs, Pete 972
Wigwam [1] 1296
Wilber, Jason 893
Wilco 138, 432, 485, 502, 541, 582, 667, 935,
    1039, 1043, 1082, 1174, **1223**, 1344
Wild Bunch 701
Wild Bunch [1] 1159
Wild Cherry 562, 1284
Wild Pair 3
Wild Swans 654
Wild Tchoupitoulas 791, **1223**
Wild, Chuck 743
Wilde Flowers 181, **1223**, 1224
Wilde, Danny 931
Wilde, Kim **1224**
Wilde, Marty 1224, 1310
Wilder, Alan 277, 300, 301
Wilder, Alec 240
Wilder, Gene 1239
Wilder, Matthew 803
Wiley, Isaac 286
Wiley, Michael 286
Wiley, Tess 1017
Wilhelm, Mike 200
Wilhoite, Orion 1020
Wilk, Brad 912
Wilkins, Ernie 59
Wilkins, Robert 1350
Wilkinson, John [1] 882
Wilkinson, Peter 190
Will to Power 1281
Will, Wildcat 830
Willett, Jason 499
Williams & Watson 949
Williams Brothers [2] 159
Williams [1] 866
Williams, Andre 226, 1015, **1224**
Williams, Andrew 189
Williams, Andy 333, 1276
Williams, Big Joe 937
Williams, Christopher 322, 379
Williams, Cliff 3
Williams, Curtis [1] 'Fitz' 850
Williams, Doc 759
Williams, Eric 108
Williams, Esther 132
Williams, Fleming 544
Williams, Freedom 170
Williams, Hank [1] 159, 191, 203, 258, 341,
    376, 487, 630, 652, 695, 787, 983, 1130
Williams, Hank [2] Jr. 409
Williams, Harvey 402
Williams, Huw 388
Williams, Jerry [1] 125, 219, 914, 937
Williams, Jez 334

Williams, Joe 44, 976, 1292
Williams, John [Film Composer] 673, 1225
Williams, John [Irish] 1299
Williams, John [Pop/Rock] 353
Williams, Johnny [2] 191, 705
Williams, Joseph [1] 1150
Williams, Lamar 17
Williams, Larry [60's] 610, 642, 973,
    1224, 1294
Williams, Larry [Horn/Piano] 1232
Williams, Lenny 1151
Williams, Leo [1] 'E-Zee-Kill' 95
Williams, Lucinda 230, 857, 893, 982, **1224**,
    1225, 1353
Williams, Maizie 125
Williams, Mars 370, 1199
Williams, Mason 1292
Williams, Maurice **1225**, 1282, 1307
Williams, Maurice & the Zodiacs 1225
Williams, McKinley 711
Williams, Michelle 304
Williams, Paul [01] 1093
Williams, Paul [02] 1093, **1225**, 1226
Williams, Paul [08] 198, 584
Williams, Pip 325
Williams, Rich [2] 610
Williams, Robbie 740, 781, 1115, **1226**, 1243
Williams, Robert [1] 181
Williams, Robert [2] Pete 1350
Williams, Ronny 1106
Williams, Scotty 1288
Williams, Senon 910
Williams, Terry 677, 949
Williams, Tex 320
Williams, Tony [Bass] 868
Williams, Tony [Drums] 976, 1329
Williams, Tony [Drums] Lifetime 975
Williams, Tony [Platters] 868
Williams, Vanessa **1226**, 1227
Williams, Victoria 175, 207, 582, **1227**, 1248
Williams, Walter [3] 818, 819
Williams, Wendy [1] O. 768, 866
Williamson, James [1] 874, 1086
Williamson, Robin 558
Williamson, Sonny Boy [I] 981, 1352
Williamson, Sonny Boy [II] 29, 708, 794,
    1253, 1308
Willing Sinners 19, 20
Willis, Bill 1294
Willis, Carol 549
Willis, Carolyn 536
Willis, Chuck 59, 147, 248, 969, **1227**,
    1289, 1305
Willis, Ike 1267
Willis, Kelly 266
Willoughby, Brian 1089
Willoughby, Rusty 396
Wills, Bob 1303, 1307
Wills, John 668
Wills, Rick [1] 426
Wills, Viola 1219
Willson, Meredith 1049
Willson-Piper, Marty 15, 214, 215, 216,
    999, 1000
Wilsey, James Calvin 564
Wilson Phillips 253, **1228**
Wilson, Alan 179
Wilson, Ann 518, 519, 674
Wilson, B.J. 893, 894
Wilson, Brian 12, 71, 72, 73, 74, 75, 92, 108,
    151, 198, 271, 315, 355, 368, 411, 525, 527,
    528, 535, 537, 578, 585, 599, 637, 638, 645,
    688, 713, 797, 842, 852, 910, 971, 999, 1045,
    1056, 1102, 1103, 1106, 1107, 1141, 1178,
    1188, 1198, 1223, **1228**, 1229, 1240, 1241,
    1299, 1321
Wilson, Carl [1] 71, 72, 73, 74, 1102
Wilson, Carl [3] 93
Wilson, Carnie 1228
Wilson, Cassandra 957
Wilson, Charles [1] 449
Wilson, Chris [1] 410
Wilson, Cindy 47
Wilson, Dan 1160
Wilson, Dennis [1] 73, 74, 75, 151
Wilson, Dennis [1] [Beach Boys] 71, 75,
    1228, 1229

Wilson, Erik 1098
Wilson, Frank [5] 534
Wilson, Gerald 44, 203
Wilson, Jackie 202, 421, 662, 718, 772, 773,
    925, 974, 1037, 1206, 1207, 1215, **1229**,
    1230, 1236, 1303, 1305, 1314, 1324, 1325
Wilson, Joe [1] 223
Wilson, Kaia 1121
Wilson, Kim 384, 915
Wilson, Leslie 678
Wilson, Matt [2] 1160
Wilson, Murry 1102, 1103
Wilson, Nancy [1] 1263
Wilson, Nancy [2] 518, 519
Wilson, Ricky [2] 47
Wilson, Robert [1] 168, 449
Wilson, Robin 465
Wilson, Ron [1] 1105
Wilson, Ruby 1298
Wilson, Teddy 1036
Wilson, Tom [1] 119, 317, 1008
Wilson, Tony [1] 540
Wilson, Wendy 1228
Wilton, Michael 907
Wimberley, Peele 245
Wimbish, Doug 663, 1242
Wimple Winch **1250**, 1322
Wincer, Paul 639
Winchester, Jesse 56, 156, 675, 706, **1230**, 1231
Wincott, Terry 21, 22
Windbreakers 322, 1343
Winders, Paul 1191
Windo, Gary 1247
Windross, Rose 1044
Windsor, Morris 530, 531
Windy & Carl 1155, **1231**
Winfrey, Oprah 1226
Winger 322, 327, **1231**, 1302
Winger, Kip 510, 1231
Wings [Paul McCartney] 359, 713, 714,
    715, 1211
Winkies **1231**, 1335
Winley, Harold 227
Winslow, Barry 960
Winstanley, Alan 161, 235, 255, 307, 685, 765,
    935, 1107
Winston, Jimmy 1027, 1028
Winter Hours **1231**
Winter [1] 1232
Winter, Edgar 121, 144, 302, 497, 716, 757,
    1232, 1291, 1333
Winter, Johnny 302, 518, 716, **1232**, 1233,
    1273, 1297, 1302, 1326, 1333
Winter, Johnny Band 302
Winter, Kurt 491, 492
Winwood, Muff 284, 285, 1051, 1233
Winwood, Steve 110, 118, 136, 230, 251, 284,
    285, 318, 389, 474, 694, 700, 701, 733, 773,
    913, 927, 1123, 1153, 1154, 1155, **1233**,
    1270, 1300, 1315, 1316, 1325
Wipers **1233**, 1340, 1341
Wire 40, 58, 62, 82, 134, 243, 275, 302, 358,
    406, 726, 740, 741, 984, 1059, **1233**, 1234,
    1278, 1279, 1280, 1283, 1337, 1339
Wire Train 351, **1234**, 1235, 1344
Wire, Nicky 692, 693, 740
Wirtz, Mark **1235**, 1291
Wise, Richie 624, 1087
Wisefield, Laurie 1235
Wiseman, Bob 117, 995
Wishart, Alan 97
Wishbone Ash **1235**, 1286
Wissert, Joseph 454
Wistanley, Alan 685
Witchman 771
Withers, Bill 488, 538, 565, 572, 574, 785,
    1235, 1236
Witherspoon, Jimmy 570, 764, 1286
Withrow, Kenny 142, 143
Wizzard [1] 358, 772, 1004, 1241, 1242
Wobble, Jah 369, 376, 824, 898, 935
Wolf [1] 1236
Wolf, Kate [1] 1353
Wolf, Kurt 131
Wolf, Peter [1] 150, 454, 455, **1236**
Wolf, Roland 193
Wolfie **1236**

Wolinski, David 831
Woloschuck, John 626
Woloschuk, John 626
Wolstencroft, Simon 393
Womack & Womack 382, 1351
Womack Brothers 247
Womack, Bobby 247, 430, 860, 1119, **1236**,
    1237, 1240, 1274, 1290
Womack, Bobby [1] 609, 975, 1236, 1237
Womack, Bobby [2] 1237
Womack, Cecil 1215
Wombles **1237**
Wonder Mike 1100
Wonder Stuff 779, **1237**, 1238
Wonder [1] 841, 944
Wonder, Stevie 44, 49, 56, 57, 108, 110, 278,
    282, 284, 348, 378, 427, 428, 430, 431, 451,
    452, 453, 454, 496, 512, 522, 572, 577, 578,
    613, 631, 714, 828, 841, 869, 879, 922, 940,
    944, 947, 962, 964, 1055, 1093, 1119, 1120,
    1183, 1184, 1186, **1238**, 1239, 1240, 1244,
    1287, 1314, 1315, 1324, 1328, 1334, 1355
Wondermints 1228, **1240**
Wonderwheel 1245
Woo, Philip 711
Wood [1] 358, 396, 772, 1125, 1153
Wood, Andrew 767, 848, 1125
Wood, Andrew [Mother Love Bone] 1125
Wood, Art 1081
Wood, Bill 57
Wood, Brad 361, 857, 985, 1130, 1149,
    1192, 1216
Wood, Brenton **1240**, 1275, 1276
Wood, Chris [Bass] 1153, 1154
Wood, Chris [Saxophone] 1153, 1154
Wood, Danny 792
Wood, Ed 1178
Wood, Grant 62
Wood, John 298
Wood, Pete 336
Wood, Peter 335
Wood, Ron 84, 98, 99, 265, 312, 385, 951,
    1027, 1070, 1079, 1081, **1240**, 1241
Wood, Roy 355, 358, 359, 772, 773, 784,
    1241, 1242
Woodenspoon 990
Woodentops **1242**
Woodley, Bruce 990
Woods, Bobby 937
Woods, Danny 195
Woods, Gay 1071
Woods, Jimmy 688
Woods, Lesley 42
Woods, Peter 954
Woods, Terry 871, 1071
Woodson, Craig 1175
Woodson, Elbert 925
Woodward, Kaye 69
Woodward, Keren 60
Woody's Truck Stop 784
Woolfson, Eric 844, 845
Workman, Lyle 585
World Class Wreckin' Cru 553, 1300
World Party 1208, **1242**
Wormworth, James 988
Worrell, Bernie 314, 440, 441, 442, 470, 842,
    843, 1107, 1117, 1242
Wrath, Billy 769
Wratten, Robert 402
Wray, Link 16, 1149, **1243**, 1273, 1282, 1292,
    1294, 1297, 1301, 1308, 1309
Wray, Link & the Wraymen 1243
Wray, Lucky 1294
Wray, Vernon 1243
Wreckless Eric 727, **1243**, 1244, 1278, 1285,
    1295, 1335
Wreckx N Effect **1244**
Wright [1] [Arranger] 852
Wright, Adrian 545
Wright, Aggi 846
Wright, Alex 1171
Wright, Andy 1013
Wright, Betty **1244**, 1284, 1299
Wright, Charles **1244**, 1334
Wright, Charles & the Watts 103rd Street
    Rhythm 1244
Wright, Denny 329

Wright, Edna 536
Wright, Gary 473, 605, 831, **1245**
Wright, John [1] 75
Wright, Johnny 51, 1163
Wright, Kate 773
Wright, Martin 1076
Wright, O.V. **1245**, 1283
Wright, Patricia 272
Wright, Paul 402, 403
Wright, Richard [1] 66, 861, 862
Wright, Rik 862
Wright, Shannon **1245**, 1246
Wright, Simon 316
Wright, Stevie 349
Wright, Syreeta 1238
Wright, Tim 368
Wright, Tim [1] 851
Wright, Vance 1023
Wright, Wilbo 1171
Wu All Stars 553
Wu Syndicate 1246
Wu Tang Clan 365, 376, 458, 464, 554, 702,
    722, 731, 819, 820, 898, 911, 912, 939, 970,
    1018, **1246**
Wu, Reuben 638
Wurster, Jon 948
Wyatt, Johnny 1219
Wyatt, Robert 45, 66, 182, 208, 473, 476,
    703, 1038, 1039, 1223, 1224, **1246**, 1247,
    1329, 1331
Wydler, Thomas 193, 194
Wygal, Doug 1343
Wyld, Bob 688
Wylde, Zakk 832
Wylie & the Wild West Show 253
Wylie, Alan 35
Wylie, Daniel 253
Wylie, Pete 1122, 1197
Wylie, Pete & Wah! The Mongrel 1197
Wyman, Bill 949, 950, 952, 1275
Wynans, Reese 1186
Wyndorf, Dave 757
Wynette, Tammy 627, 638, 1217, 1351
Wynn, Steve [1] 63, 241, 337, 485, 541, 667,
    673, **1248**
Wynn, Toby 678
Wynne, Philippe 237, 794, 1055
Wysocki, Jon 1067

X

X Ray Spex 954, 993, **1250**, 1278, 1279, 1337
X [1] 21, 43, 53, 109, 245, 361, 493, 642, 775,
    921, 1089, **1249**, 1250, 1279, 1280, 1336,
    1338, 1340
X, Dexter 691
X., Petey 948
Xanadu 305
XBXRX 783
Xenakis, Iannis 7, 1289
XL 702

Xscape 833
XTC 65, 76, 88, 95, 121, 160, 190, 225, 250,
    295, 306, 320, 338, 339, 355, 400, 655, 717,
    795, 818, 828, 874, 889, 896, 964, 1012,
    1250, 1251, 1252, 1278, 1290, 1338, 1339,
    1345, 1346, 1347

Y

Yachts 727, **1253**, 1295
Yale, Brian 702
Yama Motor 131
Yamamoto, Hiro 1044, 1045
Yamamoto, Moog 154
Yamazaki, Iwao 463
Yancey, Mama 696
Yang, Naomi 446, 447
Yankovic, Weird Al 302
Yanni 371
Yanovsky, Zalman 153, 691
Yarbrough, Glenn 986
Yardbirds 9, 30, 84, 92, 98, 99, 114, 119, 124,
    134, 198, 218, 219, 240, 249, 257, 264, 272,
    305, 306, 310, 473, 476, 564, 565, 576, 595,
    621, 657, 694, 695, 702, 708, 745, 768, 784,
    792, 807, 857, 932, 964, 980, 989, 996,
    1001, 1054, 1134, 1171, 1172, 1216, **1253**,
    1254, 1264, 1277, 1284, 1309, 1310, 1315,
    1316, 1317, 1318, 1320, 1322, 1323, 1326,
    1337, 1352
Yardbyrds 1076, 1112
Yashiki, Gota 1013
Yates, Peter 402
Yates, Russell 760, 761
Yaz 300, 372, 373, 827, 1100, **1254**
Yazoo 300, 372, 1254
Yearwood, Trisha 893, 1030
Yeats, Robbie 1191
Yeats, W.B. 764
Yella [1] 350
Yello 1142, **1254**, 1255
Yellow Balloon 227, 1296
Yellow Magic Orchestra 579, 684, 899
Yellowjackets 382
Yelvington, Malcolm 1295
Yes [1] 39, 40, 105, 135, 143, 144, 157, 292,
    338, 363, 364, 420, 429, 458, 515, 587, 611,
    617, 618, 743, 922, 986, 1005, 1077, 1147,
    1155, 1162, 1201, 1231, 1235, **1255**, 1256,
    1257, 1291, 1296, 1331, 1332
Yester, Jerry 41, 153, 1199
Yester, Jim 41
Yeston, Maury 1094
Yo La Tengo 357, 478, 599, 779, 806, 868, 963,
    981, 1018, 1118, **1257**, 1258, 1280
Yoakam, Dwight 21, 109, 117, 675, 720, 1294
Yoho, Monte 834
York, Don 996
York, John 167
York, Melissa 1121
York, Peter 284, 285, 1300

Yorke, Thom [1] 55, 687, 911
Yorke, Thom [2] 101, 511
Yoshimi 130, 131
Yoshinaga, Sugar 154
Yost, Dennis 223
Yothu Yindi 1342
Youlden, Chris 979, 980
Young Fresh Fellows 396, 531, 591
Young Ginns 783
Young Gods 466
Young Marble Giants 77, 446, 656, **1258**
Young MC 1147, 1185, **1258**
Young Rascals 291, 688
Young, Angus 3, 4, 5, 274, 484, 1341
Young, Astrid 1263
Young, Colin 426
Young, Earl 536, 732
Young, Gary 847
Young, George [1] 349, 1341
Young, George [2] 4, 349
Young, James [1] 925
Young, James [Styx] 1097
Young, Jesse Colin 355, **1258**, 1259, 1263
Young, LaMonte 337, 1048, 1056, 1289
Young, Larry 253, 975
Young, Malcolm 3, 4, 1341
Young, Neil 23, 24, 62, 77, 94, 129, 133, 155,
    157, 158, 167, 185, 193, 216, 221, 256, 259,
    264, 269, 270, 315, 337, 354, 355, 361, 380,
    399, 486, 490, 506, 524, 529, 551, 555, 559,
    565, 640, 654, 665, 668, 673, 677, 681, 719,
    731, 751, 815, 831, 848, 855, 864, 910, 926,
    972, 1082, 1107, 1116, 1123, 1227, 1232,
    1248, 1257, **1259**, 1260, 1261, 1262, 1269,
    1270, 1285, 1327, 1328, 1343, 1344, 1354
Young, Neil & Crazy Horse 337
Young, Neil & The Shocking Pinks 1262
Young, Paul [1] **1263**
Young, Paul [2] 735, 736
Young, Pegi 1263
Young, Reggie [1] 937
Young, Rusty 666, 869, 870
Young, Starleana 1020
Young, Steve 81, 347, 705
Young-Holt Unlimited 1309, 1329
Youngberg, Rob 671
Youngbloods 559, 583, 671, 707, 1259, **1263**
Younger, Rob 910, 911, 1341, 1342
Yount, Dick 507
Youth Brigade [1] 1279
Youth [1] 272, 616, 617, 716, 824
Yow, David 586, 587
Yule, Billy 1189
Yule, Doug 24, 1189
Yuro, Timi **1263**

Z

Z., David 122
Zaakir 608
Zaentz, Saul 117, 421

Zager & Evans 1195
Zajkowski, Tony 671
Zakary Thaks **1264**, 1321
Zakatek, Lenny 844, 845
Zander, Robin 204, 205, 335, 519, 877, 1339
Zanes, Dan 295
Zanes, Warren 295
Zapp 171, 1284
Zappa, Dweezil 599
Zappa, Frank 88, 119, 126, 153, 173, 178, 180,
    181, 226, 258, 262, 305, 328, 393, 394, 397,
    417, 459, 474, 478, 501, 647, 659, 743, 745,
    751, 867, 888, 892, 900, 923, 935, 938, 958,
    997, 1141, 1149, 1162, 1165, 1181, 1216,
    1264, 1265, 1266, 1267, 1268, 1297, 1307,
    1329, 1330, 1337, 1348
Zappa, Frank & the Mothers of Invention 179,
    251, 258, 306, 417, 671, 996, 1264, 1265,
    1266, 1267, 1268, 1323
Zaremba, Peter 195, 415, 416
Zaremba, Peter Love Delegation 415
Zarr, Fred 464s
Zawinul, Joe 430
Zax, Andy 351
Ze, Tom 778
Zedek, Thalia 241
Zehringer, Rick 716
Zeitgeist 930
Zekley, Gary 226, 227
Zelenko, Mike 703
Zender, Stuart 577
Zephyr 122, 123, 576
Zero Boys 1280
Zero, Jimmy 287
Zeros [1] 1279
Zevon, Warren 410, 523, 955, 1165, **1269**,
    1270, 1282, 1285
Ziegler, Suzi 447
Ziggy [1] 134
Zimmer, Hans 279
Zincavage, Frank 954
Zippers 1066
Ziter, Chris 376
Znuff, Chip 370
Zolitin, Cynthia 1146
Zombie, Rob 1219
Zombies 34, 35, 67, 68, 346, 395, 470, 472, 476,
    645, 694, 780, 790, 976, 999, 1016, 1059,
    1165, 1172, 1188, 1207, 1216, 1236, 1240,
    1270, 1271, 1280, 1298, 1317, 1318,
    1320, 1329
Zoom, Billy 1249
Zorn, John 130, 259, 470, 498, 745
Zounds 680
Zucchero 1263
Zuiderwijk, Cesar 470
Zuill, Bobby 979
Zumpano 189
ZZ Top 123, 151, 375, 719, 720, 773, **1271**,
    1272, 1326, 1333

More *ALL MUSIC GUIDES* from BACKBEAT BOOKS

All Music Guide
Fourth Edition

"The most useful single volume your money can buy." –Mojo

Get the ultimate record guide for every style of music, from rock to rap, country to reggae, avant-garde jazz to folk. Thoroughly revised and updated, this guide reviews 20,000 recordings by 4,000 performers in 16 major genres.
Softcover, 1,491 pages, 30 charts, ISBN 0-87930-627-0, $34.95

All Music Guide to Electronica

"Well researched…incredibly reader-friendly." –Billboard

Discover the most electrifying recordings with the irresistible rhythm of house, the engulfing pulse of techno, and the lush twirl of trance. You get 5,000 album reviews, 1,200 artist bios, historical essays and "music maps," online resources, and more.
Softcover, 688 pages, ISBN 0-87930-628-9, $24.95

All Music Guide to the Blues
Second Edition

"Easily the best blues guide." –Real Blues

Reissues…compilations…live recordings…new releases…new players…soundtracks…everybody's got the blues. This guide takes you straight to 6,000 great blues recordings by 900 artists – from 1920s Delta blues to 1990s Chicago electric. Plus you get a special section on the blues influence in jazz, and coverage of seminal gospel performers and recordings.
Softcover, 658 pages, 30 charts, ISBN 0-87930-548-7, $22.95

All Music Guide to Jazz
Third Edition

"An excellent resource for scholars, devotees, and casual listeners alike." –Jazz Notes

Start or fine-tune a sizzling jazz collection with this definitive reference. It zeroes in on 18,000 recordings by 1,700 musicians in all key styles and eras: ragtime, New Orleans jazz, classic jazz, swing, bop, Dixieland revival, cool jazz, Latin jazz, fusion, avant-garde, and more.
Softcover, 1,378 pages, 52 charts, ISBN 0-87930-530-4, $29.95

All Music Guide to Country

"A definite must for any serious music collector." –Country Song Roundup

This is the comprehensive guide to the entire spectrum of country music – from the Grand Ole Opry to the sounds of today's Nashville superstars. Designed for devoted fans and newcomers alike, this book covers 5,500 cream-of-the-crop recordings by 1,000 top country artists.
Softcover, 611 pages, 14 charts, ISBN 0-87930-475-8, $22.95

AVAILABLE AT FINE BOOK AND MUSIC STORES EVERYWHERE. OR CONTACT:

Backbeat Books • 6600 Silacci Way • Gilroy, CA 95020 USA • **Phone Toll Free: (866) 222-5232**
Fax: (408) 848-5784 • E-mail: backbeat@rushorder.com • Web: www.backbeatbooks.com